SKY SPORTS

FOOTBALL YEARBOOK 2010-2011

EDITORS: GLENDA ROLLIN AND **JACK ROLLIN**

D0264554

headline

First published in 2010
by HEADLINE PUBLISHING GROUP

1

Front cover photographs: (left) Andrei Arshavin (Arsenal) – *Julian Finney/Getty Images*; (centre and background) Frank Lampard (Chelsea) – *Sean Dempsey/PA Wire/Press Association Images*; (right) Ryan Giggs (Manchester United) – *Offside/Rex Features*

Spine photograph: Steven Gerrard, England v. USA, FIFA World Cup 2010 – *Back Page Images/Rex Features*

Back cover photographs: (above) – Gareth Barry (Manchester City) – *Laurence Griffiths/Getty Images;* (below) Kris Boyd (Rangers) and Scott Brown (Celtic) – *Ian MacNicol/Getty Images*

Cataloguing in Publication Data is available from the British Library

ISBN 978 0 7553 6106 9   (Hardback)
ISBN 978 0 7553 6107 6   (Trade paperback)

Typeset by Wearset Ltd, Boldon, Tyne and Wear

Printed and bound in the UK by
CPI Mackays, Chatham ME5 8TD

HEADLINE PUBLISHING GROUP
An Hachette UK Company
338 Euston Road
London NW1 3BH

www.headline.co.uk
www.hachette.co.uk

CONTENTS

INTERNATIONAL FOOTBALL

NON-LEAGUE FOOTBALL

INFORMATION AND RECORDS

FOREWORD

After another busy season of Sky Sports News and Gillette Soccer Specials, I packed my bags for the World Cup in South Africa in June and naturally I made room for my *Sky Sports Football Yearbook*.

As it is in our west London studio, so it was in our temporary Cape Town base; you have to do your research and it has to be spot on. The Yearbook was a constant source of reference and now the tournament is history you'll find the World Cup section of the 41st edition to be as complete and comprehensive as you'd expect from this editorial institution.

The shows I'm involved in can appear a smooth operation to the viewer. But we do have a little help from our friends in the production gallery. On our week night Soccer Specials, for example, the flow of information is constant and frenetic. It's up to me to deliver scores and breaking stories to fans sitting on the edge of their sofas quickly and accurately. This is where the Yearbook comes in. Our colleagues behind the scenes are often available with a useful nugget of information to illustrate and illuminate the stories unfolding. If you had a quick glance into the gallery during these shows you'd see a stack of well-thumbed Yearbooks ready for reference. They play an important role week in, week out across our football programming, just as they do among the broader football community.

So as we brace ourselves for our biggest ever season of live football on Sky Sports, the arrival of the Yearbook offers reassurance as well as an essential source of reference. It's also the surest signal that kick-off is just around the corner!

Ed Chamberlin, Sky Sports

Ed Chamberlin

INTRODUCTION

The 41st edition of the Yearbook, our eighth with sponsors Sky Sports, features complete coverage of the 2010 World Cup with a report of the final tournament plus detailed match statistics from South Africa as well as the qualifying stages. These include results, line-ups and goal scorers for all 32 finalists in their preliminary games.

Once again our comprehensive review of both the Champions League and new Europa League is unrivalled with every qualifying game and those in the latter stages given the same fulsome overall treatment.

The Daily Round-up of events has been increased by popular request as our intention to provide more information which is totally new to the edition each year continues to expand. It is stressed these are diary notes which are compiled as they happen and may be overturned by subsequent happenings.

As ever our domestic duties in providing line-ups of Premier League, Football League, Scottish Premier League and Scottish League matches have not been neglected. As an added attraction our main league tables include easy-to-read notes on which clubs were promoted or relegated in the previous season.

In the pages devoted to each Premier League and Football League club, it may be that the strip for the new season had not been announced before going to press. In these instances the colours in use during the previous season have been repeated. Honours represent champions, cup winners and the respective runners-up positions.

Because it has been necessary to cut back on much of the purely historical information which rarely changes from edition to edition in order to promote new material, the International Appearances section for England, Scotland, Northern Ireland, Wales and the Republic of Ireland again has the name of the player with the end of the season in which he was given his first cap plus all the clubs for whom he has played while earning such honours.

However, as another innovation, all players who played for these five countries in 2009–10 are picked out in bold type which makes for easy reference when checking on who appeared. All appearances include those made by England players in the 2010 World Cup finals in South Africa.

The frequently referred to Players Directory also includes honours achieved by those who appeared in the tournament in the southern hemisphere. Indeed there were more than 100 players either with Premier League clubs or the Football League who were spread around most of the competing nations.

The latest list of such honours is included in this section along with personal details of all the domestic players who have won similar representation for their countries at the various levels to which they are referred.

Again the invaluable nature of the cross reference A to Z which accompanies this section enables the reader to quickly find any such player's club. In the club-by-club pages which contain the line-ups of all league matches appearances are split into starting line-ups and those who were brought on as substitutes. However, in the Players Directory the total of these two figures appears.

· Throughout the book players sent off are designated thus ▪, substitutes in the club pages are 12, 13 and 14 with 15 for the substitute goalkeeper. Squad numbers are not used.

In addition to competitions already mentioned there are sections devoted to Welsh, Irish, Women's football, schools, reserve team, academies, referees and the leading non-league competitions as well as the work of the chaplains at clubs. On a wider scale the main tournaments outside the UK at club and national level are not forgotten. The International Directory itself features Europe in some depth as well as every FIFA country's international record for the previous year.

The Editors would like to express their appreciation to those clubs who responded to queries raised, to Tony Brown for sequences and instances of match results in the Records Section and Ian Nannestad for the obituaries. As always thanks are also due to John English, for his conscientious proof reading.

ACKNOWLEDGEMENTS

Additionally the Editors are also keen to express appreciation to the following individuals and organisations for their co-operation: David Barber at the Football Association, David C Thomson (Scottish League), Dr Malcolm Brodie, Rev. Nigel Sands, Ken Goldman, Grahame Lloyd, Marshall Gillespie, Sean Creedon, Bob Bannister, Martin Cooper and Alan Platt. Many thanks, too, for Rhea Halford (Headline) as the invaluable link between the Editors and the publisher.

Special mention as well for the indefatigable, ebullient and loquacious Lorraine Jerram, for her generosity, clinical expertise, constant support, determined resilience, patience, endearing sincerity, perspicacity and appreciation, not to forget her unfailing humour, stoicism, quick-wit, courtesy, quiet consideration and understated authority.

Finally sincere thanks to John Anderson, Simon Dunnington, Geoff Turner, Brian Tait and the staff at Wearset for their much appreciated efforts in the production of the book throughout the year.

EDITORIAL

We should have known not to be carried away on a tide of pre-World Cup hysteria. Even Piers Morgan for one was unsure of our ultimate success. These people are aware of the big events. The rest of us can promote our twenty-twenty vision with that visionary gift of hindsight. Sadly the media led the way voicing its post-exit concerns with the traditional wringing of hands and gnashing of teeth.

Helpful suggestions were plentiful, like sacking the manager, all the players involved, implementing a winter break (tricky as even the Met Office can't forecast bad weather), more coaches to be bussed in, blaming the Premier League and banning all the foreigners. Does this include Scots, Welsh and Irish?

For Fabio Capello reeling from his personal nightmare of early elimination it must have felt like the bad dream of an IT wizard with a blocked Blog. Facebook pages stuck together, a blank iPod and a silent Twitter. But after only a few days and a wave of the FA wand, it was – with echoes of Pinewood – "Carry on Fabio!"

A year ago in this editorial there was detailed reference to the march of Germany at all levels of the game. Last season's Bundesliga had the advantage of some clubs using the controversial Jabulana ball and were aware of its shortcomings. As usual we underestimated the Germans.

All well and good remembering we once beat them in that World Cup final – even the FA's address is PO Box 1966 – and also a more recent and memorable 5-1 victory, but living in past times has little or no future.

Of course it was unfortunate that a legitimate goal by Frank Lampard was not given when the ball was clearly a foot over the line. This was no Geoff Hurst on the goal line job – a real goal. Where was a Russian – actually from Azerbaijan – linesman with incredible eyesight when you needed him? Even Paul the pundit octopus changed nationality from being English to German.

FIFA has consistently refused to introduce technology to solve such problems. Yet they have hinted at change. Even so the Europa League experiment of another official behind the goal could have been used if they feared progress. Their reaction after the furore which followed England's defeat was much as expected. In a similar vein to rounding up the usual suspects or when in doubt arrest a vagrant, in this case it was packing off the offending referee and linesman back home.

It is not all bad news on the England front. The various youth levels had their successes which it is only right and proper that we highlight in this edition. However, it should be underlined that invariably our youngsters are used to playing at a higher level at a younger age than many of those in opposing teams. The problems clearly arise afterwards.

You must also remember that half of the present generation has been brought up with a Government which has discouraged competitive sport, producing a philosophy which is against winners. How one immediately reverses this ideology is tricky, too.

Dare one have the audacity to mention the "f" word? In this instance it refers to flair. All the coaching in the world will not be able to produce this commodity in journeymen footballers. One can look back on Pele's illustrious career and recall the wisdom of one of his earliest coaches, Waldemar de Brito. Just one session with Pele made him realise the best way to nurture his talent was to let him do his own thing. But for every Pele there are thousands without such ability.

The innocent team at a penalty is now made to appear the guilty party because taker cannot feint in his run-up. This is just another piece of legislative nonsense in keeping with the award of a penalty, now a prize to be offered equally to victims or perpetrators. That of course is the penalty shoot-out. How much longer before the step-over is banned along with the drag back, because it is unfair to the opposition? Is time running out before football becomes a total non-contact sport?

On the specifics of penalty shoot-outs, this again illustrates the change of attitude towards spot kicks. Why should a team who has had a player sent off during the match be allowed a full complement of five kickers? If further sanctions included one less for every two yellow cards handed out to players, there would be a totally different attitude to teams playing out time and hoping for the best from the shoot-out. Why such penalties anyway? Continued play is good enough for tennis players, so what works at Wimbledon should be ok for Milton Keynes and far beyond.

Nationwide's most amusing television advert in which Fabio Capello is nonplussed by a spectator asking for his autograph while his wheelchair bound companion proceeds to nutmeg one of his defenders and score a spectacular goal with a somersault kick, climbs back into his seat then refuses the gift of a signed shirt, clearly expected England to go all the way to the final triumph. As to the advertisement comment of "Do you follow the football at all?" The jury might be out for a time musing over that one.

SKY SPORTS FOOTBALL YEARBOOK HONOURS

In 2008–09 for the first time since the inception of the *Sky Sports Football Yearbook* team of the season, the FWA members chose players in a 4-3-3 formation; however, for 2009–10 it reverted to 4-4-2.

Sky Sports Football Yearbook Team of the Season 2009–10

Joe Hart
(Manchester C)

Branislav Ivanovic *(Chelsea)*	Thomas Vermaelen *(Arsenal)*	Michael Dawson *(Tottenham H)*	Ashley Cole *(Chelsea)*

James Milner *(Aston Villa)*	Frank Lampard *(Chelsea)*	Cesc Fabregas *(Arsenal)*	Florent Malouda *(Chelsea)*

Didier Drogba *(Chelsea)*   Wayne Rooney *(Manchester U)*

Manager:
Roy Hodgson *(Fulham)*

Substitutes:
Jamie Carragher *(Liverpool)*
Gareth Bale *(Tottenham H)*
Carlos Tevez *(Manchester C)*

Manchester United's Wayne Rooney wins the Football Writers' Association Footballer of the Year award.
(Action Images/Andrew Boyers)

FOOTBALL AWARDS 2010

FOOTBALLER OF THE YEAR

The Football Writers' Association Sir Stanley Matthews Trophy for the Footballer of the Year was awarded to Wayne Rooney of Manchester United and England. Didier Drogba of Chelsea was runner-up and Carlos Tevez of Manchester City, came third.

Past Winners

1947–48 Stanley Matthews (Blackpool), 1948–49 Johnny Carey (Manchester U), 1949–50 Joe Mercer (Arsenal), 1950–51 Harry Johnston (Blackpool), 1951–52 Billy Wright (Wolverhampton W), 1952–53 Nat Lofthouse (Bolton W), 1953–54 Tom Finney (Preston NE), 1954–55 Don Revie (Manchester C), 1955–56 Bert Trautmann (Manchester C), 1956–57 Tom Finney (Preston NE), 1957–58 Danny Blanchflower (Tottenham H), 1958–59 Syd Owen (Luton T), 1959–60 Bill Slater (Wolverhampton W) 1960–61 Danny Blanchflower (Tottenham H), 1961–62 Jimmy Adamson (Burnley), 1962–63 Stanley Matthews (Stoke C), 1963–64 Bobby Moore (West Ham U), 1964–65 Bobby Collins (Leeds U), 1965–66 Bobby Charlton (Manchester U), 1966–67 Jackie Charlton (Leeds U), 1967–68 George Best (Manchester U), 1968–69 Dave Mackay (Derby Co) shared with Tony Book (Manchester C), 1969–70 Billy Bremner (Leeds U), 1970–71 Frank McLintock (Arsenal), 1971–72 Gordon Banks (Stoke C), 1972–73 Pat Jennings (Tottenham H), 1973–74 Ian Callaghan (Liverpool), 1974–75 Alan Mullery (Fulham), 1975–76 Kevin Keegan (Liverpool), 1976–77 Emlyn Hughes (Liverpool), 1977–78 Kenny Burns (Nottingham F), 1978–79 Kenny Dalglish (Liverpool), 1979–80 Terry McDermott (Liverpool), 1980–81 Frans Thijssen (Ipswich T), 1981–82 Steve Perryman (Tottenham H), 1982–83 Kenny Dalglish (Liverpool), 1983–84 Ian Rush (Liverpool), 1984–85 Neville Southall (Everton), 1985–86 Gary Lineker (Everton), 1986–87 Clive Allen (Tottenham H), 1987–88 John Barnes (Liverpool), 1988–89 Steve Nicol (Liverpool), 1989–90 John Barnes (Liverpool), 1990–91 Gordon Strachan (Leeds U), 1991–92 Gary Lineker (Tottenham H), 1992–93 Chris Waddle (Sheffield W), 1993–94 Alan Shearer (Blackburn R), 1994–95 Jurgen Klinsmann (Tottenham H), 1995–96 Eric Cantona (Manchester U), 1996–97 Gianfranco Zola (Chelsea), 1997–98 Dennis Bergkamp (Arsenal), 1998–99 David Ginola (Tottenham H), 1999–2000 Roy Keane (Manchester U), 2000–01 Teddy Sheringham (Manchester U), 2001–02 Robert Pires (Arsenal), 2002–03 Thierry Henry (Arsenal), 2003–04 Thierry Henry (Arsenal), 2004–05 Frank Lampard (Chelsea), 2005–06 Thierry Henry (Arsenal), 2006–07 Cristiano Ronaldo (Manchester U), 2007–08 Cristiano Ronaldo (Manchester U), 2008–09 Ryan Giggs (Manchester U), 2009–10 Wayne Rooney (Manchester U).

THE PFA AWARDS 2010

Player of the Year: Wayne Rooney, Manchester U and England.
Young Player of the Year: James Milner, Aston Villa and England.
Merit Award: Lucas Radebe, South Africa.

OTHER AWARDS

EUROPEAN FOOTBALLER OF THE YEAR 2009

Lionel Messi, Barcelona and Argentina

WORLD PLAYER OF THE YEAR 2009

Lionel Messi, Barcelona and Argentina

WOMEN'S PLAYER OF THE YEAR 2009

Marta, Los Angeles Sol and Santos, Brazil

SCOTTISH PFA PLAYER OF THE YEAR AWARDS 2010

Player of the Year: Steven Davis, Rangers and Northern Ireland.
Young Player of the Year: Danny Wilson, Rangers.
First Division Player of the Year: Adam Rooney, Inverness CT.
Second Division Player of the Year: Rory McAllister, Brechin C.
Third Division Player of the Year: Robbie Winters, Livingston.
Manager of the Year: Walter Smith, Rangers.

SCOTTISH FOOTBALL WRITERS' ASSOCIATION 2010

Player of the Year: David Weir, Rangers and Scotland.
Young Player of the Year: Danny Wilson, Rangers.
Manager of the Year: Walter Smith, Rangers.

DAILY ROUND-UP 2009–10

JULY 2009
Eriksson tied in at Notts … Bobby Robson dies at 76.

1   Real's Benzema swoop flat foots Sir Alex. Pearce defends his touchline passion. Man C is still hoping for Eto'o and Tevez. Inter wants Ricardo Carvalho and Deco for free. Two Ch Lge qualifiers played!

2   Sir Alex gets Owen for nothing. Now Real may pip Chelsea for Ribery, but Blues may get Zhirkov. Eureka! Europa League (E Lge) kicks off and Lisburn Distillery and Linfield look goners, Sligo, too, but Llanelli shake Motherwell and The New Saints are praying for better second leg.

3   Man C is to up the ante for Terry. Wiseacres get jobs as ambassadors – Dalglish at Liverpool, Cottee at West Ham. Paul Ince is back as MK Dons boss.

4   Chopra move to Cardiff is a £4m club record.

5   England plan friendly v Brazil in Doha for November and wants high altitude training camp as WC prelude.

6   Ronaldo unveiling attracts 80,000 fans in Madrid pound for pound.

7   Sheff Utd's Kenny forced in battle to prove drug innocence. Swiss are to rescue Saints. Jo goes back to Everton – on loan again.

8   After Valencia, Owen signings, it's a triple with Gabriel Obertan in £3m move to Old Trafford from Bordeaux.

9   What the E Lge? Distillery, Linfield, Sligo, The New Saints all crash and 'Well turn tables on Llanelli. The Swiss regime quickly disposes of manager Wotte.

10 Man C loses out on Eto'o, but still retain Terry hopes. Kroenke increases stake in Arsenal.

11 Sunderland spends £3.5m of the Chopra money on Man U Campbell.

12 Chelsea makes Arnesen their sporting director. Olympic Stadium will not figure in any WC 2018 plans.

13 Tevez moves next door to Man C – only the eleventh since Meredith so to do from Old Trafford – and it costs £25m. Unrest at Newcastle as club awaits new owner. Real will have to pay £30m for Xabi Alonso. Hartson is facing more cancer treatment.

14 Middle-men in transfer deals will be revealed by the PL this coming season. Kinnear may return as Toon boss. Ch Lge: Rhyl hits for four by Partizans. E Lge: Crusaders battle to draw with Rabotnicki.

15 The Becks boy upsets LA after revealing his yearning for PL again. Ch Lge: Glentoran suffer six-hit in Haifa, but Bohs do well to hold the Red Bulls in Salzburg.

16 Man U expects to take £23.5m more in sponsorship and make £80m extra from shirt deal with AON. Ribery going nowhere says Bayern coach Van Gaal as he designs his diamond-shaped formation around him. E Lge: Falkirk edge Vaduz, Derry hold Skonto in Riga, but Motherwell go a goal down at Flamurtari and Bangor suffer two goal deficit away to Honka while St Pat's surprisingly held by Valletta. England Ladies are beaten by Iceland in Colchester.

17 Now it's the bird for Becks LA return. Man U cancels Indonesia trip after bombings. Pardew is apponted manager of Southampton.

18 Owen scores winner on debut in Kuala Lumpur!

19 Rosicky comeback from injury might save Arsenal a replacement. The Becks argues with fan after more abuse in draw with AC Milan.

20 Owen gets another goal but Rooney unhappy about rough stuff. Real and one-half Ronaldo win in Ireland against Shamrock, 11,000 present at Tallaght Stadium.

21 Eriksson back in English football (courtesy of unknown Qatar money-men) as D of F at – Notts County! Nasri injury upsets Arsenal. PL is to monitor Pompey's new chairman Sulaiman Al Fahim. Ch Lge: Rhyl eighth-some reel against the Partizans and go out by twelve goals. Euro U-19s: England held by Swiss.

22 Liverpool renegotiating loan with RBS. Vassell goes on Turkey trot to Ankaragucu. Four players banned from betting after FA investigation. Cardiff unveils new ground in draw with Celtic. Ch Lge: Bohs edged out, Glentoran lose mightily by ten over two legs to Maccabi Haifa.

23 Liverpool supporters groups aim to raise money to buy the club on Barcelona lines. Old boy Henry tells Arsenal to encourage youth. Redknapp backs Man C for title! E Lge: Falkirk (800 fans making trip) ousted by Vaduz aet; Bangor, Crusaders losers, too, but Derry, eight-goal Motherwell and St Pat's go through.

24 Pompey draws with Barca and want to sign Vieira. Macheda, still 17, lights up Man U in front of 64,000 South Koreans. Becks is fined £600 by LA. It's another draw for England U-19s – with Ukraine. Gerrard cleared in brawl – there's a surprise!

25 England Ladies U-19s win the Euro crown against Sweden. Scots start with Alba Cup! – Stranraer top scorers with four! Terry is on the brink of staying – or going. Newcastle loses friendly six goals at Orient!

26 Terry will stay with better deal. Disquiet at Arsenal over sale of Adebayor. Debt deal will sort out Liverpool finances. Crouch is heading to Spurs.

27 Sky replaces Setanta with FA deals. Crouch goes to WHL for £10m in five-year agreement. Ibrahimovic Inter to Barca £45m, Eto'o makes the reverse journey. England creates U-19 score record beating Slovenia 7-1 to make semi-final.

28 Ancelotti wants to shake up the Chelsea playing formations. Ronaldo scores first goal for Real. Hargreaves is still having treatment.

29 Man C's latest capture is Toure at £16m. Newcastle flogs Martins to Wolfsburg for £9m. Ch Lge: Celtic shocked by Dynamo Moscow at Parkhead. Boa Morte suffers injury in Asia Trophy tournament in China as Hammers lose to Spurs while Hull beats Beijing Guoan in s/o.

30 Man U add another forward Mame Biram Diouf from Molde. Vieira may return to Arsenal. Bent is unhappy over delay in move to Sunderland. England U-19s go extra time to beat one-over-the-eight (nine-man) France to reach Euro final. E Lge: Fulham's impressive debut in Lithuania against Vetra, but Aberdeen hit for five by Sigma, Motherwell for three by Steaua and Derry just edged at CSKA Sofia. Attwell – ref of Reading no goal fame – is in charge of Vojvodina – FK Austria tie.

31 Death of Sir Bobby Robson at 76; the man who came closest to Sir Alf Ramsey's World Cup feat. Spurs win the Asia Cup beating Hull, Hammers take third place.

AUGUST
Six-hit Gunners open fire … Burnley surprises MU … Spurs on a roll.

1   Big Al goes back to BBC – no Toon job? CIS Cup starts with 61 goals – high fives for five: Dundee, Dunfermline, Partick, Ross Co and St Johnstone – 15 ties.

2 Euro U-19 final: England lose to home team Ukraine. CIS Cup: East Stirling hit three – St Mirren double it and Mehmet gets his own nap hand.

3 Lescott tug-of-war involves Man C with Everton. Is Xabi Alonso on move to Real at last? Delph expected to join Villa for £6m.

4 Ch Lge: McClaren woe as Sporting's last gasp ends Twente hopes; Maccabi Haifa three goals down score four to oust Aktobe. Alonso moves to Real for £34m, to boost the Spaniards spending to over £200m this summer.

5 Under-siege Toon may get a Moat to save them as money-man Barry of that ilk steps in with Kinnear back as boss? Ch Lge: Celtic wins in Moscow to end six-year away travel misery in Europe – their first ever after losing first home leg. Liverpool is quick to replace Alonso with Alberto Aquilani for £20m from Roma. Sunderland bags Bent in record £10m capture from Spurs, but Chelsea frustrated over Pirlo. Gunners are under-fire from ex-directors. Livingston demoted to Scots Div 3 through breach of insolvency rule. Airdrie U and Cowdenbeath promoted to Div 1 and Div 2 respectively.

6 E Lge: Fulham doubles its advantage, Motherwell almost as poor again, Aberdeen better away but make it two Scottish departures while Derry are edged out and only St Pat's on away goals carry flag for Republic interest. Relegated Chester hit by 25-point penalty. Man U promotes gk Foster as No.1.

7 Championship (FLC) starts with Sheff U in no goals affair at relegated Boro. Ch Lge draw: Arsenal faces Celtic. E Lge play-off round pair Hearts away to Dinamo Zagreb, Everton hosting Sigma Olomouc in Group 1, Fulham v Russians Amkar in Group 2 and Aston Villa away to Rapid Vienna. Livi refuse to play at East Stirling!

8 FLC: Chopra has a brace in four-play for Cardiff; Derby celebrates first home fixture for seven years edging promoted Posh with 33,010 present. Yorks derby at Sheff Wed attracts 30,644 for the draw with Barnsley – one of six such in the division. Newcastle levels at West Bromwich and sub gk Krul earns plaudits. Davidson pen equaliser in 94th min rescues PNE. F1: Norwich suffers sensational worst home defeat to Colchester whose 7-1 is their best ever away – even Canaries Delia gets the bird. High-five for Gillingham with Simeon Jackson bags three goals. Saints knock off one pt off deficit and Davis saves a Millwall pen. Brighton first home fixture for ten years is a loss. F2: Sven works his magic as Notts hit five, too, Hughes grabbing a treble. Golden oldies on target: Warne, 38, for Rotherham, Hayles, 37, for Cheltenham. New boys Burton lose, but Torquay win. First goal: Morgan (Shots) 3 mins. Overall best FL opening gates since 1963: over 450,000. SL: seven red cards (four in BSP, three in FL). BSP: AFC Dons fight back to hold Luton (4488), but Oxford have best gate (6405). On-the-brink Chester refused permission to play at Grays!

9 C Shield: Ancelotti annexes early pot after stirring encounter, four shared goals but 4-1 to the good for Chelsea on the shoot-out following Rooney's last gasp leveller for Man U, but Ballack escapes after raised arm on Evra. FLC: boot camp ended does nothing for Ipswich laced up at Coventry.

10 C Cup: Leeds win opener at Darlo. Foster is out of England contention with a knock. Shearer continues to be talk of the Toon.

11 U-21s: England draw in Groningen ahead of big Dutch game while Irish lose in Portugal. C Cup: Plenty of goals – QPR, Preston and Reading five each, foursomes for Millwall, Swindon, Tranmere, Peterborough – even Norwich (Holt hat trick) at Yeovil! But Saturday's seven-up boys Colchester lose at home to Orient. Bigger names crash, too, with Derby beaten by Rotherham and Port Vale overcoming Sheff U. Sven's lads also exit courtesy of visiting Doncaster. Wickham, 16, gets two for Ipswich who need pens to oust Shrews – mercifully the only tie thus decided.

12 Defoe double – Dutch draw, work remains in progress towards WC finals. In that same competition four goals in Scots game – sadly all scored by Norway. Croatia keeps in touch with win in Belarus. Friendly defeat for Wales in Montenegro, the Republic by the Aussies in Dublin and Israel manages a draw in N Ireland. U-21s: Welsh in fine win over Hungary. Bendtner swaps shirt 26 for 52 and faces a likely £10,000 fine over replica sales. C Cup: Forest easy over Bradford.

13 O'Leary is not for Newcastle. Daily Telegraph says of 595 PL players only 41.7 percent are English with 68 different nationalities represented. Spurs Bentley is on drink driving charge.

14 Norwich fire Gunn. Sven signs Schmeichel from Man City for record club fee. Everton are holding on to Lescott.

15 PL opens with six away wins and Arsenal's sensational six-gun salvo at Goodison Park, to equal the competition's best away day opening margin and Everton's worst start. Moneybags Man C actually win on travel at Blackburn (Adebayor paying off some of transfer with a stunner) – heralding a new era at Eastlands? Grey day for Hull's Brown at Chelsea Blues who need a Drogba fluke to save Ancelotti's red face. Stoke hand new boys Burnley (only three were alive in 1976) a reminder of top flight fare and Hammers dictate terms at promoted Wolves, too. Bent straightens out Sunderland at Bolton. Zamora's rear end deflection gives Fulham the edge at Portsmouth. Villa booed off as Wigan lifts the three points (Rodallega fine volley as well). FLC: No Hawk-Eye, just blind indifference to using technology as Palace denied a goal in single goal defeat at Bristol C. Ameobi hits his first ever treble to raise spirits on up-for-sale Newcastle. Two games played but only Coventry, winners at Barnsley, have maximum points! F1: Million pound man Lambert makes in three goals in three games (one for Bristol R) but Saints taken out at Huddersfield. Norwich manage a draw at Exeter, Tranmere scores four. F2: Burton get into the swing of it now with five goals against Morecambe, but Torquay on the receiving end of Daggers high five. Rochdale's ten have sucker punch pen in injury time to beat Shots. Crewe rows in with four at Grimsby, so do Notts. Windass fluffs Darlo pen. SPL: Rangers (home), Celtic (away) make predictable winning starts. SL: Even Livi is in action and ten-man Brechin beats Cowden. BSP: Chester play, too, but chucks two goal lead to let Cambridge in. Gateshead make Luton go for the points.

16 Spurs defenders become goal scoring winners over disappointing Liverpool. Rooney's goal for Man U condemns third promotion team Birmingham to weekend defeat. Palace blunder-whistler Shoebridge is dropped for next game and Warnock gets an apology from ref supreme Hackett – but no replay.

17 Now Hackett wants Hawk-Eye on goal-line! Norwich is lining up a replacement for departed Gunn. SPL: Cadamarteri double on debut sparks Dundee U over Hearts.

18 Ch Lge: Lucky Arsenal but they still beat Celtic at Parkhead. PL: Chelsea give Sunderland a goal start and win – Lampard's 132nd goal equalling Jimmy Greaves, is their fifth highest marksman. Wolves win the W formation at Wigan. Benitez may face rap over ref comment. Injured Ashbee seeks surgery in USA to save career. FLC: Palace shake off City nightmare to win at Ipswich, Chopra hat-trick sends Cardiff top as Coventry only draws. F1: New Norwich boss Paul Lambert (ex-Colchester of 7-1 fame!) watches as Canaries lose to Brentford's Bees. But there is another 7-1 as Huddersfield takes it out on Brighton. Soton remains on a loser at Swindon. F2: Another five for Daggers (Benson foursome) to go ahead as Shrews wilt. Torquay wins promoted-teams battle at Burton. BSP: Four-play for AFC Dons, Mansfield and leaders Oxford. Altrincham go second. Alba: Partick gets five at Forfar!

19 Blake's heaven of a priceless goal for Burnley and Jensen's pen save from Carrick sends Man U into defeat. Liverpool including a Bolt-like effort from Gerrard leads foursome rout of Stoke. Birmingham learns quickly but has to thank James for gifting late pen as Pompey has takeover worries. Fame is the Spur as Tottenham hit Hull for five

Arsenal's Thomas Vermaelen scores his team's second goal in the 6-1 thrashing of Everton in the opening-day fixture at Goodison Park. (PA Photos)

(Defoe three) to head affairs. Lescott trains alone at Everton. Ch Lge: Lyon five shakes Anderlecht. FLC: Ameobi can't stop scoring, Toon can't stop winning, but Duff goes to Fulham for £4m. F2: Crisis for Sven? – Notts lose at Chesterfield.

20   E Lge: Everton on song sinking Sigma Olomouc, Fulham (Johnson injury) ease against Amkar, but Villa quickly concedes in 16 seconds to Rapid, Hearts hit for four in Zagreb and St Pat's ship three to Steaua. Bankers hold the purse strings at Liverpool. Even the hacks are homing in on Wenger's prediction of a European League.

21   Defoe defended by Redknapp over alleged police harassment. Terry breaks with agent. Man C expects to sign Lescott. Moat edging nearer Toon takeover. F1: Millwall day out at Southend yields a point.

22   Diaby's first double on his 100th Gunners outing shoots Arsenal to the top in four-play win over cellar dwellers Pompey. Centurion Rooney makes it 100, 101 and even Owen scores in Man U goals in a five star whitewash of Wigan – their worst PL result. Not so dozy Jozy Altidore – ex-swine flu victim – sets up Algerian Kamel Ghilas to give pig sick Trotters the hump at Hull. Adebayor continues to bale out wasteful Man C in beating Wolves. Blackburn's 1000th top flight game but they fail to keep up with the two-goal Sunderland Jones boy. First goalless PL game of the season at Birmingham, but visit of Stoke draws only 21,604, eight thousand short of capacity. FLC: Toon tramples Palace – Warnock unhappy with ref again. Four for Sheff W – their first win. Reading's worst start in 12 years. £1m Gallagher in action for Leicester but Fryatt nets the points. F1: Charlton, Leeds only 100 percent teams. Baker three in Stockport's best goal in seven win at nine-man Brighton. New boss Lambert sees Norwich get five goals. Saints knock another pt off deficit. Stewart hits career 200th goal for Exeter win at Carlisle. F2: Notts put Daggers in their place (second). No-score Bradford get odd goal in nine win at Cheltenham. Stunned Shots hit by sudden death of Chairman John McGinty, 72, beat Accrington. First win for Grimsby. SPL: Celtic five against St J, with £3m Fortune twice on the score-sheet. SL: No 100 percent teams after only three matches. BSP: Chester holds up Luton. Gateshead wins at Crawley. Oxford, Mansfield are first and second. New boys AFC Dons go fourth.

23   Spurs – equalling best ever start 1960-61 – winners at West Ham – Cole scoring and gifting a leveller, Chelsea at Fulham in Thames-side derby go above Arsenal and Burnley make it more misery for Everton with an Elliott goal. FLC: Cardiff recaptures top spot with threesome against Bristol C. F2: Rochdale old-boy Le Fondre does in old mates for Rotherham. SPL: Lucky Gers as Boyd comes off the bench to score first-touch controversial pen for ten-man Rangers at Hearts. Calum Davenport stabbed Saturday morning along with his mother may never play again.

24   Flaky Liverpool beaten at Anfield by Villa. Sol Campbell joins the Sven revolution at Notts. Storrie still hopes for Pompey takeover. Man City expects to land Lescott at last for £24m and get Sylvinho for free from Barca. C Cup: Sunderland put Norwich in their place. Toon takeover delayed.

25   Serious violence at West Ham, before, during and after win over Millwall. Other C Cup events see Swansea have three sent off, two injured and yet game not abandoned in Scunthorpe win: Forest give Boro goal start and win. Wolves need shoot-out to beat Swindon. Women's Euro: England lose to Italy. CIS Cup: Ross knocks out Hamilton. Ch Lge: Lyon's Lopez ends Anderlecht interest with hat trick. BSP: Tamworth surprise Wrexham.

26   Ch Lge: Eduardo accused of diving as Celtic bow out at Arsenal. C Cup: Blackpool four-play shakes Wigan, Spurs get five at Donny, Newcastle has to fight back to beat Huddersfield. Sulaiman Al Fahim, the man from Dubai – once involved with Man C – is takeover winner at Portsmouth. CIS Cup: St J get six at Arbroath.

27   Ch Lge draw: Brits avoid each other – Chelsea may have toughest draw in Porto group. E Cup: Villa (missed pen), Fulham and Hearts win but go out, Everton draw is enough. St Pat's are also victims. Dinamo Bucharest fans who invaded pitch at home – club given 3-0 deficit, win in Liberec after shoot-out! Is this punishment? Platini threatening PL clubs over debts. Hammers nail £6m Alessandro Diamanti. Villa gets Dunne from Man C.

28   UEFA charges Eduardo over dive to Wenger fury. Daily Telegraph reveals Spurs (!) as biggest spenders in last five years – £301m. Shevy leaves the Bridge at last free to Dynamo Kiev. Messi and other midget marvels help Barca win the Super Cup against Shakhtar. Millwall draws again.

29   Table-topping Chelsea "Pensioners" average age 29 years 291 days hit three in seven minutes either side of the break to beat Burnley. Own goal Diaby day disaster heads it to Man Utd after Rooney pen, but Wenger wobbly over disallowed goal and sent to stands. Spurs dig deep with sub Crouch and last minute Lennon snatching it over Birmingham but Modric fracture injury. Gerrard – naturally – is Liver good to edge out ten-man Bolton. Goal-shy Kitson splits the verdict for Stoke over Sunderland. Hull gets a point at Wolves thanks to Turner goal-line save. Blackburn and Hammers go quietly goalless. FLC: Tyson goal and corner flag wave starts a riot as Forest just holds on to beat the Rams. Boro concede first goals and lose out to Bristol C. Reading's win at Barnsley signals end of Simon Davey's reign there. Ten-man Preston holds Ipswich. Donny surprise Cardiff. Sub Cotterill's pen nabs a point against Baggies for Sheff U. F1: Charlton four-play at Tranmere. Saints unhappy as Stockport pen snatches two points from them. Leeds seven League and Cup wins equals 1973 start. Easter comes early at Exeter – hits two in six minutes for MK Dons. F2: Injury-time winner floors Notts at Barnet. One-time shelf-stacker Hanson wraps it up for Bradford against Torquay. Grimsby late wobbly, too, with two sent off in time added on as Shots win. Three in eleven mins and Burton have to hang on against Northampton. Daggers back on top. SPL: Rangers have Hamilton nailed at the bottom. SL: Forfar five (Ross Campbell 3) and clear lead in Div 3, away day win for Raith at Dunfermline to lead Div 1 but Partick high five over Morton. Alloa is ahead on goal difference from Stirling in Div 2. BSP: AFC Dons og is Oxford winner. Real field seven newcomers, Ronaldo pen and just edge La Coruna. Inter flay AC in Milan derby by four goals. Ex-Real Robben two for Bayern after £22m move. FA Cup: Enfield 1893 up-to-date with seven goals and seven different scorers.

30   Adebayor pays off more of his transfer with the Man C goal at rock-bottom Pompey. Everton leave it to a late pen in pen-in Wigan. Out of sorts Villa needs og start to help beat Fulham. SPL: Celtic benefit from an alleged dive beating ten-man Hibs. St J levels late to thwart Hearts.

31   Activity in the market place as window closing in. FLC: Guthrie is winner for top team Toon over Leicester. Posh held by Palace. Wenger receives apology for banishment from ref supremo. Women's Euro: Draw for England against Sweden ensures progress. BSP: Tubbs trio lifts Salisbury, but Oxford held by FGR, Mansfield by Kettering. AFC Dons go third after win at Grays.

SEPTEMBER

Spending down ... England sees off Croatia ... Pompey in crisis ... Another Giggs milestone.

1   Quiet draw of window curtains – Dunne, Man City – Villa £6m; Johnny Heitinga, Real – Everton £6m; Collins, West Ham – Villa £5m; Mike Williamson, Watford – Pompey £3m; Collins, Sunderland – Stoke £2.75m head the list as total spending is £100m down on previous year. Eduardo gets two-game ban for the dive. Benitez may face touchline ban. E.ON will cut off FA sponsorship. JPT: Chesterfield gets five at Burton. BSP: Luton scores three against Crawley.

2   Peter Jackson out at Lincoln, Aidy Boothroyd in at Colchester.

3   Chelsea banned from signing players until January 2011 after alleged snatching of Gael Kakuta from Lens in 2007. Arsenal is unhappy over Eduardo ban. Forest and Derby charged. Women's Euro: England beat Finns to reach semis.

4   Foreigners to blame for diving – says Terry ahead of Slovenia match. Burley shrugs off underlying Scots worry. Worthington is upbeat for Polish venture. Republic aims to put Aussie rout behind them in Cyprus. England U-21s win in Macedonia, Wales beats Italy but N.Ireland loses to Czechs. Maradona's Argy job is on the line as Brazil waits. Arnesen may be first casualty at the Bridge over ban. F1: Barnard threesome as Shrimpers net Orient. F2: Morecambe chucks three goal lead in Rochdale draw. Barnet give Northampton goal start and win.

5   WC: Suddenly Scots are in with a chance after beating Macedonia as Norway drop a point against Iceland. Northern Ireland have excellent draw in Poland. Republic are so 40-goal Keane in Cyprus. Ten-man Croatia edge Belarus, Ukraine hits five against Andorra. Elsewhere Portugal is held to a draw in Denmark so Sweden goes above them. Spain wacks Belgium for five and misses a pen. Romania holds up France who has Ribery on bench. AC Milan's Kaladze's two ogs give it to Italy! Ghana qualifies for finals. Brazil sees off Maradona's Argentina. Friendlies: England need "diver" Rooney's pen to set off win over Slovenia. Germany beat South Africa and Holland ease against Japan. F1: Saints unable to beat ten-man Colchester. Six out of six for Charlton and Leeds the only two 100 percent teams in the FL and United's start is better than 1973 and 1969's 13 home wins in a row. F2: Port Vale four play hits ten-man Grimsby. Burton holds Notts. Shots rally to hit two and level late with Hereford. Cash-crisis Accrington wins at Bury. Is Mark Robins on the way from Rotherham to Barnsley? Vase: Seven of the worst caning for debutants Canning. BSP: Cambridge seven, too, against FGR, Rushden six at ten-man Barrow. Claridge, 43, plays for beaten Weymouth.

6   Euro Women: England beats Holland in extra time to reach final. Alba: Annan, Inverness, Ross and Dundee reach semis.

7   Bilic mind games do not distract England. Buoyant Burley and Butcher as Scots prepare for Dutch crunch. Trapattoni challenges Republic's beyond the fringe men. Tough one for Wales as the Russia is calling. Irish needs win over Slovakia to aid hopes. Man U to take stern steps against Le Havre claim over Paul Pogba. Sheff U's Kenny gets nine-month ban for drug failure. Benitez whines over the Liverpool whiners. Germany will face England Women in Euro final. WAG Cheryl Cole may buy Toon. Brian Kidd is Man C technical director-manager.

8   One goal enough for Republic to see off South Africa. U-21s: England draws in Greece, but Northern Ireland left cold as Iceland hits them for six. BSP: Luton beaten at Oxford – 10,613 present! Tamworth moves up to fifth place. Now Fiorentina complain about a Man U signing, Man C get one, too, from Rennes. Leeds calls for points to be deducted on "snatchers."

9   WC: Passage to South Africa – Capello's high five-star outfit sees off Croatia. But Scots wilt as Dutch make it eight out of eight. Northern Ireland fails in front of goal and face daunting task in Prague. Russians see off Wales. Spain qualifies for the finals. Now Paraguay beats Argentina to reach South Africa. Goals galore as Israel, Czechs get seven each. Poland sacks Beenhakker. U-21s Republic draws in Estonia. Tony Pulis leaves Thais for Stoke No.2. Robins becomes a Tyke.

10   FA relief as England qualifies. England Ladies bravely battle but well beaten by Germany. Juande Ramos replaces Zico at CSKA Moscow.

11   Mystery over Tevez transfer figure – it could have been £47m! More good news: Capello is cleared on Italian tax probe. F1: Higgs saves pen and Leeds record at Southend. F2: Stanley puts misery on Darlo.

12   Adebayor stamps his authority but also plants a foot on Van Persie as five-in-a-row Man C (best for 23 years) is becoming a force. Drogba's leveller at Stoke is the PL's 100th of the season, the Malouda winner in the 95th min of a 103 min game. Defoe under 50 secs but Spurs see the Man U Reds win despite Scholes seeing a red of his own. Rovers ravage Wolves. £66m Sunderland Black Cats paw almost toothless Tigers. Israeli Benayoun's hat-trick revives Liverpool 1990 title reminder of Ronnie Rosenthal treble as Burnley bemoan soft goal surrender. Cahill confirms Pompey's worst start to a season as Bolton win. Rodallega rebound for Wigan robs Green and

Hammers of a point. FLC: Sunny day for Scunny at Selhurst as four goals bring Palace gloom. Foxy bingo as Fryatt double for Leicester – his 50th City goal – edges Blackpool for first time in 43 years. Top men WBA owe it to switch Cech to plunder Pilgrims. Keane is in crisis at Ipswich after they are beaten at Boro. F1: Grand draw for Soton at Charlton but it's win they need. Ageing Forster, 36, hits two goals for Brighton at Carlisle. Boss Barnes comes under fire at Tranmere. Ten-man Yeovil manage a point. F2: Boertien's 200th League game rescues Burton at Bradford. Bournemouth is top of the pile under young boss Howe, 31. Hughes scores hat-trick for Notts in another five goal effort. Hayles, 37, hits winner for Cheltenham. SPL: Celtic home to Dundee U, ten-man Rangers away to Motherwell, are both held. SL: Ross take clean lead in Div 1; Alloa beat Stirling in top of the table clash in Div 2; Annan clip leaders Forfar in Div 3 but game off as motorway fire traps Stranraer on way to Berwick. BSP: Oxford seven points clear after win at Wrexham in ten-a-side. FA Cup: goals galore – sixes for Sutton Coldfield, Rugby, Spennymoor, Dartford. Kendal hit nine – Alex Taylor and Carl Osman trebles. Ryan O'Toole all four for Uxbridge. Lingfield and Badshot Lea share eight goals.

13   Villa leaves it late to win un-pretty Birmingham derby at City. Fulham comes from behind to heap more misery on Everton and Moyes is unhappy. FLC: Toon gets ahead at Cardiff and stay there. SPL: Hamilton gets its first win against ten-finishing Hibs.

14   Eduardo ban is scrubbed. PL to bale out any clubs in crisis and will limit squads to 25 senior players of whom just 17 can be over 21 years of age and not "local talent" – that is three years trained at a home club – for 2010-11. Liverpool is to benefit from new bank sponsorship. Man C pleads for Adebayor. All go for Michael Ngoo as the 16 year old goes from Southend to Liverpool in a likely £250k deal.

15   Ch Lge: Scholes seals Man U win at Besiktas, but subbed Rooney throws a wobbly. Anelka does the Drogba bit – and scores winner against Porto. Ronaldo gets a couple of Real's five. FLC: Baggies carry on at the top via Donny. Boro also scores three at Sheff W, but Preston suffers three of their own at Scunny. Ipswich is still seeking victory after another draw. Hearts move away from the lower reaches against Killie.

16   Ch Lge: The Eduardo show: he gives away a goal before "kneeing" the winner at Standard. Flying Kuyt brings Debrecen down to earth for Liverpool. Barca held at Inter. FLC: Blackpool beach Toon at last, but ten-man Cardiff make Reading groan. The Brady bunch will quit Birmingham after takeover. PL donates £1m to 68 BSP clubs after loss of Setanta cash.

17   Three-match ban for Adebayor as Fabregas reveals it may have been a book of stamps after all! E Lge: Fringe benefits of a draw for Fulham at CSKA Sofia. Four goals for struggling Everton is a Greek tragedy for AEK. Celtic surprised by Hapoel. Extra officials behind goals – jury is out after twelve group experiments in E Lge. Mourinho says that Italy and Spain are the new PL!

18   War of words explodes ahead of Mancunian derby. Giggs with 811 outings, 149 goals – 99 in PL – awaits his 30th such encounter. Villa axes Reo-Coker. FLC: United wins Sheffield derby, odd goal in five after three goal lead. Maradona owes the Italian tax man.

19   Batttered face, but Torres' brace edges out plucky Hammers for Liverpool. Vermaelen (two) is now Arsenal's top-scorer with four overall as four-play on the day wrecks Wigan – only two Englishmen start, both Latics. Pompey free-fall continues – six of the worst – as Villa's two take care of them. Burnley's Portsmouth reject Nugent is at the double to end Sunderland hopes of a point. Bolton needs a pen to write a draw down with Stoke. Hull – one win in last 14 at home – succumbs to Brum. FLC: High five Baggies bury Boro at the Riverside, home reject Brunt starring, too. Palace of varieties: now they beat Derby. Toon is back on the goal standard. Loanee Simpson gives Cardiff ache for QPR. Watford, Leicester share six goals, so do Ipswich with Donny as Keane still seeks to end Tractor Boys worst start for 45 years. F1: Saints are praised for two pens and first win. Leeds is clear ahead in 15th home win in succession. First home wins for Stockport, Oldham. Norwich just prevents another Charlton win. F2: Erratic Notts fail to wise up at Morecambe in Campbell bow. Bournemouth plough on at Darlo's expense. Chesterfield hit four against Macc. SPL: Killie hold Rangers in ten-a-side. SL: Ross, Stirling (leapfrogging Alloa) and Forfar are divisional leaders. BSP: Oxford is still setting the pace, Stevenage, Tamworth in pursuit as top five all win. Spain: Messi celebrates new contract with two for Barca against Atletico Madrid. FIFA is to probe 15 PL transfers.

20   Derby day drama at Old Trafford: record seven goals (all British!), a City leveller in the 90th minute and Owen United's winner in the 96th! Hughes rage over ref Atkinson's and fourth-man Wiley's signal of four added mins in a time warp but Sir Alex having said it should have been six or seven-nil, was happy with three points. Even so Chelsea stays ahead of the game taking three off Spurs who claimed a pen. Saha so good as his double lifts Everton over Blackburn. Wolves edge Fulham to move up, too. PL weekend goal haul is 34, only two fewer than last week. SPL: Celtic regains leadership but needs third min of injury time to take out Hearts. JM sent to stands as Inter climbs to third.

21   Thanksgiving service for Sir Bobby Robson. Bellamy for whacking a pitch invader, Neville goading away fans, may face suspensions. Man U off the hook over Fiorentina youngster. Spurs injury list continues to grow. Diouf faces racist abuse charge. Reo-Coker is back in the Villa fold.

22   C Cup: Posh takes the shine off Toon. Liverpool attracts 38,168 to Leeds and leave all Ngoo with a win. Blackpool pushes Stoke to the wire (96th min!) for a best of seven goals success. Young Gunners two is too good for Baggies. Pompey wins at Carlisle. Barnsley surprise Burnley. Scunny need extra time to overturn Port Vale, as do Bolton against the Hammers. Early strikes help Sunderland land the Brummies. Rovers return from Forest with victory. CIS Cup: Dundee carries SL flag into quarter-finals at Dons expense. BSP: Oxford's first defeat at Mansfield, but Stevenage held by Grays, Tamworth at Altrincham, so Kettering's win over Barrow shoots them third. Luton is well beaten at Wrexham. The great escape for Bellamy and Neville as FA also dismisses action on a crowd coin incident. Has Sol quit Notts already?

23   C Cup: second strings have plenty of bow shots with ten-man Man U targeting Wolves, Chelsea benefiting from Cole J return and Crouch leading Spurs to a five-star show at Preston with a hat-trick. Man C needs extra time to overcome Fulham and an early Villa strike puts Cardiff out of action. Everton hits another foursome at leaky Hull. CIS Cup: Celtic easily at Falkirk, Rangers just at QofS and Hearts pen is the Dunfermline downfall. Carlos Yeung takes over at Birmingham. Bryan Robson is the Thailand coach. Wenger issues warning over Under-18 transfer ban – six of their C Cup squad would have been ineligible!

24   Pompey's Hart faces crisis. Wenger is to carry on managing. Government targets FA. Jagielka threatened with knife and robbed at home.

25   Pompey's CEO Storrie on brink of quitting. Van Persie admits to "failure to stand up." UEFA will investigate 40 suspect cup matches and FK Pobeda from Macedonia already banned eight years for match-fixing. Eight goals as Stanley hits Crewe for five of them.

26   Chelsea's run (23 unbeaten) ends in Cech mate given to Wigan gk sees red and the Latics record their first win over the big four in 35 attempts, despite Drogba's 100th goal. Man U go top as Giggs comes on in 813th outing to inspire win at Stoke, O'Shea scoring on his 350th appearance. Spurs marksman is Keane as four-goal mustard in

Crouch-absent five goals over Burnley. Torres hits scintillating form with hat-trick in six of the best for Liverpool rout over poor Hull the Anfield team's 22 goals best since 1895-96. Mannone heroics and a non-diving performance and goal from Van Persie keeps Arsenal flowing at Fulham. Ten-man Blackburn gives Villa an early goal – Agbonlahor naturally – and achieves the points. The "Yeung" ones start at Birmingham by losing to Bolton as the Sullivan-Brady era ends after 17 years. Pompey now seven reverse on the trot after Everton visit. FLC: Sir Bobby Robson day at Ipswich as the Toon raiders plunder four goals and make the Tractor Boys worst start in 73 years. Preston is first winner at Leicester in a year. QPR make it five goals and misery for Barnsley who last won there January 1950 – 5-0! There is joy for Warnock and Palace after the win at West Bromwich. Esajas wings it for the Owls over the Bluebirds and nine Swans still blunt the Blades. Donny's nine also get a point at Scunny. F1: MK Dons unhappy with late Leeds winner. Saints salvage a point at Carlisle. It's a first home win for the Orient. Brentford goes seven without a win and Norwich fans upset by goalie's red. F2: Best ever start for Bournemouth. Ronnie Moore back at Rotherham helm watches them win. No boss Northampton five defeats in a row. Darlo scrape a point by boss man Todd goes. Forty yard trajectory seals Shots four goal win over Cheltenham. SPL: Season over? Celtic open four pt gap as Rangers go 293 mins without a goal in draw with Dons. Ten-man Dundee U wins at St Johnstone. SL: Dundee beats Ross, so QofS go top in Div 1. Stirling three pts clear in Div 2 and Berwick's second win in a week leave them four ahead in Div 3. BSP: Luton's ten-men are odd goal in seven winners at Cambridge. Oxford is still in pole position at Gateshead. FA Cup: Odd spot 1: 20 red cards: PL 2, FL 12, SPL 1, SL 2, BSP 3. Odd spot 2: Ref Singh limps off for second time this season. FA Cup: Bad luck Badshot Lea as ten-goal Ashford Town (Middx) hit its best competition score. FIFA World U-20: Uruguay 1 England 0. Spain: Real and Barca still 100 percent. Italy: JM woe as Sampdoria beat them to go top.

27   Black Cats paw it over the Wolves five times on McCarthy's return as PL weekend goals tally 33. FLC: Forest's minimal fire extinguishes Plymouth. BSP: The North Wales derby leaves Wrexham and Chester goalless. Anfield's Saudi link emerges again. Millwall and West Ham face FA charges. Notts Trust men revealed.

28   Another Hammer blow as Tevez is two-goal star for Man C. McAllister is possible Pompey No.2. Arsenal expects to collect big when Highbury Square money rolls in.

29   Ch Lge: Fiorentina flourish finishes Liverpool off early and Rafa rages. Late strikes are enough for Arsenal over Olympiakos. Rangers wiped out by Sevilla's second-half swamp. FLC: Chopra foursome in Cardiff's six-goal thrashing of Derby. Ipswich chucks a two-goal lead to share six goals at Sheff U so Plymouth winners at Peterborough get off the bottom. Baggies ambushed at Barnsley. Lowest Riverside gate of 18,577 sees another Boro reverse as Leicester prevails. Reading surprises at Preston. F1: Leeds held up by Carlisle, Charlton dumped at Colchester. Saints are beaten by Bristol R who consolidate third place. F2: Hereford beats Bournemouth as Rochdale benefits at Darlo, Rotherham slip up at lowly Northampton and Daggers are blunted at Barnet. Rodgers is a three-some hero for Notts at Lincoln. FL is to end Coca Cola association. BSP: Stevenage edges Luton before Hatters gate of 8,223. World U-20s and England suffering from Nile delta bug lets in four against Ghana!

30   Ch Lge: Man U relies on Giggs' 150th strike to start to keep Wolfsburg at bay. Out of sorts Chelsea still manage an Anelka winner in Nicosia. Milan is surprised by Zurich, but Real and a two-goal Ronaldo effort defeats Marseille. FLC: QPR poses Newcastle with drawing question. Pompey players await pay.

OCTOBER
WC 2018 bid worries ... Centuries for Given, Kilbane .... Beach ball fiasco ... Chelsea looking good.

1   E Lge: Everton edges it away to BATE, Fulham at home to Basle, but Celtic held at Parkhead by Rapid. Adebayor fined £25,000 and two-match ban. Four Accrington and one Bury player lose betting appeal. Sky Sports Victory Shield starts with Scots winning in Northern Ireland.

2   Keegan awarded £2m in damages over Newcastle signing Gonzalez without his say so. Is Redknapp on way back to Pompey as brothers of a Saudi family stump up some rescue dosh? Ancelotti: there is no crisis at Chelsea. Liverpool ponders poor Ch Lge performance. Bye, bye England U-20s after draw with Uzbekistan.

3   Foster gaffe then ninety-two min og leveller by the younger Ferdinand but Sir Alex wants more time as both sides blow the whistle on ref Wiley, pushing 50 – the Knight's best pal two weeks ago – who wrongly red cards ex- Man U Richardson to thwart Sunderland. Pompey gains victory at last after eight games and 720 mins in its worst start in 79 years, thanks to a French-Algerian on loan from a Portuguese club and stoic James who is no Jessie in goal. All square at Bolton as Spurs share four goals. Hull's first of the season downs Wigan. One-time Liverpool mascot Fletcher helps Burnley to become first PL newcomers to win initial four home games and best such in top flight since 1982-83. FLC: Newcastle robbed of plain pen by ref Salisbury so Bristol C gets a goalless draw and PNE and WBA do the same. Bug-hit Watford suffers Cardiff surge. Palace fires on four cylinders. Ipswich loses again. Reading's home curse added to by old boy Lita for Boro. Nine man QPR sunk by Swans to delight of ex-Rangers boss Sousa. F1: Still maroon Leeds held by Charlton in first re-match for Civer. Red letter day for Saints with four goal lift off and in the black for points at last. Norwich hits five goals. McGleish scores against Wycombe, his third ex-club to suffer thus as Orient win. Tranmere boss Barnes sees poorest result for five years as Henry hat trick sparks five-goal Millwall. F2: Bournemouth draws to Rotherham closes gap after winning at Crewe. Chris Sutton gets a boss-debut win for Lincoln over Shots. Seventh draw in eight games for Morecambe. SPL: St Mirren achieves first League win at new ground to beat Hearts. St J off the bottom beating Hamilton. Hibs second for the time being in draw with Dundee U. SL: With Alba cup on Sunday and high winds postponing matches, Partick are new leaders in Div 1 and Albion in Div 3 as Berwick lose at home to Forfar. Highland League sensation: Fort William – one pt only last season – wins a match, first away since 2006-07! BSP: Boss-seeking Luton edges Tamworth. Oxford held at Barrow so Kettering cut its lead against Eastbourne. Trophy: Born-again Halifax win best of seven score at Trafford. Radcliffe six goals, doubles Mickleover score. Vase: Brislington eight, Cambridge Regional College seven and six goals each for Welton, Wimborne and Daisy Hill. Barca's one goal is enough, Inter is back on top and Leverkusen remains unbeaten, but Bordeaux suffer first defeat since March so Lyon regains leadership.

4   Perfect celebration for Wenger as Arsenal's longest serving 13-year manager after Rovers lead twice and ship six, but Sam A is unhappy about a pen not given – also eight different scorers. Old boy Henry was in attendance. Chelsea wears down Liverpool in the second half to regain leadership. Everton and Stoke share two goals – West Ham and Fulham four, too, after old-man Cottagers surrender late leveller. Redknapp waves away offshore account rumours. It's an Internet game only for England v Ukraine. SPL: Rangers keep unbeaten tag with two early goals to hold off Celtic comeback. Alba semis: Dundee take three off Annan, Inverness CT edges Ross near the break. Real minus Ronaldo is beaten. No goals again for slipping Bayern.

5   Dunne shines for Villa against old Man C mates, Barry gets the bird in reverse, but Bellamy's 99th strike equals it all. Cracks at Liverpool – ownership and manager? FA ask question of Sir Alex. Eriksson denies the old England

WAG factor. Pompey: Ali Al-Faraj is latest owner. Mutu fine is suspended. Auld Firm ref admits to Celtic pen error. Defoe is on a speeding charge. Top of the table Bournemouth is in debt and only 13 fit players.

6   Napoli sacks Donadoni and seeks Zola power. Everton's Baxter is on drug suspicion, Villa's Osbourne on alleged robbery. Bullard scores on comeback game for Hull reserves. JPT: A third of ties decided by shoot-outs.

7   WC 2018 bid: clouds gathering from at least one-anti English source – Jack Warner. Portugal worried about qualifying for 2010 finals, Argentina faced with Maradona threatening to quit. Ex-Man U chairman Martin Edwards expresses concern over club's current debt. Mystery men behind several FL clubs are to be investigated. Coyle, 43, plays for Burnley reserves. Pompey appoints Avram Grant as DofF – Hart's job is safe. Steve Staunton is Darlo boss until the end of the season, so is Ian Sampson at Northampton.

8   Cannavaro drug bust over insect bite remedy! FA dismisses WC warning. Becks will return on loan to AC Milan. Briatore's future at QPR is in the balance. Hargreaves nears Man U return.

9   Iron fist in the iron glove – that's England's boss FC ahead of internet only Ukraine game. U-21s: England doubles Macedonia's three goals. Republic held by Georgia. F1: Now Saints win away at Southend! Barnes sacked by Tranmere, Taylor leaves Wycombe.

10   WC 2010: One over the eight is a game too far for England as flares from Ukraine descend, a Rio-Green foul up and the first gk red; Shevy only hits woodwork from the pen, but still it's a single goal local win. Fever pitch excitement as Republic snatches a draw from the jaws of victory against Italy who thus qualify; so it's play-off time for the wearing of the green. Wails for Wales in Finland but Bellamy's 17th goal is fifth in country ranking. Klose's 50th goal helps ten-man Germany to get through as Hiddink and Co head Russia for the lottery, too. Danes clinch final spot after edging Swedes. Serbia's five against Romania lift them to S.Africa, but five for France is only for play-offs. Arsenal's Senderos scores twice for Swiss. Super sub Drogba hits 39th goal in 57 Ivory Coast games to see them through. Argies scrape a win over Peru, Forlan last gasp pen gives Uruguay win in Ecuador. NZ gets a draw in Bahrain. U-21s: Wales beat Bosnia, Scots edge Belarus late on. Sir Alex says sorry to Wiley. F1: Charlton creep pt nearer inactive Leeds as Oldham draws. Rhodes heads eight-min treble in Huddersfield foursome. F2: Daggers move nearer to beaten Bournemouth after Darlo lose again. Four goals scored by Accrington. Card sharp ref Bratt takes tally to 22 yellows in three games and adds a wrong red in Shrews v Port Vale. SL Div 1: Jocky Scott's Dees cut the Thistle down, so Q of S goes top. Div 2: Stirling held, but still lead. Div 3: Albion stay ahead. BSP: Five goals Oxford maintain nine-pt advantage. AFC Dons are also five hitters. FA Cup: Chelmsford attracts 1830 to Dartford and register four goals. Craig Henney is three-timer for lowly Aylesbury in Bucks derby edging Chesham. Adam Webster is four score man as Hinckley Knitters sew up Cambridge City. Northwich Mark Danks hits three (five last round, too).

11   Internet viewers listed as half a million. Notts held and manager McParland is booed despite climb to fifth place in F2. England U-19s win game two against Slovenia.

12   Now Sir Alex pens an apology. Injuries hit England squad. More 2018 fears. McParland axed by the Eriksson regime. More misery for Tranmere, they are beaten by Stockport. Wise is in at Chalfont! Cannavaro cleared.

13   Eriksson tempted by North Korea offer. Given and Kilbane are on brink of their 100th Republic caps. Benitez escapes touchline ban. Waddock quits Shots for Wycombe. U21s: Republic snatch draw with Swiss, Northern Ireland lose to Iceland. Peterhead is off bottom of Div 2, Livingston still climbing in Div 3. World U-20s: Ghana to meet Brazil in final.

14   WC 2010: Crouch early and late as three-goal England ease past Belarus and sub Becks gets man of the match! Ukraine celebrates edging out Croatia from play-offs with six goals against Andorra. Sweden fails to reach play-offs as Portuguese take the runners-up spot. Swiss held by Israel but qualify and it's Greece for the play-offs. Slovakia and Slovenia both win away but finish in that order. Northern Ireland ends programme with draw in Czech Republic. Already there but Germans need last gasp for draw with Finns. Wales finish with a win in Liechtenstein. Spain's perfect ten as five goals underline it in Bosnia the surprise runners-up. Given and Kilbane become century makers as the Republic draws with Montenegro. There are hat-tricks in this group for Berbatov (Bulgaria) and Gilardino (Italy). Argentina just edge nine-man Uruguay to qualify, their hosts having to play-off with Costa Rica now. U-21s: Perfect three out of three for England as Slovakia is beaten. SL: Dundee chucks a two-goal lead to draw at Ayr. Clyde surprises Arbroath in Div 2. Sven is not for North Korea. Aldershot appoints Jason Dodd as caretaker-manager.

15   Speculation rises whether Crouch and Owen will not make South Africa. Round-up of other qualifiers sees USA, Mexico and Honduras as definitely through. Becks may be England's only hope for WC 2018 bid. Birmingham promised more money for players by new owners. Sky Sports Victory Shield sees England edge Wales.

16   Maradona faces ban following after-match burst of obscenities. Macc wins at Cheltenham. World U-20s: Hungary takes third place on pens over Costa Rica, but winners are ten-man Ghana the first Africans to win it in another s-o with Brazil.

17   Battered Benitez bugged by Black Cats Bent's ballooning beach ball bouncer (courtesy of Reds fan!) as Liverpool makes worse start to a championship-chasing season since 1963-64. Literal head-banger (off post) Terry rages over defensive errors which cost headed goals points against Villa. Arsenal score-line flatters just a trifle against Birmingham. Not much to spare for Man U in clipping the Trotters – an own goal and a first for Valencia. Ten-man finishing Pompey (fifth home defeat poorest since Man U 1930-31 in top flight) back to losing ways as Spurs edge them despite Defoe dismissal. Beattie duo upsets Hammers for Stoke. Everton scratch late draw with ten-finishing Wolves. FLC: Four in a row Forest chop Newcastle. Loanee Seip does in his Argyle mates for Blackpool. Boro is beaten again at home. QPR racks up four goals against PNE. Boyd equals Posh consecutive appearance record with equalising goal at Bristol C. Only winless FL team Ipswich draw yet again. Rejected two-goal Thomas lifts the Baggies. F1: Caretaker Parry sees Tranmere take out ten-man Brighton. Charlton rallies to top it all. Saints on a roll and Connolly debut goal. Waddock scrapes a draw as Wycombe hold Colchester. Harris hat trick – his career eighth – as Millwall humble Stockport. F2: Darlo first win as Thomas scores on his bow. Veteran Warrington holds up Notts for Rotherham. Caretaker Dodd sees Shots lose home record to Bury. Top three: Bournemouth, Dagenham and Rochdale all win.

18   Blackburn wins the battle of the "only one local lad (ex-Claret Dunn) 43 years since last Lancs Bs affair" as Burnley early and late strikes are not enough. Man C's ten-men hold Wigan to a draw. Grimsby sack boss Newell. Raul's 711th record game for Real sees him score twice.

19   Fulham beats Hull and Bullard gets the bird on Tigers return. Leeds grateful for Norwich goalie gaffe to resume leadership. Are cracks appearing at Anfield? Sir Alex wants personal hearing. Eriksson for Sweden now is the latest. Windass retires. West Ham disputes FA charges.

20   Ch Lge: Lyon lay it in for Liverpool in injury time. AZ foils Arsenal win in a similar time frame. Rangers hammered by visiting Unirea in game of oggy, oggy, oggy! Rubin rub it in on Barca. FLC: Newcastle slips up at Scunny. Baggies are beaten by old boy Beattie for Swansea, so Cardiff and Boro both move closer, but victory does not save Southgate's job at the Riverside. Ipswich stunned again by Watford leveller at the death. Forest continues

winning ways. QPR hits Reading four times in ten-a-side match. Notts new owners are cleared and Eriksson is staying. Martin Allen is sent on gardening leave at Cheltenham after alleged night club incident. BSP: Luton and York, Stevenage and Wrexham involved in draws.

21   Ch Lge: Chelsea awesome foursome takes out Atletico and Lampard overtakes Jimmy Greaves scoring record. Man U just need one on CSKA's plastic. Pato pair pares it for AC Milan in Madrid seven-goal thriller despite Raul's Muller-equalling 66th Euro goal for Real. Bordeaux edges Bayern but squander two pens against nine-finishing opponents. Bullet-proof vests for German players in South Africa!

22   E Lge: Benfica stuff the Everton Toffees five times. Fulham held by late Roma strike. Celtic add to Scots misery by losing at home to Hamburg. Wenger on 60th birthday looks ahead to Arsenal presents this season. FA signing-up foreigners for WC bid. Pompey's Storrie in Customs allegations has club backing.

23   Watford's four is enough to swat the Owls with loan star Lansbury getting two. Barclays dig deeper for PL sponsorship – £82.25m over three years. South Africa who ditched manager Joel Santana, persuades Carlos Alberto Parreira to return.

24   Four in 16 s-h mins bring Rovers to their knees as Chelsea's high five puts them ahead of the pack; Lampard's 36th PL home goal against different opponents. Stoke – with 11th hour Simonsen standout – achieves its best result in the capital for 28 years with Whelan snatching win at injury-hit Spurs with four mins left and Harry "Totter" R failing to persuade Lennon to limp on for last 12 regardless. A Jensen gaffe then sees off as Burnley loses home record to Wigan, with hot-Rodallega getting a brace. Sunderland only starts playing when it's too late at Birmingham. Hull and Pompey share only third goalless draw of the PL season. Villa is first to reach 200th PL draw in local derby at Wolves. FLC: Toon leaves it to 92nd min to clip Donny. A Whittingham treble sparks Cardiff to best of seven goals at Sheff U. Coventry – no progs before game – no goals afterwards with WBA. Four goals scored again by rampant Rangers, despite Dickov's 100th career League goal for Derby. F1: Lions tame Leeds as last unbeaten record goes at Millwall, but crowd in bother. Saints make it five games with no loss as Connolly seals it with another late effort. First Kent derby for 28 years as Gills and Addicks draw. F2: Schmeichel pen save helps towards Notts win. Five players share Chesterfield goals. Port Vale is unbeaten in six. Spot kick saves ten Daggers from defeat. Cobblers nail three goals in 20 mns. Bournemouth pile more gloom on Grimsby. SPL: Rangers held by Hibs. SL: Dundee hit the front as Ross and the Jags share four goals. Stirling held by Clyde in Div 2. S Cup: South of Scotland woe as Annan run out of steam to Cove's ten and Stranraer's ten are shunted by Locos. FA Cup: Harry Arter scores three of Woking's five at Hendon. Stourbridge (133 years trying), Paulton both reach first round for first time. Eastleigh scores five to Dover's three to make it such a milestone treble.

25   Liverpool lives again! In a ten-a-side ending N'Gog cements unfit Torres strike to leave Man U all agog. Arsenal squanders two-goal lead at West Ham and draw against ten-finishing Hammers. Dodgy defending Man C does the same with visiting Fulham (Zamora miss of the season!) and Bolton almost achieve the same kind of draw with Everton, but manage a winning third goal via kidney-transplant Klasnic to celebrate first home win and boss man Megson's second anniversary. Blackburn warns of swine flu outbreak as a French game is off.

26   Gordon Strachan moves into Boro job. Leicester's away day brings success at Reading. Becks LA team is heading for title?

27   C Cup: Man U stiffs win at Barnsley, but crowd problems persist. Swine flu-ridden Rovers still manage to make Posh pig sick. Pompey's Piquionne is in peak form as team famed for lack of goals hits Stoke for four. Villa edges Sunderland in a s-o after Guzan pen save from Jones near the end. Spurs shake off recent disappointment to defeat Everton. F1: Leeds takes it out on Bristol R – four times. FA Cup replays: Eight games, 36 goals! Chester, Kidderminster, Eastbourne and Crawley are among casualties. CIS: Last SL team Dundee beaten by Rangers, St J surprises Dundee U and St Mirren ease over Motherwell. Wigan's Martinez in Spanish press interview hits out at Sir Alex clan of Allardyce and Bruce. Bolton is hit by flu. Newcastle is not for sale. Hans Backe is new Notts boss.

28   C Cup: A Liverpool of sorts loses to an Arsenal of similar strength. Chelsea gets four against Bolton, Man C hits high five over Scunthorpe. CIS: Celtic's ten are surprised by Hearts. Confusion arises at Hull over fate of chairman and manager. Southend faces administration and Accrington needs help, too. Pompey may lose TV money to pay for debts. Davenport pleads not guilty to assault on his sister.

29   Hull manager Brown may follow his chairman Duffen out of KC Stadium. Pompey's Hart was unaware of transfer ban. Sir Alex hits out at England friendly fixtures. Marlon King jailed for 18 months for assault and chucked out by Wigan. Gerrard faces another operation. PL worried over falling attendances. Martinez attempts to repair the damage. Sky Sports Victory Shield: Scots win in Wales.

30   Fryatt cooks Rangers home record as Leicester go second on goal difference. Late man Barnard is again the Shrimpers winner against the Gills. Conlon in another late show salvages a Grimsby point in Stanley draw. Pompey loan eases debt worry. Jewell may be next Hull boss if Brown fails.

31   Wheels come off for Liverpool firing on two less players in losing to vintage Fulham, despite injury-hit Torres becoming first in PL to hit ten. Arsenal's two in 50 secs ensures the North London derby with Spurs. Ding dong Dindane hat trick as Pompey continue four play at Wigan's expense. Chelsea make Bolton ten pay in the second half as four-play is repeated against them. Four goals shared between Stoke and Wolves (two down) plus ten-man Sunderland (26th such in PL with no win) and West Ham. Below par Man U finish off Blackburn (robbed of a goal) in s/h. Alexander, 38, hits his 69th successful spot kick in 900th overall game and adds a second as Burnley as Hull – wrongly red award by calamity Jones – slumps. Friedel's 200th PL game and Villa draw at Everton (O'Neill no boss loss there). FLC: Ipswich win at last – against injury/illness hit Derby. Strachan starts with defeat for Boro at home to Argyle (Green Army!). Donny and Blackpool share six. Swansea goes nine unbeaten. WBA regain goal standard with five over Watford. Reading is relieved by win at Coventry. Boss Boothroyd suffers first Colchester reverse at Millwall. F1: Leeds keeps up the four goal habit, but Charlton goes down at Carlisle. Lambert rescues Saints. Boyd's 100th in career as Hartlepool shares six at Brighton. Wycombe chucks two-goal lead to lose to Walsall. F2: Home-groan Bournemouth rocked by ten-man Rochdale's four goals. Cheltenham suffers similarly at feet of Crewe. Macc again loses two-goal lead in Bradford draw. BSP: Oxford increases lead as Kettering and Stevenage draw with each other, Mansfield, too, while Luton loses. SPL: Celtic takes advantage of Rangers inactivity to beat Killie, Hibs, too, late strikes helping second place against nine-finishing Dons. SL: Q of S regains Div 1 lead as Dundee draws at Fifers. Stirling is surprised by Peterhead. Livi goes top of Div 3. Trophy: sixth heaven for Tonbridge Angels, Nuneaton, too. Jamie Richards hat trick for Boreham Wood. Spain: Barca is held, Real wins.

NOVEMBER
Chelsea beats Man U ... Scots slumping ... "Hand of Frog" robs Republic ... Nine alive for Spurs.

1   The Brummie ten men hold Man C who creep into fourth place. Cardiff caught at the death by Forest leveller. Huddersfield moves to sixth place at Oldham. Russell Slade axed by Brighton. SPL: Rangers lead nullified by waterlogged pitch at Dundee U. Weekend red tally: 26 – PL 9! FL 4, SPL 4, SL 3, S Cup 3, BSP: 3.

2   Own goal and Harper heroics enough for Toon to take out Sheff U. Platini is in another attack on PL club finances and says Drogba will be a better player after his ban, but Chelsea still wants to have their transfer one overturned. Liverpool's injury list grows. Becks is back at AC Milan. Ipswich debt rises to £35m.

3   Ch Lge: Chelsea just held at the death by Atletico Madrid, but qualifies along with Man U two down to CSKA Moscow before Daddy Roo comes on to help out in levelling, but Sir Alex spots worst ever booking of Fletcher. Ronaldinho rescues AC Milan against Real. Marseille hits six, Bayern loses again. QPR and Palace share a point each. Accrington is safe! Curbishley gets £1m compensation from West Ham.

4   Ch Lge: Liverpool strikes late, but Lyon later, as qualification hangs by a thread. Rangers also caught in a draw. Arsenal hit four against AZ. Barca not looking too clever after Rubin hold them in the draw group where Inter win in Kiev. PL: Down to ten men, Villa loses player and game at West Ham. FA's handbag gift policy for WC 2018 may backfire as Warner hands his back. Shots caretaker Dodd will take over Saints Academy after cup tie.

5   E Lge: Everton second best to Benfica at Goodison, Fulham's nine overpowered by Roma. Celtic is goalless but not bottomless. Bolton chairman wants two-tier PL. Stan Kroenke is gaining more control at Arsenal. Ben Gourlay moves up at Chelsea into Kenyon role. Sky Sports Victory Shield: England hits two against the Irish.

6   FA Cup: Huddersfield six-hit sends Daggers packing. Notts edges Bradford, Saints hold off Bristol R. FLC: Coventry's ten lose at Derby. Carry-on spending Chelsea – as ban is suspended.

7   Foursome Gunners get serious (36 goals is PL start) helped by couple of ogs at Wolves to go second. Burnley throws away two-goal lead at Man C (Bellamy's 100th Lge goal in fifth draw for them) to share six. High five Villa makes its mark on Trotters. Weak pen mars Bent's return to WHL but Gomes only gets yellow for it as lucky Spurs go fourth. Pompey scores first at Rovers but three in 20 s/h mins (two for flu boy Roberts) changes it. FLC: Strachan's Boro still losing, this one at Palace. Toon fans rage over ground name – sportsdirect.com – and team takes it out on Posh. Swans wing it in Welsh derby over Bluebirds. Another draw for Ipswich comes at Reading. Scunny sub Slocombe suffers in debut in goal at Blackpool. Baggies crucially win at Leicester. FA Cup: Shocks with Bath washing out Grimsby, Kettering winning at Hartlepool, York edging Crewe, Oxford with best age 6344 clipping Yeovil and Staines' Ali C (Chaaban) responsible for the big upset at Shrewsbury. Eight goals, three pens and ten-a-side as Wycombe, Brighton are to fight again. Rochdale three down at Luton draws. Wroe hat trick for Torquay, but Martin is four goal man for Norwich's seven (its best since eight 20 years ago v Sutton) at plucky Paulton. Late goals give Gateshead, Stevenage replays at Brentford and home to Port Vale respectively. Stockport puts five past Tooting. SPL: 18 secs Boyd goal puts Rangers on track against St Mirren. Div 1: Top four are all winners. Div 2: Stirling loses to Alloa, so Cowden goes top. Div 3: Livi six at Elgin. Spain: Henry the first for Barca this season.

8   Chelsea give Man U, Rooney and Sir Alex the Blues as another debatable free kick goes against the champions. Ref Atkinson becomes the latest in the line of officials off the Old Trafford Christmas Card list. Hull sub Vennegoor saves his boss with an injury-time winner over ten-man Stoke. Hammers lose at home again to Everton. Fulham takes a point at Wigan. FA Cup: Outstanding Northwich put the Addicks on a slab. Burton pushed all the way by Oxford City. Weadstone not disgraced in losing to Rotherham. SPL: Bonny Bairns share six with Celtic.

9   Another diving controversy, but it gives Liverpool a life-line pen equaliser against Birmingham. FLC: Two spot kicks and Sheff Utd draws at Barnsley. FA Cup: AFC Dons downed at Millwall. Aldershot appoints Kevin Dillon as manager.

10   Ronaldo out of play-offs. Robinho will stay at Man C. Newcastle fans want to buy the club. Gus Poyet is appointed at Brighton. German goalkeeper Robert Enke commits suicide at train track. JPT: Accrington, Bradford, Carlisle and Leeds make Northern semis, Hereford, MK Dons and Norwich the Southern version. Spurs make a profit of £33.4m. FA faces cuts over Wembley drain on finance.

11   Crisis time for WC bid. Sir Alex remains on the backs of the whistlers. FA Cup: Luton surprises Rochdale. JPT: Saints clip the Addicks for semi place.

12   Two-match ban, £20,000 fine for Sir Alex. Lampard suffers injury blow. WC 2018 backroom team cut to size. Cudicini injured in motor cycle crash. Lord Mawhinney is to quit League job. Rangers announce £30m debt, while they and Celtic turned down by PL.

13   England gets prissy over landing rights in Qatar ahead of the friendly with Brazil. Ireland faces day of destiny part one against France, but Stephen of that ilk has abandoned them. Wales and Scotland will meet at the new Cardiff City Stadium. U-21s: Irish get a last minute leveller against Germany. JM wants to return to English football, as might Hiddink if Russia fails.

14   WC round-up: Dublin sees deflected goal, dejected Irish as French leave one up. Portugal just leads post-hitting Bosnia. "Bilya boy" double as Russians edge the late-goal Slovenia, too. Ukraine is happy with draw in Greece. New Zealand reigns over Bahrain one goal from Fallon, pen save by Paston to qualify. No-go for Gabon as defeat in Togo means Cameroon is heading for South Africa after victory in Morocco. Goal down Nigeria pips Tunisia – losers in Mozambique – so Super-Eagles fly south, too, after winning in Kenya. Injury-time, last minute drama as Egypt beats Algeria 2-0 to force play-off as both finish level on everything! Friendly fire: No oasis or desert storm for England B boys lead by Daddy Roo palmed off by sauntering penalty-missing Brazil. Wales is three times better than sad Scotland. Serbia just does enough in Belfast to beat the Irish. U-21s: England wins in the rain at Wembley over Portugal. It's a fourth qualifying draw for Republic in Georgia. Four cheers Scots in Azer. F1: Charlton strikes five for first time in ten years to beat MK Dons. Huddersfield is a six-hit over woeful Wycombe. Loanee Bostock double for the Bees holds the Lions. Manager Mark Cooper has quit Kettering for Posh. F2: Daggers top it at Stanley. Lester two in two mins for Chesterfield rocks Rochdale. Ref Salisbury sends off two benched subs as Lincoln – Cheltenham finish level but with three reds overall. SL: Dundee and Queens settle for no goals. Weather hit Vase but Spennymoor, Bridlington, Witney and Peacehaven & T are all high-fivers.

15   Maradona's reporter rage in Uruguay earns him £14,750 fine and two month ban, as Uruguay takes a slender lead in WC p-o in Costa Rica. Becks in MLS final sparks ticket boom. L1: Poyet starts with Brighton winning at Soton. Van Persie adds to growing Arsenal injury list.

16   Burley axed by Scots. Chelsea's injury list grows, too.

17   French continue to un-love coach Domenech. After big trouble in Cairo, play-off between Egypt and Algeria looks another powder keg. Chelsea is to pursue £40m Aguero (Atletico Madrid). Liverpool plans mini-clearout. FA Cup: Brentford five hits Gateshead, Vale dents Stevenage, Tranmere surprises Orient as does Carlisle at Morecambe. Millwall announces £3.5m loss. U-21s: England is held in Lithuania, Republic loses in Armenia and N Ireland at home to Czechs.

18   WC furore as Henry's "Hand of Frog" gives France aggregate win. Is it luck of the Irish? You're having a laugh. Portugal wins in Bosnia without Ronaldo, Beaten Russians finish with nine men. Greeks have a word for it in Ukraine – winning. Algeria edges Egypt out amid massive police presence. Uruguay becomes last qualifier despite Costa Rica's leveller. FA Cup: Poyet's Brighton is still rolling at Wycombe's expense. Liverpool pays money for a 14 year old Dave Moli from Luton.

19 Clamour for France – Republic replay grows. England will be top sees for Euro 2012. PL is not to fund WC 2018 bid. Birmingham battle of past and present owners looms. Sky Sports Victory Shield: Wales double beats N Ireland.

20 Now Henry wants a replay! Two hundred European matches face match-fixing probe. FLC: Swans late winners over Rams. L1: Barnard the 90 min-plus pen man nips it over MK Dons for Shrimpers.

21 Four-play Chelsea, minus a few stars, round-up the Wolves in 10th home clean sheet in a row as in 1927 and gives sub bow to ex-dispute boy Kakuta, 18. Man U with on-fire Fletcher rumble to another win over Everton. Arsenal's straight 13-unbeaten streak ends in a Bent winner for Sunderland, but pen appeal fails. Villa has a late leveller at Burnley. "Wannabies" Liverpool and Man City share four goals. Fulham bows to Bowyer at Birmingham – whose 11th goal has brought 15 pts! Six goals at Hull after Hammers PL season record of two in first 11 mins is overturned until parity is restored. Allardyce has heart op. McPhail has cancer treatment. FLC: Baggies pop Bristol C Robins into their satchel. Loanee and ex-Hornet Helguson has Watford buzzing again. Injury time triumphs for Tykes over Cardiff and Leicester on Plymouth. Reading, last to win at home does so edging Blackpool. L1: Ex-Poole striker Craig Austin pockets win for Swindon at Carlisle. Akpo Sodje saves pt for Charlton at Yeovil after brother Sam's 11th career red. Leeds beach Brighton. Orient gain revenge over Tranmere for cup defeat. L2: Rochdale's two in three mins rock the Daggers. Bournemouth wins at Macc after conceding first – a rare such event in their year. Chesterfield hits five against Darlo. Shots snatch pt as first to stop Notts home scoring. SPL: Rangers finish Killie in one half. Falkirk closes on Hamilton after beating them. SL: Morton continues improvement at Airdrie. Cowden holds Stirling and stays top in Div 2. Livi is still ahead of affairs in Div 3. BSP: Cambridge comes back to draw at Luton. Oxford, Stevenage wins again. Kettering loses to Kiddy. Mansfield draw, York enters play-off berth. Trophy: Woking hits six. Chelmsford and Hornchurch share eight. Dave Syers hat trick for born-again Farsley. Vase: New Mills score six. Spain: Barca held, so Real Madrid goes top. Inter is eight pts clear in Italy but new leaders in France as Auxerre goes in front.

22 White "Hot" Lane as Tottenham bury nine against Wigan with Defoe five goals in second half and a perfect hat trick their biggest win for 32 years. Rovers aided by bizarre own goal in winning at Bolton. Stoke add to Pompey's bottom trouble. Tayside triumphs as Dundee Utd catch Celtic at the death and Dundee gives Caley two-goals start and then beats them in Alba final.

23 FIFA crisis meeting over hooray Henry. Wigan players offer to repay 400 fans for trip to Spurs. Toon back on top of FLC after it wins at Preston. Becks battles but his LA loses final.

24 Ch Lge: Liverpool wins but E Lge beckons as Fiorentina does the same to go on after beating qualifying Lyon. Arsenal twosome sees off Standard to reach knock-out stage. Barca comes to life against Inter. Alas for Rangers not even E Lge as Stuttgart consigns them to bottom. Hart gets cut out by Pompey. L1: Leeds held up by Orient until last minute. Charlton, Colchester and Norwich record wins but Huddersfield lose. At the bottom there are victories for Tranmere, Wycombe and Southampton. Carlisle beats MK Dons by the odd goal in seven. L2: Rochdale, Rotherham cut Bournemouth's lead as they are Daggers drawn! Cheltenham hits five, Morecambe four away at Darlo. Neil Woods, new Grimsby boss starts with loss against Bradford. SL Livi playing catch up beat Albion to move further ahead in Div 3. BSP: Top three Oxford, Stevenage, York all win, but Kettering suffers another defeat. Sir Dave Richards pulls out of WC 2018 bid team.

25 Ch Lge: Chelsea wins away to Porto, but both qualify. Man U surprised by Rustu gk heroics for Besiktas ending 23 home games in it without defeat, but as Wolfsburg loses to CSKA they go through, too. Ronaldo back for Real and they top Group C. PL: Dempsey double dumps Blackburn for Fulham's threesome. Hull's three in 19 mins forestalls Everton fight back on the day Toffees are turned down for new ground. UEFA names SK Tirana, Vllaznia (both Albania), Dinaburg (Latvia), Ljubljana (Slovenia) and Honved (Hungary) as clubs involved in match-fixing. Call for Lineker to save 2018 WC bid.

26 Clamour by clubs wanting to sign up for WC. Now Everton turned down for a ground share with Liverpool. Surprise, surprise Avram Grant is appointed manager of Pompey. Women's World Cup sees England hit three put the trots on Turkey. Montpellier has five players with swine flu. Notts not out of the wood over ownership. Sky Sports Victory Shield: England takes title in Scotland again.

27 Wenger attacks Chelsea's reprieve over the Kakuta ok. World's two richest starting line-ups Barca £309m v Real Madrid £322 play at the weekend. PM Gordon Brown rescues England's WC bid?

28 Rooney treble (2 pens), Giggs 100th PL goal on eve of 36th birthday as Man U gives Grant a baptism of fire power at Pompey. Hammers hit five against away wobblers Burnley but have just two goals to spare at the end having squandered all of their goals to the chagrin of the locals. Tottenham still clings to third place after draw at Villa as vet Friedel holds them up. Wigan comes back from Spurs disaster to beat City boss Bruce and his Black Cats. Man C held in PL equalling seven draws in a row and Hull's pen man Bullard apes boss Brown pitch lecture! Blackburn day after manager Sam's ope release share no quarter with Stoke, Fulham, too, is held by Bolton. FLC: Warnock celebrates his 100th Palace League game as Watford is banished. Forest goes ten unbeaten now. Henderson hat trick lifts Sheff U spirits at Bristol C. Toon finish Swans off early ending visitors eleven match unbeaten run. Baggies foursome grounds the Owls. Barnsley halted by rain after skating it at Plymouth. FA Cup: Few shocks but Al C is again the Staines hero as Millwall is forced to replay. MK Dons three-goal rally beats Exeter by the odd goal in seven. Non-league survivors to next round: Forest Green and York while Oxford and Barrow as are Luton with Rotherham in replays. Odd spot: Bournemouth, Oxford shares same gate size – 6082. SPL: Celtic has it over St Mirren while Rangers suffer at the Dons. Dundee U finishes with nine men in Motherwell draw. S Cup: Irvine Meadow become their first junior league team to beat seniors when ousting Arbroath. Brechin forced to share eight goals with Wick Academy. BSP: Stevenage takes advantage of Oxford's cup involvement to go two points nearer the leaders. Chester game abandoned when protesting crowd invades pitch – with them leading!

29 Couple of "Drogs" and an og, so it's goodbye Arsenal for Chelsea. Merseyside derby goes to the Reds at Goodison, chiefly thanks to Reina. Now the tally is 12 goals 18 pts for Bowyer inspired Birmingham in Wolves defeat. FLC: First away day fillip for Ipswich – at Cardiff! Boss man gk Harper holds up Leeds until leveller at Kettering. Blatter in support for Henry and blames ref!

30 PL clubs pay agents £70m a year. Clarke 22 secs strike for Blackpool but PNE level in derby game. FIFA will study Republic plea for extra WC place. Concerns are raised over building delays for Brazil 2014.

DECEMBER
England "kind" WC draw ... Liverpool in the toils ... Man C sacks Hughes ... All-foreign game!

1 C Cup: Gibson duo dents Spurs for Man U. Pompey throws early gift and loses to Villa. L1: Leeds, Charlton, Norwich are all winners and Bristol R edges into play-off section. Tranmere shares six goals at Huddersfield. Saints go out of the drop zone. F2: Rare high five for Shots as Daggers are jiggered. Rochdale overtakes Bournemouth as the Cherries draw at Barnet. BSP: Oxford leaves it late at Crawley, but Stevenage flounders at

Ebbsfleet. S Cup: emphatic replay win is hoisted for Raith at Peterhead. Messi is European Player of the Year as La Liga personnel get nod over PL entries. Moyes pledges his Everton commitment.

2   C Cup: Crisis club Chelsea, concede three goals in Blackburn draw then Ballack, Kakuta have pens saved by Robinson in losing shoot-out. Wenger dismisses defeat at Man C as he writes off the competition. E Lge: Everton wins in Athens to enter knock-out stage. Celtic has a victory but goes out. Becks proving the front runner for 2018 bid. Sir Alex regrets opting out of FA Cup ten years to help England WC bid. England seeded for South Africa, France and Portugal fail. Blatter criticises Henry! BSP: Kettering wins at Luton to go fourth.

3   Republic might receive "moral award." WC winners will get record £18m. E Lge: Fulham still hanging in there after edging CSKA. Eriksson's future at Notts is in question. Pompey delays paying players back money.

4   WC draw: lucky England gets USA, Algeria and Slovenia. Jolly "Group of Death" puts Brazil in with North Korea, Ivory Coast and Portugal. Loan helps to pay for Pompey wages. Shots awarded F and C performance of the week for dumping Daggers.

5   "Wannabies" edge the "Wobblers" as Man C's gk is "Given" to saving Lamps pussy foot spot kick to deny six-yellows Chelsea a point, while Adebayor scores at both ends and Terry limps off. Gibson strikes again for make-do-and-mend Man U – Scholes, too, his 99th – as part of a foursome at West Ham celebrating Sir Alex's 1300th game in charge. Arsenal celebrates 100th Emirates game to ease out Stoke. Villa three goals, three points Hull with Bullard injuring left knee now. Liverpool in a blank at Blackburn the sixth PL goalless of the season on Gerrard's 500th outing. Pompey wins and even writes off a pen against Burnley. Wigan's usual second half collapse lets in Birmingham (21 pts from 15 goals now). Wolves leapfrog the Trotters in the danger zone with one "offside" goal and a Milijas blaster. FLC: Down to ten Toon but another win dismisses Watford. Cox gives "hand" Baggies a late leveller at Derby. No-pay Palace turned over by Donny. Strachan joy as Boro hit five at QPR for his first bonus win. Owls lose again to Reading and Laws joins the sack race speculation. Rare start Earnshaw nets a proper hat trick as Forest fire five in routing Leicester. L1: Leeds share four goals with Huddersfield but have 36,723 watching. Charlton celebrates 17 years back at The Valley by clipping the Shrimpers with the same single goal win. Byfield's strikes his 100th career goal for Walsall but Saints go marching on. L2: Rochdale keeps in top form against Macc. Last gasp og gives Bournemouth victory over Shrews. Jevons 25 sec start motivates Morecambe to sixth win on the trot at Port Vale. Now it's seven defeats in a row for Stockport losers at Wycombe. SPL: McDonald (unsettled?) kick starts Celtic win over Dons. Boyd hits 150th and 151st goals in Rangers win at Falkirk. SL: Caley's nine get a draw at QoS's ten. Dundee five points clear in Div 1. S Cup: Sten stun Cove with five. BSP: Oxford, Stevenage move on and York sets club record eighth successive win to go third. Vase: Willand hits six goals. Bundesliga: Leverkusen club record 15 unbeaten. JM worry as Inter loses to Juve. Ronaldo misses pen, scores and gets sent off – all in eight minutes!

6   Everton claws back two goals for a draw with Spurs. "Zamora" of that for Fulham as it singularly scratches out another away defeat for Black Cats. Nine without a win is Coventry's lot. Tunnel collision after Hamilton beats nine Hearts, another three red-carded! Stuttgart appoints ex-Spurs boss Gross as coach.

7   Man U has a crisis in defence – midfield men to take over. Real, Bayern, AC Milan and Juve represents a foursome ensure of Ch Lge qualification. There are five candidates for FIFA World Player of the Year: Iniesta, Messi and Xavi from Barca, Ronaldo and Kaka from Real. Capello is to spearhead new coaching direction. Bust-up at Stoke has involving Beattie and boss man Pulis. Alleged assault concerns Carroll of Newcastle. Russian players accused of partying before crucial tie with Slovenia. Everton new ground hope is revived. QPR downed at Watford. S Cup: Livi fogged off in Clyde lead.

8   Ch Lge: Owen to the rescue with hat trick for Man U who keep Wolfsburg away from the knock-out door. Now Apoel manages to score two goals at Chelsea (Kakuta their youngest in Ch Lge 18 years 170 days) in a draw. Ronald double enables Real to go through at Marseille. Ronaldinho pen gives AC Milan a qualifying draw in Zurich, but Bayern's foursome in Italy spells the end for Juve. FA Cup: Luton surprises Rotherham, Stanley clip Barnet, Leeds need extra time for high five against Kettering, Barrow tips out Oxford and Shots taken out by Tranmere. Stockport tie is off again. FA signs cup deal with ESPN. FLC: Gk Carson's butt for a red card and Cardiff makes Baggies prickly at The Hawthorns. Cash-strapped Palace gets four goals at Reading. Boro, Leicester are both beaten at home. S Cup: Alloa, Brechin are both replay winners. Magilton is under the spotlight in QPR hot seat.

9   Ch Lge: Liverpool loses at home – of course, Arsenal away (with youngest ever Ch Lge average age 21 years 154 days) and naturally Rangers completes its sixth without a victory. Inter's double strike lifts JM spirits. Last 16: Bordeaux, Bayern, Man U, CSKA Moscow, Real, AC Milan, Chelsea, Porto, Fiorentina, Lyon, Barcelona, Inter, Sevilla, Stuttgart, Arsenal and Olympiakos. Liverpool is heading for E League among others. FA Cup: Staines slips four at Millwall. FLC: Newcastle inflicts tenth successive reverse for Coventry. Magilton reported in alleged fracas with Buzsaky. S Cup: now Livi held in reprise.

10   Hammers Ashton has to quit and may sue over injury sustained in England training clash with Wright-Phillips three years ago. Pompey may be forced to download players. Notts up for sale and Sven may decide to leave if buy-out flops. Plymouth appoints Paul Mariner as manager.

11   Harry scraps Spurs Xmas party. PFA tries to dissuade Ashton from legal action. Cheltenham and Martin Allen part company. Colchester wins at Brighton to go third.

12   No case for the defence as Chelsea concede three at set pieces and land Everton with a point. Villa wins at Old Trafford for the first time in 26 years, Rooney booked for diving and also hits the bar while Sir Alex unhappy over short injury span. Tenth game unbeaten Man C (Bellamy unlucky red) shares joy of six goals with Bolton. The Trotters thrice led. Bouncing Bowyer buries old mates Hammers for Brum's club record equalling PL win plus seventh unbeaten match. Burnley retains home record in Fulham draw, Kaboul's 93rd leveller for Pompey at Sunderland then sees red for getting "shirty." Figueroa 60.59 yard free kick foils Sorensen who later saves Rodallega pen in two-all draw between Stoke and Wigan. Hull and Blackburn go blankety-blank. Resurgent Wolves have best top-flight win in London for 30 years and first at Spurs since 1973. FLC: Seven thousand travelling Toons have to suffer late draw at Barnsley. Eastwood treble strike makes Coventry's day and ends nightmare run as Posh, Plymouth, Sheff W (ten games no win and 527 mins no goals) all lose. Ipswich 29-secs opener and move out of the bottom three against Blackpool. Birthday boy Porter carries Derby to win at Watford. Forest wins at Swansea. L1: Leeds held goalless at Brentford. Ten man Stockport, eight on the spin losers, hit again by Charlton. Southend gives Hartlepool two goals start and beat them. Saints ease over Tranmere. Norwich forced to share six at Yeovil. First win in eight for Oldham. L2: Seven wins in a row Morecambe's finest five including three in ten mins League success shocks Bournemouth. Shots go for a Burton in six-goal slaughter, Pearson grabbing a hat trick. Torquay high five, too, over Darlo, is their eighth for eleven years. Rotherham's Roberts hits 45 yard free-kick in local derby success at Bradford. Notts are beaten at home by Accrington. First victory in seven games notched up for Macc. SPL: Fortune smiles on Celtic over Motherwell. Rangers win over St J and Boyd is just five off Larsson record goals. SL: Dundee recovers from Ayr lead. Cowden, Stirling are both away day winners. Livi sur-

prised by Forfar so East Stirling closes gap. Trophy: Bug-hit Cambridge flours Luton, Forest Green, Grays are BSP casualties to the W formations at Woking and Worcester. Barca needs late pen in Spain.

13 Mersey misery moves on as Wenger h-t rage helps Arsenal turn it around thanks to og and Arshavin blaster at Liverpool. Cardiff adds to Boro home woes. Manager Laws is cut at Hillsborough. Lehmann sent off for Stuttgart.

14 Silver lining for Hammers as Gold and Sullivan offer £50m? Cox saves Baggies after battling Rangers draw.

15 Ten-change Wolves wimp out at Man U. Trotters tread more grief into West Ham. Now Villa goes third at tenman Sunderland. Heady days for sixth place Birmingham after Jerome double against Blackburn fifth straight and club record PL win and best sequence in top flight for 36 years. Backe resigns at Notts. Man C to pursue ref Clattenburg's alleged bias against Bellamy. FA Cup: Tie finally settled at Macclesfield, as Stockport crashes to fourgoal Torquay. JPT: Carlisle, Leeds plus Soton (pens) and MK Dons through to area finals. SPL: Playing catch-up Rangers win at Dundee U. SL: Stirling held, so Cowden move ahead in Div 2. Ex-Liverpool legend Alan A'Court dies at 75.

16 Lamps pen edges edgy Chelsea over Pompey. Torres is the difference as Liverpool on Shankly's 50th anniversary day returns to winning ways against Wigan – just. Spurs ends Man C "unbeaten run" to put pressure on Sparky Hughes. Wenger rants over Wolves stance after Arsenal held at Burnley. E Lge: Zamora goals leave Basle faulty. Reading axes Rodgers, QPR relieve Magilton of position. Les Parry is given Tranmere to end of season. Gazza arrested for D and D. Barca given bye to semis in WCC beat Atlante. Twelve sites now for 2018 hope.

17 Link to Hiddink is rumour at Man C. Paul Hart is in at QPR with Mick Harford. E Lge: Everton rest players and BATE wins there. Celtic gives Rapid three goal starts and catches up with them.

18 Ch Lge draw: Man U gets Becks at AC Milan. JM returns for Inter at Chelsea and Porto meets Arsenal. E Lge draw: Fulham plays Shakhtar, Everton v Sporting, Liverpool meets Unirea. Benitez wants PL fixtures to the reversed half-way through season. Grimsby ends Morecambe run with a draw. Redknapp annoyed over Spurs private party.

19 Santa C gives Man C a double pre-Xmas present but Hughes still gets sacking as Sunderland and 405 mins of no away goals just lose by the odd one in seven. Robert Mancini takes over reins at Eastlands. Fulham hoist their 100th PL win and easily lower, injury-ravaged (Fletcher centre-back) Man U's colours. Arsenal close on Sir Alex's team with three goals off Hull but Nasri stamp on Garcia sparks altercation. Carew scores for the good ship Villa sailing on 373 mins without shipping a goal. Crouch double keeps Spurs ticking at Blackburn but Harry R faces taxing time. Pompey hit PL's 500th (Belhadj) of the season and another fine mess for Liverpool with Mascherano first in PL with two reds this time. FLC: 3 frozen off. Fiery Forest 14 no loss. Swans swoop on awful managerless ten-no-win Owls, now 617 mins goalless. Posh on boss Cooper's birthday off the bottom as Plymouth hit it losing to Coventry. Snappy Sharp is on goal standard again for Donny. Reading's Church salvages a point late at Bristol C then sees second yellow for celebrating. L1: 1 frozen off. Leeds edges Saints depriving them of 11 post-war unbeaten away run. Charlton have to share eight goals with ten-man Millwall (Morison hat trick includes one og!) Norwich has crucial win – seventh on the trot at home – over Huddersfield. Swindon in again thankful for its Austin. Stockport loses again, but Tranmere beat Bristol R. Shearer pen save helps ten-man Wycombe draw with Oldham. L2: all frozen off except Rochdale foursome over Shrews. SPL: 1 frozen off. Rangers hit 'Well for six. Hibs 12 no loss, topples the Dons. SL: 11 frozen off. Dundee, Ross both win. Only Queen's Park edging Montrose survive in Div 3 with Div 2 wipe- out. BSP: Completely frozen off!

20 West Ham and Chelsea share pens, courtesy of spot-king whistler Dean, Hammers one unfair but Lamps made to takes his three times for encroachment!, Now nine change Wolves rocket to 12th place after beating Burnley. Birmingham gets a point at Everton whose eighth home try without a win equalled their 1972 record. Tyne-Tees derby is watched by close on 50,000 and goes Toon way as Boro plummet to 14th. Celtic find burden of ten-man after half an hour costs defeat against Hearts.

21 Man C and Mancini have different timeline on when he was approached. FA backs Terry over ticket deal allegations. Secret Xmas party so the Spurs players have to donate to charity. England will play Egypt. Messi is World Player of the Year. Wigan and Bournemouth games are frozen off.

22 CEO Cook at Man C reveals last summer shortlist for Hughes disposal! Torres backs under-fire Rafa, Ancelotti does same for Terry. Arsenal, Hull will face FA wrath. Lewes beats weather and Hampton & R in Trophy replay. Mark Yates is appointed at Cheltenham. Busby Babe and Munich survivor Albert Scanlon dies at 74.

23 Pompey may be forced to sell players. Craig Levein is appointed as Scotland manager.

24 Already a host of Boxing Day fixtures succumb to the weather and almost the entire SL programme is wiped out.

25 Sir Alex takes swipe at Man C over "Sparky" departure. Billy Davies, Forest manager, wants a winter break.

26 Defence ok now, but first no score in 24 as Chelsea blank it (Malouda two yellows) at Brum ten no loss and denied a goal for wrong off side. Roberto M starts where Hughes left – with a win, Tevez making one and acrobatically scoring another to put a spoke in Stoke. Liverpool finally nails the ten Wolves. Spurs owe it to Gomes at Fulham in another scoreless one. Bent scores for Black Cats but Toffees stick it out to level. Wigan and Blackburn share two goals as do Burnley and Bolton in another Lancs derby. Hammers move out of bottom three as Pompey are left there. FLC: 1 off. Owls and Mags share four goals ending Sheff W's 554 mins drought. Baggies move nearer Toon with second half win over Posh. Forest 15 no loss maintains best English away record unbeaten in 12, but escape "hands" incident. Boro (late finishing ten) beats Scunny (early losing player) for Strachan's first home bonus. Plymouth end eight hour goal famine at Cardiff (11 years no Boxing Day win), but QPR end eight year BD curse edging Bristol C. Donny concede first goal in 457 mins and lose at Coventry. L1: 3 off. Holt hits 20th Norwich goal. Leeds 6 pts clear after beating Hartlepool. Nine men Charlton scrape a point against Swindon – Sam Sodje's 14th career red. Saints climb to tenth over ten man Exeter with best FL gate 30,890. L2: 4 off. Born again Grant double strike lifts Shots against Barnet. Lester pen miss costs Chesterfield at Lincoln. Accrington fifth win in a row ends Morecambe run. Rochdale held at Crewe, so Bournemouth take advantage at Cheltenham. SPL: 1 off. Celtic Accies to go a point behind inactive Rangers. SL: ten-man Dundee draw at Caley, Partick and QofS also share – 13 others all off! BSP: 3 off. Stevenage wins at ten-man Cambridge (4439) to close on Oxford. York third and AFC Dons go fourth. Stuart Pearce offers to sponsor old club Wealdstone's No. 3 shirt for ten years.

27 Man U take Hull out, but not that easily. For Arsenal against Villa, super-sub Fabregas has delightful double ending in injury again.

28 "Drog and og" for uncertain Chelsea (JM watching) rescue pts against Fulham. Two-goal Tevez again the tormentor as Man C silence the Wolves. Ten-man burden finally too much for Burnley at Everton, but controversy over Yakubu off side when much-injured Vaughan returns for first touch goal. Bent double lands a point for Sunderland at Blackburn. Birmingham (Hart stancout) equals best since 1907-08 with 11th unbeaten game at Stoke. Tottenham holds on to fourth place to give Hammers the derby day claret and blues. FLC: 2 off. Cardiff four up in 38 mins manages a draw with gutsy Posh! The Scunny nine are overtaken by WBA. Forest is still creating havoc in 16th unbeaten. Plymouth can't stop winning! Ipswich's two-goal Stead courtesy of "bail" over red card query

brings victory. Newcastle front men let them down against Derby in goalless draw. L1: 2 off. Top (Leeds) at Tail (Stockport) ends as expected. Ten Brentford Bees hold the Charlton Addicks. Seventh goal in seven games is the call for Millwall's Morison. Murray "mints" it with four-timer for Brighton (3 in 24 mins) at Wycombe. Soton unseated at Colchester. L2: 3 off. Four-timers Rochdale, Bournemouth (with a pen), Notts (with Hughes eight-minute treble) are all winners but Accrington run ends at hands of visiting Bury. Welcome win for Cheltenham at Dagenham. BSP: 3 off. Oxford concede late leveller at Salisbury. AFC Dons draw at Stevenage. Ademeno three in four mins for Crawley at Grays.

29   Added time but Liverpool fastest-to-fifty striker Torres still seals it at Villa. Megson on knife-edge as Bolton concedes two goals to keep Hull in the Hunt(!) with a point. Dons v Bairns is off for frost in SPL. Preston sacks Alan Irvine.

30   High five for Man U takes toll of Wigan. Pompey, unpaid, facing winding-up, too, is taken out by Arsenal in first PL game with 22 foreigners starting! Abramovich turns loans into equity to balance Chelsea's books. Megson is out at Bolton. Baby Fergie is mentioned for both Preston and Bolton jobs! SPL: Boyd has five of Rangers seven v Dundee U and beats Larsson record.

31   Ferdinand on the road to recovery, O'Shea sidelined for longer now. Curbishley is Bolton rumour.

JANUARY
FA Cup: Leeds axe Man U ... African Cup tragedy ... Weather hits hard ... Chester on the brink.

1   Football League to make clubs ensure all games are played regardless of weather from 2010-11! Everton sends back Jo to Man C after his unscheduled Brazil visit. Scottish programme already looks to be a white-out.

2   FA Cup, 3 off, no shocks, but no-pay Pompey will be sent to Coventry for replay, Earnshaw wastes pen so Birmingham fight another day as Forest go 17 unbeaten and Liverpool only manage a draw at McDermott's Reading with even Torres heading wide as rookie sub gk Hamer flaps. No boss Preston pans Colchester with seven up, their best since 1966 and Parkin gets three. Everton pushed all the way by Carlisle. Wigan (only 5335) gives Hull goal start then hit four. Other four-timers Spurs (35,862 best of round) whack poor Posh, boss-less Bolton send Lincoln spinning four times as well. Barrow boys (backed by 8000) wheeled away at Sunderland. York, held up in snow, take early lead at Stoke before losing. Villa beats ten-man Blackburn in low key affair. Two "froggy" subs and one of them N'Guessan again hits the winning goal (see Aug 8) for Foxes over Swans. Scarf-face RM sees much changed Man C (remember Mwaruwari?) edges it at Boro. Slick Rickie Lambert's 20th of season helps Saints tops the Hatters. Owl-ighting Warnock joy as unpaid Palace gets a dividend at Sheff W. "Fulzam" beats plucky Swindon. Coyle likely farewell as Burnley wins at MK Dons. Toon fans (2376) see no goals at Plymouth. Derby draws at Millwall. Brighton – 16 years since last past 3rd round – win sea-side game at Torquay. Scunny success as Hayes hits old Tykes mates. Ipswich clips nine-man Blackpool by the sea, too. Toothless Terriers bow to "bug-shrugger" Dorrans for WBA. L1:2 off. Norwich keeps it up at Wycombe. L2: 4 off. Bournemouth gets shaken by the Cobblers – third time in five months. SPL: 2 off. Dons win at Dundee U. St Mirren go ninth after beating Killie. SL; all off! Barca held by Villarreal.

3   FA Cup: I off, one big shock: Leeds beats Man U (worst 3rd for 26 years), as one-time windscreen man Beckford fits them up at Old Trafford, where they last won in 1981. Hammers have a half-time lead then Arsenal eventually assumes late control. Chelsea high five ends Watford dream. QPR earns a replay at Sheff U. One goal is it for unconvincing Wolves at Tranmere. SPL: Rangers cling to draw at Celtic to stay top. Edinburgh derby finishes all square in ten-a-side. SL: Dundee (ten from h-t) flips fixture with Airdrie and loses home record!

4   Sir Alex will wield the axe. Pompey banned from signings. SL: Partick beats Morton.

5   Three up Stoke holds on after Fulham fights back. C Cup: Blackburn off for safety reasons. AFC Dons – Wrexham hit by frozen pitch. Notts need more wonga to keep Sven. Man City post £92.6m loss. Becks is eager at AC Milan. Pompey men are waiting for December wages.

6   Sheikh Mansour bin Zayed al-Nahyan writes off £394.5m of Man C debts as RM moves in for Vieira comeback, while their C Cup tie with Utd neighbours is snowed off. Meanwhile snow outside Emirates calls off Bolton PL game for Arsenal. Zamora has dislocated collarbone. Liverpool's Johnson is likely to be out until March with knee injury. Baby Fergie (Darren) takes charge at Preston.

7   Pompey pays up its players. Chelsea may go for Aguero. Becks in shining form for Milan shirt. Everton lands Landon Donovan, Becks LA colleague.

8   As Togo bus is ambushed with fatalities, doubts over African Nations Cup carrying on. Vieira is paraded at Man C. Man U's £699m debt may prevent signings. Sol talked about for a return to Arsenal! FLC and a match on! Eighteen-match unbeaten Forest eases to victory at The Hawthorns. Coyle is installed at Bolton. Atletico winger Maxi Rodriguez heads for Liverpool as Dossena is flogged to Napoli. Irvine gets a new job quickly – at Sheff W. FL reveals gates average up 10,441 as opposed to 10,101 by December 2009.

9   Wintry weather winds wreck contenders: Rosicky deflection saves Everton victory and on-a-roll Birmingham holds on to early lead against Man U, grateful for an og, but there is an icy scream from Sir Alex over ref Clattenburg's dismissal of Fletcher and short o/t. FLC: 7 off. Taxing times for Cardiff and now held by Blackpool. Coventry's improvement continues. Scunny routs the Rams. L1: 10 off. Leeds brought back to reality by stuffy Wycombe leveller. Holt's double strike for Norwich and journey's end after 12 hour trip to beaten Exeter. L2, BSP, SL, Trophy – all off! L2 Cup: 10 off. Hibs put Irvine Meadow out to pasture. Dundee U needs drummed out over ineligible Woods despite Dunfermline's seven goal stun of Sten.

10   FLC: Ipswich og gift at Leicester but Foxes level it. S Cup: The-man Accies ache over late Rangers pen in share of six. ANC: Mali trailing four goals in 79 mins fight back to draw at the death against Angola, but Togo contingent flies home. Dodgy email threatens Boy Hicks at Liverpool.

11   Tevez the terrible takes treble chance as Man C goes fourth with four-play against Blackburn. Next door, Glazers take £23m out of Man U. Hicks Jnr chucks in his hand. Sheff W appoints Alan Irvine as manager. ANC: Malawi upsets fancied Algeria and Ivory Coast held by Burkina Faso.

12   FA Cup: Pompey just escapes at Coventry with og at the death equalizer and extra time winner. Fourteenth unbeaten Birmingham chops the Forest. Derby needs pens to take care of the Lions. Blades cut the Rangers down to size. Cardiff just denied win at late-levelling Bristol C. Sol Campbell gets half a game for Arsenal stiffs. Leicester chairman Mandaric caught up in Pompey finances probe. SPL: St Mirren wins again over Dons to go seventh. ANC: Egypt eases over Nigeria and Benin levels with Mozambique.

13   FA Cup: A Long night for Reading after Liverpool leads but loses (fifth at home this season) in extra time as Torres (knee) and Gerrard (hamstring) get themselves injured to pile pressure on Rafa. "Long old poke for Plymouth at Newcastle" ends with Lovenkrands hat trick for the Toon. SPL: Dundee U's win puts more misery on Accies. ANC: Gabon surprises Cameroon, Zambia and Tunisia draw, but Togo now disqualified! Brian Laws

Peter Lovenkrands of Newcastle United and Jonas Olsson of West Bromwich Albion contest possession in the battle at the top of the Championship at St James' Park. Lovenkrands scored Newcastle's second in the 2-2 draw. Both teams went on to gain promotion to the Premier League. (PA Photos)

      ousted by the Owls, takes over at Burnley. Man U hopeful of raising more cash interest. Suitors hover around West Ham.

14   C Cup semi: Milner enables Villa to take a useful lead at Blackburn. Harry R has a tax problem again. QPR loses Hart after just five games! Dunfermline bounced out of S Cup will appeal. ANC: Algeria brings Mali down to earth and Angola does not make same mistake against Malawi.

15   No James move to Stoke to ease Pompey cash crisis. Briatore is to sell stake in QPR. ANC: Ivory Coast first to reach quarter-finals to put Ghana in jeopardy.

16   PL; 1 off (Pompey). Seven-up Chelsea – their first in PL, best at top level for 49 years – slaughter Black Cats and Cole A hits 18,000th PL goal. Burnley share worst away record with Darlo and lose after an hour's resistance against unimpressive Man U despite their three goals (V d Sar at 39 years, 79 days is their oldest post-war player). Liverpool huffs and puffs and get caught by Stoke's 90th Huth after lucky strike opener – but denied by ref and woodwork later. Honeymoon period ends for RM as Man C taken out by Everton. Harry R's 500th PL game but Spurs held by Hull and Myhill. Wigan wins at Wolves in ten-a-side finish, with McCarthy at 19 years, 65 days the season's second youngest PL scorer after Ramsey. FLC: Forest 18 League no loss wins Jekyll and Hyde performance against Reading who miss a pen – Camp guessing Howard's way from the spot. Ipswich nets a 97th min winner when ref had signalled four extra – so Coventry is not happy. New boss Irvine gets plaudits with first win in 13 for Sheff W at Barnsley. Boro ring the changes but still lose at Sheff U. Baby Fergie loses first for PNE at Bristol C. L1: 3 off. Harley is streets ahead for Exeter over Leeds. Ninety-second min Lambert deflected free off Trotter puts Saints ahead, 93rd Trotter levels for MK Dons in high five at Hartlepool. Sweet revenge fit is or Norwich at Colchester in another nap hand. Austin is still sparking for Swindon. Charlton heaps more pressure on Wycombe. L2 6 off. Bury away day at Bournemouth is bracing. Daggers are up to third. Injury-hit Chesterfield is grateful for loan star Conlon. Grimsby 17 no win miss a pen against ten-man Cheltenham. SPL: Accies with no win over Rangers since 1938 – lose again! Bairns hold Celtic at Parkhead. Killie stays in the toils. SL: 9 off. Stranraer two up in seven mins go 4-2 down then win with last minute goal at 5-4! BSP: Oxford shunted by Tamworth. AFC Dons clip the Stags. Brodie hits 23rd and 24th goals for York. Vase: 11 off, four on and produce 24 goals while Dawlish and Gresley share eight and get abandoned! ANC: Egypt record 15th unbeaten in come back over Mozambique. Real loses to Bilbao so Barca goes 5 pts ahead. Leverkusen is back at Bundesliga head.

17   Coyle springs life into Bolton but it's absolutely Fabregas who upstages them for Arsenal. No League win in nine run ends for Blackburn over Fulham. Hammers dig deep for goalless draw at Villa. SL: Dundee twice denies Dunfermline equalising as others forced to play catch-up. Pompey transfer ban is still on. Beckford withdraws transfer request at Leeds. ANC: Cameroon edges Zambia, Gabon draws with Tunisia.

18   Newcastle and WBA share four goals in top v third place game, but Northern Rock sponsorship deal at Toon is criticised. Is it asset-stripping or just pay back time for Glazers at Man U? Becks boy sticks his knife into Man C.

With the Fernandes bid failed, David Sullivan gains control of £110m in debt West Ham for £20m. Van Nistelrooy is on point of a UK return. No FIFA punishment for Henry. ANC: Angola and Algeria in goalless draw, but both qualify. Mali beating Malawi is the "losers" group game.

19   C Cup: Two-goal terror Tevez taunts old mates as the Blue Moon rises at Eastlands in the first leg semi, with the sun setting for Man U. FA Cup: Accrington, Doncaster and Notts all march on but Cardiff needs an og to end Bristol C replay hopes. FLC: Wednesday wins again! L2: Late Shots deny Dale. Darlo ends misery with victory at Rotherham in game between longest without playing. JPT: Leeds downturn continues at home to Carlisle. S Cup: Celtic edges home at Morton, Rangers need extra time to take out Accies. ANC: Ghana secures quarter-final spot. Burton C of E is now a runner. Sol Campbell is to sue Pompey.

20   Arsenal gives Bolton two goals start and delightfully beats them, but Gallas challenge on Mark Davies enrages Coyle. Liverpool lives again as Kuyt double finishes Spurs. C Cup: Villa make it to Wembley but after blistering see-saw with buoyant Blackburn ends 6-4 to the midlanders. JPT: Saints take lead at MK Dons. S Cup: Soutar pen save helps Dundee win at Livi. Stirling is also through against Albion in replay. ANC: Egypt and Algeria both enter the last eight.

21   Tevez launches attack on Man U amid fears of crowd trouble in second leg. Gallas will escape censure. UEFA wants to crack down on debt. Bond issue at Man U is a winner. WC finalists are lining up security guards. ANC: Zambia and Cameroon complete the qualifiers.

22   Hull seeks agent fees recoup. Tevez and Neville are warned by the FA after exchange of views on derby day.

23   FA Cup: Resurgent Reading digs deep and long to oust Burnley. Two-goal born-again Beckford keeps his nerve with an overtime pen after Defoe's spot kick is saved by Ankergren, so Leeds get another bite at Spurs. Newcastle's 14-game unbeaten run ends but Baggies are given two controversial pens by ref Linnington who denies Toon the same, the Mags claiming a dodgy goal and suspect red card, too! Pompey is able to put aside cash crisis to retrieve win over Sunderland. Debt-ridden Notts frighten Wigan to get another chance. Cardiff Bluebirds have fifth game in 15 days but 92nd and 93rd min goals fox Leicester. Fifteen no loss Brum's bandwagon rolls on at Everton. Accrington finds ten men are not enough to hold disappointing Fulham. Brighton is not disgraced at Villa. Bolton is two-good for Sheff U. Saints relish Thomas 30 yarder and go on to beat Ipswich. Seven-change Wolves have to replay with Palace. Baby Fergie's home debut at PNE ends in defeat as Chelsea make the 5th round for the 12th consecutive time, but Carter's levelling miss is costly. Sub McEveley arrives in time for Derby over Donny. FL: Rooney is not only four (3 in last eight) for Man U, but is the club as Hull sinks. FLC: 1 off. Boro held by Swansea and 16,847 is Riverside's lowest. Third in a row for Sheff W! L1: Eight goals in ten games! Norwich equals club record ten on the spin at home despite Holt red. Stockport rings the changes and stops the 12 defeat rot in drawing at Carlisle. L2: O'Grady hat trick sparks clear leaders Rochdale in rocking Robins at Cheltenham. Eighteen no win Grimsby loses at Rotherham. Shots deal blow to Bournemouth in card-sharp hit. Two-down Burton wins at Torquay. SPL: Rangers need a late Little sub to rescue pt against ten-man Hearts (two yellow Nade). Killie loses again at Aberdeen. Hibs hit Acccies for five. SL: Dundee held at QofS, so Ross edges Ayr and closes gap. Cowden slips up at Dumbarton, but East Fife share six with Stirling. Livi needs an overtime leveller to thwart Stranraer, as East Stirling goes level at the top. BSP: Long gives Kettering short shrift at Stevenage. Oxford nets four at Grays. York (9 no loss), Mansfield are both winners.

24   FA Cup: Gunners fire power ends at Stoke on Campbell return to leave just Chelsea of "Big Four" in it. Even Robinho scores for Man C in win at Scunthorpe. SPL: Four "aways" for Dundee Utd at Falkirk and Celtic at ten-man St J. ANC: Ghana, Algeria into semis as Angola and Ivory Coast miss out. Inter finishing with ten men still beats AC Milan for JM delight and Ronaldinho has pen saved by Julio Cesar. Ronaldo scores twice then sees red for Real.

25   Charlton suffers first defeat at home to Orient. S Cup: Raith's ten are unable to beat Airdrie. Egypt, Algeria (on shoot-out) edge into semis over Cameroon and Zambia – Ahmed Hassan's 170th cap for the Egyptians. Gaddafi's boy is a likely Pompey saviour! Notts seek £2m in a hurry.

26   Spurs firm on fourth place as Fulham slip up. Liverpool held by the Wolves. Coyle's Trotters clip old Burnley mates. It's a point for Pompey- with transfer ban likely to ease – against West Ham, who hopes to sign McCarthy from Rovers. Rio Ferdinand is facing FA wrath and Sir Alex bans Sky from meeting. But Man U is to sign Smalling at £7m. Palace enters administration. FLC: Cardiff 6th game in 18 days manages to find six goals at Bristol C! Forest (19 no loss) fire five over QPR who have never won there. WBA leaves it late at Ipswich for a point. Boro gets four at Donny! Baby Fergie returns to Posh and has the points for PNE. L1: Leeds are back to wearing worn out League form in crashing at Swindon, as Norwich assume top spot at come back time at Walsall. Colchester dents MK Dons. Strugglers Stockport draws again, Tranmere wins. L2: Notts hoping for more investment get a dividend at Dagenham. Vale holds Rochdale at Spotland. BSP: Kettering moves up at Gateshead. SPL: Valuable point for Killie at Hamilton. Livi is back to winning in Div 3. S Cup: Fifers reprieve game at Sten needs extra time for their winner.

27   C Cup: Red sky over Manchester, Blue Moon fading as Tevez strives to lift them, Rooney does better, so Man U hits the final. PL: A Bridge too far for Birmingham as their 15 game run ends at Chelsea. Arsenal held at "long-ball" Villa (Wenger version) and Vermaelen is injured. Black Cats stuffed by the Toffees at Goodison. Wigan loses again, only one win in seven now, as it is back-to-back wins for Blackburn. FLC: Newcastle gift-wrapped win against cash-strapped Palace. Owls come unstuck at Scunny. Reading appoints McDermott as manager. Chester faces tax bill. SPL: Rangers take giant step towards title as they win at St Mirren and Celtic slip up to Hibs at home. Dons win at Hearts puts Laszlo job on line. S Cup: Raith wins replay at Airdrie.

28   Rio appeal ends in four-match ban. ANC: Egypt takes its revenge on Algeria and meets Ghana in final after they edge Nigeria. Pompey is to sell players without boss man Grant's knowledge. Ex-Chelsea Gudjohnsen falls in line for Spurs. Palace has 10 pts deducted. Vermaelen is not too badly injured. Mutu fails another drug test!

29   Terry's future as England skipper remains in doubt after affair revealed. Kroenke grip on Arsenal is increased. Chester players call off strike after payment. Juve chases Benitez.

30   Headliner Terry brought to booking but heads the winner for Chelsea at Burnley. Birmingham (tenth goal in 12 homers) unchanged starting XI eleven games on trot, deprives Spurs of a win in stoppage time. Flying Kuyt's 49th Liverpool goal lifts Liverpool over Bolton. Fulham with five defeats on the spin find Villa a problem at the Cottage. Everton's late winner at Wigan deepens Latics gloom. Hammers and Blackburn (claiming a pen) finish all square. Wolves twice lead at Hull (first Lge goal in 203 mins) in another draw. FLC: 1 off. Ten Foxes hold Newcastle scoreless. Ram raid does for ex-boss Billy Davies and Forest in stormy affair. Palace knocks off three points of deficit with Posh struggling again. Lucky pen helps WBA over Sheff U. Ten-man Boro gets a point with Bristol C. One win in 13 and QPR loses to Scunthorpe. Late winning Cardiff shows against Donny in sixth game in 18 days. L1: 1 off. Paynter 44 secs for Swindon against his ex- Southend mates, but Shrimpers share four goals in the end. Stockport 100 days and 15 Lge games no win lose at Soton. Slipping Charlton gift og to Tranmere in another draw. Loanee Nathan Eccleston, 19, debut winner for Huddersfield against Yeovil missing pen. Leeds and

Beckford on form again see off Colchester. Wycombe eight no win needs two pens for victory at Bristol R. L2: 3 off. Ten man Vale hits Hereford. Shots gift Grimsby og, level it, then Proudlock fires spot kick over the bar late as the Mariners settle for 20th game without a win. No win in 14 for Barnet. Bournemouth revives at Crewe. SPL: Rangers, Celtic both win while Killie and Dundee Urd share eight goals. SL: Ross deal Dundee a blow at Dens Park. Montrose celebrate first win of the season at 20th time at Berwick. East Stirling again levels up on points with Livi. BSP: Rushden race to six goals at Hayes. Trophy: Holders Stevenage takes out Dover. Workington surprises AFC Dons. York and Oxford are both through. ANC: Nigeria beats Algeria for third spot.

31 Rooney's 100th PL goal as Man U makes it a little more difficult for Arsenal at the Emirates. Man C sees the return of Adebayor in low-key win over Pompey. ANC: Egypt wins the final with Ghana. HM Government puts in its "tuppence" worth in the Terry affair.

FEBRUARY
Terry loses England armband ... Only Chelsea left of "Big Four" Cup ... Man U ends San Siro hoodoo ... and wins Carling.

1 Deadline day: Adam Johnson, Boro to Man C, £6m; Scott McDonald, Celtic to Boro, £3.6m; Begovic, Pompey to Stoke, £3.25m; Victor Moses, Palace to Wigan, £2.5m; Benni McCarthy, Blackburn to West Ham, £2.25m; Lee Miller, Aberdeen to Boro, £500,000; Christopher Buchtmann, Liverpool to Fulham, £100,000; Robbie Keane, Spurs to Celtic, loan. PL: Sunderland and Stoke find no goals on view. L2: Bury edges Rochdale to move into third place. Posh axes Cooper after 13 games. FA passes buck to Capello over Terry issue.

2 Hull holds Chelsea and Terry for valuable point. FA Cup: Butterfield spreads it for Palace with three goals in six minutes to floor Wolves. FLC: Watford's first win in two months catches Sheff U. L1: 1 off. Charlton drops two more points at Walsall. Orient hits Bristol R for five. L2: 1 off. Bournemouth posts another win at Rotherham. BSP: Wrexham surprises Mansfied, while York is held at Histon. CIS semi: St Mirren shakes Hearts. SPL: Celtic are Keane enough, but Killie keener as loan star Maguire gives them first win in nine years at home against the Bhoys. Bairns shake Aberdeen and dump Accies to the bottom. Derby and Forest face brawl punishment. Jim Gannon is appointed by Posh.

3 FA Cup: Defiant Defoe does in doughty Leeds with a Spurs hat trick. PL: Pompey with fourth different owner this season, still manages to lose at Fulham. FLC: Bednar double sends Blackpool packing to restore Baggies to second place. CIS semi: Rangers account for St Johnstone. West Ham looking to save money. Notts deal collapses.

4 Capello arrives for Terry talks. Chelsea off the hook at least with Kakuta after deal with Lens on transfers is lifted for them. Private life revelations now hit Grant at Pompey.

5 Twelve decisive minutes and Terry loses armband to Ferdinand. Newcastle romps it with high five over Cardiff in club's record 15th unbeaten game.

6 Oggy, oggy, oggy! Three (nine for season) deflections and it's high five for table-topping Man U against doomed Pompey, but green and gold (Newton Heath colours) campaign grows at Old Trafford. Liverpool hits fourth place! Kuyt with 50th goal is again the difference in the bruising ten-a-side 213th Merseyside derby. Spurs drop down a place in goalless draw with Villa. Fulham finishes similarly at Bolton after Elmander miss and Kevin Davies on 500th League game is denied a goal by ref Clattenburg. Hull leaps to 14th with first win in eleven games by beating slumping Man C. Stoke's long ball shortens Blackburn expectations on Pulis 300th in charge of City. Burnley gives boss Laws his first win and consigns West Ham to bottom three. Eleven in a row without a win causes Sunderland concern in draw with Sheff U. Eleven PL teams face the drop! FLC: WBA wins at Plymouth despite ten men and missed pen. Sheff W boils with rage as ref Kettle awards Forest a pen. Nine-man QPR even lose at Peterborough. Palace second half revival ends ten-man Scunny hopes. Twenty-two secs debut goal for Murphy but Ipswich draws for 15th time with Boro. Another ten-man outfit Reading (Mills against old mates) wins at Doncaster. Yet another losing to a red card triumphs as Barnsley edges Watford. L1: Top of the tree Norwich slip up after 16 unbeaten games with sub "old reliable" Harris marking 300th Millwall outing with a winner. Leeds held at the death by Hartlepool, Charlton scraps a point late on at Swindon. Stockport 16 without a win sees lead swallowed up by MK Dons. L2: As Bournemouth is held, Rochdale increases lead to six points. Bury keeps pace, too, as Bradford where boss McCall considers quitting. Northampton unbeaten in ten games blunts the Daggers. Sad Shots end Barnet's 13 no win run. Hughes 22nd goal for Notts as Grimsby goes club record 20 without a win. S Cup: Rangers held at St Mirren. Six players share nine goals for Ross as Stirling (home ground under threat) goes off the goal standard. Tayside joy as Dundee U wins at St Johnstone and Dundee clips Ayr. Killie takes out Caley but after a tussle. Hibs hit Montrose for five. Raith earn replay with Aberdeen. SL: East Stirling continues to chase Livi – held by Forfar – by beating Berwick. Another few away goals for Stranraer! BSP: Stevenage finishes with nine men at Tamworth and loses. Oxford held. York win at Kettering is their 11th undefeated.

7 Drogba at the double and Arsenal are set packing as Chelsea resumes at the head of affairs. Unchanged melody for Birmingham, but soloist sub Phillips is the two-goal hero as Wolves are tamed. S Cup: Fifers lead Celtic before order is restored. Euro 2012 draw: England get Wales, Switzerland, Bulgaria and Montenegro; the Republic finds itself with Slovakia, Macedonia, Armenia and Andorra; Northern Ireland with Italy, Serbia, Slovenia, Estonia, Faeroes while Scotland faces Spain, Czech Republic, Lithuania and Liechtenstein. Finals are in Poland and Ukraine who are excused qualifying.

8 Bradford and McCall agree to part. Pompey seeks postponement of court day and Cardiff is confident of avoiding a wind-up. Colchester is more at home in the sand than Southend!

9 Dindane rescues a point for ten-man Portsmouth with Grant sent to the stands as Sunderland end with two short. Burnley, who doesn't do away games, stops Fulham's rot at the Cottage. "Thud and blunder" as Wigan and Stoke divide it. Johnson starting from the off in second game gives Man C wake up call against Bolton. FLC: Shock, Horror! Newcastle crashes at Derby, so Baggies nab top spot against Scunny. Forest fades at Coventry. Cardiff heaps more problems onto Posh. Swans shine at the Palace. L1: Tranmere pulls Gillingham into the bottom four. L2: Notts surprised at Bournemouth, Bury clip Macclesfield and Northampton ends Stanley run. JPT: Carlisle shakes Leeds in penalty shoot-out (but post-match trouble) to meet Soton in final, the Saints taking out MK Dons. BSP: Oxford slips up at Luton, so Stevenage takes advantage over Mansfield. Unpaid Chester players refuse to fulfil fixture at FGR. SL: Alloa leap frogs Cowden at the top of Div 2, Livi consolidates in Div 3. Terry will be allowed to spend more quality time with family.

10 "Saha-ronara" as his two Everton goals send Terry on beach leave and Chelsea back empty handed. Man U's second highest scorer – Oggy – gives the ten men a point at Villa to close gap on leaders to just one. Arsenal capitalizes by beating Liverpool as Rafa claims a pen. Own goal ends ten-man Hull hopes at Blackburn. Wolves complete a double over Spurs and first at home since 1981. Hammers with first win in six, climb to 14th place as G and S owners celebrate against former club Birmingham, who changed team. Pompey is given extra time by the courts.

SPL: Celtic makes a little ground on Rangers after beating Hearts. Rangers only draw at Motherwell. Struggle Killie, Hamilton wins away at Falkirk and Dundee U. SL: East Stirling closes gap on Livi by defeating Elgi Chester fans may form breakaway club.

11   Ashley Cole is out for three months with broken ankle, Giggs misses Wembley with a broken arm. Eriksson qui Notts as takeover happens at Meadow Lane. Chester handed seven-day ban. Hull settles legal dispute out c court. Leeds Carnegie beats Everton in Women's PL Cup final.

12   Eriksson writes off £2.5m owed by Notts. Cobblers runs ends at last as Shots nail their ten men. Bridge wants play for England again.

13   FA Cup: "Big Four" survivors Chelsea go foursome after an hour to overcome battling Cardiff. Ridgewell is aga. the last man standing for Birmingham in victory at Derby. "King" James rules ok for Pompey against the Saints a cash-strapped Portsmouth wins the bragging rights late on at St Mary's. Kebe hits FA Cup proper fastest recor goal in nine seconds for Reading but Albion still bags a draw. Man C squanders a gift as Stoke draw with trad mark throw of the sub Delap dice. FLC: Swansea riles as Toon leveller Carroll escapes card. Plymouth secure first win at Barnsley for 18 years. Gallagher achieves first hat trick in Leicester high five. Blackwell celebrates tw years at Sheff U with a win. Forest cut down again by Donny. L1: Leeds scrapes draw at Orient with an og in th fourth minute of time added. Austin powers Swindon to a draw in tenth undefeated. First home goal in 601 mir for Brighton but still four months there without a League win! Harris is again the main man for Millwall. Carlisl is a five-star winner over MK Dons. L2: Daggers put Bournemouth to the sword. Bury slips up at Chesterfield. L Fondre hits the 22 goal mark for Rotherham, his best yet. Grimsby makes it 21 without a win but get a point. SPL Celtic forced to share eight goals at Aberdeen. SL: Ross fights back to draw with Dunfermline in Div 1. Allo extends lead to four points in Div 2. In Div 3 Livi, two down to Annan, rallies to win.

14   FA Cup: Warnock likely on the carpet again after "lino" complaints following crucial corner as Palace draws wit Villa. Spurs miss pen – fourth out of six (loaned out Keane only scorer!) – so need to replay Bolton. Fulham four some puts Notts in their place and Sven seeks employment. Rangers treble over Hibs puts them ten pts clear o Celtic. Season over? PL thinking of play-offs for fourth place. Ex-Man U's Forlan helps Atletico Madrid firs down for Barca. Inter seven pts clear.

15   Charlton falters again at Bristol R and loses Basey with broken leg.

16   Ch Lge: Roo shakes, rallies and rules Man U to end 52 years of not scoring at the San Siro. Makoun magic fror 25 yards a Lyon lays Real Madrid low. E Lge: Everton edges Sporting but loses Fellaini with ankle injury. PL: Ma C limps into fourth place with late leveller at Stoke. FLC: Cardiff and WBA (top again) draw, Forest beats She U's ten-men, Derby hits PNE for five in eight goal thriller and Posh wins against Ipswich! L1: Leeds slip up in firs home defeat to Walsall, Colchester wins at Yeovil. BSP: Oxford puts Rushden on the spot to lead by three p with game in hand. S Cup: Raith stuns the Dons at Pittodrie in replay. Peter Taylor is appointed by Bradforc Dave Kevan gets Notts job to season's end.

17   Ch Lge: Comedy of errors starring Fabianski in goal for Arsenal and "Calamity" Hansson of "Hand of Frog fame as ref so Porto beat the Gunners and spoil Campbell's comeback goal. Klose holds his hand up to offsid winner for Bayern from Fiorentina. PL: Another goalless draw for Lancs rivals Wigan and Bolton on poor pitch FLC: Newcastle back on top after foursome against Coventry who led, while Palace dip again to Reading a Warnock is rumoured to be finding a job elsewhere. L2: Notts held by Grimsby and Hughes sees added time re S Cup: Boyd digs Rangers out against St Mirren. SPL: St J hits five against ten finishing Hibs. Curbishley get Hammers compensation. Tax man looks at Pompey. Shakhtar players turned away at Harrods!

18   E Lge: Fulham have something in store against Donetsk – a super strike from Zamora. Liverpool scrapes a late winner through N'Gog as Unirea concede just once. Wolves given suspended sentence for fielding weak team Man U. FIFA admits to WC ticket hike. Blatter faces leadership challenge. Conference clubs are likely to ditc Chester.

19   Chelsea cracks the whip over off-field misbehaviour. Wenger hits out at Hansson performance. Pompey seek extra time to sell players. Briatore quits at QPR. Bury edges Shrewsbury to go second.

20   Moyes' men make it Mersey misery for Man U on another Rooney revisit to Everton. Cech mate at one end Drogby duo at the other, star as Chelsea denies Wanderers at the Wolves den. Arsenal keeps in the hunt a "lucky" (?) Black Cats suffer 13th since last PL win. Back-to-back wins for Hammers as ten-man Hull rival. On the-brink Pompey topples over in the last minute to ten-man Stoke (Diao first goal in six years). FLC: Hughton' homers have Preston in their pockets as the Toon march on. Swans peck at the Rams but too much "animal" mis behaviour. Rangers win at last. Club record nine wins in succession at home for Forest. Clean sheet and win fo Ipswich. Injury-hit Cardiff is downed by Barnsley's Bogdanovic. Coventry pushes Palace into deeper trouble. L1 First win in six for Charlton – first in 17 games and four months for Stockport! Leeds 95th min leveller and spark fly with Brighton. Nine games and it's no loss for Huddersfield. Two-goal Barnard allows Saints to trample ove ten-man Norwich. Gills end ten games no win sequence. Seven matches since last win for Southend. Tranmer moves out of drop zone. Wycombe achieves double over pen-missing Millwall as Kelly hits debut winner. L2 Grimsby makes it 23 and club record no win in another draw. Veteran Alsop, 36, equals Cheltenham League goal record with 38th to end six game no win. Chesterfield scores three in last ten mins at Darlo. Hereford chucks two goal advantage to Burton's 96th min winner. Rochdale leaves it late against the Daggers. SPL: Rangers rage ove St J pitch postponement as Keane lifts Celtic. Falkirk shakes Aberdeen. SL: Paton puts Partick in their place a Dundee just win. All off in Div 2, but Livi wins crucially at East Stirling. Trophy last four: Kiddy knocks ou Oxford. Stevenage late winner hits Workington. Salisbury edges Tamworth. Barrow v York is off. BSP: AFC Dons win at Luton (7736). Third successive draw for JM boys as Inter finishes with nine, Sampdoria with ten Henry is on target for Barca. Leaders Bayern are held.

21   Spurs back to fourth but only after Defoe "off-side" goal and Ruskie Pavlyuchenko double floors Wigan. Fear o losing duo Man C and Liverpool settle for no goals. Burnley, Bolton with new bosses bounced out by Villa's high five – after O'Neill rant – and Blackburn in another Lancs derby respectively. Zamora's 89th min goal edges Brum but Capello had left Fulham by then. FLC: Baggies beaten at Bristol C after leading. SPL: Hearts put more pres sure on Accies. England's WC HQ is a building site. Ronaldo sparks Real's six-hit effort over Villarreal. Lev erkusen's 23 unbeaten run is Bundesliga record.

22   RM may be in Man C unrest mix and return of Tevez awaited. Chelsea emphasises good conduct off the field i essential. Steve Bruce fined for ref rant, Derby and Swansea for brawl. Ronaldo (the fat one) is to retire in 2011. Pompey retains hopes of another buyer. Rotherham and Shrews draw, but Disley breaks ankle.

23   Ch Lge: Barca draws in Stuttgart, Bordeaux more direct at Olympiakos. E Lge: Benfica is foursome against Hertha. Rooney is at the double – who else – as Man U beats West Ham, but worries over Rio's fitness. Pompey is heading for administration, but Notts, who appoint Steve Cotterill as boss, may be in the clear. FLC: Leicester wins at Donny, Scunny and Ipswich draw. L1: 2 off. Norwich back from the dead against Southend, Becchio brace buoys Leeds, Charlton bows to Brighton. L2: 2 off. Rochdale stunned by Bradford. Another point for Grimsby 24

games without a win and ten-finishing. Daggers turn tables on Shots after two down. BSP: 2 off. Oxford defeats ten-man AFC Dons to go six points clear.

24   Ch Lge: Advantage JM as Inter edges Chelsea (Cech injured). Sevilla holds CSKA in Moscow. FA Cup: More woe for Man C, Adebayor sees red and the Blue Moon sinks late at Stoke. Reading prevails over Albion in extra time to reach last eight for first time in 83 years, but ends in melee. Palace blows it at Villa Park in match of three pens. Another Ruskie double as Spurs ease over Bolton. Chesterfield goes fourth in L2. BSP: Stevenage has crucial win at Wrexham. Administration seems almost a gift for Pompey now!

25   Bridge's span for England ends with resignation. Adebayor is banned for four games. Midweek idea for FA Cup looks a loser. Eriksson and Hoddle chase Nigeria job. E Lge: Everton crashes out at Sporting, but Gerrard hits record 33 goals in Europe mark away to Unirea and Fulham holds Shakhtar in Donetsk, two English clubs carry on.

26   Arsenal cuts debt to £190m. Chester City chucked out of Conference! Ten-man Shrimpers dip out to the Addicks in the dying moments.

27   Blues Battle of the Bridges – Wayne and Stamford – Ballack and Belletti banished, Terry (boycotted by W Bridge) baited by brace-man Bellamy and two-goal Tevez as Man C completes first double over Chelsea for 52 years and go fourth. Arsenal anger over horror tackle by England call-up Shawcross as Ramsey's right ankle is broken as ten-man Stoke suffer late defeat. Stricken Pompey gains second away win at Burnley. Not dog eats dog, but Trotters end 550 goalless minutes to bite Wolves at Bolton. Brum's McFadden leaves Wigan on the spot with pen that was not. FLC: Carroll, with court day behind him, helps Newcastle in win at Watford. Eight unbeaten Leicester gains revenge on Forest. WBA comeback edges Derby. Cardiff slips up again at Preston. Goalie Stockdale comedy gaffe aids Sheff U over Plymouth. High five Reading ground the Owls. L1: All square in fine West Yorkshire derby with Huddersfield and Leeds. Oldham stopped by Norwich's Holt. Saints nap hand hits Walsall. Brighton with worst home record gives Poyet a home win. Four up Stockport almost let Wycombe in. L2: Grimmer for Grimsby, 25 no win now. New boss Cotterill (nearly not let in by gateman!) sees Westcarr's first hat-trick as five-goal Notts show Hereford Bulls the door. "Seb the sub" Harris ex-Yankie college boy has Northampton's winner. One goal is enough for Rochdale and Rotherham (Le Fondre's 24th) at Macc and Burton respectively. Bournemouth loses to Shrewsbury in fixture. SPL; Dons with worst home record go eight points adrift of the cut against ten-man Hearts. SL: 8 off. Alloa beats Peterhead, but own goal confusion has media with reverse score! Ross slips up to the Jags. BSP: York goes west at home to Eastbourne. Vase: W for away day: Whitehawk, Whitley Bay and Wroxham all win. Spain: Ronaldo inspires five-goal Real, while Barca leaves it late.

28   C Cup Final: Rooney comes on and makes the Man U winner after Vidic controversially stays on the field despite conceding Villa's penalty. PL: Spurs reclaim fourth place but lose Huddlestone injured against Everton, whose Donovan misses equaliser. It is goalless for Sunderland – 14 no win now – and Fulham at Stadium of Light. Torres starts and finishes off Blackburn for Liverpool. SPL: Brown sees red for the bhoys in Green and blue is the colour as Rangers with late scrambled winner, go ten pts clear with game in hand. Season over? Last surviving Newcastle 1951 FA Cup winner Charlie Crowe dies at 85.

MARCH
Wembley not pitch perfect … Fulham E League hopefuls … Another FA Crisis … Rooney injury worry.

1   FA urged to cut up rough over Wembley pitch. South Africa boss tips England for WC. "Red Knights" supporting Green and Gold aim for Man U takeover. There are still taxing times ahead for Pompey. Neil Warnock gets the QPR job, fifth boss this season. Highbury clock to tick again at the Emirates next term. Bruce job is safe at Sunderland.

2   Gerrard will lead England against Egypt. Terry faces irate fans. Robinho (remember him?) lifts Brazil team with a goal against Republic at the Emirates (of course). U21s: N Ireland wins in San Marino, Scots held by Azers. L1: Five again for rampant Saints as even Huddersfield crumble. L2: Rochdale back winning as Rotherham suffers there. BSP: Stevenage hits six at Eastbourne, Ten-man Oxford sat at Cambridge. Trophy: Barrow beats York to reach semis. "Rent-a-boss" Paul Hart is new Palace manager. Pompey's latest owner (Chainral) promises £15m lifeline. Keith Alexander, 53, Macclesfield manager dies.

3   England survive goal down, Terry boos and sub Crouch gets a couple against Egypt as Baines fits No. 3 spot ok. Levein sees new Scots beat Czechs, N Ireland loses in Albania as Craigan hits woodwork twice, Elmander beats Wales for Sweden. England's WC opponents fare: USA edged out by Dutch, Algeria concedes three to Serbia, but Slovenia is foursome over Qatarr. Elsewhere, Spain wins in France, Argies in Germany. Man U attacks "Red Knights." Tevez has a pop at Terry. U21s: England loses to Greece in Doncaster and may not progress. Armenia surprises the Republic. BSP: Rushden climbs to fourth at Histor.

4   South Africa's president Jacob Zuma attempts to push aside fears over WC safety. Capello plans England strategy. PL scraps play-off idea. Man U's consortium in revolt gets more dosh backing.

5   Owen is out for season. Rooney injured knee remains a worry but Sir Alex is unconcerned over "Red Knights" issue. Wembley pitch will be re-laid (fifth time in a year).

6   FA Cup: Paucity-ridden off the pitch, Pompey's pair man Piquionne sends Birmingham packing, though Brummies denied clear goal on day FIFA writes off technology. Fulham and Spurs are to try again after goalless draw. PL: Scholes 100th PL goal (19th so to do and eighth for one club) fires Man U to top at Wolves. Arsenal takes out Burnley but Fabregas injured. West Ham concedes first home goal in 399 mins and crucially loses to ten-man Bolton. FLC: Six for Newcastle but only after red card for Barnsley keeper. Five star Donny at Bristol C. W and H boss-swap works as QPR beats Sheff U. Forest's tenth home win in a row and they go second, but Swans denied a pen. L1: Norwich increases lead to seven points beating Yeovil. Leeds, one win in seven, is held by Brentford, but Charlton defeats Stockport. Swindon hammered at home by Bristol R. Millwall fights back to 93rd min leveller at ten-man Walsall. O'Donovan hits treble for Huddersfield against slumping Southend – his earlier loan club. Saints – first defeat in eight – edged out at Tranmere. L2: Rochdale held by Lincoln. Chesterfield ride luck at thrice-woodwork hitting Cheltenham to win. Small squad Bournemouth lifted by the win over Morecambe. Grimsby ends 26 no win game sequence against Shrewsbury. Torquay's fifth unbeaten makes it five defeats in a row for Darlo. SPL: Rangers fight back to defeat St Mirren as Walter Smith advocates 18-team league. SL: Div 1: Two down Dundee levels with Caley, but Ross gains ground on them. Div 2: Cowden six hitters close gap on drawing Alloa. Nine Warriors hold Arbroath for Sten. Div 3: Lynch scores trio for East Stirling. BSP: Stevenage climbs on top over Crawley. Vase: Barwell into semis after Ancients lose.

7   FA Cup: Chelsea at the double over Stoke and Terry holds his head high for one goal. Reading starts with a Long, Long brace of goals but Villa ties it up with four in the second half and a Carew hat trick. PL: Five more holes in the Hull at Everton as the good ship City is still adrift. SPL: Keane double as Celtic wins at Falkirk. Ronaldo helps Real Madrid to the top. Inter held at home by Genoa.

Fernando Torres of Liverpool drives past Sunderland's Paulo da Silva during the 3-0 Premier League win at Anfield.
Torres scored twice and Glen Johnson was also on the scoresheet. (Action Images/Alex Morton)

8   Fourth place Liverpool? – You're having a laugh as they slip up to Rodallega at Wigan (first such win over them) with Gerrard and Torres among yellow cards. Colchester held by Brighton. Hereford sacks Trewick so Turner takes over again. Chester is axed from the BSP.

9   Ch Lge: Five-star Gunners (Bendtner treble) put Porto out of their misery. Bayern edged in Florence but go through on away goals. PL: Birmingham revenges itself on Pompey. Bent hat trick ends Sunderland sorrow of 14 no wins. Gerrard will escape censure. England players bugged. FLC: Sheffield sags as United lose to Posh's Mikhail-Smith 100th career goal and Wednesday goes down to the Baggies. QPR is unable to stop winning, but Palace loses at home to Bristol C. Murphy's law rules for Ipswich, unbeaten in 12 at home, as Cardiff fails. L1: Leeds is foursome at Tranmere. Millwall, MK Dons are both winners. L2: Notts keep chipping away with wins, Grimsby back to losing. BSP: Oxford in a daze as ten-man Hayes wins there, so four-goal Stevenage takes over at the top. Luton goes third but York slips up. SPL: Rangers in no danger it seems coasting at Killie. SL: Ross loses ground at Raith, but Cowden cuts Alloa's lead in Div 2 to three points with game in hand. East Fife's nine holds Clyde.

10   Ch Lge: Roo-two leads AC Milan a merry dance on Becks return to Old Trafford as Man U hits four. Real Madrid bows out to Lyon despite Ronaldo's early strike. PL: Burnley held by Stoke. FLC: Derby loses two goalies, one injured, one red, Savage dons the jersey but Reading hits them for four. Cardiff, Southend face taxing issues, Chester wound-up and record expunged, but fans to start new club. Pompey sacks 85 staff but keeps £35k a month Storrie. Capello hopes for WC semis.

11   E Lge: Hazard lights up Lille as the Liver boys trail late. Fulham will have to retrieve a two-goal deficit from Juve. Sporting's nine men hold Atletico Madrid. It's not all Greek for Standard away to Panathinaikos. Hamburg has a two-goal cushion over Anderlecht while the three other ties are level pegging: Benfica and Marseille, Rubin and Wolfsburg plus Valencia and Werder. "Red Knights" aim to court Becks. Pompey's finances are still being scrutinised.

12   Storrie quits Pompey, but stays as consultant. Greg Clarke appointed as FL chairman. Derby is not for sale. Woodgate undergoes groin op to save career. Farsley Celtic is finally wound up. JM unhappy ahead of Chelsea clash as Inter loses at Catania.

13   Chelsea overcomes Hammers leveller and finishes with four-timer. "Lucky" Arsenal snatches 93rd min winner at ten-man Hull as Gunners are tied on pts with leaders but a game more played. Born-again "Payly" pairs it again (14 of last 17 Spurs goals) as Tottenham hold fourth place against Blackburn. Even Muamba scores as Bolton hits four over Wigan. There is no good fortune for Burnley as Wolves snatch it with a deflection. Birmingham just preserves run of 11 no home defeats as Gardner digs deep to level with Everton. No March wind of change for O'Neill's poor month record in goalless at Stoke. FLC: Tees-Tyne derby sees four goals shared. Second spot WBA goes five clear of Forest – edged at PNE – by clipping Blackpool. One goal is enough for Leicester over Cardiff. Posh wins at Watford to close gap at bottom. Warnock is joyful over QPR draw at his "team" Sheff U. Boy Wickham, 16, is Ipswich's youngest League scorer for 26 years with winner over Scunny. L1: Norwich ends FL's only unbeaten home record at Huddersfield. Leeds slips up again at Soton. Millwall clobbers Charlton for four (17,632, best at New Den since 2002). L2: Rochdale's away success at Shrewsbury leaves them nine pts clear. Cheltenham's 6-5 special win at Burton sees Pook treble (94th min winner). Another trio for Richards (of five for PV) as Chesterfield suffers worst at home since 1976. SC: Keane hat trick for Celtic ends Killie interest. Dundee

finds Raith too strong, but Ross earns replay at Hibs. SPL: Falkirk crucially loses to St J. SL: Caley closes on Dundee. Alloa, Cowden keep winning in Div 2. McColm scores all three goals for Stranraer. BSP: Rushden rolls on with eight goal demolition of Gateshead. Oxford held by Kettering. Trophy semis: Stevenage shakes Kiddy with five away goals. Barrow takes slender lead at Salisbury.

14 Thirty-two goal flash forward Rooney twosome sends Man U back to top as Fulham are beaten. Game of two halves as Sunderland is caught at the death by one-time fan Johnson for Man C. S Cup: Rangers coasting it seemed before Dundee U hit two for a replay. Becks Achilles tendon tears in AC Milan win, to end his WC hopes.

15 Torres double sparks Liverpool's fourth place hopes in foursome over Pompey. Bournemouth does well to draw at Notts. Capello will give Becks a WC role. Hull sacks boss man Brown, with Dowie favourite. FL is to receive £7m deal from npower. JM is cool over Stamford Bridge return.

16 Ch Lge: Chelsea lost, Special won as Inter's virtual 4-2-4 baffles Ancelotti and it's ko by Eto'o with Drogba's two yellows leaving the Blues red faced. CSKA surprises Sevilla to go through. PL: Villa aided by an og wins at Wigan. FLC; It is a crucial win for WBA at Swansea as Forest slips up at Barnsley – sixth away on the trot. Cardiff also makes ground at Coventry. Ten-man Palace loses to Leicester and QPR goes down at improving Reading. L1: Austin breaks Saints hearts for Swindon. Crisis club Stockport trails to Oldham. L2: Rotherham is edged out at Accrington. SPL: More misery for Aberdeen at St Johnstone. SL: It's a significant draw for Alloa at Cowden in table-topping clash in Div 2. Livi held at Annan (604 present) in Div 3. BSP: Stevenage, Luton and York are the crucial winning teams. Gerrard will escape another censure over his clash with Pompey's Brown.

17 Ch Lge: Messi magic as Barca buries Stuttgart for four goals. Bordeaux' ten overcome Olympiakos' nine. FLC: Double-barrelled Carroll in Toon as Newcastle beats Scunny. L1: Exeter leaves it late for win over Bristol R. SL: Dundee manages a point at Ayr. Div 3: E Stirling keeps hoping as they score three over Albion. Nine pts deduction hits Stockport. Man U heads for Indian sponsorship. Iain Dowie is appointed at Hull. FA Youth Cup semi: Chelsea takes away win at Blackburn.

18 E Lge: By jove, by Juve by-passed by virulent Fulham who retrieved the deficit after conceding in 98 seconds, the Italians finishing with nine players. Two-goal Torres to the rescue for Liverpool after Gerrard's pen levels with Lille. Hamburg edged out by still go on as cc Wolfsburg the Germans. Away goals see Atletico and Valencia through, but Benfica surprises Marseille on the coast. Standard eases over Panathinaikos. Gary Johnson and Bristol C part company.

19 Ch Lge draw: Arsenal will face Barca, Man U paired with Bayern. Inter is down to meet CSKA while the two French teams Lyon and Bordeaux are in direct opposition. E Lge: Fulham will host Wolfsburg to start with while Liverpool is due to meet Benfica away first leg. Sir Alex hits out at "dysfunctional" FA over Gerrard. Defoe has an injury worry.

20 New boy Gunners lose Vermaelen to a dodgy red, Almunia saves Diamanti pen but Arsenal still beats West Ham. Injury-hit Spurs keep the fourth spot at ten-man Stoke who get ref Dean's 15th pen award but are unhappy over the card issue. Villa – only PL team unbeaten in 2010 – struggles to a midland derby point with two goals (both off-side?) from Carew against Wolves. Everton with 7th home win in a row moves up after beating ten-finishing Bolton whose boss Coyle is unhappy. Benni two goals in eleven mins, hoists Black Cats to 12th as Birmingham loses. Wigan's added time goal puts the skids under Burnley. Pompey even gives Hull a two-goal start and catches them cold in the last two mins. FLC; WBA manages maximum points from four games in eleven days as PNE loses. Yet Newcastle stays top with Carroll's 15th goal helping to draw at Bristol C after Gerken gets in a pickle. No bus for Posh team and they arrive in cars to lose at Forest (11th successive home win). Loan star Murphy D on target for Ipswich but Barnsley gk Steele gifts it. Scunny achieves first win in six. L1: Norwich held at Swindon. Jeers for Charlton from best of season 26,034, held by the Gills. Ten-man Walsall beats Colchester. Lambert hat trick sends his total to 30 as Saints erase MK Dons. Wycombe throws two-goal lead in draw with Exeter. Two down Southend with ten-man, levels with Carlisle. L2: Notts climb to second after winning at Crewe as 91st min winner for Grimsby dumps Bournemouth. Two-goal Rochdale hits four at Accrington to stay ahead. Two-goal Somma springs it for Lincoln at Torquay. Five wins in a row for Northampton. Darlo (1463) suffers 12th home defeat. SPL: Ninth goal in nine games for Keane as Celtic takes out St J. Hearts edge Edinburgh derby over Hibs. SL: Nose-diving Dundee crashes at cellar dwellers Airdrie and sack boss Jocky Scott. Alloa extends Div 2 lead with late goals beating Sten. Div 3 Livi beats Stranraer to lead by 11 points. BSP: One down at the interval, Luton sinks Ebbsfleet with six. Mansfield scores five at Histon. Trophy: Barrow edging Salisbury and Stevenage drawing with Kiddy will contest the final.

21 Man U goes top after Torres gives Liverpool the lead only for Rooney (later limping) to follow up Reina's pen save from him and Park has the winner. Rafa is unhappy with the spot kick. Chelsea held at Blackburn trickles down to third. Tevez inspires Man C at Fulham as the Blue Moon rises to the fifth quadrant. FLC: Leicester lets a two-goal lead dwindle away in Coventry craw. Cardiff stays above the cut after Watford victory. BSP: Wilder worries as Oxford fails to beat Tamworth. CIS Final: Rangers come to life – only when down to nine men – beat St Mirren. Steve Staunton is sacked by Darlington. Dundee appoints QoS duo Gordon Chisholm and Billy Dodds to lead them.

22 FA in another crisis as CEO Ian Watmore is "no more" having resigned. Torres escapes scuffing penalty spot before Rooney shot on Sunday. Steven Taylor suffers broken jaw in training spit with Carroll at Newcastle. Leeds slip up yet again as Millwall score twice there. Chelsea reaches FA Youth Cup final taking four off Blackburn.

23 Hammer horror as Wolves take a chunk out of their hopes and fans turn on them. FLC: Fives for Blackpool, Bristol C as Swans and Tykes are beaten. That man Carroll is again Toon winner. Forest equals Clough's 12 successive home wins in defeat of Palace. Scunny takes four off Posh. Ipswich is surprised by Argyle. L1: Colchester shares six with Brentford. Southend end nightmare run to beat Walsall. L2 Notts held at Bradford, another defeat for Darlo. BSP: Grays make Stevenage go all the way. S Cup: Joy for Ross as they edge Hibs to meet Celtic in semi-final. SPL: St J foils Falkirk in a draw. SL: Dundee fails to beat ten-man QoS! Alloa keeps ahead in Div 2. Alex Horne is temporary CEO at FA. Rafa wants Torres to calm down after five yellows in seven games. Worry over unsold WC tickets.

24 FA Cup: Spurs sub standard is the key to win over one-goal leading Fulham. PL: Chelsea takes it out on Pompey after another James gaffe in high five rout. Hand-bagging between M and M sees Mancini and Moyes banished to the stands as Everton end Man C's home record. Villa's March scare continues in a draw with Sunderland. Birmingham is Dunn-for as Blackburn edges them with his two goals. FLC: Baggies need just one goal over Coventry for fifth successive win, Cardiff held by Sheff U, Reading wins way at Leicester. L2: Bristol R on way to fourth place. Auld Firm disaster as Rangers lose S Cup replay at Dundee U in the dying moments and Celtic crashes by four clear goals at St Mirren! Hibs pile more misery on Killie. SL: Ten-man Stranraer edges S of Scots derby with Annan in dying seconds. BSP: Oxford held at Rushden after gifting an og. Inter marches on in Italy.

25   Everton – City problems mount as news of directors box confrontation emerges. Ricardo Carvalho is out for season, but Hargreaves on way back for Man U. Wenger states priority is season, not his contract. Celtic sacks Mowbray, leaving Lennon in charge. Friday night will start England's 2012 Euro qualification v Bulgaria at Wembley. Wigan supreme wants PL to run England team. England women beat Austria in WC qualifier.

26   Internal strife reigns at West Ham. Moyes comes to Mancini aid. PL sensing wounded FA goes for the kill. UEFA threatens to end PL's money-men. Bournemouth boosted by transfer embargo being lifted.

27   No Roo but Man U equals Chelsea's early season foursome win at Bolton after Terry-led (325th club record as skipper) Blues had hit another super seven with Lamps lighting up the Bridge over troubled Villa with his 151st strike – overtaking legends Osgood and Bentley to enter third in the Chelsea pecking order. Sub Phillips nips in for a Birmingham dead heat by a nose deflection (his 250th overall goal) to thwart Arsenal. Fourth place is still looking good for Tottenham (ex-Pompey pair scoring) as Portsmouth suffers again. Hammer horror mark 2 with Zola on the brink of giving up as Stoke made it West Ham's club record sixth PL loss in a row. Bullard puts old mates Fulham on the spot for Hull. It's goalless again at Molineux (only ten home goals) in a stalemate with Everton. FLC: Baggies made to fight for point at Reading. Palace with an injury list mounting forced to bow to Cardiff. QPR rallies to draw at PNE. Keane said to be on the brink at Ipswich manages a draw at Swansea. Weale gaffe spins Leicester out at Derby. L1: Tip-top Norwich nabs crucial victory over stuttering Leeds. Five for Millwall catches United on pts. Southend lose added time goal in best of seven win for Bristol R. Wycombe scrapes valuable draw at Colchester. Charlton is held at Huddersfield. L2: Dagnall trio for Rochdale as the leaders collect another four goals to aid Grimsby's woes, but Darlo causes a stir with a win at Shrews, as do Shots at Bury. Notts leave it late to keep second spot. Daggers share six with Bantams at Bradford. Bournemouth zooms back to winning ways against Stanley. SPL: Rangers on song again at Hearts. Keane double revives Celtic. SL: Ross Co and Dundee level it, so Caley goes top in Div 1. BSP: Stevenage remains the team to beat leaving Oxford to play catch-up after both win. Luton seven goals in 35 mins finish Hayes with eight. Money note: JM on £11m pa at Inter! Vase semi: Six goals shared by Barwell and Whitley Bay.

28   Tor-Tor Torres at the double as Black Cats are put out at Liverpool. Burnley blisters over Blackburn "dive" and pen as this Lancs derby day ends in its Turf Moor defeat. Scunny welcomes slender win at Sheff U. JPT: Saints canonize the trophy with emphatic foursome over Carlisle. Vase semi: Wroxham two goals lead at Whitehawk. Welsh PL: The New Saints edge Llanelli in table-topper, seven pts ahead but three games more played. Eriksson is off the dole – i/c of Ivory Coast!

29   Wigan's Caldwell sees red then treble Man "Tevez" C revives fourth place chances. FLC: Newcastle adds to Forest's current away day blues. Labour party election pledge to allow fans to own clubs may be up the pole. Zola aims to see West Ham job through.

30   Ch Lge: Early striking Rooney suffers with ankle injury as Bayern strikes back late to beat Man U. Lyon wins all-Froggy tie with two goals to spare over Bordeaux. FLC: Crucial wins for Cardiff over Leicester near top, Palace at Watford at other end. L2: Stanley's game with Barnet hits water. SPL: Shocks for Rangers at St J, whacked with a foursome. SL: Dundee dumped at Dunfermline gives Caley (three goals to the good over ten-man Ross) the edge in promotion race. 4 off and another abandoned. Arsenal is to risk Fabregas. Drogba banned for two Euro games. JM may to turn back on Italy? O'Neill could be on the brink? Dog bites man (Maradona)!

31   Ch Lge: Gutsy Gunners force draw after being outplayed by Barca, but Fabregas breaks his leg. Inter may rue missed chances in slender lead over CSKA Moscow. Rooney will miss a month. Crucial win for Dundee U at Hibs consolidates third place. Gosling knee injury may keep him out for nine months at Everton. Ofcom's stance over TV funding is likely to affect the game's finances.

APRIL
Messi four floors Arsenal ... Skint Pompey reach Cup Final ... Newcastle back in Premier ... Inter beats Barca.

1   E Lge: Rafa riles over two pens and a Babel red as Benfica fire-crackers rule in Lisbon after early Liverpool lead. Fulham allows Wolfsburg to sneak an away goal after two-goal lead. Hamburg takes slender lead over Standard and twice leading Atletico Madrid lets Valencia level its tie. L1: Soton digs deep for late equaliser at Brighton in coastal issue. England women and Spain to their conquests. Drogba may need a hernia op. There is no Rooney fracture. Darlington appoints Simon Davey as manager. Hammers No.2 Steve Clarke might replace Zola in the summer.

2   Berbatov will bear Man U attack against Chelsea. FLC: Baggies deposit three at Leicester's expense. Blackpool enjoys foursome reel at Scunthorpe. L1: Tranmere surprises Norwich after Canaries gk is carded as does Exeter against Colchester. Millwall is held by Brentford. L2: Best of seven goals edges it for ten-man Morecambe over Crewe. Ten-man Grimsby suffers another reverse. BSP: Hayes achieves double over faltering ten-man Oxford. RM hints at return to Italy JM fuels his own departure.

3   Drogba's "offside" goal clinches it for Chelsea after Macheda "handles" Man U back in contention – so Joe Cole's back-flick is the one legitimate effort at Old Trafford as the Blues complete a double. Black Cats Bent double (36 secs opener two quicker than Defoe!) but the joke is on Harry R despite Gomes two-pen saves from the same ex-Spur (his third such). Evening sees Blue Moon rising above Tottenham with six-hitting as soggy, sinking Burnley so Man C goes fourth – first PL team to score five in first half plus three goals in first seven mins equals Spurs v Oldham 1993! Arsenal's customary added time (third in last six) is enough to paw over Wolves. Villa and O'Neill welcome April with victory at Bolton. Stoke moves to tenth easing over Hull, leapfrogging Blackburn (sixth goalless draw) at injury-ridden Pompey. FLC: Newcastle recovers from early an early strike from Posh, but Forest delay Toon promotion with draw at Bristol C. Chopra axes Swans in added time – first such Cardiff win since 1993. Charlton edges it at flapping MK Dons. Four defeats and Leeds still in a spin as United crumbles to Swindon at Elland Road. Rhodes 21st goal of the season helps Huddersfield win at Wycombe. One in eleven wins and another defeat against Hartlepool costs Geraint Williams his Orient job. Ipswich clips ten-man Reading. Ward injury as Sheff U draws derby with Barnsley. L2: Chesterfield surprises Rochdale. Pitman surfaces with his 20th Lge goal – best for Cherries for 38 years – as Bournemouth. Young early pen save aids Shots pt at Macc. Darlo wins away – again! Bury buried at five-star Notts. Alsop jets Cheltenham scoring record with 39th goal. SPL: Rangers (21 games since January) move 13 pts clear after beating Hamilton. Falkirk puts 'Well down for crucial win. SL: Caley 94th min winner keeps them four pts ahead with Dundee, Ross also winners. Witteveen hits hat trick for Morton over Q of S in six-share. Annan stuns Livi in Div 3. BSP: In-form Luton eight in a row upsets the odds at Stevenage (first home defeat). Grays relegated by Kettering draw. Vase: Whitley Bay and Wroxham for the Wembley final. Barca under-strength still scores four. Inter stays one pt ahead. Bayern goes top in Bundesliga as does Lyon in France.

4   Pursuit of fourth place looks unlikely for Liverpool drawing at Birmingham. Zola delights with a West Ham pt at Everton. Fulham fans unhappy despite a comeback win over Wigan. SPL: Keane is again the Celtic winner at

Hibs. Killie moves up a place beating the Dons. Real takes over top spot in Spain as Ronaldo hits 18th Lge goal in their 12th successive win. Auxerre misses chance to go top in France with a draw – three pts separate top six.

FLC: Squandering Forest held by Cardiff so Newcastle achieves promotion before beating Sheff U! WBA snatches draw at ten-man Watford. Leicester ends four defeats on the trot with four pasting of QPR. Sheff W is in the drop zone after Bristol C wins there. Posh will play in L1 next season after draw at Barnsley. O'Neil left out of Boro because £1m appearance money looms due to Pompey! L1: Norwich (Holt's 30th goal, first by Canary for 46 years) edges Stockport and Swindon (Paynter's 25th goal) stays in second spot after beating ten-man Tranmere and Millwall grateful for an og at Colchester maintains third place. Welcome win for Leeds at Yeovil, courtesy of skipper Naylor. Bottom five teams all lose and Crient appoints Russell Slade as manager. L2: Rochdale held by Bournemouth, so Notts – with ex-Salop captain Davies scoring – move nearer with a win at free-fall Shrewsbury. Rotherham is out to three strikes at Aldershot. Darlo loses at home, but Grimsby and Cheltenham are both away winners. Forty-one year old Furlong races to two goals, misses a pen, too, as Barnet surprises Chesterfield. SFL: Dundee U consolidates third place at St J. BSP: Stevenage wins at AFC Dons, Luton hits Grays for six and Oxford scrapes a win over Salisbury.

Ch Lge: Mercurial midget Messi massacres Arsenal with four goal five star display after Barca concedes early. Inter completes whitewash in Moscow over ten-man CSKA. L1: More misery for a struggler as Oldham loses at Huddersfield. SL: Giant strike for Caley at Morton as Ross is held. Livi leaves it late to edge Montrose.

Ch Lge: Rooney starts, scores, limps off and Man U (Rafael two yellows) chucks three goal lead to bow out as Robben hoodwinks them with a classic away goal for Bayern. Both English clubs are out and Sir Alex wails "typical Germans." Bordeaux beat Lyon but not enough to survive SPL: Rangers extends its lead in defeating the Scottish Dons (Aberdeen) while in the BSP York whacks five past the AFC variety! SL: Alloa takes another step towards promotion in Div 2.

E Lge: St George fights back as Fulham completes the double over Wolfsburg and Liverpool retrieves deficit with foursome – Torres getting two. Atletico knocks out Valencia on away goals, Hamburg eases again over Standard. Man U signs Chicharito (Little Pea) a £10m deal worth more than peanuts. Derby fined £50,000 for failure to control players, Swans £15,000 half suspended for same.

Pompey appoints David Lampitt as CEO from FA post. Liverpool may give chairman post to Martin Broughton from BA. Pompey fearful of reaching FA Cup final over payments to players! WPL: Llanelli held at Aberystwyth.

FA Cup semis: New Wembley "home" for Chelsea's Drogba – fifth goal in six outings – ends Villa hopes but O'Neill fury over Terry tackle on Milner and ref Webb pen refusal. PL: Burnley wins away! Alexander (885th game at 38) the great saint king (73rd of 78) adds another two as Hull is holed and Pompey relegated by it. Ilan crucially half volleys West Ham up to 16th against Sunderland. FLC: WBA's 23rd consecutive scoring match and 101st goal of the season lifts them at Donny and up to PL. Meanwhile four-goal Newcastle strolls on at the top. Reading holds Cardiff scoreless. Boss Davies at three goal Forest is eyeing third uplift with three different clubs. Sheff U ends five no-win run. Preston secures place in FLC. Winning Warnock returns to Palace with QPR. Swans downed at Bristol C. Losers Sheff W, Plymouth are still in the toils. L1: Colchester ends eight-game no-win to stun Swindon. Pardew does in old Charlton mates with Soton. Millwall four play hits the Gills. First win in nine for Wycombe. Stockport relegated by Yeovil. Chris Martin saves a point for Norwich. Leeds pile more problems onto Southend. L2: Torquay tanks Rochdale with five-goal salvo. It is a poor away day for Bournemouth at Lincoln. Notts landing unbeaten in 13 may be at the top after all. Gk red card sees Bury buried with five conceded at Chesterfield. Grimsby clings to survival with another away win. Shrewsbury debutant super-sub Tom Bradshaw, 17, is two-goal match winner. Darlo is on the brink. S Cup: Sensation as Dingwall Staggies from Ross defeat Celtic! SPL: Hearts secure sixth place beating Falkirk, now menaced near the foot. Falkirk edges St Mirren to draw level. Caley, Dundee, Dunfermline are all Div 1 winners. Alloa slips up in Div 2 with Stirling on the move, too. Forfar surprises Livi to go second. BSP: Stevenage four points clear with game in hand of Luton. Spain: Messi helps Barca to win at Real Madrid. Inter held at Fiorentina.

FA Cup semis: Dire straits Pompey sinks Spurs in extra time. PL: Blue Moon rises again (three in five mins again) with five star win over Brummies to go fourth. Not a goal between the other three games as Rooney-less Man U held at Blackburn, Liverpool fails to beat Fulham at Anfield and the stats at Stoke concern Delap's 27 throws and 26 passes at Wolves. S Cup semi sees Dundee U beat Raith to play Ross in final. SPL: Aberdeen still toiling against St J. Ranieri's Roma overtakes JM's Inter in Italy!

Life's a serial pitch at Wembley 10 in three years £1.25m. Shares are trading at Arsenal and it's not all bull. Torres is back in Spain for treatment. Exeter denied by added time og at Swindon. Stirling makes ground in SL Div 2.

Bolton's Coyle recoils as ref Probert fails to spot two "hands" as Chelsea edges closer to the title. Newcastle adds another win at Reading. L1: Five for Saints at Bristol R. Leeds, Charlton win, but Norwich loses at Orient and Millwall held at Tranmere. Valuable win obtained for Wycombe at Tranmere. L2: Notts takes over at the top as Darlo shakes Rochdale but are relegated to BSP! Rotherham's ten beat Northampton's nine men. Shots slip up to Torquay. Chris Roy named as FA Cup Final ref. BSP: Luton hits three-goal Histon for six and Oxford fails to beat Cambridge. SPL: Celtic beats Motherwell but only 27,750 turn up. SL: Livi held at Berwick. Arsenal welcomes Van Persie back after injury. Hunt is out for rest of season at Hull.

Rose is the thorn in Arsenal's side after 29.2 yard 69.7 min effort digs out Spurs despair to victory. Villa snatches two-all draw with a late og against Everton. Another scoreless effort involves Wigan and scratching around for players Pompey. SPL: Ten-man Dundee U holds Rangers on eve of League's split. Bates rages at Leeds over Aussie takeover rumours. Southend gets seven-day reprieve in court. BSP: Giant step for Stevenage at Altrincham – four point lead with game in hand over Luton. Barca lead in Spain is six points.

Gunners spiked at all levels – trophy room, fans and boardroom. FA Cup in midweek would suit ESPN. Birmingham faces financial inquiry as PL insists on new code for owners. Rooney is tipped for PFA title. Mancini is unhappy about Atkinson as ref for Mancunian derby – again seven added mins last time! Liverpool is up for sale.

Huddersfield dents Millwall unbeaten. Ince resigns at MK Dons but will stay to season's end. FA Youth Cup: Villa's edges Newcastle to reach final. Inter reclaims top spot beating Juve.

Man U is back – 92 mins 43 secs and Scholes hits the only goal to damage Man C's fourth hopes and revive their own title ones. Blues Terry sees two yellow become a red and Spurs get the green light in another derby day shock against Chelsea. Sunderland pushes Burnley nearer to the exit and Bent has scored half of the Black Cats 46 goals. Cahill is again Everton's winner as Arteta receives a card at Blackburn. Hull at Birmingham, Wolves (17th no score) at Fulham adds to the growing list of PL goalless draws. First time this season Bolton win after trailing with Taylor two in three minutes at Stoke. FLC: Pl-off spots: Baggies win ends Boro chance, but Cardiff ensures one at QPR. Blackpool is two points behind Swansea (winners over Barnsley) after beating third place Forest. Leicester consolidates hitting Watford for four. Reading goes to a plus goal difference with six against Posh and can still make it with Bristol C caught by a Hooper hat trick for Scunny. Including two of bottom three, nine clubs are in the relegation area. Ipswich manages club record 19th draw. L1 p-o spots: Norwich promoted at Charlton year

after being relegated there! Leeds grabbed by the Gills, Swindon held by Walsall, Colchester slips up at Hartlepool and ten Saints hit late winner at Yeovil. Elsewhere, Orient wins, Tranmere beats ten-man Exeter, resurgent Wycombe gets added time winner at MK Dons, but Southend bow to Brighton. Only three teams in the division have no interest! L2 p-o spots: Notts and Rochdale (after 41 years) are both promoted. Bournemouth assured a least of a place beats Darlo and seven points separate nine teams! Grimsby looks BSP candidate as Cheltenham needs a point after draw at Rotherham, as does Lincoln, while Barnet requires two. BSP: Stevenage is promoted to the FL after being denied in 1996. Luton, Oxford, Rushden and York are in the play-offs. SPL; Celtic keep Rangers waiting for title by beating Hibs. SL; Caley moves step nearer to Div 1 title and promotion by beating Dunfermline. Alloa slips up again so Stirling edges nearer. Livingston is champions of Div 3. Ten-man Barca is held by Espanyol. Robben scores three of Bayern seven.

18   Arsenal throws two-goal lead at Wigan to concede three in last ten and concede winner in 91st min. Villa's fourth place dream is revived at Pompey. FLC: Steel city derby all square does neither any down or up favours. SPL Rangers restore 11 pt lead beating ten-man Hearts. Torres out for season may miss WC, too. 11th Wembley pitch is started. UEFA plans no-fly alternatives for semis. Roma takes over in Italy. McClaren's Twente waits on brink of Dutch title treat. Real M is only point behind Barca now.

19   Liverpool's turn to go fourth chasing as win concerns West Ham. Newcastle is FLC champions and relegates Plymouth. Sex scandal hits France. Mutu gets nine-month drug ban! Lens agrees to let Dindane play in Pompey's final. Scottish FA CEO Smith resigns. Partick and Raith are goalless.

20   Ch Lge semis: Two-day coach trip and poor fare for Barca as JM's Inter stalls the Catalans in their tracks, with better tactics. Becks to lead England's backroom back-up for WC. Pompey could be £119m in debt. Essien is out for the season. QPR puts pressure on Watford. Tranmere edged out at Brentford, Oldham gets a point at Soton. Cheltenham manages a point – the hard way v Darlo, three goals down! Notts win table-topper with Rochdale (10,536). BSP: Stevenage wins at Gateshead. SL: Stirling win at Clyde relegates the Bully Wee.

21   Ch Lge semis: Robben strike gives Bayern the goal advantage over Lyon. PL: Hull ships another brace as Villa aim for fourth place. Southend goes two up. SL: Dundee loses at Raith, so Caley regains SPL spot. Airdrie only two points adrift of Ayr after win there.

22   E Lge semis: Liverpool 24 hour journey ends with Forlan (ex-Man U) scoring the only goal for Atletico Madrid. Fulham succeeds with a goalless draw at Hamburg in a seven hour fewer trek. N'Zogbia has a sub for his driving test! Coppell is new Bristol C boss, Millen as assistant. Parachute money is diverted to creditors, so no Euro happy landings for Pompey.

23   Carry-on Sir Alex! Birmingham CEO Michael Dunford resigns. Grant is furious over Pompey's Euro snub. England beats Scots at U-18 level. DJ Campbell arrested.

24   No Rooney (groin), but two-pen Giggs (836th game) takes the strain for Man U to send Spurs to defeat (67th winless away v Big Four). Arsenal blanked out of title contention as Man C shares no goals. Parker special (first at home) delivery posts Hammers likely survival winner against Wigan. Another early Black Cats Bent effort is enough to spin ten-man Hull (Bullard hits post pen) nearer the drop. First Wolves home strike in 11 weeks (7 hours 50 mins) grabs Blackburn draw. Two down Pompey fights back for Bolton draw. FLC: Ipswich almost blows the Toon trophy celebrations bubbles (52,181 new FLC record) with added time leveller, but Newcastle (16th unbeaten) stays unbeaten at home beating 103 year club record. Either Blackpool (winners at Posh) or Swansea (losers at Sheff U) are for play-offs. Leicester is there at PNE. Forest wins again but Davies unsure of job? Cardiff (Whittingham first to 20 goals) shoves Sheff W nearer drop. Donny edges Scunny in best of sever. Watford gets crucial win over Reading. F1: Leeds (automatic?) drives four past eight MK Dons. P-o: Millwall's Morison hits 20th goal. Swindon draw menaces Wycombe. Charlton gets a point at Exeter and six different Huddersfield scorers shatter Stockport. Colchester held by Tranmere are out of contention. F2: Cash-strapped Bournemouth wins promotion with same 19 players relegated with last season! Nine still in race for play-offs! Grimsby clings to life in win at Darlo as Barnet suffers. SPL: Falkirk (Accies Paixao stuffing) and Killie (beaten by Buddies) fight out bottom place. SL: Caley celebrates with seven different marksmen at Ayr. Stirling overtakes Alloa with another win over Clyde in Div 2. BSP: Forest G R relegated along with Ebbsfleet. Another home win for JM's Inter. Barca wins without Messi, but Real is close. Schalke catches Bayern.

25   Seven-up (3rd time and best top flight) strikes for Chelsea against Stoke as Simonsen suffers dislocated shoulder. Fulham rest players at Everton and are pipped. Birmingham rages over pen that wasn't as Villa takes the derby day. Liverpool foursome floors Burnley to FLC. Rangers settle the SPL title with three games to go beating Hibs as Celtic defeats ten-man Dundee U. Rooney (better fitness news) gets PFA award, Milner young player, Merit Lucas Radebe.

26   Wenger is to receive some serious "wonga." Palace draws with WBA to set up last game at Sheff W to decide relegation! SL: Airdrie wins at Raith to catch Ayr at the foot.

27   Ch Lge: Olic treble breaks Lyon hearts for Bayern to reach final. Solano denies assault charge. Loosemores final TNS beats Rhyl.

28   Ch Lge: JM masterminds Inter's ten-man resistance to Barca's passing fancy securing a passage to the final. Could it be Hey Juve for Rafa? Fulham waits on Zamora. Hull may exploit loophole to avoid pts deduction. Barnet sacks boss Hendon.

29   E Lge: Goal down Fulham anything but craven at the Cottage earns final spot, but Atletico's Forlan leaves Liverpool forlorn in extra time. Capello is top of the rich managers list. Tevez may be leaving Man C. FA Youth Cup final: Advantage Chelsea as they draw at Villa in first leg.

30   Sir Alex calls on Liverpool to beat Chelsea, with Rafa on brink of Juve move. Roy Hodgson will be Manager of the Year. Shrewsbury sacks Simpson. England U-18s beaten by Republic. Oxford Univ beats Cambridge in s/o.

MAY

Chelsea champs and Cup … Brave Fulham loses … Triesman topples … Mourinho masterclass.

1   May the fourth … Spurs (Huddlestone talisman scorer, 12 such games no loss), Man C lead the race as Bolton, Villa (out of running) are respective losers. "Zombie" Pompey still shows life again over Wolves with Utaka hitting 1000th PL goal of season. Jensen's og is 41st of season (PL record) as Burnley is edge out at Birmingham (only two home defeats best since one in 1906–07), yet Burnley might be in E Lge by Fair Play! Stoke – Everton 26th goalless draw but Toffees rage over "no" goal, so no Euro despite tenth no loss. L1: Norwich gets three – goals and points at Bristol R. Auto/p-o: Leeds slip up at The Valley courtesy of og for Charlton, Millwall totters at Tranmere (given chance of survival), Swindon edges Brentford, Huddersfield clips Colchester. Relegation: Wycombe goes "west" at the Orient (old boy McGleish scoring!). In peril: Exeter crucial point at Hartlepool (still facing possible deduction of points), Gillingham snatch win over Soton. L2: Notts take title in five-goal style over surviving Cheltenham (11,331). Rotherham goalless at Crewe and Shots three in six mins after trailing to Lincoln are in the p-os. Hoping: Losers still in the chase are Bury, Chesterfield, Port Vale and Northampton. Winners like-

wise are Dagenham and Morecambe. Relegation: Grimsby gives itself lifeline beating Barnet. SPL: Boyd's 100th SPL goal at last as Rangers win at Dundee U. Celtic's 6th win in a row. Hearts nip Hibs in Euro place chase. St Mirren draws with Falkirk as Killie stumbles at home to St J. SL: Drawing Stirling is Div 2 champions on goal difference despite Alloa win. Albion held by Strarraer, so Queen's Park stay in p-os. Messi has two goals for Barca. Roma back on top over inactive Inter. Muller three as Bayern nears title. Bangor beats Pt Talbot in Welsh Cup Final.

2 Liverpool labours without the watching Torres with Chelsea in pole position after Gerrard back pass gaffe marks the first cross. Nani keeps Man U in the running at Sunderland with chances missed, too. Mix and match Fulham has odd goal in five win over West Ham (first such for 44 years). FLC: Blackpool point is enough against Bristol C to stay in p-os as Swans have last gasp goal disallowed and earlier no pen award against Doncaster. Champions Newcastle registers 102 points. Relegation: Palace (Hart's last i/c) sends Sheff W down in draw at Hillsborough, but pitch invasion sparks trouble. McClaren clinches Dutch title with Twente. Inter back on top after win away to Lazio. Ronaldo heads late winner for Real.

3 Goalie lapses and Arsenal loses at Blackburn and cost Wigan win though draw sends Hull down. BSP: Oxford eases to final over Rushden, York repeats single goal win at Luton but sparks crowd trouble. Women's FA Cup Final: Everton surprises Arsenal.

4 Coleman sacked by Coventry. SPL: Celtic beats Rangers for seven in a row wins. Chelsea bids for Torres. FA Youth Cup: Chelsea defeats Villa.

5 Man C eclipsed for fourth place by Spurs. Fulham edged out by Stoke. Ronaldo hits first Real treble. SPL: Motherwell and Hibs share twelve goals! Crucial win for Killie. SL p-os: Brechin clips Airdrie, Cowden levels late with Alloa, Arbroath scores four at Queen's Park and Forfar nips it at East Stirling. Italian Cup Final: Inter beats Roma.

6 Barry injury worries Capello. Mancini receives vote of confidence. Glazers dig heels in at Old Trafford. Rafa may still go. Wenger will spend. Pompey owes £138m. Hartlepool deducted three points. Oldham axes boss Penny, Mariner reverts to coach at Plymouth. "Skint" five-goal Oleg Salenko (WC 1994) is to sell his Golden Boot.

7 Carragher comes to England fold. Chelsea and Man U prepare for last PLstand. Liverpool posts £54.9m loss and debts of £351m. Harry Redknapp is Manager of the Year! Zola balanced on knife edge at Upton Park.

8 FLC: Blackpool edges the first leg against Forest. F1: Ten-man Leeds (Gradel off) recovers to automatically snatch last such place with Beckford winner after Bristol R lead. So Millwall enjoy only three such mins of joy before settling for play-off with victory over Swindon. Gillingham (don't do away wins) crash down and out at Wycombe – of all places! Hartlepool survives instead. Norwich ends season as it started – losing – but have the title. F2: Morecambe shoots to fourth place as play-off save Shots lose. Daggers also confirm a slot. Grimsby fails at Burton to BSP exit but fans riot. Barnet beats Rochdale to stay. Trophy: Ten-man Barrow boys wheel Stevenage (finishing with nine, one red) out, but it's back to Wembley via gaining Euro spot at Dundee U. Celtic makes it eighth win in a row at Hearts. Inter, Roma still chasing Serie A title as are Barca, Real Madrid in La Liga. Louis Van Gaal wins with Bayern Munich.

9 Chelsea champions in style, revenge defeat at Wigan and leave ten-man Latics behind the eight ball as records tumble at the Bridge: most PL and club goals 103, highest Blues League win, first team post-war to score seven or more four times; greatest goal margin, etc! Drogba treble makes him leading marksman on 29. Anti-climax it is for Man U at Old Trafford despite foursome over Stoke. Four-goal Arsenal (83 best PL season) takes out Fulham. Sloppy Spurs (two up) concede four to relegated Burnley. Birmingham (only one win in last 10) finish 9th – it's best at the top for 51 years in losing at Bolton. Wolves scatter the nine finishing Black Cats of Sunderland. Pompey denied "good" goal at Everton and ose in the 94th minute. Mr Og helps Blackburn win at Villa. Hull and Liverpool play out another goalless draw to deny the Reds their 2000th League success, but "Baby" Jack Robinson 16 years 250 days is their youngest. Drawing West Ham blunt Man C but Manager Zola is on a knife-edge. FLC: p-o: Whittingham the midfield marksman is Cardiff's winner at Leicester. SPL: Motherwell catch Rangers with two late goals in six sharing, but it is not enough to prevent Hibs gaining Euro spot at Dundee U. Celtic makes it eighth win in a row at Hearts. Inter, Roma still chasing Serie A title as are Barca, Real Madrid in La Liga. Louis Van Gaal wins with Bayern Munich.

10 Focus on Capello re-role for Rooney, Beckham, web site ratings. FA wants new PM to champion WC 2018. Terry gets "champagne" text from JM! MK Dons appoint Karl Robinson, 29, manager. Mark Stimson leaves Gillingham. Tony Adams gets Azer job with Qabala. FL agrees to PL new parachute plan.

11 FLC: p-o: DJ Campbell spins Forest out with a hat trick for Blackpool. Capello's 30 raise questions and FA unhappy with his web. Zola axed by Hammers. Is Pardew next for chop? Ronaldinho is left out of Brazil squad.

12 E Lge final: Forlan wins the F factor over Fulham with a double as Atletico Madrid take the extra time to seal it. FLC p-o: Cardiff owes it to Marshall in shoot-out to thwart Leicester come back. Terry injured in training. O'Neill is safe at Villa. SL p-o: no goals in first leg for Cowden, Brechin or Arbroath, Forfar.

13 Becks is main man for WC coaching role. Rooney looks to boss job one day. Foy joy as Cup Final ref Chris will complete set of major finals: C Cup, Com Sad and Trophy.

14 FL1 p-o: Ex-brickie Austin powers Swindon to edge home against Charlton. Ubiquitous Becks leads 2018 bid! Cup previews rich men v paupers. Zola will sue West Ham, Grant may get his job!

15 FA Cup final; Drogba (second player after Rush to score in three different finals) bends free kick to clip inside of post to clinch Chelsea's double; Ashley Cole secures record sixth (out of seven) winners' medals; But Daley's poor pen for Pompey who becomes sixth relegated losers might have changed history, though Chelsea find woodwork irresistible (five such including Kalou from four yards) – "post" traumatic stress! Lamps is even spot "off" too. F1: Millwall is denied two pen claims in goalless at Huddersfield. F2: Shots man of the match Brown backpass gaffe is advantage Rotherham. S Cup final: Tannadice Terrors stunt the Staggies from Ross Co so Dundee U celebrates in Centenary year. Triesman gaffe over ref bribing fears could end WC bid. Death announced of Swansea's Besian Idrizaj at 22.

16 Triesman out, Sheepshanks/Burden are stand-ins for now with Geoff Thompson leading the 2018 bid. F2 p-o: Great Scott (Josh) foursome as Daggers s'ab the Morecambe Shrimps six times for record win. BSP: Oxford bear back in the League after four years easing to win over York Inter wins in Italy, Barca in Spain. SL p-o: Cowden hits three at Brechin to get the lift up while Forfar double achieves the same over Arbroath.

17 FIFA to investigate "Tries-gate" as FA enters damage limitation. England trip to Austria tests altitude attitude. Ballack out of WC after Boateng tackle in final. F1: Ten-side ends with Charlton's Bailey missing pen in s/o and Swindon earning FLC spot.

18 Fabregas is to quit Arsenal for Barca. England will practice penalties. Lineker quits as Mail on Sunday columnist over sting. WC 2018 bid undiminished by ill-judged Lord T. L1: Millwall twosome sees off Huddersfield. England U-17 Euro qualifier starts with Czechs beaten. U-21: Wales loses in Austria.

19   Carragher returns to England fold. Fabregas price is £45m, but Barca gets Villa £35m from Valencia. Man C tries for Milner at £20m. F2 p-o: Rotherham double sees off Shots.

20   Capello feels the heat, Grant puts himself out at Pompey. Interpol brought in by FIFA over "Tries-gate." Howard Webb is given Ch Lge final. MK Dons appoint Dietmar Hamann as player-manager. Colchester loses Aidy Boothroyd to Coventry job. Sports Minister Hugh Robertson warns FA over next chairman. F2 p-o: Morecambe for pride snatches Daggers win but D & R for Wembley. England Ladies spank Maltesers six times.

21   Win or lose, JM may head for Real job after Ch Lge final. Capello may go for 4-2-3-1 formation. First Wenger signing of the close season is Marouane Chamakh free from Bordeaux. WC 2018 bidders will see Blatter. U-17s: England adds Jamaica to victims. Andy Hessenthaler is new Gillingham boss.

22   Ch Lge final: Two goal Millito makes Mourinho mighty in Madrid, so it's bye-bye Bayern. FLC p-o final: Blackpool beaches Cardiff in game worth £90m to winners.

23   FL announces increase in gates to 17.1m a rise of over four percent over 2008-09 with Championship netting 9.9m – better than Serie A! Wales is beaten in Croatia.

24   England beat Mexico but leaves Capello with problems. U-17s: England edges Turkey to top group. Mourinho men are finalizing his move to Real.

25   Blackpool will have to make do with capacity of 12,000. UEFA plans to limit PL spending take shape. Republic edges Paraguay in friendly match. Peter Houston confirmed as Dundee U boss.

26   Manuel Pellegrini's dismissal at Real Madrid opens door for JM. Grant is nearer to Hammers job. N Ireland loses to Turkey in USA.

27   WC top tickets trail in sales. Gerrard has in injury scare, but Barry hopeful. Alex Horne appointed FA General Secretary. U-17s beat France in semis and face Spain. Birmingham adds 6ft 8in striker Nikola Zigic to roster from Valencia (£6m).

28   Republic hits England WC oppos Algeria for three. FIFA finds no substance in Triesman tales. Real will pay £6.8m to Inter for JM. Shane Duffy has successful op on liver damaged in training! Allan Moore is new Morton boss.

29   Capello contract needs killing on as Inter looms. L1 p-o: Robinson wrecks the Swindon Robins as Millwall make it. N-L crisis as Merthyr, Northwich, Chester, Grays, Salisbury all face uncertainty.

30   Grazie in Graz! FC is grateful for a couple of Japanese ogs to nip them in front in last friendly run-out. W formation (Wisdom and Wickham) as England beats Spain in U-17 final. F2 p-o: Daggers just find cutting edge over Rotherham at Wembley.

31   Is Capello coming on board? He prepares to ditch seven from squad. Everton signs Beckford free. JM installed at RM. Palace gates may shut. John Ward gets Colchester job. Jimmy Calderwood leaves Kilmarnock.

JUNE

WC shocks as holders Italy and 2006 runners-up France crash out ... England fails to reach last eight ... Capello anxious to stay on.

1   Walcott, Bent, Adam Johnson, Baines, Parker, Dawson and Huddlestone are left out of England squad. Palace escapes extinction. Stimson gets Barnet job, Dickov at Oldham. Bullard for Celtic, Iwelumo for Burnley.

2   Capello signals stay for England. Benitez is on way out at Anfield. Real Madrid wants to sign Gerrard. Eight-panelled World Cup ball is disliked by goalies. Torres remains resting injury. Taxman is keen to change game's financial rules. Baggies get Ibanez (Atletico Madrid) free.

3   Kingmaker Dalglish is Liverpool favourite. England's first game will be on a good pitch. Grant takes over at West Ham. Fabregas comes back for Spain in win over South Korea. Everton only pink away from home.

4   Rio Ferdinand injures left knee and is out of WC, Dawson recalled and Gerrard skipper. Drogba may also miss finals. Is Hodgson for Liverpool? Craig Short is Notts boss. Fox moves from Colchester to Norwich £250,000.

5   USA v Aussies, Algeria v UAE and Slovenia v New Zealand, all win their latest warm-up games. Drogba has operation on his arm. Robben injury hits Dutch camp.

6   Simon, Brazil ref for England v USA was suspended last season! Warm-up game ends in stampede and injuries. Rafa for Inter? Family Glazers hit by more debt.

7   Swearing Rooney booked as 21 English warm-up (Cole J stays on) in 3-0 v Platinum Stars. Kaka wants Brazil to improve. Benitez will take backroom staff to Inter post.

8   Cole J, Ballack released by Chelsea. Dalglish for Anfield? WC worries over Rooney temper. Nani out injured. Robben misses opener. Corporate sales are poor. Torres is back scoring in warm-up. FL to restrict teams to 25 players over 21, ten must be home grown.

9   WC ball kicked – out of touch! Capello frowns on snappers. A ref is out injured. Hodgson is favoured for Liverpool job. Everton signs Joao Silva, Das Avas striker.

10   Troops send England team "good luck" DVD. PM Cameron backs 2018 bid, Aussies drop out. Caviar ordered for WAGS. Zola and West Ham reached amicable settlement.

11   WC starts: all square in Group A, South Africa lead levelled by Mexico, but Mphela hits post; Uruguay finishes with ten (Lodeiro two yellows) and holds France goalless. Graham Turner returns as boss of Shrewsbury Town.

12   Argies with all possession, acres of space, no urgency and Nigeria close to levelling. Lively South Korea's invention is too much for Greek plodders. Decent opener skipper Gerrard (ITV HD missed it!) finishing then ghastly Green gaffe and post hit apiece as USA draws with England, too.

13   Group of goal gaffes as ten Algerians spill it to Slovenia. Ghana's Gyan pens win over ten Serbs and then hits post. Formidable Germans light it up firing four over Cahill harshly carded for plucky overrun Aussies.

14   Bizarre 50 secs s/h og takes stuffing out of Danes for Dutch treat. Nippy Japs in top gear and Honda scores to thwart Cameroon. Italy forced to step it up to get a point against Paraguay's headed opener. Beckenbauer hits out at "long ball" England.

15   Gutsy NZ Kiwis bear fruit with peach of an equaliser against Slovakia. Ronaldo and Portugal unhappy with Sven's Ivorians approach in another goalless encounter. Intricate Brazil steps up to pace and two goals but stoic North Korea pulls one back. There have been four sell-outs so far. Eighteen days after being appointed as Dover boss, Ian Hendon quits to Gills assistant.

16   Chile raise the tempo and give Honduras a single goal hammering. First upset: "Hop Swiss" use route one and rebound to score only goal against all-pressure Spain (Torres on as a sub).

17   Fluent Argies turn the screw against spirited South Koreans for foursome (Higuain treble). Another gk spill as Nigeria's ten are edged out by Greece. Mexicans take out poor French. George Burley is appointed manager of Crystal Palace, Ryan Kidd replaces Simon Davey at Darlo.

18   Off-day Germans lose Klose to two yellows, Podolski has pen saved and Serbs get the points. Yanks fight back to level after being two down and denied a winner. England lacking drive, has no answers, little idea in goalless draw with Algeria – happy birthday Fabio Capello! Pompey out of administration and Steve Cotterill is new manager.

19 Holland just edges Japan with another goalie fumble and ten-man Aussies (Kewell arm) find Ghana keeper in similar distress during another draw. Danes put out woefully weak finishing Cameroon – first to go home. Anelka also banished by France after rant at manager. Rooney forced to apologise to fans for his comments. Rumours of unrest persist in the camp and Capello likely to quit if there is no qualification.

20 Paraguay is two goals too slick for lack-lustre Slovakia. NZ hold the holders Italy despite obvious off-side goal, Kiwis conceding a pen in the upset of the tournament. Brazil, slow start, step up hit three (one via an arm), Ivorians reply through Drogba then get Kaka sent off. Nasty ending as Brazil make last 16. Terry hits out at boss man. It's a revolt in French camp.

21 Portugal explodes with seven-goal salvo against poor defending N Korea. Chile squanders chances before edging ten-man Swiss. Villa double (then he misses pen) as Spain defeats meagre Honduras, but Torres off key again, chucking three chances and subbed. Peace breaks out in England camp.

22 France in disarray bowing out with ten-men to South Africa who become the first hosts not to progress from group stage. Uruguay edges Mexico, but both move on. Argies finish off the Greeks Yakubu – miss of the stage – costs Nigeria in draw with South Korea who go through. Hereford appoints Simon Davey as manager.

23 Defoe earns his call up and England edges Slovenia with it. Yanks – with Bill Clinton watching – grateful again to Donovan with 92nd min effort, then Algeria's Yakia sent off and they join Slovenes homeward. Ozil brings sigh of relief for Germany over Ghana, but both in last 16 despite Aussies win over wasteful Serbia. Now England faces its old Deutschland foe. Aldershot transfer Donnelly for club record £200,000. Peter Reid steps in at Plymouth.

24 Holders Italy – only play when they're losing – still loses to Slovakia. Lippi blames himself for the early exit. Defensive NZ holds Paraguay scoreless and retires unbeaten! Sorensen bad day at the office from free-kicks, so Danish dynamite a forgotten tag as snappy Japs race on via Honda and co. Robben enters to aid Dutch to last 16, edging Cameroon out.

25 Scrappy scrap and Brazil and Portugal settle for level. Ivory Coast hits N Korea for three in group also-rans affair. Spain more like Euro 2008 but Torres still off form, just have enough over ten-man Chile as both progress. Swiss miss out along with scoreless Honduras. Draw: Uru v SK, USA v Gha, Holl v Slov, Br v Ch, Arg v Mex, Ger v Eng, Para v Jap, Sp v Port. Cowdenbeath appoints Jimmy Nicholl as manager. Les Parry to carry on at Tranmere.

26 Suarez double for Uruguay fends off battling display by South Korea in pouring rain. Yanks don't come back this time and then it's route one for Ghana winner over the Route 66 boys.

27 Shades of 1966 again for England as Lampard clearly scores leveller at two-each but no official near enough to see it and Germany marches on to hit four. Blatant off-side goal as Argies hit a threesome with Mexicans giving their best in defeat.

28 Capello wants to stay on. Dutch with 1 to 11 on their shirts edge the numbers game with Slovakia whose response was too late to count. Brazil is now finding its rhythm against Chile.

29 Paraguay needs a shoot-out to dispose of Japan after scoreless two hours, Komano the unfortunate bar-hitting. Iberia's local derby and Spain rules with Villa the match-winner again and Portugal's Ricardo Costa sent off late. Stars:Torres pulled off and Ronaldo anonymous Back at the ranch FA divided over Capello. Nigel Pearson gets Hull job.

30 Gerrard and Rooney pull out of skills contest. Pro Capello camp increases. Man C spends £24m on David Silva (Valencia). Hodgson nears Anfield. Are stars losing their glitter in WC?

JULY
Axe falls on Brazil heads ... Torres snubs Hodgson ... Spain is WC winner.

1 Inquest continues over England's performance. Hodgson settles in at Anfield. The Europa League starts! TNS wins, Dundalk, Llanelli and Portadown draw, Glentoran, Port Talbot lose first legs.

2 Capello is given the thumbs up. Brazil beaten by the Dutch, disintegrate after leading and Felipe Melo caps own goal with being dismissed. Ghana robbed of a goal in dramatic climax by Suarez handball then Gyan hits bar from the spot. The Africans lead had been levelled by Forlan free kick. Uruguay then wins the shoot-out with Abreu's cheeky clincher. Chelsea signs Benayoun for £5.5m. Man C to add Yaya Toure for £30m having spent £11.5m on Jerome Boateng.

3 Germans effect demolition job on Argentina in four-star win. It's a story of two pens in a minute, Paraguay missing, Spain scoring but not on retake. Eventually Villa via both posts houses Spanish win. Dunga and co are sacked by Brazil. At Southend, too, Tilson is washed out.

4 Nationwide will abandon England sponsorship. England may be represented in WC final by Whistler Webb. Paul Sturrock is new Southend boss.

5 As Torres stalls over Hodgson approach, Chelsea may move in. Sir Alex forecasts Rooney will dominate 2014 WC. Boyd moves from Rangers to Middlesbrough.

6 WC semi: two in three minutes off the post turn game Dutch way after another Forlan equaliser for Uruguay. WC 2018 bid is alleged back on track. Hawk-Eye could be back too in contention.

7 WC semi: skipper is head man for Spain as patience pays princely for Puyol against Germany. Arsenal reinforces defence with £8.5m Laurent Koscielny from Lorient – not the O's! Eriksson and Bilic are mentioned for Fulham. Paulo Sousa gets Leicester job. Notts are in financial clear.

8 Howard Webb is WC final ref with Mike Mullarkey and Darren Cann as assistants – Spain does not approve. Europa casualties: Llanelli, Glentoran, Port Talbot but victors: Dundalk and Portadown.

9 Platini faints and goes to hospital. WC final labelled as Beauty (Spain) v the Beast (Holland). FIFA denies Nigeria involved in match-fixing. Ricardo Carvalho is heading for Inter.

10 Third place for Germany, thanks to spilling shot-stopper Muslera in the Uruguayan goal, despite Forlan for once failing to rescue his team, hitting the bar with the last kick. Platini is out of hospital. Paul the German (English-born) octopus predicts a Spanish victory.

11 No joy in Jo'burg as Webb tries to master Dutch aggression and Spanish retaliation, flashing 14 yellow and one red card to Johnny Heitinga. Mercifully, Andres Iniesta ends it with a 116th minute goal for Spain. Paul was right again!

ENGLISH LEAGUE TABLES 2009–10

(P) *Promoted into division at end of 2008–09 season.*   (R) *Relegated into division at end of 2008–09 season.*

BARCLAYS PREMIER LEAGUE 2009–10

			Home					Away					Total						
		P	W	D	L	F	A	W	D	L	F	A	W	D	L	F	A	GD	Pts
1	Chelsea	38	17	1	1	68	14	10	4	5	35	18	27	5	6	103	32	71	86
2	Manchester U	38	16	1	2	52	12	11	3	5	34	16	27	4	7	86	28	58	85
3	Arsenal	38	15	2	2	48	15	8	4	7	35	26	23	6	9	83	41	42	75
4	Tottenham H	38	14	2	3	40	12	7	5	7	27	29	21	7	10	67	41	26	70
5	Manchester C	38	12	4	3	41	20	6	9	4	32	25	18	13	7	73	45	28	67
6	Aston Villa	38	8	8	3	29	16	9	5	5	23	23	17	13	8	52	39	13	64
7	Liverpool	38	13	3	3	43	15	5	6	8	18	20	18	9	11	61	35	26	63
8	Everton	38	11	6	2	35	21	5	7	7	25	28	16	13	9	60	49	11	61
9	Birmingham C (P)	38	8	9	2	19	13	5	2	12	19	34	13	11	14	38	47	–9	50
10	Blackburn R	38	10	6	3	28	18	3	5	11	13	37	13	11	14	41	55	–14	50
11	Stoke C	38	7	6	6	24	21	4	8	7	10	27	11	14	13	34	48	–14	47
12	Fulham	38	11	3	5	27	15	1	7	11	12	31	12	10	16	39	46	–7	46
13	Sunderland	38	9	7	3	32	19	2	4	13	16	37	11	11	16	48	56	–8	44
14	Bolton W	38	6	6	7	26	31	4	3	12	16	36	10	9	19	42	67	–25	39
15	Wolverhampton W (P)	38	5	6	8	13	22	4	5	10	19	34	9	11	18	32	56	–24	38
16	Wigan Ath	38	6	7	6	19	24	3	2	14	18	55	9	9	20	37	79	–42	36
17	West Ham U	38	7	5	7	30	29	1	6	12	17	37	8	11	19	47	66	–19	35
18	Burnley (P)	38	7	5	7	25	30	1	1	17	17	52	8	6	24	42	82	–40	30
19	Hull C	38	6	6	7	22	29	0	6	13	12	46	6	12	20	34	75	–41	30
20	Portsmouth*	38	5	3	11	24	32	2	4	13	10	34	7	7	24	34	66	–32	19

Portsmouth deducted 9 points.

COCA-COLA CHAMPIONSHIP 2009–10

			Home					Away					Total						
		P	W	D	L	F	A	W	D	L	F	A	W	D	L	F	A	GD	Pts
1	Newcastle U (R)	46	18	5	0	56	13	12	7	4	34	22	30	12	4	90	35	55	102
2	WBA (R)	46	16	3	4	48	21	10	10	3	41	27	26	13	7	89	48	41	91
3	Nottingham F	46	18	2	3	45	13	4	11	8	20	27	22	13	11	65	40	25	79
4	Cardiff C	46	12	6	5	37	20	10	4	9	36	34	22	10	14	73	54	19	76
5	Leicester C (P)	46	13	6	4	40	18	8	7	8	21	27	21	13	12	61	45	16	76
6	Blackpool¶	46	13	6	4	46	22	6	7	10	28	36	19	13	14	74	58	16	70
7	Swansea C	46	10	10	3	21	12	7	8	8	19	25	17	18	11	40	37	3	69
8	Sheffield U	46	12	8	3	37	20	5	6	12	25	35	17	14	15	62	55	7	65
9	Reading	46	10	7	6	39	22	7	5	11	29	41	17	12	17	68	63	5	63
10	Bristol C	46	10	10	3	38	34	5	8	10	18	31	15	18	13	56	65	–9	63
11	Middlesbrough (R)	46	9	8	6	25	21	7	6	10	33	29	16	14	16	58	50	8	62
12	Doncaster R	46	9	7	7	32	29	6	8	9	27	29	15	15	16	59	58	1	60
13	QPR	46	8	9	6	36	28	6	6	11	22	37	14	15	17	58	65	–7	57
14	Derby Co	46	12	3	8	37	32	3	8	12	16	31	15	11	20	53	63	–10	56
15	Ipswich T	46	8	11	4	24	23	4	9	10	26	38	12	20	14	50	61	–11	56
16	Watford	46	10	6	7	36	26	4	6	13	25	42	14	12	20	61	68	–7	54
17	Preston NE	46	9	10	4	35	26	4	5	14	23	47	13	15	18	58	73	–15	54
18	Barnsley	46	8	7	8	25	29	6	5	12	28	40	14	12	20	53	69	–16	54
19	Coventry C	46	8	9	6	27	29	5	6	12	20	35	13	15	18	47	64	–17	54
20	Scunthorpe U (P)	46	10	7	6	40	32	4	3	16	22	52	14	10	22	62	84	–22	52
21	Crystal Palace*	46	8	5	10	24	27	6	12	5	26	26	14	17	15	50	53	–3	49
22	Sheffield W	46	8	6	9	30	31	3	8	12	19	38	11	14	21	49	69	–20	47
23	Plymouth Arg	46	5	6	12	20	30	6	2	15	23	38	11	8	27	43	68	–25	41
24	Peterborough U (P)	46	6	5	12	32	37	2	5	16	14	43	8	10	28	46	80	–34	34

Crystal Palace deducted 10 points. ¶ Blackpool promoted via play-offs.

COCA-COLA LEAGUE 1 2009–10

		Home					Away					Total						
		P	W	D	L	F	A	W	D	L	F	A	W	D	L	F	A	GD	Pts
1	Norwich C (R)	46	17	3	3	43	22	12	5	6	41	25	29	8	9	89	47	42	95
2	Leeds U	46	14	6	3	41	19	11	5	7	33	25	25	11	10	77	44	33	86
3	Millwall¶	46	17	5	1	48	15	7	8	8	28	29	24	13	9	76	44	32	85
4	Charlton Ath (R)	46	14	6	3	41	22	9	9	5	30	26	23	15	8	71	48	23	84
5	Swindon T	46	13	8	2	42	25	9	8	6	31	32	22	16	8	73	57	16	82
6	Huddersfield T	46	14	8	1	52	22	9	3	11	30	34	23	11	12	82	56	26	80
7	Southampton* (R)	46	15	5	3	48	21	8	9	6	37	26	23	14	9	85	47	38	73
8	Colchester U	46	15	5	3	37	21	5	7	11	27	31	20	12	14	64	52	12	72
9	Brentford (P)	46	9	12	2	34	21	5	8	10	21	31	14	20	12	55	52	3	62
10	Walsall	46	10	8	5	36	26	6	6	11	24	37	16	14	16	60	63	-3	62
11	Bristol R	46	13	3	7	32	30	6	2	15	27	40	19	5	22	59	70	-11	62
12	Milton Keynes D	46	10	5	8	31	28	7	4	12	29	40	17	9	20	60	68	-8	60
13	Brighton & HA	46	7	4	12	26	30	8	10	5	30	30	15	14	17	56	60	-4	59
14	Carlisle U	46	10	4	9	34	28	5	9	9	29	38	15	13	18	63	66	-3	58
15	Yeovil T	46	9	7	7	36	26	4	7	12	19	33	13	14	19	55	59	-4	53
16	Oldham Ath	46	7	7	9	23	28	6	6	11	16	29	13	13	20	39	57	-18	52
17	Leyton Orient	46	10	6	7	35	25	3	6	14	18	38	13	12	21	53	63	-10	51
18	Exeter C (P)	46	9	10	4	30	20	2	8	13	18	40	11	18	17	48	60	-12	51
19	Tranmere R	46	11	3	9	30	32	3	6	14	15	40	14	9	23	45	72	-27	51
20	Hartlepool U*	46	10	6	7	33	26	4	5	14	26	41	14	11	21	59	67	-8	50
21	Gillingham (P)	46	12	8	3	35	15	0	6	17	13	49	12	14	20	48	64	-16	50
22	Wycombe W (P)	46	6	7	10	26	31	4	8	11	30	45	10	15	21	56	76	-20	45
23	Southend U	46	7	10	6	29	27	3	3	17	22	45	10	13	23	51	72	-21	43
24	Stockport Co	46	2	6	15	21	51	3	4	16	14	44	5	10	31	35	95	-60	25

*Southampton deducted 10 points, Hartlepool United deducted 3 points. ¶ Millwall promoted via play-offs.

COCA-COLA LEAGUE 2 2009–10

		Home					Away					Total						
		P	W	D	L	F	A	W	D	L	F	A	W	D	L	F	A	GD	Pts
1	Notts Co	46	16	6	1	58	14	11	6	6	38	17	27	12	7	96	31	65	93
2	Bournemouth	46	16	3	4	33	16	9	5	9	28	28	25	8	13	61	44	17	83
3	Rochdale	46	14	3	6	45	20	11	4	8	37	28	25	7	14	82	48	34	82
4	Morecambe	46	14	6	3	44	24	6	7	10	29	40	20	13	13	73	64	9	73
5	Rotherham U	46	10	9	4	29	18	11	1	11	26	34	21	10	15	55	52	3	73
6	Aldershot T	46	12	7	4	43	24	8	5	10	26	32	20	12	14	69	56	13	72
7	Dagenham & R¶	46	15	2	6	46	27	5	10	8	23	31	20	12	14	69	58	11	72
8	Chesterfield	46	14	3	6	38	27	7	4	12	23	35	21	7	18	61	62	-1	70
9	Bury	46	11	6	6	29	23	8	6	9	25	36	19	12	15	54	59	-5	69
10	Port Vale	46	8	8	7	32	25	9	9	5	29	25	17	17	12	61	50	11	68
11	Northampton T (R)	46	9	9	5	29	21	9	4	10	33	32	18	13	15	62	53	9	67
12	Shrewsbury T	46	10	6	7	30	20	7	6	10	25	34	17	12	17	55	54	1	63
13	Burton Alb (P)	46	9	5	9	38	34	8	6	9	33	37	17	11	18	71	71	0	62
14	Bradford C	46	8	8	7	28	27	8	6	9	31	35	16	14	16	59	62	-3	62
15	Accrington S	46	11	1	11	38	39	7	6	10	24	35	18	7	21	62	74	-12	61
16	Hereford U (R)	46	12	4	7	32	25	5	4	14	22	40	17	8	21	54	65	-11	59
17	Torquay U (P)	46	9	6	8	34	24	5	9	9	30	31	14	15	17	64	55	9	57
18	Crewe Alex (R)	46	7	4	12	35	36	8	6	9	33	37	15	10	21	68	73	-5	55
19	Macclesfield T	46	7	8	8	27	28	5	10	8	22	30	12	18	16	49	58	-9	54
20	Lincoln C	46	9	7	7	25	26	4	4	15	17	39	13	11	22	42	65	-23	50
21	Barnet	46	8	10	5	30	18	4	2	17	17	45	12	12	22	47	63	-16	48
22	Cheltenham T (R)	46	5	8	10	34	38	5	10	8	20	33	10	18	18	54	71	-17	48
23	Grimsby T	46	4	9	10	25	36	5	8	10	20	35	9	17	20	45	71	-26	44
24	Darlington	46	3	3	17	14	40	5	3	15	19	47	8	6	32	33	87	-54	30

¶ Dagenham & R promoted via play-offs.

FOOTBALL LEAGUE PLAY-OFFS 2009–10

■ *Denotes player sent off.*

CHAMPIONSHIP FIRST LEG

Saturday, 8 May 2010

Blackpool (1) 2 *(Southern 26, Adam 57 (pen))*
Nottingham F (1) 1 *(Cohen 13)*   11,805

Blackpool: Gilks; John-Baptiste, Crainey, Southern, Coleman, Evatt, Adam, Taylor-Fletcher (Burgess), Ormerod (Bannan), Campbell (Dobbie), Vaughan.
Nottingham F: Camp; Gunter, Perch, Wilson, Morgan, Majewski (McGoldrick), Anderson, McKenna, Tyson (MgGugan), Blackstock (Earnshaw), Cohen.

Sunday, 9 May 2010

Leicester C (0) 0
Cardiff C (0) 1 *(Whittingham 78)*   29,165

Leicester C: Weale; Solano, Berner, King A, Bruce, Hobbs, Spearing, Wellens (N'Guessan), Waghorn (Kermorgant), Gallagher, Dyer (Fryatt).
Cardiff C: Marshall; Kennedy, McNaughton, Burke (Etuhu), Hudson, Blake, Whittingham, McPhail, Bothroyd, Chopra (McCormack), Ledley.

CHAMPIONSHIP SECOND LEG

Tuesday, 11 May 2010

Nottingham F (1) 3 *(Earnshaw 7, 66, Adebola 90)*
Blackpool (0) 4 *(Campbell 56, 76, 79, Dobbie 72)*   28,358

Nottingham F: Camp; Gunter, Perch (McGoldrick), Wilson, Morgan, Majewski, Tyson, McKenna (Adebola), Earnshaw, Blackstock (Anderson), Cohen.
Blackpool: Gilks; John-Baptiste, Crainey, Southern, Coleman, Evatt, Adam (Edwards), Taylor-Fletcher (Burgess), Ormerod (Dobbie), Campbell, Vaughan.

Wednesday, 12 May 2010

Cardiff C (1) 2 *(Chopra 21, Whittingham 69 (pen))*
Leicester C (2) 3 *(Fryatt 25, Hudson 36 (og), King 49)*   26,033

Cardiff C: Marshall; Kennedy, McNaughton (Quinn), Whittingham (McCormack), Hudson, Blake, Burke (Etuhu), McPhail, Bothroyd, Chopra, Ledley.

Leicester C: Weale; Solano, Berner, King A, Bruce, Hobbs, Dyer (Waghorn), Wellens, Howard, Fryatt (Kermorgant), Gallagher (Spearing).
aet; Cardiff C won 4-3 on penalties.

CHAMPIONSHIP FINAL (at Wembley)

Saturday, 22 May 2010

Blackpool (3) 3 *(Adam 13, Taylor-Fletcher 41, Ormerod 45)*
Cardiff C (2) 2 *(Chopra 9, Ledley 37)*   82,244

Blackpool: Gilks; Coleman, Crainey, Southern, John-Baptiste, Evatt, Adam, Taylor-Fletcher (Burgess), Ormerod (Dobbie), Campbell, Vaughan (Bannan).
Cardiff C: Marshall; McNaughton (Gerrard), Kennedy, Whittingham, Hudson, Blake, Burke (McCormack), McPhail, Bothroyd (Etuhu), Chopra, Ledley.
Referee: A. Marriner (West Midlands).

LEAGUE 1 FIRST LEG

Friday, 14 May 2010

Swindon T (0) 2 *(Austin 52, Ward 60)*
Charlton Ath (0) 1 *(Burton 65)*   13,560

Swindon T: Lucas; Amankwaah (Darby), Sheehan, Douglas, Cuthbert, Greer, McGovern, O'Brien (Timlin), Ward, Austin (Pericard), Ferry.
Charlton Ath: Randolph; Richardson, Borrowdale, Bailey, Sodje S, Dailly, Semedo, Racon, Mooney (Forster), Burton (Sodje A), Sam (Wagstaff).

Saturday, 15 May 2010

Huddersfield T (0) 0
Millwall (0) 0   14,654

Huddersfield T: Smithies; Peltier, Clarke T (Williams), Drinkwater (Collins), Clarke P, Trotman, Pilkington, Kay, Rhodes, Novak, Roberts.
Millwall: Forde; Smith, Barron, Trotter, Robinson, Ward, Abdou, Laird, Morison, Harris (Alexander), Craig.

Millwall's Darren Ward (left) shrugs off Charlie Austin of Swindon Town during the League 1 Play-off Final at Wembley. Millwall won 1-0 with a first-half goal from Paul Robinson. (Action Images/Tony O'Brien)

Dagenham & Redbridge's Danny Green celebrates scoring their second goal in the League 2 Play-off Final against Rotherham United at Wembley. The Daggers ran out 3-2 winners. (PA Photos)

LEAGUE 1 SECOND LEG

Monday, 17 May 2010

Charlton Ath (2) 2 *(Ferry 27 (og), Mooney 45)*
Swindon T (0) 1 *(Ward 74)*   21,521
Charlton Ath: Randolph; Richardson, Borrowdale, Bailey, Llera, Dailly, Semedo, Reid (Racon), Mooney (Forster), Burton, Sam (Wagstaff).
Swindon T: Lucas (Smith); Darby, Lescinel, Douglas, Cuthbert, Green, McGovern, Ward, Paynter (O'Brien), Austin, Ferry (Amankwaah).
aet; Swindon T won 5-4 on penalties.

Tuesday, 18 May 2010

Millwall (1) 2 *(Morison 23, Robinson 82)*
Huddersfield T (0) 0   15,463
Millwall: Forde; Smith, Barron, Trotter, Robinson, Ward, Craig, Abdou, Morison, Harris (Alexander), Schofield.
Huddersfield T: Smithies; Peltier, Williams, Drinkwater, Clarke P, Trotman (Clarke N), Pilkington (Eccleston), Kay, Rhodes (Robinson), Novak, Roberts.

LEAGUE 1 FINAL (at Wembley)

Saturday, 29 May 2010

Millwall (1) 1 *(Robinson 39)*
Swindon T (0) 0   73,108
Millwall: Forde; Barron, Craig (Frampton), Trotter, Robinson, Ward, Batt (Hackett), Abdou, Morison, Harris, Schofield.
Swindon T: Lucas; Amankwaah, Lescinel, Douglas, Cuthbert, Sheehan (Darby), McGovern (O'Brien), Ward, Paynter (Pericard), Austin, Ferry.
Referee: C. Webster (Tyne & Wear).

LEAGUE 2 FIRST LEG

Saturday, 15 May 2010

Aldershot T (0) 0
Rotherham U (0) 1 *(Le Fondre 38)*   5470
Aldershot T: Young (Jaimez-Ruiz); Herd, Sandell, Halls, Brown, Charles, Jackson (Spencer), Donnelly, Morgan M, Morgan D, Straker.
Rotherham U: Warrington; Lynch, Gunning, Mills, Sharps, Fenton, Law, Harrison, Taylor R, Le Fondre, Ellison.

Sunday, 16 May 2010

Dagenham & R (2) 6 *(Benson 4, 66, Scott 35, 48, 54, 69)*
Morecambe (0) 0   4566
Dagenham & R: Roberts; Ogogo, McCrory, Arber, Doe (Uddin), Vincelot, Green, Nurse, Benson, Scott, Gain (Tejan-Sie).
Morecambe: Roche; Moss (Curtis), Parrish, Artell, Haining, Bentley (Panther), Wilson, Drummond, Duffy, Mullin, Hunter (Jevons).

LEAGUE 2 SECOND LEG

Wednesday, 19 May 2010

Rotherham U (1) 2 *(Le Fondre 43, Ellison 68)*
Aldershot T (0) 0   7082
Rotherham U: Warrington; Lynch, Gunning, Fenton, Sharps, Mills, Law (Warne), Harrison, Taylor R (Broughton), Le Fondre, Ellison.
Aldershot T: Jaimez-Ruiz; Herd, Charles (Spencer), Halls, Brown, Winfield, Jackson (Hudson), Donnelly, Morgan M, Morgan D, Straker.

Thursday, 20 May 2010

Morecambe (0) 2 *(Duffy 81, Artell 90)*
Dagenham & R (0) 1 *(Benson 85)*   4972
Morecambe: Roche; Moss, Wilson, Artell, Parrish, Stanley, Duffy, Drummond, Jevons, Mullin, Curtis.
Dagenham & R: Roberts; Ogogo, McCrory, Arber, Doe, Vincelot, Green (Montgomery), Nurse, Benson, Scott (Walsh), Gain.

LEAGUE 2 FINAL (at Wembley)

Sunday, 30 May 2010

Dagenham & R (1) 3 *(Benson 38, Green 56, Nurse 70)*
Rotherham U (1) 2 *(Taylor R 39, 61)*   32,054
Dagenham & R: Roberts; Ogogo, McCrory, Arber, Doe, Vincelot, Green, Nurse (Montgomery), Benson, Scott (Walsh), Gain.
Rotherham U: Warrington; Lynch, Gunning, Mills (Marshall), Sharps, Fenton, Law, Harrison, Taylor R, Le Fondre, Ellison (Bell-Baggie).
Referee: J. Linington (Isle of Wight).

LEADING GOALSCORERS 2009–10

	League	Carling Cup	FA Cup	Other	Total
BARCLAYS PREMIERSHIP					
Only goals scored in the same division are included.					
Didier Drogba *(Chelsea)*	29	2	3	3	37
Wayne Rooney *(Manchester U)*	26	2	0	6	34
Darren Bent *(Sunderland)*	24	0	1	0	25
Carlos Tevez *(Manchester C)*	23	6	0	0	29
Frank Lampard *(Chelsea)*	22	0	3	2	27
Jermain Defoe *(Tottenham H)*	18	1	5	0	24
Fernando Torres *(Liverpool)*	18	0	0	4	22
Cesc Fabregas *(Arsenal)*	15	0	0	4	19
Emmanuel Adebayor *(Manchester C)*	14	0	0	0	14
Gabriel Agbonlahor *(Aston Villa)*	13	2	1	0	16
Louis Saha *(Everton)*	13	0	0	2	15
Florent Malouda *(Chelsea)*	12	1	2	0	15
Dimitar Berbatov *(Manchester U)*	12	0	0	0	12
In order of total goals:					
Bobby Zamora *(Fulham)*	8	0	3	9	20
COCA-COLA CHAMPIONSHIP					
Peter Whittingham *(Cardiff C)*	20	2	1	2	25
Nicky Maynard *(Bristol C)*	20	1	0	0	21
Gary Hooper *(Scunthorpe U)*	19	1	0	0	20
Andy Carroll *(Newcastle U)*	17	0	2	0	19
Kevin Nolan *(Newcastle U)*	17	1	0	0	18
Michael Chopra *(Cardiff C)*	16	1	2	2	21
Gylfi Sigurdsson *(Reading)*	16	1	3	0	20
Charlie Adam *(Blackpool)*	16	1	0	2	19
Darren Ambrose *(Crystal Palace)*	15	2	3	0	20
Robert Earnshaw *(Nottingham F)*	15	0	0	2	17
Billy Sharp *(Sheffield U on loan to Doncaster R)*	15	1	0	0	16
(Carling Cup goal for Sheffield U)					
Danny Graham *(Watford)*	14	0	0	0	14
COCA-COLA LEAGUE 1					
Rickie Lambert *(Southampton)*	30	1	2	3	36
(including one League goal for Bristol R)					
Billy Paynter *(Swindon T)*	26	2	1	0	29
Jermaine Beckford *(Leeds U)*	25	0	5	1	31
Grant Holt *(Norwich C)*	24	3	3	0	30
Lee Barnard *(Southampton)*	24	2	0	0	26
(Includes 15 League and 2 Carling Cup goals for Southend U)					
Steve Morison *(Millwall)*	20	0	2	1	23
Jordan Rhodes *(Huddersfield T)*	19	3	1	0	23
Charlie Austin *(Swindon T)*	19	0	0	1	20
Chris Martin *(Norwich C)*	17	0	4	2	23
Ian Harte *(Carlisle U)*	16	1	1	0	18
Luciano Becchio *(Leeds U)*	15	0	2	0	17
Charlie MacDonald *(Brentford)*	15	0	2	0	17
Adam Lallana *(Southampton)*	15	2	1	2	20
COCA-COLA LEAGUE 2					
Lee Hughes *(Notts Co)*	30	0	3	0	33
Brett Pitman *(Bournemouth)*	26	0	1	1	28
Adam Le Fondre *(Rotherham U)*	25	0	2	3	30
Chris O'Grady *(Rochdale)*	22	0	0	0	22
Shaun Harrad *(Burton Alb)*	21	0	1	0	22
Chris Dagnall *(Rochdale)*	20	0	0	0	20
Mark Richards *(Port Vale)*	19	2	0	1	22
Phil Jevons *(Morecambe on loan from Huddersfield T)*	18	0	1	0	19
Ryan Lowe *(Bury)*	18	0	0	0	18
Paul Benson *(Dagenham & R)*	17	0	1	4	22
Adebayo Akinfenwa *(Northampton T)*	17	0	0	0	17

Other matches consist of European games, J Paint Trophy, Community Shield and Football League play-offs. Players listed in order of League goals total.

REVIEW OF THE SEASON

Viewed in isolation Chelsea's successful capturing of the Premier League title would have masked the real scenario. With all six victories against the other three teams in the so-called "Big Four" – namely Arsenal, Liverpool and Manchester United – scoring twelve in the process and conceding just one goal, overall registering 103 goals with an amazing difference of 71 between those for and against, one would have expected the championship to have been wrapped up long before its finale. Not a bit of it as it went down to the wire with just a point separating the top two teams.

Reigning champions Manchester United hosted Stoke City, while the leaders Chelsea were at home to Wigan Athletic, who had beaten them 3-1 in September. But with thirteen goals better difference, Chelsea were unlikely to lose the title if they lost and United only managed a draw. In the event United scored four, Chelsea doubled it.

Yet on 21 March the top of the table had Manchester United four points ahead after beating Liverpool 2-1 while Chelsea, lying third with a game in hand, were held 1-1 at Blackburn Rovers. The crucial match was on 3 April at Old Trafford and with Wayne Rooney out injured, Chelsea won 2-1 to snatch a two point lead. Chelsea had one more blip when beaten 2-1 at Tottenham Hotspur and the last chance for Manchester United was that their old rivals Liverpool could stop Chelsea on 2 May. It was a vain hope.

In addition to their eight goals against Wigan, Chelsea hit seven on three occasions. They never lost two games in succession. They called upon the services of thirty players though none was ever-present. Not surprisingly they had four players in double figures among the goals. Didier Drogba was top scorer in the Premier League with 29 goals, Frank Lampard managed 22 – with ten penalties among them – Florent Malouda had a dozen and Nicolas Anelka hit eleven. Carlo Ancelotti in his first season in English football had masterminded the entire effort and had the FA Cup as a bonus, too.

As has been said before, even second place is a huge disappointment to some teams and particularly Manchester United who had just the Carling Cup success over Aston Villa to add to the trophy cabinet. Rooney missed half a dozen games with injury and it certainly cost him the leading scorer slot, though he still finished with 26. Moreover there was no Champions League joy.

Ten points behind even United, Arsenal finished in third place. Briefly on Saturday night 20 March the Gunners were top, before their two rivals wee due to play on the following day. Devastating on their day but just as likely to perform below expectations, on four separate occasions they lost two in a row. Yes, one might have predicted a stronger challenge.

However, fourth place was something of a triumph for Tottenham Hotspur whose successes over Chelsea and Manchester City in the last five matches ensured a coveted slot in the Champions League. City were edged out after a bright start which started to fade even in a run of ten undefeated games as it included eight draws! At the helm Mark Hughes gave way to Roberto Mancini.

Aston Villa had also entertained thoughts of fourth place but the goals dried up at the turn of the year for a time. Yet for Liverpool there was arguably the most disappointment of any Premier League team. Fernando Torres suffered from injuries and missed sixteen matches. He did contribute an invaluable eighteen goals when he was playing. Even a second chance in the Europa League ended unsuccessfully after faltering in the Champions League. At season's end, Rafa Benitez departed Anfield.

Champions Chelsea's Didier Drogba scores his first of three and his sides fifth in the 8-0 demolition of Wigan at Stamford Bridge on the final day of the season. (Action Images/John Sibley)

Only two points behind their Mersey rivals, Everton had a better second half to the season and performed well enough to be in the Europa League. They finished the term with an unbeaten run of eleven games.

Birmingham City were frugal to the extreme, scarcely wasting a goal when you see thirty-eight of them produced 50 points and ninth place. Twelve unbeaten matches into January was the highlight of their season. Blackburn Rovers never managed a run of three consecutive wins and were involved in seven goalless draws.

Stoke City also found goal scoring a problem area, failing to average one per game, yet achieving 47 points and eleventh place, one better than the previous season. Fulham's domestic efforts were overshadowed by their magnificent showing in the Europa League in which a marathon nineteen matches culminated with being edged out in added time in the final. Roy Hodgson was rightly acclaimed as Manager of the Year.

For a team which endured fourteen matches without a win mid-season, Sunderland were a surprise thirteenth, due mostly to others below them having even poorer runs. Darren Bent scored half of their goals.

Bolton Wanderers, having captured Owen Coyle, Burnley's manager, scratched around for goals on their own behalf. Sixteen times they were non-scorers, chiefly in the second half of the season, again surviving through the adversity of more lowly life.

Newly promoted Wolverhampton Wanderers scraped together just thirty-two goals but again it yielded a precious point per game to guarantee safety. Seventeen times they failed to score, yet beating Burnley on 20 December, so tight was the bottom of the table, took them up to twelfth.

Wigan Athletic, made to suffer by Chelsea as previously mentioned, found themselves punished severely in another game when crashing 9-1 at Tottenham Hotspur on 22 November. Thirty-seven goals of their own succeeded in keeping them just out of the relegation zone throughout.

But it was a close run outcome for West Ham United, second from bottom at the half-way stage and hovering in peril, too, thereafter until two wins in the last five outings pulled them out of danger.

Not as fortunate was the fate of Burnley, Hull City and Portsmouth. Wins for all three were rarities. Newcomers Burnley began early beating Manchester United but won only three games in the second half of the season. Hull contrived just two more wins after the end of November and hit only thirty-four goals. Portsmouth, in financial meltdown and with points deducted, remained rooted to the cellar, yet courageously reached the FA Cup final.

Championship honours for Newcastle United, back in the top flight after one season and apart from a stutter in late September it always looked a likely event in the making. Three periods of outright wins instilled confidence and staying unbeaten for the last seventeen – and overall, too, at home – was the pinnacle.

Promotion was secured on 5 April when West Bromwich Albion were held to a draw at Watford and Newcastle still had five games to play. The Baggies joined the elevation five days later after winning at Doncaster Rovers. Curiously, too, their worst spell came around the same time as the one which hit United.

However they had to contend with a mid-season surge from Nottingham Forest which, yes, you guessed correctly, began in late September and extended to nineteen matches, a fine improvement having been nineteenth when it started!

But the play-offs ended Forest's ambition as it did both Cardiff City and Leicester City, respectively fourth and fifth on the same number of points. Cardiff, erratic at times put in their best challenge from mid-March and stayed in the play-off zone. Leicester made sure, too, in the last weeks after suffering four straight defeats to end with five successive wins.

The remaining play-off spot went to Blackpool, who appeared out of contention in mid-March. It came down to a last game decider. Blackpool were entertaining Bristol City, Swansea City – affected by the Ides of March, too, and incredibly scratching just 40 goals all season – the other contestant for the slot at home to Doncaster. Just a point separated the two teams and both games were drawn, giving Blackpool the nod.

Blackpool took care of Forest, Cardiff just edged Leicester and it was Blackpool who defeated Cardiff at Wembley to join the Premier League for the first time.

Sheffield United went eight games without a win until mid-November which floored a bright enough start. Reading looked relegation material before a determined revival in the second half of the season even produced thoughts of the play-offs.

Tottenham Hotspur's Peter Crouch scores the late winner in Spurs' 1-0 victory over Manchester City at the City of Manchester Stadium. The win sealed Tottenham's fourth place in the Premier League and a place in the Champions League. (PA Photos)

Manchester United's Jonny Evans with a strong challenge on Emile Heskey of Aston Villa during the Carling Cup Final at Wembley. Although Villa took an early lead through Milner, United fought back to win 2-1 with goals from Michael Owen and Wayne Rooney. (Action Images/Andrew Couldridge)

Bristol City disappointed from late October and a late comeback was too little, too late for them. Middlesbrough, still third in October, found changes of personnel did nothing to improve prospects on the field. Doncaster, with only one victory out of the opening dozen, turned it round but needed a grandstand finish.

Queens Park Rangers scrambled just one win from mid-November until Boxing Day, a depressing sequence of fourteen matches. Yet had Ipswich Town managed to turn half of their twenty draws into wins, it would have guaranteed a play-off berth.

For Derby County, the bottom half of the table was ever present, five games undefeated their best into April and 40 players called upon during the campaign. Eighth in November, Watford needed a sustained effort to extricate the dangerous position and the last two wins were crucial.

The promise shown by Preston North End in the opening phase which saw them third at one stage, faded and they had to be grateful for isolated successes. Barnsley, with just one point from the first possible eighteen, climbed to ninth in early February but failed to win any of the last ten.

Coventry City slumped alarmingly from early March when win bonuses disappeared, yet their problems had initially appeared in October. Scunthorpe United only once achieved three wins in a row but it proved a blessing in March as they won only once more.

Extreme financial worries and a subsequent loss of ten points through administration threatened Crystal Palace on and off the field – one day eighth, the next twentieth. But losing only once in the last seven and amazingly drawing at Sheffield Wednesday on the last day to save themselves and relegate the home team provided a dramatic finale.

For Wednesday it was not entirely unexpected. Goals were hard to come by and three wins in a row from mid-January was the high spot. They were joined in relegation by Plymouth Argyle and Peterborough United. Plymouth were even poorer in attack and never recovered from starting without a win until late September. Peterborough were demoted after a draw at Barnsley on 5 April, victory at Plymouth purely academic on match 46.

Though not a unique situation Norwich City began the 2009–10 League season losing 7-1 at home to East Anglian neighbours Colchester United, ending it beaten on their own doorstep by Carlisle yet in between won more matches than any other team in the four divisions and became champions.

Oddly enough it was the 5-0 revenge win at Colchester in January which pushed them to the front and there they remained. Yet for months Leeds United had seem unlikely to be caught. Until the end of December they had lost just once at Millwall. Points continued to be dropped and it seemed the play-offs would be their only hope. But five wins from the last seven secured the second automatic place.

Perhaps it was fitting that Millwall, in third place after they had completed the double over Leeds, should have won through in the play-offs beating Swindon Town in the final having accounted for Huddersfield Town.

Millwall had started the season none too confidently but lost only three times in the last half of it. In contrast, fellow South Londoners Charlton Athletic shot off with six consecutive wins but in January cracks began to appear. They lost to Swindon on penalties.

The Wiltshire team, who themselves twice defeated Leeds, even reached second place in early April before dropping valuable points. Free-scoring at times, Huddersfield's problem was inconsistency.

With the ten-point deficit hanging over them all season, Southampton did extremely well to finish as high as seventh. In fact after a worrying two months at the beginning, they improved tremendously and had Oldham Athletic not forced a draw at St Mary's in April the incentive to go on might have secured the play-offs.

Despite that sensational opening to the campaign, Colchester had a miserable time of it from the end of February when they won only twice more. Brentford's ninth placing was as high as they managed all season, though as draw champions of the division with twenty such, it was not difficult to understand.

Walsall slipped up in December with a run of eight games without a win and stayed middle of the table from then on. Bristol Rovers, too, faced similar concerns at the same time and also found goals had dried up.

Milton Keynes Dons had looked good play-off material before mid-March when they failed to win another match. Brighton & Hove Albion, with the poorest home record in the division, still pulled themselves away from the relegation zone.

Carlisle United were never able to put more than two wins in a row together for any significant movement after dragging themselves away from the drop area, while Yeovil Town succeeded in achieving the same duo feat just twice.

Oldham's best sequence came in September. Thereafter wins here and there proved enough to stave off relegation. Leyton Orient, too, flirted dangerously with the foot of the table but three wins in the last five helped. Exeter City were another in similar peril but nine games without defeat provided the lifeline.

Not that there was much breathing space for any of those so involved. Tranmere Rovers had to move smartly in the last weeks as did Hartlepool United, hit late with a three point deduction. Even then only goal difference kept them safe at the expense of Gillingham.

On the last day of drama, Exeter and Tranmere were winners, and Gillingham losers while Hartlepool grabbed a point. Thus three points had separated seven clubs at the final analysis, leaving Wycombe Wanderers, Southend United and Stockport County to join Gillingham into League Two.

Gillingham, nine matches, no wins and only three goals, spelled out disaster on the horizon in mid-February. Wycombe, trailing badly all season, produced four wins from their last six outings, but it had come much too late. Southend with financial worries and only two wins from January were heading out from March and cash-strapped Stockport County suffered a club record twelve consecutive defeats into the New Year.

Notts County won the League Two title, though they had endured a fiscal farce earlier in the season. They lost just once at home and only once in the last twenty. However, it was Rochdale's decline which assisted them. In the end they only made it in third place. In nine outings they scored just three goals for four points!

Bournemouth, with transfer restrictions imposed, had last season's squad but stuck gamely to the task and were rewarded with second place after a useful start. From the play-offs Dagenham & Redbridge emerged winners, taking out Rotherham United in the final after hitting six in one semi-final against Morecambe who had come through on the rails to qualify. Plucky Aldershot Town had been edged out by Rotherham.

Again it was tough at the top with six points separating the last eight at the final whistle. Chesterfield's highest was third in March, but Bury drifted away from mid-February and Port Vale slipped up in their last two matches when a play-off spot seemed likely.

Northampton Town disappeared from the radar from April after several promising runs while Shrewsbury Town's demise began a month earlier having been fifth at one stage. Burton Albion in their first season produced some outstanding performances but lacked consistency and Bradford City disappointed with a mid-table look throughout.

Accrington Stanley lost momentum after one point from a possible twenty-seven, Hereford United – sixteen without a win – finished on a firmer note with seven wins in ten and Torquay United fought back well when still in the bottom four in mid-April.

Crewe Alexandra's reasonable opening was not maintained and only one win came from April. Macclesfield Town endured ten games without a win into March while Lincoln City, weak in attack hovered dangerously throughout.

A run of six defeats in a row left Barnet on the edge but secured their status on the last day beating Rochdale, while Grimsby Town, who had beaten Barnet a week earlier, lost at Burton having suffered a club record twenty-five games without a win until March.

So Grimsby were relegated, but Cheltenham Town avoided the drop in spite of being unable to win any of their last six matches. Alas for Darlington, their Blue Square Premier membership had been achieved in early in April. They also used 53 players. Newcomers Stevenage and returnees Oxford United were promoted.

Premiership bound Blackpool's Brett Omerod scores the winner just before half-time in a thrilling
Championship Play-off Final against Cardiff City at Wembley. Blackpool won 3-2 after twice falling behind.
(PA Photos)

THE FA CHARITY SHIELD WINNERS 1908–2009

Year	Match	Score	Year	Match	Score
1908	Manchester U v QPR	4-0 after 1-1 draw	1967	Manchester U v Tottenham H	3-3*
1909	Newcastle U v Northampton T	2-0	1968	Manchester C v WBA	6-1
1910	Brighton v Aston Villa	1-0	1969	Leeds U v Manchester C	2-1
1911	Manchester U v Swindon T	8-4	1970	Everton v Chelsea	2-1
1912	Blackburn R v QPR	2-1	1971	Leicester C v Liverpool	1-0
1913	Professionals v Amateurs	7-2	1972	Manchester C v Aston Villa	1-0
1920	WBA v Tottenham H	2-0	1973	Burnley v Manchester C	1-0
1921	Tottenham H v Burnley	2-0	1974	Liverpool† v Leeds U	1-1
1922	Huddersfield T v Liverpool	1-0	1975	Derby Co v West Ham U	2-0
1923	Professionals v Amateurs	2-0	1976	Liverpool v Southampton	1-0
1924	Professionals v Amateurs	3-1	1977	Liverpool v Manchester U	0-0*
1925	Amateurs v Professionals	6-1	1978	Nottingham F v Ipswich T	5-0
1926	Amateurs v Professionals	6-3	1979	Liverpool v Arsenal	3-1
1927	Cardiff C v Corinthians	2-1	1980	Liverpool v West Ham U	1-0
1928	Everton v Blackburn R	2-1	1981	Aston Villa v Tottenham H	2-2*
1929	Professionals v Amateurs	3-0	1982	Liverpool v Tottenham H	1-0
1930	Arsenal v Sheffield W	2-1	1983	Manchester U v Liverpool	2-0
1931	Arsenal v WBA	1-0	1984	Everton v Liverpool	1-0
1932	Everton v Newcastle U	5-3	1985	Everton v Manchester U	2-0
1933	Arsenal v Everton	3-0	1986	Everton v Liverpool	1-1*
1934	Arsenal v Manchester C	4-0	1987	Everton v Coventry C	1-0
1935	Sheffield W v Arsenal	1-0	1988	Liverpool v Wimbledon	2-1
1936	Sunderland v Arsenal	2-1	1989	Liverpool v Arsenal	1-0
1937	Manchester C v Sunderland	2-0	1990	Liverpool v Manchester U	1-1*
1938	Arsenal v Preston NE	2-1	1991	Arsenal v Tottenham H	0-0*
1948	Arsenal v Manchester U	4-3	1992	Leeds U v Liverpool	4-3
1949	Portsmouth v Wolverhampton W	1-1*	1993	Manchester U† v Arsenal	1-1
1950	World Cup Team v Canadian Touring Team	4-2	1994	Manchester U v Blackburn R	2-0
1951	Tottenham H v Newcastle U	2-1	1995	Everton v Blackburn R	1-0
1952	Manchester U v Newcastle U	4-2	1996	Manchester U v Newcastle U	4-0
1953	Arsenal v Blackpool	3-1	1997	Manchester U† v Chelsea	1-1
1954	Wolverhampton W v WBA	4-4*	1998	Arsenal v Manchester U	3-0
1955	Chelsea v Newcastle U	3-0	1999	Arsenal v Manchester U	2-1
1956	Manchester U v Manchester C	1-0	2000	Chelsea v Manchester U	2-0
1957	Manchester U v Aston Villa	4-0	2001	Liverpool v Manchester U	2-1
1958	Bolton W v Wolverhampton W	4-1	2002	Arsenal v Liverpool	1-0
1959	Wolverhampton W v Nottingham F	3-1	2003	Manchester U† v Arsenal	1-1
1960	Burnley v Wolverhampton W	2-2*	2004	Arsenal v Manchester U	3-1
1961	Tottenham H v FA XI	3-2	2005	Chelsea v Arsenal	2-1
1962	Tottenham H v Ipswich T	5-1	2006	Liverpool v Chelsea	2-1
1963	Everton v Manchester U	4-0	2007	Manchester U† v Chelsea	1-1
1964	Liverpool v West Ham U	2-2*	2008	Manchester U† v Portsmouth	0-0
1965	Manchester U v Liverpool	2-2*	2009	Chelsea† v Manchester U	2-2
1966	Liverpool v Everton	1-0			

* *Each club retained shield for six months.*   † *Won on penalties.*

THE FA COMMUNITY SHIELD 2009

Chelsea (0) 2, Manchester United (1) 2

Chelsea won 4-1 on penalties.

At Wembley Stadium, 9 August 2009, attendance 85,896

Chelsea: Cech; Ivanovic (Bosingwa 45), Cole A, Mikel (Ballack 65), Terry, Ricardo Carvalho, Essien, Lampard, Anelka (Kalou 83), Drogba, Malouda (Deco 77).
Scorers: Ricardo Carvalho 52, Lampard 71.

Manchester United: Foster; O'Shea (Fabio 76), Evra, Carrick, Ferdinand, Evans J, Park (Giggs 75), Fletcher (Scholes 75), Berbatov (Owen 75), Rooney, Nani (Valencia 62).
Scorers: Nani 10, Rooney 90.

Chelsea won 4-1 on penalties: Lampard scored; Giggs saved; Ballack scored; Carrick scored; Drogba scored; Evra saved; Kalou scored.

Referee: C. Foy (Merseyside).

ACCRINGTON STANLEY FL Championship 2

FOUNDATION

Accrington Football Club, founder members of the Football League in 1888, were not connected with Accrington Stanley. In fact both clubs ran concurrently between 1891 when Stanley were formed and 1895 when Accrington FC folded. Actually Stanley Villa was the original name, those responsible for forming the club living in Stanley Street and using the Stanley Arms as their meeting place. They became Accrington Stanley in 1893. In 1894–95 they joined the Accrington & District League, playing at Moorhead Park. Subsequently they played in the North-East Lancashire Combination and the Lancashire Combination before becoming founder members of the Third Division (North) in 1921, two years after moving to Peel Park. In 1962 they resigned from the Football League, were wound up, reformed 1963, disbanded in 1966 only to restart as Accrington Stanley (1968), returning to the Lancashire Combination in 1970.

The Fraser Eagle Stadium, Livingstone Road, Accrington, Lancashire BB5 5BX.

Telephone: (0871) 434 1968.

Ticket Office: (01254) 356 950/(01254) 336 954.

Fax: (01254) 356 951.

Website: www.accringtonstanley.co.uk

Email: info@accringtonstanley.co.uk

Ground Capacity: 5,057.

Record Attendance: 4,368 v Colchester U, FA Cup 1st rd, 3 January 2004.

Pitch Measurements: 111yds × 72yds.

Chairman: Ilyas Khan.

President: Peter Marsden.

Managing Directory: David O'Neill.

Secretary: Hannah Bailey.

Manager: John Coleman.

Assistant Manager: Jimmy Bell.

Physio: Joe Hinnigan.

Club Nickname: 'Reds'.

Colours: All red.

Change Colours: All yellow.

Year Formed: 1891, reformed 1968.

Turned Professional: 1919.

HONOURS

Football League: Division 3 (N) – Runners-up 1954–55, 1957–58.

Conference: Champions 2005–06.

FA Cup: 4th rd 1927, 1937, 1959.

Football League Cup: never past 2nd rd.

Northern Premier League: Champions 2002–03.

Northern League: Division 1 – Champions 1999–2000.

North West Counties: Runners-up 1986–87.

Cheshire County League: Division 2 – Champions 1980–81; Runners-up 1979–80.

Lancashire Combination: Champions 1973–74, 1977–78; Runners-up 1971–72, 1975–76.

Lancashire Combination Cup: Winners 1971–72, 1972–73, 1973–74, 1976–77.

Grounds: 1891, Moorhead Park; 1897, Bell's Ground; 1919, Peel Park; 1970, Crown Inn.

First Football League Game: 27 August 1921, Division 3 (N), v Rochdale (a) L 3-6 – Tattersall; Newton, Baines, Crawshaw, Popplewell, Burkinshaw, Oxley, Makin, Green (1), Hosker (2), Hartles.

sky SPORTS FACT FILE

Centre-forward Jim Blakeney, signed from Spen Juniors by Accrington Stanley in 1937, scored three hat-tricks for the reserves in a month. In the first team he impressed so much that Arsenal signed him a year later where he scored four hat-tricks in their reserves 1938–39.

Record League Victory: 8–0 v New Brighton, Division 3 (N), 17 March 1934 – Maidment; Armstrong (pen), Price, Dodds, Crawshaw, McCulloch, Wyper, Lennox (2), Cheetham (4), Leedham (1), Watson.

Record Cup Victory: 7–0 v Spennymoor U, FA Cup 2nd rd, December 1938 – Tootill; Armstrong, Whittaker, Latham, Curran, Lee, Parry (2), Chadwick, Jepson (3), McLoughlin (2), Barclay.

Record Defeat: 9–1 v Lincoln C, Division 3 (N), 3 March 1951.

Most League Points (2 for a win): 61, Division 3 (N), 1954–55.

Most League Points (3 for a win): 61, FL 2, 2009–10.

Most League Goals: 96, Division 3 (N), 1954–55.

Highest League Scorer in Season: George Stewart, 35, Division 3 (N), 1955–56; George Hudson, 35, Division 4, 1960–61.

Most League Goals in Total Aggregate: George Stewart, 136, 1954–58.

Most League Goals in One Match: 5, Billy Harker v Gateshead, Division 3 (N), 16 November 1935; George Stewart v Gateshead, Division 3 (N), 27 November 1954.

Most Capped Player: Romuald Boco, 19 (39), Benin.

Most League Appearances: Jim Armstrong, 260, 1927–34.

Youngest League Player: Ian Gibson, 15 years 358 days, v Norwich C, 23 March 1959.

Record Transfer Fee Received: £180,000 from Ipswich T for Gary Roberts, January 2007.

Record Transfer Fee Paid: £85,000 to Swansea C for Ian Craney, January 2008

Football League Record: 1921 Original Member of Division 3 (N); 1958–60 Division 3; 1960–62 Division 4; 2006– FL 2.

MANAGERS

William Cronshaw c.1894
John Haworth 1897–1910
Johnson Haworth c.1916
Sam Pilkingson 1919–24
  (Tommy Booth p-m 1923–24)
Ernie Blackburn 1924–32
Amos Wade 1932–35
John Hacking 1935–49
Jimmy Porter 1949–51
Walter Crook 1951–53
Walter Galbraith 1953–58
George Eastham snr 1958–59
Harold Bodle 1959–60
James Harrower 1960–61
Harold Mather 1962–63
Jimmy Hinksman 1963–64
Terry Neville 1964–65
Ian Bryson 1965
Danny Parker 1965–66
Gerry Keenan
Gary Pierce
Dave Thornley
Phil Staley
Eri Whalley
Stan Allen 1995–96
Tony Greenwood 1996–98
Billy Rodaway 1998
Wayne Harrison 1998–99
John Coleman May 1999–

LATEST SEQUENCES

Longest Sequence of League Wins: 7, 27.12.1954 – 5.2.1955.

Longest Sequence of League Defeats: 9, 8.3.1030 – 21.4.1930.

Longest Sequence of League Draws: 4, 10.9.1927 – 27.9.1927.

Longest Sequence of Unbeaten League Matches: 11, 27.11.1954 – 5.2.1955.

Longest Sequence Without a League Win: 18, 17.9.1938 – 31.12.1938.

Successive Scoring Runs: 22 from 14.11.1936.

Successive Non-scoring Runs: 5 from 15.3.1930.

TEN YEAR LEAGUE RECORD

		P	W	D	L	F	A	Pts	Pos
2000-01	U Pr	44	18	10	16	72	67	64	9
2001-02	U Pr	44	21	9	14	89	64	72	6
2002-03	U Pr	44	30	10	4	97	44	100	1
2003-04	Conf	42	15	13	14	68	61	58	10
2004-05	Conf	42	18	11	13	72	58	65	10
2005-06	Conf	42	28	7	7	76	45	91	1
2006-07	FL 2	46	13	11	22	70	81	50	20
2007-08	FL 2	46	16	3	27	49	83	51	17
2008-09	FL 2	46	13	11	22	42	59	50	16
2009-10	FL 2	46	18	7	21	62	74	61	15

DID YOU KNOW ?

Jack Hacking was appointed player-coach by Accrington Stanley at the start of 1935–36, an unusual move as he was a goalkeeper. After a distinguished career and having England international credentials, he stayed at Peel Park to become a long-serving manager.

ACCRINGTON STANLEY 2009–10 LEAGUE RECORD

Match No.	Date	Venue	Opponents	Result	H/T Score	Lg Pos.	Goalscorers	Attendance
1	Aug 8	A	Rotherham U	L 0-1	0-0	—		10,25
2	15	H	Lincoln C	W 1-0	0-0	11	Kempson [51]	149
3	18	H	Northampton T	L 0-3	0-2	—		156
4	22	A	Aldershot T	L 1-3	0-2	21	Edwards [48]	227
5	29	H	Shrewsbury T	L 1-3	0-1	23	Symes [67]	144
6	Sept 5	A	Bury	W 2-0	0-0	18	Grant 2 [83, 85]	308
7	11	H	Darlington	W 2-1	1-0	—	Procter [21], Kee [84]	322
8	19	A	Hereford U	L 0-2	0-1	16		201
9	25	H	Crewe Alex	W 5-3	2-1	—	Grant 2 [3, 49], Symes 2 [5, 77], Procter [68]	276
10	29	A	Port Vale	D 2-2	0-1	—	Edwards (pen) [82], Procter [90]	432
11	Oct 3	A	Chesterfield	L 0-1	0-0	14		310
12	10	H	Cheltenham T	W 4-0	0-0	13	Turner [54], Edwards (pen) [59], Grant 2 [62, 68]	184
13	17	H	Bournemouth	L 0-1	0-0	14		185
14	24	A	Rochdale	W 2-1	1-0	14	Grant [45], Symes [70]	320
15	30	H	Grimsby T	D 2-2	1-1	—	King G [5], Edwards (pen) [68]	432
16	Nov 14	H	Dagenham & R	L 0-1	0-1	14		153
17	21	A	Bradford C	D 1-1	0-1	14	Symes [56]	11,17
18	Dec 1	A	Burton Alb	W 2-0	0-0	14	Kee [45], Symes [76]	202
19	5	H	Torquay U	W 4-2	2-1	12	Edwards (pen) [39], Procter [40], Joyce [56], Grant [70]	135
20	12	H	Notts Co	W 2-1	0-0	11	Symes [60], Ryan [74]	585
21	26	A	Morecambe	W 2-1	0-0	9	Edwards 2 (1 pen) [56, 62 (p)]	347
22	28	H	Bury	L 2-4	1-0	11	Symes [14], McConville [69]	313
23	Jan 26	A	Aldershot T	W 2-1	1-0	—	Procter [30], Kee [75]	127
24	30	A	Shrewsbury T	W 1-0	1-0	10	Grant [26]	531
25	Feb 6	H	Morecambe	W 3-2	1-1	8	Grant 2 [29, 62], Ryan [83]	237
26	9	A	Northampton T	L 0-4	0-1	—		320
27	13	A	Macclesfield T	D 0-0	0-0	12		172
28	16	H	Lincoln C	L 1-2	1-0	—	Grant [30]	277
29	20	H	Bradford C	W 2-0	0-0	8	Miles 2 [54, 86]	339
30	27	A	Torquay U	L 1-2	0-0	12	Symes [69]	250
31	Mar 6	H	Notts Co	L 0-3	0-1	14		212
32	9	H	Macclesfield T	D 1-1	0-0	—	Kee [65]	121
33	13	A	Barnet	W 2-1	0-1	12	Edwards [59], Kee [84]	155
34	16	H	Rotherham U	W 2-1	1-0	—	Symes [18], Ryan [79]	144
35	20	H	Rochdale	L 2-4	0-0	12	Symes [61], Miles [65]	302
36	23	H	Burton Alb	L 0-2	0-1	—		127
37	27	A	Bournemouth	L 0-2	0-1	14		541
38	Apr 3	A	Dagenham & R	L 1-3	1-2	14	Grant [5]	203
39	5	H	Grimsby T	L 2-3	2-0	14	Kee [38], Symes [44]	183
40	10	A	Darlington	D 0-0	0-0	14		154
41	13	H	Port Vale	L 1-2	0-1	—	Grant [52]	220
42	17	H	Hereford U	L 1-2	0-1	15	Symes (pen) [48]	142
43	24	A	Crewe Alex	L 1-5	0-1	17	Brayford (og) [85]	381
44	27	A	Barnet	W 1-0	0-0	—	Kee [70]	126
45	May 1	H	Chesterfield	W 2-0	0-0	13	Kee 2 [70, 88]	247
46	8	A	Cheltenham T	D 1-1	1-1	15	Turner [24]	385

Final League Position: 15

GOALSCORERS

League (62): Grant 14, Symes 13 (1 pen), Kee 9, Edwards 8 (5 pens), Procter 5, Miles 3, Ryan 3, Turner 2, Joyce 1, Kempson 1, King G 1, McConville 1, own goal 1.
Carling Cup (3): Grant 1, Mullin 1, Symes 1.
FA Cup (7): Symes 3, Grant 2, Miles 1, Ryan 1.
J Paint Trophy (7): Symes 2, Edwards 1, Grant 1, King G 1, Winnard 1, own goal 1.

Martin A 7	Winnard D 44	Ryan J 36+3	King C 1	Kempson D 40	Edwards P 46	Joyce L 36+5	Grant R 41+1	Kee B 15+22	Mullin P 4	Miles J 32+4	McConville S 14+14	Turner C 11+13	Symes M 39+2	Procter A 44	King G 3+5	Murphy P 5+6	Dunbavin J 27	Lees T 39	Black A —+1	Bouzanis D 12+2	Flynn J 6+2	Mullin J 1+2	McCarten J 1	Richardson L 2	Match No.
1	2	3	4[1]	5	6	7	8[2]	9[3]	10	11	12	13	14												1
1	2	3		5	6	7	8		10	11	12			4	9[1]										2
1	2	3		5	6	7	8	9[1]	10	11	12			4											3
1	2[1]	3		5	6	7	8	13	10[3]	11	9[2]		14	4	12										4
1	2	3		5	6	7	8	12		11	9[1]		10	4											5
	2			5	6[1]	7	8			11		9	10	4	12		1	3							6
	2			5	6	7	8	12		11[1]		9	10	4			1	3							7
	2			5	6	7	8	12		11[2]		9[1]	10	4	13	14	14	3[3]							8
1	2	9[1]		5	6	7	8[2]	13		11	12		10	4				3							9
1	2	9		5	6	7[1]	8	12		11		13	10	4				3[2]							10
	2	9[1]		5	6	12	8	7[2]		11		13	10	4			1	3							11
	2			5[1]	6	10	8[2]	7		11[3]		9		4	3	12	1	3	14						12
	2	12		5		7	8[1]	10		11	13	9		4	6[2]		1	3							13
	2	11		5	6	7	8	12				9[1]	10	4			1	3							14
	2	10		5	6	7	8	12				9		4	11[1]		1	3							15
	2	8[1]		5	6	7		10		11[2]	12	9		4	13		1	3							16
	2	8		5	6[1]			10		12	11	7	9	4			1	3							17
	2	8		5	6	7		10		11		9		4			1	3							18
	2	8		5		7	11[1]	10		12		9			3		1				6				19
	2	8		5	6	7	11	9[1]		12			10				1	3							20
	2	8		5	6	7	11[1]	12				9	10				1	3							21
	2	8		5	6	7[1]	11	12		13		9[2]	10				1	3			1				22
	2	8		5		7		9		12		11[1]	10	4			1	3			6				23
	2	8		5	6	7		9		12		11	10[1]	4			1	3							24
	2	8		5	6	4	9	12		11[1]		7	10				1	3							25
	2	8[3]		5	6[2]	7	9	12		14		10	4	11[1]			1	3			13				26
	2	8		5	6		9	12		11[1]	7[2]	13	10	4			1	3							27
	2	8		5	6		9			11	7		10	4			1	3							28
	2	8		5	6	7	9			11			10	4			1	3							29
	2	8		5	6	7[1]	9			11		12	10	4			1	3							30
	2	8[2]		5	6	7[1]	9			11		12	10	4			1	3			13				31
	2	8[1]		5	6	12		9		11[2]	13	7	10	4			1	3							32
	2	12		5	6	7		9[2]		11[6]	13	8[1]	10	4	1[8]			3		15					33
	2	8		5	6	7				11[1]			10	4				3			1	12			34
	2	8		5	6	7[1]	12	9		11[2]	14	13	10[4]	4				3		1					35
	2	8		5	6	7	10	9		11	13			4[1]	12		1	3[2]							36
	2	8		5	6	7	10[3]	9[2]		11	13	12		4[1]	14		1	3							37
	2	13		5		14	11	9[3]		8	12		4		6[1]		1	3			7	10[2]			38
	2	8[1]		5	6	12	11	9[3]		14	13	7[2]	10	4			1	3					3		39
	2	8		5	6	7	11	9[1]		12			10	4			1	3							40
	2	8[2]		5	6	7[1]	9	12		11		13	10	4			1	3							41
	2	8		5	6	7[1]	9	12		11[2]		13	10	4			1	3							42
	2	8		5[6]	6	7[1]	9	12		11[2]		13	10	4			1[8]	3		15					43
	2			5[1]	6		9	13				7[2]	10	4	12		1	3			11				44
				5	14		9	13		12		7[2]	8[1]	10	4[3]	6	1				11		2		45
				5			9	13				7[2]	1.	10	4	6[1]	1				8	12	2		46

FA Cup

First Round	Salisbury C	(h)	2-1	
Second Round	Barnet	(h)	2-2	
		(a)	1-0	
Third Round	Gillingham	(h)	1-0	
Fourth Round	Fulham	(h)	1-3	

Carling Cup

First Round	Walsall	(h)	2-1
Second Round	QPR	(a)	1-2

J Paint Trophy

First Round	Oldham Ath	(a)	2-1
Second Round	Shrewsbury T	(h)	2-0
Northern Quarter-Final	Bury	(h)	3-2
Northern Semi-Final	Leeds U	(a)	0-2

ALDERSHOT TOWN   FL Championship 2

FOUNDATION

It was through the initiative of Councillor Jack White, a local newsagent, who immediately captured the interest of the Town Clerk D. Llewellyn Griffiths, that Aldershot Town was formed in 1926. Having established a limited liability company under the chairmanship of Norman Clinton, an Aldershot resident and chairman of the Hampshire County FA, they rented the Recreation Ground from the Aldershot Borough Council. Admitted to the Southern League for 1927–28, they were elected to the Football League in 1932 but were removed from the competition in March 1992 and their record expunged. Re-formed almost immediately as Aldershot Town Football Club.

The EBB Stadium at the Recreation Ground, High Street, Aldershot GU11 1TW.

Telephone: 01252 320211.

Fax: 01252 324347.

Ticket Office: 01252 320211.

Website: www.theshots.co.uk

Ground capacity: 7,100.

Record Attendance: 19,138 v Carlisle U, FA Cup 4th rd (replay), 28 January 1970.

Pitch Measurements: 117yd × 75yd.

Acting Chairman: John Leppard.

Chief Executive: Peter Duffy.

Secretary: Bob Green.

Manager: Kevin Dillon.

Assistant Manager: Gary Owers.

Physio: Nick Brink.

Colours: All red shirts with blue sleeves, red shorts with blue and white trim, red stockings with blue and white trim.

Change Colours: All black with red, blue and white trim.

Year Formed: 1926.

Turned Professional: 1927. *Ltd Co.:* 1927.

Previous Names: 1926, Aldershot Town; c.1937 Aldershot; 1992, Aldershot Town.

Club nickname: 'The Shots'.

Ground: 1927, Recreation Ground.

First Football League Game: 27 August 1932, Division 3 (S), v Southend U (h) L 1–2 – Robb; Wade, McDougall, Lawson, Spence, Middleton, Proud, White, Gamble, Douglas, Fishlock (1).

HONOURS

Football League: Best season: 8th, Division 3, 1973–74.

FA Cup: Best season: 5th rd, 1932–33, 5th rd replay, 1978–79.

Football League Cup: Best season: 3rd rd replay, 1984–85.

Blue Square Premier League: Champions 2007–08.

Conference: Runners-up 2003–04.

Isthmian League Division 3: Champions 1992–93.

Isthmian First Division Champions: 1997–98.

Isthmian League Premier Division: Champions 2002–03.

Hampshire Senior Cup: Winners 1928, 1999, 2000, 2002, 2003, 2007.

Setanta Shield: Winners 2008.

sky SPORTS FACT FILE

On 1 December 2009 Aldershot Town won 5–2 at Dagenham & Redbridge, who were then lying fourth in League Two. This result gave the Shots the best performance of the week anywhere in the country and was rewarded with a presentation at the Recreation Ground.

Record League Victory: 8–1 v Gateshead, Division 4, 13 September 1958 – Marshall; Henry, Jackson, Mundy, Price, Gough, Walters, Stepney (3), Lacey (3), Matthews (2), Tyrer.

Record Cup Victory: 7–0 v Chelmsford, FA Cup, 1st rd, 28 November 1931 – Robb; Twine, McDougall (1), Norman Wilson, Gardiner, Middleton (1), Blackbourne, Stevenson (1), Thom (3), Hopkins (1), Edgar.

7–0 v Newport (IW), FA Cup, 2nd rd, 8 December 1945 – Reynolds; Horton, Sheppard, Ray, White, Summerbee, Sinclair, Hold (1), Brooks (5), Fitzgerald, Hobbs (1).

N.B. 11–1 v Kingstonian, FA Cup, 4th qual rd, 16 November 1929 – Mobbs; Thomas, McDougall, Norman Wilson, Gardiner, Middleton (2), Young (1), Common (1), Horton (2), Hopkins (3), Edgar (2).

Record Defeat: – 1–10 v Southend U, Leyland Daf Cup, Pr rd, 6 November 1990.

Most League Points: (2 for a win): 57, Division 4, 1978–79.

Most League Points (3 for a win): 75, Division 4, 1983–84.

Most League Goals: 83, Division 4, 1963–64.

Highest League Scorer in Season: John Dungworth, 26, Division 4, 1978–79.

Most League Goals in Total Aggregate: Jack Howarth, 171, 1965–71 and 1972–77.

Most Capped Player: Louie Soares, 3, Barbados.

Most League Appearances: Murray Brodie, 461, 1970–83.

Youngest League Player: Clive Jackman, 16 years 135 days v Leyton Orient, 16 April 1953.

Record Transfer Fee Received: £150,000 from Wolverhampton W for Tony Lange, July 1989.

Record Transfer Fee Paid: £54,000 to Portsmouth for Colin Garwood, February 1980.

Football League Record: 1932 Elected to Division 3 (S); 1958–73 Division 4; 1973–76 Division 3; 1976–87 Division 4; 1987–89 Division 3; 1989–92 Division 4; 1992–93 Isthmian League Division 3; 1993–94 Isthmian League Division 2; 1994–98 Isthmian League Division 1; 1998–2003 Isthmian League Premier Division; 2003–08 Conference; 2008– FL 2.

MANAGERS
Angus Seed 1927–37
Bill McCracken 1937–49
Gordon Clark 1950–55
Harry Evans 1955–59
Dave Smith 1959–71
(GM from 1967)
Tommy McAnearney 1967–68
Jimmy Melia 1968–72
Tommy McAnearney 1972–81
Len Walker 1981–84
Ron Harris (GM) 1984–85
Len Walker 1985–91
Brian Talbot 1991–92
Ian McDonald 1992
Steve Wignall 1992–95
Steve Wigley 1995–97
George Borg 1997–2002
Terry Brown 2002–07
Gary Waddock 2007–09
Kevin Dillon November 2009–

LATEST SEQUENCES

Longest Sequence of League Wins: 5, 16.9.1961 – 2.10.61.

Longest Sequence of League Defeats: 9, 20.11.1965 – 5.2.1966.

Longest Sequence of League Draws: 6, 6.10.1962 – 27.10.1962.

Longest Sequence of Unbeaten League Matches: 13, 26.3.1966 – 3.9.1966.

Longest Sequence Without a League Win: 17, 10.10.1936 – 30.1.1937.

Successive Scoring Runs: 29 from 1.4.1961.

Successive Non-scoring Runs: 6 from 22.3.1988.

TEN YEAR LEAGUE RECORD

		P	W	D	L	F	A	Pts	Pos
2000-01	Isth PR	41	21	11	9	73	39	74	2
2001-02	Isth PR	42	22	7	13	76	51	73	3
2002-03	Isth PR	46	33	6	7	81	36	105	1
2003-04	Conf	42	20	10	12	80	67	70	5
2004-05	Conf	42	21	10	11	68	52	73	4
2005-06	Conf	42	16	6	20	61	74	54	13
2006-07	Conf	46	18	11	17	64	62	65	9
2007-08	B Sq Pr	46	31	8	7	82	48	101	1
2008-09	FL 2	46	14	12	20	59	80	54	15
2009-10	FL 2	46	20	12	14	69	56	72	6

DID YOU KNOW ?

On 12 February 2010 Aldershot Town won 3–0 at Northampton Town, the Cobblers having remained unbeaten in their previous eleven League games. Then on 27 February their 1–0 win at Chesterfield saw the end of their undefeated six-match sequence.

ALDERSHOT TOWN 2009–10 LEAGUE RECORD

Match No.	Date		Venue	Opponents	Result	H/T Score	Lg Pos.	Goalscorers	Attendance
1	Aug	8	H	Darlington	W 3-1	2-0	—	Morgan M [3], Sandell [30], Soares [47]	2866
2		15	A	Rochdale	L 0-1	0-0	9		2465
3		18	A	Bournemouth	L 0-1	0-0	—		5556
4		22	H	Accrington S	W 3-1	2-0	10	Donnelly 2 [8, 90], Morgan M [22]	2276
5		29	A	Grimsby T	W 2-1	1-0	7	Donnelly 2 [27, 49]	3757
6	Sept	5	H	Hereford U	D 2-2	0-1	7	Hylton [86], Morgan M [87]	3094
7		12	H	Port Vale	D 1-1	1-1	8	Soares [38]	3406
8		19	A	Crewe Alex	W 2-1	1-1	5	Donnelly [33], Hudson [66]	3661
9		26	H	Cheltenham T	W 4-1	1-0	4	Winfield [34], Charles [69], Morgan M [73], Donnelly [90]	2964
10		29	A	Torquay U	D 1-1	0-0	—	Morgan M (pen) [48]	2271
11	Oct	3	A	Lincoln C	L 0-1	0-0	8		4131
12		10	H	Morecambe	W 4-1	1-0	6	Morgan M [14], Stanley (og) [47], Hudson [67], Soares [80]	2974
13		17	H	Bury	L 2-3	1-1	6	Winfield [9], Soares [71]	3196
14		24	A	Shrewsbury T	L 1-3	1-2	10	Soares [4]	5417
15		31	A	Rotherham U	D 0-0	0-0	10		3002
16	Nov	14	H	Macclesfield T	D 0-0	0-0	10		2646
17		21	A	Notts Co	D 0-0	0-0	11		6500
18		24	H	Northampton T	W 2-1	0-1	—	Donnelly (pen) [80], Morgan M [89]	2761
19	Dec	1	A	Dagenham & R	W 5-2	1-1	—	Charles [30], Sandell [52], Morgan M [59], Jackson [77], Soares [90]	1876
20		5	H	Chesterfield	W 1-0	0-0	6	Charles [68]	2977
21		12	A	Burton Alb	L 1-6	0-4	8	Grant [67]	2547
22		26	H	Barnet	W 4-0	1-0	5	Grant 2 [36, 59], Sandell [65], Donnelly (pen) [77]	3231
23	Jan	19	A	Rochdale	D 1-1	0-0	—	Soares [87]	2453
24		23	H	Bournemouth	W 2-1	1-0	6	Sandell [21], Straker [87]	4387
25		26	A	Accrington S	L 1-2	0-1	—	Sandell (pen) [59]	1279
26		30	H	Grimsby T	D 1-1	0-1	8	Hylton [68]	3195
27	Feb	6	A	Barnet	L 0-3	0-0	9		2145
28		12	A	Northampton T	W 3-0	1-0	—	Morgan M 2 [12, 75], Hudson [68]	4718
29		16	A	Hereford U	L 0-2	0-2	—		1576
30		20	H	Notts Co	D 1-1	1-0	10	Bozanic [45]	4016
31		23	H	Dagenham & R	L 2-3	1-0	—	Hudson [22], Donnelly [51]	2053
32		27	A	Chesterfield	W 1-0	0-0	10	Hylton [64]	3827
33	Mar	2	H	Bradford C	W 1-0	0-0	—	Charles [54]	2311
34		6	H	Burton Alb	L 0-2	0-2	9		2784
35		13	A	Bradford C	L 1-2	1-2	10	Straker [8]	11,272
36		20	H	Shrewsbury T	W 2-0	1-0	10	Bozanic [29], Morgan M [74]	2681
37		23	A	Darlington	W 2-1	2-0	—	Brown [25], Morgan M [41]	1296
38		27	A	Bury	W 2-1	1-0	7	Donnelly 2 (1 pen) [30 (p), 56]	2795
39	Apr	3	A	Macclesfield T	D 1-1	0-1	7	Donnelly (pen) [76]	1428
40		5	H	Rotherham U	W 3-0	1-0	5	Morgan D [16], Morgan M [62], Howell [87]	3573
41		10	A	Port Vale	D 1-1	0-0	4	Morgan D [53]	5399
42		13	H	Torquay U	L 0-2	0-2	—		3652
43		17	A	Crewe Alex	D 1-1	1-1	6	Harding [41]	2966
44		24	H	Cheltenham T	W 2-1	0-1	5	Donnelly (pen) [48], Morgan D [90]	3386
45	May	1	H	Lincoln C	W 3-1	0-0	5	Morgan M 2 [69, 75], Morgan D [73]	4506
46		8	A	Morecambe	L 0-1	0-0	6		5268

Final League Position: 6

GOALSCORERS

League (69): Morgan M 15 (1 pen), Donnelly 13 (5 pens), Soares 7, Sandell 5 (1 pen), Charles 4, Hudson 4, Morgan D 4, Grant 3, Hylton 3, Bozanic 2, Straker 2, Winfield 2, Brown 1, Harding 1, Howell 1, Jackson 1, own goal 1.
Carling Cup (1): Morgan M 1 (pen).
FA Cup (3): Bozanic 1, Donnelly 1, Soares 1.
J Paint Trophy (2): Hudson 1, Soares 1.
Play-Offs (0).

Jaimez-Ruiz M 30	Herd B 33 + 1	Sandell A 29	Halls J 10 + 6	Blackburn C 36 + 6	Hinshelwood A 13 + 2	Soares L 28 + 8	Harding B 28 + 5	Morgan M 36 + 4	Donnelly S 42 + 1	Hudson K 24 + 10	Chalmers L 19 + 4	Hylton D 5 + 16	Grant J 5 + 12	Winfield D 19 + 6	Connolly R — + 3	Charles A 32 + 1	Straker A 35 + 2	Parret D 4	German A 2 + 1	Hopkinson B — + 1	Masters C — + 1	Jackson M 18 + 4	Bozanic U 19 + 6	Henderson S 8	Howell D — + 3	Spencer D 3 + 9	Riza O — + 1	Brown A 12	Morgan D 8 + 1	Young J 8 + 1	Match No.
1	2	3	4	6	5	7	8^1	9^2	10^3	11	12	13	14																		1
1		3	4	5	6	7	8	9	10	11	2^1				12																2
1		3	4	5	2	7^2	8	9	10^1	11				12		6	13														3
1		3	4	2	5	7	8^1	9^2	10^3	11	12	13	14			6															4
1		3	4	2	5	7	8	9	10^1	11	12					6															5
1		3	4	2	5^2	7	8^1	9	10	11		13	12			6															6
1	3^1	4	2				7	9	10	11		8^2				6	13	5	12												7
1			4		2		7	9	10	11	12					6	5	3	8^1												8
1			12		2		7	9	10	11	4					6	5	3	8^1												9
1	2		4			12	7	9	10^1	11	8					6	5	3													10
1	2				5		7	9	10	11^1	4			12		6		3	8												11
1	2				5		8	9	10^3	11^1	4	13	12			6		3			7^2	14									12
1^6	2		12		5^1		11	9	10		4	13				6		3	8^2	7	15										13
1	2	8^3	13		5^2		7	9	10	11^1	4					6^1	2	3				14									14
1	2	3		5		7	8	9^1	10		4		12			6	11														15
1	2	3		5^1		7	8	9	10		4^2	13	12			6	11														16
1	2	3		5		7^3	8	9^2	10		4^1	13	12	14		6	11														17
1	2	3		5		7^3	8	9	10		4^2	13	12	14		6	11^1														18
1	2	3		5			8	9^3	10^2		4		12	14		6	11					7^1	13								19
1	2	3		5			8	9	10		4^1		12	14		6	11^2					7^3	13								20
1	2			5		7	8		10^2		4	13	12			6^1	3					9	11^1								21
1	2	3		5			8^2	9^3	10		4^1		12	14		6	11					7	13								22
1	2	3		5			8	9	10		4^2	13	12			6	11^1					7^3	14								23
1	2	3		5				9	10^2	11^1	4	13		14		6	12					7^3	8								24
1	2	3		5			8	9			4	13	12	14		6	11^1					7^3	10^2								25
1	2	3		5				9^2	10	11^3	4	13	12	14		6						7^1	8								26
	2	3		5			8^3	9^2	10		4	13	12			6						7^1	11	1	14						27
	2	3		5			8	9^3	10		4	13	12	14		6^2	11						7	1							28
	2	3		5			8	9	10^2		4^3	13	12	14		6	11						7	1							29
	2	3		5				9	10		4		12			6	11					7^1	8	1							30
	2	3^2		5				9^1	10		4	13	12	14		6	11^3					7	8	1							31
	2	3		5		7^1		9^2	10		4					6	11					12	8	1	13						32
	2	3		5^1		7^3		9	10		4		12			6	11^2					14	8	1	13						33
	2	3^3		5		7^2		9	10		4					6	11					12	3^1	1	13	14					34
1	2	3		5				9^3	10^2	11	4	13				6	3					7^1	12			14					35
1	2			5				9^3	10^2		4	13		14		3	11					7^1	8					6	12		36
1	2			5				9^3	10		4	13		14		3^1	11					7^2	8					6	12		37
1^1	2			5		7		9^6	10		4	13				3							8^2			12		6	11^1	15	38
	2			5			8	9	10		4	13	12				3					7^1						6	11^2	1	39
	2			5			8^2	9	10		4		12	14			3^1					7^3				13		6	11	1	40
	2^2			5			8^1	9^3	10		4	13	12	14			3					7						6	11	1	41
	2			5			8	9^1	10		4	13		14			3					7^2	12					6	11^3	1	42
	2			5			8	9	10^3		4^1	13		14			3					7^2						6	11	1	43
	2	3					8	9			4	13		14		6						7^3	12			10^1		5^2	11	1	44
	2	3^3					8	9			4	13		14		6						7^1	12			10^2		5	11	1	45
	2						8	9^2		11^1	4^2			14		6	3					7	12			10		5	13	1	46

FA Cup
First Round   Bury   (h)   2-0
Second Round   Tranmere R   (a)   0-0
                             (h)   1-2

Carling Cup
First Round   Bristol R   (a)   1-2

J Paint Trophy
Second Round   Hereford U   (a)   2-2
Play-Offs
Semi-Final   Rotherham U (h)   0-1
                             (a)   0-2

ARSENAL   FA Premiership

FOUNDATION

Formed by workers at the Royal Arsenal, Woolwich in 1886, they began as Dial Square (name of one of the workshops), and included two former Nottingham Forest players, Fred Beardsley and Morris Bates. Beardsley wrote to his old club seeking help and they provided the new club with a full set of red jerseys and a ball. The club became known as the 'Woolwich Reds' although their official title soon after formation was Woolwich Arsenal.

Emirates Stadium, Highbury House, 75 Drayton Park, Islington, London N5 1BU.

Telephone: (0207) 619 5003.

Fax: (0207) 704 4001.

Ticket Office: (0207) 619 5000.

Website: www.arsenal.com

Email: contactafc@arsenal.com

Ground Capacity: 60,361.

Record Attendance: 73,295 v Sunderland, Div 1, 9 March 1935.

At Wembley: 73,707 v RC Lens, UEFA Champions League, 25 November 1998.

At Highbury: 60,162 v Manchester U, FA Premier League, 3 November 2007.

Pitch Measurements: 105m × 68m.

Chairman: Peter Hill-Wood.

Acting Managing Director: Ken Friar OBE.

Secretary: David Miles.

Manager: Arsène Wenger.

Assistant Manager: Pat Rice.

Physio: Colin Lewin.

Colours: Red shirts with white trim, white shorts, white stockings with red tops.

Change Colours: Yellow shirts with black sleeves, black shorts, yellow stockings with black trim.

Year Formed: 1886.

Turned Professional: 1891.

Ltd Co: 1893.

Previous Names: 1886, Dial Square; 1886, Royal Arsenal; 1891, Woolwich Arsenal; 1914 Arsenal.

Club Nickname: 'Gunners'.

HONOURS

FA Premier League: Champions 1997–98, 2001–02, 2003–04. Runners-up 1998–99, 1999–2000, 2000–01, 2002–03, 2004–05.

Football League: Division 1 – Champions 1930–31, 1932–33, 1933–34, 1934–35, 1937–38, 1947–48, 1952–53, 1970–71, 1988–89, 1990–91; Runners-up 1925–26, 1931–32, 1972–73; Division 2 – Runners-up 1903–04.

FA Cup: Winners 1930, 1936, 1950, 1971, 1979, 1993, 1998, 2002, 2003, 2005; Runners-up 1927, 1932, 1952, 1972, 1978, 1980, 2001.

Double performed: 1970–71, 1997–98, 2001–02.

Football League Cup: Winners 1987, 1993; Runners-up 1968, 1969, 1988, 2007.

European Competitions: Fairs Cup: 1963–64, 1969–70 (winners), 1970–71. *European Cup:* 1971–72, 1991–92. *UEFA Champions League:* 1998–99, 1999–2000, 2000–01, 2001–02, 2002–03, 2003–04, 2004–05, 2005–06 (runners-up), 2006–07, 2007–08 (q-f), 2008–09 (s-f), 2009–10. *UEFA Cup:* 1978–79, 1981–82, 1982–83, 1996–97, 1997–98, 1999–2000 (runners-up). *European Cup-Winners' Cup:* 1979–80 (runners-up), 1993–94 (winners), 1994–95 (runners-up). *Super Cup:* 1994 (runners up).

sky SPORTS FACT FILE

In February 2008 Jack Wilshere made a scoring reserve debut for Arsenal against West Ham United. He became their youngest League player on 13 September aged 16 years 256 days against Blackburn Rovers and hit his first senior goal ten days later v Sheffield United.

Grounds: 1886, Plumstead Common; 1887, Sportsman Ground; 1888, Manor Ground; 1890, Invicta Ground; 1893, Manor Ground; 1913, Highbury; 2006, Emirates Stadium.

First Football League Game: 2 September 1893, Division 2, v Newcastle U (h) D 2–2 – Williams; Powell. Jeffrey; Devine, Buist, Howat; Gemmell, Henderson, Shaw (1), Elliott (1), Booth.

Record League Victory: 12–0 v Loughborough T, Division 2, 12 March 1900 – Orr; McNichol, Jackson; Moir, Dick (2), Anderson (1); Hunt, Cottrell (2), Main (2), Gaudie (3), Tennant (2).

Record Cup Victory: 11–1 v Darwen, FA Cup 3rd rd, 9 January 1932 – Moss; Parker, Hapgood; Jones, Roberts, John; Hulme (2), Jack (3), Lambert (2), James, Bastin (4).

Record Defeat: 0–8 v Loughborough T, Division 2, 12 December 1896.

Most League Points (2 for a win): 66, Division 1, 1930–31.

Most League Points (3 for a win): 90, FA Premier League, 2003–04.

Most League Goals: 127, Division 1, 1930–31.

Highest League Scorer in Season: Ted Drake, 42, 1934–35.

Most League Goals in Total Aggregate: Thierry Henry, 174, 1999–2007.

Most League Goals in One Match: 7, Ted Drake v Aston Villa, Division 1, 14 December 1935.

Most Capped Player: Thierry Henry, 81 (123), France.

Most League Appearances: David O'Leary, 558, 1975–93.

Youngest League Player: Jack Wilshere, 16 years 256 days v Blackburn R, 13 September 2008.

Record Transfer Fee Received: £25,000,000 from Manchester C for Emmanuel Adebayor, July 2009.

Record Transfer Fee Paid: £12,800,000 to Marseille for Samir Nasri, July 2008.

Football League Record: 1893 Elected to Division 2; 1904–13 Division 1; 1913–19 Division 2; 1919–92 Division 1; 1992– FA Premier League.

MANAGERS

Sam Hollis 1894–97
Tom Mitchell 1897–98
George Elcoat 1898–99
Harry Bradshaw 1899–1904
Phil Kelso 1904–08
George Morrell 1908–15
Leslie Knighton 1919–25
Herbert Chapman 1925–34
George Allison 1934–47
Tom Whittaker 1947–56
Jack Crayston 1956–58
George Swindin 1958–62
Billy Wright 1962–66
Bertie Mee 1966–76
Terry Neill 1976–83
Don Howe 1984–86
George Graham 1986–95
Bruce Rioch 1995–96
Arsène Wenger September 1996–

LATEST SEQUENCES

Longest Sequence of League Wins: 14, 10.2.2002 – 18.8.2002.

Longest Sequence of League Defeats: 7, 12.2.1977 – 12.3.1977.

Longest Sequence of League Draws: 6, 4.3.1961 – 1.4.1961.

Longest Sequence of Unbeaten League Matches: 49, 7.5.2003 – 24.10.2004.

Longest Sequence Without a League Win: 23, 28.9.1912 – 1.3.1913.

Successive Scoring Runs: 55 from 19.5.2001.

Successive Non-scoring Runs: 6 from 25.2.1987.

TEN YEAR LEAGUE RECORD

		P	W	D	L	F	A	Pts	Pcs
2000-01	PR Lge	38	20	10	8	63	38	70	2
2001-02	PR Lge	38	26	9	3	79	36	87	1
2002-03	PR Lge	38	23	9	6	85	42	78	2
2003-04	PR Lge	38	26	12	0	73	26	90	1
2004-05	PR Lge	38	25	8	5	87	36	83	2
2005-06	PR Lge	38	20	7	11	68	31	67	4
2006-07	PR Lge	38	19	11	8	63	35	68	4
2007-08	PR Lge	38	24	11	3	74	31	83	3
2008-09	PR Lge	38	20	12	6	68	37	72	4
2009-10	PR Lge	38	23	6	9	83	41	75	3

DID YOU KNOW ?

On 13 December 2009 Arsenal became the fifth team to reach 7,000 goals since entering the Football League with their first goal in a 2–1 win at Liverpool, against one of the previous teams to achieve the feat, the others being Aston Villa, Manchester United and Wolverhampton Wanderers.

ARSENAL 2009–10 LEAGUE RECORD

Match No.	Date	Venue	Opponents	Result	H/T Score	Lg Pos.	Goalscorers	Attendance
1	Aug 15	A	Everton	W 6-1	3-0	—	Denilson [26], Vermaelen [37], Gallas [41], Fabregas 2 [48, 69], Eduardo [89]	39,309
2	22	H	Portsmouth	W 4-1	2-1	3	Diaby 2 [18, 21], Gallas [51], Ramsey [68]	60,049
3	29	A	Manchester U	L 1-2	1-0	6	Arshavin [40]	75,095
4	Sept 12	A	Manchester C	L 2-4	0-1	9	Van Persie [62], Rosicky [88]	47,339
5	19	H	Wigan Ath	W 4-0	1-0	7	Vermaelen 2 [25, 49], Eboue [59], Fabregas [90]	59,103
6	26	A	Fulham	W 1-0	0-0	5	Van Persie [52]	25,700
7	Oct 4	H	Blackburn R	W 6-2	3-2	4	Vermaelen [17], Van Persie [33], Arshavin [37], Fabregas [57], Walcott [75], Bendtner [89]	59,431
8	17	A	Birmingham C	W 3-1	2-1	4	Van Persie [16], Diaby [18], Arshavin [84]	60,082
9	25	A	West Ham U	D 2-2	2-0	3	Van Persie [16], Gallas [37]	34,442
10	31	H	Tottenham H	W 3-0	2-0	3	Van Persie 2 [42, 60], Fabregas [43]	60,103
11	Nov 7	A	Wolverhampton W	W 4-1	3-0	2	Zubar (og) [28], Craddock (og) [35], Fabregas [45], Arshavin [66]	28,937
12	21	A	Sunderland	L 0-1	0-0	3		44,918
13	29	H	Chelsea	L 0-3	0-2	4		60,067
14	Dec 5	H	Stoke C	W 2-0	1-0	3	Arshavin [26], Ramsey [79]	60,048
15	13	A	Liverpool	W 2-1	0-1	3	Johnson (og) [50], Arshavin [58]	43,853
16	16	A	Burnley	D 1-1	1-1	—	Fabregas [7]	21,309
17	19	H	Hull C	W 3-0	1-0	3	Denilson [45], Eduardo [59], Diaby [80]	60,006
18	27	H	Aston Villa	W 3-0	0-0	3	Fabregas 2 [65, 81], Diaby [90]	60,056
19	30	A	Portsmouth	W 4-1	2-0	—	Kaboul (og) [27], Nasri [42], Ramsey [69], Song Billong [81]	20,404
20	Jan 9	H	Everton	D 2-2	1-1	—	Osman (og) [28], Rosicky [90]	60,053
21	17	A	Bolton W	W 2-0	1-0	3	Fabregas [28], Merida Perez [78]	23,893
22	20	H	Bolton W	W 4-2	1-2	—	Rosicky [43], Fabregas [52], Vermaelen [66], Arshavin [85]	59,084
23	27	A	Aston Villa	D 0-0	0-0	—		39,601
24	31	H	Manchester U	L 1-3	0-2	3	Vermaelen [80]	60,091
25	Feb 7	A	Chelsea	L 0-2	0-2	3		41,794
26	10	H	Liverpool	W 1-0	0-0	—	Diaby [72]	60,045
27	20	H	Sunderland	W 2-0	1-0	3	Bendtner [27], Fabregas (pen) [90]	60,083
28	27	A	Stoke C	W 3-1	1-1	3	Bendtner [32], Fabregas (pen) [89], Vermaelen [90]	27,011
29	Mar 6	H	Burnley	W 3-1	1-0	—	Fabregas [34], Walcott [60], Arshavin [90]	60,043
30	13	A	Hull C	W 2-1	1-1	3	Arshavin [14], Bendtner [90]	25,023
31	20	A	West Ham U	W 2-0	1-0	2	Denilson [5], Fabregas (pen) [83]	60,077
32	27	H	Birmingham C	D 1-1	0-0	3	Nasri [81]	27,039
33	Apr 3	H	Wolverhampton W	W 1-0	0-0	3	Bendtner [90]	60,067
34	14	A	Tottenham H	L 1-2	0-1	—	Bendtner [85]	36,041
35	18	A	Wigan Ath	L 2-3	1-0	3	Walcott [41], Silvestre [48]	22,113
36	24	H	Manchester C	D 0-0	0-0	3		60,086
37	May 3	A	Blackburn R	L 1-2	1-1	—	Van Persie [13]	26,138
38	9	H	Fulham	W 4-0	3-0	3	Arshavin [21], Van Persie [26], Baird (og) [37], Vela [84]	60,039

Final League Position: 3

GOALSCORERS

League (83): Fabregas 15 (3 pens), Arshavin 10, Van Persie 9, Vermaelen 7, Bendtner 6, Diaby 6, Denilson 3, Gallas 3, Ramsey 3, Rosicky 3, Walcott 3, Eduardo 2, Nasri 2, Eboue 1, Merida Perez 1, Silvestre 1, Song Billong 1, Vela 1, own goals 6.
Carling Cup (4): Bendtner 1, Merida 1, Vela 1, Watt 1.
FA Cup (3): Denilson 1, Eduardo 1, Ramsey 1.
Champions League (26): Bendtner 5 (1 pen), Fabregas 4 (1 pen), Nasri 3, Arshavin 2, Eboue 2, Eduardo 2 (1 pen), Campbell 1, Denilson 1, Diaby 1, Gallas 1, Van Persie 1, Vermaelen 1, Walcott 1, own goal 1.

Almunia M 29	Sagna B 31+4	Clichy G 23+1	Song Billong A 25+1	Vermaelen T 33	Gallas W 26	Denilson 19+1	Fabregas F 26+1	Bendtner N 13+10	Van Persie R 14+2	Arshavin A 25+5	Eboue E 17+8	Eduardo 13+11	Ramsey A 7+11	Gibbs K 3	Diaby V 26+3	Merida Perez F —+4	Rosicky T 14+11	Mannone V 5	Walcott T 12+11	Wilshere J —+1	Nasri S 22+4	Traore A 9	Vela C 1+10	Silvestre M 9+3	Eastmond C 2+2	Campbell S 10+1	Fabianski L 4	Djourou J —+1	Lansbury H —+1	Match No.
1	2	3		4	5	6	7	8²	9¹	10³	11	12	13	14																1
1				5	6	4	8¹	14	10	11²	2	9³	12		3		7	13												2
1	2	3	8	5	6	4²		12	10	9³	7¹	13	14		11															3
1	2²	3	7³	5	6	4¹	8	9	10		13	14			11		12													4
	2	3	4	5	6		8	13	10		7²	9³	12		11¹		14	1												5
	2	3	4	5	6		8	9	10²	11¹	13		7		12	1														6
	2	3	4	5	6		8³	13	10	9²		14		7		11¹	1	12												7
	13			4	5	6		8		10	12	2³			3	11		9²	1	7¹	14									8
	2	3	4	5	6		8	12	10	9	7¹	13			11²		1													9
1	2	3	4	5	6		8	9¹	10³	7²	13	12	14		11															10
1	2	12	5	6		8		10	7²		9³	4	3	11¹	14				13											11
1	2		4	5	6	8		12		9³	7¹				10²		13		11	3	14									12
1	2	7¹	5	6	4	8		10		9²					14		12		11³	3	13									13
1	2		5	6	4	8		9	7²		13				10¹				11	3	12	14								14
1	2	7	5	6	4	8		10³		14		12					9¹		11	3		13								15
1	2		4	5	6		8¹		9		13	12	10				7²		11		3									16
1		7	5	6	4		10³	2	9²	12	8				13		11¹		14	3										17
1	2	7	5	6	4¹	12²		10		9¹	13				8		14		11	3										18
1	2		4	5	6			10²		9¹	7				8	12			11³	3	13		14							19
1	2			5	6	4³		10		9²	7¹				8	14	12		11	3	13									20
1	2	13		5	6	8		7		9³					11	12	10²			3	14		4¹							21
1	2	3		5	6	4	8		7		9³				11¹		10²	14		13	12									22
1	2	3		5¹	6	4	8	13		7		9²	11		10³			14				12								23
1	2²	3	7	5	6	4¹	8	14		10	13				9³		12		11											24
1	2³	3	4	5	6		8	12		7	14				10²		13		9¹	11										25
1	14	3	4	5	6		8	9¹		7²	2				10		12		13	11¹										26
1	13	3	4	5		14	8	9		2³		7			12		10²	11¹			6									27
1	2	3	4	5			8	9		7²	14	10¹			12		13	11³					6							28
1		3			4	8¹	9³	13	2	14					12		10²	7		11			6							29
1	2	3		5		4	9		10	7¹	13				8		12	11²					6							30
1	13	3	7	5⁴	4	8	9¹	10³	2	14					12			11²					6							31
1	2	3	6		4	8	9	12							11		10¹	7²	13				5							32
1	2	8²	5		4	12			7¹	9³					10		11	13		14	3	6								33
1	2²	3	5¹		4²	9	14		7						8		10	13		12		6								34
	2	3			9	14		12							8	13	10²	7¹	11			6	4³	5	1					35
	2	3	4		13	9		12							8		10²	7¹	11			6		5	1					36
	2				10	12	7²	13							4			8	11	3	9¹	6		5	1					37
	2	3			10	9²	7								4			8³	11		13	6¹		5	1	12	14			38

FA Cup
Third Round   West Ham U   (a) 2-1
Fourth Round   Stoke C   (a) 1-3

Carling Cup
Third Round   WBA   (h) 2-0
Fourth Round   Liverpool   (h) 2-1
Quarter-Final   Manchester C   (a) 0-3

Champions League
Play-Off	Celtic	(a)	2-0
		(h)	3-1
Group H	Standard Liege	(a)	3-2
	Olympiakos	(h)	2-0
	AZ	(a)	1-1
		(h)	4-1
	Standard Liege	(h)	2-0
	Olympiakos	(a)	0-1
Knock-Out Round	Porto	(a)	1-2
		(h)	5-0
Quarter-Final	Barcelona	(h)	2-2
		(a)	1-4

ASTON VILLA   FA Premiership

FOUNDATION

Cricketing enthusiasts of Villa Cross Wesleyan Chapel, Aston, Birmingham decided to form a football club during the winter of 1874–75. Football clubs were few and far between in the Birmingham area and in their first game against Aston Brook St Mary's Rugby team they played one half rugby and the other soccer. In 1876 they were joined by a Scottish soccer enthusiast George Ramsay who was immediately appointed captain and went on to lead Aston Villa from obscurity to one of the country's top clubs in a period of less than 10 years.

Villa Park, Birmingham B6 6HE.
Telephone: (0121) 327 2299.
Fax: (0121) 322 2107.
Ticket Office/Consumer Sales: (0800) 612 0970.
Website: www.avfc.co.uk
Email: postmaster@avfc.co.uk
Ground Capacity: 42,582.
Record Attendance: 76,588 v Derby Co, FA Cup 6th rd, 2 March 1946.
Pitch Measurements: 115yd × 75yd.
Chairman: Randolph Lerner.
Secretary: Sharon Barnhurst.
Manager: Martin O'Neill.
Assistant Managers: John Robertson, Steve Walford.
Physio: Alan Smith.
Colours: Claret body, blue sleeve shirts, white shorts, sky blue stockings.
Change Colours: White shirts with blue trim, blue shorts, white stockings.
Third Kit: White shirts with thin claret pinstripe, blue shorts, white stockings.
Year Formed: 1874.
Turned Professional: 1885.
Ltd Co.: 1896.
Public Ltd Company: 1969.
Club Nickname: 'The Villans'.
Grounds: 1874, Wilson Road and Aston Park (also used Aston Lower Grounds for some matches); 1876, Wellington Road, Perry Barr; 1897, Villa Park.

HONOURS

FA Premier League: Runners-up 1992–93.
Football League: Division 1 – Champions 1893–94, 1895–96, 1896–97, 1898–99, 1899–1900, 1909–10, 1980–81; Runners-up 1888–89, 1902–03, 1907–08, 1910–11, 1912–13, 1913–14, 1930–31, 1932–33, 1989–90; Division 2 – Champions 1937–38, 1959–60; Runners-up 1974–75, 1987–88; Division 3 – Champions 1971–72.
FA Cup: Winners 1887, 1895, 1897, 1905, 1913, 1920, 1957; Runners-up 1892, 1924, 2000.
Double Performed: 1896–97.
Football League Cup: Winners 1961, 1975, 1977, 1994, 1996; Runners-up 1963, 1971, 2010.
European Competitions: *European Cup:* 1981–82 (winners), 1982–83. *UEFA Cup:* 1975–76, 1977–78, 1983–84, 1990–91, 1993–94, 1994–95, 1996–97, 1997–98, 1998–99, 2001–02, 2008–09. *Europa Legue:* 2009–10. *World Club Championship:* 1982. *European Super Cup:* 1982–83 (winners). *Intertoto Cup:* 2000, 2001 (winners), 2002, 2008 (winners).

First Football League Game: 8 September 1888, Football League, v Wolverhampton W (a) D 1–1 – Warner; Cox, Coulton; Yates, H. Devey, Dawson; A. Brown, Green (1), Allen, Garvey, Hodgetts.

sky SPORTS FACT FILE

On 12 December 2009 Aston Villa won 1–0 against Manchester United at Old Trafford. It was their first win at the ground since 5 November 1983 when two goals from Peter Withe gave Villa a 2–1 win. United finished fourth that season, Villa were tenth in Division One.

Record League Victory: 12–2 v Accrington S, Division 1, 12 March 1892 – Warner; Evans, Cox; Harry Devey, Jimmy Cowan, Baird; Athersmith (1), Dickson (2), John Devey (4), L. Campbell (4), Hodgetts (1).

Record Cup Victory: 13–0 v Wednesbury Old Ath, FA Cup 1st rd, 30 October 1886 – Warner; Coulton, Simmonds; Yates, Robertson, Burton (2); R. Davis (1), A. Brown (3), Hunter (3), Loach (2), Hodgetts (2).

Record Defeat: 1–8 v Blackburn R, FA Cup 3rd rd, 16 February 1889.

Most League Points (2 for a win): 70, Division 3, 1971–72.

Most League Points (3 for a win): 78, Division 2, 1987–88.

Most League Goals: 128, Division 1, 1930–31.

Highest League Scorer in Season: 'Pongo' Waring, 49, Division 1, 1930–31.

Most League Goals in Total Aggregate: Harry Hampton, 215, 1904–15.

Most League Goals in One Match: 5, Harry Hampton v Sheffield W, Division 1, 5 October 1912; 5, Harold Halse v Derby Co, Division 1, 19 October 1912; 5, Len Capewell v Burnley, Division 1, 29 August 1925; 5, George Brown v Leicester C, Division 1, 2 January 1932; 5, Gerry Hitchens v Charlton Ath, Division 2, 18 November 1959.

Most Capped Player: Steve Staunton 64 (102), Republic of Ireland.

Most League Appearances: Charlie Aitken, 561, 1961–76.

Youngest League Player: Jimmy Brown, 15 years 349 days v Bolton W, 17 September 1969.

Record Transfer Fee Received: £12,600,000 from Manchester U for Dwight Yorke, August 1998.

Record Transfer Fee Paid: £12,000,000 to Newcastle U for James Milner, August 2008; £12,000,000 to Middlesbrough for Stewart Downing, July 2009.

Football League Record: 1888 Founder Member of the League; 1936–38 Division 2; 1938–59 Division 1; 1959–60 Division 2; 1960–67 Division 1; 1967–70 Division 2; 1970–72 Division 3; 1972–75 Division 2; 1975–87 Division 1; 1987–88 Division 2; 1988–92 Division 1; 1992– FA Premier League.

MANAGERS

George Ramsay 1884–1926
(Secretary-Manager)
W. J. Smith 1926–34
(Secretary-Manager)
Jimmy McMullan 1934–35
Jimmy Hogan 1936–44
Alex Massie 1945–50
George Martin 1950–53
Eric Houghton 1953–58
Joe Mercer 1958–64
Dick Taylor 1964–67
Tommy Cummings 1967–68
Tommy Docherty 1968–70
Vic Crowe 1970–74
Ron Saunders 1974–82
Tony Barton 1982–84
Graham Turner 1984–86
Billy McNeill 1986–87
Graham Taylor 1987–90
Dr Jozef Venglos 1990–91
Ron Atkinson 1991–94
Brian Little 1994–98
John Gregory 1998–2002
Graham Taylor OBE 2002–03
David O'Leary 2003–06
Martin O'Neill August 2006–

LATEST SEQUENCES

Longest Sequence of League Wins: 9, 15.10.1910 – 10.12.1910.

Longest Sequence of League Defeats: 11, 23.3.1963 – 4.5.1963.

Longest Sequence of League Draws: 6, 12.9.1981 – 10.10.1981.

Longest Sequence of Unbeaten League Matches: 15, 12.3.1949 – 27.8.1949.

Longest Sequence Without a League Win: 12, 27.12.1986 – 25.3.1987.

Successive Scoring Runs: 35 from 10.11.1895.

Successive Non-scoring Runs: 5 from 29.2.1992.

TEN YEAR LEAGUE RECORD

		P	W	D	L	F	A	Pts	Pos
2000-01	PR Lge	38	13	15	10	46	43	54	8
2001-02	PR Lge	38	12	14	12	46	47	50	8
2002-03	PR Lge	38	12	9	17	42	47	45	16
2003-04	PR Lge	38	15	11	12	48	44	56	6
2004-05	PR Lge	38	12	11	15	45	52	47	10
2005-06	PR Lge	38	10	12	16	42	55	42	16
2006-07	PR Lge	38	11	17	10	43	41	50	11
2007-08	PR Lge	38	16	12	10	71	51	60	6
2008-09	PR Lge	38	17	11	10	54	48	62	6
2009-10	PR Lge	38	17	13	8	52	39	64	6

DID YOU KNOW ?

Eric Houghton became the first Aston Villa winger to achieve the feat of scoring double figures in ten successive seasons up to and including 1938–39. His total number of League goals in the period was 160 and his best came in 1930–31 with 30.

ASTON VILLA 2009–10 LEAGUE RECORD

Match No.	Date	Venue	Opponents	Result	H/T Score	Lg Pos.	Goalscorers	Attendance
1	Aug 15	H	Wigan Ath	L	0-2	0-1	—	35,578
2	24	A	Liverpool	W	3-1	2-0	—	Lucas (og) [34], Davies [45], Young A (pen) [75]	43,667
3	30	H	Fulham	W	2-0	1-0	8	Pantsil (og) [3], Agbonlahor [59]	32,917
4	Sept 13	A	Birmingham C	W	1-0	0-0	6	Agbonlahor [85]	25,196
5	19	H	Portsmouth	W	2-0	2-0	5	Milner (pen) [34], Agbonlahor [43]	35,979
6	26	A	Blackburn R	L	1-2	1-1	7	Agbonlahor [3]	25,172
7	Oct 5	H	Manchester C	D	1-1	1-0	—	Dunne [15]	37,924
8	17	H	Chelsea	W	2-1	1-1	6	Dunne [32], James M Collins [52]	39,047
9	24	A	Wolverhampton W	D	1-1	0-0	7	Agbonlahor [79]	28,734
10	31	A	Everton	D	1-1	0-1	7	Carew [46]	36,648
11	Nov 4	A	West Ham U	L	1-2	0-1	—	Young A [52]	30,024
12	7	H	Bolton W	W	5-1	2-1	5	Young A [5], Agbonlahor [43], Carew [53], Milner [72], Cuellar [75]	38,101
13	21	A	Burnley	D	1-1	0-1	5	Heskey [86]	21,178
14	28	H	Tottenham H	D	1-1	1-0	6	Agbonlahor [10]	39,866
15	Dec 5	H	Hull C	W	3-0	2-0	5	Dunne [13], Milner [29], Carew (pen) [88]	39,748
16	12	A	Manchester U	L	1-0	1-0	4	Agbonlahor [21]	75,130
17	15	A	Sunderland	W	2-0	1-0	—	Heskey [24], Milner [61]	34,821
18	19	H	Stoke C	W	1-0	0-0	4	Carew [61]	35,852
19	27	A	Arsenal	L	0-3	0-0	4		60,056
20	29	H	Liverpool	L	0-1	0-0	—		42,788
21	Jan 17	H	West Ham U	D	0-0	0-0	6		35,646
22	27	H	Arsenal	D	0-0	0-0	—		39,601
23	30	A	Fulham	W	2-0	2-0	7	Agbonlahor 2 [40, 44]	25,408
24	Feb 6	A	Tottenham H	D	0-0	0-0	7		35,899
25	10	H	Manchester U	D	1-1	1-1	—	Cuellar [19]	42,788
26	21	H	Burnley	W	5-2	1-1	7	Young A [32], Downing 2 [56, 58], Heskey [61], Agbonlahor [68]	38,709
27	Mar 13	A	Stoke C	D	0-0	0-0	7		27,598
28	16	A	Wigan Ath	W	2-1	1-1	—	McCarthy (og) [25], Milner [63]	16,186
29	20	H	Wolverhampton W	D	2-2	1-2	7	Carew 2 [16, 82]	37,562
30	24	H	Sunderland	D	1-1	1-1	—	Carew [30]	37,473
31	27	A	Chelsea	L	1-7	1-2	7	Carew [29]	41,825
32	Apr 3	A	Bolton W	W	1-0	1-0	7	Young A [11]	21,111
33	14	H	Everton	D	2-2	0-1	—	Agbonlahor [72], Jagielka (og) [90]	38,729
34	18	A	Portsmouth	W	2-1	1-1	6	Carew [16], Delfouneso [82]	16,523
35	21	A	Hull C	W	2-0	1-0	—	Agbonlahor [13], Milner (pen) [76]	23,842
36	25	H	Birmingham C	W	1-0	0-0	5	Milner (pen) [83]	42,788
37	May 1	A	Manchester C	L	1-3	1-2	6	Carew [16]	47,102
38	9	H	Blackburn R	L	0-1	0-0	6		41,799

Final League Position: 6

GOALSCORERS

League (52): Agbonlahor 13, Carew 10 (1 pen), Milner 7 (3 pens), Young A 5 (1 pen), Dunne 3, Heskey 3, Cuellar 2, Downing 2, James M Collins 1, Davies 1, Delfouneso 1, own goals 4.
Carling Cup (13): Milner 4 (2 pens), Agbonlahor 2, Heskey 2, Young A 2, Downing 1, Warnock 1, own goal 1.
FA Cup (15): Carew 6 (4 pens), Delfouneso 2, Young A 2, Agbonlahor 1, James M Collins 1, Cuellar 1, Delph 1, Petrov 1.
Europa League (2): Carew 1, Milner 1 (pen).

Friedel B 38	Beye H 5+1	Shorey N 3	Delph F 4+4	Davies C 2	Cuellar C 36	Milner J 36	Petrov S 37	Agbonlahor G 35+1	Heskey E 16+15	Young A 37	Sidwell S 12+13	Albrighton M —+3	Delfouneso N —+9	Reo-Coker N 6+4	Clark C 1	Carew J 22+11	Warnock A 30	Dunne R 35	Collins James M 26+1	Young L 14+2	Gardner C —+1	Downing S 23+2	Match No.
1	2^2	3	4^1	5	6	7	8	9^1	10	11	12	13	14										1
1	2	3			6	7	8	9	12	10^1	4			11				5					2
1	2	3			6	7	8	9		10	4			11^1	5	12							3
1					2	7	8	9		10	4			11^1		12	3	5	6				4
1			13		2	7	8	9	12^2	11	4					10^1	3	5	6				5
1			4^1		2	7	8	9	12	11						10	3	5	6				6
1					2	7	8	9	13	11^1	4			12		10^2	3	5	6				7
1					2	7	8	9	12	11	4					10^1	3	5	6				8
1					2	7	8	9	12	11	4					10^1	3	5	6				9
1					2	7^1	8^2	9	10	11	4			13		12	3	5	6				10
1	2					7	8^1	9	12	11	4			13		10^2	3	5	6				11
1			14			7^1	8^2	9	12	11	4			6^3		10	3	5	13	2			12
1					6	7	8	9	13	11	4^1					10	3	5	12	2^2			13
1	2				6	7	8	9	13	11	4^1			12		10^5	3	5					14
1					6	7	8	9	10^1	11						12	3	5	4	2			15
1					4	7	8	9	10^2	11			14			13	3^1	5	12	2		6^5	16
1					4	7	8	9^1	10	11						12	3	5		2		6	17
1					4	7	8	9	10^1	11	13					12	3	5		2		6^2	18
1			13		4	7	8	9	10^1	11						12	3	5		2^2		6	19
1					4	7	8	9	13		12			6^1		10	3	5		2		11^2	20
1					2	7	8	9	10^1	11						13	3	5	4			6	21
1			12		2	7	8	9	10^1	11							3	5	4			6	22
1					2	7	8	9	10	11							3	5	4			6	23
1					2	7	8	9	10^1	11	13					13	3	5	4			6^2	24
1			11^1		2	7	8^2	9	10					13		13	3	5	4			6	25
1					2	7	8	9^1	10^2	11^3	14			13		13	3	5	4			5	26
1					2	7	8	9		11	12					10^1	3	5	4			3	27
1					2	7	8	9^1	13	11	12					10^2	3	5	4			5	28
1					2	7	8	9	13	11	12					10	3	5^1	4			6^2	29
1					2	7^2	8	9^1	13	11	12					10	3	5	4			6	30
1			14			7	8^1	9^3	13	11	4					10^2	3	5	6	2	12		31
1			7^2		2		8	9	13	11	12					10^1	3	5	4			6	32
1					2	7	8	9		11	12					10	3^1	5	4			6	33
1					2	7	8	9^2	13	11	12					10^1	3	5	4			6	34
1					2	7	8^1	9	13	11	12					10^2	3	5	4			6	35
1					2	7	8	9		11	12					10^1	3	5	4			6	36
1					2	7	8	9	13	11	12					10^2	3^1	5	4			6	37
1					2	7	8	9^3	13	11	14					10^2	3^1	5	4		12	6	38

FA Cup

Third Round	Blackburn R	(h)	3-1
Fourth Round	Brighton & HA	(h)	3-2
Fifth Round	Crystal Palace	(a)	2-2
		(h)	3-1
Sixth Round	Reading	(a)	4-2
Semi-Final	Chelsea		0-3
(at Wembley).			

Carling Cup

Third Round	Cardiff C	(h)	1-0
Fourth Round	Sunderland	(a)	0-0
Quarter-Final	Portsmouth	(a)	4-2
Semi-Final	Blackburn R	(a)	1-0
		(h)	6-4
Final	Manchester U		1-2
(at Wembley).			

Europa League

Play-Off	Rapid Vienna	(a)	0-1
		(h)	2-1

BARNET   FL Championship 2

FOUNDATION

Barnet Football Club was formed in 1888 as an amateur organisation and they played at a ground in Queen's Road until they disbanded in 1901. A club known as Alston Works FC was then formed and they played at Totteridge Lane until changing to Barnet Alston FC in 1906. They moved to their present ground a year later, combining with The Avenue to form Barnet and Alston in 1912. The club progressed to senior amateur football by way of the Athenian and Isthmian Leagues, turning professional in 1965. It was as a Southern League and Conference club that they made their name.

Underhill Stadium, Barnet Lane, Barnet, Herts EN5 2DN.

Telephone: (020) 8441 6932.

Fax: (020) 8447 0655.

Ticket Office: 0208 449 6325.

Website: www.barnetfc.com

Email: info@barnetfc.com

Ground Capacity: 5,345.

Record Attendance: 11,026 v Wycombe Wanderers, FA Amateur Cup 4th Round 1951–52.

Record Receipts: £31,202 v Portsmouth, FA Cup 3rd Round, 5 January 1991.

Pitch Measurements: 100m × 64m.

Chairman: Anthony Kleanthous.

Group Finance Director: Andrew Adie.

Manager: Mark Stimson.

Physio: Mark Stein.

Colours: All black with amber trim.

Change Colours: White shirts with black trim, red shorts, red stockings.

Year Formed: 1888.

Turned Professional: 1965.

Previous Name: 1906, Barnet Alston FC; 1919, Barnet.

Club Nickname: The Bees.

Grounds: 1888, Queens Road; 1901, Totteridge Lane; 1907, Barnet Lane.

First Football League Game: 17 August 1991, Division 4, v Crewe Alex (h) L 4–7 – Phillips; Blackford, Cooper (Murphy), Horton, Bodley (Stein), Johnson, Showler, Carter (2), Bull (2), Lowe, Evans.

HONOURS

Football League: Division 2 best season: 24th, 1993–94.

FA Amateur Cup: Winners 1946.

FA Trophy: Runners-up 1972.

GM Vauxhall Conference: Winners 1990–91. *Conference:* Winners 2004–05

FA Cup: 4th rd, 2007, 2008.

League Cup: best season: 3rd rd, 2006.

sky SPORTS FACT FILE

The first Chinese team to visit the United Kingdom was Sing Tao Sports Club from the Hong Kong League. En route in Asia they had played 24 matches, winning 21 and drawing another. Barnet beat them 5–3 on 20 September 1947 in a fine exhibition of football.

Record League Victory: 7–0 v Blackpool, Division 3, 11 November 2000 – Naisbitt; Stockley, Sawyers, Niven (Brown), Heald, Arber (1), Currie (3), Doolan, Richards (2) (McGleish), Cottee (1) (Riza), Toms.

Record Cup Victory: 6–1 v Newport Co, FA Cup 1st rd, 21 November 1970 – McClelland; Lye, Jenkins, Ward, Embery, King, Powell (1), Ferry, Adams (1), Gray, George (3), (1 og).

Record Defeat: 1–9 v Peterborough U, Division 3, 5 September 1998.

Most League Points (3 for a win): 79, Division 3, 1992–93.

Most League Goals: 81, Division 4, 1991–92.

Highest League Scorer in Season: Dougie Freedman, 24, Division 3, 1994–95.

Most League Goals in Total Aggregate: Sean Devine, 47, 1995–99.

Most League Goals in One Match: 4, Dougie Freedman v Rochdale, Division 3, 13 September 1994; 4, Lee Hodges v Rochdale, Division 3, 8 April 1996.

Most Capped Player: Ken Charlery, 4, St Lucia.

Most League Appearances: Paul Wilson, 263. 1991–2000.

Youngest League Player: Kieran Adams, 17 years 71 days v Mansfield T, 31 December 1994.

Record Transfer Fee Received: £800,000 from Crystal Palace for Dougie Freedman, September 1995.

Record Transfer Fee Paid: £130,000 to Peterborough U for Greg Heald, August 1997.

Football League Record: 1991 Promoted to Division 4 from GMVC; 1991–92 Division 4; 1992–93 Division 3; 1993–94 Division 2; 1994–2001 Division 3; 2001–05 Conference; 2005– FL 2.

MANAGERS

Lester Finch
George Wheeler
Dexter Adams
Tommy Coleman
Gerry Ward
Gordon Ferry
Brian Kelly
Bill Meadows 1976–79
Barry Fry 1979–85
Roger Thompson 1985
Don McAllister 1985–86
Barry Fry 1986–93
Edwin Stein 1993
Gary Phillips (Player–Manager) 1993–94
Ray Clemence 1994–96
Alan Mullery (Director of Football) 1996–97
Terry Bullivant 1997
John Still 1997–2000
Tony Cottee 2000–01
John Still 2001–02
Peter Shreeves 2002–03
Martin Allen 2003–04
Paul Fairclough 2004–08
Ian Hendon 2008–10
Mark Stimson June 2010–

LATEST SEQUENCES

Longest Sequence of League Wins: 6, 28.8.1993 – 25.9.1999.

Longest Sequence of League Defeats: 11, 8.5.1993 – 2.10.1993.

Longest Sequence of League Draws: 4, 22.1.1994 – 12.2.1994.

Longest Sequence of Unbeaten League Matches: 12, 5.12.1992 – 2.3.1993.

Longest Sequence Without a League Win: 14, 24.4.1993 – 10.10.1993.

Successive Scoring Runs: 12 from 19.3.1995.

Successive Non-scoring Runs: 5 from 12.2.2000.

TEN YEAR LEAGUE RECORD

		P	W	D	L	F	A	Pts	Pos
2000-01	Div 3	46	12	9	25	67	81	45	24
2001-02	Conf	42	19	10	13	64	43	67	5
2002-03	Conf	42	13	14	15	65	63	53	11
2003-04	Conf	42	19	14	9	60	43	71	4
2004-05	Conf	42	26	8	8	90	44	86	1
2005-06	FL 2	46	12	18	16	44	57	54	18
2006-07	FL 2	46	16	11	19	55	70	59	14
2007-08	FL 2	46	16	12	18	56	63	60	12
2008-09	FL 2	46	11	15	20	56	74	48	17
2009-10	FL 2	46	12	12	22	47	63	48	21

DID YOU KNOW ?

Oscar Linkson was a locally born full-back and an outstanding teenager for Barnet Alston. After leaving the club he played for another amateur side The Pirates on tour where he was spotted by Manchester United and was duly signed as a professional in 1908.

BARNET 2009–10 LEAGUE RECORD

Match No.	Date	Venue	Opponents	Result	H/T Score	Lg Pos.	Goalscorers	Attendance
1	Aug 8	A	Lincoln C	L 0-1	0-0	—		3753
2	15	H	Shrewsbury T	D 2-2	2-1	18	Hyde J 2 (1 pen) [30, 44 (p)]	1835
3	18	H	Morecambe	W 2-0	1-0	—	Furlong [3], Jarrett (pen) [83]	1298
4	22	A	Torquay U	W 1-0	1-0	7	Adomah [26]	2856
5	29	H	Notts Co	W 1-0	0-0	4	Hyde J [89]	2858
6	Sept 4	A	Northampton T	W 3-1	0-1	4	Deen [51], Furlong [66], O'Flynn [71]	4206
7	12	A	Macclesfield T	D 1-1	1-1	4	Morgan (og) [41]	1125
8	19	H	Bradford C	D 2-2	0-1	4	O'Flynn [56], Hughes [61]	2282
9	26	A	Rotherham U	L 0-3	0-2	8		3823
10	29	H	Dagenham & R	W 2-0	2-0	—	Furlong [21], O'Flynn (pen) [45]	2093
11	Oct 3	H	Grimsby T	W 3-0	2-0	4	O'Flynn (pen) [11], Adomah [16], Bolasie [67]	2497
12	10	A	Rochdale	L 1-2	0-2	7	Hyde J [84]	2648
13	17	A	Burton Alb	L 0-2	0-1	9		2935
14	24	A	Darlington	W 3-0	0-0	6	Yakubu [62], Deverdics [80], Bolasie [82]	2313
15	31	A	Chesterfield	L 0-1	0-0	8		3585
16	Nov 14	H	Hereford U	D 0-0	0-0	8		1965
17	21	H	Port Vale	D 0-0	0-0	8		1939
18	24	A	Cheltenham T	L 1-5	1-2	—	O'Flynn [13]	2331
19	Dec 1	H	Bournemouth	D 1-1	1-1	—	O'Flynn [15]	2030
20	5	A	Bury	L 0-2	0-1	13		2511
21	12	H	Crewe Alex	L 1-2	1-1	15	Sinclair [40]	1841
22	26	A	Aldershot T	L 0-4	0-1	15		3231
23	28	H	Northampton T	D 0-0	0-0	16		2237
24	Jan 16	H	Lincoln C	L 1-2	0-1	—	Yakubu [75]	1810
25	23	A	Morecambe	L 1-2	1-1	18	Lockwood (pen) [34]	1558
26	26	H	Torquay U	D 1-1	1-0	—	Sawyer [15]	1331
27	30	A	Notts Co	L 0-2	0-2	18		6444
28	Feb 6	H	Aldershot T	W 3-0	0-0	17	Hyde M [56], O'Flynn 2 [63, 85]	2145
29	9	A	Shrewsbury T	L 0-2	0-2	—		4328
30	13	H	Cheltenham T	D 1-1	1-1	17	Adomah [35]	1667
31	20	A	Port Vale	W 2-0	1-0	16	O'Flynn 2 [8, 84]	4571
32	23	A	Bournemouth	L 0-3	0-0	—		4019
33	27	H	Bury	D 0-0	0-0	17		1949
34	Mar 6	A	Crewe Alex	D 2-2	2-1	17	O'Flynn [23], Lockwood [29]	3551
35	13	H	Accrington S	L 1-2	1-0	18	O'Flynn (pen) [32]	1559
36	20	A	Darlington	W 2-1	2-0	18	Livermore [23], Adomah [32]	1463
37	27	H	Burton Alb	D 1-1	1-1	19	Hughes [45]	1842
38	Apr 3	A	Hereford U	L 1-2	1-1	20	Rose (og) [43]	2146
39	5	H	Chesterfield	W 3-1	3-1	19	Furlong 2 [34, 45], Hyde J [42]	1916
40	10	H	Macclesfield T	L 1-2	0-0	20	Upson [90]	1433
41	13	A	Dagenham & R	L 1-4	1-1	—	Hyde J [45]	2004
42	17	A	Bradford C	L 1-2	1-0	22	Adomah [28]	11,138
43	24	A	Rotherham U	L 0-1	0-1	22		1884
44	27	A	Accrington S	L 0-1	0-0	—		1268
45	May 1	A	Grimsby T	L 0-2	0-0	22		7033
46	8	H	Rochdale	W 1-0	0-0	21	Jarrett [90]	4638

Final League Position: 21

GOALSCORERS

League (47): O'Flynn 12 (3 pens), Hyde J 6 (1 pen), Adomah 5, Furlong 5, Bolasie 2, Hughes 2, Jarrett 2 (1 pen), Lockwood 2 (1 pen), Yakubu 2, Deen 1, Deverdics 1, Hyde M 1, Livermore 1, Sawyer 1, Sinclair 1, Upson 1, own goals 2.
Carling Cup (0).
FA Cup (5): O'Flynn 3 (1 pen), Hyde M 1, Yakubu 1.
J Paint Trophy (3): Hyde J 1, O'Flynn 1, Yakubu 1.

Cole J 46	O'Neill R 11 + 4	Gillet K 31 + 6	Hughes M 40 + 1	Yakubu I 25	Leach D 12 + 1	Adomah A 37 + 8	Hyde M 41	Furlong P 31 + 7	Jarrett A 33 + 12	Bolasie Y 14 + 8	Hyde J 17 + 17	Charles E — + 3	Deverdics N 4 + 12	Deen A 12 + 4	Tabiri J 2 + 3	Kamdjo C 14 + 1	O'Flynn J 31 + 5	Devera J 31 + 2	Breen G 25	Lockhart-Adams K — + 1	Butcher C 3	McAllister C 4 + 1	Sinclair D 2 + 1	Sawyer L 4 + 3	Lockwood M 19	Livermore D 11 + 3	Wright B — + 3	Upson E 5 + 4	Hart D — + 1	James C — + 2	Medley L — + 1	Vilhete N 1 + 1	Match No.
1	2	3	4	5	6	7	8	9²	10	11¹	12	13																					1
1	2	3	11¹	5	6	7	4	9	10²	13	8		12																				2
1	2	3¹		5	6	7	4	9	10	14	8³					11²	12	13															3
1	2³		11	5		7¹	4	9	10	12	8²	13				6	14	3															4
1	2		11	5	6	7	4	9	8¹	12	13					3	10²																5
1	2		11	5		7¹	4	9	12	8	10²					3	6	13															6
1	2²		11	5		7¹	4	9	12	8	14					3	5	10³	13														7
1	2²	12	11	5	14	4	7	8³	9							3¹	5	10	13														8
1	5		11	5	4	7¹	9³	8	12	13			6²	14		10	2																9
1		3	11	5		7	4	9	13	8²	12					10¹	2	6															10
1		3	11	5		7²	4¹	9	13	8	12					14	10³	2	6														11
1	12	3	11	5		7²	4	9	13	8	14					10³	2¹	6															12
1	3³			5	14	4	9²	7	8	12		10		11¹	2	13		6															13
1	3		11	5		7	4²	9		8	12	13		10¹	2	6																	14
1	3¹		11	5		7	4	9	13	8²	10³		12	14		2	6																15
1	3		11	5		7²	4¹	9	13	8	12	2				6	10																16
1	3		11	5	6	12	4	9²	7	8¹	13		2			10																	17
1	3³		11	5	6	12	4	9²	7	8¹	13		2			10					14												18
1	3		11	5		7	4	12	8		13		2			10²						6	9¹										19
1	3	6⁴	5		7³	4	14	8¹	12	13			11	2		10							9²										20
1	3	11	5	6		4	13	8	12	14			10³	2								6	9¹	7¹									21
1	3	11	5		7	9	12	8					4³	2		10²					6	3	14										22
1	6	3	11	5¹	13	4	8	14					12			10³	2					9²	7⁸										23
1	6	3¹	11²	5		7	4	14		8		9		12		10³	2							13									24
1		11			6	12	4¹	9	8		10²					13	2	5					7	3									25
1	12		11	5¹		13	4	9	8	14			10³	2		6						7²	3										26
1		3	11			7	4	9²	8		13			12		9	2	6				13¹	5										27
1		3	11			7¹	4	13	8²		10³			9		2	6					14	5	12									28
1		3	11³			12	4	13	14		10²			9		2	6					7¹	5	8									29
1	3					7	4			8		10¹				9	2	6					12	5	11								30
1	13					7²	4	9¹	8		12					3	10	2	6					5	11								31
1	12	11				7	4	8²	10		13					3	9¹	2						5	6								32
1	14	13				7	4¹	8	10		12					3	9	2	6					5³	11²								33
1		10				7	4	8	12							3	9	2	6					5	11¹								34
1		11¹				7	4	8	10²		13					3	9²	2	6					5		13							35
1	12	10				7	4	8¹			13					3	9²	2	6					5	11								36
1	13	10				7	4²	9	8³							3¹		2	6					5	11	12	14						37
1	3	10				7		9¹	8³		13							2	6					5	11²	12	4	14					38
1	3	11				7¹	4	9	8³		10²							2	6					5	13	12	14						39
1	3	11	6			7	4¹	9	8²		10							2						5	12	13							40
1	3	11¹	4⁸	7			9	13	10²		12	8						2						5		6							41
1	13	3				7²	4	9	8		12							2	6					5	11	10¹							42
1	14	3	11¹			13	7	4	9	8						10		2³	6					5	12								43
1	3²	11	6		7		9	12								10		2	5					8		4¹		13					44
1	3	11				7	4²	9	8¹		13					10³		2						5	6			12			14		45
1	3	11				7	4	14	12							9³		2						5	6	10²			8¹				46

FA Cup

First Round	Darlington	(h)	3-1
Second Round	Accrington S	(a)	2-2
		(h)	0-1

Carling Cup

First Round	Watford	(h)	0-2

J Paint Trophy

First Round	Millwall	(h)	2-0
Second Round	Charlton Ath	(a)	1-4

BARNSLEY   FL Championship

FOUNDATION

Many clubs owe their inception to the church and Barnsley
are among them, for they were formed in 1887 by the
Rev. T. T. Preedy, curate of Barnsley St Peter's and went
under that name until it was dropped in 1897 a year before
being admitted to the Second Division of the Football League.

Oakwell Stadium, Grove Street, Barnsley,
South Yorkshire S71 1ET.
Telephone: (01226) 211 211.
Fax: (01226) 211 444.
Ticket Office: (0871) 22 66 777.
Website: www.barnsleyfc.co.uk
Email: thereds@barnsleyfc.co.uk
Ground Capacity: 23,186.
Record Attendance: 40,255 v Stoke C, FA Cup 5th rd,
15 February 1936.
Pitch Measurements: 110yd × 73yd.
Owner: Patrick Cryne.
Director: Barry Taylor.
General Manager/Secretary: Albert Donald Rowing.
Manager: Mark Robins. *Assistant Manager:* John Breckin.
Physio: Chris Burton.
Colours: Red shirts with white trim, white shorts, red stockings.
Change Colours: Black shirts, mustard shorts, mustard stockings.
Year Formed: 1887.
Turned Professional: 1888.
Ltd Co.: 1899.
Previous Name: 1887, Barnsley St Peter's; 1897, Barnsley.
Club Nickname: 'The Tykes', 'Reds' or 'Colliers'.
Ground: 1887, Oakwell.
First Football League Game: 1 September 1898, Division 2, v Lincoln C (a) L 0–1 – Fawcett;
McArtney, Nixon; King, Burleigh, Porteous; Davis, Lees, Murray, McCullough, McGee.
Record League Victory: 9–0 v Loughborough T, Division 2, 28 January 1899 – Greaves; McArtney,
Nixon; Porteous, Burleigh, Howard; Davis (4), Hepworth (1), Lees (1), McCullough (1), Jones (2).
9–0 v Accrington S, Division 3 (N), 3 February 1934 – Ellis; Cookson, Shotton; Harper, Henderson,
Whitworth; Spence (2), Smith (1), Blight (4), Andrews (1), Ashton (1).
Record Cup Victory: 6–0 v Blackpool, FA Cup 1st rd replay, 20 January 1910 – Mearns; Downs, Ness;
Glendinning, Boyle (1), Utley; Bartrop, Gadsby (1), Lillycrop (2), Tufnell (2), Forman. 6–0 v
Peterborough U, League Cup 1st rd 2nd leg, 15 September 1981 – Horn; Joyce, Chambers, Glavin (2),
Banks, McCarthy, Evans, Parker (2), Aylott (1), McHale, Barrowclough (1).

HONOURS

Football League: Division 1 –
Runners-up 1996–97; Division 3 (N) –
Champions 1933–34, 1938–39,
1954–55; Runners-up 1953–54;
Division 3 – Runners-up 1980–81;
Division 4 – Runners-up 1967–68.
FA Cup: Winners 1912; Runners-up
1910.
Football League Cup: best season:
5th rd, 1982.

sky SPORTS FACT FILE

Harry Davis was the first Barnsley player to score a hat-
trick and then four goals. On 3 November 1898 he hit
three against Gainsborough Trinity in the FA Cup and
this was followed in the League on 28 January 1899 with
his four-timer in an 8–0 win over Loughborough.

Record Defeat: 0–9 v Notts Co, Division 2, 19 November 1927.

Most League Points (2 for a win): 67, Division 3 (N), 1938–39.

Most League Points (3 for a win): 82, Division 1, 1999–2000.

Most League Goals: 118, Division 3 (N), 1933–34.

Highest League Scorer in Season: Cecil McCormack, 33, Division 2, 1950–51.

Most League Goals in Total Aggregate: Ernest Hine, 123, 1921–26 and 1934–38.

Most League Goals in One Match: 5, Frank Eaton v South Shields, Division 3 (N), 9 April 1927; 5, Peter Cunningham v Darlington, Division 3 (N), 4 February 1933; 5, Beau Asquith v Darlington, Division 3 (N), 12 November 1938; 5, Cecil McCormack v Luton T, Division 2, 9 September 1950.

Most Capped Player: Gerry Taggart, 35 (50), Northern Ireland.

Most League Appearances: Barry Murphy, 514, 1962–78.

Youngest League Player: Reuben Noble-Lazarus, 15 years 45 days v Ipswich T, 30 September 2008.

Record Transfer Fee Received: £4,500,000 from Blackburn R for Ashley Ward, December 1998.

Record Transfer Fee Paid: £1,500,000 to Partizan Belgrade for Georgi Hristov, July 1997.

Football League Record: 1898 Elected to Division 2; 1932–34 Division 3 (N); 1934–38 Division 2; 1938–39 Division 3 (N); 1946–53 Division 2; 1953–55 Division 3 (N); 1955–59 Division 2; 1959–65 Division 3; 1965–68 Division 4; 1968–72 Division 3; 1972–79 Division 4; 1979–81 Division 3; 1981–92 Division 2; 1992–97 Division 1; 1997–98 FA Premier League; 1998–2002 Division 1; 2002–04 Division 2; 2004–06 FL 1; 2006– FL C.

LATEST SEQUENCES

Longest Sequence of League Wins: 10, 5.3.1955 – 23.4.1955.

Longest Sequence of League Defeats: 9, 14.3 1953 – 25.4.1953.

Longest Sequence of League Draws: 7, 28.3.1911 – 22.4.1911.

Longest Sequence of Unbeaten League Matches: 21, 1.1.1934 – 5.5.1934.

Longest Sequence Without a League Win: 26, 13.12.1952 – 25.8.1953.

Successive Scoring Runs: 44 from 2.10.1926.

Successive Non-scoring Runs: 6 from 7.10.1899.

MANAGERS

Arthur Fairclough 1898–1901
(Secretary-Manager)
John McCartney 1901–04
(Secretary-Manager)
Arthur Fairclough 1904–12
John Hastie 1912–14
Fercy Lewis 1914–19
Peter Sant 1919–26
John Commins 1926–29
Arthur Fairclough 1929–30
Brough Fletcher 1930–37
Angus Seed 1937–53
Tim Ward 1953–60
Johnny Steele 1960–71
(continued as General Manager)
John McSeveney 1971–72
Johnny Steele *(General Manager)*
1972–73
Jim Iley 1973–78
Allan Clarke 1978–80
Norman Hunter 1980–84
Bobby Collins 1984–85
Allan Clarke 1985–89
Mel Machin 1989–93
Viv Anderson 1993–94
Danny Wilson 1994–98
John Hendrie 1998–99
Dave Bassett 1999–2000
Nigel Spackman 2001
Steve Parkin 2001–02
Glyn Hodges 2002–03
Gudjon Thordarson 2003–04
Paul Hart 2004–05
Andy Ritchie 2005–06
Simon Davey 2007–10
(caretaker from November 2006)
Mark Robins September 2009–

TEN YEAR LEAGUE RECORD

		P	W	D	L	F	A	Pts	Pos
2000-01	Div 1	46	15	9	22	49	62	54	16
2001-02	Div 1	46	11	15	20	59	86	48	23
2002-03	Div 2	46	13	13	20	51	64	52	19
2003-04	Div 2	46	15	17	14	54	58	62	12
2004-05	FL 1	46	14	19	13	69	64	61	13
2005-06	FL 1	46	18	18	10	62	44	72	5
2006-07	FL C	46	15	5	26	53	85	50	20
2007-08	FL C	46	14	13	19	52	65	55	18
2008-09	FL C	46	13	13	20	45	58	52	20
2009-10	FL C	46	14	12	20	53	69	54	18

DID YOU KNOW ?

Despite an indifferent start to the 1954–55 season in which they lost six of their first seventeen League games and failed to score six times, Barnsley won the championship of the Third Division (North) with four points to spare over runners-up Accrington Stanley.

BARNSLEY 2009–10 LEAGUE RECORD

Match No.	Date	Venue	Opponents	Result	H/T Score	Lg Pos.	Goalscorers	Attendance
1	Aug 8	A	Sheffield W	D	2-2	0-2	—	Butterfield [59], Macken [76]	30,644
2	15	H	Coventry C	L	0-2	0-1	21		12,552
3	18	H	Preston NE	L	0-3	0-2	—		11,850
4	22	A	Leicester C	L	0-1	0-0	24		21,799
5	29	H	Reading	L	1-3	1-1	24	Gray A [11]	11,116
6	Sept 12	A	Watford	L	0-1	0-0	24		12,613
7	15	A	Derby Co	W	3-2	1-1	—	Hammill [36], Gray A [57], Anderson [89]	27,609
8	19	H	Swansea C	D	0-0	0-0	22		11,596
9	26	A	QPR	L	2-5	0-3	22	Foster [51], Gray A [56]	12,025
10	29	H	WBA	W	3-1	2-0	—	Hammill [14], Hume (pen) [32], Martis (og) [80]	12,191
11	Oct 3	H	Ipswich T	W	2-1	1-1	20	Hume [8], Macken [90]	12,224
12	17	A	Doncaster R	W	1-0	0-0	19	Hammill [74]	12,708
13	20	A	Nottingham F	L	0-1	0-0	—		20,395
14	24	H	Bristol C	L	2-3	0-2	20	Bogdanovic [62], Hammill [90]	11,314
15	31	A	Peterborough U	W	2-1	2-1	17	Bogdanovic [26], Macken [39]	8556
16	Nov 9	H	Sheffield U	D	2-2	0-0	—	Anderson [53], Bogdanovic [74]	12,998
17	21	H	Cardiff C	W	1-0	0-0	15	Dickinson [90]	11,903
18	Dec 5	A	Blackpool	W	2-1	0-0	15	Vaughan (og) [85], Gray A (pen) [88]	8108
19	9	H	Scunthorpe U	D	1-1	0-0	—	Colace [53]	11,657
20	12	H	Newcastle U	D	2-2	0-1	16	Hallfredsson [52], Hassell [87]	20,079
21	19	A	Crystal Palace	D	1-1	1-0	16	Bogdanovic [19]	14,279
22	28	H	Middlesbrough	W	2-1	0-1	15	Foster [49], Colace [59]	18,001
23	Jan 9	A	Coventry C	L	1-3	0-2	—	Macken [50]	15,015
24	16	H	Sheffield W	L	1-2	1-2	16	Hallfredsson [7]	17,477
25	26	H	Leicester C	W	1-0	0-0	—	Colace [77]	12,065
26	30	A	Reading	L	0-1	0-1	15		15,580
27	Feb 2	A	Preston NE	W	4-1	2-1	—	Anderson [8], Hart (og) [41], Gray A [69], Rodriguez [90]	12,453
28	6	H	Watford	W	1-0	0-0	9	Hallfredsson [55]	11,739
29	9	A	Middlesbrough	L	1-2	0-2	—	Colace [65]	17,775
30	13	H	Plymouth Arg	L	1-3	1-0	12	Colace [45]	11,661
31	16	H	Scunthorpe U	L	1-2	0-0	—	Bogdanovic [78]	5648
32	20	A	Cardiff C	W	2-0	2-0	11	Bogdanovic 2 [9, 12]	19,753
33	27	H	Blackpool	W	1-0	0-0	11	Hume [75]	12,347
34	Mar 6	A	Newcastle U	L	1-6	0-1	11	Bogdanovic [83]	44,464
35	13	H	Crystal Palace	D	0-0	0-0	13		11,416
36	16	H	Nottingham F	W	2-1	1-0	—	Bogdanovic 2 (1 pen) [12, 65 (p)]	13,174
37	20	A	Ipswich T	L	0-1	0-1	12		20,558
38	23	A	Bristol C	L	3-5	2-2	—	Colace [3], Bogdanovic [25], Gray A [81]	13,009
39	27	H	Doncaster R	L	0-1	0-1	15		14,188
40	30	A	Plymouth Arg	D	0-0	0-0	—		7243
41	Apr 3	A	Sheffield U	D	0-0	0-0	16		24,808
42	5	H	Peterborough U	D	2-2	1-1	15	Hume 2 [7, 84]	11,290
43	10	H	Derby Co	D	0-0	0-0	15		13,034
44	17	A	Swansea C	L	1-3	1-2	17	Moore [35]	15,139
45	24	H	QPR	L	0-1	0-1	18		11,944
46	May 2	A	WBA	D	1-1	0-0	18	Colace [59]	25,297

Final League Position: 18

GOALSCORERS

League (53): Bogdanovic 11 (1 pen), Colace 7, Gray A 6 (1 pen), Hume 5 (1 pen), Hammill 4, Macken 4, Anderson 3, Hallfredsson 3, Foster 2, Butterfield 1, Dickinson 1, Hassell 1, Moore 1, Rodriguez 1, own goals 3.
Carling Cup (6): Bogdanovic 3 (1 pen), Anderson 1, Colace 1, Macken 1.
FA Cup (0).

Steele L 39	Hassell B 22 + 2	Kozluk R 12 + 2	Butterfield J 10 + 10	Moore D 33 + 2	Foster S 42	Campbell-Ryce J 8 + 5	Anderson 25 + 6	Odejayi K 2 + 3	Macken J 27 + 4	Devaney M 6 + 5	Bogdanovic D 20 + 9	Hammill A 31 + 8	Hume I 17 + 18	Sodje O — + 1	Potter L 12 + 2	El Haimour M 2	Hallfredsson E 22 + 5	Gray A 19 + 11	Colace R 41	Preece D 5 + 1	Thompson O 1	Gray J 1 + 4	Doyle N 32 + 2	Shotton R 30	Dickinson C 27 + 1	Bialkowski B 2	Adam J — + 2	Teixeira F 14	Rodriguez J 1 + 5	Trippier K 3	Noble-Lazarus R — + 2	Taylor A — + 1	Match No.
1	2	3	4	5	6	7	8	9	10	11[1]	12																						1
1	2	3[4]	4[3]	5	6	7	8	9[1]	10[2]	11	12	13	14																				2
1	2		4[3]	5	3	7	8	9	13	14	12	11[1]	10[2]			6																	3
1	2[1]	12		5	6	7	8		13		11[2]		14		10[3]		3	4	9														4
1	2			5	6	7		14	10[2]	11[1]	13	12					3	4	9				8[3]										5
	3	2		5	6	7[1]	8	13[3]	11		12	14					4	9		1	10[2]												6
	3	2	7	5	6		13		12			11	10[1]				4[2]	9	8	1													7
		2	7[1]	5	6		4		13			3[2]	10					9	8	1	11	12											8
	12		7[1]		6	13	4		3				10				9[2]	8	1	11		2	5										9
			4	6	13	7[1]		10				3	9[2]				8		12	11	2	5	1										10
		13	4	6	7[1]		10				3	9					12	8[2]		14	11[3]	2	5	1									11
1			13	5	6		12		10[3]		11	9					7[1]	14	8				2[2]	3	4								12
1				5	6	7[3]		10[1]	14	11	9[2]		4				12		8				3	2	3								13
1		14		5	6	7[2]	13	12	11		9[1]		4				10		8[3]				2	3									14
1		14	5	6	7		10	9[1]	11[2]	12	8						13						3[3]	2	4								15
1	2		5			8	10[1]	9[2]	11	12	13	7	4										6	3									16
1	2				6	4	10	9[1]	11	12	8		7										3	5									17
1	3	2		5	14		10[2]	9[1]	11	12	7[3]	13	8										4	6									18
1	2	12	5[1]	14	8[3]		10	9[2]	11	13		7											4	3	6								19
1	5		2		8[1]		9[2]	12	13	11	10	7					11	10	7				4	3	6								20
1	4		5		8[2]		9[1]	13	12	7	10	11					7	10	11				3	2	6								21
1	3	2	12	5	6		8		9	11[1]	4	10					4	10	7														22
1	2	14	5	6	8[1]		10		9[2]	12	13	7					7		11				4[3]	3									23
1			5	6	12		10[2]		9[3]	11	14	8[1]	13				8[1]	13	7				4	2	3								24
1	2[1]	12	5				8		10[2]	11	9	13					13		7				4	3	6								25
1			5	6			8[2]		10[1]	12	11[3]	9	13				13		7				4	2	3			14					26
1			5	6			8[1]					11	10				11	10	9				4	2	3			7	12				27
1			5	6			8[1]					11	10				11	10	9				4	2[4]	3			7	12				28
1			5	6			4[1]					13	14				11[2]	10	8				2	3				8	7[3]				29
1			5	6			13					12	11				10		4				2	3				8[1]	9[2]	7			30
1	12		5	6			4[2]					13	11				10[3]	9					2	3				8	14	7[1]			31
1	4			5			10[1]					9[2]	11		3		12	7					2		6			8	13				32
1	2			5			10					9[1]	11	12			11[1]	10[2]	7				4	3	6			7					33
1[1]	2			5			8[6]		12	13		11	10[2]	9	15		4	6	3									7					34
	2	14		5			10					9	11	12	13		8	1	5[2]				4	6[1]				7[3]					35
1	6			5			10					9[2]	11	13		4	12		7				3	2				8					36
1	6	14		5			10[1]					9	12			4	11[2]		7				3[3]	2				8	13				37
1	6			5	14		10[1]					9	13			4	11[2]	12	7				3	2				8[3]					38
1	13			5	6	7[3]			12			11				4	14	10	9				3[2]	2				8[1]					39
1				5	6		10[1]					9[2]	11	13		4	8	12	7				3	2									40
1		2		5	6		12		13			11	9[2]		4		8[1]	10	7				3										41
1	2	4[1]	5	6			13		10[3]	7[2]		11	9		3		14	8					12										42
1	2	14		5			10		12			9[2]	11[1]	6			13	8					4	3				7[3]					43
1	13		5	4		7[3]						11	9[1]	6			10	8					3[2]	2				12		14			44
1	2	7	5	4			10		12			11[1]	9	6[2]				8					3[3]	13						14			45
1	4	7	5[1]				10		11			9		12		8							3	2	6								46

FA Cup
Third Round   Scunthorpe U   (a)   0-1

Carling Cup
First Round   Lincoln C   (a)   1-0
Second Round   Reading   (a)   2-1
Third Round   Burnley   (h)   3-2
Fourth Round   Manchester U   (h)   0-2

BIRMINGHAM CITY   FA Premiership

FOUNDATION

In 1875, cricketing enthusiasts who were largely members of Trinity Church, Bordesley, determined to continue their sporting relationships throughout the year by forming a football club which they called Small Heath Alliance. For their earliest games played on waste land in Arthur Street, the team included three Edden brothers and two James brothers.

St Andrews Stadium, Birmingham B9 4RL.
Telephone: 0844 557 1875.
Fax: 0844 557 1975.
Ticket Office: (0844) 557 1875 (then option 2).
Website: www.bcfc.com
Email: reception@bcfc.com
Ground Capacity: 30,079.
Record Attendance: 66,844 v Everton, FA Cup 5th rd, 11 February 1939.
Pitch Measurements: 101m × 68m.
President: Carson Yeung.
Vice-president: Michael Wiseman.
Chairman: Vico Hui.
Vice-chairman: Peter Pannu.
Secretary: Julia Shelton.
Manager: Alex McLeish.
First Team Coaches: Roy Aitken, Andy Watson.
Physio: Tim Williamson.
Colours: Blue shirts with white trim, white shorts, blue stockings.
Change Colours: All black.
Year Formed: 1875.
Turned Professional: 1885.
Ltd Co.: 1888.
Previous Names: 1875, Small Heath Alliance; 1888, dropped 'Alliance'; 1905, Birmingham; 1945, Birmingham City.
Club Nickname: 'Blues'.
Grounds: 1875, waste ground near Arthur St; 1877, Muntz St, Small Heath; 1906, St Andrews.
First Football League game: 3 September 1892, Division 2, v Burslem Port Vale (h) W 5–1 – Charsley; Bayley, Speller; Ollis, Jenkyns, Devey; Hallam (1), Edwards (1), Short (1), Wheldon (2), Hands.
Record League Victory: 12–0 v Walsall T Swifts, Division 2, 17 December 1892 – Charsley; Bayley, Jones; Ollis, Jenkyns, Devey; Hallam (2), Walton (3), Mobley (3), Wheldon (2), Hands (2). 12–0 v Doncaster R, Division 2, 11 April 1903 – Dorrington; Goldie, Wassell; Beer, Dougherty (1), Howard; Athersmith (1), Leonard (3), McRoberts (1), Wilcox (4), Field (1). Aston, (1 og).

HONOURS

Football League: FL C – Runners-up 2006–07, 2008–09; Division 2 – Champions 1892–93, 1920–21, 1947–48, 1954–55, 1994–95; Runners-up 1893–94, 1900–01, 1902–03, 1971–72, 1984–85; Division 3 Runners-up 1991–92.
FA Cup: Runners-up 1931, 1956.
Football League Cup: Winners 1963; Runners-up 2001.
Leyland Daf Cup: Winners 1991.
Auto Windscreens Shield: Winners 1995.
European Competitions: European Fairs Cup: 1955–58, 1958–60 (runners-up), 1960–61 (runners-up), 1961–62.

sky SPORTS FACT FILE

The Birmingham City team when still known as Small Heath were particularly harsh on Burton Wanderers in early FA Cup matches. In 1885–86 they beat them 9–2 with Eddie Stanley scoring four goals and in 1888–89 it was 9–0 with the Devey brothers Ted and Will each scoring four times.

Record Cup Victory: 9–2 v Burton W, FA Cup 1st rd, 31 October 1885 – Hedges; Jones, Evetts (1): F. James, Felton, A. James (1); Davenport (2), Stanley (4), Simms, Figures, Morris (1).

Record Defeat: 1–9 v Sheffield W, Division 1, 13 December 1930. 1–9 v Blackburn R, Division 1, 5 January 1895.

Most League Points (2 for a win): 59, Division 2, 1947–48.

Most League Points (3 for a win): 89, Division 2, 1994–95.

Most League Goals: 103, Division 2, 1893–94 (only 28 games)

Highest League Scorer in Season: Joe Bradford, 29, Division 1, 1927–28.

Most League Goals in Total Aggregate: Joe Bradford, 249, 1920–35.

Most League Goals in One Match: 5, Walter Abbott v Darwen, Division 2, 26 November, 1898; 5, John McMillan v Blackpool, Division 2, 2 March 1901; 5, James Windridge v Glossop, Division 2, 23 January 1915.

Most Capped Player: Maik Taylor, 50 (83). Northern Ireland.

Most League Appearances: Frank Womack, 491, 1908–28.

Youngest League Player: Trevor Francis, 16 years 7 months v Cardiff C, 5 September 1970.

Record Transfer Fee Received: £6,800,000 from Liverpool for Jermaine Pennant, July 2006.

Record Transfer Fee Paid: £8,500,000 to Santos Laguna for Christian Benitez, July 2009.

Football League Record: 1892 Elected to Division 2; 1894–96 Division 1; 1896–1901 Division 2; 1901–02 Division 1; 1902–03 Division 2; 1903–08 Division 1; 1908–21 Division 2; 1921–39 Division 1; 1946–48 Division 2; 1948–50 Division 1; 1950–55 Division 2; 1955–65 Division 1; 1965–72 Division 2; 1972–79 Division 1; 1979–80 Division 2; 1980–84 Division 1; 1984–85 Division 2; 1985–86 Division 1; 1986–89 Division 2; 1989–92 Division 3; 1992–94 Division 1; 1994–95 Division 2; 1995–2002 Division 1; 2002–06 FA Premier League; 2006–07 FL C; 2007–08 FA Premier League; 2008–09 FL C; 2009– FA Premier League.

MANAGERS

Alfred Jones 1892–1908
(Secretary-Manager)
Alec Watson 1908–10
Bob McRoberts 1910–15
Frank Richards 1915–23
Billy Beer 1923–27
William Harvey 1927–28
Leslie Knighton 1928–33
George Liddell 1933–39
Harry Storer 1945–48
Bob Brocklebank 1949–54
Arthur Turner 1954–58
Pat Beasley 1959–60
Gil Merrick 1960–64
Joe Mallett 1965
Stan Cullis 1965–70
Fred Goodwin 1970–75
Willie Bell 1975–77
Sir Alf Ramsay 1977–78
Jim Smith 1978–82
Ron Saunders 1982–86
John Bond 1986–87
Garry Pendrey 1987–89
Dave Mackay 1989–91
Lou Macari 1991
Terry Cooper 1991–93
Barry Fry 1993–96
Trevor Francis 1996–2001
Steve Bruce 2001–07
Alex McLeish November 2007–

LATEST SEQUENCES

Longest Sequence of League Wins: 13, 17.12.1892 – 16.9.1893.

Longest Sequence of League Defeats: 8, 28.9.1985 – 23.11.1985.

Longest Sequence of League Draws: 8, 18.9.1990 – 23.10.1990.

Longest Sequence of Unbeaten League Matches: 20, 3.9.1994 – 2.1.1995.

Longest Sequence Without a League Win: 17, 28.9.1985 – 18.1.1986.

Successive Scoring Runs: 24 from 24.9.1892.

Successive Non-scoring Runs: 6 from 1.10.1949.

TEN YEAR LEAGUE RECORD

		P	W	D	L	F	A	Pts	Pos
2000-01	Div 1	46	23	9	14	59	48	78	5
2001-02	Div 1	46	21	13	12	70	49	76	5
2002-03	PR Lge	38	13	9	16	41	49	48	13
2003-04	PR Lge	38	12	14	12	43	48	50	10
2004-05	PR Lge	38	11	12	15	40	46	45	12
2005-06	PR Lge	38	8	10	20	28	50	34	18
2006-07	FL C	46	26	8	12	67	42	86	2
2007-08	PR Lge	38	8	11	19	46	62	35	19
2008-09	FL C	46	23	14	9	54	37	83	2
2009-10	PR Lge	38	13	11	14	38	47	50	9

DID YOU KNOW ?

In 2009–10 Birmingham City established a record for the most successive Premier League matches with the same starting eleven. The twelve-game sequence began on 21 November in a 1–0 win over Fulham and ended after beating Wolverhampton Wanderers 2–1 on 7 February.

BIRMINGHAM CITY 2009–10 LEAGUE RECORD

Match No.	Date	Venue	Opponents	Result		H/T Score	Lg Pos.	Goalscorers	Attendance
1	Aug 16	A	Manchester U	L	0-1	0-1	—		75,062
2	19	H	Portsmouth	W	1-0	0-0	—	McFadden (pen) [90]	19,922
3	22	H	Stoke C	D	0-0	0-0	8		21,694
4	29	A	Tottenham H	L	1-2	0-0	12	Bowyer [75]	35,318
5	Sept 13	H	Aston Villa	L	0-1	0-0	15		25,196
6	19	A	Hull C	W	1-0	0-0	11	O'Connor [75]	23,759
7	26	H	Bolton W	L	1-2	0-1	14	Phillips [84]	28,671
8	Oct 3	A	Burnley	L	1-2	0-0	14	Larsson [90]	20,102
9	17	A	Arsenal	L	1-3	1-2	17	Bowyer [38]	60,082
10	24	H	Sunderland	W	2-1	1-0	15	Ridgewell [37], McFadden [48]	21,723
11	Nov 1	H	Manchester C	D	0-0	0-0	14		21,462
12	9	A	Liverpool	D	2-2	2-1	—	Benitez [26], Jerome [45]	42,560
13	21	H	Fulham	W	1-0	1-0	13	Bowyer [16]	23,659
14	29	A	Wolverhampton W	W	1-0	1-0	11	Bowyer [3]	26,668
15	Dec 5	A	Wigan Ath	W	3-2	0-1	9	Larsson 2 [61, 72], Benitez [66]	18,797
16	12	H	West Ham U	W	1-0	0-0	8	Bowyer [52]	28,203
17	15	H	Blackburn R	W	2-1	1-0	—	Jerome 2 [12, 48]	23,187
18	20	A	Everton	D	1-1	1-1	7	Larsson [22]	33,660
19	26	H	Chelsea	D	0-0	0-0	8		28,958
20	28	A	Stoke C	W	1-0	0-0	7	Jerome [50]	27,211
21	Jan 9	H	Manchester U	D	1-1	1-0	—	Jerome [39]	28,907
22	27	A	Chelsea	L	0-3	0-2	—		41,293
23	30	H	Tottenham H	D	1-1	0-0	8	Ridgewell [90]	27,238
24	Feb 7	H	Wolverhampton W	W	2-1	0-1	8	Phillips 2 [80, 85]	24,165
25	10	A	West Ham U	L	0-2	0-1	—		34,458
26	21	A	Fulham	L	1-2	1-0	10	Baird (og) [3]	21,758
27	27	H	Wigan Ath	W	1-0	1-0	8	McFadden (pen) [45]	25,921
28	Mar 9	A	Portsmouth	W	2-1	2-0	—	Jerome 2 [16, 42]	18,465
29	13	A	Everton	D	2-2	1-2	8	Jerome [26], Gardner [51]	24,579
30	20	A	Sunderland	L	1-3	0-2	9	Jerome [60]	37,962
31	24	A	Blackburn R	L	1-2	0-1	—	McFadden [55]	23,856
32	27	H	Arsenal	D	1-1	0-0	9	Phillips [90]	27,039
33	Apr 4	H	Liverpool	D	1-1	0-0	9	Ridgewell [56]	27,909
34	11	A	Manchester C	L	1-5	1-3	—	Jerome [42]	45,209
35	17	H	Hull C	D	0-0	0-0	9		26,669
36	25	A	Aston Villa	L	0-1	0-0	9		42,788
37	May 1	H	Burnley	W	2-1	2-0	9	Jerome [29], Benitez [41]	24,578
38	9	A	Bolton W	L	1-2	0-1	9	McFadden [76]	22,863

Final League Position: 9

GOALSCORERS

League (38): Jerome 11, Bowyer 5, McFadden 5 (2 pens), Larsson 4, Phillips 4, Benitez 3, Ridgewell 3, Gardner 1, O'Connor 1, own goal 1.
Carling Cup (2): Bowyer 1, Carsley 1.
FA Cup (5): Ferguson 2, Benitez 1, Dann 1, Ridgewell 1.

Hart J 36	Carr S 35	Vignal G 6+2	Carsley L 3+4	Queudrue F 6	Johnson R 38	Larsson S 26+7	Ferguson B 37	Jerome C 32	McFadden J 32+4	Fahey K 18+16	O'Connor G 5+5	Benitez C 21+9	O'Shea J —+1	Parnaby S 6+2	Phillips K 2+17	Bowyer L 34+1	McSheffrey G 1+4	Tainio T 5+1	Dann S 30	Ridgewell L 30+1	Taylor Maik 2	Johnson D —+1	Michel 3+6	Gardner C 10+3	Match No.
1	2	3	4²	5	6	7³	8	9¹	10	11	12	13	14												1
1	2	3¹		5	6	7	4	9²	11	8	10³	14			12	13									2
1	2			5	6	13	4		11	8	10	12			3	9¹	7²								3
1	2	11¹		5	6	7²	4	9	10	12					3	8	13								4
1			12²	5	6	7	4	9¹		3	10³	14		2	13	8		11							5
1	2					6		7				3	12		9	5	8	11¹	10	4					6
1	2	5²			6	7		11				3	12		9	13	8	10¹		4					7
1	2	5¹			6	13		11				9	3²		10	14	8	7³	4	12					8
1	2	4³			6	7	8	9¹	10²	12		14			11	13			5	3					9
1	2	14			6	7³	4	9²	11¹	12		10				8	13		5	3					10
	2				6	7	4¹	9²	11¹	12		10			13	8			5	3	1				11
1	2	13	12		6	7		9	11²			10³			4	14	8¹		5	3					12
1	2				6	7	4	9	11	12		10¹				8			5	3					13
1	2				6	7	4	9	11	12		10¹				8			5	3					14
1	2				6	7	4	9¹	11	12		10				8			5	3					15
1	2				6	7	4	9	11²	12		10¹			13	8			5	3					16
1	2				6	7	4	9	11	12		10				8			5	3					17
1	2	13			6	7	4	9	11	12		10²				8			5	3					18
1	2				6	7²	4	9	11	12		10				8	13		5	3					19
1	2				6	7¹	4	9	11	12		10				8			5	3					20
1	2				6	7¹	4	9	11	12		10				8			5	3					21
1	2				6	7	4	9¹	11	12		10				8			5	3		13			22
1	2				6	7¹	4	9	11	12		10				8²			5	3		13			23
1	2				6	7²	4	9	11³	14		10¹			12	8			5	3		13			24
1	2				6		4	9	11¹	12		10				8²			5	3		13	7		25
1	2				6	7¹	4³	9²	11			10			13	8			5	3		14	12		26
1	2²				6	7	4	9³	11	12		10¹				8			5	3		14	13		27
1	2¹	13			6		4	9	11	12		10³			14	8			5	3			7²		28
1	2				6		4	9	11	12		10²			13	8			5	3			7¹		29
1	2				6		4	9	11¹	12		10²			13	8			5	3		14	7²		30
1	2				6		4	9²	11³	12		10			13	8			5	3		14	7¹		31
1	2				6		4	9	11¹	12		10¹			13	8			5	3			7		32
1	2				6		4	9	11	12		10¹				8			5	3			7		33
	2¹				6		4	9³	11²	12		10			13	8			5	3	1	14	7		34
1	2				6		4	9	11²	12		10¹			13	8			5	3			7		35
1	2	3¹			6	7²	8	9	11	12		10			13				5			14		4³	36
1		3	14		6	7	4	9³	11¹			10		2²	13	8			5				12		37
1	2	3			6	7¹	4	9	11	12		10²			13	8			5						38

FA Cup

Third Round	Nottingham F	(a)	0-0	
		(h)	1-0	
Fourth Round	Everton	(a)	2-1	
Fifith Round	Derby Co	(a)	2-1	
Sixth Round	Portsmouth	(a)	0-2	

Carling Cup

Second Round	Southampton	(a)	2-1
Third Round	Sunderland	(a)	0-2

BLACKBURN ROVERS   FA Premiership

FOUNDATION

It was in 1875 that some Public School old boys called a meeting at which the Blackburn Rovers club was formed and the colours blue and white adopted. The leading light was John Lewis, later to become a founder of the Lancashire FA, a famous referee who was in charge of two FA Cup Finals, and a vice-president of both the FA and the Football League.

Ewood Park, Blackburn, Lancs BB2 4JF.

Telephone: 0871 702 1875.

Fax: (01254) 671 042.

Ticket Office: 0871 222 1444.

Website: www.rovers.co.uk

Email: enquiries@rovers.co.uk

Ground Capacity: 31,367.

Record Attendance: 62,522 v Bolton W, FA Cup 6th rd, 2 March 1929.

Pitch Measurements: 105m × 65.8m.

Chairman: John Williams.

Vice-chairman: David Brown.

Managing Director: Tom Finn.

Secretary: Andrew Pincher.

Manager: Sam Allardyce.

Assistant Manager: Neil McDonald.

Physio: Dave Fevre.

Colours: Blue and white halved shirts, white shorts, blue stockings.

Change Colours: All red with black trim.

Year Formed: 1875.

Turned Professional: 1880.

Ltd Co.: 1897.

Club Nickname: Rovers.

Grounds: 1875, all matches played away; 1876, Oozehead Ground; 1877, Pleasington Cricket Ground; 1878, Alexandra Meadows; 1881, Leamington Road; 1890, Ewood Park.

First Football League Game: 15 September 1888, Football League, v Accrington (h) D 5–5 – Arthur; Beverley, James Southworth; Douglas, Almond, Forrest; Beresford (1), Walton, John Southworth (1), Fecitt (1), Townley (2).

Record League Victory: 9–0 v Middlesbrough, Division 2, 6 November 1954 – Elvy; Suart, Eckersley; Clayton, Kelly, Bell; Mooney (3), Crossan (2), Briggs, Quigley (3), Langton (1).

HONOURS

FA Premier League: Champions 1994–95; Runners-up 1993–94.

Football League: Division 1 – Champions 1911–12, 1913–14; Runners-up 2000–01; Division 2 – Champions 1938–39; Runners-up 1957–58; Division 3 – Champions 1974–75; Runners-up 1979–80.

FA Cup: Winners 1884, 1885, 1886, 1890, 1891, 1928; Runners-up 1882, 1960.

Football League Cup: Winners 2002.

Full Members' Cup: Winners 1987.

European Competitions: European Cup: 1995–96. UEFA Cup: 1994–95, 1998–99, 2002–03, 2003–04, 2006–07, 2007–08. Intertoto Cup: 2007

sky SPORTS FACT FILE

In 1911–12, when Blackburn Rovers won their first championship title, the team made an indifferent start to the season, winning just two of their opening five matches. A run of eleven games unbeaten at the turn of the year was the turning point.

Record Cup Victory: 11–0 v Rossendale, FA Cup 1st rd, 13 October 1884 – Arthur; Hopwood, McIntyre; Forrest, Blenkhorn, Lofthouse; Sowerbutts (2), J. Brown (1), Fecitt (4), Barton (3), Birtwistle (1).

Record Defeat: 0–8 v Arsenal, Division 1, 25 February 1933.

Most League Points (2 for a win): 60, Division 3, 1974–75.

Most League Points (3 for a win): 91, Division 1, 2000–01.

Most League Goals: 114, Division 2, 1954–55.

Highest League Scorer in Season: Ted Harper, 43, Division 1, 1925–26.

Most League Goals in Total Aggregate: Simon Garner, 168, 1978–92.

Most League Goals in One Match: 7, Tommy Briggs v Bristol R, Division 2, 5 February 1955.

Most Capped Player: Henning Berg, 58 (100), Norway.

Most League Appearances: Derek Fazackerley, 596, 1970–86.

Youngest League Player: Harry Dennison, 16 years 155 days v Bristol C, 8 April 1911.

Record Transfer Fee Received: £18,000,000 from Manchester C for Roque Santa Cruz, June 2009.

Record Transfer Fee Paid: £7,500,000 to Manchester U for Andy Cole, December 2001.

Football League Record: 1888 Founder Member of the League; 1936–39 Division 2; 1946–48 Division 1; 1948–58 Division 2; 1958–66 Division 1; 1966–71 Division 2; 1971–75 Division 3; 1975–79 Division 2; 1979–80 Division 3; 1980–92 Division 2; 1992–99 FA Premier League; 1999–2001 Division 1; 2001– FA Premier League.

LATEST SEQUENCES

Longest Sequence of League Wins: 8, 1.3.1980 – 7.4.1980.

Longest Sequence of League Defeats: 7, 12.3.1966 – 16.4.1966.

Longest Sequence of League Draws: 5, 11.10.1975 – 1.11.1975.

Longest Sequence of Unbeaten League Matches: 23, 30.9.1987 – 27.3.1988.

Longest Sequence Without a League Win: 16, 11.11.1978 – 24.3.1979.

Successive Scoring Runs: 32 from 24.4.1954.

Successive Non-scoring Runs: 4 from 12.12.1908.

MANAGERS

Thomas Mitchell 1884–96
(Secretary-Manager)
J. Walmsley 1896–1903
(Secretary-Manager)
R. B. Middleton 1903–25
Jack Carr 1922–26
*(Team Manager under
Middleton to 1925)*
Bob Crompton 1926–30
(Hon. Team Manager)
Arthur Barritt 1931–36
(had been Secretary from 1927)
Reg Taylor 1936–38
Bob Crompton 1938–41
Eddie Hapgood 1944–47
Will Scott 1947
Jack Bruton 1947–49
Jackie Bestall 1949–53
Johnny Carey 1953–58
Dally Duncan 1958–60
Jack Marshall 1960–67
Eddie Quigley 1967–70
Johnny Carey 1970–71
Ken Furphy 1971–73
Gordon Lee 1974–75
Jim Smith 1975–78
Jim Iley 1978
John Pickering 1978–79
Howard Kendall 1979–81
Bobby Saxton 1981–86
Don Mackay 1987–91
Kenny Dalglish 1991–95
Ray Harford 1995–97
Roy Hodgson 1997–98
Brian Kidd 1998–99
Tony Parkes 1999–2000
Graeme Souness 2000–04
Mark Hughes 2004–08
Paul Ince 2008
Sam Allardyce December 2008–

TEN YEAR LEAGUE RECORD

		P	W	D	L	F	A	Pts	Pos
2000-01	Div 1	46	26	13	7	76	39	91	2
2001-02	PR Lge	38	12	10	16	55	51	46	10
2002-03	PR Lge	38	16	12	10	52	43	60	6
2003-04	PR Lge	38	12	8	18	51	59	44	15
2004-05	PR Lge	38	9	15	14	32	43	42	15
2005-06	PR Lge	38	19	6	13	51	42	63	6
2006-07	PR Lge	38	15	7	16	52	54	52	10
2007-08	PR Lge	38	15	13	10	50	48	58	7
2008-09	PR Lge	38	10	11	17	40	60	41	15
2009-10	PR Lge	38	13	11	14	41	55	50	10

DID YOU KNOW ?

Herbie Arthur was the first Blackburn Rovers player to be capped by England. A wing-half when signed in 1880 he became a goalkeeper. In a snowstorm-affected game against Burnley he stayed alone on the pitch, delaying a goal kick to ensure abandonment!

BLACKBURN ROVERS 2009–10 LEAGUE RECORD

Match No.	Date	Venue	Opponents		Result	H/T Score	Lg Pos.	Goalscorers	Attendance
1	Aug 15	H	Manchester C	L	0-2	0-1	—		29,584
2	22	A	Sunderland	L	1-2	1-1	18	Givet [21]	37,106
3	29	H	West Ham U	D	0-0	0-0	18		23,421
4	Sept 12	H	Wolverhampton W	W	3-1	1-0	14	Diouf [19], Roberts Jason [56], Dunn [64]	24,845
5	20	A	Everton	L	0-3	0-1	18		35,546
6	26	H	Aston Villa	W	2-1	1-1	15	Samba [24], Dunn (pen) [88]	25,172
7	Oct 4	A	Arsenal	L	2-6	2-3	16	N'Zonzi [4], Dunn [30]	59,431
8	18	A	Burnley	W	3-2	3-1	12	Dunn [9], Di Santo [21], Chimbonda [43]	26,689
9	24	A	Chelsea	L	0-5	0-1	16		40,836
10	31	A	Manchester U	L	0-2	0-0	17		74,658
11	Nov 7	H	Portsmouth	W	3-1	0-1	14	Roberts Jason 2 [53, 86], Nelsen [73]	23,110
12	22	A	Bolton W	W	2-0	1-0	11	Dunn [32], Ricketts (og) [73]	21,777
13	25	A	Fulham	L	0-3	0-1	—		21,414
14	28	H	Stoke C	D	0-0	0-0	13		25,143
15	Dec 5	H	Liverpool	D	0-0	0-0	12		29,660
16	12	H	Hull C	D	0-0	0-0	12		24,124
17	15	A	Birmingham C	L	1-2	0-1	—	Nelsen [69]	23,187
18	19	H	Tottenham H	L	0-2	0-1	13		26,490
19	26	A	Wigan Ath	D	1-1	1-0	12	McCarthy [30]	20,243
20	28	H	Sunderland	D	2-2	0-0	13	Pedersen [53], Diouf [77]	25,656
21	Jan 11	A	Manchester C	L	1-4	0-2	—	Pedersen [71]	40,292
22	17	H	Fulham	W	2-0	1-0	12	Samba [25], Nelsen [54]	21,287
23	27	H	Wigan Ath	W	2-1	1-0	—	Pedersen [20], Kalinic [76]	22,190
24	30	A	West Ham U	D	0-0	0-0	10		33,093
25	Feb 6	A	Stoke C	L	0-3	0-2	12		27,386
26	10	H	Hull C	W	1-0	0-0	—	Olsson [16]	23,518
27	21	H	Bolton W	W	3-0	1-0	12	Kalinic [41], Roberts Jason [73], Givet [84]	23,888
28	28	A	Liverpool	L	1-2	1-2	12	Andrews (pen) [40]	42,795
29	Mar 13	H	Tottenham H	L	1-3	0-1	12	Samba [80]	35,474
30	21	H	Chelsea	D	1-1	0-1	12	Diouf [70]	25,554
31	24	H	Birmingham C	W	2-1	1-0	—	Dunn 2 [5, 67]	23,856
32	28	A	Burnley	W	1-0	1-0	10	Dunn (pen) [20]	21,546
33	Apr 3	A	Portsmouth	D	0-0	0-0	11		16,207
34	11	H	Manchester U	D	0-0	0-0	—		29,912
35	17	H	Everton	L	2-3	0-1	12	N'Zonzi [69], Roberts Jason [81]	27,022
36	24	A	Wolverhampton W	D	1-1	1-0	11	Nelsen [28]	28,967
37	May 3	H	Arsenal	W	2-1	1-1	—	Dunn [43], Samba [68]	26,138
38	9	A	Aston Villa	W	1-0	0-0	10	Dunne (og) [84]	41,799

Final League Position: 10

GOALSCORERS

League (41): Dunn 9 (2 pens), Roberts Jason 5, Nelsen 4, Samba 4, Diouf 3, Pedersen 3, Givet 2, Kalinic 2, N'Zonzi 2, Andrews 1 (pen), Chimbonda 1, Di Santo 1, McCarthy 1, Olsson 1, own goals 2.
Carling Cup (16): Kalinic 4 (1 pen), McCarthy 3 (1 pen), Emerton 2, Pedersen 2, Dunn 1, Hoilett 1, Olsen 1, Reid 1 (pen), Salgado 1.
FA Cup (1): Kalinic 1.

Robinson P 35	Jacobsen L 11 + 2	Warnock S 1	Andrews K 22 + 10	Givet G 33 + 1	Samba C 30	Diouf E 24 + 2	N'Zonzi S 33	Roberts Jason 15 + 14	McCarthy B 7 + 7	Pedersen M 27 + 6	Hoilett D 8 + 15	Gallagher P — + 1	Di Santo F 15 + 7	Nelsen R 25 + 3	Kalinic N 14 + 12	Olsson M 19 + 2	Chimbonda P 22 + 2	Grella V 10 + 5	Dunn D 20 + 5	Emerton B 17 + 7	Salgado M 16 + 5	Reid S 1 + 3	Brown J 3 + 1	Jones P 7 + 2	Basturk Y 1	Hanley G 1	Linganzi A 1	Match No.
1	2	3	4^2	5	6	7^1	8	9^3	10	11	12	13	14															1
1	2		4	3	6	7^3	8	9	14	11				10^1	5^2	12	13											2
1	2		4	5	6		8^1	9^2		11	12			13			3	7	10									3
1	2^3		4	5	6^2	10		9		11^1				13			3	7	8	12	14							4
1			4	5^1	6	10		9		11^2				13	12	14	3	7	8		2^3							5
1	2		13		6^3	10^2	4			11^1				9	5		3	7^4	8	12	14							6
1	2		11	5		10	4	13^3	12	14				9		E	3		8^2	7^1								7
1	2		7	14	6	10^2	4		12	11				9^1	5		3^3		8	13								8
1	2^2		4	3		10	8	9^1		11^3	14			5	12	6			7	13								9
1			8^1	3	6	10	4		14		12			9^2	5	13	2		11^3	7								10
1			14	3	6	10^2	4	12	13	11^1				9^3	5		2		8	7								11
1	12		3^1		6	11	4	10	13					9^2	5		2	14	8^3	7								12
1	3		4		6	11			10^1	13				9^2	5	12	2	7	8									13
1			11^2	3	6	10^3	4	12		14				9	5		2	13	8^1	7								14
1			14	3	6	11^1	4		10^2		12			9^3	5	13	2		8	7								15
1	12		3		6		4	14	10^2		8			9^3	5	13	2		11^1	7								16
1	12		3		6		8^2	4	10^3	14	11	13		5	9		2		7^1									17
1	3				6		4	14	10	12	8^3			9^2	5	13	2		7		11^1							18
1	12		8	3	6		4	13	10	14	7			9^2	5		2^1				11^3							19
1			8	3	6	14	4	9^1	10^2	11	7^3			12	5	13	2											20
1	2		10^1	3	6		4		11	12				9^2	5	13	14		8^3	7								21
1	13		3^1		6		4		10	12				5	9^3		2		7^2	14	8^3							22
1			3		10^2	4	14		11		8^1			13	5	9^3	6		2	7	12							23
1	12		3		6	10^3	8	13	11	14				5	9^2		4		2	7^1								24
1	12		3		6		4^3		11					9^1	5	10	8	2^2	7	13	14							25
1			8	3		10	4		12	11				5	9^2	6	2		7^1	13								26
1			8	3		10	4	13		11			7^2	5^1	9^3	6	2	12	14									27
1			8	3	6	10	4^2		14	11			7^3	9	5^1	12	2	13										28
1^6	12	5^2	6				4			11				13		9	10	2		8	7^1	3	15					29
	7		5	10	4^3	13			11	14				9^2	6					8^1	12	2	1	3				30
	7		5	10^2	4	12			11	13				9^1	6					8^3	14	2	1	3				31
			4	5	10^1	7		9^2		11		13		6	14					8	12	2^3	1	3				32
1			6	4	10^2	7^1	9			11	13			14	5				12	8^9	2		3					33
1			6	4^1	14	10				11	12			9	5^3		8	13	7^2		2		3					34
1			8^2		6			7	12	11^1	13		14	5	9		4^3	10			2		3					35
1	13		6					7	10^3	11			14	5	9^2		4	12			2		3		8^1			36
1			10	3	6			9		11	12			5			4		7^1	8^2	2		13					37
1	9		3^2		5	10^3		12		7				6	8	14	2	13								4	11^1	38

FA Cup

Third Round	Aston Villa	(a)	1-3

Carling Cup

Second Round	Gillingham	(a)	3-1
Third Round	Nottingham F	(a)	1-0
Fourth Round	Peterborough U	(h)	5-2
Quarter-Final	Chelsea	(h)	3-3
Semi-Final	Aston Villa	(h)	0-1
		(a)	4-6

BLACKPOOL   FA Premiership

FOUNDATION

Old boys of St John's School who had formed themselves into a
football club decided to establish a club bearing the name of their
town and Blackpool FC came into being at a meeting at the
Stanley Arms Hotel in the summer of 1887. In their first season
playing at Raikes Hall Gardens, the club won both the Lancashire
Junior Cup and the Fylde Cup.

Bloomfield Road, Seasiders Way, Blackpool FY1 6JJ.

Telephone: (0871) 6221 953.

Fax: (01253) 405 011.

Ticket Office: (0871) 6221 953.

Website: www.blackpoolfc.co.uk

Email: info@blackpoolfc.co.uk

Ground Capacity: 9,491.

Record Attendance: 38,098 v Wolverhampton W,
Division 1, 17 September 1955.

Pitch Measurements: 110yd × 74yd.

Chairman: Karl Oyston.

Secretary: Matt Williams.

Manager: Ian Holloway.

First Team Coach: Steve Thompson.

Physio: Phil Horner.

HONOURS

Football League: Division 1 –
Runners-up 1955–56; Division 2 –
Champions 1929–30; Runners-up
1936–37, 1969–70; Division 4 –
Runners-up 1984–85.

FA Cup: Winners 1953; Runners-up
1948, 1951.

Football League Cup: Semi-final 1962.

Anglo-Italian Cup: Winners 1971;
Runners-up 1972.

LDV Vans Trophy: Winners 2002,
2004.

Colours: Tangerine shirts with white trim, white shorts, tangerine stockings with white tops.

Change Colours: White shirts with tangerine trim, tangerine shorts, white stockings.

Year Formed: 1887.

Turned Professional: 1887.

Ltd Co.: 1896.

Previous Name: 'South Shore' combined with Blackpool in 1899, twelve years after the latter had
been formed on the breaking up of the old 'Blackpool St John's' club.

Club Nickname: 'The Seasiders'.

Grounds: 1887, Raikes Hall Gardens; 1897, Athletic Grounds; 1899, Raikes Hall Gardens; 1899,
Bloomfield Road.

First Football League game: 5 September 1896, Division 2, v Lincoln C (a) L 1–3 – Douglas; Parr,
Bowman; Stuart, Stirzaker, Norris; Clarkin, Donnelly, R. Parkinson, Mount (1), J. Parkinson.

Record League Victory: 7–0 v Reading, Division 2, 10 November 1928 – Mercer; Gibson, Hamilton,
Watson, Wilson, Grant, Ritchie, Oxberry (2), Hampson (5), Tufnell, Neal. 7–0 v Preston NE (away),
Division 1, 1 May 1948 – Robinson; Shimwell, Crosland; Buchan, Hayward, Kelly; Hobson, Munro (1),
McIntosh (5), McCall, Rickett (1). 7–0 v Sunderland, Division 1, 5 October 1957 – Farm; Armfield,
Garrett, Kelly (J), Gratrix, Kelly (H), Matthews, Taylor (2), Charnley (2), Durie (2), Perry (1).

sky SPORTS FACT FILE

When wing-half George Farrow joined Second Division
Blackpool in 1936 he had completed five years in all four
Football League divisions: Stockport County (Third
Division North), Wolverhampton Wanderers (Division
One) and Bournemouth (Division Three South).

Record Cup Victory: 7–1 v Charlton Ath, League Cup 2nd rd, 25 September 1963 – Harvey; Armfield, Martin; Crawford, Gratrix, Cranston; Lea, Ball (1), Charnley (4), Durie (1), Oates (1).

Record Defeat: 1–10 v Small Heath, Division 2, 2 March 1901 and v Huddersfield T, Division 1, 13 December 1930.

Most League Points (2 for a win): 58, Division 2, 1929–30 and Division 2, 1967–68.

Most League Points (3 for a win): 86, Division 4, 1984–85.

Most League Goals: 98, Division 2, 1929–30.

Highest League Scorer in Season: Jimmy Hampson, 45, Division 2, 1929–30.

Most League Goals in Total Aggregate: Jimmy Hampson, 248, 1927–38.

Most League Goals in One Match: 5, Jimmy Hampson v Reading, Division 2, 10 November 1928; 5, Jimmy McIntosh v Preston NE, Division 1, 1 May 1948.

Most Capped Player: Jimmy Armfield, 43, England.

Most League Appearances: Jimmy Armfield, 568, 1952–71.

Youngest League Player: Matty Kay, 16 years 32 days v Scunthorpe U, 13 November 2005.

Record Transfer Fee Received: £1,750,000 from Southampton for Brett Ormerod, December 2001.

Record Transfer Fee Paid: £275,000 to Millwall for Chris Malkin, October 1996.

Football League Record: 1896 Elected to Division 2; 1899 Failed re-election; 1900 Re-elected; 1900–30 Division 2; 1930–33 Division 1; 1933–37 Division 2; 1937–67 Division 1; 1967–70 Division 2; 1970–71 Division 1; 1971–78 Division 2; 1978–81 Division 3; 1981–85 Division 4; 1985–90 Division 3; 1990–92 Division 4; 1992–2000 Division 2; 2000–01 Division 3; 2001–04 Division 2; 2004–07 FL 1; 2007–10 FL C; 2010– FA Premier League.

MANAGERS

Tom Barcroft 1903–33
  (Secretary-Manager)
John Cox 1909–11
Bill Norman 1919–23
Maj. Frank Buckley 1923–27
Sid Beaumont 1927–28
Harry Evans 1928–33
  (Hon. Team Manager)
Alex 'Sandy' Macfarlane 1933–35
Joe Smith 1935–58
Ronnie Suart 1958–67
Stan Mortensen 1967–69
Les Shannon 1969–70
Bob Stokoe 1970–72
Harry Potts 1972–76
Allan Brown 1976–78
Bob Stokoe 1978–79
Stan Ternent 1979–80
Alan Ball 1980–81
Allan Brown 1981–82
Sam Ellis 1982–89
Jimmy Mullen 1989–90
Graham Carr 1990
Bill Ayre 1990–94
Sam Allardyce 1994–96
Gary Megson 1996–97
Nigel Worthington 1997–99
Steve McMahon 2000–04
Colin Hendry 2004–05
Simon Grayson 2005–08
Ian Holloway May 2009–

LATEST SEQUENCES

Longest Sequence of League Wins: 9, 21.11.1936 – 1.1.1937.
Longest Sequence of League Defeats: 8, 25.11.1898 – 7.1.1899.
Longest Sequence of League Draws: 5, 4.12.1976 – 1.1.1977.
Longest Sequence of Unbeaten League Matches: 17, 6.4.1968 – 21.9.1968.
Longest Sequence Without a League Win: 19, 19.12.1970 – 24.4.1971.
Successive Scoring Runs: 33 from 23.2.1929.
Successive Non-scoring Runs: 5 from 12.4.1975.

TEN YEAR LEAGUE RECORD

		P	W	D	L	F	A	Pts	Pos
2000-01	Div 2	46	22	6	18	74	58	72	7
2001-02	Div 2	46	14	14	18	66	69	56	16
2002-03	Div 2	46	15	13	18	56	64	58	13
2003-04	Div 2	46	16	11	19	58	65	59	14
2004-05	FL 1	46	15	12	19	54	59	57	16
2005-06	FL 1	46	12	17	17	56	64	53	19
2006-07	FL 1	46	24	11	11	76	49	83	3
2007-08	FL C	46	12	18	16	59	64	54	19
2008-09	FL C	46	13	17	16	47	58	56	16
2009-10	FL C	46	19	13	14	74	58	70	6

DID YOU KNOW ?

On 2 May 2010 Blackpool secured the last play-off place in the Football League Championship with a 1–1 draw against Bristol City. It was the 57th anniversary of the "Matthews" FA Cup final success and the attendance of 12,296 was the highest at home for 32 years.

BLACKPOOL 2009–10 LEAGUE RECORD

Match No.	Date	Venue	Opponents	Result	H/T Score	Lg Pos.	Goalscorers	Attendance
1	Aug 8	A	QPR	D	1-1	1-0	—	Burgess [37]	14,013
2	15	H	Cardiff C	D	1-1	1-1	13	Evatt [45]	7698
3	18	H	Derby Co	D	0-0	0-0	—		8056
4	22	A	Watford	D	2-2	0-1	13	John-Baptiste [56], Taylor-Fletcher [72]	12,745
5	29	H	Coventry C	W	3-0	1-0	10	Adam (pen) [13], Burgess [59], Taylor-Fletcher [71]	8239
6	Sept 12	A	Leicester C	L	1-2	1-1	12	Adam [31]	22,827
7	16	H	Newcastle U	W	2-1	1-1	—	Ormerod [45], Euell [65]	9647
8	19	H	Nottingham F	W	1-0	1-0	7	Adam [19]	23,487
9	26	H	Peterborough U	W	2-0	2-0	5	Euell [3], Bouazza [11]	7728
10	29	A	Bristol C	L	0-2	0-1	—		13,673
11	Oct 3	A	Crystal Palace	L	1-4	0-2	9	John-Baptiste [53]	15,749
12	17	H	Plymouth Arg	W	2-0	1-0	5	Seip [31], Vaughan [64]	7765
13	20	H	Sheffield U	W	3-0	0-0	—	Seip [60], Euell [69], Adam [82]	8042
14	24	A	Swansea C	D	0-0	0-0	7		14,724
15	31	A	Doncaster R	D	3-3	1-1	6	Ormerod [21], Emmanuel-Thomas [62], Burgess [77]	10,312
16	Nov 7	H	Scunthorpe U	W	4-1	0-0	5	Evatt [59], Adam [64], Burgess [70], John-Baptiste [89]	7727
17	21	H	Reading	L	1-2	0-0	7	Ormerod [58]	15,945
18	30	H	Preston NE	D	1-1	1-1	—	Clarke [1]	9861
19	Dec 5	H	Barnsley	L	1-2	0-0	8	Adam (pen) [72]	8108
20	8	A	Middlesbrough	W	3-0	2-0	—	Taylor-Fletcher 2 [21, 26], Adam [83]	18,089
21	12	A	Ipswich T	L	1-3	0-2	7	Evatt [67]	19,831
22	26	A	Derby Co	W	2-0	1-0	7	Buxton (og) [38], Ormerod [79]	30,313
23	Jan 9	A	Cardiff C	D	1-1	0-1	—	Adam [46]	19,147
24	16	H	QPR	D	2-2	1-0	9	Adam [9], Taylor-Fletcher [77]	7600
25	19	H	Sheffield W	L	1-2	0-0	—	Adam [90]	8007
26	23	A	Watford	W	3-2	1-1	—	Adam [17], Southern [89], Ormerod [90]	6855
27	30	A	Coventry C	D	1-1	0-0	7	Bannan [69]	16,019
28	Feb 3	H	WBA	L	2-3	1-2	—	Southern [25], Dobbie [80]	8510
29	6	H	Leicester C	L	1-2	0-1	8	Dobbie [89]	8484
30	9	A	Sheffield W	L	0-2	0-0	—		19,058
31	13	A	Preston NE	D	0-0	0-0	7		19,840
32	16	H	Middlesbrough	W	2-0	1-0	—	Ormerod [30], Campbell [90]	7936
33	20	H	Reading	W	2-0	1-0	7	Campbell [41], Adam [74]	7147
34	27	A	Barnsley	L	0-1	0-0	8		12,347
35	Mar 6	H	Ipswich T	W	1-0	0-0	7	Euell [54]	8635
36	13	A	WBA	L	2-3	1-1	7	Adam [6], Ormerod [72]	21,592
37	16	H	Sheffield U	L	0-3	0-2	—		22,555
38	20	H	Crystal Palace	D	2-2	0-2	9	Adam [47], Burgess [89]	9702
39	23	H	Swansea C	W	5-1	2-0	—	Ormerod 2 [13, 68], Evatt [45], Burgess [50], Taylor-Fletcher [82]	9149
40	27	A	Plymouth Arg	W	2-0	0-0	7	Adam [78], Dobbie [82]	10,614
41	Apr 2	A	Scunthorpe U	W	4-2	1-0	—	Wright A (og) [22], Coleman [77], Campbell 2 [82, 85]	7508
42	5	H	Doncaster R	W	2-0	1-0	7	Campbell [27], Dobbie [67]	9701
43	10	A	Newcastle U	L	1-4	0-2	7	Ormerod [85]	47,010
44	17	H	Nottingham F	W	3-1	1-0	7	Adam (pen) [32], Campbell 2 [54, 84]	11,164
45	24	A	Peterborough U	W	1-0	1-0	6	Campbell [11]	7812
46	May 2	H	Bristol C	D	1-1	0-1	6	Ormerod [54]	12,296

Final League Position: 6

GOALSCORERS

League (74): Adam 16 (3 pens), Ormerod 11, Campbell 8, Burgess 6, Taylor-Fletcher 6, Dobbie 4, Euell 4, Evatt 4, John-Baptiste 3, Seip 2, Southern 2, Bannan 1, Bouazza 1, Clarke 1, Coleman 1, Emmanuel-Thomas 1, Vaughan 1, own goals 2.
Carling Cup (9): Burgess 2, Adam 1, Clarke 1, Demontagnac 1, Nardiello 1, Nowland 1, Taylor-Fletcher 1, Vaughan 1.
FA Cup (1): Ormerod 1.
Play-Offs (9): Campbell 3, Adam 2 (1 pen), Dobbie 1, Ormerod 1, Southern 1, Taylor-Fletcher 1.

Rachubka P 20	John-Baptiste A 42	Crainey S 41	Southern K 43+2	Edwards R 19+2	Evatt I 35+1	Adam C 41+2	Euell J 23+10	Burgess B 20+15	Taylor-Fletcher G 26+6	Vaughan D 37+4	Clarke B 9+9	Omerod B 27+9	Nardiello D 1+4	Demontagnac I 1+7	Eardley N 22+2	Emmanuel-Thomas J 6+5	Bangura A 2+7	Bouazza H 11+8	Eastham A —+1	Gilks M 26	Seip M 7	Martin J 4+2	Bannan B 8+12	Butler A 4+3	Cold D 1	Campbell D 14+1	Dobbie S 6+10	Husband S 1+2	Coleman S 9	Match No.
1	2	3	4	5	6	7	8	9	10^2	11^1	12	13																		1
1	2	3	4	5	6	7	8		10^2	11		9^1	12	13																2
1	2		4	5	6	7^2	8		10^3	11^1	14	9	13	3	12															3
1	2	3	4		6	7	8^1	12	10^2	11	13	14			5	9^2														4
1		3	4	5	6	11^3	8	9^1	7^2	13	10				2	12	14													5
1		3	4^3	5	6	11	8^2	9	14	12	10^1				2	7	13													6
1	5	3	4		6	7^2	8			11		10			2	13	12	9^1												7
1	5	3	4	12	6^1	7	8			11	14	10^3			2	13		9^2												8
1	5	3	4		6	7^3	8	13		11		10^2			2^1	14	9	12												9
1	5	3	4		6	7^3	8	10^2		11	12	13			2	14		9^1												10
1	5	3	4		6	7	8	12		11	13	10^2			2^3	14														11
	2	3^1	4		6	7	13	9^3	11	10^2	14	12				8				1	5									12
	2	3	12		8	10^2	13	9	4^3	5	7	11^1		14						1	6									13
	2	3	4	12	7^2	10	13	11	9			5^1		14		8^2				1	6									14
	2	3	4		6	8	9	12	11	10^1		7								1	5									15
	2	3	4		6	7^1	12	9	10^2	13		11^1		14		8^3				1	5									16
	2	3^1	4^2		6	7	8	9	14	11	13	10^3								1	5	12								17
	2	3	4		6	7^3	12	9^1		11		10^2		13		8				1	5		14							18
	2	3	4	5		7	12	9	14	11		10^2			6	8^3				1			13							19
1	2	3	4	5^1	6	7	14		10^3	11		9			12	13							8^2							20
	3	12	5	6	13	10			9	11^4		14			2	4^1	7^3						8^2							21
1	2^1	3	4	12	6	7^2	8	9^3	10			11		13	5	14														22
1	2		4			7		10	8^1	11		9^2		12		5						3	13	6						23
1	2	3	4		6	7	14	12	10^3	11^2		9		13	5								8^1							24
1	2	3	12		6	7	8^2	9	13	11^3		10			4^1	5							14							25
1	2	3	4		6^3	7	12	10^1	11	9		14		13	5								8^2							26
1	2	3	4	5	6	7^2	12	10	11	9^4		13				8														27
1		3	4	5	6	7		9^3	14	11		8^2		12								2^1	10	13						28
	2	3	4		6^2	7	12	10		11		13			5					1			8^1			9				29
1	2	3	4^2	5		8	12		9	11^3		14			6									10		7^1	13			30
	2	3	4	5	6		9	7	11	8										1						10				31
	2	3	4	5^4	6	7		8^1	11^2	9^3		14								1				12		10	13			32
	2	3	4		6	7	13	8^1	11	9^2		12								1			5			10^3	14			33
	2	3	4		6	7	14	9^3	11	10^2		13								1			5			8^1	12			34
	2		4	5		7	8	13		11	12				6					1		3^2				10	9^1			35
	2		4	5		7	8	14		11	12				6					1		3^2	13			10	9^1			36
	2	3	4^2	5		7	8^3	13		11		9			6^1					1			14	12		10				37
	2	3	4		6	7	12	14		10^2		13								1			8^3			9	11^1	5		38
	2	3	4		6	7^3	13	11^3	8	10^1		9								1			12	14				5		39
	2	3^1	4		6	7	8^3	11	9	10^2										1			12	14		13		5		40
	2		4		6	7	11	9^3	13	10^2		12								1		3	14			8^1		5		41
	2	3	4		6	7		8	11	9^1										1						10	12	5		42
	2	3	4		6	7	9^2	8^1	11^3	13										1			14			10	12	5		43
	2	3	4		6	7	13	8^3	11^1	9^2										1			14			10	12	5		44
	2	3	4		6	7	14	8^1	11	9^2										1			13			10^3	12	5		45
	2	3	4		6	7	14	8^3	11^2	9										1			13			10^1	12	5		46

FA Cup
Third Round   Ipswich T   (h)   1-2

Carling Cup
First Round   Crewe Alex   (a)   2-1
Second Round   Wigan Ath   (h)   4-1
Third Round   Stoke C   (a)   3-4

Play-Offs
Semi-Final   Nottingham F   (h)   2-1
                                         (a)   4-3
Final   Cardiff C   3-2
(at Wembley).

BOLTON WANDERERS FA Premiership

FOUNDATION

In 1874 boys of Christ Church Sunday School, Blackburn Street, led by their master Thomas Ogden, established a football club which went under the name of the school and whose president was Vicar of Christ Church. Membership was 6d (two and a half pence). When their president began to lay down too many rules about the use of church premises, the club broke away and formed Bolton Wanderers in 1877, holding their earliest meetings at the Gladstone Hotel.

The Reebok Stadium, Burnden Way, Lostock, Bolton BL6 6JW.

Telephone: (0844) 871 2932. *Fax:* (01204) 673 773.

Ticket Office: (0844) 871 2932.

Website: www.bwfc.co.uk

Email: reception@bwfc.co.uk

Ground Capacity: 28,101.

Record Attendance: 69,912 v Manchester C, FA Cup 5th rd, 18 February 1933.

Pitch Measurements: 105m × 68m.

Chairman: Phil A. Gartside.

Chief Executive: Allan Duckworth.

Vice-chairman: Brett Warburton.

Secretary: Simon Marland.

Manager: Owen Coyle.

Assistant Manager: Sandy Stewart.

Physio: Nick Worth.

HONOURS

Football League: Division 1 – Champions 1996–97. Division 2 – Champions 1908–09, 1977–78; Runners-up 1899–1900, 1904–05, 1910–11, 1934–35, 1992–93; Division 3 – Champions 1972–73.

FA Cup: Winners 1923, 1926, 1929, 1958; Runners-up 1894, 1904, 1953.

Football League Cup: Runners-up 1995, 2004.

Freight Rover Trophy: Runners-up 1986.

Sherpa Van Trophy: Winners 1989.

European Competitions: UEFA Cup: 2005–06, 2007–08.

Colours: White shirts with blue body trim, blue shorts, white stockings.

Change Colours: Blue shirts with red trim, white shorts, blue stockings.

Year Formed: 1874. *Turned Professional:* 1880. *Ltd Co.:* 1895.

Previous Name: 1874, Christ Church FC; 1877, Bolton Wanderers.

Club Nickname: 'The Trotters'.

Grounds: Park Recreation Ground and Cockle's Field before moving to Pike's Lane ground 1881; 1895, Burnden Park; 1997, Reebok Stadium.

First Football League Game: 8 September 1888, Football League, v Derby Co (h) L 3–6 – Harrison; Robinson, Mitchell; Roberts, Weir, Bullough, Davenport (2), Milne, Coupar, Barbour, Brogan (1).

Record League Victory: 8–0 v Barnsley, Division 2, 6 October 1934 – Jones; Smith, Finney; Goslin, Atkinson, George Taylor; George T. Taylor (2), Eastham, Milsom (1), Westwood (4), Cook, (1 og).

sky SPORTS FACT FILE

On 4 December 1993 in an FA Cup second round tie, Bolton Wanderers beat Lincoln City 3–1 at Sincil Bank, with Owen Coyle scoring one goal. On 2 January 2010 Burnley, managed by Coyle, defeated Lincoln 4–0 in a third round tie. Days later he became Bolton's manager.

Record Cup Victory: 13–0 v Sheffield U, FA Cup 2nd rd, 1 February 1890 – Parkinson; Robinson (1), Jones; Bullough, Davenport, Roberts; Rushton, Brogan (3), Cassidy (5), McNee, Weir (4).

Record Defeat: 1–9 v Preston NE, FA Cup 2nd rd, 10 December 1887.

Most League Points (2 for a win): 61, Division 3, 1972–73.

Most League Points (3 for a win): 98, Division 1, 1996–97.

Most League Goals: 100, Division 1, 1996–97.

Highest League Scorer in Season: Joe Smith, 38, Division 1, 1920–21.

Most League Goals in Total Aggregate: Nat Lofthouse, 255, 1946–61.

Most League Goals in One Match: 5, Tony Caldwell v Walsall, Division 3, 10 September 1983.

Most Capped Player: Mark Fish, 34 (62), South Africa.

Most League Appearances: Eddie Hopkinson, 519, 1956–70.

Youngest League Player: Ray Parry, 15 years 267 days v Wolverhampton W, 13 October 1951.

Record Transfer Fee Received: £15,000,000 from Chelsea for Nicolas Anelka, January 2008.

Record Transfer Fee Paid: £8,200,000 to Toulouse for Johan Elmander, July 2008.

Football League Record: 1888 Founder Member of the League; 1899–1900 Division 2; 1900–03 Division 1; 1903–05 Division 2; 1905–08 Division 1; 1908–09 Division 2; 1909–10 Division 1; 1910–11 Division 2; 1911–33 Division 1; 1933–35 Division 2; 1935–64 Division 1; 1964–71 Division 2; 1971–73 Division 3; 1973–78 Division 2; 1978–80 Division 1; 1980–83 Division 2; 1983–87 Division 3; 1987–88 Division 4; 1988–92 Division 3; 1992–93 Division 2; 1993–95 Division 1; 1995–96 FA Premier League; 1996–97 Division 1; 1997–98 FA Premier League; 1998–2001 Division 1; 2001– FA Premier League.

LATEST SEQUENCES

Longest Sequence of League Wins: 11, 5.11.1904 – 2.1.1905.

Longest Sequence of League Defeats: 11, 7.4.1902 – 18.10.1902.

Longest Sequence of League Draws: 6, 25.1.1913 – 8.3.1913.

Longest Sequence of Unbeaten League Matches: 23, 13.10.1990 – 9.3.1991.

Longest Sequence Without a League Win: 26, 7.4.1902 – 10.1.1903.

Successive Scoring Runs: 24 from 22.11.1996.

Successive Non-scoring Runs: 5 from 3.1.1898.

MANAGERS

Tom Rawthorne 1874–85
(Secretary)
J. J. Bentley 1885–86
(Secretary)
W. G. Struthers 1886–87
(Secretary)
Fitzroy Norris 1887
(Secretary)
J. J. Bentley 1887–95
(Secretary)
Harry Downs 1895–96
(Secretary)
Frank Brettell 1896–98
(Secretary)
John Somerville 1898–1910
Will Settle 1910–15
Tom Mather 1915–19
Charles Foweraker 1919–44
Walter Rowley 1944–50
Bill Ridding 1951–68
Nat Lofthouse 1968–70
Jimmy McIlroy 1970
Jimmy Meadows 1971
Nat Lofthouse 1971
(then Admin. Manager to 1972)
Jimmy Armfield 1971–74
Ian Greaves 1974–80
Stan Anderson 1980–81
George Mulhall 1981–82
John McGovern 1982–85
Charlie Wright 1985
Phil Neal 1985–92
Bruce Rioch 1992–95
Roy McFarland 1995–96
Colin Todd 1996–99
Sam Allardyce 1999–2007
Sammy Lee 2007
Gary Megson 2007–09
Owen Coyle January 2010–

TEN YEAR LEAGUE RECORD

		P	W	D	L	F	A	Pts	Pos
2000-01	Div 1	46	24	15	7	76	45	87	3
2001-02	PR Lge	38	9	13	16	44	62	40	16
2002-03	PR Lge	38	10	14	14	41	51	44	17
2003-04	PR Lge	38	14	11	13	48	56	53	8
2004-05	PR Lge	38	16	10	12	49	44	58	6
2005-06	PR Lge	38	15	11	12	49	41	56	8
2006-07	PR Lge	38	16	8	14	47	52	56	7
2007-08	PR Lge	38	9	10	19	36	54	37	16
2008-09	PR Lge	38	11	8	19	41	53	41	13
2009-10	PR Lge	38	10	9	19	42	67	39	14

DID YOU KNOW ?

On 6 March 2010 Kevin Davies continued his scoring rate for Bolton Wanderers at the expense of West Ham United in a 2–1 win at Upton Park. It was his seventh goal in six League and Cup matches against them in four seasons. All six ended in Bolton victories, too.

BOLTON WANDERERS 2009–10 LEAGUE RECORD

Match No.	Date	Venue	Opponents	Result	H/T Score	Lg Pos.	Goalscorers	Attendance
1	Aug 15	H	Sunderland	L	0-1	0-1	—		22,247
2	22	A	Hull C	L	0-1	0-0	17		22,999
3	29	H	Liverpool	L	2-3	1-1	19	Davies K [33], Cohen [47]	23,284
4	Sept 12	A	Portsmouth	W	3-2	2-1	18	Cohen [13], Taylor (pen) [41], Cahill [89]	17,564
5	19	H	Stoke C	D	1-1	0-0	17	Taylor (pen) [89]	20,265
6	26	A	Birmingham C	W	2-1	1-0	13	Cohen [10], Lee [86]	28,671
7	Oct 3	H	Tottenham H	D	2-2	1-1	13	Gardner [3], Davies K [69]	21,305
8	17	A	Manchester U	L	1-2	0-2	14	Taylor [75]	75,103
9	25	H	Everton	W	3-2	2-1	12	Lee [16], Cahill [27], Klasnic [86]	21,547
10	31	H	Chelsea	L	0-4	0-1	15		22,680
11	Nov 7	A	Aston Villa	L	1-5	1-2	16	Elmander [44]	38,101
12	22	H	Blackburn R	L	0-2	0-1	18		21,777
13	28	A	Fulham	D	1-1	1-0	18	Klasnic [35]	23,554
14	Dec 5	A	Wolverhampton W	L	1-2	0-1	19	Elmander [79]	27,362
15	12	H	Manchester C	D	3-3	2-2	19	Klasnic 2 [11, 53], Cahill [43]	22,735
16	15	H	West Ham U	W	3-1	0-0	—	Lee [64], Klasnic [77], Cahill [88]	17,849
17	26	A	Burnley	D	1-1	1-0	18	Taylor [29]	21,761
18	29	H	Hull C	D	2-2	1-0	—	Klasnic [20], Davies K [61]	20,696
19	Jan 17	A	Arsenal	L	0-2	0-1	19		23,893
20	20	A	Arsenal	L	2-4	2-1	—	Cahill [7], Taylor (pen) [28]	59,084
21	26	H	Burnley	W	1-0	1-0	—	Lee [35]	23,986
22	30	A	Liverpool	L	0-2	0-1	16		43,413
23	Feb 6	H	Fulham	D	0-0	0-0	17		22,289
24	9	A	Manchester C	L	0-2	0-1	—		42,016
25	17	A	Wigan Ath	D	0-0	0-0	—		18,089
26	21	H	Blackburn R	L	0-3	0-1	18		23,888
27	27	H	Wolverhampton W	W	1-0	1-0	15	Knight [45]	21,261
28	Mar 6	A	West Ham U	W	2-1	2-0	—	Davies K [10], Wilshere [16]	33,824
29	9	A	Sunderland	L	0-4	0-1	—		36,087
30	13	H	Wigan Ath	W	4-0	1-0	13	Elmander [10], Davies K (pen) [48], Muamba [53], Taylor [69]	20,053
31	20	A	Everton	L	0-2	0-0	14		36,503
32	27	H	Manchester U	L	0-4	0-1	15		25,370
33	Apr 3	H	Aston Villa	L	0-1	0-1	15		21,111
34	13	A	Chelsea	L	0-1	0-1	—		40,539
35	17	A	Stoke C	W	2-1	0-1	14	Taylor 2 [85, 88]	27,250
36	24	H	Portsmouth	D	2-2	2-0	14	Klasnic [26], Davies K [28]	20,526
37	May 1	A	Tottenham H	L	0-1	0-1	14		35,852
38	9	H	Birmingham C	W	2-1	1-0	14	Davies K [33], Klasnic [60]	22,863

Final League Position: 14

GOALSCORERS

League (42): Klasnic 8, Taylor 8 (3 pens), Davies K 7 (1 pen), Cahill 5, Lee 4, Cohen 3, Elmander 3, Gardner 1, Knight 1, Muamba 1, Wilshere 1.
Carling Cup (4): Cahill 1, Davies K 1, Davies M 1, Elmander 1.
FA Cup (7): Cahill 1, Davies K 1, Davies M 1, Elmander 1, Lee 1, Steinsson 1, own goal 1.

Jaaskelainen J 38	Ricketts S 25+2	Robinson P 24+1	Davis S 3	Knight Z 35	Cahill G 29	McCann G 5+6	Muamba F 35+1	Elmander J 15+10	Davies K 37	Taylor M 29+8	Lee C 27+7	Ward D —+2	Davies M 5+12	Samuel J 12+1	Cohen T 26+1	Basham C 2+6	Steinsson G 25+2	Mustapha R —+1	Klasnic I 12+15	Gardner R 11+10	O'Brien A 6	Weiss V 3+10	Wilshere J 13+1	Holden S 1+1	Match No.
1	2	3	4	5	6	7^1	8	9^2	10	11	12	13													1
1	2	3^2	4	5	6		8	9^1	10	11	12	14	7^3	13											2
1	2		4^4	5	6		8^0	9^1	10	11				3	7^2	12	13	14							3
1	2^1			5	6	14	8		10	9		11^2	3	7^3	12	4		13							4
1	2			5	6	11	8^2		10	9			3	7		4^1		13	12						5
1	2			5	6	13	8		10	11	12		3	7				9^1	4^2						6
1	2			5	6	12	8^1		10	11^2	9^3	13	3	7				14	4						7
1	2			5	6		8^3		10	11	9^1	13	3	4^2	14			12	7						8
1	2			5	6		8		10	11	9^2		3	4	13			12	7^1						9
1	2	13		5	6		4^3	9	10		11^2	14	3^4	8	7^8			12							10
1	2^2	3		5	6		4	12	10	11	9		8^1		13			7							11
1	2				6	8^1	4		9^1	10	11	14	13	3					12	7^2	5				12
1					6	8	12		10	11		13	3	4^2		2		9^1	7	5					13
1				6	4		12			11	10		3^1	8		2		9	7	5					14
1		3		5	6		4^2	12	10	11	8	13		7		2		9^1						15
1		3		5	6		4		10	11^1	8			7	13	2		9^2	12					16
1		3		5	6				10	11	8^2	12		7	4	2		9^1	13					17
1		3		5	6		12	4	10	11	8			7		2		9^1						18
1		3		5	6	12	4^1	14	10	11	8			7^2		2		9^2	13					19
1	14	3^3		5	6	12	4		10	11	9^2		7^1	8		2		13						20
1		3		5	6		4	12	10	11^2	8^3		7			2		9^1	13		14			21
1		3		5	6		4^3	14	10	11^2	8		7			2		9^1	12		13			22
1	2	3		5		4	12		10	9^3	8		7^1					11	13	6^2	14			23
1		3		5	6		4	9	10	13	8			7^2		2		12	11^1					24
1		3		5	6		4	9	10	11^3	8^1	13		7^2		2		12			14			25
1		3		5	6		4^1	9^3	10	11^2	8	12				2		14	7		13			26
1		3		5	6		4	9^1	10	13	8^3					2		12			14	11^2	7	27
1		3		5	6		4	9^1	10	13	8			11^*		2		12				7^2		28
1	6^8	3		5		4^1	9^2	10	14	8						2		13	7^3		12	11		29
1		3		5		4	9	10^3	12	8^2				11		2		14		6	13	7^1		30
1	12	3		5		4	9^1	10	13	8		14	11^3	2^*						6		7^2		31
1	2			5	6		4	9^1	10	13	8			3^*	11^2			12				7		32
1	2	3		5	6		4	9^1	10	14	8^3				11^2			12			3	7		33
1	7	3		5	6		4	12	10	11	9^2				2			13				8^1		34
1	7^1	3		5	6		4^3		10	11	9^2	14			2			12			3	8		35
1		3		5	6		4	13	10	11	12	14			2			9^2			7^1	8^3		36
1		3		5	6		4^3	12	10	7	13				2			9^2	14			11^1	8	37
1		3		5	6		4		10	7^2	13				2			9	14			11^1	8^3 12	38

FA Cup

Third Round	Lincoln C	(h)	4-0
Fourth Round	Sheffield U	(a)	2-0
Fifth Round	Tottenham H	(h)	1-1
		(a)	0-4

Carling Cup

Second Round	Tranmere R	(a)	1-0
Third Round	West Ham U	(h)	3-1
Fourth Round	Chelsea	(a)	0-4

AFC BOURNEMOUTH FL Championship 1

FOUNDATION

There was a Bournemouth FC as early as 1875, but the present club arose out of the remnants of the Boscombe St John's club (formed 1890). The meeting at which Boscombe FC came into being was held at a house in Gladstone Road in 1899. They began by playing in the Boscombe and District Junior League.

Dean Court, Kings Park, Bournemouth, Dorset BH7 7AF.

Telephone: (01202) 726 300.

Fax: (01202) 726 373.

Ticket Office: (01202) 726 338.

Website: www.afcb.co.uk

Email: enquiries@afcb.co.uk

Ground Capacity: 10,375 (with temporary stand, 9,776 without).

Record Attendance: 28,799 v Manchester U, FA Cup 6th rd, 2 March 1957.

Pitch Measurements: 105m × 78m.

Chairman: Eddie Mitchell.

Chief Executive: Neill Blake.

Secretary: Neil Vacher (Football Administrator).

Manager: Eddie Howe.

Assistant Manager: Jason Tindall.

Physio: Steve Hard.

Colours: Red shirts with thin black vertical stripes, black shorts, black stockings.

Change Colours: All black with red trim.

Year Formed: 1899.

Turned Professional: 1910.

Ltd Co.: 1914.

Previous Names: 1890, Boscombe St Johns; 1899, Boscombe FC; 1923, Bournemouth & Boscombe Ath FC; 1971, AFC Bournemouth.

Club Nickname: 'Cherries'.

Grounds: 1899, Castlemain Road, Pokesdown; 1910, Dean Court.

First Football League Game: 25 August 1923, Division 3 (S), v Swindon T (a) L 1–3 – Heron; Wingham, Lamb; Butt, C. Smith, Voisey; Miller, Lister (1), Davey, Simpson, Robinson.

Record League Victory: 7–0 v Swindon T, Division 3 (S), 22 September 1956 – Godwin; Cunningham, Keetley; Clayton, Crosland, Rushworth; Siddall (1), Norris (2), Arnott (1), Newsham (2), Cutler (1). 10–0 win v Northampton T at start of 1939–40 expunged from the records on outbreak of war.

HONOURS

Football League: Division 3 – Champions 1986–87; Division 3 (S) – Runners-up 1947–48; Division 4 – Runners-up 1970–71.

FA Cup: best season: 6th rd, 1957.

Football League Cup: best season: 4th rd, 1962, 1964.

Associate Members' Cup: Winners 1984.

Auto Windscreens Shield: Runners-up 1998.

sky SPORTS FACT FILE

Baven Penton was the first professional player employed by Boscombe FC in January 1912. He cost the princely sum of £10 for his transfer! He scored nine of the club's first twelve FA Cup goals – all away from home as their ground was considered unfit for the competition.

Record Cup Victory: 11–0 v Margate, FA Cup 1st rd, 20 November 1971 – Davies; Machin (1), Kitchener, Benson, Jones, Powell, Cave (1), Boyer, MacDougall (9 incl. 1p), Miller, Scott (De Garis).

Record Defeat: 0–9 v Lincoln C, Division 3, 18 December 1982.

Most League Points (2 for a win): 62, Division 3, 1971–72.

Most League Points (3 for a win): 97, Division 3, 1986–87.

Most League Goals: 88, Division 3 (S), 1956–57.

Highest League Scorer in Season: Ted MacDougall, 42, 1970–71.

Most League Goals in Total Aggregate: Ron Eyre, 202, 1924–33.

Most League Goals in One Match: 4, Jack Russell v Clapton Orient, Division 3 (S), 7 January 1933; 4, Jack Russell v Bristol C, Division 3 (S), 28 January 1933; 4, Harry Mardon v Southend U, Division 3 (S), 1 January 1938; 4, Jack McDonald v Torquay U, Division 3 (S), 8 November 1947; 4, Ted MacDougall v Colchester U, 18 September 1970; 4, Brian Clark v Rotherham U, 10 October 1972; 4, Luther Blissett v Hull C, 29 November 1988; 4, James Hayter v Bury, Division 2, 21 October 2000.

Most Capped Player: Gerry Peyton, 7 (33), Republic of Ireland.

Most League Appearances: Steve Fletcher, 514, 1992–2007; 2008–09.

Youngest League Player: Jimmy White, 15 years 321 days v Brentford, 30 April 1958.

Record Transfer Fee Received: £800,000 from Everton for Joe Parkinson, March 1994 and £800,000 from Ipswich T for Matt Holland, July 1997.

Record Transfer Fee Paid: £210,000 to Gillingham for Gavin Peacock, August 1989.

Football League Record: 1923 Elected to Division 3 (S) and remained a Third Division club for record number of years until 1970; 1970–71 Division 4; 1971–75 Division 3; 1975–82 Division 4; 1982–87 Division 3; 1987–90 Division 2; 1990–92 Division 3; 1992–2002 Division 2; 2002–03 Division 3; 2003–04 Division 2; 2004–08 FL 1; 2008–10 FL 2; 2010– FL 1.

MANAGERS

Vincent Kitcher 1914–23
(Secretary-Manager)
Harry Kinghorn 1923–25
Leslie Knighton 1925–28
Frank Richards 1928–30
Billy Birrell 1930–35
Bob Crompton 1935–36
Charlie Bell 1936–39
Harry Kinghorn 1939–47
Harry Lowe 1947–50
Jack Bruton 1950–56
Fred Cox 1956–58
Don Welsh 1958–61
Bill McGarry 1961–63
Reg Flewin 1963–65
Fred Cox 1965–70
John Bond 1970–73
Trevor Hartley 1974–75
John Benson 1975–78
Alec Stock 1979–80
David Webb 1980–82
Don Megson 1983
Harry Redknapp 1983–92
Tony Pulis 1992–94
Mel Machin 1994–2000
Sean O'Driscoll 2000–06
Kevin Bond 2006–08
Jimmy Quinn 2008
Eddie Howe January 2009–

LATEST SEQUENCES

Longest Sequence of League Wins: 7, 22.8.1970 – 23.9.1970.

Longest Sequence of League Defeats: 7, 13.8.1994 – 13.9.1994.

Longest Sequence of League Draws: 5, 25.4.2000 – 12.8.2000.

Longest Sequence of Unbeaten League Matches: 18, 6.3.1982 – 28.8.1982.

Longest Sequence Without a League Win: 14, 6.3.1974 – 27.4.1974.

Successive Scoring Runs: 31 from 28.10.2000.

Successive Non-scoring Runs: 6 from 1.2.1975.

TEN YEAR LEAGUE RECORD

		P	W	D	L	F	A	Pts	Pos
2000-01	Div 2	46	20	13	13	79	55	73	7
2001-02	Div 2	46	10	14	22	56	71	44	21
2002-03	Div 3	46	20	14	12	60	48	74	4
2003-04	Div 2	46	17	15	14	56	51	66	9
2004-05	FL 1	46	20	10	16	77	64	70	8
2005-06	FL 1	46	12	19	15	49	53	55	17
2006-07	FL 1	46	13	13	20	50	64	52	19
2007-08	FL 1	46	17	7	22	62	72	48*	21
2008-09	FL 2	46	17	12	17	59	51	46†	21
2009-10	FL 2	46	25	8	13	61	44	83	2

*10 pts deducted; †17 points deducted.

DID YOU KNOW ?

In 1923–24 during Bournemouth's first season in the Football League, Hugh Davey while missing eight matches managed to score exactly half of the club's total. His 20 goals were also remarkable because the team only scored in 23 of the fixtures involved.

AFC BOURNEMOUTH 2009–10 LEAGUE RECORD

Match No.	Date	Venue	Opponents	Result	H/T Score	Lg Pos.	Goalscorers	Attendance
1	Aug 8	A	Bury	W 3-0	2-0	—	Pitman [17], Robinson [39], Molesley [50]	2998
2	15	H	Rotherham U	W 1-0	1-0	2	Garry [45]	5091
3	18	H	Aldershot T	W 1-0	0-0	—	Pearce [48]	5556
4	22	A	Northampton T	L 0-2	0-1	4		4102
5	29	H	Crewe Alex	W 1-0	0-0	3	Feeney [51]	4563
6	Sept 5	A	Torquay U	W 2-1	0-0	2	Pitman [49], Fletcher [87]	3881
7	12	H	Lincoln C	W 3-1	2-1	1	Pitman [7], Igoe 2 [20, 61]	5385
8	19	A	Darlington	W 2-0	1-0	1	Pitman 2 (1 pen) [15, 83 (p)]	1999
9	26	H	Burton Alb	W 1-0	0-0	1	Pitman [86]	6327
10	29	A	Hereford U	L 1-2	0-0	—	Fletcher [60]	2104
11	Oct 3	A	Port Vale	D 0-0	0-0	—		4905
12	10	H	Chesterfield	L 1-2	0-2	1	Hollands [75]	5896
13	17	A	Accrington S	W 1-0	0-0	1	Hollands [76]	1858
14	24	H	Grimsby T	W 3-1	2-0	1	Connell [27], Linwood (og) [34], Pitman [87]	5270
15	31	H	Rochdale	L 0-4	0-1	1		6378
16	Nov 14	A	Bradford C	D 1-1	1-1	2	Pitman [33]	11,732
17	21	A	Macclesfield T	W 2-1	1-1	1	Pitman 2 [45, 78]	1413
18	24	H	Dagenham & R	D 0-0	0-0	—		6881
19	Dec 1	A	Barnet	D 1-1	1-1	—	Pitman [44]	2030
20	5	H	Shrewsbury T	W 1-0	0-0	2	Coughlan (og) [85]	4652
21	12	A	Morecambe	L 0-5	0-3	2		2034
22	26	A	Cheltenham T	W 1-0	0-0	2	Feeney [57]	4114
23	28	H	Torquay U	W 2-1	0-0	2	Feeney [84], Pitman (pen) [90]	7626
24	Jan 2	H	Northampton T	L 0-2	0-2	—		5715
25	16	H	Bury	L 1-2	0-2	—	Pitman [90]	4516
26	23	A	Aldershot T	L 1-2	0-1	2	Pitman (pen) [61]	4387
27	30	A	Crewe Alex	W 2-1	1-0	2	Fletcher [22], Robinson [63]	3741
28	Feb 2	A	Rotherham U	W 3-1	0-1	—	Pitman [47], Hollands 2 [59, 67]	3180
29	6	H	Cheltenham T	D 0-0	0-0	2		5259
30	9	H	Notts Co	W 2-1	2-0	—	Hollands 2 [2, 35]	5472
31	13	A	Dagenham & R	L 0-1	0-1	2		2215
32	20	H	Macclesfield T	D 1-1	0-0	3	Connell [85]	4549
33	23	H	Barnet	W 3-0	0-0	—	Fletcher [59], Pitman 2 [61, 76]	4019
34	27	A	Shrewsbury T	L 0-1	0-0	2		6061
35	Mar 6	A	Morecambe	W 1-0	1-0	2	Robinson [18]	5103
36	15	H	Notts Co	D 2-2	0-1	—	Pitman [50], Goulding [90]	6120
37	20	A	Grimsby T	L 2-3	1-1	3	Bradbury [42], Feeney [62]	4428
38	27	H	Accrington S	W 2-0	1-0	3	Feeney [18], Pitman [79]	5413
39	Apr 3	A	Bradford C	W 1-0	1-0	3	Pitman [41]	6239
40	5	A	Rochdale	D 0-0	0-0	3		5027
41	10	A	Lincoln C	L 1-2	0-1	3	Pitman [70]	3040
42	13	H	Hereford U	W 2-1	1-0	—	Pitman 2 (1 pen) [32 (p), 77]	6128
43	17	A	Darlington	W 2-0	0-0	3	Robinson [56], Pitman (pen) [71]	6464
44	24	A	Burton Alb	W 2-0	0-0	3	Pitman [86], Connell [90]	3977
45	May 1	H	Port Vale	W 4-0	0-0	2	Pitman [53], Connell 2 [76, 81], McQuoid [86]	9055
46	8	A	Chesterfield	L 1-2	1-0	2	Talbot (og) [42]	4998

Final League Position: 2

GOALSCORERS

League (61): Pitman 26 (5 pens), Hollands 6, Connell 5, Feeney 5, Fletcher 4, Robinson 4, Igoe 2, Bradbury 1, Garry 1, Goulding 1, McQuoid 1, Molesley 1, Pearce 1, own goals 3.
Carling Cup (0).
FA Cup (4): Connell 2, Igoe 1, Pitman 1.
J Paint Trophy (3): Connell 1, Hollands 1, Pitman 1.

Jalal S 44	Bradbury L 43 + 1	Cummings W 27 + 7	Molesley M 10	Pearce J 39	Guyett S 6 + 3	Igoe S 15 + 6	Robinson A 43 + 1	Pitman B 46	Fletcher S 31 + 14	Feeney L 44	Partington J 4 + 7	Bartley M 24 + 10	Goulding J 3 + 14	Garry R 33 + 1	McQuoid J 9 + 20	Connell A 19 + 19	Hollands D 37 + 2	Webb G — + 1	Edgar A 2 + 1	Stockley J — + 2	Thomas D 1 + 1	Stech M 1	Wiggins R 19	Cooper S 6	Match No.
1	2	3	4	5	6[1]	7	8	9	10[3]	11[2]	12	13	14												1
1	2	3	4	5	12	7[3]	8	9[2]	10	11		13			6[1]	14									2
1	2	3	4	5	12	7	8	9[3]	10	11[2]		13			6[1]	14									3
1	2	3	4	5	6	7[2]	8	9	10[3]	11[1]			14			13	12[2]								4
1	10	3	4	5	13	7[2]	6	9[3]	11	8[1]	12				2	14									5
1	2[2]	3	4	5		7[3]	8	9	12	11		13			6	10[1]	14								6
1	2	3	4[1]	5		7[3]	8	9	10	11[2]	12				6	14	13								7
1	2	3	8[2]	5		7		9	10[1]	11[3]				6	13	15	4		14						8
1	2	3		5	6	7		9	10	11					8[1]	12	4								9
1	2[2]	3		5	6	7		9	10	11[1]				8	13	12	4								10
1	2	3		5		7		9	12	11				13	6[2]	10[1]	4	8							11
1	12	3		5		7		9	10	11				6[2]	2[3]	13	4	8[1]	14						12
1	2	3	8[2]	5		7		9	10[1]	11[3]	13	14			6	2	4								13
1	2	3	8[1]	5		7		9	13	11[3]				6	14	10[2]	4			12					14
1	2	3		5		7		9	10[1]	11	12				6	8	4								15
1	2	3		5		7		9	12	11				8	6	10[1]	4								16
1	2	3		5	13	7		9	12	11[2]				8	6	10[1]	4								17
		3		5	2	7		9	12	11[3]				8	6	13	4								18
1	2	3		5		7	8	9	12	11[2]				6	13	10[1]	4								19
1	2	3		5		7	8[1]	9	13	11	12				6	10[2]	4			15					20
	2	3		5	12			9	10[2]	11[3]			14	7[4]	6	8[6]	4				1				21
1	2			5	6	7[1]		9	12	11	8			10[2]	3	13[1]	4								22
1	2	3		5				9	12	11	7		14	10[1]	6[3]	13	4								23
1	2			5		7[2]	8	9	12	11	3			13	6	10[1]	4								24
1	2	3[3]		5		7[2]	8	9	12	11			10[1]	6	13	14	4								25
1	2	3		5		7[1]	8	9	10	11	12			13	6		4[2]								26
1	2			5			8	9	10	11				7[1]	6	12	4						3		27
1	2			5			8	9	10	11[2]			13	6	7[1]	12	4						3		28
1	2			5			8	9	10[3]	11	12[2]			13	6	14	4						3		29
1	2	13		5			8	9	10	11[2]				7[1]	6	12	4						3		30
1	2			5			8	9	10	11[1]				7	5	12	4						3		31
1	2			5			8	9	10[1]	11				6	13	7[2]	4						3		32
1	2	14		5			8	9	10	11[2]				7[3]	6	12	4						3		33
1	2		5				8	9	10[1]	11	12			6[2]	4	7				13			3		34
1	2	13	12				8	9	10	11[2]				6	5	7[1]	4						3		35
1	2			5			8	9	10[1]	11				6	12	5	4						3		36
1	2						8	9[3]	10	11	13			6	5	12[2]	4						3		37
1	2	14	13				8	9	10[2]	11[3]				6	7[1]	12	4						3	5	38
1	2						8	9	10	11				6	5	12	4						3	7[1]	39
1	2[1]			5		12	8	9	14	11		13		7	6[2]	10[3]	4						3		40
1	2			5		7[1]	8	9	12	11				6	13	10[2]	4						3		41
1	2	14		5		12	8	9	10[2]	11[3]				6	13	7[1]	4						3		42
1	2			5			8	9	10[2]	11[1]			14	7[3]	12	13	4						3	6	43
1	2	14		5			8	9	10[3]	11[1]				7[2]	12	13	4						3	6	44
	2	14		5			8	9	10[1]	11				7[2]	13	12	4				1		3[3]	6	45
1	2	3[2]		5			8	9	10[2]	11[1]			13	7	14	12	4							6	46

FA Cup
First Round   Chesterfield   (a)   3-1
Second Round   Notts Co   (h)   1-2

Carling Cup
First Round   Millwall   (a)   0-4

J Paint Trophy
First Round   Yeovil T   (h)   2-1
Second Round   Northampton T   (a)   1-2

BRADFORD CITY FL Championship 2

FOUNDATION

Bradford was a rugby stronghold around the turn of the century but after Manningham RFC held an archery contest to help them out of financial difficulties in 1903, they were persuaded to give up the handling code and turn to soccer. So they formed Bradford City and continued at Valley Parade. Recognising this as an opportunity of spreading the dribbling code in this part of Yorkshire, the Football League immediately accepted the new club's first application for membership of the Second Division.

Coral Window Stadium, Valley Parade, Bradford, West Yorkshire BD8 7DY.

Telephone: (01274) 773 355.

Fax: (01274) 773 356.

Ticket Office: (01274) 770 012.

Website: www.bradfordcityfc.co.uk

Email: bradfordcityfc@compuserve.com

Ground Capacity: 25,136.

Record Attendance: 39,146 v Burnley, FA Cup 4th rd, 11 March 1911.

Pitch Measurements: 113yd × 70yd.

Joint Chairmen: Julian Rhodes and Mark Lawn.

Director of Operations: David Baldwin.

Football Club Secretary: Kath Brown.

Manager: Peter Taylor.

Assistant Manager: Wayne Jacobs.

Physio: Damian Buck.

Colours: Claret and amber striped shirts with claret sleeves, black shorts, black stockings.

Change Colours: All white with black trimmed sleeves.

Year Formed: 1903.

Turned Professional: 1903.

Ltd Co.: 1908.

Club Nickname: 'The Bantams'.

Ground: 1903, Valley Parade.

First Football League Game: 1 September 1903, Division 2, v Grimsby T (a) L 0–2 – Seymour; Wilson, Halliday; Robinson, Millar, Farnall; Guy, Beckram, Forrest, McMillan, Graham.

Record League Victory: 11–1 v Rotherham U, Division 3 (N), 25 August 1928 – Sherlaw; Russell, Watson; Burkinshaw (1), Summers, Bauld; Harvey (2), Edmunds (3), White (3), Cairns, Scriven (2).

Record Cup Victory: 11–3 v Walker Celtic, FA Cup 1st rd (replay), 1 December 1937 – Parker; Rookes, McDermott; Murphy, Mackie, Moore; Bagley (1), Whittingham (1), Deakin (4 incl. 1p), Cooke (1), Bartholomew (4).

HONOURS

Football League: Division 1 – Runners-up 1998–99; Division 2 – Champions 1907–08; Division 3 – Champions 1984–85; Division 3 (N) – Champions 1928–29; Division 4 – Runners-up 1981–82.

FA Cup: Winners 1911.

Football League Cup: best season: 5th rd, 1965, 1989.

European Competitions: *Intertoto Cup:* 2000.

sky SPORTS FACT FILE

In 1906 Jimmy Roberts just beat Jimmy Conlin to become the first full international for Bradford City by five days. Full-back Roberts played for Wales against Ireland, while outside-left Conlin turned out for England against Scotland.

Record Defeat: 1–9 v Colchester U, Division 4, 30 December 1961.

Most League Points (2 for a win): 63, Division 3 (N), 1928–29.

Most League Points (3 for a win): 94, Division 3, 1984–85.

Most League Goals: 128, Division 3 (N), 1928–29.

Highest League Scorer in Season: David Layne, 34, Division 4, 1961–62.

Most League Goals in Total Aggregate: Bobby Campbell, 121, 1981–84, 1984–86.

Most League Goals in One Match: 7, Albert Whitehurst v Tranmere R, Division 3 (N), 6 March 1929.

Most Capped Player: Jamie Lawrence, (24), Jamaica.

Most League Appearances: Cec Podd, 502, 1970–84.

Youngest League Player: Robert Cullingford, 16 years 141 days v Mansfield T, 22 April 1970.

Record Transfer Fee Received: £2,000,000 from Newcastle U for Des Hamilton, March 1997 and £2,000,000 from Newcastle U for Andrew O'Brien, March 2001.

Record Transfer Fee Paid: £2,500,000 to Leeds U for David Hopkins, July 2000.

Football League Record: 1903 Elected to Division 2; 1908–22 Division 1; 1922–27 Division 2; 1927–29 Division 3 (N); 1929–37 Division 2; 1937–61 Division 3; 1961–69 Division 4; 1969–72 Division 3; 1972–77 Division 4; 1977–78 Division 3; 1978–82 Division 4; 1982–85 Division 3; 1985–90 Division 2; 1990–92 Division 3; 1992–96 Division 2; 1996–99 Division 1; 1999–2001 FA Premier League; 2001–04 Division 1; 2004–07 FL 1; 2007– FL 2.

LATEST SEQUENCES

Longest Sequence of League Wins: 10, 26.11.1983 – 3.2.1984.

Longest Sequence of League Defeats: 8, 21.1.1933 – 11.3.1933.

Longest Sequence of League Draws: 6, 30.1.1976 – 13.3.1976.

Longest Sequence of Unbeaten League Matches: 21, 11.1.1969 – 2.5.1969.

Longest Sequence Without a League Win: 16, 28.8.1948 – 20.11.1948.

Successive Scoring Runs: 30 from 26.12.1961.

Successive Non-scoring Runs: 7 from 18.4.1925.

MANAGERS

Robert Campbell 1903–05
Peter O'Rourke 1905–21
David Menzies 1921–26
Colin Veitch 1926–28
Peter O'Rourke 1928–30
Jack Peart 1930–35
Dick Ray 1935–37
Fred Westgarth 1938–43
Bob Sharp 1943–46
Jack Barker 1946–47
John Milburn 1947–48
David Steele 1948–52
Albert Harris 1952
Ivor Powell 1952–55
Peter Jackson 1955–61
Bob Brocklebank 1961–64
Bill Harris 1965–66
Willie Watson 1966–69
Grenville Hair 1967–68
Jimmy Wheeler 1968–71
Bryan Edwards 1971–75
Bobby Kennedy 1975–78
John Napier 1978
George Mulhall 1978–81
Roy McFarland 1981–82
Trevor Cherry 1982–87
Terry Dolan 1987–89
Terry Yorath 1989–90
John Docherty 1990–91
Frank Stapleton 1991–94
Lennie Lawrence 1994–95
Chris Kamara 1995–98
Paul Jewell 1998–2000
Chris Hutchings 2000
Jim Jefferies 2000–01
Nicky Law 2002–03
Bryan Robson 2003–04
Colin Todd 2004–07
Stuart McCall 2007–10
Peter Taylor February 2010

TEN YEAR LEAGUE RECORD

		P	W	D	L	F	A	Pts	Pos
2000-01	PR Lge	38	5	11	22	30	70	26	20
2001-02	Div 1	46	15	10	21	69	76	55	15
2002-03	Div 1	46	14	10	22	51	73	52	19
2003-04	Div 1	46	10	6	30	38	69	36	23
2004-05	FL 1	46	17	14	15	64	62	65	11
2005-06	FL 1	46	14	19	13	51	49	61	11
2006-07	FL 1	46	11	14	21	47	65	47	22
2007-08	FL 2	46	17	11	18	63	61	62	10
2008-09	FL 2	46	18	13	15	66	55	67	9
2009-10	FL 2	46	16	14	16	59	62	62	14

DID YOU KNOW ?

In 1928–29 when Bradford City won the championship of Division Three (North), Albert Whitehurst only appeared in the last third of the season but managed to score 24 goals in just 15 League games including one spell of finding the net in six successive matches.

BRADFORD CITY 2009–10 LEAGUE RECORD

Match No.	Date	Venue	Opponents	Result	H/T Score	Lg Pos.	Goalscorers	Attendance
1	Aug 8	A	Notts Co	L	0-5	0-3	—	9396
2	15	H	Port Vale	D	0-0	0-0	22	11,333
3	18	H	Lincoln C	L	0-2	0-0	—	11,242
4	22	A	Cheltenham T	W	5-4	3-3	19	O'Brien J [2], Evans G [7], Townsend (og) [71], Hanson [20], Williams [50]	3073
5	29	H	Torquay U	W	2-0	1-0	14	Hanson [45], Brandon [90]	11,123
6	Sept 5	A	Shrewsbury T	W	2-1	2-0	9	Evans G [16], Flynn [35]	5525
7	12	H	Burton Alb	D	1-1	1-0	12	Evans G [24]	11,439
8	19	A	Barnet	D	2-2	1-0	11	Hanson [14], Rehman [70]	2282
9	26	H	Chesterfield	W	3-0	1-0	9	Flynn [23], Neilson [55], Brandon [86]	11,664
10	29	A	Morecambe	D	0-0	0-0	—		3116
11	Oct 3	A	Northampton T	D	2-2	0-0	9	Ramsden [50], Boulding M [54]	4391
12	10	H	Crewe Alex	L	2-3	1-2	11	Boulding M [44], Hanson [69]	11,757
13	17	A	Dagenham & R	L	1-2	1-1	13	Flynn [18]	2446
14	24	H	Hereford U	W	1-0	1-0	12	Evans G [41]	11,107
15	31	A	Macclesfield T	D	2-2	0-2	12	Hanson [58], Williams [66]	2526
16	Nov 14	H	Bournemouth	D	1-1	1-1	12	Evans G [42]	11,732
17	21	H	Accrington S	D	1-1	1-0	12	Edwards (og) [21]	11,176
18	24	A	Grimsby T	W	3-0	1-0	—	Whaley [24], Williams [60], Hanson [82]	3646
19	Dec 1	H	Rochdale	L	0-3	0-2	—		11,472
20	5	A	Darlington	W	1-0	1-0	11	Williams [23]	2744
21	12	H	Rotherham U	L	2-4	1-2	14	Bullock [19], Flynn [46]	11,578
22	28	H	Shrewsbury T	L	1-3	1-2	15	Hanson [20]	11,522
23	Jan 2	H	Cheltenham T	D	1-1	1-0	—	O'Brien J [35]	10,831
24	19	A	Bury	L	1-2	1-2	—	Sodje (og) [23]	2930
25	23	A	Lincoln C	L	1-2	0-2	16	Boulding M [62]	3803
26	30	A	Torquay U	W	2-1	0-1	16	Evans G 2 [82, 90]	2592
27	Feb 6	H	Bury	L	0-1	0-0	16		11,965
28	13	H	Grimsby T	D	0-0	0-0	16		11,321
29	20	A	Accrington S	L	0-2	0-0	18		3396
30	23	A	Rochdale	W	3-1	1-1	—	Clarke [10], Threlfall [80], Evans G [87]	3055
31	27	H	Darlington	W	1-0	1-0	16	Hanson [26]	11,532
32	Mar 2	A	Aldershot T	L	0-1	0-0	—		2311
33	6	A	Rotherham U	W	2-1	0-0	16	Flynn [60], Hanson [90]	4185
34	9	A	Port Vale	L	1-2	1-0	—	Threlfall [12]	3728
35	13	H	Aldershot T	W	2-1	2-1	16	Hanson [14], Daley [22]	11,272
36	20	A	Hereford U	L	0-2	0-1	16		1926
37	23	H	Notts Co	D	0-0	0-0	—		11,630
38	27	H	Dagenham & R	D	3-3	1-0	16	Hanson 2 [2, 67], Kendall [82]	11,064
39	Apr 3	A	Bournemouth	L	0-1	0-1	16		6239
40	5	H	Macclesfield T	L	1-2	0-1	17	Oliver [47]	11,395
41	10	A	Burton Alb	D	1-1	0-0	18	Oliver [59]	2648
42	13	H	Morecambe	W	2-0	0-0	—	Rehman [69], Bolder [90]	11,027
43	17	A	Barnet	W	2-1	0-1	14	O'Brien L [79], Flynn [90]	11,138
44	24	A	Chesterfield	D	1-1	0-0	14	Evans G [75]	4109
45	May 1	H	Northampton T	W	2-0	1-0	15	Evans G 2 [12, 81]	12,403
46	8	A	Crewe Alex	W	1-0	0-0	14	Kendall [67]	5172

Final League Position: 14

GOALSCORERS

League (59): Hanson 12, Evans G 11, Flynn 6, Williams 4, Boulding M 3, Brandon 2, Kendall 2, O'Brien J 2, Oliver 2, Rehman 2, Threlfall 2, Bolder 1, Bullock 1, Clarke 1, Daley 1, Neilson 1, O'Brien L 1, Ramsden 1, Whaley 1, own goals 3.

Carling Cup (0).

FA Cup (1): Boulding M 1.

J Paint Trophy (6): Flynn 2, Boulding M 1, Brandon 1, Hanson 1, Neilson 1.

Eastwood S 22	Ramsden S 30+1	O'Brien L 39+4	Flynn M 41+1	Rehman Z 36+2	Clarke M 20+1	Brandon C 14+6	Bullock L 41	Boulding M 9+12	Thorne P 4+3	Colbeck J 3+2	Williams S 36+3	Evans G 38+5	Hanson J 33+1	O'Brien J 15+8	Neilson S 18+5	Osborne L 5+7	Bateson J 14+7	Sharry L —+1	Boulding R —+2	Whaley S 5+1	Daley O 6+8	McLaughlin J 7	Horne L —+1	Glennon M 17	Threlfall R 17	McCammon M 2+2	Grant G 7+4	Bolder A 14	Oliver L 7	Kendall R 2+4	Harrison R —+1	Dean L —+1	Match No.
1	2	3	4	5	6¹	7²	8	9	10	11³	12	13	14																				1
1	2	3	8	5		7³		9¹	10	14	6	12	11	4²	13																		2
1	2	3	8	5		7²	4¹	13	10³	12	6	9	11	14																			3
1	2	3	8	5			4			7	6	9	11	10																			4
1	2	3	8	5		12	4			7²	6	9	11	10¹	13																		5
1	2	3	8	5			4				6	9	11	10²	7¹	12	13																6
1	2	3	8	5		11¹	4	13			6	9	10		7²	12																	7
1	2¹	3	8	5			4				6	9	10	11	7		12																8
1		3	8³	5		12	4	13			6	9²	10	11¹	7	2	14																9
1		3	8	5			4				6	9⁴	10	11	7	2																	10
1	10	3	8	5		12	4	9			6			11¹	7	2																	11
1	2	6	8	5		7¹	4	9			3		10	11²	12	13																	12
1	2	3	4	5	14	12	8				6³	9	10	11¹	7²	13																	13
1		3	4	5		7¹	6⁴				11	9	10	12	8	2																	14
1		3	4	5		8¹		12			6	9	10	11	7	2																	15
1		3	4	6	5	10	8				7	9¹		11		2	12																16
1	2	3	4	5		7²	8	13			6	9	10	11¹			12																17
1	2	3	4	5			8				6	9	10	11		7																	18
1	2	3	4	5¹			8	14			6	9³	10	11²	13	12	7																19
1	2	3	4		5		8	9¹			6	12	10	13²	11		7²																20
1	5	3	4		6	13	8	9¹				12	10	14	11³	2	7⁸																21
1		3	4	5⁴			8³					12	9	10	14	11¹	2	7³	13														22
	2	3	4	5		7²	8				6⁸	9	10	14¹									13	1	12								23
	2	3	4	5	6	7²		10				9¹			8					11	13		12	1									24
	2	3	4	5¹	6	7	8	12			13	9³		14		10²				11				1									25
	2	3	4	13	5	7²	8	9	14		6¹	12		10³						11				1									26
	2	3	4	5	6		8²	9	12		11	10	13			7¹								1									27
	2	3	4	5	6	14	8	12	9¹		11²	10				7³	13							1									28
	2	3	4	5³	6	7¹	8	12	14			9	10	11²	13									1									29
	2	3	4	13	6		8	12			7	9	10	11¹										1		5²							30
	2	3²	4		6		8	12			7	9	11				13							1	5	10¹							31
	2	3¹	4		6		8				7	9³	11	13			12							1	5	10²	14						32
	2	3	4		6		8				7	9	10											1	5	11							33
	2	3¹	4		5		8	14			7	9²	10				12							1	6	13	11³						34
	2¹	3	4		5		8					9					12					7²		1		11	13	10	6				35
			4		6		8²	9³	10							2	12							1	3	13	7¹	11	5	14			36
		3	4	5¹							7	9	10				12							1	2	11²	8	6	13				37
		3	4²	5							7	9	10	13	14		11¹							1	2³		8	6	12				38
		3¹		5			4				7	9	10¹		13	14								1	2	12	8	6	11²				39
		3¹		5			4³				7	9		11	13									1	2	12	8	6	10²	14			40
		13		5			4				3	9		11	12		6							1		2	7²	8	10				41
				5			4				3	9		11¹		10	6							1		2	7	8		12			42
	13	12		5			4				3	9		11¹		10	6							1		2	7²	8					43
	13	11		5	6		4				3	9		10¹									12	1		2	7²	8					44
12		11		5¹	6		4				3	9		10										1		2	7	8					45
	2	13	8	5			4				3	9¹		14	10									1		6	7³	11²		12			46

FA Cup
First Round — Notts Co — (a) 1-2

Carling Cup
First Round — Nottingham F — (a) 0-3

J Paint Trophy
First Round — Rochdale — (a) 2-1
Second Round — Notts Co — (h) 2-2
Northern Quarter-Final — Port Vale — (h) 2-2
Northern Semi-Final — Carlisle U — (a) 0-3

BRENTFORD   FL Championship 1

FOUNDATION

Formed as a small amateur concern in 1889 they were very
successful in local circles. They won the championship of the West
London Alliance in 1893 and a year later the West Middlesex
Junior Cup before carrying off the Senior Cup in 1895. After
winning both the London Senior Amateur Cup and the Middlesex
Senior Cup in 1898 they were admitted to the Second Division of
the Southern League.

*Griffin Park, Braemar Road, Brentford, Middlesex
TW8 0NT.*

Telephone: 0845 3456 442.

Fax: (0208) 568 9940.

Ticket Office: 0845 3456 442.

Website: www.brentfordfc.co.uk

E-mail: enquiries@brentfordfc.co.uk

Ground Capacity: 12,400.

Record Attendance: 38,678 v Leicester C, FA Cup 6th rd,
26 February 1949.

Pitch Measurements: 111yd × 74yd.

Chairman: Greg Dyke.

Chief Executive Officer: Andrew Mills.

Secretary: Lisa Hall.

Manager: Andy Scott.

Assistant Manager: Terry Bullivant.

Physio: George Cooper.

HONOURS

Football League: Division 1 best
season: 5th, 1935–36; Division 2 –
Champions 1934–35; Division 3 –
Champions 1991–92, 1998–99;
Division 3 (S) – Champions 1932–33,
Runners-up 1929–30, 1957–58;
Division 4 – Champions 1962–63;
FL 2 – Champions 2008–09.

FA Cup: best season: 6th rd, 1938,
1946, 1949, 1989.

Football League Cup: best season:
4th rd, 1983.

Freight Rover Trophy: Runners-up
1985.

LDV Vans Trophy: Runners-up 2001.

Colours: White shirts with red sleeves and black trim underneath, four separated red vertical stripes
on body, black shorts, black stockings.

Change Colours: Black shirts with gold trim, black shorts with gold trim, black stockings.

Year Formed: 1889.

Turned Professional: 1899.

Ltd Co.: 1901.

Club Nickname: 'The Bees'.

Grounds: 1889, Clifden Road; 1891, Benns Fields, Little Ealing; 1895, Shotters Field; 1898, Cross
Road, S. Ealing; 1900, Boston Park; 1904, Griffin Park.

First Football League Game: 28 August 1920, Division 3, v Exeter C (a) L 0–3 – Young; Hodson,
Rosier, Elliott J, Levitt, Amos, Smith, Thompson, Spreadbury, Morley, Henery.

Record League Victory: 9–0 v Wrexham, Division 3, 15 October 1963 – Cakebread; Coote, Jones;
Slater, Scott, Higginson; Summers (1), Brooks (2), McAdams (2), Ward (2), Hales (1), (1 og).

Record Cup Victory: 7–0 v Windsor & Eton (away), FA Cup 1st rd, 20 November 1982 – Roche;
Rowe, Harris (Booker), McNichol (1), Whitehead, Hurlock (2), Kamara, Joseph (1), Mahoney (3),
Bowles, Roberts. *N.B.* 8–0 v Uxbridge, FA Cup, 3rd Qual rd, 31 October 1903.

sky SPORTS FACT FILE

Wally Bragg was a 17-year-old winger when he made his
First Division debut for Brentford against Grimsby
Town on 29 March 1947. But he became a centre-half
and was still making first team appearances as a right-
back with the club ten years later.

Record Defeat: 0–7 v Swansea T, Division 3 (S), 8 November 1924; v Walsall, Division 3 (S), 19 January 1957; v Peterborough U, 24 November 2007.

Most League Points (2 for a win): 62, Division 3 (S), 1932–33 and Division 4, 1962–63.

Most League Points (3 for a win): 85, Division 2, 1994–95, Division 3, 1998–99 and FL 2, 2008–09.

Most League Goals: 98, Division 4, 1962–63.

Highest League Scorer in Season: Jack Holliday, 38, Division 3 (S), 1932–33.

Most League Goals in Total Aggregate: Jim Towers, 153, 1954–61.

Most League Goals in One Match: 5, Jack Holliday v Luton T, Division 3 (S), 28 January 1933; 5, Billy Scott v Barnsley, Division 2, 15 December 1934; 5, Peter McKennan v Bury, Division 2, 18 February 1949.

Most Capped Player: John Buttigieg, 22 (98), Malta.

Most League Appearances: Ken Coote, 514, 1949–64.

Youngest League Player: Danis Salman, 15 years 248 days v Watford, 15 November 1975.

Record Transfer Fee Received: £2,500,000 from Wimbledon for Hermann Hreidarsson, October 1999.

Record Transfer Fee Paid: £750,000 to Crystal Palace for Hermann Hreidarsson, September 1998.

Football League Record: 1920 Original Member of Division 3; 1921–33 Division 3 (S); 1933–35 Division 2; 1935–47 Division 1; 1947–54 Division 2; 1954–62 Division 3 (S); 1962–63 Division 4; 1963–66 Division 3; 1966–72 Division 4; 1972–73 Division 3; 1973–78 Division 4; 1978–92 Division 3; 1992–93 Division 1; 1993–98 Division 2; 1998–99 Division 3; 1999–04 Division 2; 2004–07 FL 1; 2007–09 FL 2; 2009– FL 1.

LATEST SEQUENCES

Longest Sequence of League Wins: 9, 30.4.1932 – 24.9.1932.

Longest Sequence of League Defeats: 9, 20.10.1928 – 25.12.1928.

Longest Sequence of League Draws: 5, 16.3.1957 – 6.4.1957.

Longest Sequence of Unbeaten League Matches: 26, 20.2.1999 – 16.10.1999.

Longest Sequence Without a League Win: 18, 9.9.2006 – 26.12.2006.

Successive Scoring Runs: 26 from 4.3.1963.

Successive Non-scoring Runs: 7 from 7.3.2000.

MANAGERS

Will Lewis 1900–03
(Secretary-Manager)
Dick Molyneux 1902–06
W. G. Brown 1906–08
Fred Halliday 1908–12, 1915–21, 1924–26
(only Secretary to 1922)
Ephraim Rhodes 1912–15
Archie Mitchell 1921–24
Harry Curtis 1926–49
Jackie Gibbons 1949–52
Jimmy Bain 1952–53
Tommy Lawton 1953
Bill Dodgin Snr 1953–57
Malcolm Macdonald 1957–65
Tommy Cavanagh 1965–66
Billy Gray 1966–67
Jimmy Sirrel 1967–69
Frank Blunstone 1969–73
Mike Everitt 1973–75
John Docherty 1975–76
Bill Dodgin Jnr 1976–80
Fred Callaghan 1980–84
Frank McLintock 1984–87
Steve Perryman 1987–90
Phil Holder 1990–93
David Webb 1993–97
Eddie May 1997
Micky Adams 1997–98
Ron Noades 1998–2000
Ray Lewington 2001
Steve Coppell 2001–02
Wally Downes 2002–04
Martin Allen 2004–06
Leroy Rosenior 2006
Scott Fitzgerald 2006–07
Terry Butcher 2007
Andy Scott December 2007–

TEN YEAR LEAGUE RECORD

		P	W	D	L	F	A	Pts	Pos
2000-01	Div 2	46	14	17	15	56	70	59	14
2001-02	Div 2	46	24	11	11	77	43	83	3
2002-03	Div 2	46	14	12	20	47	56	54	16
2003-04	Div 2	46	14	11	21	52	69	53	17
2004-05	FL 1	46	22	9	15	57	60	75	4
2005-06	FL 1	46	20	16	10	72	52	76	3
2006-07	FL 1	46	8	13	25	40	79	37	24
2007-08	FL 2	46	17	8	21	52	70	59	14
2008-09	FL 2	46	23	16	7	65	36	85	1
2009-10	FL 1	46	14	20	12	55	52	62	9

DID YOU KNOW ?

Left-winger Jose Gallego was the first player from Spain to play in the First Division. His family were Basque refugees who fled the country in 1939 after the Civil War. He was signed by Brentford from Abbey United (now Cambridge United) in 1946.

BRENTFORD 2009–10 LEAGUE RECORD

Match No.	Date	Venue	Opponents	Result	H/T Score	Lg Pos.	Goalscorers	Attendance
1	Aug 8	A	Carlisle U	W 3-1	1-1	—	Weston 2 [12, 47], Wood [64]	6367
2	15	H	Brighton & HA	D 0-0	0-0	—		6950
3	18	H	Norwich C	W 2-1	0-0	—	Dickson [51], Hunt [71]	7395
4	22	A	Southampton	D 1-1	0-0	—	Taylor [83]	19,169
5	29	H	Oldham Ath	D 1-1	1-0	—	O'Connor (pen) [43]	5125
6	Sept 5	A	Charlton Ath	L 0-2	0-2	—		16,399
7	12	A	Huddersfield T	D 0-0	0-0	9		12,020
8	19	H	Bristol R	L 1-3	0-3	11	MacDonald [58]	6528
9	26	A	Yeovil T	L 0-2	0-1	15		4249
10	29	H	Southend U	W 2-1	0-1	—	O'Connor 2 (2 pens) [69, 90]	5578
11	Oct 3	H	Swindon T	L 2-3	0-2	14	Cort [77], MacDonald [82]	6471
12	9	A	Hartlepool U	D 0-0	0-0	—		3105
13	17	A	Leyton Orient	L 1-2	1-1	17	Cort [4]	4781
14	24	H	Stockport Co	W 2-0	1-0	15	MacDonald [45], Weston [70]	5045
15	31	A	Exeter C	L 0-3	0-2	16		5355
16	Nov 14	H	Millwall	D 2-2	2-1	16	Bostock 2 [9, 25]	6408
17	21	H	Walsall	D 1-1	1-0	16	Strevens [11]	4492
18	24	A	Wycombe W	L 0-1	0-0	—		5181
19	Dec 1	H	Colchester U	W 1-0	1-0	—	MacDonald [15]	4200
20	5	A	Tranmere R	L 0-1	0-0	18		4839
21	12	H	Leeds U	D 0-0	0-0	17		9031
22	19	A	Milton Keynes D	W 1-0	0-0	14	MacDonald [67]	9520
23	26	A	Gillingham	W 1-0	1-0	11	Strevens [42]	7019
24	28	H	Charlton Ath	D 1-1	0-0	11	Cort [49]	8387
25	Jan 16	H	Carlisle U	W 3-1	1-0	10	Weston 2 [31, 55], Dickson [90]	5089
26	23	A	Norwich C	L 0-1	0-0	10		24,979
27	26	A	Southampton	D 1-1	0-1	—	Legge [83]	6501
28	Feb 6	H	Gillingham	W 4-0	3-0	10	MacDonald 2 (2 pens) [10, 33], Weston 2 [35, 79]	6036
29	13	H	Wycombe W	D 1-1	0-1	10	Weston [75]	5740
30	20	A	Walsall	L 1-2	1-1	11	MacDonald [17]	3616
31	Mar 6	H	Leeds U	D 1-1	0-0	14	Strevens [60]	25,445
32	13	H	Milton Keynes D	D 3-3	1-1	15	Wood [27], Strevens [70], Cort [90]	5209
33	16	A	Brighton & HA	L 0-3	0-1	—		5539
34	20	A	Stockport Co	W 1-0	0-0	15	MacDonald [46]	3707
35	23	A	Colchester U	D 3-3	2-2	—	Hunt [13], Legge [17], MacDonald [57]	3915
36	27	H	Leyton Orient	W 1-0	1-0	12	Grabban [43]	6369
37	30	A	Oldham Ath	W 3-2	1-1	—	MacDonald 2 [30, 69], Balkestein [64]	2833
38	Apr 2	A	Millwall	D 1-1	1-0	—	Cort [32]	14,025
39	5	H	Exeter C	D 0-0	0-0	11		6017
40	10	H	Huddersfield T	W 3-0	0-0	9	MacDonald 2 (1 pen) [71 (p), 84], Grabban [82]	5209
41	13	A	Southend U	D 2-2	1-0	—	MacDonald [21], Cort [62]	6838
42	17	A	Bristol R	D 0-0	0-0	11		6048
43	20	A	Tranmere R	W 2-1	0-0	—	O'Connor [49], Strevens [86]	4341
44	24	H	Yeovil T	D 1-1	0-1	10	Saunders [76]	5395
45	May 1	A	Swindon T	L 2-3	1-2	10	Hunt [33], Strevens [60]	10,465
46	8	H	Hartlepool U	D 0-0	0-0	9		6893

Final League Position: 9

GOALSCORERS

League (55): MacDonald 15 (3 pens), Weston 8, Cort 6, Strevens 6, O'Connor 4 (3 pens), Hunt 3, Bostock 2, Dickson 2, Grabban 2, Legge 2, Wood 2, Balkestein 1, Saunders 1, Taylor 1.
Carling Cup (0).
FA Cup (8): MacDonald 2, Weston 2, Cort 1, Legge 1, O'Connor 1, Strevens 1.
J Paint Trophy (0).

Price L 13	Foster D 32 + 4	Dickson R 26 + 1	O'Connor K 43	Phillips M 19 + 3	Bennett A 11 + 2	Saunders S 15 + 11	Hunt D 18 + 6	Cort C 16 + 12	Wood S 37 + 6	Weston M 32 + 8	Osborne K 13 + 6	Kabba S 3 + 7	Taylor C 8 + 4	Bean M 25 + 6	Wilson J 13	MacDonald C 39 + 1	Bull N 5 + 1	Legge L 28 + 1	Bostock J 9	Strevens B 20 + 5	Szczesny W 28	Balkestein P 14	Murphy R 1 + 4	Smith T 8	Diagouraga T 20	Akinde J 2	Ainsworth L 1 + 8	Grabban L 7	Blake R — + 1	Moore S — + 1	Match No.
1	2	3	4	5	6	7	8^1	9	10	11^2	12	13																			1
1	2	3	4	5	6	7^1	8^2	9	10^3	11		14	12	13																	2
1	2	3	4	5	6^1	7^3	8	9	10	11^2	12	13	14																		3
1	2	3	4	5		7^2	8	9	10	11^1		13	12			6															4
1	2		4	5		7	8	9	10	11^1			12		3	6															5
1	2^1		4	5		7	8	9	10	11			12		3^2	6	13														6
1			4	5	6	12	8^2	7	11						9^1	3	13	2	10												7
1			4	5	6	13	8^2	7	11^1						9	3	12	2	10												8
13			4	5	6	11^2		7	12						9^1	3^3	8	2	10	1	14										9
3			4	5	6	11			7^1	9			12			8	2	10	1												10
		3	4	5	6	11		9	7^1	12						8	2	10	1												11
	2	3	4	5^1	6	7		9	11^2	13	12					8		10	1												12
	2	3	4	5	6			9	11^1	12					7	8		10	1												13
1	2	3	4	5		13	8	9	11^1	12					7^2		6	10													14
1	2	3	4	5^1		13		9	11^3	14	12				7^2	8	6	10													15
1	2^1	3	4		6					11				12	8	5	10			7	9										16
		3	4							12	11	2	13		8	5	10^2		7	9	1	6									17
	2		4					14	11					5	13	8	3^6		7^3	9	1	6	12^2								18
	2	3	4				14	13	11						8^2	10^1		5	7^3	9	1	6	12								19
	2	3	4				14	13	11^2						8^3	10^1		5	7	9^1	1	6	12								20
	2	3	4				12	11	13						8	10^1		5	7^2	9^1	1	6									21
	2	3^2	4				11	13	12						8	10		5	7^1	9	1	6									22
1	2		4			13	12	7^1		3	11				8	10^8		5^2		9^3		6	14								23
1	2	3	4			14		12	11^2	13					8			5	7^3	9		6	10^1								24
	2	3	4				12	11		13					8	10		6	7^1	9	1			5							25
	2	3	6				12	9	11						8	10		5		1					7	4^1					26
	2	3	4			13		12	7^1	11					8	10		5	9^2	1		6									27
	2	3	4			7^1		13		11					10^2			5	14	1					6	8	9^3	12			28
	2	3^2	8			7^1		14	13	11					10			5		1					6	4	9^3	12			29
	2		8	6		7^1		13		11					10			5^2	9	1					3	4	12				30
14	3	8	5^3			12		7	11^2				13		10			2	9^1	1					6	4					31
	3	4	5			12		7	11						10			2	9^1	1					8	6					32
	2	3	8	6¹	12^8			14		7^2	11				10			5	9^3						4	13					33
	2	3^2	8			13				7	11	6		12	10			5	9						4^1						34
		4						2	12	7	11	3		8	10			5	9						6						35
		4				7^1	13		3	11				8	10			5	12		2				6		9^2				36
13		4				14	3		7^2	11				8^1	10			5	12		2				6		9^3				37
	3^1	7^2				13	9	12	11	4				8	10^3			5			2				6	14					38
		3				7	11^2	4						8	10			5	13		2				6	12	9^1				39
4			12			7	3	11	2					8	10			5	1						6	9^1					40
13			12	3		7	11	6^2					8^1	10	15	5		1^6	2						4	9					41
	2	8	3			7	11^1	6						10	5			1	4						12	9					42
	2	3				7^1	8	11	4					10	5			12	1						6	13	9^2				43
		11	13	8^2	3		4	2						10	5			9	1						6	7^1	12				44
	2	8	13			7	11^2	5						12	10			6	9	1		3^1				4					45
	2	13	4	12		3^2		7	11	5					10			6^1	9	1^6					8			15			46

FA Cup

First Round	Gateshead	(a)	2-2
		(h)	5-2
Second Round	Walsall	(h)	1-0
Third Round	Doncaster R	(h)	0-1

Carling Cup

First Round	Bristol C	(h)	0-1

J Paint Trophy

First Round	Norwich C	(a)	0-1

BRIGHTON & HOVE ALBION FL Championship 1

FOUNDATION

A professional club Brighton United was formed in November 1897 at the Imperial Hotel, Queen's Road, but folded in March 1900 after less than two seasons in the Southern League at the County Ground. An amateur team Brighton & Hove Rangers was then formed by some prominent United supporters and after one season at Withdean, decided to turn semi-professional and play at the County Ground. Rangers were accepted into the Southern League but then also folded June 1901. John Jackson the former United manager organised a meeting at the Seven Stars public house, Ship Street on 24 June 1901 at which a new third club Brighton & Hove United was formed. They took over Rangers' place in the Southern League and pitch at County Ground. The name was changed to Brighton & Hove Albion before a match was played because of objections by Hove FC.

Withdean Stadium, Tongdean Lane, Brighton, East Sussex BN1 5JD.
Telephone: (01273) 695 400 (admin office 44 North Road, Brighton).
Fax: (01273) 648 179 (admin office 44 North Road, Brighton).
Ticket Office: (0845) 496 1901 (128 Queen's Road).
Website: www.seagulls.co.uk
Email: seagulls@bhafc.co.uk
Ground Capacity: 8,850.
Record Attendance: 36,747 v Fulham, Division 2, 27 December 1958 (at Goldstone Ground).
Pitch Measurements: 110yd × 70yd.
Chairman: Tony Bloom.
Managing Director: Ken Brown.
Chief Executive: Martin Perry.
Secretary: Derek J. Allan.
Manager: Gus Poyet.
Assistant Manager: Mauricio Taricco. *Physio:* Jim Joyce.
Colours: Blue and white striped shirts, white sleeves with blue trim, white shorts, white stockings.
Change Colours: Yellow and navy blue striped shirts with blue sleeves, navy blue shorts, navy blue stockings.
Year Formed: 1901. *Turned Professional:* 1901. *Ltd Co.:* 1904.
Grounds: 1901, County Ground; 1902, Goldstone Ground; 1997, groundshare at Gillingham FC; 1999, Whithdean Stadium.
Club Nickname: 'The Seagulls'.
First Football League Game: 28 August 1920, Division 3, v Southend U (a) L 0–2 – Hayes; Woodhouse, Little; Hall, Comber, Bentley; Longstaff, Ritchie, Doran, Rodgerson, March.

HONOURS

Football League: Division 1 best season: 13th, 1981–82; Division 2 – Champions 2001–02; Runners-up 1978–79; Division 3 (S) – Champions 1957–58; Runners-up 1953–54, 1955–56; Division 3 – Champions 2000–01; Runners-up 1971–72, 1976–77, 1987–88; Division 4 – Champions 1964–65.

FA Cup: Runners-up 1983.

Football League Cup: best season: 5th rd, 1979.

sky SPORTS FACT FILE

On 5 December 2009 Brighton & Hove Albion gave a debut in goal to Peter Brezovan after a week's trial. He was only told of his selection the previous day. He not only kept a clean sheet but saved a penalty at Exeter City but Albion won with a last-minute goal.

Record League Victory: 9–1 v Newport Co, Division 3 (S), 18 April 1951 – Ball; Tennant (1p), Mansell (1p); Willard, McCoy, Wilson; Reed, McNichol (4), Garbutt, Bennett (2), Keene (1). 9–1 v Southend U, Division 3, 27 November 1965 – Powney; Magill, Baxter; Leck, Gall, Turner; Gould (1), Collins (1), Livesey (2), Smith (3), Goodchild (2).

Record Cup Victory: 10–1 v Wisbech, FA Cup 1st rd, 13 November 1965 – Powney; Magill, Baxter; Collins (1), Gall, Turner; Gould, Smith (2), Livesey (3), Cassidy (2), Goodchild (1), (1 og).

Record Defeat: 0–9 v Middlesbrough, Division 2, 23 August 1958.

Most League Points (2 for a win): 65, Division 3 (S), 1955–56 and Division 3, 1971–72.

Most League Points (3 for a win): 92, Division 3, 2000–01.

Most League Goals: 112, Division 3 (S), 1955–56.

Highest League Scorer in Season: Peter Ward, 32, Division 3, 1976–77.

Most League Goals in Total Aggregate: Tommy Cook, 114, 1922–29.

Most League Goals in One Match: 5, Jack Doran v Northampton T, Division 3 (S), 5 November 1921; 5, Adrian Thorne v Watford, Division 3 (S), 30 April 1958.

Most Capped Player: Steve Penney, 17, Northern Ireland.

Most League Appearances: 'Tug' Wilson, 509, 1922–36.

Youngest League Player: Ian Chapman, 16 years 259 days v Birmingham C, 14 February 1987.

Record Transfer Fee Received: £1,500,000 from Tottenham H for Bobby Zamora, July 2003 and £1,500,000 from Celtic for Adam Virgo, July 2005.

Record Transfer Fee Paid: £500,000 to Manchester U for Andy Ritchie, October 1980.

Football League Record: 1920 Original Member of Division 3; 1921–58 Division 3 (S); 1958–62 Division 2; 1962–63 Division 3; 1963–65 Division 4; 1965–72 Division 3; 1972–73 Division 2; 1973–77 Division 3; 1977–79 Division 2; 1979–83 Division 1; 1983–87 Division 2; 1987–88 Division 3; 1988–96 Division 2; 1996–2001 Division 3; 2001–02 Division 2; 2002–03 Division 1; 2003–04 Division 2; 2004–06 FL C; 2006– FL 1.

MANAGERS

John Jackson 1901–05
Frank Scott-Walford 1905–08
John Robson 1908–14
Charles Webb 1919–47
Tommy Cook 1947
Don Welsh 1947–51
Billy Lane 1951–61
George Curtis 1961–63
Archie Macaulay 1963–68
Fred Goodwin 1968–70
Pat Saward 1970–73
Brian Clough 1973–74
Peter Taylor 1974–76
Alan Mullery 1976–81
Mike Bailey 1981–82
Jimmy Melia 1982–83
Chris Cattlin 1983–86
Alan Mullery 1986–87
Barry Lloyd 1987–93
Liam Brady 1993–95
Jimmy Case 1995–96
Steve Gritt 1996–98
Brian Horton 1998–99
Jeff Wood 1999
Micky Adams 1999–2001
Peter Taylor 2001–02
Martin Hinshelwood 2002
Steve Coppell 2002–03
Mark McGhee 2003–06
Dean Wilkins 2006–08
Micky Adams 2008–09
Russell Slade 2009
Gus Poyet November 2009–

LATEST SEQUENCES

Longest Sequence of League Wins: 9, 2.10.1926 – 20.11.1926.
Longest Sequence of League Defeats: 12, 17.8.2002 – 26.10.2002.
Longest Sequence of League Draws: 6, 16.2.1980 – 15.3.1980.
Longest Sequence of Unbeaten League Matches: 16, 8.10.1930 – 28.1.1931.
Longest Sequence Without a League Win: 15, 21.10.1972 – 27.1.1973
Successive Scoring Runs: 31 from 4.2.1956.
Successive Non-scoring Runs: 6 from 8.11.1924.

TEN YEAR LEAGUE RECORD

		P	W	D	L	F	A	Pts	Pos
2000-01	Div 3	46	28	8	10	73	35	92	1
2001-02	Div 2	46	25	15	6	66	42	90	1
2002-03	Div 1	46	11	12	23	49	67	45	23
2003-04	Div 2	46	22	11	13	64	43	77	4
2004-05	FL C	46	13	12	21	40	65	51	20
2005-06	FL C	46	7	17	22	39	71	38	24
2006-07	FL 1	46	14	11	21	49	58	53	18
2007-08	FL 1	46	19	12	15	58	50	69	7
2008-09	FL 1	46	13	13	20	55	70	52	16
2009-10	FL 1	46	15	14	17	56	60	59	13

DID YOU KNOW ?

On 28 December 2009 Brighton & Hove Albion won 5–2 away to Wycombe Wanderers. Glenn Murray, who was included because of a suspension to another forward, scored four goals. Earlier in the season Brighton had knocked Wycombe out in an FA Cup replay.

BRIGHTON & HOVE ALBION 2009–10 LEAGUE RECORD

Match No.	Date	Venue	Opponents	Result	H/T Score	Lg Pos.	Goalscorers	Attendance
1	Aug 8	H	Walsall	L	0-1	0-1	—		6504
2	15	A	Brentford	D	0-0	0-0	17		6950
3	18	A	Huddersfield T	L	1-7	1-3	—	Dickinson [34]	11,269
4	22	H	Stockport Co	L	2-4	1-1	23	Forster [28], Dickinson [59]	5270
5	28	A	Millwall	D	1-1	0-1	23	Forster [70]	10,138
6	Sept. 5	H	Wycombe W	W	1-0	0-0	21	Forster [75]	5895
7	12	A	Carlisle U	W	2-0	1-0	15	Forster 2 [4, 66]	5368
8	19	H	Southend U	L	2-3	2-2	19	Forster 2 [21, 40]	6287
9	26	A	Bristol R	D	1-1	0-0	21	Tunnicliffe [56]	8098
10	Oct 3	H	Milton Keynes D	L	0-1	0-1	21		6419
11	10	A	Yeovil T	D	2-2	2-1	21	Crofts [6], Dickinson [41]	4412
12	13	H	Gillingham	W	2-0	1-0	—	Bennett [24], Elphick [78]	5960
13	17	A	Tranmere R	L	1-2	0-1	19	Murray (pen) [78]	5250
14	24	H	Oldham Ath	L	0-2	0-0	21		6205
15	31	H	Hartlepool U	D	3-3	2-3	20	Dickinson [27], Forster 2 [39, 48]	5694
16	Nov 15	A	Southampton	W	3-1	2-1	19	Murray 2 [16, 22], Crofts [86]	21,932
17	21	A	Leeds U	L	0-3	0-2	20		7615
18	24	A	Norwich C	L	1-4	0-2	—	Tunnicliffe [61]	24,670
19	Dec 1	H	Charlton Ath	L	0-2	0-2	—		6769
20	5	A	Exeter C	W	1-0	0-0	21	Crofts [90]	5456
21	11	H	Colchester U	L	1-2	1-2	—	Dicker [42]	5898
22	19	A	Swindon T	L	1-2	1-1	21	Forster [38]	7068
23	26	H	Leyton Orient	D	0-0	0-0	21		6690
24	28	A	Wycombe W	W	5-2	1-2	20	Murray 4 [36, 56, 70, 80], Forster [49]	6126
25	Jan 16	A	Walsall	W	2-1	2-1	18	Murray [8], Forster [37]	3450
26	26	A	Stockport Co	D	1-1	0-0	—	Crofts [90]	3636
27	30	A	Millwall	L	0-1	0-0	20		6610
28	Feb 6	A	Leyton Orient	D	1-1	1-0	21	Murray [10]	6027
29	9	H	Huddersfield T	D	0-0	0-0	—		4711
30	13	H	Norwich C	L	1-2	1-0	21	Bennett [21]	7258
31	20	A	Leeds U	D	1-1	0-0	22	Murray (pen) [77]	24,120
32	23	A	Charlton Ath	W	2-1	1-0	—	Calderon [36], Bennett [78]	17,508
33	27	H	Exeter C	W	2-0	1-0	16	Elphick [26], Dicker [49]	6952
34	Mar 8	A	Colchester U	D	0-0	0-0	—		3914
35	13	H	Swindon T	L	0-1	0-0	18		6946
36	16	A	Brentford	W	3-0	1-0	—	Murray [33], Virgo [89], Forster (pen) [90]	5539
37	20	A	Oldham Ath	W	2-0	1-0	14	Bennett [40], Worthington (og) [57]	4059
38	27	H	Tranmere R	W	3-0	2-0	13	Murray [7], Crofts [30], Barnes [81]	6812
39	Apr 1	H	Southampton	D	2-2	1-1	—	Bennett [12], Barnes [66]	7784
40	5	A	Hartlepool U	L	0-2	0-0	14		3466
41	10	H	Carlisle U	L	1-2	0-1	13	Elphick [85]	6673
42	13	A	Gillingham	D	1-1	1-0	—	El-Abd [5]	7977
43	17	A	Southend U	W	1-0	1-0	14	Barnes [15]	8503
44	24	H	Bristol R	W	2-1	1-1	13	Barnes [17], Bennett (pen) [90]	6922
45	May 1	A	Milton Keynes D	D	0-0	0-0	13		12,023
46	8	H	Yeovil T	W	1-0	1-0	13	Bennett [44]	7323

Final League Position: 13

GOALSCORERS

League (56): Forster 13 (1 pen), Murray 12 (2 pens), Bennett 7 (1 pen), Crofts 5, Barnes 4, Dickinson 4, Elphick 3, Dicker 2, Tunnicliffe 2, Calderon 1, El-Abd 1, Virgo 1, own goal 1.
Carling Cup (0).
FA Cup (12): Forster 3 (2 pens), Bennett 2, Crofts 2, Dickinson 2, Murray 2 (1 pen), Elphick 1.
J Paint Trophy (0).

Kuipers M 20	Whing A 9	Virgo A 20+5	Wright M 2+2	Elphick T 43+1	Wright J 4+2	Cox D 9+12	Navarro A 31+5	Dickinson L 17+10	Thornhill M 3+4	Crofts A 44	McLeod K 2+3	Forster N 23+4	Murray G 25+7	El-Abd A 33+2	Smith J 1+1	Smith G 5+1	Tunnicliffe J 17	Bennett E 43	Hawkins C —+1	Dicker G 33+9	Hart G 1+16	Davies A 7	Davies C —+5	Hoyte G 16+2	McNulty J 5+3	Brezovan P 20	Painter M 18+1	Calderon I 19	Carole S 7+2	Holroyd C 5+8	LuaLua K 9+2	Barnes A 4+4	Hendrie L 6+2	Arismendi D 3+3	Dunk L 1	Walker M 1	Caskey J —+1	Match No.
1	2	3	4	5	6	7¹	8	9³	10²	11	12	13	14																									1
1	2	3	4²	5	6¹	7	8	9	14	11	10³	13	12																									2
1█	2	3		5		7	8²	9¹	13	4	10	12		6	11⁶	15																						3
	2	3	12	5█		7²	8	9		4		10³		1			6	11¹	13█	14																		4
1	2	3	12			7¹	8²	9		4		10³		5			6	11		13	14																	5
1	2¹	3	12		13		9			4		10³		5			6	11		8	14	7²																6
1	3	2					9¹	13		4		10		5			6	11²		8	12	7																7
1	3	2	12				9²			4		10³		5			6	11		8	14	7¹	13															8
1	3█	2	12		13		9¹			4		10³		5			6	11		8	14	7²																9
1		2	3				9	12		4		10	13	5█			6	11		8²		7¹																10
1		3	13				9¹			4		10	12				6	11		8		7²	2															11
1	3	5				12	4	7		10¹	9²						11			8	13		2	6														12
1	3	5	12	13		14	4²	7		9█							11			8	10³		2	6¹														13
1	2	5				12	11¹	9²		4	10						6			7	8	13	3															14
	12	5¹		13			9			4	10			6	1	3	11			8		7²	2															15
1	2	5		7¹	14	13	4	10³	9	6				3		11²		8	12																			16
	2¹	5		7²	12		4	13	10	9	6³			1	3	11		8		14																		17
	2³	5		7¹		9	4	12	10²	6				1	3	11		8		13	14																	18
		5		7	13		4	10²	9	6¹				3	11	8³		14	2	12																		19
		5	14	7	12		4	10³	9¹	6				3	11	8²		2	13	1																		20
		5	14	7³	13		4	10	9	6¹				3	11	8		2²	12	1																		21
		5	12	7²	13		4	10	9³	6				3¹	11	8		14	2	1																		22
		5	13	7²	9		4█	10³	12	6¹				3	11			14	2	8	1																	23
	12	5		7³	4¹		10²	9	6	14				11		8	13		2	3	1																	24
1	2	5		7		12	4	10¹	9					11		8						3	6															25
1	6	5		7		12	4	10	9					11		8¹						3	2²	13														26
1	6	5		12		7¹	13	4	10²	9				11		8						3³	2	14														27
1	6	5		7			10	4	9¹	11				8		12						3	2															28
1	6	5		8			10¹	4	12	11				13								3	2	7²	9													29
1	6	5		8³			4	10	11	13				14								3	2	12	9²	7¹												30
	6█	5		7			4	9	13	11¹				8		12								1			3	2	10²									31
		5		7			4	10¹	6	11				8		13								1			3	2	12	9²								32
		5		7			4	9²	6	11				8		13								1			3	2	12	10¹								33
		5		7			4	9	6	11				8										1			3	2	12	10¹								34
		5		7¹			4	13	9	6				11		8								1			3	2	12	10								35
	14	5		7³			4	13	9	6				11		8								1			3	2	12²	10¹								36
	12	5		10¹			4	9	6	11				8		13								1			3	2	7²									37
	14	5		10			4	9¹	6	11				8³										1			3	2	7²	12	13							38
		5		10³			4	9²	6	11				8										1			3	2	7¹	12	13	14						39
		5		10⁹			4		6	11		7		3										1			2	7²	13	12	9	4¹	14					40
		5		10			4		6	11		8²		3¹										1			2	12	7	9	13							41
	5			13			4	9	6	11		14		3										1			2	7¹	12	8³	10²							42
		5		12			4	9	6	11		13	14											1			3	2³	8	7²	10¹							43
		5		8³			4	12█	6	11		13		2										1			3	9¹	10	7²	14							44
		5		13			4	6³	10	12			2											1	14		11²	9	7¹	8█	3							45
		5		10			4³	6	11	14		2		3													7¹	9²	12	8					1	13		46

FA Cup

First Round	Wycombe W	(a)	4-4
		(h)	2-0
Second Round	Rushden & D	(h)	3-2
Third Round	Torquay U	(a)	1-0
Fourth Round	Aston Villa	(a)	2-3

Carling Cup

First Round	Swansea C	(a)	0-3

J Paint Trophy

Second Round	Leyton Orient	(a)	0-1

BRISTOL CITY
FL Championship

FOUNDATION

The name Bristol City came into being in 1897 when the Bristol South End club, formed three years earlier, decided to adopt professionalism and apply for admission to the Southern League after competing in the Western League. The historic meeting was held at The Albert Hall, Bedminster. Bristol City employed Sam Hollis from Woolwich Arsenal as manager and gave him £40 to buy players. In 1900 they merged with Bedminster, another leading Bristol club.

Ashton Gate Stadium, Bristol BS3 2EJ.

Telephone: (0871) 222 6666.

Fax: (0117) 9630 700.

Ticket Office: 0871 222 6666 (option 1).

Website: www.bcfc.co.uk

Email: enquiries@bcfc.co.uk

Ground Capacity: 21,804.

Record Attendance: 43,335 v Preston NE, FA Cup 5th rd, 16 February 1935.

Pitch Measurements: 115yd × 75yd.

Chairman: Steve Lansdown.

Vice-chairman: Keith Dawe.

Chief Executive: Colin Sexstone.

Secretary: Michelle McDonald.

Manager: Steve Coppell.

Assistant Manager: Keith Millen.

Physio: Nick Dawes.

Colours: Red shirts with white trim, white shorts, red stockings.

Change Colours: White shirts with red trim, red shorts, white stockings.

Year Formed: 1894.

Turned Professional: 1897.

Ltd Co.: 1897. Bristol City Football Club Ltd.

Previous Name: 1894, Bristol South End; 1897, Bristol City.

Club Nickname: 'Robins'.

Grounds: 1894, St John's Lane; 1904, Ashton Gate.

First Football League Game: 7 September 1901, Division 2, v Blackpool (a) W 2–0 – Moles; Tuft, Davies; Jones, McLean, Chambers; Bradbury, Connor, Boucher, O'Brien (2), Flynn.

Record League Victory: 9–0 v Aldershot, Division 3 (S), 28 December 1946 – Eddols; Morgan, Fox; Peacock, Roberts, Jones (1); Chilcott, Thomas, Clark (4 incl. 1p), Cyril Williams (1), Hargreaves (3).

HONOURS

Football League: Division 1 – Runners-up 1906–07; Division 2 – Champions 1905–06; Runners-up 1975–76, 1997–98; FL 1 – Runners-up 2006–07; Division 3 (S) – Champions 1922–23, 1926–27, 1954–55; Runners-up 1937–38; Division 3 – Runners-up 1964–65, 1989–90.

FA Cup: Runners-up 1909.

Football League Cup: Semi-final 1971, 1989.

Welsh Cup: Winners 1934.

Anglo-Scottish Cup: Winners 1978.

Freight Rover Trophy: Winners 1986; Runners-up 1987.

Auto Windscreens Shield: Runners-up 2000.

LDV Vans Trophy: Winners 2003.

sky SPORTS FACT FILE

The ever-present need to secure finance in the pre-war era was familiar to clubs like Bristol City. But they unexpectedly received £3,750 from Manchester City for teenage inside-left Jimmy Heale in 1933, who subsequently became a prolific wartime marksman at Maine Road.

Record Cup Victory: 11–0 v Chichester C, FA Cup 1st rd, 5 November 1960 – Cook; Collinson, Thresher; Connor, Alan Williams, Etheridge; Tait (1), Bobby Williams (1), Atyeo (5), Adrian Williams (3), Derrick, (1 og).

Record Defeat: 0–9 v Coventry C, Division 3 (S), 28 April 1934.

Most League Points (2 for a win): 70, Division 3 (S), 1954–55.

Most League Points (3 for a win): 91, Division 3, 1989–90

Most League Goals: 104, Division 3 (S), 1926–27.

Highest League Scorer in Season: Don Clark, 36, Division 3 (S), 1946–47.

Most League Goals in Total Aggregate: John Atyeo, 314, 1951–66.

Most League Goals in One Match: 6, Tommy 'Tot' Walsh v Gillingham, Division 3 (S), 15 January 1927.

Most Capped Player: Billy Wedlock, 26, England.

Most League Appearances: John Atyeo, 597, 1951–66.

Youngest League Player: Marvin Brown, 16 years 105 days v Bristol R, 17 October 1999.

Record Transfer Fee Received: £3,000,000 from Wolverhampton W for Ade Akinbiyi, September 1999.

Record Transfer Fee Paid: £2,250,000 to Crewe Alex for Nicky Maynard, August 2008.

Football League Record: 1901 Elected to Division 2; 1906–11 Division 1; 1911–22 Division 2; 1922–23 Division 3 (S); 1923–24 Division 2; 1924–27 Division 3 (S); 1927–32 Division 2; 1932–55 Division 3 (S); 1955–60 Division 2; 1960–65 Division 3; 1965–76 Division 2; 1976–80 Division 1; 1980–81 Division 2; 1981–82 Division 3; 1982–84 Division 4; 1984–90 Division 3; 1990–92 Division 2; 1992–95 Division 1; 1995–98 Division 2; 1998–99 Division 1; 1999–04 Division 2; 2004–07 FL 1; 2007– FL C.

MANAGERS

Sam Hollis 1897–99
Bob Campbell 1899–1901
Sam Hollis 1901–05
Harry Thickett 1905–10
Frank Bacon 1910–11
Sam Hollis 1911–13
George Hedley 1913–17
Jack Hamilton 1917–19
Joe Palmer 1919–21
Alex Raisbeck 1921–29
Joe Bradshaw 1929–32
Bob Hewison 1932–49
   (under suspension 1938–39)
Bob Wright 1949–50
Pat Beasley 1950–58
Peter Doherty 1958–60
Fred Ford 1960–67
Alan Dicks 1967–80
Bobby Houghton 1980–82
Roy Hodgson 1982
Terry Cooper 1982–88
   (Director from 1983)
Joe Jordan 1988–90
Jimmy Lumsden 1990–92
Denis Smith 1992–93
Russell Osman 1993–94
Joe Jordan 1994–97
John Ward 1997–98
Benny Lennartsson 1998–99
Tony Pulis 1999
Tony Fawthrop 2000
Danny Wilson 2000–04
Brian Tinnion 2004–05
Gary Johnson 2005–2010
Steve Coppell April 2010–

LATEST SEQUENCES

Longest Sequence of League Wins: 14, 9.9.1905 – 2.12.1905.

Longest Sequence of League Defeats: 7, 3.10.1970 – 7.11.1970.

Longest Sequence of League Draws: 4, 6.11.1999 – 27.11.1999.

Longest Sequence of Unbeaten League Matches: 24, 9.9.1905 – 10.2.1906.

Longest Sequence Without a League Win: 15, 29.4.1933 – 4.11.1933.

Successive Scoring Runs: 25 from 26.12.1905.

Successive Non-scoring Runs: 6 from 10.9.1910.

TEN YEAR LEAGUE RECORD

		P	W	D	L	F	A	Pts	Pos
2000-01	Div 2	46	18	14	14	70	56	68	9
2001-02	Div 2	46	21	10	15	68	53	73	7
2002-03	Div 2	46	24	11	11	79	48	83	3
2003-04	Div 2	46	23	13	10	58	37	82	3
2004-05	FL 1	46	18	16	12	74	57	70	7
2005-06	FL 1	46	18	11	17	66	62	65	9
2006-07	FL 1	46	25	10	11	63	39	85	2
2007-08	FL C	46	20	14	12	54	53	74	4
2008-09	FL C	46	15	16	15	54	54	61	10
2009-10	FL C	46	15	18	13	56	65	63	10

DID YOU KNOW ?

On 4 May 1912 Bristol City defeated Bristol Rovers 3–1 in the Titanic Disaster Fund match. They repeated this local derby success on 11 May 1946 in the Bolton Disaster Fund game, this time with a 7–1 win, with six different players sharing the goal scoring.

BRISTOL CITY 2009–10 LEAGUE RECORD

Match No.	Date	Venue	Opponents	Result	H/T Score	Lg Pos.	Goalscorers	Attendance
1	Aug 8	A	Preston NE	D 2-2	0-0	—	Hartley (pen) [49], Clarkson [58]	13,025
2	15	H	Crystal Palace	W 1-0	0-0	6	Maynard [89]	14,603
3	18	H	QPR	W 1-0	0-0	—	Maynard [78]	14,571
4	23	A	Cardiff C	L 0-3	0-2	10		20,853
5	29	H	Middlesbrough	W 2-1	0-0	5	Maynard 2 [63, 90]	14,402
6	Sept 12	A	Coventry C	D 1-1	0-1	7	Maynard [48]	16,449
7	15	A	Swansea C	D 0-0	0-0	—		12,859
8	19	H	Scunthorpe U	D 1-1	0-0	10	Saborio [50]	14,203
9	26	A	Derby Co	L 0-1	0-0	11		27,144
10	29	A	Blackpool	W 2-0	1-0	—	Maynard [28], Haynes [57]	13,673
11	Oct 3	A	Newcastle U	D 0-0	0-0	8		43,326
12	17	H	Peterborough U	D 1-1	1-0	9	Skuse [31]	13,833
13	20	H	Plymouth Arg	W 3-1	0-0	—	Haynes [73], McCombe [76], Maynard [79]	15,021
14	24	A	Barnsley	W 3-2	2-0	5	Maynard [26], Sno [42], Elliott [75]	11,314
15	31	H	Sheffield W	D 1-1	0-0	5	Maynard [59]	15,005
16	Nov 7	A	Nottingham F	D 1-1	0-0	7	Haynes [90]	21,467
17	21	A	WBA	L 1-4	0-2	10	Hartley [83]	23,444
18	28	H	Sheffield U	L 2-3	0-2	12	Carey [53], Saborio [90]	14,637
19	Dec 5	D	Ipswich T	D 0-0	0-0	11		14,287
20	8	A	Leicester C	W 3-1	2-0	—	Sproule [19], Skuse [29], Sno [76]	19,349
21	12	A	Doncaster R	L 0-1	0-1	9		9572
22	19	H	Reading	D 1-1	1-0	9	Hartley (pen) [13]	14,366
23	26	A	QPR	L 1-2	0-2	12	Maynard [57]	13,534
24	28	H	Watford	D 2-2	2-1	12	Haynes [38], Hartley [45]	16,035
25	Jan 16	H	Preston NE	W 4-2	2-1	10	Haynes [2], Fontaine [12], Carey [58], Sno [90]	13,146
26	26	H	Cardiff C	L 0-6	0-4	—		13,825
27	30	A	Middlesbrough	D 0-0	0-0	10		17,865
28	Feb 6	A	Coventry C	D 1-1	0-0	11	Clarkson [83]	13,852
29	9	A	Watford	L 0-2	0-2	—		12,179
30	13	A	Sheffield U	L 0-2	0-0	15		22,613
31	16	H	Leicester C	D 1-1	0-0	12	Clarkson [89]	13,746
32	21	A	WBA	W 2-1	0-1	12	Iwelumo [55], Johnson [59]	14,374
33	27	A	Ipswich T	D 0-0	0-0	12		20,302
34	Mar 6	H	Doncaster R	L 2-5	2-4	15	Orr 2 [9, 15]	13,401
35	9	A	Crystal Palace	W 1-0	0-0	—	Iwelumo [73]	12,844
36	13	A	Reading	L 0-2	0-2	14		17,900
37	16	A	Plymouth Arg	L 2-3	0-2	—	Maynard 2 [58, 78]	9289
38	20	H	Newcastle U	D 2-2	2-0	16	Nyatanga [10], Maynard [44]	19,144
39	23	H	Barnsley	W 5-3	2-2	—	Haynes 2 [2, 63], Maynard 2 [43, 56], Hartley (pen) [76]	13,009
40	27	A	Peterborough U	W 1-0	0-0	13	Clarkson [71]	6445
41	Apr 3	H	Nottingham F	D 1-1	1-1	11	Fontaine [3]	16,125
42	5	A	Sheffield W	W 1-0	0-0	9	Maynard [81]	19,688
43	10	H	Swansea C	W 1-0	0-0	9	Maynard [84]	14,719
44	17	A	Scunthorpe U	L 0-3	0-1	11		5430
45	24	H	Derby Co	W 2-1	1-0	10	Maynard 2 (1 pen) [3, 79 (p)]	15,835
46	May 2	A	Blackpool	D 1-1	1-0	10	Maynard [16]	12,296

Final League Position: 10

GOALSCORERS

League (56): Maynard 20 (1 pen), Haynes 7, Hartley 5 (3 pens), Clarkson 4, Sno 3, Carey 2, Fontaine 2, Iwelumo 2, Orr 2, Saborio 2, Skuse 2, Elliott 1, Johnson 1, McCombe 1, Nyatanga 1, Sproule 1.
Carling Cup (1): Maynard 1.
FA Cup (1): Williams 1.

Gerken D 39	Orr B 38 + 1	McAllister J 31 + 2	Fontaine L 31 + 5	Nyatanga L 33 + 4	Carey L 36 + 1	Elliott M 33 + 6	Clarkson D 10 + 16	Haynes D 29 + 9	Maynard N 40 + 2	Hartley P 36 + 4	Williams G 2 + 12	Skuse C 39 + 4	Sproule 18 + 22	McCombe J 13 + 3	Akinde J — + 7	Velicka A — + 1	Johnson L 18 + 10	Wilson B 3	Saborio A 11 + 8	Sno E 16 + 8	Basso A 4	Campbell-Ryce J 13 + 1	Agyemang P 5 + 2	Iwelumo C 7	Maierhofer E 1 + 2	Ribeiro C 5	Henderson S 3	Sawyer G 2	Match No.
1	2	3	4	5	6	7	8^2	9^3	10	11^1	12	13	14																1
1	2	3	13	5		7		9^1	10	8^2		4	11	6	12														2
1	2	3^2	12	5		7	8	9	10	11		4^1		6			13^3	14											3
1		3	5			7	8^1	9^3	10	11	13		14		6	12			2^2	4									4
1		3	5		4	7		9^3	10^2	11		8	13	6	12				2										5
1	12	3	5		4	7			10	11^3		8^2		6			13		2^1	9	14								6
	2	3	5^2	13			4^1	14		11		12	7	6			8		9	10^3	1								7
	2	3	5			4			10	11^1		12	13	6			8		9^2	7	1								8
	2	3	5	12		4		13	10	11			14	6			8^2		9^1	7^3	1								9
	2	3			5	6	4		12	10^2		13	11				8		9^1	7	1								10
1	2	3^1			5	6	4		13	10		14	11		12		8^3		9^2	7									11
1	2	3			5	6	7		12	10	14	13	4^2				8		9^1	11^3									12
1	2	3			5^2	12			11	10		7	13	4	14	6			9^1	8^3									13
1	2^1	3			5	6	7		9^3	10		13	12		4		8		14	11^2									14
1		3			5	6^1	7		9^3	10	13		4	14	2		8^2		12	11									15
1		3^3			5	6	7	14	8	10	2	12	4		13				9^2	11^1									16
1		3^1			5	6	7^2	13	9	10	11	12	4			2	14			8^3									17
1		3^3	14		5	7		9	10	11		6^1	12	2			4	13	8^2										18
	1	3	2	5		7^1	13	9^3	10	11		4	12				6		14	8^2									19
1	2	3^2	6	5		12		9	10	11^1		4	7	13			14		8^3										20
1	2	3	6	5^2		8^2		9	10	11	12	4	7^1				14		13										21
1	2	3	6	5	4	12^2	9^3		10	11	13	7					14		8^1										22
1	2	3	5		6		12	9^3	10	11	7^1	4	14				8^2		13										23
1	2	3	12	5	6	7	8^1	9^2	10^3	11		4	13				14												24
1	2	3	5	6	8		13	9^1	10^2	11^3		4	7				12		14										25
1	2	3^1	5	12	6		13	9^2	10	11^3		4					14					7	8						26
1	2		4	5^3	6		12	13	10^2	11		8^1	14									7	9						27
1	2	3	4	5^3	6	7		14	12	10^1		11	13						8^2			9							28
1	2	3^1	4	5	6				12	10			7	13			8			11^2		9							29
1	2		4	5	3		12	14	13	11			7^1				6^3		8			9^2		10					30
1	2		4	5	3		7			11			9^2				13		6^1			8	12	10					31
1	2		4	5	3		7			11^1			9^2		12		14		6	13		8^3		10					32
1	2		4	5	3	8		9^3		11^2			12				6		14			7^1	13	10					33
1	2		4	5	3		13	9^1	10^3	11			14				6		8			7^2	12						34
1	2	13	6	5	3				10^2	11		4			12				8			7			9^1				35
1	2	14	6^3	5	3		12		10^1	11		4					13		8			7			9^2				36
1	2	3^2	6	14	5	8		13	10	11^1		4			12							7^4	9^3						37
1	2	3^1	5	6		8		9^3	10	11		4	13						12			7							38
1	2		6	5		8^1	13	9^3	10^2	11		4			14		12					7				3			39
1	2		6	5		8^2	12	9	10	11^2		4			14		13					7				3			40
1	2		6	5		8	13	9^2	10^3	11		4^1					12					7			14	3			41
	2		6	5	3	8	14	9^2	10^2	11^1		4					12					7	13				1		42
	2		6	5	3	8	13	9^2	10	11^3		4					12					7^1	14				1		43
	2		6	5	3	7	13	9^2	10	11^3		4					12					8^1	14				1		44
1	2		5	6		8		9^1	10	11^3		4					13		14			7^2	12					3	45
1	2	14	5	6		8	10	9^3		11^2		4^1					13					7	12					3	46

FA Cup
Third Round Cardiff C (h) 1-1
  (a) 0-1

Carling Cup
First Round Brentford (a) 1-0
Second Round Carlisle U (h) 0-2

BRISTOL ROVERS   FL Championship 1

FOUNDATION

Bristol Rovers were formed at a meeting in Stapleton Road, Eastville, in 1883. However, they first went under the name of the Black Arabs (wearing black shirts). Changing their name to Eastville Rovers in their second season, they won the Gloucestershire Senior Cup in 1888–89. Original members of the Bristol & District League in 1892, this eventually became the Western League and Eastville Rovers adopted professionalism in 1897.

The Memorial Stadium, Filton Avenue, Horfield, Bristol BS7 0BF.

Telephone: (0117) 909 6648.

Fax: (0117) 907 4312.

Ticket Office: (0117) 909 8848.

Website: www.bristolrovers.co.uk

Email: rodwesson@bristolrovers.co.uk; dave@bristolrovers.co.uk

Ground Capacity: 11,626.

Record Attendance: 12,011 v WBA, FA Cup 6th rd, 9 March 2008 (Memorial Stadium). 9,464 v Liverpool, FA Cup 4th rd, 8 February 1992 (Twerton Park). 38,472 v Preston NE, FA Cup 4th rd, 30 January 1960 (Eastville).

Pitch Measurements: 110yd × 73yd 6in.

Chairman: Nick Higgs.

Secretary: Rod Wesson.

First Team Manager: Paul Trollope.

Physio: Phil Kite.

Colours: Blue and white quarters, white shorts, white stockings.

Change Colours: Black and gold quartered shirts, black shorts, gold stockings.

Year Formed: 1883. *Turned Professional:* 1897. *Ltd Co.:* 1896.

Previous Names: 1883, Black Arabs; 1884, Eastville Rovers; 1897, Bristol Eastville Rovers; 1898, Bristol Rovers. *Club Nickname:* 'Pirates'.

Grounds: 1883, Purdown; Three Acres, Ashley Hill; Rudgeway, Fishponds; 1897, Eastville; 1986, Twerton Park; 1996, The Memorial Stadium.

First Football League Game: 28 August 1920, Division 3, v Millwall (a) L 0–2 – Stansfield; Bethune, Panes; Boxley, Kenny, Steele; Chance, Bird, Sims, Bell, Palmer.

Record League Victory: 7–0 v Brighton & HA, Division 3 (S), 29 November 1952 – Hoyle; Bamford, Fox; Pitt, Warren, Sampson; McIlvenny, Roost (2), Lambden (1), Bradford (1), Petherbridge (2), (1 og). 7–0 v Swansea T, Division 2, 2 October 1954 – Radford; Bamford, Watkins; Pitt, Muir, Anderson; Petherbridge, Bradford (2), Meyer, Roost (1), Hooper (2), (2 og). 7–0 v Shrewsbury T, Division 3, 21 March 1964 – Hall; Hillard, Gwyn Jones; Oldfield, Stone (1), Mabbutt; Jarman (2), Brown (1), Biggs (1p), Hamilton, Bobby Jones (2).

HONOURS

Football League: Division 2 best season: 4th, 1994–95; Division 3 (S) – Champions 1952–53; Division 3 – Champions 1989–90; Runners-up 1973–74.

FA Cup: best season: 6th rd, 1951, 1958, 2008.

Football League Cup: best season: 5th rd, 1971, 1972.

J Paint Trophy: Runners-up 2007.

sky SPORTS FACT FILE

In 1956–57 five Bristol Rovers forwards reached double figures in goals during League matches. Alfie Biggs was leading scorer with 17 goals, followed by Peter Hooper and Dai Ward each with 16, plus Geoff Bradford and Barrie Meyer with eleven each.

Record Cup Victory: 6–0 v Merthyr Tydfil, FA Cup 1st rd, 14 November 1987 – Martyn; Alexander (Dryden), Tanner Hibbitt, Twentyman, Jones, Holloway, Meacham (1), White (2), Penrice (3) (Reece), Purnell.

Most League Points (2 for a win): 64, Division 3 (S), 1952–53.

Most League Points (3 for a win): 93, Division 3, 1989–90.

Most League Goals: 92, Division 3 (S), 1952–53.

Highest League Scorer in Season: Geoff Bradford, 33, Division 3 (S), 1952–53.

Most League Goals in Total Aggregate: Geoff Bradford, 242, 1949–64.

Most League Goals in One Match: 4, Sidney Leigh v Exeter C, Division 3 (S), 2 May 1921; 4, Jonah Wilcox v Bournemouth, Division 3 (S), 12 December 1925; 4, Bill Culley v QPR, Division 3 (S), 5 March 1927; 4, Frank Curran v Swindon T, Division 3 (S), 25 March 1939; 4, Vic Lambden v Aldershot, Division 3 (S), 29 March 1947; 4, George Petherbridge v Torquay U, Division 3 (S), 1 December 1951; 4, Vic Lambden v Colchester U, Division 3 (S), 14 May 1952; 4, Geoff Bradford v Rotherham U, Division 2, 14 March 1959; 4, Robin Stubbs v Gillingham, Division 2, 10 October 1970; 4, Alan Warboys v Brighton & HA, Division 3, 1 December 1973; 4, Jamie Cureton v Reading, Division 2, 16 January 1999.

Most Capped Player: Vitalijs Astafjevs, 31 (159), Latvia.

Most League Appearances: Stuart Taylor, 546, 1966–80.

Youngest League Player: Ronnie Dix, 15 years 173 days v Charlton Ath, 25 February 1928.

Record Transfer Fee Received: £2,100,000 from Fulham for Barry Hayles, November 1998 and £2,100,000 from WBA for Jason Roberts, July 2000.

Record Transfer Fee Paid: £375,000 to QPR for Andy Tillson, November 1992.

Football League Record: 1920 Original Member of Division 3; 1921–53 Division 3 (S); 1953–62 Division 2; 1962–74 Division 3; 1974–81 Division 2; 1981–90 Division 3; 1990–92 Division 2. 1992–93 Division 1; 1993–2001 Division 2; 2001–04 Division 3; 2004–07 FL 2; 2007– FL 1.

MANAGERS

Alfred Homer 1899–1920
(continued as Secretary to 1928)
Ben Hall 1920–21
Andy Wilson 1921–26
Joe Palmer 1926–29
Dave McLean 1929–30
Albert Prince-Cox 1930–36
Percy Smith 1936–37
Brough Fletcher 1938–49
Bert Tann 1950–68 *(continued as General Manager to 1972)*
Fred Ford 1968–69
Bill Dodgin Snr 1969–72
Don Megson 1972–77
Bobby Campbell 1978–79
Harold Jarman 1979–80
Terry Cooper 1980–81
Bobby Gould 1981–83
David Williams 1983–85
Bobby Gould 1985–87
Gerry Francis 1987–91
Martin Dobson 1991
Dennis Rofe 1992
Malcolm Allison 1992–93
John Ward 1993–96
Ian Holloway 1996–2001
Garry Thompson 2001
Gerry Francis 2001
Garry Thompson 2001–02
Ray Graydon 2002–04
Ian Atkins 2004–05
Paul Trollope September 2005–

LATEST SEQUENCES

Longest Sequence of League Wins: 12, 18.10.1952 – 17.1.1953.
Longest Sequence of League Defeats: 8, 26.10.2002 – 21.12.2002.
Longest Sequence of League Draws: 5, 1.11.1975 – 22.11.1975.
Longest Sequence of Unbeaten League Matches: 32, 7.4.1973 – 27.1.1974.
Longest Sequence Without a League Win: 20, 5.4.1980 – 1.11.1980.
Successive Scoring Runs: 26 from 26.3.1927.
Successive Non-scoring Runs: 6 from 14.10.1922.

TEN YEAR LEAGUE RECORD

		P	W	D	L	F	A	Pts	Pos
2000-01	Div 2	46	12	15	19	53	57	51	21
2001-02	Div 3	46	11	12	23	40	60	45	23
2002-03	Div 3	46	12	15	19	50	57	51	20
2003-04	Div 3	46	14	13	19	50	61	55	15
2004-05	FL 2	46	13	21	12	60	57	60	12
2005-06	FL 2	46	17	9	20	59	67	60	12
2006-07	FL 2	46	20	12	14	49	42	72	6
2007-08	FL 1	46	12	17	17	45	53	53	16
2008-09	FL 1	46	17	12	17	79	61	63	11
2009-10	FL 1	46	19	5	22	59	70	62	11

DID YOU KNOW ?

The most appearances made by a Bristol Rovers player during their Southern League days was the record of goalkeeper Arthur Cartlidge between 1901 and 1909. His total of 258 plus 25 FA Cup outings included four seasons when he was an ever present.

BRISTOL ROVERS 2009–10 LEAGUE RECORD

Match No.	Date	Venue	Opponents	Result	H/T Score	Lg Pos.	Goalscorers	Attendance
1	Aug 8	H	Leyton Orient	L	1-2	1-1	—	Lambert [44]	7745
2	15	A	Stockport Co	W	2-0	2-0	9	Osei-Kuffour [3], Coles [8]	4084
3	18	A	Hartlepool U	W	2-1	2-1	—	Lescott [39], Osei-Kuffour [45]	3137
4	22	H	Huddersfield T	W	1-0	0-0	4	Hughes (pen) [84]	6952
5	29	A	Wycombe W	L	1-2	1-1	7	Lines [26]	5214
6	Sept 5	H	Millwall	W	2-0	1-0	4	Hughes (pen) [26], Lines [63]	6038
7	12	H	Oldham Ath	W	1-0	0-0	3	Osei-Kuffour [90]	6674
8	19	A	Brentford	W	3-1	3-0	3	Dickson 2 [11, 27], Lescott [41]	6528
9	26	H	Brighton & HA	D	1-1	0-0	3	Osei-Kuffour [68]	8098
10	29	A	Southampton	W	3-2	1-1	—	Dickson [42], Osei-Kuffour [65], Williams [90]	19,724
11	Oct 3	A	Norwich C	L	1-5	1-4	3	Hughes (pen) [26]	24,117
12	17	A	Southend U	L	1-2	0-1	5	Grant (og) [56]	6853
13	24	H	Yeovil T	L	1-2	0-0	6	Dickson [46]	7812
14	27	H	Leeds U	L	0-4	0-1	—		11,448
15	31	A	Milton Keynes D	L	1-2	0-0	9	Duffy [90]	9711
16	Nov 14	H	Carlisle U	W	3-2	1-1	8	Osei-Kuffour [35], Hughes [62], Lines [90]	5862
17	21	A	Gillingham	W	2-1	1-1	7	Lines [17], Hughes (pen) [81]	6210
18	24	A	Charlton Ath	L	2-4	1-2	—	Hughes (pen) [41], Lines [56]	15,885
19	Dec 1	H	Exeter C	W	1-0	1-0	—	Duffy [34]	7313
20	5	A	Colchester U	L	0-1	0-1	7		4942
21	12	A	Swindon T	W	3-0	3-0	6	Williams [11], Hughes [13], Osei-Kuffour [34]	7613
22	19	A	Tranmere R	L	0-2	0-1	7		4755
23	28	A	Millwall	L	0-2	0-0	9		10,014
24	Jan 19	A	Huddersfield T	D	0-0	0-0	—		12,624
25	23	H	Hartlepool U	W	2-0	1-0	9	Lines [3], Duffy [66]	5794
26	30	H	Wycombe W	L	2-3	2-1	9	Lines 2 [40, 44]	6688
27	Feb 2	A	Leyton Orient	L	0-5	0-1	—		2931
28	6	A	Walsall	D	0-0	0-0	9		3886
29	9	H	Walsall	L	0-1	0-1	—		5919
30	15	H	Charlton Ath	W	2-1	1-0	—	Elliott [14], Heffernan [64]	7624
31	20	A	Gillingham	L	0-1	0-0	10		5302
32	27	H	Colchester U	W	3-2	1-1	9	Blizzard [16], Osei-Kuffour [67], Lines [79]	6023
33	Mar 2	H	Stockport Co	W	1-0	1-0	—	Hughes [30]	5322
34	6	A	Swindon T	W	4-0	3-0	9	Osei-Kuffour [25], Heffernan [39], Lines [45], Hughes [61]	10,341
35	13	H	Tranmere R	D	0-0	0-0	9		6477
36	17	A	Exeter C	L	0-1	0-0	—		5269
37	20	H	Yeovil T	W	3-0	3-0	9	Osei-Kuffour 2 [4, 41], Heffernan [37]	5968
38	27	H	Southend U	W	4-3	2-2	8	Osei-Kuffour [34], Hughes 2 (1 pen) [38 (p), 52], Grant (og) [90]	6476
39	Apr 2	A	Carlisle U	L	1-3	0-0	—	Heffernan [57]	5407
40	5	H	Milton Keynes D	W	1-0	0-0	8	Osei-Kuffour [56]	6406
41	10	A	Oldham Ath	L	1-2	0-0	8	Osei-Kuffour [77]	3769
42	13	H	Southampton	L	1-5	1-2	—	Hughes (pen) [24]	8607
43	17	H	Brentford	D	0-0	0-0	9		6048
44	24	A	Brighton & HA	L	1-2	1-1	9	Williams [11]	6922
45	May 1	H	Norwich C	L	0-3	0-2	9		8836
46	8	A	Leeds U	L	1-2	0-0	11	Duffy [48]	38,234

Final League Position: 11

GOALSCORERS

League (59): Osei-Kuffour 14, Hughes 12 (7 pens), Lines 10, Dickson 4, Duffy 4, Heffernan 4, Williams 3, Lescott 2, Blizzard 1, Coles 1, Elliott 1, Lambert 1, own goals 2.
Carling Cup (3): Duffy 2 (1 pen), Elliott 1.
FA Cup (2): Duffy 1, Hughes 1 (pen).
J Paint Trophy (0).

Forster F 4	Regan C 32 + 3	Lescott A 23 + 1	Campbell S 46	Coles D 36	Anthony B 37	Pipe D 5 + 2	Lines C 41 + 1	Lambert R 1	Osei-Kuffour J 42	Hughes J 44	Blizzard D 22 + 12	Duffy D 15 + 15	Hunt B — + 2	Williams A 18 + 25	Evans R 3	Swallow R 6 + 17	Andersen M 39	Wright M 19 + 5	Dickson C 10 + 4	Elliott S 21	Reece C 5 + 9	Raldwin P 6	Brown W 3 + 1	Heffernan P 11	Jones D 17	Richards Elliot — + 5	Match No.
1	2	3	4	5	6	7	8[1]	9	10	11[2]	12	13															1
1	2	3	4	5	6	7	8		10	11			9[1]	12													2
1	2	3	4	5	6	7[2]	8		10	11	13		9[1]	12													3
1	2	3	4	5	6	7	8		10[2]	11	13		9[1]	12													4
	2	3[2]	4	5	6	7	8		10	11			9[1]	12			1	13									5
	2	3	4	5	6	13	8		10[3]	11	14		9[1]	12			1	7[2]									6
	2	3	4	5	6	12	8[3]		10	11	14		9[2]	13			1	7[1]									7
	2	3	4	5	6		8		10[2]	11	13			12			1	7	9[1]								8
	2	3[1]	4	5	6		8		10	11	12	13	14				1	7[1]	9[2]								9
	2	3	4	5	6		8		10[3]	11	14	13	12				1	7[1]	9[2]								10
	2	3	4	5	6		8[2]		10	11	13	14	12				1	7[1]	9[3]								11
	2	3	4	5			8		10	11[1]	14	12	13				1	7[2]	9[3]	6							12
	2	3[3]	4	5	6		8[1]		10	11	12	13	14				1	7[2]	9								13
	2	3	4	5					10	11	7[1]	12	8[3]				1	13	9[2]	6	14						14
	2	3	4	5	12				10	11[3]	7[1]	14	9[2]				1	8	13	6							15
	2		4	5	6		8		10	11[2]	7[3]	3		12		13	1	9[1]	14								16
	2[2]	4	3		6	7	8		10[3]	11	12	3					1	14	9[1]		5						17
		4	2		6		8		10	11	7[2]	3[1]	9				1					13		5			18
	2	4		5			8		10	11		3[2]	9[3]	12		3	1	7[1]	14	6							19
	2	4		5			8		10	11		3[1]	9[2]	14		2	1	7[3]	13	6							20
	2	3	4				8		10[1]	11	13		9[2]				1	7[3]	12	6	14	5					21
	2	3[3]	4				8		10	11	14			12		13	1	7[1]	9[2]	6		5					22
	2	3[2]	4	5			8		10	11	13	7[1]	9	12			1			6							23
	2	3	4	5	6		8		10	11			9[1]	12			1	7									24
	2	3	4	5	6		8		10	11[2]			9[1]	12		14	1	7[3]	13								25
	2	3[2]	4	5	6		8		10	11			9	12		13	1	7[1]									26
	2	3[1]	4[2]	5	6		8		10	11	13		9	12			1	7[3]	14								27
	2		4		6				10	11		3	9				1	8		7		5					28
		4		5					10	11		3	9	12		13	1	7[2]	2	6[1]	12				3		29
	14	4	2	5			8[3]		10[1]	11	7[2]			12			1				6	13			3	3	30
	3	4		5			8[1]			11	7		9[2]	12			1				6	13	2		13		31
	13	4	2	5			8		10	11[3]	7[2]			12		14	1				6			9[1]	3		32
		4	2	5			8		10[2]	11	7[1]			12			1				6	13		9	3		33
		4	2	5			8		10	11	7			12			1				6			9[1]	3		34
		4	2	5[1]			8		10	11	7[2]			13			1				6		12	9	3		35
		4	2	5			8		10	11[1]	7			12			1				6			9	3		36
		4	2	5			8		10	11	7			12			1				6			9[1]	3		37
	13	4	2	5[2]			8		10	11	7[1]			12			1				6			9	3		38
	2	4			7				10	11		3[2]	8[1]			13	1				6		12	9	5		39
	2	4		5			8		10	11	7[2]	9[1]		12			1				6	13			3		40
		4	2	5			8		10	11	7[2]	9[1]		12		13	1				6				3		41
	12	4	2	5			8		10	11	7	9					1				6[1]				3		42
	3	4	2				8		10[1]	11	7	9		12			1				6[2]	5			13		43
	2	4		5[4]			8		10[2]	11	7[1]	9					1				6	13	12		3		44
	2	4		5			8		10	11	7	9[1]					1				6		12		3		45
	2	4		5	6		8		10	11	7	9[2]		12			1								3	13	46

FA Cup
First Round   Southampton   (h)   2-3

Carling Cup
First Round   Aldershot T   (h)   2-1
Second Round   Cardiff C   (a)   1-3

J Paint Trophy
First Round   Hereford U   (a)   0-0

BURNLEY   FL Championship

FOUNDATION

On 18 May 1882 Burnley (Association) Football Club was still known as Burnley Rovers as members of that Rugby Club had decided on that date to play Association Football in the future. It was only a matter of days later that the members met again and decided to drop Rovers from the club's name.

Turf Moor, Harry Potts Way, Burnley, Lancashire BB10 4BX.

Telephone: 0871 221 1882.

Fax: (01282) 700 014.

Ticket Office: 0871 221 1914.

Website: www.burnleyfc.com

Email: info@burnleyfc.com

Ground Capacity: 22,610.

Record Attendance: 54,775 v Huddersfield T, FA Cup 3rd rd, 23 February 1924.

Pitch Measurements: 112yd × 70yd.

Chairman: Barry Kilby.

Vice-chairman: Ray Ingleby.

Manager: Brian Laws.

Assistant Manager: Russ Wilcox.

Football Secretary: Pauline Scott.

Physio: Andy Mitchell.

Colours: Claret shirts with blue sleeves, white shorts, claret stockings.

Change Colours: White shirts, light blue shorts, light blue stockings.

Year Formed: 1882.

Turned Professional: 1883. *Ltd Co.:* 1897.

Previous Name: 1882, Burnley Rovers; 1882, Burnley.

Club Nickname: 'The Clarets'.

Grounds: 1882, Calder Vale; 1883, Turf Moor.

HONOURS

Football League: Division 1 – Champions 1920–21, 1959–60; Runners-up 1919–20, 1961–62; Division 2 – Champions 1897–98, 1972–73; Runners-up 1912–13, 1946–47, 1999–2000; Division 3 – Champions 1981–82; Division 4 – Champions 1991–92. Record 30 consecutive Division 1 games without defeat 1920–21.

FA Cup: Winners 1914; Runners-up 1947, 1962.

Football League Cup: Semi-final 1961, 1969, 1983, 2009.

Anglo–Scottish Cup: Winners 1979.

Sherpa Van Trophy: Runners-up 1988.

European Competitions: *European Cup:* 1960–61. *European Fairs Cup:* 1966–67.

First Football League Game: 8 September 1888, Football League, v Preston NE (a) L 2–5 – Smith; Lang, Bury, Abrahams, Friel, Keenan, Brady, Tait, Poland (1), Gallocher (1), Yates.

Record League Victory: 9–0 v Darwen, Division 1, 9 January 1892 – Hillman; Walker, McFettridge, Lang, Matthews, Keenan, Nicol (3), Bowes, Espie (1), McLardie (3), Hill (2).

Record Cup Victory: 9–0 v Crystal Palace, FA Cup 2nd rd (replay), 10 February 1909 – Dawson; Barron, McLean; Cretney (2), Leake, Moffat; Morley, Ogden, Smith (3), Abbott (2), Smethams (1). 9–0 v New Brighton, FA Cup 4th rd, 26 January 1957 – Blacklaw; Angus, Winton; Seith, Adamson, Miller; Newlands (1), McIlroy (3), Lawson (3), Cheesebrough (1), Pilkington (1). 9–0 v Penrith, FA Cup 1st rd, 17 November 1984 – Hansbury; Miller, Hampton, Phelan, Overson (Kennedy), Hird (3 incl. 1p), Grewcock (1), Powell (2), Taylor (3), Biggins, Hutchison.

---

sky SPORTS FACT FILE

Amateur centre-forward Tommy Lawton, already a senior debutant for Burnley, signed professional forms on Friday 9 October 1936, in the mill offices of chairman Tom Clegg. The following day he scored in 20 seconds, the first of three goals against Tottenham Hotspur.

Record Defeat: 0–10 v Aston Villa, Division 1, 29 August 1925 and v Sheffield U, Division 1, 19 January 1929.

Most League Points (2 for a win): 62, Division 2, 1972–73.

Most League Points (3 for a win): 88, Division 2, 1999–2000.

Most League Goals: 102, Division 1, 1960–61.

Highest League Scorer in Season: George Beel, 35, Division 1, 1927–28.

Most League Goals in Total Aggregate: George Beel, 179, 1923–32.

Most League Goals in One Match: 6, Louis Page v Birmingham C, Division 1, 10 April 1926.

Most Capped Player: Jimmy McIlroy, 51 (55), Northern Ireland.

Most League Appearances: Jerry Dawson, 522, 1907–28.

Youngest League Player: Tommy Lawton, 16 years 174 days v Doncaster R, 28 March 1936.

Record Transfer Fee Received: £3,250,000 from Glasgow Rangers for Kyle Lafferty, June 2008.

Record Transfer Fee Paid: £2,000,000 to Reading for Andre Bikey, July 2009.

Football League Record: 1888 Original Member of the Football League; 1897–98 Division 2; 1898–1900 Division 1; 1900–13 Division 2; 1913–30 Division 1; 1930–47 Division 2; 1947–71 Division 1; 1971–73 Division 2; 1973–76 Division 1; 1976–80 Division 2; 1980–82 Division 3; 1982–83 Division 2; 1983–85 Division 3; 1985–92 Division 2; 1992–94 Division 2; 1994–95 Division 1; 1995–2000 Division 2; 2000–04 Division 1; 2004–09 FL C; 2009–10 FA Premier League; 2010– FL C.

LATEST SEQUENCES

Longest Sequence of League Wins: 10, 16.11.1912 – 18.1.1913.

Longest Sequence of League Defeats: 8, 2.1.1995 – 25.2.1995.

Longest Sequence of League Draws: 6, 21.2.1931 – 28.3.1931.

Longest Sequence of Unbeaten League Matches: 30, 6.9.1920 – 25.3.1921.

Longest Sequence Without a League Win: 24, 16.4.1979 – 17.11.1979.

Successive Scoring Runs: 27 from 13.2.1926.

Successive Non-scoring Runs: 6 from 9.8.1997.

MANAGERS

Harry Bradshaw 1894–99
(Secretary-Manager from 1897)
Club Directors 1899–1900
J. Ernest Mangnall 1900–03
(Secretary-Manager)
Spen Whittaker 1903–10
(Secretary-Manager)
John Haworth 1910–24
(Secretary-Manager)
Albert Pickles 1925–31
(Secretary-Manager)
Tom Bromilow 1932–35
Selection Committee 1935–45
Cliff Britton 1945–48
Frank Hill 1948–54
Alan Brown 1954–57
Billy Dougall 1957–58
Harry Potts 1958–70
(General Manager to 1972)
Jimmy Adamson 1970–76
Joe Brown 1976–77
Harry Potts 1977–79
Brian Miller 1979–83
John Bond 1983–84
John Benson 1984–85
Martin Buchan 1985
Tommy Cavanagh 1985–86
Brian Miller 1986–89
Frank Casper 1989–91
Jimmy Mullen 1991–96
Adrian Heath 1996–97
Chris Waddle 1997–98
Stan Ternent 1998–2004
Steve Cotterill 2004–07
Owen Coyle 2007–10
Brian Laws January 2010–

TEN YEAR LEAGUE RECORD

		P	W	D	L	F	A	Pts	Pos
2000-01	Div 2	46	21	9	16	50	54	72	7
2001-02	Div 1	46	21	12	13	70	62	75	7
2002-03	Div 1	46	15	10	21	65	89	55	16
2003-04	Div 1	46	13	14	19	60	77	53	19
2004-05	FL C	46	15	15	16	38	39	60	13
2005-06	FL C	46	14	12	20	46	54	54	17
2006-07	FL C	46	15	12	19	52	49	57	15
2007-08	FL C	46	16	14	16	60	67	62	13
2008-09	FL C	46	21	13	12	72	60	76	5
2009-10	PR Lge	38	8	6	24	42	82	30	18

DID YOU KNOW ?

On 19 August 2009 in their first meeting in 23 years, Burnley defeated Manchester United 1–0 at Turf Moor in their initial Premier League home fixture. Goalkeeper Brian Jensen saved a penalty for Burnley and Robbie Blake on 19 minutes was the all-important goal scorer.

BURNLEY 2009–10 LEAGUE RECORD

Match No.	Date	Venue	Opponents		Result	H/T Score	Lg Pos.	Goalscorers	Attendance
1	Aug 15	A	Stoke C	L	0-2	0-2	—		27,385
2	19	H	Manchester U	W	1-0	1-0	—	Blake [19]	20,872
3	23	H	Everton	W	1-0	1-0	7	Elliott [34]	19,983
4	29	A	Chelsea	L	0-3	0-1	10		40,906
5	Sept 12	A	Liverpool	L	0-4	0-2	12		43,817
6	19	H	Sunderland	W	3-1	1-1	9	Alexander (pen) [13], Nugent 2 [67, 86]	20,196
7	26	A	Tottenham H	L	0-5	0-2	11		35,462
8	Oct 3	H	Birmingham C	W	2-1	0-0	9	Fletcher [53], Bikey [62]	20,102
9	18	A	Blackburn R	L	2-3	1-3	10	Blake [5], Eagles [90]	26,689
10	24	H	Wigan Ath	L	1-3	1-1	11	Fletcher [4]	19,430
11	31	H	Hull C	W	2-0	1-0	10	Alexander 2 (1 pen) [20 (p), 77]	20,219
12	Nov 7	A	Manchester C	D	3-3	2-1	10	Alexander (pen) [19], Fletcher [32], McDonald [87]	47,205
13	21	H	Aston Villa	D	1-1	1-0	10	Caldwell [9]	21,178
14	28	A	West Ham U	L	3-5	0-3	12	Fletcher 2 [68, 74], Eagles [90]	34,003
15	Dec 5	A	Portsmouth	L	0-2	0-0	13		17,822
16	12	H	Fulham	D	1-1	0-0	13	Elliott [60]	18,397
17	16	H	Arsenal	D	1-1	1-1	—	Alexander (pen) [28]	21,309
18	20	A	Wolverhampton W	L	0-2	0-1	14		27,410
19	26	H	Bolton W	D	1-1	0-1	13	Nugent [56]	21,761
20	28	A	Everton	L	0-2	0-0	14		39,419
21	Jan 16	A	Manchester U	L	0-3	0-1	15		75,120
22	26	A	Bolton W	L	0-1	0-1	—		23,986
23	30	H	Chelsea	L	1-2	0-1	18	Fletcher [50]	21,131
24	Feb 6	H	West Ham U	W	2-1	1-0	15	Nugent [14], Fox Danny [55]	21,001
25	9	A	Fulham	L	0-3	0-2	—		23,005
26	21	A	Aston Villa	L	2-5	1-1	19	Fletcher [10], Paterson [90]	38,709
27	27	H	Portsmouth	L	1-2	1-1	19	Paterson [31]	19,714
28	Mar 6	A	Arsenal	L	1-3	0-1	—	Nugent [50]	60,043
29	10	H	Stoke C	D	1-1	0-1	—	Nugent [52]	20,323
30	13	A	Wolverhampton W	L	1-2	0-1	18	Thompson [73]	21,217
31	20	A	Wigan Ath	L	0-1	0-0	18		18,498
32	28	H	Blackburn R	L	0-1	0-1	19		21,546
33	Apr 3	H	Manchester C	L	1-6	0-5	19	Fletcher [71]	21,330
34	10	A	Hull C	W	4-1	1-1	—	Paterson [35], Alexander 2 (2 pens) [64, 70], Elliott [90]	24,369
35	17	A	Sunderland	L	1-2	0-2	19	Thompson [82]	41,341
36	25	H	Liverpool	L	0-4	0-0	19		21,553
37	May 1	A	Birmingham C	L	1-2	0-2	19	Thompson [87]	24,578
38	9	H	Tottenham H	W	4-2	1-2	18	Elliott [42], Cork [54], Paterson [71], Thompson [88]	21,161

Final League Position: 18

GOALSCORERS

League (42): Fletcher 8, Alexander 7 (6 pens), Nugent 6, Elliott 4, Paterson 4, Thompson 4, Blake 2, Eagles 2, Bikey 1, Caldwell 1, Cork 1, Fox Danny 1, McDonald 1.
Carling Cup (4): Fletcher 3, Eagles 1.
FA Cup (2): Alexander 1 (pen), Fletcher 1.

Jensen B 38	Mears T 38	Kalvenes C 3 + 3	Alexander G 33	Carlisle C 27	Jordan S 23 + 2	Blake R 20 + 11	McCann C 7	Fletcher S 35	Paterson M 17 + 6	Elliott W 34 + 4	Thompson S 1 + 19	Eagles C 20 + 14	Guerrero F — + 7	Bikey A 26 + 2	Gudjonsson J 1 + 9	McDonald K 15 + 11	Nugent D 20 + 10	Caldwell S 12 + 1	Penny D — + 1	Duff M 10 + 1	Edgar D 2 + 2	Niimani F — + 2	Cort L 15	Fox Danny 13 + 1	Cork J 8 + 3	Match No.
1	2	3	4¹	5	6	7³	8	9	10²	11	12	13	14													1
1	2		4¹	5	3	7	8	9³	10²	11	14	13		6	12											2
1	2		4	5	3	9²	8	7³	10¹	11	14	12	13	6												3
1	2		4²	5	3	9³	8	7	10¹	11		14		6	12	13										4
1	2		4³	5	3	9¹	8	7	10²	11		12		6	14		13									5
1	2		4	5	3	9	8¹	7³	10²	11		14		6	12		13									6
1	2		4	5	3	9¹		7²		11	13	12	14	6	8		10¹									7
1	2	14	8	5	3	9⁵		7¹		11	13	12		6		10²	4									8
1	2		7	5	3	10		9¹		11	13	12		6³	14	8²	4									9
1⁶	2		8	5	3	10¹		9		11	7			4²		13	12	6	15							10
1	2		8	5	3	10¹		9²		11	7³	14		6		12	13	4								11
1	2		8	5	3	10²		9		11	7³			6¹	12	13	14	4								12
1	2		8	5	3	10³		9²		11	7¹			6	14	12	13	4								13
1	2	13	8³	5	3¹	10²		9		11	7			6	14	12	4⁸									14
1	2		4	5	3	10¹		9		11	12	7²	13	6		8										15
1	2		8	5	3	10¹		9		11	7³	14		6²		13	12	4								16
1	2		8	5	3	14		9³		11	7²			6¹	12	10	13	4								17
1	2		8	5¹	3			9		11	7			6²	14	10	13	4³		12						18
1	2		8		3	12		9¹		11	7			6		4	10			5						19
1	2	12	8		3⁸	14		9²		11³	13	7		6		4	10¹			5						20
1	2		4		3	14		9¹		11	12	7³		13		8²	10			5	6					21
1	2	3	4²	5		8¹		9	13	11	7³			12	10		6			14						22
1	2	3¹		5		10³		9	13	11	14	7		6		8²				12		4				23
1	2			5		10¹		9	12	11	14			6		7	8³			13		4	3²			24
1	2			5		9		14	11²		12			6		8	10³			7			4¹	3	13	25
1	2			5		9³		14	12		7			6		8¹	10²			13			4	3	11	26
1	2			5		8³		9	10	11²	14	12		6¹		7							4	3	13	27
1	2	8²		5		9³		12	14	7				13		11¹	10						6	3	4	28
1	2	8		5	14	9		13	11²	7				12		10							6	3³	4¹	29
1	2	8		5	12	13		9	11	14	7³			6²		10							4	3¹		30
1	2	7			3	12		9¹	10²	11	13			6		8				4			5			31
1	2	4³			3¹	13		9	10²	11	14			7		8				6			5	12		32
1	2	4				10²		9³	14	12	7			11¹		8				5			6	3	13	33
1	2	7				9²		10	11	14	13			8³		12				5¹			6	3	4	34
1	2	8				13		9	10¹	11	12	7				5							6	3	4²	35
1	2	7¹				12		9	10²	11	14	13				8³				5			6	3	4	36
1	2	7³				12		9²	10	11	13	14				8¹				5			6	3	4	37
1	2	7				12		9²	10³	11	13	14		6		8¹				5				3	4	38

FA Cup

Third Round	Milton Keynes D	(a)	2-1	
Fourth Round	Reading	(a)	0-1	

Carling Cup

Second Round	Hartlepool U	(a)	2-1	
Third Round	Barnsley	(a)	2-3	

BURTON ALBION   FL Championship 2

FOUNDATION

Once upon a time there were three Football League clubs bearing the name Burton. Then there was none. In reality it had been two. Originally Burton Swifts and Burton Wanderers competed in it until 1901 when they amalgamated to form Burton United. This club disbanded in 1910. There was no senior club representing the town until 1924 when Burton Town, formerly known as Burton All Saints played in the Birmingham & District League, subsequently joining the Midland League in 1935–36. When the Second World War broke out the club fielded a team in a truncated version of the Birmingham & District League taking over from the club's reserves. But it was not revived in peacetime. So it was not until a further decade that a club bearing the name of Burton reappeared. Founded in 1950 Burton Albion made progress from the Birmingham & District League, too, then into the Southern League and because of its geographical situation later had spells in the Northern Premier League. In April 2009 Burton Albion restored the name of the town to the Football League competition as champions of the Blue Square Premier League.

Pirelli Stadium, Princess Way, Burton-on-Trent, Staffordshire DE13 0AR.

Telephone: (01283) 565 938.

Fax: (01283) 523 199.

Website: www.burtonalbionfc.co.uk

Email: bafc@burtonalbionfc.co.uk

Ground Capactiy: 6,350 (2,034 seated).

Record attendance: 6,192 v Oxford U, Blue Square Premier, 17 April 2009.

Chairman: Ben Robinson.

Football Secretary: Fleur Robinson.

Manager: Paul Peschisolido.

Assistant Manager: Gary Rowett.

Physio: TBC.

Colours: Yellow shirts with black insert, black shorts, black stockings.

Change Colours: White shirts with blue trim, blue shorts, blue stockings.

HONOURS

Conference: Champions 2008–09. *FA Cup:* 3rd rd 1956, 1985, 2006. *FA Trophy:* Runners-up 1986–87. *Southern League Premier Division:* Runners-up 1999–2000, 2000–01. *Division 1 (North):* Runners-up 1971–72, 1973–74. *Shared Cup:* 2000. *Southern League Cup:* Winners 1964, 1997, 2000; Runners-up 1989. *Northern Premier League:* Champions 2001–02. *Northern Premier League Shield:* 1983. *Challenge Cup:* Winners 1983; Runners-up 1987. *President's Cup:* Runners-up 1983, 1986. *Birmingham Senior Cup:* Winners 1954, 1997; Runners-up 1970, 1971, 1987. *Staffordshire Senior Cup:* Winners 1956; Runners-up 1977. *Midland Floodlit Cup:* Winners 1976; Runners-up 1973.

sky SPORTS FACT FILE

On 12 December 2009 Burton Albion recorded their highest Football League score in defeating Aldershot Town 6–1. Greg Pearson also became the first Burton player to hit a hat-trick in the competition. Then on 6 March they completed the double 2–0 at the Recreation Ground.

Year Formed: 1950.

Club nickname: Brewers.

Grounds: 1950, Wellington Street; 1958, Eton Park; 2005, Pirelli Stadium.

First Football League Game: 8 August 2009, FL 2, v Shrewsbury T (a) L 1–3 – Redmond; Edworthy, Boertien, Austin, Branston, McGrath, Maghoma, Penn, Phillips (Stride), Walker, Shroot (Pearson) (1).

Record League Victory: 6-1 v Aldershot T, FL 2, 12 December 2009 – Krysiak; James, Boertien, Stride, Webster, McGrath, Jackson, Penn, Kabba (2), Pearson (3) (Harrad) (1), Gilroy (Maghoma).

Record Cup Victory: 12–1 v Coalville T, Birmingham Senior Cup, 6 September 1954.

Record Defeat: 0–10 v Barnet, Southern League, 7 February 1970.

Most League Points (3 for a win): 62, FL 2, 2009–10.

Most League Goals: 71, FL 2, 2009–10.

Highest League Scorer in Season: Shaun Harrad, 21, 2009–10.

Most League Goals in One Match: 3, Greg Pearson v Aldershot T, FL 2, 12 December 2009.

Most Capped Player: Jacques Maghoma, 1, DR Congo.

Most League Appearances: John McGrath, 45, 2009–10.

Record Transfer Fee Received: £130,000 from Crewe Alex for John Brayford, September 2008.

Record Transfer Fee Paid: £20,000 to Kidderminster H for Russell Penn, July 2009.

Football League Record: Promoted from Blue Square Premier 2008–09; 2009– FL 2.

MANAGERS

Reg Weston
Sammy Crooks 1957
Eddie Shimwell 1958
Bill Townsend 1959–62
Peter Taylor 1962–65
Richie Norman
Reg Gutteridge
Harold Bodle 1974–76
Ian Storey-Moore 1978–81
Neil Warnock 1981–86
Brian Fidler 1986–88
Vic Halom 1988
Bobby Hope 1988
Chris Wright 1988–89
Ken Blair 1989–90
Frank Upton (caretaker) 1990
Steve Powell 1990–91
Brian Fidler 1991–92
Brian Kenning 1992–94
John Barton 1994–98
Nigel Clough 1998–2009
Roy McFarland 2009
Paul Peschisolido May 2009–

LATEST SEQUENCES

Longest Sequence of League Wins: 3, 4.10 2009 – 17.10.2009.

Longest Sequence of League Defeats: 2, 19.9.2009 – 26.9.2009.

Longest Sequence of League Draws: 2, 5.9.2009 – 12.9.2009.

Longest Sequence of Unbeaten League Matches: 5, 23.1.2010 – 9.2.2010.

Longest Sequence Without a League Win: 7, 27.3.2010 – 24.4.2010.

Successive Scoring Runs: 13 from 5.12.2009.

Successive Non-scoring Runs: 2 from 19.9.2009.

TEN YEAR LEAGUE RECORD

		P	W	D	L	F	A	Pts	Pos
2000-01	SLPL	42	25	13	4	76	36	88	2
2001-02	UNI	44	31	11	2	106	30	104	1
2002-03	Conf	42	13	10	19	52	77	49	16
2003-04	Conf	42	15	7	20	57	59	51*	14
2004-05	Conf	42	13	11	18	50	66	50	16
2005-06	Conf	42	16	12	14	50	52	60	9
2006-07	Conf	46	22	9	15	52	47	75	6
2007-08	B Sq Pr	46	23	12	11	79	56	81	5
2008-09	B Sq Pr	46	27	7	12	81	52	88	1
2009-10	FL 2	46	17	11	18	71	71	62	13

*1 pt deducted.

DID YOU KNOW ?

Stan Round scored six goals for Burton Albion against Hinckley Athletic in an 8–1 win during a Southern League First Division match in 1964–65. His total for the season was 30 in League and Cup games. He had been signed from Hinckley where he had been their top scorer.

BURTON ALBION 2009–10 LEAGUE RECORD

Match No.	Date	Venue	Opponents	Result	H/T Score	Lg Pos.	Goalscorers	Attendance
1	Aug 8	A	Shrewsbury T	L	1-3	0-1	—	Pearson [62]	6438
2	15	H	Morecambe	W	5-2	3-1	8	Pearson 2 (1 pen) [3, 54 (p)], Penn [16], Harrad [38], McGrath [75]	2342
3	18	H	Torquay U	L	0-2	0-2	—		2670
4	22	A	Lincoln C	W	2-0	1-0	11	Austin [23], Penn [90]	3590
5	29	H	Northampton T	W	3-2	3-0	8	Harrad [2], Simpson 2 [7, 11]	3321
6	Sept 5	A	Notts Co	D	1-1	0-0	8	Walker [84]	8891
7	12	A	Bradford C	D	1-1	0-1	10	Boertien [74]	11,439
8	19	H	Dagenham & R	L	0-1	0-1	12		2689
9	26	A	Bournemouth	L	0-1	0-0	14		6327
10	29	H	Macclesfield T	D	1-1	1-1	—	Pearson [37]	2332
11	Oct 4	H	Rochdale	W	1-0	1-0	12	Walker [3]	3119
12	10	A	Grimsby T	W	2-1	2-1	10	Corbett [10], Phillips [31]	4002
13	17	H	Barnet	W	2-0	1-0	8	Maghoma [8], Austin [78]	2935
14	24	A	Chesterfield	L	2-5	0-2	11	Webster [79], Harrad [90]	4218
15	31	H	Bury	D	0-0	0-0	11		3373
16	Nov 14	A	Darlington	L	0-1	0-1	11		2404
17	21	H	Hereford U	W	3-2	0-0	10	Harrad 2 (1 pen) [50, 64 (p)], Webster [87]	2796
18	24	A	Crewe Alex	L	1-2	0-2	—	Walker [90]	3446
19	Dec 1	H	Accrington S	L	0-2	0-1	—		2027
20	5	A	Rotherham U	D	2-2	0-1	15	Webster [65], Pearson [85]	3177
21	12	H	Aldershot T	W	6-1	4-0	12	Pearson 3 (1 pen) [31 (p), 39, 45], Kabba 2 [43, 72], Harrad [84]	2547
22	28	H	Notts Co	L	1-4	1-2	14	Kabba [38]	5801
23	Jan 16	H	Shrewsbury T	D	1-1	0-1	—	Pearson [75]	3139
24	19	A	Port Vale	L	1-3	1-2	—	Harrad (pen) [15]	4458
25	23	A	Torquay U	W	3-2	1-2	15	Penn [31], Harrad [56], Taylor [84]	2629
26	27	H	Lincoln C	W	1-0	1-0	—	Taylor [1]	2109
27	30	A	Northampton T	D	1-1	0-0	14	Harrad [53]	4552
28	Feb 6	H	Port Vale	W	1-0	1-0	12	Maghoma [39]	4644
29	9	A	Cheltenham T	W	1-0	1-0	—	Harrad [7]	2593
30	12	H	Crewe Alex	L	1-2	1-1	—	Harrad [28]	2985
31	16	A	Morecambe	L	2-3	2-1	—	Maghoma [23], Harrad [41]	1537
32	20	A	Hereford U	W	4-3	1-1	9	Harrad [9], Taylor [60], Webster [66], James [90]	2253
33	27	H	Rotherham U	L	0-1	0-0	13		3568
34	Mar 6	A	Aldershot T	W	2-0	2-0	11	Parkes [9], Kabba [26]	2784
35	13	H	Cheltenham T	L	5-6	2-0	14	Harrad 2 (1 pen) [2, 32 (p)], Townsend (og) [58], Kabba 2 [72, 85]	2500
36	20	H	Chesterfield	D	2-2	1-1	14	Penn [40], Pearson [90]	3696
37	23	A	Accrington S	W	2-0	1-0	—	Harrad [27], Pearson [79]	1270
38	27	A	Barnet	D	1-1	1-1	12	Pearson [18]	1842
39	Apr 3	H	Darlington	L	1-2	1-2	13	Pearson (pen) [45]	2779
40	5	A	Bury	L	0-3	0-1	13		2710
41	10	H	Bradford C	D	1-1	0-0	13	Harrad [82]	2648
42	13	A	Macclesfield T	D	1-1	0-1	—	Tipton (og) [58]	1588
43	17	A	Dagenham & R	L	1-2	1-0	13	Harrad [22]	1891
44	24	H	Bournemouth	L	0-2	0-0	13		3977
45	May 1	A	Rochdale	W	2-1	0-0	14	Taylor [62], Harrad (pen) [66]	3749
46	8	H	Grimsby T	W	3-0	2-0	13	Pearson [10], Harrad 2 [37, 58]	5510

Final League Position: 13

GOALSCORERS

League (71): Harrad 21 (4 pens), Pearson 14 (3 pens), Kabba 6, Penn 4, Taylor 4, Webster 4, Maghoma 3, Walker 3, Austin 2, Simpson 2, Boertien 1, Corbett 1, James 1, McGrath 1, Parkes 1, Phillips 1, own goals 2.
Carling Cup (1): Phillips 1.
FA Cup (3): Austin 1, Harrad 1 (pen), Maghoma 1.
J Paint Trophy (1): McGrath 1.

Redmond S 3	Edworthy M 1	Boertien P 33+1	Austin R 18	Branston G 18+1	McGrath J 44+1	Maghoma J 24+11	Penn R 34+6	Phillips J 19+5	Walker R 10+7	Shroot R 4+3	Stride D 5+4	Pearson G 24+18	Krysiak A 38	Corbett A 32+2	Harrad S 35+7	Simpson M 20+4	James T 42	Goodfellow M —+3	Makofo S —+2	Webster A 18+6	Cadogan K 2	Gilroy K 4+4	Brown A 1	Kabba S 18+5	Jackson R 4+1	Taylor C 23+1	Thompson O 1+1	Poole K 5+1	Parkes T 21+1	Boco R 3+5	Kelly S 2+2	Match No.
1	2	3	4	5	6	7	8	9[1]	10	11[2]	12	13																				1
		3	4	5	6	7	8	11[2]	13			9	1	2	10[1]	12																2
		3[2]	4	5	6	7	8[1]	11	12	13		9	1	2	10																	3
		3	4	5	6	13	12	11[1]				9[2]	1		7	10	3	2														4
		3	4	5	6	12	11[2]			13		9[1]	1		7	10	3	2														5
		3	4	5	6	14	12	11[1]	13			9	1		7	10[3]	3[2]	2														6
		3	4	5	6	11[3]		13	12			9[2]	1		7[1]	10	3	2	14													7
		3	4	5[1]	6	13		9	11[3]	12	14	1		7[2]	10[1]	3	2															8
		3	4		6[3]	14	7	13	9[1]	11[2]	5	12	1		10		8	2														9
		3	4		6		7[1]		9	11	5	10	1			12	8	2														10
		3	4	5	6	12	14	11[3]	9[1]			10[2]	1		7		8	2	13													11
		3[2]	2	5	6	14		7	9[3]			10[1]	1	11	12	8	4		13													12
			2	5	12	7	13	9[2]	10			8[1]	1	11		6	4		3													13
			2	5	6	7[3]	12		10[2]			9	1	11[1]	13	8	4	14	3													14
			2	5		7	8	9	11[1]			12	1		10	6	4		3													15
			2	5	6	7[2]		11	9			12	1		10[1]	8	4	13	3													16
			2	5	6		8	9		13		11	1		10	7	4		3	11[2]	12											17
			2	5	6	13	8	9[1]	14			12	1		10[3]	1	4		3	7[2]												18
1		3		5	6	13	8	7[1]				12			10	12	4					2	9									19
1		3			7		8					4	10		12		5			6			11	9	2							20
		3		6	12	8						4	10[2]		13		2			5			11[1]	9	7							21
		3[1]	13	7		8	12					5[2]	10[3]		1		14			2			7[1]	9	4							22
		3	5[1]	6	13	8						10	1	12		4	4						11[1]	9	2[3]	7[2]						23
		3		6	11	8		12[6]				9[1]	1[1]	2	10		5							7	4	15						24
		3		6	9[1]	8						2	10		5	12	4							7		1	11					25
				6	11	8						12	1	2	10		5			4				9[1]	7		3					26
				6	11	8						12	1	2	10		5			4				9[1]	7		3					27
				6	11	8	12					1	2	10[2]		5	4							9	7[1]	13	3					28
				6	11	8	12					13	1	2	10[2]		5	4						9	7[1]		3					29
				6	11	8[1]	12	14				13	1	2	10[3]		5	4						9[2]	7		3					30
		3		6	11							13	1	2[3]	10		5	4						9	12	7[1]		8				31
		14		6	11		8[1]	13				9[2]	1	2	10		5	4[1]	12						7[3]		3					32
		3		6	11	8[1]						13	1	2	10		4							9	7[2]		5	12				33
		3		6	11[2]	8						12	1	2	10[1]		4			14				3	7[3]		5	13				34
		3		6	11[1]	8						1	2	10		4								3	7		5	12				35
		3		6		8	11[2]					12	1	2	10		5	13						3[1]	7		4					36
		3		6		8	11[2]					9[3]	1	2	10		4	13							7[1]		5	12	14			37
		3		6		8	11[1]					9[2]	1	2	10		4	12						13	7		5					38
		3		6[3]		8	11[1]					9	1	2	10[2]	12	4			14				13	7		5					39
				6	14	8						11	1	2[1]	13		5			4				3[2]	7		12	10[3]	3			40
		3		6	11	8						9[1]	1	2	10		5							12	7		4					41
		3		6	11	8[1]						13	1	2	10	12	4							9[2]	7		5					42
		3		6	11	8						12		2	10[2]	9	4							13	7[1]	1	5[3]	14				43
		3		6	11[2]	8						9		2[1]	10[3]	7								14	12	1	5	13	4			44
		3		6		8						14	13	10	11[2]	4	12							9	2[1]	1	5	7[3]				45
		3		6		8[1]						9		10	11	4	12							2	1	5	7					46

FA Cup

First Round	Oxford C	(h)	3-2
Second Round	Gillingham	(a)	0-1

Carling Cup

First Round	Reading	(a)	1-5

J Paint Trophy

First Round	Chesterfield	(h)	1-5

BURY

FL Championship 2

FOUNDATION

A meeting at the Waggon & Horses Hotel, attended largely by members of Bury Wesleyans and Bury Unitarians football clubs, decided to form a new Bury club. This was officially formed at a subsequent gathering at the Old White Horse Hotel, Fleet Street, Bury on 24 April 1885.

Gigg Lane, Bury, Lancs BL9 9HR.

Telephone: (08445) 790009.

Fax: (0161) 764 5521.

Ticket Office: (08445) 790009.

Website: www.buryfc.co.uk

Email: info@buryfc.co.uk

Ground Capacity: 11,669.

Record Attendance: 35,000 v Bolton W, FA Cup 3rd rd, 9 January 1960.

Pitch Measurements: 112yd × 72yd.

Secretary: Jill Neville.

Directors: Mark Catlin, Brian Fenton, Jeremy Rothwell, Margaret Ladkin.

Manager: Alan Knill.

Assistant Manager: Chris Brass.

Physio: Tom Walsh.

Colours: Black and blue halved shirts, white shorts, black stockings

Change Colours: Red and white striped shirts, black shorts, black stockings.

Year Formed: 1885.

Turned Professional: 1885.

Ltd Co.: 1897.

Club Nickname: 'Shakers'.

Ground: 1885, Gigg Lane.

HONOURS

Football League: Division 1 best season: 4th, 1925–26; Division 2 – Champions 1894–95, 1996–97; Runners-up 1923–24; Division 3 – Champions 1960–61; Runners-up 1967–68.

FA Cup: Winners 1900, 1903.

Football League Cup: Semi-final 1963.

First Football League Game: 1 September 1894, Division 2, v Manchester C (h) W 4–2 – Lowe; Gillespie, Davies; White, Clegg, Ross; Wylie, Barbour (2), Millar (1), Ostler (1), Plant.

Record League Victory: 8–0 v Tranmere R, Division 3, 10 January 1970 – Forrest; Tinney, Saile; Anderson, Turner, McDermott; Hince (1), Arrowsmith (1), Jones (4), Kerr (1), Grundy, (1 og).

Record Cup Victory: 12–1 v Stockton, FA Cup 1st rd (replay), 2 February 1897 – Montgomery; Darroch, Barbour; Hendry (1), Clegg, Ross (1); Wylie (3), Pangbourn, Millar (4), Henderson (2), Plant, (1 og).

Record Defeat: 0–10 v Blackburn R, FA Cup pr rd, 1 October 1887. 0–10 v West Ham U, Milk Cup 2nd rd 2nd leg, 25 October 1983.

sky SPORTS FACT FILE

The first player to be capped for a country outside of the British Isles while playing for Bury was Lutel James, a forward signed from Hyde United in 1997–98. He gained his full international recognition playing for St Kitts and Nevis.

Most League Points (2 for a win): 68, Division 3, 1960–61.

Most League Points (3 for a win): 84, Division 4, 1984–85 and Division 2, 1996–97.

Most League Goals: 108, Division 3, 1960–61.

Highest League Scorer in Season: Craig Madden, 35, Division 4, 1981–82.

Most League Goals in Total Aggregate: Craig Madden, 129, 1978–86.

Most League Goals in One Match: 5, Eddie Quigley v Millwall, Division 2, 15 February 1947; 5, Ray Pointer v Rotherham U, Division 2, 2 October 1965.

Most Capped Player: Bill Gorman, 11 (13), Republic of Ireland and (4), Northern Ireland.

Most League Appearances: Norman Bullock, 506, 1920–35.

Youngest League Player: Brian Williams, 16 years 133 days v Stockport Co, 18 March 1972.

Record Transfer Fee Received: £1,100,000 from Ipswich T for David Johnson, November 1997.

Record Transfer Fee Paid: £200,000 to Ipswich T for Chris Swailes, November 1997 and £200,000 to Swindon T for Darren Bullock, February 1999.

Football League Record: 1894 Elected to Division 2; 1895–1912 Division 1; 1912–24 Division 2; 1924–29 Division 1; 1929–57 Division 2; 1957–61 Division 3; 1961–67 Division 2; 1967–68 Division 3; 1968–69 Division 2; 1969–71 Division 3; 1971–74 Division 4; 1974–80 Division 3; 1980–85 Division 4; 1985–96 Division 3; 1996–97 Division 2; 1997–99 Division 1; 1999–2002 Division 2; 2002–04 Division 3; 2004– FL 2.

LATEST SEQUENCES

Longest Sequence of League Wins: 9, 26.9.1960 – 19.11.1960.

Longest Sequence of League Defeats: 8, 18.8.2001 – 25.9.2001.

Longest Sequence of League Draws: 6, 6.3.1999 – 3.4.1999.

Longest Sequence of Unbeaten League Matches: 18, 4.2.1961 – 29.4.1961.

Longest Sequence Without a League Win: 19, 1.4.1911 – 2.12.1911.

Successive Scoring Runs: 24 from 1.9.1894.

Successive Non-scoring Runs: 6 from 11.1.1969.

MANAGERS

T. Hargreaves 1887
(Secretary-Manager)
H. S. Hamer 1887–1907
(Secretary-Manager)
Archie Montgomery 1907–15
William Cameron 1919–23
James Hunter Thompson 1923–27
Percy Smith 1927–30
Arthur Paine 1930–34
Norman Bullock 1934–38
Charlie Dean 1938–44
Jim Porter 1944–45
Norman Bullock 1945–49
John McNeil 1950–53
Dave Russell 1953–61
Bob Stokoe 1961–65
Bert Head 1965–66
Les Shannon 1966–69
Jack Marshall 1969
Colin McDonald 1970
Les Hart 1970
Tommy McAnearney 1970–72
Alan Brown 1972–73
Bobby Smith 1973–77
Bob Stokoe 1977–78
David Hatton 1978–79
Dave Connor 1979–80
Jim Iley 1980–84
Martin Dobson 1984–89
Sam Ellis 1989–90
Mike Walsh 1990–95
Stan Ternent 1995–98
Neil Warnock 1998–99
Andy Preece 2000–04
Graham Barrow 2004–05
Chris Casper 2005–08
Alan Knill February 2008–

TEN YEAR LEAGUE RECORD

		P	W	D	L	F	A	Pts	Pos
2000-01	Div 2	46	16	10	20	45	59	58	16
2001-02	Div 2	46	11	11	24	43	75	44	22
2002-03	Div 3	46	18	16	12	57	56	70	7
2003-04	Div 3	46	15	11	20	54	64	56	12
2004-05	FL 2	46	14	16	16	54	54	58	17
2005-06	FL 2	46	12	17	17	45	57	52*	19
2006-07	FL 2	46	13	11	22	46	61	50	21
2007-08	FL 2	46	16	11	19	58	61	59	13
2008-09	FL 2	46	21	15	10	63	43	78	4
2009-10	FL 2	46	19	12	15	54	59	69	9

*1 pt deducted.

DID YOU KNOW ?

Financial consideration forced Bury to sell Jack Lythgoe just after the Great War. He was transferred to Nottingham Forest for £500, a sum which helped the finances at the club. Signed in 1914 he was top scorer and during wartime regional football hit over 50 goals.

BURY 2009–10 LEAGUE RECORD

Match No.	Date	Venue	Opponents	Result	H/T Score	Lg Pos.	Goalscorers	Attendance
1	Aug 8	H	Bournemouth	L 0-3	0-2	—		2998
2	15	A	Darlington	W 1-0	0-0	15	Robertson [59]	2310
3	18	A	Hereford U	W 3-1	1-1	—	Jones [10], Lowe 2 [53, 86]	2321
4	22	H	Grimsby T	L 0-1	0-1	14		2799
5	29	A	Rochdale	L 0-3	0-0	18		4534
6	Sept 5	H	Accrington S	L 0-2	0-0	19		3082
7	12	H	Cheltenham T	L 0-1	0-0	20		2130
8	19	A	Port Vale	W 1-0	1-0	17	Lowe [8]	5461
9	26	H	Lincoln C	W 2-0	0-0	13	Lowe [85], Worrall [90]	2554
10	29	A	Crewe Alex	W 3-2	2-1	—	Elliott [22], Lowe [41], Dawson (pen) [86]	3534
11	Oct 3	H	Torquay U	D 1-1	1-0	11	Jones [38]	2524
12	10	H	Northampton T	D 2-2	2-0	12	Worrall [29], Lowe [33]	2863
13	17	A	Aldershot T	W 3-2	1-1	11	Barry-Murphy [39], Dawson [74], Sodje [76]	3196
14	24	H	Rotherham U	W 2-1	0-1	9	Lowe [48], Baker [84]	3496
15	31	A	Burton Alb	D 0-0	0-0	9		3373
16	Nov 14	H	Notts Co	D 3-3	2-2	9	Nardiello [9], Morrell [19], Dawson [50]	3602
17	21	A	Shrewsbury T	D 1-1	1-0	9	Nardiello [29]	5070
18	24	A	Chesterfield	W 2-1	0-0	9	Morrell 2 [56, 71]	2504
19	Dec 1	A	Morecambe	L 0-3	0-0	—		1875
20	5	H	Barnet	W 2-0	1-0	8	Nardiello (pen) [45], Worrall [82]	2511
21	12	A	Dagenham & R	L 1-3	1-1	9	Nardiello [45]	1915
22	28	A	Accrington S	W 4-2	0-1	9	Jones [53], Morrell 2 [55, 75], Lowe [90]	3138
23	Jan 2	A	Grimsby T	D 1-1	0-0	—	Lowe (pen) [90]	3463
24	16	A	Bournemouth	W 2-1	2-0	—	Dawson [9], Worrall [39]	4516
25	19	H	Bradford C	W 2-1	2-1	—	Jones [17], Lowe (pen) [32]	2930
26	23	H	Hereford U	W 1-0	1-0	3	Jones [2]	2797
27	Feb 1	H	Rochdale	W 1-0	0-0	—	Lowe [78]	6528
28	6	A	Bradford C	W 1-0	0-0	3	Morrell [52]	11,965
29	9	H	Macclesfield T	W 2-1	1-1	—	Lowe (pen) [29], Bishop [79]	2169
30	13	A	Chesterfield	L 0-1	0-0	3		4122
31	19	H	Shrewsbury T	W 1-0	0-0	—	Lowe (pen) [71]	3720
32	23	H	Morecambe	D 0-0	0-0	—		2222
33	27	A	Barnet	D 0-0	0-0	3		1949
34	Mar 6	H	Dagenham & R	D 0-0	0-0	4		2886
35	9	H	Darlington	D 1-1	1-1	—	Lowe (pen) [42]	2123
36	13	A	Macclesfield T	L 0-2	0-1	3		2740
37	20	A	Rotherham U	L 0-1	0-0	6		3521
38	27	H	Aldershot T	L 1-2	0-1	6	Bishop (pen) [87]	2795
39	Apr 3	A	Notts Co	L 0-5	0-1	8		7005
40	5	H	Burton Alb	W 3-0	1-0	7	James (og) [9], Morrell 2 [76, 86]	2710
41	10	A	Cheltenham T	L 2-5	0-1	8	Lowe 2 (1 pen) [80 (p), 82]	3071
42	13	A	Crewe Alex	W 3-0	1-0	—	Morrell [30], Lowe [48], Bishop [88]	2178
43	17	H	Port Vale	D 1-1	0-1	5	Sodje [82]	4570
44	24	A	Lincoln C	L 0-1	0-0	6		3403
45	May 1	H	Torquay U	L 0-3	0-1	8		3492
46	8	A	Northampton T	D 1-1	1-0	9	Lowe [45]	5234

Final League Position: 9

GOALSCORERS

League (54): Lowe 18 (6 pens), Morrell 9, Jones 5, Dawson 4 (1 pen), Nardiello 4 (1 pen), Worrall 4, Bishop 3 (1 pen), Sodje 2, Baker 1, Barry-Murphy 1, Elliott 1, Robertson 1, own goal 1.
Carling Cup (0).
FA Cup (0).
J Paint Trophy (4): Jones 2, Racchi 1, Worrall 1.

Brown W 41	Scott P 26+4	Buchanan D 37+1	Racchi D 10+12	Futcher B 29+3	Sodje E 39	Dawson S 45	Jones M 36+5	Carlton D 1+6	Lowe R 34+5	Barry-Murphy B 46	Worrall D 34+6	Johnson S 1+3	Rouse D 1+3	Robertson J 4	Morrell A 25+7	Cresswell R 24+4	Bishop A 12+13	Newey T 29+3	Baker R 7+7	Elliot T 7+9	Belford C 5+2	Nardiello D 6	Hewson S 1+6	Parker K 2	Poole J 4+5	Match No.
1	2	3	4[1]	5	6	7	8[2]	9	10[3]	11	12	13	14													1
1	2	3		5	6	4	11		10[1]	8	7[2]	13			9	12										2
1	2	3	13	5	6	4	11[2]		10[3]	8	7	14			9[1]	12										3
1	2[2]	3[1]	13	5	6	4	11		10	8	7				9[3]	12	14									4
1	2	11[3]		5	6	4			10[1]	8	7		14		9[2]	12	13	3								5
1	2			5	6	4			12	8	7[2]	11[3]	14		9[1]		10	3	13							6
1	2	13		5	6	4	12		9	8	7[2]				E	10	3	11[1]								7
1	2	13		14	6	4	7[3]		9[1]	8					E	10	3	11[2]	12							8
1	2			5	6	4	7		9	8	12					10[2]	3	11[1]	13							9
1	2	13			6	4	7		9[2]	8	12				E		3	11[1]	10							10
1	2				6	4	7		9	8	12				E		3	11[1]	10							11
1	2			5		4	11		10	8	7				E		3		9							12
1	13	2	12		6	4	8[1]		10[2]	11	7				E		3		9							13
1[6]		2	4		6	7	11		10	8					E		3	12	9[1]			15				14
1	13	2	9[2]	12	6[1]	4	8		10	7					E		3	11								15
1		2	7		6	4	11			8					9	5	3			10						16
1	13	2	7[1]		6	4	11			8	12				9[2]	5	3			10						17
1		2	7[2]	12	6	4	11			8	13				9	5[1]	3	14		10[3]						18
1		2	11	5	6	4			12	8	7				9		3			10						19
1		2	11[2]	5	6	4			12	8	7				9		3	13		10[1]						20
1		2	11[1]	5	6	4	12		13	8	7				9		3			10[2]						21
1		2	12	5	6	4	11		10	8	7[1]				9		3									22
1	12	2	13	5	6	4[1]	11		10	8	7				9		3[2]									23
1	2	3	13	5	6	4	11		10	8	7[2]				9[1]			12								24
1	2	3		5	6	4	11		10	8	7				9											25
1	2	3		5	6	4	11		10	8	7				9[1]			12								26
1	2	3		5	6[1]	4	11		10[3]	8	7[2]				9	12	13	14								27
1	2			5	6	4	11[1]		10[3]	8	7				9[2]	14	13	3			12					28
1	2			5	6	4	11[2]		10[3]	8	7				9[1]		12	3			13					29
1	2			5	6	4[1]	11		10[3]	8	7				9[2]		13	3	14		12					30
1	2			5	6	4[2]	11		10[3]	8	7				9[1]		12	3	14		13					31
1	2	13		5		6	11		10	8					9[1]	4	12	3					7[2]			32
1		2	13	5		6	11[2]		10[3]	8	7				9[1]	4	12	3					14			33
1		2		5		4	11[2]		10	8	7				9[1]	6	12	3					13			34
1		2		5		4	11		9	8	7[2]				6	10[1]	3	12					13			35
1		2	13	5	6	4[3]			9	8	7			14		10[1]	3[2]	11	12							36
1		2	13	5	6[1]	4	11[2]			8	7				14	12	3	10							9[1]	37
	2[1]	3		5		4	11[2]			8	7				6	13	12	9					10[3]		14	38
1	2	3		5		4	12		13	8	7[1]				9[3]	6	10[2]	14					11			39
1	2	3			6	4	13	14		8	7				9[1]	5	10[3]	12					11[2]			40
1[4]	2	3			6	4	13		9	8	7[1]				12	5	10[2]					15	11[6]			41
	2	3			6	4[1]	11		10	8	7[3]				9[2]	5	13	12			1		14			42
	2	3			6	4	11	14	10[3]	8	7[2]				9[1]	5	12				1		13			43
	2[3]	3			6	4	11[2]	12		8	7				9	5	10[1]	14			1		13			44
	2	3			6	4	11[2]		13	8	7[1]				9	5	10				1		12			45
	2	3		5		4	13		12	10[3]	8				9[2]	6	11[1]	14			1				7[8]	46

FA Cup
First Round — Aldershot T — (a) — 0-2

Carling Cup
First Round — WBA — (h) — 0-2

J Paint Trophy
First Round — Walsall — (a) — 0-0
Second Round — Tranmere R — (h) — 2-1
Northern Quarter-Final — Accrington S — (a) — 2-3

CARDIFF CITY
FL Championship

FOUNDATION

Credit for the establishment of a first class professional football club in such a rugby stronghold as Cardiff, is due to members of the Riverside club formed in 1899 out of a cricket club of that name. Cardiff became a city in 1905 and in 1908 the South Wales and Monmouthshire FA granted Riverside permission to call themselves Cardiff City. The club turned professional under that name in 1910.

Cardiff City Stadium, Leckwith Road, Cardiff CF11 8AZ.

Telephone: (0845) 365 1115.

Fax: (0845) 365 1116.

Ticket Office: 0845 345 1400.

Website: www.cardiffcityfc.co.uk

Email: club@cardiffcityfc.co.uk

Ground Capacity: 26,828.

Record Attendance: 62,634, Wales v England, 17 October 1959 (at Ninian Park); 26,055 v Leicester C, FL C Play-Off semi-final 2nd leg 12 May 2010 (at Cardiff City Stadium).

Club Record Attendance: 57,893 v Arsenal, Division 1, 22 April 1953.

Pitch Measurements: 110yd × 75yd.

Chairman: Dato Chan Tien Ghee.

Secretary: Jason Turner.

Manager: Dave Jones. *Assistant Manager:* Terry Burton.

Physio: Sean Connely BHSc MCSP, SRP.

Colours: Blue shirts with yellow trim, white shorts, white stockings.

Change Colours: Yellow shirts, blue shorts, blue stockings.

Year Formed: 1899. *Turned Professional:* 1910.

Ltd Co.: 1910.

Previous Names: 1899, Riverside; 1902, Riverside Albion; 1908, Cardiff City.

Club Nickname: 'Bluebirds'.

Grounds: Riverside, Sophia Gardens, Old Park and Fir Gardens. 1910, Ninian Park; 2009, Cardiff City Stadium.

First Football League Game: 28 August 1920, Division 2, v Stockport Co (a) W 5–2 – Kneeshaw; Brittan, Leyton; Keenor (1), Smith, Hardy; Grimshaw (1), Gill (2), Cashmore, West, Evans (1).

Record League Victory: 9–2 v Thames, Division 3 (S), 6 February 1932 – Farquharson; E. L. Morris, Roberts; Galbraith, Harris, Ronan; Emmerson (1), Keating (1), Jones (1), McCambridge (1), Robbins (5).

HONOURS

Football League: Division 1 – Runners-up 1923–24; Division 2 – Runners-up 1920–21, 1951–52, 1959–60; Division 3 (S) – Champions 1946–47; Division 3 – Champions 1992–93. Runners-up 1975–76, 1982–83, 2000–01; Division 4 – Runners-up 1987–88.

FA Cup: Winners 1927 (only occasion the Cup has been won by a club outside England); Runners-up 1925, 2008.

Football League Cup: Semi-final 1966.

Welsh Cup: Winners 22 times (joint record).

Charity Shield: Winners 1927.

European Competitions: European Cup-Winners' Cup: 1964–65, 1965–66, 1967–68 (semi-finalists), 1968–69, 1969–70, 1970–71, 1971–72, 1973–74, 1974–75, 1976–77, 1977–78, 1988–89, 1992–93, 1993–94.

sky SPORTS FACT FILE

On 14 April 1923 Cardiff City were forced to field six reserve players against Sheffield United because of international calls. Three first team regulars were playing for Wales, two more for Ireland, while a sixth was fielded by Scotland against England. Cardiff still won 1–0!

Record Cup Victory: 8–0 v Enfield, FA Cup 1st rd, 28 November 1931 – Farquharson; Smith, Roberts; Harris (1), Galbraith, Ronan; Emmerson (2), Keating (3); O'Neill (2), Robbins, McCambridge.

Record Defeat: 2–11 v Sheffield U, Division 1, 1 January 1926.

Most League Points (2 for a win): 66, Division 3 (S), 1946–47.

Most League Points (3 for a win): 86, Division 3, 1982–83.

Most League Goals: 95, Division 3, 2000–01.

Highest League Scorer in Season: Robert Earnshaw, 31, Division 2, 2002–03.

Most League Goals in Total Aggregate: Len Davies, 128, 1920–31.

Most League Goals in One Match: 5, Hugh Ferguson v Burnley, Division 1, 1 September 1928; 5, Walter Robbins v Thames, Division 3 (S), 6 February 1932; 5, William Henderson v Northampton T, Division 3 (S), 22 April 1933.

Most Capped Player: Alf Sherwood, 39 (41), Wales.

Most League Appearances: Phil Dwyer, 471, 1972–85.

Youngest League Player: Bob Adams, 15 years 355 days v Southend U, 18 February 1933.

Record Transfer Fee Received: £5,000,000 from Sunderland for Michael Chopra, August 2006; £5,000,000 from Arsenal for Aaron Ramsey, June 2008; £5,000,000 from Birmingham C for Roger Johnson, June 2009.

Record Transfer Fee Paid: £3,000,000 to Sunderland for Michael Chopra, July 2009.

Football League Record: 1920 Elected to Division 2; 1921–29 Division 1; 1929–31 Division 2; 1931–47 Division 3 (S); 1947–52 Division 2; 1952–57 Division 1; 1957–60 Division 2; 1960–62 Division 1; 1962–75 Division 2; 1975–76 Division 3; 1976–82 Division 2; 1982–83 Division 3; 1983–85 Division 2; 1985–86 Division 3; 1986–88 Division 4; 1988–90 Division 3; 1990–92 Division 4; 1992–93 Division 3; 1993–95 Division 2; 1995–99 Division 3; 1999–2000 Division 2; 2000–01 Division 3; 2001–03 Division 2; 2003–04 Division 1; 2004– FL C.

MANAGERS

Davy McDougall 1910–11
Fred Stewart 1911–33
Bartley Wilson 1933–34
B. Watts-Jones 1934–37
Bill Jennings 1937–39
Cyril Spiers 1939–46
Billy McCandless 1946–48
Cyril Spiers 1948–54
Trevor Morris 1954–58
Bill Jones 1958–62
George Swindin 1962–64
Jimmy Scoular 1964–73
Frank O'Farrell 1973–74
Jimmy Andrews 1974–78
Richie Morgan 1978–81
Graham Williams 1981–82
Len Ashurst 1982–84
Jimmy Goodfellow 1984
Alan Durban 1984–86
Frank Burrows 1986–89
Len Ashurst 1989–91
Eddie May 1991–94
Terry Yorath 1994–95
Eddie May 1995
Kenny Hibbitt *(Chief Coach)* 1995
Phil Neal 1996
Russell Osman 1996–97
Kenny Hibbitt 1996–98
Frank Burrows 1998–99
Billy Ayre 1999–2000
Bobby Gould 2000
Alan Cork 2000–02
Lennie Lawrence 2002–05
Dave Jones May 2005–

LATEST SEQUENCES

Longest Sequence of League Wins: 9, 26.10.1946 – 28.12.1946.

Longest Sequence of League Defeats: 7, 4.11.1933 – 25.12.1933.

Longest Sequence of League Draws: 6, 29.11.1980 – 17.1.1981.

Longest Sequence of Unbeaten League Matches: 21, 21.9.1946 – 1.3.1947.

Longest Sequence Without a League Win: 15, 21.11.1936 – 6.3.1937.

Successive Scoring Runs: 23 from 24.10.1992.

Successive Non-scoring Runs: 8 from 20.12.1952.

TEN YEAR LEAGUE RECORD

		P	W	D	L	F	A	Pts	Pos
2000-01	Div 3	46	23	13	10	95	58	82	2
2001-02	Div 2	46	23	14	9	75	50	83	4
2002-03	Div 2	46	23	12	11	68	43	81	6
2003-04	Div 1	46	17	14	15	68	58	65	13
2004-05	FL C	46	13	15	18	48	51	54	16
2005-06	FL C	46	16	12	18	58	59	60	11
2006-07	FL C	46	17	13	16	57	53	64	13
2007-08	FL C	46	16	16	14	59	55	64	12
2008-09	FL C	46	19	17	10	65	53	74	7
2009-10	FL C	46	22	10	14	73	54	76	4

DID YOU KNOW ?

Cardiff City signed 17 new professionals at the start of 1934–35. No fewer than eight of these were in the team for the opening match against Charlton Athletic. Goals from old hand Reg Keating and new boy Harold Riley gave Cardiff a 2–1 win.

CARDIFF CITY 2009–10 LEAGUE RECORD

Match No.	Date	Venue	Opponents	Result	H/T Score	Lg Pos.	Goalscorers	Attendance
1	Aug 8	H	Scunthorpe U	W 4-0	3-0	—	Chopra 2 [21, 45], Bothroyd [31], Whittingham (pen) [90]	22,264
2	15	A	Blackpool	D 1-1	1-1	2	Chopra [12]	7698
3	18	A	Plymouth Arg	W 3-1	1-0	—	Chopra 3 (1 pen) [4, 80, 85 (p)]	11,918
4	23	H	Bristol C	W 3-0	2-0	1	McCombe (og) [37], Chopra [45], Rae [66]	20,853
5	29	H	Doncaster R	L 0-2	0-2	2		9742
6	Sept13	H	Newcastle U	L 0-1	0-1	8		25,630
7	16	A	Reading	W 1-0	0-0	—	Burke [58]	16,687
8	19	H	QPR	L 0-2	0-2	6		20,121
9	26	A	Sheffield W	L 1-3	1-1	9	Whittingham (pen) [16]	18,959
10	29	H	Derby Co	W 6-1	2-0	—	Whittingham [16], Chopra 4 [36, 57, 62, 75], Burke [63]	18,670
11	Oct 3	A	Watford	W 4-0	2-0	4	Whittingham 2 (1 pen) [24 (p), 66], Matthews [41], Bothroyd [67]	13,895
12	17	H	Crystal Palace	D 1-1	1-1	3	Whittingham [19]	21,457
13	20	H	Coventry C	W 2-0	1-0	—	Gerrard [5], Whittingham (pen) [60]	19,038
14	24	A	Sheffield U	W 4-3	2-2	2	Bothroyd [41], Whittingham 3 (1 pen) [45 (p), 60, 85]	25,021
15	Nov 1	H	Nottingham F	D 1-1	0-0	2	Bothroyd [63]	20,413
16	7	A	Swansea C	L 2-3	2-2	3	Bothroyd [32], Hudson [35]	18,209
17	21	A	Barnsley	L 0-1	0-0	5		11,903
18	29	H	Ipswich T	L 1-2	1-0	7	Whittingham [35]	19,463
19	Dec 5	H	Preston NE	W 1-0	0-0	5	Burke [55]	18,735
20	8	A	WBA	W 2-0	1-0	—	Burke [18], Whittingham [85]	20,742
21	13	A	Middlesbrough	W 1-0	0-0	3	Burke [61]	17,232
22	26	H	Plymouth Arg	L 0-1	0-0	5		24,010
23	28	A	Peterborough U	D 4-4	4-0	24	Ledley 2 [6, 23], Bothroyd [34], Whittingham [38]	9796
24	Jan 9	H	Blackpool	D 1-1	1-0	—	Hudson [9]	19,147
25	16	A	Scunthorpe U	D 1-1	0-1	5	Whittingham [82]	5032
26	26	A	Bristol C	W 6-0	4-0	—	Whittingham [19], McCormack 2 [23, 57], Chopra 2 [24, 46], Fontaine (og) [43]	13,825
27	30	H	Doncaster R	W 2-1	1-0	4	Chopra [9], Bothroyd [90]	19,730
28	Feb 5	A	Newcastle U	L 1-5	0-3	—	Wildig [89]	44,028
29	9	H	Peterborough U	W 2-0	1-0	—	Burke [30], Gerrard [78]	17,686
30	16	H	WBA	D 1-1	1-1	—	Whittingham (pen) [8]	20,758
31	20	H	Barnsley	L 0-2	0-2	5		19,753
32	27	A	Preston NE	L 0-3	0-1	6		11,777
33	Mar 6	H	Middlesbrough	W 1-0	1-0	6	Bothroyd [3]	19,803
34	9	A	Ipswich T	L 0-2	0-1	—		19,997
35	13	A	Leicester C	L 0-1	0-1	6		22,767
36	16	A	Coventry C	W 2-1	1-1	—	Burke [41], Whittingham (pen) [90]	16,038
37	21	H	Watford	W 3-1	1-0	6	McCormack [7], Whittingham [63], Burke [78]	20,130
38	24	H	Sheffield U	D 1-1	1-0	—	Bothroyd [45]	18,715
39	27	A	Crystal Palace	W 2-1	1-0	4	Gyepes [4], Burke [67]	13,464
40	30	H	Leicester C	W 2-1	2-0	—	McCormack [10], Whittingham [45]	20,438
41	Apr 3	H	Swansea C	W 2-1	1-1	4	Chopra 2 [42, 90]	25,130
42	5	A	Nottingham F	D 0-0	0-0	4		22,185
43	10	H	Reading	D 0-0	0-0	4		21,248
44	17	A	QPR	W 1-0	0-0	4	Ledley [80]	12,832
45	24	H	Sheffield W	W 3-2	1-1	4	Whittingham [17], Bothroyd 2 [54, 81]	23,304
46	May 2	A	Derby Co	L 0-2	0-0	4		31,102

Final League Position: 4

GOALSCORERS

League (73): **Whittingham** 20 (7 pens), **Chopra** 16 (1 pen), **Bothroyd** 11, **Burke** 9, **McCormack** 4, **Ledley** 3, **Gerrard** 2, **Hudson** 2, **Gyepes** 1, **Matthews** 1, **Rae** 1, **Wildig** 1, own goals 2.
Carling Cup (6): **Whittingham** 2, **Bothroyd** 1 (pen), **Chopra** 1, **Magennis** 1, **Rae** 1.
FA Cup (7): **Chopra** 2, **Bothroyd** 1, **Burke** 1, **McCormack** 1, **Whittingham** 1, own goal 1.
Play-Offs (5): **Chopra** 2, **Whittingham** 2 (1 pen), **Ledley** 1.

Marshall D 43	Quinn P 16+6	Kennedy M 25+5	Gerrard A 39	Hudson M 26+1	Whittingham P 41	McCormack R 21+13	McPhail S 21	Bothroyd J 40	Chopra M 36+5	Ledley J 27+2	Rae G 28+9	Burke C 38+6	Magennis J 1+8	Capaldi T 10+5	Matthews A 24+8	Comminges M 1+1	Etuhu K 7+9	Taiwo S 2+6	Scimeca R 2+2	Feeney W 1+8	McNaughton K 20+1	Gyepes G 16	Enckelman P 3+1	Wildig A 4+7	Blake D 15+3	Morris A —+1	Match No.
1	2	3	4	5	6	7	8	9^3	10^2	11^1	12	13	14														1
1	2^3		4	5	6	7^1	8^2	9	10	11	13	12		3	14												2
1		6		5			8	9^1	10^2	11	4	7	12	3^4	2	13											3
1	2	6		5			8	9^2	10^1	11	4	7	13	3			12										4
1		6		5			8^2	9^1	10	11	4	7^3	14	3	2		12	13									5
1	2	6		5			8^1	9	10	11	4	7		3			12										6
1	12	2	6	5		8		4^9	9	10^2	11^3	13	7		3^1		14										7
1	3	2	6	5		8^1		9^3	10	11	12	7	13				4^2	14									8
1		2^1	6	5	8			9	10	11^4	4	7^2	13	12	3												9
1	2	6	5	8		11^1		9	10^3		4^2	7	14	3			12	13									10
1	12	2^1	6	5	8	14	11	9	10^3	13	4^2	7		3													11
1	3	4	5	6	12			9^1	10	11	8	7^2		2					13								12
1	3	4	5	6		8		9	10	11		7		2													13
1	3	4	5	6	13	8^1		9	10	11	12	7^2		2													14
1	3	4	5	6		8^1		9	10	11	12	7		2													15
1	3		5	6		10		9		8	4	7	11^1	2			12										16
1	12	3		5	8	9^2		10	11	4	7			13	2^1	6											17
1^0		3		5	8	13		9	10	11	4^2	7^1		2		12				6	15						18
1	2	12	4^1	5	8	13		9	10^2	11^3	14	7						6	3								19
1	2	14	6	5	11	13			10		4	7		9^2		8^1		3^3		12							20
1	2		6	5	8^2	14		9	10	11	4	7			12	13^3		3^1									21
1	2^3		5	6	8	13		9	10^2	11	4	7^1		14	12			3									22
1	12		5	6	8	10^2		9^3	13	11	4	7		2	14			3^1									23
1	2		5	6	8	9^3			14	11	4	7^2	10^1	13			12	3									24
1	13		5	6	8	12		9	10	11		7^1		2^2				3		4							25
1		3	5		7^3	8		9^2	10	11	4^1	14		2				13		6		12					26
1		3^2	5		8	11		9	10		4^1	7^3		2		14		13		6		14	4	12			27
1	13	5		11	7	8^3		9^1	10		12			2^2				3		6		14	4				28
1	3	5		11		8^2		9^3	10		7				13		14	2	6		12	4^1					29
1	2	5			8^1	12		9	10		4	7						3	6			11^4	13				30
	2	5^2			8	12		9	10		4	7		13				3	6	1	11^1						31
2^2	12	5			11	8		9	10		4	7		13				3	6^1	1							32
1		5			11^1			9	10		4	7		12	2			3	6		8						33
1		5			11			9	10		4	7		12	2^1			3	6		8						34
1		6	5		11	10	8	9			12	7			2^1			3			4						35
1	13	6	5		11	10	8	9			12	7			2^2			3^1			4						36
1	2	3^1			11	10^3	8	9^2	14		4	7		12				13	5		6						37
1	2				11	10^1	8	9	12		4	7		3					5		6						38
1	2	12			11	14	8		10^3		4	7		3^1			9^2		13		5						39
1	2	5^2			11	9	8				4	7		13	12		10^3		14		5^4			3^1			40
1		5			7	11^2	8^3	9	10	12	4^1			3	2		13						14	6			41
1	3	5			7	8		9	10	11				2			4^1						12	6			42
1	3	5			7	12	8	9	10^1	11^2	13						4^3		2			14	6				43
1	2	5		6	10^1	8		9	12	11	7			7^2			13		3				4				44
1		5	12	7			8^3	9	10	11				13	3		4^2		2			14	6^1				45
	2		5	10				8^3	9^1	11			4	12	3	13	8^2	7^3		9^1		3	1	11		14	46

FA Cup

Third Round	Bristol C	(a)	1-1
		(h)	1-0
Fourth Round	Leicester C	(h)	4-2
Fifth Round	Chelsea	(a)	1-4

Carling Cup

First Round	Dagenham & R	(h)	3-1
Second Round	Bristol R	(h)	3-1
Third Round	Aston Villa	(a)	0-1

Play-Offs

Semi-Final	Leicester C	(a)	1-0
		(h)	2-3
Final	Blackpool		2-3
(at Wembley).			

CARLISLE UNITED   FL Championship 1

FOUNDATION

Carlisle United came into being in 1903 through the amalgamation of Shaddongate United and Carlisle Red Rose. The new club was admitted to the Second Division of the Lancashire Combination in 1905–06, winning promotion the following season. Devonshire Park was officially opened on 2 September 1905, when St Helens Town were the visitors. Despite defeat in a disappointing 3-2 start, a respectable mid-table position was achieved.

Brunton Park, Warwick Road, Carlisle CA1 1LL.
Telephone: (01228) 526 237.
Fax: (01228) 554 141.
Ticket Office: (0844) 371 1921.
Website: www.carlisleunited.co.uk
Email: enquiries@carlisleunited.co.uk
Ground Capacity: 16,981.
Record Attendance: 27,500 v Birmingham C, FA Cup 3rd rd, 5 January 1957 and v Middlesbrough, FA Cup 5th rd, 7 February 1970.
Pitch Measurements: 114yd × 74yd.
Chairman: Andrew Jenkins.
Managing Director: John Nixon.
Secretary: Sarah McKnight.
Manager: Greg Abbott.
Assistant Manager: Graham Kavanagh.
Physio: Neil Dalton.
Colours: Blue shirts with white and red trim, white shorts, white stockings.
Change Colours: All red with blue trim on sleeves.
Year Formed: 1903.   *Ltd Co.:* 1921.
Previous Name: 1903, Shaddongate United; 1904, Carlisle United.
Club Nicknames: 'Cumbrians' or 'The Blues'.
Grounds: 1903, Milholme Bank; 1905, Devonshire Park; 1909, Brunton Park.

HONOURS

Football League: Division 1 best season: 22nd, 1974–75; Division 3 – Champions 1964–65, 1994–95; Runners-up 1981–82; Division 4 – Runners-up 1963–64; FL 2 – Champions 2005–06.
FA Cup: best season: 6th rd 1975.
Football League Cup: Semi-final 1970.
Auto Windscreens Shield: Winners 1997; Runners-up 1995.
LDV Vans Trophy: Runners-up 2003, 2006.
Johnstone's Paint Trophy: Runners-up 2010

First Football League Game: 25 August 1928, Division 3 (N), v Accrington S (a) W 3–2 – Prout; Coulthard, Cook; Harrison, Ross, Pigg; Agar (1), Hutchison, McConnell (1), Ward (1), Watson.

Record League Victory: 8–0 v Hartlepool U, Division 3 (N), 1 September 1928 – Prout; Smiles, Cook; Robinson (1) Ross, Pigg; Agar (1), Hutchison (1), McConnell (4), Ward (1), Watson. 8–0 v Scunthorpe U, Division 3 (N), 25 December 1952 – MacLaren; Hill, Scott; Stokoe, Twentyman, Waters; Harrison (1), Whitehouse (5), Ashman (2), Duffett, Bond.

Record Cup Victory: 6–0 v Shepshed Dynamo, FA Cup 1st rd, 16 November 1996 – Caig; Hopper, Archdeacon (pen), Walling, Robinson, Pounewatchy, Peacock (1), Conway (1) (Jansen), Smart (McAlindon (1)), Hayward, Aspinall (Thorpe), (2 og).

sky SPORTS FACT FILE

Joe Laidlaw was not only the sole ever-present player in the Carlisle United team during its 1973–74 promotion to the First Division, but scored the first, decisive goal against Aston Villa on 27 April which clinched the rise in status.

Record Defeat: 1–11 v Hull C, Division 3 (N), 14 January 1939.

Most League Points (2 for a win): 62, Division 3 (N), 1950–51.

Most League Points (3 for a win): 91, Division 3, 1994–95.

Most League Goals: 113, Division 4, 1963–64.

Highest League Scorer in Season: Jimmy McConnell, 42, Division 3 (N), 1928–29.

Most League Goals in Total Aggregate: Jimmy McConnell, 126, 1928–32.

Most League Goals in One Match: 5, Hugh Mills v Halifax T, Division 3 (N), 11 September 1937; 5, Jim Whitehouse v Scunthorpe U, Division 3 (N), 25 December 1952.

Most Capped Player: Eric Welsh, 4, Northern Ireland.

Most League Appearances: Allan Ross, 466, 1963–79.

Youngest League Player: John Slaven, 16 years 162 days v Scunthorpe U, 16 March 2002.

Record Transfer Fee Received: £1,500,000 from Crystal Palace for Matt Jansen, February 1998.

Record Transfer Fee Paid: £140,000 to Blackburn R for Joe Garner, August 2007.

Football League Record: 1928 Elected to Division 3 (N); 1958–62 Division 4; 1962–63 Division 3; 1963–64 Division 4; 1964–65 Division 3; 1965–74 Division 2; 1974–75 Division 1; 1975–77 Division 2; 1977–82 Division 3; 1982–86 Division 2; 1986–87 Division 3; 1987–92 Division 4; 1992–95 Division 3; 1995–96 Division 2; 1996–97 Division 3; 1997–98 Division 2; 1998–04 Division 3; 2004–05 Conference; 2005–06 FL 2; 2006– FL 1.

LATEST SEQUENCES

Longest Sequence of League Wins: 7, 18.2.06 – 8.4.06.

Longest Sequence of League Defeats: 12, 27.9.2003 – 13.12.2003.

Longest Sequence of League Draws: 6, 11.2.1978 – 11.3.1978

Longest Sequence of Unbeaten League Matches: 19, 1.10.1994 – 11.2.1995.

Longest Sequence Without a League Win: 14, 19.1.1935 – 19.4.1935.

Successive Scoring Runs: 26 from 23.8.1947.

Successive Non-scoring Runs: 5 from 24.8.1968.

MANAGERS

Harry Kirkbride 1904–05 *(Secretary-Manager)*
McCumiskey 1905–06 *(Secretary-Manager)*
Jack Houston 1906–08 *(Secretary-Manager)*
Bert Stansfield 1908–10
Jack Houston 1910–12
Davie Graham 1912–13
George Bristow 1913–30
Billy Hampson 1930–33
Bill Clarke 1933–35
Robert Kelly 1935–36
Fred Westgarth 1936–38
David Taylor 1938–40
Howard Harkness 1940–45
Bill Clark 1945–46 *(Secretary-Manager)*
Ivor Broadis 1946–49
Bill Shankly 1949–51
Fred Emery 1951–58
Andy Beattie 1958–60
Ivor Powell 1960–63
Alan Ashman 1963–67
Tim Ward 1967–68
Bob Stokoe 1968–70
Ian MacFarlane 1970–72
Alan Ashman 1972–75
Dick Young 1975–76
Bobby Moncur 1976–80
Martin Harvey 1980
Bob Stokoe 1980–85
Bryan 'Pop' Robson 1985
Bob Stokoe 1985–86
Harry Gregg 1986–87
Cliff Middlemass 1987–91
Aidan McCaffery 1991–92
David McCreery 1992–93
Mick Wadsworth *(Director of Coaching)* 1993–96
Mervyn Day 1996–97
David Wilkes and John Halpin *(Directors of Coaching)*, and Michael Knighton 1997–99
Nigel Pearson 1998–99
Keith Mincher 1999
Martin Wilkinson 1999–2000
Ian Atkins 2000–01
Roddy Collins 2001–02; 2002–03
Paul Simpson 2003–06
Neil McDonald 2006–07
John Ward 2007–08
Greg Abbott December 2008–

TEN YEAR LEAGUE RECORD

		P	W	D	L	F	A	Pts	Pos
2000-01	Div 3	46	11	15	20	42	65	48	22
2001-02	Div 3	46	12	16	18	49	56	52	17
2002-03	Div 3	46	13	10	23	52	78	49	22
2003-04	Div 3	46	12	9	25	46	69	45	23
2004-05	Conf	42	20	13	9	74	37	73	3
2005-06	FL 2	46	25	11	10	84	42	86	1
2006-07	FL 1	46	19	11	16	54	55	68	8
2007-08	FL 1	46	23	11	12	64	46	80	4
2008-09	FL 1	46	12	14	20	56	69	50	20
2009-10	FL 1	46	15	13	18	63	66	58	14

DID YOU KNOW ?

On 27 January 1968 in an FA Cup third round tie, Carlisle United won 1–0 away to Newcastle United in front of a big crowd of 56,569 including some 8,000 visiting supporters. The only goal of the match was scored by Tommy Murray, the smallest player on the field.

CARLISLE UNITED 2009–10 LEAGUE RECORD

Match No.	Date		Venue	Opponents	Result		H/T Score	Lg Pos.	Goalscorers	Attendance
1	Aug	8	H	Brentford	L	1-3	1-1	—	Harte (pen) [17]	6367
2		15	A	Millwall	D	0-0	0-0	18		9055
3		18	A	Stockport Co	W	2-1	1-1	—	Hurst [13], Anyinsah [65]	4009
4		22	H	Exeter C	L	0-1	0-0	17		5156
5		29	A	Leyton Orient	D	2-2	1-0	16	Robson [42], Thirlwell [90]	3546
6	Sept	5	H	Tranmere R	W	3-0	0-0	9	Anyinsah [59], Livesey [67], Harte [77]	5269
7		12	H	Brighton & HA	L	0-2	0-1	12		5368
8		19	A	Oldham Ath	L	0-2	0-1	17		4268
9		26	H	Southampton	D	1-1	0-0	18	Dobie [69]	7000
10		29	A	Leeds U	D	1-1	0-1	—	Dobie [75]	19,673
11	Oct	3	A	Walsall	D	2-2	1-1	19	Robson [44], Keogh [90]	3572
12		10	H	Norwich C	L	0-1	0-1	19		6825
13		17	A	Yeovil T	L	1-3	0-2	21	Harte (pen) [54]	4333
14		24	H	Southend U	W	2-1	1-1	18	Pericard [11], Anyinsah [80]	4551
15		31	H	Charlton Ath	W	3-1	1-1	15	Harte [41], Kavanagh 2 [63, 83]	6077
16	Nov	14	A	Bristol R	L	2-3	1-1	18	Harte [21], Keogh [72]	5862
17		21	H	Swindon T	L	0-1	0-1	19		4339
18		24	A	Milton Keynes D	W	4-3	3-2	—	Hurst [5], Pericard 2 [17, 20], Anyinsah [67]	9459
19	Dec	1	H	Hartlepool U	W	3-2	1-1	—	Harte [33], Taiwo [52], Robson [63]	4109
20		5	A	Gillingham	D	0-0	0-0	12		7214
21		12	H	Wycombe W	W	1-0	1-0	11	Pericard [45]	4528
22		28	A	Tranmere R	D	0-0	0-0	15		6313
23	Jan	16	A	Brentford	L	1-3	0-1	17	Harte (pen) [81]	5089
24		23	H	Stockport Co	D	0-0	0-0	16		4966
25		26	A	Exeter C	W	3-2	2-0	—	Anyinsah 2 [33, 44], Offiong [90]	4106
26		30	H	Leyton Orient	D	2-2	2-0	12	Anyinsah [14], Harte [42]	4687
27	Feb	2	A	Colchester U	L	1-2	1-0	—	Harte [24]	3903
28		6	A	Huddersfield T	D	1-1	0-0	15	Marshall [83]	14,132
29		13	H	Milton Keynes D	W	5-0	2-0	15	Harte [21], Robson [39], Duffy [63], Dobie [71], Anyinsah [74]	4930
30		16	H	Huddersfield T	L	1-2	0-1	—	Anyinsah [90]	5236
31		20	A	Swindon T	L	0-2	0-1	13		7704
32		23	A	Hartlepool U	L	1-4	1-3	—	Dobie [10]	2975
33		27	H	Gillingham	W	2-0	1-0	13	Harte 2 (1 pen) [41, 52 (p)]	4646
34	Mar	6	A	Wycombe W	D	0-0	0-0	12		4876
35		9	H	Millwall	L	1-3	0-1	—	Livesey [89]	3853
36		13	H	Colchester U	W	2-1	0-0	12	Marshall [68], Price [73]	4469
37		16	H	Yeovil T	W	1-0	0-0	—	Clayton [66]	3731
38		20	A	Southend U	D	2-2	2-2	11	Dobie [6], Marshall [13]	6384
39	Apr	2	H	Bristol R	W	3-1	0-0	—	Harte 2 (2 pens) [56, 72], Price [61]	5407
40		5	A	Charlton Ath	L	0-1	0-1	12		17,229
41		10	A	Brighton & HA	W	2-1	1-0	12	Harte [33], Madine [88]	6673
42		13	H	Leeds U	L	1-3	1-1	—	Keogh [43]	8728
43		17	H	Oldham Ath	L	1-2	0-0	13	Madine [69]	4484
44		24	A	Southampton	L	2-3	1-1	14	Harte [45], Madine [90]	18,908
45	May	1	H	Walsall	D	1-1	1-1	14	Price [29]	5114
46		8	A	Norwich C	W	2-0	2-0	14	Madine [1], Price [7]	25,181

Final League Position: 14

GOALSCORERS

League (63): Harte 16 (6 pens), Anyinsah 9, Dobie 5, Madine 4, Pericard 4, Price 4, Robson 4, Keogh 3, Marshall 3, Hurst 2, Kavanagh 2, Livesey 2, Clayton 1, Duffy 1, Offiong 1, Taiwo 1, Thirlwell 1.
Carling Cup (4): Dobie 2, Harte 1 (pen), Madine 1.
FA Cup (7): Hurst 2, Pericard 2, Anyinsah 1, Harte 1, Keogh 1.
J Paint Trophy (17): Dobie 3, Kavanagh 3, Robson 3, Clayton 1, Anyinsah 1, Bridge-Wilkinson 1, Hurst 1, Keogh 1, Madine 1, Murphy 1.

Pidgeley L 17	Raven D 14 + 2	Harte I 45	Thirlwell P 24 + 4	Livesey D 38	Keogh R 41	Taylor C 1	Taiwo T 30 + 5	Anyinsah J 20 + 8	Kavanagh G 28 + 1	Robson M 39	Bridge-Wilkinson M 6 + 13	Dobie S 24 + 15	Madine G 6 + 14	Hurst K 30 + 3	Rothery G — + 1	Murphy P 12 + 4	Offiong R 2 + 13	Horwood E 31 + 1	Pericard V 10	Clayton A 28	Kane T 1 + 3	Collin A 29	Aldred T 4 + 1	Duffy D 7 + 1	Marshall B 11 + 9	Price J 8 + 1	Bowman R — + 6	Gillespie M — + 1	Match No.
1	2	3	4¹	5	6	7	8²	9³	10	11	12	13	14																1
1	2	3		5	6		8	9	4	11		7¹	10	12															2
1	2	3		5	6		8¹	9	4	11	12	10		7²	13														3
1	2	3		5			8	9¹	4	11		10	12	7		6													4
1	2	3	4	5			8¹	9		12	10²	13	7			6³	14												5
1	2	3	4	5			9²	8³	11	14	10¹	13	7		6	12													6
1	2	3	4	5			14	9	8³	11		10¹	13	7²		6	12												7
1	2	3	4	5			13	12	8¹	11		10³	14	7		6	9²												8
1	2	3	4	5	6		10	8		11		12		7		9¹													9
1	2	3		5	6		10²	8	9	11	4¹	12	7		13														10
1	2	3	5²	6			10	8	4	11	13	9¹	7		12														11
1		3	2	5			10	8	4¹	11	12	9	7		13	6²													12
1		3		2	5	6	4	8¹		11	7	9	12		13	2²	10												13
1		3		2	5		8	12	4	11		9		7¹		6	10												14
1		3		2	5		8	12	4	11	13	9		7¹		6	10²												15
1		5		2	6		8	7²	4	11		12		13		3	10¹	9											16
1		6		2	5¹		11²	8	4	7		12		14		3	10³	9	13										17
		6		2	5		8¹	12	4	11				7		3	10	9¹											18
		6		2	5		8	9	4	11				12		7¹	3	10											19
		6		2¹	5		8		4²	11		13				7	12	3	10	9									20
		6		2²	5			8	11			12		7		4¹	3	10	9		13								21
		6		2	5			13	8	11		12		7²		4¹	3	10	9										22
		6	13	2	5		8²	10	4	11	14	9		7¹		12	3³												23
		6		2	5		8	10	4¹	11		12⁴	14	7²		13	3³	9											24
		6	4	2	5			10¹		11	13		8	7²		12	3	9											25
		6	4	2	5			10¹		11	13		8	7²		12	3	9											26
		6	4	2	5					8¹	11			7²		12	3	9				10	13						27
		6¹	4	2	5					8³	11	13		7²	12		3	9				10	14						28
		3	4³	2	5		14	12		11²		8¹		7		6		9				10	13						29
		3	4²	2	5		14	12		11		10¹		7³		6		9				7	10²						30
		3	4	2	5			8		7¹	11	14		13		6		9³		1		12	10²						31
		3	4²	2	5		13			11		10		7³		6¹	12	9		1		8	14						32
		6	12	2	5		4¹			11		10		7²			3	9		1		8	13						33
		6	13	2	5		4²			11		10		7			3	9		1		8¹	12						34
		6		2	5		8³			4	11	14	10¹	7²		12	3	9		1		13							35
		6	13	2	5		8⁴			4²	11			7¹			3	9		1		12	10						36
		6	4	2³	5				8²	11	12		13			14	3	9		1		7¹	10						37
		5	4		2					11	13	8¹	12			6	3	9		1		7	10²						38
		5	4		2		7					11¹	12⁴	14			3	9	5	1	6	8	10³	13					39
			4²		2		7					8	12				3	9²	14	1	6	11	10¹	13					40
		5	4		2		7					8²	12				3	9³	14	1	6	11	10¹	13					41
	13	5	4¹		2		7					12	8³	10			3	9		1		6²	11		14				42
	6	5	4¹		2		7					8²	12	10			3	9		1			11		13				43
	13	6¹	4	2²	5		7					8¹	11	10			3				14	1			9	12			44
	2	6	4		5		7						12	10			3			9		1			11¹	8²	13		45
	2	6	4		5			13				8	12	11			3			9		1³			10²	7¹		15	46

CHARLTON ATHLETIC   FL Championship 1

FOUNDATION

The club was formed on 9 June 1905, by a group of 14- and 15-year-old youths living in streets by the Thames in the area which now borders the Thames Barrier. The club's progress through local leagues was so rapid that after the First World War they joined the Kent League where they spent a season before turning professional and joining the Southern League in 1920. A year later they were elected to the Football League's Division 3 (South).

The Valley, Floyd Road, Charlton, London SE7 8BL.
Telephone: (020) 8333 4000.
Fax: (020) 8333 4001.
Ticket Office: (0871) 226 1905.
Website: www.cafc.co.uk
Email: info@cafc.co.uk
Ground Capacity: 27,111.
Record Attendance: 75,031 v Aston Villa, FA Cup 5th rd, 12 February 1938 (at The Valley).
Pitch Measurements: 101.5m × 65.8m.
Chairman: Richard Murray.
Deputy Chairman: Martin Simons.
Chief Executive: Steve Waggott.
Football Secretary: Chris Parkes.
Manager: Phil Parkinson.
Assistant Manager: Tim Breaker.
Physio: Steve Allen.
Colours: Red shirts with white trim, white shorts, white stockings with red tops.
Change Colours: Black and blue striped shirts, black shorts, blue stockings.
Year Formed: 1905.
Turned Professional: 1920.
Ltd Co.: 1919.
Club Nickname: 'Addicks'.
Grounds: 1906, Siemen's Meadow; 1907, Woolwich Common; 1909, Pound Park; 1913, Horn Lane; 1920, The Valley; 1923, Catford (The Mount); 1924, The Valley; 1985, Selhurst Park; 1991, Upton Park; 1992, The Valley.
First Football League Game: 27 August 1921, Division 3 (S), v Exeter C (h) W 1–0 – Hughes; J Mitchell, Goodman; Dowling (1), Hampson, Dunn; Castle, Bailey, Halse, Green, Wilson.
Record League Victory: 8–1 v Middlesbrough, Division 1, 12 September 1953 – Bartram; Campbell, Ellis; Fenton, Ufton, Hammond; Hurst (2), O'Linn (2), Leary (1), Firmani (3), Kiernan.

HONOURS

Football League: Division 1 – Champions 1999–2000; Runners-up Division 2 – Runners-up 1935–36, 1985–86; Division 3 (S) – Champions 1928–29, 1934–35.
FA Cup: Winners 1947; Runners-up 1946.
Football League Cup: Quarter-final 2007.
Full Members' Cup: Runners-up 1987.

sky SPORTS FACT FILE

On 5 December 2009 Charlton Athletic celebrated the 17th anniversary of the club's return to The Valley with a 1–0 win over Southend United. An interested spectator at the ground was Colin Walsh who had hit the winning goal against Portsmouth on 5 December 1992.

Record Cup Victory: 7–0 v Burton A, FA Cup 3rd rd, 7 January 1956 – Bartram; Campbell, Townsend; Hewie, Ufton, Hammond; Hurst (1), Gauld (1), Leary (3), White, Kiernan (2).

Record Defeat: 1–11 v Aston Villa, Division 2, 14 November 1959.

Most League Points (2 for a win): 61, Division 3 (S), 1934–35.

Most League Points (3 for a win): 91, Division 1, 1999–2000.

Most League Goals: 107, Division 2, 1957–58.

Highest League Scorer in Season: Ralph Allen, 32, Division 3 (S), 1934–35.

Most League Goals in Total Aggregate: Stuart Leary, 153, 1953–62.

Most League Goals in One Match: 5, Wilson Lennox v Exeter C, Division 3 (S), 2 February 1929; 5, Eddie Firmani v Aston Villa, Division 1, 5 February 1955; 5, John Summers v Huddersfield T, Division 2, 21 December 1957; 5, John Summers v Portsmouth, Division 2, 1 October 1960.

Most Capped Player: Jonatan Johansson, 42 (103), Finland.

Most League Appearances: Sam Bartram, 579, 1934–56.

Youngest League Player: Jonjo Shevley, 16 years 59 days v Burnley, 26 April 2008.

Record Transfer Fee Received: £16,500,000 from Tottenham H for Darren Bent, May 2007

Record Transfer Fee Paid: £5,380,000 to Ipswich T for Darren Bent, June 2005.

Football League Record: 1921 Elected to Division 3 (S); 1929–33 Division 2; 1933–35 Division 3 (S); 1935–36 Division 2; 1936–57 Division 1; 1957–72 Division 2; 1972–75 Division 3; 1975–80 Division 2; 1980–81 Division 3; 1981–86 Division 2; 1986–90 Division 1; 1990–92 Division 2; 1992–98 Division 1; 1998–99 FA Premier League; 1999–2000 Division 1; 2000–07 FA Premier League; 2007–09 FL C; 2009– FL 1.

MANAGERS
Walter Rayner 1920–25
Alex Macfarlane 1925–27
Albert Lindon 1928
Alex Macfarlane 1928–32
Albert Lindon 1932–33
Jimmy Seed 1933–56
Jimmy Trotter 1956–61
Frank Hill 1961–65
Bob Stokoe 1965–67
Eddie Firmani 1967–70
Theo Foley 1970–74
Andy Nelson 1974–79
Mike Bailey 1979–81
Alan Mullery 1981–82
Ken Craggs 1982
Lennie Lawrence 1982–91
Steve Gritt/Alan Curbishley 1991–95
Alan Curbishley 1995–2006
Iain Dowie 2006
Les Reed 2006
Alan Pardew 2006–08
Phil Parkinson November 2008–

LATEST SEQUENCES

Longest Sequence of League Wins: 12, 26.12.1999 – 7.3.2000.

Longest Sequence of League Defeats: 10, 11.4.1990 – 15.9.1990.

Longest Sequence of League Draws: 6, 13.12.1992 – 16.1.1993.

Longest Sequence of Unbeaten League Matches: 15, 4.10.1980 – 20.12.1980.

Longest Sequence Without a League Win: 18, 18.8.2008 – 17.1.2009.

Successive Scoring Runs: 25 from 26.12.1935.

Successive Non-scoring Runs: 5 from 6.9.1922.

TEN YEAR LEAGUE RECORD

		P	W	D	L	F	A	Pts	Pos
2000-01	PR Lge	38	14	10	14	50	57	52	9
2001-02	PR Lge	38	10	14	14	38	49	44	14
2002-03	PR Lge	38	14	7	17	45	56	49	12
2003-04	PR Lge	38	14	11	13	51	51	53	7
2004-05	PR Lge	38	12	10	16	42	58	46	11
2005-06	PR Lge	38	13	8	17	41	55	47	13
2006-07	PR Lge	38	8	10	20	34	60	34	19
2007-08	FL C	46	17	13	16	63	58	64	11
2008-09	FL C	46	8	15	23	52	74	39	24
2009-10	FL 1	46	23	15	8	71	48	84	4

DID YOU KNOW ?

In 1923 Charlton Athletic temporarily quit The Valley and moved to Catford. On 22 December they played a goalless draw against Northampton Town at The Mount. For the occasion Charlton wore light and dark blue stripes, the colours of the Catford Southend club.

CHARLTON ATHLETIC 2009–10 LEAGUE RECORD

Match No.	Date	Venue	Opponents	Result	H/T Score	Lg Pos.	Goalscorers	Attendance
1	Aug 8	H	Wycombe W	W 3-2	2-1	—	Dailly [20], Bailey [23], Llera [50]	16,552
2	15	A	Hartlepool U	W 2-0	2-0	—	Burton [23], Bailey [27]	4408
3	18	A	Leyton Orient	W 2-1	0-1	—	Shelvey [64], Burton [84]	7376
4	22	H	Walsall	W 2-0	1-0	—	Llera [30], Wagstaff [72]	15,306
5	29	A	Tranmere R	W 4-0	2-0	—	Sam 2 [24, 49], Semedo [26], Bailey [68]	5417
6	Sept 5	H	Brentford	W 2-0	2-0	—	Burton [11], Sam [30]	16,399
7	12	H	Southampton	D 1-1	0-1	1	Burton [49]	19,441
8	19	A	Norwich C	D 2-2	2-1	2	Burton [18], Shelvey [40]	24,018
9	26	H	Exeter C	W 2-1	1-0	2	Bailey [43], McLeod [87]	16,867
10	29	A	Colchester U	L 0-3	0-2	—		7098
11	Oct 3	A	Leeds U	D 0-0	0-0	2		31,838
12	10	H	Oldham Ath	D 0-0	0-0	2		16,441
13	17	H	Huddersfield T	W 2-1	1-1	1	Sodje S [8], McLeod [49]	16,991
14	24	A	Gillingham	D 1-1	0-0	2	Nutter (og) [79]	10,304
15	31	A	Carlisle U	L 1-3	1-1	2	Burton (pen) [45]	6077
16	Nov 14	H	Milton Keynes D	W 5-1	2-1	2	Mooney [13], Bailey [21], Sam [65], Sodje S [73], Burton [76]	17,188
17	21	A	Yeovil T	D 1-1	0-1	2	Sodje A [56]	5632
18	24	H	Bristol R	W 4-2	2-1	—	Mooney [4], Burton (pen) [16], Bailey [68], Sodje A [86]	15,885
19	Dec 1	A	Brighton & HA	W 2-0	2-0	—	Burton [29], Wagstaff [37]	6769
20	5	H	Southend U	W 1-0	1-0	2	Burton [25]	17,445
21	12	A	Stockport Co	W 2-1	1-0	2	Sodje S [13], Wagstaff [74]	4277
22	19	A	Millwall	D 4-4	2-2	2	Morison (og) [85], Burton 2 (2 pens) [31, 38], Bailey [47]	19,105
23	26	H	Swindon T	D 2-2	2-2	2	Shelvey [38], Llera [90]	17,977
24	28	A	Brentford	D 1-1	0-0	2	Bailey (pen) [58]	8387
25	Jan 16	A	Wycombe W	W 2-1	1-0	3	Shelvey [11], Bailey [77]	6123
26	19	H	Hartlepool U	W 2-1	1-0	—	Mooney [31], Wagstaff [79]	14,636
27	25	H	Leyton Orient	L 0-1	0-0	—		15,955
28	30	A	Tranmere R	D 1-1	0-0	3	Bailey [57]	16,168
29	Feb 2	A	Walsall	D 1-1	1-1	—	Burton (pen) [45]	3417
30	6	A	Swindon T	D 1-1	0-0	3	Bailey [90]	9552
31	15	A	Bristol R	L 1-2	0-1	—	Racon [90]	7624
32	20	H	Yeovil T	W 2-0	1-0	4	Reid [29], Mooney [54]	15,991
33	23	H	Brighton & HA	L 1-2	0-1	—	Sodje A [90]	17,508
34	26	A	Southend U	W 2-1	0-1	—	Sodje A [73], Reid [90]	9724
35	Mar 6	H	Stockport Co	W 2-0	2-0	3	Huntington (og) [7], Sodje A [10]	16,609
36	13	A	Millwall	L 0-4	0-1	3		17,632
37	20	H	Gillingham	D 2-2	1-2	3	Richardson [31], Mooney [60]	20,024
38	27	A	Huddersfield T	D 1-1	0-0	5	Reid [58]	14,459
39	Apr 3	H	Milton Keynes D	W 1-0	0-0	5	Forster (pen) [65]	10,869
40	5	H	Carlisle U	W 1-0	1-0	5	Sodje S [44]	17,229
41	10	A	Southampton	L 0-1	0-1	5		23,061
42	13	H	Colchester U	W 1-0	1-0	—	Forster [21]	17,427
43	17	A	Norwich C	L 0-1	0-1	5		20,023
44	24	A	Exeter C	D 1-1	0-0	5	Reid [72]	6835
45	May 1	H	Leeds U	W 1-0	0-0	5	Naylor (og) [88]	23,198
46	8	A	Oldham Ath	W 2-0	1-0	4	Bailey [23], Llera [48]	5686

Final League Position: 4

GOALSCORERS

League (71): Burton 13 (5 pens), Bailey 12 (1 pen), Mooney 5, Sodje A 5, Llera 4, Reid 4, Sam 4, Shelvey 4, Sodje S 4, Wagstaff 4, Forster 2 (1 pen), McLeod 2, Dailly 1, Racon 1, Richardson 1, Semedo 1, own goals 4.
Carling Cup (0).
FA Cup (0).
J Paint Trophy (5): Bailey 1, McKenzie 1, McLeod 1, Tuna 1, Wagstaff 1.
Play-Offs (3): Burton 1, Mooney 1, own goal 1.

Elliot R 33	Richardson F 37+1	Youga K 18	Bailey N 43+1	Llera M 23+2	Dailly C 44	Shelvey J 19+5	Racon T 36	Sam L 40+3	Burton D 35+4	Semedo J 35+3	Gray A —+2	McLeod 13+8	Solly C 2+7	Wagstaff S 9+21	Spring M 7+5	Tuna T —+1	Sodje S 24+3	Bassey G 14+5	McKenzie L —+12	Mooney D 20+8	Ikeme C 4	Omozusi F 7+2	Sodje A 10+15	Dickson C 1+4	Reid K 11+6	Randolph D 9+2	Jackson J 4	Borrowdale G 10	Forster N 8	Match No.
1	2	3	4	5	6	7	8	9^2	10^1	11	12	13																		1
1	2	3	4	5^1	6	7^2	8	9	10	11		13		12																2
1	2	3	4	5	6	7	8	9^1	10	11				12																3
1	2	3	4	5	6	7	8	9^1	10	11					12															4
1	2	3	4	5	6	7^2	8	9	10	11^1				12	13															5
1	2	3	4	5	6	7^2	8	9	10	11		13		12																6
1	2	3	4	5	6	7	8	9^1	10	11				12																7
1	2	3	4	5	6	7^2	8	9^1	10	11		12		13																8
1	2	3	4	5	6	7^3	8^2	9	10^1			12		13	11		14													9
1	2	3	4	5^2	6	7	8	9	10					12	11^1		13													10
1	2	3	4		6	7	8^3	9^1	10			13		12	11		5	14												11
1	2	3	8	6	5	7^1	4	9^3	10^2			12		14	11		13													12
1	2	3	4	5	8	7^2	10	12	9^3			13		11^1			6	14												13
1	2^1	3	4	5	8	11^3	9	7	10^2	14		6		12	13															14
	3	4	5	12	8	11	9	7^1	10^3	6		13		14							1	2^2								15
	2^1	3	4	5	8	11	10^2	7	6	12		13		9^3			14				1									16
	3	4	12	5		8^2	11	10	7	6^4		2		9^1			13				1									17
	3^1	4	5	6	7^2	8	10	11		13		2		9^3							1	12	14							18
1			4		6	7	10^1	8		13	11			5	3		9^2			2		12								19
1	2^1		4		6	8^3	7	10		11	14			5	3		9^2			12		13								20
1			4		6	8^2	10^1	7		11	13			5	3		9			2		12								21
1			4		6	8^3	10	7		11^2	14			5	3	13	9^1			2		12								22
1		4	5		7^3	10^8	8	13	11					6^4	3		12			2^8		9^1	14							23
1		4	5	12		8		6		7^1	11			3	13		2			9		10^2								24
1	13	4	5	6	11	8	10^3	7						3	14		9^1	1		2^8		12								25
1	2	4	5	6	11^1	8^2	10	7		14				3	12		9^3					13								26
1	2	4	5	6	11	8	10^2	7^1		12				3	13		9^3					14								27
1^0	2	4	6		8^1	10	7	13		5	3	12	9				11^2	15												28
1	2	4	6		8	13	10			3^3	11^2		5	14	12		9			9^1		7								29
1	2	4	6	10	8^2		14	12	13	11^1			5	3^3						9		7								30
1	2	4	6		8	11	10	7^3		12			5	3^1			13			9^2		14								31
1	2	4	5	6		11^2	3^1	10		12							9					7	8							32
1	2^2	4	5	6	8	3	10^1			14		13	9							12		7	11^3							33
1	2	4	5	6	8	7^3	3^1			14		13	9^2				10			12		11								34
1	2	4	5	6	8	3^2	13			12	14		9				10^3			7		11^1								35
1	2	4	5	6	8^1	12	13	3		7	14		9				10^2	11^3												36
1^0	2	4	6		8^2	11	10^1	7		5			9				12	13	15			3								37
	2	5	7		6		12	11		4			9				13			8			1		3^1	10^2				38
	2	5	14	4	12		7			11^1	6		9^3				13			8			1		3	10^2				39
	2	13	6	9^3	4	11	7			5	14		12				8^1						1		3	10^2				40
	2	4	6	14	9	11	7^2			5	13		12				8^3			1					3	10^1				41
	2	4	6	8^1	11^3	7	14	12		5	13		9										1		3	10^2				42
	2	4^3	6	14	8	11	12	7^2		5			9^1				13						1		3	10				43
	2	4	13	6	8^1	11^3	10	7		14	5^2		12										1		3	9				44
	2	4	6	8^1	11	10^2	7			5	14		12	13									1		3	9^3				45
	2	4	5	6	8	11^1	10	7^2			12	13					9^3			14			1		3					46

FA Cup
First Round   Northwich Vic   (a)   0-1

Carling Cup
First Round   Hereford U   (a)   0-1

J Paint Trophy
Second Round   Barnet   (h)   4-1
Southern Quarter-Final   Southampton   (a)   1-2

Play-Offs
Semi-Final   Swindon T   (a)   1-2
                               (h)   2-1

CHELSEA   FA Premiership

FOUNDATION

Chelsea may never have existed but for the fact that Fulham rejected an offer to rent the Stamford Bridge ground from Mr H. A. Mears who had owned it since 1904. Fortunately he was determined to develop it as a football stadium rather than sell it to the Great Western Railway and got together with Frederick Parker, who persuaded Mears of the financial advantages of developing a major sporting venue. Chelsea FC was formed in 1905, and when admission to the Southern League was denied, they immediately gained admission to the Second Division of the Football League.

Stamford Bridge, Fulham Road, London SW6 1HS.
Telephone: 0871 984 1955.
Fax: (020) 7381 4831.
Ticket Office: 0871 984 1905.
Website: www.chelseafc.com
Ground Capacity: 41,841.
Record Attendance: 82,905 v Arsenal, Division 1, 12 October 1935.
Pitch Measurements: 103m × 67m.
Chairman: Bruce Buck.
Director: Eugene Tenenbaum.
Chief Executive: Ron Gourlay.
Secretary: David Barnard.
Manager: Carlo Ancelotti.
Assistant First Team Coaches: Ray Wilkins, Bruno Demichelis and Paul Clement.
Fitness Coach: Glen Driscoll.
Colours: Reflex blue shirt, reflex blue shorts, white stockings with blue trim.
Change Colours: Blue and black hooped shirts with yellow trim, black shorts with yellow trim, black stockings with yellow tops.
Year Formed: 1905.
Turned Professional: 1905.
Ltd Co.: 1905.
Club Nickname: 'The Blues'.
Ground: 1905, Stamford Bridge.
First Football League Game: 2 September 1905, Division 2, v Stockport Co (a) L 0–1 – Foulke; Mackie, McEwan; Key, Harris, Miller; Moran, J. T. Robertson, Copeland, Windridge, Kirwan.

HONOURS

FA Premier League: Champions 2004–05, 2005–06. Runners-up 2003–04, 2006–07, 2007–08, 2009–10.

Football League: Division 1 – Champions 1954–55; Division 2 – Champions 1983–84, 1988–89; Runners-up 1906–07, 1911–12, 1929–30, 1962–63, 1976–77.

FA Cup: Winners 1970, 1997, 2000, 2007, 2009, 2010. Runners-up 1915, 1967, 1994, 2002.

Football League Cup: Winners 1965, 1998, 2005, 2007; Runners-up 1972, 2008.

Full Members' Cup: Winners 1986.

Zenith Data Systems Cup: Winners 1990.

European Competitions: *Champions League:* 1999–2000, 2003–04 (semi-finals), 2004–05 (semi-finals), 2005–06, 2006–07 (semi-finals), 2007–08 (runners-up), 2008–09 (semi-finals), 2009–10. *European Fairs Cup:* 1958–60, 1965–66, 1968–69. *European Cup-Winners' Cup:* 1970–71 (winners), 1971–72, 1994–95, 1997–98 (winners), 1998–99 (semi-finals). *UEFA Cup:* 2000–01, 2001–02, 2002–03. *Super Cup:* 1998–99 (winners).

sky SPORTS FACT FILE

On 16 January 2010 Chelsea beat Sunderland 7–2. It was their highest score in the top flight since defeating West Bromwich Albion 7–1 on 3 December 1960 when Jimmy Greaves scored five times. Ashley Cole's goal against Sunderland was the Premier League's 18,000th.

Record League Victory: 8-0 v Wigan Ath, FA Premier League, 9 May 2010 – Cech; Ivanovic (Belletti), Cole A (1), Ballack (Matic), Terry, Alex, Kalou (1) (Cole J), Lampard (pen), Anelka (2), Drogba (3, 1 pen), Malouda.

Record Cup Victory: 13–0 v Jeunesse Hautcharage, ECWC, 1st rd 2nd leg, 29 September 1971 – Bonetti; Boyle, Harris (1), Hollins (1p), Webb (1), Hinton, Cooke, Baldwin (3), Osgood (5), Hudson (1), Houseman (1).

Record Defeat: 1–8 v Wolverhampton W, Division 1, 26 September 1953.

Most League Points (2 for a win): 57, Division 2, 1906–07.

Most League Points (3 for a win): 99, Division 2, 1988–89.

Most League Goals: 103, FA Premier League, 2009–10.

Highest League Scorer in Season: Jimmy Greaves, 41, 1960–61.

Most League Goals in Total Aggregate: Bobby Tambling, 164, 1958–70.

Most League Goals in One Match: 5, George Hilsdon v Glossop, Division 2, 1 September 1906; 5, Jimmy Greaves v Wolverhampton W, Division 1, 30 August 1958; 5, Jimmy Greaves v Preston NE, Division 1, 19 December 1959; 5, Jimmy Greaves v WBA, Division 1, 3 December 1960; 5, Bobby Tambling v Aston Villa, Division 1, 17 September 1966; 5, Gordon Durie v Walsall, Division 2, 4 February 1989.

Most Capped Player: Frank Lampard, 80 (82), England.

Most League Appearances: Ron Harris, 655, 1962–80.

Youngest League Player: Ian Hamilton, 16 years 138 days v Tottenham H, 18 March 1967.

Record Transfer Fee Received: £12,000,000 from Rangers for Tore Andre Flo, November 2000; £12,000,000 from Manchester C for Wayne Bridge, January 2009.

Record Transfer Fee Paid: £29,500,000 to AC Milan for Andriy Shevchenko, June 2006.

Football League Record: 1905 Elected to Division 2; 1907–10 Division 1; 1910–12 Division 2; 1912–24 Division 1; 1924–30 Division 2; 1930–62 Division 1; 1962–63 Division 2; 1963–75 Division 1; 1975–77 Division 2; 1977–79 Division 1; 1979–84 Division 2; 1984–88 Division 1; 1988–89 Division 2; 1989–92 Division 1; 1992– FA Premier League.

MANAGERS

John Tait Robertson 1905–07
David Calderhead 1907–33
Leslie Knighton 1933–39
Billy Birrell 1939–52
Ted Drake 1952–61
Tommy Docherty 1961–67
Dave Sexton 1967–74
Ron Suart 1974–75
Eddie McCreadie 1975–77
Ken Shellito 1977–78
Danny Blanchflower 1978–79
Geoff Hurst 1979–81
John Neal 1981–85 *(Director to 1986)*
John Hollins 1985–88
Bobby Campbell 1988–91
Ian Porterfield 1991–93
David Webb 1993
Glenn Hoddle 1993–96
Ruud Gullit 1996–98
Gianluca Vialli 1998–2000
Claudio Ranieri 2000–04
Jose Mourinho 2004–07
Avram Grant 2007–08
Luiz Felipe Scolari 2008–09
Guus Hiddink 2009
Carlo Ancelotti June 2009–

LATEST SEQUENCES

Longest Sequence of League Wins: 11, 25.4.2009 – 20.9.2009.
Longest Sequence of League Defeats: 7, 1.11.1952 – 20.12.1952.
Longest Sequence of League Draws: 6, 20.8.1969 – 13.9.1969.
Longest Sequence of Unbeaten League Matches: 40, 23.10.2004 – 29.10.2005.
Longest Sequence Without a League Win: 21, 3.11.1987 – 2.4.1988.
Successive Scoring Runs: 27 from 29.10.1988.
Successive Non-scoring Runs: 9 from 14.3.1981.

TEN YEAR LEAGUE RECORD

		P	W	D	L	F	A	Pts	Pos
2000-01	PR Lge	38	17	10	11	68	45	61	6
2001-02	PR Lge	38	17	13	8	66	38	64	6
2002-03	PR Lge	38	19	10	9	68	38	67	4
2003-04	PR Lge	38	24	7	7	67	30	79	2
2004-05	PR Lge	38	29	8	1	72	15	95	1
2005-06	PR Lge	38	29	4	5	72	22	91	1
2006-07	PR Lge	38	24	11	3	64	24	83	2
2007-08	PR Lge	38	25	10	3	65	26	85	2
2008-09	PR Lge	38	25	8	5	68	24	83	3
2009-10	PR Lge	38	27	5	6	103	32	86	1

DID YOU KNOW ?

When Chelsea clinched the Premier League championship on 9 May 2010, their 8–0 win over Wigan Athletic was the best League win. It was the fourth time they had scored at least seven in the season, the best since Arsenal in the First Division in 1934–35.

CHELSEA 2009–10 LEAGUE RECORD

Match No.	Date	Venue	Opponents	Result	H/T Score	Lg Pos.	Goalscorers	Attendance
1	Aug 15	H	Hull C	W 2-1	1-1	—	Drogba 2 [37,90]	41,597
2	18	A	Sunderland	W 3-1	0-1	—	Ballack [52], Lampard (pen) [61], Deco [70]	41,179
3	23	A	Fulham	W 2-0	1-0	2	Drogba [39], Anelka [76]	25,404
4	29	H	Burnley	W 3-0	1-0	1	Anelka [45], Ballack [47], Cole A [52]	40,906
5	Sept12	A	Stoke C	W 2-1	1-1	1	Drogba [45], Malouda [90]	27,440
6	20	H	Tottenham H	W 3-0	1-0	1	Cole A [32], Ballack [58], Drogba [63]	41,623
7	26	A	Wigan Ath	L 1-3	0-1	2	Drogba [47]	18,542
8	Oct 4	H	Liverpool	W 2-0	0-0	1	Anelka [60], Malouda [90]	41,732
9	17	A	Aston Villa	L 1-2	1-1	2	Drogba [15]	39,047
10	24	H	Blackburn R	W 5-0	1-0	1	Givet (og) [20], Lampard 2 (pen) [48,59 (p)], Essien [52], Drogba [64]	40,836
11	31	A	Bolton W	W 4-0	1-0	1	Lampard (pen) [45], Deco [61], Ivanovic [82], Drogba [90]	22,680
12	Nov 8	H	Manchester U	W 1-0	0-0	1	Terry [76]	41,836
13	21	H	Wolverhampton W	W 4-0	3-0	1	Malouda [5], Essien 2 [12,22], Cole J [56]	41,786
14	29	A	Arsenal	W 3-0	2-0	1	Drogba 2 [41,86], Vermaelen (og) [45]	60,067
15	Dec 5	A	Manchester C	L 1-2	1-1	1	Adebayor (og) [8]	47,348
16	12	H	Everton	D 3-3	2-2	1	Drogba 2 [18,59], Anelka [23]	41,579
17	16	H	Portsmouth	W 2-1	1-0	—	Anelka [23], Lampard (pen) [79]	40,137
18	20	A	West Ham U	D 1-1	0-1	1	Lampard (pen) [61]	33,388
19	26	A	Birmingham C	D 0-0	0-0	1		28,958
20	28	H	Fulham	W 2-1	0-1	1	Drogba [73], Smalling (og) [75]	41,805
21	Jan 16	A	Sunderland	W 7-2	4-0	1	Anelka 2 [8,65], Malouda [17], Cole A [22], Lampard 2 [34,90], Ballack [52]	41,776
22	27	H	Birmingham C	W 3-0	2-0	1	Malouda [5], Lampard 2 [32,90]	41,293
23	30	A	Burnley	W 2-1	1-0	1	Anelka [27], Terry [82]	21,131
24	Feb 2	A	Hull C	D 1-1	1-1	—	Drogba [42]	24,957
25	7	H	Arsenal	W 2-0	2-0	1	Drogba 2 [8,23]	41,794
26	10	A	Everton	L 1-2	1-1	1	Malouda [17]	36,411
27	20	A	Wolverhampton W	W 2-0	1-0	1	Drogba 2 [40,67]	28,978
28	27	H	Manchester C	L 2-4	1-1	1	Lampard 2 (1 pen) [42,90 (p)]	41,814
29	Mar 13	H	West Ham U	W 4-1	1-1	2	Alex [16], Drogba 2 [56,90], Malouda [77]	41,755
30	21	A	Blackburn R	D 1-1	1-0	3	Drogba [6]	25,554
31	24	A	Portsmouth	W 5-0	1-0	1	Drogba 2 [32,77], Malouda 2 [50,60], Lampard [90]	18,753
32	27	H	Aston Villa	W 7-1	2-1	2	Lampard 4 (2 pens) [15,44 (p),62 (p),90], Malouda 2 [57,68], Kalou [83]	41,825
33	Apr 3	A	Manchester U	W 2-1	1-0	1	Cole J [20], Drogba [79]	75,217
34	13	H	Bolton W	W 1-0	1-0	—	Anelka [43]	40,539
35	17	A	Tottenham H	L 1-2	0-2	1	Lampard [90]	35,814
36	25	H	Stoke C	W 7-0	3-0	1	Kalou 3 [24,31,68], Lampard 2 (1 pen) [44 (p),81], Sturridge [87], Malouda [89]	41,013
37	May 2	A	Liverpool	W 2-0	1-0	1	Drogba [33], Lampard [54]	44,375
38	9	H	Wigan Ath	W 8-0	2-0	1	Anelka 2 [6,56], Lampard (pen) [32], Kalou [54], Drogba 3 (1 pen) [63,68 (p),80], Cole A [90]	41,383

Final League Position: 1

GOALSCORERS

League (103): Drogba 29 (1 pen), Lampard 22 (10 pens), Malouda 12, Anelka 11, Kalou 5, Ballack 4, Cole A 4, Essien 3, Cole J 2, Deco 2, Terry 2, Alex 1, Ivanovic 1, Sturridge 1, own goals 4.
Carling Cup (8): Kalou 3, Drogba 2, Deco 1, Malouda 1, Paulo Ferreira 1.
FA Cup (17): Sturridge 4, Drogba 3, Lampard 3, Malouda 2, Anelka 1, Ballack 1, Kalou 1, Terry 1, own goal 1.
Champions League (12): Anelka 3, Drogba 3, Kalou 3, Essien 1, Lampard 1, own goal 1.
Community Shield (2): Lampard 1, Ricardo Carvalho 1.

Cech P 34	Bosingwa J 8	Cole A 25+2	Mikel J 21+4	Terry J 37	Ricardo Carvalho 22	Essien M 13+1	Lampard F 36	Anelka N 31+2	Drogba D 31+1	Malouda F 26+7	Ballack M 26+6	Deco 14+5	Kalou S 11+12	Ivanovic B 25+3	Sturridge D 2+11	Shevchenko A —+1	Hutchinson S —+2	Belletti J 4+7	Borini F —+4	Hilario 2+1	Cole J 14+12	Paulo Ferreira 11+2	Bruma J —+2	Alex 13+3	Kakuta G —+1	Matic N —+2	Zhirkov Y 10+7	Turnbull R 2	Van Aanholt P —+2	Match No.
1	2	3	4^{1}	5	6	7	8	9^{1}	10	11^{2}	12	13	14																	1
1	2	3		5	4		8	9^{2}	12	7	11^{3}	10^{1}	6	13		$^{*}4$														2
1	2^{2}	3	4	5	6		8^{1}	9	10	11	7	12				13														3
1	2^{1}	3	14	5	6	4	8	9	10^{2}			7^{3}	11	13				12												4
1	2	3	4^{3}	5	13	8	12	9	11	7^{2}		10^{1}	6			14														5
1	2	3	12	5	6	4	8	9^{3}	10^{2}	11	7^{1}	13						14												6
1^{1}	2^{2}	3	4^{1}	5	6	7	8	9	10	11^{6}		13						12	15											7
		3		5	6	4	8	9	10	12	7	11^{1}	2						1											8
1	2^{1}	3		5	6	4	8	9	10	11^{2}		7	12					13												9
1				5	6^{2}	4	8	9	10	7			3	14		2^{1}		11^{3}	12	$^{*}3$										10
1				5	6	4	8	9	10		7	11	3			2														11
1	3			5	6	4	8	9^{3}	10^{2}		7	11^{1}	13	2				12			14									12
1	3	4	5		7		9^{1}		11^{2}			10^{3}		2	14	8				6	12	13								13
1	3^{2}	4	5	6	7	8	9	10^{3}	14	12		2						11^{1}	13											14
1	3	13	5^{3}	6^{1}	4	8	9	10	14	7^{2}	11	2				12														15
1	3	4^{3}	5	6^{2}		8	9	10	12	7		2				13	14	11^{1}												16
1	3	4^{2}	5		8	9		13	7	11^{1}	10^{3}	2		14		12			6											17
1	3	12	5	6	8		9	11^{2}	4		10^{1}	2	13			7^{3}					14									18
1	3	4^{3}	5		8^{2}		10	11^{1}	14		12	2	9^{1}		7			13			6									19
1	14	4^{2}	5	6	8		10		7		9	12	13					11	2^{1}			3^{3}								20
1	3^{2}		5^{1}	6	8	9		11	7		2					4		10			12	13								21
1	3		5	6	8	9^{2}		11	7	4		2	13					10^{1}			12									22
1	3^{2}		5		8	9		11	7	13		2	12					10^{1}			6	4								23
1	13		5	6	8	9^{3}	10	11	7^{1}	4		2	14					12				3^{2}								24
1	3	4	5	6	8	9^{2}	10^{3}	11	7^{1}		14	2						13			12									25
1	3^{1}	4^{3}	5	6	8	9^{2}	10	11	12		13	2	14								7									26
1		4	5			9	10	11	8			6						7	2	12		3^{1}								27
1		4^{1}	5	6^{3}	8	9	10	3	7^{8}		14	2	13		12^{*}	1	11^{2}													28
1		4	5		8	9^{1}	10	11^{3}	7		14	3^{2}					12	2		6		13	1							29
1		4	5		8	9^{3}	10	11		13	7^{2}	3^{1}	14						2		6		12	1						30
1		4	5	6^{1}	8		10	11	7			9^{2}						13	2		12	3^{3}	14							31
1		4	5		8	9		11	12	7	7^{1}	13						10^{2}	2		6	3^{3}	14							32
1		4	5		8	9^{1}	12	11	14	7^{3}	13							10^{2}	2		6	3								33
1		4	5		8	9^{1}	10	12	7	11^{2}	13							2			6	3								34
1		4^{1}	5^{8}		8	13	9	11	12	7		14						10^{3}	2^{2}		6	3								35
1	3			8	9^{3}	10	11	4		7^{1}	5	14	13					12	2^{2}		6									36
1	3		5		8	9^{2}	10	11	4		7^{1}	2						13			6		12							37
1	3		5		8	9	10	11	4^{3}		7^{2}	2^{1}		12				13			6	14								38

FA Cup

Third Round	Watford	(h)	5-0
Fourth Round	Preston NE	(a)	2-0
Fifth Round	Cardiff C	(h)	4-1
Sixth Round	Stoke C	(h)	2-0
Semi-Final	Aston Villa		3-0
(at Wembley).			
Final	Portsmouth		1-0
(at Wembley).			

Carling Cup

Third Round	QPR	(h)	1-0
Fourth Round	Bolton W	(h)	4-0
Quarter-Final	Blackburn R	(a)	3-3

Community Shield

	Manchester U	2-2
(at Wembley).		

Champions League

Group D	Porto	(h)	1-0
	Apoel	(a)	1-0
	Atletico Madrid	(h)	4-0
		(a)	2-2
	Porto	(a)	1-0
	Apoel	(h)	2-2
Knock-out Round	Internazionale	(a)	1-2
		(h)	0-1

CHELTENHAM TOWN   FL Championship 2

FOUNDATION

Although a scratch team representing Cheltenham played a match against Gloucester in 1884, the earliest recorded match for Cheltenham Town FC was a friendly against Dean Close School on 12 March 1892. The School won 4–3 and the match was played at Prestbury (half a mile from Whaddon Road). Cheltenham Town played Wednesday afternoon friendlies at a local cricket ground until entering the Mid Gloucester League. In those days the club played in deep red coloured shirts and were nicknamed 'the Rubies'. The club moved to Whaddon Lane for season 1901–02 and changed to red and white colours two years later.

The Abbey Business Stadium, Whaddon Road, Cheltenham, Gloucestershire GL52 5NA.

Telephone: (01242) 573 558.

Fax: (01242) 224 675.

Ticket Office: (01242) 573 558 (option 1).

Website: www.ctfc.com

Email: info@ctfc.com

Ground Capacity: 7,136.

Record Attendance: at Whaddon Road: 8,326 v Reading, FA Cup 1st rd, 17 November 1956; at Cheltenham Athletic Ground: 10,389 v Blackpool, FA Cup 3rd rd, 13 January 1934.

Pitch Measurements: 112yd × 72yd.

Chairman: Paul Baker.

Vice-chairman: Colin Farmer.

Secretary: Paul Godfrey.

Manager: Mark Yates.

Assistant Manager: Jon Schofield.

Physio: Ian Weston.

Colours: All red with white trim.

Change Colours: All black with red trim.

Year Formed: 1892.

Turned Professional: 1932.

Ltd Co.: 1937.

Club Nickname: 'The Robins'.

Grounds: Pre-1932, Agg-Gardner's Recreation Ground; Whaddon Lane; Carter's Lane; 1932, Wadden Road.

HONOURS

Football League: Best Season Division 3 2001–02 (4th).

FA Cup: best season: 5th rd 2002.

Football League Cup: never past 2nd rd.

Football Conference: Champions 1998–99, runners-up 1997–98.

Trophy: Winners 1997–98.

Southern League: Champions 1984–85; *Southern League Cup:* Winners 1957–58, runners-up 1968–69, 1984–85; *Southern League Merit Cup:* Winners 1984–85; *Southern League Championship Shield:* Winners 1985.

Gloucestershire Senior Cup: Winners 1998–99; *Gloucestershire Northern Senior Professional Cup:* Winners 30 times; *Midland Floodlit Cup:* Winners 1985–86, 1986–87, 1987–88; *Mid Gloucester League:* Champions 1896–97; *Gloucester and District League:* Champions 1902–03, 1905–06; *Cheltenham League:* Champions 1910–11, 1913–14; *North Gloucestershire League:* Champions 1913–14; *Gloucestershire Northern Senior League:* Champions 1928–29, 1932–33; *Gloucestershire Northern Senior Amateur Cup:* Winners 1929–30, 1930–31, 1932–33, 1933–34, 1934–35; *Leamington Hospital Cup:* Winners 1934–35.

sky SPORTS FACT FILE

In four seasons with Charlton Athletic and another at Queens Park Rangers, centre-forward Stan Prior had never managed to score in an FA Cup tie. However, on moving to Cheltenham Town in the Southern League he forced a replay against Cardiff City on 26 November 1938.

Record League Victory: 11–0 v Bourneville Ath, Birmingham Combination, 29 April 1933 – Davis; Jones, Williams; Lang (1), Blackburn, Draper; Evans, Hazard (4). Haycox (4), Goodger (1), Hill (1).

Record Cup Victory: 12–0 v Chippenham R, FA Cup 3rd qual. rd, 2 November 1935 – Bowles; Whitehouse, Williams; Lang, Devonport (1), Partridge (2); Perkins, Hackett, Jones (4), Black (4), Griffiths (1).

Record Defeat: 0–7 v Crystal Palace, League Cup 2nd rd, 2 October 2002.
N.B. 1–10 v Merthyr T, Southern League, 8 March 1952.

Most League Points (2 for a win): 60, Southern League Division 1, 1963–64.

Most League Points (3 for a win): 78, Division 3, 2001–02.

Most League Goals: 66, Division 3, 2001–02.

Highest League Scorer in Season: Julian Alsop, 20, Division 3, 2001–02.

Most League Goals in Total Aggregate: Martin Devaney, 38, 1999–2005.

Most Capped Player: Grant McCann, 7 (28), Northern Ireland.

Most League Appearances: Jamie Victory, 258, 1999–.

Record Transfer Fee Received: £400,000 from Colchester U for Steve Gillespie, July 2008.

Record Transfer Fee Paid: £50,000 to West Ham U for Grant McCann, January 2003 and £50,000 to Stoke C for Brian Wilson, March 2004.

Football League Record: 1999 Promoted to Division 3; 2002 Division 2; 2003–04 Division 3; 2004–06 FL 2; 2006–09 FL 1; 2009– FL 2.

MANAGERS

George Blackburn 1932–34
George Carr 1934–37
Jimmy Brain 1937–48
Cyril Dean 1948–50
George Summerbee 1950–52
William Raeside 1952–53
Arch Anderson 1953–58
Ron Lewin 1958–60
Peter Donnelly 1960–61
Tommy Cavanagh 1961
Arch Anderson 1961–65
Harold Fletcher 1965–66
Bob Etheridge 1966–73
Willie Penman 1973–74
Dennis Allen 1974–79
Terry Paine 1979
Alan Grundy 1979–82
Alan Wood 1982–83
John Murphy 1983–88
Jim Barron 1988–90
John Murphy 1990
Dave Lewis 1990–91
Ally Robertson 1991–92
Lindsay Parsons 1992–95
Chris Robinson 1995–97
Steve Cotterill 1997–2002
Graham Allner 2002–03
Bobby Gould 2003
John Ward 2003–07
Keith Downing 2007–08
Martin Allen 2008–09
Mark Yates December 2009–

LATEST SEQUENCES

Longest Sequence of League Wins: 4, 29.4.2006 – 8.8.2006.

Longest Sequence of League Defeats: 7, 27.1.2009 – 28.2.2009.

Longest Sequence of League Draws: 5, 5.4.2003 – 21.4.2003.

Longest Sequence of Unbeaten League Matches: 16, 1.12.2001 – 12.3.2002.

Longest Sequence Without a League Win: 14, 20.12.2008 – 7.3.2009.

Successive Scoring Runs: 17 from 16.2.2008.

Successive Non-scoring Runs: 4 from 12.9.1999.

TEN YEAR LEAGUE RECORD

		P	W	D	L	F	A	Pts	Pos
2000-01	Div 3	46	18	14	14	59	52	68	9
2001-02	Div 3	46	21	15	10	66	49	78	4
2002-03	Div 2	46	10	18	18	53	68	48	21
2003-04	Div 3	46	14	14	18	57	71	56	14
2004-05	FL 2	46	16	12	18	51	54	60	14
2005-06	FL 2	46	19	15	12	65	53	72	5
2006-07	FL 1	46	15	9	22	49	61	54	17
2007-08	FL 1	46	13	12	21	42	64	51	19
2008-09	FL 1	46	9	12	25	51	91	39	23
2009-10	FL 2	46	10	18	18	54	71	48	22

DID YOU KNOW ?

In 1957–58 Cheltenham Town were a free-scoring Southern League team hitting 115 goals, Peter Cleland scoring 39 and Danny Fowler 31. In one month the team scored nine goals on three separate occasions. They finished sixth in the championship.

CHELTENHAM TOWN 2009–10 LEAGUE RECORD

Match No.	Date	Venue	Opponents	Result		H/T Score	Lg Pos.	Goalscorers	Attendance
1	Aug 8	H	Grimsby T	W	2-1	0-1	—	Ridley [56], Hayles [68]	3654
2	15	A	Hereford U	D	1-1	0-0	5	Hammond [59]	3280
3	18	A	Rochdale	W	1-0	0-0	—	Alsop [90]	2311
4	22	H	Bradford C	L	4-5	3-3	8	Hammond [4], Townsend [12], Richards 2 [43, 89]	3073
5	29	A	Darlington	D	1-1	1-0	9	Richards [32]	1840
6	Sept 5	H	Dagenham & R	D	1-1	0-0	11	Townsend [81]	2969
7	12	A	Bury	W	1-0	0-0	7	Hayles [90]	2130
8	19	H	Rotherham U	D	1-1	0-1	9	Alsop [85]	3088
9	26	A	Aldershot T	L	1-4	0-1	10	Richards (pen) [65]	2964
10	29	H	Shrewsbury T	L	1-2	0-0	—	Hayles [60]	2928
11	Oct 3	H	Notts Co	D	1-1	0-1	13	Hammond [75]	4134
12	10	A	Accrington S	L	0-4	0-0	17		1843
13	16	H	Macclesfield T	L	1-2	0-2	—	Hammond [69]	2930
14	24	A	Port Vale	D	1-1	0-1	20	Pook [66]	4979
15	31	H	Crewe Alex	L	0-4	0-2	21		3124
16	Nov 14	A	Lincoln C	D	1-1	1-0	21	Richards [12]	3008
17	21	A	Morecambe	L	0-1	0-1	21		1567
18	24	H	Barnet	W	5-1	2-1	—	Gallinagh [21], Marshall 2 [37, 86], Richards [55], Yakubu (og) [88]	2331
19	Dec 1	A	Torquay U	L	0-3	0-2	—		2122
20	5	H	Northampton T	D	2-2	2-1	20	Hayles 2 [22, 30]	2824
21	12	A	Chesterfield	L	0-1	0-1	21		3145
22	26	H	Bournemouth	L	0-1	0-0	22		4114
23	28	A	Dagenham & R	W	2-0	1-0	21	Richards [45], Low [66]	2028
24	Jan 2	A	Bradford C	D	1-1	0-1	—	Richards (pen) [54]	10,831
25	16	A	Grimsby T	D	0-0	0-0	—		3334
26	23	H	Rochdale	L	1-4	0-1	22	Townsend [89]	3460
27	Feb 6	A	Bournemouth	D	0-0	0-0	22		5259
28	9	H	Burton Alb	L	0-1	0-1	—		2593
29	13	A	Barnet	D	1-1	1-1	22	Thornhill [20]	1667
30	20	H	Morecambe	W	2-1	1-0	21	Alsop [33], Thornhill [59]	2806
31	23	H	Torquay U	D	1-1	1-0	—	Hayles [34]	2607
32	27	A	Northampton T	L	1-2	0-0	22	Watkins [78]	4428
33	Mar 2	H	Hereford U	L	0-1	0-1	—		3273
34	6	H	Chesterfield	L	0-1	0-1	22		3006
35	13	A	Burton Alb	W	6-5	0-2	22	Richards 2 [54, 89], Elito [56], Pook 3 [84, 87, 90]	2500
36	20	H	Port Vale	D	1-1	1-1	22	Elito [40]	3503
37	27	A	Macclesfield T	L	0-1	0-0	22		1572
38	Apr 3	H	Lincoln C	W	1-0	0-0	22	Alsop [50]	3708
39	5	A	Crewe Alex	W	2-1	1-0	22	Richards 2 (1 pen) [25, 71 (p)]	3488
40	10	H	Bury	W	5-2	1-0	22	Richards (pen) [37], Thornhill [46], Low 2 [52, 85], Hayles [86]	3071
41	13	A	Shrewsbury T	D	0-0	0-0	—		4967
42	17	A	Rotherham U	D	0-0	0-0	20		3478
43	20	A	Darlington	D	3-3	1-3	—	Pook [29], Richards [46], Elito [64]	2836
44	24	H	Aldershot T	L	1-2	1-0	21	Richards (pen) [14]	3386
45	May 1	A	Notts Co	L	0-5	0-4	21		11,331
46	8	H	Accrington S	D	1-1	1-1	22	Low [9]	3856

Final League Position: 22

GOALSCORERS

League (54): Richards 15 (5 pens), Hayles 7, Pook 5, Alsop 4, Hammond 4, Low 4, Elito 3, Thornhill 3, Townsend 3, Marshall 2, Gallinagh 1, Ridley 1, Watkins 1, own goal 1.
Carling Cup (1): Hammond 1.
FA Cup (1): Lewis 1.
J Paint Trophy (1): Low 1.

Brown Scott P 46	Bird D 35 + 2	Ridley L 26 + 1	Pook M 31 + 4	Duff S 11	Diallo D 17 + 1	Hutton D 14 + 11	Gallinagh A 35 + 4	Richards J 39 + 5	Hammond E 14 + 10	Bozanic O 4	Hayles B 23 + 16	Alsop J 21 + 20	Townsend M 34	Denton T 1 + 1	Haynes K 6 + 7	Artus F 7	Watkins M 4 + 9	Low J 35 + 4	Lewis T 9 + 6	Eyjolfsson H 4	Cox S 1	Rose R 1	Marshall B 6	Labadie J 11	Pipe D 7 + 1	Eastham A 18 + 2	Andrew D 9 + 1	Thornhill M 16 + 1	Lee J — + 1	Lescott A 7 + 1	Elito M 12	Almond L 2 + 2	Brown Scott — + 1	Match No.
1	2	3	4	5	6	7	8	9	10²	11¹	12	13																						1
1	2	3	4¹	5	12	13	8	7	9		11²	10³	6		14																			2
1	2³	3		5	4	13	8	7	9²	11	12	14	6	10¹																				3
1	2	3	5¹	4	7	8	10	9³	11²	12	14	6		13																				4
1	2	3		4	7¹	5	10		9³	13	6	14	8	11²	12																			5
1	2	3		4	12	5²	11¹	9	10	6	7³	8	13	14																				6
1	2	3		4	13	5	11	14	9	10²	6	8³	7¹	12																				7
1	2	3		4	11	5³	9²	13	10	6	8¹	12	7	14																				8
1	2	3	12	4		5¹	11	9	13	10²	6	8³	14	7																				9
1	2	3	8	4	5¹		11²	9	10	12	6		7	13																				10
1	2	3	8	4	12	5	11¹	9	10	13	6		7²																					11
1			4				12	5	8²	10	9	13	6¹		7		2	14		3	11³													12
1	2	3¹	4	6			5	10	9	13	8		11³		12	14	7²																	13
1	2		4	6			12	9	13	10¹	5		8	7	11²	3																		14
1	2	4¹		5	13			10	12	9	6	14	8²	7	11	3³																		15
1	2	3	14	5		12	9	13	11³	10²	6¹		4	8			7																	16
1	2	7²		6	14	5	9³		13	12	4		3	10¹			11	8																17
1	2		6	5	9		10			4	12	3	11				7¹	8																18
1	2		6	5	9³	14		10	13		4¹		3	11²			7	8	12															19
1	2			5	9		8¹	10			12	3	6				11		7	4														20
1	2³			5	12	14	10	9¹		13		3	6				11²	8	7	4														21
1	3²	4¹		11			9	10	12	5		13	2					8	7	6														22
1	13	3¹	12	11	4	9		10	5	14			2					8²	7³	6														23
1	2		4	11¹	6	9		12	10	5								8	7	3														24
1		12		11¹	5	9			10	6			2					8	7	4⁴	3													25
1	12			11¹	5	9³	13		14	10²			2					8	7		3	4												26
1	2	7			5	9	10²			6			11¹	4	12			8			3		13											27
1	2	4		14	5	9¹	10²		12	13	6		11³	7				8			3⁴													28
1	2	3	4		5	14	12	9³	10	6	13		7	11¹							8²													29
1	2	3	4		14	5	12	13	9¹	10²	6		7									11	8³											30
1	2	3	4		11³	5		13		9²	10		7	12							6	14	8¹											31
1	2	3³	4		11	5	9¹	10²		12	13		14	7							8	6												32
1	2¹	3	4		11²	5³	13	14		9	10		12	7							6		8											33
1		3²	4				10			9¹	12	5	13	7							6		8			2	11							34
1		12	4				10	5²	9		13	6		2¹							7		3	11										35
1	2		8	5				9				12	6								3	11		4	7	10¹								36
1	7²		8		13			9³		14	12	5		2							6		4	3	11	10¹								37
1	2	3	4	5			13	9¹		12	10		7								8				11²									38
1	2		8	4			5	9		10²			7									12	3	11					13					39
1	2	3	8		5		12	9		13	10²	6³	7								14		4¹	11										40
1	2		8	6			5	9		10¹	12		7									4	3	11										41
1	2¹		8	4			5	9		10²	13		7								6	3	12	11										42
1		3	4	5¹			12	9		14	10³		13	7²							6		8	2	11									43
1		4					5	9		10¹	12	6		7							3		8	2	11									44
1		3	4				2	9		10¹		5		7							6		8	12	11									45
1		3¹	4				5	9³		13	10²	6		7									8	2	11						14	12		46

FA Cup
First Round   Torquay U   (a)   1-3

Carling Cup
First Round   Southend U   (h)   1-2

J Paint Trophy
First Round   Torquay   (h)   1-3

CHESTERFIELD   FL Championship 2

FOUNDATION

Chesterfield are fourth only to Stoke, Notts County and Nottingham Forest in age for they can trace their existence as far back as 1866, although it is fair to say that they were somewhat casual in the first few years of their history playing only a few friendlies a year. However, their rules of 1871 are still in existence showing an annual membership of 2s (10p), but it was not until 1891 that they won a trophy (the Barnes Cup) and followed this a year later by winning the Sheffield Cup, Barnes Cup and the Derbyshire Junior Cup.

The Recreation Ground, Saltergate, Chesterfield, Derbyshire S40 4SX.
Telephone: (01246) 209 765.
Fax: (01246) 556 799.
Ticket Office: (01246) 209 765.
Website: www.chesterfield-fc.co.uk
Email: reception@chesterfield-fc.co.uk
Ground Capacity: 8,502.
Record Attendance: 30,968 v Newcastle U, Division 2, 7 April 1939.
Pitch Measurements: 111yd × 71yd.
Chairman: Barrie Hubbard.
Vice-chairman: David C. Jones.
Managing Director: Mike Warner.
Finance Director: Alan Walters.
Manager: John Sheridan.
Assistant Manager: Tommy Wright.
Physio: Jamie Hewitt.
Colours: Blue shirts with white trim, white shorts, white stockings.
Change Colours: Red shirts with white sleeves, red shorts, red stockings.
Year Formed: 1866.
Turned Professional: 1891.
Ltd Co: 1871.
Previous Name: 1867, Chesterfield Town; 1919, Chesterfield.
Club Nicknames: 'Blues' or 'Spireites'.
Grounds: 1867, Drill Field; 1871, Recreation Ground.
First Football League Game: 2 September 1899, Division 2, v Sheffield W (a) L 1–5 – Hancock; Pilgrim, Fletcher; Ballantyne, Bell, Downie; Morley, Thacker, Gooing, Munday (1), Geary.
Record League Victory: 10–0 v Glossop NE, Division 2, 17 January 1903 – Clutterbuck; Thorpe, Lerper; Haig, Banner, Thacker; Tomlinson (2), Newton (1), Milward (3), Munday (2), Steel (2).
Record Cup Victory: 5–0 v Wath Ath (a), FA Cup 1st rd, 28 November 1925 – Birch; Saxby, Dennis; Wass, Abbott, Thompson; Fisher (1), Roseboom (1), Cookson (2), Whitfield (1), Hopkinson.

HONOURS

Football League: Division 2 best season: 4th, 1946–47; Division 3 (N) – Champions 1930–31, 1935–36; Runners-up 1933–34; Division 4 – Champions 1969–70, 1984–85.

FA Cup: Semi-final 1997.

Football League Cup: best season: 4th rd, 1965, 2007.

Anglo-Scottish Cup: Winners 1981.

sky SPORTS FACT FILE

Chesterfield owed their Third Division (North) championship victory in 1930–31 to a flourishing finish to the season in which they won the last six matches scoring 26 goals and ending with an 8–1 success against Gateshead to celebrate the title.

Record Defeat: 0–10 v Gillingham, Division 3, 5 September 1987.

Most League Points (2 for a win): 64, Division 4, 1969–70.

Most League Points (3 for a win): 91, Division 4, 1984–85.

Most League Goals: 102, Division 3 (N), 1930–31.

Highest League Scorer in Season: Jimmy Cookson, 44, Division 3 (N), 1925–26.

Most League Goals in Total Aggregate: Ernie Moss, 161, 1969–76, 1979–81 and 1984–86.

Most League Goals in One Match: 4, Jimmy Cookson v Accrington S, Division 3 (N), 16 January 1926; 4, Jimmy Cookson v Ashington, Division 3 (N), 1 May 1926; 4, Jimmy Cookson v Wigan Borough, Division 3 (N), 4 September 1926; 4, Tommy Lyon v Southampton, Division 2, 3 December 1938.

Most Capped Player: Walter McMillen, 4 (7), Northern Ireland; Mark Williams, 4 (30), Northern Ireland.

Most League Appearances: Dave Blakey, 613, 1948–67.

Youngest League Player: Dennis Thompson, 16 years 160 days v Notts Co, 26 December 1950.

Record Transfer Fee Received: £750,000 from Southampton for Kevin Davies, May 1997.

Record Transfer Fee Paid: £250,000 to Watford for Jason Lee, August 1998.

Football League Record: 1899 Elected to Division 2; 1909 failed re-election; 1921–31 Division 3 (N); 1931–33 Division 2; 1933–36 Division 3 (N); 1936–51 Division 2; 1951–58 Division 3 (N); 1958–61 Division 3; 1961–70 Division 4; 1970–83 Division 3; 1983–85 Division 4; 1985–89 Division 3; 1989–92 Division 3; 1992–95 Division 3; 1995–2000 Division 2; 2000–01 Division 3; 2001–04 Division 2; 2004–07 FL 1; 2007– FL 2.

LATEST SEQUENCES

Longest Sequence of League Wins: 10, 6.9.1933 – 4.11.1933.

Longest Sequence of League Defeats: 9, 22.10.1960 – 27.12.1960.

Longest Sequence of League Draws: 8, 26.11.2005 – 2.1.2006.

Longest Sequence of Unbeaten League Matches: 21, 26.12.1994 – 29.4.1995.

Longest Sequence Without a League Win: 18, 11.9.1999 – 3.1.2000.

Successive Scoring Runs: 46 from 25.12.1929.

Successive Non-scoring Runs: 7 from 23.9.1977.

MANAGERS

E. Russell Timmeus 1891–95
  (Secretary-Manager)
Gilbert Gillies 1895–1901
E. F. Hind 1901–02
Jack Hoskin 1902–06
W. Furness 1906–07
George Swift 1907–10
G. H. Jones 1911–13
R. L. Weston 1913–17
T. Callaghan 1919
J. J. Caffrey 1920–22
Harry Hadley 1922
Harry Parkes 1922–27
Alec Campbell 1927
Ted Davison 1927–32
Bill Harvey 1932–38
Norman Bullock 1938–45
Bob Brocklebank 1945–48
Bobby Marshall 1948–52
Ted Davison 1952–58
Duggie Livingstone 1958–62
Tony McShane 1962–67
Jimmy McGuigan 1967–73
Joe Shaw 1973–76
Arthur Cox 1976–80
Frank Barlow 1980–83
John Duncan 1983–87
Kevin Randall 1987–88
Paul Hart 1988–91
Chris McMenemy 1991–93
John Duncan 1993–2000
Nicky Law 2000–02
Dave Rushbury 2002–03
Roy McFarland 2003–07
Lee Richardson 2007–09
John Sheridan June 2009–

TEN YEAR LEAGUE RECORD

		P	W	D	L	F	A	Pts	Pos
2000-01	Div 3	46	25	14	7	79	42	80*	3
2001-02	Div 2	46	13	13	20	53	65	52	18
2002-03	Div 2	46	14	8	24	43	73	50	20
2003-04	Div 2	46	12	15	19	49	71	51	20
2004-05	FL 1	46	14	15	17	55	62	57	17
2005-06	FL 1	46	14	14	18	63	73	56	16
2006-07	FL 1	46	12	11	23	45	53	47	21
2007-08	FL 2	46	19	12	15	76	56	69	8
2008-09	FL 2	46	16	15	15	62	57	63	10
2009-10	FL 2	46	21	7	18	61	62	70	8

9 pts deducted.

DID YOU KNOW ?

In 1928–29 Chesterfield signed a Jack Lee from Newcastle United and a Jack Lee from Arsenal. The following season with a Sam Taylor already on the playing staff they added another Sam Taylor as player-coach! All four players were forwards.

CHESTERFIELD 2009-10 LEAGUE RECORD

Match No.	Date	Venue	Opponents	Result	H/T Score	Lg Pos.	Goalscorers	Attendance
1	Aug 8	A	Torquay U	L 0-2	0-1	—		3966
2	15	H	Northampton T	W 1-0	1-0	14	McDermott [32]	3700
3	19	H	Notts Co	W 2-1	0-0	—	Lowry 2 (2 pens) [78, 80]	6196
4	22	A	Shrewsbury T	D 1-1	0-1	9	Lowry [67]	5086
5	29	H	Morecambe	D 1-1	0-0	10	Lester [75]	3210
6	Sept 5	A	Rotherham U	L 1-3	1-0	15	Lowry (pen) [21]	4458
7	12	A	Dagenham & R	L 1-2	0-1	16	McDermott [86]	2034
8	19	H	Macclesfield T	W 4-1	4-0	13	Small [4], Lester [32], Lowry [37], McDermott [45]	3138
9	26	A	Bradford C	L 0-3	0-1	15		11,664
10	30	H	Grimsby T	W 3-2	1-0	—	Niven [30], Lester [54], McDermott [89]	3329
11	Oct 3	H	Accrington S	W 1-0	0-0	10	Small [90]	3104
12	10	A	Bournemouth	W 2-1	2-0	9	Talbot 2 [15, 45]	5896
13	17	A	Hereford U	L 0-1	0-0	10		2574
14	24	H	Burton Alb	W 5-2	2-0	8	Hall [13], Allott [24], Lester [81], Talbot [89], McDermott [90]	4218
15	31	H	Barnet	W 1-0	0-0	6	Boden [64]	3585
16	Nov 14	A	Rochdale	W 3-2	2-0	5	Lester 2 [25, 28], Perkins [63]	3011
17	21	H	Darlington	W 5-2	2-0	5	Page [37], Allott [45], Djilali [67], Boden 2 [89, 90]	3460
18	24	A	Bury	L 1-2	0-0	—	Small [90]	2504
19	Dec 2	H	Crewe Alex	L 2-3	0-2	—	Talbot [73], Lester [89]	3267
20	5	A	Aldershot T	L 0-1	0-0	7		2977
21	12	H	Cheltenham T	W 1-0	1-0	5	Lester [42]	3145
22	26	A	Lincoln C	L 1-2	0-2	6	Boden [83]	4604
23	Jan 2	A	Shrewsbury T	L 0-1	0-1	—		3601
24	16	H	Torquay U	W 1-0	0-0	—	Conlon [72]	3215
25	23	A	Northampton T	D 0-0	0-0	8		4513
26	26	A	Rotherham U	L 0-1	0-0	—		4951
27	30	A	Morecambe	W 1-0	1-0	7	Gritton [18]	1967
28	Feb 6	H	Lincoln C	W 2-1	1-0	7	Green [19], Conlon [50]	3573
29	9	A	Port Vale	W 2-1	2-0	—	Downes [10], Green [31]	4090
30	13	H	Bury	W 1-0	0-0	6	Boden [58]	4122
31	20	A	Darlington	W 3-2	0-1	4	Whaley [80], Talbot [81], Byrne (og) [87]	2209
32	24	A	Crewe Alex	W 1-0	1-0	—	Talbot [27]	3278
33	27	H	Aldershot T	L 0-1	0-0	4		3827
34	Mar 6	A	Cheltenham T	W 1-0	1-0	3	Conlon (pen) [41]	3006
35	9	A	Notts Co	L 0-1	0-1	—		7341
36	13	H	Port Vale	L 0-5	0-2	5		4138
37	20	A	Burton Alb	D 2-2	1-1	5	Demontagnac [34], Boden [61]	3696
38	27	H	Hereford U	L 1-2	0-0	5	Conlon (pen) [81]	3593
39	Apr 3	H	Rochdale	W 2-0	0-0	5	Conlon 2 (2 pens) [68, 83]	4471
40	5	A	Barnet	L 1-3	1-3	6	Small [14]	1916
41	10	H	Dagenham & R	D 2-2	0-1	6	Demontagnac [69], Conlon (pen) [89]	3588
42	13	A	Grimsby T	D 2-2	0-1	—	Lester 2 [65, 75]	5648
43	17	H	Macclesfield T	L 0-2	0-2	8		2143
44	24	H	Bradford C	D 1-1	0-0	9	Demontagnac [52]	4109
45	May 1	A	Accrington S	L 0-2	0-0	10		2475
46	8	H	Bournemouth	W 2-1	0-1	8	Lester [80], Niven [90]	4998

Final League Position: 8

GOALSCORERS
League (61): Lester 11, Conlon 7 (5 pens), Boden 6, Talbot 6, Lowry 5 (3 pens), McDermott 5, Small 4, Demontagnac 3, Allott 2, Green 2, Niven 2, Djilali 1, Downes 1, Gritton 1, Hall 1, Page 1, Perkins 1, Whaley 1, own goal 1.
Carling Cup (1): Currie 1 (pen).
FA Cup (1): Lester 1.
J Paint Trophy (9): Talbot 4, Small 2, Bowery 1, Currie 1 (pen), Lowry 1.

Crossley M 4	Picken P 20+1	Austin K 14+5	Niven D 28+11	Page R 38+1	Breckin I 41+1	Lowry J 13	Allott M 45	Talbot D 26+4	McDermott D 13+2	Currie D 2+2	Gritton M 2+7	Bowery J 2+8	Lee T 42	Lester J 27+2	Gray D 16+3	Robertson G 8+2	Small W 24+3	Boden S 5+30	Harsley P — +3	Perkins D 11+2	Little M 12	Hall D 5+2	Djilali K 8	Lewis I — +1	Morris 17	Somma D 1+2	Downes A 7	Goodall A 17	Green D 10	Conlon B 15+4	Artus F 2+1	Rundle A 12+4	Boshell D 3+6	Madine G 2+2	Whaley S 5+1	Whing A 9+2	Demontagnac I 10	Match No.
1	2	3	4¹	5	6	7	8	9	10	11²	12	13																										1
	2	3	4¹	5	6	7	8	11²	10				1	9	12	13																						2
	2	3	4	5	6	7	8	11¹	10²		12		1	9		13																						3
	2	3	4	5	6	7	8	11¹	10		12	13	1	9²																								4
	2	3	4³	5	6	7	8	11	10¹				1	9²			12	13	14																			5
	2		4¹	5	6	7²	8	10	12				1	9		3	11	13																				6
	2		4²	5	6	7	8	10¹	12	14			1	9³		3	11	13																				7
	2¹	13	4	5	6	7²	8		10³	14			1	9	12	3	11																					8
	2		4²	5		7	8		10¹	14		9³	1		12	6	3	11	13																			9
	2		4²	5	6	7	8		10				1	9	12	3	11¹	13																				10
	2		4¹	5	6	7	8	13	10				1	9²		3	11				12																	11
	2	13		5	6	7	8	10²	11		12		1	9¹						4		3																12
	2	13		5	6²	7²	8	10	11				1	9¹			12			4		3																13
		13	7¹		6		8	10	11				1	9³	2	12				4		3	5²															14
			4¹		6		8	10	11				1	9	2	12				7		3	5															15
	2			5	6		8	10					1	9		11¹	12			4		3			7													16
	2	12		5	6		8	10³					1	9		11²	13		4¹		3			7	14													17
	2	13		5	6		8	10					1	9¹		11	12		4²		3			7														18
		14		5	6		8³	13					1	9		11¹	12		4	2			7			3	10²											19
	13			5	6		8	10³					1	9²		11¹	12		4	2			7			3	14											20
1	2	12		5	6		8							9¹		11²	13		4		3			7	10													21
1	2¹	14		5	6		8³	12						9		11²	13		4		3			7	10													22
1	2²		4		6		8	10¹						14	9		13	3	11³	13		3		7	12	5												23
			6	5¹			8			13			1	11			10								12		7²	2	3	4	9							24
			6¹	5			8			13			1	11			10										7²	2	3	4	9	12						25
			6	5			8						1	9	11		12											2	3	7	10	4						26
		12	14	5	6		8			10³			1	11			13											3	3¹	7	9²	4■						27
			4	5	14		8			10¹			1	7			12											2	3	6²	9³	11	13					28
		12²	13	5	6		8						1	9			7³	14										2¹	3	4	10	11						29
			4	5	6		8	13					1	7			12											3	2	9¹		11		10²				30
		12		5	6		8	9					1	7			13					2¹						3	4³		11		10²	14				31
				5	6		8	9					1	7			12											3	2	10¹	11		4					32
		12		5	6		8	9					1	7			14	13										3	2¹	10²	11³		4					33
		2		5	6		8						1	9			7¹	12										3		10²	11	13	4		14			34
		4¹		5	6		8	9					1	7³			11	12										3		10²	11		13		2	14		35
		4¹		5	6		8	9					1				7³	13										3■			11²	12	14	10	2			36
	3			5	6		7	9					1				11	12												10¹	13	4			2	8²		37
4				5	6		8	9					1				11²	10¹										3		12	13				2	7		38
3		5	12		6		8						1			10²	7³	14						13						9	11				2¹	4		39
5		3	4		6		10¹							1	14		7	12												9²	11³	13			2	8		40
		3	4¹		6		10							1	9		7	14					5³						12	11²	13			2	8		41
		4¹		5	6		8				13	11	1	9			10²									3					12			2	7		42
	5		12	6		10					13	11	1	9³			7²	14								3¹						4		2	8		43
	2²		4		6		8	10¹					1	9	3		12			5										13	11³				14	7		44
		4	5	6		10							1	9²	2		7¹	13							3				12	14	11³				8		45
	3	4	5	6		8	11²				12		1	9													10¹			13				2	7		46

FA Cup
First Round — Bournemouth (h) 1-3

Carling Cup
First Round — Scunthorpe U (a) 1-2

J Paint Trophy
First Round — Burton Alb (a) 5-1
Second Round — Huddersfield T (h) 3-3
Northern Quarter-Final — Carlisle U (h) 1-3

COLCHESTER UNITED   FL Championship 1

FOUNDATION

Colchester United was formed in 1937 when a number of enthusiasts of the much older Colchester Town club decided to establish a professional concern as a limited liability company. The new club continued at Layer Road which had been the amateur club's home since 1909.

Weston Homes Community Stadium, United Way, Colchester, Essex CO4 5UP.

Telephone: (01206) 755 100.

Fax: (01206) 755 112.

Ticket Office: (0845) 437 9089.

Website: www.cu-fc.com

Email: caroline@colchesterunited.net

Ground Capacity: 10,000.

Record Attendance: 19,072 v Reading, FA Cup 1st rd, 27 November 1948.

Pitch Measurements: 106m × 68m.

Executive Chairman: Robbie Cowling.

Vice-chairman: Richard Cowling.

Football Secretary: Caroline Pugh.

Manager: John Ward.

Assistant Manager: Joe Dunne.

Physio: Tony Flynn.

Colours: Royal blue and white striped shirts with white sleeves, royal blue shorts, white stockings.

Change Colours: All black.

Year Formed: 1937.

Turned Professional: 1937.

Ltd Co.: 1937.

Club Nickname: 'The U's'.

Grounds: 1937, Layer Road; 2008, Eston Homes Community Stadium.

First Football League Game: 19 August 1950, Division 3 (S), v Gillingham (a) D 0–0 – Wright; Kettle, Allen; Bearryman, Stewart, Elder; Jones, Curry, Turner, McKim, Church.

Record League Victory: 9–1 v Bradford C, Division 4, 30 December 1961 – Ames; Millar, Fowler; Harris, Abrey, Ron Hunt; Foster, Bobby Hunt (4), King (4), Hill (1), Wright.

HONOURS

Football League: FL 1 – Runners-up 2005–06; Division 4 – Runners-up 1961–62.

FA Cup: best season: 6th rd, 1971.

Football League Cup: best season: 5th rd, 1975.

Auto Windscreens Shield: Runners-up 1997.

GM Vauxhall Conference: Winners 1991–92.

FA Trophy: Winners 1992.

sky SPORTS FACT FILE

On 8 August 2009 Colchester United won 7–1 at Norwich City. It was United's best away victory. Within ten days Paul Lambert left Colchester to become manager at Carrow Road. In 1938–39 Colchester had beaten City Reserves 5–1 there in a Southern League Cup match.

Record Cup Victory: 9-1 v Leamington, FA Cup 1st rd, 5 November 2005 – Davison; Stockley (Garcia), Duguid, Brown (1), Chilvers, Watson (1), Halford (1), Izzet (Dannsi (2), Iwelumo (1) (Williams), Cureton (2), Yeates (1).

Record Defeat: 0–8 v Leyton Orient, Division 4, 15 October 1988.

Most League Points (2 for a win): 60, Division 4, 1973–74.

Most League Points (3 for a win): 81, Division 4, 1982–83.

Most League Goals: 104, Division 4, 1961–62.

Highest League Scorer in Season: Bobby Hunt, 38, Division 4, 1961–62.

Most League Goals in Total Aggregate: Martyn King, 130, 1956–64.

Most League Goals in One Match: 4, Bobby Hunt v Bradford C, Division 4, 30 December 1961; 4, Martyn King v Bradford C, Division 4, 30 December 1961; 4, Bobby Hunt v Doncaster R, Division 4, 30 April 1962.

Most Capped Player: Bela Balogh, 2 (9), Hungary.

Most League Appearances: Micky Cook, 613, 1969–84.

Youngest League Player: Lindsay Smith, 16 years 218 days v Grimsby T, 24 April 1971.

Record Transfer Fee Received: £2,500,000 from Reading for Greg Halford, January 2007.

Record Transfer Fee Paid: £400,000 to Cheltenham T for Steve Gillespie, July 2008.

MANAGERS

Ted Fenton 1946–48
Jimmy Allen 1948–53
Jack Butler 1953–55
Benny Fenton 1955–63
Neil Franklin 1963–68
Dick Graham 1968–72
Jim Smith 1972–75
Bobby Roberts 1975–82
Allan Hunter 1982–83
Cyril Lea 1983–86
Mike Walker 1986–87
Roger Brown 1987–88
Jock Wallace 1989
Mick Mills 1990
Ian Atkins 1990–91
Roy McDonough 1991–94
George Burley 1994
Steve Wignall 1995–99
Mick Wadsworth 1999
Steve Whitton 1999–2003
Phil Parkinson 2003–06
Geraint Williams July 2006–08
Paul Lambert 2008–10
John Ward May 2010

Football League Record: 1950 Elected to Division 3 (S); 1958–61 Division 3; 1961–62 Division 4; 1962–65 Division 3; 1965–66 Division 4; 1966–68 Division 3; 1968–74 Division 4; 1974–76 Division 3; 1976–77 Division 4; 1977–81 Division 3; 1981–90 Division 4; 1990–92 GM Vauxhall Conference; 1992–98 Division 3; 1998–04 Division 2; 2004–06 FL 1; 2006–08 FL C; 2008– FL 1.

LATEST SEQUENCES

Longest Sequence of League Wins: 7, 29.11.1968 – 1.2.1969.

Longest Sequence of League Defeats: 8, 9.10.1954 – 4.12.1954.

Longest Sequence of League Draws: 6, 21.3.1977 – 11.4.1977.

Longest Sequence of Unbeaten League Matches: 20, 22.12.1956 – 19.4.1957.

Longest Sequence Without a League Win: 20, 2.3.1968 – 31.8.1968.

Successive Scoring Runs: 24 from 15.9.1962.

Successive Non-scoring Runs: 5 from 7.4.1981.

TEN YEAR LEAGUE RECORD

		P	W	D	L	F	A	Pts	Pos
2000-01	Div 2	46	15	12	19	55	59	57	17
2001-02	Div 2	46	15	12	19	65	76	57	15
2002-03	Div 2	46	14	16	16	52	56	58	12
2003-04	Div 2	46	17	13	16	52	56	64	11
2004-05	FL 1	46	14	17	15	60	50	59	15
2005-06	FL 1	46	22	13	11	58	40	79	2
2006-07	FL C	46	20	9	17	70	56	69	10
2007-08	FL C	46	7	17	22	62	86	38	24
2008-09	FL 1	46	18	9	19	58	58	63	12
2009-10	FL 1	46	20	12	14	64	52	72	8

DID YOU KNOW ?

In the transitional season of 1945–46 Colchester United had to call upon the services of 81 different players during their Southern League and Cup matches. Even so, one player managed to figure in all 30 such matches, right-back Bill Bower.

COLCHESTER UNITED 2009–10 LEAGUE RECORD

Match No.	Date	Venue	Opponents	Result	H/T Score	Lg Pos.	Goalscorers	Attendance
1	Aug 8	A	Norwich C	W 7-1	5-0	—	Lisbie 2 [10, 38], Platt 2 [13, 19], Fox [22], Perkins [76], Vernon [90]	25,217
2	15	H	Yeovil T	W 2-1	2-0	1	Fox [9], Vincent [18]	4263
3	18	H	Gillingham	W 2-1	1-1	—	Vernon [38], Lisbie [66]	4849
4	22	A	Milton Keynes D	L 1-2	0-1	3	Vernon [69]	8633
5	29	H	Leeds U	L 1-2	0-0	5	Lisbie (pen) [57]	8810
6	Sept 5	A	Southampton	D 0-0	0-0	7		17,070
7	12	A	Swindon T	D 1-1	1-1	6	Vincent [21]	6621
8	19	H	Hartlepool U	W 2-0	1-0	5	Lisbie 2 (2 pens) [45, 47]	4259
9	26	A	Tranmere R	D 1-1	1-1	5	O'Toole [37]	5314
10	29	H	Charlton Ath	W 3-0	2-0	—	Llera (og) [29], Odejayi 2 [31, 57]	7098
11	Oct 3	H	Huddersfield T	W 1-0	0-0	4	Odejayi [80]	5154
12	10	A	Leyton Orient	W 1-0	0-0	3	Odejayi [54]	5410
13	17	A	Wycombe W	D 1-1	1-0	4	Odejayi [23]	5394
14	24	H	Walsall	W 2-1	1-1	3	Lisbie 2 (1 pen) [26, 61 (p)]	4880
15	31	A	Millwall	L 1-2	1-0	4	Wordsworth [18]	10,036
16	Nov 14	H	Exeter C	D 2-2	1-2	3	Platt 2 [41, 85]	5208
17	21	A	Oldham Ath	D 2-2	1-0	4	Fox [12], Odejayi [50]	3607
18	24	H	Stockport Co	W 2-0	2-0	—	Lisbie [10], Platt [15]	3818
19	Dec 1	A	Brentford	L 0-1	0-1	—		4200
20	5	H	Bristol R	W 1-0	1-0	4	Lisbie [30]	4942
21	11	A	Brighton & HA	W 2-1	2-1	—	Ifil [9], Wordsworth [14]	5898
22	26	A	Southend U	W 2-1	0-0	4	Ifil [46], Wordsworth [57]	10,329
23	28	H	Southampton	W 2-1	1-0	4	Wordsworth [23], Gillespie [75]	8514
24	Jan 16	H	Norwich C	L 0-5	0-2	4		10,064
25	23	A	Gillingham	D 0-0	0-0	4		4948
26	26	H	Milton Keynes D	W 2-0	1-0	—	Lisbie [18], Prutton [67]	3601
27	30	A	Leeds U	L 0-2	0-1	4		23,425
28	Feb 2	H	Carlisle U	W 2-1	0-1	—	Platt [61], Odejayi [90]	3903
29	8	H	Southend U	W 2-0	1-0	—	Wordsworth 2 [3, 62]	6466
30	13	A	Stockport Co	D 2-2	2-1	4	Prutton [10], Wordsworth [18]	3642
31	16	A	Yeovil T	W 1-0	1-0	—	Odejayi [38]	3469
32	20	A	Oldham Ath	W 1-0	0-0	3	Batth [64]	5321
33	27	A	Bristol R	L 2-3	1-1	4	O'Toole [21], Odejayi [89]	6023
34	Mar 8	H	Brighton & HA	D 0-0	0-0	—		3914
35	13	A	Carlisle U	L 1-2	0-0	5	Platt [66]	4469
36	20	A	Walsall	L 0-1	0-0	6		3510
37	23	H	Brentford	D 3-3	2-2	—	Hunt (og) [32], Wordsworth [45], Prutton [76]	3915
38	27	H	Wycombe W	D 1-1	0-0	6	Henderson [59]	5593
39	Apr 2	A	Exeter C	L 0-2	0-1	—		6297
40	5	H	Millwall	L 1-2	0-1	7	Lisbie [50]	7393
41	10	H	Swindon T	W 3-0	1-0	7	Vincent [24], Wordsworth 2 [69, 90]	5111
42	13	A	Charlton Ath	L 0-1	0-1	—		17,427
43	17	A	Hartlepool U	L 1-3	1-2	7	Henderson [8]	3126
44	24	H	Tranmere R	D 1-1	1-1	8	Wordsworth [4]	4353
45	May 1	A	Huddersfield T	L 1-2	0-1	8	Hackney [76]	17,950
46	8	H	Leyton Orient	W 1-0	0-0	8	Lisbie (pen) [90]	5751

Final League Position: 8

GOALSCORERS

League (64): Lisbie 13 (5 pens), Wordsworth 11, Odejayi 9, Platt 7, Fox 3, Prutton 3, Vernon 3, Vincent 3, Henderson 2, Ifil 2, O'Toole 2, Batth 1, Gillespie 1, Hackney 1, Perkins 1, own goals 2.
Carling Cup (1): Hackney 1.
FA Cup (5): Hackney 1, Gillespie 1, Odejayi 1, O'Toole 1, Platt 1.
J Paint Trophy (1): Platt 1.

Williams B 46	Beevers L 4	Tierney M 41	Fox D 15 + 3	Baldwin P 6 + 1	Okuonghae M 44	Vincent A 15 + 4	Hammond D 2	Platt C 36 + 5	Lisbie K 35 + 6	Hackney S 9 + 8	Izzet K 31 + 6	Perkins D — + 5	Vernon S 4 + 3	Thomas J — + 4	Wordsworth A 36 + 5	Maybury A 1 + 1	White J 38 + 1	O'Toole J 30 + 1	Heath M 13 + 5	Guy J — + 1	Batth D 16 + 1	Odejayi K 19 + 9	Gillespie S 8 + 22	Bender Thomas — + 1	Ifil P 15 + 12	Elito M — + 3	Lockwood M 1	Payne J 2 + 1	Reid P 10 + 2	Henderson I 6 + 7	Ribeiro C 2	Prutton D 18 + 1	Queudrue F 3	Match No.
1	2	3	4	5	6	7¹	8	9	10³	11²	12	13	14																					1
1	2	3	4	5	6	7	8		10¹	11²	12	13	14																					2
1	2	3	4	5	6	7¹			10³	11²	8	13	9	12	14																			3
1	2¹	3	4	5	6	7			10	11²	8	13	9³	14	12																			4
1		3	4³	5	6	7²		12	10	11	8	13	9¹	14	2																			5
1		3		5¹	6	7		9²	10		8⁕				13		4	2	11		12													6
1		3	13		6	7¹		9	10³		8				14		4	2	11		5	12²												7
1		3	7		6			9	10³		4²				2		11	5			3¹	12	13		14									8
1		3	7¹		6			9³	10		12				4		2	11	13		5²	3	14											9
1		3			6²			9¹	10	7					4³		2	11	13		5	3	12		14									10
1		3			6			9¹	10²	7					4		2	11			5	3	12		13									11
1		3	4					9	10³	8	6				2¹		7	14			5	11²	13		12									12
1		3	4					9	10²	8	6				2		7				5	11¹	2		13									13
1					6			9³	10	13	8				2		7				5	11	4		12			3¹		4²				14
1		3			6			9²	10	12	4				2		7				5³	11	3		8¹					14				15
1		3	11		6			9		7					8³		5		4		10²	13	2¹		14⁕			12						16
1		3⁕	4²		6			9³	10¹		13				8		2	7			5	11	12		14									17
1			4³		6			9²	10	12	14				8¹		5	7			11	13	2		3									18
1		3	4		6			9	10		8				2²		7				1	13	12		5									19
1		3	4¹		6			9	10³		13				12		8	5	7		4	2²	11											20
1		3			6			9¹	10²	12	8				11		5	7			3	14	2³		4									21
1		3			6			10²	12	14	8				13		11	5	7		9¹	2³	4											22
1		3	12		6			10³	8¹		13				11		5	7	14		9²	2³	4											23
1		3	7²	12	6			9	10	8					11		5³	3			4¹	2								14⁕				24
1		3			6			9²	13	4					8		7				10¹	12	2					5	11					25
1		3			6			9	10³	4					8		12	7	2		14	5²							11¹	13				26
1		3			6			9²	10³	8					11		5	7	2		12	13	4¹	14										27
1		3			6			9		4					8		5	11	2		12	10¹			13							7²		28
1		3			6			9		4					8³		5	11¹	2		10²	13	12		14							7		29
1		3			6			9¹		4					8		5	11	2		10		12									7		30
1		3			6			9		4					8		5	11	2		10¹		12									7		31
1		3						9	12	4					8		11	2		6	10¹		5									7		32
1		3			12			9	14	8					6		11	2			4³	13	10²		5¹							7		33
1		3			6	13		9²	12	4					8		5	11¹	2		10³	14										7		34
1		3	4		6	11²		14	9						12		5	2			10³	13	8¹									7		35
1		3			6	10¹		9	4						8		5	11	2		12²	13										7		36
1		3			6			9	10	4					8		5	2			12	3	11¹									7		37
1		3			6	14		9³	8	4					12		5	13			10²	2	11¹									7	3	38
1		3			6	14		9²	8	4					12		5	11			13	2³	10¹									7		39
1		3			6	10²		9	11	4					8		2	12			13		5¹									7		40
1		3			6	10²		9¹	11	4					8		2	5			12	13										7		41
1		3	14		6	10		12	8⁕	4²					2		11¹	5			9³	13										7		42
1		3			6	10¹		9	8	12	4				2²		5	13			11											7		43
1		3			6	10¹		11	13	4²	8				2		14	9³			5	12										7⁕		44
1		3	11		6	13		10	7²	4					8		2	12			5	9¹										7		45
1		3			6	10³		13	12	11²	4				8		2	9¹			14	5										7		46

FA Cup

First Round	Bromley	(a)	4-0
Second Round	Hereford U	(a)	1-0
Third Round	Preston NE	(a)	0-7

Carling Cup

First Round	Leyton Orient	(h)	1-2

J Paint Trophy

First Round	Gillingham	(a)	1-1

COVENTRY CITY FL Championship

FOUNDATION

Workers at Singers' cycle factory formed a club in 1883. The first success of Singers' FC was to win the Birmingham Junior Cup in 1891 and this led in 1894 to their election to the Birmingham and District League. Four years later they changed their name to Coventry City and joined the Southern League in 1908 at which time they were playing in blue and white quarters.

The Ricoh Arena, Phoenix Way, Foleshill, Coventry CV6 6GE.
Telephone: (0844) 873 1883.
Fax: 0870 421 1988.
Ticket Office: (0844) 873 1883 (option 1).
Website: www.ccfc.co.uk
Email: info@ccfc.co.uk
Ground Capacity: 32,609.
Record Attendance: 51,455 v Wolverhampton W, Division 2, 29 April 1967 (at Highfield Road). 31,407 v Chelsea, FA Cup 6th rd, 7 March 2009 (at Ricoh Arena).
Pitch Measurements: 110yd × 75yd.
Chairman: Ray Ranson.
Vice-chairman: Gary Hoffman.
Secretary: Pam Hindson.
Manager: Aidy Boothroyd.
Assistant Manager: Steve Harrison.
Physio: Michael McBride.
Colours: Sky blue shirts with grey horizontal stripes, white shorts, sky blue stockings.
Change Colours: Green shirts with black vertical stripes, black shorts and stockings.
Year Formed: 1883. *Turned Professional:* 1893. *Ltd Co.:* 1907.
Previous Name: 1883, Singers FC; 1898, Coventry City FC.
Club Nickname: 'Sky Blues'.
Grounds: 1883, Binley Road; 1887, Stoke Road; 1899, Highfield Road; 2005, Ricoh Arena.
First Football League Game: 30 August 1919, Division 2, v Tottenham H (h) L 0–5 – Lindon; Roberts, Chaplin, Allan, Hawley, Clarke, Sheldon, Mercer, Sambrooke, Lowes, Gibson.
Record League Victory: 9–0 v Bristol C, Division 3 (S), 28 April 1934 – Pearson; Brown, Bisby; Perry, Davidson, Frith; White (2), Lauderdale, Bourton (5), Jones (2), Lake.
Record Cup Victory: 8–0 v Rushden & D, League Cup 2nd rd, 2 October 2002 – Debec; Caldwell, Quinn, Betts (1p); Konjic (Shaw), Davenport, Pipe, Safri (Stanford), Mills (2) (Bothroyd (2)), McSheffery (3), Partridge.
Record Defeat: 2–10 v Norwich C, Division 3 (S), 15 March 1930.
Most League Points (2 for a win): 60, Division 4, 1958–59 and Division 3, 1963–64.

HONOURS

Football League: Division 1 best season: 6th, 1969–70; Division 2 – Champions 1966–67; Division 3 – Champions 1963–64; Division 3 (S) – Champions 1935–36; Runners-up 1933–34; Division 4 – Runners-up 1958–59.

FA Cup: Winners 1987.

Football League Cup: Semi-final 1981, 1990.

European Competitions: European Fairs Cup: 1970–71.

sky SPORTS FACT FILE

In 1959–60 Coventry City became the last winners of the Southern Professional Floodlit Cup. They beat Southend United and Fulham both after replays, Southampton in the semi-final and West Ham United in the final in which Ron Hewitt notched both goals in a 2–1 success.

Most League Points (3 for a win): 66, Division 1, 2001–02.

Most League Goals: 108, Division 3 (S), 1931–32.

Highest League Scorer in Season: Clarrie Bourton, 49, Division 3 (S), 1931–32.

Most League Goals in Total Aggregate: Clarrie Bourton, 171, 1931–37.

Most League Goals in One Match: 5, Clarrie Bourton v Bournemouth, Division 3 (S), 17 October 1931; 5, Arthur Bacon v Gillingham, Division 3 (S), 30 December 1933.

Most Capped Player: Magnus Hedman, 44 (58), Sweden.

Most League Appearances: Steve Ogrizovic, 507, 1984–2000.

Youngest League Player: Ben Mackey, 16 years 167 days v Ipswich T, 12 April 2003.

Record Transfer Fee Received: £13,000,000 from Internazionale for Robbie Keane, July 2000.

Record Transfer Fee Paid: £6,500,000 to Wolverhampton W for Robbie Keane, August 1999; £6,500,000 to Norwich C for Craig Bellamy, August 2000.

Football League Record: 1919 Elected to Division 2; 1925–26 Division 3 (N); 1926–36 Division 3 (S); 1936–52 Division 2; 1952–58 Division 3 (S); 1958–59 Division 4; 1959–64 Division 3; 1964–67 Division 2; 1967–92 Division 1; 1992–2001 FA Premier League; 2001–04 Division 1; 2004– FL C.

LATEST SEQUENCES

Longest Sequence of League Wins: 6, 25.4.1964 – 5.9.1964.

Longest Sequence of League Defeats: 9, 30.8.1919 – 11.10.1919.

Longest Sequence of League Draws: 6, 1.11.2003 – 29.11.2003.

Longest Sequence of Unbeaten League Matches: 25, 26.11.1966 – 13.5.1967.

Longest Sequence Without a League Win: 19, 30.8.1919 – 20.12.1919.

Successive Scoring Runs: 25 from 10.9.1966.

Successive Non-scoring Runs: 11 from 11.10.1919.

MANAGERS

H. R. Buckle 1909–10
Robert Wallace 1910–13
(Secretary-Manager)
Frank Scott-Walford 1913–15
William Clayton 1917–19
H. Pollitt 1919–20
Albert Evans 1920–24
Jimmy Kerr 1924–28
James McIntyre 1928–31
Harry Storer 1931–45
Dick Bayliss 1945–47
Billy Frith 1947–48
Harry Storer 1948–53
Jack Fairbrother 1953–54
Charlie Elliott 1954–55
Jesse Carver 1955–56
George Raynor 1956
Harry Warren 1956–57
Billy Frith 1957–61
Jimmy Hill 1961–67
Noel Cantwell 1967–72
Bob Dennison 1972
Joe Mercer 1972–75
Gordon Milne 1972–81
Dave Sexton 1981–83
Bobby Gould 1983–84
Don Mackay 1985–86
George Curtis 1986–87
(became Managing Director)
John Sillett 1987–90
Terry Butcher 1990–92
Don Howe 1992
Bobby Gould 1992–93
Phil Neal 1993–95
Ron Atkinson 1995–96
(became Director of Football)
Gordon Strachan 1996–2001
Roland Nilsson 2001–02
Gary McAllister 2002–04
Eric Black 2004
Peter Reid 2004–05
Micky Adams 2005–07
Iain Dowie 2007
Chris Coleman 2008–10
Aidy Boothroyd May 2010–

TEN YEAR LEAGUE RECORD

		P	W	D	L	F	A	Pts	Pos
2000-01	PR Lge	38	8	10	20	36	63	34	19
2001-02	Div 1	46	20	6	20	59	53	66	11
2002-03	Div 1	46	12	14	20	46	62	50	20
2003-04	Div 1	46	17	14	15	67	54	65	12
2004-05	FL C	46	13	13	20	61	73	52	19
2005-06	FL C	46	16	15	15	62	65	63	8
2006-07	FL C	46	16	8	22	47	62	56	17
2007-08	FL C	46	14	11	21	52	64	53	21
2008-09	FL C	46	13	15	18	47	58	54	17
2009-10	FL C	46	13	15	18	47	64	54	19

DID YOU KNOW ?

While still known as Singers, forerunners of Coventry City, centre-forward Frank Mobley created an amazing goal-scoring run in Cup matches during 1891–92. In sixteen ties he fired in 26 goals including a six and two fives when the club was playing as an amateur club.

COVENTRY CITY 2009–10 LEAGUE RECORD

Match No.	Date	Venue	Opponents	Result	H/T Score	Lg Pos.	Goalscorers	Attendance
1	Aug 9	H	Ipswich T	W 2-1	2-1	—	Morrison 2 [10, 24]	16,279
2	15	A	Barnsley	W 2-0	1-0	1	Best [8], Morrison [81]	12,552
3	18	A	Doncaster R	D 0-0	0-0	—		9484
4	22	H	Swansea C	L 0-1	0-0	8		16,307
5	29	A	Blackpool	L 0-3	0-1	12		8239
6	Sept 12	H	Bristol C	D 1-1	1-0	11	Best [18]	16,449
7	15	H	Sheffield U	W 3-2	1-1	—	Best [12], Morrison [50], Cranie [60]	14,426
8	19	A	Preston NE	L 2-3	1-0	11	Clingan [19], Morrison [90]	11,230
9	26	H	Middlesbrough	D 2-2	0-2	13	Morrison [78], Best [90]	16,771
10	29	A	Watford	W 3-2	1-2	—	Clingan [14], Best 2 [67, 84]	13,034
11	Oct 3	H	Leicester C	D 1-1	1-0	11	Clingan [38]	22,209
12	17	A	Sheffield W	L 0-2	0-2	15		20,026
13	20	A	Cardiff C	L 0-2	0-1	—		19,038
14	24	H	WBA	D 0-0	0-0	15		20,871
15	31	H	Reading	L 1-3	0-1	16	Eastwood [64]	15,165
16	Nov 6	A	Derby Co	L 1-2	1-0	—	Best [4]	26,511
17	21	H	Crystal Palace	D 1-1	0-0	18	Best [47]	18,400
18	28	A	QPR	D 2-2	1-1	17	Best [16], Wood [81]	13,712
19	Dec 6	A	Scunthorpe U	L 0-1	0-1	20		5013
20	9	H	Newcastle U	L 0-2	0-1	—		21,688
21	12	H	Peterborough U	W 3-2	2-0	19	Eastwood 3 [34, 35, 72]	15,190
22	19	A	Plymouth Arg	W 1-0	0-0	17	Eastwood [72]	8347
23	26	H	Doncaster R	W 1-0	0-0	16	Morrison (pen) [85]	19,221
24	28	A	Nottingham F	L 0-2	0-1	17		28,608
25	Jan 9	H	Barnsley	W 3-1	2-0	—	Eastwood [24], Clingan [27], Morrison [90]	15,031
26	16	A	Ipswich T	L 2-3	1-1	15	Morrison [2], Wood [89]	20,135
27	26	A	Swansea C	D 0-0	0-0	—		13,868
28	30	H	Blackpool	D 1-1	0-0	14	John-Baptiste (og) [83]	16,019
29	Feb 6	A	Bristol C	D 1-1	0-0	17	Bell [47]	13,852
30	9	H	Nottingham F	W 1-0	1-0	—	Eastwood [25]	18,225
31	13	H	QPR	W 1-0	1-0	—	Deegan [10]	15,247
32	17	A	Newcastle U	L 1-4	1-1	—	Morrison [35]	39,334
33	20	A	Crystal Palace	W 1-0	0-0	10	Bell [86]	13,333
34	27	H	Scunthorpe U	W 2-1	0-0	10	Stead [55], Clingan [68]	16,197
35	Mar 6	A	Peterborough U	W 1-0	1-0	8	Stead [24]	10,469
36	13	H	Plymouth Arg	D 1-1	0-1	8	McIndoe [49]	18,127
37	16	H	Cardiff C	L 1-2	1-1	—	Morrison [32]	16,038
38	21	A	Leicester C	D 2-2	0-2	10	McPake [54], Deegan [87]	23,093
39	24	A	WBA	L 0-1	0-1	—		22,140
40	27	H	Sheffield W	D 1-1	0-0	12	Wood [79]	17,608
41	Apr 3	H	Derby Co	L 0-1	0-1	13		17,630
42	5	A	Reading	L 0-3	0-3	14		17,435
43	10	A	Sheffield U	L 0-1	0-0	17		23,603
44	17	H	Preston NE	D 1-1	1-1	16	Eastwood [19]	15,822
45	24	A	Middlesbrough	D 1-1	0-0	16	Gunnarsson [58]	27,721
46	May 2	H	Watford	L 0-4	0-2	19		19,103

Final League Position: 19

GOALSCORERS

League (47): Morrison 11 (1 pen), Best 9, Eastwood 8, Clingan 5, Wood 3, Bell 2, Deegan 2, Stead 2, Cranie 1, Gunnarsson 1, McIndoe 1, McPake 1, own goal 1.
Carling Cup (0).
FA Cup (2): Bell 1, Best 1.

Westwood K 44	Osbourne I 12 + 3	Van Aanholt P 19 + 1	Clingan S 32 + 2	Turner B 13	Wright S 38	Bell D 20 + 8	Gunnarsson A 34 + 6	Morrison C 38 + 8	Best L 25 + 2	McIndoe M 36 + 2	Clarke J 6 + 6	Ward E 4 + 4	Eastwood F 21 + 15	Cranie M 38 + 2	Grandison J 1 + 2	Jeffers S – + 4	Cork J 20 + 1	McKenzie L – + 1	Hall M 7 + 1	Cain A – + 2	Hussey C 1 + 7	Madine G – + 9	Konstantopoulos D 2 + 1	Barnett L 19 + 1	Wood R 22 + 2	McPake J 17	Deegan G 9 + 8	Baker C 14 + 8	Sears F 3 + 7	Stead J 9 + 1	Match No.
1	2	3	4	5	6	7¹	8	9	10³	11²	12	13	14																		1
1	7	6	4	5	2		8	9	10²	11				3¹	12	13															2
1	7	6	4	5	2		8	9	10	11				3																	3
1	7¹	6	4	5	2		8	9	10³	11²			14	3			12	13													4
1		6	4	5	2		8	9¹	10	11			12	3			7														5
1	8¹		4	5	2	13		9	10	11			12	3			7²		6												6
1	8		4	5	2	13		9¹	10	11	12			3			7		6²												7
1	8		4	5	2¹			9	10	11	12		14	3³			7²	13	6												8
1	8²	13	4	5¹	2		12	9	10	11			14	3			7		6¹												9
1	14	5	4		2		8³	9	10	11²	3¹	6	13	12			7														10
1	12	5	4¹		2		8	9	10		6	11	3				7														11
1	2	3		5	7		8¹	9	10	11²			6	12			4		13												12
1	2	3²		5	7	12		9	10¹	11			8	6			4			13											13
1⁰	2	3		6	7	12		9		11	8¹		10²	5			4				13	15									14
	12	3³		5			8²	9	13	11¹	6		10	2	7		4		14		1										15
	2	3¹			14	8		9	10	12	7¹	5	11³	4²			13		1		6										16
1		3			2	7	8	9¹	10	11				4					12		6	5									17
1		3¹			6⁸	7²	8³	9	10	11	12		13	4				14		2	5										18
1						7	9	10	11²				8	3			4	5¹	12	13	2	6									19
1	3				13	7³	9	10	11		5¹		8	6	12		4²		⁻4	2											20
1	3	14		5	7¹	8	12	10²	11		9³	6		4					⁻3	2											21
1	3					8	7	13	10³	11	12		9²	5			4		⁻4	2		6¹									22
1	3					7	8	13	10³	11			9²	5			4		⁻4	2	12	6¹									23
1	3	13				7¹	8	9	10³	11			12	5			4²		⁻4	2	6										24
1	4			3	7²	8³	14	10	11¹				9	5						2				6	12	13					25
1	4	2³		7	14		9	12	11				10¹	3										5	6	8²	13				26
1	4	2		7	8	14		10	11²				3											12	5	6¹	13	9²			27
1	4	2		7²	8¹	13		10³	11				14	3										5	6	12	9				28
1	4	2		7	8		9		11				10¹	3										5	6	12	13				29
1	4	2		7²	8¹		9		11				10	3										5	6	8	7	12			30
1	4	2					9¹		11				10	3										2⁴	5	10³	7	13	12		31
1	4	6		14		9²			11				8¹	3										5	6	13	7		10		32
1	4	2	12	8		9²			11¹					3										2⁴	6	12	7		10¹		33
1	4	5		8		9²			11				13	3							3			6	12	7	13	10			34
1	4¹	2		8		9²			11				5	3							12			6	12	7	13	10			35
1	4	2¹		8²		9³			11				14	5										3	6	⁻3	7		10		36
1		2		12	4	9³			11¹				13	5										3	6	8	7	14	10²		37
1	4	2		8¹	12	9			13				5	3										3	6	11	7³	14	10²		38
1	4	2³		8¹		13			10				5	14										3	6	11	7	12	9²		39
1	4		12		13				11²				5	2¹					14					3	6	8	7	10	9³		40
1	4	3	12	8¹	9								5²	13										2	6	11³	7	14	10		41
1	4	2	7²	8	9				12					3¹										5	14	6¹	11	13	10		42
1	4	2	7	8	9	13	14		12					3³										5	6		11²	10¹			43
1	4	2	7	8	9				11¹				10²	5	3									6	3		12				44
1	4	3¹	7²	8	9				11	12			10	5			4							2	6		13				45
1	4¹	3²	7	8	9				11	13			10³	5			4							2	6		12				46

FA Cup
Third Round Portsmouth (a) 1-1 / (h) 1-2

Carling Cup
First Round Hartlepool U (h) 0-1

CREWE ALEXANDRA   FL Championship 2

FOUNDATION

The first match played at Crewe was on 1 December 1877 against Basford, the leading North Staffordshire team of that time. During the club's history they have also played in a number of other leagues including the Football Alliance, Football Combination, Lancashire League, Manchester League, Central League and Lancashire Combination. Two former players, Aaron Scragg in 1899 and Jackie Pearson in 1911, had the distinction of refereeing FA Cup finals. Pearson was also capped for England against Ireland in 1892.

The Alexandra Stadium, Gresty Road, Crewe, Cheshire CW2 6EB.

Telephone: (01270) 213 014.

Fax: (01270) 216 320.

Ticket Office: (01270) 252 610.

Website: www.crewealex.net

Email: info@crewealex.net

Ground Capacity: 10,107.

Record Attendance: 20,000 v Tottenham H, FA Cup 4th rd, 30 January 1960.

Pitch Measurements: 112m × 74m.

Chairman: John Bowler.

Vice-chairman: Norman Hassall.

Business Operations Manager: Alison Bowler.

Finance Operations Manager: Andrew Blakemore.

Manager: Dario Gradi MBE.

Assistant Manager: Steve Davis.

Physio: Rob Sharp.

Colours: Red shirts with white trim, white shorts, red stockings.

Change Colours: White shirts with tangerine trim, tangerine shorts, tangerine stockings.

Year Formed: 1877.

Turned Professional: 1893.

Ltd Co.: 1892.

Club Nickname: 'Railwaymen'.

Ground: 1898, Gresty Road.

First Football League Game: 3 September 1892, Division 2, v Burton Swifts (a) L 1–7 – Hickton; Moore, Cope; Linnell, Johnson, Osborne; Bennett, Pearson (1), Bailey, Barnett, Roberts.

Record League Victory: 8–0 v Rotherham U, Division 3 (N), 1 October 1932 – Foster; Pringle, Dawson; Ward, Keenor (1), Turner (1); Gillespie, Swindells (1), McConnell (2), Deacon (2), Weale (1).

HONOURS

Football League: Division 2 – Runners-up 2002–03.

FA Cup: Semi-final 1888.

Football League Cup: never past 3rd round.

Welsh Cup: Winners 1936, 1937.

sky SPORTS FACT FILE

Goalkeeper Edward Henry Hickton was the first Crewe Alexandra player to complete 100 League and Cup matches for the club. His association with them had started even earlier when they were initially in the Combination and later the Football Alliance.

Record Cup Victory: 8–0 v Hartlepool U, Auto Windscreens Shield 1st rd, 17 October 1995 – Gayle; Collins (1), Booty, Westwood (Unsworth), Macauley (1), Whalley (1), Garvey (1), Murphy (1), Savage (1) (Rivers (1p)), Lennon, Edwards, (1 og). 8–0 v Doncaster R, LDV Vans Trophy 3rd rd, 10 November 2002 – Bankole; Wright, Walker, Foster, Tierney; Lunt (1), Brammer, Sorvel, Vaughan (1) (Bell); Ashton (3) (Miles), Jack (2) (Jones (1)).

Record Defeat: 2–13 v Tottenham H, FA Cup 4th rd replay, 3 February 1960.

Most League Points (2 for a win): 59, Division 4, 1962–63.

Most League Points (3 for a win): 86, Division 2, 2002–03.

Most League Goals: 95, Division 3 (N), 1931–32.

Highest League Scorer in Season: Terry Harkin, 35, Division 4, 1964–65.

Most League Goals in Total Aggregate: Bert Swindells, 126, 1928–37.

Most League Goals in One Match: 5, Tony Naylor v Colchester U, Division 3, 24 April 1993.

Most Capped Player: Clayton Ince, 38 (79), Trinidad & Tobago.

Most League Appearances: Tommy Lowry, 436, 1966–78.

Youngest League Player: Steve Walters, 16 years 119 days v Peterborough U, 6 May 1988.

Record Transfer Fee Received: £3,400,000 from Norwich C for Dean Ashton, January 2005.

Record Transfer Fee Paid: £650,000 to Torquay U for Rodney Jack, June 1998.

Football League Record: 1892 Original Member of Division 2; 1896 Failed re-election; 1921 Re-entered Division (N); 1958–63 Division 4; 1963–64 Division 3; 1964–68 Division 4; 1968–69 Division 3; 1969–89 Division 4; 1989–91 Division 3; 1991–92 Division 4; 1992–94 Division 3; 1994–97 Division 2; 1997–2002 Division 1; 2002–03 Division 2; 2003–04 Division 1; 2004–06 FL C; 2006–09 FL 1; 2009– FL 2.

MANAGERS

W. C. McNeill 1892–94
(Secretary-Manager)
J. G. Hall 1895–96
(Secretary-Manager)
R. Roberts *(1st team Secretary-Manager)* 1897
J. B. Blomerley 1898–1911
(Secretary-Manager, continued as Hon. Secretary to 1925)
Tom Bailey *(Secretary only)* 1925–38
George Lillycrop *(Trainer)* 1938–44
Frank Hill 1944–48
Arthur Turner 1948–51
Harry Catterick 1951–53
Ralph Ward 1953–55
Maurice Lindley 1956–57
Willie Cook 1957–58
Harry Ware 1958–60
Jimmy McGuigan 1960–64
Ernie Tagg 1964–71
(continued as Secretary to 1972)
Dennis Viollet 1971
Jimmy Melia 1972–74
Ernie Tagg 1974
Harry Gregg 1975–78
Warwick Rimmer 1978–79
Tony Waddington 1979–81
Arfon Griffiths 1981–82
Peter Morris 1982–83
Dario Gradi 1983–2007
Steve Holland 2007–08
Gudjon Thordarson 2008–09
Dario Gradi October 2009–

LATEST SEQUENCES

Longest Sequence of League Wins: 7, 30.4.1994 – 3.9.1994

Longest Sequence of League Defeats: 10, 16.4.1979 – 22.8.1979.

Longest Sequence of League Draws: 5, 31.8.1987 – 18.9.1987.

Longest Sequence of Unbeaten League Matches: 17, 25.3.1995 – 16.9.1995.

Longest Sequence Without a League Win: 30, 22.9.1956 – 6.4.1957.

Successive Scoring Runs: 26 from 7.4.1934.

Successive Non-scoring Runs: 9 from 6.11.1974.

TEN YEAR LEAGUE RECORD

		P	W	D	L	F	A	Pts	Pos
2000-01	Div 1	46	15	10	21	47	62	55	14
2001-02	Div 1	46	12	13	21	47	76	49	22
2002-03	Div 2	46	25	11	10	76	40	86	2
2003-04	Div 1	46	14	11	21	57	66	53	18
2004-05	FL C	46	12	14	20	66	86	50	21
2005-06	FL C	46	9	15	22	57	86	42	22
2006-07	FL 1	46	17	9	20	66	72	60	13
2007-08	FL 1	46	12	14	20	47	65	50	20
2008-09	FL 1	46	12	10	24	59	82	46	22
2009-10	FL 2	46	15	10	21	68	73	55	18

DID YOU KNOW ?

During 1938–39, Crewe Alexandra had four different players who scored hat-tricks – Leo Stevens (twice), Arthur Rice, Matt Johnson and Fred Chandler. Stevens and Rice actually hit four goals in a game. All four players registered double-figure goal totals.

CREWE ALEXANDRA 2009–10 LEAGUE RECORD

Match No.	Date	Venue	Opponents	Result	H/T Score	Lg Pos.	Goalscorers	Attendance
1	Aug 8	H	Dagenham & R	L	1-2	0-1	—	Moore [72]	3936
2	15	A	Grimsby T	W	4-0	2-0	7	Zola 2 [34, 45], Jones (pen) [47], Moore [90]	5007
3	18	A	Darlington	W	1-0	0-0	—	Zola [87]	1821
4	22	H	Hereford U	W	1-0	1-0	3	Jones [37]	3731
5	29	A	Bournemouth	L	0-1	0-0	6		4563
6	Sept 5	H	Macclesfield T	W	2-1	1-1	5	Zola [12], Grant [85]	4151
7	12	A	Shrewsbury T	L	0-2	0-1	6		6204
8	19	H	Aldershot T	L	1-2	1-1	10	Miller [16]	3661
9	25	A	Accrington S	L	3-5	1-2	—	Grant 2 [43, 82], Murphy [90]	2764
10	29	H	Bury	L	2-3	1-2	—	Worley [39], Zola [73]	3534
11	Oct 3	H	Rotherham U	L	2-3	1-1	17	Schumacher [6], Zola [51]	4253
12	10	A	Bradford C	W	3-2	2-1	15	Zola 2 [8, 23], Schumacher [65]	11,757
13	17	H	Port Vale	L	1-2	1-1	16	Miller [34]	6943
14	24	A	Notts Co	L	0-2	0-1	18		6545
15	31	A	Cheltenham T	W	4-0	2-0	15	Zola 2 [29, 73], Schumacher [37], Shelley [69]	3124
16	Nov 14	H	Morecambe	L	1-2	0-2	20	Schumacher [77]	4113
17	21	A	Northampton T	D	2-2	2-0	17	Donaldson [14], Johnson (og) [43]	3876
18	24	H	Burton Alb	W	2-1	2-0	—	Donaldson [12], Grant [19]	3446
19	Dec 2	A	Chesterfield	W	3-2	2-0	—	Donaldson [25], Westwood [35], Murphy [84]	3267
20	5	H	Lincoln C	D	0-0	0-0	14		3632
21	12	A	Barnet	W	2-1	1-1	13	Grant [25], Donaldson [67]	1841
22	26	H	Rochdale	D	2-2	0-0	12	Westwood [71], Tootle [77]	5563
23	28	A	Macclesfield T	L	1-4	0-3	12	Zola [64]	3449
24	Jan 16	A	Dagenham & R	L	0-2	0-2	—		1951
25	19	A	Hereford U	D	1-1	0-1	—	Donaldson [49]	1367
26	23	H	Darlington	W	3-0	3-0	11	Zola 2 [25, 34], Grant [30]	3717
27	30	A	Bournemouth	L	1-2	0-1	15	Murphy [66]	3741
28	Feb 2	H	Torquay U	D	1-1	0-1	—	Miller [90]	3421
29	6	A	Rochdale	L	0-2	0-1	15		3164
30	12	A	Burton Alb	W	2-1	1-1	—	Miller [27], Donaldson [84]	2985
31	20	H	Northampton T	W	3-2	1-1	14	Westwood 2 [16, 66], Walton [69]	4036
32	24	H	Chesterfield	L	0-1	0-1	—		3278
33	27	A	Lincoln C	D	1-1	0-0	15	Miller [84]	3110
34	Mar 6	H	Barnet	D	2-2	1-2	15	Donaldson 2 [13, 82]	3551
35	9	H	Grimsby T	W	4-2	2-2	—	Moore [29], Grant [35], Westwood [55], Donaldson [90]	3272
36	13	A	Torquay U	D	1-1	0-1	15	Donaldson [85]	2507
37	20	A	Notts Co	L	0-1	0-0	15		5003
38	27	A	Port Vale	W	1-0	0-0	15	Miller (pen) [60]	7232
39	Apr 2	A	Morecambe	L	3-4	2-0	—	Grant [17], Miller [30], Donaldson [63]	2347
40	5	H	Cheltenham T	L	1-2	0-1	15	Martin [90]	3488
41	10	H	Shrewsbury T	L	0-3	0-1	15		4283
42	13	A	Bury	L	0-3	0-1	—		2178
43	17	A	Aldershot T	D	1-1	1-1	18	Donaldson [1]	2966
44	24	H	Accrington S	W	5-1	1-0	16	Zola 2 [5, 90], Donaldson [62], Westwood [70], Grant [81]	3810
45	May 1	A	Rotherham U	D	0-0	0-0	18		4142
46	8	H	Bradford C	L	0-1	0-0	18		5172

Final League Position: 18

GOALSCORERS

League (68): Zola 15, Donaldson 13, Grant 9, Miller 7 (1 pen), Westwood 6, Schumacher 4, Moore 3, Murphy 3, Jones 2 (1 pen), Martin 1, Shelley 1, Tootle 1, Walton 1, Worley 1, own goal 1.
Carling Cup (1): Zola 1.
FA Cup (2): Grant 1, Zola 1.
J Paint Trophy (1): Zola 1.

Button D 10	Brayford J 45	Jones B 10 + 1	Schumacher S 27 + 5	O'Donnell D 27	Ada P 16 + 2	Donaldson C 28 + 9	Mitchel-King M 31 + 1	Elding A 4 + 6	Zola C 30 + 4	Grant J 41 + 2	Miller S 22 + 11	Bailey J 20 + 1	Moore B 13 + 19	Worley H 21 + 2	Verma A 5 + 2	Westwood A 34 + 2	Legdins A 6	Walton S 26 + 5	Murphy L 24 + 8	Collis S 1	Bogdan A 1	Leitch-Smith A — + 1	Shelley D 7 + 12	Phillips S 28	Tootle M 26 + 2	Martin C 1 + 5	Stokes C 2	Gardner D — + 2	Davis H — + 1	Match No.
1	2	3	4²	5	6¹	7³	8	9	10	11	12	13	14																	1
1	2	3	4³	5		12	8	13	10²	11¹	9	6	7	14																2
1	2	3	4	5		12	8	13	10	11¹		9²	6	7																3
	2	3	4²	5	14	8	12	10	11¹		9³	6	7	13	1															4
	2	3	4³	5	11¹	8	9	10	13	14	12	6	7²		1															5
1	2	3	4	5			9²	10	11	13	8	6	12	7¹																6
1	2	3	4²	5		13	10	11	12		9	6	8¹	7																7
1	2	3	14	5		8²	10	11	9³		12	6	4¹	7	13															8
	2	3	4	5¹		8	10	11	9		12	6		7²	13	1														9
	2	3⁴		5⁴		8	10	11²	9¹		12	6	4	7		1	13													10
1	2	8¹	3			10³	11	9	5	14	6		4	12	7²		13													11
1	2	7	5		6	12	10	11²	9¹	4	13		8						3											12
1	2	13	7	5	6	12	10¹	11	9	8	14		4²						3³											13
1	2		4	5	10¹	6	11³	13	8	12	14	7		9²					3											14
	2	4¹	5	13	6	10²	11	9³	8	14	7		1	12					3											15
	2¹	12	5	14	6	10³	11		8	9	4	7	13						3²	1										16
		7¹	2		9	6	10	11			5		4	8					12				1	3						17
	2				5	9	6	10	11¹		12		7	4	8								1	3						18
	2				5	9	6	10¹	11²		12		7	4	8				13				1	3						19
	2				5	9	6	10	11		12		7	4	8²				13				1	3						20
	2				5	9	6	10	11				7¹	4	8				12				1	3						21
	2				5	9	6	10	11¹		12		7	4	8								1	3						22
	2	8	5		9			12	13	10²	4		7		11				6¹				1	3						23
	2	8	5		9	6		10²		12	7		4	11¹					13				1	3						24
	2	8	5		10	6		9¹		12	7		4	11				1						3²	13					25
	2	8	5		9²	6¹	10	11³	13		12		7	4					14				1	3						26
	2	8	5¹		9³		10	11	14			6	7²	4	13								1	3	12					27
	2	8	5		9²		10	11	13	14	6		7	4³	12								1	3						28
	2	8	5			10¹	14	9		12	6		7	4²	11³				13				1	3						29
	2		5	12		11	10¹	8	9	6		3	4	7²									1		13					30
	2		5	13		11	10²	8	9	6		3	4	7¹									1		12					31
	2		5	12		11	10¹	8²	9	6		7	4	13									1	3						32
	2		5	12		11	10	8	9	6		7	4										1	3¹						33
	2		5	10		11²	9	8	12	6		7	4¹	13									1	3						34
	2	13	5	8	6	11²	10	4	9	7													1	3¹	12⁴					35
	2	7³	5	10	6	12²	11	9	4	8¹								14	13				1			3				36
	2	12	5	10	6	11	9	4¹		3⁴				8								1		13	7²					37
	2	7	5	14	10	6	11²	9¹	4					8				13	1				3³		12					38
	2	7	5		10	6	11¹	9	4					13	8²			12	1				3							39
	2	4	5²		10	6	12	11	9	7					8¹							1	3	13					40
4		7			9	6	10	11³	14	8²	12			5	13							1	3	2¹					41
	2	7			10	6	12	11	9¹			5	4	8								1	3						42
	2		12	10	6¹	9	11		5²			7	4	8				13	1				3							43
	2		5	10²	13	9	11	7		1	4	8	6¹					3					12							44
	2	13	5	10		9	11¹	12	8²			6	1	4	7								3							45
	2		5	10		9	11²	8				6	1	4¹	7			13					3			12				46

CRYSTAL PALACE FL Championship

FOUNDATION

There was a Crystal Palace club as early as 1861 but the present organisation was born in 1905 after the formation of a club by the company that controlled the Crystal Palace (building), had been rejected by the FA who did not like the idea of the Cup Final hosts running their own club. A separate company had to be formed and they had their home on the old Cup Final ground until 1915.

Selhurst Park Stadium, Whitehorse Lane, London SE25 6PU.

Telephone: (020) 8768 6000.

Fax: (020) 8771 5311.

Ticket Office: 0871 200 0071.

Website: www.cpfc.co.uk

Email: info@cpfc.co.uk

Ground Capacity: 26,225.

Record Attendance: 51,482 v Burnley, Division 2, 11 May 1979.

Pitch Measurements: 110yd × 74yd.

Co-Chairmen: Steve Parish and Martin Long.

Chief Executive: Phil Alexander.

Assistant Secretary: Christine Dowdeswell.

Manager: George Burley.

Assistant Manager: Dougie Freedman.

Physio: Stewart Wardle.

Colours: Red and blue striped shirts, blue shorts, blue stockings.

Change Colours: White shirt with one blue and one red diagonal stripe, white shorts, white stockings.

Year Formed: 1905.

Turned Professional: 1905.

Ltd Co.: 1905.

Club Nickname: 'The Eagles'.

Grounds: 1905, Crystal Palace; 1915, Herne Hill; 1918, The Nest; 1924, Selhurst Park.

First Football League Game: 28 August 1920, Division 3, v Merthyr T (a) L 1–2 – Alderson; Little, Rhodes; McCracken, Jones, Feebury; Bateman, Conner, Smith, Milligan (1), Whibley.

Record League Victory: 9–0 v Barrow, Division 4, 10 October 1959 – Rouse; Long, Noakes; Truett, Evans, McNichol; Gavin (1), Summersby (4 incl. 1p), Sexton, Byrne (2), Colfar (2).

Record Cup Victory: 8–0 v Southend U, Rumbelows League Cup 2nd rd (1st leg), 25 September 1989 – Martyn; Humphrey (Thompson (1)), Shaw, Pardew, Young, Thorn, McGoldrick, Thomas, Bright (3), Wright (3), Barber (Hodges (1)).

HONOURS

Football League: Division 1 – Champions 1993–94; Division 2 – Champions 1978–79; Runners-up 1968–69; Division 3 – Runners-up 1963–64; Division 3 (S) – Champions 1920–21; Runners-up 1928–29, 1930–31, 1938–39; Division 4 – Runners-up 1960–61.

FA Cup: Runners-up 1990.

Football League Cup: Semi-final 1993, 1995, 2001.

Zenith Data Systems Cup: Winners 1991.

European Competition: Intertoto Cup: 1998.

sky SPORTS FACT FILE

In 1960–61 Arthur Rowe, famous for his "push and run" guidance of Tottenham Hotspur a decade before, became manager of Crystal Palace. He masterminded the team's promotion to the Third Division as runners-up to newcomers Peterborough United.

Record Defeat: 0–9 v Burnley, FA Cup 2nd rd replay, 10 February 1909. 0–9 v Liverpool, Division 1, 12 September 1990.

Most League Points (2 for a win): 64, Division 4, 1960–61.

Most League Points (3 for a win): 90, Division 1, 1993–94.

Most League Goals: 110, Division 4, 1960–61.

Highest League Scorer in Season: Peter Simpson, 46, Division 3 (S), 1930–31.

Most League Goals in Total Aggregate: Peter Simpson, 153, 1930–36.

Most League Goals in One Match: 6, Peter Simpson v Exeter C, Division 3 (S), 4 October 1930.

Most Capped Player: Aleksandrs Kolinko, 23 (83), Latvia.

Most League Appearances: Jim Cannon, 571, 1973–88.

Youngest League Player: John Bostock, 15 years 287 days v Watford, 29 October 2007.

Record Transfer Fee Received: £8,500,000 from Everton for Andy Johnson, May 2006.

Record Transfer Fee Paid: £2,750,000 to RC Strasbourg for Valerien Ismael, January 1998.

Football League Record: 1920 Original Members of Division 3; 1921–25 Division 2; 1925–58 Division 3 (S); 1958–61 Division 4; 1961–64 Division 3; 1964–69 Division 2; 1969–73 Division 1; 1973–74 Division 2; 1974–77 Division 3; 1977–79 Division 2; 1979–81 Division 1; 1981–89 Division 2; 1989–92 Division 1; 1992–93 FA Premier League; 1993–94 Division 1; 1994–95 FA Premier League; 1995–97 Division 1; 1997–98 FA Premier League; 1998–2004 Division 1; 2004–05 FA Premier League; 2005– FL C.

LATEST SEQUENCES

Longest Sequence of League Wins: 8, 9.2.1921 – 26.3.1921.

Longest Sequence of League Defeats: 8, 10.1.1998 – 14.3.1998.

Longest Sequence of League Draws: 5, 21.9.2002 – 19.10.2002.

Longest Sequence of Unbeaten League Matches: 18, 22.2.1969 – 13.8.1969.

Longest Sequence Without a League Win: 20, 3.3.1962 – 8.9.1962.

Successive Scoring Runs: 24 from 27.4.1929.

Successive Non-scoring Runs: 9 from 19.11.1994.

MANAGERS

John T. Robson 1905–07
Edmund Goodman 1907–25
(had been Secretary since 1905 and afterwards continued in this position to 1933)
Alex Maley 1925–27
Fred Mavin 1927–30
Jack Tresadern 1930–35
Tom Bromilow 1935–36
R. S. Moyes 1936
Tom Bromilow 1936–39
George Irwin 1939–47
Jack Butler 1947–49
Ronnie Rooke 1949–50
Charlie Slade and Fred Dawes *(Joint Managers)* 1950–51
Laurie Scott 1951–54
Cyril Spiers 1954–58
George Smith 1958–60
Arthur Rowe 1960–62
Dick Graham 1962–66
Bert Head 1966–72 *(continued as General Manager to 1973)*
Malcolm Allison 1973–76
Terry Venables 1976–80
Ernie Walley 1980
Malcolm Allison 1980–81
Dario Gradi 1981
Steve Kember 1981–82
Alan Mullery 1982–84
Steve Coppell 1984–93
Alan Smith 1993–95
Steve Coppell *(Technical Director)* 1995–96
Dave Bassett 1996–97
Steve Coppell 1997–98
Attilio Lombardo 1998
Terry Venables *(Head Coach)* 1998–99
Steve Coppell 1999–2000
Alan Smith 2000–01
Steve Bruce 2001
Trevor Francis 2001–03
Steve Kember 2003
Iain Dowie 2003–06
Peter Taylor 2006–07
Neil Warnock 2007–10
Paul Hart 2010
George Burley June 2010–

TEN YEAR LEAGUE RECORD

		P	W	D	L	F	A	Pts	Pos
2000-01	Div 1	46	12	13	21	57	70	49	21
2001-02	Div 1	46	20	6	20	70	62	66	10
2002-03	Div 1	46	14	17	15	59	52	59	14
2003-04	Div 1	46	21	10	15	72	61	73	6
2004-05	PR Lge	38	7	12	19	41	62	33	18
2005-06	FL C	46	21	12	13	67	48	75	6
2006-07	FL C	46	18	11	17	59	51	65	12
2007-08	FL C	46	18	17	11	58	42	71	5
2008-09	FL C	46	15	12	19	52	55	57	15
2009-10	FL C	46	14	17	15	50	53	49*	21

* 10 pts deducted.

DID YOU KNOW ?

On 2 February 2010 Crystal Palace beat Wolverhampton Wanderers 3–1 in an FA Cup fourth round replay. Danny Butterfield, normally a full-back but playing in midfield, scored a six-minute hat-trick in the second half, the fastest achieved in the club's history.

CRYSTAL PALACE 2009–10 LEAGUE RECORD

Match No.	Date	Venue	Opponents	Result	H/T Score	Lg Pos.	Goalscorers	Attendance
1	Aug 8	H	Plymouth Arg	D 1-1	0-1	—	Lee [63]	14,358
2	15	A	Bristol C	L 0-1	0-0	18		14,603
3	18	A	Ipswich T	W 3-1	0-0	—	Ambrose 2 [49, 50], Danns [69]	20,348
4	22	H	Newcastle U	L 0-2	0-2	14		20,643
5	31	A	Peterborough U	D 1-1	0-0	—	Lee [64]	8473
6	Sept 12	H	Scunthorpe U	L 0-4	0-1	19		12,912
7	19	H	Derby Co	W 1-0	0-0	16	Ambrose [55]	12,760
8	26	A	WBA	W 1-0	0-0	14	N'Diaye [63]	21,007
9	29	H	Sheffield W	D 0-0	0-0	—		12,476
10	Oct 3	H	Blackpool	W 4-1	2-0	12	Lee [4], Danns [32], Ambrose [66], N'Diaye [89]	15,749
11	17	A	Cardiff C	D 1-1	1-1	14	Hudson (og) [13]	21,457
12	20	A	Leicester C	L 0-2	0-0	—		22,220
13	24	H	Nottingham F	D 1-1	1-0	14	Ambrose [40]	15,692
14	31	H	Preston NE	D 1-1	1-1	13	Ambrose [37]	12,558
15	Nov 3	A	QPR	D 1-1	0-1	—	Ambrose (pen) [62]	14,377
16	7	H	Middlesbrough	W 1-0	0-0	13	Ambrose [65]	15,321
17	21	A	Coventry C	D 1-1	1-0	13	Ambrose [28]	18,400
18	28	H	Watford	W 3-0	2-0	11	Moses [2], Lee [6], Ambrose [54]	14,085
19	Dec 5	H	Doncaster R	L 0-3	0-1	13		13,985
20	8	A	Reading	W 4-2	3-1	—	Clyne [7], Ambrose [44], Moses 2 [45, 88]	16,629
21	12	A	Sheffield U	L 0-2	0-1	13		25,510
22	19	H	Barnsley	D 1-1	0-1	11	Moses [51]	14,279
23	26	H	Ipswich T	W 3-1	1-1	9	Fonte [38], Danns [58], Moses [90]	16,496
24	28	A	Swansea C	D 0-0	0-0	9		18,794
25	Jan 16	A	Plymouth Arg	W 1-0	1-0	8	Moses [17]	9318
26	27	A	Newcastle U	L 0-2	0-1	—		37,886
27	30	H	Peterborough U	W 2-0	1-0	20	Danns 2 [28, 65]	14,699
28	Feb 6	A	Scunthorpe U	W 2-1	0-0	16	Ambrose [63], Danns [90]	7543
29	9	H	Swansea C	L 0-1	0-1	—		12,328
30	17	H	Reading	L 1-3	0-1	—	Scannell [55]	13,259
31	20	H	Coventry C	L 0-1	0-0	22		13,333
32	27	A	Doncaster R	D 1-1	0-1	21	Djilali [67]	9779
33	Mar 6	H	Sheffield U	W 1-0	1-0	21	Lee [23]	13,455
34	9	H	Bristol C	L 0-1	0-0	—		12,844
35	13	A	Barnsley	D 0-0	0-0	20		11,416
36	16	A	Leicester C	L 0-1	0-0	—		12,721
37	20	A	Blackpool	D 2-2	2-0	22	Carle [3], Ambrose [34]	9702
38	23	A	Nottingham F	L 0-2	0-1	—		20,025
39	27	H	Cardiff C	L 1-2	0-1	22	Hill [58]	13,464
40	30	H	Watford	W 3-1	1-0	—	John [31], Scannell [51], Danns [66]	15,134
41	Apr 3	A	Middlesbrough	D 1-1	1-1	22	N'Diaye [45]	18,428
42	5	H	Preston NE	W 3-1	1-1	20	Danns [40], Ambrose [50], Andrew [84]	16,642
43	10	H	QPR	L 0-2	0-1	21		20,430
44	17	A	Derby Co	D 1-1	0-1	21	John [86]	30,255
45	26	H	WBA	D 1-1	1-1	—	Reid S (og) [17]	17,798
46	May 2	A	Sheffield W	D 2-2	1-1	21	Lee [24], Ambrose [63]	37,121

Final League Position: 21

GOALSCORERS

League (50): Ambrose 15 (1 pen), Danns 8, Lee 6, Moses 6, N'Diaye 3, John 2, Scannell 2, Andrew 1, Carle 1, Clyne 1, Djilali 1, Fonte 1, Hill 1, Hudson 1, own goals 2.
Carling Cup (2): Ambrose 2 (1 pen).
FA Cup (10): Butterfield 3, Ambrose 3 (1 pen), Andrew 1, Danns 1, Ertl 1, Lee 1.

Speroni J 45	Clyne N 19+3	Hill C 43	Danns N 41+1	McCarthy P 20	Lawrence M 14+4	Moses V 14+4	Derry S 46	John S 7+9	N'Diaye A 12+14	Sears F 11+7	Lee A 33+9	Ambrose D 44+2	Scannell S 11+15	Butterfield D 36+1	Fonte J 22	Flahavan D 1	Smith R —+5	Ertl J 29+4	Carle N 14+8	Hills L 10+9	Davis C 19+2	Andrew C 13+14	Djilali K 2+6	Zaha W —+1	Match No.
1	2	3	4^2	5	6	7^3	8	9^1	10	11	12	13	14												1
1		3	4	5	12	13	8		7	11	9^3	10^2	14		2^1			6							2
1		3	4	5			8		7	11	9	10			2			6							3
		3	4^2	5	12		8		7	11^1	9	10	13		2	1		6							4
1		3	4	5^1	12	8			7^1	10	9	11^2			2			6				13			5
1		3	4		5^2	8		7	13	9^1	11^3	12			2			6				14			6
1		3	4	5		8			9	11	10^1				2			6	7	12					7
1		3	4	5		9^2	8		7	12	11^1	10^2	2		6					13					8
1		3	4	5		9^2	8		7^1	10	11^2	12	2		6		14		13						9
1	6	3	4	5			8		13	10^2	11^3	9^1	2		7			12	14						10
1		3	4	5		7^1	8	14	10	12	9^3	11^2	13		2			6							11
1		3	4	5			8	13	10^3	11	9^2	12			2			6		7		14			12
1		3	4	5	12		8	13	10^1	9^2	7^3				2			6	11	14					13
1	3^2		4			9	8	13	10^3	11					2		6	12	7	14	5				14
1		3	4^3			8	9^2	10^1	12	13	11				2			6	7	14	5				15
1		3	4^1			8	13	9^2	10	11					2			6	7	12	5				16
1		3	4^3			8	13	14	9^2	10^1	11				2			6	7		5	12			17
1		3	4			9^2	8		14		10^1	11^3			2		13	6	7		5	12			18
1		3	4^1			9	8^3		12		10^2	11			2			6	7	14	5	13			19
1	2	3	4			9^3	8		13	14	12	11^2			5			6	7			10^1			20
1	13	3	4			9	8		14	10	11^1	12	2^2					6	7^3		5				21
1	2	3	4			11	8			9^2	10^1	7						6	12			13	5		22
1	2	3	4			11	8			9^1	10^2	7						6	12			5	13		23
1	2	3	4^3			9^2	8		13	12	11	14						6	7			5	10^6		24
1	2	3	4			9^1	8	13			10^2	11^3	14						7		6	5	12		25
1	2	3	4	12			8			14	7		5					11^1	10^3	6^2		9	13		26
1	2	3	10				8			9^2	7^3	14	5					4	11^1	6	12	13			27
1	2	3	10	6^3		4				9^2	7		8^1					11	14	5	13	12			28
1	2	3	8			4				9^2	11	14	6^1					7	10^3	5		12	13		29
1	2	3	8^1			4		14		13	11	12	6^1					7	10^3	5		9^2			30
1	2	3		6		4				9	8	10^1						7	11^2	5	13	12			31
1	2	3		6		4				9	7		8					13	10	12^2	5	14	11^3		32
1	2	3				4		12		10	11^2	14	6					7	8^3	13	5	9^1			33
1	2	3	12	5		4	13			10	11^1		6					7	8^2	13	5	9			34
1	2	3	8	5		4	14			9^2	7		6					12	10^1			13	11^2		35
1	2^1	3	8	12		4				10^2	11^3	14	6					7		13	5^1	9			36
1		3	8	5		4		12		9	11		6					7	10^1	2					37
1		3	8	5^1		4	9^2			10^3	11	12	2^1					7		6	13	14			38
1		3	6	5		4	9^1			11	10							7		2		8		12	39
1		8	5	12		4^1	9^2	13		7	11^3							2	14	3^4	6	10			40
1		8	5	6		4	10			9^2	11	12						2	7^1		3	13			41
1		3	8	5	6	4		9			7	11^1						2	12			10			42
1	12	3	8	5	6	4		9		13^3	7	11	2^2					14				10^1			43
1	12	3	9	5	8		13	14		10	11	4						2^3	7^2	6^1					44
1		3	8^1	5	6^3	4	13	14		12	11	10^1	2					7^2				9			45
1		3		5	6	4	13	12		9^2	11	10^3	2					7			14	8^1			46

FA Cup

Third Round	Sheffield W	(a)	2-1
Fourth Round	Wolverhampton W	(a)	2-2
		(h)	3-1
Fifth Round	Aston Villa	(h)	2-2
		(a)	1-3

Carling Cup

First Round	Torquay U	(h)	2-1
Second Round	Manchester C	(h)	0-2

DAGENHAM & REDBRIDGE   FL Championship 1

FOUNDATION

The roots of Dagenham & Redbridge live firmly in the Essex side of the Greater London area. Though only formed in 1992 their complex origins date back to the 19th century involving Ilford (founded 1881) and Leytonstone (1886) who merged in 1979 to form Leytonstone-Ilford. They and Walthamstow Avenue (1900) joined together in 1988 to becom Redbridge Forest who in turn merged with Dagenham FC (1949) in 1992. Victoria Road has existed as a football ground since 1917. Initially used by Sterling Works, in the summer of 1955 Briggs Sports vacated the premises and Dagenham FC moved in and the pitch was enclosed.

The London Borough of Barking and Dagenham Stadium, Victoria Road, Dagenham, Essex RM10 7XL.

Telephone: (0208) 592 1549.

Fax: (020) 8593 7227.

Ticket Office: (020) 8592 1549 (extension 21).

Website: www.daggers.co.uk

Email: info@daggers.co.uk

Ground Capacity: 6,007.

Record Attendance: 4,791 v Shrewsbury T, FL 2, 2 May 2009.

Pitch Measurements: 100m × 64.5m.

Chairman: David J. Andrews.

Vice-chairman: David E. Ward.

Managing Director: Stephen R. Thompson.

Secretary: Terry Grover.

Manager: John L. Still.

Assistant Manager: Terry W. Harris.

Physio: John Gowens.

Colours: Red shirts with blue sleeves and red trim, blue shorts, blue stockings.

Change Colours: All yellow.

Year Formed: 1992.

Ground: 1992, Victoria Road.

Club Nickname: The Daggers.

First Football League Game: 11 August 2007, FL 2 v Stockport Co (a) L 0–1 – Roberts; Foster, Griffiths, Rainford, Uddin, Boardman, Saunders (Strevens), Southam, Benson (Moore), Nurse, Sloma (Huke).

MANAGERS

John Still 1992–94
Dave Cusack 1994–95
Graham Carr 1995–96
Ted Hardy 1996–99
Garry Hill 1999–2004
John Still April 2004–

sky SPORTS FACT FILE

In successive home League matches, Dagenham & Redbridge scored five goals. They beat Torquay United 5–3 on 15 August 2009 and three days later defeated Shrewsbury Town 5–0. In the latter game, Paul Benson scored four of the goals.

Record League Victory: 6–0 v Chester C, FL 2, 9 August 2008 – Roberts; Okuonghae, Griffiths, Arber, Uddin, Taiwo, Saunders (2), Green (1) (Southam), Benson (1) (Nurse), Strevens (1p) (Nwokeji (1)), Gain.

Record Defeat: 0–9 v Hereford U, Conference, 27 February 2004.

Most League Points (3 for a win): 72, FL 2, 2009–10.

Most League Goals: 77, FL 2, 2008–09.

Highest League Scorer in Season: Paul Benson, 28, Conference, 2006–07.

Most League Goals in Total Aggregate: 40, Paul Benson, 2007–.

Most League Goals in One Match: 4, Paul Benson v Shrewsbury T, FL 2, 18 August 2009.

Most Capped Player: Jon Nurse, 4, Barbados.

Most League Appearances: Tony Roberts, 132, 2007–.

Youngest League Player: Dominic Green, 18 years 93 days v Brentford, 2 October 2007.

Record Transfer Fee Received: £200,000 from Cardiff C for Solomon Taiwo, August 2009.

Record Transfer Fee Paid: £20,000 to Plymouth Arg for Damien McCrory, February 2010.

Football League Record: Promoted from Conference 2006–07; FL 2 2007–10; FL 1 2010–.

LATEST SEQUENCES

Longest Sequence of League Wins: 5, 12.2.2008 – 1.3.2008.

Longest Sequence of League Defeats: 4, 27.10.2007 – 17.11.2007.

Longest Sequence of League Draws: 2, 22.3.2008 – 24.3.2008.

Longest Sequence of Unbeaten League Matches: 6, 6.12.2008 – 17.1.2009.

Longest Sequence Without a League Win: 9, 6.10.2007 – 4.12.2007.

Successive Scoring Runs: 16 from 12.4.2008.

Successive Non-scoring Runs: 3 from 12.1.2008.

HONOURS

FA Cup: best season: 3rd rd, 2008.

Conference: Champions – 2006–07. Runners-up – 2001–02.

Isthmian League (Premier): Champions 1999–2000.

Essex Senior Cup: Winners – 1997–98, 2000–01. Runners-up 2001–02.

AS DAGENHAM FC
FA Trophy: Winners 1979–80; Runners-up 1976–77. *Amateur Cup:* Runners-up 1969–70, 1970–71.

AS ILFORD
FA Amateur Cup: Winners 1929, 1930. *Isthmian League:* Champions 1906–07, 1920–21, 1921–22.

AS LEYTONSTONE
FA Amateur Cup: Winners 1947, 1948, 1968. *Isthmian League:* Champions 1918–19, 1937–38, 1938–39, 1946–47, 1947–48, 1949–50, 1950–51, 1951–52, 1965–66.

AS LEYTONSTONE/ILFORD
Isthmian League: Champions 1981–82, 1988–89.

AS WALTHAMSTOW AVENUE
FA Amateur Cup: Winners 1952, 1961. *Isthmian League:* Champions 1945–46, 1948–49, 1952–53, 1954–55. *Athenian League:* Champions 1929–30, 1932–33, 1933–34, 1937–38, 1938–39.

AS REDBRIDGE FOREST
Isthmian League: Winners 1990–91.

TEN YEAR LEAGUE RECORD

		P	W	D	L	F	A	Pts	Pos
2000-01	Conf	42	23	8	11	71	54	77	3
2001-02	Conf	42	24	12	8	70	47	84	3
2002-03	Conf	42	21	9	12	71	59	72	5
2003-04	Conf	42	15	9	18	59	64	54	13
2004-05	Conf	42	19	8	15	68	60	65	11
2005-06	Conf	42	16	19	16	63	59	58	10
2006-07	Conf	46	28	11	7	93	48	95	1
2007-08	FL 2	46	13	10	23	49	70	49	20
2008-09	FL 2	46	19	11	16	77	53	68	8
2009-10	FL 2	46	20	12	14	69	58	72	7

DID YOU KNOW ?

When Dagenham & Redbridge paid the club's then record transfer fee for striker Paul Gibb from Purfleet in the 1997–98 season, the team finished fourth. Third the following season, they then won the Isthmian Premier League with Gibb scoring 63 League goals in the three seasons.

DAGENHAM & REDBRIDGE 2009–10 LEAGUE RECORD

Match No.	Date	Venue	Opponents	Result	H/T Score	Lg Pos.	Goalscorers	Attendance
1	Aug 8	A	Crewe Alex	W 2-1	1-0	—	Nurse [43], Benson [74]	3936
2	15	H	Torquay U	W 5-3	1-0	3	Gain [18], Green 2 [55, 56], Scott [66], Thomas [90]	1804
3	18	H	Shrewsbury T	W 5-0	4-0	—	Benson 4 [20, 26, 39, 70], Griffiths [37]	1683
4	22	A	Notts Co	L 0-3	0-2	2		6562
5	29	H	Lincoln C	W 3-0	1-0	1	Nurse 2 [13, 72], Green [57]	1810
6	Sept 5	A	Cheltenham T	D 1-1	0-0	3	Benson [49]	2969
7	12	H	Chesterfield	W 2-1	1-0	2	Antwi [25], Benson [48]	2034
8	19	A	Burton Alb	W 1-0	1-0	2	Benson [4]	2689
9	26	H	Morecambe	D 1-1	1-0	2	Scott [37]	1770
10	29	A	Barnet	L 0-2	0-2	—		2093
11	Oct 3	A	Hereford U	D 1-1	0-0	3	Thomas [83]	2253
12	10	·H	Darlington	W 2-0	2-0	2	Green [17], Scott [18]	1981
13	17	H	Bradford C	W 2-1	1-1	2	Benson [8], Ogogo [72]	2446
14	24	A	Macclesfield T	D 2-2	0-1	2	Thomas [79], Arber (pen) [90]	1574
15	31	H	Port Vale	D 1-1	0-1	3	Scott [88]	2003
16	Nov 14	A	Accrington S	W 1-0	1-0	1	Arber [39]	1538
17	21	H	Rochdale	L 1-2	1-0	3	Gain [3]	2235
18	24	A	Bournemouth	D 0-0	0-0	—		6881
19	Dec 1	H	Aldershot T	L 2-5	1-1	—	Arber (pen) [40], Ofori-Twumasi [53]	1876
20	5	A	Grimsby T	D 1-1	0-1	5	Nurse [60]	3090
21	12	H	Bury	W 3-1	1-1	4	Benson 2 [18, 78], Ofori-Twumasi [90]	1915
22	26	A	Northampton T	L 0-1	0-0	4		4108
23	28	H	Cheltenham T	L 0-2	0-1	5		2028
24	Jan 16	H	Crewe Alex	W 2-0	2-0	—	Scott [35], Green [41]	1951
25	23	A	Shrewsbury T	L 1-2	1-2	7	Benson [6]	4812
26	26	H	Notts Co	L 0-3	0-1	—		1916
27	Feb 6	A	Northampton T	L 0-1	0-0	10		2206
28	9	A	Rotherham U	L 0-2	0-2	—		2604
29	13	H	Bournemouth	W 1-0	1-0	10	Arber (pen) [39]	2215
30	20	A	Rochdale	L 1-3	1-1	13	Scott [10]	3153
31	23	A	Aldershot T	W 3-2	0-1	—	Benson 2 [66, 72], Scott [85]	2053
32	27	H	Grimsby T	W 2-0	0-0	9	Scott [49], Green [86]	2190
33	Mar 2	A	Torquay U	D 0-0	0-0	—		2140
34	6	A	Bury	D 0-0	0-0	10		2886
35	13	H	Rotherham U	L 0-1	0-0	11		1862
36	16	A	Lincoln C	D 1-1	1-0	—	Nurse [33]	2457
37	20	H	Macclesfield T	W 3-1	0-1	8	Green 2 [51, 87], Ogogo [71]	3721
38	27	A	Bradford C	D 3-3	0-1	9	Nurse [69], Williams (og) [75], Oliver (og) [90]	11,064
39	Apr 3	H	Accrington S	W 3-1	2-1	9	Benson [7], Gain [41], Green [53]	2031
40	5	A	Port Vale	L 1-3	1-1	11	Pack [15]	4572
41	10	A	Chesterfield	D 2-2	1-0	11	Green 2 (1 pen) [27 (p), 50]	3588
42	13	H	Barnet	W 4-1	1-1	—	Green 2 (2 pens) [5, 67], Benson [80], Scott [82]	2004
43	17	H	Burton Alb	W 2-1	0-1	7	Vincelot Romain [52], Montgomery [80]	1891
44	24	A	Morecambe	L 0-1	0-0	11		2100
45	May 1	H	Hereford U	W 2-1	1-0	7	Benson [35], Montgomery [90]	2663
46	8	A	Darlington	W 2-0	1-0	7	Nurse [31], Scott [76]	2720

Final League Position: 7

GOALSCORERS

League (69): Benson 17, Green 13 (3 pens), Scott 10, Nurse 7, Arber 4 (3 pens), Gain 3, Thomas 3, Montgomery 2, Ofori-Twumasi 2, Ogogo 2, Antwi 1, Griffiths 1, Pack 1, Vincelot Romain 1, own goals 2.
Carling Cup (1): Scott 1.
FA Cup (1): Benson 1.
J Paint Trophy (1): Scott 1.
Play-Offs (10): Benson 4, Scott 4, Green 1, Nurse 1.

Roberts T 46	Doe S 40+2	Griffiths S 13	Arber M 41	Antwi W 19	Taiwo S 4	Green D 45+1	Thurgood S 17	Benson P 45	Nurse J 30+8	Gain P 43	Thomas W 3+20	Ogogo A 27+3	Scott J 36+4	Montgomery G 4+13	Bingham B —+2	Spiller D 7+3	Tejan-Sie T 1+2	Lockwood M 4	Dean H —+1	Ofori-Twumasi N 8	Miller A 8	Currie D b+11	Day J 8	Pack M 17	Vincelot Romain 7+2	McCrory D 20	Walsh P —+9	Carlos J —+1	Folly Y 5+2	Uddin A 3+3	Match No.
1	2	3	4	5	6	7[1]	8	9	10[2]	11	12	13																			1
1	2	3	4	5	8	7	6	9		11	12	10[1]																			2
1	2	3	4	5	8	7[2]	6	9		11	12	10[1]	13																		3
1	2	3	4	5	8	7[1]	6	9	12	11	13	10[2]																			4
1	2	3	4	5		7[1]	6	9	8[2]		10	12	13																		5
1	2	3	4	5		7[1]	6	9	8	11		10	12																		6
1	2	3	4	5		7[2]	6	9	8[1]	11	13	10[3]	12	14																	7
1	2	3	4	5		7	6	9	8[2]	11	12	10[1]	13																		8
1	2	3	4	5		7	6	9		11		8																			9
1	2[3]	3	4	5		7[1]	6	9	8	11	12	14	10[2]	13																	10
1		3	4	5		7[2]	6	9	13	11	12	2	10[1]			8															11
1		3	4	5		7	6	9	11	13		2	10[2]			8[1]	12														12
1	12	3[1]	4	5		6	8	9	10[2]	11		2		13		7															13
1	2[2]		4	5		7	6	9	8	11	10[1]	3[1]	12	13																	14
1	2[3]		4	5		6	8	9	10[2]	11	7[1]		12	13		3	14														15
1	2		4			7	6	9	10	11	12					5	3	8[1]													16
1	2			5		7[2]	6[1]	9	12	11	13	14	10[2]			4	3	8													17
1	2			5		8		9	10	11						6	3	4	7												18
1			4	5		7[1]		9	10	11				12		3	6	8	2												19
1	12		4	5[1]		7		9	10	11						3	6	8	2												20
1	2		4			7		9	10	11		12				3	6	8[1]	5												21
1	2		4			7[1]		9	8	11	12	10				3	6		5												22
1	2		4			7[2]		9	8[1]	13	10	11				3	6	12	5												23
1	2		4			7		9	13	11		3	10[2]	12		6						5	8[1]								24
1	2[?]		4			7[1]		9		11	12	3	10[3]		6[2]							13	5	8	14						25
1	2		4			7[3]		9		11	13	3	10[2]	14	6							12	5	8[1]							26
1	2		4			13		9	8[3]	11	10[1]	5	12			7[?]							6		3	14					27
1	2		4			7		9	8[2]	11		5	10[1]	13									6		3	12					28
1	2		4			7[1]		9	12	11		5	10	8									6		3						29
1	2		4			7		9[2]	11	12		2	10	8[1]									6		3	13					30
1	5		4			7		9	8[1]	11	13	2	10	12									6		3						31
1	5		4			7[2]		9	13	11	14	2	10[2]	8[1]									6		3		12				32
1	5		4			7[3]		9	8[3]	11	14	2	10[1]	12								12	6[2]		3		13				33
1	5		4			7		9		11		2	10										6		3		8				34
1	5		4			7		9				2	10	8[1]								12	6[2]		3	13	11				35
1	5		4			7		9	8[1]			2	10	12								12	6		3		11				36
1	5[2]		4			7		9	12	11	13	2	10[3]										6[1]		3	14	8				37
1	5		4			7[3]		9	12	11		2	10[2]	14								14	6		3	13	8[1]				38
1	5[1]		4[2]			7		9	8	11		2	10										6	13	3			12			39
1						7[1]		9	8	11		2	10[2]	13								13	6	4	3	12		5			40
1	6					7		9	8	11		2	10[1]											4	3	12		5			41
1	6					7		9	8	11[1]		2	10		12									4	3			5			42
1	5		4			7[2]		9	8	11		2	10[1]	12								13		6	3						43
1	5[1]		4			7[3]		9[2]	8	11		2	10	14								14		6	3	13		12			44
1	5		4			7[3]		9	8[2]	11		2	10[1]	12										6	3	13		14			45
1	5		4			7		9	8[1]	11		2	10	12								12		6	3						46

FA Cup
First Round   Huddersfield T   (a)   1-6

Carling Cup
First Round   Cardiff C   (a)   1-3

J Paint Trophy
First Round   Milton Keynes D   (a)   1-3

Play-Offs
Semi-Final   Morecambe   (h)   6-0
                          (a)   1-2
Final   Rotherham U   3-2
(at Wembley).

DARLINGTON   Blue Square Premier

FOUNDATION

A football club was formed in Darlington as early as 1861 but the present club began in 1883 and reached the final of the Durham Senior Cup in their first season, losing to Sunderland in a replay after complaining that they had suffered from intimidation in the first. On 5 April 1884, Sunderland had defeated Darlington 4-3. Darlington's objection was upheld by the referee and the replay took place on 3 May. The new referee for the match was Major Marindin, appointed by the Football Association to ensure fair play. Sunderland won 2-0. The following season Darlington won this trophy and for many years were one of the leading amateur clubs in their area.

Northern Echo Darlington Arena, Neasham Road, Darlington DL2 1DL.

Telephone: (01325) 387 000.

Fax: (01325) 387 050.

Ticket Office: 0871 855 1883.

Website: www.darlington-fc.net

Email: reception@darlington-fc.net

Ground Capacity: 25,000.

Record Attendance: 21,023 v Bolton W, League Cup 3rd rd, 14 November 1960.

Pitch Measurements: 112yd × 74yd.

Chairman: Raj Singh.

Finance Director: Andy Wilson. *Secretary:* Lisa Charlton.

Manager: Mark Cooper. *Assistant Manager:* Richard Dryden.

Physio: Will Short.

Colours: White shirts, black sleeves with white trim, black shorts with white trim, black and white hooped stockings.

Change Colours: Yellow shirts with red design, yellow shorts, yellow stockings.

Year Formed: 1883. *Turned Professional:* 1908. *Ltd Co.:* 1891.

Grounds: 1918, Feethams Ground; 2003, Reynolds Arena, Hurworth Moor.

Club Nickname: 'The Quakers'.

First Football League Game: 27 August 1921, Division 3 (N), v Halifax T (h) W 2–0 – Ward; Greaves, Barbour; Dickson (1), Sutcliffe, Malcolm; Dolphin, Hooper (1), Edmunds, Wolstenholme, Winship.

Record League Victory: 9–2 v Lincoln C, Division 3 (N), 7 January 1928 – Archibald; Brooks, Mellen; Kelly, Waugh, McKinnell; Cochrane (1), Gregg (1), Ruddy (3), Lees (3), McGiffen (1).

HONOURS

Football League: Division 2 best season: 15th, 1925–26; Division 3 (N) – Champions 1924–25; Runners-up 1921–22; Division 4 – Champions 1990–91; Runners-up 1965–66.

FA Cup: best season: 5th rd, 1958.

Football League Cup: best season: 5th rd, 1968.

GM Vauxhall Conference: Champions 1989–90.

sky SPORTS FACT FILE

Darlington won the Third Division (North) Cup in 1933–34, beating Stockport County 4–3 in the final played at Old Trafford with an attendance of 4,640. The Quakers were still trailing 3–2 in the 86th minute before scoring twice to turn likely defeat into victory.

Record Cup Victory: 7–2 v Evenwood T, FA Cup 1st rd, 17 November 1956 – Ward; Devlin, Henderson; Bell (1p), Greener, Furphy; Forster (1), Morton (3), Tulip (2), Davis, Moran.

Record Defeat: 0–10 v Doncaster R, Division 4, 25 January 1964.

Most League Points (2 for a win): 59, Division 4, 1965–66.

Most League Points (3 for a win): 85, Division 4, 1984–85.

Most League Goals: 108, Division 3 (N), 1929–30.

Highest League Scorer in Season: David Brown, 39, Division 3 (N), 1924–25.

Most League Goals in Total Aggregate: Alan Walsh, 90, 1978–84.

Most League Goals in One Match: 5, Tom Ruddy v South Shields, Division 2, 23 April 1927; 5, Maurice Wellock v Rotherham U, Division 3 (N), 15 February 1930.

Most Capped Player: Franz Burgmeier, 7 (58), Liechtenstein.

Most League Appearances: Ron Greener, 442, 1955–68.

Youngest League Player: Curtis Main, 15 years 318 days v Peterborough U, 3 May 2008.

Record Transfer Fee Received: £400,000 from Dundee U for Jason De Vos, October 1998.

Record Transfer Fee Paid: £100,000 to Boston U for Julian Joachim, September 2006 and £100,000 to Swansea C for Pawel Abbott, July 2007.

Football League Record: 1921 Original Member of Division 3 (N); 1925–27 Division 2; 1927–58 Division 3 (N); 1958–66 Division 4; 1966–67 Division 3; 1967–85 Division 4; 1985–87 Division 3; 1987–89 Division 4; 1989–90 GM Vauxhall Conference; 1990–91 Division 4; 1991–2004 Division 3; 2004–10 FL 2; 2010– Blue Square Premier.

LATEST SEQUENCES

Longest Sequence of League Wins: 6, 6.2.2000 – 7.3.2000.

Longest Sequence of League Defeats: 8, 31.8.1985 – 19.10.1985.

Longest Sequence of League Draws: 5, 31.12.1988 – 28.1.1989.

Longest Sequence of Unbeaten League Matches: 17, 27.4.1968 – 19.10.1968.

Longest Sequence Without a League Win: 19, 27.4.1988 – 8.11.1988.

Successive Scoring Runs: 22 from 3.12.1932.

Successive Non-scoring Runs: 7 from 5.9.1975.

MANAGERS

Tom McIntosh 1902–11
W. L. Lane 1911–12
(Secretary-Manager)
Dick Jackson 1912–19
Jack English 1919–28
Jack Fairless 1928–33
George Collins 1933–36
George Brown 1936–38
Jackie Carr 1938–42
Jack Surtees 1942
Jack English 1945–46
Bill Forrest 1946–50
George Irwin 1950–52
Bob Gurney 1952–57
Dick Duckworth 1957–60
Eddie Carr 1960–64
Lol Morgan 1964–66
Jimmy Greenhalgh 1966–68
Ray Yeoman 1968–70
Len Richley 1970–71
Frank Brennan 1971
Ken Hale 1971–72
Allan Jones 1972
Ralph Brand 1972–73
Dick Conner 1973–74
Billy Horner 1974–76
Peter Madden 1976–78
Len Walker 1978–79
Billy Elliott 1979–83
Cyril Knowles 1983–87
Dave Booth 1987–89
Brian Little 1989–91
Frank Gray 1991–92
Ray Hankin 1992
Billy McEwan 1992–93
Alan Murray 1993–95
Paul Futcher 1995
David Hodgson/Jim Platt
(Director of Coaching) 1995
Jim Platt 1995–96
David Hodgson 1996–2000
Gary Bennett 2000–01
Tommy Taylor 2001–02
Mick Tait 2003
David Hodgson 2003–06
Dave Penney 2006–09
Colin Todd 2009–10
Steve Staunton 2010
Simon Davey 2010
Ryan Kidd 2010
Mark Cooper June 2010–

TEN YEAR LEAGUE RECORD

		P	W	D	L	F	A	Pts	Pos
2000-01	Div 3	46	12	13	21	44	56	49	20
2001-02	Div 3	46	15	11	20	60	71	56	15
2002-03	Div 3	46	12	18	16	58	59	54	14
2003-04	Div 3	46	14	11	21	53	61	53	18
2004-05	FL 2	46	20	12	14	57	49	72	8
2005-06	FL 2	46	16	15	15	58	52	63	8
2006-07	FL 2	46	17	14	15	52	56	65	11
2007-08	FL 2	46	22	12	12	67	40	78	6
2008-09	FL 2	46	20	12	14	61	44	62*	12
2009-10	FL 2	46	8	6	32	33	87	30	24

*10 pts deducted.

DID YOU KNOW ?

In 1948–49 the record attendance at Feethams was broken three times from 12,868. In successive home games it went from 14,590 to 15,326 until on 12 March 1949 the visit of Hull City coincided with a crowd of 17,978. Darlington finished in fourth place.

DARLINGTON 2009–10 LEAGUE RECORD

Match No.	Date	Venue	Opponents	Result	H/T Score	Lg Pos.	Goalscorers	Attendance
1	Aug 8	A	Aldershot T	L 1-3	0-2	—	Dowson 85	2866
2	15	H	Bury	L 0-1	0-0	23		2310
3	18	H	Crewe Alex	L 0-1	0-0	—		1821
4	22	A	Port Vale	L 0-1	0-1	24		4561
5	29	H	Cheltenham T	D 1-1	0-1	24	Gall 71	1840
6	Sept 5	A	Lincoln C	L 0-3	0-2	24		3005
7	11	A	Accrington S	L 1-2	0-1	—	Gall 59	3228
8	19	H	Bournemouth	L 0-2	0-1	24		1999
9	26	A	Grimsby T	D 1-1	0-1	24	Main 81	4704
10	29	H	Rochdale	L 0-2	0-0	—		1748
11	Oct 3	H	Macclesfield T	L 0-1	0-1	24		1763
12	10	A	Dagenham & R	L 0-2	0-2	24		1981
13	17	H	Shrewsbury T	W 2-1	1-1	24	Devitt 26, Thomas 56	1958
14	24	A	Barnet	L 0-3	0-0	24		2313
15	31	A	Hereford U	L 1-2	0-1	24	Collins 72	2238
16	Nov 14	H	Burton Alb	W 1-0	1-0	24	Main 7	2404
17	21	A	Chesterfield	L 2-5	0-2	24	Collins 59, Hogg 87	3460
18	24	H	Morecambe	L 0-4	0-0	—		1698
19	Dec 1	A	Notts Co	L 0-4	0-3	—		4606
20	5	H	Bradford C	L 0-1	0-1	24		2744
21	12	A	Torquay U	L 0-5	0-3	24		2434
22	Jan 19	A	Rotherham U	W 2-1	0-0	—	Purcell 47, Smith G 63	3234
23	23	A	Crewe Alex	L 0-3	0-3	24		3717
24	26	H	Northampton T	L 1-2	1-0	—	Purcell 29	1694
25	Feb 6	A	Rotherham U	W 2-0	1-0	24	Purcell 19, Waite 52	2231
26	9	H	Lincoln C	D 1-1	1-0	—	Dempsey 38	1697
27	13	A	Morecambe	L 0-2	0-1	24		1741
28	20	H	Chesterfield	L 2-3	1-0	24	Purcell 2 27, 53	2209
29	27	A	Bradford C	L 0-1	0-1	24		11,532
30	Mar 2	H	Port Vale	L 1-3	1-0	—	Purcell 6	1582
31	6	H	Torquay U	L 1-3	0-2	24	Main 54	1819
32	9	A	Bury	D 1-1	1-1	—	Purcell (pen) 32	2123
33	13	A	Northampton T	L 0-2	0-2	24		4755
34	20	H	Barnet	L 1-2	0-2	24	Breen (og) 57	1463
35	23	H	Aldershot T	L 1-2	0-2	—	Arnison 85	1296
36	27	A	Shrewsbury T	W 2-0	1-0	24	Purcell 6, Diop 87	5081
37	Apr 3	A	Burton Alb	W 2-1	2-1	24	Gray 22, White 32	2779
38	5	H	Hereford U	L 0-1	0-0	24		2131
39	10	H	Accrington S	D 0-0	0-0	24		1545
40	13	A	Rochdale	W 1-0	1-0	—	Mulligan 35	5371
41	17	A	Bournemouth	L 0-2	0-0	24		6464
42	20	A	Cheltenham T	D 3-3	3-1	—	Purcell 2, Eastham (og) 5, Diop 27	2836
43	24	H	Grimsby T	L 0-2	0-2	24		1911
44	27	H	Notts Co	L 0-5	0-1	—		2112
45	May 1	A	Macclesfield T	W 2-0	1-0	24	Miller 9, Smith M 79	1716
46	8	H	Dagenham & R	L 0-2	0-1	24		2720

Final League Position: 24

GOALSCORERS

League (33): Purcell 9 (1 pen), Main 3, Collins 2, Diop 2, Gall 2, Arnison 1, Dempsey 1, Devitt 1, Dowson 1, Gray 1, Hogg 1, Miller 1, Mulligan 1, Smith G 1, Smith M 1, Thomas 1, Waite 1, White 1, own goals 2.
Carling Cup (0).
FA Cup (1): Diop 1.
J Paint Trophy (2): Convery 1, Thorpe 1.

Knight D 7 / Redmond S 19	Arnison P 17 + 1	Bower M 12 + 1	Smith G 32 + 2	Foster S 15 + 1	Miller I 40	Convery M 9 + 12	Lumsdon C 2 / Milne A 12 + 1	Thorpe L 7 + 1	Windass D 3 + 3 / Burn D 2 + 2	Smith J 22 + 2	Plummer M 5 + 3 / Dempsey G 24	Chandler J 12 + 2 / White A 23 + 1	Dowson D 6 + 4 / Waite G 14	Main C 12 + 14	Porritt N 4 + 1 / Purcell T 22	Cook J 4 + 1 / Harsley P 3	Bains R 3 + 1 / Deane P — + 10	Gall K 9 + 1	Bennett J 3 + 1 / Madden S 13 + 2	Gray J 10 + 17	Hoult R 6 / Byrne R 2 + 2	Kane T 4	Devitt J 5 + 1 / Chisholm R 2 + 1	Groves D 8 + 8	Barnett M 4	Whelan N 2 + 1 / Moore C 8 + 3	Thomas S 7	Barnes C 4 + 2 / Smith M 3 + 4	Liversedge N 13	Davis D 5 / McReady J 3 + 1	Collins J 5 + 2	Diop M 18 + 5	Mulligan N 10 + 6	Giddings S 22	Hogg J 5	Jones A 1 / Marshall J — + 3	Hall D 3	*Match No.*
1	2	3	4	5^{1}	6	7^{3}	8	9^{2}	10	11	12	13	14																									1
1	2	3	7	6	5	12	8^{1}	9	13	11^{2}		4	10^{3}	14																								2
1	2^{1}	3	7		5			9		13	6	4	10^{3}	14	8	1[illegible]	12																					3
1		3	7		5			9^{2}	10^{1}		6	4	13	14	8^{3}	1[illegible]	2	12																				4
1		3	7^{2}	6	5				10^{3}		12	4	14		8	1[illegible]	2^{1}	9	13																			5
1		3	7	6	5					12	2	4	10^{3}	14	8^{2}	1[illegible]		9		13																		6
1		3^{1}	7		5	8^{3}			13	11	2	4	10^{2}		14	1[illegible]	6	9																				7
			7^{1}	6	5	8^{3}			13	11		4	10^{2}					9		14	1	2	3	12														8
			7	6	5	13				11		4	10^{1}	12				9	8^{2}		1	2	3															9
			7	6	5	12				11			13	10				9	8		1	2	3^{1}	4^{2}														10
	13		7	6	5	14		10^{1}		11				12				9	8^{3}		1	2^{2}	3	4														11
	2		7	5	6	13				11^{3}		8		12				9			1		14	4^{2}	3	10^{1}												12
	2		7^{2}	5	6					11		8		12				9^{1}			1		4		3		10	13										13
	2			5	6^{1}	14				11^{2}	12	7		13											3		8	10^{3}	1	4	9							14
	2^{1}			5		8^{2}				11	6	4													3		9^{3}	12	1	7	10	13	14					15
			7	5	6							14		10						13				12			9	3	1	4^{3}		11^{2}	8^{1}	2				16
			7^{1}	5	6					11^{3}				10^{2}						12							9	3	1	4	13		14	2	8			17
				5	6					11										13				14			10^{1}	3	1	7^{2}	4	12	9^{3}	2	8			18
					5			12		11						[illegible]				13				6			9^{1}				8	10^{2}		3	4	1	2	19
		5				14	6	9		11^{3}				13		[illegible]				8^{2}									1		12	10^{1}		3	4		2	20
		5^{1}	7		6^{2}			10^{3}	12	11						[illegible]				13									1		3	14		2	4		9	21
	2		7^{3}	14	6					11	4	5	8	12	9^{1}		13												1			10^{2}		3				22
	2^{1}		7^{2}		6					11^{3}	4	5	8		9		14		13	12									1			10		3				23
1					6					11	4^{2}	5	7	8^{1}	9		12		3	14						13^{3}						10		2				24
1					6					11^{3}	4	5	7	8^{2}	9		12		3	14												10^{1}	13	2				25
1					6					11^{2}	4	5	9	8^{3}	7		13		3	12												10^{1}	14	2				26
1					6					11	4^{3}	5^{2}	8	10^{1}	9		12		3	14	13												7	2				27
1			12		5						6^{1}		8		9		14		3	11^{3}	4			13								10	7^{2}	2				28
1					4						6	12	8	14	9		13		5	11^{3}	2^{1}											10	7^{2}	3				29
1			12		6						4	5	8		9				3	7^{2}			13	11^{3}								10		2				30
1					6				7^{3}		4	5	8^{1}	10^{2}	9		12		3	14			11									13		2				31
1			7		6						4	5	8	11	9				3	12												10		2^{1}				32
1			7		6		2				4^{1}	5	8	11^{2}	9		14		3	12						13						10^{3}						33
1			7		6		4					5	8	14	9				3	12			2^{1}			10^{2}						13^{3}						34
1	2		7		4		5				3^{1}	6	8	12	9					13						11						10^{2}						35
1	2		7		6	12	5				8	4			9					3^{1}						11^{2}						10	13					36
1	2		7		4	12	5				3	6		8^{1}	9					11						10												37
1	2		7^{3}		6	14	5				3^{2}	4		10	9					8				13		11^{1}		12										38
1	2		7		6	14					4	5^{2}			9					8	13					11^{3}		12				10^{1}		3				39
1	2^{1}	13	7		6	10	12^{2}				4	5			9					8						14							11^{3}	3				40
1			7		6	10					4^{1}	5			9				3	8^{3}				12		14		13					11^{2}	2				41
1		6	7				3				4	5			9^{1}									8		11		12				10		2				42
		6	7			13	3				4	5			9				14					8^{1}					1	12		10	11^{2}	2^{3}				43
		5^{2}				10	3		13		4	2							6					8				9	1	7			11^{1}			12		44
	2		7^{2}		6	8	3				4	5												13		10^{1}		9^{3}	1	11			12			14		45
	2		7^{2}			8	3		4		6	5												12				9	1	11			10^{1}			13		46

FA Cup
First Round Barnet (a) 1-3

Carling Cup
First Round Leeds U (h) 0-1

J Paint Trophy
First Round Lincoln C (h) 1-0
Second Round Leeds U (a) 1-2

DERBY COUNTY   FL Championship

FOUNDATION

Derby County was formed by members of the Derbyshire County Cricket Club in 1884, when football was booming in the area and the cricketers thought that a football club would help boost finances for the summer game. To begin with, they sported the cricket club's colours of amber, chocolate and pale blue, and went into the game at the top immediately entering the FA Cup.

Pride Park Stadium, Derby DE24 8XL.
Telephone: 0871 472 1884.
Fax: (01332) 667 519.
Ticket Office: 0871 472 1884.
Website: www.dcfc.co.uk
Email: derby.county@dcfc.co.uk
Ground Capacity: 33,597.
Record Attendance: Baseball Ground: 41,826 v Tottenham H, Division 1, 20 September 1969. Pride Park: 33,475 Derby Co Legends v Rangers 9 in a Row Legends, 1 May 2006 (Ted McMinn Benefit).
Pitch Measurements: 100.58m × 67.66m.
Chairman of GSC and Club Chairman: Andy Appleby.
Vice-chairman of GSC and Vice Club Chairman: Lionel Margolick.
President and Chief Executive: Tom Glick.
Secretary: Clare Morris.
Manager: Nigel Clough.
Coaches: Gary Crosby, Andy Garner, Martin Taylor, Johnny Metgod.
Physio: Neil Sullivan.
Colours: White shirts with black trim, black shorts with white trim, white stockings with black trim.
Change Colours: Black shirts with white trim, grey shorts with black and white trim, black stockings with grey and white trim.
Year Formed: 1884. *Turned Professional:* 1884. *Ltd Co.:* 1896.
Club Nickname: 'The Rams'.
Grounds: 1884, Racecourse Ground; 1895, Baseball Ground; 1997, Pride Park.
First Football League Game: 8 September 1888, Football League, v Bolton W (a) W 6–3 – Marshall; Latham, Ferguson, Williamson; Monks, W. Roulstone; Bakewell (2), Cooper (2), Higgins, H. Plackett, L. Plackett (2).
Record League Victory: 9–0 v Wolverhampton W, Division 1, 10 January 1891 – Bunyan; Archie Goodall, Roberts; Walker, Chalmers, Roulstone (1); Bakewell, McLachlan, Johnny Goodall (1), Holmes (2), McMillan (5). 9–0 v Sheffield W, Division 1, 21 January 1899 – Fryer; Methven, Staley; Cox, Archie Goodall, May; Oakden (1), Bloomer (6), Boag, McDonald (1), Allen, (1 og).

HONOURS

Football League: Division 1 – Champions 1971–72, 1974–75; Runners-up 1895–96, 1929–30, 1935–36, 1995–96; Division 2 – Champions 1911–12, 1914–15, 1968–69, 1986–87; Runners-up 1925–26; Division 3 (N) Champions 1956–57; Runners-up 1955–56.
FA Cup: Winners 1946; Runners-up 1898, 1899, 1903.
Football League Cup: Semi-final 1968.
Texaco Cup: Winners 1972.
European Competitions: European Cup: 1972–73, 1975–76. UEFA Cup: 1974–75, 1976–77. Anglo-Italian Cup: Runners-up 1993.

sky SPORTS FACT FILE

Although Derby County did not win the FA Cup during the period in question, from 1896 to 1904 their record in the competition was a remarkably good one. They managed to appear in the final three times and on four other occasions reached the semi-final stage.

Record Cup Victory: 12–0 v Finn Harps, UEFA Cup 1st rd 1st leg, 15 September 1976 – Moseley; Thomas, Nish, Rioch (1), McFarland, Todd (King), Macken, Gemmill, Hector (5), George (3), James (3).

Record Defeat: 2–11 v Everton, FA Cup 1st rd, 1889–90.

Most League Points (2 for a win): 63, Division 2, 1968–69 and Division 3 (N), 1955–56 and 1956–57.

Most League Points (3 for a win): 84, Division 3, 1985–86, Division 3, 1986–87 and FL C, 2006–07.

Most League Goals: 111, Division 3 (N), 1956–57.

Highest League Scorer in Season: Jack Bowers, 37, Division 1, 1930–31; Ray Straw, 37 Division 3 (N), 1956–57.

Most League Goals in Total Aggregate: Steve Bloomer, 292, 1892–1906 and 1910–14.

Most League Goals in One Match: 6, Steve Bloomer v Sheffield W, Division 1, 2 January 1899.

Most Capped Player: Deon Burton, 42 (59), Jamaica.

Most League Appearances: Kevin Hector, 486, 1966–78 and 1980–82.

Youngest League Player: Lee Holmes, 15 years 268 days v Grimsby T, 26 December 2002.

Record Transfer Fee Received: £7,000,000 rising to £9,000,000 for Seth Johnson from Leeds U. October 2001.

Record Transfer Fee Paid: £3,500,000 to Norwich C for Robert Earnshaw, June 2007.

Football League Record: 1888 Founder Member of the Football League; 1907–12 Division 2; 1912–14 Division 1; 1914–15 Division 2; 1915–21 Division 1; 1921–26 Division 2; 1926–53 Division 1; 1953–55 Division 2; 1955–57 Division 3 (N); 1957–69 Division 2; 1969–80 Division 1; 1980–84 Division 2; 1984–86 Division 3; 1986–87 Division 2; 1987–91 Division 1; 1991–92 Division 2; 1992–96 Division 1; 1996–2002 FA Premier League; 2002–04 Division 1; 2004–07 FL C; 2007–08 FA Premier League; 2008– FL C.

MANAGERS

W. D. Clark 1896–1900
Harry Newbould 1900–06
Jimmy Methven 1906–22
Cecil Potter 1922–25
George Jobey 1925–41
Ted Magner 1944–46
Stuart McMillan 1946–53
Jack Barker 1953–55
Harry Storer 1955–62
Tim Ward 1962–67
Brian Clough 1967–73
Dave Mackay 1973–76
Colin Murphy 1977
Tommy Docherty 1977–79
Colin Addison 1979–82
Johnny Newman 1982
Peter Taylor 1982–84
Roy McFarland 1984
Arthur Cox 1984–93
Roy McFarland 1993–95
Jim Smith 1995–2001
Colin Todd 2001–02
John Gregory 2002–03
George Burley 2003–05
Phil Brown 2005–06
Billy Davies 2006–07
Paul Jewell 2007–08
Nigel Clough January 2009–

LATEST SEQUENCES

Longest Sequence of League Wins: 9, 15.3.1969 – 19.4.1969.

Longest Sequence of League Defeats: 8, 12.12.1987 – 10.2.1988.

Longest Sequence of League Draws: 6, 26.3.1927 – 18.4.1927.

Longest Sequence of Unbeaten League Matches: 22, 8.3.1969 – 20.9.1969.

Longest Sequence Without a League Win: 36, 22.9.2007 – 30.8.2008.

Successive Scoring Runs: 29 from 3.12.1960.

Successive Non-scoring Runs: 8 from 30.10.1920.

TEN YEAR LEAGUE RECORD

		P	W	D	L	F	A	Pts	Pos
2000-01	PR Lge	38	10	12	16	37	59	42	17
2001-02	PR Lge	38	8	6	24	33	63	30	19
2002-03	Div 1	46	15	7	24	55	74	52	18
2003-04	Div 1	46	13	13	20	53	67	52	20
2004-05	FL C	46	22	10	14	71	60	76	4
2005-06	FL C	46	10	20	16	53	67	50	20
2006-07	FL C	46	25	9	12	62	46	84	3
2007-08	PR Lge	38	1	8	29	20	89	11	20
2008-09	FL C	46	14	12	20	55	67	54	18
2009-10	FL C	46	15	11	20	53	63	56	14

DID YOU KNOW ?

On 23 October 1948 when Derby County met Chelsea at the Baseball Ground they conceded their first goal in 458 minutes in the 2–1 win. Their unbeaten 16-match run continued until 13 November from the start of the season in which just 12 goals were conceded.

DERBY COUNTY 2009–10 LEAGUE RECORD

Match No.	Date	Venue	Opponents	Result	H/T Score	Lg Pos.	Goalscorers	Attendance
1	Aug 8	H	Peterborough U	W 2-1	1-0	—	Addison 4, Teale 87	33,010
2	15	A	Scunthorpe U	L 2-3	1-2	9	Green 20, Commons (pen) 60	7352
3	18	A	Blackpool	D 0-0	0-0	—		8056
4	22	H	Plymouth Arg	W 2-1	1-1	9	Buxton 40, Addison 90	26,186
5	29	A	Nottingham F	L 2-3	0-3	11	Morgan (og) 51, Livermore 82	28,143
6	Sept 12	H	Sheffield U	L 0-1	0-0	15		28,441
7	15	H	Barnsley	L 2-3	1-1	—	Hulse 27, Barker 90	27,609
8	19	A	Crystal Palace	L 0-1	0-0	17		12,760
9	26	H	Bristol C	W 1-0	0-0	16	Teale 85	27,144
10	29	A	Cardiff C	L 1-6	0-2	—	Hulse 47	18,670
11	Oct 3	H	Sheffield W	W 3-0	1-0	17	Croft 17, McEveley 65, Hulse (pen) 90	30,116
12	17	A	Leicester C	D 0-0	0-0	17		28,875
13	20	A	Middlesbrough	L 0-2	0-1	—		17,459
14	24	H	QPR	L 2-4	2-1	19	Dickov 10, Savage 36	30,135
15	31	A	Ipswich T	L 0-1	0-0	20		20,299
16	Nov 6	H	Coventry C	W 2-1	0-1	—	Hulse 2 49, 62	26,511
17	20	A	Swansea C	L 0-1	0-0	—		17,804
18	28	H	Reading	W 2-1	0-1	16	Green 60, Hulse 73	30,174
19	Dec 5	H	WBA	D 2-2	1-0	17	Dickov 42, Campbell 90	30,127
20	8	A	Preston NE	D 0-0	0-0	—		11,755
21	12	A	Watford	W 1-0	0-0	17	Porter 77	14,063
22	19	H	Doncaster R	L 0-2	0-1	18		28,734
23	26	A	Blackpool	L 0-2	0-1	18		30,313
24	28	A	Newcastle U	D 0-0	0-0	18		47,505
25	Jan 9	A	Scunthorpe U	L 1-4	0-2	—	Williams (og) 59	28,106
26	16	A	Peterborough U	W 3-0	1-0	18	Davies (pen) 45, Campbell 2 48, 75	10,280
27	26	A	Plymouth Arg	L 0-1	0-0	—		7996
28	30	H	Nottingham F	W 1-0	0-0	18	Hulse 78	32,674
29	Feb 6	A	Sheffield U	D 1-1	1-0	18	Savage 17	25,300
30	9	H	Newcastle U	W 3-0	1-0	—	Hulse 40, Commons (pen) 59, Barker 64	28,607
31	16	A	Preston NE	W 5-3	1-1	—	Jones (og) 34, Commons 50, Hulse 2 64, 77, Barker 68	26,993
32	20	H	Swansea C	L 0-1	0-0	15		31,024
33	27	A	WBA	L 1-3	0-0	16	Porter 49	23,335
34	Mar 6	H	Watford	W 2-0	1-0	14	Tonge 12, Porter 77	29,492
35	10	A	Reading	L 1-4	1-2	—	Sunu 21	14,096
36	13	A	Doncaster R	L 1-2	0-1	18	Hulse 74	11,858
37	16	H	Middlesbrough	D 2-2	0-1	—	Porter 67, Tonge 74	27,143
38	20	A	Sheffield W	D 0-0	0-0	18		21,827
39	23	A	QPR	D 1-1	0-1	—	Barker 67	12,569
40	27	H	Leicester C	W 1-0	1-0	17	King A (og) 19	30,259
41	Apr 3	A	Coventry C	W 1-0	1-0	15	Barker 20	17,630
42	5	H	Ipswich T	L 1-3	0-1	16	Hulse 83	28,137
43	10	A	Barnsley	D 0-0	0-0	16		13,034
44	17	H	Crystal Palace	D 1-1	1-0	15	Anderson 6	30,255
45	24	A	Bristol C	L 1-2	0-1	17	Pearson 86	15,835
46	May 2	H	Cardiff C	W 2-0	0-0	14	McEveley 48, David J Martin 62	31,102

Final League Position: 14

GOALSCORERS

League (53): Hulse 12 (1 pen), Barker 5, Porter 4, Campbell 3, Commons 3 (2 pens), Addison 2, Dickov 2, Green 2, McEveley 2, Savage 2, Teale 2, Tonge 2, Anderson 1, Buxton 1, Croft 1, Davies 1 (pen), Livermore 1, David J Martin 1, Pearson 1, Sunu 1, own goals 4.
Carling Cup (1): Teale 1.
FA Cup (4): McEveley 2, Commons 1, Davies 1.

Bywater S 42	Connolly P 17+4	Moxey D 27+3	Savage R 45+1	Ball C —+1	Buxton J 19	Connolly R —+1	Addison M 10+3	Croft L 14+5	Green P 30+3	Davies S 7+11	Pearson S 34+3	Teale G 21+7	Commons K 11+9	Pringle B 1+4	McEveley J 28+5	Hulse R 30+7	Barker S 33+2	Varney L —+1	Livermore J 11+5	Dickov P 10+6	Leacock D 13+4	Vaughan J 2	Hendrie L 4+5	Stoor F 10+1	Mendy A —+1	Mills G —+2	Hughes B 3	Campbell D 6+2	Porter C 11+10	Hunt N 20+1	Johnson L 4	Anderson R 9+6	Tonge M 18	Vidal J —+1	Martin David J 2+9	Sunu G 6+3	Deeney S 2+1	Martin David E 2	Cywka T 4+1	Match No.
1	2	3	4	5	6	7^2	8^1	9^3	10	11	12	13	14																											1
1	2^3	3	4	5	6	7	8^2		10	11	12				9^1	13	14																							2
1	2	3	4	5	6	7^1	12			8	11	10^3			14	9^2		13																						3
1	2	3	4	5	6	7^2	14	9^1	10	11	13				12				8^3																					4
1	2	3	4	5^3	6		12	13		7	11	10^1			9				8^2	14																				5
1	2	3	4		6		8^2	10^1		7	11	13			9	5^3			12		14																			6
1	2	3	4		6		8^2			13	11	10			9^1	5			7	12																				7
1	2	3	4		6		8^2			12	11	13			9		14		7^1	5^2	10																			8
1	2	3	4		6^3		8			12	11				9	14			7^1	5^2	10	13																		9
1		3	4				8^2				11		13			9^3	12		7	14	5^1			10	2															10
1		3	4^3				8^2				11		13		2	9			7	10^1				12	5	14														11
1	14	3	4				7^1				11	10	13		9		2		8		6			12^2	5^3															12
1	2	11	4				13					7^3	10^1		3^2	9	6		8	12	5				·4															13
1	2	3	4				8			13	14	11			9	6			12	10^3				5^1				7^2												14
1	2	3	4				12					10^2	7			6			11	9				5	·3	8														15
1		3	4				12	13				7^3	8		11	9	6		14	13^3	2^1			5																16
1	12	3	4				8					11^2	8^2		13	9	6		10^3	14	2			5^1							7									17
1	14		4				12					7^3	8		11	3	9		6	13	10^1			5^2																18
1		3	4				7^1						6		9				10^2	2			12	5			13													19
1	2	3	4									7	13	11	14	5			9^3	6^1				8^5	12				10	14										20
1	2	3	4									7	13	11	14	5			9^2					8^5	6				10^1	12										21
1	2	4^3										14	7		8	11			10^2	6									9^1	12										22
1	2	3^4	4		6							7^1			8	11			5	13									10^2	12										23
1	2		8	6	3					4			11		12	5^3	9		13										10^2			7^1								24
1	14	3	4	5	6					7^2	13	8		12		9													10^1	2^3	11									25
1		3	4^2	5						8	9^1	11		13			6^3												10^1	12	2	7	14							26
1	12	4	2							7	13	8		14		3^3	9^1	8^1											10^2	5	11^1									27
1		4	2							7		10	12	11^2		3	9^3	8^1											14	5	8^1	13								28
1		4	2							7		10^1	12	8^2		3	9^3	8^1											13	5		14	11							29
1		4^2	5							7		8		10^1		3	9^3	8^1											14	5		13	11	12	14					30
1		4^3	2							7		8^1		10^2		3	9	8^1											14	5		13	11	12						31
1	14	4	2							7		8^2		10^1		3^4	9	8^1											10^1	5		11			12^2					32
1		3^3	4	2						7	12	8			14		3^4												10^1	5		13	11	11^2	14					33
1		3	4	5						7	12	8					9^1	3^4											10^3	2		13	11^2	14						34
1^0			4	5						7	13	8					3	9^2	3^4											2		11			12	10^1	15^8			35
1			4^2	5^3						7	10^1	8					3	9	3^4											14	2		11			13	12		1		36
			4^1							7		8					3	9	5		13									12	2^2		6	11		14	10^3		1	37
1			12							7	14	8					3	9^3	5		13									11	2^2		6	4			10^1			38
1			4							7	13	8					3	14	6		12									10^3	2^2		5	11			9^3			39
1			4							7	9^1	8					3	12	6		2									10			5	11						40
1			4							7	13	8	14				3	9^3	6		2^1									10	12		5	11^3						41
1			4							7	9^2	$8^?$					3	12	5											10	2^1		6	11^3		13		14	42
1			4							7	10^1						3	9	5											2			6	11	12			8	43
1			4							8	12						3	12	6										9	2		6	10	11				7^1	44
	13		4										8	12			3		5											10^3	2		6^2	11	14	9^1	1	7	45
		3	4	13					14			12	11^1	10	5		6													2			8		9^3		1	7^2	46

FA Cup

Third Round	Millwall	(a)	1-1
		(h)	1-1
Fourth Round	Doncaster R	(h)	1-0
Fifth Round	Birmingham C	(h)	1-2

Carling Cup

| First Round | Rotherham U | (a) | 1-2 |

DONCASTER ROVERS   FL Championship

FOUNDATION

In 1879, Mr Albert Jenkins assembled a team to play a match against the Yorkshire Institution for the Deaf. The players remained together as Doncaster Rovers, joining the Midland Alliance in 1889 and the Midland Counties League in 1891.

Keepmoat Stadium, Stadium Way, Lakeside, Doncaster, South Yorkshire DN4 5JW.
Telephone: (01302) 764 664.
Fax: (01302) 363 525.
Ticket Office: (01302) 762 576.
Website: www.doncasterroversfc.co.uk
Email: info@doncasterroversfc.co.uk
Ground Capacity: 15,231.
Record Attendance: 37,149 v Hull C, Division 3 (N), 2 October 1948.
Pitch Measurements: 100m × 70m.
Chairman: John Ryan.
Vice-chairman: Dick Watson.
Chief Executive/Secretary: David Morris.
Manager: Sean O'Driscoll.
Assistant Manager: Richard O'Kelly.
Physio: John Dickens.
Colours: Red and white hooped shirts, red sleeves with black trim, black shorts with red trim, black stockings with red tops.
Change Colours: Black shirts with red trim, red shorts, red stockings.
Year Formed: 1879. *Turned Professional:* 1885.
Ltd Co.: 1905 & 1920.
Club Nickname: 'Rovers'.

HONOURS

Football League: Best season 2007–08. Division 3 Champions 2003–04; Division 3 (N) Champions – 1934–35, 1946–47, 1949–50; Runners-up: 1937–38, 1938–39; Division 4 Champions 1965–66, 1968–69; Runners-up: 1983–84.

FA Cup: best season 5th rd, 1952, 1954, 1955, 1956.

Football League Cup: best season: 5th rd, 1976.

J Paint Trophy: Winners 2007.

Football Conference: Champions 2002–03

Sheffield County Cup: Winners 1891, 1912, 1936, 1938, 1956, 1968, 1976, 1986.

Midland Counties League: Champions 1897, 1899.

Conference Trophy: Winners 1999, 2000.

Sheffield & Hallamshire Senior Cup: Winners 2001, 2002.

Grounds: 1880–1916, Intake Ground; 1920, Benetthorpe Ground; 1922, Low Pasture, Belle Vue; 2007, Keepmoat Stadium.
First Football League Game: 7 September 1901, Division 2, v Burslem Port Vale (h) D 3–3 – Eggett; Simpson, Layton; Longden, Jones, Wright, Langham, Murphy, Price, Goodson (2), Bailey (1).
Record League Victory: 10–0 v Darlington, Division 4, 25 January 1964: Potter; Raine, Meadows, Windross (1), White, Ripley (2), Robinson, Book (2), Hale (4), Jeffrey, Broadbent (1).
Record Cup Victory: 7–0 v Blyth Spartans, FA Cup 1st rd, 27 November 1937: Imrie; Shaw, Rodgers, McFarlane, Bycroft, Cyril Smith, Burton (1), Killourhy (4), Morgan (2), Malam, Dutton.

sky SPORTS FACT FILE

Midland League winners in 1893–94, Doncaster Rovers won two FA Cup ties beating Wath Athletic 6-1 and Parkgate United 8-1. Billy Linward (five goals) and "Dutch" Gladwin (seven goals) became the first two to score a hat-trick in the competition for the club.

Record Defeat: 0–12 v Small Heath, Division 2, 11 April 1903.

Most League Points (2 for a win): 72, Division 3 (N), 1946–47.

Most League Points (3 for a win): 92, Division 3, 2003–04.

Most League Goals: 123, Division 3 (N), 1946–47.

Highest League Scorer in Season: Clarrie Jordan, 42, Division 3 (N), 1946–47.

Most League Goals in Total Aggregate: Tom Keetley, 180, 1923–29.

Most League Goals in One Match: 6, Tom Keetley v Ashington, Division 3 (N), 16 February 1929.

Most Capped Player: Len Graham, 14, Northern Ireland.

Most League Appearances: Fred Emery, 417, 1925–36.

Youngest League Player: Alick Jeffrey, 15 years 229 days v Fulham, 15 September 1954.

Record Transfer Fee Received: £2,000,000 from Reading for Matthew Mills, July 2009.

Record Transfer Fee Paid: £300,000 to Manchester C for Matthew Mills, July 2008.

Football League Record: 1901 Elected to Division 2; 1903 Failed re-election; 1904 Re-elected; 1905 Failed re-election; 1923 Re-elected to Division 3 (N); 1935–37 Division 2; 1937–47 Division 3 (N); 1947–48 Division 2; 1948–50 Division 3 (N); 1950–58 Division 2; 1958–59 Division 3; 1959–66 Division 4; 1966–67 Division 3; 1967–69 Division 4; 1969–71 Division 3; 1971–81 Division 4; 1981–83 Division 3; 1983–84 Division 4; 1984–88 Division 3; 1988–92 Division 4; 1992–98 Division 3; 1998–2003 Conference; 2003–04 Division 3; 2004–08 FL 1; 2008– FL C.

LATEST SEQUENCES

Longest Sequence of League Wins: 10, 22.1.1947 – 4.4.1947.

Longest Sequence of League Defeats: 9, 14.1.1905 – 1.4.1905.

Longest Sequence of League Draws: 4, 29.10.1932 – 19.11.1932.

Longest Sequence of Unbeaten League Matches: 20, 26.12.1968 – 12.4.1969.

Longest Sequence Without a League Win: 20, 9.8.1997 – 29.11.1997.

Successive Scoring Runs: 27 from 10.11.1934.

Successive Non-scoring Runs: 7 from 27.9.1947.

MANAGERS

Arthur Porter 1920–21
Harry Tufnell 1921–22
Arthur Porter 1922–23
Dick Ray 1923–27
David Menzies 1928–36
Fred Emery 1936–40
Bill Marsden 1944–46
Jackie Bestall 1946–49
Peter Doherty 1949–58
Jack Hodgson & Sid Bycroft
    (*Joint Managers*) 1958
Jack Crayston 1958–59
    (*continued as Secretary-Manager to 1961*)
Jackie Bestall (TM) 1959–60
Norman Curtis 1960–61
Danny Malloy 1961–62
Oscar Hold 1962–64
Bill Leivers 1964–66
Keith Kettleborough 1966–67
George Raynor 1967–68
Lawrie McMenemy 1968–71
Morris Setters 1971–74
Stan Anderson 1975–78
Billy Bremner 1978–85
Dave Cusack 1985–87
Dave Mackay 1987–89
Billy Bremner 1989–91
Steve Beaglehole 1991–93
Ian Atkins 1994
Sammy Chung 1994–96
Kerry Dixon (*Player–Manager*) 1996–97
Dave Cowling 1997
Mark Weaver 1997–98
Ian Snodin 1998–99
Steve Wignall 1999–2001
Dave Penney 2002–06
Sean O'Driscoll September 2006–

TEN YEAR LEAGUE RECORD

		P	W	D	L	F	A	Pts	Pos
2000-01	Conf.	42	15	13	14	47	43	58	9
2001-02	Conf.	42	18	13	11	68	46	67	4
2002-03	Conf.	42	22	12	8	73	47	78	3
2003-04	Div 3	46	27	11	8	79	37	92	1
2004-05	FL 1	46	16	18	12	65	60	66	10
2005-06	FL 1	46	20	9	17	55	51	69	8
2006-07	FL 1	46	16	15	15	52	47	63	11
2007-08	FL 1	46	23	11	12	65	41	80	3
2008-09	FL C	46	17	7	22	42	53	58	14
2009-10	FL C	46	15	15	16	59	58	60	12

DID YOU KNOW ?

Joe Lievesley, 18, made his debut at centre-forward for Doncaster Rovers against Accrington Stanley on 31 August 1929. But he was injured after five minutes and did not play again until February – yet still managed to finish as top scorer with 12 goals.

DONCASTER ROVERS 2009–10 LEAGUE RECORD

Match No.	Date	Venue	Opponents	Result	H/T Score	Lg Pos.	Goalscorers	Attendance
1	Aug 8	A	Watford	D	1-1	1-1	—	Hayter [38]	15,636
2	15	H	Preston NE	D	1-1	0-1	14	Lockwood [80]	10,070
3	18	H	Coventry C	D	0-0	0-0	—		9484
4	22	A	Middlesbrough	L	0-2	0-1	17		22,041
5	29	H	Cardiff C	W	2-0	2-0	14	Lockwood [13], Hayter [17]	9742
6	Sept 12	A	Reading	D	0-0	0-0	14		15,697
7	15	A	WBA	L	1-3	1-1	—	Fairhurst [7]	22,184
8	19	H	Ipswich T	D	3-3	1-0	15	Fairhurst [13], Woods M [74], Fortune [84]	10,711
9	26	A	Scunthorpe U	D	2-2	1-0	18	Woods M (pen) [13], Sharp [61]	7945
10	29	H	Swansea C	D	0-0	0-0	—		8833
11	Oct 3	A	Sheffield U	D	1-1	1-0	18	Hayter [45]	26,211
12	17	H	Barnsley	L	0-1	0-0	20		12,708
13	20	H	Peterborough U	W	3-1	2-1	—	Sharp [17], Shiels [21], Shackell [85]	9288
14	24	A	Newcastle U	L	1-2	1-0	18	Shiels [18]	43,949
15	31	H	Blackpool	D	3-3	1-1	19	Woods M [5], Sharp 2 [46, 90]	10,312
16	Nov 7	A	Plymouth Arg	L	1-2	1-1	20	Shiels [29]	9420
17	21	H	QPR	W	2-0	0-0	16	Sharp [53], Shiels [65]	10,821
18	28	A	Nottingham F	L	1-4	0-1	18	Sharp [82]	22,035
19	Dec 5	A	Crystal Palace	W	3-0	1-0	16	Sharp [41], Woods M [62], Hayter [78]	13,985
20	8	H	Sheffield W	W	1-0	0-0	—	Sharp [78]	12,825
21	12	H	Bristol C	W	1-0	1-0	15	Sharp [12]	9572
22	19	A	Derby Co	W	2-0	1-0	10	Sharp [21], Coppinger [90]	28,734
23	26	A	Coventry C	L	0-1	0-0	14		19,221
24	Jan 16	H	Watford	W	2-1	0-0	12	Shiels [50], Roberts [83]	10,504
25	26	H	Middlesbrough	L	1-4	0-2	—	Mutch [83]	10,794
26	30	A	Cardiff C	L	1-2	0-1	13	Roberts [65]	19,730
27	Feb 6	H	Reading	L	1-2	0-1	17	Sharp (pen) [81]	8827
28	9	A	Leicester C	D	0-0	0-0	—		18,928
29	13	H	Nottingham F	W	1-0	1-0	14	Sharp [31]	12,768
30	16	A	Sheffield W	W	2-0	1-0	—	Ward [40], O'Connor (og) [64]	22,252
31	20	A	QPR	L	1-2	0-1	13	Hayter [51]	11,178
32	23	H	Leicester C	L	0-1	0-1	—		11,027
33	27	H	Crystal Palace	D	1-1	1-0	14	Coppinger [37]	9779
34	Mar 6	A	Bristol C	W	5-2	4-2	12	Emmanuel-Thomas 2 [2, 43], Orr (og) [61], Sharp 2 [12, 34]	13,401
35	9	A	Preston NE	D	1-1	1-1	—	Hayter [29]	11,942
36	13	H	Derby Co	W	2-1	1-0	11	Sharp (pen) [15], Emmanuel-Thomas [69]	11,858
37	16	A	Peterborough U	W	2-1	0-0	—	Roberts [67], Oster [90]	6773
38	20	H	Sheffield U	D	1-1	1-0	8	Hayter [5]	13,026
39	23	H	Newcastle U	L	0-1	0-0	—		14,850
40	27	A	Barnsley	W	1-0	1-0	8	Coppinger [35]	14,188
41	Apr 3	H	Plymouth Arg	L	1-2	0-0	9	Coppinger [58]	10,179
42	5	A	Blackpool	L	0-2	0-1	11		9701
43	10	H	WBA	L	2-3	0-2	12	Emmanuel-Thomas [47], Hayter [85]	12,708
44	17	A	Ipswich T	D	1-1	0-0	12	Shiels (pen) [83]	19,943
45	24	H	Scunthorpe U	W	4-3	2-1	12	Emmanuel-Thomas [22], Mutch [45], Hayter [58], Martis [89]	12,124
46	May 2	A	Swansea C	D	0-0	0-0	12		17,630

Final League Position: 12

GOALSCORERS

League (59): Sharp 15 (2 pens), Hayter 9, Shiels 6 (1 pen), Emmanuel-Thomas 5, Coppinger 4, Woods M 4 (1 pen), Roberts 3, Fairhurst 2, Lockwood 2, Mutch 2, Fortune 1, Martis 1, Oster 1, Shackell 1, Ward 1, own goals 2.
Carling Cup (2): Coppinger 1, Woods M 1 (pen).
FA Cup (1): O'Connor 1.

Sullivan N 45	Chambers J 43	Roberts G 40+2	Lockwood A 10+6	Hird S 21+15	Stock B 15	Shiels D 25+13	Woods M 21+3	Hayter J 29+9	Heffernan P 6+11	Spicer J 9+11	Coppinger J 38+1	Oster J 36+4	O'Connor J 33+5	Shackell J 20+1	Fortune Q 3+3	Wilson M 29+0	Guy L 1+12	Sharp B 32+1	Fairhurst W 2+4	Webster B 1+4	Dumbuya M —+3	Gillett S 10+1	Smith B 1+1	Mutch J 5+12	McDaid S —+1	Martis S 13+1	Ward E 6	Emmanuel-Thomas J 12+2	Match No.
1	2	3	4	5	6	7¹	8	9	10²	11³	12	13	14																1
1	2	3	4	14	6	12	8	9	10²	11¹	7³	13				5													2
1	2	3²	4	13	6	10	8³	9			12		7	11¹		5	14												3
1	2	3	4		6	10¹		9	12	13	7	11²				5	14	8³											4
1	2	3	4	12	6		8	9	11²	10¹	7³					5		3	14										5
1	2	3	4	12	6		8	9³	11¹	10²	7					5		13	14										6
1	2	3¹	4		6³	13	8		11		7²	12	5			4		10	9										7
1	2	3	4	6²		12	8		14	11³	7					5	13	10	9¹										8
1	2	3	4	6		8		14			9¹	7⁴	13			5⁸	11²	10⁵	12										9
1	2	3	4	5		7	8³	9¹	13	11			14			6		10²	12										10
1	2	3²		5		7	8	9	13	11³			3	4		6¹		10	14										11
1	2	3²		5		10¹	8	9	14		7		4			13	11	12				6³							12
1	2			5		11	8	9²		14	7¹	13	6	4		12	10³					3							13
1	2		6			9	8	13			7²	12	11	5	4	14	10³					3¹							14
1	2	3		5		9³	8	13	14		7	11²		4		12	10					6¹							15
1	2	3¹		5		11³	8⁴		13	12	9	7	4			14	10					6²							16
1	2	3		5		9²			14	7	11³	4	12	8¹³	13	10						6							17
1⁰		3		5		9²	8	13		7	11¹	4	2			12	10					6	15						18
1	2	3	14			8	6³	9	13	7²	11¹	5	4			12	10												19
1	2	3	14			8²	6¹	9		7	11³	5	4			13	10					12							20
1	2	3	12			9¹		13	14	7	11³	5	4			6	10²					8							21
1	2	3	12			9¹		13		7	11²	5	4			8	14	10³				6							22
1	2	3²				9¹	12		14	7	11	5	4			8³	13	10				6							23
1	2	3	12	6²	9			13	7³	11	5	4¹			8	10	14												24
1	2	3	5²			8	11¹	7³		6			4	9	10	13					12	14							25
1	2	3	5	6	9³	12			7¹	11²	4				8	10	14					3							26
1	2	3	12	6	9³	14			7	11	4				8¹	13	10								5¹				27
1	2	3	12	6			9		7	11¹	8				4	10								5					28
1	2		12	6			9		7	11³	8	3¹			4	10		13				4	5²						29
1	2		5	6¹	14		9		7³	11	4				8	13	13²					12			3				30
1	2	13	5	6³	12		9		7²	11	4				8¹	10						14			3				31
1	2	3		9¹		12		14	7	11	6				4²	13	10				8³			5					32
1	2	3	5	14			9¹		7	11²	6				8³	10					13			4	12				33
1	2	3	5	12			9		14	7¹	11	4			6³	10					13			8²					34
1	2	3		12	13	9			7¹	11	5				4	10²								6		8			35
1	2	3		13	9²				7³	11	5				4	10					14			12	6	8¹			36
1	2¹	3	13	5	9²	4			7	11	12					10								6		8			37
1	2	3		13		12	8²	9	7³	11	5				4							14	6	10¹					38
1	2	3²		10³	4	9	13		11	5	7¹		8									14	6	12					39
1	2	3	12	13	9				7	11	5				4	10¹						6	8²						40
1	2¹	3³	14	12	10²	9			7	11	5				4						13	6	8						41
1	2	3		13		9	10		7¹	11²	5				4						12	6	8						42
1	2¹	3	12	13		9	10³		11	5	4		14			7²	6	8											43
1	2	3	13	12	9	10³			11	5	4²		14			7¹	6	8											44
1		3	14	5	10¹	12	9	13	7		4		2			11³	6	8²											45
	3	12	5	11¹		9	13	7	2		4		1⁴	1	8	6	10²												46

FA Cup
Third Round · Brentford · (a) · 1-0
Fourth Round · Derby Co · (a) · 0-1

Carling Cup
First Round · Notts Co · (a) · 1-0
Second Round · Tottenham H · (h) · 1-5

EVERTON

FA Premiership

FOUNDATION

St Domingo Church Sunday School formed a football club in 1878 which played at Stanley Park. Enthusiasm was so great that in November 1879 they decided to expand membership and changed the name to Everton playing in black shirts with a scarlet sash and nicknamed the 'Black Watch'. After wearing several other colours, royal blue was adopted in 1901.

Goodison Park, Goodison Road, Liverpool L4 4EL.

Telephone: (0871) 663 1878.

Fax: (0151) 286 9112.

Ticket Office: (0871) 663 1878

Website: www.evertonfc.com

Email: everton@evertonfc.com

Ground Capacity: 40,158.

Record Attendance: 78,299 v Liverpool, Division 1, 18 September 1948.

Pitch Measurements: 100.48m × 68m.

Chairman: Bill Kenwright CBE.

Deputy Chairman: Jon Woods.

Chief Executive: Robert Elstone.

Secretary: David Harrison.

Manager: David Moyes.

Assistant Manager: Steve Round.

Fitness Coach: Dave Billows.

Colours: Blue shirts with white trim, white shorts, white stockings.

Change Colours: Pink shirts with blue trim, black shorts, black stockings.

Year Formed: 1878.

Turned Professional: 1885.

Ltd Co.: 1892.

Previous Name: 1878, St Domingo FC; 1879, Everton.

Club Nickname: 'The Toffees'.

Grounds: 1878, Stanley Park; 1882, Priory Road; 1884, Anfield Road; 1892, Goodison Park.

First Football League Game: 8 September 1888, Football League, v Accrington (h) W 2–1 – Smalley; Dick, Ross; Holt, Jones, Dobson; Fleming (2), Waugh, Lewis, E. Chadwick, Farmer.

HONOURS

Football League: Division 1 – Champions 1890–91, 1914–15, 1927–28, 1931–32, 1938–39, 1962–63, 1969–70, 1984–85, 1986–87; Runners-up 1889–90, 1894–95, 1901–02, 1904–05, 1908–09, 1911–12, 1985–86; Division 2 – Champions 1930–31; Runners-up 1953–54.

FA Cup: Winners 1906, 1933, 1966, 1984, 1995; Runners-up 1893, 1897, 1907, 1968, 1985, 1986, 1989, 2009.

Football League Cup: Runners-up 1977, 1984.

League Super Cup: Runners-up 1986.

Simod Cup: Runners-up 1989.

Zenith Data Systems Cup: Runners-up 1991.

European Competitions: European Cup: 1963–64, 1970–71. European Cup-Winners' Cup: 1966–67, 1984–85 (winners), 1995–96. European Fairs Cup: 1962–63, 1964–65, 1965–66. Champions League: 2005–06. UEFA Cup: 1975–76, 1978–79, 1979–80, 2005–06, 2007–08, 2008–09. Europa League: 2009–10.

---

sky SPORTS FACT FILE

Everton played 28 FA Cup matches at Goodison Park from 1976–77 to 1986–87 and remained unbeaten. During this run they won the FA Cup once, finished runners-up on two occasions and were semi-finalists twice more.

Record League Victory: 9–1 v Manchester C, Division 1, 3 September 1906 – Scott; Balmer, Crelley; Booth, Taylor (1), Abbott (1); Sharp, Bolton (1), Young (4), Settle (2), George Wilson. 9–1 v Plymouth Arg, Division 2, 27 December 1930 – Coggins; Williams, Cresswell; McPherson, Griffiths, Thomson; Critchley, Dunn, Dean (4), Johnson (1), Stein (4).

Record Cup Victory: 11–2 v Derby Co, FA Cup 1st rd, 18 January 1890 – Smalley; Hannah, Doyle (1); Kirkwood, Holt (1), Parry; Latta, Brady (3), Geary (3), Chadwick, Millward (3).

Record Defeat: 4–10 v Tottenham H, Division 1, 11 October 1958.

Most League Points (2 for a win): 66, Division 1, 1969–70.

Most League Points (3 for a win): 90, Division 1, 1984–85.

Most League Goals: 121, Division 2, 1930–31.

Highest League Scorer in Season: William Ralph 'Dixie' Dean, 60, Division 1, 1927–28 (All-time League record).

Most League Goals in Total Aggregate: William Ralph 'Dixie' Dean, 349, 1925–37.

Most League Goals in One Match: 6, Jack Southworth v WBA, Division 1, 30 December 1893.

Most Capped Player: Neville Southall, 92, Wales.

Most League Appearances: Neville Southall, 578, 1981–98.

Youngest League Player: James Vaughan, 16 years 271 days v Crystal Palace, 10 April 2005.

Record Transfer Fee Received: £25,000,000 rising to £29,000,000 from Manchester U for Wayne Rooney, August 2004.

Record Transfer Fee Paid: £15,000,000 to Standard Liège for Marouane Fellaini, September 2008.

Football League Record: 1888 Founder Member of the Football League; 1930–31 Division 2; 1931–51 Division 1; 1951–54 Division 2; 1954–92 Division 1; 1992– FA Premier League.

LATEST SEQUENCES

Longest Sequence of League Wins: 12, 24.3.1894 – 13.10.1894.

Longest Sequence of League Defeats: 6, 26.12.1996 – 29.1.1997.

Longest Sequence of League Draws: 5, 4.5.1977 – 16.5.1977.

Longest Sequence of Unbeaten League Matches: 20, 29.4.1978 – 16.12.1978.

Longest Sequence Without a League Win: 14, 6.3.1937 – 4.9.1937.

Successive Scoring Runs: 40 from 15.3.1930.

Successive Non-scoring Runs: 6 from 3.3.1951.

MANAGERS

W. E. Barclay 1888–89
  (Secretary-Manager)
Dick Molyneux 1889–1901
  (Secretary-Manager)
William C. Cuff 1901–18
  (Secretary-Manager)
W. J. Sawyer 1918–19
  (Secretary-Manager)
Thomas H. McIntosh 1919–35
  (Secretary-Manager)
Theo Kelly 1936–48
Cliff Britton 1948–56
Ian Buchan 1956–58
Johnny Carey 1958–61
Harry Catterick 1961–73
Billy Bingham 1973–77
Gordon Lee 1977–81
Howard Kendall 1981–87
Colin Harvey 1987–90
Howard Kendall 1990–93
Mike Walker 1994
Joe Royle 1994–97
Howard Kendall 1997–98
Walter Smith 1998–2002
David Moyes March 2002–

TEN YEAR LEAGUE RECORD

		P	W	D	L	F	A	Pts	Pos
2000-01	PR Lge	38	11	9	18	45	59	42	16
2001-02	PR Lge	38	11	10	17	45	57	43	15
2002-03	PR Lge	38	17	8	13	48	49	59	7
2003-04	PR Lge	38	9	12	17	45	57	39	17
2004-05	PR Lge	38	18	7	13	45	46	61	4
2005-06	PR Lge	38	14	8	16	34	49	50	11
2006-07	PR Lge	38	15	13	10	52	36	58	6
2007-08	PR Lge	38	19	8	11	55	33	65	5
2008-09	PR Lge	38	17	12	9	55	37	63	5
2009-10	PR Lge	38	16	13	9	60	49	61	8

DID YOU KNOW ?

When centre-half Tom (always TG) Jones was transferred from Wrexham to Everton in October 1936 he was following in the path of another Welshman and defender Tom Griffiths who had made the same journey ten years earlier. Both won Welsh international honours.

EVERTON 2009–10 LEAGUE RECORD

Match No.	Date	Venue	Opponents	Result	H/T Score	Lg Pos.	Goalscorers	Attendance
1	Aug 15	H	Arsenal	L	1-6	0-3	—	Saha [90]	39,309
2	23	A	Burnley	L	0-1	0-1	20		19,983
3	30	H	Wigan Ath	W	2-1	0-0	16	Saha [62], Baines (pen) [90]	35,122
4	Sept 13	A	Fulham	L	1-2	1-0	19	Cahill [33]	24,191
5	20	H	Blackburn R	W	3-0	1-0	13	Saha 2 [22, 54], Yobo [58]	35,546
6	26	A	Portsmouth	W	1-0	1-0	9	Saha [42]	18,116
7	Oct 4	H	Stoke C	D	1-1	0-0	10	Osman [55]	36,753
8	17	H	Wolverhampton W	D	1-1	0-0	11	Bilyaletdinov [88]	39,319
9	25	H	Bolton W	L	2-3	1-2	14	Saha [32], Fellaini [55]	21,547
10	31	H	Aston Villa	D	1-1	1-0	13	Bilyaletdinov [45]	36,648
11	Nov 8	A	West Ham U	W	2-1	1-0	12	Saha [27], Gosling [64]	32,466
12	21	A	Manchester U	L	0-3	0-1	14		75,169
13	25	A	Hull C	L	2-3	0-3	—	Zayatte (og) [49], Saha (pen) [65]	24,685
14	29	A	Liverpool	L	0-2	0-1	16		39,652
15	Dec 6	H	Tottenham H	D	2-2	0-0	15	Saha [78], Cahill [86]	34,003
16	12	A	Chelsea	D	3-3	2-2	15	Cech (og) [12], Yakubu [45], Saha [63]	41,579
17	20	H	Birmingham C	D	1-1	1-1	15	Bilyaletdinov [5]	33,660
18	26	A	Sunderland	D	1-1	0-0	14	Fellaini [85]	46,990
19	28	H	Burnley	W	2-0	0-0	11	Vaughan [83], Pienaar [90]	39,419
20	Jan 9	A	Arsenal	D	2-2	1-1	—	Osman [12], Pienaar [81]	60,053
21	16	H	Manchester C	W	2-0	2-0	10	Pienaar [36], Saha (pen) [45]	37,378
22	27	H	Sunderland	W	2-0	2-0	—	Cahill [6], Donovan [19]	32,163
23	30	A	Wigan Ath	W	1-0	0-0	9	Cahill [84]	16,869
24	Feb 6	A	Liverpool	L	0-1	0-0	9		44,316
25	10	H	Chelsea	W	2-1	1-1	—	Saha 2 [33, 75]	36,411
26	20	H	Manchester U	W	3-1	1-1	8	Bilyaletdinov [19], Gosling [76], Rodwell [90]	39,448
27	28	H	Tottenham H	L	1-2	0-2	10	Yakubu [55]	35,912
28	Mar 7	H	Hull C	W	5-1	2-1	—	Arteta 2 [17, 39], Garcia (og) [51], Donovan [82], Rodwell [86]	34,682
29	13	A	Birmingham C	D	2-2	2-1	9	Anichebe [19], Yakubu [22]	24,579
30	20	H	Bolton W	W	2-0	0-0	8	Arteta [72], Pienaar [89]	36,503
31	24	A	Manchester C	W	2-0	1-0	—	Cahill [33], Arteta [85]	45,708
32	27	A	Wolverhampton W	D	0-0	0-0	8		28,995
33	Apr 4	H	West Ham U	D	2-2	1-0	8	Bilyaletdinov [24], Yakubu [85]	37,451
34	14	A	Aston Villa	D	2-2	1-0	—	Cahill 2 [23, 74]	38,729
35	17	A	Blackburn R	W	3-2	1-0	8	Arteta (pen) [4], Yakubu [79], Cahill [90]	27,022
36	25	H	Fulham	W	2-1	0-1	8	Smalling (og) [50], Arteta (pen) [90]	35,578
37	May 1	A	Stoke C	D	0-0	0-0	8		27,579
38	9	H	Portsmouth	W	1-0	0-0	8	Bilyaletdinov [90]	38,730

Final League Position: 8

GOALSCORERS

League (60): Saha 13 (2 pens), Cahill 8, Arteta 6 (2 pens), Bilyaletdinov 6, Yakubu 5, Pienaar 4, Donovan 2, Fellaini 2, Gosling 2, Osman 2, Rodwell 2, Anichebe 1, Baines 1 (pen), Vaughan 1, Yobo 1, own goals 4.
Carling Cup (4): Gosling 1, Jo 1, Osman 1, Yakubu 1.
FA Cup (4): Baines 1 (pen), Cahill 1, Osman 1, Vaughan 1.
Europa League (14): Pienaar 3, Distin 2, Rodwell 2, Saha 2, Bilyaletdinov 1, Cahill 1, Fellaini 1, Jo 1, Yobo 1.

Howard T 38	Hibbert T 17+3	Baines L 37	Yobo J 14+3	Lescott J 1	Neville P 22+1	Osman L 25+1	Cahill T 33	Jo 6+9	Fellaini M 20+3	Pienaar S 30	Saha L 26+7	Gosling D 3+8	Rodwell J 17+9	Distin S 29	Bilyaletdinov D 16+7	Heitinga J 29+2	Yakubu A 9+16	Neill L 10+2	Coleman S —+3	Agard K —+1	Vaughan J —+8	Donovan L 7+3	Baxter J —+2	Arteta M 11+2	Anichebe V 6+5	Senderos P 1+1	Jagielka P 11+1	Match No.
1	2¹	3	4	5	6	7²	8	9⁸	10	11	12	13	14															1
1	2	3	4		5	7	8	12	10¹	11	9	6																2
1	2	3	4		6	7¹	10	13	12	11³	9²		8	5	14													3
1	2	3	4		6¹	7²	10	9²	13	11		8	5	12	14													4
1	13	3	4			7³	10²	12	8	11	9¹	14	6	5	2													5
1	13	3	4			7²	10	14	8	11¹	9³		6	5	12	2												6
1	6	3				7²	10	13	8		9	11	5	4¹	2	12												7
1	6¹	3	4			7³	11	13	14		9²		8	5	10	2	12											8
1	3						11	9	8		10	7	4	5		2¹		6	12									9
1		3	4				10	13	8¹		12		11	6	7⁸	2	9²	5										10
1	7	3	4				11		10		9¹	8²	6	5		2	12	13										11
1	14	3	4				10²	13	8		9³	7¹	11	6		2	12	5										12
1		3	4				8	13		11	9	12	7²	6		2	10¹	5										13
1	5	3	4³				10²	9⁶	8	11	12			6	7	2	13	14										14
1	2	3	4¹				10	9³	8	11	14		7²	6		13	5	12										15
1	4	3					10¹	8	11	9²		7		6		2	12	5	13									16
1	4	3				7²	10		8	11	9			6¹		2	12	5	13									17
1	4	3				7¹	10		8	11	9²			6		2	12	5	13									18
1	4	3				12	7	10¹	8	11				6²		2	9	5	13									19
1		3			4	7	6		8	11	9²			12	2		5		13	10¹								20
1		3			4		7		8	11	9²			5¹	6	2		12			13	10³ 14						21
1		3			4	7	6		8	11³	9²			5		2					13	10¹		12	14			22
1		3			4	7	6		8	11	9²			2		13						10¹		12	5			23
1		3			4	7²	6		8¹	11⁸	9³			5		2	13					10		12	14			24
1		3			4	7	8		9³	13	12	5		6²	2							10		11¹	14			25
1		3			4	7			8²	9	12	13	5	6¹	2							10		⁸1				26
1		3			4	7¹			8		6³	5		2	9				14		13			⁸1	10²	12		27
1		3			4	7¹			8³		14	12	5	2	9						13			⁸1	10²		6	28
1		3			4		8²		7		14	13	5	2	9¹						12			11	10³		6	29
1		3			4	14	8²		7	13		5	12	2	9³									11	10¹		6	30
1		3	13		4	7	10		8	9¹	12	5		2										11²			6	31
1		3			4	7²	10		11	9¹	13	8³	5	14	2									12			6	32
1		3			4	7²	10		11	9	13	5	8¹	²2		12											6	33
1		3	14		4	7	10		11	13		12	5	8²	2¹	9²											6	34
1	2²	3	14		4		10		7	9³		5	8¹	13										11	12		6	35
1	2	3			4²		10		8	13		5	7¹	9³							14	11	12				6	36
1		3	2		4	7¹	8			9²		12	5	14		13								11	10³		6	37
1	2	3				7			8	9		4¹	5	13	14	12								11³	10²		6	38

FA Cup
Third Round   Carlisle U   (h)   3-1
Fourth Round   Birmingham C   (h)   1-2

Carling Cup
Third Round   Hull C   (a)   4-0
Fourth Round   Tottenham H   (a)   0-2

Europa League
Play-Off   Sigma Olomouc   (h)   4-0
                       (a)   1-1

Group I   AEK Athens   (h)   4-0
         BATE Borisov   (a)   2-1
         Benfica   (a)   0-5
                 (h)   0-2
         AEK Athens   (a)   1-0
         BATE Borisov   (h)   0-1
Second Round   Sporting   (h)   2-1
                   (a)   0-3

EXETER CITY   FL Championship 1

FOUNDATION

Exeter City was formed in 1904 by the amalgamation of St Sidwell's United and Exeter United. The club first played in the East Devon League and then the Plymouth & District League. After an exhibition match between West Bromwich Albion and Woolwich Arsenal which was held to test interest as Exeter was then a rugby stronghold, it was decided to form Exeter City. At a meeting at the Red Lion Hotel in 1908, the club turned professional.

St James Park, Stadium Way, Exeter EX4 6PX.

Telephone: (01392) 411 243.

Fax: (01392) 413 959.

Website: www.exetercityfc.co.uk

Email: reception@exetercityfc.co.uk

Training Ground: (01395) 232784.

Ground Capacity: 8,830.

Record Attendance: 20,984 v Sunderland, FA Cup 6th rd (replay), 4 March 1931.

Record Receipts: £59,862.98 v Aston Villa, FA Cup 3rd rd, 8 January 1994.

Pitch Measurements: 114yd × 73yd.

Chairman: Edward Chorlton.

Vice-chairman: Julian Tagg.

Club Secretary: Mike Radford.

Manager: Paul Tisdale.

Sports Medicine: Ian Andrews.

Colours: Red and white striped shirts, red sleeves, white shorts, white stockings.

Change Colours: All black with red trim.

Year Formed: 1904.

Turned Professional: 1908.

Ltd Co.: 1908.

Club Nickname: 'The Grecians'.

Ground: 1904, St James Park.

First Football League Game: 28 August 1920, Division 3, v Brentford (h) W 3–0 – Pym; Coleburne, Feebury (1p); Crawshaw, Carrick, Mitton; Appleton, Makin, Wright (1), Vowles (1), Dockray.

Record League Victory: 8–1 v Coventry C, Division 3 (S), 4 December 1926 – Bailey; Pollard, Charlton; Pullen, Pool, Garrett; Purcell (2), McDevitt, Blackmore (2), Dent (2), Compton (2). 8–1 v Aldershot, Division 3 (S), 4 May 1935 – Chesters; Gray, Miller; Risdon, Webb, Angus; Jack Scott (1), Wrightson (1), Poulter (3), McArthur (1), Dryden (1), (1 og).

HONOURS

Football League: Division 3 best season: 8th, 1979–80; Division 3 (S) – Runners-up 1932–33; Division 4 – Champions 1989–90; Runners-up 1976–77. FL 2 – Runners-up 2008–09.

FA Cup: best season: 6th rd replay, 1931, 6th rd 1981.

Football League Cup: never beyond 4th rd.

Division 3 (S) Cup: Winners 1934.

sky SPORTS FACT FILE

The first leading goal scorer for Exeter City was the Revd Edward Reid, a Canadian-born curate at St John's Church! In 1904–05 he scored 16 goals in eleven matches including firing all five goals against 111 Battery, Royal Artillery in the East Devon League.

Record Cup Victory: 14–0 v Weymouth, FA Cup 1st qual rd, 3 October 1908 – Fletcher; Craig, Bulcock; Amble⁻, Chadwick, Wake; Parnell (1), Watson (1), McGuigan (4), Bell (6), Copestake (2).

Record Defeat: 0–9 v Notts Co, Division 3 (S), 16 October 1948. 0–9 v Northampton T, Division 3 (S), 12 April 1958.

Most League Points (2 for a win): 62, Division 4, 1976–77.

Most League Points (3 for a win): 89, Division 4, 1989–90

Most League Goals: 88, Division 3 (S), 1932–33.

Highest League Scorer in Season: Fred Whitlow, 33, Division 3 (S), 1932–33.

Most League Goals in Total Aggregate: Tony Kellow, 129, 1976–78, 1980–83, 1985–88.

Most League Goals in One Match: 4, Harold 'Jazzo' Kirk v Portsmouth, Division 3 (S), 3 March 1923; 4, Fred Dent v Bristol R, Division 3 (S), 5 November 1927; 4, Fred Whitlow v Watford, Division 3 (S), 29 October 1932.

Most Capped Player: Dermot Curtis, 1 (17), Eire.

Most League Appearances: Arnold Mitchell, 495, 1952–66.

Youngest League Player: Cliff Bastin, 16 years 31 days v Coventry C, 14 April 1928.

Record Transfer Fee Received: £500,000 from Manchester C for Martin Phillips, November 1995.

Record Transfer Fee Paid: £65,000 to Blackpool for Tony Kellow, March 1980.

Football League Record: 1920 Elected to Division 3; 1921–58 Division 3 (S); 1958–64 Division 4; 1964–66 Division 3; 1966–77 Division 4; 1977–84 Division 3; 1984–90 Division 4; 1990–92 Division 3; 1992–94 Division 2; 1994–2003 Division 3; 2003–08 Conference; 2008–09 FL 2; 2009– FL 1.

MANAGERS

Arthur Chadwick 1910–22
Fred Mavin 1923–27
Dave Wilson 1928–29
Billy McDevitt 1929–35
Jack English 1935–39
George Roughton 1945–52
Norman Kirkman 1952–53
Norman Dodgin 1953–57
Bill Thompson 1957–58
Frank Broome 1958–60
Glen Wilson 1960–62
Cyril Spiers 1962–63
Jack Edwards 1963–65
Ellis Stuttard 1965–66
Jock Basford 1966–67
Frank Broome 1967–69
Johnny Newman 1969–76
Bobby Saxton 1977–79
Brian Godfrey 1979–83
Gerry Francis 1983–84
Jim Iley 1984–85
Colin Appleton 1985–87
Terry Cooper 1988–91
Alan Ball 1991–94
Terry Cooper 1994–95
Peter Fox 1995–2000
Noel Blake 2000–01
John Cornforth 2001–02
Neil McNab 2002–03
Gary Peters 2003
Eamonn Dolan 2003–04
Alex Inglethorpe 2004–06
Paul Tisdale June 2006–

LATEST SEQUENCES

Longest Sequence of League Wins: 7, 23.4.1977 – 20.8.1977.

Longest Sequence of League Defeats: 7, 14.1.1984 – 25.2.1984.

Longest Sequence of League Draws: 6, 13.9.1986 – 4.10.1986.

Longest Sequence of Unbeaten League Matches: 13, 23.8.1986 – 25.10.1986.

Longest Sequence Without a League Win: 18, 21.2.1995 – 19.8.1995.

Successive Scoring Runs: 22 from 15.9.1958.

Successive Non-scoring Runs: 6 from 24.11.1923.

TEN YEAR LEAGUE RECORD

		P	W	D	L	F	A	Pts	Pos
2000-01	Div 3	46	12	14	20	40	58	50	19
2001-02	Div 3	46	14	13	19	48	73	55	16
2002-03	Div 3	46	11	15	20	50	64	48	23
2003-04	Conf	42	19	12	11	71	51	69	6
2004-05	Conf	42	20	11	11	71	50	71	6
2005-06	Conf	42	18	9	15	65	48	63	7
2006-07	Conf	46	22	12	12	67	48	78	5
2007-08	B Sq Pr	46	22	17	7	83	58	83	4
2008-09	FL 2	46	22	13	11	65	50	79	2
2009-10	FL 1	46	11	18	17	48	60	51	18

DID YOU KNOW ?

Exeter City won the 1933–34 Third Division (South) Cup beating neighbours Torquay United 1–0 at Plymouth's Home Park in their eighth match of the competition. Stan Hurst was the scorer. They had had a marathon semi-final with two replays against Brighton & Hove Albion.

EXETER CITY 2009–10 LEAGUE RECORD

Match No.	Date		Venue	Opponents		Result	H/T Score	Lg Pos.	Goalscorers	Attendance
1	Aug	8	A	Leeds U	L	1-2	0-1	—	Russell [73]	27,681
2		15	H	Norwich C	D	1-1	0-0	16	Logan [60]	6357
3		18	H	Yeovil T	D	1-1	1-0	—	Stam (og) [14]	6650
4		22	A	Carlisle U	W	1-0	0-0	10	Stewart (pen) [73]	5156
5		29	A	Milton Keynes D	L	1-2	0-2	15	Corr [51]	5333
6	Sept	5	A	Gillingham	L	0-3	0-1	20		5107
7		12	A	Leyton Orient	D	1-1	0-1	20	Noone [79]	4703
8		19	H	Tranmere R	W	2-1	1-0	15	Stansfield 2 [25, 54]	4901
9		26	A	Charlton Ath	L	1-2	0-1	20	Cozic [90]	16,867
10		29	H	Swindon T	D	1-1	0-0	—	Logan [87]	5337
11	Oct	3	H	Hartlepool U	W	3-1	1-1	13	Harley [34], Fleetwood [62], Dunne [90]	4706
12		10	A	Huddersfield T	L	0-4	0-2	16		13,438
13		17	A	Walsall	L	0-3	0-2	20		4063
14		24	H	Wycombe W	D	1-1	0-1	19	Corr [90]	5227
15		31	H	Brentford	W	3-0	2-0	17	Cozic [7], Tully [45], Noone [69]	5355
16	Nov	14	A	Colchester U	D	2-2	2-1	17	Fleetwood [6], Harley [45]	5208
17		21	A	Stockport Co	W	3-1	1-0	15	Harley [39], Stansfield [89], Logan [90]	4101
18		24	H	Millwall	D	1-1	0-1	—	Stansfield [88]	5732
19	Dec	1	A	Bristol R	L	0-1	0-1	—		7313
20		5	H	Brighton & HA	L	0-1	0-0	17		5456
21		12	A	Oldham Ath	L	0-2	0-0	21		6230
22		19	H	Southend U	W	1-0	1-0	18	Stansfield [17]	4839
23		26	A	Southampton	L	1-3	0-2	19	Taylor M [68]	30,890
24		28	H	Gillingham	D	1-1	0-0	18	Duffy [68]	5761
25	Jan	9	A	Norwich C	L	1-3	0-1	—	Stewart [81]	24,955
26		16	H	Leeds U	W	2-0	1-0	15	Harley 2 [4, 83]	8549
27		23	A	Yeovil T	L	1-2	1-2	17	Stansfield [22]	6282
28		26	H	Carlisle U	L	2-3	0-2	—	Stansfield [79], Harley [89]	4106
29		30	A	Milton Keynes D	D	1-1	0-0	18	Corr [90]	8740
30	Feb	6	H	Southampton	D	1-1	0-1	18	Taylor M [49]	7654
31		13	A	Millwall	L	0-1	0-0	19		9104
32		20	H	Stockport Co	L	0-1	0-0	21		4990
33		27	A	Brighton & HA	L	0-2	0-1	22		6952
34	Mar	6	H	Oldham Ath	D	1-1	0-0	21	Harley (pen) [60]	4997
35		13	A	Southend U	D	0-0	0-0	21		6761
36		17	H	Bristol R	W	1-0	0-0	—	Dunne [90]	5269
37		20	A	Wycombe W	D	2-2	0-0	21	Sercombe [66], Logan [89]	5054
38		27	H	Walsall	W	2-1	1-0	18	Taylor M [4], Harley (pen) [58]	5887
39	Apr	2	A	Colchester U	W	2-0	1-0	—	Fleetwood [33], Harley (pen) [90]	6297
40		5	A	Brentford	D	0-0	0-0	17		6017
41		10	H	Leyton Orient	D	0-0	0-0	16		5522
42		12	A	Swindon T	D	1-1	1-0	—	Dunne [41]	8753
43		17	A	Tranmere R	L	1-3	0-1	20	Fleetwood [85]	5466
44		24	H	Charlton Ath	D	1-1	0-0	19	Friend [59]	6835
45	May	1	A	Hartlepool U	D	1-1	1-0	20	Taylor M [37]	3983
46		8	H	Huddersfield T	W	2-1	1-1	18	Taylor M [22], Harley [82]	8383

Final League Position: 18

GOALSCORERS

League (48): Harley 10 (3 pens), Stansfield 7, Taylor M 5, Fleetwood 4, Logan 4, Corr 3, Dunne 3, Cozic 2, Noone 2, Stewart 2 (1 pen), Duffy 1, Friend 1, Russell 1, Sercombe 1, Tully 1, own goal 1.
Carling Cup (0).
FA Cup (7): Corr 3, Taylor M 2, Stansfield 1, own goal 1.
J Paint Trophy (1): Fleetwood 1.

Jones P 26	Duffy R 41 + 1	Golbourne S 30 + 4	Russell A 27 + 2	Seaborne D 17 + 2	Taylor M 46	Edwards R 17 + 4	Harley R 43 + 1	Stewart M 36 + 5	Corr B 17 + 17	Cozic B 21 + 8	McAllister C — + 4	Sercombe L 25 + 3	Norwood J 2 + 1	Tully S 36 + 2	Archibald-Henville T 13 + 2	Logan N 4 + 30	Saunders N 2 + 4	Jansson O 7	Fleetwood S 16 + 11	Dunne J 18 + 5	Noone C 7	Stansfield A 19 + 8	Marriott A 13	Burnell J 4 + 4	Haber M 3 + 2	Watson B — + 1	Friend G 13	Taylor R 3 + 4	Match No.
1	2	3	4	5	6	7¹	8	9⁴	10³	11²	12	13	14																1
1	2		4		6		8		10	11¹	12			7	9²	3	5			13									2
1	2	14	4		6		8		10	11¹	12			7	9²	3²	5			13									3
1	2		4		6	14	8	9²	10³	11¹		7				3	5		12	13									4
1	2	11¹	4	14	6			9³	10			13		7		3	5	2	8²										5
	2	14	4	13	6²		8		10	12				7	3¹	5		1	9	11³									6
	2	3	4		6		8		10		12	13		7¹			5	1	9²	11									7
	2	3	4		6	13	8		10	12			14			5		1	9¹	11²	7³								8
	2	3	4		6	11	8		10³			14			5	3		1	9²	7¹									9
	2			3	6		8		11¹	10²	7			5³	4	1	13	4	9	2									10
	2		7	3	6	5¹	8		12	10				14		1		9²	4	11³	3								11
	2		8	3	6	5	7¹		13	10²	12			14		1		9³	4	11	4								12
2⁴	3	4¹	5	6		7	14	8²	11					12	13			10³		9	1								13
	2	4⁵		6	5		13	10	8					3	12	14		11²	7		9¹	1							14
	3	4	5	6		13	12	10⁴	8					2				9¹	7	11²	1								15
	3	4	5	6		7	10	11	8					2				9¹		12	1								16
	3	4	5	6		8	10¹	11³	7					2	13	14		9²		12	1								17
12	3	4	5	6		8	10³	11	7¹					2	14			9²		13	1								18
	2	4	11	5	6		8	14	12	7²				3				10	13	9³	1								19
	2	3	4¹		6		8	10	11³	7				5	12			9²	14	13	1								20
	2	3	4	5	6		8¹	10³	11²	7				12		14	13			9	1								21
1	2	4	11¹	5	6		13	8	10⁴					7	3	5²			12		9								22
1	2³	7	11¹	4	6		8		10²	13				3	5▪				12	14	9								23
1	2	4	13	5	6		8		10	7²				3		12			14	11¹	9³								24
1	2	4	11¹	5	6		8		12	7			14	3		13			10²		9⁵								25
1	2	5	11		6	4¹	8		10	7²			12	3		14			13		9⁵								26
1	2	4	11		6		8		12	10²	7			3		5²	14		13		9²								27
1	2	5	11		6		8	13	10²	7¹		4		3		12			9										28
	2	5	11²		6	7³	8	13	10¹			4		3		12			9³		1	▪4							29
	2	5			6	7	8	10		12		4		3		13			9³	1	11¹								30
	2	5			6	7	8	10▪	9¹	12²		4		3		11			14		1	11³							31
	2	5	13		6	7	8					4²		3		11		9¹			1		10³	12	14				32
1	2²	5			6	8	7	10¹				4		3		12	11	13	14			9³							33
1	2	5			6		8	12				4		3		13	14		7³	9²		10¹					11		34
1	2	5			6		8					4		3		12			13	7	9²				10¹		11		35
1	2				6	5	8			10¹		4		3²		12			7			9³	13	14			11		36
1	2	14			6	5	8	13	10			4		3		12			7¹			9²					11³		37
1	2				6	5	8	10¹	9			4		3		12			7								11		38
1	2				6	5¹	8	10²	9			4		3		13			12	7							11		39
1	2	5			6		8			10¹		4		3		13³			9²	7			14				11	12	40
1	2	5			6		8	13	10			4		3					9¹	7²							11	12	41
1	2	5			6		8	10¹	12			4		3		14			7²				13				11	9³	42
1	2²	5			6		8	10	9¹	13		4		3³		14			7▪								11	12	43
1	2	12			6	5	8	10²		14		4		3¹		9										7³	11	13	44
1	2				6	5³	8	12	13			4		3		9²			14	7							11	10¹	45
1	2	5			6	13	8	12	9³	7¹		4		3		14											11	10²	46

FA Cup

First Round	Nuneaton T	(a)	4-0
Second Round	Milton Keyens D	(a)	3-4

Carling Cup

First Round	QPR	(h)	0-5

J Paint Trophy

Second Round	Swindon T	(h)	1-1

FULHAM

FA Premiership

FOUNDATION

Churchgoers were responsible for the foundation of Fulham, which first saw the light of day as Fulham St Andrew's Church Sunday School FC in 1879. They won the West London Amateur Cup in 1887 and the championship of the West London League in its initial season of 1892–93. The name Fulham had been adopted in 1888.

Craven Cottage, Stevenage Road, London SW6 6HH
Telephone: 0870 442 1222.
Fax: 0870 442 0236 (Motspur Park).
Ticket Office: 0870 442 1234.
Website: www.fulhamfc.co.uk
Email: enquiries@fulhamfc.com
Ground Capacity: 26,600.
Record Attendance: 49,335 v Millwall, Division 2, 8 October 1938.
Pitch Measurements: 100m × 65m.
Chairman: Mohamed Al Fayed.
Vice-chairman: Omar Fayed.
Chief Executive: Alistair Mackintosh.
Secretary: Darren Preston.
Manager: Ray Lewington (caretaker).
Assistant Manager: Mike Kelly.
Head of Sports Medicine and Exercise Science: Mark Taylor.
Colours: White shirts with black trim, black shorts, white stockings.
Change Colours: Red shirts with black trim, black shorts, black stockings.
Year Formed: 1879.
Turned Professional: 1898.
Ltd Co.: 1903.
Reformed: 1987.
Previous Name: 1879, Fulham St Andrew's; 1888, Fulham.
Club Nickname: 'Cottagers'.
Grounds: 1879, Star Road, Fulham; c.1883, Eel Brook Common, 1884, Lillie Road; 1885, Putney Lower Common; 1886, Ranelagh House, Fulham; 1888, Barn Elms, Castelnau; 1889, Purser's Cross (Roskell's Field), Parsons Green Lane; 1891, Eel Brook Common; 1891, Half Moon, Putney; 1895, Captain James Field, West Brompton; 1896, Craven Cottage.
First Football League Game: 3 September 1907, Division 2, v Hull C (h) L 0–1 – Skene; Ross, Lindsay; Collins, Morrison, Goldie; Dalrymple, Freeman, Bevan, Hubbard, Threlfall.
Record League Victory: 10–1 v Ipswich T, Division 1, 26 December 1963 – Macedo; Cohen, Langley; Mullery (1), Keetch, Robson (1); Key, Cook (1), Leggat (4), Haynes, Howfield (3).
Record Cup Victory: 7–0 v Swansea C, FA Cup 1st rd, 11 November 1995 – Lange; Jupp (1), Herrera, Barkus (Brooker (1)), Moore, Angus, Thomas (1), Morgan, Brazil (Hamill), Conroy (3) (Bolt), Cusack (1).

HONOURS

Football League: Division 1 – Champions 2000–01; Division 2 – Champions 1948–49, 1998–99; Runners-up 1958–59; Division 3 (S) – Champions 1931–32; Division 3 – Runners-up 1970–71, 1996–97.
FA Cup: Runners-up 1975.
Football League Cup: best season: 5th rd, 1968, 1971, 2000.
European Competitions: UEFA Cup: 2002–03. *Intertoto Cup:* 2002 (winners). *Europa League:* 2009–10 (runners-up).

sky SPORTS FACT FILE

On 19 December 2009 Fulham entertained Manchester United at Craven Cottage. The resulting 3–0 win was their 100th such achieved in the Premier League. Earlier in the week they had qualified for the knock-out stages of the Europa League beating Basle away 3–2.

Record Defeat: 0–10 v Liverpool, League Cup 2nd rd 1st leg, 23 September 1986.

Most League Points (2 for a win): 60, Division 2, 1958–59 and Division 3, 1970–71.

Most League Points (3 for a win): 101, Division 2, 1998–99. 101, Division 1, 2000–01.

Most League Goals: 111, Division 3 (S), 1931–32.

Highest League Scorer in Season: Frank Newton, 43, Division 3 (S), 1931–32.

Most League Goals in Total Aggregate: Gordon Davies, 159, 1978–84, 1986–91.

Most League Goals in One Match: 5, Fred Harrison v Stockport Co, Division 2, 5 September 1908; 5, Bedford Jezzard v Hull C, Division 2, 8 October 1955; 5, Jimmy Hill v Doncaster R, Division 2, 15 March 1958; 5, Steve Earle v Halifax T, Division 3, 16 September 1969.

Most Capped Player: Johnny Haynes, 56, England.

Most League Appearances: Johnny Haynes, 594, 1952–70.

Youngest League Player: Matthew Briggs, 16 years 65 days v Middlesbrough, 13 May 2007.

Record Transfer Fee Received: £11,500,000 from Manchester U for Louis Saha, January 2004.

Record Transfer Fee Paid: £11,500,000 to Lyon for Steve Marlet, August 2001.

Football League Record: 1907 Elected to Division 2; 1928–32 Division 3 (S); 1932–49 Division 2; 1949–52 Division 1; 1952–59 Division 2; 1959–68 Division 1; 1968–69 Division 2; 1969–71 Division 3; 1971–80 Division 2; 1980–82 Division 2; 1982–86 Division 2; 1986–92 Division 3; 1992–94 Division 2; 1994–97 Division 3; 1997–99 Division 2; 1999–2001 Division 1; 2001– FA Premier League.

LATEST SEQUENCES

Longest Sequence of League Wins: 12, 7.5.2000 – 18.10.2000.

Longest Sequence of League Defeats: 11, 2.12.1961 – 24.2.1962.

Longest Sequence of League Draws: 6, 14.10.1995 – 18.11.1995.

Longest Sequence of Unbeaten League Matches: 15, 26.1.1999 – 13.4.1999.

Longest Sequence Without a League Win: 15, 25.2.1950 – 23.8.1950.

Successive Scoring Runs: 26 from 28.3.1931.

Successive Non-scoring Runs: 6 from 21.8.1971.

MANAGERS

Harry Bradshaw 1904–09
Phil Kelso 1909–24
Andy Ducat 1924–26
Joe Bradshaw 1926–29
Ned Liddell 1929–31
Jim McIntyre 1931–34
Jimmy Hogan 1934–35
Jack Peart 1935–48
Frank Osborne 1948–64
(was Secretary-Manager or General Manager for most of this period and Team Manager 1953–56)
Bill Dodgin Snr 1949–53
Duggie Livingstone 1956–58
Bedford Jezzard 1958–64
(General Manager for last two months)
Vic Buckingham 1965–68
Bobby Robson 1968
Bill Dodgin Jnr 1968–72
Alec Stock 1972–76
Bobby Campbell 1976–80
Malcolm Macdonald 1980–84
Ray Harford 1984–96
Ray Lewington 1986–90
Alan Dicks 1990–91
Don Mackay 1991–94
Ian Branfoot 1994–96
(continued as General Manager)
Micky Adams 1996–97
Ray Wilkins 1997–98
Kevin Keegan 1998–99
(Chief Operating Officer)
Paul Bracewell 1999–2000
Jean Tigana 2000–03
Chris Coleman 2003–07
Lawrie Sanchez 2007
Roy Hodgson 2007–10

TEN YEAR LEAGUE RECORD

		P	W	D	L	F	A	Pts	Pos
2000-01	Div 1	46	30	11	5	90	32	101	1
2001-02	PR Lge	38	10	14	14	36	44	44	13
2002-03	PR Lge	38	13	9	16	41	50	48	14
2003-04	PR Lge	38	14	10	14	52	46	52	9
2004-05	PR Lge	38	12	8	18	52	60	44	13
2005-06	PR Lge	38	14	6	18	48	58	48	12
2006-07	PR Lge	38	8	15	15	38	60	39	16
2007-08	PR Lge	38	8	12	18	38	60	36	17
2008-09	PR Lge	38	14	11	13	39	34	53	7
2009-10	PR Lge	38	12	10	16	39	46	46	12

DID YOU KNOW ?

Although Danny Shea arrived at Fulham after the Great War in the twilight of a distinguished career, he was fondly remembered for his midfield artistry. His last League game for the club was his 100th on 5 May 1923. A Londoner, he had been capped on two occasions for England.

FULHAM 2009–10 LEAGUE RECORD

Match No.	Date	Venue	Opponents	Result	H/T Score	Lg Pos.	Goalscorers	Attendance
1	Aug 15	A	Portsmouth	W	1-0	1-0	—	Zamora [13]	17,510
2	23	H	Chelsea	L	0-2	0-1	12		25,404
3	30	A	Aston Villa	L	0-2	0-1	15		32,917
4	Sept 13	H	Everton	W	2-1	0-1	10	Konchesky [57], Duff [79]	24,191
5	20	A	Wolverhampton W	L	1-2	0-1	14	Murphy (pen) [66]	27,670
6	26	H	Arsenal	L	0-1	0-0	17		25,700
7	Oct 4	A	West Ham U	D	2-2	0-1	15	Murphy (pen) [47], Gera [57]	32,612
8	19	H	Hull C	W	2-0	1-0	—	Zamora [43], Kamara [64]	22,943
9	25	A	Manchester C	D	2-2	0-0	13	Duff [62], Dempsey [68]	44,906
10	31	H	Liverpool	W	3-1	1-1	11	Zamora [24], Nevland [73], Dempsey [87]	25,700
11	Nov 8	A	Wigan Ath	D	1-1	1-1	11	Dempsey (pen) [39]	16,172
12	21	A	Birmingham C	L	0-1	0-1	12		23,659
13	25	H	Blackburn R	W	3-0	1-0	—	Nevland [43], Dempsey 2 [67, 88]	21,414
14	28	H	Bolton W	D	1-1	0-1	10	Duff [75]	23,554
15	Dec 6	H	Sunderland	W	1-0	1-0	8	Zamora [7]	23,168
16	12	A	Burnley	D	1-1	0-0	9	Zamora [50]	18,397
17	19	H	Manchester U	W	3-0	1-0	9	Murphy [22], Zamora [46], Duff [75]	25,700
18	26	H	Tottenham H	D	0-0	0-0	9		25,679
19	28	A	Chelsea	L	1-2	1-0	9	Gera [4]	41,805
20	Jan 5	A	Stoke C	L	2-3	0-3	—	Duff [61], Dempsey [85]	25,104
21	17	A	Blackburn R	L	0-2	0-1	9		21,287
22	26	A	Tottenham H	L	0-2	0-1	—		35,467
23	30	H	Aston Villa	L	0-2	0-2	11		25,408
24	Feb 3	H	Portsmouth	W	1-0	0-0	—	Greening [74]	21,934
25	6	A	Bolton W	D	0-0	0-0	10		22,289
26	9	H	Burnley	W	3-0	2-0	—	Murphy [23], Elm [31], Zamora [54]	23,005
27	21	A	Birmingham C	W	2-1	0-1	9	Duff [59], Zamora [90]	21,758
28	28	A	Sunderland	D	0-0	0-0	9		40,192
29	Mar 14	A	Manchester U	L	0-3	0-0	10		75,207
30	21	H	Manchester C	L	1-2	0-2	10	Murphy (pen) [75]	25,359
31	27	A	Hull C	L	0-2	0-1	12		24,361
32	Apr 4	H	Wigan Ath	W	2-1	0-1	12	Okaka Chuka [47], Hangeland [58]	22,730
33	11	A	Liverpool	D	0-0	0-0	—		42,331
34	17	H	Wolverhampton W	D	0-0	0-0	10		25,597
35	25	A	Everton	L	1-2	1-0	12	Nevland [36]	35,578
36	May 2	H	West Ham U	W	3-2	1-0	10	Dempsey [46], Cole (og) [58], Okaka Chuka [79]	24,201
37	5	H	Stoke C	L	0-1	0-0	—		20,831
38	9	A	Arsenal	L	0-4	0-3	12		60,039

Final League Position: 12

GOALSCORERS

League (39): Zamora 8, Dempsey 7 (1 pen), Duff 6, Murphy 5 (3 pens), Nevland 3, Gera 2, Okaka Chuka 2, Elm 1, Greening 1, Hangeland 1, Kamara 1, Konchesky 1, own goal 1.
Carling Cup (1): Gera 1.
FA Cup (9): Zamora 3, Duff 2, Davies 1, Gera 1, Nevland 1, Okaka Chuka 1.
Europa League (31): Zamora 9, Gera 6 (1 pen), Johnson A 3, Davies 2, Dempsey 2, Etuhu 2, Hangeland 2, Murphy 2 (1 pen), Duff 1, Kamara 1 (pen), Seol 1.

Schwarzer M 37	Pantsil J 22	Konchesky P 27	Murphy D 25	Hughes A 34	Hangeland B 32	Gera Z 19+8	Etuhu D 14+6	Johnson A 7+1	Zamora B 27	Dempsey C 27+2	Nevland E 12+11	Seol K —+2	Duff D 30+2	Kamara D 5+4	Baird C 29+3	Greening J 15+8	Johnson E —+2	Stockdale D 1	Davies S 12+5	Dikgacoi K 7+5	Riise B 5+7	Kelly S J+1	Smalling C 9+3	Kallio T —+1	Elm D 3+7	Shorey N 9	Okaka Chuka S 3+8	Stoor F —+2	Match No.
1	2	3	4	5	6	7^2	8	9	10^1	11	12	13																	1
1	2	3	4^2	5	6	7^1	8		10^3	9	14		11	12	13														2
1	2	3		5	6		8		10	9^1			11	4		7	12												3
	2	3	4	5	6		8	9^2	10	11					7^1	13		1	12										4
1	2	3^2	4	5	6		8^3	9	10	11^1					7	14	13		12										5
1	2	3	4	5	6	12	8^2	9	10	11					7^1		13												6
1	2	3	4	5	6	7		9^1		11^3				10^2	12	13			8^4	14									7
1	2	3	4^1	5	6	13			10	11	14		8^2	9^1	7	12													8
1	2			5	6				10	11		12	7	9^1	4	8							3						9
1	2	3		5	6	13	14		10	11	12		7^1	9^2	4	8^3													10
1	2	3		5	6	13	12		10	11	9^2		7		4	8^1													11
1		3		5	6	11	13		10	9			12		7^2	8			4				2^1						12
1	2	3		5	6	12	13		10^1	11	9		7^3		4	8^2			14										13
1	2^1	3		5	6	11^2			10	9			7		4	8^2			12	13									14
1	2	3		5	6	12			10	11	9^1		7		4	8^2			13										15
1	2	3		5	6	12			10	11	9^1		7		4	8													16
1	2	3	8^2	5	6	11			10^3	9	14		7^1		4	12			13										17
1	2	3	4	5	6	11			10	9			7		8														18
1	2^1	3	4	5		11^2	12	13	10	9			7^3		8						14		6						19
1		3	4	5	6^1	11		9^3	10^2	13	14		7		8							2	12						20
1		3^1	4	5	6	11		9	10^2	13			7		8								2		2				21
1			4	2	6	9^1			10^3				11	13	3				12	8	7^1		5		14				22
1	2				6	12			10	9^2			7	8	11^1	14					3^1		5		13				23
1			4	5	6				10^3		13		7		8	11			12		2^1		14		3		9^2		24
1			4	5	6			12		9^2			7		2	11			8^1		14		10^3		3		13		25
1			4	5	6	8			10^3				7^2		2	12			11^1	13			9		3		14		26
1		4^2	5	6		8			10				7		2	11^1			12	13					3				27
1		4^1	5	6		9	8		10^2				7		2				12	11						13	3		28
1			4	5	6^2	9			10	8^1	14		12		7	13			11^1		2				3				29
1		3	4	5	6^2		8		10^1	12			7		2^3				11	14		6			13				30
1	2				6		9		8					4	13				11	10^2	7		5			3	12		31
1		3	4^3	5	6		9	8					7	13					12		8				7^1		5	14	32
1		3	4^2	5	6		8		10^1	9			7		2	11^3					13	14			12				33
1		3	4	5					9	8	10		7		2				11				6						34
1	2								11	9^1			5		8				7	4	6		12		3		10^2	13	35
1	2	3							10^2	9			5		7	11^1			8^1		4		6		13		12		36
1	2^2	3	4	5	6	9	8		10	12		7^1							11								13		37
1	2^2								11^3	9			5		8	7	4^1		13		6		12		3	10	14		38

FA Cup

Third Round	Swindon T	(h)	1-0
Fourth Round	Accrington S	(a)	3-1
Fifth Round	Notts Co	(h)	4-0
Sixth Round	Tottenham H	(h)	0-0
		(a)	1-3

Carling Cup

Third Round	Manchester C	(a)	1-2

Europa League

Third Qualifying Round	Vetra	(a)	3-0
		(h)	3-0
Play-Off	Amkar	(h)	3-1
		(a)	0-1
Group E	CSKA Sofia	(a)	1-1
	Basle	(h)	1-0
	Roma	(h)	1-1
		(a)	1-2
	CSKA Sofia	(h)	1-0
	Basle	(a)	3-2
Second Round	Shakhtar Donetsk	(h)	2-1
		(a)	1-1
Third Round	Juventus	(a)	1-3
		(h)	4-1
Quarter-Final	Wolfsburg	(h)	2-1
		(a)	1-0
Semi-Final	Hamburg	(a)	0-0
		(h)	2-1
Final (in Hamburg).	Atletico Madrid		1-2

GILLINGHAM   FL Championship 2

FOUNDATION

The success of the pioneering Royal Engineers of Chatham excited the interest of the residents of the Medway Towns and led to the formation of many clubs including Excelsior. After winning the Kent Junior Cup and the Chatham District League in 1893, Excelsior decided to go for bigger things and it was at a meeting in the Napier Arms, Brompton, in 1893 that New Brompton FC came into being, buying and developing the ground which is now Priestfield Stadium. Changed name to Gillingham in 1913, when they also changed their strip from black and white stripes to predominantly blue.

KRBS Priestfield Stadium, Redfern Avenue, Gillingham, Kent ME7 4DD.

Telephone: (01634) 300 000.

Fax: (01634) 850 986.

Ticket Office: (01634) 300 000 (option 3).

Website: www.gillinghamfootballclub.com

Email: info@priestfield.com

Ground Capacity: 11,440.

Record Attendance: 23,002 v QPR, FA Cup 3rd rd, 10 January 1948.

Pitch Measurements: 110yd × 70yd.

Chairman: Paul D. P. Scally.

Vice-chairman: Michael Anderson.

Secretary: Gwen Poynter.

Manager: Andy Hessenthaler.

Assistant Manager: Ian Hendon.

Physio: Steve Allen.

Colours: Blue shirts with white sleeves, blue shorts, blue stockings.

Change Colours: Yellow shirts with blue sleeves, yellow shorts, yellow stockings.

Year Formed: 1893.

Turned Professional: 1894.

Ltd Co.: 1893.

Previous Name: 1893, New Brompton; 1913, Gillingham.

Club Nickname: 'The Gills'.

Ground: 1893, Priestfield Stadium.

First Football League Game: 28 August 1920, Division 3, v Southampton (h) D 1–1 – Branfield; Robertson, Sissons; Battiste, Baxter, Wigmore; Holt, Hall, Gilbey (1), Roe, Gore.

HONOURS

Football League: Best season 1999–2000. Division 3 – Runners-up 1995-96; Division 4 – Champions 1963–64; Runners-up 1973–74.

FA Cup: best season: 6th rd, 2000.

Football League Cup: best season: 4th rd, 1964, 1997.

sky SPORTS FACT FILE

The highest number of goals scored in a Football League match involving Gillingham occurred on 17 January 1951 when they defeated Exeter City 9–4. In 1894–95 during the club's first season in the Southern League they had defeated Chesham 9–0.

Record League Victory: 10–0 v Chesterfield, Division 3, 5 September 1987 – Kite; Haylock, Pearce, Shipley (2) (Lillis), West, Greenall (1), Pritchard (2), Shearer (2), Lovell, Elsey (2), David Smith (1).

Record Cup Victory: 10–1 v Gorleston, FA Cup 1st rd, 16 November 1957 – Brodie; Parry, Hannaway; Riggs, Boswell, Laing; Payne, Fletcher (2), Saunders (5), Morgan (1), Clark (2).

Record Defeat: 2–9 v Nottingham F, Division 3 (S), 18 November 1950.

Most League Points (2 for a win): 62, Division 4, 1973–74.

Most League Points (3 for a win): 85, Division 2, 1999–2000

Most League Goals: 90, Division 4, 1973–74.

Highest League Scorer in Season: Ernie Morgan, 31, Division 3 (S), 1954–55; Brian Yeo, 31, Division 4, 1973–74.

Most League Goals in Total Aggregate: Brian Yeo, 135, 1963–75.

Most League Goals in One Match: 6, Fred Cheesmur v Merthyr T, Division 3 (S), 26 April 1930.

Most Capped Player: Mamady Sidibe, 7 (12), Mali.

Most League Appearances: John Simpson, 571, 1957–72.

Youngest League Player: Luke Freeman, 15 years 247 days v Hartlepool U, 24 November 2007.

Record Transfer Fee Received: £1,500,000 from Manchester C for Robert Taylor, November 1999.

Record Transfer Fee Paid: £600,000 to Reading for Carl Asaba, August 1998.

Football League Record: 1920 Original Member of Division 3; 1921 Division 3 (S); 1938 Failed re-election; Southern League 1938–44; Kent League 1944–46; Southern League 1946–50; 1950 Re-elected to Division 3 (S); 1958–64 Division 4; 1964–71 Division 3; 1971–74 Division 4; 1974–89 Division 3; 1989–92 Division 4; 1992–96; Division 3; 1996–2000 Division 2; 2000–04 Division 1; 2004–05 FL C; 2005–08 FL 1; 2008–09 FL 2; 2009–10 FL 1; 2010– FL 2.

LATEST SEQUENCES

Longest Sequence of League Wins: 7, 18.12.1954 – 29.1.1955.

Longest Sequence of League Defeats: 10, 20.9.1988 – 5.11.1988.

Longest Sequence of League Draws: 5, 28.3.1993 – 18.9.1993.

Longest Sequence of Unbeaten League Matches: 20, 13.10.1973 – 10.2.1974.

Longest Sequence Without a League Win: 15, 1.4.1972 – 2.9.1972.

Successive Scoring Runs: 20 from 31.10.1959.

Successive Non-scoring Runs: 6 from 11.2 1961.

MANAGERS

W. Ironside Groombridge
1896–1906 *(Secretary-Manager)*
(previously Financial Secretary)
Steve Smith 1906–08
W. I. Groombridge 1908–19
(Secretary-Manager)
George Collins 1919–20
John McMillan 1920–23
Harry Curtis 1923–26
Albert Hoskins 1926–29
Dick Hendrie 1929–31
Fred Mavin 1932–37
Alan Ure 1937–38
Bill Harvey 1938–39
Archie Clark 1939–58
Harry Barratt 1958–62
Freddie Cox 1962–65
Basil Hayward 1966–71
Andy Nelson 1971–74
Len Ashurst 1974–75
Gerry Summers 1975–81
Keith Peacock 1981–87
Paul Taylor 1988
Keith Burkinshaw 1988–89
Damien Richardson 1989–92
Glenn Roeder 1992–93
Mike Flanagan 1993–95
Neil Smillie 1995
Tony Pulis 1995–99
Peter Taylor 1999–2000
Andy Hessenthaler 2000–04
Stan Ternent 2004–05
Neale Cooper 2005
Ronnie Jepson 2005–07
Mark Stimson 2007–10
Andy Hessenthaler May 2010–

TEN YEAR LEAGUE RECORD

		P	W	D	L	F	A	Pts	Pos
2000-01	Div 1	46	13	16	17	61	66	55	13
2001-02	Div 1	46	18	10	18	64	67	64	12
2002-03	Div 1	46	16	14	16	56	65	62	11
2003-04	Div 1	46	14	9	23	48	67	51	21
2004-05	FL C	46	12	14	20	45	66	50	22
2005-06	FL 1	46	16	12	18	50	64	60	14
2006-07	FL 1	46	17	8	21	56	77	59	16
2007-08	FL 1	46	11	13	22	44	73	46	22
2008-09	FL 2	46	21	12	13	58	55	75	5
2009-10	FL 1	46	12	14	20	48	64	50	21

DID YOU KNOW ?

On 1 September 1937 Newport Pagnell-born ex-Watford inside-right Cyril Walker made a scoring League debut for Gillingham against Newport County. After just five weeks with the Gills he was snapped up by Sheffield Wednesday, a significant loss to the Kent club.

GILLINGHAM 2009–10 LEAGUE RECORD

Match No.	Date		Venue	Opponents	Result		H/T Score	Lg Pos.	Goalscorers	Attendance
1	Aug	8	H	Swindon T	W	5-0	1-0	—	Bentley [12], Jackson 3 [51, 85, 87], Miller [72]	6852
2		15	A	Tranmere R	L	2-4	1-1	8	Weston [34], Barcham [54]	5590
3		18	A	Colchester U	L	1-2	1-1	—	Weston [11]	4849
4		22	H	Hartlepool U	L	0-1	0-0	20		4969
5		29	A	Walsall	D	0-0	0-0	18		3331
6	Sept	5	H	Exeter C	W	3-0	1-0	11	Jackson 2 (1 pen) [5 (p), 46], Rooney [78]	5107
7		12	H	Millwall	W	2-0	2-0	8	Barcham [6], Weston [40]	8097
8		19	A	Leeds U	L	1-4	0-2	9	Barcham [50]	21,026
9		26	H	Norwich C	D	1-1	1-0	9	Jackson (pen) [36]	7550
10	Oct	3	A	Southampton	L	1-4	1-3	17	Rooney [27]	19,457
11		10	H	Wycombe W	W	3-2	2-1	11	Gowling [16], Weston [44], Jackson [77]	5316
12		13	A	Brighton & HA	L	0-2	0-1	—		5960
13		17	A	Milton Keynes D	L	0-2	0-0	16		11,764
14		24	H	Charlton Ath	D	1-1	0-0	16	Jackson [82]	10,304
15		30	A	Southend U	L	0-1	0-0	—		7830
16	Nov	14	H	Oldham Ath	W	1-0	0-0	15	Weston (pen) [61]	4787
17		21	A	Bristol R	L	1-2	1-1	18	Barcham [40]	6210
18		24	H	Yeovil T	W	1-0	1-0	—	Jackson (pen) [10]	4450
19	Dec	1	A	Leyton Orient	L	1-3	1-2	—	Weston [20]	3183
20		5	H	Carlisle U	D	0-0	0-0	16		7214
21		12	A	Huddersfield T	L	1-2	1-2	18	Jackson [3]	13,844
22		19	H	Stockport Co	W	3-1	3-0	16	Oli [8], Brandy [27], Nutter [34]	4769
23		26	H	Brentford	L	0-1	0-1	17		7019
24		28	A	Exeter C	D	1-1	0-0	17	Lewis [70]	5761
25	Jan	16	A	Swindon T	L	1-3	0-1	19	Palmer [88]	6773
26		23	H	Colchester U	D	0-0	0-0	18		4948
27		26	A	Hartlepool U	D	1-1	0-0	—	Jackson [70]	2465
28		30	H	Walsall	D	0-0	0-0	19		4796
29	Feb	6	A	Brentford	L	0-4	0-3	20		6036
30		9	H	Tranmere R	L	0-1	0-0	—		3840
31		13	A	Yeovil T	D	0-0	0-0	20		3853
32		20	H	Bristol R	W	1-0	0-0	16	Jackson [90]	5302
33		23	A	Leyton Orient	D	1-1	1-0	—	Dickson [8]	4753
34		27	A	Carlisle U	L	0-2	0-1	18		4646
35	Mar	6	H	Huddersfield T	W	2-0	1-0	18	Jackson 2 [7, 46]	5388
36		13	A	Stockport Co	D	0-0	0-0	17		3894
37		20	H	Charlton Ath	D	2-2	2-1	19	Barcham [33], Oli [45]	20,024
38		27	H	Milton Keynes D	D	2-2	1-2	17	Miller [20], Barcham [65]	5465
39	Apr	3	A	Oldham Ath	L	0-1	0-0	21		3486
40		5	H	Southend U	W	3-0	0-0	18	Oli [47], Howe [74], Barcham [85]	7657
41		10	A	Millwall	L	0-4	0-2	21		13,174
42		13	H	Brighton & HA	D	1-1	0-1	—	Miller [49]	7977
43		17	H	Leeds U	W	3-2	3-1	19	Miller [8], Bentley [30], Naylor (og) [33]	9649
44		24	A	Norwich C	L	0-2	0-0	20		25,227
45	May	1	H	Southampton	W	2-1	1-0	19	Howe [19], Gowling [51]	9504
46		8	A	Wycombe W	L	0-3	0-1	21		7110

Final League Position: 21

GOALSCORERS

League (48): Jackson 14 (3 pens), Barcham 7, Weston 6 (1 pen), Miller 4, Oli 3, Bentley 2, Gowling 2, Howe 2, Rooney 2, Brandy 1, Dickson 1, Lewis 1, Nutter 1, Palmer 1, own goal 1.
Carling Cup (3): Jackson 2 (1 pen), Barcham 1.
FA Cup (4): Weston 2, Bentley 1, Brandy 1.
J Paint Trophy (1): Jackson 1 (pen).

Julian A 30	Fuller B 35+1	Nutter J 32+3	Weston C 36+3	Gowling J 29+1	Richards G 16	Bentley M 34+2	Payne J 14+5	Jackson S 34+8	Barcham A 38+4	Miller A 22+4	Erskine J —+4	Yussuff R 2+6	McCammon M 3+11	Palmer C 16+4	Oli D 23+13	Royce S 16+1	Jackman D 21+1	Maher K 21+5	Rooney L 2+11	Lewis S 16+4	Fry M 11	Vernon S 1	Brandy F 5+2	Wynter T 4+4	Dennehy D 19	Howe R 18	Plummer T 2	Walker J 2+3	Dickson C 4+5	Match No.
1	2	3	4	5	6	7[1]	8[2]	9[3]	10	11	12	13	14																	1
1	2	3	4	5	6	7[2]	8[1]	9	10	11			13	12																2
1	2	3	4	5	6	7[1]	8	9	10	11	12																			3
1	2	3	4	5	6	7[2]	8	9	10	11[1]			13		12	15														4
	2[2]	3	4	5		7		9	8	13			10	12	11[1]	1	6[3]	14												5
	2	13	4	5		7		9	8[3]				10[1]	3	11[2]	1	6	12	14											6
	2	14	4[2]	5		7		9	10	13				3	11[1]	1	6[3]	8	12											7
	2		4[3]	5		7	13	9	10		12			3	11[1]	1	6	8[2]	14											8
	2	12	4	5		7	13	9[3]	10[2]	14				3	11	1	6	8[1]												9
	2		4	5		7	12		10	13				3	11	1	6[1]	8	9[2]											10
	2	3	4	5	6	7		9	8	11[1]					10[2]	1		13	12											11
	2	3	4	5	6[3]	7	8[2]	9	10	11[1]			14		12	1		13												12
	2	3	4	5		7		9	10						12	1	13	11[2]	6	8[1]										13
	2	3	4	5		7		9	10		12				11[1]	1		8	6											14
	2	3[2]	4	5		7		9	10					13	11[1]	1	12	8	6											15
		3	4	5		7			10					2	12	1	11	8[1]	6				3							16
	2		4[1]	5		7	12		10	13				3		1		8	11	6			9[2]							17
	2		4	5		7			10	11				3	12	1		8	6				9[1]							18
13	3	4	5			2[3]		9	8				10[1]	14		1		7	11[2]	6			12							19
	2		4	5		7[1]		9	10	13				3	12	1		8[2]	11	6										20
1	3		4[2]	5				9	10		12		13	2	11[3]		7	14		8[1]					6					21
1	2	3	4[3]			8	13	5					14		12		7	10[1]	11	6			9[2]							22
1	2	3[1]	4	5[4]		7		9	13								6[2]	11	8	10			12							23
1	2	3				7		9[2]	11	13				5	10		4	8	6[1]				12							24
1	2	3	13	5	6[3]			9	11					4	10		7[1]	8[2]	12				14							25
1	2		5	4		7		9					13		10[2]		12						3		6	8		11[1]		26
1	2		5	4		7		9					13		10[2]		12						3		6	8		11[1]		27
1	2	12	4[3]	5		7		9	10	13			14				3[2]	8[1]	11						6					28
1	2	12	4[1]	5		8		9	11[3]				14				7	13					3		6				10[2]	29
1	2	8[3]	7[2]	5				9	11	13				3	12		4	10[1]							6				14	30
1	2	3		5		8		12	13	11[2]					10		4	7							6	9[1]				31
1	2	3		5		8[3]		13	14	11					12		4	7[1]							6	9[2]			10	32
1	2[1]	3		5				9	14	11			13		12		4	7[3]							6	8[2]			10	33
1		3		5				9	13	11				2[1]	12		4	7[2]	14						6	8			10[3]	34
1		3	4	5				9	10	11				2	12			7							6	8[1]				35
1		3	4	5				9[1]	10	11				2	12			7					13		6	8[2]				36
1		3	4[1]	5	14			12	10	11				2	9[3]			7					13		6	8[2]				37
1		3	4[1]	2					10	11				5	9[4]		6	7					12			8				38
1		3	4	5					10	11				2				7	9[1]				12		6	8				39
1	7	3	4[2]	5				12	10	11				8[1]	2		13	14							6	9[3]				40
1	7	3	12	5[2]				13	9	8				11	2		14	4							6[1]	10[3]				41
1	7	3	4	5[4]				13	10	11[2]				8	2		12								6[1]	9[3]	12	14		42
1	7[1]	3	4[2]	5				12	13	10			11	8	2										6	9				43
1		3	4	5		7		12	10	11				8	2[1]										6	9				44
1		3	4	5	6				8[1]	10			11	2				7					12			9				45
1		3	4	5	6			9	8	11				2				7[1]			12					10[2]		13		46

FA Cup

First Round	Southend U	(h)	3-0	
Second Round	Burton Alb	(h)	1-0	
Third Round	Accrington S	(a)	0-1	

Carling Cup

First Round	Plymouth Arg	(h)	2-1
Second Round	Blackburn R	(h)	1-3

J Paint Trophy

First Round	Colchester U	(h)	1-1
Second Round	Norwich C	(h)	0-1

GRIMSBY TOWN Blue Square Premier

FOUNDATION

Grimsby Pelham FC, as they were first known, came into being at a meeting held at the Wellington Arms in September 1878. Pelham is the family name of big landowners in the area, the Earls of Yarborough. The receipts for their first game amounted to 6s. 9d. (approx. 39p). After a year, the club name was changed to Grimsby Town.

Blundell Park, Cleethorpes, North East Lincolnshire DN35 7PY.

Telephone: (01472) 605 050.

Fax: (01472) 693 665.

Ticket Office: (01472) 605 050.

Website: www.gtfc.co.uk

Email: mailbox@gtfc.co.uk

Ground Capacity: 9,106.

Record Attendance: 31,657 v Wolverhampton W, FA Cup 5th rd, 20 February 1937.

Pitch Measurements: 111yd × 75yd.

Chairman: John Fenty.

Vice-chairman: Mike Parker.

Chief Executive/Secretary: Ian Fleming.

Manager: Neil Woods.

Frist Team Coach: Chris Casper.

Physio: Dave Moore.

Colours: Black and white striped shirts, black shorts, white stockings.

Change Colours: All blue.

Year Formed. 1878. *Turned Professional:* 1890. *Ltd Co.:* 1890.

Previous Name: 1878, Grimsby Pelham; 1879, Grimsby Town.

Club Nickname: 'The Mariners'.

Grounds: 1880, Clee Park; 1889, Abbey Park; 1899, Blundell Park.

First Football League Game: 3 September 1892, Division 2, v Northwich Victoria (h) W 2–1 – Whitehouse; Lundie, T. Frith; C. Frith, Walker, Murrell; Higgins, Henderson, Brayshaw, Riddoch (2), Ackroyd.

Record League Victory: 9–2 v Darwen, Division 2, 15 April 1899 – Bagshaw; Lockie, Nidd; Griffiths, Bell (1), Nelmes; Jenkinson (3), Richards (1), Cockshutt (3), Robinson, Chadburn (1).

Record Cup Victory: 8–0 v Darlington, FA Cup 2nd rd, 21 November 1885 – G. Atkinson; J. H. Taylor, H. Taylor; Hall, Kimpson, Hopewell; H. Atkinson (1), Garnham, Seal (3), Sharman, Monument (4).

HONOURS

Football League: Division 1 best season: 5th, 1934–35; Division 2 – Champions 1900–01, 1933–34; Runners-up 1928–29; Division 3 (N) – Champions 1925–26, 1955–56; Runners-up 1951–52; Division 3 – Champions 1979–80; Runners-up 1961–62; Division 4 – Champions 1971–72; Runners-up 1978–79; 1989–90.

FA Cup: Semi-finals, 1936, 1939.

Football League Cup: best season: 5th rd, 1980, 1985.

League Group Cup: Winners 1982.

Auto Windscreen Shield: Winners 1998.

Johnstone's Paint Trophy: Runners-up 2008.

sky SPORTS FACT FILE

On Boxing Day 1933 Grimsby Town beat Manchester United 7–3. On Christmas Day they had won 3–1 at Old Trafford with Pat Glover scoring a hat-trick. That season Grimsby were Second Division champions, United escaping relegation by a point.

Record Defeat: 1–9 v Arsenal, Division 1, 28 January 1931.

Most League Points (2 for a win): 68, Division 3 (N), 1955–56.

Most League Points (3 for a win): 83, Division 3, 1990–91.

Most League Goals: 103, Division 2, 1933–34.

Highest League Scorer in Season: Pat Glover, 42, Division 2, 1933–34.

Most League Goals in Total Aggregate: Pat Glover, 180, 1930–39.

Most League Goals in One Match: 6, Tommy McCairns v Leicester Fosse, Division 2, 11 April 1896.

Most Capped Player: Pat Glover, 7, Wales.

Most League Appearances: John McDermott, 647, 1987– 2007.

Youngest League Player: Tony Ford, 16 years 143 days v Walsall, 4 October 1975.

Record Transfer Fee Received: £1,500,000 from Everton for John Oster, July 1997.

Record Transfer Fee Paid: £500,000 to Preston NE for Lee Ashcroft, August 1998.

Football League Record: 1892 Original Member of Division 2; 1901–03 Division 1; 1903 Division 2; 1910 Failed re-election; 1911 re-elected Division 2; 1920–21 Divis on 3; 1921–26 Division 3 (N); 1926–29 Division 2; 1929–32 Division 1; 1932–34 Division 2; 1934–48 Division 1; 1948–51 Division 2; 1951–56 Division 3 (N); 1956–59 Division 2; 1959–62 Division 3; 1962–64 Division 2; 1964–68 Division 3; 1968–72 Division 4; 1972–77 Division 3; 1977–79 Division 4; 1979–80 Division 3; 1980–87 Division 2; 1987–88 Division 3; 1988–90 Division 4; 1990–91 Division 3; 1991–92 Division 2; 1992–97 Division 1; 1997–98 Division 2; 1998–2003 Division 1; 2003–04 Division 2; 2004–10 FL 2; 2010– Blue Square Premier.

LATEST SEQUENCES

Longest Sequence of League Wins: 11, 19.1.1952 – 29.3.1952.

Longest Sequence of League Defeats: 9, 30.11.1907 – 18.1.1908.

Longest Sequence of League Draws: 5, 6.2.1965 – 6.3.1965.

Longest Sequence of Unbeaten League Matches: 19, 16.2.1980 – 30.8.1980.

Longest Sequence Without a League Win: 22, 24.3.2008 – 1.11.2008.

Successive Scoring Runs: 33 from 6.10.1928.

Successive Non-scoring Runs: 6 from 11.3.2000.

MANAGERS

H. N. Hickson 1902–20
(Secretary-Manager)
Haydn Price 1920
George Fraser 1921–24
Wilf Gillow 1924–32
Frank Womack 1932–36
Charles Spencer 1937–51
Bill Shankly 1951–53
Billy Walsh 1954–55
Allenby Chilton 1955–59
Tim Ward 1960–62
Tom Johnston 1962–64
Jimmy McGuigan 1964–67
Don McEvoy 1967–68
Bill Harvey 1968–69
Bobby Kennedy 1969–71
Lawrie McMenemy 1971–73
Ron Ashman 1973–75
Tom Casey 1975–76
Johnny Newman 1976–79
George Kerr 1979–82
David Booth 1982–85
Mike Lyons 1985–87
Bobby Roberts 1987–88
Alan Buckley 1988–94
Brian Laws 1994–96
Kenny Swain 1997
Alan Buckley 1997–2000
Lennie Lawrence 2000–01
Paul Groves 2001–04
Nicky Law 2004
Russell Slade 2004–06
Graham Rodger 2006
Alan Buckley 2006–08
Mike Newell 2008–09
Neil Woods November 2009–

TEN YEAR LEAGUE RECORD

		P	W	D	L	F	A	Pts	Pos
2000-01	Div 1	46	14	10	22	43	62	52	18
2001-02	Div 1	46	12	14	20	50	72	50	19
2002-03	Div 1	46	9	12	25	48	85	39	24
2003-04	Div 2	46	13	11	22	55	81	50	21
2004-05	FL 2	46	14	16	16	51	52	58	18
2005-06	FL 2	46	22	12	12	64	44	78	4
2006-07	FL 2	46	17	8	21	57	73	59	15
2007-08	FL 2	46	15	10	21	55	66	55	16
2008-09	FL 2	46	9	14	23	51	69	41	22
2009-10	FL 2	46	9	17	20	45	71	44	23

DID YOU KNOW ?

The average utility player's experience pales in comparison with Adam Ogilvie of Grimsby Town He appeared as a full-back, half-back and from 1889–90 had two or so seasons in goal! Returned to the outfield, he then moved on to become Blackburn Rovers goalkeeper!

GRIMSBY TOWN 2009–10 LEAGUE RECORD

Match No.	Date	Venue	Opponents	Result	H/T Score	Lg Pos.	Goalscorers	Attendance
1	Aug 8	A	Cheltenham T	L 1-2	1-0	—	Conlon [35]	3654
2	15	H	Crewe Alex	L 0-4	0-2	24		5007
3	18	H	Rotherham U	L 1-2	0-0	—	Sweeney [64]	4156
4	22	A	Bury	W 1-0	1-0	20	Conlon [20]	2799
5	29	H	Aldershot T	L 1-2	0-1	22	Conlon [81]	3757
6	Sept 5	A	Port Vale	L 0-1	0-1	23		5056
7	12	H	Hereford U	W 1-0	0-0	21	North [88]	3173
8	19	A	Torquay U	W 2-0	0-0	—	Nicholson (og) [47], Sweeney [65]	2575
9	26	H	Darlington	D 1-1	1-0	17	Atkinson [21]	4704
10	30	A	Chesterfield	L 2-3	0-1	—	Proudlock [70], Sweeney [87]	3329
11	Oct 3	A	Barnet	L 0-3	0-2	22		2497
12	10	H	Burton Alb	L 1-2	1-2	22	Jones [4]	4002
13	17	H	Rochdale	L 0-2	0-1	23		3754
14	24	A	Bournemouth	L 1-3	0-2	23	Linwood [50]	5270
15	30	A	Accrington S	D 2-2	1-1	—	Forbes [14], Conlon [90]	4325
16	Nov 14	A	Northampton T	D 0-0	0-0	23		4028
17	21	A	Lincoln C	D 0-0	0-0	23		4981
18	24	H	Bradford C	L 0-3	0-1	—		3646
19	28	A	Macclesfield T	D 0-0	0-0	—		1409
20	Dec 5	H	Dagenham & R	D 1-1	1-0	23	Coulson [36]	3090
21	12	A	Shrewsbury T	D 0-0	0-0	23		4850
22	18	H	Morecambe	D 1-1	0-0	—	Sweeney [67]	3119
23	28	A	Port Vale	L 1-2	0-2	23	Conlon (pen) [90]	4401
24	Jan 2	H	Bury	D 1-1	0-0	—	Akpa Akpro [60]	3463
25	16	H	Cheltenham T	D 0-0	0-0	—		3334
26	23	A	Rotherham U	L 1-2	0-2	23	Fletcher [90]	3751
27	30	A	Aldershot T	D 1-1	1-0	23	Grant (og) [6]	3195
28	Feb 6	H	Notts Co	L 0-1	0-0	23		4452
29	13	A	Bradford C	D 0-0	0-0	23		11,321
30	17	A	Notts Co	D 1-1	1-1	—	Devitt [45]	5163
31	20	H	Lincoln C	D 2-2	1-1	23	Peacock 2 [38, 46]	6395
32	23	A	Macclesfield T	D 1-1	1-0	—	Devitt [42]	4813
33	27	A	Dagenham & R	L 0-2	0-0	23		2190
34	Mar 6	H	Shrewsbury T	W 3-0	1-0	23	Sinclair 2 (1 pen) [45 (p), 57], Akpa Akpro [64]	3651
35	9	A	Crewe Alex	L 2-4	2-2	—	Akpa Akpro [32], Sinclair [41]	3272
36	13	A	Morecambe	D 1-1	0-1	23	Coulson [59]	1882
37	20	H	Bournemouth	W 3-2	1-1	23	Devitt [27], Coulson [61], Chambers [90]	4428
38	27	A	Rochdale	L 1-4	1-3	23	Chambers [43]	4724
39	Apr 2	H	Northampton T	L 1-2	1-1	—	Coulson [42]	6482
40	5	A	Accrington S	W 3-2	0-2	23	Hudson [56], Coulson [59], Devitt [61]	1839
41	10	A	Hereford U	W 1-0	1-0	23	Devitt [18]	2143
42	13	H	Chesterfield	D 2-2	1-0	—	Wright T [28], Akpa Akpro [57]	5648
43	17	H	Torquay U	L 0-3	0-0	23		5702
44	24	A	Darlington	W 2-0	2-0	23	Lancashire [20], Akpa Akpro [45]	1911
45	May 1	H	Barnet	W 2-0	0-0	23	Atkinson [59], Hudson [90]	7033
46	8	A	Burton Alb	L 0-3	0-2	23		5510

Final League Position: 23

GOALSCORERS

League (45): Akpa Akpro 5, Conlon 5 (1 pen), Coulson 5, Devitt 5, Sweeney 4, Sinclair 3 (1 pen), Atkinson 2, Chambers 2, Hudson 2, Peacock 2, Fletcher 1, Forbes 1, Jones 1, Lancashire 1, Linwood 1, North 1, Proudlock 1, Wright T 1, own goals 2.
Carling Cup (0).
FA Cup (0).
J Paint Trophy (3): Sweeney 2, Proudlock 1.

Colgan N 35	Stockdale R 8	Widdowson J 36 + 2	Bennett R 13	Atkinson R 37	Sweeney P 36 + 4	Hudson M 11 + 5	Jones C 6 + 1	Boshell D 5 + 1	Proudlock A 14 + 13	Conlon B 7 + 9	Hegarty N 5 + 4	Akpa Akpro J 26 + 10	Devitt J 15	Fuller J 2 + 3	Forecast T 4	Leary M 19 + 9	North D 9 + 8	Oxley M 3	Clarke J 9 + 4	Bore P 37 + 3	Linwood P 23 + 5	Lillis J 4	Stirling J 2 + 2	Heywood M 1	Forbes A 8 + 5	Wood B 7 + 1	Jarman N 2 + 5	Mendy A 1	Magennis J 1 + 1	Shahin J 4 + 1	Lancashire O 24 + 1	McCrory D 10	Featherstone N 7 + 1	Coulson M 28 + 1	Wright B 1 + 1	Cowan-Hall P — + 3	Fletcher W 1 + 5	Chambers A 2 + 2	Sinclair D 16	Wright T 13 + 1	Peacock L 14 + 3	Match No.
1	2	3	4	5	6	7¹	8	9	10	11²	12	13																														1
	2	3	6	5	8			9	14	11²	10³	13	7¹	12	1	4																										2
	2	3	6	5	8			9	11		10⁶	13	7		1	4²	12																									3
	2	3	6	5	8³		14	9	11²		10	13	7¹		1	4	12																									4
	2	3	6	5	8			9	11		10	13⁴	7¹		1	4²	12																									5
	2	3	6		8			9	11				7¹			4¹	12	1				5																				6
	2	3	6	5	8			9	11				7⁸			4	12	1																								7
	2	3	6	5	8		14	9	11¹		10³	13	7⁸			4	12	1																								8
		3	6	5	8³		14	9²			10	13	7¹			4	12				2	1	1¹																			9
1		3	6	5	8			9¹	11		10		7			4	12				2																					10
1		3	6	5	8		14⁸	9	11		10³		7²	13		4	12				2¹																					11
1		3	6	5			14	9³	11¹		10²		7	13		4	12				2				8																	12
1				5				9³	10²					13		4	12			7	2				6¹	3	8	11														13
1		3			8	14	4	9³	10²							12				7	2				6	5	11				13											14
1		3			8		4	9³	10²							13			6¹	7	2					5	11				14		12									15
1		3	6⁶		8			9¹	11²							12			4	7	2³					5					14		10				13					16
1		3¹			8			9¹								12			4	7	2				6	5	11				14		10²				13					17
1			6					9³	11¹							12			4	7	2				5					14	3		8				13		10²			18
1			6			14		9³	11							12			4	7	2				5					13	3		8¹						10²			19
1			6					9³	10¹				14			12			4	7	2				5					13	3		8²						11			20
1			6		8			9³	10¹					13		14			4	7	2				5¹					12	3		11³									21
1			6	5				9¹	10²					12		4				7	2					3				8			11				13					22
1	12		6¹		8			9	10²							4				7	2					3				5			11³	14								23
1			6	5				9²	10¹					12		4				7	2					3							8	11			13					24
1			6	5				9¹	10³							4	14			7	2					3							8²	11			13	12				25
1		3	6	5				9²								4	12			7	2				8								10	11¹			13					26
1		3	4	5				9¹	10					14		12				7	2				6								8³	11²			13					27
1		3	4	5				9²	10¹			13		14		12				7	2				6								8	11³								28
1		3	4	5	8			9²	10³			13				12				7	2				6									11¹			14					29
1		3	4	5	8			9³	10²			13		14		12				7	2				6									11 / 11¹								30
1		3	8					9	10¹					12		4				7	2				6						5			11								31
1		3	8				14	9³	10²					12		4			6¹	7	2									13²	5			11								32
		3	8					9	10²					13		4¹	12			7	2	1			6³						5		14	11								33
1		3	4				14	9³	10					13		12			6²	7	2¹										5			11³							8	34
1		3	4²	5				9	10					14		12			6¹	7	2									13				11							8	35
1		3		5				9	10¹					13		4			6²	7	2									12				11							8	36
1		3	6					9	10					13		4²	12			7	2		5											11¹				8				37
1		3	4					9	10					13		12				7	2		5³		6¹		14						8²	11								38
		3	4		8¹			9	10³					12		6		1		7	2				6¹						5⁶			11²								39
		3	2		8		14	9	10³					12		4		1		7	13				6¹						5			11²								40
1		3			8			9	10¹					12		4				7	2				6						5			11								41
1		3			8			9	10¹					12		4				7	2				6						5			11								42
1		3	12		8			9	10¹					13		4				7	2				6¹						5			11								43
1		3	6¹		8			9³	10					14		4				7	2				13						5²			11								44
1		3			8			9	10¹					13		4				7	2				6²		14				5			11³						12		45
1		3	12		8			9	10					13		4²				7	2				6¹						5			11								46

FA Cup
First Round — Bath C — (h) — 0-2

Carling Cup
First Round — Tranmere R — (a) — 0-4

J Paint Trophy
Second Round — Hartlepool U — (a) — 2-0
Northern Quarter-Final — Leeds U — (a) — 1-3

HARTLEPOOL UNITED   FL Championship 1

FOUNDATION

The inspiration for the launching of Hartlepool United was the West Hartlepool club which won the FA Amateur Cup in 1904–05. They had been in existence since 1881 and their Cup success led in 1908 to the formation of the new professional concern which first joined the North-Eastern League. In those days they were Hartlepools United and won the Durham Senior Cup in their first two seasons.

Victoria Park, Clarence Road, Hartlepool TS24 8BZ.
Telephone: (01429) 272 584.
Fax: (01429) 863 007.
Ticket Office: (01429) 272 584 (option 2).
Website: www.hartlepoolunited.co.uk
Email: enquires@hartlepoolunited.co.uk
Ground Capacity: 7,630.
Record Attendance: 17,426 v Manchester U, FA Cup 3rd rd, 5 January 1957.
Pitch Measurements: 110yd × 74yd.
Chairman: Ken Hodcroft.
Chief Executive: Russ Green.
Senior Administrator: Maureen Smith.
Director of Sport: Chris Turner.
Physio: James Haycock.

HONOURS

Football League: FL 2 – Runners-up 2006–07; Division 3 – Runners-up 2002–03; Division 3 (N) – Runners-up 1956–57.
FA Cup: best season: 4th rd, 1955, 1978, 1989, 1993, 2005, 2009.
Football League Cup, best season: 4th rd, 1975.

Colours: Broad blue and white striped shirts with blue sleeves, blue shorts, white stockings.
Change Colours: Tangerine shirts with white trim, black shorts, tangerine stockings with white tops.
Year Formed: 1908.
Turned Professional: 1908.
Ltd Co.: 1908.
Previous Names: 1908, Hartlepools United; 1968, Hartlepool; 1977, Hartlepool United.
Club Nickname: 'The Pool'.
Ground: 1908, Victoria Park.
First Football League Game: 27 August 1921, Division 3 (N), v Wrexham (a) W 2–0 – Gill; Thomas, Crilly; Dougherty, Hopkins, Short; Kessler, Mulholland (1), Lister (1), Robertson, Donald.
Record League Victory: 10–1 v Barrow, Division 4, 4 April 1959 – Oakley; Cameron, Waugh; Johnson, Moore, Anderson; Scott (1), Langland (1), Smith (3), Clark (2), Luke (2), (1 og).
Record Cup Victory: 6–0 v North Shields, FA Cup 1st rd, 30 November 1946 – Heywood; Brown, Gregory; Spelman, Lambert, Jones; Price, Scott (2), Sloan (4), Moses, McMahon; 6–0 v Gainsborough Trinity (a), FA Cup 1st rd, 10 November 2007 – Budtz; McCunnie, Humphreys, Liddle (1) (Antwi), Nelson, Clark, Moore (1), Sweeney, Barker (2) (Monkhouse), Mackay (Porter 1), Brown (1).
Record Defeat: 1–10 v Wrexham, Division 4, 3 March 1962.

sky SPORTS FACT FILE

On 20 April 1910 in a North-Western League match, Hartlepools United defeated Workington 12–0, James Hogg netting nine times himself. United also managed to miss a penalty kick that was awarded to them.

Most League Points (2 for a win): 60, Division 4, 1967–68.

Most League Points (3 for a win): 88, FL 2, 2006–07.

Most League Goals: 90, Division 3 (N), 1956–57.

Highest League Scorer in Season: William Robinson, 28, Division 3 (N), 1927–28; Joe Allon, 28, Division 4, 1990–91.

Most League Goals in Total Aggregate: Ken Johnson, 98, 1949–64.

Most League Goals in One Match: 5, Harry Simmons v Wigan Borough, Division 3 (N), 1 January 1931; 5, Bobby Folland v Oldham Ath, Division 3 (N), 15 April 1961.

Most Capped Player: Ambrose Fogarty, 1 (11), Republic of Ireland.

Most League Appearances: Wattie Moore, 447, 1948–64.

Youngest League Player: David Foley, 16 years 105 days v Port Vale, 25 August 2003.

Record Transfer Fee Received: £750,000 from Ipswich T for Tommy Miller, July 2001.

Record Transfer Fee Paid: £75,000 to Northampton for Chris Freestone, March 1993; £75,000 to Notts Co for Gary Jones, March 1999; £75,000 to Mansfield T for Darrell Clarke, July 2001.

Football League Record: 1921 Original Member of Division 3 (N); 1958–68 Division 4; 1968–69 Division 3; 1969–91 Division 4; 1991–92 Division 3; 1992–94 Division 2; 1994–2003 Division 3; 2003–04 Division 2; 2004–06 FL 1; 2006–07 FL 2; 2007– FL 1.

LATEST SEQUENCES

Longest Sequence of League Wins: 9, 18.11.2006 – 1.1.2007.

Longest Sequence of League Defeats: 8, 27.1.1993 – 27.2.1993.

Longest Sequence of League Draws: 5, 24.2.2001 – 17.3.2001.

Longest Sequence of Unbeaten League Matches: 23, 18.11.2006 – 30.3.2007.

Longest Sequence Without a League Win: 18, 9.1.1993 – 3.4.1993.

Successive Scoring Runs: 27 from 18.11.2006.

Successive Non-scoring Runs: 11 from 9.1.1993.

MANAGERS

Alfred Priest 1908–12
Percy Humphreys 1912–13
Jack Manners 1913–20
Cecil Potter 1920–22
David Gordon 1922–24
Jack Manners 1924–27
Bill Norman 1927–31
Jack Carr 1932–35
  (had been Player-Coach since 1931)
Jimmy Hamilton 1935–43
Fred Westgarth 1943–57
Ray Middleton 1957–59
Bill Robinson 1959–62
Allenby Chilton 1962–63
Bob Gurney 1963–64
Alvan Williams 1964–65
Geoff Twentyman 1965
Brian Clough 1965–67
Angus McLean 1967–70
John Simpson 1970–71
Len Ashurst 1971–74
Ken Hale 1974–76
Billy Horner 1976–83
Johnny Duncan 1983
Mike Docherty 1983
Billy Horner 1984–86
John Bird 1986–88
Bobby Moncur 1988–89
Cyril Knowles 1989–91
Alan Murray 1991–93
Viv Busby 1993
John MacPhail 1993–94
David McCreery 1994–95
Keith Houchen 1995–96
Mick Tait 1996–99
Chris Turner 1999–2002
Mike Newell 2002–03
Neale Cooper 2003–05
Martin Scott 2005–06
Danny Wilson 2006–08
Chris Turner December 2008–

TEN YEAR LEAGUE RECORD

		P	W	D	L	F	A	Pts	Pos
2000-01	Div 3	46	21	14	11	71	54	77	4
2001-02	Div 3	46	20	11	15	74	48	71	7
2002-03	Div 3	46	24	13	9	71	51	85	2
2003-04	Div 2	46	20	13	13	76	61	73	6
2004-05	FL 1	46	21	8	17	76	66	71	6
2005-06	FL 1	46	11	17	18	44	59	50	21
2006-07	FL 2	46	26	10	10	65	40	88	2
2007-08	FL 1	46	15	9	22	63	66	54	15
2008-09	FL 1	46	13	11	22	66	79	50	19
2009-10	FL 1	46	14	11	21	59	67	50*	20

*3 pts deducted.

DID YOU KNOW ?

Wing-half Frank Stamper was born in West Hartlepool but joined Hartlepools United from Colchester United in August 1949. Goalkeeper Ralph Guthrie had a similar birthplace but had been signed from Arsenal in 1956. They both played in the successful 1956–57 team.

HARTLEPOOL UNITED 2009–10 LEAGUE RECORD

Match No.	Date	Venue	Opponents	Result	H/T Score	Lg Pos.	Goalscorers	Attendance
1	Aug 8	A	Milton Keynes D	D	0-0	0-0	—	8965
2	15	H	Charlton Ath	L	0-2	0-2	19	4408
3	18	H	Bristol R	L	1-2	1-2	—	Behan [31]	3137
4	22	A	Gillingham	W	1-0	0-0	18	Brown [65]	4969
5	29	H	Norwich C	L	0-2	0-1	21		4470
6	Sept 4	A	Oldham Ath	W	3-0	2-0	14	Brown [21], McSweeney [37], Behan [60]	4014
7	12	H	Wycombe W	D	1-1	0-0	13	Boyd [79]	3326
8	19	A	Colchester U	L	0-2	0-1	18		4259
9	26	H	Walsall	W	3-0	1-0	11	Monkhouse 2 [25, 50], Larkin [75]	3334
10	29	A	Stockport Co	D	2-2	0-2	—	Boyd [51], Behan [75]	3780
11	Oct 3	A	Exeter C	L	1-3	1-1	15	Behan [23]	4706
12	9	H	Brentford	D	0-0	0-0	—		3105
13	17	A	Swindon T	W	2-0	2-0	13	Brown [2], Monkhouse [30]	7096
14	24	H	Tranmere R	W	1-0	1-0	10	Hartley [43]	3428
15	31	A	Brighton & HA	D	3-3	3-2	11	Boyd [6], Monkhouse [43], Jones [45]	5694
16	Nov 14	H	Leyton Orient	W	1-0	0-0	9	Boyd [81]	3119
17	21	A	Huddersfield T	L	1-2	1-0	12	Liddle [18]	12,518
18	24	H	Southampton	L	1-3	1-1	—	Monkhouse [16]	3818
19	Dec 1	A	Carlisle U	L	2-3	1-1	—	Bjornsson [5], Monkhouse [90]	4109
20	5	H	Millwall	W	3-0	3-0	11	Hartley [12], Boyd [22], Bjornsson [29]	3153
21	12	A	Southend U	L	2-3	2-0	12	Boyd [8], Grant (og) [31]	7737
22	19	H	Yeovil T	D	1-1	0-1	11	Monkhouse [67]	2778
23	26	A	Leeds U	L	1-3	1-2	14	Bjornsson [25]	30,191
24	Jan 2	H	Oldham Ath	W	2-1	2-0	—	Jones [32], Monkhouse [40]	2634
25	16	H	Milton Keynes D	L	0-5	0-2	12		3211
26	19	A	Charlton Ath	L	1-2	0-1	—	Behan (pen) [51]	14,636
27	23	A	Bristol R	L	0-2	0-1	14		5794
28	26	H	Gillingham	D	1-1	0-0	—	Austin [79]	2465
29	30	A	Norwich C	L	1-2	1-2	16	Austin [28]	25,506
30	Feb 6	H	Leeds U	D	2-2	0-1	16	Boyd [71], Sweeney [90]	5115
31	20	H	Huddersfield T	L	0-2	0-1	20		4452
32	23	H	Carlisle U	W	4-1	3-1	—	Jones 2 [6, 74], Sweeney [28], Gamble [42]	2975
33	27	A	Millwall	L	0-1	0-1	17		10,818
34	Mar 6	H	Southend U	W	3-0	2-0	15	O'Donovan 3 [16, 32, 90]	3299
35	13	A	Yeovil T	L	0-4	0-2	16		4169
36	19	A	Tranmere R	D	0-0	0-0	—		5409
37	23	A	Southampton	L	2-3	1-2	—	Monkhouse [10], Austin [57]	18,072
38	27	H	Swindon T	L	0-1	0-1	20		3536
39	Apr 3	A	Leyton Orient	W	3-1	3-0	18	Liddle 2 [22, 39], O'Donovan [27]	3604
40	5	H	Brighton & HA	W	2-0	0-0	16	O'Donovan [54], Monkhouse [70]	3466
41	10	A	Wycombe W	L	0-2	0-0	17		4342
42	13	H	Stockport Co	W	3-0	1-0	—	Gamble [14], Monkhouse [56], O'Donovan [90]	2869
43	17	H	Colchester U	W	3-1	2-1	15	Brown [11], O'Donovan 2 (1 pen) [19, 85 (p)]	3126
44	24	A	Walsall	L	1-3	1-2	16	O'Donovan [27]	3457
45	May 1	H	Exeter C	D	1-1	0-1	16	Behan [80]	3983
46	8	A	Brentford	D	0-0	0-0	20		6893

Final League Position: 20

GOALSCORERS

League (59): Monkhouse 11, O'Donovan 9 (1 pen), Boyd 7, Behan 6 (1 pen), Brown 4, Jones 4, Austin 3, Bjornsson 3, Liddle 3, Gamble 2, Hartley 2, Sweeney 2, Larkin 1, McSweeney 1, own goal 1.
Carling Cup (2): Boyd 2.
FA Cup (0).
J Paint Trophy (0).

Flinders S 46	Haslam S 15	Hartley P 38	Sweeney A 32+10	Collins S 44	Liddle G 40	McSweeney L 24+7	Jones R 22+11	Behan D 21+8	Fredriksen J 4+8	Monkhouse A 43	Brown J 19+13	Rowell J —+6	Boyd A 25+15	Austin N 36+3	Foley D —+2	Larkin C 10+12	Bjornsson A 10+8	Humphreys R 33+5	Greulich B —+4	Clark B 6+5	Cherel J 1	Gamble J 22	O'Donovan R 15	Mackay M —+1	Power A —+2	Match No.
1	2	3	4	5	6	7	8^1	9	10^2	11	12	13														1
1	2	3^2	4	5	6	7		9	8^3	11	12	13	10^1	14												2
1	2	3	4	5	6	7^2		9	8^3	11	10^1	14	12	13												3
1	2	3	4	5	6	7	12	9^2	8^1	11	10^3	13	14													4
1	2	3	4	5	6	7^2	8^3	9	14	11	12	13				10^1										5
1	2	3	4	5	6	7^3	8^2	9	13	11	14		12			10^1										6
1	2	3^3	4	5	6	7	8	9^2		11	10^1	13	14			12										7
1	2	3	4	5	6	7^1	8	9^3		11	12	14				10	13									8
1		3	4^3	5	6			9^1		7	10	14	8^2	2		13	12	11								9
1		3	4	5	6			9^2		7	10^1		8	2		12	13	11								10
1		3	4	5	6			9		7^1	12	13	8^3	2		10^2	14	11								11
1		3	4	5	6			9^2		7	12		8^1	2		10	13	11								12
1		3	14	5	6			9^1		7	13	12	8^3	2		10^2	4	11								13
1		3	14	5	6			9^3		7	13	12	8^2	2		10^1	4	11								14
1		3	12	5	6		8^2	9^3	4^1	7			10	2		13	11	14								15
1		3		5	6		4	9^1	12	7			8^1	2		10	11									16
1		3		5	6	13	4	12		7			8	2		9^2	10^1	11								17
1		3		5	6		4^8	9^1		7			8	2		10	11	12								18
1		3	4	5	6	8		13		7			10^2	2	12	9^1	11^3		14							19
1		3	4	5	6	8^1		12		7			10^3	2		9	11^2	13	14							20
1		3	2^2	5	6	8	4	13	7^1				10			9	11		12^8							21
1		3	2	4	5	8^1	6			7	12	10				9	11									22
1		3	4	5	6^1	7^3	8	13			10		9	2		14	11^2		12							23
1		3^8				13^3	8	14		7	10^2			2		12	9^1	11		6	5					24
1			4		6	3^2	12			7						10	2	13		5		9^1	11			25
1	3		4	5	6	13	9^1			7				12	2	10		11^2				8				26
1	3		4	5	6	12	9^2			7				13	2	10		11^1				8				27
1		3	4	5	6	12	9^2			7				13	2	10		11^1				8				28
1		3	4	5	6	12	9^2			7				13	2	10		11^1				8				29
1		3	4	5	6	13	12			7				9	2	10^1		11^2				8				30
1		3	4^3	5	6	8	9^1			7	13			10^2	2	12	14					11				31
1		3	4	5	6	14	7			12				9^1	2	10^2		13				8	11^3			32
1		3	4^3	5	6		7	13		14				9^1	2	10^2		12				8	11			33
1		3	4	5	6		8^1	14		7	12			9^3	2			13					11^2	10		34
1		3	4	5		13	8^1			7^3	12			9^2	2			14				11	10			35
1		3	4	5		12	13			7				9^2	2^1			11		6		8	10			36
1		3^1	4	5		8	13			7	12				2			11^2		6		9	10^3	14		37
1			4^3	5		8	7^2			11^1	12	13	14	2		3				6		9	10			38
1	3		13	5	6	4				7	12			2		9^1		11^2				8^3	10^1	14		39
1	3		13	5	6	4				7	12			2		9^1		11^2				8	10^3	14		40
1	3		13	5		4^3				7	12			2		14	9^1	11		6		8^2	10			41
1	3	6	14	5^1		4^3				7			9^2	13	2			11		12		8	10			42
1		3	12	5	6	4	13			7			9^3	14	2			11^1				8^2	10			43
1		3	12	5	6	4	13			7			9^3	14	2			11^1				8^2	10			44
1		3	13	5	6	4^1	12			7			9^3	14	2			11				8^2	10			45
1		3	14	5	6	4^1	12	13		7			9^2	2				11				8^3	10			46

FA Cup
First Round   Kettering T   (h)   0-1

Carling Cup
First Round   Coventry C   (a)   1-0
Second Round   Burnley   (h)   1-2

J Paint Trophy
Second Round   Grimsby T   (h)   0-2

HEREFORD UNITED   FL Championship 2

FOUNDATION

Two local teams RAOC and St Martins amalgamated in 1924 under the chairmanship of Dr. E.W. Maples to form Hereford United and joined the Birmingham Combination. The first game at Edgar Street was against Atherstone Town on 24 August 1924, the visitors winnning 3-2. The players used the Wellington Hotel as a changing room. They graduated to the Birmingham League four years later and the Southern League in 1939.

Athletic Ground, Edgar Street, Hereford HR4 9JU.

Telephone: (08442) 761 939.

Fax: (08442) 761 982.

Ticket Office: (08442) 761 939.

Website: www.herefordunited.co.uk

Email: hufc1939@hotmail.com

Ground capacity: 7,149.

Record Attendance: 18,114 v Sheffield W, FA Cup 3rd rd, 4 January 1958.

Pitch measurements: 100m × 72m.

Chairman: David Keyte.

Vice-chairman: Tim Russon.

Manager: Simon Davey.

Assistant Manager: Andy Fensome.

Physio: Jamie Pitman.

Colours: White shirts with black trim, black shorts, white stockings.

Change colours: All tangerine.

Year Formed: 1924.

Turned Professional: 1924.

Ltd Co.: 1939.

Club Nickname: 'United'.

Ground: 1924, Edgar Street.

HONOURS

Football League: Division 2 best season: 22nd, 1976–77; Division 3 – Champions 1975–76; Division 4 – Runners-up 1972–73.
FA Cup: best season: 4th rd, 1972, 1974, 1977, 1982, 1990, 1992, 2008.
Football League Cup: best season: 3rd rd, 1975.
Welsh Cup: Winners 1990.
Conference (runners-up): 2003–04, 2004–05.

First Football League game: 12 August 1972, Division 4, v Colchester U (a) L 0-1 – Potter; Mallender, Naylor; Jones, McLaughlin, Tucker; Slattery, Hollett, Owen, Radford, Wallace.

sky SPORTS FACT FILE

The election of Hereford United to the Football League was a close-run thing in 1972. At the AGM they tied with Barrow who were seeking re-election to the Fourth Division. In the re-run Hereford received 29 votes to Barrow's 20 and decided to become a full-time club.

Record League Victory: 6–0 v Burnley (away), Division 4, 24 January 1987 – Rose; Rodgerson, Devine, Halliday, Pejic, Dalziel, Harvey (1p), Wells, Phillips (3), Kearns (2), Spooner.

Record Cup Victory: 6–1 v QPR, FA Cup 2nd rd, 7 December 1957 – Sewell; Tomkins, Wade; Masters, Niblett, Horton (2p); Reg Bowen (1), Clayton (1), Fidler, Williams (1), Cyril Beech (1).

Record Defeat: 0–7 v Middlesbrough, Coca-Cola Cup 2nd rd, 1st leg, 18 September 1996.

Most League Points (2 for a win): 63, Division 3, 1975–76.

Most League Points (3 for a win): 88, FL 2, 2007–08.

Most League Goals: 86, Division 3, 1975–76.

Highest League Scorer in Season: Dixie McNeil, 35, 1975–76.

Most League Goals in Total Aggregate: Stewart Phillips, 93, 1980–88, 1990–91.

Most Capped Player: Trevor Benjamin, 2, Jamaica.

Most League Appearances: Mel Pejic, 412, 1980–92.

Record Transfer Fee Received: £440,000 from QPR for Darren Peacock, December 1990.

Record Transfer Fee Paid: £80,000 to Walsall for Dean Smith, June 1994.

Football League Record: 1972 Elected to Division 4; 1973–76 Division 3; 1976–77 Division 2; 1977–78 Division 3; 1978–92 Division 4; 1992–97 Division 3; 1997–2006 Vauxhall Conference; 2006–08 FL 2; 2008–09 FL 1; 2009– FL 2.

MANAGERS

Eric Keen 1939
George Tranter 1948–49
Alex Massie 1952
George Tranter 1953–55
Joe Wade 1956–62
Ray Daniels 1962–63
Bob Dennison 1963–67
John Charles 1967–71
Colin Addison 1971–74
John Sillett 1974–78
Mike Bailey 1978–79
Frank Lord 1979–82
Tommy Hughes 1982–83
Johnny Newman 1983–87
Ian Bowyer 1987–90
Colin Addison 1990–91
John Sillett 1991–92
Greg Downs 1992–94
John Layton 1994–95
Graham Turner 1995–2009
John Trewick 2009–10
Graham Turner 2010
Simon Davey June 2010–

LATEST SEQUENCES

Longest Sequence of League Wins: 6, 2.4.1996 – 20.4.1996.

Longest Sequence of League Defeats: 8, 7.2.1987 – 18.3.1987.

Longest Sequence of League Draws: 6, 12.4.1975 – 23.8.1975.

Longest Sequence of Unbeaten League Matches: 14, 21.10.1972 – 17.1.1973.

Longest Sequence Without a League Win: 13, 19.11.1977 – 25.2.1978.

Successive Scoring Runs: 23 from 20.9.1975.

Successive Non-scoring Runs: 6 from 10.3.2007.

TEN YEAR LEAGUE RECORD

		P	W	D	L	F	A	Pts	Pos
2000-01	Conf	42	14	15	13	60	46	57	11
2001-02	Conf	42	14	10	18	50	53	52	17
2002-03	Conf	42	19	7	16	64	51	64	6
2003-04	Conf	42	28	7	7	103	44	91	2
2004-05	Conf	42	21	11	10	68	41	74	2
2005-06	Conf	42	22	14	6	59	33	80	2
2006-07	FL 2	46	14	13	19	45	53	55	16
2007-08	FL 2	46	26	10	10	72	41	88	3
2008-09	FL 1	46	9	7	30	42	79	34	24
2009-10	FL 2	46	17	8	21	54	65	59	16

DID YOU KNOW ?

In 1982–83 Hereford United were forced to call upon the services of no fewer than seven goalkeepers during the pre-season and League competition which followed. They included John Jackson, a 40-year-old who thus became the oldest player to represent the club.

HEREFORD UNITED 2009–10 LEAGUE RECORD

Match No.	Date	Venue	Opponents	Result	H/T Score	Lg Pos.	Goalscorers	Attendance
1	Aug 8	A	Morecambe	D 2-2	1-1	—	Pugh 2 [39, 90]	2119
2	15	H	Cheltenham T	D 1-1	0-0	16	Godsmark [76]	3280
3	18	H	Bury	L 1-3	1-1	—	Constantine [15]	2321
4	22	A	Crewe Alex	L 0-1	0-1	22		3731
5	29	H	Port Vale	D 2-2	1-0	20	Pugh [36], Plummer (pen) [80]	2434
6	Sept 5	A	Aldershot T	D 2-2	1-0	21	Plummer 2 (1 pen) [4 (p), 78]	3094
7	12	A	Grimsby T	L 0-1	0-0	23		3173
8	19	H	Accrington S	W 2-0	1-0	20	King [6], Valentine [67]	2013
9	26	A	Rochdale	L 1-4	1-2	21	Pugh [23]	2620
10	29	A	Bournemouth	W 2-1	0-0	—	Pugh 2 [50, 77]	2104
11	Oct 3	H	Dagenham & R	D 1-1	0-0	20	Walker [80]	2253
12	10	A	Rotherham U	D 1-1	0-1	20	McCallum [90]	3452
13	17	H	Chesterfield	W 1-0	0-0	18	Valentine (pen) [58]	2574
14	24	A	Bradford C	L 0-1	0-1	19		11,107
15	31	H	Darlington	W 2-1	1-0	17	Lowe [41], Jones D [47]	2238
16	Nov 14	A	Barnet	D 0-0	0-0	16		1965
17	21	A	Burton Alb	L 2-3	0-0	18	Constantine 2 [61, 76]	2796
18	24	H	Shrewsbury T	W 2-1	2-1	—	Valentine (pen) [5], McCallum [30]	2913
19	Dec 1	A	Northampton T	W 3-1	1-1	—	Jones D [16], Manset [57], King [74]	3524
20	5	H	Notts Co	L 0-2	0-1	19		2727
21	12	A	Macclesfield T	L 1-3	0-2	17	Constantine [90]	1406
22	26	A	Torquay U	L 0-1	0-1	19		3792
23	Jan 19	A	Crewe Alex	D 1-1	1-0	—	Constantine [42]	1367
24	23	A	Bury	L 0-1	0-1	20		2797
25	30	A	Port Vale	L 0-2	0-1	21		4686
26	Feb 2	H	Lincoln C	W 2-0	1-0	—	McCallum 2 [29, 55]	1429
27	6	H	Torquay U	W 1-0	1-0	18	McCallum [22]	2123
28	13	A	Shrewsbury T	L 1-3	1-2	18	Constantine [5]	6098
29	16	H	Aldershot T	W 2-0	2-0	—	McCallum [27], Blackburn (og) [35]	1576
30	20	H	Burton Alb	L 3-4	1-1	17	Pugh [28], Lunt [55], McQuilkin [59]	2253
31	23	H	Northampton T	L 0-2	0-1	—		1266
32	27	A	Notts Co	L 0-5	0-1	18		6036
33	Mar 2	A	Cheltenham T	W 1-0	1-0	—	Green [25]	3273
34	6	H	Macclesfield T	L 0-2	0-1	18		1919
35	12	A	Lincoln C	L 1-3	1-2	—	Pugh [42]	6012
36	16	H	Morecambe	L 0-1	0-1	—		1208
37	20	H	Bradford C	W 2-0	1-0	19	Manset [33], Jervis [81]	1926
38	27	A	Chesterfield	W 2-1	0-0	17	Jervis (pen) [48], Pugh [63]	3593
39	Apr 3	H	Barnet	W 2-1	1-1	17	McQuilkin [29], Breen (og) [69]	2146
40	5	A	Darlington	W 1-0	0-0	16	Pugh [74]	2131
41	10	H	Grimsby T	L 0-1	0-1	16		2143
42	13	A	Bournemouth	L 1-2	0-1	—	Pugh [90]	6128
43	17	A	Accrington S	W 2-1	1-0	17	McCallum 2 [35, 90]	1420
44	24	H	Rochdale	W 2-1	0-0	15	King [52], Valentine [61]	1975
45	May 1	A	Dagenham & R	L 1-2	0-1	17	Pugh [62]	2663
46	8	H	Rotherham U	W 3-0	2-0	16	Manset [4], Jones D [21], Pugh [90]	3005

Final League Position: 16

GOALSCORERS

League (54): Pugh 13, McCallum 8, Constantine 6, Valentine 4 (2 pens), Jones D 3, King 3, Manset 3, Plummer 3 (2 pens), Jervis 2 (1 pen), McQuilkin 2, Godsmark 1, Green 1, Lowe 1, Lunt 1, Walker 1, own goals 2.
Carling Cup (2): Godsmark 1, Plummer 1 (pen).
FA Cup (2): Manset 1, Valentine 1 (pen).
J Paint Trophy (4): Constantine 2, Manset 1, Walker 1.

Bartlett A 45+1	Green R 31	Valentine R 40	Dennehy D 6+1	Jones D 40+1	Lunt K 42	Pugh M 39+1	Southam G 5+1	Morris L 5+7	Constantine L 25+10	Godsmark J 7+1	Gwynne S 21+5	Done M 7+13	Tolley J 6+4	McQuilkin J 20+2	Rose R 22+3	Lowe K 17+2	Plummer T 4+1	Jones C 1	Jackson M 2+3	McCallum G 20+7	Blanchett D 13	Marshall M 8	King C 22+4	Walker J 6	Manset M 16+13	Sonko E 5+5	Mutch J 3	Wedderburn N 3	Elford-Alliyu L 1	Downing P 6	Weir T 3	Adamson C 1	Preston D 4	Young L 5+1	Jervis J 5+2	Ajdarevic A —+1	Match No.
1	2	3[1]	4	5	6	7	8[2]	9	10	11[3]	12	13	14																								1
1	2	3	4[2]	5	6		12	9	10	8			11[1]		7	13																					2
1	2	3[4]	4		6	11	7	9[1]	10[2]	8		12	13					5																			3
1	2		4	5	6	7[1]			10[2]	8[3]	12					3				9	11	13	14														4
1	2		4	5		7	12		10[2]	8[1]	11	6				3				9			13														5
1	2	3		5	6	7	8		10[1]	13	11					4				9[2]			12														6
1		3		5	6	7	8[1]			13	11	12				4	2			9			10[2]														7
1	2	3		5	6	7								11		12				10[1]	4	8	9														8
1	2[6]	3		5	6	7[1]								11	12						4	8	9	10													9
1		3	12	5	6	7								11			2				4[1]	8	9	10													10
1	2	3	4	5	6	7								11								8	9	10													11
1	2	3		5	6	8[3]					7[2]								14	4	11[3]		9		10	12	13										12
1	2	3			6	7														4	5	8	9	10[1]	11	12											13
1	2	3			6	7						13								4	5	8	9	11[2]	10[1]	12											14
1		3		5	6	7[2]						13	11[1]				2			4		8	9		10	12											15
1	7[1]	3		5	6				10							12				4		8	2		9	11											16
1	3[1]			5	6		13		10							12				11	2[2]	7	4		9	8											17
1	2	3		5	6				10		7					8				11[1]	4		9		12												18
1	4	3		5		7			10[1]			6					2		12				9		8	11											19
1	2[1]	3		5		7			14		13	12				6[2]			4		9[3]		10					8	11								20
1		3		5	6	7			13		14	8				2			12	4			9[2]		10[1]			11[3]									21
1	2	3[3]		5	6	7			10		8[2]	13				11[1]			14				9[1]		12	4											22
1		3		5	6	7			10		12	11[3]				4			8[1]	2			13		9[2]	14											23
1		3		5	6	8			10		7					11[2]			4	2			13		9[1]	12											24
1		3[8]		5	6	8			7							11[3]	4[1]		12	2			14		13							9[2]					25
1				5	6	8			10		7					4				11			9								2	3					26
1				5	6	7			10[2]		2					8				12			11		9						3	4[1]					27
1				5	6	7			10		3					11				8			9[1]		12						2	4					28
1		3		5	6	7			13		10[1]					2				8			9		11[2]							4					29
1		3		5	6	7			12		10[2]					2				8			9		11[1]							4					30
1	2	3		5	6	7			9[1]		10[2]					12				11			4		8										13		31
15					13	6	7		12		10[6]					2[2]				9[1]			11		3					5[8]	1[4]		4				32
1	2	3			6	7			10[2]							9[1]	5	13		8[1]			12	11									4				33
1	2	3				9		13	10		7		6[1]			5[2]				8			12	11									4				34
1	2	3		5	6	7			10[2]		12					11				8			9[1]	12									4				35
1	2	3		5	6	7			10		13					11	4			8[1]			12	9[2]													36
1	2	3		5	6	7			13							11	4			8[1]			9[2]											10	12		37
1	2	3		5	6	7			12	13						8	4						9[1]											11[2]	10		38
1	2	3		5	6	7			14		12					8	4						9[3]											10[1]	11[2]	13	39
1	2	3		5	6	7			14	13	12					11[2]	4						9[3]											8[1]	10		40
1	2	3		5	6	7					12					11	4						9											8[1]	10[2]		41
1	2	3		5	6	7			10		8[2]					13	4			11[3]			14												12	9[1]	42
1		3		5	6	7			12							11	4		2	8			10[2]		9[1]											13	43
1	2	3		5	6	7			13		12					11	4			8			10[2]		9[1]												44
1	2	3		5	6	7			12							11	4			8			10[1]		9												45
1	2	3		5	6	7			10							11	4			8			9														46

FA Cup

First Round	Sutton U	(h)	2-0
Second Round	Colchester U	(h)	0-1

Carling Cup

First Round	Charlton Ath	(h)	1-0
Second Round	Portsmouth	(a)	1-4

J Paint Trophy

First Round	Bristol R	(h)	0-0
Second Round	Aldershot T	(h)	2-2
Southern Quarter-Final	Leyton Orient	(a)	1-1
Southern Semi-Final	Milton Keynes D	(h)	1-4

HUDDERSFIELD TOWN FL Championship 1

FOUNDATION

A meeting, attended largely by members of the Huddersfield & District FA, was held at the Imperial Hotel in 1906 to discuss the feasibility of establishing a football club in this rugby stronghold. However, it was not until a man with both the enthusiasm and the money to back the scheme came on the scene, that real progress was made. This benefactor was Mr Hilton Crowther and it was at a meeting at the Albert Hotel in 1908, that the club formally came into existence with a capital of £2,000 and joined the North-Eastern League.

The Galpharm Stadium, Stadium Way, Leeds Road, Huddersfield HD1 6PX.

Telephone: 0870 4444 677.

Fax: (01484) 484 101.

Ticket Office: 0870 4444 552.

Website: www.htafc.com

Email: info@htafc.com

Ground Capacity: 24,554.

Record Attendance: 67,037 v Arsenal, FA Cup 6th rd, 27 February 1932 (at Leeds Road); 23,678 v Liverpool, FA Cup 3rd rd, 12 December 1999 (at Alfred McAlpine Stadium).

Pitch Measurements: 115yd × 76yd.

Chairman: Dean Hoyle.

Secretary: Ann Hough.

Manager: Lee Clark.

Assistant Manager: Terry McDermott.

Physio: Dave Buckby.

HONOURS

Football League: Division 1 – Champions 1923–24, 1924–25, 1925–26; Runners-up 1926–27, 1927–28, 1933–34; Division 2 – Champions 1969–70; Runners-up 1919–20, 1952–53; Division 4 – Champions 1979–80.

FA Cup: Winners 1922; Runners-up 1920, 1928, 1930, 1938.

Football League Cup: Semi-final 1968.

Autoglass Trophy: Runners-up 1994.

Colours: Blue and white striped shirts, white shorts, blue stockings.

Change Colours: Red and black striped shirts, red shorts, red stockings.

Year Formed: 1908. *Turned Professional:* 1908. *Ltd Co.:* 1908. *Club Nickname:* 'The Terriers'.

Grounds: 1908, Leeds Road; 1994, The Alfred McAlpine Stadium (renamed the Galpharm Stadium 2004).

First Football League Game: 3 September 1910, Division 2, v Bradford PA (a) W 1–0 – Mutch; Taylor, Morris; Beaton, Hall, Bartlett; Blackburn, Wood, Hamilton (1), McCubbin, Jee.

Record League Victory: 10–1 v Blackpool, Division 1, 13 December 1930 – Turner; Goodall, Spencer; Redfern, Wilson, Campbell; Bob Kelly (1), McLean (4), Robson (3), Davies (1), Smailes (1).

Record Cup Victory: 7–0 v Lincoln U, FA Cup 1st rd, 16 November 1991 – Clarke; Trevitt, Charlton, Donovan (2), Mitchell, Doherty, O'Regan (1), Stapleton (1) (Wright), Roberts (2), Onuora (1), Barnett (Ireland). *N.B.* 11–0 v Heckmondwike (a), FA Cup pr rd, 18 September 1909 – Doggart; Roberts, Ewing; Hooton, Stevenson, Randall; Kenworthy (2), McCreadie (1), Foster (4), Stacey (4), Jee.

sky SPORTS FACT FILE

On 6 August 2008 Huddersfield Town staged a Centenary match against Arsenal at the Galpharm Stadium. The attendance of 19,044 was the highest for a pre-season fixture there and the best crowd since 20,042 at Leeds Road for the visit of Independiente in 1954.

Record Defeat: 1–10 v Manchester C, Division 2, 7 November 1987.

Most League Points (2 for a win): 66, Division 4, 1979–80.

Most League Points (3 for a win): 82, Division 3, 1982–83.

Most League Goals: 101, Division 4, 1979–80.

Highest League Scorer in Season: Sam Taylor, 35, Division 2, 1919–20; George Brown, 35, Division 1, 1925–26.

Most League Goals in Total Aggregate: George Brown, 142, 1921–29.

Most League Goals in One Match: 5, Dave Mangnall v Derby Co, Division 1, 21 November 1931; 5, Alf Lythgoe v Blackburn R, Division 1, 13 April 1935.

Most Capped Player: Jimmy Nicholson, 31 (41), Northern Ireland.

Most League Appearances: Billy Smith, 520, 1914–34.

Youngest League Player: Denis Law, 16 years 303 days v Notts Co, 24 December 1956.

Record Transfer Fee Received: £2,750,000 from Ipswich T for Marcus Stewart, February 2000.

Record Transfer Fee Paid: £1,200,000 to Bristol R for Marcus Stewart, July 1996.

Football League Record: 1910 Elected to Division 2; 1920–52 Division 1; 1952–53 Division 2; 1953–56 Division 1; 1956–70 Division 2; 1970–72 Division 1; 1972–73 Division 2; 1973–75 Division 3; 1975–80 Division 4; 1980–83 Division 3; 1983–88 Division 2; 1988–92 Division 3; 1992–95 Division 2; 1995–2001 Division 1; 2001–03 Division 2; 2003–04 Division 3; 2004– FL 1.

LATEST SEQUENCES

Longest Sequence of League Wins: 11, 5.4.1920 – 4.9.1920.

Longest Sequence of League Defeats: 7, 8.10.1955 – 19.11.1955.

Longest Sequence of League Draws: 6, 3.3.1987 – 3.4.1987.

Longest Sequence of Unbeaten League Matches: 27, 24.1.1925 – 17.10.1925.

Longest Sequence Without a League Win: 22, 4.12.1971 – 29.4.1972.

Successive Scoring Runs: 27 from 12.3.2005.

Successive Non-scoring Runs: 7 from 22.1.1972.

MANAGERS

Fred Walker 1908–10
Richard Pudan 1910–12
Arthur Fairclough 1912–19
Ambrose Langley 1919–21
Herbert Chapman 1921–25
Cecil Potter 1925–26
Jack Chaplin 1926–29
Clem Stephenson 1929–42
David Steele 1943–47
George Stephenson 1947–52
Andy Beattie 1952–56
Bill Shankly 1956–59
Eddie Boot 1960–64
Tom Johnston 1964–68
Ian Greaves 1968–74
Bobby Collins 1974
Tom Johnston 1975–78
(had been General Manager since 1975)
Mike Buxton 1978–86
Steve Smith 1986–87
Malcolm Macdonald 1987–88
Eoin Hand 1988–92
Ian Ross 1992–93
Neil Warnock 1993–95
Brian Horton 1995–97
Peter Jackson 1997–99
Steve Bruce 1999–2000
Lou Macari 2000–02
Mick Wadsworth 2002–03
Peter Jackson 2003–07
Andy Ritchie 2007–08
Stan Ternent 2008
Lee Clark December 2008–

TEN YEAR LEAGUE RECORD

		P	W	D	L	F	A	Pts	Pos
2000-01	Div 1	46	11	15	20	48	57	48	22
2001-02	Div 2	46	21	15	10	65	47	78	6
2002-03	Div 2	46	11	12	23	39	61	45	22
2003-04	Div 3	46	23	12	11	68	52	81	4
2004-05	FL 1	46	20	10	16	74	65	70	9
2005-06	FL 1	46	19	16	11	72	59	73	4
2006-07	FL 1	46	14	17	15	60	69	59	15
2007-08	FL 1	46	20	6	20	50	62	66	10
2008-09	FL 1	46	18	14	14	62	65	68	9
2009-10	FL 1	46	23	11	12	82	56	80	6

DID YOU KNOW ?

Herbert Chapman made one of his shrewdest signings when he secured 30-year-old inside-forward Clem Stephenson from Aston Villa in March 1921. A master tactician, the player was still thought to be past his best, but three championships later it was a different story.

HUDDERSFIELD TOWN 2009–10 LEAGUE RECORD

Match No.	Date	Venue	Opponents	Result	H/T Score	Lg Pos.	Goalscorers	Attendance
1	Aug 8	A	Southend U	D 2-2	0-1	—	Pilkington [71], Rhodes [79]	8059
2	15	H	Southampton	W 3-1	0-0	4	Rhodes 2 [50, 68], Kay [82]	12,449
3	18	H	Brighton & HA	W 7-1	3-1	—	Kay [21], Clarke P [35], Novak (pen) [43], Roberts [64], Drinkwater [69], Robinson 2 [73, 90]	11,269
4	22	A	Bristol R	L 0-1	0-0	7		6952
5	29	H	Yeovil T	W 2-1	1-1	4	Robinson [33], Collins [65]	12,646
6	Sept 5	A	Milton Keynes D	W 3-2	0-0	3	Rhodes [55], Robinson [60], Kay [78]	9772
7	12	H	Brentford	D 0-0	0-0	4		12,020
8	19	A	Millwall	L 1-3	0-2	6	Rhodes [85]	8502
9	26	H	Stockport Co	D 0-0	0-0	6		12,020
10	29	A	Walsall	L 1-2	0-0	—	Robinson [47]	3419
11	Oct 3	A	Colchester U	L 0-1	0-0	9		5154
12	10	H	Exeter C	W 4-0	2-0	8	Novak [17], Rhodes 3 [44, 49, 52]	13,438
13	17	A	Charlton Ath	L 1-2	1-1	8	Pilkington [38]	16,991
14	24	H	Leyton Orient	W 4-0	1-0	7	Roberts [45], Clarke N [57], Collins [74], Rhodes [90]	13,396
15	Nov 1	A	Oldham Ath	W 1-0	0-0	6	Williams [59]	8569
16	14	H	Wycombe W	W 6-0	2-0	6	Clarke P 2 [21, 63], Roberts [28], Pilkington [49], Duberry (og) [82], Robinson (pen) [84]	14,869
17	21	H	Hartlepool U	W 2-1	0-1	3	Hartley (og) [56], Williams [66]	12,518
18	24	A	Swindon T	L 1-2	1-1	—	Novak [28]	6630
19	Dec 1	H	Tranmere R	D 3-3	1-1	—	Novak [6], Collins [58], Kay [81]	13,509
20	5	A	Leeds U	D 2-2	0-1	5	Novak [48], Rhodes [78]	36,723
21	12	A	Gillingham	W 2-1	2-1	5	Novak [40], Rhodes [45]	13,844
22	19	A	Norwich C	L 0-3	0-0	5		25,004
23	28	H	Milton Keynes D	W 1-0	1-0	5	Pilkington [27]	16,086
24	Jan 16	H	Southend U	W 2-1	1-0	5	Rhodes 2 [44, 63]	14,200
25	19	A	Bristol R	D 0-0	0-0	—		12,624
26	30	A	Yeovil T	W 1-0	1-0	7	Eccleston [23]	4110
27	Feb 6	H	Carlisle U	D 1-1	0-0	7	Pilkington [50]	14,132
28	9	A	Brighton & HA	D 0-0	0-0	—		4711
29	13	H	Swindon T	D 2-2	1-2	7	Clarke P [8], Kay [50]	14,610
30	16	A	Carlisle U	W 2-1	1-0	—	Novak [6], Rhodes [56]	5236
31	20	A	Hartlepool U	W 2-0	1-0	6	Roberts (pen) [17], Trotman [66]	4452
32	23	A	Tranmere R	W 2-0	1-0	—	Novak 2 [8, 48]	5793
33	27	H	Leeds U	D 2-2	1-0	6	Pilkington [13], Roberts [85]	21,764
34	Mar 2	A	Southampton	L 0-5	0-3	—		19,821
35	6	A	Gillingham	L 0-2	0-1	7		5388
36	13	H	Norwich C	L 1-3	1-0	7	Trotman [3]	17,959
37	20	A	Leyton Orient	W 2-0	1-0	7	Rhodes [26], Robinson [68]	4119
38	27	H	Charlton Ath	D 1-1	0-0	7	Rhodes [53]	14,459
39	Apr 3	A	Wycombe W	W 2-1	1-0	6	Rhodes [22], Robinson [52]	5288
40	6	H	Oldham Ath	W 2-0	1-0	6	Robinson 2 [38, 90]	14,561
41	10	A	Brentford	L 0-3	0-0	6		5209
42	13	A	Walsall	W 4-3	2-0	6	Robinson (pen) [22], Rhodes [45], Kay [89], Novak [90]	14,396
43	16	H	Millwall	W 1-0	1-0	—	Clarke P [39]	16,050
44	24	A	Stockport Co	W 6-0	2-0	6	Pilkington [2], Robinson [37], Rhodes [68], Drinkwater [85], Roberts [89], Novak (pen) [90]	6887
45	May 1	H	Colchester U	W 2-1	1-0	6	Robinson (pen) [17], Novak [90]	17,950
46	8	A	Exeter C	L 1-2	1-1	6	Roberts [2]	8383

Final League Position: 6

GOALSCORERS

League (82): Rhodes 19, Robinson 13 (3 pens), Novak 12 (2 pens), Pilkington 7, Roberts 7 (1 pen), Kay 6, Clarke P 5, Collins 3, Drinkwater 2, Trotman 2, Williams 2, Clarke N 1, Eccleston 1, own goals 2.
Carling Cup (6): Rhodes 3, Robinson 3 (1 pen).   *FA Cup (7):* Novak 2, Roberts 2, Clarke N 1, Rhodes 1, Williams 1.
J Paint Trophy (5): Pilkington 2, Clarke N 1, Clarke P 1, Simpson 1.   *Play-Offs (0).*

Smithies A 46	Peltier L 42	Williams R 13+4	Collins M 23+5	Clarke P 46	Butler A 10+1	Pilkington A 42+1	Kay A 38+2	Robinson T 17+20	Simpson R 4+9	Roberts G 40+3	Clarke T 15+6	Novak L 24+13	Rhodes J 43+2	Skarz J 14+1	Drinkwater D 2/+6	Ainsworth L 2+9	Goodwin J 3+2	Clarke N 15+2	Berrett J 2+7	Heffernan D 15	Trotman N 2i	Eccleston N 4+7	Pearce K —+1	Match No.
1	2	3	4^6	5	6	7	8		9^2	10^3	11^1	12	13	14										1
1	2			5	6	7	8	12		11^2	4	9^1	10^3	3	13	14								2
1	2			5	6	7	8^2	12	14	11	4	9^1	10^3	3	13									3
1	2			5	6	7^3	8^1	12		11	4	13	10^2	3	9	14								4
1	2		4	5	6	7	8^3	9	13		12	10^1		3	11^{12}	14								5
1	2		4^1	5	6	7	8	9	13	12		10^2		3	11									6
1	2	13		5	6	7	8^2	9^1	14	4	12	10^3		3	11									7
1	2	8		5	6	7			9^2	4^1		13	10	3	11^3	14	12							8
1	2			5	6	7	8	9		4^1	13	10^2		3	11	12								9
1	2			5	6	7^1	8	9	13	12		10^2		3	11	4								10
1	2	5^8	13	14		8	9^1	10		12		3	11^2		4^3		6	7						11
1	2	3	4^3	5		7	8	13		11^1		10	9^2	14	12		6							12
1	2^3	3	4	5		7	8	13		11^1		10^2	9		12		6	14						13
1	2	3	4	5		7^2	8	12		11		10^1	9		13		6							14
1	2	3	4	5		7^2	8	12		11		10^1	9		13		6							15
1	2	3	4	5		7	8	12		11		10^1	9				6							16
1	2	3	4	5		7	8	12		11		10^1	9				6							17
1	2	3	4	5		7	8	13		11^1		10^2	9		12		6							18
1	2	3^1	4	5		7	8	12		11		10	9^2	13			6							19
1	2		4	5		7	8	12		11		10	9^1	3			6							20
1	2		4	5			8			11		10	9	3	7^1		6							21
1	2		4	5		7		13		11	12	10^2	9	3	8^1		6							22
1	2			5		7	8	12		11^2	4	10^1	9	3	13		6							23
1	2	3		5		7	8^1	13	14	11	4	10^2	9^3		12		6							24
1	2	3	14	5		7	8	12	13	11^3		10^1	9^2		4		6							25
1	2			5		8		14		11^3	4	12	9		7^2			13	3	6		10^1		26
1	2	13		5		7	8	14		11	4^1		9^3		12				3	6		10		27
1	2	3	4^3	5		7	8			10^1		13	12		11		14			6		9^2		28
1	2		4	5		7	8	12		11		10	9^1						3	6				29
1	2			5		7	8			11^1		10	9		6			3	4	12				30
1	2			5		7	8			11^2	12	10	9		6			3	4	13				31
1	2			5		7	8			11		10	9		4			3	6					32
1	2^1			5		7	8^2			11	12	10	9		4			3	6					33
1				5		7	8	14		11^2	2	10^3	9		4			3	6	13		12		34
1		3^3	12	5		7^2	8^1	14	13	2		10	9		4					6		11^8		35
1	2		6	5		7		12		11		10^2	9^1		8			13	3	4				36
1	2		4^3	5		7	12	10		11^2	14		9^1		8			13	3	6				37
1	2		4	5		7		10		11			9		8				3	6				38
1	2		4	5		7	13	10^1		11^2			9		8				3	6		12		39
1	2		4^2	5		7^3		10		11	12		9^1		8			13	3	6		14		40
1		13	4	5				10		11	2		9		8			7^1	3	6		12		41
1				5		7	8	10		11	2	12	9^1		4				3	6				42
1	2^2	13		5		7	8	10^3		11	3	12	9^1		4			14		6				43
1	2			5		7	8	10		11	3	13	9^2		4			12		6^1				44
1	2			5		7^2	8	10^1		11	3	12	9		4					6		13		45
1	2	13	12	5		7	8	10		11	3^2		9		4^1					6				46

FA Cup

First Round	Dagenham & R	(h)	6-1
Second Round	Port Vale	(a)	1-0
Third Round	WBA	(h)	0-2

Play-Offs

Semi-Final	Millwall	(h)	0-0
		(a)	0-2

Carling Cup

First Round	Stockport Co	(h)	3-1
Second Round	Newcastle U	(a)	3-4

J Paint Trophy

First Round	Rotherham U	(a)	2-1
Second Round	Chesterfield	(a)	3-3

HULL CITY   FL Championship

FOUNDATION

The enthusiasts who formed Hull City in 1904 were brave men indeed. More than that they were audacious for they immediately put the club on the map in this Rugby League fortress by obtaining a three-year agreement with the Hull Rugby League club to rent their ground! They had obtained quite a number of conversions to the dribbling code, before the Rugby League forbade the use of any of their club grounds by Association Football clubs. By that time, Hull City were well away having entered the FA Cup in their initial season and the Football League, Second Division after only a year.

The Circle, The KC Stadium, Walton Street, Hull, East Yorkshire HU3 6HU.

Telephone: (01482) 504 600.

Fax: (01482) 304 882.

Ticket Office: (01482) 505 600.

Website: www.hullcityafc.net

Email: info@hulltigers.com

Ground Capacity: 25,404.

Record Attendance: KC Stadium: 25,512 v Sunderland, FL C, 28 October 2007. Boothferry Park: 55,019 v Manchester U, FA Cup 6th rd, 26 February 1949.

Pitch Measurements: 100.5m × 67.5m.

Chairman: Russell Bartlett.

Football Secretary: Phil Hough.

Manager: Nigel Pearson.

Assistant Manager: Craig Shakespeare.

Physio: Simon Maltby.

Colours: Black and amber striped shirts, black shorts, amber stockings with black hoops.

Change Colours: All blue with black trim.

Year Formed: 1904. *Turned Professional:* 1905.

Ltd Co.: 1905.

Club Nickname: 'The Tigers'.

Grounds: 1904, Boulevard Ground (Hull RFC); 1905, Anlaby Road (Hull CC); 1944, Boulevard Ground; 1946, Boothferry Park; 2002, Kingston Communications Stadium.

First Football League Game: 2 September 1905, Division 2, v Barnsley (h) W 4–1 – Spendiff; Langley, Jones; Martin, Robinson, Gordon (2); Rushton, Spence (1), Wilson (1), Howe, Raisbeck.

Record League Victory: 11–1 v Carlisle U, Division 3 (N), 14 January 1939 – Ellis; Woodhead, Dowen; Robinson (1), Blyth, Hardy; Hubbard (2), Richardson (2), Dickinson (2), Davies (2), Cunliffe (2).

HONOURS

Football League: Best season 2007–08, Championship 1 runners-up 2004–05; Division 3 (N) – Champions 1932–33, 1948–49; Division 3 – Champions 1965–66; Runners-up 1958–59, 2003–04; Division 4 – Runners-up 1982–83.

FA Cup: Semi-final 1930.

Football League Cup: best season: 4th, 1974, 1976, 1978.

Associate Members' Cup: Runners-up 1984.

sky SPORTS FACT FILE

On 31 August 1946 Hull City drew 0–0 with Lincoln City on the opening day of the season at the new Boothferry Park ground watched by 25,586, a then record League crowd. On Christmas Day 1948 it was broken in terms of their League gates at 49,655 against Rotherham United.

Record Cup Victory: 8–2 v Stalybridge Celtic (a), FA Cup 1st rd, 26 November 1932 – Maddison; Goldsmith, Woodhead; Gardner, Hill (1), Denby; Forward (1), Duncan, McNaughton (1), Wainscoat (4), Sargeant (1).

Record Defeat: 0–8 v Wolverhampton W, Division 2, 4 November 1911.

Most League Points (2 for a win): 69, Division 3, 1965–66.

Most League Points (3 for a win): 90, Division 4, 1982–83.

Most League Goals: 109, Division 3, 1965–66.

Highest League Scorer in Season: Bill McNaughton, 39, Division 3 (N), 1932–33.

Most League Goals in Total Aggregate: Chris Chilton, 193, 1960–71.

Most League Goals in One Match: 5, Ken McDonald v Bristol C, Division 2, 17 November 1928; 5, Simon 'Slim' Raleigh v Halifax T, Division 3 (N), 26 December 1930.

Most Capped Player: Theo Whitmore, 28 (105), Jamaica.

Most League Appearances: Andy Davidson, 520, 1952–67.

Youngest League Player: Matthew Edeson, 16 years 63 days v Fulham, 10 October 1992.

Record Transfer Fee Received: £2,000,000 from Sunderland for Michael Turner, September 2009.

Record Transfer Fee Paid: £5,000,000 to Fulham for Jimmy Bullard, January 2009.

Football League Record: 1905 Elected to Division 2; 1930–33 Division 3 (N); 1933–36 Division 2; 1936–49 Division 3 (N); 1949–56 Division 2; 1956–58 Division 3 (N); 1958–59 Division 3; 1959–60 Division 2; 1960–66 Division 3; 1966–78 Division 2; 1978–81 Division 3; 1981–83 Division 4; 1983–85 Division 3; 1985–91 Division 2; 1991–92 Division 3; 1992–96 Division 2; 1996–2004 Division 3; 2004–05 FL 1; 2005–08 FL C; 2008–10 FA Premier League; 2010– FL C.

LATEST SEQUENCES

Longest Sequence of League Wins: 10, 23.2.1966 – 20.4.1966.

Longest Sequence of League Defeats: 8, 7.4.1934 – 8.9.1934.

Longest Sequence of League Draws: 5, 30.3.1929 – 15.4.1929.

Longest Sequence of Unbeaten League Matches: 19, 13.3.2001 – 22.9.2001.

Longest Sequence Without a League Win: 27, 27.3.1989 – 4.11.1989.

Successive Scoring Runs: 26 from 10.4.1990.

Successive Non-scoring Runs: 6 from 13.11.1920.

MANAGERS

James Ramster 1904–05
  (Secretary-Manager)
Ambrose Langley 1905–13
Harry Chapman 1913–14
Fred Stringer 1914–16
David Menzies 1916–21
Percy Lewis 1921–23
Bill McCracken 1923–31
Haydn Green 1931–34
John Hill 1934–36
David Menzies 1936
Ernest Blackburn 1936–46
Major Frank Buckley 1946–48
Raich Carter 1948–51
Bob Jackson 1952–55
Bob Brocklebank 1955–61
Cliff Britton 1961–70
  (continued as General Manager to 1971)
Terry Neill 1970–74
John Kaye 1974–77
Bobby Collins 1977–78
Ken Houghton 1978–79
Mike Smith 1979–82
Bobby Brown 1982
Colin Appleton 1982–84
Brian Horton 1984–88
Eddie Gray 1988–89
Colin Appleton 1989
Stan Ternent 1989–91
Terry Dolan 1991–97
Mark Hateley 1997–98
Warren Joyce 1998–2000
Brian Little 2000–02
Jan Molby 2002
Peter Taylor 2002–06
Phil Parkinson 2006
Phil Brown *(after caretaker role December 2006)* 2007–10
Ian Dowie *(consultant)* 2010
Nigel Pearson June 2010–

TEN YEAR LEAGUE RECORD

		P	W	D	L	F	A	Pts	Pos
2000-01	Div 3	46	19	17	10	47	39	74	6
2001-02	Div 3	46	16	13	17	57	51	61	11
2002-03	Div 3	46	14	17	15	58	53	59	13
2003-04	Div 3	46	25	13	8	82	44	88	2
2004-05	FL 1	46	26	8	12	80	53	86	2
2005-06	FL C	46	12	16	18	49	55	52	18
2006-07	FL C	46	13	10	23	51	67	49	21
2007-08	FL C	46	21	12	13	65	47	75	3
2008-09	PR Lge	38	8	11	19	39	64	35	17
2009-10	PR Lge	38	6	12	20	34	75	30	19

DID YOU KNOW ?

In 1924–25 and despite missing six games, Paddy Mills scored exactly half of the 50 League goals scored by Hull City. He also managed four of the seven in the FA Cup. In two spells with the club he topped 100 League goals alone for the Tigers.

HULL CITY 2009–10 LEAGUE RECORD

Match No.	Date	Venue	Opponents	Result		H/T Score	Lg Pos.	Goalscorers	Attendance
1	Aug 15	A	Chelsea	L	1-2	1-1	—	Hunt [28]	41,597
2	19	H	Tottenham H	L	1-5	1-3	—	Hunt [25]	24,735
3	22	H	Bolton W	W	1-0	0-0	14	Ghilas [61]	22,999
4	29	A	Wolverhampton W	D	1-1	1-0	14	Geovanni [3]	27,906
5	Sept 12	A	Sunderland	L	1-4	1-1	17	Zayatte [43]	38,997
6	19	H	Birmingham C	L	0-1	0-0	19		23,759
7	26	A	Liverpool	L	1-6	1-2	19	Geovanni [15]	44,392
8	Oct 3	H	Wigan Ath	W	2-1	0-0	18	Vennegoor [60], Geovanni [66]	22,822
9	19	A	Fulham	L	0-2	0-1	—		22,943
10	24	H	Portsmouth	D	0-0	0-0	18		23,720
11	31	A	Burnley	L	0-2	0-1	18		20,219
12	Nov 8	H	Stoke C	W	2-1	0-1	17	Olofinjana [62], Vennegoor [90]	24,516
13	21	H	West Ham U	D	3-3	3-2	16	Bullard 2 (1 pen) [27, 45 (p)], Zayatte [44]	24,909
14	25	H	Everton	W	3-2	3-0	—	Hunt [9], Dawson [20], Marney [28]	24,685
15	28	A	Manchester C	D	1-1	0-1	15	Bullard (pen) [82]	46,394
16	Dec 5	A	Aston Villa	L	0-3	0-2	16		39,748
17	12	H	Blackburn R	D	0-0	0-0	16		24,124
18	19	A	Arsenal	L	0-3	0-1	17		60,006
19	27	H	Manchester U	L	1-3	0-1	19	Fagan (pen) [59]	24,627
20	29	A	Bolton W	D	2-2	0-1	—	Hunt 2 [71, 78]	20,696
21	Jan 16	A	Tottenham H	D	0-0	0-0	18		35,729
22	23	A	Manchester U	L	0-4	0-1	—		73,933
23	30	H	Wolverhampton W	D	2-2	1-0	19	Vennegoor [11], Hunt (pen) [52]	24,957
24	Feb 2	H	Chelsea	D	1-1	1-1	—	Mouyokolo [30]	24,957
25	6	H	Manchester C	W	2-1	1-0	14	Altidore [31], Boateng [54]	24,959
26	10	A	Blackburn R	L	0-1	0-1	—		23,518
27	20	A	West Ham U	L	0-3	0-1	17		33,971
28	Mar 7	A	Everton	L	1-5	1-2	—	Cairney [32]	34,682
29	13	H	Arsenal	L	1-2	1-1	19	Bullard (pen) [28]	25,023
30	20	A	Portsmouth	L	2-3	1-1	19	Folan 2 [27, 73]	16,513
31	27	H	Fulham	W	2-0	1-0	18	Bullard (pen) [16], Fagan [48]	24,361
32	Apr 3	A	Stoke C	L	0-2	0-1	18		27,604
33	10	H	Burnley	L	1-4	1-1	—	Kilbane [3]	24,369
34	17	A	Birmingham C	D	0-0	0-0	18		26,669
35	21	H	Aston Villa	L	0-2	0-1	—		23,842
36	24	H	Sunderland	L	0-1	0-1	18		25,012
37	May 3	A	Wigan Ath	D	2-2	1-1	—	Atkinson [42], Cullen [64]	20,242
38	9	H	Liverpool	D	0-0	0-0	19		25,030

Final League Position: 19

GOALSCORERS

League (34): Hunt 6 (1 pen), Bullard 5 (4 pens), Geovanni 3, Vennegoor 3, Fagan 2 (1 pen), Folan 2, Zayatte 2, Altidore 1, Atkinson 1, Boateng 1, Cairney 1, Cullen 1, Dawson 1, Ghilas 1, Kilbane 1, Marney 1, Mouyokolo 1, Olofinjana 1.
Carling Cup (3): Altidore 1, Cairney 1, Geovanni 1.
FA Cup (1): Geovanni 1.

Myhill B 27	Mouyokolo S 19+2	Dawson A 35	Olofinjana S 11+8	Gardner A 24	Turner M 4	Mendy B 15+6	Marney D 15+1	Folan C 7+1	Boateng G 26+3	Hunt S 27	Barmby N 6+14	Ghilas K 6+7	Geovanni 16+10	Cousin D 1+2	Zayatte K 21+2	Kilbane K 15+6	Altidore J 16+12	Fagan C 20+5	McShane P 26+1	Sonko 19	Vennegoor J 17+14	Cooper L 1+1	Bullard J 13+1	Garcia R 14+4	Duke M 11	Cairney T 10+1	Zaki A 2+4	Cullen M 2+1	Atkinson W 2	Match No.
1	2	3	4	5	6	7^3	8^1	9	10	11^2	12	13	14																	1
1	2^2	3	4	5	6	7		9	8^3	11	13	14	12	10^1																2
1		3	4	5	6			9^1	13	10			7^3	8^2	2	11	12	14												3
1	5	3	4		6			9^1		10	14		7^2	8^3	2	11	12	13												4
1		3	4				14			10			7^2	8	6	11^3	13	9^1	2	5	12									5
1		3	4				14	7^2		11	13	12		8	6			9^1	2	5	10^5									6
1		3							12		6	9	7	8^3	13	11^1	14		2	5	10	4								7
1	14	3	13				4				9		7^1	12	6^2	11			2	5	10^5									8
1		3					14				9^2		7^1	8	6	11	13		2	5	10^5	12								9
1		3	4	5		7^1	8^3				9^2	12	14	11	6				2		10			13						10
		3	4	5		13	8				9^3	14	7		6	11^4	12		2^1		10^2				1					11
		3	4	5		2					14	11	12		6	10^2	9^3				13		8	7^1	1					12
		3		5		2^4	4				11^3			14	6	10^2	9	12			13		8	7^1	1					13
		3		5			7			4	11	13		10^3	6	14	9^1		2		12		8^2	1						14
		3		5			4^2			12	11	13		10^1	6		9^2		2		14		8	7	1					15
		3		5			7^3			4	10	13			6		9^2	12	2		14		8^1	11	1					16
1		3	13	5			7^3			4	10			11	6		12	9^2	2		14		8^1							17
1		4	12	5			14				3	9	11^1			10^2	13	6		7	2		8^2							18
1		3	4	5			11				2^2	9		14	13	6		10^3	7		12		8^1							19
1		3	4^3	5			7				2	9	12		14	6		10^1	11		13		8^2							20
1	14	3		5						4	9	10^1		8^2	6	12			7	2	13		1^3							21
1		3		5			12			4	9	10^1	13	8^3	6	14			7	2			1^2							22
1	3	6		5		7^2			8	11					9^1			2	10		1^3				4	12				23
1	3	6		5					8	11			14	13	9^2	7	2^3		10^8						4	12				24
1	3	6	13	5					8^2	11			14		9^1	7	2		10^2						4	12				25
1	3	6^3	12	5					8^4	11			14		9	7	2^2		10^2						4	13				26
1	3	6	14	5					8	11^1	12				13	7^4	2		10						4^2	9^3				27
1	2								11		10^1		12		6	3	13		5	14	8^2	7			4	9^9				28
1	3	5				2	7	4^6					6^{14}	9^3	11				10^2	12	8	13								29
1	3	6^2				2	4	7	12				11		9	5			10^1				8	13						30
1	3	13				2			4		11	9^1	7	5	6	12			8^2	10										31
1	2					11	6^1	9^2	4				12		3	13	7	5	14		8^{10}									32
1	3	6^1				7			4	12	13		11	9	10^3	2^2	5	14	8											33
	3	6							4				11	12	7	2	5	10^1	8				1	9						34
	3	6	14						4				13	11^3	12	7	2	5	10^1	8			1	9^2						35
	3	6		5		2	10	4^3		7^2	11				9^6	13			8^1				1	12	14					36
	3	6		5		7	12	4					11			10^1			1	8			9	2						37
	3	6		5		2		4			12				11^1	13			10^2				1	8		9	7			38

FA Cup
Third Round Wigan Ath (a) 1-4

Carling Cup
Second Round Southend U (h) 3-1
Third Round Everton (h) 0-4

IPSWICH TOWN   FL Championship

FOUNDATION

Considering that Ipswich Town only reached the Football League in 1938, many people outside of East Anglia may be surprised to learn that this club was formed at a meeting held in the Town Hall as far back as 1878 when Mr T. C. Cobbold, MP, was voted president. Originally it was the Ipswich Association FC to distinguish it from the older Ipswich Football Club which played rugby. These two amalgamated in 1888 and the handling game was dropped in 1893.

Portman Road, Ipswich, Suffolk IP1 2DA.

Telephone: (01473) 400 500.

Fax: (01473) 400 040.

Ticket Office: 0844 8011 555.

Website: www.itfc.co.uk

Email: enquiries@itfc.co.uk

Ground Capacity: 30,311.

Record Attendance: 38,010 v Leeds U, FA Cup 6th rd, 8 March 1975.

Pitch Measurements: 102.46m × 66m.

Chairman: Marcus Evans.

Chief Executive: Simon Clegg CBE.

Secretary: Sally Webb.

Manager: Roy Keane.

First Team Coach: Tony Loughlan.

Physio: Matt Byard.

Colours: Blue shirts with white trim, white shorts, blue stockings.

Change Colours: Black shirts with white trim, black shorts and stockings.

Year Formed: 1878.

Turned Professional: 1936.

Ltd Co.: 1936.

Club Nicknames: 'Blues' or 'Town' or 'Tractor Boys'.

Grounds: 1878, Broom Hill and Brook's Hall; 1884, Portman Road.

Record League Victory: 7–0 v Portsmouth, Division 2, 7 November 1964 – Thorburn; Smith, McNeil; Baxter, Bolton, Thompson; Broadfoot (1), Hegan (2), Baker (1), Leadbetter, Brogan (3). 7–0 v Southampton, Division 1, 2 February 1974 – Sivell; Burley, Mills (1), Morris, Hunter, Beattie (1), Hamilton (2), Viljoen, Johnson, Whymark (2), Lambert (1) (Woods). 7–0 v WBA, Division 1, 6 November 1976 – Sivell; Burley, Mills, Talbot, Hunter, Beattie (1), Osborne, Wark (1), Mariner (1) (Bertschin), Whymark (4), Woods.

HONOURS

Football League: Division 1 – Champions 1961–62; Runners-up 1980–81, 1981–82; Division 2 – Champions 1960–61, 1967–68, 1991–92; Division 3 (S) – Champions 1953–54, 1956–57.

FA Cup: Winners 1978.

Football League Cup: Semi-final 1982, 1985.

Texaco Cup: Winners 1973.

European Competitions: European Cup: 1962–63. *European Cup-Winners' Cup:* 1978–79. *UEFA Cup:* 1973–74, 1974–75, 1975–76, 1977–78, 1979–80, 1980–81 (winners), 1981–82, 1982–83, 2001–02, 2002–03.

sky SPORTS FACT FILE

In 1938 Ipswich Town secured several notable players: Mick Burns, Preston North End's 1937 FA Cup final goalkeeper, England winger Ellis Rimmer from Sheffield Wednesday, Manchester City full-back Billy Dale and Trevor Morris, later to become Welsh FA secretary.

First Football League Game: 27 August 1938, Division 3 (S), v Southend U (h) W 4–2 – Burns; Dale, Parry; Perrett, Fillingham, McLuckie; Williams, Davies (1), Jones (2), Alsop (1), Little.

Record Cup Victory: 10–0 v Floriana, European Cup prel. rd, 25 September 1962 – Bailey; Malcolm, Compton; Baxter, Laurel, Elsworthy (1); Stephenson, Moran (2), Crawford (5), Phillips (2), Blackwood.

Record Defeat: 1–10 v Fulham, Division 1, 26 December 1963.

Most League Points (2 for a win): 64, Division 3 (S), 1953–54 and 1955–56.

Most League Points (3 for a win): 87, Division 1, 1999–2000.

Most League Goals: 106, Division 3 (S), 1955–56.

Highest League Scorer in Season: Ted Phillips, 41, Division 3 (S), 1956–57.

Most League Goals in Total Aggregate: Ray Crawford, 204, 1958–63 and 1966–69.

Most League Goals in One Match: 5, Alan Brazil v Southampton, Division 1, 16 February 1981.

Most Capped Player: Allan Hunter, 47 (53), Northern Ireland.

Most League Appearances: Mick Mills, 591, 1966–82.

Youngest League Player: Jason Dozzell, 16 years 56 days v Coventry C, 4 February 1984.

Record Transfer Fee Received: £6,000,000 from Newcastle U for Kieron Dyer, July 1999 and £6,000,000 from Arsenal for Richard Wright, July 2001.

Record Transfer Fee Paid: £5,000,000 to Sampdoria for Matteo Sereni, August 2001.

Football League Record: 1938 Elected to Division 3 (S); 1954–55 Division 2; 1955–57 Division 3 (S); 1957–61 Division 2; 1961–64 Division 1; 1964–68 Division 2; 1968–86 Division 1; 1986–92 Division 2; 1992–95 FA Premier League; 1995–2000 Division 1; 2000–02 FA Premier League; 2002–04 Division 1; 2004– FL C.

MANAGERS

Mick O'Brien 1936–37
Scott Duncan 1937–55
  (continued as Secretary)
Alf Ramsey 1955–63
Jackie Milburn 1963–64
Bill McGarry 1964–68
Bobby Robson 1969–82
Bobby Ferguson 1982–87
Johnny Duncan 1987–90
John Lyall 1990–94
George Burley 1994–2002
Joe Royle 2002–06
Jim Magilton 2006–09
Roy Keane April 2009–

LATEST SEQUENCES

Longest Sequence of League Wins: 8, 23.9.1953 – 31.10.1953.

Longest Sequence of League Defeats: 10, 4.9.1954 – 16.10.1954.

Longest Sequence of League Draws: 7, 10.11.1990 – 21.12.1990.

Longest Sequence of Unbeaten League Matches: 23, 8.12.1979 – 26.4.1980.

Longest Sequence Without a League Win: 21, 28.8.1963 – 14.12.1963.

Successive Scoring Runs: 31 from 7.3.2004.

Successive Non-scoring Runs: 7 from 28.2.1995.

TEN YEAR LEAGUE RECORD

		P	W	D	L	F	A	Pts	Pos
2000-01	PR Lge	38	20	6	12	57	42	66	5
2001-02	PR Lge	38	9	9	20	41	64	36	18
2002-03	Div 1	46	19	13	14	80	64	70	7
2003-04	Div 1	46	21	10	15	84	72	73	5
2004-05	FL C	46	24	13	9	85	56	85	3
2005-06	FL C	46	14	14	18	53	66	56	15
2006-07	FL C	46	18	8	20	64	59	62	14
2007-08	FL C	46	18	15	13	65	56	69	8
2008-09	FL C	46	17	15	14	62	53	66	9
2009-10	FL C	46	12	20	14	50	61	56	15

DID YOU KNOW ?

In 1923–24 Ipswich Town produced a regular match-day programme for the first time on 16 February, though others had appeared spasmodically. That same season the local Saturday evening newspaper the Green'Un appeared for the first time on 8 September.

IPSWICH TOWN 2009–10 LEAGUE RECORD

Match No.	Date	Venue	Opponents	Result		H/T Score	Lg Pos.	Goalscorers	Attendance
1	Aug 9	A	Coventry C	L	1-2	1-2	—	Walters [28]	16,279
2	15	H	Leicester C	D	0-0	0-0	19		22,454
3	18	H	Crystal Palace	L	1-3	0-0	—	Bruce [62]	20,348
4	22	A	WBA	L	0-2	0-2	23		19,390
5	29	H	Preston NE	D	1-1	1-1	22	Walters [45]	19,454
6	Sept 12	A	Middlesbrough	L	1-3	0-1	23	Walters (pen) [90]	19,742
7	15	H	Nottingham F	D	1-1	1-0	—	Leadbitter [1]	21,130
8	19	A	Doncaster R	D	3-3	0-1	23	Colback [66], Priskin [77], Martin [78]	10,711
9	26	H	Newcastle U	L	0-4	0-3	23		27,059
10	29	A	Sheffield U	D	3-3	2-1	—	Walters [24], Leadbitter [34], McAuley [70]	28,366
11	Oct 3	A	Barnsley	L	1-2	1-1	24	Rosenior [45]	12,224
12	17	H	Swansea C	D	1-1	1-1	24	Counago [15]	19,667
13	20	H	Watford	D	1-1	1-0	—	McAuley [5]	19,283
14	24	A	Plymouth Arg	D	1-1	0-1	24	Stead [68]	10,875
15	31	H	Derby Co	W	1-0	0-0	24	Wright D [86]	20,299
16	Nov 7	A	Reading	D	1-1	1-0	23	Stead [9]	19,053
17	21	H	Sheffield W	D	0-0	0-0	23		19,636
18	29	A	Cardiff C	W	2-1	0-1	22	Walters [73], Stead [85]	19,463
19	Dec 5	A	Bristol C	D	0-0	0-0	22		14,287
20	8	H	Peterborough U	D	0-0	0-0	—		19,975
21	12	H	Blackpool	W	3-1	2-0	20	Stead [1], Colback [45], McAuley [71]	19,831
22	26	A	Crystal Palace	L	1-3	1-1	21	Peters [19]	16,496
23	28	H	QPR	W	3-0	1-0	19	Walters [4], Stead 2 [63, 78]	25,349
24	Jan 10	A	Leicester C	D	1-1	1-1	—	McGivern (og) [1]	20,758
25	16	H	Coventry C	W	3-2	1-1	19	John [42], Colback [52], Counago [90]	20,135
26	26	H	WBA	D	1-1	0-0	—	Leadbitter (pen) [68]	19,574
27	30	A	Preston NE	L	0-2	0-0	21		12,087
28	Feb 6	H	Middlesbrough	D	1-1	1-0	21	Murphy D [1]	21,243
29	9	A	QPR	W	2-1	2-0	—	Norris [8], Murphy D [38]	10,940
30	16	A	Peterborough U	L	1-3	1-0	—	Murphy D [9]	9428
31	20	A	Sheffield W	W	1-0	1-0	19	Edwards [15]	21,641
32	23	A	Scunthorpe U	D	1-1	0-0	—	Healy D [75]	5828
33	27	H	Bristol C	D	0-0	0-0	17		20,302
34	Mar 6	A	Blackpool	L	0-1	0-0	19		8635
35	9	H	Cardiff C	W	2-0	1-0	—	Murphy D 2 [18, 58]	19,997
36	13	H	Scunthorpe U	W	1-0	0-0	17	Wickham [90]	19,378
37	16	A	Watford	L	1-2	0-1	—	Colback [68]	13,996
38	20	H	Barnsley	W	1-0	1-0	15	Murphy D [4]	20,558
39	23	H	Plymouth Arg	L	0-2	0-1	—		19,316
40	27	A	Swansea C	D	0-0	0-0	16		14,902
41	Apr 3	H	Reading	W	2-1	2-0	14	McAuley [41], Walters [45]	21,403
42	5	A	Derby Co	W	3-1	1-0	13	McAuley [4], Edwards [81], Wickham [90]	28,137
43	10	A	Nottingham F	L	0-3	0-0	13		23,459
44	17	H	Doncaster R	D	1-1	0-0	13	Wickham [72]	19,943
45	24	A	Newcastle U	D	2-2	1-1	14	Wickham [42], Walters [90]	52,181
46	May 2	H	Sheffield U	L	0-3	0-1	14		23,003

Final League Position: 15

GOALSCORERS

League (50): Walters 8 (1 pen), Murphy D 6, Stead 6, McAuley 5, Colback 4, Wickham 4, Leadbitter 3 (1 pen), Counago 2, Edwards 2, Bruce 1, Healy D 1, John 1, Martin 1, Norris 1, Peters 1, Priskin 1, Rosenior 1, Wright D 1, own goal 1.
Carling Cup (4): Wickham 2, Priskin 1, Quinn 1.
FA Cup (3): Colback 1, Counago 1, Garvan 1.

Wright R 12	Bruce A 12+1	Delaney D 36	Peters J 22+10	McAuley G 40+1	Balkestein P 8+1	Walters J 43	Norris D 24	Martin L 9+7	Stead J 13+9	Trotter L 11+1	Garvan O 14+11	Priskin T 9+8	Wickham C 9+17	Wright D 25+1	Healy C 3	Quinn A 8+11	Smith T 11+3	Colback J 29+8	Counago P 11+16	Rosenior L 26+3	Edwards C 21+7	Leadbitter G 36+2	Begovic A 6	Juhn S 5+2	Lee-Barrett A 12+1	Murphy D 18	Healy D 5+7	Murphy B 16	O'Connor S 11+1	Clark B -+3	Eastman T 1	Brown T -+1	Match No.
1	2	3	4^2	5	6	7		8^1	9	10^3	11	12	13	14																			1
1		3	4	5	6	7		9^3	10^2	11	14	12	13	2		8^1																	2
1	2	3		5	6	7		9^1	13	4	12	10^2	11			8^3	14																3
1	5				6	7		9	10^2	11	4^1	14	8^3	2			13	3	12														4
1	2			5	6	7		8^1	12	4		9^2	14			13	3	11	10^3														5
1	6	3^3	4	5		9		14			12		13			11^2	10^1	2	7	8													6
1	6	4	12	5^1		9		8	10	14			11^1			13		2^3	7^2	3													7
1	5	4	12			9^2		8			14		11^2	6	13	10	2	7^1	3														8
1	5^1	4^2	13		6	9		8			10^3		12	11	14	2	7	3															9
1		4	5		9^3	13	12	8		10^1		11^2	6		14	2	7	3															10
1		4	5		9	14	13	8		10^1		11^2	6		12	2	7^2	3															11
		4^2	5		9	13		8^3			12		11^1	6	14	10	2		7	1													12
		12	5		9^3	11^1		4			13	2		14	6		10^2	3	7	8	1												13
12		4	5^1		9			14			2		13	6	11	10^3	3^2	7	8	1													14
	5	6	14		9			10^2	4^1		12		2		11		13	3	7^5	8	1												15
	5	6	12		9			10^2			8		2		11^2	14	13	3	7^1	4	1												16
5^1	6		12		9^3			11^2	14	4	10		2		13		3	7	8	1													17
16	6		5	11		12		4	10^1		2		13		3	7^5	8				9	15											18
	6		5	7		10^2		4		2		11^3		14	12	3	13	8		9^1	1												19
	6		5	11^2		10^3		4	13	14		2		12		3	7	8		9^1	1												20
	6	7^1	5		9^2			10	4		2		12		3	13	8			1													21
	6	8	5		9^8			4^2		12	2	10^3	13		11	14	3	7		1													22
	6	4	5		11	2^2		10		12	14		13		3	7	8	9^3	1														23
2^1	3	4	5	6	9	7		13	10^2		11^3		12		8	14	1																24
	3	6	5		9	7^1	14	4^3	12		11	13	2		8	10^2	1																25
	6	4	5	13		7	10^3	14	2^2		11	9^1	3	12	8		1																26
	3	4^1	5	6		7	10^3	12	9^2		11	13	2		8	14	1																27
	6		5		8	7	14	13	2^2		11	12	3		1	9^3	10^1																28
	3	2	5		9	7	14	4^1		11	10^2	12	6		1	8^3	13																29
	3	12	5		9	7	4^1	13	11	14	2	6^2	1	8	10^3																		30
	3		5		9	8	12	2	11	7^5	4	10^1	1	6																			31
	3	14	5		9	8^1	13	2	11	7^5	4	10^2	12	1	6																		32
	3		5		9	6	14	12	11	13	2	7^5	4	10^1	8^2	1																	33
	3	6	5		9	8^3	12	11	14	2	7^5	4	10^1	13	1																		34
	3		5		9	7	4	13	2	11	12	10^5	8^1	1	6																		35
	3^8		5		9	7	4^2	12	2	11	8^3	1^4	10^1	13	1	6																	36
	3		5		9	12	4^1	10^3	11	14	2	6	8^1	13	1	7																	37
	3	13	5		9	6	12	2	11	10^1	7^2	14	8^3	1	4																		38
	3		5		9	6^2	12	2	11	10^3	7^1	13	8	14	1	4																	39
	6	3	5		9	7	2	11	1^2	4	10	1	8^1																				40
	6	3	5		9	7^3	14	12	2	11	13	4	8^2	10^1	1																		41
	6	2^1	5		9	7	10	12	14	11	1^2	4	8^3	1	3^3																		42
	3^2	2	5		9	7	10^3	13	11^1	12	1^2	6	8	14	1	4																	43
	13	5		9	7^2	12	10^3	2	6	11	3	8^8	1	4	14																		44
	3	5		9	7	12	10	2^1	4	11	13	6^3	8^8	1	14																		45
	3	5		9	7^2	4	10	6^1	11^3	8	1	12	13	2^8	14																		46

FA Cup

Third Round	Blackpool	(a)	2-1
Fourth Round	Southampton	(a)	1-2

Carling Cup

First Round	Shrewsbury T	(a)	3-3
Second Round	Peterborough U	(a)	1-2

LEEDS UNITED   FL Championship

FOUNDATION

Immediately the Leeds City club (founded in 1904) was wound up by the FA in October 1919, following allegations of illegal payments to players, a meeting was called by a Leeds solicitor, Mr Alf Masser, at which Leeds United was formed. They joined the Midland League playing their first game in that competition in November 1919. It was in this same month that the new club had discussions with the directors of a virtually bankrupt Huddersfield Town who wanted to move to Leeds in an amalgamation. But Huddersfield survived even that crisis.

Elland Road, Leeds, West Yorkshire LS11 0ES.

Telephone: (0871) 334 1919.

Fax: (0113) 367 6050.

Ticket Office: 0871 334 1992.

Website: www.leedsunited.com

Email: reception@leedsunited.com

Ground Capacity: 39,457.

Record Attendance: 57,892 v Sunderland, FA Cup 5th rd (replay), 15 March 1967.

Pitch Measurements: 115yd × 76yd.

Chairman: Ken Bates.

Chief Executive: Shaun Harvey.

Manager: Simon Grayson.

Assistant Managers: Glynn Snodin, Ian Miller.

Physio: Harvey Sharman.

Colours: White shirts, white shorts, white stockings with yellow trim.

Change Colours: Yellow shirts with blue trim, yellow shorts, yellow stockings.

Year Formed: 1919, as Leeds United after disbandment (by FA order) of Leeds City (formed in 1904).

Turned Professional: 1920.

Ltd Co.: 1920.

Club Nickname: 'The Whites'.

Ground: 1919, Elland Road.

First Football League Game: 28 August 1920, Division 2, v Port Vale (a) L 0–2 – Down; Duffield, Tillotson; Musgrove, Baker, Walton; Mason, Goldthorpe, Thompson, Lyon, Best.

HONOURS

Football League: Division 1 – Champions 1968–69, 1973–74, 1991–92; Runners-up 1964–65, 1965–66, 1969–70, 1970–71, 1971–72; Division 2 – Champions 1923–24, 1963–64, 1989–90; Runners-up 1927–28, 1931–32, 1955–56; FL 1 – Runners-up 2009–10.

FA Cup: Winners 1972; Runners-up 1965, 1970, 1973.

Football League Cup: Winners 1968; Runners-up 1996.

European Competitions: European Cup: 1969–70, 1974–75 (runners-up). *Champions League:* 1992–93, 2000–01 (semi-finalists). *European Cup-Winners' Cup:* 1972–73 (runners-up). *European Fairs Cup:* 1965–66, 1966–67 (runners-up), 1967–68 (winners), 1968–69, 1970–71 (winners). *UEFA Cup:* 1971–72, 1973–74, 1979–80, 1995–96, 1998–99, 1999–2000 (semi-finalists), 2001–02, 2002–03.

sky SPORTS FACT FILE

Dave Mangnall was Leeds United's third choice centre-forward. The other two were injured. He was tried in the stiffs and scored ten in the 13–1 win over Stockport County reserves! He made his first team debut on 28 September 1929 and stayed until Tom Jennings was fit.

Record League Victory: 8–0 v Leicester C, Division 1, 7 April 1934 – Moore; George Milburn, Jack Milburn; Edwards, Hart, Copping; Mahon (2), Firth (2), Duggan (2), Furness (2), Cochrane.

Record Cup Victory: 10–0 v Lyn (Oslo), European Cup 1st rd 1st leg, 17 September 1969 – Sprake; Reaney, Cooper, Bremner (2), Charlton, Hunter, Madeley, Clarke (2), Jones (3), Giles (2) (Bates), O'Grady (1).

Record Defeat: 1–8 v Stoke C, Division 1, 27 August 1934.

Most League Points (2 for a win): 67, Division 1, 1968–69.

Most League Points (3 for a win): 86, FL 1, 2009–10.

Most League Goals: 98, Division 2, 1927–28.

Highest League Scorer in Season: John Charles, 42, Division 2, 1953–54.

Most League Goals in Total Aggregate: Peter Lorimer, 168, 1965–79 and 1983–86.

Most League Goals in One Match: 5, Gordon Hodgson v Leicester C, Division 1, 1 October 1938.

Most Capped Player: Lucas Radebe, 58 (70), South Africa.

Most League Appearances: Jack Charlton, 629, 1953–73.

Youngest League Player: Peter Lorimer, 15 years 289 days v Southampton, 29 September 1962.

Record Transfer Fee Received: £30,000,000 from Manchester U for Rio Ferdinand, July 2002.

Record Transfer Fee Paid: £18,000,000 to West Ham United for Rio Ferdinand, November 2000.

MANAGERS

Dick Ray 1919–20
Arthur Fairclough 1920–27
Dick Ray 1927–35
Bill Hampson 1935–47
Willis Edwards 1947–48
Major Frank Buckley 1948–53
Raich Carter 1953–58
Bill Lambton 1958–59
Jack Taylor 1959–61
Don Revie OBE 1961–74
Brian Clough 1974
Jimmy Armfield 1974–78
Jock Stein CBE 1978
Jimmy Adamson 1978–80
Allan Clarke 1980–82
Eddie Gray MBE 1982–85
Billy Bremner 1985–88
Howard Wilkinson 1988–96
George Graham 1996–98
David O'Leary 1998–2002
Terry Venables 2002–03
Peter Reid 2003
Eddie Gray *(Caretaker)* 2003–04
Kevin Blackwell 2004–06
Dennis Wise 2006–08
Gary McAllister 2008
Simon Grayson December 2008–

Football League Record: 1920 Elected to Division 2; 1924–27 Division 1; 1927–28 Division 2; 1928–31 Division 1; 1931–32 Division 2; 1932–47 Division 1; 1947–56 Division 2; 1956–60 Division 1; 1960–64 Division 2; 1964–82 Division 1; 1982–90 Division 2; 1990–92 Division 1; 1992–2004 FA Premier League; 2004–07 FL C; 2007–10 FL 1; 2010– FL C.

LATEST SEQUENCES

Longest Sequence of League Wins: 9, 26.9.1931 – 21.11.1931.

Longest Sequence of League Defeats: 6, 28.12.2003 – 7.2.2004.

Longest Sequence of League Draws: 5, 19.4.1997 – 9.8.1997.

Longest Sequence of Unbeaten League Matches: 34, 26.10.1968 – 26.8.1969.

Longest Sequence Without a League Win: 17, 1.2.1947 – 26.5.1947.

Successive Scoring Runs: 30 from 27.8.1927.

Successive Non-scoring Runs: 6 from 30.1.1982.

TEN YEAR LEAGUE RECORD

		P	W	D	L	F	A	Pts	Pos
2000-01	PR Lge	38	20	8	10	64	43	68	4
2001-02	PR Lge	38	18	12	8	53	37	66	5
2002-03	PR Lge	38	14	5	19	58	57	47	15
2003-04	PR Lge	38	8	9	21	40	79	33	19
2004-05	FL C	46	14	18	14	49	52	60	14
2005-06	FL C	46	21	15	10	57	38	78	5
2006-07	FL C	46	13	7	26	46	72	36*	24
2007-08	FL 1	46	27	10	9	72	38	76†	5
2008-09	FL 1	46	26	6	14	77	49	84	4
2009-10	FL 1	46	25	11	10	77	44	86	2

*10 pts deducted; †15 pts deducted.

DID YOU KNOW ?

On 3 January 2010 Leeds United visited Old Trafford for an FA Cup third round tie against Manchester United. They won 1–0, their first success there since 1981 when on 28 February they won by the same score line with a second-half goal from Brian Flynn.

LEEDS UNITED 2009–10 LEAGUE RECORD

Match No.	Date	Venue	Opponents	Result	H/T Score	Lg Pos.	Goalscorers	Attendance
1	Aug 8	H	Exeter C	W 2-1	1-0	—	Beckford 2 [13, 88]	27,681
2	15	A	Wycombe W	W 1-0	0-0	3	Becchio [61]	8400
3	18	A	Walsall	W 2-1	0-0	—	Johnson [83], Beckford [86]	8483
4	22	H	Tranmere R	W 3-0	2-0	2	Johnson [14], Beckford [35], Becchio [86]	21,692
5	29	A	Colchester U	W 2-1	0-0	2	Johnson [47], Beckford [64]	8810
6	Sept 5	H	Stockport Co	W 2-0	2-0	2	Grella [9], Michalik [37]	22,870
7	11	A	Southend U	D 0-0	0-0	—		10,123
8	19	H	Gillingham	W 4-1	2-0	1	Johnson 2 [14, 28], Howson [46], Beckford [80]	21,026
9	26	A	Milton Keynes D	W 1-0	0-0	1	Snodgrass [90]	16,713
10	29	H	Carlisle U	D 1-1	1-0	—	Beckford [30]	19,673
11	Cct 3	H	Charlton Ath	D 0-0	0-0	1		31,838
12	19	H	Norwich C	W 2-1	1-1	—	Johnson [15], Beckford [90]	19,912
13	24	A	Millwall	L 1-2	1-1	1	Kisnorbo [12]	14,165
14	27	H	Bristol R	W 4-0	1-0	—	Beckford 2 [9, 65], Vokes [55], Kandol [87]	11,448
15	31	H	Yeovil T	W 4-0	1-0	1	Johnson [42], Gradel [69], Beckford [79], Kandol [84]	24,482
16	Nov 21	A	Brighton & HA	W 3-0	2-0	1	Snodgrass [27], Beckford [43], Kilkenny [90]	7615
17	24	H	Leyton Orient	W 1-0	0-0	—	Gradel [89]	19,744
18	Dec 1	A	Oldham Ath	W 2-0	1-0	—	Kilkenny [37], Becchio [82]	7793
19	5	H	Huddersfield T	D 2-2	1-0	1	Snodgrass [2], Gradel [66]	36,723
20	12	A	Brentford	D 0-0	0-0	1		9031
21	19	H	Southampton	W 1-0	0-0	1	Snodgrass [77]	25,948
22	26	H	Hartlepool U	W 3-1	2-1	1	Beckford 2 [38, 69], Becchio [45]	30,191
23	28	A	Stockport Co	W 4-2	1-1	1	Snodgrass [2], Beckford 2 [67, 90], Bromby [87]	7768
24	Jan 9	H	Wycombe W	D 1-1	1-0	—	Howson [4]	24,383
25	16	A	Exeter C	L 0-2	0-1	1		8549
26	26	A	Swindon T	L 0-3	0-1	—		14,508
27	30	H	Colchester U	W 2-0	1-0	2	Beckford 2 (1 pen) [38 (p), 55]	23,425
28	Feb 6	A	Hartlepool U	D 2-2	1-0	2	Becchio 2 [23, 78]	5115
29	13	A	Leyton Orient	D 1-1	0-0	2	Daniels (og) [90]	8013
30	16	H	Walsall	L 1-2	0-0	—	McSheffrey [54]	18,941
31	20	A	Brighton & HA	D 1-1	0-0	2	Snodgrass [90]	24,120
32	23	H	Oldham Ath	W 2-0	0-0	—	Becchio 2 [54, 61]	17,635
33	27	A	Huddersfield T	D 2-2	0-1	2	Howson [61], Becchio [66]	21,764
34	Mar 6	H	Brentford	D 1-1	0-0	2	Beckford [72]	25,445
35	9	A	Tranmere R	W 4-1	3-1	2	Snodgrass [9], Beckford 2 (1 pen) [16 (p), 65], Becchio [34]	8346
36	13	A	Southampton	L 0-1	0-1	2		30,794
37	22	H	Millwall	L 0-2	0-1	—		21,348
38	27	A	Norwich C	L 0-1	0-0	2		25,445
39	Apr 3	A	Swindon T	L 0-3	0-1	4		27,881
40	5	A	Yeovil T	W 2-1	2-0	4	Naylor 2 [29, 34]	6308
41	10	H	Southend U	W 2-0	0-0	4	Gradel [60], Becchio [83]	21,650
42	13	A	Carlisle U	W 3-1	1-1	2	Becchio 2 [13, 51], Gradel [47]	8728
43	17	A	Gillingham	L 2-3	1-3	2	Becchio [45], Beckford (pen) [87]	9649
44	24	H	Milton Keynes D	W 4-1	2-1	2	Becchio [13], Gradel [33], Beckford 2 (1 pen) [80, 86 (p)]	25,964
45	May 1	A	Charlton Ath	L 0-1	0-0	2		23,198
46	8	H	Bristol R	W 2-1	0-0	2	Howson [69], Beckford [63]	38,234

Final League Position: 2

GOALSCORERS

League (77): Beckford 25 (4 pens), Becchio 15, Johnson 7, Snodgrass 7, Gradel 6, Howson 4, Kandol 2, Kilkenny 2, Naylor 2, Bromby 1, Grella 1, Kisnorbo 1, McSheffrey 1, Michalik 1, Vokes 1, own goal 1.
Carling Cup (3): Snodgrass 2, Showunmi 1.
FA Cup (12): Beckford 5 (1 pen), Grella 3, Becchio 2, Howson 1, Kandol 1.
J Paint Trophy (11): Crowe 2, Kilkenny 2, Beckford 1, Ephraim 1, Grella 1, Kandol 1, Robinson 1, Snodgrass 1, own goal 1.

Higgs S 19	Crowe J 16+1	Parker B 2+2	Doyle M 42	Rui Marques M 5	Kisnorbo P 29	Johnson B 26+10	Howson J 39+6	Beckford J 38+4	Becchio L 32+5	Snodgrass R 40+4	Hughes A 38+1	Robinson A —+6	Showunmi E —+7	Prutton D 1+5	Killkenny N 24+11	Grella M 3+14	Michalik L 7+6	Bromby L 31+1	Ankergren C 27+2	Naylor R 29	Vokes S 8	Kandol T —+10	Gradel M 11+21	White A 4+4	Capaldi T 3	Ephraim H 1+2	Lowry S 11	McSheffrey G 9+1	Dickov P 1+3	Collins N 9	Watt S 1+5	Match No
1	2	3¹	4	5	6	7²	8	9	10³	11	12	13	14																			1
1	2		4	5	6	7	8	9	10²	11¹	3	13	12																			2
1	2		4¹	5	6	7	8	9	10	11³	3²	13			14	12																3
1	2		4¹	5	6	7	8	9³	10	11²	3	13			12	14																4
1	2		4	5²	6	7	8	9	10³	11¹	3		14	12			13															5
1	2		4¹			7	8		10	11	3	13	14		12	9³	6	5²														6
1	2¹		4		6	7	8	9	10³	11²	3				13	14	12	5														7
1	2¹		4		6	7	8	9	10³	11²	3				12	14	13	5														8
1⁶	2¹		4		6	7	8	9		11		3²	13		10	12		5	15													9
			4		6	7	8²	9	10³	11	3				5¹	1	2															10
			4		6	7	8	9	10¹				3²	13	12			5	1	2												11
1⁶	2		4			7	8	9		11²	6				5	15	3	10¹	12	13												12
			4³		3	7	8	9		11²	6		14		5	1	2	10¹	12	13												13
			4¹		6	7	8	9²		11	3				12		5	1	2	10	14	13										14
			3²		6	7	8	9³		11	4¹				13		5	1	2	10	14	12										15
			4		3	11¹	9³		7	2		13	12	8			6	5	1	10²		14										16
			2		6		8³	9		11	3²			7	14	4	5	1	10¹		13	12										17
	2					8		13	12					7	4	14	6	5	1	10²		9³		3	11¹							18
	2		7			8		9	12	11³					4¹		6	5	1	10²		13		3	14							19
	14		2		6		8³	9	10¹		11				4		5	1		12	7²	13		3								20
			4		6	13	8²	9¹	10	11	3				7			5	1	2		12										21
			3¹		6	12	8	9	10²	11	7				4			5	1	2³		14	13									22
			3¹		6	7	12	9	10³	11²	8				4			5	1	2		14	13									23
	2		3		6	7²	8	9	10³	11¹					4	14		1	5			12	13									24
			3¹		6	7	12	9	10²	11	8				4	14		5	1	2³		13										25
	2¹		4		6	11³	8	9	12	10	3				7²	13	5	1		14												26
			3			12	8	9	10	11					6	5	1	4	13			2¹	7²									27
			4			13	8	9¹	10	12					6	2	1	3		7		5	11²									28
	2					11	13		10	9³					4²	12	5	1	3			7¹	14			6	8					29
	2					7	14	9	10²	8¹					4³	13	5	1	3			12				6	11					30
			2		5	7²	8¹	9	13	14	11				4		1	3				12				6	10³					31
			4		5	13	8	9²	10³	11	7				14		1	2				12	3¹			6						32
			3		5	12	4	9	10²	11	8						1	2		13						6	7¹					33
			3		6	14	4	9	10³	11	7¹				12	5	1	2					2²				8	13				34
			3		5		4	9³	10²	11¹	7					12	1	2		13	6						8	14				35
			3		5		4	9³	10³	11	7	13				12	1	2		14	6¹						8²					36
			3²		6¹	7³	4		10	11	8	13					5	1	2		14	12						9				37
1			3			13	4	9	10¹	11	7³	8²	12				2	14⁴					6						5			38
1	12	3²				4	9		11	7		8	10³				2¹			13			6		14	5						39
1		3				12	4	9²		10	7	8				5	2		11									6	13			40
1		3				12	4	9²	13	10³	7¹	8				5	2		11									6	14			41
1		3					4	12	10²	9	7	8	13			5	2		11¹									6				42
1	12	3					4	13	10³	9²	7¹	8				5	2		11									6	14			43
1		3¹				7	12	13	10	11²	6	4					2		9			14						5	8³			44
1		3²				7		12	10	11¹	8³	4	14				2		9		6						5	13				45
1		3				7	12	9³	10²	14	8	4				5			11⁸		6¹						2	13				46

FA Cup

First Round	Oldham Ath	(a)	2-0
Second Round	Kettering T	(a)	1-1
		(h)	5-1
Third Round	Manchester U	(a)	1-0
Fourth Round	Tottenham H	(a)	2-2
		(h)	1-3

Carling Cup

First Round	Darlington	(a)	1-0
Second Round	Watford	(h)	2-1
Third Round	Liverpool	(h)	0-1

J Paint Trophy

Second Round	Darlington	(h)	2-1
Northern Quarter-Final	Grimsby T	(h)	3-1
Northern Semi-Final	Accrington S	(h)	2-0
Northern Final	Carlisle U	(h)	1-2
		(a)	3-2

LEICESTER CITY   FL Championship

FOUNDATION

In 1884 a number of young footballers who were mostly old boys of Wyggeston School, held a meeting at a house on the Roman Fosse Way and formed Leicester Fosse FC. They collected 9d (less than 4p) towards the cost of a ball, plus the same amount for membership. Their first professional, Harry Webb from Stafford Rangers, was signed in 1888 for 2s 6d (12p) per week, plus travelling expenses.

Walkers Stadium, Filbert Way, Leicester LE2 7FL.
Telephone: 0844 815 6000.
Fax: (0116) 229 4549.
Ticket Office: 0844 815 5000.
Website: www.lcfc.co.uk
Email: customer.relations@lcfc.co.uk
Ground Capacity: 32,312.
Record Attendance: 47,298 v Tottenham H, FA Cup 5th rd, 18 February 1928.
Pitch Measurements: 110yd × 74yd.
Chairman: Milan Mandaric.
Chief Executive: Lee Hoos.
Secretary: Andrew Neville.
Manager: Paulo Sousa.
Assistant Manager: Bruno Oliveira.
Physio: Dave Rennie.
Colours: Blue shirts with white trim, white shorts, blue stockings with white trim.
Change Colours: Black shirts with one diagonal light blue stripe, black shorts, black stockings.
Year Formed: 1884.
Turned Professional: 1888.   *Ltd Co:* 1897.
Previous Name: 1884, Leicester Fosse; 1919, Leicester City.
Club Nickname: 'Foxes'.
Grounds: 1884, Victoria Park; 1887, Belgrave Road; 1888, Victoria Park; 1891, Filbert Street; 2002, Walkers Stadium.
First Football League Game: 1 September 1894, Division 2, v Grimsby T (a) L 3–4 – Thraves; Smith, Bailey; Seymour, Brown, Henrys; Hill, Hughes, McArthur (1), Skea (2), Priestman.
Record League Victory: 10–0 v Portsmouth, Division 1, 20 October 1928 – McLaren; Black, Brown; Findlay, Carr, Watson; Adcock, Hine (3), Chandler (6), Lochhead, Barry (1).
Record Cup Victory: 8–1 v Coventry C (a), League Cup 5th rd, 1 December 1964 – Banks; Sjoberg, Norman (2); Roberts, King, McDerment; Hodgson (2), Cross, Goodfellow, Gibson (1), Stringfellow (2), (1 og).

HONOURS

Football League: Division 1 – Runners-up 1928–29; Division 2 – Champions 1924–25, 1936–37, 1953–54, 1956–57, 1970–71, 1979–80; Runners-up 1907–08; FL 1 – Champions 2008–09.

FA Cup: Runners-up 1949, 1961, 1963, 1969.

Football League Cup: Winners 1964, 1997, 2000; Runners-up 1965, 1999.

European Competitions: European Cup-Winners' Cup: 1961–62. *UEFA Cup:* 1997–98, 2000–01.

sky SPORTS FACT FILE

Leicester City have been unusual in recording high-scoring drawn matches. In the First Division it was 6–6 with Arsenal (1930), Premier League 4–4 with Aston Villa (1995), and two in the FA Cup 5–5 with Tottenham Hotspur (1914) and 5–5 with Luton Town (1949).

Record Defeat: 0–12 (as Leicester Fosse) v Nottingham F, Division 1, 21 April 1909.

Most League Points (2 for a win): 61, Division 2, 1956–57.

Most League Points (3 for a win): 96, FL 1, 2008–09.

Most League Goals: 109, Division 2, 1956–57.

Highest League Scorer in Season: Arthur Rowley, 44, Division 2, 1956–57.

Most League Goals in Total Aggregate: Arthur Chandler, 259, 1923–35.

Most League Goals in One Match: 6, John Duncan v Port Vale, Division 2, 25 December 1924; 6, Arthur Chandler v Portsmouth, Division 1, 20 October 1928.

Most Capped Player: John O'Neill, 39, Northern Ireland.

Most League Appearances: Adam Black, 528, 1920–35.

Youngest League Player: Dave Buchanan, 16 years 192 days v Oldham Ath, 1 January 1979.

Record Transfer Fee Received: £11,000,000 from Liverpool for Emile Heskey, March 2000.

Record Transfer Fee Paid: £5,000,000 to Wolverhampton W for Ade Akinbiyi, July 2000.

Football League Record: 1894 Elected to Division 2; 1908–09 Division 1; 1909–25 Division 2; 1925–35 Division 1; 1935–37 Division 2; 1937–39 Division 1; 1946–54 Division 2; 1954–55 Division 1; 1955–57 Division 2; 1957–69 Division 1; 1969–71 Division 2; 1971–78 Division 1; 1978–80 Division 2; 1980–81 Division 1; 1981–83 Division 2; 1983–87 Division 1; 1987–92 Division 2; 1992–94 Division 1; 1994–95 FA Premier League; 1995–96 Division 1; 1996–2002 FA Premier League; 2002–03 Division 1; 2003–04 FA Premier League; 2004–08 FL C; 2008–09 FL 1; 2009– FL C.

LATEST SEQUENCES

Longest Sequence of League Wins: 7, 28.2.1993 – 27.3.1993.

Longest Sequence of League Defeats: 8, 17.3.2001 – 28.4.2001.

Longest Sequence of League Draws: 6, 21.8.1976 – 18.9.1976.

Longest Sequence of Unbeaten League Matches: 23, 1.11.2008 – 7.3.2009.

Longest Sequence Without a League Win: 18, 12.4.1975 – 1.11.1975.

Successive Scoring Runs: 31 from 12.11.1932.

Successive Non-scoring Runs: 7 from 21.11.1987.

MANAGERS

Frank Gardner 1884–92
Ernest Marson 1892–94
J. Lee 1894–95
Henry Jackson 1895–97
William Clark 1897–98
George Johnson 1898–1912
Jack Bartlett 1912–14
Louis Ford 1914–15
Harry Linney 1915–19
Peter Hodge 1919–26
Willie Orr 1926–32
Peter Hodge 1932–34
Arthur Lochhead 1934–36
Frank Womack 1936–39
Tom Bromilow 1939–45
Tom Mather 1945–46
John Duncan 1946–49
Norman Bullock 1949–55
David Halliday 1955–58
Matt Gillies 1958–68
Frank O'Farrell 1968–71
Jimmy Bloomfield 1971–77
Frank McLintock 1977–78
Jock Wallace 1978–82
Gordon Milne 1982–86
Bryan Hamilton 1986–87
David Pleat 1987–91
Gordon Lee 1991
Brian Little 1991–94
Mark McGhee 1994–95
Martin O'Neill 1995–2000
Peter Taylor 2000–01
Dave Bassett 2001–02
Micky Adams 2002–04
Craig Levein 2004–06
Robert Kelly 2006–07
Martin Allen 2007
Gary Megson 2007
Ian Holloway 2007–08
Nigel Pearson June 2008–10
Paulo Sousa July 2010–

TEN YEAR LEAGUE RECORD

		P	W	D	L	F	A	Pts	Pos
2000-01	PR Lge	38	14	6	18	39	51	48	13
2001-02	PR Lge	38	5	13	20	30	64	28	20
2002-03	Div 1	46	26	14	6	73	40	92	2
2003-04	PR Lge	38	6	15	17	48	65	33	18
2004-05	FL C	46	12	21	13	49	46	57	15
2005-06	FL C	46	13	15	18	51	59	54	16
2006-07	FL C	46	13	14	19	49	64	53	19
2007-08	FL C	46	12	16	18	42	45	52	22
2008-09	FL 1	46	27	15	4	84	39	96	1
2009-10	FL C	46	21	13	12	61	45	76	5

DID YOU KNOW

In 1922 Leicester City signed the Duncan brothers John and Tom from Raith Rovers. John Duncan scored twice on his debut and was also a constructive midfield player, his brother a right-winger. Tom Duncan's daughter Elsie later married Don Revie.

LEICESTER CITY 2009–10 LEAGUE RECORD

Match No.	Date	Venue	Opponents	Result	H/T Score	Lg Pos.	Goalscorers	Attendance
1	Aug 8	H	Swansea C	W 2-1	0-1	—	Waghorn [69], N'Guessan [72]	26,171
2	15	A	Ipswich T	D 0-0	0-0	7		22,454
3	18	A	Sheffield U	D 1-1	0-0	—	Fryatt [52]	26,069
4	22	H	Barnsley	W 1-0	0-0	7	Fryatt [54]	21,799
5	31	A	Newcastle U	L 0-1	0-0	—		38,813
6	Sept 12	H	Blackpool	W 2-1	1-1	6	Fryatt 2 [26, 58]	22,827
7	15	H	Peterborough U	D 1-1	0-1	—	Fryatt (pen) [47]	21,485
8	19	A	Watford	D 3-3	2-0	9	Fryatt 2 (1 pen) [20 (p), 40], N'Guessan [90]	14,647
9	26	H	Preston NE	L 1-2	0-1	10	Berner [90]	20,623
10	29	A	Middlesbrough	W 1-0	0-0	—	Dyer [83]	18,577
11	Oct 3	A	Coventry C	D 1-1	0-1	7	Waghorn [71]	22,209
12	17	H	Derby Co	D 0-0	0-0	8		28,875
13	20	H	Crystal Palace	W 2-0	0-0	—	Gallagher 2 [59, 81]	22,220
14	26	A	Reading	W 1-0	1-0	—	Waghorn [45]	18,192
15	30	A	QPR	W 2-1	1-1	—	Fryatt 2 [37, 64]	17,082
16	Nov 7	H	WBA	L 1-2	0-2	6	Berner [90]	28,748
17	21	H	Plymouth Arg	W 1-0	0-0	3	King A [90]	27,174
18	28	A	Scunthorpe U	D 1-1	1-0	3	Waghorn [3]	6884
19	Dec 5	A	Nottingham F	L 1-5	0-2	4	Waghorn (pen) [64]	28,626
20	8	H	Bristol C	L 1-3	0-2	—	Fryatt [90]	19,349
21	12	H	Sheffield W	W 3-0	2-0	5	Howard [8], King A 2 [25, 73]	22,236
22	26	H	Sheffield U	W 2-1	2-0	4	Morrison [26], Fryatt (pen) [35]	23,999
23	Jan 10	H	Ipswich T	D 1-1	1-1	—	Howard [38]	20,758
24	16	A	Swansea C	L 0-1	0-1	7		15,037
25	26	A	Barnsley	L 0-1	0-0	—		12,065
26	30	H	Newcastle U	D 0-0	0-0	8		29,067
27	Feb 6	A	Blackpool	W 2-1	1-0	6	N'Guessan [15], Dyer [78]	8484
28	9	H	Doncaster R	D 0-0	0-0	—		18,928
29	13	H	Scunthorpe U	W 5-1	4-0	6	Morrison [6], Gallagher 3 [16, 25, 73], Waghorn [34]	21,626
30	16	A	Bristol C	D 1-1	0-0	—	Dyer [90]	13,746
31	20	A	Plymouth Arg	D 1-1	1-1	6	Arnason (og) [32]	11,581
32	23	A	Doncaster R	W 1-0	1-0	—	Waghorn [12]	11,027
33	27	H	Nottingham F	W 3-0	0-0	5	Berner [68], Gallagher [79], King A [81]	31,759
34	Mar 6	A	Sheffield W	L 0-2	0-1	5		21,647
35	13	H	Cardiff C	W 1-0	1-0	5	Waghorn [29]	22,767
36	16	A	Crystal Palace	W 1-0	0-0	—	Berner [53]	12,721
37	21	H	Coventry C	D 2-2	2-0	4	King A 2 [4, 19]	23,093
38	24	H	Reading	L 1-2	1-1	—	Waghorn [40]	20,108
39	27	A	Derby Co	L 0-1	0-1	6		30,259
40	30	A	Cardiff C	L 1-2	0-2	—	Howard [62]	20,438
41	Apr 2	A	WBA	L 0-3	0-2	—		23,334
42	5	H	QPR	W 4-0	2-0	6	King A [5], Waghorn 2 [45, 50], Howard [78]	22,079
43	10	A	Peterborough U	W 2-1	1-0	5	Howard [40], King A [66]	9651
44	17	H	Watford	W 4-1	2-0	5	Waghorn (pen) [36], Gallagher [41], Spearing [51], Vaughan [67]	24,765
45	24	A	Preston NE	W 1-0	0-0	5	King A [63]	14,926
46	May 2	H	Middlesbrough	W 2-0	1-0	5	Kermorgant [41], Wellens (pen) [86]	30,223

Final League Position: 5

GOALSCORERS

League (61): Waghorn 12 (2 pens), Fryatt 11 (3 pens), King A 9, Gallagher 7, Howard 5, Berner 4, Dyer 3, N'Guessan 3, Morrison 2, Kermorgant 1, Spearing 1, Vaughan 1, Wellens 1 (pen), own goal 1.
Carling Cup (3): Adams 1, Fryatt 1, N'Guessan 1.
FA Cup (4): N'Guessan 2, King A 1, Morrison 1.
Play-Offs (3): Fryatt 1, King A 1, own goal 1.

Weale C 45	Morrison M 30 + 1	Berner B 34 + 1	King A 37 + 6	Brown W 38 + 1	Hobbs J 44	Oakley M 37 + 1	Wellens R 41	Howard S 17 + 19	Fryatt M 26 + 3	Dyer L 25 + 8	N'Guessan D 16 + 11	Waghorn M 27 + 16	Adams N 1 + 17	Neilson R 19	Gallagher P 31 + 10	Dickov P — + 1	Tunchev A 1 + 1	Kermorgant Y 9 + 11	Campbell D — + 3	McGivern R 9 + 3	O'Neill I — + 1	Powell C 2	Solano N 6 + 5	Bruce A 2 + 1	Logan C 1 + 1	Vaughan J 2 + 6	Spearing J 6 + 1	Match No.
1	2	3	4¹	5	6		7	8	9	10²	11³	12	13	14														1
1		3	12	5	6	4	8	9	10²	7³	11¹	13	14	2														2
1		3	14	5	6	4	8	9¹	10	13	7	12³	11²	2														3
1		3	13	5	6	4	8	10³	11¹	7	12	2	9²	14														4
1		3		5	6	4	8	11	10²	12	7³	13	14	2	9¹													5
1		3	12	5	6	4	8	9²	10³	11¹	7	13		2	14													6
1		3	12	5¹	6	4	8	9	10³	7²	14		2	11	13													7
1		3	7	5	6	4	8¹	9	10³	13	14	12	2	11²														8
1		3		5		4	8³	9¹	10	12	7²	13	2	11	6	14												9
1	2	3	8	5	6	4		12	10¹	7	13	14	11³		9²													10
1	2	3	8	5	6	4		13	10²	7	14	11¹	9²	12														11
1	2	3	4	5	6	7	8	9	10¹	11²	12	13																12
1		4	5	6	7	8	9²	10³	11¹	13	3	12	14	2														13
1	14	4	5	6	7	8	13	10¹	9²	3	11³	12	2															14
1	3	4	5	6	7	8	10¹	11	9²	2	12	13																15
1	3	4²	5	6	7¹	8	14	10	11³	9	2	12	13															16
1	3	4	5	6		8	13	10³	12	9¹	14	2	11	7²														17
1	3	4	5	6		8	13	10²	12	9¹	2	7	11															18
1	14	3	4	5	6	8	12	10²	13	9	2³	11¹																19
1	2		4	5	6	7	8	12	11¹	9⁴	10	3																20
1	2	3¹	4	5	6	7	8	9³	10	11²	13	14	12															21
1	2		4		6¹	7	8	9	10	11²	5	13	3	12														22
1	6		4	5		7	8¹	9³	10	11²	13	2	12	14	3													23
1	2		4	5	6	7		12	10²	11³	14	13	8	9¹	3													24
1	2		14	5	6	4	8	13	12	11³	9²	7	10¹					3										25
1	2	3	4	5	6	7	8⁴	13	10³	12	9²	11¹				14												26
1	2	3	4	5	6	8		13	10	12	11³	9¹	7²				14											27
1	2	3	4	5	6	7	8	14	10¹	13	11³	12	5⁴²?															28
1	2¹	3	4	5	6	7²	8		11	14	9	10³	13	12														29
1	2	3	4	5	6	7²	8		11	14	9¹	13	10³	12														30
1	2	3	4	5	6	7	8		11		9¹	10²	12	13														31
1	2	3	4	5	6		8		11	10²	9	13	12	7¹														32
1	2	3	4	5	6	7	8¹	13	11		9³	14	10²	12														33
1⁶	2	3¹	4	5	6	7	8	12	11		9	10²	13	12	5¹	13	15											34
1	2	3	4		6	7²	8	14	11		9³	10	12	5¹	13													35
1	5	3	4		6	7	8	12	11²	13	9¹	14	10³	2														36
1	5		4	13	6	7	8	14	11		9³	10¹	12	3	2²													37
1	5		4		6	7¹	8		11	13	9	10²	3	2	12													38
1	2		4	5	6	7³	8	13	11	14	9²	12	10¹	3														39
1	5		4		6		8	12	11¹	9²	14	3³	10	2	13	7												40
1	5	3	4		6	7³	8	10	11²	9¹	14	2	12	13														41
1	2	3	4	5	6		8¹	10		9²	12	11	13	7														42
1	2	3	4	5	6	13	8	10		9¹	14	11³	12	7²														43
1	2	3	4	5	6		8²	10⁴		9³	13	11¹	14	12	7													44
1	2¹	3	4	5	6			11²	14	9	13	8	12	10³	7													45
				6		4		12	14	11²	13	10¹	8	3	2	5	1	9³	7									46

FA Cup

Third Round	Swansea C	(h)	2-1
Fourth Round	Cardiff C	(a)	2-4

Carling Cup

First Round	Macclesfield T	(a)	2-0
Second Round	Preston NE	(a)	1-2

Play-Offs

Semi-Final	Cardiff C	(h)	0-1
		(a)	3-2

LEYTON ORIENT   FL Championship 1

FOUNDATION

There is some doubt about the foundation of Leyton Orient, and, indeed, some confusion with clubs like Leyton and Clapton over their early history. As regards the foundation, the most favoured version is that Leyton Orient was formed originally by members of Homerton Theological College who established Glyn Cricket Club in 1881 and then carried on through the following winter playing football. Eventually many employees of the Orient Shipping Line became involved and so the name Orient was chosen in 1888.

Matchroom Stadium, Brisbane Road, Leyton, London E10 5NF.

Telephone: 0871 310 1881.

Fax: 0871 310 1882.

Ticket Office: 0871 310 1883.

Website: www.leytonorient.com

Email: info@leytonorient.net

Ground Capacity: 9,300

Record Attendance: 34,345 v West Ham U, FA Cup 4th rd, 25 January 1964.

Pitch Measurements: 110yd × 76yd.

Chairman: Barry Hearn.

Vice-chairman: Eddie Hearn.

Chief Executive: Matthew Porter.

Secretary: Lindsey Martin.

Manager: Russell Slade.

Assistant Manager: Kevin Nugent.

Physio: Dave Appanah.

Colours: Red shirts with white insert and striped sleeves, red shorts, red stockings.

Change Colours: All blue.

Year Formed: 1881. *Turned Professional:* 1903.   *Ltd Co.:* 1906.

Previous Names: 1881, Glyn Cricket and Football Club; 1886, Eagle Football Club; 1888, Orient Football Club; 1898, Clapton Orient; 1946, Leyton Orient; 1966, Orient; 1987, Leyton Orient.

Club Nickname: 'The O's'.

Grounds: 1884, Glyn Road; 1896, Whittles Athletic Ground; 1900, Millfields Road; 1930, Lea Bridge Road; 1937, Brisbane Road.

First Football League Game: 2 September 1905, Division 2, v Leicester Fosse (a) L 1–2 – Butler; Holmes, Codling; Lamberton, Boden, Boyle; Kingaby (1), Wootten, Leigh, Evenson, Bourne.

Record League Victory: 8–0 v Crystal Palace, Division 3 (S), 12 November 1955 – Welton; Lee, Earl; Blizzard, Aldous, McKnight; White (1), Facey (3), Burgess (2), Heckman, Hartburn (2). 8–0 v Rochdale, Division 4, 20 October 1987 – Wells; Howard, Dickenson (1), Smalley (1), Day, Hull, Hales (2), Castle (Sussex), Shinners (2), Godfrey (Harvey), Comfort (2). 8–0 v Colchester U,

HONOURS

Football League: Division 1 best season: 22nd, 1962–63; Division 2 – Runners-up 1961–62; Division 3 – Champions 1969–70; Division 3 (S) – Champions 1955–56; Runners-up 1954–55.

FA Cup: Semi-final 1978.

Football League Cup: best season: 5th rd, 1963.

sky SPORTS FACT FILE

On the last day of the 1959–60 season Eddie Brown hit his 200th career League goal playing for Leyton Orient against Middlesbrough in a 2–2 draw. Three weeks earlier Tommy Johnston had reached his double century in his lengthy service in a 2–0 victory over Liverpool.

Division 4, 15 October 1988 – Wells; Howard, Dickenson, Hales (1p), Day (1), Sitton (1), Baker (1), Ward, Hull (3), Juryeff, Comfort (1). 8–0 v Doncaster R, Division 3, 28 December 1997 – Hyde; Channing, Naylor, Smith (1p), Hicks, Clark, Ling, Joseph R, Griffiths (3) (Harris), Richards (2) (Baker (1)), Inglethorpe (1) (Simpson).

Record Cup Victory: 9–2 v Chester, League Cup 3rd rd, 15 October 1962 – Robertson; Charlton. Taylor; Gibbs, Bishop, Lea; Deeley (1), Waites (3), Dunmore (2), Graham (3), Wedge.

Record Defeat: 0–8 v Aston Villa, FA Cup 4th rd, 30 January 1929.

Most League Points (2 for a win): 66, Division 3 (S), 1955–56.

Most League Points (3 for a win): 81, FL 2, 2005–06.

Most League Goals: 106, Division 3 (S). 1955–56.

Highest League Scorer in Season: Tom Johnston, 35, Division 2, 1957–58.

Most League Goals in Total Aggregate: Tom Johnston. 121, 1956–58, 1959–61.

Most League Goals in One Match: 4, Wally Leigh v Bradford C, Division 2, 13 April 1906; 4, Albert Pape v Oldham Ath, Division 2, 1 September 1924; 4, Peter Kitchen v Millwall, Division 3, 21 April 1984.

Most Capped Players: Tunji Banjo, 7 (7), Nigeria; John Chiedozie, 7 (9), Nigeria; Tony Grealish, 7 (45), Republic of Ireland.

Most League Appearances: Peter Allen. 432, 1965–78.

Youngest League Player: Paul Went, 15 years 327 days v Preston NE, 4 September 1965.

Record Transfer Fee Received: £1,000,000 from Fulham for Gabriel Zakuani, July 2006.

Record Transfer Fee Paid: £175,000 to Wigan Ath for Paul Beesley, October 1989.

Football League Record: 1905 Elected to Division 2; 1929–56 Division 3 (S); 1956–62 Division 2; 1962–63 Division 1; 1963–66 Division 2; 1966–70 Division 3; 1970–82 Division 2; 1982–85 Division 3; 1985–89 Division 4; 1989–92 Division 3; 1992–95 Division 2; 1995–2004 Division 3; 2004–06 FL 2; 2006– FL 1.

LATEST SEQUENCES

Longest Sequence of League Wins: 10, 21.1.1956 – 30.3.1956.

Longest Sequence of League Defeats: 9, 1.4.1995 – 6.5.1995.

Longest Sequence of League Draws: 6, 30.11.1974 – 28.12.1974.

Longest Sequence of Unbeaten League Matches: 13, 30.10.1954 – 19.2.1955.

Longest Sequence Without a League Win: 23, 6.10.1962 – 13.4.1963.

Successive Scoring Runs: 24 from 3.5.2003.

Successive Non-scoring Runs: 8 from 19.11.1994.

MANAGERS

Sam Omerod 1905–06
Ike Ivenson 1906
Billy Holmes 1907–22
Peter Proudfoot 1922–29
Arthur Grimsdell 1929–30
Peter Proudfoot 1930–31
Jimmy Seed 1931–33
David Pratt 1933–34
Peter Proudfoot 1935–39
Tom Halsey 1939
Bill Wright 1939–45
Willie Hall 1945
Bill Wright 1945–46
Charlie Hewitt 1946–48
Neil McBain 1948–49
Alec Stock 1949–59
Les Gore 1959–61
Johnny Carey 1961–63
Benny Fenton 1963–64
Dave Sexton 1965
Dick Graham 1966–68
Jimmy Bloomfield 1968–71
George Petchey 1971–77
Jimmy Bloomfield 1977–81
Paul Went 1981
Ken Knighton 1981–83
Frank Clark 1983–91
  (Managing Director)
Peter Eustace 1991–94
Chris Turner/John Sitton 1994–95
Pat Holland 1995–96
Tommy Taylor 1996–2001
Paul Brush 2001–03
Martin Ling 2004–09
Geraint Williams 2009–10
Russell Slade April 2010–

TEN YEAR LEAGUE RECORD

		P	W	D	L	F	A	Pts	Pos
2000-01	Div 3	46	20	15	11	59	51	75	5
2001-02	Div 3	46	13	13	20	55	71	52	18
2002-03	Div 3	46	14	11	21	51	61	53	18
2003-04	Div 3	46	13	14	19	48	65	53	19
2004-05	FL 2	46	16	15	15	65	67	63	11
2005-06	FL 2	46	22	15	9	67	51	81	3
2006-07	FL 1	46	12	15	19	61	77	51	20
2007-08	FL 1	46	16	12	18	49	63	60	14
2008-09	FL 1	46	15	11	20	45	57	56	14
2009-10	FL 1	46	13	12	21	53	63	51	17

DID YOU KNOW ?

When the Prince of Wales attended Clapton Orient's home match against Notts County on 30 April 1921 it was the first time a member of the Royal family had attended a Football League match. Orient won 3–0 with goals from Tommy Dixon, Jack Forrest and Ernie Gillatt.

LEYTON ORIENT 2009–10 LEAGUE RECORD

Match No.	Date		Venue	Opponents	Result		H/T Score	Lg Pos.	Goalscorers	Attendance
1	Aug	8	A	Bristol R	W	2-1	1-1	—	Melligan [40], Smith [67]	7745
2		15	H	Oldham Ath	L	1-2	1-1	12	Jarvis [31]	4061
3		18	H	Charlton Ath	L	1-2	1-0	—	Mkandawire [27]	7376
4		22	A	Yeovil T	D	3-3	2-2	14	McGleish [5], Townsend [42], Jarvis [61]	3827
5		29	H	Carlisle U	D	2-2	0-1	13	McGleish 2 (1 pen) [48 (p), 85]	3546
6	Sept	4	A	Southend U	L	0-3	0-0	19		8836
7		12	H	Exeter C	D	1-1	1-0	19	Stewart (og) [26]	4703
8		19	A	Stockport Co	L	1-2	0-0	21	Mkandawire [88]	4091
9		26	H	Millwall	W	1-0	0-0	19	Townsend [57]	5255
10		29	A	Norwich C	L	0-4	0-0	—		23,981
11	Oct	3	A	Wycombe W	W	1-0	0-0	16	McGleish [77]	4798
12		10	H	Colchester U	L	0-1	0-0	18		5410
13		17	H	Brentford	W	2-1	1-1	15	McGleish [36], Foster (og) [65]	4781
14		24	A	Huddersfield T	L	0-4	0-1	17		13,396
15		31	H	Southampton	D	2-2	1-0	18	Mkandawire [2], Trotman (og) [56]	7544
16	Nov	14	A	Hartlepool U	L	0-1	0-0	20		3119
17		21	H	Tranmere R	W	2-1	1-1	17	McGleish 2 [24, 70]	4620
18		24	A	Leeds U	L	0-1	0-0	—		19,744
19	Dec	1	A	Gillingham	W	3-1	2-1	—	Jarvis [4], Thornton [28], Smith [49]	3183
20		5	A	Swindon T	L	2-3	0-0	19	Thornton 2 [67, 90]	6815
21		12	H	Milton Keynes D	L	1-2	1-0	20	McGleish [17]	3959
22		19	A	Walsall	D	2-2	2-0	20	Jarvis [2], Mkandawire [29]	3616
23		26	A	Brighton & HA	D	0-0	0-0	20		6690
24		28	A	Southend U	L	1-2	0-0	21	Chambers [57]	5680
25	Jan	19	H	Yeovil T	W	2-0	1-0	—	Mkandawire [14], McGleish [79]	2669
26		25	A	Charlton Ath	W	1-0	0-0	—	McGleish [48]	15,955
27		30	A	Carlisle U	D	2-2	0-2	17	Jarvis [59], Livesey (og) [77]	4687
28	Feb	2	H	Bristol R	W	5-0	1-0	—	Purches [26], Jarvis [51], Andersen (og) [62], Demetriou [71], Tehoue [89]	2931
29		6	H	Brighton & HA	D	1-1	0-1	11	McGleish [53]	6027
30		13	H	Leeds U	D	1-1	0-0	13	Mkandawire [83]	8013
31		20	A	Tranmere R	L	1-2	0-2	14	Tehoue [86]	5357
32		23	A	Gillingham	D	1-1	0-1	—	Mkandawire [72]	4753
33		27	H	Swindon T	D	0-0	0-0	15		4574
34	Mar	6	A	Milton Keynes D	L	0-1	0-1	16		14,323
35		9	A	Oldham Ath	L	0-2	0-1	—		3126
36		13	H	Walsall	W	2-0	0-0	14	Thornton 2 [63, 73]	3685
37		20	A	Huddersfield T	L	0-2	0-1	16		4119
38		27	A	Brentford	L	0-1	0-1	16		6369
39	Apr	3	H	Hartlepool U	L	1-3	0-3	19	Patulea [84]	3604
40		5	A	Southampton	L	1-2	1-1	20	Spicer [2]	21,559
41		10	A	Exeter C	D	0-0	0-0	19		5522
42		13	H	Norwich C	W	2-1	2-1	—	Thornton 2 [3, 29]	7520
43		17	H	Stockport Co	W	2-0	0-0	18	Jarvis [53], Lichaj [80]	4373
44		24	A	Millwall	L	1-2	0-0	18	Chorley [90]	13,011
45	May	1	H	Wycombe W	W	2-0	0-0	18	Jarvis [78], McGleish [90]	5918
46		8	A	Colchester U	L	0-1	0-0	17		5751

Final League Position: 17

GOALSCORERS
League (53): McGleish 12 (1 pen), Jarvis 8, Mkandawire 7, Thornton 7, Smith 2, Tehoue 2, Townsend 2, Chambers 1, Chorley 1, Demetriou 1, Lichaj 1, Melligan 1, Patulea 1, Purches 1, Spicer 1, own goals 5.
Carling Cup (2): Milligan 1, Patulea 1.
FA Cup (1): Ashworth 1.
J Paint Trophy (2): Demetriou 1, Patulea 1.

Jones J 36	Purches S 30+1	Daniels C 40+1	Chorley B 42	Mkandawire T 43	Thornton S 28+2	Meligan J 14+2	Smith J 34+6	McGleish S 36+6	Jarvis R 34+8	Demetriou J 29+10	Scowcroft J 13+13	Townsend A 17+5	Patulea A 4+17	Morris G 10+1	Ashworth L 7+3	Chambers A 26+3	O'Leary K 1+2	Pires L —+8	Cave-Brown A 12+4	Summerfield L 14	Baker H —+4	Briggs M 1	Adams N 6	Tehoue J 5+11	Doran A 6	Lichaj E 9	Spicer J 9	Match No.
1	2	3	4	5	6	7	8	9^1	10	11	12																	1
1	2	3	4	5	6	7^1	8	9^2	10^3	11	13	12	14															2
1	2	3	4	5	6^3	7^2	8	12	10	11	9^1	14	13															3
1	2	3	4	5		7	6	10^2	12	11	9^1	8	13															4
	2	3		5		7	6	10	9^2	11		8^1	13	1	4	12												5
	2	3		5		7^3	6	10	9			8^1	12	1	4	11^2	13	14										6
	2^1	3	4^3	5		7	6	10		11	9		14	1		8^2	13		12									7
1	2^1	3	4	5		7	6	10^3		11	9	13	14			8^2			12									8
1		3	4	5		7	6	13	10^2	11^1	9	12							2	8								9
1		3	4	5		7^4	6	12	10	13	9^1	11^2							2	8								10
1		3	4	5			6	9	10^1	7	11	12							2	8								11
1^6		3	4	5			6	10	11^1	9^2	7	13	15			12			2	8								12
12		3	4	5		13	6	9	10^2	7	11			1					2^1	8								13
		3^1	4	5		12	6	9^2	10^3	7	13	11	14	1					2	8								14
	2	3	4	5^1		7	6	10^3	14	13	11	9^3		1		12				8								15
	2	3	4				8^1	6^2	10		11	9	13	1	5	12					7							16
	2	3	4	5	6		8	9	10^1		11	12		1							7							17
1	2	3	4	5	6		11	9^1	13	12	10					8					7^2							18
1	2	3	4	5	6^1		8	9	10^2	12	11	13									7							19
1	2	3	4	5^4	6		8^1	13	12	11	9^2	10^3	14								7							20
1	2	3	4		6		8^2	9	10^1	13	11	12			5						7							21
1	2		4	5	6	7		9	10^1	11					12	3	8											22
1	2	3	4	5	6	7^3		10^1	13	11	9^2					8			12		14							23
1			4	5		7^2	8	10	13	11	9^1				2	6			12		3							24
1	2	3		5	8^1		12	9	10^2	11					4	6								7	13			25
1	2	3	4	5	8			9^1	10	11						6							7	12				26
1	2	3	4	5	8		13	10^2	11	9^1						6							7	12				27
1	2	3	4	5	8		14	9^2	10^1	11	12					6							7^3	13				28
1	2	3	4	5	8			9^2	10^1	11	13					6							7	12				29
1	2	3	4	5	6^2		13	9^1	10	11						8							7	12				30
1	2	3	4	5	6^1		8	9^2	10^3	11	12					7	14							13				31
1	2	3	4	5	12		7	13	8	11	14					6^1							10^2	9^3				32
1	2		4	5	12		8	9^2	7	11						6^1			3				13	10				33
1	2		4	5	6^3		8	9^1	10	11	12					14			3				13	7^2				34
1	2	3		5			8	14	13	11^3	9				6	4					12		10^2	7^1				35
	2^1	3	4	5	6			9	13	11				1		8			12				10^2	7				36
	3	4	5		8			9	12	11^1	14			1		6			2		13		10^3	7^2				37
1		3	4	5	6		14		12	11^1	9	13				8^3							10^2			2	7	38
1		3	4	5	6		14	9^2	10	11	13					8^3			12							2	7^1	39
1		3^3	4	5			8	10^1	11	9	13					6			14				12^2			2	7	40
1	2	12	4	5			8	10	11^1	13	9^3					14			6					3		7^2		41
1		3	4	5	6		8	9	10^1	11	12															2	7	42
1		3	4	5	6		8	9	10	12						11										2	7^1	43
1		3	4	5	6		8	9^2	10^2	12	13					7	14									2	11^1	44
1		3	4	5	6^2		8	9	10^3	12	14					7							13			2	11^1	45
1			4		6		8^1	9^2	10	12	13					$5^□$	7		3							2	11	46

FA Cup

First Round	Tranmere R	(a)	1-1	
		(h)	0-1	

Carling Cup

First Round	Colchester U	(a)	2-1
Second Round	Stoke C	(h)	0-1

J Paint Trophy

Second Round	Brighton & HA	(h)	1-0
Southern Quarter-Final	Hereford U	(h)	1-1

LINCOLN CITY

FL Championship 2

FOUNDATION

The original Lincoln Football Club was established in the early 1860s and was one of the first provisional clubs to affiliate to the Football Association. In their early years, they regularly played matches against the famous Sheffield Club and later became known as Lincoln Lindum. The present organisation was formed at a public meeting held in the Monson Arms Hotel in June 1884 and won the Lincolnshire Cup in only their third season. They were founder members of the Midland League in 1889 and that competition's first champions.

Sincil Bank Stadium, Sincil Bank, Lincoln LN5 8LD.
Telephone: (01522) 880 011.
Fax: (01522) 880 020.
Ticket Office: (01522) 880 011.
Website: www.redimps.com
Email: lcfc@redimps.com
Ground Capacity: 10,120.
Record Attendance: 23,196 v Derby Co, League Cup 4th rd, 15 November 1967.
Pitch Measurements: 100m × 65m.
Chairman: Bob Dorrian.
Vice-chairman: Chris Travers.
Chief Executive: Dave Roberts.
Football Secretary: Fran Martin.
Manager: Chris Sutton.
Assistant Manager: Ian Pearce.
Physio: Michael Wait.

HONOURS

Football League: Division 2 best season: 5th, 1901–02; Division 3 (N) – Champions 1931–32, 1947–48, 1951–52; Runners-up 1927–28, 1930–31, 1936–37; Division 4 – Champions 1975–76; Runners-up 1980–81.

FA Cup: best season: 1st rd of Second Series (5th rd equivalent), 1887, 2nd rd (5th rd equivalent), 1890, 1902.

Football League Cup: best season: 4th rd, 1968.

GM Vauxhall Conference: Champions 1987–88.

Colours: Red and white striped shirts, black shorts, red stockings.
Change Colours: Grey shirts with dark blue sleeves, dark blue shorts, dark blue stockings.
Year Formed: 1884.
Turned Professional: 1892.
Ltd Co.: 1895.
Club Nickname: 'The Red Imps'.
Grounds: 1883, John O'Gaunt's; 1894, Sincil Bank.
First Football League Game: 3 September 1892, Division 2, v Sheffield U (a) L 2–4 – W. Gresham; Coulton, Neill; Shaw, Mettam, Moore; Smallman, Irving (1), Cameron (1), Kelly, J. Gresham.
Record League Victory: 11–1 v Crewe Alex, Division 3 (N), 29 September 1951 – Jones; Green (1p), Varney; Wright, Emery, Grummett (1); Troops (1), Garvey, Graver (6), Whittle (1), Johnson (1).
Record Cup Victory: 8–1 v Bromley, FA Cup 2nd rd, 10 December 1938 – McPhail; Hartshorne, Corbett; Bean, Leach, Whyte (1); Hancock, Wilson (1), Ponting (3), Deacon (1), Clare (2).

sky SPORTS FACT FILE

Twenty-eight-year-old goalkeeper Dan McPhail was signed by Lincoln City from Portsmouth in 1931 and became a consistent and reliable servant completing 309 League appearances until 1939. It included an initial run of 105 consecutive matches.

Record Defeat: 3–11 v Manchester C, Division 2, 23 March 1895.

Most League Points (2 for a win): 74, Division 4, 1975–76.

Most League Points (3 for a win): 77, Division 3, 1981–82.

Most League Goals: 121, Division 3 (N), 1951–52.

Highest League Scorer in Season: Allan Hall, 41, Division 3 (N), 1931–32.

Most League Goals in Total Aggregate: Andy Graver, 143, 1950–55 and 1958–61.

Most League Goals in One Match: 6, Frank Keetley v Halifax T, Division 3 (N), 16 January 1932; 6, Andy Graver v Crewe Alex, Division 3 (N), 29 September 1951.

Most Capped Player: Gareth McAuley, 5 (21), Northern Ireland.

Most League Appearances: Grant Brown, 407, 1989–2002.

Youngest League Player: Shane Nicholson, 16 years 172 days v Burnley, 22 November 1986.

Record Transfer Fee Received: £750,000 from Liverpool for Jack Hobbs, August 2005.

Record Transfer Fee Paid: £75,000 to Carlisle U for Dean Walling, October 1997 and £75,000 to Bury for Tony Battersby, August 1998.

Football League Record: 1892 Founder member of Division 2. Remained in Division 2 until 1920 when they failed re-election but also missed seasons 1908–09 and 1911–12 when not re-elected. 1921–32 Division 3 (N); 1932–34 Division 2; 1934–48 Division 3 (N); 1948–49 Division 2; 1949–52 Division 3 (N); 1952–61 Division 2; 1961–62 Division 3; 1962–76 Division 4; 1976–79 Division 3; 1979–81 Division 4; 1981–86 Division 3; 1986–87 Division 4; 1987–88 GM Vauxhall Conference; 1988–92 Division 4; 1992–98 Division 3; 1998–99 Division 2; 1999–2004 Division 3; 2004– FL 2.

MANAGERS

David Calderhead 1900–07
John Henry Strawson 1907–14
(had been Secretary)
George Fraser 1919–21
David Calderhead Jnr. 1921–24
Horace Henshall 1924–27
Harry Parkes 1927–36
Joe McClelland 1936–46
Bill Anderson 1946–65
(General Manager to 1966)
Roy Chapman 1965–66
Ron Gray 1966–70
Bert Loxley 1970–71
David Herd 1971–72
Graham Taylor 1972–77
George Kerr 1977–78
Willie Bell 1977–78
Colin Murphy 1978–85
John Pickering 1985
George Kerr 1985–87
Peter Daniel 1987
Colin Murphy 1987–90
Allan Clarke 1990
Steve Thompson 1990–93
Keith Alexander 1993–94
Sam Ellis 1994–95
Steve Wicks *(Head Coach)* 1995
John Beck 1995–98
Shane Westley 1998
John Reames 1998–99
Phil Stant 2000–01
Alan Buckley 2001–02
Keith Alexander 2002–06
John Schofield 2006–07
Peter Jackson 2007–09
Chris Sutton October 2009–

LATEST SEQUENCES

Longest Sequence of League Wins: 10, 1.9.1930 – 18.10.1930.

Longest Sequence of League Defeats: 12, 21.9.1896 – 9.1.1897.

Longest Sequence of League Draws: 5, 21.2.1981 – 7.3.1981.

Longest Sequence of Unbeaten League Matches: 18, 11.3.1980 – 13.9.1980.

Longest Sequence Without a League Win: 19, 22.8.1978 – 23.12.1978.

Successive Scoring Runs: 37 from 1.3.1930.

Successive Non-scoring Runs: 5 from 15.11.1913.

TEN YEAR LEAGUE RECORD

		P	W	D	L	F	A	Pts	Pos
2000-01	Div 3	46	12	15	19	58	66	51	18
2001-02	Div 3	46	10	16	20	44	62	46	22
2002-03	Div 3	46	18	16	12	46	37	70	6
2003-04	Div 3	46	19	17	10	68	47	74	7
2004-05	FL 2	46	20	12	14	64	47	72	6
2005-06	FL 2	46	15	21	10	65	53	66	7
2006-07	FL 2	46	21	11	14	70	59	74	5
2007-08	FL 2	46	18	4	24	61	77	58	15
2008-09	FL 2	46	14	17	15	53	52	59	13
2009-10	FL 2	46	13	11	22	42	65	50	20

DID YOU KNOW ?

Fifty-seven points in successive seasons for Lincoln City but the difference was missing promotion and then gaining it in 1931–32. Having led the table for most of 1930–31 they were denied by one point. The next season they made it – on goal average!

LINCOLN CITY 2009-10 LEAGUE RECORD

Match No.	Date	Venue	Opponents	Result	H/T Score	Lg Pos.	Goalscorers	Attendance
1	Aug 8	H	Barnet	W 1-0	0-0	—	Kovacs [59]	3753
2	15	A	Accrington S	L 0-1	0-0	12		1498
3	18	A	Bradford C	W 2-0	0-0	—	Howe (pen) [62], Fagan [63]	11,242
4	22	H	Burton Alb	L 0-2	0-1	13		3590
5	29	A	Dagenham & R	L 0-3	0-1	17		1810
6	Sept 5	H	Darlington	W 3-0	2-0	12	Howe 2 [3, 30], Fagan [55]	3005
7	12	A	Bournemouth	L 1-3	1-2	14	Fagan [26]	5385
8	19	H	Shrewsbury T	L 0-2	0-1	15		3234
9	26	A	Bury	L 0-2	0-0	19		2554
10	29	A	Notts Co	L 0-3	0-2	—		5527
11	Oct 3	H	Aldershot T	W 1-0	0-0	18	Torres [83]	4131
12	10	A	Macclesfield T	W 1-0	0-0	16	Howe (pen) [70]	2006
13	17	A	Northampton T	L 0-1	0-0	19		4341
14	24	H	Torquay U	D 0-0	0-0	17		3604
15	31	A	Morecambe	L 1-3	0-2	19	Howe [79]	1701
16	Nov 14	H	Cheltenham T	D 1-1	0-1	20	Clarke J [48]	3008
17	21	H	Grimsby T	D 0-0	0-0	20		4981
18	24	A	Rotherham U	L 0-2	0-1	—		2901
19	Dec 1	A	Port Vale	L 1-2	0-1	—	Martin (og) [47]	2569
20	5	A	Crewe Alex	D 0-0	0-0	22		3632
21	12	H	Rochdale	L 1-3	1-2	22	Herd [23]	3293
22	26	H	Chesterfield	W 2-1	2-0	21	Hughton [25], Facey [29]	4604
23	Jan 16	A	Barnet	W 2-1	1-0	—	Hughton [30], John-Lewis [90]	1810
24	23	A	Bradford C	W 2-1	2-0	19	Herd [31], Gilmour [37]	3803
25	27	A	Burton Alb	L 0-1	0-1	—		2109
26	Feb 2	A	Hereford U	L 0-2	0-1	—		1429
27	6	A	Chesterfield	L 1-2	0-1	20	Swaibu [65]	3573
28	9	A	Darlington	D 1-1	0-1	—	Hone [90]	1697
29	13	H	Rotherham U	L 1-2	0-1	20	Lennon [77]	4152
30	16	H	Accrington S	W 2-1	0-1	—	Lennon [83], Kempson (og) [90]	2779
31	20	A	Grimsby T	D 2-2	1-1	19	Herd [4], Gilmour [60]	6395
32	23	A	Port Vale	L 0-4	0-3	—		3231
33	27	H	Crewe Alex	D 1-1	0-0	19	Somma [46]	3110
34	Mar 6	A	Rochdale	D 1-1	1-0	21	Herd [27]	3453
35	12	H	Hereford U	W 3-1	2-1	—	Somma [11], Saunders 2 [20, 70]	6012
36	16	H	Dagenham & R	D 1-1	0-1	—	Somma [68]	2457
37	20	A	Torquay U	W 3-2	1-1	17	Somma 2 [9, 57], Hughton [53]	2547
38	27	H	Northampton T	D 1-1	0-0	18	Saunders [54]	3964
39	Apr 3	A	Cheltenham T	L 0-1	0-0	19		3708
40	5	H	Morecambe	L 1-3	0-1	20	Hughton [66]	3109
41	10	H	Bournemouth	W 2-1	1-0	19	Somma 2 [23, 82]	3040
42	13	A	Notts Co	L 1-3	1-1	—	Lennon [4]	7501
43	17	A	Shrewsbury T	L 0-1	0-0	21		4932
44	24	H	Bury	W 1-0	0-0	20	Somma [80]	3403
45	May 1	A	Aldershot T	L 1-3	0-0	20	Somma [57]	4506
46	8	H	Macclesfield T	D 0-0	0-0	20		3291

Final League Position: 20

GOALSCORERS

League (42): Somma 9, Howe 5 (2 pens), Herd 4, Hughton 4, Fagan 3, Lennon 3, Saunders 3, Gilmour 2, Clarke J 1, Facey 1, Hone 1, John-Lewis 1, Kovacs 1, Swaibu 1, Torres 1, own goals 2.
Carling Cup (0).
FA Cup (6): Clarke J 3, Brown 1, Fagan 1, Torres 1.
J Paint Trophy (0).

Burch R 46	Hughton C 41	Heath J 3 +1	Kovacs J 14	Swaibu M 29 +5	Butcher R 10 +5	Oakes S 11 +5	Clarke J 14 +6	Connor P 8 +7	Somma D 14	Fagan C 10 +3	Brown A 14 +3	Stephens D 3	Coleman-Carr L —+1	Clarke S 21 +8	Howe R 14 +3	Kerr S 36 +3	John-Lewis L 7 +17	Hutchinson A —+10	Bennett L —+1	Adams N —+2	Torres S 7 +1	Hone D 16 +1	Watts A 18	Pulis A 7	Pearce I 5 +5	Lichaj E 6	Baker N 17 +1	Smith K 4 +1	Gordon M 4 +1	Herd C 20	Facey D 9 +1	Gilmour B 14 +2	Green P 13 +2	Anderson J 23	Saunders M 17 +1	Uwezu M —+2	Keltie C 9 +2	Lennon S 15 +4	Broughton D 7	Match No.
1	2	3¹	4	5	6	7²	8	9	10³	11	12	13	14																											1
1	2	3	4	5	8		7¹		9²	11					6	10	12	13																						2
1	2		4	5	8⁹	7²		9			3				10	11	6¹	13	12	14																				3
1	2		4	5	6	7²		9			3				10	11	8¹	12		13																				4
1	2		4	5	6	8²	7¹	9			3				10	11	13	12																						5
1	2		4	5	6	7²	9¹	12			3		14		10	11³	8	13																						6
1	2		4	5	6	7	9²				3				10	11	8¹	12	13																					7
1	2		4	5	6²	13	12	9³			3				10	11	8	14			7¹																			8
1	2³		4	5		12	14	9²			3			8¹	10	11		13			7	6																		9
1	2			5		13	9¹	14			3			8	10	11²	4³	12			7	6																		10
1	2			9	11¹						3			8	10	12					7	6	5																	11
1	14		5	10	8³	12					2			11	9	13					7³	6	3	4¹																12
1	4		10	11¹	13						3			2	9	12					7	6³	5	8²	14															13
1	2		12	8¹	14									10	9²						5	3	7	13	6	4	11³													14
1	2		5			14								10³	13	11	9				12	6¹	4	7		3⁴	8²													15
1			4	5	13	10		9	3⁴					11²							8¹		6			7	12	2												16
1	11		4	13		10		9¹						12		6					5⁵	7				3	8	2												17
1	2		4	12		9			12					10	13	6						8¹		5	7	11²	3													18
1	7					10¹					12			11		6³							2	14	5	4	3²		8	9	13									19
1	11		5			10²			12					8		6	13						2			4	3¹		7	9										20
1	11		5		13	10¹			14					8²		6³	12						2			4	3		7	9										21
1	2	5		12		8								13		6							4			3¹			7	9	10²	11								22
1	11															6	13						4						5	7	9²	8¹	2	3	10	12				23
1	11													13		6	14						4						5	7²	9³	8¹	2	3	10	12				24
1	10		12						14							6	13						4						5¹	7	9²11	2	3			8³				25
1	11		12		7²									14		6	9						4⁵						5¹	13	10	2	3		8				26
1	11²		5						14					8		6	12				4								7¹	9³10	2	3		13					27
1	11²		5					9								6	12				4	2							7	10¹	8	3		13					28
1	11		5⁴		8²			9¹								6	12				4³	2	14						7	10	3		13						29
1	11				8²											6	14					2	12		3¹				7	10³	4	13	5	9					30
1	11		12													6	13								5⁵	2			7	8²	3	10	4	9					31
1	11		5											14		6²	12						4						7³	8	3	10	13	2	9¹				32
1	11		5		10											6							4						7		3	8	12	2¹	9				33
1	11		5	10		13								12		6							2						7¹		3	8	4	9²					34
1	11		5¹	10		14								7		6					12		2²						13	4	8	3	9³						35
1	11		5	10										7		6					4								12	3	8¹	2	9						36
1	11		5	10		9								7		6					4								2	8		3							37
1	11		5	12	10	9¹								6		7													2	4	8	3							38
1	2		5	10	9¹									6	12						13		7						4	3	8	11²							39
1	11		5	10	12									8									6					7²	2	3¹	9	4							40
1	11		5	10	13									8¹									6					7²	2	3	9	4	12						41
1		5⁴		10										12		8							6		13	7¹		2	3	9²	4	11							42
1					14	10	13							4		6³	12				5²					3				8¹	2		9	7	11				43
1	11					10					2					6	12				5								9¹	3	8	4	7						44
1	2					10		4								6		12			5								7¹	3	9	8	11						45
1	2			12	10¹		4									6	9²				5								13	3	8	11¹	7						46

FA Cup

First Round	AFC Telford U	(a)	3-1
Second Round	Northwich Vic	(a)	3-1
Third Round	Bolton W	(a)	0-4

Carling Cup

First Round	Barnsley	(h)	0-1

J Paint Trophy

First Round	Darlington	(a)	0-1

LIVERPOOL   FA Premiership

FOUNDATION

But for a dispute between Everton FC and their landlord at Anfield in 1892, there may never have been a Liverpool club. This dispute persuaded the majority of Evertonians to quit Anfield for Goodison Park, leaving the landlord, Mr John Houlding, to form a new club. He originally tried to retain the name 'Everton' but when this failed, he founded Liverpool Association FC on 15 March 1892.

Anfield Stadium, Anfield Road, Liverpool L4 0TH.

Telephone: (0151) 260 1433.

Fax: (0151) 260 8813.

Ticket Office: (0151) 260 8680.

Website: www.liverpoolfc.tv

Email: customercontact@liverpoolfc.tv or customerservices@liverpoolfc.tv

Ground Capacity: 45,522.

Record Attendance: 61,905 v Wolverhampton W, FA Cup 4th rd, 2 February 1952.

Pitch Measurements: 101m × 68m.

Chairman: Martin Broughton.

Managing Director: Christian Purslow.

Directors: George Gillett Jnr and Tom Hicks.

Secretary: Ian Silvester.

Manager: Roy Hodgson.

Assistant Manager: Sammy Lee.

Physio: Rob Price.

Colours: All red with white trim.

Change Colours: All black with yellow trim.

Year Formed: 1892.

Turned Professional: 1892.

Ltd Co.: 1892.

Club Nicknames: 'Reds' or 'Pool'.

Ground: 1892, Anfield.

First Football League Game: 2 September 1893, Division 2, v Middlesbrough Ironopolis (a) W 2–0 – McOwen; Hannah, McLean; Henderson, McQue (1), McBride; Gordon, McVean (1), M. McQueen, Stott, H. McQueen.

HONOURS

Football League: Division 1 – Champions 1900–01, 1905–06, 1921–22, 1922–23, 1946–47, 1963–64, 1965–66, 1972–73, 1975–76, 1976–77, 1978–79, 1979–80, 1981–82, 1982–83, 1983–84, 1985–86, 1987–88, 1989–90 (Liverpool have a record number of 18 League Championship wins); Runners-up 1898–99, 1909–10, 1968–69, 1973–74, 1974–75, 1977–78, 1984–85, 1986–87, 1988–89, 1990–91, 2001–02; Division 2 – Champions 1893–94, 1895–96, 1904–05, 1961–62; FA Premier League – Runners-up 2001–02, 2008–09.

FA Cup: Winners 1965, 1974, 1986, 1989, 1992, 2001, 2006; Runners-up 1914, 1950, 1971, 1977, 1988, 1996.

Football League Cup: Winners 1981, 1982, 1983, 1984, 1995, 2001, 2003; Runners-up 1978, 1987, 2005.

League Super Cup: Winners 1986.

European Competitions: European Cup: 1964–65, 1966–67, 1973–74, 1976–77 (winners), 1977–78 (winners), 1978–79, 1979–80, 1980–81 (winners), 1981–82, 1982–83, 1983–84 (winners), 1984–85 (runners-up). *Champions League:* 2001–02, 2002–03, 2004–05 (winners), 2005–06, 2006–07 (runners-up), 2007–08 (s-f), 2008–09 (q-f), 2009–10. *European Cup-Winners' Cup:* 1965–66 (runners-up), 1971–72, 1974–75, 1992–93, 1996–97 (s-f). *European Fairs Cup:* 1967–68, 1968–69, 1969–70, 1970–71. *UEFA Cup:* 1972–73 (winners), 1975–76 (winners), 1991–92, 1995–96, 1997–98, 1998–99, 2000–01 (winners), 2002–03, 2003–04. *Europa League* 2009–10. *Super Cup:* 1977 (winners), 1978, 1984, 2001 (winners), 2005 (winners). *World Club Championship:* 1981 (runners-up), 1984 (runners-up). *FIFA Club World Championship:* 2005 (runners-up).

sky SPORTS FACT FILE

Foreign imports are prevalent in the Premier League these days. But Liverpool could boast of a unique record more than sixty years ago. Between August 1925 and October 1945 they engaged on a professional basis eleven players born in South Africa.

Record League Victory: 10–1 v Rotherham T, Division 2, 18 February 1896 – Storer; Goldie, Wilkie; McCartney, McQue, Holmes; McVean (3), Ross (2), Allan (4), Becton (1), Bradshaw.

Record Cup Victory: 11–0 v Stromsgodset Drammen, ECWC 1st rd 1st leg, 17 September 1974 – Clemence; Smith (1), Lindsay (1p), Thompson (2), Cormack (1), Hughes (1), Boersma (2), Hall, Heighway (1), Kennedy (1), Callaghan (1).

Record Defeat: 1–9 v Birmingham C, Division 2, 11 December 1954.

Most League Points (2 for a win): 68, Division 1, 1978–79.

Most League Points (3 for a win): 90, Division 1, 1987–88.

Most League Goals: 106, Division 2, 1895–96.

Highest League Scorer in Season: Roger Hunt, 41, Division 2, 1961–62.

Most League Goals in Total Aggregate: Roger Hunt, 245, 1959–69.

Most League Goals in One Match: 5, Andy McGuigan v Stoke C, Division 1, 4 January 1902; 5, John Evans v Bristol R, Division 2, 15 September 1954; 5, Ian Rush v Luton T, Division 1, 29 October 1983.

Most Capped Player: Steven Gerrard, 84, England.

Most League Appearances: Ian Callaghan, 640, 1960–78

Youngest League Player: Jack Robinson, 16 years 250 days v Hull C, 9 May 2010.

Record Transfer Fee Received: £34,000,000 from Real Madrid for Xabi Alonso, August 2009.

Record Transfer Fee Paid: £22,000,000 to Atletico Madrid for Fernando Torres, July 2007.

Football League Record: 1893 Elected to Division 2; 1894–95 Division 1; 1895–96 Division 2; 1896–1904 Division 1; 1904–05 Division 2; 1905–54 Division 1; 1954–62 Division 2; 1962–92 Division 1; 1992– FA Premier League.

MANAGERS

W. E. Barclay 1892–96
Tom Watson 1896–1915
David Ashworth 1920–23
Matt McQueen 1923–28
George Patterson 1928–36
 (continued as Secretary)
George Kay 1936–51
Don Welsh 1951–56
Phil Taylor 1956–59
Bill Shankly 1959–74
Bob Paisley 1974–83
Joe Fagan 1983–85
Kenny Dalglish 1985–91
Graeme Souness 1991–94
Roy Evans 1994–98
 (then Joint Manager)
Gerard Houllier 1998–2004
Rafael Benitez 2004–10
Roy Hodgson June 2010

LATEST SEQUENCES

Longest Sequence of League Wins: 12, 21.4.1990 – 6.10.1990.

Longest Sequence of League Defeats: 9, 29.4.1899 – 14.10.1899.

Longest Sequence of League Draws: 6, 19.2.1975 – 19.3.1975.

Longest Sequence of Unbeaten League Matches: 31, 4.5.1987 – 16.3.1988.

Longest Sequence Without a League Win: 14, 12.12.1953 – 20.3.1954.

Successive Scoring Runs: 29 from 27.4.1957.

Successive Non-scoring Runs: 5 from 22.12.1906.

TEN YEAR LEAGUE RECORD

		P	W	D	L	F	A	Pts	Pos
2000-01	PR Lge	38	20	9	9	71	39	69	3
2001-02	PR Lge	38	24	8	6	67	30	80	2
2002-03	PR Lge	38	18	10	10	61	41	64	5
2003-04	PR Lge	38	16	12	10	55	37	60	4
2004-05	PR Lge	38	17	7	14	52	41	58	5
2005-06	PR Lge	38	25	7	6	57	25	82	3
2006-07	PR Lge	38	20	8	10	57	27	68	3
2007-08	PR Lge	38	21	13	4	67	28	76	4
2008-09	PR Lge	38	25	11	2	77	27	86	2
2009-10	PR Lge	38	18	9	11	61	35	63	7

DID YOU KNOW ?

On 29 December 2009 Fernando Torres scored into added time at Aston Villa to become the fastest Liverpool goal scorer to reach 50 League goals for the club in 72 games. Sam Raybould (1902) and Albert Stubbins (1948) jointly held the previous record in 80 matches.

LIVERPOOL 2009–10 LEAGUE RECORD

Match No.	Date	Venue	Opponents	Result	H/T Score	Lg Pos.	Goalscorers	Attendance
1	Aug 16	A	Tottenham H	L	1-2	0-1	—	Gerrard (pen) [56]	35,935
2	19	H	Stoke C	W	4-0	2-0	—	Torres [4], Johnson [45], Kuyt [78], N'Gog [90]	44,318
3	24	H	Aston Villa	L	1-3	0-2	—	Torres [72]	43,667
4	29	A	Bolton W	W	3-2	1-1	7	Johnson [41], Torres [56], Gerrard [83]	23,284
5	Sept12	H	Burnley	W	4-0	2-0	5	Benayoun 3 [27, 61, 82], Kuyt [41]	43,817
6	19	A	West Ham U	W	3-2	2-2	3	Torres 2 [20, 75], Kuyt [41]	34,658
7	26	H	Hull C	W	6-1	2-1	3	Torres 3 [12, 28, 47], Gerrard [61], Babel 2 [88, 90]	44,392
8	Oct 4	A	Chelsea	L	0-2	0-0	5		41,732
9	17	A	Sunderland	L	0-1	0-1	8		47,327
10	25	H	Manchester U	W	2-0	0-0	5	Torres [65], N'Gog [90]	44,188
11	31	A	Fulham	L	1-3	1-1	6	Torres [42]	25,700
12	Nov 9	H	Birmingham C	D	2-2	1-2	—	N'Gog [13], Gerrard (pen) [71]	42,560
13	21	H	Manchester C	D	2-2	0-0	7	Skrtel [50], Benayoun [77]	44,164
14	29	A	Everton	W	2-0	1-0	5	Yobo (og) [12], Kuyt [80]	39,652
15	Dec 5	A	Blackburn R	D	0-0	0-0	7		29,660
16	13	H	Arsenal	L	1-2	1-0	7	Kuyt [41]	43,853
17	16	H	Wigan Ath	W	2-1	1-0	—	N'Gog [9], Torres [79]	41,116
18	19	A	Portsmouth	L	0-2	0-1	8		20,534
19	26	H	Wolverhampton W	W	2-0	0-0	7	Gerrard [62], Benayoun [70]	41,956
20	29	A	Aston Villa	W	1-0	0-0	—	Torres [90]	42,788
21	Jan 16	A	Stoke C	D	1-1	0-0	7	Kyrgiakos [57]	27,247
22	20	H	Tottenham H	W	2-0	1-0	—	Kuyt 2 (1 pen) [6, 90 (p)]	42,016
23	26	A	Wolverhampton W	D	0-0	0-0	—		28,763
24	30	H	Bolton W	W	2-0	1-0	5	Kuyt [37], Davies K (og) [70]	43,413
25	Feb 6	H	Everton	W	1-0	0-0	4	Kuyt [55]	44,316
26	10	A	Arsenal	L	0-1	0-0	—		60,045
27	21	A	Manchester C	D	0-0	0-0	6		47,203
28	28	H	Blackburn R	W	2-1	2-1	6	Gerrard [20], Torres [44]	42,795
29	Mar 8	A	Wigan Ath	L	0-1	0-1	—		17,427
30	15	H	Portsmouth	W	4-1	3-0	—	Torres 2 [26, 77], Babel [28], Aquilani [32]	40,316
31	21	A	Manchester U	L	1-2	1-1	6	Torres [5]	75,216
32	28	H	Sunderland	W	3-0	2-0	5	Torres 2 [3, 60], Johnson [32]	43,121
33	Apr 4	A	Birmingham C	D	1-1	0-0	6	Gerrard [47]	27,909
34	11	H	Fulham	D	0-0	0-0	—		42,331
35	19	H	West Ham U	W	3-0	2-0	—	Benayoun [19], N'Gog [29], Green (og) [59]	37,697
36	25	A	Burnley	W	4-0	0-0	7	Gerrard 2 [52, 59], Rodriguez [74], Babel [90]	21,553
37	May 2	H	Chelsea	L	0-2	0-1	7		44,375
38	9	A	Hull C	D	0-0	0-0	7		25,030

Final League Position: 7

GOALSCORERS

League (61): Torres 18, Gerrard 9 (2 pens), Kuyt 9 (1 pen), Benayoun 6, N'Gog 5, Babel 4, Johnson 3, Aquilani 1, Kyrgiakos 1, Rodriguez 1, Skrtel 1, own goals 3.
Carling Cup (2): Insua 1, N'Gog 1.
FA Cup (2): Gerrard 1, own goal 1.
Champions League (5): Benayoun 2, Babel 1, Kuyt 1, N'Gog 1.
Europa League (14): Torres 4, Gerrard 2 (1 pen), Agger 1, Aquilaini 1, Babel 1, Benayoun 1, Kuyt 1, Lucas 1, Mascherano 1, N'Gog 1.

Reina J 38	Johnson G 24+1	Insua E 30+1	Mascherano J 31+3	Carragher J 37	Skrtel M 16+3	Kuyt D 35+2	Lucas 32+3	Torres F 20+2	Gerrard S 32+1	Babel R 9+16	Benayoun Y 19+11	Ayala D 2+3	Voronin A 1+7	Riera A 9+3	N'Gog D 10+14	Kyrgiakos S 13+1	Dossena A 1+1	Degen P 3+4	Fabio Aurelio 8+6	Agger D 23	Spearing J 1+2	Eccleston N —+1	Aquilani A 9+9	El Zhar N 1+2	Pacheco D —+4	Rodriguez M 14+3	Darby S —+1	Kelly M —+1	Robinson J —+1	Match No.
1	2	3	4	5	6²	7³	8	9	10	11¹	12	13	14																	1
1	2	3	4	5		10²	7	9³	8¹	11			6	12	13	14														2
1	2	3	4	5	6	10	7¹	9	8	13	11²	12																		3
1	2	3	4²	5		10³	7	9	8	12	13			11¹	6	14														4
1	2¹	3		5	6	10²	4	9³	8		7	13	11	14	12															5
1	2	3	4	5	6	10¹	11	9³	8	12	7²	14	13																	6
1	2	3	13	5	6	10	4	9¹	8²	12	7³	14	11																	7
1¹	2	3³	4	5	6	10	7²	9	8	13	12	11	14																	8
1	2		13	5	6¹	10	8	11³	7	12	14									3	4		9							9
1	2	3	4⁴	5	13	10	8	9¹	7²	12	11					6														10
1		3	4	5⁴		11³	8	9¹	12	7²	14	10	2	6⁴	13															11
1	2	3	4		6	10	8³	12	13	7²	11¹				9	5							14							12
1	3	4	2		6	10	7	8	11²	13³	9	12	14						5¹											13
1	2	3	4	5		10	7	8		12	13	9		11²																14
1	2	3	4	5		10	11	8	7²		9¹	12				6							13							15
1	2³		4¹	5		10	11	9	8	7²	13	14							6	3			12							16
1	3	11	5	4		10	12	13	8	7³	9	2¹							6				14							17
1	2	3²	7	5	10	11³	9	8		12						4¹	13		6				14							18
1	2	3		5	12	11	9	8	7³							4¹			6				14			10²				19
1	2²	3		5	13	10	4	9	8	12	7³	14							6							11¹				20
1	3	8		5	6	10	11	9²								2			13	4¹			7			12				21
1	3	8		5	6	10	11	9²								12				2			4³			7¹	13	14		22
1	3	4	5	6		10	11	8	9¹							12				2						7				23
1	3	4	5	6		10	12	8	14	11²	9³									2			13			7¹				24
1	3	4	5		13	10³	11	8	12	9¹									6	2⁴			14			7²				25
1	3	4	2		6	10	11²	8	13	9									5				12			7				26
1	3	4	2			10³	9	13	8	11²	12								5				14			7¹				27
1	12	4	2		10	11	9³	8	13	7²	14								5	3¹			6							28
1	12	3	4	5	10³	11¹	9	8	14	7²									6	2			13							29
1	2¹	3	4	5			8²	9³	10	11	13	14							6							7			12	30
1	2	3	4	5		10¹	11³	9	8	13	14								6				12			7²				31
1	2	3	4	5		10¹	9²	8³	11	13									6				12	14		7				32
1	6	3		5		10³	11	9¹	8	13	7²									2			12	14		4				33
1	2	4	5		12		8	11²	13	9³									6	3			10¹	14		7				34
1	2	12	5		10	11	8¹	14	7²	9³									6	3			13			4				35
1	2	4	5		10¹	13	8³	11	12	3									6²				9	14		7				36
1	2		5²		10	11	8	12	7	13	14		3						6				9³			4¹				37
1	2		5		10	7	8	11³	12				3						6				4²	9¹	13				14	38

MACCLESFIELD TOWN   FL Championship 2

FOUNDATION

From the mid-19th Century until 1874, Macclesfield Town FC played under rugby rules. In 1891 they moved to the Moss Rose and finished champions of the Manchester & District League in 1906 and 1908. By 1911, they had carried off the Cheshire Senior Cup five times. Macclesfield were founder members of the Cheshire County League in 1919.

Moss Rose Ground, London Road, Macclesfield, Cheshire SK11 7SP.

Telephone: (01625) 264 686.

Fax: (01625) 264 692.

Ticket Office: (01625) 264 686.

Website: www.mtfc.co.uk

Email: office@mtfc.co.uk

Ground Capacity: 6,141.

Record Attendance: 9,008 v Winsford U, Cheshire Senior Cup 2nd rd, 4 February 1948.

Pitch Measurements: 100m × 60m.

Chairman: Mike Rance.

Vice-chairman: Andy Scott.

Company Secretary: Barrie Darcey.

Manager: Gary Simpson.

Assistant Manager: Glyn Chamberlain.

Physio: Nick Reid.

Colours: Blue shirts with white design, white shorts, blue stockings.

Change Colours: Black shirts with one yellow sleeve, black shorts, yellow stockings.

Year formed: 1874.

Club Nickname: 'The Silkmen'.

Grounds: 1874, Rostron Field; 1891, Moss Rose.

First Football League Game: 9 August 1997, Division 3, v Torquay U (h) W 2–1 – Price; Tinson, Rose, Payne (Edey), Howarth, Sodje (1), Askey, Wood, Landon (1) (Power), Mason, Sorvel.

HONOURS

Football League: Division 3 – Runners-up 1997–98.

FA Cup: best season: 3rd rd, 1968, 1988, 2002, 2003, 2004, 2007, 2009.

Football League Cup: never past 2nd rd.

Vauxhall Conference: Champions 1994–95, 1996–97.

FA Trophy: Winners 1969–70, 1995–96; Runners-up 1988–89.

Bob Lord Trophy: Winners 1993–94; Runners-up 1995–96, 1996–97.

Vauxhall Conference Championship Shield: Winners 1996, 1997, 1998.

Northern Premier League: Winners 1968–69, 1969–70, 1986–87; Runners-up 1984–85.

Northern Premier League Challenge Cup: Winners 1986–87; Runners-up 1969–70, 1970–71, 1982–83.

Northern Premier League Presidents Cup: Winners 1986–87; Runners-up 1984–85.

Cheshire Senior Cup: Winners 20 times; Runners-up 11.

sky SPORTS FACT FILE

In 1933–34 Albert Valentine had a brief but spectacular season with Macclesfield Town who scored 142 League goals alone. His contribution was a staggering 84 including fifteen hat-tricks. He moved to Halifax Town in the summer and was equally successful there.

Record League Victory: 6–0 v Stockport Co, FL 1, 26 December 2005 – Fettis; Harsley, Sandwith, Morley, Swailes (Teague), Navarro, Whitaker (Miles (1)), Bullock (1), Parkin (2), Wijnhard (2) (Townson), McIntyre.

Record Win: 15–0 v Chester St Marys, Cheshire Senior Cup 2nd rd, 16 February 1886.

Record Defeat: 1–13 v Tranmere R reserves, 3 May 1929.

Most League Points (3 for a win): 82, Division 3, 1997–98.

Most League Goals: 66, Division 3, 1999–2000.

Highest League Scorer in Season: Jon Parkin, 22, FL 2, 2004–05.

Most League Goals in Total Aggregate: Matt Tipton, 45, 2002–05; 2006–07.

Most Capped Player: George Abbey, 10, Nigeria.

Most League Appearances: Darren Tinson, 263, 1997–2003.

Youngest League Player: Peter Griffiths, 18 years 44 days v Reading, 26 September 1998.

Record Transfer Fee Received: £300,000 from Stockport Co for Rickie Lambert, April 2002.

Record Transfer Fee Paid: £40,000 to Bury for Danny Swailes, January 2005.

Football League Record: 1997 Promoted to Division 3; 1998–99 Division 2; 1999–2004 Division 3; 2004– FL 2.

MANAGERS

Since 1967
Keith Goalen 1967–68
Frank Beaumont 1968–72
Billy Haydock 1972–74
Eddie Brown 1974
John Collins 1974
Willie Stevenson 1974
John Collins 1975–76
Tony Coleman 1976
John Barnes 1976
Brian Taylor 1976
Dave Connor 1976–78
Derek Partridge 1978
Phil Staley 1978–80
Jimmy Williams 1980–81
Brian Booth 1981–85
Neil Griffiths 1985–86
Roy Campbell 1986
Peter Wragg 1986–93
Sammy McIlroy 1993–2000
Peter Davenport 2000
Gil Prescott 2001
David Moss 2001–03
John Askey 2003–04
Brian Horton 2004–06
Paul Ince 2006–07
Ian Brightwell 2007–08
Keith Alexander 2008–10
Gary Simpson April 2010–

LATEST SEQUENCES

Longest Sequence of League Wins: 6, 25.1.2005 – 26.2.2005.

Longest Sequence of League Defeats: 6, 26.12.1998 – 6.2.1999.

Longest Sequence of League Draws: 5, 5.5.2007 – 1.9.2007.

Longest Sequence of Unbeaten League Matches: 8, 16.10.1999 – 27.11.1999.

Longest Sequence Without a League Win: 19, 5.8.2006 – 25.11.2006.

Successive Scoring Runs: 14 from 11.10.2003.

Successive Non-scoring Runs: 5 from 18.12.1998.

TEN YEAR LEAGUE RECORD

		P	W	D	L	F	A	Pts	Pos
2000-01	Div 3	46	14	14	18	51	62	56	14
2001-02	Div 3	46	15	13	18	41	52	58	13
2002-03	Div 3	46	14	12	20	57	63	54	16
2003-04	Div 3	46	13	13	20	54	69	52	20
2004-05	FL 2	46	22	9	15	60	49	75	5
2005-06	FL 2	46	12	18	16	60	71	54	17
2006-07	FL 2	46	12	12	22	55	77	48	22
2007-08	FL 2	46	11	17	18	47	64	50	19
2008-09	FL 2	46	13	8	25	45	77	47	20
2009-10	FL 2	46	12	18	16	49	58	54	19

DID YOU KNOW ?

To celebrate the occasion of Macclesfield Town gaining their historic promotion to Division Two in May 1998, a special beer was produced by Titanic Brewery for the local Beer Festival and was aptly named "Mad Macc's Two".

MACCLESFIELD TOWN 2009–10 LEAGUE RECORD

Match No.	Date	Venue	Opponents	Result	H/T Score	Lg Pos.	Goalscorers	Attendance
1	Aug 8	A	Northampton T	D	0-0	0-0	—	4064
2	15	H	Notts Co	L	0-4	0-2	21	2785
3	18	H	Port Vale	W	2-0	1-0	—	Tipton [6], Bencherif [68]	3433
4	22	A	Morecambe	D	2-2	1-0	16	Tipton (pen) [12], Draper [58]	1757
5	29	H	Rotherham U	L	1-3	1-2	19	Tipton [45]	1972
6	Sept 5	A	Crewe Alex	L	1-2	1-1	20	Sappleton [32]	4151
7	12	H	Barnet	D	1-1	1-1	19	Sappleton [12]	1125
8	19	A	Chesterfield	L	1-4	0-4	23	Bencherif [79]	3138
9	26	H	Torquay U	W	2-1	0-0	20	Bencherif 2 [61, 66]	1745
10	29	A	Burton Alb	D	1-1	1-1	—	Sinclair [14]	2332
11	Oct 3	A	Darlington	W	1-0	1-0	15	Smith J (og) [15]	1763
12	10	H	Lincoln C	L	0-1	0-0	18		2006
13	16	A	Cheltenham T	W	2-1	2-0	—	Sappleton [27], Rooney [43]	2930
14	24	H	Dagenham & R	D	2-2	1-0	16	Tipton (pen) [30], Sappleton [66]	1574
15	31	H	Bradford C	D	2-2	2-0	18	Daniel [4], Bencherif [41]	2526
16	Nov 14	A	Aldershot T	D	0-0	0-0	17		2646
17	21	H	Bournemouth	L	1-2	1-1	19	Brisley [35]	1413
18	28	H	Grimsby T	D	0-0	0-0	—		1409
19	Dec 5	A	Rochdale	L	0-3	0-2	19		3003
20	12	H	Hereford U	W	3-1	2-0	18	Sinclair 2 [43, 68], Wright [45]	1406
21	26	A	Shrewsbury T	D	2-2	2-1	20	Brown [43], Daniel [45]	5942
22	28	H	Crewe Alex	W	4-1	3-0	17	Wright [4], Bolland [13], Daniel [30], Sappleton [90]	3449
23	Jan 20	H	Northampton T	L	0-2	0-1	—		1035
24	23	A	Port Vale	D	0-0	0-0	17		5167
25	26	H	Morecambe	D	2-2	1-0	—	Lindfield [38], Sappleton [83]	1046
26	Feb 6	H	Shrewsbury T	L	0-1	0-0	19		2058
27	9	A	Bury	L	1-2	1-1	—	Butcher [26]	2169
28	13	H	Accrington S	D	0-0	0-0	19		1729
29	20	A	Bournemouth	D	1-1	0-0	20	Brown [62]	4549
30	23	A	Grimsby T	D	1-1	0-1	—	Butcher [58]	4813
31	27	H	Rochdale	L	0-1	0-0	21		2462
32	Mar 2	A	Notts Co	L	0-1	0-1	—		4672
33	6	A	Hereford U	W	2-0	1-0	20	Sappleton [16], Sinclair [62]	1919
34	9	A	Accrington S	D	1-1	0-0	—	Tipton (pen) [78]	1210
35	13	H	Bury	W	2-0	1-0	17	Wright [30], Lindfield [57]	2740
36	20	A	Dagenham & R	L	1-3	1-0	20	Bell [33]	3721
37	23	A	Rotherham U	L	1-3	1-1	—	Wright [25]	2873
38	27	H	Cheltenham T	W	1-0	0-0	20	Wright [89]	1572
39	Apr 3	H	Aldershot T	D	1-1	1-0	18	Brown [17]	1428
40	5	A	Bradford C	W	2-1	1-0	18	Sinclair [40], Wright [61]	11,395
41	10	A	Barnet	W	2-1	0-0	17	Sinclair [54], Bell [89]	1433
42	13	H	Burton Alb	D	1-1	1-0	—	Brown [3]	1588
43	17	H	Chesterfield	W	2-0	2-0	16	Sinclair [32], Mukendi [38]	2143
44	24	A	Torquay U	L	0-1	0-0	19		2570
45	May 1	H	Darlington	L	0-2	0-1	19		1716
46	8	A	Lincoln C	D	0-0	0-0	19		3291

Final League Position: 19

GOALSCORERS

League (49): Sappleton 7, Sinclair 7, Wright 6, Bencherif 5, Tipton 5 (3 pens), Brown 4, Daniel 3, Bell 2, Butcher 2, Lindfield 2, Bolland 1, Brisley 1, Draper 1, Mukendi 1, Rooney 1, own goal 1.
Carling Cup (0).
FA Cup (0).
J Paint Trophy (2): Brisley 1, Rooney 1.

Brain J 41	Brisley S 29 + 4	Tremarco C 27 + 2	Bolland P 17 + 10	Bencherif H 19	Morgan P 35 + 1	Rooney J 14 + 11	Draper R 28 + 1	Sinclair E 33 + 9	Wright B 25 + 14	Daniel C 34 + 4	Tipton M 11 + 20	Reid 34 + 3	Bell L 37 + 5	Wilson K — + 4	Veiga J 5	Sappleton R 18 + 6	Brown N 37 + 1	Thomas M — + 4	Hessey S 27	Lindfield C 12 + 6	Butcher R 8	Mills G — + 1	Lowe M 7 + 3	Mukendi V 8 + 1	Match No.
1	2	3	4	5	6	7^1	8	9^2	10	11	12	13													1
1		3	4	6	5	8	7^1	13	10^2	11	9^3	2	12	14											2
1	4	3		6	5		7		10	11	9^1	2	8	12											3
1	4	3	8	6	5		7	12	10	11^2	9^1	2	13												4
	4^2	3	8^1	6	5	14	7	13		11	9^3	2	12		1	10									5
	4	3		6	5		7	12		11	9^1	2	8^2		1	10	13								6
		3		6	5	14	7	13	12	11^2	9^3	2	8		1	10^1	4								7
	2	3		6	5	13	7	12	14	11^2	9		8^1		1	10^3	4								8
1	14	3		6	5	12	7	10^1	11^3	9^2		2	8			13	4								9
1		3		6	5^1	9	8	7	10	11		2					4			12					10
1	14	3		5	6		9^2	7^3	10^1	11		2	8			12	4			13					11
1	5	3	14	6		11		9^1	10^2	7	13	2	8^3			12	4								12
1	5	3		6		7^1	13	9	12	11		2	8			10^2	4								13
1	5	3		6^1		13	7	9	14	11	12^8	2	8			10^3	4^2								14
1	2	3		6	5		9	4	10	7	11		8												15
1	4	3	14	6	5		7	9^2	13	11^3	12	2	8			10^1									16
1	4	3		6	5	11^2	7	9	12	13	14	2	8^3			10^1									17
1	4	3	14	6			7	9^2	10^1	11	13	2	8^3			12	5								18
1	4^8	3	13	6^2	5		8	9^3	12	11	14	2				10^1	7								19
1		3	7		5	14	8^2	9^1	10	11^3	12	2				4	13		6						20
1		3		6	5		7	9^1	10	11		2	12				8		4						21
1	12	3^3		6	5		7	9^1	10^2	11		2	14			13	8		4						22
	2^2	3	8		5	12		9^1	10^3	11	14	7				10^2	6		4						23
1		3	8		5			9^3	13	11^1	14	2	7			10^2	6		4	12					24
1		3	8		5^1		13		12	11^2		2	7			10	6		4	9					25
1	12		4^1		5	14		9^2	13	11		2	7			10	3		6^3	8					26
1					5			9^3	12	3	14	2	7			10^1	4		6	8^2	11	13			27
1	3						8	12	4	11		2	7				5		6	9^1	10				28
1	3	14					8	13	12	11		2	7^3			10^2	5		6	9^1	8				29
1	3						8		9^1	11	12	2	4			10	5		6		7				30
1	3	14					8^3		9^1	11^2	12	2	4			10	5		6	13	7				31
1		13			5		8	12	14	11		2	6^2			10^3	3		4	9^1	7				32
1	2		12		5		8	9	13	11^1			6			10^2	3		4		7				33
1	3	11^2			5	13	8	9			12		6			2			4	10^1	7^3		14		34
1	3				5	7	8	9^2	10	11^1			6			2			4	12			13		35
1	3	12			5	7^1	8	9	11		13		6			2^2			4	10					36
1	6	3^1	13		5		8	10^2	11		14		7			2			4	9^2			12		37
1	3			6	5		8^1	10^3	11	14	13	7				2			4	9^2				12	38
1	3				5	8^1		9^2	10		12		6			2			4	13			7	11	39
1	3	6^1			5			9^2	10	13	12	7				2			4				8	11	40
1	3^1				5	12		9	10		8	6				2			4				7	11	41
1					5	7^1		9		8^2	2	6	12			3			4	13			10	11	42
1					5			9^2	13	8^1	2	6	12			3			4	10			7	11	43
1			12		5			9^2	8	14	13	2	7			6			4^3	10^1			3	11	44
1	3^3	14	6				13	9		12	8	2	7			5	4			10^2	11				45
	3	6					8	9		11		2	7^2		1		5	13	4	12				0^1	46

FA Cup
First Round — Milton Keynes D — (a) — 0-1

Carling Cup
First Round — Leicester C — (h) — 0-2

J Paint Trophy
Second Round — Carlisle U — (a) — 2-4

MANCHESTER CITY   FA Premiership

FOUNDATION

Manchester City was formed as a Limited Company in 1894 after their predecessors Ardwick had been forced into bankruptcy. However, many historians like to trace the club's lineage as far back as 1880 when St Mark's Church, West Gorton added a football section to their cricket club. They amalgamated with Gorton Athletic in 1884 as Gorton FC. Because of a change of ground they became Ardwick in 1887.

The City of Manchester Stadium, SportCity, Manchester M11 3FF.
Telephone: 0870 062 1894.
Fax: (0161) 438 7999.
Ticket Office: 0870 062 1894 (option 2).
Website: www.mcfc.co.uk
Email: mcfc@mcfc.co.uk
Ground Capacity: 47,726.
Record Attendance: (at Maine Road) 84,569 v Stoke C, FA Cup 6th rd, 3 March 1934 (British record for any game outside London or Glasgow); (at City of Manchester Stadium) 47,304 v Chelsea, FA Premier League, 28 February 2004.
Pitch Measurements: 105m × 68m.
Chairman: Khaldoon Al Mubarak.
Chief Executive: Garry Cook.
Secretary: Rebecca Firth.
Manager: Roberto Mancini.
Assistant Manager: Brian Kidd.
Fitness Coach: Ivan Carminati.
Colours: Sky blue shirts with white detail, white shorts with sky blue detail, white stockings with sky blue tops.
Change Colours: Black shirts with yellow trim, black shorts, black stockings.
Year Formed: 1887 as Ardwick FC; 1894 as Manchester City.
Turned Professional: 1887 as Ardwick FC. *Ltd Co.:* 1894.
Previous Names: 1887, Ardwick FC (formed through the amalgamation of West Gorton and Gorton Athletic, the latter having been formed in 1880); 1894, Manchester City.
Club Nicknames: 'Blues' or 'The Citizens'.
Grounds: 1880, Clowes Street; 1881, Kirkmanshulme Cricket Ground; 1882, Queens Road; 1884, Pink Bank Lane; 1887, Hyde Road (1894–1923 as City); 1923, Maine Road; 2003, City of Manchester Stadium.
First Football League Game: 3 September 1892, Division 2, v Bootle (h) W 7–0 – Douglas; McVickers, Robson; Middleton, Russell, Hopkins; Davies (3), Morris (2), Angus (1), Weir (1), Milarvie.
Record League Victory: 10–1 v Huddersfield T, Division 2, 7 November 1987 – Nixon; Gidman, Hinchcliffe, Clements, Lake, Redmond, White (3), Stewart (3), Adcock (3), McNab (1), Simpson.

HONOURS

Football League: Division 1 – Champions 1936–37, 1967–68, 2001–02; Runners-up 1903–04, 1920–21, 1976–77, 1999–2000; Division 2 – Champions 1898–99, 1902–03, 1909–10, 1927–28, 1946–47, 1965–66; Runners-up 1895–96, 1950–51, 1987–88.
FA Cup: Winners 1904, 1934, 1956, 1969; Runners-up 1926, 1933, 1955, 1981.
Football League Cup: Winners 1970, 1976; Runners-up 1974.
European Competitions: European Cup: 1968–69. *European Cup-Winners' Cup:* 1969–70 (winners), 1970–71. *UEFA Cup:* 1972–73, 1976–77, 1977–78, 1978–79, 2003–04, 2008–09.

sky SPORTS FACT FILE

On 8 December 1934 Manchester City were away to Preston North End. With the score 2–2 goalkeeper Frank Swift was carried off injured. Outside-left Eric Brook took over and saved a penalty from Jackie Palethorpe. City were inspired and went on to win 4–2.

Record Cup Victory: 10–1 v Swindon T, FA Cup 4th rd, 29 January 1930 – Barber; Felton, McCloy; Barrass, Cowan, Heinemann; Toseland, Marshall (5), Tait (3), Johnson (1), Brook (1).

Record Defeat: 1–9 v Everton, Division 1. 3 September 1906.

Most League Points (2 for a win): 62, Division 2, 1946–47.

Most League Points (3 for a win): 99, Division 1, 2001–02.

Most League Goals: 108, Division 2, 1926–27, 108, Division 1, 2001–02.

Highest League Scorer in Season: Tommy Johnson, 38, Division 1, 1928–29.

Most League Goals in Total Aggregate: Tommy Johnson, 158, 1919–30.

Most League Goals in One Match: 5, Fred Williams v Darwen, Division 2, 18 February 1899; 5, Tom Browell v Burnley, Division 2, 24 October 1925; 5, Tom Johnson v Everton, Division 1, 15 September 1928; 5, George Smith v Newport Co, Division 2, 14 June 1947.

Most Capped Player: Colin Bell, 48, England.

Most League Appearances: Alan Oakes, 565, 1959–76.

Youngest League Player: Glyn Pardoe, 15 years 314 days v Birmingham C, 11 April 1962.

Record Transfer Fee Received: £21,000,000 from Chelsea for Shaun Wright-Phillips, July 2005.

Record Transfer Fee Paid: £32,500,000 to Real Madrid for Robinho, September 2008.

Football League Record: 1892 Ardwick elected founder member of Division 2; 1894 Newly-formed Manchester C elected to Division 2; Division 1 1899–1902, 1903–09, 1910–26, 1928–38, 1947–50, 1951–63, 1966–83, 1985–87, 1989–92; Division 2 1902–03, 1909–10, 1926–28, 1938–47, 1950–51, 1963–66, 1983–85, 1987–89; 1992–96 FA Premier League; 1996–98 Division 1; 1998–99 Division 2; 1999–2000 Division 1; 2000–01 FA Premier League; 2001–02 Division 1; 2002– FA Premier League.

LATEST SEQUENCES

Longest Sequence of League Wins: 9, 8.4.1912 – 28.9.1912.

Longest Sequence of League Defeats: 8, 23.8.1995 – 14.10.1995.

Longest Sequence of League Draws: 6, 5.4.1913 – 6.9.1913.

Longest Sequence of Unbeaten League Matches: 22, 16.11.1946 – 19.4.1947.

Longest Sequence Without a League Win: 17, 26.12.1979 – 7.4.1980.

Successive Scoring Runs: 44 from 3.10.1936.

Successive Non-scoring Runs: 6 from 30.1.1971.

MANAGERS

Joshua Parlby 1893–95
(Secretary-Manager)
Sam Omerod 1895–1902
Tom Maley 1902–06
Harry Newbould 1906–12
Ernest Magnall 1912–24
David Ashworth 1924–25
Peter Hodge 1926–32
Wilf Wild 1932–46
(continued as Secretary to 1950)
Sam Cowan 1946–47
John 'Jock' Thomson 1947–50
Leslie McDowall 1950–63
George Poyser 1963–65
Joe Mercer 1965–71
(continued as General Manager to 1972)
Malcolm Allison 1972–73
Johnny Hart 1973
Ron Saunders 1973–74
Tony Book 1974–79
Malcolm Allison 1979–80
John Bond 1980–83
John Benson 1983
Billy McNeill 1983–86
Jimmy Frizzell 1986–87
(continued as General Manager)
Mel Machin 1987–89
Howard Kendall 1990
Peter Reid 1990–93
Brian Horton 1993–95
Alan Ball 1995–96
Steve Coppell 1996
Frank Clark 1996–98
Joe Royle 1998–2001
Kevin Keegan 2001–05
Stuart Pearce 2005–07
Sven-Göran Eriksson 2007–08
Mark Hughes 2008–09
Roberto Mancini December 2009–

TEN YEAR LEAGUE RECORD

		P	W	D	L	F	A	Pts	Pos
2000-01	PR Lge	38	8	10	20	41	65	34	18
2001-02	Div 1	46	31	6	9	108	52	99	1
2002-03	PR Lge	38	15	6	17	47	54	51	9
2003-04	PR Lge	38	9	14	15	55	54	41	16
2004-05	PR Lge	38	13	13	12	47	39	52	8
2005-06	PR Lge	38	13	4	21	43	48	43	15
2006-07	PR Lge	38	11	9	18	29	44	42	14
2007-08	PR Lge	38	15	10	13	45	53	55	9
2008-09	PR Lge	38	15	5	18	58	50	50	10
2009-10	PR Lge	38	18	13	7	73	45	67	5

DID YOU KNOW ?

On 27 February 2010 Manchester City won 4–2 at Chelsea, exactly equalling their last win there in 1992–93. It was their first goal at the venue in ten years and first double over them since 1957–58 when they won 3–2 and coupled it with a 5–2 success at Maine Road.

MANCHESTER CITY 2009–10 LEAGUE RECORD

Match No.	Date	Venue	Opponents	Result	H/T Score	Lg Pos.	Goalscorers	Attendance
1	Aug 15	A	Blackburn R	W 2-0	1-0	—	Adebayor [3], Ireland [90]	29,584
2	22	H	Wolverhampton W	W 1-0	1-0	5	Adebayor [17]	47,287
3	30	A	Portsmouth	W 1-0	1-0	4	Adebayor [30]	17,826
4	Sept 12	H	Arsenal	W 4-2	1-0	3	Richards [20], Bellamy [74], Adebayor [80], Wright-Phillips [84]	47,339
5	20	A	Manchester U	L 3-4	1-1	4	Barry [16], Bellamy 2 [52, 90]	75,065
6	28	H	West Ham U	W 3-1	2-1	—	Tevez 2 [5, 61], Petrov [31]	42,745
7	Oct 5	A	Aston Villa	D 1-1	0-1	—	Bellamy [67]	37,924
8	18	A	Wigan Ath	D 1-1	0-1	5	Petrov [47]	20,005
9	25	H	Fulham	D 2-2	0-0	6	Lescott [54], Petrov [60]	44,906
10	Nov 1	A	Birmingham C	D 0-0	0-0	4		21,462
11	7	H	Burnley	D 3-3	1-2	6	Wright-Phillips [43], Toure [55], Bellamy [58]	47,205
12	21	A	Liverpool	D 2-2	0-0	6	Adebayor [69], Ireland [76]	44,164
13	28	H	Hull C	D 1-1	1-0	7	Wright-Phillips [45]	46,382
14	Dec 5	H	Chelsea	W 2-1	1-1	6	Adebayor [37], Tevez [56]	47,348
15	12	A	Bolton W	D 3-3	2-2	6	Tevez 2 [28, 77], Richards [45]	22,735
16	16	A	Tottenham H	L 0-3	0-1	—		35,891
17	19	H	Sunderland	W 4-3	3-2	6	Santa Cruz 2 [4, 69], Tevez (pen) [12], Bellamy [35]	44,735
18	26	H	Stoke C	W 2-0	2-0	6	Petrov [28], Tevez [45]	47,325
19	28	A	Wolverhampton W	W 3-0	1-0	6	Tevez 2 [33, 86], Garrido [69]	28,957
20	Jan 11	H	Blackburn R	W 4-1	2-0	—	Tevez 3 [7, 49, 90], Richards [39]	40,292
21	16	A	Everton	L 0-2	0-2	5		37,378
22	31	H	Portsmouth	W 2-0	2-0	6	Adebayor [40], Kompany [45]	44,015
23	Feb 6	A	Hull C	L 1-2	0-1	6	Adebayor [59]	24,959
24	9	H	Bolton W	W 2-0	1-0	—	Tevez (pen) [31], Adebayor [73]	42,016
25	16	A	Stoke C	D 1-1	0-0	—	Barry [85]	26,778
26	21	H	Liverpool	D 0-0	0-0	5		47,203
27	27	A	Chelsea	W 4-2	1-1	5	Tevez 2 (1 pen) [45, 76 (p)], Bellamy 2 [51, 87]	41,814
28	Mar 14	A	Sunderland	D 1-1	0-1	5	Johnson A [90]	41,398
29	21	A	Fulham	W 2-1	2-0	5	Santa Cruz [7], Tevez [36]	25,359
30	24	H	Everton	L 0-2	0-1	—		45,708
31	29	H	Wigan Ath	W 3-0	0-0	5	Tevez 3 [72, 74, 84]	43,534
32	Apr 3	A	Burnley	W 6-1	5-0	4	Adebayor 2 [4, 45], Bellamy [5], Tevez [7], Vieira [20], Kompany [58]	21,330
33	11	H	Birmingham C	W 5-1	3-1	—	Tevez 2 (1 pen) [38 (p), 40], Adebayor 2 [43, 88], Onuoha [74]	45,209
34	17	H	Manchester U	L 0-1	0-0	5		47,019
35	24	A	Arsenal	D 0-0	0-0	6		60,086
36	May 1	H	Aston Villa	W 3-1	2-1	5	Tevez (pen) [41], Adebayor [43], Bellamy [89]	47,102
37	5	H	Tottenham H	L 0-1	0-0	—		47,370
38	9	A	West Ham U	D 1-1	1-1	5	Wright-Phillips [21]	34,989

Final League Position: 5

GOALSCORERS

League (73): Tevez 23 (5 pens), Adebayor 14, Bellamy 10, Petrov 4, Wright-Phillips 4, Richards 3, Santa Cruz 3, Barry 2, Ireland 2, Kompany 2, Garrido 1, Johnson A 1, Lescott 1, Onuoha 1, Toure 1, Vieira 1.
Carling Cup (15): Tevez 6 (1 pen), Wright-Phillips 2, Barry 1, Ireland 1, Johnson M 1, Lescott 1, Santa Cruz R 1, Toure 1, Weiss 1.
FA Cup (7): Bellamy 1, Mwaruwari 1, Onuoha 1, Petrov 1, Robinho 1, Sylvinho 1, Wright-Phillips 1.

Given S 35	Richards M 19+4	Bridge W 23	Barry G 34	Toure K 31	Dunne R 2	Wright-Phillips S 19+11	Ireland S 16+6	Adebayor E 25+1	Robinho 6+4	Bellamy C 26+6	Tevez C 32+3	De Jong N 30+4	Lescott J 17+1	Zabaleta P 23+4	Petrov M 8+8	Santa Cruz R 6+13	Johnson M —+1	Kompany V 21+4	Onuoha N 5+5	Sylvinho 6+4	Garrido J 7+2	Mwaruwari B 1+1	Boyata A 1+2	Johnson A 14+2	Vieira P 8+5	Ibrahim A —+1	Nimely-Tchuimeni A —+1	Cunningham G —+2	Nielsen G —+1	Fulop M 3	Match No.
1	2	3	4	5	6	7	8	9	10^1	11	12																				1
1	2	3	4	5	6	7	8	9	10^2	12	11^1	13																			2
1	2^1	3	4	5		7	8^2	9		11	10	13	6	12																	3
1	2	3	4	5		7	11^1	9		10		8	6			12															4
1	2	3	4	5		7	11			9	10	8^1	6			12															5
1		3	4^2	5		7^1			9	10	8	6	2	11	12	13															6
1		3	4	5		7	12	9		11	10^2	8^1	6	2		13															7
1	5	3	4			7^2	13	9^1		10^3	8	6	2^4	11	14			12													8
1	2	3	4	5^3		12	13	9		11	10	8^2	6			7^1		14													9
1		3	4	5		7	12			11	10	8^1	5	2	13	9^2		6													10
1		3	4	5		7	8	9		11	10^1		6	2	12																11
1		3	4^2	5^1		7	11	9		10	13	8	6	2		12															12
1	2	3		5		7	8	9^1	10^2	13	11	4	6			12															13
1	2^1	3^2	4	5		7		9	10^3	11	8	6	14			13	12														14
1	2		4	5		7^1	12	9^3	13	11^4	10		6		14	14		8^2	3												15
1	2		4	5		7		9	10^1	11	8^2	13				12		6	3												16
1	2^1		4	5		7^2	8	11^3	10		12	14	9			13		6	3												17
1	12		4	5			11		9^2	13	10^3	8	2			7		6						3^1	14						18
1	3		4	5			11^1		13	9	10^3	8	2			7^2		6						14	12						19
1	5		4				12		11^1	10	8	2				7^3		13		6			3	9^2	14						20
1	5		4				14		13^3	11	10	8	2			7^1		9^2		6			3	12							21
1			4	5			11		9	14	10	8	2^1			7^3		6^2	12				3	13							22
1	3^3		4	5		7^1		9		11^2	10	8	2			14								6	12	13					23
1	3^2		4	5^1		13		9		10	8	12	2			6		14						11^3	7						24
1	2^2		4	5		12		9		8	6	13	14	10		3^1								11^3	7						25
1	3		4			7^1	10^2	9		12	8	5	2			6								11		13					26
1	5	3^2	4			12		9		10^3	8	6	2			13		7		14				11^1							27
1	5^2	3^1	4			11^3		9		10	8	6	2			12		7						14	13						28
1		4	5			13		11^3	10	12	2			9^1		6	14			3				7^2	8						29
1	5^3	4	6			12	7^1	9	10	8	2			13		3								11^2	14						30
1		5				7^1	9	12	10^3	8	2			6	14	13	3^5							11	4						31
1		4	2			9^2	11	10^3	12				13	6	5	3^1								7	8	14					32
1		4	2	12		9	11^1	10^2	8				13	6	5	3								7^3	14						33
1	3	4	2	13	14	9^2	11	10	8^3				6	5										7^1	12						34
1	12	3^1	4	5		13		9	10	8	2			6										11	7^2			15			35
	13	3		5		12		9	11	10^2	8	2		6										7^1	4				1		36
	3	4^1	5	13		9		11^3	10	8	2		14	6										7^2	12				1		37
	13	5		7		9		12	8	2	10^2		6	3^1										11^3	4		14		1		38

FA Cup

Third Round	Middlesbrough	(a)	1-0
Fourth Round	Scunthorpe U	(a)	4-2
Fifth Round	Stoke C	(h)	1-1
		(a)	1-3

Carling Cup

Second Round	Crystal Palace	(a)	2-0
Third Round	Fulham	(h)	2-1
Fourth Round	Scunthorpe U	(h)	5-1
Quarter-Final	Arsenal	(h)	3-0
Semi-Final	Manchester U	(h)	2-1
		(a)	1-3

MANCHESTER UNITED   FA Premiership

FOUNDATION

Manchester United was formed as comparatively recently as 1902 after their predecessors, Newton Heath, went bankrupt. However, it is usual to give the date of the club's foundation as 1878 when the dining room committee of the carriage and waggon works of the Lancashire and Yorkshire Railway Company formed Newton Heath L and YR Cricket and Football Club. They won the Manchester Cup in 1886 and as Newton Heath FC were admitted to the Second Division in 1892.

Old Trafford, Sir Matt Busby Way, Manchester M16 0RA.

Telephone: (0161) 868 8000.

Fax: (0161) 868 8804.

Ticket Office: (0161) 868 8000.

Website: www.manutd.com

Email: enquiries@manutd.co.uk

Ground Capacity: 75,769.

Record Attendance: 76,962 Wolverhampton W v Grimsby T, FA Cup semi-final, 25 March 1939.

Club Record Attendance: 76,098 v Blackburn R, FA Premier League, 31 March 2007.

Pitch Measurements: 105m × 68m.

Co-Chairmen: Joel and Avram Glazer.

Chief Executive: David Gill.

Secretary: John Alexander.

Manager: Sir Alex Ferguson CBE.

Assistant Manager: Mick Phelan.

Physio: Rob Swire.

Colours: Red shirts with black chevron, white shorts with red side panels, black stockings.

Change Colours: All black with light blue chevron on shirts.

Year Formed: 1878 as Newton Heath LYR; 1902, Manchester United.

Turned Professional: 1885. *Ltd Co.:* 1907.

Previous Name: 1880, Newton Heath; 1902, Manchester United.

Club Nickname: 'Red Devils'.

Grounds: 1880, North Road, Monsall Road; 1893, Bank Street; 1910, Old Trafford (played at Maine Road 1941–49).

HONOURS

FA Premier League – Champions 1992–93, 1993–94, 1995–96, 1996–97, 1998–99, 1999–2000, 2000–01, 2002–03, 2006–07, 2007–08, 2008–09; Runners-up 1994–95, 1997–98, 2005–06, 2009–10.

Football League: Division 1 – Champions 1907–08, 1910–11, 1951–52, 1955–56, 1956–57, 1964–65, 1966–67; Runners-up 1946–47, 1947–48, 1948–49, 1950–51, 1958–59, 1963–64, 1967–68, 1979–80, 1987–88, 1991–92. Division 2 – Champions 1935–36, 1974–75; Runners-up 1896–97, 1905–06, 1924–25, 1937–38.

FA Cup: Winners 1909, 1948, 1963, 1977, 1983, 1985, 1990, 1994, 1996, 1999, 2004; Runners-up 1957, 1958, 1976, 1979, 1995, 2005, 2007.

Football League Cup: Winners 1992, 2006, 2009, 2010; Runners-up 1983, 1991, 1994, 2003.

European Competitions: European Cup: 1956–57 (s-f), 1957–58 (s-f), 1965–66 (s-f), 1967–68 (winners), 1968–69 (s-f). Champions League: 1993–94, 1994–95, 1996–97 (s-f), 1997–98, 1998–99 (winners), 1999–2000, 2000–01, 2001–02 (s-f), 2002–03, 2003–04, 2004–05, 2005–06, 2006–07 (s-f), 2007–08 (winners), 2008–09 (runners-up), 2009–10. European Cup-Winners' Cup: 1963–64, 1977–78, 1983–84, 1990–91 (winners). 1991–92. Inter Cities Fairs Cup: 1964–65. UEFA Cup: 1976–77, 1980–81, 1982–83, 1984–85, 1992–93, 1995–96. Super Cup: 1991 (winners), 1999 (runners-up), 2008 (runners-up). Inter-Continental Cup: 1999 (winners), 1968 (runners-up). FIFA World Club Cup: 2008 (winners).

sky SPORTS FACT FILE

On 28 November 2009 Ryan Giggs, on the eve of his 36th birthday, scored his 100th Premier League goal as Manchester United beat Portsmouth 4–1 at Fratton Park. United won 4-1 with Wayne Rooney scoring a hat-trick including two penalties.

First Football League Game: 3 September 1892, Division 1, v Blackburn R (a) L 3–4 – Warner; Clements, Brown; Perrins, Stewart, Erentz; Farman (1), Coupar (1), Donaldson (1), Carson, Mathieson.

Record League Victory (as Newton Heath): 10–1 v Wolverhampton W, Division 1, 15 October 1892 – Warner; Mitchell, Clements; Perrins, Stewart (3), Erentz; Farman (1), Hood (1), Donaldson (3), Carson (1), Hendry (1).

Record League Victory (as Manchester U): 9–0 v Ipswich T, FA Premier League, 4 March 1995 – Schmeichel; Keane (1) (Sharpe), Irwin, Bruce (Butt), Kanchelskis, Pallister, Cole (5), Ince (1), McClair, Hughes (2), Giggs.

Record Cup Victory: 10–0 v RSC Anderlecht, European Cup prel. rd 2nd leg, 26 September 1956 – Wood; Foulkes, Byrne; Colman, Jones, Edwards; Berry (1), Whelan (2), Taylor (3), Viollet (4), Pegg.

Record Defeat: 0–7 v Blackburn R, Division 1, 10 April 1926; 0–7 v Aston Villa, Division 1, 27 December 1930; 0–7 v Wolverhampton W, Division 2, 26 December 1931.

Most League Points (2 for a win): 64, Division 1, 1956–57.

Most League Points (3 for a win): 92, FA Premier League, 1993–94.

Most League Goals: 103, Division 1, 1956–57 and 1958–59.

Highest League Scorer in Season: Dennis Viollet, 32, 1959–60.

Most League Goals in Total Aggregate: Bobby Charlton, 199, 1956–73.

Most Capped Player: Bobby Charlton, 106, England.

Most League Appearances: Bobby Charlton, 606, 1956–73.

Youngest League Player: Jeff Whitefoot, 16 years 105 days v Portsmouth, 15 April 1950.

Record Transfer Fee Received: £80,000,000 from Real Madrid for Cristiano Ronaldo, June 2009.

Record Transfer Fee Paid: £30,750,000 to Tottenham H for Dimitar Berbatov, September 2008.

Football League Record: 1892 Newton Heath elected to Division 1; 1894–1906 Division 2; 1906–22 Division 1; 1922–25 Division 2; 1925–31 Division 1; 1931–36 Division 2; 1936–37 Division 1; 1937–38 Division 2; 1938–74 Division 1; 1974–75 Division 2; 1975–92 Division 1; 1992– FA Premier League.

LATEST SEQUENCES

Longest Sequence of League Wins: 14, 15.10.1904 – 3.1.1905.

Longest Sequence of League Defeats: 14, 26.4.1930 – 25.10.1930.

Longest Sequence of League Draws: 6, 30.10.1988 – 27.11.1988.

Longest Sequence of Unbeaten League Matches: 29, 26.12 1998 – 25.9.1999.

Longest Sequence Without a League Win: 16, 19.4.1930 – 25.10.1930.

Successive Scoring Runs: 36 from 3.12.2007.

Successive Non-scoring Runs: 5 from 22.2.1902.

MANAGERS

J. Ernest Mangnall 1903–12
John Bentley 1912–14
John Robson 1914–21
  (Secretary-Manager from 1916)
John Chapman 1921–26
Clarence Hilditch 1926–27
Herbert Bamlett 1927–31
Walter Crickmer 1931–32
Scott Duncan 1932–37
Walter Crickmer 1937–45
  (Secretary-Manager)
Matt Busby 1945–69
  (continued as General Manager then Director)
Wilf McGuinness 1969–70
Sir Matt Busby 1970–71
Frank O'Farrell 1971–72
Tommy Docherty 1972–77
Dave Sexton 1977–81
Ron Atkinson 1981–86
Sir Alex Ferguson November 1986–

TEN YEAR LEAGUE RECORD

		P	W	D	L	F	A	Pts	Pos
2000-01	PR Lge	38	24	8	6	79	31	80	1
2001-02	PR Lge	38	24	5	9	87	45	77	3
2002-03	PR Lge	38	25	8	5	74	34	83	1
2003-04	PR Lge	38	23	6	9	64	35	75	3
2004-05	PR Lge	38	22	11	5	58	26	77	3
2005-06	PR Lge	38	25	8	5	72	34	83	2
2006-07	PR Lge	38	28	5	5	83	27	89	1
2007-08	PR Lge	38	27	6	5	80	22	87	1
2008-09	PR Lge	38	28	6	4	68	24	90	1
2009-10	PR Lge	38	27	4	7	86	28	85	2

DID YOU KNOW ?

On 23 January 2010 Wayne Rooney scored all four goals for Manchester United against Hull City. Eight days later he hit his 100th Premier League goal against Arsenal. It was his 119th overall (in 267 games), beating Cristiano Ronaldo's tally at the club by one goal (292 games).

MANCHESTER UNITED 2009–10 LEAGUE RECORD

Match No.	Date	Venue	Opponents	Result	H/T Score	Lg Pos.	Goalscorers	Atten-dance
1	Aug 16	H	Birmingham C	W 1-0	1-0	—	Rooney [34]	75,062
2	19	A	Burnley	L 0-1	0-1	—		20,872
3	22	A	Wigan Ath	W 5-0	0-0	4	Rooney 2 [56, 65], Berbatov [58], Owen [85], Nani [90]	18,164
4	29	H	Arsenal	W 2-1	0-1	3	Rooney (pen) [59], Diaby (og) [64]	75,095
5	Sept 12	A	Tottenham H	W 3-1	2-1	2	Giggs [25], Anderson [41], Rooney [78]	35,785
6	20	H	Manchester C	W 4-3	1-1	2	Rooney [2], Fletcher 2 [49, 80], Owen [90]	75,065
7	26	A	Stoke C	W 2-0	0-0	1	Berbatov [62], O'Shea [77]	27,500
8	Oct 3	H	Sunderland	D 2-2	0-1	2	Berbatov [51], Ferdinand (og) [90]	75,114
9	17	H	Bolton W	W 2-1	2-0	1	Knight (og) [5], Valencia [33]	75,103
10	25	A	Liverpool	L 0-2	0-0	2		44,188
11	31	H	Blackburn R	W 2-0	0-0	2	Berbatov [55], Rooney [87]	74,658
12	Nov 8	A	Chelsea	L 0-1	0-0	3		41,836
13	21	H	Everton	W 3-0	1-0	2	Fletcher [35], Carrick [67], Valencia [76]	75,169
14	28	A	Portsmouth	W 4-1	1-1	2	Rooney 3 (2 pens) [25 (p), 48, 54 (p)], Giggs [87]	20,482
15	Dec 5	A	West Ham U	W 4-0	1-0	2	Scholes [45], Gibson [61], Valencia [70], Rooney [72]	34,980
16	12	H	Aston Villa	L 0-1	0-1	2		75,130
17	15	H	Wolverhampton W	W 3-0	2-0	—	Rooney (pen) [30], Vidic [43], Valencia [66]	73,709
18	19	A	Fulham	L 0-3	0-1	2		25,700
19	27	A	Hull C	W 3-1	1-0	2	Rooney [45], Dawson (og) [73], Berbatov [82]	24,627
20	30	H	Wigan Ath	W 5-0	3-0	—	Rooney [28], Carrick [32], Rafael [45], Berbatov [50], Valencia [75]	74,560
21	Jan 9	A	Birmingham C	D 1-1	0-1	—	Dann (og) [63]	28,907
22	16	H	Burnley	W 3-0	0-0	2	Berbatov [64], Rooney [69], Biram Diouf [90]	75,120
23	23	H	Hull C	W 4-0	1-0	2	Rooney 4 [8, 82, 86, 90]	73,933
24	31	A	Arsenal	W 3-1	2-0	2	Nani [33], Rooney [37], Park [52]	60,091
25	Feb 6	H	Portsmouth	W 5-0	2-0	2	Rooney [40], Vanden Borre (og) [45], Carrick [59], Berbatov [62], Wilson (og) [69]	74,684
26	10	A	Aston Villa	D 1-1	1-1	—	James M Collins (og) [23]	42,788
27	20	A	Everton	L 1-3	1-0	2	Berbatov [16]	39,448
28	23	H	West Ham U	W 3-0	1-0	—	Rooney 2 [38, 55], Owen [80]	73,797
29	Mar 6	A	Wolverhampton W	W 1-0	0-0	—	Scholes [72]	28,883
30	14	H	Fulham	W 3-0	0-0	1	Rooney 2 [46, 84], Berbatov [89]	75,207
31	21	H	Liverpool	W 2-1	1-1	1	Rooney [12], Park [60]	75,216
32	27	A	Bolton W	W 4-0	1-0	1	Samuel (og) [38], Berbatov 2 [69, 78], Gibson [82]	25,370
33	Apr 3	H	Chelsea	L 1-2	0-1	2	Macheda [81]	75,217
34	11	A	Blackburn R	D 0-0	0-0	—		29,912
35	17	A	Manchester C	W 1-0	0-0	2	Scholes [90]	47,019
36	24	H	Tottenham H	W 3-1	0-0	2	Giggs 2 (2 pens) [58, 86], Nani [81]	75,268
37	May 2	A	Sunderland	W 1-0	1-0	2	Nani [28]	47,641
38	9	H	Stoke C	W 4-0	2-0	2	Fletcher [31], Giggs [38], Higginbotham (og) [54], Park [84]	75,316

Final League Position: 2

GOALSCORERS

League (86): Rooney 26 (4 pens), Berbatov 12, Giggs 5 (2 pens), Valencia 5, Fletcher 4, Nani 4, Carrick 3, Owen 3, Park 3, Scholes 3, Gibson 2, Anderson 1, Biram Diouf 1, Macheda 1, O'Shea 1, Rafael 1, Vidic 1, own goals 10.
Carling Cup (11): Gibson 2, Owen 2, Rooney 2, Welbeck 2, Carrick 1, Giggs 1, Scholes 1.
FA Cup (0).
Champions League (21): Rooney 5, Owen 4, Scholes 3, Nani 2, Valencia 2, Carrick 1, Fletcher 1, Gibson 1, Giggs 1, Park 1.
Community Shield (2): Nani 1, Rooney 1.

Foster B 9	Fabio 1+4	Evra P 37+1	Fletcher D 29+1	O'Shea J 12+3	Evans J 18	Valencia L 29+5	Scholes P 24+4	Berbatov D 24+9	Rooney W 32	Nani 19+4	Giggs R 20+5	Owen M 5+14	Brown W 18+1	Carrick M 22+8	Park J 10+7	Anderson 10+4	Neville G 15+2	Vidic N 24	Gibson D 6+9	Ferdinand R 12+1	Welbeck D 1+4	Van der Sar E 21	Obertan G 1+6	Rafael 8	Kuszczak T 8	De Laet R 2	Biram Diouf M —+5	Macheda F 1+4	Hargreaves 0—+1	Match No.
1	2	3	4	5	6³	7	8	9²	10	11¹	12	13	14																	1
1		3		2	6	12		13	10		11	9²	5³	4	7	8¹	14													2
1		3	4	13	5²	7	8³	9	10¹	11		12					2	6	14											3
1		3	8	2		7¹		13	10	11	9²		5	4	12		6													4
1		3	7	2		8¹	9¹	10	13	11		12		4²	6		5													5
1		3	7	2		12		9²	10		11	13		14	8¹	4³	6	5												6
1		3	4	2		7	8³	9	10²	11¹	12	13		14			6	5												7
1		3	4²	2	5	13	8¹	9	10	11			14		12		6		7³											8
	3¹		12	6	7	14	9		11	10²		4		8³	2		5	13	1											9
	3		2		7	8¹	9²	10	13	11	12		4			6⁸	5	1												10
	3		2	6	7		9²	10	11¹		13	5	4	8			1	12												11
	3	9	2	6	7		10		11²	12	5	4	8¹				1	13												12
	3	8		7	12		10²	11	9	5	4³		6	14			1	13	2¹											13
	3	10		7	8	9		11		5	4¹	12	2	6								1								14
	3	6		7	10	13	9³	11	14	5	12		4	2¹		8²						1								15
	3	10		7		13	9	11¹	12	5	4	2²	8³	6	14							1								16
	3	12		7	8	9	10³		14	4		5¹	6	13		11²						1	2							17
12	3	5		7	8	13	10		9³	4	11		6²	14								1	2¹							18
	3	8		7¹		9	10	11²	5	4	12		6			13	2	1												19
14	3³	8		7		9²	10		5	4	11	12	6¹		13		2	1												20
	3	8⁸	6	7	10²		9	12	5	4	11¹					2	1	13												21
	3		6	7	8	9³	10²	11	13	5	4¹	12	2			1		14												22
14	3³	4	6		8¹	13	10	11	9²		7		12	5		1	2													23
	3	8	6	13		9¹	14	10	11³	12	5	4	7²			1	2													24
	3	8¹	6	7		9³	10²	11		14	5	4		2	12	1		13												25
	3	7	6	12		8¹	13	10	11⁸	9²	5	4				1	2													26
	3	8	6	7³	12	9¹	10		14	5	4	11²	2			1	¹3													27
1	3		7	8	9³	10²		13	5	12	4¹	2	6	11											14					28
	3		7	8	9		11³		2¹	4	14	12	6	10²	5	1									13					29
13	3	8		7¹		9	10	11		4	12		2²	6		5		1												30
	3	10		7	13		9	11¹	12		4	8²	2	6		5		1												31
	3	4²	5	7	8	9		11	10³		12		2	6	13	1											14			32
	3	10³		7	8²	9		12	11			4¹	2	6	14	5	1										13			33
	14		3³	7	4	9		11	10¹			13	2	6	12	5	1										8²			34
	3	4	5	7³	9	13	10²	12	11			2	6	8¹		1	14													35
	3²	4	13	5	7¹	8	9		11	10	12		6			2²								14						36
	3	4²	2	5		8	9¹	10	7³	11	12		6	13														14		37
	3	4			8¹	9²	10³	7	11		14		2	6	12	5												13		38

FA Cup

Third Round	Leeds U	(h)	0-1

Champions League

Group B	Besiktas	(a)	1-0
	Wolfsburg	(h)	2-1
	CSKA Moscow	(a)	1-0
		(h)	3-3
	Besiktas	(h)	0-1
	Wolfsburg	(a)	3-1
Knock-Out Round	AC Milan	(a)	3-2
		(h)	4-0
Quarter-Final	Bayern Munich	(a)	1-2
		(h)	3-2

Carling Cup

Third Round	Wolverhampton W	(h)	1-0
Fourth Round	Barnsley	(a)	2-0
Quarter-Final	Tottenham H	(h)	2-0
Semi-Final	Manchester C	(a)	1-2
		(h)	3-1
Final	Aston Villa		2-1

(at Wembley).

Community Shield

	Chelsea	2-2

(at Wembley).

MIDDLESBROUGH

FL Championship

FOUNDATION

A previous belief that Middlesbrough Football Club was founded at a tripe supper at the Corporation Hotel has proved to be erroneous. In fact, members of Middlesbrough Cricket Club were responsible for forming it at a meeting in the gymnasium of the Albert Park Hotel in 1875.

Riverside Stadium, Middlesbrough TS3 6RS.

Telephone: (0844) 499 6789.

Fax: (01642) 757 690.

Ticket Office: (0844) 499 1234

Website: www.mfc.co.uk

Email: enquiries@mfc.co.uk

Ground Capacity: 35,100.

Record Attendance: Ayresome Park: 53,536 v Newcastle U, Division 1, 27 December 1949. Riverside Stadium: 34,814 v Newcastle U, FA Premier League, 5 March 2003.

Pitch Measurements: 105m × 68m.

Chairman: Steve Gibson.

Chief Executive: Keith Lamb.

Secretary: Karen Nelson.

Manager: Gordon Strachan.

Assistant Manager: Garry Pendrey.

Physio: Grant Downie.

Colours: Red shirts with white design and one white sleeve, white shorts with red trim, white stockings.

Change Colours: All light blue with white trim on shirts, black stockings.

Year Formed: 1876; reformed 1986.

Turned Professional: 1889; became amateur 1892, and professional again, 1899.

Ltd Co: 1892. *Club Nickname:* 'Boro'.

Grounds: 1877, Old Archery Ground, Albert Park; 1879, Breckon Hill; 1882, Linthorpe Road Ground; 1903, Ayresome Park; 1995, Riverside Stadium.

First Football League Game: 2 September 1899, Division 2, v Lincoln C (a) L 0–3 – Smith; Shaw, Ramsey; Allport, McNally, McCracken; Wanless, Longstaffe, Gettins, Page, Pugh.

Record League Victory: 9–0 v Brighton & HA, Division 2, 23 August 1958 – Taylor; Bilcliff, Robinson; Harris (2p), Phillips, Walley; Day, McLean, Clough (5), Peacock (2), Holliday.

Record Cup Victory: 7–0 v Hereford U, Coca-Cola Cup 2nd rd, 1st leg, 18 September 1996 – Miller; Fleming (1), Branco (1), Whyte, Vickers, Whelan, Emerson (1), Mustoe, Stamp, Juninho, Ravanelli (4).

HONOURS

Football League: Division 1 – Champions 1994–95; Runners-up 1997–98; Division 2 – Champions 1926–27, 1928–29, 1973–74; Runners-up 1901–02, 1991–92; Division 3 – Runners-up 1966–67, 1986–87.

FA Cup: Runners-up 1997.

Football League Cup: Winners 2004; Runners-up 1997, 1998.

Amateur Cup: Winners 1895, 1898.

Anglo-Scottish Cup: Winners 1976.

Zenith Data Systems Cup: Runners-up 1990.

European Competitions: UEFA Cup: 2004–05, 2005–06 (runners-up).

sky SPORTS FACT FILE

Ronnie Dicks rendered loyal service to Middlesbrough for 15 years. From wartime regional football in 1943 while in the Army he missed the next three seasons. Starting as a winger, then inside-forward, wing-half, full-back and centre-half, he made over 350 appearances.

Record Defeat: 0–9 v Blackburn R, Division 2, 6 November 1954.

Most League Points (2 for a win): 65, Division 2, 1973–74.

Most League Points (3 for a win): 94, Division 3, 1986–87.

Most League Goals: 122, Division 2, 1926–27.

Highest League Scorer in Season: George Camsell, 59, Division 2, 1926–27 (Second Division record).

Most League Goals in Total Aggregate: George Camsell, 325, 1925–39.

Most League Goals in One Match: 5, John Wilkie v Gainsborough T, Division 2, 2 March 1901; 5, Andy Wilson v Nottingham F, Division 1, 6 October 1923; 5, George Camsell v Manchester C, Division 2, 25 December 1926; 5, George Camsell v Aston Villa, Division 1, 9 September 1935; 5, Brian Clough v Brighton & HA, Division 2, 22 August 1958.

Most Capped Player: Wilf Mannion, 26, England.

Most League Appearances: Tim Williamson, 563, 1902–23.

Youngest League Player: Stephen Bell, 16 years 323 days v Southampton, 30 January 1982; Sam Lawrie, 16 years 323 days v Arsenal, 3 November 1951.

Record Transfer Fee Received: £12,000,000 from Atletico Madrid for Juninho, July 1997; £12,000,000 from Aston Villa for Stewart Downing, July 2009.

Record Transfer Fee Paid: £12,000,000 to Heerenveen for Afonso Alves, January 2008.

Football League Record: 1899 Elected to Division 2; 1902–24 Division 1; 1924–27 Division 2; 1927–28 Division 1; 1928–29 Division 2; 1929–54 Division 1; 1954–66 Division 2; 1966–67 Division 3; 1967–74 Division 2; 1974–82 Division 1; 1982–86 Division 2; 1986–87 Division 3; 1987–88 Division 2; 1988–89 Division 1; 1989–92 Division 2; 1992–93 FA Premier League; 1993–95 Division 1; 1995–97 FA Premier League; 1997–98 Division 1; 1998–2009 FA Premier League; 2009– FL C.

MANAGERS

John Robson 1899–1905
Alex Mackie 1905–06
Andy Aitken 1906–09
J. Gunter 1908–10
  (Secretary-Manager)
Andy Walker 1910–11
Tom McIntosh 1911–19
Jimmy Howie 1920–23
Herbert Bamlett 1923–26
Peter McWilliam 1927–34
Wilf Gillow 1934–44
David Jack 1944–52
Walter Rowley 1952–54
Bob Dennison 1954–63
Raich Carter 1963–66
Stan Anderson 1966–73
Jack Charlton 1973–77
John Neal 1977–81
Bobby Murdoch 1981–82
Malcolm Allison 1982–84
Willie Maddren 1984–86
Bruce Rioch 1986–90
Colin Todd 1990–91
Lennie Lawrence 1991–94
Bryan Robson 1994–2001
Steve McClaren 2001–06
Gareth Southgate 2006–2009
Gordon Strachan October 2009–

LATEST SEQUENCES

Longest Sequence of League Wins: 9, 16.2.1974 – 6.4.1974.

Longest Sequence of League Defeats: 8, 26.12.1995 – 17.2.1996.

Longest Sequence of League Draws: 8, 3.4.1971 – 1.5.1971.

Longest Sequence of Unbeaten League Matches: 24, 8.9.1973 – 19.1.1974.

Longest Sequence Without a League Win: 19, 3.10.1981 – 5.3.1982.

Successive Scoring Runs: 26 from 21.9.1946.

Successive Non-scoring Runs: 5 from 17.1.2009.

TEN YEAR LEAGUE RECORD

		P	W	D	L	F	A	Pts	Pos
2000-01	PR Lge	38	9	15	14	44	44	42	14
2001-02	PR Lge	38	12	9	17	35	47	45	12
2002-03	PR Lge	38	13	10	15	48	44	49	11
2003-04	PR Lge	38	13	9	16	44	52	48	11
2004-05	PR Lge	38	14	13	11	53	46	55	7
2005-06	PR Lge	38	12	9	17	48	58	45	14
2006-07	PR Lge	38	12	10	16	44	49	46	12
2007-08	PR Lge	38	10	12	16	43	53	42	13
2008-09	PR Lge	38	7	11	20	28	57	32	19
2009-10	FL C	46	16	14	16	58	50	62	11

DID YOU KNOW ?

George Washington Elliott was one of several Middlesbrough centre-forwards who won international honours. He played his entire career there from 1910, retiring 15 years later. Scored 213 League and Cup goals for them and once hit eleven in a reserve game.

MIDDLESBROUGH 2009–10 LEAGUE RECORD

Match No.	Date	Venue	Opponents	Result	H/T Score	Lg Pos.	Goalscorers	Attendance
1	Aug 7	H	Sheffield U	D 0-0	0-0	—		23,541
2	15	A	Swansea C	W 3-0	1-0	4	Johnson A [32], Emnes [52], Tuncay [62]	16,201
3	18	A	Scunthorpe U	W 2-0	1-0	—	Johnson A 2 (1 pen) [28, 53 (p)]	8274
4	22	H	Doncaster R	W 2-0	1-0	2	Tuncay [17], Lita [71]	22,041
5	29	A	Bristol C	L 1-2	0-0	3	Johnson A (pen) [80]	14,402
6	Sept 12	H	Ipswich T	W 3-1	1-0	3	O'Neil [17], Aliadiere 2 [66, 85]	19,742
7	15	A	Sheffield W	W 3-1	1-1	3	Purse (og) [19], Aliadiere [49], Johnson A [85]	21,722
8	19	H	WBA	L 0-5	0-3	3		22,725
9	26	A	Coventry C	D 2-2	2-0	4	St Ledger-Hall [40], Williams R [45]	16,771
10	29	H	Leicester C	L 0-1	0-0	—		18,577
11	Oct 3	A	Reading	W 2-0	1-0	3	St Ledger-Hall [12], Lita [55]	17,638
12	17	H	Watford	L 0-1	0-1	4		18,957
13	20	H	Derby Co	W 2-0	1-0	—	Johnson A 2 (1 pen) [22 (p), 59]	17,459
14	24	A	Preston NE	D 2-2	1-0	4	O'Neil [43], Johnson A [67]	16,116
15	31	H	Plymouth Arg	L 0-1	0-0	7		21,141
16	Nov 7	A	Crystal Palace	L 0-1	0-0	10		15,321
17	21	H	Nottingham F	D 1-1	1-0	11	Lita [5]	22,710
18	28	A	Peterborough U	D 2-2	1-0	10	Kitson 2 [28, 58]	10,772
19	Dec 5	A	QPR	W 5-1	1-0	6	Kitson [31], Lita 2 (1 pen) [50 (p), 60], O'Neil [75], Yeates [87]	13,949
20	8	H	Blackpool	L 0-3	0-2	—		18,089
21	13	H	Cardiff C	L 0-1	0-0	11		17,232
22	20	A	Newcastle U	L 0-2	0-1	14		49,644
23	26	H	Scunthorpe U	W 3-0	2-0	10	Johnson A (pen) [11], Williams R [45], Aliadiere [46]	20,647
24	28	A	Barnsley	L 1-2	1-0	11	Hoyte [23]	18,001
25	Jan 16	A	Sheffield U	L 0-1	0-0	13		23,974
26	23	H	Swansea C	D 1-1	0-0	—	Flood [58]	16,847
27	26	A	Doncaster R	W 4-1	2-0	—	Johnson A 2 [30, 90], Franks [45], Lita [66]	10,794
28	30	H	Bristol C	D 0-0	0-0	9		17,865
29	Feb 6	A	Ipswich T	D 1-1	0-1	10	Wheater [62]	21,243
30	9	H	Barnsley	W 2-1	2-0	—	Killen [24], O'Neil [35]	17,775
31	13	H	Peterborough U	W 1-0	1-0	8	Robson [7]	18,412
32	16	A	Blackpool	L 0-2	0-1	—		7936
33	20	A	Nottingham F	L 0-1	0-0	9		25,498
34	27	H	QPR	W 2-0	2-0	9	Robson 2 (2 pens) [39, 45]	17,568
35	Mar 6	A	Cardiff C	L 0-1	0-1	10		19,803
36	13	H	Newcastle U	D 2-2	1-1	10	Robson [36], McDonald [74]	27,342
37	16	A	Derby Co	D 2-2	1-0	—	Robson [15], Lita [90]	27,143
38	20	H	Reading	D 1-1	0-0	11	Killen [47]	17,082
39	23	H	Preston NE	W 2-0	1-0	—	Killen [29], Franks [90]	16,974
40	27	A	Watford	D 1-1	0-1	9	Lita [55]	14,038
41	Apr 3	H	Crystal Palace	D 1-1	1-1	8	McDonald [15]	18,428
42	5	A	Plymouth Arg	W 2-0	1-0	8	McManus [22], Franks [90]	11,770
43	10	H	Sheffield W	W 1-0	1-0	8	McDonald [40]	19,932
44	17	A	WBA	L 0-2	0-1	8		22,548
45	24	H	Coventry C	D 1-1	0-0	8	McDonald [52]	27,721
46	May 2	A	Leicester C	L 0-2	0-1	11		30,223

Final League Position: 11

GOALSCORERS

League (58): Johnson A 11 (4 pens), Lita 8 (1 pen), Robson 5 (2 pens), Aliadiere 4, McDonald 4, O'Neil 4, Franks 3, Killen 3, Kitson 3, St Ledger-Hall 2, Tuncay 2, Williams R 2, Emnes 1, Flood 1, Hoyte 1, McManus 1, Wheater 1, Yeates 1, own goal 1.
Carling Cup (1): Johnson A 1.
FA Cup (0).

Coyne D 22+1	McMahon T 20+1	Grounds J 16+4	Williams R 31+1	Huth R 4	Wheater D 42	Yeates M 11+8	Digard D 4+5	Emnes M 12+4	Aliadiere J 16+4	Johnson A 25+1	O'Neil G 35+1	Lita L 23+17	Tuncay S —+3	Franks J 9+14	Arca J 26+8	Hoyte J 23+7	Taylor A 8+4	Hines S 2	St Ledger-Hall S 14+1	Folan C —+1	Jones B 24	Bennett J 10+2	Pogatetz E 13	Bent M 3+4	Osbourne 19	Kitson D 6	Riggott C 4+2	Williams L 2+2	Flood W 11	Killen C 15+2	Robson B 18	McManus S 16	Miller L 6+4	Naughton K 12+3	McDonald S 12+1	Walker J 1	O'Shea J 1+1	Match No
1	2	3	4	5	6	7	8^1	9^2	10	11	12	13																										1
1	2	3	4	5	6	7^3		9^1	11	8	10^2	12	13	14																								2
1	2	3	4	5	6	7^2		9	11^3	8	10^3	12	13	14																								3
1	2	3	4	5	6	7^2		9^1	13	11	10^3	12		8			14																					4
1	2		5	4	6	7		9^1	12	11	10	8		3																								5
1	2	12	4		6	14		9	13	11	7	10^2			8^3		3^1		5																				6
1	2^2	3	4		6			9^1	10	11	7^3	12			8^2				5	13																		7
1	2	3	4		6	7	13	9^3	10^1	11	14				8^2				5	12																		8
	13		4		6	14		9^1	10	11^3	7	12			8	2			5		1	3^2																9
	2		4		6	13	14	9^1	10	11	7	12			8^2				5		1	3^1																10
	2		4		6	7^1		13	10	11	8	9^2			12				5		1	3^1																11
	2				6	7^2	8		10	11	4	9			13^1	12			5		1	3^1																12
			4		6	12	8^1	13	10^2	11	7	9				2			5		1	3																13
			4		6		8	10^1	11	7	9	12			2				5		1	3																14
	13		4		6	14		9^1	11	7	10	8^3		2					5		1	3^2	12															15
	3		4		6			11	7	9^2	13	12	2^1						5		1		10	8														16
			4		6	13		11	7	9^3	14	8^2							5		1	3	12^2	2	10^1													17
	2		4		7^1			11		10	8	9^2			12				5		1	6	3	9														18
			4		6	11	12	7^1	10		8								5		1	3	2	9														19
12		2^1	6	13	14			11	4^2	9	8^3								5		1	3	7	10														20
3	2		4		7		13	11^2	12										5		1	6	10	8	9^1													21
	2		4		7	13		8	10^3	14	11^2	3							1		5	12	6	9^1														22
1	2		4		6	13		10^1	11^2	8	9^4				3							5^3	12	7	14													23
1	2		4		6			11	7		9^1	8	3									10		5	12													24
1	2		6					10^1	12	8		13	3										4	5	7^2	9	11											25
1	2^1	14	6					11	4	9^2	8	3			2								5^3	13	7	10												26
1	5	3	6					11	4	9^2	12	9^1	8^2	2^3	14							3			7	10												27
1	5	3	6					11	4	9^2	13	12	2^1												7	10	8^4											28
1		3	6					8	13	12		2	4^1												7	10^2		5	9	11									29
	3							4		9	3								1		5				7	10^1	11	6	12	2^2	8							30
1			5					12		14	9	3									3				7		11	6	10^1	2	8^3	4^2							31
1	3^2		5					10	4	9^1	12	2													7		8	6	13		11								32
1			5					10^1	4	12	13	8^2										3			7		11	6		2	9								33
1			5					10^1	4	9^3	12	14		13								2^2			7	8	11	6		3								34
1	12		5					10^2	4	9		8		2											7^1	13	11	6		3									35
1	7		5					4		8		2													10^1	11	6	12	3	9									36
1	4^8		5					7	13	8^3	-2	2													10^2	11	6	14	3^1	9									37
	3		5			14		4	13	7^3	8	2^1									1		6		10	11				12	9^2								38
	4		5					14	9		2	13									1	7^1	3^2		10	11	6	8^3	12										39
	4		5			7	12	13	8^2	2	3									1					10	11	6	9^1										40
	4^3		5			7	13	9	2	3^1											1				10^2	11	6	12	8						14			41
	4		5			9^1	14	8	2	1		13									11		6		10^2	3	12								7^3			42
	4		5			9	7	8	2	1											11		6		3	10												43
	5^2	4^3				7	12	14	8	2	1										13				10^1	11	6	9^1		8								44
	4					10^2		12	13	2	1	3										5	7		11	6	9^1		8									45
15	5					9	4		11	2	1^8	3													7^6	10		3	8									46

FA Cup
Third Round   Manchester C   (h)   0-1

Carling Cup
Second Round   Nottingham F   (a)   1-2

MILLWALL

FOUNDATION

Formed in 1885 as Millwall Rovers by employees of Morton & Co, a jam and marmalade factory in West Ferry Road. The founders were predominantly Scotsmen. Their first headquarters was The Islanders pub in Tooke Street, Millwall. Their first trophy was the East End Cup in 1887.

The Den, Zampa Road, London SE16 3LN.

Telephone: (020) 7232 1222.

Fax: (020) 7231 3663.

Ticket Office: (020) 7231 9999.

Website: www.millwallfc.co.uk

Email: questions@millwallplc.com

Ground Capacity: 19,734.

Record Attendance: 20,093 v Arsenal, FA Cup 3rd rd, 10 January 1994.

Pitch Measurements: 105m × 68m.

Chairman: John G Berylson.

Executive Deputy Chairman: Heather Rabbatts.

Chief Executive: Andy Ambler.

Secretary: Yvonne Haines.

Manager: Kenny Jackett.

Assistant Manager: Joe Gallen.

Physio: Bobby Bacic.

Colours: All blue with white detail on shirts.

Change Colours: Red and black striped shirts, black shorts, black stockings.

HONOURS

Football League: Division 1 best season: 3rd, 1993–94; Division 2 – Champions 1987–88, 2000–01; Division 3 (S) – Champions 1927–28, 1937–38; Runners-up 1952–53; Division 3 – Runners–up 1965–66, 1984–85; Division 4 – Champions 1961–62; Runners-up 1964–65.

FA Cup: Runners-up 2004; Semi-final 1900, 1903, 1937 (first Division 3 side to reach semi-final).

Football League Cup: best season: 5th rd, 1974, 1977, 1995.

Football League Trophy: Winners 1983.

Auto Windscreens Shield: Runners-up 1999.

European Competitions: UEFA Cup: 2004–05.

Year Formed: 1885. *Turned Professional:* 1893. *Ltd Co.:* 1894.

Previous Names: 1885, Millwall Rovers; 1889, Millwall Athletic; 1899, Millwall; 1985, Millwall Football & Athletic Company.

Club Nickname: 'The Lions'.

Grounds: 1885, Glengall Road, Millwall; 1886, Back of 'Lord Nelson'; 1890, East Ferry Road; 1901, North Greenwich; 1910, The Den, Cold Blow Lane; 1993, The Den, Bermondsey.

First Football League Game: 28 August 1920, Division 3, v Bristol R (h) W 2–0 – Lansdale; Fort, Hodge; Voisey (1), Riddell, McAlpine; Waterall, Travers, Broad (1), Sutherland, Dempsey.

Record League Victory: 9–1 v Torquay U, Division 3 (S), 29 August 1927 – Lansdale, Tilling, Hill, Amos, Bryant (3), Graham, Chance, Hawkins (3), Landells (1), Phillips (2), Black. 9–1 v Coventry C, Division 3 (S), 19 November 1927 – Lansdale, Fort, Hill, Amos, Collins (1), Graham, Chance, Landells (4), Cock (2), Phillips (2), Black.

Record Cup Victory: 7–0 v Gateshead, FA Cup 2nd rd, 12 December 1936 – Yuill; Ted Smith, Inns; Brolly, Hancock, Forsyth; Thomas (1), Mangnall (1), Ken Burditt (2), McCartney (2), Thorogood (1).

sky SPORTS FACT FILE

Left-winger Alf Geddes had an outstanding record for Millwall in FA Cup matches between 1894–95 and 1898–99. He played in fifteen ties during the period and scored eleven goals including a run of seven consecutive games when he was on the score sheet in each one.

Record Defeat: 1–9 v Aston Villa, FA Cup 4th rd, 28 January 1946.

Most League Points (2 for a win): 65, Division 3 (S), 1927–28 and Division 3, 1965–66.

Most League Points (3 for a win): 93, Division 2, 2000–01.

Most League Goals: 127, Division 3 (S), 1927–28.

Highest League Scorer in Season: Richard Parker, 37, Division 3 (S), 1926–27.

Most League Goals in Total Aggregate: Neil Harris, 114, 1995–2004; 2006–.

Most League Goals in One Match: 5, Richard Parker v Norwich C, Division 3 (S), 28 August 1926.

Most Capped Player: Eamonn Dunphy, 22 (23), Republic of Ireland.

Most League Appearances: Barry Kitchener, 523, 1967–82.

Youngest League Player: Moses Ashikodi, 15 years 240 days v Brighton & HA, 22 February 2003.

Record Transfer Fee Received: £2,300,000 from Liverpool for Mark Kennedy, March 1995.

Record Transfer Fee Paid: £800,000 to Derby Co for Paul Goddard, December 1989.

Football League Record: 1920 Original Members of Division 3; 1921 Division 3 (S); 1928–34 Division 2; 1934–38 Division 3 (S); 1938–48 Division 2; 1948–58 Division 3 (S); 1958–62 Division 4; 1962–64 Division 3; 1964–65 Division 4; 1965–66 Division 3; 1966–75 Division 2; 1975–76 Division 3; 1976–79 Division 2; 1979–85 Division 3; 1985–88 Division 2; 1988–90 Division 1; 1990–92 Division 2; 1992–96 Division 1; 1996–2001 Division 2; 2001–04 Division 1; 2004–06 FL C; 2006–10 FL 1; 2010– FL C.

LATEST SEQUENCES

Longest Sequence of League Wins: 10, 10.3.1928 – 25.4.1928.

Longest Sequence of League Defeats: 11, 10.4.1929 – 16.9.1929.

Longest Sequence of League Draws: 5, 22.12.1973 – 12.1.1974.

Longest Sequence of Unbeaten League Matches: 19, 22.8.1959 – 31.10.1959.

Longest Sequence Without a League Win: 20, 26.12.1989 – 5.5.1990.

Successive Scoring Runs: 22 from 8.12.1923.

Successive Non-scoring Runs: 6 from 20.12.1947.

MANAGERS

F. B. Kidd 1894–99
(Hon. Treasurer/Manager)
E. R. Stopher 1899–1900
(Hon. Treasurer/Manager)
George Saunders 1900–11
(Hon. Treasurer/Manager)
Herbert Lipsham 1911–19
Robert Hunter 1919–33
Bill McCracken 1933–36
Charlie Hewitt 1936–40
Bill Voisey 1940–44
Jack Cock 1944–48
Charlie Hewitt 1948–56
Ron Gray 1956–57
Jimmy Seed 1958–59
Reg Smith 1959–61
Ron Gray 1961–63
Billy Gray 1963–66
Benny Fenton 1966–74
Gordon Jago 1974–77
George Petchey 1978–80
Peter Anderson 1980–82
George Graham 1982–86
John Docherty 1986–90
Bob Pearson 1990
Bruce Rioch 1990–92
Mick McCarthy 1992–96
Jimmy Nicholl 1996–97
John Docherty 1997
Billy Bonds 1997–98
Keith Stevens May 1998–2000
(then Joint Manager)
(plus Alan McLeary 1999–2000)
Mark McGhee 2000–03
Dennis Wise 2003–05
Steve Claridge 2005
Colin Lee 2005–06
Nigel Spackman 2006
Willie Donachie 2006–07
Kenny Jackett November 2007–

TEN YEAR LEAGUE RECORD

		P	W	D	L	F	A	Pts	Pos
2000-01	Div 2	46	28	9	9	89	38	93	1
2001-02	Div 1	46	22	11	13	69	48	77	4
2002-03	Div 1	46	19	9	18	59	69	66	9
2003-04	Div 1	46	18	15	13	55	48	69	10
2004-05	FL C	46	18	12	16	51	45	66	10
2005-06	FL C	46	8	17	21	35	61	40	23
2006-07	FL 1	46	19	9	18	59	62	66	10
2007-08	FL 1	46	14	10	22	45	60	52	17
2008-09	FL 1	46	25	7	14	63	53	82	5
2009-10	FL 1	46	24	13	9	76	44	85	3

DID YOU KNOW

On 6 February 2010 Millwall ended the 16-match unbeaten run by Norwich City. The winning goal was scored by substitute Neil Harris. It was his 130th goal for the club on his 300th appearance in what was his testimonial season for the New Den club.

MILLWALL 2009–10 LEAGUE RECORD

Match No.	Date	Venue	Opponents	Result	H/T Score	Lg Pos.	Goalscorers	Attendance
1	Aug 8	A	Southampton	D 1-1	0-0	—	Abdou [67]	20,103
2	15	H	Carlisle U	D 0-0	0-0	14		9055
3	18	H	Oldham Ath	W 2-0	1-0	—	Martin [12], Harris [90]	7369
4	21	A	Southend U	D 0-0	0-0	8		8435
5	28	H	Brighton & HA	D 1-1	1-0	9	Price [6]	10,138
6	Sept 5	A	Bristol R	L 0-2	0-1	13		6038
7	12	A	Gillingham	L 0-2	0-2	16		8097
8	19	H	Huddersfield T	W 3-1	2-0	10	Hackett [13], Harris [14], Morison [50]	8502
9	26	A	Leyton Orient	L 0-1	0-0	12		5255
10	29	H	Yeovil T	D 0-0	0-0	—		6617
11	Oct 3	H	Tranmere R	W 5-0	4-0	10	Henry 3 [6, 27, 85], Frampton [9], Morison [23]	8046
12	10	A	Swindon T	D 1-1	0-1	10	Schofield [82]	7222
13	17	A	Stockport Co	W 4-0	3-0	9	Robinson [18], Harris 3 [23, 37, 68]	4394
14	24	H	Leeds U	W 2-1	1-1	8	Harris [3], Alexander [83]	14,165
15	31	H	Colchester U	W 2-1	0-1	7	Dunne [66], Henry [90]	10,036
16	Nov 14	H	Brentford	D 2-2	1-2	7	Robinson [15], Henry [89]	6408
17	21	H	Wycombe W	L 0-2	0-0	8		9728
18	24	A	Exeter C	D 1-1	1-0	—	Martin (pen) [21]	5732
19	Dec 1	H	Milton Keynes D	W 3-2	2-0	—	Frampton [11], Hackett [20], Morison [90]	7883
20	5	A	Hartlepool U	L 0-3	0-3	10		3153
21	12	H	Walsall	W 2-1	0-1	8	Morison 2 [59, 76]	8174
22	19	A	Charlton Ath	D 4-4	2-2	8	Morison 2 [12, 27], Martin [81], Schofield [90]	19,105
23	26	A	Norwich C	L 0-2	0-1	9		25,242
24	28	H	Bristol R	W 2-0	0-0	7	Morison [62], Baldwin (og) [90]	10,014
25	Jan 16	A	Southampton	D 1-1	0-0	8	Trotter [90]	11,524
26	23	A	Oldham Ath	W 1-0	0-0	8	Harris (pen) [57]	3656
27	26	H	Southend U	W 2-0	1-0	—	Schofield [45], Batt [64]	7612
28	30	A	Brighton & HA	W 1-0	0-0	6	Morison [49]	6610
29	Feb 6	A	Norwich C	W 2-1	1-1	5	Craig [25], Harris [51]	14,374
30	13	H	Exeter C	W 1-0	0-0	6	Harris [81]	9104
31	20	A	Wycombe W	L 0-1	0-1	7		5774
32	23	A	Milton Keynes D	W 3-1	1-0	—	Schofield [19], Harris 2 [61, 85]	10,610
33	27	H	Hartlepool U	W 1-0	1-0	7	Harris [9]	10,818
34	Mar 6	A	Walsall	D 2-2	1-2	6	Morison [29], Dunne [90]	3835
35	9	A	Carlisle U	W 3-1	1-0	—	Morison 2 [12, 78], Schofield [90]	3853
36	13	H	Charlton Ath	W 4-0	1-0	4	Ward [44], Dailly (og) [74], Morison 2 [76, 81]	17,632
37	22	A	Leeds U	W 2-0	1-0	—	Morison [11], Batt [80]	21,348
38	27	H	Stockport Co	W 5-0	3-0	3	Swailes (og) [27], Morison [42], Schofield [45], Huntington (og) [58], Obika [69]	11,116
39	Apr 2	H	Brentford	D 1-1	0-1	3	Robinson [75]	14,025
40	5	A	Colchester U	W 2-1	1-0	3	Morison [43], Batth (og) [78]	7393
41	10	H	Gillingham	W 4-0	2-0	3	Batt [27], Craig [35], Schofield [60], Harris [68]	13,174
42	13	A	Yeovil T	D 1-1	0-1	—	Obika [90]	4713
43	16	A	Huddersfield T	L 0-1	0-1	—		16,050
44	24	H	Leyton Orient	W 2-1	0-0	3	Robinson [69], Morison (pen) [80]	13,011
45	May 1	A	Tranmere R	L 0-2	0-1	3		8694
46	8	H	Swindon T	W 3-2	1-1	3	Morison 2 (1 pen) [14 (p), 73], Greer (og) [32]	17,083

Final League Position: 3

GOALSCORERS

League (76): Morison 20 (2 pens), Harris 13 (1 pen), Schofield 7, Henry 5, Robinson 4, Batt 3, Martin 3 (1 pen), Craig 2, Dunne 2, Frampton 2, Hackett 2, Obika 2, Alexander 1, Abdou 1, Price 1, Trotter 1, Ward 1, own goals 6.
Carling Cup (5): Harris 4, Alexander 1.
FA Cup (11): Morison 2, Price 2, Schofield 2, Dunne 1, Grabban 1, Harris 1, Robinson 1, Smith 1.
J Paint Trophy (0).
Play-Offs (3): Robinson 2, Morison 1.

Forde D 46	Dunne A 29 + 3	Smith J 30 + 1	Bolder A 5 + 6	Frampton A 20 + 1	Barron S 12 + 11	Hackett C 34 + 6	Abdou N 43	Morison S 42 + 7	Alexander G 8 + 7	Martin D 16 + 4	Fuseini A 10 + 5	Price J 5 + 10	Harris N 21 + 11	Friend G 4 + 2	Craig T 29 + 1	Laird M 17 + 3	Hughes-Mason K — + 1	Grimes A 2 + 2	Schofield D 28 + 8	Marquis J — + 1	Ward D 30 + 1	Henry J 6 + 3	Robinson P 34	Grabban L 5 + 6	Trotter L 20	Batt S 10 + 6	Obika J — + 12	Match No.
1	2	3	4^1	5	6	7	8	9	10	11^2	12	13^3	14															1
1	2	3		5	6	7^2		9	10^1	12	4	13	8	11														2
1	14	2	8^3	5		7^2		9^1	10	11	4	13	12	3	6													3
1		2	8	5		13		10	11	7	9^1	12		3	6	4^2												4
1	5	2		6	3	7		10	11^2	8^1	9^3		13		4	12	14											5
1	5	2		6	3	7		10^2	11^1	8		12		9	4	13												6
1		2	11^1	5		13	7	9	14	12			10^3	3		4^2			6				8					7
1	4	2		5		11^3	7	9^1		3	8		10	14					13				6			8^2		8
1	2	3		5		11^1	7	9^2	13	12	4^3		10						14				6			8		9
1	2	3		5		13	7	9^1	12	11^3	4		10						14				6			8^2		10
1	2		5	3		13	7	9	10	11^1				6	4				12							8^2		11
1	2		5^1	3		14	7	9	10^1	11^2			12	6	4				13							8^3		12
1	2	3	13			7	8^2	9^3	14			12	10^1	6	4				11						5			13
1	2	3				7	8	9^1	12			13	10^2	6	4				11						5			14
1	2	3				7^1	8	9^2				13	10	6	4				11		12				5			15
1	2	3^1				7^2	8	14				9^9	10	6	4			11		2	13				5			16
1	2		12			7	8	9^3	13			10			3^1	4^2		14	11		6		5					17
1	12	2^1		3		7	8	9				11^2	13			4			10		6		5					18
1	2		12	3		7^3	8	9				11^2	14			4^1			10		6		5		13			19
1	2	14	4^1	3^1		7^2	11	9					13						10		6	8	5	12				20
1	2	3	14	6			8	9			11^2		13						4^3		7^1	10		5	12			21
1	2	3	14	6^1			8	9			11	7					2		4^3		13		5	10^2				22
1	2		13	6^3	14		8	9				7^1	12						3^4		11		5	10^2				23
1		2	14	6			7	8	9			11^2	10^1						3^4		13		5	12				24
1	2					3	7	8	9				12						11		6		5	10^1	4			25
1	2						8	9			11		13^3	10^1	3				7		6		5	12^2	4			26
1	2					7	8	9							3						6		5	4	10			27
1	12	2^1		13		7	8	9				11^2			3						6		5	4	10			28
1	2			3		7	8	9					12		11						6		5	10^1	4			29
1	2			12		7	8	9					10		3^1						6		5	4	11^2	13		30
1	2			3^1		7	8	9^2					12		1				13		6		5	4	10^3	14		31
1	2			12		7^1	8	9	13				10^3		3				11^2		6		5	4		14		32
1	2			13		7	8	9					10^2		3				11^1		6		5	4	12			33
1	2			13		7	8^3	9					10^1		3				11		6^2		5	4	12	14		34
1	2			13		7^2	8	9							3				11		6		5	4	10^1	12		35
1	2			14		7^3	8	9^2					12		3				11		6		5	4	10^1	13		36
1	2					7	8	9					10^1		3				11		6		5	4	12			37
1	2			14		7	8^3	9^1					10^2		3				11		6		5	4	12	13		38
1	2					7^1	8	9					10		3				11		6		5	4	12			39
1	2					7^2	8	9^1					10		3				11		6		5	4	12	13		40
1	2			14		7	8	9^1					12		3				11		6		5	4^3	10^3	13		41
1	2			12	14	8	9						10^2		3				11		6		5	4^1	7^3	13		42
1	2					7^2	8	9^2	14				13		3	4			11		6		5		10^1	12		43
1	2			3		7^1	8	9	12		13		10			4^2			11		6		5					44
1	2		4	3^1		7^2	11	9^2	13				10								6		5	12	8		14	45
1	2			3		7	8	9					12			13					6		5	10^2	4		11^1	46

FA Cup
First Round — AFC Wimbledon (h) 4-1
Second Round — Staines T (a) 1-1
(h) 4-0
Third Round — Derby Co (h) 1-1
(a) 1-1

Carling Cup
First Round — Bournemouth (h) 4-0
Second Round — West Ham U (a) 1-3

J Paint Trophy
First Round — Barnet (a) 0-2

Play-Offs
Semi-Final — Huddersfield T (a) 0-0
(h) 2-0
Final — Swindon T 1-0
(at Wembley).

MILTON KEYNES DONS FL Championship 1

FOUNDATION

Old boys from Central School formed this club as Wimbledon Old Centrals in 1889. Their earliest successes were in the Clapham League before switching to the Southern Suburban League in 1902. In July 2004 Wimbledon became MK Dons and relocated to Milton Keynes.

Stadiummk, Stadium Way West, Milton Keynes MK1 1ST.

Telephone: (01908) 622 922.

Fax: (01908) 622 933.

Ticket Office: (01908) 622 900.

Website: www.mkdons.com

Email: info@mkdons.com

Ground Capacity: 21,189.

Record Attendance: 30,115 v Manchester U, FA Premier League, 9 May 1993 (at Selhurst Park).

Pitch Measurements: 105m × 68m.

Chairman: Pete Winkelman.

Head of Football Operations: Kirstine Nicholson.

Manager: Karl Robinson.

Assistant Manager: John Gorman.

Physio: Simon Crampton.

Colours: White shirts with black sleeves, white shorts, white stockings with black tops.

Change Colours: Red shirts with white sleeves, red shorts, red stockings with white tops.

Year Formed: 1889.

Turned Professional: 1964.

Ltd Co.: 1964.

Previous Names: 1899, Wimbledon Old Centrals; 1905, Wimbledon; 2004, Milton Keynes Dons.

Grounds: 1899, Plough Lane; 1991, Selhurst Park; 2003, The National Hockey Stadium; 2007, Stadiummk.

Club Nicknames: 'The Dons', 'The Crazy Gang'.

First Football League Game: 20 August 1977, Division 4, v Halifax T (h) D 3–3 – Guy; Bryant (1), Galvin, Donaldson, Aitken, Davies, Galliers, Smith, Connell (1), Holmes, Leslie (1).

HONOURS

As Wimbledon
FA Premier League: best season: 6th, 1993–94.
Football League: Division 3 – Runners-up 1983–84; Division 4 – Champions 1982–83.
FA Cup: Winners 1988.
Football League Cup: Semi-final 1996–97, 1998–99.
League Group Cup: Runners-up 1982.
Amateur Cup: Winners 1963; Runners-up 1935, 1947.
European Competitions: *Intertoto Cup:* 1995.
As Milton Keynes Dons
Football League: FL 2 – Champions 2007–08.
Johnstone's Paint Trophy: Winners 2008.

sky SPORTS FACT FILE

On 29 August 2009 the seasons appeared to stand on their heads when MK Dons visited Exeter City. With a spring in his step Jermaine Easter opened the scoring for Milton Keynes with a goal in the 33rd second and added another five minutes later in the resultant 2–1 win.

Record League Victory: 6–0 v Newport Co, Division 3,
3 September 1983 – Beasant; Peters, Winterburn, Galliers,
Morris, Hatter, Evans (2), Ketteridge (1), Cork (3 incl. 1p),
Downes, Hodges (Driver).

Record Cup Victory: 7–2 v Windsor & Eton, FA Cup 1st rd,
22 November 1980 – Beasant; Jones, Armstrong, Galliers,
Mick Smith (2), Cunningham (1), Ketteridge, Hodges,
Leslie, Cork (1), Hubbick (3).

Record Defeat: 0–8 v Everton, League Cup 2nd rd,
29 August 1978.

Most League Points (2 for a win): 61, Division 4, 1978–79.

Most League Points (3 for a win): 98, Division 4, 1982–83;
as MK Dons 97, FL 2, 2007–08

Most League Goals: 97, Division 3, 1983–84; as MK Dons
83, FL 1, 2008–09.

Highest League Scorer in Season: Alan Cork, 29, 1983–84.

Most League Goals in Total Aggregate: Alan Cork, 145,
1977–92.

Most League Goals in One Match: 4, Alan Cork v
Torquay U, Division 4, 28 February 1979.

Most Capped Player: Kenny Cunningham, 40 (72), Republic of Ireland. As MK Dons – Ali Gerba
(29), Canada.

Most League Appearances: Alan Cork, 430, 1977–92.

Youngest League Player: Kevin Gage, 17 years 15 days v Bury, 2 May 1981.

Record Transfer Fee Received: £7,000,000 from Newcastle U for Carl Cort, July 2000.

Record Transfer Fee Paid: £7,500,000 to West Ham U for John Hartson, January 1999.
Football League Record: 1977 Elected to Division 4; 1979–80 Division 3; 1980–81 Division 4;
1981–82 Division 3; 1982–83 Division 4; 1983–84 Division 3; 1984–86 Division 2; 1986–92 Division 1;
1992–2000 FA Premier League; 2000–04 Division 1; 2004–06 FL 1; 2006–08 FL 2; 2008– FL 1.

MANAGERS

Les Henley 1955–71
Mike Everitt 1971–73
Dick Graham 1973–74
Allen Batsford 1974–78
Dario Gradi 1978–81
Dave Bassett 1981–87
Bobby Gould 1987–90
Ray Harford 1990–91
Peter Withe 1991
Joe Kinnear 1992–99
Egil Olsen 1999–2000
Terry Burton 2000–02
Stuart Murdock 2002–04
Danny Wilson 2004–06
Martin Allen 2006–07
Paul Ince 2007–08
Roberto Di Matteo 2008–09
Paul Ince 2009–10
Karl Robinson May 2010–

LATEST SEQUENCES (as Milton Keynes Dons)

Longest Sequence of League Wins: 8, 7.9.2007 – 20.10.2007.

Longest Sequence of League Defeats: 4, 10.8.2004 – 28.8.2004.

Longest Sequence of League Draws: 4, 21.2.2009 – 10.3.2009.

Longest Sequence of Unbeaten League Matches: 18, 29.1.2008 – 3.5.2008.

Longest Sequence Without a League Win: 11, 13.3.2010 – .

Successive Scoring Runs: 18 from 7.4.2007.

Successive Non-scoring Runs: 4, 17.12.2005–2.1.2006.

TEN YEAR LEAGUE RECORD

		P	W	D	L	F	A	Pts	Pos
2000-01	Div 1	46	17	18	11	71	50	69	8
2001-02	Div 1	46	18	13	15	63	57	67	9
2002-03	Div 1	46	18	11	17	76	73	65	10
2003-04	Div 1	46	8	5	33	41	89	29	24
2004-05	FL 1	46	12	15	19	54	68	51	20
2005-06	FL 1	46	12	14	20	45	66	50	22
2006-07	FL 2	46	25	9	12	76	58	84	4
2007-08	FL 2	46	29	10	7	82	37	97	1
2008-09	FL 1	46	26	9	11	83	47	87	3
2009-10	FL 1	46	17	9	20	60	68	60	12

DID YOU KNOW ?

The one remaining MK Dons
player in 2009–10 who had
previously appeared for
Wimbledon was Dean
Lewington, now the club
captain. He made his debut
for the old club as a substitute
against Sheffield Wednesday
at Hillsborough on 5 April
2003.

MILTON KEYNES DONS 2009–10 LEAGUE RECORD

Match No.	Date	Venue	Opponents	Result	H/T Score	Lg Pos.	Goalscorers	Attendance
1	Aug 8	H	Hartlepool U	D	0-0	0-0	—		8965
2	15	A	Swindon T	D	0-0	0-0	15		6692
3	18	A	Tranmere R	W	1-0	0-0	—	Ibehre [81]	5744
4	22	H	Colchester U	W	2-1	1-0	6	Easter (pen) [22], Carrington [58]	8633
5	29	A	Exeter C	W	2-1	2-0	3	Easter 2 [1, 6]	5333
6	Sept 5	H	Huddersfield T	L	2-3	0-0	5	Johnson [47], Easter [58]	9772
7	14	H	Norwich C	W	2-1	0-1	—	Puncheon [57], Leven (pen) [77]	10,354
8	19	A	Wycombe W	W	1-0	1-0	4	Doumbe [44]	6127
9	26	H	Leeds U	L	0-1	0-0	4		16,713
10	29	A	Oldham Ath	L	1-2	0-1	—	Brill (og) [87]	3630
11	Oct 3	A	Brighton & HA	W	1-0	0-0	5	Easter [49]	6419
12	10	H	Walsall	W	1-0	1-0	4	Easter [32]	8919
13	17	H	Gillingham	W	2-0	0-0	3	Easter [61], Wilbraham [90]	11,764
14	24	A	Southampton	L	1-3	1-0	4	Puncheon [45]	21,387
15	31	H	Bristol R	W	2-1	0-0	3	Leven (pen) [71], Puncheon [89]	9711
16	Nov 14	A	Charlton Ath	L	1-5	1-2	4	Wilbraham [10]	17,188
17	20	A	Southend U	L	1-2	1-1	—	Baldock S [14]	6957
18	24	H	Carlisle U	L	3-4	2-3	—	Chadwick 2 [36, 37], Baldock S [47]	9459
19	Dec 1	A	Millwall	L	2-3	0-2	—	Easter 2 [46, 80]	7883
20	5	H	Yeovil T	D	2-2	1-2	9	Baldock S [4], Leven (pen) [66]	8965
21	12	A	Leyton Orient	W	2-1	0-1	7	Morgan [79], Quashie [89]	3959
22	19	H	Brentford	L	0-1	0-0	8		9520
23	26	H	Stockport Co	W	4-1	2-0	5	Puncheon 2 [25, 92], Easter [28], Quashie [49]	9661
24	28	A	Huddersfield T	L	0-1	0-1	8		16,086
25	Jan 16	A	Hartlepool U	W	5-0	2-0	7	Easter [4], Liddle (og) [22], Leven [54], Baldock S [77], Puncheon [82]	3211
26	23	H	Tranmere R	W	1-0	1-0	7	Puncheon [7]	9438
27	26	A	Colchester U	L	0-2	0-1	—		3601
28	30	H	Exeter C	D	1-1	0-0	8	Baldock S [50]	8740
29	Feb 6	A	Stockport Co	W	3-1	1-1	8	Easter [24], Wilbraham [56], Townsend [74]	3720
30	13	A	Carlisle U	L	0-5	0-2	8		4930
31	20	H	Southend U	W	3-1	1-0	8	Carrington 2 [18, 49], Townsend [80]	9801
32	23	H	Millwall	L	1-3	0-1	—	Wilbraham [53]	10,610
33	27	A	Yeovil T	L	0-1	0-1	8		3844
34	Mar 6	H	Leyton Orient	W	1-0	1-0	8	Carrington [31]	14,323
35	9	H	Swindon T	W	2-1	2-0	—	Wilbraham [2], Tunnicliffe [37]	8764
36	13	A	Brentford	D	3-3	1-1	8	Wilbraham 2 [11, 89], Easter (pen) [55]	5209
37	20	A	Southampton	L	0-3	0-0	8		10,570
38	27	A	Gillingham	D	2-2	2-1	9	McCracken [18], Easter [45]	5465
39	Apr 3	H	Charlton Ath	L	0-1	0-0	9		10,869
40	5	A	Bristol R	L	0-1	0-0	10		6406
41	10	A	Norwich C	D	1-1	1-0	10	Wilbraham [20]	24,888
42	13	A	Oldham Ath	D	0-0	0-0	—		8528
43	17	H	Wycombe W	L	2-3	1-1	10	Wilbraham 2 [45, 75]	10,561
44	24	A	Leeds U	L	1-4	1-2	11	Lewington [19]	25,964
45	May 1	H	Brighton & HA	D	0-0	0-0	11		12,023
46	8	A	Walsall	L	1-2	1-0	12	Powell Daniel [26]	4772

Final League Position: 12

GOALSCORERS

League (60): Easter 14 (2 pens), Wilbraham 10, Puncheon 7, Baldock S 5, Carrington 4, Leven 4 (3 pens), Chadwick 2, Quashie 2, Townsend 2, Doumbe 1, Ibehre 1, Johnson 1, Lewington 1, McCracken 1, Morgan 1, Powell Daniel 1, Tunnicliffe 1, own goals 2.
Carling Cup (1): Easter 1 (pen).
FA Cup (6): Baldock S 2, Devaney 1, Easter 1, Gobern L 1, Morgan 1.
J Paint Trophy (13): Baldock S 3 (1 pen), Easter 3, Wilbraham 2, Carrington 1, Doran 1, Lewington 1, Puncheon 1, Randall 1.

Gueret W 43	Doumbe S 29 + 4	Howell L 17 + 12	Powell Darren 19 + 5	McCracken D 41	Woodards D 23 + 6	Chadwick L 39 + 1	Carrington M 15 + 5	Easter J 32 + 4	Johnson J 12 + 5	Puncheon J 23 + 1	Baldock G — + 1	Gobern L 7 + 13	Bridges M — + 1	Lewington D 42	Gleeson S 26 + 3	Davis S 6 + 5	Ibehre J 3 + 7	Partridge R 1 + 3	Baldock S 11 + 9	Leven P 26 + 5	Wilbraham A 31 + 4	Morgan D 1 + 8	Doran A 2 + 2	Gobern O — + 1	Swailes D 2	Devaney M 4 + 1	Quashie N 6 + 1	Stirling J 1 + 8	Townsend A 8 + 1	Randall M 12 + 4	Tunnicliffe J 9	Rae A 2 + 1	Flanagan T — + 1	O'Hanlon S 3 + 3	Chicksen A 4 + 2	Searle S 3	Powell Daniel 2	Collins C 2	Match No.
1	2	4	3	5	6	7¹	8	9²	10	11	12	13																											1
1	6¹	4	12	5	2³	7		9	10	11				3²	8	13	14																						2
1		2	4¹	5	12	7	6²	9	10²	11				8	3	13	14																						3
1	12	2		5	4	7¹	6	9³	10²	11				8	3	13	14																						4
1	12	2		5	4	7	6	9²	10¹	11³				3	8	13	14																						5
1	6	2		5	4¹	7³	12²	9	10	11	14			3	8	13																							6
1	6		2	5		7²		10	11	4³				3	8		9¹	14		12	13																		7
1	6	14	2	5		7³		10	11	4²				3	8		9¹		13	12																			8
1	6	14	2	5		7³		10	11¹	4¹				3	8		13		12	9²																			9
1	6	11²	2³	5		7¹	13		12					3	8		10		4	9	14																		10
1	6	14	2	5			10²	11³						3	8	13		7¹		4	9	12																	11
1	6	12	3	5¹			9	7³	11	13				2²					14	4	10		8																12
1	2	6		5			9²	13	11	12				3	7				4³	10		8¹	14																13
1	2		6	5			10³	9¹	11	7²				3	8				14	4	13	12																	14
1	2	13		6			9¹		11					3	8³				12	4	10	14		5	7²														15
1	2		6	5	13	7¹		12	11	8³				3²	14		9		4	10																			16
1	2	4²	6	5		8³	13	12	14	11				3					9¹		10					7													17
1	2	4¹		5		8³		13	14	11				3					9		10				6	7²	12												18
1		13	6	5		2²	8¹		10					11					3		9	14	12					7³	4										19
1		2		6		5	8¹		11					3	13				9	7	10						12	4²											20
1	2	4³	5			14	8¹	10		11	12			3	7				9²			13				6													21
1	2	8¹	14	5	12	7²		9		11	13			3						6	10						4³												22
1	2		12	5¹	4	7		9²		11				3	8				13	14	10					6²													23
1	2			5	4	7¹		13			10¹			3	8				12	11	9					6²	14												24
1	2			5	4	7¹		9³		11				3	8				14	6²	10								12	13									25
1	4			5	2¹	14		9²		11³				3	7				13	6	10								12	8									26
1	4¹			5	2	10³	6			13				3	7				14		9								12²	11	8²								27
1		4¹		5	2		7²	12	14					3	8				9³	6	10								11	13									28
1	6		5¹	2				10²						3	7				9³	4	8	13							12	11									29
1					9				12					3	7	2²				4	10	E¹							5³	11		6	13	14					30
1	13			5¹	2²	7	8	9³		14				3						4	10								12	11	6								31
1				5	2²	7¹	8	9						3						4	10	12							13	11	6								32
1				5	2²	7¹		9						3					8	4	10								11		6				13				33
1				5	2	7¹	8	9³						3						4	10	12							14	11	6²				13				34
1	13	14		5	2¹	7	8	9						3						4	10								12²	11³	6								35
1	13			5	2²	7	8	9³						3	12					4	10	12								11¹	6								36
1	2			5		7	8¹	9²			13			3	12					4	10									11	6								37
1	2³			5	13	11			8²					3	7					4	10								14	6¹					12				38
1	2			5	14	7	12	9						3	11					4¹	10								13						6³	8²			39
	2¹	12	13	5	6²	11	4	9						3	7¹						10								8								1		40
1		12	2		8	7²	6	9						3	13					4	10¹	10⁸							11					5					41
1	2	12	13		6	7	8	9						3						10¹									11		4³			5²	14				42
1	2	12		5	6²	7	8¹							3	13					9	10								11					4					43
1	2¹	8	6	5¹		7²		9		12				3						10¹	4⁸								11					13					44
	2	5				7				13	12			3	4														10	11⁸		6	1	8²	9¹				45
	2	4	5			7		10						13	3	12													8¹			6	1	11	9²				46

FA Cup

First Round	Macclesfield T	(h)	1-0
Second Round	Exeter C	(h)	4-3
Third Round	Burnley	(h)	1-2

Carling Cup

| First Round | Swindon T | (h) | 1-4 |

J Paint Trophy

First Round	Dagenham & R	(h)	3-1
Second Round	Southend U	(h)	2-0
Southern Quarter-Final	Northampton T	(h)	3-1
Southern Semi-Final	Hereford U	(a)	4-1
Southern Final	Southampton	(h)	0-1
		(a)	1-3

MORECAMBE   FL Championship 2

FOUNDATION

Several attempts to start a senior football club in a rugby stronghold finally succeeded on 7 May 1920 at the West View Hotel, Morecambe and a team competed in the Lancashire Combination for 1920–21. The club shared with a local cricket club at Woodhill Lane for the first season and a crowd of 3,000 watched the first game. The club moved to Roseberry Park the name of which was changed to Christie Park after J.B. Christie who as President had purchased the ground.

Globe Arena, Christie Way, Westgate, Morecambe LA4 4TB.

Telephone: (01524) 598 393.

Website: www.morecambefc.com

Email: info@globearena.co.uk

Ground Capacity: 6,402.

Record Attendance: 9,383 v Weymouth, FA Cup 3rd rd, 6 January 1962.

Chairman: Peter McGuigan.

Vice-chairman: Graham Hodgson.

Chief Executive: Rod Taylor.

Secretary: Neil Marsdin.

Manager: Sammy McIlroy.

Assistant Manager: Mark Lillis.

Physio: Simon Farnworth.

Colours: Red shirts with black trim, white shorts, red stockings.

Change Colours: All royal blue with black trim.

Year Formed: 1920.

Club Nickname: The Shrimps.

Grounds: 1920, Woodhill Lane; 1921, Christie Park; 2010, Globe Arena.

HONOURS

FA Cup: best season: 3rd rd, 1962, 2001, 2003.

League Cup: best season: 3rd rd, 2008.

Northern Premier League: Runners-up – 1994–95.

Presidents Cup: Winners – 1991–92.

FA Trophy: Winners 1973–74.

Lancs Senior Cup: Winners 1967–68.

Lancs Combination: Champions – 1924–25, 1961–62, 1962–63, 1967–68. Runners-up – 1925–26.

Lancs Combination Cup: Winners – 1926–27, 1945–46, 1964–65, 1966–67, 1967–68. Runners-up – 1923–24, 1924–25, 1962–63.

Lancs Junior Cup: Winners – 1927, 1928, 1962, 1963, 1969, 1986, 1987, 1994, 1996, 1999, 2004.

sky SPORTS FACT FILE

On 12 December 2009 Morecambe defeated Bournemouth 5–0. It was the club's best result since joining the Football League and was their seventh win in succession, which represented another club record. Three of the goals came in a ten-minute spell in the first half.

First Football League game: 11 August 2007, FL 2, v Barnet (h) D 0–0 – Lewis; Yates, Adams, Artell, Bentley, Stanley, Baker (Burns), Sorvel, Twiss (Newby), Curtis, Hunter (Thompson).

Record League Victory: 5-0 v AFC Bournemouth, FL 2, 12 December 2009 – Roche; Parrish, Wilson (1), Artell, Haining, Stanley (1), Hunter (Duffy (1)), Twiss, Jevons (pen) (Wainwright), Mullin (Curtis), Drummond (1).

Most League Points (3 for a win): 73, FL 2, 2009–10.

Most League Goals: 73, FL 2, 2009–10.

Highest League Scorer in Season: Phil Jevons, 18, 2009–10.

Most League Goals in Total Aggregate: Stuart Drummond, 21, 2007–.

Most League Goals in One Match: 3, Jon Newby v Rotherham U, FL 2, 29 March 2008.

Most League Appearances: Jim Bentley, 116, 2007–.

Record Transfer Fee Received: undisclosed from Rushden & D for Justin Jackson, June 2000.

Record Transfer Fee Paid: undisclosed to Southport for Carl Baker, July 2007.

Football League Record: 2006–07 Promoted from Conference; 2007– FL2.

MANAGERS

Jimmy Milne 1947–48
Albert Dainty 1955–56
Ken Horton 1956–61
Joe Dunn 1961–64
Geoff Twentyman 1964–65
Ken Waterhouse 1965–69
Ronnie Clayton 1969–70
Gerry Irving/Ronnie Mitchell 1970
Ken Waterhouse 1970–72
Dave Roberts 1972–75
Alan Spavin 1975–76
Johnny Johnson 1976–77
Tommy Ferber 1977–78
Mick Hogarth 1978–79
Don Curbage 1979–81
Jim Thompson 1981
Les Rigby 1981–84
Sean Gallagher 1984–85
Joe Wojciechowicz 1985–88
Eric Whalley 1988
Billy Wright 1988–89
Lawrie Milligan 1989
Bryan Griffiths 1989–93
Leighton James 1994
Jim Harvey 1994–2006
Sammy McIlroy May 2006–

LATEST SEQUENCES

Longest Sequence of League Wins: 7, 31.10.2009 – 12.12.2009.

Longest Sequence of League Defeats: 4, 23.2.2008 – 12.3.2008.

Longest Sequence of League Draws: 4, 13.9.2008 – 4.10.2008.

Longest Sequence of Unbeaten League Matches: 12, 31.1.2009 – 21.3.2009.

Longest Sequence Without a League Win: 10, 5.4.2008 – 30.8.2008.

Successive Scoring Runs: 16 from 3.10.2009.

Successive Non-scoring Runs: 2 from 15.1.2008.

TEN YEAR LEAGUE RECORD

		P	W	D	L	F	A	Pts	Pos
2000-01	Conf	42	11	12	19	64	66	45	19
2001-02	Conf	42	17	11	14	63	67	62	6
2002-03	Conf	42	23	9	10	86	42	78	2
2003-04	Conf	42	20	7	15	66	66	67	7
2004-05	Conf	42	19	14	9	69	50	71	7
2005-06	Conf	42	22	8	12	68	41	74	5
2006-07	Conf	46	23	12	11	64	46	81	3
2007-08	FL 2	46	16	12	18	59	63	60	11
2008-09	FL 2	46	15	18	13	53	56	63	11
2009-10	FL 2	46	20	13	13	73	64	73	4

DID YOU KNOW ?

The 2009–10 "End of an Era" season at Morecambe marked the end of the club's association with its long-standing Christie Park. The new campaign will produce new headquarters at the Globe Arena, ninety years after the club's formation in 1920.

MORECAMBE 2009–10 LEAGUE RECORD

Match No.	Date	Venue	Opponents	Result	H/T Score	Lg Pos.	Goalscorers	Attendance
1	Aug 8	H	Hereford U	D	2-2	1-1	—	Stanley [43], Drummond [57]	2119
2	15	A	Burton Alb	L	2-5	1-3	20	Craney [17], Jevons [62]	2342
3	18	A	Barnet	L	0-2	0-1	—		1298
4	22	H	Macclesfield T	D	2-2	0-1	23	Twiss [49], Artell [81]	1757
5	29	A	Chesterfield	D	1-1	0-0	21	Jevons (pen) [79]	3210
6	Sept 4	H	Rochdale	D	3-3	3-0	22	Jevons 2 [33, 42], Craney [38]	2367
7	12	A	Rotherham U	D	0-0	0-0	22		3172
8	19	H	Notts Co	W	2-1	1-0	19	Bentley [36], Mullin [52]	3335
9	26	A	Dagenham & R	D	1-1	0-1	18	Jevons (pen) [62]	1770
10	29	H	Bradford C	D	0-0	0-0	—		3116
11	Oct 3	H	Shrewsbury T	D	1-1	1-1	21	Drummond [23]	2105
12	10	A	Aldershot T	L	1-4	0-1	21	Mullin [90]	2974
13	17	A	Torquay U	D	2-2	1-1	21	Duffy [24], Mullin [47]	2614
14	24	H	Northampton T	L	2-4	2-1	21	Jevons (pen) [26], Drummond [40]	2041
15	31	H	Lincoln C	W	3-1	2-0	20	Drummond [19], Jevons (pen) [42], Mullin [54]	1701
16	Nov 14	A	Crewe Alex	W	2-1	2-0	21	Bentley [7], Jevons [37]	4113
17	21	H	Cheltenham T	W	1-0	1-0	15	Wilson [24]	1567
18	24	A	Darlington	W	4-0	0-0	—	Jevons [56], Wilson [64], Drummond [80], Curtis [85]	1698
19	Dec 1	H	Bury	W	3-0	0-0	—	Jevons 2 (1 pen) [60 (p), 81], Futcher (og) [68]	1875
20	5	A	Port Vale	W	2-0	2-0	10	Jevons [1], Mullin [39]	4679
21	12	H	Bournemouth	W	5-0	3-0	7	Drummond [15], Stanley [23], Wilson [25], Jevons (pen) [50], Duffy [90]	2034
22	18	A	Grimsby T	D	1-1	0-0	—	Mullin [60]	3119
23	26	H	Accrington S	L	1-2	0-0	8	Hunter [69]	3478
24	28	A	Rochdale	L	1-4	0-2	10	Curtis [84]	4309
25	Jan 23	H	Barnet	W	2-1	1-1	10	Drummond [4], Duffy [78]	1558
26	26	A	Macclesfield T	D	2-2	0-1	—	Drummond [52], Haining [64]	1046
27	30	H	Chesterfield	L	0-1	0-1	11		1967
28	Feb 6	A	Accrington S	L	2-3	1-1	13	Artell 2 [17, 54]	2372
29	13	H	Darlington	W	2-0	1-0	13	Jevons [9], Mullin [58]	1741
30	16	A	Burton Alb	W	3-2	1-2	—	Drummond [28], Jevons [72], Mullin [85]	1537
31	20	A	Cheltenham T	L	0-2	0-1	11		2806
32	23	A	Bury	D	0-0	0-0	—		2222
33	27	H	Port Vale	W	1-0	1-0	11	Jevons [20]	2064
34	Mar 6	A	Bournemouth	L	0-1	0-1	12		5103
35	13	H	Grimsby T	D	1-1	1-0	13	Mullin [41]	1882
36	16	A	Hereford U	W	1-0	1-0	—	Bentley [24]	1208
37	20	A	Northampton T	L	0-2	0-1	13		4210
38	27	H	Torquay U	W	2-0	1-0	10	Mullin [8], Stanley [90]	1734
39	Apr 2	H	Crewe Alex	W	4-3	0-2	—	Jevons [53], Curtis [87], Mullin [89], Artell [90]	2347
40	5	A	Lincoln C	W	3-1	1-0	9	Stanley [17], Mullin [82], Curtis [90]	3109
41	10	H	Rotherham U	W	2-0	0-0	7	Jevons [57], Hackney [69]	2337
42	13	A	Bradford C	L	0-2	0-0	—		11,027
43	17	H	Notts Co	L	1-4	0-3	10	Artell [73]	8500
44	24	H	Dagenham & R	W	1-0	0-0	8	Moss [86]	2100
45	May 1	A	Shrewsbury T	W	3-2	2-1	6	Duffy [9], Artell 2 [15, 62]	5340
46	8	H	Aldershot T	W	1-0	0-0	4	Hunter [72]	5268

Final League Position: 4

GOALSCORERS

League (73): Jevons 18 (6 pens), Mullin 12, Drummond 9, Artell 7, Curtis 4, Duffy 4, Stanley 4, Bentley 3, Wilson 3, Craney 2, Hunter 2, Hackney 1, Haining 1, Moss 1, Twiss 1, own goal 1.
Carling Cup (1): Twiss 1.
FA Cup (2): Duffy 1, Jevons 1.
J Paint Trophy (2): Curtis 1, Hunter 1.
Play-Offs (2): Artell 1, Duffy 1.

Roche B 42	Wilson L 41	Moss D 13+3	Haining W 28+4	Adams D 15+2	McLachlan F 1	Drummond S 41+2	Twiss M 18+8	Jevons P 40	Craney I 16	Duffy M 24+11	Stanley C 31+9	Bentley J 27+1	McStay H —+2	Artell D 33+4	Wainwright N 5+12	Panther M 14+5	Curtis W 9+26	Mullin P 36+2	Hunter G 26+5	Parrish A 34+1	Davies S 1	Smith B 3	Taylor A —+3	Hackney S 8	Match No.
1	3	4	5	6	7^1	8	9	10	11	2	12														1
1	7	2^1	5^3	3^2		8	9	10	11	12^4	6	4	13	14											2
1	3	2		5		7	9	10	6					4	11		8	12							3
1	7	2	3			8	9	10^1	6^2	13	5			4			11	12							4
1	7	2	3			8	9^1	10	6		5			4			11	12							5
1	7	2	3			8	13	10^2	6^1		5			4			11	9	12						6
1	7		3			8		10^1	6^2	13	5			4			11	9	2						7
1	7^1		3			8	13	10^3	6		12	5		4			11^2	14	9	2					8
1	7		3			8		10	6^2	13	5			4^1			11	9	2	12					9
1	7	3^1				8	13	10^2	6	14		5	12				11	9	2^3	4					10
1	7		3^4			8	14	10^2	6^1	12	11	5					13	9^3	2	4					11
	3					11	10		6	12	8	5		4^1			9	7	2	1					12
	3^2		7			8	12	10^1	6	2	13	5		4			9	11			1				13
	3^1		6			7		9	8	2^3	14	5		4			12	10^2	11		1	13			14
	3		7			4	13	10^1		6	5			8			12	9^2	11	2	1				15
1	3	12				11	10	7		6	5^1	4	13				9^2	8	2						16
1	3	5				11	10	8^1		6		4	12			13	9^2	7	2						17
1	3	5				7	8^3	10		13	6	4	14				12	9^1	11^2	2					18
1	3	5				8	7^1	10		13	6	4	14				12	9^2	11^3	2					19
1	3	5				8	7^1	10			6	4					12	9	11	2					20
1	3	5				8	7	10^2		12	6	4	13				14	9^3	11^1	2					21
1	3	5				6	7	10^2		12	8^1	4	13				9	11	2						22
1	3	5				8	7	9^1		12	6	4	14				13	10^2	11^3	2					23
1	3	5				8	10^1		7	6	13	4^2					9	11	2				12		24
1		3	8			4	7	10^1	11	6		5	12	9					2						25
1	3	5				8	11	10^1	7	6		4	12	9					2						26
1	3	5				8	7	10	11	6		4	13	9^1	12				2^2						27
1	3	5				11	12	10^2	9^1	6		4	7^2	8	13	14			2						28
1	3	5	12			8		9	11	6		4	7^1		10				2						29
1	3	5	12			8	9^2	7^1	6			4	13	14	10^3	11			2						30
1	3^3	5	7			8^1	9	12	6			4	14	13	10^2	11			2						31
1	3	5				13	9^1	7	6	4			8	12	10	11^2			2						32
1	3	5				13	9^2	7	6	4			8	12	10	11^1			2						33
1	3	5				13	9	7^1	6	4			8	12	10	11^2			2						34
1	3	5				6	9^1		11	14	4		13	8^3	12	10			2			7^2			35
1	3	5				6	9^1		11^3	12	4		13	8	14	10			2			7^2			36
1	3	5^1				6	9		11^2		4	12		8	13	10			2			7			37
1	3^3	14				6	9		11	12	5	4		8^1	13	10			2			7^2			38
1	3	14	5^1			8	9		11^3	6	4		12	13	10				2^4			7^2			39
1	3	2				8	9^2		6	5	4	12		11	10	13						7^1			40
1	3	14	5			8	9		11^2	6	4^1	12		10	13	2^3						7			41
1	3	5				8	9		11	6	4	12		10		2						7^1			42
1		2	5			8			11	6^1	4	7		9	10^2	12	3		13						43
1		2	13			8^2			11^1	6	5	4	12	14	9^3	10	7	3							44
1	7^1	2	13			8			9	6	5	4	12	10	11	3									45
1	7	2	12			8			9	6^1	5	4		10	11	3									46

FA Cup
First Round   Carlisle U   (a)   2-2
                           (h)   0-1

Carling Cup
First Round   Preston NE   (a)   1-5

J Paint Trophy
First Round   Carlisle U   (h)   2-2

Play-Offs
Semi-Final   Dagenham & R   (a)   0-6
                                 (h)   2-1

NEWCASTLE UNITED   FA Premiership

FOUNDATION

It stemmed from a newly formed club called Stanley in 1881.
In October 1882 they changed their name to Newcastle East End to
avoid confusion with two other local clubs, Stanley Nops and
Stanley Albion. Shortly afterwards another club Rosewood merged
with them. Newcastle West End had been formed in August 1882
and they played on a pitch which was part of the Town Moor.
Moved to Brandling Park 1885 and St James' Park 1886 (home of
Newcastle Rangers). West End went out of existence after a bad
run and the remaining committee men invited East End to move to
St James' Park. They accepted and, at a meeting in Bath Lane Hall
in 1892, changed their name to Newcastle United.

St James' Park, Newcastle-upon-Tyne NE1 4ST.
Telephone: (0191) 201 8400.
Fax: (0191) 201 8600.
Ticket Office: (0844) 372 1892.
Website: www.nufc.co.uk
Email: admin@nufc.co.uk
Ground Capacity: 52,387.
Record Attendance: 68,386 v Chelsea, Division 1,
3 September 1930.
Pitch Measurements: 105m × 68m.
Managing Director: Derek Llambias.
Manager: Chris Hughton.
First Team Coach: Colin Calderwood.
Physio: Derek Wright.
Colours: Black and white striped shirts, black shorts with
white trim, black stockings with white trim.
Change Colours: All blue with white trim.
Year Formed: 1881.
Turned Professional: 1889.
Ltd Co.: 1890.
Previous Names: 1881, Stanley; 1882, Newcastle East
End; 1892, Newcastle United.
Club Nickname: 'The Magpies'.
Grounds: 1881, South Byker; 1886, Chillingham Road, Heaton; 1892, St James' Park.
First Football League Game: 2 September 1893, Division 2, v Royal Arsenal (a) D 2–2 – Ramsay;
Jeffery, Miller; Crielly, Graham, McKane; Bowman, Crate (1), Thompson, Sorley (1), Wallace.
Graham and not Crate scored according to some reports.

HONOURS

FA Premier League: Runners-up
1995–96, 1996–97; *Football League:*
Division 1 – Champions 1904–05,
1906–07, 1908–09, 1926–27, 1992–93;
Division 2 – Champions 1964–65;
Runners-up 1897–98, 1947–48; FL C –
Champions 2009–10.
FA Cup: Winners 1910, 1924, 1932,
1951, 1952, 1955; Runners-up 1905,
1906, 1908, 1911, 1974, 1998, 1999.
Football League Cup: Runners-up 1976.
Texaco Cup: Winners 1974, 1975.
*European Competitions: Champions
League:* 1997–98, 2002–03, 2003–04.
European Fairs Cup: 1968–69 (winners),
1969–70, 1970–71. *UEFA Cup:* 1977–78,
1994–95, 1996–97, 1999–2000, 2003–04
(semi-final), 2004–05, 2006–07.
European Cup Winners' Cup: 1998–99.
Anglo-Italian Cup: Winners 1972–73.
Intertoto Cup: 2001 (runners-up), 2005,
2006 (winners).

sky SPORTS FACT FILE

In the previous nine seasons to the 2009–10 campaign,
Newcastle United had been the only club to break into
the so-called "Big Four" clubs on as many as two
occasions. They achieved fourth place in 2001–02 and
finished third the following season.

Record League Victory: 13–0 v Newport Co, Division 2,
5 October 1946 – Garbutt; Cowell, Graham; Harvey,
Brennan, Wright; Milburn (2), Bentley (1), Wayman (4),
Shackleton (6), Pearson.

Record Cup Victory: 9–0 v Southport (at Hillsborough),
FA Cup 4th rd, 1 February 1932 – McInroy; Nelson,
Fairhurst; McKenzie, Davidson, Weaver (1); Boyd (1),
Jimmy Richardson (3), Cape (2), McMenemy (1), Lang (1).

Record Defeat: 0–9 v Burton Wanderers, Division 2,
15 April 1895.

Most League Points (2 for a win): 57, Division 2, 1964–65.

Most League Points (3 for a win): 102, FL C, 2009–10.

Most League Goals: 98, Division 1, 1951–52.

Highest League Scorer in Season: Hughie Gallacher, 36,
Division 1, 1926–27.

Most League Goals in Total Aggregate: Jackie Milburn,
177, 1946–57.

Most League Goals in One Match: 6, Len Shackleton v
Newport Co, Division 2, 5 October 1946.

Most Capped Player: Shay Given, 82 (103), Republic of
Ireland.

Most League Appearances: Jim Lawrence, 432, 1904–22.

Youngest League Player: Steve Watson, 16 years 223 days v
Wolverhampton W, 10 November 1990.

Record Transfer Fee Received: £13,650,000 from Real
Madrid for Jonathan Woodgate, August 2004.

Record Transfer Fee Paid: £16,000,000 to Real Madrid for
Michael Owen, September 2005.

Football League Record: 1893 Elected to Division 2;
1898–1934 Division 2; 1934–48 Division 2; 1948–61
Division 1; 1961–65 Division 2; 1965–78 Division 1; 1978–84
Division 2; 1984–89 Division 1; 1989–92 Division 2; 1992–93
Division 1; 1993–2009 FA Premier League; 2009–10 FL C;
2010– FA Premier League.

MANAGERS

Frank Watt 1895–32
(Secretary-Manager)
Andy Cunningham 1930–35
Tom Mather 1935–39
Stan Seymour 1939–47
(Hon. Manager)
George Martin 1947–50
Stan Seymour 1950–54
(Hon. Manager)
Duggie Livingstone 1954–56
Stan Seymour 1956–58
(Hon. Manager)
Charlie Mitten 1958–61
Norman Smith 1961–62
Joe Harvey 1962–75
Gordon Lee 1975–77
Richard Dinnis 1977
Bill McGarry 1977–80
Arthur Cox 1980–84
Jack Charlton 1984
Willie McFaul 1985–88
Jim Smith 1988–91
Ossie Ardiles 1991–92
Kevin Keegan 1992–97
Kenny Dalglish 1997–98
Ruud Gullit 1998–99
Sir Bobby Robson 1999–2004
Graeme Souness 2004–06
Glenn Roeder 2006–07
Sam Allardyce 2007–08
Kevin Keegan 2008
Joe Kinnear 2008–09
Alan Shearer 2009
Chris Hughton October 2009–

LATEST SEQUENCES

Longest Sequence of League Wins: 13, 25.4.1992 – 18.10.1992.
Longest Sequence of League Defeats: 10, 23.8.1977 – 15.10.1977.
Longest Sequence of League Draws: 4, 20.1.1990 – 24.2.1990.
Longest Sequence of Unbeaten League Matches: 17, 13.2.2010 – .
Longest Sequence Without a League Win: 21, 14.1.1978 – 23.8.1978.
Successive Scoring Runs: 25 from 15.4.1939.
Successive Non-scoring Runs: 6 from 31.12.1938.

TEN YEAR LEAGUE RECORD

		P	W	D	L	F	A	Pts	Pos
2000-01	PR Lge	38	14	9	15	44	50	51	11
2001-02	PR Lge	38	21	8	9	74	52	71	4
2002-03	PR Lge	38	21	6	11	63	48	69	3
2003-04	PR Lge	38	13	17	8	52	40	56	5
2004-05	PR Lge	38	10	14	14	47	57	44	14
2005-06	PR Lge	38	17	7	14	47	42	58	7
2006-07	PR Lge	38	11	10	17	38	47	43	13
2007-08	PR Lge	38	11	10	17	45	65	43	12
2008-09	PR Lge	38	7	13	18	40	59	34	18
2009-10	FL C	46	30	12	4	90	35	102	1

DID YOU KNOW ?

On 9 January 1957 in a third
round FA Cup replay against
Manchester City, Newcastle
United found themselves
three down in thirty minutes.
With four minutes remaining
it was 3–3 but in extra time
United were again losing
before finally winning 5–4
despite being a player short.

NEWCASTLE UNITED 2009–10 LEAGUE RECORD

Match No.	Date	Venue	Opponents	Result	H/T Score	Lg Pos.	Goalscorers	Attendance
1	Aug 8	A	WBA	D 1-1	0-1	—	Duff 55	23,502
2	15	H	Reading	W 3-0	1-0	3	Ameobi 3 (1 pen) 38, 61, 75 (p)	36,944
3	19	H	Sheffield W	W 1-0	1-0	—	Ameobi 15	43,904
4	22	A	Crystal Palace	W 2-0	2-0	3	Nolan 2, Taylor R 21	20,643
5	31	H	Leicester C	W 1-0	0-0	—	Guthrie 52	38,813
6	Sept 13	A	Cardiff C	W 1-0	1-0	1	Coloccini 18	25,630
7	16	A	Blackpool	L 1-2	1-1	—	Carroll 40	9647
8	19	H	Plymouth Arg	W 3-1	1-0	2	Taylor S 6, Nolan 61, Carroll 84	42,898
9	26	A	Ipswich T	W 4-0	3-0	1	Nolan 3 30, 32, 51, Taylor R 34	27,059
10	30	H	QPR	D 1-1	0-1	—	Harewood 70	38,923
11	Oct 3	H	Bristol C	D 0-0	0-0	1		43,326
12	17	A	Nottingham F	L 0-1	0-1	2		29,155
13	20	A	Scunthorpe U	L 1-2	0-0	—	Nolan 65	8921
14	24	H	Doncaster R	W 2-1	0-1	1	Carroll 67, Nolan 90	43,949
15	Nov 2	A	Sheffield U	W 1-0	0-0	—	Morgan (og) 54	26,536
16	7	H	Peterborough U	W 3-1	2-0	1	Gutierrez 15, Carroll 18, Simpson 52	43,067
17	23	A	Preston NE	W 1-0	0-0	—	Nolan 74	16,924
18	28	H	Swansea C	W 3-0	3-0	1	Harewood 2 6, 28, Lovenkrands 21	42,616
19	Dec 5	H	Watford	W 2-0	1-0	1	Lovenkrands 20, Pancrate 83	43,050
20	9	A	Coventry C	W 2-0	1-0	—	Ameobi 45, Ranger 82	21,688
21	12	A	Barnsley	D 2-2	1-0	1	Nolan 6, Harewood 78	20,079
22	20	H	Middlesbrough	W 2-0	1-0	1	Harewood 16, Ameobi 59	49,644
23	26	A	Sheffield W	D 2-2	2-1	1	Nolan 19, Ameobi 22	30,030
24	28	H	Derby Co	D 0-0	0-0	1		47,505
25	Jan 18	H	WBA	D 2-2	1-1	—	Guthrie 25, Lovenkrands 54	39,291
26	27	H	Crystal Palace	W 2-0	1-0	1	Derry (og) 20, Ranger 90	37,886
27	30	A	Leicester C	D 0-0	0-0	1		29,067
28	Feb 5	H	Cardiff C	W 5-1	3-0	1	Carroll 2 3, 15, Gyepes (og) 6, Lovenkrands 2 69, 82	44,028
29	9	A	Derby Co	L 0-3	0-0	—		28,607
30	13	A	Swansea C	D 1-1	0-0	1	Carroll 67	15,188
31	17	H	Coventry C	W 4-1	1-1	—	Routledge 37, Carroll 53, Lovenkrands (pen) 70, Taylor R 90	39,334
32	20	H	Preston NE	W 3-0	1-0	1	Lovenkrands 3, Nolan 55, Taylor R 90	45,525
33	27	A	Watford	W 2-1	1-0	1	Coloccini 4, Carroll 50	17,120
34	Mar 6	H	Barnsley	W 6-1	1-0	1	Lovenkrands 2 (1 pen) 44 (p), 48, Guthrie 2 50, 69, Gutierrez 90, Nolan 71	44,464
35	13	A	Middlesbrough	D 2-2	1-1	1	Lovenkrands 16, Carroll 82	27,342
36	17	H	Scunthorpe U	W 3-0	2-0	—	Carroll 2 10, 55, Lovenkrands 22	39,301
37	20	A	Bristol C	D 2-2	0-2	1	Gutierrez 71, Carroll 75	19,144
38	23	A	Doncaster R	W 1-0	0-0	—	Carroll 59	14,850
39	29	H	Nottingham F	W 2-0	0-0	—	Ameobi 71, Jose Enrique 90	45,987
40	Apr 3	A	Peterborough U	W 3-2	1-1	1	Nolan 45, Barton 48, Ameobi 58	12,877
41	5	H	Sheffield U	W 2-1	1-1	1	Lovenkrands (pen) 45, Nolan 73	48,270
42	10	A	Blackpool	W 4-1	2-0	1	Gutierrez 12, Carroll 36, Nolan 62, Routledge 77	47,010
43	13	H	Reading	W 2-1	2-0	—	Nolan 2 20, 42	23,163
44	19	A	Plymouth Arg	W 2-0	2-0	—	Carroll 20, Routledge 28	13,111
45	24	H	Ipswich T	D 2-2	1-1	1	Carroll 26, Ameobi (pen) 84	52,181
46	May 2	A	QPR	W 1-0	0-0	1	Lovenkrands 71	16,819

Final League Position: 1

GOALSCORERS

League (90): Carroll 17, Nolan 17, Lovenkrands 13 (3 pens), Ameobi 10 (2 pens), Harewood 5, Guthrie 4, Gutierrez 4, Taylor R 4, Routledge 3, Coloccini 2, Ranger 2, Barton 1, Duff 1, Jose Enrique 1, Pancrate 1, Simpson 1, Taylor S 1, own goals 3.
Carling Cup (4): Ameobi 1 (pen), Geremi 1, Guthrie 1, Nolan 1.
FA Cup (5): Lovenkrands 3, Carroll 2.

Harper S 45	Taylor R 19+12	Jose Enrique 33+1	Nolan K 44	Coloccini F 37	Taylor S 21	Gutierrez J 34+3	Smith A 31+1	Ameobi S 11+7	Carroll A 33+6	Duff D 1	Barton J 8+7	Ranger N 4+21	Krul T 1+2	Xisco —+2	Ouremi J 3+4	LuaLua K —+1	Simpson D 39	Guthrie D 36+2	Butt N 10+7	Donaldson R —+2	Vuckic H —+2	Kadar T 8+7	Lovenkrands P 19+10	Khizanishvili Z 6+1	Harewood M 9+6	Tozer B —+1	Pancrate F 5+11	Williamson M 16	Routledge W 15+2	Van Aanholt P 7	Hall F 7	Best L 6+7	Match No.
1^6	2	3	4	5	6	7	8	9^2	10^1	11	12	13		15																			1
1	2	3	4	5	6	7	8^2	9^1	10		11^3			12	13	14																	2
1	11^3	3	4	5	6	7	8	9^2	10^1			13		12			2	14															3
1	11^1	3	4	5	6	7^3	8	9				13		14			2	10^2	12														4
1	5	3	4		6			9^1	10		11^3			14			2	8^2	12	13	14												5
1	7^2	3	4	5	6	10^4	11^3		9					14			2	8^1				13	12										6
1	7^1	3	4	5	6				9		11^3	14		13			2	8^2	10				12										7
1	12	3	4	5	6		8		9		11^2	14			7		2^1	13					10^3										8
1	7^3	3	4	5^2	6		8	9	10^1														13	2	12								9
1		3	4		6	12	8	9			10^2						2	7^3	11^1				14	5	13								10
1		3	4		6	11^1	8				12	13					2	7^2					10	5	9								11
1	2	3	4			12	8		10			13					6	7					11^1	5	9^2								12
1	2	3	4			11	10		9			13				7^1	6	8^2					5	12									13
1	2	3	11			7^2			10		12						8	4	6				5^4	9^1	13								14
1	6	3	11	5		7^2	10		9		12						2^1	4	3				13										15
1	12	3	4	5	6	7^1	11		9^3			13					2	8	14				10^2										16
1		3	4	5	6	7^3	11		10^1		12						2^2	8	13	14	9												17
1^0		3	4	5	6	7	10					12		15			2	8^2					11		9^1		13						18
1		3	4^5	5	6	7	10				12						2	8^3	13				11^2		9^1	14							19
1	14	3		5	6	7	10	9^2				13					2	4					11^1		12		8^3						20
1	2	3^3	11	5	6	7^1	10	9				13						4					14	12			8^2						21
1		3	4	5	6	7	11^1		10^3			13					2	8	12					9^2			14						22
1		3	11	5	6	7^1	10^2					13					2	8	4				14		9^3		12						23
1	6^2	3	8	5	4	7	10	12	9^1			14					2						11^3				13						24
1	13	3	4	5	6	7	10	9^1	12								2^2	8					11										25
1	3^1		4	5		7^3	10	9				14						8				6	11^2				12	2	13				26
1		3	11^2	5			10^1	9			12							8	4								13	2	7	6			27
1	13		4			11^2		9									2	8	14				12					6	7	3	5^3	10^1	28
1	4						11	14	13		9^3						2	8					12					6	7	3^1	5	10^2	29
1			4	5			10	9									2	8	11^1										7	3	6	12	30
1	14		4	5		11^2		9									2	8					10^1				13	6	7^3	3		12	31
1	13		4	5		7^2	10	9									2	8^3					11^1		14			6		3		12	32
1	13		4	5		7^2	11	9			12						2	8^3					14					6		3		10^1	33
1	14	3^1	4	5			11	9^2									2	8				12	10					7	6			13	34
1	12		4	5		7		9									3	8	13				10^2				11^3	6				14	35
1	3^1		4	5			11	9^2				14					2	8	13				10^3					7		6		12	36
1		3	4	5			11	9									2	8					12					7		6^1		10	37
1		3	10	5			11	9			12						2	8^1	4			6					13		7^2				38
1		3	4	5			11		9^1		12	13					2	8					10^2					6	7				39
1		3	4	5			14	9^2	10		8^3						2	13									7^1	6	12		11		40
1	14	3	4	5			11	9			12	13					2	8^2					10^1					6	7^3				41
1	12		4^2	5			11	9			13	14					2^3	8	3^1				10					6	7				42
1		3	12	4	5^1		11	9	10			14					2	8^3	13									6	7^2				43
1		3	4^1					9^2	10	11	13						2	8				14						6	7		5^3	12	44
1		3	4^3	5			11	9			12	13					2	8^2				14	10^1					6	7				45
		3		5			11	9^3			13	4	1				2	8^2				14	12					6	7			10^1	46

FA Cup

Third Round	Plymouth Arg	(a)	0-0	
		(h)	3-0	
Fourth Round	WBA	(a)	2-4	

Carling Cup

Second Round	Huddersfield T	(h)	4-3
Third Round	Peterborough U	(a)	0-2

NORTHAMPTON TOWN   FL Championship 2

FOUNDATION

Formed in 1897 by school teachers connected with the
Northampton and District Elementary Schools' Association, they
survived a financial crisis at the end of their first year when they
were £675 in the red and became members of the Midland League
– a fast move indeed for a new club. They achieved Southern
League membership in 1901.

Sixfields Stadium, Upton Way, Northampton NN5 5QA.

Telephone: (01604) 683 700.

Fax: (01604) 751 613.

Ticket Office: (01604) 683 777.

Website: www.ntfc.co.uk

Email: gareth.willsher@ntfc.tv

Ground Capacity: 7,300.

Record Attendance: (at County Ground): 24,523 v
Fulham, Division 1, 23 April 1966; (at Sixfields Stadium):
7,557 v Manchester C, Division 2, 26 September 1998.

Pitch Measurements: 116yd × 72yd.

Chairman: David Cardoza.

Secretary: Norman Howells.

Manager: Ian Sampson.

Assistant Manager: Malcolm Crosby.

Physio: Stuart Barker.

Colours: Claret shirts, white shorts, white stockings.

Change Colours: Light blue shirts, white shorts, light blue stockings.

Year Formed: 1897.

Turned Professional: 1901.

Ltd Co.: 1901.

Grounds: 1897, County Ground; 1994, Sixfields Stadium.

Club Nickname: 'The Cobblers'.

First Football League Game: 28 August 1920, Division 3, v Grimsby T (a) L 0–2 – Thorpe; Sproston,
Hewison; Jobey, Tomkins, Pease; Whitworth, Lockett, Thomas, Freeman, MacKechnie.

Record League Victory: 10–0 v Walsall, Division 3 (S), 5 November 1927 – Hammond; Watson, Jeffs;
Allen, Brett, Odell; Daley, Smith (3), Loasby (3), Hoten (1), Wells (3).

Record Cup Victory: 10–0 v Sutton T, FA Cup prel rd, 7 December 1907 – Cooch; Drennan,
Lloyd Davies, Tirrell (1), McCartney, Hickleton, Badenock (3), Platt (3), Lowe (1), Chapman (2),
McDiarmid.

HONOURS

Football League: Division 1 best
season: 21st, 1965–66; Division 2 –
Runners-up 1964–65; Division 3 –
Champions 1962–63; Division 3 (S) –
Runners-up 1927–28, 1949–50;
Division 4 – Champions 1986–87;
Runners-up 1975–76; FL 2 – Runners-
up 2005–06.

FA Cup: best season: 5th rd, 1934,
1950, 1970.

Football League Cup: best season:
5th rd, 1965, 1967.

sky SPORTS FACT FILE

Former Arsenal centre-forward Ted Bowen scored 114
League goals for Northampton Town at the impressive
rate of three goals every five games. He even scored a
hat-trick on his debut against Norwich City on 4
February 1928 in a 4–3 away win.

Record Defeat: 0–11 v Southampton, Southern League, 28 December 1901.

Most League Points (2 for a win): 68, Division 4, 1975–76.

Most League Points (3 for a win): 99, Division 4, 1986–87.

Most League Goals: 109, Division 3, 1962–63 and Division 3 (S), 1952–53.

Highest League Scorer in Season: Cliff Holton, 36, Division 3, 1961–62.

Most League Goals in Total Aggregate: Jack English, 135, 1947–60.

Most League Goals in One Match: 5, Ralph Hoten v Crystal Palace, Division 3 (S), 27 October 1928.

Most Capped Player: Edwin Lloyd Davies, 12 (16), Wales.

Most League Appearances: Tommy Fowler, 521, 1946–61.

Youngest League Player: Adrian Mann, 16 years 297 days v Bury, 5 May 1984.

Record Transfer Fee Received: £265,000 from Watford for Richard Hill, July 1987.

Record Transfer Fee Paid: £165,000 to Oldham Ath for Josh Low, July 2003.

Football League Record: 1920 Original Member of Division 3; 1921 Division 3 (S); 1958–61 Division 4; 1961–63 Division 3; 1963–65 Division 2; 1965–66 Division 1; 1966–67 Division 2; 1967–69 Division 3; 1969–76 Division 4; 1976–77 Division 3; 1977–87 Division 4; 1987–90 Division 3; 1990–92 Division 4; 1992–97 Division 3; 1997–99 Division 2; 1999–2000 Division 3; 2000–03 Division 2; 2003–04 Division 3; 2004–06 FL 2; 2006–09 FL 1; 2009– FL 2.

LATEST SEQUENCES

Longest Sequence of League Wins: 8, 27.8.1960 – 19.9.1960.

Longest Sequence of League Defeats: 8, 26.10.1935 – 21.12.1935.

Longest Sequence of League Draws: 6, 18.9.1983 – 15.10.1983.

Longest Sequence of Unbeaten League Matches: 21, 27.9.1986 – 6.2.1987.

Longest Sequence Without a League Win: 18, 26.3.1969 – 20.9.1969.

Successive Scoring Runs: 27 from 23.8.1986.

Successive Non-scoring Runs: 7 from 7.4.1939.

MANAGERS

Arthur Jones 1897–1907
(Secretary-Manager)
Herbert Chapman 1907–12
Walter Bull 1912–13
Fred Lessons 1913–19
Bob Hewison 1920–25
Jack Tresadern 1925–30
Jack English 1931–35
Syd Puddefoot 1935–37
Warney Cresswell 1937–39
Tom Smith 1939–49
Bob Dennison 1949–54
Dave Smith 1954–59
David Bowen 1959–67
Tony Marchi 1967–68
Ron Flowers 1968–69
Dave Bowen 1969–72
(continued as General Manager and Secretary to 1985 when joined the board)
Billy Baxter 1972–73
Bill Dodgin Jnr 1973–76
Pat Crerand 1976–77
Bill Dodgin Jnr 1977
John Petts 1977–78
Mike Keen 1978–79
Clive Walker 1979–80
Bill Dodgin Jnr 1980–82
Clive Walker 1982–84
Tony Barton 1984–85
Graham Carr 1985–90
Theo Foley 1990–92
Phil Chard 1992–93
John Barnwell 1993–95
Ian Atkins 1995–99
Kevin Wilson 1999–2001
Kevan Broadhurst 2001–03
Terry Fenwick 2003
Martin Wilkinson 2003
Colin Calderwood 2003–06
John Gorman 2006
Stuart Gray 2007–09
Ian Sampson October 2009–

TEN YEAR LEAGUE RECORD

		P	W	D	L	F	A	Pts	Pos
2000-01	Div 2	46	15	12	19	46	59	57	18
2001-02	Div 2	46	14	7	25	54	79	49	20
2002-03	Div 2	46	10	9	27	40	79	39	24
2003-04	Div 3	46	22	9	15	58	51	75	6
2004-05	FL 2	46	20	12	14	62	51	72	7
2005-06	FL 2	46	22	17	7	63	37	83	2
2006-07	FL 1	46	15	14	17	48	51	59	14
2007-08	FL 1	46	17	15	14	60	55	66	9
2008-09	FL 1	46	12	13	21	61	65	49	21
2009-10	FL 2	46	18	13	15	62	53	67	11

DID YOU KNOW ?

In 1924–25 Northampton Town appointed Jack Tresadern as player-manager. A former West Ham United and Burnley player, he had won two full caps for England but unusually had never been a full-time professional, combining the game with duties as a shipping clerk.

NORTHAMPTON TOWN 2009–10 LEAGUE RECORD

Match No.	Date		Venue	Opponents	Result		H/T Score	Lg Pos.	Goalscorers	Attendance
1	Aug	8	H	Macclesfield T	D	0-0	0-0	—		4064
2		15	A	Chesterfield	L	0-1	0-1	19		3700
3		18	A	Accrington S	W	3-0	2-0	—	Guinan[3], Akinfenwa (pen)[18], McKay[78]	1561
4		22	H	Bournemouth	W	2-0	1-0	6	Akinfenwa[6], Marshall[84]	4102
5		29	A	Burton Alb	L	2-3	0-3	12	Guinan[72], Gilligan (pen)[81]	3321
6	Sept	4	H	Barnet	L	1-3	1-0	16	Marshall[30]	4206
7		12	A	Notts Co	L	2-5	1-2	17	Dyer[10], Holt[89]	7154
8		19	H	Rochdale	L	1-2	0-1	21	Gilligan[64]	4048
9		26	A	Shrewsbury T	L	0-3	0-1	22		5548
10		29	H	Rotherham U	W	3-1	1-0	—	Gilligan[10], Herbert[46], Sharps (og)[58]	4017
11	Oct	3	H	Bradford C	D	2-2	0-0	19	Dyer[77], Johnson[90]	4391
12		10	A	Bury	D	2-2	0-2	19	Herbert[66], Akinfenwa[74]	2863
13		17	H	Lincoln C	W	1-0	0-0	17	Guinan[72]	4341
14		24	A	Morecambe	W	4-2	1-2	15	Guinan[4], Holt[70], Johnson[79], Akinferwa[84]	2041
15		31	A	Torquay U	L	0-1	0-0	16		2732
16	Nov	14	H	Grimsby T	D	0-0	0-0	15		4028
17		21	H	Crewe Alex	D	2-2	0-2	16	Akinfenwa 2[51,62]	3876
18		24	A	Aldershot T	L	1-2	1-0	—	Guttridge[18]	2761
19	Dec	1	H	Hereford U	L	1-3	1-1	—	Gilligan[1]	3524
20		5	A	Cheltenham T	D	2-2	1-2	18	Akinfenwa 2[23,47]	2824
21		12	H	Port Vale	D	1-1	0-1	20	Akinfenwa (pen)[51]	4132
22		26	H	Dagenham & R	W	1-0	0-0	18	McKay[88]	4108
23		28	A	Barnet	D	0-0	0-0	18		2237
24	Jan	2	A	Bournemouth	W	2-0	2-0	—	Guttridge[5], Gilligan[16]	5715
25		20	A	Macclesfield T	W	2-0	1-0	—	Guttridge[23], Akinfenwa[76]	1035
26		23	H	Chesterfield	D	0-0	0-0	14		4513
27		26	A	Darlington	W	2-1	0-1	—	McKay[55], Gilligan[70]	1694
28		30	H	Burton Alb	D	1-1	0-0	13	Holt[88]	4552
29	Feb	6	A	Dagenham & R	W	1-0	0-0	11	Johnson[71]	2206
30		9	H	Accrington S	W	4-0	1-0	—	Akinfenwa[10], McKay 2[57,61], Guttridge[66]	3206
31		12	H	Aldershot T	L	0-3	0-1	—		4718
32		20	A	Crewe Alex	L	2-3	1-1	12	Gilligan[45], Akinfenwa[57]	4036
33		23	A	Hereford U	W	2-0	1-0	—	McKay[29], Akinfenwa[67]	1266
34		27	H	Cheltenham T	W	2-1	0-0	8	Akinfenwa[52], Harris[86]	4428
35	Mar	6	A	Port Vale	W	3-1	3-1	8	Akinfenwa[3], Osman[44], McKay[45]	4861
36		13	H	Darlington	W	2-0	2-0	7	Johnson[20], Osman[39]	4755
37		20	A	Morecambe	W	2-0	1-0	7	Davis[2], Gilligan[51]	4210
38		27	A	Lincoln C	D	1-1	0-0	8	Johnson[84]	3964
39	Apr	2	A	Grimsby T	W	2-1	1-1	—	Davis[18], Akinfenwa[68]	6482
40		5	H	Torquay U	D	0-0	0-0	8		5515
41		10	H	Notts Co	L	0-1	0-0	9		5647
42		13	A	Rotherham U	L	0-1	0-0	—		3325
43		17	A	Rochdale	L	0-1	0-1	11		5025
44		24	H	Shrewsbury T	W	2-0	0-0	10	McKay[54], Thornton[82]	5019
45	May	1	A	Bradford C	L	0-2	0-1	11		12,403
46		8	H	Bury	D	1-1	0-1	11	Akinfenwa[90]	5234

Final League Position: 11

GOALSCORERS

League (62): Akinfenwa 17 (2 pens), Gilligan 8 (1 pen), McKay 8, Johnson 5, Guinan 4, Guttridge 4, Holt 3, Davis 2, Dyer 2, Herbert 2, Marshall 2, Osman 2, Harris 1, Thornton 1, own goal 1.
Carling Cup (0).
FA Cup (4): Guttridge 2, Gilligan 1 (pen), own goal 1.
J Paint Trophy (5): Guinan 3, Gilligan 2 (2 pens).

Dunn C 29	McCready C 13+1	Marshall B 11+4	Dyer A 4+16	Hinton C 38+2	Beckwith D 37+1	Gilligan R 41+1	Osman A 26+4	McKay B 29+11	Akinfenwa A 36+4	Holt A 31	Guinan S 19+9	Rodgers P 24+7	Curtis J 18+1	Rose R —+1	Threlfall R 1+3	Boden L 4	Mulligan G 2+7	Benjamin J 2+1	Brown S 2	Gutridge L 24+7	Johnson J 30	Herbert C 8+15	Davis L 13+4	Gilbert P 30	Kanyuka P 3	Walker J 3	Harris S —+9	Swailes D 3	O'Flynn S —+5	Thornton K 4+7	Lumley B 2	Steele J 13	Match No.
1	2	3	4^2	5^1	6	7	8	9	10	11	12	13																					1
1	4	7^3		5^1	6	12	8	13	10	11	9^2	2	3	14																			2
1	4	7		5	6	8		12	10^1	11	9	2	3																				3
1	4	7	12	5	6	8^1		13	10^2	11	9	2	3^1		14																		4
1	4	7		5^1	6	8		13	10	11	9	2^2			14	3^3	12																5
1	4	7		5^1	6	8	12		9	11		2				2	3^2	10	13														6
		$4^■$	7^2	5	14	6	8		9^1	12	11	10^3			2	13	3		1														7
		7	9^2	5	6	8	4^1		10	11^1	12	2				3^3	14		1	13													8
1	13	12		5	6	8			9^1	11	10	2^1								7^2	4	3	14										9
1	13	7		5	6^2	8	12		14	11	9^3	2								4	3		10^1										10
1	6	7	14	5		8		13		11	9	2^3					12			4^1	3		10^2										11
1	6	8^1		5			12	14	13	11^1	10^2	3	2							4	7	9											12
1	13			5	6	8		9^1	12	11	10^2	7	2							4	3												13
1	12			5	6	8		13	10	11	9^2	7	2^1							4	3												14
1	6	12		5		7^3			10^2	11	9	8	2^1	13						4	3	14											15
1	2				7			14	10^1	11	9^3	12	8^2							4	3	13	5^4	6									16
1	2				6				10^2	11	9^1	5					12			8	3		4			7	13						17
1	2^3	13	14		4				10^1	11	9	5					12			8^2	3					6	7						18
1		12		5		7	8^3		10^2	11	9				13						3	14		2		4^3						6	19
1		5	13	7			8^1	10	11		14	12	4								3		9^3	2			6^2						20
1		6		7				13	10		8	2						12	11		3	9^2	3^1				5						21
1		5		6	7			14	13	10	11			4^3	2^1					12	8	9^2	3										22
1	13	5		6	7	8		12	10			2							11^2	4		9^1	3										23
1	12	5		6	7	8		9^1	10^2	11										4	8	13	2										24
1		5		6	7	8		9^1	10^2	11										4	8	12	2						13				25
1		5		6	7	8		9^1	10^2	11										4	8	12	2						13				26
1		5		6	7^3	8		9	10^1	11							14			4	8	12	2^2							13			27
1		5		6	7	8^2	9			11	11^2						14			4	8	10^1	2							12 13			28
1		5		6	7	8		9^1	10	11^2		13								4	8		2							12			29
1	14	5		6	7^3	8	9		10^1											4	8	13	2							11^2			30
1		5		6	7	8		9^2	10^1			14								4	8	12	2^3							13 $11^■$			31
	12	5		6	7	8^3	9^2	10												4	3	13	11^1	2		14				1		1	32
	13	5	6			8	9	10^1					4^3	3							7	14	11^2	2		12				1		1	33
	13	5	6			8	9	10^1					4^3	3							7	14	11^2	2		12					1	1	34
		5	6	4	8		9^1	10					7^3							13	3	14	11^2	2		12						1	35
	11	5	6			8	9	10				3								12	4		7^1	2								1	36
		5	6	4^1	8		9^2	10			13	3								12	7		11	2								1	37
	14	5	6		7	8	9^2	10			13	4^3								12	3		11^1	2								1	38
	13	5	6		7	8	9^1	10			12									4	3		11^2	2								1	39
		5	6		7	8	9^2	10^1												4	3	13	11^3	2		14						1	40
	13	5	6		7^2	8	9^1			10		11^1								4	3			2		14				12		1	41
		$5^■$	6		7	8	9^2			10^3		11^1								$4^■$	3	13		2		14				12		1	42
	14			5	7	8	9^1	11	10												12	3	4^2	2		13			6^1			1	43
	14			5	7	8	9	10^2	11	12		3^1									6		4^3	2						13		1	44
		$5^■$		7	8	9^2	10^2	11	12	6											3	14	4	2^1						13		1	45
		5		7		9^2	10	11				6^1								12	3	13	8	2						4		1	46

FA Cup
First Round — Fleetwood T — (h) 2-1
Second Round — Southampton — (h) 2-3

Carling Cup
First Round — Southampton — (a) 0-2

J Paint Trophy
First Round — Wycombe W — (a) 2-2
Second Round — Bournemouth — (h) 2-1
Southern Quarter-Final — Milton Keynes D — (a) 1-3

NORWICH CITY   FL Championship

FOUNDATION

Formed in 1902, largely through the initiative of two local schoolmasters who called a meeting at the Criterion Cafe, they were shocked by an FA Commission which in 1904 declared the club professional and ejected them from the FA Amateur Cup. However, this only served to strengthen their determination. New officials were appointed and a professional club established at a meeting in the Agricultural Hall in March 1905.

Carrow Road, Norwich NR1 1JE.

Telephone: (01603) 760 760.

Fax: (01603) 613 886.

Ticket Office: (0844) 826 1902.

Website: www.canaries.co.uk

Email: reception@ncfc-canaries.co.uk

Ground Capacity: 26,034.

Record Attendance: 43,984 v Leicester C, FA Cup 6th rd, 30 March 1963.

Pitch Measurements: 105m × 67m.

Joint Majority Shareholders: Delia Smith and Michael Wynn Jones.

Chairman: Alan Bowkett.

Deputy Chairman: Michael Foulger.

Chief Executive: David McNally.

Director of Finance and Operations: Sam Gordon.

Secretary: Kevan Platt.

Manager: Paul Lambert.

Assistant Manager: Ian Culverhouse.

Physio: Neal Reynolds.

Colours: Yellow shirts with green trim, green shorts, yellow stockings.

Change Colours: All white with green trim on shirts.

Year Formed: 1902. *Turned Professional:* 1905. *Ltd Co.:* 1905.

Club Nickname: 'The Canaries'.

Grounds: 1902, Newmarket Road; 1908, The Nest, Rosary Road; 1935, Carrow Road.

First Football League Game: 28 August 1920, Division 3, v Plymouth Arg (a) D 1–1 – Skermer; Gray, Gadsden; Wilkinson, Addy, Martin; Laxton, Kidger, Parker, Whitham (1), Dobson.

Record League Victory: 10–2 v Coventry C, Division 3 (S), 15 March 1930 – Jarvie; Hannah, Graham; Brown, O'Brien, Lochhead (1); Porter (1), Anderson, Hunt (5), Scott (2), Slicer (1).

HONOURS

FA Premier League: best season: 3rd 1992–93.

Football League: Division 1 – Champions 2003–04; Division 2 – Champions 1971–72, 1985–86; Division 3 (S) – Champions 1933–34; Division 3 – Runners-up 1959–60.

FA Cup: Semi-finals 1959, 1989, 1992.

Football League Cup: Winners 1962, 1985; Runners-up 1973, 1975.

European Competitions: UEFA Cup: 1993–94.

sky SPORTS FACT FILE

On 7 November 2009 Norwich City won 7–0 at Paulton Rovers in an FA Cup first round tie. Chris Martin scored four in the club's best win in it since 28 January 1989 when Malcolm Allen scored four goals, Robert Fleck a hat-trick and Trevor Putney once in an 8–0 win over Sutton United.

Record Cup Victory: 8–0 v Sutton U, FA Cup 4th rd, 28 January 1989 – Gunn; Culverhouse, Bowen, Butterworth, Linighan, Townsend (Crook), Gordon, Fleck (3), Allen (4), Phelan, Putney (1).

Record Defeat: 2–10 v Swindon T, Southern League, 5 September 1908.

Most League Points (2 for a win): 64, Division 3 (S), 1950–51.

Most League Points (3 for a win): 95, FL 1, 2009–10.

Most League Goals: 99, Division 3 (S), 1952–53.

Highest League Scorer in Season: Ralph Hunt, 31, Division 3 (S), 1955–56.

Most League Goals in Total Aggregate: Johnny Gavin, 122, 1945–54, 1955–58.

Most League Goals in One Match: 5, Tommy Hunt v Coventry C, Division 3 (S), 15 March 1930; 5, Roy Hollis v Walsall, Division 3 (S), 29 December 1951.

Most Capped Player: Mark Bowen, 35 (41), Wales.

Most League Appearances: Ron Ashman, 592, 1947–64

Youngest League Player: Ryan Jarvis, 16 years 282 days v Walsall, 19 April 2003.

Record Transfer Fee Received: £7,250,000 from West Ham U for Dean Ashton, January 2006.

Record Transfer Fee Paid: £3,400,000 to Crewe Alex for Dean Ashton, January 2005.

Football League Record: 1920 Original Member of Division 3; 1921 Division 3 (S): 1934–39 Division 2; 1946–58 Division 3 (S); 1958–60 Division 3; 1960–72 Division 2; 1972–74 Division 1; 1974–75 Division 2; 1975–81 Division 1; 1981–82 Division 2; 1982–85 Division 1; 1985–86 Division 2; 1986–92 Division 1; 1992–95 FA Premier League; 1995–2004 Division 1; 2004–05 FA Premier League; 2005–09 FL C; 2009–10 FL 1; 2010– FL C.

LATEST SEQUENCES

Longest Sequence of League Wins: 10, 23.11.1985 – 25.1.1986.

Longest Sequence of League Defeats: 7, 1.4.1995 – 6.5.1995.

Longest Sequence of League Draws: 7, 15.1.1994 – 26.2.1994.

Longest Sequence of Unbeaten League Matches: 20, 31.3.1950 – 30.12.1950.

Longest Sequence Without a League Win: 25, 22.9.1956 – 23.2.1957.

Successive Scoring Runs: 25 from 31.8.1963.

Successive Non-scoring Runs: 5 from 21.2.1925.

MANAGERS

John Bowman 1905–07
James McEwen 1907–08
Arthur Turner 1909–10
Bert Stansfield 1910–15
Major Frank Buckley 1919–20
Charles O'Hagan 1920–21
Albert Gosnell 1921–26
Bert Stansfield 1926
Cecil Potter 1926–29
James Kerr 1929–33
Tom Parker 1933–37
Bob Young 1937–39
Jimmy Jewell 1939
Bob Young 1939–45
Cyril Spiers 1946–47
Duggie Lochhead 1947–50
Norman Low 1950–55
Tom Parker 1955–57
Archie Macaulay 1957–61
Willie Reid 1961–62
George Swindin 1962
Ron Ashman 1962–66
Lol Morgan 1966–69
Ron Saunders 1969–73
John Bond 1973–80
Ken Brown 1980–87
Dave Stringer 1987–92
Mike Walker 1992–94
John Deehan 1994–95
Martin O'Neill 1995
Gary Megson 1995–96
Mike Walker 1996–98
Bruce Rioch 1998–2000
Bryan Hamilton 2000
Nigel Worthington 2001–06
Peter Grant 2006–07
Glenn Roeder 2007–09
Bryan Gunn 2009
Paul Lambert August 2009–

TEN YEAR LEAGUE RECORD

		P	W	D	L	F	A	Pts	Pos
2000-01	Div 1	46	14	12	20	46	58	54	15
2001-02	Div 1	46	22	9	15	60	51	75	6
2002-03	Div 1	46	19	12	15	60	49	69	8
2003-04	Div 1	46	28	10	8	79	39	94	1
2004-05	PR Lge	38	7	12	19	42	77	33	19
2005-06	FL C	46	18	8	20	56	65	62	9
2006-07	FL C	46	16	9	21	56	71	57	16
2007-08	FL C	46	15	10	21	49	59	55	17
2008-09	FL C	46	12	10	24	57	70	46	22
2009-10	FL 1	46	29	8	9	89	47	95	1

DID YOU KNOW ?

On 16 January 2010 Norwich City went to Colchester United seeking revenge for a 7–1 defeat at home on the opening day of the season. They won 5–0 and manager Paul Lambert could claim to have been in charge of both the winners in these two East Anglian derby games.

NORWICH CITY 2009–10 LEAGUE RECORD

Match No.	Date	Venue	Opponents	Result	H/T Score	Lg Pos.	Goalscorers	Attendance
1	Aug 8	H	Colchester U	L	1-7	0-5	—	McDonald [72]	25,217
2	15	A	Exeter C	D	1-1	0-0	22	Berthel Askou [52]	6357
3	18	A	Brentford	L	1-2	0-0	—	Tudur Jones [90]	7395
4	22	H	Wycombe W	W	5-2	3-1	19	Holt 2 [16, 71], Smith [25], Otsemobor [35], Berthel Askou [49]	23,428
5	29	A	Hartlepool U	W	2-0	1-0	10	Nelson [27], Hughes [64]	4470
6	Sept 5	A	Walsall	D	0-0	0-0	10		23,041
7	14	A	Milton Keynes D	L	1-2	1-0	—	Martin C [1]	10,354
8	19	H	Charlton Ath	D	2-2	1-2	14	Hoolahan [44], Holt [90]	24,018
9	26	A	Gillingham	D	1-1	0-1	14	Russell [90]	7550
10	29	H	Leyton Orient	W	4-0	0-0	10	Martin C [75], Holt [78], Spillane [81], Cureton [90]	23,981
11	Oct 3	H	Bristol R	W	5-1	4-1	7	Martin C [9], Hoolahan (pen) [31], Holt 2 [33, 40], Cureton [90]	24,117
12	10	A	Carlisle U	W	1-0	1-0	6	Hoolahan [42]	6825
13	19	A	Leeds U	L	1-2	1-1	—	Holt [38]	19,912
14	24	H	Swindon T	W	1-0	1-0	5	Martin C [32]	24,959
15	31	A	Stockport Co	W	3-1	1-0	5	Holt 2 [16, 90], Hoolahan (pen) [69]	5218
16	Nov 14	H	Tranmere R	W	2-0	0-0	5	Hoolahan (pen) [60], Doherty [80]	25,025
17	21	H	Southampton	D	2-2	0-1	5	Hoolahan [54], Hughes [75]	21,362
18	24	H	Brighton & HA	W	4-1	2-0	—	Holt [3], Hoolahan [22], Elphick (og) [69], Martin C [82]	24,670
19	Dec 1	A	Southend U	W	3-0	0-0	—	Holt 2 (1 pen) [68, 90 (p)], Smith [77]	8732
20	5	H	Oldham Ath	W	2-0	2-0	3	Holt [21], Hoolahan [32]	24,404
21	12	A	Yeovil T	D	3-3	0-1	3	Martin C [60], Doherty [65], Russell [90]	4964
22	19	H	Huddersfield T	W	3-0	0-0	3	Hoolahan [57], Martin C [74], Doherty [79]	25,004
23	26	H	Millwall	W	2-0	1-0	3	Hoolahan [28], Holt [68]	25,242
24	Jan 2	A	Wycombe W	W	1-0	0-0	—	Smith [77]	7171
25	9	H	Exeter C	W	3-1	1-0	—	Holt 2 [8, 82], Martin C [77]	24,955
26	16	A	Colchester U	W	5-0	2-0	2	Martin C 2 [16, 45], Doherty [49], Johnson [81], Holt [90]	10,064
27	23	A	Brentford	W	1-0	0-0	1	Martin C [77]	24,979
28	26	A	Walsall	W	2-1	0-1	—	Martin C [77], McDonald [86]	5022
29	30	H	Hartlepool U	W	2-1	2-1	1	McDonald [27], Rose [32]	25,506
30	Feb 6	A	Millwall	L	1-2	1-1	1	Martin C [4]	14,374
31	13	A	Brighton & HA	W	2-1	0-1	1	Holt [80], Doherty [84]	7258
32	20	A	Southampton	L	0-2	0-1	1		23,103
33	23	H	Southend U	W	2-1	0-1	—	Johnson 2 [78, 90]	24,824
34	27	A	Oldham Ath	W	1-0	0-0	1	Holt [53]	5344
35	Mar 6	H	Yeovil T	W	3-0	1-0	1	Hoolahan [3], Holt [69], Martin C [75]	24,868
36	13	A	Huddersfield T	W	3-1	0-1	1	Holt [69], Elliott 2 [74, 85]	17,959
37	20	A	Swindon T	D	1-1	0-0	1	Holt [52]	11,972
38	27	H	Leeds U	W	1-0	0-0	1	Martin C [89]	25,445
39	Apr 2	A	Tranmere R	L	1-3	0-3	—	Holt [58]	6263
40	5	H	Stockport Co	W	2-1	2-1	1	McNamee [3], Holt [26]	25,353
41	10	H	Milton Keynes D	D	1-1	0-1	1	Martin C [90]	24,888
42	13	A	Leyton Orient	L	1-2	1-2	1	Smith [19]	7520
43	17	A	Charlton Ath	W	1-0	1-0	1	Nelson [34]	20,023
44	24	H	Gillingham	W	2-0	0-0	1	Russell [74], Nelson [82]	25,227
45	May 1	A	Bristol R	W	3-0	2-0	1	Martin C [31], Johnson [45], Hughes [68]	8836
46	8	H	Carlisle U	L	0-2	0-2	1		25,181

Final League Position: 1

GOALSCORERS

League (89): Holt 24 (1 pen), Martin C 17, Hoolahan 11 (3 pens), Doherty 5, Johnson 4, Smith 4, Hughes 3, McDonald 3, Nelson 3, Russell 3, Berthel Askou 2, Cureton 2, Elliott 2, McNamee 1, Otsemobor 1, Rose 1, Spillane 1, Tudur Jones 1, own goal 1.
Carling Cup (5): Holt 3, Hoolahan 2 (1 pen).
FA Cup (8): Martin C 4, Holt 3, Hoolahan 1.
J Paint Trophy (4): Martin C 2, Doherty 1, McDonald 1.

Theoklitos M 1	Otsemobor J 12+1	Drury A 35	Gill M 5+3	Nelson M 28+3	Doherty G 38	Tudur Jones O 2+1	Whaley S 3	Martin C 36+6	Holt G 39	Hoolahan W 36+1	Adeyemi T 2+9	McDonald C 4+13	Alnwick B 3	Spillane M 10+3	Berthel Askou J 21+1	Lappin S 42+2	Hughes S 12+17	McVeigh P 4+5	Smith K 36+1	Cureton J 3+3	Foretor F 28	Daley L 3+4	Russell D 34+1	Rudd D 4+3	Francomb G 2	Martin R 26	McNamee A 7+10	Johnson O 4+13	Whitbread Z 1+3	Rose M 11+1	Elliott S 4+6	Match No.
1	2	3	4¹	5	6	7	8	9²	10	11	12	13																				1
		3	4		6	13	8	14	10³	11¹	7²	9	1	2	5	12																2
14	3	4²			6	7	8¹	12	10	11		9	1	2³	5		13															3
2	3							10	14	13	12	1	6	5	11	4¹	7	8³	9²													4
2	3		6					10		12	14		5	11	4	7¹	8³	9²		13												5
2	3		6					10		13			5	11	4	7¹	8³	9²		12	14											6
2	3²		6³			7	10		13		14	5	11	4¹	12	8		9														7
2	3²					12	10	7		14	6	5	11	13	8³		9¹	4														8
2¹	3					10	7		13	6	5	11	12		8²	I¹	9⁶	4	15													9
	3		2		13	10³	7		6	5	11	12	9²	8	14		4¹	1														10
	3		2		9	10³	7		6¹	5	11	13	12	8	14		4²	1														11
	3		2		9²	10	7	12	13	5	11			8		I	4		6¹													12
2	3	12	6		9	10	7			5	11	8¹			I	4																13
	3	14	6		9²	10	7			5	11		12	8³	13	I	4	2¹														14
	2	3¹	14	4	9	10	7²	12	13	5	11³			8		I	6															15
2	3		5		9	10	7			6	11			8		I	4															16
2	3		5		9	10	7¹	12		6	11²	13		8		I	4															17
2	3		6		9	10²	7	14	13	5	11	12		8¹		I	4²															18
	3¹	14	6		9	10	7²	12		5	11	4		8³		I	13		2													19
	3		6		9¹	10	7²			5	11			8		I	12	4	2	13												20
	3		6		9	10	7¹	12		5	11	13		8²		I	4		2													21
	3	5	6		9	10	7	8¹			11	12				I	4		2													22
2	3	12	5		9	10	7³	13			11	8²				I	4		6	14												23
	3	5	6		9	10	7				11		8		I	4		2														24
	3	5	6		9	10	7¹				11		8		I	4		2	12													25
	3	5	6		9²	10	7¹				11³	14		8		I	4		2	12	13											26
	3	5	6		9	10⁸	7²				11		8		I	4		2¹	13	12												27
	3¹	5	6		9		7	14			11	12		8²		I	4		2	13	10³											28
		5	6		9		7	10¹			11		8		I	4		2	12		3											29
		5	6		9		7³	10²			11		8¹		I	4		2	12	13	14	3										30
		5²	6		9	10	7²		14		11		8¹		I	4		2	12	13		3										31
		5¹	6		9	10	7				11²	13	8	1		4⁸		2	12			3										32
		5	6		9	10	7				11	8²	13	1				2	4	12		3										33
		5	6		9²	10	7¹		13		11	12	8	1				2	4²	14		3										34
	14	5	6		9²	10¹	7³				11		8	1				2	4	12		3	13									35
		5	6		9¹	10	7				11		8	1		4		2				3	12									36
		5	6		9¹	10	7				11²	13	8	1		4		2				3	12									37
	3	5	6		12	10	7²				11	14	8³		I	4		2	13				9¹									38
	3	5	6		12	10	7				11⁶	8²			1⁸		4	15	2	13			9¹									39
	3	5			9¹	10					11	13	8²			4	1	2	7	12	6											40
	3	5	6		9	10					11		8²			4	1	2	7¹	12			13									41
	3	5	6		9			13			11¹	14	8		I	4		2	12	10³			7²									42
	3	5	6		9²				7		11	8			I	4		2		10¹		12	13									43
		5	6		9	10³			2		13	11²	8		I	4			7¹	14		3	12									44
	7	5²	6		9				2	·4	11³	8	13		I				3	12		4	10¹									45
	3		6		9		7				5	11¹	12	8		1⁶		4	15	2	13	10²										46

FA Cup

| First Round | Paulton R | (a) | 7-0 |
| Second Round | Carlisle U | (a) | 1-3 |

Carling Cup

| First Round | Yeovil T | (a) | 4-0 |
| Second Round | Sunderland | (h) | 1-4 |

J Paint Trophy

First Round	Brentford	(h)	1-0
Second Round	Gillingham	(a)	1-0
Southern Quarter-Final	Swindon T	(a)	0-0
Southern Semi-Final	Southampton	(a)	2-2

NOTTINGHAM FOREST FL Championship

FOUNDATION

One of the oldest football clubs in the world, Nottingham Forest was formed at a meeting in the Clinton Arms in 1865. Known originally as the Forest Football Club, the game which first drew the founders together was 'shinney', a form of hockey. When they determined to change to football in 1865, one of their first moves was to buy a set of red caps to wear on the field.

The City Ground, Nottingham NG2 5FJ.
Telephone: (0115) 982 4444.
Fax: (0115) 982 4455.
Ticket Office: 0871 226 1980.
Website: www.nottinghamforest.co.uk
Email: info@nottinghamforest.co.uk
Ground Capacity: 30,576.
Record Attendance: 49,946 v Manchester U, Division 1, 28 October 1967.
Pitch Measurements: 112yd × 76yd.
Chairman: Nigel Doughty.
Chief Executive: Mark Arthur.
Finance Director: John Pelling.
Manager: Billy Davies.
Assistant Manager: David Kelly.
Physios: Steve Devine, Andy Hunt.
Colours: Red shirt with white trim, white shorts, red stockings.
Change Colours: Black and blue halved shirts with red trim, blue shorts, blue stockings.
Year Formed: 1865.
Turned Professional: 1889. *Ltd Co.:* 1982.
Club Nickname: 'Reds'.
Grounds: 1865, Forest Racecourse; 1879, The Meadows; 1880, Trent Bridge Cricket Ground; 1882, Parkside, Lenton; 1885, Gregory, Lenton; 1890, Town Ground; 1898, City Ground.

First Football League Game: 3 September 1892, Division 1, v Everton (a) D 2–2 – Brown; Earp, Scott; Hamilton, A. Smith, McCracken; McCallum, W. Smith, Higgins (2), Pike, McInnes.

Record League Victory: 12–0 v Leicester Fosse, Division 1, 12 April 1909 – Iremonger; Dudley, Maltby; Hughes (1), Needham, Armstrong; Hooper (3), Marrison, West (3), Morris (2), Spouncer (3 incl. 1p).

Record Cup Victory: 14–0 v Clapton (away), FA Cup 1st rd, 17 January 1891 – Brown; Earp, Scott; A. Smith, Russell, Jeacock; McCallum (2), 'Tich' Smith (1), Higgins (5), Lindley (4), Shaw (2).

Record Defeat: 1–9 v Blackburn R, Division 2, 10 April 1937.

HONOURS

Football League: Division 1 – Champions 1977–78, 1997–98; Runners-up 1966–67, 1978–79; FL 1 – Runners-up 2007–08. Division 2 – Champions 1906–07, 1921–22; Runners-up 1956–57; Division 3 (S) – Champions 1950–51.
FA Cup: Winners 1898, 1959; Runners-up 1991.
Football League Cup: Winners 1978, 1979, 1989, 1990; Runners-up 1980, 1992.
Anglo-Scottish Cup: Winners 1977;
Simod Cup: Winners 1989.
Zenith Data Systems Cup: Winners: 1992.
European Competitions: *European Cup:* 1978–79 (winners), 1979–80 (winners), 1980–81. *European Fairs Cup:* 1961–62, 1967–68. *UEFA Cup:* 1983–84, 1984–85, 1995–96. *Super Cup:* 1979–80 (winners), 1980–81 (runners-up). *World Club Championship:* 1980.

sky SPORTS FACT FILE

In 1965 Nottingham Forest became the third Football League club to celebrate its centenary. A match was arranged against Valencia ending in a 1–1 draw. Before the event Arsenal presented the club with a set of shirts in a reciprocal gesture dating back to the 1886 occasion.

Most League Points (2 for a win): 70, Division 3 (S), 1950–51.

Most League Points (3 for a win): 94, Division 1, 1997–98.

Most League Goals: 110, Division 3 (S), 1950–51.

Highest League Scorer in Season: Wally Ardron, 36, Division 3 (S), 1950–51.

Most League Goals in Total Aggregate: Grenville Morris, 199, 1898–1913.

Most League Goals in One Match: 4, Enoch West v Sunderland, Division 1, 9 November 1907; 4, Tommy Gibson v Burnley, Division 2, 25 January 1913; 4, Tom Peacock v Port Vale, Division 2, 23 December 1933; 4, Tom Peacock v Barnsley, Division 2, 9 November 1935; 4, Tom Peacock v Port Vale, Division 2, 23 November 1935; 4, Tom Peacock v Doncaster R, Division 2, 26 December 1935; 4, Tommy Capel v Gillingham, Division 3 (S), 18 November 1950; 4, Wally Ardron v Hull C, Division 2, 26 December 1952; 4, Tommy Wilson v Barnsley, Division 2, 9 February 1957; 4, Peter Withe v Ipswich T, Division 1, 4 October 1977.

Most Capped Player: Stuart Pearce, 76 (78), England.

Most League Appearances: Bob McKinlay, 614, 1951–70.

Youngest League Player: Craig Westcarr, 16 years 257 days v Burnley, 13 October 2001.

Record Transfer Fee Received: £8,500,000 from Liverpool for Stan Collymore, June 1995.

Record Transfer Fee Paid: £3,500,000 to Celtic for Pierre van Hooijdonk, March 1997.

Football League Record: 1892 Elected to Division 1; 1906–07 Division 2; 1907–11 Division 1; 1911–22 Division 2; 1922–25 Division 1; 1925–49 Division 2; 1949–51 Division 3 (S); 1951–57 Division 2; 1957–72 Division 1; 1972–77 Division 2; 1977–92 Division 1; 1992–93 FA Premier League; 1993–94 Division 1; 1994–97 FA Premier League; 1997–98 Division 1; 1998–99 FA Premier League; 1999–2004 Division 1; 2004–05 FL C; 2005–08 FL 1; 2008– FL C.

MANAGERS

Harry Radford 1889–97
  (Secretary-Manager)
Harry Haslam 1897–1909
  (Secretary-Manager)
Fred Earp 1909–12
Bob Masters 1912–25
John Baynes 1925–29
Stan Hardy 1930–31
Noel Watson 1931–36
Harold Wightman 1936–39
Billy Walker 1939–60
Andy Beattie 1960–63
Johnny Carey 1963–68
Matt Gillies 1969–72
Dave Mackay 1972
Allan Brown 1973–75
Brian Clough 1975–93
Frank Clark 1993–96
Stuart Pearce 1996–97
Dave Bassett 1997–98 *(previously General Manager from February)*
Ron Atkinson 1998–99
David Platt 1999–2001
Paul Hart 2001–04
Joe Kinnear 2004
Gary Megson 2005
Colin Calderwood 2006–08
Billy Davies January 2009–

LATEST SEQUENCES

Longest Sequence of League Wins: 7, 9.5.1979 – 1.9.1979.

Longest Sequence of League Defeats: 14, 21.3.1913 – 27.9.1913.

Longest Sequence of League Draws: 7, 29.4.1978 – 2.9.1978.

Longest Sequence of Unbeaten League Matches: 42, 26.11.1977 – 25.11.1978.

Longest Sequence Without a League Win: 19, 8.9.1998 – 16.1.1999.

Successive Scoring Runs: 22 from 28.3.1931.

Successive Non-scoring Runs: 7 from 13.12.2003.

TEN YEAR LEAGUE RECORD

		P	W	D	L	F	A	Pts	Pos
2000-01	Div 1	46	20	8	18	55	53	68	11
2001-02	Div 1	46	12	18	16	50	51	54	16
2002-03	Div 1	46	20	14	12	82	50	74	6
2003-04	Div 1	46	15	15	16	61	58	60	14
2004-05	FL C	46	9	17	20	42	66	44	23
2005-06	FL 1	46	19	12	15	67	52	69	7
2006-07	FL 1	46	23	13	10	65	41	82	4
2007-08	FL 1	46	22	16	8	64	32	82	2
2008-09	FL C	46	13	14	19	50	65	53	19
2009-10	FL C	46	22	13	11	65	40	79	3

DID YOU KNOW ?

On 16 February 2010 Robert Earnshaw scored for Nottingham Forest in the fourth minute of the Championship match against Sheffield United. It registered his 150th career League goal in what was his 340th Football League appearance starting with Cardiff City.

NOTTINGHAM FOREST 2009–10 LEAGUE RECORD

Match No.	Date	Venue	Opponents	Result	H/T Score	Lg Pos.	Goalscorers	Attendance
1	Aug 8	A	Reading	D	0-0	0-0	—	19,640
2	15	H	WBA	L	0-1	0-0	20	22,794
3	18	H	Watford	L	2-4	1-1	—	Blackstock [45], Adebola [87]	19,232
4	22	A	QPR	D	1-1	0-1	20	McGoldrick [57]	13,058
5	29	H	Derby Co	W	3-2	3-0	16	Majewski [1], Blackstock [28], Tyson [43]	28,143
6	Sept 12	A	Sheffield W	D	1-1	1-1	16	Blackstock [2]	25,270
7	15	A	Ipswich T	D	1-1	0-1	—	Earnshaw [59]	21,130
8	19	H	Blackpool	L	0-1	0-1	19		23,487
9	27	A	Plymouth Arg	W	1-0	1-0	19	Gunter [45]	14,792
10	30	H	Scunthorpe U	W	2-0	0-0	—	Chambers [71], Blackstock [76]	18,332
11	Oct 3	A	Peterborough U	W	2-1	0-0	10	Majewski [51], Anderson [56]	12,711
12	17	H	Newcastle U	W	1-0	1-0	7	Blackstock [45]	29,155
13	20	H	Barnsley	W	1-0	0-0	—	Moussi [90]	20,395
14	24	A	Crystal Palace	D	1-1	0-1	9	McGoldrick [48]	15,692
15	Nov 1	A	Cardiff C	D	1-1	0-0	9	McGugan [90]	20,413
16	7	H	Bristol C	D	1-1	0-0	8	Morgan [86]	21,467
17	21	A	Middlesbrough	D	1-1	0-1	9	Earnshaw [73]	22,710
18	28	H	Doncaster R	W	4-1	1-0	4	Roberts (og) [18], Morgan [59], Earnshaw [77], McGugan [80]	22,035
19	Dec 5	H	Leicester C	W	5-1	2-0	3	Earnshaw 3 [12, 32, 49], Anderson [54], Adebola [77]	28,626
20	8	A	Sheffield U	D	0-0	0-0	—		26,490
21	12	H	Swansea C	W	1-0	0-0	4	McGoldrick [35]	16,690
22	19	H	Preston NE	W	3-0	2-0	3	McKenna [16], Adebola [25], McGugan [81]	21,582
23	26	A	Watford	D	0-0	0-0	3		17,086
24	28	H	Coventry C	W	2-0	1-0	3	Earnshaw [42], Blackstock [78]	28,608
25	Jan 8	A	WBA	W	3-1	1-0	—	Blackstock [18], Majewski [53], Cohen [58]	22,873
26	16	H	Reading	W	2-1	2-0	2	Anderson [11], Earnshaw [41]	27,635
27	26	H	QPR	W	5-0	3-0	—	Earnshaw 2 [18, 21], Blackstock (pen) [32], Cohen [49], Perch [78]	23,293
28	30	A	Derby Co	L	0-1	0-0	2		32,674
29	Feb 6	H	Sheffield W	W	2-1	1-0	3	Blackstock 2 (1 pen) [24 (p), 80]	27,900
30	9	A	Coventry C	L	0-1	0-1	—		18,225
31	13	A	Doncaster R	L	0-1	0-1	3		12,768
32	16	H	Sheffield U	W	1-0	1-0	—	Earnshaw [4]	22,076
33	20	H	Middlesbrough	W	1-0	0-0	2	Cohen [72]	25,498
34	27	A	Leicester C	L	0-3	0-0	3		31,759
35	Mar 6	H	Swansea C	W	1-0	0-0	2	Chambers [90]	25,012
36	13	A	Preston NE	L	2-3	0-3	3	Blackstock (pen) [57], Earnshaw [76]	14,426
37	16	A	Barnsley	L	1-2	0-1	—	Blackstock [78]	13,174
38	20	H	Peterborough U	W	1-0	1-0	3	Earnshaw [13]	24,582
39	23	H	Crystal Palace	W	2-0	1-0	—	Morgan [45], Tyson [62]	20,025
40	29	A	Newcastle U	L	0-2	0-0	—		45,987
41	Apr 3	A	Bristol C	D	1-1	1-1	3	Moussi [29]	16,125
42	5	H	Cardiff C	D	0-0	0-0	3		22,185
43	10	H	Ipswich T	W	3-0	0-0	3	Chambers [47], Moussi [57], Earnshaw [76]	23,459
44	17	A	Blackpool	L	1-3	0-1	3	Garner [65]	11,164
45	24	A	Plymouth Arg	W	3-0	2-0	3	Earnshaw [19], N'Gala (og) [34], Anderson [90]	22,602
46	May 2	H	Scunthorpe U	D	2-2	2-0	3	Garner [17], Boyd [43]	8119

Final League Position: 3

GOALSCORERS

League (65): Earnshaw 15, Blackstock 12 (3 pens), Anderson 4, Adebola 3, Chambers 3, Cohen 3, Majewski 3, McGoldrick 3, McGugan 3, Morgan 3, Moussi 3, Garner 2, Tyson 2, Boyd 1, Gunter 1, McKenna 1, Perch 1, own goals 2.
Carling Cup (5): Anderson 1, Blackstock 1, Chambers 1, McGugan 1, Majewski 1.
FA Cup (0).
Play-Offs (4): Earnshaw 2, Adebola 1, Cohen 1.

Camp L 45	Gunter C 44	Lynch J 9 + 1	Chambers L 17 + 6	Morgan W 44	Majewski R 31 + 4	McKenna P 35	Adebola D 13 + 20	McGoldrick D 18 + 15	Cohen C 44	Garner J 14 + 4	Earnshaw R 20 + 12	Tyson N 17 + 16	McCleary G 1 + 23	Anderson P 33 + 4	McGugan L 6 + 12	Blackstock D 30 + 9	Moussi G 21 + 6	Wilson K 35	Shorey N 9	Perch J 14 + 3	Boyd D 5 + 1	Smith P 1	Match No.
1	2	3	4	5	6	7	9	10[1]	11[2]	8[3]	12	13	14										1
1	2	3		5	4[1]	6	9[3]		11	8	13	10		7[2]	12	14							2
1	2	3		5	12	6	14	13	11	9	8			7[2]	4[1]	10[3]							3
1	2	3[1]	4	5	6	8	9[2]	10[3]	11	7		14	12			13							4
1	2		4	5	6	7	12	8[3]	3	11[2]	14	9	13			10[1]							5
1	2	7	4	5		6	13	9[2]	3	11[1]		12	8	14		10[3]							6
1	2	7	4	5		6	12	9	3	11[2]	13		14	8[3]		10[1]							7
1	2	7	4	5		6	13	9[2]	3	10[3]	8			14	12	11[1]							8
1	2	13		5	7	6	11[3]		3	9[1]		8		12		10	14	4[2]					9
1	2	14	4	5	7[2]	6		12	3	9[1]		8[3]		11		10	13						10
1	2		4	5	7[3]	6		9[2]	3		12	8	13	11		10	14						11
1	2			5	11[1]	8[3]		12	3	14		9		7[3]	13	10	4	6					12
1	2			5	12	8	13	9	3	14		11[1]		7[2]		10[3]	4[5]	6					13
1	2	13		5		8	9	10	3	14		11[3]	12	7[1]	4[2]			6					14
1	2			5	6[1]	8	12	10	3	9[2]		13		7	14	11[3]	4						15
1	2			5	6[1]	11	12	9[3]	3	10[3]	14	13		7		8	4						16
1	2			5		6	9[3]	10[1]	3	8[2]	12	13		7		14	11	4					17
1	2			5	6[2]	8	12	14		9[3]		11		7	13	10[1]		4	3				18
1	2			5	6[1]	8	13		11	9	12	14		7[3]		10[2]		4	3				19
1	2	4		5		8	13		7	9[3]	14	12	11[1]			10[2]		6	3				20
1	2			5	6	8	10[2]	9	7		12	14	11[3]			13		4	3				21
1	2			5	4[1]	8	9		11		10[2]	14	12	7[2]	13			6	3				22
1	2	4				6	9[2]	10[3]	11		14	12		7[1]	8	13		5	3				23
1	2			5	8[3]	6	13		11		9[2]	7[1]	12		14	10		4	3				24
1	2			5	6[3]	8	13		11		12			7		10[2]	9[1]	4	3	14			25
1	2	13		5	6[2]	8			11	9[1]	14			7		10[3]		4	3[4]	12			26
1	2	13		5[2]	6	8	14		11	9	12			7[1]		10[3]		4		3			27
1	2			5	6[3]	8	12		11	9[1]				7[2]	4	10	13	4		3			28
1	2			5		8	13	14		9[2]	7[1]			12		10[3]	11	6		3			29
1	2			5	6	8		13	3	9[1]	12			7[2]	4	10	11[3]	4		3			30
1	2			5	11[2]	7	9	13	4			10[3]	12[8]		8[1]	14		6		3			31
1	2			5	6[3]	8		13	11	9[2]	12			7[1]		10	14	4		3			32
1	2			5	6[3]	8	13	12	11	9[1]				7[2]		10	14	4		3			33
1	2			5	6[2]	8		13	11	9	12			7[1]		10		4		3			34
1	2	4		5	9[2]	6[1]		13	3			14		7[3]	2	10	8				11		35
1	2	12		5			14	9	3	13				7[3]	8[1]	10	4	6			11[2]		36
1	2			5	6		9[2]		8	10	12	14		13	7[3]	4		3	11[1]				37
1	2	12		5	6[2]		14	11		9[3]		13	7	10	8	4		3[3]					38
1	2	4		5	8[1]			14	3	9[2]	13	12	7[3]		10	11	6						39
1	2			5	8[2]			14	11	13	9[1]	12	7		10[3]	4	6	3					40
1	2	4	5			9[1]	8	11	12		13	14			7	6		3[3]	10[2]				41
1	2	3	5	6[1]			13	11		9[2]	8	12			10	7	4						42
1	2	4[1]	5	13				3		9	8[3]		7[2]		10	11	6		12	14			43
	2[2]	4	5			8[1]	9[2]	11	10	13	14			12	7	6	3						44
1	2			5	6		13	11[1]	9	8[3]		12	4	10[2]	7	4	3						45
	2	4		14			13	10		9[2]		12	7[1]	8[3]		6	5			3	11	1	46

FA Cup
Third Round   Birmingham C   (h)   0-0
                                   (a)   0-1

Carling Cup
First Round   Bradford C   (h)   3-0
Second Round   Middlesbrough   (h)   2-1
Third Round   Blackburn R   (h)   0-1

Play-Offs
Semi-Final   Blackpool   (a)   1-2
                                   (h)   3-4

NOTTS COUNTY

FL Championship 1

FOUNDATION

According to the official history of Notts County 'the true date of Notts' foundation has to be the meeting at the George Hotel on 7 December 1864'. However, there is documented evidence of continuous play from 1862, when club members played organised matches amongst themselves in The Park in Nottingham.

Meadow Lane Stadium, Meadow Lane, Nottingham NG2 3HJ.

Telephone: (0115) 952 9000.

Fax: (0115) 955 3994.

Ticket Office: (0115) 955 7204.

Website: www.nottscountyfc.co.uk

Email: office@nottscountyfc.co.uk

Ground Capacity: 20,300.

Record Attendance: 47,310 v York C, FA Cup 6th rd, 12 March 1955.

Pitch Measurements: 113yd × 72yd.

Chairman: Ray Trew.

Chief Executive: James Rodwell.

Secretary and General Manager: Tony Cuthbert.

Manager: Craig Short.

Assistant Manager: Dave Kevan.

Physio: Paul Godfrey.

Colours: Black and white striped shirts, black shorts, black stockings.

Change Colours: All blue.

Year Formed: 1862* (*see Foundation*). *Turned Professional:* 1885. *Ltd Co.:* 1890.

Club Nickname: 'Magpies'.

HONOURS

Football League: Division 1 best season: 3rd, 1890–91, 1900–01; Division 2 – Champions 1896–97, 1913–14, 1922–23; Runners-up 1894–95, 1980–81; Division 3 (S) – Champions 1930–31, 1949–50; Runners-up 1936–37; Division 3 – Champions 1997–98; Runners-up 1972–73; Division 4 – Champions 1970–71; Runners-up 1959–60.

FA Cup: Winners 1894; Runners-up 1891.

Football League Cup: best season: 5th rd, 1964, 1973, 1976.

Anglo-Italian Cup: Winners 1995; Runners-up 1994.

Grounds: 1862, The Park; 1864, The Meadows; 1877, Beeston Cricket Ground; 1880, Castle Ground; 1883, Trent Bridge; 1910, Meadow Lane.

First Football League Game: 15 September 1888, Football League, v Everton (a) L 1–2 – Holland; Guttridge, McLean; Brown, Warburton, Shelton; Hodder, Harker, Jardine, Moore (1), Wardle.

Record League Victory: 11–1 v Newport Co, Division 3 (S), 15 January 1949 – Smith; Southwell, Purvis; Gannon, Baxter, Adamson; Houghton (1), Sewell (4), Lawton (4), Pimbley, Johnston (2).

Record Cup Victory: 15–0 v Rotherham T (at Trent Bridge), FA Cup 1st rd, 24 October 1885 – Sherwin; Snook, H. T. Moore; Dobson (1), Emmett (1), Chapman; Gunn (1), Albert Moore (2), Jackson (3), Daft (2), Cursham (4), (1 og).

Record Defeat: 1–9 v Blackburn R, Division 1, 16 November 1889. 1–9 v Aston Villa, Division 1, 29 September 1888. 1–9 v Portsmouth, Division 2, 9 April 1927.

sky SPORTS FACT FILE

In 1934 Notts County signed three players from Swansea Town called Jones. Only one of them, Fred Jones, played a first team game. Another, Bryn, an amateur, was capped at this level for Wales against Scotland that season, while Maldwyn had been a reserve at Swansea.

Most League Points (2 for a win): 69, Division 4, 1970–71.

Most League Points (3 for a win): 99, Division 3, 1997–98.

Most League Goals: 107, Division 4, 1959–60.

Highest League Scorer in Season: Tom Keetley, 39, Division 3 (S), 1930–31.

Most League Goals in Total Aggregate: Les Bradd, 125, 1967–78.

Most League Goals in One Match: 5, Robert Jardine v Burnley, Division 1, 27 October 1888; 5, Daniel Bruce v Port Vale, Division 2, 26 February 1895; 5, Bertie Mills v Barnsley, Division 2, 19 November 1927.

Most Capped Player: Kevin Wilson, 15 (42), Northern Ireland.

Most League Appearances: Albert Iremonger, 564, 1904–26.

Youngest League Player: Tony Bircumshaw, 16 years 54 days v Brentford, 3 April 1961.

Record Transfer Fee Received: £2,500,000 from Derby Co for Craig Short, September 1992.

Record Transfer Fee Paid: £800,000 to Manchester C for Kasper Schmeichel, July 2009.

Football League Record: 1888 Founder Member of the Football League; 1893–97 Division 2; 1897–1913 Division 1; 1913–14 Division 2; 1914–20 Division 1; 1920–23 Division 2; 1923–26 Division 1; 1926–30 Division 2; 1930–31 Division 3 (S); 1931–35 Division 2; 1935–50 Division 3 (S); 1950–58 Division 2; 1958–59 Division 3; 1959–60 Division 4; 1960–64 Division 3; 1964–71 Division 4; 1971–73 Division 3; 1973–81 Division 2; 1981–84 Division 1; 1984–85 Division 2; 1985–90 Division 3; 1990–91 Division 2; 1991–95 Division 1; 1995–97 Division 2; 1997–98 Division 3; 1998–2004 Division 2; 2004–10 FL 2; 2010– FL 1.

LATEST SEQUENCES

Longest Sequence of League Wins: 10, 3.12.1997 – 31.1.1998.

Longest Sequence of League Defeats: 7, 3.9.1983 – 16.10.1983.

Longest Sequence of League Draws: 6, 16.8.2008 – 20.9.2008.

Longest Sequence of Unbeaten League Matches: 19, 26.4.1930 – 6.12.1930.

Longest Sequence Without a League Win: 20, 3.12.1996 – 31.3.1997.

Successive Scoring Runs: 35 from 26.4.1930.

Successive Non-scoring Runs: 5 from 30.11.1912.

MANAGERS

Albert Fisher 1913–27
Horace Henshall 1927–34
Charlie Jones 1934
David Pratt 1935
Percy Smith 1935–36
Jimmy McMullan 1936–37
Harry Parkes 1938–39
Tony Towers 1939–42
Frank Womack 1942–43
Major Frank Buckley 1944–46
Arthur Stollery 1946–49
Eric Houghton 1949–53
George Poyser 1953–57
Tommy Lawton 1957–58
Frank Hill 1958–61
Tim Coleman 1961–63
Eddie Lowe 1963–65
Tim Coleman 1965–66
Jack Burkitt 1966–67
Andy Beattie *(General Manager)* 1967
Billy Gray 1967–68
Jack Wheeler *(Caretaker Manager)* 1968–69
Jimmy Sirrel 1969–75
Ron Fenton 1975–77
Jimmy Sirrel 1978–82 *(continued as General Manager to 1984)*
Howard Wilkinson 1982–83
Larry Lloyd 1983–84
Richie Barker 1984–85
Jimmy Sirrel 1985–87
John Barnwell 1987–88
Neil Warnock 1989–93
Mick Walker 1993–94
Russell Slade 1994–95
Howard Kendall 1995
Colin Murphy 1995 *(continued as General Manager to 1996)*
Steve Thompson 1996
Sam Allardyce 1997–99
Gary Brazil 1999–2000
Jocky Scott 2000–01
Gary Brazil 2001
Billy Dearden 2002–04
Gary Mills 2004
Ian Richardson 2004–05
Gudjon Thordarson 2005–06
Steve Thompson 2006–07
Ian McParland 2007–09
Hans Backe 2009
Steve Cotterill 2010
Craig Short June 2010–

TEN YEAR LEAGUE RECORD

		P	W	D	L	F	A	Pts	Pos
2000-01	Div 2	46	19	12	15	62	66	69	8
2001-02	Div 2	46	13	11	22	59	71	50	19
2002-03	Div 2	46	13	16	17	62	70	55	15
2003-04	Div 2	46	10	12	24	50	78	42	23
2004-05	FL 2	46	13	13	20	46	62	52	19
2005-06	FL 2	46	12	16	18	48	63	52	21
2006-07	FL 2	46	16	14	16	55	53	62	13
2007-08	FL 2	46	10	18	18	37	53	48	21
2008-09	FL 2	46	11	14	21	49	69	47	19
2009-10	FL 2	46	27	12	7	96	31	93	1

DID YOU KNOW ?

Of all players who made a solitary appearance for Notts County, surely the one with the highest credentials was Sol Campbell on 19 September 2009 at Morecambe. He had made 485 League appearances with Tottenham Hotspur, Arsenal and Portsmouth and had 73 England caps.

NOTTS COUNTY 2009–10 LEAGUE RECORD

Match No.	Date	Venue	Opponents	Result	H/T Score	Lg Pos.	Goalscorers	Attendance
1	Aug 8	H	Bradford C	W 5-0	3-0	—	Davies [17], Hughes 3 (1 pen) [40, 43 (p), 54], Moloney [86]	9396
2	15	A	Macclesfield T	W 4-0	2-0	1	Ravenhill [13], Hunt [45], Wright (og) [50], Westcarr [90]	2785
3	19	A	Chesterfield	L 1-2	0-0	—	Edwards [83]	6196
4	22	H	Dagenham & R	W 3-0	2-0	1	Hughes [43], Hawley [45], Jackson [63]	6562
5	29	A	Barnet	L 0-1	0-0	5		2858
6	Sept 5	H	Burton Alb	D 1-1	0-0	6	Hawley [54]	8891
7	12	H	Northampton T	W 5-2	2-1	5	Ritchie 2 [23, 65], Hughes 3 (1 pen) [44, 61, 75 (p)]	7154
8	19	A	Morecambe	L 1-2	0-1	8	Davies [71]	3335
9	26	H	Port Vale	W 3-1	2-1	7	Hughes 2 (1 pen) [16, 45 (p)], Collins (og) [58]	7561
10	29	A	Lincoln C	W 3-0	2-0	—	Rodgers 3 [1, 25, 89]	5527
11	Oct 3	A	Cheltenham T	D 1-1	1-0	6	Rodgers [26]	4134
12	11	H	Torquay U	D 2-2	2-1	5	Westcarr [12], Davies [33]	8812
13	17	A	Rotherham U	D 0-0	0-0	5		5738
14	24	A	Crewe Alex	W 2-0	1-0	4	Rodgers [28], Westcarr [66]	6545
15	31	H	Shrewsbury T	D 1-1	0-1	4	Lee [85]	7562
16	Nov 14	A	Bury	D 3-3	2-2	6	Hughes 2 [26, 39], Ritchie [77]	3602
17	21	H	Aldershot T	D 0-0	0-0	6		6500
18	24	A	Rochdale	L 1-2	1-2	—	Davies [35]	2779
19	Dec 1	H	Darlington	W 4-0	3-0	—	Rodgers [12], Hughes 2 [14, 79], Davies [17]	4606
20	5	A	Hereford U	W 2-0	1-0	4	Westcarr [31], Edwards [51]	2727
21	12	H	Accrington S	L 1-2	0-0	6	Hughes (pen) [82]	5855
22	28	A	Burton Alb	W 4-1	2-1	4	Ravenhill [13], Hughes 3 (1 pen) [45, 48, 53 (p)]	5801
23	Jan 26	A	Dagenham & R	W 3-0	1-0	—	Davies [44], Hughes [47], Ogogo (og) [85]	1916
24	30	A	Barnet	W 2-0	2-0	5	Hawley [5], Davies [25]	6444
25	Feb 6	A	Grimsby T	W 1-0	0-0	4	Hughes [69]	4452
26	9	A	Bournemouth	L 1-2	0-2	—	Bishop [50]	5472
27	17	H	Grimsby T	D 1-1	1-1	—	Hughes [18]	5163
28	20	A	Aldershot T	D 1-1	0-1	7	Davies [90]	4016
29	27	H	Hereford U	W 5-0	1-0	7	Westcarr 3 (1 pen) [34, 56, 73 (p)], Rodgers 2 (1 pen) [89 (p), 90]	6036
30	Mar 2	H	Macclesfield T	W 1-0	1-0	—	Clapham [18]	4672
31	6	A	Accrington S	W 3-0	1-0	5	Davies [29], Hughes [48], Rodgers [55]	2123
32	9	H	Chesterfield	W 1-0	1-0	—	Davies [20]	7341
33	15	H	Bournemouth	D 2-2	1-0	—	Hughes 2 [22, 54]	6120
34	20	A	Crewe Alex	W 1-0	0-0	2	Edwards [51]	5003
35	23	A	Bradford C	D 0-0	0-0	—		11,630
36	27	H	Rotherham U	W 1-0	0-0	2	Rodgers [89]	9015
37	Apr 3	H	Bury	W 5-0	1-0	2	Edwards [4], Westcarr [52], Davies [60], Hughes [66], Facey [81]	7005
38	5	A	Shrewsbury T	W 1-0	1-0	2	Davies [36]	6287
39	10	A	Northampton T	W 1-0	0-0	2	Davies [47]	5647
40	13	A	Lincoln C	W 3-1	1-1	—	Hughes [1], Lee [65], Facey [87]	7501
41	17	H	Morecambe	W 4-1	3-0	1	Hughes 2 [7, 18], Ravenhill [14], Davies [77]	8500
42	20	H	Rochdale	W 1-0	0-0	—	Hughes [30]	10,536
43	24	A	Port Vale	L 1-2	1-2	1	Lee [25]	7459
44	27	A	Darlington	W 5-0	1-0	—	Jackson [33], Edwards [70], Westcarr [75], Fodgers 2 [78, 81]	2112
45	May 1	H	Cheltenham T	W 5-0	4-0	—	Lee [21], Hughes 2 [22, 31], Davies [25], Rodgers [81]	11,331
46	8	A	Torquay U	D 0-0	0-0	1		5124

Final League Position: 1

GOALSCORERS

League (96): Hughes 30 (5 pens), Davies 15, Rodgers 13 (1 pen), Westcarr 9 (1 pen), Edwards 5, Lee 4, Hawley 3, Ravenhill 3, Ritchie 3, Facey 2, Jackson 2, Bishop 1, Clapham 1, Hunt 1, Moloney 1, own goals 3.
Carling Cup (0).
FA Cup (10): Hughes 3, Hunt 2, Davies 1, Hawley 1, Jackson 1, Westcarr 1, own goal 1.
J Paint Trophy (2): Facey 1, Westcarr 1.

Houtt R 3+1	Moloney B 18	Hunt S 32	Ravenhill R 40	Lee G 31+1	Thompson J 38+2	Westcarr C 33+9	Bishop N 39+4	Hughes L 39	Rodgers L 27+15	Davies B 45	Hamshaw M 2+18	Clapham J 17+13	Hawley K 14+17	Edwards M 37+3	Jackson J 20+4	Schmeichel K 43	Ritchie M 12+4	Facey D 7+11	Campbell S 1	Jones D 7	Akinbiyi A 1+9	Fox N —+1	Canham S —1	Match No.
1	2	3	4	5	6	7^1	8	9^3	10	11^2	12	13	14											1
1	2	3	4	5^1	6	7	8^2	9	10^3	11		13	14	12										2
1	2	3	4	5	6	7^2	8	9	10^1	11		13		12										3
	2	3	4	5	6	7	8^1	9	10^2	11^3	12	13	14			1								4
	2	3	4	5	6	7^2	8	9	10^1	11	12	13				1								5
	2	3^1	4^2	5	6	7	8	9	10	11	12	13				1								6
	2	3	4^3	5	6	7	8	9^1	10^2	11	12	13	14			1								7
	2	3	4^2	5	6	7	8	9	10^1	11	12	13				1								8
	2	3	4	5	6	7^1		9^3	10^2	11	12	13	14			1								9
	2	3	4^1	5	6	7		9	10^3	11^2	12	13	14			1								10
	2	3	4^2	5	6	7		9	10^1	11	12	13				1								11
	2	3	4	5	6	7	8^2	9	10^1	11	12	13				1								12
	2	3^2	4	5	6	7	8	9^3	10	11	12	13		4^1		1								13
	2	3	4	5	6	7	8^9	9^1	10^2	11	12		14	3		1								14
	2	3	4	5	6^2	7	8^1	9	10	11	12			3		1								15
	2^3	3	4^1	5	6	7	8	9	10^2	11	12		14			1								16
	2	3	4	5	6	7	8^1	9	10	11	12					1								17
	2	3	4	5^1	6	7	8^3	9	10^2	11	12	13	14			1								18
	2	3	4	5	6	7^2	8^3	9	10^1	11	12	13	14			1								19
	2	3	4	5	6	7^2	8	9	10^1	11	12	13				1								20
	2	3	4^3	5	6	7^1	8	9	10^2	11	12	13	14			1								21
	2	3	4	5	6	7^2	8	9	10	11^3	12	13	14			1								22
	2	3	4		6	7^1	8	9^2	10	11^3	12	3	14	5		1								23
	2	3	4^1	5		7	8	9^2	10^3	11	12	13		10	4	1								24
	2	3	4	5	6	7^1	8	9^3	10	11^2	12	13	14			1								25
	2^2	3	4	5	6	7^1	8	9	10	11	12	13				1								26
	2	3	4	5	6^1	7	8	9^8	10^2	11	12	13				1								27
	2	3	4	5	6	7^1	8	9	10	11	12					1								28
	2	3	4	5	6	7^3	8	9^2	10^1	11	12	13	14			1								29
	2	3^1	4	5	6	7	8	9	10^2	11^3	12	3	14			1								30
	2	3	4^2	5	6	7	8^1	9^3	10	11	12	13		4		1								31
	2	3	4	5	6	7	8^2	9^3	10^1	11	12	13	14			1								32
	2	3	4	5	6	7^1	8	9^2	10	11	12	13				1								33
	2	3	4	5	6	7	8^1	9	10^2	11	12					1								34
	2	3	4	5	6	7	8	9^1	10^2	11	12	3				1								35
	2	3	4	5	6	7	8	9	10^2	11	12	13				1								36
	2	3	4	5	6	7	8	9	10^3	11^1	12	13	14			1								37
	2	3	4	5	6	7	8^1	9	10^2	11	12	13				1								38
	2	3	4	5	6	7	8	9	10^1	11	12					1								39
	2	3	4	5	6	7	8^3	9^2	10	11^1	12	13	14			1								40
	2	3	4^1	5	6	7	8	9^2	10	11	12	13	14			1								41
	2	3	4	5	6	7	8	9	10	11						1								42
	2	3	4	5	6	7	8	9^3	10^2	11^1	12	13	14			1								43
	2	3	4	5	6	7	8^1	9^3	10	11^2	12	13	14											44
15	2	3	4	5	6	7	8	9^1	10^2	11	12	13				16								45
	2	3	4	5	6	7	8^1	9^2	10	11	12	13				1								46

FA Cup

First Round	Bradford C	(h)	2-1
Second Round	Bournemouth	(a)	2-1
Third Round	Forest Green R	(h)	2-1
Fourth Round	Wigan Ath	(h)	2-2
		(a)	2-0
Fifth Round	Fulham	(a)	0-4

Carling Cup

First Round	Doncaster R	(h)	0-1

J Paint Trophy

Second Round	Bradford C	(a)	2-2

OLDHAM ATHLETIC   FL Championship 1

FOUNDATION

It was in 1895 that John Garland, the landlord of the Featherstall and Junction Hotel, decided to form a football club. As Pine Villa they played in the Oldham Junior League. In 1899 the local professional club, Oldham County, went out of existence and one of the liquidators persuaded Pine Villa to take over their ground at Sheepfoot Lane and change their name to Oldham Athletic.

Boundary Park, Furtherwood Road, Oldham OL1 2PA.

Telephone: (0161) 624 4972.

Fax: (0161) 627 5915. ,

Ticket Office: (0161) 785 5150.

Website: www.oldhamathletic.co.uk

Email: enquiries@oldhamathletic.co.uk

Ground Capacity: 13,624.

Record Attendance: 46,471 v Sheffield W, FA Cup 4th rd, 25 January 1930.

Pitch Measurements: 106yd × 72yd.

Chairman: Simon Blitz.

Managing Director: Simon Corney.

Chief Executive/Secretary: Alan Hardy.

Manager: Paul Dickov.

Assistant Manager: Gerry Taggart.

Physio: Marc Czuczman.

Colours: Blue shirts with white sleeves, white shorts, white stockings.

Change Colours: Black shirts with tangerine sleeves, black shorts, black stockings.

Year Formed: 1895.

Turned Professional: 1899.

Ltd Co.: 1906.

Previous Name: 1895, Pine Villa; 1899, Oldham Athletic.

Club Nickname: 'The Latics'.

Grounds: 1895, Sheepfoot Lane; 1900, Hudson Field; 1906, Sheepfoot Lane; 1907, Boundary Park.

First Football League Game: 9 September 1907, Division 2, v Stoke (a) W 3–1 – Hewitson; Hodson, Hamilton; Fay, Walders, Wilson; Ward, W. Dodds (1), Newton (1), Hancock, Swarbrick (1).

Record League Victory: 11–0 v Southport, Division 4, 26 December 1962 – Bollands; Branagan, Marshall; McCall, Williams, Scott; Ledger (1), Johnstone, Lister (6), Colquhoun (1), Whitaker (3).

HONOURS

Football League: Division 1 – Runners-up 1914–15; Division 2 – Champions 1990–91; Runners-up 1909–10; Division 3 (N) – Champions 1952–53; Division 3 – Champions 1973–74; Division 4 – Runners-up 1962–63.

FA Cup: Semi-final 1913, 1990, 1994.

Football League Cup: Runners-up 1990.

sky SPORTS FACT FILE

On the eve of 1913–14, Oldham Athletic secured the services of Charlie Roberts, the outstanding 30-year-old England international centre-half from Manchester United for £1,750. He had made over 250 League appearances for the Old Trafford club.

Record Cup Victory: 10–1 v Lytham, FA Cup 1st rd, 28 November 1925 – Gray; Wynne, Grundy; Adlam, Heaton, Naylor (1), Douglas, Pynegar (2), Ormston (2), Barnes (3), Watson (2).

Record Defeat: 4–13 v Tranmere R, Division 3 (N), 26 December 1935.

Most League Points (2 for a win): 62, Division 3, 1973–74.

Most League Points (3 for a win): 88, Division 2, 1990–9_.

Most League Goals: 95, Division 4, 1962–63.

Highest League Scorer in Season: Tom Davis, 33, Division 3 (N), 1936–37.

Most League Goals in Total Aggregate: Roger Palmer, 141, 1980–94.

Most League Goals in One Match: 7, Eric Gemmell v Chester, Division 3 (N), 19 January 1952.

Most Capped Player: Gunnar Halle, 24 (64), Norway.

Most League Appearances: Ian Wood, 525, 1966–80.

Youngest League Player: Wayne Harrison, 15 years 11 months v Notts Co, 27 October 1984.

Record Transfer Fee Received: £1,700,000 from Aston Villa for Earl Barrett, February 1992.

Record Transfer Fee Paid: £750,000 to Aston Villa for Ian Olney, June 1992.

Football League Record: 1907 Elected to Division 2; 1910–23 Division 1; 1923–35 Division 2; 1935–53 Division 3 (N); 1953–54 Division 2; 1954–58 Division 3 (N); 1958–63 Division 4; 1963–69 Division 3; 1969–71 Division 4; 1971–74 Division 3; 1974–91 Division 2; 1991–92 Division 1; 1992–94 FA Premier League; 1994–97 Division 1; 1997–2004 Division 2; 2004– FL 1.

MANAGERS

David Ashworth 1906–14
Herbert Bamlett 1914–21
Charlie Roberts 1921–22
David Ashworth 1923–24
Bob Mellor 1924–27
Andy Wilson 1927–32
Jimmy McMullan 1933–34
Bob Mellor 1934–45
  (continued as Secretary to 1953)
Frank Womack 1945–47
Billy Wootton 1947–50
George Hardwick 1950–56
Ted Goodier 1956–58
Norman Dodgin 1958–60
Jack Rowley 1960–63
Les McDowall 1963–65
Gordon Hurst 1965–66
Jimmy McIlroy 1966–68
Jack Rowley 1968–69
Jimmy Frizzell 1970–82
Joe Royle 1982–94
Graeme Sharp 1994–97
Neil Warnock 1997–98
Andy Ritchie 1998–2001
Mick Wadsworth 2001–02
Iain Dowie 2002–03
Brian Talbot 2004–05
Ronnie Moore 2005–06
John Sheridan 2006–09
Joe Royle 2009
Dave Penney 2009–10
Paul Dickov June 2010–

LATEST SEQUENCES

Longest Sequence of League Wins: 10, 12.1.1974 – 12.3.1974.

Longest Sequence of League Defeats: 8, 15.12.1934 – 2.2.1935.

Longest Sequence of League Draws: 5, 26.12.1982 – 15.1.1983.

Longest Sequence of Unbeaten League Matches: 20, 1.5.1990 – 10.11.1990.

Longest Sequence Without a League Win: 17, 4.9.1920 – 18.12.1920.

Successive Scoring Runs: 25 from 15.1.1927.

Successive Non-scoring Runs: 6 from 4.2.1922.

TEN YEAR LEAGUE RECORD

		P	W	D	L	F	A	Pts	Pos
2000-01	Div 2	46	15	13	18	53	65	58	15
2001-02	Div 2	46	18	16	12	77	65	70	9
2002-03	Div 2	46	22	16	8	68	38	82	5
2003-04	Div 2	46	12	21	13	66	60	57	15
2004-05	FL 1	46	14	10	22	60	73	52	19
2005-06	FL 1	46	18	11	17	58	60	65	10
2006-07	FL 1	46	21	12	13	69	47	75	6
2007-08	FL 1	46	18	13	15	58	46	67	8
2008-09	FL 1	46	16	17	13	66	65	65	10
2009-10	FL 1	46	13	13	20	39	57	52	16

DID YOU KNOW ?

Centre-forward Stewart Littlewood arrived from Port Vale in a £1,300 transfer and player exchange deal to save Oldham Athletic from relegation in January 1929 with 12 goals in 18 appearances. After a total of 45 goals he went back to Port Vale in March 1931 for £1,550.

OLDHAM ATHLETIC 2009–10 LEAGUE RECORD

Match No.	Date		Venue	Opponents	Result	H/T Score	Lg Pos.	Goalscorers	Atten- dance
1	Aug	8	H	Stockport Co	D 0-0	0-0	—		6918
2		15	A	Leyton Orient	W 2-1	1-1	7	Abbott 2 (1 pen) [12, 59 (p)]	4061
3		18	A	Millwall	L 0-2	0-1	—		7369
4		22	H	Swindon T	D 2-2	1-0	11	Marrow [37], Lee [90]	4229
5		29	A	Brentford	D 1-1	0-1	11	Blackman [52]	5125
6	Sept	4	H	Hartlepool U	L 0-3	0-2	16		4014
7		12	A	Bristol R	L 0-1	0-0	21		6674
8		19	H	Carlisle U	W 2-0	1-0	16	Abbott [13], Parker [52]	4268
9		26	A	Southend U	W 1-0	0-0	8	Abbott (pen) [76]	6979
10		29	H	Milton Keynes D	W 2-1	1-0	—	Sheehan [8], Parker [70]	3630
11	Oct	3	H	Yeovil T	D 0-0	0-0	8		4208
12		10	A	Charlton Ath	D 0-0	0-0	9		16,441
13		17	H	Southampton	L 1-3	0-2	12	Abbott [65]	5341
14		24	A	Brighton & HA	W 2-0	0-0	9	Abbott [57], Hazell [81]	6205
15	Nov	1	H	Huddersfield T	L 0-1	0-0	13		8569
16		14	A	Gillingham	L 0-1	0-0	14		4787
17		21	H	Colchester U	D 2-2	0-1	14	Taylor (pen) [63], Brooke [88]	3607
18		24	A	Walsall	L 0-3	0-2	—		3191
19	Dec	1	A	Leeds U	L 0-2	0-1	—		7793
20		5	A	Norwich C	L 0-2	0-2	20		24,404
21		12	H	Exeter C	W 2-0	0-0	16	Smalley [51], Heffernan [59]	6230
22		19	A	Wycombe W	D 2-2	1-1	19	Whitaker [45], Hazell [51]	4160
23	Jan	2	A	Hartlepool U	L 1-2	0-2	—	Abbott [88]	2634
24		20	H	Tranmere R	D 0-0	0-0	—		3688
25		23	H	Millwall	L 0-1	0-0	21		3656
26	Feb	6	A	Tranmere R	W 1-0	1-0	19	Abbott [41]	5518
27		9	A	Swindon T	L 2-4	0-2	—	Colbeck [79], Price [90]	6183
28		13	H	Walsall	W 1-0	0-0	18	Abbott [78]	3968
29		20	A	Colchester U	L 0-1	0-0	19		5321
30		23	A	Leeds U	L 0-2	0-0	—		17,635
31		27	H	Norwich C	L 0-1	0-0	21		5344
32	Mar	6	A	Exeter C	D 1-1	0-0	20	Gregan [81]	4997
33		9	H	Leyton Orient	W 2-0	1-0	—	Smalley [20], Stephens [49]	3126
34		13	H	Wycombe W	D 2-2	1-1	19	Hazell [29], Abbott (pen) [90]	3846
35		16	H	Stockport Co	W 1-0	1-0	—	Abbott (pen) [25]	4283
36		20	A	Brighton & HA	L 0-2	0-1	17		4059
37		30	H	Brentford	L 2-3	1-1	—	Abbott 2 [22, 82]	2833
38	Apr	3	H	Gillingham	W 1-0	0-0	17	Guy [59]	3486
39		6	A	Huddersfield T	L 0-2	0-1	—		14,561
40		10	H	Bristol R	W 2-1	0-0	16	Guy [48], Smalley [88]	3769
41		13	A	Milton Keynes D	D 0-0	0-0	—		8528
42		17	A	Carlisle U	W 2-1	0-0	16	Guy [55], Stephens [64]	4484
43		20	A	Southampton	D 0-0	0-0	—		18,366
44		24	H	Southend U	D 2-2	2-1	15	Whitaker [2], Black [43]	4225
45	May	1	A	Yeovil T	L 0-3	0-2	17		4513
46		8	H	Charlton Ath	L 0-2	0-1	16		5686

Final League Position: 16

GOALSCORERS

League (39): Abbott 13 (4 pens), Guy 3, Hazell 3, Smalley 3, Parker 2, Stephens 2, Whitaker 2, Black 1, Blackman 1, Brooke 1, Colbeck 1, Gregan 1, Heffernan 1, Lee 1, Marrow 1, Price 1, Sheehan 1, Taylor 1 (pen).
Carling Cup (0).
FA Cup (0).
J Paint Trophy (1): Whitaker 1.

Brill D 28	Marrow A 26+6	Gilbert P 5	Furman D 32+6	Gregan S 46	Hazell R 41	Holdsworth A 11+1	Worthington J 11+5	Abbott P 38+1	Parker K 17+10	Taylor C 27+5	Alessandra L —+1	Whitaker D 31+10	Byfield D —+3	Lomax K 11+4	Blackman N 6+6	Lee K 16+8	Sheehan A 8	Colbeck J 18+9	Brooke R 2+13	Smalley D 23+6	Flahavan D 18	Hills L 3	Jacobson J 14+1	Black P 12+1	Heffernan P 4	Stephens D 24+2	Rowney C —+1	Timar K 2	Goodwin J 8	Eaves T —+15	Price J 7	Nardiello D 2	Millar K 2+4	Guy L 12	Aijofree H 1	Match No.
1	2	3	4	5	6	7[1]	8	9	10[3]	11[2]	12	13	14																							1
1	2[1]	3	4	5	6	7	8	9[2]	10[3]	11		13	14	12																						2
1	2	3	4	5	6	7[1]	8	9	10	11		12																								3
1	2	3	13	5	6	7	8[3]	9	10[1]	11[2]		12				4	14																			4
1	2	3	8	5	6	7		9	10	11						4[1]	12																			5
1	2	13		5	6	7	8[2]	9	10	3[1]	12					4	11																			6
1	2		8	5	6	7[1]		9	14	3[2]	12	13		10[3]		4	11																			7
1			8	5	6			9	10[2]	3	7	2			12	4	11[1]	13																		8
1	12		8	5	6			9	10[2]	3	7	2			13	4	11[1]																			9
1	11		8	5	6			9[2]	10[1]	3	7	2			12	4	13																			10
1	11		8[2]	5	6		12	9	10	3[3]	7	2[1]				4	13	14																		11
1	3		4	5	6	7		9	10[1]	8		2			12		11																			12
1	2		4	5	6	8[1]		9	10	7	3	13			12		11[2]																			13
1	11		4	5	6	14		9	10[2]	12	7[1]	2			13	3	8[3]																			14
1			4	5	6	7		9	10[2]	3		12	13		2	11[1]		8																		15
	10		4	5	6	7			12	11[3]	3[1]	9			14	13		8[2]	1	2																16
	10			5	6	2			13	11		4			9	7		12	8[2]	1			3[1]													17
			4	5	6[2]	2			14	11		13	9[1]		7	10		8[3]	1		3*	12														18
	3		4[3]	5		8[2]				11	2	*3	7		12	10[1]		1	6	9	14															19
			4[2]	5					12	11	2		7	13	10	1		3	6	9[1]	8															20
	6		12	5					13	11	2		7[2]	14	8	1		3	10[1]	9[3]	4															21
	3		4	5	6					2			7	11[1]	12	10	1			9[2]	8	13														22
1			5			14			13	3		12	7	11[3]	10[1]	9[2]	2			8		4	6													23
1	12		5	6		9	13	7[3]	3[2]					14	10		2			8	4[1]	11														24
1			4	5	6	9[1]	11[2]	3						12	10		2			8		7	13													25
1	14		4	5	6		9[2]	13	12	3[1]					10		2			8[3]		7	11													26
1	13		4[2]	5	6		9[1]			3[1]					14		10			2		7	8	11												27
1			4[1]	5	6		9			3	12				13		10[2]			2		7	8	11												28
1	3		4	5	6		9[3]			7					12		10[2]			2		7		11												29
1	3		4[2]	5	6		9[3]			7	13				12		10[1]			2		8		14	11											30
1			4	5	6		9	12	7			3			11[1]		13			2		8			10[2]											31
1			4[2]	5	6		9		3	13			7		14		12			2		8			11[1]	10[3]										32
1				5	6	14	9[2]		7[3]	3			4		12		10			2		8		13	11[1]											33
1		12		5	6		9	11[1]	7	3			4				10[2]			2[3]		8		13		14										34
	3[2]		4	5	6	13	9[3]	7		12			8				10	1			2			14				11[1]								35
			4	5	6	7[2]	9		11	3[1]			8				12	1			2			13				10								36
				5	6	7[1]	9		3	12	2[2]		4				14	1			8			13				10[3]	11							37
1	14			5	6	7[1]	9[2]		3	12			4								2	8			13				10[3]	11						38
	14		4[3]	5	6		9[2]		3[1]	11			7*	13			1				2	8			12				10							39
	3		14	5	6		9[3]	11[1]		4			7[2]	12	1						2	8			13				10							40
1	3		4	5	6		9[2]			2			7	11[1]	14	12	1				8			13				10[3]								41
	3[1]		4	5	6	13	9[3]			2			7				10	1			12	8			14				11[2]							42
	3		4[1]	5	6	7	9[2]			14			8				10	1			2	12			13				11[3]							43
	3[2]		14	5	6		9[1]			7			4				10	1			2	8[3]			13	12	11									44
11[1]				5			13	9	12	3			7[3]					1			2	8		4[2]				14	10	6						45
				5	6		9[1]		7	3							13	10[3]	1		2	8			4	12			14	11[2]						46

FA Cup
First Round   Leeds U   (h)   0-2

Carling Cup
First Round   Carlisle U   (a)   0-1

J Paint Trophy
First Round   Accrington S   (h)   1-2

OXFORD UNITED   FL Championship 2

The Kassam Stadium, Grenoble Road, Oxford OX4 4XP.

Telephone: (01865) 337 500.

Fax: (01865) 337 501.

Ticket Office: (01865) 337 533.

Website: www.oufc.co.uk

Email: admin@oufc.co.uk

Ground Capacity: 12,500.

Record Attendance: 22,730 v Preston NE, FA Cup 6th rd, 29 February 1964.

Pitch Measurements: 115yd × 71yd.

Chairman: Kelvin Thomas.

General Manager/Club Secretary: Mick Brown.

Manager: Chris Wilder.

First Team Coach: Mickey Lewis.

Physios: Charlie Greig, Jon Brown.

Colours: Yellow shirts, blue shorts, blue stockings.

Change Colours: All white.

Year Formed: 1893.

Turned Professional: 1949.

Ltd Co.: 1949.

Club Nickname: 'The U's'.

Previous Names: 1893, Headington; 1894, Headington United; 1960, Oxford United.

Grounds: 1893, Headington Quarry; 1894, Wootten's Field; 1898, Sandy Lane Ground; 1902, Britannia Field; 1909, Sandy Lane; 1910, Quarry Recreation Ground; 1914, Sandy Lane; 1922, The Paddock Manor Road; 1925, Manor Ground; 2001, The Kassam Stadium.

First Football League Game: 18 August 1962, Division 4, v Barrow (a) L 2–3 – Medlock; Beavon, Quartermain; R. Atkinson, Kyle, Jones; Knight, G. Atkinson (1), Houghton (1), Cornwell, Colfar.

Record League Victory: 7–0 v Barrow, Division 4, 19 December 1964 – Fearnley; Beavon, Quartermain; R. Atkinson (1), Kyle, Jones; Morris, Booth (3), Willey (1), G. Atkinson (1), Harrington (1).

HONOURS

Football League: Division 1 best season: 12th, 1997–98; Division 2 – Champions 1984–85; Runners-up 1995–96; Division 3 – Champions 1967–68, 1983–84; Division 4 – Promoted 1964–65 (4th).

FA Cup: best season: 6th rd, 1964 (shared record for 4th Division club).

Football League Cup: Winners 1986.

sky SPORTS FACT FILE

Harry Thompson, the first professional player-manager of the then Headington United, had been an inside-forward once transferred to Sunderland from Wolverhampton Wanderers for £7,500 in 1938. But he finished his playing career with Headington playing at centre-half.

Record Cup Victory: 9–1 v Dorchester T, FA Cup 1st rd, 11 November 1995 – Whitehead; Wood (2), Ford M (1), Smith, Elliott, Gilchrist, Rush (1), Massey (Murphy), Moody (3), Ford R (1), Angel (Beauchamp (1)).

Record Defeat: 0–7 v Sunderland, Division 1, 19 September 1998.

Most League Points (2 for a win): 61, Division 4, 1964–65.

Most League Points (3 for a win): 95, Division 3, 1983–84.

Most League Goals: 91, Division 3, 1983–84.

Highest League Scorer in Season: John Aldridge, 30, Division 2, 1984–85.

Most League Goals in Total Aggregate: Graham Atkinson, 77, 1962–73.

Most League Goals in One Match: 4, Tony Jones v Newport Co, Division 4, 22 September 1962; 4, Arthur Longbottom v Darlington, Division 4, 26 October 1963; 4, Richard Hill v Walsall, Division 2, 26 December 1988; 4, John Durnin v Luton T, 14 November 1992.

Most Capped Player: Jim Magilton, 18 (52), Northern Ireland.

Most League Appearances: John Shuker, 478, 1962–77.

Youngest League Player: Jason Seacole, 16 years 149 days v Mansfield T, 7 September 1976.

Record Transfer Fee Received: £1,600,000 from Leicester C for Matt Elliott, January 1997.

Record Transfer Fee Paid: £475,000 to Aberdeen for Dean Windass, August 1998.

Football League Record: 1962 Elected to Division 4; 1965–68 Division 3; 1968–76 Division 3; 1976–84 Division 3; 1984–85 Division 2; 1985–88 Division 1; 1988–92 Division 2; 1992–94 Division 1; 1994–96 Division 2; 1996–99 Division 1; 1999–2001 Division 2; 2001–04 Division 3; 2004–06 FL2; 2006–10 Conference; 2010– FL 2.

MANAGERS

Harry Thompson 1949–58
  (Player-Manager) 1949-51
Arthur Turner 1959–69
  (continued as General Manager to 1972)
Ron Saunders 1969
Gerry Summers 1969–75
Mick Brown 1975–79
Bill Asprey 1979–80
Ian Greaves 1980–82
Jim Smith 1982–85
Maurice Evans 1985–88
Mark Lawrenson 1988
Brian Horton 1988–93
Denis Smith 1993–97
Malcolm Crosby 1997
Malcolm Shotton 1998–99
Denis Smith 2000
David Kemp 2000–01
Mark Wright 2001
Ian Atkins 2001–04
Graham Rix 2004
Ramon Diaz 2004–05
Brian Talbot 2005–2006
Darren Patterson 2006
Jim Smith 2006–07
Darren Patterson 2007–08
Chris Wilder December 2008–

LATEST SEQUENCES

Longest Sequence of League Wins: 6, 6.4 1985 – 24.4.1985.

Longest Sequence of League Defeats: 7, 4.5.1991 – 7.9.1991.

Longest Sequence of League Draws: 5, 7.10.1978 – 28.10.1978.

Longest Sequence of Unbeaten League Matches: 20, 17.3.1984 – 29.9.1984.

Longest Sequence Without a League Win: 27, 14.11.1987 – 27.8.1988.

Successive Scoring Runs: 17 from 10.9.1983.

Successive Non-scoring Runs: 6 from 26.3.1988.

TEN YEAR LEAGUE RECORD

		P	W	D	L	F	A	Pts	Pos
2000-01	Div 2	46	7	6	33	53	100	27	24
2001-02	Div 3	46	11	14	21	53	62	47	21
2002-03	Div 3	46	19	12	15	57	47	69	8
2003-04	Div 3	46	18	17	11	55	44	71	9
2004-05	FL 2	46	16	11	19	50	63	59	15
2005-06	FL 2	46	11	16	19	43	57	49	23
2006-07	Conf	46	22	15	9	66	33	81	2
2007-08	B Sq Pr	46	20	11	15	56	48	71	9
2008-09	B Sq Pr	46	24	10	12	72	51	77*	7
2009-10	B Sq Pr	44	25	11	8	64	31	86	3

* 5 points deducted.

DID YOU KNOW ?

Oxford United had the best individual attendance in the Blue Square Premier League last season when entertaining Luton Town on 8 September 2009. United won 2–0 with goals from Constable and Cook and suffered only one defeat in the first 18 League games.

PETERBOROUGH UNITED   FL Championship 1

London Road Stadium, London Road, Peterborough PE2 8AL.

Telephone: (01733) 563 947.

Fax: (01733) 344 140.

Ticket Office: (01733) 865 674.

Website: www.theposh.com

Email: info@theposh.com

Ground Capacity: 15,460.

Record Attendance: 30,096 v Swansea T, FA Cup 5th rd, 20 February 1965.

Pitch Measurements: 112yd × 71yd.

Chairman: Darragh MacAnthony.

Chief Executive: Bob Symns.

Director of Football and Club Secretary: Barry Fry.

Manager: Gary Johnson.

Assistant Manager: Nicky Eaden.

Physio: Peter Corder.

Colours: Blue shirts with white design, white shorts, white stockings.

Change Colours: Green and white striped shirts with green sleeves, black shorts, green stockings.

Year Formed: 1934.

Turned Professional: 1934.

Ltd Co.: 1934.

Club Nickname: 'The Posh'.

Ground: 1934, London Road Stadium.

First Football League Game: 20 August 1960, Division 4, v Wrexham (h) W 3–0 – Walls; Stafford, Walker; Rayner, Rigby, Norris; Hails, Emery (1), Bly (1), Smith, McNamee (1).

Record League Victory: 9–1 v Barnet (a) Division 3, 5 September 1998 – Griemink; Hooper (1), Drury (Farell), Gill, Bodley, Edwards, Davies, Payne, Grazioli (5), Quinn (2) (Rowe), Houghton (Etherington) (1).

HONOURS

Football League: Division 1 best season: 10th, 1992–93; Division 2 1991–92 (play-offs); FL 1 – Runners-up 2008–09; FL 2 – Runners-up 2007–08; Division 4 – Champions 1960–61, 1973–74.

FA Cup: best season: 6th rd, 1965.

Football League Cup: Semi-final 1966.

sky SPORTS FACT FILE

On 28 December 2009 Peterborough United were losing 4–0 at home to Cardiff City after 38 minutes before staging a remarkable comeback. Still trailing after 51 minutes and 4–2 down with 22 minutes remaining, they secured a 4–4 draw with two goals in the last minute.

Record Cup Victory: 9-1 v Rushden T, FA Cup 1st quard, 6 October 1945 – Hilliard; Bryan, Parrott, Warner, Hobbs, Woods, Polhill (1), Fairchild, Laxton (6), Tasker (1), Rodgers (1).

Record Defeat: 1–8 v Northampton T, FA Cup 2nd rd (2nd replay), 18 December 1946.

Most League Points (2 for a win): 66, Division 4, 1960–61.

Most League Points (3 for a win): 92, FL 2, 2007–08.

Most League Goals: 134, Division 4, 1960–61.

Highest League Scorer in Season: Terry Bly, 52, Division 4, 1960–61.

Most League Goals in Total Aggregate: Jim Hall, 122, 1967–75.

Most League Goals in One Match: 5, Guiliano Grazioli v Barnet, Division 3, 5 September 1998.

Most Capped Player: Craig Morgan, 19 (20), Wales.

Most League Appearances: Tommy Robson, 482, 1968–81.

Youngest League Player: Matthew Etherington, 15 years 262 days v Brentford, 3 May 1997.

Record Transfer Fee Received: £700,000 from Tottenham H for Simon Davies, December 1999.

Record Transfer Fee Paid: £500,000 to Grimsby T for Ryan Bennett, January 2010.

Football League Record: 1960 Elected to Division 4; 1961–68 Division 3, when they were demoted for financial irregularities; 1968–74 Division 4; 1974–79 Division 3; 1979–91 Division 4; 1991–92 Division 3; 1992–94 Division 1; 1994–97 Division 2; 1997–2000 Division 3; 2000–04 Division 2; 2004–05 FL 1; 2005–08 FL 2; 2008–09 FL 1; 2009–10 FL C; 2010– FL 1.

LATEST SEQUENCES

Longest Sequence of League Wins: 9, 1.2.1992 – 14.3.1992.

Longest Sequence of League Defeats: 8, 12.1.2008 – 12.4.2008.

Longest Sequence of League Draws: 8, 18.12.1971 – 12.2.1972.

Longest Sequence of Unbeaten League Matches: 17, 17.12.1960 – 8.4.1961.

Longest Sequence Without a League Win: 17, 23.9.1978 – 30.12.1978.

Successive Scoring Runs: 33 from 20.9.1960.

Successive Non-scoring Runs: 6 from 13.8.2002.

MANAGERS

Jock Porter 1934–36
Fred Taylor 1936–37
Vic Poulter 1937–38
Sam Haden 1938–48
Jack Blood 1948–50
Bob Gurney 1950–52
Jack Fairbrother 1952–54
George Swindin 1954–58
Jimmy Hagan 1958–62
Jack Fairbrother 1962–64
Gordon Clark 1964–67
Norman Rigby 1967–69
Jim Iley 1969–72
Noel Cantwell 1972–77
John Barnwell 1977–78
Billy Hails 1978–79
Peter Morris 1979–82
Martin Wilkinson 1982–83
John Wile 1983–86
Noel Cantwell 1986–88 *(continued as General Manager)*
Mick Jones 1988–89
Mark Lawrenson 1989–90
Dave Booth 1990–91
Chris Turner 1991–92
Lil Fuccillo 1992–93
John Still 1994–95
Mick Halsall 1995–96
Barry Fry 1996–2005
Mark Wright 2005–06
Keith Alexander 2006–07
Darren Ferguson 2007–09
Mark Cooper 2009–10
Gary Johnson April 2010–

TEN YEAR LEAGUE RECORD

		P	W	D	L	F	A	Pts	Pos
2000-01	Div 2	46	15	14	17	61	66	59	12
2001-02	Div 2	46	15	10	21	64	59	55	17
2002-03	Div 2	46	14	16	16	51	54	58	11
2003-04	Div 2	46	12	16	18	58	58	52	18
2004-05	FL 1	46	9	12	25	49	73	39	23
2005-06	FL 2	46	17	11	18	57	49	62	9
2006-07	FL 2	46	18	11	17	70	61	65	10
2007-08	FL 2	46	28	8	10	84	43	92	2
2008-09	FL 1	46	26	11	9	78	54	89	2
2009-10	FL C	46	8	10	28	46	80	34	24

DID YOU KNOW ?

Financial problems forced Peterborough United to transfer full-back Arthur Jefferson to Queens Park Rangers in 1935–36 in what was his first season with the club. He moved for the princely sum of £50 and went on to enjoy a career lasting 20 years and ending at Aldershot.

PETERBOROUGH UNITED 2009–10 LEAGUE RECORD

Match No.	Date		Venue	Opponents	Result		H/T Score	Lg Pos.	Goalscorers	Attendance
1	Aug	8	A	Derby Co	L	1-2	0-1	—	Boyd (pen) [84]	33,010
2		15	H	Sheffield W	D	1-1	0-1	17	Mackail-Smith [61]	10,747
3		18	H	WBA	L	2-3	1-3	—	Mackail-Smith [45], McLean [53]	8752
4		22	A	Preston NE	L	0-2	0-2	22		11,549
5		31	H	Crystal Palace	D	1-1	0-0	—	Batt [53]	8473
6	Sept	12	A	QPR	D	1-1	1-1	21	McLean [16]	11,814
7		15	A	Leicester C	D	1-1	1-0	—	Boyd (pen) [32]	21,485
8		19	H	Reading	W	3-2	0-2	18	Mackail-Smith [48], McLean [54], Boyd [90]	8521
9		26	A	Blackpool	L	0-2	0-2	20		7728
10		29	H	Plymouth Arg	L	1-2	0-0	—	Mackail-Smith [86]	7114
11	Oct	3	H	Nottingham F	L	1-2	0-0	23	McLean [50]	12,711
12		17	A	Bristol C	D	1-1	0-1	22	Boyd [90]	13,833
13		20	A	Doncaster R	L	1-3	1-2	—	McLean [32]	9288
14		24	H	Scunthorpe U	W	3-0	2-0	21	Boyd 2 (1 pen) [25, 78 (p)], Mackail-Smith [45]	8051
15		31	A	Barnsley	L	1-2	1-2	23	Boyd (pen) [24]	8556
16	Nov	7	A	Newcastle U	L	1-3	0-2	24	Keates [79]	43,067
17		21	A	Sheffield U	L	0-1	0-1	24		25,144
18		28	H	Middlesbrough	D	2-2	0-1	24	Boyd [54], Batt [76]	10,772
19	Dec	5	H	Swansea C	D	2-2	0-0	24	Whelpdale [55], McLean [90]	7312
20		8	A	Ipswich T	D	0-0	0-0	—		19,975
21		12	A	Coventry C	L	2-3	0-2	24	Mackail-Smith 2 [66, 71]	15,190
22		19	H	Watford	W	2-1	1-0	23	Frecklington [9], Geohaghon [78]	7723
23		26	A	WBA	L	0-2	0-0	24		24,924
24		28	H	Cardiff C	D	4-4	0-4	24	Simpson 2 [51, 90], Lee [68], Boyd [89]	9796
25	Jan	16	H	Derby Co	L	0-3	0-1	24		10,280
26		23	A	Sheffield W	L	1-2	0-1	—	Livermore [76]	24,882
27		26	H	Preston NE	L	0-1	0-1	—		7134
28		30	A	Crystal Palace	L	0-2	0-1	24		14,699
29	Feb	6	H	QPR	W	1-0	1-0	24	McLean [9]	8933
30		9	A	Cardiff C	L	0-2	0-1	—		17,686
31		13	A	Middlesbrough	L	0-1	0-1	24		18,412
32		16	H	Ipswich T	W	3-1	0-1	—	Dickinson [47], Frecklington [63], Morgan [85]	9428
33		27	A	Swansea C	L	0-1	0-1	24		16,175
34	Mar	6	H	Coventry C	L	0-1	0-1	24		10,469
35		9	H	Sheffield U	W	1-0	1-0	—	Mackail-Smith [40]	6674
36		13	A	Watford	W	1-0	0-0	24	Dickinson [51]	16,591
37		16	H	Doncaster R	L	1-2	0-0	—	Lee [55]	6773
38		20	A	Nottingham F	L	0-1	0-1	24		24,582
39		23	A	Scunthorpe U	L	0-4	0-3	—		4995
40		27	H	Bristol C	L	0-1	0-0	24		6445
41	Apr	3	H	Newcastle U	L	2-3	1-1	24	Green [11], Dickinson [76]	12,877
42		5	A	Barnsley	D	2-2	1-1	24	Bennett [5], Rowe [77]	11,290
43		10	H	Leicester C	L	1-2	0-1	24	Rowe [63]	9651
44		17	A	Reading	L	0-6	0-4	24		15,982
45		24	H	Blackpool	L	0-1	0-1	24		7812
46	May	2	A	Plymouth Arg	W	2-1	0-1	24	Mackail-Smith 2 [63, 69]	8557

Final League Position: 24

GOALSCORERS

League (46): Mackail-Smith 10, Boyd 9 (4 pens), McLean 7, Dickinson 3, Batt 2, Frecklington 2, Lee 2, Rowe 2, Simpson 2, Bennett 1, Geohaghon 1, Green 1, Keates 1, Livermore 1, Morgan 1, Whelpdale 1.
Carling Cup (10): Boyd 3, Frecklington 2, Mackail-Smith 1, McLean 1, Rowe 1, Whelpdale 1, Williams 1.
FA Cup (0).

Lewis J 43	Lee C 28+5	Williams T 14+1	Coutts P 13+3	Morgan C 33+1	Zakuani G 28+1	Rowe T 26+6	Keates D 2+4	Mackail-Smith C 39+4	McLean A 30+5	Boyd G 32	Frecklington L 26+9	Batt S 5+15	Diagouraga T 18+1	Green D 6+5	Martin R 8+2	Whelpdale C 27+2	Day J 2+3	Pearce K —+2	Rose D 4+2	McKeown J 2+2	Amos B 1	Bennett R 20+2	Griffiths S 20	Simpson J 8+13	Geohaghon E 17+2	Gilbert K 7+3	Livermore J 9	McLeod I 2+2	Reid R 5+8	Wright B —+4	Dickinson L 9	Koranteng N 3+1	Little M 9	Torres S 7+2	Mills D 1+2	McCrae R —+2	Andrew D 2	Match No.
1	2	3	4	5	6	7²	8¹	9	10	11	12	13																										1
1	2	3	4	5	6	7¹		9²	10	11	12	8	13																									2
1	2	3¹	4	5³	6	14		9	10	11	13	7	8²	12																								3
1		3¹	4	5	6	12		9	10	11	13	7³	8²	14	2																							4
1	14	3³	12	5	6	13		9	10	11	8	7²	4¹		2																							5
1		3		5	6	12		9	10	11¹	8	13	4		2	7²																						6
1		3	12	5	6	13		9	10	11	8²		4		2	7¹																						7
1		3³	8	5	6	12		9	10	11	4¹				2	7²	14																					8
1		3	8¹	5	6²			9	10	11			14			7³	2	12	13																			9
1		8³	12	5				9	10	11	13		4			7²	2	3¹	14	6																		10
1⁶		3	8¹	5	6			9	10	11	12	13	4		2	7²				15																		11
1		3¹		5	6	8²		9³	10	11	13		4	14		7	12	2																				12
1	14		12	5	6	8		9	10	11³	13		4¹			7	2	3²																				13
1	2	3³	12	5	6	8	14	9²	10	11			4			7¹	13																					14
		3		5	6²			9	10	11	8		4			7¹	2				1		12	13														15
1	6	13	12	5				9	10	11	8		14			7³	4¹					3	2²															16
1	2		12		6			9	10	11	8		4²			7¹						5	3	13														17
1			12		6¹	7²		9	10	11	8	13	4									5	2	3														18
1				5				9	10	11	8		4			7						2	3	6														19
1			4²	5		14		9³	10	11	8	12	13			7¹						6	2	3														20
1			4²	5				9	10	11	8	13				7¹						6	2	12	3													21
1			4		6	12		9	10	11	8¹					7						5	2	3														22
1			4²	12	6³	14		9	10	11	8	13				7¹						2	3	5														23
1⁶	8		4	5				9	10²	11	12		2			7			15			3	13		6¹													24
1	12		8²	5				9	13	11	4											3	14	2	6		7¹	10³										25
1	6							9	13	11¹	12		14					2				8	3	5		7	10²	4³										26
1	6							9	13	10³						7²						5	2	8	3	4	12	11¹	14									27
1	6	3						9²	12	11	8¹					7						5	10		2	4	13											28
1	2¹	3	5				8	9²	10	11³	14					7						3	12		4	13												29
1	3²			5	6			9	10	11						7						2	13		12	4												30
1	2²	3¹	5			4		14	10³	9	8					7						6	13			11	12											31
1			5			2		9¹	13	11	8					7						6	4		3	12	10²											32
1	4¹		5	14	6			8								7	2²						3³	13	11	5	2		12	10²								33
1	11		5	6	2			13	10²		8					4	7¹					12									9	3						34
1	4		5	6	2			9	10²		8¹		7										13						11	3	12							35
1	4		5	6	7			9	10³							3²	13	12					2	13	8		12	10¹	14	11		2	8¹					36
1	7		5	6	4			9														3¹		6	2²				12			4	11					37
1	10		5	8				9	13							7						3¹		6	2²			10²				4	11					38
1	4			6	2			9	8													12	5					10²			3¹	11³						39
1	4			6	2			9	8		7¹											3	11³	5	12			13		10²			14					40
1	7³			6	4			12	8							10²						14	3	13	5	2			9		11¹							41
				6	7	14		8	9		1											5²	3	10	4		2¹		12					8¹				42
1	7				5			2	9	11												6	3	10	4				12									43
1	10			5	6²		2	9	8		14					7						4	13	11¹							3³		12					44
					4		2	9								7¹					1	5	8				12	10³	11²	3			14	13	6	45	
1					7		5	9	3													6	8				12	10¹	11	2				4				46

PLYMOUTH ARGYLE — FL Championship 1

FOUNDATION

The club was formed in September 1886 as the Argyle Football Club by former public and private school pupils who wanted to continue playing the game. The meeting was held in a room above the Borough Arms (a Coffee House), Bedford Street, Plymouth. It was common then to choose a local street/terrace as a club name and Argyle or Argyll was a fashionable name throughout the land due to Queen Victoria's great interest in Scotland.

Home Park, Plymouth, Devon PL2 3DQ.
Telephone: (01752) 562 561.
Fax: (01752) 606 167.
Ticket Office: 0845 338 7232.
Website: www.pafc.co.uk
Email: argyle@pafc.co.uk
Ground Capacity: 21,118.
Record Attendance: 43,596 v Aston Villa, Division 2, 10 October 1936.
Pitch Measurements: 112yd × 73yd.
Chairman: Sir Roy Gardner.
Deputy Chairman: Paul Stapleton.
Chief Executive: Michael Dunford.
Secretary: Carole Rowntree.
Manager: Peter Reid.
First Team Coach: Paul Mariner.
Physio: Paul Atkinson. *Prozone and Fitness Coach:* Scott Russell.
Colours: Dark green shirts with white design, white shorts, white stockings with green design.
Change Colours: White shirts with dark green design, green shorts, green stockings with white design.
Year Formed: 1886.
Turned Professional: 1903.
Ltd Co.: 1903.
Previous Name: 1886, Argyle Athletic Club; 1903, Plymouth Argyle.
Club Nickname: 'The Pilgrims'.
Ground: 1886, Home Park.
First Football League Game: 28 August 1920, Division 3, v Norwich C (h) D 1–1 – Craig; Russell, Atterbury; Logan, Dickinson, Forbes; Kirkpatrick, Jack, Bowler, Heeps (1), Dixon.
Record League Victory: 8–1 v Millwall, Division 2, 16 January 1932 – Harper; Roberts, Titmuss; Mackay, Pullan, Reed; Grozier, Bowden (2), Vidler (3), Leslie (1), Black (1), (1 og). 8–1 v Hartlepool U (a), Division 2, 7 May 1994 – Nicholls; Patterson (Naylor), Hill, Burrows, Comyn, McCall (1), Barlow, Castle (1), Landon (3), Marshall (1), Dalton (2).

HONOURS

Football League: Division 2 – Champions 2003–04; Division 3 (S) – Champions 1929–30, 1951–52; Runners-up 1921–22. 1922–23, 1923–24, 1924–25, 1925–26, 1926–27 (record of six consecutive years); Division 3 – Champions 1958–59, 2001–02; Runners-up 1974–75, 1985–86.
FA Cup: Semi-final 1984.
Football League Cup: Semi-final 1965, 1974.

sky SPORTS FACT FILE

On 28 November 1936 Plymouth Argyle won 3–1 at Tottenham Hotspur. It was their eleventh successive game unbeaten and had produced 19 points from a possible 22. They finished fifth in the Second Division.

Record Cup Victory: 6–0 v Corby T, FA Cup 3rd rd, 22 January 1966 – Leiper; Book, Baird; Williams, Nelson, Newman; Jones (1), Jackson (1), Bickle (3), Piper (1), Jennings.

Record Defeat: 0–9 v Stoke C, Division 2, 17 December 1960.

Most League Points (2 for a win): 68, Division 3 (S), 1929–30.

Most League Points (3 for a win): 102, Division 3, 2001–02.

Most League Goals: 107, Division 3 (S), 1925–26 and 1951–52.

Highest League Scorer in Season: Jack Cock, 32, Division 3 (S), 1926–27.

Most League Goals in Total Aggregate: Sammy Black, 180, 1924–38.

Most League Goals in One Match: 5, Wilf Carter v Charlton Ath, Division 2, 27 December 1960.

Most Capped Player: Moses Russell, 20 (23), Wales.

Most League Appearances: Kevin Hodges, 530, 1978–92.

Youngest League Player: Lee Phillips, 16 years 43 days v Gillingham, 29 October 1996.

Record Transfer Fee Received: £3,000,000 from Hull C for Peter Halmosi, July 2008.

Record Transfer Fee Paid: £500,000 to Cardiff C for Steve MacLean, January 2008; £500,000 to QPR for Simon Walton, August 2008.

Football League Record: 1920 Original Member of Division 3; 1921–30 Division 3 (S); 1930–50 Division 2; 1950–52 Division 3 (S); 1952–56 Division 2; 1956–58 Division 3 (S); 1958–59 Division 3; 1959–68 Division 2; 1968–75 Division 2; 1975–77 Division 2; 1977–86 Division 3; 1986–95 Division 2; 1995–96 Division 3; 1996–98 Division 2; 1998–2002 Division 3; 2002–04 Division 2; 2004–10 FL C; 2010– FL 1.

LATEST SEQUENCES

Longest Sequence of League Wins: 9, 8.3.1986 – 12.4.1986.

Longest Sequence of League Defeats: 9, 12.10.1963 – 7.12.1963.

Longest Sequence of League Draws: 5, 26.2.2000 – 14.3.2000.

Longest Sequence of Unbeaten League Matches: 22, 20.4.1929 – 21.12.1929.

Longest Sequence Without a League Win: 13, 27.4.1963 – 2.10.1963.

Successive Scoring Runs: 39 from 15.4.1939.

Successive Non-scoring Runs: 5 from 20.9.1947.

MANAGERS

Frank Brettell 1903–05
Bob Jack 1905–06
Bill Fullerton 1906–07
Bob Jack 1910–38
Jack Tresadern 1938–47
Jimmy Rae 1948–55
Jack Rowley 1955–60
Neil Dougall 1961
Ellis Stuttard 1961–63
Andy Beattie 1963–64
Malcolm Allison 1964–65
Derek Ufton 1965–68
Billy Bingham 1968–70
Ellis Stuttard 1970–72
Tony Waiters 1972–77
Mike Kelly 1977–78
Malcolm Allison 1978–79
Bobby Saxton 1979–81
Bobby Moncur 1981–83
Johnny Hore 1983–84
Dave Smith 1984–88
Ken Brown 1988–90
David Kemp 1990–92
Peter Shilton 1992–95
Steve McCall 1995
Neil Warnock 1995–97
Mick Jones 1997–98
Kevin Hodges 1998–2000
Paul Sturrock 2000–04
Bobby Williamson 2004–05
Tony Pulis 2005–06
Ian Holloway 2006–07
Paul Sturrock 2007–09
Paul Mariner 2009–10
Peter Reid June 2010–

TEN YEAR LEAGUE RECORD

		P	W	D	L	F	A	Pts	Pos
2000-01	Div 3	46	15	13	18	54	61	58	12
2001-02	Div 3	46	31	9	6	71	28	102	1
2002-03	Div 2	46	17	14	15	63	52	65	8
2003-04	Div 2	46	26	12	8	85	41	90	1
2004-05	FL C	46	14	11	21	52	64	53	17
2005-06	FL C	46	13	17	16	39	46	56	14
2006-07	FL C	46	17	16	13	63	52	67	11
2007-08	FL C	46	17	13	16	60	50	64	10
2008-09	FL C	46	13	12	21	44	57	51	21
2009-10	FL C	46	11	8	27	43	68	41	23

DID YOU KNOW ?

On 13 January 1934 in a third round FA Cup tie at Home Park watched by 44,500, Plymouth Argyle took the lead against Huddersfield Town in the 20th minute. They held on to the lead until conceding an equaliser in the 88th minute.

PLYMOUTH ARGYLE 2009–10 LEAGUE RECORD

Match No.	Date	Venue	Opponents	Result	H/T Score	Lg Pos.	Goalscorers	Attendance
1	Aug 8	A	Crystal Palace	D 1-1	1-0	—	Timar [5]	14,358
2	15	H	QPR	D 1-1	0-1	15	Gorkss (og) [90]	11,588
3	18	H	Cardiff C	L 1-3	0-1	—	Gow (pen) [90]	11,918
4	22	A	Derby Co	L 1-2	1-1	19	Judge (pen) [17]	26,186
5	29	H	Sheffield W	L 1-3	0-1	21	Gow [80]	10,228
6	Sept 12	A	WBA	L 1-3	1-2	22	Mackie [12]	22,190
7	15	H	Watford	L 0-1	0-1	—		8703
8	19	A	Newcastle U	L 1-3	0-1	24	Duguid [50]	42,898
9	27	H	Nottingham F	L 0-1	0-1	24		14,792
10	29	A	Peterborough U	W 2-1	0-0	—	Mackie [63], Fallon [69]	7114
11	Oct 3	H	Scunthorpe U	W 2-1	0-0	22	Fallon [57], Judge (pen) [76]	9780
12	17	A	Blackpool	L 0-2	0-1	23		7765
13	20	A	Bristol C	L 1-3	0-0	—	Mackie [75]	15,021
14	24	H	Ipswich T	D 1-1	1-0	23	Fletcher [22]	10,875
15	31	A	Middlesbrough	W 1-0	0-0	22	Mackie [64]	21,141
16	Nov 7	H	Doncaster R	W 2-1	1-1	21	Judge [26], Fallon [71]	9420
17	21	A	Leicester C	L 0-1	0-0	22		27,174
18	Dec 5	H	Sheffield U	L 0-1	0-0	23		9231
19	8	A	Swansea C	L 0-1	0-0	—		14,004
20	12	A	Preston NE	L 0-2	0-2	23		12,231
21	19	H	Coventry C	L 0-1	0-0	24		8347
22	26	A	Cardiff C	W 1-0	0-0	23	Sawyer [84]	24,010
23	28	H	Reading	W 4-1	1-0	22	Judge 2 (1 pen) [13 (p), 63], Arnason [59], Barnes [84]	12,091
24	Jan 16	A	Crystal Palace	L 0-1	0-1	23		9318
25	26	A	Derby Co	W 1-0	0-0	—	Mackie [82]	7996
26	30	A	Sheffield W	L 1-2	1-2	23	Fallon [24]	22,590
27	Feb 6	H	WBA	L 0-1	0-0	23		12,053
28	9	A	Reading	L 1-2	0-0	—	Fletcher [68]	15,484
29	13	A	Barnsley	W 3-1	0-1	23	Fletcher [64], Mackie [74], Fallon [83]	11,661
30	16	H	Swansea C	D 1-1	0-0	—	Johnson D [87]	9185
31	20	H	Leicester C	D 1-1	1-1	23	Noone [39]	11,581
32	27	A	Sheffield U	L 3-4	0-2	23	Bolasie [48], Mason [56], Mackie [85]	24,886
33	Mar 6	H	Preston NE	D 1-1	0-1	23	Johnson D (pen) [71]	9582
34	9	A	QPR	L 0-2	0-1	—		12,013
35	13	A	Coventry C	D 1-1	1-0	23	Arnason [45]	18,127
36	16	H	Bristol C	W 3-2	2-0	—	Clark [31], Wright-Phillips [45], Fletcher [90]	9289
37	20	A	Scunthorpe U	L 1-2	1-1	23	Mackie [28]	5153
38	23	A	Ipswich T	W 2-0	1-0	—	Wright-Phillips [34], Mason [78]	19,316
39	27	H	Blackpool	L 0-2	0-0	23		10,614
40	30	H	Barnsley	D 0-0	0-0	—		7243
41	Apr 3	A	Doncaster R	W 2-1	0-0	23	Mason [67], Wright-Phillips [90]	10,179
42	5	H	Middlesbrough	L 0-2	0-1	23		11,770
43	10	A	Watford	L 0-1	0-0	23		14,246
44	19	H	Newcastle U	L 0-2	0-2	—		13,111
45	24	A	Nottingham F	L 0-3	0-2	23		22,602
46	May 2	H	Peterborough U	L 1-2	1-0	23	Wright-Phillips [31]	8557

Final League Position: 23

GOALSCORERS

League (43): Mackie 8, Fallon 5, Judge 5 (3 pens), Fletcher 4, Wright-Phillips 4, Mason 3, Arnason 2, Gow 2 (1 pen), Johnson D 2 (1 pen), Barnes 1, Bolasie 1, Clark 1, Duguid 1, Noone 1, Sawyer 1, Timar 1, own goal 1.
Carling Cup (1): Summerfield 1.
FA Cup (0).

Larrieu R 25	Summerfield L 9+3	McNamee D 6+3	Fletcher C 41	Timar K 6+1	Seip M 5	Paterson J 11+1	Mackie J 42	MacLean S 3	Fallon R 25+8	Sawyer G 28+1	Duguid K 40+2	Judge A 28+9	Sheridan C 5+8	Noone C 3+14	Gow A 8+6	Arnason K 32	Clark C 28+9	Johnson R 23+2	Blake D 5+2	Wright-Phillips B 12+3	Lowry S 13	Gray D 12	Chester J 2+1	Barnes A 3+4	Folly Y 4+3	Mason J 5+14	Barker C 10+4	Stockdale D 21	Johnson D 20	Cooper K —+7	Bolasie Y 8+8	Eckersley R 7	N'Gala B 9	Leonard R —+1	Bhasera O 7	Match No.
1	2²	3	4		5	6	7	8	9¹	10	11	12	13																							1
1	2		4	5	6	7³	8	9¹	10	3	14	11²	12	13																						2
1	2		4	5	6	7	8	10	3	11²	9¹	13	12																							3
1	13	2	4		6	8	10¹	9	3	7²	11³			5	12	14																				4
1			4		6	8	10	3	11	9	7	5		2																						5
1	6²		4	14	8	10	9³	3	7	13	11	5	12	2¹																						6
1	2	4	5	10	14	3	7	12	9³	11²	6	8¹	13																							7
1	4	10	13	3	7	12	9	11¹	6	8²	2	5																								8
1	4	10	3	7	13	9	11³	6¹	8²	14	2	5	12																							9
1	4	11	10¹	9	3	7	12	8	2	5	6																									10
1	4	11²	10³	9	3	7	12	14	13	8¹	2	5	6																							11
1	4	5	8	10	9²	2³	7	14	12	13	11¹	3	6																							12
1	4	5	10	12	3	7	8²	14	13	11³	2	6	9¹																							13
1	4	11¹	10	9³	2	7	8	14	5	12	13⁸	3	6²																							14
1	8	10	2	7	11¹	9²	4	12	3	5	13	6																								15
1	10	9³	2	7	8²	12	11¹	5	13	3	6	14	4																							16
1	4	9¹	10	13	2	7³	8	11²	5	12	14	3	6																							17
1	4	9	2³	7	11	13	12	14	6	3	5	8²	10¹																							18
1	8	10	9	3³	7	11	14	4	12	13	2⁴	5²	6¹																							19
1	8	12	11	9	3²	7	6	13	4	2	5	10¹																								20
1	4	10	9	7	8²	12	13	6	3¹	11	2	5																								21
1	8	4	10	9²	2	11	7¹	6	3	5					13	12																				22
1	8³	4	10	9²	2	11	7¹	12	6	3	5				13	14																				23
1	8²	13	4³	9	2	7	6	12	5	11					10¹	14	3																			24
	8	13	4	10	9	3	2	7¹	12	5	11²	6³						14	1																	25
	8²	4	10	9	3	2	7¹	13	5	11	6		12						1																	26
		12	4		9	10²	3	2¹	8³	14	6	11	5							1	7	13														27
		2³	4	10	9¹	3	8²	13	5	11	6		14							7	12															28
		4	10	9	2	8¹	5	11	6				3	1	7		12																			29
	8¹	4	10	9²	2	5	11	6	14	3³		1	7	13	12																					30
		4	10	9¹	2	8	5	11²	6	12		3	1	7	13																					31
	14	8	10	9²	2	11¹	4	3	5³	13	6	1	7	12																						32
	11¹	8	10	13	2	12	5	3²	9	6	1	7	4																							33
		4	10	9²	2	11	8¹	5	13	6	12	3	1	7																						34
		8	10	12	2	5	3	9²	13	6	9¹	1	7	11	4¹																					35
		8	10	2	13	5	3²	4	9¹	6	9²	1	7	11																						36
		4	10	14	11	5	3²	9³	13	12	1	7	8	2¹																						37
		8	10	2	12	3	6	9²	13	5¹	1	7	11	4																						38
	12²	8¹	10	2	6³	3	5	9	14	1	7	11	4	13																						39
		10	2	6²	13	11	5	9³	12	1	7	14	8¹	4	3																					40
		10	2	6²	11	5	9	12	1	7	13	8¹	4	3																						41
		10	13	2	6²	11	5	9¹	3	1	7	12	4	3																						42
		10	2	12	11	5	9	13	1	7	14	8²	6¹	4	3³																					43
	8	10	11	6	5	9¹	12	1	7	13	2	4	3²																							44
	8	11	5³	12	6¹	9²	10	14	7	13	2	4	3																							45
1	8	13	2³	6	5	11²	9	10	12	7	14	4	3¹																							46

FA Cup
Third Round   Newcastle U   (h)   0-0
(a)   0-3

Carling Cup
First Round   Gillingham   (a)   1-2

PORTSMOUTH   FL Championship

FOUNDATION

At a meeting held in his High Street, Portsmouth offices in 1898, solicitor Alderman J. E. Pink and five other business and professional men agreed to buy some ground close to Goldsmith Avenue for £4,950 which they developed into Fratton Park in record breaking time. A team of professionals was signed up by manager Frank Brettell and entry to the Southern League obtained for the new club's September 1899 kick-off.

Fratton Park, Frogmore Road, Portsmouth, Hampshire PO4 8RA.

Telephone: (02392) 731 204.

Fax: (02392) 734 129.

Ticket Office: (0844) 847 1898.

Website: www.pompeyfc.co.uk

Email: info@pompeyfc.co.uk

Ground Capacity: 20,688.

Record Attendance: 51,385 v Derby Co, FA Cup 6th rd, 26 February 1949.

Pitch Measurements: 100m × 65m.

Chief Executive: David Lampitt.

Joint Administrators: Andrew Andronikou, Michael Kiely, Peter Kubik.

Secretary: Paul Weld.

Manager: Steve Cotterill.

First Team Coaches: Paul Groves, Ian Woan.

Physio: Gary Sadler MCSP, SROP.

Colours: Blue shirts with white trim, white shorts, red stockings.

Change Colours: White shirts with maroon trim, maroon shorts, maroon stockings.

Year Formed: 1898.

Turned Professional: 1898.

Ltd Co.: 1898.

Club Nickname: 'Pompey'.

Ground: 1898, Fratton Park.

First Football League Game: 28 August 1920, Division 3, v Swansea T (h) W 3–0 – Robson; Probert, Potts; Abbott, Harwood, Turner; Thompson, Stringfellow (1), Reid (1), James (1), Beedie.

Record League Victory: 9–1 v Notts Co, Division 2, 9 April 1927 – McPhail; Clifford, Ted Smith; Reg Davies (1), Foxall, Moffat; Forward (1), Mackie (2), Haines (3), Watson, Cook (2).

Record Cup Victory: 7–0 v Stockport Co, FA Cup 3rd rd, 8 January 1949 – Butler; Rookes, Ferrier; Scoular, Flewin, Dickinson; Harris (3), Barlow, Clarke (2), Phillips (2), Froggatt.

HONOURS

Football League: Division 1 – Champions 1948–49, 1949–50, 2002–03; Division 2 – Runners-up 1926–27, 1986–87; Division 3 (S) – Champions 1923–24; Division 3 – Champions 1961–62, 1982–83.

FA Cup: Winners 1939, 2008; Runners-up 1929, 1934, 2010.

Football League Cup: best season: 5th rd, 1961, 1986.

European Competitions: UEFA Cup: 2008–09.

sky SPORTS FACT FILE

On 19 December 2009 Portsmouth defeated Liverpool 2–0 at Fratton Park. The opening goal scored by Nadir Belhadj was the 500th Premier League goal of the season. It placed Pompey on 14 points equal with West Ham United but still bottom on fewest goals scored.

Record Defeat: 0–10 v Leicester C, Division 1, 20 October 1928.

Most League Points (2 for a win): 65, Division 3, 1961–62.

Most League Points (3 for a win): 98, Division 1, 2002–03.

Most League Goals: 97, Division 1, 2002–03.

Highest League Scorer in Season: Guy Whittingham, 42, Division 1, 1992–93.

Most League Goals in Total Aggregate: Peter Harris, 194, 1946–60.

Most League Goals in One Match: 5, Alf Strange v Gillingham, Division 3, 27 January 1923; 5, Peter Harris v Aston Villa, Division 1, 3 September 1958.

Most Capped Player: Jimmy Dickinson, 48, England.

Most League Appearances: Jimmy Dickinson, 764, 1946–65.

Youngest League Player: Clive Green, 16 years 259 days v Wrexham, 21 August 1976.

Record Transfer Fee Received: £20,000,000 from Real Madrid for Lassana Diarra, January 2009.

Record Transfer Fee Paid: Reported fee of £11,000,000 to Liverpool for Peter Crouch, July 2008.

Football League Record: 1920 Original Member of Division 3; 1921 Division 3 (S); 1924–27 Division 2; 1927–59 Division 1; 1959–61 Division 2; 1961–62 Division 3; 1962–76 Division 2; 1976–78 Division 3; 1978–80 Division 4; 1980–83 Division 3; 1983–87 Division 2; 1987–88 Division 1; 1988–92 Division 2; 1992–2003 Division 1; 2003–10 FA Premier League; 2010– FL C.

LATEST SEQUENCES

Longest Sequence of League Wins: 7, 17.8.2002 – 17.9.2002.

Longest Sequence of League Defeats: 9, 21.10.1975 – 6.12.1975.

Longest Sequence of League Draws: 5, 16.12.2000 – 13.1.2001.

Longest Sequence of Unbeaten League Matches: 15, 18.4.1924 – 18.10.1924.

Longest Sequence Without a League Win: 25, 29.11.1958 – 22.8.1959.

Successive Scoring Runs: 23 from 30.8.1930.

Successive Non-scoring Runs: 6 from 14.1.1939.

MANAGERS

Frank Brettell 1898–1901
Bob Blyth 1901–04
Richard Bonney 1905–08
Bob Brown 1911–20
John McCartney 1920–27
Jack Tinn 1927–47
Bob Jackson 1947–52
Eddie Lever 1952–58
Freddie Cox 1958–61
George Smith 1961–70
Ron Tindall 1970–73
   (General Manager to 1974)
John Mortimore 1973–74
Ian St John 1974–77
Jimmy Dickinson 1977–79
Frank Burrows 1979–82
Bobby Campbell 1982–84
Alan Ball 1984–89
John Gregory 1989–90
Frank Burrows 1990–91
Jim Smith 1991–95
Terry Fenwick 1995–98
Alan Ball 1998–99
Tony Pulis 2000
Steve Claridge 2000–01
Graham Rix 2001–02
Harry Redknapp 2002–04
Velimir Zajec 2004–05
Alain Perrin 2005
Harry Redknapp 2005–08
Tony Adams 2008–09
Paul Hart 2009
Avram Grant 2009–10
Steve Cotterill June 2010–

TEN YEAR LEAGUE RECORD

		P	W	D	L	F	A	Pts	Pos
2000-01	Div 1	46	10	19	17	47	59	49	20
2001-02	Div 1	46	13	14	19	60	72	53	17
2002-03	Div 1	46	29	11	6	97	45	98	1
2003-04	PR Lge	38	12	9	17	47	54	45	13
2004-05	PR Lge	38	10	9	19	43	59	39	16
2005-06	PR Lge	38	10	8	20	37	62	38	17
2006-07	PR Lge	38	14	12	12	45	42	54	9
2007-08	PR Lge	38	16	9	13	48	40	57	8
2008-09	PR Lge	38	10	11	17	38	57	41	14
2009-10	PR Lge	38	7	7	24	34	66	19*	20

9 pts deducted.

DID YOU KNOW ?

On 2 September 1899 Portsmouth opened their Southern League account against Chatham. A goal by Nobby Clarke was enough to give them the points. An unusual feature of the match was that Pompey used a substitute during it!

PORTSMOUTH 2009–10 LEAGUE RECORD

Match No.	Date	Venue	Opponents		Result	H/T Score	Lg Pos.	Goalscorers	Attendance
1	Aug 15	H	Fulham	L	0-1	0-1	—		17,510
2	19	A	Birmingham C	L	0-1	0-0	—		19,922
3	22	A	Arsenal	L	1-4	1-2	19	Kaboul [37]	60,049
4	30	H	Manchester C	L	0-1	0-1	20		17,826
5	Sept 12	H	Bolton W	L	2-3	1-2	20	Kaboul [25], Boateng [63]	17,564
6	19	A	Aston Villa	L	0-2	0-2	20		35,979
7	26	H	Everton	L	0-1	0-1	20		18,116
8	Oct 3	A	Wolverhampton W	W	1-0	1-0	20	Yebda [19]	29,023
9	17	H	Tottenham H	L	1-2	0-2	20	Boateng [59]	20,821
10	24	A	Hull C	D	0-0	0-0	20		23,720
11	31	H	Wigan Ath	W	4-0	2-0	20	Dindane 3 (1 pen) [35, 65, 90 (p)], Piquionne [45]	18,212
12	Nov 7	A	Blackburn R	L	1-3	1-0	20	O'Hara [15]	23,110
13	22	A	Stoke C	L	0-1	0-0	20		27,069
14	28	H	Manchester U	L	1-4	1-1	20	Boateng (pen) [32]	20,482
15	Dec 5	H	Burnley	W	2-0	0-0	20	Hreidarsson [65], Dindane [84]	17,822
16	12	A	Sunderland	D	1-1	0-1	20	Kaboul [90]	37,578
17	16	A	Chelsea	L	1-2	0-1	—	Piquionne [51]	40,137
18	19	H	Liverpool	W	2-0	1-0	20	Belhadj [33], Piquionne [82]	20,534
19	26	A	West Ham U	L	0-2	0-1	20		33,686
20	30	H	Arsenal	L	1-4	0-2	—	Belhadj [74]	20,404
21	Jan 26	H	West Ham U	D	1-1	0-0	—	Webber [76]	18,322
22	31	A	Manchester C	L	0-2	0-2	20		44,015
23	Feb 3	A	Fulham	L	0-1	0-0	—		21,934
24	6	A	Manchester U	L	0-5	0-2	20		74,684
25	9	H	Sunderland	D	1-1	0-1	—	Dindane [90]	16,242
26	20	H	Stoke C	L	1-2	1-0	20	Piquionne [35]	17,208
27	27	H	Burnley	W	2-1	1-1	20	Piquionne [25], Yebda (pen) [76]	19,714
28	Mar 9	H	Birmingham C	L	1-2	0-2	20	Kanu [90]	18,465
29	15	A	Liverpool	L	1-4	0-3	20	Belhadj [88]	40,316
30	20	H	Hull C	W	3-2	1-1	20	Smith [37], O'Hara [88], Kanu [89]	16,513
31	24	H	Chelsea	L	0-5	0-1	—		18,753
32	27	A	Tottenham H	L	0-2	0-2	20		35,870
33	Apr 3	H	Blackburn R	D	0-0	0-0	20		16,207
34	14	A	Wigan Ath	D	0-0	0-0	20		14,323
35	18	H	Aston Villa	L	1-2	1-1	20	Brown [9]	16,523
36	24	H	Bolton W	D	2-2	0-2	20	Dindane 2 [54, 68]	20,526
37	May 1	H	Wolverhampton W	W	3-1	2-1	20	Dindane [20], Utaka [39], Brown [67]	19,213
38	9	A	Everton	L	0-1	0-0	20		38,730

Final League Position: 20

GOALSCORERS

League (34): Dindane 8 (1 pen), Piquionne 5, Belhadj 3, Boateng 3 (1 pen), Kaboul 3, Brown 2, Kanu 2, O'Hara 2, Yebda 2 (1 pen), Hreidarsson 1, Smith 1, Utaka 1, Webber 1.
Carling Cup (13): Piquionne 3, Kanu 2, Webber 2, Dindane 1, Hughes 1, Kranjcar 1, Utaka 1, Vanden Borre 1, own goal 1.
FA Cup (13): Piquionne 3, Boateng 2 (1 pen), Utaka 2, Belhadj 1, Dindane 1, Mokoena 1, O'Hara 1, Owusu-Abeyie 1, own goal 1.

James D 25	Kaboul Y 19	Belhadj N 16+3	Mokoena A 21+2	Distin S 3	Wilson M 28	Utaka J 10+8	Diop P 9+3	Piquionne F 26+8	Mullins H 15+3	Kranjcar N 4	Kanu N 6+17	Nugent D —+3	Vanden Borre A 15+4	Basinas A 7+5	Begovic A 8+1	Brown M 22+2	Hughes R 9+1	Smith T 12+4	Ben Haim T 21+1	Boateng K 20+2	O'Hara J 25+1	Yebda H 15+3	Webber D 4+13	Dindane A 18+1	Finnan S 20+1	Ashdown J 5+1	Hreidarsson H 17	Owusu-Abeyie Q 3+7	Ricardo Rocha 10	Sowah L 3+2	Ward J 1+2	Ritchie M 1+1	Match No.
1	2	3	4	5	6	7^2	8^1	9	10	11	12	13																					1
1	2	3	4	5	6	13	8^1	9^3	10	11	14							7^2	12														2
1^0	2	3	4	5	6^2	7		9	8	11	10^1	12	13		15																		3
	5	3	4			12		9^2	6	11	13	14	2			1	7	8^3	10^1														4
1	5	3	4					9				2			1	7		10^2	6	8	11^1	12	13										5
1	5	3	4					9^1		12		2			1	7		10^2	6	8	11	13											6
1	5		4^1	3					13			2			7^2		10^3	6	8	11	12	14	9										7
1	5	13		3					14						7		10^3	6	4	11	8^1	12	9^1	2									8
1	3	13	4^2		7	14		12							6^8		10^1	5	8		11		9	2^3									9
1	3		4	6				12									10^1	5	8	11	7		9	2									10
1	3	12		4				9^2	14		13				6			5	8	11	7^2		10	2^1									11
1	3		4^2	7				9			13	2			6	12	5	8	11			10¹											12
2				7				12	4^2	9					3			5	8	11	13	10^1		1	6								13
2			3	13				9^1			12				1	4		14	5	8	11	7^2	10^3		6								14
			4					13		12					1	3		10^1	5	8^2	11	7		9	2		6						15
1	2^8		3	14	12			9^1								4^3	8	5		11	7^2	13	10		6								16
		4^3		3	14	10^1	9^2	7							1		12	5	8	11		13	2		6								17
	4	3					9^2	12	13						1	8		5	10^1	11	7			2	6								18
	4	3^1			14		9	8	13						1	7^3		5	12	11		10^2	2		6								19
	7	3	4^1				9		13		12			1	14	10^3		5	8^2	11			2	6									20
3		4	11	7			9^2	6^1					12	10	1			8		13		2	5										21
1			3	7	14		4^3			2	10					5	8	11		9^2	12		6^1	13									22
1	3		6				9^1						8^2			5	4	11	7	12	10	2			13								23
1	3		6				9^2	8		2^1				7		5	12	11^5	14	10					13	4							24
1	13		6	4^1	9			12		8						5		11	7^3	14	0	2^3			3^8								25
1	3		6	13	4	9^1		12										11	7^2	14	0	2^3	5	8									26
1	3			4	12	14	9						13					11^2	7	10^3	2		6	8^1	5^8								27
1	3		4^1				9		14		13		7^3		5			11	8^2	10	2	6	12										28
	3	12	4	8^1	9								7					11^2	14	10	2	1	6^2	13	5								29
1	3	8^1	4		9	2		12			14			10				11	13			6	7^2	5^3									30
1	6^3		4		9	8	14				13		7	10^2				11			2		3	12	5^1								31
1^6	6			9	4	10	5	8^2	7	11							12		2	15	3^1	13											32
	6		7^2	13	4	9	2^8	10	3	8^1					11						1				5	12							33
	6		4	7	8	13	2	9	6	10							1				1				5^1	12	3	11^2				34
1	6		4	7	8^3		9^1	2					5		12	10^2	11								3	13	14						35
1	6		7	12				2					4	8	10			11^1	9					5	3								36
1	6^2		7	14	9			5					4	11^3	13		8				10^1	2			3	12							37
	6^2	11^1	7	8	9^3	4		3	14					13	10	12					2	1		5									38

FA Cup

Third Round	Coventry C	(h)	1-1
		(a)	2-1
Fourth Round	Sunderland	(h)	2-1
Fifth Round	Southampton	(a)	4-1
Sixth Round	Birmingham C	(h)	2-0
Semi-Final	Tottenham H		2-0
(at Wembley).			
Final	Chelsea		0-1
(at Wembley).			

Carling Cup

Second Round	Hereford U	(h)	4-1
Third Round	Carlisle U	(a)	3-1
Fourth Round	Stoke C	(h)	4-0
Quarter-Final	Aston Villa	(h)	2-4

PORT VALE   FL Championship 2

FOUNDATION

Formed in 1876 as Port Vale, adopting the prefix 'Burslem' in 1884 upon moving to that part of the city. It was dropped in 1909.

Vale Park, Hamil Road, Burslem, Stoke-on-Trent ST6 1AW.

Telephone: (01782) 655 800.

Fax: (01782) 834 981.

Ticket Office: (01782) 655 832.

Website: www.port-vale.co.uk

Email: enquiries@port-vale.co.uk

Ground Capacity: 18,982.

Record Attendance: 49,768 v Aston Villa, FA Cup 5th rd, 20 February 1960.

Pitch Measurements: 114yd × 75yd.

Chairman/Chief Executive: Bill Bratt.

Vice-chairman: Peter Jackson.

Secretary: Bill Lodey.

Manager: Micky Adams.

Assistant Manager: Geoff Horsfield.

Physio: John Bower.

Colours: White shirts with black trim, black shorts with white trim, white stockings.

Change Colours: Black shirts with black and white sleeves, white shorts, black stockings.

Year Formed: 1876.

Turned Professional: 1885.

Ltd Co.: 1911.

Previous Names: 1876, Port Vale; 1884, Burslem Port Vale; 1909, Port Vale.

Club Nickname: 'Valiants'.

Grounds: 1876, Limekin Lane, Longport; 1881, Westport; 1884, Moorland Road, Burslem; 1886, Athletic Ground, Cobridge; 1913, Recreation Ground, Hanley; 1950, Vale Park.

First Football League Game: 3 September 1892, Division 2, v Small Heath (a) L 1–5 – Frail; Clutton, Elson; Farrington, McCrindle, Delves; Walker, Scarratt, Bliss (1), Jones. (Only 10 men).

Record League Victory: 9–1 v Chesterfield, Division 2, 24 September 1932 – Leckie; Shenton, Poyser; Sherlock, Round, Jones; McGrath, Mills, Littlewood (6), Kirkham (2), Morton (1).

Record Cup Victory: 7–1 v Irthlingborough, FA Cup 1st rd, 12 January 1907 – Matthews; Dunn, Hamilton; Eardley, Baddeley, Holyhead; Carter, Dodds (2), Beats, Mountford (2), Coxon (3).

Record Defeat: 0–10 v Sheffield U, Division 2, 10 December 1892. 0–10 v Notts Co, Division 2, 26 February 1895.

HONOURS

Football League: Division 2 – Runners-up 1993–94; Division 3 (N) – Champions 1929–30, 1953–54; Runners-up 1952–53; Division 4 – Champions 1958–59.

FA Cup: Semi-final 1954, when in Division 3.

Football League Cup: best season: 4th rd 2007.

Autoglass Trophy: Winners 1993.

Anglo-Italian Cup: Runners-up 1996.

LDV Vans Trophy: Winners 2001.

sky SPORTS FACT FILE

In three of four successive matches during 1908–09, centre-forward Tim Coleman scored four goals in each for Port Vale in the North Staffordshire and District League. He actually started the season as the club's right-back. Despite this scoring achievement, he reverted to defence.

Most League Points (2 for a win): 69, Division 3 (N), 1953–54.

Most League Points (3 for a win): 89, Division 2, 1992–93.

Most League Goals: 110, Division 4, 1958–59.

Highest League Scorer in Season: Wilf Kirkham 38, Division 2, 1926–27.

Most League Goals in Total Aggregate: Wilf Kirkham, 154, 1923–29, 1931–33.

Most League Goals in One Match: 6, Stewart Littlewood v Chesterfield, Division 2, 24 September 1922.

Most Capped Player: Chris Birchall, 22 (36), Trinidad & Tobago.

Most League Appearances: Roy Sproson, 761, 1950–72

Youngest League Player: Malcolm McKenzie, 15 years 347 days v Newport Co, 12 April 1966.

Record Transfer Fee Received: £2,000,000 from Wimbledon for Gareth Ainsworth, October 1998.

Record Transfer Fee Paid: £500,000 to York C for Jon McCarthy, August 1995 and £500,000 to Lincoln C for Gareth Ainsworth, September 1997.

Football League Record: 1892 Original Member of Division 2. Failed re-election in 1896; Re-elected 1898; Resigned 1907; Returned in Oct, 1919, when they took over the fixtures of Leeds City; 1929–30 Division 3 (N); 1930–36 Division 2; 1936–38 Division 3 (N); 1938–52 Division 3 (S); 1952–54 Division 3 (N); 1954–57 Division 2; 1957–58 Division 3 (S); 1958–59 Division 4; 1959–65 Division 3; 1965–70 Division 4; 1970–78 Division 3; 1978–83 Division 4; 1983–84 Division 3; 1984–86 Division 4; 1986–89 Division 3; 1989–94 Division 2; 1994–2000 Division 1; 2000–04 Division 2; 2004–08 FL 1; 2008– FL 2.

LATEST SEQUENCES

Longest Sequence of League Wins: 8, 8.4.1893 – 30.9.1893.

Longest Sequence of League Defeats: 9, 9.3.1957 – 20.4.1957.

Longest Sequence of League Draws: 6, 26.4.1981 – 12.9.1981.

Longest Sequence of Unbeaten League Matches: 19, 5.5.1969 – 8.11.1969.

Longest Sequence Without a League Win: 17, 7.12.1991 – 21.3.1992.

Successive Scoring Runs: 22 from 12.9.1992.

Successive Non-scoring Runs: 4 from 10.2.1896.

MANAGERS

Sam Gleaves 1896–1905
(Secretary-Manager)
Tom Clare 1905–11
A. S. Walker 1911–12
H. Myatt 1912–14
Tom Holford 1919–24
(continued as Trainer)
Joe Schofield 1924–30
Tom Morgan 1930–32
Tom Holford 1932–35
Warney Cresswell 1936–37
Tom Morgan 1937–38
Billy Frith 1945–46
Gordon Hodgson 1946–51
Ivor Powell 1951
Freddie Steele 1951–57
Norman Low 1957–62
Freddie Steele 1962–65
Jackie Mudie 1965–67
Sir Stanley Matthews
(General Manager) 1965–68
Gordon Lee 1968–74
Roy Sproson 1974–77
Colin Harper 1977
Bobby Smith 1977–78
Dennis Butler 1978–79
Alan Bloor 1979
John McGrath 1980–83
John Rudge 1984–99
Brian Horton 1999–2004
Martin Foyle 2004–07
Lee Sinnott 2007–08
Dean Glover 2008–09
Micky Adams June 2009–

TEN YEAR LEAGUE RECORD

		P	W	D	L	F	A	Pts	Pos
2000-01	Div 2	46	16	14	16	55	49	62	11
2001-02	Div 2	46	16	10	20	51	62	58	14
2002-03	Div 2	46	14	11	21	54	70	53	17
2003-04	Div 2	46	21	10	15	73	63	73	7
2004-05	FL 1	46	17	5	24	49	59	56	18
2005-06	FL 1	46	16	12	18	49	54	60	13
2006-07	FL 1	46	18	6	22	64	65	60	12
2007-08	FL 1	46	9	11	26	47	81	38	23
2008-09	FL 2	46	13	9	24	44	66	48	13
2009-10	FL 2	46	17	17	12	61	50	68	10

DID YOU KNOW ❓

In 1951–52 the veteran former Stoke City and England centre-forward Freddie Steele became player-manager of Port Vale. From 12 January the playing performances improved dramatically and Vale were able to finish the season in a respectable 13th position.

PORT VALE 2009–10 LEAGUE RECORD

Match No.	Date	Venue	Opponents	Result	H/T Score	Lg Pos.	Goalscorers	Attendance
1	Aug 8	H	Rochdale	D	1-1	0-0	—	Richards (pen) [75]	6158
2	15	A	Bradford C	D	0-0	0-0	17		11,333
3	18	A	Macclesfield T	L	0-2	0-1	—		3433
4	22	H	Darlington	W	1-0	1-0	15	Richards [29]	4561
5	29	A	Hereford U	D	2-2	0-1	16	Dodds [49], Taylor R [53]	2434
6	Sept 5	H	Grimsby T	W	4-0	1-0	10	Dodds [43], Richards [68], Heywood (og) [87], Collins [90]	5056
7	12	A	Aldershot T	D	1-1	1-1	13	Taylor R [23]	3406
8	19	H	Bury	L	0-1	0-1	14		5461
9	26	A	Notts Co	L	1-3	1-2	16	Richards (pen) [44]	7561
10	29	H	Accrington S	D	2-2	1-0	—	Dodds [5], Fraser [86]	4326
11	Oct 3	H	Bournemouth	D	0-0	0-0	16		4905
12	10	A	Shrewsbury T	W	1-0	1-0	14	McCombe [45]	7096
13	17	A	Crewe Alex	W	2-1	1-1	12	Richards [45], Taylor K [80]	6943
14	24	H	Cheltenham T	D	1-1	1-0	13	Richards [9]	4979
15	31	A	Dagenham & R	D	1-1	1-0	13	Dodds [38]	2003
16	Nov 14	H	Rotherham U	L	1-2	1-1	13	Prosser [36]	4788
17	21	A	Barnet	D	0-0	0-0	13		1939
18	24	H	Torquay U	D	2-2	1-1	—	Loft [11], Taylor R [76]	3996
19	Dec 1	H	Lincoln C	W	2-1	1-0	—	Richards [40], Dodds [59]	2569
20	5	A	Morecambe	L	0-2	0-2	16		4679
21	12	A	Northampton T	D	1-1	1-0	16	Richards (pen) [45]	4132
22	28	A	Grimsby T	W	2-1	2-0	13	Rigg [7], Taylor R [41]	4401
23	Jan 19	H	Burton Alb	W	3-1	2-1	—	Richards 2 (1 pen) [7, 85 (p)], Rigg [25]	4458
24	23	H	Macclesfield T	D	0-0	0-0	12		5167
25	26	A	Rochdale	D	0-0	0-0			3081
26	30	H	Hereford U	W	2-0	1-0	12	Davies [9], Richards [90]	4686
27	Feb 6	A	Burton Alb	L	0-1	0-1	14		4644
28	9	A	Chesterfield	L	1-2	0-2	—	Davies [49]	4090
29	13	A	Torquay U	W	2-1	1-0	14	Haldane [42], Richards [67]	2563
30	20	H	Barnet	L	0-2	0-1	15		4571
31	23	H	Lincoln C	W	4-0	3-0	—	Pearce (og) [1], Taylor R [3], Davies [15], McCombe [69]	3231
32	27	A	Morecambe	L	0-1	0-1	14		2064
33	Mar 2	A	Darlington	W	3-1	0-1	—	Loft [67], Dodds [72], Haldane [81]	1582
34	6	H	Northampton T	L	1-3	1-3	13	Loft [5]	4861
35	9	H	Bradford C	W	2-1	0-1	—	Richards [50], Taylor R [78]	3728
36	13	A	Chesterfield	W	5-0	2-0	9	Taylor R [19], Richards 3 [44, 51, 79], Davies (pen) [85]	4138
37	20	A	Cheltenham T	D	1-1	1-1	11	McCombe [8]	3503
38	27	H	Crewe Alex	L	0-1	0-0	13		7232
39	Apr 3	A	Rotherham U	W	2-1	0-0	11	Davies [59], Richards [62]	3721
40	5	H	Dagenham & R	W	3-1	1-1	10	Haldane [43], Taylor R [74], Davies [78]	4572
41	10	A	Aldershot T	D	1-1	0-0	10	Rigg [72]	5399
42	13	A	Accrington S	W	2-1	1-0	—	Davies [35], Taylor K [65]	2205
43	17	A	Bury	D	1-1	1-0	9	Richards (pen) [30]	4570
44	24	H	Notts Co	W	2-1	2-1	7	Richards [20], Taylor K [30]	7459
45	May 1	A	Bournemouth	L	0-4	0-0	9		9055
46	8	H	Shrewsbury T	D	1-1	0-1	10	Richards (pen) [77]	8467

Final League Position: 10

GOALSCORERS

League (61): Richards 20 (6 pens), Taylor R 8, Davies 7 (1 pen), Dodds 6, Haldane 3, Loft 3, McCombe 3, Rigg 3, Taylor K 3, Collins 1, Fraser 1, Prosser 1, own goals 2.
Carling Cup (4): Richards 2, Taylor K 1, Taylor R 1.
FA Cup (2): Dodds 1, Yates 1.
J Paint Trophy (5): Dodds 1, Haldane 1, McCombe 1, Richards 1, Taylor R 1.

Martin C 39	Stockley S 8 + 1	Taylor K 38 + 3	Collins L 45	McCombe J 37 + 3	Owen G 40	Griffith A 38 + 2	Loft D 21 + 11	Richards M 45 + 1	Taylor R 25 + 14	Horsfield G 1 + 8	Lawrie J — + 3	Fraser T 33 + 5	Dodds L 33 + 11	Jorgensen C — + 4	Yates A 25 + 7	McCrory D 2 + 3	Haldane L 29 + 8	Richman S — + 5	Howland D — + 4	Jarrett J 7 + 2	Guy J — + 3	Prosser L 2	Glover D — + 3	Rigg S 9 + 17	Davies C 22 + 2	Anyon J 7	Morsy S — + 1	Match No.
1	2^1	3	4	5	6	7^2	8	9	11	10^1	12	13	14															1
1	2	3	4	5	6	7^2	8^3	9	10^1	12		11	14	13														2
1	2^2	3	4	5	6	7^1	8	9	10	12		11^3	14	13														3
1		3	4	5	6		8^2	9^3	10^1	14	12	11			7	13	2											4
1			4	5	6		8	9	10^1	12		11			7^2	13	2	3										5
1			4	5	6	13	8^3	9	10^1			11			7^2		2	3	12	14								6
1		3	4	5	6	13	8^1	9^3	10	14		11			7^2		2		12									7
1		3	4	5	6		8^3	9	10			11			7^2	2^1		12	13	14								8
1	2^3	3	4	5^1	6^2	7		9	10			11	12			13	8	14										9
1	13	3	4	5	6	7	2^1	9	10^2			11				8^3		14	12									10
1		3	4	5	6	7	2^1	9^2		13		11	10^3					14	12		8							11
1	2^3	3	4	5	6	8^1		9				11	10^2		14		7			13	12							12
1	2	3	4	5	6	7^1		9	12				10^1				11^2				8	13						13
1	2	3		5	6	7^1		9	13			12	10^3				11^2			8	14	4						14
1	2	3	4	5	6			9	12			11	10				7^1			8								15
1		3	4	5		7		9	12			8	10		2		11^1						6					16
1		3	4	5	6	2	7^2	9	11^1			8^4	10^3				12		13				14					17
1		3	4	5	6^2	2	7	9	13			11^1			14		10			8^3			12					18
1		3	6	5		2^1	7^2	9	11				10			12	8^3	13	4				14					19
1		3	6	5		2	7^1	9	11	14		8^3	10			12			4^2				13					20
1		3	4	5^4	6	2^1	12	9	11			8	10		7													21
1		3	5		6	4		9	11^4	12		8	10		2								7^1					22
1	3^2	5	13	6	4		9					8	10		2		11						7^1	12				23
1		3	5		6	4		9	12			8	10^1		2		11						13	7^2				24
1		3	5		6	4		9	12			8	10^1		2		7						13	11^2				25
1		3	5		6	4^2	14	9				8	10^3		2		7^4	13						12	11^1			26
1		3^3	5		6	4^2		9	11	14		8	7^1		2				12					13	10			27
1		3	5	12	6^1	4^3		9	13			8	14		2		11^2							7	10			28
1		3	5	6		4^2	13	9				8	12		2		11							7^1	10			29
1		3	5	6		7		9	13			4^3	12		2		11^1	14						8	10^2			30
		5	4	6			9	3^9				8^2	7		2		11^1	14						12	10	1	13	31
	12	5	4	6		3^2	14	9	10			7			2^1		11^2							13	8	1		32
		3	4	5^1	6	2	14	9	7^3			10			12		11							13	8^2	1		33
		3^1	5	12	6	4	8	9				14	10^2		2		11^3							7	13	1		34
	12	5	3	6	4			9	7			8			2^1		11							13	10^2	1		35
		3	5	2	6	4	13	9^1	7^2			8	12				11^3							14	10	1		36
		3	4	5	6	2	13	9	7^1			8^2	12				11^3							14	10	1		37
		3	4	5^1	6	2	13	9	7^2			8			12		11^3							14	10	1		38
1		3^3	4	5	6	2	13	9				8^2	7		14		12							11	10^1			39
1		3	5	6	4	12		9	13			8^1	7^2		2		11^3							14	10			40
1		3	5	6	4	12		9	14			8^1	7		2		11^2							13	10^3			41
1		3	4	5	6	2	11	12	7			9					13							8^2	10^1			42
1		3	4	5	6	2	7	9	8^1			12					11^2							13	10			43
1		3	6	5		4	8	9	12			14	7^1		2		11^2							13	10^3			44
1		3	6	5		4^1	8	9	14			12	7^2		2		11^3							13	10			45
1	13	3		5^2	6	4	7^1	9	14			12			2		11							8	10^3			46

FA Cup

First Round	Stevenage B	(h)	1-1
		(a)	1-0
Second Round	Huddersfield T	(h)	0-1

Carling Cup

First Round	Sheffield U	(a)	2-1
Second Round	Sheffield W	(h)	2-0
Third Round	Scunthorpe U	(a)	0-2

J Paint Trophy

Second Round	Stockport Co	(h)	3-1
Northern Quarter-Final	Bradford C	(a)	2-2

PRESTON NORTH END   FL Championship

FOUNDATION

North End Cricket and Rugby Club which was formed in 1863, indulged in most sports before taking up soccer in about 1879. In 1881 they decided to stick to football to the exclusion of other sports and even a 16–0 drubbing by Blackburn Rovers in an invitation game at Deepdale, a few weeks after taking this decision, did not deter them for they immediately became affiliated to the Lancashire FA.

Deepdale Stadium, Sir Tom Finney Way, Deepdale, Preston PR1 6RU.

Telephone: (0844) 856 1964.

Fax: (01772) 693 366.

Ticket Office: (0844) 856 1966.

Website: www.pne.com

Email: enquiries@pne.com

Ground Capacity: 23,408.

Record Attendance: 42,684 v Arsenal, Division 1, 23 April 1938.

Pitch Measurements: 110yd × 77yd.

Chairman: Derek Shaw.

Deputy Chairman: David Taylor.

Secretary: Janet Parr.

Manager: Darren Ferguson.

Assistant Manager: Kevin Russell.

Physio: Matthew Jackson.

Colours: White shirts, blue shorts, white stockings.

Change Colours: Red shirts with blue sleeves, red shorts, red stockings.

Year Formed: 1881.

Turned Professional: 1885. *Ltd Co.:* 1893.

Club Nicknames: 'The Lilywhites' or 'North End'.

Ground: 1881, Deepdale.

First Football League Game: 8 September 1888, Football League, v Burnley (h) W 5–2 – Trainer; Howarth, Holmes; Robertson, W. Graham, J. Graham; Gordon (1), Ross (2), Goodall, Dewhurst (2), Drummond.

Record League Victory: 10–0 v Stoke, Division 1, 14 September 1889 – Trainer; Howarth, Holmes; Kelso, Russell (1), Graham; Gordon, Jimmy Ross (2), Nick Ross (3), Thomson (2), Drummond (2).

Record Cup Victory: 26–0 v Hyde, FA Cup 1st rd, 15 October 1887 – Addision; Howarth, Nick Ross; Russell (1), Thomson (5), Graham (1); Gordon (5), Jimmy Ross (8), John Goodall (1), Dewhurst (3), Drummond (2).

Record Defeat: 0–7 v Blackpool, Division 1, 1 May 1948.

Most League Points (2 for a win): 61, Division 3, 1970–71.

HONOURS

Football League: Division 1 – Champions 1888–89 (first champions) 1889–90; Runners-up 1890–91, 1891–92, 1892–93, 1905–06, 1952–53, 1957–58; Division 2 – Champions 1903–04, 1912–13, 1950–51, 1999–2000; Runners-up 1914–15, 1933–34; Division 3 – Champions 1970–71, 1995–96; Division 4 – Runners-up 1986–87.

FA Cup: Winners 1889, 1938; Runners-up 1888, 1922, 1937, 1954, 1964.

Football League Cup: best season: 4th rd, 2003.

Double Performed: 1888–89.

Football League Cup: best season: 4th rd, 1963, 1966, 1972, 1981.

sky SPORTS FACT FILE

On 4 May 1935 Andy Beattie made his debut for Preston North End against West Bromwich Albion at outside-left in a goalless draw at The Hawthorns. He had to wait until 1936–37 for his next senior outing as a wing-half and then became a fixture at full-back until 1946–47.

Most League Points (3 for a win): 95, Division 2, 1999–2000.
Most League Goals: 100, Division 2, 1927–28 and Division 1, 1957–58.
Highest League Scorer in Season: Ted Harper, 37, Division 2, 1932–33.
Most League Goals in Total Aggregate: Tom Finney, 187, 1946–60.
Most League Goals in One Match: 4, Jimmy Ross v Stoke, Division 1, 6 October 1888; 4, Nick Ross v Derby Co, Division 1, 11 January 1890; 4, George Drummond v Notts Co, Division 1, 12 December 1891; 4, Frank Becton v Notts Co, Division 1, 31 March 1893; 4, George Harrison v Grimsby T, Division 2, 3 November 1928; 4, Alex Reid v Port Vale, Division 2, 23 February 1929; 4, James McClelland v Reading, Division 2, 6 September 1930; 4, Dick Rowley v Notts Co, Division 2, 16 April 1932; 4, Ted Harper v Burnley, Division 2, 29 August 1932; 4, Ted Harper v Lincoln C, Division 2, 11 March 1933; 4, Charlie Wayman v QPR, Division 2, 25 December 1950; 4, Alex Bruce v Colchester U, Division 3, 28 February 1978.
Most Capped Player: Tom Finney, 76, England.
Most League Appearances: Alan Kelly, 447, 1961–75.
Youngest League Player: Steve Doyle, 16 years 166 days v Tranmere R, 15 November 1974.
Record Transfer Fee Received: £6,000,000 from Portsmouth for David Nugent, August 2007.
Record Transfer Fee Paid: £1,500,000 to Manchester U for David Healy, December 2000.
Football League Record: 1888 Founder Member of League; 1901–04 Division 2; 1904–12 Division 1; 1912–13 Division 2; 1913–14 Division 1; 1914–15 Division 2; 1919–25 Division 1; 1925–34 Division 2; 1934–49 Division 1; 1949–51 Division 2; 1951–61 Division 1; 1961–70 Division 2; 1970–71 Division 3; 1971–74 Division 2; 1974–78 Division 3; 1978–81 Division 2; 1981–85 Division 3; 1985–87 Division 4; 1987–92 Division 3; 1992–93 Division 2; 1993–96 Division 3; 1996–2000 Division 2; 2000–04 Division 1; 2004– FL C.

MANAGERS

Charlie Parker 1906–15
Vincent Hayes 1919–23
Jim Lawrence 1923–25
Frank Richards 1925–27
Alex Gibson 1927–31
Lincoln Hayes 1931–32
Run by committee 1932–36
Tommy Muirhead 1936–37
Run by committee 1937–49
Will Scott 1949–53
Scot Symon 1953–54
Frank Hill 1954–56
Cliff Britton 1956–61
Jimmy Milne 1961–68
Bobby Seith 1968–70
Alan Ball Sr 1970–73
Bobby Charlton 1973–75
Harry Catterick 1975–77
Nobby Stiles 1977–81
Tommy Docherty 1981
Gordon Lee 1981–83
Alan Kelly 1983–85
Tommy Booth 1985–86
Brian Kidd 1986
John McGrath 1986–90
Les Chapman 1990–92
Sam Allardyce 1992 (*Caretaker*)
John Beck 1992–94
Gary Peters 1994–98
David Moyes 1998–2002
Kelham O'Hanlon 2002
(*Caretaker*)
Craig Brown 2002–04
Billy Davies 2004–06
Paul Simpson 2006–07
Alan Irvine 2007–09
Darren Ferguson January 2010–

LATEST SEQUENCES

Longest Sequence of League Wins: 14, 25.12.1950 – 27.3.1951.
Longest Sequence of League Defeats: 8, 22.9.1984 – 27.10.1984.
Longest Sequence of League Draws: 6, 24.2.1979 – 20.3.1979.
Longest Sequence of Unbeaten League Matches: 23, 8.9.1888 – 14.9.1889.
Longest Sequence Without a League Win: 15, 14.4.1923 – 20.10.1923.
Successive Scoring Runs: 30 from 15.11.1952.
Successive Non-scoring Runs: 6 from 8.4.1897.

TEN YEAR LEAGUE RECORD

		P	W	D	L	F	A	Pts	Pos
2000-01	Div 1	46	23	9	14	64	52	78	4
2001-02	Div 1	46	20	12	14	71	59	72	8
2002-03	Div 1	46	16	13	17	68	70	61	12
2003-04	Div 1	46	15	14	17	69	71	59	15
2004-05	FL C	46	21	12	13	67	58	75	5
2005-06	FL C	46	20	20	6	59	30	80	4
2006-07	FL C	46	22	8	16	64	53	74	7
2007-08	FL C	46	15	11	20	50	56	56	15
2008-09	FL C	46	21	11	14	66	54	74	6
2009-10	FL C	46	13	15	18	58	73	54	17

DID YOU KNOW ?

On 2 January 2010 Preston North End defeated Colchester United 7–0 in a third round FA Cup tie. It was the club's highest score since 7 May 1966 when they beat Cardiff City 9–0 in the Second Division. Ernie Hannigan and Brian Godfrey both scored hat-tricks.

PRESTON NORTH END 2009–10 LEAGUE RECORD

Match No.	Date	Venue	Opponents	Result	H/T Score	Lg Pos.	Goalscorers	Attendance
1	Aug 8	H	Bristol C	D	2-2	0-0	—	Parkin [82], Davidson (pen) [90]	13,025
2	15	A	Doncaster R	D	1-1	1-0	11	Brown [28]	10,070
3	18	A	Barnsley	W	3-0	2-0	—	Parry [11], Mellor [32], Parkin [72]	11,850
4	22	H	Peterborough U	W	2-0	2-0	5	Mellor [8], Jones [30]	11,549
5	29	A	Ipswich T	D	1-1	1-1	6	Wallace [12]	19,454
6	Sept 12	H	Swansea C	W	2-0	1-0	4	Mellor [27], Elliott [89]	12,854
7	15	A	Scunthorpe U	L	1-3	0-2	—	Parkin [58]	5383
8	19	H	Coventry C	W	3-2	0-1	4	Brown 2 [50, 68], Mellor [55]	11,230
9	26	A	Leicester C	W	2-1	1-0	3	Mellor [41], Chaplow [66]	20,623
10	29	H	Reading	L	1-2	0-2	—	Parkin (pen) [85]	10,987
11	Oct 3	H	WBA	D	0-0	0-0	5		11,180
12	17	A	QPR	L	0-4	0-1	6		12,810
13	20	A	Sheffield W	W	2-1	1-1	—	Mellor [20], Parkin [55]	20,882
14	24	H	Middlesbrough	D	2-2	0-1	8	Parry [61], Jones [90]	16,116
15	31	H	Crystal Palace	D	1-1	1-1	8	Wallace [35]	12,558
16	Nov 7	A	Watford	L	0-2	0-2	11		13,524
17	23	H	Newcastle U	L	0-1	0-0	—		16,924
18	30	A	Blackpool	D	1-1	1-1	—	Wallace [38]	9861
19	Dec 5	A	Cardiff C	L	0-1	0-0	14		18,735
20	8	H	Derby Co	D	0-0	0-0	—		11,755
21	12	H	Plymouth Arg	W	2-0	2-0	12	Chaplow [10], Wallace [26]	12,231
22	19	A	Nottingham F	L	0-3	0-2	15		21,582
23	28	A	Sheffield U	L	0-1	0-0	16		25,231
24	Jan 16	A	Bristol C	L	2-4	1-2	17	Brown [27], Wallace [90]	13,146
25	26	A	Peterborough U	W	1-0	1-0	—	Mellor [34]	7134
26	30	H	Ipswich T	W	2-0	0-0	11	Collins N [64], Welbeck [64]	12,087
27	Feb 2	H	Barnsley	L	1-4	1-2	—	Welbeck [27]	12,453
28	6	A	Swansea C	L	0-2	0-1	13		14,659
29	9	H	Sheffield U	W	2-1	1-0	—	James [10], Parkin [71]	10,270
30	13	H	Blackpool	D	0-0	0-0	11		19,840
31	16	A	Derby Co	L	3-5	1-1	—	Parkin [10], Sedgwick [62], Brown [90]	26,993
32	20	A	Newcastle U	L	0-3	0-1	16		45,525
33	27	A	Cardiff C	W	3-0	1-0	13	Parkin 2 (1 pen) [30 (p), 54], Brown [86]	11,777
34	Mar 6	A	Plymouth Arg	D	1-1	1-0	13	St Ledger-Hall [18]	9582
35	9	A	Doncaster R	D	1-1	1-1	—	Mellor [42]	11,942
36	13	H	Nottingham F	W	3-2	3-0	12	Wallace [20], Davidson (pen) [28], James [32]	14,426
37	16	H	Sheffield W	D	2-2	1-0	—	Mellor [29], Coutts [53]	12,311
38	20	H	WBA	L	2-3	2-3	14	St Ledger-Hall [15], Mellor [43]	21,343
39	23	A	Middlesbrough	L	0-2	0-1	—		16,974
40	27	H	QPR	D	2-2	1-0	14	Jones [37], Davidson (pen) [56]	12,080
41	Apr 3	H	Watford	D	1-1	0-1	17	Davidson [53]	12,534
42	5	A	Crystal Palace	L	1-3	1-1	17	Treacy [8]	16,642
43	10	A	Scunthorpe U	W	3-2	1-0	14	Parkin [28], Jones [86], Treacy [90]	12,441
44	17	A	Coventry C	D	1-1	1-1	14	Davidson (pen) [37]	15,822
45	24	H	Leicester C	L	0-1	0-0	15		14,926
46	May 2	A	Reading	L	1-4	0-2	17	Wallace [64]	19,239

Final League Position: 17

GOALSCORERS

League (58): Mellor 10, Parkin 10 (2 pens), Wallace 7, Brown 6, Davidson 5 (4 pens), Jones 4, Chaplow 2, James 2, Parry 2, St Ledger-Hall 2, Treacy 2, Welbeck 2, Collins N 1, Coutts 1, Elliott 1, Sedgwick 1.
Carling Cup (8): Brown 4, Elliott 1, Mellor 1, Nicholson 1, Trottman 1.
FA Cup (7): Parkin 3 (1 pen), Brown 1, Carter 1, Sedgwick 1, own goal 1.

Lonergan A 45	Jones B 42+2	Davidson C 25+2	Chaplow R 29+2	St Ledger-Hall S 30	Mawene Y 18+1	Parry P 12+5	Sumulikoski V 9+6	Parkin J 26+17	Mellor N 29+10	Wallace R 40+1	Brown C 24+19	Nicholson B 3+1	Sedgwick C 25+9	Chilvers L 20+3	Carter D 11+12	Elliott S 3+6	Nolan E 15+4	Hart M 10+1	Collins N 19+2	Tonge M 7	Mayor D 4+3	Welbeck D 8	Treacy K 8+9	Coutts P 13	James M 17+1	Williams T 8+2	Ward E 4	Barton A 1	Henderson W 1+1	Proctor J —+1	Match No.
1	2	3	4	5	6	7	8²	9	10¹	11	12	13																			1
1	2	3	4	5	6¹	10³		13	11²	9	8	7	12	14																	2
1	2	3		5		7¹	8	9²	10³	11	13		12	6	4	14															3
1	2	3	4	5		13		9³	10²	11	14	8¹	7	6	12																4
1	2	3¹	4	5³		7²	8	9¹	11	10	13		6				12	14													5
1	2		4	5		7²	13	9³	11¹	10	12		6	8	14		3														6
1	2		4	5		8	9²	13	11¹	12	7³		6	14	10		3														7
1	2		4²			13	14	9¹	11	10³	6		8	12			3		5												8
1	2		4			8		9	11	10	7		6				3		5												9
1	2		4¹	14		8	13	9	11	10	7²	6³	·2				3		5												10
1	2		4²	6		13	12	9	11	10¹	7		8				3		5												11
1	2		4	6		12	8²	14	10	11	9³		7¹	13			3	5													12
1	2		4			9	10¹	11	12	7	5		8				3	6													13
1	2	12				7	4¹	9	10³	11	13		5	8²	14		3	6													14
1	2		4			7³	12	13	10	11	9²		14	5	8¹		3	6													15
1	2	3¹				12	8	9	10²	11	14		7³	5		13	6	4													16
1	2	3²	4		6¹	7		14	10	9	11³	12	13				5	8													17
1	2		4			12		13	10³	11¹	9²		7	14	6		5	8													18
1	2	3	4			7¹		9²	12	11	13		14	5	10³		6	8													19
1	2¹	3	4			14		9³	10	11	13		7	5	12		6	8	8²												20
1		3	4³			7²	14	9¹	12	11	10	13	5	2			6	8													21
1	2	3³	4			7¹		13	12	11	9²		10	5	14		6	8													22
1	2	3¹	4	5		7²	13	9¹	14	12	11			10			6	8													23
1	12	3	4³	5				9²	13	11	10		7	8	2¹		6		14												24
1	7	3¹	4	5	6			13	10²	11	9			12								8³									25
1	2		4	5	6¹			13	10²	11³	9		14		7	3	12					8									26
1	2		4¹	5	6¹			14	10²	11³	9		12		7	3	6					8	13								27
1	2			5	6			12	10²	13	9				14		7³	3				8	11¹	4							28
1	2			5	6			10	11²	14					7¹	13		3				8	12	4	9³						29
1	2			5	6			10	11	12					7¹			3				8	4	9							30
1	2			5				9²	11	12					7¹			6				8	13	4	10	3					31
1	2			5	6			9	13	11					7¹							8²	·2	4	10	3					32
1	2			5	6			9³	10²	11	14		13		12							7¹	4¹	8	3						33
1	2		4	5	6			9	10²	11¹	13		12		14							7³		8	3						34
1	2	12	4³	5	6			9	10	7	13						13		·1²		8	14			3¹						35
1	2	3	13	5	6¹			10²	11	9	7³		12		14								14		4	8					36
1	2	3		5				12	10	11³	9¹		7²	6		13						13	14		4	8					37
1		3	4	5				12	10	11	9²		7¹	6		2							13			8					38
1	12	3	4	5				13	10	11	9²		6		7	2¹										8					39
1	2	3	4	5				9²	10	11	13		12		7¹											8		6			40
1	2	3		5	6			10²	13	11	9		7¹		12										4	8					41
1	2	12		5				9	10	13	11¹		7												4	8	3²	6			42
1	2	3		5				9²	12	13					11¹					8³			7		4	10	14	6	11¹		43
1	2	3		5				9		11			6							8			7¹		4	10	12				44
1⁶	2	3		5				9²	12	11	13		8							8			7¹		10	4	6		15		45
	2	3		5	6			12		11	9³	4¹								8²			13		10	7		1		14	46

FA Cup
Third Round — Colchester U — (h) — 7-0
Fourth Round — Chelsea — (h) — 0-2

Carling Cup
First Round — Morecambe — (h) — 5-1
Second Round — Leicester C — (h) — 2-1
Third Round — Tottenham H — (h) — 1-5

QUEENS PARK RANGERS FL Championship

FOUNDATION

There is an element of doubt about the date of the foundation of this club, but it is believed that in either 1885 or 1886 it was formed through the amalgamation of Christchurch Rangers and St Jude's Institute FC. The leading light was George Wodehouse, whose family maintained a connection with the club until comparatively recent times. Most of the players came from the Queen's Park district so this name was adopted after a year as St Jude's Institute.

Loftus Road Stadium, South Africa Road, Shepherds Bush, London W12 7PJ.

Telephone: (020) 8743 0262

Fax: (020) 8749 0994

Ticket Office: 08444 777007

Website: www.qpr.co.uk

Ground Capacity: 18,682.

Record Attendance: 35,353 v Leeds U, Division 1, 27 April 1974.

Pitch Measurements: 110yd × 73yd.

Chairman: Gianni Paladini.

Deputy Managing Director: Ali Russell.

Manager: Neil Warnock.

Assistant Manager: Mick Jones.

Physio: Nigel Cox.

Colours: Blue and white hooped shirts, white shorts, white stockings.

Change Colours: All red with blue design on shirts.

Year Formed: 1885* (*see Foundation*).

Turned Professional: 1898. *Ltd Co.:* 1899.

Previous Name: 1885, St Jude's; 1887, Queens Park Rangers. *Club Nicknames:* 'Rangers' or 'Rs'.

Grounds: 1885* (*see Foundation*), Welford's Fields; 1888–99; London Scottish Ground, Brondesbury, Home Farm, Kensal Rise Green, Gun Club Wormwood Scrubs, Kilburn Cricket Ground; 1899, Kensal Rise Athletic Ground; 1901, Latimer Road, Notting Hill; 1904, Agricultural Society, Park Royal; 1907, Park Royal Ground; 1917, Loftus Road; 1931, White City; 1933, Loftus Road; 1962, White City; 1963, Loftus Road.

First Football League Game: 28 August 1920, Division 3, v Watford (h) L 1–2 – Price; Blackman, Wingrove; McGovern, Grant, O'Brien; Faulkner, Birch (1), Smith, Gregory, Middlemiss.

Record League Victory: 9–2 v Tranmere R, Division 3, 3 December 1960 – Drinkwater; Woods, Ingham; Keen, Rutter, Angell; Lazarus (2), Bedford (2), Evans (2), Andrews (1), Clark (2).

Record Cup Victory: 8–1 v Bristol R (away), FA Cup 1st rd, 27 November 1937 – Gilfillan; Smith, Jefferson; Lowe, James, March; Cape, Mallett, Cheetham (3), Fitzgerald (3) Bott (2). 8–1 v Crewe Alex, Milk Cup 1st rd, 3 October 1983 – Hucker; Neill, Dawes, Waddock (1), McDonald (1), Fenwick, Micklewhite (1), Stewart (1), Allen (1), Stainrod (3), Gregory.

HONOURS

Football League: Division 1 – Runners-up 1975–76; Division 2 – Champions 1982–83; Runners-up 1967–68, 1972–73, 2003–04; Division 3 (S) – Champions 1947–48; Runners-up 1946–47; Division 3 – Champions 1966–67.

FA Cup: Runners-up 1982.

Football League Cup: Winners 1967; Runners-up 1986. (In 1966–67 won Division 3 and Football League Cup).

European Competitions: UEFA Cup: 1976–77, 1984–85.

sky SPORTS FACT FILE

Arthur Chandler, a centre-forward, who had played for Hampstead Town and Handley-Page, joined Queens Park Rangers in their first season in the Football League. In 1923 he was transferred to Leicester City for a then club record fee of £3,000.

Record Defeat: 1–8 v Mansfield T, Division 3, 15 March 1965. 1–8 v Manchester U, Division 1, 19 March 1969.

Most League Points (2 for a win): 67, Division 3, 1966–67.

Most League Points (3 for a win): 85, Division 2, 1982–83.

Most League Goals: 111, Division 3, 1961–62.

Highest League Scorer in Season: George Goddard, 37, Division 3 (S), 1929–30.

Most League Goals in Total Aggregate: George Goddard, 172, 1926–34.

Most League Goals in One Match: 4, George Goddard v Merthyr T, Division 3 (S), 9 March 1929; 4, George Goddard v Swindon T, Division 3 (S), 12 April 1930; 4, George Goddard v Exeter C, Division 3 (S), 20 December 1930; 4, George Goddard v Watford, Division 3 (S), 19 September 1931; 4, Tom Cheetham v Aldershot, Division 3 (S), 14 September 1935; 4, Tom Cheetham v Aldershot, Division 3 (S), 12 November 1938.

Most Capped Player: Alan McDonald, 52, Northern Ireland.

Most League Appearances: Tony Ingham, 519, 1950–63.

Youngest League Player: Frank Sibley, 16 years 97 days v Bristol C, 10 March 1964.

Record Transfer Fee Received: £6,000,000 from Newcastle U for Les Ferdinand, June 1995.

Record Transfer Fee Paid: £2,350,000 to Stoke C for Mike Sheron, July 1997.

Football League Record: 1920 Original Members of Division 3; 1921–48 Division 3 (S); 1948–52 Division 2; 1952–58 Division 3 (S); 1958–67 Division 3; 1967–68 Division 2; 1968–69 Division 1; 1969–73 Division 2; 1973–79 Division 1; 1979–83 Division 2; 1983–92 Division 1; 1992–96 FA Premier League; 1996–2001 Division 1; 2001–04 Division 2; 2004– FL C.

LATEST SEQUENCES

Longest Sequence of League Wins: 8, 7.11.1931 – 28.12.1931.

Longest Sequence of League Defeats: 9, 25.2.1969 – 5.4.1969.

Longest Sequence of League Draws: 6, 29.1.2000 – 5.3.2000.

Longest Sequence of Unbeaten League Matches: 20, 11.3.1972 – 23.9.1972.

Longest Sequence Without a League Win: 20, 7.12.1968 – 7.4.1969.

Successive Scoring Runs: 33 from 9.12.1961.

Successive Non-scoring Runs: 6 from 18.3.1939.

MANAGERS

James Cowan 1906–13
Jimmy Howie 1913–20
Ned Liddell 1920–24
Will Wood 1924–25
   (had been Secretary since 1903)
Bob Hewison 1925–31
John Bowman 1931
Archie Mitchell 1931–33
Mick O'Brien 1933–35
Billy Birrell 1935–39
Ted Vizard 1939–44
Dave Mangnall 1944–52
Jack Taylor 1952–59
Alec Stock 1959–65
   (General Manager to 1968)
Bill Dodgin Jnr 1968
Tommy Docherty 1968
Les Allen 1968–71
Gordon Jago 1971–74
Dave Sexton 1974–77
Frank Sibley 1977–78
Steve Burtenshaw 1978–79
Tommy Docherty 1979–80
Terry Venables 1980–84
Gordon Jago 1984
Alan Mullery 1984
Frank Sibley 1984–85
Jim Smith 1985–88
Trevor Francis 1988–90
Don Howe 1990–91
Gerry Francis 1991–94
Ray Wilkins 1994–96
Stewart Houston 1996–97
Ray Harford 1997–98
Gerry Francis 1998–2001
Ian Holloway 2001–06
Gary Waddock 2006
John Gregory 2006–07
Luigi Di Canio 2007–08
Iain Dowie 2008
Paulo Sousa 2008–09
Jim Magilton 2009
Paul Hart 2009–10
Neil Warnock March 2010–

TEN YEAR LEAGUE RECORD

		P	W	D	L	F	A	Pts	Pos
2000-01	Div 1	46	7	19	20	45	75	40	23
2001-02	Div 2	46	19	14	13	60	49	71	8
2002-03	Div 2	46	24	11	11	69	45	83	4
2003-04	Div 2	46	22	17	7	80	45	83	2
2004-05	FL C	46	17	11	18	54	58	62	11
2005-06	FL C	46	12	14	20	50	65	50	21
2006-07	FL C	46	14	11	21	54	68	53	18
2007-08	FL C	46	14	16	16	60	66	58	14
2008-09	FL C	46	15	16	15	42	44	61	11
2009-10	FL C	46	14	15	17	58	65	57	13

DID YOU KNOW ?

Queens Park Rangers won their first trophy against local rivals Fulham. On 24 July 1893 in the final of the West London Observer Challenge Cup, they allowed a two-goal lead to lapse and needed extra time before winning 3–2, with William Ward scoring the decisive goal.

QUEENS PARK RANGERS 2009–10 LEAGUE RECORD

Match No.	Date		Venue	Opponents	Result	H/T Score	Lg Pos.	Goalscorers	Attendance
1	Aug	8	H	Blackpool	D 1-1	0-1	—	Ramage [86]	14,013
2		15	A	Plymouth Arg	D 1-1	1-0	16	Helguson [43]	11,588
3		18	A	Bristol C	L 0-1	0-0	—		14,571
4		22	H	Nottingham F	D 1-1	1-0	16	Leigertwood [25]	13,058
5		29	A	Scunthorpe U	W 1-0	1-0	15	Taarabt [3]	5866
6	Sept	12	H	Peterborough U	D 1-1	1-1	13	Routledge [34]	11,814
7		19	A	Cardiff C	W 2-0	2-0	12	Simpson 2 [19, 40]	20,121
8		26	H	Barnsley	W 5-2	3-0	8	Leigertwood [7], Buzsaky 2 [15, 39], Watson [67], Simpson [79]	12,025
9		30	A	Newcastle U	D 1-1	1-0	—	Watson [7]	38,923
10	Oct	3	A	Swansea C	L 0-2	0-0	13		14,444
11		17	H	Preston NE	W 4-0	1-0	10	Taarabt [11], Buzsaky (pen) [63], Simpson [74], Routledge [85]	12,810
12		20	H	Reading	W 4-1	2-0	—	Buzsaky [31], Simpson [39], Vine [71], Agyemang [83]	11,900
13		24	A	Derby Co	W 4-2	1-2	6	Taarabt [40], Mahon [47], Simpson [59], Buzsaky (pen) [90]	30,135
14		30	H	Leicester C	L 1-2	1-1	—	Taarabt [33]	17,082
15	Nov	3	H	Crystal Palace	D 1-1	1-0	—	Buzsaky (pen) [19]	14,377
16		7	A	Sheffield W	W 2-1	1-1	4	Simpson [10], Gorkss [82]	19,491
17		21	A	Doncaster R	L 0-2	0-0	6		10,821
18		28	H	Coventry C	D 2-2	1-1	5	Simpson [35], Buzsaky [69]	13,712
19	Dec	5	H	Middlesbrough	L 1-5	0-1	9	Agyemang [53]	13,949
20		7	A	Watford	L 1-3	1-1	—	Agyemang [33]	15,058
21		14	A	WBA	D 2-2	0-0	—	Olsson (og) [56], Gorkss [62]	21,565
22		19	H	Sheffield U	D 1-1	1-1	10	Leigertwood [2]	12,639
23		26	A	Bristol C	W 2-1	2-0	8	Simpson [31], Leigertwood [40]	13,534
24		28	A	Ipswich T	L 0-3	0-1	10		25,349
25	Jan	16	A	Blackpool	D 2-2	0-1	11	Taarabt (pen) [55], Connolly [84]	7600
26		26	A	Nottingham F	L 0-5	0-3	—		23,293
27		30	H	Scunthorpe U	L 0-1	0-0	12		13,105
28	Feb	6	A	Peterborough U	L 0-1	0-1	14		8933
29		9	H	Ipswich T	L 1-2	0-2	—	Simpson [66]	10,940
30		13	A	Coventry C	L 0-1	0-1	17		15,247
31		20	H	Doncaster R	W 2-1	1-0	17	German [25], Simpson [76]	11,178
32		27	A	Middlesbrough	L 0-2	0-2	20		17,568
33	Mar	6	H	WBA	W 3-1	2-1	16	Simpson [13], Connolly [18], Buzsaky [67]	14,578
34		9	H	Plymouth Arg	W 2-0	1-0	—	Taarabt (pen) [36], Stewart [49]	12,013
35		13	A	Sheffield U	D 1-1	0-1	15	Taarabt [49]	23,456
36		16	A	Reading	L 0-1	0-0	—		16,886
37		20	H	Swansea C	D 1-1	0-0	17	German [78]	15,502
38		23	A	Derby Co	D 1-1	1-1	—	Cook [45]	12,569
39		27	A	Preston NE	D 2-2	0-1	18	Ramage [57], Priskin [66]	12,080
40	Apr	3	H	Sheffield W	D 1-1	1-0	18	Faurlin [23]	13,405
41		5	A	Leicester C	L 0-4	0-2	18		22,079
42		10	A	Crystal Palace	W 2-0	1-0	18	Buzsaky [11], Gorkss [60]	20,430
43		17	H	Cardiff C	L 0-1	0-0	18		12,832
44		20	H	Watford	W 1-0	1-0	—	Buzsaky (pen) [38]	13,171
45		24	A	Barnsley	W 1-0	1-0	13	Leigertwood [27]	11,944
46	May	2	H	Newcastle U	L 0-1	0-0	13		16,819

Final League Position: 13

GOALSCORERS

League (58): Simpson 12, Buzsaky 10 (4 pens), Taarabt 7 (2 pens), Leigertwood 5, Agyemang 3, Gorkss 3, Connolly 2, German 2, Ramage 2, Routledge 2, Watson 2, Cook 1, Faurlin 1, Helguson 1, Mahon 1, Priskin 1, Stewart 1, Vine 1, own goal 1.
Carling Cup (7): Routledge 4 (1 pen), Ephraim 2, Pellicori 1.
FA Cup (3): Buzsaky 1 (pen), Simpson 1, Stewart 1.

Cerny R 29	Ramage P 29+4	Borrowdale G 18+3	Mahon G 5+2	Hall F 12+2	Gorkss K 40+1	Routledge W 25	Rowlands M 5+1	Helguson H 3+2	Taarabt A 32+9	Balanta A 1+3	Vine R 8+23	Buzsaky A 29+10	Agyemang P 5+12	Leigertwood M 39+1	Ephraim H 16+6	Faurlin A 36+5	Stewart D 30	Pellicori A 1+7	Connolly M 17+2	Simpson J 34+5	Watson B 16	Ainsworth G —+1	Williams T 5	Reid S 1+1	Ikeme C 17	German A 5+8	Hill M 15+1	Quashie N 4	Cook L 8+8	Priskin T 13	Bent M 2+1	Tosic D 5	Parker J 1+3	Oastler J —+1	Brown L —+1	Rose R —+1	Match No.
1	2	3	4	5	6	7	8[3]	9[1]	10	11[2]	12	13	14																								1
1	2	3	4	5	6	7		9[1]	10[3]	14	11[2]	12	8	13																							2
1	2	3		5		7	14	10[1]			12	11	9[2]	8		4[3]	6	13																			3
1	2	3	5[1]	12		7		9	10[3]		13	14		8		4	6	11[2]																			4
1	2	3	14	5		7	13	10[1]			12		8	11	4[3]		6	9[2]																			5
1		3				7	12		10[2]		13	14	8	11[3]	4[1]	5		6	9	2																	6
1		3			6	7	11		10[2]		4	13	8		5	12		9[1]	2																		7
1		3			6	7[1]	11		12		10[2]	4	8	13	5	14		9[3]	2																		8
1		3			6	7	11		12		10[2]	4	8		5			9[1]	2																		9
1		3			6	7	11[4]		13		10[1]	4[2]	8		12	5	14		9[3]	2[4]																	10
1	3	2	8		6	7[3]			10		13	4[1]	12		11	5			9[2]	14																	11
1	3	2	13		6	7			10[3]		12	4[2]	14		11	5			9[1]	8[4]																	12
1	3[1]	2	8		6	7			10[2]		13	4	14	12	11	5			9[3]																		13
1	3[2]	2	12		6	7			10[3]		13	4	14	8	11	5[1]			9																		14
1	2			5	6	7			10[1]		12	4[3]	13	8	14	11			9[2]	3																	15
1	2	11	5[1]	6		7			10[3]		14	4[2]		8	13			12	9	3																	16
1					6	7			12			11[12]	13	8	10[1]		14	5	9[3]	4		3	2														17
1	2		5			7			10[1]			4		8	11			6	9	3			12														18
1	2			5	6	7[3]			10		12	4[1]	13	8	11		14		9[2]	3																	19
1	2	5			6	7[2]			12		10[1]	14	9	8[3]	11	3			13	4																	20
1	2	14			6	7			10[1]			9[2]	8		12	5	13		11[2]	4	3																21
1	2				6	7			10		12		9	8		5			11[1]	4	3																22
1	2	13		5	6	7			10[2]		12	8		11[11]		14			9[3]	4	3																23
1	2				6	7			10[2]		13	11[1]	12	8		5			9	4	3																24
	13		2[2]		6	7			10			4[1]	9	8	12	11[3]	5		3					1	14												25
	12				6				10		14	4		8	13	11[2]	5[1]		2	9[3]				1		3	7										26
					6				8[2]	14	10[1]	4[3]		2		11			3	9				1	13	5	7	12									27
	2[4]				6				14					8[4]	12	11			3	13				1		5	4[1]	7[3]	9[2]	10							28
					6				14		12	13		7[3]	8	5			2	9				1		3	4[2]	11	10[1]								29
	2				6				13			8[2]			7	5			4	10				1		²2	3	11	9[1]								30
	2[1]	13			6				12		14	8			7	5			4[2]	10				1		9[3]	3	11									31
	2	12			6				14			4			9[3]	5				10				1		7[2]	3[1]	11	13								32
	13				6				11[2]		14	12		4	7[1]	8	5		2	10				1		3		9[3]									33
					6				11[1]		14	12		4	7[2]	8	5		2	10[3]				1		3		13	9								34
					6				11[1]			12		4	7[2]	8	5		2	10				1		3		13	9								35
	12				6				11[11]					4	7	8	5[4]		2	10				1	13	3			9[2]								36
	2				6				10		14	8[1]		4	7[3]	11	5							1	12	3		13	9[2]								37
	2				6				8		10			4	14	7	5		3[1]	9[3]				1	13	12	11[2]										38
	2				6				8[2]		12	13		4	7	11	5			10[1]				1	10[1]	3		9									39
	2				6				8		14			4	7[2]	11	5			10[1]				1	12	3		13	9[3]								40
	2				6				10		13	12		4	7	8	5			9[2]				1	3		11[1]										41
1	2				6				10[2]			8		4	7	11	5[1]		12							9	3		13			3	13				42
1	5				6				11			4		2	7[2]	8	10[1]		14							12	9[3]		3	13							43
1	3				6				11[1]	10	4[2]			2	7	8	14								9[3]	12		5		13							44
1	3				6				4			2		7[2]	8	12			9[1]	13						10[3]	5	11	14								45
1	3[4]				6				4			2		7[2]	8	10										11[1]	9	13	5	12					13		46

FA Cup
Third Round Sheffield U (a) 1-1
  (h) 2-3

Carling Cup
First Round Exeter C (a) 5-0
Second Round Accrington S (h) 2-1
Third Round Chelsea (a) 0-1

READING   FL Championship

FOUNDATION

Reading was formed as far back as 1871 at a public meeting held at the Bridge Street Rooms. They first entered the FA Cup as early as 1877 when they amalgamated with the Reading Hornets. The club was further strengthened in 1889 when Earley FC joined them. They were the first winners of the Berks and Bucks Cup in 1878–79.

Madejski Stadium, Junction 11, M4, Reading, Berkshire RG2 0FL.

Telephone: (0118) 968 1100.

Fax: (0118) 968 1101.

Ticket Office: (0844) 249 1871.

Website: www.readingfc.co.uk

Email: customerservice@readingfc.co.uk

Ground Capacity: 24,082.

Record Attendance: Madejski Stadium: 24,122 v Aston Villa, Premiershp, 10 February 2007. Elm Park: 33,042 v Brentford, FA Cup 5th rd, 19 February 1927.

Pitch Measurements: 105m × 68m.

Chairman: Sir John Madejski OBE, DL.

Vice-chairman: Ian Wood-Smith.

Chief Executive: Nigel Howe.

Secretary: Sue Hewett.

Director of Football: Nick Hammond

Manager: Brian McDermott.

First Team Coach: Nigel Gibbs.

Physio: Luke Anthony.

HONOURS

FA Premier League: Best season – 8th 2006–07.
Football League: FL C – Champions 2005–06; Division 1 – Runners-up 1994–95; Division 2 – Champions 1993–94; Runners-up 2001–02; Division 3 – Champions 1985–86; Division 3 (S) – Champions 1925–26; Runners-up 1931–32, 1934–35, 1948–49, 1951–52; Division 4 – Champions 1978–79.
FA Cup: Semi-final 1927.
Football League Cup: best season: 5th rd, 1996.
Simod Cup: Winners 1988.

Colours: Blue and white hooped shirts, blue shorts, blue stockings.

Change Colours: White shirts, green shorts, white stockings.

Year Formed: 1871. *Turned Professional:* 1895. *Ltd Co.:* 1895.

Club Nickname: 'The Royals'.

Grounds: 1871, Reading Recreation; Reading Cricket Ground; 1882, Coley Park; 1889, Caversham Cricket Ground; 1896, Elm Park; 1998, Madejski Stadium.

First Football League Game: 28 August 1920, Division 3, v Newport Co (a) W 1–0 – Crawford; Smith, Horler; Christie, Mavin, Getgood; Spence, Weston, Yarnell, Bailey (1), Andrews.

Record League Victory: 10–2 v Crystal Palace, Division 3 (S), 4 September 1946 – Groves; Glidden, Gulliver; McKenna, Ratcliffe, Young; Chitty, Maurice Edelston (3), McPhee (4), Barney (1), Deverell (2).

sky SPORTS FACT FILE

Formerly known as the "Biscuitmen", Reading had at least one player with the perfect credentials to be involved with the club. Harry Holmes worked at Huntley & Palmers factory and scored on his debut against Newport County on 4 September 1920.

Record Cup Victory: 6–0 v Leyton, FA Cup 2nd rd, 12 December 1925 – Duckworth; Eggo, McConnell; Wilson, Messer, Evans; Smith (2), Braithwaite (1), Davey (1), Tinsley, Robson (2).

Record Defeat: 0–18 v Preston NE, FA Cup 1st rd, 1893–94.

Most League Points (2 for a win): 65, Division 4, 1978–79.

Most League Points (3 for a win): 106, Championship, 2005–06.

Most League Goals: 112, Division 3 (S), 1951–52.

Highest League Scorer in Season: Ronnie Blackman, 39, Division 3 (S), 1951–52.

Most League Goals in Total Aggregate: Ronnie Blackman, 158, 1947–54.

Most League Goals in One Match: 6, Arthur Bacon v Stoke C, Division 2, 3 April 1931.

Most Capped Player: Kevin Doyle, 26 (35), Northern Ireland.

Most League Appearances: Martin Hicks, 500, 1978–91.

Youngest League Player: Peter Castle, 16 years 49 days v Watford, 30 April 2003.

Record Transfer Fee Received: £6,500,000 from Wolverhampton W for Kevin Doyle, June 2009.

Record Transfer Fee Paid: Undisclosed to Nantes for Emerse Fae, August 2007.

Football League Record: 1920 Original Member of Division 3; 1921–26 Division 3 (S); 1926–31 Division 2; 1931–58 Division 3 (S); 1958–71 Division 3; 1971–76 Division 4; 1976–77 Division 3; 1977–79 Division 4; 1979–83 Division 3; 1983–84 Division 4; 1984–86 Division 3; 1986–88 Division 2; 1988–92 Division 3; 1992–94 Division 2; 1994–98 Division 1; 1998–2002 Division 2; 2002–04 Division 1; 2004–06 FL C; 2006–08 FA Premier League; 2008– FL C.

MANAGERS

Thomas Sefton 1897–1901
  (Secretary-Manager)
James Sharp 1901–02
Harry Matthews 1902–20
Harry Marshall 1920–22
Arthur Chadwick 1923–25
H. S. Bray 1925–26
  (Secretary only since 1922 and 1926–35)
Andrew Wylie 1926–31
Joe Smith 1931–35
Billy Butler 1935–39
John Cochrane 1939
Joe Edelston 1939–47
Ted Drake 1947–52
Jack Smith 1952–55
Harry Johnston 1955–63
Roy Bentley 1963–69
Jack Mansell 1969–71
Charlie Hurley 1972–77
Maurice Evans 1977–84
Ian Branfoot 1984–89
Ian Porterfield 1989–91
Mark McGhee 1991–94
Jimmy Quinn/Mick Gooding 1994–97
Terry Bullivant 1997–98
Tommy Burns 1998–99
Alan Pardew 1999–2003
Steve Coppell 2003–09
Brendan Rodgers 2009
Brian McDermott December 2009–

LATEST SEQUENCES

Longest Sequence of League Wins: 13, 17.8.1985 – 19.10.1985.

Longest Sequence of League Defeats: 8, 29.12.2007 – 24.2.2008.

Longest Sequence of League Draws: 6, 23.3.2002 – 20.4 2002.

Longest Sequence of Unbeaten League Matches: 33, 9.8.2005 – 14.2.2006.

Longest Sequence Without a League Win: 14, 30.4.1927 – 29.10.1927.

Successive Scoring Runs: 32 from 1.10.1932.

Successive Non-scoring Runs: 6 from 13.4.1925.

TEN YEAR LEAGUE RECORD

		P	W	D	L	F	A	Pts	Pos
2000-01	Div 2	46	25	11	10	86	52	86	3
2001-02	Div 2	46	23	15	8	70	43	84	2
2002-03	Div 1	46	25	4	17	61	46	79	4
2003-04	Div 1	46	20	10	16	55	57	70	9
2004-05	FL C	46	19	13	14	51	44	70	7
2005-06	FL C	46	31	13	2	99	32	106	1
2006-07	PR Lge	38	16	7	15	52	47	55	8
2007-08	PR Lge	38	10	6	22	41	66	36	18
2008-09	FL C	46	21	14	11	72	40	77	4
2009-10	FL C	46	17	12	17	68	63	63	9

DID YOU KNOW ?

In 1950–51 Ronnie Blackman scored 52 goals in all matches for Reading. They comprised 35 Football League, 5 FA Cup, 7 friendly and 5 reserve games. The following season he hit 39 in League alone in just 41 matches. His career at Elm Park yielded 158 League goals.

READING 2009–10 LEAGUE RECORD

Match No.	Date	Venue	Opponents	Result	H/T Score	Lg Pos.	Goalscorers	Attendance
1	Aug 8	H	Nottingham F	D	0-0	0-0	—		19,640
2	15	A	Newcastle U	L	0-3	0-1	23		36,944
3	18	A	Swansea C	D	0-0	0-0	—		12,775
4	22	H	Sheffield U	L	1-3	1-1	21	Mills [13]	16,025
5	29	A	Barnsley	W	3-1	1-1	17	Pearce [29], Hunt N 2 (1 pen) [53 (p), 54]	11,116
6	Sept 12	H	Doncaster R	D	0-0	0-0	17		15,697
7	16	H	Cardiff C	L	0-1	0-0	—		16,687
8	19	A	Peterborough U	L	2-3	2-0	21	Sigurdsson [30], Church [42]	8521
9	26	A	Watford	D	1-1	1-0	21	Rasiak [7]	18,147
10	29	A	Preston NE	W	2-1	2-0	—	Church [34], Kebe [43]	10,987
11	Oct 3	H	Middlesbrough	L	0-2	0-1	21		17,638
12	17	A	WBA	L	1-3	1-1	21	Mills [6]	20,935
13	20	A	QPR	L	1-4	0-2	—	Howard [86]	11,900
14	26	H	Leicester C	L	0-1	0-1	—		18,192
15	31	A	Coventry C	W	3-1	1-0	21	Rasiak 2 [1, 72], McAnuff [54]	15,165
16	Nov 7	H	Ipswich T	D	1-1	0-1	22	Church [47]	19,053
17	21	H	Blackpool	W	2-1	0-0	20	Sigurdsson [52], Rasiak [82]	15,945
18	28	A	Derby Co	L	1-2	0-0	21	Sigurdsson [56]	30,174
19	Dec 5	A	Sheffield W	W	2-0	0-0	19	Rasiak [49], Cisse [67]	22,090
20	8	H	Crystal Palace	L	2-4	1-3	—	Pearce [31], Sigurdsson (pen) [80]	16,629
21	12	H	Scunthorpe U	D	1-1	1-0	21	Rasiak [16]	15,274
22	19	A	Bristol C	D	1-1	0-1	20	Church [90]	14,366
23	26	H	Swansea C	D	1-1	1-1	17	Sigurdsson [45]	19,608
24	28	A	Plymouth Arg	L	1-4	0-1	20	Sigurdsson [62]	12,091
25	Jan 16	A	Nottingham F	L	1-2	0-2	21	Kebe [90]	27,635
26	26	A	Sheffield U	L	0-3	0-2	—		24,009
27	30	H	Barnsley	W	1-0	1-0	22	Long [29]	15,580
28	Feb 6	A	Doncaster R	W	2-1	1-0	22	Long [39], Howard [77]	8827
29	9	H	Plymouth Arg	W	2-1	0-0	—	Long 2 (1 pen) [51, 90 (p)]	15,484
30	17	A	Crystal Palace	W	3-1	1-0	—	Church 2 [23, 81], Kebe [47]	13,259
31	20	A	Blackpool	L	0-2	0-1	20		7147
32	27	H	Sheffield W	W	5-0	2-0	18	Kebe 2 [42, 71], Rasiak 2 [45, 65], Church [52]	17,573
33	Mar 10	H	Derby Co	W	4-1	2-1	—	Long [8], Kebe [34], Bertrand [69], Church [84]	14,096
34	13	H	Bristol C	W	2-0	2-0	16	Sigurdsson 2 [12, 22 (p)]	17,900
35	16	H	QPR	W	1-0	0-0	—	Sigurdsson (pen) [86]	16,886
36	20	A	Middlesbrough	D	1-1	0-0	13	Wheater (og) [63]	17,082
37	24	A	Leicester C	W	2-1	1-1	—	Kebe [16], Sigurdsson (pen) [90]	20,108
38	27	H	WBA	D	1-1	1-0	11	Sigurdsson [9]	20,515
39	Apr 3	A	Ipswich T	L	1-2	0-2	12	Sigurdsson [90]	21,403
40	5	H	Coventry C	W	3-0	3-0	12	Rasiak [15], Church (pen) [22], Kebe [40]	17,435
41	10	A	Cardiff C	D	0-0	0-0	11		21,248
42	13	A	Newcastle U	L	1-2	0-2	—	Simpson (og) [72]	23,163
43	17	H	Peterborough U	W	6-0	4-0	9	Pearce [3], Sigurdsson 2 (1 pen) [25 (p), 76], McAnuff [29], Kebe [44], Long [59]	15,982
44	20	A	Scunthorpe U	D	2-2	0-0	—	Pearce [48], Sigurdsson (pen) [72]	5299
45	24	A	Watford	L	0-3	0-1	11		15,949
46	May 2	H	Preston NE	W	4-1	2-0	9	Kebe [12], McAnuff [17], Sigurdsson [72], Church [90]	19,239

Final League Position: 9

GOALSCORERS

League (68): Sigurdsson 16 (6 pens), Church 10 (1 pen), Kebe 10, Rasiak 9, Long 6 (1 pen), Pearce 4, McAnuff 3, Howard 2, Hunt N 2 (1 pen), Mills 2, Bertrand 1, Cisse 1, own goals 2.
Carling Cup (6): Bignall 2, Mooney 2, Sigurdsson 1, own goal 1.
FA Cup (11): Long 3, Sigurdsson 3 (1 pen), Church 2, Kebe 2, Howard 1.

Federici A 46	Rosenior L 5	Bertrand R 44	Cisse K 14+3	Pearce A 24+1	Karacan J 19+8	Robson-Kanu H 4+13	Tabb J 27+1	Church S 22+14	Davies S 3+1	Kebe J 30+12	Long S 22+9	Hunt N 5+5	Harper J —+3	Mills M 22+1	Henry J 1+2	Sigurdsson G 32+6	Gunnarsson B 18+8	Rasiak G 14+15	Antonio M —+1	Cummings S 8	O'Dea D 7+1	Howard B 30+4	Matejovsky M 13+2	Ingimarsson I 25	McAnuff J 36	Griffin A 21	Thorvaldsson G 2+2	Bignall N —+1	Khizanishvili Z 12+3	Match No.
1	2	3	4	5	6	7¹	8	9	10	11	12																			1
1	2	3	4	5	6	12	7³	9¹	8	11²	10	13	14																	2
1	2	3	4	5	8²	11	14	9	10¹		12	13		6	7³															3
1	2	3¹	4¹	5	8			9	10²	11	12	13	14	6	7															4
1	2	3		5	8			9²	10³	11¹	12	13	14	6	7		4													5
1		3	14	5	8²			9			10	13				7¹	4³					2	12	6	11					6
1		3		5	8²			10¹			12	13				7	9					2	4	6	11					7
1		3		5	12			8³	10²			13	14			7	9					2	4⁹	6	11					8
1		3	4	5	8²						10	13	14			7¹	9					2	12	6	11³					9
1		3	13	5	8¹			9³			10		14			7	4²					2	12	6	11					10
1		3		5	8			9			10¹	13				7²	4					2	12	6	11					11
1		3¹		5	8			9²		11	10	13	14			7	4³					2	12	6						12
1		3¹	14		8			9³		11²	10	13				7	4					2	12	5⁴						13
1		3		5				9²		11	12	13				7¹	4	10				2		6	8					14
1		3	4	5				9¹			12	13				7	8	10				2		6	11²					15
1		3	13	5	8			9			12		14			7³	4	10¹				2		6	11²					16
1		3	14	5	8			9²			12	13				7¹	4	10				2		6	11³					17
1		3	13⁴	5	8			9²			12		14			7	4	10³				2		6	11¹					18
1		3	4	5	8			9¹			12	13				7		10				2		6	11²					19
1		3⁴	4	5	8			9			12	13				7		10				2		6	11¹					20
1		3	4	5	8			9			12					7		10				2		6	11¹					21
1		3	4	5	8			9³			12	13	14⁴			7		10				2¹		6	11²					22
1		3	14	5	8			9¹			12	13				7	4	10²				2		6⁵	11					23
1		3		5	8			9			12	13				7	4	10²				2		6⁷	11					24
1		3	4	5	8			9²			12	13	14			7³		10						6	11¹	2				25
1		3	4³	5	8¹			9			12	13	14			7		10²						6	11	2				26
1		3	4²	5	8			9¹				13				7		10					12	6	11	2				27
1		3	4	5⁸	8			9				13	14			7		10³					12²	6	11¹	2				28
1		3	4¹	5	8			9²				13				7		10					12	6	11	2				29
1		3	4	5	8			9²				13				7		10¹					12	6	11	2				30
1		3	4³	5	8¹			9²				13	14			7		10					12	6	11	2				31
1		3	4	5	8³			9¹				13	14			7²		10					12	6	11	2				32
1		3		5	8			9				13	14			7		10¹					12	4²	11	2³			6	33
1		3		5	8			9¹								7		10					12	4	11	2			6	34
1		3		5	8			9²				13				7		10					12	4¹	11	2			6	35
1		3		5	8			9								7		10					12	4	11	2			6¹	36
1		3		5	8		14	9²				13				7		10					12	4	11¹	2			6²	37
1		3		5	8			9¹								7		10					12	4	11²·13	2			6	38
1		3		5⁹	8¹		14	9²				13				7		10					12	4	11³	2			6	39
1		3		5	8		14	9				13				7³		10²					12	4	11	2			6¹	40
1		3		5	8			9¹				13				7		10						4	11²·12	2			6	41
1		3		5	8²		14	9³			12	13				7		10						4	11¹	2			6	42
1		3		5	8¹		14	9			12	13				7		10						4²	11³	2			6	43
1		3		5	8			9¹			12	13				7		10						4	11	2			6²	44
1		3		5	8		14	9²			12					7³		10						4	11¹·13	2			6	45
1		3	4	5	8		14	9³			12	13				7		10							11	2²			6¹	46

FA Cup

Third Round	Liverpool	(h)	1-1
		(a)	2-1
Fourth Round	Burnley	(h)	1-0
Fifth Round	WBA	(h)	2-2
		(a)	3-2
Sixth Round	Aston Villa	(h)	2-4

Carling Cup

First Round	Burton Alb	(h)	5-1
Second Round	Barnsley	(h)	1-2

ROCHDALE

FL Championship 1

FOUNDATION

Considering the love of rugby in their area, it is not surprising that Rochdale had difficulty in establishing an Association Football club. The earlier Rochdale Town club formed in 1900 went out of existence in 1907 when the present club was immediately established and joined the Manchester League, before graduating to the Lancashire Combination in 1908.

Spotland Stadium, Willbutts Lane, Rochdale OL11 5DS.

Telephone: (0844) 826 1907.

Ticket Office: (0844) 826 1907.

Website: www.rochdaleafc.co.uk

Email: office@rochdaleafc.co.uk

Ground Capacity: 9,223.

Record Attendance: 24,231 v Notts Co, FA Cup 2nd rd, 10 December 1949.

Pitch Measurements: 114yd × 76yd.

Chairman: Chris Dunphy.

Chief Executive/Secretary: Colin Garlick.

Manager: Keith Hill.

Assistant Manager: David Flitcroft.

Physio: Andy Thorpe.

Colours: Black and blue striped shirts, white shorts, blue stockings with black tops.

Change Colours: Purple shirts with white sleeves and purple trim, purple shorts, purple stockings with white tops.

Year Formed: 1907.

Turned Professional: 1907.

Ltd Co.: 1910.

Club Nickname: 'The Dale'.

Ground: 1907, St Clements Playing Fields (original name Spotland).

First Football League Game: 27 August 1921, Division 3 (N), v Accrington Stanley (h) W 6–3 – Crabtree; Nuttall, Sheehan; Hill, Farrer, Yarwood; Hoad, Sandiford, Dennison (2), Owens (3), Carney (1).

Record League Victory: 8–1 v Chesterfield, Division 3 (N), 18 December 1926 – Hill; Brown, Ward; Hillhouse, Parkes, Braidwood; Hughes, Bertram, Whitehurst (5), Schofield (2), Martin (1).

Record Cup Victory: 8–2 v Crook T, FA Cup 1st rd, 26 November 1927 – Moody; Hopkins, Ward; Braidwood, Parkes, Barker; Tompkinson, Clennell (3) Whitehurst (4), Hall, Martin (1).

HONOURS

Football League: Division 3 best season: 9th, 1969–70; Division 3 (N) – Runners-up 1923–24, 1926–27.

FA Cup: best season: 5th rd, 1990, 2003.

Football League Cup: Runners-up 1962 (record for 4th Division club).

---

sky SPORTS FACT FILE

Albert Smith, an outside-left signed for Rochdale from Bradford Park Avenue in 1910, gave yeoman service to the club. With wartime matches included he made over 450 appearances, went to Grimsby Town in 1919 and returned four years later as player-coach.

Record Defeat: 1–9 v Tranmere R, Division 3 (N), 25 December 1931.

Most League Points (2 for a win): 62, Division 3 (N), 1923–24.

Most League Points (3 for a win): 82, FL 2, 2009–10.

Most League Goals: 105, Division 3 (N), 1926–27.

Highest League Scorer in Season: Albert Whitehurst, 44, Division 3 (N), 1926–27.

Most League Goals in Total Aggregate: Reg Jenkins, 119, 1964–73.

Most League Goals in One Match: 6, Tommy Tippett v Hartlepools U, Division 3 (N), 21 April 1930.

Most Capped Player: Leo Bertos, 6 (31), New Zealand.

Most League Appearances: Gary Jones, 379, 1998–2001; 2003–.

Youngest League Player: Zac Hughes, 16 years 105 days v Exeter C, 19 September 1987.

Record Transfer Fee Received: £400,000 from West Ham U for Stephen Bywater, August 1998.

Record Transfer Fee Paid: £150,000 to Stoke C for Paul Connor, March 2001.

Football League Record: 1921 Elected to Division 3 (N); 1958–59 Division 3; 1959–69 Division 4; 1969–74 Division 3; 1974–92 Division 4; 1992–2004 Division 3; 2004–10 FL 2; 2010– FL 1.

LATEST SEQUENCES

Longest Sequence of League Wins: 8, 29.9.1969 – 3.11.1969.

Longest Sequence of League Defeats: 17, 14.11.1931 – 12.3.1932.

Longest Sequence of League Draws: 6, 17.8.1968 – 14.9.1968.

Longest Sequence of Unbeaten League Matches: 20, 15.9.1923 – 19.1.1924.

Longest Sequence Without a League Win: 28, 14.11.1931 – 29.8.1932.

Successive Scoring Runs: 29 from 8.1.1927.

Successive Non-scoring Runs: 9 from 14.3.1980.

MANAGERS

Billy Bradshaw 1920
Run by committee 1920–22
Tom Wilson 1922–23
Jack Peart 1923–30
Will Cameron 1930–31
Herbert Hopkinson 1932–34
Billy Smith 1934–35
Ernest Nixon 1935–37
Sam Jennings 1937–38
Ted Goodier 1938–52
Jack Warner 1952–53
Harry Catterick 1953–58
Jack Marshall 1958–60
Tony Collins 1960–68
Bob Stokoe 1967–68
Len Richley 1968–70
Dick Conner 1970–73
Walter Joyce 1973–76
Brian Green 1976–77
Mike Ferguson 1977–78
Doug Collins 1979
Bob Stokoe 1979–80
Peter Madden 1980–83
Jimmy Greenhoff 1983–84
Vic Halom 1984–86
Eddie Gray 1986–88
Danny Bergara 1988–89
Terry Dolan 1989–91
Dave Sutton 1991–94
Mick Docherty 1995–96
Graham Barrow 1996–99
Steve Parkin 1999–2001
John Hollins 2001–02
Paul Simpson 2002–03
Alan Buckley 2003–04
Steve Parkin 2004–06
Keith Hill January 2007–
(caretaker from December 2006)

TEN YEAR LEAGUE RECORD

		P	W	D	L	F	A	Pts	Pos
2000-01	Div 3	46	18	17	11	59	48	71	8
2001-02	Div 3	46	21	15	10	65	52	78	5
2002-03	Div 3	46	12	16	18	63	70	52	19
2003-04	Div 3	46	12	14	20	49	58	50	21
2004-05	FL 2	46	16	18	12	54	48	66	9
2005-06	FL 2	46	14	14	18	66	69	56	14
2006-07	FL 2	46	18	12	16	70	50	66	9
2007-08	FL 2	46	23	11	12	77	54	80	5
2008-09	FL 2	46	19	13	14	70	59	70	6
2009-10	FL 2	46	25	7	14	82	48	82	3

DID YOU KNOW ?

Rochdale struck a purple patch midway through the 1920s. In 1923–24 they were runners-up to Wolverhampton Wanderers just one point adrift and subsequently finished sixth, third and runners-up again in the next few seasons. In 1926–27 their average gate was 7,095.

ROCHDALE 2009–10 LEAGUE RECORD

Match No.	Date	Venue	Opponents	Result	H/T Score	Lg Pos.	Goalscorers	Attendance
1	Aug 8	A	Port Vale	D	1-1	0-0	—	Thompson [66]	6158
2	15	H	Aldershot T	W	1-0	0-0	6	Kennedy T (pen) [90]	2465
3	18	H	Cheltenham T	L	0-1	0-0	—		2311
4	23	A	Rotherham U	L	1-2	1-1	18	Dagnall [45]	3602
5	29	H	Bury	W	3-0	0-0	13	Thompson [59], Dagnall [73], Kennedy T (pen) [81]	4534
6	Sept 4	H	Morecambe	D	3-3	0-3	13	Dagnall [48], Thompson [64], Stephens [76]	2367
7	12	H	Torquay U	W	2-1	1-0	9	Dagnall 2 [25, 76]	2407
8	19	A	Northampton T	W	2-1	1-0	6	O'Grady [19], Buckley [68]	4048
9	26	H	Hereford U	W	4-1	2-1	5	Dagnall [19], Whaley [45], Buckley [80], Dawson [83]	2620
10	29	A	Darlington	W	2-0	0-0	—	Buckley [60], O'Grady [81]	1748
11	Oct 4	A	Burton Alb	L	0-1	0-1	7		3119
12	10	H	Barnet	W	2-1	2-0	4	Dagnall [11], Kennedy T (pen) [45]	2648
13	17	A	Grimsby T	W	2-0	1-0	3	Rundle [24], O'Grady [85]	3754
14	24	H	Accrington S	L	1-2	0-1	3	Dagnall [90]	3206
15	31	A	Bournemouth	W	4-0	1-0	2	Dagnall [45], O'Grady 2 [63, 72], Whaley [69]	6378
16	Nov 14	H	Chesterfield	L	2-3	0-2	3	O'Grady [49], Dawson [52]	3011
17	21	H	Dagenham & R	W	2-1	0-1	2	Higginbotham [70], Dawson [72]	2235
18	24	H	Notts Co	W	2-1	2-1	—	Dagnall (pen) [41], O'Grady [45]	2779
19	Dec 1	A	Bradford C	W	3-0	2-0	—	Dagnall 2 [12, 28], O'Grady [58]	11,472
20	5	H	Macclesfield T	W	3-0	2-0	1	Atkinson [30], Wiseman [33], Taylor [90]	3003
21	12	A	Lincoln C	W	3-1	2-1	1	O'Grady [36], Dawson [45], Thompson [59]	3293
22	19	H	Shrewsbury T	W	4-0	2-0	—	Dawson 2 [8, 53], O'Grady 2 [38, 67]	2596
23	26	A	Crewe Alex	D	2-2	0-0	1	Dawson [53], Higginbotham [74]	5563
24	28	H	Morecambe	W	4-1	2-0	1	O'Grady [12], Dagnall [22], Atkinson 2 [72, 86]	4309
25	Jan 19	A	Aldershot T	D	1-1	0-0	—	Dagnall [74]	2453
26	23	A	Cheltenham T	W	4-1	1-0	1	O'Grady 3 [18, 49, 90], Dawson [56]	3460
27	26	H	Port Vale	D	0-0	0-0	—		3081
28	Feb 1	A	Bury	L	0-1	0-0	—		6528
29	6	H	Crewe Alex	W	2-0	1-0	1	O'Grady [8], Tootle (og) [46]	3164
30	20	H	Dagenham & R	W	3-1	1-1	1	Obadeyi [9], Jones G [83], O'Grady [90]	3153
31	23	H	Bradford C	L	1-3	1-1	1	Dagnall [45]	3055
32	27	A	Macclesfield T	W	1-0	0-0	1	O'Grady [60]	2462
33	Mar 2	H	Rotherham U	W	4-0	1-0	—	Dagnall [9], Green (og) [64], Dawson [71], O'Grady [74]	3502
34	6	A	Lincoln C	D	1-1	0-1	1	Dagnall [70]	3453
35	13	A	Shrewsbury T	W	1-0	0-0	1	Thompson [62]	6081
36	20	A	Accrington S	W	4-2	0-0	1	Jones G 2 [67, 72], O'Grady [83], Higginbotham [90]	3025
37	27	H	Grimsby T	W	4-1	3-1	1	Thompson [17], Dagnall 3 [20, 41, 90]	4724
38	Apr 3	A	Chesterfield	L	0-2	0-0	1		4471
39	5	H	Bournemouth	D	0-0	0-0	1		5027
40	10	A	Torquay U	L	0-5	0-3	1		3093
41	13	H	Darlington	L	0-1	0-1	—		5371
42	17	H	Northampton T	W	1-0	1-0	2	O'Grady [23]	5025
43	20	A	Notts Co	L	0-1	0-1	—		10,536
44	24	A	Hereford U	L	1-2	0-0	2	Jones G [62]	1975
45	May 1	H	Burton Alb	L	1-2	0-0	3	O'Grady [79]	3749
46	8	A	Barnet	L	0-1	0-0	3		4638

Final League Position: 3

GOALSCORERS

League (82): O'Grady 22, Dagnall 20 (1 pen), Dawson 9, Thompson 6, Jones G 4, Atkinson 3, Buckley 3, Higginbotham 3, Kennedy T 3 (3 pens), Whaley 2, Obadeyi 1, Rundle 1, Stephens 1, Taylor 1, Wiseman 1, own goals 2.
Carling Cup (0).
FA Cup (3): Thompson 2, Dawson 1.
J Paint Trophy (1): Dawson 1.

Arthur K 15	Wiseman S 33+3	Kennedy T 44	Jones G 32+2	Stanton N 37+1	Dawson C 40+2	Thompson J 27+9	Kennedy J 40+2	Dagnall C 45	Buckley W 12+3	Rundle A 6+6	Shaw J —+1	Le Fondre A —+1	Flynn M 7+3	Holness M 7+4	Spencer S —+4	O'Grady C 43	Higginbotham K 6+23	Stephens D 3+3	Whaley S 8+1	McArdle R 17+3	Manga M —+2	Lillis J 1	Heaton T 12	Taylor J 23	Atkinson W 15	Toner C 7+6	Glover D —+2	Haworth A 3+4	Fielding F 18	Obadeyi T 5+6	Gray R —+2	Match No.
1	2	3	4	5	6	7	8	9¹	10²	11	12	13																				1
1	13	3	4	5⁴	6	7	8	9	10	11¹			2²	12																		2
1		3	4		6	7	8	9		11¹			2	5		10	12															3
1		3	4	5	6	7²	8	9	11¹	12			2			10	13															4
1		3	4		6	7	8	9	11				2	5		10																5
1	12	3	4³		6	7	8	9	11				2¹	5		10²	13	14														6
1	2	3	4	5	6	7	8	9	11¹	12						10																7
1	2	3	4	5	6	7¹	8	9¹	11							10			13	12												8
1	2	3	4	5	6	12	8	9	11							10				7¹												9
1	2	3	4	5	6	11¹	8	9	12							10				7												10
1	2	3	4	5	6¹	13	8	9²	11					12	14	10³				7¹												11
1	2	3	4	5	6	12	8	9	11¹	14			13			10				7³												12
1		3	4¹		6	13	8	9³	11²				2			10	12			7					5¹	14						13
1	14	3			6	12	8	9	11¹				2			10²		4		7					5¹	13						14
		3		2⁶	6	7	8	9²					12			10	13			11		1		4¹	5							15
	2	3	7²		6		8	9	12				13	14		10³	11¹	4		5			1									16
	2	3			6		8	9³	12				4			10	13			5			1	7	11²	14						17
	2			5	3		8	9	11²				4			10	12						1	6	7¹	13						18
	2	3		5	4	7¹	8	9								10	12						1	6	11							19
	2	3		5	6		8	9¹								10	11						1	4	7	12						20
	2	3		5	6	7	8	9¹								10	12						1	4	11							21
	2	3		5	6	7¹	8	9								10²	12						1	4	11	13						22
		3	13	5	6	7¹	8	9					2			10	12						1	4²	11							23
		3	2		6	7²	8	9¹					13			10	12			5			1	4	11							24
	2	3		5	6	7	8	9	11¹							10	12						1	4								25
	2	3		5	6	7¹	8	9					13			10	12						1	4	11²							26
	2	3²	12	5	6	7	8¹	9							14	10	13						1	4	11³							27
	2	3		5	6	7¹	8	9								10³	13							4	11²			14	1	12		28
	2	3	7	5¹	6			9								10	13		12					4	11				1	8²		29
	2	3	4	5	6	13		9								10	12							7²	8³			14	1	11¹		30
	2	3	4	5	6			9								10	12							7	8²			13	1	11¹		31
	2¹	3	4²	12	6		8	9								10				5				7	11³	13			1	14		32
		3	7	2	6¹		8	9	12							10				E				11	4				1			33
		3	7	2	6	13	8	9								10	12			E				11²	4¹				1			34
	2	3	4	5		12	8	9								10	11¹			E				7					1			35
	2	3	4	5		11²	8¹	9								10	12			E				7¹	13				1			36
	2	3	7	5		11	8	9								10¹	12			E				4					1			37
	2	3	7	5²	14	11³	8¹	9								10	12			E				4				1	13			38
	2	3	7	5			8	9								10	11¹			E				4				1	12			39
	2¹	3³	7	5	13	11	8	9						14		10	12			E				4²				1				40
	2	3	6	5	4	11		9								10	12							7				1	8¹			41
	2	3	6	5¹	4	7		9								10	11²		12						8	13		1				42
	2	3	4	5	6	11²	8	9³								10	12							7¹				13	1	14		43
	2	3	4		6	12	8³	9								10	13			E							14	7²	1	11¹		44
1	2	3	4	5	6	12	13	9³								10	11							7²	8¹		14					45
	6	2	4	11	8		3	9								10²				E				7¹					1	12	13	46

FA Cup
First Round   Luton T   (a)   3-3
                     (h)   0-2

Carling Cup
First Round   Sheffield W   (a)   0-3

J Paint Trophy
First Round   Bradford C   (h)   1-2

ROTHERHAM UNITED   FL Championship 2

FOUNDATION

Rotherham were formed in 1870 before becoming Town in the late 1880s. Thornhill United were founded in 1877 and changed their name to Rotherham County in 1905. The Town amalgamated with Rotherham County to form Rotherham United in 1925.

Don Valley Stadium, Worksop Road, Sheffield, South Yorkshire S9 3TL.
Telephone: (08444) 140 737.
Fax: (08444) 140 744.
Ticket Office: (08444) 140 737.
Website: www.themillers.co.uk
Email: office@rotherhamunited.net
Ground Capacity: 25,000.
Record Attendance: 25,170 v Sheffield U, Division 2, 13 December 1952 (at Millmoor); 7,082 v Aldershot T, FL 2 Play-offs semi-final 2nd leg, 19 May 2010 (at Don Valley).
Pitch Measurements. 108yd × 72yd.
Chairman: Tony Stewart.
Chief Operating Officer: Paul Douglas.
Manager: Ronnie Moore.
Assistant Manager: Jimmy Mullen.
Physio: Denis Circuit.

HONOURS

Football League: Division 2 – runners-up 2000–01; Division 3 – Champions 1980–81; Runners-up 1999–2000; Division 3 (N) – Champions 1950–51; Runners-up 1946–47, 1947–48, 1948–49; Division 4 – Champions 1988–89; Runners-up 1991–92.

FA Cup: best season: 5th rd, 1953, 1968.

Football League Cup: Runners-up 1961.

Auto Windscreens Shield: Winners 1996.

Colours: Red shirts with white design, white shorts, red stockings.
Change Colours: All sky blue with white trim.
Year Formed: 1870. *Turned Professional:* 1905. *Ltd Co.:* 1920.
Club Nickname: 'The Merry Millers'.
Previous Names: 1877, Thornhill United; 1905, Rotherham County; 1925, amalgamated with Rotherham Town under Rotherham United.
Grounds: 1870, Red House Ground; 1907, Millmoor; 2008, Don Valley Stadium.
First Football League Game: 2 September 1893,.Division 2, Rotherham T v Lincoln C (a) D 1–1 – McKay; Thickett, Watson; Barr, Brown, Broadhead; Longden, Cutts, Leatherbarrow, McCormick, Pickering, (1 og). 30 August 1919, Division 2, Rotherham Co v Nottingham F (h) W 2–0 – Branston; Alton, Baines; Bailey, Coe, Stanton; Lee (1), Cawley (1), Glennon, Lees, Lamb.
Record League Victory: 8–0 v Oldham Ath, Division 3 (N), 26 May 1947 – Warnes; Selkirk, Ibbotson; Edwards, Horace Williams, Danny Williams; Wilson (2), Shaw (1), Ardron (3), Guest (1), Hainsworth (1).
Record Cup Victory: 6–0 v Spennymoor U, FA Cup 2nd rd, 17 December 1977 – McAlister; Forrest, Breckin, Womble, Stancliffe, Green, Finney, Phillips (3), Gwyther (2) (Smith), Goodfellow, Crawford (1). 6–0 v Wolverhampton W, FA Cup 1st rd, 16 November 1985 – O'Hanlon; Forrest, Dungworth, Gooding (1), Smith (1), Pickering, Birch (2), Emerson, Tynan (1), Simmons (1), Pugh. 6–0 v Kings Lynn, FA Cup 2nd rd, 6 December 1997 – Mimms; Clark, Hurst (Goodwin), Garner (1) (Hudson) (1), Warner (Bass), Richardson (1), Berry (1), Thompson, Druce (1), Glover (1), Roscoe.
Record Defeat: 1–11 v Bradford C, Division 3 (N), 25 August 1928.

sky SPORTS FACT FILE

Wally Ardron celebrated the birth of his son on 13 September 1947 by scoring four goals for Rotherham United in a 7–2 win over Carlisle United. On the 13 September 1948 he marked the boy's first birthday by scoring all four goals in a 4–1 win over Hartlepools United.

Most League Points (2 for a win): 71, Division 3 (N), 1950–51.

Most League Points (3 for a win): 91, Division 2, 2000–01.

Most League Goals: 114, Division 3 (N), 1946–47.

Highest League Scorer in Season: Wally Ardron, 38, Division 3 (N), 1946–47.

Most League Goals in Total Aggregate Gladstone Guest, 130, 1946–56.

Most League Goals in One Match: 4, Roland Bastow v York C, Division 3 (N), 9 November 1935; 4, Roland Bastow v Rochdale, Division 3 (N), 7 March 1936; 4, Wally Ardron v Crewe Alex, Division 3 (N), 5 October 1946; 4, Wally Ardron v Carlisle U, Division 3 (N), 13 September 1947; 4, Wally Ardron v Hartlepools U, Division 3 (N), 13 October 1948; 4, Ian Wilson v Liverpool, Division 2, 2 May 1955; 4, Carl Gilbert v Swansea C, Division 3, 28 September 1971; 4, Carl Airey v Chester, Division 3, 31 August 1987; 4, Shaun Goater v Hartlepool U, Division 3, 9 April 1994; 4, Lee Glover v Hull C, Division 3, 28 December 1997; 4, Darren Byfield v Millwall, Division 1, 10 August 2002.

Most Capped Player: Shaun Goater, 14 (36), Bermuda

Most League Appearances: Danny Williams, 459, 1946–62.

Youngest League Player: Kevin Eley, 16 years 72 days v Scunthorpe U, 15 May 1984.

Record Transfer Fee Received: £850,000 from Cardiff C for Alan Lee, August 2003.

Record Transfer Fee Paid: £150,000 to Millwall for Tony Towner, August 1980; £150,000 to Port Vale for Lee Glover, August 1996; £150,000 to Burnley for Alan Lee, September 2000; £150,000 to Reading for Martin Butler, September 2003. £150,000 to Crewe Alex for Tom Pope, June 2009.

MANAGERS

Billy Heald 1925–29 *(Secretary only for long spell)*
Stanley Davies 1929–30
Billy Heald 1930–33
Reg Freeman 1934–52
Andy Smailes 1952–58
Tom Johnston 1958–62
Danny Williams 1962–65
Jack Mansell 1965–67
Tommy Docherty 1967–68
Jimmy McAnearney 1968–73
Jimmy McGuigan 1973–79
Ian Porterfield 1979–81
Emlyn Hughes 1981–83
George Kerr 1983–85
Norman Hunter 1985–87
Dave Cusack 1987–88
Billy McEwan 1988–91
Phil Henson 1991–94
Archie Gemmill/John McGovern 1994–96
Danny Bergara 1996–97
Ronnie Moore 1997–2005
Mick Harford 2005
Alan Knill 2005–07
Mark Robins 2007–09
Ronnie Moore September 2009–

Football League Record: 1893 Rotherham Town elected to Division 2; 1896 Failed re-election; 1919 Rotherham County elected to Division 2; 1923–51 Division 3 (N); 1951–68 Division 2; 1968–73 Division 3; 1973–75 Division 4; 1975–81 Division 3; 1981–83 Division 2; 1983–88 Division 3; 1988–89 Division 4; 1989–91 Division 3; 1991–92 Division 4; 1992–97 Division 2; 1997–2000 Division 3; 2000–01 Division 2; 2001–04 Division 1; 2004–05 FL C; 2005–07 FL 1; 2007– FL 2.

LATEST SEQUENCES

Longest Sequence of League Wins: 9, 2.2.1982 – 6.3.1982.

Longest Sequence of League Defeats: 8, 7.4.1956 – 18.8.1956.

Longest Sequence of League Draws: 6, 13.10.1969 – 22.11.1969.

Longest Sequence of Unbeaten League Matches: 18, 13.10.1969 – 7.2.1970.

Longest Sequence Without a League Win: 21, 9.5.2004 – 20.11.2004.

Successive Scoring Runs: 30 from 3.4.1954.

Successive Non-scoring Runs: 6 from 21.8.2004.

TEN YEAR LEAGUE RECORD

		P	W	D	L	F	A	Pts	Pos
2000-01	Div 2	46	27	10	9	79	55	91	2
2001-02	Div 1	46	10	19	17	52	66	49	21
2002-03	Div 1	46	15	14	17	62	62	59	15
2003-04	Div 1	46	13	15	18	53	61	54	17
2004-05	FL C	46	5	14	27	35	69	29	24
2005-06	FL 1	46	12	16	18	52	62	52	20
2006-07	FL 1	46	13	9	24	58	75	38	23
2007-08	FL 2	46	21	11	14	62	58	64*	9
2008-09	FL 2	46	21	12	13	60	46	58†	14
2009-10	FL 2	46	21	10	15	55	52	73	5

*10 pts deducted; †17 points deducted.

DID YOU KNOW?

Outside-right Charlie Ramsden was signed by Rotherham United from South Normanton Colliery in November 1925. In the following season he made 36 consecutive League and Cup appearances and was snapped up by Manchester United in the summer months.

ROTHERHAM UNITED 2009–10 LEAGUE RECORD

Match No.	Date	Venue	Opponents	Result	H/T Score	Lg Pos.	Goalscorers	Attendance
1	Aug 8	H	Accrington S	W 1-0	0-0	—	Warne [89]	10,254
2	15	A	Bournemouth	L 0-1	0-1	13		5091
3	18	A	Grimsby T	W 2-1	0-0	—	Le Fondre (pen) [53], Cummins [67]	4156
4	23	H	Rochdale	W 2-1	1-1	5	Le Fondre [43], Warne [61]	3602
5	29	A	Macclesfield T	W 3-1	2-1	2	Le Fondre [24], Pope [37], Harrison [87]	1972
6	Sept 5	H	Chesterfield	W 3-1	0-1	1	Harrison [68], Le Fondre [73], Ellison [81]	4458
7	12	H	Morecambe	D 0-0	0-0	3		3172
8	19	A	Cheltenham T	D 1-1	1-0	3	Le Fondre [45]	3088
9	26	H	Barnet	W 3-0	2-0	3	Ellison [5], Law [25], Le Fondre [60]	3823
10	29	A	Northampton T	L 1-3	0-1	—	Le Fondre (pen) [79]	4017
11	Oct 3	A	Crewe Alex	W 3-2	1-1	2	Ellison [15], Le Fondre (pen) [58], Broughton [85]	4253
12	10	H	Hereford U	D 1-1	1-0	3	Le Fondre [11]	3452
13	17	H	Notts Co	D 0-0	0-0	4		5738
14	24	A	Bury	L 1-2	1-0	5	Ellison [45]	3496
15	31	H	Aldershot T	D 0-0	0-0	5		3002
16	Nov 14	H	Port Vale	W 2-1	1-1	4	Brogan [31], Law [90]	4788
17	21	A	Torquay U	W 2-0	0-0	4	Ellison [85], Le Fondre [90]	2551
18	24	H	Lincoln C	W 2-0	1-0	—	Le Fondre 2 [37, 82]	2901
19	Dec 1	A	Shrewsbury T	L 0-2	0-1	—		4522
20	5	H	Burton Alb	D 2-2	1-0	3	Le Fondre 2 (1 pen) [39 (p), 63]	3177
21	12	A	Bradford C	W 4-2	2-1	3	Ellison 2 [30, 37], Roberts [78], Broughton [88]	11,578
22	Jan 19	H	Darlington	L 1-2	0-0	—	Roberts [78]	3234
23	23	H	Grimsby T	W 2-1	2-0	4	Le Fondre 2 [9, 38]	3751
24	26	A	Chesterfield	W 1-0	0-0	—	Pope [90]	4951
25	Feb 2	A	Bournemouth	L 1-3	0-0	—	Pope [26]	3180
26	6	A	Darlington	L 0-2	0-1	5		2231
27	9	H	Dagenham & R	W 2-0	2-0	—	Le Fondre 2 (1 pen) [11, 35 (p)]	2604
28	13	A	Lincoln C	W 2-1	1-0	4	Le Fondre (pen) [14], Roberts [65]	4152
29	19	H	Torquay U	D 1-1	1-0	—	Harrison [20]	3339
30	22	H	Shrewsbury T	D 1-1	1-1	—	Le Fondre (pen) [12]	2869
31	27	A	Burton Alb	W 1-0	0-0	5	Le Fondre [52]	3568
32	Mar 2	A	Rochdale	L 0-4	0-1	—		3502
33	6	H	Bradford C	L 1-2	0-0	6	Le Fondre (pen) [89]	4185
34	13	A	Dagenham & R	W 1-0	0-0	6	Le Fondre [61]	1862
35	16	A	Accrington S	L 1-2	0-1	—	Walker [56]	1440
36	20	H	Bury	W 1-0	0-0	4	Walker [80]	3521
37	23	A	Macclesfield T	W 3-1	1-1	—	Harrison [12], Le Fondre (pen) [81], Broughton [83]	2873
38	27	H	Notts Co	L 0-1	0-0	4		9015
39	Apr 3	H	Port Vale	L 1-2	0-0	4	Walker [81]	3721
40	5	A	Aldershot T	L 0-3	0-1	4		3573
41	10	A	Morecambe	L 0-2	0-0	5		2337
42	13	A	Northampton T	W 1-0	0-0	—	Le Fondre (pen) [65]	3325
43	17	H	Cheltenham T	D 0-0	0-0	4		3478
44	24	A	Barnet	W 1-0	1-0	4	Ellison [34]	1884
45	May 1	H	Crewe Alex	D 0-0	0-0	4		4142
46	8	A	Hereford U	L 0-3	0-2	5		3005

Final League Position: 5

GOALSCORERS

League (55): Le Fondre 25 (10 pens), Ellison 8, Harrison 4, Broughton 3, Pope 3, Roberts 3, Walker 3, Law 2, Warne 2, Brogan 1, Cummins 1.
Carling Cup (5): Pope 2, Cummins 1, Ellison 1, Warne 1.
FA Cup (5): Le Fondre 2, Brogan 1, Broughton 1, Ellison 1.
J Paint Trophy (1): Le Fondre 1.
Play-Offs (5): Le Fondre 2, Taylor R 2, Ellison 1.

Warrington A 46	Lynch M 21+2	Green J 14+5	Mills P 34+3	Sharps I 44	Fenton N 34+1	Taylor J 2	Law N 41+1	Pope T 26+9	Taylor R 3+16	Ellison K 36+3	Harrison D 32+5	Liddell A —+2	Warne P 8+6	Tonge D 18+3	Le Fondre A 43+1	Cummins M 6+9	Joseph M 11+4	Broughton D 6+10	Nicholas A 7	Brogan S 1+4	Roberts G 11+2	Rundle A 4	Gunning G 21	Marshall M 13+9	Walker J 15	McAllister C 7+1	Bell-Baggie A 2+9	Match No.
1	2	3	4	5	6	7¹	8	9	10⁵	11²	12	13	14															1
1		3	8	5	6	11²	4	9³	14	7¹					10	2	12	13										2
1		3¹	8	5²	6		11	9			4		14	7³	10	2	13	12										3
1		3	8		6		11	9			12		4	7²	10¹	2	13	5										4
1		3	8		6		11	9¹	13				4	7	10²	2	12	5										5
1		3	8		6		11	12			9		4	7¹	10	2		5										6
1		3	8		6¹	12	11²	14	7³	9	4		13		10	2		5										7
1		3	8	6	5		11	7¹	12	9	4				10	2												8
1	13	3	8	6	5		11	7¹	12	9	4		14		10³	2²												9
1		3	8²	6	5		11	7¹	12	9	4				10	2	13											10
1		3	8	6	5		11	7¹		9	4				10	2	12											11
1		3	8	5	6¹		11	7²		9	4				10	2	12	13										12
1	12		8	5	6●	7		13		11	4		14		10³	2			9²	3¹								13
1			6	5			11	7¹	12	9	4				10	2	8			3								14
1			8	5	6		7¹			9	4		11		10	2			12	3								15
1			7	5	6		4	13		11¹			8		10	2			9²	3	12							16
1	2		4²	5	6		7	14	9³	11			8¹		10				3	12	13							17
1	2			5	6		7	9	13	8	12				10				3		4¹	11²						18
1	2			5	6		7	9		8³	12				10		13		3²	14	4	11¹						19
1	2			5	6●		7	9		8					10	12			3		4	11¹						20
1		3	6	5			7				8	12			10		2	9			4	11¹						21
1		3	6	5			8	13	14	11³	4¹				10	12	2	9²			7							22
1			6	5			8	9²		11	12				10	7	2				4¹		3	13				23
1			6	5			8	9		11²					10	7	2				4		3¹	13				24
1			6	5			7²	9	13	11³					10	8	2¹				4		3	14				25
1			6¹	5	2		7	9					4³		11	10	8²	13			12		3	14				26
1	2			5	6		7	9¹	12	11²	4				10						8		3	13				27
1	2			5	6		7	9¹	12	11	4				10						8		3					28
1	2			5	6		7	9³	13	11²	4				10		14	8●					3¹					29
1	2			5	6		7	9²	12	11	4				10	8¹							3	13				30
1	2	13		5	6		7	9¹		11					10²								3	12	8			31
1	2	12		5¹	6		7	9³	13	11²	4				10								3	14	8			32
1	2	13		5	6		7¹	9	14	11	4				10								3²	12	8			33
1	2²	12		5	6			14		11¹	4		13		10		3							8	7	9³		34
1	2			5	6			12		11¹	4				10	3								8²	7	9	13	35
1		12		5	6¹		8²			4					10			14					2	11³	7	9	13	36
1	12			6	5		7			4					3¹	10		14					2	11	8²	9³	13	37
1	2			6	5		7			4					10		12						3	11	8	9¹		38
1	2			6	5		7²	12		4					10								3	11	8	9¹	13	39
1		6		5³	2			12		13	4				10		14						3	11²	8	9¹	7	40
1	2²	13	3	5	6		12			14	4				10		9³							11	8		7¹	41
1		6	5	2			7¹			11	4●				10								3	9	8	7¹		42
1	2	12	4	5	6		7			11					10								3¹	9³	8²	14	13	43
1	2		6	5	3		7			11	14				10	13							4	9³	8¹		12²	44
1	2		4	5	6		7			11					10	12							3	9²	8¹		13	45
1	2		6²	5	4		7³			11	8		12		13		9¹						3	10			14	46

FA Cup

First Round	Wealdstone	(a)	3-2
Second Round	Luton T	(h)	2-2
		(a)	0-3

Carling Cup

First Round	Derby Co	(h)	2-1
Second Round	WBA	(a)	3-4

J Paint Trophy

First Round	Huddersfield T	(h)	1-2

Play-Offs

Semi-Final	Aldershot T	(a)	1-0
		(h)	2-0
Final	Dagenham & R		2-3
(at Wembley)			

SCUNTHORPE UNITED FL Championship

FOUNDATION

The year of foundation for Scunthorpe United has often been quoted as 1910, but the club can trace its history back to 1899 when Brumby Hall FC, who played on the Old Showground, consolidated their position by amalgamating with some other clubs and changing their name to Scunthorpe United. The year 1910 was when that club amalgamated with North Lindsey United as Scunthorpe and Lindsey United. The link is Mr W. T. Lockwood whose chairmanship covers both years.

Glanford Park, Doncaster Road, Scunthorpe DN15 8TD.

Telephone: (0871) 221 1899.

Fax: (01724) 857 986.

Ticket Office: (0871) 221 1899 (option 1).

Website: www.scunthorpe-united.co.uk

Email: admin@scunthorpe-united.co.uk

Ground Capacity: 9,088.

Record Attendance: Old Showground: 23,935 v Portsmouth, FA Cup 4th rd, 30 January 1954. Glanford Park: 8,906 v Nottingham F, FL 1, 10 March 2007.

Pitch Measurements: 112yd × 72yd.

Chairman: Steve Wharton.

Vice-chairman: Rex Garton.

Manager: Nigel Adkins B.Sc (Hons).

Assistant Manager: Andy Crosby.

Physio: Alex Dalton.

Colours: Claret shirts with light blue sleeves, white shorts, claret stockings.

Change Colours: White shirts with blue inserts and claret cuffs on sleeves, white shorts, white stockings.

Year Formed: 1899.

Turned Professional: 1912.

Ltd Co.: 1912.

Club Nickname: 'The Iron'.

Previous Names: Amalgamated first with Brumby Hall then North Lindsey United to become Scunthorpe & Lindsey United, 1910; 1958 Scunthorpe United.

Grounds: 1899, Old Showground; 1988, Glanford Park.

First Football League Game: 19 August 1950, Division 3 (N), v Shrewsbury T (h) D 0–0 – Thompson; Barker, Brownsword; Allen, Taylor, McCormick; Mosby, Payne, Gorin, Rees, Boyes.

Record League Victory: 8–1 v Luton T, Division 3, 24 April 1965 – Sidebottom; Horstead, Hemstead;

HONOURS

Football League: FL 1 – Champions 2006–07; FL 2 – Runners-up 2004–05; Division 3 (N) – Champions 1957–58.

FA Cup: best season: 5th rd, 1958, 1970.

Football League Cup: never past 3rd rd.

Johnstone's Paint Trophy: Runners-up 2008–09.

sky SPORTS FACT FILE

In 1938–39 Scunthorpe United had a team which bristled with former Football League players. One of the most famous was the club's player-manager Tom Jones. A former Welsh international full-back, he had served Manchester United well over a period of 13 years.

Smith, Neale, Lindsey; Bramley (1); Scott, Thomas (5), Mahy (1), Wilson (1). 8–1 v Torquay U (a), Division 3, 28 October 1995 – Samways; Housham. Wilson, Ford (1), Knill (1), Hope (Nicholson), Thornber, Bullimore (Wash), McFarlane (4) (Young), Eyre (2), Paterson.

Record Cup Victory: 9–0 v Boston U, FA Cup 1st rd, 21 November 1953 – Malan; Hubbard, Brownsword; Sharpe, White, Bushby; Mosby (1), Haigh (3), Whitfield (2), Gregory (1), Mervyn Jones (2).

Record Defeat: 0–8 v Carlisle U, Division 3 (N), 25 December 1952.

Most League Points (2 for a win): 66, Division 3 (N), 1956–57, 1957–58.

Most League Points (3 for a win): 91, FL 1, 2006–07.

Most League Goals: 88, Division 3 (N), 1957–58.

Highest League Scorer in Season: Barrie Thomas, 31, Division 2, 1961–62.

Most League Goals in Total Aggregate: Steve Cammack, 110, 1979–81, 1981–86.

Most League Goals in One Match: 5, Barrie Thomas v Luton T, Division 3, 24 April 1965.

Most Capped Player: Grant McCann, 10 (28), Northern Ireland.

Most League Appearances: Jack Brownsword, 595, 1950–65.

Youngest League Player: Mike Farrell, 16 years 240 days v Workington, 8 November 1975.

Record Transfer Fee Received: £2,000,000 from Sheffield U for Billy Sharp, July 2007.

Record Transfer Fee Paid: £425,000 to Stoke C for Martin Paterson, July 2007.

Football League Record: 1950 Elected to Division 3 (N); 1958–64 Division 2; 1964–68 Division 3; 1968–72 Division 4; 1972–73 Division 3; 1973–83 Division 4; 1983–84 Division 3; 1984–92 Division 4; 1992–99 Division 3; 1999–2000 Division 2; 2000–04 Division 3; 2004–05 FL 2; 2005–07 FL 1; 2007–08 FL C; 2008–09 FL 1; 2009– FL C.

MANAGERS

Harry Allcock 1915–53
  (Secretary-Manager)
Tom Crilly 1936–37
Bernard Harper 1946–48
Leslie Jones 1950–51
Bill Corkhill 1952–56
Ron Suart 1956–58
Tony McShane 1959
Bill Lambton 1959
Frank Soo 1959–60
Dick Duckworth 1960–64
Fred Goodwin 1964–66
Ron Ashman 1967–73
Ron Bradley 1973–74
Dick Rooks 1974–76
Ron Ashman 1976–81
John Duncan 1981–83
Allan Clarke 1983–84
Frank Barlow 1984–87
Mick Buxton 1987–91
Bill Green 1991–93
Richard Money 1993–94
David Moore 1994–96
Mick Buxton 1996–97
Brian Laws 1997–2004; 2004–06
Nigel Adkins December 2006–

LATEST SEQUENCES

Longest Sequence of League Wins: 7, 27.1.2007 – 3.3.2007.

Longest Sequence of League Defeats: 8, 29.11.1997 – 20.1.1998.

Longest Sequence of League Draws: 6, 2.1.1984 – 25.2.1984.

Longest Sequence of Unbeaten League Matches: 19, 22.12.2006 – 6.4.2007.

Longest Sequence Without a League Win: 14, 22.3.1975 – 6.9.1975.

Successive Scoring Runs: 24 from 13.1.2007.

Successive Non-scoring Runs: 7 from 19.4.1975.

TEN YEAR LEAGUE RECORD

		P	W	D	L	F	A	Pts	Pos
2000-01	Div 3	46	18	11	17	62	52	65	10
2001-02	Div 3	46	19	14	13	74	56	71	8
2002-03	Div 3	46	19	15	12	68	49	72	5
2003-04	Div 3	46	11	16	19	69	72	49	22
2004-05	FL 2	46	22	14	10	69	42	80	2
2005-06	FL 1	46	15	15	16	68	73	60	12
2006-07	FL 1	46	26	13	7	73	35	91	1
2007-08	FL C	46	11	13	22	46	69	46	23
2008-09	FL 1	46	22	10	14	82	63	76	6
2009-10	FL C	46	14	10	22	62	84	52	20

DID YOU KNOW ?

In 1954–55 premier striker Gordon Brown (23 goals) and John Gregory (22) contributed over half of the 83 League goals scored by Scunthorpe United. But Jack Hubbard with a four-timer and Jimmy Whitfield with a hat-trick made their own telling contributions to the total.

SCUNTHORPE UNITED 2009–10 LEAGUE RECORD

Match No.	Date	Venue	Opponents	Result	H/T Score	Lg Pos.	Goalscorers	Attendance
1	Aug 8	A	Cardiff C	L	0-4	0-3	—	22,264
2	15	H	Derby Co	W	3-2	2-1	10	Hooper 2 [17, 44], Woolford [82]	7352
3	18	H	Middlesbrough	L	0-2	0-1	—	8274
4	22	A	Sheffield W	L	0-4	0-3	18		20,215
5	29	H	QPR	L	0-1	0-1	20		5866
6	Sept 12	A	Crystal Palace	W	4-0	1-0	18	Forte [4], Hayes [58], Togwell [66], O'Connor [68]	12,912
7	15	H	Preston NE	W	3-1	2-0	—	McCann [12], Hooper 2 [42, 53]	5383
8	19	A	Bristol C	D	1-1	0-0	13	McCann [90]	14,203
9	26	H	Doncaster R	D	2-2	0-1	15	Byrne [72], McCann (pen) [90]	7945
10	30	A	Nottingham F	L	0-2	0-0	—		18,332
11	Oct 3	A	Plymouth Arg	L	1-2	0-0	19	Hooper (pen) [75]	9780
12	17	H	Sheffield U	W	3-1	1-0	18	McCann 2 [22, 59], Hayes [53]	7599
13	20	H	Newcastle U	W	2-1	0-0	—	Woolford 2 [53, 79]	8921
14	24	A	Peterborough U	L	0-3	0-2	16		8051
15	31	A	Swansea C	L	0-2	0-1	18		5201
16	Nov 7	A	Blackpool	L	1-4	0-0	19	Hayes [51]	7727
17	21	A	Watford	L	0-3	0-2	21		13,241
18	28	H	Leicester C	D	1-1	0-1	20	Woolford [90]	6884
19	Dec 6	H	Coventry C	W	1-0	1-0	18	Hooper [30]	5013
20	9	A	Barnsley	D	1-1	0-0	—	Hayes [58]	11,657
21	12	A	Reading	D	1-1	0-1	18	Hooper [80]	15,274
22	26	A	Middlesbrough	L	0-3	0-2	20		20,647
23	28	H	WBA	L	1-3	0-1	21	Jones [47]	7221
24	Jan 9	A	Derby Co	W	4-1	2-0	—	Hooper [14], Thompson 2 [45, 80], Forte [89]	28,106
25	16	H	Cardiff C	D	1-1	1-0	20	O'Connor [11]	5032
26	27	H	Sheffield W	W	2-0	1-0	—	Hooper [2], McCann [77]	7038
27	30	A	QPR	W	1-0	0-0	16	Thompson [74]	13,105
28	Feb 6	H	Crystal Palace	L	1-2	0-0	19	Mirfin [84]	7543
29	9	A	WBA	L	0-2	0-1	—		23,146
30	13	A	Leicester C	L	1-5	0-4	21	Hayes [54]	21,626
31	16	H	Barnsley	W	2-1	0-0	—	Hooper [50], Hayes [90]	5648
32	20	H	Watford	D	2-2	1-0	18	Hooper 2 (1 pen) [42, 90 (p)]	5411
33	23	H	Ipswich T	D	1-1	0-0	—	Byrne [70]	5828
34	27	A	Coventry C	L	1-2	0-0	19	McCann [83]	16,197
35	Mar 13	H	Ipswich T	L	0-1	0-0	22		19,378
36	17	A	Newcastle U	L	0-3	0-2	—		39,301
37	20	A	Plymouth Arg	W	2-1	1-1	20	Thompson [32], Woolford [65]	5153
38	23	H	Peterborough U	W	4-0	3-0	—	Hayes [15], Thompson 2 [25, 64], Togwell [44]	4995
39	28	A	Sheffield U	W	1-0	1-0	19	Hayes [45]	23,005
40	Apr 2	H	Blackpool	L	2-4	0-1	—	McCann (pen) [48], Hooper [86]	7508
41	5	A	Swansea C	L	0-3	0-1	19		14,830
42	10	A	Preston NE	L	2-3	0-1	20	Thompson 2 [64, 72]	12,441
43	17	H	Bristol C	W	3-0	1-0	19	Hooper 3 [19, 55, 70]	5430
44	20	H	Reading	D	2-2	0-0	—	Hooper [82], Sparrow [89]	5299
45	24	A	Doncaster R	L	3-4	1-2	20	Hooper 2 [19, 84], Hayes [53]	12,124
46	May 2	H	Nottingham F	D	2-2	0-2	20	Canavan [49], Thompson [87]	8119

Final League Position: 20

GOALSCORERS

League (62): Hooper 19 (2 pens), Hayes 9, Thompson 9, McCann 8 (2 pens), Woolford 5, Byrne 2, Forte 2, O'Connor 2, Togwell 2, Canavan 1, Jones 1, Mirfin 1, Sparrow 1.
Carling Cup (7): Hayes 2, Canavan 1, Forte 1, Hooper 1 (pen), McCann 1, Sparrow 1.
FA Cup (3): Hayes 2, own goal 1.

Murphy J 40	Byrne C 34 + 2	Morris 12 + 1	Togwell S 33 + 8	Mirfin D 37	Jones R 28	Sparrow M 22 + 8	McCann G 36 + 6	Hayes P 45	Hooper G 31 + 4	Woolford M 29 + 11	Wright J 24 + 11	Forte J 6 + 22	O'Connor M 23 + 9	Wright A 13 + 6	Williams M 37	Spence J 9	Thompson G 22 + 14	Canavan N 4 + 3	Lillis J 6 + 2	Friend G 6 + 2	N'Gala B - + 2	Slocombe S - + 1	May D - + 1	Moloney B 1 + 2	McDermott D 4 + 5	Raynes M 12	Milne K 4	McNulty J 2 + 1	Match No.
1	2	3	4³	5	6	7²	8	9	10¹	11	12	13	14																1
1	5	14			6	7	8¹	9	10²	11	12	13	4³	2	3														2
1	5				6	7²	8	9	10	11	12		4¹	2	3		13												3
1	5	14			6¹	7	8³	9	10	11		13	4²	2	3		12												4
1	5		8¹		6	7³		9	10	11	12	13	4²	2	3		14												5
1	8			5	6	7		9	10³	11²	12	14	4¹	2	3		13												6
1	13	14	8¹	5	6	7		9	10	11	12		4²	2	3														7
1	8	14		5	6	7		9	10¹	11³	12	13	4²	2	3														8
1	12		8³	5	6¹	7		9	10²	11		13	4	2	3		14												9
1⁶	6		8²	5		7		9	10	11¹	12		4	2	3		13	15											10
	6	3	8	5³		4²	11¹	9	10	12	7	14	2		13				1										11
1	2		4	5	6	7³	8	9	10²	11¹	12	13			3		14												12
1	2		4	5	6	7	8³	9	10	11³	12	14			3		13												13
1	2		4¹		6	7²	8	9	10	11	12	14			3	5³	13												14
1	2		4	5	6	7	8¹	9³	10	11²	12	13	14		3														15
1⁸	2		4	5	6	7	8⁶	9²	10	11¹		13			3						12	15							16
	2		4	5	6¹	7²	8	9	10	11	12				3		13		1										17
1	2		4¹	5	6	7	8	9³	10	11	12				3		13												18
1⁶	2		4	5	6	7	8	9²	10¹	11	12				3		13	15											19
1	2		4	5	6	7	8	9	10³	11		13	14		3¹						12²								20
	2¹		4²	5	6	7	8	9	10³	11	12	13	14		3														21
1	2⁸			5	6	7³	8	9¹	10	11	14	13			3						12								22
1	4	2	5		6	7¹	8⁸	9	10⁸	14	12²				3		11³							13					23
	2	12	5		6	7	8	9	10²	11¹	14	13	4³		3				1										24
	2		6²	5		7	8	9	10³	11¹	12	13	14		3				1										25
1	2		4	5	6²	7	8	9	10³	11¹	12	14			3										13				26
1	2		4	5¹	6	7	8	9	10³	11²	12	14			3										13				27
1	2		4³	5	6	7¹	8	9	10		12	14			3⁸										13	11²			28
1	2⁸	12	4³	5	6	7	8	9	13	14	11				3¹										10²				29
1			4	2	6	7	8	9	10	11					3											5			30
1		3	4²	2	6	7	8³	9	10	11	13	12	14													5³			31
1	2	12		5		7	8²	9	10	11¹	14	4³			3		13									6			32
1	2		4	5		7		9	10	11¹	12				3		8									6			33
1	2		4¹	5		7³		9	10	11²	8	14			3		12								13	6			34
1	2⁸		4	5		10	8²	9¹		11	13	12			3		7								13	6			35
1	12			6		11		9²	14		7³	10	2¹		3	8	4								13	5			36
1			4	2		7		9¹	10	11	12				3	8	6									5			37
1			4	2		7²		9	10	11¹		13	8		3	6	14								12		5³		38
1			4	2¹		8²		9		11	14	13	7		3	6	12								10³	5			39
1			4³			10²	8	9	13	11¹	14	2	3			7									12	6	5	6	40
1	2					11²	4	9³	13	14	7		3¹		10	6								8	5		12	41
1	2		5			7	4	9	10²	11¹	12		13			8									6		3		42
1	2	12	5			7	4	9	10¹	11				3		8									6			43
1	2	13	5			7	4	9²	10	11	12			8			6	3¹											44
1	2	12	5¹			7	4	9	10	11²	13	14		8			6³								3				45
	2		4	5		12	8	9¹	10²	11		13					7	3	1								6		46

FA Cup

Third Round	Barnsley	(h)	1-0
Fourth Round	Manchester C	(h)	2-4

Carling Cup

First Round	Chesterfield	(h)	2-1
Second Round	Swansea C	(a)	2-1
Third Round	Port Vale	(h)	2-0
Fourth Round	Manchester C	(a)	1-5

SHEFFIELD UNITED   FL Championship

FOUNDATION

In March 1889, Yorkshire County Cricket Club formed Sheffield United six days after an FA Cup semi-final between Preston North End and West Bromwich Albion had finally convinced Charles Stokes, a member of the cricket club, that the formation of a professional football club would prove successful at Bramall Lane. The United's first secretary, Mr J. B. Wostinholm was also secretary of the cricket club.

Bramall Lane Ground, Cherry Street, Bramall Lane, Sheffield S2 4SU.
Telephone: (0871) 995 1899.
Fax: 0871 663 2430.
Ticket Office: (0871) 995 1889.
Website: www.sufc.co.uk
Email: info@sufc.co.uk
Ground Capacity: 32,500.
Record Attendance: 68,287 v Leeds U, FA Cup 5th rd, 15 February 1936.
Pitch Measurements: 101.1m × 62.2m.
Chairman: Kevin McCabe.
Vice-chairman: Chris Steer.
Chief Executive: Trevor Birch.
Secretary: Donna Fletcher.
Manager: Kevin Blackwell.
Assistant Manager: Sam Ellis.
Physio: Paul Teather.
Colours: Red and white striped shirts with red sleeves, black shorts, black stockings.
Change Colours: White shirts with red trim, white shorts, white stockings.
Year Formed: 1889. *Turned Professional:* 1889. *Ltd Co.:* 1899.
Club Nickname: 'The Blades'.
Ground: 1889, Bramall Lane.
First Football League Game: 3 September 1892, Division 2, v Lincoln C (h) W 4–2 – Lilley; Witham, Cain; Howell, Hendry, Needham (1); Wallace, Dobson, Hammond (3), Davies, Drummond.
Record League Victory: 10–0 v Burslem Port Vale (a), Division 2, 10 December 1892 – Howlett; Witham, Lilley; Howell, Hendry, Needham; Drummond (1), Wallace (1), Hammond (4), Davies (2), Watson (2).
Record Cup Victory: 6–1 v Lincoln C, League Cup, 22 August 2000 – Tracey; Uhlenbeek, Weber, Woodhouse (Ford), Murphy, Sandford, Devlin (pen), Ribeiro (Santos), Bent (3), Kelly (1) (Thompson), Jagielka, og (1). 6–1 v Loughborough, FA Cup 4th qualifying rd, 6 December 1890; 6–1 v Scarborough (a), FA Cup 1st qualifying rd, 5 October 1889.
Record Defeat: 0–13 v Bolton W, FA Cup 2nd rd, 1 February 1890.

HONOURS

Football League: FL C – Runners-up 2005–06; Division 1 – Champions 1897–98; Runners-up 1896–97, 1899–1900; Division 2 – Champions 1952–53; Runners-up 1892–93, 1938–39, 1960–61, 1970–71, 1989–90; Division 4 – Champions 1981–82.
FA Cup: Winners 1899, 1902, 1915, 1925; Runners-up 1901, 1936.
Football League Cup: semi-final 2003.

sky SPORTS FACT FILE

As a youngster Jack Smith's family emigrated to the USA. Jack started playing soccer with the locals but since none of them had much idea about goalkeeping he went in goal. Back in England his career blossomed as Sheffield United's No.1 from 1930 to 1949.

Most League Points (2 for a win): 60, Division 2, 1952–53.

Most League Points (3 for a win): 96, Division 4, 1981–82.

Most League Goals: 102, Division 1, 1925–26.

Highest League Scorer in Season: Jimmy Dunne, 41, Division 1, 1930–31.

Most League Goals in Total Aggregate: Harry Johnson, 205, 1919–30.

Most League Goals in One Match: 5, Harry Hammond v Bootle, Division 2, 26 November 1892; 5, Harry Johnson v West Ham U, Division 1, 26 December 1927.

Most Capped Player: Billy Gillespie, 25, Northern Ireland.

Most League Appearances: Joe Shaw, 629, 1948–66.

Youngest League Player: Steve Hawes, 17 years 47 days v WBA, 2 September 1995.

Record Transfer Fee Received: £4,000,000 from Everton for Phil Jagielka, July 2007.

Record Transfer Fee Paid: £4,000,000 to Everton for James Beattie, August 2007.

Football League Record: 1892 Elected to Division 2; 1893–1934 Division 1; 1934–39 Division 2; 1946–49 Division 1; 1949–53 Division 2; 1953–56 Division 1; 1955–61 Division 2; 1961–68 Division 1; 1968–71 Division 2; 1971–76 Division 1; 1976–79 Division 2; 1979–81 Division 3; 1981–82 Division 4; 1982–84 Division 3; 1984–88 Division 2; 1988–89 Division 3; 1989–90 Division 2; 1990–92 Division 1; 1992–94 FA Premier League; 1994–2004 Division 1; 2004–06 FL C; 2006–07 FA Premier League; 2007– FL C.

MANAGERS

J. B. Wostinholm 1889–99
    (Secretary-Manager)
John Nicholson 1899–1932
Ted Davison 1932–52
Reg Freeman 1952–55
Joe Mercer 1955–58
Johnny Harris 1959–68
    *(continued as General Manager
    to 1970)*
Arthur Rowley 1968–69
Johnny Harris *(General Manager
    resumed Team Manager duties)*
    1969–73
Ken Furphy 1973–75
Jimmy Sirrel 1975–77
Harry Haslam 1978–81
Martin Peters 1981
Ian Porterfield 1981–86
Billy McEwan 1986–88
Dave Bassett 1988–95
Howard Kendall 1995–97
Nigel Spackman 1997–98
Steve Bruce 1998–99
Adrian Heath 1999
Neil Warnock 1999–2007
Bryan Robson 2007–08
Kevin Blackwell February 2008–

LATEST SEQUENCES

Longest Sequence of League Wins: 8, 14.9.1960 – 22.10.1960.

Longest Sequence of League Defeats: 7, 19.8.1975 – 20.9.1975.

Longest Sequence of League Draws: 6, 6.5.2001 – 8.9.2001.

Longest Sequence of Unbeaten League Matches: 22, 2.9.1899 – 13.1.1900.

Longest Sequence Without a League Win: 19, 27.9.1975 – 7.2 1976.

Successive Scoring Runs: 34 from 30.3.1956.

Successive Non-scoring Runs: 6 from 4.12.1993.

TEN YEAR LEAGUE RECORD

		P	W	D	L	F	A	Pts	Pos
2000-01	Div 1	46	19	11	16	52	49	68	10
2001-02	Div 1	46	15	15	16	53	54	60	13
2002-03	Div 1	46	23	11	12	72	52	80	3
2003-04	Div 1	46	20	11	15	65	56	71	8
2004-05	FL C	46	18	13	15	57	56	67	8
2005-06	FL C	46	26	12	8	76	46	90	2
2006-07	PR Lge	38	10	8	20	32	55	38	18
2007-08	FL C	46	17	15	14	56	51	66	9
2008-09	FL C	46	22	14	10	64	39	80	3
2009-10	FL C	46	17	14	15	62	55	65	8

DID YOU KNOW ?

In 1935 the eleven Sheffield United players who had won the FA Cup twenty years earlier were widespread. Five were licensees, three in business, one an ex-League manager, another coaching at a school while Bill Brelsford remained as the club's assistant trainer.

SHEFFIELD UNITED 2009–10 LEAGUE RECORD

Match No.	Date	Venue	Opponents	Result	H/T Score	Lg Pos.	Goalscorers	Attendance
1	Aug 7	A	Middlesbrough	D 0-0	0-0	—		23,541
2	15	H	Watford	W 2-0	1-0	—	Ward [12], Evans [63]	24,638
3	18	H	Leicester C	D 1-1	0-0	—	Treacy [66]	26,069
4	22	A	Reading	W 3-1	1-1	—	Quinn S [42], Ward [62], Cotterill [90]	16,025
5	29	H	WBA	D 2-2	0-0	—	Evans [56], Cotterill (pen) [88]	25,169
6	Sept 12	A	Derby Co	W 1-0	0-0	5	Kilgallon [80]	28,441
7	15	A	Coventry C	L 2-3	1-1	—	Ward [31], Harper [76]	14,426
8	18	H	Sheffield W	W 3-2	3-0	—	Ward [7], Henderson [15], Buxton (og) [42]	29,210
9	26	A	Swansea C	L 1-2	0-0	6	Quinn S [73]	14,324
10	29	A	Ipswich T	D 3-3	1-2	—	Henderson 2 [9, 77], Morgan [90]	28,366
11	Oct 3	H	Doncaster R	D 1-1	0-1	6	Cresswell [65]	26,211
12	17	A	Scunthorpe U	L 1-3	0-1	11	Evans [51]	7599
13	20	A	Blackpool	L 0-3	0-0	—		8042
14	24	H	Cardiff C	L 3-4	2-2	13	Henderson 2 [43, 45], Harper [90]	25,021
15	Nov 2	H	Newcastle U	L 0-1	0-0	—		26,536
16	9	A	Barnsley	D 2-2	0-0	—	Henderson 2 (2 pens) [61, 83]	12,998
17	21	H	Peterborough U	W 1-0	1-0	14	Camara [42]	25,144
18	28	A	Bristol C	W 3-2	2-0	14	Henderson 3 [30, 33, 90]	14,637
19	Dec 5	A	Plymouth Arg	W 1-0	0-0	10	Harper [88]	9231
20	8	H	Nottingham F	D 0-0	0-0	—		26,490
21	12	H	Crystal Palace	W 2-0	1-0	8	Williamson [21], Quinn S [90]	25,510
22	19	A	QPR	D 1-1	1-1	7	Cresswell [8]	12,639
23	26	A	Leicester C	L 1-2	0-2	11	Camara [47]	23,999
24	28	H	Preston NE	W 1-0	0-0	7	Ward [86]	25,231
25	Jan 16	H	Middlesbrough	W 1-0	0-0	6	Cresswell [56]	23,974
26	26	H	Reading	W 3-0	2-0	—	Fortune [12], Cresswell [42], Morgan [80]	24,009
27	30	A	WBA	L 1-3	0-2	6	Henderson (pen) [49]	22,193
28	Feb 2	A	Watford	L 0-3	0-1	—		13,076
29	6	H	Derby Co	D 1-1	0-1	7	Williamson [90]	25,300
30	9	A	Preston NE	L 1-2	0-1	—	Yeates [81]	10,270
31	13	A	Bristol C	W 2-0	0-0	7	Camara [49], Henderson [62]	22,613
32	16	A	Nottingham F	L 0-1	0-1	—		22,076
33	27	H	Plymouth Arg	W 4-3	2-0	7	Camara [7], Ward 2 [35, 47], Cresswell [80]	24,886
34	Mar 6	A	Crystal Palace	L 0-1	0-1	9		13,455
35	9	A	Peterborough U	L 0-1	0-1	—		6674
36	13	H	QPR	D 1-1	1-0	9	Cresswell [44]	23,456
37	16	H	Blackpool	W 3-0	2-0	—	Cresswell 2 [1, 66], Montgomery [43]	22,555
38	20	A	Doncaster R	D 1-1	0-1	7	Harper [88]	13,026
39	24	H	Cardiff C	D 1-1	0-1	—	Quinn S [67]	18,715
40	28	H	Scunthorpe U	L 0-1	0-1	10		23,005
41	Apr 3	H	Barnsley	D 0-0	0-0	10		24,808
42	5	A	Newcastle U	L 1-2	1-1	10	Cresswell [22]	48,270
43	10	H	Coventry C	W 1-0	0-0	10	Cresswell [47]	23,603
44	18	A	Sheffield W	D 1-1	0-1	10	Williamson [60]	35,485
45	24	H	Swansea C	W 2-0	0-0	9	Cresswell [62], De Vries (og) [90]	25,966
46	May 2	A	Ipswich T	W 3-0	1-0	8	Yeates [34], Evans [56], Cresswell [63]	23,003

Final League Position: 8

GOALSCORERS

League (62): Cresswell 12, Henderson 12 (3 pens), Ward 7, Camara 4, Evans 4, Harper 4, Quinn S 4, Williamson 3, Cotterill 2 (1 pen), Morgan 2, Yeates 2, Fortune 1, Kilgallon 1, Montgomery 1, Treacy 1, own goals 2.
Carling Cup (1): Sharp 1.
FA Cup (4): Cresswell 2, Ward 1, Williamson 1.

Bunn M 31+1	Walker K 26	Taylor A 22+4	Montgomery N 39	Morgan C 37	Kilgallon M 21	France R 3+6	Quinn S 38+6	Henderson D 28+4	Howard B 3+1	Treacy K 12+4	Cotterill D 3+11	Evans C 21+12	Ward J 25+3	Reid K —+7	Harper J 31+3	Stewart J 15+8	Davies A 7+1	Little G 7+9	Cresswell R 28+3	Williamson L 14+6	Bennett I 4+1	Camara H 9+14	Fortune J 3+2	Geary D 5+2	Ikeme C 2	Kallio T 8	Seip M 5+1	Yeates M 11+9	Nosworthy N 19	Bartley K 10+4	Connolly P 7	Simonsen S 7	Lowton M 1+1	Kenny P 2	Naysmith G 2	Match No.
1	2	3	4	5	6	7	8	9	10^2	11^1	12	13																								1
1	2	3	4	5	6		14	9	8	7^2	12	10^3	11^1	13																						2
1	2	3	4	5	6	12	9	8^1	7^2	14	10	11^3	13																							3
1	2	3	4	5	6	13	8	9	7^1	12	10^2	11																								4
1	2	3	4	5	6	8	9	14	7^1	12	10^2	11^3	13																							5
1	2	3	4	5	6	14	8^3	9^1	7^2	13	12	10			11																					6
1	2	3^1	4	5	6		8^1	9		7^2	13	12	10		11	14																				7
1	2	3	4	5		13	14	9		7^3	12^2	8	10^1		11						6															8
1	2	3^1	4	5	6		8^2	9		7^1	10	12			11	14				13																9
1	2	3^1	4	5	6^1		8	9		7^2	10				11			12	13	14																10
1	2		4^1	5			12	8	9	13	14	10^2				3	6	7^3	11																	11
1	2	14		5	6^1		11	9		13		10		12	8	3^3	4	7^2																		12
1	2	3		5	6	7^1	8	9		12	11^3	13			4				10^2	14																13
	2	3^1		5	6		8	9		11	13	10^3			4	12		7^2		1	14															14
	2^1			5	6	12	8	10		7	13	9^3			11	3^2	4			1	14															15
15	2				6^1		8	10		7^2		9	11		4		5			1^1	13	3	12													16
1	2			5	6	13	3			12		9	8^3	14	11	4			7^2	10^3																17
	2		4	5	6		8	9			10^2	13	11^3	12	3		7^1	14		1																18
	2		4	5	6		8			12	10		11	13			9^2	7^1		1	3															19
1	2	3	4	5	6		8^2	9^1		10		11	13		7			12																		20
1	2	3		5	6		8			9^1	10^2		11	12		7	4	13																		21
1	2		4	5	6		8				10		11	3		9					7															22
1	2^2	3^1	4^3	5	6		8				14	10	11	7		9			12		·3															23
1	14		4	5	6		8^1				9	10^3		2	13	11	12	7^2		3																24
1	2	3	4	5		7	14				9^2	13	11		10^3	8^1		12			6															25
1	2	3^1	4	5			8	13			9^2	10^3	11	12	7			6					14													26
1	2		4	5			8^2	9^1			10		11	3	7			12^6			13															27
1			4	5^1			8	9^3			14	10^2		11	3			7		12	2			13	6											28
1^6			4				8	9^1			10^2		12		6			11	2	15	13		3	7	5											29
			4				8^1	14				9^2	12					11^3	10	1	13		2	3		7	5	6								30
1			4				12	9^2				10						13	8	11^1	2		3	7		5	6									31
1			4				12	9^8				14	10					13	8^3	11^2	2^1		3	7		5	6									32
1			4	5			12	10				13	14					9^3	8	11^1			3	7^2		2	6									33
1			4	5			11^1					14	10	13				9	8^2	12			3	7^3		2	6									34
1			4	5			13					9^1	10^2	7	3			11	8^3	12				14		2	6									35
1			4	5			8	12				11^1	3		13	9		10					6	7^2	2											36
1			4				8	10				12	3		9^1			11					6	7	5	13	2^2									37
	14		4				8					11	3		12	9		10^3					6^2	7^1	5	13	2	1								38
	3^3	8					11					10	4^1		7	9	13		12					5	6	2	1	14								39
	3	4					8	10				11^1	14		9	13	$||2^2$		7^3					5	6	2	1									40
	12	4	5				8	9				10^2			3^1		7^3	11	14					13	6	2^8	1									41
	3	4	5				11	9				8			12	10^2	7^1						6^3	13		2	14	1								42
	3	4	5				11^2	9				8			7^1	10			12					13	6		2	1								43
	3^2	4	5				8	10				11^1			14	9		7^3	2					6	13		2	1								44
		4	5				8^1					13			11			7	9		0^2			14	12		2	6					1		3^3	45
		4	5									10			11			12	9						7		2^1	6				8	1	3		46

FA Cup

Third Round	QPR	(h)	1-1
		(a)	3-2
Fourth Round	Bolton W	(a)	0-2

Carling Cup

First Round	Port Vale	(h)	1-2

SHEFFIELD WEDNESDAY FL Championship 1

FOUNDATION

Sheffield being one of the principal centres of early Association Football, this club was formed as long ago as 1867 by the Sheffield Wednesday Cricket Club (formed 1825) and their colours from the start were blue and white. The inaugural meeting was held at the Adelphi Hotel and the original committee included Charles Stokes who was subsequently a founder member of Sheffield United.

Hillsborough, Sheffield S6 1SW.
Telephone: (0871) 995 1867.
Fax: (0114) 221 2122.
Ticket Office: (0871) 900 1867.
Website: www.swfc.co.uk
Email: enquiries@swfc.co.uk
Ground Capacity: 39,812.
Record Attendance: 72,841 v Manchester C, FA Cup 5th rd, 17 February 1934.
Pitch Measurements: 110yd × 71yd.
Interim Chairman: Howard Wilkinson.
Chief Executive: Nick Parker.
Operations Manager: John Rutherford
Manager: Alan Irvine.
Assistant Manager: Rob Kelly.
Physios: Paul Smith, Mark Palmer.
Colours: Blue and white striped shirts, black shorts, blue stockings.
Change Colours: Yellow shirts, blue shorts, blue stockings.
Year Formed: 1867 (fifth oldest League club).
Turned Professional: 1887.
Ltd Co.: 1899.
Former Names: The Wednesday until 1929.
Club Nickname: 'The Owls'.

HONOURS

Football League: Division 1 – Champions 1902–03, 1903–04, 1928–29, 1929–30; Runners-up 1960–61; Division 2 – Champions 1899–1900, 1925–26, 1951–52, 1955–56, 1958–59; Runners-up 1949–50, 1983–84.
FA Cup: Winners 1896, 1907, 1935; Runners-up 1890, 1966, 1993.
Football League Cup: Winners 1991; Runners-up 1993.
European Competitions: European Fairs Cup: 1961–62, 1963–64. *UEFA Cup:* 1992–93. *Intertoto Cup:* 1995.

Grounds: 1867, Highfield; 1869, Myrtle Road; 1877, Sheaf House; 1887, Olive Grove; 1899, Owlerton (since 1912 known as Hillsborough). Some games were played at Endcliffe in the 1880s. Until 1895 Bramall Lane was used for some games.
First Football League Game: 3 September 1892, Division 1, v Notts Co (a) W 1–0 – Allan; Tom Brandon (1), Mumford; Hall, Betts, Harry Brandon; Spiksley, Brady, Davis, R. N. Brown, Dunlop.
Record League Victory: 9–1 v Birmingham, Division 1, 13 December 1930 – Brown; Walker, Blenkinsop; Strange, Leach, Wilson; Hooper (3), Seed (2), Ball (2), Burgess (1), Rimmer (1).
Record Cup Victory: 12–0 v Halliwell, FA Cup 1st rd, 17 January 1891 – Smith; Thompson, Brayshaw; Harry Brandon (1), Betts, Cawley (2); Winterbottom, Mumford (2), Bob Brandon (1), Woolhouse (5),

sky SPORTS FACT FILE

Charlie Tomlinson scored the fastest goal for Sheffield Wednesday. It was on 22 October 1949 at Preston North End and it took just twelve seconds to achieve, the goal being enough to win the match. He was in his second spell at the club, the first from school in 1935.

Ingram (1).

Record Defeat: 0–10 v Aston Villa, Division 1, 5 October 1912.

Most League Points (2 for a win): 62, Division 2, 1958–59.

Most League Points (3 for a win): 88, Division 2, 1983–84.

Most League Goals: 106, Division 2, 1958–59.

Highest League Scorer in Season: Derek Dooley, 46, Division 2, 1951–52.

Most League Goals in Total Aggregate: Andrew Wilson, 199, 1900–20.

Most League Goals in One Match: 6, Doug Hunt v Norwich C, Division 2, 19 November 1938.

Most Capped Player: Nigel Worthington, 50 (66), Northern Ireland.

Most League Appearances: Andrew Wilson, 501, 1900–20.

Youngest League Player: Peter Fox, 15 years 269 days v Orient, 31 March 1973.

Record Transfer Fee Received: £2,750,000 from Blackburn R for Paul Warhurst, September 1993.

Record Transfer Fee Paid: £4,500,000 to Celtic for Paolo Di Canio, August 1997.

Football League Record: 1892 Elected to Division 1; 1899–1900 Division 2; 1900–20 Division 1; 1920–26 Division 2; 1926–37 Division 1; 1937–50 Division 2; 1950–51 Division 1; 1951–52 Division 2; 1952–55 Division 1; 1955–56 Division 2; 1956–58 Division 1; 1958–59 Division 2; 1959–70 Division 1; 1970–75 Division 2; 1975–80 Division 3; 1980–84 Division 2; 1984–90 Division 1; 1990–91 Division 2; 1991–92 Division 1; 1992–2000 FA Premier League; 2000–03 Division 1; 2003–04 Division 2; 2004–05 FL 1; 2005–10 FL C; 2010– FL 1.

LATEST SEQUENCES

Longest Sequence of League Wins: 9, 23.4.1904 – 15.10.1904.

Longest Sequence of League Defeats: 8, 9.9.2000 – 17.10.2000.

Longest Sequence of League Draws: 7, 15.3.2008 – 14.4.2008.

Longest Sequence of Unbeaten League Matches: 19, 10.12.1960 – 8.4.1961.

Longest Sequence Without a League Win: 20, 11.1.1975 – 30.8.1975.

Successive Scoring Runs: 40 from 14.11.1959.

Successive Non-scoring Runs: 8 from 8.3.1975.

MANAGERS

Arthur Dickinson 1891–1920
  (Secretary-Manager)
Robert Brown 1920–33
Billy Walker 1933–37
Jimmy McMullan 1937–42
Eric Taylor 1942–58
  (continued as General Manager to 1974)
Harry Catterick 1958–61
Vic Buckingham 1961–64
Alan Brown 1964–68
Jack Marshall 1968–69
Danny Williams 1969–71
Derek Dooley 1971–73
Steve Burtenshaw 1974–75
Len Ashurst 1975–77
Jackie Charlton 1977–83
Howard Wilkinson 1983–88
Peter Eustace 1988–89
Ron Atkinson 1989–91
Trevor Francis 1991–95
David Pleat 1995–97
Ron Atkinson 1997–98
Danny Wilson 1998–2000
Peter Shreeves (Acting) 2000
Paul Jewell 2000–01
Peter Shreeves 2001
Terry Yorath 2001–02
Chris Turner 2002–04
Paul Sturrock 2004–06
Brian Laws 2006–09
Alan Irvine January 2010–

TEN YEAR LEAGUE RECORD

		P	W	D	L	F	A	Pts	Pos
2000-01	Div 1	46	15	8	23	52	71	53	17
2001-02	Div 1	46	12	14	20	49	71	50	20
2002-03	Div 1	46	10	16	20	56	73	46	22
2003-04	Div 2	46	13	14	19	48	64	53	16
2004-05	FL 1	46	19	15	12	77	59	72	5
2005-06	FL C	46	13	13	20	39	52	52	19
2006-07	FL C	46	20	11	15	70	66	71	9
2007-08	FL C	46	14	13	19	54	55	55	16
2008-09	FL C	46	16	13	17	51	58	61	12
2009-10	FL C	46	11	14	21	49	69	47	22

DID YOU KNOW ?

Sheffield Wednesday played their first match at Olive Grove on 12 September 1887. It was a Monday. Invitations to Preston North End and Aston Villa having been turned down, Blackburn Rovers provided the opposition. Trailing three down, Wednesday drew 4–4.

SHEFFIELD WEDNESDAY 2009–10 LEAGUE RECORD

Match No.	Date	Venue	Opponents	Result		H/T Score	Lg Pos.	Goalscorers	Attendance
1	Aug 8	H	Barnsley	D	2-2	2-0	—	Johnson [9], Gray [38]	30,644
2	15	A	Peterborough U	D	1-1	1-0	12	O'Connor [21]	10,747
3	19	A	Newcastle U	L	0-1	0-1	—		43,904
4	22	H	Scunthorpe U	W	4-0	3-0	11	Wood R [6], Johnson [12], Tudgay [34], Potter [58]	20,215
5	29	A	Plymouth Arg	W	3-1	1-0	8	Wood R [33], Tudgay 2 (1 pen) [72 (p), 90]	10,228
6	Sept 12	H	Nottingham F	D	1-1	1-1	9	Tudgay [39]	25,270
7	15	H	Middlesbrough	L	1-3	1-1	—	Varney [2]	21,722
8	18	A	Sheffield U	L	2-3	0-3	—	Tudgay [46], Esajas [65]	29,210
9	26	H	Cardiff C	W	3-1	1-1	12	Esajas [4], Varney [48], Clarke [80]	18,959
10	29	A	Crystal Palace	D	0-0	0-0	—		12,476
11	Oct 3	A	Derby Co	L	0-3	0-1	16		30,116
12	17	H	Coventry C	W	2-0	2-0	13	Purse [4], Clarke (pen) [20]	20,026
13	20	H	Preston NE	L	1-2	1-1	—	Gray [38]	20,882
14	23	A	Watford	L	1-4	1-2	—	Tudgay [45]	14,591
15	31	A	Bristol C	D	1-1	0-0	14	Varney [75]	15,005
16	Nov 7	H	QPR	L	1-2	1-1	14	Johnson [13]	19,491
17	21	A	Ipswich T	D	0-0	0-0	17		19,636
18	28	H	WBA	L	0-4	0-3	19		20,824
19	Dec 5	H	Reading	L	0-2	0-0	21		22,090
20	8	A	Doncaster R	L	0-1	0-0	—		12,825
21	12	H	Leicester C	L	0-3	0-2	22		22,236
22	19	H	Swansea C	L	0-2	0-2	22		18,329
23	26	H	Newcastle U	D	2-2	1-2	22	Varney [14], O'Connor [59]	30,030
24	Jan 16	A	Barnsley	W	2-1	2-1	22	Spurr [3], Johnson [21]	17,844
25	19	A	Blackpool	W	2-1	0-0	—	Soares [71], Clarke [84]	8007
26	23	H	Peterborough U	W	2-1	1-0	8	Tudgay 2 [45, 67]	24,882
27	27	A	Scunthorpe U	L	0-2	0-1	—		7038
28	30	H	Plymouth Arg	W	2-1	2-1	19	Varney 2 [24, 42]	22,590
29	Feb 6	A	Nottingham F	L	1-2	0-1	20	Varney [73]	27,900
30	9	H	Blackpool	W	2-0	1-0	—	O'Connor [3], Potter [50]	19,058
31	16	H	Doncaster R	L	0-2	0-1	—		22,252
32	20	H	Ipswich T	L	0-1	0-1	21		21,641
33	27	A	Reading	L	0-5	0-2	22		17,573
34	Mar 6	H	Leicester C	W	2-0	1-0	22	Clarke 2 [6, 61]	21,647
35	9	A	WBA	L	0-1	0-0	—		20,458
36	13	A	Swansea C	D	0-0	0-0	21		14,167
37	16	A	Preston NE	D	2-2	0-1	—	Miller [57], Tudgay [60]	12,311
38	20	H	Derby Co	D	0-0	0-0	21		21,827
39	24	H	Watford	W	2-1	0-0	—	Nolan [56], Varney [89]	18,449
40	27	A	Coventry C	D	1-1	0-0	20	Varney [67]	17,608
41	Apr 3	A	QPR	D	1-1	0-1	20	Soares [77]	13,405
42	5	H	Bristol C	L	0-1	0-0	22		19,688
43	10	A	Middlesbrough	L	0-1	0-1	22		19,932
44	18	H	Sheffield U	D	1-1	1-0	22	Potter [41]	35,485
45	24	A	Cardiff C	L	2-3	1-1	22	Johnson [15], Tudgay [78]	23,304
46	May 2	H	Crystal Palace	D	2-2	1-1	22	Clarke [43], Purse [87]	37,121

Final League Position: 22

GOALSCORERS

League (49): Tudgay 10 (1 pen), Varney 9, Clarke 6 (1 pen), Johnson 5, O'Connor 3, Potter 3, Esajas 2, Gray 2, Purse 2, Soares 2, Wood R 2, Miller 1, Nolan 1, Spurr 1.
Carling Cup (3): Johnson 2, Esajas 1.
FA Cup (1): own goal 1.

Grant L 46	Buxton L 28	Spurr T 46	Potter D 46	Wood R 10 + 1	Purse D 39	Gray M 27 + 3	O'Connor J 44	Jeffers F 1 + 12	Tudgay M 41 + 2	Johnson J 29 + 5	Esajas E 5 + 15	Beevers M 32 + 3	McAllister S 5 + 7	Miller T 10 + 10	Hinds R 7 + 4	Varney L 32 + 7	Sodje A — + 11	Clarke L 18 + 18	Simek F 9 + 3	Soares T 17 + 8	Feeney W 1 + 1	Nolan E 14	Match No.
1	2	3	4	5	6	7	8	9¹	10	11¹²	12	13											1
1	2	3	4³	5	6	11	8		10	9²	13		7¹	12	14								2
1	2	3	4	5	6	11¹	8³	14	10	9	13		7²	12									3
1	2	3	4	5	6	11¹	8³	13	10	7¹	12		14			9³							4
1	2	3	4	5	6	11¹	8		10	7²	12	13		14		9³							5
1	2	3	4	5³	6	11	10¹	7	14	13			8²			9		12					6
1	2	3	4		6	11³	10	7	5¹	13			8²	12		9	14						7
1	2	3	4	5	6	11	8³		10	7¹	12		14			9²		13					8
1	2	3	4	5	6	11	8		10¹	14	7³					9²		13		12			9
1	2	3	4	5	6	11	8		12	14	7³					9¹		13		10²			10
1	2	3	4	5	6	11	8³		9	12	7¹		14		13					10²			11
1	2	3	4		6	7²	8			11³		5	13	14		9		12		10¹			12
1	2	3	4		6	7³	8²	14		11		5	13			9		12		10¹			13
1	2	3	4		6	7²	8¹		10	11³	13	5		12		9	14						14
1	5	3	4				8		10	11			7¹		6	9		12	2				15
1	5	3			8	12	7		10	11³		13	4²		6	9		14	2¹				16
1	5	3	4			7	8		10	11¹					6	9		12	2				17
1	5	3¹	4			7	8		10³	11²	12		6		14	9			2	13			18
1	2	3	4			7¹	8		10	12	11¹²	6	5			9³		13		14			19
1	5	3	4		6	8³			10	11²	13		7			9¹		12	2	14			20
1	5	3	4²		6	13	8		10	11¹			7		14	9³		12	2				21
1	2²	3	4		6	8		12	10	11³		5	7¹		14	9		13					22
1		3	4		6	8			10	11¹	12	5				9²		13	2	7			23
1	2	3	4		6	7	8			9	11¹		5					12		10			24
1	2	3²	4		6	7			10	9	11¹		5					13		12		8	25
1	2	3	4		6	7				11	9		5					12		10¹		8	26
1	2	3	4		6	11³	7³			9	13		5					12	14	10		8¹	27
1	2¹	3	4		6	11	7			9			5			10		13	12			8²	28
1		3	4		6	11³	7			9	13		5			10		12	2			8¹	29
1		3	4		6	7			11	9			5			10¹		12	2			8	30
1		3	4		6	7²	8			9	13		5			10		12	2	11¹			31
1		3	4			7¹		8	9	11¹²		5	13	6	10			12	2				32
1		3	4			7²	8³	9				5	14	13	6	10		12		11¹		2	33
1		3¹	4		6			8	9		7²		5			11	13	10³		12	14	2	34
1		3	4		6				11²	13		7¹	5			8	10	9		12		2	35
1		3	4		6				11	12		7	5			8		10¹		9		2	36
1		3	4		6				11	9		7¹	5			8	10²	13		12		2	37
1		3	4		6¹				11³	13		9	14	5		8	12	10²		7		2	38
1		3	4		6			14	11	13		9	5			8¹	10³	12		7²		2	39
1		3	4		6			12	11	13		9	5			8	10²			7¹		2	40
1	2	3	4²		6				11	9	12		5			10¹		13		7		8	41
1		3	4¹		6				11	12		9	5			10	8			7		2	42
1		3	4		6				11¹	13	9²	8	12	5		10				7		2	43
1		3	4		6				8	9		7	5			10	11¹	12				2	44
1		3	4		6				11	13		9	7¹	14	5	10³		12		8²		2	45
1		3	4		6				11¹²	14		9	7	13	5	10	8¹	12				2³	46

FA Cup
Third Round   Crystal Palace   (h)   1-2

Carling Cup
First Round   Rochdale   (h)   3-0
Second Round   Port Vale   (a)   0-2

SHREWSBURY TOWN   FL Championship 2

FOUNDATION

Shrewsbury School having provided a number of the early England and Wales international players it is not surprising that there was a Town club as early as 1876 which won the Birmingham Senior Cup in 1879. However, the present Shrewsbury Town club was formed in 1886 and won the Welsh FA Cup as early as 1891.

Greenhous Meadow, Oteley Road, Shrewsbury SY2 6ST.

Telephone: (01743) 289 177.

Fax: (01743) 246 972.

Ticket Office: (01743) 273 943.

Website: www.shrewsburytown.com

Email: ian@shrewsburytown.co.uk

Ground Capacity: 10,000.

Record Attendance: 18,917 v Walsall, Division 3, 26 April 1961 (Gay Meadow); 8,429 v Bury, FL 2 Play-off semi-final, 7 May 2009 (ProStar Stadium).

Pitch Measurements: 114yd × 73yd.

Chairman: Roland Wycherley.

Vice-chairman: Keith Sayfritz.

Secretary/General Manager: Jonathan Harris.

Manager: Graham Turner.

First Team Coach: John Trewick.

Physio: Nathan Ring.

Colours: All blue with yellow and red design.

Change Colours: All black with red and white design on shirts.

Year Formed: 1886.

Turned Professional: 1896.

Ltd Co.: 1936.

Club Nickname: 'Town', 'Blues' or 'Salop'. The name 'Salop' is a colloquialism for the county of Shropshire. Since Shrewsbury is the only club in Shropshire, cries of 'Come on Salop' are frequently used!

Grounds: 1886, Old Racecourse Ground; 1889, Ambler's Field; 1893, Sutton Lane; 1895, Barracks Ground; 1910, Gay Meadow; 2007, New Meadow.

First Football League Game: 19 August 1950, Division 3 (N), v Scunthorpe U (a) D 0–0 – Egglestone; Fisher, Lewis; Wheatley, Depear, Robinson; Griffin, Hope, Jackson, Brown, Barker.

Record League Victory: 7–0 v Swindon T, Division 3 (S), 6 May 1955 – McBride; Bannister, Skeech; Wallace, Maloney, Candlin; Price, O'Donnell (1), Weigh (4), Russell, McCue (2); 7–0 v Gillingham, FL 2, 13 September 2008 – Daniels; Herd, Tierney, Davies (2), Jackson (1) (Langmead), Coughlan (1), Cansdell-Sherriff (1), Thornton, Hibbert (1) (Hindmarch), Holt (pen), McIntyre (Ashton).

HONOURS

Football League: Division 2 best season: 8th, 1983–84, 1984–85; Division 3 – Champions 1978–79, 1993–94; Division 4 – Runners-up 1974–75.

FA Cup: best season: 6th rd, 1979, 1982.

Football League Cup: Semi-final 1961.

Welsh Cup: Winners 1891, 1938, 1977, 1979, 1984, 1985; Runners-up 1931, 1948, 1980.

Auto Windscreens Shield: Runners-up 1996.

sky SPORTS FACT FILE

In 1935–36 Shrewsbury Town signed Bill Hewitson from Oldham Athletic. Despite missing a few matches with injury he amassed 71 League and Cup goals for the club including a six, four fours and six hat-tricks. He was lost to the club in the summer when York City signed him.

Record Cup Victory: 11–2 v Marine, FA Cup 1st rd, 11 November 1995 – Edwards, Seabury (Dempsey (1)), Withe (1), Evans (1), Whiston (2), Scott (1), Woods, Stevens (1), Spink (3) (Anthrobus), Walton, Berkley, (1 og).

Record Defeat: 1–8 v Norwich C, Division 3 (S), 13 September 1952; 1–8 v Coventry C, Division 3, 22 October 1963.

Most League Points (2 for a win): 62, Division 4, 1974–75.

Most League Points (3 for a win): 79, Division 3, 1993–94.

Most League Goals: 101, Division 4, 1958–59.

Highest League Scorer in Season: Arthur Rowley, 38, Division 4, 1958–59.

Most League Goals in Total Aggregate: Arthur Rowley, 152, 1958–65 (thus completing his League record of 434 goals).

Most League Goals in One Match: 5, Alf Wood v Blackburn R, Division 3, 2 October 1971.

Most Capped Player: Jimmy McLaughlin, 5 (12), Northern Ireland; Bernard McNally, 5, Northern Ireland.

Most League Appearances: Mickey Brown, 418, 1986–91; 1992–94; 1996–2001.

Youngest League Player: Graham French, 16 years 177 days v Reading, 30 September 1961.

Record Transfer Fee Received: £600,000 from Manchester C for Joe Hart, May 2006.

Record Transfer Fee Paid: £170,000 to Nottingham F for Grant Holt, June 2008.

Football League Record: 1950 Elected to Division 3 (N); 1951–58 Division 3 (S); 1958–59 Division 4; 1959–74 Division 3; 1974–75 Division 4; 1975–79 Division 3; 1979–89 Division 2; 1989–94 Division 3; 1994–97 Division 2; 1997–2003 Division 3; 2003–04 Conference; 2004– FL 2.

MANAGERS

W. Adams 1905–12
  (Secretary-Manager)
A. Weston 1912–34
  (Secretary-Manager)
Jack Roscamp 1934–35
Sam Ramsey 1935–36
Ted Bousted 1936–40
Leslie Knighton 1945–49
Harry Chapman 1949–50
Sammy Crooks 1950–54
Walter Rowley 1955–57
Harry Potts 1957–58
Johnny Spuhler 1958
Arthur Rowley 1958–68
Harry Gregg 1968–72
Maurice Evans 1972–73
Alan Durban 1974–78
Richie Barker 1978
Graham Turner 1978–84
Chic Bates 1984–87
Ian McNeill 1987–90
Asa Hartford 1990–91
John Bond 1991–93
Fred Davies 1994–97
  (previously Caretaker-Manager 1993–94)
Jake King 1997–99
Kevin Ratcliffe 1999–2003
Jimmy Quinn 2003–04
Gary Peters 2004–08
Paul Simpson 2008–10
Graham Turner June 2010–

LATEST SEQUENCES

Longest Sequence of League Wins: 7, 28.10.1995 – 16.12.1995.

Longest Sequence of League Defeats: 11, 9.4.2003 – 14.8.2004.

Longest Sequence of League Draws: 6, 30.10.1963 – 14.12.1963.

Longest Sequence of Unbeaten League Matches: 16, 30.10.1993 – 26.2.1994.

Longest Sequence Without a League Win: 18, 8.3.2003 – 14.8.2004.

Successive Scoring Runs: 28 from 7.9.1960.

Successive Non-scoring Runs: 6 from 1.1.1991.

TEN YEAR LEAGUE RECORD

		P	W	D	L	F	A	Pts	Pos
2000-01	Div 3	46	15	10	21	49	65	55	15
2001-02	Div 3	46	20	10	16	64	53	70	9
2002-03	Div 3	46	9	14	23	62	92	41	24
2003-04	Conf.	42	20	14	8	67	42	74	3
2004-05	FL 2	46	11	16	19	48	53	49	21
2005-06	FL 2	46	16	13	17	55	55	61	10
2006-07	FL 2	46	18	17	11	68	46	71	7
2007-08	FL 2	46	12	14	20	56	65	50	18
2008-09	FL 2	46	17	18	11	61	44	69	7
2009-10	FL 2	46	17	12	17	55	54	63	12

DID YOU KNOW ?

In 1936–37, just one season on from the Hewitson experience, enter Ernie Breeze, a full-back from Port Vale. A skipper and penalty expert, he was tried out at centre-forward against Bangor and in an 11–1 win he rattled in six goals including one from another spot kick.

SHREWSBURY TOWN 2009–10 LEAGUE RECORD

Match No.	Date	Venue	Opponents	Result	H/T Score	Lg Pos.	Goalscorers	Attendance
1	Aug 8	H	Burton Alb	W 3-1	1-0	—	Robinson [10], Hibbert [49], Labadie [83]	6438
2	15	A	Barnet	D 2-2	1-2	4	Elder [2], Hibbert [57]	1835
3	18	A	Dagenham & R	L 0-5	0-4	—		1683
4	22	H	Chesterfield	D 1-1	1-0	17	Leslie [31]	5086
5	29	A	Accrington S	W 3-1	1-0	11	Leslie (pen) [18], Langmead [50], Hibbert [82]	1447
6	Sept 5	H	Bradford C	L 1-2	0-2	14	Hibbert [70]	5525
7	12	H	Crewe Alex	W 2-0	1-0	11	Hibbert [29], Labadie [69]	6204
8	19	A	Lincoln C	W 2-0	1-0	7	Robinson [29], Hibbert (pen) [76]	3234
9	26	H	Northampton T	W 3-0	1-0	6	Robinson [22], Labadie [50], Langmead [54]	5548
10	29	A	Cheltenham T	W 2-1	0-0	—	Hibbert [72], Labadie [74]	2928
11	Oct 3	A	Morecambe	D 1-1	1-1	5	Labadie [8]	2105
12	10	H	Port Vale	L 0-1	0-1	8		7096
13	17	A	Darlington	L 1-2	1-1	7	Neal L [2]	1958
14	24	H	Aldershot T	W 3-1	2-1	7	Fairhurst [32], Neal L [45], Elder [60]	5417
15	31	A	Notts Co	D 1-1	1-0	7	Devitt [30]	7562
16	Nov 14	H	Torquay U	D 1-1	0-0	7	Hibbert [81]	5072
17	21	H	Bury	D 1-1	0-1	7	Coughlan [90]	5070
18	24	A	Hereford U	L 1-2	1-2	—	Fairhurst [45]	2913
19	Dec 1	H	Rotherham U	W 2-0	1-0	—	Fairhurst [43], Devitt [88]	4522
20	5	A	Bournemouth	L 0-1	0-0	9		4652
21	12	H	Grimsby T	D 0-0	0-0	10		4850
22	19	A	Rochdale	L 0-4	0-2	—		2596
23	26	H	Macclesfield T	D 2-2	1-2	10	Fairhurst [44], Hibbert [90]	5942
24	28	A	Bradford C	W 3-1	2-1	8	Dunfield [11], McIntyre (pen) [45], Hibbert [79]	11,522
25	Jan 2	A	Chesterfield	W 1-0	1-0	—	Hibbert [38]	3601
26	16	A	Burton Alb	D 1-1	1-0	—	Hibbert [27]	3139
27	23	H	Dagenham & R	W 2-1	2-1	5	Hibbert [13], Leslie [45]	4812
28	30	H	Accrington S	L 0-1	0-1	6		5319
29	Feb 6	A	Macclesfield T	W 1-0	0-0	6	Leslie [54]	2058
30	9	H	Barnet	W 2-0	2-0	—	Disley [12], Leslie [28]	4328
31	13	H	Hereford U	W 3-1	2-1	5	Langmead [15], Cansdell-Sherriff [24], Coughlan [79]	6098
32	19	A	Bury	L 0-1	0-0	—		3720
33	22	A	Rotherham U	D 1-1	1-1	—	Leslie [45]	2869
34	27	H	Bournemouth	W 1-0	0-0	6	Dunfield [49]	6061
35	Mar 6	A	Grimsby T	L 0-3	0-1	7		3651
36	13	H	Rochdale	L 0-1	0-0	8		6081
37	20	A	Aldershot T	L 0-2	0-1	9		2681
38	27	H	Darlington	L 0-2	0-1	11		5081
39	Apr 3	A	Torquay U	L 1-2	1-0	12	Bevan (og) [29]	3094
40	5	H	Notts Co	L 0-1	0-1	12		6287
41	10	A	Crewe Alex	W 3-0	1-0	12	Hibbert [30], Bradshaw 2 [86, 90]	4283
42	13	H	Cheltenham T	D 0-0	0-0	—		4967
43	17	A	Lincoln C	W 1-0	0-0	12	Bright [83]	4932
44	24	A	Northampton T	L 0-2	0-0	14	.	5019
45	May 1	H	Morecambe	L 2-3	1-2	12	Van den Broek [33], Bradshaw [48]	5340
46	8	A	Port Vale	D 1-1	1-0	12	Bright [11]	8467

Final League Position: 12

GOALSCORERS

League (55): Hibbert 14 (1 pen), Leslie 6 (1 pen), Labadie 5, Fairhurst 4, Bradshaw 3, Langmead 3, Robinson 3, Bright 2, Coughlan 2, Devitt 2, Dunfield 2, Elder 2, Neal L 2, Cansdell-Sherriff 1, Disley 1, McIntyre 1 (pen), Van den Broek 1, own goal 1.
Carling Cup (3): Cansdell-Sherriff 1, Hibbert 1, Robinson 1.
FA Cup (0).
J Paint Trophy (0).

Neal C 7	Holden D 37	McIntyre K 43+2	Murray P 25+2	Coughlan G 36	Langmead K 44	Disley C 16+2	Labadie J 11+2	Hibbert D 37+1	Elder N 9+10	Robinson J 15+19	Riza O 1+7	Simpson J 14+4	Gray A —+4	Cansdell-Sherriff S 41	Bright K 4+22	Leslie S 21+13	Dunfield T 28+2	Phillips S 11	Neal L 21+8	Hooman H 1+1	Devitt J 8+1	Fairhurst W 10	Arestidou A 2	Button D 26	Taylor J —+2	Taylor D 2+1	Skarz J 20	Cureton J 10+2	Van den Broek B 5+6	Bradshaw T 1+5	Match No.
1	2	3	4	5	6	7	8	9[2]	10[3]	11[1]	12	13	14																		1
1	2	3	8[1]	5	6	4	12	9[3]	10[2]	7			14		11	13															2
1	2	3		5[1]	4	8		9	10[3]	7	12[2]		13		11		14														3
1	2	13	7	5	6	4	8[2]	9	10[1]	12				3[1]		11	14														4
	2	13	7	5	6	4[1]	8	9[3]	10[2]	12				3		14	11[1]					1									5
	2		7	5	6		8	9	10[2]	13	12		4[3]	3	14	11[1]						1									6
	2	11	7[2]	5	6		8	9[3]	13	10[3]			4[1]	3	12	14						1									7
	2	11	7	5	6		8	9[3]	14	10[1]			4[2]	3	12							1								13	8
	2[2]	11	7[1]	5	6		8	9		10[3]			4	3	14							1								12	9
	2	11	7	5	6		8	9[3]	13	10[2]			4[1]	3	14							1								12	10
	2	11	7	5	6		8[8]	9	14	10[2]			4[1]	3	13							1								12	11
	2	11	7	5[4]	6			9[3]	13	10[2]	8[1]			3	14	12						1							4		12
	2	11	4[3]		6	8		12		10[1]		13		3	9[2]	14			1					7	5						13
	2	11	4	5	6			10	12				14	3		13			1	7[2]				8[2]	9[1]						14
	2	11	4	5	6	13		9[3]	14	12				3					1	7				8[2]	10[1]						15
1	2	11	7	5	6			9		12				3	13	8			4[1]	10[2]											16
	2	11	4	5	6			9[2]	14	13	12			3		8	7[1]			10[3]			1								17
	2	11	8	5	6			9[2]	14	12	13			3		7			4[1]	10[3]			1								18
	2	11	8[2]	5	6			9[1]	12	13				3		14	7		4	10[3]				1							19
	2	11	8	5	6			9[1]		13				3	12	7			4	10[2]				1							20
	2	3	11[1]	5	6	12		10[2]	13				14	8	7				4	9[3]				1							21
	2	11		5	6	8		13		14	10[2]			3		7			12	4[1]	9[3]			1							22
	2	11	8[2]	5	6	7		9		12				3		4			13	10[1]				1							23
	2	11		5	6	7		9						3	8	10			4					1							24
	2[8]	11		5	6	8		9[2]						3	13	10	7		4[1]					1		12					25
		3	12	5[1]	6	8		9		2		13			10[2]	7			4					1	[1]1						26
	2[1]	11			6	8[2]		9	10				5		13	7			4					1			3	12			27
		11			6	8[1]		9	10[3]	2		13	12		7				4[2]					1	14	5	3				28
		11		5	10	8[2]		9	12	2		13	7	6					4[1]					1			3				29
		11		5	10	8		9[2]	12	2		13	7	6					4[1]					1			3				30
		11		5	10	8[1]		9	12	2			7	6					4					1			3				31
		11		5	10	8		9[3]	13	2		14	7	6[1]					4[2]					1			3	12			32
		11	4[1]	5	6	12[2]		9[3]	8	2		14	7	13										1			3	10			33
	2	11		5	6			9	12					8[1]	7				4					1			3	10			34
		11	2	5	6			9	12					7[1]	8				4					1			3	10[2]	13		35
		11		5	6			9	14	2[8]		12	13	7					4[1]					1			3	10[3]	8[2]		36
	2	11	8	5	6			12						9[3]	7[2]	4			13					1			3	14	10[1]		37
	2	11	8[1]		6			9	7					5	12	4			13					1			3	10[2]			38
	2	11	10			8		12	7[2]					5	14	6	4[3]							1			3	9[1]	13		39
	2	11	12	5				9[3]		8				6	14	7[1]	4							1			3	10[3]	13		40
	2	11	5[1]					9		8[3]				6	12	7	4							1			3	10[2]	14	13	41
	2	11	6					9[3]		8[2]				5	13	7	4[1]							1			3	10	12	14	42
	2	11	6					9[3]		4				5	14	8	7[2]							1			3	10[1]	13	12	43
	2	11	10					9		4[1]				5	13	8	7							1			3[2]		6	12	44
1	2	11	6					13	10[1]					5	9	8	7										3		4[2]	12	45
1	2	11	6											5	9	8	7										3		4	10	46

FA Cup
First Round   Staines T   (h)   0-1

Carling Cup
First Round   Ipswich T   (h)   3-3

J Paint Trophy
Second Round   Accrington S   (a)   0-2

SOUTHAMPTON   FL Championship 1

FOUNDATION

The club was formed by members of the St Mary's Church of England Young Men's Association at a meeting of the Y.M.A. in November 1885 and it was named as such. For the sake of brevity this was usually shortened to St Mary's Y.M.A. The rector Canon Albert Basil Orme Wilberforce was elected president. The name was changed to plain St Mary's during 1887–88 and did not become Southampton St Mary's until 1894, the inaugural season in the Southern League.

St Mary's Stadium, Britannia Road, Southampton SO14 5FP.

Telephone: (0845) 688 9448.

Fax: (0845) 688 9445

Ticket Office: (0845) 688 9288.

Website: www.saintsfc.co.uk

Email: sfc@saintsfc.co.uk

Ground Capacity: 32,689.

Record Attendance: 32,104 v Liverpool, FA Premier League, 18 January 2003.

Pitch Measurements: 112yd × 72yd.

Chairman: Nicola Cortese.

Football Secretary: Ros Wheeler.

Manager: Alan Pardew.

Assistant Manager: Dean Wilkins.

Physio: Mo Gimpel.

Colours: White shirts with diagonal red stripe, white shorts, black stockings.

Change Colours: Dark blue shirts, yellow shorts, yellow stockings.

HONOURS

Football League: Division 1 – Runners-up 1983–84; Division 2 – Runners-up 1965–66, 1977–78; Division 3 (S) – Champions 1921–22; Division 3 – Champions 1959–60: Runners-up 1920–21.

FA Cup: Winners 1976; Runners-up 1900, 1902, 2003.

Football League Cup: Runners-up 1979.

Zenith Data Systems Cup: Runners-up 1992.

Johnstone's Paint Trophy: Winners 2009–10.

European Competitions: European Fairs Cup: 1969–70. UEFA Cup: 1971–72, 1981–82, 1982–83, 1984–85, 2003–04. European Cup-Winners' Cup: 1976–77.

Year Formed: 1885. *Turned Professional:* 1894. *Ltd Co.:* 1897.

Previous Name: 1885, St Mary's Young Men's Association; 1887–88, St Mary's; 1894–95 Southampton St Mary's; 1897, Southampton.

Club Nickname: 'The Saints'.

Grounds: 1885, 'The Common' (from 1887 also used the County Cricket Ground and Antelope Cricket Ground); 1889, Antelope Cricket Ground; 1896 The County Cricket Ground; 1898, The Dell; 2001, St Mary's.

First Football League Game: 28 August 1920, Division 3, v Gillingham (a) D 1–1 – Allen; Parker, Titmuss; Shelley, Campbell, Turner; Barratt, Dominy (1), Rawlings, Moore, Foxall.

Record League Victory: 9–3 v Wolverhampton W, Division 2, 18 September 1965 – Godfrey; Jones, Williams; Walker, Knapp, Huxford; Paine (2), O'Brien (1), Melia, Chivers (4), Sydenham (2).

sky SPORTS FACT FILE

Perhaps their geographical proximity to the continent was a contributory factor in Southampton transferring three players to French clubs in the early 1930s. Inside-left Peter Dougal and half-backs George Harkus and Harold Rivers made the trip.

Record Cup Victory: 7–1 v Ipswich T, FA Cup 3rd rd, 7 January 1961 – Reynolds; Davies, Traynor, Conner, Page, Huxford, Paine (1), O'Brien (3 incl. 1p), Reeves, Mulgrew (2), Penk (1).

Record Defeat: 0–8 v Tottenham H, Division 2, 28 March 1936; 0–8 v Everton, Division 1, 20 November 1971.

Most League Points (2 for a win): 61, Division 3 (S), 1921–22 and Division 3, 1959–60.

Most League Points (3 for a win): 77, Division 1, 1983–84.

Most League Goals: 112, Division 3 (S), 1957–58.

Highest League Scorer in Season: Derek Reeves, 39, Division 3, 1959–60.

Most League Goals in Total Aggregate: Mike Channon, 185, 1966–77, 1979–82.

Most League Goals in One Match: 5, Charlie Wayman v Leicester C, Division 2, 23 October 1948.

Most Capped Player: Peter Shilton, 49 (125), England.

Most League Appearances: Terry Paine, 713, 1956–74.

Youngest League Player: Theo Walcott, 16 years 143 days v Wolverhampton W, 6 August 2005.

Record Transfer Fee Received: Up to £10,000,000 from Arsenal for Theo Walcott, January 2006.

Record Transfer Fee Paid: £4,000,000 to Derby Co for Rory Delap, July 2001.

Football League Record: 1920 Original Member of Division 3; 1921–22 Division 3 (S); 1922–53 Division 2; 1953–58 Division 3 (S); 1958–60 Division 3; 1960–66 Division 2; 1966–74 Division 1; 1974–78 Division 2; 1978–92 Division 1; 1992–2005 FA Premier League; 2005–09 FL C; 2009– FL 1.

LATEST SEQUENCES

Longest Sequence of League Wins: 6, 3.3.1992 – 4.4.1992.

Longest Sequence of League Defeats: 5, 16.8.1998 – 12.9.1998.

Longest Sequence of League Draws: 8, 29.8.2005 – 15.10.2005.

Longest Sequence of Unbeaten League Matches: 19, 5.9.1921 – 31.12.1921.

Longest Sequence Without a League Win: 20, 30.8.1969 – 27.12.1969.

Successive Scoring Runs: 28 from 10.2.2008.

Successive Non-scoring Runs: 5 from 1.9.1937.

MANAGERS

Cecil Knight 1894–95
(Secretary-Manager)
Charles Robson 1895–97
Er Arnfield 1897–1911
(Secretary-Manager)
(continued as Secretary)
George Swift 1911–12
Er Arnfield 1912–19
Jimmy McIntyre 1919–24
Arthur Chadwick 1925–31
George Kay 1931–36
George Gross 1936–37
Tom Parker 1937–43
J. R. Sarjantson stepped down
from the board to act as
Secretary-Manager 1943–47
with the next two listed being
team Managers during this
period
Arthur Dominy 1943–46
Bill Dodgin Snr 1946–49
Sid Cann 1949–51
George Roughton 1952–55
Ted Bates 1955–73
Lawrie McMenemy 1973–85
Chris Nicholl 1985–91
Ian Branfoot 1991–94
Alan Ball 1994–95
Dave Merrington 1995–96
Graeme Souness 1996–97
Dave Jones 1997–2000
Glenn Hoddle 2000–01
Stuart Gray 2001
Gordon Strachan 2001–04
Paul Sturrock 2004
Steve Wigley 2004
Harry Redknapp 2004–05
George Burley 2005–08
Nigel Pearson 2008
Jan Poortvliet 2008–09
Mark Wotte 2009
Alan Pardew July 2009–

TEN YEAR LEAGUE RECORD

		P	W	D	L	F	A	Pts	Pos
2000-01	PR Lge	38	14	10	14	40	48	52	10
2001-02	PR Lge	38	12	9	17	46	54	45	11
2002-03	PR Lge	38	13	13	12	43	46	52	8
2003-04	PR Lge	38	12	11	15	44	45	47	12
2004-05	PR Lge	38	6	14	18	45	66	32	20
2005-06	FL C	46	13	19	14	49	50	58	12
2006-07	FL C	46	21	12	13	77	53	75	6
2007-08	FL C	46	13	15	18	56	72	54	20
2008-09	FL C	46	10	15	21	46	69	45	23
2009-10	FL 1	46	23	14	9	85	47	73*	7

*10 pts deducted.

DID YOU KNOW

On 25 August 1945 the Football League South match between Southampton and Plymouth Argyle ended in a 5–5 draw. Two of the Saints goals were scored from centre-forward by a certain Alf Ramsey!

SOUTHAMPTON 2009–10 LEAGUE RECORD

Match No.	Date	Venue	Opponents	Result	H/T Score	Lg Pos.	Goalscorers	Attendance
1	Aug 8	H	Millwall	D	1-1	0-0	—	Paterson [51]	20,103
2	15	A	Huddersfield T	L	1-3	0-0	24	Lambert [53]	12,449
3	18	A	Swindon T	L	0-1	0-1	—		11,673
4	22	H	Brentford	D	0-0	0-0	24	Harding [73]	19,169
5	29	A	Stockport Co	D	1-1	1-0	24	Lambert (pen) [45]	4680
6	Sept 5	H	Colchester U	D	0-0	0-0	24		17,070
7	12	A	Charlton Ath	D	1-1	1-0	24	Lallana [42]	19,441
8	19	H	Yeovil T	W	2-0	1-0	24	Lambert 2 (2 pens) [19, 52]	19,907
9	26	A	Carlisle U	D	1-1	0-0	24	Jaidi [90]	7000
10	29	H	Bristol R	L	2-3	1-1	—	Lallana [34], Lambert [46]	19,724
11	Oct 3	H	Gillingham	W	4-1	3-1	24	Lambert [13], Papa Waigo [35], Lallana 2 [46, 74]	19,457
12	9	A	Southend U	W	3-1	3-1	—	Trotman [6], Lallana 2 [32, 45]	8281
13	17	A	Oldham Ath	W	3-1	2-0	23	Hammond [12], Lambert [23], Connolly [82]	5341
14	24	H	Milton Keynes D	W	3-1	0-1	22	Hammond [56], Lambert [74], Connolly [90]	21,387
15	31	A	Leyton Orient	D	2-2	0-1	22	Lambert 2 [74, 84]	7544
16	Nov 15	H	Brighton & HA	L	1-3	1-2	22	Lambert (pen) [44]	21,932
17	21	H	Norwich C	D	2-2	1-0	22	Lallana [11], Connolly [65]	21,362
18	24	A	Hartlepool U	W	3-1	1-1	—	Lallana 2 [29, 53], Lambert [82]	3818
19	Dec 1	H	Wycombe W	W	1-0	1-0	—	Lambert [41]	16,402
20	5	A	Walsall	W	3-1	2-0	15	Connolly [32], Hammond [38], Lambert [65]	5681
21	12	H	Tranmere R	W	3-0	0-0	14	Harding [51], Lambert 2 (1 pen) [64 (p), 70]	19,800
22	19	A	Leeds U	L	0-1	0-0	15		25,948
23	26	H	Exeter C	W	3-1	2-0	12	James [14], Trotman [38], Papa Waigo [88]	30,890
24	28	A	Colchester U	L	1-2	0-1	13	Lambert (pen) [90]	8514
25	Jan 16	A	Millwall	D	1-1	0-0	13	Lambert [89]	11,524
26	26	A	Brentford	D	1-1	1-0	—	James [4]	6501
27	30	H	Stockport Co	W	2-0	0-0	11	Lambert [63], Papa Waigo [69]	18,308
28	Feb 6	A	Exeter C	D	1-1	1-0	12	Lallana [37]	7654
29	20	A	Norwich C	W	2-0	1-0	12	Barnard 2 [33, 77]	23,103
30	23	A	Wycombe W	D	0-0	0-0	—		6232
31	27	H	Walsall	W	5-1	3-1	11	Puncheon [8], Barnard 2 [33, 36], Lambert [61], Lallana [89]	20,461
32	Mar 2	H	Huddersfield T	W	5-0	3-0	—	Lambert [16], Barnard [24], Puncheon [34], Hammond [76], Papa Waigo [84]	19,821
33	6	A	Tranmere R	L	1-2	1-1	10	Barnard [12]	6187
34	13	H	Leeds U	W	1-0	1-0	10	Harding [25]	30,794
35	16	H	Swindon T	L	0-1	0-0	—		20,752
36	20	A	Milton Keynes D	W	3-0	0-0	10	Lambert 3 (1 pen) [48, 69 (p), 76]	10,570
37	23	H	Hartlepool U	W	3-2	2-1	—	Barnard [13], Lambert [38], Papa Waigo [56]	18,072
38	Apr 1	A	Brighton & HA	D	2-2	1-1	—	Hammond [41], Barnard [89]	7784
39	5	A	Leyton Orient	W	2-1	1-1	9	Lallana 2 [41, 54]	21,559
40	10	H	Charlton Ath	W	1-0	1-0	9	Antonio [34]	23,061
41	13	A	Bristol R	W	5-1	2-1	—	Lambert 2 [43, 45], Schneiderlin [53], Lallana [73], Puncheon [75]	8607
42	17	A	Yeovil T	W	1-0	0-0	8	Barnard [90]	7484
43	20	H	Oldham Ath	D	0-0	0-0	—		18,366
44	24	H	Carlisle U	W	3-2	1-1	7	Antonio 2 [46, 52], Lambert [46]	18,908
45	May 1	A	Gillingham	L	1-2	0-1	7	Connolly [65]	9504
46	8	H	Southend U	W	3-1	0-0	7	Lambert 2 (1 pen) [58, 85 (p)], Lallana [90]	25,289

Final League Position: 7

GOALSCORERS

League (85): Lambert 30 (8 pens), Lallana 15, Barnard 9, Connolly 5, Hammond 5, Papa Waigo 5, Antonio 3, Harding 3, Puncheon 3, James 2, Trotman 2, Jaidi 1, Paterson 1, Schneiderlin 1.
Carling Cup (3): Lallana 2, Lambert 1.
FA Cup (10): Antonio 2, Connolly 2, Lambert 2, Hammond 1, Lallana 1, Papa Waigo 1, Thomas 1.
J Paint Trophy (14): Papa Waigo 4, Lambert 3 (1 pen), Antonio 2, Lallana 2, Harding 1, Thomas 1, own goal 1.

Davis K 40	Murty G 5 + 1	Harding D 42	Wotton P 12 + 14	Perry C 11 + 1	Thomas W 10 + 5	Schneiderlin M 35 + 2	Paterson M 4 + 3	Saganowski M 3 + 3	James L 28 + 2	Thomson J — + 4	Gillett S — + 2	Gobern O — + 4	Lambert R 44 + 1	Rasiak G 1 + 2	Mellis J 7 + 5	Lancashire O 1 + 1	Hammond D 40	Trotman N 17 + 1	Mills J 8 + 8	Jaidi R 26 + 1	Papa Waigo N 11 + 24	Holmes L 2 + 3	Antonio M 14 + 14	Connolly D 9 + 11	Bialkowski B 6 + 1	Otsemobor J 19	Seaborne D 11 + 5	Fonte J 21	Barnard L 14 + 6	Puncheon J 19	Oxlade-Chamberlain A — + 2	McNish C — + 1	Martin A 2	Match No.
1	2	3	4	5	6	7	8^1	9^3	10	11^2	12	13	14																					1
1	2	3	4	5^3	6	7	8^2		11^1	12			9	10	13	14																		2
1		3	4^1		6	7	8	10^2	12	2		13	9^3	14	11	5^3																		3
1		3		5		7	8	10^2	12	2	13		9^3	14	11^1		4	6																4
1		3		5	8	7		12	10^1	2			9		11		4	6																5
1		3	5^3	8	7	14	10^2		2	13			9		11^1		4	6	12															6
1		3	5^1	8	7^3	10			2				9		13		4	6	11^2	12	14													7
1		3	14	8^3	7	11^1		10^2	2				9				4	6	8^1	5	12	13												8
1		3		7	11				2				9		10^2		4	6	8^1	5	12	13												9
1		3	14	7	11^3		13		2				9		10^1		4	6	12	5	8^2													10
1		3	11		7^1	14			2	12			9^3		10		4	6		5	8^2	13													11
1		3	11^2	13	7	8^3			2				9				4	6	14	5	10^1		12											12
1		3	4		7^3	8^2			2				9				11	6	14	5	10^1		12	13										13
1		3	4^1		7^3	8			2				9				11	6	14	5	10^2		12	13										14
1		3	4^1		10	8			2				9				11	6		5	7^2		13	12										15
1		3^3		12	7	8			2				9				4	6^1	14	5	13		11^2	10										16
1^6	2	3			7^3	8			2				9^2	14			4	6		5	13		11^1	10										17
1	2	3	13		7	8^1			2				9				11	6		5			12	10^1	15									18
	2	3	13	6		7	8^3		4^2				9		14		11			5	10^1		12		1									19
	2	3	13	6		7	8^2	14	4				9^3				11			5			12	10^1	1									20
		3	12	6		8	2^1		7				9^3	14			4			5	13		11	10^2	1									21
		3		6	4^2	7			2		13	9	9				8	14		5	11^1		12	10^3	1									22
		3	13	5		7^1	8		2				9				4	6	12^2		14		11	10^3	1									23
		3		6	10	8^1			2		14	9					7	4^3		5	13		11^2	12	1									24
1		3	12		10^3	8			7^2				9				11^1			14	4	13				2	5	6						25
1		4			7	12			8^1				9					3		14	13	11^3				2	5	6	10^2					26
1		4			8								9					3		12	7	11				2	5	6	10^1					27
1			13	7	8				4^2				9					3		10^1		12				2^3	5	6	14	11				28
1		3			7	8^1							9				4			5		12				2		6	10	11				29
1		3	12		14	8^3							9				4			5	13		7^1			2		6	10^1	11				30
1		3		13	7	8							9^3				4			5^2	12		14			2		6	10^1	11				31
1		3			7	8							9^3				4			5^2	12					2	13	6	10^3	11	14			32
1		3^1			7^2	8							9				4			5	13		14			2	12	6	10^3	11				33
1		3		12	7	8							9				4			5	13					2^1		6	10^1	11				34
1		3		5^2	7	8			13				9				4^3			2	12		14					6	10^1	11				35
1		3	14		7	8^3							9^1				4	2		12			13			5	6	10^2	11				36
1		3	12			8^1							9^2				4	2		7			13			5	6	10	11				37
1		3	8^3		10								9				4			5^1	13		7^2			2	12	6	14	11				38
1		3	14			8^3							9				4			5^1		13				2	12	6	10^2	11				39
1		3	13		10	8							9^2				4						7^1			2	5	6	12	11				40
1		3			10	8							9^2				4				12		7^3	14		2	5	6	13	11^1				41
1		3	8^1		10	8^4							9				4^3				14		7^1	13		2^2	5	6	12	11				42
1		3	8^1		7				12^2				9				4				14		13			2	5	6	10^1	11				43
1		3			10								9^3				4				8		7^1	13		2	5	6	14	11^2	12			44
1					8^2				3				12				4		5		14		9			2	13	6^1	10^3	11		7		45
1		3	13		10								9				4			5	12		7^1	8^2		2			11^3	14		6		46

FA Cup

First Round	Bristol R	(a)	3-2
Second Round	Northampton T	(a)	3-2
Third Round	Luton T	(h)	1-0
Fourth Round	Ipswich T	(h)	2-1
Fifth Round	Portsmouth	(h)	1-4

Carling Cup

First Round	Northampton T	(h)	2-0
Second Round	Birmingham C	(h)	1-2

J Paint Trophy

Second Round	Torquay U	(h)	2-2
Southern Quarter-Final	Charlton Ath	(h)	2-1
Southern Semi-Final	Norwich C	(h)	2-2
		(a)	1-0
Southern Final	Milton Keynes D	(h)	3-1
Final	Carlisle U	(a)	4-1
(at Wembley).			

SOUTHEND UNITED   FL Championship 2

FOUNDATION

The leading club in Southend around the turn of the century was Southend Athletic, but they were an amateur concern. Southend United was a more ambitious professional club when they were founded in 1906, employing Bob Jack as secretary-manager and immediately joining the Second Division of the Southern League.

Roots Hall Stadium, Victoria Avenue, Southend-on-Sea, Essex SS2 6NQ.

Telephone: (01702) 304 050.

Fax: (01702) 304 124.

Ticket Office: (08444) 770 077.

Website: www.southendunited.co.uk

Email: info@southend-united.co.uk

Ground Capacity: 12,260.

Record Attendance: 31,090 v Liverpool, FA Cup 3rd rd, 10 January 1979.

Pitch Measurements: 110yd × 76yd.

Chairman: Ronald Martin.

Chief Executive: Geoffrey King.

Secretary: Mrs Helen Norbury.

Manager: Paul Sturrock.

Assistant Manager: Tommy Widdrington.

Physio: John Stannard.

Club Nickname: 'The Blues' or 'The Shrimpers'.

Colours: Navy blue shirts with white collar, navy blue shorts, white stockings.

Change Colours: Maroon shirts with white trim, maroon shorts, maroon stockings.

Year Formed: 1906.

Turned Professional: 1906. *Ltd Co.:* 1919.

Grounds: 1906, Roots Hall, Prittlewell; 1920, Kursaal; 1934, Southend Stadium; 1955, Roots Hall Football Ground.

First Football League Game: 28 August 1920, Division 3, v Brighton & HA (a) W 2–0 – Capper; Reid, Newton; Wileman, Henderson, Martin; Nicholls, Nuttall, Fairclough (2), Myers, Dorsett.

Record League Victory: 9–2 v Newport Co, Division 3 (S), 5 September 1936 – McKenzie; Nelson, Everest (1); Deacon, Turner, Carr; Bolan, Lane (1), Goddard (4), Dickinson (2), Oswald (1).

Record Cup Victory: 10–1 v Golders Green, FA Cup 1st rd, 24 November 1934 – Moore; Morfitt, Kelly; Mackay, Joe Wilson, Carr (1); Lane (1), Johnson (5), Cheesmuir (2), Deacon (1), Oswald. 10–1 v Brentwood, FA Cup 2nd rd, 7 December 1968 – Roberts; Bentley, Birks; McMillan (1) Beesley, Kurila; Clayton, Chisnall, Moore (4), Best (5), Hamilton. 10–1 v Aldershot, Leyland Daf Cup Prel rd, 6 November 1990 – Sansome; Austin, Powell, Cornwell, Prior (1), Tilson (3), Cawley, Butler, Ansah (1), Benjamin (1), Angell (4).

HONOURS

Football League: FL 1 – Champions 2005–06; Division 1 best season: 13th, 1994–95; Division 3 – Runners-up 1990–91; Division 4 – Champions 1980–81; Runners-up 1971–72, 1977–78.

FA Cup: best season: old 3rd rd, 1921; 5th rd, 1926, 1952, 1976, 1993.

Football League Cup: Quarter final 2007.

LDV Vans Trophy: Runners-up 2004, 2005.

sky SPORTS FACT FILE

Jack French a right-back joined Southend United from Middlesbrough in 1925. His nephew also called Jack was two months old at the time. The youngster went on to make the same journey from the Middlesbrough club to United in February 1947 playing as a wing-half.

Record Defeat: 1–9 v Brighton & HA, Division 3, 27 November 1965.

Most League Points (2 for a win): 67, Division 4, 1980–81.

Most League Points (3 for a win): 85, Division 3, 1990–91.

Most League Goals: 92, Division 3 (S), 1950–51.

Highest League Scorer in Season: Jim Shankly, 31, 1928–29; Sammy McCrory, 1957–58, both in Division 3 (S).

Most League Goals in Total Aggregate: Roy Hollis, 122, 1953–60.

Most League Goals in One Match: 5, Jim Shankly v Merthyr T, Division 3 (S), 1 March 1930.

Most Capped Player: George Mackenzie, 9, Eire.

Most League Appearances: Sandy Anderson, 452, 1950–63.

Youngest League Player: Phil O'Connor, 16 years 76 days v Lincoln C, 26 December 1969.

Record Transfer Fee Received: £4,200,000 from Nottingham F for Stan Collymore, June 1993.

Record Transfer Fee Paid: £750,000 to Crystal Palace for Stan Collymore, November 1992.

Football League Record: 1920 Original Member of Division 3; 1921–58 Division 3 (S); 1958–66 Division 3; 1966–72 Division 4; 1972–76 Division 3; 1976–78 Division 4; 1978–80 Division 3; 1980–81 Division 4; 1981–84 Division 3; 1984–87 Division 4; 1987–89 Division 3; 1989–90 Division 4; 1990–91 Division 3; 1991–92 Division 2; 1992–97 Division 1; 1997–98 Division 2; 1998–2004 Division 3; 2004–05 FL 2; 2005–06 FL 1; 2006–07 FL C; 2007–10 FL 1; 2010– FL 2.

LATEST SEQUENCES

Longest Sequence of League Wins: 8, 29.8.2005 – 9.10.2005.

Longest Sequence of League Defeats: 6, 29.8.1987 – 19.9.1987.

Longest Sequence of League Draws: 6, 30.1.1982 – 19.2.1982.

Longest Sequence of Unbeaten League Matches: 16, 20.2.1932 – 29.8.1932.

Longest Sequence Without a League Win: 17, 31.12.1983 – 14.4.1984.

Successive Scoring Runs: 24 from 23.3.1929.

Successive Non-scoring Runs: 6 from 28.10.1933.

MANAGERS

Bob Jack 1906–10
George Molyneux 1910–11
O. M. Howard 1911–12
Joe Bradshaw 1912–19
Ned Liddell 1919–20
Tom Mather 1920–21
Ted Birnie 1921–34
David Jack 1934–40
Harry Warren 1946–56
Eddie Perry 1956–60
Frank Broome 1960
Ted Fenton 1961–65
Alvan Williams 1965–67
Ernie Shepherd 1967–69
Geoff Hudson 1969–70
Arthur Rowley 1970–76
Dave Smith 1976–83
Peter Morris 1983–84
Bobby Moore 1984–86
Dave Webb 1986–87
Dick Bate 1987
Paul Clark 1987–88
Dave Webb *(General Manager)* 1988–92
Colin Murphy 1992–93
Barry Fry 1993
Peter Taylor 1993–95
Steve Thompson 1995
Ronnie Whelan 1995–97
Alvin Martin 1997–99
Alan Little 1999–2000
David Webb 2000–01
Rob Newman 2001–03
Steve Wignall 2003–04
Steve Tilson 2004–10
Paul Sturrock July 2010–

TEN YEAR LEAGUE RECORD

		P	W	D	L	F	A	Pts	Pos
2000-01	Div 3	46	15	18	13	55	53	63	11
2001-02	Div 3	46	15	13	18	51	54	58	12
2002-03	Div 3	46	17	3	26	47	59	54	17
2003-04	Div 3	46	14	12	20	51	63	54	17
2004-05	FL 2	46	22	12	12	65	46	78	4
2005-06	FL 1	46	23	13	10	72	43	82	1
2006-07	FL C	46	10	12	24	47	80	42	22
2007-08	FL 1	46	22	10	14	70	55	76	6
2008-09	FL 1	46	21	8	17	58	61	71	8
2009-10	FL 1	46	10	13	23	51	72	43	23

DID YOU KNOW ?

Southend United had ground problems in both World Wars. In the first the original Roots Hall was cultivated for allotments. The club had two weeks to find a new home and move to The Kursaal. In the Second World War the Greyhound Stadium was occupied by the Army.

SOUTHEND UNITED 2009–10 LEAGUE RECORD

Match No.	Date	Venue	Opponents	Result	H/T Score	Lg Pos.	Goalscorers	Attendance
1	Aug 8	H	Huddersfield T	D 2-2	1-0	—	Barnard (pen) [14], Moussa [56]	8059
2	15	A	Walsall	D 2-2	0-1	13	Barnard [66], Freedman [80]	3658
3	18	A	Wycombe W	D 1-1	1-1	—	Christophe [45]	4607
4	21	H	Millwall	D 0-0	0-0	13		8435
5	29	A	Swindon T	L 1-2	0-1	19	Scannell [80]	6417
6	Sept 4	H	Leyton Orient	W 3-0	0-0	12	Barnard 3 (1 pen) [59 (p), 78, 90]	8836
7	11	H	Leeds U	D 0-0	0-0	—		10,123
8	19	A	Brighton & HA	W 3-2	2-2	—	Barnard [8], O'Donovan [27], Laurent [90]	6287
9	26	A	Oldham Ath	L 0-1	0-0	10		6979
10	29	A	Brentford	L 1-2	1-0	—	Francis [9]	5578
11	Oct 3	A	Stockport Co	W 2-0	0-0	11	Barnard 2 (1 pen) [57 (p), 90]	4102
12	9	H	Southampton	L 1-3	1-3	—	Friend [27]	8281
13	17	H	Bristol R	W 2-1	1-0	10	Barnard 2 [13, 48]	6853
14	24	A	Carlisle U	L 1-2	1-1	13	Laurent [42]	4551
15	30	H	Gillingham	W 1-0	0-0	—	Barnard [90]	7830
16	Nov 14	A	Yeovil T	L 0-1	0-0	13		3906
17	20	H	Milton Keynes D	W 2-1	1-1	—	Wilbraham (og) [24], Barnard (pen) [90]	6957
18	24	A	Tranmere R	L 0-2	0-1	—		4317
19	Dec 1	H	Norwich C	L 0-3	0-0	—		8732
20	5	A	Charlton Ath	L 0-1	0-1	14		17,445
21	12	H	Hartlepool U	W 3-2	0-2	13	Laurent [49], Barnard 2 [56, 74]	7737
22	19	A	Exeter C	L 0-1	0-1	13		4839
23	26	H	Colchester U	L 1-2	0-0	16	Barnard [76]	10,329
24	28	A	Leyton Orient	W 2-1	0-0	12	Barrett [59], McCormack [74]	5680
25	Jan 16	A	Huddersfield T	L 1-2	0-1	14	Spencer [90]	14,200
26	23	H	Wycombe W	D 1-1	0-0	13	McCormack [60]	6675
27	26	A	Millwall	L 0-2	0-1	—		7612
28	30	H	Swindon T	D 2-2	0-2	15	Spencer [85], Baldwin [89]	6669
29	Feb 8	A	Colchester U	L 0-2	0-1	—		6466
30	13	H	Tranmere R	D 1-1	1-0	16	Vernon (pen) [15]	6382
31	20	A	Milton Keynes D	L 1-3	0-1	18	Paterson [89]	9801
32	23	A	Norwich C	L 1-2	1-0	—	Vernon [45]	24,824
33	26	H	Charlton Ath	L 1-2	1-0	—	Paterson [31]	9724
34	Mar 6	A	Hartlepool U	L 0-3	0-2	22		3299
35	13	H	Exeter C	D 0-0	0-0	22		6761
36	20	H	Carlisle U	D 2-2	2-2	22	Moussa [25], Barrett [28]	6384
37	23	H	Walsall	W 3-0	1-0	—	Moussa 2 [19, 89], Spencer [51]	6432
38	27	A	Bristol R	L 3-4	2-2	22	Vernon 2 (1 pen) [5 (p), 57], Spencer [12]	6476
39	Apr 3	H	Yeovil T	D 0-0	0-0	22		6854
40	5	A	Gillingham	L 0-3	0-0	22		7657
41	10	A	Leeds U	L 0-2	0-0	22		21,650
42	13	H	Brentford	D 2-2	0-1	—	Laurent 2 [56, 61]	6838
43	17	H	Brighton & HA	L 0-1	0-1	23		8503
44	24	A	Oldham Ath	D 2-2	1-2	23	Laurent [6], M'Voto [75]	4225
45	May 1	H	Stockport Co	W 2-1	0-0	22	Crawford [75], McCormack [89]	7145
46	8	A	Southampton	L 1-3	0-0	23	Moussa [56]	25,289

Final League Position: 23

GOALSCORERS

League (51): Barnard 15 (4 pens), Laurent 6, Moussa 5, Spencer 4, Vernon 4 (2 pens), McCormack 3, Barrett 2, Paterson 2, Baldwin 1, Christophe 1, Crawford 1, Francis 1, Freedman 1, Friend 1, M'Voto 1, O'Donovan 1, Scannell 1, own goal 1.
Carling Cup (3): Barnard 2, Moussa 1.
FA Cup (0).
J Paint Trophy (0).

Mildenhall S 44	Francis S 45	White J 5	Christophe J 31 + 5	Heath M 4	Barrett A 41	Grant A 38	McCormack A 40 + 1	Barnard L 25	Laurent F 28 + 7	Moussa F 41 + 2	Betsy K — + 2	Freedman D 9 + 11	Walker J 2 + 11	Sawyer L — + 6	Revell A 1 + 2	M'Voto J 15 + 2	Scannell D 15 + 10	Herd J 17 + 3	O'Donovan R 3 + 1	Sankofa O 10 + 2	Friend G 5 + 1	O'Keefe S 3 + 4	Morrison S 8	Malone S 15 + 2	Ihehre J 4	Joyce 12	Spencer S 5 + 7	Paterson M 9 + 7	Baldwin P 18	Vernon S 17	Watt S 4	Crawford H 2 + 5	Milner M — + 1	Match No.
1	2	3	4¹	5	6	7	8	9²	10⁵	11	12	13	14																					1
1	2	3	4¹	5	6	7³	8	9		11	14	13	10²	12																				2
1	2	3	4	5	6	7	8	9		11		10¹			12																			3
1	2	3	4	5	6	7	8	9		11		10¹			12																			4
1	2	5	4■		6	7	8	9²	12	11		10¹				3	13																	5
1	2				6	7	8³	9	10²	4		13	14	12		3	11¹	5																6
1	2		4		6	7¹	8	9	10²	11		12				5	13	3																7
1	2		4		6	7	8	9			14	11				5¹	3²	10³	12	13														8
1	2		4³		6	7²	8	9		11		13	14	12		10¹	5	3																9
1	2		4³		6	7	8	9²	12	11		13	14			10¹	5	3																10
1	2		12		6	7¹	8	9	10	4		11					5	3																11
1	2		14		6	7	8³	9	10²	4		11¹	12			13	5	3																12
1	2		4		5	7	6	9	10¹	11³		8²	12			13	14	3																13
1	2		4		5	7	6	9	10	11		8¹					3	12																14
1	2		4		5	7	6	9	11	8		10					3																	15
1	2		4		3	7	6	9	11	8		10¹	12					5■																16
1	2		4		5	7	6	9	10	11		8¹				12	3																	17
1	2		4		6		8	9	11²	7		10¹	13			12					5	3												18
1	2		4		5		8	9	7¹	12		13				11²					6	3	10											19
1	2				5	7	8	9	11	4²		12				13					6	3	10¹											20
1			4		5	2²	8	9	11¹	7		13				12					6	3	10											21
1	2				5	7	8²	9	11	4		12				13					6	3¹	10■											22
	2		4¹		5	7	8	9	10	11²		12				13					6	3	1											23
	2		13		5	7¹	4	9	10²	8		12				11					6	3	1											24
1	2		12		6	7¹	4	9³	10	8		14	11²			5	3					13												25
1	2				6	7²	4		10	8	12	14	11³			5	3					13	9¹											26
1	2	11			6	7²	4			8	13	9				5¹	12	3				14	10³											27
1	2	11			6	7³		10	8¹	3²	12	14					4					13					5	9						28
1	2	4			6		8	7								5	11					3		10¹	12			9						29
1	2	4			6	12		8²	7			13				3	11						13				5	9	10¹					30
1	2	4²			6		8	11¹	14	13						3	7						12				5	10	9³				31
1	2	8			6	7		11²								5¹	10	13				3					12	4	9					32
1	2	4■			6	7		13	12							3	11³					14					8¹	5	10	9²				33
1	2				6		4■	9	7							3¹	11					12					13	10²	5	8				34
1	2				6	7		9	4							11						3					12	10¹	5	8				35
1	2				6■	7	8		4	11						3		12									10¹	5	9					36
1	2					7	8		4							11¹	3	6	12								10²	5	9		13			37
1	2	11			6	4	8		7■								3										10	5	9					38
1	2	4			6	7	8	12									3					11˙				10²	13	5	9³	14				39
1	2	8²			6	7		10³								3	4	13								11¹	12	5	9	14				40
1	2	8			6	7		12								13	3	4	1˙							10¹	5	9²						41
1	2	4				7	8	10	11							5	3											5	9					42
1	2	4¹				7	8	10	11							5	3					13				5	9²	12						43
1	2	13			6¹	7	8	10²	4							12	3					11³				5	9	14						44
1	2					7	8	4								6	3	1˙				12					5	9¹	10					45
1	2					7	8	4								6	3	1˙˙				10	5					9	12					46

FA Cup
First Round   Gillingham   (a)   0-3

Carling Cup
First Round   Cheltenham T   (a)   2-1
Second Round   Hull C   (a)   1-3

J Paint Trophy
Second Round   Milton Keynes D   (a)   0-2

STEVENAGE
FL Championship 2

FOUNDATION

There have been several clubs associated with town of Stevenage. Stevenage Town was formed in 1884. They absorbed Stevenage Rangers in 1955 and later played at Broadhall Way. The club went into liquidation in 1968 and Stevenage Athletic was formed, but they, too, followed a similar path in 1976. Then Stevenage Borough was founded. The Broadhall Way pitch was dug up and remained unused for three years. Thus the new club started its life in the modest surrounds of the King George V playing fields with a roped-off ground in the Chiltern League. A change of competition followed to the Wallspan Southern Combination and by 1980 the club returned to the council-owned Broadhall Way when "Borough" was added to the name. Entry into the United Counties League was so successful the League and Cup were won in the first season. On to the Isthmian League Division Two and the climb up the pyramid continued. In 1995–96 Stevenage Borough won the Conference but was denied a place in the Football League as the ground did not measure up to the competition's standards. Subsequent improvements changed this and the 7,100 capacity venue became one of the best appointed grounds in non-league football. After winning elevation to the Football League the club dropped Borough from its title.

Lamex Stadium, Broadhall Way, Stevenage, Herts SG2 8RH.

Telephone: 01438 223223.

Fax: 01438 743611.

Website: stevenageboro.fc.com

Ground Capacity: 6,546

Record Attendance: 6,489 v Kidderminster H, Conference, 25 January 1997.

Chairman: Phil Wallace

Chief Executive: Bob Makin

Secretary: Roger Austin

Manager: Graham Westley

MANAGERS

Paul Fairclough 1990–98
Steve Wignall 2000–01
Graham Westley 2001–02
Mark Stimson 2006–07
Peter Taylor 2007–08
Graham Westley May 2008–

sky SPORTS FACT FILE

Stevenage Borough reached the fourth round of the FA Cup in 1997–98. On 25 January they drew 1–1 with Newcastle United at Broadhall Way to force a replay. At St James' Park they were unlucky to lose 2–1, Alan Shearer's first goal clearly not crossing the line!

Assistant Manager: John Dreyer

Sports Therapist: Paul Dando

Nickname: The Boro

Grounds: 1976, King George V playing fields; 1980, Broadhall Way.

Colours: White shirts, red shorts, red stockings with white tops

Change Colours: All blue.

Year Formed: 1976.

Record Victory: 11-1 v British Timken Ath 1980–81

Record Defeat: 0-7 v Southwick 1987–88.

Most Appearances: Mike Smith, 466, 1992–2001, 2003–04.

Most Goals: Martin Gittings, 230, 1980–95

Most Goals in One Season: Martin Gittings, 40, 1991–92

Record Transfer Fee Received: £260,000 from Peterborough U for George Boyd, January 2007.

Record Transfer Fee Paid: £20,000 to Hereford United for Richard Leadbetter, February 1999

HONOURS

Blue Square Premier League: Champions 2009–10.

Conference: Champions 1995–96.

FA Trophy: Winners 2007, 2009. Runners-up 2002, 2010.

Herts Senior Cup: Winners 2009.

Isthmian League Premier Division: Champions 1993–94.

Isthmian League Division 1 Champions: 1991–92.

Isthmian League Division 2 North Champions: 1985–86, 1990–91.

United Counties League Division 1: Champions 1980–81.

United Counties League Cup: Winners 1981.

TEN YEAR LEAGUE RECORD

		P	W	D	L	F	A	Pts	Pos
2000-01	Conf	42	15	18	9	71	61	63	7
2001-02	Conf	42	15	10	17	57	60	55	11
2002-03	Con	42	14	10	18	61	55	52	12
2003-04	Conf	42	18	9	15	58	52	63	8
2004-05	Conf	42	22	6	14	65	52	72	5
2005-06	Conf	42	19	12	11	62	47	69	6
2006-07	Conf	46	20	10	16	76	66	70	8
2007-08	B Sq Pr	46	24	7	15	82	55	79	6
2008-09	B Sq Pr	46	23	12	11	73	54	81	5
2009-10	B Sq Pr	44	30	9	5	79	24	99	1

DID YOU KNOW ?

On 17 April 2010 Stevenage Borough won 2–0 at Kidderminster Harriers to ensure promotion to the Football League. Two matches were still to play, the removal of Chester City having reduced the competition to 44 matches to deprive them of a competition points record.

STOCKPORT COUNTY   FL Championship 2

FOUNDATION

Formed at a meeting held at Wellington Road South by members of Wycliffe Congregational Chapel in 1883, they called themselves Heaton Norris Rovers until changing to Stockport County in 1890, a year before joining the Football Combination.

Edgeley Park, Hardcastle Road, Edgeley, Stockport, Cheshire SK3 9DD.

Telephone: (0161) 286 8888 (ext 257).

Fax: (0161) 429 7392.

Ticket Office: 0845 688 5799.

Website: www.stockportcounty.com

Email: stockport.county@btinternet.com

Ground Capacity: 10,641.

Record Attendance: 27,833 v Liverpool, FA Cup 5th rd, 11 February 1950.

Pitch Measurements: 104m × 66m.

Chairman: Alwin Thompson.

Business Operations Manager: Rachael Moss.

Manager: Paul Simpson.

Assistant Manager: Peter Ward.

Physio: Rodger Wylde.

Colours: Reflex blue shirts with one broad white band, reflex blue shorts, white stockings.

Change Colours: All black.

Year Formed: 1883.

Turned Professional: 1891.

Ltd Co.: 1908.

Previous Names: 1883, Heaton Norris Rovers; 1888, Heaton Norris; 1890, Stockport County.

Club Nicknames: 'County' or 'Hatters'.

Grounds: 1883, Heaton Norris Recreation Ground; 1884, Heaton Norris Wanderers Cricket Ground; 1885, Chorlton's Farm, Chorlton's Lane; 1886, Heaton Norris Cricket Ground; 1887, Wilkes' Field, Belmont Street; 1889, Nursery Inn, Green Lane; 1902, Edgeley Park.

First Football League Game: 1 September 1900, Division 2, v Leicester Fosse (a) D 2–2 – Moores; Earp, Wainwright; Pickford, Limond, Harvey; Stansfield, Smith (1), Patterson, Foster, Betteley (1).

Record League Victory: 13–0 v Halifax T, Division 3 (N), 6 January 1934 – McGann; Vincent (1p), Jenkinson; Robinson, Stevens, Len Jones; Foulkes (1), Hill (3), Lythgoe (2), Stevenson (2), Downes (4).

Record Cup Victory: 5–0 v Lincoln C, FA Cup 1st rd, 11 November 1995 – Edwards; Connelly, Todd, Bennett, Flynn, Gannon (Dinning), Beaumont, Oliver, Ware, Eckhardt (3), Armstrong (1) (Mike), Chalk, (1 og).

Record Defeat: 1–8 v Chesterfield, Division 2, 19 April 1902.

HONOURS

Football League: Division 1 best season: 8th, 1997–98; Division 2 – Runners-up 1996–97; Division 3 (N) – Champions 1921–22, 1936–37; Runners-up 1928–29, 1929-30, 1996–97; Division 4 – Champions 1966–67; Runners-up 1990–91.

FA Cup: best season: 5th rd, 1935, 1950, 2001.

Football League Cup: Semi-final 1997.

Autoglass Trophy: Runners-up 1992, 1993.

sky SPORTS FACT FILE

Among the Stockport County players who returned to the club after the Great War was goalkeeper Harry Hardy who survived being captured and spending some months as a Prisoner of War in Germany. He went on to win a championship medal with the club in 1921–22.

Most League Points (2 for a win): 64, Division 4, 1966–67.

Most League Points (3 for a win): 85, Division 2, 1993–94.

Most League Goals: 115, Division 3 (N), 1933–34.

Highest League Scorer in Season: Alf Lythgoe, 46, Division 3 (N), 1933–34.

Most League Goals in Total Aggregate: Jack Connor, 132, 1951–56.

Most League Goals in One Match: 5, Joe Smith v Southport, Division 3 (N), 7 January 1928; 5, Joe Smith v Lincoln C, Division 3 (N), 15 September 1928; 5, Frank Newton v Nelson, Division 3 (N), 21 September 1929; 5, Alf Lythgoe v Southport, Division 3 (N), 25 August 1934; 5, Billy McNaughton v Mansfield T, Division 3 (N), 14 December 1935; 5, Jack Connor v Workington, Division 3 (N), 8 November 1952; 5, Jack Connor v Carlisle U, Division 3 (N), 7 April 1956.

Most Capped Player: Jarkko Wiss, 9 (43), Finland.

Most League Appearances: Andy Thorpe, 489, 1978–86. 1988–92.

Youngest League Player: Paul Turnbull, 16 years 97 days v Wrexham, 30 April 2005.

Record Transfer Fee Received: £1,600,000 from Middlesbrough for Alun Armstrong, February 1998.

Record Transfer Fee Paid: £800,000 to Nottingham F for Ian Moore, July 1998.

Football League Record: 1900 Elected to Division 2; 1904 Failed re-election; 1905–21 Division 2; 1921–22 Division 3 (N); 1922–26 Division 2; 1926–37 Division 3 (N); 1937–38 Division 2; 1938–58 Division 3 (N); 1958–59 Division 3; 1959–67 Division 4; 1967–70 Division 3; 1970–91 Division 4; 1991–92 Division 3; 1992–97 Division 2; 1997–2002 Division 1; 2002–04 Division 2; 2004–05 FL 1; 2005–08 FL 2; 2008–10 FL 1; 2010– FL 2.

LATEST SEQUENCES

Longest Sequence of League Wins: 9, 13.1.2007 – 3.3.2007.

Longest Sequence of League Defeats: 10, 24.11.2001 – 13.01.2002.

Longest Sequence of League Draws: 7, 17.3.1989 – 14.4.1989.

Longest Sequence of Unbeaten League Matches: 18, 28.1.1933 – 28.8.1933.

Longest Sequence Without a League Win: 19, 28.12.1999 – 22.4.2000.

Successive Scoring Runs: 27 from 20.10.2007.

Successive Non-scoring Runs: 7 from 10.3.1923.

MANAGERS

Fred Stewart 1894–1911
Harry Lewis 1911–14
David Ashworth 1914–19
Albert Williams 1919–24
Fred Scotchbrook 1924–26
Lincoln Hyde 1926–31
Andrew Wilson 1932–33
Fred Westgarth 1934–36
Bob Kelly 1936–38
George Hunt 1938–39
Bob Marshall 1939–49
Andy Beattie 1949–52
Dick Duckworth 1952–56
Billy Moir 1956–60
Reg Flewin 1960–63
Trevor Porteous 1963–65
Bert Trautmann
  (General Manager) 1965–66
Eddie Quigley *(Team
  Manager)* 1965–66
Jimmy Meadows 1966–69
Wally Galbraith 1969–70
Matt Woods 1970–71
Brian Doyle 1972–74
Jimmy Meadows 1974–75
Roy Chapman 1975–76
Eddie Quigley 1976–77
Alan Thompson 1977–78
Mike Summerbee 1978–79
Jimmy McGuigan 1979–82
Eric Webster 1982–85
Colin Murphy 1985
Les Chapman 1985–86
Jimmy Melia 1986
Colin Murphy 1986–87
Asa Hartford 1987–89
Danny Bergara 1989–95
Dave Jones 1995–97
Gary Megson 1997–99
Andy Kilner 1999–2001
Carlton Palmer 2001–03
Sammy McIlroy 2003–04
Chris Turner 2004–05
Jim Gannon 2006–09
Gary Ablett 2009–10
Paul Simpson July 2010–

TEN YEAR LEAGUE RECORD

		P	W	D	L	F	A	Pts	Pos
2000-01	Div 1	46	11	18	17	58	65	51	19
2001-02	Div 1	46	6	8	32	42	102	26	24
2002-03	Div 2	46	15	10	21	65	70	55	14
2003-04	Div 2	46	11	19	16	62	70	52	19
2004-05	FL 1	46	6	8	32	49	98	26	24
2005-06	FL 2	46	11	19	16	57	78	52	22
2006-07	FL 2	46	21	8	17	65	54	71	8
2007-08	FL 2	46	24	10	12	72	54	82	4
2008-09	FL 1	46	16	12	18	59	57	50*	18
2009-10	FL 1	46	5	10	31	35	95	25	24

* 10 points deducted.

DID YOU KNOW ?

In 1972–73 Stockport County met West Ham United in a League Cup tie at Edgeley Park. A penalty from Tommy Spratt and a goal from Malcolm Russell was enough to knock the First Division team out of the competition.

STOCKPORT COUNTY 2009–10 LEAGUE RECORD

Match No.	Date	Venue	Opponents	Result	H/T Score	Lg Pos.	Goalscorers	Attendance
1	Aug 8	A	Oldham Ath	D	0-0	0-0	—		6918
2	15	H	Bristol R	L	0-2	0-2	20		4084
3	18	H	Carlisle U	L	1-2	1-1	—	Keogh (og) [14]	4009
4	22	A	Brighton & HA	W	4-2	1-1	15	Baker 3 (1 pen) [30, 54, 66 (p)], Johnson O [86]	5270
5	29	H	Southampton	D	1-1	0-1	14	Baker (pen) [90]	4680
6	Sept 5	A	Leeds U	L	0-2	0-2	18		22,870
7	12	A	Yeovil T	D	2-2	2-1	18	Baker 2 (1 pen) [22 (p), 45]	3519
8	19	H	Leyton Orient	W	2-1	0-0	13	Bignall [49], Tansey [77]	4091
9	26	A	Huddersfield T	D	0-0	0-0	13		12,020
10	29	H	Hartlepool U	D	2-2	2-0	—	Bignall [16], Raynes [17]	3780
11	Oct 3	H	Southend U	L	0-2	0-0	20		4102
12	12	A	Tranmere R	W	1-0	0-0	—	Baker (pen) [67]	5645
13	17	H	Millwall	L	0-4	0-3	18		4394
14	24	A	Brentford	L	0-2	0-1	20		5045
15	31	H	Norwich C	L	1-3	0-1	21	Thompson, P [82]	5218
16	Nov 14	A	Walsall	L	0-2	0-1	21		4143
17	21	A	Exeter C	L	1-3	0-1	21	Rose [81]	4101
18	24	A	Colchester U	L	0-2	0-2	—		3818
19	Dec 5	A	Wycombe W	L	1-2	0-0	24	Baker [64]	4343
20	12	H	Charlton Ath	L	1-2	0-1	24	Elliot (og) [90]	4277
21	19	A	Gillingham	L	1-3	0-3	24	Rose [65]	4769
22	26	A	Milton Keynes D	L	1-4	0-2	24	Thompson, P [76]	9661
23	28	H	Leeds U	L	2-4	1-1	24	Baker [12], Mullins [61]	7768
24	Jan 19	H	Swindon T	L	0-1	0-0	—		3281
25	23	A	Carlisle U	D	0-0	0-0	24		4966
26	26	H	Brighton & HA	D	1-1	0-0	—	Pilkington [58]	3636
27	30	A	Southampton	L	0-2	0-0	24		18,308
28	Feb 6	H	Milton Keynes D	L	1-3	1-1	24	Donnelly [11]	3720
29	13	H	Colchester U	D	2-2	1-2	24	Ibehre 2 [22, 77]	3642
30	20	A	Exeter C	W	1-0	0-0	24	Johnson J [77]	4990
31	23	A	Swindon T	L	1-4	1-2	—	Tansey [45]	7063
32	27	H	Wycombe W	W	4-3	2-0	24	Partridge [22], Donnelly 2 [23, 60], Johnson J [53]	3740
33	Mar 2	A	Bristol R	L	0-1	0-1	—		5322
34	6	A	Charlton Ath	L	0-2	0-2	24		16,609
35	13	H	Gillingham	D	0-0	0-0	24		3894
36	16	H	Oldham Ath	L	0-1	0-1	—		4283
37	20	H	Brentford	L	0-1	0-0	24		3707
38	27	A	Millwall	L	0-5	0-3	24		11,116
39	Apr 3	H	Walsall	D	1-1	1-0	24	Ibehre (pen) [19]	3580
40	5	A	Norwich C	L	1-2	1-2	24	Ibehre [12]	25,353
41	10	H	Yeovil T	L	1-3	0-2	24	Donnelly [82]	3587
42	13	A	Hartlepool U	L	0-3	0-1	—		2869
43	17	A	Leyton Orient	L	0-2	0-0	24		4373
44	24	H	Huddersfield T	L	0-6	0-2	24		6887
45	May 1	A	Southend U	L	1-2	0-0	24	Ibehre [71]	7145
46	8	H	Tranmere R	L	0-3	0-1	24		7208

Final League Position: 24

GOALSCORERS

League (35): Baker 9 (4 pens), Ibehre 5 (1 pen), Donnelly 4, Bignall 2, Johnson J 2, Rose 2, Tansey 2, Thompson, P 2, Johnson O 1, Mullins 1, Partridge 1, Pilkington 1, Raynes 1, own goals 2.
Carling Cup (1): Poole 1.
FA Cup (5): Turnbull 2, Baker 1 (pen), Poole 1, Thompson P 1.
J Paint Trophy (5): Baker 3, Bignall 1, Bridcutt 1.

Williams O 44	Mullins J 36	Havern G 7	Turnbull P 24+6	Rose M 24	Raynes M 24+1	Baker C 19+1	Tansey G 25+7	Thompson P 14+8	Johnson O 4+12	Poole D 29+7	Pilkington D 10+19	Edwards D —+1	Vincent J 30+4	Bridcutt L 15	Griffin A 9+9	Bignall N 11	Huntington P 26	Ribeiro C 7	McNeil M 4+1	Perkins D 22	Swailes D 20	Johnson J 14+2	Ibehre J 20	Partridge R 20+2	Rowe D —+4	Sadler M 20	Donnelly G 16+3	Halls A 8+3	Fisher T —+1	Barnes S 2	Rigby L 2	Match No.
1	2	3	4	5	6	7	8	9	10[1]	11	12																					1
1	2	3	4	5	6	7	8	9[2]	10[1]	11	12	13																				2
1	2	3	12	5	6	10	4	9	13	11[2]	8		7[1]																			3
1	2	3	14	5	6	10[3]	4	9[2]	13	11	8[1]				7	12																4
1	2	3	12	5	6[1]	10	4	9	13,11	8[2]			7																			5
1	2	3		5		10	4	14	12	11[2]	8[1]		7	6	13	9[3]																6
1	2	3		5		10	4	13	12	11			7[1]	8		9[2]	6															7
1	2			5	3	10[2]	4	12		11	13		7	8		9[1]	6															8
1	2			5	3	10	4	13		11	12		7[1]	8		9[2]	6															9
1	2			5	3	10	4	12		11			7[1]	6		9	8															10
1	2			5	3	10	4	13		11[1]	12		7[2]	8		9	6[8]															11
1	2			3	5	10	8	9[1]	12	7			11	4			6															12
1	2			3	5	10	8[1]	9	13	7[3]	12		11[2]	4	14		6															13
1	2		8	3	5		11[1]		12	7[2]	10			4	13	9	6															14
1	2		8	3	5	10		11	13	7[1]	12			4		9[2]	6															15
1		8[1]	6	5	11	12	10	14	7[2]	13			3	4	2	9[3]																16
1	2		8	6	5	12	4	10		7[1]	13		11		3[2]		9															17
1	2		8	3	5	10		9		12	7[2]		11	4	7[1]		6															18
1	2		14	3	5	11	8	12	7[2]		10		4[3]		9[1]		6	13														19
1		6		5	11[8]		8	12	7[2]	13			4	2	9[1]		3	10														20
1	3		8	2	13		4	9[2]	11	7[3]	12		6[1]	14			5	10														21
1	6		7	2	5		4	12	9[1]	14	13	10[3]	3		11[2]	8																22
1	2		4		5	8		9[1]	12	7[4]			11	3			6	10														23
1	2		3	5		12				11[1]	8									4	6	7	9	10								24
1	3		2	5						11	8									4	6	7	9[8]	10								25
1	3[1]		8	2	5	12				7			11	13						4	6	10[2]	9[1]	14								26
1		8		5				11	7[1]	3	12									4	6	10	9[1]		2	13						27
1	4			8		7[2]	12	13	3	5										11	6		9[1]		2	10						28
1	2	8[2]		4			13	12		5											6	7[1]	10	9		3	11					29
1	2			4		12				13							5			7	6	8[2]	9	11		3	10[1]					30
1	2			7		13	12			5										4	6	8	9	11[3]		3	10[2]					31
1	2[1]			12		14			7	13							5			4	6	8[2]	9	11[3]		3	10					32
1		6				8[8]		11	2	5										4		7[1]	9	12		3	10[2]	13				33
1		8		7						5										4	6		9	11		2	10	3				34
1	2	7		8						5										4	6		9	11[1]	12	3	10					35
1	2	8[2]		13		7				5										4	6[8]		9	11[3]	14	3	10[1]	12				36
1	2			8[1]		7		12		5										4			9	11[2]		3	10	6	13			37
1	2	8						11[1]		5										4	6	7	9	10		3	12					38
1	2	12						11		5										4[1]	6	7	9	8		3	10					39
1	2			14		13		8[3]		5[1]										4	6	7[2]	9	11		3	10	12				40
1	2	13		12[2]		7		8[1]												4	6		9	11	14	3	10[3]	5				41
1		8				7[1]		13		5										4	6	12	9	11[2]		3	10	2				42
1		8				14	12	11[1]												4		7[3]	9	13		3	10[2]	2		6		43
1		8				12	13													4	6	7[1]	9	11[2]		3	10	5		2		44
1		8				10[2]	12	7				5								4	6		9	11[1]		3	13	2			1	45
1		8						11	10	7[1]		5								4	6	12	9			3		2			1	46

FA Cup
First Round   Tooting & M   (h)   5-0
Second Round   Torquay U   (h)   0-4

Carling Cup
First Round   Huddersfield T   (a)   1-3

J Paint Trophy
First Round   Crewe Alex   (a)   4-1
Second Round   Port Vale   (a)   1-3

STOKE CITY FA Premiership

FOUNDATION

The date of the formation of this club has long been in doubt. The year 1863 was claimed, but more recent research by Wade Martin has uncovered nothing earlier than 1868, when a couple of Old Carthusians, who were apprentices at the local works of the old North Staffordshire Railway Company, met with some others from that works, to form Stoke Ramblers. It should also be noted that the old Stoke club went bankrupt in 1908 when a new club was formed.

Britannia Stadium, Stanley Matthews Way, Stoke-on-Trent, Staffs ST4 4EG.

Telephone: (0871) 663 2008.

Fax: (01782) 592 210.

Ticket Office: (0871) 663 2008.

Website: www.stokecityfc.com

Email: info@stokecityfc.com

Ground Capacity: 28,383.

Record Attendance: 51,380 v Arsenal, Division 1, 29 March 1937 (at Victoria Ground).

Pitch Measurements: 100m × 64m.

Chairman: Peter Coates.

Chief Executive: Tony Scholes.

Club Secretary: Eddie Harrison.

Manager: Tony Pulis.

First Team Coaches: Mark O'Connor, Gerry Francis.

Physio: Chris Banks.

Colours: Red and white striped shirts with red sleeves and shoulders, white shorts, white stockings.

Change Colours: All black with red trim on shirt.

Year Formed: 1863* (*see Foundation*). *Turned Professional:* 1885. *Ltd Co.:* 1908.

Previous Names: 1868, Stoke Ramblers; 1870, Stoke; 1925, Stoke City.

Club Nickname: 'The Potters'.

Grounds: 1875, Sweeting's Field; 1878, Victoria Ground (previously known as the Athletic Club Ground); 1997, Britannia Stadium.

First Football League Game: 8 September 1888, Football League, v WBA (h) L 0–2 – Rowley; Clare, Underwood; Ramsey, Shutt, Smith; Sayer, McSkimming, Staton, Edge, Tunnicliffe.

Record League Victory: 10–3 v WBA, Division 1, 4 February 1937 – Doug Westland; Brigham, Harbot; Tutin, Turner (1p), Kirton; Matthews, Antonio (2), Freddie Steele (5), Jimmy Westland, Johnson (2).

Record Cup Victory: 7–1 v Burnley, FA Cup 2nd rd (replay), 20 February 1896 – Clawley; Clare, Eccles; Turner, Grewe, Robertson; Willie Maxwell, Dickson, A. Maxwell (3), Hyslop (4), Schofield.

HONOURS

Football League: Division 1 best season: 4th, 1935–36, 1946–47; FL C – Runners-up 2007–08; Division 2 – Champions 1932–33, 1962–63, 1992–93; Runners-up 1921–22; Division 3 (N) – Champions 1926–27.

FA Cup: Semi-finals 1899, 1971, 1972.

Football League Cup: Winners 1972; Runners-up 1964.

Autoglass Trophy: Winners: 1992.

Auto Windscreens Shield: Winners: 2000.

European Competitions: UEFA Cup: 1972–73, 1974–75.

sky SPORTS FACT FILE

To supplement fixtures in the Birmingham League in 1909–10, Stoke City also competed in the Southern League (Division Two, Western Section). They won all ten games, scoring 49 and conceding just nine. They also won the play-off with Hastings 6–0 for the overall title.

Record Defeat: 0–10 v Preston NE, Division 1,
14 September 1889.

Most League Points (2 for a win): 63, Division 3 (N), 1926–27.

Most League Points (3 for a win): 93, Division 2, 1992–93.

Most League Goals: 92, Division 3 (N). 1926–27.

Highest League Scorer in Season: Freddie Steele, 33,
Division 1, 1936–37.

Most League Goals in Total Aggregate: Freddie Steele,
142, 1934–49.

Most League Goals in One Match: 7, Neville Coleman v
Lincoln C, Division 2, 23 February 1957.

Most Capped Player: Gordon Banks, 36 (73), England.

Most League Appearances: Eric Skeels, 506, 1958–76.

Youngest League Player: Peter Bullock, 16 years 163 days v
Swansea C, 19 April 1958.

Record Transfer Fee Received: £3,000,000 from
Manchester U for Ritchie De Laat, January 2009;
£3,000,000 from Hull C for Seyi Olofinjana, August 2009.

Record Transfer Fee Paid: £5,500,000 to Reading for Dave
Kitson, July 2008.

Football League Record: 1888 Founder Member of
Football League; 1890 Not re-elected; 1891 Re-elected;
relegated in 1907, and after one year in Division 2, resigned
for financial reasons; 1919 re-elected to Division 2; 1922–23
Division 1; 1923–26 Division 2; 1926–27 Division 3 (N);
1927–33 Division 2; 1933–53 Division 1; 1953–63 Division 2;
1963–77 Division 1; 1977–79 Division 2; 1979–85 Division 1;
1985–90 Division 2; 1990–92 Division 3; 1992–93 Division 2;
1993–98 Division 1; 1998–2002 Division 2; 2002–04
Division 1; 2004–08 FL C; 2008– FA Premier League.

LATEST SEQUENCES

Longest Sequence of League Wins: 8, 30.3.1895 – 21.9.1895.

Longest Sequence of League Defeats: 11, 6.4.1985 –
17.8.1985.

Longest Sequence of League Draws: 5, 21.3.1987 –
11.4.1987.

Longest Sequence of Unbeaten League Matches: 25,
5.9.1992 – 20.2.1993.

Longest Sequence Without a League Win: 17, 22.4.1939 – 14.10.1989.

Successive Scoring Runs: 21 from 24.12.1921.

Successive Non-scoring Runs: 8 from 29.12.1984.

MANAGERS

Tom Slaney 1874–83
  (Secretary-Manager)
Walter Cox 1883–84
  (Secretary-Manager)
Harry Lockett 1884–90
Joseph Bradshaw 1890–92
Arthur Reeves 1892–95
William Rowley 1895–97
H. D. Austerberry 1897–1908
A. J. Barker 1908–14
Peter Hodge 1914–15
Joe Schofield 1915–19
Arthur Shallcross 1919–23
John 'Jock' Rutherford 1923
Tom Mather 1923–35
Bob McGrory 1935–52
Frank Taylor 1952–60
Tony Waddington 1960–77
George Eastham 1977–78
Alan A'Court 1978
Alan Durban 1978–81
Richie Barker 1981–83
Bill Asprey 1984–85
Mick Mills 1985–89
Alan Ball 1989–91
Lou Macari 1991–93
Joe Jordan 1993–94
Lou Macari 1994–97
Chic Bates 1997–98
Chris Kamara 1998
Brian Little 1998–99
Gary Megson 1999
Gudjon Thordarson 1999–2002
Steve Cotterill 2002
Tony Pulis 2002–05
Johan Boskamp 2005–06
Tony Pulis June 2006–

TEN YEAR LEAGUE RECORD

		P	W	D	L	F	A	Pts	Pos
2000-01	Div 2	46	21	14	11	74	49	77	5
2001-02	Div 2	46	23	11	12	67	40	80	5
2002-03	Div 1	46	12	14	20	45	69	50	21
2003-04	Div 1	46	18	12	16	58	55	66	11
2004-05	FL C	46	17	10	19	36	38	61	12
2005-06	FL C	46	17	7	22	54	63	58	13
2006-07	FL C	46	19	16	11	62	41	73	8
2007-08	FL C	46	21	16	9	69	55	79	2
2008-09	PR Lge	38	12	9	17	38	55	45	12
2009-10	PR Lge	38	11	14	13	34	48	47	11

DID YOU KNOW ?

Seven goals in three matches
for Freddie Steele on
England's 1937 Scandinavian
tour but on his return found
he had lost his boots. Goals
were scarce in League games
wearing another pair. A
search at home revealed them
and he hit a hat-trick against
West Bromwich Albion.

STOKE CITY 2009–10 LEAGUE RECORD

Match No.	Date	Venue	Opponents	Result	H/T Score	Lg Pos.	Goalscorers	Attendance
1	Aug 15	H	Burnley	W 2-0	2-0	—	Shawcross [19], Jordan (og) [33]	27,385
2	19	A	Liverpool	L 0-4	0-2	—		44,318
3	22	A	Birmingham C	D 0-0	0-0	9		21,694
4	29	H	Sunderland	W 1-0	1-0	5	Kitson [43]	27,091
5	Sept 12	H	Chelsea	L 1-2	1-1	8	Diagne-Faye [32]	27,440
6	19	A	Bolton W	D 1-1	0-0	10	Kitson [53]	20,265
7	26	H	Manchester U	L 0-2	0-0	12		27,500
8	Oct 4	A	Everton	D 1-1	0-0	11	Huth [50]	36,753
9	17	H	West Ham U	W 2-1	1-1	9	Beattie 2 (1 pen) [11 (p), 69]	27,026
10	24	A	Tottenham H	W 1-0	0-0	9	Whelan [86]	36,031
11	31	H	Wolverhampton W	D 2-2	2-0	9	Beattie [17], Etherington [44]	27,500
12	Nov 8	A	Hull C	L 1-2	1-0	9	Etherington [29]	24,516
13	22	H	Portsmouth	W 1-0	0-0	9	Fuller [74]	27,069
14	28	A	Blackburn R	D 0-0	0-0	9		25,143
15	Dec 5	A	Arsenal	L 0-2	0-1	11		60,048
16	12	H	Wigan Ath	D 2-2	1-1	11	Tuncay [37], Shawcross [74]	26,728
17	19	A	Aston Villa	L 0-1	0-0	11		35,852
18	26	A	Manchester C	L 0-2	0-2	11		47,325
19	28	H	Birmingham C	L 0-1	0-0	12		27,211
20	Jan 5	H	Fulham	W 3-2	3-0	—	Tuncay [12], Diagne-Faye [34], Sidibe [37]	25,104
21	16	A	Liverpool	D 1-1	0-0	11	Huth [90]	27,247
22	Feb 1	A	Sunderland	D 0-0	0-0	—		35,078
23	6	H	Blackburn R	W 3-0	2-0	11	Higginbotham [8], Sidibe [45], Etherington [67]	27,386
24	9	A	Wigan Ath	D 1-1	0-1	—	Tuncay [74]	16,033
25	16	H	Manchester C	D 1-1	0-0	—	Whelan [72]	26,778
26	20	A	Portsmouth	W 2-1	0-1	11	Huth [50], Diao [90]	17,208
27	27	H	Arsenal	L 1-3	1-1	11	Pugh [8]	27,011
28	Mar 10	A	Burnley	D 1-1	1-0	—	Tuncay [23]	20,323
29	13	A	Aston Villa	D 0-0	0-0	11		27,598
30	20	H	Tottenham H	L 1-2	0-0	11	Etherington (pen) [64]	27,575
31	27	A	West Ham U	W 1-0	0-0	11	Fuller [69]	34,564
32	Apr 3	H	Hull C	W 2-0	1-0	10	Fuller [6], Lawrence [90]	27,604
33	11	A	Wolverhampton W	D 0-0	0-0	—		28,455
34	17	H	Bolton W	L 1-2	1-0	11	Kitson [13]	27,250
35	25	A	Chelsea	L 0-7	0-3	13		41,013
36	May 1	H	Everton	D 0-0	0-0	12		27,579
37	5	A	Fulham	W 1-0	0-0	—	Etherington [83]	20,831
38	9	A	Manchester U	L 0-4	0-2	11		75,316

Final League Position: 11

GOALSCORERS

League (34): Etherington 5 (1 pen), Tuncay 4, Beattie 3 (1 pen), Fuller 3, Huth 3, Kitson 3, Diagne-Faye 2, Shawcross 2, Sidibe 2, Whelan 2, Diao 1, Higginbotham 1, Lawrence 1, Pugh 1, own goal 1.
Carling Cup (5): Etherington 1, Fuller 1, Griffiin 1, Higginbotham 1, Kitson 1.
FA Cup (10): Fuller 4, Etherington 1, Kitson 1, Shawcross 1, Tuncay 1, Whitehead 1, own goal 1.

Sorensen T 33	Wilkinson A 21+4	Higginbotham D 23+1	Whitehead D 33+3	Shawcross R 27+1	Diagne-Faye A 30+1	Lawrence L 14+11	Delap R 34+2	Beattie J 11+11	Fuller R 22+13	Etherington M 33+1	Kitson D 10+8	Whelan G 25+8	Cresswell R 1+1	Pugh D 1+6	Tuncay S 13+17	Huth R 30+2	Collins D 22+3	Simonsen S 2+1	Diao S 11+5	Sidibe M 19+5	Moult L —+1	Begovic A 3+1	Match No.
1	2	3	4	5	6	7	8	9¹	10³	11²	12	13	14										1
1	2	3	4³	5	6	12	7	9¹	13	11	8	10²	14										2
1	2	3	13	5	6	7	8	9¹	10	11²	12	4											3
1	2	3	12	5	6	7	8	10²	11¹	9³	4				13	14							4
1⁶	2		11	3	6		8	10¹	12			9²	7		¹3	5	4	15					5
1	2	3		6	12	8	14	10³	11¹	9²	7				13		5	4					6
1	2¹	3	6	7³	8	13		11		9²	10				14	¹2	5	4					7
1	2	3	6		8	9	10²	11	13	12							5	4	7¹				8
1		4	5	6	12	8¹	9³	10	11	14	13					2	3		7²				9
	2	14	4	5	6		7¹	9²	10³	11		12			13		3	1	8				10
1	2		4	5	6	14	8³	9¹	10²	11		7			13	3				12			11
1	14		4	5	6⁸		8	9¹	10²	11	12	7			13³	2	3						12
1	2		4	5		13	8	9²	10³	11					14	6	3		7¹	12			13
1	3		4	5¹	12	7		13	10³	11					14	2	6		8	9²			14
1	3			6		7²	8³	12	13	11		14			10	2	5		4	9¹			15
1	2	3	4	6		8	13	9²	11		12				10	5				7¹			16
1	2	3	4			13	14	11		7²					10		5		8¹	9³			17
1	2¹	3	4		6		13	14	11	7					10³	12	5		8	9²			18
1		3	4	5	6	7²	8	9¹	12	11					10	2				13			19
	3	4	5	6	7³	8²		12	11	13					10¹	2		1	14	9			20
1	13	13	4	5	6²	12	7¹	14	11	10					10	2			8	9³			21
1	12	3	7	5	6¹	14		13	11	4					10²	2			8³	9			22
1	6	3	4	5		7	8³	13	10¹	11		14			12	2				9²			23
1	2	3	7	6		13	8¹	14	12	11		4			10³	5				9²			24
1	3¹		7	5	6⁸	11²	8	14	10³		4					2	12		13	9			25
1	3⁸		7	5			11		10²	13		4			8¹	2	6		12	9			26
1	3	8²	5⁸	6¹	13	11		10³		4		7	14		2	12				9			27
1	3		4	6	7¹	8		11	12		13	10³	2	5						9²	14		28
1	3	4	6		8	13	11	12	7		10²	2	5							9¹			29
1	3	7⁸	6		8	10	11	9²	4¹		13	2	5							12			30
1	12	3	6¹	7	8	14	11³	10²	4		13	2	5							9			31
1	3	13	6	7	8	10¹	11	9³	4²		12	2	5							14			32
1	3	7	6	13	8	11	10¹	4	12		2	5								9²			33
1	3	11	6	7¹	8	14	13	12	9³	4	10²	2	5										34
1⁶	3	7	12	6¹	8	10	11	9²	4		13	2	5									15	35
	6	3	7	5		14	8¹	10	11³	4	12	13	2		9²							1	36
	6	3	7	5		14	8	10³	11²	4	12	2	13		9¹							1	37
	6	3¹	7²	5		8	10	11		4	12	2	13	14	9²							1	38

FA Cup

Third Round	York C	(h)	3-1	
Fourth Round	Arsenal	(h)	3-1	
Fifth Round	Manchester C	(a)	1-1	
		(h)	3-1	
Sixth Round	Chelsea	(a)	0-2	

Carling Cup

Second Round	Leyton Orient	(a)	1-0	
Third Round	Blackpool	(h)	4-3	
Fourth Round	Portsmouth	(a)	0-4	

SUNDERLAND

FA Premiership

FOUNDATION

A Scottish schoolmaster named James Allan, working at Hendon Board School, took the initiative in the foundation of Sunderland in 1879 when they were formed as The Sunderland and District Teachers' Association FC at a meeting in the Adults School, Norfolk Street. Due to financial difficulties, they quickly allowed members from outside the teaching profession and so became Sunderland AFC in October 1880.

Stadium of Light, Sunderland, Tyne and Wear SR5 1SU.
Telephone: (0871) 911 1200.
Fax: (0191) 551 5123.
Ticket Office: (0871) 911 1973.
Website: www.safc.com
Email: enquiries@safc.com
Ground Capacity: 49,000.
Record Attendance: Stadium of Light: 48,353 v Liverpool, FA Premier League, 13 April 2002. FA Premier League figure (46,062). Roker Park: 75,118 v Derby Co, FA Cup 6th rd replay, 8 March 1933.
Pitch Measurements: 105m × 68m.
Chairman: Niall Quinn.
Chief Executive: Steve Walton.
Club Secretary: Margaret Byrne.
Manager: Steve Bruce.
Assistant Manager: Eric Black.
Head of Sports Therapy: Pete Friar.

HONOURS

Football League: FL C – Champions 2004–05, 2006–07; Division 1 – Champions 1891–92, 1892–93, 1894–95, 1901–02, 1912–13, 1935–36, 1995–96, 1998–99; Runners-up 1893–94, 1897–98, 1900–01, 1922–23, 1934–35; Division 2 – Champions 1975–76; Runners-up 1963–64, 1979–80. Division 3 – Champions 1987–88.

FA Cup: Winners 1937, 1973; Runners-up 1913, 1992.

Football League Cup: Runners-up 1985.

European Competitions: European Cup-Winners' Cup: 1973–74.

Colours: Red and white striped shirts, black shorts, black stockings with red tops.
Change Colours: Stone shirts with burgundy trim, stone shorts, stone stockings with burgundy tops.
Year Formed: 1879. *Turned Professional:* 1886. *Ltd Co.:* 1906.
Club Nickname: Black Cats.
Previous Name: 1879, Sunderland and District Teacher's AFC; 1880, Sunderland.
Grounds: 1879, Blue House Field, Hendon; 1882, Groves Field, Ashbrooke; 1883, Horatio Street; 1884, Abbs Field, Fulwell; 1886, Newcastle Road; 1898, Roker Park; 1997, Stadium of Light.
First Football League Game: 13 September 1890, Football League, v Burnley (h) L 2–3 – Kirtley; Porteous, Oliver; Wilson, Auld, Gibson; Spence (1), Miller, Campbell (1), Scott, D. Hannah.
Record League Victory: 9–1 v Newcastle U (a), Division 1, 5 December 1908 – Roose; Forster, Melton; Daykin, Thomson, Low; Mordue (1), Hogg (3), Brown, Holley (3), Bridgett (2).
Record Cup Victory: 11–1 v Fairfield, FA Cup 1st rd, 2 February 1895 – Doig; McNeill, Johnston; Dunlop, McCreadie (1), Wilson; Gillespie (1), Millar (5), Campbell, Hannah (3), Scott (1).

sky SPORTS FACT FILE

In 1925 Sunderland signed Dave Halliday from Dundee. He scored ten times in the first four games and raced to hit a century of First Division goals in only 101 games which earned him a then First Division record. He went on to top 150 before joining Arsenal.

Record Defeat: 0–8 v Sheff Wed, Division 1, 26 December 1911. 0–8 v West Ham U, Division 1, 19 October 1968. 0–8 v Watford, Division 1, 25 September 1982.

Most League Points (2 for a win): 61, Division 2, 1963–64.

Most League Points (3 for a win): 105, Division 1, 1998–99 (Football League Record).

Most League Goals: 109, Division 1, 1935–36.

Highest League Scorer in Season: Dave Halliday, 43, Division 1, 1928–29.

Most League Goals in Total Aggregate: Charlie Buchan, 209, 1911–25.

Most League Goals in One Match: 5, Charlie Buchan v Liverpool, Division 1, 7 December 1919; 5, Bobby Gurney v Bolton W, Division 1, 7 December 1935; 5, Dominic Sharkey v Norwich C, Division 2, 20 February 1962.

Most Capped Player: Charlie Hurley, 38 (40), Republic of Ireland.

Most League Appearances: Jim Montgomery, 537, 1962–77.

Youngest League Player: Derek Forster, 15 years 184 days v Leicester C, 22 August 1964.

Record Transfer Fee Received: £5,500,000 from Leeds U for Michael Bridges, July 1999.

Record Transfer Fee Paid: £10,000,000 to Tottenham H for Darren Bent, August 2009.

Football League Record: 1890 Elected to Division 1; 1958–64 Division 2; 1964–70 Division 1; 1970–76 Division 2; 1976–77 Division 1; 1977–80 Division 2; 1980–85 Division 1; 1985–87 Division 2; 1987–88 Division 3; 1988–90 Division 2; 1990–91 Division 1; 1991–92 Division 2; 1992–96 Division 1; 1996–97 FA Premier League; 1997–99 Division 1; 1999–2003 FA Premier League; 2003–04 Division 1; 2004–05 FL C; 2005–06 FA Premier League; 2006–07 FL C; 2007– FA Premier League.

MANAGERS

Tom Watson 1888–96
Bob Campbell 1896–99
Alex Mackie 1899–1905
Bob Kyle 1905–28
Johnny Cochrane 1928–39
Bill Murray 1939–57
Alan Brown 1957–64
George Hardwick 1964–65
Ian McColl 1965–68
Alan Brown 1968–72
Bob Stokoe 1972–76
Jimmy Adamson 1976–78
Ken Knighton 1979–81
Alan Durban 1981–84
Len Ashurst 1984–85
Lawrie McMenemy 1985–87
Denis Smith 1987–91
Malcolm Crosby 1992–93
Terry Butcher 1993
Mick Buxton 1993–95
Peter Reid 1995–2002
Howard Wilkinson 2002–03
Mick McCarthy 2003–06
Niall Quinn 2006
Roy Keane 2006–08
Ricky Sbragia 2008–09
Steve Bruce June 2009–

LATEST SEQUENCES

Longest Sequence of League Wins: 13, 14.11.1891 – 2.4.1892.

Longest Sequence of League Defeats: 17, 18.1.2003 – 16.8.2003.

Longest Sequence of League Draws: 6, 26.3.1949 – 19.4.1949.

Longest Sequence of Unbeaten League Matches: 19, 3.5.1998 – 14.11.1998.

Longest Sequence Without a League Win: 22, 21.12.2002 – 16.8.2003.

Successive Scoring Runs: 29 from 8.11.1997.

Successive Non-scoring Runs: 10 from 27.11.1976.

TEN YEAR LEAGUE RECORD

		P	W	D	L	F	A	Pts	Pos
2000-01	PR Lge	38	15	12	11	46	41	57	7
2001-02	PR Lge	38	10	10	18	29	51	40	17
2002-03	PR Lge	38	4	7	27	21	65	19	20
2003-04	Div 1	46	22	13	11	62	45	79	3
2004-05	FL C	46	29	7	10	76	41	94	1
2005-06	PR Lge	38	3	6	29	26	69	15	20
2006-07	FL C	46	27	7	12	76	47	88	1
2007-08	PR Lge	38	11	6	21	36	59	39	15
2008-09	PR Lge	38	9	9	20	34	54	36	16
2009-10	PR Lge	38	11	11	16	48	56	44	13

DID YOU KNOW ?

On 18 May 1890 half-back Hugh Wilson signed a contract to play for Samuel Tyzack, the club's treasurer rather than Sunderland AFC. He was given a £70 signing-on fee plus the then equivalent of £1.25 a game as well as match bonuses for drawing and winning.

SUNDERLAND 2009–10 LEAGUE RECORD

Match No.	Date	Venue	Opponents		Result	H/T Score	Lg Pos.	Goalscorers	Attendance
1	Aug 15	A	Bolton W	W	1-0	1-0	—	Bent [5]	22,247
2	18	H	Chelsea	L	1-3	1-0	—	Bent [18]	41,179
3	22	H	Blackburn R	W	2-1	1-1	6	Jones 2 [32, 53]	37,106
4	29	A	Stoke C	L	0-1	0-1	9		27,091
5	Sept 12	H	Hull C	W	4-1	1-1	7	Bent 2 (1 pen) [13 (p), 66], Zayatte (og) [75], Reid [49]	38,997
6	19	A	Burnley	L	1-3	1-1	8	Bent [39]	20,196
7	27	H	Wolverhampton W	W	5-2	1-0	8	Bent (pen) [6], Jones 2 (1 pen) [48 (p), 70], Turner [73], Mancienne (og) [89]	37,566
8	Oct 3	A	Manchester U	D	2-2	1-0	7	Bent [7], Jones [58]	75,114
9	17	H	Liverpool	W	1-0	1-0	7	Bent [5]	47,327
10	24	A	Birmingham C	L	1-2	0-1	8	Turner [82]	21,723
11	31	H	West Ham U	D	2-2	1-2	8	Reid [39], Richardson [76]	39,033
12	Nov 7	A	Tottenham H	L	0-2	0-1	8		35,955
13	21	A	Arsenal	W	1-0	0-0	8	Bent [71]	44,918
14	28	H	Wigan Ath	L	0-1	0-0	8		20,447
15	Dec 6	A	Fulham	L	0-1	0-1	10		23,168
16	12	H	Portsmouth	D	1-1	1-0	10	Bent [23]	37,578
17	15	H	Aston Villa	L	0-2	0-1	—		34,821
18	19	A	Manchester C	L	3-4	2-3	10	Mensah [16], Henderson [24], Jones [62]	44,735
19	26	H	Everton	D	1-1	1-0	10	Bent [17]	46,990
20	28	A	Blackburn R	D	2-2	0-0	10	Bent 2 [52, 65]	25,656
21	Jan 16	A	Chelsea	L	2-7	0-4	13	Zenden [56], Bent [90]	41,776
22	27	A	Everton	L	0-2	0-2	—		32,163
23	Feb 1	H	Stoke C	D	0-0	0-0	—		35,078
24	6	H	Wigan Ath	D	1-1	0-1	13	Jones [64]	38,350
25	9	A	Portsmouth	D	1-1	1-0	—	Bent (pen) [12]	16,242
26	20	A	Arsenal	L	0-2	0-1	14		60,083
27	28	H	Fulham	D	0-0	0-0	14		40,192
28	Mar 9	H	Bolton W	W	4-0	1-0	—	Campbell [1], Bent 3 (1 pen) [64, 74 (p), 88]	36,087
29	14	H	Manchester C	D	1-1	1-0	14	Jones [9]	41,398
30	20	A	Birmingham C	W	3-1	2-0	13	Bent 2 [5, 11], Campbell [88]	37,962
31	24	A	Aston Villa	D	1-1	1-1	—	Campbell [22]	37,473
32	28	A	Liverpool	L	0-3	0-2	13		43,121
33	Apr 3	H	Tottenham H	W	3-1	2-0	13	Bent 2 (1 pen) [1, 29 (p)], Zenden [86]	43,184
34	10	A	West Ham U	L	0-1	0-0	—		34,685
35	17	H	Burnley	W	2-1	2-0	13	Campbell [25], Bent [41]	41,341
36	24	A	Hull C	W	1-0	1-0	10	Bent [7]	25,012
37	May 2	H	Manchester U	L	0-1	0-1	11		47,641
38	9	A	Wolverhampton W	L	1-2	1-1	13	Jones [8]	28,971

Final League Position: 13

GOALSCORERS

League (48): Bent 24 (5 pens), Jones 9 (1 pen), Campbell 4, Reid 2, Turner 2, Zenden 2, Henderson 1, Mensah 1, Richardson 1, own goals 2.
Carling Cup (6): Reid 2, Campbell 1, Henderson 1, Tainio 1, own goal 1.
FA Cup (4): Campbell 2, Bent 1, Malbranque 1.

Fulop M 12+1	Bardsley P 18+8	McCartney G 20+5	Cattermole L 19+3	Ferdinand A 19+5	Collins D 3	Malbranque S 30+1	Cana L 29+2	Jones K 24+8	Bent D 38	Richardson K 28+1	Henderson J 23+10	Campbell F 19+12	Leadbitter G —+1	Reid A 18+3	Nosworthy N 7+3	Gordon C 26	Turner M 29	Mensah J 14+2	Da Silva P 12+4	Zenden B 1+19	Healy D —+3	Murphy D 2+1	Moylor D 9+1	Kilgallon M 6+1	Hutton A 11	Mwaruwari B 1+7	Colback J —+1	Match No.
1	2	3	4	5	6	7[1]	8	9	10	11[2]	12	13																1
1	2	3	4[2]	5	6		8	9[1]	10	11[3]	7	12	13	14														2
1	2	3[1]	4	5	6	7[2]	8	9	10[3]	11	13	14			12													3
	2	3	4[3]	5		7[1]	8	9	10	11[2]	14	12		13	6	1												4
	2[2]		4	5		7[3]	8	12	10[1]	3		9		11		1	6	13	14									5
	2	3		5		7[1]	8	12	10	11	13	9[2]		4		1	6											6
		14	11[1]	13		7	8	9	10[3]	3	12			4		1	6	5	2[2]									7
	2	14	11	5		7[3]	8	9[2]	10	3[4]	12	13		4[1]		1	6											8
	2	3[1]	4[2]	5		7	8	9[3]	10	12	14			11		1	6		13									9
	2	14		5		7[3]	4[1]	9	10	3	12	8[2]		11		1	6		13									10
		12				7[1]	6	9[4]	10	3		8		11	5	1	2	4										11
15	2[2]	3	13			7[1]		10	11		8	9			4	1[6]	5	6	12									12
1	2	3	14			7[1]	4		10	11		8	12				5	9[2]	6[3]	13								13
1	2	3[2]				7[1]	4		10	11		8	12				5	9	6[3]	14	13							14
1	2		6[1]			7[2]	4	9[2]	10	3		8		13			5	11	12	14								15
1	3				13		4	9[1]	10[2]	7	8	11				5	2	6	12									16
1	13	3	12			4[4]	9[3]	10	11	7[1]	8					2	5[2]	14	6									17
1		3	4			7[1]	12	10	13	11	9[2]	8				2	5[4]	6[3]	14									18
1	2	3				7[1]	4	9	10	11		8	13				6[2]	5	12									19
1	2	3				4		10	11	9		6					5	8	7									20
1	2	3				7[1]	6	9	10	11	13						5	12	8[2]	4								21
		3	8[2]			4	12	10	11[1]	9		13				1	5[3]	2	14	7	6							22
		3	8[3]			7[1]	4	9	10	14	12	11[2]				1	5	2	13	6								23
		3	8			4	9	10	7[1]	11[2]						1	5	12		6			2		13			24
	14	3	8[4]			7[1]	4	9	10[3]	11[2]						1	5		12	13[8]		6	2					25
	14	3[3]		5			4	9[2]	10	11[1]		8				1	6	7	12						2	13		26
	14	7[1]	6				4	9[2]	10	11		8				1	5	3[3]	12						2	13		27
	12	8[1]	5			7[3]	4	9	10	11						1	6	3[2]	13						2	14		28
	14		5			7[2]	9[1]		10	11	12	8[3]				1	6	3	13			4	2					29
	12	14	6			7[3]		10	11	13	8					1	5	3[1]				4	2	9[2]				30
		4	6			7[2]	13		10	11	8	9				1	5	3[1]	12			4	2					31
	2	8[1]	6			7[2]	4	13	10	3	11[3]	9				1	5		12	14								32
	14	8	6			7[1]		13	10[2]	3	11	9[3]				1	5		4	12		2						33
		4	6			7[2]	12		10	11	8	9				1	5		3[3]	13		2[1]				14		34
		12				7		9	10[3]	3	11	8				1	5	6[1]		13		4[2]				2	14	35
	13		12			7[2]	14	9[3]	10	3	11	8				1	5[1]			13		4	6			2[8]		36
	2	13				7	4	14	10	3	11[3]	9				1	5	6[1]					8[2]	12				37
						7[3]	4[2]	9	10	3	11[1]	8				1	5[8]		12			6			2	13	14[4]	38

FA Cup

Round	Opponent		Score
Third Round	Barrow	(h)	3-0
Fourth Round	Portsmouth	(a)	1-2

Carling Cup

Round	Opponent		Score
Second Round	Norwich C	(a)	4-1
Third Round	Birmingham C	(h)	2-0
Fourth Round	Aston Villa	(h)	0-0

SWANSEA CITY   FL Championship

FOUNDATION

The earliest Association Football in Wales was played in the Northern part of the country and no international took place in the South until 1894, when a local paper still thought it necessary to publish an outline of the rules and an illustration of the pitch markings. There had been an earlier Swansea club, but this has no connection with Swansea Town (now City) formed at a public meeting in June 1912.

Liberty Stadium, Morfa, Landore, Swansea SA1 2FA.
Telephone: (01792) 616 600.
Fax: (01792) 616 606.
Ticket Office: (0870) 040 0004.
Website: www.swanseacity.net
Email: info@swanseacityfc.co.uk
Ground Capacity: 20,520.
Record Attendance: 32,796 v Arsenal, FA Cup 4th rd, 17 February 1968 (at Vetch Field).
Pitch Measurements: 115yd × 74yd.
Chairman: Huw Jenkins.
Vice-chairman: Leigh Dineen.
Secretary: Jackie Rockey.
Manager: TBC.
Assistant Manager: TBC.
Physio: Richard Buchanan.
Colours: All white.
Change Colours: All black with white and black hooped stockings.
Year Formed: 1912. *Turned Professional:* 1912.
Ltd Co.: 1912.
Previous Name: 1912, Swansea Town; 1970, Swansea City.
Club Nicknames: 'The Swans', 'The Jacks'.
Grounds: 1912, Vetch Field; 2005, Liberty Stadium.
First Football League Game: 28 August 1920, Division 3, v Portsmouth (a) L 0–3 – Crumley; Robson, Evans; Smith, Holdsworth, Williams; Hole, I. Jones, Edmundson, Rigsby, Spottiswood.
Record League Victory: 8–0 v Hartlepool U, Division 4, 1 April 1978 – Barber; Evans, Bartley, Lally (1) (Morris), May, Bruton, Kevin Moore, Robbie James (3 incl. 1p), Curtis (3), Toshack (1), Chappell.
Record Cup Victory: 12–0 v Sliema W (Malta), ECWC 1st rd 1st leg, 15 September 1982 – Davies; Marustik, Hadziabdic (1), Irwin (1), Kennedy, Rajkovic (1), Loveridge (2) (Leighton James), Robbie James, Charles (2), Stevenson (1), Latchford (1) (Walsh (3)).

HONOURS

Football League: Division 1 best season: 6th, 1981–82; FL 1 – Champions 2007–08; Division 3 (S) – Champions 1924–25, 1948–49; Division 3 – Champions 1999–2000.
FA Cup: Semi-finals 1926, 1964.
Football League Cup: best season: 4th rd, 1965, 1977, 2009.
Welsh Cup: Winners 11 times; Runners-up 8 times.
Autoglass Trophy: Winners 1994, 2006.
Football League Trophy: Winners 2006.
European Competitions: *European Cup-Winners' Cup:* 1961–62, 1966–67, 1981–82, 1982–83, 1983–84, 1989–90, 1991–92.

sky SPORTS FACT FILE

In October 2000 Swansea City signed Giovanni Savarese, a 29-year-old Venezuelan international forward. He scored twice on his debut against Stoke City and in what proved to be his only season with the club registered 12 goals in 31 League appearances.

Record Defeat: 0–8 v Liverpool, FA Cup 3rd rd, 9 January 1990. 0–8 v Monaco, ECWC, 1st rd 2nd leg, 1 October 1991.

Most League Points (2 for a win): 62, Division 3 (S), 1948–49.

Most League Points (3 for a win): 92, FL 1, 2007–08.

Most League Goals: 90, Division 2, 1956–57.

Highest League Scorer in Season: Cyril Pearce, 35, Division 2, 1931–32.

Most League Goals in Total Aggregate: Ivor Allchurch, 166, 1949–58, 1965–68.

Most League Goals in One Match: 5, Jack Fowler v Charlton Ath, Division 3S, 27 December 1924.

Most Capped Player: Ivor Allchurch, 42 (68), Wales.

Most League Appearances: Wilfred Milne, 585, 1919–37.

Youngest League Player: Nigel Dalling, 15 years 289 days v Southport, 6 December 1974.

Record Transfer Fee Received: £2,000,000 from Wigan Ath for Jason Scotland, July 2009.

Record Transfer Fee Paid: £400,000 to Stockport Co for Ashley Williams, May 2008.

Football League Record: 1920 Original Member of Division 3; 1921–25 Division 3 (S); 1925–47 Division 2; 1947–49 Division 3 (S); 1949–65 Division 2; 1965–67 Division 3; 1967–70 Division 4; 1970–73 Division 3; 1973–78 Division 4; 1978–79 Division 3; 1979–81 Division 2; 1981–83 Division 1; 1983–84 Division 2; 1984–86 Division 3; 1986–88 Division 4; 1988–92 Division 3; 1992–96 Division 2; 1996–2000 Division 3; 2000–01 Division 2; 2001–04 Division 3; 2004–05 FL 2; 2005–08 FL 1; 2008– FL C.

LATEST SEQUENCES

Longest Sequence of League Wins: 9, 27.11.1999 – 22.01.2000.

Longest Sequence of League Defeats: 9, 26.1.1991 – 19.3.1991.

Longest Sequence of League Draws: 8, 25.11.2008 – 28.12.2008.

Longest Sequence of Unbeaten League Matches: 19, 19.10.1970 – 9.3.1971.

Longest Sequence Without a League Win: 15, 25.3.1989 – 2.9.1989.

Successive Scoring Runs: 27 from 28.8.1947.

Successive Non-scoring Runs: 6 from 6.2.1996.

MANAGERS

Walter Whittaker 1912–14
William Bartlett 1914–15
Joe Bradshaw 1919–26
Jimmy Thomson 1927–31
Neil Harris 1934–39
Haydn Green 1939–47
Bill McCandless 1947–55
Ron Burgess 1955–58
Trevor Morris 1958–65
Glyn Davies 1965–66
Billy Lucas 1967–69
Roy Bentley 1969–72
Harry Gregg 1972–75
Harry Griffiths 1975–77
John Toshack 1978–83
   (resigned October re-appointed in December) 1983–84
Colin Appleton 1984
John Bond 1984–85
Tommy Hutchison 1985–86
Terry Yorath 1986–89
Ian Evans 1989–90
Terry Yorath 1990–91
Frank Burrows 1991–95
Bobby Smith 1995
Kevin Cullis 1996
Jan Molby 1996–97
Micky Adams 1997
Alan Cork 1997–98
John Hollins 1998–2001
Colin Addison 2001–02
Nick Cusack 2002
Brian Flynn 2002–04
Kenny Jackett 2004–07
Roberto Martinez 2007–09
Paulo Sousa 2009–10

TEN YEAR LEAGUE RECORD

		P	W	D	L	F	A	Pts	Pos
2000-01	Div 2	46	8	13	25	47	73	37	23
2001-02	Div 3	46	13	12	21	53	77	51	20
2002-03	Div 3	46	12	13	21	48	65	49	21
2003-04	Div 3	46	15	14	17	58	61	59	10
2004-05	FL 2	46	24	8	14	62	43	80	3
2005-06	FL 1	46	18	17	11	78	55	71	6
2006-07	FL 1	46	20	12	14	69	53	72	7
2007-08	FL 1	46	27	11	8	82	42	92	1
2008-09	FL C	46	16	20	10	63	50	68	8
2009-10	FL C	46	17	18	11	40	37	69	7

DID YOU KNOW ?

The legendary Wilf Milne, famous at Swansea Town for scoring for the first time (a penalty) in his 501st League game, went on to notch a total of seven in the competition. But only one of these was from open play against Norwich City in 1934–35 – and he added a penalty!

SWANSEA CITY 2009–10 LEAGUE RECORD

Match No.	Date		Venue	Opponents	Result		H/T Score	Lg Pos.	Goalscorers	Atten- dance
1	Aug	8	A	Leicester C	L	1-2	1-0	—	Williams [17]	26,171
2		15	H	Middlesbrough	L	0-3	0-1	24		16,201
3		18	H	Reading	D	0-0	0-0	—		12,775
4		22	A	Coventry C	W	1-0	0-0	15	Williams [69]	16,307
5		29	H	Watford	D	1-1	0-0	18	Tate [90]	14,172
6	Sept	12	A	Preston NE	L	0-2	0-1	20		12,854
7		15	H	Bristol C	D	0-0	0-0	—		12,859
8		19	A	Barnsley	D	0-0	0-0	20		11,596
9		26	H	Sheffield U	W	2-1	0-0	17	Trundle (pen) [52], Butler [82]	14,324
10		29	A	Doncaster R	D	0-0	0-0	—		8833
11	Oct	3	H	QPR	W	2-0	0-0	14	Gower [74], Trundle [85]	14,444
12		17	A	Ipswich T	D	1-1	1-1	16	Beattie [7]	19,667
13		20	A	WBA	W	1-0	0-0	—	Beattie [50]	21,022
14		24	H	Blackpool	D	0-0	0-0	12		14,724
15		31	A	Scunthorpe U	W	2-0	1-0	11	Beattie [32], Van der Gun [67]	5201
16	Nov	7	H	Cardiff C	W	3-2	2-2	9	Dyer [9], Pratley 2 [16, 61]	18,209
17		20	H	Derby Co	W	1-0	0-0	—	Bessone [81]	17,804
18		28	A	Newcastle U	L	0-3	0-3	6		42,616
19	Dec	5	A	Peterborough U	D	2-2	0-0	7	Trundle 2 [84, 89]	7312
20		8	H	Plymouth Arg	W	1-0	0-0	—	Trundle [52]	14,004
21		12	H	Nottingham F	L	0-1	0-1	6		16,690
22		19	A	Sheffield W	W	2-0	2-0	5	Pratley 2 [5, 36]	18,329
23		26	A	Reading	D	1-1	1-1	6	Pratley [36]	19,608
24		28	H	Crystal Palace	D	0-0	0-0	6		18,794
25	Jan	16	H	Leicester C	W	1-0	1-0	4	Pintado [32]	15,037
26		23	A	Middlesbrough	D	1-1	0-0	—	Pintado [47]	16,847
27		26	H	Coventry C	D	0-0	0-0	—		13,868
28	Feb	6	H	Preston NE	W	2-0	1-0	5	Cotterill [35], Williams [48]	14,659
29		9	A	Crystal Palace	W	1-0	1-0	—	Kuqi [14]	12,328
30		13	H	Newcastle U	D	1-1	0-0	4	Cotterill [56]	15,188
31		16	A	Plymouth Arg	D	1-1	0-0	—	Pratley [46]	9185
32		20	A	Derby Co	W	1-0	0-0	4	Kuqi [66]	31,024
33		27	H	Peterborough U	W	1-0	1-0	4	Cotterill (pen) [19]	16,175
34	Mar	6	A	Nottingham F	L	0-1	0-0	4		25,012
35		9	A	Watford	W	1-0	1-0	—	Kuqi [18]	12,907
36		13	H	Sheffield W	D	0-0	0-0	4		14,167
37		16	H	WBA	L	0-2	0-0	—		17,774
38		20	A	QPR	D	1-1	0-0	5	Dyer [57]	15,502
39		23	A	Blackpool	L	1-5	0-2	—	Van der Gun [84]	9149
40		27	H	Ipswich T	D	0-0	0-0	5		14,902
41	Apr	3	A	Cardiff C	L	1-2	1-1	5	Orlandi [28]	25,130
42		5	H	Scunthorpe U	W	3-0	1-0	5	Edgar [27], Williams [51], Kuqi [80]	14,830
43		10	A	Bristol C	L	0-1	0-0	6		14,719
44		17	H	Barnsley	W	3-1	2-1	6	Williams [23], Kuqi [28], Pratley [72]	15,139
45		24	A	Sheffield U	L	0-2	0-0	7		25,966
46	May	2	H	Doncaster R	D	0-0	0-0	7		17,630

Final League Position: 7

GOALSCORERS

League (40): Pratley 7, Kuqi 5, Trundle 5 (1 pen), Williams 5, Beattie 3, Cotterill 3 (1 pen), Dyer 2, Pintado 2, Van der Gun 2, Bessone 1, Butler 1, Edgar 1, Gower 1, Orlandi 1, Tate 1.
Carling Cup (4): Dobbie 3, Monk 1.
FA Cup (1): Cotterill 1.

De Vries D 46	Rangel A 37 + 1	Tate A 39	Britton L 35 + 1	Monk G 22 + 1	Williams A 45 + 1	Allen J 13 + 8	Macdonald S 2 + 1	Pintado G 16 + 16	Dyer N 37 + 3	Gower M 25 + 6	Lopez J 7 + 5	Orlandi A 22 + 8	Dobbie S 4 + 2	Thomas C — + 1	Richards J 10 + 5	Morgan K 1 + 2	Bond C 1	Collins M 1	Painter M 4	Beattie C 12 + 11	Trundle L 2 + 17	Idrizaj B 1 + 3	Van der Gun C 20 + 5	Bessone F 21	Bodde F 9 + 16	Butler T 9 + 16	Pratley D 33 + 3	Cotterill D 14 + 7	Serran A 3 + 3	Bauza G 3 + 3	Kuqi S 14 + 6	Edgar D 5	Match No.
1	2³	3	4	5	6	7¹	8²	9	10	11	12	13	14																				1
1	2	3	4	5	6		8²	14	10	11¹		7³	9	12	13																		2
1	2	3	4	5	6		13	12	10²	11³		7	9¹	14	8																		3
1	2	3	4	5	6			14	10	11	13	7²	9³		12	8¹																	4
1		5	4¹		6			10²	11	8	7³			13		2	3	9	12	14													5
1		5	4		6			14	10	11	8²	7		2			3³	12	9¹	13													6
1		5	14		6	4³		9	10	8	7²			2			12			11	3	13											7
1	2	3	4	5	6			9³	10	8¹		7					14			11²		12	13										8
1	2	3		5	6			9	10⁴	8	7⁸			13				12²			4³	11¹	14										9
1	2	3		5	6			9²		8³			13	11		4	1⁰		14				7	12									10
1	2	3	4	5	6			10	8	14		9²			1⁰	12						7¹	11³										11
1	2	3	4		6			10²	7³	12	8¹			14			6				5	13	11										12
1	2	3	4		6	14		10²	7³					12			5¹	6		8			13	11									13
1	2	3	4		6			14	12	7							6²	13		8¹	5		10¹	11									14
1	2	3	4	5	6	8²		14		7¹	13						6⁹			10			12	11									15
1	2	3	4		6	8²		12	7³			13					6⁹			10	5		14	11									16
1	2	3	4		6	12			8			7¹					6⁹	14		10²	5		13	11									17
1	2	3	4		6	14		12	8			7					6⁹			10²	5		11³	13									18
1	2				6			9	12		4	7						14		10³	5		8¹	11²	13	3							19
1	2	3	4		6	8²		12	10			14						13	9¹		5		11	7³									20
1	2	3	4³		6			14	8			7					6⁹	12		10²	5		11	13									21
1	2	3			5			9³	8¹		6²	7								10	4		12	11		13	14					22
1	2	3	4		6	13		9³	8			7²						14		10¹	5		12	11									23
1		3	4	12	6	8¹		9³	13			14								10²	5		7	11		2⁹							24
1	2	3	4	5	14	8¹		9³	10						1⁹						6²		11	7	12								25
1		3	4	5	6	8³		9²	10¹	14					1⁹						2		12	11	7								26
1	2			5	6	12		9³	10²			3¹	7					13			4		8	11				14					27
1		3	4	5	6	8³		9¹	10			14									2		13	11	7²		12						28
1		3	4³	5	6	13		14	9²	7¹		8									2		11	12		10							29
1	12	3		5	6	8		13	9³			4									2¹		14	11	7		10²						30
1	2	3		5	6	14		9		13		4³		8					1³¹				7²	11			12						31
1	2	5			6	8²		13⁴	3³	12		4¹		9									14	11	7		10						32
1	2	5	4		6			7	12					9			1⁴	13			8²		11¹	3			10³						33
1	2	3	4		6			8¹	7			5					1³				12		9²	11			10						34
1	2	3	4²		6				7			5					9¹		14	8			13	11			12	10³					35
1	2	3	4		6				7			5					9²	14		12			10¹	11	8³			13					36
1	2	3	4³	5	6			9²	7¹								1²			8			11	13			14	10					37
1	2	5	4		6			9²	7³			8					1⁴			12			13		3¹		11	10					38
1	2	5	4²		6			14	11	7		13								9			12	3¹			8	10³					39
1	2	5	4³		6	13		9¹	12			7²								14			8	11				10	3				40
1	2	5	4		6			9²	8¹	14		7											10³	11	12			13	3				41
1	2			5	6	4²		14	8	7										13			12	11			9¹	10³	3				42
1	2¹			5	6	4		9	10²			7										13		11	8³	12		14	3				43
1			4	5	6				7¹	12										13			9	3	14	11	8¹	2		10²			44
1	2		4	5	6			8¹	7	13										14			9³	3			11²	12		10			45
1	2		4³	5	6			12	9	7¹										1³	14						11	8		10²	3		46

FA Cup
Third Round   Leicester C   (a)   1-2

Carling Cup
First Round   Brighton & HA   (h)   3-0
Second Round   Scunthorpe U   (h)   1-2

SWINDON TOWN   FL Championship 1

The County Ground, County Road, Swindon, Wiltshire SN1 2ED.

Telephone: 0871 423 6433.

Fax: (0844) 880 1112.

Ticket Office: 0871 223 2300.

Website: www.swindontownfc.co.uk

Email: brianp@swindontownfc.co.uk

Ground Capacity: 14,700.

Record Attendance: 32,000 v Arsenal, FA Cup 3rd rd, 15 January 1972.

Pitch Measurements: 110yd × 75yd.

Chairman: Andrew Fitton.

Chief Executive: Nicholas Watkins.

Secretary: Louise Fletcher.

Manager: Danny Wilson.

Assistant Manager: Peter Shirtliff.

Physio: Dick Mackey.

Colours: Red shirts with white inserts, red shorts with white inserts, red stockings with shite inserts.

Change Colours: All white with blue inserts.

Year Formed: 1881* (*see Foundation*).

Turned Professional: 1894.

Ltd Co.: 1894.

Club Nickname: 'Robins'.

Grounds: 1881, The Croft; 1896, County Ground.

First Football League Game: 28 August 1920, Division 3, v Luton T (h) W 9–1 – Nash; Kay, Macconachie; Langford, Hawley, Wareing; Jefferson (1), Fleming (4), Rogers, Batty (2), Davies (1), (1 og).

Record League Victory: 9–1 v Luton T, Division 3 (S), 28 August 1920 – Nash; Kay, Macconachie; Langford, Hawley, Wareing; Jefferson (1), Fleming (4), Rogers, Batty (2), Davies (1), (1 og).

HONOURS

Football League: Best season 1992–93. Division 2 – Champions 1995–96; Division 3 – Runners-up 1962–63, 1968–69; Division 4 – Champions 1985–86 (with record 102 points).

FA Cup: Semi-finals 1910, 1912.

Football League Cup: Winners 1969.

Anglo-Italian Cup: Winners 1970.

sky SPORTS FACT FILE

In 1922–23 Swindon Town signed Jack Evans, a Walsall winger. He scored 14 League and Cup goals and was sold on to Sheffield United for a then club record fee of £300. He returned via Stoke City and Northwich Victoria in 1925–26 and this time scored 25 goals for the club.

Record Cup Victory: 10–1 v Farnham U Breweries (away), FA Cup 1st rd (replay), 28 November 1925 – Nash; Dickenson, Weston, Archer, Bew, Adey; Denyer (2), Wall (1), Richardson (4), Johnson (3), Davies.

Record Defeat: 1–10 v Manchester C, FA Cup 4th rd (replay), 25 January 1930.

Most League Points (2 for a win): 64, Division 3, 1968–69.

Most League Points (3 for a win): 102, Division 4, 1985–86.

Most League Goals: 100, Division 3 (S), 1926–27.

Highest League Scorer in Season: Harry Morris, 47, Division 3 (S), 1926–27.

Most League Goals in Total Aggregate: Harry Morris, 216, 1926–33.

Most League Goals in One Match: 5, Harry Morris v QPR, Division 3 (S), 18 December 1926; 5, Harry Morris v Norwich C, Division 3 (S), 26 April 1930; 5, Keith East v Mansfield T, Division 3, 20 November 1965.

Most Capped Player: Rod Thomas, 30 (50), Wales.

Most League Appearances: John Trollope, 770, 1960–80.

Youngest League Player: Paul Rideout, 16 years 107 days v Hull C, 29 November 1980.

Record Transfer Fee Received: £1,500,000 from Manchester C for Kevin Horlock, January 1997; £1,500,000 from WBA for Simon Cox, July 2009.

Record Transfer Fee Paid: £800,000 to West Ham U for Joey Beauchamp, August 1994.

Football League Record: 1920 Original Member of Division 3; 1921–58 Division 3 (S); 1958–63 Division 3; 1963–65 Division 2; 1965–69 Division 3; 1969–74 Division 2; 1974–82 Division 3; 1982–86 Division 4; 1986–87 Division 3; 1987–92 Division 2; 1992–93 Division 1; 1993–94 FA Premier League; 1994–95 Division 1; 1995–96 Division 2; 1996–2000 Division 1; 2000–04 Division 2; 2004–06 FL 1; 2006–07 FL 2; 2007– FL 1.

MANAGERS

Sam Allen 1902–33
Ted Vizard 1933–39
Neil Harris 1939–41
Louis Page 1945–53
Maurice Lindley 1953–55
Bert Head 1956–65
Danny Williams 1965–69
Fred Ford 1969–71
Dave Mackay 1971–72
Les Allen 1972–74
Danny Williams 1974–78
Bobby Smith 1978–80
John Trollope 1980–83
Ken Beamish 1983–84
Lou Macari 1984–89
Ossie Ardiles 1989–91
Glenn Hoddle 1991–93
John Gorman 1993–94
Steve McMahon 1994–99
Jimmy Quinn 1999–2000
Colin Todd 2000
Andy King 2000–01
Roy Evans 2001
Andy King 2002–06
Iffy Onuora 2006
Dennis Wise 2006
Paul Sturrock 2006–07
Maurice Malpas 2008
Danny Wilson December 2008–

LATEST SEQUENCES

Longest Sequence of League Wins: 8, 12.1.1986 – 15.3.1986.

Longest Sequence of League Defeats: 8, 29.8.2005 – 8.10.2005.

Longest Sequence of League Draws: 6, 22.11.1991 – 28.12.1991.

Longest Sequence of Unbeaten League Matches: 22, 12.1.1986 – 23.8.86.

Longest Sequence Without a League Win: 19, 30.10.1999 – 4.3.2000.

Successive Scoring Runs: 31 from 17.4.1926.

Successive Non-scoring Runs: 5 from 16.11.1963.

TEN YEAR LEAGUE RECORD

		P	W	D	L	F	A	Pts	Pos
2000-01	Div 2	46	13	13	20	47	65	52	20
2001-02	Div 2	46	15	14	17	46	56	59	13
2002-03	Div 2	46	16	12	18	59	63	60	10
2003-04	Div 2	46	20	13	13	76	58	73	5
2004-05	FL 1	46	17	12	17	66	68	63	12
2005-06	FL 1	46	11	15	20	46	65	48	23
2006-07	FL 2	46	25	10	11	58	38	85	3
2007-08	FL 1	46	16	13	17	63	56	61	13
2008-09	FL 1	46	12	17	17	68	71	53	15
2009-10	FL 1	46	22	16	8	73	57	82	5

DID YOU KNOW ?

Jimmy Hogan was given a free transfer by Fulham suffering from a gammy leg. Cured by a bonesetter, he wrote to Norwich City for a trial but received no reply. Signed by Swindon Town, he scored four times against Norwich in a 10–2 win in the Southern League.

SWINDON TOWN 2009–10 LEAGUE RECORD

Match No.	Date	Venue	Opponents	Result	H/T Score	Lg Pos.	Goalscorers	Attendance
1	Aug 8	A	Gillingham	L 0-5	0-1	—		6852
2	15	H	Milton Keynes D	D 0-0	0-0	21		6692
3	18	H	Southampton	W 1-0	1-0	—	Morrison [9]	11,673
4	22	A	Oldham Ath	D 2-2	0-1	12	McGovern [83], Paynter [90]	4229
5	29	H	Southend U	W 2-1	1-0	8	Cuthbert [21], Obadeyi [79]	6417
6	Sept 5	A	Yeovil T	W 1-0	1-0	6	Forbes (og) [41]	4807
7	12	H	Colchester U	D 1-1	1-1	5	Obadeyi [45]	6621
8	19	A	Walsall	D 1-1	0-1	7	Paynter (pen) [80]	4148
9	26	H	Wycombe W	D 1-1	1-0	7	Amankwaah [17]	6929
10	29	A	Exeter C	D 1-1	0-0	—	Amankwaah [53]	5337
11	Oct 3	A	Brentford	W 3-2	2-0	6	Revell 2 [8, 79], Hutchinson [21]	6471
12	10	H	Millwall	D 1-1	1-0	7	Cuthbert [15]	7222
13	17	H	Hartlepool U	L 0-2	0-2	7		7096
14	24	A	Norwich C	L 0-1	0-1	11		24,959
15	31	A	Tranmere R	W 4-1	2-0	8	Paynter 2 [34, 39], McNamee [65], Ferry [90]	5811
16	Nov 21	A	Carlisle U	W 1-0	1-0	9	Austin [3]	4339
17	24	A	Huddersfield T	W 2-1	1-1	—	Paynter [24], Austin [58]	6630
18	Dec 5	H	Leyton Orient	W 3-2	0-0	6	Paynter (pen) [51], Austin 2 [76, 85]	6815
19	12	A	Bristol R	L 0-3	0-3	9		7613
20	19	H	Brighton & HA	W 2-1	1-1	6	Paynter (pen) [31], Austin [54]	7068
21	26	A	Charlton Ath	D 2-2	0-1	7	Austin [56], Paynter [74]	17,977
22	28	H	Yeovil T	W 3-1	2-1	6	Paynter [13], Austin [22], Ward [46]	8509
23	Jan 16	H	Gillingham	W 3-1	1-0	6	Austin [38], Cuthbert [52], Paynter (pen) [74]	6773
24	19	A	Stockport Co	W 1-0	0-0	—	Paynter (pen) [73]	3281
25	26	H	Leeds U	W 3-0	1-0	6	Austin [13], Paynter 2 (1 pen) [60, 63 (p)]	14,508
26	30	A	Southend U	D 2-2	2-0	5	Paynter [1], Austin [10]	6669
27	Feb 6	H	Charlton Ath	D 1-1	0-0	6	Amankwaah [65]	9552
28	9	H	Oldham Ath	W 4-2	2-0	—	Paynter 2 (1 pen) [44, 45 (p)], Austin [48], Ward [58]	6183
29	13	A	Huddersfield T	D 2-2	2-1	5	Austin [10], Ward [27]	14,610
30	20	H	Carlisle U	W 2-0	1-0	5	Austin [31], Paynter [54]	7704
31	23	H	Stockport Co	W 4-1	2-1	—	Ward [4], Paynter 2 [45, 79], Ferry [74]	7063
32	27	A	Leyton Orient	D 0-0	0-0	5		4574
33	Mar 6	A	Bristol R	L 0-4	0-3	5		10,341
34	9	A	Milton Keynes D	L 1-2	0-2	—	Ward [90]	8764
35	13	A	Brighton & HA	W 1-0	0-0	6	Austin [69]	6946
36	16	A	Southampton	W 1-0	0-0	—	Austin [56]	20,752
37	20	H	Norwich C	D 1-1	0-0	4	Greer [90]	11,972
38	27	A	Hartlepool U	W 1-0	1-0	4	Austin [22]	3536
39	Apr 3	A	Leeds U	W 3-0	1-0	2	Paynter 2 [43, 48], Austin [55]	27,881
40	5	H	Tranmere R	W 3-0	2-0	2	Gordon (og) [10], Paynter (pen) [37], Austin [56]	9495
41	10	A	Colchester U	L 0-3	0-1	2		5111
42	12	A	Exeter C	D 1-1	0-1	—	Taylor M (og) [90]	8753
43	17	H	Walsall	D 1-1	0-1	4	Austin [55]	8467
44	24	A	Wycombe W	D 2-2	0-1	4	Paynter [48], Sheehan [80]	7459
45	May 1	H	Brentford	W 3-2	2-1	4	Paynter 2 [8, 58], Ward [45]	10,465
46	8	A	Millwall	L 2-3	1-1	5	Ward [3], Paynter [85]	17,083

Final League Position: 5

GOALSCORERS

League (73): Paynter 26 (8 pens), Austin 19, Ward 7, Amankwaah 3, Cuthbert 3, Ferry 2, Obadeyi 2, Revell 2, Greer 1, Hutchinson 1, McGovern 1, McNamee 1, Morrison 1, Sheehan 1, own goals 3.
Carling Cup (4): Paynter 2, McGovern 1, own goal 1.
FA Cup (2): Greer 1, Paynter 1.
J Paint Trophy (1): McNamee 1.
Play-Offs (3): Ward 2, Austin 1.

Lucas D 41	Cuthbert S 39	Amankwaah K 33+3	Douglas J 43	Morrison S 8+1	Greer G 43+1	Lescinel J 27+6	Timlin M 6+15	Paynter B 37+5	O'Brien A 3+6	McNamee A 14+3	Macklin L 1+8	Marshall M 1+6	McGovern J 45	Obadeyi T 9+3	Kennedy C 4+4	Ferry S 40	Hutchinson B 6+4	Smith P 5+1	Revell A 7+3	Peacock L —+4	Austin C 29+4	Easton C 2+10	Sheehan A 22	Ward D 24+4	Pericard V 2+12	Ritchie M —+4	Darby S 12	Noble F 3+5	Match No.
1	2¹	3	4	5	6	7	8	9	10²	11	12	13																	1
1		2	4	5	6	3	8²	9	13	11	7¹		10	12															2
1		2	4	5	6	3	8	9		11¹	12		7	10²	13														3
1		2	4	5	6	3²	8¹	9	14	11³	12		7	10	13														4
1	5	2	4		6	3	14	9	13	11²			7	12			8³	10¹											5
1	5	2	4		6	3	14	9		11¹	13		7	12			8³	10²											6
	5	2	4		6	3	14	13		12			7	9			8³	10¹	1	11²									7
1	5	2	4	6		3¹		10		12	13		7	9	14		8³			11²									8
1	5	2	4		6	3³	12	10		13			7²	9	14		8¹			11									9
1	5	2	4		6		14	10²		11³			7	9¹	3		8	12	13										10
1	5	2	4		6		13	14		11²	12		7		3		8	10¹		9³									11
1	5	2	4⁸		6	13	12	14		11²			7		3		8	10¹		9³									12
1	2	3		6	12		14			11			7	10	5¹	4	8³			9²	13								13
1	5	2		6	3	8		11¹					7	10²		4	12			9³	14	3							14
1	5	2		6	3	8¹	9³		11				7	10²		4			14	3	12								15
1	5	2	4		6	3	13	9		11²			7			8			12		0¹								16
1	5	2	4		6	3		9		11			7			8			12		0¹								17
1	5	2	4		6	3		9¹					7			8			0	1¹	12								18
1	5	2	8		6	3¹		9	12	14			7			11³			0²		4	13							19
1	5	2¹	8		6	12	13	9	11²				7			4			0		3								20
1	5	2	8		6	3¹		9	12				7			11²	13		0³		4	14							21
1	5	2	8		6		9	4¹					7			11			13	0²	3	12							22
1	5	2	4		6	12		9³					7			11	14		0²		3¹	8	13						23
1	5	2	4		6	3		9					7			11			0			3	8						24
1	5	2	4		6	3		9					7			11			0¹			3	8	12					25
	5	2	4		6	3	12	9					7			11	1		0¹			3	8						26
1	5	2	4		6	3		9		12			7			11			0¹			3	8						27
	5	2	4		6	3		9³			14		7¹			11	1		0²	12		3	8	13					28
1	5	2	4		6	3		9					7			11²			0¹	13		3	8	12					29
1	5	2	4	14	6³			9²					7			11¹			0³	12	3	8	13						30
1	5	2⁴	4	6				9					7			11			0³	13	3	8¹	14	12					31
1	5		4	2	6			9					7			11¹			0²	12	3	8¹	13	14					32
1	5	2	4		6			9					7			11²			0¹		3	8	12	13					33
1	5	2³	4		6¹	13	14	9					7			11			2		3	8	10²						34
1⁶	5		4		6			12					7			11	15		0	13	3	8²	9¹		2				35
	5¹		4		6	12	14			8²	7		11⁸	1			0			3	9¹			13	2				36
		4		6	3	12		13	7				1				0³	11¹	5	8	14			2	9²				37
1		4		6	3	13	12		7				11				0²	14	2	8³			5	9¹					38
1	5		4		6	3		9²					7			11			0	12		8¹			2	13			39
1	5		4		6		14	9¹			13	7				11³			0		3	8²			2	12			40
1	5		4		6			9					7			11²			0²		3	8	12	13	2¹				41
1	5²	12	4		6			9					7			11			0		3	8	13		2¹				42
1	5		4		6	12		9					7			11¹			0²		3	8¹⁴			2	13			43
1	5	14	4		6			9		12			7			11²			0	13	3	8¹			2³				44
1		4		6	3			9					7				2	11	2	8			5	10¹					45
1	13	4		6	3		9	12					7¹			11			0³		2	8		5²	14				46

FA Cup

First Round	Woking	(h)	1-0
Second Round	Wrexham	(a)	1-0
Third Round	Fulham	(a)	0-1

Carling Cup

First Round	Milton Keynes D	(a)	4-1
Second Round	Wolverhampton W	(a)	0-0

J Paint Trophy

Second Round	Exeter C	(a)	1-1
Southern Quarter-Final	Norwich C	(h)	0-0

Play-Offs

Semi-Final	Charlton Ath	(h)	2-1
		(a)	1-2
Final	Millwall		0-1
(at Wembley).			

TORQUAY UNITED   FL Championship 2

FOUNDATION

The idea of establishing a Torquay club was agreed by old boys of Torquay College and Torbay College, while sitting in Princess Gardens listening to the band. A proper meeting was subsequently held at Tor Abbey Hotel at which officers were elected. This was on 1 May 1899 and the club's first competition was the Eastern League (later known as the East Devon League). As an amateur club it played at Teignmouth Road, Torquay Recreation Ground and Cricket Field Road before settling down for four years at Torquay Cricket Ground where the rugby club now plays. They became Torquay United in 1921 after merging with Babbacombe FC.

Plainmoor Ground, Torquay, Devon TQ1 3PS.

Telephone: (01803) 328 666.

Fax: (01803) 323 976.

Ticket Office: (01803) 328 666.

Website: www.torquayunited.com

Email: reception@torquayunited.com

Ground Capacity: 6,117.

Record Attendance: 21,908 v Huddersfield T, FA Cup 4th rd, 29 January 1955.

Pitch Measurements: 110yd × 74yd.

Chairman: Simon Baker.

Vice-chairman: Paul Bristow.

Secretary: Ann Sandford.

Manager: Paul Buckle.

First Team Coach: Shaun North.

Physio: Pete Morgan.

Colours: All yellow with blue inserts.

Change Colours: All white with blue design, tangerine cuffs and stocking tops.

Year Formed: 1899.

Turned Professional: 1921.

Ltd Co.: 1921.

Previous Name: 1910, Torquay Town; 1921, Torquay United.

Club Nickname: 'The Gulls'.

Grounds: 1899, Teignmouth Road; 1900, Torquay Recreation Ground; 1904, Cricket Field Road; 1906, Torquay Cricket Ground; 1910, Plainmoor Ground.

First Football League Game: 27 August 1927, Division 3 (S), v Exeter C (h) D 1–1 – Millsom; Cook, Smith; Wellock, Wragg, Connor, Mackey, Turner (1), Jones, McGovern, Thomson.

Record League Victory: 9–0 v Swindon T, Division 3 (S), 8 March 1952 – George Webber; Topping,

HONOURS

Football League: Division 3 (S) – Runners-up 1956–57.

FA Cup: best season: 4th rd, 1949, 1955, 1971, 1983, 1990, 2009.

Football League Cup: never past 3rd rd.

Sherpa Van Trophy: Runners-up 1989.

sky SPORTS FACT FILE

The first Torquay United player to go on and win international honours was Ralph Birkett, an outside-right from Newton Abbot and signed from Dartmouth United. He was transferred to Arsenal and was capped for England against Ireland on 19 October 1935.

Ralph Calland; Brown, Eric Webber, Towers; Shaw (1), Marchant (1), Northcott (2), Collins (3), Edds (2).

Record Cup Victory: 7–1 v Northampton T, FA Cup 1st rd, 14 November 1959 – Gill; Penford, Downs; Bettany, George Northcott, Rawson; Baxter, Cox, Tommy Northcott (1), Bond (3), Pym (3).

Record Defeat: 2–10 v Fulham, Division 3 (S), 7 September 1931. 2–10 v Luton T, Division 3 (S), 2 September 1933.

Most League Points (2 for a win): 60, Division 4, 1959–60.

Most League Points (3 for a win): 81, Division 3, 2003–04.

Most League Goals: 89, Division 3 (S), 1956–57.

Highest League Scorer in Season: Sammy Collins, 40, Division 3 (S), 1955–56.

Most League Goals in Total Aggregate: Sammy Collins, 204, 1948–58.

Most League Goals in One Match: 5, Robin Stubbs v Newport Co, Division 4, 19 October 1963.

Most Capped Player: Tony Bedeau, 4, Grenada.

Most League Appearances: Dennis Lewis, 443, 1947–59.

Youngest League Player: David Byng, 16 years 36 days v Walsall, 14 August 1993.

Record Transfer Fee Received: £400,000 from Crystal Palace for Matthew Greg, October 1998.

Record Transfer Fee Paid: £75,000 to Peterborough U for Leon Constantine, December 2004.

Football League Record: 1927 Elected to Division 3 (S); 1958–60 Division 4; 1960–62 Division 3; 1962–66 Division 4; 1966–72 Division 3; 1972–91 Division 4; 1991–2004 Division 3; 2004–05 FL 1; 2005–07 FL 2; 2007–09 Blue Square Pr; 2009– FL 2.

LATEST SEQUENCES

Longest Sequence of League Wins: 8, 24.1.1998 – 3.3.1998.

Longest Sequence of League Defeats: 8, 30.9.1995 – 18.11.1995.

Longest Sequence of League Draws: 8, 25.10.1969 – 13.12.1969.

Longest Sequence of Unbeaten League Matches: 15, 5.5.1990 – 3.11.1990.

Longest Sequence Without a League Win: 19, 23.9.2006 – 20.1.2007.

Successive Scoring Runs: 19 from 3.10.1953.

Successive Non-scoring Runs: 7 from 8.1.1972.

MANAGERS

Percy Mackrill 1927–29
A. H. Hoskins 1929
  (Secretary-Manager)
Frank Womack 1929–32
Frank Brown 1932–38
Alf Steward 1938–40
Billy Butler 1945–46
Jack Butler 1946–47
John McNeil 1947–50
Bob John 1950
Alex Massie 1950–51
Eric Webber 1951–65
Frank O'Farrell 1965–68
Alan Brown 1969–71
Jack Edwards 1971–73
Malcolm Musgrove 1973–76
Mike Green 1977–81
Frank O'Farrell 1981–82
  (continued as General Manager to 1983)
Bruce Rioch 1982–84
Dave Webb 1984–85
John Sims 1985
Stuart Morgan 1985–87
Cyril Knowles 1987–89
Dave Smith 1989–91
John Impey 1991–92
Ivan Golac 1992
Paul Compton 1992–93
Don O'Riordan 1993–95
Eddie May 1995–96
Kevin Hodges *(Head Coach)* 1996–98
Wes Saunders 1998–2001
Roy McFarland 2001–02
Leroy Rosenior 2002–06
Ian Atkins 2006
Lubos Kubik 2006–07
Keith Curle 2007
Leroy Rosenior 2007
Paul Buckle June 2007–

TEN YEAR LEAGUE RECORD

		P	W	D	L	F	A	Pts	Pos
2000-01	Div 3	46	12	13	21	52	77	49	21
2001-02	Div 3	46	12	15	19	46	63	51	19
2002-03	Div 3	46	16	18	12	71	71	66	9
2003-04	Div 3	46	23	12	11	68	44	81	3
2004-05	FL 1	46	12	15	19	55	79	51	21
2005-06	FL 2	46	13	13	20	53	66	52	20
2006-07	FL 2	46	7	14	25	36	63	35	24
2007-08	B Sq Pr	46	26	8	12	83	57	86	3
2008-09	B Sq Pr	46	23	14	9	72	47	83	4
2009-10	FL 2	46	14	15	17	64	55	57	17

DID YOU KNOW ?

Dean Edwards was the first Torquay United player to score a goal at Wembley. It was in the Sherpa Van Trophy against Bolton Wanderers in May 1989. Signed from neighbours Exeter City, he made over 100 League appearances in just over three seasons at Plainmoor.

TORQUAY UNITED 2009–10 LEAGUE RECORD

Match No.	Date	Venue	Opponents	Result	H/T Score	Lg Pos.	Goalscorers	Attendance
1	Aug 8	H	Chesterfield	W 2-0	1-0	—	Rendell [15], Mansell [71]	3966
2	15	A	Dagenham & R	L 3-5	0-1	10	Wroe (pen) [62], Benyon [81], Carayol [87]	1804
3	18	A	Burton Alb	W 2-0	2-0	—	Rendell [26], Benyon [37]	2670
4	22	H	Barnet	L 0-1	0-1	12		2856
5	29	A	Bradford C	L 0-2	0-1	15		11,123
6	Sept 5	H	Bournemouth	L 1-2	0-0	17	Todd [64]	3881
7	12	A	Rochdale	L 1-2	0-1	18	Hargreaves [90]	2407
8	19	H	Grimsby T	L 0-2	0-0	22		2575
9	26	A	Macclesfield T	L 1-2	0-0	23	Benyon [51]	1745
10	29	H	Aldershot T	D 1-1	0-0	—	Sills [84]	2271
11	Oct 3	H	Bury	D 1-1	0-1	23	Benyon [59]	2524
12	11	A	Notts Co	D 2-2	1-2	23	Ellis [43], Sills [77]	8812
13	17	H	Morecambe	D 2-2	1-1	22	Wroe (pen) [19], Carlisle [54]	2614
14	24	A	Lincoln C	D 0-0	0-0	22		3604
15	31	H	Northampton T	W 1-0	0-0	22	Hargreaves [83]	2732
16	Nov 14	A	Shrewsbury T	D 1-1	0-0	22	Hargreaves [78]	5072
17	21	H	Rotherham U	L 0-2	0-0	22		2551
18	24	A	Port Vale	D 2-2	1-1	—	Wroe [17], Rendell [67]	3996
19	Dec 1	H	Cheltenham T	W 3-0	2-0	—	Zebroski [6], Rendell [38], Thomson [48]	2122
20	5	A	Accrington S	L 2-4	1-2	21	Wroe (pen) [10], Zebroski [82]	1351
21	12	H	Darlington	W 5-0	3-0	19	Zebroski 2 [17, 69], Carlisle [31], Rendell [45], Benyon [77]	2434
22	26	H	Hereford U	W 1-0	1-0	17	Wroe (pen) [19]	3792
23	28	A	Bournemouth	L 1-2	0-0	19	Rendell [63]	7626
24	Jan 16	A	Chesterfield	L 0-1	0-0	—		3215
25	23	H	Burton Alb	L 2-3	2-1	21	Rendell [8], Robertson [15]	2629
26	26	A	Barnet	D 1-1	0-1	—	Furlong (og) [85]	1331
27	30	H	Bradford C	L 1-2	1-0	20	Robertson [15]	2592
28	Feb 2	A	Crewe Alex	D 1-1	1-0	—	Zebroski [7]	3421
29	6	A	Hereford U	L 0-1	0-1	21		2123
30	13	H	Port Vale	L 1-2	0-1	21	Benyon [58]	2563
31	19	A	Rotherham U	D 1-1	0-1	—	Benyon [85]	3339
32	23	A	Cheltenham T	D 1-1	0-1	—	Carayol [89]	2607
33	27	H	Accrington S	W 2-1	0-0	20	Mansell [50], Kempson (og) [90]	2503
34	Mar 2	H	Dagenham & R	D 0-0	0-0	—		2140
35	6	A	Darlington	W 3-1	2-0	19	Ellis [10], O'Kane [46], Carayol [85]	1819
36	13	H	Crewe Alex	D 1-1	1-0	21	Rendell [38]	2507
37	20	H	Lincoln C	L 2-3	1-1	21	Wroe [29], Zebroski [76]	2547
38	27	A	Morecambe	L 0-2	0-1	21		1734
39	Apr 3	H	Shrewsbury T	W 2-1	0-1	21	Ellis [47], Rendell [61]	3094
40	5	A	Northampton T	D 0-0	0-0	21		5515
41	10	H	Rochdale	W 5-0	3-0	21	Rendell [29], Benyon 2 [31, 35], Wroe (pen) [62], Carayol [77]	3093
42	13	A	Aldershot T	W 2-0	2-0	—	Benyon [17], Rendell [36]	3652
43	17	A	Grimsby T	W 3-0	0-0	19	Wroe (pen) [54], Benyon [62], Carayol [71]	5702
44	24	H	Macclesfield T	W 1-0	0-0	18	Wroe [86]	2570
45	May 1	A	Bury	W 3-0	1-0	16	Carayol [37], Stevens [88], Rendell [90]	3492
46	8	H	Notts Co	D 0-0	0-0	17		5124

Final League Position: 17

GOALSCORERS

League (64): Rendell 12, Benyon 11, Wroe 9 (6 pens), Carayol 6, Zebroski 6, Ellis 3, Hargreaves 3, Carlisle 2, Mansell 2, Robertson 2, Sills 2, O'Kane 1, Stevens 1, Thomson 1, Todd 1, own goals 2.
Carling Cup (1): Sills 1.
FA Cup (7): Benyon 3, Wroe 3 (2 pens), Rendell 1.
J Paint Trophy (5): Stevens 2, Benyon 1, Sills 1, Wroe 1 (pen).

	Bevan S 17+1	Mansell L 35+4	Nicholson K 23+4	Hargreaves C 21+2	Robertson C 45	Todd C 9	Carlisle W 20+4	Wroe N 45	Rendell S 28+7	Sills T 12+6	Stevens D 16+11	Hodges L 2+3	Benyon E 31+14	Charnock K 22+2	Carayol M 11+9	Brough M —+1	Thompson T 17+7	Poke M 28+1	Williams M 1+3	Ellis M 25+2	Mills D —+2	Thomson J 13+2	Smith A 16	Zebroski C 30	O'Kane E 5+11	Cox S 1+2	Branston G 16	Camara M 2	Barnes A 6	Macklin L 3+1	Rowe-Turner L 5+1	Collis S 1	Match No.
	1	2	3	4	5	6	7	8	9^2	10	11^1	12	13																				1
	1		3	4	2	5	7		8^3	9^2	10	11^1		12	6	13	14																2
	1	13	3	4	2	5	7^2	8	9^1	12	11^3	14	10	6																			3
	1	12	3	4	2	5^1	13	8	9^3	14	7^2		10	6	11																		4
	1		3	4	2	5	11	8	12	10	7^2		9^1	6	13																		5
	1		3	4^3	2	5	11	8	13	10^2	7	12	9	6^1		14																	6
			3	14	2	5	11	8	10		7^2	4^1	9^3		13		6	1	12														7
			3^1	4	2	5^2	13	8	10^3	14	7		9		12		1	11	6														8
			4	2	5	11	8	8^1		10	7^2	3	9^3		14		1	12	6	13													9
		5	3	4	2		11	8	12	10^8	7		9^1				1		6														10
		5	3	4	2		11	8	10		7		9				1		6														11
		2	3	4	5		8		10		9	11		7	1				6														12
		2	3	4	5	12	8	11^1	10	13	9^3		7^2	1		6	14																13
		2	3	4	5		7	8	10	11		6	9	1																			14
		2	3	4	5		7	8	13	10	12		9^2	6	1			11^1															15
		2	3	4	5		7		10^3	11^1	12	6^8	9	1	14	13		8^2															16
		2			5		7^3	8	13	10^2	14		9^1		4	1	6		12	3	11		5^2	11^3									17
		2		4	5		7^8	8	10^2	13			9^1		12	1	6			3	11												18
		2	14	4	3		7	8	9		12		13				1		6		10^1	5^2	11^3										19
		2	13	4	3		8^1	9^3	14			12	6				7^1			10		5^2	11										20
		2^3	14	4	5		7^1	8	9^2	12	13	6					1			11		3	10										21
		2		3	7		8	12					9^1	6			11	1				4	5	10									22
		2	13	3			7	8	9				12	6			11^2	1				4^1	5	10									23
		2		4^2	5		7	8	9				12	6				1				11	3	10^1	13								24
		2		4	5^3			8	10		12		9^1	6				1	14			7^2	3	11	13								25
		2^1			5			8	10		13		9^2	6			7	1				4^5	3	11	14	12							26
		2			5			4	10^1		7		9	6			8	1					3	11	12								27
		14			3			8			7^2		9^3	2^1			11	1				4	6	10	13	12	5						28
		13			3			8			14		12				11^2	1				4	6	10	9^3	2	5						29
	15	2			3			8			13		12	4					16^1			7^1	6	10	11^2		5	3	9				30
	1	2			3			8					13	14			7^3		4					10			5	6^1	9	11^2	12		31
	1				3			8					9	13			7		6		12			11			5	10^1	4^2	2			32
	1	4			3		12	8					9^2	13		14			6					11			5	13^3	7^1	2			33
	1	2			6			8					12	13		7			4					10	11^2		5	3		3			34
	1	2			6			8	14				13	12		7^2			4					10	11^3		5	3^1		3			35
	1	2			6		7	8	10				9^1	12					4						1		5			3			36
	1	2	12		3			8	10				9^2		7				4^1			6		1			5		13				37
	1	2			3			8	10				12		7				4			6		1	9^1		5						38
	1	2	3		6			8	10		12		9^2	13	7^1				4					1			5						39
	1	2	3		6			8	10				9		7				4					1			5						40
	1^6	2	3		6			8	10		12		9^2		7				15					1	13		5						41
		2	3		6			8	10				9^2		7^1		12	1	4					1	13		5						42
		2	3		6			8	10^3				9^1	12	7^2		13	1	4					1	14		5^8						43
		2	3		6			8	10				9	5	7^2			1	4					1	12								44
		2	3		6			8	10		13		9^2	5	7^2			1	4					1	12								45
		2	3		6			8	10				7^1		9	5			4					1	12							1	46

FA Cup

First Round	Cheltenham T	(h)	3-1
Second Round	Stockport Co	(a)	4-0
Third Round	Brighton & HA	(h)	0-1

Carling Cup

First Round	Crystal Palace	(a)	1-2

J Paint Trophy

First Round	Cheltenham T	(a)	3-1
Second Round	Southampton	(a)	2-2

TOTTENHAM HOTSPUR   FA Premiership

FOUNDATION

The Hotspur Football Club was formed from an older cricket club in 1882. Most of the founders were old boys of St John's Presbyterian School and Tottenham Grammar School. The Casey brothers were well to the fore as the family provided the club's first goalposts (painted blue and white) and their first ball. They soon adopted the local YMCA as their meeting place, but after a couple of moves settled at the Red House, which is still their headquarters, although now known simply as 748 High Road.

White Hart Lane, Bill Nicholson Way, 748 High Road, Tottenham, London N17 0AP.

Telephone: (0844) 499 5000.

Fax: (020) 8365 5005.

Ticket Office: 0844 844 0102.

Website: www.tottenhamhotspur.com

Email: website@tottenhamhotspur.com

Ground Capacity: 36,534.

Record Attendance: 75,038 v Sunderland, FA Cup 6th rd. 5 March 1938.

Pitch Measurements: 100m × 67m.

Executive Chairman: Daniel Levy.

Secretary: Darren Eales.

Manager: Harry Redknapp.

Assistant Manager: Kevin Bond.

Head of Medical Services: Wayne Diesel.

Colours: White shirts with black and yellow trim, black shorts, white stockings.

Change Colours: All black with yellow trim.

Year Formed: 1882.

Turned Professional: 1895.

Ltd Co.: 1898.

Previous Name: 1882, Hotspur Football Club; 1884, Tottenham Hotspur.

Club Nickname: 'Spurs'.

Grounds: 1882, Tottenham Marshes; 1888, Northumberland Park; 1899, White Hart Lane.

First Football League Game: 1 September 1908, Division 2, v Wolverhampton W (h) W 3–0 – Hewitson; Coquet, Burton; Morris (1), D. Steel, Darnell; Walton, Woodward (2), Macfarlane, R. Steel, Middlemiss.

Record League Victory: 9–0 v Bristol R, Division 2, 22 October 1977 – Daines; Naylor, Holmes,

HONOURS

Football League: Division 1 – Champions 1950–51, 1960–61; Runners-up 1921–22, 1951–52, 1956–57, 1962–63; Division 2 – Champions 1919–20, 1949–50; Runners-up 1908–09, 1932–33.

FA Cup: Winners 1901 (as non-League club), 1921, 1961, 1962, 1967, 1981, 1982, 1991; Runners-up 1987.

Football League Cup: Winners 1971, 1973, 1999, 2008; Runners-up 1982, 2002, 2009.

European Competitions: European Cup: 1961–62. European Cup-Winners' Cup: 1962–63 (winners), 1963–64, 1967–68, 1981–82, 1982–83, 1991–92. UEFA Cup: 1971–72 (winners), 1972–73, 1973–74 (runners-up), 1983–84 (winners), 1984–85, 1999–2000, 2006–07, 2007–08, 2008–09. Intertoto Cup: 1995.

sky SPORTS FACT FILE

On 22 November 2009 Tottenham Hotspur defeated Wigan Athletic 9–1 to record the club's biggest win for 32 years. Jermain Defoe scored five second-half goals including a perfect hat-trick. It was only the second time a team had scored nine in the Premier League.

Hoddle (1), McAllister, Perryman, Pratt, McNab, Moores (3), Lee (4), Taylor (1).

Record Cup Victory: 13–2 v Crewe Alex, FA Cup 4th rd (replay), 3 February 1960 – Brown; Hills, Henry; Blanchflower, Norman, Mackay; White, Harmer (1), Smith (4), Allen (5), Jones (3 incl. 1p).

Record Defeat: 0–8 v Cologne, UEFA Intertoto Cup, 22 July 1995.

Most League Points (2 for a win): 70, Division 2, 1919–20.

Most League Points (3 for a win): 77, Division 1, 1984–85.

Most League Goals: 115, Division 1, 1960–61.

Highest League Scorer in Season: Jimmy Greaves, 37, Division 1, 1962–63.

Most League Goals in Total Aggregate: Jimmy Greaves, 220, 1961–70.

Most League Goals in One Match: 5, Ted Harper v Reading, Division 2, 30 August 1930; 5, Alf Stokes v Birmingham C, Division 1, 18 September 1957; 5, Bobby Smith v Aston Villa, Division 1, 29 March 1958.

Most Capped Player: Pat Jennings, 74 (119), Northern Ireland.

Most League Appearances: Steve Perryman, 655, 1969–86.

Youngest League Player: Ally Dick, 16 years 301 days v Manchester C, 20 February 1982.

Record Transfer Fee Received: £30,750,000 from Manchester U for Dimitar Berbatov, September 2008.

Record Transfer Fee Paid: £17,000,000 to Blackburn R for David Bentley, July 2008.

Football League Record: 1908 Elected to Division 2; 1909–15 Division 1; 1919–20 Division 2; 1920–28 Division 1; 1928–33 Division 2; 1933–35 Division 1; 1935–50 Division 2; 1950–77 Division 1; 1977–78 Division 2; 1978–92 Division 1; 1992– FA Premier League.

MANAGERS

Frank Brettell 1898–99
John Cameron 1899–1906
Fred Kirkham 1907–08
Peter McWilliam 1912–27
Billy Minter 1927–29
Percy Smith 1930–35
Jack Tresadern 1935–38
Peter McWilliam 1938–42
Arthur Turner 1942–46
Joe Hulme 1946–49
Arthur Rowe 1949–55
Jimmy Anderson 1955–58
Bill Nicholson 1958–74
Terry Neill 1974–76
Keith Burkinshaw 1976–84
Peter Shreeves 1984–86
David Pleat 1986–87
Terry Venables 1987–91
Peter Shreeves 1991–92
Doug Livermore 1992–93
Ossie Ardiles 1993–94
Gerry Francis 1994–97
Christian Gross *(Head Coach)* 1997–98
George Graham 1998–2001
Glenn Hoddle 2001–03
David Pleat *(Caretaker)* 2003–04
Jacques Santini 2004
Martin Jol 2004–07
Juande Ramos 2007–08
Harry Redknapp October 2008–

LATEST SEQUENCES

Longest Sequence of League Wins: 13, 23.4.1960 – 1.10.1960.

Longest Sequence of League Defeats: 7, 1.1.1994 – 27.2.1994.

Longest Sequence of League Draws: 6, 9.1.1999 – 27.2.1999.

Longest Sequence of Unbeaten League Matches: 22, 31.8.1949 – 31.12.1949.

Longest Sequence Without a League Win: 16, 29.12.1934 – 13.4.1935.

Successive Scoring Runs: 32 from 24.2.1962.

Successive Non-scoring Runs: 6 from 28.12.1985.

TEN YEAR LEAGUE RECORD

		P	W	D	L	F	A	Pts	Pos
2000-01	PR Lge	38	13	10	15	47	54	49	12
2001-02	PR Lge	38	14	8	16	49	53	50	9
2002-03	PR Lge	38	14	8	16	51	62	50	10
2003-04	PR Lge	38	13	6	19	47	57	45	14
2004-05	PR Lge	38	14	10	14	47	41	52	9
2005-06	PR Lge	38	18	11	9	53	38	65	5
2006-07	PR Lge	38	17	9	12	57	54	60	5
2007-08	PR Lge	38	11	13	14	66	61	46	11
2008-09	PR Lge	38	14	9	15	45	45	51	8
2009-10	PR Lge	38	21	7	10	67	41	70	4

DID YOU KNOW ?

On 5 May 2010 Tottenham Hotspur won 1–0 at Manchester City to secure fourth place in the Premier League and entry into the Champions League. It represented the club's highest finishing position since placing third in the First Division at the end of 1989–90.

TOTTENHAM HOTSPUR 2009–10 LEAGUE RECORD

Match No.	Date	Venue	Opponents	Result	H/T Score	Lg Pos.	Goalscorers	Attendance
1	Aug 16	H	Liverpool	W 2-1	1-0	—	Assou-Ekotto [44], Bassong [59]	35,935
2	19	A	Hull C	W 5-1	3-1	—	Defoe 3 [10, 45, 90], Palacios [14], Keane [78]	24,735
3	23	A	West Ham U	W 2-1	0-0	1	Defoe [54], Lennon [79]	33,095
4	29	H	Birmingham C	W 2-1	0-0	2	Crouch [72], Lennon [90]	35,318
5	Sept 12	H	Manchester U	L 1-3	1-2	4	Defoe [1]	35,785
6	20	A	Chelsea	L 0-3	0-1	6		41,623
7	26	H	Burnley	W 5-0	2-0	4	Keane 4 (1 pen) [18 (p), 74, 77, 87], Jenas [33]	35,462
8	Oct 3	A	Bolton W	D 2-2	1-1	3	Kranjcar [34], Corluka [73]	21,305
9	17	A	Portsmouth	W 2-1	2-0	3	King [29], Defoe [45]	20,821
10	24	H	Stoke C	L 0-1	0-0	4		36,031
11	31	A	Arsenal	L 0-3	0-2	5		60,103
12	Nov 7	H	Sunderland	W 2-0	1-0	4	Keane [12], Huddlestone [68]	35,955
13	22	A	Wigan Ath	W 9-1	1-0	4	Crouch [9], Defoe 5 [51, 54, 58, 69, 87], Lennon [64], Bentley [68], Kranjcar [90]	35,650
14	28	A	Aston Villa	D 1-1	0-1	3	Dawson [77]	39,866
15	Dec 6	A	Everton	D 2-2	0-0	4	Defoe [47], Dawson [59]	34,003
16	12	H	Wolverhampton W	L 0-1	0-1	5		36,012
17	16	H	Manchester C	W 3-0	1-0	—	Kranjcar 2 [37, 90], Defoe [54]	35,891
18	19	A	Blackburn R	W 2-0	1-0	5	Crouch 2 [45, 83]	26,490
19	26	H	Fulham	D 0-0	0-0	5		25,679
20	28	H	West Ham U	W 2-0	1-0	4	Modric [11], Defoe [81]	35,994
21	Jan 16	H	Hull C	D 0-0	0-0	4		35,729
22	20	A	Liverpool	L 0-2	0-1	—		42,016
23	26	H	Fulham	W 2-0	1-0	—	Crouch [27], Bentley [60]	35,467
24	30	A	Birmingham C	D 1-1	0-0	4	Defoe [69]	27,238
25	Feb 6	H	Aston Villa	D 0-0	0-0	5		35,899
26	10	A	Wolverhampton W	L 0-1	0-1	—		27,992
27	21	A	Wigan Ath	W 3-0	1-0	4	Defoe [27], Pavlyuchenko 2 [84, 90]	16,165
28	28	H	Everton	W 2-1	2-0	4	Pavlyuchenko [11], Modric [28]	35,912
29	Mar 13	H	Blackburn R	W 3-1	1-0	4	Defoe [45], Pavlyuchenko 2 [55, 85]	35,474
30	20	A	Stoke C	W 2-1	0-0	4	Gudjohnsen [46], Kranjcar [77]	27,575
31	27	H	Portsmouth	W 2-0	2-0	4	Crouch [27], Kranjcar [41]	35,870
32	Apr 3	A	Sunderland	L 1-3	0-2	5	Crouch [72]	43,184
33	14	H	Arsenal	W 2-1	1-0	—	Rose [10], Bale [47]	36,041
34	17	H	Chelsea	W 2-1	2-0	4	Defoe (pen) [15], Bale [44]	35,814
35	24	A	Manchester U	L 1-3	0-0	4	King [70]	75,268
36	May 1	H	Bolton W	W 1-0	1-0	4	Huddlestone [38]	35,852
37	5	A	Manchester C	W 1-0	0-0	—	Crouch [82]	47,370
38	9	A	Burnley	L 2-4	2-1	4	Bale [3], Modric [32]	21,161

Final League Position: 4

GOALSCORERS

League (67): Defoe 18 (1 pen), Crouch 8, Keane 6 (1 pen), Kranjcar 6, Pavlyuchenko 5, Bale 3, Lennon 3, Modric 3, Bentley 2, Dawson 2, Huddlestone 2, King 2, Assou-Ekotto 1, Bassong 1, Corluka 1, Gudjohnsen 1, Jenas 1, Palacios 1, Rose 1.
Carling Cup (12): Crouch 4, Huddlestone 2, Keane 2, Bentley 1, Defoe 1, O'Hara 1, Pavlyuchenko 1.
FA Cup (17): Defoe 5, Pavlyuchenko 4, Kranjcar 2, Bentley 1, Crouch 1, Gudjohnsen 1, Keane 1 (pen), own goals 2.

Gomes H 31	Corluka V 29	Assou-Ekotto B 29 + 1	Palacios W 29 + 4	Bassong S 25 + 3	King L 19 + 1	Lennon A 20 + 2	Huddlestone T 33	Defoe J 31 + 3	Keane R 15 + 5	Modric L 21 + 4	Crouch P 21 + 17	O'Hara J — + 2	Pavlyuchenko R 8 + 8	Hutton A 1 + 7	Bentley D 11 + 4	Cudicini C 6 + 1	Naughton K — + 1	Jenas J 9 + 10	Kranjcar N 19 + 5	Bale G 19 + 6	Dawson M 25 + 4	Woodgate J 3	Giovani — + 1	Kaboul Y 8 + 2	Gudjohnsen E 3 + 8	Livermore J — + 1	Walker K 2	Rose D 1	Alnwick B 1	Match No.
1	2	3	4	5	6	7	8	9^3	10^1	11^2	12	13	14																	1
1^6	6	3	4	5		7	8	9	10^1	11^2	12			2	13	15														2
	2	3	4	5	6	7	8	9^3	10^1	11^2	12	13				1	14													3
	2	3	4	5	6^1	7	8	9^3	10	11^2	13		14	12		1														4
	2^2	3	4^1	5		7	8	9	10^3		11		13			1		12	14											5
	2	3	4	5^3	6^1	7	8	9^2	10		13		12			1		11	14											6
	2	3	4	5^3		7^2	6	9	10		12					1		8	11											7
	2	3	4	5		7	6	12	10^1		9					1		8	11											8
1	2	3	13	5	6	7	4^3	9^4	10^1		12							8	11^2		14									9
1	2	3	4	6		7	8^3		10^2	9		13						14	11		12	5^3								10
1	2^3	3	4	5	6		7^1		10^2	9		13	14	11				8		12										11
1	2	3	4			6^1		7	10	11^2	9							8	13		12	5								12
1	2	3^2	4^3	13		7^1	8	10		9			12		14	11		5	5											13
1	2	3	4^1	5		7	8	10	13	9					12	11^2		6												14
1	2	3^1	4^3	5		7	8	10		9		14			13	11^2	12	6												15
1	2	3	4^1			7	8	9	10^2	12	13			11^3		6		14												16
1	2	3^1	4	5		7	8	10^2		9					12	11	13	6												17
1	2	3	4^1	5		7^3	8	10^2	13	9		14		12	11		6													18
1	2	3	4	5^3	14	7		13	10^2	12	9		8	11^1		6														19
1	2	3^2	4		5	7^3	8	10		11^1	9		14	12	13		6													20
1	2		4^1	5			8	9	10^2	11	13		12	7		6														21
1	2^1		4	14	6^3			10	13	11	9		12		8	7^2		5												22
1	2			6		8	10^1	12	11	9			7					5												23
1	2			4	6		8	10^1	12	11	9		7^2		13			5												24
1	2			4	6		8	10	11	9			7					5												25
1		12	5			4	10		14	13		7		8^1	11^3		6			2	9^2									26
1	2		4	12	6^1		8	10^3		13	9	14	7		11^2		5													27
1	2		4	5		8^1	10^2		11	14		9^3		7		6			12	13										28
1	2	3	4	5			10^1		8^2	12	9				7	1	6			13										29
1	2	3					8	9	10^1					7^2	1	4		6	12	13										30
1		13	5			4		8	9	14	7			11^2		6^1		12	10^9	2										31
1	2^1	4	5				13	8	14	9^3	7^2		12	1				6	10	3										32
1	3		6			4	10^2	8	14	9^3	12			1		5		2	13			7^1								33
1	3		5			4	10^1	8	13	9^2	7			1		6		2	12											34
1	2	4		6	13	8	10^1		11	14		9^3		7^2		5			12											35
1	2		6	13	8	10^1		11	12		9^3		7^2		5			4	14											36
1		3	14	6	7^1	4	10^2		8^3	9	13	12				1		5		2										37
		3	13	6	7	4^2	10^1	8	9^3	12						1		5		2	14					1				38

FA Cup

Third Round	Peterborough U	(h)	4-0
Fourth Round	Leeds U	(h)	2-2
		(a)	3-1
Fifth Round	Bolton W	(a)	1-1
		(h)	4-0
Sixth Round	Fulham	(a)	0-0
		(h)	3-1
Semi-Final	Portsmouth		0-2

(at Wembley).

Carling Cup

Second Round	Doncaster R	(a)	5-1
Third Round	Preston NE	(a)	5-1
Fourth Round	Everton	(h)	2-0
Quarter-Final	Manchester U	(a)	0-2

TRANMERE ROVERS   FL Championship 1

FOUNDATION

Formed in 1884 as Belmont they adopted their present title the following year and eventually joined their first league, the West Lancashire League in 1889–90, the same year as their first success in the Wirral Challenge Cup. The club almost folded in 1899–1900 when all the players left en bloc to join a rival club, but they survived the crisis and went from strength to strength winning the 'Combination' title in 1907–08 and the Lancashire Combination in 1913–14. They joined the Football League in 1921 from the Central League.

Prenton Park, Prenton Road West, Birkenhead, Merseyside CH42 9PY.

Telephone: (0871) 221 2001.

Fax: (0151) 608 6144.

Ticket Office: (0871) 221 2001.

Website: www.tranmererovers.co.uk

Email: info@tranmererovers.co.uk

Ground Capacity: 16,587.

Record Attendance: 24,424 v Stoke C, FA Cup 4th rd, 5 February 1972.

Pitch Measurements: 100yd × 70yd.

Chairman: Peter Johnson.

Chief Executive/Secretary: Mick Horton.

Manager: Les Parry.

Assistant Manager: Kevin Summerfield.

Head of Youth/Centre of Excellence Manager: Shaun Garnett.

Physio: Steve Walker.

Colours: White shirts, white shorts, blue and white hooped stockings.

Change Colours: Light green shirts, light green shorts, black and light green hooped stockings.

Year Formed: 1884.

Turned Professional: 1912.

Ltd Co.: 1920.

Previous Name: 1884, Belmont AFC; 1885, Tranmere Rovers.

Club Nickname: 'The Rovers'.

Grounds: 1884, Steeles Field; 1887, Ravenshaws Field/Old Prenton Park; 1912, Prenton Park.

First Football League Game: 27 August 1921, Division 3 (N), v Crewe Alex (h) W 4–1 – Bradshaw; Grainger, Stuart (1); Campbell, Milnes (1), Heslop; Moreton, Groves (1), Hyam, Ford (1), Hughes.

Record League Victory: 13–4 v Oldham Ath, Division 3 (N), 26 December 1935 – Gray; Platt, Fairhurst; McLaren, Newton, Spencer; Eden, MacDonald (1), Bell (9), Woodward (2), Urmson (1).

HONOURS

Football League Division 1 best season: 4th, 1992–93; Division 3 (N) – Champions 1937–38; Division 4 – Runners-up 1988–89.

FA Cup: best season: 6th rd, 2000, 2001, 2004.

Football League Cup: Runners-up, 2000.

Welsh Cup: Winners 1935; Runners-up 1934.

Leyland Daf Cup: Winners 1990; Runners-up 1991.

sky SPORTS FACT FILE

In the Football League (Mercantile Credit) Centenary Festival at Wembley in April 1988, Tranmere Rovers did well to beat Wimbledon 1–0, Newcastle United (43,000) 2–0 and only lose to Nottingham Forest in the semi-final on penalties after a 2–2 draw.

Record Cup Victory: 13–0 v Oswestry U. FA Cup 2nd prel rd, 10 October 1914 – Ashcroft; Stevenson, Bullough, Hancock, Taylor, Holden (1), Moreton (1), Cunningham (2), Smith (5), Leck (3), Gould (1).

Record Defeat: 1–9 v Tottenham H, FA Cup 3rd rd (replay), 14 January 1953.

Most League Points (2 for a win): 60, Division 4, 1964–65.

Most League Points (3 for a win): 80, Division 4, 1988–89; Division 3, 1989–90; Division 2, 2002–03.

Most League Goals: 111, Division 3 (N), 1930–31.

Highest League Scorer in Season: Bunny Bell, 35, Division 3 (N), 1933–34.

Most League Goals in Total Aggregate: Ian Muir, 142, 1985–95.

Most League Goals in One Match: 9, Bunny Bell v Oldham Ath, Division 3 (N), 26 December 1935.

Most Capped Player: John Aldridge, 30 (69), Republic of Ireland.

Most League Appearances: Harold Bell, 595, 1946–64 (incl. League record 401 consecutive appearances).

Youngest League Player: Iain Hume, 16 years 167 days v Swindon T, 15 April 2000.

Record Transfer Fee Received: £2,500,000 from WBA for Jason Koumas, August 2002.

Record Transfer Fee Paid: £450,000 to Aston Villa for Shaun Teale, August 1995.

Football League Record: 1921 Original Member of Division 3 (N): 1938–39 Division 2; 1946–58 Division 3 (N); 1958–61 Division 3; 1961–67 Division 4; 1967–75 Division 3; 1975–76 Division 4; 1976–79 Division 3; 1979–89 Division 4; 1989–91 Division 3; 1991–92 Division 2; 1992–2001 Division 1; 2001–04 Division 2; 2004– FL 1.

MANAGERS

Bert Cooke 1912–35
Jackie Carr 1935–36
Jim Knowles 1936–39
Bill Ridding 1939–45
Ernie Blackburn 1946–55
Noel Kelly 1955–57
Peter Farrell 1957–60
Walter Galbraith 1961
Dave Russell 1961–69
Jackie Wright 1969–72
Ron Yeats 1972–75
John King 1975–80
Bryan Hamilton 1980–85
Frank Worthington 1985–87
Ronnie Moore 1987
John King 1987–96
John Aldridge 1996–2001
Dave Watson 2001–02
Ray Mathias 2002–03
Brian Little 2003–06
Ronnie Moore 2006–09
John Barnes 2009
Les Parry October 2009–

LATEST SEQUENCES

Longest Sequence of League Wins: 9, 9.2.1990 – 19.3.1990.

Longest Sequence of League Defeats: 8, 29.10.1938 – 17.12.1938.

Longest Sequence of League Draws: 5, 25.12.1997 – 31.1.1998.

Longest Sequence of Unbeaten League Matches: 18, 16.3.1970 – 4.9.1970.

Longest Sequence Without a League Win: 16, 8.11.1969 – 14.3.1970.

Successive Scoring Runs: 32 from 24.2.1934.

Successive Non-scoring Runs: 7 from 20.12.1997.

TEN YEAR LEAGUE RECORD

		P	W	D	L	F	A	Pts	Pos
2000-01	Div 1	46	9	11	26	46	77	38	24
2001-02	Div 2	46	16	15	15	63	60	63	12
2002-03	Div 2	46	23	11	12	66	57	80	7
2003-04	Div 2	46	17	16	13	59	56	67	8
2004-05	FL 1	46	22	13	11	73	55	79	3
2005-06	FL 1	46	13	15	18	50	52	54	18
2006-07	FL 1	46	18	13	15	58	53	67	9
2007-08	FL 1	46	18	11	17	52	47	65	11
2008-09	FL 1	46	21	11	14	62	49	74	7
2009-10	FL 1	46	14	9	23	45	72	51	19

DID YOU KNOW ?

While Tranmere Rovers have had several international players appear for Scotland, Wales and Ireland, the nearest they have had to an England equivalent was when Len Kieran – 359 League and Cup appearances to his credit – played for England B in 1950.

TRANMERE ROVERS 2009–10 LEAGUE RECORD

Match No.	Date		Venue	Opponents	Result		H/T Score	Lg Pos.	Goalscorers	Attendance
1	Aug	8	A	Yeovil T	L	0-2	0-1	—		4349
2		15	H	Gillingham	W	4-2	1-1	11	Thomas-Moore 2 [5, 90], Welsh [48], Gornell [73]	5590
3		18	H	Milton Keynes D	L	0-1	0-0	—		5744
4		22	A	Leeds U	L	0-3	0-2	21		21,692
5		29	H	Charlton Ath	L	0-4	0-2	22		5417
6	Sept	5	A	Carlisle U	L	0-3	0-0	23		5269
7		12	H	Walsall	L	2-3	1-1	23	Shuker [11], Mahon [61]	4858
8		19	A	Exeter C	L	1-2	0-1	23	Ricketts [63]	4901
9		26	H	Colchester U	D	1-1	1-1	23	Welsh [35]	5314
10		29	A	Wycombe W	W	1-0	1-0	—	Thomas-Moore [16]	3899
11	Oct	3	A	Millwall	L	0-5	0-4	22		8046
12		12	H	Stockport Co	L	0-1	0-0	—		5645
13		17	H	Brighton & HA	W	2-1	1-0	22	Edds [36], Welsh [66]	5250
14		24	A	Hartlepool U	L	0-1	0-1	23		3428
15		31	H	Swindon T	L	1-4	0-2	23	Shuker [78]	5811
16	Nov	14	A	Norwich C	L	0-2	0-0	23		25,025
17		21	A	Leyton Orient	L	1-2	1-1	24	Barnett [29]	4620
18		24	H	Southend U	W	2-0	1-0	—	Goodison [10], Gornell [72]	4317
19	Dec	1	A	Huddersfield T	D	3-3	1-1	—	Thomas-Moore [8], Curran [60], Ricketts [85]	13,509
20		5	H	Brentford	W	1-0	0-0	23	Curran [60]	4839
21		12	A	Southampton	L	0-3	0-0	23		19,800
22		19	H	Bristol R	W	2-0	1-0	22	Curran [29], Edds [56]	4755
23		28	H	Carlisle U	D	0-0	0-0	22		6313
24	Jan	20	A	Oldham Ath	D	0-0	0-0	—		3688
25		23	A	Milton Keynes D	L	0-1	0-1	22		9438
26		26	H	Yeovil T	W	2-1	0-0	—	Thomas-Moore [48], Taylor [52]	4584
27		30	A	Charlton Ath	D	1-1	0-0	22	Sodje S (og) [50]	16,168
28	Feb	6	H	Oldham Ath	L	0-1	0-1	22		5518
29		9	A	Gillingham	W	1-0	0-0	—	Thomas-Moore [68]	3840
30		13	A	Southend U	D	1-1	0-1	22	Goodison [48]	6382
31		20	H	Leyton Orient	W	2-1	2-0	17	Thomas-Moore [27], Sordell [35]	5357
32		23	H	Huddersfield T	L	0-2	0-1	—		5793
33	Mar	6	H	Southampton	W	2-1	1-1	19	Broomes [3], Thomas-Moore (pen) [65]	6187
34		9	H	Leeds U	L	1-4	1-3	—	Welsh [19]	8346
35		13	A	Bristol R	D	0-0	0-0	20		6477
36		19	H	Hartlepool U	D	0-0	0-0	—		5409
37		27	A	Brighton & HA	L	0-3	0-2	21		6812
38	Apr	2	H	Norwich C	W	3-1	3-0	—	Thomas-Moore 2 (2 pens) [6, 12], Curran [31]	6263
39		5	A	Swindon T	L	0-3	0-2	21		9495
40		10	A	Walsall	L	1-2	1-1	21	Smith (og) [27]	3841
41		13	H	Wycombe W	L	0-3	0-1	—		4956
42		17	H	Exeter C	W	3-1	1-0	21	Curran [43], Labadie [59], Edds [88]	5466
43		20	A	Brentford	L	1-2	0-0	—	Labadie [82]	4341
44		24	A	Colchester U	D	1-1	1-1	21	Thomas-Moore [6]	4353
45	May	1	H	Millwall	W	2-0	1-0	21	Thomas-Moore (pen) [45], Robinson [66]	8694
46		8	A	Stockport Co	W	3-0	1-0	19	Goodison [38], Thomas-Moore [53], Labadie [76]	7208

Final League Position: 19

GOALSCORERS

League (45): Thomas-Moore 13 (4 pens), Curran 5, Welsh 4, Edds 3, Goodison 3, Labadie 3, Gornell 2, Ricketts 2, Shuker 2, Barnett 1, Broomes 1, Mahon 1, Robinson 1, Sordell 1, Taylor 1, own goals 2.
Carling Cup (4): Curran 1, Edds 1, McLaren 1, Thomas-Moore 1 (pen).
FA Cup (4): Gornell 1, Shuker 1, Taylor 1, Thomas-Moore 1.
J Paint Trophy (1): Curran 1.

Daniels L 37	Logan S 32+1	Cresswell A 13+1	Taylor A 27+6	Gunning G 6	McLaren P 36+2	Shaker C 16+10	Welsh J 44+1	Thomas-Moore I 41+2	Curran C 38+5	Mahon A 8+8	Fraughan R 1+5	Gornell T 18+9	Goodison I 44	Edds G 24+11	Ricketts M 7+5	Broomes M 31	Bain K —+10	Collister J 1+2	Carole S 4	Bakayogo Z 30	Martin D 3	Barnett C 1+6	Sordell M 6+2	McCready C 8	O'Neill L 4	Savage B 10+3	Robinson A 3+2	Gordon B 4	Labadie J 5+4	Gulacsi P 5	Match No.
1	2	3	4	5	6	7	8	9	10²	11¹	12	13																			1
1	2	3		5	6	7	8	9	10¹	11²		12	4	13																	2
1	2	3	12	5	6	7	8	9³	10	11²		14	4¹	13																	3
1	2	3	12	5¹	6	7³	8	9	10²	11		14	4	13																	4
1	2	3		5	6	7²	8	9		11¹	14	10³	4	13	12																5
1	2ᵃ	3²	12	5	6	7³	8	9	13	10¹	14		4	11																	6
1⁶		3	12		6	7²	8		10	2			4	11	9	5¹	13	15													7
	2	3	12		6		8		10			13	4	11¹	9³	5	14	1	7²												8
1	2	3			6	7¹	8		10²	11		13	4	12	9³	5	14														9
1	2	3			6	7¹	8		10	11²		13	4	12	9	5															10
1	2	3	14		6	7¹	8		10³	11		13	4	12	9²	5ᵃ															11
1ᵃ	2				6	7	8	9	10²	11⁶	12	13	4¹			5		15		3											12
	2				6	7¹	8²	9	10	11		13	4			5				3	1	12									13
	2				6	12	8²	9	10³	11¹			4		7	5	14			3	1	13ᵃ									14
	2				6¹	12	8	9	10²	11		13	4		7	5				3	1										15
1	2				6	7³	8		10²	11	12	13	4		9¹	5	14			3											16
1	12	3			6	7	8	9³	10²	11		13	4¹		14	5					2ᵃ										17
1	2				6¹	7	8	9	10	11²	12	13	4			5				3											18
1	2				6	7	8	9²	10	11¹			4			5				3		12	13								19
1	2				6	7	8	9	10	11¹			4		12	5				3											20
1	2				6	7³	8	9	10	11²	14	13	4¹		12	5				3											21
1	2		4		6	7	8	9	10	11						5			7	3											22
1	2		4		6		8	9	10	11¹				12		5			7	3											23
1	2				6	7	8	9	10	11			4			5				3											24
1	2				6	7	8	9	10	11			4¹	12		5				3											25
1	2				6	7	8	9	10	11			4			5				3											26
1	2		4		6¹	7²	8	9	10	11		13		12		5				3ᵃ											27
1	2	3	4		6	7²	8	9	10³	11¹				13		5						14	12								28
1	2		4¹		6	7	8	9	10			13		12		5				3			11²								29
1	2				6	7	8	9	10				4	12		5				3			11¹								30
1					6	7	8²	9	10				4	12		5				3		13	11¹		2						31
1					6	7²	8	9	10			13	4¹	14		5				3		12	11³		2						32
1					6	7	8²	9	10			13	4			5				3			11¹		2	12					33
1					6	7	8	9	10			13	4³	14		5				3			11¹		2²	12					34
1	2		4		6	7	8	9	10							5				3ᵃ						11					35
1	2	3		5	6	7²	8	9¹	10³			13	4	12		5						14				11					36
1					6	7			10				4¹			5				3			12		2	11		8ᵃ	9		37
1					6	7	8	9	10				4¹			5				3					2	11		12			38
1					6	7³		9²	10¹				4			5				3			12		2	11ᵃ	13	8	14		39
1					6	7		9	10²				4			5				3¹					2	11	13	8	12		40
1			4		6	7³	8	9	10²			13				5				3		14	12		2¹	11					41
					6	7		9	10				4¹			5				3			12		2	11²	13	8		1	42
					6	7		9	10				4			5				3			12		2²	11¹	13	8		1	43
	2				6	7		9	10¹				4			5				3			12			11		8		1	44
	2				6	7		9	10¹			13	4	12		5				3						11		8²		1	45
	2				6	7		9	10¹				4	12		5				3						11		8		1	46

FA Cup

First Round	Leyton Orient	(h)	1-1	
		(a)	1-0	
Second Round	Aldershot T	(h)	0-0	
		(a)	2-1	
Third Round	Wolverhampton W	(h)	0-1	

Carling Cup

First Round	Grimsby T	(h)	4-0
Second Round	Bolton W	(h)	0-1

J Paint Trophy

Second Round	Bury	(a)	1-2

WALSALL   FL Championship 1

FOUNDATION

Two of the leading clubs around Walsall in the 1880s were Walsall Swifts (formed 1877) and Walsall Town (formed 1879). The Swifts were winners of the Birmingham Senior Cup in 1881, while the Town reached the 4th round (5th round modern equivalent) of the FA Cup in 1883. These clubs amalgamated as Walsall Town Swifts in 1888, becoming simply Walsall in 1895.

Banks's Stadium, Bescot Crescent, Walsall WS1 4SA.
Telephone: (01922) 622 791.
Fax: (01922) 613 202.
Ticket Office: (01922) 651 414/416.
Website: www.saddlers.co.uk
Email: info@walsallfc.co.uk
Ground Capacity: 11,300.
Record Attendance: 11,037 v Wolverhampton W, Division 1, 11 January 2003.
Pitch Measurements: 110yd × 73yd.
Chairman: Jeff Bonser.
Secretary: Roy Whalley.
Manager: Chris Hutchings.
Assistant Manager: Martin O'Connor.
Physio: Jon Whitney.
Colours: Red shirts with black trim, red shorts, red stockings with black tops.
Change Colours: Laser green shirts with red trim and blue sleeves, laser green shorts, laser green stockings.
Year Formed: 1888. *Turned Professional:* 1888.
Ltd Co.: 1921.
Previous Names: Walsall Swifts (founded 1877) and Walsall Town (founded 1879) amalgamated in 1888 as Walsall Town Swifts; 1895, Walsall.
Club Nickname: 'The Saddlers'.
Grounds: 1888, Fellows Park; 1990, Bescot Stadium.
First Football League Game: 3 September 1892, Division 2, v Darwen (h) L 1–2 – Hawkins; Withington, Pinches; Robinson, Whitrick, Forsyth; Marshall, Holmes, Turner, Gray (1), Pangbourn.
Record League Victory: 10–0 v Darwen, Division 2, 4 March 1899 – Tennent; E. Peers (1), Davies; Hickinbotham, Jenkyns, Taggart; Dean (3), Vail (2), Aston (4), Martin, Griffin.
Record Cup Victory: 7–0 v Macclesfield T (a), FA Cup 2nd rd, 6 December 1997 – Walker; Evans, Marsh, Viveash (1), Ryder, Peron, Boli (2 incl. 1p) (Ricketts), Porter (2), Keates, Watson (Platt), Hodge (2 incl. 1p).
Record Defeat: 0–12 v Small Heath, 17 December 1892. 0–12 v Darwen, 26 December 1896, both Division 2.

HONOURS

Football League: Division 2: Runners-up, 1998–99; FL 2 – Champions 2006–07; Division 3 – Runners-up 1960–61, 1994–95; Division 4 – Champions 1959–60; Runners-up 1979–80.

FA Cup: best season: 5th rd, 1939, 1975, 1978, 1987, 2002, 2003 and last 16 1889.

Football League Cup: Semi-final 1984.

sky SPORTS FACT FILE

On 28 October 1931 Walsall visited Holland and met a Netherlands FA XI. They did well to draw 3–3 with goals from Bert Turner, David Prentice and Billy Bradford, the club's long-serving half-back who went on to complete more than 300 League appearances for them.

Most League Points (2 for a win): 65, Division 4, 1959–60.

Most League Points (3 for a win): 89, FL 2, 2006–07.

Most League Goals: 102, Division 4, 1959–60.

Highest League Scorer in Season: Gilbert Alsop, 40, Division 3 (N), 1933–34 and 1934–35.

Most League Goals in Total Aggregate: Tony Richards, 184, 1954–63; Colin Taylor, 184, 1958–63, 1964–68, 1969–73.

Most League Goals in One Match: 5, Gilbert Alsop v Carlisle U, Division 3 (N), 2 February 1935; 5, Bill Evans v Mansfield T, Division 3 (N), 5 October 1935; 5, Johnny Devlin v Torquay U, Division 3 (S), 1 September 1949.

Most Capped Player: Mick Kearns, 15 (18), Republic of Ireland.

Most League Appearances: Colin Harrison, 467, 1964–82.

Youngest League Player: Geoff Morris, 16 years 218 days v Scunthorpe U, 14 September 1965.

Record Transfer Fee Received: £750,000 from Coventry C for Scott Dann, January 2008.

Record Transfer Fee Paid: £175,000 to Birmingham C for Alan Buckley, June 1979.

Football League Record: 1892 Elected to Division 2; 1895 Failed re-election; 1896–1901 Division 2; 1901 Failed re-election; 1921 Original Member of Division 3 (N); 1927–31 Division 3 (S); 1931–36 Division 3 (N); 1936–58 Division 3 (S); 1958–60 Division 4; 1960–61 Division 3; 1961–63 Division 2; 1963–79 Division 3; 1979–80 Division 4; 1980–88 Division 3; 1988–89 Division 2; 1989–90 Division 3; 1990–92 Division 4; 1992–95 Division 3; 1995–99 Division 2; 1999–2000 Division 1; 2000–01 Division 2; 2001–04 Division 1; 2004–06 FL 1; 2006–07 FL 2; 2007– FL 1.

LATEST SEQUENCES

Longest Sequence of League Wins: 7, 10.10.1959 – 21.11.1959.

Longest Sequence of League Defeats: 15, 29.10.1988 – 4.2.1989.

Longest Sequence of League Draws: 5, 7.5.1988 – 17.9 1988.

Longest Sequence of Unbeaten League Matches: 21, 6.11.1979 – 22.3.1980.

Longest Sequence Without a League Win: 18, 15.10.1988 – 4.2.1989.

Successive Scoring Runs: 27 from 9.2.1928.

Successive Non-scoring Runs: 5 from 8.10.1927.

MANAGERS

H. Smallwood 1888–91
 (Secretary-Manager)
A. G. Burton 1891–93
J. H. Robinson 1893–95
C. H. Ailso 1895–96
 (Secretary-Manager)
A. E. Parsloe 1896–97
 (Secretary-Manager)
L. Ford 1897–98 *(Secretary-Manager)*
G. Hughes 1898–99
 (Secretary-Manager)
L. Ford 1899–1901
 (Secretary-Manager)
J. E. Shutt 1908–13
 (Secretary-Manager)
Haydn Price 1914–20
Joe Burchell 1920–26
David Ashworth 1926–27
Jack Torrance 1927–28
James Kerr 1928–29
Sid Scholey 1929–30
Peter O'Rourke 1930–32
Bill Slade 1932–34
Andy Wilson 1934–37
Tommy Lowes 1937–44
Harry Hibbs 1944–51
Tony McPhee 1951
Brough Fletcher 1952–53
Major Frank Buckley 1953–55
John Love 1955–57
Billy Moore 1957–64
Alf Wood 1964
Reg Shaw 1964–68
Dick Graham 1968
Ron Lewin 1968–69
Billy Moore 1969–72
John Smith 1972–73
Doug Fraser 1973–77
Dave Mackay 1977–78
Alan Ashman 1978
Frank Sibley 1979
Alan Buckley 1979–86
Neil Martin *(Joint Manager with Buckley)* 1981–82
Tommy Coakley 1986–88
John Barnwell 1989–90
Kenny Hibbitt 1990–94
Chris Nicholl 1994–97
Jan Sorensen 1997–98
Ray Graydon 1998–2002
Colin Lee 2002–04
Paul Merson 2004–06
Kevin Broadhurst 2006
Richard Money 2006–08
Jimmy Mullen 2008–09
Chris Hutchings January 2009–

TEN YEAR LEAGUE RECORD

		P	W	D	L	F	A	Pts	Pos
2000-01	Div 2	46	23	12	11	79	50	81	4
2001-02	Div 1	46	13	12	21	51	71	51	18
2002-03	Div 1	46	15	9	22	57	69	54	17
2003-04	Div 1	46	13	12	21	45	65	51	22
2004-05	FL 1	46	16	12	18	65	69	60	14
2005-06	FL 1	46	11	14	21	47	70	47	24
2006-07	FL 2	46	25	14	7	66	34	89	1
2007-08	FL 1	46	16	16	14	52	46	64	12
2008-09	FL 1	46	17	10	19	61	66	61	13
2009-10	FL 1	46	16	14	16	60	63	62	10

DID YOU KNOW ?

Dave Massart, signed from Birmingham City at the beginning of 1947–48, scored hat-tricks in each of his first three home League games for Walsall against Exeter City, Leyton Orient and Southend United. After amassing 23 goals in 27 outings he was transferred to Bury.

WALSALL 2009–10 LEAGUE RECORD

Match No.	Date	Venue	Opponents	Result	Score	H/T	Lg Pos.	Goalscorers	Attendance
1	Aug 8	A	Brighton & HA	W	1-0	1-0	—	Whing (og) [30]	6504
2	15	H	Southend U	D	2-2	1-0	6	Jones [11], Parkin (pen) [90]	3658
3	18	H	Leeds U	L	1-2	0-0	—	Parkin (pen) [79]	8483
4	22	A	Charlton Ath	L	0-2	0-1	16		15,306
5	29	H	Gillingham	D	0-0	0-0	17		3331
6	Sept 5	A	Norwich C	D	0-0	0-0	15		23,041
7	12	A	Tranmere R	W	3-2	1-1	10	Byfield [45], Deeney 2 [47, 83]	4858
8	19	H	Swindon T	D	1-1	1-0	12	Deeney [8]	4148
9	26	A	Hartlepool U	L	0-3	0-1	16		3334
10	29	H	Huddersfield T	W	2-1	0-0	—	Byfield (pen) [66], Mattis [87]	3419
11	Oct 3	H	Carlisle U	D	2-2	1-1	12	Byfield [33], Jones [74]	3572
12	10	A	Milton Keynes D	L	0-1	0-1	14		8919
13	17	H	Exeter C	W	3-0	2-0	11	Jones 2 [29, 45], Deeney [70]	4063
14	24	A	Colchester U	L	1-2	1-1	14	Byfield [28]	4880
15	31	A	Wycombe W	W	3-2	0-2	12	Jones [55], Hughes M [80], Nicholls [83]	5046
16	Nov 14	H	Stockport Co	W	2-0	1-0	10	Richards [37], Byfield [56]	4143
17	21	A	Brentford	D	1-1	0-1	10	Jones [68]	4492
18	24	H	Oldham Ath	W	3-0	2-0	—	Deeney 2 [20, 80], Jones [45]	3191
19	Dec 1	A	Yeovil T	W	3-1	2-1	—	Byfield [5], Jones [20], Parkin [89]	3508
20	5	H	Southampton	L	1-3	0-2	8	Byfield [66]	5681
21	12	A	Millwall	L	1-2	1-0	10	Smith [8]	8174
22	19	H	Leyton Orient	D	2-2	0-2	10	Deeney 2 [46, 57]	3616
23	Jan 16	H	Brighton & HA	L	1-2	1-2	11	Richards [26]	3450
24	26	H	Norwich C	L	1-2	1-0	—	Deeney [35]	5022
25	30	A	Gillingham	D	0-0	0-0	13		4796
26	Feb 2	H	Charlton Ath	D	1-1	1-1	—	Deeney [32]	3417
27	6	A	Bristol R	D	0-0	0-0	13		3886
28	9	A	Bristol R	W	1-0	1-0	—	Taundry [32]	5919
29	13	A	Oldham Ath	L	0-1	0-0	14		3968
30	16	A	Leeds U	W	2-1	0-0	—	Mattis [46], McDonald [81]	18,941
31	20	H	Brentford	W	2-1	1-1	9	Nicholls [35], Deeney [84]	3616
32	23	H	Yeovil T	L	0-1	0-1	—		2929
33	27	A	Southampton	L	1-5	1-3	10	Richards [3]	20,461
34	Mar 6	A	Millwall	D	2-2	2-1	11	Nicholls [12], Taundry [27]	3835
35	13	A	Leyton Orient	L	0-2	0-0	13		3685
36	20	H	Colchester U	W	1-0	0-0	12	Byfield [90]	3510
37	23	A	Southend U	L	0-3	0-1	—		6432
38	27	A	Exeter C	L	1-2	0-1	14	Gray [62]	5887
39	Apr 3	A	Stockport Co	D	1-1	0-1	14	Gray [47]	3580
40	5	H	Wycombe W	W	2-1	2-0	13	Smith [7], Gray [22]	3618
41	10	H	Tranmere R	W	2-1	1-1	13	Smith [35], Byfield [70]	3841
42	13	A	Huddersfield T	L	3-4	0-2	—	Deeney 2 [63, 69], Nicholls [83]	14,396
43	17	A	Swindon T	D	1-1	1-0	12	Jones [44]	8467
44	24	H	Hartlepool U	W	3-1	2-1	12	Gray [7], Deeney [28], Taundry [76]	3457
45	May 1	A	Carlisle U	D	1-1	1-1	15	Byfield [2]	5114
46	8	H	Milton Keynes D	W	2-1	0-1	10	Richards [47], Smith [86]	4772

Final League Position: 10

GOALSCORERS

League (60): Deeney 14, Byfield 10 (1 pen), Jones 9, Gray 4, Nicholls 4, Richards 4, Smith 4, Parkin 3 (2 pens), Taundry 3, Mattis 2, Hughes M 1, McDonald 1, own goal 1.
Carling Cup (1): Nicholls 1.
FA Cup (1): Jones 1.
J Paint Trophy (0).

Ince C 24+1	Weston R 23+4	Vincent J 37+1	Richards M 39+1	Hughes M 24+2	Smith M 30+3	Jones S 25+5	Mattis D 34	Parkin S 7+17	Deeney T 42	Till P 18+10	Bradley M 19+9	Taundry R 24+6	Nicholls A 20+17	Westlake D 20+2	Roberts S 1	Byfield D 31+6	Gilmartin R 22	McDonald C 24+2	O'Keefe J 8+5	Sansara N 17	Gray J 17+1	Adkins S —+1	Match No.
1	2	3	4	5	6	7^2	8	9	10^3	11^1	12	13	14										1
1		3	4	5	6	7^1	8^5	9	10	11^2		12	13	2									2
1		3	4^1	5	6	7^2		9	10	11		8	12	13	2								3
1		3	4	5	6	7^1	8	9	10	11^2		12	13	2									4
1	13	3	4^1		6	7	8	9	10	11^3		12		2	5^2	14							5
		3	4		6		8	12	10^1	11		7	13	2		9^2	1	5					6
		3	4		6		8		10			7^1	11	2		9	1	5	12				7
13		3	4	6			8	12	10^1			7	11	2		9	1	5^2					8
12		3	4	6		13	8	14	10			7	11^2	2		9^3	1	5^1					9
2		3	4	6		13	8	12	10			7	11^2			9^1	1	5					10
2		3	4	6			12	8	13	10			7	11^1		9^2	1	5					11
2	3	4	6	12		11^2	8	14	10^3	13	7					9	1	5^1					12
15	2	3	4	5	6	7	8	12	10^2		11		13			9^1	1^G						13
1	2		4	5	6		8		10	7	11		12			9			3				14
1	2		4	3	6	12			10	7^2	11	8^1	13			9			5				15
1	2		4	3	6	7	8		10		11					9			5				16
1	2		4	3	6	7	8	12	10^1		11					9			5				17
1	2		4	3	6	7^2		12	10^3	13	8		14			9^1			11	5			18
1	2		4^1	3	6	7	8	13	10^3		11		14			9^2			12	5			19
1	2		4	3	6	7	8	12	10		11^1					9				5			20
1	2	12	4	3	6		8	9		7^2	11		13			10				5^8			21
1	2	3	4		6		8		10	7	11					9				5			22
1			4	3	6		8	13	10	7^2	11^1		2			9			12	5			23
1	2	3	4		6		8^1	13	10	7^2	11					9		5	12				24
1	2	3	4		6		8		10	7^2	11^1	12	13			9		5					25
1	2^1	3	4			8	14	10^8	7^2		6	13	12			9^3		11		5			26
1		3	4^1			8	10		7^2	13	6	12	2			9		11		5			27
1		3	4			8		9	7		6	10	2					11		5			28
1		3	4			8		10	7		6^3	9^2	2		13			11	14	5	12		29
1		3	4			8		9	7^1	12	6	10	2					5			11		30
1		3	4	12		8^2		10		13	6	11	2^1			9		5			7		31
1		3	4	5		8		10			6	8				9		11	7		2^1	12	32
13	3	3	4		12		10			5	8	2^1			9^2	1	11	7		6		33
2^1	3	4^8	13		9^2		10			6	11^3	12		14	1	5	7			8		34
3			7	7^1			10	12	14	4	9^2	2		13	1	11	8^3	5^1	6				35
	3	12	5^8	11^3	8		10	14		4	9^2			13	1	2	7^1		6			36
	3	4^2	12	7	8^3		10	13	14	5	9			1	6^8	2^1		11				37
4	3		6	7^2			10	13		2	9			12	1		8^1	5^1	11				38
2	3		6	7^1	8	13	10^8		14	4	12			9^2	1		5^1	11^3					39
2	3		5	6	7^2	8	12			13	4	10^1			9	1		11					40
	3		5	6	7	8	13		12		4	10^1	2		9^2	1		11					41
	3		5^8	6	7^1	8^3	10		14	4	13	2		9^2	1	12		11^1					42
	3	4		6	7^1		10	12		8	9	2			1	5		1^1					43
	3	4		6	7^1		10	12		8	9				1	5		1^1					44
2	3	4	12	6	7^2		10	13		8				9	1	5^1		1^1					45
	3	4	5	6	7^2		10			8	12	2		9^1	1	13		1^1					46

FA Cup
First Round   Stourbridge   (a)   1-0
Second Round   Brentford   (a)   0-1

Carling Cup
First Round   Accrington S   (a)   1-2

J Paint Trophy
First Round   Bury   (h)   0-0

WATFORD

FL Championship

FOUNDATION

The club was formed as Watford Rovers in 1881. The name was changed to West Herts in 1893 and then the name Watford was adopted after rival club Watford St Mary's was absorbed in 1898.

Vicarage Road Stadium, Vicarage Road, Watford, Hertsfordshire, WD18 0ER.

Telephone: 0844 856 1881.

Fax: (01923) 496 001.

Ticket Office: 0844 856 1881.

Website: www.watfordfc.com

Email: yourvoice@watfordfc.com

Ground Capacity: 19,920.

Record Attendance: 34,099 v Manchester U, FA Cup 4th rd (replay), 3 February 1969.

Pitch Measurements: 114 yd × 73yd.

Chairman: Graham Taylor OBE.

Chief Executive: Julian Winter.

Secretary: Michelle Ives.

Manager: Malky Mackay.

Assistant Manager: Sean Dyche.

First Team Coach: David Kerslake.

Head of Medicine: Richard Collinge.

Colours: Yellow shirts with red and black trim, black shorts, yellow stockings.

Change Colours: All black.

Year Formed: 1881.

Turned Professional: 1897.

Ltd Co.: 1909.

Club Nickname: 'The Hornets'.

Previous Names: 1881, Watford Rovers; 1893, West Herts; 1898, Watford.

Grounds: 1883, Vicarage Meadow, Rose and Crown Meadow; 1889, Colney Butts; 1890, Cassio Road; 1922, Vicarage Road.

First Football League Game: 28 August 1920, Division 3, v QPR (a) W 2–1 – Williams; Horseman, F. Gregory; Bacon, Toone, Wilkinson; Bassett, Ronald (1), Hoddinott, White (1), Waterall.

Record League Victory: 8–0 v Sunderland, Division 1, 25 September 1982 – Sherwood; Rice, Rostron, Taylor, Terry, Bolton, Callaghan (2), Blissett (4), Jenkins (2), Jackett, Barnes.

Record Cup Victory: 10–1 v Lowestoft T, FA Cup 1st rd, 27 November 1926 – Yates; Prior, Fletcher (1); F. Smith, 'Bert' Smith, Strain; Stephenson, Warner (3), Edmonds (3), Swan (1), Daniels (1), (1 og).

HONOURS

Football League: Division 1 – Runners-up 1982–83: Division 2 – Champions 1997–98; Runners-up 1981–82; Division 3 – Champions 1968–69; Runners-up 1978–79; Division 4 – Champions 1977–78.

FA Cup: Runners-up 1984, semi-finals 1970, 1984, 1987, 2003, 2007.

Football League Cup: Semi-final 1979.

European Competitions: UEFA Cup: 1983–84.

sky SPORTS FACT FILE

Robbie Slaughter played for both West Herts and Watford St Mary's before two seasons with the amalgamated Watford in the Second Division of the Southern League. In the 1899–1900 championship winning season the team won all ten of its home fixtures.

Record Defeat: 0–10 v Wolverhampton W, FA Cup 1st rd (replay), 24 January 1912.

Most League Points (2 for a win): 71, Division 4, 1977–78.

Most League Points (3 for a win): 88, Division 2, 1997–98.

Most League Goals: 92, Division 4, 1959–60.

Highest League Scorer in Season: Cliff Holton, 42, Division 4, 1959–60.

Most League Goals in Total Aggregate: Luther Blissett, 148, 1976–83, 1984–88, 1991–92.

Most League Goals in One Match: 5, Eddie Mummery v Newport Co, Division 3 (S), 5 January 1924.

Most Capped Player: John Barnes, 31 (79), England and Kenny Jackett, 31, Wales.

Most League Appearances: Luther Blissett, 415, 1976–83, 1984–88, 1991–92.

Youngest League Player: Keith Mercer, 16 years 125 days v Tranmere R, 16 February 1973.

Record Transfer Fee Received: £9,600,000 from Aston V for Ashley Young, January 2007.

Record Transfer Fee Paid: £3,250,000 to WBA for Nathan Ellington, August 2007.

Football League Record: 1920 Original Member of Division 3; 1921–58 Division 3 (S); 1958–60 Division 4; 1960–69 Division 3; 1969–72 Division 2; 1972–75 Division 3; 1975–78 Division 4; 1978–79 Division 3; 1979–82 Division 2; 1982–88 Division 1; 1988–92 Division 2; 1992–96 Division 1; 1996–98 Division 2; 1998–99 Division 1; 1999–2000 FA Premier League; 2000–04 Division 1; 2004–06 FL C; 2006–07 FA Premier League; 2007– FL C.

MANAGERS

John Goodall 1903–10
Harry Kent 1910–26
Fred Pagnam 1926–29
Neil McBain 1929–37
Bill Findlay 1938–47
Jack Bray 1947–48
Eddie Hapgood 1948–50
Ron Gray 1950–51
Haydn Green 1951–52
Len Goulden 1952–55
    (General Manager to 1956)
Johnny Paton 1955–56
Neil McBain 1956–59
Ron Burgess 1959–63
Bill McGarry 1963–64
Ken Furphy 1964–71
George Kirby 1971–73
Mike Keen 1973–77
Graham Taylor 1977–87
Dave Bassett 1987–88
Steve Harrison 1988–90
Colin Lee 1990
Steve Perryman 1990–93
Glenn Roeder 1993–96
Kenny Jackett 1996–97
Graham Taylor 1997–2001
Gianluca Vialli 2001–02
Ray Lewington 2002–05
Adrian Boothroyd 2005–08
Brendan Rodgers 2008–09
Malky Mackay June 2009–

LATEST SEQUENCES

Longest Sequence of League Wins: 7, 28.8.2000 – 14.10.2000.

Longest Sequence of League Defeats: 9, 26.12.1972 – 27.2.1973.

Longest Sequence of League Draws: 7, 30.11.1996 – 27.1.1997.

Longest Sequence of Unbeaten League Matches: 22, 1.10.1996 – 1.3.1997.

Longest Sequence Without a League Win: 19, 27.11.1971 – 8.4.1972.

Successive Scoring Runs: 22 from 20.8.1985.

Successive Non-scoring Runs: 7 from 18.12.1971.

TEN YEAR LEAGUE RECORD

		P	W	D	L	F	A	Pts	Pos
2000-01	Div 1	46	20	9	17	76	67	69	9
2001-02	Div 1	46	16	11	19	62	56	59	14
2002-03	Div 1	46	17	9	20	54	70	60	13
2003-04	Div 1	46	15	12	19	54	68	57	16
2004-05	FL C	46	12	16	18	52	59	52	18
2005-06	FL C	46	22	15	9	77	53	81	3
2006-07	PR Lge	38	5	13	20	29	59	28	20
2007-08	FL C	46	18	16	12	62	56	70	6
2008-09	FL C	46	16	10	20	68	72	58	13
2009-10	FL C	46	14	12	20	61	68	54	16

DID YOU KNOW ?

In 1927–28 Joe Groome, an amateur centre-forward, made an immediate impact in his only full season with Watford. He scored 14 goals in only 16 League appearances. Previously with Apsley Town, he had also assisted Northampton Town and hit two goals on his debut there.

WATFORD 2009–10 LEAGUE RECORD

Match No.	Date		Venue	Opponents	Result		H/T Score	Lg Pos.	Goalscorers	Attendance
1	Aug	8	H	Doncaster R	D	1-1	1-1	—	Graham [27]	15,636
2		15	A	Sheffield U	L	0-2	0-1	22		24,638
3		18	A	Nottingham F	W	4-2	1-1	—	Graham [31], Williamson M [78], Smith [80], Cleverley [90]	19,232
4		22	H	Blackpool	D	2-2	1-0	12	Smith [24], Cleverley [63]	12,745
5		29	A	Swansea C	D	1-1	0-0	13	Graham [66]	14,172
6	Sept	12	H	Barnsley	W	1-0	0-0	12	Graham [54]	12,613
7		15	A	Plymouth Arg	W	1-0	1-0	—	Cleverley [4]	8703
8		19	H	Leicester C	D	3-3	0-2	8	Graham [58], Helguson 2 [60, 77]	14,647
9		26	A	Reading	D	1-1	0-1	7	Graham [66]	18,147
10		29	H	Coventry C	L	2-3	2-1	—	Cleverley [21], Hoskins [37]	13,034
11	Oct	3	H	Cardiff C	L	0-4	0-2	15		13,895
12		17	A	Middlesbrough	W	1-0	1-0	12	Cleverley [26]	18,957
13		20	A	Ipswich T	D	1-1	0-1	—	Ellington [90]	19,283
14		23	H	Sheffield W	W	4-1	2-1	—	Mariappa [21], Lansbury 2 [26, 61], Harley [54]	14,591
15		31	A	WBA	L	0-5	0-2	12		21,421
16	Nov	7	H	Preston NE	W	2-0	2-0	12	Helguson [9], Cleverley [33]	13,524
17		21	H	Scunthorpe U	W	3-0	2-0	8	Helguson 2 [19, 22], Graham [48]	13,241
18		28	A	Crystal Palace	L	0-3	0-2	9		14,085
19	Dec	5	A	Newcastle U	L	0-2	0-1	12		43,050
20		7	H	QPR	W	3-1	1-1	—	Doyley [43], Cowie [56], Cleverley [90]	15,058
21		12	H	Derby Co	L	0-1	0-0	10		14,063
22		19	A	Peterborough U	L	1-2	0-1	12	Eustace [49]	7723
23		26	H	Nottingham F	D	0-0	0-0	13		17,086
24		28	A	Bristol C	D	2-2	1-2	13	Cleverley [43], Eustace [90]	16,035
25	Jan	16	A	Doncaster R	L	1-2	0-0	14	Helguson (pen) [90]	10,504
26		23	A	Blackpool	L	2-3	1-1	—	Lansbury [27], Cleverley [79]	6855
27	Feb	2	H	Sheffield U	W	3-0	1-0	—	Cleverley [39], Helguson [55], Cowie [74]	13,076
28		6	A	Barnsley	L	0-1	0-0	12		11,739
29		9	H	Bristol C	W	2-0	2-0	—	Helguson [14], Taylor [34]	12,179
30		20	A	Scunthorpe U	D	2-2	0-1	14	Graham [64], Eustace [89]	5411
31		27	H	Newcastle U	L	1-2	0-1	15	Hoskins [90]	17,120
32	Mar	6	A	Derby Co	L	0-2	0-1	17		29,492
33		9	H	Swansea C	L	0-1	0-1	—		12,907
34		13	H	Peterborough U	L	0-1	0-0	19		16,591
35		16	H	Ipswich T	W	2-1	1-0	—	Lansbury [7], Hoskins [77]	13,996
36		21	A	Cardiff C	L	1-3	0-1	19	Helguson [90]	20,130
37		24	A	Sheffield W	L	1-2	0-0	—	Cleverley [67]	18,449
38		27	H	Middlesbrough	D	1-1	0-0	21	Eustace [21]	14,038
39		30	H	Crystal Palace	L	1-3	0-1	—	Graham [83]	15,134
40	Apr	3	A	Preston NE	D	1-1	1-0	21	Buckley [35]	12,534
41		5	H	WBA	D	1-1	0-0	21	Graham [85]	14,555
42		10	H	Plymouth Arg	W	1-0	0-0	19	Helguson [50]	14,246
43		17	A	Leicester C	L	1-4	0-2	20	Taylor [78]	24,765
44		20	A	QPR	L	0-1	0-1	—		13,171
45		24	H	Reading	W	3-0	1-0	19	Graham 2 [30, 55], Helguson [47]	15,949
46	May	2	A	Coventry C	W	4-0	2-0	16	Graham 2 (1 pen) [16 (pl), 78], Lansbury [17], Sordell [81]	19,103

Final League Position: 16

GOALSCORERS

League (61): Graham 14 (1 pen), Cleverley 11, Helguson 11 (1 pen), Lansbury 5, Eustace 4, Hoskins 3, Cowie 2, Smith 2, Taylor 2, Buckley 1, Doyley 1, Ellington 1, Harley 1, Mariappa 1, Sordell 1, Williamson M 1.
Carling Cup (3): Severin 1, Sordell 1, Williamson M 1.
FA Cup (0).

Loach S 46	Mariappa A 46	Doyley L 43 + 1	Severin S 4 + 5	DeMerit J 25 + 2	Williamson M 4	McAnuff J 3	Jenkins R 21 + 3	Graham D 37 + 9	Smith T 4	Cowie D 40 + 1	Hoskins W 5 + 13	Ellington N 2 + 15	Sordell M 1 + 5	Harley J 20 + 18	Bryan M 1 + 6	Cleverley T 33	Eustace J 39 + 3	Lansbury H 34 + 3	Hodson L 29 + 2	Bennett D 8 + 2	Cathcart C 12	Helguson H 26 + 3	Henderson I — + 13	Oshodi Eddie — + 1	Taylor M 17 + 2	McGinn S 2 + 7	Buckley W 4 + 2	Massey G — + 1	Match No.
1	2	3	4	5	6	7¹	8	9	10	11	12																		1
1	2	3	4	5	6	7²	8	9³	10¹	11	12	13	14																2
1	2	3	4²	5	6	7¹	8	9³	10	11	12	13	14																3
1	2	3	4¹	5	6		8	9	10	11³	12	13	7²	14															4
1	2	3		5			8	9³	10¹	11	12	13	14			7²	4		6										5
1	2	3		5			8	9	10¹	11²	12	13				7	4		6										6
1	2	3		5			8³	9	10¹	11²	12	13	14			7	4		6										7
1	2	3		5			8	9	10¹	11³		13	14			7	4		6			5			12²				8
1	2	3		5			8	9	10¹	11²	12⁴	13				7	4		6			5							9
1	2	3						9	7¹	6			10²			11	8	12	4³		5		13	14					10
1	2	3					8²	9	7³	11		12	14				6	13	4	5									11
1	2	3						9	10	11	12		4			7¹		8	6		5								12
1	2	3						9	10	11	12	6	13				4¹	8²	7		5								13
1	2	3	14					9	10¹	11²		13	4³			7	12	8	6		5								14
1	2	3	14					9²	11¹	13		4				7	8³	10	6		5	12							15
1	2	3						9³	11	12	13		7²			4	8	6			5	10¹	14						16
1	2	3						10³	11	12	13	14	7¹			4	8	6			5	9²							17
1	2	3						9		12		7¹				11	4	8	6		5	10²	13						18
1	2	3						9¹	11	12						7	4	8²	6		5	10	13						19
1	2	3	14	12				9	11	10²		8³				7	4		6	5¹		13							20
1	2	3	13	5				9¹	11³	12	8²					7	4		6			10	14						21
1	2	3	12	5				9		13		6¹				11	7	8²	4			10							22
1	2	3		5				9²	11¹	12						7	4	8	6			10	13						23
1	2	3		5				9	11	12						7	4	8¹	6²			10	13						24
1	2	3		5				9¹	11²	12	13					7	4	8	6³			10	14						25
1	2	3		5				10	14	11¹						12	7	4	8³	6² 13		9							26
1	2	3		5				10³	12	11	13					14	7¹	4	8			9²			6				27
1	2	3²		5				10¹	12	11	13						4	8				9			6				28
1	2	3		5				13	9¹	11							4	8²				10	12		6				29
1	2	3		5					9	11	12					7⁴	4	8				10¹			6				30
1	2	3		5					9	11²	12					7¹	4	8				10			6		13		31
1	2	3³		5					9	11	12					7²	4	8				10¹ 14			6		13		32
1	2²	3		5					14	9	11					7¹	4	8³	13			10			6		12		33
1	2³	3		5						9¹	11²	12					4	8				10	13		6		14		34
1	2	3		5				13	12	11	9²		14			7	4	8³				10¹			6				35
1	2	3					8¹	13	11³	9²						7	4					10			6	12	14		36
1	2	3		5			8²	12	11³	9¹	13					7	4					10			6		14		37
1	2	3		5					12	11						7	4	8				10			6		9¹		38
1	2	3		5					12	11¹	13					7	4	8				10			6²		9		39
1	2	3							12	14			11			7	4	8³	13	5		10			6²		9¹		40
1	2	3¹	12						10	11	14			9⁴		7³	4		6	5							13	8²	41
1	2			5			8²	9³	11	14						4	7	6				10¹	12		13	3			42
1	2		5²				10	9	11³			6	14			4	8	7¹	3			12			13				43
1	2	12						10³	9		13	11	14			4	8	7	5¹			6	3²						44
1	2	3						9	11	13	7					4	8	5¹ 12				10²			6				45
1	2	3						9²	11	12	7	10¹				4³	8	6							5 14		13		46

FA Cup
Third Round   Chelsea   (a)   0-5

Carling Cup
First Round   Barnet   (a)   2-0
Second Round   Leeds U   (a)   1-2

WEST BROMWICH ALBION FA Premiership

FOUNDATION

There is a well known story that when employees of Salter's Spring Works in West Bromwich decided to form a football club, they had to send someone to the nearby Association Football stronghold of Wednesbury to purchase a football. A weekly subscription of 2d (less than 1p) was imposed and the name of the new club was West Bromwich Strollers.

The Hawthorns, West Bromwich, West Midlands B71 4LF.

Telephone: 0871 271 1100.

Fax: 0871 271 9861.

Ticket Office: 0871 271 9780.

Website: www.wbafc.co.uk

Email: enquiries@wbafc.co.uk

Ground Capacity: 28,003.

Record Attendance: 64,815 v Arsenal, FA Cup 6th rd, 6 March 1937.

Pitch Measurements: 115yd × 74yd.

Chairman: Jeremy Peace.

Legal Counsel/Secretary: Richard Garlick.

Head Coach: Roberto Di Matteo.

Assistant Head Coach: Eddie Newton.

Physio: Richie Rawlins.

Colours: Navy blue and white striped shirts, white shorts, white stockings.

Change Colours: Red shirts with blue trim, blue shorts, blue stockings.

Year Formed: 1878.

Turned Professional: 1885.

Ltd Co.: 1892.

Plc: 1996.

Previous Name: 1878, West Bromwich Strollers; 1881, West Bromwich Albion.

Club Nicknames: 'Throstles', 'Baggies', 'Albion'.

Grounds: 1878, Coopers Hill; 1879, Dartmouth Park; 1881, Bunns Field, Walsall Street; 1882, Four Acres (Dartmouth Cricket Club); 1885, Stoney Lane; 1900, The Hawthorns.

First Football League Game: 8 September 1888, Football League, v Stoke (a) W 2–0 – Roberts; J. Horton, Green; E. Horton, Perry, Bayliss; Bassett, Woodhall (1), Hendry, Pearson, Wilson (1).

Record League Victory: 12–0 v Darwen, Division 1, 4 April 1892 – Reader; J. Horton, McCulloch; Reynolds (2), Perry, Groves; Bassett (3), McLeod, Nicholls (1), Pearson (4), Geddes (1), (1 og).

HONOURS

Football League: Division 1 – Champions 1919–20; Runners-up 1924–25, 1953–54, 2001–02, 2003–04. FL C – Champions 2007–08; Runners-up 2009–10. Division 2 – Champions 1901–02, 1910–11; Runners-up 1930–31, 1948–49.

FA Cup: Winners 1888, 1892, 1931, 1954, 1968; Runners-up 1886, 1887, 1895, 1912, 1935.

Football League Cup: Winners 1966; Runners-up 1967, 1970.

European Competitions: *European Cup-Winners' Cup:* 1968–69. *European Fairs Cup:* 1966–67. *UEFA Cup:* 1978–79, 1979–80, 1981–82.

sky SPORTS FACT FILE

On 21 December 1907 when West Bromwich Albion entertained Lincoln City, five goals were scored in eleven minutes during the last quarter of an hour's play. Albion, who had already scored from two penalties in the match, missed another in this period but won 5–2.

Record Cup Victory: 10–1 v Chatham (away), FA Cup 3rd rd, 2 March 1889 – Roberts; J. Horton, Green; Timmins (1), Charles Perry, E. Horton; Bassett (2), Perry (1), Bayliss (2), Pearson, Wilson (3), (1 og).

Record Defeat: 3–10 v Stoke C, Division 1, 4 February 1937.

Most League Points (2 for a win): 60, Division 1, 1919–20.

Most League Points (3 for a win): 91, FL C, 2009–10.

Most League Goals: 105, Division 2, 1929–30.

Highest League Scorer in Season: William 'Ginger' Richardson, 39, Division 1, 1935–36.

Most League Goals in Total Aggregate: Tony Brown, 218, 1963–79.

Most League Goals in One Match: 6, Jimmy Cookson v Blackpool, Division 2, 17 September 1927.

Most Capped Player: Stuart Williams, 33 (43), Wales.

Most League Appearances: Tony Brown, 574, 1963–80.

Youngest League Player: Charlie Wilson, 16 years 73 days v Oldham Ath, 1 October 1921.

Record Transfer Fee Received: £8,000,000 from Aston Villa for Curtis Davies, July 2008.

Record Transfer Fee Paid: £4,700,000 to Mallorca for Borja Valero, August 2008.

Football League Record: 1888 Founder Member of Football League; 1901–02 Division 2; 1902–04 Division 1; 1904–11 Division 2; 1911–27 Division 1; 1927–31 Division 2; 1931–38 Division 1; 1938–49 Division 2; 1949–73 Division 1; 1973–76 Division 2; 1976–86 Division 1; 1986–91 Division 2; 1991–92 Division 3; 1992–93 Division 2; 1993–2002 Division 1; 2002–03 FA Premier League; 2003–04 Division 1; 2004–06 FA Premier League; 2006–08 FL C; 2008–09 FA Premier League; 2009–10 FL C; 2010– FA Premier League.

LATEST SEQUENCES

Longest Sequence of League Wins: 11, 5.4.1930 – 8.9.1930.

Longest Sequence of League Defeats: 11, 28.10.1995 – 26.12.1995.

Longest Sequence of League Draws: 5, 30.8.1999 – 3.10 1999.

Longest Sequence of Unbeaten League Matches: 17, 7.9.1957 – 7.12.1957.

Longest Sequence Without a League Win: 15, 16.10.2004 – 25.9.2004.

Successive Scoring Runs: 36 from 26.4.1958.

Successive Non-scoring Runs: 4 from 15.2.1913.

MANAGERS

Louis Ford 1890–92
(Secretary-Manager)
Henry Jackson 1892–94
(Secretary-Manager)
Edward Stephenson 1894–95
(Secretary-Manager)
Clement Keys 1895–96
(Secretary-Manager)
Frank Heaven 1896–1902
(Secretary-Manager)
Fred Everiss 1902–48
Jack Smith 1948–52
Jesse Carver 1952
Vic Buckingham 1953–59
Gordon Clark 1959–61
Archie Macaulay 1961–63
Jimmy Hagan 1963–67
Alan Ashman 1967–71
Don Howe 1971–75
Johnny Giles 1975–77
Ronnie Allen 1977
Ron Atkinson 1978–81
Ronnie Allen 1981–82
Ron Wylie 1982–84
Johnny Giles 1984–85
Ron Saunders 1986–87
Ron Atkinson 1987–88
Brian Talbot 1988–91
Bobby Gould 1991–92
Ossie Ardiles 1992–93
Keith Burkinshaw 1993–94
Alan Buckley 1994–97
Ray Harford 1997
Denis Smith 1997–2000
Brian Little 2000
Gary Megson 2000–04
Bryan Robson 2004–06
Tony Mowbray 2006–09
Roberto Di Matteo June 2009–

TEN YEAR LEAGUE RECORD

		P	W	D	L	F	A	Pts	Pos
2000-01	Div 1	46	21	11	14	60	52	74	6
2001-02	Div 1	46	27	8	11	61	29	89	2
2002-03	PR Lge	38	6	8	24	29	65	26	19
2003-04	Div 1	46	25	11	10	64	42	86	2
2004-05	PR Lge	38	6	16	16	36	61	34	17
2005-06	PR Lge	38	7	9	22	31	58	30	19
2006-07	FL C	46	22	10	14	81	55	76	4
2007-08	FL C	46	23	12	11	88	55	81	1
2008-09	PR Lge	38	8	8	22	36	67	32	20
2009-10	FL C	46	26	13	7	89	48	91	2

DID YOU KNOW ?

Five days after Manchester U had taken a 1–0 lead over Real Madrid in the 1968 European Cup they met West Bromwich Albion at The Hawthorns. Albion won 6–3 with a Jeff Astle treble. The Baggies had beaten Birmingham City 2–0 in the FA Cup semi-final two days earlier!

WEST BROMWICH ALBION 2009–10 LEAGUE RECORD

Match No.	Date	Venue	Opponents	Result	H/T Score	Lg Pos.	Goalscorers	Attendance
1	Aug 8	H	Newcastle U	D 1-1	1-0	—	Martis [39]	23,502
2	15	A	Nottingham F	W 1-0	0-0	8	Cohen (og) [53]	22,794
3	18	A	Peterborough U	W 3-2	3-1	—	Moore 2 [3, 34], Brunt [41]	8752
4	22	H	Ipswich T	W 2-0	2-0	4	Mulumbu [10], Koren [38]	19,390
5	29	A	Sheffield U	D 2-2	0-0	1	Bednar 2 [54, 60]	25,169
6	Sept 12	H	Plymouth Arg	W 3-1	2-1	2	Martis [34], Cech 2 [40, 86]	22,190
7	15	H	Doncaster R	W 3-1	1-1	—	Olsson 2 [19, 65], Wood [85]	22,184
8	19	A	Middlesbrough	W 5-0	3-0	1	Brunt 2 [17, 31], Mulumbu [42], Bednar [62], Thomas [89]	22,725
9	26	H	Crystal Palace	L 0-1	0-0	2		21,007
10	29	A	Barnsley	L 1-3	0-2	—	Brunt [88]	12,191
11	Oct 3	A	Preston NE	D 0-0	0-0	2		11,180
12	17	H	Reading	W 3-1	1-1	1	Thomas 2 [29, 65], Mulumbu [87]	20,935
13	20	A	Swansea C	L 0-1	0-0	—		21,022
14	24	A	Coventry C	D 0-0	0-0	3		20,871
15	31	H	Watford	W 5-0	2-0	1	Olsson [5], Dorrans (pen) [18], Moore [49], Zuiverloon [63], Cox [68]	21,421
16	Nov 7	A	Leicester C	W 2-1	2-0	2	Dorrans [37], Jara [40]	28,748
17	21	H	Bristol C	W 4-1	2-0	1	Thomas [3], Brunt [12], Carey (og) [47], Cox [4E]	23,444
18	28	A	Sheffield W	W 4-0	3-0	2	Cox 2 [23, 30], Thomas [38], Brunt [85]	20,824
19	Dec 5	A	Derby Co	D 2-2	0-1	2	Cox [82], Dorrans [89]	30,127
20	8	H	Cardiff C	L 0-2	0-1	—		20,742
21	14	H	QPR	D 2-2	0-0	—	Thomas [67], Cox [90]	21,565
22	26	H	Peterborough U	W 2-0	0-0	2	Moore [61], Bennett (og) [67]	24,924
23	28	A	Scunthorpe U	W 3-1	1-0	2	Dorrans 2 (1 pen) [19, 66 (p)], Zuiverloon [86]	7221
24	Jan 8	H	Nottingham F	L 1-3	0-1	—	Bednar [64]	22,873
25	18	A	Newcastle U	D 2-2	1-1	—	Olsson [13], Bednar [46]	39,291
26	26	A	Ipswich T	D 1-1	0-0	—	Brunt [90]	19,574
27	30	H	Sheffield U	W 3-1	2-0	3	Dorrans (pen) [19], Bednar [30], Thomas [50]	22,193
28	Feb 3	A	Blackpool	W 3-2	2-1	—	Bednar 2 [29, 40], Dorrans (pen) [63]	8510
29	6	A	Plymouth Arg	W 1-0	0-0	2	Cox [66]	12,053
30	9	H	Scunthorpe U	W 2-0	1-0	—	Bednar [13], Zuiverloon [86]	23,146
31	16	A	Cardiff C	D 1-1	1-1	—	Zuiverloon [45]	20,758
32	21	A	Bristol C	L 1-2	1-0	3	Dorrans [24]	14,374
33	27	H	Derby Co	W 3-1	0-0	2	Brunt 2 [67, 77], Cox [83]	23,335
34	Mar 6	A	QPR	L 1-3	1-2	3	Brunt [36]	14,578
35	9	H	Sheffield W	W 1-0	0-0	—	Koren [79]	20,458
36	13	H	Blackpool	W 3-2	1-1	2	Miller [13], Koren [53], Dorrans (pen) [78]	21,592
37	16	A	Swansea C	W 2-0	0-0	—	Dorrans (pen) [79], Miller [89]	17,774
38	20	H	Preston NE	W 3-2	3-2	2	Watson [7], Brunt [9], Dorrans [33]	21,343
39	24	H	Coventry C	W 1-0	1-0	—	Reid S [22]	22,140
40	27	A	Reading	D 1-1	0-1	2	Tamas [96]	20,515
41	Apr 2	H	Leicester C	W 3-0	2-0	—	Morrison [38], Koren 2 [45, 85]	23,334
42	5	A	Watford	D 1-1	0-0	2	Brunt [90]	14,555
43	10	A	Doncaster R	W 3-2	2-0	2	Dorrans [31], Brunt [45], Bednar [73]	12,708
44	17	H	Middlesbrough	W 2-0	1-0	2	Cox [45], Bednar [55]	22,548
45	26	A	Crystal Palace	D 1-1	1-1	—	Tamas [21]	17,798
46	May 2	H	Barnsley	D 1-1	0-0	2	Dorrans [90]	25,297

Final League Position: 2

GOALSCORERS

League (89): Brunt 13, Dorrans 13 (6 pens), Bednar 11, Cox 9, Thomas 7, Koren 5, Moore 4, Olsson 4, Zuiverloon 4, Mulumbu 3, Cech 2, Martis 2, Miller 2, Tamas 2, Jara 1, Morrison 1, Reid S 1, Watson 1, Wood 1, own goals 3.
Carling Cup (6): Beattie 2, Dorrans 2, Cox 1, own goal 1.
FA Cup (10): Dorrans 3 (2 pens), Koren 3, Mattock 1, Olsson 1, Thomas 1, Wood 1.

Carson S 43	Zuiverloon G 26+4	Cech M 29+4	Olsson J 43	Martis S 10+3	Mulumbu Y 35+5	Koren R 26+8	Greening J 2	Moore L 23+3	Wood C 6+12	Brunt C 39+1	Dorrans G 42+3	Cox S 17+11	Mattock J 26+3	Beattie C —+3	Barnett L —+2	Cummings S 3	Thomas J 22+5	Borja Valero —+1	Bednar R 21+6	Reid R —+4	Teixeira F 1+8	Jara G 20+2	Meite A 16+4	Thorne G —+1	Kiely D 3+2	Tamas G 23	Miller 14+11	Slory A 1+5	Nouble F 3	Watson B 6+1	Morrison J 5+6	Reid S 10	Barnes G 1+8	Match No.
1	2	3	4	5	6	7^1	8	9	10^2	11	12	13																						1
1	2^2	14	4	5	6	7^1	8	9		10^3	11		3	12	13																			2
1	7^2	4	5	6	12	9^3	10^1	8	11^8		3	14				2	13																	3
1	11	4	5	6	8^3	9	10	7^1		3^2	13					2	12	14																4
1	11	4	5	6	8	9^1		12		3						2	7^2		10	13														5
1	2	7	4	5	6	12		13	8^3	11	9^1	3					14		10^2															6
1	2	7^1	4	5	6	9		13	8^2	11		3					12		10^3		4													7
1	2		4	5	6	12		9^1	14	8^3	11		3^2	13			7		10															8
1	2^1		4	5	7	8^3		9^2	14	11	12	3					10	13					6											9
1	2		4	5	6^1	7^3		9^2	8	11	13	3					10	14					12											10
1	2	8^2	4	14	7^3	12		9^1		11		3					10	13					5	6										11
1	2	3^2	4		6			9^3	12	11		8					7		10^1		3		5	14										12
1	2	3^1	4		6	13		9^2	10	11	14	8^3					7				2		5											13
1	2	13	4		8	10^1		9^3	14	11		3					7^2				2		5	8										14
1	2	6			9			12	11	10	3						7^1				8	5	4											15
1	2	13	6		12			9^3	8	11	10^1	3					7^2	14				5	4											16
1	2	12	6		13	14		9	8	11^2	10^3	3^1					7					5	4											17
1	2	3	6		12			9^2	13	8	11	10^3					7^1					5	4	14										18
1	2	3	6					9^2		8	7	10	11^1					13		2	5	4												19
1^8	2	3^6	6		7^1					8	11	10					9			2	5	4		15										20
	2^2		6					9^1	12	8	11	10^2	3				7	13			5	4		1										21
	2		6	14				9^3	13	8	11	10^2	3				7^1			2	5	4		1										22
	2	3	6	14	13			9	12	8	11^2	10^1					7				5	4		1										23
1	2	6			13			9^1		8	11	10^3	3^2				7		12		5				4	14								24
1		2	3		4	10		8		11							7		9^1		5				3	12								25
1		2	3		4^3	10^1		8		11	14						7^2		9	3	5				3	12								26
1	13	2	3		4	10^1		8		11	12	14					7^3		9		5^2				3									27
1	14	2	3		4	10		8^2		11							7^1		9^2		5				3	13	12							28
1	2				4^1			13		8	11	10^3	3				7^8		9^2		12	5			3		14							29
1	14		6		4	7^1				8^3	11	12	3						9			5			2		13	10^2						30
1	2		6		4^1			9	13	8	11	12	3									5					7^8	10						31
1	2^3		6		4	7^2		14		8	11	13	3						9			5					12	10^1						32
1		2	3		14	10^1		9^2		8	11	13					7					6			5					4^3	12			33
1		2^1	3		4					8	13	9					7								5	12				6	11^2	10		34
1		3	6		8	12		9^2		10	11						7^1								5	13					4^3	2	14	35
1		3	6		8	4				10^3	11								13						5	9^2		14	2^1	7	12			36
1	12	2	3^1		8	7		9^2		10^3	11											6			5	13		4				14		37
1	2	3			8	7^1		13		10^3	11											6			5	9^2		4	14			12		38
1			8		6^3	13		10^1		11		3					14								5	2	9^2		4		7	12		39
1		5	8^1					9^2		11	14	3					7								2	12		4	6³	10	13		40
1		2	3^3		8	4				10	11	14					13						12		5	9^2		6		7^1			41
1	2^1	3	6		8	4^3				10	11						9						12		5	14		13		7^2			42
1		3	6		8	4		7		11	10^1						9^2								5	13				2	12		43
1^6		2	3		6	4		8		11	10^1						9^2						15		5	13		12	7				44
1		3	6^2		4	7^1		8		11^3	10						9						13		5					14	2	12	45
1		3^1	6		4	7		8		11	10^2	12					9								5	14				13	2^3		46

FA Cup

Third Round	Huddersfield T	(a)	2-0
Fourth Round	Newcastle U	(h)	4-2
Fifth Round	Reading	(a)	2-2
		(h)	2-3

Carling Cup

First Round	Bury	(a)	2-0
Second Round	Rotherham U	(h)	4-3
Third Round	Arsenal	(a)	0-2

WEST HAM UNITED   FA Premiership

FOUNDATION

Thames Iron Works FC was formed by employees of this famous shipbuilding company in 1895 and entered the FA Cup in their initial season at Chatham and the London League in their second. The committee wanted to introduce professional players, so Thames Iron Works was wound up in June 1900 and relaunched a month later as West Ham United.

The Boleyn Ground, Upton Park, Green Street, London E13 9AZ.

Telephone: (020) 8548 2748.

Fax: (020) 8548 2758.

Ticket Office: 0871 222 2700.

Website: www.whufc.co.uk

Email: yourcomments@westhamunited.co.uk

Ground Capacity: 35,303.

Record Attendance: 42,322 v Tottenham H, Division 1, 17 October 1970.

Pitch Measurements: 100.58m × 66.84m.

Joint Chairmen: David Sullivan and David Gold.

Vice-chairman: Karren Brady.

Secretary: Peter Barnes.

Manager: Avram Grant.

First Team Coach: Kevin Keen.

Physio: Andy Rolls.

Colours: Claret shirts with blue trim, white shorts, claret stockings.

Change Colours: Dark blue shirts with broad royal blue stripe, dark blue shorts, dark blue stockings.

Year Formed: 1895.

Turned Professional: 1900.

Ltd Co.: 1900.

Previous Name: 1895, Thames Iron Works FC; 1900, West Ham United.

Club Nicknames: 'The Hammers', 'The Irons'.

Grounds: 1895, Memorial Recreation Ground, Canning Town; 1904, Boleyn Ground.

First Football League Game: 30 August 1919, Division 2, v Lincoln C (h) D 1–1 – Hufton; Cope, Lee; Lane, Fenwick, McCrae; D. Smith, Moyes (1), Puddefoot, Morris, Bradshaw.

HONOURS

Football League: Division 2 – Champions 1957–58, 1980–81; Runners-up 1922–23, 1990–91.
FA Cup: Winners 1964, 1975, 1980; Runners-up 1923, 2006.
Football League Cup: Runners-up 1966, 1981.
European Competitions: European Cup-Winners' Cup: 1964–65 (winners), 1965–66, 1975–76 (runners-up), 1980–81. *UEFA Cup:* 1999–2000; 2006–07. *Intertoto Cup:* 1999 (winners).

---

sky SPORTS FACT FILE

Stan Earle and George Webb were two West Ham United players to win England amateur international honours and then play for the full professional national team. Earle played in the 1920s while Webb, who remained as an amateur, was active in the previous decade.

Record League Victory: 8–0 v Rotherham U, Division 2,
8 March 1958 – Gregory; Bond, Wright; Malcolm, Brown,
Lansdowne; Grice, Smith (2), Keeble (2), Dick (4),
Musgrove. 8–0 v Sunderland, Division 1, 19 October 1968 –
Ferguson; Bonds, Charles; Peters, Stephenson, Moore (1);
Redknapp, Boyce, Brooking (1), Hurst (6), Sissons.

Record Cup Victory: 10–0 v Bury, League Cup 2nd rd
(2nd leg), 25 October 1983 – Parkes; Stewart (1), Walford,
Bonds (Orr), Martin (1), Devonshire (2), Allen, Cottee (4),
Swindlehurst, Brooking (2), Pike.

Record Defeat: 2–8 v Blackburn R, Division 1,
26 December 1963.

Most League Points (2 for a win): 66, Division 2, 1980–81.

Most League Points (3 for a win): 88, Division 1, 1992–93.

Most League Goals: 101, Division 2, 1957–58.

Highest League Scorer in Season: Vic Watson, 42,
Division 1, 1929–30.

Most League Goals in Total Aggregate: Vic Watson, 298, 1920–35.

Most League Goals in One Match: 6, Vic Watson v Leeds U, Division 1, 9 February 1929;
6, Geoff Hurst v Sunderland, Division 1, 19 October 1968.

Most Capped Player: Bobby Moore, 108, England.

Most League Appearances: Billy Bonds, 663, 1967–88.

Youngest League Player: Billy Williams, 16 years 221 days v Blackpool, 6 May 1922.

Record Transfer Fee Received: £18,000,000 from Leeds U for Rio Ferdinand, November 2000.

Record Transfer Fee Paid: £7,500,000 to Liverpool for Craig Bellamy, July 2007.

Football League Record: 1919 Elected to Division 2; 1923–32 Division 1; 1932–58 Division 2;
1958–78 Division 1; 1978–81 Division 2; 1981–89 Division 1; 1989–91 Division 2; 1991–93 Division 1;
1993–2003 FA Premier League; 2003–04 Division 1; 2004–05 FL C; 2005– FA Premier League.

MANAGERS

Syd King 1902–32
Charlie Paynter 1932–50
Ted Fenton 1950–61
Ron Greenwood 1961–74
 *(continued as General Manager
 to 1977)*
John Lyall 1974–89
Lou Macari 1989–90
Billy Bonds 1990–94
Harry Redknapp 1994–2001
Glenn Roeder 2001–03
Alan Pardew 2003–06
Alan Curbishley 2006–08
Gianfranco Zola 2008–10
Avram Grant May 2010–

LATEST SEQUENCES

Longest Sequence of League Wins: 9, 19.10.1985 – 14.12.1985.

Longest Sequence of League Defeats: 9, 28.3.1932 – 29.8.1932.

Longest Sequence of League Draws: 5, 15.10.2003 – 1.11.2003.

Longest Sequence of Unbeaten League Matches: 27, 27.12.80 – 10.10.81.

Longest Sequence Without a League Win: 17, 31.1.1976 – 21.8.1976.

Successive Scoring Runs: 27 from 5.10.1957.

Successive Non-scoring Runs: 5 from 1.5.1971.

TEN YEAR LEAGUE RECORD

		P	W	D	L	F	A	Pts	Pos
2000-01	PR Lge	38	10	12	16	45	50	42	15
2001-02	PR Lge	38	15	8	15	48	57	53	7
2002-03	PR Lge	38	10	12	16	42	59	42	18
2003-04	Div 1	46	19	17	10	67	45	74	4
2004-05	FL C	46	21	10	15	66	56	73	6
2005-06	PR Lge	38	16	7	15	52	55	55	9
2006-07	PR Lge	38	12	5	21	35	59	41	15
2007-08	PR Lge	38	13	10	15	42	50	49	10
2008-09	PR Lge	38	14	9	15	42	45	51	9
2009-10	PR Lge	38	8	11	19	47	66	35	17

DID YOU KNOW ?

West Ham United can claim
to have had four "one-game-
wonders", all forwards, who
scored on their only Football
League appearances. They
were Robert Allen (1919–20),
Cliff Ette (1933–34) plus Dick
Bell and Cliff Hubbard
(1938–39) who both played in
wartime regional games.

WEST HAM UNITED 2009–10 LEAGUE RECORD

Match No.	Date	Venue	Opponents	Result		H/T Score	Lg Pos.	Goalscorers	Attendance
1	Aug 15	A	Wolverhampton W	W	2-0	1-0	—	Noble [22], Upson [69]	28,674
2	23	H	Tottenham H	L	1-2	0-0	11	Cole [49]	33,095
3	29	A	Blackburn R	D	0-0	0-0	11		23,421
4	Sept 12	A	Wigan Ath	L	0-1	0-0	13		17,142
5	19	H	Liverpool	L	2-3	2-2	16	Diamanti (pen) [29], Cole [45]	34,658
6	28	A	Manchester C	L	1-3	1-2	—	Cole [24]	42,745
7	Oct 4	H	Fulham	D	2-2	1-0	19	Cole [16], Stanislas [90]	32,612
8	17	A	Stoke C	L	1-2	1-1	19	Upson [34]	27,026
9	25	H	Arsenal	D	2-2	0-2	19	Cole [74], Diamanti (pen) [80]	34,442
10	31	A	Sunderland	D	2-2	2-1	19	Franco [30], Cole [36]	39,033
11	Nov 4	H	Aston Villa	W	2-1	1-0	—	Noble (pen) [45], Hines [90]	30,024
12	8	H	Everton	L	1-2	0-1	18	Stanislas [65]	32,466
13	21	A	Hull C	D	3-3	2-3	17	Franco [5], Collison [11], Da Costa [69]	24,909
14	28	H	Burnley	W	5-3	3-0	17	Collison [18], Stanislas [33], Cole (pen) [43], Franco [51], Jimenez (pen) [64]	34,003
15	Dec 5	H	Manchester U	L	0-4	0-1	17		34,980
16	12	A	Birmingham C	L	0-1	0-0	18		28,203
17	15	A	Bolton W	L	1-3	0-0	—	Diamanti [69]	17,849
18	20	H	Chelsea	D	1-1	1-0	19	Diamanti (pen) [45]	33,388
19	26	H	Portsmouth	W	2-0	1-0	17	Diamanti (pen) [23], Kovac [89]	33,686
20	28	A	Tottenham H	L	0-2	0-1	17		35,994
21	Jan 17	A	Aston Villa	D	0-0	0-0	16		35,646
22	26	A	Portsmouth	D	1-1	0-0	—	Upson [52]	18,322
23	30	A	Blackburn R	D	0-0	0-0	15		33,093
24	Feb 6	A	Burnley	L	1-2	0-1	18	Ilan [81]	21,001
25	10	H	Birmingham C	W	2-0	1-0	—	Diamanti [45], Cole [67]	34,458
26	20	H	Hull C	W	3-0	1-0	13	Behrami [3], Cole [59], Faubert [90]	33,971
27	20	A	Manchester U	L	0-3	0-1	—		73,797
28	Mar 6	H	Bolton W	L	1-2	0-2	—	Diamanti [88]	33,824
29	13	A	Chelsea	L	1-4	1-1	16	Parker [30]	41,755
30	20	A	Arsenal	L	0-2	0-1	17		60,077
31	23	H	Wolverhampton W	L	1-3	0-1	—	Franco [90]	33,988
32	27	H	Stoke C	L	0-1	0-0	17		34,564
33	Apr 4	A	Everton	D	2-2	0-1	17	Da Costa [60], Ilan [87]	37,451
34	10	H	Sunderland	W	1-0	0-0	—	Ilan [51]	34,685
35	19	A	Liverpool	L	0-3	0-2	—		37,697
36	24	H	Wigan Ath	W	3-2	2-1	17	Ilan [31], Kovac [45], Parker [77]	33,057
37	May 2	A	Fulham	L	2-3	0-1	17	Cole [61], Franco [90]	24,201
38	9	H	Manchester C	D	1-1	1-1	17	Boa Morte [17]	34,989

Final League Position: 17

GOALSCORERS

League (47): Cole 10 (1 pen), Diamanti 7 (4 pens), Franco 5, Ilan 4, Stanislas 3, Upson 3, Collison 2, Da Costa 2, Kovac 2, Noble 2 (1 pen), Parker 2, Behrami 1, Boa Morte 1, Faubert 1, Hines 1, Jimenez 1 (pen).
Carling Cup (4): Stanislaus 2 (1 pen), Hines 1, Ilunga 1.
FA Cup (1): Diamanti 1.

Green R 38	Faubert J 32+1	Ilunga H 16	Parker S 30+1	Upson M 33	Collins J 3	Noble M 25+2	Jimenez L 6+5	Cole C 26+4	Dyer K 4+6	Collison J 19+3	Spector J 22+5	Stanislas J 11+15	Noble F 3+5	Kovac R 27+4	Hines Z 5+8	Gabbidon D 8+2	Tomkins J 22+1	Behrami V 24+3	Diamanti A 18+9	Da Costa M 12+3	Franco G 18+7	Kurucz P —+1	Sears F —+1	McCarthy B 2+3	Mido 5+4	Ilan 6+5	Daprela F 4+3	Boa Morte L 1	Spence J —+1	Match No.
1	2	3^1	4	5	6	7	8	9^3	10^2	11	12	13	14																	1
1	2		4^2	5	6	7	8^1	9		11^3	3	10	14	12	13															2
1	2		4	5	6	7	8^1	9	12	11^2	3	10		13																3
1	2		4	5		7^3		9		11^2	14			8^1	10	3	6	12	13											4
1	2	3	4	5^1		7		9	14					13	11	12	6	8^1	10^3											5
1	2	3	4			7	8^2	9				13		11^1	12		6	10	5											6
1	2	3	4^1	5		7	8	9				13		11^2			6	12	10											7
1	2	3		5		6		9		11^3		13		8^2	12		4	7	10^1		14									8
1		3	8^4	5		6^1		9		11	2			14	13		4	7^3	12		10^2									9
1		3		5		6		9		11	2			6^4	13		4	7^1	12		10^2									10
1	2	3^1	8	5		6	14	9^2		11	12			13			7			4	10^3									11
1	2		8	5		6^2				11	3	12		9			7	13		4	10									12
1	2		4	5		13	9			11		10		12	6		7^1		3		8^2									13
1	14	3	8							13	9^2			11^3	2	7	4	12	6		5	10^1								14
1^6		3	8							13	11	2	7	4^2	9^1	5	6		12		10^3	15								15
1	2	3^1	4			7^8				12	13			11^2	14	8^1	5	6	10		9									16
1	2	3	4							7^1	11^2	12		8		5	6	10	13		9									17
1	7	3	4	5		6				11				8		2^1	12	10			9									18
1	2	3	8	5		6^1	12			11				14	7		4	13	10^2		9^3									19
1	2	3^2	8^1	5		12				11^3	13	14		6			4	7	10		9									20
1	2		4^1	5		8				11	3	13	9^3	10^2			6	7	12	14										21
1	2			5		6		12		11	3	14	9^1	8		4^2	7	10^3	13					14						22
1	2	13	5			6^2		12		11	3		9	8^1		4	7^2	10						14						23
1	2		4	5		8^3		9		11^2	3	13					6	7							10^1	12	14			24
1	2	3^1	4	5		14^3		9			12			8			6	7	10						11^2	13				25
1	2		4	5				9^2		14	3			8			6	7	10^3		11^1				13	12				26
1	2			5		6		11	14	13	3			8			4	7	10^3		9^1				12					27
1	2^1		4	5		6		11	14	13	3			8^3			6	7	10		9^2				13					28
1			4	5				12	11^1	3	13			8	6			7	14						9^2	10^3	2			29
1			5			13		12		3	11			6^2			4	7	10		9^1			14	8^3		2			30
1	2		4	5				11		12	13			8^2			6^1	7	10		14			9^3			3			31
1	2		4	5		8^2		10	11^1	6							7	12	3					14	9^3	13				32
1	2		4	5		7		10		3	11^2			8	13			6							9^1	12				33
1	2			5		4		9		3	11^1			8			7			6	12				10^2	13				34
1	2			5		4		9^2		3^3	11^1			8			7			6	12			13	10	14				35
1	2		8	5		4^2		9		3				$\cdot1$			7			6	12				10^1	13				36
1	2^1		8	5		4		9		3	14			$\cdot1$			7^3	13	6	12					10^2					37
1	2		4	5				9^2			13			7				11^3	6	12						10	3	8^1	14	38

FA Cup
Third Round   Arsenal   (h)   1-2

Carling Cup
Second Round   Millwall   (h)   3-1
Third Round   Bolton W   (a)   1-3

WIGAN ATHLETIC   FA Premiership

FOUNDATION

Following the demise of Wigan Borough and their resignation from the Football League in 1931, a public meeting was called in Wigan at the Queen's Hall in May 1932 at which a new club, Wigan Athletic, was founded in the hope of carrying on in the Football League. With this in mind, they bought Springfield Park for £2,250, but failed to gain admission to the Football League until 46 years later.

The DW Stadium, Robin Park Complex, Newtown, Wigan, Lancashire WN5 0UZ.

Telephone: (01942) 774 000.

Fax: (01942) 770 477.

Ticket Office: (0871) 663 3552.

Website: www.wiganathletic.tv

Email: s.hayton@wiganathletic.com

Ground Capacity: 25,138.

Record Attendance: 27,526 v Hereford U, 12 December 1953 (at Springfield Park).

Pitch Measurements: 105m × 68m.

Chairman: David Whelan.

Vice-chairman: Phillip Williams.

Chief Executive: Brenda Spencer.

Secretary: Stuart Hayton.

Manager: Roberto Martinez.

Assistant Manager: Graeme Jones.

Physios: Alex Cribley and Neil Fitzhenry.

Colours: Blue and white striped shirts with blue sleeves, blue shorts, white stockings.

Change Colours: Orange shirts with black trim, black shorts, black stockings.

Year Formed: 1932.

Grounds: 1932, Springfield Park; 1999, JJB Stadium (renamed the DW Stadium in 2009).

Club Nickname: 'The Latics'.

First Football League Game: 19 August 1978, Division 4, v Hereford U (a) D 0–0 – Brown; Hinnigan, Gore, Gillibrand, Ward, Davids, Corrigan, Purdie, Houghton, Wilkie, Wright.

Record League Victory: 7–1 v Scarborough, Division 3, 11 March 1997 – Butler L, Butler J, Sharp (Morgan), Greenall, McGibbon (Biggins (1)), Martinez (1), Diaz (2), Jones (Lancashire (1)), Lowe (2), Rogers, Kilford.

Record Cup Victory: 6–0 v Carlisle U (away), FA Cup 1st rd, 24 November 1934 – Caunce; Robinson, Talbot; Paterson, Watson, Tufnell; Armes (2), Robson (1), Roberts (2), Felton, Scott (1).

HONOURS

Football League: Championship – Runners-up 2004–05; Division 2 Champions, 2002–03; Division 3 Champions, 1996–97.

FA Cup: best season: 6th rd, 1987.

Football League Cup: Runners up: 2006.

Freight Rover Trophy: Winners 1985.

Auto Windscreens Shield: Winners 1999.

sky SPORTS FACT FILE

On 4 February 1970 Wigan Athletic beat Darwen 11–1 in a Lancashire Challenge Trophy tie. The game saw Tony McLoughlin score seven of the goals including a perfect hat-trick. He was making his first appearance for three months after a ban imposed for playing Sunday football!

Record Defeat: 1–6 v Bristol R, Division 3, 3 March 1990.

Most League Points (2 for a win): 55, Division 4, 1978–79 and 1979–80.

Most League Points (3 for a win): 100, Division 2, 2002–03.

Most League Goals: 84, Division 3, 1996–97.

Highest League Scorer in Season: Graeme Jones, 31, Division 3, 1996–97.

Most League Goals in Total Aggregate: Andy Liddell, 70, 1998–2004.

Most League Goals in One Match: Not more than three goals by one player.

Most Capped Players: Kevin Kilbane, 22 (103), Republic of Ireland; Henri Camara, 22 (89), Senegal.

Most League Appearances: Kevin Langley, 317, 1981–86, 1990–94.

Youngest League Player: Steve Nugent, 16 years 132 days v Leyton Orient, 16 September 1989.

Record Transfer Fee Received: £15,250,000 from Manchester U for Antonio Valencia, June 2009.

Record Transfer Fee Paid: £6,000,000 to Newcastle U for Charles N'Zogbia, February 2009.

Football League Record: 1978 Elected to Division 4; 1982–92 Division 3; 1992–93 Division 2; 1993–97 Division 3; 1997–2003 Division 2; 2003–04 Division 1; 2004–05 FL C; 2005– FA Premier League.

LATEST SEQUENCES

Longest Sequence of League Wins: 11, 2.11.2002 – 18.1.2003.

Longest Sequence of League Defeats: 8, 13.12.2006 – 30.1.2007.

Longest Sequence of League Draws: 6, 11.12.2001 – 5.1.2002.

Longest Sequence of Unbeaten League Matches: 25, 8.5.1999 – 3.1.2000.

Longest Sequence Without a League Win: 14, 9.5.1989 – 17.10.1989.

Successive Scoring Runs: 24 from 27.4.1996.

Successive Non-scoring Runs: 4 from 15.4.1995.

MANAGERS

Charlie Spencer 1932–37
Jimmy Milne 1946–47
Bob Pryde 1949–52
Ted Goodier 1952–54
Walter Crook 1954–55
Ron Suart 1955–56
Billy Cooke 1956
Sam Barkas 1957
Trevor Hitchen 1957–58
Malcolm Barrass 1958–59
Jimmy Shirley 1959
Pat Murphy 1959–60
Allenby Chilton 1960
Johnny Ball 1961–63
Allan Brown 1963–66
Alf Craig 1966–67
Harry Leyland 1967–68
Alan Saunders 1968
Ian McNeill 1968–70
Gordon Milne 1970–72
Les Rigby 1972–74
Brian Tiler 1974–76
Ian McNeill 1976–81
Larry Lloyd 1981–83
Harry McNally 1983–85
Bryan Hamilton 1985–86
Ray Mathias 1986–89
Bryan Hamilton 1989–93
Dave Philpotts 1993
Kenny Swain 1993–94
Graham Barrow 1994–95
John Deehan 1995–98
Ray Mathias 1998–99
John Benson 1999–2000
Bruce Rioch 2000–01
Steve Bruce 2001
Paul Jewell 2001–07
Chris Hutchings 2007
Steve Bruce 2007–09
Roberto Martinez June 2009–

TEN YEAR LEAGUE RECORD

		P	W	D	L	F	A	Pts	Pos
2000-01	Div 2	46	19	18	9	53	42	75	6
2001-02	Div 2	46	16	16	14	66	51	64	10
2002-03	Div 2	46	29	13	4	68	25	100	1
2003-04	Div 1	46	18	17	11	60	45	71	7
2004-05	FL C	46	25	12	9	79	35	87	2
2005-06	PR Lge	38	15	6	17	45	52	51	10
2006-07	PR Lge	38	10	8	20	37	59	38	17
2007-08	PR Lge	38	10	10	18	34	51	40	14
2008-09	PR Lge	38	12	9	17	34	45	45	11
2009-10	PR Lge	38	9	9	20	37	79	36	16

DID YOU KNOW ?

On 26 September 2009 Wigan Athletic achieved their first win in the Premier League against the so-called "Big Four" clubs in 35 such attempts. They beat Chelsea 3–1 to end the London club's run of 23 unbeaten matches dating back to the previous season.

WIGAN ATHLETIC 2009–10 LEAGUE RECORD

Match No.	Date	Venue	Opponents	Result	H/T Score	Lg Pos.	Goalscorers	Attendance
1	Aug 15	A	Aston Villa	W 2-0	1-0	—	Rodallega [31], Koumas [56]	35,578
2	18	H	Wolverhampton W	L 0-1	0-1	—		16,661
3	22	H	Manchester U	L 0-5	0-0	15		18,164
4	30	A	Everton	L 1-2	0-0	17	Scharner [57]	35,122
5	Sept 12	H	West Ham U	W 1-0	0-0	11	Rodallega [55]	17,142
6	19	A	Arsenal	L 0-4	0-1	15		59,103
7	26	H	Chelsea	W 3-1	1-0	10	Bramble [16], Rodallega (pen) [53], Scharner [90]	18,542
8	Oct 3	A	Hull C	L 1-2	0-0	12	Sinclair [87]	22,822
9	18	H	Manchester C	D 1-1	1-0	13	N'Zogbia [45]	20,005
10	24	A	Burnley	W 3-1	1-1	10	Rodallega 2 [11, 51], Boyce [76]	19,430
11	31	A	Portsmouth	L 0-4	0-2	12		18,212
12	Nov 8	H	Fulham	D 1-1	1-1	13	Boyce [13]	16,172
13	22	A	Tottenham H	L 1-9	0-1	15	Scharner [57]	35,650
14	28	H	Sunderland	W 1-0	0-0	14	Rodallega [76]	20,447
15	Dec 5	H	Birmingham C	L 2-3	1-0	14	N'Zogbia [33], Gomez [89]	18,797
16	12	A	Stoke C	D 2-2	1-1	14	Boyce [15], Figueroa [72]	26,728
17	16	A	Liverpool	L 1-2	0-1	—	N'Zogbia [90]	41,116
18	26	H	Blackburn R	D 1-1	0-1	16	Rodallega [53]	20,243
19	30	A	Manchester U	L 0-5	0-3	—		74,560
20	Jan 16	A	Wolverhampton W	W 2-0	0-0	14	McCarthy [60], N'Zogbia [73]	27,604
21	27	A	Blackburn R	L 1-2	0-1	—	Caldwell [57]	22,190
22	30	H	Everton	L 0-1	0-0	14		16,869
23	Feb 6	A	Sunderland	D 1-1	1-0	16	Diame [20]	38,350
24	9	H	Stoke C	D 1-1	1-0	—	Scharner [14]	16,033
25	17	H	Bolton W	D 0-0	0-0	—		18,089
26	21	H	Tottenham H	L 0-3	0-1	15		16,165
27	27	A	Birmingham C	L 0-1	0-1	16		25,921
28	Mar 8	H	Liverpool	W 1-0	1-0	—	Rodallega [35]	17,427
29	13	A	Bolton W	L 0-4	0-1	15		20,053
30	16	H	Aston Villa	L 1-2	1-1	—	Caldwell [27]	16,186
31	20	H	Burnley	W 1-0	0-0	15	Rodallega [90]	18,498
32	29	A	Manchester C	L 0-3	0-0	—		43,534
33	Apr 4	A	Fulham	L 1-2	1-0	16	Scotland [34]	22,730
34	14	H	Portsmouth	D 0-0	0-0	—		14,323
35	18	A	Arsenal	W 3-2	0-1	15	Watson [80], Bramble [89], N'Zogbia [90]	22,113
36	24	A	West Ham U	L 2-3	1-2	16	Spector (og) [4], Rodallega [52]	33,057
37	May 3	H	Hull C	D 2-2	1-1	—	Moses [30], Gohouri [90]	20,242
38	9	A	Chelsea	L 0-8	0-2	16		41,383

Final League Position: 16

GOALSCORERS

League (37): Rodallega 10 (1 pen), N'Zogbia 5, Scharner 4, Boyce 3, Bramble 2, Caldwell 2, Diame 1, Figueroa 1, Gohouri 1, Gomez 1, Koumas 1, McCarthy 1, Moses 1, Scotland 1, Sinclair 1, Watson 1, own goal 1.
Carling Cup (1): Amaya 1.
FA Cup (6): N'Zogbia 2, McCarthy 1, Scotland 1, Sinclair 1, Watson 1.

Kirkland C 32	Melchiot M 32	Figueroa H 27+4	Thomas H 27+4	Bramble T 35	Scharner P 30+8	N'Zogbia C 35+1	Brown M 2	Rodallega H 38	Gomez J 11+12	Koumas J 6+2	Sinclair S 1+17	Cho W 1+3	Scotland J 14+18	Diame M 34	McCarthy J 19+1	Pollitt M 2+2	Boyce E 23+1	King M —+3	Kapo O —+1	Edman E 2+1	Caldwell G 16	Stojkovic V 4	Moreno M 9+3	Moses V 2+12	Gohouri S 4+1	Watson B 4+1	Match No.
1	2	3	4	5	6	7^1	8	9^3	10	11^2	12	13	14														1
1	2	3	4	5	6	7	8^1	9	10	11^2	13		12														2
1	2	3	4	5	6	7^2		9	10	11^1	12		13	8^3	14												3
	2	3	4^2	5	8	7		9^3	10	11^1	12	13	14			1	6										4
1	2	3	4	5	12	7		9^2	10^3				13	8^1	11		6										5
1	2	3	4	5	12	7		9^3	10^2				13	8^1	11		6										6
1	2	3	4	5	8	7		9					12	10^1	11		6										7
1	2	3	4^3	5	8^1	7^2		9	12		13		14	10	11		6										8
1	2	3	4	5	8^1	7		9	12					10	11		6										9
1	2	3^1	4	5	8^2	7		9	12					10	11		6	13									10
1	2	3	4	5	8^1	7		9^2	12					10	11		6	13									11
1	2	3^1	4	5	8	7		9	12		13			10^2	11		6										12
1	2^2	3^1	4^1	5	8	7		9	12			13		10	11		6										13
1	2	3	4	5	8	7		9	12					10^1	11		6										14
1^6	2	3	4	5	8	7		9	12			13		10	11^1	15	6^2										15
1	2	3	4	5	8^2	7		9	10		12	13			1^1		6^1										16
1	2	3	4	5	8	7		9			12	13		10^2	1^{11}		6										17
1	2	3	4	5	8	7		9						10	11		6										18
1^6	2	3	4^2	5	8	7^1		9	10		12				11	15	6	$1^?$									19
1	2	3	4^5	5	8^1	7		9	12			13		10^2	11		6										20
	2^1	3	4^3	5	8	7		9	12				14	10^2	11		6	1									21
	2	3	4^3	5	8	7		9	12	11^1			14	10^2			5	5	1								22
1		3	4	2	8^1	7		9^2						10	11		6				5		12	13			23
1		3	2		6	7		9	12	11^3	13			10^2			8^1				5		4	14			24
1	2	3	5^1		6	7		9	12					11			8				4		10^2	13			25
1	2	3	4^1		6	7		9			13			11			8				5		10^2	12			26
1	2	3	4	5	8^1	7^2		9	12				14	10^3	11		6							13			27
1		3	2	13	6	7		9^3					14	10^1	11^2		8				5		4	12			28
1		3	2	14	6^1	7		9^3	12		13			10^2	11		8				5		4				29
1		3	4	2	13	7^1		9					14	10	11		8^2				5^3		12				30
1	2	3	4^2	5	7^1			9	12					10	11		8				6		13				31
	2	3	4^1	5	8	7		9^2	12				14	10^3	11		7				6^4	1	13				32
1	2	3	5	4	7^3			9			13			10^1	6		8						11^2	12		14	33
1	2	3	5	6^1	7			9						10^2	11		8						12	13		4	34
1	2	3	5	13	7			9						11			8						10^1	12	4	6^2	35
1	2	3	5	13	7^2			9					14	11^3			8						10^1	12	6	4	36
	2	3	14		7^2			9	12		13			11^3	8^1						5	1	10		6	4	37
	2	3	12	13	7			9^3						11^2	10	1	6				5^4		14	8		4^1	38

FA Cup

Third Round	Hull C	(h)	4-1	
Fourth Round	Notts Co	(a)	2-2	
		(h)	0-2	

Carling Cup

Second Round	Blackpool	(a)	1-4

WOLVERHAMPTON WANDERERS FA Premiership

FOUNDATION

Enthusiasts of the game at St Luke's School, Blakenhall formed a club in 1877. In the same neighbourhood a cricket club called Blakenhall Wanderers had a football section. Several St Luke's footballers played cricket for them and shortly before the start of the 1879–80 season the two amalgamated and Wolverhampton Wanderers FC was brought into being.

Molineux Stadium, Waterloo Road, Wolverhampton WV1 4QR.

Telephone: (0871) 222 2220.

Fax: (01902) 687 006.

Ticket Office: (0871) 222 1877.

Website: wolves.co.uk

Email: info@wolves.co.uk

Ground Capacity: 28,565.

Record Attendance: 61,315 v Liverpool, FA Cup 5th rd, 11 February 1939.

Pitch Measurements: 110yd × 75yd.

Chairman: Steve Morgan OBE.

Chief Executive: Jez Moxey.

Secretary: Richard Skirrow.

Manager: Mick McCarthy.

Assistant Manager: Terry Connor.

Physio: Alan Peauchamp.

Colours: Gold shirts with black trim, black shorts, gold stockings.

Change Colours: All black with gold trim.

Year Formed: 1877* (*see Foundation*).

Turned Professional: 1888.

Ltd Co.: 1923 (but current club is WWFC (1986) Ltd).

Previous Names: 1879, St Luke's combined with Wanderers Cricket Club to become Wolverhampton Wanderers (1923) Ltd. New limited companies followed in 1982 and 1986 (current).

Club Nickname: 'Wolves'.

Grounds: 1877, Windmill Field; 1879, John Harper's Field; 1881, Dudley Road; 1889, Molineux.

First Football League Game: 8 September 1888, Football League, v Aston Villa (h) D 1–1 – Baynton; Baugh, Mason; Fletcher, Allen, Lowder; Hunter, Cooper, Anderson, White, Cannon, (1 og).

Record League Victory: 10–1 v Leicester C, Division 1, 15 April 1938 – Sidlow; Morris, Dowen; Galley, Cullis, Gardiner; Maguire (1), Horace Wright, Westcott (4), Jones (1), Dorsett (4).

HONOURS

Football League: Division 1 – Champions 1953–54, 1957–58, 1958–59; Runners-up 1937–38, 1938–39, 1949–50, 1954–55, 1959–60; Division 2 – Champions 1931–32, 1976–77; Runners-up 1966–67, 1982–83; FL C – Champions 2008–09; Division 3 (N) – Champions 1923–24; Division 3 – Champions 1988–89; Division 4 – Champions 1987–88.

FA Cup: Winners 1893, 1908, 1949, 1960; Runners-up 1889, 1896, 1921, 1939.

Football League Cup: Winners 1974, 1980.

Texaco Cup: Winners 1971.

Sherpa Van Trophy: Winners 1988.

European Competitions: European Cup: 1958–59, 1959–60. European Cup-Winners' Cup: 1960–61. UEFA Cup: 1971–72 (runners-up), 1973–74, 1974–75, 1980–81.

sky SPORTS FACT FILE

On 12 December 2009 Wolverhampton Wanderers won 1–0 at White Hart Lane. It was their first win on Tottenham Hotspur's ground since 24 November 1973 when goals by Geoff Palmer, Barry Powell and Kenny Hibbitt gave them a 3–1 victory.

Record Cup Victory: 14–0 v Crosswell's Brewery, FA Cup 2nd rd, 13 November 1886 – I. Griffiths; Baugh, Mason; Pearson, Allen (1), Lowder; Hunter (4), Knight (2), Brodie (4), 3. Griffiths (2), Wood. Plus one goal 'scrambled through'.

Record Defeat: 1–10 v Newton Heath, Division 1, 15 October 1892.

Most League Points (2 for a win): 64, Division 1, 1957–58.

Most League Points (3 for a win): 92, Division 3, 1988–89.

Most League Goals: 115, Division 2, 1931–32.

Highest League Scorer in Season: Dennis Westcott, 38, Division 1, 1946–47.

Most League Goals in Total Aggregate: Steve Bull, 250, 1986–99.

Most League Goals in One Match: 5, Joe Butcher v Accrington, Division 1, 19 November 1892; 5, Tom Phillipson v Barnsley, Division 2, 26 April 1926; 5, Tom Phillipson v Bradford C, Division 2, 25 December 1926; 5, Billy Hartill v Notts Co, Division 2, 12 October 1929; 5, Billy Hartill v Aston Villa, Division 1, 3 September 1934.

Most Capped Player: Billy Wright, 105, England (70 consecutive).

Most League Appearances: Derek Parkin, 501, 1967–82.

Youngest League Player: Jimmy Mullen, 16 years 43 days v Leeds U, 18 February 1939.

Record Transfer Fee Received: £6,000,000 from Coventry C for Robbie Keane, August 1999.

Record Transfer Fee Paid: £6,500,000 to Reading for Kevin Doyle, June 2009; £6,500,000 to Burnley for Steven Fletcher, June 2010.

MANAGERS

George Worrall 1877–85
  (Secretary-Manager)
John Addenbrooke 1885–1922
George Jobey 1922–24
Albert Hoskins 1924–26
  (had been Secretary since 1922)
Fred Scotchbrook 1926–27
Major Frank Buckley 1927–44
Ted Vizard 1944–48
Stan Cullis 1948–64
Andy Beattie 1964–65
Ronnie Allen 1966–68
Bill McGarry 1968–76
Sammy Chung 1976–78
John Barnwell 1978–81
Ian Greaves 1982
Graham Hawkins 1982–84
Tommy Docherty 1984–85
Bill McGarry 1985
Sammy Chapman 1985–86
Brian Little 1986
Graham Turner 1986–94
Graham Taylor 1994–95
Mark McGhee 1995–98
Colin Lee 1998–2000
Dave Jones 2001–04
Glenn Hoddle 2004–06
Mick McCarthy July 2006–

Football League Record: 1888 Founder Member of Football League: 1906–23 Division 2; 1923–24 Division 3 (N); 1924–32 Division 2; 1932–65 Division 1; 1965–67 Division 2; 1967–76 Division 1; 1976–77 Division 2; 1977–82 Division 1; 1982–83 Division 2; 1983–84 Division 1; 1984–85 Division 2; 1985–86 Division 3; 1986–88 Division 4; 1988–89 Division 3; 1989–92 Division 2; 1992–2003 Division 1; 2003–04 FA Premier League; 2004–09 FL C; 2009– FA Premier League.

LATEST SEQUENCES

Longest Sequence of League Wins: 8, 15.10.1988 – 26.11.1988.
Longest Sequence of League Defeats: 8, 5.12.1981 – 13.2.1982.
Longest Sequence of League Draws: 6, 22.4.1995 – 20.8.1995.
Longest Sequence of Unbeaten League Matches: 21, 15.1.2005 – 13.8.2005.
Longest Sequence Without a League Win: 19, 1.12.1984 – 6.4.1985.
Successive Scoring Runs: 41 from 20.12.1958.
Successive Non-scoring Runs: 7 from 2.2.1985.

TEN YEAR LEAGUE RECORD

1999-2000	Div 1	46	21	11	14	64	48	74	7
2000-01	Div 1	46	14	13	19	45	48	55	12
2001-02	Div 1	46	25	11	10	76	43	86	3
2002-03	Div 1	46	20	16	10	81	44	76	5
2003-04	PR Lge	38	7	12	19	38	77	33	20
2004-05	FL C	46	15	21	10	72	59	66	9
2005-06	FL C	46	16	19	11	50	42	67	7
2006-07	FL C	46	22	10	14	59	56	76	5
2007-08	FL C	46	18	16	12	53	48	70	7
2008-09	FL C	46	27	9	10	80	52	90	1
2009-10	PR Lge	38	9	11	18	32	56	38	15

DID YOU KNOW ?

In 1923–24 when Wolverhampton Wanderers became champions of the Third Division (North), goalkeeper Noel George kept 23 clean sheets in the 42 matches played. The team conceded only 27 goals during the entire campaign.

WOLVERHAMPTON WANDERERS 2009–10 LEAGUE RECORD

Match No.	Date	Venue	Opponents	Result	H/T Score	Lg Pos.	Goalscorers	Attendance
1	Aug 15	H	West Ham U	L	0-2	0-1	—		28,674
2	18	A	Wigan Ath	W	1-0	1-0	—	Keogh [6]	16,661
3	22	A	Manchester C	L	0-1	0-1	13		47,287
4	29	H	Hull C	D	1-1	0-1	13	Stearman [46]	27,906
5	Sept 12	A	Blackburn R	L	1-3	0-1	16	Maierhofer [88]	24,845
6	20	H	Fulham	W	2-1	1-0	12	Doyle [18], Edwards [50]	27,670
7	27	A	Sunderland	L	2-5	0-1	16	Mensah (og) [50], Doyle [55]	37,566
8	Oct 3	H	Portsmouth	L	0-1	0-1	17		29,023
9	17	A	Everton	D	1-1	0-0	15	Doyle [76]	39,319
10	24	H	Aston Villa	D	1-1	0-0	17	Ebanks-Blake (pen) [83]	28,734
11	31	A	Stoke C	D	2-2	0-2	16	Craddock 2 [46, 64]	27,500
12	Nov 7	A	Arsenal	L	1-4	0-3	19	Craddock [89]	28,937
13	21	A	Chelsea	L	0-4	0-3	19		41,786
14	29	H	Birmingham C	L	0-1	0-1	19		26,668
15	Dec 5	H	Bolton W	W	2-1	1-0	18	Craddock [3], Milijas [63]	27,362
16	12	A	Tottenham H	W	1-0	1-0	17	Doyle [3]	36,012
17	15	A	Manchester U	L	0-3	0-2	—		73,709
18	20	H	Burnley	W	2-0	1-0	12	Milijas [15], Doyle [50]	27,410
19	26	A	Liverpool	L	0-2	0-0	15		41,956
20	28	H	Manchester C	L	0-3	0-1	16		28,957
21	Jan 16	A	Wigan Ath	L	0-2	0-0	17		27,604
22	26	H	Liverpool	D	0-0	0-0	—		28,763
23	30	A	Hull C	D	2-2	0-1	17	Gardner A (og) [49], Jarvis [67]	24,957
24	Feb 7	A	Birmingham C	L	1-2	1-0	19	Doyle [42]	24,165
25	10	H	Tottenham H	W	1-0	1-0	—	David Jones [27]	27,992
26	20	H	Chelsea	L	0-2	0-1	16		28,978
27	27	A	Bolton W	L	0-1	0-1	17		21,261
28	Mar 6	H	Manchester U	L	0-1	0-0	—		28,883
29	13	A	Burnley	W	2-1	1-0	17	Jarvis [26], Carlisle (og) [47]	21,217
30	20	H	Aston Villa	D	2-2	2-1	16	Craddock [23], Milner (og) [38]	37,562
31	23	A	West Ham U	W	3-1	1-0	—	Doyle [28], Zubar [58], Jarvis [61]	33,988
32	27	H	Everton	D	0-0	0-0	14		28,995
33	Apr 3	A	Arsenal	L	0-1	0-0	14		60,067
34	11	H	Stoke C	D	0-0	0-0	—		28,455
35	17	A	Fulham	D	0-0	0-0	16		25,597
36	24	H	Blackburn R	D	1-1	0-1	15	Ebanks-Blake [81]	28,967
37	May 1	A	Portsmouth	L	1-3	1-2	15	Doyle [35]	19,213
33	9	H	Sunderland	W	2-1	1-1	15	Doyle (pen) [10], Guedioura [78]	28,971

Final League Position: 15

GOALSCORERS

League (32): Doyle 9 (1 pen), Craddock 5, Jarvis 3, Ebanks-Blake 2 (1 pen), Milijas 2, Edwards 1, Guedioura 1, David Jones 1, Keogh 1, Maierhofer 1, Stearman 1, Zubar 1, own goals 4.
Carling Cup (0).
FA Cup (4): Henry 1, Jarvis 1, David Jones 1, Zubar 1.

Hennessey W 13	Foley K 23 + 2	Ward S 18 + 4	Milijas N 12 + 7	Mancienne M 22 + 8	Craddock J 33	Halford G 12 + 3	Henry K 34	Keogh A 8 + 5	Ebanks-Blake S 12 + 11	Jarvis M 30 + 4	Stearman R 12 + 4	Vokes S — + 5	Edwards D 16 + 4	Jones David 16 + 4	Surman A 3 + 4	Elokobi G 17 + 5	Doyle K 33 + 1	Hill M 2	Berra C 32	Maierhofer S 1 + 7	Castillo S 7 + 1	Kightly M 3 + 6	Zubar R 23	Iwelumo C 2 + 13	Hahnemann M 25	Friend G 1	Guedioura A 7 + 7	Mujangi Bia G 1 + 2	Match No.
1	2[2]	3	4[3]	5[1]	6	7	8	9	10	11	12	13	14																1
1		3	11[1]	5	6	7[2]	8	9[3]		10	2	14	4	12	13														2
1		3[3]	11[2]	5	6	7[1]	8	9		10	2	14	4	12	13														3
1			11	5	6	7	8	9[1]			2		4	12		3	10												4
1			11[2]	5		7[1]	8	9			2	14	4	12		14	10[3]	3	6	13									5
1				5			2	8	9	13	4[3]			7[1]		3	10[2]		6	12	11	14							6
1				5			2	8	9[2]	13	4			7		3	10[3]		6	14	11[1]	12							7
1	2[1]			5			7	8	9[2]	13	4			11		3[3]	10		6	14		12							8
1				6	2[2]	8		10[3]	12				11			3	9		5	14	13	7[1]	4						9
1		12		6	13	8		10[3]					4[1]			3	9		5		11	7[2]	2	14					10
1		13		6		8		12					4			3[1]	10		5	14	11[2]	7	2	9[3]					11
1		11[2]	14	6		8		10	13	2			4[3]				9		5		7[1]	12	3						12
1				6	3	8	13	9[2]	10	2			4	11			5			7[1]	12								13
	14	13	4[3]	6	3[1]	8		10	11	2			7				9		5	12[2]					1				14
	3	11	13	6		8		10[1]	7	2			4[2]				9		5	12					1				15
	12	3	11[2]	13	6		8		10	7	2[3]		4[1]				9		5			14	1						16
	7				6[3]			13					14	11	3	4	5[1]	8		2	12	1	10[2]						17
	2	3	11[1]	12	6		8		10	7[2]	4			14			9[3]		5			13	1						18
	2	3[4]	11[2]	13	6		8		10[3]	7	4			12			9[1]		5			14	1						19
	2[3]			4	6		8		13	14	12				11	3	10[2]		5[1]			7	9	1					20
	2	3	11[3]	6		8			10[2]	7[1]	4[4]			12	14		9		5			13	1						21
	7	3	10[1]	4	6		8			11[2]					12		9		5			2	1	13					22
	7[1]	3[3]		6	5		8			10[2]					12		11		9			4	2	1	13	14			23
	7[2]	3		6	5		8			14				11[3]		10[1]	13		9			4	2	1	12				24
	7	3[1]	14	13	5		8			11[3]					6	12	9		4			2	1	10[2]					25
	7[1]	3		5	12		8		13	11[2]					6[3]		9		4			2	1	10	14				26
	7[2]	3		5			8	13	12	11					6		9		4			2	1	10[1]					27
	7	3[2]		5			8	13	12	11[3]	14				6		9		4			2	1	10[1]					28
	7	3	12	5		8	13	14		11[3]					6[2]		9		4			2	1	10[1]					29
	7	3[2]	13	5		8				11[3]					6	12	9		4			2	14	1	10[1]				30
	7	12		6[3]	5	13	8		10[1]					11		3	9		4			2[2]	1	14					31
	7	13		6[1]	5		8		10[2]					11		3	9[3]		4			2	14	1	12				32
	7	14		6	5		8[4]	13		11[3]			12	10[1]		3	9[2]		4			2	1						33
	7		13	6	5		11			8[1]	10[2]					3	9		4			2	12	1					34
	7		13	6	5		11[3]			8[1]	10[2]					3	9		4			2	14	1	12				35
	7[3]	11	13	6[2]	5			14								11	3	9	4			2	12	1					36
	7[3]			6[2]	5	8	13			11						3	9		4			2	12	1	14	10[1]			37
	14			5	8		10	11[3]		12	6[1]					3	9[2]		4			2	13	1	7				38

FA Cup

Third Round	Tranmere R	(a)	1-0
Fourth Round	Crystal Palace	(h)	2-2
		(a)	1-3

Carling Cup

Second Round	Swindon T	(h)	0-0
Third Round	Manchester U	(a)	0-1

WYCOMBE WANDERERS FL Championship 2

FOUNDATION

In 1887 a group of young furniture trade workers called a meeting at the Steam Engine public house with the aim of forming a football club and entering junior football. It is thought that they were named after the famous FA Cup winners, The Wanderers who had visited the town in 1877 for a tie with the original High Wycombe club. It is also possible that they played informally before their formation, although there is no proof of this.

Adams Park, Hillbottom Road, Sands, High Wycombe HP12 4HJ.

Telephone: (01494) 472 100.

Fax: (01494) 527 633.

Ticket Office: (01494) 472 100.

Website: www.wwfc.com

Email: wwfc@wwfc.com

Ground Capacity: 10,000.

Record Attendance: 9,921 v Fulham, FA Cup 3rd rd, 9 January 2002.

Pitch Measurements: 115yd × 75yd.

Owner: Steve Hayes.

Chairman: Ivor L. Beeks.

Vice-chairman: Brian Kane.

Secretary: Keith Allen.

Manager: Gary Waddock.

Assistant Manager: Martin Kuhl.

Physio: Shay Connolly.

Colours: Light blue and dark blue quartered shirts, dark blue shorts, light blue stockings.

Change Colours: All black with white trim.

Year Formed: 1887.

Turned Professional: 1974.

Club Nicknames: 'Chairboys' (after High Wycombe's tradition of furniture making), 'The Blues'.

Grounds: 1887, The Rye; 1893, Spring Meadow; 1895, Loakes Park; 1899, Daws Hill Park; 1901, Loakes Park; 1990, Adams Park.

First Football League Game: 14 August 1993, Division 3 v Carlisle U (a) D 2–2: Hyde; Cousins, Horton (Langford), Kerr, Crossley, Ryan, Carroll, Stapleton, Thompson, Scott, Guppy (1) (Hutchinson), (1 og).

Record League Victory: 5–0 v Burnley, Division 2, 15 April 1997 – Parkin; Cousins, Bell, Kavanagh, McCarthy, Forsyth, Carroll (2p) (Simpson), Scott (Farrell), Stallard (1), McGavin (1) (Read (1)), Brown.

HONOURS

Football League: Division 2 best season: 6th, 1994–95.

FA Amateur Cup: Winners 1931.

FA Trophy: Winners 1991, 1993.

GM Vauxhall Conference: Winners 1992–93.

FA Cup: semi-final 2001.

Football League Cup: semi-final 2007.

sky SPORTS FACT FILE

Six days after Leeds United had beaten Manchester United 1–0 at Old Trafford in the FA Cup third round, Wycombe Wanderers met the victors at Elland Road in a League One match. Despite conceding a goal as early as the fourth minute the bottom-placed team earned a draw.

Record Cup Victory: 5–0 v Hitchin T (a), FA Cup 2nd rd, 3 December 1994 – Hyde; Cousins, Brown, Crossley, Evans, Ryan (1), Carroll, Bell (1), Thompson, Garner (3) (Hemmings), Stapleton (Langford).

Record Defeat: 0-7 v Shrewsbury T, Johnstone's Paint Trophy, 7 October 2008.

Most League Points (3 for a win): 78, Division 2, 1994–95; 78, FL 2, 2007–08; 78, FL 2, 2008–09.

Most League Goals: 72, FL 2, 2005–06.

Highest League Goalscorer in Season: Scott McGleish, 25, 2007–08.

Most League Goals in Total Aggregate: Nathan Tyson, 42, 2004–06.

Most League Goals in One Match: 3, Miquel Desouza v Bradford C, Division 2, 2 September 1995; 3, John Williams v Stockport Co, Division 2, 24 February 1996; 3, Mark Stallard v Walsall, Division 2, 21 October 1997; 3, Sean Devine v Reading, Division 2, 2 October 1999; 3, Sean Divine v Bury, Division 2, 26 February 2000; 3, Nathan Tyson v Lincoln C, FL 2, 5 March 2005; 3, Nathan Tyson v Kidderminster H, FL 2, 2 April 2005; 3, Nathan Tyson v Stockport Co, FL 2, 10 September 2005; 3, Kevin Betsy v Mansfield T, FL 2, 24 September 2005; 3, Scott McGleish v Mansfield T, FL 2, 8 January 2008.

Most Capped Player: Mark Rogers, 7, Canada.

Most League Appearances: Steve Brown, 371, 1994–2004.

Youngest League Player: Ikechi Anya, 16 years 279 days v Scunthorpe U, 8 October 2004.

Record Transfer Fee Received: £600,000 from Nottingham F for Nathan Tyson, January 2006.

Record Transfer Fee Paid: £200,000 to Barnet for Sean Devine, 15 April 1999.

Football League Record: 1993 Promoted to Division 3 from GM Vauxhall Conference; 1993–94 Division 3; 1994–2004 Division 2; 2004–09 FL 2; 2009–10 FL 1; 2010– FL 2.

MANAGERS

First coach appointed 1951.
Prior to Brian Lee's appointment in 1969 the team was selected by a Match Committee which met every Monday evening.

James McCormack 1951–52
Sid Cann 1952–61
Graham Adams 1961–62
Don Welsh 1962–64
Barry Darvill 1964–68
Brian Lee 1969–76
Ted Powell 1976–77
John Reardon 1977–78
Andy Williams 1978–80
Mike Keen 1980–84
Paul Bence 1984–86
Alan Gane 1986–87
Peter Suddaby 1987–88
Jim Kelman 1988–90
Martin O'Neill 1990–95
Alan Smith 1995–96
John Gregory 1996–98
Neil Smillie 1998–99
Lawrie Sanchez 1999–2003
Tony Adams 2003–04
John Gorman 2004–06
Paul Lambert 2006–08
Peter Taylor 2008–09
Gary Waddock October 2009–

LATEST SEQUENCES

Longest Sequence of League Wins: 6, 19.8.2006 – 16.9 2006.
Longest Sequence of League Defeats: 6, 18.3.2006 – 17.4.2006.
Longest Sequence of League Draws: 5, 24.1.2004 – 21.2.2004.
Longest Sequence of Unbeaten League Matches: 21, 6.8.2005 – 10.12.2005.
Longest Sequence Without a League Win: 13, 16.8.2003 – 18.10.2003 and 10.1.2004 – 20.3.2004.
Successive Scoring Runs: 15 from 28.12.2004.
Successive Non-scoring Runs: 5 from 15.10.1996.

TEN YEAR LEAGUE RECORD

		P	W	D	L	F	A	Pts	Pos
2000-01	Div 2	46	15	14	17	46	53	59	13
2001-02	Div 2	46	17	13	16	58	64	64	11
2002-03	Div 2	46	13	13	20	59	66	52	13
2003-04	Div 2	46	6	19	21	50	75	37	24
2004-05	FL 2	46	17	14	15	58	52	65	10
2005-06	FL 2	46	18	17	11	72	56	71	3
2006-07	FL 2	46	16	14	16	52	47	62	12
2007-08	FL 2	46	22	12	12	56	42	78	7
2008-09	FL 2	46	20	18	8	54	33	78	3
2009-10	FL 1	46	10	15	21	56	76	45	22

DID YOU KNOW ?

Although Wycombe Wanderers spent only two seasons in the Spartan League from 1919–20, they had a remarkable record in it. From a total of 42 League games they lost just twice and drew three times. They rattled up 222 goals and conceded just 53 in gaining two titles.

WYCOMBE WANDERERS 2009–10 LEAGUE RECORD

Match No.	Date	Venue	Opponents	Result	H/T Score	Lg Pos.	Goalscorers	Attendance
1	Aug 8	A	Charlton Ath	L	2-3	1-2	—	Zebroski 2 [43, 74]	16,552
2	15	H	Leeds U	L	0-1	0-0			8400
3	18	H	Southend U	D	1-1	1-1	—	Harrold [40]	4607
4	22	A	Norwich C	L	2-5	1-3	—	Pittman [39], Harrold [46]	23,428
5	29	H	Bristol R	W	2-1	1-1	—	Phillips [36], Pittman [80]	5214
6	Sept 5	H	Brighton & HA	L	0-1	0-0	—		5895
7	12	A	Hartlepool U	D	1-1	0-0	22	Beavon [50]	3326
8	19	H	Milton Keynes D	L	0-1	0-1	22		6127
9	26	A	Swindon T	D	1-1	0-1	22	Chambers [89]	6929
10	29	A	Tranmere R	L	0-1	0-1	—		3899
11	Oct 3	H	Leyton Orient	L	0-1	0-0	23		4798
12	10	A	Gillingham	L	2-3	1-2	23	Woodman [27], Bentley (og) [62]	5316
13	17	H	Colchester U	D	1-1	0-0	24	Pittman [87]	5394
14	24	A	Exeter C	D	1-1	1-0	24	Harrold (pen) [42]	5227
15	31	H	Walsall	L	2-3	2-0	24	Davies 2 [14, 37]	5046
16	Nov 14	A	Huddersfield T	L	0-6	0-2	24		14,869
17	21	A	Millwall	W	2-0	0-0	23	Westwood [56], Betsy [72]	9728
18	24	H	Brentford	W	1-0	0-0	—	Harrold (pen) [48]	5181
19	Dec 1	A	Southampton	L	0-1	0-1	—		16,402
20	5	H	Stockport Co	W	2-1	0-0	22	Westwood [74], Davies [83]	4343
21	12	A	Carlisle U	L	0-1	0-1	22		4528
22	19	H	Oldham Ath	D	2-2	1-1	23	Akinde [9], Harrold (pen) [88]	4160
23	26	A	Yeovil T	L	0-4	0-1	23		5055
24	28	H	Brighton & HA	L	2-5	2-1	23	Pittman [27], Mousinho [40]	6126
25	Jan 2	H	Norwich C	L	0-1	0-0	—		7171
26	9	A	Leeds U	D	1-1	0-1	—	Pittman [63]	24,383
27	16	H	Charlton Ath	L	1-2	0-1	23	Pittman [64]	6123
28	23	A	Southend U	D	1-1	0-0	23	Payne [64]	6675
29	30	A	Bristol R	W	3-2	1-2	23	Harrold (pen) [15], Revell (pen) [48], Beavon [80]	6688
30	Feb 6	H	Yeovil T	L	1-4	0-1	23	Harrold [50]	4793
31	13	A	Brentford	D	1-1	1-0	23	Betsy [27]	5740
32	20	H	Millwall	W	1-0	1-0	23	Kelly [45]	5774
33	23	H	Southampton	D	0-0	0-0	—		6232
34	27	A	Stockport Co	L	3-4	0-2	23	Phillips 2 [67, 70], Williams (og) [85]	3740
35	Mar 6	A	Carlisle U	D	0-0	0-0	23		4876
36	13	A	Oldham Ath	D	2-2	1-1	23	Harrold (pen) [42], Betsy [49]	3846
37	20	H	Exeter C	D	2-2	0-0	23	Ainsworth [55], Beavon [61]	5054
38	27	A	Colchester U	D	1-1	0-0	23	Ainsworth [90]	5593
39	Apr 3	H	Huddersfield T	L	1-2	0-1	23	Keates [73]	5288
40	5	A	Walsall	L	1-2	0-2	23	Hinshelwood [78]	3618
41	10	H	Hartlepool U	W	2-0	0-0	23	Pittman [66], Phillips [88]	4342
42	13	A	Tranmere R	W	3-0	1-0	—	Revell 2 [15, 69], Bloomfield [86]	4956
43	17	A	Milton Keynes D	W	3-2	1-1	22	Revell 2 [29, 64], Betsy [90]	10,561
44	24	H	Swindon T	D	2-2	1-0	22	Bloomfield [45], Revell [75]	7459
45	May 1	A	Leyton Orient	L	0-2	0-0	23		5918
46	8	H	Gillingham	W	3-0	1-0	22	Phillips [45], Bennett [64], Betsy [72]	7110

Final League Position: 22

GOALSCORERS

League (56): Harrold 8 (5 pens), Pittman 7, Revell 6 (1 pen), Betsy 5, Phillips 5, Beavon 3, Davies 3, Ainsworth 2, Bloomfield 2, Westwood 2, Zebroski 2, Akinde 1, Bennett 1, Chambers 1, Hinshelwood 1, Keates 1, Kelly 1, Mousinho 1, Payne 1, Woodman 1, own goals 2.
Carling Cup (0).
FA Cup (4): Harrold 2 (1 pen), Davies 1, Pittman 1.
J Paint Trophy (2): Pittman 2 (1 pen).

Shearer S 29	Smith A 3	Woodman C 44	Mousinho J 37+2	Duberry M 18	Westwood C 28	Green S 10+3	Montrose L 11+3	Harrold M 29+7	Zebroski C 12+3	Phillips M 18+18	Oliver L 19+4	Pittman J 21+20	Beavon S 14+11	Westlake I 7+2	Johnson L 5	Moncur T 4	Pack M 7+1	Betsy K 35+4	Hunt L 26+1	Chambers A —+3	Davies S 14+1	Bloomfield M 8+6	Doherty T 11+1	Young J 1	Akinde J 4+2	Ainsworth G 12+2	Harris D —+2	Hinshelwood A 13	Keates D 13	Payne J 3	Revell A 11+4	Heaton T 16	McLeod K 8+3	Kelly J 9	Bennett A 6	Match No.
1	2	3	4	5	6[1]	7[2]	8	9[9]	10	11	12	13	14																							1
1	2[3]	3	4	5		14	8	9[2]	10	11	6	12	13	7[1]																						2
1	2[1]	3	4	5		13	8	9[3]	10	11	6	12	14	7[2]																						3
1		3	4	5		2	11	8[1]	9	10	12	7			6																					4
1		3	4	5			11	9[1]	10	8	6	13	12	7[2]		2																				5
1		3	4	5			11[1]	9	10	8	6	12		7[2]		2[3]	13	14																		6
1		3	4	5			11[2]	9[1]	10	8	6	13				2	7	12																		7
1		3	4[1]	5			11	9[3]	10	14	6	13	8[2]			2	7	12																		8
1		3	4	5			11[3]	9[2]	10	12	6		14				7	8	2[1]	13																9
1		3	4	5			11[3]	9[2]	10	12	6		14				7	8	2[1]	13																10
1		3	4	5		12	11[1]	9	10[2]		6	13	14				7	8	2[3]																	11
1		3	4[2]	5	6	13	11[1]	9	10		12						7	8	2[3]	14																12
1		3	4[2]	5	6			9	10[3]	11		13	14				7[1]	8	2	12																13
1		3	4[3]	5	6	13		9	10	11[2]	12		14				7	8[1]	2																	14
1		3	4	5	6			9[2]	10	11[1]	12	13					7	8	2																	15
		3	4	5	6			9	10[1]	11	12						7	8	2					1												16
1		3	4	5	6		8	9[1]	10	11	12						7		2																	17
1		3	4	5	6		8	9[2]	10[1]	11	12	13					7		2																	18
1		3	4	5	6		8[1]	9	10[2]	11[3]	12	13	14				7		2																	19
1		3	4	5	6			9[1]	10	11	12						7		2		8															20
1		3	4	5	6[1]			9[2]	10	11	12	13					7		2		8															21
1		3		5	6			9[2]	10[8]		12	13					7	11[1]	2		8		4													22
1		3		5	6[3]			9[2]	10[1]		12	13	14				7	11	2		8		4													23
1		3		5	6			9	10[2]		12	13					7	11	2[1]		8		4													24
1		3			6			9	10[3]		12	13	14				7	11[2]	2		8		4			5[1]										25
1		3			6			9	10								7	11	2		8		4			5										26
1		3	4[1]		6			9	10		12	13					7	11[2]	2		8					5										27
1		3			6			9	10		12						7	11	2				4			5					8[1]					28
1		3			6			9			12	13					7	11[2]	2				4			5					10[1]		8			29
1		3			6			9			12						7	11	2				4			5[1]					10		8			30
		3			6			9[1]			12						7	11	2				4			5					10	1	8			31
		3			6			9[2]			12[8]	13	14				7	11[1]	2				4			5					10[3]	1	8			32
		3	8		6			9									7		2				4			5					10	1	11			33
		3[2]	8[3]		6			9			12	13	14				7		2				4			5					10[1]	1	11			34
		3	8					9	10[2]		12	13					7		2				4			5						1	11[1]		6	35
		3	8					9[1]	10[3]		12	13	14						2				4			7[2]			5			1	11		6	36
		3	8		6			9[1]	10[2]		12	13							2				4			7			5			1	11			37
		3	8[1]		6			9[3]	10[2]		12	13	14						2				4			7			5			1	11			38
		3	8		6[2]			9[3]	10		12	13	14						2[1]				4			7			5			1	11			39
		3	8		6[3]			9	10[1]		12	13	14						2[2]				4			7			5			1	11			40
		3	4		6			9[2]			12	13						11	2		8					7			5[1]		10	1				41
		3	4	5	6			9[1]			12	13	14					11	2		8					7[2]					10[3]	1				42
		3	4	5	6[2]			9[1]			12	13						11	2		8					7					10	1				43
		3	4[2]	5	6			9[1]			12	13						11	2		8					7					10	1				44
		3	4	5[3]	6[1]			9[2]			12	13	14					11	2		8					7					10	1				45
		3	4		6			9	10		12	13					7[1]	11	2		8[2]								5			1				46

FA Cup
First Round   Brighton & HA   (h)   4-4
                              (a)   0-2

Carling Cup
First Round   Peterborough U   (h)   0-4

J Paint Trophy
First Round   Northampton T   (h)   2-2

YEOVIL TOWN — FL Championship 1

Huish Park, Lufton Way, Yeovil, Somerset BA22 8YF.

Telephone: (01935) 423 662.

Fax: (01935) 473 956.

Ticket Office: (01935) 847 888.

Website: www.ytfc.net

Email: jcotton@ytfc.net

Ground Capacity: 9,665.

Record Attendance: 9,527 v Leeds U, FL 1, 25 April 2008 (16,318 v Sunderland at Huish).

Pitch Measurements: 110m × 69m.

Chairman: John R. Fry.

Chief Executive: Martyn Starnes.

Secretary: Jean Cotton.

Manager: Terry Skiverton.

Assistant Manager: Nathan Jones.

Physio: Simon Baker.

Colours: Green and white hooped shirts with green sleeves and black trim, white shorts, white stockings.

Change Colours: Black shirts with one green sleeve, green shorts, black stockings.

Year Formed: 1895.

Turned Professional: 1921.

Ltd Co.: 1923.

Club Nickname: 'Glovers'.

Previous Names: 1895, Yeovil Casuals; 1907, Yeovil Town; 1915, Yeovil & Petters United; 1946, Yeovil Town.

HONOURS

FL Championship 2 winners 2004–05.

Conference: Champions 2002–03.

FA Cup: 5th rd 1949.

League Cup: never past 2nd rd.

Southern League: Champions 1954–55, 1963–64, 1970–71; Runners-up: 1923–24, 1931–32, 1934–35, 1969–70, 1972–73.

Southern League Cup: Winners 1948–49, 1954–55, 1960–61, 1965–66; Runners-up: 1946–47, 1955–56.

Isthmian League: Winners 1987–88; Runners-up: 1985–86, 1986–87, 1996–97.

AC Delco Cup: Winners 1987–88.

Bob Lord Trophy: Winners 1989–90.

FA Trophy: Winners 2002.

London Combination: Runners-up 1930–31, 1932–33.

sky SPORTS FACT FILE

Yeovil Town can claim to have recorded two scores of ten goals during their time in the Southern League. In 1955–56 they defeated Kidderminster Harriers and followed this up with a similar victory over Bedford Town in 1960–61.

Grounds: 1895, Pen Mill Ground; 1921, Huish; 1990, Huish Park.

First Football League Game: 9 August 2003, Division 3 v Rochdale (a) W 3-1: Weale; Williams (Lindegaard), Crittenden, Lockwood, O'Brien, Pluck (Rodrigues), Gosling (El Kholti), Way, Jackson, Gall (2), Johnson (1).

Record League Victory: 10–0 v Kidderminster H, Southern League, 27 December 1955. 10–0 v Bedford T, Southern League, 4 March 1961.

Record Cup Victory: 12–1 v Westbury United, FA Cup 1st qual rd, 1923–24.

Record Defeat: 0–8 v Manchester United, FA Cup 5th rd, 12 February 1949.

Most League Points (3 for a win): 83, FL 2, 2004–05.

Most League Goals: 90, FL 2, 2004–05.

Highest League Goalscorer in Season: Phil Jevons, 27, 2004–05

Most League Goals in Total Aggregate: Phil Jevons, 42, 2004–06

Most Capped Player: Andrejs Stolcers, 1 (81) Latvia and Arron Davies, 1, Wales.

Most League Appearances: Terry Skiverton, 195, 2003–09.

Record Transfer Fee Received: Undisclosed from Nottingham F for Arron Davies, July 2007.

Record Transfer Fee Paid: Undisclosed to Atletico Penarol de Rafaela (Argentina) for Pablo Bastianini, August 2005.

Football League Record: 2003 Promoted to Division 3 from Conference; 2003–04 Division 3; 2004–05 FL 2; 2005– FL 1.

LATEST SEQUENCES

Longest Sequence of League Wins: 7, 7.12.2004 – 15.1.2005.

Longest Sequence of League Defeats: 5, 29.10.05 – 6.12.05.

Longest Sequence of Unbeaten League Matches: 7, 7.12.2004 – 15.1.2005.

Longest Sequence Without a League Win: 6, 6.8.05 – 29.8.05.

Successive Scoring Runs: 22 from 30.10.2004.

Successive Non-scoring Runs: 3 from 21.1.2006.

MANAGERS

Jack Gregory 1922–28
Tommy Lawes 1928–29
Dave Pratt 1929–33
Louis Page 1933–35
Dave Halliday 1935–38
Billy Kingdon 1938–46
Alec Stock 1946–49
George Patterson 1949–51
Harry Lowe 1951–53
Ike Clarke 1953–57
Norman Dodgin 1957
Jimmy Baldwin 1957–60
Basil Hayward 1960–64
Glyn Davies 1964–65
Joe McDonald 1965–67
Ron Saunders 1967–69
Mike Hughes 1969–72
Cecil Irwin 1972–75
Stan Harland 1975–81
Barry Lloyd 1978–81
Malcolm Allison 1981
Jimmy Giles 1981–83
Trevor Finnigan/Mike Hughes 1983
Steve Coles 1983–84
Ian McFarlane 1984
Gerry Gow 1984–87
Brian Hall 1987–90
Clive Whitehead 1990–91
Steve Rutter 1991–93
Brian Hall 1994–95
Graham Roberts 1995–98
Colin Lippiatt 1998–99
Steve Thompson 1999–2000
Dave Webb 2000
Gary Johnson 2001–05
Steve Thompson 2005–06
Russell Slade 2006–09
Terry Skiverton February 2009–

TEN YEAR LEAGUE RECORD

		P	W	D	L	F	A	Pts	Pos
2000-01	Conf.	42	24	8	10	73	50	80	2
2001-02	Conf.	42	19	13	10	66	53	70	3
2002-03	Conf.	42	28	11	3	100	37	95	1
2003-04	Div 3	46	23	5	18	70	57	74	8
2004-05	FL 2	46	25	8	13	90	65	83	1
2005-06	FL 1	46	15	11	20	54	62	56	15
2006-07	FL 1	46	23	10	13	55	39	79	5
2007-08	FL 1	46	14	10	22	38	59	52	18
2008-09	FL 1	46	12	15	19	41	66	51	17
2009-10	FL 1	46	13	14	19	55	59	53	15

DID YOU KNOW ?

In the same 1960–61 season Yeovil Town added to their many FA Cup exploits when they were drawn away to promotion-bound Walsall in the first round. Yeovil won 1–0 with a goal from leading scorer Dave Taylor. It was Walsall's only home defeat in the season.

YEOVIL TOWN 2009–10 LEAGUE RECORD

Match No.	Date	Venue	Opponents	Result	H/T Score	Lg Pos.	Goalscorers	Attendance
1	Aug 8	H	Tranmere R	W 2-0	1-0	—	Bowditch [23], Tomlin (pen) [76]	4349
2	15	A	Colchester U	L 1-2	0-2	10	Mason [82]	4263
3	18	A	Exeter C	D 1-1	0-1	—	Mason [72]	6650
4	22	H	Leyton Orient	D 3-3	2-2	9	Tomlin (pen) [11], Obika [40], Schofield [52]	3827
5	29	A	Huddersfield T	L 1-2	1-1	12	Murtagh [6]	12,646
6	Sept 5	H	Swindon T	L 0-1	0-1	17		4807
7	12	H	Stockport Co	D 2-2	1-2	17	Tomlin [33], Williams S [68]	3519
8	19	A	Southampton	L 0-2	0-1	20		19,907
9	26	H	Brentford	W 2-0	1-0	17	Alcock [25], Welsh [51]	4249
10	29	A	Millwall	D 0-0	0-0	—		6617
11	Oct 3	A	Oldham Ath	D 0-0	0-0	18		4208
12	10	H	Brighton & HA	D 2-2	1-2	14	Murray 2 (1 pen) [45, 82 (p)]	4412
13	17	H	Carlisle U	W 3-1	2-0	14	Mason 2 [13, 43], Murtagh [87]	4333
14	24	A	Bristol R	W 2-1	0-0	12	Obika [61], Forbes [64]	7812
15	31	A	Leeds U	L 0-4	0-1	14		24,482
16	Nov 14	H	Southend U	W 1-0	0-0	12	Bowditch [76]	3906
17	21	H	Charlton Ath	D 1-1	1-0	13	Obika [44]	5632
18	24	A	Gillingham	L 0-1	0-1	—		4450
19	Dec 1	H	Walsall	L 1-3	1-2	—	Obika [30]	3508
20	5	A	Milton Keynes D	D 2-2	2-1	13	Bowditch [1], Macdonald [17]	8965
21	12	H	Norwich C	D 3-3	1-0	15	Bowditch [21], Macdonald [67], Obika [89]	4964
22	19	A	Hartlepool U	D 1-1	1-0	17	Williams S [33]	2778
23	26	H	Wycombe W	W 4-0	1-0	13	Murtagh [36], Kalala [71], Obika [74], Williams S [87]	5055
24	28	A	Swindon T	L 1-3	1-2	14	Tomlin [27]	8509
25	Jan 19	A	Leyton Orient	L 0-2	0-1	—		2669
26	23	H	Exeter C	W 2-1	2-1	12	Stam [6], Mason [41]	6282
27	26	A	Tranmere R	L 1-2	0-0	—	Mason (pen) [90]	4584
28	30	H	Huddersfield T	L 0-1	0-1	14		4110
29	Feb 6	A	Wycombe W	W 4-1	1-0	14	Bowditch 2 [16, 67], Welsh [52], Tudur Jones [60]	4793
30	13	H	Gillingham	D 0-0	0-0	14		3853
31	16	H	Colchester U	L 0-1	0-1	—		3469
32	20	A	Charlton Ath	L 0-2	0-1	15		15,991
33	23	A	Walsall	W 1-0	1-0	—	Williams S [5]	2929
34	27	H	Milton Keynes D	W 1-0	1-0	12	Macdonald [23]	3844
35	Mar 6	A	Norwich C	L 0-3	0-1	13		24,868
36	13	H	Hartlepool U	W 4-0	2-0	11	Tomlin (pen) [20], Williams G [36], Collins (og) [50], Bowditch [71]	4169
37	16	A	Carlisle U	L 0-1	0-0	—		3731
38	20	A	Bristol R	L 0-3	0-3	13		5968
39	Apr 3	A	Southend U	D 0-0	0-0	15		6854
40	5	H	Leeds U	L 1-2	0-2	15	Bowditch [66]	6308
41	10	A	Stockport Co	W 3-1	2-0	14	Bowditch [21], Williams G 2 [32, 74]	3587
42	13	H	Millwall	D 1-1	1-0	—	Bowditch [26]	4713
43	17	H	Southampton	L 0-1	0-0	17		7484
44	24	A	Brentford	D 1-1	1-0	17	Tomlin (pen) [3]	5395
45	May 1	H	Oldham Ath	W 3-0	1-0	15	Tomlin [18], Williams G 2 [83, 89]	4513
46	8	A	Brighton & HA	L 0-1	0-1	15		7323

Final League Position: 15

GOALSCORERS

League (55): Bowditch 10, Tomlin 7 (4 pens), Mason 6 (1 pen), Obika 6, Williams G 5, Williams S 4, Macdonald 3, Murtagh 3, Murray 2 (1 pen), Welsh 2, Alcock 1, Forbes 1, Kalala 1, Schofield 1, Stam 1, Tudur Jones 1, own goal 1.
Carling Cup (0).
FA Cup (0).
J Paint Trophy (1): Obika 1.

McCarthy A 44	Forbes T 35+3	Jones N 18	Stam S 18	Caulker S 44	Mason R 26+2	O'Callaghan G 7+5	Welsh A 28+14	Bowditch D 26+4	Tomlin G 29+6	Schofield D 4	Murray S 10+10	McCollin A —+2	Williams S 28+6	Smith N 27+7	Obika J 13+9	Alcock C 39+3	Murtagh K 13+14	Hutchins D 4+3	Lindegaard A 2+3	Kalala J 32+2	Martin R 2+1	Macdonald S 31	Davies C 2+2	Tudur Jones O 6	Davies A 4+6	Downes A 2+3	Williams G 7+1	Davies S 4	Ayling L 1+3	Match No.
1	2	3	4	5	6	7	8^1	9^3	10^2	11	12	13	14																	1
1	2	3	4	5	6	7	8^1		10^2	11				9	12	13														2
1	12		4^1	5	6	7	8^2	13	11					9		3	10^3	2	14											3
1	4	3		5		7	8	9^1	11^2	13			12			10	2	6^3	14											4
1	4	3^1		5	8^3	14	12	9^2	11				13	7	10	2	6													5
1	4	3		5	8		11^3	9			12	9^1	7	10	2^2	6	13	14												6
1^*	4	3	2	5	8	13	11^6	9			12		10^1		6^2				15											7
1	4	3		5	8		11^1	9			10	12	2	6				1												8
1	4	3		5	8	13	11^2	9			10^1	14	2				6	12												9
1	4	3		5		13	11	9			10		2^1	14	12		6	8^3												10
1	4	3		5	10^1		11^3	9	12		14		13	2^2		6	8													11
1	4	3			6	11		10^1	8		9	12	2	5																12
1	2	3		5	10^1	11		7^2	9		4	13		8	6	12														13
1	2	3		5	10	11^2		8^1	9		12	6	13	4																14
1	2	3		5	8^2	11^1		10	9	4	12	13	6																	15
1		2	5	10^3	4	11^1	12	13	8^2		9	3	14	6																16
1	13	2	5	11		8^1	12	6^2	14	9	3	10^3	4																	17
1		6	5	10	11^2	13	14	4^1	12	9^3	2	3	8																	18
1	4		5	10	3	7^1	12	8	13	14	9^2	2	11^3	6																19
1	4		5	11^1	12		8^2	10	9	3	13	2	6																	20
1	3		5	8		7^1	10	9	6	12	2	1	4																	21
1		6	5	8^2		11	10^1	13	9	3	12	2									4									22
1		6	5	8^3	14	11^1	10^2	13	9	3	12	2	4																	23
14		6^3	5	8	13	10	12	9^2	3	11	2	4	1																	24
1	3	6	5	11^2	13	10	12	14	9^3	2	4^1	8																		25
1	3	6	5	4^1	13	11^3	10	14	9^2	2	12	8																		26
1	3	6	5	12	13	10^3	9	11^2	14	2	4^1	8																		27
1	3	6	5	11^2	13	10^1	12	9	2	8																				28
1	2	6^3	5	7	11	10^2	13	9^1	3	12	14	8	4																	29
1	2	6^1	5	11^2	7	9		10	3	12	13	8	4																	30
1	2	6^1	5		7	10		9	3	12		11	4	8																31
1	4		5		7^1	10	12	9	3		2	14	13	11	6^3	6^2														32
1	4		5		11	10^1		9	3		2		7	8	6^1	12														33
1	4		5	12	13	11^1	10^3	9	3		2	14	7	6	6^2															34
1	4		5	11^2	12		10^3	9	3		2	14	7	6	8^1	13														35
1	4		5		13	8^2	10^3	14	9	3		2	12	7^1	6	$11^■$														36
1	4		5		12	9	10^2	7^1	11	3		2		6	13	8														37
1	4		5		13	11	10	9^1	3		2		7	6	12	8^2														38
1	4		5		12	11	10		3		2	6^2		8	9^1	7	13													39
1	4		5		12	9	10		3		2		7	6	11	8^1														40
1	4		5		8^2	9^1	10^3	14	3		2	13	7	6	12	11														41
1	4		5		6^1	9	10		3		2	12	7	8	12	11														42
1	4		5		6	9^1	10		3		2	12	7	8	11															43
1	4		5		8^2	9	10		3		2	6	7		13	11^1	12													44
1	4		5		6	9	10^1		3		2	8	7		12	11^2	13													45
1	4	5			7^3	9		11	3		2	8	13		14	10^1	12	6^2												46

FA Cup
First Round   Oxford U   (a)   0-1

Carling Cup
First Round   Norwich C   (h)   0-4

J Paint Trophy
First Round   Bournemouth   (a)   1-2

ENGLISH LEAGUE PLAYERS DIRECTORY

Players listed represent those with their clubs during the 2009–10 season.

Players are listed alphabetically on pages 552–558.
The number alongside each player corresponds to the team number heading. (Abalimba, Medi 32 = team 32 (Derby Co))

ACCRINGTON S (1)

BLACK, Adam (F)   1   0
H: 6 1   W: 11 00   b.Liverpool 24-5-92
Source: Scholar.

2009–10	Accrington S	1	0	1 0

BURTON, Alan (M)   0   0
H: 6 0   W: 11 00   b.Blackpool 22-2-91
Source: Scholar.

2009–10	Accrington S	0	0

DUNBAVIN, Ian (G)   173   0
H: 6 1   W: 12 10   b.Knowsley 27-5-80
Source: Trainee.

1998–99	Liverpool	0	0	
1999–2000	Liverpool	0	0	
1999–2000	Shrewsbury T	7	0	
2000–01	Shrewsbury T	22	0	
2001–02	Shrewsbury T	34	0	
2002–03	Shrewsbury T	33	0	
2003–04	Shrewsbury T	0	0	96 0
From Halifax T.				
2006–07	Accrington S	23	0	
2007–08	Accrington S	23	0	
2008–09	Accrington S	4	0	
2009–10	Accrington S	27	0	77 0

EDWARDS, Phil (D)   156   10
H: 5 8   W: 11 03   b.Bootle 8-11-85
Source: Scholar.

2005–06	Wigan Ath	0	0	
2006–07	Accrington S	33	1	
2007–08	Accrington S	31	1	
2008–09	Accrington S	46	0	
2009–10	Accrington S	46	8	156 10

GRANT, Robert (M)   65   15
H: 5 11   W: 12 00   b.Blackpool 27-3-87
Source: Scholar.

2006–07	Accrington S	1	0	
2007–08	Accrington S	7	0	
2008–09	Accrington S	15	1	
2009–10	Accrington S	42	14	65 15

JOYCE, Luke (M)   67   3
H: 5 11   W: 12 03   b.Bolton 9-7-87
Source: Scholar.

2005–06	Wigan Ath	0	0	
2005–06	Carlisle U	0	0	
2006–07	Carlisle U	16	1	
2007–08	Carlisle U	3	1	
2008–09	Carlisle U	7	0	26 2
2009–10	Accrington S	41	1	41 1

KEMPSON, Darran (D)   90   2
H: 6 2   W: 13 00   b.Blackpool 6-12-84
Source: Scholar.

2004–05	Preston NE	0	0	
From Morecambe.				
2006–07	Crewe Alex	7	0	7 0
2006–07	Bury	12	0	12 0
2007–08	Shrewsbury T	23	0	
2007–08	*Accrington S*	8	1	
2008–09	Shrewsbury T	0	0	23 0
2009–10	Accrington S	40	1	48 2

KING, Chris (D)   28   0
H: 5 8   W: 10 01   b.Liverpool 14-11-80

2008–09	Accrington S	27	0	
2009–10	Accrington S	1	0	28 0

KING, Gary (M)   19   2
H: 5 10   W: 11 04   b.Grimsby 27-1-90
Source: Scholar.

2007–08	Lincoln C	6	1	
2008–09	Lincoln C	5	0	
2009–10	Lincoln C	0	0	11 1
2009–10	Accrington S	8	1	8 1

McCONVILLE, Sean (F)   33   1
H: 5 11   W: 11 09   b.Burscough 6-3-89
Source: Skelmersdale U.

2008–09	Accrington S	5	0	
2009–10	Accrington S	28	1	33 1

MILES, John (F)   235   28
H: 5 10   W: 10 08   b.Fazackerley 28-9-81
Source: Trainee.

1998–99	Liverpool	0	0	
1999–2000	Liverpool	0	0	
2000–01	Liverpool	0	0	
2001–02	Liverpool	0	0	
2001–02	Stoke C	1	0	1 0
2002–03	Crewe Alex	5	1	5 1
2002–03	Macclesfield T	8	4	
2003–04	Macclesfield T	29	6	
2004–05	Macclesfield T	30	3	
2005–06	Macclesfield T	25	4	
2006–07	Macclesfield T	30	4	122 21
2007–08	Accrington S	16	0	
2007–08	*Milton Keynes D*	12	0	12 0
2008–09	Accrington S	43	3	
2009–10	Accrington S	36	3	95 6

MULLIN, John (M)   407   31
H: 6 0   W: 11 10   b.Bury 11-8-75
Source: School.

1992–93	Burnley	0	0	
1993–94	Burnley	6	1	
1994–95	Burnley	12	1	
1995–96	Sunderland	10	1	
1996–97	Sunderland	10	1	
1997–98	Sunderland	6	0	
1997–98	*Preston NE*	7	0	7 0
1997–98	*Burnley*	6	0	
1998–99	Sunderland	9	2	35 4
1999–2000	Burnley	37	5	
2000–01	Burnley	36	3	
2001–02	Burnley	4	0	101 10
2001–02	Rotherham U	34	2	
2002–03	Rotherham U	34	3	
2003–04	Rotherham U	38	4	
2004–05	Rotherham U	31	1	
2005–06	Rotherham U	43	2	180 12
2006–07	Tranmere R	40	5	
2007–08	Tranmere R	10	0	50 5
2008–09	Accrington S	31	0	
2009–10	Accrington S	3	0	34 0

MURPHY, Peter (M)   15   0
H: 6 0   W: 11 10   b.Liverpool 13-2-90
Source: Scholar.

2007–08	Accrington S	2	0	
2008–09	Accrington S	3	0	
2009–10	Accrington S	10	0	15 0

PROCTER, Andy (M)   167   21
H: 6 0   W: 12 04   b.Blackburn 13-3-83
Source: Great Harwood T.

2006–07	Accrington S	43	3	
2007–08	Accrington S	43	10	
2008–09	Accrington S	37	3	
2009–10	Accrington S	44	5	167 21

RICHARDSON, Leam (D)   193   1
H: 5 7   W: 11 04   b.Leeds 19-11-79
Source: Trainee.

1997–98	Blackburn R	0	0	
1998–99	Blackburn R	0	0	
1999–2000	Blackburn R	0	0	
2000–01	Bolton W	12	0	
2001–02	Bolton W	1	0	
2001–02	*Notts Co*	21	0	21 0
2002–03	Bolton W	0	0	13 0
2002–03	*Blackpool*	20	0	20 0
2003–04	Blackpool	28	0	
2004–05	Blackpool	23	0	71 0
2006–07	Accrington S	38	0	
2007–08	Accrington S	37	1	

2008–09	Accrington S	11	0	
2009–10	Accrington S	2	0	88 1

RYAN, James (M)   87   13
H: 5 8   W: 11 08   b.Maghull 6-9-88
Source: Scholar. *Honours:* Eire Under-21.

2006–07	Liverpool	0	0	
2007–08	Liverpool	0	0	
2007–08	*Shrewsbury T*	4	0	4 0
2008–09	Accrington S	44	10	
2009–10	Accrington S	39	3	83 13

SYMES, Michael (F)   149   33
H: 6 3   W: 12 04   b.Gt Yarmouth 31-10-83
Source: Scholar.

2001–02	Everton	0	0	
2002–03	Everton	0	0	
2003–04	Everton	0	0	
2003–04	*Crewe Alex*	4	1	4 1
2004–05	Bradford C	12	2	
2004–05	*Darlington*	0	0	
2005–06	Bradford C	3	1	
2005–06	*Stockport Co*	1	0	1 0
2006–07	Bradford C	0	0	15 3
2006–07	Shrewsbury T	33	9	
2007–08	Shrewsbury T	21	3	
2007–08	*Macclesfield T*	14	1	14 1
2008–09	Shrewsbury T	8	2	62 14
2008–09	Bournemouth	5	0	5 0
2008–09	*Accrington S*	7	1	
2009–10	Accrington S	41	13	48 14

TURNER, Chris (F)   47   2
H: 5 10   W: 11 10   b.Manchester 12-8-90
Source: Scholar.

2007–08	Accrington S	1	0	
2008–09	Accrington S	22	0	
2009–10	Accrington S	24	2	47 2

WINNARD, Dean (D)   44   0
H: 5 9   W: 10 04   b.Wigan 20-8-89

2006–07	Blackburn R	0	0	
2007–08	Blackburn R	0	0	
2008–09	Blackburn R	0	0	
2009–10	Accrington S	44	0	44 0

ALDERSHOT T (2)

BLACKBURN, Chris (D)   86   0
H: 6 0   W: 12 00   b.Crewe 2-8-82
Source: Scholarship.

1999–2000	Chester C	1	0	1 0
From Morecambe.				
2007–08	Swindon T	7	0	7 0
2008–09	Aldershot T	36	0	
2009–10	Aldershot T	42	0	78 0

BROWN, Aaron (D)   40   4
H: 6 4   W: 14 07   b.Birmingham 23-6-83
Source: Stafford R, Tamworth.

2005–06	Reading	0	0	
2005–06	*Bournemouth*	4	0	4 0
2006–07	Reading	0	0	
2007–08	Walsall	0	0	
2007–08	Reading	0	0	
From Redditch U.				
2008–09	Yeovil T	23	3	23 3
From AFC Telford U, Truro C.				
2009–10	Burton Alb	1	0	1 0
2009–10	Aldershot T	12	1	12 1

CHALMERS, Lewis (M)   46   1
H: 6 0   W: 12 04   b.Manchester 4-2-86
Source: Altrincham.

2008–09	Aldershot T	23	1	
2009–10	Aldershot T	23	0	46 1

CHARLES, Anthony (D)   131   6
H: 6 1   W: 12 07   b.Isleworth 11-3-81
Source: Brook House.

1999–2000	Crewe Alex	0	0	
From Brookhouse.				
2000–01	Crewe Alex	0	0	
From Hayes, Aldershot T, Farnborough T				
2004–05	Barnet	0	0	
2005–06	Barnet	40	0	
2006–07	Barnet	17	0	57 0
2008–09	Aldershot T	41	2	
2009–10	Aldershot T	33	4	74 6

CLEMENT, Jordan (G)   0   0
H: 6 1   W: 12 08   b.Chertsey 6-12-93
Honours: From Scholar.

2009–10	Aldershot T	0	0

CONNOLLY, Reece (F)   3   0
H: 6 0   W: 11 09   b.Frimley 22-1-92
Source: Scholar.

2009–10	Aldershot T	3	0	3 0

DONNELLY, Scott (M)   76   14
H: 5 8   W: 11 10   b.Hammersmith 25-12-87
Source: Scholar.

2004–05	QPR	2	0	
2005–06	QPR	8	0	
2006–07	QPR	3	0	13 0
From Wealdstone.				
2008–09	Aldershot T	20	1	
2009–10	Aldershot T	43	13	63 14

GRANT, John (F)   78   10
H: 5 11   W: 10 08   b.Manchester 9-8-81
Source: Trainee.

1999–2000	Crewe Alex	4	0	
2000–01	Crewe Alex	2	0	
2001–02	Crewe Alex	1	0	7 0
2001–02	*Rushden & D*	0	0	
From Here U, Telfd U				
2004–05	Shrewsbury T	19	2	19 2
From Halifax T.				
2008–09	Aldershot T	35	5	
2009–10	Aldershot T	17	3	52 8

HALLS, John (M)   131   3
H: 6 0   W: 11 11   b.Islington 14-2-82
Source: Scholar. *Honours:* England Youth, Under-20.

2000–01	Arsenal	0	0	
2001–02	Arsenal	0	0	
2001–02	*Colchester U*	6	0	6 0
2002–03	Arsenal	0	0	
2003–04	Arsenal	0	0	
2003–04	Stoke C	34	0	
2004–05	Stoke C	22	0	
2005–06	Stoke C	13	2	69 2
2005–06	Reading	1	1	
2006–07	Reading	0	0	
2007–08	Reading	1	0	
2007–08	*Preston NE*	4	0	4 0
2007–08	*Crystal Palace*	5	0	5 0
2007–08	*Sheffield U*	6	0	6 0
2008–09	Reading	0	0	2 1
2008–09	Brentford	23	0	23 0
2009–10	Aldershot T	16	0	16 0

HARDING, Ben (M)   113   10
H: 5 10   W: 11 02   b.Carshalton 6-9-84
Source: Scholar.

2001–02	Wimbledon	0	0	
2002–03	Wimbledon	0	0	
2003–04	Wimbledon	15	0	15 0
2004–05	Milton Keynes D	26	4	
2005–06	Milton Keynes D	10	2	
2006–07	Milton Keynes D	0	0	36 6
2008–09	Aldershot T	29	3	
2009–10	Aldershot T	33	1	62 4

HERD, Ben (D)   177   3
H: 5 9   W: 10 12   b.Welwyn 21-6-85
Source: Scholar.

2002–03	Watford	0	0	
2003–04	Watford	0	0	
2004–05	Watford	0	0	
2005–06	Shrewsbury T	46	2	
2006–07	Shrewsbury T	31	1	
2007–08	Shrewsbury T	45	0	
2008–09	Shrewsbury T	21	0	143 3
2009–10	Aldershot T	34	0	34 0

HODKINSON, Bobby (M)   1   0
H: 5 8   W: 13 06   b.Plymouth 3-7-90
Source: Plymouth Arg Scholar, Aldershot T.

2009–10	Aldershot T	1	0	1 0

HOWELL, Dean (D)   29   1
H: 6 1   W: 12 05   b.Burton-on-Trent 29-1-80
Source: Trainee.

1999–2000	Notts Co	1	0	1 0
2000–01	Crewe Alex	1	0	1 0
2000–01	*Rochdale*	3	0	3 0
From Southport, Morecambe, Halifax T				
2005–06	Colchester U	4	0	4 0
From Halifax, Weymouth, Grays, Rushden				
2008–09	Aldershot T	14	0	
2008–09	*Bury*	3	0	3 0
2009–10	Aldershot T	3	1	17 1

HUDSON, Kirk (F)   78   15
H: 5 8   W: 10 00   b.Rochford 12-12-86
Source: Ipswich T Scholar, Celtic.

2005–06	Bournemouth	1	0	1 0
2008–09	Aldershot T	43	11	
2009–10	Aldershot T	34	4	77 15

HYLTON, Danny (F)   50   8
H: 6 0   W: 11 13   b.London 25-2-89
Source: Youth.

2008–09	Aldershot T	29	5	
2009–10	Aldershot T	21	3	50 8

JAIMEZ-RUIZ, Mikhael (G)   44   0
H: 6 0   W: 12 02   b.Merida 12-7-84
Source: Northwood. *Honours:* Venezuela 1 full cap.

2008–09	Aldershot T	14	0	
2009–10	Aldershot T	30	0	44 0

MASTERS, Clark (G)   13   0
H: 6 3   W: 13 12   b.Hastings 31-5-87
Source: Scholar.

2005–06	Brentford	0	0	
2006–07	Brentford	11	0	
2007–08	Brentford	1	0	12 0
2008–09	Southend U	0	0	
2009–10	Southend U	0	0	
2009–10	Aldershot T	1	0	1 0

MEKKI, Adam (M)   0   0
H: 5 9   W: 11 00   b.Chester 24-6-92
Honours: From Scholar

2009–10	Aldershot T	0	0

MORGAN, Marvin (F)   72   21
H: 6 4   W: 12 08   b.Manchester 13-4-83
Source: Wealdstone, Yeading, Woking.

2008–09	Aldershot T	32	6	
2009–10	Aldershot T	40	15	72 21

RIZA, Omer (F)   91   18
H: 5 9   W: 11 00   b.Edmonton 8-11-79
Source: Trainee.

1998–99	Arsenal	0	0	
1999–2000	Arsenal	0	0	
1999–2000	West Ham U	0	0	
2000–01	West Ham U	0	0	
2000–01	*Barnet*	10	4	10 4
2000–01	*Cambridge U*	12	3	
2001–02	West Ham U	0	0	
2002–03	Cambridge U	46	11	58 14
2003–04	Denizli	0	0	
2004–05	Denizli	0	0	
2005–06	Denizli	0	0	
2006–07	Trabzonspor	12	0	
2007–08	Trabzonspor	0	0	12 0
2008–09	Shrewsbury T	2	0	
2009–10	Shrewsbury T	8	0	10 0
2009–10	Aldershot T	1	0	1 0

SANDELL, Andy (M)   94   10
H: 5 11   W: 11 09   b.Calne 8-9-83
Source: Bath C.

2005–06	Bristol R	0	0	
2006–07	Bristol R	36	3	
2008–09	Bristol R	0	0	36 3
From Salisbury C.				
2008–09	Aldershot T	29	2	
2009–10	Aldershot T	29	5	58 7

SOARES, Louie (D)   92   11
H: 5 11   W: 13 05   b.Reading 8-1-85
Source: Scholar. *Honours:* Barbados 3 full caps.

2004–05	Reading	0	0	
2004–05	Bristol R	1	0	1 0
2005–06	Barnet	20	1	20 1
2008–09	Aldershot T	35	3	
2009–10	Aldershot T	36	7	71 10

SPENCER, Damien (F)   260   37
H: 6 1   W: 14 00   b.Ascot 19-9-81
Source: Scholarship.

1999–2000	Bristol C	9	1	
2000–01	Bristol C	4	0	
2000–01	*Exeter C*	6	0	6 0
2001–02	Bristol C	0	0	13 1
2002–03	Cheltenham T	30	6	
2003–04	Cheltenham T	36	9	
2004–05	Cheltenham T	41	8	
2005–06	Cheltenham T	46	3	
2006–07	Cheltenham T	27	3	
2007–08	Cheltenham T	30	3	
2008–09	Cheltenham T	14	3	
2008–09	*Brentford*	5	1	5 1
2009–10	Cheltenham T	0	0	224 35
From Kettering T.				
2009–10	*Aldershot T*	12	0	12 0

STRAKER, Anthony (D)   69   2
H: 5 9   W: 11 11   b.Ealing 23-9-88
Source: Crystal Palace Scholar.

2008–09	Aldershot T	32	0	
2009–10	Aldershot T	37	2	69 2

WINFIELD, Dave (D)   35   2
H: 6 3   W: 13 08   b.Aldershot 24-2-88
Source: Youth.

2008–09	Aldershot T	10	0	
2009–10	Aldershot T	25	2	35 2

YOUNG, Jamie (G)   69   0
H: 5 11   W: 13 00   b.Brisbane 25-8-85
Source: Scholar. *Honours:* England Youth, Under-20.

2003–04	Reading	1	0	
2004–05	Reading	0	0	
2005–06	Reading	0	0	1 0
2005–06	*Rushden & D*	20	0	20 0
2006–07	Wycombe W	19	0	
2007–08	Wycombe W	4	0	
2008–09	Wycombe W	15	0	
2009–10	Wycombe W	1	0	39 0
2009–10	Aldershot T	9	0	9 0

ARSENAL (3)

AFOBE, Benik (F)   0   0
b.Leyton 12-2-93
Source: Scholar. *Honours:* England Youth.

2009–10	Arsenal	0	0

ALMUNIA, Manuel (G)   236   0
H: 6 3   W: 13 00   b.Pamplona 19-5-77

1996–97	Osasuna B	2	0	
1997–98	Osasuna B	31	0	
1998–99	Osasuna B	13	0	46 0
1999–2000	*Cartagena*	3	0	3 0
2000–01	Sabadell	25	0	25 0
2000–01	Celta Vigo	0	0	
2001–02	Celta Vigo	0	0	
2001–02	*Eibar*	35	0	35 0
2002–03	*Recreativo*	2	0	2 0
2003–04	Albacete	24	0	24 0
2004–05	Arsenal	10	0	
2005–06	Arsenal	0	0	
2006–07	Arsenal	1	0	
2007–08	Arsenal	29	0	
2008–09	Arsenal	32	0	
2009–10	Arsenal	29	0	101 0

ARSHAVIN, Andrei (F)   280   67
H: 5 8   W: 9 11   b.St Petersburg 29-5-81
Honours: Russia 51 full caps, 16 goals.

1999	Zenit	0	0	
2000	Zenit	10	0	
2001	Zenit	29	4	
2002	Zenit	30	4	
2003	Zenit	27	5	
2004	Zenit	28	6	

2005	Zenit	29	9		
2006	Zenit	28	7		
2007	Zenit	30	10		
2008	Zenit	27	6	**238**	**51**
2008–09	Arsenal	12	6		
2009–10	Arsenal	30	10	**42**	**16**

AYLING, Luke (D) **4** **0**
H: 5 11　W: 10 08　b.London 25-8-91

| 2009–10 | Arsenal | 0 | 0 | | |
| 2009–10 | Yeovil T | 4 | 0 | **4** | **0** |

BARAZITE, Nacer (M) **30** **1**
H: 6 2　W: 13 01　b.Arnhem 27-5-90
Source: Scholar. Honours: Holland Youth.

2007–08	Arsenal	0	0		
2008–09	Arsenal	0	0		
2008–09	Derby Co	30	1	**30**	**1**
2009–10	Arsenal	0	0		

BARTLEY, Kyle (D) **14** **0**
H: 5 11　W: 11 00　b.Manchester 22-5-91
Source: Scholar.

2008–09	Arsenal	0	0		
2009–10	Arsenal	0	0		
2009–10	Sheffield U	14	0	**14**	**0**

BENDTNER, Nicklas (F) **123** **31**
H: 6 2　W: 13 00　b.Copenhagen 16-1-88
Source: Scholar. Honours: Denmark Youth,
Under-21, 35 full caps, 12 goals.

2005–06	Arsenal	0	0		
2006–07	Arsenal	0	0		
2006–07	Birmingham C	42	11	**42**	**11**
2007–08	Arsenal	27	5		
2008–09	Arsenal	31	9		
2009–10	Arsenal	23	6	**81**	**20**

CAMPBELL, Sol (D) **497** **20**
H: 6 2　W: 15 07　b.Plaistow 18-9-74
Source: Trainee. Honours: England Youth,
Under-21, B, 73 full caps, 1 goal.

1992–93	Tottenham H	1	1		
1993–94	Tottenham H	34	0		
1994–95	Tottenham H	30	0		
1995–96	Tottenham H	31	1		
1996–97	Tottenham H	38	0		
1997–98	Tottenham H	34	0		
1998–99	Tottenham H	37	6		
1999–2000	Tottenham H	29	0		
2000–01	Tottenham H	21	2	**255**	**10**
2001–02	Arsenal	31	2		
2002–03	Arsenal	33	2		
2003–04	Arsenal	35	1		
2004–05	Arsenal	16	0		
2005–06	Arsenal	20	2		
2006–07	Portsmouth	32	1		
2007–08	Portsmouth	31	1		
2008–09	Portsmouth	32	0		
2009–10	Portsmouth	0	0	**95**	**2**
2009–10	Notts Co	1	0	**1**	**0**
2009–10	Arsenal	11	0	**146**	**8**

CLICHY, Gaël (D) **154** **1**
H: 5 9　W: 10 04　b.Toulouse 26-7-85
Source: Cannes. Honours: France Under-21,
B, 5 full caps.

2003–04	Arsenal	12	0		
2004–05	Arsenal	15	0		
2005–06	Arsenal	7	0		
2006–07	Arsenal	27	0		
2007–08	Arsenal	38	0		
2008–09	Arsenal	31	1		
2009–10	Arsenal	24	0	**154**	**1**

COQUELIN, Francis (M) **0** **0**
H: 5 10　W: 11 08　b.Laval 13-5-91
Source: Laval.

| 2008–09 | Arsenal | 0 | 0 | | |
| 2009–10 | Arsenal | 0 | 0 | | |

CRUISE, Tom (D) **0** **0**
H: 6 1　W: 12 08　b.London 9-3-91
Source: Scholar. Honours: England Youth.

| 2008–09 | Arsenal | 0 | 0 | | |
| 2009–10 | Arsenal | 0 | 0 | | |

DENILSON (M) **92** **6**
H: 5 10　W: 10 10　b.Sao Paulo 16-2-88
Honours: Brazil Youth, Under-20.

2005	Sao Paulo	10	0		
2006	Sao Paulo	2	0	**12**	**0**
2006–07	Arsenal	10	0		

2007–08	Arsenal	13	0		
2008–09	Arsenal	37	3		
2009–10	Arsenal	20	3	**80**	**6**

DIABY, Vassiriki (M) **102** **13**
H: 6 2　W: 12 04　b.Paris 11-5-86
Honours: France Youth, Under-21, 7 full
caps.

2004–05	Auxerre	5	0		
2005–06	Auxerre	5	1	**10**	**1**
2005–06	Arsenal	12	1		
2006–07	Arsenal	12	1		
2007–08	Arsenal	15	1		
2008–09	Arsenal	24	3		
2009–10	Arsenal	29	6	**92**	**12**

DJOUROU, Johan (D) **59** **0**
H: 6 2　W: 12 05　b.Ivory Coast 18-1-87
Source: Scholar. Honours: Switzerland Youth,
Under-20, Under-21, 24 full caps, 1 goal.

2004–05	Arsenal	0	0		
2005–06	Arsenal	7	0		
2006–07	Arsenal	21	0		
2007–08	Arsenal	2	0		
2007–08	Birmingham C	13	0	**13**	**0**
2008–09	Arsenal	15	0		
2009–10	Arsenal	1	0	**46**	**0**

EASTMOND, Craig (D) **4** **0**
H: 6 0　W: 11 11　b.Wandsworth 9-12-90
Source: Scholar.

| 2009–10 | Arsenal | 4 | 0 | **4** | **0** |

EBOUE, Emmanuel (D) **189** **8**
H: 5 10　W: 11 08　b.Abidjan 4-6-83
Source: Academie JM Guillou. Honours:
Ivory Coast 45 full caps, 1 goal.

2002–03	Beveren	23	0		
2003–04	Beveren	30	2		
2004–05	Beveren	17	2	**70**	**4**
2004–05	Arsenal	1	0		
2005–06	Arsenal	18	0		
2006–07	Arsenal	24	0		
2007–08	Arsenal	23	0		
2008–09	Arsenal	28	3		
2009–10	Arsenal	25	1	**119**	**4**

EDUARDO (F) **167** **89**
H: 5 10　W: 10 03　b.Rio 25-2-83
Source: Bangu. Honours: Croatia Under-21,
29 full caps, 18 goals.

2001–02	Dinamo Zagreb	4	0		
2002–03	Inter Zapresic	15	10	**15**	**10**
2003–04	Dinamo Zagreb	24	9		
2004–05	Dinamo Zagreb	22	10		
2005–06	Dinamo Zagreb	29	20		
2006–07	Dinamo Zagreb	32	34	**111**	**73**
2007–08	Arsenal	17	4		
2008–09	Arsenal	0	0		
2009–10	Arsenal	24	2	**41**	**6**

EMMANUEL-THOMAS, Jay (M) **25** **6**
H: 5 9　W: 11 05　b.Forest Gate 27-12-90
Source: Scholar. Honours: England Youth.

2008–09	Arsenal	0	0		
2009–10	Arsenal	0	0		
2009–10	Blackpool	11	1	**11**	**1**
2009–10	Doncaster R	14	5	**14**	**5**

EVINA, Cedric (D) **0** **0**
b.Cameroon 16-11-91
Source: Scholar.

| 2009–10 | Arsenal | 0 | 0 | | |

FABIANSKI, Lukasz (G) **66** **0**
H: 6 3　W: 13 01　b.Costrzyn nad Odra
18-4-85
Honours: Poland Under-21, 15 full caps.

2005–06	Legia	30	0		
2006–07	Legia	23	0	**53**	**0**
2007–08	Arsenal	3	0		
2008–09	Arsenal	6	0		
2009–10	Arsenal	4	0	**13**	**0**

FABREGAS, Francesc (M) **187** **32**
H: 5 11　W: 11 01　b.Vilessoc de Mar 4-5-87
Source: Barcelona. Honours: Spain Youth,
Under-21, 54 full caps, 6 goals.

2003–04	Arsenal	0	0		
2004–05	Arsenal	33	2		
2005–06	Arsenal	35	3		
2006–07	Arsenal	38	2		
2007–08	Arsenal	32	7		

| 2008–09 | Arsenal | 22 | 3 | | |
| 2009–10 | Arsenal | 27 | 15 | **187** | **32** |

FREEMAN, Luke (F) **1** **0**
H: 6 0　W: 10 00　b.London 22-3-92
Source: Scholar.

2007–08	Gillingham	1	0	**1**	**0**
2008–09	Arsenal	0	0		
2009–10	Arsenal	0	0		

FRIMPONG, Emmanuel (M) **0** **0**
H: 5 11　W: 10 07　b.Ghana 10-1-92
Source: Scholar.

| 2008–09 | Arsenal | 0 | 0 | | |
| 2009–10 | Arsenal | 0 | 0 | | |

GALLAS, William (D) **363** **26**
H: 6 0　W: 12 12　b.Asnieres 17-8-77
Honours: France Under-21, 83 full caps, 5
goals.

1996–97	Caen	18	0	**18**	**0**
1997–98	Marseille	3	0		
1998–99	Marseille	30	0		
1999–2000	Marseille	22	0		
2000–01	Marseille	30	2	**85**	**2**
2001–02	Chelsea	30	1		
2002–03	Chelsea	38	4		
2003–04	Chelsea	29	0		
2004–05	Chelsea	28	2		
2005–06	Chelsea	34	5		
2006–07	Chelsea	0	0	**159**	**12**
2006–07	Arsenal	21	3		
2007–08	Arsenal	31	4		
2008–09	Arsenal	23	2		
2009–10	Arsenal	26	3	**101**	**12**

GIBBS, Kieran (M) **18** **0**
H: 5 10　W: 10 02　b.Lambeth 26-9-89
Source: Scholar. Honours: England Youth,
Under-21.

2007–08	Arsenal	0	0		
2007–08	Norwich C	7	0	**7**	**0**
2008–09	Arsenal	8	0		
2009–10	Arsenal	3	0	**11**	**0**

GILBERT, Kerrea (D) **75** **1**
H: 5 6　W: 11 03　b.Hammersmith 28-2-87
Source: Scholar. Honours: England Youth.

2005–06	Arsenal	2	0		
2006–07	Arsenal	0	0		
2006–07	Cardiff C	24	0	**24**	**0**
2007–08	Arsenal	0	0		
2007–08	Southend U	5	0	**5**	**0**
2008–09	Arsenal	0	0		
2008–09	Leicester C	34	1	**34**	**1**
2009–10	Arsenal	0	0	**2**	**0**
2009–10	Peterborough U	10	0	**10**	**0**

HENDERSON, Conor (M) **0** **0**
H: 6 1　W: 11 13　b.Sidcup 8-9-91
Source: Scholar. Honours: Eire Youth.

| 2008–09 | Arsenal | 0 | 0 | | |
| 2009–10 | Arsenal | 0 | 0 | | |

HOYTE, Gavin (D) **26** **0**
H: 5 11　W: 11 00　b.Waltham Forest 6-6-90
Source: Scholar. Honours: England Youth,
Under-20.

2007–08	Arsenal	0	0		
2008–09	Arsenal	1	0		
2008–09	Watford	7	0	**7**	**0**
2009–10	Arsenal	0	0	**1**	**0**
2009–10	Brighton & HA	18	0	**18**	**0**

LANSBURY, Henri (M) **54** **9**
H: 6 0　W: 13 06　b.Enfield 12-10-90
Source: Scholar. Honours: England Youth,
Under-21.

2007–08	Arsenal	0	0		
2008–09	Arsenal	0	0		
2008–09	Scunthorpe U	16	4	**16**	**4**
2009–10	Arsenal	1	0	**1**	**0**
2009–10	Watford	37	5	**37**	**5**

MANNONE, Vito (G) **8** **0**
H: 6 0　W: 11 08　b.Desio 2-3-88
Source: Atalanta.

2005–06	Arsenal	0	0		
2006–07	Arsenal	0	0		
2006–07	Barnsley	2	0	**2**	**0**
2007–08	Arsenal	0	0		
2008–09	Arsenal	1	0		
2009–10	Arsenal	5	0	**6**	**0**

McDERMOTT, Sean (G) 0 0
b.Kristiansand 30-5-93
Source: Scholar. *Honours:* Eire Youth.

| 2009–10 | Arsenal | 0 | 0 | | |

MERIDA PEREZ, Fran (M) 6 1
H: 5 11 W: 13 00 b.Barcelona 4-3-90
Source: Scholar.

2006–07	Arsenal	0	0		
2007–08	Arsenal	0	0		
2008–09	Arsenal	2	0		
2009–10	Arsenal	4	1	6	1

MIQUEL, Ignasi (D) 0 0
b.Barcelona 28-9-92
Source: Scholar.

| 2009–10 | Arsenal | 0 | 0 | | |

MURPHY, Rhys (F) 5 0
H: 6 1 W: 11 13 b.Shoreham 6-11-90
Honours: England Youth.

2007–08	Arsenal	0	0		
2008–09	Arsenal	0	0		
2009–10	Arsenal	0	0		
2009–10	Brentford	5	0	5	0

NASRI, Samir (M) 176 19
H: 5 9 W: 11 11 b.Marseille 26-6-87
Honours: France Youth, Under-21, 15 full caps, 2 goals.

2004–05	Marseille	24	1		
2005–06	Marseille	30	1		
2006–07	Marseille	37	3		
2007–08	Marseille	30	6	121	11
2008–09	Arsenal	29	6		
2009–10	Arsenal	26	2	55	8

NORDTVEIT, Havard (D) 26 0
H: 6 2 W: 11 09 b.Vats 21-6-90
Honours: Norway Youth.

2007	Haugesund	9	0	9	0
2007–08	Arsenal	0	0		
2008–09	Arsenal	0	0		
2009	Lillestrom	17	0	17	0
2009–10	Arsenal	0	0		

OZYAKUP, Oguzhan (M) 0 0
b.Zaandam 23-9-92
Source: AZ.

| 2009–10 | Arsenal | 0 | 0 | | |

RAMSEY, Aaron (M) 43 4
H: 5 9 W: 10 07 b.Caerphilly 26-12-90
Source: School. *Honours:* Wales Youth, Under-21, 11 full caps, 2 goals.

2006–07	Cardiff C	1	0		
2007–08	Cardiff C	15	1	16	1
2008–09	Arsenal	9	0		
2009–10	Arsenal	18	3	27	3

RANDALL, Mark (M) 28 0
H: 6 0 W: 12 12 b.Milton Keynes 28-9-89
Source: Scholar.

2006–07	Arsenal	0	0		
2007–08	Arsenal	1	0		
2007–08	Burnley	10	0	10	0
2008–09	Arsenal	1	0		
2009–10	Arsenal	0	0	2	0
2009–10	Milton Keynes D	16	0	16	0

ROSICKY, Tomas (M) 259 39
H: 5 10 W: 10 10 b.Prague 4-10-80
Honours: Czech Republic Under-21, 71 full caps, 19 goals.

1998–99	Sparta Prague	3	0		
1999–2000	Sparta Prague	24	5		
2000–01	Sparta Prague	14	3	41	8
2000–01	Borussia Dortmund	15	0		
2001–02	Borussia Dortmund	30	5		
2002–03	Borussia Dortmund	30	3		
2003–04	Borussia Dortmund	19	2		
2004–05	Borussia Dortmund	27	4		
2005–06	Borussia Dortmund	28	5	149	19
2006–07	Arsenal	26	3		
2007–08	Arsenal	18	6		
2008–09	Arsenal	0	0		
2009–10	Arsenal	25	3	69	12

SAGNA, Bakari (D) 186 1
H: 5 10 W: 11 05 b.Sens 14-2-83
Source: Auxerre B. *Honours:* France Under-21, 23 full caps.

2003–04	Auxerre	0	0		
2004–05	Auxerre	26	0		
2005–06	Auxerre	23	0		
2006–07	Auxerre	38	0	87	0
2007–08	Arsenal	29	1		
2008–09	Arsenal	35	0		
2009–10	Arsenal	35	0	99	1

SENDEROS, Philippe (D) 106 7
H: 6 1 W: 13 10 b.Geneva 14-2-85
Honours: Switzerland Youth, Under-20, Under-21, 41 full caps, 5 goals.

2001–02	Servette	0	0		
2002–03	Servette	23	3	26	3
2003–04	Arsenal	0	0		
2004–05	Arsenal	13	0		
2005–06	Arsenal	20	2		
2006–07	Arsenal	14	0		
2007–08	Arsenal	17	2		
2008–09	Arsenal	0	0		
2008–09	AC Milan	14	0	14	0
2009–10	Arsenal	0	0	64	4
2009–10	Everton	2	0	2	0

SHEA, James (G) 0 0
H: 5 11 W: 12 00 b.Islington 16-6-91
Source: Scholar.

| 2009–10 | Arsenal | 0 | 0 | | |

SILVESTRE, Mikael (D) 342 10
H: 6 0 W: 13 12 b.Chambray les Tours 9-8-77
Honours: France Youth, Under-21, 40 full caps, 2 goals.

1995–96	Rennes	1	0		
1996–97	Rennes	16	0		
1997–98	Rennes	32	0	49	0
1998–99	Internazionale	18	1	18	1
1999–2000	Manchester U	31	0		
2000–01	Manchester U	30	1		
2001–02	Manchester U	35	0		
2002–03	Manchester U	34	1		
2003–04	Manchester U	34	0		
2004–05	Manchester U	35	2		
2005–06	Manchester U	33	1		
2006–07	Manchester U	14	1		
2007–08	Manchester U	3	0	249	6
2008–09	Arsenal	14	2		
2009–10	Arsenal	12	1	26	3

SIMPSON, Jay (M) 93 19
H: 5 11 W: 13 04 b.Enfield 1-12-88
Source: Scholar.

2007–08	Arsenal	0	0		
2007–08	Millwall	41	6	41	6
2008–09	Arsenal	0	0		
2008–09	WBA	13	1	13	1
2009–10	Arsenal	0	0		
2009–10	QPR	39	12	39	12

SONG BILLONG, Alexandre (M) 85 2
H: 5 11 W: 12 04 b.Douala 9-9-87
Source: Bastia. *Honours:* France Youth, Cameroon Youth. Cameroon 24 full caps.

2005–06	Arsenal	5	0		
2006–07	Arsenal	2	0		
2006–07	Charlton Ath	12	0	12	0
2007–08	Arsenal	9	0		
2008–09	Arsenal	31	1		
2009–10	Arsenal	26	1	73	2

SUNU, Gilles (F) 9 1
H: 5 11 W: 11 00 b.Chateauroux 30-3-91
Source: Scholar.

2007–08	Arsenal	0	0		
2008–09	Arsenal	0	0		
2009–10	Arsenal	0	0		
2009–10	Derby Co	9	1	9	1

SZCZESNY, Wojciech (G) 28 0
H: 5 10 W: 11 11 b.Warsaw 18-4-90
Source: Scholar. *Honours:* Poland 1 full cap.

2007–08	Arsenal	0	0		
2008–09	Arsenal	0	0		
2009–10	Arsenal	0	0		
2009–10	Brentford	28	0	28	0

TRAORE, Armand (D) 31 1
H: 6 1 W: 12 12 b.Paris 8-10-89
Source: Monaco. *Honours:* France Youth.

2006–07	Arsenal	0	0		
2007–08	Arsenal	3	0		
2008–09	Arsenal	0	0		
2008–09	Portsmouth	19	1	19	1
2009–10	Arsenal	9	0	12	0

VAN PERSIE, Robin (F) 192 62
H: 6 0 W: 11 00 b.Rotterdam 6-8-83
Source: Excelsior. *Honours:* Holland Under-21, 51 full caps, 19 goals.

2001–02	Feyenoord	10	0		
2002–03	Feyenoord	23	8		
2003–04	Feyenoord	23	6	61	14
2004–05	Arsenal	25	5		
2005–06	Arsenal	24	5		
2006–07	Arsenal	22	11		
2007–08	Arsenal	15	7		
2008–09	Arsenal	28	11		
2009–10	Arsenal	15	9	131	48

VELA, Carlos (F) 89 13
H: 5 9 W: 10 05 b.Cancun 1-3-89
Source: Guadalajara. *Honours:* Mexico Youth, Under-20, 29 full caps, 9 goals.

2005–06	Arsenal	0	0		
2006–07	Arsenal	0	0		
2006–07	Salamanca	31	8	31	8
2007–08	Osasuna	33	3	33	3
2007–08	Arsenal	0	0		
2008–09	Arsenal	14	1		
2009–10	Arsenal	11	1	25	2

VERMAELEN, Thomas (D) 145 16
H: 6 0 W: 11 11 b.Kapellen 14-11-85
Source: Ekeren, Antwerp. *Honours:* Belgium Under-21, 28 full caps, 1 goal.

2003–04	Ajax	1	0		
2004–05	RKC Waalwijk	13	2	13	2
2005–06	Ajax	24	3		
2006–07	Ajax	23	0		
2007–08	Ajax	20	0		
2008–09	Ajax	31	4	99	9
2009–10	Arsenal	33	7	33	7

WALCOTT, Theo (F) 107 13
H: 5 9 W: 11 01 b.Compton 16-3-89
Source: Scholar. *Honours:* England Youth, Under-21, B, 11 full caps, 3 goals.

2005–06	Southampton	21	4	21	4
2005–06	Arsenal	0	0		
2006–07	Arsenal	16	0		
2007–08	Arsenal	25	4		
2008–09	Arsenal	22	0		
2009–10	Arsenal	23	3	86	9

WATT, Sanchez (M) 10 0
H: 5 11 W: 12 00 b.London 14-2-91
Source: Scholar. *Honours:* England Youth.

2008–09	Arsenal	0	0		
2009–10	Arsenal	0	0		
2009–10	Southend U	4	0	4	0
2009–10	Leeds U	6	0	6	0

WILSHERE, Jack (M) 16 1
H: 5 7 W: 11 03 b.Stevenage 1-1-92
Source: Scholar. *Honours:* England Youth, Under-21.

2008–09	Arsenal	0	0		
2009–10	Arsenal	1	0	2	0
2009–10	Bolton W	14	1	14	1

Scholars
Aneke, Chukwuemeka Ademola Amachi; Boateng, Daniel; Brislen-Hall, George; Deacon, Roarie; Hajrovic, Sead; Meade, Jernade Ronnel; Yennaris, Nicholas.

ASTON VILLA (4)

AGBONLAHOR, Gabriel (F) 166 45
H: 5 11 W: 12 05 b.Birmingham 13-10-86
Source: Scholar. *Honours:* England Under-20, Under-21, 3 full caps.

2005–06	Aston Villa	9	1		
2005–06	Watford	2	0	2	0
2005–06	Sheffield W	8	0	8	0
2006–07	Aston Villa	38	9		
2007–08	Aston Villa	37	11		
2008–09	Aston Villa	36	11		
2009–10	Aston Villa	36	13	156	45

ALBRIGHTON, Marc (M)   3   0
H: 6 2 W: 12 06 b.Sutton Coldfield 18-11-89
Source: Scholar. *Honours:* England Youth, Under-20.

| 2008–09 | Aston Villa | 0 | 0 | | |
| 2009–10 | Aston Villa | 3 | 0 | 3 | 0 |

BAKER, Nathan (D)   18   0
H: 6 2 W: 11 11 b.23-4-91
Source: Scholar. *Honours:* England Youth.

2008–09	Aston Villa	0	0		
2009–10	Aston Villa	0	0		
2009–10	*Lincoln C*	18	0	18	0

BANNAN, Barry (D)   30   2
H: 5 10 W: 10 08 b.Glasgow 1-12-89
Source: Scholar. *Honours:* Scotland Under-21.

2008–09	Aston Villa	0	0		
2008–09	*Derby Co*	10	1	10	1
2009–10	Aston Villa	0	0		
2009–10	*Blackpool*	20	1	20	1

BEVAN, David (G)   0   0
H: 6 2 W: 13 00 b.Cork 24-6-89
Source: Scholar.

2007–08	Aston Villa	0	0		
2008–09	Aston Villa	0	0		
2009–10	Aston Villa	0	0		

BEYE, Habib (D)   320   11
H: 6 0 W: 12 06 b.Paris 19-10-77
Honours: Senegal 45 full caps, 1 goal.

1997–98	Paris St Germain	0	0		
1998–99	Strasbourg	23	0		
1999–2000	Strasbourg	33	1		
2000–01	Strasbourg	31	3		
2001–02	Strasbourg	20	3		
2002–03	Strasbourg	26	1		
2003–04	Strasbourg	1	0	134	8
2003–04	Marseille	22	0		
2004–05	Marseille	37	1		
2005–06	Marseille	29	1		
2006–07	Marseille	36	0		
2007–08	Marseille	4	0	128	2
2007–08	Newcastle U	29	1		
2008–09	Newcastle U	23	0	52	1
2009–10	Aston Villa	6	0	6	0

CAREW, John (F)   317 120
H: 6 5 W: 14 11 b.Lorenskog 5-9-79
Source: Lorenskog. *Honours:* Norway Youth, Under-21, 84 full caps, 22 goals.

1998	Valerenga	18	7		
1999	Valerenga	15	7	33	14
1999	Rosenborg	8	10		
2000	Rosenborg	10	8	18	18
2000–01	Valencia	37	11		
2001–02	Valencia	15	1		
2002–03	Valencia	32	8	84	20
2003–04	Roma	20	8	20	8
2004–05	Besiktas	24	13	24	13
2005–06	Lyon	26	9		
2006–07	Lyon	9	1	35	10
2006–07	Aston Villa	11	3		
2007–08	Aston Villa	32	13		
2008–09	Aston Villa	27	11		
2009–10	Aston Villa	33	10	103	37

CLARK, Ciaran (D)   1   0
H: 6 2 W: 12 00 b.Harrow 26-9-89
Source: Scholar. *Honours:* England Youth, Under-20.

| 2008–09 | Aston Villa | 0 | 0 | | |
| 2009–10 | Aston Villa | 1 | 0 | 1 | 0 |

COLLINS, James M (D)   147   6
H: 6 2 W: 14 05 b.Newport 23-8-83
Source: Scholar. *Honours:* Wales Youth, Under-21, 34 full caps, 2 goals.

2000–01	Cardiff C	3	0		
2001–02	Cardiff C	7	1		
2002–03	Cardiff C	2	0		
2003–04	Cardiff C	20	1		
2004–05	Cardiff C	34	1	66	3
2005–06	West Ham U	14	2		
2006–07	West Ham U	16	0		
2007–08	West Ham U	3	0		
2008–09	West Ham U	18	0		
2009–10	West Ham U	3	0	54	2
2009–10	Aston Villa	27	1	27	1

COLLINS, James S (F)   7   2
H: 6 2 W: 13 08 b.Coventry 1-12-90
Source: Scholar. *Honours:* Eire Under-21.

2008–09	Aston Villa	0	0		
2009–10	Aston Villa	0	0		
2009–10	*Darlington*	7	2	7	2

CUELLAR, Carlos (D)   260   12
H: 6 3 W: 13 03 b.Madrid 23-8-81

2000–01	Calahorra	27	0	27	0
2001–02	Numancia	23	1		
2002–03	Numancia	39	3	62	4
2003–04	Osasuna	5	0		
2004–05	Osasuna	14	0		
2005–06	Osasuna	29	1		
2006–07	Osasuna	23	1	71	2
2007–08	Rangers	36	4	36	4
2008–09	Aston Villa	28	0		
2009–10	Aston Villa	36	2	64	2

DAVIES, Curtis (D)   170   7
H: 6 2 W: 11 13 b.Waltham Forest 15-3-85
Source: Scholar. *Honours:* England Under-21.

2003–04	Luton T	6	0		
2004–05	Luton T	44	1		
2005–06	Luton T	6	1	56	2
2005–06	WBA	33	2		
2006–07	WBA	32	0		
2007–08	WBA	0	0	65	2
2007–08	*Aston Villa*	12	1		
2008–09	Aston Villa	35	1		
2009–10	Aston Villa	2	1	49	3

DELFOUNESO, Nathan (F)   13   1
H: 6 1 W: 12 04 b.Birmingham 2-2-91
Source: Scholar. *Honours:* England Youth, Under-21.

2007–08	Aston Villa	0	0		
2008–09	Aston Villa	4	0		
2009–10	Aston Villa	9	1	13	1

DELPH, Fabian (D)   52   6
H: 5 8 W: 11 00 b.Bradford 5-5-91
Source: Scholar. *Honours:* England Under-21.

2006–07	Leeds U	1	0		
2007–08	Leeds U	1	0		
2008–09	Leeds U	42	6	44	6
2009–10	Aston Villa	8	0	8	0

DEVINE, Daniel (M)   0   0
b.Dublin 8-5-93
Honours: From Scholar

| 2009–10 | Aston Villa | 0 | 0 | | |

DOWNING, Stewart (M)   213   22
H: 5 11 W: 10 04 b.Middlesbrough 22-7-84
Source: Scholar. *Honours:* England Youth, Under-21, B, 23 full caps.

2001–02	Middlesbrough	3	0		
2002–03	Middlesbrough	2	0		
2003–04	Middlesbrough	20	0		
2003–04	*Sunderland*	7	3	7	3
2004–05	Middlesbrough	35	5		
2005–06	Middlesbrough	12	1		
2006–07	Middlesbrough	34	2		
2007–08	Middlesbrough	38	9		
2008–09	Middlesbrough	37	0	181	17
2009–10	Aston Villa	25	2	25	2

DUNNE, Richard (D)   391   11
H: 6 2 W: 15 10 b.Dublin 21-9-79
Source: Trainee. *Honours:* Eire Schools, Youth, Under-21, B, 58 full caps, 7 goals.

1996–97	Everton	7	0		
1997–98	Everton	3	0		
1998–99	Everton	16	0		
1999–2000	Everton	31	0		
2000–01	Everton	3	0	60	0
2000–01	Manchester C	25	0		
2001–02	Manchester C	43	1		
2002–03	Manchester C	25	0		
2003–04	Manchester C	29	0		
2004–05	Manchester C	35	2		
2005–06	Manchester C	32	3		
2006–07	Manchester C	38	1		
2007–08	Manchester C	36	0		
2008–09	Manchester C	31	1		
2009–10	Manchester C	2	0	296	8
2009–10	Aston Villa	35	3	35	3

FORRESTER, Harry (F)   0   0
H: 5 9 W: 11 03 b.Milton Keynes 2-1-91

2007–08	Aston Villa	0	0		
2008–09	Aston Villa	0	0		
2009–10	Aston Villa	0	0		

FRIEDEL, Brad (G)   427   1
H: 6 3 W: 14 00 b.Lakewood 18-5-71
Honours: USA 82 full caps.

1996	Columbus Crew	9	0		
1997	Columbus Crew	29	0	38	0
1997–98	Liverpool	11	0		
1998–99	Liverpool	12	0		
1999–2000	Liverpool	2	0		
2000–01	Liverpool	0	0	25	0
2000–01	Blackburn R	27	0		
2001–02	Blackburn R	36	0		
2002–03	Blackburn R	37	0		
2003–04	Blackburn R	36	1		
2004–05	Blackburn R	38	0		
2005–06	Blackburn R	38	0		
2006–07	Blackburn R	38	0		
2007–08	Blackburn R	38	0	288	1
2008–09	Aston Villa	38	0		
2009–10	Aston Villa	38	0	76	0

GARDNER, Gary (M)   0   0
b.Solihull 29-6-92
Source: Scholar. *Honours:* England Youth, Under-20.

| 2009–10 | Aston Villa | 0 | 0 | | |

GUZAN, Brad (G)   80   0
H: 6 4 W: 14 11 b.Chicago 9-9-84
Honours: USA 16 full caps.

2005	Chivas USA	24	0		
2006	Chivas USA	13	0		
2007	Chivas USA	27	0		
2008	Chivas USA	15	0	79	0
2008–09	Aston Villa	1	0		
2009–10	Aston Villa	0	0	1	0

HALFHUID, Arsenio (D)   0   0
H: 6 2 W: b.Voorburg 9-11-91
Source: Excelsior.

| 2008–09 | Aston Villa | 0 | 0 | | |
| 2009–10 | Aston Villa | 0 | 0 | | |

HAREWOOD, Marlon (F)   379 109
H: 6 1 W: 13 07 b.Hampstead 25-8-79
Source: Trainee.

1996–97	Nottingham F	0	0		
1997–98	Nottingham F	0	0		
1998–99	Nottingham F	23	1		
1998–99	*Ipswich T*	6	1	6	1
1999–2000	Nottingham F	34	4		
2000–01	Nottingham F	33	3		
2001–02	Nottingham F	28	11		
2002–03	Nottingham F	44	20		
2003–04	Nottingham F	19	12	182	51
2003–04	West Ham U	28	13		
2004–05	West Ham U	45	17		
2005–06	West Ham U	37	14		
2006–07	West Ham U	32	3	142	47
2007–08	Aston Villa	23	5		
2008–09	Aston Villa	6	0		
2008–09	*Wolverhampton W*	5	0	5	0
2009–10	Aston Villa	0	0	29	5
2009–10	*Newcastle U*	15	5	15	5

HERD, Chris (M)   35   6
H: 5 9 W: 11 04 b.Melbourne 4-4-89
Source: Scholar.

2007–08	Aston Villa	0	0		
2007–08	*Port Vale*	11	2	11	2
2007–08	*Wycombe W*	4	0	4	0
2008–09	Aston Villa	0	0		
2009–10	Aston Villa	0	0		
2009–10	*Lincoln C*	20	4	20	4

HESKEY, Emile (F)   499 113
H: 6 2 W: 13 12 b.Leicester 11-1-78
Source: Trainee. *Honours:* England Youth, Under-21, B, 62 full caps, 7 goals.

1994–95	Leicester C	1	0		
1995–96	Leicester C	30	7		
1996–97	Leicester C	35	10		
1997–98	Leicester C	35	10		
1998–99	Leicester C	30	6		
1999–2000	Leicester C	23	7	154	40
1999–2000	Liverpool	12	3		
2000–01	Liverpool	36	14		

2001–02	Liverpool	35	9		
2002–03	Liverpool	32	6		
2003–04	Liverpool	35	7	150	39
2004–05	Birmingham C	34	10		
2005–06	Birmingham C	34	4	68	14
2006–07	Wigan Ath	34	8		
2007–08	Wigan Ath	28	4		
2008–09	Wigan Ath	20	3	82	15
2008–09	Aston Villa	14	2		
2009–10	Aston Villa	31	3	45	5

HOGG, Jonathan (M) 5 1
H: 5 7 W: 10 05 b.Middlesbrough 6-12-88
Source: Scholar.

2007–08	Aston Villa	0	0		
2008–09	Aston Villa	0	0		
2009–10	Aston Villa	0	0		
2009–10	*Darlington*	5	1	5	1

LICHAJ, Eric (M) 15 1
H: 5 11 W: 12 07 b.Denwers Grove 17-11-88
Source: Univ of North Carolina, Chicago Magic.

2007–08	Aston Villa	0	0		
2008–09	Aston Villa	0	0		
2009–10	Aston Villa	0	0		
2009–10	*Lincoln C*	6	0	6	0
2009–10	*Leyton Orient*	9	1	9	1

LOWRY, Shane (D) 24 0
H: 6 1 W: 13 01 b.Perth 12-6-89
Source: Scholar. *Honours:* Eire Under-21.

2007–08	Aston Villa	0	0		
2008–09	Aston Villa	0	0		
2009–10	Aston Villa	0	0		
2009–10	*Plymouth Arg*	13	0	13	0
2009–10	*Leeds U*	11	0	11	0

MILNER, James (M) 247 24
H: 5 9 W: 11 00 b.Leeds 4-1-86
Source: Trainee. *Honours:* FA Schools, Youth, England Under-20, Under-21, 11 full caps.

2002–03	Leeds U	18	2		
2003–04	Leeds U	30	3	48	5
2003–04	Swindon T	6	2	6	2
2004–05	Newcastle U	25	1		
2005–06	Newcastle U	3	0		
2005–06	*Aston Villa*	27	1		
2006–07	Newcastle U	35	3		
2007–08	Newcastle U	29	2		
2008–09	Newcastle U	2	0	94	6
2008–09	Aston Villa	36	3		
2009–10	Aston Villa	36	7	99	11

O'HALLORAN, Stephen (D) 14 0
H: 6 0 W: 11 07 b.Cork 29-11-87
Source: Scholar. *Honours:* Eire Under-21, 2 full caps.

2005–06	Aston Villa	0	0		
2006–07	Aston Villa	0	0		
2006–07	*Wycombe W*	11	0	11	0
2007–08	Aston Villa	0	0		
2007–08	*Southampton*	1	0	1	0
2008–09	Aston Villa	0	0		
2008–09	*Swansea C*	2	0	2	0
2009–10	Aston Villa	0	0		

OSBOURNE, Isaiah (M) 36 0
H: 6 2 W: 12 07 b.Birmingham 5-11-87
Source: Scholar.

2005–06	Aston Villa	0	0		
2006–07	Aston Villa	11	0		
2007–08	Aston Villa	8	0		
2008–09	Aston Villa	0	0		
2008–09	*Nottingham F*	8	0	8	0
2009–10	Aston Villa	0	0	19	0
2009–10	*Middlesbrough*	9	0	9	0

PARISH, Elliot (G) 0 0
H: 6 2 W: 13 00 b.Northampton 20-5-90
Source: Scholar. *Honours:* England Youth, Under-20.

2008–09	Aston Villa	0	0		
2009–10	Aston Villa	0	0		

PETROV, Stilian (M) 397 60
H: 5 11 W: 11 09 b.Sofia 5-7-79
Source: FC Montana. *Honours:* Bulgaria 94 full caps, 8 goals.

1997–98	CSKA Sofia	10	0		
1998–99	CSKA Sofia	29	3	39	3
1999–2000	Celtic	29	2		
2000–01	Celtic	28	7		
2001–02	Celtic	27	6		
2002–03	Celtic	34	12		
2003–04	Celtic	35	6		
2004–05	Celtic	37	11		
2005–06	Celtic	37	13	227	53
2006–07	Aston Villa	30	2		
2007–08	Aston Villa	28	1		
2008–09	Aston Villa	36	1		
2009–10	Aston Villa	37	0	131	4

REO-COKER, Nigel (M) 250 18
H: 5 8 W: 12 03 b.Southwark 14-5-84
Source: Scholar. *Honours:* England Youth, Under-20, Under-21.

2001–02	Wimbledon	1	0		
2002–03	Wimbledon	32	2		
2003–04	Wimbledon	32	4	58	6
2003–04	West Ham U	15	2		
2004–05	West Ham U	39	3		
2005–06	West Ham U	31	5		
2006–07	West Ham U	35	1	120	11
2007–08	Aston Villa	36	0		
2008–09	Aston Villa	26	1		
2009–10	Aston Villa	10	0	72	1

SALIFOU, Moustapha (M) 67 3
H: 5 11 W: 10 12 b.Lome 1-6-83
Source: Modele de Lome. *Honours:* Togo 46 full caps, 6 goals.

2002–03	Oberhausen	11	1		
2003–04	Oberhausen	6	0		
2004–05	Oberhausen	16	0	33	1
2005–06	Stade Brest	7	0	7	0
2006–07	FC Wil	19	2		
2007–08	FC Wil	4	0	23	2
2007–08	Aston Villa	4	0		
2008–09	Aston Villa	0	0		
2009–10	Aston Villa	0	0	4	0

SHOREY, Nicky (D) 324 12
H: 5 9 W: 10 08 b.Romford 19-2-81
Source: Trainee. *Honours:* England B, 2 full caps.

1999–2000	Leyton Orient	7	0		
2000–01	Leyton Orient	8	0	15	0
2000–01	Reading	0	0		
2001–02	Reading	32	0		
2002–03	Reading	43	2		
2003–04	Reading	35	2		
2004–05	Reading	44	3		
2005–06	Reading	40	2		
2006–07	Reading	37	1		
2007–08	Reading	36	2	267	12
2008–09	Aston Villa	21	0		
2009–10	Aston Villa	3	0	24	0
2009–10	*Nottingham F*	9	0	9	0
2009–10	*Fulham*	9	0	9	0

SIDWELL, Steve (M) 266 41
H: 5 10 W: 11 00 b.Wandsworth 14-12-82
Source: Scholar. *Honours:* England Under-20, Under-21.

2001–02	Arsenal	0	0		
2001–02	*Brentford*	30	4	30	4
2002–03	Arsenal	0	0		
2002–03	*Brighton & HA*	12	5	12	5
2002–03	Reading	13	2		
2003–04	Reading	43	8		
2004–05	Reading	44	5		
2005–06	Reading	33	10		
2006–07	Reading	35	4	168	29
2007–08	Chelsea	15	0	15	0
2008–09	Aston Villa	16	3		
2009–10	Aston Villa	25	0	41	3

SIEGRIST, Benjamin (G) 0 0
H: 6 4 W: 13 05 b.Basle 31-1-92
Source: Scholar.

2008–09	Aston Villa	0	0		
2009–10	Aston Villa	0	0		

WARNOCK, Stephen (D) 214 10
H: 5 7 W: 11 09 b.Ormskirk 12-12-81
Source: Trainee. *Honours:* England Schools, Youth, 1 full cap.

1998–99	Liverpool	0	0		
1999–2000	Liverpool	0	0		
2000–01	Liverpool	0	0		
2001–02	Liverpool	0	0		
2002–03	Liverpool	0	0		
2002–03	*Bradford C*	12	1	12	1
2003–04	Liverpool	0	0		
2003–04	*Coventry C*	44	3	44	3
2004–05	Liverpool	19	0		
2005–06	Liverpool	20	1		
2006–07	Liverpool	1	0	40	1
2006–07	Blackburn R	13	1		
2007–08	Blackburn R	37	1		
2008–09	Blackburn R	37	3		
2009–10	Blackburn R	1	0	88	5
2009–10	Aston Villa	30	0	30	0

WEIMANN, Andreas (F) 0 0
H: 5 9 W: 11 09 b.Vienna 5-8-91
Source: Scholar.

2008–09	Aston Villa	0	0		
2009–10	Aston Villa	0	0		

WILLIAMS, Derrick (D) 0 0
b.Germany 17-1-93
Source: Scholar.

2009–10	Aston Villa	0	0		

YOUNG, Ashley (M) 221 42
H: 5 10 W: 10 03 b.Stevenage 9-7-85
Source: Juniors. *Honours:* England Under-21, 7 full caps.

2002–03	Watford	0	0		
2003–04	Watford	5	3		
2004–05	Watford	34	0		
2005–06	Watford	39	13		
2006–07	Watford	20	3	98	19
2006–07	Aston Villa	13	2		
2007–08	Aston Villa	37	9		
2008–09	Aston Villa	36	7		
2009–10	Aston Villa	37	5	123	23

YOUNG, Luke (D) 330 6
H: 6 0 W: 12 04 b.Harlow 19-7-79
Source: Trainee. *Honours:* England Youth, Under-21, 7 full caps.

1997–98	Tottenham H	0	0		
1998–99	Tottenham H	15	0		
1999–2000	Tottenham H	20	0		
2000–01	Tottenham H	23	0	58	0
2001–02	Charlton Ath	34	0		
2002–03	Charlton Ath	32	0		
2003–04	Charlton Ath	24	0		
2004–05	Charlton Ath	36	2		
2005–06	Charlton Ath	32	1		
2006–07	Charlton Ath	29	1	187	4
2007–08	Middlesbrough	31	1	35	1
2008–09	Aston Villa	34	1		
2009–10	Aston Villa	16	0	50	1

Scholars
Berry, Durrell Joel; Cameron, Courtney Lee; Carruthers, Samir Badre; Deeney, Ellis John Paul; Flanagan, Calum Ress; Johnson, Daniel Anthony; Lampkin, Jason Severiano; Nelson-Addy, Ebby; Stieber, Andras; Taylor, Connor; Ward, Charles Patrick.

BARNET (5)

ADOMAH, Albert (F) 112 19
H: 6 1 W: 11 08 b.Harrow 13-12-87
Source: Harrow Borough.

2007–08	Barnet	22	5		
2008–09	Barnet	45	9		
2009–10	Barnet	45	5	112	19

BREEN, Gary (D) 552 13
H: 6 3 W: 13 03 b.Hendon 12-12-73
Source: Charlton Ath. *Honours:* Eire Under-21, 63 full caps, 7 goals.

1991–92	Maidstone U	19	0	19	0
1992–93	Gillingham	29	0		
1993–94	Gillingham	22	0	51	0
1994–95	Peterborough U	44	1		
1995–96	Peterborough U	25	0	69	1
1995–96	Birmingham C	18	1		
1996–97	Birmingham C	22	1	40	2
1996–97	Coventry C	9	0		
1997–98	Coventry C	30	1		
1998–99	Coventry C	25	0		
1999–2000	Coventry C	21	0		
2000–01	Coventry C	31	1		
2001–02	Coventry C	30	0	146	2
2002–03	West Ham U	14	0	14	0
2003–04	Sunderland	32	4		
2004–05	Sunderland	40	2		

2005–06	Sunderland	35	1	107	7
2006–07	Wolverhampton W	40	1		
2007–08	Wolverhampton W	19	0	59	1
2008–09	Barnet	22	0		
2009–10	Barnet	25	0	47	0

CHARLES, Elliott (F)   8 0
H: 6 2 W: 13 00 b.Enfield 23-12-90
Source: Scholar.

2008–09	Barnet	5	0		
2009–10	Barnet	3	0	8	0

COLE, Jake (G)   62 0
H: 6 2 W: 13 00 b.Hammersmith 11-9-85
Source: Scholar.

2005–06	QPR	3	0		
2006–07	QPR	3	0		
2007–08	QPR	0	0		
2008–09	QPR	0	0	6	0
2008–09	Barnet	10	0		
2009–10	Barnet	46	0	56	0

DEEN, Ahmed (M)   49 1
H: 5 9 W: 11 05 b.Sierra Leone 30-6-85
Source: Leicester C Scholar. Honours: Sierra Leone 10 full caps.

2004–05	Peterborough U	5	0	5	0

From Aldershot T, St Albans C.

2008–09	Macclesfield T	28	0		
2009–10	Macclesfield T	0	0	28	0
2009–10	Barnet	16	1	16	1

DEVERA, Joe (D)   134 1
H: 6 2 W: 12 00 b.Southgate 6-2-87

2005–06	Barnet	0	0		
2006–07	Barnet	26	0		
2007–08	Barnet	41	0		
2008–09	Barnet	34	1		
2009–10	Barnet	33	0	134	1

DEVERDICS, Nicky (M)   76 5
H: 5 11 W: 12 04 b.Gateshead 24-11-87
Source: Newcastle U Scholar, Gateshead.

2006–07	Gretna	6	1		
2007–08	Gretna	25	2	31	3
2008–09	Barnet	29	1		
2009–10	Barnet	16	1	45	2

FURLONG, Paul (F)   580 185
H: 6 0 W: 13 11 b.Wood Green 1-10-68
Source: Enfield.

1991–92	Coventry C	37	4	37	4
1992–93	Watford	41	19		
1993–94	Watford	38	18	79	37
1994–95	Chelsea	36	10		
1995–96	Chelsea	28	3	64	13
1996–97	Birmingham C	43	10		
1997–98	Birmingham C	25	15		
1998–99	Birmingham C	29	13		
1999–2000	Birmingham C	19	11		
2000–01	Birmingham C	4	0		
2000–01	*QPR*	3	1		
2001–02	Birmingham C	11	1		
2001–02	*Sheffield U*	4	2	4	2
2002–03	Birmingham C	0	0	131	50
2002–03	QPR	33	13		
2003–04	QPR	36	16		
2004–05	QPR	40	18		
2005–06	QPR	37	7		
2006–07	QPR	22	2	171	57
2007–08	Luton T	32	8	32	8
2008–09	Southend U	3	0	3	0
2008–09	*Barnet*	21	9		
2009–10	Barnet	38	5	59	14

GILLET, Kenny (M)   100 0
H: 5 10 W: 12 04 b.Bordeaux 3-1-86
Source: Caen.

2007–08	Barnet	31	0		
2008–09	Barnet	32	0		
2009–10	Barnet	37	0	100	0

HART, Danny (M)   6 1
H: 5 10 W: 11 09 b.London 26-4-89
Source: Boreham Wood.

2007–08	Barnet	2	0		
2008–09	Barnet	3	1		
2009–10	Barnet	1	0	6	1

HUGHES, Mark (M)   184 8
H: 5 10 W: 12 05 b.Dungannon 16-9-83
Source: Scholar. Honours: Northern Ireland Schools, Youth, Under-21, Under-23, 2 full caps.

2001–02	Tottenham H	0	0		
2002–03	Tottenham H	0	0		
2003–04	Tottenham H	0	0		
2004–05	Tottenham H	0	0		
2004–05	*Northampton T*	3	0	3	0
2004–05	*Oldham Ath*	27	0		
2005–06	Oldham Ath	33	1		
2006–07	Oldham Ath	0	0	60	1

From Thurrock.

2006–07	Chesterfield	2	1	2	1

From Stevenage B.

2007–08	Chester C	43	4		
2008–09	Chester C	26	0	69	4
2008–09	Barnet	9	0		
2009–10	Barnet	41	2	50	2

HYDE, Jake (F)   34 6
H: 6 1 W: 12 02 b.Maidenhead 1-7-90
Source: Scholar.

2007–08	Swindon T	0	0		
2008–09	Swindon T	0	0		
2009–10	Barnet	34	6	34	6

HYDE, Micah (M)   567 39
H: 5 10 W: 11 02 b.Newham 10-11-74
Source: Trainee. Honours: Jamaica 16 full caps, 1 goal.

1993–94	Cambridge U	18	2		
1994–95	Cambridge U	27	0		
1995–96	Cambridge U	24	4		
1996–97	Cambridge U	38	7	107	13
1997–98	Watford	40	4		
1998–99	Watford	44	2		
1999–2000	Watford	34	3		
2000–01	Watford	26	6		
2001–02	Watford	39	4		
2002–03	Watford	37	4		
2003–04	Watford	33	1	253	24
2004–05	Burnley	38	1		
2005–06	Burnley	41	0		
2006–07	Burnley	23	0	102	1
2006–07	Peterborough U	18	0		
2007–08	Peterborough U	37	0		
2008–09	Peterborough U	9	0	64	0
2009–10	Barnet	41	1	41	1

JAMES, Chris (M)   23 5
H: 5 11 W: 10 12 b.Wellington 4-7-87
Source: Fulham. Honours: England Youth, New Zealand Under-20, 12 full caps.

2008	Tampere U	19	4	19	4
2008	*TPV*	1	0	1	0
2008	*Ilves*	1	1	1	1
2009–10	Barnet	2	0	2	0

JARRETT, Albert (M)   110 5
H: 6 1 W: 10 07 b.Sierra Leone 23-10-84
Source: Dulwich Hamlet. Honours: Sierra Leone 5 full caps.

2003–04	Wimbledon	0	0		
2003–04	Wimbledon	9	0	9	0
2004–05	Brighton & HA	12	1		
2005–06	Brighton & HA	11	0	23	1
2005–06	*Swindon T*	6	0	6	0
2006–07	Watford	1	0		
2006–07	*Boston U*	5	2	5	2
2006–07	*Milton Keynes D*	5	0	5	0
2007–08	Watford	0	0		
2008–09	Watford	0	0	1	0
2008–09	Gillingham	16	0	16	0
2009–10	Barnet	45	2	45	2

KAMDJO, Clovis (D)   15 0
H: 5 11 W: 12 02 b.Cameroon 15-12-90
Source: Reading Youth. Honours: Cameroon Youth.

2009–10	Barnet	15	0	15	0

LEACH, Daniel (D)   13 0
H: 6 3 W: 12 10 b.Redcliffe 5-1-86
Source: Queensland Academy, Brisbane Toro, Brisbane Strikers, Oregon State Univ, Portland Timbers.

2009–10	Barnet	13	0	13	0

LIVERMORE, David (M)   366 19
H: 5 11 W: 12 02 b.Edmonton 20-5-80
Source: Trainee.

1998–99	Arsenal	0	0		
1999–2000	Millwall	32	2		
2000–01	Millwall	39	3		
2001–02	Millwall	43	0		
2002–03	Millwall	41	2		
2003–04	Millwall	36	1		
2004–05	Millwall	41	2		
2005–06	Millwall	41	2	273	12
2006–07	Hull C	25	4		
2007–08	Hull C	20	1	45	5
2007–08	*Oldham Ath*	10	1	10	1
2008–09	Brighton & HA	16	0		
2008–09	*Luton T*	8	0	8	0
2009–10	Brighton & HA	0	0	16	0
2009–10	Barnet	14	1	14	1

LOCKHART-ADAMS, Kofi (F)   1 0
H: 12 13 b.London 9-10-92
Source: Scholar.

2009–10	Barnet	1	0	1	0

MEDLEY, Luke (F)   28 3
H: 6 1 W: 13 03 b.Greenwich 21-6-89
Source: Tottenham H Scholar.

2007–08	Bradford C	9	2	9	2
2008–09	Barnet	18	1		
2009–10	Barnet	1	0	19	1

O'FLYNN, John (F)   70 29
H: 5 11 W: 11 11 b.Cobh 11-7-82
Source: Peterborough U Scholar, Cork C. Honours: Eire Under-21.

2008–09	Barnet	34	17		
2009–10	Barnet	36	12	70	29

O'NEILL, Ryan (D)   15 0
H: 6 0 W: 12 13 b.Dungannon 19-1-91
Source: Scholar.

2007–08	West Ham U	0	0		
2008–09	West Ham U	0	0		
2009–10	Barnet	15	0	15	0

SAWYER, Lee (M)   36 3
H: 5 10 W: 10 03 b.Leytonstone 10-9-89
Source: Scholar. Honours: England Youth.

2007–08	Chelsea	0	0		
2008–09	Chelsea	0	0		
2008–09	*Southend U*	12	1		
2008–09	*Coventry C*	2	0	2	0
2008–09	*Wycombe W*	9	1	9	1
2009–10	Chelsea	0	0		
2009–10	*Southend U*	6	0	18	1
2009–10	Barnet	7	1	7	1

TABIRI, Joe (M)   12 0
H: 5 9 W: 11 09 b.Kingsbury 16-10-89

2008–09	Barnet	7	0		
2009–10	Barnet	5	0	12	0

VILHETE, Mauro (M)   2 0
H: 5 8 W: 11 09 b.Rio de Mauro 10-5-93
Source: Scholar.

2009–10	Barnet	2	0	2	0

YAKUBU, Ismail (D)   146 9
H: 6 1 W: 13 09 b.Kano 8-4-85
Source: Trainee.

2005–06	Barnet	26	1		
2006–07	Barnet	29	1		
2007–08	Barnet	28	2		
2008–09	Barnet	38	3		
2009–10	Barnet	25	2	146	9

BARNSLEY (6)

ADAM, Jamil (M)   3 0
H: 5 10 W: 10 00 b.Bolton 5-6-91
Source: Scholar.

2007–08	Barnsley	1	0		
2008–09	Barnsley	0	0		
2009–10	Barnsley	2	0	3	0

ANDERSON (M)   156 9
H: 6 2 W: 12 11 b.Sao Paulo 29-8-82
Honours: Brazil 4 full caps.

2003	Santiago Wanderers	18	2	18	2
2003–04	Santander	8	0		
2004–05	Santander	30	2	38	2

2005–06	Malaga	15	0	15	0
2006–07	Everton	1	0		
2007–08	Everton	0	0	1	0
2007–08	Barnsley	20	0		
2008–09	Barnsley	33	2		
2009–10	Barnsley	31	3	84	5

BOGDANOVIC, Daniel (F) 45 16
H: 6 2 W: 11 02 b.Misurata 26-3-80
Source: Sliema W, Naxxar Lions, Valletta, Marsaxlokk, Cisco Roma, Lokomotiv Sofia.
Honours: Malta 27 full caps, 1 goal.

2008–09	Barnsley	16	5		
2009–10	Barnsley	29	11	45	16

BUTTERFIELD, Jacob (D) 26 1
H: 5 10 W: 11 00 b.Manchester 10-6-90
Source: Scholar.

2007–08	Barnsley	3	0		
2008–09	Barnsley	3	0		
2009–10	Barnsley	20	1	26	1

COLACE, Roberto (M) 75 7
H: 5 10 W: 11 07 b.Buenos Aires 6-1-84
Honours: Argentina Youth.

2008–09	Barnsley	34	0		
2009–10	Barnsley	41	7	75	7

COULSON, Michael (F) 45 5
H: 5 10 W: 10 00 b.Scarborough 4-4-88
Source: Scarborough.

2006–07	Barnsley	2	0		
2007–08	Barnsley	12	0		
2008–09	Barnsley	2	0		
2009–10	Barnsley	0	0	16	0
2009–10	*Grimsby T*	29	5	29	5

DEVANEY, Martin (M) 358 53
H: 5 11 W: 12 00 b.Cheltenham 1-6-80
Source: Trainee.

1997–98	Coventry C	0	0		
1998–99	Coventry C	0	0		
1999–2000	Cheltenham T	26	6		
2000–01	Cheltenham T	34	10		
2001–02	Cheltenham T	25	1		
2002–03	Cheltenham T	40	6		
2003–04	Cheltenham T	40	5		
2004–05	Cheltenham T	38	10	203	38
2005–06	Watford	0	0		
2005–06	Barnsley	38	6		
2006–07	Barnsley	41	5		
2007–08	Barnsley	34	4		
2008–09	Barnsley	26	0		
2009–10	Barnsley	11	0	150	15
2009–10	*Milton Keynes D*	5	0	5	0

DOYLE, Nathan (M) 88 0
H: 5 11 W: 12 06 b.Derby 12-1-87
Source: Scholar. *Honours:* England Youth, Under-20.

2003–04	Derby Co	2	0		
2004–05	Derby Co	3	0		
2005–06	Derby Co	4	0		
2005–06	*Notts Co*	12	0	12	0
2006–07	Derby Co	0	0	9	0
2006–07	*Bradford C*	28	0	28	0
2006–07	Hull C	1	0		
2007–08	Hull C	1	0		
2008–09	Hull C	3	0		
2009–10	Hull C	0	0	5	0
2009–10	Barnsley	34	0	34	0

EL HAIMOUR, Mounir (M) 80 13
H: 5 9 W: 10 03 b.Limoges 29-10-80

2000–01	Chatellerault	0	0		
2001–02	Chatellerault	0	0		
2002–03	Champagne Sports	22	12	22	12
2003–04	Yverdon	0	0		
2004	*Alania*	9	0	9	0
2004–05	Yverdon	0	0		
2005–06	Yverdon	0	0		
2006–07	Schaffhausen	26	1	26	1
2006–07	*Chateauroux*	1	0	1	0
2007–08	Neuchatel Xamax	4	0	4	0
2008–09	Barnsley	16	0		
2009–10	Barnsley	2	0	18	0

FOSTER, Stephen (D) 356 21
H: 6 0 W: 11 05 b.Warrington 10-9-80
Source: Trainee. *Honours:* England Schools.

1998–99	Crewe Alex	1	0		
1999–2000	Crewe Alex	0	0		
2000–01	Crewe Alex	30	0		

2001–02	Crewe Alex	34	5		
2002–03	Crewe Alex	35	4		
2003–04	Crewe Alex	45	2		
2004–05	Crewe Alex	34	1		
2005–06	Crewe Alex	39	3	218	15
2006–07	Burnley	17	0		
2007–08	Burnley	0	0	17	0
2007–08	Barnsley	41	1		
2008–09	Barnsley	38	3		
2009–10	Barnsley	42	2	121	6

GRAY, Andy (F) 401 91
H: 6 1 W: 13 00 b.Harrogate 15-11-77
Source: Trainee. *Honours:* Scotland Youth, B, 2 full caps.

1995–96	Leeds U	15	0		
1996–97	Leeds U	7	0		
1997–98	Leeds U	0	0		
1997–98	*Bury*	6	1	6	1
1998–99	Leeds U	0	0	22	0
1998–99	Nottingham F	8	0		
1998–99	*Preston NE*	5	0	5	0
1998–99	*Oldham Ath*	4	0	4	0
1999–2000	Nottingham F	22	0		
2000–01	Nottingham F	18	0		
2001–02	Nottingham F	16	1	64	1
2002–03	Bradford C	44	15		
2003–04	Bradford C	33	5	77	20
2003–04	Sheffield U	14	9		
2004–05	Sheffield U	43	15		
2005–06	Sheffield U	1	1	58	25
2005–06	Sunderland	21	1	21	1
2005–06	Burnley	9	3		
2006–07	Burnley	35	14		
2007–08	Burnley	25	11	69	28
2007–08	Charlton Ath	16	2		
2008–09	Charlton Ath	27	7		
2009–10	Charlton Ath	2	0	45	9
2009–10	Barnsley	30	6	30	6

HALLFREDSSON, Emil (M) 95 13
H: 6 1 W: 13 01 b.Iceland 29-6-84
Honours: Iceland Under-21, 29 full caps,1 goal.

2004	FH	16	4	16	4
2004–05	Tottenham H	0	0		
2005–06	Tottenham H	0	0		
2006	*Malmo*	19	5	19	5
2006–07	Tottenham H	0	0		
2007	*Lyn*	1	0	1	0
2007–08	*Reggina*	32	1	32	1

On loan from Reggina.

2009–10	Barnsley	27	3	27	3

HAMMILL, Adam (M) 113 7
H: 5 11 W: 11 07 b.Liverpool 25-1-88
Source: Scholar. *Honours:* England Youth.

2005–06	Liverpool	0	0		
2006–07	Liverpool	0	0		
2006–07	*Dunfermline Ath*	13	1	13	1
2007–08	Liverpool	0	0		
2007–08	*Southampton*	25	0	25	0
2008–09	Liverpool	0	0		
2008–09	*Blackpool*	22	1	22	1
2008–09	*Barnsley*	14	1		
2009–10	Liverpool	0	0		
2009–10	Barnsley	39	4	53	5

HASSELL, Bobby (D) 350 8
H: 5 10 W: 12 00 b.Derby 4-6-80
Source: Trainee.

1997–98	Mansfield T	9	0		
1998–99	Mansfield T	3	0		
1999–2000	Mansfield T	11	1		
2000–01	Mansfield T	40	1		
2001–02	Mansfield T	43	1		
2002–03	Mansfield T	20	0		
2003–04	Mansfield T	34	0	160	3
2004–05	Barnsley	39	0		
2005–06	Barnsley	28	2		
2006–07	Barnsley	39	2		
2007–08	Barnsley	20	0		
2008–09	Barnsley	40	0		
2009–10	Barnsley	24	1	190	5

HUME, Iain (F) 322 74
H: 5 7 W: 11 02 b.Brampton 31-10-83
Source: Juniors. *Honours:* Canada Youth, Under-20, 28 full caps, 2 goals.

1999–2000	Tranmere R	3	0		
2000–01	Tranmere R	10	0		

2001–02	Tranmere R	14	0		
2002–03	Tranmere R	35	6		
2003–04	Tranmere R	40	10		
2004–05	Tranmere R	42	15		
2005–06	Tranmere R	6	1	150	32
2005–06	Leicester C	37	9		
2006–07	Leicester C	45	13		
2007–08	Leicester C	40	11	122	33
2008–09	Barnsley	15	4		
2009–10	Barnsley	35	5	50	9

KOZLUK, Rob (D) 319 2
H: 5 8 W: 10 02 b.Mansfield 5-8-77
Source: Trainee. *Honours:* England Under-21.

1995–96	Derby Co	0	0		
1996–97	Derby Co	0	0		
1997–98	Derby Co	9	0		
1998–99	Derby Co	7	0	16	0
1998–99	Sheffield U	10	0		
1999–2000	Sheffield U	39	0		
2000–01	Sheffield U	27	0		
2000–01	*Huddersfield T*	14	0	14	0
2001–02	Sheffield U	8	0		
2002–03	Sheffield U	32	1		
2003–04	Sheffield U	42	1		
2004–05	Sheffield U	9	0		
2004–05	*Preston NE*	1	0	1	0
2005–06	Sheffield U	27	0		
2006–07	Sheffield U	19	0	213	2
2007–08	Barnsley	24	0		
2008–09	Barnsley	37	0		
2009–10	Barnsley	14	0	75	0

MACKEN, Jon (F) 390 80
H: 5 11 W: 12 04 b.Manchester 7-9-77
Source: Trainee. *Honours:* England Youth. Eire 1 full cap.

1996–97	Manchester U	0	0		
1997–98	Preston NE	29	6		
1998–99	Preston NE	42	8		
1999–2000	Preston NE	44	22		
2000–01	Preston NE	38	19		
2001–02	Preston NE	31	8	184	63
2001–02	Manchester C	8	5		
2002–03	Manchester C	5	0		
2003–04	Manchester C	15	1		
2004–05	Manchester C	23	1	51	7
2005–06	Crystal Palace	24	2		
2006–07	Crystal Palace	1	0	25	2
2006–07	*Ipswich T*	14	4	14	4
2006–07	Derby Co	8	0		
2007–08	Derby Co	3	0	11	0
2007–08	Barnsley	29	7		
2008–09	Barnsley	45	9		
2009–10	Barnsley	31	4	105	20

MOORE, Darren (D) 557 31
H: 6 2 W: 15 07 b.Birmingham 22-4-74
Source: Trainee. *Honours:* Jamaica 3 full caps.

1991–92	Torquay U	5	1		
1992–93	Torquay U	31	2		
1993–94	Torquay U	37	2		
1994–95	Torquay U	30	3	103	8
1995–96	Doncaster R	35	2		
1996–97	Doncaster R	41	5	76	7
1997–98	Bradford C	18	0		
1998–99	Bradford C	44	3		
1999–2000	Bradford C	0	0	62	3
1999–2000	Portsmouth	10	1		
2000–01	Portsmouth	32	1		
2001–02	Portsmouth	2	0	59	2
2001–02	WBA	32	2		
2002–03	WBA	29	2		
2003–04	WBA	22	2		
2004–05	WBA	16	0		
2005–06	WBA	5	0	104	6
2005–06	Derby Co	14	1		
2006–07	Derby Co	35	2		
2007–08	Derby Co	31	0	80	3
2008–09	Barnsley	38	1		
2009–10	Barnsley	35	1	73	2

NOBLE-LAZARUS, Reuben (F) 4 0
H: 5 11 W: 13 07 b.Huddersfield 16-8-93
Source: Youth.

2008–09	Barnsley	2	0		
2009–10	Barnsley	2	0	4	0

POTTER, Luke (D)   15   0
H: 6 2 W: 12 07 b.Barnsley 13-7-89
Source: Scholar.

2006–07	Barnsley	1	0	
2007–08	Barnsley	0	0	
2008–09	Barnsley	0	0	
2009–10	Barnsley	14	0	15 0

PREECE, David (G)   241   0
H: 6 2 W: 11 11 b.Sunderland 28-8-76
Source: Sunderland Scholar.

1994–95	Sunderland	0	0	
1995–96	Sunderland	0	0	
1996–97	Sunderland	0	0	
1997–98	Darlington	45	0	
1998–99	Darlington	46	0	91 0
1999–2000	Aberdeen	10	0	
2000–01	Aberdeen	2	0	
2001–02	Aberdeen	8	0	
2002–03	Aberdeen	16	0	
2003–04	Aberdeen	36	0	
2004–05	Aberdeen	17	0	89 0
2005–06	Silkeborg	32	0	
2006–07	Silkeborg	23	0	
2007–08	Silkeborg	0	0	55 0
2008–09	Odense	0	0	
2009–10	Barnsley	6	0	6 0

SODJE, Onome (F)   1   0
H: 6 0 W: 10 12 b.Warri 17-7-88
Source: Charlton Ath, Gravesend & N, York C.

2009–10	Barnsley	1	0	1 0

To Senica January 2010.

STEELE, Luke (G)   104   0
H: 6 2 W: 12 00 b.Peterborough 24-9-84
Source: Scholar. *Honours:* England Youth, Under-20.

2001–02	Peterborough U	2	0	2 0
2001–02	Manchester U	0	0	
2002–03	Manchester U	0	0	
2003–04	Manchester U	0	0	
2004–05	Manchester U	0	0	
2004–05	Coventry C	32	0	
2005–06	Manchester U	0	0	
2006–07	WBA	0	0	
2006–07	Coventry C	5	0	37 0
2007–08	WBA	2	0	2 0
2007–08	*Barnsley*	14	0	
2008–09	Barnsley	10	0	
2009–10	Barnsley	39	0	63 0

TAYLOR, Alistair (M)   1   0
H: 6 1 W: 10 06 b.Sheffield 13-9-91
Source: Scholar.

2009–10	Barnsley	1	0	1 0

THOMPSON, O'Neil (D)   49   0
H: 6 4 W: 13 00 b.Kingston 11-8-80
Source: Boys Town. *Honours:* Jamaica 21 full caps, 1 goal.

2007	Notodden	22	1	
2008	Notodden	14	0	
2009	Notodden	10	0	46 1
2009–10	Barnsley	1	0	1 0
2009–10	*Burton Alb*	2	0	2 0

BIRMINGHAM C (7)

BENITEZ, Christian (F)   171   63
H: 5 6 W: 10 12 b.Esmereldas 1-5-86
Honours: Ecuador 32 full caps, 10 goals.

2004	El Nacional	1	0	
2005	El Nacional	29	6	
2006	El Nacional	38	16	
2007–08	El Nacional	15	7	83 29
2007–08	Santos Laguna	40	17	
2008–09	Santos Laguna	18	14	58 31
2009–10	Birmingham C	30	3	30 3

BENT, Marcus (F)   475   93
H: 6 2 W: 13 03 b.Hammersmith 19-5-78
Source: Trainee. *Honours:* England Under-21.

1995–96	Brentford	12	1	
1996–97	Brentford	34	3	
1997–98	Brentford	24	4	70 8
1997–98	Crystal Palace	16	5	
1998–99	Crystal Palace	12	0	28 5
1998–99	Port Vale	15	0	
1999–2000	Port Vale	8	1	23 1
1999–2000	Sheffield U	32	15	
2000–01	Sheffield U	16	5	48 20
2000–01	Blackburn R	28	8	
2001–02	Blackburn R	9	0	37 8
2001–02	Ipswich T	25	9	
2002–03	Ipswich T	32	11	
2003–04	Ipswich T	4	1	61 21
2003–04	*Leicester C*	33	9	33 9
2004–05	Everton	37	6	
2005–06	Everton	18	1	55 7
2005–06	Charlton Ath	13	2	
2006–07	Charlton Ath	30	1	
2007–08	Charlton Ath	3	1	46 4
2007–08	Wigan Ath	31	7	31 7
2008–09	Birmingham C	33	3	
2009–10	Birmingham C	0	0	33 3
2009–10	*Middlesbrough*	7	0	7 0
2009–10	*QPR*	3	0	3 0

BOWYER, Lee (M)   431   62
H: 5 9 W: 10 12 b.Canning Town 3-1-77
Source: Trainee. *Honours:* England Youth, Under-21, 1 full cap.

1993–94	Charlton Ath	0	0	
1994–95	Charlton Ath	5	0	
1995–96	Charlton Ath	41	8	46 8
1996–97	Leeds U	32	4	
1997–98	Leeds U	25	3	
1998–99	Leeds U	35	9	
1999–2000	Leeds U	33	5	
2000–01	Leeds U	38	9	
2001–02	Leeds U	25	5	
2002–03	Leeds U	15	3	203 38
2002–03	West Ham U	10	0	
2003–04	Newcastle U	24	2	
2004–05	Newcastle U	27	3	
2005–06	Newcastle U	28	1	79 6
2006–07	West Ham U	20	0	
2007–08	West Ham U	15	4	
2008–09	West Ham U	6	0	51 4
2008–09	*Birmingham C*	17	1	
2009–10	Birmingham C	35	5	52 6

BUTLAND, Jack (G)   0   0
H: 6 4 W: 12 00 b.Clevedon 10-3-93
Source: Scholar. *Honours:* England Youth.

2009–10	Birmingham C	0	0

CARR, Stephen (D)   352   8
H: 5 9 W: 11 13 b.Dublin 29-8-76
Source: Trainee. *Honours:* Eire Schools, Youth, Under-21, 44 full caps.

1993–94	Tottenham H	1	0	
1994–95	Tottenham H	0	0	
1995–96	Tottenham H	0	0	
1996–97	Tottenham H	26	0	
1997–98	Tottenham H	38	0	
1998–99	Tottenham H	37	0	
1999–2000	Tottenham H	34	3	
2000–01	Tottenham H	28	3	
2001–02	Tottenham H	0	0	
2002–03	Tottenham H	30	0	
2003–04	Tottenham H	32	1	226 7
2004–05	Newcastle U	26	1	
2005–06	Newcastle U	19	0	
2006–07	Newcastle U	23	0	
2007–08	Newcastle U	10	0	
2008–09	Newcastle U	0	0	78 1
2008–09	Birmingham C	13	0	
2009–10	Birmingham C	35	0	48 0

CARSLEY, Lee (M)   445   33
H: 5 10 W: 12 04 b.Birmingham 28-2-74
Source: Trainee. *Honours:* Eire 39 full caps.

1992–93	Derby Co	0	0	
1993–94	Derby Co	0	0	
1994–95	Derby Co	23	2	
1995–96	Derby Co	35	1	
1996–97	Derby Co	24	0	
1997–98	Derby Co	34	1	
1998–99	Derby Co	22	1	138 5
1998–99	Blackburn R	8	0	
1999–2000	Blackburn R	30	10	
2000–01	Blackburn R	8	0	46 10
2000–01	Coventry C	21	2	
2001–02	Coventry C	26	2	47 4
2001–02	Everton	8	1	
2002–03	Everton	24	3	
2003–04	Everton	21	2	
2004–05	Everton	36	4	
2005–06	Everton	5	0	
2006–07	Everton	38	1	
2007–08	Everton	34	1	166 12
2008–09	Birmingham C	41	2	
2009–10	Birmingham C	7	0	48 2

DANN, Scott (D)   136   10
H: 6 2 W: 12 00 b.Liverpool 14-2-87
Source: Scholar. *Honours:* England Under-21.

2004–05	Walsall	1	0	
2005–06	Walsall	0	0	
2006–07	Walsall	30	4	
2007–08	Walsall	28	3	59 7
2007–08	Coventry C	16	0	
2008–09	Coventry C	31	3	47 3
2009–10	Birmingham C	30	0	30 0

DOYLE, Colin (G)   41   0
H: 6 5 W: 14 05 b.Cork 12-8-85
Honours: Eire Youth, Under-21, 1 full cap.

2004–05	Birmingham C	1	0	
2004–05	*Chester C*	0	0	
2004–05	*Nottingham F*	3	0	3 0
2005–06	Birmingham C	0	0	
2005–06	*Millwall*	14	0	14 0
2006–07	Birmingham C	19	0	
2007–08	Birmingham C	3	0	
2008–09	Birmingham C	2	0	
2009–10	Birmingham C	0	0	24 0

ESPINOZA, Giovanny (D)   378   16
H: 6 1 W: 14 12 b.Charguayaco 12-4-77
Honours: Ecuador 90 full caps, 2 goals.

1995	Aucas	0	0	
1996	Aucas	0	0	
1997	Aucas	17	1	
1998	Aucas	34	0	
1999	Aucas	36	0	
2000	Aucas	36	0	
2001	Aucas	14	2	
2001–02	Monterrey	6	0	6 0
2002	Aucas	24	3	161 6
2003	LDU Quito	34	1	
2004	LDU Quito	36	2	
2005	LDU Quito	42	2	
2006	LDU Quito	32	4	144 9
2006–07	Vitesse	10	0	
2007–08	Vitesse	17	0	27 0
2008	Cruzeiro	25	1	25 1
2009	Barcelona SC	15	0	15 0
2009–10	Birmingham C	0	0	

FAHEY, Keith (M)   197   26
H: 5 10 W: 12 07 b.Dublin 15-1-83
Honours: Eire 2 full caps.

1999–2000	Aston Villa	0	0	
2000–01	Aston Villa	0	0	
2001–02	Aston Villa	0	0	
2002–03	Aston Villa	0	0	
2003	St Patrick's Ath	0	0	
2004	St Patrick's Ath	33	5	
2005	St Patrick's Ath	14	3	
2005	Drogheda U	14	2	
2006	Drogheda U	8	0	22 2
2006	St Patrick's Ath	13	3	
2007	St Patrick's Ath	32	1	
2008	St Patrick's Ath	30	8	122 20
2008–09	Birmingham C	19	4	
2009–10	Birmingham C	34	0	53 4

FERGUSON, Barry (M)   363   47
H: 5 7 W: 9 10 b.Glasgow 2-2-78
Source: Rangers SABC. *Honours:* Scotland Under-21, 45 full caps, 3 goals.

1994–95	Rangers	0	0	
1995–96	Rangers	0	0	
1996–97	Rangers	1	0	
1997–98	Rangers	7	0	
1998–99	Rangers	23	1	
1999–2000	Rangers	31	4	
2000–01	Rangers	30	2	
2001–02	Rangers	22	1	
2002–03	Rangers	36	16	
2003–04	Rangers	3	0	
2003–04	Blackburn R	15	1	
2003–04	Blackburn R	21	2	36 3
2004–05	Rangers	13	2	
2005–06	Rangers	32	4	
2006–07	Rangers	32	4	
2007–08	Rangers	38	7	

2008–09	Rangers	22	2	290	44
2009–10	Birmingham C	37	0	37	0

FOSTER, Ben (G) 104 0
H: 6 2 W: 12 08 b.Leamington Spa 3-4-83
Source: Racing Club Warwick. *Honours:*
England 4 full caps.

2000–01	Stoke C	0	0		
2001–02	Stoke C	0	0		
2002–03	Stoke C	0	0		
2003–04	Stoke C	0	0		
2004–05	Stoke C	0	0		
2004–05	*Kidderminster H*	2	0	2	0
2004–05	*Wrexham*	17	0	17	0
2005–06	Manchester U	0	0		
2005–06	*Watford*	44	0		
2006–07	Manchester U	0	0		
2006–07	*Watford*	29	0	73	0
2007–08	Manchester U	1	0		
2008–09	Manchester U	2	0		
2009–10	Manchester U	9	0	12	0
2009–10	Birmingham C	0	0		

GARDNER, Craig (M) 72 6
H: 5 10 W: 11 13 b.Solihull 25-11-86
Source: Scholar. *Honours:* England Under-21.

2004–05	Aston Villa	0	0		
2005–06	Aston Villa	8	0		
2006–07	Aston Villa	13	2		
2007–08	Aston Villa	23	3		
2008–09	Aston Villa	14	0		
2009–10	Aston Villa	1	0	59	5
2009–10	Birmingham C	13	1	13	1

JEROME, Cameron (F) 219 58
H: 6 1 W: 13 06 b.Huddersfield 14-8-86
Honours: England Under-21.

2004–05	Cardiff C	29	6		
2005–06	Cardiff C	44	18	73	24
2005–06	Birmingham C	0	0		
2006–07	Birmingham C	38	7		
2007–08	Birmingham C	33	7		
2008–09	Birmingham C	43	9		
2009–10	Birmingham C	32	11	146	34

JERVIS, Jake (F) 7 2
H: 6 3 W: 12 13 b.Birmingham 17-9-91
Source: Scholar.

2009–10	Birmingham C	0	0		
2009–10	*Hereford U*	7	2	7	2

JOHNSON, Roger (D) 314 31
H: 6 3 W: 11 00 b.Ashford 28-4-83
Source: Trainee.

1999–2000	Wycombe W	1	0		
2000–01	Wycombe W	0	0		
2001–02	Wycombe W	7	1		
2002–03	Wycombe W	33	3		
2003–04	Wycombe W	28	2		
2004–05	Wycombe W	42	6		
2005–06	Wycombe W	45	7	157	19
2006–07	Cardiff C	32	2		
2007–08	Cardiff C	42	5		
2008–09	Cardiff C	45	5	119	12
2009–10	Birmingham C	38	0	38	0

KRYSIAK, Artur (G) 45 0
H: 6 1 W: 12 00 b.Lodz 11-8-89
Source: LKS Lodz. *Honours:* Poland Youth.

2006–07	Birmingham C	0	0		
2007–08	*Gretna*	4	0	4	0
2007–08	Birmingham C	0	0		
2008–09	Birmingham C	0	0		
2008–09	*Motherwell*	1	0	1	0
2008–09	*Swansea C*	2	0	2	0
2009–10	Birmingham C	0	0		
2009–10	*Burton Alb*	38	0	38	0

LARSSON, Sebastian (M) 152 15
H: 5 11 W: 11 02 b.Eskilstuna 6-6-85
Source: Trainee. *Honours:* Sweden Under-21,
21 full caps.

2002–03	Arsenal	0	0		
2003–04	Arsenal	0	0		
2004–05	Arsenal	0	0		
2005–06	Arsenal	3	0		
2006–07	Arsenal	0	0	3	0
2006–07	Birmingham C	43	4		
2007–08	Birmingham C	35	6		
2008–09	Birmingham C	38	1		
2009–10	Birmingham C	33	4	149	15

McFADDEN, James (M) 250 50
H: 6 0 W: 12 11 b.Glasgow 14-4-83
Honours: Scotland Under-21, B, 45 full caps,
15 goals.

2000–01	Motherwell	6	0		
2001–02	Motherwell	24	10		
2002–03	Motherwell	30	13		
2003–04	Motherwell	3	3	63	26
2003–04	Everton	23	0		
2004–05	Everton	23	1		
2005–06	Everton	32	5		
2006–07	Everton	19	2		
2007–08	Everton	12	2	109	11
2007–08	Birmingham C	12	4		
2008–09	Birmingham C	30	4		
2009–10	Birmingham C	36	5	78	13

McSHEFFREY, Gary (F) 268 72
H: 5 8 W: 10 06 b.Coventry 13-8-82
Source: Trainee. *Honours:* England Youth,
Under-20.

1998–99	Coventry C	1	0		
1999–2000	Coventry C	3	0		
2000–01	Coventry C	0	0		
2001–02	*Stockport Co*	5	1	5	1
2001–02	Coventry C	8	1		
2002–03	Coventry C	29	4		
2003–04	Coventry C	19	11		
2003–04	*Luton T*	18	9		
2004–05	Coventry C	37	12		
2004–05	*Luton T*	5	1	23	10
2005–06	Coventry C	43	15		
2006–07	Coventry C	3	1	143	44
2006–07	Birmingham C	40	13		
2007–08	Birmingham C	32	3		
2008–09	Birmingham C	6	0		
2008–09	*Nottingham F*	4	0	4	0
2009–10	Birmingham C	5	0	83	16
2009–10	*Leeds U*	10	1	10	1

MICHEL (M) 181 9
H: 6 0 W: 11 05 b.Pola de Lena 9-11-85

2004–05	Gijon B	3	2	33	2
2005–06	Gijon	24	1		
2006–07	Gijon	35	3		
2007–08	Gijon	36	3		
2008–09	Gijon	30	0		
2009–10	Gijon	14	0	139	7
2009–10	Birmingham C	9	0	9	0

MURPHY, David (D) 174 7
H: 6 1 W: 12 03 b.Hartlepool 1-3-84
Source: Scholar. *Honours:* England Youth.

2001–02	Middlesbrough	1	0		
2002–03	Middlesbrough	8	0		
2003–04	Middlesbrough	0	0	13	0
2003–04	*Barnsley*	10	2	10	2
2004–05	Hibernian	27	1		
2005–06	Hibernian	30	1		
2006–07	Hibernian	33	0		
2007–08	Hibernian	12	1	107	4
2007–08	Birmingham C	14	1		
2008–09	Birmingham C	30	0		
2009–10	Birmingham C	0	0	44	1

MUTCH, Jordon (M) 20 2
H: 5 9 W: 10 03 b.Birmingham 2-12-91
Source: Derby Co. *Honours:* England Youth.

2007–08	Birmingham C	0	0		
2008–09	Birmingham C	0	0		
2009–10	Birmingham C	0	0		
2009–10	*Hereford U*	3	0	3	0
2009–10	*Doncaster R*	17	2	17	2

O'CONNOR, Garry (F) 189 57
H: 6 1 W: 12 02 b.Edinburgh 7-5-83
Honours: Scotland Under-21, 16 full caps, 4
goals.

2000–01	Hibernian	1	0		
2001–02	Hibernian	4	1		
2002–03	Hibernian	19	10		
2003–04	Hibernian	24	6		
2004–05	Hibernian	35	13		
2005–06	Hibernian	24	11	107	41
2006	Lokomotiv Moscow	24	7		
2007	Lokomotiv Moscow	9	0	33	7
2007–08	Birmingham C	23	2		
2008–09	Birmingham C	16	6		
2009–10	Birmingham C	10	1	49	9

O'SHEA, Jay (M) 78 15
H: 5 9 W: 12 00 b.Dunlaoghdrie 10-8-88
Honours: Eire Under-21.

2007	Bray Wanderers	27	4	27	4
2008	Galway United	29	8		
2009	Galway United	19	3	48	11
2009–10	Birmingham C	1	0	1	0
2009–10	*Middlesbrough*	2	0	2	0

PARNABY, Stuart (M) 139 2
H: 5 11 W: 11 00 b.Durham 19-7-82
Source: Trainee. *Honours:* England Youth,
Under-20, Under-21.

1999–2000	Middlesbrough	0	0		
2000–01	Middlesbrough	0	0		
2000–01	*Halifax T*	6	0	6	0
2001–02	Middlesbrough	0	0		
2002–03	Middlesbrough	21	0		
2003–04	Middlesbrough	13	0		
2004–05	Middlesbrough	19	0		
2005–06	Middlesbrough	20	2		
2006–07	Middlesbrough	18	0	91	2
2007–08	Birmingham C	13	0		
2008–09	Birmingham C	21	0		
2009–10	Birmingham C	8	0	42	0

PHILLIPS, Kevin (F) 480 219
H: 5 7 W: 11 00 b.Hitchin 25-7-73
Source: Baldock T. *Honours:* England B,
8 full caps.

1994–95	Watford	16	9		
1995–96	Watford	27	11		
1996–97	Watford	16	4	59	24
1997–98	Sunderland	43	29		
1998–99	Sunderland	26	23		
1999–2000	Sunderland	36	30		
2000–01	Sunderland	34	14		
2001–02	Sunderland	37	11		
2002–03	Sunderland	32	6	208	113
2003–04	Southampton	34	12		
2004–05	Southampton	30	10	64	22
2005–06	Aston Villa	23	4		
2006–07	Aston Villa	0	0	23	4
2006–07	WBA	36	16		
2007–08	WBA	35	22	71	38
2008–09	Birmingham C	36	14		
2009–10	Birmingham C	19	4	55	18

PRESTON, Dan (D) 4 0
H: 5 11 W: 12 04 b.Birmingham 26-9-91

2009–10	Birmingham C	0	0		
2009–10	*Hereford U*	4	0	4	0

QUEUDRUE, Franck (D) 271 17
H: 6 1 W: 12 01 b.Paris 27-8-78
Source: Meaux. *Honours:* France B.

1999–2000	Lens	16	1		
2000–01	Lens	24	1		
2001–02	Lens	2	0	42	2
2001–02	Middlesbrough	28	2		
2002–03	Middlesbrough	31	1		
2003–04	Middlesbrough	31	0		
2004–05	Middlesbrough	31	5		
2005–06	Middlesbrough	29	3	150	11
2006–07	Fulham	29	1	29	1
2007–08	Birmingham C	16	0		
2008–09	Birmingham C	25	3		
2009–10	Birmingham C	6	0	47	3
2009–10	*Colchester U*	3	0	3	0

RIDGEWELL, Liam (D) 186 11
H: 5 10 W: 10 03 b.Bexley 21-7-84
Source: Scholar. *Honours:* England Youth,
Under-20, Under-21.

2001–02	Aston Villa	0	0		
2002–03	Aston Villa	0	0		
2002–03	*Bournemouth*	5	0	5	0
2003–04	Aston Villa	11	0		
2004–05	Aston Villa	15	0		
2005–06	Aston Villa	32	5		
2006–07	Aston Villa	21	1	79	6
2007–08	Birmingham C	35	1		
2008–09	Birmingham C	36	1		
2009–10	Birmingham C	31	3	102	5

SAMMONS, Ashley (M) 0 0
b.Solihull 10-11-91
Source: Scholar. *Honours:* England Youth.

2008–09	Birmingham C	0	0		
2009–10	Birmingham C	0	0		

SHROOT, Robin (M) 12 0
H: 5 9 W: 11 05 b.London 26-3-88
Source: Staines T, AFC Wimbledon, Harrow Borough. Honours: Northern Ireland Under-21.

2008–09	Birmingham C	0	0	
2008–09	Walsall	5	0	5 0
2009–10	Birmingham C	0	0	
2009–10	Burton Alb	7	0	7 0

TAYLOR, Maik (G) 486 0
H: 6 4 W: 14 02 b.Hildesheim 4-9-71
Source: Farnborough T. Honours: Northern Ireland Under-21, B, 83 full caps.

1995–96	Barnet	45	0	
1996–97	Barnet	25	0	70 0
1996–97	Southampton	18	0	
1997–98	Southampton	0	0	18 0
1997–98	Fulham	28	0	
1998–99	Fulham	46	0	
1999–2000	Fulham	46	0	
2000–01	Fulham	44	0	
2001–02	Fulham	1	0	
2002–03	Fulham	19	0	
2003–04	Fulham	0	0	184 0
2003–04	Birmingham C	34	0	
2004–05	Birmingham C	38	0	
2005–06	Birmingham C	34	0	
2006–07	Birmingham C	27	0	
2007–08	Birmingham C	34	0	
2008–09	Birmingham C	45	0	
2009–10	Birmingham C	2	0	214 0

VIGNAL, Gregory (D) 103 6
H: 5 9 W: 11 06 b.Montpellier 19-7-81
Source: Montpellier Herault SC.

2000–01	Liverpool	6	0	
2001–02	Liverpool	4	0	
2002–03	Liverpool	1	0	11 0
2002–03	Bastia	15	0	15 0
2003–04	Rennes	5	0	5 0
2004–05	Rangers	30	3	30 3
2005–06	Portsmouth	14	0	
2006–07	Portsmouth	0	0	14 0
2007–08	Southampton	20	3	
2008–09	Southampton	0	0	20 3
2009–10	Birmingham C	8	0	8 0

Scholars
Asante, Akwasi; Bogle, Omar; Dunphy, Jamie; Fleet. Reece; Gombala, Julius; Hronec, Jacub; Hubbins, Luke Anthony; Hutchison, Graham William Robert McDonald; Kerr, Fraser; Newbury, Adam Lee; Ntambwe, Brice; Preston, Daniel Sean; Rowe, Luke Jonothan.

BLACKBURN R (8)

ALEY, Zach (M) 0 0
b. 17-8-91
Source: Scholar.

2009–10	Blackburn R	0	0	

ANDREWS, Keith (M) 265 26
H: 6 0 W: 12 04 b.Dublin 13-9-80
Source: Trainee. Honours: Eire Youth, 15 full caps, 1 goal.

1997–98	Wolverhampton W	0	0	
1998–99	Wolverhampton W	0	0	
1999–2000	Wolverhampton W	2	0	
2000–01	Wolverhampton W	22	0	
2000–01	Oxford U	4	1	4 1
2001–02	Wolverhampton W	11	0	
2002–03	Wolverhampton W	9	0	
2003–04	Wolverhampton W	1	0	
2003–04	Stoke C	16	0	16 0
2003–04	Walsall	10	2	10 2
2004–05	Wolverhampton W	20	0	65 0
2005–06	Hull C	26	0	
2006–07	Hull C	3	0	29 0
2006–07	Milton Keynes D	34	6	
2007–08	Milton Keynes D	41	12	
2008–09	Milton Keynes D	1	0	76 18
2008–09	Blackburn R	33	4	
2009–10	Blackburn R	32	1	65 5

BANTON, Jason (F)
Source: Scholar.

2009–10	Blackburn R	0	0	

BASTURK, Yildiray (M) 280 39
H: 5 6 W: 10 12 b.Herne 24-12-78
Honours: Turkey 49 full caps, 3 goals.

1996–97	Wattenscheid	0	0	
1997–98	Bochum	17	1	
1998–99	Bochum	28	1	
1999–2000	Bochum	30	7	
2000–01	Bochum	29	4	104 13
2001–02	Leverkusen	30	3	
2002–03	Leverkusen	26	3	
2003–04	Leverkusen	17	2	73 8
2004–05	Hertha Berlin	25	7	
2005–06	Hertha Berlin	27	6	
2006–07	Hertha Berlin	19	1	71 14
2007–08	Stuttgart	26	4	
2008–09	Stuttgart	4	0	
2009–10	Stuttgart	1	0	31 4
2009–10	Blackburn R	1	0	1 0

BOWEN, Jordan (M) 0 0
Source: Scholar.

2008–09	Blackburn R	0	0	
2009–10	Blackburn R	0	0	

BROWN, Jason (G) 135 0
H: 6 0 W: 15 07 b.Southwark 18-5-82
Source: Charlton Ath Scholar. Honours: Wales Youth, Under-21, 2 full caps.

2000–01	Gillingham	0	0	
2001–02	Gillingham	10	0	
2002–03	Gillingham	39	0	
2003–04	Gillingham	22	0	
2004–05	Gillingham	16	0	
2005–06	Gillingham	39	0	126 0
2006–07	Blackburn R	1	0	
2007–08	Blackburn R	0	0	
2008–09	Blackburn R	4	0	
2009–10	Blackburn R	4	0	9 0

BUNN, Mark (G) 125 0
H: 6 0 W: 12 02 b.Camden 16-11-84
Source: Scholar.

2004–05	Northampton T	0	0	
2005–06	Northampton T	0	0	
2006–07	Northampton T	42	0	
2007–08	Northampton T	45	0	
2008–09	Northampton T	3	0	90 0
2008–09	Blackburn R	0	0	
2008–09	Leicester C	3	0	3 0
2009–10	Blackburn R	0	0	
2009–10	Sheffield U	32	0	32 0

CHIMBONDA, Pascal (D) 295 15
H: 5 10 W: 11 05 b.Les Abymes 21-2-79
Source: Port Louis. Honours: Guadeloupe 3 full caps, France 1 full cap.

1999–2000	Le Havre	2	0	
2000–01	Le Havre	32	1	
2001–02	Le Havre	27	2	
2002–03	Le Havre	24	2	85 5
2003–04	Bastia	31	1	
2004–05	Bastia	36	3	67 4
2005–06	Wigan Ath	37	2	
2006–07	Wigan Ath	1	0	38 2
2006–07	Tottenham H	33	1	
2007–08	Tottenham H	32	2	
2008–09	Sunderland	13	0	13 0
2008–09	Tottenham H	3	0	68 3
2009–10	Blackburn R	24	1	24 1

DIOUF, El Hadji (F) 320 47
H: 5 11 W: 11 11 b.Dakar 15-1-81
Honours: Senegal 57 full caps, 16 goals.

1998–99	Sochaux	15	0	15 0
1999–2000	Rennes	28	1	28 1
2000–01	Lens	28	8	
2001–02	Lens	26	10	54 18
2002–03	Liverpool	29	3	
2003–04	Liverpool	26	0	
2004–05	Liverpool	0	0	55 3
2004–05	Bolton W	27	9	
2005–06	Bolton W	20	3	
2006–07	Bolton W	33	5	
2007–08	Bolton W	34	4	114 21
2007–08	Sunderland	14	0	14 0
2008–09	Blackburn R	14	1	
2009–10	Blackburn R	26	3	40 4

DORAN, Aaron (M) 13 0
H: 5 7 W: 11 13 b.Ireland 13-5-91
Source: Scholar. Honours: Eire Youth.

2007–08	Blackburn R	0	0	
2008–09	Blackburn R	3	0	
2009–10	Blackburn R	0	0	3 0
2009–10	Milton Keynes D	4	0	4 0
2009–10	Leyton Orient	6	0	6 0

DUNN, David (M) 274 48
H: 5 9 W: 12 03 b.Gt Harwood 27-12-79
Source: Trainee. Honours: England Youth, Under-21, 1 full cap.

1997–98	Blackburn R	0	0	
1998–99	Blackburn R	15	1	
1999–2000	Blackburn R	22	2	
2000–01	Blackburn R	42	12	
2001–02	Blackburn R	29	7	
2002–03	Blackburn R	28	8	
2003–04	Birmingham C	21	2	
2004–05	Birmingham C	11	2	
2005–06	Birmingham C	12	2	
2006–07	Birmingham C	11	1	58 7
2006–07	Blackburn R	11	0	
2007–08	Blackburn R	31	1	
2008–09	Blackburn R	15	1	
2009–10	Blackburn R	23	9	216 41

EMERTON, Brett (M) 401 36
H: 6 1 W: 13 05 b.Bankstown 22-2-79
Honours: Australia Youth, Under-20, Under-23, 75 full caps, 17 goals.

1996–97	Sydney Olympic	18	2	
1997–98	Sydney Olympic	24	3	
1998–99	Sydney Olympic	21	2	
1999–2000	Sydney Olympic	31	9	94 16
2000–01	Feyenoord	28	2	
2001–02	Feyenoord	31	6	
2002–03	Feyenoord	33	3	92 11
2003–04	Blackburn R	37	2	
2004–05	Blackburn R	37	4	
2005–06	Blackburn R	30	1	
2006–07	Blackburn R	34	0	
2007–08	Blackburn R	33	1	
2008–09	Blackburn R	20	1	
2009–10	Blackburn R	24	0	215 9

FIELDING, Frank (G) 89 0
H: 5 11 W: 12 00 b.Blackburn 4-4-88
Source: Scholar. Honours: England Youth, Under-21.

2006–07	Blackburn R	0	0	
2007–08	Blackburn R	0	0	
2007–08	Wycombe W	36	0	36 0
2008–09	Blackburn R	0	0	
2008–09	Northampton T	12	0	12 0
2008–09	Rochdale	23	0	
2009–10	Blackburn R	0	0	
2009–10	Rochdale	18	0	41 0

FLYNN, Johnny (D) 8 0
H: 5 10 W: 11 00 b.Ballymena 18-11-89
Source: Ballymena U. Honours: Northern Ireland Under-21.

2007–08	Blackburn R	0	0	
2008–09	Blackburn R	0	0	
2009–10	Blackburn R	0	0	
2009–10	Accrington S	8	0	8 0

GIVET, Gael (D) 255 10
H: 5 11 W: 11 11 b.Arles 9-10-81
Honours: France 13 full caps.

2000–01	Monaco	1	0	
2001–02	Monaco	23	2	
2002–03	Monaco	23	1	
2003–04	Monaco	33	2	
2004–05	Monaco	34	0	
2005–06	Monaco	32	2	
2006–07	Monaco	32	1	178 8
2007–08	Marseille	29	0	
2008–09	Marseille	0	0	29 0
2008–09	Blackburn R	14	0	
2009–10	Blackburn R	34	2	48 2

GRELLA, Vince (M) 300 7
H: 6 0 W: 12 06 b.Melbourne 5-10-79
Honours: Australia Under-20, Under-23, 46 full caps.

1996–97	Canberra Cosmos	14	1	14 1
1997–98	Carlton SC	22	2	
1998–99	Carlton SC	1	0	23 2

1998–99	Empoli	5	0	
1999-2000	Empoli	0	0	
1999-2000	Ternana	9	0	
2000–01	Ternana	18	0	27 0
2001–02	Empoli	32	0	
2002–03	Empoli	31	1	
2003–04	Empoli	24	0	
2004–05	Empoli	0	0	92 0
2004–05	Parma	23	0	
2005–06	Parma	35	1	
2006–07	Parma	26	1	84 2
2007–08	Torino	28	1	28 1
2008–09	Blackburn R	17	0	
2009–10	Blackburn R	15	0	32 0

GUNNING, Gavin (D)   27 0
H: 6 0 W: 12 06 b.Dublin 26-1-91
Source: Scholar. Honours: Eire Youth, Under-21.

2007–08	Blackburn R	0	0	
2008–09	Blackburn R	0	0	
2009–10	Blackburn R	0	0	
2009–10	*Tranmere R*	6	0	6 0
2009–10	*Rotherham U*	21	0	21 0

HANLEY, Grant (D)   1 0
H: 6 2 W: 12 00 b.Dumfries 20-11-91
Source: Scholar. Honours: Scotland Youth.

2008–09	Blackburn R	0	0	
2009–10	Blackburn R	1	0	1 0

HAWORTH, Andrew (M)   7 0
H: 5 11 W: 11 10 b.Lancaster 28-11-88
Source: Scholar.

2007–08	Blackburn R	0	0	
2008–09	Blackburn R	0	0	
2009–10	Blackburn R	0	0	
2009–10	*Rochdale*	7	0	7 0

HITCHCOCK, Tom (F)   0 0
Source: Scholar.

2009–10	Blackburn R	0	0	

HOILETT, David (M)   23 0
H: 5 8 W: 11 00 b.Ottawa 5-6-90
Source: Scholar.

2008–09	Blackburn R	0	0	
2009–10	Blackburn R	23	0	23 0

JACOBSEN, Lars (D)   267 6
H: 5 11 W: 12 02 b.Odense 29-9-79
Honours: Denmark Youth, Under-21, 34 full caps.

1996–97	Odense	5	0	
1997–98	Odense	15	0	
1998–99	Odense	0	0	
1999-2000	Odense	27	1	
2000–01	Odense	32	0	
2001–02	Odense	32	1	111 2
2002–03	Hamburg II	5	0	
2002–03	Hamburg	12	1	
2003–04	Hamburg II	1	0	6 0
2003–04	Hamburg	10	0	22 1
2003–04	FC Copenhagen	13	0	
2004–05	FC Copenhagen	27	0	
2005–06	FC Copenhagen	33	3	
2006–07	FC Copenhagen	30	0	103 3
2007–08	Nuremberg	7	0	7 0
2008–09	Everton	5	0	5 0
2009–10	Blackburn R	13	0	13 0

JONES, Phil (D)   9 0
H: 5 11 W: 11 02 b.Preston 21-2-92
Source: Scholar. Honours: England Youth.

2009–10	Blackburn R	9	0	9 0

JUDGE, Alan (F)   54 7
H: 5 6 W: 11 03 b.Dublin 11-11-88
Honours: Eire Under-21.

2006–07	Blackburn R	0	0	
2007–08	Blackburn R	0	0	
2008–09	Blackburn R	0	0	
2008–09	*Plymouth Arg*	17	2	
2009–10	Blackburn R	0	0	
2009–10	*Plymouth Arg*	37	5	54 7

KALINIC, Nikola (F)   105 40
H: 6 2 W: 12 11 b.Olin 5-1-88
Honours: Croatia Youth, Under-21, 3 full caps.

2005–06	Hajduk Split	6	0	
2006–07	Sibenik	8	3	8 3
2006–07	Pula 1856	12	3	12 3

2007–08	Hajduk Split	25	17	
2008–09	Hajduk Split	28	15	59 32
2009–10	Blackburn R	26	2	26 2

KEAN, Jake (G)   0 0
b.Derby 4-2-91
Honours: From Scholar.

2009–10	Blackburn R	0	0	

KHIZANISHVILI, Zurab (D)   213 6
H: 6 1 W: 12 08 b.Tbilisi 6-10-81
Honours: Georgia 65 full caps, 1 gcal.

1998–99	Dynamo Tbilisi B	17	3	17 3
1998–99	Dynamo Tbilisi	2	1	2 1
1999-2000	Tbilisi	9	0	9 0
1999-2000	Lokomotivi	5	1	
2000–01	Lokomotivi	11	0	16 1
2000–01	Dundee	18	0	
2001–02	Dundee	18	0	
2002–03	Dundee	19	0	43 0
2003–04	Rangers	26	0	
2004–05	Rangers	16	0	
2005–06	Rangers	0	0	42 0
2005–06	*Blackburn R*	26	1	
2006–07	Blackburn R	18	0	
2007–08	Blackburn R	13	0	
2008–09	Blackburn R	5	0	
2009–10	Blackburn R	0	0	62 1
2009–10	*Newcastle U*	7	0	7 0
2009–10	*Reading*	15	0	15 0

KNOWLES, James (M)   0 0
H: 5 9 W: 11 00 b. 6-4-93
Source: Scholar.

2009–10	Blackburn R	0	0	

LINGANZI, Amine (M)   4 0
H: 6 1 W: 10 00 b.Alger 16-11-89

2008–09	St Etienne	3	0	
2009–10	St Etienne	0	0	3 0
2009–10	Blackburn R	1	0	1 0

LOWE, Jason (M)   0 0
Source: Scholar.

2009–10	Blackburn R	0	0	

MARROW, Alex (M)   32 1
H: 6 1 W: 13 00 b.Ashton 21-1-90

2007–08	Blackburn R	0	0	
2008–09	Blackburn R	0	0	
2009–10	Blackburn R	0	0	
2009–10	*Oldham Ath*	32	1	32 1

MARSHALL, Marcus (F)   22 0
H: 5 10 W: 11 06 b.Hammersmith 7-10-89

2007–08	Blackburn R	0	0	
2008–09	Blackburn R	0	0	
2009–10	Blackburn R	0	0	
2009–10	*Rotherham U*	22	0	22 0

N'ZONZI, Steven (M)   70 3
H: 6 3 W: 11 11 b.Paris 15-12-88
Honours: France Under-21.

2007–08	Amiens	3	0	
2008–09	Amiens	34	1	37 1
2009–10	Blackburn R	33	2	33 2

NELSEN, Ryan (D)   224 12
H: 5 11 W: 14 02 b.Christchurch, NZ 18-10-77
Honours: New Zealand Under-23, 43 full caps, 7 goals.

2001	DC United	19	0	
2002	DC United	20	4	
2003	DC United	25	1	
2004	DC United	17	2	81 7
2004–05	Blackburn R	15	0	
2005–06	Blackburn R	31	0	
2006–07	Blackburn R	12	0	
2007–08	Blackburn R	22	0	
2008–09	Blackburn R	35	1	
2009–10	Blackburn R	28	4	143 5

OLSSON, Martin (D)   32 1
H: 5 7 W: 12 12 b.Sweden 17-5-88
Source: Hogaborg. Honours: Sweden Under-21, 1 full cap, 2 goals.

2005–06	Blackburn R	0	0	
2006–07	Blackburn R	0	0	
2007–08	Blackburn R	2	0	
2008–09	Blackburn R	9	0	
2009–10	Blackburn R	21	1	32 1

PEDERSEN, Morten (F)   355 72
H: 5 11 W: 11 00 b.Vadso 8-9-81
Honours: Norway Youth, Under-21, 58 full caps, 13 goals.

1997	Norlid	21	0	
1998	Pola	20	4	20 4
1999	Norlid	19	0	40 0
2000	Tromso	10	3	
2001	Tromso	26	5	
2002	Tromso	23	18	
2003	Tromso	26	8	
2004	Tromso	18	7	103 41
2004–05	Blackburn R	19	4	
2005–06	Blackburn R	34	9	
2006–07	Blackburn R	36	6	
2007–08	Blackburn R	37	4	
2008–09	Blackburn R	33	1	
2009–10	Blackburn R	33	3	192 27

POTTS, Michael (F)   0 0
b. 26-11-91
Source: Scholar.

2008–09	Blackburn R	0	0	
2009–10	Blackburn R	0	0	

REID, Steven (M)   264 25
H: 6 0 W: 12 07 b.Kingston 10-3-81
Source: Trainee. Honours: England Youth. Eire Under-21, 23 full caps, 2 goals.

1997–98	Millwall	1	0	
1998–99	Millwall	25	0	
1999-2000	Millwall	21	0	
2000–01	Millwall	37	7	
2001–02	Millwall	35	5	
2002–03	Millwall	20	6	139 18
2003–04	Blackburn R	16	0	
2004–05	Blackburn R	28	2	
2005–06	Blackburn R	34	4	
2006–07	Blackburn R	3	0	
2007–08	Blackburn R	24	0	
2008–09	Blackburn R	4	0	
2009–10	Blackburn R	4	0	113 6
2009–10	*QPR*	2	0	2 0
2009–10	*WBA*	10	1	10 1

RIGTERS, Maceo (F)   79 5
H: 5 10 W: 14 07 b.Amsterdam 22-1-84
Honours: Holland Under-21.

2005–06	NAC Breda	24	2	
2006–07	NAC Breda	32	3	56 5
2007–08	Blackburn R	2	0	
2007–08	*Norwich C*	2	0	2 0
2008–09	Blackburn R	0	0	
2008–09	*Barnsley*	19	0	19 0
2009–10	Blackburn R	0	0	2 0

ROBERTS, Jason (F)   386 126
H: 6 0 W: 14 01 b.Park Royal 25-1-78
Source: Hayes. Honours: Grenada 22 full caps, 12 goals.

1997–98	Wolverhampton W	0	0	
1997–98	*Torquay U*	14	6	14 6
1997–98	*Bristol C*	3	1	3 1
1998–99	Bristol R	37	16	
1999-2000	Bristol R	41	22	78 38
2000–01	WBA	43	14	
2001–02	WBA	14	7	
2002–03	WBA	32	3	
2003–04	WBA	0	0	89 24
2003–04	Portsmouth	10	1	10 1
2003–04	Wigan Ath	14	8	
2004–05	Wigan Ath	45	21	
2005–06	Wigan Ath	34	8	93 37
2006–07	Blackburn R	18	4	
2007–08	Blackburn R	26	3	
2008–09	Blackburn R	26	7	
2009–10	Blackburn R	29	5	99 19

ROBINSON, Paul (G)   302 1
H: 6 1 W: 14 07 b.Beverley 15-10-79
Source: Trainee. Honours: England Under-21, 41 full caps.

1996–97	Leeds U	0	0	
1997–98	Leeds U	0	0	
1998–99	Leeds U	5	0	
1999-2000	Leeds U	0	0	
2000–01	Leeds U	16	0	
2001–02	Leeds U	0	0	
2002–03	Leeds U	38	0	
2003–04	Leeds U	36	0	95 0
2003–04	Tottenham H	0	0	

2004–05	Tottenham H	36	0		
2005–06	Tottenham H	38	0		
2006–07	Tottenham H	38	1		
2007–08	Tottenham H	25	0	137	1
2008–09	Blackburn R	35	0		
2009–10	Blackburn R	35	0	70	0

SALGADO, Michel (D)   421   9
H: 5 9   W: 11 11   b.Galicia 22-10-75
Honours: Spain Youth, Under-20, Under-21, 53 full caps.

1992–93	Celta Vigo B	20	1		
1993–94	Celta Vigo B	0	0	20	1
1994–95	Celta Vigo	14	0		
1995–96	Celta Vigo	18	0		
1996–97	Salamanca	36	1	36	1
1997–98	Celta Vigo	25	0		
1998–99	Celta Vigo	35	3	92	3
1999–2000	Real Madrid	29	0		
2000–01	Real Madrid	28	1		
2001–02	Real Madrid	35	0		
2002–03	Real Madrid	35	0		
2003–04	Real Madrid	35	1		
2004–05	Real Madrid	30	2		
2005–06	Real Madrid	27	0		
2006–07	Real Madrid	16	0		
2007–08	Real Madrid	8	0		
2008–09	Real Madrid	9	0	252	4
2009–10	Blackburn R	21	0	21	0

SAMBA, Christopher (D)   166   14
H: 6 5   W: 13 03   b.Creteil 28-3-84
Source: Issy-les-Moulineaux, Rouen.
Honours: Congo 20 full caps.

2001–02	Sedan	1	0		
2002–03	Sedan	0	0		
2003–04	Sedan	3	0	4	0
2004–05	Hertha Berlin	0	0		
2004–05	Hertha Berlin II	16	3		
2005–06	Hertha Berlin	12	0		
2005–06	Hertha Berlin II	12	1		
2006–07	Hertha Berlin	8	0	20	0
2006–07	Hertha Berlin II	2	0	30	4
2006–07	Blackburn R	14	2		
2007–08	Blackburn R	33	2		
2008–09	Blackburn R	35	2		
2009–10	Blackburn R	30	4	112	10

SANTA CRUZ, Julio (F)   0   0
H: 6 0   W: 12 04   b.Asuncion 12-5-90
Source: Cerro Porteno.

2008–09	Blackburn R	0	0
2009–10	Blackburn R	0	0

VAN HEERDEN, Elrio (M)   83   6
H: 5 6   W: 10 03   b.Johannesburg 11-7-83
Honours: South Africa 33 full caps, 3 goals.

2002–03	FC Copenhagen	0	0		
2003–04	FC Copenhagen	1	1		
2004–05	FC Copenhagen	6	0		
2005–06	FC Copenhagen	19	4	26	5
2005–06	Club Brugge	10	0		
2006–07	Club Brugge	22	1		
2007–08	Club Brugge	8	0		
2008–09	Club Brugge	17	0	57	1
2009–10	Blackburn R	0	0		

Transferred to Sivas January 2010.

VASTIC, Tony (F)   0   0
b. 17-1-93
Source: Blackburn R Academy.

2009–10	Blackburn R	0	0

Scholars
Ajagbe, Damilola Mubarak; Billington,
Alexander Ross; Evans, Micah; Lindsay,
Cameron; Morris, Joshua Francis; Murray,
Thomas David; O'Connor, Callum Anthony;
O'Connor, Anthony Dean; Parry, Andrew
James; Pearson, Matthew Joe; Ramm,
Jackson Wayne.

BLACKPOOL (9)

ADAM, Charlie (M)   154   38
H: 6 1   W: 12 00   b.Dundee 10-12-85
Honours: Scotland Under-21, B, 4 full caps.

2004–05	Rangers	1	0		
2004–05	*Ross Co*	10	2	10	2
2005–06	Rangers	1	0		
2005–06	*St Mirren*	29	5	29	5
2006–07	Rangers	32	11		
2007–08	Rangers	16	2		
2008–09	Rangers	9	0	59	13
2008–09	Blackpool	13	2		
2009–10	Blackpool	43	16	56	18

ALMOND, Louis (F)   4   0
H: 5 11   W: 12 00   b.Blackburn 15-8-90
Source: Scholar.

2009–10	Blackpool	0	0		
2009–10	*Cheltenham T*	4	0	4	0

BANGURA, Alhassan (M)   77   1
H: 5 11   W: 10 07   b.Freetown 24-1-88
Source: Scholar. *Honours:* Sierra Leone 1 full cap.

2004–05	Watford	2	0		
2005–06	Watford	35	1		
2006–07	Watford	16	0		
2007–08	Watford	7	0		
2008–09	Watford	2	0		
2008–09	*Brighton & HA*	6	0	6	0
2009–10	Watford	0	0	62	1
2009–10	Blackpool	9	0	9	0

BOUAZZA, Hameur (F)   176   18
H: 5 10   W: 12 01   b.Evry 22-2-85
Source: Scholar. *Honours:* Algeria 15 full caps, 2 goals.

2003–04	Watford	9	1		
2004–05	Watford	28	1		
2005–06	Watford	14	1		
2005–06	*Swindon T*	13	2	13	2
2006–07	Watford	32	6	83	9
2007–08	Fulham	20	1		
2008–09	Fulham	0	0		
2008–09	*Charlton Ath*	25	4	25	4
2008–09	*Birmingham C*	16	1	16	1
2009–10	Fulham	0	0	20	1
2009–10	Blackpool	19	1	19	1

BURGESS, Ben (F)   294   84
H: 6 3   W: 14 04   b.Buxton 9-11-81
Source: Trainee. *Honours:* Eire Youth, Under-21.

1998–99	Blackburn R	0	0		
1999–2000	Blackburn R	2	0		
2000–01	Blackburn R	0	0		
2000–01	*Northern Spirit*	27	16	27	16
2001–02	Blackburn R	0	0	2	0
2001–02	*Brentford*	43	17	43	17
2002–03	*Stockport Co*	19	4	19	4
2002–03	*Oldham Ath*	7	0	7	0
2002–03	Hull C	7	4		
2003–04	Hull C	44	18		
2004–05	Hull C	2	0		
2005–06	Hull C	14	2		
2006–07	Hull C	3	0	70	24
2006–07	Blackpool	27	2		
2007–08	Blackpool	35	9		
2008–09	Blackpool	29	6		
2009–10	Blackpool	35	6	126	23

CLARKE, Billy (F)   114   22
H: 5 7   W: 10 01   b.Cork 13-12-87
Source: Scholar. *Honours:* Eire Youth, Under-21.

2004–05	Ipswich T	0	0		
2005–06	Ipswich T	2	0		
2005–06	*Colchester U*	6	0	6	0
2006–07	Ipswich T	27	3		
2007–08	Ipswich T	20	0		
2007–08	*Falkirk*	8	1	8	1
2008–09	Ipswich T	0	0		
2008–09	*Darlington*	20	8	20	8
2008–09	*Northampton T*	5	3	5	3
2008–09	*Brentford*	8	6	8	6
2009–10	Blackpool	18	1	18	1

COID, Danny (D)   264   9
H: 5 11   W: 11 07   b.Liverpool 3-10-81
Source: Trainee.

1998–99	Blackpool	1	0		
1999–2000	Blackpool	21	1		
2000–01	Blackpool	46	1		
2001–02	Blackpool	27	3		
2002–03	Blackpool	36	1		
2003–04	Blackpool	35	3		
2004–05	Blackpool	13	0		
2005–06	Blackpool	13	0		
2006–07	Blackpool	18	0		
2007–08	Blackpool	13	0		
2008–09	Blackpool	18	0		
2009–10	Blackpool	1	0	264	9

CRAINEY, Stephen (D)   196   1
H: 5 9   W: 9 11   b.Glasgow 22-6-81
Honours: Scotland B, Under-21, 6 full caps.

1999–2000	Celtic	9	0		
2000–01	Celtic	2	0		
2001–02	Celtic	15	0		
2002–03	Celtic	13	0		
2003–04	Celtic	2	0	41	0
2003–04	Southampton	5	0	5	0
2004–05	Leeds U	9	0		
2005–06	Leeds U	24	0		
2006–07	Leeds U	19	0	52	0
2007–08	Blackpool	40	1		
2008–09	Blackpool	17	0		
2009–10	Blackpool	41	0	98	1

DEMONTAGNAC, Ishmel (F)   101   12
H: 5 10   W: 11 05   b.London 15-6-88
Source: Charlton Ath Scholar. *Honours:* England Youth.

2005–06	Walsall	24	2		
2006–07	Walsall	19	1		
2007–08	Walsall	30	3		
2008–09	Walsall	10	3		
2009–10	Walsall	0	0	83	9
2009–10	Blackpool	8	0	8	0
2009–10	*Chesterfield*	10	3	10	3

EARDLEY, Neal (M)   137   10
H: 5 11   W: 11 10   b.Llandudno 6-11-88
Source: Scholar. *Honours:* Wales Under-21, 13 full caps.

2005–06	Oldham Ath	1	0		
2006–07	Oldham Ath	33	0		
2007–08	Oldham Ath	42	6		
2008–09	Oldham Ath	34	2		
2009–10	Oldham Ath	0	0	113	10
2009–10	Blackpool	24	0	24	0

EASTHAM, Ashley (D)   21   0
H: 6 3   W: 12 06   b.Preston 22-3-91
Source: Scholar.

2009–10	Blackpool	1	0	1	0
2009–10	*Cheltenham T*	20	0	20	0

EDWARDS, Rob (D)   183   5
H: 6 1   W: 11 10   b.Telford 25-12-82
Source: Trainee. *Honours:* Wales Youth, 15 full caps.

1999–2000	Aston Villa	0	0		
2000–01	Aston Villa	0	0		
2001–02	Aston Villa	0	0		
2002–03	Aston Villa	8	0		
2003–04	Aston Villa	0	0	8	0
2003–04	*Crystal Palace*	7	1	7	1
2003–04	*Derby Co*	11	1	11	1
2004–05	Wolverhampton W	17	0		
2005–06	Wolverhampton W	42	0		
2006–07	Wolverhampton W	33	0		
2007–08	Wolverhampton W	8	1	100	1
2008–09	Blackpool	36	2		
2009–10	Blackpool	21	0	57	2

EUELL, Jason (F)   392   84
H: 5 11   W: 11 13   b.Lambeth 6-2-77
Source: Trainee. *Honours:* England Youth, Under-21, Jamaica 3 full caps, 1 goal.

1995–96	Wimbledon	9	2		
1996–97	Wimbledon	7	2		
1997–98	Wimbledon	19	4		
1998–99	Wimbledon	33	10		
1999–2000	Wimbledon	37	4		
2000–01	Wimbledon	36	19	141	41
2001–02	Charlton Ath	36	11		
2002–03	Charlton Ath	36	10		
2003–04	Charlton Ath	31	10		
2004–05	Charlton Ath	26	2		
2005–06	Charlton Ath	10	1		
2006–07	Charlton Ath	0	0	139	34
2006–07	Middlesbrough	17	0		
2007–08	Middlesbrough	0	0	17	0
2007–08	Southampton	38	3		
2008–09	Southampton	24	2	62	5
2009–10	Blackpool	33	4	33	4

EVATT, Ian (D)   298   14
H: 6 3   W: 13 12   b.Coventry 19-11-81
Source: Trainee.

1998–99	Derby Co	0	0

1999–2000	Derby Co	0	0		
2000–01	Derby Co	1	0		
2001–02	*Northampton T*	11	0	11	0
2001–02	Derby Co	3	0		
2002–03	Derby Co	30	0	34	0
2003–04	Chesterfield	43	5		
2004–05	Chesterfield	41	4	84	9
2005–06	QPR	27	0		
2006–07	QPR	0	0	27	0
2006–07	Blackpool	44	0		
2007–08	Blackpool	29	0		
2008–09	Blackpool	33	1		
2009–10	Blackpool	36	4	142	5

GILKS, Matthew (G)   211   0
H: 6 3 W: 13 12 b.Rochdale 4-6-82
Source: Scholar.

2000–01	Rochdale	3	0		
2001–02	Rochdale	19	0		
2002–03	Rochdale	20	0		
2003–04	Rochdale	12	0		
2004–05	Rochdale	30	0		
2005–06	Rochdale	46	0		
2006–07	Rochdale	46	0	176	0
2007–08	Norwich C	0	0		
2008–09	Blackpool	5	0		
2008–09	*Shrewsbury T*	4	0	4	0
2009–10	Blackpool	26	0	31	0

HALSTEAD, Mark (G)   0   0
H: 6 3 W: 14 00 b.Blackpool 1-1-90
Source: Scholar.

| 2009–10 | Blackpool | 0 | 0 | | |

HUSBAND, Stephen (M)   15   0
H: 6 0 W: 12 13 b.Dunfermline 29-10-90

2006–07	Cowdenbeath	5	0	5	0
2007–08	Hearts	0	0		
2008–09	Hearts	0	0		
2009–10	Hearts	0	0		
2009–10	*Livingston*	7	0	7	0
2009–10	Blackpool	3	0	3	0

JOHN-BAPTISTE, Alex (D)   237   9
H: 6 0 W: 11 11 b.Sutton-in-Ashfield 31-1-86
Source: Scholar.

2002–03	Mansfield T	4	0		
2003–04	Mansfield T	17	0		
2004–05	Mansfield T	41	1		
2005–06	Mansfield T	41	1		
2006–07	Mansfield T	46	3		
2007–08	Mansfield T	25	0	174	5
2008–09	Blackpool	21	1		
2009–10	Blackpool	42	3	63	4

MARTIN, Joe (M)   22   0
H: 6 0 W: 12 13 b.Dagenham 29-11-88
Source: Scholar. *Honours:* England Youth.

2005–06	Tottenham H	0	0		
2006–07	Tottenham H	0	0		
2007–08	Tottenham H	0	0		
2007–08	*Blackpool*	1	0		
2008–09	Blackpool	15	0		
2009–10	Blackpool	6	0	22	0

NARDIELLO, Daniel (F)   158   37
H: 5 11 W: 11 04 b.Coventry 22-10-82
Source: Trainee. *Honours:* Wales 3 full caps.

1999–2000	Manchester U	0	0		
2000–01	Manchester U	0	0		
2001–02	Manchester U	0	0		
2002–03	Manchester U	0	0		
2003–04	Manchester U	0	0		
2003–04	*Swansea C*	4	0	4	0
2003–04	*Barnsley*	16	7		
2004–05	Manchester U	0	0		
2004–05	*Barnsley*	28	7		
2005–06	Barnsley	34	5		
2006–07	Barnsley	30	9		
2007–08	*QPR*	8	0	8	0
2007–08	*Barnsley*	11	2	119	30
2008–09	Blackpool	2	0		
2008–09	*Hartlepool U*	12	3	12	3
2009–10	Blackpool	5	0	7	0
2009–10	*Bury*	4	6	4	6
2009–10	*Oldham Ath*	2	0	2	0

ORMEROD, Brett (F)   370   87
H: 5 11 W: 11 12 b.Blackburn 18-10-76
Source: Blackburn R Trainee, Accrington S.

1996–97	Blackpool	4	0		
1997–98	Blackpool	9	2		
1998–99	Blackpool	40	8		
1999–2000	Blackpool	13	5		
2000–01	Blackpool	41	17		
2001–02	Blackpool	21	13		
2001–02	Southampton	18	1		
2002–03	Southampton	31	5		
2003–04	Southampton	22	5		
2004–05	Southampton	9	0		
2004–05	*Leeds U*	6	0	6	0
2004–05	*Wigan Ath*	6	2	6	2
2005–06	Scunthorpe	19	1	99	12
2005–06	Preston NE	15	4		
2006–07	Preston NE	29	8		
2007–08	Preston NE	18	1		
2007–08	*Nottingham F*	13	2	13	2
2008–09	Preston NE	0	0	62	13
2008–09	*Oldham Ath*	5	0	5	0
2008–09	Blackpool	15	2		
2009–10	Blackpool	36	11	179	58

RACHUBKA, Paul (G)   227   0
H: 6 1 W: 13 05 b.San Luis Opispo 21-5-81
Source: Trainee. *Honours:* England Youth, Under-20.

1999–2000	Manchester U	0	0		
2000–01	Manchester U	1	0		
2001–02	Manchester U	0	0	1	0
2001–02	*Oldham Ath*	16	0	16	0
2002–03	Charlton Ath	0	0		
2003–04	Charlton Ath	0	0		
2003–04	*Huddersfield T*	13	0		
2004–05	Charlton Ath	0	0		
2004–05	*Milton Keynes D*	4	0	4	0
2004–05	*Northampton T*	10	0	10	0
2005–06	*Huddersfield T*	29	0		
2005–06	Huddersfield T	34	0		
2006–07	Huddersfield T	0	0	76	0
2006–07	*Peterborough U*	4	0	4	0
2006–07	*Blackpool*	8	0		
2007–08	Blackpool	46	0		
2008–09	Blackpool	42	0		
2009–10	Blackpool	20	0	116	0

SOUTHERN, Keith (M)   284   24
H: 5 10 W: 12 06 b.Gateshead 24-4-81
Source: Trainee.

1998–99	Everton	0	0		
1999–2000	Everton	0	0		
2000–01	Everton	0	0		
2001–02	Everton	0	0		
2002–03	Everton	0	0		
2002–03	Blackpool	38	1		
2003–04	Blackpool	28	2		
2004–05	Blackpool	27	6		
2005–06	Blackpool	42	2		
2006–07	Blackpool	39	5		
2007–08	Blackpool	30	3		
2008–09	Blackpool	35	3		
2009–10	Blackpool	45	2	284	24

TAYLOR-FLETCHER, Gary (F)   300   66
H: 6 0 W: 11 00 b.Liverpool 4-6-81
Source: Northwich Vic. *Honours:* England Schools.

2000–01	Hull C	5	0	5	0
2001–02	Leyton Orient	9	0		
2002–03	Leyton Orient	12	1	21	1
2003–04	Lincoln C	42	16		
2004–05	Lincoln C	58	11	80	27
2005–06	Huddersfield T	43	10		
2006–07	Huddersfield T	39	11	82	21
2007–08	Blackpool	42	6		
2008–09	Blackpool	38	5		
2009–10	Blackpool	32	6	112	17

VAUGHAN, David (M)   266   18
H: 5 7 W: 11 00 b.Rhuddlan 18-2-83
Source: Scholar. *Honours:* Wales Youth, Under-21, 17 full caps, 1 goal.

2000–01	Crewe Alex	1	0		
2001–02	Crewe Alex	13	0		
2002–03	Crewe Alex	32	3		
2003–04	Crewe Alex	31	0		
2004–05	Crewe Alex	44	5		
2005–06	Crewe Alex	34	5		
2006–07	Crewe Alex	29	4		
2007–08	Crewe Alex	1	0	185	18
2007–08	*Real Sociedad*	7	1	7	1
2008–09	Blackpool	33	1		
2009–10	Blackpool	41	1	74	2

BOLTON W (10)

AL-HABSI, Ali (G)   72   0
H: 6 4 W: 12 06 b.Oman 30-12-81
Source: Al-Nasser, Al-Mudhaibi. *Honours:* Oman 70 full caps.

2003	Lyn	13	0		
2004	Lyn	24	0		
2005	Lyn	25	0	62	0
2005–06	Bolton W	0	0		
2006–07	Bolton W	0	0		
2007–08	Bolton W	10	0		
2008–09	Bolton W	0	0		
2009–10	Bolton W	0	0	10	0

BASHAM, Chris (M)   32   1
H: 5 11 W: 12 08 b.Stafford 20-7-88
Source: Scholar.

2007–08	Bolton W	0	0		
2007–08	*Rochdale*	13	0	13	0
2008–09	Bolton W	11	1		
2009–10	Bolton W	8	0	19	1

BOGDAN, Adam (G)   1   0
H: 6 4 W: 14 02 b.Budapest 27-9-87
Source: Vasas.

2007–08	Bolton W	0	0		
2008–09	Bolton W	0	0		
2009–10	Bolton W	0	0		
2009–10	*Crewe Alex*	1	0	1	0

CAHILL, Gary (D)   146   12
H: 6 2 W: 12 06 b.Dronfield 19-12-85
Source: Trainee. *Honours:* England Youth, Under-20, Under-21.

2003–04	Aston Villa	0	0		
2004–05	Aston Villa	0	0		
2004–05	*Burnley*	27	1	27	1
2005–06	Aston Villa	7	1		
2006–07	Aston Villa	20	0		
2007–08	*Sheffield U*	16	2	16	2
2007–08	Bolton W	13	0		
2008–09	Bolton W	33	3		
2009–10	Bolton W	29	5	75	8

COHEN, Tamir (M)   153   11
H: 5 11 W: 11 09 b.Israel 4-3-84
Honours: Israel Youth, Under-21, 15 full caps.

2002–03	Maccabi Tel Aviv	13	0		
2003–04	Maccabi Tel Aviv	30	2		
2004–05	Maccabi Tel Aviv	22	2		
2005–06	Maccabi Tel Aviv	16	0		
2006–07	Maccabi Tel Aviv	3	0	84	4
2006–07	Maccabi Netanya	15	1		
2007–08	Maccabi Netanya	13	1	28	2
2007–08	Bolton W	10	1		
2008–09	Bolton W	4	1		
2009–10	Bolton W	27	3	41	5

CONNOLLY, Mark (D)   0   0
H: 6 1 W: 12 01 b.Monaghan 16-12-91
Source: Wolverhampton W Scholar. *Honours:* Eire Youth

| 2009–10 | Bolton W | 0 | 0 | | |

DAVIES, Kevin (F)   515   98
H: 6 0 W: 12 10 b.Sheffield 26-3-77
Source: Trainee. *Honours:* England Youth, Under-21.

1993–94	Chesterfield	24	4		
1994–95	Chesterfield	41	11		
1995–96	Chesterfield	50	4		
1996–97	Chesterfield	54	3	129	22
1996–97	Southampton	0	0		
1997–98	Southampton	25	9		
1998–99	Blackburn R	21	1		
1999–2000	Blackburn R	2	0	23	1
1999–2000	Southampton	23	6		
2000–01	Southampton	27	1		
2001–02	Southampton	23	2		
2002–03	Southampton	9	1	107	19
2002–03	*Millwall*	9	3	9	3
2003–04	Bolton W	38	9		
2004–05	Bolton W	35	8		
2005–06	Bolton W	37	7		
2006–07	Bolton W	30	8		
2007–08	Bolton W	32	3		

Season	Club	A	G	Tot A	Tot G
2008–09	Bolton W	38	11		
2009–10	Bolton W	37	7	247	53

DAVIES, Mark (M)   61 2
H: 5 11   W: 11 08   b.Wolverhampton 18-2-88
Source: Scholar. Honours: England Youth.

Season	Club	A	G	Tot A	Tot G
2004–05	Wolverhampton W	0	0		
2005–06	Wolverhampton W	20	1		
2006–07	Wolverhampton W	7	0		
2007–08	Wolverhampton W	0	0		
2008–09	Wolverhampton W	0	0	27	1
2008–09	Leicester C	7	1	7	1
2008–09	Bolton W	10	0		
2009–10	Bolton W	17	0	27	0

DAVIS, Sean (M)   275 16
H: 5 10   W: 11 00   b.Clapham 20-9-79
Source: Trainee. Honours: England Under-21.

Season	Club	A	G	Tot A	Tot G
1996–97	Fulham	1	0		
1997–98	Fulham	0	0		
1998–99	Fulham	6	0		
1999–2000	Fulham	26	0		
2000–01	Fulham	40	6		
2001–02	Fulham	30	0		
2002–03	Fulham	28	3		
2003–04	Fulham	24	5	155	14
2004–05	Tottenham H	15	0		
2005–06	Tottenham H	0	0	15	0
2005–06	Portsmouth	17	1		
2006–07	Portsmouth	31	0		
2007–08	Portsmouth	22	0		
2008–09	Portsmouth	32	1		
2009–10	Portsmouth	0	0	102	2
2009–10	Bolton W	3	0	3	0

ELMANDER, Johan (F)   329 83
H: 6 1   W: 11 13   b.Alingsas 27-5-81
Honours: Sweden Under-21, 47 full caps, 13 goals.

Season	Club	A	G	Tot A	Tot G
1997	Holmalund	5	0		
1998	Holmalund	19	5	24	5
1999	Orgryte	18	2		
2000	Orgryte	21	2	39	4
2000–01	Feyenoord	16	2		
2001–02	Feyenoord	22	1		
2002	Djurgaarden	8	5		
2002–03	Feyenoord	1	0	39	3
2003	Djurgaarden	11	7	19	12
2003–04	NAC Breda	31	7	31	7
2004–05	Brondby	27	9		
2005–06	Brondby	31	13	58	22
2006–07	Toulouse	32	11		
2007–08	Toulouse	32	11	64	22
2008–09	Bolton W	30	5		
2009–10	Bolton W	25	3	55	8

GARDNER, Ricardo (D)   333 20
H: 5 9   W: 11 00   b.St Andrews 25-9-78
Source: Harbour View. Honours: Jamaica 109 full caps, 9 goals.

Season	Club	A	G	Tot A	Tot G
1998–99	Bolton W	30	2		
1999–2000	Bolton W	29	5		
2000–01	Bolton W	32	3		
2001–02	Bolton W	31	3		
2002–03	Bolton W	32	2		
2003–04	Bolton W	22	0		
2004–05	Bolton W	33	0		
2005–06	Bolton W	30	0		
2006–07	Bolton W	18	0		
2007–08	Bolton W	26	0		
2008–09	Bolton W	29	4		
2009–10	Bolton W	21	1	333	20

HOLDEN, Stuart (M)   89 15
H: 5 10   W: 11 07   b.Aberdeen 1-8-85
Source: Clemson Tigers. Honours: USA 15 full caps, 2 goals.

Season	Club	A	G	Tot A	Tot G
2005–06	Sunderland	0	0		
2006	Houston Dynamo	13	1		
2007	Houston Dynamo	21	5		
2008	Houston Dynamo	27	3		
2009	Houston Dynamo	26	6	87	15
2009–10	Bolton W	2	0	2	0

HUNT, Nicky (D)   160 1
H: 6 1   W: 13 07   b.Westhoughton 3-9-83
Source: Scholar. Honours: England Under-21.

Season	Club	A	G	Tot A	Tot G
2000–01	Bolton W	1	0		
2001–02	Bolton W	0	0		
2002–03	Bolton W	0	0		
2003–04	Bolton W	31	1		
2004–05	Bolton W	29	0		
2005–06	Bolton W	20	0		
2006–07	Bolton W	33	0		
2007–08	Bolton W	14	0		
2008–09	Bolton W	0	0		
2008–09	Birmingham C	11	0	11	0
2009–10	Bolton W	0	0	128	1
2009–10	Derby Co	21	0	21	0

JAASKELAINEN, Jussi (G)   539 0
H: 6 3   W: 12 10   b.Vaasa 19-4-75
Honours: Finland Youth, Under-21, 55 full caps.

Season	Club	A	G	Tot A	Tot G
1992	MP	6	0		
1993	MP	6	0		
1994	MP	26	0		
1995	MP	26	0	64	0
1996	VPS	27	0		
1997	VPS	27	0	54	0
1997–98	Bolton W	0	0		
1998–99	Bolton W	34	0		
1999–2000	Bolton W	34	0		
2000–01	Bolton W	27	0		
2001–02	Bolton W	34	0		
2002–03	Bolton W	38	0		
2003–04	Bolton W	38	0		
2004–05	Bolton W	36	0		
2005–06	Bolton W	38	0		
2006–07	Bolton W	38	0		
2007–08	Bolton W	28	0		
2008–09	Bolton W	38	0		
2009–10	Bolton W	38	0	421	0

KLASNIC, Ivan (F)   302 89
H: 6 1   W: 12 00   b.Hamburg 29-1-80
Honours: Croatia Under-21, 38 full caps, 12 goals.

Season	Club	A	G	Tot A	Tot G
1997–98	St Pauli	8	0		
1998–99	St Pauli	24	8		
1999–2000	St Pauli	32	8		
2000–01	St Pauli	31	10	95	26
2001–02	Werder Bremen	23	1		
2002–03	Werder Bremen	13	2		
2003–04	Werder Bremen	29	13		
2004–05	Werder Bremen	28	10		
2005–06	Werder Bremen	30	15		
2006–07	Werder Bremen	13	1		
2007–08	Werder Bremen	16	7	152	49
2008–09	Nantes	28	6	28	6
2009–10	Bolton W	27	8	27	8

KNIGHT, Zat (D)   233 6
H: 6 6   W: 15 02   b.Solihull 2-5-80
Source: Rushall Olympic. Honours: England Under-21, 2 full caps.

Season	Club	A	G	Tot A	Tot G
1998–99	Fulham	0	0		
1999–2000	Fulham	0	0		
1999–2000	Peterborough U	8	0	8	0
2000–01	Fulham	0	0		
2001–02	Fulham	10	0		
2002–03	Fulham	17	0		
2003–04	Fulham	31	0		
2004–05	Fulham	35	1		
2005–06	Fulham	30	0		
2006–07	Fulham	23	2		
2007–08	Fulham	4	0	150	3
2007–08	Aston Villa	27	1		
2008–09	Aston Villa	13	1		
2009–10	Aston Villa	0	0	40	2
2009–10	Bolton W	35	1	35	1

LAINTON, Robert (G)   0 0
H: 6 2   W: 12 06   b.Ashton-under-Lyne 12-10-89
Source: Scholar.

Season	Club	A	G	Tot A	Tot G
2009–10	Bolton W	0	0		

LEE, Chung Yong (M)   85 14
H: 5 11   W: 10 09   b.Seoul 2-7-88
Honours: South Korea 28 full caps, 5 goals.

Season	Club	A	G	Tot A	Tot G
2006	FC Seoul	2	0		
2007	FC Seoul	15	3		
2008	FC Seoul	20	5		
2009	FC Seoul	14	2	51	10
2009–10	Bolton W	34	4	34	4

McCANN, Gavin (M)   312 12
H: 5 11   W: 11 00   b.Blackpool 10-1-78
Source: Trainee. Honours: England 1 full cap.

Season	Club	A	G	Tot A	Tot G
1995–96	Everton	0	0		
1996–97	Everton	0	0		
1997–98	Everton	11	0		
1998–99	Everton	0	0	11	0
1998–99	Sunderland	11	0		
1999–2000	Sunderland	24	4		
2000–01	Sunderland	22	3		
2001–02	Sunderland	29	0		
2002–03	Sunderland	30	1	116	8
2003–04	Aston Villa	28	0		
2004–05	Aston Villa	20	1		
2005–06	Aston Villa	32	1		
2006–07	Aston Villa	30	1	110	3
2007–08	Bolton W	31	1		
2008–09	Bolton W	33	0		
2009–10	Bolton W	11	0	75	1

MUAMBA, Fabrice (M)   145 3
H: 6 1   W: 11 10   b.DR Congo 6-4-88
Source: Scholar. Honours: England Youth, Under-21.

Season	Club	A	G	Tot A	Tot G
2005–06	Arsenal	0	0		
2006–07	Arsenal	0	0		
2006–07	Birmingham C	34	0		
2007–08	Birmingham C	37	2	71	2
2008–09	Bolton W	38	0		
2009–10	Bolton W	36	1	74	1

MUSTAPHA, Riga (F)   230 55
H: 5 10   W: 11 00   b.Accra 10-10-81
Honours: Holland Under-21.

Season	Club	A	G	Tot A	Tot G
1998–99	Vitesse	1	0		
1999–2000	Vitesse	7	0		
2000–01	Roosendaal	8	0	8	0
2001–02	Vitesse	6	1		
2002–03	Vitesse	17	0	31	1
2003–04	Sparta Rotterdam	32	4		
2004–05	Sparta Rotterdam	36	22	68	26
2005–06	Levante	38	11		
2006–07	Levante	33	9		
2007–08	Levante	34	8	105	28
2008–09	Bolton W	17	0		
2009–10	Bolton W	1	0	18	0

O'BRIEN, Andy (D)   357 10
H: 6 2   W: 11 13   b.Harrogate 29-6-79
Source: Trainee. Honours: England Youth, Under-21, Eire Under-21, 26 full caps, 1 goal.

Season	Club	A	G	Tot A	Tot G
1996–97	Bradford C	22	2		
1997–98	Bradford C	26	0		
1998–99	Bradford C	31	0		
1999–2000	Bradford C	36	1		
2000–01	Bradford C	18	0	133	3
2000–01	Newcastle U	9	1		
2001–02	Newcastle U	34	2		
2002–03	Newcastle U	26	0		
2003–04	Newcastle U	28	1		
2004–05	Newcastle U	23	2	120	6
2005–06	Portsmouth	29	0		
2006–07	Portsmouth	3	0		
2007–08	Portsmouth	0	0	32	0
2007–08	Bolton W	32	0		
2008–09	Bolton W	34	1		
2009–10	Bolton W	6	0	72	1

O'BRIEN, Joey (M)   65 2
H: 5 11   W: 10 13   b.Dublin 17-2-86
Source: Scholar. Honours: Eire Youth Under-21, 3 full caps.

Season	Club	A	G	Tot A	Tot G
2004–05	Bolton W	1	0		
2004–05	Sheffield W	15	2	15	2
2005–06	Bolton W	23	0		
2006–07	Bolton W	0	0		
2007–08	Bolton W	19	0		
2008–09	Bolton W	7	0		
2009–10	Bolton W	0	0	50	0

O'HALLORAN, Michael (F)   0 0
H: 6 2
Source: Scholar.

Season	Club	A	G	Tot A	Tot G
2009–10	Bolton W	0	0		

OBADEYI, Temitope (F)   26 3
H: 5 10   W: 11 09   b.Coventry 29-10-89
Source: Coventry C. Honours: England Youth, Under-20.

Season	Club	A	G	Tot A	Tot G
2006–07	Bolton W	0	0		
2007–08	Bolton W	0	0		
2008–09	Bolton W	3	0		
2009–10	Bolton W	0	0	3	0
2009–10	Swindon T	12	2	12	2
2009–10	Rochdale	11	1	11	1

RICKETTS, Sam (D) 271 3
H: 6 1 W: 12 01 b.Aylesbury 11-10-81
Source: Trainee. *Honours:* Wales 38 full caps.

1999-2000	Oxford U	0	0		
2000-01	Oxford U	14	0		
2001-02	Oxford U	29	1		
2002-03	Oxford U	2	0	45	1
From Telford U					
2004-05	Swansea C	42	0		
2005-06	Swansea C	44	1	86	1
2006-07	Hull C	40	1		
2007-08	Hull C	44	0		
2008-09	Hull C	29	0		
2009-10	Hull C	0	0	113	1
2009-10	Bolton W	27	0	27	0

SAMUEL, JLloyd (D) 248 2
H: 5 11 W: 11 04 b.Trinidad 29-3-81
Source: Charlton Ath Trainee. *Honours:* England Youth, Under-20, Under-21.

1998-99	Aston Villa	0	0		
1999-2000	Aston Villa	9	0		
2000-01	Aston Villa	3	0		
2001-02	*Gillingham*	8	0	8	0
2001-02	Aston Villa	23	0		
2002-03	Aston Villa	38	0		
2003-04	Aston Villa	38	2		
2004-05	Aston Villa	35	0		
2005-06	Aston Villa	19	0		
2006-07	Aston Villa	4	0	169	2
2007-08	Bolton W	20	0		
2008-09	Bolton W	38	0		
2009-10	Bolton W	13	0	71	0

SHERIDAN, Sam (M) 0 0
H: 5 11 W: 11 10 b.Manchester 30-11-89
Source: Scholar.

| 2009-10 | Bolton W | 0 | 0 | | |

SHITTU, Dan (D) 265 27
H: 6 2 W: 16 03 b.Lagos 2-9-80
Honours: Nigeria 30 full caps.

1999-2000	Charlton Ath	0	0		
2000-01	Charlton Ath	0	0		
2000-01	*Blackpool*	17	2	17	2
2001-02	Charlton Ath	0	0		
2001-02	QPR	27	2		
2002-03	QPR	43	7		
2003-04	QPR	20	0		
2004-05	QPR	34	4		
2005-06	QPR	45	4	169	17
2006-07	Watford	30	1		
2007-08	Watford	39	7	69	8
2008-09	Bolton W	10	0		
2009-10	Bolton W	0	0	10	0

STEINSSON, Gretar Rafn (D) 238 25
H: 6 2 W: 16 03 b.Siglufjordur 9-1-82
Honours: Iceland 38 full caps, 4 goals.

1999	IA Akranes	0	0		
2000	IA Akranes	13	0		
2001	IA Akranes	18	6		
2002	IA Akranes	17	2		
2003	IA Akranes	11	2		
2004	IA Akranes	17	2	76	12
2004-05	Young Boys	14	3		
2005-06	Young Boys	7	0	21	3
2005-06	AZ	20	4		
2006-07	AZ	25	1		
2007-08	AZ	16	2	61	7
2007-08	Bolton W	16	0		
2008-09	Bolton W	37	3		
2009-10	Bolton W	27	0	80	3

TAYLOR, Matthew (D) 395 60
H: 5 11 W: 12 03 b.Oxford 27-11-81
Source: Trainee. *Honours:* England Youth, Under-21.

1998-99	Luton T	0	0		
1999-2000	Luton T	41	4		
2000-01	Luton T	45	1		
2001-02	Luton T	43	11	129	16
2002-03	Portsmouth	35	7		
2003-04	Portsmouth	30	0		
2004-05	Portsmouth	32	1		
2005-06	Portsmouth	34	6		
2006-07	Portsmouth	35	8		
2007-08	Portsmouth	13	1	179	23
2007-08	Bolton W	16	3		
2008-09	Bolton W	34	10		
2009-10	Bolton W	37	8	87	21

VAZ TE, Ricardo (F) 64 3
H: 6 2 W: 12 05 b.Lisbon 1-10-86
Source: Trainee. *Honours:* Portugal Youth, Under-20, Under-21.

2003-04	Bolton W	1	0		
2004-05	Bolton W	7	0		
2005-06	Bolton W	22	3		
2006-07	Bolton W	25	0		
2006-07	Hull C	6	0	6	0
2007-08	Bolton W	1	0		
2008-09	Bolton W	2	0		
2009-10	Bolton W	0	0	58	3

WARD, Danny (F) 30 7
H: 5 11 W: 12 05 b.Bradford 11-12-91
Source: Leeds U.

2008-09	Bolton W	0	0		
2009-10	Bolton W	2	0	2	0
2009-10	*Swindon T*	28	7	28	7

Scholars
Battersby, Nathan Paul; Bennett, Rhys Gordon; Blakeman, Adam John; Burns, Andrew John; Campbell, Javlon; Duyile, Raphael; Eckersley, Thomas Scott; Irwin, Liam Joseph; Lynch, Jay MacGregor, Graeme Douglas; McGeechan, Maison Sean; McQuade, Alexander Michael; Mooy, Aaron Frank; Odelusi, Oluwasanmi; Proudfoot, Lewis Steven; Riley, Joseph; Sampson, Jack; Stayte, Ryan; Turner, Thomas David.

BOURNEMOUTH (11)

BARTLEY, Marvyn (M) 87 2
H: 6 1 W: 12 04 b.Reading 4-7-86
Source: Hampton & Richmond B.

2007-08	Bournemouth	20	1		
2008-09	Bournemouth	33	1		
2009-10	Bournemouth	34	0	87	2

BRADBURY, Lee (F) 495 92
H: 6 0 W: 12 07 b.Isle of Wight 3-7-75
Source: Cowes. *Honours:* England Under-21.

1995-96	Portsmouth	12	0		
1995-96	*Exeter C*	14	5	14	5
1996-97	Portsmouth	42	15		
1997-98	Manchester C	27	7		
1998-99	Manchester C	13	3	40	10
1998-99	Crystal Palace	22	4		
1998-99	*Birmingham C*	7	0	7	0
1999-2000	Crystal Palace	10	2	32	6
1999-2000	Portsmouth	35	10		
2000-01	Portsmouth	39	10		
2001-02	Portsmouth	22	7		
2002-03	Portsmouth	3	1		
2002-03	*Sheffield W*	11	3	11	3
2003-04	Portsmouth	0	0	153	43
2003-04	*Derby Co*	7	0	7	0
2003-04	*Walsall*	8	1	8	1
2004-05	Oxford U	41	4		
2005-06	Oxford U	22	5	63	9
2005-06	Southend U	15	1		
2006-07	Southend U	31	4		
2007-08	Southend U	1	0	47	5
2007-08	Bournemouth	35	3		
2008-09	Bournemouth	34	6		
2009-10	Bournemouth	44	1	113	10

CONNELL, Alan (F) 214 41
H: 6 0 W: 12 00 b.Enfield 5-2-83
Source: Ipswich T Trainee.

2002-03	Bournemouth	13	6		
2003-04	Bournemouth	7	0		
2004-05	Bournemouth	34	2		
2005-05	*Torquay U*	22	7	22	7
2006-07	*Hereford U*	44	9	44	9
2007-08	Brentford	42	12		
2008-09	Brentford	2	0	44	12
2008-09	Bournemouth	2	0		
2009-10	Bournemouth	38	5	104	13

COOPER, Shaun (D) 175 1
H: 5 10 W: 10 05 b.Newport (IW) 5-10-83
Source: School.

2000-01	Portsmouth	0	0		
2001-02	Portsmouth	7	0		
2002-03	Portsmouth	0	0		
2003-04	Portsmouth	0	0		
2003-04	*Leyton Orient*	9	0	9	0
2004-05	Portsmouth	0	0		
2004-05	*Kidderminster H*	10	0	10	0
2005-06	Portsmouth	0	0	7	0
2005-06	Bournemouth	35	0		
2006-07	Bournemouth	33	0		
2007-08	Bournemouth	38	1		
2008-09	Bournemouth	37	0		
2009-10	Bournemouth	6	0	149	1

CUMMINGS, Warren (D) 248 7
H: 5 9 W: 11 05 b.Aberdeen 15-10-80
Source: Trainee. *Honours:* Scotland Under-21, 1 full cap.

1999-2000	Chelsea	0	0		
2000-01	Chelsea	0	0		
2000-01	*Bournemouth*	10	1		
2000-01	WBA	3	0		
2001-02	Chelsea	0	0		
2001-02	*WBA*	14	0	17	0
2002-03	Chelsea	0	0		
2002-03	Bournemouth	20	0		
2003-04	Bournemouth	42	2		
2004-05	Bournemouth	30	2		
2005-06	Bournemouth	0	0		
2006-07	Bournemouth	31	0		
2007-08	Bournemouth	32	2		
2008-09	Bournemouth	32	0		
2009-10	Bournemouth	34	0	231	7

FEENEY, Liam (M) 59 8
H: 5 10 W: 12 02 b.Hammersmith 21-1-87
Source: Salisbury C.
On loan from Salisbury C.

2008-09	Southend U	1	0	1	0
2008-09	Bournemouth	14	3		
2009-10	Bournemouth	44	5	58	8

FLETCHER, Steve (F) 629 105
H: 6 2 W: 14 09 b.Hartlepool 26-7-72
Source: Trainee.

1990-91	Hartlepool U	14	2		
1991-92	Hartlepool U	18	2	32	4
1992-93	Bournemouth	31	4		
1993-94	Bournemouth	36	6		
1994-95	Bournemouth	40	6		
1995-96	Bournemouth	7	1		
1996-97	Bournemouth	35	7		
1997-98	Bournemouth	42	12		
1998-99	Bournemouth	39	8		
1999-2000	Bournemouth	36	7		
2000-01	Bournemouth	45	9		
2001-02	Bournemouth	2	0		
2002-03	Bournemouth	35	5		
2003-04	Bournemouth	41	9		
2004-05	Bournemouth	36	9		
2005-06	Bournemouth	27	4		
2006-07	Bournemouth	41	1		
2007-08	Chesterfield	38	5	38	5
From Crawley T.					
2008-09	Bournemouth	21	4		
2009-10	Bournemouth	45	4	559	96

GARRY, Ryan (D) 68 1
H: 6 0 W: 11 05 b.Hornchurch 29-9-83
Source: Scholar. *Honours:* England Youth, Under-20.

2001-02	Arsenal	0	0		
2002-03	Arsenal	1	0		
2003-04	Arsenal	0	0		
2004-05	Arsenal	0	0		
2005-06	Arsenal	0	0		
2006-07	Arsenal	0	0	1	0
2007-08	Bournemouth	8	0		
2008-09	Bournemouth	25	0		
2009-10	Bournemouth	34	1	67	1

GOULDING, Jeff (F) 44 4
H: 6 2 W: 11 11 b.Sutton 13-5-84
Source: Croydon, Egham T, Aldershot T, Hayes, Yeading, Fisher Ath.

| 2008-09 | Bournemouth | 27 | 3 | | |
| 2009-10 | Bournemouth | 17 | 1 | 44 | 4 |

GUYETT, Scott (D) 145 2
H: 6 2 W: 13 06 b.Ascot 20-1-76
Source: Brisbane C, Gresley R, Southport.

2001-02	Oxford U	22	0	22	0
From Chester C.					
2004-05	Yeovil T	18	2		
2005-06	Yeovil T	21	0		
2006-07	Yeovil T	16	0		
2007-08	Yeovil T	34	0	89	2

2008–09	Bournemouth	25	0
2009–10	Bournemouth	9	0	34	0

HOLLANDS, Danny (M)   161 18
H: 6 0   W: 11 11   b.Ashford 6-11-85
Source: Trainee.

2003–04	Chelsea	0	0
2004–05	Chelsea	0	0
2005–06	Chelsea	0	0
2005–06	*Torquay U*	10	1	10	1
2006–07	Bournemouth	33	1
2007–08	Bournemouth	37	4
2008–09	Bournemouth	42	6
2009–10	Bournemouth	39	6	151	17

IGOE, Sammy (M)   458 32
H: 5 6   W: 10 00   b.Staines 30-9-75
Source: Trainee.

1993–94	Portsmouth	0	0
1994–95	Portsmouth	1	0
1995–96	Portsmouth	22	0
1996–97	Portsmouth	40	2
1997–98	Portsmouth	31	3
1998–99	Portsmouth	40	5
1999–2000	Portsmouth	26	1	160	11
1999–2000	Reading	6	0
2000–01	Reading	31	6
2001–02	Reading	35	1
2002–03	Reading	15	0	87	7
2002–03	*Luton T*	2	0	2	0
2003–04	Swindon T	36	5
2004–05	Swindon T	43	4	79	9
2005–06	Millwall	5	0	5	0
2005–06	Bristol R	11	1
2006–07	Bristol R	40	1
2007–08	Bristol R	21	0	72	2
2007–08	*Hereford U*	4	0	4	0
2008–09	Bournemouth	28	1
2009–10	Bournemouth	21	2	49	3

INGS, Danny (M)   0 0
H: 5 10   W: 11 07   b.Winchester 1-8-92
Source: Scholar.

2009–10	Bournemouth	0	0

JALAL, Shwan (G)   105 0
H: 6 2   W: 14 02   b.Baghdad 14-8-83
Source: Hastings T.

2001–02	Tottenham H	0	0
2002–03	Tottenham H	0	0
2003–04	Tottenham H	0	0
From Woking.			
2006–07	*Sheffield W*	0	0
2006–07	Peterborough U	1	0
2007–08	Peterborough U	7	0
2007–08	*Morecambe*	12	0	12	0
2008–09	Peterborough U	0	0	8	0
2008–09	Bournemouth	41	0
2009–10	Bournemouth	44	0	85	0

McQUOID, Josh (M)   52 1
H: 5 9   W: 10 10   b.Southampton 15-12-89
Source: Scholar. *Honours:* Northern Ireland Under-21, B.

2006–07	Bournemouth	2	0
2007–08	Bournemouth	5	0
2008–09	Bournemouth	16	0
2009–10	Bournemouth	29	1	52	1

MOLESLEY, Mark (M)   39 5
H: 6 1   W: 12 07   b.Hillingdon 11-3-81
From Hayes, Cam C, Ald T, Steve B, Grays

2008–09	Bournemouth	29	4
2009–10	Bournemouth	10	1	39	5

PARTINGTON, Joe (M)   28 2
H: 5 11   W: 11 13   b.Portsmouth 1-4-90
Source: Scholar. *Honours:* Wales Youth, Under-21.

2007–08	Bournemouth	6	1
2008–09	Bournemouth	11	1
2009–10	Bournemouth	11	0	28	2

PEARCE, Jason (D)   116 4
H: 5 11   W: 12 00   b.Hillingdon 6-12-87
Source: Scholar.

2006–07	Portsmouth	0	0
2007–08	Bournemouth	33	1
2008–09	Bournemouth	44	2
2009–10	Bournemouth	39	1	116	4

PITMAN, Brett (M)   172 55
H: 6 0   W: 11 00   b.Jersey 31-1-88

2005–06	Bournemouth	19	1
2006–07	Bournemouth	29	5
2007–08	Bournemouth	39	6
2008–09	Bournemouth	39	17
2009–10	Bournemouth	46	26	172	55

PRYCE, Ryan (G)   5 0
H: 6 0   W: 11 09   b.Bournemouth 20-9-89
Source: Scholar.

2007–08	Bournemouth	4	0
2008–09	Bournemouth	1	0
2009–10	Bournemouth	0	0	5	0

ROBINSON, Anton (M)   61 5
H: 5 9   W: 10 03   b.Harrow 17-2-86
Source: Millwall Scholar.
From Ex C, Eastb B, Fish A, Weymouth.

2008–09	Bournemouth	17	1
2009–10	Bournemouth	44	4	61	5

STOCKLEY, Jayden (F)   2 0
H: 6 2   W: 12 07   b.Poole 10-10-93
Source: School.

2009–10	Bournemouth	2	0	2	0

THOMAS, Dan (G)   2 0
H: 6 2   W: 13 01   b.Poole 1-9-91
Source: School.

2009–10	Bournemouth	2	0	2	0

WEBB, George (M)   2 0
H: 5 10   W: 11 06   b.Poole 1-5-91

2008–09	Bournemouth	1	0
2009–10	Bournemouth	1	0	2	0

BRADFORD C (12)

BATESON, Jonathan (D)   21 0
H: 6 1   W: 12 04   b.Blackburn 20-9-89
Source: Blackburn R.

2008–09	Blackburn R	0	0
2009–10	Blackburn R	0	0
2009–10	Bradford C	21	0	21	0

BOULDING, Mick (F)   332 90
H: 5 10   W: 11 05   b.Sheffield 8-2-76
Source: Hallam.

1999–2000	Mansfield T	33	6
2000–01	Mansfield T	33	6
2001–02	Mansfield T	0	0
2001–02	Grimsby T	35	11
2002–03	Aston Villa	0	0
2002–03	*Sheffield U*	6	0	6	0
2002–03	Grimsby T	12	4
2003–04	Grimsby T	27	12	74	27
2003–04	Barnsley	14	0
2004–05	Barnsley	29	10	35	10
2004–05	*Cardiff C*	4	0	4	0
2005–06	Rotherham U	0	0
2006–07	Mansfield T	39	5
2007–08	Mansfield T	43	21	148	38
2008–09	Bradford C	44	12
2009–10	Bradford C	21	3	65	15

BOULDING, Rory (F)   23 0
H: 6 0   W: 12 02   b.Sheffield 21-7-88
Source: Ilkeston T.

2006–07	Mansfield T	9	0
2007–08	Mansfield T	11	0	20	0
2008–09	Bradford C	1	0
2009–10	Bradford C	2	0	3	0

BRANDON, Chris (M)   317 35
H: 5 8   W: 10 00   b.Bradford 7-4-76
Source: Bradford PA.

1999–2000	Torquay U	42	5
2000–01	Torquay U	2	0
2001–02	Torquay U	27	3	71	8
2002–03	Chesterfield	36	7
2003–04	Chesterfield	43	4	79	11
2004–05	Huddersfield T	44	6
2005–06	Huddersfield T	40	3
2006–07	Huddersfield T	23	1
2006–07	*Blackpool*	5	2	5	2
2007–08	Huddersfield T	28	2	135	12
2008–09	Bradford C	7	0
2009–10	Bradford C	20	2	27	2

BULLOCK, Lee (M)   349 40
H: 6 0   W: 11 04   b.Stockton 22-5-81
Source: Trainee.

1999–2000	York C	24	0
2000–01	York C	33	3
2001–02	York C	40	8
2002–03	York C	39	6
2003–04	York C	35	7	171	24
2003–04	*Cardiff C*	11	3
2004–05	Cardiff C	21	3	32	6
2005–06	Hartlepool U	31	4
2006–07	Hartlepool U	25	1
2007–08	Hartlepool U	1	0	57	5
2007–08	*Mansfield T*	5	0	5	0
2007–08	*Bury*	8	0	8	0
2007–08	Bradford C	12	1
2008–09	Bradford C	23	3
2009–10	Bradford C	41	1	76	5

CARSON, Rory (M)   0 0
H: 5 10   W: 11 06   b.County Donegal 31-12-90
Source: Scholar.

2009–10	Bradford C	0	0

CLARKE, Matthew (D)   328 19
H: 6 3   W: 13 00   b.Leeds 18-12-80
Source: Wolverhampton W Trainee.

1999–2000	Halifax T	19	0
2000–01	Halifax T	19	1
2001–02	Halifax T	31	1	69	2
2002–03	Darlington	38	3
2003–04	Darlington	45	4
2004–05	Darlington	43	3
2005–06	Darlington	43	3
2006–07	Bradford C	8	0
2006–07	*Darlington*	2	0	171	13
2007–08	Bradford C	17	1
2008–09	Bradford C	42	2
2009–10	Bradford C	21	1	88	4

CONVEY, Matthew (G)   0 0
H: 6 1   W: 11 12   b.Oman 5-11-89
Source: Scholar.

2008–09	Bradford C	0	0
2009–10	Bradford C	0	0

DALEY, Omar (M)   117 10
H: 5 10   W: 11 03   b.Kingston, Jamaica 25-4-81
Source: Portmore U. *Honours:* Jamaica Under-20, 56 full caps, 5 goals.

2003–04	Reading	6	0	6	0
2004–05	Preston NE	14	0	14	0
From Charleston B, Portmore U.			
2006–07	Bradford C	14	2
2007–08	Bradford C	41	4
2008–09	Bradford C	28	3
2009–10	Bradford C	14	1	97	10

DEAN, Luke (F)   1 0
H: 5 9   W: 11 00   b.Bradford 1-8-89
Source: Scholar.

2009–10	Bradford C	1	0	1	0

EVANS, Gary (F)   125 30
H: 6 0   W: 12 08   b.Macclesfield 26-4-88
Source: Crewe Alex.

2007–08	Macclesfield T	42	7
2008–09	Macclesfield T	40	12	82	19
2009–10	Macclesfield T	43	11	43	11

FLYNN, Michael (M)   236 34
H: 5 10   W: 13 04   b.Newport 17-10-80
Source: Barry T.

2002–03	Wigan Ath	17	1
2003–04	Wigan Ath	8	0
2004–05	Wigan Ath	13	1	38	2
2004–05	*Blackpool*	6	0
2004–05	Gillingham	16	3
2005–06	Gillingham	36	6
2006–07	Gillingham	45	10	97	19
2007–08	Blackpool	28	3	34	3
2008–09	*Darlington*	0	0
2008–09	Huddersfield T	25	4	25	4
2009–10	Bradford C	42	6	42	6

GLENNON, Matty (G)   279 0
H: 6 2   W: 14 08   b.Stockport 8-10-78
Source: Trainee.

1997–98	Bolton W	0	0
1998–99	Bolton W	0	0

1999–2000	Bolton W	0	0		
1999–2000	Port Vale	0	0		
1999–2000	*Stockport Co*	0	0		
2000–01	Bolton W	0	0		
2000–01	*Bristol R*	1	0	1	0
2000–01	*Carlisle U*	29	0		
2001–02	Hull C	26	0		
2002–03	Hull C	9	0	35	0
2002–03	Carlisle U	32	0		
2003–04	Carlisle U	44	0		
2004–05	Carlisle U	0	0	105	0
2005–06	St Johnstone	12	0	12	0
2006–07	Huddersfield T	46	0		
2007–08	Huddersfield T	45	0		
2008–09	Huddersfield T	18	0		
2009–10	Huddersfield T	0	0	109	0
2009–10	Bradford C	17	0	17	0

GRANT, Gavin (F) 35 1
H: 5 11 W: 12 04 b.Middlesex 27-3-84
Source: Tooting & Mitcham U.

2005–06	Gillingham	10	1	10	1
2005–06	Millwall	0	0		
2006–07	Millwall	4	0		
2007–08	Millwall	0	0	4	0
2008–09	Wycombe W	10	0		
2009–10	Wycombe W	0	0	10	0
2009–10	Bradford C	11	0	11	0

HANSON, James (F) 34 12
H: 6 4 W: 12 04 b.Bradford 9-11-87
Source: Eccleshill U, Guiseley.

2009–10	Bradford C	34	12	34	12

HARRISON, Ryan (M) 1 0
H: 5 10 W: 12 02 b.Leeds 13-10-91
Source: Scholar.

2009–10	Bradford C	1	0	1	0

HORNE, Louis (M) 1 0
H: 6 2 W: 12 07 b.Bradford 28-5-91
Source: Scholar.

2009–10	Bradford C	1	0	1	0

McLAUGHLIN, Jon (G) 8 0
H: 6 2 W: 13 00 b.Edinburgh 9-9-87
Source: Harrogate Railway.

2008–09	Bradford C	1	0		
2009–10	Bradford C	7	0	8	0

NEILSON, Scott (M) 23 1
H: 6 0 W: 12 10 b.Enfield 15-5-87
Source: Cambridge C.

2009–10	Bradford C	23	1	23	1

O'BRIEN, Luke (D) 80 2
H: 5 9 W: 12 01 b.Halifax 11-9-88
Source: Scholar.

2007–08	Bradford C	2	0		
2008–09	Bradford C	35	1		
2009–10	Bradford C	43	1	80	2

O'BRIEN, Jamie (M) 23 2
H: 6 0 W: 11 08 b.Dublin 28-9-87
Source: Cherry Orchard, Birmingham C Scholar, Barnsley.

2009–10	Bradford C	23	2	23	2

O'LEARY, Stephen (M) 88 7
H: 6 0 W: 11 09 b.Barnet 12-2-85
Source: Scholar. Honours: Eire Youth.

2003–04	Luton T	5	1		
2004–05	Luton T	17	1		
2005–06	Luton T	0	0		
2005–06	*Tranmere R*	21	3	21	3
2006–07	Luton T	7	1		
2007–08	Luton T	16	0	45	3
2008–09	Hereford U	15	1	15	1
2009–10	Bradford C	7	0	7	0

OSBORNE, Leon (F) 15 0
H: 5 10 W: 10 10 b.Doncaster 28-10-89
Source: Scholar.

2006–07	Bradford C	1	0		
2007–08	Bradford C	0	0		
2008–09	Bradford C	2	0		
2009–10	Bradford C	12	0	15	0

RAMSDEN, Simon (D) 212 7
H: 6 0 W: 12 06 b.Bishop Auckland 17-12-81
Source: Scholar.

2000–01	Sunderland	0	0		
2001–02	Sunderland	0	0		
2002–03	Sunderland	0	0		
2002–03	*Notts Co*	32	0	32	0
2003–04	Sunderland	0	0		
2004–05	Grimsby T	25	0		
2005–06	Grimsby T	12	0	37	0
2005–06	Rochdale	15	1		
2006–07	Rochdale	34	3		
2007–08	Rochdale	35	2		
2008–09	Rochdale	28	0	112	6
2009–10	Bradford C	31	1	31	1

REHMAN, Zesh (D) 149 4
H: 6 2 W: 12 08 b.Birmingham 14-10-83
Source: Scholar. Honours: Eng and Youth, Pakistan 6 full caps.

2001–02	Fulham	0	0		
2002–03	Fulham	0	0		
2003–04	Fulham	1	0		
2003–04	*Brighton & HA*	11	2		
2004–05	Fulham	17	0		
2005–06	Fulham	3	0	21	0
2005–06	*Norwich C*	5	0	5	0
2006–07	QPR	25	0		
2006–07	*Brighton & HA*	8	0	19	2
2007–08	QPR	21	0		
2008–09	QPR	0	0	46	0
2008–09	*Blackpool*	3	0	3	0
2008–09	*Bradford C*	17	0		
2009–10	Bradford C	38	2	55	2

SHARRY, Luke (M) 2 0
H: 5 10 W: 12 12 b.Leeds 9-3-90
Source: Scholar.

2008–09	Bradford C	1	0		
2009–10	Bradford C	1	0	2	0

THORNE, Peter (F) 485 170
H: 6 1 W: 13 13 b.Manchester 21-6-73
Source: Trainee.

1991–92	Blackburn R	0	0		
1992–93	Blackburn R	0	0		
1993–94	Blackburn R	0	0		
1993–94	*Wigan Ath*	11	0	11	0
1994–95	Blackburn R	0	0		
1994–95	Swindon T	20	5		
1995–96	Swindon T	26	10		
1996–97	Swindon T	31	8	77	27
1997–98	Stoke C	36	12		
1998–99	Stoke C	34	5		
1999–2000	Stoke C	45	24		
2000–01	Stoke C	38	16		
2001–02	Stoke C	5	4	158	65
2001–02	Cardiff C	26	8		
2002–03	Cardiff C	46	13		
2003–04	Cardiff C	23	13		
2004–05	Cardiff C	31	12	126	46
2005–06	Norwich C	21	1		
2006–07	Norwich C	15	0	36	1
2007–08	Bradford C	33	14		
2008–09	Bradford C	37	17		
2009–10	Bradford C	7	0	77	31

WETHERALL, David (D) 506 30
H: 6 3 W: 13 12 b.Sheffield 14-3-71
Source: School. Honours: England Schools.

1989–90	Sheffield W	0	0		
1990–91	Sheffield W	0	0		
1991–92	Leeds U	1	0		
1992–93	Leeds U	13	1		
1993–94	Leeds U	32	1		
1994–95	Leeds U	38	3		
1995–96	Leeds U	34	4		
1996–97	Leeds U	29	0		
1997–98	Leeds U	34	3		
1998–99	Leeds U	21	0	202	12
1999–2000	Bradford C	38	2		
2000–01	Bradford C	18	1		
2001–02	Bradford C	19	2		
2002–03	Bradford C	17	0		
2003–04	Bradford C	34	1		
2004–05	Bradford C	45	4		
2005–06	Bradford C	46	5		
2006–07	Bradford C	41	1		
2007–08	Bradford C	46	2		
2008–09	Bradford C	0	0		
2009–10	Bradford C	0	0	304	18

WILLIAMS, Steve (D) 39 4
H: 6 4 W: 13 06 b.Preston 24-4-87
Source: Charnock Richard, Chorley, Bamber Bridge, Hyde U, Fleetwood T, Bamber Bridge.

2009–10	Bradford C	39	4	39	4

BRENTFORD (13)

BEAN, Marcus (M) 194 14
H: 5 11 W: 11 06 b.Hammersmith 2-11-84
Source: Scholar.

2002–03	QPR	7	0		
2003–04	QPR	31	1		
2004–05	QPR	20	1		
2004–05	Swansea C	8	0		
2005–06	QPR	9	0	67	2
2005–06	Swansea C	9	1	17	1
2005–06	Blackpool	17	1		
2006–07	Blackpool	6	0		
2007–08	Blackpool	0	0	23	1
2007–08	*Rotherham U*	12	1	12	1
2008–09	Brentford	44	9		
2009–10	Brentford	31	0	75	9

BENNETT, Alan (D) 84 3
H: 6 2 W: 12 08 b.Kilkenny 4-10-81
Honours: Eire Under-21, B, 2 full caps.

2006–07	Reading	0	0		
2007–08	Reading	0	0		
2007–08	Southampton	10	0	10	0
2007–08	Brentford	11	1		
2008–09	Reading	0	0		
2008–09	Brentford	44	1		
2009–10	Brentford	13	0	68	2
2009–10	Wycombe W	6	1	6	1

BLAKE, Ryan (D) 1 0
H: 5 10 W: 10 10 b.Kingston 8-12-91
Source: Scholar. Honours: Northern Ireland Youth.

2009–10	Brentford	1	0	1	0

BULL, Nikki (G) 36 0
H: 6 2 W: 12 08 b.Hastings 2-10-81
Source: Scholarship.

1999–2000	QPR	0	0		
2000–01	QPR	0	0		
2001–02	QPR	0	0		
2008–09	Aldershot T	30	0	30	0
2009–10	Brentford	6	0	6	0

CORT, Carl (D) 249 62
H: 6 4 W: 12 04 b.Southwark 1-11-77
Source: Trainee. Honours: England Under-21.

1996–97	Wimbledon	1	0		
1996–97	*Lincoln C*	6	1	6	1
1997–98	Wimbledon	22	4		
1998–99	Wimbledon	16	3		
1999–2000	Wimbledon	34	9	73	16
2000–01	Newcastle U	13	6		
2001–02	Newcastle U	8	1		
2002–03	Newcastle U	1	0		
2003–04	Newcastle U	0	0	22	7
2003–04	Wolverhampton W	16	5		
2004–05	Wolverhampton W	37	15		
2005–06	Wolverhampton W	31	11		
2006–07	Wolverhampton W	10	0	94	31
2007–08	Leicester C	14	0		
2008–09	Leicester C	0	0	14	0
2008–09	Norwich C	12	1	12	1
2009–10	Brentford	28	6	28	6

DICKSON, Ryan (M) 111 4
H: 5 10 W: 11 05 b.Saltash 14-12-86
Source: Scholar.

2004–05	Plymouth Arg	3	0		
2005–06	Plymouth Arg	0	0		
2006–07	Plymouth Arg	0	0		
2006–07	*Torquay U*	9	1	9	1
2007–08	Plymouth Arg	0	0	5	0
2007–08	Brentford	31	0		
2008–09	Brentford	39	1		
2009–10	Brentford	27	2	97	3

FOSTER, Danny (D) 106 3
H: 5 10 W: 12 10 b.Enfield 23-9-84
Source: Trainee.

2002–03	Tottenham H	0	0		

2003–04	Tottenham H	0	0		
2004–05	Tottenham H	0	0		
2005–06	Tottenham H	0	0		
2006–07	Tottenham H	0	0		
2007–08	Dagenham & R	32	1		
2008–09	Dagenham & R	38	2	70	3
2009–10	Brentford	36	0	36	0

HUNT, David (M)   213 11
H: 5 11 W: 11 09 b.Dulwich 10-9-82
Source: Scholar.

2002–03	Crystal Palace	2	0	2	0
2003–04	Leyton Orient	38	1		
2004–05	Leyton Orient	27	0	65	1
2004–05	Northampton T	4	0		
2005–06	Northampton T	40	3		
2006–07	Northampton T	29	0	73	3
2007–08	Shrewsbury T	27	2		
2008–09	Shrewsbury T	2	0	29	2
2008–09	.Brentford	20	2		
2009–10	Brentford	24	3	44	5

KABBA, Steven (F)   187 34
H: 5 10 W: 11 03 b.Lambeth 7-3-81
Source: Trainee.

1999–2000	Crystal Palace	1	0		
2000–01	Crystal Palace	1	0		
2001–02	Crystal Palace	4	0		
2001–02	Luton T	3	0	3	0
2002–03	Crystal Palace	4	1	10	1
2002–03	Grimsby T	13	6	13	6
2002–03	Sheffield U	25	7		
2003–04	Sheffield U	1	0		
2004–05	Sheffield U	11	2		
2005–06	Sheffield U	34	9		
2006–07	Sheffield U	7	0	78	18
2006–07	Watford	11	0		
2007–08	Watford	14	1		
2008–09	Watford	0	0	25	1
2008–09	*Blackpool*	17	2	17	2
2008–09	*Oldham Ath*	8	0	8	0
2009–10	Brentford	10	0	10	0
2009–10	*Burton Alb*	23	6	23	6

LEGGE, Leon (D)   29 2
H: 6 1 W: 11 02 b.London 28-4-85
Source: Eastbourne UA, Hailsham T, Lewes, Tonbridge Angels.

2009–10	Brentford	29	2	29	2

MACDONALD, Charlie (F)   128 36
H: 5 8 W: 12 10 b.Southwark 13-2-81
Source: Trainee.

1998–99	Charlton Ath	0	0		
1999–2000	Charlton Ath	3	0		
2000–01	Charlton Ath	3	0		
2000–01	*Cheltenham T*	8	2	8	2
2001–02	Charlton Ath	2	1		
2001–02	*Torquay U*	5	0	5	0
2001–02	*Colchester U*	4	1	4	1
2002–03	Charlton Ath	0	0		
2003–04	Charlton Ath	0	0		
2004–05	Charlton Ath	0	0		
2005–06	Charlton Ath	0	0		
2006–07	Charlton Ath	0	0	8	1
2007–08	Southend U	25	1	25	1
2008–09	Brentford	38	16		
2009–10	Brentford	40	15	78	31

MOORE, Simon (G)   1 0
H: 6 3 W: 12 02 b.Isle of Wight 19-5-90
Source: Farnborough T.

2009–10	Brentford	1	0	1	0

O'CONNOR, Kevin (F)   344 29
H: 5 11 W: 12 00 b.Blackburn 24-2-82
Source: Trainee. *Honours:* Eire Youth, Under-21.

1999–2000	Brentford	6	0		
2000–01	Brentford	11	1		
2001–02	Brentford	25	0		
2002–03	Brentford	45	5		
2003–04	Brentford	43	1		
2004–05	Brentford	37	2		
2005–06	Brentford	30	7		
2006–07	Brentford	39	6		
2007–08	Brentford	37	3		
2008–09	Brentford	28	0		
2009–10	Brentford	43	4	344	29

OSBORNE, Karleigh (D)   94 5
H: 6 2 W: 12 04 b.Southall 19-3-88
Source: Scholar.

2004–05	Brentford	1	0		
2005–06	Brentford	1	0		
2006–07	Brentford	21	0		
2007–08	Brentford	29	1		
2008–09	Brentford	23	4		
2009–10	Brentford	19	0	94	5

PHILLIPS, Mark (D)   130 2
H: 6 2 W: 11 00 b.Lambeth 27-1-82
Source: Scholarship.

1999–2000	Millwall	0	0		
2000–01	Millwall	0	0		
2001–02	Millwall	1	0		
2002–03	Millwall	7	0		
2003–04	Millwall	0	0		
2004–05	Millwall	25	1		
2005–06	Millwall	22	0		
2006–07	Millwall	12	0		
2006–07	*Darlington*	8	0	8	0
2007–08	Millwall	0	0	67	1
2008–09	Brentford	33	1		
2009–10	Brentford	22	0	55	1

SAUNDERS, Sam (M)   88 15
H: 5 6 W: 11 04 b.London 29-10-82
Source: Welling U, Hastings T, Ashford T, Carshalton Ath.

2007–08	Dagenham & R	22	0		
2008–09	Dagenham & R	40	14	62	14
2009–10	Brentford	26	1	26	1

STREVENS, Ben (M)   186 44
H: 6 1 W: 12 00 b.Edgware 24-5-80
Source: Wingate & Finchley.

1998–99	Barnet	0	0		
1999–2000	Barnet	6	0		
2000–01	Barnet	28	4		
2001–02	Barnet	0	0		
2002–03	Barnet	0	0		
2003–04	Barnet	0	0		
2004–05	Barnet	0	0		
2005–06	Barnet	35	5		
2006–07	Barnet	0	0	69	9

From Crawley T.

2007–08	Dagenham & R	46	15		
2008–09	Dagenham & R	46	14	92	29
2009–10	Brentford	25	6	25	6

TAYLOR, Cleveland (M)   274 23
H: 5 8 W: 10 07 b.Leicester 9-9-83
Source: Scholar. *Honours:* Jamaica Youth.

2001–02	Bolton W	0	0		
2002–03	Bolton W	0	0		
2002–03	*Exeter C*	3	0	3	0
2003–04	Bolton W	0	0		
2003–04	Scunthorpe U	20	3		
2004–05	Scunthorpe U	44	6		
2005–06	Scunthorpe U	45	3		
2006–07	Scunthorpe U	45	3		
2007–08	Scunthorpe U	20	0	174	15
2007–08	Carlisle U	18	0		
2008–09	Carlisle U	42	3		
2009–10	Carlisle U	1	0	61	3
2009–10	Brentford	12	1	12	1
2009–10	*Burton Alb*	24	4	24	4

WESTON, Myles (F)   113 11
H: 5 11 W: 12 05 b.Lewisham 12-3-88
Source: Scholar.

2006–07	Charlton Ath	0	0		
2006–07	*Notts Co*	4	0		
2007–08	Notts Co	25	0		
2008–09	Notts Co	44	3	73	3
2009–10	Brentford	40	8	40	8

WOOD, Sam (M)   83 3
H: 6 0 W: 11 05 b.London 9-8-86
Source: Bromley.

2008–09	Brentford	40	1		
2009–10	Brentford	43	2	83	3

BRIGHTON & HA (14)

BREZOVAN, Peter (G)   113 0
H: 6 6 W: 14 13 b.Bratislava 9-12-79
Source: PS Bratislava, Vinohrady, Devin, Slovan Breclav, Zigma Olomouc. *Honours:* Slovakia U-21.

2002–03	Brno	10	0		
2003–04	Brno	2	0		
2004–05	Inter Bratislava	8	0	8	0
2005–06	Brno	7	0	19	0
2006–07	Swindon T	14	0		
2007–08	Swindon T	31	0		
2008–09	Swindon T	21	0	66	0
2009–10	Brighton & HA	20	0	20	0

BRINKHURST, Steve (M)   0 0
H: 5 9 W: 11 11 b.Lewes 28-12-91
Source: Scholar.

2009–10	Brighton & HA	0	0	

CALDERON, Inigo (D)   224 9
H: 5 10 W: 12 02 b.Vitoria 4-1-82

2002–03	Alaves B	35	1		
2003–04	Alaves B	33	0	68	1
2004–05	Alicante	25	0		
2005–06	Alicante	31	4		
2006–07	Alicante	28	1	84	5
2007–08	Alaves	20	0		
2008–09	Alaves	33	2	53	2
2009–10	Brighton & HA	19	1	19	1

CAROLE, Sebastien (M)   128 6
H: 5 7 W: 11 05 b.Pontoise 8-9-82
Source: Monaco.

2003–04	West Ham U	1	0	1	0
2004–05	Chateauroux	11	1	11	1
2005–06	Brighton & HA	40	2		
2006–07	Leeds U	17	0		
2007–08	Leeds U	28	3		
2008–09	Leeds U	0	0	45	3
2008–09	*Darlington*	6	0	6	0
2008–09	Brighton & HA	12	0		
2009–10	*Tranmere R*	4	0	4	0
2009–10	Brighton & HA	9	0	61	2

CASKEY, Jake (M)   1 0
H: 5 10 W: 10 00 b.Southend 1-6-94
Source: Hull C.

2009–10	Brighton & HA	1	0	1	0

COOK, Steve (D)   2 0
H: 6 1 W: 12 13 b.Hastings 19-4-91
Source: Scholar.

2008–09	Brighton & HA	0	0		
2009–10	Brighton & HA	0	0	2	0

COX, Dean (M)   146 16
H: 5 4 W: 9 08 b.Cuckfield 12-8-87
Source: Scholar.

2005–06	Brighton & HA	1	0		
2006–07	Brighton & HA	42	6		
2007–08	Brighton & HA	42	4		
2008–09	Brighton & HA	40	4		
2009–10	Brighton & HA	21	0	146	16

CROFTS, Andrew (D)   227 22
H: 5 10 W: 12 09 b.Chatham 29-5-84
Source: Trainee. *Honours:* Wales Youth, Under-21, 13 full caps.

2000–01	Gillingham	1	0		
2001–02	Gillingham	0	0		
2002–03	Gillingham	8	0		
2003–04	Gillingham	8	0		
2004–05	Gillingham	27	2		
2005–06	Gillingham	45	2		
2006–07	Gillingham	43	8		
2007–08	Gillingham	41	5		
2008–09	Gillingham	9	0	174	17
2008–09	*Peterborough U*	9	0	9	0
2009–10	Brighton & HA	44	5	44	5

DAVIES, Craig (F)   173 31
H: 6 2 W: 13 05 b.Burton-on-Trent 9-1-86
Source: Manchester City. *Honours:* Wales Youth, Under-21, 5 full caps.

2004–05	Oxford U	28	6		
2005–06	Oxford U	20	2	48	8
2005–06	Verona	0	0		
2006–07	Wolverhampton W	23	0	23	0
2007–08	Oldham Ath	32	10		

2008–09	Oldham Ath	12	0	44 10
2008–09	*Stockport Co*	9	5	9 5
2008–09	Brighton & HA	16	1	
2009–10	Brighton & HA	5	0	21 1
2009–10	*Yeovil T*	4	0	4 0
2009–10	*Port Vale*	24	7	24 7

DICKER, Gary (M) 174 8
H: 6 0 W: 12 00 b.Dublin 31-7-86
Honours: Eire Under-21.

2004	UCD	9	1	
2005	UCD	31	2	
2006	UCD	28	2	68 5
2006–07	Birmingham C	0	0	
2007–08	Stockport Co	30	0	
2008–09	Stockport Co	25	0	55 0
2008–09	*Brighton & HA*	9	1	
2009–10	Brighton & HA	42	2	51 3

DICKINSON, Liam (F) 158 50
H: 6 4 W: 11 07 b.Salford 4-10-85
Source: Woodley Sports.

2005–06	Stockport Co	21	7	
2006–07	Stockport Co	33	7	
2007–08	Stockport Co	40	19	94 33
2008–09	*Huddersfield T*	13	6	13 6
2008–09	*Blackpool*	7	4	7 4
2008–09	*Leeds U*	8	0	8 0
2008–09	*Derby Co*	0	0	
2009–10	Brighton & HA	27	4	27 4
2009–10	*Peterborough U*	9	3	9 3

DUNK, Lewis (D) 1 0
H: 6 3 W: 12 02 b.Brighton 1-12-91
Source: Scholar.

2009–10	Brighton & HA	1	0	1 0

EL-ABD, Adam (D) 199 3
H: 5 10 W: 13 05 b.Brighton 11-9-84
Source: Scholar.

2003–04	Brighton & HA	11	0	
2004–05	Brighton & HA	16	0	
2005–06	Brighton & HA	29	0	
2006–07	Brighton & HA	42	1	
2007–08	Brighton & HA	35	1	
2008–09	Brighton & HA	31	0	
2009–10	Brighton & HA	35	1	199 3

ELPHICK, Tommy (M) 126 6
H: 5 11 W: 11 07 b.Brighton 7-9-87
Source: Scholar.

2005–06	Brighton & HA	1	0	
2006–07	Brighton & HA	3	0	
2007–08	Brighton & HA	39	2	
2008–09	Brighton & HA	39	1	
2009–10	Brighton & HA	44	3	126 6

FORSTER, Nicky (F) 596 189
H: 5 9 W: 11 05 b.Caterham 8-9-73
Source: Horley T. *Honours*: England Under-21.

1992–93	Gillingham	26	6	
1993–94	Gillingham	41	18	67 24
1994–95	Brentford	46	24	
1995–96	Brentford	38	5	
1996–97	Brentford	25	10	109 39
1996–97	Birmingham C	7	3	
1997–98	Birmingham C	28	3	
1998–99	Birmingham C	33	5	68 12
1999–2000	Reading	36	10	
2000–01	Reading	9	1	
2001–02	Reading	42	19	
2002–03	Reading	40	16	
2003–04	Reading	30	7	
2004–05	Reading	30	7	187 60
2005–06	Ipswich T	20	7	
2006–07	Ipswich T	4	1	24 8
2006–07	Hull C	35	5	35 5
2007–08	Brighton & HA	41	15	
2008–09	Brighton & HA	30	12	
2009–10	Brighton & HA	27	13	98 40
2009–10	*Charlton Ath*	8	2	8 2

HART, Gary (F) 370 44
H: 5 9 W: 12 03 b.Harlow 21-9-76
Source: Stansted.

1998–99	Brighton & HA	44	12	
1999–2000	Brighton & HA	43	9	
2000–01	Brighton & HA	45	7	
2001–02	Brighton & HA	39	4	
2002–03	Brighton & HA	36	4	
2003–04	Brighton & HA	42	3	
2004–05	Brighton & HA	26	2	
2005–06	Brighton & HA	35	1	
2006–07	Brighton & HA	25	2	
2007–08	Brighton & HA	7	0	
2008–09	Brighton & HA	11	0	
2009–10	Brighton & HA	17	0	370 44

HAWKINS, Colin (D) 261 20
H: 6 1 W: 12 06 b.Galway 17-8-77
Honours: Eire Youth, Under-20, Under-21.

1995–96	Coventry C	0	0	
1996–97	Coventry C	0	0	
1997–98	St Patrick's Ath	32	4	
1998–99	St Patrick's Ath	26	7	
1999–2000	St Patrick's Ath	27	2	85 13
From Doncaster R				
2001–02	Bohemians	9	1	
2002–03	Bohemians	21	2	
2003	Bohemians	30	1	
2004	Bohemians	29	1	89 5
2005	Shelbourne	26	0	
2006	Shelbourne	25	2	51 2
2006–07	Coventry C	13	0	
2007–08	Coventry C	0	0	13 0
2007–08	*Chesterfield*	5	0	5 0
2008–09	Brighton & HA	17	0	
2009–10	Brighton & HA	1	0	18 0

HOLROYD, Chris (F) 60 4
H: 5 11 W: 12 03 b.Macclesfield 24-10-86
Source: Crewe Alex Scholar.

2005–06	Chester C	0	0	
2006–07	Chester C	22	0	
2007–08	Chester C	25	4	
2008–09	Chester C	0	0	47 4
From Cambridge U.				
2009–10	Brighton & HA	13	0	13 0

KUIPERS, Michels (G) 266 0
H: 6 2 W: 14 03 b.Amsterdam 26-6-74
Source: SDW Amsterdam

1998–99	Bristol R	1	0	
1999–2000	Bristol R	0	0	1 0
2000–01	Brighton & HA	34	0	
2001–02	Brighton & HA	39	0	
2002–03	Brighton & HA	21	0	
2003–04	Brighton & HA	10	0	
2003–04	*Hull C*	3	0	3 0
2004–05	Brighton & HA	30	0	
2005–06	Brighton & HA	5	0	
2005–06	*Boston U*	15	0	15 0
2006–07	Brighton & HA	14	0	
2007–08	Brighton & HA	46	0	
2008–09	Brighton & HA	28	0	
2009–10	Brighton & HA	20	0	247 0

McNULTY, Jim (D) 87 3
H: 6 1 W: 12 00 b.Liverpool 13-2-85
Source: Scholar. *Honours*: Scotland Youth.

2003–04	Wrexham	0	0	
2004–05	Wrexham	0	0	
2005–06	Wrexham	0	0	
2006–07	Macclesfield T	15	0	
2007–08	Macclesfield T	19	1	34 1
2007–08	Stockport Co	11	0	
2008–09	Stockport Co	26	1	37 1
2009–10	Brighton & HA	8	0	13 1
2009–10	*Scunthorpe U*	3	0	3 0

MURRAY, Glenn (F) 168 63
H: 6 1 W: 12 12 b.Maryport 25-9-83
Source: Wilmington Hammerheads, Workington.

2005–06	Carlisle U	26	3	
2006–07	Carlisle U	1	0	27 3
2006–07	*Stockport Co*	11	3	11 3
2006–07	Rochdale	31	16	
2007–08	Rochdale	23	9	54 25
2007–08	Brighton & HA	21	9	
2008–09	Brighton & HA	23	11	
2009–10	Brighton & HA	32	12	76 32

NAVARRO, Alan (M) 246 9
H: 5 10 W: 11 07 b.Liverpool 21-5-81
Source: Trainee.

1998–99	Liverpool	0	0	
1999–2000	Liverpool	0	0	
2000–01	Liverpool	0	0	
2000–01	Crewe Alex	8	1	
2001–02	Liverpool	0	0	
2001–02	Crewe Alex	7	0	15 1
2001–02	Tranmere R	21	1	
2002–03	Tranmere R	5	0	
2003–04	Tranmere R	19	0	
2004–05	Tranmere R	0	0	
2004–05	*Chester C*	3	0	3 0
2004–05	*Macclesfield T*	11	1	
2005–06	Tranmere R	0	0	45 1
From Accrington S.				
2005–06	Macclesfield T	27	0	
2006–07	Macclesfield T	32	2	70 3
2007–08	Milton Keynes D	39	3	
2008–09	Milton Keynes D	38	1	77 4
2009–10	Brighton & HA	36	0	36 0

SMITH, Graeme (G) 153 0
H: 6 1 W: 12 04 b.Edinburgh 8-6-83

2003–04	Rangers	0	0	
2003–04	*Ross Co*	20	0	20 0
2004–05	Rangers	0	0	
2005–06	Motherwell	30	0	
2006–07	Motherwell	24	0	
2007–08	Motherwell	36	0	
2008–09	Motherwell	37	0	127 0
2009–10	Brighton & HA	6	0	6 0

SMITH, Jamie (M) 2 0
H: 5 6 W: 10 07 b.Leytonstone 16-9-89
Source: Leytonstone.

2009–10	Brighton & HA	2	0	2 0

TUNNICLIFFE, James (D) 67 3
H: 6 4 W: 12 03 b.Denton 17-1-89
Source: Scholar.

2005–06	Stockport Co	1	0	
2006–07	Stockport Co	5	0	
2007–08	Stockport Co	5	0	
2008–09	Stockport Co	30	0	41 0
2009–10	Brighton & HA	17	2	17 2
2009–10	*Milton Keynes D*	9	1	9 1

VIRGO, Adam (D) 204 15
H: 6 2 W: 13 12 b.Brighton 25-1-83
Source: Juniors. *Honours*: Scotland B.

2000–01	Brighton & HA	6	0	
2001–02	Brighton & HA	6	0	
2002–03	Brighton & HA	3	0	
2002–03	*Exeter C*	9	0	9 0
2003–04	Brighton & HA	22	1	
2004–05	Brighton & HA	36	8	
2005–06	Celtic	10	0	
2006–07	Celtic	0	0	10 0
2006–07	Coventry C	15	1	
2007–08	Coventry C	0	0	15 1
2007–08	Colchester U	36	1	36 1
2008–09	Brighton & HA	36	3	
2009–10	Brighton & HA	25	1	134 13

WALKER, Mitch (G) 1 0
H: 6 2 W: 13 00 b.St Albans 24-9-91
Source: Scholar.

2009–10	Brighton & HA	1	0	1 0

WHING, Andrew (D) 220 2
H: 6 0 W: 12 00 b.Birmingham 20-9-84
Source: Scholar.

2002–03	Coventry C	14	0	
2003–04	Coventry C	28	1	
2004–05	Coventry C	16	1	
2005–06	Coventry C	32	0	
2006–07	Coventry C	16	0	106 2
2006–07	*Brighton & HA*	12	0	
2007–08	Brighton & HA	42	0	
2008–09	Brighton & HA	40	0	
2009–10	Brighton & HA	9	0	103 0
2009–10	*Chesterfield*	11	0	11 0

WRIGHT, Jake (D) 7 0
H: 5 10 W: 11 07 b.Keighley 11-3-86
Source: Scholar.

2005–06	Bradford C	1	0	
2006–07	Bradford C	0	0	
2007–08	Bradford C	0	0	
2008–09	Bradford C	0	0	1 0
2009–10	Brighton & HA	6	0	6 0

BRISTOL C (15)

AKINDE, John (F) 33 9
H: 6 2 W: 10 01 b.Gravesend 8-7-89
Source: Ebbsfleet U.

2008–09	Bristol C	7	1	

2008–09	Wycombe W	11	7		
2009–10	Bristol C	7	0	14	1
2009–10	Wycombe W	6	1	17	8
2009–10	Brentford	2	0	2	0

ARTUS, Frankie (M) 20 3
H: 6 0 W: 11 02 b.Bristol 27-9-88
Source: Scholar.

2005–06	Bristol C	0	0		
2006–07	Bristol C	0	0		
2007–08	Bristol C	0	0		
2008–09	Brentford	1	0	1	0
2008–09	Cheltenham T	9	3		
2009–10	Bristol C	0	0		
2009–10	Cheltenham T	7	0	16	3
2009–10	Chesterfield	3	0	3	0

BASSO, Adriano (G) 165 0
H: 6 1 W: 11 07 b.Jundiai 18-4-75
Source: Woking.

2005–06	Bristol C	29	0		
2006–07	Bristol C	45	0		
2007–08	Bristol C	44	0		
2008–09	Bristol C	43	0		
2009–10	Bristol C	4	0	165	0

BLACKMAN, Andre (D) 0 0
H: 5 11 W: 11 05 b.Lambeth 10-11-90
Source: Arsenal, Tottenham H, Portsmouth Youth.

| 2009–10 | Bristol C | 0 | 0 | | |

CAMPBELL-RYCE, Jamal (M) 235 16
H: 5 7 W: 12 03 b.Lambeth 6-4-83
Source: Scholar. *Honours:* Jamaica 20 full caps.

2002–03	Charlton Ath	1	0		
2002–03	Leyton Orient	17	2	17	2
2003–04	Charlton Ath	2	0		
2003–04	Wimbledon	4	0	4	0
2004–05	Charlton Ath	0	0	3	0
2004–05	Chesterfield	14	0	14	0
2004–05	Rotherham U	24	0		
2005–06	Rotherham U	7	0	31	0
2005–06	Southend U	13	0		
2005–06	Colchester U	4	0	4	0
2006–07	Southend U	43	2		
2007–08	Southend U	2	0	58	2
2007–08	Barnsley	37	3		
2008–09	Barnsley	40	9		
2009–10	Barnsley	13	0	90	12
2009–10	Bristol C	14	0	14	0

CAREY, Louis (D) 523 12
H: 5 10 W: 11 00 b.Bristol 20-1-77
Source: Trainee. *Honours:* Scotland Under-21.

1995–96	Bristol C	23	0		
1996–97	Bristol C	42	0		
1997–98	Bristol C	38	0		
1998–99	Bristol C	41	0		
1999–2000	Bristol C	22	0		
2000–01	Bristol C	46	3		
2001–02	Bristol C	35	0		
2002–03	Bristol C	24	1		
2003–04	Bristol C	41	1		
2004–05	Coventry C	23	0	23	0
2004–05	Bristol C	14	0		
2005–06	Bristol C	38	3		
2006–07	Bristol C	38	2		
2007–08	Bristol C	33	0		
2008–09	Bristol C	28	0		
2009–10	Bristol C	37	2	500	12

CLARKSON, David (F) 247 53
H: 5 10 W: 10 03 b.Belshill 10-9-85
Honours: Scotland Under 21, B.

2002–03	Motherwell	19	3		
2003–04	Motherwell	38	12		
2004–05	Motherwell	35	3		
2005–06	Motherwell	32	4		
2006–07	Motherwell	29	2		
2007–08	Motherwell	35	12		
2008–09	Motherwell	33	13	221	49
2009–10	Bristol C	26	4	26	4

COLLIS, Steve (G) 84 0
H: 6 3 W: 12 05 b.Harrow 18-3-81
Source: Barnet Juniors.

1999–2000	Barnet	0	0		
2000–01	Nottingham F	0	0		
2001–02	Nottingham F	0	0		
2003–04	Yeovil T	11	0		
2004–05	Yeovil T	9	0		
2005–06	Yeovil T	23	0	43	0
2006–07	Southend U	1	0		
2007–08	Southend U	20	0	21	0
2008–09	Crewe Alex	18	0		
2009–10	Crewe Alex	1	0	19	0
2009–10	Bristol C	0	0		
2009–10	Torquay U	1	0	1	0

EDWARDS, Joe (D) 0 0
H: 5 8 W: 11 07 b.Gloucester 31-10-90
Source: Scholar.

| 2009–10 | Bristol C | 0 | 0 | | |

ELLIOTT, Marvin (M) 256 12
H: 6 0 W: 12 02 b.Wandsworth 15-9-84
Source: Scholar.

2001–02	Millwall	0	0		
2002–03	Millwall	1	0		
2003–04	Millwall	21	0		
2004–05	Millwall	41	1		
2005–06	Millwall	39	2		
2006–07	Millwall	42	0	144	3
2007–08	Bristol C	45	5		
2008–09	Bristol C	28	3		
2009–10	Bristol C	39	1	112	9

FONTAINE, Liam (D) 187 5
H: 5 11 W: 11 09 b.Beckenham 7-1-86
Source: Trainee. *Honours:* England Youth, Under-20.

2003–04	Fulham	0	0		
2004–05	Fulham	1	0		
2004–05	Yeovil T	15	0		
2005–06	Fulham	0	0	1	0
2005–06	Yeovil T	10	0	25	0
2005–06	Bristol C	15	0		
2006–07	Bristol C	30	0		
2007–08	Bristol C	38	1		
2008–09	Bristol C	42	2		
2009–10	Bristol C	36	2	161	5

GERKEN, Dean (G) 155 0
H: 6 3 W: 12 08 b.Rochford 22-5-85
Source: Scholar.

2003–04	Colchester U	1	0		
2004–05	Colchester U	13	0		
2005–06	Colchester U	7	0		
2006–07	Colchester U	27	0		
2007–08	Colchester U	40	0		
2008–09	Colchester U	21	0	109	0
2008–09	Darlington	7	0	7	0
2009–10	Bristol C	39	0	39	0

HARTLEY, Paul (M) 465 82
H: 5 8 W: 10 05 b.Glasgow 19-10-76
Honours: Scotland Under-21, 25 full caps, 1 goal.

1994–95	Hamilton A	16	0		
1995–96	Hamilton A	31	11	47	11
1996–97	Millwall	44	4	44	4
1997–98	Raith R	30	10	30	10
1998–99	Hibernian	12	5		
1999–2000	Hibernian	24	1	36	6
2000–01	St Johnstone	23	2		
2001–02	St Johnstone	32	4		
2002–03	St Johnstone	33	6	88	12
2003–04	Hearts	30	3		
2004–05	Hearts	33	11		
2005–06	Hearts	34	14		
2006–07	Hearts	21	3	118	31
2006–07	Celtic	10	0		
2007–08	Celtic	27	0		
2008–09	Celtic	25	3	62	3
2009–10	Bristol C	40	5	40	5

HAYNES, Danny (F) 157 26
H: 5 11 W: 12 04 b.London 19-1-88
Source: Scholar. *Honours:* England Youth.

2005–06	Ipswich T	19	3		
2006–07	Ipswich T	31	7		
2006–07	Millwall	5	2	5	2
2007–08	Ipswich T	40	7		
2008–09	Ipswich T	24	0	114	17
2009–10	Bristol C	38	7	38	7

HENDERSON, Stephen (G) 13 0
H: 6 3 W: 11 00 b.Dublin 2-5-88
Source: Scholar. *Honours:* Eire Under-21.

2005–06	Aston Villa	0	0		
2006–07	Aston Villa	0	0		
2007–08	Bristol C	1	0		
2008–09	Bristol C	1	0		
2009–10	Bristol C	3	0	5	0
2009–10	Aldershot T	8	0	8	0

JACKSON, Marlon (F) 27 1
H: 5 11 W: 11 12 b.Bristol 6-12-90
Source: Scholar.

2009–10	Bristol C	0	0		
2009–10	Hereford U	5	0	5	0
2009–10	Aldershot T	22	1	22	1

JOHNSON, Lee (M) 277 24
H: 5 6 W: 10 07 b.Newmarket 7-6-81
Source: Trainee.

1998–99	Watford	0	0		
1999–2000	Watford	0	0		
2000–01	Brighton & HA	0	0		
2000–01	Brentford	0	0		
2001–02	Brentford	0	0		
2003–04	Yeovil T	45	5		
2004–05	Yeovil T	44	7		
2005–06	Yeovil T	26	2	115	14
2005–06	Hearts	4	0	4	0
2006–07	Bristol C	42	5		
2007–08	Bristol C	40	1		
2008–09	Bristol C	44	3		
2009–10	Bristol C	28	1	154	10
2009–10	Derby Co	4	0	4	0

MAYNARD, Nicky (F) 144 62
H: 5 11 W: 11 00 b.Winsford 11-12-86
Source: Scholar.

2005–06	Crewe Alex	1	1		
2006–07	Crewe Alex	31	16		
2007–08	Crewe Alex	27	14	59	31
2008–09	Bristol C	43	11		
2009–10	Bristol C	42	20	85	31

McALLISTER, Jamie (D) 388 3
H: 5 10 W: 11 00 b.Glasgow 26-4-78
Honours: Scotland

1995–96	Q of S	2	0		
1996–97	Q of S	6	0		
1997–98	Q of S	15	0		
1998–99	Q of S	27	0	50	0
1999–2000	Aberdeen	34	0		
2000–01	Aberdeen	25	0		
2001–02	Aberdeen	29	0		
2002–03	Aberdeen	29	0	117	0
2003–04	Livingston	34	1	34	1
2004–05	Hearts	30	0		
2005–06	Hearts	17	0	47	0
2006–07	Bristol C	31	1		
2007–08	Bristol C	41	0		
2008–09	Bristol C	35	1		
2009–10	Bristol C	33	0	140	2

McCOMBE, Jamie (D) 269 17
H: 6 5 W: 12 05 b.Scunthorpe 1-1-83
Source: Scholar.

2001–02	Scunthorpe U	17	0		
2002–03	Scunthorpe U	31	1		
2003–04	Scunthorpe U	15	0	63	1
2003–04	Lincoln C	8	0		
2004–05	Lincoln C	41	3		
2005–06	Lincoln C	38	4	87	7
2006–07	Bristol C	41	4		
2007–08	Bristol C	34	3		
2008–09	Bristol C	28	1		
2009–10	Bristol C	16	1	119	9

NYATANGA, Lewin (D) 162 7
H: 6 2 W: 12 08 b.Burton 18-8-88
Source: Scholar. *Honours:* Wales Under-21, 33 full caps.

2005–06	Derby Co	24	1		
2006–07	Derby Co	7	1		
2006–07	Sunderland	11	0	11	0
2006–07	Barnsley	10	1		
2007–08	Derby Co	2	1		
2007–08	Barnsley	41	1	51	2
2008–09	Derby Co	30	1	63	4
2009–10	Bristol C	37	1	37	1

ORR, Bradley (M) 233 12
H: 6 0 W: 11 11 b.Liverpool 1-11-82
Source: Scholar.

2001–02	Newcastle U	0	0		
2002–03	Newcastle U	0	0		
2003–04	Newcastle U	0	0		

2003–04	Burnley	4	0	4 0
2004–05	Bristol C	37	0	
2005–06	Bristol C	38	1	
2006–07	Bristol C	35	4	
2007–08	Bristol C	42	4	
2008–09	Bristol C	38	1	
2009–10	Bristol C	39	2	229 12

PLUMMER, Tristan (F)   12 3
H: 5 6   W: 10 07   b.Bristol 30-1-90
Source: Scholar. *Honours:* England Youth.

2007–08	Bristol C	0	0	
2008–09	Bristol C	0	0	
2008–09	*Luton T*	5	0	5 0
2009–10	Bristol C	0	0	
2009–10	*Hereford U*	5	3	5 3
2009–10	*Gillingham*	2	0	2 0

RIBEIRO, Christian (D)   14 0
H: 5 11   W: 12 02   b.Neath 14-12-89
Source: Scholar. *Honours:* Wales Youth, Under-21, 1 full cap.

2006–07	Bristol C	0	0	
2007–08	Bristol C	0	0	
2008–09	Bristol C	0	0	
2009–10	Bristol C	5	0	5 0
2009–10	*Stockport Co*	7	0	7 0
2009–10	*Colchester U*	2	0	2 0

SABORIO, Alvaro (F)   106 38
H: 6 0   W: 12 02   b.Ciudad Quesada 25-3-82
Source: Dep Saprissa. *Honours:* Costa Rica 55 full caps, 22 goals.

2006–07	Sion	31	14	
2007–08	Sion	34	17	
2008–09	Sion	22	5	87 36
2009–10	Bristol C	19	2	19 2

SKUSE, Cole (M)   188 6
H: 6 1   W: 11 05   b.Bristol 29-3-86
Source: Scholar.

2004–05	Bristol C	7	0	
2005–06	Bristol C	38	2	
2006–07	Bristol C	42	0	
2007–08	Bristol C	25	0	
2008–09	Bristol C	33	2	
2009–10	Bristol C	43	2	188 6

SNO, Evander (M)   87 8
H: 6 1   W: 12 08   b.Dordrecht 9-4-87
Honours: Holland Under-21, Under-23.

2005–06	Feyenoord	0	0	
2005–06	NAC Breda	14	0	14 0
2006–07	Celtic	18	1	
2007–08	Celtic	12	0	30 1
2008–09	Ajax	19	4	19 4
2009–10	Bristol C	24	3	24 3

SPROULE, Ivan (M)   172 17
H: 5 8   W: 11 09   b.Castlederg 18-2-81
Source: Omagh Town, Institute. *Honours:* Northern Ireland 11 full caps, 1 goal.

2005–06	Hibernian	32	4	
2006–07	Hibernian	32	7	64 11
2007–08	Bristol C	40	2	
2008–09	Bristol C	38	3	
2009–10	Bristol C	30	1	108 6

TRUNDLE, Lee (F)   320 117
H: 6 0   W: 11 06   b.Liverpool 10-10-76
Source: Rhyl.

2000–01	Wrexham	14	8	
2001–02	Wrexham	36	8	
2002–03	Wrexham	44	11	94 27
2003–04	Swansea C	31	16	
2004–05	Swansea C	42	22	
2005–06	Swansea C	36	20	
2006–07	Swansea C	34	19	
2007–08	Bristol C	35	5	
2008–09	Bristol C	19	2	
2008–09	*Leeds U*	10	1	10 1
2009–10	Bristol C	0	0	54 7
2009–10	*Swansea C*	19	5	162 82

VELICKA, Andrius (F)   253 116
H: 6 1   W: 12 08   b.Kaunas 5-4-79
Honours: Lithuania 21 full caps, 2 goals.

1996–97	Kaunas	5	0	
1997–98	Kaunas	9	3	
1998–99	Kaunas	9	1	
1999	Kaunas	10	0	
2000	Kaunas	30	26	
2001	Kaunas	14	5	
2002	Kaunas	21	13	
2002	Anzhi	5	1	5 1
2003	Kaunas	3	0	
2003	Irtysh	12	0	12 0
2004	Kaunas	18	0	
2005	Kaunas	27	13	
2006	Kaunas	23	14	169 89
2006–07	Hearts	27	3	
2007–08	Hearts	20	11	47 19
2008	Viking	11	3	11 3
2008–09	Rangers	8	4	
2009–10	Rangers	0	0	8 4

On loan from Rangers.

2009–10	Bristol C	1	0	1 0

WILLIAMS, Gavin (M)   176 23
H: 5 10   W: 11 05   b.Pontypridd 20-6-80
Source: Hereford U. *Honours:* Wales 2 full caps.

2003–04	Yeovil T	42	9	
2004–05	Yeovil T	13	2	
2004–05	West Ham U	10	1	
2005–06	West Ham U	0	0	10 1
2005–06	Ipswich T	12	1	
2006–07	Ipswich T	29	2	
2007–08	Ipswich T	13	0	54 3
2008–09	Bristol C	35	3	
2009–10	Bristol C	14	0	49 3
2009–10	*Yeovil T*	8	5	63 16

WILSON, Brian (D)   191 15
H: 5 10   W: 11 00   b.Manchester 9-5-83
Source: Scholar.

2001–02	Stoke C	1	0	
2002–03	Stoke C	3	0	
2003–04	Stoke C	2	0	6 0
2003–04	Cheltenham T	14	0	
2004–05	Cheltenham T	43	3	
2005–06	Cheltenham T	43	0	
2006–07	Cheltenham T	25	2	125 14
2006–07	Bristol C	19	0	
2007–08	Bristol C	18	1	
2008–09	Bristol C	20	0	
2009–10	Bristol C	3	0	60 1

WILSON, James (D)   29 0
H: 6 2   W: 11 05   b.Chepstow 26-2-89
Source: Scholar. *Honours:* Wales Youth, Under-21.

2005–06	Bristol C	0	0	
2006–07	Bristol C	0	0	
2007–08	Bristol C	0	0	
2008–09	*Brentford*	14	0	
2009–10	Bristol C	0	0	2 0
2009–10	*Brentford*	13	0	27 0

BRISTOL R (16)

ANTHONY, Byron (D)   110 3
H: 6 1   W: 11 02   b.Newport 20-9-84
Source: Scholar. *Honours:* Wales Youth, Under-21.

2003–04	Cardiff C	0	0	
2004–05	Cardiff C	0	0	
2005–06	Cardiff C	0	0	
2006–07	Bristol R	23	0	
2007–08	Bristol R	20	1	
2008–09	Bristol R	30	2	
2009–10	Bristol R	37	0	110 3

BLIZZARD, Dominic (M)   136 7
H: 6 2   W: 12 04   b.High Wycombe 2-9-83
Source: Scholar.

2001–02	Watford	0	0	
2002–03	Watford	0	0	
2003–04	Watford	2	1	
2004–05	Watford	17	1	
2005–06	Watford	10	0	
2006–07	Watford	0	0	29 2
2006–07	Stockport Co	7	0	
2006–07	*Milton Keynes D*	8	0	8 0
2007–08	Stockport Co	2	0	
2008–09	Stockport Co	31	3	65 4
2009–10	Bristol R	34	1	34 1

BOOTH, George (M)   0 0

2009–10	Bristol R	0	0	

CAMPBELL, Stuart (M)   434 14
H: 5 10   W: 10 08   b.Corby 9-12-77
Source: Trainee. *Honours:* Scotland Under-21.

1996–97	Leicester C	10	0	
1997–98	Leicester C	11	0	
1998–99	Leicester C	12	0	
1999–2000	Leicester C	4	0	
1999–2000	Birmingham C	2	0	2 0
2000–01	Leicester C	0	0	37 0
2000–01	Grimsby T	38	2	
2001–02	Grimsby T	33	3	
2002–03	Grimsby T	45	6	
2003–04	Grimsby T	39	1	155 12
2004–05	Bristol R	25	0	
2005–06	Bristol R	38	1	
2006–07	Bristol R	41	1	
2007–08	Bristol R	46	0	
2008–09	Bristol R	44	0	
2009–10	Bristol R	46	0	240 2

CLARKE, Ollie (M)   0 0

2009–10	Bristol R	0	0	

COLES, Danny (D)   247 8
H: 6 1   W: 11 05   b.Bristol 31-10-81
Source: Scholarship.

1999–2000	Bristol C	1	0	
2000–01	Bristol C	2	0	
2001–02	Bristol C	23	0	
2002–03	Bristol C	39	2	
2003–04	Bristol C	45	2	
2004–05	Bristol C	38	1	148 5
2005–06	Hull C	9	0	
2006–07	Hull C	21	0	
2007–08	Hull C	1	0	31 0
2007–08	*Hartlepool U*	3	0	3 0
2007–08	Bristol R	24	1	
2008–09	Bristol R	5	1	
2009–10	Bristol R	36	1	65 3

COOPER, Mark (D)   0 0
b. 2-1-92

2009–10	Bristol R	0	0	

DUFFY, Darryl (F)   208 61
H: 5 11   W: 12 01   b.Glasgow 16-4-84
Honours: Scotland Under-21, B.

2003–04	Rangers	1	0	1 0
2003–04	*Brechin C*	8	3	8 3
2004–05	Falkirk	35	17	
2005–06	Falkirk	21	9	56 26
2005–06	Hull C	15	3	
2006–07	Hull C	9	0	24 3
2006–07	*Hartlepool U*	10	5	10 5
2006–07	Swansea C	8	5	
2007–08	Swansea C	20	1	28 6
2008–09	Bristol R	43	13	
2009–10	Bristol R	30	4	73 17
2009–10	*Carlisle U*	8	1	8 1

ELLIOTT, Steve (D)   319 17
H: 6 1   W: 14 00   b.Derby 29-10-78
Source: Trainee. *Honours:* England Under-21.

1996–97	Derby Co	0	0	
1997–98	Derby Co	3	0	
1998–99	Derby Co	11	0	
1999–2000	Derby Co	20	0	
2000–01	Derby Co	6	0	
2001–02	Derby Co	6	0	
2002–03	Derby Co	23	1	
2003–04	Derby Co	4	0	73 1
2003–04	Blackpool	28	0	28 0
2004–05	Bristol R	41	2	
2005–06	Bristol R	45	2	
2006–07	Bristol R	39	5	
2007–08	Bristol R	33	3	
2008–09	Bristol R	39	3	
2009–10	Bristol R	21	1	218 16

EVANS, Rhys (G)   245 0
H: 6 1   W: 13 12   b.Swindon 27-1-82
Source: Trainee. *Honours:* England Schools, Youth, Under-20, Under-21.

1998–99	Chelsea	0	0	
1999–2000	Chelsea	0	0	
1999–2000	*Bristol R*	4	0	
2000–01	Chelsea	0	0	
2001–02	Chelsea	0	0	
2001–02	*QPR*	11	0	11 0

2002–03	Chelsea	0	0		
2002–03	*Leyton Orient*	7	0	7	0
2003–04	Swindon T	41	0		
2004–05	Swindon T	45	0		
2005–06	Swindon T	32	0	118	0
2006–07	Blackpool	32	0		
2007–08	Blackpool	0	0	32	0
2007–08	*Bradford C*	4	0		
2007–08	Millwall	21	0	21	0
2008–09	Bradford C	45	0		
2009–10	Bradford C	0	0	49	0
2009–10	Bristol R	3	0	7	0

GREEN, Mike (G) 0 0
H: 6 1 W: 13 01 b.Bristol 23-7-89
Source: Scholar.

2006–07	Bristol R	0	0
2007–08	Bristol R	0	0
2008–09	Bristol R	0	0
2009–10	Bristol R	0	0

HUGHES, Jeff (D) 217 28
H: 6 1 W: 11 00 b.Larne 29-5-85
Source: Larne Tech Old Boys. *Honours:*
Northern Ireland Under-21, 2 full caps.

2003–04	Larne	21	1		
2004–05	Larne	29	0	50	1
2005–06	Lincoln C	22	2		
2006–07	Lincoln C	41	6	63	8
2007–08	Crystal Palace	10	0	10	0
2007–08	*Peterborough U*	7	1	7	1
2008–09	Bristol R	43	6		
2009–10	Bristol R	44	12	87	18

HUNT, Ben (F) 14 0
H: 6 1 W: 12 07 b.Southwark 23-1-90
Source: West Ham U Scholar.

| 2008–09 | Bristol R | 12 | 0 | | |
| 2009–10 | Bristol R | 2 | 0 | 14 | 0 |

LESCOTT, Aaron (M) 329 6
H: 5 8 W: 10 09 b.Birmingham 2-12-78
Source: Trainee. *Honours:* England Schools.

1996–97	Aston Villa	0	0		
1997–98	Aston Villa	0	0		
1998–99	Aston Villa	0	0		
1999–2000	Aston Villa	0	0		
1999–2000	*Lincoln C*	5	0	5	0
2000–01	Aston Villa	0	0		
2000–01	Sheffield W	30	0		
2001–02	Sheffield W	7	0	37	0
2001–02	Stockport Co	17	0		
2002–03	Stockport Co	41	1		
2003–04	Stockport Co	14	0	72	1
2003–04	*Bristol R*	8	0		
2004–05	Bristol R	26	0		
2005–06	Bristol R	37	0		
2006–07	Bristol R	34	0		
2007–08	Bristol R	34	0		
2008–09	Bristol R	44	3		
2009–10	Bristol R	24	2	207	5
2009–10	*Cheltenham T*	8	0	8	0

LINES, Chris (M) 125 17
H: 6 2 W: 12 00 b.Bristol 30-11-85
Source: Youth.

2005–06	Bristol R	4	0		
2006–07	Bristol R	7	0		
2007–08	Bristol R	27	3		
2008–09	Bristol R	45	4		
2009–10	Bristol R	42	10	125	17

McKENNA, Jack (M) 0 0
| 2009–10 | Bristol R | 0 | 0 |

OSEI-KUFFOUR, Jo (F) 325 80
H: 5 8 W: 11 11 b.Edmonton 17-11-81
Source: Scholar.

2000–01	Arsenal	0	0		
2001–02	Arsenal	0	0		
2001–02	*Swindon T*	11	2	11	2
2002–03	Torquay U	30	5		
2003–04	Torquay U	41	10		
2004–05	Torquay U	34	6		
2005–06	Torquay U	43	8	148	29
2006–07	Brentford	39	12	39	12
2007–08	Bournemouth	42	12		
2008–09	Bournemouth	2	0	44	12
2008–09	Bristol R	41	11		
2009–10	Bristol R	42	14	83	25

PHILLIPS, Steve (G) 432 0
H: 6 1 W: 11 10 b.Bath 6-5-78
Source: Paulton R.

1996–97	Bristol C	0	0		
1997–98	Bristol C	0	0		
1998–99	Bristol C	15	0		
1999–2000	Bristol C	21	0		
2000–01	Bristol C	42	0		
2001–02	Bristol C	22	0		
2002–03	Bristol C	46	0		
2003–04	Bristol C	46	0		
2004–05	Bristol C	46	0		
2005–06	Bristol C	19	0	257	0
2006–07	Bristol R	44	0		
2007–08	Bristol R	46	0		
2008–09	Bristol R	46	0		
2009–10	Bristol R	0	0	136	0
2009–10	*Shrewsbury T*	11	0	11	0
2009–10	*Crewe Alex*	28	0	28	0

PIPE, David (M) 256 8
H: 5 9 W: 12 01 b.Caerphilly 5-11-83
Source: Scholar. *Honours:* Wales Youth,
Under-21, 1 full cap.

2000–01	Coventry C	0	0		
2001–02	Coventry C	0	0		
2002–03	Coventry C	21	1		
2003–04	Coventry C	0	0	21	1
2003–04	Notts Co	18	0		
2004–05	Notts Co	41	2		
2005–06	Notts Co	43	2		
2006–07	Notts Co	39	0	141	4
2007–08	Bristol R	40	2		
2008–09	Bristol R	39	1		
2009–10	Bristol R	7	0	86	3
2009–10	*Cheltenham T*	8	0	8	0

REECE, Charlie (M) 16 0
H: 5 11 W: 11 03 b.Birmingham 8-9-88
Source: Scholar.

2007–08	Bristol R	1	0		
2008–09	Bristol R	1	0		
2009–10	Bristol R	14	0	16	0

REGAN, Carl (D) 251 3
H: 5 11 W: 11 12 b.Liverpool 14-1-80
Source: Trainee. *Honours:* England Youth.

1997–98	Everton	0	0		
1998–99	Everton	0	0		
1999–2000	Everton	0	0		
2000–01	Barnsley	27	0		
2001–02	Barnsley	10	0		
2002–03	Barnsley	0	0	37	0
2002–03	Hull C	38	0		
2003–04	Hull C	0	0		
2004–05	Hull C	0	0	38	0
2004–05	Chester C	6	0		
2005–06	Chester C	41	0	47	0
2006–07	Macclesfield T	38	2		
2007–08	Macclesfield T	20	0	58	2
2007–08	Milton Keynes D	9	1		
2008–09	Milton Keynes D	27	0	36	1
2009–10	Bristol R	35	0	35	0

RICHARDS, Eliot (M) 5 0
H: 5 9 W: 11 09 b.Merthyr Tydfil 1-9-91
Source: Scholar.

| 2009–10 | Bristol R | 5 | 0 | 5 | 0 |

RIGG, Sean (F) 83 5
H: 5 9 W: 12 01 b.Bristol 1-10-88
Source: Forest Green R.

2006–07	Bristol R	18	1		
2007–08	Bristol R	31	1		
2008–09	Bristol R	8	0		
2009–10	Bristol R	0	0	57	2
2009–10	*Port Vale*	26	3	26	3

SWALLOW, Ben (M) 23 0
H: 5 8 W: 10 10 b.Barry 20-10-89
Source: Scholar.

| 2009–10 | Bristol R | 23 | 0 | 23 | 0 |

TYRRELL, James (D) 0 0
H: 6 2 W: 13 04 b.Oxford 26-4-89
Honours: From Scholar

| 2009–10 | Bristol R | 0 | 0 |

WILLIAMS, Andy (F) 155 18
H: 5 11 W: 11 09 b.Hereford 14-8-86
Source: Pershore College.

2006–07	Hereford U	41	8		
2007–08	Bristol R	41	4		
2008–09	Bristol R	4	1		
2008–09	*Hereford U*	26	2	67	10
2009–10	Bristol R	43	3	88	8

WRIGHT, Mark (M) 218 27
H: 5 11 W: 11 00 b.Wolverhampton
24-2-82
Source: Scholar.

2000–01	Walsall	4	0		
2001–02	Walsall	0	0		
2002–03	Walsall	5	0		
2003–04	Walsall	11	2		
2004–05	Walsall	37	2		
2005–06	Walsall	30	2		
2006–07	Walsall	37	3	124	9
2007–08	Milton Keynes D	34	13		
2008–09	Milton Keynes D	32	5	66	18
2009–10	Brighton & HA	4	0	4	0
2009–10	Bristol R	24	0	24	0

BURNLEY (17)

ALEXANDER, Graham (D) 783 102
H: 5 10 W: 12 07 b.Coventry 10-10-71
Source: Trainee. *Honours:* Scotland B, 40 full
caps.

1989–90	Scunthorpe U	0	0		
1990–91	Scunthorpe U	1	0		
1991–92	Scunthorpe U	36	5		
1992–93	Scunthorpe U	41	5		
1993–94	Scunthorpe U	41	4		
1994–95	Scunthorpe U	40	4	159	18
1995–96	Luton T	37	1		
1996–97	Luton T	45	2		
1997–98	Luton T	39	8		
1998–99	Luton T	29	4	150	15
1998–99	Preston NE	10	0		
1999–2000	Preston NE	46	6		
2000–01	Preston NE	34	5		
2001–02	Preston NE	45	6		
2002–03	Preston NE	45	10		
2003–04	Preston NE	45	9		
2004–05	Preston NE	42	7		
2005–06	Preston NE	40	3		
2006–07	Preston NE	42	6		
2007–08	Preston NE	3	0	352	52
2007–08	Burnley	43	1		
2008–09	Burnley	46	9		
2009–10	Burnley	33	7	122	17

ANDERSON, Chris (M) 0 0
H: 5 11 W: 10 02 b.Burnley 2-10-90
Source: Scholar.

| 2009–10 | Burnley | 0 | 0 |

BIKEY, Andre (D) 117 8
H: 6 0 W: 12 08 b.Douala 8-1-85
Source: Espanyol, Marco. *Honours:*
Cameroon 24 full caps, 1 goal.

2003–04	Pacos de Ferreira	2	0	2	0
2004–05	Dep Aves	0	0		
2005	Shinnik	11	1	11	1
2005	Loko Moscow	9	0		
2006	Loko Moscow	5	0	14	0
2006–07	Reading	15	0		
2007–08	Reading	22	3		
2008–09	Reading	25	3		
2009–10	Reading	0	0	62	6
2009–10	Burnley	28	1	28	1

BLAKE, Robbie (F) 562 144
H: 5 9 W: 12 00 b.Middlesbrough 4-3-76
Source: Trainee.

1994–95	Darlington	9	0		
1995–96	Darlington	29	11		
1996–97	Darlington	30	10	68	21
1996–97	Bradford C	5	0		
1997–98	Bradford C	34	8		
1998–99	Bradford C	39	16		
1999–2000	Bradford C	28	2		
2000–01	Bradford C	21	4		
2000–01	*Nottingham F*	11	1	11	1
2001–02	Bradford C	26	10	153	40
2001–02	Burnley	10	0		
2002–03	Burnley	41	13		
2003–04	Burnley	45	19		
2004–05	Burnley	24	10		
2004–05	Birmingham C	11	2	11	2

2005–06	Leeds U	41	11		
2006–07	Leeds U	36	8	77	19
2007–08	Burnley	45	9		
2008–09	Burnley	46	8		
2009–10	Burnley	31	2	242	61

CALDWELL, Steven (D)   236 11
H: 6 2   W: 13 12   b.Stirling 12-9-80
Source: Trainee. *Honours:* Scotland Youth, Under-21, B, 10 full caps.

1997–98	Newcastle U	0	0		
1998–99	Newcastle U	0	0		
1999–2000	Newcastle U	0	0		
2000–01	Newcastle U	9	0		
2001–02	Newcastle U	0	0		
2001–02	Blackpool	6	0	6	0
2001–02	*Bradford C*	9	0	9	0
2002–03	Newcastle U	14	1		
2003–04	Newcastle U	5	0	28	1
2003–04	*Leeds U*	13	1	13	1
2004–05	Sunderland	41	4		
2005–06	Sunderland	24	0		
2006–07	Sunderland	11	0	76	4
2006–07	Burnley	17	0		
2007–08	Burnley	29	2		
2008–09	Burnley	45	2		
2009–10	Burnley	13	1	104	5

CARLISLE, Clarke (D)   361 25
H: 6 2   W: 14 11   b.Preston 14-10-79
Source: Trainee. *Honours:* England Under-21.

1997–98	Blackpool	11	2		
1998–99	Blackpool	39	1		
1999–2000	Blackpool	43	4	93	7
2000–01	QPR	27	3		
2001–02	QPR	0	0		
2002–03	QPR	36	2		
2003–04	QPR	33	1	96	6
2004–05	Leeds U	35	4	35	4
2005–06	Watford	32	3		
2006–07	Watford	4	0		
2006–07	*Luton T*	5	0	5	0
2007–08	Watford	0	0	36	3
2007–08	Burnley	33	2		
2008–09	Burnley	36	3		
2009–10	Burnley	27	0	96	5

CORT, Leon (D)   331 36
H: 6 3   W: 13 01   b.Bermondsey 11-9-79
Source: Dulwich H.

1997–98	Millwall	0	0		
1998–99	Millwall	0	0		
1999–2000	Millwall	0	0		
2000–01	Millwall	0	0		
2001–02	Southend U	45	4		
2002–03	Southend U	46	6		
2003–04	Southend U	46	1	137	11
2004–05	Hull C	44	6		
2005–06	Hull C	42	4	86	10
2006–07	Crystal Palace	37	7		
2007–08	Crystal Palace	12	0	49	7
2007–08	Stoke C	33	8		
2008–09	Stoke C	11	0		
2009–10	Stoke C	0	0	44	8
2009–10	Burnley	15	0	15	0

DUFF, Michael (D)   374 16
H: 6 1   W: 11 08   b.Belfast 11-1-78
Source: Trainee. *Honours:* Northern Ireland 22 full caps.

1999–2000	Cheltenham T	31	2		
2000–01	Cheltenham T	39	5		
2001–02	Cheltenham T	45	3		
2002–03	Cheltenham T	44	2		
2003–04	Cheltenham T	42	0	201	12
2004–05	Burnley	42	0		
2005–06	Burnley	41	0		
2006–07	Burnley	44	2		
2007–08	Burnley	8	1		
2008–09	Burnley	27	1		
2009–10	Burnley	11	0	173	4

EAGLES, Chris (M)   153 19
H: 5 10   W: 11 07   b.Hemel Hempstead 19-11-85
Source: Trainee. *Honours:* England Youth.

2003–04	Manchester U	0	0		
2004–05	Manchester U	0	0		
2004–05	*Watford*	13	1		
2005–06	Manchester U	0	0		
2005–06	*Sheffield W*	25	3	25	3
2005–06	*Watford*	17	3	30	4
2006–07	Manchester U	2	1		
2006–07	*NEC Nijmegen*	15	1	15	1
2007–08	Manchester U	2	0	6	1
2008–09	Burnley	43	8		
2009–10	Burnley	34	2	77	10

EASTON, Brian (D)   114 2
H: 6 0   W: 12 00   b.Glasgow 5-3-88
Honours: Scotland Under-21, B.

2006–07	Hamilton A	31	1		
2007–08	Hamilton A	36	0		
2008–09	Hamilton A	35	1		
2009–10	Burnley	0	0		
2009–10	Hamilton A	12	0	114	2

ECKERSLEY, Richard (D)   9 0
H: 5 9   W: 11 09   b.Worsley 12-3-89
Source: Scholar.

2006–07	Manchester U	0	0		
2007–08	Manchester U	0	0		
2008–09	Manchester U	2	0		
2009–10	Manchester U	0	0	2	0
2009–10	Burnley	0	0		
2009–10	*Plymouth Arg*	7	0	7	0

EDGAR, David (D)   28 3
H: 6 2   W: 12 13   b.Ontario 19-5-87
Source: Scholar. *Honours:* Canada Youth, Under-20.

2005–06	Newcastle U	0	0		
2006–07	Newcastle U	3	1		
2007–08	Newcastle U	5	0		
2008–09	Newcastle U	11	1		
2009–10	Newcastle U	0	0	19	2
2009–10	Burnley	4	0	4	0
2009–10	*Swansea C*	5	1	5	1

ELLIOTT, Wade (M)   424 48
H: 5 10   W: 10 03   b.Southampton 14-12-78
Source: Bashley.

1999–2000	Bournemouth	12	3		
2000–01	Bournemouth	36	9		
2001–02	Bournemouth	46	4		
2002–03	Bournemouth	44	4		
2003–04	Bournemouth	39	3		
2004–05	Bournemouth	43	4	220	31
2005–06	Burnley	36	3		
2006–07	Burnley	42	4		
2007–08	Burnley	45	2		
2008–09	Burnley	42	4		
2009–10	Burnley	38	4	204	17

FLETCHER, Steven (F)   191 51
H: 6 1   W: 12 00   b.Shrewsbury 26-3-87
Honours: Scotland Under-20, Under-21, B, 7 full caps, 1 goal.

2003–04	Hibernian	5	0		
2004–05	Hibernian	20	5		
2005–06	Hibernian	34	8		
2006–07	Hibernian	31	6		
2007–08	Hibernian	32	13		
2008–09	Hibernian	34	11	156	43
2009–10	Burnley	35	8	35	8

FLETCHER, Wes (F)   6 1
H: 5 11   W: 12 06   b.Ormskirk 28-2-90
Source: Scholar.

2008–09	Burnley	0	0		
2009–10	Burnley	0	0		
2009–10	*Grimsby T*	6	1	6	1

FOX, Danny (D)   196 14
H: 5 11   W: 12 06   b.Crewe 29-5-86
Source: Scholar. *Honours:* England Under-21, Scotland 1 full cap.

2004–05	Everton	0	0		
2004–05	*Stranraer*	11	1	11	1
2005–06	Walsall	33	0		
2006–07	Walsall	44	3		
2007–08	Walsall	22	3	99	6
2007–08	Coventry C	18	1		
2008–09	Coventry C	39	5		
2009–10	Coventry C	0	0	57	6
2009–10	Celtic	15	0	15	0
2009–10	Burnley	14	1	14	1

GUDJONSSON, Joey (M)   258 28
H: 5 9   W: 12 04   b.Akranes 25-5-80
Honours: Iceland Youth, Under-21, 34 full caps, 1 goal.

1998–99	Genk	5	0	5	0
1999–2000	MVV	19	5	19	5
2000–01	RKC	31	4	31	4
2001–02	Betis	11	0	11	0
2002–03	Aston Villa	11	2	11	2
2003–04	Wolverhampton W	11	0	11	0
2004–05	Leicester C	35	2		
2005–06	Leicester C	42	8	77	10
2006–07	AZ	5	0	5	0
2006–07	Burnley	11	0		
2007–08	Burnley	28	1		
2008–09	Burnley	39	6		
2009–10	Burnley	10	0	88	7

GUERRERO, Fernando (M)   22 4
H: 5 7   W: 11 00   b.Quito 30-9-89
Source: Castilla, Emelec (loan). *Honours:* Ecuador 1 full cap.

| 2009 | Indep. del Valle | 15 | 4 | 15 | 4 |

On loan from Independiente del Valle.

| 2009–10 | Burnley | 7 | 0 | 7 | 0 |

HARVEY, Alex-Ray (M)   0 0
H: 5 7   W: 10 09   b.Burnley 4-4-90
Source: Scholar.

| 2009–10 | Burnley | 0 | 0 | | |

HOSKIN, Benjamin (D)   0 0
H: 5 11   W: 11 02   b.Blackburn 8-10-90
Source: Scholar.

| 2009–10 | Burnley | 0 | 0 | | |

JENSEN, Brian (G)   292 0
H: 6 1   W: 12 04   b.Copenhagen 8-6-75
Source: Hvidovre, B93.

1997–98	AZ	0	0		
1998–99	AZ	1	0	1	0
1999–2000	WBA	12	0		
2000–01	WBA	33	0		
2001–02	WBA	1	0		
2002–03	WBA	0	0	46	0
2003–04	Burnley	46	0		
2004–05	Burnley	27	0		
2005–06	Burnley	39	0		
2006–07	Burnley	31	0		
2007–08	Burnley	19	0		
2008–09	Burnley	45	0		
2009–10	Burnley	38	0	245	0

JORDAN, Stephen (D)   137 0
H: 6 1   W: 13 00   b.Warrington 6-3-82
Source: Scholarship.

1998–99	Manchester C	0	0		
1999–2000	Manchester C	0	0		
2000–01	Manchester C	0	0		
2001–02	Manchester C	0	0		
2002–03	Manchester C	1	0		
2002–03	*Cambridge U*	11	0	11	0
2003–04	Manchester C	2	0		
2004–05	Manchester C	19	0		
2005–06	Manchester C	18	0		
2006–07	Manchester C	13	0	53	0
2007–08	Burnley	21	0		
2008–09	Burnley	27	0		
2009–10	Burnley	25	0	73	0

KALVENES, Christian (D)   147 7
H: 6 0   W: 11 11   b.Bergen 8-3-77

2000	Sogndal	6	0		
2001	Sogndal	22	3		
2002	Sogndal	18	0		
2003	Sogndal	21	1	67	4
2004	Brann	0	0		
2005	Brann	4	0		
2006	Brann	1	0	5	0
2006–07	Dundee U	29	1		
2007–08	Dundee U	19	1	48	2
2008–09	Burnley	21	1		
2009–10	Burnley	6	0	27	1

KUDIERSKY, Nikolaus (D)   0 0
H: 6 1   W: 13 04   b.Tameside 15-2-91
Source: Scholar.

| 2009–10 | Burnley | 0 | 0 | | |

LONG, Kevin (D)   16 0
H: 6 3   W: 13 01   b.Cork 18-8-90

| 2009 | Cork City | 16 | 0 | 16 | 0 |
| 2009–10 | Burnley | 0 | 0 | | |

LYNCH, Chris (D) 10 0
H: 6 3 W: 15 06 b.Blackburn 31-1-91
Source: Scholar.
2009–10	Burnley	0	0	
2009–10	*Chester C*	10	0	**10 0**

MACDONALD, Alex (F) 16 1
H: 5 7 W: 11 04 b.Warrington 14-4-90
Source: Scholar. *Honours:* Scotland Youth.
2007–08	Burnley	2	0	
2008–09	Burnley	3	0	
2009–10	Burnley	0	0	**5 0**
2009–10	*Falkirk*	11	1	**11 1**

MARNEY, Dean (M) 160 11
H: 5 10 W: 11 09 b.Barking 31-1-84
Source: Scholar. *Honours:* England Under-21.
2002–03	Tottenham H	0	0	
2002–03	*Swindon T*	9	0	**9 0**
2003–04	Tottenham H	3	0	
2003–04	*QPR*	2	0	**2 0**
2004–05	Tottenham H	5	2	
2004–05	*Gillingham*	3	0	**3 0**
2005–06	Tottenham H	0	0	**8 2**
2005–06	*Norwich C*	13	0	**13 0**
2006–07	Hull C	37	2	
2007–08	Hull C	41	6	
2008–09	Hull C	31	0	
2009–10	Hull C	16	1	**125 9**
2009–10	Burnley	0	0	

McCANN, Chris (M) 147 18
H: 6 1 W: 11 11 b.Dublin 21-7-87
Source: Scholar. *Honours:* Eire Youth.
2005–06	Burnley	23	2	
2006–07	Burnley	38	5	
2007–08	Burnley	35	5	
2008–09	Burnley	44	6	
2009–10	Burnley	7	0	**147 18**

McDONALD, Kevin (M) 142 16
H: 6 2 W: 13 03 b.Carnoustie 4-11-88
Honours: Scotland Youth, Under-21.
2005–06	Dundee	26	3	
2006–07	Dundee	31	2	
2007–08	Dundee	34	9	**91 14**
2008–09	Burnley	25	1	
2009–10	Burnley	26	1	**51 2**

MEARS, Tyrone (D) 159 6
H: 5 11 W: 11 10 b.Stockport 18-2-83
Source: Manchester C Juniors.
2000–01	Manchester C	0	0	
2001–02	Manchester C	1	0	**1 0**
2002–03	Preston NE	22	1	
2003–04	Preston NE	12	1	
2004–05	Preston NE	4	0	
2005–06	Preston NE	32	2	**70 4**
2006–07	West Ham U	5	0	**5 0**
2006–07	Derby Co	13	1	
2007–08	Derby Co	25	1	
2008–09	Derby Co	3	0	**41 2**
2008–09	*Marseille*	4	0	**4 0**
2009–10	Burnley	38	0	**38 0**

NIMANI, Frederic (F) 49 8
H: 6 4 W: 13 10 b.Marseille 8-10-88
Honours: On loan from Monaco. France Under-21.
2006–07	Monaco	3	1	
2007–08	Monaco	0	0	
2007–08	*Lorient*	2	0	**2 0**
2007–08	*Sedan*	6	0	**6 0**
2008–09	Monaco	28	6	
2009–10	Monaco	8	1	**39 8**
2009–10	Burnley	2	0	**2 0**

PATERSON, Martin (F) 136 36
H: 5 9 W: 10 11 b.Tunstall 13-5-87
Source: Scholar. *Honours:* Northern Ireland Youth, Under-21,11 full caps.
2004–05	Stoke C	3	0	
2005–06	Stoke C	3	0	
2006–07	Stoke C	9	1	**15 1**
2006–07	*Grimsby T*	15	6	**15 6**
2007–08	Scunthorpe U	40	13	**40 13**
2008–09	Burnley	43	12	
2009–10	Burnley	23	4	**66 16**

PENNY, Diego (G) 181 0
H: 6 5 W: 12 00 b.Lima 22-4-84
Honours: Peru 6 full caps.
2004	Cor Bolognesi	39	0	
2005	Cor Bolognesi	47	0	
2006	Cor Bolognesi	38	0	
2007	Cor Bolognesi	40	0	
2008	Cor Bolognesi	15	0	**179 0**
2008–09	Burnley	1	0	
2009–10	Burnley	1	0	**2 0**

RODRIGUEZ, Jay (F) 43 6
H: 6 0 W: 12 00 b.Burnley 27-7-89
Source: Scholar.
2007–08	Burnley	1	0	
2007–08	*Stirling Alb*	11	3	**11 3**
2008–09	Burnley	25	2	
2009–10	Burnley	0	0	**26 2**
2009–10	*Barnsley*	6	1	**6 1**

THOMPSON, Steven (F) 342 62
H: 6 2 W: 12 05 b.Paisley 14-10-78
Source: Dundee U BC. *Honours:* Scotland Under-21, 16 full caps, 3 goals.
1996–97	Dundee U	1	0	
1997–98	Dundee U	8	0	
1998–99	Dundee U	15	1	
1999–2000	Dundee U	27	1	
2000–01	Dundee U	31	4	
2001–02	Dundee U	32	6	
2002–03	Dundee U	20	6	**134 18**
2002–03	Rangers	8	2	
2003–04	Rangers	16	8	
2004–05	Rangers	19	5	
2005–06	Rangers	14	2	**57 17**
2005–06	Cardiff C	14	4	
2006–07	Cardiff C	43	6	
2007–08	Cardiff C	36	5	
2008–09	Cardiff C	4	1	**97 16**
2008–09	Burnley	34	7	
2009–10	Burnley	20	4	**54 11**

VAN DER SCHAAF, Remco (D) 230 10
H: 6 01 W: 12 02 b.Groningen 28-2-79
Honours: Holland Under-21.
1997–98	Vitesse	3	0	
1998–99	Vitesse	22	0	
1999–2000	Vitesse	14	1	
1999–2000	Fortuna Sittard	4	0	**4 0**
2000–01	Vitesse	26	0	
2001–02	Vitesse	27	4	
2002–03	PSV Eindhoven	17	0	
2003–04	PSV Eindhoven	18	0	
2004–05	PSV Eindhoven	4	0	**39 0**
2005–06	Vitesse	27	2	
2006–07	Vitesse	14	0	
2007–08	Vitesse	29	3	**162 10**
2008–09	Burnley	1	0	
2008–09	*Brondby*	10	0	**10 0**
2009–10	Burnley	0	0	**1 0**
2009–10	*Brondby*	14	0	**24 0**

WEAVER, Nick (G) 272 0
H: 6 4 W: 14 07 b.Sheffield 2-3-79
Source: Trainee. *Honours:* England Under-21.
1995–96	Mansfield T	1	0	
1996–97	Mansfield T	0	0	**1 0**
1996–97	Manchester C	0	0	
1997–98	Manchester C	0	0	
1998–99	Manchester C	45	0	
1999–2000	Manchester C	45	0	
2000–01	Manchester C	31	0	
2001–02	Manchester C	25	0	
2002–03	Manchester C	0	0	
2003–04	Manchester C	0	0	
2004–05	Manchester C	1	0	
2005–06	Manchester C	0	0	
2005–06	*Sheffield W*	14	0	**14 0**
2006–07	Manchester C	25	0	**172 0**
2007–08	Charlton Ath	45	0	
2008–09	Charlton Ath	22	0	**67 0**
2009–10	Dundee U	18	0	**18 0**
2009–10	Burnley	0	0	

Scholars
Edwards, Stephen Matthew; Jackson, Josef; Lazaar, Mehdi; Lynch, David Christopher; McKee, Joseph John Paul; Overson, Dean James; Taylor, James; Taylor, Thomas; Williams, Edward; Wilson, Ross Strachan; Woods, Curtis; Yadolahi, Neil.

BURTON ALB (18)

AUSTIN, Ryan (D) 18 2
H: 6 2 W: 12 09 b.Stoke 15-11-84
Source: Scholar.
2004–05	Crewe Alex	0	0	
2009–10	Burton Alb	18	2	**18 2**

BOCO, Romuald (F) 51 3
H: 5 10 W: 10 12 b.Bernay 8-7-85
Source: Niort. *Honours:* Benin 39 full caps, 9 goals.
2006–07	Accrington S	32	3	
2007–08	Accrington S	11	0	
2008–09	Accrington S	0	0	**43 3**
2009–10	Burton Alb	8	0	**8 0**

BOERTIEN, Paul (D) 227 4
H: 5 10 W: 11 02 b.Haltwhistle 21-1-79
Source: Trainee.
1996–97	Carlisle U	0	0	
1997–98	Carlisle U	9	0	
1998–99	Carlisle U	8	1	**17 1**
1998–99	Derby Co	1	0	
1999–2000	Derby Co	2	0	
1999–2000	*Crewe Alex*	2	0	**2 0**
2000–01	Derby Co	8	1	
2001–02	Derby Co	32	0	
2002–03	Derby Co	42	1	
2003–04	Derby Co	18	0	
2003–04	*Notts Co*	5	0	**5 0**
2004–05	Derby Co	0	0	
2005–06	Derby Co	0	0	
2006–07	Derby Co	11	0	**114 2**
2006–07	*Chesterfield*	4	0	**4 0**
2007–08	Walsall	20	0	
2008–09	Walsall	31	0	**51 0**
2009–10	Burton Alb	34	1	**34 1**

BRANSTON, Guy (D) 280 18
H: 6 1 W: 15 01 b.Leicester 9-1-79
Source: Trainee.
1997–98	Leicester C	0	0	
1997–98	*Colchester U*	12	1	
1998–99	Leicester C	0	0	
1998–99	*Colchester U*	1	0	**13 1**
1998–99	*Plymouth Arg*	7	1	**7 1**
1999–2000	Leicester C	0	0	
1999–2000	*Lincoln C*	4	0	**4 0**
1999–2000	*Rotherham U*	30	4	
2000–01	Rotherham U	41	6	
2001–02	Rotherham U	10	1	
2002–03	Rotherham U	15	2	
2003–04	Rotherham U	8	0	**104 13**
2003–04	*Wycombe W*	9	0	**9 0**
2003–04	*Peterborough U*	14	0	
2004–05	Sheffield W	11	0	**11 0**
2004–05	*Peterborough U*	4	1	
2004–05	Oldham Ath	7	1	
2005–06	Oldham Ath	38	1	**45 2**
2006–07	Peterborough U	24	0	
2007–08	Peterborough U	2	0	**44 1**
2007–08	*Rochdale*	4	0	**4 0**
2007–08	*Northampton T*	3	0	**3 0**
2007–08	Notts Co	1	0	**1 0**
2009–10	Burton Alb	19	0	**19 0**
	From Kettering T.			
2009–10	*Torquay U*	16	0	**16 0**

CORBETT, Andy (F) 42 1
H: 6 0 W: 11 07 b.Worcester 20-2-82
2000–01	Kidderminster H	6	0	
2001–02	Kidderminster H	2	0	**8 0**
	From Solihull B, Nuneaton B.			
2009–10	Burton Alb	34	1	**34 1**

EDWORTHY, Marc (D) 447 2
H: 5 10 W: 11 11 b.Barnstaple 24-12-72
Source: Trainee.
1990–91	Plymouth Arg	0	0	
1991–92	Plymouth Arg	15	0	
1992–93	Plymouth Arg	15	0	
1993–94	Plymouth Arg	12	0	
1994–95	Plymouth Arg	27	1	**69 1**
1995–96	Crystal Palace	44	0	
1996–97	Crystal Palace	45	0	
1997–98	Crystal Palace	34	0	
1998–99	Crystal Palace	3	0	**126 0**

1998–99	Coventry C	22	0		
1999–2000	Coventry C	10	0		
2000–01	Coventry C	24	1		
2001–02	Coventry C	20	0	76	1
2002–03	Wolverhampton W	22	0	22	0
2003–04	Norwich C	43	0		
2004–05	Norwich C	28	0	71	0
2005–06	Derby Co	30	0		
2006–07	Derby Co	38	0		
2007–08	Derby Co	9	0	77	0
2008–09	Leicester C	5	0	5	0
2009–10	Burton Alb	1	0	1	0

GILROY, Keith (F) 16 1
H: 5 10 W: 11 04 b.Sligo 8-7-83
Honours: Eire Youth, Under-21.

2001–02	Sligo R	6	1	6	1
2002–03	Middlesbrough	0	0		
2003–04	Middlesbrough	0	0		
2004–05	Middlesbrough	0	0		
From Scarborough.					
2004–05	Darlington	2	0	2	0
2009–10	Burton Alb	8	0	8	0

GOODFELLOW, Marc (M) 123 15
H: 5 10 W: 11 00 b.Swadlincote 20-9-81

1998–99	Stoke C	0	0		
1999–2000	Stoke C	0	0		
2000–01	Stoke C	7	0		
2001	IBV	5	0	5	0
2001–02	Stoke C	23	5		
2002–03	Stoke C	20	1		
2003–04	Stoke C	4	0	54	6
2003–04	Bristol C	15	4		
2004–05	Bristol C	5	0	20	4
2004–05	Port Vale	5	0	5	0
2004–05	Swansea C	6	3		
2004–05	Colchester U	5	1	5	1
2005–06	Swansea C	11	0	17	3
2005–06	Grimsby T	10	1	10	1
2006–07	Bury	4	0	4	0
2009–10	Burton Alb	3	0	3	0

HARRAD, Shaun (F) 71 22
H: 5 10 W: 12 04 b.Nottingham 11-12-84
Source: Scholar.

2002–03	Notts Co	5	0		
2003–04	Notts Co	8	0		
2004–05	Notts Co	16	1	29	1
2009–10	Burton Alb	42	21	42	21

JACKSON, Richard (D) 199 0
H: 5 8 W: 12 10 b.Whitby 18-4-80
Source: Trainee.

1997–98	Scarborough	2	0		
1998–99	Scarborough	20	0	22	0
1998–99	Derby Co	0	0		
1999–2000	Derby Co	2	0		
2000–01	Derby Co	2	0		
2001–02	Derby Co	7	0		
2002–03	Derby Co	21	0		
2003–04	Derby Co	36	0		
2004–05	Derby Co	19	0		
2005–06	Derby Co	26	0		
2006–07	Derby Co	5	0	118	0
2007–08	Luton T	29	0	29	0
From Whitby T.					
2008–09	Hereford U	25	0	25	0
2009–10	Burton Alb	5	0	5	0

JAMES, Tony (D) 42 1
H: 5 10 W: 13 06 b.Abergavenny 9-10-78
Source: WBA Scholar, Hereford U, Weymouth.

| 2009–10 | Burton Alb | 42 | 1 | 42 | 1 |

KELLY, Shaun (D) 61 0
H: 6 1 W: 11 04 b.Southampton 4-7-86
Source: Scholar.

2006–07	Chester C	2	0		
2007–08	Chester C	10	0		
2008–09	Chester C	27	1		
2009–10	Chester C	18	1	57	2
2009–10	Burton Alb	4	0	4	0

KNOWLES, James (F) 0 0
H: 5 9 W: 11 04 b.Sheffield 7-6-90
Source: Scholar.

| 2009–10 | Burton Alb | 0 | 0 | | |

MAGHOMA, Jacques (M 35 3
H: 5 9 W: 11 06 b.Lubumbashi 23-10-87
Source: Scholar. Honours: DR Congo 1 full cap.

2005–06	Tottenham H	0	0		
2006–07	Tottenham H	0	0		
2007–08	Tottenham H	0	0		
2008–09	Tottenham H	0	0		
2009–10	Burton Alb	35	3	35	3

MAKOFO, Serge (M) 3 0
H: 5 11 W: 12 06 b.Kinshasa 22-10-86
Source: Scholar.

| 2004–05 | Milton Keynes D | 1 | 0 | 1 | 0 |
| 2009–10 | Burton Alb | 2 | 0 | 2 | 0 |

McGRATH, John (M) 86 1
H: 5 10 W: 10 04 b.Limerick 27-3-80
Source: Belvedere. Honours: Eire Under-21.

1999–2000	Aston Villa	0	0		
2000–01	Aston Villa	3	0		
2001–02	Aston Villa	0	0		
2002–03	Aston Villa	0	0	3	0
2003–04	Doncaster R	11	0		
2004–05	Doncaster R	0	0	11	0
2004–05	Shrewsbury T	8	0	8	0
2004–05	Kidderminster H	19	0	19	0
From Weymouth, Tamworth.					
2005–06	Limerick	0	0		
2009–10	Burton Alb	45	1	45	1

PEARSON, Greg (F) 67 15
H: 6 0 W: 12 00 b.Birmingham 3-4-85
Source: Trainee.

2003–04	West Ham U	0	0		
2004–05	West Ham U	0	0		
2004–05	Lincoln C	3	0	3	0
2005–06	Rushden & D	22	1	22	1
From Bishop's Stortford.					
2009–10	Burton Alb	42	14	42	14

PENN, Russ (M) 40 4
H: 5 11 W: 12 13 b.Dudley 8-11-85
Source: Scunthorpe U, Kidderminster H.
Honours: England C.

| 2009–10 | Burton Alb | 40 | 4 | 40 | 4 |

PHILLIPS, Jimmy (M) 24 1
H: 5 7 W: 10 00 b.Stoke 20-9-89
Source: Scholar.

| 2008–09 | Stoke C | 0 | 0 | | |
| 2009–10 | Burton Alb | 24 | 1 | 24 | 1 |

POOLE, Kevin (G) 313 0
H: 5 10 W: 12 11 b.Bromsgrove 21-7-63
Source: Apprentice.

1981–82	Aston Villa	0	0		
1982–83	Aston Villa	0	0		
1983–84	Aston Villa	0	0		
1984–85	Aston Villa	7	0		
1984–85	Northampton T	3	0	3	0
1985–86	Aston Villa	11	0		
1986–87	Aston Villa	10	0	28	0
1987–88	Middlesbrough	1	0		
1988–89	Middlesbrough	12	0		
1989–90	Middlesbrough	21	0		
1990–91	Middlesbrough	0	0	34	0
1990–91	Hartlepool U	12	0	12	0
1991–92	Leicester C	42	0		
1992–93	Leicester C	19	0		
1993–94	Leicester C	14	0		
1994–95	Leicester C	36	0		
1995–96	Leicester C	45	0		
1996–97	Leicester C	7	0	163	0
1997–98	Birmingham C	1	0		
1998–99	Birmingham C	36	0		
1999–2000	Birmingham C	18	0		
2000–01	Birmingham C	1	0		
2001–02	Birmingham C	0	0	56	0
2001–02	Bolton W	3	0		
2002–03	Bolton W	0	0		
2003–04	Bolton W	0	0		
2004–05	Bolton W	2	0	5	0
2005–06	Derby Co	6	0	6	0
2009–10	Burton Alb	6	0	6	0

SIMPSON, Michael (M) 475 25
H: 5 8 W: 10 12 b.Nottingham 28-2-74
Source: Trainee.

1992–93	Notts Co	0	0		
1993–94	Notts Co	6	1		
1994–95	Notts Co	19	2		
1995–96	Notts Co	23	0		
1996–97	Notts Co	1	0	49	3
1996–97	Plymouth Arg	12	0	12	0
1996–97	Wycombe W	20	1		
1997–98	Wycombe W	21	0		
1998–99	Wycombe W	33	4		
1999–2000	Wycombe W	43	0		
2000–01	Wycombe W	45	3		
2001–02	Wycombe W	43	1		
2002–03	Wycombe W	42	5		
2003–04	Wycombe W	38	2	285	16
2004–05	Leyton Orient	45	2		
2005–06	Leyton Orient	45	1		
2006–07	Leyton Orient	15	1	105	4
2008–09	Burton Alb	24	2	24	2

STRIDE, Darren (D) 9 0
H: 5 11 W: 13 07 b.Burton 29-9-75
Source: Scholar.

| 2009–10 | Burton Alb | 9 | 0 | 9 | 0 |

WALKER, Richard (F) 322 81
H: 6 0 W: 12 04 b.Sutton Coldfield 8-11-77
Source: Trainee.

1995–96	Aston Villa	0	0		
1996–97	Aston Villa	0	0		
1997–98	Aston Villa	1	0		
1998–99	Aston Villa	0	0		
1998–99	Cambridge U	21	3	21	3
1999–2000	Aston Villa	5	2		
2000–01	Aston Villa	0	0		
2000–01	Blackpool	18	3		
2001–02	Aston Villa	0	0	6	2
2001–02	Wycombe W	12	3	12	3
2001–02	Blackpool	21	8		
2002–03	Blackpool	32	4		
2003–04	Blackpool	9	0	80	15
2003–04	Northampton T	12	4	12	4
2003–04	Oxford U	4	0	4	0
2004–05	Bristol R	27	10		
2005–06	Bristol R	46	20		
2006–07	Bristol R	46	12		
2007–08	Bristol R	24	4		
2008–09	Bristol R	0	0	143	46
2008–09	Shrewsbury T	27	5	27	5
2009–10	Burton Alb	17	3	17	3

WEBSTER, Aaron (D) 24 4
H: 6 1 W: 12 00 b.Derby 19-12-80
Source: Youth.

| 2009–10 | Burton Alb | 24 | 4 | 24 | 4 |

BURY (19)

BAKER, Richie (M) 107 7
H: 5 10 W: 11 05 b.Burnley 29-12-87
Source: Preston NE Scholar.

2006–07	Bury	39	5		
2007–08	Bury	32	1		
2008–09	Bury	22	0		
2009–10	Bury	14	1	107	7

BARRY-MURPHY, Brian (M) 392 16
H: 5 10 W: 13 01 b.Cork 27-7-78
Honours: Eire Youth, Under-21.

1995–96	Cork City	13	0		
1996–97	Cork City	25	0		
1997–98	Cork City	15	1		
1998–99	Cork City	27	1	80	2
1999–2000	Preston NE	1	0		
2000–01	Preston NE	14	0		
2001–02	Preston NE	4	0		
2001–02	Southend U	8	1	8	1
2002–03	Preston NE	2	0	21	0
2002–03	Hartlepool U	7	0	7	0
2002–03	Sheffield W	17	0		
2003–04	Sheffield W	41	0	58	0
2004–05	Bury	45	6		
2005–06	Bury	40	3		
2006–07	Bury	14	0		
2007–08	Bury	31	1		
2008–09	Bury	42	2		
2009–10	Bury	46	1	218	13

BELFORD, Cameron (G) 9 0
H: 6 1 W: 11 10 b.Nuneaton 16-10-88

2006–07	Coventry C	0	0		
2007–08	Bury	1	0		
2008–09	Bury	1	0		
2009–10	Bury	7	0	9	0

BISHOP, Andy (F) 209 63
H: 6 0 W: 10 10 b.Stone 19-10-82
Source: Scholar.

Season	Club				
2002–03	Walsall	0	0		
2002–03	*Kidderminster H*	29	5		
2003–04	*Kidderminster H*	11	2	40	7
2003–04	*Rochdale*	10	1	10	1
2003–04	*Yeovil T*	5	2	5	2
From York C.					
2006–07	Bury	43	15		
2007–08	Bury	44	19		
2008–09	Bury	42	16		
2009–10	Bury	25	3	154	53

BROWN, Wayne (G) 267 0
H: 6 0 W: 13 11 b.Southampton 14-1-77
Source: Trainee.

Season	Club				
1993–94	Bristol C	1	0		
1994–95	Bristol C	0	0		
1995–96	Bristol C	0	0	1	0
From Weston-S-Mare					
1996–97	Chester C	2	0		
1997–98	Chester C	13	0		
1998–99	Chester C	23	0		
1999–2000	Chester C	46	0		
2000–01	Chester C	0	0		
2001–02	Chester C	0	0		
2004–05	Chester C	23	0		
2005–06	Chester C	0	0	107	0
2006–07	Hereford U	39	0		
2007–08	Hereford U	44	0	83	0
2008–09	Bury	35	0		
2009–10	Bury	41	0	76	0

BUCHANAN, David (M) 186 0
H: 5 7 W: 11 03 b.Rochdale 6-5-86
Source: Scholar. *Honours:* Northern Ireland Youth, Under-21.

Season	Club				
2004–05	Bury	3	0		
2005–06	Bury	23	0		
2006–07	Bury	41	0		
2007–08	Bury	35	0		
2008–09	Bury	46	0		
2009–10	Bury	38	0	186	0

CARLTON, Danny (F) 75 9
H: 5 11 W: 12 04 b.Leeds 22-12-83
Source: Morecambe.

Season	Club				
2007–08	Carlisle U	31	0		
2008–09	Carlisle U	12	3	43	3
2008–09	*Morecambe*	8	2	8	2
2008–09	*Darlington*	17	4	17	4
2009–10	Bury	7	0	7	0

CRESSWELL, Ryan (D) 77 2
H: 5 9 W: 10 05 b.Rotherham 22-12-87
Source: Scholar.

Season	Club				
2006–07	Sheffield U	0	0		
2007–08	Sheffield U	0	0		
2007–08	*Rotherham U*	3	0	3	0
2007–08	*Morecambe*	2	0	2	0
2007–08	*Macclesfield T*	19	1	19	1
2008–09	Bury	25	1		
2009–10	Bury	28	0	53	1

DAWSON, Stephen (M) 205 10
H: 5 9 W: 11 09 b.Dublin 4-12-85
Source: Scholar. *Honours:* Eire Under-21.

Season	Club				
2003–04	Leicester C	0	0		
2004–05	Leicester C	0	0		
2005–06	Mansfield T	40	1		
2006–07	Mansfield T	34	1		
2007–08	Mansfield T	43	2	117	4
2008–09	Bury	43	2		
2009–10	Bury	45	4	88	6

FUTCHER, Ben (D) 295 20
H: 6 7 W: 12 05 b.Manchester 20-2-81
Source: Trainee.

Season	Club				
1999–2000	Oldham Ath	5	0		
2000–01	Oldham Ath	5	0		
2001–02	Oldham Ath	0	0	10	0
From Stalybridge C, Doncaster R					
2002–03	Lincoln C	43	8		
2003–04	Lincoln C	43	2		
2004–05	Lincoln C	35	3	121	13
2005–06	Boston U	14	0	14	0
2005–06	Grimsby T	15	2		
2006–07	Grimsby T	4	0	19	2
2006–07	Peterborough U	25	3	25	3
2007–08	Bury	40	0		
2008–09	Bury	34	2		
2009–10	Bury	32	0	106	2

JOHNSON, Simon (F) 186 22
H: 5 9 W: 11 09 b.West Bromwich 9-3-83
Source: Scholar. *Honours:* England Youth, Under-20.

Season	Club				
2000–01	Leeds U	0	0		
2001–02	Leeds U	0	0		
2002–03	Leeds U	4	0		
2002–03	*Hull C*	12	2	12	2
2003–04	Leeds U	5	0		
2003–04	*Blackpool*	4	1	4	1
2004–05	Leeds U	2	0	11	0
2004–05	*Sunderland*	5	0	5	0
2004–05	*Doncaster R*	11	3	11	3
2004–05	*Barnsley*	11	2	11	2
2005–06	Darlington	42	7		
2006–07	Darlington	24	2	66	9
2007–08	Hereford U	33	5		
2008–09	Hereford U	29	0	62	5
2009–10	Bury	4	0	4	0

JONES, Mike (M) 110 11
H: 5 11 W: 12 04 b.Birkenhead 15-8-87
Source: Scholar.

Season	Club				
2005–06	Tranmere R	1	0		
2006–07	Tranmere R	0	0		
2006–07	*Shrewsbury T*	13	1	13	1
2007–08	Tranmere R	9	1	10	1
2008–09	Bury	46	4		
2009–10	Bury	41	5	87	9

LOWE, Ryan (F) 329 83
H: 5 10 W: 12 08 b.Liverpool 18-9-78
Source: Burscough.

Season	Club				
2000–01	Shrewsbury T	30	4		
2001–02	Shrewsbury T	38	7		
2002–03	Shrewsbury T	39	9		
2003–04	Shrewsbury T	0	0		
2004–05	Shrewsbury T	30	3	137	23
2004–05	Chester C	8	4		
2005–06	Chester C	32	10		
2005–06	Crewe Alex	0	0		
2006–07	Crewe Alex	37	8		
2007–08	Crewe Alex	27	4	64	12
2008–09	*Stockport Co*	4	0	4	0
2008–09	*Chester C*	45	16	85	30
2009–10	Bury	39	18	39	18

MORRELL, Andy (F) 359 96
H: 5 11 W: 12 00 b.Doncaster 28-9-74
Source: Newcastle Blue Star.

Season	Club				
1998–99	Wrexham	7	0		
1999–2000	Wrexham	13	1		
2000–01	Wrexham	20	3		
2001–02	Wrexham	25	2		
2002–03	Wrexham	45	34	110	40
2003–04	Coventry C	30	9		
2004–05	Coventry C	34	6		
2005–06	Coventry C	34	2		
2006–07	Coventry C	0	0	98	17
2007–08	Blackpool	40	16		
2007–08	Blackpool	38	5	78	21
2008–09	Bury	41	9		
2009–10	Bury	32	9	73	18

NEWEY, Tom (D) 264 7
H: 5 10 W: 10 02 b.Sheffield 31-10-82
Source: Scholar.

Season	Club				
2000–01	Leeds U	0	0		
2001–02	Leeds U	0	0		
2002–03	Leeds U	0	0		
2002–03	*Cambridge U*	6	0		
2002–03	*Darlington*	7	1	7	1
2003–04	Leyton Orient	34	2		
2004–05	Leyton Orient	20	1	54	3
2004–05	*Cambridge U*	16	0	22	0
2005–06	Grimsby T	38	1		
2006–07	Grimsby T	43	1		
2007–08	Grimsby T	42	1		
2008–09	Grimsby T	24	0		
2008–09	*Rochdale*	2	0	2	0
2009–10	Grimsby T	0	0	147	3
2009–10	Bury	32	0	32	0

RACCHI, Danny (D) 49 0
H: 5 8 W: 10 04 b.Halifax 22-11-87
Source: Scholar.

Season	Club				
2006–07	Huddersfield T	3	0		
2007–08	Huddersfield T	3	0	6	0
2008–09	Bury	21	0		
2009–10	Bury	22	0	43	0

ROUSE, Domaine (F) 12 0
H: 5 6 W: 10 10 b.Stretford 4-7-89
Source: Scholar.

Season	Club				
2006–07	Bury	2	0		
2007–08	Bury	6	0		
2008–09	Bury	0	0		
2009–10	Bury	4	0	12	0

SCOTT, Paul (D) 245 15
H: 5 11 W: 12 00 b.Wakefield 5-11-79
Source: Trainee.

Season	Club				
1998–99	Huddersfield T	0	0		
1999–2000	Huddersfield T	0	0		
2000–01	Huddersfield T	0	0		
2001–02	Huddersfield T	0	0		
2002–03	Huddersfield T	13	0		
2003–04	Huddersfield T	19	2		
2004–05	Huddersfield T	0	0	32	2
2004–05	Bury	23	0		
2005–06	Bury	41	2		
2006–07	Bury	46	2		
2007–08	Bury	40	6		
2008–09	Bury	33	3		
2009–10	Bury	30	0	213	13

SODJE, Efe (D) 431 29
H: 6 1 W: 12 00 b.Greenwich 5-10-72
Source: Delta Steel Pioneer, Stevenage Bor.
Honours: Nigeria 9 full caps, 1 goal.

Season	Club				
1997–98	Macclesfield T	41	3		
1998–99	Macclesfield T	42	3	83	6
1999–2000	Luton T	9	0	9	0
1999–2000	Colchester U	3	0	3	0
2000–01	Crewe Alex	32	0		
2001–02	Crewe Alex	36	2		
2002–03	Crewe Alex	30	1	98	3
2003–04	Huddersfield T	39	4		
2004–05	Huddersfield T	28	1	67	5
2004–05	Yeovil T	6	2		
2005–06	Yeovil T	19	1	25	3
2005–06	Southend U	13	1		
2006–07	Southend U	24	1	37	2
2007–08	Gillingham	13	0	13	0
2007–08	*Bury*	16	1		
2008–09	Bury	41	7		
2009–10	Bury	39	2	96	10

WORRALL, David (M) 54 4
H: 6 0 W: 11 03 b.Manchester 12-6-90
Source: Scholar.

Season	Club				
2006–07	Bury	1	0		
2007–08	Bury	0	0		
2007–08	WBA	0	0		
2008–09	*Accrington S*	4	0	4	0
2008–09	*Shrewsbury T*	9	0	9	0
2009–10	WBA	0	0		
2009–10	Bury	40	4	41	4

CARDIFF C (20)

BLAKE, Darcy (M) 51 0
H: 5 10 W: 12 05 b.Caerphilly 13-12-88
Source: Scholar. *Honours:* Wales Youth, Under-21.

Season	Club				
2005–06	Cardiff C	1	0		
2006–07	Cardiff C	10	0		
2007–08	Cardiff C	8	0		
2008–09	Cardiff C	7	0		
2009–10	Cardiff C	18	0	44	0
2009–10	*Plymouth Arg*	7	0	7	0

BOTHROYD, Jay (F) 265 56
H: 6 3 W: 14 13 b.Islington 7-5-82
Source: Trainee. *Honours:* England Schools, Youth, Under-20, Under-21.

Season	Club				
1999–2000	Arsenal	0	0		
2000–01	Coventry C	8	0		
2001–02	Coventry C	31	6		
2002–03	Coventry C	33	8	72	14
2003–04	*Perugia*	26	4	26	4
2004–05	Blackburn R	11	1	11	1
2005–06	Charlton Ath	18	2	18	2
2006–07	Wolverhampton W	33	9		
2007–08	Wolverhampton W	22	3	55	12
2007–08	*Stoke C*	4	0	4	0
2008–09	Cardiff C	39	12		
2009–10	Cardiff C	40	11	79	23

BURKE, Chris (M)   153 21
H: 5 9   W: 10 10   b.Glasgow 2-12-83
Honours: Scotland Under-21, B, 2 full caps.

Season	Club				
2001–02	Rangers	2	1		
2002–03	Rangers	0	0		
2003–04	Rangers	20	3		
2004–05	Rangers	12	0		
2005–06	Rangers	27	3		
2006–07	Rangers	22	2		
2007–08	Rangers	11	2		
2008–09	Rangers	1	0	95	11
2008–09	Cardiff C	14	1		
2009–10	Cardiff C	44	9	58	10

CAPALDI, Tony (D)   206 12
H: 6 0   W: 11 08   b.Porsgrunn 12-8-81
Source: Trainee. *Honours:* Northern Ireland
Youth, Under-21, 22 full caps.

Season	Club				
1999–2000	Birmingham C	0	0		
2000–01	Birmingham C	0	0		
2001–02	Birmingham C	0	0		
2002–03	Birmingham C	0	0		
2002–03	Plymouth Arg	1	0		
2003–04	Plymouth Arg	33	7		
2004–05	Plymouth Arg	35	2		
2005–06	Plymouth Arg	41	3		
2006–07	Plymouth Arg	31	0	141	12
2007–08	Cardiff C	44	0		
2008–09	Cardiff C	3	0		
2009–10	Cardiff C	15	0	62	0
2009–10	Leeds U	3	0	3	0

CHOPRA, Michael (F)   219 78
H: 5 9   W: 10 10   b.Newcastle 23-12-83
Source: Scholar. *Honours:* England Youth,
Under-20, Under-21.

Season	Club				
2000–01	Newcastle U	0	0		
2001–02	Newcastle U	0	0		
2002–03	Newcastle U	1	0		
2002–03	*Watford*	5	5	5	5
2003–04	Newcastle U	6	0		
2003–04	*Nottingham F*	5	0	5	0
2004–05	Newcastle U	1	0		
2004–05	*Barnsley*	39	17	39	17
2005–06	Newcastle U	13	1	21	1
2006–07	Cardiff C	42	22		
2007–08	Sunderland	33	6		
2008–09	Sunderland	6	2	39	8
2008–09	*Cardiff C*	27	9		
2009–10	Cardiff C	41	16	110	47

COMMINGS, Miguel (D)   157 0
H: 5 9   W: 11 03   b.Les Abymes 16-3-82

Season	Club				
2002–03	Amiens	12	0	12	0
2003–04	Reims	29	0		
2004–05	Reims	21	0		
2005–06	Reims	11	0		
2006–07	Reims	13	0	74	0
2007–08	Swindon T	40	0	40	0
2008–09	Cardiff C	30	0		
2009–10	Cardiff C	1	0	31	0

DENNEHY, Darren (D)   29 0
H: 6 3   W: 11 11   b.Republic of Ireland
21-9-88
Source: Scholar. *Honours:* Eire Under-21.

Season	Club				
2005–06	Everton	0	0		
2006–07	Everton	0	0		
2007–08	Everton	0	0		
2008–09	Cardiff C	0	0		
2008–09	*Hereford U*	3	0		
2009–10	Cardiff C	0	0		
2009–10	*Hereford U*	7	0	10	0
2009–10	*Gillingham*	19	0	19	0

ENCKELMAN, Peter (G)   165 0
H: 6 2   W: 12 05   b.Turku 10-3-77
Source: TPS Turku. *Honours:* Finland
Under-21, 12 full caps.

Season	Club				
1995	TPS Turku	6	0		
1996	TPS Turku	24	0		
1997	TPS Turku	25	0		
1998	TPS Turku	24	0	79	0
1998–99	Aston Villa	0	0		
1999–2000	Aston Villa	10	0		
2000–01	Aston Villa	0	0		
2001–02	Aston Villa	9	0		
2002–03	Aston Villa	33	0		
2003–04	Aston Villa	0	0	52	0
2003–04	Blackburn R	2	0		
2004–05	Blackburn R	1	0		
2005–06	Blackburn R	0	0		
2006–07	Blackburn R	0	0		
2007–08	Blackburn R	0	0	2	0
2007–08	Cardiff C	16	0		
2008–09	Cardiff C	12	0		
2009–10	Cardiff C	4	0	32	0

FEENEY, Warren (F)   270 70
H: 5 8   W: 12 04   b.Belfast 17-1-81
Source: Trainee. *Honours:* Northern Ireland
Schools, Youth, Under-21, 34 full caps, 5
goals.

Season	Club				
1997–98	Leeds U	0	0		
1998–99	Leeds U	0	0		
1999–2000	Leeds U	0	0		
2000–01	Leeds U	0	0		
2000–01	Bournemouth	10	4		
2001–02	Bournemouth	57	15		
2002–03	Bournemouth	21	7		
2003–04	Bournemouth	40	12	108	36
2004–05	Stockport Co	31	15	31	15
2004–05	Luton T	6	0		
2005–06	Luton T	42	6		
2006–07	Luton T	29	2	77	8
2006–07	*Cardiff C*	6	0		
2007–08	Cardiff C	5	0		
2007–08	*Swansea C*	10	5	10	5
2008–09	*Dundee U*	23	6	23	6
2008–09	Cardiff C	0	0		
2009–10	Cardiff C	9	0	20	0
2009–10	*Sheffield W*	1	0	1	0

GERRARD, Anthony (D)   202 9
H: 6 2   W: 13 07   b.Liverpool 6-2-86
Source: Scholar. *Honours:* Eire Youth.

Season	Club				
2004–05	Everton	0	0		
2004–05	Walsall	8	0		
2005–06	Walsall	34	0		
2006–07	Walsall	35	1		
2007–08	Walsall	44	3		
2008–09	Walsall	42	3	163	7
2009–10	Cardiff C	39	2	39	2

GYEPES, Gabor (D)   192 15
H: 6 3   W: 13 10   b.Hungary 26-6-81
Honours: Hungary 26 full caps, 1 goal.

Season	Club				
1999–2000	Ferencvaros	2	0		
2000–01	Ferencvaros	29	2		
2001–02	Ferencvaros	33	3		
2002–03	Ferencvaros	17	2		
2003–04	Ferencvaros	7	0		
2004–05	Ferencvaros	26	5	114	12
2005–06	Wolverhampton W	20	0		
2006–07	Wolverhampton W	0	0	20	0
2007–08	Northampton T	13	0		
2008–09	Northampton T	2	0	15	0
2008–09	Cardiff C	27	2		
2009–10	Cardiff C	16	1	43	3

HUDSON, Mark (D)   205 12
H: 6 1   W: 12 01   b.Guildford 30-3-82
Source: Trainee.

Season	Club				
1998–99	Fulham	0	0		
1999–2000	Fulham	0	0		
2000–01	Fulham	0	0		
2001–02	Fulham	0	0		
2002–03	Fulham	0	0		
2003–04	Fulham	0	0		
2003–04	*Oldham Ath*	15	0	15	0
2003–04	*Crystal Palace*	14	0		
2004–05	Crystal Palace	7	1		
2005–06	Crystal Palace	15	0		
2006–07	Crystal Palace	39	4		
2007–08	Crystal Palace	45	3	120	7
2008–09	Charlton Ath	43	3	43	3
2009–10	Cardiff C	27	2	27	2

KENNEDY, Mark (M)   433 32
H: 5 11   W: 11 09   b.Dublin 15-5-76
Source: Belvedere, Trainee. *Honours:* Eire
Schools, Youth, Under-21, 34 full caps, 3
goals.

Season	Club				
1992–93	Millwall	1	0		
1993–94	Millwall	12	4		
1994–95	Millwall	30	5	43	9
1994–95	Liverpool	6	0		
1995–96	Liverpool	4	0		
1996–97	Liverpool	5	0		
1997–98	Liverpool	1	0	16	0
1997–98	*QPR*	8	2	8	2
1997–98	Wimbledon	4	0		
1998–99	Wimbledon	17	0	21	0
1999–2000	Manchester C	41	8		
2000–01	Manchester C	25	0	66	8
2001–02	Wolverhampton W	35	5		
2002–03	Wolverhampton W	31	3		
2003–04	Wolverhampton W	31	2		
2004–05	Wolverhampton W	30	0		
2005–06	Wolverhampton W	40	2	167	12
2006–07	Crystal Palace	38	1		
2007–08	Crystal Palace	8	0	46	1
2008–09	Cardiff C	36	0		
2009–10	Cardiff C	30	0	66	0

LEDLEY, Joe (M)   226 25
H: 6 0   W: 11 07   b.Cardiff 23-1-87
Source: Scholar. *Honours:* Wales Youth,
Under-21, 32 full caps, 2 goals.

Season	Club				
2004–05	Cardiff C	28	3		
2005–06	Cardiff C	42	3		
2006–07	Cardiff C	46	2		
2007–08	Cardiff C	41	10		
2008–09	Cardiff C	40	4		
2009–10	Cardiff C	29	3	226	25

MAGENNIS, Josh (F)   11 0
H: 6 2   W: 14 07   b.Bangor 15-8-90
Source: Scholar. *Honours:* Northern Ireland
Under-21, 2 full caps.

Season	Club				
2009–10	Cardiff C	9	0	9	0
2009–10	*Grimsby T*	2	0	2	0

MARSHALL, David (G)   172 0
H: 6 3   W: 13 04   b.Glasgow 5-3-85
Source: Celtic Youth. *Honours:* Scotland
Youth, Under-21, B, 5 full caps.

Season	Club				
2003–04	Celtic	11	0		
2004–05	Celtic	18	0		
2005–06	Celtic	4	0		
2006–07	Celtic	2	0	35	0
2006–07	Norwich C	2	0		
2007–08	Norwich C	46	0		
2008–09	Norwich C	46	0	94	0
2008–09	Cardiff C	0	0		
2009–10	Cardiff C	43	0	43	0

MATTHEWS, Adam (M)   32 1
H: 5 10   W: 11 02   b.Swansea 13-1-92
Source: Scholar. *Honours:* Wales Under-21.

Season	Club				
2008–09	Cardiff C	0	0		
2009–10	Cardiff C	32	1	32	1

McCORMACK, Ross (F)   150 42
H: 5 9   W: 11 00   b.Glasgow 18-8-86
Honours: Scotland Youth, Under-21, B, 5 full
caps, 1 goal.

Season	Club				
2003–04	Rangers	2	1		
2004–05	Rangers	1	0		
2005–06	Rangers	8	1	11	2
2005–06	Doncaster R	19	4	19	4
2006–07	Motherwell	12	2		
2007–08	Motherwell	36	9	48	11
2008–09	Cardiff C	38	21		
2009–10	Cardiff C	34	4	72	25

McNAUGHTON, Kevin (D)   312 4
H: 5 10   W: 10 06   b.Dundee 28-8-82
Honours: Scotland Under-21, 4 full caps.

Season	Club				
1999–2000	Aberdeen	2	0		
2000–01	Aberdeen	33	0		
2001–02	Aberdeen	34	0		
2002–03	Aberdeen	22	1		
2003–04	Aberdeen	17	0		
2004–05	Aberdeen	35	2		
2005–06	Aberdeen	34	0	175	3
2006–07	Cardiff C	42	0		
2007–08	Cardiff C	35	1		
2008–09	Cardiff C	39	0		
2009–10	Cardiff C	21	0	137	1

McPHAIL, Stephen (M)   304 10
H: 5 8   W: 11 04   b.Westminster 9-12-79
Source: Trainee. *Honours:* Eire Youth, B,
Under-21, 10 full caps, 1 goal.

Season	Club				
1995–97	Leeds U	0	0		
1997–98	Leeds U	10	0		
1998–99	Leeds U	17	0		
1999–2000	Leeds U	24	2		
2000–01	Leeds U	7	0		
2001–02	Leeds U	1	0		
2001–02	*Millwall*	3	0	3	0
2002–03	Leeds U	13	0		
2003–04	Leeds U	12	1	78	3

2003–04	Nottingham F	14	0	14	0
2004–05	Barnsley	36	2		
2005–06	Barnsley	34	2	70	4
2006–07	Cardiff C	43	0		
2007–08	Cardiff C	43	3		
2008–09	Cardiff C	32	0		
2009–10	Cardiff C	21	0	139	3

MORRIS, Aaron (D) 1 0
H: 6 1 W: 12 05 b.Cardiff 30-12-89
Source: Scholar. *Honours:* Wales Youth, Under-21.

2008–09	Cardiff C	0	0		
2009–10	Cardiff C	1	0	1	0

OWUSU-ABEYIE, Quincy (F) 88 9
H: 5 11 W: 11 10 b.Amsterdam 15-4-86
Source: Scholar. *Honours:* Holland Youth, Under-21, Ghana 15 full caps, 1 goal.

2003–04	Arsenal	0	0		
2004–05	Arsenal	1	0		
2005–06	Arsenal	4	0	5	0
2006	Spartak Moscow	15	1		
2007–08	Spartak Moscow	6	0		
2007–08	*Celta Vigo*	20	4	20	4
2008–09	Birmingham C	19	2	19	2
2008–09	Cardiff C	5	0		
2009	Spartak Moscow	8	2	29	3
2009–10	Cardiff C	0	0	5	0
2009–10	*Portsmouth*	10	0	10	0

QUINN, Paul (D) 183 3
H: 6 0 W: 11 04 b.Wishaw 21-7-85

2002–03	Motherwell	4	0		
2003–04	Motherwell	26	0		
2004–05	Motherwell	23	0		
2005–06	Motherwell	18	0		
2006–07	Motherwell	26	0		
2007–08	Motherwell	31	2		
2008–09	Motherwell	33	1	161	3
2009–10	Cardiff C	22	0	22	0

RAE, Gavin (D) 363 32
H: 5 11 W: 10 04 b.Aberdeen 28-11-77
Source: Hermes J. *Honours:* Scotland Under-21, 13 full caps.

1995–96	Dundee	6	0		
1996–97	Dundee	17	2		
1997–98	Dundee	6	0		
1998–99	Dundee	30	1		
1999–2000	Dundee	35	4		
2000–01	Dundee	32	4		
2001–02	Dundee	36	6		
2002–03	Dundee	37	4		
2003–04	Dundee	13	2	212	23
2003–04	Rangers	10	2		
2004–05	Rangers	0	0		
2005–06	Rangers	8	0		
2006–07	Rangers	10	1	28	3
2007–08	Cardiff C	45	4		
2008–09	Cardiff C	41	1		
2009–10	Cardiff C	37	1	123	6

SCIMECA, Riccardo (D) 358 16
H: 6 1 W: 12 09 b.Leamington Spa 13-6-75
Source: Scholar. *Honours:* England Under-21, B.

1993–94	Aston Villa	0	0		
1994–95	Aston Villa	0	0		
1995–96	Aston Villa	17	0		
1996–97	Aston Villa	17	0		
1997–98	Aston Villa	21	0		
1998–99	Aston Villa	18	2	73	2
1999–2000	Nottingham F	38	0		
2000–01	Nottingham F	36	4		
2001–02	Nottingham F	37	0		
2002–03	Nottingham F	40	3	151	7
2003–04	Leicester C	29	1	29	1
2004–05	WBA	33	0		
2005–06	WBA	2	0	35	0
2006–07	Cardiff C	18	1		
2006–07	Cardiff C	35	5		
2007–08	Cardiff C	9	0		
2008–09	Cardiff C	4	0		
2009–10	Cardiff C	4	0	70	6

TAIWO, Soloman (M) 62 4
H: 6 1 W: 13 02 b.Lagos 29-4-85
Source: Sutton U.

2007–08	Dagenham & R	10	0		
2008–09	Dagenham & R	40	4		
2009–10	Dagenham & R	4	0	54	4
2009–10	Cardiff C	8	0	8	0

WHITTINGHAM, Peter (D) 208 33
H: 5 10 W: 9 13 b.Nuneaton 8-9-84
Source: Trainee. *Honours:* England Youth, Under-20, Under-21.

2002–03	Aston Villa	4	0		
2003–04	Aston Villa	32	0		
2004–05	Aston Villa	13	1		
2004–05	*Burnley*	7	0	7	0
2005–06	Aston Villa	4	0		
2005–06	*Derby Co*	11	0	11	0
2006–07	Aston Villa	3	0	56	1
2006–07	Cardiff C	19	4		
2007–08	Cardiff C	41	5		
2008–09	Cardiff C	33	3		
2009–10	Cardiff C	41	20	134	32

WILDIG, Aaron (M) 11 1
H: 5 9 W: 11 02 b.Hereford 26-1-90
Source: Scholar.

2009–10	Cardiff C	11	1	11	1

CARLISLE U (21)

ALDRED, Tom (D) 5 0
H: 6 2 W: 13 02 b.Bolton 11-9-90
Source: Scholar.

2008–09	Carlisle U	0	0		
2009–10	Carlisle U	5	0	5	0

ANYINSAH, Joe (M) 94 16
H: 5 8 W: 11 00 b.Bristol 8-10-84
Source: Scholar.

2001–02	Bristol C	0	0		
2002–03	Bristol C	0	0		
2003–04	Bristol C	0	0		
2004–05	Bristol C	7	0	7	0
2005–06	Preston NE	3	0		
2005–06	*Bury*	3	0	3	0
2006–07	Preston NE	3	0		
2007–08	Preston NE	0	0		
2007–08	*Carlisle U*	12	3		
2007–08	*Crewe Alex*	8	0	8	0
2008–09	Preston NE	0	0	6	0
2008–09	*Brighton & HA*	11	0	11	0
2008–09	Carlisle U	19	4		
2009–10	Carlisle U	28	9	59	16

BOWMAN, Ryan (F) 6 0
H: 6 2 W: 12 00 b.Carlisle 30-11-91
Source: Scholar.

2009–10	Carlisle U	6	0	6	0

BRIDGE-WILKINSON, Marc (M) 328 56
H: 5 6 W: 11 00 b.Coventry 16-3-79
Source: Trainee.

1996–97	Derby Co	0	0		
1997–98	Derby Co	0	0		
1998–99	Derby Co	1	0		
1998–99	*Carlisle U*	7	0		
1999–2000	Derby Co	0	0	1	0
2000–01	Port Vale	42	9		
2001–02	Port Vale	19	6		
2002–03	Port Vale	31	9		
2003–04	Port Vale	32	7	124	31
2004–05	Stockport Co	22	2	22	2
2004–05	*Bradford C*	12	3		
2005–06	Bradford C	36	5		
2006–07	Bradford C	39	4	87	12
2007–08	Carlisle U	45	6		
2008–09	Carlisle U	23	5		
2009–10	Carlisle U	19	0	94	11

BURNS, Michael (D) 1 0
H: 5 10 W: 11 07 b.Huyton 4-10-88
Source: Liverpool Scholar.

2007–08	Bolton W	0	0		
2008–09	Bolton W	0	0		
2008–09	Carlisle U	1	0		
2009–10	Carlisle U	0	0	1	0

COLLIN, Adam (G) 29 0
H: 6 2 W: 12 00 b.Carlisle 9-12-84
Source: Trainee.

2003–04	Newcastle U	0	0		
2003–04	*Oldham Ath*	0	0		
2003–04	Doncaster R	0	0		
2004–05	Doncaster R	0	0		
2005–06	Doncaster R	0	0		
2006–07	Doncaster R	0	0		
2007–08	Doncaster R	0	0		
2008–09	Doncaster R	0	0		
2009–10	Carlisle U	29	0	29	0

COOK, Andy (F) 0 0
H: 6 1 W: 11 04 b.Bishop Auckland 18-10-90
Source: Scholar.

2008–09	Carlisle U	0	0		
2009–10	Carlisle U	0	0		

DOBIE, Scott (F) 393 63
H: 6 1 W: 12 05 b.Workington 10-10-78
Source: Trainee. *Honours:* Scotland 6 full caps, 1 goal.

1996–97	Carlisle U	2	1		
1997–98	Carlisle U	23	0		
1998–99	Carlisle U	33	6		
1998–99	*Clydebank*	6	0	6	0
1999–2000	Carlisle U	34	7		
2000–01	Carlisle U	44	10		
2001–02	WBA	43	10		
2002–03	WBA	31	5		
2003–04	WBA	31	5		
2004–05	WBA	5	1	110	21
2004–05	Millwall	16	3	16	3
2004–05	Nottingham F	12	1		
2005–06	Nottingham F	8	2		
2006–07	Nottingham F	19	0		
2007–08	Nottingham F	2	0	41	3
2007–08	Carlisle U	15	4		
2008–09	Carlisle U	30	3		
2009–10	Carlisle U	39	5	220	36

GILLESPIE, Mark (G) 1 0
H: 6 3 W: 13 07 b.Newcastle 27-3-92
Source: Scholar.

2009–10	Carlisle U	1	0	1	0

HARTE, Ian (D) 303 46
H: 5 11 W: 12 06 b.Drogheda 31-8-77
Source: Trainee. *Honours:* Eire 63 full caps, 11 goals.

1995–96	Leeds U	4	0		
1996–97	Leeds U	14	2		
1997–98	Leeds U	12	0		
1998–99	Leeds U	35	4		
1999–2000	Leeds U	33	6		
2000–01	Leeds U	29	7		
2001–02	Leeds U	36	5		
2002–03	Leeds U	27	3		
2003–04	Leeds U	23	1	213	28
2004–05	Levante	24	1		
2005–06	Levante	0	0		
2006–07	Levante	6	0	30	1
2007–08	Sunderland	8	0	8	0
2008–09	Blackpool	4	0	4	0
2008–09	Carlisle U	3	1		
2009–10	Carlisle U	45	16	48	17

HORWOOD, Evan (D) 121 1
H: 6 0 W: 10 06 b.Billingham 10-3-86
Source: Scholar.

2004–05	Sheffield U	0	0		
2004–05	*Stockport Co*	10	0	10	0
2005–06	Sheffield U	0	0		
2005–06	*Scunthorpe U*	0	0		
2005–06	*Chester C*	1	0	1	0
2006–07	Sheffield U	0	0		
2006–07	*Darlington*	20	0	20	0
2007–08	Sheffield U	0	0		
2007–08	*Gretna*	15	1	15	1
2007–08	Carlisle U	19	0		
2008–09	Carlisle U	24	0		
2009–10	Carlisle U	32	0	75	0

HURST, Kevan (M) 183 14
H: 5 10 W: 11 07 b.Chesterfield 27-8-85
Source: Sheffield U Scholar.

2003–04	*Boston U*	7	1	7	1
2004–05	Sheffield U	1	0		
2004–05	*Stockport Co*	14	1	14	1
2005–06	Sheffield U	0	0		
2005–06	*Chesterfield*	37	4		
2006–07	Sheffield U	0	0	1	0
2006–07	*Chesterfield*	25	3	62	7
2006–07	*Scunthorpe U*	13	0		
2007–08	Scunthorpe U	33	1		
2008–09	Scunthorpe U	20	2	66	3
2009–10	Carlisle U	33	2	33	2

KANE, Tony (D) — 24 0
H: 5 11 W: 11 00 b.Belfast 29-8-87
Source: Scholar. Honours: Eire Under-21, Northern Ireland Youth, Under-21.

Season	Club	A	G	Tot A	Tot G
2004-05	Blackburn R	0	0		
2005-06	Blackburn R	0	0		
2006-07	Blackburn R	0	0		
2006-07	Stockport Co	4	0		
2007-08	Blackburn R	0	0		
2008-09	Blackburn R	0	0		
2008-09	Stockport Co	3	0	7	0
2008-09	Carlisle U	9	0		
2009-10	Carlisle U	4	0	13	0
2009-10	Darlington	4	0	4	0

KAVANAGH, Graham (M) — 536 76
H: 5 10 W: 13 03 b.Dublin 2-12-73
Source: Home Farm. Honours: Eire Schools, Youth, Under-21, B, 16 full caps, 1 goal.

Season	Club	A	G	Tot A	Tot G
1991-92	Middlesbrough	0	0		
1992-93	Middlesbrough	10	0		
1993-94	Middlesbrough	11	2		
1993-94	Darlington	5	0	5	0
1994-95	Middlesbrough	7	0		
1995-96	Middlesbrough	7	1		
1996-97	Middlesbrough	0	0	35	3
1996-97	Stoke C	38	4		
1997-98	Stoke C	44	5		
1998-99	Stoke C	36	11		
1999-2000	Stoke C	45	7		
2000-01	Stoke C	43	8	206	35
2001-02	Cardiff C	43	13		
2002-03	Cardiff C	44	5		
2003-04	Cardiff C	27	7		
2004-05	Cardiff C	28	3	142	28
2004-05	Wigan Ath	11	0		
2005-06	Wigan Ath	35	0		
2006-07	Wigan Ath	2	0	48	0
2006-07	Sunderland	14	1		
2007-08	Sunderland	0	0		
2007-08	Sheffield W	23	2	23	2
2008-09	Sunderland	0	0	14	1
2008-09	Carlisle U	34	5		
2009-10	Carlisle U	29	2	63	7

KEOGH, Richard (D) — 142 8
H: 6 0 W: 11 02 b.Harlow 11-8-86
Source: Scholar. Honours: Eire Under-21.

Season	Club	A	G	Tot A	Tot G
2004-05	Stoke C	0	0		
2005-06	Bristol C	9	1		
2005-06	Wycombe W	3	0	3	0
2006-07	Bristol C	31	2		
2007-08	Bristol C	0	0	40	3
2007-08	Huddersfield T	9	1	9	1
2007-08	Carlisle U	7	0		
2007-08	Cheltenham T	10	0	10	0
2008-09	Carlisle U	32	1		
2009-10	Carlisle U	41	3	80	4

LAKELAND, Simon (D) — 0 0
H: 5 9 W: 9 12 b.Preston 13-8-91
Source: Scholar.

Season	Club	A	G
2009-10	Carlisle U	0	0

LIVESEY, Danny (D) — 204 13
H: 6 3 W: 13 01 b.Salford 31-12-84
Source: Trainee.

Season	Club	A	G	Tot A	Tot G
2002-03	Bolton W	2	0		
2003-04	Bolton W	0	0		
2003-04	Notts Co	11	0	11	0
2003-04	Rochdale	13	0	13	0
2004-05	Bolton W	0	0	2	0
2004-05	Blackpool	1	0	1	0
2005-06	Carlisle U	36	4		
2006-07	Carlisle U	31	1		
2007-08	Carlisle U	45	6		
2008-09	Carlisle U	27	0		
2009-10	Carlisle U	38	2	177	13

MADINE, Gary (F) — 61 5
H: 6 1 W: 12 00 b.Gateshead 24-8-90
Source: Scholar.

Season	Club	A	G	Tot A	Tot G
2007-08	Carlisle U	11	0		
2008-09	Carlisle U	14	1		
2008-09	Rochdale	3	0	3	0
2009-10	Carlisle U	20	4	45	5
2009-10	Coventry C	9	0	9	0
2009-10	Chesterfield	4	0	4	0

MURPHY, Peter (M) — 300 11
H: 5 10 W: 12 10 b.Dublin 27-10-80
Source: Trainee. Honours: Eire Youth, Under-21, 1 full cap.

Season	Club	A	G	Tot A	Tot G
1998-99	Blackburn R	0	0		
1999-2000	Blackburn R	0	0		
2000-01	Blackburn R	0	0		
2000-01	Halifax T	21	1	21	1
2001-02	Blackburn R	0	0		
2001-02	Carlisle U	40	0		
2002-03	Carlisle U	40	2		
2003-04	Carlisle U	35	1		
2004-05	Carlisle U	0	0		
2005-06	Carlisle U	44	2		
2006-07	Carlisle U	40	2		
2007-08	Carlisle U	35	3		
2008-09	Carlisle U	28	0		
2009-10	Carlisle U	16	0	279	10

OFFIONG, Richard (F) — 136 42
H: 5 11 W: 12 02 b.South Shields 17-12-83
Source: Scholar. Honours: England Youth, Under-20.

Season	Club	A	G	Tot A	Tot G
2001-02	Newcastle U	0	0		
2002-03	Newcastle U	0	0		
2002-03	Darlington	7	2	7	2
2002-03	Motherwell	9	0	9	0
2003-04	Newcastle U	0	0		
2003-04	York C	4	0	4	0
2004-05	Newcastle U	0	0		
2005-06	Doncaster R	5	0	5	0
2006-07	Hamilton A	29	14		
2007-08	Hamilton A	34	19		
2008-09	Hamilton A	30	6		
2009-10	Hamilton A	1	0	94	39
2009-10	Carlisle U	15	1	15	1
2009-10	Ostersund	2	0	2	0

PIDGELEY, Lenny (G) — 101 0
H: 6 4 W: 14 09 b.Isleworth 7-2-84
Source: Scholar. Honours: England Under-20.

Season	Club	A	G	Tot A	Tot G
2003-04	Chelsea	0	0		
2003-04	Watford	27	0	27	0
2004-05	Chelsea	1	0		
2005-06	Chelsea	0	0	2	0
2005-06	Millwall	0	0		
2006-07	Millwall	42	0		
2007-08	Millwall	13	0		
2008-09	Millwall	0	0	55	0
2009-10	Carlisle U	17	0	17	0

RAVEN, David (D) — 148 1
H: 6 0 W: 11 04 b.Birkenhead 10-3-85
Source: Scholar. Honours: England Youth, Under-20.

Season	Club	A	G	Tot A	Tot G
2001-02	Liverpool	0	0		
2002-03	Liverpool	0	0		
2003-04	Liverpool	0	0		
2004-05	Liverpool	1	0		
2005-06	Liverpool	0	0	1	0
2005-06	Tranmere R	11	0	11	0
2006-07	Carlisle U	36	0		
2007-08	Carlisle U	43	1		
2008-09	Carlisle U	41	0		
2009-10	Carlisle U	16	0	136	1

ROBSON, Matty (D) — 174 13
H: 5 10 W: 11 02 b.Durham 23-1-85
Source: Scholar.

Season	Club	A	G	Tot A	Tot G
2002-03	Hartlepool U	0	0		
2003-04	Hartlepool U	23	1		
2004-05	Hartlepool U	27	2		
2005-06	Hartlepool U	19	1		
2006-07	Hartlepool U	20	2		
2007-08	Hartlepool U	17	1		
2008-09	Hartlepool U	29	2	135	9
2009-10	Carlisle U	39	4	39	4

ROTHERY, Gavin (M) — 2 0
H: 5 9 W: 10 12 b.Morley 22-9-87
Source: Scholar. Honours: England Youth.

Season	Club	A	G	Tot A	Tot G
2005-06	Leeds U	0	0		
From York C.					
2008-09	Carlisle U	1	0		
2009-10	Carlisle U	1	0	2	0

TAIWO, Tom (M) — 39 1
H: 5 8 W: 10 07 b.Leeds 27-2-90
Source: Scholar.

Season	Club	A	G	Tot A	Tot G
2007-08	Chelsea	0	0		
2008-09	Chelsea	0	0		
2008-09	Port Vale	4	0	4	0
2009-10	Chelsea	0	0		
2009-10	Carlisle U	35	1	35	1

THIRLWELL, Paul (M) — 245 6
H: 5 11 W: 12 08 b.Springwell 13-2-79
Source: Trainee. Honours: England Under-21.

Season	Club	A	G	Tot A	Tot G
1996-97	Sunderland	0	0		
1997-98	Sunderland	0	0		
1998-99	Sunderland	2	0		
1999-2000	Sunderland	8	0		
1999-2000	Swindon T	12	0	12	0
2000-01	Sunderland	5	0		
2001-02	Sunderland	14	0		
2002-03	Sunderland	19	0		
2003-04	Sunderland	29	0	77	0
2004-05	Sheffield U	30	1	30	1
2005-06	Derby Co	21	0		
2006-07	Derby Co	0	0	21	0
2007-08	Carlisle U	30	0		
2007-08	Carlisle U	13	0		
2008-09	Carlisle U	34	4		
2009-10	Carlisle U	28	1	105	5

CHARLTON ATH (22)

BAILEY, Nicky (M) — 221 46
H: 5 10 W: 12 06 b.Hammersmith 10-6-84
Source: Sutton U.

Season	Club	A	G	Tot A	Tot G
2005-06	Barnet	45	7		
2006-07	Barnet	44	5	89	12
2007-08	Southend U	44	9		
2008-09	Southend U	1	0	45	9
2008-09	Charlton Ath	43	13		
2009-10	Charlton Ath	44	12	87	25

BASEY, Grant (D) — 54 1
H: 6 2 W: 13 12 b.Farnborough 30-11-88
Source: Scholar. Honours: Wales Under-21.

Season	Club	A	G	Tot A	Tot G
2007-08	Charlton Ath	8	1		
2007-08	Brentford	8	0	8	0
2008-09	Charlton Ath	19	0		
2009-10	Charlton Ath	19	0	46	1

BURTON, Deon (F) — 469 107
H: 5 9 W: 11 09 b.Ashford 25-10-76
Source: Trainee. Honours: Jamaica 51 full caps, 9 goals.

Season	Club	A	G	Tot A	Tot G
1993-94	Portsmouth	2	0		
1994-95	Portsmouth	7	2		
1995-96	Portsmouth	32	7		
1996-97	Portsmouth	21	1		
1996-97	Cardiff C	5	2	5	2
1997-98	Derby Co	29	3		
1998-99	Derby Co	21	9		
1998-99	Barnsley	3	0	3	0
1999-2000	Derby Co	19	4		
2000-01	Derby Co	32	5		
2001-02	Derby Co	17	1		
2001-02	Stoke C	12	2	12	2
2002-03	Derby Co	7	3	125	25
2002-03	Portsmouth	15	4		
2003-04	Portsmouth	1	0	78	14
2003-04	Walsall	3	0	3	0
2003-04	Swindon T	4	1	4	1
2004-05	Brentford	40	10	40	10
2005-06	Rotherham U	24	12	24	12
2005-06	Sheffield W	17	3		
2006-07	Sheffield W	42	12		
2007-08	Sheffield W	40	7		
2008-09	Sheffield W	17	1	116	23
2008-09	Charlton Ath	3	0		
2009-10	Charlton Ath	39	13	59	18

DAILLY, Christian (D) — 513 31
H: 6 1 W: 12 10 b.Dundee 23-10-73
Source: 'S' Form. Honours: Scotland Schools, Youth, Under-21, B, 67 full caps, 6 goals.

Season	Club	A	G	Tot A	Tot G
1990-91	Dundee U	18	5		
1991-92	Dundee U	8	0		
1992-93	Dundee U	14	4		
1993-94	Dundee U	38	4		
1994-95	Dundee U	33	4		
1995-96	Dundee U	30	1	141	18
1996-97	Derby Co	36	3		
1997-98	Derby Co	30	1		
1998-99	Derby Co	1	0	67	4
1998-99	Blackburn R	17	0		

1999–2000	Blackburn R	43	4		
2000–01	Blackburn R	10	0	70	4
2000–01	West Ham U	12	0		
2001–02	West Ham U	38	0		
2002–03	West Ham U	26	0		
2003–04	West Ham U	43	2		
2004–05	West Ham U	3	0		
2005–06	West Ham U	22	0		
2006–07	West Ham U	14	0		
2007–08	West Ham U	0	0	158	2
2007–08	*Southampton*	11	0	11	0
2007–08	Rangers	13	2		
2008–09	Rangers	9	0	22	2
2009–10	Charlton Ath	44	1	44	1

DICKSON, Chris (F) 66 12
H: 5 11 W: 11 09 b.East Dulwich 28-12-84
Source: Dulwich H. Honours: Ghana 1 full cap.

2006–07	Charlton Ath	0	0		
2007–08	Charlton Ath	2	0		
2007–08	*Crewe Alex*	3	0	3	0
2007–08	*Gillingham*	12	7		
2008–09	Charlton Ath	21	0		
2009–10	Charlton Ath	5	0	28	0
2009–10	*Bristol R*	14	4	14	4
2009–10	*Gillingham*	9	1	21	8

ELLIOT, Rob (G) 68 0
H: 6 3 W: 14 10 b.Chatham 30-8-86
Source: Scholar.

2004–05	Charlton Ath	0	0		
2004–05	*Notts Co*	4	0	4	0
2005–06	Charlton Ath	0	0		
2006–07	Charlton Ath	0	0		
2006–07	*Accrington S*	7	0	7	0
2007–08	Charlton Ath	1	0		
2008–09	Charlton Ath	23	0		
2009–10	Charlton Ath	33	0	57	0

FLEETWOOD, Stuart (F) 91 13
H: 5 10 W: 12 07 b.Gloucester 23-4-86
Source: Scholar. Honours: Wales Youth, Under-21.

2003–04	Cardiff C	2	0		
2004–05	Cardiff C	6	0		
2005–06	Cardiff C	0	0	8	0
2006–07	Hereford U	27	3	27	3
2006–07	*Accrington S*	3	0	3	0
2008–09	Charlton Ath	0	0		

From Forest Green R.

2008–09	*Cheltenham T*	6	2	6	2
2008–09	*Brighton & HA*	11	1	11	1
2008–09	*Exeter C*	9	3		
2009–10	Charlton Ath	0	0		
2009–10	*Exeter C*	27	4	36	7

HOLDEN, Luke (M) 0 0
b.Liverpool 24-11-88
On loan from Rhyl.

2009–10	Charlton Ath	0	0		

LLERA, Miguel (D) 111 12
H: 6 3 W: 13 12 b.Seville 7-8-79
Source: Recretivo B, San Fernando (loan), Alicante.

2005–06	Gimnastic	27	3		
2006–07	Gimnastic	12	2	39	5
2007–08	Heracles	13	1	13	1
2008–09	Milton Keynes D	34	2	34	2
2009–10	Charlton Ath	25	4	25	4

MAMBO, Yado (D) 0 0
H: 6 3 W: 13 01 b.Kilburn 22-10-91
Source: Scholar.

2009–10	Charlton Ath	0	0	0	0

McKENZIE, Leon (F) 345 92
H: 5 11 W: 12 11 b.Croydon 17-5-78
Source: Trainee.

1995–96	Crystal Palace	12	0		
1996–97	Crystal Palace	21	2		
1997–98	Crystal Palace	3	0		
1997–98	*Fulham*	3	0	3	0
1998–99	Crystal Palace	16	1		
1998–99	*Peterborough U*	14	8		
1999–2000	Crystal Palace	25	4		
2000–01	Crystal Palace	8	0	85	7
2000–01	Peterborough U	30	13		
2001–02	Peterborough U	30	18		
2002–03	Peterborough U	11	5		
2003–04	Peterborough U	19	9	104	53
2003–04	Norwich C	18	9		
2004–05	Norwich C	37	7		
2005–06	Norwich C	20	4		
2006–07	Norwich C	4	0	79	20
2006–07	Coventry C	31	7		
2007–08	Coventry C	11	2		
2008–09	Coventry C	19	3		
2009–10	Coventry C	1	0	62	12
2009–10	Charlton Ath	12	0	12	0

McLEOD, Izale (F) 206 63
H: 6 1 W: 11 02 b.Birmingham 15-10-84
Source: Scholar. Honours: England Under-21.

2002–03	Derby Co	29	3		
2003–04	Derby Co	10	1	39	4
2003–04	*Sheffield U*	7	0	7	0
2004–05	Milton Keynes D	43	16		
2005–06	Milton Keynes D	39	17		
2006–07	Milton Keynes D	34	21	116	54
2007–08	Charlton Ath	18	1		
2007–08	*Colchester U*	2	0	2	0
2008–09	Charlton Ath	2	0		
2008–09	*Millwall*	7	2	7	2
2009–10	Charlton Ath	11	2	31	3
2009–10	*Peterborough U*	4	0	4	0

MOUTAOUAKIL, Yassin (D) 34 0
H: 5 10 W: 11 05 b.Nice 18-7-86
Honours: France Youth, Under-21.

2006–07	Chateauroux	0	0		
2007–08	Charlton Ath	10	0		
2008–09	Charlton Ath	11	0		
2009–10	Charlton Ath	0	0	21	0
2009–10	*Motherwell*	13	0	13	0

RACON, Thierry (M) 95 7
H: 5 10 W: 10 02 b.Villeneuve-St-Georges 1-5-84

2004–05	Lorient	28	3	28	3
2005–06	Guingamp	0	0		
2006–07	Guingamp	0	0		
2007–08	Charlton Ath	4	0		
2007–08	*Brighton & HA*	8	0	8	0
2008–09	Charlton Ath	19	3		
2009–10	Charlton Ath	36	1	59	4

RANDOLPH, Darren (G) 44 0
H: 6 2 W: 14 00 b.Dublin 12-5-87
Source: Ardmore R Scholar, Eire B, Under-21.

2004–05	Charlton Ath	0	0		
2005–06	Charlton Ath	0	0		
2006–07	Charlton Ath	1	0		
2006–07	*Gillingham*	3	0	3	0
2007–08	Charlton Ath	1	0		
2007–08	*Bury*	14	0	14	0
2008–09	Charlton Ath	1	0		
2008–09	*Hereford U*	13	0	13	0
2009–10	Charlton Ath	11	0	14	0

RICHARDSON, Frazer (D) 200 5
H: 5 11 W: 11 12 b.Rotherham 29-10-82
Source: Trainee. Honours: England Youth, Under-20.

1999–2000	Leeds U	0	0		
2000–01	Leeds U	0	0		
2001–02	Leeds U	0	0		
2002–03	Leeds U	0	0		
2002–03	*Stoke C*	7	0		
2003–04	Leeds U	4	0		
2003–04	*Stoke C*	6	1	13	1
2004–05	Leeds U	38	1		
2005–06	Leeds U	23	1		
2006–07	Leeds U	22	0		
2007–08	Leeds U	39	1		
2008–09	Leeds U	23	0	149	3
2009–10	Charlton Ath	38	1	38	1

SAM, Lloyd (F) 135 6
H: 5 10 W: 11 00 b.Leeds 27-9-84
Honours: England Youth, Under-20.

2002–03	Charlton Ath	0	0		
2003–04	Charlton Ath	0	0		
2003–04	*Leyton Orient*	10	0	10	0
2004–05	Charlton Ath	1	0		
2005–06	Charlton Ath	2	0		
2006–07	Charlton Ath	7	0		
2006–07	*Sheffield W*	4	0	4	0
2006–07	*Southend U*	2	0	2	0
2007–08	Charlton Ath	28	2		
2008–09	Charlton Ath	38	0		
2009–10	Charlton Ath	43	4	119	6

SEMEDO, Jose (D) 148 3
H: 6 0 W: 12 08 b.Setubal 11-1-85
Honours: Portugal Under-21.

2004–05	Sporting Lisbon	0	0		
2004–05	*Casa Pia*	34	2	34	2
2005–06	*Feirense*	18	0	18	0
2006–07	*Cagliari*	3	0	3	0
2007–08	Charlton Ath	37	0		
2008–09	Charlton Ath	18	0		
2009–10	Charlton Ath	38	1	93	1

SINCLAIR, Dean (M) 131 14
H: 5 10 W: 11 03 b.St Albans 17-12-84
Source: Scholar.

2002–03	Norwich C	2	0		
2003–04	Norwich C	0	0	2	0
2004–05	Barnet	0	0		
2005–06	Barnet	44	2		
2006–07	Barnet	42	6		
2007–08	Charlton Ath	0	0		
2007–08	*Cheltenham T*	12	1		
2007–08	Charlton Ath	0	0		
2008–09	*Cheltenham T*	3	0	15	1
2008–09	*Grimsby T*	9	1		
2009–10	Charlton Ath	0	0		
2009–10	*Barnet*	3	1	89	9
2009–10	*Grimsby T*	16	3	25	4

SODJE, Akpo (F) 162 37
H: 6 2 W: 12 08 b.Greenwich 31-1-81
Source: QPR, Stevenage B, Margate, Gravesend & N, Erith & Belvedere.

2004–05	Huddersfield T	7	0	7	0
2004–05	Darlington	7	1		
2005–06	Darlington	36	8	43	9
2006–07	Port Vale	43	14		
2007–08	Port Vale	3	0	46	14
2007–08	Sheffield W	19	7		
2008–09	Sheffield W	11	2		
2009–10	Sheffield W	11	0	41	9
2009–10	Charlton Ath	25	5	25	5

SODJE, Sam (D) 153 19
H: 6 0 W: 12 00 b.Greenwich 29-5-79
Source: Stevenage B, Margate. Honours: Nigeria 4 full caps.

2004–05	Brentford	40	7		
2005–06	Brentford	43	5	83	12
2006–07	Reading	3	0		
2006–07	*WBA*	7	1	7	1
2007–08	Reading	0	0		
2007–08	*Charlton Ath*	27	2		
2008–09	Reading	0	0		
2008–09	*Watford*	1	0	1	0
2008–09	*Leeds U*	5	0	5	0
2009–10	Reading	0	0	3	0
2009–10	Charlton Ath	27	4	54	6

SOLLY, Chris (D) 10 0
H: 5 8 W: 10 07 b.Rochester 20-1-91
Source: Scholar.

2008–09	Charlton Ath	1	0		
2009–10	Charlton Ath	9	0	10	0

SPRING, Matthew (M) 402 47
H: 5 11 W: 12 05 b.Harlow 17-11-79
Source: Trainee.

1997–98	Luton T	12	0		
1998–99	Luton T	45	3		
1999–2000	Luton T	45	6		
2000–01	Luton T	41	4		
2001–02	Luton T	42	6		
2002–03	Luton T	41	5		
2003–04	Luton T	24	1		
2004–05	Leeds U	13	1		
2005–06	Leeds U	0	0	13	1
2005–06	Watford	39	8		
2006–07	Watford	6	0	45	8
2006–07	Luton T	14	1		
2007–08	Luton T	44	9		
2008–09	Luton T	0	0	308	35
2008–09	*Sheffield U*	11	1	11	1
2008–09	Charlton Ath	13	2		
2009–10	Charlton Ath	12	0	25	2

STAVRINOU, Alex (M) 0 0
H: 5 9 W: 11 12 b.Harlow 13-9-90
Source: Scholar.

2009–10	Charlton Ath	0	0		

TUNA, Tamer (F)   3   0
H: 5 9   W: 11 05   b.Bexley 19-10-91
Source: Scholar.

| 2008–09 | Charlton Ath | 2 | 0 | | |
| 2009–10 | Charlton Ath | 1 | 0 | 3 | 0 |

WAGSTAFF, Scott (F)   39   4
H: 5 10   W: 10 03   b.Maidstone 31-3-90
Source: Scholar.

2007–08	Charlton Ath	2	0		
2008–09	Charlton Ath	2	0		
2008–09	*Bournemouth*	5	0	5	0
2009–10	Charlton Ath	30	4	34	4

YOUGA, Kelly (D)   96   2
H: 6 1   W: 12 00   b.Bangui 22-9-85
Source: Lyon.

2005–06	Charlton Ath	0	0		
2005–06	*Bristol C*	4	0	4	0
2006–07	Charlton Ath	0	0		
2006–07	*Bradford C*	11	0	11	0
2007–08	Charlton Ath	11	0		
2007–08	*Scunthorpe U*	19	1	19	1
2008–09	Charlton Ath	33	1		
2009–10	Charlton Ath	18	0	62	1

CHELSEA (23)

ALEX (D)   215   28
H: 6 2   W: 14 00   b.Niteroi 17-6-82
Honours: Brazil 17 full caps.

2002	Santos	25	3		
2003	Santos	34	9		
2004	Santos	4	0	63	12
2004–05	PSV Eindhoven	27	3		
2005–06	PSV Eindhoven	28	2		
2006–07	PSV Eindhoven	29	6	84	11
2007–08	Chelsea	28	2		
2008–09	Chelsea	24	2		
2009–10	Chelsea	16	1	68	5

ANELKA, Nicolas (F)   418   143
H: 6 1   W: 13 03   b.Versailles 14-3-79
Honours: France Youth, Under-21, 69 full caps, 14 goals.

1995–96	Paris St Germain	2	0		
1996–97	Paris St Germain	8	1		
1996–97	Arsenal	4	0		
1997–98	Arsenal	26	6		
1998–99	Arsenal	35	17	65	23
1999–2000	Real Madrid	19	2	19	2
2000–01	Paris St Germain	27	8		
2001–02	Paris St Germain	12	2	49	11
2001–02	Liverpool	20	4	20	4
2002–03	Manchester C	38	14		
2003–04	Manchester C	32	16		
2004–05	Manchester C	19	7	89	37
2004–05	Fenerbahce	14	4		
2005–06	Fenerbahce	25	10	39	14
2006–07	Bolton W	35	11		
2007–08	Bolton W	18	10	53	21
2007–08	Chelsea	14	1		
2008–09	Chelsea	37	19		
2009–10	Chelsea	33	11	84	31

BALLACK, Michael (M)   403   109
H: 6 2   W: 12 08   b.Gorlitz 26-9-76
Source: Motor Karl-Marx-Stadt. *Honours:* Germany Under-21, 98 full caps, 42 goals.

1995–96	Chemnitzer	15	0		
1996–97	Chemnitzer	34	10	49	10
1997–98	Kaiserslautern A	17	8	17	8
1997–98	Kaiserslautern	16	0		
1998–99	Kaiserslautern	30	4	46	4
1999–2000	Leverkusen	23	3		
2000–01	Leverkusen	27	7		
2001–02	Leverkusen	29	17	79	27
2002–03	Bayern Munich	26	10		
2003–04	Bayern Munich	28	7		
2004–05	Bayern Munich	27	13		
2005–06	Bayern Munich	26	13	107	43
2006–07	Chelsea	26	5		
2007–08	Chelsea	18	7		
2008–09	Chelsea	29	1		
2009–10	Chelsea	32	4	105	17

BELLETTI, Juliano (D)   276   20
H: 5 9   W: 10 12   b.Casaval 20-6-76
Honours: Brazil 23 full caps, 2 goals.

1994	Cruzeiro	5	0		
1995	Cruzeiro	17	0	22	0
1996	Sao Paulo	13	1		
1997	Sao Paulo	12	1		
1998	Sao Paulo	4	1		
1999	Atletico Mineiro	17	5	17	5
2000	Sao Paulo	11	0		
2001	Sao Paulo	14	1		
2002	Sao Paulo	0	0	54	4
2002–03	Villarreal	31	3		
2003–04	Villarreal	28	3	59	6
2004–05	Barcelona	31	0		
2005–06	Barcelona	26	0		
2006–07	Barcelona	13	0	70	0
2007–08	Chelsea	23	2		
2008–09	Chelsea	20	3		
2009–10	Chelsea	11	0	54	5

BERTRAND, Ryan (D)   126   1
H: 5 10   W: 11 00   b.Southwark 5-8-89
Source: Scholar. *Honours:* England Youth, Under-21.

2006–07	Chelsea	0	0		
2006–07	*Bournemouth*	5	0	5	0
2007–08	Chelsea	0	0		
2007–08	*Oldham Ath*	21	0	21	0
2007–08	*Norwich C*	18	0		
2008–09	Chelsea	0	0		
2008–09	*Norwich C*	38	0	56	0
2009–10	Chelsea	0	0		
2009–10	*Reading*	44	1	44	1

BORINI, Fabio (F)   4   0
H: 5 10   W: 11 02   b.Bentivoglio 23-3-91
Source: Scholar.

| 2008–09 | Chelsea | 0 | 0 | | |
| 2009–10 | Chelsea | 4 | 0 | 4 | 0 |

BOSINGWA, Jose (D)   201   5
H: 6 0   W: 12 08   b.Kinshasa 24-8-82
Honours: Portugal Under-21, 23 full caps.

2000–01	Freamunde	11	0	11	0
2001–02	Boavista	15	0		
2002–03	Boavista	26	0	41	0
2003–04	Porto	13	1		
2004–05	Porto	25	1		
2005–06	Porto	21	0		
2006–07	Porto	25	0		
2007–08	Porto	23	1	107	3
2008–09	Chelsea	34	2		
2009–10	Chelsea	8	0	42	2

BRIDCUTT, Liam (M)   30   0
H: 5 9   W: 11 07   b.Reading 8-5-89
Source: Scholar.

2007–08	Chelsea	0	0		
2007–08	*Yeovil T*	9	0	9	0
2008–09	Chelsea	0	0		
2008–09	*Watford*	6	0	6	0
2009–10	Chelsea	0	0		
2009–10	*Stockport Co*	15	0	15	0

BRUMA, Jeffrey (D)   2   0
H: 6 1   W: 12 00   b.Rotterdam 13-11-91
Source: Feyenoord. *Honours:* Holland Under-21.

| 2009–10 | Chelsea | 2 | 0 | 2 | 0 |

CECH, Petr (G)   312   0
H: 6 5   W: 14 07   b.Plzen 20-5-82
Honours: Czech Republic Youth, Under-20, Under-21, 72 full caps.

1998–99	Viktoria Plzen	0	0		
1999–2000	Chmel	1	0		
2000–01	Chmel	25	0	27	0
2001–02	Sparta Prague	25	0	26	0
2002–03	Rennes	37	0		
2003–04	Rennes	38	0	75	0
2004–05	Chelsea	35	0		
2005–06	Chelsea	34	0		
2006–07	Chelsea	20	0		
2007–08	Chelsea	26	0		
2008–09	Chelsea	35	0		
2009–10	Chelsea	34	0	184	0

CLIFFORD, Conor (M)   0   0
H: 5 8   W: 10 08   b.Dublin 1-10-91
Source: Scholar. *Honours:* Eire Youth, Under-21.

| 2008–09 | Chelsea | 0 | 0 | | |
| 2009–10 | Chelsea | 0 | 0 | | |

COLE, Ashley (D)   281   15
H: 5 8   W: 10 05   b.Stepney 20-12-80
Source: Trainee. *Honours:* England Schools, Youth, Under-21, B, 82 full caps.

1998–99	Arsenal	0	0		
1999–2000	Arsenal	1	0		
1999–2000	*Crystal Palace*	14	1	14	1
2000–01	Arsenal	17	3		
2001–02	Arsenal	29	2		
2002–03	Arsenal	31	1		
2003–04	Arsenal	32	0		
2004–05	Arsenal	35	2		
2005–06	Arsenal	11	0		
2006–07	Arsenal	0	0	156	8
2006–07	Chelsea	23	0		
2007–08	Chelsea	27	1		
2008–09	Chelsea	34	1		
2009–10	Chelsea	27	4	111	6

COLE, Joe (M)   309   37
H: 5 9   W: 11 09   b.Romford 8-11-81
Source: Trainee. *Honours:* England Schools, Youth, Under-21, B, 56 full caps, 10 goals.

1998–99	West Ham U	8	0		
1999–2000	West Ham U	22	1		
2000–01	West Ham U	30	5		
2001–02	West Ham U	30	0		
2002–03	West Ham U	36	4	126	10
2003–04	Chelsea	35	1		
2004–05	Chelsea	28	8		
2005–06	Chelsea	34	7		
2006–07	Chelsea	13	0		
2007–08	Chelsea	33	7		
2008–09	Chelsea	14	2		
2009–10	Chelsea	26	2	183	27

CORK, Jack (D)   115   3
H: 6 0   W: 10 12   b.Carshalton 25-6-89
Source: Scholar. *Honours:* England Youth, Under-20, Under-21.

2006–07	Chelsea	0	0		
2006–07	*Bournemouth*	7	0	7	0
2007–08	Chelsea	0	0		
2007–08	*Scunthorpe U*	34	2	34	2
2008–09	Chelsea	0	0		
2008–09	*Southampton*	23	0	23	0
2008–09	*Watford*	19	0	19	0
2009–10	Chelsea	0	0		
2009–10	*Coventry C*	21	0	21	0
2009–10	*Burnley*	11	1	11	1

DECO (M)   355   65
H: 5 9   W: 11 07   b.Sao Paulo 27-8-77
Honours: Portugal 75 full caps, 5 goals.

1995–96	Corinthians	2	0	2	0
1996–97	Alverca	32	13	32	13
1997–98	Porto	6	0		
1997–98	Salgueiros	12	2	12	2
1998–99	Porto	6	0		
1999–2000	Porto	23	1		
2000–01	Porto	31	6		
2001–02	Porto	30	13		
2002–03	Porto	30	10		
2003–04	Porto	28	2	154	32
2004–05	Barcelona	35	8		
2005–06	Barcelona	29	3		
2006–07	Barcelona	30	1		
2007–08	Barcelona	18	1	112	13
2008–09	Chelsea	24	3		
2009–10	Chelsea	19	2	43	5

DI SANTO, Franco (F)   85   14
H: 6 4   W: 13 01   b.Mendoza 7-4-89
Source: Audax Italiano. *Honours:* Argentina Under-20.

2006	Audax Italiano	18	6		
2007	Audax Italiano	37	7	55	13
2007–08	Chelsea	0	0		
2008–09	Chelsea	8	0		
2009–10	Chelsea	0	0	8	0
2009–10	*Blackburn R*	22	1	22	1

DJALO, Aliu (M) — 0 0
b.Bissau 5-2-92
Source: Scholar.

Season	Club	Apps	Gls		
2009–10	Chelsea	0	0		

DROGBA, Didier (F) — 310 133
H: 6 2　W: 14 05　b.Abidjan 11-3-78
Honours: Ivory Coast 71 full caps, 42 goals.

Season	Club	Apps	Gls		
1998–99	Le Mans	2	0		
1999–2000	Le Mans	30	6		
2000–01	Le Mans	11	0		
2001–02	Le Mans	21	5	64	11
2001–02	Guingamp	11	3		
2002–03	Guingamp	34	17	45	20
2003–04	Marseille	35	18	35	18
2004–05	Chelsea	26	10		
2005–06	Chelsea	29	12		
2006–07	Chelsea	36	20		
2007–08	Chelsea	19	8		
2008–09	Chelsea	24	5		
2009–10	Chelsea	32	29	166	84

ESSIEN, Michael (M) — 253 32
H 5 10　W: 13 06　b.Accra 3-12-82
Source: Liberty Accra. Honours: Ghana 51 full caps, 9 goals.

Season	Club	Apps	Gls		
2000–01	Bastia	13	1		
2001–02	Bastia	24	4		
2002–03	Bastia	29	6	66	11
2003–04	Lyon	34	3		
2004–05	Lyon	37	4	71	7
2005–06	Chelsea	31	2		
2006–07	Chelsea	33	2		
2007–08	Chelsea	27	6		
2008–09	Chelsea	11	1		
2009–10	Chelsea	14	3	116	14

GORDON, Ben (D) — 4 0
H: 5 11　W: 12 06　b.Bradford 2-3-91
Source: Scholar.

Season	Club	Apps	Gls		
2008–09	Chelsea	0	0		
2009–10	Chelsea	0	0		
2009–10	Tranmere R	4	0	4	0

HILARIO (G) — 251 2
H: 6 2　W: 13 05　b.San Pedro da Cova 21-10-75
Honours: Portugal Under-21, B, 1 full cap.

Season	Club	Apps	Gls		
1994–95	Naval	27	0	27	0
1995–96	Academica	33	2		
1996–97	Porto	18	0		
1997–98	Porto	3	0		
1998–99	Amadora	27	0	27	0
1999–2000	Porto	19	0		
2000–01	Porto	0	0		
2001–02	Varzim	24	0	24	0
2002–03	Porto	0	0	40	0
2002–03	Academica	10	0	43	2
2003–04	Nacional	29	0		
2004–05	Nacional	32	0		
2005–06	Nacional	11	0	72	0
2006–07	Chelsea	11	0		
2007–08	Chelsea	3	0		
2008–09	Chelsea	1	0		
2009–10	Chelsea	3	0	18	0

HUTCHINSON, Sam (M) — 3 0
H: 6 0　W: 11 07　b.Windsor 3-8-89
Source: Scholar. Honours: England Youth.

Season	Club	Apps	Gls		
2005–07	Chelsea	1	0		
2007–08	Chelsea	0	0		
2008–09	Chelsea	0	0		
2009–10	Chelsea	2	0	3	0

IVANOVIC, Branislav (M) — 172 13
H: 6 0　W: 12 04　b.Sremska Mitreovica 22-2-84
Honours: Serbia Under-21, 34 full caps, 4 goals.

Season	Club	Apps	Gls		
2002–03	Sremska	19	2	19	2
2003–04	OFK Belgrade	13	0		
2004–05	OFK Belgrade	27	2		
2005–06	OFK Belgrade	15	3	55	5
2006	Lokomotiv Moscow	28	2		
2007	Lokomotiv Moscow	26	3	54	5
2007–08	Chelsea	16	0		
2008–09	Chelsea	28	1	44	1

KAKUTA, Gael (F) — 1 0
H: 5 8　W: 10 03　b.Lille 21-6-91
Source: Lens. Honours: Chelsea Scholar.

Season	Club	Apps	Gls		
2008–09	Chelsea	0	0		
2009–10	Chelsea	1	0	1	0

KALOU, Salomon (F) — 191 64
H: 6 0　W: 12 02　b.Oume 5-8-85
Source: Oume, ASEC Abidjan. Honours: Ivory Coast 35 full caps, 11 goals.

Season	Club	Apps	Gls		
2003–04	Excelsior	11	4	11	4
2003–04	Feyenoord	2	0		
2004–05	Feyenoord	31	20		
2005–06	Feyenoord	34	15	67	35
2006–07	Chelsea	33	7		
2007–08	Chelsea	30	7		
2008–09	Chelsea	27	6		
2009–10	Chelsea	23	5	113	25

LAMPARD, Frank (M) — 477 130
H: 6 0　W: 14 02　b.Romford 20-6-78
Source: Trainee. Honours: England Youth, Under-21, B, 82 full caps, 20 goals.

Season	Club	Apps	Gls		
1994–95	West Ham U	0	0		
1995–96	West Ham U	2	0		
1995–96	Swansea C	9	1	9	1
1996–97	West Ham U	13	0		
1997–98	West Ham U	31	5		
1998–99	West Ham U	38	5		
1999–2000	West Ham U	34	7		
2000–01	West Ham U	30	7	148	24
2001–02	Chelsea	37	5		
2002–03	Chelsea	38	6		
2003–04	Chelsea	38	10		
2004–05	Chelsea	38	13		
2005–06	Chelsea	35	16		
2006–07	Chelsea	37	11		
2007–08	Chelsea	24	10		
2008–09	Chelsea	37	12		
2009–10	Chelsea	36	22	320	105

MAGNAY, Carl (D) — 4 0
H: 6 0　W: 11 13　b.Durham 27-1-89
Honours: Northern Ireland Under-21.

Season	Club	Apps	Gls		
2006–07	Chelsea	0	0		
2007–08	Chelsea	0	0		
2008–09	Chelsea	0	0		
2008–09	Milton Keynes D	2	0	2	0
2008–09	Northampton T	2	0	2	0
2009–10	Chelsea	0	0		

MALOUDA, Florent (M) — 374 65
H: 6 0　W: 11 06　b.Cayenne 13-6-80
Honours: France 57 full caps, 4 goals.

Season	Club	Apps	Gls		
1996–97	Chateauroux	2	0		
1997–98	Chateauroux	1	0		
1998–99	Chateauroux	28	3		
1999–2000	Chateauroux	28	2	59	5
2000–01	Guingamp	23	1		
2001–02	Guingamp	32	4		
2002–03	Guingamp	37	10	92	15
2003–04	Lyon	35	4		
2004–05	Lyon	37	5		
2005–06	Lyon	31	6		
2006–07	Lyon	35	10	138	25
2007–08	Chelsea	21	2		
2008–09	Chelsea	31	6		
2009–10	Chelsea	33	12	85	20

MANCIENNE, Michael (D) — 102 0
H: 6 0　W: 11 09　b.Isleworth 8-1-88
Source: Scholar. Honours: England Youth, Under-21.

Season	Club	Apps	Gls		
2005–06	Chelsea	0	0		
2006–07	Chelsea	0	0		
2006–07	QPR	28	0		
2007–08	Chelsea	0	0		
2007–08	QPR	30	0	58	0
2008–09	Chelsea	4	0		
2008–09	Wolverhampton W	10	0		
2009–10	Chelsea	0	0	4	0
2009–10	Wolverhampton W	30	0	40	0

MATIC, Nemanja (M) — 85 4
H: 6 4　W: 12 13　b.Sabac 1-8-88
Honours: Serbia Under-21, 2 full caps.

Season	Club	Apps	Gls		
2005–06	Jedinstvo	7	0		
2006–07	Jedinstvo	9	0	16	0
2006–07	Kosice	13	1		
2007–08	Kosice	25	1		
2008–09	Kosice	29	2	67	4
2009–10	Chelsea	2	0	2	0

MELLIS, Jacob (D) — 12 0
H: 6 0　W: 11 08　b.Nottingham 8-1-91
Source: Scholar. Honours: England Youth.

Season	Club	Apps	Gls		
2008–09	Chelsea	0	0		
2009–10	Chelsea	0	0		
2009–10	Southampton	12	0	12	0

MIKEL, John Obi (M) — 116 1
H: 6 0　W: 13 05　b.Plateau State 22-4-87
Source: Plateau U. Honours: Nigeria Youth, 34 full caps, 2 goals.

Season	Club	Apps	Gls		
2005	Lyn	6	1	6	1
2006–07	Chelsea	22	0		
2007–08	Chelsea	29	0		
2008–09	Chelsea	34	0		
2009–10	Chelsea	25	0	110	0

MITROVIC, Marko (F) — 0 0
b.Malmo 27-6-92
Source: Malmo.

Season	Club	Apps	Gls		
2009–10	Chelsea	0	0		

OFORI-TWUMASI, Nana (D) — 8 2
H: 5 8　W: 11 09　b.Accra 15-5-90
Source: Scholar. Honours: England Under-20.

Season	Club	Apps	Gls		
2007–08	Chelsea	0	0		
2008–09	Chelsea	0	0		
2009–10	Chelsea	0	0		
2009–10	Dagenham & R	8	2	8	2

PAIM, Fabio (F) — 0 0
b.Portugal 15-2-88
On loan from Sporting Lisbon.

Season	Club	Apps	Gls		
2008–09	Chelsea	0	0		
2009–10	Chelsea	0	0		

PAULO FERREIRA (D) — 277 4
H: 6 0　W: 11 13　b.Cascais 18-1-79
Honours: Portugal Under-21, 62 full caps.

Season	Club	Apps	Gls		
1997–98	Estoril	1	0		
1998–99	Estoril	16	0		
1999–2000	Estoril	18	2	35	2
2000–01	Vitoria Setubal	34	2		
2001–02	Vitoria Setubal	34	0	68	2
2002–03	Porto	30	0		
2003–04	Porto	32	0	62	0
2004–05	Chelsea	29	0		
2005–06	Chelsea	21	0		
2006–07	Chelsea	24	0		
2007–08	Chelsea	18	0		
2008–09	Chelsea	7	0		
2009–10	Chelsea	13	0	112	0

PHILLIP, Adam (F) — 0 0
b.Carshalton 19-6-91
Source: Scholar.

Season	Club	Apps	Gls		
2009–10	Chelsea	0	0		

PHILLISKIRK, Daniel (M) — 0 0
H: 5 10　W: 11 05　b.Oldham 10-4-91
Source: Scholar.

Season	Club	Apps	Gls		
2008–09	Chelsea	0	0		
2009–10	Chelsea	0	0		

RAJKOVIC, Slobodan (D) — 97 3
H: 6 5　W: 14 00　b.Belgrade 3-3-89
Honours: Serbia Under-21, 2 full caps.

Season	Club	Apps	Gls		
2004–05	OFK Belgrade	26	1		
2005–06	Chelsea	0	0		
2005–06	OFK Belgrade	25	0		
2006–07	Chelsea	0	0		
2006–07	OFK Belgrade	11	0	62	1
2007–08	Chelsea	0	0		
2007–08	PSV Eindhoven	13	0	13	0
2008–09	Chelsea	0	0		
2008–09	Twente	8	1	8	1
2009–10	Chelsea	0	0		
2009–10	Twente	14	1	22	2

RICARDO CARVALHO (D) — 283 14
H: 6 0　W: 12 04　b.Amarante 18-5-78
Honours: Portugal Under-21, 67 full caps, 4 goals.

Season	Club	Apps	Gls		
1996–97	Leca	0	0		
1997–98	Leca	22	1	22	1
1998–99	Porto	0	0		
1999–2000	Vitoria Setubal	25	2	25	2
2000–01	Alverca	29	1	29	1
2001–02	Porto	25	0		
2002–03	Porto	17	1		
2003–04	Porto	29	2	72	3

2004–05	Chelsea	25	1		
2005–06	Chelsea	24	1		
2006–07	Chelsea	31	3		
2007–08	Chelsea	21	1		
2008–09	Chelsea	12	1		
2009–10	Chelsea	22	0	135	7

SALA, Jacopo (M)   0   0
b.Bergamo 5-12-91
Source: Scholar.
| 2009–10 | Chelsea | 0 | 0 | | |

SEBEK, Jan (G)   0   0
H: 6 4   W: 12 13   b.Plana 31-1-91
Source: Scholar.
| 2009–10 | Chelsea | 0 | 0 | | |

SINCLAIR, Scott (F)   72   6
H: 5 10   W: 10 00   b.Bath 26-3-89
Source: Bristol R Schoolboy, England Youth.
2004–05	Bristol R	2	0	2	0
2005–06	Chelsea	0	0		
2006–07	Chelsea	2	0		
2006–07	Plymouth Arg	15	2	15	2
2007–08	Chelsea	1	0		
2007–08	QPR	9	1	9	1
2007–08	Charlton Ath	3	0	3	0
2007–08	Crystal Palace	6	2	6	2
2008–09	Chelsea	2	0		
2008–09	Birmingham C	14	0	14	0
2009–10	Chelsea	5	0		
2009–10	Wigan Ath	18	1	18	1

STOCH, Miroslav (F)   39   10
H: 5 6   W: 10 01   b.Nitra 19-10-89
Source: Scholar. *Honours:* Slovakia Under-21,
16 full caps, 1 goal.
2005–06	Nitra	3	0	3	0
2006–07	Chelsea	0	0		
2007–08	Chelsea	0	0		
2008–09	Chelsea	4	0		
2009–10	Chelsea	0	0	4	0
2009–10	Twente	32	10	32	10

STURRIDGE, Daniel (F)   34   6
H: 6 2   W: 12 00   b.Manchester 1-9-89
Source: Scholar. *Honours:* England Youth,
Under-21.
2006–07	Manchester C	2	0		
2007–08	Manchester C	3	1		
2008–09	Manchester C	16	4		
2009–10	Manchester C	0	0	21	5
2009–10	Chelsea	13	1	13	1

TAYLOR, Rhys (G)   0   0
H: 6 2   W: 12 08   b.Neath 7-4-90
Honours: Wales Under-21.
2007–08	Chelsea	0	0		
2008–09	Chelsea	0	0		
2009–10	Chelsea	0	0		

TERRY, John (D)   315   19
H: 6 1   W: 14 02   b.Barking 7-12-80
Source: Trainee. *Honours:* England
Under-21, 64 full caps, 6 goals.
1997–98	Chelsea	0	0		
1998–99	Chelsea	2	0		
1999–2000	Chelsea	4	0		
1999–2000	Nottingham F	6	0	6	0
2000–01	Chelsea	22	1		
2001–02	Chelsea	33	1		
2002–03	Chelsea	20	3		
2003–04	Chelsea	33	2		
2004–05	Chelsea	36	3		
2005–06	Chelsea	36	4		
2006–07	Chelsea	28	1		
2007–08	Chelsea	23	1		
2008–09	Chelsea	35	1		
2009–10	Chelsea	37	2	309	19

TORE, Gokhan (M)   0   0
H: 5 9   W: 11 09   b.Cologne 20-1-92
Source: Leverkusen.
| 2008–09 | Chelsea | 0 | 0 | | |
| 2009–10 | Chelsea | 0 | 0 | | |

TURNBULL, Ross (G)   93   0
H: 6 4   W: 15 00   b.Bishop Auckland 4-1-85
Source: Trainee. *Honours:* England Youth,
Under-20.
2002–03	Middlesbrough	0	0		
2003–04	Middlesbrough	0	0		
2003–04	Darlington	1	0	1	0

2003–04	Barnsley	3	0		
2004–05	Middlesbrough	0	0		
2004–05	Bradford C	2	0	2	0
2004–05	Barnsley	23	0	26	0
2005–06	Middlesbrough	2	0		
2005–06	Crewe Alex	29	0	29	0
2006–07	Middlesbrough	0	0		
2007–08	Middlesbrough	3	0		
2007–08	Cardiff C	6	0	6	0
2008–09	Middlesbrough	22	0		
2009–10	Middlesbrough	0	0	27	0
2009–10	Chelsea	2	0	2	0

VAN AANHOLT, Patrick (D)   29   0
H: 5 9   W: 10 08   b.S'Hertogenbosch 3-7-88
2007–08	Chelsea	0	0		
2008–09	Chelsea	0	0		
2009–10	Chelsea	2	0	2	0
2009–10	Coventry C	20	0	20	0
2009–10	Newcastle U	7	0	7	0

VAN HOMOET, Jeffrey (D)   0   0
b.Rotterdam 13-11-91
Source: Scholar.
| 2009–10 | Chelsea | 0 | 0 | | |

WALKER, Sam (G)   0   0
H: 6 5   W: 14 00   b.Gravesend 2-10-91
Source: Scholar.
| 2009–10 | Chelsea | 0 | 0 | | |

WOODS, Michael (M)   0   0
H: 5 0   W: 12 07   b.York 6-4-90
Source: Scholar. *Honours:* England Youth.
Scotland B.
2006–07	Chelsea	0	0		
2007–08	Chelsea	0	0		
2008–09	Chelsea	0	0		
2009–10	Chelsea	0	0		

ZHIRKOV, Yuri (M)   157   15
H: 6 1   W: 11 11   b.Tambov 20-8-83
Honours: Russia 34 full caps.
2004	CSKA Moscow	25	6		
2005	CSKA Moscow	20	2		
2006	CSKA Moscow	27	1		
2007	CSKA Moscow	29	2		
2008	CSKA Moscow	28	3		
2009	CSKA Moscow	11	1	140	15
2009–10	Chelsea	17	0	17	0

Scholars
Ashton, James; Clifford, Billy; Deen-Conteh,
Abdul Aziz; Devyne, Booby; Ince, Rohan;
Lalkovic, Milan; McEachran, Joshua; Na
Bangna, Buomesca Tue; Prosenik, Philipp;
Rodgers, Anton; Samparo, Ben Jordan;
Saville, George Alan.

CHELTENHAM T (24)

ALSOP, Julian (F)   322   65
H: 6 4   W: 15 02   b.Nuneaton 28-5-73
Source: Nuneaton, VS Rugby, RC Warwick,
Tamworth, Halesowen T.
1996–97	Bristol R	16	3		
1997–98	Bristol R	17	1	33	4
1997–98	Swansea C	12	3		
1998–99	Swansea C	41	10		
1999–2000	Swansea C	37	3	90	16
2000–01	Cheltenham T	39	5		
2001–02	Cheltenham T	41	20		
2002–03	Cheltenham T	37	10		
2003–04	Oxford U	29	5		
2004–05	Oxford U	5	0	34	5
2004–05	Northampton T	7	1	7	1
2009–10	Cheltenham T	41	4	158	39

BIRD, David (M)   249   8
H: 5 9   W: 12 00   b.Gloucester 26-12-84
Source: Cinderford T.
2001–02	Cheltenham T	0	0		
2002–03	Cheltenham T	14	0		
2003–04	Cheltenham T	24	0		
2004–05	Cheltenham T	34	0		
2005–06	Cheltenham T	36	1		
2006–07	Cheltenham T	31	2		
2007–08	Cheltenham T	46	4		
2008–09	Cheltenham T	27	1		
2009–10	Cheltenham T	37	0	249	8

BROWN, Scott (M)   106   6
H: 5 9   W: 10 03   b.Runcorn 8-5-85
Source: Scholar. *Honours:* England Youth.
2001–02	Everton	0	0		
2002–03	Everton	0	0		
2003–04	Everton	0	0		
2004–05	Bristol C	19	0		
2005–06	Bristol C	29	1		
2006–07	Bristol C	15	4	63	5
2006–07	Cheltenham T	4	0		
2007–08	Cheltenham T	20	0		
2008–09	Cheltenham T	0	0		
2008–09	Port Vale	18	1		
2009–10	Port Vale	0	0	18	1
2009–10	Cheltenham T	1	0	25	0

BROWN, Scott P (G)   93   0
H: 6 2   W: 13 01   b.Wolverhampton 26-4-85
Source: Wolverhampton W Trainee.
From Welshpool T
2003–04	Bristol C	0	0		
2004–05	Cheltenham T	0	0		
2005–06	Cheltenham T	1	0		
2006–07	Cheltenham T	11	0		
2007–08	Cheltenham T	0	0		
2008–09	Cheltenham T	35	0		
2009–10	Cheltenham T	46	0	93	0

DIALLO, Drissa (D)   185   5
H: 6 1   W: 11 13   b.Nouadhibou 4-1-73
Honours: Guinea full caps.
2002–03	Burnley	14	1	14	1
2003–04	Ipswich T	19	0		
2004–05	Ipswich T	26	0	45	0
2005–06	Sheffield W	11	0	11	0
2006–07	Milton Keynes D	40	0		
2007–08	Milton Keynes D	30	2		
2008–09	Milton Keynes D	0	0	70	2
2008–09	Cheltenham T	27	2		
2009–10	Cheltenham T	18	0	45	2

DUFF, Shane (D)   193   2
H: 6 1   W: 11 13   b.Wroughton 2-4-82
Source: Juniors. *Honours:* Northern Ireland
Under-21.
2000–01	Cheltenham T	0	0		
2001–02	Cheltenham T	0	0		
2002–03	Cheltenham T	18	0		
2003–04	Cheltenham T	15	1		
2004–05	Cheltenham T	45	1		
2005–06	Cheltenham T	20	0		
2006–07	Cheltenham T	34	0		
2007–08	Cheltenham T	30	0		
2008–09	Cheltenham T	20	0		
2009–10	Cheltenham T	11	0	193	2

EMERY, Josh (M)   1   0
H: 5 6   W: 10 10   b.Ledbury 30-9-90
Source: Scholar.
| 2008–09 | Cheltenham T | 1 | 0 | | |
| 2009–10 | Cheltenham T | 0 | 0 | 1 | 0 |

GALLINAGH, Andy (D)   106   2
H: 5 8   W: 11 08   b.Sutton Coldfield 16-3-85
Source: Stratford T.
2004–05	Cheltenham T	0	0		
2005–06	Cheltenham T	1	0		
2006–07	Cheltenham T	1	0		
2007–08	Cheltenham T	26	0		
2008–09	Cheltenham T	39	1		
2009–10	Cheltenham T	39	1	106	2

HAMMOND, Elvis (F)   146   19
H: 5 10   W: 11 02   b.Accra 6-10-80
Source: Trainee. *Honours:* Ghana 1 full cap.
1999–2000	Fulham	0	0		
2000–01	Fulham	0	0		
2001–02	Fulham	0	0		
2001–02	Bristol R	7	0	7	0
2002–03	Fulham	10	0		
2003–04	Fulham	0	0		
2003–04	Norwich C	4	0	4	0
2004–05	Fulham	0	0	11	0
2004–05	RBC Roosendaal	14	2	14	2
2005–06	Fulham	0	0		
2005–06	Leicester C	33	3		
2006–07	Leicester C	31	5		
2007–08	Leicester C	0	0	64	8
2008–09	Cheltenham T	22	5		
2009–10	Cheltenham T	24	4	46	9

HAYLES, Barry (F)   437 120
H: 5 10   W: 12 11   b.Lambeth 17-5-72
Source: Stevenage Bor. *Honours:* Jamaica 10 full caps.

1997–98	Bristol R	45	23	
1998–99	Bristol R	17	9	62 32
1998–99	Fulham	30	8	
1999–2000	Fulham	35	5	
2000–01	Fulham	35	18	
2001–02	Fulham	35	8	
2002–03	Fulham	14	1	
2003–04	Fulham	26	4	175 44
2004–05	Sheffield U	4	0	4 0
2004–05	Millwall	32	12	
2005–06	Millwall	23	4	55 16
2006–07	Plymouth Arg	39	13	
2007–08	Plymouth Arg	23	2	62 15
2007–08	Leicester C	18	2	
2008–09	Leicester C	10	0	28 2
2008–09	*Cheltenham T*	12	4	
2009–10	Cheltenham T	39	7	51 11

HAYNES, Kyle (D)   17 0
H: 5 11   W: 11 02   b.Wolverhampton 29-12-91
Source: Scholar.

2008–09	Cheltenham T	4	0
2009–10	Cheltenham T	13	0	17 0

HUTTON, David (M)   32 1
H: 5 5   W: 10 10   b.Enfield 4-12-89
Source: Scholar.

2008–09	Tottenham H	0	0
2008–09	*Cheltenham T*	7	1
2009–10	Cheltenham T	25	0	32 1

LEE, Jake (F)   4 0
H: 6 0   W: 12 07   b.Cirencester 18-9-91
Source: Scholar.

2008–09	Cheltenham T	3	0
2009–10	Cheltenham T	1	0	4 0

LEWIS, Theo (F)   17 0
H: 5 10   W: 10 12   b.Oxford 10-8-91
Source: Scholar.

2008–09	Cheltenham T	2	0
2009–10	Cheltenham T	15	0	17 0

LOW, Josh (M)   328 32
H: 6 2   W: 14 03   b.Bristol 15-2-79
Source: Trainee. *Honours:* Wales Youth, Under-21.

1995–96	Bristol R	1	0	
1996–97	Bristol R	3	0	
1997–98	Bristol R	10	0	
1998–99	Bristol R	8	0	22 0
1999–2000	Leyton Orient	5	1	5 1
1999–2000	Cardiff C	17	2	
2000–01	Cardiff C	36	4	
2001–02	Cardiff C	22	0	
2002–03	Cardiff C	0	0	75 6
2002–03	Oldham Ath	21	3	21 3
2003–04	Northampton T	33	3	
2004–05	Northampton T	34	7	
2005–06	Northampton T	35	5	102 15
2006–07	Leicester C	16	0	16 0
2006–07	Peterborough U	19	1	
2007–08	Peterborough U	15	2	
2008–09	Peterborough U	0	0	34 3
2008–09	Cheltenham T	14	0	
2009–10	Cheltenham T	39	4	53 4

POOK, Michael (M)   144 8
H: 5 11   W: 11 10   b.Swindon 22-10-85
Source: Scholar.

2003–04	Swindon T	0	0	
2004–05	Swindon T	5	0	
2005–06	Swindon T	30	0	
2006–07	Swindon T	38	2	
2007–08	Swindon T	22	1	
2008–09	Swindon T	14	0	109 3
2009–10	Cheltenham T	35	5	35 5

PUDDY, Will (G)   0 0
H: 5 10   W: 11 07   b.Warminster 4-10-87
Source: Scholar.

2005–06	Cheltenham T	0	0
2006–07	Cheltenham T	0	0
2007–08	Cheltenham T	0	0
2008–09	Cheltenham T	1	0
2009–10	Cheltenham T	0	0	1 0

RICHARDS, Justin (F)   79 16
H: 5 11   W: 11 00   b.Sandwell 16-10-80
Source: Trainee.

1998–99	WBA	1	0	
1999–2000	WBA	0	0	
2000–01	WBA	0	0	1 0
2000–01	Bristol R	7	0	
2001–02	Bristol R	1	0	
2002–03	Bristol R	8	0	16 0
2002–03	*Colchester U*	2	0	2 0

From Stevenage B, Woking.

2006–07	Peterborough U	13	1	13 1
2006–07	*Boston U*	3	0	3 0
2009–10	Cheltenham T	44	15	44 15

From Kidderminster H.

RIDLEY, Lee (D)   183 3
H: 5 9   W: 11 11   b.Scunthorpe 5-12-81
Source: Scholar.

2000–01	Scunthorpe U	2	0	
2001–02	Scunthorpe U	4	0	
2002–03	Scunthorpe U	11	0	
2003–04	Scunthorpe U	18	1	
2004–05	Scunthorpe U	44	0	
2005–06	Scunthorpe U	3	1	
2006–07	Scunthorpe U	18	0	100 2
2007–08	Cheltenham T	8	0	
2007–08	*Darlington*	6	0	6 0
2007–08	*Lincoln C*	15	0	15 0
2008–09	Cheltenham T	27	0	
2009–10	Cheltenham T	27	1	62 1

TABOR, Jordan (D)   0 0
H: 5 10   W: 12 06   b.Oxford 9-9-90
Source: Chelsea Scholar.

2009–10	Cheltenham T	0	0

TOWNSEND, Michael (D)   147 6
H: 6 1   W: 13 12   b.Walsall 17-5-86
Source: Wolverhampton W scholar.

2004–05	Cheltenham T	0	0
2005–06	Cheltenham T	31	0
2006–07	Cheltenham T	30	1
2007–08	Cheltenham T	13	1
2008–09	Cheltenham T	26	1
2008–09	*Barnet*	13	0	13 0
2009–10	Cheltenham T	34	3	134 6

WATKINS, Marley (M)   25 1
H: 5 10   W: 10 04   b.London 17-10-90
Source: Scholar.

2008–09	Cheltenham T	12	0
2009–10	Cheltenham T	13	1	25 1

CHESTERFIELD (25)

ALLOTT, Mark (M)   507 51
H: 5 11   W: 11 07   b.Middleton 3-10-77
Source: Trainee.

1995–96	Oldham Ath	0	0
1996–97	Oldham Ath	5	1
1997–98	Oldham Ath	22	2
1998–99	Oldham Ath	41	7
1999–2000	Oldham Ath	32	10
2000–01	Oldham Ath	39	7
2001–02	Oldham Ath	15	4
2001–02	Chesterfield	21	4
2002–03	Chesterfield	33	0
2003–04	Chesterfield	40	2
2004–05	Chesterfield	45	2
2005–06	Chesterfield	43	3
2006–07	Chesterfield	39	0
2007–08	Oldham Ath	42	4
2008–09	Oldham Ath	45	3	241 38
2009–10	Chesterfield	45	2	266 13

AUSTIN, Kevin (D)   477 5
H: 6 1   W: 14 08   b.Hackney 12-2-73
Source: Saffron Walden. *Honours:* Trinidad & Tobago 1 full cap.

1993–94	Leyton Orient	30	0	
1994–95	Leyton Orient	39	2	
1995–96	Leyton Orient	40	1	109 3
1996–97	Lincoln C	44	1	
1997–98	Lincoln C	46	0	
1998–99	Lincoln C	39	1	129 2
1999–2000	Barnsley	3	0	
2000–01	Barnsley	0	0	3 0
2000–01	*Brentford*	3	0	3 0

2001–02	Cambridge U	6	0	6 0
2002–03	Bristol R	33	0	
2003–04	Bristol R	23	0	56 0
2004–05	Swansea C	42	0	
2005–06	Swansea C	26	0	
2006–07	Swansea C	30	0	
2007–08	Swansea C	19	0	117 0
2008–09	Chesterfield	35	0	
2009–10	Chesterfield	19	0	54 0

BODEN, Scott (F)   46 8
H: 5 11   W: 11 00   b.Sheffield 19-12-89
Source: IFK Marlehamn.

2008–09	Chesterfield	11	2
2009–10	Chesterfield	35	6	46 8

BOSHELL, Danny (M)   217 13
H: 5 11   W: 11 09   b.Bradford 30-5-81
Source: Trainee.

1998–99	Oldham Ath	0	0	
1999–2000	Oldham Ath	8	0	
2000–01	Oldham Ath	18	1	
2001–02	Oldham Ath	4	0	
2002–03	Oldham Ath	2	0	
2003–04	Oldham Ath	22	0	
2004–05	Oldham Ath	16	1	70 2
2004–05	*Bury*	6	0	6 0
2005–06	Stockport Co	33	1	33 1
2006–07	Grimsby T	29	2	
2007–08	Grimsby T	40	6	
2008–09	Grimsby T	24	2	
2009–10	Grimsby T	6	0	99 10
2009–10	Chesterfield	9	0	9 0

BOWERY, Jordan (F)   13 0
H: 6 1   W: 12 00   b.Nottingham 2-7-91
Source: Scholar.

2008–09	Chesterfield	3	0
2009–10	Chesterfield	10	0	13 0

BRECKIN, Ian (D)   625 26
H: 6 2   W: 13 05   b.Rotherham 24-2-75
Source: Trainee.

1993–94	Rotherham U	10	0	
1994–95	Rotherham U	41	2	
1995–96	Rotherham U	39	1	
1996–97	Rotherham U	42	3	132 6
1997–98	Chesterfield	43	1	
1998–99	Chesterfield	44	2	
1999–2000	Chesterfield	38	1	
2000–01	Chesterfield	45	3	
2001–02	Chesterfield	42	1	
2002–03	Wigan Ath	9	0	
2003–04	Wigan Ath	45	0	
2004–05	Wigan Ath	42	0	96 0
2005–06	Nottingham F	46	8	
2006–07	Nottingham F	46	3	
2007–08	Nottingham F	28	1	
2008–09	Nottingham F	23	0	143 12
2009–10	Chesterfield	42	0	254 8

CONLON, Barry (F)   432 121
H: 6 3   W: 14 00   b.Drogheda 1-10-78
Source: QPR Trainee. *Honours:* Eire Under-21.

1997–98	Manchester C	7	0	
1997–98	*Plymouth Arg*	13	2	13 2
1998–99	Manchester C	0	0	7 0
1998–99	Southend U	34	7	34 7
1999–2000	York C	40	11	
2000–01	York C	8	0	48 11
2000–01	*Colchester U*	26	8	26 8
2001–02	Darlington	35	10	
2002–03	Darlington	41	15	
2003–04	Darlington	39	14	
2004–05	Barnsley	24	6	
2005–06	Barnsley	11	1	35 7
2005–06	*Rotherham U*	3	1	3 1
2006–07	Darlington	19	6	134 45
2006–07	Mansfield T	17	6	17 6
2007–08	Bradford C	42	7	
2008–09	Bradford C	30	10	72 17
2008–09	*Grimsby T*	8	5	
2009–10	Grimsby T	16	5	24 10
2009–10	Chesterfield	19	7	19 7

CROSSLEY, Mark (G)   451 1
H: 6 3   W: 15 09   b.Barnsley 16-6-69
Source: Trainee. *Honours:* England Under-21, B, Wales B. 8 full caps.

1987–88	Nottingham F	0	0
1988–89	Nottingham F	2	0

1989–90	Nottingham F	8	0		
1989–90	*Manchester U*	0	0		
1990–91	Nottingham F	38	0		
1991–92	Nottingham F	36	0		
1992–93	Nottingham F	37	0		
1993–94	Nottingham F	37	0		
1994–95	Nottingham F	42	0		
1995–96	Nottingham F	38	0		
1996–97	Nottingham F	33	0		
1997–98	Nottingham F	0	0		
1997–98	*Millwall*	13	0	13	0
1998–99	Nottingham F	12	0		
1999–2000	Nottingham F	20	0	303	0
2000–01	Middlesbrough	5	0		
2001–02	Middlesbrough	18	0		
2002–03	Middlesbrough	0	0	23	0
2002–03	*Stoke C*	12	0	12	0
2003–04	Fulham	1	0		
2004–05	Fulham	6	0		
2005–06	Fulham	13	0		
2006–07	Fulham	0	0	20	0
2006–07	*Sheffield W*	17	1	17	1
2007–08	Oldham Ath	38	0		
2008–09	Oldham Ath	21	0	59	0
2009–10	Chesterfield	4	0	4	0

DOWNES, Aaron (D)   165 10
H: 6 2   W: 13 02   b.Mudgee 15-5-85
Honours: Australia Youth, Under-20, Under-21, Under-23.

2004–05	Chesterfield	9	2		
2005–06	Chesterfield	22	0		
2006–07	Chesterfield	45	3		
2007–08	Chesterfield	40	2		
2008–09	Chesterfield	42	2		
2009–10	Chesterfield	7	1	165	10

GOODALL, Alan (D)   194 12
H: 5 7   W: 11 08   b.Birkenhead 2-12-81
Source: Bangor C.

2004–05	Rochdale	34	2		
2005–06	Rochdale	40	3		
2006–07	Rochdale	46	3	120	8
2007–08	Luton T	29	1	29	1
2008–09	Chesterfield	28	3		
2009–10	Chesterfield	17	0	45	3

GRAY, Dan (M)   44 0
H: 6 0   W: 11 00   b.Mansfield 23-11-89
Source: Scholar.

2008–09	Chesterfield	25	0		
2009–10	Chesterfield	19	0	44	0

GRITTON, Martin (F)   313 63
H: 6 1   W: 12 02   b.Glasgow 1-6-78
Source: Porthleven.

1998–99	Plymouth Arg	2	0		
1999–2000	Plymouth Arg	30	6		
2000–01	Plymouth Arg	10	1		
2001–02	Plymouth Arg	2	0		
2002–03	Plymouth Arg	0	0	44	7
2002–03	Torquay U	43	13		
2003–04	Torquay U	31	4		
2004–05	Torquay U	19	6	93	23
2004–05	Grimsby T	23	4		
2005–06	Grimsby T	26	2	49	6
2005–06	Lincoln C	10	1		
2006–07	Lincoln C	17	2	27	3
2006–07	*Mansfield T*	19	6	19	6
2007–08	Macclesfield T	31	8		
2008–09	Macclesfield T	21	5	52	13
2008–09	Chesterfield	20	4		
2009–10	Chesterfield	9	1	29	5

HALL, Danny (D)   156 3
H: 6 0   W: 12 02   b.Ashton-under-Lyne 14-11-83
Source: Scholar.

2002–03	Oldham Ath	2	0		
2003–04	Oldham Ath	31	1		
2004–05	Oldham Ath	21	0		
2005–06	Oldham Ath	10	0	64	1
2006–07	Shrewsbury T	27	0		
2007–08	Shrewsbury T	15	0	42	0
2007–08	*Gretna*	15	0	15	0
2008–09	Chesterfield	25	1		
2009–10	Chesterfield	7	1	32	2
2009–10	*Darlington*	3	0	3	0

HARSLEY, Paul (M)   435 36
H: 5 8   W: 11 05   b.Scunthorpe 29-5-78
Source: Trainee.

1996–97	Grimsby T	0	0		
1997–98	Scunthorpe U	15	1		
1998–99	Scunthorpe U	34	0		
1999–2000	Scunthorpe U	46	3		
2000–01	Scunthorpe U	33	1	128	5
2001–02	Halifax T	45	11	45	11
2002–03	Northampton T	45	2		
2003–04	Northampton T	14	0	59	2
2003–04	Macclesfield T	16	2		
2004–05	Macclesfield T	46	3		
2005–06	Macclesfield T	45	6	107	11
2006–07	Port Vale	32	1		
2007–08	Port Vale	41	5	73	6
2008–09	Chesterfield	17	1		
2009–10	Chesterfield	3	0	20	1
2009–10	*Darlington*	3	0	3	0

LEE, Tommy (G)   144 0
H: 6 2   W: 12 00   b.Keighley 3-1-86
Source: Scholar.

2005–06	Manchester U	0	0		
2005–06	*Macclesfield T*	11	0		
2006–07	Macclesfield T	34	0		
2007–08	Macclesfield T	18	0	63	0
2007–08	*Rochdale*	11	0	11	0
2008–09	Chesterfield	28	0		
2009–10	Chesterfield	42	0	70	0

LESTER, Jack (F)   465 117
H: 5 9   W: 12 08   b.Sheffield 8-10-75
Source: Trainee. *Honours:* England Schools.

1994–95	Grimsby T	7	0		
1995–96	Grimsby T	5	0		
1996–97	Grimsby T	22	5		
1996–97	*Doncaster R*	11	1	11	1
1997–98	Grimsby T	40	4		
1998–99	Grimsby T	33	4		
1999–2000	Grimsby T	26	4	133	17
1999–2000	Nottingham F	15	2		
2000–01	Nottingham F	19	7		
2001–02	Nottingham F	32	5		
2002–03	Nottingham F	33	7		
2003–04	Sheffield U	32	12		
2004–05	Sheffield U	12	0	44	12
2004–05	Nottingham F	3	1		
2005–06	Nottingham F	38	5		
2006–07	Nottingham F	35	6	175	33
2007–08	Chesterfield	36	23		
2008–09	Chesterfield	37	20		
2009–10	Chesterfield	29	11	102	54

LEWIS, Terrell (F)   1 0
H: 5 8   W: 11 00   b.Brent 13-8-88
Source: Chalfont St Peter.

2009–10	Chesterfield	1	0	1	0

LOWRY, Jamie (D)   105 11
H: 6 0   W: 12 00   b.Newquay 18-3-87
Source: Scholar.

2006–07	Chesterfield	8	0		
2007–08	Chesterfield	42	6		
2008–09	Chesterfield	42	0		
2009–10	Chesterfield	13	5	105	11

MALAK, Matt (G)   0 0
H: 6 3   W: 12 00   b.Doncaster 23-9-90
Source: Scholar.

2009–10	Chesterfield	0	0		

NIVEN, Derek (M)   256 17
H: 5 11   W: 12 05   b.Falkirk 12-12-83
Source: Stenhousemuir.

2000–01	Raith R	1	0	1	0
2001–02	Bolton W	0	0		
2002–03	Bolton W	0	0		
2003–04	Bolton W	0	0		
2003–04	Chesterfield	22	1		
2004–05	Chesterfield	38	1		
2005–06	Chesterfield	42	5		
2006–07	Chesterfield	45	3		
2007–08	Chesterfield	38	3		
2008–09	Chesterfield	31	2		
2009–10	Chesterfield	39	2	255	17

PAGE, Robert (D)   475 6
H: 6 0   W: 12 05   b.Llwynpia 3-9-74
Source: Trainee. *Honours:* Wales Schools, Youth, Under-21, B, 41 full caps.

1992–93	Watford	0	0		
1993–94	Watford	4	0		
1994–95	Watford	5	0		
1995–96	Watford	19	0		
1996–97	Watford	36	0		
1997–98	Watford	41	0		
1998–99	Watford	39	0		
1999–2000	Watford	36	1		
2000–01	Watford	36	1		
2001–02	Watford	0	0	216	2
2001–02	Sheffield U	43	0		
2002–03	Sheffield U	34	0		
2003–04	Sheffield U	30	1	107	1
2004–05	Cardiff C	9	0	9	0
2004–05	Coventry C	9	0		
2005–06	Coventry C	32	1		
2006–07	Coventry C	29	0		
2007–08	Coventry C	0	0	70	1
2007–08	Huddersfield T	18	1	18	1
2008–09	Chesterfield	16	0		
2009–10	Chesterfield	39	1	55	1

PICKEN, Phil (D)   162 2
H: 5 9   W: 10 07   b.Droylsden 12-11-85
Source: Scholar.

2004–05	Manchester U	0	0		
2005–06	Manchester U	0	0		
2005–06	*Chesterfield*	32	1		
2006–07	Chesterfield	39	1		
2007–08	Chesterfield	37	0		
2008–09	Chesterfield	11	0		
2008–09	Notts Co	22	0	22	0
2009–10	Chesterfield	21	0	140	2

ROBERTSON, Gregor (D)   172 4
H: 6 0   W: 12 04   b.Edinburgh 19-1-84
Honours: Scotland Under-21.

2000–01	Nottingham F	0	0		
2001–02	Nottingham F	0	0		
2002–03	Nottingham F	0	0		
2003–04	Nottingham F	16	0		
2004–05	Nottingham F	20	0	36	0
2005–06	Rotherham U	35	1		
2006–07	Rotherham U	18	0	53	1
2007–08	Chesterfield	35	1		
2008–09	Chesterfield	38	2		
2009–10	Chesterfield	10	0	83	3

RUNDLE, Adam (F)   261 27
H: 5 8   W: 11 02   b.Durham 8-7-84
Source: Scholar.

2001–02	Darlington	12	0		
2002–03	Darlington	5	0	17	0
2002–03	Carlisle U	21	1		
2003–04	Carlisle U	23	0		
2004–05	Carlisle U	0	0	44	1
2004–05	Mansfield T	18	4		
2005–06	Mansfield T	35	5	53	9
2006–07	Rochdale	29	4		
2007–08	Rochdale	42	5		
2008–09	Rochdale	44	7		
2009–10	Rochdale	12	1	127	17
2009–10	*Rotherham U*	4	0	4	0
2009–10	Chesterfield	16	0	16	0

SMALL, Wade (M)   199 24
H: 5 8   W: 11 05   b.Croydon 23-2-84
Source: Scholar.

2003–04	Wimbledon	27	1	27	1
2004–05	Milton Keynes D	44	10		
2005–06	Milton Keynes D	28	1	72	11
2006–07	Sheffield W	20	2		
2007–08	Sheffield W	29	4		
2008–09	Sheffield W	19	1		
2008–09	*Blackpool*	5	1	5	1
2009–10	Sheffield W	0	0	68	7
2009–10	Chesterfield	27	4	27	4

TALBOT, Drew (F)   128 16
H: 5 10   W: 11 00   b.Barnsley 19-7-86
Source: Trainee.

2003–04	Sheffield W	0	0		
2004–05	Sheffield W	21	4		
2005–06	Sheffield W	0	0		
2006–07	Sheffield W	8	0	29	4
2006–07	*Scunthorpe U*	3	1	3	1
2006–07	Luton T	15	3		
2007–08	Luton T	27	0		
2008–09	Luton T	7	0	49	3
2008–09	*Chesterfield*	17	2		
2009–10	Chesterfield	30	6	47	8

COLCHESTER U (26)

BALDWIN, Pat (D) 216 2
H: 6 3 W: 12 07 b.City of London 12-11-82
Source: Chelsea Academy.

2002–03	Colchester U	19	0	
2003–04	Colchester U	4	0	
2004–05	Colchester U	38	0	
2005–06	Colchester U	25	0	
2006–07	Colchester U	38	1	
2007–08	Colchester U	26	0	
2008–09	Colchester U	35	0	
2009–10	Colchester U	7	0	192 1
2009–10	*Bristol R*	6	0	6 0
2009–10	*Southend U*	18	1	18 1

BEEVERS, Lee (D) 242 12
H: 6 2 W: 11 07 b.Doncaster 4-12-83
Source: Scholar. *Honours:* Wales Youth, Under-21.

2000–01	Ipswich T	0	0	
2001–02	Ipswich T	0	0	
2002–03	Ipswich T	0	0	
2002–03	*Boston U*	1	0	
2003–04	*Boston U*	40	2	
2004–05	*Boston U*	31	1	72 3
2004–05	Lincoln C	8	0	
2005–06	Lincoln C	33	1	
2006–07	Lincoln C	44	5	
2007–08	Lincoln C	37	1	
2008–09	Lincoln C	44	2	166 9
2009–10	Colchester U	4	0	4 0

BENDER, Tom (D) 1 0
H: 6 3 W: 12 00 b.Harlow 19-1-93
Source: Scholar. *Honours:* Wales Youth.

2009–10	Colchester U	1	0	1 0

COUSINS, Mark (G) 11 0
H: 6 2 W: 12 02 b.Chelmsford 9-1-87
Source: Scholar.

2005–06	Colchester U	0	0	
2006–07	Colchester U	0	0	
2007–08	Colchester U	2	0	
2008–09	Colchester U	9	0	
2009–10	Colchester U	0	0	11 0

ELITO, Medy (M) 31 4
H: 6 2 W: 13 00 b.Kinshasa 20-3-90
Source: Scholar. *Honours:* England Youth.

2007–08	Colchester U	11	1	
2008–09	Colchester U	5	0	
2009–10	Colchester U	3	0	19 1
2009–10	*Cheltenham T*	12	3	12 3

FOX, David (M) 116 10
H: 5 9 W: 11 08 b.Leek 13-12-83
Source: Scholar. *Honours:* England Youth, Under-20.

2000–01	Manchester U	0	0	
2001–02	Manchester U	0	0	
2002–03	Manchester U	0	0	
2003–04	Manchester U	0	0	
2004–05	Manchester U	0	0	
2004–05	*Shrewsbury T*	4	1	4 1
2005–06	Manchester U	0	0	
2005–06	Blackpool	7	1	
2006–07	Blackpool	37	4	
2007–08	Blackpool	28	1	
2008–09	Blackpool	22	0	94 6
2009–10	Colchester U	18	3	18 3

GILLESPIE, Steven (F) 145 35
H: 5 9 W: 11 02 b.Liverpool 4-6-84
Source: Liverpool Scholar.

2004–05	Bristol C	8	0	
2004–05	*Cheltenham T*	12	5	
2005–06	Bristol C	4	1	12 1
2005–06	Cheltenham T	14	5	
2006–07	Cheltenham T	23	5	
2007–08	Cheltenham T	37	14	86 29
2008–09	Colchester U	17	4	
2009–10	Colchester U	30	1	47 5

GUY, Jamie (M) 64 4
H: 6 1 W: 13 00 b.Barking 1-8-87
Source: Scholar.

2004–05	Colchester U	2	0	
2005–06	Colchester U	2	0	
2006–07	Colchester U	32	3	
2007–08	Colchester U	11	0	
2008–09	Colchester U	4	0	
2008–09	*Dagenham & R*	9	1	9 1
2009–10	Colchester U	1	0	52 3
2009–10	*Port Vale*	3	0	3 0

HACKNEY, Simon (M) 155 19
H: 5 8 W: 9 13 b.Manchester 5-2-84
Source: Woodley Sports.

2005–06	Carlisle U	30	6	
2006–07	Carlisle U	18	2	
2007–08	Carlisle U	43	8	
2008–09	Carlisle U	22	1	113 17
2008–09	Colchester U	17	0	
2009–10	Colchester U	17	1	34 1
2009–10	*Morecambe*	8	1	8 1

HEATH, Matt (D) 190 12
H: 6 4 W: 13 13 b.Leicester 1-11-81
Source: Scholar.

2000–01	Leicester C	0	0	
2001–02	Leicester C	5	0	
2002–03	Leicester C	11	3	
2003–04	Leicester C	13	0	
2003–04	*Stockport Co*	8	0	8 0
2004–05	Leicester C	22	3	51 6
2005–06	Coventry C	25	1	
2006–07	Coventry C	7	0	32 1
2006–07	Leeds U	26	3	
2007–08	Leeds U	26	1	52 4
2007–08	*Colchester U*	5	0	
2008–09	Colchester U	14	0	
2008–09	*Brighton & HA*	6	1	6 1
2009–10	Colchester U	18	0	37 0
2009–10	*Southend U*	4	0	4 0

HENDERSON, Ian (F) 146 10
H: 5 10 W: 11 06 b.Thetford 25-1-85
Source: Scholar. *Honours:* England Youth, Under-20.

2002–03	Norwich C	20	1	
2003–04	Norwich C	19	4	
2004–05	Norwich C	3	0	
2005–06	Norwich C	24	1	
2006–07	Norwich C	2	0	68 6
2006–07	*Rotherham U*	18	1	18 1
2007–08	Northampton T	23	0	
2008–09	Northampton T	3	0	26 0
2008–09	*Luton T*	19	1	19 1
2009–10	Colchester U	13	2	13 2
2009–10	*Ankaragucu*	2	0	2 0

IFIL, Phil (D) 84 2
H: 5 10 W: 12 02 b.Willesden 18-11-86
Honours: England Youth, Under-20.

2004–05	Tottenham H	2	0	
2005–06	Tottenham H	0	0	
2005–06	*Millwall*	16	0	16 0
2006–07	Tottenham H	1	0	
2007–08	Tottenham H	0	0	3 0
2007–08	*Southampton*	12	0	12 0
2007–08	Colchester U	20	0	
2008–09	Colchester U	6	0	
2009–10	Colchester U	27	2	53 2

IZZET, Kem (M) 336 18
H: 5 7 W: 10 05 b.Mile End 29-9-80
Source: Trainee.

1998–99	Charlton Ath	0	0	
1999–2000	Charlton Ath	0	0	
2000–01	Charlton Ath	0	0	
2000–01	Colchester U	6	1	
2001–02	Colchester U	40	3	
2002–03	Colchester U	45	8	
2003–04	Colchester U	44	3	
2004–05	Colchester U	4	0	
2005–06	Colchester U	33	0	
2006–07	Colchester U	45	1	
2007–08	Colchester U	39	1	
2008–09	Colchester U	43	1	
2009–10	Colchester U	37	0	336 18

KNUDSEN, Morten (D) 17 0
b.Norway 27-10-86

2009	*Notodden*	17	0	17 0
2009–10	Colchester U	0	0	

LOCKWOOD, Matt (D) 443 53
H: 5 11 W: 11 10 b.Southend 17-10-76
Source: Trainee.

1994–95	QPR	0	0	
1995–96	QPR	0	0	
1996–97	Bristol R	39	1	
1997–98	Bristol R	24	0	63 1
1998–99	Leyton Orient	37	3	
1999–2000	Leyton Orient	41	6	
2000–01	Leyton Orient	32	7	
2001–02	Leyton Orient	24	2	
2002–03	Leyton Orient	43	5	
2003–04	Leyton Orient	25	2	
2004–05	Leyton Orient	43	6	
2005–06	Leyton Orient	42	8	
2006–07	Leyton Orient	41	11	328 50
2007–08	Nottingham F	11	0	11 0
2008–09	Colchester U	5	0	
2008–09	*Barnet*	12	0	
2009–10	Colchester U	1	0	6 0
2009–10	*Dagenham & R*	4	0	4 0
2009–10	*Barnet*	19	2	31 2

MAYBURY, Alan (D) 250 7
H: 5 8 W: 11 08 b.Dublin 8-8-78
Source: Trainee. *Honours:* Eire Youth, Under-21, B, 10 full caps.

1995–96	Leeds U	1	0	
1996–97	Leeds U	0	0	
1997–98	Leeds U	12	0	
1998–99	Leeds U	0	0	
1998–99	*Reading*	8	0	8 0
1999–2000	Leeds U	0	0	
2000–01	Leeds U	0	0	
2000–01	*Crewe Alex*	6	0	6 0
2001–02	Leeds U	1	0	14 0
2001–02	Hearts	27	0	
2002–03	Hearts	35	2	
2003–04	Hearts	33	2	
2004–05	Hearts	15	0	110 4
2004–05	Leicester C	17	2	
2005–06	Leicester C	40	1	
2006–07	Leicester C	27	0	
2007–08	Leicester C	1	0	
2008–09	Leicester C	0	0	85 3
2008–09	Colchester U	25	0	
2009–10	Colchester U	2	0	27 0

O'TOOLE, John (M) 97 13
H: 6 2 W: 13 07 b.Harrow 30-9-88
Honours: Eire Under-21.

2007–08	Watford	35	3	
2008–09	Watford	22	7	
2008–09	*Sheffield U*	9	1	9 1
2009–10	Watford	0	0	57 10
2009–10	Colchester U	31	2	31 2

ODEJAYI, Kayode (F) 260 44
H: 6 2 W: 12 02 b.Ibadan 21-2-82
Source: Scholar. *Honours:* Nigeria 1 full cap.

1999–2000	Bristol C	3	0	
2000–01	Bristol C	3	0	
2001–02	Bristol C	0	0	
2002–03	Bristol C	0	0	6 0
2003–04	Cheltenham T	30	5	
2004–05	Cheltenham T	32	1	
2005–06	Cheltenham T	41	11	
2006–07	Cheltenham T	45	13	148 30
2007–08	Barnsley	39	3	
2008–09	Barnsley	28	1	
2008–09	*Scunthorpe U*	6	1	6 1
2009–10	Barnsley	5	0	72 4
2009–10	Colchester U	28	9	28 9

OKUONGHAE, Magnus (D) 121 3
H: 6 3 W: 13 04 b.Nigeria 16-2-86
Source: Scholar.

2003–04	Rushden & D	1	0	
2004–05	Rushden & D	4	0	
2005–06	Rushden & D	21	1	
2006–07	Rushden & D	0	0	22 1
2007–08	Dagenham & R	10	0	
2008–09	Dagenham & R	45	2	55 2
2009–10	Colchester U	44	0	44 0

PERKINS, David (D) 136 11
H: 5 6 W: 11 06 b.St Asaph 21-6-82

2007–08	Rochdale	18	0	
2007–08	Rochdale	40	4	58 4
2008–09	Colchester U	38	5	
2009–10	Colchester U	5	1	43 6
2009–10	*Chesterfield*	13	1	13 1
2009–10	*Stockport Co*	22	0	22 0

PLATT, Clive (F) 484 95
H: 6 4 W: 12 07 b.Wolverhampton 27-10-77
Source: Trainee.

1995-96	Walsall	4	2		
1996-97	Walsall	1	0		
1997-98	Walsall	20	1		
1998-99	Walsall	7	1		
1999-2000	Walsall	0	0	32	4
1999-2000	Rochdale	41	9		
2000-01	Rochdale	43	8		
2001-02	Rochdale	43	7		
2002-03	Rochdale	42	6	169	30
2003-04	Notts Co	19	3	19	3
2003-04	Peterborough U	18	2		
2004-05	Peterborough U	19	4	37	6
2004-05	Milton Keynes D	20	3		
2005-06	Milton Keynes D	40	6		
2006-07	Milton Keynes D	42	18	102	27
2007-08	Colchester U	41	8		
2008-09	Colchester U	43	10		
2009-10	Colchester U	41	7	125	25

PRUTTON, David (M) 321 19
H: 5 10 W: 13 00 b.Hull 12-9-81
Source: Trainee. *Honours:* England Youth, Under-21.

1998-99	Nottingham F	0	0		
1999-2000	Nottingham F	34	2		
2000-01	Nottingham F	42	1		
2001-02	Nottingham F	43	3		
2002-03	Nottingham F	24	1		
2002-03	Southampton	12	0		
2003-04	Southampton	27	1		
2004-05	Southampton	23	1		
2005-06	Southampton	17	0		
2006-07	Southampton	3	1	82	3
2006-07	*Nottingham F*	12	2	155	9
2007-08	Leeds U	43	4		
2008-09	Leeds U	16	0		
2009-10	Leeds U	6	0	65	4
2009-10	Colchester U	19	3	19	3

RAFTER, Michael (M) 0 0

| 2008-09 | Colchester U | 0 | 0 | | |
| 2009-10 | Colchester U | 0 | 0 | | |

REID, Paul (D) 225 7
H: 6 2 W: 11 08 b.Carlisle 18-2-82
Source: Trainee. *Honours:* England Youth, Under-20.

1998-99	Carlisle U	0	0		
1999-2000	Carlisle U	19	0		
2000-01	Rangers	0	0		
2001-02	Rangers	0	0		
2001-02	*Preston NE*	1	1	1	1
2002-03	Rangers	0	0		
2002-03	Northampton T	19	0		
2003-04	Northampton T	33	2	52	2
2004-05	Barnsley	41	3		
2005-06	Barnsley	33	0		
2006-07	Barnsley	37	0		
2007-08	Barnsley	3	0	114	3
2007-08	*Carlisle U*	1	0	20	0
2008-09	Colchester U	26	1		
2009-10	Colchester U	12	0	38	1

THOMAS, Joel (F) 30 0
H: 6 1 W: 12 04 b.Caen 30-6-87
Honours: On loan to Hamilton A.

| 2008-09 | Hamilton A | 26 | 0 | 26 | 0 |
| 2009-10 | Colchester U | 4 | 0 | 4 | 0 |

TIERNEY, Marc (D) 183 2
H: 5 11 W: 11 04 b.Manchester 7-9-86
Source: Trainee.

2003-04	Oldham Ath	2	0		
2004-05	Oldham Ath	11	0		
2005-06	Oldham Ath	19	0		
2006-07	Oldham Ath	5	0	37	0
2006-07	Shrewsbury T	18	0		
2007-08	Shrewsbury T	43	1		
2008-09	Shrewsbury T	18	0	79	1
2008-09	Colchester U	26	1		
2009-10	Colchester U	41	0	67	1

VERNON, Scott (F) 237 57
H: 6 1 W: 11 06 b.Manchester 13-12-83
Source: Scholar.

2002-03	Oldham Ath	8	1		
2003-04	Oldham Ath	45	12		
2004-05	Oldham Ath	22	7	75	20
2004-05	Blackpool	4	3		
2005-06	Blackpool	17	1		
2005-06	Colchester U	7	1		
2006-07	Blackpool	38	11		
2007-08	Blackpool	15	4	74	19
2007-08	Colchester U	17	5		
2008-09	Colchester U	33	4		
2008-09	*Northampton T*	6	1	6	1
2009-10	Colchester U	7	3	64	13
2009-10	*Gillingham*	1	0	1	0
2009-10	*Southend U*	17	4	17	4

VINCENT, Ashley (F) 135 12
H: 5 10 W: 11 08 b.Oldbury 26-5-85
Source: Wolverhampton W Scholar.

2004-05	Cheltenham T	26	1		
2005-06	Cheltenham T	13	2		
2006-07	Cheltenham T	5	0		
2007-08	Cheltenham T	38	5		
2008-09	Cheltenham T	29	3	110	8
2008-09	Colchester U	6	1		
2009-10	Colchester U	19	3	25	4

WHITE, John (D) 162 0
H: 6 0 W: 12 01 b.Maldon 26-7-86
Source: Scholar.

2004-05	Colchester U	20	0		
2005-06	Colchester U	35	0		
2006-07	Colchester U	16	0		
2007-08	Colchester U	21	0		
2008-09	Colchester U	26	0		
2009-10	Colchester U	39	0	157	0
2009-10	*Southend U*	5	0	5	0

WILLIAMS, Ben (G) 226 0
H: 6 0 W: 13 01 b.Manchester 27-8-82
Source: Scholar. *Honours:* England Schools.

2001-02	Manchester U	0	0		
2002-03	Manchester U	0	0		
2002-03	Coventry C	0	0		
2002-03	Chesterfield	14	0	14	0
2003-04	Manchester U	0	0		
2003-04	Crewe Alex	10	0		
2004-05	Crewe Alex	23	0		
2005-06	Crewe Alex	17	0		
2006-07	Crewe Alex	39	0		
2007-08	Crewe Alex	46	0	135	0
2008-09	Carlisle U	31	0	31	0
2009-10	Colchester U	46	0	46	0

WORDSWORTH, Anthony (M) 74 14
H: 6 1 W: 12 00 b.Camden 3-1-89
Source: Scholar.

2007-08	Colchester U	3	0		
2008-09	Colchester U	30	3		
2009-10	Colchester U	41	11	74	14

COVENTRY C (27)

BAKER, Carl (M) 106 22
H: 6 2 W: 12 06 b.Prescot 26-12-82
Source: Southport.

2007-08	Morecambe	42	10	42	10
2008-09	Stockport Co	22	3		
2009-10	Stockport Co	20	9	42	12
2009-10	Coventry C	22	0		

BELL, David (M) 258 20
H: 5 10 W: 11 05 b.Kettering 21-1-84
Source: Trainee. *Honours:* Eire Youth, Under-21.

2001-02	Rushden & D	0	0		
2002-03	Rushden & D	30	3		
2003-04	Rushden & D	37	1		
2004-05	Rushden & D	40	3		
2005-06	Rushden & D	14	3	121	10
2005-06	Luton T	9	0		
2006-07	Luton T	34	3		
2007-08	Luton T	32	4	75	7
2007-08	*Leicester C*	6	0	6	0
2008-09	Norwich C	19	0	19	0
2008-09	Coventry C	9	1		
2009-10	Coventry C	28	2	37	3

CAIN, Ashley (M) 7 0
H: 6 2 W: 12 06 b.Nuneaton 27-9-90
Source: Scholar.

| 2008-09 | Coventry C | 5 | 0 | | |
| 2009-10 | Coventry C | 2 | 0 | 7 | 0 |

CAMERON, Nathan (D) 0 0
H: 6 2 W: 12 04 b.Birmingham 21-11-91
Source: Scholar.

| 2009-10 | Coventry C | 0 | 0 | | |

CLARKE, Jordan (D) 12 0
H: 6 0 W: 11 02 b.Coventry 19-11-91
Source: Scholar. *Honours:* England Youth.

| 2009-10 | Coventry C | 12 | 0 | 12 | 0 |

CLINGAN, Sammy (M) 195 15
H: 5 11 W: 11 06 b.Belfast 13-1-84
Source: Scholar. *Honours:* Northern Ireland Schools, Youth, Under-21, Under-23, 24 full caps.

2001-02	Wolverhampton W	0	0		
2002-03	Wolverhampton W	0	0		
2003-04	Wolverhampton W	0	0		
2004-05	Wolverhampton W	0	0		
2004-05	*Chesterfield*	15	2		
2005-06	Wolverhampton W	0	0		
2005-06	*Chesterfield*	21	1	36	3
2005-06	Nottingham F	15	0		
2006-07	Nottingham F	28	0		
2007-08	Nottingham F	42	1	85	1
2008-09	Norwich C	40	6		
2009-10	Norwich C	0	0	40	6
2009-10	Coventry C	34	5	34	5

CRANIE, Martin (D) 98 1
H: 6 1 W: 12 09 b.Yeovil 23-9-86
Source: Scholar. *Honours:* England Youth, Under-20, Under-21.

2003-04	Southampton	1	0		
2004-05	Southampton	3	0		
2004-05	*Bournemouth*	3	0	3	0
2005-06	Southampton	11	0		
2006-07	Southampton	1	0	16	0
2006-07	*Yeovil T*	12	0	12	0
2007-08	Portsmouth	2	0		
2007-08	*QPR*	6	0	6	0
2008-09	Portsmouth	0	0		
2008-09	*Charlton Ath*	19	0	19	0
2009-10	Portsmouth	0	0	2	0
2009-10	Coventry C	40	1	40	1

DEEGAN, Gary (M) 117 14
H: 5 9 W: 11 11 b.Dublin 28-9-87

2005-06	Shelbourne	0	0		
2006	Kilkenny City	18	4	18	4
2007	Longford Town	30	3	30	3
2008	Galway	17	0	17	0
2008	Bohemians	12	3	12	3
2009	Bohemains	23	2	23	2
2009-10	Coventry C	17	2	17	2

DOYLE, Micky (M) 289 19
H: 5 10 W: 11 00 b.Dublin 8-7-81
Source: Celtic. *Honours:* Eire Under-21, 1 full cap.

2003-04	Coventry C	40	5		
2004-05	Coventry C	44	2		
2005-06	Coventry C	44	0		
2006-07	Coventry C	40	3		
2007-08	Coventry C	42	7		
2008-09	Coventry C	37	2		
2009-10	Coventry C	0	0	247	19
2009-10	*Leeds U*	42	0	42	0

EASTWOOD, Freddy (F) 228 68
H: 5 11 W: 12 04 b.Epsom 29-10-83
Source: West Ham U Trainee, Grays Ath.
Honours: Wales 10 full caps, 4 goals.

2004-05	Southend U	33	19		
2005-06	Southend U	40	23		
2006-07	Southend U	42	11	115	53
2007-08	Wolverhampton W	31	3	31	3
2008-09	Coventry C	46	4		
2009-10	Coventry C	36	8	82	12

GIDDINGS, Stuart (M) 40 0
H: 6 0 W: 11 08 b.Coventry 27-3-86
Source: Scholar. *Honours:* England Youth.

2003-04	Coventry C	1	0		
2004-05	Coventry C	12	0		
2005-06	Coventry C	2	0		
2006-07	Coventry C	1	0		
2007-08	Coventry C	0	0		
2007-08	*Oldham Ath*	2	0	2	0
2008-09	Coventry C	0	0		
2009-10	Coventry C	0	0	16	0
2009-10	*Darlington*	22	0	22	0

GRANDISON, Jermaine (D)   5   0
H: 6 4   W: 13 03   b.Birmingham 15-12-90
Source: Scholar.

2008–09	Coventry C	2	0		
2009–10	Coventry C	3	0	5	0

GUNNARSSON, Aron (M)   81   2
H: 5 9   W: 11 00   b.Akureyri 22-9-89
Honours: Iceland Under-21, 17 full caps.

2007–08	AZ	1	0	1	0
2008–09	Coventry C	40	1		
2009–10	Coventry C	40	1	80	2

HALL, Marcus (D)   350   7
H: 6 1   W: 12 02   b.Coventry 24-3-76
Source: Trainee. *Honours:* England Under-21, B.

1994–95	Coventry C	5	0		
1995–96	Coventry C	25	0		
1996–97	Coventry C	13	0		
1997–98	Coventry C	25	1		
1998–99	Coventry C	5	0		
1999–2000	Coventry C	9	0		
2000–01	Coventry C	21	0		
2001–02	Coventry C	29	1		
2002–03	Nottingham F	1	0	1	0
2002–03	Stoke C	24	0		
2003–04	Stoke C	35	0		
2004–05	Stoke C	20	1	79	1
2004–05	Coventry C	10	0		
2005–06	Coventry C	39	0		
2006–07	Coventry C	40	0		
2007–08	Coventry C	18	0		
2008–09	Coventry C	23	0		
2009–10	Coventry C	8	0	270	2

HUSSEY, Chris (D)   8   0
H: 5 10   W: 10 03   b.Hammersmith 2-1-89
Source: AFC Wimbledon.

2009–10	Coventry C	8	0	8	0

IRELAND, Daniel (G)   0   0
H: 6 2   W: 13 00   b.Sydney 20-1-89
Source: Academy.

2007–08	Coventry C	0	0
2008–09	Coventry C	0	0
2009–10	Coventry C	0	0

JEFFERS, Shaun (F)   4   0
H: 6 1   W: 11 03   b.Bedford 14-4-92
Source: Scholar.

2009–10	Coventry C	4	0	4	0

KONSTANTOPOULOS, Dimitrios (G) 151 0
H: 6 4   W: 14 02   b.Kalamata 29-11-78
Source: Farense. *Honours:* Greece Under-21.

2003–04	Hartlepool U	0	0		
2004–05	Hartlepool U	25	0		
2005–06	Hartlepool U	46	0		
2006–07	Hartlepool U	46	0	117	0
2007–08	Coventry C	21	0		
2008–09	Coventry C	0	0		
2008–09	Swansea C	4	0	4	0
2008–09	Cardiff C	6	0	6	0
2009–10	Coventry C	3	0	24	0

McINDOE, Michael (M)   344   48
H: 5 8   W: 11 00   b.Edinburgh 2-12-79
Source: Trainee. *Honours:* Scotland B.

1997–98	Luton T	0	0		
1998–99	Luton T	22	0		
1999–2000	Luton T	17	0	39	0
From Hereford, Yeovil					
2003–04	Doncaster R	45	10		
2004–05	Doncaster R	44	10		
2005–06	Doncaster R	33	8	122	28
2005–06	Derby Co	8	0	8	0
2006–07	Barnsley	18	4	18	4
2006–07	Wolverhampton W	27	3	27	3
2007–08	Bristol C	45	6		
2008–09	Bristol C	45	6		
2009–10	Bristol C	0	0	90	12
2009–10	Coventry C	40	1	40	1

McPAKE, James (D)   133   10
H: 6 2   W: 12 08   b.Airdrie 2-6-84

2003–04	Livingston	1	0		
2004–05	Livingston	15	2		
2005–06	Livingston	15	0		
2005–06	Morton	11	2	11	2
2006–07	Livingston	33	3		
2007–08	Livingston	19	0		

2008–09	Livingston	18	2	101	7
2008–09	Coventry C	4	0		
2009–10	Coventry C	17	1	21	1

MORRISON, Clinton (F)   459 138
H: 6 0   W: 12 00   b.Tooting 14-5-79
Source: Trainee. *Honours:* Eire Under-21, 36 full caps, 9 goals.

1996–97	Crystal Palace	0	0		
1997–98	Crystal Palace	1	1		
1998–99	Crystal Palace	37	12		
1999–2000	Crystal Palace	29	13		
2000–01	Crystal Palace	45	14		
2001–02	Crystal Palace	45	22		
2002–03	Birmingham C	28	6		
2003–04	Birmingham C	32	4		
2004–05	Birmingham C	26	4		
2005–06	Birmingham C	1	0	87	14
2005–06	Crystal Palace	40	13		
2006–07	Crystal Palace	41	12		
2007–08	Crystal Palace	43	16	281	103
2008–09	Coventry C	45	10		
2009–10	Coventry C	46	11	91	21

OSBOURNE, Isaac (M)   124   0
H: 5 10   W: 11 11   b.Birmingham 22-6-86
Source: Scholar.

2002–03	Coventry C	2	0		
2003–04	Coventry C	0	0		
2004–05	Coventry C	9	0		
2005–06	Coventry C	10	0		
2006–07	Coventry C	19	0		
2006–07	Crewe Alex	2	0	2	0
2007–08	Coventry C	42	0		
2008–09	Coventry C	25	0		
2009–10	Coventry C	15	0	122	0

TURNER, Ben (D)   67   0
H: 6 4   W: 14 04   b.Birmingham 21-1-88
Source: Scholar. *Honours:* England Youth.

2005–06	Coventry C	1	0		
2006–07	Coventry C	1	0		
2006–07	Peterborough U	8	0	8	0
2006–07	Oldham Ath	1	0	1	0
2007–08	Coventry C	19	0		
2008–09	Coventry C	24	0		
2009–10	Coventry C	13	0	58	0

WARD, Elliot (D)   161 16
H: 6 2   W: 13 00   b.Harrow 19-1-85
Source: Scholar.

2001–02	West Ham U	0	0		
2002–03	West Ham U	0	0		
2003–04	West Ham U	0	0		
2004–05	West Ham U	11	0		
2004–05	Bristol R	3	0	3	0
2005–06	West Ham U	4	0	15	0
2005–06	Plymouth Arg	16	1	16	1
2006–07	Coventry C	39	3		
2007–08	Coventry C	37	6		
2008–09	Coventry C	33	5		
2009–10	Coventry C	8	0	117	14
2009–10	Doncaster R	6	1	6	1
2009–10	Preston NE	4	0	4	0

WESTWOOD, Keiren (G)   217   0
H: 6 1   W: 13 10   b.Manchester 23-10-84
Source: Scholar. *Honours:* Eire 5 full caps.

2001–02	Manchester C	0	0	
2002–03	Manchester C	0	0	
2003–04	Manchester C	0	0	
2003–04	Oldham Ath	0	0	
2004–05	Manchester C	0	0	
2005–06	Manchester C	0	0	
2005–06	Carlisle U	35	0	
2006–07	Carlisle U	46	0	
2007–08	Carlisle U	46	0	127	0
2008–09	Coventry C	46	0	
2009–10	Coventry C	44	0	90	0

WILSON, Callum (M)   0   0
H: 5 11   W: 10 06   b.Coventry 27-2-92
Source: Scholar.

2009–10	Coventry C	0	0

WOOD, Richard (D)   195 10
H: 6 3   W: 12 13   b.Wakefield 5-7-85
Source: Scholar.

2002–03	Sheffield W	3	1
2003–04	Sheffield W	12	0
2004–05	Sheffield W	34	1
2005–06	Sheffield W	30	1

2006–07	Sheffield W	12	0		
2007–08	Sheffield W	27	2		
2008–09	Sheffield W	42	0		
2009–10	Sheffield W	11	2	171	7
2009–10	Coventry C	24	3	24	3

WRIGHT, Stephen (D)   200   2
H: 6 0   W: 12 06   b.Liverpool 8-2-80
Source: Trainee. *Honours:* England Youth, Under-21.

1997–98	Liverpool	0	0		
1998–99	Liverpool	0	0		
1999–2000	Liverpool	0	0		
1999–2000	Crewe Alex	23	0	23	0
2000–01	Liverpool	2	0		
2001–02	Liverpool	12	0	14	0
2002–03	Sunderland	26	0		
2003–04	Sunderland	22	1		
2004–05	Sunderland	39	1		
2005–06	Sunderland	2	0		
2006–07	Sunderland	3	0		
2007–08	Sunderland	0	0	92	2
2007–08	Stoke C	16	0	16	0
2008–09	Coventry C	17	0		
2009–10	Coventry C	38	0	55	0

CREWE ALEX (28)

ADA, Patrick (D)   18   0
H: 6 0   W: 13 05   b.Yaounde 14-1-85
Source: Redbridge, Barnet, St Albans C, Exeter C, Histon.

2009–10	Crewe Alex	18	0	18	0

BAILEY, James (M)   46   0
H: 6 0   W: 12 05   b.Bollington 18-9-88
Source: Scholar.

2006–07	Crewe Alex	0	0		
2007–08	Crewe Alex	1	0		
2008–09	Crewe Alex	24	0		
2009–10	Crewe Alex	21	0	46	0

BRAYFORD, John (D)   81   2
H: 5 8   W: 11 02   b.Stoke 29-12-87
Source: Burton Alb.

2008–09	Crewe Alex	36	2		
2009–10	Crewe Alex	45	0	81	2

CLEMENTS, Chris (M)   0   0
H: 5 9   W: 10 05   b.Birmingham 6-2-90
Source: Scholar.

2008–09	Crewe Alex	0	0
2009–10	Crewe Alex	0	0

CONNERTON, Jordan (F)   0   0
b.Lancaster 2-10-89
Source: Lancaster C, Chorley, Kendal, Lancaster C.

2009–10	Crewe Alex	0	0

DAVIS, Harry (D)   1   0
H: 6 2   W: 12 04   b.Burnley 24-9-91
Source: Scholar.

2009–10	Crewe Alex	1	0	1	0

DONALDSON, Clayton (F)   93   24
H: 6 1   W: 11 07   b.Bradford 7-2-84
Source: Scholar.

2002–03	Hull C	2	0		
2003–04	Hull C	0	0		
2004–05	Hull C	0	0	2	0
From York C					
2007–08	Hibernian	17	5	17	5
2008–09	Crewe Alex	37	6		
2009–10	Crewe Alex	37	13	74	19

ELDING, Anthony (F)   122 34
H: 6 1   W: 12 02   b.Boston 16-4-82
Source: Trainee.

2002–03	Boston U	0	0		
From Stevenage B, Kettering T.					
2006–07	Boston U	19	5	27	5
2006–07	Stockport Co	20	11		
2007–08	Stockport Co	25	13	45	24
2007–08	Leeds U	9	1	9	1
2008–09	Crewe Alex	16	1		
2008–09	Lincoln C	15	3	15	3
2009–10	Crewe Alex	10	0	26	1

GARDNER, Danny (F)   2   0
H: 6 1   W: 12 08   b.Manchester 30-11-89

2009–10	Crewe Alex	2	0	2	0

GRANT, Joel (F)   78 11
H: 6 0   W: 12 01   b.Hammersmith 26-8-87
Source: Scholar.

2005–06	Watford	7	0	
2006–07	Watford	0	0	7 0

From Aldershot T.

2008–09	Crewe Alex	28	2	
2009–10	Crewe Alex	43	9	71 11

JONES, Billy (D)   155 8
H: 6 1   W: 11 05   b.Chatham 26-3-83
Source: Trainee.

2000–01	Leyton Orient	1	0	
2001–02	Leyton Orient	16	0	
2002–03	Leyton Orient	24	0	
2003–04	Leyton Orient	31	0	
2004–05	Leyton Orient	0	0	72 0
2004–05	Kidderminster H	12	0	
2005–06	Kidderminster H	0	0	
2006–07	Kidderminster H	0	0	12 0
2007–08	Crewe Alex	22	0	
2008–09	Crewe Alex	38	6	
2009–10	Crewe Alex	11	2	71 8

LEGZDINS, Adam (G)   6 0
H: 6 1   W: 14 02   b.Stafford 28-11-86
Source: Scholar.

2006–07	Birmingham C	0	0	
2007–08	Birmingham C	0	0	
2008–09	Crewe Alex	0	0	
2009–10	Crewe Alex	6	0	6 0

LEITCH-SMITH, AJ (F)   19 5
H: 5 11   W: 12 04   b.Crewe 6-3-90
Source: Scholar.

2008–09	Crewe Alex	0	0	
2009	IBV	18	5	18 5
2009–10	Crewe Alex	1	0	1 0

MARTIN, Carl (D)   6 1
H: 5 8   W: 10 07   b.London 24-10-86
Source: Wealdstone.

2009–10	Crewe Alex	6	1	6 1

MELLOR, Kelvin (D)   0 0
H: 5 10   W: 11 09   b.Copenhagen 5-4-90
Source: Nantwich T.

2007–08	Crewe Alex	0	0	
2008–09	Crewe Alex	0	0	
2009–10	Crewe Alex	0	0	

MILLER, Shaun (F)   88 15
H: 5 10   W: 11 08   b.Alsager 25-9-87
Source: Scholar.

2006–07	Crewe Alex	7	3	
2007–08	Crewe Alex	15	1	
2008–09	Crewe Alex	33	4	
2009–10	Crewe Alex	33	7	88 15

MITCHEL-KING, Mat (D)   32 0
H: 6 4   W: 13 00   b.Cambridge 12-9-83
Source: Cambridge C, Mildenhall T, Histon.

2009–10	Crewe Alex	32	0	32 0

MOORE, Byron (M)   101 9
H: 6 0   W: 10 06   b.Stoke 24-8-88
Source: Scholar.

2006–07	Crewe Alex	0	0	
2007–08	Crewe Alex	33	3	
2008–09	Crewe Alex	36	3	
2009–10	Crewe Alex	32	3	101 9

MURPHY, Luke (M)   41 4
H: 6 1   W: 11 05   b.Alsager 21-10-89
Source: Scholar.

2008–09	Crewe Alex	9	1	
2009–10	Crewe Alex	32	3	41 4

O'DONNELL, Daniel (D)   103 3
H: 6 2   W: 11 11   b.Liverpool 10-3-86
Source: Scholar.

2004–05	Liverpool	0	0	
2005–06	Liverpool	0	0	
2006–07	Liverpool	0	0	
2006–07	Crewe Alex	25	1	
2007–08	Crewe Alex	27	1	
2008–09	Crewe Alex	24	1	
2009–10	Crewe Alex	27	0	103 3

SARCEVIC, Antoni (M)   0 0
H: 5 10   W: 11 00   b. 13-3-92
Source: Woodley Sports.

2009–10	Crewe Alex	0	0	

SCHUMACHER, Steven (M)   194 20
H: 5 10   W: 11 00   b.Liverpool 30-4-84
Source: Scholar. Honours: England Youth.

2000–01	Everton	0	0	
2001–02	Everton	0	0	
2002–03	Everton	0	0	
2003–04	Everton	0	0	
2003–04	Carlisle U	4	0	4 0
2004–05	Bradford C	43	6	
2005–06	Bradford C	30	2	
2006–07	Bradford C	44	6	117 13
2007–08	Crewe Alex	26	1	
2008–09	Crewe Alex	15	2	
2009–10	Crewe Alex	32	4	73 7

SHELLEY, Danny (D)   22 1
H: 5 9   W: 10 08   b.Stoke 29-12-90
Source: Scholar.

2008–09	Crewe Alex	3	0	
2009–10	Crewe Alex	19	1	22 1

STOKES, Chris (M)   2 0
H: 5 7   W: 10 04   b.Trowbridge 8-3-91

2009–10	Crewe Alex	2	0	2 0

TITCHINER, Alex (F)   0 0
H: 6 4   W: 13 12   b.Wales 13-6-91

2009–10	Crewe Alex	0	0	

TOOTLE, Matt (D)   28 1
H: 5 9   W: 11 00   b.Knowsley 11-10-90
Source: Scholar.

2009–10	Crewe Alex	28	1	28 1

WESTWOOD, Ashley (D)   38 6
H: 5 10   W: 11 00   b.Nantwich 1-4-90
Source: Scholar.

2008–09	Crewe Alex	2	0	
2009–10	Crewe Alex	36	6	38 6

ZOLA, Calvin (F)   182 41
H: 6 3   W: 14 06   b.Kinshasa 31-12-84
Source: Scholar.

2001–02	Newcastle U	0	0	
2002–03	Newcastle U	0	0	
2003–04	Newcastle U	0	0	
2003–04	Oldham Ath	25	5	25 5
2004–05	Tranmere R	15	2	
2005–06	Tranmere R	22	4	
2006–07	Tranmere R	29	5	
2007–08	Tranmere R	30	5	96 16
2008–09	Crewe Alex	27	5	
2009–10	Crewe Alex	34	15	61 20

CRYSTAL PALACE (29)

AMBROSE, Darren (M)   234 41
H: 6 0   W: 11 00   b.Harlow 29-2-84
Source: Scholar. Honours: England Youth,
Under-20, Under-21.

2001–02	Ipswich T	1	0	
2002–03	Ipswich T	29	8	
2002–03	Newcastle U	1	0	
2003–04	Newcastle U	24	2	
2004–05	Newcastle U	12	3	37 5
2005–06	Charlton Ath	28	3	
2006–07	Charlton Ath	26	3	
2007–08	Charlton Ath	37	7	
2008–09	Charlton Ath	21	0	112 13
2008–09	Ipswich T	9	0	39 8
2009–10	Crystal Palace	46	15	46 15

ANDREW, Calvin (F)   109 8
H: 6 0   W: 12 11   b.Luton 19-12-86
Source: Scholar.

2004–05	Luton T	8	0	
2005–06	Luton T	1	1	
2005–06	Grimsby T	8	1	8 1
2005–06	Bristol C	3	0	3 0
2006–07	Luton T	7	1	
2007–08	Luton T	39	2	55 4
2008–09	Crystal Palace	7	0	
2008–09	Brighton & HA	9	2	9 2
2009–10	Crystal Palace	27	1	34 1

BUTTERFIELD, Danny (D)   368 9
H: 5 10   W: 11 06   b.Boston 21-11-79
Source: Trainee. Honours: England Youth.

1997–98	Grimsby T	7	0	
1998–99	Grimsby T	12	0	

1999–2000	Grimsby T	29	0	
2000–01	Grimsby T	30	1	
2001–02	Grimsby T	46	2	124 3
2002–03	Crystal Palace	46	1	
2003–04	Crystal Palace	45	4	
2004–05	Crystal Palace	7	0	
2005–06	Crystal Palace	13	0	
2006–07	Crystal Palace	28	0	
2007–08	Crystal Palace	30	0	
2008–09	Crystal Palace	26	1	
2008–09	Charlton Ath	12	0	12 0
2009–10	Crystal Palace	37	0	232 6

CADOGAN, Kieron (M)   6 1
H: 6 4   W: 12 07   b.Tooting 3-8-90
Source: Scholar.

2007–08	Crystal Palace	0	0	
2008–09	Crystal Palace	4	1	
2009–10	Crystal Palace	0	0	4 1
2009–10	Burton Alb	2	0	2 0

CARLE, Nick (F)   257 31
H: 5 9   W: 12 04   b.Sydney 23-11-81
Honours: Australia Youth, Under-20,
Under-23, 12 full caps.

1997–98	Sydney Olympic	16	3	
1998–99	Sydney Olympic	11	3	
1999–2000	Sydney Olympic	24	1	
2000–01	Sydney Olympic	23	2	
2001–02	Sydney Olympic	12	3	86 12
2001–02	Troyes	5	0	
2002–03	Troyes	0	0	5 0
2003–04	Marconi Stallions	24	6	
2004	Ryde City	7	1	7 1
2004–05	Marconi Stallions	0	0	24 6
2005–06	Newcastle U Jets	22	3	
2006–07	Newcastle U Jets	23	4	45 7
2007–08	Genclerbirligi	14	1	14 1
2007–08	Bristol C	17	0	17 0
2008–09	Crystal Palace	37	3	
2009–10	Crystal Palace	22	1	59 4

CLYNE, Nathaniel (D)   48 1
H: 5 9   W: 10 07   b.Stockwell 5-4-91
Source: Scholar. Honours: England Youth.

2008–09	Crystal Palace	26	0	
2009–10	Crystal Palace	22	1	48 1

DANNS, Neil (M)   194 35
H: 5 10   W: 10 12   b.Liverpool 23-11-82
Source: Scholar.

2000–01	Blackburn R	0	0	
2001–02	Blackburn R	0	0	
2002–03	Blackburn R	2	0	
2003–04	Blackpool	12	2	12 2
2003–04	Blackburn R	1	0	
2003–04	Hartlepool U	9	1	9 1
2004–05	Blackburn R	0	0	3 0
2004–05	Colchester U	32	11	
2005–06	Colchester U	41	8	73 19
2006–07	Birmingham C	29	3	
2007–08	Birmingham C	2	0	31 3
2007–08	Crystal Palace	4	0	
2008–09	Crystal Palace	20	2	
2009–10	Crystal Palace	42	8	66 10

DAVIS, Claude (D)   170 4
H: 6 3   W: 14 04   b.Kingston, Jam 6-3-79
Source: Portmore U. Honours: Jamaica 64 full
caps, 2 goals.

2003–04	Preston NE	22	1	
2004–05	Preston NE	32	0	
2005–06	Preston NE	40	3	94 4
2006–07	Sheffield U	21	0	21 0
2007–08	Derby Co	19	0	
2008–09	Derby Co	8	0	
2008–09	Crystal Palace	7	0	
2009–10	Derby Co	0	0	27 0
2009–10	Crystal Palace	21	0	28 0

DERRY, Shaun (M)   476 11
H: 5 10   W: 10 13   b.Nottingham 6-12-77
Source: Trainee.

1995–96	Notts Co	12	0	
1996–97	Notts Co	39	2	
1997–98	Notts Co	28	2	79 4
1997–98	Sheffield U	12	0	
1998–99	Sheffield U	26	0	
1999–2000	Sheffield U	34	0	72 0
1999–2000	Portsmouth	9	1	
2000–01	Portsmouth	28	0	
2001–02	Portsmouth	12	0	49 1

Season	Club				
2002–03	Crystal Palace	39	1		
2003–04	Crystal Palace	37	2		
2004–05	Crystal Palace	7	0		
2004–05	*Nottingham F*	7	0	7	0
2004–05	Leeds U	7	2		
2005–06	Leeds U	41	0		
2006–07	Leeds U	23	1		
2007–08	Leeds U	0	0	71	3
2007–08	Crystal Palace	30	0		
2008–09	Crystal Palace	39	0		
2009–10	Crystal Palace	46	0	198	3

DJILALI, Kieran (M) 22 2
H: 6 3 W: 13 02 b.London 1-1-91
Source: Scholar.

Season	Club				
2008–09	Crystal Palace	6	0		
2009–10	Crystal Palace	8	1	14	1
2009–10	*Chesterfield*	8	1	8	1

ERTL, Johannes (D) 162 6
H: 6 2 W: 12 08 b.Graz 13-11-82
Honours: Austria 7 full caps.

Season	Club				
2003–04	*Kalzdorf*	11	3	11	3
2004–05	Sturm Graz	26	0		
2005–06	Sturm Graz	27	0		
2006–07	Sturm Graz	5	0	58	0
2006–07	FK Austria	24	1		
2007–08	FK Austria	24	2	48	3
2008–09	Crystal Palace	12	0		
2009–10	Crystal Palace	33	0	45	0

FLAHAVAN, Darryl (G) 311 0
H: 5 11 W: 12 05 b.Southampton 9-9-77
Source: Trainee.
From Woking.

Season	Club				
2000–01	Southend U	29	0		
2001–02	Southend U	41	0		
2002–03	Southend U	41	0		
2003–04	Southend U	37	0		
2004–05	Southend U	28	0		
2005–06	Southend U	43	0		
2006–07	Southend U	46	0		
2007–08	Southend U	26	0	291	0
2008–09	Crystal Palace	1	0		
2008–09	*Leeds U*	0	0		
2009–10	Crystal Palace	1	0	2	0
2009–10	*Oldham Ath*	18	0	18	0

HILL, Clint (D) 351 25
H: 6 0 W: 11 06 b.Liverpool 19-10-78
Source: Trainee.

Season	Club				
1997–98	Tranmere R	14	0		
1998–99	Tranmere R	33	4		
1999–2000	Tranmere R	29	5		
2000–01	Tranmere R	34	5		
2001–02	Tranmere R	30	2	140	16
2002–03	Oldham Ath	17	1	17	1
2003–04	Stoke C	12	0		
2004–05	Stoke C	32	1		
2005–06	Stoke C	13	0		
2006–07	Stoke C	18	2		
2007–08	Stoke C	5	0	80	3
2007–08	Crystal Palace	28	3		
2008–09	Crystal Palace	43	1		
2009–10	Crystal Palace	43	1	114	5

HILLS, Lee (D) 50 1
H: 5 10 W: 11 11 b.Croydon 3-4-90
Source: Scholar. *Honours:* England Youth.

Season	Club				
2007–08	Crystal Palace	12	1		
2008–09	Crystal Palace	14	0		
2008–09	*Colchester U*	2	0	2	0
2009–10	Crystal Palace	19	0	45	1
2009–10	*Oldham Ath*	3	0	3	0

JOHN, Stern (F) 399 133
H: 6 1 W: 12 13 b.Tunapuna 30-10-76
Honours: Trinidad & Tobago 109 full caps, 69 goals.

Season	Club				
1998	Columbus Crew	27	26		
1999	Columbus Crew	28	18	55	44
1999–2000	Nottingham F	17	3		
2000–01	Nottingham F	29	2		
2001–02	Nottingham F	26	13	72	18
2001–02	Birmingham C	15	7		
2002–03	Birmingham C	30	5		
2003–04	Birmingham C	29	4		
2004–05	Birmingham C	3	0	77	16
2004–05	Coventry C	30	11		
2005–06	Coventry C	25	10		
2005–06	*Derby Co*	7	0	7	0
2006–07	Coventry C	23	5	78	26
2006–07	Sunderland	15	4		
2007–08	Sunderland	1	1	16	5
2007–08	Southampton	40	19		
2008–09	Southampton	7	0	47	19
2008–09	*Bristol C*	24	2	24	2
2009–10	Crystal Palace	16	2	16	2
2009–10	*Ipswich T*	7	1	7	1

LAWRENCE, Matt (D) 483 6
H: 6 1 W: 12 12 b.Northampton 19-6-74
Source: Grays Ath. *Honours:* England Schools.

Season	Club				
1995–96	Wycombe W	3	0		
1996–97	Wycombe W	13	1		
1996–97	Fulham	15	0		
1997–98	Fulham	43	0		
1998–99	Wycombe W	1	0	59	0
1998–99	Wycombe W	34	2		
1999–2000	Wycombe W	29	2	79	5
1999–2000	Millwall	9	0		
2000–01	Millwall	45	0		
2001–02	Millwall	26	0		
2002–03	Millwall	33	0		
2003–04	Millwall	36	0		
2004–05	Millwall	44	0		
2005–06	Millwall	31	0	224	0
2006–07	Crystal Palace	34	0		
2007–08	Crystal Palace	37	1		
2008–09	Crystal Palace	32	0		
2009–10	Crystal Palace	18	0	121	1

LEE, Alan (F) 398 93
H: 6 2 W: 13 09 b.Galway 21-8-78
Source: Trainee. *Honours:* Eire Under-21, 10 full caps.

Season	Club				
1995–96	Aston Villa	0	0		
1996–97	Aston Villa	0	0		
1997–98	Aston Villa	0	0		
1998–99	Aston Villa	0	0		
1998–99	*Torquay U*	7	2	7	2
1998–99	*Port Vale*	11	2	11	2
1999–2000	Burnley	15	0		
2000–01	Burnley	0	0	15	0
2000–01	Rotherham U	31	13		
2001–02	Rotherham U	38	9		
2002–03	Rotherham U	41	15		
2003–04	Rotherham U	1	0	111	37
2003–04	Cardiff C	23	3		
2004–05	Cardiff C	38	5		
2005–06	Cardiff C	25	2	86	10
2005–06	Ipswich T	14	4		
2006–07	Ipswich T	41	16		
2007–08	Ipswich T	45	11		
2008–09	Ipswich T	3	0	103	31
2008–09	Crystal Palace	16	3		
2008–09	*Norwich C*	7	2	7	2
2009–10	Crystal Palace	42	6	58	9

McCARTHY, Patrick (D) 166 8
H: 6 2 W: 13 07 b.Dublin 31-5-83
Source: Scholar. *Honours:* Eire Youth, B, Under-21.

Season	Club				
2000–01	Manchester C	0	0		
2001–02	Manchester C	0	0		
2002–03	Manchester C	0	0		
2002–03	*Boston U*	12	0	12	0
2002–03	*Notts Co*	6	0	6	0
2003–04	Manchester C	0	0		
2004–05	Manchester C	0	0		
2004–05	Leicester C	12	0		
2005–06	Leicester C	38	2		
2006–07	Leicester C	22	1	72	3
2007–08	Charlton Ath	29	2	29	2
2008–09	Crystal Palace	27	3		
2009–10	Crystal Palace	20	0	47	3

N'DIAYE, Alassane (M) 26 3
H: 6 4 W: 14 02 b.Audincourt 25-2-90
Source: Scholar.

Season	Club				
2008–09	Crystal Palace	0	0		
2009–10	Crystal Palace	26	3	26	3

PINNEY, Nathaniel (F) 1 0
H: 6 0 W: 12 05 b.South Norwood 16-11-90
Source: Scholar.

Season	Club				
2008–09	Crystal Palace	1	0		
2009–10	Crystal Palace	0	0	1	0

SCANNELL, Sean (F) 74 6
H: 5 9 W: 11 07 b.Cork 21-3-89
Source: Scholar. *Honours:* Eire Youth, Under-21.

Season	Club				
2007–08	Crystal Palace	23	2		
2008–09	Crystal Palace	25	2		
2009–10	Crystal Palace	26	2	74	6

SMITH, Ryan (M) 73 1
H: 5 10 W: 11 00 b.Islington 10-11-86
Source: Scholar. *Honours:* England Youth, Under-21.

Season	Club				
2004–05	Arsenal	0	0		
2005–06	Arsenal	0	0		
2005–06	Leicester C	17	1	17	1
2006–07	Derby Co	15	0	15	0
2006–07	Millwall	6	0		
2007–08	Millwall	16	0		
2008–09	Millwall	1	0	23	0
2008–09	Southampton	13	0		
2009–10	Southampton	0	0	13	0
2009–10	Crystal Palace	5	0	5	0

SPERONI, Julian (G) 245 0
H: 6 0 W: 11 00 b.Buenos Aires 18-5-79
Honours: Argentina Under-20, Under-21.

Season	Club				
1999–2000	Platense	2	0		
2000–01	Platense	0	0	2	0
2001–02	Dundee	17	0		
2002–03	Dundee	38	0		
2003–04	Dundee	37	0	92	0
2004–05	Crystal Palace	6	0		
2005–06	Crystal Palace	4	0		
2006–07	Crystal Palace	5	0		
2007–08	Crystal Palace	46	0		
2008–09	Crystal Palace	45	0		
2009–10	Crystal Palace	45	0	151	0

THOMAS, Simon (F) 10 1
H: 5 6 W: 12 02 b.Stratford 21-7-84
Source: Thurrock, Aveley, Wivenhoe T, Redbridge, Boreham Wood.

Season	Club				
2008–09	Crystal Palace	1	0		
2008–09	*Rotherham U*	2	0	2	0
2009–10	Crystal Palace	0	0	1	0
2009–10	*Darlington*	7	1	7	1

WYNTER, Alex (M) 0 0
H: 6 0 W: 13 04 b.Beckenham 15-9-93
Source: Youth.

Season	Club			
2009–10	Crystal Palace	0	0	

ZAHA, Wilfred (F) 1 0
H: 5 11 W: 10 05 b.Ivory Coast 10-11-92
Source: Scholar.

Season	Club				
2009–10	Crystal Palace	1	0	1	0

DAGENHAM & R (30)

ANTWI, Will (D) 65 2
H: 6 2 W: 12 08 b.Epsom 19-10-82
Source: Scholar. *Honours:* Ghana 1 full cap.

Season	Club				
2002–03	Crystal Palace	4	0		
2003–04	Crystal Palace	0	0	4	0

From Aldershot T

Season	Club				
2005–06	Wycombe W	5	0		
2006–07	Wycombe W	25	1		
2007–08	Wycombe W	6	0		
2008–09	Wycombe W	6	0	42	1
2009–10	Dagenham & R	19	1	19	1

ARBER, Mark (D) 408 32
H: 6 1 W: 11 09 b.Johannesburg 9-10-77
Source: Trainee.

Season	Club				
1995–96	Tottenham H	0	0		
1996–97	Tottenham H	0	0		
1997–98	Tottenham H	0	0		
1998–99	Tottenham H	0	0		
1998–99	Barnet	35	2		
1999–2000	Barnet	45	6		
2000–01	Barnet	45	7		
2001–02	Barnet	0	0	125	15
2002–03	Peterborough U	25	2		
2003–04	Peterborough U	44	3		
2004–05	Oldham Ath	14	1	14	1
2004–05	Peterborough U	21	0		
2005–06	Peterborough U	46	2		
2006–07	Peterborough U	34	1		
2007–08	Peterborough U	0	0	170	8
2007–08	*Dagenham & R*	16	1		

2008–09	Dagenham & R	42	3		
2009–10	Dagenham & R	41	4	99	8

BENSON, Paul (F)   **100 40**
H: 6 1   W: 11 01   b.Rochford 12-10-79
Source: White Notley.

2007–08	Dagenham & R	22	6		
2008–09	Dagenham & R	33	17		
2009–10	Dagenham & R	45	17	100	40

BINGHAM, Billy (D)   **2 0**
H: 5 11   W: 11 02   b.London 15-7-90
Source: Crystal Palace.

2008–09	Dagenham & R	0	0		
2009–10	Dagenham & R	2	0	2	0

CARLOS, Joao (M)   **1 0**
H: 5 10   W: 12 05   b.Rio Tinto 17-7-87
Source: Aveley.

2009–10	Dagenham & R	1	0	1	0

CURRIE, Darren (M)   **551 60**
H: 5 11   W: 12 07   b.Hampstead 29-11-74
Source: Trainee.

1993–94	West Ham U	0	0		
1994–95	West Ham U	0	0		
1994–95	*Shrewsbury T*	17	2		
1995–96	West Ham U	0	0		
1995–96	Leyton Orient	10	0	10	0
1995–96	Shrewsbury T	13	2		
1996–97	Shrewsbury T	37	2		
1997–98	Shrewsbury T	16	4	83	10
1997–98	*Plymouth Arg*	7	0	7	0
1998–99	Barnet	38	4		
1999–2000	Barnet	44	5		
2000–01	Barnet	45	10	127	19
2001–02	Wycombe W	46	3		
2002–03	Wycombe W	38	4		
2003–04	Wycombe W	42	7	126	14
2004–05	Brighton & HA	22	2	22	2
2004–05	Ipswich T	24	3		
2005–06	Ipswich T	46	5		
2006–07	Ipswich T	13	1	83	9
2006–07	*Coventry C*	8	0	8	0
2006–07	*Derby Co*	7	1	7	1
2007–08	Luton T	31	2	31	2
2008–09	Chesterfield	27	3		
2009–10	Chesterfield	4	0	31	3
2009–10	Dagenham & R	16	0	16	0

DEAN, Harlee (M)   **1 0**
H: 6 0   W: 11 10   b.Basingstoke 26-7-91
Source: Scholar.

2008–09	Dagenham & R	0	0		
2009–10	Dagenham & R	1	0	1	0

DEMETRIOU, Stephen (M)   **0 0**
b.Redbridge

2009–10	Dagenham & R	0	0		

DOE, Scott (D)   **42 0**
H: 6 0   W: 11 06   b.Reading 6-11-88
Source: Weymouth, Kettering T.

2009–10	Dagenham & R	42	0	42	0

GAIN, Peter (M)   **390 34**
H: 5 9   W: 11 07   b.Hammersmith 11-11-76
Source: Trainee.

1995–96	Tottenham H	0	0		
1996–97	Tottenham H	0	0		
1997–98	Tottenham H	0	0		
1998–99	Tottenham H	0	0		
1998–99	Lincoln C	4	0		
1999–2000	Lincoln C	32	2		
2000–01	Lincoln C	24	5		
2001–02	Lincoln C	42	2		
2002–03	Lincoln C	43	5		
2003–04	Lincoln C	42	7		
2004–05	Lincoln C	40	0	227	21
2005–06	Peterborough U	37	3		
2006–07	Peterborough U	34	6		
2007–08	Peterborough U	0	0	71	9
2007–08	Dagenham & R	18	1		
2008–09	Dagenham & R	31	0		
2009–10	Dagenham & R	43	3	92	4

GREEN, Danny (M)   **46 13**
H: 5 11   W: 12 00   b.Harlow 9-7-88
Source: Bishop's Stortford.

2006–07	Northampton T	0	0		
2007–08	Northampton T	0	0		
2008–09	Northampton T	0	0		
2009–10	Dagenham & R	46	13	46	13

McCRORY, Damien (M)   **47 0**
H: 6 2   W: 12 10   b.Limerick 22-2-90
Honours: Eire Youth.

2008–09	*Plymouth Arg*	0	0		
2008–09	*Port Vale*	12	0		
2009–10	*Plymouth Arg*	0	0		
2009–10	*Port Vale*	5	0	17	0
2009–10	*Grimsby T*	10	0	10	0
2009–10	Dagenham & R	20	0	20	0

MONTGOMERY, Graeme (M)   **22 2**
H: 6 1   W: 12 00   b.Dagenham 3-3-88
Source: Wealdstone.

2008–09	Dagenham & R	5	0		
2009–10	Dagenham & R	17	2	22	2

NURSE, Jon (F)   **102 12**
H: 5 9   W: 12 04   b.Barbados 28-3-81
Source: Stevenage B. *Honours:* Barbados 4 full caps.

2007–08	Dagenham & R	30	1		
2008–09	Dagenham & R	34	4		
2009–10	Dagenham & R	38	7	102	12

NWOKEJI, Mark (F)   **16 3**
H: 5 11   W: 11 05   b.London 30-1-82
Source: Harlow T, Leatherhead, Chesham U, Walton & Hersham, St Albans C, Staines T.

2008–09	Dagenham & R	16	3		
2009–10	Dagenham & R	0	0	16	3

OGOGO, Abu (D)   **39 3**
H: 5 8   W: 10 02   b.Epsom 3-11-89
Source: Scholar.

2007–08	*Arsenal*	0	0		
2008–09	*Arsenal*	0	0		
2008–09	*Barnet*	9	1	9	1
2009–10	Dagenham & R	30	2	30	2

ROBERTS, Tony (G)   **262 0**
H: 6 0   W: 13 11   b.Holyhead 4-3-69
Source: Trainee. *Honours:* Wales Under-21, 2 full caps.

1987–88	QPR	1	0		
1988–89	QPR	0	0		
1989–90	QPR	5	0		
1990–91	QPR	12	0		
1991–92	QPR	1	0		
1992–93	QPR	28	0		
1993–94	QPR	16	0		
1994–95	QPR	31	0		
1995–96	QPR	5	0		
1996–97	QPR	13	0		
1997–98	QPR	10	0	122	0
1998–99	Millwall	8	0	8	0

From St Albans C.

2007–08	Dagenham & R	43	0		
2008–09	Dagenham & R	43	0		
2009–10	Dagenham & R	46	0	132	0

SCOTT, Josh (F)   **40 10**
H: 6 1   W: 12 00   b.London 10-5-85
Source: Hayes, Hayes & Yeading U.

2009–10	Dagenham & R	40	10	40	10

SPILLER, Danny (M)   **147 7**
H: 5 8   W: 11 00   b.Maidstone 10-10-81
Source: Trainee.

2000–01	Gillingham	0	0		
2001–02	Gillingham	1	0		
2002–03	Gillingham	10	0		
2003–04	Gillingham	39	6		
2004–05	Gillingham	22	0		
2005–06	Gillingham	32	0		
2006–07	Gillingham	25	0	129	6
2007–08	Millwall	6	1		
2008–09	Millwall	2	0		
2009–10	Millwall	0	0	8	1
2009–10	Dagenham & R	10	0	10	0

TEJAN-SIE, Thomas (M)   **4 0**
H: 5 6   W: 11 08   b.London 25-11-88
Source: Leicester C Scholar, Wingate & Finchley.

2007–08	Dagenham & R	0	0		
2008–09	Dagenham & R	1	0		
2009–10	Dagenham & R	3	0	4	0

THOMAS, Wesley (F)   **28 3**
H: 5 10   W: 11 00   b.Barking 23-1-87
Source: QPR Youth, Waltham Forest, Thurrock, Fisher Ath.

2008–09	Dagenham & R	5	0		

2009–10	Dagenham & R	23	3	28	3

THURGOOD, Stuart (M)   **108 1**
H: 5 8   W: 12 03   b.Enfield 4-11-81
From Shimizu S-Pulse

2000–01	Southend U	13	1		
2001–02	Southend U	39	0		
2002–03	Southend U	27	0		
2003–04	Southend U	0	0	79	1

From Grays Ath

2007–08	Gillingham	12	0		
2008–09	Gillingham	0	0	12	0
2009–10	Dagenham & R	17	0	17	0

UDDIN, Anwar (D)   **83 2**
H: 5 11   W: 11 10   b.Whitechapel 1-11-81
Source: West Ham U Scholar.

2001–02	West Ham U	0	0		
2001–02	Sheffield W	0	0		
2002–03	Bristol R	18	1		
2003–04	Bristol R	1	0		
2004–05	Bristol R	0	0		
2005–06	Bristol R	0	0		
2006–07	Bristol R	0	0	19	1
2007–08	Dagenham & R	41	1		
2008–09	Dagenham & R	17	0		
2009–10	Dagenham & R	6	0	64	1

VINCELOT, Romain (M)   **75 2**
H: 5 9   W: 11 02   b.Poitiers 29-10-85
Source:

2004–05	Chamois Niortais	3	0	3	0
2005–06	Chemois Niortais	28	1		
2006–07	Chemois Niortais	9	0		
2007–08	Chemois Niortais	6	0	43	1
2008–09	Gueugnon	20	0	20	0
2009–10	Dagenham & R	9	1	9	1

WALSH, Phil (F)   **9 0**
H: 6 3   W: 13 04   b.Hartlepool 4-2-84
Source: Dorchester T.

2009–10	Dagenham & R	9	0	9	0

DARLINGTON (31)

ARNISON, Paul (D)   **217 5**
H: 5 10   W: 10 12   b.Hartlepool 18-9-77
Source: Trainee.

1995–96	Newcastle U	0	0		
1996–97	Newcastle U	0	0		
1997–98	Newcastle U	0	0		
1998–99	Newcastle U	0	0		
1999–2000	Newcastle U	0	0		
1999–2000	Hartlepool U	8	1		
2000–01	Hartlepool U	27	1		
2001–02	Hartlepool U	19	0		
2002–03	Hartlepool U	19	1		
2003–04	Hartlepool U	4	0	77	3
2003–04	Carlisle U	26	1		
2004–05	Carlisle U	0	0		
2005–06	Carlisle U	41	0		
2006–07	Carlisle U	11	0		
2007–08	Carlisle U	17	0	95	1
2008–09	Bradford C	27	0	27	0
2009–10	Darlington	18	1	18	1

BAINS, Rikki (D)   **9 0**
H: 6 1   W: 13 00   b.Coventry 3-2-88
Source: Scholar.

2006–07	Coventry C	0	0		
2006–07	Accrington S	3	0	3	0

From Tamworth, Corby.

2008–09	Macclesfield T	2	0		
2009–10	Macclesfield T	0	0	2	0
2009–10	Darlington	4	0	4	0

BARNES, Corey (F)   **9 0**
H: 5 8   W: 10 08   b.Sunderland 1-1-92
Source: Scholar.

2008–09	Darlington	3	0		
2009–10	Darlington	6	0	9	0

BENNETT, James (M)   **4 0**
H: 5 10   W: 12 03   b.Beverley 4-9-88
Source: Scholar.

2006–07	Hull C	0	0		
2007–08	Hull C	0	0		
2008–09	Hull C	0	0		
2008–09	*Lincoln C*	0	0		
2009–10	Darlington	4	0	4	0

BOWER, Mark (D)   296 15
H: 5 10   W: 11 00   b.Bradford 23-1-80
Source: Trainee.

Season	Club				
1997–98	Bradford C	3	0		
1998–99	Bradford C	0	0		
1999–2000	Bradford C	0	0		
1999–2000	York C	15	1		
2000–01	Bradford C	0	0		
2000–01	York C	21	1	36	2
2001–02	Bradford C	10	2		
2002–03	Bradford C	37	0		
2003–04	Bradford C	14	0		
2004–05	Bradford C	46	2		
2005–06	Bradford C	45	2		
2006–07	Bradford C	46	3		
2007–08	Bradford C	27	3		
2008–09	Bradford C	3	0	231	14
2008–09	Luton T	16	1	16	1
2009–10	Darlington	13	0	13	0

BURN, Dan (D)   4 0
H: 6 6   W: 13 00   b.Blyth 9-5-92
Source: Scholar.

2009–10	Darlington	4	0	4	0

BYRNE, Ritchie (D)   82 1
H: 6 1   W: 12 05   b.Dublin 24-9-81
Honours: Eire B.

2003–04	Dunfermline Ath	13	0		
2004–05	Dunfermline Ath	6	0	19	0
2004–05	Aberdeen	13	1		
2005–06	Aberdeen	19	0		
2006–07	Aberdeen	5	0		
2007–08	Aberdeen	13	0	50	1
2008–09	Oldham Ath	4	0	4	0
2008–09	Inverness CT	0	0		
2008–09	St Johnstone	5	0	5	0
2009–10	Darlington	4	0	4	0

CHISHOLM, Ross (M)   58 1
H: 5 9   W: 11 07   b.Irvine 14-1-88

2006–07	Hibernian	6	0		
2007–08	Hibernian	18	0		
2008–09	Hibernian	19	0	43	0
2009	Shamrock R	12	1	12	1
2009–10	Darlington	3	0	3	0

CONVERY, Mark (M)   97 3
H: 5 6   W: 10 05   b.Newcastle 29-5-81
Source: Trainee.

1998–99	Sunderland	0	0		
1999–2000	Sunderland	0	0		
2000–01	Sunderland	0	0		
2000–01	Darlington	11	0		
2001–02	Darlington	17	1		
2002–03	Darlington	0	0		
2003–04	Darlington	25	2		
2004–05	Darlington	23	0		
2005–06	Darlington	0	0		
2006–07	Darlington	0	0		
2007–08	Darlington	0	0		
2008–09	Darlington	0	0		
2009–10	Darlington	21	0	97	3

DEANE, Patrick (F)   11 0
H: 5 11   W: 12 08   b.Perth 16-4-90

2009–10	Montrose	1	0	1	0
2009–10	Darlington	10	0	10	0

DEMPSEY, Gary (M)   175 11
H: 5 9   W: 10 04   b.Wexford 15-1-81
Source: Bray W, Waterford.

2002–03	Dunfermline Ath	31	1		
2003–04	Dunfermline Ath	33	5		
2004–05	Dunfermline Ath	17	0	81	6
2004–05	Aberdeen	4	0		
2005–06	Aberdeen	24	0		
2006–07	Aberdeen	26	2	54	2
2007–08	Yeovil T	16	2		
2008–09	Yeovil T	0	0	16	2
2009–10	Darlington	24	1	24	1

DIOP, Mor (F)   23 2
H: 6 0   W: 13 07   b.Paris 29-9-88
Source: Metalurgs Donetsk, Stal (loan), Beerschot, Apollon, PAEEK (loan), Elvissa-Ibiza.

2009–10	Darlington	23	2	23	2

FOSTER, Steve (D)   451 11
H: 6 1   W: 13 00   b.Mansfield 3-12-74
Source: Trainee.

1993–94	Mansfield T	5	0	5	0

From Telford U, Woking

1997–98	Bristol R	34	0		
1998–99	Bristol R	43	1		
1999–2000	Bristol R	43	1		
2000–01	Bristol R	44	4		
2001–02	Bristol R	33	1	197	7
2002–03	Doncaster R	0	0		
2003–04	Doncaster R	44	1		
2004–05	Doncaster R	34	1		
2005–06	Doncaster R	17	0	95	2
2005–06	Scunthorpe U	18	0		
2006–07	Scunthorpe U	44	0	62	0
2007–08	Darlington	42	2		
2008–09	Darlington	34	0		
2009–10	Darlington	16	0	92	2

GALL, Kevin (F)   273 29
H: 5 9   W: 10 08   b.Merthyr 4-2-82
Source: Trainee. *Honours:* Wales Schools, Youth, Under-21.

1998–99	Newcastle U	0	0		
1999–2000	Newcastle U	0	0		
2000–01	Newcastle U	0	0		
2000–01	Bristol R	10	2		
2001–02	Bristol R	31	3		
2002–03	Bristol R	9	0	50	5
2003–04	Yeovil T	43	8		
2004–05	Yeovil T	43	3		
2005–06	Yeovil T	37	2	123	13
2006–07	Carlisle U	45	8		
2007–08	Carlisle U	21	1		
2007–08	Darlington	8	0		
2008–09	Carlisle U	0	0		
2008–09	Lincoln C	9	0	9	0
2008–09	Port Vale	7	0	7	0
2009–10	Carlisle U	0	0	66	9
2009–10	Darlington	10	2	18	2

GRAY, Josh (F)   32 1
H: 6 1   W: 11 12   b.South Shields 22-7-91
Source: Scholar.

2008–09	Darlington	5	0		
2009–10	Darlington	27	1	32	1

GROVES, Danny (M)   17 0
H: 6 2   W: 12 00   b.Darlington 12-10-90
Source: Scholar.

2008–09	Darlington	1	0		
2009–10	Darlington	16	0	17	0

JONES, Ashlee (G)   1 0
H: 6 1   W: 12 07   b.Rushden 4-8-87
Source: Rushden & D, Potters Bar T, Fisher Ath, Crawley T, Wycombe W, Rushden & D.

2009–10	Darlington	1	0	1	0

KNIGHT, David (G)   12 0
H: 6 0   W: 11 07   b.Sunderland 15-1-87
Source: Scholar. *Honours:* England Youth.

2004–05	Middlesbrough	0	0		
2005–06	Middlesbrough	0	0		
2005–06	Darlington	3	0		
2006–07	Middlesbrough	0	0		
2006–07	Oldham Ath	2	0	2	0
2007–08	Swansea C	0	0		
2008–09	Middlesbrough	0	0		
2009–10	Darlington	7	0	10	0

LIVERSEDGE, Nick (G)   13 0
H: 6 1   W: 11 07   b.Huddersfield 18-7-88
Source: Scholar.

2007–08	Darlington	0	0		
2008–09	Darlington	0	0		
2009–10	Darlington	13	0	13	0

LUMSDON, Chris (M)   235 23
H: 5 11   W: 10 06   b.Newcastle 15-12-79
Source: Trainee.

1997–98	Sunderland	1	0		
1998–99	Sunderland	0	0		
1999–2000	Sunderland	1	0		
1999–2000	Blackpool	6	1	6	1
2000–01	Sunderland	0	0		
2000–01	Crewe Alex	16	0	16	0
2001–02	Sunderland	0	0	2	0
2001–02	Barnsley	32	7		
2002–03	Barnsley	25	3		
2003–04	Barnsley	28	3		

2004–05	Barnsley	0	0	85	13
2005–06	Carlisle U	38	7		
2006–07	Carlisle U	39	2		
2007–08	Carlisle U	40	0		
2008–09	Carlisle U	7	0	124	9
2009–10	Darlington	2	0	2	0

MADDEN, Simon (D)   15 0
H: 5 9   W: 11 10   b.Dublin 1-5-88
Source: Shelbourne.

2005–06	Leeds U	0	0		
2006–07	Leeds U	0	0		
2007–08	Leeds U	0	0		
2008–09	Leeds U	0	0		
2009–10	Leeds U	0	0		
2009–10	Darlington	15	0	15	0

MAIN, Curtis (F)   45 5
H: 5 9   W: 12 02   b.South Shields 20-6-92
Source: Scholar.

2007–08	Darlington	1	0		
2008–09	Darlington	18	2		
2009–10	Darlington	26	3	45	5

MARSHALL, Jordan (F)   3 0
H: 5 11   W: 11 09   b.Gateshead 10-5-93
Source: Scholar.

2009–10	Darlington	3	0	3	0

McREADY, John (M)   4 0
H: 5 10   W: 11 07   b.South Shields 1-7-92
Source: Scholar.

2009–10	Darlington	4	0	4	0

MILLER, Ian (M)   109 5
H: 6 2   W: 12 02   b.Colchester 23-11-83

2006–07	Ipswich T	1	0		
2006–07	Boston U	12	0	12	0
2006–07	Darlington	7	1		
2007–08	Ipswich T	0	0	1	0
2007–08	Darlington	28	2		
2008–09	Darlington	21	1		
2009–10	Darlington	40	1	96	5

MOORE, Chris (M)   11 0
H: 5 9   W: 12 00   b.Newcastle 17-1-84
Source: Whitley Bay.

2009–10	Darlington	11	0	11	0

MULLIGAN, Nathan (M)   16 1
H: 5 10   W: 11 07   b.Ingleby Barwick 23-8-83
Source: Norton & Stockton Ancients.

2009–10	Darlington	16	1	16	1

PLUMMER, Matt (D)   8 0
H: 6 1   W: 12 01   b.Hull 18-1-89
Source: Scholar.

2006–07	Hull C	0	0		
2007–08	Hull C	0	0		
2008–09	Hull C	0	0		
2009–10	Darlington	8	0	8	0

PURCELL, Tadgh (F)   102 27
H: 5 11   W: 11 08   b.Dundrum 9-2-85
Source: UCD, Kilkenny City.

2007	Shamrock R	28	12		
2008	Shamrock R	28	4		
2009	Shamrock R	24	2	80	18
2009–10	Darlington	22	9	22	9

SMITH, Gary (M)   149 10
H: 5 8   W: 10 09   b.Middlesbrough 30-1-84
Source: Trainee.

2002–03	Middlesbrough	0	0		
2003–04	Middlesbrough	0	0		
2003–04	Wimbledon	11	3	11	3
2004–05	Milton Keynes D	23	1		
2005–06	Milton Keynes D	25	3		
2006–07	Milton Keynes D	23	1	71	5
2007–08	Brentford	29	1		
2008–09	Brentford	4	0	33	1
2009–10	Darlington	34	1	34	1

SMITH, Jeff (M)   187 9
H: 5 11   W: 11 10   b.Middlesbrough 28-6-80
Source: Trainee.

1998–99	Hartlepool U	3	0		
1999–2000	Hartlepool U	0	0	3	0

From Bishop Auckland

2000–01	Bolton W	0	0		
2001–02	Macclesfield T	8	2	8	2
2001–02	Bolton W	1	0		
2002–03	Bolton W	0	0		

2003–04	Bolton W	0	0	2	0
2003–04	Scunthorpe U	1	0	1	0
2003–04	Rochdale	1	0	1	0
2003–04	Preston NE	5	0	5	0
2004–05	Port Vale	34	1		
2005–06	Port Vale	27	1		
2006–07	Port Vale	27	3	88	5
2006–07	Carlisle U	17	1		
2007–08	Carlisle U	22	1		
2008–09	Carlisle U	16	0	55	2
2009–10	Darlington	24	0	24	0

SMITH, Michael (F)   7   1
H: 5 11 W: 11 02 b.Wallsend 17-10-91
Source: Scholar.

2009–10	Darlington	7	1	7	1

THORPE, Lee (F)   438   98
H: 6 0 W: 11 06 b.Wolverhampton 14-12-75
Source: Trainee.

1993–94	Blackpool	1	0		
1994–95	Blackpool	1	0		
1995–96	Blackpool	1	0		
1996–97	Blackpool	9	0	12	0
1997–98	Lincoln C	44	14		
1998–99	Lincoln C	38	8		
1999–2000	Lincoln C	42	16		
2000–01	Lincoln C	31	7		
2001–02	Lincoln C	37	13	192	58
2001–02	Leyton Orient	0	0		
2002–03	Leyton Orient	38	8		
2003–04	Leyton Orient	17	4	55	12
2003–04	*Grimsby T*	6	0	6	0
2003–04	Bristol R	10	1		
2004–05	Bristol R	25	3	35	4
2004–05	Swansea C	15	3		
2005–06	Swansea C	3	0	18	3
2005–06	*Peterborough U*	6	0	6	0
2005–06	Torquay U	10	3		
2006–07	Torquay U	41	8	51	11
2007–08	Brentford	19	4	19	4
2007–08	Rochdale	8	1		
2008–09	Rochdale	28	5	36	6
2009–10	Darlington	8	0	8	0

WAITE, Gareth (M)   14   1
H: 6 1 W: 13 01 b.Stockton 16-2-86
Source: Spennymoor T.

2009–10	Darlington	14	1	14	1

WHELAN, Noel (F)   321   60
H: 6 2 W: 12 03 b.Leeds 30-12-74
Source: Trainee. *Honours:* England Under-21.

1992–93	Leeds U	1	0		
1993–94	Leeds U	16	0		
1994–95	Leeds U	23	7		
1995–96	Leeds U	8	0	48	7
1995–96	Coventry C	21	8		
1996–97	Coventry C	35	6		
1997–98	Coventry C	21	6		
1998–99	Coventry C	31	10		
1999–2000	Coventry C	26	1	134	31
2000–01	Middlesbrough	27	1		
2001–02	Middlesbrough	19	4		
2002–03	Middlesbrough	15	1	61	6
2002–03	*Crystal Palace*	8	3	8	3
2003–04	Millwall	15	4	15	4
2003–04	Derby Co	8	0	8	0
2004–05	Aberdeen	20	4	20	4
2005–06	Boston U	15	4	15	4
2005–06	Livingston	8	1	8	1
2006–07	Dunfermline Ath	1	0	1	0

From Harrogate T.

2009–10	Darlington	3	0	3	0

WHITE, Alan (D)   438   23
H: 6 0 W: 13 04 b.Darlington 22-3-76
Source: Derby Co Schoolboy.

1994–95	Middlesbrough	0	0		
1995–96	Middlesbrough	0	0		
1996–97	Middlesbrough	0	0		
1997–98	Middlesbrough	0	0		
1997–98	Luton T	28	1		
1998–99	Luton T	33	1		
1999–2000	Luton T	19	1	80	3
1999–2000	Colchester U	4	0		
2000–01	Colchester U	37	0		
2001–02	Colchester U	33	3		
2002–03	Colchester U	41	0		
2003–04	Colchester U	33	1	143	4
2004–05	Leyton Orient	26	0	26	0
2004–05	Boston U	11	0		
2005–06	Boston U	37	4	48	4
2005–07	Notts Co	35	5	35	5
2005–07	*Peterborough U*	7	3	7	3
2007–08	Darlington	35	1		
2008–09	Darlington	40	2		
2009–10	Darlington	24	1	99	4

WINDASS, Dean (F)   634   199
H: 5 10 W: 12 03 b.North Ferriby 1-4-69
Source: N Ferriby U.

1991–92	Hull C	32	6		
1992–93	Hull C	41	7		
1993–94	Hull C	43	23		
1994–95	Hull C	44	17		
1995–96	Hull C	16	4		
1995–96	Aberdeen	20	6		
1996–97	Aberdeen	29	10		
1997–98	Aberdeen	24	5	73	21
1998–99	Oxford U	33	15	33	15
1998–99	Bradford C	12	3		
1999–2000	Bradford C	38	10		
2000–01	Bradford C	24	3		
2000–01	Middlesbrough	8	2		
2001–02	Middlesbrough	27	1		
2001–02	*Sheffield W*	2	0	2	0
2002–03	Middlesbrough	2	0	37	3
2002–03	Sheffield U	20	6	20	6
2003–04	Bradford C	36	6		
2004–05	Bradford C	41	27		
2005–06	Bradford C	40	16		
2006–07	Bradford C	25	11	216	76
2006–07	Hull C	18	8		
2007–08	Hull C	37	11		
2008–09	Hull C	5	1	236	77
2008–09	*Oldham Ath*	11	1	11	1
2009–10	Darlington	6	0	6	0

DERBY CO (32)

ABALIMBA, Medi (M)   0   0
Source: Southend U.

2009–10	Derby Co	0	0		

ADDISON, Miles (D)   44   3
H: 6 2 W: 13 03 b.London 7-1-89
Source: Scholar. *Honours:* England Under-21.

2005–06	Derby Co	2	0		
2006–07	Derby Co	0	0		
2007–08	Derby Co	1	0		
2008–09	Derby Co	28	1		
2009–10	Derby Co	13	2	44	3

ANDERSON, Russell (D)   308   19
H: 5 11 W: 10 09 b.Aberdeen 25-10-78
Source: Dyce J. *Honours:* Scotland Under-21, 11 full caps.

1996–97	Aberdeen	14	0		
1997–98	Aberdeen	26	0		
1998–99	Aberdeen	16	0		
1999–2000	Aberdeen	34	1		
2000–01	Aberdeen	0	0		
2001–02	Aberdeen	24	1		
2002–03	Aberdeen	33	2		
2003–04	Aberdeen	25	5		
2004–05	Aberdeen	31	1		
2005–06	Aberdeen	36	6		
2006–07	Aberdeen	35	2	274	18
2007–08	Sunderland	1	0		
2007–08	*Plymouth Arg*	14	0	14	0
2008–09	Sunderland	0	0		
2008–09	*Burnley*	4	0	4	0
2009–10	Sunderland	0	0	1	0
2009–10	Derby Co	15	1	15	1

ATKINS, Ross (G)   0   0
H: 6 0 W: 12 01 b.Derby 3-11-89
Source: Scholar.

2008–09	Derby Co	0	0		
2009–10	Derby Co	0	0		

BALL, Callum (F)   1   0
H: 6 1 W: 10 03 b.Leicester 8-10-92
Source: Scholar.

2009–10	Derby Co	1	0	1	0

BARKER, Shaun (D)   292   17
H: 6 2 W: 12 08 b.Nottingham 19-9-82
Source: Scholar.

2002–03	Rotherham U	11	0		
2003–04	Rotherham U	36	2		
2004–05	Rotherham U	33	2		
2005–06	Rotherham U	43	3	123	7
2006–07	Blackpool	45	3		
2007–08	Blackpool	46	2		
2008–09	Blackpool	43	0	134	5
2009–10	Derby Co	35	5	35	5

BUXTON, Jake (D)   170   6
H: 6 1 W: 13 05 b.Sutton-in-Ashfield 4-3-85
Source: Scholar.

2002–03	Mansfield T	3	0		
2003–04	Mansfield T	9	1		
2004–05	Mansfield T	30	1		
2005–06	Mansfield T	39	0		
2006–07	Mansfield T	30	1		
2007–08	Mansfield T	40	2		
2008–09	Mansfield T	0	0	151	5

From Burton Alb.

2008–09	Derby Co	0	0		
2009–10	Derby Co	19	1	19	1

BYWATER, Steve (G)   224   0
H: 6 2 W: 12 10 b.Manchester 7-6-81
Source: Trainee. *Honours:* England Youth, Under-20, Under-21.

1997–98	Rochdale	0	0		
1998–99	West Ham U	0	0		
1999–2000	West Ham U	4	0		
1999–2000	Wycombe W	2	0	2	0
1999–2000	*Hull C*	4	0	4	0
2000–01	West Ham U	1	0		
2001–02	West Ham U	0	0		
2001–02	Wolverhampton W	0	0		
2001–02	*Cardiff C*	0	0		
2002–03	West Ham U	0	0		
2003–04	West Ham U	17	0		
2004–05	West Ham U	36	0		
2005–06	West Ham U	1	0		
2005–06	*Coventry C*	14	0	14	0
2006–07	West Ham U	0	0	59	0
2006–07	Derby Co	37	0		
2007–08	Derby Co	18	0		
2007–08	*Ipswich T*	17	0	17	0
2008–09	Derby Co	31	0		
2009–10	Derby Co	42	0	128	0

COMMONS, Kris (M)   233   45
H: 5 6 W: 9 08 b.Mansfield 30-8-83
Source: Scholar. *Honours:* Scotland 6 full caps.

2000–01	Stoke C	0	0		
2001–02	Stoke C	0	0		
2002–03	Stoke C	8	1		
2003–04	Stoke C	33	4	41	5
2004–05	Nottingham F	30	6		
2005–06	Nottingham F	37	8		
2006–07	Nottingham F	32	9		
2007–08	Nottingham F	39	9	138	32
2008–09	Derby Co	34	5		
2009–10	Derby Co	20	3	54	8

CONNOLLY, Paul (D)   230   2
H: 6 0 W: 11 09 b.Liverpool 29-9-83
Source: Scholar.

2000–01	Plymouth Arg	1	0		
2001–02	Plymouth Arg	0	0		
2002–03	Plymouth Arg	2	0		
2003–04	Plymouth Arg	29	0		
2004–05	Plymouth Arg	19	0		
2005–06	Plymouth Arg	31	0		
2006–07	Plymouth Arg	38	0		
2007–08	Plymouth Arg	42	1	162	1
2008–09	Derby Co	40	1		
2009–10	Derby Co	21	0	61	1
2009–10	*Sheffield U*	7	0	7	0

CONNOLLY, Ryan (M)   1   0
H: 5 10 W: 10 04 b.Castlebar 13-1-92
Source: Scholar.

2009–10	Derby Co	1	0	1	0

CROFT, Lee (F) 177 11
H: 5 11 W: 13 00 b.Wigan 21-6-85
Source: Scholar. Honours: England Youth, Under-20.

2002–03	Manchester C	0	0	
2003–04	Manchester C	0	0	
2004–05	Manchester C	7	0	
2004–05	*Oldham Ath*	12	0	12 0
2005–06	Manchester C	21	1	28 1
2006–07	Norwich C	36	3	
2007–08	Norwich C	41	1	
2008–09	Norwich C	41	5	118 9
2009–10	Derby Co	19	1	19 1

DAVIES, Steve (F) 97 9
H: 6 0 W: 12 00 b.Liverpool 29-12-87
Source: Scholar.

2005–06	Tranmere R	22	2	
2006–07	Tranmere R	28	1	
2007–08	Tranmere R	10	2	60 5
2008–09	Derby Co	19	3	
2009–10	Derby Co	18	1	37 4

DEENEY, Saul (G) 52 0
H: 6 0 W: 12 13 b.Londonderry 12-3-83
Source: Scholar. Honours: Eire Youth, Under-21.

2000–01	Notts Co	0	0	
2001–02	Notts Co	0	0	
2002–03	Notts Co	7	0	
2003–04	Notts Co	3	0	
2004–05	Notts Co	32	0	
2005–06	Notts Co	0	0	
2006–07	Notts Co	7	0	
2007–08	Notts Co	0	0	
2008–09	Notts Co	0	0	49 0
2009–10	Derby Co	3	0	3 0

GREEN, Paul (M) 260 30
H: 5 9 W: 10 02 b.Pontefract 10-4-83
Source: Scholar. Honours: Eire 2 full caps, 1 goal.

2003–04	Doncaster R	43	8	
2004–05	Doncaster R	42	7	
2005–06	Doncaster R	34	3	
2006–07	Doncaster R	41	2	
2007–08	Doncaster R	38	5	198 25
2008–09	Derby Co	29	3	
2009–10	Derby Co	33	2	62 5

HANSON, Mitch (D) 5 0
H: 5 1 W: 13 07 b.Derby 2-9-88
Source: Scholar.

2007–08	Derby Co	0	0	
2008–09	Derby Co	0	0	
2008–09	*Notts Co*	5	0	5 0
2009–10	Derby Co	0	0	

HENDRIE, Lee (M) 328 32
H: 5 10 W: 11 00 b.Birmingham 18-5-77
Source: Trainee. Honours: England Youth, Under-21, B, 1 full cap.

1993–94	Aston Villa	0	0	
1994–95	Aston Villa	0	0	
1995–96	Aston Villa	3	0	
1996–97	Aston Villa	4	0	
1997–98	Aston Villa	17	3	
1998–99	Aston Villa	32	3	
1999–2000	Aston Villa	29	1	
2000–01	Aston Villa	32	6	
2001–02	Aston Villa	29	2	
2002–03	Aston Villa	27	4	
2003–04	Aston Villa	32	2	
2004–05	Aston Villa	29	5	
2005–06	Aston Villa	16	1	
2006–07	Aston Villa	1	0	251 27
2006–07	*Stoke C*	28	3	28 3
2007–08	Sheffield U	12	1	
2007–08	*Leicester C*	9	1	9 1
2008–09	Sheffield U	5	0	
2008–09	*Blackpool*	6	0	6 0
2009–10	Sheffield U	0	0	17 1
2009–10	Derby Co	9	0	9 0
2009–10	*Brighton & HA*	8	0	8 0

HULSE, Rob (F) 337 109
H: 6 1 W: 12 04 b.Crewe 25-10-79
Source: Trainee.

1998–99	Crewe Alex	0	0	
1999–2000	Crewe Alex	4	0	
2000–01	Crewe Alex	33	11	
2001–02	Crewe Alex	41	12	
2002–03	Crewe Alex	38	22	116 46
2003–04	WBA	33	10	
2004–05	WBA	5	0	38 10
2004–05	*Leeds U*	13	6	
2005–06	Leeds U	39	12	52 18
2006–07	Sheffield U	29	8	
2007–08	Sheffield U	21	0	50 8
2008–09	Derby Co	44	15	
2009–10	Derby Co	37	12	81 27

LEACOCK, Dean (D) 114 0
H: 6 2 W: 12 04 b.Croydon 10-6-84
Source: Trainee. Honours: England Youth, Under-20.

2002–03	Fulham	0	0	
2003–04	Fulham	4	0	
2004–05	Fulham	0	0	
2004–05	*Coventry C*	13	0	13 0
2005–06	Fulham	5	0	
2006–07	Fulham	0	0	9 0
2006–07	Derby Co	38	0	
2007–08	Derby Co	26	0	
2008–09	Derby Co	11	0	
2009–10	Derby Co	17	0	92 0

McEVELEY, James (D) 156 6
H: 6 1 W: 13 03 b.Liverpool 11-2-85
Source: Trainee. Honours: England Under-20, Under-21. Scotland B, 3 full caps.

2002–03	Blackburn R	9	0	
2003–04	Blackburn R	0	0	
2003–04	*Burnley*	4	0	4 0
2004–05	Blackburn R	5	0	
2004–05	*Gillingham*	10	1	10 1
2005–06	Blackburn R	0	0	
2005–06	*Ipswich T*	19	1	19 1
2006–07	Blackburn R	4	0	18 0
2006–07	Derby Co	15	0	
2007–08	Derby Co	29	2	
2008–09	Derby Co	15	0	
2008–09	*Preston NE*	7	0	7 0
2009–10	*Charlton Ath*	6	0	6 0
2009–10	Derby Co	33	2	92 4

MENDY, Arnaud (F) 2 0
H: 6 3 W: 13 10 b.Evreux 10-2-90
Source: Rouen.

2008–09	Derby Co	0	0	
2009–10	Derby Co	1	0	1 0
2009–10	*Grimsby T*	1	0	1 0

MILLS, Greg (F) 3 0
H: 6 2 W: 13 01 b.Derby 18-9-90
Source: Scholar.

2009–10	Derby Co	2	0	2 0
2009–10	*Macclesfield T*	1	0	1 0

MOXEY, Dean (D) 73 4
H: 6 2 W: 11 00 b.Exeter 14-1-86
Source: Scholar.

2008–09	Exeter C	43	4	43 4
2009–10	Derby Co	30	0	30 0

O'BRIEN, Mark (D) 1 0
H: 5 11 W: 12 02 b.Dublin 20-11-92
Source: Cherry Orchard.

2008–09	Derby Co	1	0	
2009–10	Derby Co	0	0	1 0

PEARSON, Stephen (M) 222 20
H: 6 0 W: 11 01 b.Lanark 2-10-82
Honours: Scotland Under-21, B, 10 full caps.

2000–01	Motherwell	6	0	
2001–02	Motherwell	27	2	
2002–03	Motherwell	29	6	
2003–04	Motherwell	18	4	80 12
2003–04	Celtic	17	3	
2004–05	Celtic	8	0	
2005–06	Celtic	18	2	
2006–07	Celtic	13	1	56 6
2006–07	Derby Co	9	0	
2007–08	Derby Co	24	0	
2007–08	*Stoke C*	4	0	4 0
2008–09	Derby Co	12	1	
2009–10	Derby Co	37	1	82 2

PORTER, Chris (F) 222 76
H: 6 1 W: 12 09 b.Wigan 12-12-83
Source: School.

2002–03	Bury	2	0	
2003–04	Bury	37	9	
2004–05	Bury	32	9	71 18
2005–06	Oldham Ath	31	7	
2006–07	Oldham Ath	35	21	66 28
2007–08	Motherwell	37	14	
2008–09	Motherwell	22	9	59 23
2008–09	Derby Co	5	3	
2009–10	Derby Co	21	4	26 7

PRICE, Lewis (G) 96 0
H: 6 3 W: 13 05 b.Bournemouth 19-7-84
Source: Southampton Academy. Honours: Wales Youth, Under-21, 7 full caps.

2002–03	Ipswich T	0	0	
2003–04	Ipswich T	1	0	
2004–05	Ipswich T	8	0	
2004–05	*Cambridge U*	6	0	6 0
2005–06	Ipswich T	25	0	
2006–07	Ipswich T	34	0	68 0
2007–08	Derby Co	6	0	
2008–09	Derby Co	0	0	
2008–09	*Milton Keynes D*	2	0	2 0
2008–09	*Luton T*	1	0	1 0
2009–10	Derby Co	0	0	6 0
2009–10	*Brentford*	13	0	13 0

PRINGLE, Ben (M) 5 0
H: 5 8 W: 11 10 b.Newcastle-upon-Tyne 27-5-89
Source: Newcastle Blue Star, Morpeth T, Ilkeston T.

2009–10	Derby Co	5	0	5 0

SAVAGE, Robbie (M) 497 33
H: 5 11 W: 11 00 b.Wrexham 18-10-74
Source: Trainee. Honours: Wales Schools, Youth, Under-21, 39 full caps, 2 goals.

1993–94	Manchester U	0	0	
1994–95	Crewe Alex	6	2	
1995–96	Crewe Alex	30	7	
1996–97	Crewe Alex	41	1	77 10
1997–98	Leicester C	35	2	
1998–99	Leicester C	34	1	
1999–2000	Leicester C	35	1	
2000–01	Leicester C	33	4	
2001–02	Leicester C	35	0	172 8
2002–03	Birmingham C	33	4	
2003–04	Birmingham C	31	3	
2004–05	Birmingham C	18	4	82 11
2004–05	Blackburn R	9	0	
2005–06	Blackburn R	34	1	
2006–07	Blackburn R	21	0	
2007–08	Blackburn R	12	0	76 1
2007–08	Derby Co	16	0	
2008–09	Derby Co	22	1	
2008–09	*Brighton & HA*	6	0	6 0
2009–10	Derby Co	46	2	84 3

TEALE, Gary (F) 434 39
H: 5 11 W: 12 02 b.Glasgow 21-7-78
Honours: Scotland Under-21, B, 13 full caps.

1996–97	Clydebank	33	6	
1997–98	Clydebank	27	6	
1998–99	Clydebank	8	2	68 14
1998–99	Ayr U	23	4	
1999–2000	Ayr U	32	0	
2000–01	Ayr U	29	5	
2001–02	Ayr U	18	4	102 13
2001–02	Wigan Ath	23	1	
2002–03	Wigan Ath	38	2	
2003–04	Wigan Ath	28	2	
2004–05	Wigan Ath	37	3	
2005–06	Wigan Ath	24	0	
2006–07	Wigan Ath	12	0	162 8
2006–07	Derby Co	16	1	
2007–08	Derby Co	0	0	
2007–08	*Plymouth Arg*	12	0	12 0
2008–09	Derby Co	25	1	
2008–09	*Barnsley*	3	0	3 0
2009–10	Derby Co	28	2	87 4

VARNEY, Luke (F) 206 49
H: 5 11 W: 11 00 b.Leicester 28-9-82
Source: Quorn.

2002–03	Crewe Alex	0	0	
2003–04	Crewe Alex	8	1	
2004–05	Crewe Alex	26	4	
2005–06	Crewe Alex	27	5	
2006–07	Crewe Alex	34	17	95 27
2007–08	Charlton Ath	39	8	
2008–09	Charlton Ath	18	2	57 10
2008–09	*Sheffield W*	4	2	
2008–09	Derby Co	10	1	
2009–10	Derby Co	1	0	11 1
2009–10	*Sheffield W*	39	9	43 11

DONCASTER R (33)

BROOKER, Stephen (F)   **248 78**
H: 6 0 W: 14 00 b.Newport Pagnell 21-5-81
Source: Trainee.

Season	Club				
1999–2000	Watford	1	0		
2000–01	Watford	0	0	**1**	**0**
2000–01	Port Vale	23	8		
2001–02	Port Vale	41	9		
2002–03	Port Vale	26	5		
2003–04	Port Vale	32	8		
2004–05	Port Vale	9	5	**131**	**35**
2004–05	Bristol C	33	16		
2005–06	Bristol C	37	16		
2006–07	Bristol C	23	2		
2007–08	Bristol C	4	1		
2007–08	*Cheltenham T*	14	5	**14**	**5**
2008–09	Bristol C	4	2	**101**	**37**
2008–09	Doncaster R	1	1		
2009–10	Doncaster R	0	0	**1**	**1**

CHAMBERS, James (D)   **274 0**
H: 5 10 W: 11 11 b.West Bromwich 20-11-80
Source: Trainee. *Honours:* England Youth.

Season	Club				
1998–99	WBA	0	0		
1999–2000	WBA	12	0		
2000–01	WBA	31	0		
2001–02	WBA	5	0		
2002–03	WBA	8	0		
2003–04	WBA	17	0		
2004–05	WBA	0	0	**73**	**0**
2004–05	Watford	40	0		
2005–06	Watford	38	0		
2006–07	Watford	12	0	**90**	**0**
2006–07	*Cardiff C*	7	0	**7**	**0**
2007–08	Leicester C	24	0	**24**	**0**
2008–09	Doncaster R	37	0		
2009–10	Doncaster R	43	0	**80**	**0**

CLARKE, Robert (M)   **0 0**
H: 5 10 W: 10 10 b.Hull 30-4-91
Source: Scholar.

Season	Club		
2009–10	Doncaster R	0	0

COPPINGER, James (F)   **284 31**
H: 5 7 W: 10 03 b.Middlesbrough 10-1-81
Source: Darlington Trainee. *Honours:* England Youth.

Season	Club				
1997–98	Newcastle U	0	0		
1998–99	Newcastle U	0	0		
1999–2000	Newcastle U	0	0		
1999–2000	*Hartlepool U*	10	3		
2000–01	Newcastle U	1	0		
2001–02	Newcastle U	0	0	**1**	**0**
2001–02	*Hartlepool U*	14	2	**24**	**5**
2002–03	Exeter C	43	5		
2003–04	Exeter C	0	0	**43**	**5**
2004–05	Doncaster R	31	0		
2005–06	Doncaster R	36	5		
2006–07	Doncaster R	39	4		
2007–08	Doncaster R	39	3		
2008–09	Doncaster R	32	5		
2009–10	Doncaster R	39	4	**216**	**21**

DUMBUYA, Mustapha (D)   **3 0**
H: 5 7 W: 11 00 b.Sierra Leone 7-8-87
Source: Grays Ath.

Season	Club				
2009–10	Doncaster R	3	0	**3**	**0**

ELLIOTT, Stuart (M)   **389 116**
H: 5 10 W: 11 09 b.Belfast 23-7-78
Honours: Northern Ireland Under-21, B, 39 full caps, 4 goals.

Season	Club				
1994–95	Glentoran	0	0		
1995–96	Glentoran	1	0		
1996–97	Glentoran	8	1		
1997–98	Glentoran	22	5		
1998–99	Glentoran	31	7		
1999–2000	Glentoran	34	16	**96**	**29**
2000–01	Motherwell	33	10		
2001–02	Motherwell	37	10	**70**	**20**
2002–03	Hull C	36	12		
2003–04	Hull C	42	14		
2004–05	Hull C	36	27		
2005–06	Hull C	40	7		
2006–07	Hull C	32	5		
2007–08	Hull C	7	0	**193**	**65**
2007–08	*Doncaster R*	10	0		
2008–09	*Doncaster R*	9	0		
2008–09	*Grimsby T*	11	2	**11**	**2**
2009–10	Doncaster R	0	0	**19**	**0**

FAIRHURST, Waide (F)   **19 6**
H: 5 10 W: 10 07 b.Sheffield 7-5-89
Source: Scholar.

Season	Club				
2008–09	Doncaster R	3	0		
2009–10	Doncaster R	6	2	**9**	**2**
2009–10	*Shrewsbury T*	10	4	**10**	**4**

FORTUNE, Quinton (F)   **184 14**
H: 5 10 W: 12 09 b.Cape Town 21-5-77
Source: Kaizer Chiefs, Tottenham H schoolboy. *Honours:* South Africa Under-23, 53 full caps, 2 goals.

Season	Club				
1995–96	Mallorca	8	1	**8**	**1**
1995–96	Atletico Madrid	3	0		
1996–97	Atletico Madrid B	30	2		
1996–97	Atletico Madrid	2	0		
1997–98	Atletico Madrid B	31	1		
1997–98	Atletico Madrid	0	0		
1998–99	Atletico Madrid	2	0	**7**	**0**
1998–99	Atletico Madrid B	20	4	**81**	**7**
1999–2000	Manchester U	6	2		
2000–01	Manchester U	7	2		
2001–02	Manchester U	14	1		
2002–03	Manchester U	9	0		
2003–04	Manchester U	23	0		
2004–05	Manchester U	17	0		
2005–06	Manchester U	0	0	**76**	**5**
2006–07	Bolton W	6	0		
2007–08	Bolton W	0	0		
2008–09	Bolton W	0	0	**6**	**0**
2009–10	Doncaster R	6	1	**6**	**1**

GUY, Lewis (F)   **163 21**
H: 5 10 W: 10 07 b.Penrith 27-8-85
Source: Trainee. *Honours:* England Youth, Under-20.

Season	Club				
2002–03	Newcastle U	0	0		
2003–04	Newcastle U	0	0		
2004–05	Newcastle U	0	0		
2004–05	Doncaster R	9	3		
2005–06	Doncaster R	31	3		
2006–07	Doncaster R	36	4		
2007–08	Doncaster R	29	6		
2008–09	Doncaster R	29	2		
2008–09	*Hartlepool U*	4	0	**4**	**0**
2009–10	Doncaster R	13	0	**147**	**18**
2009–10	*Oldham Ath*	12	3	**12**	**3**

HAYTER, James (F)   **457 114**
H: 5 9 W: 10 13 b.Newport (IW) 9-4-79
Source: Trainee.

Season	Club				
1996–97	Bournemouth	2	0		
1997–98	Bournemouth	5	0		
1998–99	Bournemouth	20	2		
1999–2000	Bournemouth	31	2		
2000–01	Bournemouth	40	11		
2001–02	Bournemouth	44	7		
2002–03	Bournemouth	45	9		
2003–04	Bournemouth	44	14		
2004–05	Bournemouth	39	19		
2005–06	Bournemouth	46	20		
2006–07	Bournemouth	42	10	**358**	**94**
2007–08	Doncaster R	34	7		
2008–09	Doncaster R	27	4		
2009–10	Doncaster R	38	9	**99**	**20**

HEFFERNAN, Paul (F)   **269 82**
H: 5 10 W: 11 00 b.Dublin 29-12-81
Source: Newton.

Season	Club				
1999–2000	Notts Co	2	0		
2000–01	Notts Co	1	0		
2001–02	Notts Co	23	6		
2002–03	Notts Co	36	10		
2003–04	Notts Co	38	20	**100**	**36**
2004–05	Bristol C	27	5	**27**	**5**
2005–06	Doncaster R	26	8		
2006–07	Doncaster R	29	11		
2007–08	Doncaster R	27	7		
2008–09	Doncaster R	28	10		
2009–10	Doncaster R	17	0	**127**	**36**
2009–10	*Oldham Ath*	4	1	**4**	**1**
2009–10	*Bristol R*	11	4	**11**	**4**

HIRD, Samuel (D)   **99 1**
H: 5 7 W: 10 12 b.Askern 7-9-87
Source: Scholar.

Season	Club				
2005–06	Leeds U	0	0		
2006–07	Leeds U	0	0		
2006–07	*Doncaster R*	5	0		
2007–08	Doncaster R	4	0		
2007–08	*Grimsby T*	17	0	**17**	**0**
2008–09	Doncaster R	37	1		
2009–10	Doncaster R	36	0	**82**	**1**

LOCKWOOD, Adam (D)   **203 14**
H: 6 0 W: 12 07 b.Wakefield 26-10-81
Source: Reading Trainee.

Season	Club				
2003–04	Yeovil T	43	4		
2004–05	Yeovil T	10	0		
2005–06	Yeovil T	20	0	**73**	**4**
2005–06	*Torquay U*	9	3	**9**	**3**
2006–07	Doncaster R	44	2		
2007–08	Doncaster R	39	3		
2008–09	Doncaster R	22	0		
2009–10	Doncaster R	15	2	**121**	**7**

MARTIS, Shelton (D)   **134 6**
H: 6 0 W: 11 11 b.Willemstad 29-11-82
Honours: Netherlands Antilles 1 full cap.

Season	Club				
2002–03	Excelsior	12	0		
2003–04	Excelsior	10	0	**22**	**0**
2005–06	Darlington	40	2		
2006–07	Darlington	2	0	**42**	**2**
2006–07	Hibernian	26	0	**26**	**0**
2007–08	WBA	2	0		
2007–08	*Scunthorpe U*	3	0	**3**	**0**
2008–09	WBA	7	0		
2008–09	*Doncaster R*	5	1		
2009–10	WBA	13	2	**22**	**2**
2009–10	Doncaster R	14	1	**19**	**2**

McDAID, Sean (M)   **80 1**
H: 5 6 W: 9 08 b.Harrogate 6-3-86
Source: Trainee.

Season	Club				
2002–03	Leeds U	0	0		
2003–04	Leeds U	0	0		
2004–05	Leeds U	0	0		
2005–06	Doncaster R	35	0		
2006–07	Doncaster R	20	0		
2007–08	Doncaster R	24	1		
2008–09	Doncaster R	0	0		
2009–10	Doncaster R	1	0	**80**	**1**

O'CONNOR, James (D)   **208 3**
H: 5 10 W: 12 05 b.Birmingham 20-11-84
Source: Scholar.

Season	Club				
2003–04	Aston Villa	0	0		
2004–05	Aston Villa	0	0		
2004–05	*Port Vale*	13	0	**13**	**0**
2004–05	Bournemouth	6	0		
2005–06	Bournemouth	39	1	**45**	**1**
2006–07	Doncaster R	40	1		
2007–08	Doncaster R	40	0		
2008–09	Doncaster R	32	1		
2009–10	Doncaster R	38	0	**150**	**2**

OSTER, John (M)   **321 23**
H: 5 9 W: 10 08 b.Boston 8-12-78
Source: Trainee. *Honours:* Wales Youth, Under-21, B, 13 full caps.

Season	Club				
1996–97	Grimsby T	24	3		
1997–98	Everton	31	1		
1998–99	Everton	9	0	**40**	**1**
1999–2000	Sunderland	10	0		
2000–01	Sunderland	8	0		
2001–02	Sunderland	0	0		
2001–02	*Barnsley*	2	0	**2**	**0**
2002–03	Sunderland	3	0		
2002–03	*Grimsby T*	17	6	**41**	**7**
2003–04	Sunderland	38	5		
2004–05	Sunderland	9	0	**68**	**5**
2004–05	*Leeds U*	8	1	**8**	**1**
2004–05	*Burnley*	15	1	**15**	**1**
2005–06	Reading	33	1		
2006–07	Reading	25	1		
2007–08	Reading	18	0	**76**	**2**
2008–09	Crystal Palace	31	3	**31**	**3**
2009–10	Doncaster R	40	1	**40**	**1**

ROBERTS, Gareth (D)   **422 21**
H: 5 8 W: 11 12 b.Wrexham 6-2-78
Source: Trainee. *Honours:* Wales Under-21, B, 9 full caps.

Season	Club		
1995–96	Liverpool	0	0

Season	Club	Apps	Gls	Tot A	Tot G
1996–97	Liverpool	0	0		
1997–98	Liverpool	0	0		
1998–99	Liverpool	0	0		
1999–2000	Tranmere R	37	1		
2000–01	Tranmere R	34	0		
2001–02	Tranmere R	45	2		
2002–03	Tranmere R	37	4		
2003–04	Tranmere R	44	1		
2004–05	Tranmere R	40	3		
2005–06	Tranmere R	44	2	281	13
2006–07	Doncaster R	30	1		
2007–08	Doncaster R	37	3		
2008–09	Doncaster R	32	1		
2009–10	Doncaster R	42	3	141	8

SHIELS, Dean (F)   168 31
H: 5 11 W: 9 10 b.Magherfelt 1-2-85
Source: Arsenal Scholar. *Honours:* Northern Ireland Under-21, 9 full caps.

Season	Club	Apps	Gls	Tot A	Tot G
2002–03	Arsenal	0	0		
2003–04	Arsenal	0	0		
2004–05	Hibernian	37	5		
2005–06	Hibernian	16	2		
2006–07	Hibernian	24	7		
2007–08	Hibernian	22	7		
2008–09	Hibernian	19	3	118	24
2008–09	Doncaster R	12	1		
2009–10	Doncaster R	38	6	50	7

SMITH, Benjamin (G)   27 0
H: 6 1 W: 12 11 b.Newcastle 5-9-86
Source: Newcastle U Scholar.

Season	Club	Apps	Gls	Tot A	Tot G
2006–07	Stockport Co	0	0		
2006–07	Doncaster R	13	0		
2007–08	Doncaster R	0	0		
2007–08	*Lincoln C*	9	0	9	0
2008–09	Doncaster R	0	0		
2009–10	Doncaster R	2	0	15	0
2009–10	*Morecambe*	3	0	3	0

SPICER, John (M)   171 12
H: 5 11 W: 11 07 b.Romford 13-9-83
Source: Scholar. *Honours:* England Schools, Youth, Under-20.

Season	Club	Apps	Gls	Tot A	Tot G
2001–02	Arsenal	0	0		
2002–03	Arsenal	0	0		
2003–04	Arsenal	0	0		
2004–05	Arsenal	0	0		
2004–05	Bournemouth	39	6		
2005–06	Bournemouth	4	0	43	6
2005–06	Burnley	34	3		
2006–07	Burnley	11	1		
2007–08	Burnley	24	0	69	4
2008–09	Doncaster R	30	1		
2009–10	Doncaster R	20	0	50	1
2009–10	*Leyton Orient*	9	1	9	1

STOCK, Brian (M)   280 31
H: 5 11 W: 11 02 b.Winchester 24-12-81
Source: Trainee. *Honours:* Wales Under-21, 2 full caps.

Season	Club	Apps	Gls	Tot A	Tot G
1999–2000	Bournemouth	5	0		
2000–01	Bournemouth	1	0		
2001–02	Bournemouth	26	2		
2002–03	Bournemouth	27	2		
2003–04	Bournemouth	19	3		
2004–05	Bournemouth	41	6		
2005–06	Bournemouth	26	3	145	16
2005–06	Preston NE	6	1		
2006–07	Preston NE	2	0	8	1
2006–07	Doncaster R	36	3		
2007–08	Doncaster R	40	5		
2008–09	Doncaster R	36	6		
2009–10	Doncaster R	15	0	127	14

SULLIVAN, Neil (G)   498 0
H: 6 2 W: 12 00 b.Sutton 24-2-70
Source: Trainee. *Honours:* Scotland 28 full caps.

Season	Club	Apps	Gls	Tot A	Tot G
1988–89	Wimbledon	0	0		
1989–90	Wimbledon	0	0		
1990–91	Wimbledon	1	0		
1991–92	Wimbledon	1	0		
1991–92	*Crystal Palace*	1	0	1	0
1992–93	Wimbledon	1	0		
1993–94	Wimbledon	2	0		
1994–95	Wimbledon	11	0		
1995–96	Wimbledon	16	0		
1996–97	Wimbledon	36	0		
1997–98	Wimbledon	38	0		
1998–99	Wimbledon	38	0		
1999–2000	Wimbledon	37	0	181	0
2000–01	Tottenham H	35	0		
2001–02	Tottenham H	29	0		
2002–03	Tottenham H	0	0	64	0
2003–04	Chelsea	4	0	4	0
2004–05	Leeds U	46	0		
2005–06	Leeds U	42	0		
2006–07	Leeds U	7	0	95	0
2006–07	Doncaster R	16	0		
2007–08	Doncaster R	46	0		
2008–09	Doncaster R	46	0		
2009–10	Doncaster R	45	0	153	0

WEBSTER, Byron (D)   5 0
H: 6 5 W: 12 07 b.Leeds 13-3-87
Source: York C, Harrogate T, Whitby T, FK SIAD Most.

Season	Club	Apps	Gls	Tot A	Tot G
2009–10	Doncaster R	5	0	5	0

WILSON, Mark (M)   186 10
H: 5 10 W: 12 07 b.Scunthorpe 9-2-79
Source: Trainee. *Honours:* England Schools, Youth, Under-21.

Season	Club	Apps	Gls	Tot A	Tot G
1995–96	Manchester U	0	0		
1996–97	Manchester U	0	0		
1997–98	Manchester U	0	0		
1997–98	*Wrexham*	13	4	13	4
1998–99	Manchester U	0	0		
1999–2000	Manchester U	3	0		
2000–01	Manchester U	0	0	3	0
2001–02	Middlesbrough	10	0		
2002–03	Middlesbrough	6	0		
2002–03	*Stoke C*	4	0	4	0
2003–04	Middlesbrough	0	0		
2003–04	*Swansea C*	12	2	12	2
2003–04	*Sheffield W*	3	0	3	0
2004–05	Middlesbrough	0	0	16	0
2004–05	*Doncaster R*	3	0		
2004–05	*Livingston*	5	0	5	0
2006	Dallas	12	1	12	1
2006–07	Doncaster R	22	1		
2007–08	Doncaster R	31	1		
2008–09	Doncaster R	22	1		
2008–09	*Tranmere R*	5	0	5	0
2009–10	Doncaster R	35	0	113	3

WOODS, Gary (G)   1 0
H: 6 1 W: 11 00 b.Kettering 1-10-90
Source: Scholar.

Season	Club	Apps	Gls	Tot A	Tot G
2008–09	Manchester U	0	0		
2008–09	Doncaster R	1	0		
2009–10	Doncaster R	0	0	1	0

WOODS, Martin (M)   133 10
H: 5 11 W: 11 00 b.Airdrie 1-1-86
Source: Trainee. *Honours:* Scotland Youth, Under-21.

Season	Club	Apps	Gls	Tot A	Tot G
2002–03	Leeds U	0	0		
2003–04	Leeds U	0	0		
2004–05	Leeds U	1	0	1	0
2004–05	*Hartlepool U*	6	0	6	0
2005–06	Sunderland	7	0	7	0
2006–07	Rotherham U	36	4	36	4
2007–08	Doncaster R	15	0		
2007–08	*Yeovil T*	3	0	3	0
2008–09	Doncaster R	41	2		
2009–10	Doncaster R	24	4	80	6

EVERTON (34)

AGARD, Kieran (F)   1 0
H: 5 10 W: 10 10 b.Newham 10-10-89
Source: Scholar.

Season	Club	Apps	Gls	Tot A	Tot G
2006–07	Everton	0	0		
2007–08	Everton	0	0		
2008–09	Everton	0	0		
2009–10	Everton	1	0	1	0

AKPAN, Hope (M)   0 0
H: 6 0 W: 10 08 b.Liverpool 14-8-91
Source: Scholar.

Season	Club	Apps	Gls	Tot A	Tot G
2007–08	Everton	0	0		
2008–09	Everton	0	0		
2009–10	Everton	0	0		

ANICHEBE, Victor (F)   76 7
H: 6 1 W: 13 00 b.Nigeria 23-4-88
Source: Scholar. *Honours:* Nigeria Under-23, 5 full caps, 1 goal.

Season	Club	Apps	Gls	Tot A	Tot G
2005–06	Everton	2	1		
2006–07	Everton	19	3		
2007–08	Everton	27	1		
2008–09	Everton	17	1		
2009–10	Everton	11	1	76	7

ARTETA, Mikel (M)   280 41
H: 5 9 W: 10 08 b.San Sebastian 26-3-82
Honours: Spain Youth, Under-21.

Season	Club	Apps	Gls	Tot A	Tot G
1999–2000	Barcelona B	26	1		
2000–01	Barcelona B	16	2	42	3
2000–01	Paris St Germain	6	1		
2001–02	Paris St Germain	25	1	31	2
2002–03	Rangers	27	4		
2003–04	Rangers	23	8	50	12
2004–05	Real Sociedad	14	1	14	1
2004–05	Everton	12	1		
2005–06	Everton	29	1		
2006–07	Everton	35	9		
2007–08	Everton	28	1		
2008–09	Everton	26	5		
2009–10	Everton	13	6	143	23

BAINES, Leighton (D)   235 6
H: 5 8 W: 11 00 b.Liverpool 11-12-84
Source: Trainee. *Honours:* England Under-21, 2 full caps.

Season	Club	Apps	Gls	Tot A	Tot G
2002–03	Wigan Ath	6	0		
2003–04	Wigan Ath	26	0		
2004–05	Wigan Ath	41	1		
2005–06	Wigan Ath	37	0		
2006–07	Wigan Ath	35	3		
2007–08	Wigan Ath	0	0	145	4
2007–08	Everton	22	0		
2008–09	Everton	31	1		
2009–10	Everton	37	1	90	2

BARNETT, Moses (D)   4 0
H: 6 3 W: 13 05 b.London 3-12-90
Source: Arsenal.

Season	Club	Apps	Gls	Tot A	Tot G
2007–08	Everton	0	0		
2008–09	Everton	0	0		
2009–10	Everton	0	0		
2009–10	*Darlington*	4	0	4	0

BAXTER, Jose (F)   5 0
H: 5 10 W: 11 07 b.Bootle 7-2-92
Source: Academy. *Honours:* England Youth.

Season	Club	Apps	Gls	Tot A	Tot G
2008–09	Everton	3	0		
2009–10	Everton	2	0	5	0

BIDWELL, Jake (G)   0 0
H: 6 0 W: 11 00 b.Southport 21-3-93
Source: Scholar. *Honours:* England Youth.

Season	Club	Apps	Gls	Tot A	Tot G
2009–10	Everton	0	0		

BILYALETDINOV, Diniyar (F)   173 37
H: 6 1 W: 11 11 b.Moscow 27-2-85
Honours: Russia 33 full caps, 5 goals.

Season	Club	Apps	Gls	Tot A	Tot G
2003	Lokomotiv Moscow	0	0		
2004	Lokomotiv Moscow	25	5		
2004	*Neftekhlmik*	5	0		
2005	Lokomotiv Moscow	29	8		
2006	Lokomotiv Moscow	29	3		
2007	Lokomotiv Moscow	28	3		
2008	Lokomotiv Moscow	26	9		
2009	Lokomotiv Moscow	13	3	150	31
2009–10	Everton	23	6	23	6

CAHILL, Tim (M)   381 97
H: 5 10 W: 10 12 b.Sydney 6-12-79
Source: Sydney U. *Honours:* Western Samoa Youth, Australia Under-23, 42 full caps, 21 goals.

Season	Club	Apps	Gls	Tot A	Tot G
1997–98	Millwall	1	0		
1998–99	Millwall	36	6		
1999–2000	Millwall	45	12		
2000–01	Millwall	41	9		
2001–02	Millwall	43	13		
2002–03	Millwall	11	3		
2003–04	Millwall	40	9	217	52
2004–05	Everton	33	11		
2005–06	Everton	32	6		
2006–07	Everton	18	5		
2007–08	Everton	18	7		
2008–09	Everton	30	8		
2009–10	Everton	33	8	164	45

CASTILLO, Segundo (M)   245 38
H: 5 10 W: 12 02 b.Quito 15-5-82
Honours: Ecuador 45 full caps, 2 goals.

Season	Club	Apps	Gls	Tot A	Tot G
2000	Espoli	8	0		
2001	Espoli	28	2		
2002	Espoli	30	9	66	11

2003	El Nacional	14	0		
2004	El Nacional	32	0		
2005	El Nacional	48	8		
2006	El Nacional	19	3	113	11
2006–07	Red Star Belgrade	23	8		
2007–08	Red Star Belgrade	26	8	49	16
2008–09	Everton	9	0		
2009–10	Everton	0	0	9	0
2009–10	Wolverhampton W	8	0	8	0

COLEMAN, Seamus (D)   12   1
H: 6 4   W: 10 07   b.Donegal 11-10-88
Source: Sligo R. *Honours:* Eire Under-21, Under-23.

2008–09	Everton	0	0		
2009–10	Everton	3	0	3	0
2009–10	*Blackpool*	9	1	9	1

CRAIG, Nathan (M)   0   0
H: 6 0   W: 11 06   b.Bangor 25-10-91
Source: Scholar. *Honours:* Wales Under-21.

2008–09	Everton	0	0
2009–10	Everton	0	0

DAVIES, Adam (G)   0   0
b.Rinteln 17-7-92
Source: Scholar.

2009–10	Everton	0	0

DISTIN, Sylvain (D)   399   9
H: 6 3   W: 14 06   b.Bagnolet 16-12-77

1998–99	Tours	26	3	26	3
1999–2000	Gueugnon	33	1	33	1
2000–01	Paris St Germain	28	0	28	0
2001–02	Newcastle U	28	0	28	0
2002–03	Manchester C	34	0		
2003–04	Manchester C	38	2		
2004–05	Manchester C	38	1		
2005–06	Manchester C	31	0		
2006–07	Manchester C	37	2	178	5
2007–08	Portsmouth	36	0		
2008–09	Portsmouth	38	0		
2009–10	Portsmouth	3	0	77	0
2009–10	Everton	29	0	29	0

DONOVAN, Landon (F)   259   108
H: 5 8   W: 11 05   b.Ontario 4-3-82
Honours: USA 126 full caps, 45 goals.

1999	Bradenton Academics	0	0		
1999–2000	Leverkusen II	20	6		
2000–01	Leverkusen II	8	3	28	9
2001	San Jose E	22	7		
2002	San Jose E	20	7		
2003	San Jose E	22	12		
2004	San Jose E	23	6	87	32
2004–05	Leverkusen	7	0	7	0
2005	LA Galaxy	22	12		
2006	LA Galaxy	24	13		
2007	LA Galaxy	25	8		
2008	LA Galaxy	25	20		
2008–09	Bayern Munich	6	0	6	0
2009	LA Galaxy	25	12	121	65
2009–10	Everton	10	2	10	2

DUFFY, Shane (D)   0   0
H: 6 4   W: 12 00   b.County Derry 1-1-92
Source: Scholar. *Honours:* Northern Ireland Under-21.

2008–09	Everton	0	0
2009–10	Everton	0	0

FELLAINI, Marouane (M)   115   16
H: 6 4   W: 13 05   b.Brussels 22-11-87
Honours: Belgium 21 full caps, 3 goals.

2006–07	Standard Liege	29	0		
2007–08	Standard Liege	30	6		
2008–09	Standard Liege	3	0	62	6
2008–09	Everton	30	8		
2009–10	Everton	23	2	53	10

FORSHAW, Adam (M)   0   0
H: 6 1   W: 11 02   b.Liverpool 8-10-91
Source: Scholar.

2009–10	Everton	0	0

GOSLING, Dan (M)   44   6
H: 6 0   W: 11 00   b.Brixham 2-9-90
Source: Scholar. *Honours:* England Youth, Under-21.

2006–07	Plymouth Arg	12	2		
2007–08	Plymouth Arg	10	0	22	2

2007–08	Everton	0	0		
2008–09	Everton	11	2		
2009–10	Everton	11	2	22	4

HEITINGA, Johnny (D)   210   8
H: 5 11   W: 11 05   b.Alphen aan den Rijn 15-11-83
Honours: Holland 61 full caps, 6 goals.

2000–01	Ajax	0	0		
2001–02	Ajax	15	0		
2002–03	Ajax	1	0		
2003–04	Ajax	26	3		
2004–05	Ajax	26	1		
2005–06	Ajax	19	1		
2005–07	Ajax	32	0		
2007–08	Ajax	33	0	152	5
2008–09	Atletico Madrid	27	3	27	3
2009–10	Everton	31	0	31	0

HIBBERT, Tony (D)   201   0
H: 5 9   W: 11 05   b.Liverpool 20-2-81
Source: Trainee.

1998–99	Everton	0	0		
1999–2000	Everton	0	0		
2000–01	Everton	3	0		
2001–02	Everton	10	0		
2002–03	Everton	24	0		
2003–04	Everton	25	0		
2004–05	Everton	36	0		
2005–06	Everton	29	0		
2006–07	Everton	13	0		
2007–08	Everton	24	0		
2008–09	Everton	17	0		
2009–10	Everton	20	0	201	0

HOWARD, Tim (G)   278   0
H: 6 3   W: 14 12   b.North Brunswick 6-3-79
Honours: USA Under-21, Under-23, 55 full caps.

1998	NY/NJ MetroStars	1	0		
1999	NY/NJ MetroStars	9	0		
2000	NY/NJ MetroStars	9	0		
2001	NY/NJ MetroStars	26	0		
2002	NY/NJ MetroStars	27	0		
2003	NY/NJ MetroStars	13	0	85	0
2003–04	Manchester U	32	0		
2004–05	Manchester U	12	0		
2005–06	Manchester U	1	0		
2006–07	Manchester U	0	0	45	0
2006–07	Everton	36	0		
2007–08	Everton	36	0		
2008–09	Everton	38	0		
2009–10	Everton	38	0	148	0

JAGIELKA, Phil (D)   334   19
H: 6 0   W: 13 01   b.Manchester 17-8-82
Source: Scholar. *Honours:* England Youth, Under-20, Under-21, B, 3 full caps.

1999–2000	Sheffield U	1	0		
2000–01	Sheffield U	15	0		
2001–02	Sheffield U	23	3		
2002–03	Sheffield U	42	0		
2003–04	Sheffield U	43	3		
2004–05	Sheffield U	46	0		
2005–06	Sheffield U	46	8		
2006–07	Sheffield U	38	4	254	18
2007–08	Everton	34	1		
2008–09	Everton	34	0		
2009–10	Everton	12	0	80	1

JUTKIEWICZ, Lucas (F)   82   17
H: 6 1   W: 12 11   b.Southampton 20-3-89
Source: Scholar.

2005–06	Swindon T	5	0		
2006–07	Swindon T	33	5	38	5
2006–07	Everton	0	0		
2007–08	Everton	0	0		
2007–08	*Plymouth Arg*	3	0	3	0
2008–09	Everton	1	0		
2008–09	*Huddersfield T*	7	0	7	0
2009–10	Everton	0	0	1	0
2009–10	*Motherwell*	33	12	33	12

KINSELLA, Gerard (M)   0   0
b.Liverpool 13-11-90
Source: Scholar.

2008–09	Everton	0	0
2009–10	Everton	0	0

McALENY, Conor (F)   0   0
b.Liverpool 12-8-92
Source: Scholar.

2009–10	Everton	0	0

McARDLE, Lee (M)   0   0
Source: Scholar.

2008–09	Everton	0	0
2009–10	Everton	0	0

McCARTEN, James (D)   1   0
H: 6 3   W: 12 10   b.Netherton 8-11-90
Source: Scholar.

2008–09	Everton	0	0		
2009–10	Everton	0	0		
2009–10	*Accrington S*	1	0	1	0

MUSTAFI, Shkodran (D)   0   0
H: 6 0   W: 11 07   b.Bad Hersfeld 17-4-92
Source: Hamburg.

2009–10	Everton	0	0

NEILL, Lucas (D)   431   19
H: 6 0   W: 12 03   b.Sydney 9-3-78
Source: NSW Soccer Academy. *Honours:* Australia Under-20, Under-23, 51 full caps.

1995–96	Millwall	13	0		
1996–97	Millwall	39	3		
1997–98	Millwall	6	0		
1998–99	Millwall	35	6		
1999–2000	Millwall	31	1		
2000–01	Millwall	24	2		
2001–02	Millwall	4	1	152	13
2001–02	Blackburn R	31	1		
2002–03	Blackburn R	34	0		
2003–04	Blackburn R	32	2		
2004–05	Blackburn R	36	1		
2005–06	Blackburn R	35	1		
2006–07	Blackburn R	20	0	188	5
2006–07	West Ham U	11	0		
2007–08	West Ham U	34	0		
2008–09	West Ham U	34	1		
2009–10	West Ham U	0	0	79	1
2009–10	Everton	12	0	12	0

NEVILLE, Phil (M)   429   8
H: 5 11   W: 12 00   b.Bury 21-1-77
Source: Trainee. *Honours:* England Schools, Youth, B, 59 full caps.

1994–95	Manchester U	2	0		
1995–96	Manchester U	24	0		
1996–97	Manchester U	18	0		
1997–98	Manchester U	30	1		
1998–99	Manchester U	28	0		
1999–2000	Manchester U	29	0		
2000–01	Manchester U	29	1		
2001–02	Manchester U	28	2		
2002–03	Manchester U	25	1		
2003–04	Manchester U	31	0		
2004–05	Manchester U	19	0	263	5
2005–06	Everton	34	0		
2006–07	Everton	35	1		
2007–08	Everton	37	2		
2008–09	Everton	37	0		
2009–10	Everton	23	0	166	3

NSIALA, Aristote (D)   0   0
b.Congo 25-3-92
Source: Scholar.

2009–10	Everton	0	0

ORENUGA, Femi (M)   0   0
b.London 18-3-93
Source: Southend U.

2009–10	Everton	0	0

OSMAN, Leon (F)   221   29
H: 5 8   W: 10 09   b.Billinge 17-5-81
Source: Trainee. *Honours:* England Schools, Youth.

1998–99	Everton	0	0		
1999–2000	Everton	0	0		
2000–01	Everton	0	0		
2001–02	Everton	0	0		
2002–03	Everton	2	0		
2002–03	*Carlisle U*	12	1	12	1
2003–04	Everton	4	1		
2003–04	*Derby Co*	17	3	17	3
2004–05	Everton	29	6		
2005–06	Everton	35	3		
2006–07	Everton	34	3		
2007–08	Everton	28	4		

| 2008–09 | Everton | 34 | 6 | | |
| 2009–10 | Everton | 26 | 2 | 192 | 25 |

PIENAAR, Steven (M)   205 23
H: 5 10   W: 10 06   b.Westbury 17-3-82
Honours: South Africa 53 full caps, 2 goals.

2001–02	Ajax	8	1		
2002–03	Ajax	31	5		
2003–04	Ajax	16	3		
2004–05	Ajax	24	4		
2005–06	Ajax	15	2	94	15
2006–07	Bor Dortmund	25	0	25	0
2007–08	Everton	28	2		
2008–09	Everton	28	2		
2009–10	Everton	30	4	86	8

ROBERTS, Connor (G)   0 0
b.Wrexham 8-12-92
Source: Scholar.

| 2009–10 | Everton | 0 | 0 | | |

RODWELL, Jack (D)   47 2
H: 6 2   W: 12 08   b.Birkdale 11-3-91
Source: Scholar. *Honours:* England Youth, Under-21.

2007–08	Everton	2	0		
2008–09	Everton	19	0		
2009–10	Everton	26	2	47	2

RUDDY, John (G)   134 0
H: 6 3   W: 12 07   b.St Ives 24-10-86
Source: Scholar. *Honours:* England Youth.

2003–04	Cambridge U	1	0		
2004–05	Cambridge U	38	0	39	0
2005–06	Everton	1	0		
2005–06	Walsall	5	0	5	0
2005–06	Rushden & D	3	0	3	0
2005–06	Chester C	4	0	4	0
2006–07	Everton	0	0		
2006–07	Stockport Co	11	0		
2006–07	Wrexham	5	0	5	0
2006–07	Bristol C	1	0	1	0
2007–08	Everton	0	0		
2007–08	Stockport Co	12	0	23	0
2008–09	Everton	0	0		
2008–09	Crewe Alex	19	0	19	0
2009–10	Everton	0	0	1	0
2009–10	Motherwell	34	0	34	0

SAHA, Louis (F)   318 106
H: 6 1   W: 12 08   b.Paris 8-8-78
Honours: France Youth, Under-21, 18 full caps, 4 goals.

1997–98	Metz	21	1		
1998–99	Metz	3	0		
1998–99	Newcastle U	11	1	11	1
1999–2000	Metz	23	4	47	5
2000–01	Fulham	43	27		
2001–02	Fulham	36	8		
2002–03	Fulham	17	5		
2003–04	Fulham	21	13	117	53
2003–04	Manchester U	12	7		
2004–05	Manchester U	14	1		
2005–06	Manchester U	19	7		
2006–07	Manchester U	24	8		
2007–08	Manchester U	17	5		
2008–09	Manchester U	0	0	86	28
2008–09	Everton	24	6		
2009–10	Everton	33	13	57	19

TURNER, Iain (G)   48 0
H: 6 3   W: 12 10   b.Stirling 26-1-84
Source: Riverside BC. *Honours:* Scotland Youth, Under-21, B.

2002–03	Stirling A	14	0	14	0
2002–03	Everton	0	0		
2003–04	Everton	0	0		
2004–05	Everton	0	0		
2004–05	Doncaster R	8	0	8	0
2005–06	Everton	3	0		
2005–06	Wycombe W	3	0	3	0
2006–07	Everton	1	0		
2006–07	Crystal Palace	5	0	5	0
2006–07	Sheffield W	11	0	11	0
2007–08	Everton	0	0		
2008–09	Everton	0	0		
2008–09	Nottingham F	3	0	3	0
2009–10	Everton	0	0	4	0

VAUGHAN, James (F)   48 7
H: 5 11   W: 13 00   b.Birmingham 14-7-88
Source: Scholar. *Honours:* England Youth, Under-21.

2004–05	Everton	2	1		
2005–06	Everton	1	0		
2006–07	Everton	14	4		
2007–08	Everton	8	1		
2008–09	Everton	13	0		
2009–10	Everton	8	1	46	7
2009–10	Derby Co	2	0	2	0

WALLACE, James (M)   0 0
H: 5 11   W: 12 08   b.Fazackerly 19-12-91
Source: Scholar. *Honours:* England Youth.

| 2008–09 | Everton | 0 | 0 | | |
| 2009–10 | Everton | 0 | 0 | | |

YAKUBU, Ayegbeni (F)   281 106
H: 6 0   W: 14 07   b.Benin City 22-11-82
Source: Julius Berger. *Honours:* Nigeria Under-21, Under-23, 53 full caps, 21 goals.

1999–2000	Gil Vicente	0	0		
1999–2000	Hapoel Kfar-Sava	23	6	23	6
2000–01	Maccabi Haifa	14	3		
2001–02	Maccabi Haifa	22	13	36	16
2002–03	Portsmouth	14	7		
2003–04	Portsmouth	37	16		
2004–05	Portsmouth	30	12	81	35
2005–06	Middlesbrough	34	13		
2006–07	Middlesbrough	37	12		
2007–08	Middlesbrough	2	0	73	25
2007–08	Everton	29	15		
2008–09	Everton	14	4		
2009–10	Everton	25	5	68	24

YOBO, Joseph (D)   291 10
H: 6 1   W: 13 00   b.Kano 6-9-80
Source: Mechelen. *Honours:* Nigeria B, 70 full caps, 4 goals.

1998–99	Standard Liege	0	0		
1999–2000	Standard Liege	18	0		
2000–01	Standard Liege	30	2	48	2
2001–02	Marseille	23	0	23	0
2002–03	Everton	24	0		
2003–04	Everton	28	2		
2004–05	Everton	27	0		
2005–06	Everton	29	1		
2006–07	Everton	38	2		
2007–08	Everton	30	1		
2008–09	Everton	27	1		
2009–10	Everton	17	1	220	8

Scholars
Cummins, Adam; Dobie, Luke Jeffrey; Donegan, Thomas David; Garbutt, Luke; Murphy, Daniel; Thompson, Zac; Watson, Ryan.

EXETER C (35)

ARCHIBALD-HENVILLE, Troy (D) 34 0
H: 6 2   W: 13 03   b.Newham 4-11-88
Source: Scholar.

2007–08	Tottenham H	0	0		
2008–09	Tottenham H	0	0		
2008–09	Norwich C	0	0		
2008–09	Exeter C	19	0		
2009–10	Tottenham H	0	0		
2009–10	Exeter C	15	0	34	0

BENNETT, Scott (D)   0 0
H: 5 10   W: 12 10   b.Truro 30-11-90
Source: Scholar.

| 2008–09 | Exeter C | 0 | 0 | | |
| 2009–10 | Exeter C | 0 | 0 | | |

BURNELL, Joe (M)   253 2
H: 5 8   W: 12 00   b.Bristol 10-10-80
Source: Trainee.

1999–2000	Bristol C	17	0		
2000–01	Bristol C	23	0		
2001–02	Bristol C	30	0		
2002–03	Bristol C	44	0		
2003–04	Bristol C	17	1	131	1
2004–05	Wycombe W	24	0		
2005–06	Wycombe W	33	0	57	0
2006–07	Northampton T	24	1		
2007–08	Northampton T	33	0		
2008–09	Northampton T	40	0	57	1
2009–10	Exeter C	8	0	8	0

CORR, Barry (F)   90 13
H: 6 3   W: 12 07   b.Co Wicklow 2-4-85
Honours: Eire Youth.

2001–02	Leeds U	0	0		
2002–03	Leeds U	0	0		
2003–04	Leeds U	0	0		
2004–05	Leeds U	0	0		
2005–06	Sheffield W	0	0		
2006–07	Sheffield W	1	0	17	0
2006–07	*Bristol C*	3	0	3	0
2006–07	Swindon T	8	3		
2007–08	Swindon T	17	5		
2008–09	Swindon T	11	2	36	10
2009–10	Exeter C	34	3	34	3

COZIC, Bertrand (M)   85 3
H: 5 10   W: 12 06   b.Quimper 18-5-78
Source: Team Bath.

2003–04	Cheltenham T	7	1	7	1
From Hereford U					
2004–05	Northampton T	14	0	14	0
2004–05	Kidderminster H	15	0	15	0
From Aldershot T.					
2008–09	Exeter C	20	0		
2009–10	Exeter C	29	2	49	2

DUFFY, Richard (D)   152 3
H: 5 9   W: 10 03   b.Swansea 30-8-85
Source: Scholar. *Honours:* Wales Youth, Under-21, 13 full caps.

2002–03	Swansea C	0	0		
2003–04	Swansea C	18	1		
2003–04	Portsmouth	1	0		
2004–05	Portsmouth	0	0		
2004–05	Burnley	7	1	7	1
2004–05	Coventry C	14	0		
2005–06	Portsmouth	0	0		
2005–06	Coventry C	32	0		
2006–07	Portsmouth	0	0		
2006–07	Coventry C	13	0		
2006–07	*Swansea C*	11	0	29	1
2007–08	Portsmouth	0	0		
2007–08	*Coventry C*	2	0	61	0
2008–09	Portsmouth	0	0	1	0
2008–09	Millwall	12	0	12	0
2009–10	Exeter C	42	1	42	1

DUNNE, James (M)   23 3
H: 5 11   W: 10 12   b.Farnborough 18-9-89
Source: Scholar.

2007–08	Arsenal	0	0		
2008–09	Arsenal	0	0		
2008–09	*Nottingham F*	0	0		
2009–10	Exeter C	23	3	23	3

EDWARDS, Rob (D)   556 15
H: 6 0   W: 12 02   b.Kendal 1-1-73
Source: Trainee. *Honours:* Wales Youth, Under-21, B, 4 full caps

1989–90	Carlisle U	12	0		
1990–91	Carlisle U	36	5	48	5
1990–91	Bristol C	0	0		
1991–92	Bristol C	20	1		
1992–93	Bristol C	18	0		
1993–94	Bristol C	38	2		
1994–95	Bristol C	30	0		
1995–96	Bristol C	19	0		
1996–97	Bristol C	31	0		
1997–98	Bristol C	37	2		
1998–99	Bristol C	23	0	216	5
1999–2000	Preston NE	41	2		
2000–01	Preston NE	42	0		
2001–02	Preston NE	36	2		
2002–03	Preston NE	26	0		
2003–04	Preston NE	24	0	169	4
2004–05	Blackpool	26	1		
2005–06	Blackpool	32	0	58	1
2008–09	Exeter C	44	0		
2009–10	Exeter C	21	0	65	0

FREAR, Elliott (F)   0 0
b.Exeter 11-9-90
Source: Scholar.

| 2009–10 | Exeter C | 0 | 0 | | |

GOLBOURNE, Scott (M)   97 1
H: 5 8   W: 11 08   b.Bristol 29-2-88
Source: Scholar. *Honours:* England Youth.

2004–05	Bristol C	9	0		
2005–06	Bristol C	5	0	14	0
2005–06	Reading	1	0		

2006–07	Reading	0	0		
2006–07	Wycombe W	34	1	34	1
2007–08	Reading	1	0		
2007–08	Bournemouth	5	0	5	0
2008–09	Reading	0	0	2	0
2008–09	Oldham Ath	8	0	8	0
2009–10	Exeter C	34	0	34	0

HARLEY, Ryan (D) 77 14
H: 5 11 W: 11 00 b.Bristol 22-1-85
Source: Scholar.

2004–05	Bristol C	2	0		
2005–06	Bristol C	0	0	2	0
2008–09	Exeter C	31	4		
2009–10	Exeter C	44	10	75	14

JONES, Paul (G) 72 0
H: 6 3 W: 13 00 b.Maidstone 28-6-86
Source: Leyton Orient Scholar.

2008–09	Exeter C	46	0		
2009–10	Exeter C	26	0	72	0

LOGAN, Richard (F) 219 41
H: 6 1 W: 12 05 b.Bury St Edmunds 4-1-82
Source: Trainee. *Honours:* England Youth.

1998–99	Ipswich T	2	0		
1999–2000	Ipswich T	1	0		
2000–01	Ipswich T	0	0		
2000–01	Cambridge U	5	1	5	1
2001–02	Ipswich T	3	0		
2001–02	Torquay U	16	4	16	4
2002–03	Ipswich T	0	0	3	0
2002–03	Boston U	27	10		
2003–04	Boston U	8	0	35	10
2003–04	Peterborough U	29	7		
2004–05	Peterborough U	26	4		
2004–05	Shrewsbury T	5	1	5	1
2005–06	Peterborough U	28	4	83	15
2005–06	Lincoln C	8	2	8	2
From Weymouth.					
2008–09	Exeter C	30	4		
2009–10	Exeter C	34	4	64	8

MARRIOTT, Andy (G) 470 0
H: 6 2 W: 13 07 b.Sutton-in-Ashfield 11-10-70
Source: Trainee. *Honours:* England Schools, FA Schools, Youth, Under-21, Wales 5 full caps.

1988–89	Arsenal	0	0		
1989–90	Nottingham F	0	0		
1989–90	WBA	3	0	3	0
1989–90	Blackburn R	2	0	2	0
1989–90	Colchester U	10	0	10	0
1990–91	Nottingham F	0	0		
1991–92	Nottingham F	6	0		
1991–92	Burnley	15	0	15	0
1992–93	Nottingham F	5	0		
1993–94	Nottingham F	0	0	11	0
1993–94	Wrexham	36	0		
1994–95	Wrexham	46	0		
1995–96	Wrexham	46	0		
1996–97	Wrexham	43	0		
1997–98	Wrexham	42	0		
1998–99	Wrexham	0	0	213	0
1998–99	Sunderland	1	0		
1999–2000	Sunderland	1	0		
2000–01	Sunderland	0	0	2	0
2000–01	Wigan Ath	0	0		
2000–01	Barnsley	0	0		
2001–02	Barnsley	18	0		
2002–03	Barnsley	36	0	54	0
2002–03	Birmingham C	1	0	1	0
2003–04	Beira Mar	24	0	24	0
2004–05	Bury	19	0	19	0
2004–05	Torquay U	11	0		
2005–06	Torquay U	46	0	57	0
2006–07	Boston U	46	0		
2007–08	Boston U	0	0	46	0
2008–09	Exeter C	0	0		
2009–10	Exeter C	13	0	13	0

McALLISTER, Craig (F) 47 7
H: 6 1 W: 11 03 b.Glasgow 28-6-80
Source: Basingstoke T, Stevenage B, Woking, Grays Ath, Oxford U.

2008–09	Exeter C	30	7		
2009–10	Exeter C	4	0	34	7
2009–10	Barnet	5	0	5	0
2009–10	Rotherham U	8	0	8	0

NOBLE, David (M) 162 13
H: 6 0 W: 12 04 b.Hitchin 2-2-82
Source: Scholar. *Honours:* England Youth, Under-20, Scotland Under-21, B.

2000–01	Arsenal	0	0		
2001–02	Arsenal	0	0		
2001–02	Watford	15	1	15	1
2002–03	Arsenal	0	0		
2002–03	West Ham U	0	0		
2003–04	West Ham U	3	0	3	0
2003–04	Boston U	14	2		
2004–05	Boston U	32	3		
2005–06	Boston U	11	0	57	5
2005–06	Bristol C	24	1		
2006–07	Bristol C	26	3		
2007–08	Bristol C	26	2		
2008–09	Bristol C	9	1	85	7
2008–09	Yeovil T	2	0	2	0
2009–10	Exeter C	0	0		

NORWOOD, James (F 3 0
H: 5 9 W: 11 07 b.Eastbourne 5-9-90
Source: Eastbourne T. *Honours:* England Schools.

2009–10	Exeter C	3	0	3	0

RUSSELL, Alex (M) 477 53
H: 5 10 W: 11 07 b.Crosby 17-3-73
Source: Burscough.

1994–95	Rochdale	7	1		
1995–96	Rochdale	25	0		
1996–97	Rochdale	39	9		
1997–98	Rochdale	31	4	102	14
1998–99	Cambridge U	37	6		
1999–2000	Cambridge U	15	0		
2000–01	Cambridge U	29	2	81	8
2001–02	Torquay U	33	7		
2002–03	Torquay U	39	9		
2003–04	Torquay U	43	2		
2004–05	Torquay U	38	3	153	21
2005–06	Bristol C	27	4		
2006–07	Bristol C	28	2		
2007–08	Bristol C	1	0	56	6
2007–08	Northampton T	13	1	13	1
2007–08	Cheltenham T	13	2		
2008–09	Cheltenham T	23	0	36	2
2008–09	Exeter C	7	0		
2009–10	Exeter C	29	1	36	1

SAUNDERS, Neil (M) 23 3
H: 5 11 W: 11 02 b.Dagenham 7-5-83
Source: Watford Scholar, Harlow T.

2001–02	Watford	0	0		
2002–03	Watford	0	0		
From Barnet, Team Bath.					
2008–09	Exeter C	17	3		
2009–10	Exeter C	6	0	23	3

SERCOMBE, Liam (M) 57 3
H: 5 10 W: 10 10 b.Exeter 25-4-90

2008–09	Exeter C	29	2		
2009–10	Exeter C	28	1	57	3

SHEPHARD, Chris (M) 2 0
H: 6 3 W: 13 03 b.Exeter 25-12-88

2008–09	Exeter C	2	0		
2009–10	Exeter C	0	0	2	0

STANSFIELD, Adam (F) 96 23
H: 5 11 W: 11 02 b.Plymouth 10-9-78
Source: Elmore.

2003–04	Yeovil T	32	6	32	6
From Hereford U.					
2008–09	Exeter C	37	10		
2009–10	Exeter C	27	7	64	17

STEWART, Marcus (F) 656 199
H: 5 10 W: 11 00 b.Bristol 7-11-72
Source: Trainee. *Honours:* England Schools, Football League.

1991–92	Bristol R	33	5		
1992–93	Bristol R	38	11		
1993–94	Bristol R	29	5		
1994–95	Bristol R	27	15		
1995–96	Bristol R	44	21	171	57
1996–97	Huddersfield T	20	7		
1997–98	Huddersfield T	41	15		
1998–99	Huddersfield T	43	22		
1999–2000	Huddersfield T	29	14	133	58
1999–2000	Ipswich T	13	2		
2000–01	Ipswich T	34	19		
2001–02	Ipswich T	28	6		
2002–03	Ipswich T	3	0	75	27
2002–03	Sunderland	19	1		
2003–04	Sunderland	40	14		
2004–05	Sunderland	43	16	102	31
2005–06	Bristol C	27	5		
2005–06	Preston NE	4	0	4	0
2006–07	Bristol C	0	0	27	5
2006–07	Yeovil T	31	8		
2007–08	Yeovil T	36	4	67	12
2008–09	Exeter C	36	7		
2009–10	Exeter C	41	2	77	9

TAYLOR, Matthew (D) 77 7
H: 6 0 W: 12 04 b.Chorley 30-1-82
Source: Burscough, Rossendale U, Matlock T, Hucknall T, Guiseley, Team Bath.

2008–09	Exeter C	31	2		
2009–10	Exeter C	46	5	77	7

TULLY, Steve (D) 180 4
H: 5 10 W: 11 02 b.Paignton 10-2-80
Source: Trainee.

1997–98	Torquay U	9	0		
1998–99	Torquay U	37	2		
1999–2000	Torquay U	13	0		
2000–01	Torquay U	29	1		
2001–02	Torquay U	18	0	106	3
From Weymouth.					
2008–09	Exeter C	36	0		
2009–10	Exeter C	38	1	74	1

WATSON, Ben (F) 13 2
H: 5 10 W: 10 11 b.Shoreham 6-12-85
Source: Grays Ath.

2008–09	Exeter C	12	2		
2009–10	Exeter C	1	0	13	2

FULHAM (36)

BAIRD, Chris (D) 146 3
H: 5 10 W: 11 11 b.Ballymoney 25-2-82
Source: Scholar. *Honours:* Northern Ireland Youth, Under-21, 44 full caps.

2000–01	Southampton	0	0		
2001–02	Southampton	0	0		
2002–03	Southampton	3	0		
2003–04	Southampton	4	0		
2003–04	Walsall	10	0	10	0
2003–04	Watford	8	0	8	0
2004–05	Southampton	0	0		
2005–06	Southampton	17	0		
2006–07	Southampton	44	3	68	3
2007–08	Fulham	18	0		
2008–09	Fulham	10	0		
2009–10	Fulham	32	0	60	0

BRIGGS, Matthew (D) 2 0
H: 6 1 W: 11 12 b.Wandsworth 6-3-91
Source: School. *Honours:* England Youth, Under-20.

2006–07	Fulham	1	0		
2007–08	Fulham	0	0		
2008–09	Fulham	0	0		
2009–10	Fulham	0	0	1	0
2009–10	Leyton Orient	1	0	1	0

BROWN, Wayne (M) 41 10
H: 5 9 W: 12 05 b.Kingston 6-8-88
Source: Scholar.

2006–07	Fulham	0	0		
2007–08	Fulham	0	0		
2007–08	Brentford	11	1	11	1
2008–09	Fulham	1	0		
2009	TPS Turku	25	9	25	9
2009–10	Fulham	0	0	1	0
2009–10	Bristol R	4	0	4	0

BUCHTMANN, Christopher (M) 0 0
H: 5 8 W: 10 10 b.Mincen 25-4-92
Source: Liverpool Scholar.

2009–10	Fulham	0	0		

DAVIES, Simon (M) 332 29
H: 5 10 W: 11 07 b.Haverfordwest 23-10-79
Source: Trainee. *Honours:* Wales Youth, Under-21, B, 58 full caps, 6 goals.

1997–98	Peterborough U	6	0		
1998–99	Peterborough U	43	4		
1999–2000	Peterborough U	16	2	65	6
1999–2000	Tottenham H	3	0		

2000–01	Tottenham H	13	2		
2001–02	Tottenham H	31	4		
2002–03	Tottenham H	36	5		
2003–04	Tottenham H	17	2		
2004–05	Tottenham H	21	0	121	13
2005–06	Everton	30	1		
2006–07	Everton	15	0	45	1
2006–07	Fulham	14	2		
2007–08	Fulham	37	5		
2008–09	Fulham	33	2		
2009–10	Fulham	17	0	101	9

DEMPSEY, Clint (M) 187 47
H: 6 1 W: 12 02 b.Nacogdoches 9-3-83
Source: Furman Univ. *Honours:* USA
Under-21, 66 full caps, 19 goals.

2004	New England Rev	24	7		
2005	New England Rev	30	11		
2006	New England Rev	23	8	77	26
2006–07	Fulham	10	1		
2007–08	Fulham	36	6		
2008–09	Fulham	35	7		
2009–10	Fulham	29	7	110	21

DIKGACOI, Kagisho (M) 102 8
H: 5 11 W: 12 10 b.Brandfort 24-11-84
Honours: South Africa 39 full caps, 2 goals.

2004–05	Bloemfontein YT	10	0	10	0
2005–06	Lamontville GA	9	0		
2006–07	Lamontville GA	25	0		
2007–08	Lamontville GA	23	4		
2008–09	Lamontville GA	23	4	80	8
2009–10	Fulham	12	0	12	0

DUFF, Damien (F) 366 52
H: 5 9 W: 12 06 b.Ballyboden 2-3-79
Source: Lourdes Celtic. *Honours:* Eire
Schools, Youth, Under-20, B, 83 full caps, 7
goals.

1995–96	Blackburn R	0	0		
1996–97	Blackburn R	1	0		
1997–98	Blackburn R	26	4		
1998–99	Blackburn R	28	1		
1999–2000	Blackburn R	39	5		
2000–01	Blackburn R	32	1		
2001–02	Blackburn R	32	7		
2002–03	Blackburn R	26	9	184	27
2003–04	Chelsea	23	5		
2004–05	Chelsea	30	6		
2005–06	Chelsea	28	3	81	14
2006–07	Newcastle U	22	1		
2007–08	Newcastle U	16	0		
2008–09	Newcastle U	30	3		
2009–10	Newcastle U	1	1	69	5
2009–10	Fulham	32	6	32	6

ELM, David (M) 143 26
H: 6 3 W: 13 12 b.Johansfors 10-1-83

2004	Falkenberg	15	1		
2005	Falkenberg	27	3		
2006	Falkenberg	26	10	68	14
2007	Kalmar	21	1		
2008	Kalmar	27	7		
2009	Kalmar	17	3	65	11
2009–10	Fulham	10	1	10	1

ETHERIDGE, Neil (G) 0 0
H: 6 3 W: 14 00 b.Enfield 7-2-90
Source: Scholar.

2008–09	Fulham	0	0		
2009–10	Fulham	0	0		

ETUHU, Dickson (M) 269 25
H: 6 2 W: 13 04 b.Kano 8-6-82
Source: Scholar. *Honours:* Nigeria 17 full
caps.

1999–2000	Manchester C	0	0		
2000–01	Manchester C	0	0		
2001–02	Manchester C	12	0	12	0
2001–02	Preston NE	16	3		
2002–03	Preston NE	39	6		
2003–04	Preston NE	31	3		
2004–05	Preston NE	35	3		
2005–06	Preston NE	13	2	134	17
2005–06	Norwich C	19	0		
2006–07	Norwich C	43	6	62	6
2007–08	Sunderland	20	1		
2008–09	Sunderland	0	0	20	1
2008–09	Sunderland	21	1		
2009–10	Fulham	20	0	41	1

GERA, Zoltan (M) 325 61
H: 6 0 W: 11 11 b.Pecs 22-4-79
Source: Hakarny. *Honours:* Hungary 63 full
caps, 18 goals.

1999–2000	Pecsi	15	4	15	4
2000–01	Ferencvaros	32	7		
2001–02	Ferencvaros	27	8		
2002–03	Ferencvaros	26	6		
2003–04	Ferencvaros	30	11	115	32
2004–05	WBA	38	6		
2005–06	WBA	15	2		
2006–07	WBA	40	5		
2007–08	WBA	43	8	136	21
2008–09	Fulham	32	2		
2009–10	Fulham	27	2	59	4

HANGELAND, Brede (D) 261 11
H: 6 4 W: 13 05 b.Houston 20-6-81
Honours: Norway Under-21, 60 full caps.

2000	Vidar	0	0		
2001	Viking	22	0		
2002	Viking	26	2		
2003	Viking	26	1		
2004	Viking	14	3		
2005	Viking	26	0	114	6
2005–06	FC Copenhagen	13	1		
2006–07	FC Copenhagen	32	0		
2007–08	FC Copenhagen	18	2	63	3
2007–08	Fulham	15	0		
2008–09	Fulham	37	1		
2009–10	Fulham	32	1	84	2

HOESEN, Danny (F) 0 0
b.Eindhoven 15-1-91
Source: Fortuna Sittard.

2008–09	Fulham	0	0		
2009–10	Fulham	0	0		

HUGHES, Aaron (D) 361 4
H: 6 0 W: 11 02 b.Cookstown 8-11-79
Source: Trainee. *Honours:* Northern Ireland
Youth, B, 71 full caps.

1996–97	Newcastle U	0	0		
1997–98	Newcastle U	4	0		
1998–99	Newcastle U	14	0		
1999–2000	Newcastle U	27	2		
2000–01	Newcastle U	35	0		
2001–02	Newcastle U	34	0		
2002–03	Newcastle U	35	1		
2003–04	Newcastle U	34	0		
2004–05	Newcastle U	22	1	205	4
2005–06	Aston Villa	35	0		
2006–07	Aston Villa	19	0	54	0
2007–08	Fulham	30	0		
2008–09	Fulham	38	0		
2009–10	Fulham	34	0	102	0

JOHNSON, Andy (F) 323 106
H: 5 7 W: 10 09 b.Bedford 10-2-81
Source: Trainee. *Honours:* England Youth,
Under-20, 8 full caps.

1997–98	Birmingham C	0	0		
1998–99	Birmingham C	4	0		
1999–2000	Birmingham C	22	1		
2000–01	Birmingham C	34	4		
2001–02	Birmingham C	23	3	83	8
2002–03	Crystal Palace	28	11		
2003–04	Crystal Palace	42	27		
2004–05	Crystal Palace	37	21		
2005–06	Crystal Palace	33	15	140	74
2006–07	Everton	32	11		
2007–08	Everton	29	6	61	17
2008–09	Fulham	31	7		
2009–10	Fulham	8	0	39	7

JOHNSON, Eddie (F) 168 43
H: 6 0 W: 12 02 b.Bunnell 31-3-84
Honours: USA 41 full caps, 12 goals.

2001	Dallas Burn	10	2		
2002	Dallas Burn	14	2		
2003	Dallas Burn	22	3		
2004	Dallas Burn	26	12		
2005	Dallas Burn	15	5	87	24
2006	Kansas City Wizards	19	2		
2007	Kansas City Wizards	24	15	43	17
2007–08	Fulham	6	0		
2008–09	Fulham	0	0		
2008–09	*Cardiff C*	30	2	30	2
2009–10	Fulham	2	0	8	0

KALLIO, Toni (D) 221 24
H: 6 4 W: 13 05 b.Tampere 9-8-78
Source: HJK Helsinki. *Honours:* Finland 49
full caps, 2 goals.

1997	Jazz	1	0	1	0
1997	Tampere U	19	1		
1998	Tampere U	19	2	38	3
1998	HJK Helsinki	9	0		
2000	HJK Helsinki	19	1		
2001	HJK Helsinki	32	5		
2002	HJK Helsinki	26	7		
2003	HJK Helsinki	0	0	86	13
2004	Molde	7	2		
2005	Molde	22	3		
2006	Molde	24	1	53	6
2006–07	Young Boys	15	0		
2007–08	Young Boys	16	2	31	2
2007–08	Fulham	0	0		
2008–09	Fulham	3	0		
2009–10	Fulham	1	0	4	0
2009–10	*Sheffield U*	8	0	8	0

KAMARA, Diomansy (F) 254 59
H: 6 0 W: 11 05 b.Paris 8-11-80
Honours: Senegal 49 full caps, 9 goals.

1998–99	Red Star 93	4	0	4	0
1999–2000	Catanzaro	11	4		
2000–01	Catanzaro	23	5	34	9
2001–02	Chievo	0	0		
2001–02	Modena	24	4		
2002–03	Modena	29	5		
2003–04	Modena	29	6	82	15
2004–05	Portsmouth	25	4	25	4
2005–06	WBA	26	1		
2006–07	WBA	34	20	60	21
2007–08	Fulham	28	5		
2008–09	Fulham	12	4		
2009–10	Fulham	9	1	49	10

KELLY, Stephen (D) 160 2
H: 6 0 W: 12 04 b.Dublin 6-9-83
Source: Juniors. *Honours:* Eire Youth,
Under-21, 18 full caps.

2000–01	Tottenham H	0	0		
2001–02	Tottenham H	0	0		
2002–03	Tottenham H	0	0		
2002–03	*Southend U*	10	0	10	0
2002–03	*QPR*	7	0	7	0
2003–04	Tottenham H	11	0		
2003–04	*Watford*	13	0	13	0
2004–05	Tottenham H	17	2		
2005–06	Tottenham H	9	0	37	2
2006–07	Birmingham C	36	0		
2007–08	Birmingham C	38	0		
2008–09	Birmingham C	5	0		
2008–09	*Stoke C*	6	0	6	0
2009–10	Birmingham C	0	0	79	0
2009–10	Fulham	8	0	8	0

KONCHESKY, Paul (D) 316 8
H: 5 10 W: 11 07 b.Barking 15-5-81
Source: Trainee. *Honours:* England Youth,
Under-20, Under-21, 2 full caps.

1997–98	Charlton Ath	3	0		
1998–99	Charlton Ath	2	0		
1999–2000	Charlton Ath	8	0		
2000–01	Charlton Ath	23	0		
2001–02	Charlton Ath	34	1		
2002–03	Charlton Ath	30	3		
2003–04	Charlton Ath	21	0		
2003–04	*Tottenham H*	12	0	12	0
2004–05	Charlton Ath	28	1	149	5
2005–06	West Ham U	37	1		
2006–07	West Ham U	22	0	59	1
2007–08	Fulham	33	0		
2008–09	Fulham	36	1		
2009–10	Fulham	27	1	96	2

MARQUEZ-SANCHEZ, Christian (D) 0 0
b.Barcelona 13-1-93

2009–10	Fulham	0	0		

MARSH-BROWN, Keanu (F) 0 0
H: 5 11 W: 12 04 b.Hammersmith 10-8-92
Source: Scholar.

2009–10	Fulham	0	0		

MILSOM, Robert (D) 13 0
H: 5 10 W: 11 05 b.Redhill 2-1-87
Source: Scholar.

2005–06	Fulham	0	0		

2006–07	Fulham	0	0	
2007–08	Fulham	0	0	
2007–08	*Brentford*	6	0	6 0
2008–09	Fulham	1	0	
2008–09	*Southend U*	6	0	6 0
2009–10	Fulham	0	0	1 0

MURPHY, Danny (M) 494 76
H: 5 10 W: 11 09 b.Chester 18-3-77
Source: Trainee. *Honours:* England Schools, Youth, Under-21, 9 full caps, 1 goal.

1993–94	Crewe Alex	12	2	
1994–95	Crewe Alex	35	5	
1995–96	Crewe Alex	42	10	
1996–97	Crewe Alex	45	10	
1997–98	Liverpool	16	0	
1998–99	Liverpool	1	0	
1998–99	*Crewe Alex*	16	1	150 28
1999–2000	Liverpool	23	3	
2000–01	Liverpool	27	4	
2001–02	Liverpool	36	6	
2002–03	Liverpool	36	7	
2003–04	Liverpool	35	5	170 25
2004–05	Charlton Ath	38	3	
2005–06	Charlton Ath	18	4	56 7
2005–06	Tottenham H	10	0	
2006–07	Tottenham H	12	1	
2007–08	Tottenham H	0	0	22 1
2007–08	Fulham	33	5	
2008–09	Fulham	38	5	
2009–10	Fulham	25	5	96 15

NEVLAND, Erik (F) 306 132
H: 5 10 W: 11 12 b.Stavanger 10-11-77
Honours: Norway 8 full caps.

1996	Viking	1	0	
1997	Viking	13	5	
1997–98	Manchester U	1	0	1 0
1998	Viking	8	3	
1999	IFK Gothenburg	4	0	4 0
2000	Viking	20	14	
2001	Viking	37	18	
2002	Viking	27	23	
2003	Viking	25	11	
2004	Viking	23	6	154 80
2004–05	Groningen	20	16	
2005–06	Groningen	29	8	
2006–07	Groningen	31	13	
2007–08	Groningen	15	6	95 43
2007–08	Fulham	8	2	
2008–09	Fulham	21	4	
2009–10	Fulham	23	3	52 9

OKAKA CHUKA, Stefano (F) 83 12
H: 6 1 W: 13 01 b.Castiglion del Lago 9-8-89
Honours: Italy Youth, Under-20, Under-21.

2005–06	Roma	1	0	
2006–07	Roma	6	1	
2007–08	Roma	0	0	
2007–08	*Modena*	33	7	33 7
2008–09	Roma	9	0	23 1
2008–09	*Brescia*	16	2	16 2
2009–10	Fulham	11	2	11 2

On loan from Roma.

OMOZUSI, Elliot (D) 38 0
H: 5 11 W: 12 09 b.Hackney 15-12-88
Source: Scholar. *Honours:* England Youth.

2005–06	Fulham	0	0	
2006–07	Fulham	0	0	
2007–08	Fulham	8	0	
2008–09	Fulham	0	0	
2008–09	*Norwich C*	21	0	21 0
2009–10	Fulham	0	0	8 0
2009–10	*Charlton Ath*	9	0	9 0

PANTSIL, John (D) 207 5
H: 5 10 W: 12 08 b.Berekum 15-6-81
Source: Liberty Professionals, Berkum Arsenals. *Honours:* Ghana Youth, Under-20, 60 full caps.

2000–01	Liberty Pros	10	0	10 0
2001–02	Berekum Arsenal	12	1	12 1
2001–02	Widzew Lodz	19	1	19 1
2002–03	Maccabi Tel Aviv	17	0	
2003–04	Maccabi Tel Aviv	22	0	
2004–05	Maccabi Tel Aviv	7	0	46 0
2005–06	Hapoel Tel Aviv	15	1	
2006–07	Hapoel Tel Aviv	27	2	42 3
2006–07	West Ham U	5	0	
2007–08	West Ham U	14	0	19 0
2008–09	Fulham	37	0	
2009–10	Fulham	22	0	59 0

PAYNE, Stefan (F) 0 0
b.London 10-8-91
Source: Sutton U.

2009–10	Fulham	0	0

RIISE, Bjorn Helge (M) 146 12
H: 5 10 W: 11 11 b.Alesund 21-6-83
Honours: Norway 22 full caps, 1 goal.

2002	*Viking*	0	0	
2002–03	Standard Liege	9	0	
2003–04	Standard Liege	8	0	17 0
2004–05	FC Brussels	31	2	31 2
2005	Lillestrom	13	0	
2006	Lillestrom	25	1	
2007	Lillestrom	24	3	
2008	Lillestrom	9	0	
2009	Lillestrom	15	6	86 10
2009–10	Fulham	12	0	12 0

SAUNDERS, Matthew (M) 18 3
H: 5 11 W: 11 05 b.Chertsey 12-9-89
Source: Scholar.

2008–09	Fulham	0	0	
2009–10	Fulham	0	0	
2009–10	*Lincoln C*	18	3	18 3

SCHWARZER, Mark (G) 519 0
H: 6 4 W: 14 07 b.Sydney 6-10-72
Honours: Australia Youth, Under-20, Under-23, 78 full caps.

1990–91	Marconi Stallions	1	0	
1991–92	Marconi Stallions	9	0	
1992–93	Marconi Stallions	23	0	
1993–94	Marconi Stallions	25	0	58 0
1994–95	Dynamo Dresden	2	0	2 0
1995–96	Kaiserslautern	4	0	
1996–97	Kaiserslautern	0	0	4 0
1996–97	Bradford C	13	0	13 0
1996–97	Middlesbrough	7	0	
1997–98	Middlesbrough	35	0	
1998–99	Middlesbrough	34	0	
1999–2000	Middlesbrough	37	0	
2000–01	Middlesbrough	31	0	
2001–02	Middlesbrough	21	0	
2002–03	Middlesbrough	38	0	
2003–04	Middlesbrough	36	0	
2004–05	Middlesbrough	31	0	
2005–06	Middlesbrough	27	0	
2006–07	Middlesbrough	36	0	
2007–08	Middlesbrough	34	0	367 0
2008–09	Fulham	38	0	
2009–10	Fulham	37	0	75 0

SEOL, Ki-Hyun (F) 220 41
H: 6 0 W: 11 07 b.South Korea 8-1-79
Honours: South Korea 83 full caps, 19 goals.

2000–01	Antwerp	25	10	25 10
2001–02	Anderlecht	20	3	
2002–03	Anderlecht	32	12	
2003–04	Anderlecht	19	3	71 18
2004–05	Wolverhampton W	37	4	
2005–06	Wolverhampton W	32	4	69 8
2006–07	Reading	27	4	
2007–08	Reading	3	0	30 4
2007–08	Fulham	12	0	
2008–09	Fulham	4	1	
2008–09	*Al-Hilal*	7	0	7 0
2009–10	Fulham	2	0	18 1

SMALLING, Chris (D) 13 0
H: 6 4 W: 14 02 b.Greenwich 22-11-89
Honours: England Youth, Under-21.

2008–09	Fulham	1	0	
2009–10	Fulham	12	0	13 0

SMITH, Alex (D) 0 0
H: 5 9 W: 8 09 b. 31-10-91
Source: Scholar.

2009–10	Fulham	0	0

STOCKDALE, David (G) 86 0
H: 6 3 W: 13 04 b.Leeds 20-9-85
Source: Scholar.

2002–03	York C	1	0	
2003–04	York C	0	0	
2004–05	York C	0	0	
2005–06	York C	0	0	1 0
2006–07	Darlington	6	0	
2007–08	Darlington	41	0	47 0
2008–09	Fulham	0	0	
2008–09	*Rotherham U*	8	0	8 0
2008–09	*Leicester C*	8	0	8 0
2009–10	Fulham	1	0	1 0
2009–10	*Plymouth Arg*	21	0	21 0

STOOR, Fredrik (D) 87 2
H: 6 0 W: 12 06 b.Stockholm 28-2-84
Honours: Sweden 11 full caps.

2002	Hammarby	0	0	
2003	Hammarby	1	0	
2004	Hammarby	7	0	
2005	Hammarby	20	1	
2006	Hammarby	23	1	51 2
2007	Rosenborg	21	0	21 0
2008–09	Fulham	2	0	
2009–10	Fulham	2	0	4 0
2009–10	*Derby Co*	11	0	11 0

TROTTA, Marcello (F) 0 0
b.Santa Maria Capua 29-9-92
Source: Napoli.

2009–10	Fulham	0	0

UWEZU, Michael (M) 2 0
H: 5 6 W: 12 02 b.Nigeria 12-12-90

2008–09	Fulham	0	0	
2009–10	Fulham	0	0	
2009–10	*Lincoln C*	2	0	2 0

ZAMORA, Bobby (F) 337 116
H: 6 1 W: 11 11 b.Barking 16-1-81
Source: Trainee. *Honours:* England Under-21.

1999–2000	Bristol R	4	0	4 0
1999–2000	Brighton & HA	6	6	
2000–01	Brighton & HA	43	28	
2001–02	Brighton & HA	41	28	
2002–03	Brighton & HA	35	14	125 76
2003–04	Tottenham H	16	0	16 0
2003–04	West Ham U	17	5	
2004–05	West Ham U	34	7	
2005–06	West Ham U	34	6	
2006–07	West Ham U	32	11	
2007–08	West Ham U	13	1	130 30
2008–09	Fulham	35	2	
2009–10	Fulham	27	8	62 10

Scholars
Bangura, Suliaman; Cosgrove, Jonathan Graham; Dean, Jack; Harris, Courtney; Jorenen, Jenne; Kamau, Michael; Maloney, Robert John; Owusu-Anseh, Albert Junior; Peniket, Richard James; Pierre, Aaron; Pritchard, Joshua Philip; Reece, Matthew; Toure, Cheick Sekou.

GILLINGHAM (37)

BARCHAM, Andy (F) 100 14
H: 5 8 W: 11 10 b.Basildon 16-12-86
Source: Scholar.

2005–06	Tottenham H	0	0	
2006–07	Tottenham H	0	0	
2007–08	Tottenham H	0	0	
2007–08	*Leyton Orient*	25	1	25 1
2008–09	Tottenham H	0	0	
2008–09	Gillingham	33	6	
2009–10	Gillingham	42	7	75 13

BENTLEY, Mark (M) 242 21
H: 6 2 W: 13 04 b.Hertford 7-1-78
Source: Enfield, Aldershot T, Gravesend & N, Dagenham & R.

2003–04	Southend U	21	2	
2004–05	Southend U	39	5	
2005–06	Southend U	33	5	93 12
2006–07	Gillingham	41	4	
2007–08	Gillingham	33	2	
2008–09	Gillingham	39	1	
2009–10	Gillingham	36	2	149 9

ERSKINE, Jacob (F) 4 0
H: 6 1 W: 14 00 b.Lambeth 13-1-89
Source: Croyden Ath, Dagenham & R. From Bromley.

2009–10	Gillingham	4	0	4 0

FULLER, Barry (M) 98 1
H: 5 10 W: 11 10 b.Ashford 25-9-84
Source: Scholar.

2004–05	Charlton Ath	0	0
2005–06	Charlton Ath	0	0

2005–06	Barnet	15	1	15	1

From Stevenage B.

2007–08	Gillingham	10	0		
2008–09	Gillingham	37	0		
2009–10	Gillingham	36	0	83	0

GOWLING, Josh (D) 143 3
H: 6 3 W: 12 08 b.Coventry 29-11-83
Source: WBA Scholar.

2004–05	Herfolge	13	0	13	0
2005–06	Bournemouth	13	0		
2006–07	Bournemouth	33	1		
2007–08	Bournemouth	37	0	83	1
2008–09	Carlisle U	4	0		
2008–09	*Hereford U*	13	0	13	0
2009–10	Carlisle U	0	0	4	0
2009–10	Gillingham	30	2	30	2

JACKMAN, Danny (D) 244 15
H: 5 4 W: 10 00 b.Worcester 3-1-83
Source: Scholar.

2000–01	Aston Villa	0	0		
2001–02	Aston Villa	0	0		
2001–02	*Cambridge U*	7	1	7	1
2002–03	Aston Villa	0	0		
2003–04	Aston Villa	0	0		
2003–04	Stockport Co	27	2		
2004–05	Stockport Co	33	2	60	4
2005–06	Gillingham	42	0		
2006–07	Gillingham	31	1		
2007–08	Northampton T	39	1		
2008–09	Northampton T	43	8		
2009–10	Northampton T	0	0	82	9
2009–10	Gillingham	22	0	95	1

JACKSON, Simeon (M) 118 40
H: 5 10 W: 10 12 b.Kingston, Jamaica 28-3-87
Source: Scholar. *Honours:* Canada Youth, 10 full caps, 1 goal.

2004–05	Rushden & D	3	0		
2005–06	Rushden & D	14	5		
2005–07	Rushden & D	0	0		
2007–08	Rushden & D	0	0	17	5
2007–08	Gillingham	18	4		
2008–09	Gillingham	41	17		
2009–10	Gillingham	42	14	101	35

JULIAN, Alan (G) 50 0
H: 6 2 W: 13 07 b.Ashford 11-3-83
Source: Trainee. *Honours:* Northern Ireland Youth, Under-21.

2001–02	Brentford	0	0		
2002–03	Brentford	3	0		
2003–04	Brentford	13	0		
2004–05	Brentford	0	0		
2005–06	Brentford	0	0		
2006–07	Brentford	0	0		
2007–08	Brentford	0	0	16	0

From Stevenage B.

2008–09	Gillingham	4	0		
2009–10	Gillingham	30	0	34	0

KING, Simon (D) 164 4
H: 6 0 W: 13 00 b.Oxford 11-4-83
Source: Scholar.

2000–01	Oxford U	2	0		
2001–02	Oxford U	2	0		
2002–03	Oxford U	0	0		
2003–04	Oxford U	0	0		
2004–05	Oxford U	0	0	4	0
2005–06	Barnet	32	0		
2006–07	Barnet	43	2	75	2
2007–08	Gillingham	42	0		
2008–09	Gillingham	43	2		
2009–10	Gillingham	0	0	85	2

LEWIS, Stuart (M) 55 1
H: 5 10 W: 11 06 b.Welwyn 15-10-87
Source: Scholar. *Honours:* England Youth.

2005–06	Tottenham H	0	0		
2006–07	Tottenham H	0	0		
2006–07	Barnet	4	0	4	0

From Stevenage B.

2007–08	Gillingham	10	0		
2008–09	Gillingham	21	0		
2009–10	Gillingham	20	1	51	1

MAHER, Kevin (M) 444 23
H: 6 0 W: 12 13 b.Ilford 17-10-76
Source: Trainee. *Honours:* Eire Under-21.

1995–96	Tottenham H	0	0		
1996–97	Tottenham H	0	0		
1997–98	Tottenham H	0	0		
1997–98	Southend U	18	1		
1998–99	Southend U	34	4		
1999–2000	Southend U	24	0		
2000–01	Southend U	41	2		
2001–02	Southend U	36	5		
2002–03	Southend U	42	2		
2003–04	Southend U	42	1		
2004–05	Southend U	42	1		
2005–06	Southend U	44	1		
2006–07	Southend U	41	5		
2007–08	Southend U	19	0	383	22
2007–08	*Gillingham*	7	0		
2008–09	Oldham Ath	28	1	28	1
2009–10	Gillingham	26	0	33	0

McCAMMON, Mark (F) 248 30
H: 6 2 W: 14 05 b.Barnet 7-8-78
Source: Cambridge C. *Honours:* Barbados 5 full caps, 4 goals.

1997–98	Cambridge U	2	0		
1998–99	Cambridge U	2	0	4	0
1998–99	Charlton Ath	0	0		
1999–2000	Charlton Ath	4	0	4	0
1999–2000	*Swindon T*	4	0	4	0
2000–01	Brentford	24	3		
2001–02	Brentford	14	0		
2002–03	Brentford	37	7	75	10
2002–03	Millwall	7	2		
2003–04	Millwall	7	0		
2004–05	Millwall	8	0	22	2
2004–05	Brighton & HA	18	3		
2005–06	Brighton & HA	7	0	25	3
2005–06	*Bristol C*	11	4	11	4
2006–07	Doncaster R	22	2		
2007–08	Doncaster R	32	4	54	6
2008–09	Gillingham	31	5		
2009–10	Gillingham	14	0	45	5
2009–10	*Bradford C*	4	0	4	0

MILLER, Adam (M) 114 13
H: 5 11 W: 11 06 b.Hemel Hempstead 19-2-82
Source: Aldershot T.

2004–05	QPR	14	0		
2005–06	QPR	1	0	15	0
2005–06	*Peterborough U*	2	0	2	0

From Stevenage B

2007–08	Gillingham	28	3		
2008–09	Gillingham	35	6		
2009–10	Gillingham	26	4	89	13
2009–10	*Dagenham & R*	8	0	8	0

MURPHY, Tom (M) 0 0
H: 5 11 W: 10 12 b.Gillingham 19-12-91
Source: Scholar.

2008–09	Gillingham	0	0		
2009–10	Gillingham	0	0		

NUTTER, John (D) 105 2
H: 6 2 W: 12 10 b.Burnham 13-6-82
Source: Blackburn R Scholar.

2000–01	Wycombe W	1	0		
2001–02	Wycombe W	0	0		
2007–08	Wycombe W	0	0	1	0

From Ald'shot T, Grays Ath, Stevenage B.

2007–08	Gillingham	24	1		
2008–09	Gillingham	45	0		
2009–10	Gillingham	35	1	104	2

OLI, Dennis (F) 117 12
H: 6 0 W: 12 00 b.Newham 28-1-84

2001–02	QPR	2	0		
2002–03	QPR	18	0		
2003–04	QPR	3	0	23	0
2004–05	Swansea C	1	0	1	0
2004–05	Cambridge U	4	1		
2005–06	Cambridge U	0	0		
2006–07	Cambridge U	0	0	4	1

From Grays Ath.

2007–08	Gillingham	22	4		
2008–09	Gillingham	31	4		
2009–10	Gillingham	36	3	89	11

PALMER, Chris (M) 155 7
H: 5 7 W: 11 00 b.Derby 16-10-83
Source: Scholar.

2003–04	Derby Co	0	0		
2004–05	Notts Co	25	4		
2005–06	Notts Co	29	1	54	5
2006–07	Wycombe W	32	0		
2007–08	Wycombe W	1	0	33	0
2007–08	*Darlington*	4	0	4	0
2008–09	Walsall	44	1	44	1
2009–10	Gillingham	20	1	20	1

PAYNE, Jack (M) 21 0
H: 5 9 W: 9 02 b.Gravesend 5-12-91
Source: Scholar.

2008–09	Gillingham	2	0		
2009–10	Gillingham	19	0	21	0

RICHARDS, Garry (D) 106 5
H: 6 3 W: 13 00 b.Romford 11-6-86
Source: Scholar.

2005–06	Colchester U	15	0		
2006–07	Colchester U	5	1	20	1
2006–07	*Brentford*	10	1	10	1
2007–08	*Southend U*	10	0	10	0
2007–08	Gillingham	14	1		
2008–09	Gillingham	36	2		
2009–10	Gillingham	16	0	66	3

ROONEY, Luke (M) 13 2
H: 5 8 W: 11 07 b.Southwark 28-12-90
Source: Scholar.

2009–10	Gillingham	13	2	13	2

ROYCE, Simon (G) 359 0
H: 6 2 W: 12 10 b.Forest Gate 9-9-71
Source: Heybridge Swifts.

1991–92	Southend U	1	0		
1992–93	Southend U	3	0		
1993–94	Southend U	6	0		
1994–95	Southend U	13	0		
1995–96	Southend U	46	0		
1996–97	Southend U	43	0		
1997–98	Southend U	37	0	149	0
1998–99	Charlton Ath	8	0		
1999–2000	Charlton Ath	0	0		
2000–01	Leicester C	19	0		
2001–02	Leicester C	0	0		
2001–02	*Brighton & HA*	6	0	6	0
2001–02	*Manchester C*	0	0		
2002–03	Leicester C	0	0	19	0
2002–03	*QPR*	16	0		
2003–04	Charlton Ath	1	0		
2004–05	Charlton Ath	0	0	9	0
2004–05	*Luton T*	2	0	2	0
2004–05	*QPR*	13	0		
2005–06	QPR	30	0		
2006–07	QPR	20	0	79	0
2006–07	*Gillingham*	3	0		
2007–08	Gillingham	33	0		
2008–09	Gillingham	42	0		
2009–10	Gillingham	17	0	95	0

WALKER, James (F) 99 13
H: 5 10 W: 11 10 b.Hackney 25-11-87
Source: Scholar. *Honours:* England Youth.

2004–05	Charlton Ath	0	0		
2005–06	Charlton Ath	0	0		
2005–06	Hartlepool U	4	0	4	0
2006–07	Charlton Ath	0	0		
2006–07	*Bristol R*	4	1	4	1
2006–07	*Leyton Orient*	14	2	14	2
2006–07	Notts Co	8	0	8	0
2007–08	Charlton Ath	0	0		
2007–08	*Yeovil T*	13	3	13	3
2007–08	*Southend U*	15	4		
2008–09	Southend U	17	2		
2009–10	Southend U	13	0	45	6
2009–10	Hereford U	6	1	6	1
2009–10	Gillingham	5	0	5	0

WESTON, Curtis (M) 129 13
H: 5 11 W: 11 09 b.Greenwich 24-1-87
Source: Scholar.

2003–04	Millwall	1	0		
2004–05	Millwall	3	0		
2005–06	Millwall	0	0	4	0
2006–07	Swindon T	27	1	27	1
2007–08	Leeds U	7	1		
2007–08	*Scunthorpe U*	7	0	7	0
2008–09	Leeds U	0	0	7	1
2008–09	Gillingham	45	5		
2009–10	Gillingham	39	6	84	11

WYNTER, Tom (M) 8 0
H: 5 7 W: 11 11 b.Lewisham 20-6-90
Source: Scholar.

2008–09	Gillingham	0	0		
2009–10	Gillingham	8	0	8	0

YUSSUFF, Rashid (M)   8   0
H: 6 1   W: 10 07   b.Poplar 23-9-89

2007–08	Charlton Ath	0	0	
2008–09	Charlton Ath	0	0	
2009–10	Gillingham	8	0	8 0

GRIMSBY T (38)

AKPA AKPRO, Jean-Louis (F)   108   14
H: 6 0   W: 10 12   b.Toulouse 4-1-85

2004–05	Toulouse	13	0	
2005–06	Toulouse	14	3	
2006–07	Toulouse	10	1	
2007–08	Brest	15	2	15 2
2007–08	Toulouse	0	0	37 4
2008–09	Grimsby T	20	3	
2009–10	Grimsby T	36	5	56 8

ATKINSON, Rob (D)   102   5
H: 6 1   W: 12 00   b.Beverley 29-4-87
Source: Scholar.

2003–04	Barnsley	1	0	
2004–05	Barnsley	1	0	
2005–06	Barnsley	0	0	
2006–07	Barnsley	6	0	
2007–08	Barnsley	0	0	
2007–08	Rochdale	0	2	2 0
2007–08	Grimsby T	24	1	
2008–09	Barnsley	0	0	8 0
2008–09	Grimsby T	31	2	
2009–10	Grimsby T	37	2	92 5

BORE, Peter (M)   116   11
H: 5 11   W: 11 04   b.Grimsby 4-11-87
Source: Scholar.

2006–07	Grimsby T	32	8	
2007–08	Grimsby T	17	2	
2008–09	Grimsby T	27	1	
2009–10	Grimsby T	40	0	116 11

CLARKE, Jamie (D)   223   8
H: 6 2   W: 12 03   b.Sunderland 18-9-82
Source: Scholar.

2001–02	Mansfield T	1	0	
2002–03	Mansfield T	21	1	
2003–04	Mansfield T	12	0	34 1
2004–05	Rochdale	41	1	
2005–06	Rochdale	22	0	63 1
2005–06	Boston U	15	1	
2006–07	Boston U	37	2	52 3
2007–08	Grimsby T	29	2	
2008–09	Grimsby T	32	1	
2009–10	Grimsby T	13	0	74 3

COLGAN, Nick (G)   283   0
H: 6 1   W: 12 00   b.Drogheda 19-9-73
Source: Drogheda. Honours: Eire Schools, Youth, Under-21, B, 9 full caps.

1992–93	Chelsea	0	0	
1993–94	Chelsea	0	0	
1993–94	Crewe Alex	0	0	
1994–95	Chelsea	0	0	
1994–95	Grimsby T	0	0	
1995–96	Chelsea	0	0	
1995–96	Millwall	0	0	
1996–97	Chelsea	1	0	
1997–98	Chelsea	0	0	1 0
1997–98	Brentford	5	0	5 0
1997–98	Reading	5	0	5 0
1998–99	Bournemouth	24	0	
1999–2000	Hibernian	24	0	
2000–01	Hibernian	37	0	
2001–02	Hibernian	30	0	
2002–03	Hibernian	30	0	
2003–04	Hibernian	0	0	121 0
2003–04	Stockport Co	15	0	15 0
2004–05	Barnsley	13	0	
2005–06	Barnsley	43	0	
2006–07	Barnsley	44	0	
2007–08	Barnsley	1	0	101 0
2007–08	Ipswich T	0	0	
2008–09	Sunderland	0	0	
2009–10	Grimsby T	35	0	35 0

FORBES, Adrian (F)   330   38
H: 5 8   W: 11 10   b.Greenford 23-1-79
Source: Trainee. Honours: England Youth.

1996–97	Norwich C	10	0	
1997–98	Norwich C	33	4	
1998–99	Norwich C	15	0	
1999–2000	Norwich C	25	1	
2000–01	Norwich C	29	3	112 8
2001–02	Luton T	40	4	
2002–03	Luton T	5	1	
2003–04	Luton T	27	9	72 14
2004–05	Swansea C	40	7	
2005–06	Swansea C	29	4	69 11
2006–07	Blackpool	34	1	
2007–08	Blackpool	2	0	36 1
2007–08	Millwall	11	0	
2008–09	Millwall	2	0	13 0
2008–09	Grimsby T	15	3	
2009–10	Grimsby T	13	1	28 4

FULLER, Josh (M)   6   0
H 5 9   W: 11 00   b.Grimsby 9-2-92
Source: Scholar.

2008–09	Grimsby T	1	0	
2009–10	Grimsby T	5	0	6 0

HEGARTY, Nick (M)   92   8
H: 5 10   W: 11 00   b.Hemsworth 25-6-86
Source: Scholar.

2004–05	Grimsby T	1	0	
2005–06	Grimsby T	2	0	
2006–07	Grimsby T	15	0	
2007–08	Grimsby T	30	4	
2008–09	Grimsby T	35	4	
2009–10	Grimsby T	9	0	92 8

HEYWOOD, Matt (D)   299   12
H: 6 3   W: 14 00   b.Chatham 26-8-79
Source: Trainee.

1998–99	Burnley	13	0	
1999–2000	Burnley	0	0	
2000–01	Burnley	0	0	13 0
2000–01	Swindon T	21	2	
2001–02	Swindon T	44	3	
2002–03	Swindon T	46	1	
2003–04	Swindon T	40	1	
2004–05	Swindon T	32	1	183 8
2005–06	Bristol C	24	2	24 2
2006–07	Brentford	28	1	
2007–08	Brentford	32	1	60 2
2008–09	Grimsby T	13	0	
2009–10	Grimsby T	1	0	19 0

HUDSON, Mark (M)   221   27
H: 5 10   W: 11 03   b.Bishop Auckland 24-10-80
Source: Scholar.

1999–2000	Middlesbrough	0	0	
2000–01	Middlesbrough	3	0	
2001–02	Middlesbrough	2	0	
2002–03	Middlesbrough	0	0	5 0
2002–03	Carlisle U	15	1	15 1
2002–03	Chesterfield	24	3	
2003–04	Chesterfield	35	2	
2004–05	Chesterfield	34	4	93 9
2005–06	Huddersfield T	29	3	
2006–07	Huddersfield T	32	3	61 6
2007–08	Rotherham U	31	9	
2008–09	Rotherham U	0	0	31 9
2009–10	Blackpool	0	0	
2009–10	Grimsby T	16	2	16 2

JARMAN, Nathan (F)   64   6
H: 5 11   W: 11 03   b.Scunthorpe 19-9-86
Source: Scholar.

2004–05	Barnsley	6	0	
2005–06	Barnsley	9	0	
2005–06	Bury	2	0	2 0
2006–07	Barnsley	0	0	
2007–08	Barnsley	0	0	15 0
2007–08	Grimsby T	7	0	
2008–09	Grimsby T	33	6	
2009–10	Grimsby T	7	0	47 6

JONES, Chris (F)   14   1
H: 5 7   W: 10 00   b.Swansea 12-9-89
Honours: Wales Youth, Under-21.

2006–07	Swansea C	7	0	
2007–08	Swansea C	0	0	
2008–09	Swansea C	0	0	7 0
2009–10	Grimsby T	7	1	7 1

LEARY, Michael (M)   147   6
H: 6 0   W: 11 10   b.Ealing 17-4-83
Source: Scholar.

2001–02	Luton T	0	0	
2002–03	Luton T	0	0	
2003–04	Luton T	14	2	
2004–05	Luton T	8	0	
2005–06	Luton T	0	0	
2005–06	Bristol R	13	0	13 0
2005–06	Walsall	15	1	15 1
2006–07	Luton T	0	0	22 2
2005–07	Torquay U	2	0	2 0
2006–07	Brentford	17	0	17 0
2007–08	Barnet	22	1	
2008–09	Barnet	28	2	50 3
2009–10	Grimsby T	28	0	28 0

LINWOOD, Paul (D)   203   5
H: 6 2   W: 13 03   b.Birkenhead 24-10-83
Source: Scholar.

2001–02	Tranmere R	0	0	
2002–03	Tranmere R	0	0	
2003–04	Tranmere R	20	0	
2004–05	Tranmere R	10	0	
2005–06	Tranmere R	14	0	44 0
2005–06	Wrexham	9	0	9 0
2006–07	Chester C	37	1	
2007–08	Chester C	42	1	
2008–09	Chester C	43	2	122 4
2009–10	Grimsby T	28	1	28 1

NORTH, Danny (F)   81   17
H: 5 9   W: 12 08   b.Grimsby 7-9-87
Source: Scholar.

2004–05	Grimsby T	1	0	
2005–06	Grimsby T	1	0	
2006–07	Grimsby T	20	6	
2007–08	Grimsby T	27	9	
2008–09	Grimsby T	15	1	
2009–10	Grimsby T	17	1	81 17

PEACOCK, Lee (F)   510   122
H: 6 0   W: 12 08   b.Paisley 9-10-76
Source: Trainee. Honours: Scotland Youth, Under-21.

1993–94	Carlisle U	1	0	
1994–95	Carlisle U	7	0	
1995–96	Carlisle U	22	2	
1996–97	Carlisle U	44	9	
1997–98	Carlisle U	2	0	76 11
1997–98	Mansfield T	32	5	
1998–99	Mansfield T	45	17	
1999–2000	Mansfield T	12	7	89 29
1999–2000	Manchester C	8	0	8 0
2000–01	Bristol C	35	13	
2001–02	Bristol C	31	15	
2002–03	Bristol C	37	12	
2003–04	Bristol C	41	14	144 54
2004–05	Sheffield W	29	4	
2005–06	Sheffield W	22	2	51 6
2005–06	Swindon T	15	2	
2006–07	Swindon T	42	10	
2007–08	Swindon T	37	6	
2008–09	Swindon T	27	2	
2009–10	Swindon T	4	0	125 20
2009–10	Grimsby T	17	2	17 2

PROUDLOCK, Adam (F)   266   48
H: 6 0   W: 13 07   b.Wellington 9-5-81
Source: Trainee.

1999–2000	Wolverhampton W	0	0	
2000–01	Clyde	4	4	4 4
2000–01	Wolverhampton W	35	8	
2001–02	Wolverhampton W	19	3	
2001–02	Nottingham F	3	0	3 0
2002–03	Wolverhampton W	17	2	
2002–03	Tranmere R	5	0	5 0
2002–03	Sheffield W	5	2	
2003–04	Wolverhampton W	0	0	71 13
2003–04	Sheffield W	30	3	
2004–05	Sheffield W	14	6	
2005–06	Sheffield W	6	0	55 11
2005–06	Ipswich T	9	0	
2006–07	Ipswich T	0	0	9 0
2006–07	Stockport Co	23	3	
2007–08	Stockport Co	33	8	56 11
2008–09	Darlington	8	0	8 0
2008–09	Grimsby T	28	8	
2009–10	Grimsby T	27	1	55 9

RHOADES, Drew (G)   0   0
Source: Scholar.

2009–10	Grimsby T	0	0	

SHAHIN, Jammal (M)   5   0
H: 5 11   W: 12 01   b.Grimsby 19-12-88
Source: Armthorpe Wel.
| 2009–10 | Grimsby T | 5 | 0 | 5 | 0 |

STOCKDALE, Robbie (D)   256   3
H: 6 0   W: 11 03   b.Middlesbrough 30-11-79
Source: Trainee. *Honours:* England
Under-21. Scotland B, 5 full caps.
1997–98	Middlesbrough	1	0		
1998–99	Middlesbrough	19	0		
1999–2000	Middlesbrough	11	1		
2000–01	Middlesbrough	0	0		
2000–01	*Sheffield W*	6	0	6	0
2001–02	Middlesbrough	28	1		
2002–03	Middlesbrough	14	0		
2003–04	Middlesbrough	2	0	75	2
2003–04	*West Ham U*	7	0	7	0
2003–04	*Rotherham U*	16	1		
2004–05	Rotherham U	27	0	43	1
2004–05	Hull C	14	0		
2005–06	Hull C	0	0	14	0
2005–06	*Darlington*	3	0	3	0
2006–07	Tranmere R	36	0		
2007–08	Tranmere R	44	0	80	0
2008–09	Grimsby T	20	0		
2009–10	Grimsby T	8	0	28	0

SWEENEY, Peter (M)   166   11
H: 6 0   W: 12 11   b.Glasgow 25-9-84
Source: Scholar. *Honours:* Scotland Youth,
Under-21, B.
2001–02	Millwall	1	0		
2002–03	Millwall	5	1		
2003–04	Millwall	29	2		
2004–05	Millwall	24	2	59	5
2005–06	Stoke C	17	1		
2006–07	Stoke C	13	1		
2006–07	*Yeovil T*	8	0	8	0
2007–08	Stoke C	5	0	35	2
2007–08	*Walsall*	7	0	7	0
2007–08	Leeds U	9	0		
2008–09	Leeds U	0	0	9	0
2008–09	*Grimsby T*	8	0		
2009–10	Grimsby T	40	4	48	4

WIDDOWSON, Joe (D)   61   1
H: 6 0   W: 12 00   b.Forest Gate 28-3-89
Source: Scholar.
2007–08	*West Ham U*	0	0		
2007–08	*Rotherham U*	3	0	3	0
2008–09	West Ham U	0	0		
2008–09	*Grimsby T*	20	1		
2009–10	Grimsby T	38	0	58	1

WOOD, Bradley (D)   8   0
H: 5 9   W: 11 00   b.Leicester 2-9-91
Source: Scholar.
| 2009–10 | Grimsby T | 8 | 0 | 8 | 0 |

WRIGHT, Tommy (F)   184   34
H: 6 0   W: 12 02   b.Leicester 28-9-84
Source: Scholar. *Honours:* England Youth,
Under-20.
2001–02	Leicester C	1	0		
2002–03	Leicester C	13	2		
2003–04	Leicester C	0	0		
2003–04	*Brentford*	25	3	25	3
2004–05	Leicester C	7	0		
2005–06	Leicester C	0	0	21	2
2005–06	*Blackpool*	13	6	13	6
2005–06	Barnsley	17	1		
2006–07	Barnsley	17	1	34	2
2006–07	*Walsall*	6	2	6	2
2006–07	Darlington	13	4		
2007–08	Darlington	40	13	53	17
2008–09	Aberdeen	15	1		
2009–10	Aberdeen	3	0	18	1
2009–10	Grimsby T	14	1	14	1

HARTLEPOOL U (39)

AUSTIN, Neil (D)   249   8
H: 5 10   W: 11 09   b.Barnsley 26-4-83
Source: Trainee. *Honours:* England Youth,
Under-20.
1999–2000	Barnsley	0	0		
2000–01	Barnsley	0	0		
2001–02	Barnsley	0	0		

2002–03	Barnsley	34	0		
2003–04	Barnsley	37	0		
2004–05	Barnsley	15	0		
2005–06	Barnsley	38	0		
2006–07	Barnsley	24	0	148	0
2007–08	Darlington	29	2		
2008–09	Darlington	33	3	62	5
2009–10	Hartlepool U	39	3	39	3

BEHAN, Denis (F)   181   37
H: 6 0   W: 13 04   b.Abbeyfeale 2-1-84
Honours: Eire Under-21.
2004	Cork C	21	1		
2005	Cork C	22	4		
2006	Cork C	28	6		
2007	Cork C	30	8		
2008	Cork C	31	7		
2009	Cork C	20	5	152	31
2009–10	Hartlepool U	29	6	29	6

BJORNSSON, Armann (F)   137   26
H: 6 5   W: 14 00   b.Hafnarfjordur 7-1-81
Source: Sindri, Lillestrom (loan).
2001	Valur	14	1		
2002	Valur	14	4		
2002	*Brann*	7	3		
2003	Valur	14	4	42	9
2004	Hafnafjordur	12	3		
2005	Hafnafjordur	9	2		
2006	Hafnafjordur	15	2	36	7
2006	Brann	2	0		
2007	Brann	15	2		
2008	Brann	8	0		
2009	Brann	9	2	41	7
2009–10	Hartlepool U	18	3	18	3

BOYD, Adam (F)   294   88
H: 5 9   W: 10 12   b.Hartlepool 25-5-82
Source: Scholarship.
1999–2000	Hartlepool U	4	1		
2000–01	Hartlepool U	5	0		
2001–02	Hartlepool U	29	9		
2002–03	Hartlepool U	22	5		
2003–04	Hartlepool U	18	12		
2003–04	*Boston U*	14	4	14	4
2004–05	Hartlepool U	45	22		
2005–06	Hartlepool U	21	4		
2006–07	Luton T	19	1	19	1
2007–08	Leyton Orient	44	14		
2008–09	Leyton Orient	33	9	77	23
2009–10	Hartlepool U	40	7	184	60

BROWN, James (F)   125   27
H: 5 11   W: 11 00   b.Newcastle 3-1-87
Source: Cramlington Jun.
2004–05	Hartlepool U	0	0		
2005–06	Hartlepool U	4	1		
2006–07	Hartlepool U	36	6		
2007–08	Hartlepool U	35	10		
2008–09	Hartlepool U	18	6		
2009–10	Hartlepool U	32	4	125	27

CHEREL, Julian (M)   1   0
H: 6 5   W: 13 05   b.Caen 8-3-83
Source: Caen, Mondeville.
| 2009–10 | Hartlepool U | 1 | 0 | 1 | 0 |

CLARK, Ben (D)   170   6
H: 6 1   W: 13 11   b.Shotley Bridge 24-1-83
Source: Manchester U Trainee. *Honours:*
England Youth, Under-20.
2000–01	Sunderland	0	0		
2001–02	Sunderland	0	0		
2002–03	Sunderland	1	0		
2003–04	Sunderland	5	0		
2004–05	Sunderland	2	0	8	0
2004–05	Hartlepool U	25	0		
2005–06	Hartlepool U	32	0		
2006–07	Hartlepool U	40	3		
2007–08	Hartlepool U	19	1		
2008–09	Hartlepool U	35	2		
2009–10	Hartlepool U	11	0	162	6

COLLINS, Sam (D)   375   16
H: 6 2   W: 14 03   b.Pontefract 5-6-77
Source: Trainee.
1994–95	Huddersfield T	0	0		
1995–96	Huddersfield T	0	0		
1996–97	Huddersfield T	0	0		
1997–98	Huddersfield T	10	0		
1998–99	Huddersfield T	23	0	37	0
1999–2000	Bury	19	0		

2000–01	Bury	34	2		
2001–02	Bury	29	0	82	2
2002–03	Port Vale	44	5		
2003–04	Port Vale	43	4		
2004–05	Port Vale	33	2		
2005–06	Port Vale	15	0	135	11
2005–06	Hull C	17	0		
2006–07	Hull C	6	0		
2007–08	Hull C	0	0	23	0
2007–08	*Swindon T*	4	0	4	0
2007–08	Hartlepool U	10	2		
2008–09	Hartlepool U	40	1		
2009–10	Hartlepool U	44	0	94	3

FLINDERS, Scott (G)   98   0
H: 6 4   W: 13 00   b.Rotherham 12-5-86
Source: Scholar. *Honours:* England Youth,
Under-20.
2004–05	Barnsley	11	0		
2005–06	Barnsley	3	0	14	0
2006–07	Crystal Palace	8	0		
2006–07	*Gillingham*	9	0	9	0
2006–07	*Brighton & HA*	12	0	12	0
2007–08	Crystal Palace	0	0		
2007–08	*Yeovil T*	9	0	9	0
2008–09	Crystal Palace	0	0	8	0
2009–10	Hartlepool U	46	0	46	0

FOLEY, David (F)   98   0
H: 5 4   W: 8 09   b.South Shields 12-5-87
Source: Scholar.
2003–04	Hartlepool U	1	0		
2004–05	Hartlepool U	2	0		
2005–06	Hartlepool U	11	0		
2006–07	Hartlepool U	25	0		
2007–08	Hartlepool U	34	0		
2008–09	Hartlepool U	23	0		
2009–10	Hartlepool U	2	0	98	0

FREDRIKSEN, Jon-Andre (M)   181   26
H: 5 11   W: 12 00   b.Moss 5-4-82
2002	Moss	10	0		
2003	Moss	13	0		
2004	Moss	25	4		
2005	Moss	29	7		
2006	Moss	27	8		
2007	Moss	27	6		
2008	Moss	17	0	156	26
2009	Sarpsborg	13	0	13	0
2009–10	Hartlepool U	12	0	12	0

GAMBLE, Joe (M)   169   6
H: 5 7   W: 11 00   b.Cork 14-1-82
Honours: Eire Under-21, B, 2 full caps.
2000–01	Reading	0	0		
2001–02	Reading	6	0		
2002–03	Reading	0	0		
2003–04	Reading	0	0	7	0
2004	Cork C	16	0		
2005	Cork C	25	2		
2006	Cork C	24	0		
2007	Cork C	27	1		
2008	Cork C	25	1		
2009	Cork C	23	0	140	4
2009–10	Hartlepool U	22	2	22	2

GREULICH, Billy (F)   4   0
H: 6 3   W: 11 13   b.London 24-4-91
Source: Brandon U.
| 2009–10 | Hartlepool U | 4 | 0 | 4 | 0 |

HARTLEY, Peter (D)   51   2
H: 6 0   W: 12 06   b.Hartlepool 3-4-88
Source: Scholar.
2006–07	Sunderland	1	0		
2007–08	Sunderland	0	0		
2007–08	*Chesterfield*	12	0	12	0
2008–09	Sunderland	0	0	1	0
2009–10	Hartlepool U	38	2	38	2

HASLAM, Steven (M)   212   3
H: 5 11   W: 10 10   b.Sheffield 6-9-79
Source: Trainee. *Honours:* England Schools
Youth.
1996–97	Sheffield W	0	0		
1997–98	Sheffield W	0	0		
1998–99	Sheffield W	2	0		
1999–2000	Sheffield W	23	0		
2000–01	Sheffield W	27	1		
2001–02	Sheffield W	41	0		
2002–03	Sheffield W	26	1		
2003–04	Sheffield W	25	0	144	2

2004–05	Northampton T	3	0		
2005–06	Northampton T	0	0		
2006–07	Northampton T	0	0	3	0

From Halifax T.

2007–08	Bury	37	1		
2008–09	Bury	13	0	50	1
2009–10	Hartlepool U	15	0	15	0

HUMPHREYS, Richie (M)   492 41
H: 5 11 W: 12 07 b.Sheffield 30-11-77
Source: Trainee. *Honours:* England Youth, Under-21.

1995–96	Sheffield W	5	0		
1996–97	Sheffield W	29	3		
1997–98	Sheffield W	7	0		
1998–99	Sheffield W	19	1		
1999–2000	Sheffield W	0	0		
1999–2000	*Scunthorpe U*	6	2	6	2
1999–2000	*Cardiff C*	9	2	9	2
2000–01	Sheffield W	7	0	67	4
2000–01	Cambridge U	7	3	7	3
2001–02	Hartlepool U	46	5		
2002–03	Hartlepool U	46	11		
2003–04	Hartlepool U	46	3		
2004–05	Hartlepool U	46	3		
2005–06	Hartlepool U	46	2		
2006–07	Hartlepool U	38	3		
2006–07	*Port Vale*	7	0	7	0
2007–08	Hartlepool U	45	3		
2008–09	Hartlepool U	45	0		
2009–10	Hartlepool U	38	0	396	30

JONES, Richie (M)   88 7
H: 6 0 W: 11 00 b.Manchester 26-9-86
Source: Scholar. *Honours:* England Youth.

2004–05	Manchester U	0	0		
2005–06	Manchester U	0	0		
2006–07	Manchester U	0	0		
2006–07	*Colchester U*	6	0	6	0
2006–07	*Barnsley*	4	0	4	0
2007–08	Manchester U	0	0		
2007–08	*Yeovil T*	9	0	9	0
2008–09	Hartlepool U	36	3		
2009–10	Hartlepool U	33	4	69	7

LARKIN, Colin (F)   284 46
H: 5 9 W: 11 07 b.Dundalk 27-4-82
Source: Trainee.

1998–99	Wolverhampton W	0	0		
1999–2000	Wolverhampton W	1	0		
2000–01	Wolverhampton W	2	0		
2001–02	Wolverhampton W	0	0	3	0
2001–02	*Kidderminster H*	33	6	33	6
2002–03	Mansfield T	22	7		
2003–04	Mansfield T	37	7		
2004–05	Mansfield T	33	11	92	25
2005–06	Chesterfield	41	7		
2006–07	Chesterfield	39	4	80	11
2007–08	Northampton T	33	2		
2008–09	Northampton T	21	1		
2009–10	Northampton T	0	0	54	3
2009–10	Hartlepool U	22	1	22	1

LIDDLE, Gary (D)   166 8
H: 6 1 W: 12 06 b.Middlesbrough 15-6-86
Source: Trainee. *Honours:* England Youth.

2003–04	Middlesbrough	0	0		
2004–05	Middlesbrough	0	0		
2005–06	Middlesbrough	0	0		
2006–07	Hartlepool U	42	3		
2007–08	Hartlepool U	41	2		
2008–09	Hartlepool U	43	0		
2009–10	Hartlepool U	40	3	166	8

MACKAY, Michael (F)   49 7
H: 6 0 W: 11 06 b.Durham 11-10-82
Source: Consett.

2006–07	Hartlepool U	1	0		
2007–08	Hartlepool U	24	5		
2008–09	Hartlepool U	23	2		
2009–10	Hartlepool U	1	0	49	7

McSWEENEY, Leon (F)   78 6
H: 5 10 W: 10 11 b.Cork 19-2-83
Source: Cork C.

2001–02	Leicester C	0	0		
2002–03	Leicester C	0	0		
2003–04	Leicester C	0	0		
2004–05	Leicester C	0	0		
2005–06	Leicester C	0	0		
2006–07	Leicester C	0	0		
2007–08	Stockport Co	11	1		

2008–09	Stockport Co	36	4	47	5
2009–10	Hartlepool U	31	1	31	1

MONKHOUSE, Andy (M)   276 37
H: 6 1 W: 11 06 b.Leeds 23-10-80
Source: Trainee.

1998–99	Rotherham U	5	1		
1999–2000	Rotherham U	0	0		
2000–01	Rotherham U	12	0		
2001–02	Rotherham U	38	2		
2002–03	Rotherham U	20	0		
2003–04	Rotherham U	27	3		
2004–05	Rotherham U	14	2		
2005–06	Rotherham U	12	1	128	9
2006–07	Swindon T	10	2	10	2
2006–07	Hartlepool U	26	7		
2007–08	Hartlepool U	25	2		
2008–09	Hartlepool U	44	6		
2009–10	Hartlepool U	43	11	138	26

POWER, Alan (M)   6 0
H: 5 7 W: 11 06 b.Dublin 23-1-88
Source: Scholar. *Honours:* Éire Under-21.

2005–06	Nottingham F	0	0		
2006–07	Nottingham F	0	0		
2007–08	Nottingham F	0	0		
2008–09	Hartlepool U	4	0		
2009–10	Hartlepool U	2	0	6	0

ROWELL, Jonny (M)   12 0
H: 5 7 W: 11 02 b.Newcastle 10-9-89

2007–08	Hartlepool U	0	0		
2008–09	Hartlepool U	6	0		
2009–10	Hartlepool U	6	0	12	0

SWEENEY, Anthony (M)   253 34
H: 6 0 W: 11 07 b.Stockton 5-9-83
Source: Scholar.

2001–02	Hartlepool U	2	0		
2002–03	Hartlepool U	4	0		
2003–04	Hartlepool U	11	1		
2004–05	Hartlepool U	44	13		
2005–06	Hartlepool U	35	5		
2006–07	Hartlepool U	35	4		
2007–08	Hartlepool U	36	4		
2008–09	Hartlepool U	44	5		
2009–10	Hartlepool U	42	2	253	34

HEREFORD U (40)

ADAMSON, Chris (G)   34 0
H: 6 2 W: 13 07 b.Ashington 4-11-78
Source: Trainee.

1997–98	WBA	3	0		
1998–99	WBA	0	0		
1998–99	*Mansfield T*	2	0	2	0
1999–2000	WBA	9	0		
1999–2000	*Halifax T*	7	0	7	0
2000–01	WBA	0	0		
2001–02	WBA	0	0	12	0
2001–02	*Plymouth Arg*	1	0	1	0

From St Patrick's At

2004–05	Sheffield W	2	0		
2005–06	Sheffield W	5	0		
2006–07	Sheffield W	2	0	11	0
2007–08	Stockport Co	0	0		

From Ilkston.

2008–09	Stockport Co	0	0		
2009–10	Hereford U	0	0		

BARTLETT, Adam (G)   46 0
H: 6 0 W: 11 11 b.Newcastle-upon-Tyne 27-2-86
Source: Blyth Spartans, Kidderminster H, Cambridge U (loan). *Honours:* England C.
From Kidderminster H.

2009–10	Hereford U	45	0	46	0

CONSTANTINE, Leon (F)   283 80
H: 6 2 W: 12 00 b.Hackney 24-2-78
Source: Edgware T.

2000–01	Millwall	0	0		
2001–02	Millwall	0	0	1	0
2001–02	*Leyton Orient*	10	3	10	3
2001–02	*Partick T*	2	0	2	0
2002–03	Brentford	17	0	17	0
2003–04	*Southend U*	43	21	43	21
2004–05	Peterborough U	11	1	11	1
2004–05	Torquay U	27	9		
2005–06	Torquay U	15	1	42	10

2005–06	Port Vale	30	10		
2006–07	Port Vale	42	22		
2007–08	Port Vale	0	0	72	32
2007–08	Leeds U	4	1	4	1
2007–08	*Oldham Ath*	8	2	8	2
2008–09	Northampton T	32	3	32	3
2008–09	*Cheltenham T*	6	1	6	1
2009–10	Hereford U	35	6	35	6

DONE, Matt (M)   122 1
H: 5 10 W: 10 04 b.Oswestry 22-6-88
Source: Scholar.

2005–06	Wrexham	6	0		
2006–07	Wrexham	34	1		
2007–08	Wrexham	26	0	66	1
2008–09	Hereford U	36	0		
2009–10	Hereford U	20	0	56	0

GREEN, Ryan (M)   137 1
H: 5 7 W: 10 10 b.Cardiff 20-10-80
Source: Danes Court. *Honours:* Wales Youth, Under-21, 2 full caps.

1997–98	Wolverhampton W	0	0		
1998–99	Wolverhampton W	1	0		
1999–2000	Wolverhampton W	0	0		
2000–01	Wolverhampton W	7	0		
2000–01	*Torquay U*	10	0	10	0
2001–02	Wolverhampton W	0	0	8	0
2001–02	Millwall	13	0	13	0
2002–03	Cardiff C	0	0		
2002–03	Sheffield W	4	0	4	0

From Hereford U.

2006–07	Bristol R	33	0		
2007–08	Bristol R	12	0		
2008–09	Bristol R	26	0	71	0
2009–10	Hereford U	31	1	31	1

GWYNNE, Sam (M)   62 1
H: 5 9 W: 11 11 b.Hereford 17-12-87
Source: Scholar.

2006–07	Hereford U	0	0		
2007–08	Hereford U	15	0		
2008–09	Hereford U	21	1		
2009–10	Hereford U	26	0	62	1

JONES, Craig (M)   4 0
H: 6 1 W: 12 02 b.Hereford 12-12-89
Source: Cardiff C.

2007–08	Hereford U	0	0		
2008–09	Hereford U	3	0		
2009–10	Hereford U	1	0	4	0

JONES, Darren (D)   57 4
H: 6 0 W: 14 12 b.Newport 28-8-83
Source: Scholar. *Honours:* Wales Schools, Youth.

2000–01	Bristol C	0	0		
2001–02	Bristol C	2	0		
2002–03	Bristol C	0	0		
2003–04	Bristol C	0	0		
2003–04	*Cheltenham T*	14	1	14	1
2004–05	Bristol C	0	0		
2005–06	Bristol C	0	0		
2006–07	Bristol C	0	0		
2007–08	Bristol C	0	0		
2008–09	Bristol C	0	0	2	0
2009–10	Hereford U	41	3	41	3

LOWE, Keith (D)   98 5
H: 6 2 W: 13 00 b.Wolverhampton 13-9-85
Source: Scholar.

2004–05	Wolverhampton W	11	0		
2005–06	Wolverhampton W	3	0		
2005–06	*Burnley*	16	0	16	0
2005–06	*QPR*	1	0	1	0
2005–06	*Swansea C*	4	0	4	0
2006–07	Wolverhampton W	0	0		
2006–07	*Brighton & HA*	0	0		
2006–07	*Cheltenham T*	16	1	16	1
2007–08	Wolverhampton W	0	0		
2007–08	*Port Vale*	28	3	28	3
2008–09	Wolverhampton W	0	0	14	0
2009–10	Hereford U	19	1	19	1

LUNT, Kenny (M)   473 36
H: 5 10 W: 10 05 b.Runcorn 20-11-79
Source: Trainee. *Honours:* England Schools, Youth.

1997–98	Crewe Alex	41	2		
1998–99	Crewe Alex	18	1		
1999–2000	Crewe Alex	43	3		
2000–01	Crewe Alex	46	1		

2001–02	Crewe Alex	45	5		
2002–03	Crewe Alex	46	7		
2003–04	Crewe Alex	45	7		
2004–05	Crewe Alex	46	5		
2005–06	Crewe Alex	43	4		
2006–07	Sheffield W	37	0		
2007–08	Sheffield W	4	0		
2007–08	*Crewe Alex*	14	0		
2008–09	Sheffield W	0	0	41	0
2008–09	*Crewe Alex*	3	0	390	35
2009–10	Hereford U	42	1	42	1

MANSET, Mathieu (F) 29 3
H: 6 1 W: 13 08 b.Metz 5-8-89
Source: Le Havre.

2009–10	Hereford U	29	3	29	3

McCALLUM, Gavin (M) 27 8
H: 5 9 W: 12 00 b.Mississauga 24-8-87
Honours: Canada 1 full cap, 1 goal.

2005–06	Yeovil T	0	0		
2006–07	Yeovil T	0	0		

From Weymouth, Havant & W, Sutton U.

2009–10	Hereford U	27	8	27	8

McQUILKIN, James (F) 28 2
H: 5 8 W: 11 10 b.Belfast 9-1-89

2007–08	Zlin	4	0		
2008–09	Zlin	2	0	6	0
2009–10	Hereford U	22	2	22	2

MORRIS, Lee (F) 178 29
H: 5 10 W: 11 07 b.Blackpool 30-4-80
Source: Trainee. *Honours:* England Youth.

1997–98	Sheffield U	5	0		
1998–99	Sheffield U	20	6		
1999–2000	Sheffield U	1	0	26	6
1999–2000	Derby Co	3	0		
2000–01	Derby Co	20	0		
2000–01	*Huddersfield T*	5	1	5	1
2001–02	Derby Co	15	4		
2002–03	Derby Co	30	8		
2003–04	Derby Co	23	5	91	17
2003–04	Leicester C	0	0		
2004–05	Leicester C	10	0		
2005–06	Leicester C	0	0	10	0
2006–07	Yeovil T	33	5		
2007–08	Yeovil T	1	0		
2008–09	Yeovil T	0	0	34	5
2009–10	Hereford U	12	0	12	0

PUGH, Marc (M) 138 22
H: 5 11 W: 11 04 b.Burnley 2-4-87
Source: Scholar.

2005–06	Burnley	0	0		
2005–06	Bury	6	1		
2006–07	Bury	35	3	41	4
2007–08	Shrewsbury T	37	4		
2008–09	Shrewsbury T	7	0	44	4
2008–09	*Luton T*	4	0	4	0
2008–09	Hereford U	9	1		
2009–10	Hereford U	40	13	49	14

ROSE, Richard (D) 198 2
H: 6 0 W: 12 04 b.Pembury 8-9-82
Source: Trainee.

2000–01	Gillingham	4	0		
2001–02	Gillingham	3	0		
2002–03	Gillingham	2	0		
2002–03	*Bristol R*	9	0	9	0
2003–04	Gillingham	17	0		
2004–05	Gillingham	18	0		
2005–06	Gillingham	14	0	58	0
2006–07	Hereford U	33	1		
2007–08	Hereford U	31	1		
2008–09	Hereford U	42	0		
2009–10	Hereford U	25	0	131	2

SONKO, Edrissa (M) 202 31
H: 5 10 W: 11 05 b.Essau 23-3-80
Honours: Gambia 14 full caps, 7 goals.

2000–01	Roda JC	16	2		
2001–02	Roda JC	9	2		
2002–03	Roda JC	22	8		
2003–04	Roda JC	18	2		
2004–05	Roda JC	25	1		
2005–06	Roda JC	18	5	108	20
2006–07	Xanthi	9	1	9	1
2007–08	Walsall	37	5	37	5
2008–09	Tranmere R	38	5		
2009–10	Tranmere R	0	0	38	5
2009–10	Hereford U	10	0	10	0

SOUTHAM, Glen (M) 81 3
H: 5 7 W: 11 10 b.Enfield 27-8-80
Source: Bishop's Stortford.

2007–08	Dagenham & R	45	2		
2008–09	Dagenham & R	30	1	75	3
2009–10	Hereford U	6	0	6	0

TOLLEY, Jamie (M) 233 17
H: 6 1 W: 11 03 b.Ludlow 12-5-83
Source: Scholarship. *Honours:* Wales Under-21.

1999–2000	Shrewsbury T	2	0		
2000–01	Shrewsbury T	24	2		
2001–02	Shrewsbury T	23	1		
2002–03	Shrewsbury T	39	3		
2003–04	Shrewsbury T	0	0		
2004–05	Shrewsbury T	36	4		
2005–06	Shrewsbury T	36	4	160	14
2006–07	Macclesfield T	23	1		
2007–08	Macclesfield T	24	2		
2008–09	Macclesfield T	16	0	63	3
2009–10	Hereford U	10	0	10	0

VALENTINE, Ryan (D) 298 10
H: 5 10 W: 11 05 b.Wrexham 19-8-82
Source: Trainee. *Honours:* Wales Youth, Under-21.

1999–2000	Everton	0	0		
2000–01	Everton	0	0		
2001–02	Everton	0	0		
2002–03	Darlington	43	1		
2003–04	Darlington	40	2		
2004–05	Darlington	36	1		
2005–06	Darlington	43	0		
2006–07	Wrexham	34	2		
2007–08	Wrexham	14	0	48	2
2007–08	Darlington	17	0		
2008–09	Darlington	31	0	210	0
2009–10	Hereford U	40	4	40	4

WEIR, Tyler (M) 3 0
H: 5 10 W: 11 10 b.Hereford 21-12-90
Source: Youth.

2009–10	Hereford U	3	0	3	0

HUDDERSFIELD T (41)

AINSWORTH, Lionel (F) 87 7
H: 5 9 W: 9 10 b.Nottingham 1-10-87
Source: Scholar. *Honours:* England Youth.

2005–06	Derby Co	2	0		
2006–07	Derby Co	0	0	2	0
2006–07	*Bournemouth*	7	0	7	0
2006–07	*Wycombe W*	7	0	7	0
2007–08	Hereford U	15	4		
2007–08	Watford	8	0		
2008–09	Watford	7	0	15	0
2008–09	*Hereford U*	7	3	22	7
2008–09	Huddersfield T	14	0		
2009–10	Huddersfield T	11	0	25	0
2009–10	*Brentford*	9	0	9	0

BERRETT, James (M) 35 2
H: 5 10 W: 10 13 b.Halifax 13-1-89
Source: Scholar. *Honours:* Eire Youth, Under-21.

2006–07	Huddersfield T	2	0		
2007–08	Huddersfield T	15	1		
2008–09	Huddersfield T	9	1		
2009–10	Huddersfield T	9	0	35	2

BUTLER, Andy (D) 199 20
H: 6 0 W: 13 00 b.Doncaster 4-11-83
Source: Scholar.

2003–04	Scunthorpe U	35	2		
2004–05	Scunthorpe U	37	10		
2005–06	Scunthorpe U	16	1		
2006–07	Scunthorpe U	11	1		
2006–07	*Grimsby T*	4	0	4	0
2007–08	Scunthorpe U	36	2	135	16
2008–09	Huddersfield T	42	4		
2009–10	Huddersfield T	11	0	53	4
2009–10	*Blackpool*	7	0	7	0

CLARKE, Nathan (D) 263 8
H: 6 2 W: 12 00 b.Halifax 30-11-83
Source: Scholar.

2001–02	Huddersfield T	36	1		
2002–03	Huddersfield T	3	0		
2003–04	Huddersfield T	26	1		
2004–05	Huddersfield T	37	0		
2005–06	Huddersfield T	46	0		
2006–07	Huddersfield T	16	0		
2007–08	Huddersfield T	44	2		
2008–09	Huddersfield T	38	3		
2009–10	Huddersfield T	17	1	263	8

CLARKE, Peter (D) 299 30
H: 6 0 W: 12 00 b.Southport 3-1-82
Source: Trainee. *Honours:* England Schools, Youth, Under-20, Under-21.

1998–99	Everton	0	0		
1999–2000	Everton	0	0		
2000–01	Everton	1	0		
2001–02	Everton	7	0		
2002–03	Everton	0	0		
2002–03	*Blackpool*	16	3		
2002–03	*Port Vale*	13	1	13	1
2003–04	Everton	1	0		
2003–04	*Coventry C*	5	0	5	0
2004–05	Everton	0	0	9	0
2004–05	Blackpool	38	5		
2005–06	Blackpool	46	6	100	14
2006–07	Southend U	38	2		
2007–08	Southend U	45	4		
2008–09	Southend U	43	4	126	10
2009–10	Huddersfield T	46	5	46	5

CLARKE, Tom (D) 83 2
H: 6 0 W: 11 02 b.Halifax 21-12-87
Source: Scholar. *Honours:* England Youth.

2004–05	Huddersfield T	12	0		
2005–06	Huddersfield T	17	1		
2006–07	Huddersfield T	9	0		
2007–08	Huddersfield T	3	0		
2008–09	Huddersfield T	15	1		
2008–09	*Bradford C*	6	0	6	0
2009–10	Huddersfield T	21	0	77	2

COLLINS, Michael (M) 173 19
H: 6 0 W: 11 00 b.Halifax 30-4-86
Source: Scholar. *Honours:* Eire Youth, Under-21.

2004–05	Huddersfield T	8	0		
2005–06	Huddersfield T	17	1		
2006–07	Huddersfield T	43	4		
2007–08	Huddersfield T	41	2		
2008–09	Huddersfield T	36	9		
2009–10	Huddersfield T	28	3	173	19

CRANEY, Ian (M) 132 20
H: 5 10 W: 12 00 b.Liverpool 21-7-82
Source: Runcorn, Altrincham.

2006–07	Accrington S	18	5		
2006–07	Swansea C	27	0		
2007–08	Swansea C	1	0	28	0
2007–08	Accrington S	34	7		
2008–09	Accrington S	2	1	54	13
2008–09	Huddersfield T	34	5		
2009–10	Huddersfield T	0	0	34	5
2009–10	*Morecambe*	16	2	16	2

DENTON, Tom (F) 2 0
H: 6 6 W: 14 07 b.Shepley 24-7-89
Source: Wakefield.

2008–09	Huddersfield T	0	0		
2009–10	Huddersfield T	0	0		
2009–10	*Cheltenham T*	2	0	2	0

EASTWOOD, Simon (G) 23 0
H: 6 2 W: 13 00 b.Luton 26-6-89
Source: Scholar. *Honours:* England Youth

2005–06	Huddersfield T	0	0		
2006–07	Huddersfield T	0	0		
2007–08	Huddersfield T	0	0		
2008–09	Huddersfield T	1	0		
2009–10	Huddersfield T	0	0	1	0
2009–10	*Bradford C*	22	0	22	0

FRANKS, Lee (D) 0 0
H: 5 11 W: 12 00 b. 7-3-91
Source: Scholar.

2009–10	Huddersfield T	0	0		

GOODWIN, Jim (M) 237 14
H: 5 9 W: 12 01 b.Waterford 20-11-81
Source: Tramore. *Honours:* Eire Under-21, B, 1 full cap.

2001–02	Celtic	0	0		
2002–03	Stockport Co	33	3		
2003–04	Stockport Co	34	4		
2004–05	Stockport Co	36	0	103	7
2005–06	Scunthorpe U	13	2		

2006–07	Scunthorpe U	31	1		
2007–08	Scunthorpe U	40	3	84	6
2008–09	Huddersfield T	37	1		
2009–10	Huddersfield T	5	0	42	1
2009–10	Oldham Ath	8	0	8	0

HEFFERNAN, Dean (D) 116 11
H: 6 1 W: 12 10 b.Sydney 19-5-80
Honours: Australia 2 full caps, 1 goal.

2000	St George Saints	0	0		
2001	Sutherland SS	0	0		
2002	Sutherland SS	0	0		
2002–03	Wollongong Wolves	20	1	20	1
2003–04	Sydney U	18	1	18	1
2004	Celangor	3	0	3	0
2005	Sutherland SS	0	0		
2005–06	Central Coast M	19	7		
2007–08	Central Coast M	15	1		
2008–09	Central Coast M	6	0		
2009–10	Central Coast M	20	1	60	9
2009–10	Huddersfield T	15	0	15	0

HUNT, Jack (D) 0 0
H: 5 9 W: 11 02 b. 6-12-90
Source: Scholar.

| 2009–10 | Huddersfield T | 0 | 0 | | |

JEVONS, Phil (F) 313 103
H: 5 11 W: 12 00 b.Liverpool 1-8-79
Source: Trainee.

1996–97	Everton	0	0		
1997–98	Everton	0	0		
1998–99	Everton	1	0		
1999–2000	Everton	3	0		
2000–01	Everton	4	0	8	0
2001–02	Grimsby T	31	6		
2002–03	Grimsby T	3	0		
2002–03	Hull C	24	3	24	3
2003–04	Grimsby T	29	12	63	18
2004–05	Yeovil T	46	27		
2005–06	Yeovil T	38	15	84	42
2006–07	Bristol C	41	11		
2007–08	Bristol C	2	0	43	11
2007–08	Huddersfield T	21	7		
2008–09	Huddersfield T	23	2		
2008–09	Bury	7	2	7	2
2009–10	Huddersfield T	0	0	44	9
2009–10	Morecambe	40	18	40	18

KAY, Antony (D) 296 34
H: 5 11 W: 11 08 b.Barnsley 21-10-82
Source: Trainee. *Honours:* England Youth.

1999–2000	Barnsley	0	0		
2000–01	Barnsley	7	0		
2001–02	Barnsley	1	0		
2002–03	Barnsley	16	0		
2003–04	Barnsley	43	3		
2004–05	Barnsley	39	6		
2005–06	Barnsley	36	1		
2006–07	Barnsley	32	1	174	11
2007–08	Tranmere R	38	6		
2008–09	Tranmere R	44	11	82	17
2009–10	Huddersfield T	40	6	40	6

NOVAK, Lee (F) 37 12
H: 6 0 W: 12 04 b.Newcastle 28-9-88
Source: Gateshead.

| 2008–09 | Huddersfield T | 0 | 0 | | |
| 2009–10 | Huddersfield T | 37 | 12 | 37 | 12 |

PEARCE, Krystian (D) 62 1
H: 6 1 W: 13 05 b.Birmingham 5-1-90
Source: Scholar. *Honours:* England Youth.

2006–07	Birmingham C	0	0		
2007–08	Birmingham C	0	0		
2007–08	Port Vale	12	0	12	0
2007–08	Notts Co	8	1	8	1
2008–09	Birmingham C	0	0		
2008–09	Scunthorpe U	39	0	39	0
2009–10	Birmingham C	0	0		
2009–10	Peterborough U	2	0	2	0
2009–10	Huddersfield T	1	0	1	0

PELTIER, Lee (D) 118 1
H: 5 10 W: 12 00 b.Liverpool 11-12-86
Source: Scholar.

2004–05	Liverpool	0	0		
2005–06	Liverpool	0	0		
2006–07	Liverpool	0	0		
2006–07	Hull C	7	0	7	0
2007–08	Liverpool	0	0		
2007–08	Yeovil T	34	0		
2008–09	Yeovil T	35	1	69	1
2009–10	Huddersfield T	42	0	42	0

PILKINGTON, Anthony (M) 136 25
H: 5 11 W: 12 00 b.Blackburn 3-11-87
Source: Atherton CW. *Honours:* Eire Under-21.

2006–07	Stockport Co	24	5		
2007–08	Stockport Co	29	6		
2008–09	Stockport Co	24	5	77	16
2008–09	Huddersfield T	16	2		
2009–10	Huddersfield T	43	7	59	9

RHODES, Jordan (F) 74 29
H: 5 1 W: 11 03 b.Oldham 5-2-90
Source: Academy.

2007–08	Ipswich T	8	1		
2008–09	Ipswich T	2	0	10	1
2008–09	Rochdale	5	2	5	2
2008–09	Brentford	14	7	14	7
2009–10	Huddersfield T	45	19	45	19

RIDEHALGH, Liam (D) 0 0
H: 5 10 W: 11 05 b. 20-4-91
Source: Scholar.

| 2009–10 | Huddersfield T | 0 | 0 | | |

ROBERTS, Gary (F) 158 27
H: 5 10 W: 11 09 b.Chester 18-3-84
Source: Denbigh T, Bangor C.

2006–07	Accrington S	14	8	14	8
2006–07	Ipswich T	33	2		
2007–08	Ipswich T	21	1	54	3
2007–08	Crewe Alex	4	0	4	0
2008–09	Huddersfield T	43	9		
2009–10	Huddersfield T	43	7	86	16

ROBINSON, Theo (M) 106 33
H: 5 9 W: 10 03 b.Birmingham 22-1-89
Source: Scholar.

2005–06	Watford	1	0		
2006–07	Watford	1	0		
2007–08	Watford	0	0		
2007–08	Hereford U	43	13	43	13
2008–09	Watford	3	0	5	0
2008–09	Southend U	21	7	21	7
2009–10	Huddersfield T	37	13	37	13

SIMPSON, Robbie (F) 74 4
H: 6 1 W: 11 11 b.Stevenage 15-3-85
Source: Cambridge U.

2007–08	Coventry C	28	1		
2008–09	Coventry C	33	3	61	4
2009–10	Huddersfield C	13	0	13	0

SKARZ, Joe (D) 95 1
H: 5 10 W: 11 04 b.Huddersfield 13-7-89
Source: Scholar.

2006–07	Huddersfield T	17	0		
2007–08	Huddersfield T	27	0		
2008–09	Huddersfield T	9	1		
2008–09	Hartlepool U	7	0	7	0
2009–10	Huddersfield T	15	0	68	1
2009–10	Shrewsbury T	20	0	20	0

SMITHIES, Alex (G) 75 0
H: 6 1 W: 10 01 b.Huddersfield 25-3-90
Source: Scholar. *Honours:* England Youth.

2006–07	Huddersfield T	0	0		
2007–08	Huddersfield T	2	0		
2008–09	Huddersfield T	27	0		
2009–10	Huddersfield T	46	0	75	0

SPENCER, James (F) 0 0
Source: Scholar.

| 2008–09 | Huddersfield T | 0 | 0 | | |
| 2009–10 | Huddersfield T | 0 | 0 | | |

WILLIAMS, Robbie (D) 152 12
H: 5 10 W: 11 13 b.Pontefract 2-10-84
Source: Scholar.

2002–03	Barnsley	8	0		
2003–04	Barnsley	4	1		
2004–05	Barnsley	17	1		
2005–06	Barnsley	22	2		
2006–07	Barnsley	15	0		
2006–07	Blackpool	9	4	9	4
2007–08	Barnsley	30	0	66	4
2007–08	Huddersfield T	25	2		
2008–09	Huddersfield T	35	0		
2009–10	Huddersfield T	17	2	77	4

HULL C (42)

ALTIDORE, Josmer (F) 71 17
H: 6 1 W: 12 08 b.Livingston (USA) 6-11-89
Honours: USA 29 full caps, 9 goals.

2006	NY Red Bulls	7	3		
2007	NY Red Bulls	22	9		
2008	NY Red Bulls	8	3	37	15
2008–09	Villarreal	6	1	6	1
2008–09	Xerez	0	0		
2009–10	Hull C	28	1	28	1

ASHBEE, Ian (M) 428 20
H: 6 1 W: 13 07 b.Birmingham 6-9-76
Source: Trainee. *Honours:* England Youth.

1994–95	Derby Co	1	0		
1995–96	Derby Co	0	0		
1996–97	Derby Co	0	0	1	0
1996–97	Cambridge U	18	0		
1997–98	Cambridge U	27	1		
1998–99	Cambridge U	41	4		
1999–2000	Cambridge U	45	1		
2000–01	Cambridge U	44	3		
2001–02	Cambridge U	38	2	203	11
2002–03	Hull C	31	1		
2003–04	Hull C	39	2		
2004–05	Hull C	40	1		
2005–06	Hull C	6	0		
2006–07	Hull C	35	1		
2007–08	Hull C	42	3		
2008–09	Hull C	31	1		
2009–10	Hull C	0	0	224	9

ATKINSON, Will (M) 33 4
H: 5 10 W: 10 07 b.Driffield 14-10-88
Source: Scholar.

2006–07	Hull C	0	0		
2007–08	Hull C	0	0		
2007–08	Port Vale	4	0	4	0
2007–08	Mansfield T	12	0	12	0
2008–09	Hull C	0	0		
2009–10	Hull C	2	1	2	1
2009–10	Rochdale	15	3	15	3

BARMBY, Nick (F) 449 73
H: 5 7 W: 11 03 b.Hull 11-2-74
Source: Trainee. *Honours:* England Schools, Youth, Under-21, B, 23 full caps, 4 goals.

1991–92	Tottenham H	0	0		
1992–93	Tottenham H	22	6		
1993–94	Tottenham H	27	5		
1994–95	Tottenham H	38	9	87	20
1995–96	Middlesbrough	32	7		
1996–97	Middlesbrough	10	1	42	8
1996–97	Everton	25	4		
1997–98	Everton	30	2		
1998–99	Everton	24	3		
1999–2000	Everton	37	9	116	18
2000–01	Liverpool	26	2		
2001–02	Liverpool	6	0	32	2
2002–03	Leeds U	19	4		
2003–04	Nottingham F	6	1	6	1
2003–04	Leeds U	6	0	25	4
2004–05	Hull C	39	9		
2005–06	Hull C	26	5		
2006–07	Hull C	20	4		
2007–08	Hull C	15	1		
2008–09	Hull C	21	1		
2009–10	Hull C	20	0	141	20

BOATENG, George (M) 461 18
H: 5 9 W: 12 06 b.Nkawkaw 5-9-75
Honours: Holland Under-21, 4 full caps.

1994–95	Excelsior	9	0	9	0
1995–96	Feyenoord	24	1		
1996–97	Feyenoord	26	0		
1997–98	Feyenoord	18	0	68	1
1997–98	Coventry C	14	1		
1998–99	Coventry C	33	4	47	5
1999–2000	Aston Villa	33	2		
2000–01	Aston Villa	33	1		
2001–02	Aston Villa	37	1	103	4
2002–03	Middlesbrough	28	0		
2003–04	Middlesbrough	35	0		
2004–05	Middlesbrough	25	3		
2005–06	Middlesbrough	26	2		
2006–07	Middlesbrough	35	1		
2007–08	Middlesbrough	33	1	182	7

2008–09	Hull C	23	0	
2009–10	Hull C	29	1	**52**	**1**

BULLARD, Jimmy (M)   **265 32**
H: 5 10   W: 11 05   b.Newham 23-10-78
Source: Corinthian, Dartford, Gravesend &
N.

1998–99	West Ham U	0	0		
1999–2000	West Ham U	0	0		
2000–01	West Ham U	0	0		
2001–02	Peterborough U	40	8		
2002–03	Peterborough U	26	3	**66**	**11**
2002–03	Wigan Ath	17	1		
2003–04	Wigan Ath	46	2		
2004–05	Wigan Ath	46	3		
2005–06	Wigan Ath	36	4	**145**	**10**
2005–06	Fulham	0	0		
2006–07	Fulham	4	2		
2007–08	Fulham	17	2		
2008–09	Fulham	18	2	**39**	**6**
2008–09	Hull C	1	0		
2009–10	Hull C	14	5	**15**	**5**

CAIRNEY, Tom (M)   **11 1**
H: 6 0   W: 11 05   b.Nottingham 20-1-91
Source: Scholar. *Honours:* Scotland Youth.

2009–10	Hull C	11	1	**11**	**1**

COOPER, Liam (D)   **2 0**
H: 6 2   W: 13 07   b.Hull 30-8-91
Source: Scholar. *Honours:* Scotland Youth.

2008–09	Hull C	0	0		
2009–10	Hull C	2	0	**2**	**0**

COUSIN, Daniel (F)   **367 94**
H: 6 2   W: 12 13   b.Libreville 7-2-77
Honours: Gabon 30 full caps, 9 goals.

1997–98	Martigues	36	5	**36**	**5**
1998–99	Niort	22	1		
1999–2000	Niort	24	4	**46**	**5**
2000–01	Le Mans	29	6		
2001–02	Le Mans	33	12		
2002–03	Le Mans	33	15		
2003–04	Le Mans	33	11	**128**	**44**
2004–05	Lens	37	9		
2005–06	Lens	33	13		
2006–07	Lens	30	4		
2007–08	Lens	1	0	**101**	**26**
2007–08	Rangers	26	10	**26**	**10**
2008–09	Hull C	27	4		
2009–10	Hull C	3	0	**30**	**4**

CULLEN, Mark (F)   **3 1**
H: 5 9   W: 11 11   b.Stakeford 24-4-92
Source: Scholar.

2009–10	Hull C	3	1	**3**	**1**

DAWSON, Andy (D)   **407 16**
H: 5 9   W: 11 02   b.Northallerton 20-10-78
Source: Trainee.

1995–96	Nottingham F	0	0		
1996–97	Nottingham F	0	0		
1997–98	Nottingham F	0	0		
1998–99	Nottingham F	0	0		
1998–99	Scunthorpe U	24	0		
1999–2000	Scunthorpe U	43	2		
2000–01	Scunthorpe U	41	4		
2001–02	Scunthorpe U	44	0		
2002–03	Scunthorpe U	43	2	**195**	**8**
2003–04	Hull C	33	3		
2004–05	Hull C	34	0		
2005–06	Hull C	18	0		
2006–07	Hull C	38	2		
2007–08	Hull C	29	1		
2008–09	Hull C	25	1		
2009–10	Hull C	35	1	**212**	**8**

DEVITT, Jamie (F)   **30 8**
H: 5 10   W: 10 05   b.Dublin 6-6-90
Source: Cherry Orchard BC, Hull C Scholar.
Honours: Eire Youth.

2007–08	Hull C	0	0		
2008–09	Hull C	0	0		
2009–10	Hull C	0	0		
2009–10	Darlington	6	1	**6**	**1**
2009–10	Shrewsbury T	9	2	**9**	**2**
2009–10	Grimsby T	15	5	**15**	**5**

DUKE, Matt (G)   **37 0**
H: 5 5   W: 13 04   b.Sheffield 16-7-77
Source: Alfreton T.

1959–2000	Sheffield U	0	0		
2000–01	Sheffield U	0	0		

2001–02	Sheffield U	0	0		
2004–05	Hull C	2	0		
2005–06	Hull C	2	0		
2005–06	*Stockport Co*	3	0	**3**	**0**
2005–06	*Wycombe W*	5	0	**5**	**0**
2006–07	Hull C	1	0		
2007–08	Hull C	3	0		
2008–09	Hull C	10	0		
2009–10	Hull C	11	0	**29**	**0**

FAGAN, Craig (F)   **244 39**
H: 5 11   W: 11 11   b.Birmingham 11-12-82
Source: Scholar.

2001–02	Birmingham C	0	0		
2002–03	Birmingham C	1	0		
2002–03	*Bristol C*	6	1	**6**	**1**
2003–04	Birmingham C	0	0	**1**	**0**
2003–04	Colchester U	37	9		
2004–05	Colchester U	26	8	**63**	**17**
2004–05	Hull C	12	4		
2005–06	Hull C	41	5		
2006–07	Hull C	27	6		
2006–07	Derby Co	17	1		
2007–08	Derby Co	22	0	**39**	**1**
2007–08	*Hull C*	8	0		
2008–09	Hull C	22	3		
2009–10	Hull C	25	2	**135**	**20**

FEATHERSTONE, Nicky (F)   **16 0**
H: 5 6   W: 11 02   b.North Ferriby 22-9-88
Source: Scholar.

2006–07	Hull C	2	0		
2007–08	Hull C	6	0		
2008–09	Hull C	0	0		
2009–10	Hull C	0	0	**8**	**0**
2009–10	*Grimsby T*	8	0	**8**	**0**

FOLAN, Caleb (F)   **177 28**
H: 6 2   W: 14 07   b.Leeds 26-10-82
Source: Trainee. *Honours:* Eire 7 full caps.

1999–2000	Leeds U	0	0		
2000–01	Leeds U	0	0		
2001–02	*Rushden & D*	6	0	**6**	**0**
2001–02	*Hull C*	1	0		
2002–03	Leeds U	0	0		
2002–03	Chesterfield	13	1		
2003–04	Chesterfield	7	0		
2004–05	Chesterfield	32	6		
2005–06	Chesterfield	27	0		
2006–07	Chesterfield	23	8	**102**	**15**
2006–07	Wigan Ath	13	2		
2007–08	Wigan Ath	2	0	**15**	**2**
2007–08	Hull C	29	8		
2008–09	Hull C	15	1		
2009–10	Hull C	8	2	**53**	**11**
2009–10	*Middlesbrough*	1	0	**1**	**0**

GARCIA, Richard (F)   **195 26**
H: 5 11   W: 12 01   b.Perth 4-9-81
Source: Trainee. *Honours:* Australia
Under-23, 9 full caps.

1998–99	West Ham U	0	0		
1999–2000	West Ham U	0	0		
2000–01	West Ham U	0	0		
2000–01	*Leyton Orient*	18	4	**18**	**4**
2001–02	West Ham U	8	0		
2002–03	West Ham U	1	0		
2003–04	West Ham U	7	0		
2004–05	West Ham U	1	0	**16**	**0**
2004–05	Colchester U	24	4		
2005–06	Colchester U	22	5		
2006–07	Colchester U	36	7	**82**	**16**
2007–08	Hull C	38	5		
2008–09	Hull C	23	1		
2009–10	Hull C	18	0	**79**	**6**

GARDNER, Anthony (D)   **185 6**
H: 6 3   W: 14 00   b.Stone 19-9-80
Source: Trainee. *Honours:* England
Under-21, 1 full cap.

1998–99	Port Vale	15	1		
1999–2000	Port Vale	26	3	**41**	**4**
1999–2000	Tottenham H	0	0		
2000–01	Tottenham H	8	0		
2001–02	Tottenham H	15	0		
2002–03	Tottenham H	12	1		
2003–04	Tottenham H	33	0		
2004–05	Tottenham H	17	0		
2005–06	Tottenham H	17	0		
2006–07	Tottenham H	8	0		

2007–08	*Everton*	0	0		
2007–08	Tottenham H	4	1	**114**	**2**
2008–09	Hull C	6	0		
2009–10	Hull C	24	0	**30**	**0**

GARDNER, Steven (D)   **0 0**
H: 5 9   W: 10 09   b.Hull 12-5-90
Source: Scholar.

2008–09	Hull C	0	0		
2009–10	Hull C	0	0		

GEOVANNI (F)   **278 45**
H: 5 8   W: 10 08   b.Acaiaca 11-1-80
Honours: Brazil 4 full caps, 1 goal.

1997	Cruzeiro	7	0		
1998	America	15	1	**15**	**1**
1999	Cruzeiro	21	2		
2000	Cruzeiro	22	9		
2001–02	Barcelona	21	1		
2002–03	Barcelona	5	0	**26**	**1**
2002–03	Benfica	17	2		
2003–04	Benfica	21	5		
2004–05	Benfica	31	6		
2005–06	Benfica	25	3	**94**	**16**
2006	Cruzeiro	12	2		
2007	Cruzeiro	2	0	**64**	**12**
2007–08	Manchester C	19	3	**19**	**3**
2008–09	Hull C	34	8		
2009–10	Hull C	26	3	**60**	**11**

GHILAS, Kamel (F)   **189 52**
H: 5 10   W: 11 00   b.Marseille 9-3-84
Honours: Algeria 16 full caps, 3 goals.

2003–04	Cannes	18	0		
2004–05	Cannes	31	7		
2005–06	Cannes	35	13	**84**	**20**
2006–07	Guimaraes	29	12		
2007–08	Guimaraes	30	6	**59**	**18**
2008–09	Celta Vigo	33	13	**33**	**13**
2009–10	Hull C	13	1	**13**	**1**

HALMOSI, Peter (M)   **271 39**
H: 5 10   W: 10 12   b.Szombathely 25-9-79
Honours: Hungary 30 full caps.

1998–99	Haladas	2	0		
1999–2000	Haladas	26	2		
2000–01	Haladas	14	2		
2001–02	Haladas	38	2	**80**	**6**
2002–03	Graz	17	3	**17**	**3**
2003–04	Debrecen	29	5		
2004–05	Debrecen	28	5		
2005–06	Debrecen	26	7		
2006–07	Debrecen	14	1	**97**	**18**
2006–07	Plymouth Arg	16	4		
2007–08	Plymouth Arg	43	8	**59**	**12**
2008–09	Hull C	18	0		
2009–10	Hull C	0	0	**18**	**0**

HUGHES, Bryan (M)   **460 52**
H: 5 10   W: 11 08   b.Liverpool 19-6-76
Source: Trainee.

1993–94	Wrexham	11	0		
1994–95	Wrexham	38	9		
1995–96	Wrexham	22	0		
1996–97	Wrexham	23	3	**94**	**12**
1996–97	Birmingham C	11	0		
1997–98	Birmingham C	40	5		
1998–99	Birmingham C	28	3		
1999–2000	Birmingham C	45	10		
2000–01	Birmingham C	45	4		
2001–02	Birmingham C	31	7		
2002–03	Birmingham C	22	2		
2003–04	Birmingham C	26	3	**248**	**34**
2004–05	Charlton Ath	17	1		
2005–06	Charlton Ath	33	3		
2006–07	Charlton Ath	24	1	**74**	**5**
2007–08	Hull C	35	1		
2008–09	Hull C	6	0		
2009–10	Hull C	0	0	**41**	**1**
2009–10	*Derby Co*	3	0	**3**	**0**

HUNT, Steve (M)   **322 48**
H: 5 9   W: 10 10   b.Port Laoise 1-8-80
Source: Trainee. *Honours:* Eire Under-21, B,
25 full caps, 1 goal.

1999–2000	Crystal Palace	3	0		
2000–01	Crystal Palace	0	0	**3**	**0**
2001–02	Brentford	35	4		
2002–03	Brentford	42	7		
2003–04	Brentford	40	11		
2004–05	Brentford	19	3	**136**	**25**
2005–06	Reading	38	2		

2006–07	Reading	35	4		
2007–08	Reading	37	5		
2008–09	Reading	46	6		
2009–10	Reading	0	0	156	17
2009–10	Hull C	27	6	27	6

KENDALL, Ryan (F)   6 2
H: 5 7 W: 10 09 b.Hull 14-9-89
Source: Scholar.

2008–09	Hull C	0	0		
2009–10	Hull C	0	0		
2009–10	*Bradford C*	6	2	6	2

KILBANE, Kevin (M)   483 33
H: 6 1 W: 13 05 b.Preston 1-2-77
Source: Trainee. *Honours:* Eire Under-21, 103 full caps, 7 goals.

1993–94	Preston NE	0	0		
1994–95	Preston NE	0	0		
1995–96	Preston NE	11	1		
1996–97	Preston NE	36	2	47	3
1997–98	WBA	43	4		
1998–99	WBA	44	6		
1999–2000	WBA	19	5	106	15
1999–2000	Sunderland	20	1		
2000–01	Sunderland	30	4		
2001–02	Sunderland	28	2		
2002–03	Sunderland	30	1		
2003–04	Sunderland	5	0	113	8
2003–04	Everton	30	3		
2004–05	Everton	38	1		
2005–06	Everton	34	0		
2006–07	Everton	2	0	104	4
2006–07	Wigan Ath	31	1		
2007–08	Wigan Ath	35	1		
2008–09	Wigan Ath	10	0	76	2
2008–09	Hull C	16	0		
2009–10	Hull C	21	1	37	1

McSHANE, Paul (D)   142 7
H: 6 0 W: 11 05 b.Wicklow 6-1-86
Source: Trainee. *Honours:* Eire Youth, Under-21, 22 full caps.

2002–03	Manchester U	0	0		
2003–04	Manchester U	0	0		
2004–05	Manchester U	0	0		
2004–05	*Walsall*	4	1	4	1
2005–06	Manchester U	0	0		
2005–06	*Brighton & HA*	38	3	38	3
2006–07	WBA	32	2	32	2
2007–08	Sunderland	21	0		
2008–09	Sunderland	3	0		
2008–09	Hull C	17	1		
2009–10	Sunderland	0	0	24	0
2009–10	Hull C	27	0	44	1

MENDY, Bernard (D)   293 6
H: 5 11 W: 12 02 b.Evreux 20-8-81
Honours: France 3 full caps.

1998–99	Caen	4	0		
1999–2000	Caen	30	2	34	2
2000–01	Paris St Germain	19	0		
2001–02	Paris St Germain	21	1		
2002–03	Bolton W	21	0	21	0
2003–04	Paris St Germain	33	0		
2004–05	Paris St Germain	29	0		
2005–06	Paris St Germain	36	0		
2006–07	Paris St Germain	28	0		
2007–08	Paris St Germain	23	1	189	2
2008–09	Hull C	28	2		
2009–10	Hull C	21	0	49	2

MOUYOKOLO, Steven (D)   56 1
H: 6 3 W: 13 08 b.Mellin 24-11-87

2007–08	Gueugnon	22	0	22	0

From Chateauroux B.

2008–09	Boulogne	13	0	13	0
2009–10	Hull C	21	1	21	1

MYHILL, Boaz (G)   276 0
H: 6 3 W: 14 06 b.Modesto 9-11-82
Source: Scholar. *Honours:* England Youth, Under-20. Wales 8 full caps.

2000–01	Aston Villa	0	0		
2001–02	Aston Villa	0	0		
2001–02	Stoke C	0	0		
2002–03	Aston Villa	0	0		
2002–03	Bristol C	0	0		
2002–03	*Bradford C*	2	0	2	0
2003–04	Aston Villa	0	0		
2003–04	*Macclesfield T*	15	0	15	0
2003–04	*Stockport Co*	2	0	2	0

2003–04	Hull C	23	0		
2004–05	Hull C	45	0		
2005–06	Hull C	45	0		
2006–07	Hull C	46	0		
2007–08	Hull C	43	0		
2008–09	Hull C	28	0		
2009–10	Hull C	27	0	257	0

OLOFINJANA, Seyi (M)   206 30
H: 6 4 W: 11 10 b.Lagos 30-6-80
Source: Kwara United Ilorin. *Honours:* Nigeria 41 full caps.

2003	Brann	25	9		
2004	Brann	9	2	34	11
2004–05	Wolverhampton W	42	5		
2005–06	Wolverhampton W	13	0		
2006–07	Wolverhampton W	44	8		
2007–08	Wolverhampton W	36	3	135	16
2008–09	Stoke C	18	2		
2009–10	Stoke C	0	0	18	2
2009–10	Hull C	19	1	19	1

OXLEY, Mark (G)   3 0
H: 5 11 W: 11 05 b. 2-6-90
Source: Rotherham U Scholar. *Honours:* England Youth.

2008–09	Hull C	0	0		
2009–10	Hull C	0	0		
2009–10	*Grimsby T*	3	0	3	0

VENNEGOOR, Jan (F)   383 162
H: 6 3 W: 13 05 b.Oldenzaal 7-11-78

1996–97	Twente	12	0		
1997–98	Twente	28	4		
1998–99	Twente	34	21		
1999–2000	Twente	34	19		
2000–01	Twente	34	15	142	59
2001–02	PSV Eindhoven	34	22		
2002–03	PSV Eindhoven	32	8		
2003–04	PSV Eindhoven	30	12		
2004–05	PSV Eindhoven	28	19		
2005–06	PSV Eindhoven	32	11		
2006–07	PSV Eindhoven	1	0	157	72
2006–07	Celtic	21	13		
2007–08	Celtic	32	15		
2009–10	Celtic	0	0	53	28
2009–10	Hull C	31	3	31	3

ZAYATTE, Kamil (D)   97 4
H: 6 2 W: 13 10 b.Conakry 7-3-85
Honours: Guinea 21 full caps, 2 goals.

2005–06	Lens	0	0		
2006–07	Lens	0	1	0	
2006–07	Young Boys	18	0		
2007–08	Young Boys	23	1	41	1
2008–09	Hull C	32	1		
2009–10	Hull C	23	2	55	3

Scholars
Bennett, Thomas William; Bradley, Sonny; Cooper, Joseph; Deague, Dean East, Daniel; Emerton, Daniel James; Ford, Raymond Ashley; Fox, Joseph Charles; Holohan, Gavan; Townsend, Conor Stephen; Ward, William; Wilkinson, Daniel.

IPSWICH T (43)

AINSLEY, Jack (D)   0 0
H: 5 11 W: 11 00 b.Ipswich 17-9-90
Source: Scholar.

2009–10	Ipswich T	0	0

BALKESTEIN, Pim (D)   43 1
H: 6 3 W: 11 06 b.Gouda 29-4-87
Source: Heerenveen.

2008–09	Ipswich T	20	0		
2009–10	Ipswich T	9	0	29	0
2009–10	*Brentford*	14	1	14	1

BROWN, Troy (D)   1 0
H: 6 1 W: 12 01 b.Cardiff 17-9-90
Source: Fulham Scholar.

2009–10	Ipswich T	1	0	1	0

BRUCE, Alex (D)   153 2
H: 6 0 W: 11 06 b.Norwich 28-9-84
Source: Trainee. *Honours:* Eire B, Under-21, 2 full caps.

2002–03	Blackburn R	0	0
2003–04	Blackburn R	0	0

2004–05	Blackburn R	0	0		
2004–05	*Oldham Ath*	12	0	12	0
2004–05	Birmingham C	0	0		
2004–05	*Sheffield W*	6	0	6	0
2005–06	Birmingham C	6	0	6	0
2005–06	*Tranmere R*	11	0	11	0
2006–07	Ipswich T	41	0		
2007–08	Ipswich T	36	0		
2008–09	Ipswich T	25	1		
2009–10	Ipswich T	13	1	115	2
2009–10	*Leicester C*	3	0	3	0

CIVELLI, Luciano (M)   78 8
H: 6 2 W: 13 01 b.Buenos Aires 6-10-86

2005–06	Banfield	0	0		
2006–07	Banfield	18	0		
2007–08	Banfield	34	6		
2008–09	Banfield	17	2	70	8
2008–09	Ipswich T	8	0		
2009–10	Ipswich T	0	0	8	0

CLARK, Billy (M)   3 0
H: 5 10 W: 11 11 b.Ipswich 20-10-91
Source: Scholar.

2009–10	Ipswich T	3	0	3	0

COUNAGO, Pablo (F)   310 69
H: 5 11 W: 11 06 b.Pontevedra 9-8-79

1998–99	Numancia	13	1	13	1
1998–99	Celta Vigo	1	0		
1999–2000	Huelva	26	4	26	4
2000–01	Celta Vigo	8	0	9	0
2001–02	Ipswich T	13	0		
2002–03	Ipswich T	39	17		
2003–04	Ipswich T	29	11		
2004–05	Ipswich T	19	3		
2005–06	Malaga	27	3		
2006–07	Malaga	21	7	48	10
2007–08	Ipswich T	43	12		
2008–09	Ipswich T	44	9		
2009–10	Ipswich T	27	2	214	54

DELANEY, Damien (D)   343 8
H: 6 3 W: 14 00 b.Cork 20-7-81
Source: Cork C. *Honours:* Eire 2 full caps.

2000–01	Leicester C	5	0		
2001–02	Leicester C	3	0		
2001–02	*Stockport Co*	12	1	12	1
2001–02	*Huddersfield T*	2	0	2	0
2002–03	Leicester C	0	0	8	0
2002–03	*Mansfield T*	7	0	7	0
2002–03	Hull C	30	1		
2003–04	Hull C	46	2		
2004–05	Hull C	43	1		
2005–06	Hull C	46	0		
2006–07	Hull C	37	1		
2007–08	Hull C	22	0	224	5
2007–08	QPR	17	1		
2008–09	QPR	37	1		
2009–10	QPR	0	0	54	2
2009–10	Ipswich T	36	0	36	0

EASTMAN, Tom (D)   1 0
H: 6 3 W: 13 12 b.Colchester 21-10-91
Source: Scholar.

2009–10	Ipswich T	1	0	1	0

EDWARDS, Carlos (M)   318 38
H: 5 8 W: 11 02 b.Port of Spain 24-10-78
Source: Defence Force. *Honours:* Trinidad & Tobago 78 full caps, 4 goals.

2000–01	Wrexham	36	4		
2001–02	Wrexham	26	5		
2002–03	Wrexham	44	8		
2003–04	Wrexham	42	5		
2004–05	Wrexham	18	1	166	23
2005–06	Luton T	42	2		
2006–07	Luton T	26	6	68	8
2006–07	Sunderland	15	5		
2007–08	Sunderland	13	0		
2008–09	Sunderland	22	0		
2008–09	Wolverhampton W	6	0	6	0
2009–10	Sunderland	0	0	50	5
2009–10	Ipswich T	28	2	28	2

GARVAN, Owen (M)   164 13
H: 6 0 W: 10 07 b.Dublin 29-1-88
Source: Scholar. *Honours:* Eire Youth, Under-21.

2005–06	Ipswich T	32	3
2006–07	Ipswich T	27	1
2007–08	Ipswich T	43	2

2008–09	Ipswich T	37	7		
2009–10	Ipswich T	25	0	**164**	**13**

HEALY, Colin (M)   **169   8**
H: 6 1   W: 12 13   b.Cork 14-3-80
Source: Wilton U. *Honours:* Eire Youth,
Under-21, 13 full caps, 1 goal.

1998–99	Celtic	3	0
1999–2000	Celtic	10	1
2000–01	Celtic	11	0
2001–02	Celtic	4	0
2001–02	*Coventry C*	17	2	**17**	**2**
2002–03	Celtic	0	0	**28**	**1**
2003–04	Sunderland	20	0
2004–05	Sunderland	0	0	**20**	**0**
2005–06	Livingston	10	2	**10**	**2**
2006–07	Barnsley	8	0	**8**	**0**
2006–07	*Bradford C*	2	0	**2**	**0**
2007	Cork C	18	0
2008	Cork C	24	0
2009	Cork C	20	2	**62**	**2**
2009–10	Ipswich T	3	0	**3**	**0**
2009–10	*Falkirk*	19	1	**19**	**1**

LAMBE, Reggie (M)   **0   0**
H: 5 7   W: 10 09   b.Bermuda 4-2-91
Source: Scholar.

2009–10	Ipswich T	0	0

LEADBITTER, Grant (M)   **154   15**
H: 5 9   W: 11 06   b.Sunderland 7-1-86
Source: Trainee. *Honours:* FA Schools,
England Youth, Under-20, Under-21.

2002–03	Sunderland	0	0
2003–04	Sunderland	0	0
2004–05	Sunderland	0	0
2005–06	Sunderland	12	0
2005–06	*Rotherham U*	5	1	**5**	**1**
2006–07	Sunderland	44	7
2007–08	Sunderland	31	2
2008–09	Sunderland	23	2
2009–10	Sunderland	1	0	**111**	**11**
2009–10	Ipswich T	38	3	**38**	**3**

LEE-BARRETT, Arran (G)   **68   0**
H: 5 2   W: 14 01   b.Ipswich 28-2-84
Source: Norwich C Scholar.

2002–03	Cardiff C	0	0
2003–04	Cardiff C	0	0
2004–05	Cardiff C	0	0
2005–06	Cardiff C	0	0
From Weymouth			
2005–06	Coventry C	0	0
2007–08	Hartlepool U	18	0
2008–09	Hartlepool U	37	0
2009–10	Hartlepool U	0	0	**55**	**0**
2009–10	Ipswich T	13	0	**13**	**0**

LISBIE, Kevin (F)   **303   58**
H: 5 10   W: 11 06   b.Hackney 17-10-78
Source: Trainee. *Honours:* England Youth.
Jamaica 10 full caps, 2 goals.

1996–97	Charlton Ath	25	1
1997–98	Charlton Ath	17	1
1998–99	Charlton Ath	1	0
1998–99	Gillingham	7	4	**7**	**4**
1999–2000	Charlton Ath	0	0
1999–2000	*Reading*	2	0	**2**	**0**
2000–01	Charlton Ath	18	0
2000–01	*QPR*	2	0	**2**	**0**
2001–02	Charlton Ath	22	5
2002–03	Charlton Ath	32	4
2003–04	Charlton Ath	9	4
2004–05	Charlton Ath	17	1
2005–06	Charlton Ath	6	0
2005–06	*Norwich C*	6	1	**6**	**1**
2005–06	*Derby Co*	7	1	**7**	**1**
2006–07	Charlton Ath	8	0	**155**	**16**
2007–08	Colchester U	42	17
2008–09	Ipswich T	41	6
2009–10	Ipswich T	0	0	**41**	**6**
2009–10	*Colchester U*	41	13	**83**	**30**

MARTIN, Lee (M)   **68   5**
H: 5 10   W: 10 03   b.Taunton 9-2-87
Source: Scholar. *Honours:* England Youth.

2004–05	Manchester U	0	0
2005–06	Manchester U	0	0
2006–07	Manchester U	0	0
2006–07	*Rangers*	7	0	**7**	**0**
2006–07	*Stoke C*	13	1	**13**	**1**
2007–08	Manchester U	0	0

2007–08	*Plymouth Arg*	12	2	**12**	**2**
2007–08	*Sheffield U*	6	0	**6**	**0**
2008–09	Manchester U	1	0
2008–09	*Nottingham F*	13	1	**13**	**1**
2009–10	Manchester U	0	0	**1**	**0**
2009–10	Ipswich T	16	1	**16**	**1**

McAULEY, Gareth (D)   **222   18**
H: 6 3   W: 13 00   b.Larne 5-12-79
Source: Coleraine. *Honours:* Northern
Ireland Schools, B, 21 full caps, 1 goal.

2004–05	Lincoln C	37	3
2005–06	Lincoln C	35	5	**72**	**8**
2006–07	Leicester C	30	3
2007–08	Leicester C	44	2	**74**	**5**
2008–09	Ipswich T	35	0
2009–10	Ipswich T	41	5	**76**	**5**

McLOUGHLIN, Ian (G)   **0   0**
H: 6 3   W: 13 08   b.Ireland 9-8-91
Source: St Francis.

2008–09	Ipswich T	0	0
2009–10	Ipswich T	0	0

MURPHY, Brian (G)   **127   0**
H: 6 0   W: 13 00   b.Waterford 7-5-83
Honours: Eire Under-21.

2000–01	Manchester C	0	0
2001–02	Manchester C	0	0
2002–03	Manchester C	0	0
2002–03	*Oldham Ath*	0	0
2002–03	*Peterborough U*	1	0	**1**	**0**
From Waterford			
2003–04	Swansea C	11	0
2004–05	Swansea C	2	0
2005–06	Swansea C	0	0
2006–07	Swansea C	0	0	**13**	**0**
2007	Bohemians	29	0
2008	Bohemians	33	0
2009	Bohemians	35	0	**97**	**0**
2009–10	Ipswich T	16	0	**16**	**0**

NORRIS, David (M)   **302   33**
H: 5 7   W: 11 06   b.Stamford 22-2-81
Source: Boston U.

1999–2000	Bolton W	0	0
2000–01	Bolton W	0	0
2001–02	Bolton W	0	0
2001–02	*Hull C*	6	1	**6**	**1**
2002–03	Bolton W	0	0
2002–03	*Plymouth Arg*	33	6
2003–04	Plymouth Arg	45	5
2004–05	Plymouth Arg	35	3
2005–06	Plymouth Arg	45	2
2006–07	Plymouth Arg	41	6
2007–08	Plymouth Arg	27	5	**226**	**27**
2007–08	Ipswich T	9	1
2008–09	Ipswich T	37	3
2009–10	Ipswich T	24	1	**70**	**5**

O'CONNOR, Shane (M)   **12   0**
H: 5 9   W: 11 08   b.Cork 14-4-90
Source: Liverpool Academy.

2009–10	Ipswich T	12	0	**12**	**0**

PETERS, Jaime (M)   **93   4**
H: 5 7   W: 10 12   b.Pickering 4-5-87
Source: Moor Green. *Honours:* Canada
Youth, Under-20, Under-23, 22 full caps, 1
goal.

2005–06	Ipswich T	13	0
2006–07	Ipswich T	23	2
2007–08	Ipswich T	5	0
2007–08	*Yeovil T*	14	1	**14**	**1**
2008–09	Ipswich T	3	0
2008–09	*Gillingham*	3	0	**3**	**0**
2009–10	Ipswich T	32	1	**76**	**3**

PRISKIN, Tamas (F)   **169   43**
H: 6 2   W: 13 03   b.Komarno 27-9-86
Honours: Hungary Under-21, 25 full caps, 7
goals.

2002–03	Gyor	3	0
2003–04	Gyor	17	5
2004–05	Gyor	23	8
2005–06	Gyor	25	11	**68**	**24**
2006–07	Watford	16	2
2007–08	Watford	14	1
2007–08	*Preston NE*	5	2	**5**	**2**
2008–09	Watford	36	12
2009–10	Watford	0	0	**66**	**15**

2009–10	Ipswich T	17	1	**17**	**1**
2009–10	*QPR*	13	1	**13**	**1**

QUINN, Alan (M)   **329   30**
H: 5 9   W: 10 06   b.Dublin 13-6-79
Source: Cherry Orchard. *Honours:* Eire
Youth, Under-21, 8 full caps.

1997–98	Sheffield W	1	0
1998–99	Sheffield W	1	0
1999–2000	Sheffield W	19	3
2000–01	Sheffield W	37	2
2001–02	Sheffield W	38	2
2002–03	Sheffield W	37	5
2003–04	Sheffield W	24	4	**157**	**16**
2003–04	*Sunderland*	6	0	**6**	**0**
2004–05	Sheffield U	43	7
2005–06	Sheffield U	27	4
2006–07	Sheffield U	19	0
2007–08	Sheffield U	8	0	**97**	**11**
2007–08	Ipswich T	16	1
2008–09	Ipswich T	34	2
2009–10	Ipswich T	19	0	**69**	**3**

SMITH, Tommy (D)   **24   0**
H: 6 2   W: 12 02   b.Macclesfield 31-3-90
Source: Scholar. *Honours:* New Zealand 7 full
caps.

2007–08	Ipswich T	1	0
2008–09	Ipswich T	2	0
2009–10	Ipswich T	14	0	**16**	**0**
2009–10	*Brentford*	8	0	**8**	**0**

STEAD, Jon (F)   **272   63**
H: 6 3   W: 13 03   b.Huddersfield 7-4-83
Source: Scholar. *Honours:* England Under-21.

2001–02	Huddersfield T	0	0
2002–03	Huddersfield T	42	6
2003–04	Huddersfield T	26	16	**68**	**22**
2003–04	Blackburn R	13	6
2004–05	Blackburn R	29	2	**42**	**8**
2005–06	Sunderland	30	1
2006–07	Sunderland	5	1	**35**	**2**
2006–07	*Derby Co*	17	3	**17**	**3**
2007–08	Sheffield U	14	5
2007–08	Sheffield U	24	3
2008–09	Sheffield U	1	0	**39**	**8**
2008–09	Ipswich T	39	12
2009–10	Ipswich T	22	6	**61**	**18**
2009–10	*Coventry C*	10	2	**10**	**2**

TROTTER, Liam (M)   **72   6**
H: 6 2   W: 12 02   b.Ipswich 24-8-88
Source: Scholar.

2005–06	Ipswich T	1	0
2006–07	Ipswich T	0	0
2006–07	*Millwall*	2	0
2007–08	Ipswich T	7	1
2008–09	Ipswich T	3	1
2008–09	*Grimsby T*	15	2	**15**	**2**
2009–10	*Scunthorpe U*	12	1	**12**	**1**
2009–10	Ipswich T	12	0	**23**	**2**
2009–10	*Millwall*	20	1	**22**	**1**

UPSON, Edward (M)   **9   1**
H: 5 10   W: 11 07   b.Bury St Edmunds
21-11-89
Source: Scholar. *Honours:* England Youth.

2006–07	Ipswich T	0	0
2007–08	Ipswich T	0	0
2008–09	Ipswich T	0	0
2009–10	Ipswich T	0	0
2009–10	*Barnet*	9	1	**9**	**1**

WALTERS, Jon (F)   **262   51**
H: 6 0   W: 12 06   b.Birkenhead 20-9-83
Source: Blackburn R Scholar. *Honours:* Eire
Youth, Under-21, B.

2001–02	Bolton W	0	0
2002–03	Bolton W	4	0
2002–03	*Hull C*	11	5
2003–04	Bolton W	0	0	**4**	**0**
2003–04	*Crewe Alex*	0	0
2003–04	*Barnsley*	8	0	**8**	**0**
2003–04	Hull C	16	1
2004–05	Hull C	21	1	**48**	**7**
2004–05	*Scunthorpe U*	3	0	**3**	**0**
2005–06	Wrexham	38	5	**38**	**5**
2006–07	Chester C	26	9	**26**	**9**
2006–07	Ipswich T	16	4
2007–08	Ipswich T	40	13
2008–09	Ipswich T	36	5
2009–10	Ipswich T	43	8	**135**	**30**

WICKHAM, Connor (F) 28 4
H: 6 0 W: 14 01 b.Ipswich 31-3-93
Source: School. *Honours:* England Youth.

Season	Club	Apps	Gls	Tot Apps	Tot Gls
2008-09	Ipswich T	2	0		
2009-10	Ipswich T	26	4	28	4

WRIGHT, David (D) 381 8
H: 5 11 W: 11 01 b.Warrington 1-5-80
Source: Trainee. *Honours:* England Youth.

Season	Club	Apps	Gls	Tot Apps	Tot Gls
1997-98	Crewe Alex	3	0		
1998-99	Crewe Alex	20	1		
1999-2000	Crewe Alex	45	0		
2000-01	Crewe Alex	42	0		
2001-02	Crewe Alex	30	0		
2002-03	Crewe Alex	31	1		
2003-04	Crewe Alex	40	1	211	3
2004-05	Wigan Ath	31	0		
2005-06	Wigan Ath	2	0		
2005-06	*Norwich C*	5	0	5	0
2006-07	Wigan Ath	12	0	45	0
2006-07	Ipswich T	19	1		
2007-08	Ipswich T	41	2		
2008-09	Ipswich T	34	1		
2009-10	Ipswich T	26	1	120	5

WRIGHT, Richard (G) 377 0
H: 6 2 W: 14 04 b.Ipswich 5-11-77
Source: Trainee. *Honours:* England Schools, Youth, Under-21, 2 full caps.

Season	Club	Apps	Gls	Tot Apps	Tot Gls
1994-95	Ipswich T	3	0		
1995-96	Ipswich T	23	0		
1996-97	Ipswich T	40	0		
1997-98	Ipswich T	46	0		
1998-99	Ipswich T	46	0		
1999-2000	Ipswich T	46	0		
2000-01	Ipswich T	36	0		
2001-02	Arsenal	12	0	12	0
2002-03	Everton	33	0		
2003-04	Everton	4	0		
2004-05	Everton	7	0		
2005-06	Everton	15	0		
2006-07	Everton	1	0	60	0
2007-08	West Ham U	0	0		
2007-08	*Southampton*	7	0	7	0
2008-09	Ipswich T	46	0		
2009-10	Ipswich T	12	0	298	0

LEEDS U (44)

ANKERGREN, Casper (G) 205 0
H: 6 3 W: 14 07 b.Koge 9-11-79
Source: Koge. *Honours:* Denmark Youth, Under-21.

Season	Club	Apps	Gls	Tot Apps	Tot Gls
2001-02	Brondby	1	0		
2002-03	Brondby	16	0		
2003-04	Brondby	1	0		
2004-05	Brondby	32	0		
2005-06	Brondby	18	0		
2006-07	Brondby	18	0	86	0
2006-07	Leeds U	14	0		
2007-08	Leeds U	43	0		
2008-09	Leeds U	33	0		
2009-10	Leeds U	29	0	119	0

BECCHIO, Luciano (F) 182 60
H: 6 2 W: 13 05 b.Cordoba 28-12-83
Source: Boca Juniors.

Season	Club	Apps	Gls	Tot Apps	Tot Gls
2003-04	Mallorca B	0	0		
2004-05	Mallorca B	0	0		
2004-05	*Murcia*	16	3	16	3
2005-06	*Terrassa*	24	2	24	2
2006-07	*Barcelona Athletic*	10	0	10	0
2006-07	*Merida*	12	5		
2007-08	*Merida*	38	22	50	27
2008-09	Leeds U	45	15		
2009-10	Leeds U	37	15	82	30

BECKFORD, Jermaine (F) 148 80
H: 6 2 W: 13 02 b.London 9-12-83
Source: Wealdstone.

Season	Club	Apps	Gls	Tot Apps	Tot Gls
2005-06	Leeds U	5	0		
2006-07	Leeds U	5	0		
2006-07	*Carlisle U*	4	1	4	1
2006-07	*Scunthorpe U*	18	8	18	8
2007-08	Leeds U	40	20		
2008-09	Leeds U	34	26		
2009-10	Leeds U	42	25	126	71

BROMBY, Leigh (D) 306 12
H: 5 11 W: 11 06 b.Dewsbury 2-6-80
Honours: England Schools.

Season	Club	Apps	Gls	Tot Apps	Tot Gls
1998-99	Sheffield W	0	0		
1999-2000	Sheffield W	0	0		
1999-2000	*Mansfield T*	10	1	10	1
2000-01	Sheffield W	18	0		
2001-02	Sheffield W	26	1		
2002-03	Sheffield W	27	0		
2002-03	*Norwich C*	5	0	5	0
2003-04	Sheffield W	29	1	100	2
2004-05	Sheffield U	46	5		
2005-06	Sheffield U	35	1		
2006-07	Sheffield U	17	0		
2007-08	Sheffield U	11	0		
2007-08	Watford	16	1		
2008-09	Watford	22	0	38	1
2008-09	*Sheffield U*	12	1	121	7
2009-10	Leeds U	32	1	32	1

CROWE, Jason (D) 360 23
H: 5 9 W: 10 09 b.Sidcup 30-9-78
Source: Trainee. *Honours:* England Schools, Youth.

Season	Club	Apps	Gls	Tot Apps	Tot Gls
1995-96	Arsenal	0	0		
1996-97	Arsenal	0	0		
1997-98	Arsenal	0	0		
1998-99	Arsenal	0	0		
1998-99	*Crystal Palace*	8	0	8	0
1999-2000	Portsmouth	25	0		
2000-01	Portsmouth	23	0		
2000-01	*Brentford*	9	0	9	0
2001-02	Portsmouth	22	1		
2002-03	Portsmouth	16	4	86	5
2003-04	Grimsby T	32	0		
2004-05	Grimsby T	37	4	69	4
2005-06	Northampton T	41	2		
2006-07	Northampton T	43	3		
2007-08	Northampton T	44	4		
2008-09	Northampton T	43	5	171	14
2009-10	Leeds U	17	0	17	0

DARVILLE, Liam (D) 0 0
b. 26-10-90
Source: Scholar. *Honours:* England Youth.

Season	Club	Apps	Gls	Tot Apps	Tot Gls
2008-09	Leeds U	0	0		
2009-10	Leeds U	0	0		

DICKOV, Paul (F) 416 98
H: 5 6 W: 10 06 b.Livingston 1-11-72
Source: Trainee. *Honours:* Scotland Schools, Youth, Under-21, 10 full caps, 1 goal.

Season	Club	Apps	Gls	Tot Apps	Tot Gls
1992-93	Arsenal	3	2		
1993-94	Arsenal	1	0		
1993-94	*Luton T*	15	1	15	1
1993-94	*Brighton & HA*	8	5	8	5
1994-95	Arsenal	9	0		
1995-96	Arsenal	7	1		
1996-97	Arsenal	1	0	21	3
1996-97	Manchester C	29	5		
1997-98	Manchester C	30	9		
1998-99	Manchester C	35	10		
1999-2000	Manchester C	34	5		
2000-01	Manchester C	21	4		
2001-02	Manchester C	7	0		
2001-02	Leicester C	12	4		
2002-03	Leicester C	42	17		
2003-04	Leicester C	35	11		
2004-05	Blackburn R	29	9		
2005-06	Blackburn R	21	5	50	14
2006-07	Manchester C	16	0		
2007-08	Manchester C	0	0	172	33
2007-08	*Crystal Palace*	9	0	9	0
2007-08	*Blackpool*	11	6	11	6
2008-09	Leicester C	20	2		
2009-10	Leicester C	1	0	110	34
2009-10	*Derby Co*	16	2	16	2
2009-10	Leeds U	4	0	4	0

ELLIOTT, Tom (F) 25 1
H: 5 10 W: 11 02 b.Leeds 9-9-89
Source: School.

Season	Club	Apps	Gls	Tot Apps	Tot Gls
2006-07	Leeds U	3	0		
2007-08	Leeds U	0	0		
2008-09	Leeds U	0	0		
2008-09	*Macclesfield T*	6	0	6	0
2009-10	Leeds U	0	0	3	0
2009-10	*Bury*	16	1	16	1

GRADEL, Max (M) 93 16
H: 5 8 W: 12 03 b.Ivory Coast 30-9-87

Season	Club	Apps	Gls	Tot Apps	Tot Gls
2005-06	Leicester C	0	0		
2006-07	Leicester C	0	0		
2007-08	Leicester C	0	0		
2007-08	*Bournemouth*	34	9	34	9
2008-09	Leicester C	27	1		
2009-10	Leicester C	0	0	27	1
2009-10	Leeds U	32	6	32	6

GRELLA, Mike (F) 28 1
H: 5 11 W: 12 02 b.Glen Cove 23-1-87
Source: Duke University. *Honours:* USA Youth.

Season	Club	Apps	Gls	Tot Apps	Tot Gls
2008-09	Leeds U	11	0		
2009-10	Leeds U	17	1	28	1

HATFIELD, Will (M) 0 0
b. 10-10-91
Source: Scholar.

Season	Club	Apps	Gls	Tot Apps	Tot Gls
2009-10	Leeds U	0	0		

HIGGS, Shane (G) 266 0
H: 6 3 W: 14 06 b.Oxford 13-5-77
Source: Trainee.

Season	Club	Apps	Gls	Tot Apps	Tot Gls
1994-95	Bristol R	0	0		
1995-96	Bristol R	0	0		
1996-97	Bristol R	2	0		
1997-98	Bristol R	8	0	10	0
From Worcester C.					
1999-2000	Cheltenham T	0	0		
2000-01	Cheltenham T	1	0		
2001-02	Cheltenham T	1	0		
2002-03	Cheltenham T	10	0		
2003-04	Cheltenham T	42	0		
2004-05	Cheltenham T	46	0		
2005-06	Cheltenham T	45	0		
2006-07	Cheltenham T	36	0		
2007-08	Cheltenham T	46	0		
2008-09	Cheltenham T	10	0	237	0
2008-09	Wolverhampton W	0	0		
2009-10	Leeds U	19	0	19	0

HOWSON, Jonathan (M) 120 12
H: 5 11 W: 12 01 b.Morley 21-5-88
Source: Scholar.

Season	Club	Apps	Gls	Tot Apps	Tot Gls
2006-07	Leeds U	9	1		
2007-08	Leeds U	26	3		
2008-09	Leeds U	40	4		
2009-10	Leeds U	45	4	120	12

HUGHES, Andy (M) 487 39
H: 5 11 W: 12 01 b.Stockport 2-1-78
Source: Trainee.

Season	Club	Apps	Gls	Tot Apps	Tot Gls
1995-96	Oldham Ath	15	1		
1996-97	Oldham Ath	8	0		
1997-98	Oldham Ath	10	0	33	1
1997-98	Notts Co	15	2		
1998-99	Notts Co	30	3		
1999-2000	Notts Co	35	7		
2000-01	Notts Co	30	5	110	17
2001-02	Reading	39	6		
2002-03	Reading	43	9		
2003-04	Reading	43	3		
2004-05	Reading	41	0	166	18
2005-06	Norwich C	36	2		
2006-07	Norwich C	36	0	72	2
2007-08	Leeds U	40	1		
2008-09	Leeds U	27	0		
2009-10	Leeds U	39	0	106	1

JOHNSON, Brad (M) 136 22
H: 6 0 W: 12 10 b.Hackney 28-4-87
Source: Cambridge U Juniors.

Season	Club	Apps	Gls	Tot Apps	Tot Gls
2004-05	Cambridge U	1	0	1	0
2005-06	Northampton T	3	0		
2006-07	Northampton T	27	5		
2007-08	Northampton T	23	2	53	7
2007-08	Leeds U	21	3		
2008-09	Leeds U	15	1		
2008-09	*Brighton & HA*	10	4	10	4
2009-10	Leeds U	36	7	72	11

KANDOL, Tresor (F) 169 39
H: 6 0 W: 13 07 b.Banga 30-8-81
Source: Trainee. *Honours:* DR Congo 1 full cap.

Season	Club	Apps	Gls	Tot Apps	Tot Gls
1998-99	Luton T	4	0		
1999-2000	Luton T	4	0		
2000-01	Luton T	13	3	21	3
2001-02	Bournemouth	12	0	12	0
From Thurrock, Dagenham					

2005–06   *Darlington*   7   2   **7 2**
From Dagenham & R.
2005–06   Barnet   13   4
2006–07   Barnet   16   6   **29 10**
2006–07   Leeds U   18   1
2007–08   Leeds U   41   11
2008–09   Leeds U   0   0
2008–09   *Millwall*   18   8   **18 8**
2008–09   *Charlton Ath*   13   2   **13 2**
2009–10   Leeds U   10   2   **69 14**

KILKENNY, Neil (M)   **154 12**
H: 5 8   W: 10 08   b.Enfield 19-12-85
Source: Arsenal Trainee. *Honours:* England Youth, Under-20, Australia Under-23, 2 full caps.
2003–04   Birmingham C   0   0
2004–05   Birmingham C   0   0
2004–05   Oldham Ath   27   4
2005–06   Birmingham C   18   0
2006–07   Birmingham C   8   0
2007–08   Birmingham C   0   0   **26 0**
2007–08   *Oldham Ath*   20   1   **47 5**
2007–08   Leeds U   16   1
2008–09   Leeds U   30   4
2009–10   Leeds U   35   2   **81 7**

KISNORBO, Patrick (D)   **270 14**
H: 6 1   W: 11 11   b.Melbourne 24-3-81
Honours: Australia Schools, Under-20, Under-23, 18 full caps, 1 goal.
2000–01   South Melbourne   25   0
2001–02   South Melbourne   23   2
2002–03   South Melbourne   19   1   **67 3**
2003–04   Hearts   31   0
2004–05   Hearts   17   1   **48 1**
2005–06   Leicester C   37   1
2006–07   Leicester C   40   5
2007–08   Leicester C   41   3
2008–09   Leicester C   8   0   **126 9**
2009–10   Leeds U   29   1   **29 1**

LEES, Tom (M)   **39 0**
H: 6 1   W: 12 04   b.Warwick 28-11-90
2308–09   Leeds U   0   0
2009–10   Leeds U   0   0
2009–10   *Accrington S*   39   0   **39 0**

MARTIN, Alan (G)   **7 0**
H: 6 0   W: 11 11   b.Glasgow 1-1-89
Source: Motherwell. *Honours:* Scotland Youth, Under-21.
2007–08   Leeds U   0   0
2008–09   Leeds U   0   0
2009–10   Leeds U   0   0
2009–10   *Accrington S*   7   0   **7 0**

McCANN, Joe (M)   **0 0**
b. 11-10-92
Source: Scholar. *Honours:* England Youth.
2009–10   Leeds U   0   0

MICHALIK, Lubomir (D)   **87 5**
H: 6 4   W: 13 00   b.Cadca 13-8-83
Source: Cadca, Martin. *Honours:* Slovakia 4 full caps, 2 goals.
2005–06   Senec   8   1
2006–07   Senec   12   1   **20 2**
2006–07   *Leeds U*   7   1
2006–07   Bolton W   4   1
2007–08   Bolton W   7   0   **11 1**
2007–08   Leeds U   17   0
2008–09   Leeds U   19   0
2009–10   Leeds U   13   1   **56 2**

MILNE, Andrew (D)   **13 0**
H: 5 11   W: 11 08   b.Leeds 30-9-90
Source: Scholar. *Honours:* Scotland Youth.
2009–10   Leeds U   0   0
2009–10   *Darlington*   13   0   **13 0**

NAYLOR, Richard (D)   **386 40**
H: 6 1   W: 13 07   b.Leeds 28-2-77
Source: Trainee.
1995–96   Ipswich T   0   0
1996–97   Ipswich T   27   4
1997–98   Ipswich T   5   2
1998–99   Ipswich T   30   5
1999–2000   Ipswich T   36   8
2000–01   Ipswich T   13   1
2001–02   Ipswich T   14   1
2001–02   *Millwall*   3   0   **3 0**
2001–02   *Barnsley*   8   0   **8 0**

2002–03   Ipswich T   17   2
2003–04   Ipswich T   39   5
2004–05   Ipswich T   46   6
2005–06   Ipswich T   42   3
2006–07   Ipswich T   25   0
2007–08   Ipswich T   7   0
2008–09   Ipswich T   23   0   **324 37**
2008–09   Leeds U   22   1
2009–10   Leeds U   29   2   **51 3**

PARKER, Ben (D)   **89 0**
H: 5 11   W: 11 06   b.Pontefract 8-11-87
Source: Scholar. *Honours:* England Youth.
2004–05   Leeds U   0   0
2005–06   Leeds U   0   0
2006–07   Leeds U   0   0
2006–07   *Bradford C*   39   0   **39 0**
2007–08   Leeds U   9   0
2007–08   *Darlington*   13   0   **13 0**
2008–09   Leeds U   24   0
2009–10   Leeds U   4   0   **37 0**

ROBINSON, Andy (M)   **235 46**
H: 5 8   W: 11 04   b.Birkenhead 3-11-79
Source: Cammell Laird.
2002–03   Tranmere R   0   0
2003–04   Swansea C   37   8
2004–05   Swansea C   37   8
2005–06   Swansea C   39   12
2006–07   Swansea C   39   7
2007–08   Swansea C   40   8   **192 43**
2008–09   Leeds U   32   2
2009–10   Leeds U   6   0   **38 2**
2009–10   *Tranmere R*   5   1   **5 1**

RUI MARQUES, Manuel (D)   **206 4**
H: 5 11   W: 11 13   b.Luanda 3-9-77
Source: Benfica. *Honours:* Angola 19 full caps.
1998–99   Baden   27   0   **27 0**
1999–2000   SSV Ulm   32   0   **32 0**
2000–01   Hertha   1   0   **1 0**
2000–01   Stuttgart   12   0
2001–02   Stuttgart   23   0
2002–03   Stuttgart   12   0
2003–04   Stuttgart   0   0   **47 0**
2004–05   Maritimo   8   0   **8 0**
2005–06   Leeds U   0   0
2005–06   *Hull C*   1   0   **1 0**
2006–07   Leeds U   17   0
2007–08   Leeds U   36   3
2008–09   Leeds U   32   1
2009–10   Leeds U   5   0   **90 4**

SHEEHAN, Alan (D)   **87 5**
H: 5 11   W: 11 02   b.Athlone 14-9-86
Source: Scholar. *Honours:* Eire Youth, Under-21.
2004–05   Leicester C   1   0
2005–06   Leicester C   2   0
2006–07   Leicester C   0   0
2006–07   *Mansfield T*   10   0   **10 0**
2007–08   Leicester C   20   1   **23 1**
2007–08   *Leeds U*   10   1
2008–09   Leeds U   11   1
2008–09   *Crewe Alex*   3   0   **3 0**
2009–10   Leeds U   0   0   **21 2**
2009–10   *Oldham Ath*   8   1   **8 1**
2009–10   *Swindon T*   22   1   **22 1**

SHOWUNMI, Enoch (F)   **177 29**
H: 6 3   W: 14 11   b.Kilburn 21-4-82
Source: Willesden Constantine. *Honours:* Nigeria 2 full caps.
2003–04   Luton T   26   7
2004–05   Luton T   35   6
2005–06   Luton T   41   1   **102 14**
2006–07   Bristol C   33   10
2007–08   Bristol C   17   3   **50 13**
2007–08   *Sheffield W*   10   0   **10 0**
2008–09   Leeds U   8   2
2009–10   Leeds U   7   0   **15 2**

SNODGRASS, Robert (F)   **179 36**
H: 6 0   W: 12 02   b.Glasgow 7-9-87
Honours: Scotland Youth, Under-21.
2003–04   Livingston   0   0
2004–05   Livingston   17   2
2005–06   Livingston   27   4
2006–07   Livingston   6   0
2006–07   *Stirling A*   12   5   **12 5**
2007–08   Livingston   31   9   **81 15**

2008–09   Leeds U   42   9
2009–10   Leeds U   44   7   **86 16**

SOMMA, Davide (F)   **74 12**
H: 6 1   W: 12 13   b.Johannesburg 26-3-85
2005–06   Pro Vasto   20   2
2006–07   Pro Vasto   19   0   **39 2**
2007–08   Olbia   15   1   **15 1**
2008   San Jose Eq   3   0   **3 0**
2009–10   Leeds U   0   0
2009–10   *Chesterfield*   3   0   **3 0**
2009–10   *Lincoln C*   14   9   **14 9**

WHITE, Aidan (D)   **13 0**
H: 5 7   W: 10 00   b.Otley 10-10-91
Source: Scholar. *Honours:* England Youth.
2008–09   Leeds U   5   0
2009–10   Leeds U   8   0   **13 0**

LEICESTER C (45)

ADAMS, Nicky (F)   **127 15**
H: 5 10   W: 11 00   b.Bolton 16-10-86
Source: Scholar. *Honours:* Wales Under-21.
2005–06   Bury   15   1
2006–07   Bury   19   1
2007–08   Bury   43   12   **77 14**
2008–09   Leicester C   12   0
2008–09   *Rochdale*   14   1   **14 1**
2009–10   Leicester C   18   0   **30 0**
2009–10   *Leyton Orient*   6   0   **6 0**

AJDAREVIC, Astrit (M)   **10 1**
H: 6 1   W: 11 08   b.Kosovo 17-4-90
2006–07   Falkenberg   4   1   **4 1**
2006–07   Liverpool   0   0
2007–08   Liverpool   0   0
2008–09   Liverpool   0   0
2008–09   *Leicester C*   5   0
2009–10   Leicester C   0   0   **5 0**
2009–10   *Hereford U*   1   0   **1 0**

AMBROSICS, Robert (G)   **0 0**
H: 6 3   W: 13 00   b.Hungary 22-1-92
Honours: Hungary Youth.

BERNER, Bruno (M)   **251 13**
H: 6 1   W: 12 13   b.Zurich 21-11-77
Honours: Switzerland Youth, Under-20, Under-21, 16 full caps.
1997–98   Grasshoppers   2   0
1998–99   Grasshoppers   21   0
1999–2000   Grasshoppers   6   1
1999–2000   *Oviedo*   1   1   **1 1**
2000–01   Grasshoppers   27   1
2001–02   Grasshoppers   16   0   **72 2**
2002–03   Freiburg   31   2
2003–04   Freiburg   33   1
2004–05   Freiburg   12   0   **76 3**
2005–06   Basle   17   0
2006–07   Basle   15   0   **32 0**
2006–07   Blackburn R   1   0
2007–08   Blackburn R   2   0
2008–09   Blackburn R   0   0   **3 0**
2008–09   Leicester C   32   3
2009–10   Leicester C   35   4   **67 7**

BOLGER, Cian (D)   **0 0**
b.Ireland
Source: Scholar.
2009–10   Leicester C   0   0

BROWN, Wayne (D)   **337 11**
H: 6 0   W: 12 06   b.Barking 20-8-77
Source: Trainee.
1995–96   Ipswich T   0   0
1996–97   Ipswich T   0   0
1997–98   Ipswich T   1   0
1997–98   *Colchester U*   2   0
1998–99   Ipswich T   1   0
1999–2000   Ipswich T   25   0
2000–01   Ipswich T   4   0
2000–01   *QPR*   2   0   **2 0**
2001–02   Ipswich T   0   0
2001–02   *Wimbledon*   17   1   **17 1**
2001–02   *Watford*   11   3
2002–03   Ipswich T   9   0   **40 0**
2002–03   Watford   13   1
2003–04   Watford   12   0   **36 4**
2003–04   *Gillingham*   4   1   **4 1**

2003–04	Colchester U	16	0		
2004–05	Colchester U	40	1		
2005–06	Colchester U	38	2		
2006–07	Colchester U	46	1	142	4
2007–08	Hull C	41	1		
2008–09	Hull C	1	0	42	1
2008–09	Preston NE	6	0	6	0
2008–09	Leicester C	9	0		
2009–10	Leicester C	39	0	48	0

BURNS, Robbie (M)   2 0
H: 6 0   W: 11 12   b.Milton Keynes 15-11-90
Source: Scholar.

2008–09	Leicester C	0	0		
2008–09	Trannere R	2	0	2	0
2009–10	Leicester C	0	0		

CAMPBELL, Dudley (F)   147 42
H: 5 10   W: 11 00   b.London 12-11-81
Source: Aston Villa Trainee, QPR, Chesham U, Stevenage B, Yeading.

2005–06	Brentford	23	9	23	9
2005–06	Birmingham C	11	0		
2006–07	Birmingham C	32	9	43	9
2007–08	Leicester C	28	4		
2008–09	Leicester C	7	0		
2008–09	Blackpool	20	9		
2009–10	Leicester C	3	0	38	4
2009–10	Derby Co	8	3	8	3
2009–10	Blackpool	15	8	35	17

CHAMBERLAIN, Elliott (M)   0 0
b. 29-4-92
Source: Scholar. *Honours:* Wales Youth, Under-21.

| 2009–10 | Leicester C | 0 | 0 | | |

CHAMBERS, Ashley (F)   13 3
H: 5 10   W: 11 06   b.Leicester 1-3-90
Source: Scholar. *Honours:* England Schools, Youth.

2005–06	Leicester C	0	0		
2006–07	Leicester C	0	0		
2007–08	Leicester C	5	0		
2008–09	Leicester C	1	0		
2009–10	Leicester C	0	0	6	0
2009–10	Wycombe W	3	1	3	1
2009–10	Grimsby T	4	2	4	2

DYER, Lloyd (M)   218 32
H: 5 8   W: 10 03   b.Birmingham 13-9-82
Source: Aston Villa Juniors.

2001–02	WBA	0	0		
2002–03	WBA	0	0		
2003–04	WBA	17	2		
2003–04	Kidderminster H	7	1	7	1
2004–05	WBA	4	0		
2004–05	Coventry C	6	0	6	0
2005–06	WBA	0	0	21	2
2005–06	QPR	15	0	15	0
2005–06	Millwall	6	0	6	0
2006–07	Milton Keynes D	41	5		
2007–08	Milton Keynes D	45	11	86	16
2008–09	Leicester C	44	10		
2009–10	Leicester C	33	3	77	13

FRYATT, Matty (F)   236 77
H: 5 10   W: 11 00   b.Nuneaton 5-3-86
Source: Scholar. *Honours:* England Youth.

2002–03	Walsall	1	0		
2003–04	Walsall	11	1		
2003–04	Carlisle U	10	1	10	1
2004–05	Walsall	36	15		
2005–06	Walsall	23	11	70	27
2005–06	Leicester C	19	6		
2006–07	Leicester C	32	3		
2007–08	Leicester C	30	2		
2008–09	Leicester C	46	27		
2009–10	Leicester C	29	11	156	49

GALLAGHER, Paul (F)   205 38
H: 6 1   W: 11 00   b.Glasgow 9-8-84
Source: Trainee. *Honours:* Scotland Under-21, B, 1 full cap.

2002–03	Blackburn R	1	0		
2003–04	Blackburn R	26	3		
2004–05	Blackburn R	16	2		
2005–06	Blackburn R	4	0		
2005–06	Stoke C	37	11		
2006–07	Blackburn R	16	1		
2007–08	Blackburn R	0	0		
2007–08	Preston NE	19	1	19	1
2007–08	Stoke C	7	0	44	11
2008–09	Blackburn R	0	0		
2008–09	Plymouth Arg	40	13	40	13
2009–10	Blackburn R	1	0	61	6
2009–10	Leicester C	41	7	41	7

HOBBS, Jack (D)   100 2
H: 6 3   W: 13 05   b.Portsmouth 18-8-88
Source: Scholar. *Honours:* England Youth.

2004–05	Lincoln C	1	0	1	0
2005–06	Liverpool	0	0		
2006–07	Liverpool	0	0		
2007–08	Liverpool	2	0		
2007–08	Scunthorpe U	9	1	9	1
2008–09	Liverpool	0	0	2	0
2008–09	Leicester C	44	0		
2009–10	Leicester C	44	0	88	1

HOWARD, Steve (F)   601 181
H: 6 3   W: 15 00   b.Durham 10-5-76
Source: Tow Law T. *Honours:* Scotland B.

1995–96	Hartlepool U	39	7		
1996–97	Hartlepool U	32	8		
1997–98	Hartlepool U	43	7		
1998–99	Hartlepool U	28	5	142	27
1998–99	Northampton T	12	0		
1999–2000	Northampton T	41	10		
2000–01	Northampton T	33	8	86	18
2000–01	Luton T	12	3		
2001–02	Luton T	42	24		
2002–03	Luton T	41	22		
2003–04	Luton T	34	14		
2004–05	Luton T	40	18		
2005–06	Luton T	43	14	212	95
2006–07	Derby Co	43	16		
2007–08	Derby Co	20	1	63	17
2007–08	Leicester C	21	6		
2008–09	Leicester C	41	13		
2009–10	Leicester C	36	5	98	24

JOHN, Jorrin (F)   0 0
Source: Scholar.

| 2009–10 | Leicester C | 0 | 0 | | |

KEE, Billy (F)   37 9
H: 5 9   W: 11 04   b.Leicester 1-12-90
Honours: Northern Ireland Youth, Under-21.

| 2009–10 | Leicester C | 0 | 0 | | |
| 2009–10 | Accrington S | 37 | 9 | 37 | 9 |

KERMORGANT, Yann (F)   174 44
H: 6 0   W: 13 03   b.Vannes 8-11-81
Source: Vannes.

2004–05	Chatellerault	29	14	29	14
2005–06	Grenoble	26	6		
2006–07	Grenoble	32	10	58	16
2007–08	Reims	33	4		
2008–09	Reims	34	9	67	13
2009–10	Leicester C	20	1	20	1

KING, Andy (M)   99 19
H: 6 0   W: 11 10   b.Luton 29-10-88
Source: Scholar. *Honours:* Wales Youth, Under-21, 3 full caps.

2007–08	Leicester C	11	1		
2008–09	Leicester C	45	9		
2009–10	Leicester C	43	9	99	19

KING, Craig (F)   107 9
H: 5 11   W: 11 12   b.Chesterfield 6-10-90
Source: Scholar. *Honours:* Scotland Youth.

2005–06	The New Saints	23	2		
2006–07	The New Saints	18	1		
2007–08	The New Saints	30	3	81	6
2008–09	Leicester C	0	0		
2009–10	Leicester C	0	0		
2009–10	Hereford U	26	3	26	3

LOGAN, Conrad (G)   96 0
H: 6 2   W: 14 00   b.Letterkenny 18-4-86
Source: Scholar. *Honours:* Eire Youth.

2003–04	Leicester C	0	0		
2004–05	Leicester C	0	0		
2005–06	Leicester C	0	0		
2005–06	Boston U	13	0	13	0
2006–07	Leicester C	28	0		
2007–08	Leicester C	0	0		
2007–08	Stockport Co	34	0		
2008–09	Leicester C	0	0		
2008–09	Luton T	22	0	22	0
2008–09	Stockport Co	7	0	41	0
2009–10	Leicester C	2	0	20	0

MORRISON, Michael (D)   66 5
H: 6 0   W: 12 00   b.Bury St Edmunds 3-3-88
Source: Cambridge U.

| 2008–09 | Leicester C | 35 | 3 | | |
| 2009–10 | Leicester C | 31 | 2 | 66 | 5 |

N'GUESSAN, Dany (M)   141 23
H: 6 0   W: 12 13   b.Ivry-sur-Seine 11-8-87
Source: Auxerre, Rangers.

2006–07	Boston U	23	5	23	5
2006–07	Lincoln C	9	0		
2007–08	Lincoln C	37	7		
2008–09	Lincoln C	45	8	91	15
2009–10	Leicester C	27	3	27	3

NEILSON, Robbie (D)   240 1
H: 6 0   W: 13 01   b.Paisley 19-6-80

1999–2000	Cowdenbeath	8	0	8	0
2000–01	Hearts	18	0		
2001–02	Hearts	2	0		
2002–03	Hearts	5	0		
2002–03	Queen of the S	13	0	13	0
2003–04	Hearts	29	0		
2004–05	Hearts	35	1		
2005–06	Hearts	37	0		
2006–07	Hearts	14	0		
2007–08	Hearts	33	0		
2008–09	Hearts	27	0	200	1
2009–10	Leicester C	19	0	19	0

O'NEILL, Luke (D)   5 0
H: 6 0   W: 11 04   b.Slough 20-8-91
Source: Scholar. *Honours:* England Youth.

2008–09	Leicester C	0	0		
2009–10	Leicester C	1	0	1	0
2009–10	Tranmere R	4	0	4	0

OAKLEY, Matthew (M)   420 31
H: 5 10   W: 12 06   b.Peterborough 17-8-77
Source: Trainee. *Honours:* England Under-21.

1994–95	Southampton	1	0		
1995–96	Southampton	10	0		
1996–97	Southampton	28	3		
1997–98	Southampton	33	1		
1998–99	Southampton	22	2		
1999–2000	Southampton	31	3		
2000–01	Southampton	35	1		
2001–02	Southampton	27	1		
2002–03	Southampton	31	0		
2003–04	Southampton	7	0		
2004–05	Southampton	7	1		
2005–06	Southampton	29	2	261	14
2006–07	Derby Co	37	6		
2007–08	Derby Co	19	3	56	9
2007–08	Leicester C	20	0		
2008–09	Leicester C	45	8		
2009–10	Leicester C	38	0	103	8

PARKES, Tom (M)   22 1
H: 6 3   W: 12 05   b.Leicester 15-1-92
Source: Scholar.

2008–09	Leicester C	0	0		
2009–10	Leicester C	0	0		
2009–10	Burton Alb	22	1	22	1

PENTNEY, Carl (G)   1 0
H: 6 0   W: 12 00   b.Leicester 3-2-89

2007–08	Leicester C	0	0		
2008–09	Leicester C	1	0		
2009–10	Leicester C	0	0	1	0

POWELL, Chris (D)   667 6
H: 5 11   W: 11 12   b.Lambeth 8-9-69
Source: Trainee. *Honours:* England 5 full caps.

1987–88	Crystal Palace	0	0		
1988–89	Crystal Palace	3	0		
1989–90	Crystal Palace	0	0	3	0
1989–90	Aldershot	11	0	11	0
1990–91	Southend U	45	1		
1991–92	Southend U	44	0		
1992–93	Southend U	42	2		
1993–94	Southend U	46	0		
1994–95	Southend U	44	0		
1995–96	Southend U	27	0	248	3
1995–96	Derby Co	19	0		
1996–97	Derby Co	35	0		
1997–98	Derby Co	37	1	91	1
1998–99	Charlton Ath	38	0		
1999–2000	Charlton Ath	40	0		
2000–01	Charlton Ath	33	0		

Season	Club	Apps	Gls	Tot Apps	Tot Gls
2001–02	Charlton Ath	36	1		
2002–03	Charlton Ath	37	0		
2003–04	Charlton Ath	16	0		
2004–05	Charlton Ath	0	0		
2004–05	West Ham U	36	0	36	0
2005–06	Charlton Ath	27	0		
2006–07	Watford	15	0	15	0
2007–08	Charlton Ath	17	1	244	2
2008–09	Leicester C	17	0		
2009–10	Leicester C	2	0	19	0

SOLANO, Nolberto (M)   469 98
H: 5 8 W: 10 07 b.Callao 12-12-74
Honours: Peru 95 full caps, 20 goals.

Season	Club	Apps	Gls	Tot Apps	Tot Gls
1954–95	Sporting Cristal	38	12		
1955–96	Sporting Cristal	26	13		
1996–97	Sporting Cristal	11	7	75	32
1997–98	Boca Juniors	32	5	32	5
1998–99	Newcastle U	29	6		
1999–2000	Newcastle U	30	3		
2000–01	Newcastle U	33	6		
2001–02	Newcastle U	37	7		
2002–03	Newcastle U	31	7		
2003–04	Newcastle U	12	0		
2003–04	Aston Villa	10	0		
2004–05	Aston Villa	36	8		
2005–06	Aston Villa	3	0	49	8
2005–06	Newcastle U	29	6		
2005–07	Newcastle U	28	2		
2007–08	Newcastle U	1	0	230	37
2007–08	West Ham U	23	4	23	4
2008–09	Larissa	17	2	17	2
2009	Universitario	32	10	32	10
2009–10	Leicester C	11	0	11	0

TUNCHEV, Aleksandar (D)   233 25
H: 6 2 W: 13 03 b.Pazardzhik 10-7-81
Honours: Bulgaria 25 full caps, 1 goal.

Season	Club	Apps	Gls	Tot Apps	Tot Gls
1998–99	Pazardzhik	6	0		
1999–2000	Pazardzhik	14	2		
1999–2000	Iskar	15	1	15	1
2000–01	Pazardzhik	18	3	38	5
2001–02	Lokomotiv Plovdiv	30	3	30	3
2002–03	Lokomotiv Plovdiv	1	0		
2003–04	Lokomotiv Plovdiv	25	1		
2004–05	Lokomotiv Plovdiv	28	1		
2005–06	Lokomotiv Plovdiv	11	2	65	4
2005–06	CSKA Sofia	10	1		
2006–07	CSKA Sofia	27	7		
2007–08	CSKA Sofia	26	3	63	11
2008–09	Leicester C	20	1		
2009–10	Leicester C	2	0	22	1

VAUGHAN, James (D)   87 1
H: 5 10 W: 12 09 b.Liverpool 6-12-86
Source: Scholar.

Season	Club	Apps	Gls	Tot Apps	Tot Gls
2004–05	Tranmere R	0	0		
2005–06	Chester C	0	0		
2006–07	Chester C	6	0		
2007–08	Chester C	30	0		
2008–09	Chester C	42	0		
2009–10	Chester C	1	0	79	0
2009–10	Leicester C	8	1	8	1

VERMA, Aman (M)   7 0
H: 6 1 W: 13 00 b.Leicester 1-2-88
Source: Bedworth U, Redditch U.

Season	Club	Apps	Gls	Tot Apps	Tot Gls
2008–09	Leicester C	0	0		
2009–10	Leicester C	0	0		
2009–10	Crewe Alex	7	0	7	0

WEALE, Chris (G)   164 1
H: 6 2 W: 13 03 b.Yeovil 9-2-82
Source: Juniors.

Season	Club	Apps	Gls	Tot Apps	Tot Gls
2003–04	Yeovil T	35	0		
2004–05	Yeovil T	38	0		
2005–06	Yeovil T	25	0		
2006–07	Bristol C	1	0		
2007–08	Hereford U	1	0		
2007–08	Bristol C	3	0		
2008–09	Bristol C	5	0	9	0
2008–09	Hereford U	1	0	2	0
2008–09	Yeovil T	10	1	108	1
2009–10	Leicester C	45	0	45	0

WELLENS, Richard (M)   400 34
H: 5 9 W: 11 06 b.Manchester 26-3-80
Source: Trainee. *Honours:* England Youth.

Season	Club	Apps	Gls	Tot Apps	Tot Gls
1996–97	Manchester U	0	0		
1997–98	Manchester U	0	0		
1998–99	Manchester U	0	0		
1999–2000	Manchester U	0	0		
1999–2000	Blackpool	8	0		
2000–01	Blackpool	36	8		
2001–02	Blackpool	36	1		
2002–03	Blackpool	39	1		
2003–04	Blackpool	41	3		
2004–05	Blackpool	28	3	188	16
2005–06	Oldham Ath	45	4		
2006–07	Oldham Ath	42	4	87	8
2007–08	Doncaster R	45	6		
2008–09	Doncaster R	39	3	84	9
2009–10	Leicester C	41	1	41	1

WESOLOWSKI, James (D)   87 4
H: 5 8 W: 11 11 b.Sydney 25-8-87
Source: Scholar. *Honours:* Australia Youth, Under-20.

Season	Club	Apps	Gls	Tot Apps	Tot Gls
2004–05	Leicester C	0	0		
2005–06	Leicester C	5	0		
2006–07	Leicester C	19	0		
2007–08	Leicester C	22	0		
2008–09	Leicester C	0	0		
2008–09	Dundee U	8	0	8	0
2008–09	Cheltenham T	4	0	4	0
2009–10	Leicester C	0	0	46	0
2009–10	Hamilton A	29	4	29	4

WORLEY, Harry (D)   44 1
H: 6 3 W: 13 00 b.Warrington 25-11-88
Source: Scholar.

Season	Club	Apps	Gls	Tot Apps	Tot Gls
2005–06	Chelsea	0	0		
2006–07	Chelsea	0	0		
2006–07	Doncaster R	10	0	10	0
2007–08	Chelsea	0	0		
2007–08	Carlisle U	1	0	1	0
2007–08	Leicester C	2	0		
2008–09	Leicester C	0	0		
2008–09	Luton T	8	0	8	0
2009–10	Leicester C	0	0	2	0
2009–10	Crewe Alex	23	1	23	1

LEYTON ORIENT (46)

ASHWORTH, Luke (D)   13 0
H: 6 2 W: 12 08 b.Bolton 4-12-89

Season	Club	Apps	Gls	Tot Apps	Tot Gls
2008–09	Wigan Ath	0	0		
2008–09	Leyton Orient	3	0		
2009–10	Leyton Orient	10	0	13	0

BAKER, Harry (M)   8 0
H: 5 11 W: 12 04 b.Bexley Heath 20-9-90
Source: Scholar.

Season	Club	Apps	Gls	Tot Apps	Tot Gls
2008–09	Leyton Orient	4	0		
2009–10	Leyton Orient	4	0	8	0

CAVE-BROWN, Andrew (D)   29 0
H: 5 10 W: 12 02 b.Gravesend 5-8-88
Source: Scholar. *Honours:* Scotland Youth.

Season	Club	Apps	Gls	Tot Apps	Tot Gls
2005–06	Norwich C	0	0		
2006–07	Norwich C	0	0		
2007–08	Norwich C	0	0		
2008–09	Leyton Orient	13	0		
2009–10	Leyton Orient	16	0	29	0

CHAMBERS, Adam (D)   214 10
H: 5 10 W: 11 12 b.Sandwell 20-11-80
Source: Trainee. *Honours:* England Youth.

Season	Club	Apps	Gls	Tot Apps	Tot Gls
1998–99	WBA	0	0		
1999–2000	WBA	0	0		
2000–01	WBA	11	1		
2001–02	WBA	32	0		
2002–03	WBA	13	0		
2003–04	WBA	0	0		
2003–04	Sheffield W	11	0	11	0
2004–05	WBA	0	0	56	1
2004–05	Kidderminster H	2	0	2	0
2006–07	Leyton Orient	38	4		
2007–08	Leyton Orient	45	3		
2008–09	Leyton Orient	33	1		
2009–10	Leyton Orient	29	1	145	9

CHORLEY, Ben (D)   272 9
H: 6 3 W: 13 02 b.Sidcup 30-9-82
Source: Scholar.

Season	Club	Apps	Gls	Tot Apps	Tot Gls
2001–02	Arsenal	0	0		
2002–03	Arsenal	0	0		
2002–03	Brentford	2	0	2	0
2002–03	Wimbledon	10	0		
2003–04	Wimbledon	35	2	45	2
2004–05	Milton Keynes D	41	2		
2005–06	Milton Keynes D	26	0		
2006–07	Milton Keynes D	13	1	80	3
2006–07	Gillingham	27	1	27	1
2007–08	Tranmere R	31	1		
2008–09	Tranmere R	45	1	76	2
2009–10	Leyton Orient	42	1	42	1

DANIELS, Charlie (M)   100 5
H: 6 1 W: 12 12 b.Harlow 7-9-86
Source: Scholar.

Season	Club	Apps	Gls	Tot Apps	Tot Gls
2005–06	Tottenham H	0	0		
2006–07	Tottenham H	0	0		
2006–07	Chesterfield	2	0	2	0
2007–08	Tottenham H	0	0		
2007–08	Leyton Orient	31	2		
2008–09	Tottenham H	0	0		
2008–09	Gillingham	5	1	5	1
2008–09	Leyton Orient	21	2		
2009–10	Leyton Orient	41	0	93	4

DEMETRIOU, Jason (M)   143 10
H: 5 11 W: 10 08 b.Newham 18-11-87
Source: Scholar.

Season	Club	Apps	Gls	Tot Apps	Tot Gls
2005–06	Leyton Orient	3	0		
2006–07	Leyton Orient	15	2		
2007–08	Leyton Orient	43	3		
2008–09	Leyton Orient	43	4		
2009–10	Leyton Orient	39	1	143	10

JARVIS, Ryan (F)   148 20
H: 6 1 W: 11 11 b.Fakenham 11-7-86
Source: Scholar. *Honours:* FA Schools, England Youth.

Season	Club	Apps	Gls	Tot Apps	Tot Gls
2002–03	Norwich C	3	0		
2003–04	Norwich C	12	1		
2004–05	Norwich C	4	1		
2004–05	Colchester U	6	0	6	0
2005–06	Norwich C	4	1		
2006–07	Norwich C	5	0		
2006–07	Leyton Orient	14	6		
2007–08	Norwich C	1	0	29	3
2007–08	Kilmarnock	9	1	9	1
2007–08	Notts Co	17	2	17	2
2008–09	Leyton Orient	31	0		
2009–10	Leyton Orient	42	8	87	14

JONES, Jamie (G)   56 0
H: 6 2 W: 14 05 b.Kirkby 18-2-89
Source: Scholar.

Season	Club	Apps	Gls	Tot Apps	Tot Gls
2007–08	Everton	0	0		
2008–09	Leyton Orient	20	0		
2009–10	Leyton Orient	36	0	56	0

McGLEISH, Scott (F)   617 189
H: 5 9 W: 11 09 b.Barnet 10-2-74
Source: Edgware T.

Season	Club	Apps	Gls	Tot Apps	Tot Gls
1994–95	Charlton Ath	6	0	6	0
1994–95	Leyton Orient	6	1		
1995–96	Peterborough U	12	0		
1995–96	Colchester U	15	6		
1996–97	Peterborough U	1	0	13	0
1996–97	Cambridge U	10	7	10	7
1996–97	Leyton Orient	28	7		
1997–98	Leyton Orient	8	0		
1997–98	Barnet	37	13		
1998–99	Barnet	36	8		
1999–2000	Barnet	42	10		
2000–01	Barnet	19	5	134	36
2000–01	Colchester U	21	5		
2001–02	Colchester U	46	15		
2002–03	Colchester U	43	8		
2003–04	Colchester U	34	10	159	44
2004–05	Northampton T	44	13		
2005–06	Northampton T	42	17		
2006–07	Northampton T	25	12		
2006–07	Wycombe W	14	5		
2007–08	Wycombe W	46	25		
2008–09	Wycombe W	15	3	75	33
2008–09	Northampton T	9	1	120	43
2008–09	Wycombe W	16	6		
2009–10	Leyton Orient	42	12	100	26

MELLIGAN, John (M)   262 34
H: 5 9 W: 11 02 b.Dublin 11-2-82
Source: Trainee. *Honours:* Eire Youth, Under-21.

Season	Club	Apps	Gls	Tot Apps	Tot Gls
2000–01	Wolverhampton W	0	0		
2001–02	Wolverhampton W	0	0		
2001–02	Bournemouth	8	0	8	0
2002–03	Wolverhampton W	2	0		
2002–03	Kidderminster H	29	10		
2003–04	Wolverhampton W	0	0	2	0
2003–04	Kidderminster H	5	1	34	11

2003–04	Doncaster R	21	2	21	2
2004–05	Cheltenham T	29	2		
2005–06	Cheltenham T	42	6		
2006–07	Cheltenham T	43	7	114	15
2007–08	Leyton Orient	32	3		
2008–09	Leyton Orient	35	2		
2009–10	Leyton Orient	16	1	83	6

MIKE, Cestor (D) 0 0
b.Paris 30-4-92
Source: Youth.

2009–10	Leyton Orient	0	0

MKANDAWIRE, Tamika (D) 153 17
H: 6 1 W: 12 03 b.Malawi 28-5-83
Source: Scholar.

2002–03	WBA	0	0		
2003–04	WBA	0	0		
2006–07	Hereford U	39	2	39	2
2007–08	Leyton Orient	35	3		
2008–09	Leyton Orient	36	5		
2009–10	Leyton Orient	43	7	114	15

MORRIS, Glenn (G) 124 0
H: 6 0 W: 12 03 b.Woolwich 20-12-83
Source: Scholar.

2001–02	Leyton Orient	2	0		
2002–03	Leyton Orient	23	0		
2003–04	Leyton Orient	27	0		
2004–05	Leyton Orient	12	0		
2005–06	Leyton Orient	4	0		
2006–07	Leyton Orient	3	0		
2007–08	Leyton Orient	16	0		
2008–09	Leyton Orient	26	0		
2009–10	Leyton Orient	11	0	124	0

PATULEA, Adrian (F) 52 12
H: 5 10 W: 11 04 b.Targoviste 10-11-84
Source: Petrolul.

2008–09	Lincoln C	31	11	31	11
2009–10	Leyton Orient	21	1	21	1

PIRES, Loick (F) 15 0
H: 6 3 W: 13 02 b.Lisbon 20-11-89
Source: Scholar.

2007–08	Leyton Orient	1	0		
2008–09	Leyton Orient	6	0		
2009–10	Leyton Orient	8	0	15	0

PURCHES, Stephen (D) 354 15
H: 5 11 W: 11 13 b.Ilford 14-1-80

1998–99	West Ham U	0	0		
1999–2000	West Ham U	0	0		
2000–01	Bournemouth	34	0		
2001–02	Bournemouth	41	2		
2002–03	Bournemouth	44	3		
2003–04	Bournemouth	42	3		
2004–05	Bournemouth	14	1		
2005–06	Bournemouth	26	0		
2006–07	Bournemouth	43	1	244	10
2007–08	Leyton Orient	37	1		
2008–09	Leyton Orient	42	3		
2009–10	Leyton Orient	31	1	110	5

SCOWCROFT, James (F) 494 88
H: 6 1 W: 14 07 b.Bury St Edmunds 15-11-75
Source: Trainee. Honours: England Under-21.

1994–95	Ipswich T	0	0		
1995–96	Ipswich T	23	2		
1996–97	Ipswich T	41	9		
1997–98	Ipswich T	31	6		
1998–99	Ipswich T	32	13		
1999–2000	Ipswich T	41	13		
2000–01	Ipswich T	34	4		
2001–02	Leicester C	24	5		
2002–03	Leicester C	43	10		
2003–04	Leicester C	35	5		
2004–05	Leicester C	31	4	133	24
2004–05	*Ipswich T*	9	0	211	47
2005–06	Coventry C	41	3	41	3
2006–07	Crystal Palace	35	5		
2007–08	Crystal Palace	38	9		
2008–09	Crystal Palace	10	0	83	14
2009–10	Leyton Orient	26	0	26	0

SMITH, Jimmy (M) 107 8
H: 6 0 W: 10 03 b.Newham 7-1-87
Source: Scholar. Honours: England Youth.

2004–05	Chelsea	0	0
2005–06	Chelsea	1	0
2006–07	Chelsea	0	0
2006–07	*QPR*	29	6	29	6
2007–08	Chelsea	0	0		
2007–08	*Norwich C*	9	0	9	0
2008–09	Chelsea	0	0	1	0
2008–09	*Sheffield W*	12	0	12	0
2008–09	*Leyton Orient*	16	0		
2009–10	Leyton Orient	40	2	56	2

TEHOUE, Jonathan (F) 110 27
H: 5 8 W: 11 06 b.Paris 3-5-84

2003–04	Bastia	7	0	7	0
2004–05	Apoel	0	0		
2005–06	Virton	13	4	13	4
2006–07	FC Brussels	19	5	19	5
2007–08	Kasimpasa	15	6	15	6
2008–09	Konya	38	9	38	9
2009–10	Alfortville	2	0	2	0
2009–10	Leyton Orient	16	2	16	2

THORNTON, Sean (M) 218 24
H: 5 10 W: 11 00 b.Drogheda 18-5-83
Source: Scholar. Honours: Eire Youth, Under-21.

2001–02	Tranmere R	11	1	11	1
2002–03	Sunderland	11	1		
2002–03	*Blackpool*	3	0	3	0
2003–04	Sunderland	22	4		
2004–05	Sunderland	16	4	49	9
2005–06	Doncaster R	29	2		
2006–07	Doncaster R	30	0	59	2
2007–08	Leyton Orient	31	3		
2008–09	Leyton Orient	30	1		
2008–09	*Shrewsbury T*	5	1	5	1
2009–10	Leyton Orient	30	7	91	11

LINCOLN C (47)

ADAMS, Nathan (M) 4 0
H: 5 7 W: 11 00 b.Lincoln 6-10-91
Source: Scholar.

2008–09	Lincoln C	2	0		
2009–10	Lincoln C	2	0	4	0

ANDERSON, Joe (D) 23 0
H: 5 11 W: 11 05 b.Lincoln 13-10-89
Source: Scholar.

2008–09	Fulham	0	0		
2009–10	Fulham	0	0		
2009–10	Lincoln C	23	0	23	0

BENNETT, Lee (D) 1 0
H: 5 10 W: 12 04 b.Barnsley 19-9-90
Source: Scholar.

2009–10	Lincoln C	1	0	1	0

BROWN, Aaron (M) 300 20
H: 5 10 W: 11 11 b.Bristol 14-3-80
Source: Trainee. Honours: England Schools.

1997–98	Bristol C	0	0		
1998–99	Bristol C	14	0		
1999–2000	Bristol C	13	2		
1999–2000	*Exeter C*	5	1	5	1
2000–01	Bristol C	35	2		
2001–02	Bristol C	36	1		
2002–03	Bristol C	32	2		
2003–04	Bristol C	36	5	160	12
2004–05	QPR	1	0		
2004–05	*Torquay U*	5	0	5	0
2005–06	QPR	2	0	3	0
2005–06	*Cheltenham T*	3	0	3	0
2005–06	Swindon T	27	2		
2006–07	Swindon T	30	2	57	4
2007–08	Gillingham	11	1	11	1
2008–09	Lincoln C	39	2		
2009–10	Lincoln C	17	0	56	2

BURCH, Rob (G) 100 0
H: 6 2 W: 12 13 b.Yeovil 8-10-83
Source: Trainee. Honours: England Under-20.

2002–03	Tottenham H	0	0		
2003–04	Tottenham H	0	0		
2004–05	Tottenham H	0	0		
2004–05	*West Ham U*	0	0		
2005–06	Tottenham H	0	0		
2005–06	*Bristol C*	0	0		
2006–07	Tottenham H	0	0		
2006–07	*Barnet*	6	0	6	0
2007–08	Sheffield W	2	0	2	0
2008–09	Lincoln C	46	0		
2009–10	Lincoln C	46	0	92	0

BUTCHER, Richard (M) 290 40
H: 6 0 W: 13 01 b.Peterborough 22-1-81
Source: Kettering T.

2002–03	Lincoln C	26	3		
2003–04	Lincoln C	32	6		
2004–05	Lincoln C	46	2		
2005–06	Oldham Ath	36	4	36	4
2005–06	*Lincoln C*	4	1		
2006–07	Peterborough U	43	4	43	4
2007–08	Notts Co	46	12		
2008–09	Notts Co	34	6	80	18
2009–10	Lincoln C	15	0	123	12
2009–10	*Macclesfield T*	8	2	8	2

CLARKE, Jamie (F) 46 8
H: 5 10 W: 11 11 b.Sunderland 11-9-88
Source: Scholar.

2007–08	Blackburn R	0	0		
2008–09	Blackburn R	0	0		
2008–09	*Accrington S*	15	5	15	5
2008–09	*Rotherham U*	11	2	11	2
2009–10	Lincoln C	20	1	20	1

CLARKE, Shane (D) 68 0
H: 6 1 W: 13 03 b.Lincoln 7-11-87
Source: Scholar.

2006–07	Lincoln C	0	0		
2007–08	Lincoln C	16	0		
2008–09	Lincoln C	23	0		
2009–10	Lincoln C	29	0	68	0

CLUCAS, Sam (M) 0 0
H: 5 9 W: 10 06 b.Lincoln 25-9-90
Source: Leicester C, Nettleham.

2009–10	Lincoln C	0	0

COLEMAN-CARR, Luca (D) 2 0
H: 5 8 W: 11 02 b.Epsom 11-1-91
Source: Scholar.

2008–09	Lincoln C	1	0		
2009–10	Lincoln C	1	0	2	0

CONNOR, Paul (F) 341 70
H: 6 2 W: 11 08 b.Bishop Auckland 12-1-79
Source: Trainee.

1996–97	Middlesbrough	0	0		
1997–98	Middlesbrough	0	0		
1997–98	*Hartlepool U*	5	0	5	0
1998–99	Middlesbrough	0	0		
1998–99	Stoke C	3	2		
1999–2000	Stoke C	26	5		
2000–01	Stoke C	7	0	36	7
2000–01	*Cambridge U*	13	5	13	5
2000–01	Rochdale	14	10		
2001–02	Rochdale	17	1		
2002–03	Rochdale	39	12		
2003–04	Rochdale	24	5	94	28
2003–04	Swansea C	12	5		
2004–05	Swansea C	40	10		
2005–06	Swansea C	13	1	65	16
2005–06	Leyton Orient	16	5		
2006–07	Leyton Orient	18	2	34	7
2006–07	Cheltenham T	15	1		
2007–08	Cheltenham T	39	4		
2008–09	Cheltenham T	25	2	79	7
2009–10	Lincoln C	15	0	15	0

FAGAN, Chris (F) 13 3
H: 5 8 W: 10 05 b.Dublin 11-5-89
Source: Scholar.

2006–07	Manchester U	0	0		
2007–08	Manchester U	0	0		
2008–09	Manchester U	0	0		
2009–10	Lincoln C	13	3	13	3

GILMOUR, Brian (D) 61 4
H: 5 7 W: 10 00 b.Irvine 8-5-87
Honours: Scotland Youth, Under-20.

2005–06	Rangers	0	0		
2006–07	Rangers	0	0		
2006–07	Clyde	13	1	13	1
2007–08	Queen of the S	23	1	23	1
2008–09	Haka	9	0	9	0
2009–10	Lincoln C	16	2	16	2

GORDON, Michael (F) 24 0
H: 5 6 W: 10 04 b.Wandsworth 11-10-84
Source: Arsenal Trainee.

2002–03	Wimbledon	1	0		
2003–04	Wimbledon	18	0	19	0
2009–10	Lincoln C	5	0	5	0

GREEN, Paul (D) 100 3
H: 5 8　W: 10 04　b.Birmingham 15-4-87
Source: Scholar.
2005–06	Aston Villa	0	0
2006–07	Aston Villa	0	0
2006–07	Lincoln C	16	1
2007–08	Lincoln C	36	1
2008–09	Lincoln C	33	1
2009–10	Lincoln C	15	0	100	3

HONE, Daniel (D) 59 3
H: 6 2　W: 12 00　b.Croydon 15-9-89
Source: Scholar.
2007–08	Lincoln C	23	1
2008–09	Lincoln C	19	1
2009–10	Lincoln C	17	1	59	3

HUGHTON, Cian (D) 41 4
H: 5 8　W: 10 05　b.Enfield 25-1-89
Source: Tottenham H Scholar. Honours: Eire Under-21.
2007–08	Tottenham H	0	0
2008–09	Tottenham H	0	0
2009–10	Lincoln C	41	4	41	4

HUTCHINSON, Andrew (F) 14 1
H: 5 7　W: 12 00　b.Lincoln 10-3-92
Source: Scholar.
2008–09	Lincoln C	4	1
2009–10	Lincoln C	10	0	14	1

JOHN-LEWIS, Leneli (M) 72 8
H: 5 10　W: 11 10　b.Hammersmith 17-5-89
Source: Scholar.
2006–07	Lincoln C	0	0
2007–08	Lincoln C	21	3
2008–09	Lincoln C	27	4
2009–10	Lincoln C	24	1	72	8

KELTIE, Clark (M) 203 10
H: 5 11　W: 11 08　b.Newcastle 31-8-83
Source: Shildon.
2001–02	Darlington	1	0
2002–03	Darlington	30	3
2003–04	Darlington	31	1
2004–05	Darlington	21	0
2005–06	Darlington	24	0
2006–07	Darlington	27	1
2007–08	Darlington	27	4	161	9
2008–09	Rochdale	31	1
2009–10	Rochdale	0	0	31	1
2009–10	Lincoln C	11	0	11	0

KERR, Scott (M) 206 8
H: 5 9　W: 10 07　b.Leeds 11-12-81
Source: Scholar.
2000–01	Bradford C	1	0	1	0
2001–02	Hull C	0	0
2002–03	Hull C	0	0
2003–04	Hull C	0	0
2004–05	Hull C	0	0

From Scarborough.
2005–06	Lincoln C	41	2
2006–07	Lincoln C	44	3
2007–08	Lincoln C	36	1
2008–09	Lincoln C	45	2
2009–10	Lincoln C	39	0	205	8

KOVACS, Janos (D) 116 6
H: 6 4　W: 14 10　b.Budapest 11-9-85
Source: MTK. Honours: Hungary Under-20.
2005–06	Chesterfield	9	0
2006–07	Chesterfield	7	0
2007–08	Chesterfield	41	2	57	2
2008–09	Lincoln C	45	3
2009–10	Lincoln C	14	1	59	4

LENNON, Steven (F) 31 3
H: 5 7　W: 10 00　b.Irvine 20-1-88
2006–07	Rangers	3	0
2007–08	Rangers	0	0
2008–09	Rangers	0	0
2008–09	Partick T	9	0	9	0
2009–10	Rangers	0	0	3	0

On loan from Rangers.
2009–10	Lincoln C	19	3	19	3

MILLER, Kern (D) 1 0
H: 5 9　W: 11 03　b.Skegness 2-9-91
Source: Scholar.
2008–09	Lincoln C	1	0
2009–10	Lincoln C	0	0	1	0

MUSSELWHITE, Paul (G) 613 0
H: 6 2　W: 14 02　b.Portsmouth 22-12-68
Source: Apprentice.
1987–88	Portsmouth	0	0
1988–89	Scunthorpe U	41	0
1989–90	Scunthorpe U	29	0
1990–91	Scunthorpe U	38	0
1991–92	Scunthorpe U	24	0
1992–93	Port Vale	41	0
1993–94	Port Vale	46	0
1994–95	Port Vale	44	0
1995–96	Port Vale	39	0
1996–97	Port Vale	33	0
1997–98	Port Vale	41	0
1998–99	Port Vale	38	0
1999–2000	Port Vale	30	0	312	0
2000–01	Sheffield W	0	0
2000–01	Hull C	37	0
2001–02	Hull C	20	0
2002–03	Hull C	20	0
2003–04	Hull C	18	0	95	0
2004–05	Scunthorpe U	46	0
2005–06	Scunthorpe U	28	0
2006–07	Scunthorpe U	0	0
2007–08	Scunthorpe U	0	0
2008–09	Scunthorpe U	0	0	206	0
2009–10	Lincoln C	0	0

OAKES, Stefan (M) 271 13
H: 6 1　W: 13 07　b.Leicester 6-9-78
Source: Trainee.
1997–98	Leicester C	0	0
1998–99	Leicester C	3	0
1999–2000	Leicester C	22	1
2000–01	Leicester C	13	0
2001–02	Leicester C	21	1
2002–03	Leicester C	5	0	64	2
2002–03	Crewe Alex	7	0	7	0
2003–04	Walsall	5	0	5	0
2003–04	Notts Co	14	0
2004–05	Notts Co	31	5	45	5
2005–06	Wycombe W	37	2
2006–07	Wycombe W	35	0
2007–08	Wycombe W	34	3	106	5
2008–09	Lincoln C	28	1
2009–10	Lincoln C	16	0	44	1

PEARCE, Ian (D) 276 12
H: 6 3　W: 15 06　b.Bury St Edmunds 7-5-74
Source: School. Honours: England Youth, Under-21.
1990–91	Chelsea	1	0
1991–92	Chelsea	2	0
1992–93	Chelsea	1	0
1993–94	Chelsea	0	0	4	0
1993–94	Blackburn R	5	1
1994–95	Blackburn R	28	0
1995–96	Blackburn R	12	1
1996–97	Blackburn R	12	0
1997–98	Blackburn R	5	0	62	2
1997–98	West Ham U	30	1
1998–99	West Ham U	33	2
1999–2000	West Ham U	1	0
2000–01	West Ham U	15	1
2001–02	West Ham U	9	2
2002–03	West Ham U	30	2
2003–04	West Ham U	24	1	142	9
2003–04	Fulham	13	0
2004–05	Fulham	11	0
2005–06	Fulham	10	0
2006–07	Fulham	22	1
2007–08	Fulham	1	0
2007–08	Southampton	1	0	1	0
2008–09	Fulham	0	0	57	1
2009–10	Lincoln C	10	0	10	0

SMITH, Khano (M) 110 12
H: 6 3　W: 12 00　b.Paget 10-1-81
Honours: Bermuda 23 full caps, 7 goals.
2003	Carolina Dynamo	12	4	12	4
2003–04	Dandy Town Hornets	0	0
2004–05	Dandy Town Hornets	0	0
2005	New England Rev	23	3
2006	New England Rev	10	1
2007	New England Rev	29	2
2008	New England Rev	22	2	85	8
2009	New York Red Bulls	8	0	8	0
2009–10	Lincoln C	5	0	5	0

SWAIBU, Moses (D) 44 1
H: 6 2　W: 11 11　b.Croydon 9-5-89
Source: Scholar.
2007–08	Crystal Palace	0	0
2008–09	Crystal Palace	0	0
2008–09	Lincoln C	10	0
2009–10	Lincoln C	34	1	44	1

WATTS, Adam (D) 25 0
H: 6 1　W: 11 09　b.London 4-3-88
Source: Scholar.
2006–07	Fulham	0	0
2006–07	Milton Keynes D	2	0	2	0
2007–08	Fulham	0	0
2008–09	Fulham	0	0
2008–09	Northampton T	5	0	5	0
2009–10	Fulham	0	0
2009–10	Lincoln C	18	0	18	0

LIVERPOOL (48)

AGGER, Daniel (D) 111 8
H: 6 2　W: 12 06　b.Hvidovre 12-12-84
Honours: Denmark Youth, Under-20, Under-21, 35 full caps, 3 goals.
2004–05	Brondby	26	5
2005–06	Brondby	8	0	34	5
2005–06	Liverpool	4	0
2006–07	Liverpool	27	2
2007–08	Liverpool	5	0
2008–09	Liverpool	18	1
2009–10	Liverpool	23	0	77	3

AMOO, David (F) 0 0
H: 5 10　W: 12 03　b.London 23-4-91
Source: Millwall.
2007–08	Liverpool	0	0
2008–09	Liverpool	0	0
2009–10	Liverpool	0	0

AQUILANI, Alberto (M) 151 14
H: 6 0　W: 12 03　b.Rome 7-7-84
Honours: Italy 11 full caps, 2 goals.
2002–03	Roma	1	0
2003–04	Triestina	31	4	31	4
2004–05	Roma	29	0
2005–06	Roma	24	3
2006–07	Roma	13	1
2007–08	Roma	21	3
2008–09	Roma	14	2	102	9
2009–10	Liverpool	18	1	18	1

AYALA, Daniel (M) 5 0
H: 6 3　W: 13 03　b.Sevilla 7-11-90
2007–08	Liverpool	0	0
2008–09	Liverpool	0	0
2009–10	Liverpool	5	0	5	0

BABEL, Ryan (F) 155 25
H: 6 1　W: 12 04　b.Amsterdam 19-12-86
Honours: Holland Under-21, 39 full caps, 5 goals.
2003–04	Ajax	1	0
2004–05	Ajax	20	7
2005–06	Ajax	25	2
2006–07	Ajax	27	5	73	14
2007–08	Liverpool	30	4
2008–09	Liverpool	27	3
2009–10	Liverpool	25	4	82	11

BENAYOUN, Yossi (M) 376 107
H: 5 10　W: 11 00　b.Beer Sheva 6-6-80
Honours: Israel 78 full caps, 20 goals.
1997–98	Hapoel Beer Sheva	25	15	25	15
1998–99	Maccabi Haifa	29	16
1999–2000	Maccabi Haifa	38	19
2000–01	Maccabi Haifa	37	13
2001–02	Maccabi Haifa	26	7	130	55
2002–03	Santander	31	4
2003–04	Santander	35	7
2004–05	Santander	0	0	66	11
2005–06	West Ham U	34	5
2006–07	West Ham U	29	3	63	8
2007–08	Liverpool	32	8
2008–09	Liverpool	32	8
2009–10	Liverpool	30	6	92	18

BOUZANIS, Dean (G)   14 0
H: 6 1   W: 13 06   b.Sydney 2-10-90
Source: St George Saints, Sydney.

2007–08	Liverpool	0	0		
2008–09	Liverpool	0	0		
2009–10	Liverpool	0	0		
2009–10	*Accrington S*	14	0	14	0

BROUWER, Jordy (F)   0 0
H: 6 2   W: 12 05   b.Den Haag 26-2-88
Source: Ajax.

2006–07	Liverpool	0	0
2007–08	Liverpool	0	0
2008–09	Liverpool	0	0
2009–10	Liverpool	0	0

BRUNA, Gerardo (M)   0 0
H: 5 8   W: 10 02   b.Mendoza 29-1-91
Source: Real Madrid.

2007–08	Liverpool	0	0
2008–09	Liverpool	0	0
2009–10	Liverpool	0	0

CARRAGHER, Jamie (D)   435 3
H: 5 9   W: 12 01   b.Liverpool 28-1-78
Source: Trainee. *Honours:* England Youth, Under-21, B, 38 full caps.

1995–96	Liverpool	1	0		
1996–97	Liverpool	2	1		
1997–98	Liverpool	20	0		
1998–99	Liverpool	34	1		
1999–2000	Liverpool	36	0		
2000–01	Liverpool	34	0		
2001–02	Liverpool	33	0		
2002–03	Liverpool	35	0		
2003–04	Liverpool	22	0		
2004–05	Liverpool	38	0		
2005–06	Liverpool	36	0		
2006–07	Liverpool	35	1		
2007–08	Liverpool	35	0		
2008–09	Liverpool	38	0		
2009–10	Liverpool	37	0	435	3

CAVALIERI, Diego (G)   66 0
H: 6 3   W: 13 07   b.Sao Paulo 1-12-82

2001	Palmeiras	0	0		
2002	Palmeiras	0	0		
2003	Palmeiras	0	0		
2004	Palmeiras	3	0		
2005	Palmeiras	0	0		
2006	Palmeiras	25	0		
2007	Palmeiras	38	0		
2008	Palmeiras	0	0	66	0
2008–09	Liverpool	0	0		
2009–10	Liverpool	0	0		

COOPER, Alex (M)   0 0
H: 5 8   W: 11 08   b.Birmingham 4-11-91

| 2008–09 | Liverpool | 0 | 0 |
| 2009–10 | Liverpool | 0 | 0 |

DALLA VALLE, Lauri (F)   8 0
H: 5 9   W: 11 03   b.Kontiolahti 14-9-91
Honours: Finland Youth.

2007–08	JIPPO	8	0	8	0
2008–09	Liverpool	0	0		
2009–10	Liverpool	0	0		

DARBY, Stephen (D)   13 0
H: 5 9   W: 10 00   b.Liverpool 6-10-88
Source: Scholar. *Honours:* England Youth.

2006–07	Liverpool	0	0		
2007–08	Liverpool	0	0		
2008–09	Liverpool	0	0		
2009–10	Liverpool	1	0	1	0
2009–10	*Swindon T*	12	0	12	0

DEGEN, Philipp (D)   174 5
H: 6 0   W: 12 10   b.Holstein 15-2-83
Honours: Switzerland Under-21, 30 full caps.

2001–02	Basle	3	0		
2002–03	Basle	16	0		
2002–03	Aarau	16	0	16	0
2003–04	Basle	33	4		
2004–05	Basle	31	0	83	4
2005–06	Bor Dortmund	31	1		
2006–07	Bor Dortmund	27	0		
2007–08	Bor Dortmund	10	0	68	1
2008–09	Liverpool	0	0		
2009–10	Liverpool	7	0	7	0

DOSSENA, Andrea (D)   201 6
H: 5 11   W: 12 06   b.Lodi 11-9-81
Honours: Italy Youth, 10 full caps.

2001–02	Verona	2	0		
2002–03	Verona	21	1		
2003–04	Verona	37	1		
2004–05	Verona	39	1	99	3
2005–06	Treviso	21	0	21	0
2006–07	Udinese	28	0		
2007–08	Udinese	35	2	63	2
2008–09	Liverpool	16	1		
2009–10	Liverpool	2	0	18	1

ECCLESTON, Nathan (F)   12 1
H: 5 10   W: 12 00   b.Manchester 30-12-90
Source: Scholar.

2007–08	Liverpool	0	0		
2008–09	Liverpool	0	0		
2009–10	Liverpool	1	0	1	0
2009–10	*Huddersfield T*	11	1	11	1

EL ZHAR, Nabil (F)   21 0
H: 5 9   W: 11 05   b.Ales 27-8-86
Source: St Etienne. *Honours:* France Youth, Morocco Under-20, 8 full caps, 2 goals.

2006–07	Liverpool	3	0		
2007–08	Liverpool	0	0		
2008–09	Liverpool	15	0		
2009–10	Liverpool	3	0	21	0

ELLISON, James (F)   0 0
H: 5 10   W: 12 08   b.Liverpool 25-10-91
Source: Scholar.

| 2009–10 | Liverpool | 0 | 0 |

EMILSSON, Kristjan (M)   0 0
b.Sweden 26-4-93
Source: Scholar.

| 2009–10 | Liverpool | 0 | 0 |

FABIO AURELIO (M)   219 17
H: 5 10   W: 11 11   b.Sao Carlos 24-9-79
Honours: Brazil Youth, Under-20, Under-21.

1997	Sao Paulo	15	1		
1998	Sao Paulo	11	1		
1998	Santos	0	0		
1999	Sao Paulo	23	1		
2000	Sao Paulo	4	0	53	3
2000–01	Valencia	7	0		
2001–02	Valencia	15	1		
2002–03	Valencia	26	8		
2003–04	Valencia	2	0		
2004–05	Valencia	21	0		
2005–06	Valencia	24	2	95	11
2006–07	Liverpool	17	0		
2007–08	Liverpool	15	1		
2008–09	Liverpool	24	2		
2009–10	Liverpool	14	0	71	0

GERRARD, Steven (M)   366 80
H: 6 0   W: 12 05   b.Whiston 30-5-80
Source: Trainee. *Honours:* England Youth, Under-21, 84 full caps, 17 goals.

1997–98	Liverpool	0	0		
1998–99	Liverpool	12	0		
1999–2000	Liverpool	29	1		
2000–01	Liverpool	33	7		
2001–02	Liverpool	28	3		
2002–03	Liverpool	34	5		
2003–04	Liverpool	34	4		
2004–05	Liverpool	30	7		
2005–06	Liverpool	32	10		
2006–07	Liverpool	36	7		
2007–08	Liverpool	34	11		
2008–09	Liverpool	31	16		
2009–10	Liverpool	33	9	366	80

GULACSI, Peter (G)   23 0
H: 6 3   W: 13 01   b.Budapest 6-5-90
Source: MTK. *Honours:* Hungary Youth.

2007–08	Liverpool	0	0		
2008–09	Liverpool	0	0		
2008–09	*Hereford U*	18	0	18	0
2009–10	Liverpool	0	0		
2009–10	*Tranmere R*	5	0	5	0

HANSEN, Martin (G)   0 0
H: 6 2   W: 12 07   b.Glostrup 15-6-90
Source: Brondby.

2007–08	Liverpool	0	0		
2008–09	Liverpool	0	0		
2009–10	Liverpool	0	0		

HIGHDALE, Sean (M)   0 0
b.Liverpool 4-3-91

2007–08	Liverpool	0	0
2008–09	Liverpool	0	0
2009–10	Liverpool	0	0

INCE, Thomas (F)   0 0
H: 5 10   W: 10 05   b.Liverpool 30-1-92
Source: Scholar.

| 2009–10 | Liverpool | 0 | 0 |

INSUA, Emiliano (D)   46 0
H: 5 10   W: 12 08   b.Buenos Aires 7-1-89
Source: Boca Juniors. *Honours:* Argentina Youth, Under-20, Under-23, 1 full cap.

2006–07	Liverpool	2	0		
2007–08	Liverpool	3	0		
2008–09	Liverpool	10	0		
2009–10	Liverpool	31	0	46	0

IRWIN, Steven (D)   0 0
H: 5 8   W: 10 06   b.Liverpool 29-9-90
Source: Scholar.

2007–08	Liverpool	0	0
2008–09	Liverpool	0	0
2009–10	Liverpool	0	0

ITANDJE, Charles (G)   179 0
H: 6 3   W: 13 01   b.Paris 2-11-82
Honours: France Under-21.

2000–01	Red Star 93	9	0	9	0
2001–02	Lens	0	0		
2002–03	Lens	22	0		
2003–04	Lens	35	0		
2004–05	Lens	38	0		
2005–06	Lens	37	0		
2006–07	Lens	38	0	170	0
2007–08	Liverpool	0	0		
2008–09	Liverpool	0	0		
2009–10	Liverpool	0	0		

JOHNSON, Glen (D)   174 10
H: 6 0   W: 13 04   b.Greenwich 23-8-84
Source: Scholar. *Honours:* England Youth, Under-20, Under-21, 26 full caps, 1 goal.

2001–02	West Ham U	0	0		
2002–03	West Ham U	15	0	15	0
2002–03	*Millwall*	8	0	8	0
2003–04	Chelsea	19	3		
2004–05	Chelsea	17	0		
2005–06	Chelsea	4	0		
2006–07	Chelsea	0	0		
2006–07	*Portsmouth*	26	0		
2007–08	Chelsea	2	0	42	3
2007–08	Portsmouth	29	1		
2008–09	Portsmouth	29	3		
2009–10	Portsmouth	0	0	84	4
2009–10	Liverpool	25	3	25	3

KACANIKLIC, Alexander (M)   0 0
H: 5 11   W: 10 05   b.Sweden 13-8-91
Source: Scholar.

| 2008–09 | Liverpool | 0 | 0 |
| 2009–10 | Liverpool | 0 | 0 |

KELLY, Martin (D)   8 1
H: 6 3   W: 12 02   b.Bolton 27-4-90
Source: Scholar. *Honours:* England Youth, Under-20.

2007–08	Liverpool	0	0		
2008–09	Liverpool	0	0		
2008–09	*Huddersfield T*	7	1	7	1
2009–10	Liverpool	1	0	1	0

KOHLERT, Nicolaj (F)   0 0
H: 5 10   W: 11 00   b.Denmark 21-1-93
Honours: Denmark Youth.

| 2009–10 | Liverpool | 0 | 0 |

KUYT, Dirk (F)   402 158
H: 6 0   W: 12 02   b.Katwijk 22-7-80
Source: Quick Boys. *Honours:* Holland 70 full caps, 16 goals.

1998–99	Utrecht	28	5		
1999–2000	Utrecht	32	6		
2000–01	Utrecht	32	13		
2001–02	Utrecht	34	7		
2002–03	Utrecht	34	20	160	51
2003–04	Feyenoord	34	20		
2004–05	Feyenoord	34	29		
2005–06	Feyenoord	33	22	101	71
2006–07	Liverpool	34	12		
2007–08	Liverpool	32	3		

| 2008–09 | Liverpool | 38 | 12 | | |
| 2009–10 | Liverpool | 37 | 9 | 141 | 36 |

KYRGIAKOS, Sotirios (D)   **240**   **18**
H: 6 3 W: 14 06 b.Megalochori 23-7-79
Honours: Greece 60 full caps, 4 goals.

1998–99	Panathinaikos	0	0		
1999–2000	Agios	28	1		
2000–01	Agios	25	2	53	3
2001–02	Panathinaikos	18	1		
2002–03	Panathinaikos	24	0		
2003–04	Panathinaikos	6	1		
2004–05	Panathinaikos	12	3	60	5
2004–05	Rangers	15	0		
2005–06	Rangers	28	1	43	1
2006–07	Eintracht Frankfurt	27	5		
2007–08	Eintracht Frankfurt	24	3	51	8
2008–09	AEK Athens	19	0	19	0
2009–10	Liverpool	14	1	14	1

LUCAS (M)   **111**   **5**
H: 5 10 W: 11 09 b.Dourados 9-1-87
Honours: Brazil Under-20, 4 full caps.

2005	Gremio	3	0		
2006	Gremio	30	4	33	4
2007–08	Liverpool	18	0		
2008–09	Liverpool	25	1		
2009–10	Liverpool	35	0	78	1

MARTIN, David E (G)   **57**   **0**
H: 6 1 W: 13 04 b.Romford 22-1-86
Source: Scholar. *Honours:* England Youth, Under-20.

2003–04	Wimbledon	2	0	2	0
2004–05	Milton Keynes D	15	0		
2005–06	Milton Keynes D	0	0	15	0
2005–06	Liverpool	0	0		
2006–07	Liverpool	0	0		
2006–07	Accrington S	10	0	10	0
2007–08	Liverpool	0	0		
2008–09	Liverpool	0	0		
2008–09	Leicester C	25	0	25	0
2009–10	Liverpool	0	0		
2009–10	Tranmere R	3	0	3	0
2009–10	Leeds U	0	0		
2009–10	Derby Co	2	0	2	0

MASCHERANO, Javier (M)   **151**   **1**
H: 5 7 W: 10 05 b.San Lorenzo 8-6-84
Honours: Argentina Youth, Under-20, Under-23, 61 full caps, 2 goals.

2003–04	River Plate	21	0		
2004–05	River Plate	25	0	46	0
2005	Corinthians	7	0	7	0
2006–07	West Ham U	5	0	5	0
2006–07	Liverpool	7	0		
2007–08	Liverpool	25	1		
2008–09	Liverpool	27	0		
2009–10	Liverpool	34	0	93	1

MAVINGA, Chrys (D)   **0**   **0**
H: 5 10 W: 10 03 b.Meaux 26-5-91
Source: Paris St Germain.

| 2009–10 | Liverpool | 0 | 0 | | |

MENDY, Emmanuel (D)   **0**   **0**
H: 5 7 W: 11 09 b.Medina Gounass 30-3-90
Source: Murcia.

| 2008–09 | Liverpool | 0 | 0 | | |
| 2009–10 | Liverpool | 0 | 0 | | |

MIHAYLOV, Nikolay (G)   **44**   **0**
H: 6 3 W: 14 00 b.Bulgaria 28-6-88

2004–05	Levski	10	0		
2005–06	Levski	21	0		
2006–07	Levski	13	0	44	0
2007–08	Liverpool	0	0		
2008–09	Liverpool	0	0		

N'GOG, David (F)   **56**   **8**
H: 6 3 W: 12 04 b.Paris 1-4-89
Honours: France Youth, Under-21.

2006–07	Paris St Germain	4	0		
2007–08	Paris St Germain	14	1	18	1
2008–09	Liverpool	14	2		
2009–10	Liverpool	24	5	38	7

NEMETH, Kristian (F)   **38**   **14**
H: 5 10 W: 11 07 b.Gyor 5-1-89
Honours: Hungary 1 full cap.

| 2005–06 | MTK | 13 | 2 | | |
| 2006–07 | MTK | 24 | 12 | 37 | 14 |

2007–08	Liverpool	0	0		
2008–09	Liverpool	0	0		
2008–09	Blackpool	1	0	1	0
2009–10	Liverpool	0	0		

NGOO, Michael (F)   **0**   **0**
b.London 23-10-92
Source: Southend U.

| 2009–10 | Liverpool | 0 | 0 | | |

PACHECO, Daniel (F)   **4**   **0**
H: 5 6 W: 10 07 b.Malaga 5-1-91

2007–08	Liverpool	0	0		
2008–09	Liverpool	0	0		
2009–10	Liverpool	4	0	4	0

PALSSON, Victor (M)   **0**   **0**
H: 6 1 W: 12 09 b.Reykjavik 30-4-91
Source: Aarhus. *Honours:* Iceland Youth.

| 2008–09 | Liverpool | 0 | 0 | | |
| 2009–10 | Liverpool | 0 | 0 | | |

PEPPER, Adam (M)   **0**   **0**
H: 5 6 W: 9 04 b.Liverpool 2-12-91

| 2008–09 | Liverpool | 0 | 0 | | |
| 2009–10 | Liverpool | 0 | 0 | | |

PLESSIS, Damien (M)   **19**   **0**
H: 6 3 W: 12 02 b.Neuvy-sous-Bois 5-3-88
Honours: France Youth.

2005–06	Lyon B	7	0		
2006–07	Lyon B	9	0	16	0
2007–08	Liverpool	2	0		
2008–09	Liverpool	1	0		
2009–10	Liverpool	0	0	3	0

REINA, Jose (G)   **351**
H: 6 2 W: 14 06 b.Madrid 31-8-82
Honours: Spain Youth, Under-21, 20 full caps.

1999–2000	Barcelona	30	0	30	0
2000–01	Barcelona	19	0		
2001–02	Barcelona	11	0	30	0
2002–03	Villarreal	33	0		
2003–04	Villarreal	38	0		
2004–05	Villarreal	38	0	109	0
2005–06	Liverpool	33	0		
2006–07	Liverpool	35	0		
2007–08	Liverpool	38	0		
2008–09	Liverpool	38	0		
2009–10	Liverpool	38	0	182	0

RIERA, Alberto (M)   **272**   **33**
H: 6 1 W: 12 01 b.Manacor 15-4-82
Honours: Spain Under-21, 16 full caps, 4 goals.

2000–01	Mallorca B	31	6		
2000–01	Mallorca	3	1		
2001–02	Mallorca	8	1		
2001–02	Mallorca B	16	5	47	11
2002–03	Mallorca	35	4	46	6
2003–04	Bordeaux	32	2		
2004–05	Bordeaux	21	2	53	4
2005–06	Espanyol	8	0		
2005–06	Manchester C	15	1	15	1
2006–07	Espanyol	28	4		
2007–08	Espanyol	35	4	71	8
2008–09	Liverpool	28	3		
2009–10	Liverpool	12	0	40	3

ROBERTS, Michael (M)   **0**   **0**
b.Liverpool 5-12-91

| 2008–09 | Liverpool | 0 | 0 | | |
| 2009–10 | Liverpool | 0 | 0 | | |

ROBINSON, Jack (D)   **1**   **0**
H: 5 11 W: 10 08 b.Warrington 1-9-93
Honours: England Youth.

| 2009–10 | Liverpool | 1 | 0 | 1 | 0 |

RODRIGUEZ, Maxi (M)   **306**   **78**
H: 5 11 W: 12 06 b.Rosario 2-1-81
Honours: Argentina 41 full caps, 12 goals.

1999–2000	Newell's Old Boys	6	0		
2000–01	Newell's Old Boys	18	5		
2001–02	Newell's Old Boys	33	15	57	20
2002–03	Espanyol	37	7		
2003–04	Espanyol	37	4		
2004–05	Espanyol	37	15	111	26
2005–06	Atletico Madrid	29	10		
2006–07	Atletico Madrid	10	5		
2007–08	Atletico Madrid	35	8		
2008–09	Atletico Madrid	33	6		

| 2009–10 | Atletico Madrid | 14 | 2 | 121 | 31 |
| 2009–10 | Liverpool | 17 | 1 | 17 | 1 |

SAMA, Stephen (D)   **0**   **0**
b.Cameroon 5-3-93
Source: Scholar.

| 2009–10 | Liverpool | 0 | 0 | | |

SAN JOSE DOMINGUEZ, Mikel (D)   **0**   **0**
H: 6 0 W: 12 04 b.Pamplona 30-5-89
Source: Athletic Bilbao.

2007–08	Liverpool	0	0		
2008–09	Liverpool	0	0		
2009–10	Liverpool	0	0		

SARIC, Nikola (F)   **0**   **0**
H: 6 0 W: 11 08 b.Sarajevo 6-1-91
Source: Herfolge. *Honours:* Denmark Youth.

| 2008–09 | Liverpool | 0 | 0 | | |
| 2009–10 | Liverpool | 0 | 0 | | |

SHELVEY, Jonjo (M)   **42**   **7**
H: 6 1 W: 11 02 b.Romford 27-2-92
Source: Scholar. *Honours:* England Youth.

2007–08	Charlton Ath	2	0		
2008–09	Charlton Ath	16	3		
2009–10	Charlton Ath	24	4	42	7
2009–10	Liverpool	0	0		

SIMON, Andras (F)   **1**   **0**
H: 6 0 W: 11 05 b.Salgotarjan 30-3-90

2006–07	MTK	1	0	1	0
2007–08	Liverpool	0	0		
2008–09	Liverpool	0	0		
2009–10	Liverpool	0	0		

SKRTEL, Martin (D)   **163**   **4**
H: 6 3 W: 12 10 b.Handlova 15-12-84
Honours: Slovakia 43 full caps, 5 goals.

2002–03	Trencin	1	0		
2003–04	Trencin	34	0	35	0
2004	Zenit	7	0		
2005	Zenit	18	1		
2006	Zenit	26	1		
2007	Zenit	23	1	74	3
2007–08	Liverpool	14	0		
2008–09	Liverpool	21	0		
2009–10	Liverpool	19	1	54	1

SPEARING, Jay (D)   **10**   **1**
H: 5 6 W: 11 01 b.Wallasey 25-11-88
Source: Scholar.

2006–07	Liverpool	0	0		
2007–08	Liverpool	0	0		
2008–09	Liverpool	0	0		
2009–10	Liverpool	3	0	3	0
2009–10	Leicester C	7	1	7	1

THRELFALL, Robbie (D)   **35**   **2**
H: 5 11 W: 11 00 b.Liverpool 25-11-88
Source: Scholar. *Honours:* England Youth.

2006–07	Liverpool	0	0		
2007–08	Liverpool	0	0		
2007–08	Hereford U	9	0		
2008–09	Liverpool	0	0		
2008–09	Hereford U	3	0	12	0
2008–09	Stockport Co	2	0	2	0
2009–10	Liverpool	0	0		
2009–10	Northampton T	4	0	4	0
2009–10	Bradford C	17	2	17	2

TORRES, Fernando (F)   **253**   **131**
H: 5 9 W: 12 03 b.Madrid 20-3-84
Honours: Spain 80 full caps, 24 goals.

2002–03	Atletico Madrid	29	13		
2003–04	Atletico Madrid	35	19		
2004–05	Atletico Madrid	38	16		
2005–06	Atletico Madrid	36	13		
2006–07	Atletico Madrid	36	14	174	75
2007–08	Liverpool	33	24		
2008–09	Liverpool	24	14		
2009–10	Liverpool	22	18	79	56

VORONIN, Andrei (F)   **310**   **102**
H: 5 11 W: 11 08 b.Odessa 21-7-79
Honours: Ukraine 62 full caps, 6 goals.

1997–98	M Gladbach	7	1		
1997–98	M Gladbach II	21	3		
1998–99	M Gladbach II	14	1		
1999–2000	M Gladbach	2	0	9	1
1999–2000	M Gladbach II	21	11	56	15
2000–01	Mainz	10	1		
2000–01	Mainz II	6	6	6	6
2001–02	Mainz	34	8		

2002–03	Mainz	31	20	**75** **29**
2003–04	Cologne	19	4	**19** **4**
2004–05	Leverkusen	31	14	
2005–06	Leverkusen	29	7	
2006–07	Leverkusen	31	10	**91** **31**
2007–08	Liverpool	19	5	
2008–09	Liverpool	0	0	
2008–09	Hertha Berlin	27	11	**27** **11**
2009–10	Liverpool	8	0	**27** **5**

WEIJL, Vincent (M)   **9** **1**
H: 6 0   W: 12 04   b.Amsterdam 11-11-90
Source: Scholar.

2008–09	Liverpool	0	0	
2009–10	Liverpool	0	0	
2009–10	*Helmond Sport*	9	1	**9** **1**

WISDOM, Andre (D)   **0** **0**
b.Leeds 9-5-93
Source: Scholar. *Honours:* England Youth.

2009–10	Liverpool	0	0	

Scholars
Adorjan, Krisztian; Chamberlain, Deale;
Clair, Karl; Coady, Conor David; Flanagan,
John; Giglio, Marcus; Ihiekwe, Michael;
McGiveron, Matthew Lawrence; Roddan,
Craig; Sokolik, Jakub; Stephens, James
Edward; Whittle, Alex.

MACCLESFIELD T (49)

BELL, Lee (M)   **160** **7**
H: 5 11   W: 12 04   b.Crewe 26-1-83
Source: Scholar.

2000–01	Crewe Alex	0	0	
2001–02	Crewe Alex	0	0	
2002–03	Crewe Alex	17	1	
2003–04	Crewe Alex	3	0	
2004–05	Crewe Alex	17	0	
2005–06	Crewe Alex	17	2	
2006–07	Crewe Alex	0	0	**54** **3**
2007–08	Mansfield T	23	1	**23** **1**
2008–09	Macclesfield T	41	1	
2009–10	Macclesfield T	42	2	**83** **5**

BENCHERIF, Hamza (D)   **31** **6**
H: 5 9   W: 12 03   b.Paris 9-2-88
Source: Scholar.

2006–07	Nottingham F	0	0	
2007–08	*Lincoln C*	12	1	**12** **1**
2008–09	Nottingham F	0	0	
2009–10	Macclesfield T	19	5	**19** **5**

BOLLAND, Paul (M)   **329** **20**
H: 5 10   W: 10 12   b.Bradford 23-12-79
Source: Trainee.

1997–98	Bradford C	10	0	
1998–99	Bradford C	2	0	**12** **0**
1998–99	Notts Co	13	0	
1999–2000	Notts Co	25	1	
2000–01	Notts Co	7	0	
2001–02	Notts Co	19	0	
2002–03	Notts Co	29	3	
2003–04	Notts Co	39	1	
2004–05	Notts Co	40	1	**172** **6**
2005–06	Grimsby T	44	4	
2006–07	Grimsby T	39	5	
2007–08	Grimsby T	35	4	
2008–09	Grimsby T	0	0	**118** **13**
2009–10	Macclesfield T	27	1	**27** **1**

BRAIN, Jonny (G)   **184** **0**
H: 6 3   W: 13 05   b.Carlisle 11-2-83
Source: Newcastle U Trainee.

2003–04	Port Vale	32	0	
2004–05	Port Vale	27	0	
2005–06	Port Vale	0	0	**59** **0**
2006–07	Macclesfield T	9	0	
2007–08	Macclesfield T	29	0	
2008–09	Macclesfield T	46	0	
2009–10	Macclesfield T	41	0	**125** **0**

BRISLEY, Shaun (M)   **81** **3**
H: 6 2   W: 12 02   b.Stockport 6-5-90
Source: Scholar.

2007–08	Macclesfield T	10	2	
2008–09	Macclesfield T	38	0	
2009–10	Macclesfield T	33	1	**81** **3**

BROWN, Nat (D)   **238** **18**
H: 6 2   W: 12 05   b.Sheffield 15-6-81
Source: Trainee.

1999–2000	Huddersfield T	0	0	
2000–01	Huddersfield T	0	0	
2001–02	Huddersfield T	0	0	
2002–03	Huddersfield T	38	0	
2003–04	Huddersfield T	21	0	
2004–05	Huddersfield T	17	0	**76** **0**
2005–06	Lincoln C	39	7	
2006–07	Lincoln C	28	1	
2007–08	Lincoln C	27	0	**94** **8**

on loan from Wrexham

2008–09	Macclesfield T	30	6	
2009–10	Macclesfield T	38	4	**68** **10**

DANIEL, Colin (M)   **60** **4**
H: 5 11   W: 11 06   b.Crewe 15-2-88
Source: Eastwood T.

2006–07	Crewe Alex	0	0	
2007–08	Crewe Alex	1	0	
2008–09	Crewe Alex	13	1	**14** **1**
2008–09	*Macclesfield T*	8	0	
2009–10	Macclesfield T	38	3	**46** **3**

DRAPER, Ross (M)   **29** **1**
H: 6 3   W: 15 05   b.Wolverhampton 20-10-88
Source: Shrewsbury T, Stafford R, Hednesford T.

2009–10	Macclesfield T	29	1	**29** **1**

HESSEY, Sean (D)   **226** **2**
H: 5 11   W: 12 08   b.Whiston 19-9-78
Source: Liverpool Trainee.

1997–98	Wigan Ath	0	0	
1997–98	Leeds U	0	0	
1997–98	Huddersfield T	1	0	
1998–99	Huddersfield T	10	0	**11** **0**
1999–2000	Kilmarnock	11	0	
2000–01	Kilmarnock	6	0	
2001–02	Kilmarnock	15	0	
2002–03	Kilmarnock	5	0	
2003–04	Kilmarnock	7	1	**44** **1**
2003–04	Blackpool	6	0	**6** **0**
2004–05	Chester C	34	1	
2005–06	Chester C	19	0	
2006–07	Chester C	25	0	
2007–08	Chester C	0	0	**79** **1**
2007–08	*Macclesfield T*	25	0	
2008–09	Macclesfield T	33	0	
2009–10	Macclesfield T	27	0	**86** **0**

KIRK, Tyrone (M)   **0** **0**
H: 5 11   W: 12 00   b.Scunthorpe 2-1-84
Source: Stamford.

2009–10	Macclesfield T	0	0	

LINDFIELD, Craig (F)   **51** **6**
H: 6 0   W: 10 05   b.Wirral 7-9-88
Source: Scholar. *Honours:* England Youth.

2006–07	Liverpool	0	0	
2007–08	Liverpool	0	0	
2007–08	Notts Co	3	1	**3** **1**
2007–08	*Chester C*	7	0	**7** **0**
2008–09	Liverpool	0	0	
2008–09	*Bournemouth*	3	1	**3** **1**
2008–09	*Accrington S*	20	2	**20** **2**
2009–10	Liverpool	0	0	
2009–10	Macclesfield T	18	2	**18** **2**

LOWE, Matt (M)   **10** **0**
H: 5 8   W: 10 12   b.Stoke 20-10-90
Source: Scholar.

2009–10	Macclesfield T	10	0	**10** **0**

MORGAN, Paul (D)   **307** **3**
H: 6 0   W: 11 05   b.Belfast 23-10-78
Source: Trainee. *Honours:* Northern Ireland Under-21.

1997–98	Preston NE	0	0	
1998–99	Preston NE	0	0	
1999–2000	Preston NE	0	0	
2000–01	Preston NE	0	0	
2001–02	Lincoln C	34	1	
2002–03	Lincoln C	45	0	
2003–04	Lincoln C	41	0	
2004–05	Lincoln C	39	0	
2005–06	Lincoln C	20	0	
2006–07	Lincoln C	33	1	**212** **2**
2007–08	Bury	20	0	
2008–09	Bury	0	0	**20** **0**

2008–09	*Macclesfield T*	39	1	
2009–10	Macclesfield T	36	0	**75** **1**

MUKENDI, Vinny (F)   **10** **1**
H: 6 2   W: 12 00   b.Bury 12-3-92
Source: Scholar.

2008–09	Macclesfield T	1	0	
2009–10	Macclesfield T	9	1	**10** **1**

REID, Izak (M)   **108** **4**
H: 5 5   W: 10 05   b.Sheffield 8-7-87
Source: Scholar.

2006–07	Macclesfield T	8	0	
2007–08	Macclesfield T	25	2	
2008–09	Macclesfield T	38	2	
2009–10	Macclesfield T	37	0	**108** **4**

ROONEY, John (F)   **41** **3**
H: 5 10   W: 12 00   b.Liverpool 17-12-90
Source: Scholar.

2007–08	Macclesfield T	2	0	
2008–09	Macclesfield T	14	2	
2009–10	Macclesfield T	25	1	**41** **3**

SAPPLETON, Reneil (M)   **28** **8**
H: 5 10   W: 11 13   b.Kingston 8-12-89

2007–08	Leicester C	1	0	
2008–09	Leicester C	0	0	
2008–09	*Bournemouth*	3	1	**3** **1**
2009–10	Leicester C	0	0	**1** **0**
2009–10	Macclesfield T	24	7	**24** **7**

SINCLAIR, Emile (F)   **78** **9**
H: 6 0   W: 11 04   b.Leeds 20-12-87
Source: Scholar.

2007–08	Nottingham F	12	1	
2007–08	*Brentford*	4	0	**4** **0**
2008–09	Nottingham F	3	0	**15** **1**
2008–09	*Macclesfield T*	17	1	
2009–10	Macclesfield T	42	7	**59** **8**

THOMAS, Michael (M)   **4** **0**
H: 6 1   W: 11 00   b.Manchester 12-8-92
Source: Scholar.

2009–10	Macclesfield T	4	0	**4** **0**

TIPTON, Matt (F)   **334** **68**
H: 5 10   W: 11 02   b.Bangor 29-6-80
Source: Trainee. *Honours:* Wales Youth, Under-21.

1997–98	Oldham Ath	3	0	
1998–99	Oldham Ath	28	2	
1999–2000	Oldham Ath	29	3	
2000–01	Oldham Ath	30	5	
2001–02	Oldham Ath	22	5	**112** **15**
2001–02	Macclesfield T	13	3	
2002–03	Macclesfield T	36	10	
2003–04	Macclesfield T	38	16	
2004–05	Macclesfield T	44	12	
2005–06	Mansfield T	4	0	**4** **0**
2005–06	Bury	24	3	**24** **3**
2006–07	*Macclesfield T*	32	4	

From Hyde U, Droylsden.

2009–10	Macclesfield T	31	5	**194** **50**

TREMARCO, Carl (D)   **93** **1**
H: 5 8   W: 11 11   b.Liverpool 11-10-85
Source: Scholar.

2003–04	Tranmere R	0	0	
2004–05	Tranmere R	3	0	
2005–06	Tranmere R	18	1	
2006–07	Tranmere R	23	0	
2007–08	Tranmere R	8	0	**52** **1**
2007–08	Wrexham	10	0	
2008–09	Wrexham	0	0	**10** **0**
2008–09	*Darlington*	2	0	**2** **0**

On loan from Wrexham.

2009–10	Macclesfield T	29	0	**29** **0**

VEIGA, Jose Manuel (G)   **277** **0**
H: 6 2   W: 12 13   b.Lisbon 18-12-76
Source: Benfica. *Honours:* Cape Verde full caps.

1996–97	Alverca	14	0	
1997–98	Alverca	33	0	**47** **0**
1998–99	Levante	38	0	
1999–2000	Levante	40	0	
2000–01	Levante	30	0	
2001–02	Levante	22	0	**130** **0**
2001–02	Valladolid	0	0	
2002–03	Amadora	33	0	
2003–04	Amadora	28	0	
2004–05	Amadora	31	0	**92** **0**

2005–06	Olhance	2	0	2	0

From Tamworth, Atherstone T.

2008–09	Hereford U	1	0		
2009–10	Hereford U	0	0	1	0
2009–10	Macclesfield T	5	0	5	0

WILSON, Kyle (F)   4   0
H: 5 10 W: 11 05 b.Wirrall 14-11-85
Source: Scholar. *Honours:* England Youth.

2003–04	Crewe Alex	0	0		
2004–05	Crewe Alex	0	0		
2005–06	Crewe Alex	0	0		

From Barrow, Droyslden, FC United of Manchester.

| 2009–10 | Macclesfield T | 4 | 0 | 4 | 0 |

WRIGHT, Ben (F)   229   55
H: 6 1 W: 13 07 b.Munster 1-7-80

1998–99	Bristol C	0	0		
1999–2000	Bristol C	2	0		
2000–01	Bristol C	0	0	2	0
2001	Viking	22	0		
2002	Viking	18	1	40	1
2003	Start	30	13		
2004	Start	29	15		
2005	Start	9	1		
2006	*Moss*	11	2	11	2
2007	Start	2	0	70	29
2007–08	Lincoln C	34	15		
2008–09	Lincoln C	33	2	67	17
2009–10	Macclesfield T	39	6	39	6

MANCHESTER C (50)

ADEBAYOR, Emmanuel (F)   252   93
H: 6 4 W: 11 08 b.Lome 26-2-84
Source: Lome. *Honours:* Togo 42 full caps, 18 goals.

2001–02	Metz	10	2		
2002–03	Metz	34	13	44	15
2003–04	Monaco	31	8		
2004–05	Monaco	34	9		
2005–06	Monaco	13	1	78	18
2005–06	Arsenal	13	4		
2006–07	Arsenal	29	8		
2007–08	Arsenal	36	24		
2008–09	Arsenal	26	10	104	46
2009–10	Manchester C	26	14	26	14

BALL, David (F)   0   0
H: 6 0 W: 11 08 b.Whitefield 14-12-89
Source: Scholar.

2007–08	Manchester C	0	0		
2008–09	Manchester C	0	0		
2009–10	Manchester C	0	0		

BARRY, Gareth (M)   399   43
H: 5 11 W: 12 06 b.Hastings 23-2-81
Source: Trainee. *Honours:* England Youth, B, Under-21, 39 full caps, 2 goals.

1997–98	Aston Villa	2	0		
1998–99	Aston Villa	32	2		
1999–2000	Aston Villa	30	1		
2000–01	Aston Villa	30	0		
2001–02	Aston Villa	20	0		
2002–03	Aston Villa	35	3		
2003–04	Aston Villa	36	3		
2004–05	Aston Villa	34	7		
2005–06	Aston Villa	36	3		
2006–07	Aston Villa	35	8		
2007–08	Aston Villa	37	9		
2008–09	Aston Villa	38	5	365	41
2009–10	Manchester C	34	2	34	2

BELLAMY, Craig (F)   341   112
H: 5 9 W: 10 12 b.Cardiff 13-7-79
Source: Trainee. *Honours:* Wales Schools, Youth, Under-21, 58 full caps, 17 goals.

1996–97	Norwich C	3	0		
1997–98	Norwich C	36	13		
1998–99	Norwich C	40	17		
1999–2000	Norwich C	4	2		
2000–01	Norwich C	1	0	84	32
2000–01	Coventry C	34	6	34	6
2001–02	Newcastle U	27	9		
2002–03	Newcastle U	29	7		
2003–04	Newcastle U	16	4		
2004–05	Newcastle U	21	7	93	27
2004–05	*Celtic*	12	7	12	7
2005–06	Blackburn R	27	13	27	13

2006–07	Liverpool	27	7	27	7
2007–08	West Ham U	8	2		
2008–09	West Ham U	16	5	24	7
2008–09	Manchester C	8	3		
2009–10	Manchester C	32	10	40	13

BENALI, Ahmed (M)   0   0
b.Libya 7-2-92
Source: Scholar.

2008–09	Manchester C	0	0		
2009–10	Manchester C	0	0		

BOJINOV, Valeri (F)   130   30
H: 5 10 W: 12 04 b.Oriahovizca 15-2-86
Honours: Bulgaria 29 full caps, 7 goals.

2001–02	Lecce	2	0		
2002–03	Lecce	15	2		
2003–04	Lecce	28	3		
2004–05	Lecce	20	11	65	16
2004–05	Fiorentina	9	2		
2005–06	Fiorentina	27	6	36	8
2006–07	Juventus	18	5	18	5
2007–08	Manchester C	3	0		
2008–09	Manchester C	8	1		
2009–10	Manchester C	0	0	11	1

BOYATA, Anga (M)   3   0
H: 6 2 W: 12 00 b.Uccle 8-9-90
Source: Scholar. *Honours:* Belgium Under-21.

2008–09	Manchester C	0	0		
2009–10	Manchester C	3	0	3	0

BRIDGE, Wayne (D)   290   3
H: 5 10 W: 12 13 b.Southampton 5-8-80
Source: Trainee. *Honours:* England Youth, Under-21, 36 full caps, 1 goal.

1997–98	Southampton	0	0		
1998–99	Southampton	23	0		
1999–2000	Southampton	19	1		
2000–01	Southampton	38	0		
2001–02	Southampton	38	0		
2002–03	Southampton	34	1	152	2
2003–04	Chelsea	33	1		
2004–05	Chelsea	15	0		
2005–06	Chelsea	0	0		
2005–06	*Fulham*	12	0	12	0
2006–07	Chelsea	22	0		
2007–08	Chelsea	11	0		
2008–09	Chelsea	6	0	87	1
2008–09	Manchester C	16	0		
2009–10	Manchester C	23	0	39	0

CAICEDO, Felipe (F)   72   15
H: 6 1 W: 12 08 b.Guayaquil 5-9-88
Source: Rocafuerte. *Honours:* Ecuador 28 full caps, 3 goals.

2006–07	Basle	27	7		
2007–08	Basle	18	4	45	11
2007–08	Manchester C	10	0		
2008–09	Manchester C	17	4		
2009–10	Manchester C	0	0	27	4

CHANTLER, Chris (M)   0   0
H: 5 8 W: 11 00 b.Cheadle Hulme 16-12-90
Source: Scholar.

2009–10	Manchester C	0	0		

CLAYTON, Adam (M)   28   1
H: 5 9 W: 11 11 b.Manchester 14-1-89
Source: Scholar. *Honours:* England Under-20.

2007–08	Manchester C	0	0		
2008–09	Manchester C	0	0		
2009–10	Manchester C	0	0		
2009–10	*Carlisle U*	28	1	28	1

CUNNINGHAM, Greg (D)   2   0
H: 6 0 W: 11 00 b.Cammore 31-1-91
Source: Scholar. *Honours:* Eire 1 full cap.

2008–09	Manchester C	0	0		
2009–10	Manchester C	2	0	2	0

DE JONG, Nigel (D)   212   11
H: 5 8 W: 11 05 b.Amsterdam 30-11-84
Honours: Holland 48 full caps, 1 goal.

2002–03	Ajax	17	0		
2003–04	Ajax	32	1		
2004–05	Ajax	31	5		
2005–06	Hamburg	12	1		
2005–06	Ajax	16	2	96	8
2006–07	Hamburg	18	1		
2007–08	Hamburg	29	1		
2008–09	Hamburg	7	0	66	3

2008–09	Manchester C	16	0		
2009–10	Manchester C	34	0	50	0

ELABDELLAOUI, Omar (M)   0   0
b.Norway 5-12-91
Source: Scholar.

2009–10	Manchester C	0	0		

ETUHU, Kelvin (F)   34   3
H: 5 11 W: 11 02 b.Kano 30-5-88
Source: Scholar.

2005–06	Manchester C	0	0		
2006–07	Manchester C	0	0		
2006–07	*Rochdale*	4	2	4	2
2007–08	Manchester C	6	1		
2007–08	*Leicester C*	4	0	4	0
2008–09	Manchester C	4	0		
2009–10	Manchester C	0	0	10	1
2009–10	*Cardiff C*	16	0	16	0

GARRIDO, Javier (M)   135   3
H: 5 10 W: 11 11 b.Irun 15-3-85
Honours: Spain Under-21.

2004–05	Real Sociedad	28	0		
2005–06	Real Sociedad	33	0		
2006–07	Real Sociedad	25	1	86	1
2007–08	Manchester C	27	0		
2008–09	Manchester C	13	1		
2009–10	Manchester C	9	1	49	2

GIVEN, Shay (G)   428   0
H: 6 0 W: 13 03 b.Lifford 20-4-76
Source: Celtic. *Honours:* Eire Youth, Under-21, 103 full caps.

1994–95	Blackburn R	0	0		
1994–95	*Swindon T*	0	0		
1995–96	Blackburn R	0	0		
1995–96	*Swindon T*	5	0	5	0
1995–96	*Sunderland*	17	0	17	0
1996–97	Blackburn R	2	0	2	0
1997–98	Newcastle U	24	0		
1998–99	Newcastle U	31	0		
1999–2000	Newcastle U	14	0		
2000–01	Newcastle U	34	0		
2001–02	Newcastle U	38	0		
2002–03	Newcastle U	38	0		
2003–04	Newcastle U	38	0		
2004–05	Newcastle U	36	0		
2005–06	Newcastle U	38	0		
2006–07	Newcastle U	22	0		
2007–08	Newcastle U	19	0		
2008–09	Newcastle U	22	0	354	0
2008–09	Manchester C	15	0		
2009–10	Manchester C	35	0	50	0

GONZALEZ, David (G)   238   0
H: 6 4 b.Medellin 20-7-82
Honours: Colombia 2 full caps.

2001	At Nacional	0	0		
2002	Independiente	21	0		
2003	Independiente	38	0		
2004	Independiente	46	0		
2005	Independiente	22	0	127	0
2006	Dep Cali	35	0		
2007	Dep Cali	22	0	57	0
2007–08	Rize	24	0	24	0
2009	Huracan	30	0	30	0
2009–10	Manchester C	0	0		

GUIDETTI, John (F)   8   3
b.Stockholm 15-4-92
Source: Scholar. *Honours:* Sweden Youth, Under-21.

2009–10	Manchester C	0	0		
2009–10	*Brommapojkana*	8	3	8	3

HART, Joe (G)   149   0
H: 6 3 W: 13 03 b.Shrewsbury 19-4-87
Source: Scholar. *Honours:* England Youth, Under-21, 3 full caps.

2004–05	Shrewsbury T	6	0		
2005–06	Shrewsbury T	46	0	52	0
2006–07	Manchester C	1	0		
2006–07	*Tranmere R*	6	0	6	0
2006–07	*Blackpool*	5	0	5	0
2007–08	Manchester C	26	0		
2008–09	Manchester C	23	0		
2009–10	Manchester C	0	0	50	0
2009–10	*Birmingham C*	36	0	36	0

HELAN, Jeremy (M) 0 0
b.France 9-5-92
Source: Rennes.
2009–10 Manchester C 0 0

IBRAHIM, Abdisalam (M) 1 0
H: 6 0 W: 11 02 b.Guriceel 4-5-91
Source: Scholar.
2008–09 Manchester C 0 0
2009–10 Manchester C 1 0 **1 0**

IRELAND, Stephen (F) 138 16
H: 5 8 W: 10 07 b.Cork 22-8-86
Source: Scholar. *Honours:* Eire Youth,
Under-21, 6 full caps, 4 goals.
2005–06 Manchester C 24 0
2006–07 Manchester C 24 1
2007–08 Manchester C 33 4
2008–09 Manchester C 35 9
2009–10 Manchester C 22 2 **138 16**

JO (F) 170 49
H: 5 9 W: 11 00 b.Sao Paulo 20-3-87
Honours: Brazil Under-23, 3 full caps.
2003 Corinthians 14 1
2004 Corinthians 42 8
2005 Corinthians 25 4 **81 13**
2006 CSKA Moscow 18 14
2007 CSKA Moscow 27 13
2008 CSKA Moscow 8 3 **53 30**
2008–09 Manchester C 9 1
2008–09 Everton 12 5
2009–10 Manchester C 0 0 **9 1**
2009–10 Everton 15 0 **27 5**

JOHNSON, Adam (M) 129 19
H: 5 8 W: 10 00 b.Sunderland 14-7-87
Source: Scholar. *Honours:* England Youth,
Under-21, 1 full cap.
2004–05 Middlesbrough 0 0
2005–06 Middlesbrough 13 1
2006–07 Middlesbrough 12 0
2006–07 Leeds U 5 0 **5 0**
2007–08 Middlesbrough 19 1
2007–08 Watford 12 5 **12 5**
2008–09 Middlesbrough 26 0
2009–10 Middlesbrough 26 11 **96 13**
2009–10 Manchester C 16 1 **16 1**

JOHNSON, Michael (M) 37 2
H: 6 1 W: 12 07 b.Urmston 3-3-88
Source: Scholar. *Honours:* England Youth,
Under-21.
2005–06 Manchester C 0 0
2006–07 Manchester C 10 0
2007–08 Manchester C 23 2
2008–09 Manchester C 3 0
2009–10 Manchester C 1 0 **37 2**

KAY, Scott (D) 0 0
b.Denton 18-9-89
Source: Scholar.
2007–08 Manchester C 0 0
2008–09 Manchester C 0 0
2009–10 Manchester C 0 0

KOMPANY, Vincent (D) 149 8
H: 6 3 W: 13 05 b.Brussels 10-4-86
Honours: Belgium 31 full caps, 1 goal.
2004–05 Anderlecht 29 2
2005–06 Anderlecht 32 2 **61 4**
2006–07 Hamburg 6 0
2007–08 Hamburg 22 1
2008–09 Hamburg 1 0 **29 1**
2008–09 Manchester C 34 1
2009–10 Manchester C 25 2 **59 3**

LESCOTT, Joleon (D) 343 28
H: 6 2 W: 13 00 b.Birmingham 16-8-82
Source: Trainee. *Honours:* England Youth,
Under-20, Under-21, B, 9 full caps.
1999–2000 Wolverhampton W 0 0
2000–01 Wolverhampton W 37 2
2001–02 Wolverhampton W 44 5
2002–03 Wolverhampton W 44 1
2003–04 Wolverhampton W 41 4
2004–05 Wolverhampton W 46 1 **212 13**
2005–06 Everton 38 2
2007–08 Everton 38 8
2008–09 Everton 36 4

2009–10 Everton 1 0 **113 14**
2009–10 Manchester C 18 1 **18 1**

LOGAN, Shaleum (M) 50 2
H: 6 1 W: 12 07 b.Manchester 6-11-88
Source: Scholar.
2006–07 Manchester C 0 0
2007–08 Manchester C 0 0
2007–08 Grimsby T 5 2 **5 2**
2007–08 Scunthorpe U 4 0 **4 0**
2007–08 Stockport Co 7 0 **7 0**
2008–09 Manchester C 1 0
2009–10 Manchester C 0 0 **1 0**
2009–10 Tranmere R 33 0 **33 0**

MAK, Robert (M) 0 0
H: 5 10 W: 11 00 b.Slovakia 8-3-91
Source: Scholar.
2008–09 Manchester C 0 0
2009–10 Manchester C 0 0

MARSHALL, Paul (M) 15 1
H: 6 1 W: 12 03 b.Manchester 9-7-89
Source: Scholar. *Honours:* England Under-20.
2007–08 Manchester C 0 0
2008–09 Manchester C 0 0
2008–09 Blackpool 2 0 **2 0**
2008–09 Port Vale 13 1 **13 1**
2009–10 Manchester C 0 0

McDERMOTT, Donal (F) 25 5
H: 6 6 W: 12 00 b.Dublin 19-10-89
Source: Scholar. *Honours:* Eire Youth.
2007–08 Manchester C 0 0
2008–09 Manchester C 0 0
2008–09 Milton Keynes D 1 0 **1 0**
2009–10 Manchester C 0 0
2009–10 Chesterfield 15 5 **15 5**
2009–10 Scunthorpe U 9 0 **9 0**

McGIVERN, Ryan (D) 17 1
H: 5 10 W: 11 07 b.Newry 8-1-90
Source: Scholar. *Honours:* Northern Ireland
Youth, Under-21, B, 11 full caps.
2007–08 Manchester C 0 0
2008–09 Manchester C 0 0
2008–09 Morecambe 5 1 **5 1**
2009–10 Manchester C 0 0
2009–10 Leicester C 12 0 **12 0**

MEE, Ben (D) 0 0
H: 5 11 W: 11 09 b.Sale 21-9-89
Source: Scholar. *Honours:* England Youth,
Under-20.
2007–08 Manchester C 0 0
2008–09 Manchester C 0 0
2009–10 Manchester C 0 0

MWARUWARI, Benjamin (F) 243 63
H: 6 2 W: 12 03 b.Harare 13-8-78
Honours: Zimbabwe 30 full caps, 8 goals.
1999–2000 Jomo Cosmos 15 7
2000–01 Jomo Cosmos 30 13 **45 20**
2001–02 Grasshoppers 25 1 **25 1**
2002–03 Auxerre 27 7
2003–04 Auxerre 3 0
2004–05 Auxerre 31 11
2005–06 Auxerre 11 1 **72 19**
2005–06 Portsmouth 16 1
2006–07 Portsmouth 31 6
2007–08 Portsmouth 23 12 **70 19**
2007–08 Manchester C 13 3
2008–09 Manchester C 8 1
2009–10 Manchester C 2 0 **23 4**
2009–10 Sunderland 8 0 **8 0**

NIELSEN, Gunnar (G) 1 0
H: 6 3 W: 14 00 b.Faeroes 7-10-86
Source: Frem. *Honours:* Faeroes Under-21, 2
full caps.
2007–08 Blackburn R 0 0
2008–09 Manchester C 0 0
2009–10 Manchester C 1 0 **1 0**

NIMELY-TCHUIMENI, Alex (F) 1 0
H: 5 11 W: 11 03 b.Monrovia 11-5-91
Source: Scholar. *Honours:* Liberia
Youth, England Under-20.
2008–09 Manchester C 0 0
2009–10 Manchester C 1 0 **1 0**

ONUOHA, Nedum (D) 94 3
H: 6 2 W: 12 04 b.Warri 12-11-86
Source: Scholar. *Honours:* England Youth,
Under-20, Under-21.
2004–05 Manchester C 17 0
2005–06 Manchester C 10 0
2006–07 Manchester C 18 0
2007–08 Manchester C 16 1
2008–09 Manchester C 23 1
2009–10 Manchester C 10 1 **94 3**

PARIS, James (M) 0 0
b. 22-5-92
2009–10 Manchester C 0 0

PETROV, Martin (F) 306 62
H: 6 0 W: 12 02 b.Vratza 15-1-79
Honours: Bulgaria 78 full caps, 18 goals.
1996–97 CSKA Sofia 3 0
1997–98 CSKA Sofia 4 0 **7 0**
1998–99 Servette 12 2
1999–2000 Servette 31 9
2000–01 Servette 32 11 **75 22**
2001–02 Wolfsburg 32 6
2002–03 Wolfsburg 26 2
2003–04 Wolfsburg 28 8
2004–05 Wolfsburg 30 12 **116 28**
2005–06 Atletico Madrid 36 1
2006–07 Atletico Madrid 13 2 **49 3**
2007–08 Manchester C 34 5
2008–09 Manchester C 9 0
2009–10 Manchester C 16 4 **59 9**

POOLE, James (F) 9 0
H: 5 11 W: 12 05 b.Stockport 20-3-90
Source: Scholar.
2008–09 Manchester C 0 0
2009–10 Manchester C 0 0
2009–10 Bury 9 0 **9 0**

REDSHAW, Jack (F) 0 0
H: 5 6 W: 10 00 b. 20-1-90
Source: Scholar.
2009–10 Manchester C 0 0

RICHARDS, Micah (D) 123 5
H: 5 11 W: 13 00 b.Birmingham 24-6-88
Source: Scholar. *Honours:* England Youth,
Under-21, 11 full caps, 1 goal.
2005–06 Manchester C 13 0
2006–07 Manchester C 28 1
2007–08 Manchester C 25 0
2008–09 Manchester C 34 1
2009–10 Manchester C 23 3 **123 5**

ROBINHO (F) 240 79
H: 5 8 W: 10 00 b.Sao Vicente 25-1-84
Honours: Brazil Under-23, 79 full caps,
25 goals.
2002 Santos 24 7
2003 Santos 32 9
2004 Santos 37 21
2005 Santos 5 3 **98 40**
2005–06 Real Madrid 37 8
2006–07 Real Madrid 32 6
2007–08 Real Madrid 32 11 **101 25**
2008–09 Manchester C 31 14
2009–10 Manchester C 10 0 **41 14**

SANTA CRUZ, Roque (F) 239 60
H: 6 2 W: 13 12 b.Asuncion 16-8-81
Honours: Paraguay Under-20, 75 full caps, 21
goals.
1998–99 Olimpia 9 3 **9 3**
1999–2000 Bayern Munich 28 5
2000–01 Bayern Munich 19 5
2001–02 Bayern Munich 22 5
2002–03 Bayern Munich 14 5
2003–04 Bayern Munich 28 5
2004–05 Bayern Munich 4 0
2005–06 Bayern Munich 13 4
2006–07 Bayern Munich 24 2 **154 31**
2007–08 Blackburn R 37 19
2008–09 Blackburn R 20 4
2009–10 Blackburn R 0 0 **57 23**
2009–10 Manchester C 19 3 **19 3**

SYLVINHO (D) 327 6
H: 5 8 W: 10 07 b.Sao Paulo 12-4-74
Honours: Brazil 6 full caps.
1994 Corinthians 3 0
1995 Corinthians 13 0

1996	Corinthians	21	0		
1997	Corinthians	22	0		
1998	Corinthians	30	0		
1999	Corinthians	0	0	89	0
1999–2000	Arsenal	31	1		
2000–01	Arsenal	24	2	55	3
2001–02	Celta Vigo	23	0		
2002–03	Celta Vigo	32	1		
2003–04	Celta Vigo	29	0	84	1
2004–05	Barcelona	21	0		
2005–06	Barcelona	26	2		
2006–07	Barcelona	13	0		
2007–08	Barcelona	14	0		
2008–09	Barcelona	15	0	89	2
2009–10	Manchester C	10	0	10	0

TEVEZ, Carlos (F)   **228 95**
H: 5 8   W: 11 11   b.Cuidadela 5-2-84
Source: All Boys. *Honours:* Argentina Youth, Under-20, Under-23, 58 full caps, 11 goals.

2001–02	Boca Juniors	11	1		
2002–03	Boca Juniors	32	11		
2003–04	Boca Juniors	23	12		
2004–05	Boca Juniors	9	2	75	26
2005	Corinthians	29	20	29	20
2006–07	West Ham U	26	7	26	7
2007–08	Manchester U	34	14		
2008–09	Manchester U	29	5		
2009–10	Manchester U	0	0	63	19
2009–10	Manchester C	35	23	35	23

TOURE, Kolo (D)   **256 10**
H: 5 10   W: 13 08   b.Sokoura Bouake 19-3-81
Source: ASEC Mimosas. *Honours:* Ivory Coast 84 full caps, 3 goals.

2001–02	Arsenal	0	0		
2002–03	Arsenal	26	2		
2003–04	Arsenal	37	1		
2004–05	Arsenal	35	0		
2005–06	Arsenal	33	0		
2006–07	Arsenal	35	3		
2007–08	Arsenal	30	2		
2008–09	Arsenal	29	1		
2009–10	Arsenal	0	0	225	9
2009–10	Manchester C	31	1	31	1

TRIPPIER, Keiran (D)   **3 0**
H: 5 10   W: 11 00   b.Bury 19-9-90
Source: Scholar. *Honours:* England Youth, Under-20.

2007–08	Manchester C	0	0		
2008–09	Manchester C	0	0		
2009–10	Manchester C	0	0		
2009–10	*Barnsley*	3	0	3	0

TUTTE, Andrew (M)   **0 0**
H: 5 9   W: 10 10   b. 21-9-90
Source: Scholar. *Honours:* England Youth, Under-20.

2007–08	Manchester C	0	0
2008–09	Manchester C	0	0
2009–10	Manchester C	0	0

VESELI, Frederic (D)   **0 0**
b.Switzerland 22-11-92
Source: Scholar.

2009–10	Manchester C	0	0

VIDAL, Javan (D)   **17 0**
H: 5 10   W: 10 10   b.Manchester 10-5-89
Source: Scholar. *Honours:* England Youth, Under-20.

2007–08	Manchester C	0	0		
2008–09	Manchester C	0	0		
2008–09	*Aberdeen*	13	0	13	0
2008–09	*Grimsby T*	3	0	3	0
2009–10	Manchester C	0	0		
2009–10	*Derby Co*	1	0	1	0

VIEIRA, Patrick (M)   **441 42**
H: 6 4   W: 13 09   b.Dakar 23-6-76
Honours: France Under-21, 107 full caps, 6 goals.

1993–94	Cannes	5	0		
1994–95	Cannes	31	2		
1995–96	Cannes	13	0	49	2
1995–96	AC Milan	2	0	2	0
1996–97	Arsenal	31	2		
1997–98	Arsenal	33	2		
1998–99	Arsenal	34	3		
1999–2000	Arsenal	30	2		
2000–01	Arsenal	30	5		
2001–02	Arsenal	36	2		
2002–03	Arsenal	24	3		
2003–04	Arsenal	29	3		
2004–05	Arsenal	32	6	279	28
2005–06	Juventus	31	5	31	5
2006–07	Inter Milan	20	1		
2007–08	Inter Milan	16	3		
2008–09	Inter Milan	19	1		
2009–10	Inter Milan	12	1	67	6
2009–10	Manchester C	13	1	13	1

WABARA, Reece (D)   **0 0**
b. 28-12-91

2008–09	Manchester C	0	0
2009–10	Manchester C	0	0

WEISS, Vladimir (M)   **14 0**
H: 5 9   W: 10 10   b.Bratislava 30-11-89
Source: Scholar. *Honours:* Slovakia 12 full caps.

2007–08	Manchester C	0	0		
2008–09	Manchester C	1	0		
2009–10	Manchester C	0	0	1	0
2009–10	*Bolton W*	13	0	13	0

WOOD, James (G)   **0 0**
H: 6 0   W: 13 01   b. 10-11-91
Source: Scholar.

WRIGHT-PHILLIPS, Shaun (F)   **292 39**
H: 5 5   W: 10 01   b.Lewisham 25-10-81
Source: Scholar. *Honours:* England Under-21, 34 full caps, 6 goals.

1998–99	Manchester C	0	0		
1999–2000	Manchester C	4	0		
2000–01	Manchester C	15	0		
2001–02	Manchester C	35	8		
2002–03	Manchester C	31	1		
2003–04	Manchester C	34	7		
2004–05	Manchester C	34	10		
2005–06	Chelsea	27	0		
2006–07	Chelsea	27	2		
2007–08	Chelsea	27	2		
2008–09	Chelsea	1	0	82	4
2008–09	Manchester C	27	5		
2009–10	Manchester C	30	4	210	35

ZABALETA, Pablo (D)   **202 12**
H: 5 8   W: 10 12   b.Buenos Aires 16-1-85
Honours: Argentina Youth, Under-23, 7 full caps.

2002–03	San Lorenzo	11	0		
2003–04	San Lorenzo	27	3		
2004–05	San Lorenzo	28	5	66	8
2005–06	Espanyol	27	2		
2006–07	Espanyol	21	0		
2007–08	Espanyol	32	1	80	3
2008–09	Manchester C	29	1		
2009–10	Manchester C	27	0	56	1

Scholars
Bunn, Harry; Hippias, Emerick; Johansen, Eirik Holmen; Karius, Loris Sven; Morrissey, Conor Patrick; Robinson, Bradley; Roman Olle, Joan Angel; Skogsrud, Kim Eugen; Skogsrud, Tom Even; Smith, Thomas George; Tse, Sean Ka Keung; Zander, Nils.

MANCHESTER U (51)

AJOSE, Nicholas (F)   **0 0**
b.Bury 7-10-91
Source: Scholar.

2009–10	Manchester U	0	0

AMOS, Ben (G)   **1 0**
H: 6 1   W: 13 00   b.Macclesfield 10-4-90
Source: Scholar. *Honours:* England Youth.

2007–08	Manchester U	0	0		
2008–09	Manchester U	0	0		
2009–10	Manchester U	0	0		
2009–10	*Peterborough U*	1	0	1	0

ANDERSON (M)   **78 4**
H: 5 8   W: 10 07   b.Porto Alegre 13-4-88

2004–05	Gremio	5	1	5	1
2005–06	Porto	3	0		
2006–07	Porto	15	2	18	2
2007–08	Manchester U	24	0		
2008–09	Manchester U	17	0		
2009–10	Manchester U	14	1	55	1

BERBATOV, Dimitar (F)   **338 142**
H: 6 2   W: 12 06   b.Blagoevgrad 30-1-81
Honours: Bulgaria Under-21, 78 full caps, 48 goals.

1998–99	CSKA Sofia	11	3		
1999–2000	CSKA Sofia	27	14		
2000–01	CSKA Sofia	12	8	50	25
2000–01	Leverkusen	6	0		
2001–02	Leverkusen	24	8		
2002–03	Leverkusen	24	4		
2003–04	Leverkusen	33	16		
2004–05	Leverkusen	33	20		
2005–06	Leverkusen	34	21	154	69
2006–07	Tottenham H	33	12		
2007–08	Tottenham H	36	15		
2008–09	Tottenham H	1	0	70	27
2008–09	Manchester U	31	9		
2009–10	Manchester U	33	12	64	21

BIRAM DIOUF, Mame (F)   **78 33**
H: 6 1   W: 11 13   b.Dakar 16-12-87
Source: Diaraf. *Honours:* Senegal 3 full caps.

2007	Molde	21	9		
2008	Molde	23	7		
2009	Molde	29	16	73	32
2009–10	Manchester U	5	1	5	1

BRADY, Robert (F)   **0 0**
b.Belfast 14-1-92
Source: Scholar.

2008–09	Manchester U	0	0
2009–10	Manchester U	0	0

BRANDY, Febian (F)   **55 8**
H: 5 5   W: 10 00   b.Manchester 4-2-89
Source: Scholar. *Honours:* England Youth, Under-20.

2006–07	Manchester U	0	0		
2007–08	Manchester U	0	0		
2007–08	*Swansea C*	19	3		
2008–09	Manchester U	0	0		
2008–09	*Swansea C*	14	0	33	3
2008–09	*Hereford U*	15	4	15	4
2009–10	Manchester U	0	0		
2009–10	*Gillingham*	7	1	7	1

BROWN, Wes (D)   **225 3**
H: 6 1   W: 13 08   b.Manchester 13-10-79
Source: Trainee. *Honours:* England Schools, Youth, Under-21, 23 full caps, 1 goal.

1996–97	Manchester U	0	0		
1997–98	Manchester U	2	0		
1998–99	Manchester U	14	0		
1999–2000	Manchester U	0	0		
2000–01	Manchester U	28	0		
2001–02	Manchester U	17	0		
2002–03	Manchester U	22	0		
2003–04	Manchester U	17	0		
2004–05	Manchester U	21	1		
2005–06	Manchester U	19	0		
2006–07	Manchester U	22	0		
2007–08	Manchester U	36	1		
2008–09	Manchester U	8	1		
2009–10	Manchester U	19	0	225	3

CARRICK, Michael (M)   **330 22**
H: 6 1   W: 11 10   b.Wallsend 28-7-81
Source: Trainee. *Honours:* England Youth, Under-21, B, 22 full caps.

1998–99	West Ham U	0	0		
1999–2000	West Ham U	8	1		
1999–2000	Swindon T	6	2	6	2
1999–2000	Birmingham C	2	0	2	0
2000–01	West Ham U	33	1		
2001–02	West Ham U	30	2		
2002–03	West Ham U	30	1		
2003–04	West Ham U	35	1		
2004–05	West Ham U	0	0	136	6
2004–05	Tottenham H	29	0		
2005–06	Tottenham H	35	2	64	2
2006–07	Manchester U	33	3		
2007–08	Manchester U	31	2		
2008–09	Manchester U	28	4		
2009–10	Manchester U	30	3	122	12

CATHCART, Craig (D)   56   3
H: 6 2 W: 11 06 b.Belfast 6-2-89
Source: Scholar. *Honours:* Northern Ireland Youth, Under-21.

2005–06	Manchester U	0	0		
2006–07	Manchester U	0	0		
2007–08	Manchester U	0	0		
2007–08	Antwerp	13	2	13	2
2008–09	Manchester U	0	0		
2008–09	Plymouth Arg	31	1	31	1
2009–10	Manchester U	0	0		
2009–10	Watford	12	0	12	0

CHESTER, James (D)   8   0
H: 5 11 W: 11 04 b.Warrington 23-1-89
Source: Scholar.

2007–08	Manchester U	0	0		
2008–09	Manchester U	0	0		
2008–09	Peterborough U	5	0	5	0
2009–10	Manchester U	0	0		
2009–10	Plymouth Arg	3	0	3	0

CLEVERLEY, Tom (M)   48   13
H: 5 9 W: 10 07 b.Basingstoke 12-8-89
Source: Scholar. *Honours:* England Youth, Under-20, Under-21.

2007–08	Manchester U	0	0		
2008–09	Manchester U	0	0		
2008–09	Leicester C	15	2	15	2
2009–10	Manchester U	0	0		
2009–10	Watford	33	11	33	11

DE LAET, Ritchie (D)   3   0
H: 6 1 W: 12 02 b.Belgium 28-11-88
Source: Antwerp. *Honours:* Belgium 2 full caps.

2007–08	Stoke C	0	0		
2008–09	Stoke C	0	0		
2008–09	Manchester U	1	0		
2009–10	Manchester U	2	0	3	0

DRINKWATER, Daniel (M)   33   2
H: 5 10 W: 11 00 b.Manchester 5-3-90
Source: Scholar. *Honours:* England Youth.

2008–09	Manchester U	0	0		
2009–10	Manchester U	0	0		
2009–10	Huddersfield T	33	2	33	2

DUDGEON, Joe (D)   0   0
b.Leeds 26-11-90
Source: Scholar. *Honours:* Northern Ireland Under-21.

2009–10	Manchester U	0	0		

EIKREM, Magnus (M)   0   0
H: 5 8 W: 10 12 b.Molde 8-8-90
Source: Scholar.

2008–09	Manchester U	0	0		
2009–10	Manchester U	0	0		

EVANS, Corry (M)   0   0
H: 5 8 W: 10 12 b.Belfast 30-7-90
Source: Scholar. *Honours:* Northern Ireland Under-21, B, 4 full caps.

2007–08	Manchester U	0	0		
2008–09	Manchester U	0	0		
2009–10	Manchester U	0	0		

EVANS, Jonny (D)   82   3
H: 6 2 W: 12 02 b.Belfast 3-1-88
Source: Scholar. *Honours:* Northern Ireland Schools, Youth, Under-21, 20 full caps, 1 goal.

2004–05	Manchester U	0	0		
2005–06	Manchester U	0	0		
2006–07	Manchester U	0	0		
2006–07	Antwerp	14	2	14	2
2006–07	Sunderland	18	1		
2007–08	Manchester U	0	0		
2007–08	Sunderland	15	0	33	1
2008–09	Manchester U	17	0		
2009–10	Manchester U	18	0	35	0

EVRA, Patrice (D)   320   6
H: 5 8 W: 11 10 b.Dakar 15-5-81
Honours: France 32 full caps.

1998–99	Marsala	24	3	24	3
1999–2000	Monza	3	0	3	0
2000–01	Nice	5	0		
2001–02	Nice	34	1	39	1
2002–03	Monaco	36	1		
2003–04	Monaco	33	0		
2004–05	Monaco	36	0		
2005–06	Monaco	15	0	120	1
2005–06	Manchester U	11	0		
2006–07	Manchester U	24	1		
2007–08	Manchester U	33	0		
2008–09	Manchester U	28	0		
2009–10	Manchester U	38	0	134	1

FABIO (M)   5   0
H: 5 8 W: 10 03 b.Rio de Janeiro 9-7-90
Source: Fluminense.

2008–09	Manchester U	0	0		
2009–10	Manchester U	5	0	5	0

FERDINAND, Rio (D)   412   10
H: 6 2 W: 13 12 b.Peckham 7-11-78
Source: Trainee. *Honours:* England Youth, Under-21, B, 78 full caps, 3 goals.

1995–96	West Ham U	1	0		
1996–97	West Ham U	15	2		
1996–97	Bournemouth	10	0	10	0
1997–98	West Ham U	35	0		
1998–99	West Ham U	31	0		
1999–2000	West Ham U	33	0		
2000–01	West Ham U	12	0	127	2
2000–01	Leeds U	23	2		
2001–02	Leeds U	31	0	54	2
2002–03	Manchester U	28	0		
2003–04	Manchester U	20	0		
2004–05	Manchester U	31	0		
2005–06	Manchester U	37	3		
2006–07	Manchester U	34	0		
2007–08	Manchester U	35	2		
2008–09	Manchester U	24	0		
2009–10	Manchester U	13	0	221	6

FLETCHER, Darren (M)   163   14
H: 6 0 W: 11 09 b.Edinburgh 1-2-84
Source: Scholar. *Honours:* Scotland Under-21, B, 47 full caps, 4 goals.

2000–01	Manchester U	0	0		
2001–02	Manchester U	0	0		
2002–03	Manchester U	0	0		
2003–04	Manchester U	22	0		
2004–05	Manchester U	13	3		
2005–06	Manchester U	27	1		
2006–07	Manchester U	24	3		
2007–08	Manchester U	16	0		
2008–09	Manchester U	26	3		
2009–10	Manchester U	30	4	163	14

GIBSON, Darron (M)   39   4
H: 6 0 W: 12 04 b.Londonderry 25-10-87
Source: Scholar. *Honours:* Eire Youth, Under-21, 9 full caps.

2005–06	Manchester U	0	0		
2006–07	Manchester U	0	0		
2007–08	Manchester U	0	0		
2007–08	Wolverhampton W	21	1	21	1
2008–09	Manchester U	3	1		
2009–10	Manchester U	15	2	18	3

GIGGS, Ryan (F)   588   108
H: 5 11 W: 11 02 b.Cardiff 29-11-73
Source: School. *Honours:* England Schools, Wales Youth, Under-21, 64 full caps, 12 goals.

1990–91	Manchester U	2	1		
1991–92	Manchester U	38	4		
1992–93	Manchester U	41	9		
1993–94	Manchester U	38	13		
1994–95	Manchester U	29	1		
1995–96	Manchester U	33	11		
1996–97	Manchester U	26	3		
1997–98	Manchester U	29	8		
1998–99	Manchester U	24	3		
1999–2000	Manchester U	30	6		
2000–01	Manchester U	31	5		
2001–02	Manchester U	25	7		
2002–03	Manchester U	36	8		
2003–04	Manchester U	33	7		
2004–05	Manchester U	32	5		
2005–06	Manchester U	27	3		
2006–07	Manchester U	30	4		
2007–08	Manchester U	31	3		
2008–09	Manchester U	28	2		
2009–10	Manchester U	25	5	588	108

GILL, Oliver (D)   0   0
b.Frimley 15-9-90
Source: Scholar.

2009–10	Manchester U	0	0		

GRAY, David (F)   27   0
H: 5 11 W: 11 02 b.Edinburgh 4-5-88
Source: Scholar. *Honours:* Scotland Under-21.

2005–06	Manchester U	0	0		
2006–07	Manchester U	0	0		
2007–08	Manchester U	0	0		
2007–08	Crewe Alex	1	0	1	0
2008–09	Manchester U	0	0		
2008–09	Plymouth Arg	14	0		
2009–10	Manchester U	0	0		
2009–10	Plymouth Arg	12	0	26	0

HARGREAVES, Owen (M)   171   7
H: 5 11 W: 11 07 b.Calgary 20-1-81
Source: Calgary Foothills. *Honours:* England Under-21, B, 42 full caps.

2000–01	Bayern Munich	14	0		
2001–02	Bayern Munich	29	0		
2002–03	Bayern Munich	25	1		
2003–04	Bayern Munich	25	2		
2004–05	Bayern Munich	27	1		
2005–06	Bayern Munich	16	1		
2006–07	Bayern Munich	9	0	145	5
2007–08	Manchester U	23	2		
2008–09	Manchester U	2	0		
2009–10	Manchester U	1	0	26	2

HEATON, Tom (G)   63   0
H: 6 1 W: 13 12 b.Chester 15-4-86
Source: Trainee. *Honours:* England Youth, Under-21.

2003–04	Manchester U	0	0		
2004–05	Manchester U	0	0		
2005–06	Manchester U	0	0		
2005–06	Swindon T	14	0	14	0
2006–07	Manchester U	0	0		
2007–08	Manchester U	0	0		
2008–09	Manchester U	0	0		
2008–09	Cardiff C	21	0	21	0
2009–10	Manchester U	0	0		
2009–10	Rochdale	12	0	12	0
2009–10	Wycombe W	16	0	16	0

HEWSON, Sam (M)   17   3
H: 5 8 W: 11 00 b.Bolton 28-11-88
Source: Scholar.

2007–08	Manchester U	0	0		
2008–09	Manchester U	0	0		
2008–09	Hereford U	10	3	10	3
2009–10	Manchester U	0	0		
2009–10	Bury	7	0	7	0

HUSSAIN, Ettaz (M)   0   0
b.Oslo 27-1-93
Source: Scholar.

2009–10	Manchester U	0	0		

JAMES, Matthew (M)   18   2
H: 6 0 W: 11 12 b.Bacup 22-7-91
Source: Scholar. *Honours:* England Youth, Under-20.

2007–08	Manchester U	0	0		
2008–09	Manchester U	0	0		
2009–10	Manchester U	0	0		
2009–10	Preston NE	18	2	18	2

JOHNSTONE, Samuel (G)   0   0
b.Preston 25-3-93
Source: Scholar. *Honours:* England Youth.

2009–10	Manchester U	0	0		

KEANE, William (F)   0   0
b.Stockport 11-11-93
Source: Scholar. *Honours:* England Youth.

2009–10	Manchester U	0	0		

KING, Josh (F)   0   0
H: 5 11 W: 11 09 b.Oslo 15-1-92
Source: Scholar.

2008–09	Manchester U	0	0		
2009–10	Manchester U	0	0		

KUSZCZAK, Tomasz (G)   58   0
H: 6 3 W: 13 03 b.Krosno Odrzansia 20-3-82
Source: Uerdingen. *Honours:* Poland Youth, Under-21, 9 full caps.

2001–02	Hertha Berlin	0	0		
2002–03	Hertha Berlin	0	0		
2003–04	Hertha Berlin	0	0		
2004–05	WBA	3	0		
2005–06	WBA	28	0		

2006–07	WBA	0	0	31	0
2006–07	*Manchester U*	6	0		
2007–08	Manchester U	9	0		
2008–09	Manchester U	4	0		
2009–10	Manchester U	8	0	27	0

MACHEDA, Federico (F)   9 3
H: 6 0 W: 11 13 b.Rome 22-8-91
Source: Scholar.

2008–09	Manchester U	4	2
2009–10	Manchester U	5 1	9 3

MORRISON, Ravel (M)   0 0
b.Wythenshawe 2-2-93
Source: Scholar.

2009–10	Manchester U	0	0

NANI (M)   120 17
H: 5 9 W: 10 04 b.Amadora 17-11-86
Honours: Portugal Under-21, 36 full caps, 7 goals.

2005–06	Sporting Lisbon	29	4		
2006–07	Sporting Lisbon	29	5	58	9
2007–08	Manchester U	26	3		
2008–09	Manchester U	13	1		
2009–10	Manchester U	23	4	62	8

NEVILLE, Gary (D)   397 5
H: 5 11 W: 12 10 b.Bury 18-2-75
Source: Trainee. *Honours:* England Youth, 85 full caps.

1992–93	Manchester U	0	0		
1993–94	Manchester U	1	0		
1994–95	Manchester U	18	0		
1995–96	Manchester U	31	0		
1996–97	Manchester U	31	1		
1997–98	Manchester U	34	0		
1998–99	Manchester U	34	1		
1999–2000	Manchester U	22	0		
2000–01	Manchester U	32	1		
2001–02	Manchester U	34	0		
2002–03	Manchester U	26	0		
2003–04	Manchester U	30	2		
2004–05	Manchester U	22	0		
2005–06	Manchester U	25	0		
2006–07	Manchester U	24	0		
2007–08	Manchester U	0	0		
2008–09	Manchester U	16	0		
2009–10	Manchester U	17	0	397	5

NORWOOD, Oliver (M)   0 0
b.Burnley 12-4-91
Source: Scholar. *Honours:* Northern Ireland Under-21.

2009–10	Manchester U	0	0

O'SHEA, John (D)   246 11
H: 6 3 W: 13 07 b.Waterford 30-4-81
Source: Waterford. *Honours:* Eire Youth, Under-21, 62 full caps, 1 goal.

1998–99	Manchester U	0	0		
1999–2000	Manchester U	0	0		
1999–2000	*Bournemouth*	10	1	10	1
2000–01	Manchester U	0	0		
2001–02	Manchester U	9	0		
2002–03	Manchester U	32	0		
2003–04	Manchester U	33	2		
2004–05	Manchester U	23	2		
2005–06	Manchester U	34	1		
2006–07	Manchester U	32	4		
2007–08	Manchester U	28	0		
2008–09	Manchester U	30	0		
2009–10	Manchester U	15	1	236	10

OBERTAN, Gabriel (F)   76 4
H: 6 1 W: 12 06 b.Pantin 26-2-89
Honours: France Youth, Under-21.

2006–07	Bordeaux	17	1		
2007–08	Bordeaux	26	2		
2008–09	Bordeaux	11	0	54	3
2008–09	*Lorient*	15	1	15	1
2009–10	Manchester U	7	0	7	0

OWEN, Michael (F)   342 160
H: 5 8 W: 10 12 b.Chester 14-12-79
Source: Trainee. *Honours:* England Schools, Youth, Under-21, B, 89 full caps, 40 goals.

1996–97	Liverpool	2	1		
1997–98	Liverpool	36	18		
1998–99	Liverpool	30	18		
1999–2000	Liverpool	27	11		
2000–01	Liverpool	28	16		
2001–02	Liverpool	29	19		
2002–03	Liverpool	35	19		
2003–04	Liverpool	29	16	216	118
2004–05	Real Madrid	36	13	36	13
2005–06	Newcastle U	11	7		
2006–07	Newcastle U	3	0		
2007–08	Newcastle U	29	11		
2008–09	Newcastle U	28	8		
2009–10	Newcastle U	0	0	71	26
2009–10	Manchester U	19	3	19	3

PARK, Ji-Sung (M)   241 36
H: 5 9 W: 11 06 b.Seoul 25-2-81
Honours: South Korea 92 full caps, 13 goals.

2000	Kyoto Purple S	13	1		
2001	Kyoto Purple S	38	3		
2002	Kyoto Purple S	25	7	76	11
2002–03	PSV Eindhoven	8	0		
2003–04	PSV Eindhoven	28	6		
2004–05	PSV Eindhoven	28	7	64	13
2005–06	Manchester U	33	1		
2006–07	Manchester U	14	5		
2007–08	Manchester U	12	1		
2008–09	Manchester U	25	2		
2009–10	Manchester U	17	3	101	12

PETRUCCI, Davide (F)   0 0
b.Rome 5-10-91
Source: Scholar.

2008–09	Manchester U	0	0
2009–10	Manchester U	0	0

POGBA, Paul (M)   0 0
b.Lagny-sur-Marne 15-3-93
Source: Scholar.

2009–10	Manchester U	0	0

POSSEBON, Rodrigo (M)   3 0
H: 6 0 W: 11 13 b.Porto Alegre 13-2-89
Source: Internacional. *Honours:* Italy Youth.

2007–08	Manchester U	0	0		
2008–09	Manchester U	3	0		
2009–10	Manchester U	0	0	3	0

RAFAEL (D)   24 2
H: 6 3 W: 12 08 b.Petropolis 9-7-90
Source: Fluminense. *Honours:* Brazil Youth.

2008–09	Manchester U	16	1		
2009–10	Manchester U	8	1	24	2

ROONEY, Wayne (F)   256 106
H: 5 10 W: 12 13 b.Liverpool 24-10-85
Source: Scholar. *Honours:* FA Schools, England Youth, 64 full caps, 25 goals.

2002–03	Everton	33	6		
2003–04	Everton	34	9	67	15
2004–05	Manchester U	29	11		
2005–06	Manchester U	36	16		
2006–07	Manchester U	35	14		
2007–08	Manchester U	27	12		
2008–09	Manchester U	30	12		
2009–10	Manchester U	32	26	189	91

ROSE, Danny (M)   6 0
H: 5 7 W: 10 01 b.Bristol 21-2-88
Source: Scholar. *Honours:* England Youth.

2006–07	Manchester U	0	0		
2007–08	Manchester U	0	0		
2008–09	Manchester U	0	0		
2009–10	Manchester U	0	0		
2009–10	*Peterborough U*	6	0	6	0

SCHOLES, Paul (M)   444 101
H: 5 7 W: 11 00 b.Salford 16-11-74
Source: Trainee. *Honours:* England Youth, 66 full caps, 14 goals.

1992–93	Manchester U	0	0		
1993–94	Manchester U	0	0		
1994–95	Manchester U	17	5		
1995–96	Manchester U	26	10		
1996–97	Manchester U	24	3		
1997–98	Manchester U	31	8		
1998–99	Manchester U	31	6		
1999–2000	Manchester U	31	9		
2000–01	Manchester U	32	6		
2001–02	Manchester U	35	8		
2002–03	Manchester U	33	14		
2003–04	Manchester U	28	9		
2004–05	Manchester U	33	9		
2005–06	Manchester U	20	2		
2006–07	Manchester U	30	6		
2007–08	Manchester U	24	1		
2008–09	Manchester U	21	2		
2009–10	Manchester U	28	3	444	101

STEWART, Cameron (M)   0 0
b.Manchester 8-4-91
Source: Scholar. *Honours:* England Youth.

2009–10	Manchester U	0	0

TOSIC, Zoran (M)   83 16
H: 5 7 W: 10 10 b.Zrenjanin 24-4-87
Honours: Serbia Under-21, 21 full caps, 4 goals.

2005–06	Buducnost	7	0	7	0
2006–07	Banat Zrenjanin	25	2	25	2
2007–08	Partizan Belgrade	32	8		
2008–09	Partizan Belgrade	17	6	49	14
2008–09	Manchester U	2	0		
2009–10	Manchester U	0	0	2	0

TUNNICLIFFE, Ryan (M)   0 0
b.Bury 30-12-92
Source: Scholar.

2009–10	Manchester U	0	0

VALENCIA, Luis (M)   207 23
H: 5 10 W: 12 04 b.Lago Agrio 5-8-85
Honours: Ecuador Under-21, Under-23, 41 full caps, 6 goals.

2002	El Nacional	1	0		
2003	El Nacional	26	2		
2004	El Nacional	42	5		
2005	El Nacional	14	4	83	11
2005–06	Villarreal	2	0	2	0
2005–06	*Recreativo*	4	0	4	0
2006–07	Wigan Ath	22	1		
2007–08	Wigan Ath	31	3		
2008–09	Wigan Ath	31	3		
2009–10	Wigan Ath	0	0	84	7
2009–10	Manchester U	34	5	34	5

VAN DER SAR, Edwin (G)   572 1
H: 6 5 W: 14 11 b.Voorhout 29-10-70
Honours: Holland 130 full caps.

1990–91	Ajax	9	0		
1991–92	Ajax	1	0		
1992–93	Ajax	19	0		
1993–94	Ajax	32	0		
1994–95	Ajax	33	0		
1995–96	Ajax	33	0		
1996–97	Ajax	33	0		
1997–98	Ajax	33	1	192	1
1998–99	Juventus	34	0		
1999–2000	Juventus	32	0		
2000–01	Juventus	34	0	100	0
2001–02	Fulham	37	0		
2002–03	Fulham	19	0		
2003–04	Fulham	37	0		
2004–05	Fulham	34	0	127	0
2005–06	Manchester U	38	0		
2006–07	Manchester U	32	0		
2007–08	Manchester U	29	0		
2008–09	Manchester U	33	0		
2009–10	Manchester U	21	0	153	0

VIDIC, Nemanja (D)   260 31
H: 6 1 W: 13 02 b.Uzice 21-10-81
Honours: Serbia 48 full caps, 2 goals.

2000–01	Subotica	27	6	27	6
2001–02	Red Star Belgrade	22	2		
2002–03	Red Star Belgrade	22	5		
2003–04	Red Star Belgrade	20	5	68	12
2004	Spartak Moscow	12	2		
2005	Spartak Moscow	27	2	39	4
2005–06	Manchester U	11	0		
2006–07	Manchester U	25	3		
2007–08	Manchester U	32	1		
2008–09	Manchester U	34	4		
2009–10	Manchester U	24	1	126	9

WELBECK, Danny (F)   16 3
H: 6 1 W: 11 07 b.Manchester 26-11-90
Source: Scholar. *Honours:* England Youth, Under-21.

2007–08	Manchester U	0	0		
2008–09	Manchester U	3	1		
2009–10	Manchester U	5	0	8	1
2009–10	*Preston NE*	8	2	8	2

WOOTTON, Scott (D)   0 0
b.Birkenhead 12-9-91
Source: Scholar.

2009–10	Manchester U	0	0

Scholars
Brown, Reece; Cofie, John Erzuah; Cole, Larnell James; Devlin, Conor; Fornasier,

Michele; Fryers, Ezekiel David; Lingard, Jesse Ellis; Massacci, Alberto; McGinty, Sean Andrew; Thorpe, Thomas Joseph.

MIDDLESBROUGH (52)

ALIADIERE, Jeremie (F)   128   14
H: 6 0 W: 11 00 b.Rambouillet 30-3-83
Source: Scholar. *Honours:* France Youth, Under-21.

1999–2000	Arsenal	0	0		
2000–01	Arsenal	0	0		
2001–02	Arsenal	1	0		
2002–03	Arsenal	3	1		
2003–04	Arsenal	10	0		
2004–05	Arsenal	4	0		
2005–06	Arsenal	0	0		
2005–06	Celtic	0	0		
2005–06	West Ham U	7	0	7	0
2005–06	Wolverhampton W	14	2	14	2
2006–07	Arsenal	11	0	29	1
2007–08	Middlesbrough	29	5		
2008–09	Middlesbrough	29	2		
2009–10	Middlesbrough	20	4	78	11

ARCA, Julio (M)   290   22
H: 5 9 W: 11 13 b.Quilmes 31-1-81
Honours: Argentina Youth, Under-21.

1999–2000	Argentinos Jun	19	0		
2000–01	Argentinos Jun	17	1	36	1
2000–01	Sunderland	27	2		
2001–02	Sunderland	22	1		
2002–03	Sunderland	13	0		
2003–04	Sunderland	31	4		
2004–05	Sunderland	40	9		
2005–06	Sunderland	24	1	157	17
2006–07	Middlesbrough	21	2		
2007–08	Middlesbrough	24	2		
2008–09	Middlesbrough	18	0		
2009–10	Middlesbrough	34	0	97	4

BATES, Matthew (D)   45   1
H: 5 10 W: 12 03 b.Stockton 10-12-86
Source: Scholar. *Honours:* England Youth, Under-20.

2003–04	Middlesbrough	0	0		
2004–05	Middlesbrough	2	0		
2004–05	Darlington	4	0	4	0
2005–06	Middlesbrough	16	0		
2006–07	Middlesbrough	1	0		
2006–07	Ipswich T	2	0	2	0
2007–08	Middlesbrough	0	0		
2007–08	Norwich C	3	0	3	0
2008–09	Middlesbrough	17	1		
2009–10	Middlesbrough	0	0	36	1

BENNETT, Joe (D)   13   0
H: 5 10 W: 10 04 b.Rochdale 28-3-90
Source: Scholar. *Honours:* England Under-20.

2008–09	Middlesbrough	1	0		
2009–10	Middlesbrough	12	0	13	0

COYNE, Danny (G)   439   0
H: 6 0 W: 13 00 b.Prestatyn 27-8-73
Source: Trainee. *Honours:* Wales Schools, Youth, Under-21, B, 16 full caps.

1991–92	Tranmere R	0	0		
1992–93	Tranmere R	2	0		
1993–94	Tranmere R	5	0		
1994–95	Tranmere R	5	0		
1995–96	Tranmere R	46	0		
1996–97	Tranmere R	21	0		
1997–98	Tranmere R	16	0		
1998–99	Tranmere R	17	0		
1999–2000	Grimsby T	44	0		
2000–01	Grimsby T	46	0		
2001–02	Grimsby T	45	0		
2002–03	Grimsby T	46	0	181	0
2003–04	Leicester C	4	0	4	0
2004–05	Burnley	20	0		
2005–06	Burnley	8	0		
2006–07	Burnley	12	0	40	0
2007–08	Tranmere R	41	0		
2008–09	Tranmere R	39	0	191	0
2009–10	Middlesbrough	23	0	23	0

DIGARD, Didier (M)   120   3
H: 6 0 W: 11 13 b.Gisors 12-7-86
Honours: France Under-21.

2004–05	Le Havre	15	0		

2005–06	Le Havre	30	2		
2006–07	Le Havre	27	1	72	3
2007–08	Paris St Germain	16	0	16	0
2008–09	Middlesbrough	23	0		
2009–10	Middlesbrough	9	0	32	0

EMNES, Marvin (M)   87   10
H: 5 11 W: 10 06 b.Rotterdam 27-5-88
Honours: Holland Under-21.

2005–06	Sparta Rotterdam	11	1		
2006–07	Sparta Rotterdam	16	0		
2007–08	Sparta Rotterdam	29	8	56	9
2008–09	Middlesbrough	15	0		
2009–10	Middlesbrough	16	1	31	1

FLOOD, Willo (M)   126   5
H: 5 7 W: 10 05 b.Dublin 10-4-85
Source: Trainee. *Honours:* Eire Youth, Under-21.

2001–02	Manchester C	0	0		
2002–03	Manchester C	0	0		
2003–04	Manchester C	0	0		
2003–04	Rochdale	6	0	6	0
2004–05	Manchester C	9	1		
2005–06	Manchester C	5	0	14	1
2005–06	Coventry C	8	1	8	1
2006–07	Cardiff C	25	1		
2007–08	Cardiff C	0	0		
2007–08	Dundee U	36	1		
2008–09	Dundee U	20	0	56	1
2008–09	Cardiff C	0	0	25	1
2009–10	Celtic	6	0	6	0
2009–10	Middlesbrough	11	1	11	1

FRANKS, Jonathan (F)   24   3
H: 5 9 W: 11 03 b.Stockton 8-4-90
Source: Scholar. *Honours:* England Youth.

2007–08	Middlesbrough	0	0		
2008–09	Middlesbrough	1	0		
2009–10	Middlesbrough	23	3	24	3

GROUNDS, Jonathan (D)   43   3
H: 6 1 W: 13 10 b.Thornaby 2-2-88
Source: Scholar.

2007–08	Middlesbrough	5	0		
2008–09	Middlesbrough	2	0		
2008–09	Norwich C	16	3	16	3
2009–10	Middlesbrough	20	0	27	0

HINES, Seb (D)   8   0
H: 6 1 W: 12 02 b.Wetherby 29-5-88
Source: Scholar. *Honours:* England Youth.

2005–06	Middlesbrough	0	0		
2006–07	Middlesbrough	0	0		
2007–08	Middlesbrough	1	0		
2008–09	Middlesbrough	1	0		
2008–09	Derby Co	0	0		
2008–09	Oldham Ath	4	0	4	0
2009–10	Middlesbrough	2	0	4	0

HOYTE, Justin (D)   113   3
H: 5 11 W: 11 00 b.Waltham Forest 20-11-84
Source: Scholar. *Honours:* England Youth, Under-20, Under-21.

2002–03	Arsenal	1	0		
2003–04	Arsenal	1	0		
2004–05	Arsenal	5	0		
2005–06	Arsenal	0	0		
2005–06	Sunderland	27	1	27	1
2006–07	Arsenal	22	1		
2007–08	Arsenal	5	0	34	1
2008–09	Middlesbrough	22	0		
2009–10	Middlesbrough	30	1	52	1

JOHNSON, John (D)   41   5
H: 6 0 W: 12 00 b.Middlesbrough 16-9-88
Source: Scholar.

2007–08	Middlesbrough	0	0		
2008–09	Middlesbrough	1	0		
2008–09	Tranmere R	4	0	4	0
2009–10	Middlesbrough	0	0	1	0
2009–10	Northampton T	36	5	36	5

JONES, Brad (G)   93   0
H: 6 3 W: 12 01 b.Armadale 19-3-82
Source: Trainee. *Honours:* Australia Under-20, Under-23, 2 full caps.

1998–99	Middlesbrough	0	0		
1999–2000	Middlesbrough	0	0		
2000–01	Middlesbrough	0	0		
2001–02	Middlesbrough	0	0		
2002	Shelbourne	2	0	2	0

2002–03	Middlesbrough	0	0		
2002–03	Stockport Co	1	0	1	0
2003–04	Middlesbrough	1	0		
2003–04	Blackpool	5	0		
2003–04	Rotherham U	0	0		
2004–05	Middlesbrough	5	0		
2004–05	Blackpool	12	0	17	0
2005–06	Middlesbrough	9	0		
2006–07	Middlesbrough	2	0		
2006–07	Sheffield W	15	0	15	0
2007–08	Middlesbrough	1	0		
2008–09	Middlesbrough	16	0		
2009–10	Middlesbrough	24	0	58	0

KILLEN, Chris (F)   168   46
H: 6 1 W: 11 07 b.Wellington 8-10-81
Source: Miramar R. *Honours:* New Zealand Under-20, Under-23, 32 full caps, 11 goals.

1998–99	Manchester C	0	0		
1999–2000	Manchester C	0	0		
2000–01	Manchester C	0	0		
2000–01	Wrexham	12	3	12	3
2001–02	Port Vale	9	6	9	6
2001–02	Manchester C	3	0	3	0
2002–03	Oldham Ath	27	3		
2003–04	Oldham Ath	13	2		
2004–05	Oldham Ath	26	10		
2005–06	Oldham Ath	12	2	78	17
2005–06	Hibernian	7	3		
2006–07	Hibernian	18	13	25	16
2007–08	Celtic	20	1	20	1

On loan from Celtic.

2008–09	Norwich C	4	0		
2009–10	Norwich C	0	0	4	0
2009–10	Middlesbrough	17	3	17	3

LITA, Leroy (F)   232   69
H: 5 7 W: 11 12 b.DR Congo 28-12-84
Source: Scholar. *Honours:* England Under-21.

2002–03	Bristol C	15	2		
2003–04	Bristol C	26	5		
2004–05	Bristol C	44	24	85	31
2005–06	Reading	26	11		
2006–07	Reading	33	7		
2007–08	Reading	14	1		
2007–08	Charlton Ath	8	3	8	3
2008–09	Reading	10	1	83	20
2009–10	Norwich C	15	7	16	7
2009–10	Middlesbrough	40	8	40	8

McDONALD, Scott (F)   237   100
H: 5 7 W: 12 07 b.Dandenong 21-8-83
Honours: Australia Youth, Under-20, Under-23, 16 full caps.

1998–99	Eastern Pride	3	0	3	0
1999–2000	Southampton	0	0		
2000–01	Southampton	0	0		
2001–02	Southampton	2	0		
2002–03	Southampton	0	0	2	0
2002–03	Huddersfield T	13	1	13	1
2002–03	Bournemouth	7	1	7	1
2003–04	Wimbledon	2	0	2	0
2003–04	Motherwell	15	2		
2004–05	Motherwell	27	15		
2005–06	Motherwell	35	11		
2006–07	Motherwell	32	15	109	43
2007–08	Celtic	36	25		
2008–09	Celtic	34	16		
2009–10	Celtic	18	10	88	51
2009–10	Middlesbrough	13	4	13	4

McMAHON, Tony (D)   68   1
H: 5 10 W: 11 04 b.Bishop Auckland 24-3-86
Source: Scholar. *Honours:* England Youth.

2003–04	Middlesbrough	0	0		
2004–05	Middlesbrough	13	0		
2005–06	Middlesbrough	3	0		
2006–07	Middlesbrough	0	0		
2007–08	Middlesbrough	1	0		
2007–08	Blackpool	2	0	2	0
2008–09	Middlesbrough	13	0		
2008–09	Sheffield W	15	1	15	1
2009–10	Middlesbrough	21	0	51	0

McMANUS, Stephen (D)   166   18
H: 6 2 W: 13 00 b.Lanark 10-9-82
Honours: Scotland 22 full caps, 1 goal.

2003–04	Celtic	5	0		
2004–05	Celtic	2	0		
2005–06	Celtic	36	7		

On loan from Celtic.

Season	Club	Apps	Gls	Tot Apps	Tot Gls
2006–07	Celtic	31	2		
2007–08	Celtic	37	4		
2008–09	Celtic	31	4		
2009–10	Celtic	*8	0	150	17
2009–10	Middlesbrough	16	1	16	1

On loan from Celtic.

MIDO (F)   212 69
H: 6 2 W: 14 09 b.Cairo 23-2-83
Honours: Egypt 51 full caps, 19 goals.

Season	Club	Apps	Gls	Tot Apps	Tot Gls
1999–2000	Zamalek	4	3		
2000–01	Gent	21	11	21	11
2001–02	Ajax	24	12		
2002–03	Ajax	16	9	40	21
2002–03	Celta Vigo	8	4	8	4
2003–04	Marseille	22	7	22	7
2004–05	Roma	8	0	8	0
2004–05	Tottenham H	9	2		
2005–06	Tottenham H	27	11		
2006–07	Tottenham H	12	1	48	14
2007–08	Middlesbrough	12	2		
2008–09	Middlesbrough	13	4		
2008–09	Wigan Ath	12	2	12	2
2009–10	Zamalek	15	1	19	4
2009–10	Middlesbrough	0	0	25	6
2009–10	West Ham U	9	0	9	0

MILLER, Lee (F)   295 81
H: 6 0 W: 11 07 b.Lanark 18-5-83
Source: Form S.

Season	Club	Apps	Gls	Tot Apps	Tot Gls
2000–01	Falkirk	0	0		
2001–02	Falkirk	27	11		
2002–03	Falkirk	34	17	61	28
2003–04	Bristol C	42	8		
2004–05	Bristol C	7	0	49	8
2004–05	Hearts	18	8	18	8
2005–06	Dundee U	34	8		
2006–07	Dundee U	3	0	37	8
2006–07	Aberdeen	32	4		
2007–08	Aberdeen	36	12		
2008–09	Aberdeen	34	10		
2009–10	Aberdeen	18	3	120	29
2009–10	Middlesbrough	10	0	10	0

O'NEIL, Gary (M)   282 25
H: 5 10 W: 11 00 b.Bromley 18-5-83
Source: Scholar. *Honours:* England Youth, Under-20, Under-21.

Season	Club	Apps	Gls	Tot Apps	Tot Gls
1999–2000	Portsmouth	1	0		
2000–01	Portsmouth	10	1		
2001–02	Portsmouth	33	1		
2002–03	Portsmouth	31	3		
2003–04	Portsmouth	3	2		
2003–04	Walsall	7	0	7	0
2004–05	Portsmouth	24	2		
2004–05	Cardiff C	9	1	9	1
2005–06	Portsmouth	36	6		
2006–07	Portsmouth	35	1		
2007–08	Portsmouth	2	0	175	16
2007–08	Middlesbrough	26	0		
2008–09	Middlesbrough	29	4		
2009–10	Middlesbrough	36	4	91	8

POGATETZ, Emanuel (D)   246 6
H: 6 2 W: 13 05 b.Steinbock 16-1-83
Honours: Austria 37 full caps, 2 goals.

Season	Club	Apps	Gls	Tot Apps	Tot Gls
1999–2000	Sturm Graz	0	0		
2000–01	Karntern	33	0	33	0
2001–02	Leverkusen B	23	0		
2001–02	Leverkusen	0	0		
2002–03	Leverkusen B	3	0	26	0
2002–03	Leverkusen	0	0		
2002–03	Aarau	11	0	11	0
2003–04	Graz	31	1		
2004–05	Graz	22	1	53	2
2005–06	Middlesbrough	24	1		
2006–07	Middlesbrough	35	2		
2007–08	Middlesbrough	24	0		
2008–09	Middlesbrough	27	1		
2009–10	Middlesbrough	13	0	123	4

PORRITT, Nathan (F)   5 0
H: 5 9 W: 12 00 b.Middlesbrough 9-1-90
Source: Scholar.

Season	Club	Apps	Gls	Tot Apps	Tot Gls
2008–09	Middlesbrough	0	0		
2009–10	Middlesbrough	0	0		
2009–10	Darlington	5	0	5	0

RIGGOTT, Chris (D)   204 10
H: 6 2 W: 13 09 b.Derby 1-9-80
Source: Trainee. *Honours:* England Youth, Under-21.

Season	Club	Apps	Gls	Tot Apps	Tot Gls
1998–99	Derby Co	0	0		
1999–2000	Derby Co	1	0		
2000–01	Derby Co	31	3		
2001–02	Derby Co	37	0		
2002–03	Derby Co	22	2	91	5
2002–03	Middlesbrough	5	2		
2003–04	Middlesbrough	17	0		
2004–05	Middlesbrough	21	2		
2005–06	Middlesbrough	22	0		
2006–07	Middlesbrough	6	0		
2007–08	Middlesbrough	10	1		
2007–08	Stoke C	9	0	9	0
2008–09	Middlesbrough	17	0		
2009–10	Middlesbrough	6	0	104	5

ROBSON, Barry (M)   360 70
H: 5 11 W: 12 00 b.Inverurie 7-11-78
Honours: Scotland B, 8 full caps.

Season	Club	Apps	Gls	Tot Apps	Tot Gls
1997–98	Inverness CT	23	3		
1998–99	Inverness CT	16	0		
1999–2000	Inverness CT	4	0		
1999–2000	Forfar Ath	25	9	25	9
2000–01	Inverness CT	34	5		
2001–02	Inverness CT	24	2		
2002–03	Inverness CT	34	10	135	20
2003–04	Dundee U	28	3		
2004–05	Dundee U	36	6		
2005–06	Dundee U	31	1		
2006–07	Dundee U	29	11		
2007–08	Dundee U	21	11	145	32
2007–08	Celtic	15	2		
2008–09	Celtic	12	1		
2009–10	Celtic	10	1	37	4
2009–10	Middlesbrough	18	5	18	5

SMALLWOOD, Richard (M)   0 0
b.Redcar 29-12-90
Source: Scholar. *Honours:* England Youth.

Season	Club	Apps	Gls	Tot Apps	Tot Gls
2008–09	Middlesbrough	0	0		
2009–10	Middlesbrough	0	0		

STEELE, Jason (G)   13 0
H: 6 2 W: 12 07 b.Stockton 18-8-90
Source: Scholar. *Honours:* England Youth.

Season	Club	Apps	Gls	Tot Apps	Tot Gls
2007–08	Middlesbrough	0	0		
2008–09	Middlesbrough	0	0		
2009–10	Middlesbrough	0	0		
2009–10	Northampton T	13	0	13	0

TAYLOR, Andrew (D)   128 0
H: 5 10 W: 11 04 b.Hartlepool 1-8-86
Source: Trainee. *Honours:* England Youth, Under-20, Under-21.

Season	Club	Apps	Gls	Tot Apps	Tot Gls
2003–04	Middlesbrough	0	0		
2004–05	Middlesbrough	0	0		
2005–06	Middlesbrough	13	0		
2005–06	Bradford C	24	0	24	0
2006–07	Middlesbrough	34	0		
2007–08	Middlesbrough	19	0		
2008–09	Middlesbrough	26	0		
2009–10	Middlesbrough	12	0	104	0

WALKER, Josh (M)   40 3
H: 5 11 W: 11 13 b.Newcastle 21-2-89
Source: Scholar. *Honours:* England Schools, Youth, Under-20.

Season	Club	Apps	Gls	Tot Apps	Tot Gls
2005–06	Middlesbrough	1	0		
2006–07	Middlesbrough	0	0		
2006–07	Bournemouth	6	0	6	0
2007–08	Aberdeen	8	0	8	0
2007–08	Middlesbrough	0	0		
2008–09	Middlesbrough	6	0		
2009–10	Middlesbrough	1	0	8	0
2009–10	Northampton T	3	0	3	0
2009–10	Rotherham U	15	3	15	3

WHEATER, David (D)   139 9
H: 6 5 W: 12 12 b.Redcar 14-2-87
Source: Scholar. *Honours:* England Youth, Under-21.

Season	Club	Apps	Gls	Tot Apps	Tot Gls
2004–05	Middlesbrough	0	0		
2005–06	Middlesbrough	6	0		
2005–06	Doncaster R	7	1	7	1
2006–07	Middlesbrough	0	0		
2006–07	Wolverhampton W	1	0	1	0
2006–07	Darlington	15	2	15	2
2007–08	Middlesbrough	34	3		
2008–09	Middlesbrough	32	1		
2009–10	Middlesbrough	42	1	116	6

WILLIAMS, Rhys (D)   49 2
H: 6 2 W: 11 05 b.Perth 14-7-88
Source: Scholar. *Honours:* Wales Under-21. Australia 3 full caps.

Season	Club	Apps	Gls	Tot Apps	Tot Gls
2006–07	Middlesbrough	0	0		
2007–08	Middlesbrough	0	0		
2008–09	Middlesbrough	0	0		
2008–09	Burnley	17	0	17	0
2009–10	Middlesbrough	32	2	32	2

WILLIAMS, Luke (F)   4 0
H: 6 1 W: 11 08 b.Middlesbrough 11-6-93
Source: Scholar. *Honours:* England Youth.

Season	Club	Apps	Gls	Tot Apps	Tot Gls
2009–10	Middlesbrough	4	0	4	0

MILLWALL (53)

ABDOU, Nadjim (M)   216 8
H: 5 10 W: 11 02 b.Martigues 13-7-84

Season	Club	Apps	Gls	Tot Apps	Tot Gls
2002–03	Martigues	26	1	26	1
2003–04	Sedan	17	0		
2004–05	Sedan	32	2		
2005–06	Sedan	14	0		
2006–07	Sedan	17	0	80	2
2007–08	Plymouth Arg	31	1	31	1
2008–09	Millwall	36	3		
2009–10	Millwall	43	1	79	4

ALEXANDER, Gary (F)   407 117
H: 6 0 W: 13 04 b.Lambeth 15-8-79
Source: Trainee.

Season	Club	Apps	Gls	Tot Apps	Tot Gls
1998–99	West Ham U	0	0		
1999–2000	West Ham U	0	0		
1999–2000	Exeter C	37	16	37	16
2000–01	Swindon T	37	7	37	7
2001–02	Hull C	43	17		
2002–03	Hull C	25	6	68	23
2002–03	Leyton Orient	17	2		
2003–04	Leyton Orient	44	15		
2004–05	Leyton Orient	28	9		
2005–06	Leyton Orient	46	14		
2006–07	Leyton Orient	44	12	179	52
2007–08	Millwall	36	7		
2008–09	Millwall	35	11		
2009–10	Millwall	15	1	86	19

BARRON, Scott (D)   67 0
H: 5 9 W: 9 08 b.Preston 2-9-85
Source: Scholar.

Season	Club	Apps	Gls	Tot Apps	Tot Gls
2003–04	Ipswich T	0	0		
2004–05	Ipswich T	0	0		
2005–06	Ipswich T	15	0		
2006–07	Ipswich T	0	0	15	0
2006–07	Wrexham	3	0	3	0
2007–08	Millwall	12	0		
2008–09	Millwall	14	0		
2009–10	Millwall	23	0	49	0

BIGNOT, Marcus (D)   394 4
H: 5 7 W: 11 04 b.Birmingham 22-8-74
Source: Kidderminster H.

Season	Club	Apps	Gls	Tot Apps	Tot Gls
1997–98	Crewe Alex	42	0		
1998–99	Crewe Alex	26	0		
1999–2000	Crewe Alex	27	0	95	0
2000–01	Bristol R	26	1	26	1
2000–01	QPR	9	1		
2001–02	QPR	45	0		
2002–03	Rushden & D	33	0		
2003–04	Rushden & D	35	2	68	2
2003–04	QPR	6	0		
2004–05	QPR	43	0		
2005–06	QPR	44	0		
2006–07	QPR	33	0		
2007–08	QPR	2	0	182	1
2007–08	Millwall	22	0		
2008–09	Millwall	1	0		
2009–10	Millwall	0	0	23	0

BOLDER, Adam (M)   292 16
H: 5 9 W: 10 08 b.Hull 25-10-80
Source: Trainee.

Season	Club	Apps	Gls	Tot Apps	Tot Gls
1998–99	Hull C	1	0		
1999–2000	Hull C	19	0	20	0
1999–2000	Derby Co	0	0		
2000–01	Derby Co	2	0		
2001–02	Derby Co	11	0		
2002–03	Derby Co	45	6		
2003–04	Derby Co	24	1		

2004–05	Derby Co	36	2		
2005–06	Derby Co	35	2		
2006–07	Derby Co	13	0	**166**	**11**
2006–07	QPR	16	0		
2007–08	QPR	24	2		
2007–08	Sheffield W	13	2	**13**	**2**
2008–09	QPR	0	0	**40**	**2**
2008–09	Millwall	28	0		
2009–10	Millwall	11	0	**39**	**0**
2009–10	*Bradford C*	14	1	**14**	**1**

CRAIG, Tony (D)   **185**   **7**
H: 6 0 W: 10 03 b.Greenwich 20-4-85
Source: Scholar.

2002–03	Millwall	2	1		
2003–04	Millwall	9	0		
2004–05	Millwall	10	0		
2004–05	Wycombe W	14	0	**14**	**0**
2005–06	Millwall	28	0		
2006–07	Millwall	30	1		
2007–08	Crystal Palace	13	0	**13**	**0**
2007–08	*Millwall*	5	1		
2008–09	Millwall	44	2		
2009–10	Millwall	30	2	**158**	**7**

DUNNE, Alan (D)   **179**   **14**
H: 5 10 W: 10 13 b.Dublin 23-8-82
Source: Trainee.

1999–2000	Millwall	0	0		
2000–01	Millwall	0	0		
2001–02	Millwall	1	0		
2002–03	Millwall	4	0		
2003–04	Millwall	8	0		
2004–05	Millwall	19	3		
2005–06	Millwall	40	0		
2006–07	Millwall	32	6		
2007–08	Millwall	19	3		
2008–09	Millwall	24	0		
2009–10	Millwall	32	2	**179**	**14**

FORDE, David (G)   **115**   **0**
H: 6 3 W: 13 06 b.Galway 20-12-79
Source: Barry T.

2001–02	West Ham U	0	0		
2002–03	West Ham U	0	0		
2003–04	West Ham U	0	0		
2004–05	West Ham U	0	0		
2005–06	West Ham U	0	0		
2006–07	Cardiff C	7	0		
2007–08	Cardiff C	0	0	**7**	**0**
2007–08	*Luton T*	5	0	**5**	**0**
2007–08	*Bournemouth*	11	0	**11**	**0**
2008–09	Millwall	46	0		
2009–10	Millwall	46	0	**92**	**0**

FRAMPTON, Andrew (D)   **250**   **8**
H: 5 11 W: 10 10 b.Wimbledon 3-9-79
Source: Trainee.

1998–99	Crystal Palace	6	0		
1999–2000	Crystal Palace	9	0		
2000–01	Crystal Palace	10	0		
2001–02	Crystal Palace	2	0		
2002–03	Crystal Palace	1	0	**28**	**0**
2002–03	Brentford	15	0		
2003–04	Brentford	16	0		
2004–05	Brentford	35	0		
2005–06	Brentford	36	3		
2006–07	Brentford	32	1	**134**	**4**
2007–08	Millwall	30	1		
2008–09	Millwall	37	1		
2009–10	Millwall	21	2	**88**	**4**

FUSEINI, Ali (M)   **76**   **2**
H: 5 6 W: 9 10 b.Ghana 7-12-88
Source: Scholar.

2006–07	Millwall	7	0		
2007–08	Millwall	37	2		
2008–09	Millwall	17	0		
2009–10	Millwall	15	0	**76**	**2**

GRABBAN, Lewis (F)   **87**   **12**
H: 6 0 W: 11 03 b.Croydon 12-1-88
Source: Scholar.

2005–06	Crystal Palace	3	0		
2006–07	Crystal Palace	8	1		
2006–07	*Oldham Ath*	9	0	**9**	**0**
2007–08	Crystal Palace	2	0	**10**	**1**
2007–08	*Motherwell*	6	0	**6**	**0**
2007–08	Millwall	13	3		
2008–09	Millwall	31	6		
2009–10	Millwall	11	0	**55**	**9**
2009–10	*Brentford*	7	2	**7**	**2**

GRIMES, Ashley (M)   **25**   **2**
H: 6 0 W: 11 02 b.Swindon 9-12-86
Source: Scholar.

2006–07	Manchester C	0	0		
2006–07	*Swindon T*	4	0	**4**	**0**
2007–08	Manchester C	0	0		
2008–09	Millwall	17	2		
2009–10	Millwall	4	0	**21**	**2**

HACKETT, Chris (M)   **228**   **14**
H: 6 0 W: 12 08 b.Oxford 1-3-83
Source: Scholarship.

1999–2000	Oxford U	2	0		
2000–01	Oxford U	16	2		
2001–02	Oxford U	15	0		
2002–03	Oxford U	12	0		
2003–04	Oxford U	22	2		
2004–05	Oxford U	37	4		
2005–06	Oxford U	21	2	**125**	**9**
2005–06	*Hearts*	2	0	**2**	**0**
2006–07	Millwall	33	3		
2007–08	Millwall	6	0		
2008–09	Millwall	22	0		
2009–10	Millwall	40	2	**101**	**5**

HARRIS, Neil (F)   **420**   **130**
H: 5 10 W: 11 08 b.Orsett 12-7-77
Source: Cambridge C.

1997–98	Millwall	3	0		
1998–99	Millwall	39	15		
1999–2000	Millwall	38	25		
2000–01	Millwall	42	27		
2001–02	Millwall	21	4		
2002–03	Millwall	40	12		
2003–04	Millwall	38	9		
2004–05	Millwall	12	1		
2004–05	*Cardiff C*	3	1	**3**	**1**
2004–05	Nottingham F	13	0		
2005–06	Nottingham F	1	0		
2005–06	*Gillingham*	36	6	**36**	**6**
2006–07	Nottingham F	19	1	**33**	**1**
2006–07	Millwall	21	5		
2007–08	Millwall	27	3		
2008–09	Millwall	35	8		
2309–10	Millwall	32	13	**348**	**122**

HUGHES-MASON, Kiernon (F)   **1**   **0**
H: 5 8 W: 10 05 b.London 22-10-91
Source: Scholar.

2009–10	Millwall	1	0	**1**	**0**
2009–10	*Cheltenham T*	0	0		

LAIRD, Marc (M)   **88**   **7**
H: 6 1 W: 10 07 b.Edinburgh 23-1-86
Source: Trainee.

2003–04	Manchester C	0	0		
2004–05	Manchester C	0	0		
2005–06	Manchester C	0	0		
2006–07	Manchester C	0	0		
2006–07	*Northampton T*	6	0	**6**	**0**
2007–08	Manchester C	0	0		
2007–08	*Port Vale*	7	1	**7**	**1**
2007–08	Millwall	17	1		
2008–09	Millwall	38	5		
2009–10	Millwall	20	0	**75**	**6**

MARQUIS, John (M)   **1**   **0**
H: 6 1 W: 11 03 b.Millwall 16-5-92
Source: Scholar.

2009–10	Millwall	1	0	**1**	**0**

MARTIN, David J (M)   **100**   **10**
H: 5 9 W: 10 10 b.Erith 3-6-85
Source: Dartford.

2006–07	Crystal Palace	5	0		
2007–08	Crystal Palace	9	0	**14**	**0**
2007–08	Millwall	11	2		
2008–09	Millwall	44	4		
2009–10	Millwall	20	3	**75**	**9**
2009–10	*Derby Co*	11	1	**11**	**1**

MORISON, Steve (F)   **66**   **23**
H: 6 2 W: 13 07 b.Enfield 29-8-83
Source: Scholar.

2001–02	Northampton T	1	0		
2002–03	Northampton T	13	1		
2003–04	Northampton T	5	1		
2004–05	Northampton T	4	1	**23**	**3**

From Stevenage B.

2008–09	Millwall	1	0		
2009–10	Millwall	43	20	**43**	**20**

O'CONNOR, Patrick (M)   **0**   **0**
H: 6 1 W: 13 00 b.Croydon 5-9-90
Source: Scholar.

2008–09	Millwall	0	0		
2009–10	Millwall	0	0		

PRICE, Jason (M)   **415**   **68**
H: 6 2 W: 11 05 b.Pontypridd 12-4-77
Source: Aberaman Ath. *Honours:* Wales Under-21.

1995–96	Swansea C	0	0		
1996–97	Swansea C	2	0		
1997–98	Swansea C	34	3		
1998–99	Swansea C	28	4		
1999–2000	Swansea C	39	6		
2000–01	Swansea C	41	4	**144**	**17**
2001–02	Brentford	15	1	**15**	**1**
2001–02	Tranmere R	24	7		
2002–03	Tranmere R	25	4	**49**	**11**
2003–04	Hull C	33	9		
2004–05	Hull C	27	2		
2005–06	Hull C	12	1	**75**	**13**
2005–06	Doncaster R	11	4		
2006–07	Doncaster R	31	6		
2007–08	Doncaster R	29	7		
2008–09	Doncaster R	22	0	**93**	**17**
2008–09	*Millwall*	8	3		
2009–10	Millwall	15	1	**23**	**4**
2009–10	*Oldham Ath*	7	1	**7**	**1**
2009–10	*Carlisle U*	9	4	**9**	**4**

ROBINSON, Paul (D)   **210**   **12**
H: 6 1 W: 11 09 b.Barnet 7-1-82
Source: Scholar.

2000–01	Millwall	0	0		
2001–02	Millwall	0	0		
2002–03	Millwall	14	0		
2003–04	Millwall	9	0		
2004–05	Millwall	0	0		
2004–05	*Torquay U*	12	0	**12**	**0**
2005–06	Millwall	32	0		
2006–07	Millwall	38	3		
2007–08	Millwall	45	3		
2008–09	Millwall	26	2		
2009–10	Millwall	34	4	**198**	**12**

SCHOFIELD, Danny (M)   **327**   **51**
H: 5 10 W: 11 02 b.Doncaster 10-4-80
Source: Brodsworth.

1998–99	Huddersfield T	1	0		
1999–2000	Huddersfield T	2	0		
2000–01	Huddersfield T	1	0		
2001–02	Huddersfield T	40	8		
2002–03	Huddersfield T	30	2		
2003–04	Huddersfield T	40	8		
2004–05	Huddersfield T	33	5		
2005–06	Huddersfield T	41	9		
2006–07	Huddersfield T	35	5		
2007–08	Huddersfield T	25	2	**248**	**39**
2008–09	Yeovil T	34	4		
2009–10	Yeovil T	4	1	**43**	**5**
2009–10	Millwall	36	7	**36**	**7**

SMITH, Jack (D)   **194**   **11**
H: 5 11 W: 11 05 b.Hemel Hempstead 14-10-83
Source: Scholar.

2001–02	Watford	0	0		
2002–03	Watford	1	0		
2003–04	Watford	17	2		
2004–05	Watford	7	0	**25**	**2**
2005–06	Swindon T	38	0		
2006–07	Swindon T	41	3		
2007–08	Swindon T	21	1		
2008–09	Swindon T	38	5	**138**	**9**
2009–10	Millwall	31	0	**31**	**0**

SULLIVAN, John (G)   **13**   **0**
H: 5 10 W: 11 04 b.Brighton 8-3-88
Source: Scholar. *Honours:* England Youth.

2005–06	Brighton & HA	0	0		
2006–07	Brighton & HA	0	0		
2007–08	Brighton & HA	0	0		
2008–09	Brighton & HA	13	0	**13**	**0**
2009–10	Millwall	0	0		

WARD, Darren (D)   **365**   **13**
H: 6 3 W: 11 04 b.Kenton 13-9-78
Source: Trainee.

1995–96	Watford	1	0		
1996–97	Watford	7	0		

1997–98	Watford	0	0		
1998–99	Watford	1	0		
1999–2000	Watford	9	1		
1999–2000	QPR	14	0	14	0
2000–01	Watford	40	1		
2001–02	Watford	1	0		
2001–02	Millwall	14	0		
2002–03	Millwall	39	1		
2003–04	Millwall	46	3		
2004–05	Millwall	43	0		
2005–06	Crystal Palace	43	5		
2006–07	Crystal Palace	20	0	63	5
2007–08	Wolverhampton W	30	0		
2008–09	Wolverhampton W	1	0		
2008–09	*Watford*	9	1	68	3
2008–09	*Charlton Ath*	16	0	16	0
2009–10	Wolverhampton W	0	0	31	0
2009–10	Millwall	31	1	173	5

MILTON KEYNES D (54)

BALDOCK, Sam (F) 66 17
H:5 7　W:10 07　b.Bedford 15-3-89
Source: Scholar. *Honours:* England Under-20.

2005–06	Milton Keynes D	0	0		
2006–07	Milton Keynes D	1	0		
2007–08	Milton Keynes D	5	0		
2008–09	Milton Keynes D	40	12		
2009–10	Milton Keynes D	20	5	66	17

BALDOCK, George (M) 1 0
H:5 9　W:10 07　b.Buckingham 26-1-93
Source: Youth.

2009–10	Milton Keynes D	1	0	1	0

BRIDGES, Michael (F) 254 60
H:6 1　W:10 11　b.North Shields 5-8-78
Source: Trainee. *Honours:* England Schools, Youth, Under-21.

1995–96	Sunderland	15	4		
1996–97	Sunderland	25	3		
1997–98	Sunderland	9	1		
1998–99	Sunderland	30	8		
1999–2000	Leeds U	34	19		
2000–01	Leeds U	7	0		
2001–02	Leeds U	0	0		
2002–03	Leeds U	5	0		
2003–04	Leeds U	10	0	56	19
2003–04	*Newcastle U*	6	0	6	0
2004–05	Bolton W	0	0		
2004–05	Sunderland	19	1	98	0
2005–06	Bristol C	11	0	11	0
2005–06	Carlisle U	25	15		
2006–07	Carlisle U	5	0		
2006–07	Hull C	15	2		
2007–08	Hull C	7	0		
2008–09	Hull C	0	0	22	2
2008–09	*Carlisle U*	30	7	60	22
2009–10	Milton Keynes D	1	0	1	0

CARRINGTON, Mark (M) 49 6
H:6 0　W:11 00　b.Warrington 4-5-87
Source: Scholar.

2006–07	Crewe Alex	3	0		
2007–08	Crewe Alex	9	0		
2008–09	Crewe Alex	17	2	29	2
2009–10	Milton Keynes D	20	4	20	4

CHADWICK, Luke (M) 240 24
H:5 11　W:11 08　b.Cambridge 18-11-80
Source: Trainee. *Honours:* England Youth, Under-21.

1998–99	Manchester U	0	0		
1999–2000	Manchester U	0	0		
2000–01	Manchester U	16	2		
2001–02	Manchester U	8	0		
2002–03	Manchester U	1	0		
2002–03	*Reading*	15	1	15	1
2003–04	Manchester U	0	0	25	2
2003–04	*Burnley*	36	5	36	5
2004–05	West Ham U	32	1		
2005–06	West Ham U	0	0	32	1
2005–06	Stoke C	36	2		
2006–07	Stoke C	15	3	51	5
2007–08	Norwich C	4	1		
2007–08	Norwich C	13	1		
2008–09	Norwich C	0	0	17	2
2008–09	Milton Keynes D	24	6		
2009–10	Milton Keynes D	40	2	64	8

CHICKSEN, Adam (D) 7 0
H:5 8　W:11 09　b.Coventry 27-9-91
Source: Scholar.

2008–09	Milton Keynes D	1	0		
2009–10	Milton Keynes D	6	0	7	0

COLLINS, Charlie (F) 2 0
H:6 0　W:11 11　b.Hammersmith 22-11-91
Source: Scholar.

2009–10	Milton Keynes D	2	0	2	0

DAVIS, Sol (D) 326 3
H:5 7　W:12 04　b.Cheltenham 4-9-79
Source: Trainee.

1997–98	Swindon T	6	0		
1998–99	Swindon T	25	0		
1999–2000	Swindon T	29	0		
2000–01	Swindon T	36	0		
2001–02	Swindon T	21	0		
2002–03	Swindon T	0	0	117	0
2002–03	Luton T	34	0		
2003–04	Luton T	36	0		
2004–05	Luton T	45	2		
2005–06	Luton T	21	0		
2006–07	Luton T	24	0		
2007–08	Luton T	15	0		
2008–09	Luton T	24	1		
2009–10	Luton T	0	0	199	3
2009–10	Milton Keynes D	10	0	10	0

DOUMBE, Stephen (D) 212 7
H:6 1　W:12 05　b.Paris 28-10-79
Source: Paris St Germain. *Honours:* France Youth.

2001–02	Hibernian	0	0		
2002–03	Hibernian	12	0		
2003–04	Hibernian	33	2	45	2
2004–05	Plymouth Arg	26	2		
2005–06	Plymouth Arg	43	1		
2006–07	Plymouth Arg	29	0		
2007–08	Plymouth Arg	12	0		
2008–09	Plymouth Arg	24	1	134	4
2009–10	Milton Keynes D	33	1	33	1

EASTER, Jermaine (F) 235 65
H:5 9　W:12 02　b.Cardiff 15-1-82
Source: Trainee. *Honours:* Wales Youth, 8 full caps.

2000–01	Wolverhampton W	0	0		
2000–01	Hartlepool U	4	0		
2001–02	Hartlepool U	12	2		
2002–03	Hartlepool U	8	0		
2003–04	Hartlepool U	3	0	27	2
2003–04	*Cambridge U*	15	2		
2004–05	Cambridge U	24	6	39	8
2004–05	Boston U	9	3	9	3
2005–06	Stockport Co	19	8	19	8
2005–06	Wycombe W	15	2		
2006–07	Wycombe W	38	17		
2007–08	Wycombe W	6	2	59	21
2007–08	Plymouth Arg	32	6		
2008–09	Plymouth Arg	4	0	36	6
2008–09	*Millwall*	5	1	5	1
2008–09	*Colchester U*	5	2	5	2
2009–10	Milton Keynes D	36	14	36	14

FLANAGAN, Tom (D) 1 0
H:6 2　W:11 05　b.Hammersmith 21-10-91
Source: Scholar.

2009–10	Milton Keynes D	1	0	1	0

GLEESON, Stephen (M) 82 4
H:6 2　W:11 00　b.Dublin 3-8-88
Source: Scholar. *Honours:* Eire Youth, Under-21, 2 full caps.

2006–07	Wolverhampton W	3	0		
2006–07	*Stockport Co*	14	2		
2007–08	Wolverhampton W	0	0		
2007–08	*Hereford U*	4	0	4	0
2007–08	*Stockport Co*	6	0		
2008–09	Wolverhampton W	0	0	3	0
2008–09	*Stockport Co*	21	2	41	4
2008–09	*Milton Keynes D*	5	0		
2009–10	Milton Keynes D	29	0	34	0

GOBERN, Lewis (M) 61 4
H:5 10　W:11 07　b.Birmingham 28-1-85
Source: Scholar.

2003–04	Wolverhampton W	0	0		
2004–05	Wolverhampton W	0	0		
2004–05	*Hartlepool U*	1	0	1	0
2005–06	Wolverhampton W	1	0		

2005–06	*Blackpool*	8	1	8	1
2005–06	*Bury*	7	1	7	1
2006–07	Wolverhampton W	12	2		
2007–08	Wolverhampton W	0	0		
2008–09	Wolverhampton W	0	0	13	2
2008–09	*Colchester U*	12	0	12	0
2009–10	Milton Keynes D	20	0	20	0

GUERET, Willy (G) 279 0
H:6 1　W:13 02　b.Saint Claude 3-8-73
Source: Le Mans.

2000–01	Millwall	11	0		
2001–02	Millwall	1	0		
2002–03	Millwall	0	0		
2003–04	Millwall	2	0	14	0
2004–05	Swansea C	44	0		
2005–06	Swansea C	46	0		
2006–07	Swansea C	42	0	132	0
2007–08	Milton Keynes D	46	0		
2008–09	Milton Keynes D	44	0		
2009–10	Milton Keynes D	43	0	133	0

HOWELL, Luke (D) 53 1
H:5 10　W:10 05　b.Cuckfield 5-1-87
Source: Scholar.

2006–07	Gillingham	1	0	1	0
2007–08	Milton Keynes D	8	0		
2008–09	Milton Keynes D	15	1		
2009–10	Milton Keynes D	29	0	52	1

IBEHRE, Jabo (F) 282 52
H:6 2　W:13 13　b.Islington 28-1-83
Source: Trainee.

1999–2000	Leyton Orient	3	0		
2000–01	Leyton Orient	5	2		
2001–02	Leyton Orient	28	4		
2002–03	Leyton Orient	25	5		
2003–04	Leyton Orient	35	4		
2004–05	Leyton Orient	19	2		
2005–06	Leyton Orient	33	8		
2006–07	Leyton Orient	30	4		
2007–08	Leyton Orient	31	7	209	36
2008–09	Walsall	39	10	39	10
2009–10	Milton Keynes D	10	1	10	1
2009–10	*Southend U*	4	0	4	0
2009–10	*Stockport Co*	20	5	20	5

JOHNSON, Jemal (F) 148 20
H:5 8　W:11 09　b.New Jersey 3-5-84
Source: Scholar.

2001–02	Blackburn R	0	0		
2002–03	Blackburn R	0	0		
2003–04	Blackburn R	0	0		
2004–05	Blackburn R	3	0		
2005–06	Blackburn R	3	0		
2005–06	*Preston NE*	3	1	3	1
2005–06	*Darlington*	9	3	9	3
2006–07	Blackburn R	0	0	6	0
2006–07	Wolverhampton W	20	3		
2006–07	*Leeds U*	5	0	5	0
2007–08	Wolverhampton W	0	0	20	3
2007–08	Milton Keynes D	39	5		
2008–09	Milton Keynes D	33	5		
2009–10	Milton Keynes D	17	1	89	11
2009–10	*Stockport Co*	16	2	16	2

LEVEN, Peter (M) 178 25
H:5 11　W:12 13　b.Glasgow 27-9-83
Source: Rangers.

2004–05	Kilmarnock	32	4		
2005–06	Kilmarnock	6	0		
2006–07	Kilmarnock	27	1	65	5
2007–08	Chesterfield	42	6	42	6
2008–09	Milton Keynes D	40	10		
2009–10	Milton Keynes D	31	4	71	14

LEWINGTON, Dean (D) 288 8
H:5 11　W:11 07　b.Kingston 18-5-84
Source: Scholar.

2002–03	Wimbledon	1	0		
2003–04	Wimbledon	28	1	29	1
2004–05	Milton Keynes D	43	2		
2005–06	Milton Keynes D	44	1		
2006–07	Milton Keynes D	45	1		
2007–08	Milton Keynes D	45	0		
2008–09	Milton Keynes D	42	0		
2009–10	Milton Keynes D	42	1	259	7

McCRACKEN, David (D)   295 11
H: 6 2 W: 11 06 b.Glasgow 16-10-81
Source: Dundee U BC. *Honours:* Scotland Under-21.

1999–2000	Dundee U	2	0	
2000–01	Dundee U	9	1	
2001–02	Dundee U	19	0	
2002–03	Dundee U	25	1	
2003–04	Dundee U	32	1	
2004–05	Dundee U	24	2	
2005–06	Dundee U	34	2	
2006–07	Dundee U	33	1	178 8
2007–08	Wycombe W	37	1	
2008–09	Wycombe W	39	1	76 2
2009–10	Milton Keynes D	41	1	41 1

MORGAN, Dean (M)   257 31
H: 5 11 W: 11 06 b.Enfield 3-10-83
Source: Scholar.

2000–01	Colchester U	4	0	
2001–02	Colchester U	30	0	
2002–03	Colchester U	37	6	
2003–04	Colchester U	0	0	71 6
2003–04	Reading	13	1	
2004–05	Reading	18	2	31 3
2005–06	Luton T	36	6	
2006–07	Luton T	36	4	
2007–08	Luton T	16	1	
2007–08	Southend U	8	0	8 0
2007–08	Crewe Alex	9	1	9 1
2008–09	Luton T	0	0	
2008–09	Leyton Orient	32	5	32 5
2009–10	Luton T	0	0	88 11
2009–10	Milton Keynes D	9	1	9 1
2009–10	Aldershot T	9	4	9 4

O'HANLON, Sean (D)   224 20
H: 6 1 W: 12 05 b.Southport 2-1-83
Honours: England Schools, Youth, Under-20.

1999–2000	Everton	0	0	
2000–01	Everton	0	0	
2001–02	Everton	0	0	
2002–03	Everton	0	0	
2003–04	Everton	0	0	
2003–04	Swindon T	19	2	
2004–05	Swindon T	40	3	
2005–06	Swindon T	40	4	99 9
2006–07	Milton Keynes D	36	4	
2007–08	Milton Keynes D	43	4	
2008–09	Milton Keynes D	40	3	
2009–10	Milton Keynes D	6	0	125 11

POWELL, Daniel (F)   9 2
H: 5 11 W: 13 03 b.Luton 12-3-91
Source: Scholar.

2008–09	Milton Keynes D	7	1	
2009–10	Milton Keynes D	2	1	9 2

POWELL, Darren (D)   265 11
H: 6 2 W: 13 07 b.Hammersmith 10-3-76
Source: Hampton.

1998–99	Brentford	33	2	
1999–2000	Brentford	36	2	
2000–01	Brentford	18	1	
2001–02	Brentford	41	1	
2002–03	Crystal Palace	39	1	
2003–04	Crystal Palace	10	0	
2004–05	Crystal Palace	6	1	55 2
2004–05	West Ham U	5	1	5 1
2005–06	Southampton	25	1	
2006–07	Southampton	8	0	
2007–08	Southampton	10	1	
2008–09	Southampton	0	0	43 2
2008–09	Derby Co	6	0	6 0
2008–09	Brentford	4	0	
2009–10	Brentford	0	0	132 6
2009–10	Milton Keynes D	24	0	24 0

RAE, Alex (M)   585 114
H: 5 10 W: 11 09 b.Glasgow 30-9-69
Source: Bishopbriggs. *Honours:* Scotland Under-21, B.

1987–88	Falkirk	12	0	
1988–89	Falkirk	37	12	
1989–90	Falkirk	34	8	83 20
1990–91	Millwall	39	10	
1991–92	Millwall	38	11	
1992–93	Millwall	30	6	
1993–94	Millwall	36	13	
1994–95	Millwall	38	10	
1995–96	Millwall	37	13	218 63
1996–97	Sunderland	23	2	
1997–98	Sunderland	29	3	
1998–99	Sunderland	15	2	
1999–2000	Sunderland	26	3	
2000–01	Sunderland	18	2	
2001–02	Sunderland	3	0	114 12
2001–02	Wolverhampton W	36	7	
2002–03	Wolverhampton W	38	3	
2003–04	Wolverhampton W	33	5	107 15
2004–05	Rangers	25	1	
2005–06	Rangers	9	0	34 1
2006–07	Dundee	25	3	
2007–08	Dundee	1	0	
2008–09	Dundee	0	0	26 3
2009–10	Milton Keynes D	3	0	3 0

SEARLE, Stuart (G)   3 0
H: 6 3 W: 13 00 b.Wimbledon 27-2-79
Source: Basingstoke T.

2008–09	Watford	0	0	
2008–09	Milton Keynes D	3	0	3 0

STIRLING, Jude (D)   143 5
H: 6 2 W: 11 12 b.Enfield 29-6-82
Source: Trainee.

1999–2000	Luton T	0	0	
2000–01	Luton T	9	0	
2001–02	Luton T	1	0	10 0

From Tamworth.

2005–06	Oxford U	10	0	10 0

From Stevenage B, Hornchurch, Tamworth.

2005–06	Lincoln C	6	0	6 0
2005–07	Peterborough U	22	0	22 0
2006–07	Milton Keynes D	16	1	
2007–08	Milton Keynes D	34	2	
2008–09	Milton Keynes D	32	2	
2009–10	Milton Keynes D	9	0	91 5
2009–10	Grimsby T	4	0	4 0

WILBRAHAM, Aaron (F)   366 87
H: 6 3 W: 12 04 b.Knutsford 21-10-79
Source: Trainee.

1997–98	Stockport Co	7	1	
1998–99	Stockport Co	26	0	
1999–2000	Stockport Co	26	4	
2000–01	Stockport Co	36	12	
2001–02	Stockport Co	21	3	
2002–03	Stockport Co	15	7	
2003–04	Stockport Co	41	8	172 35
2004–05	Hull C	19	2	19 2
2004–05	Oldham Ath	2	2	4 2
2005–06	Milton Keynes D	31	4	
2005–06	Bradford C	5	1	5 1
2006–07	Milton Keynes D	32	7	
2007–08	Milton Keynes D	35	10	
2008–09	Milton Keynes D	33	16	
2009–10	Milton Keynes D	35	10	166 47

WOODARDS, Danny (M)   113 0
H: 5 11 W: 11 01 b.Forest Gate 7-10-83
Source: Trainee.

2003–04	Chelsea	0	0	
2004–05	Chelsea	0	0	
2005–06	Chelsea	0	0	

From Exeter C.

2006–07	Crewe Alex	11	0	
2007–08	Crewe Alex	36	0	
2008–09	Crewe Alex	37	0	84 0
2009–10	Milton Keynes D	29	0	29 0

MORECAMBE (55)

ADAMS, Danny (D)   353 2
H: 5 8 W: 13 08 b.Manchester 3-1-76
Source: Altrincham.

2000–01	Macclesfield T	37	0	
2001–02	Macclesfield T	39	0	
2002–03	Macclesfield T	45	1	
2003–04	Macclesfield T	27	0	148 1
2003–04	Stockport Co	12	0	
2004–05	Stockport Co	27	1	39 1
2004–05	Huddersfield T	5	0	
2005–06	Huddersfield T	40	0	
2006–07	Huddersfield T	23	0	68 0
2007–08	Morecambe	42	0	
2008–09	Morecambe	39	0	
2009–10	Morecambe	17	0	98 0

ARTELL, Dave (D)   300 26
H: 6 3 W: 14 01 b.Rotherham 22-11-80
Source: Trainee.

1999–2000	Rotherham U	1	0	
2000–01	Rotherham U	36	4	
2001–02	Rotherham U	0	0	
2002–03	Rotherham U	0	0	37 4
2002–03	Shrewsbury T	28	1	28 1
2003–04	Mansfield T	26	3	
2004–05	Mansfield T	19	2	45 5
2005–06	Chester C	37	2	
2006–07	Chester C	43	1	80 3
2007–08	Morecambe	36	3	
2008–09	Morecambe	37	3	
2009–10	Morecambe	37	7	110 13

BENTLEY, Jim (D)   116 12
H: 6 1 W: 13 00 b.Liverpool 11-6-76
Source: Trainee.

1993–94	Manchester C	0	0	
1994–95	Manchester C	0	0	
1995–96	Manchester C	0	0	
1996–97	Manchester C	0	0	
1997–98	Manchester C	0	0	
1998–99	Manchester C	0	0	
2007–08	Morecambe	43	6	
2008–09	Morecambe	45	3	
2009–10	Morecambe	28	3	116 12

CURTIS, Wayne (M)   103 11
H: 6 0 W: 12 00 b.Barrow 6-3-80
Source: Holker Old Boys.

2007–08	Morecambe	36	2	
2008–09	Morecambe	32	5	
2009–10	Morecambe	35	4	103 11

DAVIES, Scott (G)   11 0
H: 6 0 W: 11 00 b.Blackpool 27-2-87

2007–08	Morecambe	10	0	
2008–09	Morecambe	0	0	
2009–10	Morecambe	1	0	11 0

DRUMMOND, Stuart (M)   259 40
H: 6 2 W: 13 08 b.Preston 11-12-75
Source: Morecambe.

2004–05	Chester C	45	6	
2005–06	Chester C	42	6	87 12
2006–07	Shrewsbury T	44	4	
2007–08	Shrewsbury T	23	3	67 7
2007–08	Morecambe	18	2	
2008–09	Morecambe	44	10	
2009–10	Morecambe	43	9	105 21

DUFFY, Mark (M)   44 5
H: 5 9 W: 11 05 b.Liverpool 7-10-85
Source: Vauxhall M, Prescot C, Southport.

2008–09	Morecambe	9	1	
2009–10	Morecambe	35	4	44 5

HAINING, Will (D)   235 13
H: 6 0 W: 11 02 b.Glasgow 2-10-82
Source: Scholar.

2001–02	Oldham Ath	4	0	
2002–03	Oldham Ath	26	2	
2003–04	Oldham Ath	31	2	
2004–05	Oldham Ath	35	5	
2005–06	Oldham Ath	15	0	
2006–07	Oldham Ath	44	2	155 11
2007–08	St Mirren	29	1	
2008–09	St Mirren	19	0	48 1
2009–10	Morecambe	32	1	32 1

HUNTER, Garry (M)   98 4
H: 5 7 W: 10 03 b.Morecambe 1-1-85
Source: Scholar.

2007–08	Morecambe	38	1	
2008–09	Morecambe	29	1	
2009–10	Morecambe	31	2	98 4

McLACHLAN, Fraser (M)   111 4
H: 5 11 W: 12 07 b.Manchester 9-11-82
Source: Scholar.

2001–02	Stockport Co	11	1	
2002–03	Stockport Co	22	0	
2003–04	Stockport Co	20	3	
2004–05	Stockport Co	0	0	53 4
2004–05	Mansfield T	21	0	
2005–06	Mansfield T	8	0	29 0
2007–08	Morecambe	1	0	
2008–09	Morecambe	27	0	
2009–10	Morecambe	1	0	29 0

McSTAY, Henry (D) 48 1
H: 6 0　W: 11 11　b.Co Armagh 6-3-85
Source: Scholar. *Honours:* Eire Under-21.

2001–02	Leeds U	0	0	
2002–03	Leeds U	0	0	
2003–04	Leeds U	0	0	
2004–05	Leeds U	0	0	
2005–06	Leeds U	0	0	
2006–07	Leeds U	0	0	
2007–08	Antwerp	13	0	13 0
2007–08	Morecambe	13	0	
2008–09	Morecambe	20	1	
2009–10	Morecambe	2	0	35 1

MOSS, Darren (D) 274 15
H: 5 10　W: 11 00　b.Wrexham 24-5-81
Source: Trainee. *Honours:* Wales Youth, Under-21.

1998–99	Chester C	7	0	
1999–2000	Chester C	35	0	
2000–01	Chester C	0	0	42 0
2001–02	Shrewsbury T	31	2	
2002–03	Shrewsbury T	40	2	
2003–04	Shrewsbury T	0	0	
2004–05	Shrewsbury T	26	6	
2004–05	Crewe Alex	6	0	
2005–06	Crewe Alex	31	0	
2006–07	Crewe Alex	22	2	59 2
2007–08	Shrewsbury T	31	2	
2008–09	Shrewsbury T	29	0	157 12
2009–10	Morecambe	16	1	16 1

MULLIN, Paul (F) 173 45
H: 6 0　W: 12 01　b.Bury 16-3-74
Source: Clitheroe, Darwen, Radcliffe Borough.

2006–07	Accrington S	46	14	
2007–08	Accrington S	43	12	
2008–09	Accrington S	36	7 '	
2008–09	*Bradford C*	6	0	6 0
2009–10	Accrington S	4	0	129 33
2009–10	Morecambe	38	12	38 12

PANTHER, Manny (F) 82 5
H: 6 0　W: 13 07　b.Glasgow 11-5-84

2001–02	St Johnstone	7	0	
2002–03	St Johnstone	4	0	11 0
2003–04	Partick T	8	0	
2004–05	Partick T	14	2	22 2
2004–05	Brechin C	8	1	8 1
From York C.				
2008–09	Exeter C	22	2	
2009–10	Exeter C	0	0	22 2
2009–10	Morecambe	19	0	19 0

PARRISH, Andy (D) 91 1
H: 6 0　W: 11 00　b.Bolton 22-6-88
Source: Scholar.

2005–06	Bury	8	0	
2006–07	Bury	9	0	
2007–08	Bury	26	1	43 1
2008–09	Morecambe	13	0	
2009–10	Morecambe	35	0	48 0

POOLE, Matty (M) 0 0
H: 5 11　W: 12 06　b.Lancaster 22-10-90
Source: Scholar.

2009–10	Morecambe	0	0	

ROCHE, Barry (G) 227 0
H: 6 5　W: 14 08　b.Dublin 6-4-82
Source: Trainee.

1999–2000	Nottingham F	0	0	
2000–01	Nottingham F	2	0	
2001–02	Nottingham F	0	0	
2002–03	Nottingham F	1	0	
2003–04	Nottingham F	8	0	
2004–05	Nottingham F	2	0	13 0
2005–06	Chesterfield	41	0	
2006–07	Chesterfield	40	0	
2007–08	Chesterfield	45	0	126 0
2008–09	Morecambe	46	0	
2009–10	Morecambe	42	0	88 0

STANLEY, Craig (M) 105 11
H: 5 8　W: 10 08　b.Bedworth 3-3-83
Source: Scholar.

2002–03	Walsall	0	0
2003–04	Walsall	0	0
2004–05	Walsall	0	0
2005–06	Walsall	0	0
2006–07	Walsall	0	0

2007–08	Morecambe	41	2	
2008–09	Morecambe	24	5	
2009–10	Morecambe	40	4	105 11

TAYLOR, Aaron (F) 20 2
H: 5 8　W: 11 11　b.Morecambe 9-3-90

2008–09	Morecambe	17	2	
2009–10	Morecambe	3	0	20 2

TWISS, Michael (M) 120 13
H: 5 11　W: 13 03　b.Salford 28-12-77
Source: Trainee.

1996–97	Manchester U	0	0	
1997–98	Manchester U	0	0	
1998–99	*Sheffield U*	12	1	12 1
1999–2000	Manchester U	0	0	
2000–01	Port Vale	18	2	
2001–02	Port Vale	0	0	18 2
2007–08	Morecambe	36	6	
2008–09	Morecambe	28	3	
2009–10	Morecambe	26	1	90 10

WAINWRIGHT, Neil (M) 341 32
H: 6 0　W: 12 00　b.Warrington 4-11-77
Source: Trainee.

1996–97	Wrexham	0	0	
1997–98	Wrexham	11	3	11 3
1998–99	Sunderland	2	0	
1999–2000	Sunderland	0	0	
1999–2000	*Darlington*	17	4	
2000–01	Sunderland	0	0	
2000–01	*Halifax T*	13	0	13 0
2001–02	Sunderland	0	0	2 0
2001–02	Darlington	35	4	
2002–03	Darlington	33	1	
2003–04	Darlington	35	7	
2004–05	Darlington	38	4	
2005–06	Darlington	39	3	
2006–07	Darlington	41	5	
2007–08	Darlington	14	0	252 28
2007–08	*Shrewsbury T*	3	0	3 0
2007–08	*Mansfield T*	5	0	5 0
2008–09	Morecambe	38	1	
2009–10	Morecambe	17	0	55 1

WILSON, Laurence (M) 171 8
H: 5 10　W: 10 09　b.Huyton 10-10-86
Source: Scholar. *Honours:* England Youth.

2004–05	Everton	0	0	
2005–06	Everton	0	0	
2005–06	*Mansfield T*	15	1	15 1
2006–07	Chester C	41	1	
2007–08	Chester C	40	2	
2008–09	Chester C	34	1	115 4
2009–10	Morecambe	41	3	41 3

NEWCASTLE U (56)

ADJEI, Samuel (M) 0 0
H: 6 1　W: 12 00　b.Ghana 18-1-92
Source: Jonkoping.

2008–09	Newcastle U	0	0	
2009–10	Newcastle U	0	0	

AIREY, Philip (F) 0 0
b.Newcastle 14-11-91
Source: Scholar.

2009–10	Newcastle U	0	0

AMEOBI, Shola (F) 214 42
H: 6 3　W: 11 13　b.Zaria 12-10-81
Source: Trainee. *Honours:* England Under-21.

1998–99	Newcastle U	0	0	
1999–2000	Newcastle U	0	0	
2000–01	Newcastle U	20	2	
2001–02	Newcastle U	15	0	
2002–03	Newcastle U	28	5	
2003–04	Newcastle U	26	7	
2004–05	Newcastle U	31	2	
2005–06	Newcastle U	30	9	
2006–07	Newcastle U	12	3	
2007–08	Newcastle U	6	0	
2007–08	*Stoke C*	6	0	6 0
2008–09	Newcastle U	22	4	
2009–10	Newcastle U	18	10	208 42

BARTON, Joey (M) 177 18
H: 5 11　W: 12 05　b.Huyton 2-9-82
Source: Scholar. *Honours:* England Under-21, 1 full cap.

2001–02	Manchester C	0	0	
2002–03	Manchester C	7	1	
2003–04	Manchester C	28	1	
2004–05	Manchester C	31	1	
2005–06	Manchester C	31	6	
2006–07	Manchester C	33	6	130 15
2007–08	Newcastle U	23	1	
2008–09	Newcastle U	9	1	
2009–10	Newcastle U	15	1	47 3

BEST, Leon (F) 168 38
H: 6 1　W: 13 03　b.Nottingham 19-9-85
Source: Scholar. *Honours:* Eire Youth, Under-21, 7 full caps.

2004–05	Southampton	3	0	
2004–05	*QPR*	5	0	5 0
2005–06	Southampton	3	0	
2005–06	*Sheffield W*	13	2	13 2
2006–07	Southampton	9	4	15 4
2006–07	*Bournemouth*	15	3	15 3
2006–07	*Yeovil T*	15	10	15 10
2007–08	Coventry C	34	8	
2008–09	Coventry C	31	2	
2009–10	Coventry C	27	9	92 19
2009–10	Newcastle U	13	0	13 0

BUTT, Nicky (M) 428 29
H: 5 10　W: 11 05　b.Manchester 21-1-75
Source: Trainee. *Honours:* England Schools, Youth, Under-21, 39 full caps.

1992–93	Manchester U	1	0	
1993–94	Manchester U	1	0	
1994–95	Manchester U	22	1	
1995–96	Manchester U	32	2	
1996–97	Manchester U	26	5	
1997–98	Manchester U	33	3	
1998–99	Manchester U	31	2	
1999–2000	Manchester U	32	3	
2000–01	Manchester U	28	3	
2001–02	Manchester U	25	1	
2002–03	Manchester U	18	0	
2003–04	Manchester U	21	1	270 21
2004–05	Newcastle U	18	1	
2005–06	*Birmingham C*	24	3	24 3
2006–07	Newcastle U	31	1	
2007–08	Newcastle U	35	3	
2008–09	Newcastle U	33	0	
2009–10	Newcastle U	17	0	134 5

CARROLL, Andy (F) 72 21
H: 6 4　W: 11 00　b.Gateshead 6-1-89
Source: Scholar. *Honours:* England Youth, Under-21.

2006–07	Newcastle U	4	0	
2007–08	Newcastle U	4	0	
2007–08	*Preston NE*	11	1	11 1
2008–09	Newcastle U	14	3	
2009–10	Newcastle U	39	17	61 20

COLOCCINI, Fabricio (D) 289 18
H: 6 0　W: 12 04　b.Cordoba 22-1-82
Honours: Argentina 33 full caps, 1 goal.

1998–99	Boca Juniors	0	0	
1999–2000	Boca Juniors	1	0	2 1
1999–2000	AC Milan	0	0	
2000–01	AC Milan	0	0	
2000–01	San Lorenzo	19	3	19 3
2001–02	Alaves	33	6	33 6
2002–03	Atletico Madrid	27	0	27 0
2003–04	Villarreal	31	1	31 1
2004–05	AC Milan	1	0	1 0
2004–05	La Coruna	15	1	
2005–06	La Coruna	26	0	
2006–07	La Coruna	26	0	
2007–08	La Coruna	38	4	105 5
2008–09	Newcastle U	34	0	
2009–10	Newcastle U	37	2	71 2

DONALDSON, Ryan (F) 2 0
H: 5 9　W: 11 00　b.Newcastle 1-5-91
Source: Scholar. *Honours:* England Youth.

2008–09	Newcastle U	0	0	
2009–10	Newcastle U	2	0	2 0

EDMUNDSSON, Joan (F)   49   10
b.Faeroes 26-7-91
Honours: Faeroes Under-21, 2 full caps.

2008	B68	24	4	
2009	B68	25	6	49 10
2009–10	Newcastle U	0	0	

FERGUSON, Shane (D)   0   0
H: 5 9   W: 10 01   b.Derry 12-7-91
Source: Scholar. *Honours:* Northern Ireland
Under-21, B, 1 full cap.

2008–09	Newcastle U	0	0
2009–10	Newcastle U	0	0

FORSTER, Fraser (G)   48   0
H: 6 0   W: 12 00   b.Hexham 17-3-88
Source: Scholar.

2007–08	Newcastle U	0	0	
2008–09	Newcastle U	0	0	
2008–09	Stockport Co	6	0	6 0
2009–10	Newcastle U	0	0	
2009–10	Bristol R	4	0	4 0
2009–10	Norwich C	38	0	38 0

GEREMI (M)   262   21
H: 5 9   W: 11 01   b.Bafoussam 20-12-78
Source: Racing Bafoussam. *Honours:*
Cameroon 116 full caps, 13 goals.

1997	Cerro Porteno	6	0	6 0
1997–98	Genclerbirligi	28	4	
1998–99	Genclerbirligi	29	5	57 9
1999–2000	Real Madrid	20	0	
2000–01	Real Madrid	16	0	
2001–02	Real Madrid	9	0	45 0
2002–03	Middlesbrough	33	7	33 7
2003–04	Chelsea	25	1	
2004–05	Chelsea	13	0	
2005–06	Chelsea	15	2	
2006–07	Chelsea	19	1	72 4
2007–08	Newcastle U	27	1	
2008–09	Newcastle U	15	0	
2009–10	Newcastle U	7	0	49 1

GODSMARK, Jonny (M)   8   1
H: 5 6   W: 10 01   b.Guide Post 3-9-89
Source: Scholar.

2008–09	Newcastle U	0	0	
2009–10	Newcastle U	0	0	
2009–10	Hereford U	8	1	8 1

GUTHRIE, Danny (M)   100   6
H: 5 9   W: 11 06   b.Shrewsbury 18-4-87
Source: Scholar. *Honours:* England Schools,
Youth.

2004–05	Liverpool	0	0	
2005–06	Liverpool	0	0	
2006–07	Liverpool	3	0	
2006–07	Southampton	10	0	10 0
2007–08	Liverpool	0	0	3 0
2007–08	Bolton W	25	0	25 0
2008–09	Newcastle U	24	2	
2009–10	Newcastle U	38	4	62 6

GUTIERREZ, Jonas (M)   261   10
H: 6 0   W: 11 07   b.Buenos Aires 5-7-82
Honours: Argentina 19 full caps, 1 goal.

2001–02	Velez Sarsfield	17	0	
2002–03	Velez Sarsfield	21	1	
2003–04	Velez Sarsfield	27	0	
2004–05	Velez Sarsfield	33	0	98 1
2005–06	Mallorca	30	2	
2006–07	Mallorca	36	3	
2007–08	Mallorca	30	0	96 5
2008–09	Newcastle U	30	0	
2009–10	Newcastle U	37	4	67 4

HARPER, Steve (G)   173   0
H: 6 2   W: 13 10   b.Easington 14-3-75
Source: Seaham Red Star.

1993–94	Newcastle U	0	0	
1994–95	Newcastle U	0	0	
1995–96	Newcastle U	0	0	
1995–96	Bradford C	1	0	1 0
1996–97	Newcastle U	0	0	
1996–97	Stockport Co	0	0	
1997–98	Newcastle U	0	0	
1997–98	Hartlepool U	15	0	15 0
1997–98	Huddersfield T	24	0	24 0
1998–99	Newcastle U	8	0	
1999–2000	Newcastle U	18	0	
2000–01	Newcastle U	5	0	
2001–02	Newcastle U	0	0	

2002–03	Newcastle U	0	0
2003–04	Newcastle U	0	0
2004–05	Newcastle U	2	0
2005–06	Newcastle U	0	0
2006–07	Newcastle U	18	0
2007–08	Newcastle U	21	0
2008–09	Newcastle U	16	0
2009–10	Newcastle U	45	0	133	0

INMAN, Bradden (M)   0   0
H: 5 9   W: 11 03   b.Adelaide 10-12-91
Source: Scholar. *Honours:* Scotland Youth.

2009–10	Newcastle U	0	0

JOSE ENRIQUE (D)   139   2
H: 6 0   W: 12 00   b.Valencia 23-1-86
Honours: Spain Under-21.

2004–05	Levante	19	1	19 1
2005–06	Valencia	0	0	
2005–06	Celta Vigo	14	0	14 0
2006–07	Villarreal	23	0	23 0
2007–08	Newcastle U	23	0	
2008–09	Newcastle U	26	0	
2009–10	Newcastle U	34	1	83 1

KADAR, Tamas (D)   13   0
H: 6 0   W: 12 10   b.Veszprem 14-3-90

2007–08	Newcastle U	0	0	
2009–10	Newcastle U	13	0	13 0

KRUL, Tim (G)   34   0
H: 6 2   W: 11 08   b.Den Haag 3-4-88
Source: Academy. *Honours:* Holland Youth,
Under-21.

2005–06	Newcastle U	0	0	
2006–07	Newcastle U	0	0	
2007–08	Falkirk	22	0	22 0
2007–08	Newcastle U	0	0	
2008–09	Newcastle U	0	0	
2008–09	Carlisle U	9	0	9 0
2009–10	Newcastle U	3	0	3 0

LOVENKRANDS, Peter (F)   249   67
H: 5 11   W 11 02   b.Copenhagen 29-1-80
Honours: Denmark Youth, 21 full caps, 1
goal.

1998–99	AB Copenhagen	18	2	
1999–2000	AB Copenhagen	14	5	32 7
2000–01	Rangers	18	2	
2001–02	Rangers	18	2	
2002–03	Rangers	28	9	
2003–04	Rangers	25	8	
2004–05	Rangers	17	3	
2005–06	Rangers	33	14	129 36
2006–07	Schalke	24	6	
2007–08	Schalke	20	0	44 6
2008–09	Schalke	3	2	3 2
2008–09	Newcastle U	12	3	
2009–10	Newcastle U	29	13	41 16

LUALUA, Kazenga (F)   21   0
H: 5 11   W: 12 00   b.Kinshasa 10-12-90
Source: Scholar.

2007–08	Newcastle U	2	0	
2008–09	Newcastle U	3	0	
2008–09	Doncaster R	4	0	4 0
2009–10	Newcastle U	1	0	6 0
2009–10	Brighton & HA	11	0	11 0

McLAUGHLIN, Patrick (M)   0   0
H: 5 11   W: 12 01   b.Larne 14-1-91
Honours: Northern Ireland Under-21.

2007–08	Newcastle U	0	0
2008–09	Newcastle U	0	0
2009–10	Newcastle U	0	0

NOLAN, Kevin (M)   351   57
H: 6 0   W: 14 00   b.Liverpool 24-6-82
Source: Scholar. *Honours:* England Youth,
Under-20, Under-21.

1999–2000	Bolton W	4	0	
2000–01	Bolton W	31	1	
2001–02	Bolton W	35	8	
2002–03	Bolton W	33	1	
2003–04	Bolton W	37	9	
2004–05	Bolton W	36	4	
2005–06	Bolton W	36	9	
2006–07	Bolton W	31	3	
2007–08	Bolton W	33	5	
2008–09	Bolton W	20	0	296 40
2008–09	Newcastle U	11	0	
2009–10	Newcastle U	44	17	55 17

PANCRATE, Fabrice (F)   208   21
H: 6 1   W: 11 09   b.Paris 2-5-80

1999–2000	Louhans-Cuiseaux	2	0	2 0
2000–01	Guingamp	3	0	
2001–02	Guingamp	3	0	6 0
2002–03	Le Mans	28	3	
2003–04	Le Mans	36	5	
2004–05	Le Mans	0	0	64 8
2004–05	Paris St Germain	29	5	
2005–06	Paris St Germain	29	3	
2006–07	Paris St Germain	15	1	
2006–07	Betis	7	1	7 1
2007–08	Paris St Germain	0	0	
2007–08	Sochaux	18	1	18 1
2008–09	Paris St Germain	22	1	95 10
2009–10	Newcastle U	16	1	16 1

RANGER, Nile (F)   25   2
H: 6 2   W: 13 03   b.London 11-4-91
Source: Southampton Scholar. *Honours:*
England Youth.

2008–09	Newcastle U	0	0	
2009–10	Newcastle U	25	2	25 2

ROUTLEDGE, Wayne (M)   224   18
H: 5 6   W: 11 02   b.Sidcup 7-1-85
Source: Scholar. *Honours:* England Youth,
Under-20, Under-21.

2001–02	Crystal Palace	2	0	
2002–03	Crystal Palace	26	4	
2003–04	Crystal Palace	44	6	
2004–05	Crystal Palace	38	0	110 10
2005–06	Tottenham H	3	0	
2005–06	Portsmouth	13	0	13 0
2006–07	Tottenham H	0	0	
2006–07	Fulham	24	0	24 0
2007–08	Tottenham H	2	0	5 0
2007–08	Aston Villa	1	0	
2008–09	Aston Villa	1	0	2 0
2008–09	Cardiff C	9	2	9 2
2008–09	QPR	19	1	
2009–10	QPR	25	2	44 3
2009–10	Newcastle U	17	3	17 3

SIMPSON, Danny (D)   76   1
H: 5 9   W: 11 05   b.Eccles 4-1-87
Source: Scholar.

2005–06	Manchester U	0	0	
2006–07	Manchester U	0	0	
2006–07	Sunderland	14	0	14 0
2007–08	Manchester U	3	0	
2007–08	Ipswich T	8	0	8 0
2008–09	Manchester U	0	0	
2008–09	Blackburn R	12	0	12 0
2009–10	Manchester U	0	0	3 0
2009–10	Newcastle U	39	1	39 1

SMITH, Alan (F)   304   45
H: 5 10   W: 12 04   b.Rothwell 28-10-80
Source: Trainee. *Honours:* England Youth,
Under-21, B, 19 full caps, 1 goal.

1997–98	Leeds U	0	0	
1998–99	Leeds U	22	7	
1999–2000	Leeds U	26	4	
2000–01	Leeds U	33	11	
2001–02	Leeds U	23	4	
2002–03	Leeds U	33	3*	
2003–04	Leeds U	35	9	172 38
2004–05	Manchester U	31	6	
2005–06	Manchester U	21	1	
2006–07	Manchester U	9	0	61 7
2007–08	Newcastle U	33	0	
2008–09	Newcastle U	6	0	
2009–10	Newcastle U	32	0	71 0

SODERBERG, Ole (G)   0   0
H: 6 4   W: 14 07   b.Norrkoping 20-7-90
Source: BK Hacken.

2007–08	Newcastle U	0	0
2008–09	Newcastle U	0	0
2009–10	Newcastle U	0	0

TAVERNIER, James (D)   0   0
H: 5 9   W: 11 00   b.Bradford 31-10-91
Source: Scholar.

2009–10	Newcastle U	0	0

TAYLOR, Ryan (M)   195   24
H: 5 8   W: 10 04   b.Liverpool 19-8-84
Source: Scholar. *Honours:* England Youth,
Under-21.

2001–02	Tranmere R	0	0

2002–03 Tranmere R 25 1
2003–04 Tranmere R 30 5
2004–05 Tranmere R 43 8 98 14
2005–06 Wigan Ath 11 0
2006–07 Wigan Ath 16 1
2007–08 Wigan Ath 17 3
2008–09 Wigan Ath 12 2 56 6
2008–09 Newcastle U 10 0
2009–10 Newcastle U 31 4 41 4

TAYLOR, Steven (D) 138 8
H: 6 2 W: 13 01 b.Greenwich 23-1-86
Source: Trainee. *Honours:* FA Schools, Youth, England Under-20, Under-21, B.
2002–03 Newcastle U 0 0
2003–04 Newcastle U 1 0
2003–04 *Wycombe W* 6 0 6 0
2004–05 Newcastle U 13 0
2005–06 Newcastle U 12 0
2006–07 Newcastle U 27 2
2007–08 Newcastle U 31 1
2008–09 Newcastle U 27 4
2009–10 Newcastle U 21 1 132 8

TOZER, Ben (D) 3 0
H: 6 1 W: 12 11 b.Plymouth 1-3-90
Source: Scholar.
2007–08 *Swindon T* 2 0 2 0
2007–08 Newcastle U 0 0
2008–09 Newcastle U 0 0
2009–10 Newcastle U 1 0 1 0

VUCKIC, Haris (F) 7 0
H: 6 2 W: 12 02 b.Ljubljana 21-8-92
Source: Scholar. *Honours:* Slovenia Youth.
2007–08 Domzale 1 0
2008–09 Domzale 4 0 5 0
2009–10 Newcastle U 2 0 2 0

WILLIAMSON, Mike (D) 194 13
H: 6 4 W: 13 03 b.Stoke 8-11-83
Source: Trainee.
2001–02 Torquay U 3 0
2001–02 Southampton 0 0
2002–03 Southampton 0 0
2003–04 Southampton 0 0
2003–04 *Torquay U* 11 0 14 0
2003–04 *Doncaster R* 0 0
2004–05 Southampton 0 0
2004–05 Wycombe W 37 2
2005–06 Wycombe W 39 5
2006–07 Wycombe W 33 1
2007–08 Wycombe W 12 0
2008–09 Wycombe W 22 3 143 11
2008–09 Watford 17 1
2009–10 Watford 4 1 21 2
2009–10 Portsmouth 0 0
2009–10 Newcastle U 16 0 16 0

XISCO (F) 78 26
H: 6 0 W: 13 03 b.Palma 26-6-86
2004–05 La Coruna 7 2
2005–06 La Coruna 12 1
2006–07 *Vecindario* 27 13 27 13
2007–08 La Coruna 25 9 44 12
2008–09 Newcastle U 5 1
2009–10 Newcastle U 2 0 7 1

ZAMBLERA, Fabio (F) 0 0
H: 6 3 W: 14 09 b.Atalanta 7-4-90
Source: Atalanta. *Honours:* Italy Youth.
2007–08 Newcastle U 0 0
2008–09 Newcastle U 0 0
2009–10 Newcastle U 0 0

NORTHAMPTON T (57)

AKINFENWA, Adebayo (F) 227 74
H: 5 11 W: 13 07 b.Nigeria 10-5-82
2001 Atlanta 19 4
2002 Atlanta 4 1 23 5
From Barry T
2003–04 Boston U 3 0 3 0
2003–04 Leyton Orient 1 0 1 0
2003–04 Rushden & D 0 0
2003–04 Doncaster R 9 4 9 4
2004–05 Torquay U 37 14 37 14
2005–06 Swansea C 34 9
2006–07 Swansea C 25 5
2007–08 Swansea C 0 0 59 14

2007–08 Millwall 7 0 7 0
2007–08 Northampton T 15 7
2008–09 Northampton T 33 13
2009–10 Northampton T 40 17 88 37

BECKWITH, Dean (D) 134 3
H: 6 3 W: 13 04 b.Southwark 18-9-83
Source: Scholar.
2003–04 Gillingham 0 0
2004–05 Gillingham 1 0 1 0
2006–07 Hereford U 32 0
2007–08 Hereford U 38 2
2008–09 Hereford U 25 1 95 3
2009–10 Northampton T 38 0 38 0

BENJAMIN, Joe (F) 7 0
H: 5 11 W: 11 05 b.Woodford 8-10-90
Source: Scholar.
2008–09 Northampton T 4 0
2009–10 Northampton T 3 0 7 0

BROWN, Simon (G) 242 0
H: 6 2 W: 15 00 b.Chelmsford 3-12-76
Source: Trainee.
1995–96 Tottenham H 0 0
1996–97 Tottenham H 0 0
1997–98 Tottenham H 0 0
1997–98 *Lincoln C* 1 0 1 0
1998–99 Tottenham H 0 0
1998–99 *Fulham* 0 0
1999–2000 Colchester U 38 0
2000–01 Colchester U 18 0
2001–02 Colchester U 19 0
2002–03 Colchester U 27 0
2003–04 Colchester U 40 0 142 0
2004–05 Hibernian 36 0
2005–06 Hibernian 8 0
2006–07 Hibernian 4 0 48 0
2007–08 Brentford 26 0
2008–09 Brentford 1 0
2008–09 *Darlington* 22 0 22 0
2009–10 Brentford 0 0 27 0
2009–10 Northampton T 2 0 2 0

CURTIS, John (D) 250 2
H: 5 10 W: 11 07 b.Nuneaton 3-9-78
Source: Trainee. *Honours:* England Schools, Youth, Under-21, B.
1995–96 Manchester U 0 0
1996–97 Manchester U 0 0
1997–98 Manchester U 8 0
1998–99 Manchester U 4 0
1999–2000 Manchester U 1 0 13 0
1999–2000 *Barnsley* 28 2 28 2
2000–01 Blackburn R 46 0
2001–02 Blackburn R 10 0
2002–03 Blackburn R 5 0 61 0
2002–03 *Sheffield U* 12 0 12 0
2003–04 Leicester C 15 0 15 0
2003–04 Portsmouth 6 0
2004–05 Portsmouth 1 0 7 0
2004–05 *Preston NE* 12 0 12 0
2004–05 Nottingham F 11 0
2005–06 Nottingham F 27 0
2006–07 Nottingham F 41 0 79 0
2007–08 QPR 4 0
2008–09 QPR 0 0 4 0
2009–10 Northampton T 19 0 19 0

DAVIS, Liam (M) 64 6
H: 5 9 W: 11 07 b.Wandsworth 23-11-86
Source: Scholar.
2005–06 Coventry C 2 0
2006–07 Coventry C 3 0
2006–07 *Peterborough U* 7 0 7 0
2007–08 Coventry C 6 0 11 0
2008–09 Northampton T 29 4
2009–10 Northampton T 17 2 46 6

DUNN, Chris (G) 59 0
H: 6 5 W: 13 11 b.Brentwood 23-10-87
Source: Scholar.
2006–07 Northampton T 0 0
2007–08 Northampton T 1 0
2008–09 Northampton T 29 0
2009–10 Northampton T 29 0 59 0

DYER, Alex (M) 34 3
H: 5 8 W: 11 07 b.Wordsley 1-6-90
Source: Scholar.
2007–08 Northampton T 6 1

2008–09 Northampton T 8 0
2009–10 Northampton T 20 2 34 3

GILBERT, Peter (D) 163 1
H: 5 11 W: 12 00 b.Newcastle 31-7-83
Source: Scholar. *Honours:* Wales Under-21.
2001–02 Birmingham C 0 0
2002–03 Birmingham C 0 0
2003–04 Birmingham C 0 0
2003–04 Plymouth Arg 40 1
2004–05 Plymouth Arg 38 0 78 1
2005–06 Leicester C 5 0 5 0
2005–06 Sheffield W 17 0
2006–07 Sheffield W 6 0
2006–07 Doncaster R 4 0 4 0
2007–08 Sheffield W 10 0
2008–09 Sheffield W 8 0 41 0
2009–10 Oldham Ath 5 0 5 0
2009–10 Northampton T 30 0 30 0

GILLIGAN, Ryan (M) 158 19
H: 5 10 W: 11 07 b.Swindon 18-1-87
Source: Watford Scholar.
2005–06 Northampton T 23 4
2006–07 Northampton T 24 0
2007–08 Northampton T 38 4
2008–09 Northampton T 31 3
2009–10 Northampton T 42 8 158 19

GUINAN, Stephen (F) 293 56
H: 6 1 W: 13 02 b.Birmingham 24-12-75
Source: Trainee.
1992–93 Nottingham F 0 0
1993–94 Nottingham F 0 0
1994–95 Nottingham F 0 0
1995–96 Nottingham F 2 0
1995–96 *Darlington* 3 1 3 1
1996–97 Nottingham F 0 0
1996–97 *Burnley* 6 0 6 0
1997–98 Nottingham F 0 0
1997–98 *Crewe Alex* 3 0 3 0
1998–99 Nottingham F 0 0
1998–99 *Halifax T* 12 2 12 2
1998–99 *Plymouth Arg* 11 7
1999–2000 Nottingham F 1 0 7 0
1999–2000 *Scunthorpe U* 3 1 3 1
1999–2000 *Cambridge U* 6 0 6 0
1999–2000 Plymouth Arg 8 2
2000–01 Plymouth Arg 22 1
2001–02 Shrewsbury T 0 0 41 10
2002–03 Shrewsbury T 5 0
2003–04 Shrewsbury T 0 0 5 0
2004–05 Cheltenham T 43 6
2005–06 Cheltenham T 30 7
2006–07 Cheltenham T 19 0 92 13
2006–07 *Hereford U* 16 7
2007–08 Hereford U 28 3
2008–09 Hereford U 43 15 87 25
2009–10 Northampton T 28 4 28 4

GUTTRIDGE, Luke (M) 287 29
H: 5 6 W: 9 07 b.Barnstaple 27-3-82
Source: Trainee.
1999–2000 Torquay U 1 0
2000–01 Torquay U 0 0 1 0
2000–01 Cambridge U 1 1
2001–02 Cambridge U 29 2
2002–03 Cambridge U 43 3
2003–04 Cambridge U 46 11
2004–05 Cambridge U 17 0 136 17
2004–05 Southend U 5 0
2005–06 Southend U 41 5
2006–07 Southend U 17 0 63 5
2006–07 Leyton Orient 17 1 17 1
2007–08 Colchester U 14 0 14 0
2008–09 Northampton T 25 2
2009–10 Northampton T 31 4 56 6

HARRIS, Seb (F) 23 2
H: 6 3 W: 12 12 b.Michigan 5-10-87
2009 Michigan Bucks 14 1 14 1
2009–10 Northampton T 9 1 9 1

HERBERT, Courtney (F) 23 2
H: 6 2 W: 12 08 b.Northampton 25-10-88
Source: Long Buckby.
2009–10 Northampton T 23 2 23 2

HINTON, Craig (D) 366 6
H: 6 0 W: 12 00 b.Wolverhampton 26-11-77
Source: Trainee.
1996–97 Birmingham C 0 0
1997–98 Birmingham C 0 0
2000–01 Kidderminster H 46 2
2001–02 Kidderminster H 41 0
2002–03 Kidderminster H 44 0
2003–04 Kidderminster H 42 1 173 3
2004–05 Bristol R 38 0
2005–06 Bristol R 36 0
2006–07 Bristol R 30 0
2007–08 Bristol R 24 2
2008–09 Bristol R 25 1 153 5
2009–10 Northampton T 40 0 40 0

HOLT, Andy (M) 435 31
H: 6 1 W: 12 07 b.Stockport 21-5-78
Source: Trainee.
1996–97 Oldham Ath 1 0
1997–98 Oldham Ath 14 1
1998–99 Oldham Ath 43 5
1999–2000 Oldham Ath 46 3
2000–01 Oldham Ath 20 1 124 10
2000–01 Hull C 10 2
2001–02 Hull C 30 0
2002–03 Hull C 6 0
2002–03 *Barnsley* 7 0 7 0
2002–03 *Shrewsbury T* 9 0 9 0
2003–04 Hull C 25 1 71 3
2004–05 Wrexham 45 6
2005–06 Wrexham 36 3 81 9
2006–07 Northampton T 35 2
2007–08 Northampton T 36 2
2008–09 Northampton T 41 2
2009–10 Northampton T 31 3 143 9

JACOBS, Michael (M) 0 0
H: 5 9 W: 11 08 b.Northampton 23-3-92
Source: Scholar.
2009–10 Northampton T 0 0

KANYUKA, Patrick (D) 35 1
H: 6 0 W: 12 06 b.Kinshasa 19-7-87
Source: QPR Juniors.
2004–05 QPR 1 0
2005–06 QPR 0 0
2006–07 QPR 11 0
2007–08 QPR 0 0 12 0
2007–08 Swindon T 4 0
2008–09 Swindon T 16 1
2009–10 Swindon T 0 0 20 1
2009–10 Northampton T 3 0 3 0

LUMLEY, Billy (G) 2 0
H: 6 5 W: 15 00 b.Harlow 28-12-89
Source: Grays Ath.
2009–10 Northampton T 2 0 2 0

McCREADY, Chris (D) 179 3
H: 6 1 W: 12 05 b.Ellesmere Port 5-9-81
Source: Scholar.
2000–01 Crewe Alex 0 0
2001–02 Crewe Alex 1 0
2002–03 Crewe Alex 8 0
2003–04 Crewe Alex 22 0
2004–05 Crewe Alex 20 0
2005–06 Crewe Alex 25 0
2006–07 Tranmere R 42 1
2007–08 Crewe Alex 34 1
2008–09 Crewe Alex 5 1 115 2
2009–10 Northampton T 14 0 14 0
2009–10 *Tranmere R* 8 0 50 1

McKAY, Billy (F) 40 8
H: 5 9 W: 10 01 b.Corby 22-10-88
Honours: Northern Ireland Under-21.
2007–08 Leicester C 0 0
2008–09 Leicester C 0 0
2009–10 Northampton T 40 8 40 8

MULLIGAN, Gary (M) 140 19
H: 6 1 W: 12 03 b.Dublin 23-4-85
Source: Scholar.
2002–03 Wolverhampton W 0 0
2003–04 Wolverhampton W 0 0
2004–05 Wolverhampton W 0 0 1 0
2004–05 *Rushden & D* 13 3 13 3
2005–06 Sheffield U 0 0
2005–06 *Port Vale* 10 1 10 1
2005–06 Gillingham 13 1

2006–07 Gillingham 38 7
2007–08 Gillingham 30 5
2008–09 Gillingham 26 2 107 15
2009–10 Northampton T 9 0 9 0

O'FLYNN, Stephen (F) 160 58
H: 6 1 W: 13 07 b.Mallow 27-4-82
2001–02 Cork C 7 1
2002–03 Limerick 58 28
2004 Cork C 1 0 8 1
2005 Derry C 25 5
2006 Derry C 21 4 47 9
2007 Galway U 23 6
2008 Galway U 6 0 29 6
2009 Limerick 13 14 71 42
2009–10 Northampton T 5 0 5 0

OSMAN, Abdul (M) 84 5
H: 6 0 W: 1 00 b.Accra 27-2-87
Source: Hampton & Richmond B, Maidenhead U.
2007–08 Gretna 18 1 18 1
2008–09 Northampton T 36 2
2009–10 Northampton T 30 2 66 4

RODGERS, Paul (D) 42 0
H: 5 10 W: 10 10 b.Edmonton 6-10-89
Source: Scholar.
2007–08 Arsenal 0 0
2008–09 Arsenal 0 0
2008–09 *Northampton T* 11 0
2009–10 Northampton T 31 0 42 0

THORNTON, Kevin (M) 73 3
H: 5 7 W: 11 00 b.Drogheda 9-7-86
Source: Scholar. *Honours:* Eire Youth.
2003–04 Coventry C 0 0
2004–05 Coventry C 0 0
2005–06 Coventry C 16 0
2006–07 Coventry C 11 1
2007–08 Coventry C 19 1
2008–09 Coventry C 4 0
2008–09 *Brighton & HA* 12 0 12 0
2009–10 Coventry C 0 0 50 2
2009–10 Northampton T 11 1 11 1

NORWICH C (58)

ADEYEMI, Thomas (M) 11 0
H: 6 1 W: 12 04 b.Norwich 24-10-91
Source: Scholar.
2008–09 Norwich C 0 0
2009–10 Norwich C 11 0 11 0

BERTHEL ASKOU, Jens (D) 153 8
H: 6 2 W: 13 00 b.Videbaek 15-8-82
2002 Hoistebro 0 0
2003 Silkeborg 0 0
2004 Silkeborg 29 2
2005 Silkeborg 33 2
2006 Silkeborg 31 2
2006–07 Silkeborg 27 0 120 6
2007–08 Kasimpasa 11 0
2008–09 Kasimpasa 0 0 11 0
2009–10 Norwich C 22 2 22 2

CURETON, Jamie (F) 530 186
H: 5 8 W: 10 07 b.Bristol 28-8-75
Source: Trainee. *Honours:* England Youth
1992–93 Norwich C 0 0
1993–94 Norwich C 17 4
1994–95 Norwich C 17 4
1995–96 Norwich C 12 2
1995–96 *Bournemouta* 5 0 5 0
1996–97 Norwich C 0 0
1996–97 Bristol R 38 11
1997–98 Bristol R 43 13
1998–99 Bristol R 46 25
1999–2000 Bristol R 46 22
2000–01 Bristol R 1 1 174 72
2000–01 Reading 43 25
2001–02 Reading 38 15
2002–03 Reading 27 9 108 50
From Busan Icons.
2003–04 QPR 13 2
2004–05 QPR 30 4 43 6
2005–06 Swindon T 30 7 30 7
2005–06 *Colchester U* 8 4
2006–07 Colchester U 44 23 52 27
2007–08 Norwich C 41 12

2008–09 Norwich C 22 2
2008–09 *Barnsley* 8 2 8 2
2009–10 Norwich C 6 2 98 22
2009–10 *Shrewsbury T* 12 0 12 0

DALEY, Luke (F) 10 0
H: 5 11 W: 11 00 b.Northampton 10-11-89
Source: Scholar.
2007–08 Norwich C 0 0
2008–09 Norwich C 3 0
2009–10 Norwich C 7 0 10 0

DAWKIN, Josh (M) 0 0
H: 5 9 W: 10 12 b.Huntingdon 16-1-92
Source: Scholar. *Honours:* Wales Youth.
2009–10 Norwich C 0 0

DOHERTY, Gary (D) 336 27
H: 6 3 W: 13 13 b.Carndonagh 31-1-80
Source: Trainee. *Honours:* Eire Youth, Under-20, Under-21, 34 full caps, 4 goals.
1997–98 Luton T 10 0
1998–99 Luton T 20 6
1999–2000 Luton T 40 6 70 12
1999–2000 Tottenham H 2 0
2000–01 Tottenham H 22 3
2001–02 Tottenham H 7 0
2002–03 Tottenham H 15 1
2003–04 Tottenham H 17 0
2004–05 Tottenham H 1 0 64 4
2004–05 Norwich C 20 2
2005–06 Norwich C 42 1
2006–07 Norwich C 34 0
2007–08 Norwich C 34 0
2008–09 Norwich C 34 3
2009–10 Norwich C 38 5 202 11

DRURY, Adam (D) 442 5
H: 5 10 W: 11 09 b.Cambridge 29-8-78
Source: Trainee.
1995–96 Peterborough U 1 0
1996–97 Peterborough U 5 1
1997–98 Peterborough U 31 0
1998–99 Peterborough U 40 0
1999–2000 Peterborough U 42 1
2000–01 Peterborough U 29 0 148 2
2000–01 Norwich C 6 0
2001–02 Norwich C 35 0
2002–03 Norwich C 45 2
2003–04 Norwich C 42 0
2004–05 Norwich C 33 1
2005–06 Norwich C 39 0
2006–07 Norwich C 39 0
2007–08 Norwich C 9 0
2008–09 Norwich C 11 0
2009–10 Norwich C 35 0 294 3

DUMIC, Dario (D) 0 0
H: 6 4 W: 14 08 b.Bosnia 30-1-92
Source: Scholar.
2009–10 Norwich C 0 0

FRANCOMB, George (D) 2 0
H: 5 11 W: 11 07 b.London 8-9-91
Source: Scholar.
2009–10 Norwich C 2 0 2 0

GILL, Matthew (M) 259 14
H: 5 11 W: 11 10 b.Cambridge 8-11-80
Source: Trainee.
1997–98 Peterborough U 2 0
1998–99 Peterborough U 26 0
1999–2000 Peterborough U 20 1
2000–01 Peterborough U 17 1
2001–02 Peterborough U 12 2
2002–03 Peterborough U 41 1
2003–04 Peterborough U 33 0 151 5
2004–05 Notts Co 43 0
2005–06 Notts Co 14 0 57 0
2008–09 Exeter C 43 9 43 9
2009–10 Norwich C 8 0 8 0

HABERGHAM, Sam (D) 0 0
H: 6 1 W: 11 07 b.Rotherham 20-2-92
Source: Scholar.
2009–10 Norwich C 0 0

HOLT, Grant (F) 287 103
H: 6 1 W: 14 02 b.Carlisle 12-4-81
Source: Workington.
1999–2000 Halifax T 4 0
2000–01 Halifax T 2 0 6 0
From Sengkang, Barrow

2002–03	Sheffield W	7	1		
2003–04	Sheffield W	17	2	24	3
2003–04	Rochdale	14	4		
2004–05	Rochdale	40	17		
2005–06	Rochdale	21	14	75	35
2005–06	Nottingham F	19	4		
2006–07	Nottingham F	45	14		
2007–08	Nottingham F	32	3	96	21
2007–08	*Blackpool*	4	0	4	0
2008–09	Shrewsbury T	43	20	43	20
2009–10	Norwich C	39	24	39	24

HOOLAHAN, Wes (M)   275 35
H: 5 6   W: 10 03   b.Dublin 10-8-83
Honours: Eire Under-21, 1 full cap.

2001–02	Shelbourne	20	3		
2002–03	Shelbourne	23	0		
2004	Shelbourne	31	2		
2005	Shelbourne	29	4	103	9
2005–06	Livingston	16	0	16	0
2006–07	Blackpool	42	8		
2007–08	Blackpool	45	5	87	13
2008–09	Norwich C	32	2		
2009–10	Norwich C	37	11	69	13

HUGHES, Stephen (M)   249 19
H: 5 10   W: 11 04   b.Motherwell 14-11-82
Honours: Scotland Youth, Under-21, 1 full cap.

2000–01	Rangers	1	0		
2001–02	Rangers	17	1		
2002–03	Rangers	12	1		
2003–04	Rangers	22	3		
2004–05	Rangers	11	2	63	7
2004–05	Leicester C	16	1		
2005–06	Leicester C	34	3		
2006–07	Leicester C	41	3	91	7
2007–08	Motherwell	31	1		
2008–09	Motherwell	35	1	66	2
2009–10	Norwich C	29	3	29	3

JOHNSON, Oli (F)   57 11
H: 5 11   W: 12 04   b.Wakefield 6-11-87
Source: Nostell MW.

2008–09	Stockport Co	24	6		
2009–10	Stockport Co	16	1	40	7
2009–10	Norwich C	17	4	17	4

LAPPIN, Simon (M)   244 13
H: 5 11   W: 9 06   b.Glasgow 25-1-83
Honours: Scotland Under-21.

2001–02	St Mirren	1	0		
2002–03	St Mirren	34	0		
2003–04	St Mirren	24	4		
2004–05	St Mirren	34	1		
2005–06	St Mirren	35	3		
2006–07	St Mirren	24	1	152	9
2006–07	Norwich C	14	1		
2007–08	*Motherwell*	14	2	14	2
2007–08	Norwich C	15	1		
2008–09	Norwich C	5	0		
2009–10	Norwich C	44	0	78	2

MARIC, Goran (F)   40 11
H: 6 1   W: 13 08   b.Novi Sad 23-3-84
Source: Celta Vigo B.

2006–07	Las Palmas	6	0	6	0
2007–08	Celta Vigo	1	0		
2008–09	Celta Vigo	0	0	1	0
2008–09	*Barcelona B*	33	11	33	11
2009–10	Norwich C	0	0		

MARTIN, Chris (F)   107 32
H: 6 2   W: 12 06   b.Beccles 4-11-88
Source: Scholar. *Honours:* England Youth.

2006–07	Norwich C	18	4		
2007–08	Norwich C	7	0		
2008–09	Norwich C	0	0		
2008–09	*Luton T*	40	11	40	11
2009–10	Norwich C	42	17	67	21

MARTIN, Russell (M)   198 6
H: 6 0   W: 11 08   b.Brighton 4-1-86

2004–05	Wycombe W	7	0		
2005–06	Wycombe W	23	3		
2006–07	Wycombe W	42	2		
2007–08	Wycombe W	44	0	116	5
2008–09	Peterborough U	46	1		
2009–10	Peterborough U	10	0	56	1
2009–10	Norwich C	26	0	26	0

McDONALD, Cody (F)   24 4
H: 5 10   W: 11 03   b.Witham 30-5-86
Source: Dartford.

| 2008–09 | Norwich C | 7 | 1 | | |
| 2009–10 | Norwich C | 17 | 3 | 24 | 4 |

McNAMEE, Anthony (M)   192 6
H: 5 6   W: 10 03   b.Kensington 13-7-84
Source: Scholar. *Honours:* England Youth, Under-20.

2001–02	Watford	7	1		
2002–03	Watford	23	0		
2003–04	Watford	2	0		
2004–05	Watford	14	0		
2005–06	Watford	38	1		
2006–07	Watford	7	0		
2006–07	*Crewe Alex*	5	0	5	0
2007–08	Watford	0	0	91	2
2007–08	Swindon T	19	2		
2008–09	Swindon T	43	0		
2009–10	Swindon T	17	1	79	3
2009–10	Norwich C	17	1	17	1

McVEIGH, Paul (F)   274 43
H: 5 7   W: 11 00   b.Belfast 6-12-77
Source: Trainee. *Honours:* Northern Ireland Schools, Youth, Under-21, 20 full caps.

1995–96	Tottenham H	0	0		
1996–97	Tottenham H	3	1		
1997–98	Tottenham H	0	0		
1998–99	Tottenham H	0	0		
1999–2000	Tottenham H	0	0	3	1
1999–2000	Norwich C	1	0		
2000–01	Norwich C	11	1		
2001–02	Norwich C	42	8		
2002–03	Norwich C	44	14		
2003–04	Norwich C	44	5		
2004–05	Norwich C	17	1		
2005–06	Norwich C	36	7		
2006–07	Norwich C	21	0		
2006–07	*Burnley*	8	3	8	3
2007–08	Luton T	25	0		
2008–09	Luton T	13	3	38	3
2009–10	Norwich C	9	0	225	36

NELSON, Michael (D)   362 25
H: 6 2   W: 13 03   b.Gateshead 15-3-82
Source: Bishop Auckland.

2000–01	Bury	2	1		
2001–02	Bury	31	2		
2002–03	Bury	39	5	72	8
2003–04	Hartlepool U	40	3		
2004–05	Hartlepool U	43	1		
2005–06	Hartlepool U	43	2		
2006–07	Hartlepool U	42	1		
2007–08	Hartlepool U	45	2		
2008–09	Hartlepool U	46	5	259	14
2009–10	Norwich C	31	3	31	3

RUDD, Declan (G)   7 0
H: 6 3   W: 12 06   b.Norwich 16-1-91
Source: Scholar. *Honours:* England Youth, Under-20.

| 2008–09 | Norwich C | 0 | 0 | | |
| 2009–10 | Norwich C | 7 | 0 | 7 | 0 |

RUSSELL, Darel (M)   415 34
H: 5 10   W: 11 09   b.Mile End 22-10-80
Source: Trainee. *Honours:* England Youth.

1997–98	Norwich C	1	0		
1998–99	Norwich C	13	1		
1999–2000	Norwich C	33	4		
2000–01	Norwich C	41	2		
2001–02	Norwich C	23	0		
2002–03	Norwich C	21	0		
2003–04	Stoke C	46	4		
2004–05	Stoke C	45	2		
2005–06	Stoke C	37	3		
2006–07	Stoke C	43	7	171	16
2007–08	Norwich C	39	4		
2008–09	Norwich C	38	4		
2009–10	Norwich C	35	3	244	18

SMITH, Korey (M)   39 4
H: 5 9   W: 11 01   b.Hatfield 31-1-91
Source: Scholar.

| 2008–09 | Norwich C | 2 | 0 | | |
| 2009–10 | Norwich C | 37 | 4 | 39 | 4 |

SPILLANE, Michael (M)   65 4
H: 5 9   W: 11 10   b.Jersey 23-3-89
Source: Scholar. *Honours:* Eire Youth, Under-21.

2005–06	Norwich C	2	0		
2006–07	Norwich C	5	0		
2007–08	Norwich C	6	0		
2008–09	Norwich C	0	0		
2008–09	*Luton T*	39	3	39	3
2009–10	Norwich C	13	1	26	1

STEER, Jed (G)   0 0
H: 6 2   W: 14 00   b.Norwich 23-9-92
Source: Scholar.

| 2009–10 | Norwich C | 0 | 0 | | |

STEPHENS, David (D)   3 0
H: 6 3   W: 14 06   b.Welwyn 8-10-91
Source: Scholar.

| 2009–10 | Norwich C | 0 | 0 | | |
| 2009–10 | *Lincoln C* | 3 | 0 | 3 | 0 |

THEOKLITOS, Michael (G)   23 0
H: 6 2   W: 13 12   b.Melbourne 11-2-81
Source: Klingz.

| 2001–02 | Football Kingz | 20 | 0 | 20 | 0 |
| 2002–03 | Blackpool | 2 | 0 | 2 | 0 |

From Melbourne Victory.

| 2009–10 | Norwich C | 1 | 0 | 1 | 0 |

TUDUR JONES, Owain (M)   62 6
H: 6 2   W: 12 00   b.Bangor 15-10-84
Source: Bangor C. *Honours:* Wales Under-21, 4 full caps.

2005–06	Swansea C	21	3		
2006–07	Swansea C	4	0		
2007–08	Swansea C	8	0		
2008–09	Swansea C	9	0	42	3
2008–09	*Swindon T*	11	1	11	1
2009–10	Norwich C	3	1	3	1
2009–10	*Yeovil T*	6	1	6	1

WHALEY, Simon (M)   221 30
H: 5 10   W: 11 11   b.Bolton 7-6-85
Source: Scholar.

2002–03	Bury	2	0		
2003–04	Bury	10	1		
2004–05	Bury	38	3		
2005–06	Bury	23	7	73	11
2005–06	Preston NE	16	3		
2006–07	Preston NE	40	6		
2007–08	Preston NE	43	4		
2008–09	Preston NE	21	1	120	14
2008–09	*Barnsley*	4	1	4	1
2009–10	Norwich C	3	0	3	0
2009–10	*Rochdale*	9	2	9	2
2009–10	*Bradford C*	6	1	6	1
2009–10	*Chesterfield*	6	1	6	1

WHITBREAD, Zak (D)   104 3
H: 6 2   W: 12 07   b.Houston 4-3-84
Honours: USA Under-23.

2002–03	Liverpool	0	0		
2003–04	Liverpool	0	0		
2004–05	Liverpool	0	0		
2005–06	Liverpool	0	0		
2005–06	*Millwall*	25	0		
2006–07	Millwall	14	0		
2007–08	Millwall	23	3		
2008–09	Millwall	38	0		
2009–10	Millwall	0	0	100	3
2009–10	Norwich C	4	0	4	0

WIGGINS, Rhoys (D)   33 0
H: 5 8   W: 11 05   b.Uxbridge 4-11-87
Source: Scholar. *Honours:* Wales Youth, Under-21.

2006–07	Crystal Palace	0	0		
2007–08	Crystal Palace	0	0		
2008–09	Crystal Palace	1	0	1	0
2008–09	*Bournemouth*	13	0		
2009–10	Norwich C	0	0		
2009–10	*Bournemouth*	19	0	32	0

NOTTINGHAM F (59)

ADEBOLA, Dele (F)   567 129
H: 6 3   W: 12 08   b.Lagos 23-6-75
Source: Trainee.

| 1992–93 | Crewe Alex | 6 | 0 | | |

1993–94	Crewe Alex	0	0		
1994–95	Crewe Alex	30	8		
1995–96	Crewe Alex	29	8		
1996–97	Crewe Alex	32	16		
1997–98	Crewe Alex	27	7	124	39
1997–98	Birmingham C	17	7		
1998–99	Birmingham C	39	13		
1999–2000	Birmingham C	42	5		
2000–01	Birmingham C	31	6		
2001–02	Birmingham C	0	0	129	31
2001–02	*Oldham Ath*	5	0	5	0
2002–03	Crystal Palace	39	5	39	5
2003–04	Coventry C	28	2		
2003–04	*Burnley*	3	1	3	1
2004–05	Coventry C	25	5		
2004–05	Bradford C	15	3	15	3
2005–06	Coventry C	44	12		
2006–07	Coventry C	40	8		
2007–08	Coventry C	26	4	163	31
2007–08	Bristol C	17	6		
2008–09	Bristol C	39	10	56	16
2009–10	Nottingham F	33	3	33	3

ANDERSON, Paul (M) — 94 13
H: 5 9   W: 10 04   b.Leicester 23-7-88
Source: Scholar. *Honours:* England Youth.

2005–06	Hull C	0	0		
2005–06	Liverpool	0	0		
2006–07	Liverpool	0	0		
2007–08	Liverpool	0	0		
2007–08	Swansea C	31	7	31	7
2008–09	Liverpool	0	0		
2008–09	*Nottingham F*	26	2		
2009–10	Nottingham F	37	4	63	6

BENNETT, Julian (D) — 145 11
H: 6 1   W: 13 00   b.Nottingham 17-12-84
Source: Scholar.

2003–04	Walsall	1	0		
2004–05	Walsall	31	2		
2005–06	Walsall	19	1	51	3
2005–06	Nottingham F	18	2		
2006–07	Nottingham F	30	2		
2007–08	Nottingham F	34	4		
2008–09	Nottingham F	12	0		
2009–10	Nottingham F	0	0	94	8

BLACKSTOCK, Dexter (F) — 206 55
H: 6 2   W: 13 00   b.Oxford 20-5-86
Source: Scholar. *Honours:* England Youth, Under-20, Under-21.

2004–05	Southampton	9	1		
2004–05	Plymouth Arg	14	4	14	4
2005–06	Southampton	19	3	28	4
2005–06	Derby Co	9	3	9	3
2006–07	QPR	39	13		
2007–08	QPR	35	6		
2008–09	QPR	36	11	110	30
2008–09	*Nottingham F*	6	2		
2009–10	Nottingham F	39	12	45	14

BYRNE, Mark (M) — 2 0
H: 5 9   W: 11 00   b.Dublin 9-11-88

2006–07	Nottingham F	0	0		
2007–08	Nottingham F	1	0		
2008–09	Nottingham F	1	0		
2009–10	Nottingham F	0	0	2	0

CAMP, Lee (G) — 225
H: 5 11   W: 11 11   b.Derby 22-8-84
Source: Scholar. *Honours:* England Youth, Under-20, Under-21.

2002–03	Derby Co	1	0		
2003–04	Derby Co	0	0		
2003–04	*QPR*	12	0		
2004–05	Derby Co	45	0		
2005–06	Derby Co	40	0		
2006–07	Derby Co	3	0	89	0
2006–07	*Norwich C*	3	0	3	0
2006–07	*QPR*	11	0		
2007–08	QPR	46	0		
2008–09	QPR	4	0	73	0
2008–09	*Nottingham F*	15	0		
2009–10	Nottingham F	45	0	60	0

CHAMBERS, Luke (D) — 242 12
H: 6 1   W: 11 13   b.Kettering 29-8-85
Source: Scholar.

2002–03	Northampton T	1	0		
2003–04	Northampton T	24	0		
2004–05	Northampton T	27	0		
2005–06	Northampton T	43	0		

2006–07	Northampton T	29	1	124	1
2006–07	Nottingham F	14	0		
2007–08	Nottingham F	42	6		
2008–09	Nottingham F	39	2		
2009–10	Nottingham F	23	3	118	11

COHEN, Chris (M) — 218 14
H: 5 11   W: 10 11   b.Norwich 5-3-87
Source: Scholar. *Honours:* England Youth.

2003–04	West Ham U	7	0		
2004–05	West Ham U	11	0		
2005–06	*West Ham U*	0	0	18	0
2005–06	*Yeovil T*	30	1		
2006–07	Yeovil T	44	6	74	7
2007–08	Nottingham F	41	2		
2008–09	Nottingham F	41	2		
2009–10	Nottingham F	44	3	126	7

DARLOW, Karl (G) — 0 0
H: 6 1   W: 12 05   b.Northampton 8-10-90
Source: Scholar.

2009–10	Nottingham F	0	0		

EARNSHAW, Robert (F) — 355 154
H: 5 6   W: 9 09   b.Malfulira 6-4-81
Source: Trainee. *Honours:* Wales Youth, Under-21, 49 full caps, 14 goals.

1997–98	Cardiff C	5	0		
1998–99	Cardiff C	5	1		
1998–99	*Middlesbrough*	0	0		
1999–2000	Cardiff C	6	1		
1999–2000	*Morton*	3	2	3	2
2000–01	Cardiff C	36	19		
2001–02	Cardiff C	30	11		
2002–03	Cardiff C	46	31		
2003–04	Cardiff C	46	21		
2004–05	Cardiff C	4	1	178	85
2004–05	WBA	31	11		
2005–06	WBA	12	1	43	12
2005–06	Norwich C	15	8		
2006–07	Norwich C	30	19	45	27
2007–08	Derby Co	22	1	22	1
2008–09	Nottingham F	32	12		
2009–10	Nottingham F	32	15	64	27

GARNER, Joe (F) — 95 28
H: 5 10   W: 11 02   b.Blackburn 12-4-88
Source: Scholar. *Honours:* England Schools, Youth.

2004–05	Blackburn R	0	0		
2005–06	Blackburn R	0	0		
2006–07	Blackburn R	0	0		
2006–07	*Carlisle U*	18	5		
2007–08	Carlisle U	31	14	49	19
2008–09	Nottingham F	28	7		
2009–10	Nottingham F	18	2	46	9

GIBBONS, Robert (M) — 0 0
b.Dublin 8-10-91
Source: Scholar.

2008–09	Nottingham F	0	0		
2009–10	Nottingham F	0	0		

GUNTER, Chris (D) — 85 1
H: 5 11   W: 11 02   b.Newport 21-7-89
Source: Scholar. *Honours:* Wales Youth, Under-21, 22 full caps.

2006–07	Cardiff C	15	0		
2007–08	Cardiff C	13	0	28	0
2007–08	Tottenham H	2	0		
2008–09	Tottenham H	3	0	5	0
2008–09	*Nottingham F*	8	0		
2009–10	Nottingham F	44	1	52	1

HEATH, Joe (D) — 14 0
H: 5 11   W: 11 11   b.Birkenhead 4-10-88

2005–06	Nottingham F	0	0		
2006–07	Nottingham F	0	0		
2007–08	Nottingham F	0	0		
2008–09	Nottingham F	10	0		
2009–10	Nottingham F	0	0	10	0
2009–10	*Lincoln C*	4	0	4	0

LYNCH, Joel (D) — 112 2
H: 6 1   W: 12 10   b.Eastbourne 3-10-87
Source: Scholar. *Honours:* England Youth.

2005–06	Brighton & HA	16	1		
2006–07	Brighton & HA	39	0		
2007–08	Brighton & HA	22	1		
2008–09	Brighton & HA	2	0	79	2
2008–09	*Nottingham F*	23	0		
2009–10	Nottingham F	10	0	33	0

MAJEWSKI, Radoslaw (M) — 106 8
H: 5 7   W: 10 06   b.Pruszkow 15-12-86
Source: Znicz Pruszkow. *Honours:* Poland 7 full caps.

2006–07	Groclin	14	0		
2007–08	Groclin	28	4	42	4
2008–09	Polonia Warsaw	29	1	29	1
2009–10	Nottingham F	35	3	35	3

McCLEARY, Garath (F) — 71 2
H: 5 10   W: 12 06   b.Oxford 15-5-87
Source: Bromley.

2007–08	Nottingham F	8	1		
2008–09	Nottingham F	39	1		
2009–10	Nottingham F	24	0	71	2

McGOLDRICK, David (F) — 136 23
H: 6 1   W: 11 10   b.Nottingham 29-11-87
Source: Schoolboy.

2003–04	Notts Co	4	0		
2004–05	Notts Co	0	0		
2005–06	Southampton	1	0		
2005–06	*Notts Co*	6	0	10	0
2006–07	Southampton	9	0		
2006–07	*Bournemouth*	12	6	12	6
2007–08	Southampton	8	0		
2007–08	*Port Vale*	17	2	17	2
2008–09	Southampton	46	12	64	12
2009–10	Nottingham F	33	3	33	3

McGUGAN, Lewis (M) — 97 16
H: 5 9   W: 11 06   b.Long Eaton 25-10-88
Source: Scholar.

2006–07	Nottingham F	13	2		
2007–08	Nottingham F	33	6		
2008–09	Nottingham F	33	5		
2009–10	Nottingham F	18	3	97	16

McKENNA, Paul (M) — 457 31
H: 5 7   W: 11 12   b.Eccleston 20-10-77
Source: Trainee.

1995–96	Preston NE	0	0		
1996–97	Preston NE	5	1		
1997–98	Preston NE	5	0		
1998–99	Preston NE	36	0		
1999–2000	Preston NE	24	2		
2000–01	Preston NE	44	5		
2001–02	Preston NE	38	4		
2002–03	Preston NE	41	3		
2003–04	Preston NE	39	6		
2004–05	Preston NE	39	3		
2005–06	Preston NE	41	2		
2006–07	Preston NE	33	2		
2007–08	Preston NE	33	0		
2008–09	Preston NE	44	2	422	30
2009–10	Nottingham F	35	1	35	1

MOLONEY, Brendan (M) — 45 2
H: 6 1   W: 11 12   b.Enfield 18-1-89
Source: Scholar. *Honours:* Eire Under-21.

2005–06	Nottingham F	0	0		
2006–07	Nottingham F	1	0		
2007–08	Nottingham F	2	0		
2007–08	*Chesterfield*	9	1	9	1
2008–09	Nottingham F	12	0		
2009–10	Nottingham F	0	0	15	0
2009–10	*Notts Co*	18	1	18	1
2009–10	*Scunthorpe U*	3	0	3	0

MORGAN, Wes (D) — 289 11
H: 6 2   W: 14 00   b.Nottingham 21-1-84
Source: Scholar.

2002–03	Nottingham F	0	0		
2002–03	*Kidderminster H*	5	1	5	1
2003–04	Nottingham F	32	2		
2004–05	Nottingham F	43	1		
2005–06	Nottingham F	43	2		
2006–07	Nottingham F	38	0		
2007–08	Nottingham F	42	1		
2008–09	Nottingham F	42	1		
2009–10	Nottingham F	44	3	284	10

MOUSSI, Guy (M) — 133 5
H: 6 1   W: 12 11   b.Paris 23-1-85
Source:

2004–05	Angers	15	1		
2005–06	Angers	9	0		
2006–07	Angers	32	0		
2007–08	Angers	35	1	91	2
2008–09	Nottingham F	15	0		
2009–10	Nottingham F	27	3	42	3

PERCH, James (D)   **190 12**
H: 5 11   W: 11 05   b.Mansfield 29-9-85
Source: Scholar.

Season	Club				
2002–03	Nottingham F	0	0		
2003–04	Nottingham F	0	0		
2004–05	Nottingham F	22	0		
2005–06	Nottingham F	38	3		
2006–07	Nottingham F	46	5		
2007–08	Nottingham F	30	0		
2008–09	Nottingham F	37	3		
2009–10	Nottingham F	17	1	190	12

REDMOND, Shane (G)   **22 0**
H: 6 0   W: 12 10   b.Dublin 23-3-89
Source: Scholar. *Honours:* Eire Under-21.

Season	Club				
2006–07	Nottingham F	0	0		
2007–08	Nottingham F	0	0		
2008–09	Nottingham F	0	0		
2009–10	Nottingham F	0	0		
2009–10	Burton Alb	3	0	3	0
2009–10	*Darlington*	19	0	19	0

REID, James (D)   **1 0**
H: 5 10   W: 11 04   b.Ashbourne 28-2-90
Source: Scholar. *Honours:* England Youth.

Season	Club				
2007–08	Nottingham F	0	0		
2008–09	Nottingham F	1	0		
2009–10	Nottingham F	0	0	1	0

RODNEY, Nialle (F)   **0 0**
b.Nottingham 28-2-91
Source: Scholar.

Season	Club		
2008–09	Nottingham F	0	0
2009–10	Nottingham F	0	0

SMITH, Paul (G)   **222 0**
H: 6 3   W: 14 00   b.Epsom 17-12-79
Source: Walton & Hersham.

Season	Club				
1998–99	Charlton Ath	0	0		
1998–99	*Brentford*	0	0		
1999–2000	Charlton Ath	0	0		
From Carshalton Ath.					
2000–01	Brentford	2	0		
2001–02	Brentford	18	0		
2002–03	Brentford	43	0		
2003–04	Brentford	24	0	87	0
2003–04	Southampton	0	0		
2004–05	Southampton	6	0		
2005–06	Southampton	9	0	15	0
2006–07	Nottingham F	45	0		
2007–08	Nottingham F	46	0		
2008–09	Nottingham F	28	0		
2009–10	Nottingham F	1	0	120	0

THORNHILL, Matt (M)   **62 8**
H: 5 9   W: 12 00   b.Nottingham 11-10-88
Source: Scholar.

Season	Club				
2007–08	Nottingham F	14	2		
2008–09	Nottingham F	24	3		
2009–10	Nottingham F	0	0	38	5
2009–10	*Brighton & HA*	7	0	7	0
2009–10	*Cheltenham T*	17	3	17	3

TYSON, Nathan (F)   **284 78**
H: 5 10   W: 10 02   b.Reading 4-5-82
Source: Trainee. *Honours:* England Under-20.

Season	Club				
1999–2000	Reading	1	0		
2000–01	Reading	0	0		
2001–02	Reading	1	0		
2001–02	*Swansea C*	11	1	11	1
2001–02	*Cheltenham T*	8	1	8	1
2002–03	Reading	23	1		
2003–04	Reading	8	0	33	1
2003–04	Wycombe W	21	9		
2004–05	Wycombe W	42	22		
2005–06	Wycombe W	15	11	78	42
2005–06	Nottingham F	28	10		
2006–07	Nottingham F	24	7		
2007–08	Nottingham F	34	9		
2008–09	Nottingham F	35	5		
2009–10	Nottingham F	33	2	154	33

WILSON, Kelvin (D)   **218 4**
H: 6 2   W: 12 12   b.Nottingham 3-9-85
Source: Scholar.

Season	Club				
2003–04	Notts Co	3	0		
2004–05	Notts Co	41	2		
2005–06	Notts Co	34	1	78	3
2005–06	*Preston NE*	6	0		
2006–07	*Preston NE*	21	1	27	1
2007–08	Nottingham F	42	0		
2008–09	Nottingham F	36	0		
2009–10	Nottingham F	35	0	113	0

NOTTS CO (60)

AKINBIYI, Ade (F)   **503 136**
H: 6 1   W: 13 08   b.Hackney 10-10-74
Source: Trainee. *Honours:* Nigeria 1 full cap.

Season	Club				
1992–93	Norwich C	0	0		
1993–94	Norwich C	2	0		
1993–94	*Hereford U*	4	2	4	2
1994–95	Norwich C	13	0		
1994–95	*Brighton & HA*	7	4	7	4
1995–96	Norwich C	22	3		
1996–97	Norwich C	12	0	49	3
1996–97	Gillingham	19	7		
1997–98	Gillingham	44	21	63	28
1998–99	Bristol C	44	19		
1999–2000	Bristol C	3	2	47	21
1999–2000	Wolverhampton W	37	16	37	16
2000–01	Leicester C	37	9		
2001–02	Leicester C	21	2	58	11
2001–02	Crystal Palace	14	2		
2002–03	Crystal Palace	10	1		
2002–03	*Stoke C*	4	2		
2003–04	Crystal Palace	0	0	24	3
2003–04	Stoke C	30	10		
2004–05	Stoke C	29	7	63	19
2004–05	Burnley	10	4		
2005–06	Burnley	29	12		
2005–06	*Sheffield U*	15	3		
2006–07	Sheffield U	3	0	18	3
2006–07	Burnley	20	2		
2007–08	Burnley	39	8		
2008–09	Burnley	11	0	109	26
2009–10	Houston Dynamo	14	0	14	0
2009–10	Notts Co	10	0	10	0

BISHOP, Neil (M)   **126 4**
H: 6 1   W: 12 10   b.Stockton 7-8-81
Source: Billingham T, Gateshead, Spennymoor U, Whitby T, Scarborough, York C.

Season	Club				
2007–08	Barnet	39	2		
2008–09	Barnet	44	1	83	3
2009–10	Notts Co	43	1	43	1

CANHAM, Sean (F)   **24 3**
H: 6 1   W: 13 01   b.Exeter 26-9-84
Source: Exeter City Scholar, Team Bath.

Season	Club				
2008–09	Notts Co	23	3		
2009–10	Notts Co	1	0	24	3

CLAPHAM, Jamie (M)   **423 14**
H: 5 9   W: 11 09   b.Lincoln 7-12-75
Source: Trainee.

Season	Club				
1994–95	Tottenham H	0	0		
1995–96	Tottenham H	0	0		
1996–97	Tottenham H	1	0		
1996–97	*Leyton Orient*	6	0	6	0
1996–97	*Bristol R*	5	0	5	0
1997–98	Tottenham H	0	0	1	0
1997–98	Ipswich T	22	0		
1998–99	Ipswich T	46	3		
1999–2000	Ipswich T	46	2		
2000–01	Ipswich T	35	2		
2001–02	Ipswich T	32	2		
2002–03	Ipswich T	26	1	207	10
2002–03	Birmingham C	16	0		
2003–04	Birmingham C	25	0		
2004–05	Birmingham C	27	0		
2005–06	Birmingham C	16	1	84	1
2006–07	Wolverhampton W	26	0		
2007–08	Wolverhampton W	0	0	26	0
2007–08	*Leeds U*	13	0	13	0
2007–08	Leicester C	11	0		
2008–09	Leicester C	0	0	11	0
2008–09	Notts Co	40	2		
2009–10	Notts Co	30	1	70	3

DAVIES, Ben (M)   **258 54**
H: 5 7   W: 12 03   b.Birmingham 27-5-81
Source: Walsall trainee.

Season	Club				
2000–01	Kidderminster H	3	0		
2001–02	Kidderminster H	9	0	12	0
2004–05	Chester C	44	2		
2005–06	Chester C	45	7	89	9
2006–07	Shrewsbury T	43	12		
2007–08	Shrewsbury T	27	6		
2008–09	Shrewsbury T	42	12	112	30
2009–10	Notts Co	45	15	45	15

EDWARDS, Mike (D)   **418 25**
H: 6 0   W: 12 10   b.Hessle 25-4-80
Source: Trainee.

Season	Club				
1997–98	Hull C	21	0		
1998–99	Hull C	30	0		
1999–2000	Hull C	40	1		
2000–01	Hull C	42	4		
2001–02	Hull C	39	1		
2002–03	Hull C	6	0	178	6
2002–03	Colchester U	5	0	5	0
2003–04	Grimsby T	33	1	33	1
2004–05	Notts Co	9	0		
2005–06	Notts Co	46	7		
2006–07	Notts Co	45	3		
2007–08	Notts Co	19	1		
2008–09	Notts Co	43	2		
2009–10	Notts Co	40	5	202	18

FACEY, Delroy (F)   **336 60**
H: 6 0   W: 15 02   b.Huddersfield 22-4-80
Source: Trainee.

Season	Club				
1996–97	Huddersfield T	3	0		
1997–98	Huddersfield T	3	0		
1998–99	Huddersfield T	20	3		
1999–2000	Huddersfield T	2	0		
2000–01	Huddersfield T	34	10		
2001–02	Huddersfield T	13	2		
2002–03	Huddersfield T	0	0		
2002–03	*Bradford C*	6	1	6	1
2002–03	Bolton W	9	1		
2003–04	Bolton W	1	0	10	1
2003–04	*Burnley*	14	5	14	5
2003–04	WBA	9	0	9	0
2004–05	Hull C	21	4	21	4
2004–05	*Huddersfield T*	4	0	79	15
2004–05	Oldham Ath	6	0		
2005–06	Oldham Ath	3	0	9	0
2005–06	Tranmere R	37	8	37	8
2006–07	Rotherham U	40	10	40	10
2007–08	Gillingham	32	3	32	3
2007–08	*Wycombe W*	6	1	6	1
2008–09	Notts Co	45	9		
2009–10	Notts Co	18	2	63	11
2009–10	*Lincoln C*	10	1	10	1

FAIRCLOUGH, Ben (F)   **8 0**
H: 5 6   W: 9 10   b.Nottingham 18-4-89
Source: Nottingham F Scholar.

Season	Club				
2008–09	Notts Co	8	0		
2009–10	Notts Co	0	0	8	0

FOX, Nathan (M)   **1 0**
H: 5m 10   W: 12 02   b.Nottingham 16-8-93
Source: Scholar.

Season	Club				
2009–10	Notts Co	1	0	1	0

HAMSHAW, Matt (M)   **259 16**
H: 5 10   W: 11 08   b.Rotherham 1-1-82
Source: Trainee. *Honours:* England Youth, Under-20.

Season	Club				
1998–99	Sheffield W	0	0		
1999–2000	Sheffield W	0	0		
2000–01	Sheffield W	18	0		
2001–02	Sheffield W	21	0		
2002–03	Sheffield W	15	1		
2003–04	Sheffield W	0	0		
2004–05	Sheffield W	20	1	74	2
2005–06	Stockport Co	39	5	39	5
2006–07	Mansfield T	40	4		
2007–08	Mansfield T	45	2	85	6
2008–09	Notts Co	41	3		
2009–10	Notts Co	20	0	61	3

HAWLEY, Karl (F)   **183 51**
H: 5 8   W: 12 02   b.Walsall 6-12-81
Source: Scholar.

Season	Club				
2000–01	Walsall	0	0		
2001–02	Walsall	1	0		
2002–03	Walsall	0	0		
2002–03	*Raith R*	17	7		
2003–04	Walsall	0	0	1	0
2003–04	*Raith R*	11	2	28	9
2004–05	Carlisle U	0	0		
2005–06	Carlisle U	46	22		
2006–07	Carlisle U	32	12	78	34
2007–08	Preston NE	25	3		
2008–09	Preston NE	5	0	30	3
2008–09	*Northampton T*	11	2	11	2

2008–09	Colchester U	4	0	4	0
2009–10	Notts Co	31	3	31	3

HOULT, Russell (G)   433 0
H: 6 3   W: 14 09   b.Ashby 22-11-72
Source: Trainee.

1990–91	Leicester C	0	0		
1991–92	Leicester C	0	0		
1991–92	Lincoln C	2	0		
1991–92	Blackpool	0	0		
1992–93	Leicester C	10	0		
1993–94	Leicester C	0	0		
1993–94	Bolton W	4	0	4	0
1994–95	Leicester C	0	0	10	0
1994–95	Lincoln C	15	0	17	0
1994–95	Derby Co	15	0		
1995–96	Derby Co	41	0		
1996–97	Derby Co	32	0		
1997–98	Derby Co	2	0		
1998–99	Derby Co	23	0		
1999–2000	Derby Co	10	0	123	0
1999–2000	Portsmouth	18	0		
2000–01	Portsmouth	22	0	40	0
2000–01	WBA	13	0		
2001–02	WBA	45	0		
2002–03	WBA	37	0		
2003–04	WBA	44	0		
2004–05	WBA	36	0		
2005–06	WBA	1	0		
2005–06	Nottingham F	8	0	8	0
2006–07	WBA	14	0	190	0
2006–07	Stoke C	0	0		
2007–08	Stoke C	1	0	1	0
2007–08	Notts Co	14	0		
2008–09	Notts Co	16	0		
2009–10	Notts Co	4	0	34	0
2009–10	Darlington	6	0	6	0

HUGHES, Lee (F)   350 160
H: 5 10   W: 12 00   b.Smethwick 22-5-76
Source: Kidderminster H.

1997–98	WBA	37	14		
1998–99	WBA	42	31		
1999–2000	WBA	36	12		
2000–01	WBA	41	21		
2001–02	Coventry C	38	14		
2002–03	Coventry C	4	1	42	15
2002–03	WBA	23	0		
2003–04	WBA	32	11	211	89
2007–08	Oldham Ath	18	7		
2008–09	Oldham Ath	37	18	55	25
2008–09	Blackpool	3	1	3	1
2009–10	Notts Co	39	30	39	30

HUNT, Stephen (D)   134 5
H: 6 2   W: 13 00   b.Southampton 11-11-84
Source: Southampton Scholar.

2004–05	Colchester U	20	1		
2005–06	Colchester U	0	0	22	1
2006–07	Notts Co	32	1		
2007–08	Notts Co	37	2		
2008–09	Notts Co	11	0		
2009–10	Notts Co	32	1	112	4

JACKSON, Johnnie (M)   202 19
H: 6 1   W: 12 00   b.Camden 15-8-82
Source: Trainee. *Honours:* England Youth.
Under-20.

1999–2000	Tottenham H	0	0		
2000–01	Tottenham H	0	0		
2001–02	Tottenham H	0	0		
2002–03	Tottenham H	0	0		
2002–03	Swindon T	13	1	13	1
2002–03	Colchester U	8	0		
2003–04	Tottenham H	11	1		
2003–04	Coventry C	5	2	5	2
2004–05	Tottenham H	8	0		
2004–05	Watford	15	0	15	0
2005–06	Tottenham H	1	0	20	1
2005–06	Derby Co	6	0	6	0
2006–07	Colchester U	32	2		
2007–08	Colchester U	46	7		
2008–09	Colchester U	29	4		
2009–10	Colchester U	0	0	115	13
2009–10	Notts Co	24	2	24	2
2009–10	Charlton Ath	4	0	4	0

LEE, Graeme (D)   430 35
H: 6 2   W: 13 07   b.Middlesbrough 31-5-78
Source: Trainee.

1995–96	Hartlepool U	6	0		

1996–97	Hartlepool U	24	0		
1997–98	Hartlepool U	37	3		
1998–99	Hartlepool U	24	3		
1999–2000	Hartlepool U	38	7		
2000–01	Hartlepool U	6	0		
2001–02	Hartlepool U	39	4		
2002–03	Hartlepool U	45	2		
2003–04	Sheffield W	30	3		
2004–05	Sheffield W	22	1		
2005–06	Sheffield W	15	1	67	5
2005–06	Doncaster R	20	1		
2006–07	Doncaster R	39	4		
2007–08	Doncaster R	1	0	60	5
2007–08	Hartlepool U	3	0	222	19
2007–08	Sarewsbury T	5	0	5	0
2008–09	Bradford C	44	2	44	2
2009–10	Notts Co	32	4	32	4

RAVENHILL, Ricky (M)   246 20
H: 5 10   W: 11 02   b.Doncaster 16-1-81
Source: Barnsley Trainee.

2003–04	Doncaster R	36	3		
2004–05	Doncaster R	35	3		
2005–06	Doncaster R	27	3	98	9
2006–07	Chester C	3	0	3	0
2006–07	Grimsby T	17	2	17	2
2006–07	Darlington	15	1		
2007–08	Darlington	35	3		
2008–09	Darlington	38	2	88	6
2008–09	Notts Co	0	0		
2009–10	Notts Co	40	3	40	3

RODGERS, Luke (F)   303 92
H: 5 8   W: 11 00   b.Birmingham 1-1-82
Source: Trainee.

1999–2000	Shrewsbury T	6	1		
2000–01	Shrewsbury T	26	7		
2001–02	Shrewsbury T	38	22		
2002–03	Shrewsbury T	36	16		
2003–04	Shrewsbury T	0	0		
2004–05	Shrewsbury T	36	6	142	52
2005–06	Crewe Alex	26	6		
2006–07	Crewe Alex	12	3	38	9
2006–07	Port Vale	8	3		
2007–08	Port Vale	36	9		
2008–09	Port Vale	15	3	59	15
2008–09	Yeovil T	7	3	22	3
2009–10	Notts Co	42	13	42	13

SCHMEICHEL, Kasper (G)   122 0
H: 6 1   W: 13 00   b.Denmark 5-11-86
Source: Scholar. *Honours:* Denmark Youth,
Under-20, Under-21.

2003–04	Manchester C	0	0		
2004–05	Manchester C	0	0		
2005–06	Manchester C	0	0		
2005–06	Darlington	4	0	4	0
2005–06	Bury	15	0		
2006–07	Manchester C	0	0		
2006–07	Falkirk	15	0	15	0
2006–07	Bury	14	0	29	0
2007–08	Manchester C	7	0		
2007–08	Cardiff C	14	0	14	0
2007–08	Coventry C	9	0	9	0
2008–09	Manchester C	1	0		
2009–10	Manchester C	0	0	8	0
2009–10	Notts Co	43	0	43	0

THOMPSON, John (D)   223 9
H: 6 0   W: 12 01   b.Dublin 12-10-81
Source: Home Farm. *Honours:* Eire Youth,
Under-21, 1 full cap.

1999–2000	Nottingham F	0	0		
2000–01	Nottingham F	0	0		
2001–02	Nottingham F	8	0		
2002–03	Nottingham F	20	3		
2003–04	Nottingham F	32	1		
2004–05	Nottingham F	20	0		
2005–06	Nottingham F	35	3		
2006–07	Nottingham F	14	0	129	7
2006–07	Tranmere R	12	0	12	0
2007–08	Oldham Ath	7	0		
2008–09	Oldham Ath	0	0	7	0
2008–09	Notts Co	35	2		
2009–10	Notts Co	40	0	75	2

WESTCARR, Craig (F)   75 11
H: 5 11   W: 11 04   b.Nottingham 29-1-85
Source: Scholar. *Honours:* England Youth.

2001–02	Nottingham F	8	0		
2002–03	Nottingham F	11	1		

2003–04	Nottingham F	3	0		
2004–05	Nottingham F	1	0	23	1
2004–05	Lincoln C	6	1	6	1
2004–05	Milton Keynes D	4	0	4	0
From Cambridge U, Kettering T.					
2009–10	Notts Co	42	9	42	9

OLDHAM ATH (61)

ABBOTT, Pawel (F)   252 91
H: 6 2   W: 13 10   b.York 5-5-82
Source: LKS Lodz. *Honours:* Poland
Under-21.

2000–01	Preston NE	0	0		
2001–02	Preston NE	0	0		
2002–03	Preston NE	0	0		
2002–03	Bury	17	6	17	6
2003–04	Preston NE	9	2	25	6
2003–04	Huddersfield T	13	5		
2004–05	Huddersfield T	44	26		
2005–06	Huddersfield T	36	12		
2006–07	Huddersfield T	18	5	111	48
2006–07	Swansea C	18	1	18	1
2007–08	Darlington	24	9		
2008–09	Darlington	18	8	42	17
2009–10	Oldham Ath	39	13	39	13

ALESSANDRA, Lewis (F)   48 7
H: 5 9   W: 11 07   b.Oldham 8-2-89
Source: Scholar.

2007–08	Oldham Ath	15	2		
2008–09	Oldham Ath	32	5		
2009–10	Oldham Ath	1	0	48	7

ALJOFREE, Hasney (D)   249 9
H: 6 0   W: 12 00   b.Manchester 11-7-78
Source: Trainee.

1996–97	Bolton W	0	0		
1997–98	Bolton W	2	0		
1998–99	Bolton W	4	0		
1999–2000	Bolton W	8	0	14	0
2000–01	Dundee U	26	2		
2001–02	Dundee U	27	2	53	4
2002–03	Plymouth Arg	19	1		
2003–04	Plymouth Arg	24	0		
2004–05	Plymouth Arg	12	1		
2004–05	Sheffield W	2	0	2	0
2005–06	Plymouth Arg	37	1		
2006–07	Plymouth Arg	25	0	117	3
2006–07	Oldham Ath	5	0	5	0
2007–08	Swindon T	39	2		
2008–09	Swindon T	18	0		
2009–10	Swindon T	0	0	57	2
2009–10	Oldham Ath	1	0	6	0

BEMBO-LITA, Djenny (F)   0 0
H: 5 10   W: 11 05   b.Kinshasa 9-11-91
Source: Scholar.

2009–10	Oldham Ath	0	0		

BLACK, Paul (D)   18 1
H: 6 0   W: 12 10   b.Middleton 18-5-90
Source: Scholar.

2007–08	Oldham Ath	2	0		
2008–09	Oldham Ath	3	0		
2009–10	Oldham Ath	13	1	18	1

BLACKMAN, Nick (F)   29 3
H: 6 2   W: 11 08   b.Whitefield 11-11-89
Source: Scholar.

2006–07	Macclesfield T	1	0		
2007–08	Macclesfield T	11	1		
2008–09	Macclesfield T	0	0	12	1
2008–09	Blackburn R	0	0		
2008–09	Blackpool	5	1	5	1
2009–10	Blackburn R	0	0		
2009–10	Oldham Ath	12	1	12	1

BRILL, Dean (G)   117 0
H: 6 2   W: 14 05   b.Luton 2-12-85
Source: Scholar.

2003–04	Luton T	5	0		
2004–05	Luton T	0	0		
2005–06	Luton T	5	0		
2006–07	Luton T	11	0		
2006–07	Gillingham	8	0	8	0
2007–08	Luton T	37	0		
2008–09	Luton T	23	0	81	0
2009–10	Oldham Ath	28	0	28	0

BROOKE, Ryan (F)   16 2
H: 6 1 W: 11 07 b.Crewe 4-10-90
Source: Scholar.

| 2008–09 | Oldham Ath | 1 | 1 | | |
| 2009–10 | Oldham Ath | 15 | 1 | 16 | 2 |

COLBECK, Joe (M)   142 11
H: 5 10 W: 10 12 b.Bradford 29-11-86
Source: Scholar.

2004–05	Bradford C	0	0		
2005–06	Bradford C	11	0		
2006–07	Bradford C	32	0		
2007–08	Bradford C	33	6		
2007–08	*Darlington*	6	2	6	2
2008–09	Bradford C	28	2		
2009–10	Bradford C	5	0	109	8
2009–10	Oldham Ath	27	1	27	1

DAWSON, Liam (D)   0 0
b. 12-1-91
Source: Scholar.

| 2009–10 | Oldham Ath | 0 | 0 | | |

EAVES, Tom (M)   15 0
H: 6 3 W: 13 07 b.Liverpool 14-1-92
Source: Scholar.

| 2009–10 | Oldham Ath | 15 | 0 | 15 | 0 |

FLEMING, Greg (G)   48 0
H: 5 11 W: 12 09 b.Edinburgh 27-9-86
Source: Livingston. *Honours:* Scotland Under-21.

2006–07	Gretna	2	0		
2007–08	Gretna	28	0	30	0
2008–09	Oldham Ath	18	0		
2009–10	Oldham Ath	0	0	18	0

FURMAN, Dean (M)   71 4
H: 6 0 W: 11 08 b.Cape Town 22-6-88
Source: Chelsea Scholar.

2007–08	Rangers	1	0	1	0
2008–09	Bradford C	32	4	32	4
2009–10	Oldham Ath	38	0	38	0

GREGAN, Sean (M)   619 19
H: 6 2 W: 14 00 b.Guisborough 29-3-74
Source: Trainee.

1991–92	Darlington	17	0		
1992–93	Darlington	17	1		
1993–94	Darlington	23	1		
1994–95	Darlington	25	2		
1995–96	Darlington	38	0		
1996–97	Darlington	16	0	136	4
1996–97	Preston NE	21	1		
1997–98	Preston NE	35	2		
1998–99	Preston NE	41	3		
1999–2000	Preston NE	33	3		
2000–01	Preston NE	41	2		
2001–02	Preston NE	41	1	212	12
2002–03	WBA	36	1		
2003–04	WBA	43	1		
2004–05	WBA	0	0	79	2
2004–05	Leeds U	35	0		
2005–06	Leeds U	28	0		
2006–07	Leeds U	1	0	64	0
2006–07	Oldham Ath	27	0		
2007–08	Oldham Ath	15	0		
2008–09	Oldham Ath	40	0		
2009–10	Oldham Ath	46	1	128	1

HAZELL, Reuben (D)   316 12
H: 5 11 W: 12 05 b.Birmingham 24-4-79
Source: Trainee.

1996–97	Aston Villa	0	0		
1997–98	Aston Villa	0	0		
1998–99	Aston Villa	0	0		
1999–2000	Tranmere R	23	1		
2000–01	Tranmere R	13	0		
2001–02	Tranmere R	6	0	42	1
2001–02	Torquay U	19	0		
2002–03	Torquay U	46	1		
2003–04	Torquay U	19	1		
2004–05	Torquay U	0	0	84	2
2005–06	Chesterfield	33	0		
2006–07	Chesterfield	39	2		
2007–08	Chesterfield	0	0	72	2
2007–08	Oldham Ath	34	0		
2008–09	Oldham Ath	43	3		
2009–10	Oldham Ath	41	3	118	7

HOLDSWORTH, Andy (D)   243 6
H: 5 9 W: 11 02 b.Pontefract 29-1-84
Source: Scholar.

2003–04	Huddersfield T	36	0		
2004–05	Huddersfield T	40	0		
2005–06	Huddersfield T	42	1		
2006–07	Huddersfield T	35	2		
2007–08	Huddersfield T	44	3		
2008–09	Huddersfield T	34	0	231	6
2009–10	Oldham Ath	12	0	12	0

JACOBSON, Joe (D)   95 2
H: 5 11 W: 12 06 b.Cardiff 17-11-86
Source: Scholar. *Honours:* Wales Under-21.

2005–06	Cardiff C	1	0		
2006–07	Cardiff C	0	0	1	0
2006–07	*Accrington S*	6	1	6	1
2006–07	Bristol R	11	0		
2007–08	Bristol R	40	1		
2008–09	Bristol R	22	0	73	1
2009–10	Oldham Ath	15	0	15	0

LEE, Kieran (D)   39 1
H: 6 1 W: 12 00 b.Tameside 22-6-88
Source: Scholar.

2006–07	Manchester U	1	0		
2007–08	Manchester U	0	0	1	0
2007–08	*QPR*	7	0	7	0
2008–09	Oldham Ath	7	0		
2009–10	Oldham Ath	24	1	31	1

LOMAX, Kelvin (D)   92 0
H: 5 11 W: 12 03 b.Bury 12-11-86
Source: Scholar.

2003–04	Oldham Ath	1	0		
2004–05	Oldham Ath	9	0		
2005–06	Oldham Ath	0	0		
2006–07	Oldham Ath	9	0		
2007–08	Oldham Ath	21	0		
2007–08	*Rochdale*	10	0	10	0
2008–09	Oldham Ath	27	0		
2009–10	Oldham Ath	15	0	82	0

McGRATH, Phillip (M)   0 0
H: 5 9 W: 10 01 b. 7-4-92
Source: Glenavon.

| 2009–10 | Oldham Ath | 0 | 0 | | |

MILLAR, Kirk (M)   7 0
H: 5 9 W: 10 07 b.Belfast 7-7-92

| 2008–09 | Linfield | 1 | 0 | 1 | 0 |
| 2009–10 | Oldham Ath | 6 | 0 | 6 | 0 |

OJAPAH, Philip (M)   0 0
b.Liverpool 24-7-89

| 2009–10 | Oldham Ath | 0 | 0 | | |

OLLERENSHAW, Josh (G)   0 0
H: 6 5 W: 12 10 b.Manchester 5-10-90
Source: Scholar.

| 2009–10 | Oldham Ath | 0 | 0 | | |

PARKER, Keigan (F)   331 59
H: 5 7 W: 10 05 b.Livingston 8-6-82
Source: St Johnstone BC. *Honours:* Scotland Youth, Under-21.

1998–99	St Johnstone	2	0		
1999–2000	St Johnstone	10	2		
2000–01	St Johnstone	37	9		
2001–02	St Johnstone	21	1		
2002–03	St Johnstone	31	1		
2003–04	St Johnstone	31	8	132	21
2004–05	Blackpool	35	9		
2005–06	Blackpool	40	12		
2006–07	Blackpool	45	13		
2007–08	Blackpool	21	0	141	34
2008–09	Huddersfield T	20	2	20	2
2008–09	*Hartlepool U*	9	0	9	0
2009–10	Oldham Ath	27	2	27	2
2009–10	*Bury*	2	0	2	0

PURDIE, Rob (M)   123 12
H: 5 9 W: 11 00 b.Leicester 28-9-82
Source: Leicester C.

2006–07	Hereford U	44	6	44	6
2007–08	Darlington	39	0		
2008–09	Darlington	40	6	79	6
2008–09	Oldham Ath	0	0		
2009–10	Oldham Ath	0	0		

ROWNEY, Chris (M)   1 0
H: 5 6 W: 10 01 b.Oldham 14-2-91
Source: Scholar.

| 2009–10 | Oldham Ath | 1 | 0 | 1 | 0 |

SMALLEY, Deane (M)   102 10
H: 6 0 W: 11 10 b.Chadderton 5-9-88
Source: Scholar.

2006–07	Oldham Ath	2	0		
2007–08	Oldham Ath	37	2		
2008–09	Oldham Ath	34	5		
2009–10	Oldham Ath	29	3	102	10

STEPHENS, Dale (M)   41 4
H: 5 7 W: 11 04 b.Bolton 12-12-87
Source: Scholar.

2006–07	Bury	3	0		
2007–08	Bury	6	1	9	1
2008–09	Oldham Ath	0	0		
2009–10	Oldham Ath	26	2	26	2
2009–10	*Rochdale*	6	1	6	1

TAYLOR, Chris (M)   174 20
H: 5 11 W: 11 00 b.Oldham 20-12-86
Source: Scholar.

2005–06	Oldham Ath	14	0		
2006–07	Oldham Ath	44	4		
2007–08	Oldham Ath	42	5		
2008–09	Oldham Ath	42	10		
2009–10	Oldham Ath	32	1	174	20

WHITAKER, Danny (M)   337 45
H: 5 10 W: 11 00 b.Manchester 14-11-80
Source: Wilmslow Sports.

2000–01	Macclesfield T	0	0		
2001–02	Macclesfield T	16	2		
2002–03	Macclesfield T	41	10		
2003–04	Macclesfield T	36	5		
2004–05	Macclesfield T	36	2		
2005–06	Macclesfield T	42	4	171	23
2006–07	Port Vale	45	7		
2007–08	Port Vale	41	7	86	14
2008–09	Oldham Ath	39	6		
2009–10	Oldham Ath	41	2	80	8

WORTHINGTON, Jon (M)   238 12
H: 5 9 W: 11 05 b.Dewsbury 16-4-83
Source: Scholar.

2001–02	Huddersfield T	0	0		
2002–03	Huddersfield T	22	0		
2003–04	Huddersfield T	39	3		
2004–05	Huddersfield T	39	3		
2005–06	Huddersfield T	41	4		
2006–07	Huddersfield T	28	2		
2007–08	Huddersfield T	25	0		
2008–09	Huddersfield T	19	0	213	12
2008–09	*Yeovil T*	9	0	9	0
2009–10	Oldham Ath	16	0	16	0

PETERBOROUGH U (62)

ANDREW, Danny (D)   12 0
H: 5 11 W: 11 06 b.Boston 23-12-90

| 2009–10 | Peterborough U | 2 | 0 | 2 | 0 |
| 2009–10 | *Cheltenham T* | 10 | 0 | 10 | 0 |

APPIAH, Kwesi (F)   0 0
H: 5 11 W: 12 08 b.London 12-8-90
Source: Ebbsfleet U.

| 2008–09 | Peterborough U | 0 | 0 | | |
| 2009–10 | Peterborough U | 0 | 0 | | |

BATT, Shaun (F)   66 7
H: 6 3 W: 12 08 b.Harlow 22-2-87
Source: Fisher Ath.

2008–09	Peterborough U	30	2		
2009–10	Peterborough U	20	2	50	4
2009–10	*Millwall*	16	3	16	3

BENNETT, Ryan (M)   125 7
H: 6 2 W: 11 00 b.Orsett 6-3-90
Source: Scholar. *Honours:* England Youth.

2006–07	Grimsby T	5	0		
2007–08	Grimsby T	40	1		
2008–09	Grimsby T	45	5		
2009–10	Grimsby T	13	0	103	6
2009–10	Peterborough U	22	1	22	1

BLANCHETT, Danny (D)　　20　1
H: 5 11　W: 11 12　b.Wembley 12-3-88
Source: Northwood, Hendon, Harrow Borough, Cambridge C.
2006–07　Peterborough U　3　1
2007–08　Peterborough U　1　0
2008–09　Peterborough U　3　0
2009–10　Peterborough U　0　0　7　1
2009–10　*Hereford U*　13　0　13　0

BOYD, George (M)　　150　37
H: 5 10　W: 11 07　b.Chatham 2-10-85
Source: Stevenage B. *Honours:* Scotland B.
2006–07　Peterborough U　20　6
2007–08　Peterborough U　46　12
2008–09　Peterborough U　46　9
2009–10　Peterborough U　32　9　144　36
2009–10　*Nottingham F*　6　1　6　1

DAY, Jamie (M)　　110　5
H: 5 9　W: 10 07　b.Wycombe 7-5-86
Source: Scholar.
2003–04　Peterborough U　0　0
2004–05　Peterborough U　1　0
2005–06　Peterborough U　25　1
2006–07　Peterborough U　24　1
2007–08　Peterborough U　42　3
2008–09　Peterborough U　5　0
2009–10　Peterborough U　5　0　102　5
2009–10　*Dagenham & R*　8　0　8　0

DIAGOURAGA, Toumani (M)　　141　4
H: 6 2　W: 11 05　b.Corbeil-Essones 10-6-87
Source: Scholar.
2004–05　Watford　0　0
2005–06　Watford　1　0
2005–06　Swindon T　8　0　8　0
2006–07　Watford　0　0
2006–07　Rotherham U　7　0　7　0
2007–08　Watford　0　0　1　0
2007–08　Hereford U　41　2
2008–09　Hereford U　45　2　86　4
2009–10　Peterborough U　19　0　19　0
2009–10　*Brentford*　20　0　20　0

FRECKLINGTON, Lee (M)　　166　23
H: 5 8　W: 11 00　b.Lincoln 8-9-85
Source: Scholar. *Honours:* Eire B.
2003–04　Lincoln C　0　0
2004–05　Lincoln C　3　0
2005–06　Lincoln C　18　2
2006–07　Lincoln C　42　8
2007–08　Lincoln C　34　4
2008–09　Lincoln C　27　7　124　21
2008–09　Peterborough U　7　0
2009–10　Peterborough U　35　2　42　2

GEOHAGHON, Exodus (D)　　19　1
H: 6 7　W: 11 11　b.Birmingham 27-2-85
Source: Sutton Coldfield T, Bromsgrove R, Redditch U, Kettering T, England C.
2009–10　Peterborough U　19　1　19　1

GREEN, Dominic (F)　　51　5
H: 5 6　W: 11 02　b.London 5-7-89
Source: Scholar.
2007–08　Dagenham & R　12　0
2008–09　Dagenham & R　2　1　14　1
2008–09　Peterborough U　16　1
2009–10　Peterborough U　11　1　27　2
2009–10　*Chesterfield*　10　2　10　2

GRIFFITHS, Scott (D)　　118　1
H: 5 9　W: 11 08　b.London 27-11-85
Source: Aveley.
2007–08　Dagenham & R　41　0
2008–09　Dagenham & R　44　0
2009–10　Dagenham & R　13　1　98　1
2009–10　Peterborough U　20　0　20　0

HATCH, Liam (F)　　125　21
H: 6 4　W: 13 09　b.Hitchin 3-4-84
Source: Herne Bay, Gravesend & N.
2005–06　Barnet　35　2
2006–07　Barnet　31　3
2007–08　Barnet　21　6　87　11
2008–09　Peterborough U　11　2
2008–09　*Darlington*　26　8　26　8
2009–10　Peterborough U　0　0　12　2

HOWE, Rene (F)　　107　27
H: 6 0　W: 14 03　b.Bedford 22-10-86
Source: Kettering T.
2007–08　Peterborough U　15　1
2007–08　Rochdale　20　9　20　9
2008–09　Peterborough U　0　0
2008–09　Morecambe　37　10　37　10
2009–10　Peterborough U　0　0　15　1
2009–10　Lincoln C　17　5　17　5
2009–10　Gillingham　18　2　18　2

KORANTENG, Nathan (M)　　4　0
H: 6 2　W: 12 08　b.London 26-5-92
Source: Scholar.
2009–10　Peterborough U　4　0　4　0

LEE, Charlie (M)　　124　13
H: 5 11　W: 11 07　b.Whitechapel 5-1-87
Source: Scholar.
2005–06　Tottenham H　0　0
2005–06　Tottenham H　0　0
2006–07　Millwall　5　0　5　0
2007–08　Peterborough U　42　6
2008–09　Peterborough U　44　5
2009–10　Peterborough U　33　2　119　13

LEWIS, Joe (G)　　135　0
H: 6 5　W: 12 10　b.Bury St Edmunds 6-10-87
Source: Scholar. *Honours:* England Youth, Under-21.
2004–05　Norwich C　0　0
2005–06　Norwich C　0　0
2006–07　Norwich C　0　0
2006–07　Stockport Co　5　0　5　0
2007–08　Norwich C　0　0
2007–08　Morecambe　19　0　19　0
2008–09　Peterborough U　22　0
2008–09　Peterborough U　46　0
2009–10　Peterborough U　43　0　111　0

MACKAIL-SMITH, Craig (F)　　140　53
H: 6 3　W: 12 04　b.Hertford 25-2-84
Source: Dagenham & R.
2006–07　Peterborough U　15　8
2007–08　Peterborough U　36　12
2008–09　Peterborough U　46　23
2009–10　Peterborough U　43　10　140　53

McCRAE, Romone (M)　　2　0
H: 6 1　W: 12 07　b.Southwark 1-8-90
Source: Crawley T.
2009–10　Peterborough U　2　0　2　0

McKEOWN, James (G)　　6　0
H: 6 1　W: 13 07　b.Sutton Coldfield 24-7-89
Source: Scholar.
2005–06　Walsall　0　0
2006–07　Walsall　0　0
2007–08　Peterborough U　1　0
2008–09　Peterborough U　1　0
2009–10　Peterborough U　4　0　6　0

McLEAN, Aaron (F)　　178　63
H: 5 9　W: 10 10　b.Hammersmith 25-5-83
Source: Trainee.
1999–2000　Leyton Orient　3　0
2000–01　Leyton Orient　2　1
2001–02　Leyton Orient　27　1
2002–03　Leyton Orient　8　0　40　2
From Aldershot T, Grays Ath.
2006–07　Peterborough U　16　7
2007–08　Peterborough U　45　29
2008–09　Peterborough U　42　18
2009–10　Peterborough U　35　7　138　61

MILLS, Danny (F)　　5　0
H: 6 4　W: 13 02　b.Peterborough 27-11-91
Source: Crawley T.
2009–10　Peterborough U　3　0　3　0
2009–10　Torquay U　2　0　2　0

MORGAN, Craig (D)　　221　5
H: 6 0　W: 11 04　b.St Asaph 18-6-85
Source: Scholar. *Honours:* Wales Youth, Under-21, 20 full caps.
2001–02　Wrexham　2　0
2002–03　Wrexham　6　1
2003–04　Wrexham　18　0
2004–05　Wrexham　26　0
2005–06　Milton Keynes D　40　0
2006–07　Milton Keynes D　3　0　43　0
2006–07　Wrexham　1　0　53　1

2006–07　Peterborough U　23　1
2007–08　Peterborough U　41　2
2008–09　Peterborough U　27　0
2009–10　Peterborough U　34　1　125　4

RENDELL, Scott (F)　　53　16
H: 6 1　W: 13 00　b.Ashford 21-10-86
Source: Aldershot T, Reading, Crawley T, Cambridge U.
On loan from Cambridge U.
2007–08　Peterborough U　10　3
2008–09　Peterborough U　3　1
2008–09　*Yeovil T*　5　0　5　0
2009–10　Peterborough U　0　0　13　4
2009–10　*Torquay U*　35　12　35　12

ROWE, Tommy (M)　　104　15
H: 5 11　W: 12 11　b.Manchester 1-5-89
Source: Scholar.
2006–07　Stockport Co　4　0
2007–08　Stockport Co　24　6
2008–09　Stockport Co　44　7　72　13
2008–09　Peterborough U　0　0
2009–10　Peterborough U　32　2　32　2

SIMPSON, Josh (M)　　21　2
H: 5 10　W: 12 02　b.Cambridge 6-3-87
Source: Cambridge C, Cambridge U, Histon.
2009–10　Peterborough U　21　2　21　2

TORRES, Sergio (M)　　118　8
H: 6 2　W: 12 04　b.Mar del Plata 8-11-83
Source: Basingstoke T.
2005–06　Wycombe W　24　1
2006–07　Wycombe W　20　0
2007–08　Wycombe W　42　5　86　6
2008–09　Peterborough U　15　1
2009–10　Peterborough U　9　0　24　1
2009–10　Lincoln C　8　1　8　1

WHELPDALE, Chris (M)　　103　11
H: 6 0　W: 12 08　b.Harold Wood 27-1-87
Source: Billericay T.
2006–07　Peterborough U　0　0
2007–08　Peterborough U　35　3
2008–09　Peterborough U　39　7
2009–10　Peterborough U　29　1　103　11

WILLIAMS, Tom (M)　　262　4
H: 5 11　W: 12 06　b.Carshalton 8-7-80
Source: Walton & Hersham. *Honours:* Cyprus 1 full cap.
1999–2000　West Ham U　0　0
2000–01　West Ham U　0　0
2000–01　Peterborough U　2　0
2001–02　Peterborough U　34　2
2001–02　Birmingham C　4　0
2002–03　Birmingham C　0　0
2002–03　QPR　26　1
2003–04　Birmingham C　0　0　4　0
2003–04　QPR　5　0
2003–04　Peterborough U　21　1
2004–05　Barnsley　39　0　39　0
2005–06　Gillingham　13　0　13　0
2005–06　Swansea C　17　0
2006–07　Swansea C　29　0　46　0
2007–08　Wycombe W　10　0　10　0
2007–08　Peterborough U　7　0
2008–09　Peterborough U　25　0
2009–10　Peterborough U　15　0　104　3
2009–10　QPR　5　0　36　1
2009–10　Preston NE　10　0　10　0

WRIGHT, Ben (F)　　15　1
H: 6 2　W: 13 05　b.Basingstoke 20-8-88
Source: Basingstoke T, Hampton & Richmond B.
2008–09　Peterborough U　1　0
2009–10　Peterborough U　4　0　5　0
2009–10　Luton T　5　1　5　1
2009–10　Grimsby T　2　0　2　0
2009–10　Barnet　3　0　3　0

ZAKUANI, Gaby (D)　　176　4
H: 6 1　W: 12 13　b.DR Congo 31-5-86
Source: Scholar. *Honours:* DR Congo 1 full cap.
2002–03　Leyton Orient　1　0
2003–04　Leyton Orient　10　2
2004–05　Leyton Orient　33　0
2005–06　Leyton Orient　43　1　87　3
2006–07　Fulham　0　0
2006–07　Stoke C　9　0

Season	Club				
2007–08	Fulham	0	0		
2007–08	*Stoke C*	19	0	28	0
2008–09	Fulham	0	0		
2008–09	Peterborough U	32	1		
2009–10	Peterborough U	29	0	61	1

PLYMOUTH ARG (63)

ARNASON, Kari (M)   167 8
H: 6 3   W: 13 10   b.Reykjavik 13-10-82
Honours: Iceland 17 full caps, 1 goal.

Season	Club				
2001	Vikingur	5	2		
2002	Vikingur	5	1		
2003	Vikingur	16	0		
2004	Vikingur	15	0	41	3
2005	Djurgaarden	21	0		
2006	Djurgaarden	14	0	35	0
2006–07	Aarhus	14	2		
2007–08	Aarhus	25	0		
2008–09	Aarhus	12	1	51	3
2008–09	Esbjerg	8	0	8	0
2009–10	Plymouth Arg	32	2	32	2

BARKER, Chris (D)   393 3
H: 6 2   W: 13 08   b.Sheffield 2-3-80
Source: Alfreton.

Season	Club				
1998–99	Barnsley	0	0		
1999–2000	Barnsley	29	0		
2000–01	Barnsley	40	0		
2001–02	Barnsley	44	3	113	3
2002–03	Cardiff C	40	0		
2003–04	Cardiff C	39	0		
2004–05	*Stoke C*	4	0	4	0
2004–05	Cardiff C	39	0		
2005–06	Cardiff C	41	0		
2006–07	Cardiff C	0	0	159	0
2006–07	*Colchester U*	38	0	38	0
2007–08	QPR	25	0	25	0
2008–09	Plymouth Arg	40	0		
2009–10	Plymouth Arg	14	0	54	0

BARNES, Ashley (F)   36 6
H: 6 0   W: 12 00   b.Bath 30-10-89
Source: Paulton R.

Season	Club				
2006–07	Plymouth Arg	0	0		
2007–08	Plymouth Arg	0	0		
2008–09	Plymouth Arg	15	1		
2009–10	Plymouth Arg	7	1	22	2
2009–10	*Torquay U*	6	0	6	0
2009–10	*Brighton & HA*	8	4	8	4

BHASERA, Onismor (D)   125 2
H: 5 9   W: 11 13   b.Mutare 7-12-86
Honours: Zimbabwe 13 full caps.

Season	Club				
2004	Harare U	0	0		
2004–05	Tembisa Classic	14	0	14	0
2005–06	Maritzburg U	27	0		
2006–07	Maritzburg U	26	1	53	1
2007–08	Kaizer Chiefs	26	1		
2008–09	Kaizer Chiefs	25	0	51	1
2009–10	Plymouth Arg	7	0	7	0

BOLASIE, Yannick (M)   58 6
H: 6 2   W: 13 02   b.DR Congo 24-5-89

Season	Club				
2008–09	Plymouth Arg	0	0		
2008–09	*Barnet*	20	3		
2009–10	Plymouth Arg	16	1	16	1
2009–10	*Barnet*	22	2	42	5

CLARK, Chris (F)   266 9
H: 5 7   W: 10 05   b.Aberdeen 15-9-80

Season	Club				
1999–2000	Aberdeen	2	0		
2000–01	Aberdeen	24	0		
2001–02	Aberdeen	8	0		
2002–03	Aberdeen	25	1		
2003–04	Aberdeen	23	1		
2004–05	Aberdeen	31	2		
2005–06	Aberdeen	31	3		
2006–07	Aberdeen	37	1	181	8
2007–08	Plymouth Arg	12	0		
2008–09	Plymouth Arg	36	0		
2009–10	Plymouth Arg	37	1	85	1

COOPER, Kenny (F)   25 6
H: 6 6   W: 15 04   b.Baltimore 21-10-84

Season	Club				
2003–04	Manchester U	0	0		
2004–05	Manchester U	0	0		
2004–05	*Oldham Ath*	7	3	7	3
2005–06	Manchester U	0	0		
2006–07	Manchester U	0	0		
2006–07	*Nuremberg II*	11	3	11	3
2007–08	Manchester U	0	0		
2008–09	Manchester U	0	0		
2009–10	Plymouth Arg	7	0	7	0

DONNELLY, George (F)   21 4
H: 6 2   W: 13 03   b.Plymouth 28-5-88
Source: Skelmersdale U.

Season	Club				
2008–09	Plymouth Arg	2	0		
2009–10	Plymouth Arg	0	0	2	0
2009–10	*Stockport Co*	19	4	19	4

DUGUID, Karl (D)   466 44
H: 5 11   W: 11 06   b.Hitchin 21-3-78
Source: Trainee.

Season	Club				
1995–96	Colchester U	16	1		
1996–97	Colchester U	20	3		
1997–98	Colchester U	21	3		
1998–99	Colchester U	33	4		
1999–2000	Colchester U	41	12		
2000–01	Colchester U	41	5		
2001–02	Colchester U	41	4		
2002–03	Colchester U	27	3		
2003–04	Colchester U	30	2		
2004–05	Colchester U	0	0		
2005–06	Colchester U	35	0		
2006–07	Colchester U	43	5		
2007–08	Colchester U	37	0	385	42
2008–09	Plymouth Arg	39	1		
2009–10	Plymouth Arg	42	1	81	2

FALLON, Rory (F)   306 63
H: 6 2   W: 11 09   b.Gisbourne 20-3-82
Source: North Shore U. *Honours:* England Youth. New Zealand 10 full caps, 3 goals.

Season	Club				
1998–99	Barnsley	0	0		
1999–2000	Barnsley	0	0		
2000–01	Barnsley	1	0		
2001–02	Barnsley	9	0		
2001–02	*Shrewsbury T*	11	0	11	0
2002–03	Barnsley	26	7		
2003–04	Barnsley	16	4	52	11
2003–04	Swindon T	19	6		
2004–05	Swindon T	31	3		
2004–05	*Yeovil T*	6	1	6	1
2005–06	Swindon T	25	12	75	21
2005–06	Swansea C	17	4		
2006–07	Swansea C	24	8	41	12
2006–07	Plymouth Arg	15	1		
2007–08	Plymouth Arg	29	7		
2008–09	Plymouth Arg	44	5		
2009–10	Plymouth Arg	33	5	121	18

FLETCHER, Carl (M)   367 31
H: 5 10   W: 11 07   b.Camberley 7-4-80
Source: Trainee. *Honours:* Wales 36 full caps, 1 goal.

Season	Club				
1997–98	Bournemouth	1	0		
1998–99	Bournemouth	1	0		
1999–2000	Bournemouth	25	3		
2000–01	Bournemouth	43	6		
2001–02	Bournemouth	35	5		
2002–03	Bournemouth	42	1		
2003–04	Bournemouth	40	2		
2004–05	Bournemouth	6	2	193	19
2004–05	West Ham U	32	2		
2005–06	West Ham U	12	1	44	3
2005–06	*Watford*	3	0	3	0
2006–07	Crystal Palace	37	3		
2007–08	Crystal Palace	28	1		
2008–09	Crystal Palace	3	0	68	4
2008–09	*Nottingham F*	5	0	5	0
2008–09	*Plymouth Arg*	13	1		
2009–10	Plymouth Arg	41	4	54	5

FOLLY, Yoann (M)   99 0
H: 5 9   W: 11 04   b.Togo 6-6-85
Source: St Etienne. *Honours:* France Youth, Under-21. Togo 1 full cap.

Season	Club				
2003–04	Southampton	9	0		
2004–05	Southampton	3	0		
2004–05	*Nottingham F*	1	0	1	0
2004–05	*Preston NE*	2	0	2	0
2005–06	Southampton	2	0	14	0
2005–06	*Sheffield W*	14	0		
2006–07	Sheffield W	29	0		
2007–08	Sheffield W	10	0	53	0
2007–08	Plymouth Arg	4	0		
2008–09	Plymouth Arg	11	0		
2009–10	Plymouth Arg	7	0	22	0
2009–10	*Dagenham & R*	7	0	7	0

GOW, Alan (M)   207 46
H: 6 0   W: 11 00   b.Clydebank 9-10-82
Honours: Scotland B.

Season	Club				
2000–01	Clydebank	3	0		
2001–02	Clydebank	5	0	8	0
2002–03	Airdrie U	27	5		
2003–04	Airdrie U	32	12		
2004–05	Airdrie U	26	9	85	26
2005–06	Falkirk	34	6		
2006–07	Falkirk	36	7	70	13
2007–08	Rangers	0	0		

On loan from Rangers.

Season	Club				
2008–09	*Blackpool*	17	5	17	5
2008–09	Norwich C	13	0		
2009–10	Norwich C	0	0	13	0
2009–10	Plymouth Arg	14	2	14	2

HEAD, Liam (F)   0 0
H: 6 1   W: 13 05   b.Bovey 26-1-92
Source: Scholar.

Season	Club		
2008–09	Plymouth Arg	0	0
2009–10	Plymouth Arg	0	0

JOHNSON, Damien (M)   279 9
H: 5 9   W: 11 09   b.Lisburn 18-11-78
Source: Trainee. *Honours:* Northern Ireland Youth, Under-21, 56 full caps.

Season	Club				
1995–96	Blackburn R	0	0		
1996–97	Blackburn R	0	0		
1997–98	Blackburn R	0	0		
1997–98	*Nottingham F*	6	0	6	0
1998–99	Blackburn R	21	1		
1999–2000	Blackburn R	16	1		
2000–01	Blackburn R	16	0		
2001–02	Blackburn R	7	1	60	3
2001–02	Birmingham C	8	1		
2002–03	Birmingham C	30	1		
2003–04	Birmingham C	35	1		
2004–05	Birmingham C	36	0		
2005–06	Birmingham C	31	0		
2006–07	Birmingham C	26	1		
2007–08	Birmingham C	17	0		
2008–09	Birmingham C	9	0		
2008–09	Birmingham C	1	0	193	4
2009–10	Plymouth Arg	20	2	20	2

JOHNSON, Reda (M)   40 0
H: 6 2   W: 13 10   b.Marseille 21-3-88

Season	Club				
2005–06	Gueugnon	0	0		
2006–07	Gueugnon	0	0		
2007–08	Amiens	8	0		
2008–09	Amiens	7	0	15	0
2009–10	Plymouth Arg	25	0	25	0

LARRIEU, Romain (G)   284 0
H: 6 4   W: 13 01   b.Mont-de-Marsan 31-8-76
Source: Montpellier, ASOA Valence. *Honours:* France Youth.

Season	Club				
2000–01	Plymouth Arg	15	0		
2001–02	Plymouth Arg	45	0		
2002–03	Plymouth Arg	43	0		
2003–04	Plymouth Arg	6	0		
2004–05	Plymouth Arg	23	0		
2005–06	Plymouth Arg	45	0		
2006–07	Plymouth Arg	6	0		
2006–07	*Gillingham*	14	0	14	0
2007–08	Plymouth Arg	15	0		
2007–08	*Yeovil T*	6	0	6	0
2008–09	Plymouth Arg	41	0		
2009–10	Plymouth Arg	25	0	264	0

LEONARD, Ryan (D)   1 0
H: 6 0   W: 11 01   b.Chaddlewood 24-5-92
Source: Scholar.

Season	Club				
2009–10	Plymouth Arg	1	0	1	0

MACKIE, Jamie (F)   114 16
H: 5 8   W: 11 00   b.Dorking 22-9-85
Source: Leatherhead.

Season	Club				
2003–04	Wimbledon	13	0	13	0
2004–05	Milton Keynes D	3	0	3	0

From Exeter C

Season	Club				
2007–08	Plymouth Arg	13	3		
2008–09	Plymouth Arg	43	5		
2009–10	Plymouth Arg	42	8	98	16

MACLEAN, Steve (F)   200 66
H: 5 11   W: 12 06   b.Edinburgh 23-8-82
Honours: Scotland Under-21.

Season	Club				
2002–03	Rangers	3	0	3	0
2003–04	Scunthorpe U	42	23	42	23
2004–05	Sheffield W	36	18		

2005–06	Sheffield W	6	2	
2006–07	Sheffield W	41 12	83 32	
2007–08	Cardiff C	15 1	15 1	
2007–08	Plymouth Arg	17 3		
2008–09	Plymouth Arg	21 2		
2009–10	Plymouth Arg	3 0	41 5	
2009–10	*Aberdeen*	16 5	16 5	

MASON, Joe (F)   19   3
H: 5 9   W: 11 11   b.Peverell 13-5-91
Honours: Republic of Ireland Youth.

2009–10	Plymouth Arg	19 3	19 3

McNAMEE, David (D)   165   4
H: 5 11   W: 11 02   b.Glasgow 10-10-80
Source: St Mirren BC. *Honours:* Scotland B, 4 full caps.

1997–98	St Mirren	1 0	
1998–99	St Mirren	31 0	32 0
1998–99	Blackburn R	0 0	
1999–2000	Blackburn R	0 0	
2000–01	Blackburn R	0 0	
2001–02	Blackburn R	0 0	
2002–03	Livingston	12 0	
2003–04	Livingston	30 3	
2004–05	Livingston	29 1	
2005–06	Livingston	14 0	85 4
2006–07	Coventry C	16 0	
2007–08	Coventry C	13 0	29 0
2008–09	Plymouth Arg	10 0	
2009–10	Plymouth Arg	9 0	19 0

NOONE, Craig (M)   45   4
H: 6 3   W: 12 07   b.Southport 17-11-87
Source: Skelmersdale U, Burscough, Southport.

2008–09	Plymouth Arg	21 1	
2009–10	Plymouth Arg	17 1	38 2
2009–10	*Exeter C*	7 2	7 2

PATERSON, Jim (M)   250   11
H: 5 11   W: 12 13   b.Airdrie 25-9-79
Source: Dundee U BC. *Honours:* Scotland Under-21.

1998–99	Dundee U	15 0	
1999–2000	Dundee U	8 1	
2000–01	Dundee U	6 1	
2001–02	Dundee U	27 2	
2002–03	Dundee U	33 1	
2003–04	Dundee U	16 0	105 5
2004–05	Motherwell	35 3	
2005–06	Motherwell	19 1	
2006–07	Motherwell	34 1	
2007–08	Motherwell	20 0	108 5
2007–08	Plymouth Arg	8 1	
2008–09	Plymouth Arg	17 0	
2009–10	Plymouth Arg	12 0	37 1

SAWYER, Gary (D)   97   5
H: 6 0   W: 11 08   b.Bideford 5-7-85
Source: Scholar.

2004–05	Plymouth Arg	0 0	
2005–06	Plymouth Arg	0 0	
2006–07	Plymouth Arg	22 0	
2007–08	Plymouth Arg	31 1	
2008–09	Plymouth Arg	13 3	
2009–10	Plymouth Arg	29 1	95 5
2009–10	*Bristol C*	2 0	2 0

SEIP, Marcel (D)   252   10
H: 6 0   W: 11 03   b.Winschoten 5-4-82

1999–2000	Veendam	9 0	
2000–01	Veendam	18 0	27 0
2001–02	Heerenveen	6 0	
2002–03	Heerenveen	6 0	
2003–04	Heerenveen	31 1	
2004–05	Heerenveen	30 1	
2005–06	Heerenveen	28 0	95 2
2006–07	Plymouth Arg	37 2	
2007–08	Plymouth Arg	34 1	
2008–09	Plymouth Arg	41 3	
2009–10	Plymouth Arg	5 0	117 6
2009–10	*Blackpool*	7 2	7 2
2009–10	*Sheffield U*	6 0	6 0

SHERIDAN, Cillian (F)   40   4
H: 6 5   b.Baillieborough 21-2-89

2006–07	Celtic	1 0	
2007–08	Celtic	1 0	
2008–09	Celtic	12 4	
2008–09	*Motherwell*	13 0	13 0
2009–10	Celtic	0 0	14 4

On loan from Celtic.

2009–10	Plymouth Arg	13 0	13 0

SUMMERFIELD, Luke (M)   94   4
H: 6 0   W: 11 00   b.Ivybridge 6-12-87
Source: Scholar.

2004–05	Plymouth Arg	1 0	
2005–06	Plymouth Arg	0 0	
2006–07	Plymouth Arg	23 1	
2006–07	*Bournemouth*	8 1	8 1
2007–08	Plymouth Arg	7 0	
2008–09	Plymouth Arg	29 2	
2009–10	Plymouth Arg	12 0	72 3
2009–10	*Leyton Orient*	14 0	14 0

TIMAR, Krisztian (D)   158   12
H: 6 3   W: 13 08   b.Budapest 4-10-79
Source: Ferencvaros, MTK, Elore. *Honours:* Hungary Youth, Under-21, Under-23, 4 full caps.

2001–02	Videoton	31 4	
2002–03	Videoton	15 0	46 4
2003	Jozerit	0 0	
2003–04	Tatabanya	0 0	
2004–05	Nyiregyhaza	12 0	12 0
2005–06	Ferencvaros	23 3	23 3
2006–07	Plymouth Arg	9 1	
2007–08	Plymouth Arg	38 3	
2008–09	Plymouth Arg	21 0	
2009–10	Plymouth Arg	7 1	75 5
2009–10	*Oldham Ata*	2 0	2 0

WALTON, Simon (D)   119   7
H: 6 1   W: 13 05   b.Sherburn-in-Elmet 13-9-87
Source: Scholar. *Honours:* England Youth.

2004–05	Leeds U	30 3	
2005–06	Leeds U	4 0	34 3
2006–07	Charlton Ath	0 0	
2006–07	*Ipswich T*	19 3	19 3
2006–07	*Cardiff C*	6 0	6 0
2007–08	*QPR*	5 0	5 0
2007–08	*Hull C*	10 0	10 0
2008–09	Plymouth Arg	13 0	
2008–09	*Blackpool*	1 0	1 0
2009–10	Plymouth Arg	0 0	13 0
2009–10	*Crewe Alex*	31 1	31 1

WRIGHT-PHILLIPS, Bradley (M)   158   28
H: 5 10   W: 10 07   b.Lewisham 12-3-85
Source: Scholar. *Honours:* England Youth, Under-20.

2002–03	Manchester C	0 0	
2003–04	Manchester C	0 0	
2004–05	Manchester C	14 0	
2005–06	Manchester C	18 1	32 2
2006–07	Southampton	39 8	
2007–08	Southampton	39 8	
2008–09	Southampton	33 6	111 22
2009–10	Plymouth Arg	15 4	15 4

PORT VALE (64)

ANYON, Joe (G)   109   0
H: 6 1   W: 12 11   b.Poulton-le-Fylde 29-12-86
Source: Scholar.

2005–06	Port Vale	0 0	
2006–07	Port Vale	22 0	
2007–08	Port Vale	44 0	
2008–09	Port Vale	36 0	
2009–10	Port Vale	7 0	109 0

COLLINS, Lee (D)   100   2
H: 6 1   W: 11 10   b.Telford 23-9-83
Source: Scholar. *Honours:* England Youth.

2006–07	Wolverhampton W	0 0	
2007–08	Wolverhampton W	0 0	
2007–08	*Hereford U*	16 0	16 0
2008–09	Wolverhampton W	0 0	
2008–09	Port Vale	39 1	
2009–10	Port Vale	45 1	84 2

DODDS, Louis (F)   141   24
H: 5 10   W: 12 04   b.Leicester 8-10-86
Source: Scholar.

2005–06	Leicester C	0 0	
2006–07	Leicester C	0 0	
2006–07	*Rochdale*	12 2	12 2
2007–08	Leicester C	0 0	

2007–08	*Lincoln C*	41 9	41 9
2008–09	Port Vale	44 7	
2009–10	Port Vale	44 6	88 13

FRASER, Tom (M)   117   3
H: 5 10   W: 11 00   b.Brighton 5-12-87
Source: Bognor Regis T.

2006–07	Brighton & HA	28 1	
2007–08	Brighton & HA	24 0	
2008–09	Brighton & HA	27 1	79 2
2009–10	Port Vale	38 1	38 1

GLOVER, Danny (M)   43   4
H: 6 0   W: 11 02   b.Crewe 24-10-89
Source: Scholar.

2007–08	Port Vale	15 1	
2008–09	Port Vale	23 3	
2009–10	Port Vale	3 0	41 4
2009–10	*Rochdale*	2 0	2 0

GRIFFITH, Anthony (M)   88   0
H: 6 0   W: 12 00   b.Huddersfield 28-10-86
Source: Glasshoughton W.

2005–06	Doncaster R	4 0	
2005–06	*Oxford U*	0 0	
2006–07	Doncaster R	2 0	
2006–07	*Darlington*	4 0	4 0
2007–08	Doncaster R	0 0	6 0
2007–08	Port Vale	0 0	
2008–09	Port Vale	38 0	
2009–10	Port Vale	40 0	78 0

HALDANE, Lewis (F)   184   18
H: 6 0   W: 11 03   b.Trowbridge 13-3-85
Source: Scholar. *Honours:* Wales Under-21.

2003–04	Bristol R	27 5	
2004–05	Bristol R	13 0	
2005–06	Bristol R	30 3	
2006–07	Bristol R	45 6	
2006–07	Bristol R	32 1	
2008–09	Bristol R	0 0	147 15
2009–10	Port Vale	37 3	37 3

HORSFIELD, Geoff (F)   340   79
H: 6 0   W: 11 07   b.Barnsley 1-11-73

1992–93	Scarborough	6 1	
1993–94	Scarborough	6 0	12 1

From Witton Alb.

1998–99	Halifax T	10 7	10 7
1998–99	Fulham	28 15	
1999–2000	Fulham	31 7	59 22
2000–01	Birmingham C	34 7	
2001–02	Birmingham C	40 11	
2002–03	Birmingham C	31 5	
2003–04	Birmingham C	3 0	108 23
2003–04	Wigan Ath	16 7	16 7
2003–04	WBA	20 7	
2004–05	WBA	29 3	
2005–06	WBA	18 4	
2005–06	*Sheffield U*	3 0	
2006–07	WBA	0 0	67 14
2006–07	Sheffield U	0 0	
2006–07	*Leeds U*	14 2	14 2
2006–07	*Leicester C*	13 2	13 2
2007–08	Sheffield U	0 0	
2007–08	*Scunthorpe U*	12 0	12 0
2008–09	Sheffield U	0 0	3 0
2008–09	*Lincoln C*	17 1	17 1
2009–10	Port Vale	9 0	9 0

HOWLAND, David (M)   61   3
H: 5 11   W: 10 08   b.Ballynahinch 17-9-86
Source: Scholar. *Honours:* Northern Ireland Under-21.

2004–05	Birmingham C	0 0	
2005–06	Birmingham C	0 0	
2006–07	Birmingham C	0 0	
2007–08	Birmingham C	0 0	
2007–08	*Port Vale*	17 1	
2008–09	Port Vale	40 2	
2009–10	Port Vale	4 0	61 3

JARRETT, Jason (M)   253   9
H: 6 1   W: 11 10   b.Bury 14-9-79
Source: Trainee.

1998–99	Blackpool	2 0	
1999–2000	Blackpool	0 0	2 0
1999–2000	Wrexham	1 0	1 0
2000–01	Bury	25 2	
2001–02	Bury	37 2	62 4
2001–02	Wigan Ath	5 0	
2002–03	Wigan Ath	35 0	

Season	Club				
2003–04	Wigan Ath	41	1		
2004–05	Wigan Ath	14	0	95	1
2004–05	Stoke C	2	0	2	0
2005–06	Norwich C	11	0	11	0
2005–06	Plymouth Arg	7	0	7	0
2005–06	Preston NE	10	1		
2006–07	Preston NE	5	0		
2006–07	Hull C	3	0	3	0
2006–07	Leicester C	13	0	13	0
2007–08	Preston NE	0	0		
2007–08	QPR	2	0	2	0
2007–08	Oldham Ath	15	3	15	3
2008–09	Preston NE	3	0	18	1
2008–09	Brighton & HA	13	0	13	0
2009–10	Port Vale	9	0	9	0

JORGENSEN, Claus (M)   310 38
H: 5 10 W: 10 06 b.Holstebro 27-4-76
Source: Resen-Humlum, Struer BK, Holstebro, Aarhus, AC Horsens. *Honours:* Faeroes 10 full caps, 1 goal.

Season	Club				
1999–2000	Bournemouth	44	6		
2000–01	Bournemouth	43	8		
2001–02	Bradford C	18	1		
2002–03	Bradford C	32	11	50	12
2003–04	Coventry C	8	0		
2003–04	Bournemouth	17	0	104	14
2004–05	Coventry C	17	3		
2005–06	Coventry C	27	3	52	6
2006–07	Blackpool	31	2		
2007–08	Blackpool	37	4		
2008–09	Blackpool	32	0		
2009–10	Blackpool	0	0	100	6
2009–10	Port Vale	4	0	4	0

LAWRIE, James (F)   27 2
H: 6 0 W: 12 05 b.Belfast 18-12-90
Source: Scholar. *Honours:* Northern Ireland Under-21, B, 3 full caps.

Season	Club				
2007–08	Port Vale	6	0		
2008–09	Port Vale	18	2		
2009–10	Port Vale	3	0	27	2

LOFT, Doug (M)   82 5
H: 6 0 W: 12 01 b.Maidstone 25-12-86
Source: Hastings U.

Season	Club				
2005–06	Brighton & HA	3	1		
2006–07	Brighton & HA	11	1		
2007–08	Brighton & HA	13	0		
2008–09	Brighton & HA	12	0	39	2
2008–09	Dagenham & R	11	0	11	0
2009–10	Fort Vale	32	3	32	3

MALBON, Anthony (M)   1 0
H: 5 8 W: 11 00 b.Stoke 14-10-91
Source: Scholar.

Season	Club				
2008–09	Port Vale	1	0		
2009–10	Port Vale	0	0	1	0

MARTIN, Chris (G)   52 0
H: 6 0 W: 13 05 b.Mansfield 21-7-90
Source: Scholar.

Season	Club				
2007–08	Port Vale	2	0		
2008–09	Port Vale	11	0		
2009–10	Port Vale	39	0	52	0

McCOMBE, John (D)   112 5
H: 6 2 W: 13 00 b.Pontefract 7-5-85
Source: Scholar.

Season	Club				
2002–03	Huddersfield T	1	0		
2003–04	Huddersfield T	0	0		
2004–05	Huddersfield T	5	0		
2005–06	Huddersfield T	1	0		
2005–06	Torquay U	0	0		
2006–07	Huddersfield T	7	0	14	0
2007–08	Hereford U	27	0	27	0
2008–09	Port Vale	31	2		
2009–10	Port Vale	40	3	71	5

MORSY, Sam (M)   1 0
H: 5 9 W: 12 06 b.Wolverhampton 10-9-91
Source: Scholar.

Season	Club				
2009–10	Port Vale	1	0	1	0

OWEN, Gareth (D)   193 1
H: 6 1 W: 11 07 b.Cheadle 21-9-82
Source: Scholar. *Honours:* Wales Youth.

Season	Club				
2001–02	Stoke C	0	0		
2002–03	Stoke C	0	0		
2003–04	Stoke C	3	0		
2003–04	Oldham Ath	15	1		
2004–05	Stoke C	2	0	5	0
2004–05	Torquay U	5	0	5	0
2004–05	Oldham Ath	9	0		
2005–06	Oldham Ath	17	0		
2006–07	Oldham Ath	0	0	41	1
2006–07	Stockport Co	39	0		
2007–08	Stockport Co	36	0		
2008–09	Stockport Co	8	0	83	0
2008–09	Yeovil T	7	0	7	0
2008–09	Port Vale	12	0		
2009–10	Port Vale	40	0	52	0

PROSSER, Luke (M)   33 2
H: 6 2 W: 12 04 b.Enfield 28-5-88
Source: Scholar.

Season	Club				
2005–06	Port Vale	0	0		
2006–07	Port Vale	0	0		
2007–08	Port Vale	5	0		
2008–09	Port Vale	26	1		
2009–10	Port Vale	2	1	33	2

RICHARDS, Marc (F)   263 72
H: 6 2 W: 12 06 b.Wolverhampton 8-7-82
Source: Trainee. *Honours:* England Youth, Under-20.

Season	Club				
1999–2000	Blackburn R	0	0		
2000–01	Blackburn R	0	0		
2001–02	Blackburn R	0	0		
2001–02	Crewe Alex	4	0	4	0
2001–02	Oldham Ath	5	0	5	0
2001–02	Halifax T	5	0	5	0
2002–03	Blackburn R	0	0		
2002–03	Swansea C	17	7	17	7
2003–04	Northampton T	41	8		
2004–05	Northampton T	12	2		
2004–05	Rochdale	5	2	5	2
2005–06	Northampton T	0	0	53	10
2005–06	Barnsley	38	12		
2006–07	Barnsley	31	6	69	18
2007–08	Port Vale	29	5		
2008–09	Port Vale	30	10		
2009–10	Port Vale	46	20	105	35

RICHMAN, Simon (M)   48 5
H: 5 11 W: 11 12 b.Ormskirk 2-6-90
Source: Scholar.

Season	Club				
2007–08	Port Vale	6	0		
2008–09	Port Vale	37	5		
2009–10	Port Vale	5	0	48	5

STOCKLEY, Sam (D)   458 6
H: 6 0 W: 12 08 b.Tiverton 5-9-77
Source: Trainee.

Season	Club				
1996–97	Southampton	0	0		
1996–97	Barnet	21	0		
1997–98	Barnet	41	0		
1998–99	Barnet	41	0		
1999–2000	Barnet	34	1		
2000–01	Barnet	45	1	182	2
2001–02	Oxford U	41	0		
2002–03	Oxford U	0	0	41	0
2002–03	Colchester U	33	1		
2003–04	Colchester U	44	0		
2004–05	Colchester U	37	1		
2005–06	Colchester U	27	1	141	3
2005–06	Blackpool	7	0	7	0
2006–07	Wycombe W	34	1		
2007–08	Wycombe W	22	0	56	1
2008–09	Port Vale	22	0		
2009–10	Port Vale	9	0	31	0

TAYLOR, Kris (M)   191 11
H: 5 9 W: 11 05 b.Stafford 12-1-84
Source: Scholar. *Honours:* England Schools, Youth.

Season	Club				
2000–01	Manchester U	0	0		
2001–02	Manchester U	0	0		
2002–03	Manchester U	0	0		
2002–03	Walsall	0	0		
2003–04	Walsall	11	1		
2004–05	Walsall	12	2		
2005–06	Walsall	22	2		
2006–07	Walsall	35	1	80	6
2007–08	Hereford U	31	1		
2008–09	Hereford U	39	1	70	2
2009–10	Port Vale	41	3	41	3

TAYLOR, Rob (D)   59 11
H: 6 0 W: 12 08 b.Shrewsbury 16-1-85
Source: Ludlow T, Stourport Swifts, Solihull B, Redditch U, Nuneaton B.

Season	Club				
2008–09	Port Vale	20	3		
2009–10	Port Vale	39	8	59	11

YATES, Adam (D)   108 0
H: 5 10 W: 10 07 b.Stoke 28-5-83
Source: Scholar.

Season	Club				
2000–01	Crewe Alex	0	0		
2001–02	Crewe Alex	0	0		
2002–03	Crewe Alex	0	0		
2003–04	Crewe Alex	0	0		
2004–05	Crewe Alex	0	0		
2005–06	Crewe Alex	0	0		
2006–07	Crewe Alex	0	0		
2007–08	Morecambe	44	0		
2008–09	Morecambe	32	0	76	0
2009–10	Port Vale	32	0	32	0

PORTSMOUTH (65)

ASHDOWN, Jamie (G)   78 0
H: 6 1 W: 13 05 b.Reading 30-11-80
Source: Scholar.

Season	Club				
1999–2000	Reading	0	0		
2000–01	Reading	1	0		
2001–02	Reading	1	0		
2001–02	Arsenal	0	0		
2002–03	Reading	1	0		
2002–03	Bournemouth	2	0	2	0
2003–04	Reading	10	0	13	0
2003–04	Rushden & D	19	0	19	0
2004–05	Portsmouth	16	0		
2005–06	Portsmouth	17	0		
2006–07	Portsmouth	0	0		
2006–07	Norwich C	2	0	2	0
2007–08	Portsmouth	3	0		
2008–09	Portsmouth	0	0		
2009–10	Portsmouth	6	0	42	0

BASINAS, Angelos (M)   303 28
H: 5 11 W: 11 13 b.Chalkida 31-1-76
Honours: Greece 100 full caps, 7 goals.

Season	Club				
1995–96	Panathinaikos	1	0		
1996–97	Panathinaikos	1	0		
1997–98	Panathinaikos	26	1		
1998–99	Panathinaikos	21	0		
1999–2000	Panathinaikos	29	4		
2000–01	Panathinaikos	25	3		
2001–02	Panathinaikos	22	4		
2002–03	Panathinaikos	24	5		
2003–04	Panathinaikos	26	7		
2004–05	Panathinaikos	24	3		
2005–06	Panathinaikos	0	0	199	27
2005–06	Mallorca	14	0		
2006–07	Mallorca	29	0		
2007–08	Mallorca	32	1	75	1
2008–09	AEK Athens	14	0	14	0
2008–09	Portsmouth	3	0		
2009–10	Portsmouth	12	0	15	0

BELHADJ, Nadir (D)   242 12
H: 5 9 W: 10 07 b.Saint-Claude 18-6-82
Source: Lens. *Honours:* France Youth. Algeria 47 full caps, 4 goals.

Season	Club				
2002–03	Gueugnon	28	1		
2003–04	Gueugnon	36	1	64	2
2004–05	Sedan	31	1		
2005–06	Sedan	34	2		
2006–07	Sedan	37	2	102	5
2007–08	Lyon	9	0	9	0
2007–08	Lens	19	0	19	0
2008–09	Portsmouth	29	2		
2009–10	Portsmouth	19	3	48	5

BEN HAIM, Tal (D)   223 3
H: 5 11 W: 11 09 b.Rishon Le Zion 31-3-82
Source: Maccabi Tel Aviv. *Honours:* Israel Under-21, 54 full caps.

Season	Club				
2000–01	Maccabi Tel Aviv	1	0		
2001–02	Maccabi Tel Aviv	29	1		
2002–03	Maccabi Tel Aviv	0	0		
2003–04	Maccabi Tel Aviv	26	1	86	2
2004–05	Bolton W	21	1		
2005–06	Bolton W	35	0		
2006–07	Bolton W	32	0	88	0
2007–08	Chelsea	13	0	13	0
2008–09	Manchester C	9	0		
2008–09	Sunderland	5	0	5	0
2009–10	Manchester C	0	0	9	0
2009–10	Portsmouth	22	0	22	0

BOATENG, Kevin-Prince (M)   118   12
H: 6 0   W: 11 09   b.Berlin 6-3-87
Source: Reinickendorfer Fuchse. *Honours:*
Germany Under-21. Ghana 6 full caps, 1 goal.

2004–05	Hertha Berlin II	18	3
2005–06	Hertha Berlin	21	2
2005–06	Hertha Berlin II	4	1
2006–07	Hertha Berlin II	7	1	29	5
2006–07	Hertha Berlin	22	2	43	4
2007–08	Tottenham H	13	0
2008–09	Tottenham H	1	0	14	0
2008–09	*Bor Dortmund*	10	0	10	0
2009–10	Portsmouth	22	3	22	3

BROWN, Michael (M)   423   34
H: 5 9   W: 12 04   b.Hartlepool 25-1-77
Source: Trainee. *Honours:* England
Under-21.

1994–95	Manchester C	0	0
1995–96	Manchester C	21	0
1996–97	Manchester C	11	0
1996–97	*Hartlepool U*	6	1	6	1
1997–98	Manchester C	26	0
1998–99	Manchester C	31	2
1999–2000	Manchester C	0	0	89	2
1999–2000	*Portsmouth*	4	0
1999–2000	Sheffield U	24	3
2000–01	Sheffield U	36	1
2001–02	Sheffield U	36	5
2002–03	Sheffield U	40	16
2003–04	Sheffield U	15	2	151	27
2003–04	Tottenham H	17	1
2004–05	Tottenham H	24	1
2005–06	Tottenham H	9	0	50	2
2005–06	Fulham	7	0
2006–07	Fulham	34	0	41	0
2007–08	Wigan Ath	31	0
2008–09	Wigan Ath	25	0
2009–10	Wigan Ath	2	0	58	0
2009–10	Portsmouth	24	2	28	2

CIFTCI, Nadir (F)   0   0
H: 6 1   W: 13 00   b.Karacan 12-2-92
Source: Scholar.

2008–09	Portsmouth	0	0
2009–10	Portsmouth	0	0

COWAN-HALL, Paris (F)   3   0
H: 5 8   W: 11 08   b.London 5-10-90
Source: Scholar.

2008–09	Portsmouth	0	0
2009–10	Portsmouth	0	0
2009–10	*Grimsby T*	3	0	3	0

CUVELIER, Florent (M)   0   0
b.Belgium 12-9-92
Source: Scholar.

2009–10	Portsmouth	0	0

DINDANE, Aruna (F)   274   94
H: 5 8   W: 12 08   b.Abidjan 26-11-80
Honours: Ivory Coast 61 full caps, 18 goals.

1999–2000	ASEC Mimosas	22	9	22	9
2000–01	Anderlecht	26	5
2001–02	Anderlecht	28	10
2002–03	Anderlecht	23	6
2003–04	Anderlecht	25	15
2004–05	Anderlecht	29	14	131	50
2005–06	Lens	28	6
2006–07	Lens	34	11
2007–08	Lens	28	8
2008–09	Lens	12	2	102	27
2009–10	Portsmouth	19	8	19	8

DIOP, Papa Bouba (M)   223   23
H: 6 4   W: 14 12   b.Dakar 28-1-78
Source: Espoir, Jaraaf, Vevey Sports.
Honours: Senegal 63 full caps, 11 goals.

1999–2000	Neuchatel Xamax	0	0
2000–01	Neuchatel Xamax	18	4	18	4
2000–01	Grasshoppers	11	1
2001–02	Grasshoppers	18	4	29	5
2001–02	Lens	5	0
2002–03	Lens	16	3
2003–04	Lens	26	3	47	6
2004–05	Fulham	29	6
2005–06	Fulham	22	2
2006–07	Fulham	23	0
2007–08	Fulham	2	0	76	8
2007–08	Portsmouth	25	0

2008–09	Portsmouth	16	0
2009–10	Portsmouth	12	0	53	0

FINNAN, Steve (D)   450   15
H: 6 0   W: 12 03   b.Limerick 24-4-76
Source: Welling U. *Honours:* Eire Under-21,
B, 53 full caps, 2 goals.

1995–96	Birmingham C	12	1
1995–96	*Notts Co*	17	2
1996–97	Birmingham C	3	0	15	1
1996–97	Notts Co	23	0
1997–98	Notts Co	44	5
1998–99	Notts Co	13	0	97	7
1998–99	Fulham	22	2
1999–2000	Fulham	35	2
2000–01	Fulham	45	2
2001–02	Fulham	38	0
2002–03	Fulham	32	0	172	6
2003–04	Liverpool	22	0
2004–05	Liverpool	33	1
2005–06	Liverpool	33	0
2006–07	Liverpool	33	0
2007–08	Liverpool	24	0
2008–09	Liverpool	0	0	145	1
2009–10	Portsmouth	21	0	21	0

GAZET DUCHATTELIER, Ryan (M) 0
b.Richmond, A.as 17-2-91
Source: Scholar

2007–08	Portsmouth	0	0
2008–09	Portsmouth	0	0
2009–10	Portsmouth	0	0

HREIDARSSON, Hermann (D)   475   25
H: 6 3   W: 12 12   b.Reykjavik 11-7-74
Honours: Iceland Under-21, 85 full caps, 5
goals.

1993	IBV	2	0
1994	IBV	18	2
1995	IBV	18	1
1996	IBV	17	2
1997	IBV	11	0	66	5
1997–98	Crystal Palace	30	2
1998–99	Crystal Palace	7	0	37	2
1998–99	Brentford	33	4
1999–2000	Brentford	8	2	41	6
1999–2000	Wimbledon	24	1	24	1
2000–01	Wimbledon	1	0	25	1
2000–01	Ipswich T	36	1
2001–02	Ipswich T	38	1
2002–03	Ipswich T	28	0	102	2
2002–03	Charlton Ath	2	0
2003–04	Charlton Ath	33	2
2004–05	Charlton Ath	34	1
2005–06	Charlton Ath	34	0
2006–07	Charlton Ath	31	0	132	3
2007–08	Portsmouth	32	3
2008–09	Portsmouth	23	2
2009–10	Portsmouth	17	1	72	6

HUGHES, Richard (M)   263   15
H: 6 0   W: 13 03   b.Glasgow 25-6-79
Source: Atalanta. *Honours:* Scotland Youth,
Under-21, 5 full caps.

1997–98	Arsenal	0	0
1998–99	Bournemouth	44	2
1999–2000	Bournemouth	21	2
2000–01	Bournemouth	44	8
2001–02	Bournemouth	22	2	131	14
2002–03	Portsmouth	6	0
2002–03	*Grimsby T*	12	1	12	1
2003–04	Portsmouth	11	0
2004–05	Portsmouth	16	0
2005–06	Portsmouth	26	0
2006–07	Portsmouth	18	0
2007–08	Portsmouth	13	0
2008–09	Portsmouth	20	0
2009–10	Portsmouth	10	0	120	0

HUGHES, Jordan (M)   0   0
b.Belfast 27-1-91
Source: Scholar.

2009–10	Portsmouth	0	0

HURST, James (D)   0   0
b.Sutton Coldfield 31-1-92
Source: Scholar.

2008–09	Portsmouth	0	0
2009–10	Portsmouth	0	0

JAMES, David (G)   688   0
H: 6 5   W: 15 07   b.Welwyn 1-8-70
Source: Trainee. *Honours:* England Youth,
Under-21, B, 53 full caps.

1988–89	Watford	0	0
1989–90	Watford	0	0
1990–91	Watford	46	0
1991–92	Watford	43	0	89	0
1992–93	Liverpool	29	0
1993–94	Liverpool	14	0
1994–95	Liverpool	42	0
1995–96	Liverpool	38	0
1996–97	Liverpool	38	0
1997–98	Liverpool	27	0
1998–99	Liverpool	26	0	214	0
1999–2000	Aston Villa	29	0
2000–01	Aston Villa	38	0	67	0
2001–02	West Ham U	26	0
2002–03	West Ham U	38	0
2003–04	West Ham U	27	0	91	0
2003–04	Manchester C	17	0
2004–05	Manchester C	38	0
2005–06	Manchester C	38	0	93	0
2006–07	Portsmouth	38	0
2007–08	Portsmouth	35	0
2008–09	Portsmouth	36	0
2009–10	Portsmouth	25	0	134	0

KANU, Nwankwo (F)   399   95
H: 6 5   W: 12 08   b.Owerri 1-8-76
Honours: Nigeria 86 full caps, 13 goals.

1991–92	Federation Works	30	9	30	9
1992–93	Iwanyanwu	30	6	30	6
1993–94	Ajax	6	2
1994–95	Ajax	18	10
1995–96	Ajax	30	13	54	25
1996–97	Internazionale	0	0
1997–98	Internazionale	11	1
1998–99	Internazionale	1	0	12	1
1998–99	Arsenal	12	6
1999–2000	Arsenal	31	12
2000–01	Arsenal	27	3
2001–02	Arsenal	23	3
2002–03	Arsenal	16	5
2003–04	Arsenal	10	1	119	30
2004–05	WBA	28	2
2005–06	WBA	25	5	53	7
2006–07	Portsmouth	36	10
2007–08	Portsmouth	25	4
2008–09	Portsmouth	17	1
2009–10	Portsmouth	23	2	101	17

KILBEY, Tom (M)   0   0
H: 6 3   W: 13 08   b.Waltham Forest
19-10-90
Source: Millwall.

2007–08	Portsmouth	0	0
2008–09	Portsmouth	0	0
2009–10	Portsmouth	0	0

MAHOTO, Gauthier (M)   0   0
H: 5 11   W: 12 00   b.Frane 21-2-92
Source: Le Havre.

2009–10	Portsmouth	0	0

MOKOENA, Aaron (D)   202   2
H: 6 2   W: 14 00   b.Johannesburg 25-11-80
Honours: South Africa 104 full caps, 1 goal.

2000–01	Ajax	0	0
2000–01	Antwerp	6	0
2001–02	Antwerp	13	1
2002–03	Antwerp	29	1	48	2
2003–04	Genk	18	0
2004–05	Genk	12	0	30	0
2004–05	Blackburn R	16	0
2005–06	Blackburn R	22	0
2006–07	Blackburn R	27	0
2007–08	Blackburn R	18	0
2008–09	Blackburn R	18	0
2009–10	Blackburn R	0	0	101	0
2009–10	Portsmouth	23	0	23	0

MULLINS, Hayden (D)   437   22
H: 5 11   W: 11 12   b.Reading 27-3-79
Source: Trainee. *Honours:* England
Under-21.

1996–97	Crystal Palace	0	0
1997–98	Crystal Palace	0	0
1998–99	Crystal Palace	40	5
1999–2000	Crystal Palace	45	10
2000–01	Crystal Palace	41	1

2001–02	Crystal Palace	43	0		
2002–03	Crystal Palace	43	2		
2003–04	Crystal Palace	10	0	222	18
2003–04	West Ham U	27	0		
2004–05	West Ham U	37	1		
2005–06	West Ham U	35	0		
2006–07	West Ham U	30	2		
2007–08	West Ham U	34	0		
2008–09	West Ham U	17	1	180	4
2008–09	Portsmouth	17	0		
2009–10	Portsmouth	18	0	35	0

NLUNDULU, Gael (F)   0   0
H: 6 0   W: 12 04   b.Paris 29-4-92
Source: Scholar. *Honours:* France Youth.

2008–09	Portsmouth	0	0
2009–10	Portsmouth	0	0

NUGENT, Dave (F)   246   60
H: 5 11   W: 12 13   b.Liverpool 2-5-85
Source: Scholar. *Honours:* England Youth,
Under-20, Under-21, 1 full cap, 1 goal.

2001–02	Bury	5	0		
2002–03	Bury	31	4		
2003–04	Bury	26	3		
2004–05	Bury	26	11	88	18
2004–05	Preston NE	18	8		
2005–06	Preston NE	32	10		
2006–07	Preston NE	44	15	94	33
2007–08	Portsmouth	15	0		
2008–09	Portsmouth	16	3		
2009–10	Portsmouth	3	0	34	0
2009–10	*Burnley*	30	6	30	6

O'BRIEN, Liam (G)   0   0
H: 6 1   W: 12 06   b.Brent 30-11-91
Source: Scholar. *Honours:* England Youth.

2008–09	Portsmouth	0	0
2009–10	Portsmouth	0	0

PACK, Marlon (M)   25   1
H: 6 2   W: 11 09   b.Portsmouth 25-3-91
Source: Scholar.

2008–09	Portsmouth	0	0		
2009–10	Portsmouth	0	0		
2009–10	*Wycombe W*	8	0	8	0
2009–10	*Dagenham & R*	17	1	17	1

PIQUIONNE, Frederic (F)   279   63
H: 6 2   W: 12 00   b.New Caledonia 8-12-78

2000–01	Nimes	8	3	8	3
2001–02	Rennes	20	3		
2002–03	Rennes	31	10		
2003–04	Rennes	32	5	83	18
2004–05	St Etienne	37	11		
2005–06	St Etienne	34	6		
2006–07	St Etienne	18	6	89	23
2006–07	Monaco	14	5		
2007–08	Monaco	32	7	46	12
2008–09	Lyon	19	2	19	2
On loan from Lyon.					
2009–10	Portsmouth	34	5	34	5

RICARDO ROCHA (D)   251   8
H: 6 0   W: 12 08   b.Santo Tirso 3-10-78
Honours: Portugal 6 full caps.

1998–99	Famalicao	28	2	28	2
1999–2000	Braga	25	1		
2000–01	Braga	19	0		
2000–01	Braga B	8	0	8	0
2001–02	Braga	25	2	69	3
2002–03	Benfica	27	0		
2003–04	Benfica	25	0		
2004–05	Benfica	25	0		
2005–06	Benfica	26	0		
2006–07	Benfica	12	3	115	3
2006–07	Tottenham H	9	0		
2007–08	Tottenham H	5	0		
2008–09	Tottenham H	0	0	14	0
2009–10	Standard Liege	7	0	7	0
2009–10	Portsmouth	10	0	10	0

RITCHIE, Matt (M)   59   14
H: 5 8   W: 11 00   b.Gosport 10-9-89

2008–09	Portsmouth	0	0		
2008–09	*Dagenham & R*	37	11	37	11
2009–10	Portsmouth	2	0	2	0
2009–10	*Notts Co*	16	3	16	3
2009–10	*Swindon T*	4	0	4	0

SMITH, Tommy (F)   414   85
H: 5 8   W: 11 04   b.Hemel Hempstead
22-5-80
Source: Trainee. *Honours:* England Youth,
Under-21.

1997–98	Watford	1	0		
1998–99	Watford	8	2		
1999–2000	Watford	22	2		
2000–01	Watford	43	11		
2001–02	Watford	40	11		
2002–03	Watford	35	7		
2003–04	Watford	0	0		
2003–04	Sunderland	35	4	35	4
2004–05	Derby Co	42	11		
2005–06	Derby Co	43	8		
2006–07	Derby Co	5	1	90	20
2006–07	Watford	32	1		
2007–08	Watford	44	7		
2008–09	Watford	44	17		
2009–10	Watford	4	2	273	60
2009–10	Portsmouth	16	1	16	1

SOWAH, Lennard (D)   5   0
H: 6 1   W: 11 00   b.Hamburg 23-2-92
Source: St Pauli, Arsenal, Portsmouth
Scholar.

2009–10	Portsmouth	5	0	5	0

SUBOTIC, Danijel (F)   0   0
H: 6 2   W: 12 00   b.Doboj 31-1-89
Source: Basle.

2007–08	Portsmouth	0	0
2008–09	Portsmouth	0	0
2009–10	Portsmouth	0	0

TOSIC, Dusko (D)   146   7
H: 6 0   W: 12 04   b.Zrenjanin 19-1-85
Source: Proleter. *Honours:* Serbia 9 full caps,
1 goal.

2002–03	OFK Belgrade	14	0		
2003–04	OFK Belgrade	25	2		
2004–05	OFK Belgrade	24	2		
2005–06	OFK Belgrade	17	2	80	6
2005–06	Sochaux	14	0		
2006–07	Sochaux	25	1	39	1
2007–08	Werder Bremen	12	0		
2008–09	Werder Bremen	9	0		
2009–10	Werder Bremen	1	0	22	0
2009–10	Portsmouth	0	0		
2009–10	QPR	5	0	5	0

UTAKA, John (F)   230   53
H: 5 9   W: 11 02   b.Enugu 8-1-82
Source: Ismaily, Al Saad. *Honours:* Nigeria 43
full caps, 6 goals.

2002–03	Lens	36	8		
2003–04	Lens	32	4		
2004–05	Lens	34	12	102	24
2005–06	Rennes	28	11		
2006–07	Rennes	35	11	63	22
2007–08	Portsmouth	29	5		
2008–09	Portsmouth	18	1		
2009–10	Portsmouth	18	1	65	7

VANDEN BORRE, Anthony (D)   121   3
H: 6 1   W: 12 04   b.Likasi 24-10-87

2003–04	Anderlecht	8	0		
2004–05	Anderlecht	19	0		
2005–06	Anderlecht	22	3		
2006–07	Anderlecht	20	0	69	3
2007–08	Fiorentina	2	0	2	0
2007–08	Genoa	6	0		
2008–09	Genoa	25	0	31	0
2009–10	Portsmouth	19	0	19	0

WARD, Joel (D)   24   1
H: 6 2   W: 11 13   b.Emsworth 29-10-89
Source: Scholar.

2008–09	Portsmouth	0	0		
2008–09	*Bournemouth*	21	1	21	1
2009–10	Portsmouth	3	0	3	0

WEBBER, Danny (F)   207   45
H: 5 10   W: 11 04   b.Manchester 28-12-81
Source: Trainee. *Honours:* England Youth,
Under-20.

1998–99	Manchester U	0	0		
1999–2000	Manchester U	0	0		
2000–01	Manchester U	0	0		
2001–02	Manchester U	0	0		
2001–02	*Port Vale*	4	0	4	0
2001–02	*Watford*	5	2		

2002–03	Manchester U	0	0		
2002–03	*Watford*	12	2		
2003–04	Watford	27	5		
2004–05	Watford	28	12	72	21
2004–05	*Sheffield U*	7	3		
2005–06	Sheffield U	35	10		
2006–07	Sheffield U	22	3		
2007–08	Sheffield U	14	3		
2008–09	Sheffield U	36	4		
2009–10	Sheffield U	0	0	114	23
2009–10	Portsmouth	17	1	17	1

WILSON, Marc (M)   63   3
H: 6 2   W: 12 07   b.Belfast 17-8-87
Source: Scholar. *Honours:* Eire Under-21.

2005–06	Portsmouth	0	0		
2005–06	*Yeovil T*	2	0	2	0
2006–07	Portsmouth	0	0		
2006–07	*Bournemouth*	19	3		
2007–08	Portsmouth	0	0		
2007–08	*Bournemouth*	7	0	26	3
2007–08	*Luton T*	4	0	4	0
2008–09	Portsmouth	3	0		
2009–10	Portsmouth	28	0	31	0

YEBDA, Hassan (M)   81   7
H: 6 1   W: 12 02   b.Saint Maurice 14-5-84
Honours: Algeria 12 full caps.

2005–06	Laval	14	1	14	1
2006–07	Auxerre B	0	0		
2006–07	Le Mans	1	0		
2007–08	. Le Mans	23	3	24	3
2008–09	Benfica	25	1	25	1
On loan from Benfica.					
2009–10	Portsmouth	18	2	18	2

Scholars
Bennett, Daniel Jack; Goddard, Billy;
Gregory, Peter; Martin, Ellis; Nsaku, Yann;
Ryan, Perry Dean; Seeley, James; Sowah,
Lennard; Stockford, Lewis Jason; Tallack,
Lewis; Tsovolos, William; Walshe, Carl.

PRESTON NE (66)

BARTON, Adam (M)   1   0
H: 5 11   W: 12 01   b.Blackburn 7-1-91
Source: Scholar.

2008–09	Preston NE	0	0
2009–10	Preston NE	1	0	1	0

BROWN, Chris (F)   209   38
H: 6 3   W: 13 01   b.Doncaster 11-12-84
Source: Trainee. *Honours:* England Youth.

2002–03	Sunderland	0	0		
2003–04	Sunderland	0	0		
2003–04	*Doncaster R*	22	10	22	10
2004–05	Sunderland	37	5		
2005–06	Sunderland	13	1		
2005–06	*Hull C*	13	1	13	1
2006–07	Sunderland	16	3	66	9
2006–07	Norwich C	4	0		
2007–08	Norwich C	14	1	18	1
2007–08	Preston NE	17	5		
2008–09	Preston NE	30	6		
2009–10	Preston NE	43	6	90	17

CARTER, Darren (M)   188   12
H: 6 2   W: 12 11   b.Solihull 18-12-83
Source: Scholar. *Honours:* England Youth,
Under-20.

2001–02	Birmingham C	13	1		
2002–03	Birmingham C	12	0		
2003–04	Birmingham C	5	0		
2004–05	Birmingham C	15	2	45	3
2004–05	*Sunderland*	10	1	10	1
2005–06	WBA	20	1		
2006–07	WBA	33	3	53	4
2007–08	Preston NE	39	4		
2008–09	Preston NE	18	0		
2009–10	Preston NE	23	0	80	4

CHAPLOW, Richard (M)   188   17
H: 5 9   W: 9 03   b.Accrington 2-2-85
Source: Scholar. *Honours:* England Youth,
Under-20, Under-21.

2002–03	Burnley	5	0		
2003–04	Burnley	39	5		
2004–05	Burnley	21	2	65	7
2004–05	WBA	4	0		

2005–06	WBA	7	0	
2005–06	*Southampton*	11	1	11 1
2006–07	WBA	28	1	
2007–08	WBA	5	0	44 1
2007–08	Preston NE	12	3	
2008–09	Preston NE	25	3	
2009–10	Preston NE	31	2	68 8

CHILVERS, Liam (D) 226 6
H: 6 2 W: 12 03 b.Chelmsford 6-11-81
Source: Scholar.

2000–01	Arsenal	0	0	
2000–01	*Northampton T*	7	0	7 0
2001–02	Arsenal	0	0	
2001–02	*Notts Co*	9	1	9 1
2002–03	Arsenal	0	0	
2002–03	Colchester U	6	0	
2003–04	Arsenal	0	0	
2003–04	Colchester U	32	0	
2004–05	Colchester U	41	1	
2005–06	Colchester U	34	2	113 3
2006–07	Preston NE	45	2	
2007–08	Preston NE	28	0	
2008–09	Preston NE	1	0	
2009–10	Preston NE	23	0	97 2

COLLINS, Dominic (D) 0 0
b.Preston 15-4-91
Source: Scholar.

2008–09	Preston NE	0	0
2009–10	Preston NE	0	0

COLLINS, Neill (D) 251 15
H: 6 3 W: 12 07 b.Irvine 2-9-83
Honours: Scoland Under-21, B.

2000–01	Queen's Park	4	0	
2001–02	Queen's Park	28	0	32 0
2002–03	Dumbarton	33	2	
2003–04	Dumbarton	30	2	63 4
2004–05	Sunderland	11	0	
2005–06	Sunderland	0	0	
2005–06	Hartlepool U	22	0	22 0
2005–06	*Sheffield U*	2	0	2 0
2006–07	Sunderland	7	1	18 1
2006–07	Wolverhampton W	22	2	
2007–08	Wolverhampton W	39	3	
2008–09	Wolverhampton W	23	4	
2009–10	Wolverhampton W	0	0	84 9
2009–10	Preston NE	21	1	21 1
2009–10	*Leeds U*	9	0	9 0

COUTTS, Paul (M) 66 1
H: 5 9 W: 11 11 b.Aberdeen 22-7-88
Source: Cove R. *Honours:* Scotland Under-21.

2008–09	Peterborough U	37	0	
2009–10	Peterborough U	16	0	53 0
2009–10	Preston NE	13	1	13 1

DAVIDSON, Callum (D) 358 25
H: 5 10 W: 11 08 b.Stirling 25-6-76
Source: 'S' Form. *Honours:* Scotland Under-21, 19 full caps.

1994–95	St Johnstone	7	1	
1995–96	St Johnstone	2	0	
1996–97	St Johnstone	20	2	
1997–98	St Johnstone	15	1	44 4
1997–98	Blackburn R	1	0	
1998–99	Blackburn R	34	1	
1999–2000	Blackburn R	30	0	65 1
2000–01	Leicester C	28	1	
2001–02	Leicester C	30	0	
2002–03	Leicester C	30	1	
2003–04	Leicester C	13	0	101 2
2004–05	Preston NE	19	1	
2005–06	Preston NE	27	4	
2006–07	Preston NE	15	0	
2007–08	Preston NE	40	4	
2008–09	Preston NE	20	4	
2009–10	Preston NE	27	5	148 18

DOUGAN, Neil (M) 0 0
H: 5 6 W: 10 02 b.Northern Ireland 8-3-92
Source: Scholar.

2009–10	Preston NE	0	0

ELLIOTT, Stephen (F) 168 35
H: 5 8 W: 11 07 b.Dublin 6-1-84
Source: School. *Honours:* Eire Youth, Under-21, 9 full caps, 1 goal.

2000–01	Manchester C	0	0
2001–02	Manchester C	0	0
2002–03	Manchester C	0	0
2003–04	Manchester C	2	0	2 0
2004–05	Sunderland	42	15
2005–06	Sunderland	15	2
2006–07	Sunderland	24	5	81 22
2007–08	Wolverhampton W	29	4
2008–09	Wolverhampton W	0	0	29 4
2008–09	Preston NE	37	6
2009–10	Preston NE	9	1	46 7
2009–10	*Norwich C*	10	2	10 2

HART, Michael (M) 192 0
H: 5 10 W: 12 06 b.Airdrie 10-2-80

1998–99	Aberdeen	14	0	
1999–2000	Aberdeen	3	0	
1999–2000	*Livingston*	3	0	
1999–2000	*Morton*	10	0	10 0
2000–01	Aberdeen	0	0	
2000–01	Livingston	22	0	
2001–02	Livingston	21	0	
2002–03	Livingston	11	0	57 0
2002–03	Aberdeen	8	0	
2003–04	Aberdeen	11	0	
2004–05	Aberdeen	32	0	
2005–06	Aberdeen	4	0	
2006–07	Aberdeen	34	0	106 0
2007–08	Preston NE	2	0	
2008–09	Preston NE	6	0	
2009–10	Preston NE	11	0	19 0

HENDERSON, Wayne (G) 89 0
H: 5 11 W: 12 02 b.Dublin 16-9-83
Source: Scholar. *Honours:* Eire Youth, Under-21, 6 full caps.

2000–01	Aston Villa	0	0	
2001–02	Aston Villa	0	0	
2002–03	Aston Villa	0	0	
2003–04	Aston Villa	0	0	
2003–04	*Wycombe W*	3	0	3 0
2004–05	Aston Villa	0	0	
2004–05	*Notts Co*	11	0	11 0
2005–06	Aston Villa	0	0	
2005–06	Brighton & HA	32	0	
2006–07	Brighton & HA	20	0	52 0
2006–07	Preston NE	4	0	
2007–08	Preston NE	3	0	
2008–09	Preston NE	0	0	
2008–09	*Grimsby T*	14	0	14 0
2009–10	Preston NE	2	0	9 0

JONES, Billy (M) 249 15
H: 5 11 W: 13 00 b.Shrewsbury 24-3-87
Source: Scholar. *Honours:* England Youth, Under-20.

2003–04	Crewe Alex	27	1	
2004–05	Crewe Alex	20	0	
2005–06	Crewe Alex	44	6	
2006–07	Crewe Alex	41	1	132 8
2007–08	Preston NE	29	0	
2008–09	Preston NE	44	3	
2009–10	Preston NE	44	4	117 7

LONERGAN, Andrew (G) 184 1
H: 6 4 W: 13 02 b.Preston 19-10-83
Source: Scholar. *Honours:* Eire Youth, England Youth, Under-20.

2000–01	Preston NE	1	0	
2001–02	Preston NE	0	0	
2002–03	Preston NE	0	0	
2002–03	*Darlington*	2	0	2 0
2003–04	Preston NE	8	0	
2004–05	Preston NE	23	1	
2005–06	Preston NE	0	0	
2005–06	*Wycombe W*	2	0	2 0
2006–07	Preston NE	13	0	
2006–07	*Swindon T*	1	0	1 0
2007–08	Preston NE	43	0	
2008–09	Preston NE	46	0	
2009–10	Preston NE	45	0	179 1

MAWENE, Youl (D) 235 9
H: 6 2 W: 12 06 b.Caen 16-7-79

1999–2000	Lens	6	0	6 0
2000–01	Derby Co	8	0	
2001–02	Derby Co	17	1	
2002–03	Derby Co	0	0	
2003–04	Derby Co	30	0	55 1
2004–05	Preston NE	46	2	
2005–06	Preston NE	30	1	
2006–07	Preston NE	29	0	
2007–08	Preston NE	38	3	

2008–09	Preston NE	41	2	
2009–10	Preston NE	19	0	174 8

MAYOR, Danny (M) 10 0
H: 6 0 W: 11 12 b.Leyland 18-10-90
Source: Scholar.

2008–09	Preston NE	0	0	
2008–09	*Tranmere R*	3	0	3 0
2009–10	Preston NE	7	0	7 0

McLAUGHLIN, Conor (D) 0 0
H: 6 0 W: 11 02 b.Belfast 26-7-91
Source: Scholar. *Honours:* Northern Ireland Under-21.

2009–10	Preston NE	0	0

MELLOR, Neil (F) 144 35
H: 6 0 W: 13 05 b.Sheffield 4-11-82
Source: Scholar.

2001–02	Liverpool	0	0	
2002–03	Liverpool	3	0	
2003–04	Liverpool	0	0	
2003–04	*West Ham U*	16	2	16 2
2004–05	Liverpool	9	2	
2005–06	Liverpool	0	0	
2005–06	*Wigan Ath*	3	1	3 1
2006–07	Liverpool	0	0	12 2
2006–07	Preston NE	5	1	
2007–08	Preston NE	36	9	
2008–09	Preston NE	33	10	
2009–10	Preston NE	39	10	113 30

MILLER, George (M) 0 0
H: 5 9 W: 12 02 b.Eccleston 25-11-91
Source: Scholar.

2009–10	Preston NE	0	0

NICHOLSON, Barry (M) 325 39
H: 5 7 W: 9 01 b.Dumfries 24-8-78
Honours: Scotland Under-21, 3 full caps.

1995–96	Rangers	0	0	
1996–97	Rangers	0	0	
1997–98	Rangers	0	0	
1998–99	Rangers	6	0	
1999–2000	Rangers	2	0	8 0
2000–01	Dunfermline Ath	36	3	
2001–02	Dunfermline Ath	37	7	
2002–03	Dunfermline Ath	38	5	
2003–04	Dunfermline Ath	36	5	
2004–05	Dunfermline Ath	27	3	174 23
2005–06	Aberdeen	33	2	
2006–07	Aberdeen	31	6	
2007–08	Aberdeen	38	5	102 13
2008–09	Preston NE	37	3	
2009–10	Preston NE	4	0	41 3

NOLAN, Eddie (D) 69 1
H: 6 0 W: 13 05 b.Waterford 5-8-88
Source: Scholar. *Honours:* Eire Under-21, 3 full caps.

2005–06	Blackburn R	0	0	
2006–07	Blackburn R	0	0	
2006–07	*Stockport Co*	4	0	4 0
2007–08	Blackburn R	0	0	
2007–08	*Hartlepool U*	11	0	11 0
2008–09	Blackburn R	0	0	
2008–09	Preston NE	21	0	
2009–10	Preston NE	19	0	40 0
2009–10	*Sheffield W*	14	1	14 1

PARKIN, Jon (F) 314 81
H: 6 4 W: 13 07 b.Barnsley 30-12-81
Source: Scholarship.

1998–99	Barnsley	2	0	
1999–2000	Barnsley	0	0	
2000–01	Barnsley	4	0	
2001–02	Barnsley	4	0	10 0
2001–02	*Hartlepool U*	1	0	1 0
2001–02	York C	18	2	
2002–03	York C	41	10	
2003–04	York C	15	2	74 14
2003–04	Macclesfield T	12	1	
2004–05	Macclesfield T	42	22	
2005–06	Macclesfield T	11	7	65 30
2005–06	Hull C	18	5	
2006–07	Hull C	29	6	47 11
2006–07	Stoke C	6	3	
2007–08	Stoke C	29	2	
2008–09	Stoke C	0	0	35 5
2008–09	Preston NE	39	11	
2009–10	Preston NE	43	10	82 21

PARRY, Paul (M) 208 26
H: 5 11 W: 12 12 b.Chepstow 19-8-80
Source: Hereford U. *Honours:* Wales 12 full caps, 1 goal.

2003–04	Cardiff C	17	1		
2004–05	Cardiff C	24	4		
2005–06	Cardiff C	27	1		
2006–07	Cardiff C	42	6		
2007–08	Cardiff C	41	10		
2008–09	Cardiff C	40	2	191	24
2009–10	Preston NE	17	2	17	2

PROCTOR, Jamie (F) 1 0
H: 6 2 W: 12 03 b.Preston 25-3-92
Source: Scholar.

2009–10	Preston NE	1	0	1	0

SEDGWICK, Chris (M) 472 29
H: 5 11 W: 11 10 b.Sheffield 28-4-80
Source: Trainee.

1997–98	Rotherham U	4	0		
1998–99	Rotherham U	33	4		
1999–2000	Rotherham U	38	5		
2000–01	Rotherham U	21	2		
2001–02	Rotherham U	44	1		
2002–03	Rotherham U	43	1		
2003–04	Rotherham U	40	2		
2004–05	Rotherham U	20	2	243	17
2004–05	Preston NE	24	3		
2005–06	Preston NE	46	4		
2006–07	Preston NE	43	1		
2007–08	Preston NE	42	2		
2008–09	Preston NE	40	1		
2009–10	Preston NE	34	1	229	12

ST LEDGER-HALL, Sean (D) 248 12
H: 6 0 W: 11 09 b.Solihull 28-12-84
Source: Scholar. *Honours:* Eire 12 full caps, 1 goal.

2002–03	Peterborough U	1	0		
2003–04	Peterborough U	2	0		
2004–05	Peterborough U	33	0		
2005–06	Peterborough U	43	1	79	1
2006–07	Preston NE	41	1		
2007–08	Preston NE	37	1		
2008–09	Preston NE	46	5		
2009–10	Preston NE	30	2	154	9
2009–10	Middlesbrough	15	2	15	2

SUMULIKOSKI, Velice (M) 214 7
H: 6 0 W: 12 02 b.Macedonia 24-1-81
Honours: Macedonia 65 full caps, 1 goal.

1999–2000	Publikum	21	2		
2000–01	Publikum	28	1		
2001–02	Publikum	7	0	56	3
2001–02	Slovacko	13	0		
2002–03	Slovacko	29	2		
2003–04	Slovacko	13	0	55	2
2004	Zenit	25	0		
2005	Zenit	16	1		
2006	Zenit	5	0	46	1
2007–08	Ipswich T	16	1		
2008–09	Ipswich T	26	0	42	1
2009–10	Preston NE	15	0	15	0

TREACY, Keith (M) 49 3
H: 6 0 W: 13 02 b.Dublin 13-9-88
Source: Scholar. *Honours:* Eire Under-21.

2005–06	Blackburn R	0	0		
2006–07	Blackburn R	0	0		
2006–07	Stockport Co	4	0	4	0
2007–08	Blackburn R	0	0		
2008–09	Blackburn R	12	0		
2009–10	Blackburn R	0	0	12	0
2009–10	*Sheffield U*	16	1	16	1
2009–10	Preston NE	17	2	17	2

TROTMAN, Neal (D) 66 5
H: 6 3 W: 13 08 b.Levenshulme 11-3-87
Source: Burnley Scholar.

2006–07	Oldham Ath	1	0		
2007–08	Oldham Ath	17	1	18	1
2007–08	Preston NE	3	0		
2008–09	Preston NE	0	0		
2008–09	*Colchester U*	6	0	6	0
2009–10	Preston NE	0	0	3	0
2009–10	*Southampton*	18	2	18	2
2009–10	*Huddersfield T*	21	2	21	2

WALLACE, Ross (M) 170 21
H: 5 6 W: 9 12 b.Dundee 23-5-85
Source: Celtic S Form. *Honours:* Scotland Youth, Under-21, B, 1 full cap.

2001–02	Celtic	0	0		
2002–03	Celtic	0	0		
2003–04	Celtic	8	1		
2004–05	Celtic	16	0		
2005–06	Celtic	11	0		
2006–07	Celtic	2	0	37	1
2006–07	Sunderland	32	6		
2007–08	Sunderland	21	2		
2008–09	Sunderland	0	0	53	8
2008–09	Preston NE	39	5		
2009–10	Preston NE	41	7	80	12

QPR (67)

AGYEMANG, Patrick (F) 349 62
H: 6 1 W: 12 00 b.Walthamstow 29-9-80
Source: Trainee. *Honours:* Ghana 3 full caps, 1 goal.

1998–99	Wimbledon	0	0		
1999–2000	Wimbledon	0	0		
1999–2000	*Brentford*	12	0	12	0
2000–01	Wimbledon	29	4		
2001–02	Wimbledon	33	4		
2002–03	Wimbledon	33	5		
2003–04	Wimbledon	26	7	121	20
2003–04	Gillingham	20	6		
2004–05	Gillingham	13	2	33	8
2004–05	Preston NE	27	4		
2005–06	Preston NE	42	6		
2006–07	Preston NE	31	7		
2007–08	Preston NE	22	4	122	21
2007–08	QPR	17	8		
2008–09	QPR	20	2		
2009–10	QPR	17	3	54	13
2009–10	*Bristol C*	7	0	7	0

ALBERTI, Matteo (M) 12 2
H: 5 10 W: 11 05 b.Chievo Verona 4-8-88
Source: Chievo Verona.

2008–09	QPR	12	2		
2009–10	QPR	0	0	12	2

BALANTA, Angelo (F) 36 5
H: 5 10 W: 11 11 b.Colombia 1-7-90
Source: Scholar.

2007–08	QPR	11	1		
2008–09	QPR	10	1		
2008–09	*Wycombe W*	11	3	11	3
2009–10	QPR	4	0	25	2

BORROWDALE, Gary (D) 166 0
H: 6 0 W: 12 01 b.Sutton 16-7-85
Source: Scholar. *Honours:* England Youth, Under-20.

2002–03	Crystal Palace	13	0		
2003–04	Crystal Palace	23	0		
2004–05	Crystal Palace	7	0		
2005–06	Crystal Palace	30	0		
2006–07	Crystal Palace	25	0	98	0
2007–08	Coventry C	21	0		
2008–09	Coventry C	0	0	21	0
2008–09	*Colchester U*	4	0	4	0
2008–09	QPR	0	0		
2008–09	*Brighton & HA*	12	0	12	0
2009–10	QPR	21	0	21	0
2009–10	*Charlton Ath*	10	0	10	0

BROWN, Lee (M) 1 0
H: 6 0 W: 12 06 b.Farnborough 10-8-90
Source: Scholar.

2008–09	QPR	0	0		
2009–10	QPR	1	0	1	0

BUZSAKY, Akos (M) 173 20
H: 5 11 W: 11 09 b.Hungary 7-5-82
Source: MTK, Porto. *Honours:* Hungary Under-21, 19 full caps, 2 goals.

2004–05	Plymouth Arg	15	1		
2005–06	Plymouth Arg	34	4		
2006–07	Plymouth Arg	36	3		
2007–08	Plymouth Arg	11	0	96	8
2007–08	QPR	27	10		
2008–09	QPR	11	1		
2009–10	QPR	39	10	77	21

CERNY, Radek (G) 87 0
H: 6 1 W: 14 02 b.Prague 18-2-74
Source: Slavia Prague. *Honours:* Czech Republic 3 full caps.

2004–05	Tottenham H	3	0		
2005–06	Tottenham H	0	0		
2006–07	Tottenham H	0	0		
2007–08	Tottenham H	13	0	16	0
2008–09	QPR	42	0		
2009–10	QPR	29	0	71	0

CONNOLLY, Matthew (D) 95 5
H: 6 1 W: 11 03 b.Barnet 24-9-87
Source: Scholar. *Honours:* England Youth.

2005–06	Arsenal	0	0		
2006–07	Arsenal	0	0		
2006–07	*Bournemouth*	5	1	5	1
2007–08	Arsenal	0	0		
2007–08	*Colchester U*	16	2	16	2
2007–08	QPR	20	0		
2008–09	QPR	35	0		
2009–10	QPR	19	2	74	2

COOK, Lee (M) 257 20
H: 5 8 W: 11 10 b.Hammersmith 3-8-82
Source: Aylesbury U.

1999–2000	Watford	0	0		
2000–01	Watford	4	0		
2001–02	Watford	10	0		
2002–03	Watford	4	0		
2002–03	*York C*	7	1	7	1
2002–03	*QPR*	13	1		
2003–04	Watford	41	7	59	7
2004–05	QPR	42	2		
2005–06	QPR	40	4		
2006–07	QPR	37	3		
2007–08	Fulham	0	0		
2007–08	*Charlton Ath*	9	0	9	0
2008–09	Fulham	0	0		
2008–09	QPR	34	1		
2009–10	QPR	16	1	182	12

EHMER, Max (M) 0 0
b.Frankfurt 3-2-92
Source: Scholar.

2009–10	QPR	0	0		

EPHRAIM, Hogan (F) 102 5
H: 5 9 W: 10 06 b.Islington 31-3-88
Source: Scholar. *Honours:* England Youth.

2004–05	West Ham U	0	0		
2005–06	West Ham U	0	0		
2006–07	West Ham U	0	0		
2006–07	*Colchester U*	21	1	21	1
2007–08	West Ham U	0	0		
2007–08	QPR	29	3		
2008–09	QPR	27	1		
2009–10	QPR	22	0	78	4
2009–10	*Leeds U*	3	0	3	0

FAURLIN, Alejandro (M) 109 9
H: 6 1 W: 12 06 b.Argentina 9-8-86

2004	Rosario Central	1	0		
2005	Rosario Central	0	0		
2006	Rosario Central	0	0	1	0
2007	Atletico Rafaela	40	1	40	1
2008–09	Instituto	27	7	27	7
2009–10	QPR	41	1	41	1

GERMAN, Antonio (F) 19 2
H: 5 10 W: 12 03 b.Wembley 26-12-91
Source: Scholar.

2008–09	QPR	3	0		
2009–10	QPR	13	2	16	2
2009–10	*Aldershot T*	3	0	3	0

GORKSS, Kaspars (D) 233 14
H: 6 3 W: 13 05 b.Riga 6-11-81
Honours: Latvia 30 full caps, 2 goals.

2002	Auda Riga	28	0	28	0
2003	Oster	8	0		
2004	Oster	24	1	32	1
2005	Assyriska	23	0	23	0
2006	Ventspils	28	5	28	5
2006–07	Blackpool	10	0		
2007–08	Blackpool	40	5	50	5
2008–09	QPR	31	0		
2009–10	QPR	41	3	72	3

HALL, Fitz (D)   214 10
H: 6 3   W: 13 00   b.Leytonstone 20-12-80
Source: Barnet Trainee, Chesham U.

Season	Club				
2001–02	Oldham Ath	4	1		
2002–03	Oldham Ath	40	4	44	5
2003–04	Southampton	11	0	11	0
2004–05	Crystal Palace	36	2		
2005–06	Crystal Palace	39	1	75	3
2006–07	Wigan Ath	24	0		
2007–08	Wigan Ath	1	0	25	0
2007–08	QPR	14	0		
2008–09	QPR	24	2		
2009–10	QPR	14	0	52	2
2009–10	*Newcastle U*	7	0	7	0

HARRIS, Ed (D)   0 0
H: 6 1   W: 13 05   b.Roehampton 3-11-90
Source: Scholar.

2009–10	QPR	0	0		

HELGUSON, Heidar (F)   336 104
H: 5 10   W: 12 09   b.Akureyri 22-8-77
Source: Throttur. Honours: Iceland Youth, Under-21, 48 full caps, 10 goals.

Season	Club				
1998	Lillestrom	19	2		
1999	Lillestrom	25	16	44	18
1999–2000	Watford	16	6		
2000–01	Watford	33	8		
2001–02	Watford	34	6		
2002–03	Watford	30	11		
2003–04	Watford	22	8		
2004–05	Watford	39	16		
2005–06	Fulham	27	8		
2006–07	Fulham	30	4	57	12
2007–08	Bolton W	6	2		
2008–09	Bolton W	1	0	7	2
2008–09	QPR	20	5		
2009–10	QPR	5	1	25	6
2009–10	*Watford*	29	11	203	66

LEIGERTWOOD, Mikele (D)   266 15
H: 6 1   W: 11 04   b.Enfield 12-11-82
Source: Scholar.

Season	Club				
2001–02	Wimbledon	1	0		
2001–02	Leyton Orient	8	0	8	0
2002–03	Wimbledon	28	0		
2003–04	Wimbledon	27	2	56	2
2003–04	Crystal Palace	12	0		
2004–05	Crystal Palace	20	1		
2005–06	Crystal Palace	27	0	59	1
2006–07	Sheffield U	19	0		
2007–08	Sheffield U	2	0	21	0
2007–08	QPR	40	5		
2008–09	QPR	42	2		
2009–10	QPR	40	5	122	12

MAHON, Gavin (M)   399 19
H: 5 11   W: 13 07   b.Birmingham 2-1-77
Source: Trainee.

Season	Club				
1995–96	Wolverhampton W	0	0		
1996–97	Hereford U	11	1		
1997–98	Hereford U	0	0		
1998–99	Hereford U	0	0	11	1
1998–99	Brentford	29	4		
1999–2000	Brentford	37	3		
2000–01	Brentford	40	1		
2001–02	Brentford	35	0	141	8
2001–02	Watford	6	0		
2002–03	Watford	17	0		
2003–04	Watford	32	2		
2004–05	Watford	43	0		
2005–06	Watford	38	3		
2006–07	Watford	34	1		
2007–08	Watford	19	0	189	6
2007–08	QPR	16	1		
2008–09	QPR	35	2		
2009–10	QPR	7	1	58	4

OASTLER, Joe (D)   1 0
H: 5 10   W: 11 03   b.Portsmouth 3-7-90
Source: Scholar.

2008–09	QPR	0	0		
2009–10	QPR	1	0	1	0

PARKER, Josh (F)   4 0
H: 5 11   W: 12 00   b.Slough 1-12-90
Source: Scholar.

2009–10	QPR	4	0	4	0

PARMENTER, Taylor (D)   0 0
b.Bromley 5-9-92
Source: Scholar.

2009–10	QPR	0	0		

PELLICORI, Alessandro (F)   207 58
H: 5 11   W: 11 11   b.Cosenza 22-7-81

Season	Club				
1999–2000	Cosenza	1	0	1	0
2000–01	Lecce	1	0		
2001–02	Lecce	3	0	4	0
2002–03	Avellino	18	7		
2002–03	Varese	9	1	9	1
2003–04	Feggia	15	2	15	2
2003–04	Benevento	14	1	14	1
2004–05	Grosseto	35	12		
2005–06	Grosseto	18	10		
2005–06	Catanzaro	7	0	7	0
2006–07	Piacenza	9	0	9	0
2006–07	Cesena	12	3	12	3
2007–08	Avellino	38	18	56	25
2008–09	Grosseto	19	4	72	26
2009–10	QER	8	0	8	0

PUTNINS, Elvijs (G)   0 0
b.Latvia 12-4-91
Source: FK Auda. Honours: Latvia Youth.

2008–09	QPR	0	0		
2009–10	QPR	0	0		

QUASHIE, Nigel (M)   346 26
H: 6 0   W: 13 10   b.Peckham 20-7-78
Source: Trainee. Honours: England Youth, Under-21, B, Scotland 14 full caps, 1 goal.

Season	Club				
1995–96	QPR	11	0		
1996–97	QPR	13	0		
1997–98	QPR	33	3		
1998–99	QPR	0	0		
1998–99	Nottingham F	0	0		
1999–2000	Nottingham F	28	2	44	2
2000–01	Portsmouth	31	5		
2001–02	Portsmouth	35	2		
2002–03	Portsmouth	42	5		
2003–04	Portsmouth	21	1		
2004–05	Portsmouth	19	0	148	13
2004–05	Southampton	13	1		
2005–06	Southampton	24	4	37	5
2005–06	WBA	9	1		
2006–07	WBA	20	0	29	1
2006–07	West Ham U	7	0		
2007–08	West Ham U	0	0		
2008–09	West Ham U	0	0		
2008–09	Birmingham C	10	0	10	0
2008–09	Wolverhampton W	3	0	3	0
2009–10	West Ham U	0	0	7	0
2009–10	Milton Keynes D	7	2	7	2
2009–10	QPR	4	0	61	3

RAMAGE, Peter (D)   115 2
H: 6 3   W: 11 02   b.Whitley Bay 22-11-83
Source: Trainee.

Season	Club				
2003–04	Newcastle U	0	0		
2004–05	Newcastle U	4	0		
2005–06	Newcastle U	23	0		
2006–07	Newcastle U	21	0		
2007–08	Newcastle U	3	0	51	0
2008–09	QPR	31	0		
2009–10	QPR	33	2	64	2

ROSE, Romone (M)   6 0
H: 5 9   W: 11 05   b.Pennsylvania 19-1-90
Source: Scholar.

Season	Club				
2007–08	QPR	1	0		
2008–09	QPR	2	0		
2009–10	QPR	1	0	4	0
2009–10	Northampton T	1	0	1	0
2009–10	Cheltenham T	1	0	1	0

ROWLANDS, Martin (M)   343 53
H: 5 9   W: 10 10   b.Hammersmith 8-2-79
Source: Farnborough T. Honours: Eire Under-21, 5 full caps.

Season	Club				
1998–99	Brentford	36	4		
1999–2000	Brentford	40	6		
2000–01	Brentford	32	2		
2001–02	Brentford	23	7		
2002–03	Brentford	18	1	149	20
2003–04	QPR	42	10		
2004–05	QPR	35	3		
2005–06	QPR	14	2		
2006–07	QPR	29	10		
2007–08	QPR	44	6		
2008–09	QPR	24	2		
2009–10	QPR	6	0	194	33

STEWART, Damion (D)   174 10
H: 6 3   W: 13 10   b.Jamaica 18-8-80
Source: Harbour View. Honours: Jamaica 55 full caps, 3 goals.

Season	Club				
2005–06	Bradford C	23	1	23	1
2006–07	QPR	45	1		
2007–08	QPR	39	5		
2008–09	QPR	37	2		
2009–10	QPR	30	1	151	9

VINE, Rowan (F)   278 56
H: 5 11   W: 12 10   b.Basingstoke 21-9-82
Source: Scholar.

Season	Club				
2000–01	Portsmouth	2	0		
2001–02	Portsmouth	11	0		
2002–03	Portsmouth	0	0		
2002–03	Brentford	42	10	42	10
2003–04	Portsmouth	0	0		
2003–04	Colchester U	35	6	35	6
2004–05	Portsmouth	0	0	13	0
2004–05	Luton T	45	9		
2005–06	Luton T	31	10		
2006–07	Luton T	26	12	102	31
2006–07	Birmingham C	17	1		
2007–08	Birmingham C	0	0	17	1
2007–08	QPR	33	6		
2008–09	QPR	5	1		
2009–10	QPR	31	1	69	8

READING (68)

ANDERSEN, Mikkel (G)   45 0
H: 6 5   W: 12 08   b.Copenhagen 17-12-88
Source: AB Copenhagen. Honours: Denmark Youth.

Season	Club				
2006–07	Reading	0	0		
2007–08	Reading	0	0		
2008–09	Reading	0	0		
2008–09	Brentford	1	0	1	0
2008–09	Brighton & HA	5	0	5	0
2009–10	Reading	0	0		
2009–10	Bristol R	39	0	39	0

ANTONIO, Michael (M)   38 3
H: 6 0   W: 11 11   b.London 28-3-90
Source: Tooting & M.

Season	Club				
2008–09	Reading	0	0		
2008–09	Cheltenham T	9	0	9	0
2009–10	Reading	1	0	1	0
2009–10	Southampton	28	3	28	3

ARMSTRONG, Chris (D)   238 9
H: 5 9   W: 11 00   b.Newcastle 5-8-82
Source: Scholar. Honours: England Under-20. Scotland B.

Season	Club				
2000–01	Bury	22	1		
2001–02	Bury	11	0	33	1
2001–02	Oldham Ath	32	0		
2002–03	Oldham Ath	33	1	65	1
2003–04	Sheffield U	12	1		
2004–05	Sheffield U	0	0		
2005–06	Sheffield U	24	2		
2005–06	Blackpool	5	0	5	0
2006–07	Sheffield U	27	0		
2007–08	Sheffield U	32	3		
2008–09	Sheffield U	0	0	95	6
2008–09	Reading	40	1		
2009–10	Reading	0	0	40	0

BELL-BAGGIE, Abdulai (F)   11 0
H: 5 4   W: 9 10   b.Sierra Leone 28-4-92
Source: Scholar.

2009–10	Reading	0	0		
2009–10	*Rotherham U*	11	0	11	0

BIGNALL, Nicholas (F)   30 4
H: 5 10   W: 11 12   b.Reading 11-7-90
Source: Scholar.

Season	Club				
2008–09	Reading	0	0		
2008–09	Northampton T	5	1	5	1
2008–09	Cheltenham T	13	1	13	1
2009–10	Reading	1	0	1	0
2009–10	*Stockport Co*	11	2	11	2

BOZANIC, Ollie (M)   29 2
H: 6 0   W: 12 00   b.Melbourne 8-1-89
Source: Central Coast M. *Honours:* Australia Youth, Under-20.

2006-07	Reading	0	0	
2007-08	Reading	0	0	
2008-09	Reading	0	0	
2009-10	Reading	0	0	
2009-10	*Cheltenham T*	4	0	4 0
2009-10	*Aldershot T*	25	2	25 2

CHURCH, Simon (F)   76 16
H: 6 0   W: 13 04   b.Amersham 10-12-88
Source: Scholar. *Honours:* Wales Under-21, 8 full caps, 1 goal.

2007-08	Reading	0	0	
2007-08	*Crewe Alex*	12	1	12 1
2007-08	*Yeovil T*	6	0	6 0
2008-09	Reading	0	0	
2008-09	*Wycombe W*	9	0	9 0
2008-09	*Leyton Orient*	13	5	13 5
2009-10	Reading	36	10	36 10

CISSE, Kalifa (M)   123 7
H: 6 2   W: 12 11   b.Orleans 1-9-84
Source: Toulouse. *Honours:* Mali 1 full cap.

2004-05	Estoril	6	0	6 0
2005-06	Boavista	15	0	
2006-07	Boavista	27	0	42 0
2007-08	Reading	22	1	
2008-09	Reading	36	5	
2009-10	Reading	17	1	75 7

CUMMINGS, Shaun (D)   43 0
H: 6 0   W: 11 10   b.Hammersmith 25-2-89

2007-08	Chelsea	0	0	
2008-09	Chelsea	0	0	
2008-09	*Milton Keynes D*	32	0	32 0
2009-10	Chelsea	0	0	
2009-10	*WBA*	3	0	3 0
2009-10	Reading	8	0	8 0

DAVIES, Scott (M)   64 16
H: 5 11   W: 12 00   b.Aylesbury 10-3-88
Source: Scholar. *Honours:* Eire Under-21.

2006-07	Reading	0	0	
2007-08	Reading	0	0	
2008-09	Reading	0	0	
2008-09	*Aldershot T*	41	13	41 13
2009-10	Reading	4	0	4 0
2009-10	*Wycombe W*	15	3	15 3
2009-10	*Yeovil T*	4	0	4 0

FEDERICI, Adam (G)   73 1
H: 6 2   W: 14 02   b.Nowra 31-1-85
Honours: Australia Youth, Under-20, Under-21, 1 full cap.

2005-06	Reading	0	0	
2006-07	Reading	2	0	
2007-08	Reading	0	0	
2008-09	Reading	15	1	
2008-09	*Southend U*	10	0	10 0
2009-10	Reading	46	0	63 1

GUNNARSSON, Brynjar (M)   363 31
H: 6 1   W: 12 01   b.Reykjavik 16-10-75
Honours: Iceland Youth, Under-21, 74 full caps, 4 goals.

1995	KR	16	1	
1996	KR	18	0	
1997	KR	16	0	50 1
1998	Moss	5	2	5 2
1999-2000	Stoke C	22	1	
2000-01	Stoke C	46	5	
2001-02	Stoke C	23	5	
2002-03	Stoke C	40	5	
2003-04	Nottingham F	13	0	13 0
2003-04	*Stoke C*	3	0	134 16
2004-05	Watford	36	3	36 3
2005-06	Reading	29	4	
2006-07	Reading	23	3	
2007-08	Reading	20	0	
2008-09	Reading	27	2	
2009-10	Reading	26	0	125 0

HAMER, Ben (G)   65 0
H: 5 11   W: 12 04   b.Chard 20-11-87
Source: Crawley T.

2006-07	Reading	0	0	
2007-08	Reading	0	0	
2007-08	*Brentford*	20	0	
2008-09	Reading	0	0	
2008-09	*Brentford*	45	0	65 0
2009-10	Reading	0	0	

HECTOR, Michael (D)   0 0
Source: Scholar.

2009-10	Reading	0	0	

HENRY, James (M)   50 12
H: 6 1   W: 11 11   b.Reading 10-6-89
Source: Scholar. *Honours:* England Youth.

2006-07	Reading	0	0	
2006-07	*Nottingham F*	1	0	1 0
2007-08	Reading	0	0	
2007-08	*Bournemouth*	11	4	11 4
2007-08	*Norwich C*	3	0	3 0
2008-09	Reading	7	0	
2008-09	*Millwall*	16	3	
2009-10	Reading	3	0	10 0
2009-10	*Millwall*	9	5	25 8

HOWARD, Brian (M)   255 40
H: 5 8   W: 11 00   b.Winchester 23-1-83
Source: Trainee. *Honours:* England Schools, Youth, Under-20.

1999-2000	Southampton	0	0	
2000-01	Southampton	0	0	
2001-02	Southampton	0	0	
2002-03	Southampton	0	0	
2003-04	Swindon T	35	4	
2004-05	Swindon T	35	5	70 9
2005-06	Barnsley	31	5	
2006-07	Barnsley	42	8	
2007-08	Barnsley	41	13	
2008-09	Barnsley	7	1	121 27
2008-09	*Sheffield U*	26	2	
2009-10	Sheffield U	4	0	30 2
2009-10	Reading	34	2	34 2

HUNT, Noel (F)   191 44
H: 5 8   W: 11 05   b.Waterford 26-12-82
Honours: Eire Under-21, B, 3 full caps.

2002-03	Dunfermline Ath	12	1	
2003-04	Dunfermline Ath	13	2	
2004-05	Dunfermline Ath	23	1	
2005-06	Dunfermline Ath	32	4	80 8
2006-07	Dundee U	28	10	
2007-08	Dundee U	36	13	64 23
2008-09	Reading	37	11	
2009-10	Reading	10	2	47 13

INGIMARSSON, Ivar (D)   464 34
H: 6 0   W: 12 07   b.Reykjavik 20-8-77
Honours: Iceland Youth, Under-21, 30 full caps.

1995	Valur	12	0	
1996	Valur	17	2	
1997	Valur	16	3	45 5
1998	IBV	18	1	
1999	IBV	18	4	36 5
1999-2000	*Torquay U*	4	1	4 1
1999-2000	Brentford	25	1	
2000-01	Brentford	42	3	
2001-02	Brentford	46	6	113 10
2002-03	Wolverhampton W	13	2	
2002-03	*Brighton & HA*	15	0	15 0
2003-04	Wolverhampton W	0	0	13 2
2003-04	Reading	25	1	
2004-05	Reading	44	3	
2005-06	Reading	46	2	
2006-07	Reading	38	2	
2007-08	Reading	34	2	
2008-09	Reading	26	1	
2009-10	Reading	25	0	238 11

JOYCE, Danny (D)   0 0
b. 5-6-92
Source: Scholar.

2009-10	Reading	0	0	

KARACAN, Jem (M)   62 2
H: 5 10   W: 11 13   b.Lewisham 21-2-89
Source: Scholar.

2007-08	Reading	0	0	
2007-08	*Bournemouth*	13	1	13 1
2007-08	*Millwall*	7	0	7 0
2008-09	Reading	15	1	
2009-10	Reading	27	0	42 1

KEBE, Jimmy (M)   122 19
H: 6 2   W: 11 07   b.Vitry-sur-Seine 19-1-84
Honours: Mali 8 full caps, 3 goals.

2005-06	Lens	0	0	
2006-07	*Chateauroux*	18	2	18 2

KELLY, Julian (D)   16 1
H: 5 8   W: 11 04   b.London 6-9-89
Source: Arsenal Scholar.

2007-08	*Lens*	0	0	
2007-08	*Boulogne*	16	5	16 5
2007-08	Reading	5	0	
2008-09	Reading	41	2	
2009-10	Reading	42	10	88 12

2008-09	Reading	7	0	
2009-10	Reading	0	0	7 0
2009-10	*Wycombe W*	9	1	9 1

LONG, Shane (F)   130 23
H: 5 10   W: 11 02   b.Gortnahoe 22-1-87
Honours: Eire Youth, B, Under-21, 13 full caps, 3 goals.

2005	Cork C	1	0	1 0
2005-06	Reading	11	3	
2006-07	Reading	21	2	
2007-08	Reading	29	3	
2008-09	Reading	37	9	
2009-10	Reading	31	6	129 23

MATEJOVSKY, Marek (M)   140 8
H: 5 10   W: 11 00   b.Brandys nad Labem 20-12-81
Honours: Czech Republic 15 full caps, 1 goal.

2000-01	Jablonec	0	0	
2001-02	Jablonec	4	0	
2002-03	Jablonec	1	0	6 0
2003-04	Mlada Boleslav	0	0	
2004-05	Mlada Boleslav	28	1	
2005-06	Mlada Boleslav	26	5	
2006-07	Mlada Boleslav	29	0	83 6
2007-08	Reading	14	1	
2008-09	Reading	22	1	
2009-10	Reading	15	0	51 2

McANUFF, Jobi (M)   345 37
H: 5 11   W: 11 05   b.Edmonton 9-11-81
Source: Scholar. *Honours:* Jamaica 1 full cap.

2000-01	Wimbledon	0	0	
2001-02	Wimbledon	38	4	
2002-03	Wimbledon	31	4	
2003-04	Wimbledon	27	5	96 13
2003-04	West Ham U	12	1	
2004-05	West Ham U	1	0	13 1
2004-05	*Cardiff C*	43	2	43 2
2005-06	Crystal Palace	41	8	
2006-07	Crystal Palace	34	5	75 13
2007-08	Watford	39	2	
2008-09	Watford	40	3	
2009-10	Watford	3	0	82 5
2009-10	Reading	36	3	36 3

McCARTHY, Alex (G)   48 0
H: 6 4   W: 11 12   b.Guildford 3-12-89

2008-09	Reading	0	0	
2008-09	*Aldershot T*	4	0	4 0
2009-10	Reading	0	0	
2009-10	*Yeovil T*	44	0	44 0

MILLS, Matthew (D)   129 8
H: 6 3   W: 12 12   b.Swindon 14-7-86
Source: Scholar. *Honours:* England Youth.

2004-05	Southampton	0	0	
2004-05	*Coventry C*	4	0	4 0
2004-05	*Bournemouth*	12	3	12 3
2005-06	Southampton	4	0	4 0
2005-06	Manchester C	4	0	
2006-07	Manchester C	1	0	
2006-07	*Colchester U*	9	0	9 0
2007-08	Manchester C	0	0	2 0
2008-09	*Doncaster R*	34	3	
2009-10	*Doncaster R*	41	0	
2009-10	Doncaster R	0	0	75 3
2009-10	Reading	23	2	23 2

MOONEY, David (F)   141 51
H: 6 2   W: 12 06   b.Dublin 30-10-84
Source: Shamrock R, Longford T. *Honours:* Eire Under-23.

2005	Longford T	13	4	
2005	Shamrock R	14	2	14 2
2006	Longford T	21	3	
2007	Longford T	32	19	66 26
2008	Cork City	22	15	22 15
2008-09	Reading	0	0	
2008-09	*Stockport Co*	2	0	2 0
2008-09	*Norwich C*	9	3	9 3

2009–10	Reading	0	0	
2009–10	*Charlton Ath*	28	5	**28** 5

O'DEA, Darren (D)   **57** 4
H: 6 1   W: 13 01   b.Dublin 4-2-87
Honours: Eire Under-21, 2 full caps.

2006–07	Celtic	14	2	
2007–08	Celtic	6	0	
2008–09	Celtic	10	1	
2009–10	Celtic	19	1	**49** 4

On loan from Celtic.

2009–10	Reading	8	0	**8** 0

PEARCE, Alex (D)   **87** 8
H: 6 0   W: 11 10   b.Wallingford 9-11-88
Source: Scholar. *Honours:* Scotland Youth, Under-21.

2006–07	Reading	0	0	
2006–07	*Northampton T*	15	1	**15** 1
2007–08	Reading	0	0	
2007–08	*Bournemouth*	11	0	**11** 0
2007–08	*Norwich C*	11	0	**11** 0
2008–09	Reading	16	1	
2008–09	*Southampton*	9	2	**9** 2
2009–10	Reading	25	4	**41** 5

RASIAK, Grzegorz (F)   **278** 106
H: 6 3   W: 13 03   b.Szczecin 12-1-79
Source: Warta, GKS. *Honours:* Poland 37 full caps, 8 goals.

2000–01	Odra	28	9	**28** 9
2001–02	Groclin	26	14	
2002–03	Groclin	22	10	
2003–04	Groclin	18	10	**66** 34
2003–04	Siena	0	0	
2004–05	Derby Co	35	16	
2005–06	Derby Co	6	2	**41** 18
2005–06	Tottenham H	8	0	**8** 0
2005–06	Southampton	13	4	
2006–07	Southampton	39	18	
2007–08	Southampton	23	6	
2007–08	*Bolton W*	7	0	**7** 0
2008–09	Southampton	0	0	
2008–09	*Watford*	21	8	**21** 8
2009–10	Southampton	3	0	**78** 28
2009–10	Reading	29	9	**29** 9

ROBSON-KANU, Hal (F)   **59** 9
H: 5 7   W: 11 08   b.Acton 21-5-89
Honours: England Youth, Under-20. Wales Under-21, 1 full cap.

2007–08	Reading	0	0	
2007–08	*Southend U*	8	3	
2008–09	Reading	0	0	
2008–09	*Southend U*	14	2	**22** 5
2008–09	*Swindon T*	20	4	**20** 4
2009–10	Reading	17	0	**17** 0

ROSENIOR, Liam (D)   **204** 3
H: 5 10   W: 11 05   b.Wandsworth 9-7-84
Source: Scholar. *Honours:* England Youth, Under-20, Under-21.

2001–02	Bristol C	1	0	
2002–03	Bristol C	21	2	
2003–04	Bristol C	0	0	**22** 2
2003–04	Fulham	0	0	
2003–04	*Torquay U*	10	0	**10** 0
2004–05	Fulham	17	0	
2005–06	Fulham	24	0	
2006–07	Fulham	38	0	
2007–08	Fulham	0	0	**79** 0
2007–08	Reading	17	0	
2008–09	Reading	42	0	
2009–10	Reading	5	0	**64** 0
2009–10	*Ipswich T*	29	1	**29** 1

SIGURDSSON, Gylfi (M)   **58** 20
H: 6 1   W: 12 02   b.Reykjavik 9-9-89
Source: Scholar. *Honours:* Iceland Youth, Under-21, 1 full cap.

2007–08	Reading	0	0	
2008–09	Reading	0	0	
2008–09	*Shrewsbury T*	5	1	**5** 1
2008–09	*Crewe Alex*	15	3	**15** 3
2009–10	Reading	38	16	**38** 16

TABB, Jay (M)   **260** 31
H: 5 7   W: 10 00   b.Tooting 21-2-84
Source: Trainee. *Honours:* Eire Under-21.

2000–01	Brentford	2	0	
2001–02	Brentford	3	0	
2002–03	Brentford	5	0	

2003–04	Brentford	36	9	
2004–05	Brentford	40	5	
2005–06	Brentford	42	6	**128** 20
2006–07	Coventry C	31	3	
2007–08	Coventry C	42	5	
2008–09	Coventry C	22	3	**95** 11
2008–09	Reading	9	0	
2009–10	Reading	28	0	**37** 0

THORVALDSSON, Gunnar (F)   **161** 59
H: 6 0   W: 11 11   b.Vestmannaeyjar 1-4-82
Honours: Iceland 21 full caps, 5 goals.

1999	IBV	1	0	
2000	IBV	2	0	
2001	IBV	17	4	
2002	IBV	18	11	
2003	IBV	18	10	
2004	IBV	16	12	**72** 37
2004	Halmstad	6	0	
2005	Halmstad	23	16	
2006	Halmstad	9	0	**38** 16
2006–07	Hannover	7	0	**7** 0
2007	Valerenga	7	2	
2008	Valerenga	9	2	**16** 4
2008–09	Esbjerg	22	2	
2009–10	Esbjerg	2	0	**24** 2
2009–10	Reading	4	0	**4** 0

WILLIAMS, Marcus (D)   **166** 0
H: 5 8   W: 10 07   b.Doncaster 8-4-86
Source: Scholar.

2003–04	Scunthorpe U	1	0	
2004–05	Scunthorpe U	4	0	
2005–06	Scunthorpe U	29	0	
2006–07	Scunthorpe U	35	0	
2007–08	Scunthorpe U	34	0	
2008–09	Scunthorpe U	26	0	
2009–10	Scunthorpe U	37	0	**166** 0
2009–10	Reading	0	0	

ROCHDALE (69)

ARTHUR, Kenny (G)   **324** 0
H: 6 3   W: 13 08   b.Bellshill 7-12-78

1997–98	Partick T	19	0	
1998–99	Partick T	26	0	
1999–2000	Partick T	4	0	
2000–01	Partick T	34	0	
2001–02	Partick T	23	0	
2002–03	Partick T	35	0	
2003–04	Partick T	22	0	
2004–05	Partick T	35	0	
2005–06	Partick T	24	0	
2006–07	Partick T	21	0	**243** 0
2007–08	Accrington S	24	0	
2008–09	Accrington S	42	0	**66** 0
2009–10	Rochdale	15	0	**15** 0

BRIZELL, Josh (M)   **0** 0
H: 5 10   W: 12 04   b.Liverpool 15-10-91
Source: Scholar.

2009–10	Rochdale	0	0	

BROWN, Chris (D)   **0** 0
H: 6 3   W: 12 04   b.Hazel Grove 21-2-92
Source: Scholar.

2009–10	Rochdale	0	0	

DAGNALL, Chris (F)   **196** 61
H: 5 8   W: 12 03   b.Liverpool 15-4-86
Source: Scholar.

2003–04	Tranmere R	10	1	
2004–05	Tranmere R	23	6	
2005–06	Tranmere R	6	0	**39** 7
2005–06	Rochdale	21	3	
2006–07	Rochdale	37	17	
2007–08	Rochdale	14	7	
2008–09	Rochdale	40	7	
2009–10	Rochdale	45	20	**157** 54

DAWSON, Craig (D)   **42** 9
H: 6 0   W: 12 04   b.Rochdale 6-5-90
Source: Radcliffe B.

2008–09	Rochdale	0	0	
2009–10	Rochdale	42	9	**42** 9

EDWARDS, Matty (G)   **0** 0
H: 6 2   W: 12 11   b.Liverpool 22-8-90
Source: Leeds U.

2009–10	Rochdale	0	0	

FLYNN, Matthew (D)   **38** 0
H: 6 0   W: 11 08   b.Warrington 10-5-89
Source: Warrington T.

2007–08	Macclesfield T	0	0	
2008–09	Macclesfield T	28	0	
2009–10	Macclesfield T	0	0	**28** 0
2009–10	Rochdale	10	0	**10** 0

GRAY, Reece (F)   **2** 0
H: 5 7   W: 8 08   b.Oldham 1-9-92
Source: Scholar.

2009–10	Rochdale	2	0	**2** 0

HIGGINBOTHAM, Kallum (F)   **81** 7
H: 5 11   W: 10 10   b.Manchester 15-6-89

2007–08	Rochdale	33	3	
2008–09	Rochdale	7	1	
2008–09	*Accrington S*	12	0	**12** 0
2009–10	Rochdale	29	3	**69** 7

HOLNESS, Marcus (D)   **38** 0
H: 6 0   W: 12 02   b.Swinton 8-12-88
Source: Scholar.

2007–08	*Oldham Ath*	0	0	
2007–08	Rochdale	19	0	
2008–09	Rochdale	8	0	
2009–10	Rochdale	11	0	**38** 0

JONES, Gary (M)   **443** 54
H: 5 11   W: 12 05   b.Birkenhead 3-6-77
Source: Caernarfon T.

1997–98	Swansea C	8	0	**8** 0
1997–98	Rochdale	17	2	
1998–99	Rochdale	20	0	
1999–2000	Rochdale	39	7	
2000–01	Rochdale	44	8	
2001–02	Rochdale	20	5	
2001–02	Barnsley	25	1	
2002–03	Barnsley	31	1	
2003–04	Barnsley	0	0	**56** 2
2003–04	Rochdale	26	4	
2004–05	Rochdale	39	8	
2005–06	Rochdale	42	4	
2006–07	Rochdale	27	3	
2007–08	Rochdale	43	7	
2008–09	Rochdale	28	0	
2009–10	Rochdale	34	4	**379** 52

KENNEDY, Jason (M)   **148** 10
H: 6 1   W: 13 02   b.Stockton 11-9-86
Source: Scholar.

2004–05	Middlesbrough	1	0	
2005–06	Middlesbrough	3	0	
2006–07	Middlesbrough	0	0	
2006–07	*Boston U*	13	1	**13** 1
2006–07	*Bury*	12	0	**12** 0
2007–08	Middlesbrough	0	0	**0** 0
2007–08	*Livingston*	18	2	**18** 2
2007–08	*Darlington*	13	2	
2008–09	Darlington	46	5	**59** 7
2009–10	Rochdale	42	0	**42** 0

KENNEDY, Tom (D)   **275** 14
H: 5 10   W: 11 01   b.Bury 24-6-85
Source: Scholar.

2002–03	Bury	0	0	
2003–04	Bury	27	0	
2004–05	Bury	46	1	
2005–06	Bury	33	0	
2006–07	Bury	37	0	**143** 5
2007–08	Rochdale	43	2	
2008–09	Rochdale	45	4	
2009–10	Rochdale	44	3	**132** 9

MANGA, Marcus (F)   **2** 0
H: 5 9   W: 11 05   b.Cameroon 16-1-88
Source: Dinamo Bucharest.

2009–10	Rochdale	2	0	**2** 0

McARDLE, Rory (D)   **149** 5
H: 6 1   W: 11 11   b.Doncaster 1-5-87
Source: Scholar. *Honours:* Northern Ireland Youth, Under-21, 2 full caps.

2004–05	Sheffield W	0	0	
2005–06	Sheffield W	0	0	
2005–06	*Rochdale*	19	1	
2006–07	Sheffield W	1	0	**1** 0
2006–07	Rochdale	25	0	
2007–08	Rochdale	43	2	
2008–09	Rochdale	41	2	
2009–10	Rochdale	20	0	**148** 5

O'GRADY, Chris (F) 188 42
H: 6 3 W: 12 04 b.Nottingham 25-1-86
Source: Trainee. *Honours:* England Youth.

2002–03	Leicester C	1	0		
2003–04	Leicester C	0	0		
2004–05	Leicester C	0	0		
2004–05	Notts Co	9	0	9	0
2005–06	Leicester C	13	1		
2005–06	Rushden & D	22	4	22	4
2006–07	Leicester C	10	0	24	1
2007–08	Rotherham U	13	4		
2007–08	Rotherham U	38	9	51	13
2008–09	Oldham Ath	13	0		
2008–09	Bury	6	0	6	0
2008–09	Bradford C	2	0	2	0
2008–09	Stockport Co	18	2	18	2
2009–10	Oldham Ath	0	0	13	0
2009–10	Rochdale	43	22	43	22

SHAW, Jon (F) 33 3
H: 6 0 W: 13 01 b.Sheffield 10-11-83
Source: Scholar.

2002–03	Sheffield W	1	0		
2003–04	Sheffield W	14	2		
2003–04	York C	8	0	8	0
2004–05	Sheffield W	3	0	18	2

From Burton Alb, Halifax T.

2008–09	Rochdale	6	1		
2009–10	Rochdale	1	0	7	1

STANTON, Nathan (D) 376 0
H: 5 9 W: 12 06 b.Nottingham 6-5-81
Source: Trainee. *Honours:* England Youth.

1997–98	Scunthorpe U	1	0		
1998–99	Scunthorpe U	4	0		
1999–2000	Scunthorpe U	34	0		
2000–01	Scunthorpe U	38	0		
2001–02	Scunthorpe U	42	0		
2002–03	Scunthorpe U	42	0		
2003–04	Scunthorpe U	33	0		
2004–05	Scunthorpe U	21	0		
2005–06	Scunthorpe U	22	0	237	0
2006–07	Rochdale	35	0		
2007–08	Rochdale	27	0		
2008–09	Rochdale	39	0		
2009–10	Rochdale	38	0	139	0

TABERNER, Danny (M) 0 0
H: 6 2 W: 12 00 b.Bolton 17-6-93
Source: Scholar.

2009–10	Rochdale	0	0		

THOMPSON, Joe (M) 91 12
H: 6 0 W 9 07 b.Rochdale 5-3-89
Source: Scholar.

2005–06	Rochdale	1	0		
2006–07	Rochdale	13	0		
2007–08	Rochdale	11	1		
2008–09	Rochdale	30	5		
2009–10	Rochdale	36	6	91	12

TONER, Ciaran (M) 231 19
H: 6 1 W: 12 02 b.Craigavon 30-6-81
Source: Trainee. *Honours:* Northern Ireland Schools, Youth, Under-21, 2 full caps.

1999–2000	Tottenham H	0	0		
2000–01	Tottenham H	0	0		
2001–02	Tottenham H	0	0		
2001–02	Peterborough U	6	0	6	0
2001–02	Bristol R	6	0	6	0
2001–02	Leyton Orient	0	0		
2002–03	Leyton Orient	25	1		
2003–04	Leyton Orient	27	1	52	2
2004–05	Lincoln C	15	2	15	2
2004–05	Cambridge U	8	0	8	0
2005–06	Grimsby T	31	3		
2006–07	Grimsby T	33	8		
2007–08	Grimsby T	30	3	94	14
2008–09	Rochdale	37	1		
2009–10	Rochdale	13	0	50	1

WISEMAN, Scott (D) 121 2
H: 6 0 W: 11 06 b.Hull 9-10-85
Source: Scholar. *Honours:* England Youth, Under-20.

2003–04	Hull C	2	0		
2004–05	Hull C	3	0		
2004–05	Boston U	2	0	2	0
2005–06	Hull C	11	0		
2006–07	Hull C	0	0	16	0
2006–07	Rotherham U	18	1	18	1
2006–07	Darlington	10	0		
2007–08	Darlington	7	0	17	0
2008–09	Rochdale	32	0		
2009–10	Rochdale	36	1	68	1

ROTHERHAM U (70)

ANNERSON, Jamie (G) 0 0
H: 6 2 W: 13 02 b.Sheffield 21-6-88
Source: Scholar. *Honours:* England Youth.

2005–06	Sheffield U	0	0		
2006–07	Sheffield U	0	0		
2007–08	Rotherham U	0	0		
2007–08	Chesterfield	0	0		
2007–08	Sheffield U	0	0		
2008–09	Sheffield U	0	0		
2008–09	Rotherham U	0	0		
2009–10	Rotherham U	0	0		

BROGAN, Stephen (D) 61 4
H: 5 7 W: 10 04 b.Rotherham 12-4-88
Source: Scholar.

2005–06	Rotherham U	3	0		
2006–07	Rotherham U	23	0		
2007–08	Rotherham U	29	3		
2008–09	Rotherham U	1	0		
2009–10	Rotherham U	5	1	61	4

BROUGHTON, Drewe (F) 379 67
H: 6 3 W: 12 01 b.Hitchin 25-10-78
Source: Trainee.

1996–97	Norwich C	8	1		
1997–98	Norwich C	1	0		
1997–98	Wigan Ath	4	0	4	0
1998–99	Norwich C	0	0	9	1
1998–99	Brentford	1	0	1	0
1998–99	Peterborough U	25	7		
1999–2000	Peterborough U	10	1		
2000–01	Peterborough U	0	0	35	8
2000–01	Kidderminster H	19	7		
2001–02	Kidderminster H	38	8		
2002–03	Kidderminster H	37	4	94	19
2003–04	Southend U	35	2		
2004–05	Southend U	9	0	44	2
2004–05	Rushden & D	21	6		
2004–05	Wycombe W	3	0	3	0
2005–06	Rushden & D	37	10	58	16
2006–07	Chester C	14	2	14	2
2006–07	Boston U	5	2	5	2
2007–08	Milton Keynes D	13	0	13	0
2007–08	Wrexham	16	2	16	2
2008–09	Rotherham U	40	6		
2009–10	Rotherham U	16	3	56	9
2009–10	Lincoln C	7	0	7	0

CUMMINS, Michael (M) 384 46
H: 6 0 W: 13 06 b.Dublin 1-6-78
Source: Trainee. *Honours:* Eire Youth, Under-21.

1995–96	Middlesbrough	0	0		
1996–97	Middlesbrough	0	0		
1997–98	Middlesbrough	0	0		
1998–99	Middlesbrough	1	0		
1999–2000	Middlesbrough	1	0	2	0
1999–2000	Port Vale	12	1		
2000–01	Port Vale	45	2		
2001–02	Port Vale	46	8		
2002–03	Port Vale	30	4		
2003–04	Port Vale	42	4		
2004–05	Port Vale	39	2		
2005–06	Port Vale	39	10	253	31
2006–07	Darlington	39	4		
2007–08	Darlington	40	6	79	10
2008–09	Rotherham U	35	4		
2009–10	Rotherham U	15	1	50	5

ELLISON, Kevin (M) 271 44
H: 6 0 W: 12 00 b.Liverpool 23-2-79
Source: Altrincham.

2000–01	Leicester C	1	0		
2001–02	Leicester C	0	0	1	0
2001–02	Stockport Co	11	0		
2002–03	Stockport Co	23	1		
2003–04	Stockport Co	14	1	48	2
2003–04	Lincoln C	11	0	11	0
2004–05	Chester C	24	9		
2004–05	Hull C	16	1		
2005–06	Hull C	23	1	39	2
2006–07	Tranmere R	34	4	34	4
2007–08	Chester C	36	11		
2008–09	Chester C	39	8	99	28
2008–09	Rotherham U	0	0		
2009–10	Rotherham U	39	8	39	8

FENTON, Nick (D) 419 20
H: 6 0 W: 10 02 b.Preston 23-11-79
Source: Trainee. *Honours:* England Youth.

1996–97	Manchester C	0	0		
1997–98	Manchester C	0	0		
1998–99	Manchester C	15	0		
1999–2000	Manchester C	0	0		
1999–2000	Notts Co	13	1		
1999–2000	Bournemouth	8	0		
2000–01	Manchester C	0	0	15	0
2000–01	Bournemouth	5	0	13	0
2000–01	Notts Co	30	2		
2001–02	Notts Co	42	3		
2002–03	Notts Co	40	3		
2003–04	Notts Co	43	1	168	10
2004–05	Doncaster R	38	1		
2005–06	Doncaster R	25	2		
2006–07	Doncaster R	0	0	63	3
2006–07	Grimsby T	38	4		
2007–08	Grimsby T	42	2	80	6
2008–09	Rotherham U	45	1		
2009–10	Rotherham U	35	0	80	1

GREEN, Jamie (F) 59 2
H: 5 7 W: 10 07 b.Rossington 18-8-89
Source: Scholar.

2007–08	Rotherham U	9	1		
2008–09	Rotherham U	31	1		
2009–10	Rotherham U	19	0	59	2

HARRISON, Danny (M) 238 14
H: 5 11 W: 12 04 b.Liverpool 4-11-82
Source: Scholar.

2001–02	Tranmere R	1	0		
2002–03	Tranmere R	12	0		
2003–04	Tranmere R	32	2		
2004–05	Tranmere R	32	0		
2005–06	Tranmere R	35	2		
2006–07	Tranmere R	12	1	124	5
2007–08	Rotherham U	44	4		
2008–09	Rotherham U	33	1		
2009–10	Rotherham U	37	4	114	9

JOSEPH, Marc (D) 406 7
H: 6 0 W: 12 05 b.Leicester 10-11-76
Source: Trainee.

1995–96	Cambridge U	12	0		
1996–97	Cambridge U	8	0		
1997–98	Cambridge U	41	0		
1998–99	Cambridge U	29	0		
1999–2000	Cambridge U	33	0		
2000–01	Cambridge U	30	0	153	0
2001–02	Peterborough U	44	2		
2002–03	Peterborough U	17	0	61	2
2002–03	Hull C	23	0		
2003–04	Hull C	32	1		
2004–05	Hull C	29	0		
2005–06	Hull C	5	0	89	1
2005–06	Bristol C	3	0	3	0
2005–06	Blackpool	16	0		
2006–07	Blackpool	8	0	24	0
2007–08	Rotherham U	36	4		
2008–09	Rotherham U	25	0		
2009–10	Rotherham U	15	0	76	4

LAW, Nicky (M) 96 7
H: 5 10 W: 11 06 b.Nottingham 29-3-88
Source: Scholar. *Honours:* England Youth.

2005–06	Sheffield U	0	0		
2006–07	Sheffield U	4	0		
2006–07	Yeovil T	6	0	6	0
2007–08	Sheffield U	1	0		
2007–08	Bradford C	10	2		
2008–09	Sheffield U	0	0	5	0
2008–09	Bradford C	33	3	43	5
2009–10	Rotherham U	42	2	42	2

LE FONDRE, Adam (F) 205 80
H: 5 9 W: 11 04 b.Stockport 2-12-86
Source: Trainee.

2004–05	Stockport Co	20	4		
2005–06	Stockport Co	22	6		
2006–07	Stockport Co	21	7	63	17
2006–07	Rochdale	7	4		
2007–08	Rochdale	46	16		
2008–09	Rochdale	44	18		
2009–10	Rochdale	1	0	98	38
2009–10	Rotherham U	44	25	44	25

LIDDELL, Andy (F) 575 136
H: 5 7 W: 11 11 b.Leeds 28-6-73
Source: Trainee. *Honours:* Scotland
Under-21.

1990–91	Barnsley	0	0		
1991–92	Barnsley	1	0		
1992–93	Barnsley	21	2		
1993–94	Barnsley	22	1		
1994–95	Barnsley	39	13		
1995–96	Barnsley	43	9		
1996–97	Barnsley	38	8		
1997–98	Barnsley	26	1		
1998–99	Barnsley	8	0	198	34
1998–99	Wigan Ath	28	10		
1999–2000	Wigan Ath	41	8		
2000–01	Wigan Ath	37	9		
2001–02	Wigan Ath	34	18		
2002–03	Wigan Ath	37	16		
2003–04	Wigan Ath	40	9	217	70
2004–05	Sheffield U	33	3	33	3
2005–06	Oldham Ath	29	9		
2006–07	Oldham Ath	46	10		
2007–08	Oldham Ath	18	2		
2008–09	Oldham Ath	32	8	125	29
2009–10	Rotherham U	2	0	2	0

LYNCH, Mark (D) 109 2
H: 5 11 W: 11 03 b.Manchester 2-9-81
Source: Trainee.

1999–2000	Manchester U	0	0		
2000–01	Manchester U	0	0		
2001–02	Manchester U	0	0		
2001–02	*St Johnstone*	20	0	20	0
2002–03	Manchester U	0	0		
2003–04	Manchester U	0	0		
2004–05	Sunderland	11	0	11	0
2005–06	Hull C	16	0		
2006–07	Hull C	0	0	16	0
2006–07	Yeovil T	17	0		
2007–08	Yeovil T	14	0	31	0
2008–09	Rotherham U	8	2		
2009–10	Rotherham U	23	0	31	2

MILLS, Pablo (D) 224 4
H: 5 9 W: 11 04 b.Birmingham 27-5-84
Source: Trainee. *Honours:* England Youth.

2002–03	Derby Co	16	0		
2003–04	Derby Co	19	0		
2004–05	Derby Co	22	0		
2005–06	Derby Co	1	0	58	0
2005–06	*Milton Keynes D*	16	1	16	1
2005–06	Walsall	14	0	14	0
2006–07	Rotherham U	31	1		
2007–08	Rotherham U	33	1		
2008–09	Rotherham U	35	1		
2009–10	Rotherham U	37	0	136	3

NICHOLAS, Andrew (D) 157 4
H: 6 2 W: 12 08 b.Liverpool 10-10-83
Honours: Liverpool Trainee.

2003–04	Swindon T	31	1		
2004–05	Swindon T	16	0		
2004–05	*Chester C*	5	0	5	0
2005–06	Swindon T	33	0		
2006–07	Swindon T	35	2		
2007–08	Swindon T	11	1	126	4
2008–09	Rotherham U	19	0		
2009–10	Rotherham U	7	0	26	0

POPE, Tom (F) 91 20
H: 6 3 W: 11 03 b.Stoke 27-8-85
Source: Lancaster C.

2005–06	Crewe Alex	0	0		
2006–07	Crewe Alex	4	0		
2007–08	Crewe Alex	26	7		
2008–09	Crewe Alex	26	10	56	17
2009–10	Rotherham U	35	3	35	3

ROBERTS, Gary (M) 165 16
H: 5 8 W: 10 05 b.Chester 4-2-87
Source: Scholar. *Honours:* England Youth.

2003–04	Crewe Alex	2	0		
2004–05	Crewe Alex	2	0		
2005–06	Crewe Alex	33	2		
2006–07	Crewe Alex	43	3		
2007–08	Crewe Alex	42	6		
2008–09	Crewe Alex	0	0	122	11
2008–09	Yeovil T	30	2		
2009–10	Yeovil T	0	0	30	2
2009–10	Rotherham U	13	3	13	3

SHARPS, Ian (D) 330 14
H: 6 3 W: 14 07 b.Warrington 23-10-80
Source: Trainee.

1998–99	Tranmere R	1	0		
1999–2000	Tranmere R	0	0		
2000–01	Tranmere R	0	0		
2001–02	Tranmere R	29	0		
2002–03	Tranmere R	30	3		
2003–04	Tranmere R	27	1		
2004–05	Tranmere R	4	0		
2005–06	Tranmere R	39	1	170	6
2006–07	Rotherham U	38	2		
2007–08	Rotherham U	33	2		
2008–09	Rotherham U	45	4		
2009–10	Rotherham U	44	0	160	8

TAYLOR, Jason (M) 144 8
H: 6 1 W: 11 03 b.Ashton-under-Lyne
28-1-87
Source: Scholar.

2005–06	Oldham Ath	0	0		
2005–06	*Stockport Co*	9	0		
2006–07	Stockport Co	45	1		
2007–08	Stockport Co	42	4		
2008–09	Stockport Co	8	1	104	6
2008–09	Rotherham U	15	1		
2009–10	Rotherham U	2	0	17	1
2009–10	*Rochdale*	23	1	23	1

TAYLOR, Ryan (F) 105 10
H: 6 2 W: 10 10 b.Rotherham 4-5-88
Source: Scholar.

2005–06	Rotherham U	1	0		
2006–07	Rotherham U	10	0		
2007–08	Rotherham U	35	6		
2008–09	Rotherham U	33	4		
2009–10	Rotherham U	19	0	98	10
2009–10	*Exeter C*	7	0	7	0

TONGE, Dale (D) 145 1
H: 5 10 W: 10 06 b.Doncaster 7-5-85
Source: Scholar.

2003–04	Barnsley	1	0		
2004–05	Barnsley	14	0		
2005–06	Barnsley	24	0		
2006–07	Barnsley	6	0	45	0
2006–07	*Gillingham*	3	0	3	0
2007–08	Rotherham U	37	0		
2008–09	Rotherham U	39	1		
2009–10	Rotherham U	21	0	97	1

WARNE, Paul (M) 450 57
H: 5 10 W: 11 07 b.Norwich 8-5-73
Source: Wroxham.

1997–98	Wigan Ath	25	2		
1998–99	Wigan Ath	11	1	36	3
1998–99	Rotherham U	19	8		
1999–2000	Rotherham U	43	10		
2000–01	Rotherham U	44	7		
2001–02	Rotherham U	25	0		
2002–03	Rotherham U	40	1		
2003–04	Rotherham U	35	1		
2004–05	Rotherham U	24	1		
2004–05	*Mansfield T*	7	1	7	1
2005–06	Oldham Ath	40	9		
2006–07	Oldham Ath	46	9	86	18
2007–08	Yeovil T	33	1		
2008–09	Yeovil T	44	4	77	5
2009–10	Rotherham U	14	2	244	30

WARRINGTON, Andy (G) 300 0
H: 6 3 W: 12 13 b.Sheffield 10-6-76
Source: Trainee.

1994–95	York C	0	0		
1995–96	York C	6	0		
1996–97	York C	27	0		
1997–98	York C	17	0		
1998–99	York C	11	0	61	0
2003–04	Doncaster R	46	0		
2004–05	Doncaster R	34	0		
2005–06	Doncaster R	9	0		
2006–07	Doncaster R	0	0	89	0
2006–07	Bury	20	0	20	0
2007–08	Rotherham U	46	0		
2008–09	Rotherham U	38	0		
2009–10	Rotherham U	46	0	130	0

SCUNTHORPE U (71)

BOYES, Adam (F) 0 0
H: 6 2 W: 11 08 b.Lingdale 1-11-90
Source: York C.

2009–10	Scunthorpe U	0	0		

BYRNE, Cliff (D) 241 7
H: 6 0 W: 12 11 b.Dublin 27-4-82
Honours: Eire Youth, Under-21.

1999–2000	Sunderland	0	0		
2000–01	Sunderland	0	0		
2001–02	Sunderland	0	0		
2002–03	Sunderland	0	0		
2002–03	*Scunthorpe U*	13	0		
2003–04	Scunthorpe U	39	1		
2004–05	Scunthorpe U	29	1		
2005–06	Scunthorpe U	32	1		
2006–07	Scunthorpe U	24	0		
2007–08	Scunthorpe U	25	0		
2008–09	Scunthorpe U	43	2		
2009–10	Scunthorpe U	36	2	241	7

CANAVAN, Niall (D) 7 1
H: 6 3 W: 12 00 b.Leeds 11-4-91
Source: Scholar.

2009–10	Scunthorpe U	7	1	7	1

COLEMAN, Rory (D) 0 0
H: 6 0 W: 11 09 b.Rotherham 22-12-90
Source: Scholar.

2009–10	Scunthorpe U	0	0		

FORTE, Jonathan (M) 187 28
H: 6 0 W: 12 02 b.Sheffield 25-7-86
Source: Scholar. *Honours:* England Youth.
Barbados 2 full caps.

2003–04	Sheffield U	7	0		
2004–05	Sheffield U	22	1		
2005–06	Sheffield U	1	0		
2005–06	Doncaster R	13	4		
2005–06	*Rotherham U*	11	4	11	4
2006–07	Sheffield U	0	0	30	1
2006–07	*Doncaster R*	41	5	54	9
2007–08	Scunthorpe U	38	4		
2008–09	Scunthorpe U	8	0		
2008–09	*Notts Co*	18	8	18	8
2009–10	Scunthorpe U	28	2	74	6

GODDEN, Matthew (F) 0 0
b.Canterbury 29-7-91
Source: Scholar.

2009–10	Scunthorpe U	0	0		

HAYES, Paul (F) 307 74
H: 6 0 W: 12 12 b.Dagenham 20-9-83
Source: Norwich C. Scholar.

2002–03	Scunthorpe U	18	8		
2003–04	Scunthorpe U	35	2		
2004–05	Scunthorpe U	46	18		
2005–06	Barnsley	45	6		
2006–07	Barnsley	30	5	75	11
2006–07	*Huddersfield T*	4	1	4	1
2007–08	Scunthorpe U	40	8		
2008–09	Scunthorpe U	44	17		
2009–10	Scunthorpe U	45	9	228	62

HOOPER, Gary (M) 135 58
H: 5 10 W: 12 07 b.Loughton 26-1-88
Source: Grays Ath.

2006–07	Southend U	19	0		
2006–07	*Leyton Orient*	4	2	4	2
2007–08	Southend U	13	2	32	2
2007–08	*Hereford U*	19	11	19	11
2008–09	Scunthorpe U	45	24		
2009–10	Scunthorpe U	35	19	80	43

JONES, Rob (D) 201 16
H: 6 7 W: 12 02 b.Stockton 30-11-79
Source: Gateshead.

2002–03	Stockport Co	0	0		
2003–04	Stockport Co	16	2	16	2
2003–04	*Macclesfield T*	1	0	1	0
2004–05	Grimsby T	20	1		
2005–06	Grimsby T	40	4	60	5
2006–07	Hibernian	34	4		
2007–08	Hibernian	30	0		
2008–09	Hibernian	32	4	96	8
2009–10	Scunthorpe U	28	1	28	1

LILLIS, Josh (G) 27 0
H: 6 0 W: 12 08 b.Derby 24-6-87
Source: Scholar.

Season	Club	Apps	Gls	Tot A	Tot G
2006–07	Scunthorpe U	1	0		
2007–08	Scunthorpe U	3	0		
2008–09	Scunthorpe U	5	0		
2008–09	*Notts Co*	5	0	5	0
2009–10	Scunthorpe U	8	0	17	0
2009–10	*Grimsby T*	4	0	4	0
2009–10	*Rochdale*	1	0	1	0

MAY, Ben (F) 194 26
H: 6 3 W: 12 12 b.Gravesend 10-3-84
Source: Juniors.

Season	Club	Apps	Gls	Tot A	Tot G
2000–01	Millwall	0	0		
2001–02	Millwall	0	0		
2002–03	Millwall	10	1		
2002–03	*Colchester U*	6	0		
2003–04	Millwall	0	0		
2003–04	*Brentford*	41	7		
2004–05	Millwall	8	1		
2004–05	*Colchester U*	14	1	20	1
2004–05	*Brentford*	10	1	51	8
2005–06	Millwall	39	10		
2006–07	Millwall	13	2		
2007–08	Millwall	8	0	78	14
2007–08	Scunthorpe U	21	1		
2008–09	Scunthorpe U	23	2		
2009–10	Scunthorpe U	1	0	45	3

McCANN, Grant (M) 339 56
H: 5 10 W: 11 00 b.Belfast 14-4-80
Source: Trainee. *Honours:* Northern Ireland Youth, Under-21, 28 full caps, 4 goals.

Season	Club	Apps	Gls	Tot A	Tot G
1998–99	West Ham U	0	0		
1999–2000	West Ham U	0	0		
2000–01	West Ham U	1	0		
2000–01	*Notts Co*	2	0	2	0
2000–01	*Cheltenham T*	30	3		
2001–02	West Ham U	3	0		
2002–03	West Ham U	0	0	4	0
2002–03	Cheltenham T	27	6		
2003–04	Cheltenham T	43	8		
2004–05	Cheltenham T	39	4		
2005–06	Cheltenham T	39	8		
2006–07	Cheltenham T	15	5	193	34
2006–07	Barnsley	22	1		
2007–08	Barnsley	19	3	41	4
2007–08	Scunthorpe U	14	1		
2008–09	Scunthorpe U	43	9		
2009–10	Scunthorpe U	42	8	99	18

MILNE, Kenny (D) 212 12
H: 6 2 W: 12 08 b.Alloa 26-8-79
Honours: Scotland Under-21.

Season	Club	Apps	Gls	Tot A	Tot G
1997–98	Hearts	1	0		
1998–99	Hearts	0	0		
1998–99	Cowdenbeath	23	6		
1999–2000	Hearts	1	0		
2000–01	Hearts	7	0		
2001–02	Hearts	4	0	13	0
2001–02	Cowdenbeath	9	0	32	6
2002–03	Partick T	12	0		
2003–04	Partick T	25	1		
2004–05	Partick T	30	1	67	2
2005–06	Falkirk	33	2		
2006–07	Falkirk	34	1		
2007–08	Falkirk	28	1	95	4
2008–09	Scunthorpe U	1	0		
2009–10	Scunthorpe U	4	0	5	0

MIRFIN, David (D) 231 10
H: 6 3 W: 13 00 b.Sheffield 18-4-85
Source: Scholar.

Season	Club	Apps	Gls	Tot A	Tot G
2002–03	Huddersfield T	1	0		
2003–04	Huddersfield T	21	2		
2004–05	Huddersfield T	41	4		
2005–06	Huddersfield T	31	1		
2006–07	Huddersfield T	38	1		
2007–08	Huddersfield T	29	1	161	9
2008–09	Scunthorpe U	33	0		
2009–10	Scunthorpe U	37	1	70	1

MORRIS, Ian (D) 119 10
H: 6 0 W: 11 05 b.Dublin 27-2-87
Source: Scholar. *Honours:* Eire Under-21.

Season	Club	Apps	Gls	Tot A	Tot G
2003–04	Leeds U	0	0		
2004–05	Leeds U	0	0		
2005–06	Leeds U	0	0		
2005–06	*Blackpool*	30	3	30	3
2006–07	Leeds U	0	0		
2006–07	Scunthorpe U	28	3		
2007–08	Scunthorpe U	25	3		
2008–09	Scunthorpe U	20	1		
2008–09	*Carlisle U*	6	0	6	0
2009–10	Scunthorpe U	3	0	76	7
2009–10	*Chesterfield*	7	0	7	0

MURPHY, Joe (G) 279 0
H: 6 2 W: 13 04 b.Dublin 21-8-81
Source: Trainee. *Honours:* Eire Youth, Under-21, 2 full caps.

Season	Club	Apps	Gls	Tot A	Tot G
1999–2000	Tranmere R	21	0		
2000–01	Tranmere R	20	0		
2001–02	Tranmere R	22	0	63	0
2002–03	WBA	2	0		
2003–04	WBA	3	0		
2004–05	WBA	0	0	5	0
2004–05	*Walsall*	25	0		
2005–06	Sunderland	0	0		
2005–06	*Walsall*	14	0	39	0
2006–07	Scunthorpe U	45	0		
2007–08	Scunthorpe U	45	0		
2008–09	Scunthorpe U	42	0		
2009–10	Scunthorpe U	40	0	172	0

O'CONNOR, Michael (M) 119 6
H: 6 1 W: 11 08 b.Belfast 6-10-87
Source: Scholar. *Honours:* Northern Ireland Youth, Under-21, B, 9 full caps.

Season	Club	Apps	Gls	Tot A	Tot G
2005–06	Crewe Alex	2	0		
2006–07	Crewe Alex	29	0		
2007–08	Crewe Alex	23	0		
2008–09	Crewe Alex	23	3	77	3
2008–09	*Lincoln C*	10	1	10	1
2009–10	Scunthorpe U	32	2	32	2

RAYNES, Michael (D) 152 5
H: 6 4 W: 12 00 b.Wythenshawe 15-10-87
Source: Scholar.

Season	Club	Apps	Gls	Tot A	Tot G
2004–05	Stockport Co	19	0		
2005–06	Stockport Co	25	1		
2006–07	Stockport Co	9	0		
2007–08	Stockport Co	27	0		
2008–09	Stockport Co	35	3		
2009–10	Stockport Co	25	1	140	5
2009–10	Scunthorpe U	12	0	12	0

SLOCOMBE, Sam (G) 1 0
H: 6 0 W: 11 11 b.Scunthorpe 5-6-88
Source: Bottesford T.

Season	Club	Apps	Gls	Tot A	Tot G
2008–09	Scunthorpe U	0	0		
2009–10	Scunthorpe U	1	0	1	0

SPARROW, Matt (M) 336 37
H: 5 11 W: 10 06 b.Wembley 3-10-81
Source: Scholar.

Season	Club	Apps	Gls	Tot A	Tot G
1999–2000	Scunthorpe U	11	0		
2000–01	Scunthorpe U	11	4		
2001–02	Scunthorpe U	24	1		
2002–03	Scunthorpe U	42	9		
2003–04	Scunthorpe U	38	3		
2004–05	Scunthorpe U	44	5		
2005–06	Scunthorpe U	39	5		
2006–07	Scunthorpe U	29	4		
2007–08	Scunthorpe U	32	1		
2008–09	Scunthorpe U	36	4		
2009–10	Scunthorpe U	30	1	336	37

THOMPSON, Gary (M) 100 19
H: 6 0 W: 14 02 b.Kendal 24-11-80
Source: Scholar.

Season	Club	Apps	Gls	Tot A	Tot G
2007–08	Morecambe	40	7	40	7
2008–09	Scunthorpe U	24	3		
2009–10	Scunthorpe U	36	9	60	12

TOGWELL, Sam (D) 187 8
H: 5 11 W: 12 04 b.Beaconsfield 14-10-84
Source: Scholar.

Season	Club	Apps	Gls	Tot A	Tot G
2002–03	Crystal Palace	1	0		
2003–04	Crystal Palace	0	0		
2004–05	Crystal Palace	0	0		
2004–05	*Oxford U*	4	0	4	0
2004–05	*Northampton T*	8	0	8	0
2005–06	Crystal Palace	0	0	1	0
2005–06	*Port Vale*	27	2	27	2
2006–07	Barnsley	44	1		
2007–08	Barnsley	22	1	66	2
2008–09	Scunthorpe U	40	2		
2009–10	Scunthorpe U	41	2	81	4

WOOLFORD, Martyn (M) 79 9
H: 6 0 W: 11 09 b.Castleford 13-10-85
Source: Glasshoughton W, Frickley Ath, York C.

Season	Club	Apps	Gls	Tot A	Tot G
2008–09	Scunthorpe U	39	4		
2009–10	Scunthorpe U	40	5	79	9

WRIGHT, Andrew (M) 49 0
H: 6 1 W: 13 07 b.Southport 15-1-85
Source: Scholar.

Season	Club	Apps	Gls	Tot A	Tot G
2001–02	Liverpool	0	0		
2002–03	Liverpool	0	0		
2003–04	Liverpool	0	0		
2004–05	Liverpool	0	0		
2005–06	Liverpool	0	0		
2006–07	Liverpool	0	0		

From West Virginia Univ.

Season	Club	Apps	Gls	Tot A	Tot G
2007–08	Scunthorpe U	2	0		
2008–09	Scunthorpe U	28	0		
2009–10	Scunthorpe U	19	0	49	0

WRIGHT, Josh (M) 79 1
H: 6 1 W: 11 07 b.Tower Hamlets 6-11-89
Source: Scholar. *Honours:* England Youth.

Season	Club	Apps	Gls	Tot A	Tot G
2007–08	Charlton Ath	0	0		
2007–08	*Barnet*	32	1	32	1
2008–09	Charlton Ath	2	0	2	0
2008–09	*Brentford*	5	0	5	0
2008–09	*Gillingham*	5	0	5	0
2009–10	Scunthorpe U	35	0	35	0

SHEFFIELD U (72)

AKSALU, Mihkel (G) 117 0
H: 6 3 W: 12 06 b.Kuressaare 7-11-84
Honours: Estonia Under-21, 8 full caps.

Season	Club	Apps	Gls	Tot A	Tot G
2000	Kuressaare	1	0		
2001	Kuressaare	0	0		
2002	Kuressaare	0	0	1	0
2003	Emmaste	1	0		
2003	Flora	1	0		
2004	Flora	1	0		
2005	Flora	8	0		
2006	Flora	15	0		
2007	Flora	30	0		
2008	Flora	30	0		
2009	Flora	31	0	116	0
2009–10	Sheffield U	0	0		

BENNETT, Ian (G) 390 0
H: 6 0 W: 12 10 b.Worksop 10-10-71
Source: Newcastle U Trainee.

Season	Club	Apps	Gls	Tot A	Tot G
1991–92	Peterborough U	7	0		
1992–93	Peterborough U	46	0		
1993–94	Peterborough U	19	0	72	0
1993–94	Birmingham C	22	0		
1994–95	Birmingham C	46	0		
1995–96	Birmingham C	24	0		
1996–97	Birmingham C	40	0		
1997–98	Birmingham C	45	0		
1998–99	Birmingham C	10	0		
1999–2000	Birmingham C	21	0		
2000–01	Birmingham C	45	0		
2001–02	Birmingham C	18	0		
2002–03	Birmingham C	10	0		
2003–04	Birmingham C	6	0		
2004–05	Birmingham C	0	0	287	0
2004–05	*Sheffield U*	5	0		
2004–05	*Coventry C*	6	0	6	0
2005–06	Leeds U	4	0		
2006–07	Leeds U	0	0	4	0
2006–07	Sheffield U	2	0		
2007–08	Sheffield U	7	0		
2008–09	Sheffield U	0	0		
2009–10	Sheffield U	5	0	21	0

CAMARA, Henri (F) 269 85
H: 5 9 W: 10 08 b.Dakar 10-5-77
Honours: Senegal 89 full caps, 28 goals.

Season	Club	Apps	Gls	Tot A	Tot G
1999–2000	Neuchatel Xamax	20	12		
2000–01	Neuchatel Xamax	12	5	32	17
2000–01	Grasshoppers	11	3	11	3
2001–02	Sedan	25	8		
2002–03	Sedan	34	14	59	22
2003–04	Wolverhampton W	30	7		
2004–05	Wolverhampton W	0	0	30	7
2004–05	*Celtic*	18	8	18	8
2004–05	*Southampton*	13	4	13	4
2005–06	Wigan Ath	29	12		

2006–07	Wigan Ath	23	6		
2007–08	Wigan Ath	0	0		
2007–08	*West Ham U*	10	0	**10**	**0**
2008–09	Wigan Ath	17	2		
2008–09	Stoke C	4	0	**4**	**0**
2009–10	Wigan Ath	0	0	**69**	**20**
2009–10	Sheffield U	23	4	**23**	**4**

CRESSWELL, Richard (F)   **469** **105**
H: 6 0   W: 11 08   b.Bridlington 20-9-77
Source: Trainee. *Honours:* England
Under-21.

1995–96	York C	16	1		
1996–97	York C	17	0		
1996–97	*Mansfield T*	5	1	**5**	**1**
1997–98	York C	26	4		
1998–99	York C	36	16	**95**	**21**
1998–99	Sheffield W	7	1		
1999–2000	Sheffield W	20	1		
2000–01	Sheffield W	4	0	**31**	**2**
2000–01	Leicester C	8	0	**8**	**0**
2000–01	*Preston NE*	11	2		
2001–02	Preston NE	40	13		
2002–03	Preston NE	42	16		
2003–04	Preston NE	45	2		
2004–05	Preston NE	46	16		
2005–06	Preston NE	3	0	**187**	**49**
2005–06	Leeds U	16	5		
2006–07	Leeds U	22	4	**38**	**9**
2007–08	Stoke C	43	11		
2008–09	Stoke C	29	0		
2009–10	Stoke C	2	0	**74**	**11**
2009–10	Sheffield U	31	12	**31**	**12**

EVANS, Ched (F)   **77** **15**
H: 6 0   W: 12 00   b.Rhyl 28-12-88
Source: Scholar. *Honours:* Wales Under-21,
12 full caps, 2 goals.

2006–07	Manchester C	0	0		
2007–08	Manchester C	0	0		
2007–08	*Norwich C*	28	10	**28**	**10**
2008–09	Manchester C	16	1		
2009–10	Sheffield U	33	4	**33**	**4**

FORTUNE, Jon (D)   **203** **9**
H: 6 2   W: 12 12   b.Islington 23-8-80
Source: Trainee.

1998–99	Charlton Ath	0	0		
1999–2000	Charlton Ath	0	0		
1999–2000	*Mansfield T*	4	0		
2000–01	Charlton Ath	0	0		
2000–01	*Mansfield T*	14	0	**18**	**0**
2001–02	Charlton Ath	19	0		
2002–03	Charlton Ath	26	1		
2003–04	Charlton Ath	28	2		
2004–05	Charlton Ath	31	2		
2005–06	Charlton Ath	11	0		
2006–07	Charlton Ath	8	0		
2006–07	*Stoke C*	14	1	**14**	**1**
2007–08	Charlton Ath	26	2		
2008–09	Charlton Ath	17	0		
2009–10	Charlton Ath	0	0	**166**	**7**
2009–10	Sheffield U	5	1	**5**	**1**

FRANCE, Ryan (M)   **142** **6**
H: 5 11   W: 11 11   b.Sheffield 13-12-80
Source: Alfreton T.

2003–04	Hull C	28	2		
2004–05	Hull C	31	2		
2005–06	Hull C	35	2		
2006–07	Hull C	24	0		
2007–08	Hull C	13	0		
2008–09	Hull C	2	0	**133**	**6**
2009–10	Sheffield U	9	0	**9**	**0**

GEARY, Derek (D)   **211** **1**
H: 5 6   W: 10 00   b.Dublin 19-6-80
Source: Rivermont BC.

1997–98	Sheffield W	0	0		
1998–99	Sheffield W	0	0		
1999–2000	Sheffield W	0	0		
2000–01	Sheffield W	5	0		
2001–02	Sheffield W	32	0		
2002–03	Sheffield W	26	0		
2003–04	Sheffield W	41	0	**104**	**0**
2004–05	Stockport Co	13	0	**13**	**0**
2004–05	Sheffield U	19	1		
2005–06	Sheffield U	20	0		
2006–07	Sheffield U	26	0		
2007–08	Sheffield U	21	0		

2008–09	Sheffield U	1	0		
2009–10	Sheffield U	7	0	**94**	**1**

HARPER, James (M)   **349** **29**
H: 5 10   W: 11 02   b.Chelmsford 9-11-80
Source: Trainee.

1999–2000	Arsenal	0	0		
2000–01	Arsenal	0	0		
2000–01	*Cardiff C*	3	0	**3**	**0**
2000–01	Reading	12	1		
2001–02	Reading	26	1		
2002–03	Reading	36	2		
2003–04	Reading	39	1		
2004–05	Reading	41	3		
2005–06	Reading	45	7		
2006–07	Reading	38	3		
2007–08	Reading	38	6		
2008–09	Reading	34	1		
2009–10	Reading	3	0	**312**	**25**
2009–10	Sheffield U	34	4	**34**	**4**

HENDERSON, Darius (F)   **292** **74**
H: 6 3   W: 14 03   b.Sutton 7-9-81
Source: Trainee.

1999–2000	Reading	6	0		
2000–01	Reading	4	0		
2001–02	Reading	38	7		
2002–03	Reading	22	4		
2003–04	Reading	1	0	**71**	**11**
2003–04	*Brighton & HA*	10	2	**10**	**2**
2003–04	Gillingham	4	0		
2004–05	Gillingham	9	2	**36**	**9**
2004–05	*Swindon T*	6	5	**6**	**5**
2005–06	Watford	30	14		
2006–07	Watford	35	3		
2007–08	Watford	40	12	**105**	**29**
2008–09	Sheffield U	32	6		
2009–10	Sheffield U	32	12	**64**	**18**

KENNY, Paddy (G)   **411** **0**
H: 6 1   W: 14 01   b.Halifax 17-5-78
Source: Bradford PA. *Honours:* Eire 7 full
caps.

1998–99	Bury	0	0		
1999–2000	Bury	46	0		
2000–01	Bury	46	0		
2001–02	Bury	41	0		
2002–03	Bury	0	0	**133**	**0**
2002–03	Sheffield U	45	0		
2003–04	Sheffield U	27	0		
2004–05	Sheffield U	40	0		
2005–06	Sheffield U	46	0		
2006–07	Sheffield U	34	0		
2007–08	Sheffield U	40	0		
2008–09	Sheffield U	44	0		
2009–10	Sheffield U	2	0	**278**	**0**

LITTLE, Glen (M)   **387** **40**
H: 6 1   W: 13 00   b.Wimbledon 15-10-75
Source: Trainee.

1994–95	Crystal Palace	0	0		
1995–96	Crystal Palace	0	0		
1996–97	*Glentoran*	6	2	**6**	**2**
1996–97	Burnley	9	0		
1997–98	Burnley	24	4		
1998–99	Burnley	34	5		
1999–2000	Burnley	41	3		
2000–01	Burnley	34	3		
2001–02	Burnley	37	9		
2002–03	Burnley	33	5		
2002–03	*Reading*	6	1		
2003–04	Burnley	34	3	**246**	**32**
2003–04	*Bolton W*	4	0	**4**	**0**
2004–05	Reading	35	0		
2005–06	Reading	35	5		
2006–07	Reading	24	0		
2007–08	Reading	2	0		
2008–09	Portsmouth	5	0		
2008–09	*Reading*	8	0	**110**	**6**
2009–10	Portsmouth	0	0	**5**	**0**
2009–10	Sheffield U	16	0	**16**	**0**

LOWTON, Matt (M)   **2** **0**
H: 5 11   W: 12 04   b.Chesterfield 9-6-89
Source: Scholar.

2008–09	Sheffield U	0	0		
2009–10	Sheffield U	2	0	**2**	**0**

MONTGOMERY, Nick (M)   **294** **8**
H: 5 9   W: 11 08   b.Leeds 28-10-81
Source: Scholar. *Honours:* Scotland
Under-21, B.

2000–01	Sheffield U	27	0		
2001–02	Sheffield U	31	2		
2002–03	Sheffield U	23	0		
2003–04	Sheffield U	36	3		
2004–05	Sheffield U	25	1		
2005–06	Sheffield U	39	1		
2006–07	Sheffield U	26	0		
2007–08	Sheffield U	20	0		
2008–09	Sheffield U	28	0		
2009–10	Sheffield U	39	1	**294**	**8**

MORGAN, Chris (D)   **424** **20**
H: 6 1   W: 12 03   b.Barnsley 9-11-77
Source: Trainee.

1996–97	Barnsley	0	0		
1997–98	Barnsley	11	0		
1998–99	Barnsley	19	0		
1999–2000	Barnsley	37	0		
2000–01	Barnsley	40	1		
2001–02	Barnsley	42	4		
2002–03	Barnsley	36	2	**185**	**7**
2003–04	Sheffield U	32	1		
2004–05	Sheffield U	41	2		
2005–06	Sheffield U	39	3		
2006–07	Sheffield U	24	1		
2007–08	Sheffield U	25	2		
2008–09	Sheffield U	41	2		
2009–10	Sheffield U	37	2	**239**	**13**

NAYSMITH, Gary (D)   **310** **9**
H: 5 9   W: 12 01   b.Edinburgh 16-11-78
Source: Whitehill Welfare Colts. *Honours:*
Scotland Schools, Under-21, B, 46 full caps, 1
goal.

1995–96	Hearts	1	0		
1996–97	Hearts	10	0		
1997–98	Hearts	16	2		
1998–99	Hearts	26	0		
1999–2000	Hearts	35	1		
2000–01	Hearts	9	0	**97**	**3**
2000–01	Everton	20	2		
2001–02	Everton	24	0		
2002–03	Everton	28	1		
2003–04	Everton	29	2		
2004–05	Everton	11	0		
2005–06	Everton	7	0		
2006–07	Everton	15	1	**134**	**6**
2007–08	Sheffield U	38	0		
2008–09	Sheffield U	39	0		
2009–10	Sheffield U	2	0	**79**	**0**

POMARES, Carlos (D)   **0** **0**
Source: Alboraya.

2009–10	Sheffield U	0	0		

QUINN, Stephen (M)   **152** **15**
H: 5 6   W: 12 05   b.Dublin 4-4-86
Source: Trainee. *Honours:* Eire Under-21.

2005–06	Sheffield U	0	0		
2005–06	*Milton Keynes D*	15	0	**15**	**0**
2005–06	*Rotherham U*	16	0	**16**	**0**
2006–07	Sheffield U	15	2		
2007–08	Sheffield U	19	2		
2008–09	Sheffield U	43	7		
2009–10	Sheffield U	44	4	**121**	**15**

REID, Kyel (M)   **70** **7**
H: 5 10   W: 12 05   b.South London 26-11-87
Source: Scholar. *Honours:* England Youth.

2004–05	West Ham U	0	0		
2005–06	West Ham U	2	0		
2006–07	West Ham U	0	0		
2006–07	*Barnsley*	26	2	**26**	**2**
2007–08	West Ham U	1	0		
2007–08	*Crystal Palace*	2	0	**2**	**0**
2008–09	West Ham U	0	0	**3**	**0**
2008–09	*Blackpool*	7	0	**7**	**0**
2008–09	*Wolverhampton W*	8	1	**8**	**1**
2009–10	Sheffield U	7	0	**7**	**0**
2009–10	*Charlton Ath*	17	4	**17**	**4**

ROBERTSON, Jordan (F)   **65** **14**
H: 6 0   W: 12 06   b.Sheffield 12-2-88
Source: Scholar.

2006–07	Sheffield U	0	0		
2006–07	*Torquay U*	9	2	**9**	**2**
2006–07	*Northampton T*	17	3	**17**	**3**

2007–08	Sheffield U	0	0		
2007–08	*Dundee U*	14	3	14	3
2007–08	*Oldham Ath*	3	1	3	1
2008–09	Sheffield U	0	0		
2008–09	*Southampton*	10	1	10	1
2008–09	*Ferencvaros*	8	3	8	3
2009–10	Sheffield U	0	0		
2009–10	*Bury*	4	1	4	1

SHARP, Billy (F)   184   85
H: 5 9   W: 11 00   b.Sheffield 5-2-86
Source: Scholar.

2004–05	Sheffield U	2	0		
2004–05	*Rushden & D*	16	9	16	9
2005–06	Sheffield U	0	0		
2005–06	Scunthorpe U	37	23		
2006–07	Scunthorpe U	45	30	82	53
2007–08	Sheffield U	29	4		
2008–09	Sheffield U	22	4		
2009–10	Sheffield U	0	0	53	8
2009–10	*Doncaster R*	33	15	33	15

STEWART, Jordan (D)   268   10
H: 6 0   W: 12 09   b.Birmingham 3-3-82
Source: Trainee. *Honours:* England Youth, Under-21.

1999–2000	Leicester C	1	0		
1999–2000	*Bristol R*	4	0	4	0
2000–01	Leicester C	0	0		
2001–02	Leicester C	12	0		
2002–03	Leicester C	37	4		
2003–04	Leicester C	25	1		
2004–05	Leicester C	35	1	110	6
2005–06	Watford	35	0		
2006–07	Watford	31	0		
2007–08	Watford	39	2	105	2
2008–09	Derby Co	26	2		
2009–10	Derby Co	0	0	26	2
2009–10	Sheffield U	23	0	23	0

TAYLOR, Andy (D)   113   3
H: 5 11   W: 11 07   b.Blackburn 14-3-86
Source: Scholar. *Honours:* England Youth, Under-20, Under-21.

2004–05	Blackburn R	0	0		
2005–06	Blackburn R	0	0		
2005–06	*QPR*	3	0	3	0
2005–06	*Blackpool*	3	0	3	0
2006–07	Blackburn R	0	0		
2006–07	*Crewe Alex*	4	0	4	0
2006–07	*Huddersfield T*	8	0	8	0
2007–08	Blackburn R	0	0		
2007–08	Tranmere R	30	2		
2008–09	Tranmere R	39	1	69	3
2009–10	Sheffield U	26	0	26	0

WARD, Jamie (M)   145   48
H: 5 5   W: 9 04   b.Birmingham 12-5-86
Source: Scholar. *Honours:* Northern Ireland Youth, Under-21.

2003–04	Aston Villa	0	0		
2004–05	Aston Villa	0	0		
2005–06	Aston Villa	0	0		
2005–06	*Stockport Co*	9	1	9	1
2006–07	Torquay U	25	9	25	9
2006–07	Chesterfield	9	3		
2007–08	Chesterfield	35	12		
2008–09	Chesterfield	23	14	67	29
2008–09	Sheffield U	16	2		
2009–10	Sheffield U	28	7	44	9

WILLIAMSON, Lee (D)   333   20
H: 5 10   W: 10 04   b.Derby 7-6-82
Source: Trainee.

1999–2000	Mansfield T	4	0		
2000–01	Mansfield T	15	0		
2001–02	Mansfield T	46	3		
2002–03	Mansfield T	40	0		
2003–04	Mansfield T	35	0		
2004–05	Mansfield T	4	0	144	3
2004–05	*Northampton T*	37	0	37	0
2005–06	Rotherham U	37	4		
2006–07	Rotherham U	19	5	56	9
2006–07	Watford	5	0		
2007–08	Watford	32	2		
2008–09	Watford	34	2	71	4
2009–10	*Preston NE*	5	1	5	1
2009–10	Sheffield U	20	3	20	3

YEATES, Mark (F)   185   29
H: 5 8   W: 13 03   b.Dublin 11-1-85
Source: Trainee. *Honours:* Eire Youth, Under-21.

2002–03	Tottenham H	0	0		
2003–04	Tottenham H	1	0		
2003–04	*Brighton & HA*	9	0	9	0
2004–05	Tottenham H	2	0		
2004–05	*Swindon T*	4	0	4	0
2005–06	Tottenham H	0	0		
2005–06	*Colchester U*	44	5		
2006–07	Tottenham H	0	0	3	0
2006–07	*Hull C*	5	0	5	0
2006–07	*Leicester C*	9	1	9	1
2007–08	Colchester U	29	8		
2008–09	Colchester U	43	12	116	25
2009–10	*Middlesbrough*	19	1	19	1
2009–10	Sheffield U	20	2	20	2

SHEFFIELD W (73)

BEEVERS, Mark (D)   99   0
H: 6 4   W: 13 00   b.Barnsley 21-11-89
Source: Scholar. *Honours:* England Youth.

2006–07	Sheffield W	2	0		
2007–08	Sheffield W	28	0		
2008–09	Sheffield W	34	0		
2009–10	Sheffield W	35	0	99	0

BODEN, Luke (F)   23   0
H: 6 1   W: 12 00   b.Sheffield 26-11-88
Source: Scholar.

2006–07	Sheffield W	1	0		
2007–08	Sheffield W	2	0		
2008–09	Sheffield W	12	0		
2008–09	*Chesterfield*	4	0	4	0
2009–10	Sheffield W	0	0	15	0
2009–10	*Northampton T*	4	0	4	0

BUXTON, Lewis (D)   190   2
H: 6 1   W: 13 11   b.Newport (IW) 10-12-83
Source: School.

2000–01	Portsmouth	0	0		
2001–02	Portsmouth	29	0		
2002–03	Portsmouth	1	0		
2002–03	*Exeter C*	4	0	4	0
2002–03	*Bournemouth*	17	0		
2003–04	*Bournemouth*	0	0		
2003–04	*Bournemouth*	26	0	43	0
2004–05	Portsmouth	0	0	30	0
2004–05	Stoke C	16	0		
2005–06	Stoke C	32	1		
2006–07	Stoke C	1	0		
2007–08	Stoke C	4	0		
2008–09	Stoke C	0	0	53	1
2009–10	Sheffield W	28	0	60	1

CLARKE, Leon (F)   188   42
H: 6 2   W: 14 02   b.Birmingham 10-2-85
Source: Scholar.

2003–04	Wolverhampton W	0	0		
2003–04	*Kidderminster H*	4	0	4	0
2004–05	Wolverhampton W	28	7		
2005–06	Wolverhampton W	24	1		
2005–06	*QPR*	1	0	1	0
2005–06	*Plymouth Arg*	5	0	5	0
2006–07	Wolverhampton W	22	5	74	13
2006–07	Sheffield W	10	1		
2006–07	*Oldham Ath*	5	3	5	3
2007–08	Sheffield W	8	3		
2007–08	*Southend U*	16	8	16	8
2008–09	Sheffield W	29	8		
2009–10	Sheffield W	36	6	83	18

ESAJAS, Etienne (F)   92   8
H: 5 7   W: 10 03   b.Amsterdam 4-11-84
Source: Ajax.

2005–06	Vitesse	11	1		
2006–07	Vitesse	21	2	32	3
2007–08	Sheffield W	18	0		
2008–09	Sheffield W	22	3		
2009–10	Sheffield W	20	2	60	5

GRANT, Lee (G)   227   0
H: 6 3   W: 13 01   b.Hemel Hempstead 27-1-83
Source: Scholar. *Honours:* England Youth, Under-21.

2000–01	Derby Co	0	0		
2001–02	Derby Co	0	0		
2002–03	Derby Co	29	0		
2003–04	Derby Co	36	0		
2004–05	Derby Co	2	0		
2005–06	Derby Co	0	0		
2005–06	*Burnley*	1	0	1	0
2005–06	*Oldham Ath*	16	0	16	0
2006–07	Derby Co	7	0	74	0
2007–08	Sheffield W	44	0		
2008–09	Sheffield W	46	0		
2009–10	Sheffield W	46	0	136	0

GRAY, Michael (D)   534   22
H: 5 8   W: 10 07   b.Sunderland 3-8-74
Source: Trainee. *Honours:* England 3 full caps.

1992–93	Sunderland	27	2		
1993–94	Sunderland	22	1		
1994–95	Sunderland	16	0		
1995–96	Sunderland	46	4		
1996–97	Sunderland	34	3		
1997–98	Sunderland	44	2		
1998–99	Sunderland	37	2		
1999–2000	Sunderland	33	0		
2000–01	Sunderland	36	1		
2001–02	Sunderland	35	0		
2002–03	Sunderland	32	1		
2003–04	Sunderland	1	0	363	16
2003–04	*Celtic*	7	0	7	0
2003–04	Blackburn R	14	0		
2004–05	Blackburn R	9	0		
2004–05	*Leeds U*	10	0		
2005–06	Blackburn R	30	0		
2006–07	Blackburn R	11	0	64	0
2006–07	*Leeds U*	6	0	16	0
2007–08	Wolverhampton W	33	3		
2008–09	Wolverhampton W	8	1	41	4
2008–09	Sheffield W	13	0		
2009–10	Sheffield W	30	2	43	2

HINDS, Richard (D)   256   11
H: 6 2   W: 12 02   b.Sheffield 22-8-80
Source: Schoolboy.

1998–99	Tranmere R	2	0		
1999–2000	Tranmere R	6	0		
2000–01	Tranmere R	29	0		
2001–02	Tranmere R	10	0		
2002–03	Tranmere R	8	0	55	0
2003–04	Hull C	39	1		
2004–05	Hull C	6	0	45	1
2004–05	Scunthorpe U	7	0		
2005–06	Scunthorpe U	42	6		
2006–07	Scunthorpe U	42	4	93	8
2007–08	Sheffield W	38	2		
2008–09	Sheffield W	14	0		
2009–10	Sheffield W	11	0	63	2

JAMESON, Arron (G)   0   0
H: 6 3   W: 13 01   b. 7-11-89
Source: Scholar.

2008–09	Sheffield W	0	0		
2009–10	Sheffield W	0	0		

JEFFERS, Francis (F)   190   34
H: 5 10   W: 11 02   b.Liverpool 25-1-81
Source: Trainee. *Honours:* England Schools, Youth, Under-21, 1 full cap, 1 goal.

1997–98	Everton	1	0		
1998–99	Everton	15	6		
1999–2000	Everton	21	6		
2000–01	Everton	12	6		
2001–02	Arsenal	16	2		
2002–03	Arsenal	6	2		
2003–04	Arsenal	18	0	22	4
2003–04	*Everton*	18	0	67	18
2004–05	Charlton Ath	20	3		
2005–06	Charlton Ath	0	0	20	3
2005–06	*Rangers*	8	0	8	0
2006–07	Blackburn R	10	0	10	0
2006–07	*Ipswich T*	9	4	9	4
2007–08	Sheffield W	10	2		
2008–09	Sheffield W	31	3		
2009–10	Sheffield W	13	0	54	5

JOHNSON, Jermaine (M)   191 24
H: 5 11   W: 11 05   b.Kingston, Jamaica 25-6-80
Source: Tivoli Gardens. *Honours:* Jamaica 58 full caps, 9 goals.

2001–02	Bolton W	10	0		
2002–03	Bolton W	2	0		
2003–04	Bolton W	0	0	12	0
2003–04	Oldham Ath	20	5		
2004–05	Oldham Ath	19	4		
2005–06	Oldham Ath	0	0	39	9
2006–07	Bradford C	27	4	27	4
2006–07	Sheffield W	7	2		
2007–08	Sheffield W	35	1		
2008–09	Sheffield W	37	3		
2009–10	Sheffield W	34	5	113	11

LEKAJ, Rocky (M)   4 0
H: 5 10   W: 10 05   b.Kosovo 12-10-89
Source: Scholar. *Honours:* Norway Youth.

2006–07	Sheffield W	2	0
2007–08	Sheffield W	0	0
2008–09	Sheffield W	2	0
2009–10	Sheffield W	0	0	4 0

McALLISTER, Sean (M)   75 4
H: 5 8   W: 10 07   b.Bolton 15-8-87
Source: Scholar.

2005–06	Sheffield W	2	0		
2006–07	Sheffield W	6	1		
2007–08	Sheffield W	8	0		
2007–08	*Mansfield T*	7	0	7	0
2007–08	*Bury*	0	0		
2008–09	Sheffield W	40	3		
2009–10	Sheffield W	12	0	68	4

MILLER, Tommy (M)   383 79
H: 6 0   W: 11 07   b.Easington 8-1-79
Source: Trainee.

1997–98	Hartlepool U	13	1		
1998–99	Hartlepool U	34	4		
1999–2000	Hartlepool U	44	14		
2000–01	Hartlepool U	46	16		
2001–02	Hartlepool U	0	0	137	35
2001–02	Ipswich T	8	0		
2002–03	Ipswich T	30	6		
2003–04	Ipswich T	34	11		
2004–05	Ipswich T	45	13		
2005–06	Sunderland	29	3		
2006–07	Sunderland	4	0	33	3
2006–07	*Preston NE*	7	0	7	0
2007–08	Ipswich T	37	5		
2008–09	Ipswich T	32	5	186	40
2009–10	Sheffield W	20	1	20	1

MODEST, Nathan (F)   4 0
H: 5 9   W: 12 02   b. 29-9-91
Source: Scholar.

2008–09	Sheffield W	4	0
2009–10	Sheffield W	0	0	4 0

O'CONNOR, James (M)   430 30
H: 5 8   W: 11 00   b.Dublin 1-9-79
Source: Trainee. *Honours:* Eire Youth, Under-21.

1996–97	Stoke C	0	0		
1997–98	Stoke C	0	0		
1998–99	Stoke C	4	0		
1999–2000	Stoke C	42	6		
2000–01	Stoke C	44	8		
2001–02	Stoke C	43	2		
2002–03	Stoke C	43	0	176	16
2003–04	WBA	30	0		
2004–05	WBA	0	0	30	0
2004–05	Burnley	21	2		
2005–06	Burnley	46	3		
2006–07	Burnley	43	3		
2007–08	Burnley	29	3	139	11
2008–09	Sheffield W	41	0		
2009–10	Sheffield W	44	3	85	3

O'DONNELL, Richard (G)   4 0
H: 6 2   W: 13 05   b.Sheffield 12-9-88
Source: Scholar.

2007–08	Sheffield W	0	0		
2007–08	*Rotherham U*	0	0		
2008–09	*Oldham Ath*	4	0	4	0
2008–09	Sheffield W	0	0		
2009–10	Sheffield W	0	0		

POTTER, Darren (M)   131 5
H: 6 0   W: 10 08   b.Liverpool 21-12-84
Source: Scholar. *Honours:* Eire Youth, B, Under-21, 5 full caps.

2001–02	Liverpool	0	0		
2002–03	Liverpool	0	0		
2003–04	Liverpool	0	0		
2004–05	Liverpool	2	0		
2005–06	Liverpool	0	0		
2005–06	*Southampton*	10	0	10	0
2006–07	Liverpool	0	0	2	0
2006–07	Wolverhampton W	38	0		
2007–08	Wolverhampton W	18	0		
2008–09	Wolverhampton W	0	0	56	0
2008–09	Sheffield W	17	2		
2009–10	Sheffield W	46	3	63	5

PURSE, Darren (D)   454 29
H: 6 2   W: 12 08   b.Stepney 14-2-77
Source: Trainee. *Honours:* England Under-21.

1993–94	Leyton Orient	5	0		
1994–95	Leyton Orient	38	3		
1995–96	Leyton Orient	12	0	55	3
1996–97	Oxford U	31	1		
1997–98	Oxford U	28	4	59	5
1997–98	Birmingham C	8	0		
1998–99	Birmingham C	20	0		
1999–2000	Birmingham C	38	2		
2000–01	Birmingham C	37	3		
2001–02	Birmingham C	36	3		
2002–03	Birmingham C	20	1		
2003–04	Birmingham C	9	0	168	9
2004–05	WBA	22	0	22	0
2005–06	Cardiff C	39	5		
2006–07	Cardiff C	31	4		
2007–08	Cardiff C	18	1		
2008–09	Cardiff C	23	0	111	10
2009–10	Sheffield W	39	2	39	2

SIMEK, Frankie (D)   132 2
H: 6 0   W: 11 05   b.St Louis 13-10-84
Source: Trainee. *Honours:* USA 5 full caps.

2002–03	Arsenal	0	0		
2003–04	Arsenal	0	0		
2004–05	Arsenal	0	0		
2004–05	*QPR*	5	0	5	0
2004–05	*Bournemouth*	8	0	8	0
2005–06	Sheffield W	43	1		
2006–07	Sheffield W	41	1		
2007–08	Sheffield W	17	0		
2008–09	Sheffield W	6	0		
2009–10	Sheffield W	12	0	119	2

SPURR, Tommy (D)   166 5
H: 6 1   W: 11 05   b.Leeds 13-9-87
Source: Scholar.

2005–06	Sheffield W	2	0		
2006–07	Sheffield W	36	0		
2007–08	Sheffield W	41	2		
2008–09	Sheffield W	41	2		
2009–10	Sheffield W	46	1	166	5

TUDGAY, Marcus (F)   270 64
H: 5 10   W: 12 04   b.Worthing 3-2-83
Source: Trainee.

2002–03	Derby Co	8	0		
2003–04	Derby Co	29	6		
2004–05	Derby Co	34	9		
2005–06	Derby Co	21	2	92	17
2005–06	Sheffield W	18	5		
2006–07	Sheffield W	40	11		
2007–08	Sheffield W	35	7		
2008–09	Sheffield W	42	14		
2009–10	Sheffield W	43	10	178	47

SHREWSBURY T (74)

ARESTIDOU, Andreas (G)   2 0
H: 6 2   W: 13 00   b.London 6-12-89
Source: Scholar.

2007–08	Blackburn R	0	0
2008–09	Blackburn R	0	0
2009–10	Shrewsbury T	2	0	2 0

BRADSHAW, Tom (F)   6 3
H: 5 5   W: 11 02   b.Tywyn 27-7-92
Source: Aberystwyth T.

2009–10	Shrewsbury T	6	3	6 3

BRIGHT, Kris (F)   95 53
H: 6 2   W: 12 10   b.Manukau 5-9-86
Honours: New Zealand 4 full caps, 1 goal.

2005	Waitakere C	21	29	21	29
2005–06	New Zealand K	12	0	12	0
2006–07	Fortuna Sittard	11	1	11	1
2007	Kristiansund	7	11		
2008	Kristiansund	12	10	19	21
2008–09	Panserraikos	6	0	6	0
2009–10	Shrewsbury T	26	2	26	2

CANSDELL-SHERRIFF, Shane (D)   244 16
H: 5 11   W: 11 08   b.Sydney 10-11-82
Source: NSW Academy. *Honours:* Australia Youth, Under-23

1999–2000	Leeds U	0	0		
2000–01	Leeds U	0	0		
2001–02	Leeds U	0	0		
2002–03	*Rochdale*	3	0	3	0
2003–04	Aarhus	29	4		
2004–05	Aarhus	26	2		
2005–06	Aarhus	27	1	82	7
2006–07	Tranmere R	43	3		
2007–08	Tranmere R	44	3	87	6
2008–09	Shrewsbury T	31	2		
2009–10	Shrewsbury T	41	1	72	3

COUGHLAN, Graham (D)   412 39
H: 6 2   W: 13 07   b.Dublin 18-11-74
Source: Bray Wanderers.

1995–96	Blackburn R	0	0		
1996–97	Blackburn R	0	0		
1996–97	Swindon T	3	0	3	0
1997–98	Blackburn R	0	0		
1998–99	Livingston	6	0		
1999–2000	Livingston	29	0		
2000–01	Livingston	21	2	56	2
2001–02	Plymouth Arg	46	11		
2002–03	Plymouth Arg	45	5		
2003–04	Plymouth Arg	46	7		
2004–05	Plymouth Arg	43	2	177	25
2005–06	Sheffield W	33	4		
2006–07	Sheffield W	18	1	51	5
2006–07	Burnley	2	0	2	0
2007–08	Rotherham U	45	1	45	1
2008–09	Shrewsbury T	42	4		
2009–10	Shrewsbury T	36	2	78	6

DISLEY, Craig (M)   362 42
H: 5 10   W: 10 13   b.Worksop 24-8-81
Source: Trainee.

1999–2000	Mansfield T	5	0		
2000–01	Mansfield T	24	0		
2001–02	Mansfield T	36	7		
2002–03	Mansfield T	42	4		
2003–04	Mansfield T	34	5	141	16
2004–05	Bristol R	28	4		
2005–06	Bristol R	42	8		
2006–07	Bristol R	45	4		
2007–08	Bristol R	44	6		
2008–09	Bristol R	44	3	203	25
2009–10	Shrewsbury T	18	1	18	1

DUNFIELD, Terry (M)   183 9
H: 5 11   W: 12 04   b.Vancouver 20-2-82
Source: Trainee. *Honours:* Canada Under-23, England Youth. Canada 1 full cap.

1998–99	Manchester C	0	0		
1999–2000	Manchester C	0	0		
2000–01	Manchester C	1	0		
2001–02	Manchester C	0	0		
2002–03	Manchester C	0	0	1	0
2002–03	Bury	29	2		
2003–04	Bury	30	2		
2004–05	Bury	15	1		
2005–06	Bury	0	0		
2006–07	Bury	0	0	74	5
2007–08	Macclesfield T	41	1		
2008–09	Macclesfield T	20	1	61	2
2008–09	Shrewsbury T	17	0		
2009–10	Shrewsbury T	30	2	47	2

ELDER, Nathan (F)   85 14
H: 6 1   W: 13 12   b.Hornchurch 5-4-85
Source: Billericay T.

2006–07	Brighton & HA	13	1		
2007–08	Brighton & HA	9	1	22	2
2007–08	Brentford	17	4		
2008–09	Brentford	27	6	44	10
2009–10	Shrewsbury T	19	2	19	2

GRAY, Andre (F) 4　0
H: 5 10　W: 12 06　b.Shrewsbury 26-6-91
Source: Scholar.

2009–10	Shrewsbury T	4　0	4　0

HIBBERT, Dave (F) 153　33
H: 6 2　W: 12 00　b.Eccleshall 28-1-86
Source: Scholar.

2004–05	Port Vale	9　2	9　2
2005–06	Preston NE	10　0	
2006–07	Preston NE	0　0	10　0
2006–07	*Rotherham U*	21　2	21　2
2006–07	*Bradford C*	8　0	8　0
2007–08	Shrewsbury T	44　12	
2008–09	Shrewsbury T	23　3	
2009–10	Shrewsbury T	38　14	105　29

HOLDEN, Dean (D) 269　17
H: 6 1　W: 12 04　b.Salford 15-9-79
Source: Trainee. *Honours:* England Youth.

1997–98	Bolton W	0　0	
1998–99	Bolton W	0　0	
1999–2000	Bolton W	12　0	
2000–01	Bolton W	1　1	13　1
2001	*Valur*	7　0	7　0
2001–02	*Oldham Ath*	23　2	
2002–03	Oldham Ath	6　2	
2003–04	Oldham Ath	39　4	
2004–05	Oldham Ath	40　2	108　10
2005–06	Peterborough U	35　3	
2006–07	Peterborough U	21　1	56　4
2006–07	Falkirk	9　1	
2007–08	Falkirk	20　0	
2008–09	Falkirk	19　1	48　2
2009–10	Shrewsbury T	37　0	37　0

HOOMAN, Harry (D) 2　0
H: 5 11　W: 12 06　b.Worcester 27-4-91
Source: Scholar.

2009–10	Shrewsbury T	2　0	2　0

JACKSON, Mike (D) 554　37
H: 6 0　W: 13 08　b.Runcorn 4-12-73
Source: Trainee.

1991–92	Crewe Alex	1　0	
1992–93	Crewe Alex	4　0	5　0
1993–94	Bury	39　0	
1994–95	Bury	24　2	
1995–96	Bury	31　4	
1996–97	Bury	31　3	125　9
1996–97	Preston NE	7　0	
1997–98	Preston NE	40　2	
1998–99	Preston NE	44　8	
1999–2000	Preston NE	46　5	
2000–01	Preston NE	30　1	
2001–02	Preston NE	13　0	
2002–03	Preston NE	22　1	
2002–03	*Tranmere R*	6　0	
2003–04	Preston NE	43　0	245　17
2004–05	Tranmere R	43　5	
2005–06	Tranmere R	41　3	90　8
2006–07	Blackpool	43　1	
2007–08	Blackpool	25　0	68　1
2008–09	Shrewsbury T	21　2	
2009–10	Shrewsbury T	0　0	21　2

LANGMEAD, Kelvin (F) 253　21
H: 6 1　W: 12 00　b.Coventry 23-3-85
Source: Scholar.

2003–04	Preston NE	0　0	
2003–04	*Carlisle U*	11　1	11　1
2004–05	Preston NE	1　0	1　0
2004–05	*Kidderminster H*	10　1	10　1
2004–05	Shrewsbury T	28　3	
2005–06	Shrewsbury T	42　9	
2006–07	Shrewsbury T	45　3	
2007–08	Shrewsbury T	39　1	
2008–09	Shrewsbury T	33　0	
2009–10	Shrewsbury T	44　3	231　19

LESLIE, Steven (M) 84　7
H: 5 10　W: 11 02　b.Shrewsbury 5-11-87
Source: Scholar.

2005–06	Shrewsbury T	1　0	
2006–07	Shrewsbury T	5　0	
2007–08	Shrewsbury T	17　1	
2008–09	Shrewsbury T	27　0	
2009–10	Shrewsbury T	34　6	84　7

McINTYRE, Kevin (M) 239　19
H: 6 0　W: 11 10　b.Liverpool 23-12-77
Source: Trainee.

1996–97	Tranmere R	0　0	

1997–98	Tranmere R	2　0	
1998–99	Tranmere R	0　0	
1999–2000	Tranmere R	0　0	
2000–01	Tranmere R	0　0	
2001–02	Tranmere R	0　0	2　0
2004–05	Chester C	10　0	10　0
2004–05	Macclesfield T	23　0	
2005–06	Macclesfield T	44　5	
2006–07	Macclesfield T	44　9	
2007–08	Macclesfield T	23　2	134　16
2007–08	Shrewsbury T	22　2	
2008–09	Shrewsbury T	26　0	
2009–10	Shrewsbury T	45　1	93　3

MURRAY, Paul (M) 399　29
H: 5 9　W: 10 08　b.Carlisle 31-8-76
Source: Trainee. *Honours:* England Youth,
Under-21, B.

1993–94	Carlisle U	8　0	
1994–95	Carlisle U	5　0	
1995–96	Carlisle U	28　1	
1995–96	QPR	1　0	
1996–97	QPR	32　5	
1997–98	QPR	32　1	
1997–98	QPR	0　0	
1998–99	QPR	39　1	
1999–2000	QPR	30　0	
2000–01	QPR	6　0	140　7
2001–02	Southampton	0　1	0　1
2001–02	Oldham Ath	24　5	
2002–03	Oldham Ath	30　1	
2003–04	Oldham Ath	41　9	95　15
2004–05	Beira Mar	17　2	17　2
2005–06	Carlisle U	0　0	
2006–07	Carlisle U	14　1	55　2
2007–08	Gretna	32　1	32　1
2008–09	Shrewsbury T	32　2	
2009–10	Shrewsbury T	27　0	59　2

NEAL, Chris (G) 8　0
H: 6 2　W: 12 04　b.St Albans 23-10-85
Source: Scholar.

2004–05	Preston NE	1　0	
2005–06	Preston NE	0　0	
2006–07	Preston NE	0　0	
2007–08	*Morecambe*	0　0	
2007–08	Preston NE	0　0	
2008–09	Preston NE	0　0	1　0
2009–10	Shrewsbury T	7　0	7　0

NEAL, Lewis (M) 184　11
H: 5 10　W: 11 02　b.Leicester 14-7-81
Source: Juniors.

1998–99	Stoke C	0　0	
1999–2000	Stoke C	0　0	
2000–01	Stoke C	1　0	
2001–02	Stoke C	11　0	
2002–03	Stoke C	16　0	
2003–04	Stoke C	19　1	
2004–05	Stoke C	23　1	70　2
2005–06	Preston NE	24　2	
2006–07	Preston NE	24　1	
2007–08	Preston NE	17　2	
2008–09	Preston NE	0　0	65　5
2008–09	*Notts Co*	4　0	4　0
2008–09	Carlisle U	16　2	16　2
2009–10	Shrewsbury T	29　2	29　2

RICHARDS, Will (M) 0　0
H: 6 2　W: 12 04　b.Knighton 18-12-91
Source: Scholar.

2009–10	Shrewsbury T	0　0	

ROBINSON, Jake (F) 176　20
H: 5 7　W: 10 10　b.Brighton 23-10-86
Source: Scholar.

2003–04	Brighton & HA	9　0	
2004–05	Brighton & HA	10　1	
2005–06	Brighton & HA	27　1	
2006–07	Brighton & HA	38　6	
2007–08	Brighton & HA	34　4	
2008–09	Brighton & HA	5　1	123　13
2008–09	*Aldershot T*	19　4	19　4
2009–10	Shrewsbury T	34　3	34　3

SIMPSON, Jake (M) 18　0
H: 5 11　W: 12 03　b.Shrewsbury 27-10-90
Source: Blackburn R Academy.

2009–10	Shrewsbury T	18　0	18　0

TAYLOR, Danny (D) 3　0
H: 5 10　W: 9 06　b.Chester 1-9-91

2009–10	Shrewsbury T	3　0	3　0

TAYLOR, Jon (M) 2　0
H: 5 11　W: 12 04　b.Liverpool 23-12-89

2009–10	Shrewsbury T	2　0	2　0

VAN DEN BROEK, Benjamin (M) 68　11
H: 6 0　W: 13 03　b.Geleen 21-9-87

2008–09	Haarlem	35　9	
2009–10	Haarlem	22　1	57　10
2009–10	Shrewsbury T	11　1	11　1

SOUTHAMPTON (75)

ARGENT, Sam (M) 0　0
Source: Scholar.

2008–09	Southampton	0　0	
2009–10	Southampton	0　0	

BARNARD, Lee (F) 124　47
H: 5 10　W: 10 10　b.Romford 18-7-84
Source: Trainee.

2002–03	Tottenham H	0　0	
2002–03	*Exeter C*	3　0	3　0
2003–04	Tottenham H	0　0	
2004–05	Tottenham H	0　0	
2004–05	*Leyton Orient*	8　0	8　0
2004–05	*Northampton T*	5　0	5　0
2005–06	Tottenham H	3　0	
2006–07	Tottenham H	0　0	
2007–08	Tottenham H	0　0	3　0
2007–08	*Crewe Alex*	10　3	10　3
2007–08	Southend U	15　9	
2008–09	Southend U	35　11	
2009–10	Southend U	25　15	75　35
2009–10	Southampton	20　9	20　9

BIALKOWSKI, Bartosz (G) 30　0
H: 6 3　W: 12 10　b.Braniewo 6-7-87
Honours: Poland Under-20, Under-21.

2004–05	Gornik Zabrze	7　0	7　0
2005–06	Southampton	5　0	
2006–07	Southampton	8　0	
2007–08	Southampton	1　0	
2008–09	Southampton	0　0	
2009–10	Southampton	7　0	21　0
2009–10	*Barnsley*	2　0	2　0

CONNOLLY, David (F) 344　140
H: 5 9　W: 11 00　b.Willesden 6-6-77
Source: Trainee. *Honours:* Eire Under-21, 41
full caps, 9 goals.

1994–95	Watford	2　0	
1995–96	Watford	11　8	
1996–97	Watford	13　2	26　10
1997–98	Feyenoord	10　2	
1998–99	Wolverhampton W	32　6	32　6
1999–2000	Excelsior	32　29	32　29
2000–01	Feyenoord	15　5	25　7
2001–02	Wimbledon	35　18	
2002–03	Wimbledon	28　24	63　42
2003–04	West Ham U	39　10	39　10
2004–05	Leicester C	44　13	
2005–06	Leicester C	5　4	49　17
2005–06	Wigan Ath	17　1	
2006–07	Wigan Ath	2　0	19　1
2006–07	Sunderland	36　13	
2007–08	Sunderland	3　0	
2008–09	Sunderland	0　0	
2009–10	Sunderland	0　0	39　13
2009–10	Southampton	20　5	20　5

DAVIS, Kelvin (G) 503　0
H: 6 1　W: 11 05　b.Bedford 29-9-76
Source: Trainee. *Honours:* England Youth,
Under-21.

1993–94	Luton T	1　0	
1994–95	Luton T	9　0	
1994–95	*Torquay U*	2　0	2　0
1995–96	Luton T	6　0	
1996–97	Luton T	0　0	
1997–98	Luton T	32　0	
1997–98	*Hartlepool U*	2　0	2　0
1998–99	Luton T	44　0	92　0
1999–2000	Wimbledon	0　0	
2000–01	Wimbledon	45　0	
2001–02	Wimbledon	40　0	
2002–03	Wimbledon	46　0	131　0

Season	Club				
2003–04	Ipswich T	45	0		
2004–05	Ipswich T	39	0	84	0
2005–06	Sunderland	33	0	33	0
2006–07	Southampton	38	0		
2007–08	Southampton	35	0		
2008–09	Southampton	46	0		
2009–10	Southampton	40	0	159	0

DOBLE, Ryan (M)   0   0
b.Wales 1-2-91
Source: Scholar. Honours: Wales Under-21.

Season	Club				
2008–09	Southampton	0	0		
2009–10	Southampton	0	0		

FONTE, Jose (D)   183   9
H: 6 2 W: 12 08 b.Penafiel 22-12-83
Source: Sporting Lisbon, Salgueiros.
Honours: Portugal Under-21.

Season	Club				
2004–05	Felgueiros	28	1	28	1
2005–06	Setubal	15	0	15	0
2005–06	Benfica	1	0	1	0
2005–06	Pacos	11	1	11	1
2006–07	Amadora	25	1	25	1
2007–08	Crystal Palace	22	1		
2008–09	Crystal Palace	38	4		
2009–10	Crystal Palace	22	1	82	6
2009–10	Southampton	21	0	21	0

FORECAST, Tommy (G)   4   0
H: 6 2 W: 11 10 b.Newham 15-10-86
Source: Scholar.

Season	Club				
2005–06	Tottenham H	0	0		
2006–07	Tottenham H	0	0		
2007–08	Tottenham H	0	0		
2008–09	Southampton	0	0		
2009–10	Southampton	0	0		
2009–10	Grimsby T	4	0	4	0

GILLETT, Simon (M)   86   2
H: 5 6 W: 11 07 b.Oxford 6-11-85
Source: Trainee. Honours: Luxembourg full caps.

Season	Club				
2003–04	Southampton	0	0		
2004–05	Southampton	0	0		
2005–06	Southampton	0	0		
2005–06	Walsall	0	0	2	0
2006–07	Southampton	0	0		
2006–07	Blackpool	31	1	31	1
2006–07	Bournemouth	7	1	7	1
2007–08	Southampton	2	0		
2007–08	Yeovil T	4	0	4	0
2008–09	Southampton	27	0		
2009–10	Southampton	0	0	31	0
2009–10	Doncaster R	11	0	11	0

GOBERN, Oscar (M)   11   0
H: 5 11 W: 10 10 b.Birmingham 26-1-91
Source: Scholar. Honours: England Youth.

Season	Club				
2008–09	Southampton	6	0		
2009–10	Southampton	4	0	10	0
2009–10	Milton Keynes D	1	0	1	0

HAMMOND, Dean (M)   240   31
H: 6 0 W: 11 09 b.Hastings 7-3-83
Source: Scholar.

Season	Club				
2002–03	Brighton & HA	4	0		
2003–04	Brighton & HA	0	0		
2003–04	Leyton Orient	8	0	8	0
2004–05	Brighton & HA	30	4		
2005–06	Brighton & HA	41	4		
2006–07	Brighton & HA	37	8		
2007–08	Brighton & HA	24	5	136	21
2007–08	Colchester U	13	0		
2008–09	Colchester U	41	5		
2009–10	Colchester U	2	0	56	5
2009–10	Southampton	40	5	40	5

HARDING, Dan (D)   224   6
H: 6 0 W: 11 11 b.Gloucester 23-12-83
Source: Scholar. Honours: England Under-21.

Season	Club				
2002–03	Brighton & HA	1	0		
2003–04	Brighton & HA	23	0		
2004–05	Brighton & HA	43	1	67	1
2005–06	Leeds U	20	0	20	0
2006–07	Ipswich T	42	0		
2007–08	Ipswich T	30	1		
2008–09	Ipswich T	1	0	73	1
2008–09	Southend U	19	1	19	1
2008–09	Reading	3	0	3	0
2009–10	Southampton	42	3	42	3

HOLMES, Lee (M)   112   7
H: 5 8 W: 10 06 b.Mansfield 2-4-87
Source: Scholar. Honours: FA Schools, England Youth.

Season	Club				
2002–03	Derby Co	2	0		
2003–04	Derby Co	23	2		
2004–05	Derby Co	3	0		
2004–05	Swindon T	15	1	15	1
2005–06	Derby Co	18	0		
2006–07	Derby Co	0	0		
2006–07	Bradford C	16	0	16	0
2007–08	Derby Co	0	0	46	2
2007–08	Walsall	19	4	19	4
2008–09	Southampton	11	0		
2009–10	Southampton	5	0	16	0

JAIDI, Radh (D)   156   15
H: 6 2 W: 14 00 b.Tunis 30-8-75
Source: Esperance. Honours: Tunisia 101 full caps, 7 goals.

Season	Club				
2004–05	Bolton W	27	5		
2005–06	Bolton W	16	3	43	8
2006–07	Birmingham C	38	6		
2007–08	Birmingham C	18	0		
2008–09	Birmingham C	30	0		
2009–10	Birmingham C	0	0	86	6
2009–10	Southampton	27	1	27	1

JAMES, Lloyd (M)   71   2
H: 5 11 W: 11 01 b.Bristol 16-2-88
Source: Scholar. Honours: Wales Youth, Under-21.

Season	Club				
2005–06	Southampton	0	0		
2006–07	Southampton	0	0		
2007–08	Southampton	0	0		
2008–09	Southampton	41	0		
2009–10	Southampton	30	2	71	2

LALLANA, Adam (M)   93   17
H: 5 8 W: 11 05 b.St Albans 10-5-88
Source: Scholar Honours: England Youth, Under-21.

Season	Club				
2005–06	Southampton	0	0		
2006–07	Southampton	1	0		
2007–08	Southampton	5	1		
2007–08	Bournemouth	3	0	3	0
2008–09	Southampton	40	1		
2009–10	Southampton	44	15	90	17

LAMBERT, Ricky (F)   382   136
H: 6 2 W: 14 08 b.Liverpool 16-2-82
Source: Trainee.

Season	Club				
1999–2000	Blackpool	3	0		
2000–01	Blackpool	0	0	3	0
2000–01	Macclesfield T	9	0		
2001–02	Macclesfield T	35	8	44	8
2001–02	Stockport Co	0	0		
2002–03	Stockport Co	29	2		
2003–04	Stockport Co	40	12		
2004–05	Stockport Co	29	4	98	18
2004–05	Rochdale	15	6		
2005–06	Rochdale	46	22		
2006–07	Rochdale	3	0	64	28
2006–07	Bristol R	36	8		
2007–08	Bristol R	46	14		
2008–09	Bristol R	45	29		
2009–10	Bristol R	1	1	128	52
2009–10	Southampton	45	30	45	30

LANCASHIRE, Oliver (D)   38   1
H: 6 1 W: 11 10 b.Basingstoke 13-12-88
Source: Scholar.

Season	Club				
2006–07	Southampton	0	0		
2007–08	Southampton	0	0		
2008–09	Southampton	11	0		
2009–10	Southampton	2	0	13	0
2009–10	Grimsby T	25	1	25	1

MARTIN, Aaron (D)   2   0
H: 6 3 W: 11 13 b.Newport (IW) 29-9-89
Source: Eastleigh.

Season	Club				
2009–10	Southampton	2	0	2	0

McNISH, Callum (M)   1   0
H: 6 2 W: 12 06 b.Oxford 25-5-92
Source: Scholar.

Season	Club				
2008–09	Southampton	0	0		
2009–10	Southampton	1	0	1	0

MILLS, Joseph (F)   38   0
H: 5 9 W: 11 00 b.Swindon 30-10-89
Source: Scholar.

Season	Club				
2006–07	Southampton	0	0		
2007–08	Southampton	0	0		
2008–09	Southampton	8	0		
2008–09	Scunthorpe U	14	0	14	0
2009–10	Southampton	16	0	24	0

MOLYNEUX, Lee (D)   4   0
H: 5 10 W: 11 07 b.Liverpool 24-2-89
Source: Scholar. Honours: England Schools, Youth.

Season	Club				
2005–06	Everton	0	0		
2006–07	Everton	0	0		
2007–08	Everton	0	0		
2008–09	Everton	0	0		
2008–09	Southampton	4	0		
2009–10	Southampton	0	0	4	0

MURTY, Graeme (D)   437   9
H: 5 10 W: 11 10 b.Saltburn 13-11-74
Source: Trainee. Honours: Scotland B, 4 full caps.

Season	Club				
1992–93	York C	0	0		
1993–94	York C	1	0		
1994–95	York C	20	2		
1995–96	York C	35	2		
1996–97	York C	27	2		
1997–98	York C	34	1	117	7
1998–99	Reading	9	0		
1999–2000	Reading	17	0		
2000–01	Reading	23	1		
2001–02	Reading	43	0		
2002–03	Reading	44	0		
2003–04	Reading	38	0		
2004–05	Reading	41	0		
2005–06	Reading	40	1		
2006–07	Reading	23	0		
2007–08	Reading	28	0		
2008–09	Reading	0	0	306	2
2008–09	Charlton Ath	8	0	8	0
2009–10	Southampton	6	0	6	0

OTSEMOBOR, John (D)   193   6
H: 5 10 W: 12 07 b.Liverpool 23-3-83
Source: Trainee. Honours: England Youth, Under-20.

Season	Club				
1999–2000	Liverpool	0	0		
2000–01	Liverpool	0	0		
2001–02	Liverpool	0	0		
2002–03	Liverpool	0	0		
2002–03	Hull C	9	3	9	3
2003–04	Liverpool	4	0		
2003–04	Bolton W	1	0	1	0
2004–05	Liverpool	0	0	4	0
2004–05	Crewe Alex	14	1		
2005–06	Rotherham U	10	0	10	0
2005–06	Crewe Alex	16	0		
2006–07	Crewe Alex	27	0	57	1
2007–08	Norwich C	43	1		
2008–09	Norwich C	37	0		
2009–10	Norwich C	13	1	93	2
2009–10	Southampton	19	0	19	0

OXLADE-CHAMBERLAIN, Alex (M) 2   0
H: 5 11 W: 11 00 b.Portsmouth 15-8-93
Source: Scholar.

Season	Club				
2009–10	Southampton	2	0	2	0

PAPA WAIGO, N'Diaye (F)   193   38
H: 6 1 W: 11 09 b.St Louis 20-1-84
Honours: Senegal 15 full caps, 1 goal.

Season	Club				
2002–03	Verona	2	0		
2003–04	Verona	33	7		
2004–05	Verona	30	4	65	11
2005–06	Cesena	36	5		
2006–07	Cesena	35	15	71	20
2007–08	Genoa	9	0	9	0
2007–08	Fiorentina	7	2		
2008–09	Fiorentina	0	0	7	2
2008–09	Lecce	6	0	6	0
2009–10	Southampton	35	5	35	5

PERRY, Chris (D)   479   11
H: 5 8 W: 11 03 b.Carshalton 26-4-73
Source: Trainee.

Season	Club				
1991–92	Wimbledon	0	0		
1992–93	Wimbledon	0	0		
1993–94	Wimbledon	2	0		
1994–95	Wimbledon	22	0		

1995–96	Wimbledon	37	0	
1996–97	Wimbledon	37	1	
1997–98	Wimbledon	35	1	
1998–99	Wimbledon	34	0	167 2
1999–2000	Tottenham H	37	1	
2000–01	Tottenham H	32	1	
2001–02	Tottenham H	33	0	
2002–03	Tottenham H	18	1	
2003–04	Tottenham H	0	0	120 3
2003–04	Charlton Ath	29	1	
2004–05	Charlton Ath	19	1	
2005–06	Charlton Ath	28	1	76 3
2006–07	WBA	23	0	23 0
2007–08	Luton T	35	1	35 1
2007–08	*Southampton*	6	0	
2008–09	Southampton	40	2	
2009–10	Southampton	12	0	58 2

POKE, Michael (G) 33 0
H: 6 1 W: 13 12 b.Spelthorne 21-11-85
Source: Trainee.

2003–04	Southampton	0	0
2004–05	Southampton	0	0
2005–06	Southampton	0	0
2005–06	*Oldham Ath*	0	0
2005–06	*Northampton T*	0	0
2006–07	Southampton	0	0
2007–08	Southampton	4	0
2008–09	Southampton	0	0
2009–10	Southampton	0 0	4 0
2009–10	*Torquay U*	29 0	29 0

PULIS, Anthony (M) 27 0
H: 5 10 W: 10 10 b.Bristol 21-7-84
Source: Scholar. *Honours:* Wales Under-21.

2002–03	Portsmouth	0	0
2003–04	Portsmouth	0	0
2004–05	Portsmouth	0	0
2004–05	Stoke C	0	0
2004–05	*Torquay U*	3 0	3 0
2005–06	Stoke C	0	0
2005–06	*Plymouth Arg*	5 0	5 0
2006–07	Stoke C	1	0
2006–07	*Grimsby T*	9 0	9 0
2007–08	Stoke C	1	0
2007–08	*Bristol R*	1 0	1 0
2008–09	Stoke C	0 0	2 0
2008–09	Southampton	0	0
2009–10	Southampton	0	0
2009–10	*Lincoln C*	7 0	7 0

PUNCHEON, Jason (M) 188 30
H: 5 9 W: 12 05 b.Croydon 26-6-86
Source: Scholar.

2003–04	Wimbledon	8 0	8 0
2004–05	Milton Keynes D	25	1
2005–06	Milton Keynes D	1	0
2006–07	Barnet	37	5
2007–08	Barnet	41 10	78 15
2008–09	Plymouth Arg	6	0
2008–09	*Milton Keynes D*	27	4
2009–10	Plymouth Arg	0 0	6 0
2009–10	*Milton Keynes D*	24 7	77 12
2009–10	Southampton	19 3	19 3

RACINE, Aaron (D) 0 0
b.Rustington 30-10-91
Source: Scholar.

2008–09	Southampton	0	0
2009–10	Southampton	0	0

REEVES, Ben (D) 0 0
b. 19-11-91
Source: Scholar.

2008–09	Southampton	0	0
2009–10	Southampton	0	0

SAGANOWSKI, Marek (F) 344 111
H: 5 10 W: 12 04 b.Lodz 31-10-78
Honours: Poland 33 full caps, 5 goals.

1994–95	Lodz	3	0
1995–96	Lodz	29	11
1996–97	Lodz	2	1
1996–97	Hamburg	3 0	3 0
1996–97	Feyenoord	7 0	7 0
1997–98	Lodz	22	11
1998–99	Lodz	15	1
1999–2000	Lodz	24 6	95 30
2000–01	Plock	23 4	23 4
2001–02	Odra	27	2
2002–03	Odra	3 0	30 2
2002–03	Legia	17	10
2003–04	Legia	24	17
2004–05	Legia	26 14	67 41
2005–06	Guimaraes	32 12	32 12
2006–07	Troyes	6 0	6 0
2006–07	Southampton	13	10
2007–08	Southampton	30	3
2008	*Aalborg*	13 3	13 3
2008–09	Southampton	19	6
2009–10	Southampton	6 0	68 19

SAVILLE, Jack (D) 0 0
H: 6 3 W: 12 00 b.Frimley 2-4-91
Source: Scholar.

2009–10	Southampton	0	0

SCHNEIDERLIN, Morgan (M) 72 1
H: 5 11 W: 11 11 b.Obernai 8-11-89

2007–08	Strasbourg	5 0	5 0
2008–09	Southampton	30	0
2009–10	Southampton	37 1	67 1

SEABORNE, Danny (D) 68 1
H: 6 0 W: 11 10 b.Barnstaple 5-3-87

2008–09	Exeter C	33	1
2009–10	Exeter C	19 0	52 1
2009–10	Southampton	16 0	16 0

THOMAS, Wayne (D) 407 13
H: 6 2 W: 14 12 b.Gloucester 17-5-79
Source: Trainee.

1995–96	Torquay U	6	0
1996–97	Torquay U	12	0
1997–98	Torquay U	21	1
1998–99	Torquay U	44	1
1999–2000	Torquay U	40 3	123 5
2000–01	Stoke C	34	0
2001–02	Stoke C	40	2
2002–03	Stoke C	41	0
2003–04	Stoke C	39	3
2004–05	Stoke C	35 2	189 7
2005–06	Burnley	16	1
2006–07	Burnley	33	0
2007–08	Burnley	1 0	50 1
2007–08	Southampton	30	0
2008–09	Southampton	0	0
2009–10	Southampton	15 0	45 0

THOMSON, Jake (M) 35 2
H: 5 11 W: 11 05 b.Southsea 12-5-89
Source: Scholar.

2006–07	Southampton	0	0
2007–08	Southampton	0	0
2008–09	Southampton	10	0
2008–09	*Bournemouth*	6 1	6 1
2009–10	Southampton	4 0	14 0
2009–10	*Torquay U*	15 1	15 1

WOTTON, Paul (D) 449 54
H: 5 11 W: 12 00 b.Plymouth 17-8-77
Source: Trainee.

1994–95	Plymouth Arg	7	0
1995–96	Plymouth Arg	1	0
1996–97	Plymouth Arg	9	1
1997–98	Plymouth Arg	34	1
1998–99	Plymouth Arg	36	1
1999–2000	Plymouth Arg	23	0
2000–01	Plymouth Arg	42	4
2001–02	Plymouth Arg	46	5
2002–03	Plymouth Arg	43	8
2003–04	Plymouth Arg	38	9
2004–05	Plymouth Arg	40	12
2005–06	Plymouth Arg	45	8
2006–07	Plymouth Arg	22	4
2007–08	Plymouth Arg	8 1	394 54
2008–09	Southampton	29	0
2009–10	Southampton	26 0	55 0

SOUTHEND U (76)

ASANTE, Kyle (M) 0 0
H: 5 9 W: 10 10 b.Chelmsford 13-11-91
Source: Scholar.

2009–10	Southend U	0	0

BARRETT, Adam (D) 426 36
H: 5 10 W: 12 00 b.Dagenham 29-11-79
Source: Leyton Orient Trainee.

1998–99	Plymouth Arg	1	0
1999–2000	Plymouth Arg	42	3
2000–01	Plymouth Arg	9 0	52 3
2000–01	Mansfield T	8	1
2001–02	Mansfield T	29 0	37 1
2002–03	Bristol R	45	1
2003–04	Bristol R	45 4	90 5
2004–05	Southend U	43	11
2005–06	Southend U	45	3
2006–07	Southend U	28	3
2007–08	Southend U	45	6
2008–09	Southend U	45	2
2009–10	Southend U	41 2	247 27

CHRISTOPHE, Jean-Francois (M) 84 6
H: 6 1 W: 13 01 b.Creil 13-6-82
Source: Lens.

2007–08	Portsmouth	0	0
2007–08	*Bournemouth*	10 1	10 1
2007–08	*Yeovil T*	5 0	5 0
2008–09	Portsmouth	0	0
2008–09	Southend U	33	4
2009–10	Southend U	36 1	69 5

CRAWFORD, Harry (F) 7 1
H: 6 1 W: 12 04 b.Saffron Walden 10-12-91
Source: Scholar.

2009–10	Southend U	7 1	7 1

FRANCIS, Simon (D) 246 6
H: 6 0 W: 12 06 b.Nottingham 16-2-85
Source: Scholar. *Honours:* England Youth, Under-20.

2002–03	Bradford C	25	1
2003–04	Bradford C	30 0	55 1
2003–04	Sheffield U	5	0
2004–05	Sheffield U	6	0
2005–06	Sheffield U	1 0	12 0
2005–06	*Grimsby T*	5 0	5 0
2005–06	*Tranmere R*	17 1	17 1
2006–07	Southend U	40	1
2007–08	Southend U	27	2
2008–09	Southend U	45	0
2009–10	Southend U	45 1	157 4

FREEDMAN, Dougie (F) 520 160
H: 5 9 W: 12 05 b.Glasgow 21-1-74
Source: Trainee. *Honours:* Scotland Schools, Under-21, B, 2 full caps, 1 goal.

1991–92	QPR	0	0
1992–93	QPR	0	0
1993–94	QPR	0	0
1994–95	Barnet	42	24
1995–96	Barnet	5 3	47 27
1995–96	Crystal Palace	39	20
1996–97	Crystal Palace	44	11
1997–98	Crystal Palace	7	0
1997–98	Wolverhampton W	29 10	29 10
1998–99	Nottingham F	31	9
1999–2000	Nottingham F	34	9
2000–01	Nottingham F	5 0	70 18
2000–01	Crystal Palace	26	11
2001–02	Crystal Palace	40	20
2002–03	Crystal Palace	29	9
2003–04	Crystal Palace	35	13
2004–05	Crystal Palace	20	1
2005–06	Crystal Palace	34	5
2006–07	Crystal Palace	34	3
2007–08	Crystal Palace	19	1
2007–08	*Leeds U*	11 5	11 5
2008–09	Crystal Palace	0 0	327 94
2008–09	Southend U	16	5
2009–10	Southend U	20 1	36 6

GRANT, Anthony (M) 130 1
H: 5 10 W: 11 01 b.Lambeth 4-6-87
Source: Scholar. *Honours:* England Youth.

2004–05	Chelsea	1	0
2005–06	Chelsea	0	0
2005–06	*Oldham Ath*	2 0	2 0
2006–07	Chelsea	0	0
2006–07	*Wycombe W*	40 0	40 0
2007–08	Chelsea	0 0	1 0
2007–08	*Luton T*	4 0	4 0
2007–08	*Southend U*	10	0
2008–09	Southend U	35	1
2009–10	Southend U	38 0	83 1

HAZELL, Justin (M) 0 0
H: 5 9 W: 11 06 b.Leigh-on-Sea 12-1-92
Source: Scholar.

2008–09	Southend U	0	0
2009–10	Southend U	0	0

HERD, Johnny (D)   26   0
H: 5 9 W: 12 00 b.Huntingdon 3-10-89
Source: Welling U.

2008–09	Southend U	6	0		
2009–10	Southend U	20	0	26	0

JOYCE, Ian (G)   5   0
H: 6 3 W: 13 07 b.Kinnelon 12-7-85
Source: Watford.

2008–09	Southend U	3	0		
2009–10	Southend U	2	0	5	0

LAURENT, Francis (F)   56   9
H: 6 3 W: 14 00 b.Paris 6-1-86
Source: Mainz.

2008–09	Southend U	21	3		
2009–10	Southend U	35	6	56	9

McCORMACK, Alan (M)   191   20
H: 5 8 W: 11 00 b.Dublin 10-1-84
Source: Stella Maris BC.

2002–03	Preston NE	0	0		
2003–04	Preston NE	5	0		
2003–04	*Leyton Orient*	10	0	10	0
2004–05	Preston NE	3	0		
2004–05	*Southend U*	7	2		
2005–06	Preston NE	0	0		
2005–06	*Motherwell*	24	2	24	2
2006–07	Preston NE	3	0	11	0
2006–07	Southend U	22	3		
2007–08	Southend U	42	8		
2008–09	Southend U	34	2		
2009–10	Southend U	41	3	146	18

MILDENHALL, Steve (G)   314   1
H: 6 4 W: 14 01 b.Swindon 13-5-78
Source: Trainee.

1996–97	Swindon T	1	0		
1997–98	Swindon T	4	0		
1998–99	Swindon T	0	0		
1999–2000	Swindon T	5	0		
2000–01	Swindon T	23	0	33	0
2001–02	Notts Co	26	0		
2002–03	Notts Co	21	0		
2003–04	Notts Co	28	0		
2004–05	Notts Co	1	0	76	0
2004–05	Oldham Ath	6	0	6	0
2005–06	Grimsby T	46	1	46	1
2006–07	Yeovil T	46	0		
2007–08	Yeovil T	29	0	75	0
2008–09	Southend U	34	0		
2009–10	Southend U	44	0	78	0

MILNER, Marcus (M)   1   0
H: 5 10 W: 12 03 b.Kingston (Jam) 28-11-91
Source: Scholar.

2009–10	Southend U	1	0	1	0

MOUSSA, Franck (M)   99   7
H: 5 8 W: 10 08 b.Brussels 24-9-87
Source: Scholar.

2005–06	Southend U	1	0		
2006–07	Southend U	4	0		
2007–08	Southend U	16	0		
2008–09	Southend U	26	2		
2008–09	Wycombe W	9	0	9	0
2009–10	Southend U	43	5	90	7

O'KEEFE, Stuart (M)   10   0
H: 5 8 W: 10 00 b.Eye 4-3-91
Source: Ipswich T Scholar.

2008–09	Southend U	3	0		
2009–10	Southend U	7	0	10	0

OKAI, Julian (M)   0   0
H: 5 6 W: 9 11 b.Rochford 26-2-93
Source: Scholar.

2009–10	Southend U	0	0

PATERSON, Matthew (F)   34   4
H: 5 10 W: 10 10 b.Glasgow 18-10-89
Source: Scholar. *Honours:* Scotland Youth.

2008–09	Southampton	11	1		
2009–10	Southampton	7	1	18	2
2009–10	Southend U	16	2	16	2

SANKOFA, Osei (D)   73   0
H: 6 0 W: 12 02 b.London 19-3-85
Source: Scholar. *Honours:* England Youth, Under-20.

2002–03	Charlton Ath	1	0
2003–04	Charlton Ath	0	0
2004–05	Charlton Ath	0	0
2005–06	Charlton Ath	4	0

2005–06	Bristol C	8	0	8	0
2006–07	Charlton Ath	9	0		
2007–08	Charlton Ath	1	0	15	0
2007–08	Brentford	11	0	11	0
2008–09	Southend U	27	0		
2009–10	Southend U	12	0	39	0

SCANNELL, Damian (M)   55   2
H: 5 10 W: 11 07 b.Croydon 28-4-85
Source: Eastleigh.

2007–08	Southend U	9	0		
2008–09	Southend U	19	1		
2008–09	Brentford	2	0	2	0
2009–10	Southend U	25	1	53	2

SPENCER, Scott (F)   19   4
H: 5 11 W: 12 08 b.Manchester 1-1-89
Source: Oldham Ath Scholar.

2006–07	Everton	0	0		
2007–08	Everton	0	0		
2007–08	*Yeovil T*	0	0		
2007–08	*Macclesfield T*	3	0	3	0
2008–09	Everton	0	0		
2009–10	Everton	0	0		
2009–10	*Rochdale*	4	0	4	0
2009–10	Southend U	12	4	12	4

STOCKPORT CO (77)

BARNES, Sam (D)   2   0
H: 6 0 W: 11 06 b.Liverpool 16-10-91
Source: Scholar.

2009–10	Stockport Co	2	0	2	0

EDWARDS, Declan (M)   15   1
H: 5 10 W: 13 07 b.London 23-12-89

2008–09	Stockport Co	0	0		
2009	Galway U	14	1	14	1
2009–10	Stockport Co	1	0	1	0

FISHER, Tom (F)   2   0
H: 5 10 W: 11 07 b.Wythenshawe 28-6-92
Source: Scholar.

2008–09	Stockport Co	1	0		
2009–10	Stockport Co	1	0	2	0

GRIFFIN, Adam (D)   197   9
H: 5 7 W: 10 04 b.Salford 26-8-84
Source: Scholar.

2001–02	Oldham Ath	1	0		
2002–03	Oldham Ath	0	0		
2003–04	Oldham Ath	26	1		
2004–05	Oldham Ath	35	2		
2005–06	Oldham Ath	0	0	62	3
2005–06	*Oxford U*	9	0	9	0
2005–06	Stockport Co	21	2		
2006–07	Stockport Co	42	3		
2007–08	Stockport Co	28	1		
2008–09	Darlington	17	0		
2009–10	Darlington	0	0	17	0
2009–10	Stockport Co	18	0	109	6

HALLS, Andy (D)   16   0
H: 6 0 W: 12 02 b.Altrincham 20-4-92
Source: Scholar.

2008–09	Stockport Co	5	0		
2009–10	Stockport Co	11	0	16	0

HAVERN, Gianluca (F)   8   1
H: 6 1 W: 13 00 b.Manchester 24-9-88
Source: Scholar.

2006–07	Stockport Co	0	0		
2007–08	Stockport Co	1	1		
2008–09	Stockport Co	0	0		
2009–10	Stockport Co	7	0	8	1

HUNTINGTON, Paul (D)   58   3
H: 6 3 W: 12 08 b.Carlisle 17-9-87
Source: Scholar. *Honours:* England Youth.

2005–06	Newcastle U	0	0		
2006–07	Newcastle U	11	1		
2007–08	Newcastle U	0	0	11	1
2007–08	Leeds U	17	2		
2008–09	Leeds U	4	0		
2009–10	Leeds U	0	0	21	2
2009–10	Stockport Co	26	0	26	0

MAINWARING, Matty (M)   21   1
H: 5 11 W: 12 02 b.Salford 28-3-90
Source: Preston NE.

2008–09	Stockport Co	21	1		
2009–10	Stockport Co	0	0	21	1

McNEIL, Matthew (F)   88   11
H: 6 5 W: 14 03 b.Macclesfield 14-7-76
Source: Burnley, Curzon Ashton, Altrincham, Woodley Sp, Stalybridge C, Woking, Runcorn, Hyde U.

2005–06	Macclesfield T	12	1		
2006–07	Macclesfield T	35	5	47	6
2007–08	Stockport Co	17	2		
2008–09	Stockport Co	19	3		
2009–10	Stockport Co	5	0	41	5

MULLINS, John (D)   176   10
H: 5 11 W: 12 07 b.Hampstead 6-11-85
Source: Scholar.

2004–05	Reading	0	0		
2004–05	*Kidderminster H*	21	2	21	2
2005–06	Reading	0	0		
2006–07	Mansfield T	43	2		
2007–08	Mansfield T	43	2	86	4
2008–09	Stockport Co	33	3		
2009–10	Stockport Co	36	1	69	4

PARTRIDGE, Richie (M)   174   14
H: 5 8 W: 11 00 b.Dublin 12-9-80
Source: Trainee. *Honours:* Eire Youth, Under-21.

1998–99	Liverpool	0	0		
1999–2000	Liverpool	0	0		
2000–01	Liverpool	0	0		
2000–01	*Bristol R*	6	1	6	1
2001–02	Liverpool	0	0		
2002–03	Liverpool	0	0		
2002–03	*Coventry C*	27	4	27	4
2003–04	Liverpool	0	0		
2004–05	Liverpool	0	0		
2005–06	Sheffield W	18	0	18	0
2006–07	Rotherham U	33	3	33	3
2007–08	Chester C	36	5		
2008–09	Chester C	28	0	64	5
2009–10	Milton Keynes D	4	0	4	0
2009–10	Stockport Co	22	1	22	1

PILKINGTON, Danny (F)   32   1
H: 5 9 W: 11 10 b.Blackburn 25-5-90
Source: Chorley.

2008–09	Stockport Co	3	0		
2009–10	Stockport Co	29	1	32	1

POOLE, David (M)   144   9
H: 5 8 W: 12 00 b.Manchester 25-11-84
Source: Trainee.

2002–03	Manchester U	0	0		
2003–04	Manchester U	0	0		
2004–05	Manchester U	0	0		
2005–06	Yeovil T	25	2		
2006–07	Yeovil T	4	0	29	2
2006–07	Stockport Co	31	4		
2007–08	Stockport Co	22	2		
2008–09	Darlington	26	1	26	1
2009–10	Stockport Co	36	0	89	6

RIGBY, Lloyd (G)   2   0
H: 6 2 W: 12 05 b.Wigan 12-3-87
Source: Rochdale Scholar.

2009–10	Stockport Co	2	0	2	0

ROBERTS, Craig (M)   0   0
b.Bangor 28-10-91

2009–10	Stockport Co	0	0

ROSE, Michael (D)   175   10
H: 5 11 W: 12 04 b.Salford 28-7-82
Source: Trainee.

1999–2000	Manchester U	0	0		
2000–01	Manchester U	0	0		
2001–02	Manchester U	0	0		
From Hereford U					
2004–05	Yeovil T	40	1		
2005–06	Yeovil T	1	0	41	1
2005–06	*Cheltenham T*	3	0	3	0
2005–06	*Scunthorpe U*	15	0	15	0
2006–07	Stockport Co	25	3		
2007–08	Stockport Co	28	3		
2008–09	Stockport Co	27	0		
2009–10	Stockport Co	24	2	104	8
2009–10	Norwich C	12	1	12	1

ROWE, Daniel (M)   7   0
H: 6 0 W: 11 12 b.Wythenshawe 9-3-92
Source: Bolton W.

| 2008–09 | Stockport Co | 3 | 0 | | |
| 2009–10 | Stockport Co | 4 | 0 | 7 | 0 |

SWAILES, Danny (D)   324   22
H: 6 3 W: 12 06 b.Bolton 1-4-79
Source: Trainee.

1997–98	Bury	0	0		
1998–99	Bury	0	0		
1999–2000	Bury	24	3		
2000–01	Bury	11	0		
2001–02	Bury	28	1		
2002–03	Bury	39	3		
2003–04	Bury	42	5		
2004–05	Bury	20	1	164	13
2004–05	Macclesfield T	17	0		
2005–06	Macclesfield T	39	2		
2006–07	Macclesfield T	38	3		
2007–08	Macclesfield T	0	0	94	5
2007–08	Milton Keynes D	40	4		
2008–09	Milton Keynes D	1	0		
2009–10	Milton Keynes D	2	0	43	4
2009–10	*Northampton T*	3	0	3	0
2009–10	Stockport Co	20	0	20	0

TANSEY, Greg (M)   60   3
H: 6 1 W: 12 03 b.Huyton 21-11-88
Source: Scholar.

2006–07	Stockport Co	3	0		
2007–08	Stockport Co	13	0		
2008–09	Stockport Co	12	1		
2009–10	Stockport Co	32	2	60	3

THOMPSON, Peter (F)   173   94
H: 5 9 W: 13 06 b.Belfast 2-5-84
Source: Linfield. *Honours:* Northern Ireland 8 full caps.

2001–02	Linfield	1	0		
2002–03	Linfield	11	1		
2003–04	Linfield	4	0		
2004–05	Linfield	29	14		
2005–06	Linfield	29	25		
2006–07	Linfield	29	20		
2007–08	Linfield	29	29	132	89
2008–09	Stockport Co	19	3		
2009–10	Stockport Co	22	2	41	5

TURNBULL, Paul (F)   84   1
H: 6 0 W: 12 07 b.Handforth 23-1-89
Source: Scholar.

2004–05	Stockport Co	1	0		
2005–06	Stockport Co	0	0		
2006–07	Stockport Co	0	0		
2007–08	Stockport Co	19	0		
2008–09	Stockport Co	34	1		
2009–10	Stockport Co	30	0	84	1

VINCENT, James (M)   51   2
H: 5 11 W: 11 00 b.Glossop 27-9-89
Source: Scholar.

2007–08	Stockport Co	1	0		
2008–09	Stockport Co	16	2		
2009–10	Stockport Co	34	0	51	2

WILLIAMS, Owain fon (G)   77   0
H: 6 1 W: 12 09 b.Penygroes 17-3-87
Source: Scholar. *Honours:* Wales Youth, Under-21.

2005–06	Crewe Alex	0	0		
2006–07	Crewe Alex	0	0		
2007–08	Crewe Alex	0	0		
2008–09	Stockport Co	33	0		
2009–10	Stockport Co	44	0	77	0

STOKE C (78)

ARISMENDI, Diego (M)   61   2
H: 6 2 W: 12 13 b.Montevideo 25-1-88
Honours: Uruguay 2 full caps.

2006–07	Nacional	10	0		
2007–08	Nacional	21	1		
2008–09	Nacional	24	1	55	2
2009–10	Stoke C	0	0		
2009–10	*Brighton & HA*	6	0	6	0

BEATTIE, James (F)   384   125
H: 6 1 W: 13 06 b.Lancaster 27-2-78
Source: Trainee. *Honours:* England Under-21, 5 full caps.

1994–95	Blackburn R	0	0		
1995–96	Blackburn R	0	0		
1996–97	Blackburn R	1	0		
1997–98	Blackburn R	3	0	4	0
1998–99	Southampton	35	5		
1999–2000	Southampton	18	0		
2000–01	Southampton	37	11		
2001–02	Southampton	28	12		
2002–03	Southampton	38	23		
2003–04	Southampton	37	14		
2004–05	Southampton	11	3	204	68
2004–05	Everton	11	1		
2005–06	Everton	32	10		
2006–07	Everton	33	2	76	13
2007–08	Sheffield U	39	22		
2008–09	Sheffield U	23	12	62	34
2008–09	Stoke C	16	7		
2009–10	Stoke C	22	3	38	10

BEGOVIC, Asmir (G)   48   0
H: 6 5 W: 13 01 b.Trebinje 20-6-87
Source: La Louviere. *Honours:* Canada Under-20.

2006–07	Portsmouth	0	0		
2006–07	*Macclesfield T*	3	0	3	0
2007–08	Portsmouth	0	0		
2007–08	*Bournemouth*	8	0	8	0
2007–08	*Yeovil T*	2	0		
2008–09	Portsmouth	2	0		
2008–09	*Yeovil T*	14	0	16	0
2009–10	Portsmouth	9	0	11	0
2009–10	*Ipswich T*	6	0	6	0
2009–10	Stoke C	4	0	4	0

COLLINS, Danny (D)   186   4
H: 6 2 W: 11 13 b.Buckley 6-8-80
Source: Buckley T. *Honours:* Wales 7 full caps.

2004–05	Chester C	12	1	12	1
2004–05	Sunderland	14	0		
2005–06	Sunderland	23	1		
2006–07	Sunderland	38	0		
2007–08	Sunderland	36	1		
2008–09	Sunderland	35	1		
2009–10	Sunderland	3	0	149	3
2009–10	Stoke C	25	0	25	0

DAVIES, Andrew (D)   123   3
H: 6 3 W: 14 08 b.Stockton 17-12-84
Source: Scholar. *Honours:* England Youth, Under-20, Under-21.

2002–03	Middlesbrough	1	0		
2003–04	Middlesbrough	10	0		
2004–05	Middlesbrough	3	0		
2004–05	QPR	9	0	9	0
2005–06	Middlesbrough	12	0		
2005–06	*Derby Co*	23	3	23	3
2006–07	Middlesbrough	23	0		
2007–08	Middlesbrough	4	0	53	0
2007–08	Southampton	23	0		
2008–09	Southampton	0	0	23	0
2008–09	Stoke C	2	0		
2008–09	*Preston NE*	5	0	5	0
2009–10	Stoke C	0	0	2	0
2009–10	*Sheffield U*	8	0	8	0

DELAP, Rory (M)   428   28
H: 6 3 W: 13 00 b.Sutton Coldfield 6-7-76
Source: Trainee. *Honours:* Eire Under-21, B, 11 full caps.

1992–93	Carlisle U	1	0		
1993–94	Carlisle U	1	0		
1994–95	Carlisle U	3	0		
1995–96	Carlisle U	19	3		
1996–97	Carlisle U	32	4		
1997–98	Carlisle U	9	0	65	7
1997–98	Derby Co	13	0		
1998–99	Derby Co	23	0		
1999–2000	Derby Co	34	8		
2000–01	Derby Co	33	3	103	11
2001–02	Southampton	28	2		
2002–03	Southampton	24	0		
2003–04	Southampton	27	1		
2004–05	Southampton	37	2		
2005–06	Southampton	16	0	132	5
2005–06	Sunderland	6	1		
2006–07	Sunderland	6	0	12	1
2006–07	Stoke C	2	0		
2007–08	Stoke C	44	2		
2008–09	Stoke C	34	2		
2009–10	Stoke C	36	0	116	4

DIAGNE-FAYE, Aboulaye (M)   243   13
H: 6 2 W: 13 10 b.Dakar 26-2-78
Source: Ndiambour Louga. *Honours:* Senegal 34 full caps, 3 goals.

2001–02	Jeanne D'Arc	32	4	32	4
2002–03	Lens	15	0		
2003–04	Lens	19	0	34	0
2004–05	Istres	28	0	28	0
2005–06	Bolton W	27	1		
2006–07	Bolton W	32	2		
2007–08	Bolton W	1	0	60	3
2007–08	Newcastle U	22	1	22	1
2008–09	Stoke C	36	3		
2009–10	Stoke C	31	2	67	5

DIAO, Salif (M)   201   2
H: 6 1 W: 12 08 b.Kedougou 10-2-77
Honours: Senegal 39 full caps, 4 goals.

1996–97	Epinal	2	0	2	0
1996–97	Monaco	0	0		
1997–98	Monaco	12	0		
1998–99	Monaco	14	0		
1999–2000	Monaco	1	0	27	0
2000–01	Sedan	26	0		
2001–02	Sedan	22	0	48	0
2002–03	Liverpool	26	1		
2003–04	Liverpool	3	0		
2004–05	Liverpool	8	0		
2004–05	*Birmingham C*	2	0	2	0
2005–06	Liverpool	0	0		
2005–06	*Portsmouth*	11	0	11	0
2006–07	Liverpool	0	0	37	1
2006–07	Stoke C	27	0		
2007–08	Stoke C	11	0		
2008–09	Stoke C	20	0		
2009–10	Stoke C	16	1	74	1

DICKINSON, Carl (D)   93   1
H: 6 1 W: 12 04 b.Swadlincote 31-3-87
Source: Scholar.

2004–05	Stoke C	1	0		
2005–06	Stoke C	5	0		
2006–07	Stoke C	13	0		
2006–07	*Blackpool*	7	0	7	0
2007–08	Stoke C	27	0		
2008–09	Stoke C	5	0		
2008–09	*Leeds U*	7	0	7	0
2009–10	Stoke C	0	0	51	0
2009–10	*Barnsley*	28	1	28	1

ETHERINGTON, Matthew (M)   322   29
H: 5 10 W: 10 12 b.Truro 14-8-81
Source: School. *Honours:* England Youth, Under-21.

1996–97	Peterborough U	1	0		
1997–98	Peterborough U	2	0		
1998–99	Peterborough U	29	3		
1999–2000	Peterborough U	19	3	51	6
1999–2000	Tottenham H	5	0		
2000–01	Tottenham H	6	0		
2001–02	*Bradford C*	13	1	13	1
2001–02	Tottenham H	11	0		
2002–03	Tottenham H	23	1	45	1
2003–04	West Ham U	35	5		
2004–05	West Ham U	39	4		
2005–06	West Ham U	33	2		
2006–07	West Ham U	27	0		
2007–08	West Ham U	18	3		
2008–09	West Ham U	13	2	165	16
2008–09	Stoke C	14	0		
2009–10	Stoke C	34	5	48	5

FULLER, Ricardo (F)   299   86
H: 6 3 W: 12 10 b.Kingston, Jamaica 31-10-79
Source: Tivoli Gardens. *Honours:* Jamaica 60 full caps, 11 goals.

2000–01	Crystal Palace	8	0	8	0
2001–02	Hearts	27	8	27	8
From Tivoli Gardens.					
2002–03	Preston NE	18	9		
2003–04	Preston NE	38	17		
2004–05	Preston NE	2	1	58	27
2004–05	Portsmouth	31	1	31	1
2005–06	Southampton	30	9		

Season	Club	Apps	Gls	Total	
2005–06	Ipswich T	3	2	3	2
2006–07	Southampton	1	0	31	9
2006–07	Stoke C	30	10		
2007–08	Stoke C	42	15		
2008–09	Stoke C	34	11		
2009–10	Stoke C	35	3	141	39

GRIFFIN, Andy (D) — 281 6
H: 5 9 W: 10 10 b.Billinge 7-3-79
Source: Trainee. *Honours:* England Youth, Under-21.

Season	Club	Apps	Gls	Total	
1996–97	Stoke C	34	1		
1997–98	Stoke C	23	1		
1997–98	Newcastle U	4	0		
1998–99	Newcastle U	14	0		
1999–2000	Newcastle U	3	1		
2000–01	Newcastle U	19	0		
2001–02	Newcastle U	4	0		
2002–03	Newcastle U	27	1		
2003–04	Newcastle U	5	0	76	2
2004–05	Portsmouth	22	0		
2005–06	Portsmouth	22	0		
2006–07	Portsmouth	0	0	44	0
2006–07	Stoke C	33	2		
2007–08	Derby Co	15	0	15	0
2007–08	Stoke C	15	0		
2008–09	Stoke C	20	0		
2009–10	Stoke C	0	0	125	4
2009–10	*Reading*	21	0	21	0

HIGGINBOTHAM, Danny (D) — 303 19
H: 6 2 W: 13 01 b.Manchester 29-12-78
Source: Trainee.

Season	Club	Apps	Gls	Total	
1997–98	Manchester U	1	0		
1998–99	Manchester U	0	0		
1999–2000	Manchester U	3	0	4	0
2000–01	Derby Co	26	0		
2001–02	Derby Co	37	1		
2002–03	Derby Co	23	2	86	3
2002–03	Southampton	9	0		
2003–04	Southampton	27	0		
2004–05	Southampton	21	1		
2005–06	Southampton	37	3	94	4
2006–07	Stoke C	44	7		
2007–08	Stoke C	1	0		
2007–08	Sunderland	21	3		
2008–09	Sunderland	1	0	22	3
2008–09	Stoke C	28	1		
2009–10	Stoke C	24	1	97	9

HUTH, Robert (D) — 127 5
H: 6 3 W: 14 07 b.Berlin 18-8-84
Source: Scholar. *Honours:* Germany Youth, Under-21, 19 full caps, 2 goals.

Season	Club	Apps	Gls	Total	
2001–02	Chelsea	1	0		
2002–03	Chelsea	2	0		
2003–04	Chelsea	16	0		
2004–05	Chelsea	13	0		
2005–06	Chelsea	13	0	42	0
2006–07	Middlesbrough	12	1		
2007–08	Middlesbrough	13	1		
2008–09	Middlesbrough	24	0		
2009–10	Middlesbrough	4	0	53	2
2009–10	Stoke C	32	3	32	3

KITSON, Dave (F) — 287 102
H: 6 3 W: 12 07 b.Hitchin 21-1-80
Source: Arlesey.

Season	Club	Apps	Gls	Total	
2000–01	Cambridge U	8	1		
2001–02	Cambridge U	33	9		
2002–03	Cambridge U	44	20		
2003–04	Cambridge U	17	10	102	40
2003–04	Reading	17	5		
2004–05	Reading	37	19		
2005–06	Reading	34	18		
2006–07	Reading	13	2		
2007–08	Reading	34	10		
2008–09	Stoke C	16	0		
2008–09	*Reading*	10	2	145	56
2009–10	Stoke C	18	3	34	3
2009–10	*Middlesbrough*	6	3	6	3

LAWRENCE, Liam (M) — 322 67
H: 5 11 W: 12 06 b.Retford 14-12-81
Source: Trainee. *Honours:* Eire 8 full caps, 2 goals.

Season	Club	Apps	Gls	Total	
1999–2000	Mansfield T	2	0		
2000–01	Mansfield T	18	4		
2001–02	Mansfield T	32	2		
2002–03	Mansfield T	43	10		
2003–04	Mansfield T	41	18	136	34

Season	Club	Apps	Gls	Total	
2004–05	Sunderland	32	7		
2005–06	Sunderland	29	3		
2006–07	Sunderland	12	0	73	10
2006–07	Stoke C	27	5		
2007–08	Stoke C	41	14		
2008–09	Stoke C	20	3		
2009–10	Stoke C	25	1	113	23

LUND, Matthew (M) — 0 0
H: 6 0 W: 11 13 b.Stockport 21-11-90
Source: Crewe Alex.

Season	Club	Apps	Gls	Total	
2009–10	Stoke C	0	0		

MARSHALL, Ben (F) — 41 7
H: 5 11 W: 11 13 b.Salford 29-3-91
Source: Crewe Alex.

Season	Club	Apps	Gls	Total	
2009–10	Stoke C	0	0		
2009–10	*Northampton T*	15	2	15	2
2009–10	*Cheltenham T*	6	2	6	2
2009–10	*Carlisle U*	20	3	20	3

MOULT, Louis (F) — 1 0
H: 6 0 W: 13 05 b.Stoke 14-5-92
Source: Scholar.

Season	Club	Apps	Gls	Total	
2009–10	Stoke C	1	0	1	0

PUGH, Danny (M) — 157 10
H: 6 0 W: 12 10 b.Manchester 19-10-82
Source: Scholar.

Season	Club	Apps	Gls	Total	
2000–01	Manchester U	0	0		
2001–02	Manchester U	0	0		
2002–03	Manchester U	1	0		
2003–04	Manchester U	0	0	1	0
2004–05	Leeds U	38	5		
2005–06	Leeds U	12	0	50	5
2006–07	Preston NE	45	4		
2007–08	Preston NE	7	0	52	4
2007–08	Stoke C	30	0		
2008–09	Stoke C	17	0		
2009–10	Stoke C	7	1	54	1

SHAWCROSS, Ryan (D) — 99 12
H: 6 3 W: 13 13 b.Buckley 4-10-87
Source: Scholar. *Honours:* England Under-21.

Season	Club	Apps	Gls	Total	
2006–07	Manchester U	0	0		
2007–08	Manchester U	0	0		
2007–08	Stoke C	41	7		
2008–09	Stoke C	30	3		
2009–10	Stoke C	28	2	99	12

SHOTTON, Ryan (D) — 63 5
H: 6 3 W: 13 05 b.Stoke 30-9-88
Source: Scholar.

Season	Club	Apps	Gls	Total	
2006–07	Stoke C	0	0		
2007–08	Stoke C	0	0		
2008–09	Stoke C	0	0		
2008–09	*Tranmere R*	33	5	33	5
2009–10	Stoke C	0	0		
2009–10	*Barnsley*	30	0	30	0

SIDIBE, Mamady (F) — 303 41
H: 6 4 W: 12 02 b.Bamako 18-12-79
Source: CA Paris. *Honours:* Mali 12 full caps, 3 goals.

Season	Club	Apps	Gls	Total	
2001–02	Swansea C	31	7	31	7
2002–03	Gillingham	30	3		
2003–04	Gillingham	41	5		
2004–05	Gillingham	35	2	106	10
2005–06	Stoke C	42	6		
2006–07	Stoke C	43	9		
2007–08	Stoke C	35	4		
2008–09	Stoke C	22	3		
2009–10	Stoke C	24	2	166	24

SIMONSEN, Steve (G) — 238 0
H: 6 2 W: 12 04 b.South Shields 3-4-79
Source: Trainee *Honours:* England Youth, Under-21.

Season	Club	Apps	Gls	Total	
1996–97	Tranmere R	0	0		
1997–98	Tranmere R	30	0		
1998–99	Tranmere R	5	0	35	0
1998–99	Everton	0	0		
1999–2000	Everton	1	0		
2000–01	Everton	1	0		
2001–02	Everton	25	0		
2002–03	Everton	2	0		
2003–04	Everton	1	0	30	0
2004–05	Stoke C	31	0		
2005–06	Stoke C	45	0		
2006–07	Stoke C	46	0		
2007–08	Stoke C	36	0		
2008–09	Stoke C	5	0		

Season	Club	Apps	Gls	Total	
2009–10	Stoke C	3	0	166	0
2009–10	*Sheffield U*	7	0	7	0

SOARES, Tom (M) — 192 14
H: 6 0 W: 11 04 b.Reading 10-7-86
Source: Scholar *Honours:* England Youth, Under-20, Under-21.

Season	Club	Apps	Gls	Total	
2003–04	Crystal Palace	3	0		
2004–05	Crystal Palace	22	0		
2005–06	Crystal Palace	44	1		
2006–07	Crystal Palace	37	3		
2007–08	Crystal Palace	39	6		
2008–09	Crystal Palace	4	1	149	11
2008–09	Stoke C	7	0		
2008–09	*Charlton Ath*	11	1	11	1
2009–10	Stoke C	0	0	7	0
2009–10	*Sheffield W*	25	2	25	2

SONKO, Ibrahima (D) — 230 16
H: 6 3 W: 13 07 b.Bignola 22-1-81
Source: St Etienne, Grenoble. *Honours:* Senegal Under-21, 5 full caps, 1 goal.

Season	Club	Apps	Gls	Total	
2002–03	Brentford	37	5		
2003–04	Brentford	43	3	80	8
2004–05	Reading	39	1		
2005–06	Reading	46	3		
2006–07	Reading	23	1		
2007–08	Reading	16	0		
2008–09	Reading	3	3	127	8
2008–09	Stoke C	14	0		
2009–10	Stoke C	0	0	14	0
2009–10	*Hull C*	9	0	9	0

SORENSEN, Thomas (G) — 379 0
H: 6 4 W: 13 10 b.Fredericia 12-6-76
Source: Odense. *Honours:* Denmark Youth, Under-21, B, 89 full caps.

Season	Club	Apps	Gls	Total	
1998–99	Sunderland	45	0		
1999–2000	Sunderland	37	0		
2000–01	Sunderland	34	0		
2001–02	Sunderland	34	0		
2002–03	Sunderland	21	0	171	0
2003–04	Aston Villa	38	0		
2004–05	Aston Villa	36	0		
2005–06	Aston Villa	36	0		
2006–07	Aston Villa	29	0		
2007–08	Aston Villa	0	0	139	0
2008–09	Stoke C	36	0		
2009–10	Stoke C	33	0	69	0

ST LOUIS-HAMILTON, Danzelle (G) — 0 0
H: 6 5 W: 14 00 b.Stevenage 7-5-90
Source: Scholar.

Season	Club	Apps	Gls	Total	
2008–09	Stoke C	0	0		
2008–09	*Bristol R*	0	0		
2009–10	Stoke C	0	0		

TONGE, Michael (M) — 297 23
H: 6 0 W: 11 10 b.Manchester 7-4-83
Source: Scholar. *Honours:* England Youth, Under-20, Under-21.

Season	Club	Apps	Gls	Total	
2000–01	Sheffield U	2	0		
2001–02	Sheffield U	30	3		
2002–03	Sheffield U	44	6		
2003–04	Sheffield U	46	4		
2004–05	Sheffield U	34	2		
2005–06	Sheffield U	30	3		
2006–07	Sheffield U	27	2		
2007–08	Sheffield U	45	1		
2008–09	Sheffield U	4	0	262	21
2008–09	Stoke C	10	0		
2009–10	Stoke C	0	0	10	0
2009–10	*Preston NE*	7	0	7	0
2009–10	*Derby Co*	18	2	18	2

TUNCAY, Sanli (F) — 317 110
H: 5 10 W: 11 00 b.Sakarya 16-1-82
Honours: Turkey 74 full caps, 22 goals.

Season	Club	Apps	Gls	Total	
2000–01	Sakarya	31	16		
2001–02	Sakarya	35	16	66	32
2002–03	Fenerbahce	29	9		
2003–04	Fenerbahce	31	19		
2004–05	Fenerbahce	31	7		
2005–06	Fenerbahce	27	13		
2006–07	Fenerbahce	33	9	151	57
2007–08	Middlesbrough	34	8		
2008–09	Middlesbrough	33	7		
2009–10	Middlesbrough	3	2	70	17
2009–10	Stoke C	30	4	30	4

WEDDERBURN, Nathanial (M) — 12 0
H: 6 1 W: 13 05 b.Wolverhampton 30-6-91
Source: Scholar. *Honours:* England Youth.

Season	Club	Apps	Gls	Total	
2008–09	Stoke C	0	0		

2008–09	*Notts Co*	9	0	9	0
2009–10	Stoke C	0	0		
2009–10	*Hereford U*	3	0	3	0

WHELAN, Glenn (M)   228 16
H: 5 11 W: 12 07 b.Dublin 13-1-84
Source: Scholar. *Honours:* Eire Youth, Under-21, B, 20 full caps, 2 goals.

2000–01	Manchester C	0	0		
2001–02	Manchester C	0	0		
2002–03	Manchester C	0	0		
2003–04	Manchester C	0	0		
2003–04	*Bury*	13	0	13	0
2004–05	Sheffield W	36	2		
2005–06	Sheffield W	43	1		
2006–07	Sheffield W	38	7		
2007–08	Sheffield W	25	2	142	12
2007–08	Stoke C	14	1		
2008–09	Stoke C	26	1		
2009–10	Stoke C	33	2	73	4

WHITEHEAD, Dean (M)   343 22
H: 5 11 W: 12 06 b.Abingdon 12-1-82
Source: Trainee.

1999–2000	Oxford U	0	0		
2000–01	Oxford U	20	0		
2001–02	Oxford U	40	1		
2002–03	Oxford U	18	1		
2003–04	Oxford U	44	7	122	9
2004–05	Sunderland	42	5		
2005–06	Sunderland	37	3		
2006–07	Sunderland	45	4		
2007–08	Sunderland	27	1		
2008–09	Sunderland	34	0		
2009–10	Sunderland	0	0	185	13
2009–10	Stoke C	36	0	36	0

WILKINSON, Andy (D)   100 0
H: 5 11 W: 11 00 b.Stone 6-8-84
Source: Scholar.

2001–02	Stoke C	0	0		
2002–03	Stoke C	0	0		
2003–04	Stoke C	3	0		
2003–04	Stoke C	1	0		
2004–05	*Shrewsbury T*	9	0	9	0
2005–06	Stoke C	6	0		
2006–07	Stoke C	4	0		
2006–07	*Blackpool*	7	0	7	0
2007–08	Stoke C	23	0		
2008–09	Stoke C	22	0		
2009–10	Stoke C	25	0	84	0

Scholars
Foster, Zack; Harrison, Jack; Hedley, Alexander; Jackson, Nicholas William; Mitchell, Cameron Jake; Parton, David; Sinclair, Craig; Wint, Laton.

SUNDERLAND (79)

BAGNALL, Liam (D)   0 0
H: 5 11 W: 10 04 b.Newry 17-5-92
Source: Scholar.

2009–10	Sunderland	0	0

BARDSLEY, Phillip (D)   113 1
H: 5 11 W: 11 13 b.Salford 28-6-85
Source: Trainee.

2003–04	Manchester U	0	0		
2004–05	Manchester U	0	0		
2005–06	Manchester U	8	0		
2005–06	*Burnley*	6	0	6	0
2006–07	Manchester U	0	0		
2006–07	*Rangers*	5	1	5	1
2006–07	*Aston Villa*	13	0	13	0
2007–08	Manchester U	0	0	8	0
2007–08	*Sheffield U*	16	0	16	0
2007–08	Sunderland	11	0		
2008–09	Sunderland	28	0		
2009–10	Sunderland	26	0	65	0

BENT, Darren (F)   288 122
H: 5 11 W: 12 07 b.Wandsworth 6-2-84
Source: Scholar. *Honours:* England Youth, Under-21, 6 full caps.

2001–02	Ipswich T	5	1		
2002–03	Ipswich T	35	12		
2003–04	Ipswich T	37	16		
2004–05	Ipswich T	45	20	122	49
2005–06	Charlton Ath	36	18		
2006–07	Charlton Ath	32	13	68	31
2007–08	Tottenham H	27	6		
2008–09	Tottenham H	33	12		
2009–10	Tottenham H	0	0	60	18
2009–10	Sunderland	38	24	38	24

CAMPBELL, Frazier (F)   77 20
H: 5 11 W: 12 04 b.Huddersfield 13-9-87
Source: Scholar. *Honours:* England Youth, Under-21.

2005–06	Manchester U	0	0		
2006–07	Manchester U	0	0		
2007–08	Manchester U	1	0		
2007–08	*Hull C*	34	15	34	15
2008–09	Manchester U	1	0		
2008–09	*Tottenham H*	10	1	10	1
2009–10	Manchester U	0	0	2	0
2009–10	Sunderland	31	4	31	4

CANA, Lorik (M)   222 8
H: 5 11 W: 12 02 b.Prishtina 27-7-83
Honours: Albania 40 full caps, 1 goal.

2002–03	Paris St Germain	3	0		
2003–04	Paris St Germain	32	1		
2004–05	Paris St Germain	32	1		
2005–06	Paris St Germain	2	0	69	2
2005–06	Marseille	28	1		
2006–07	Marseille	33	2		
2007–08	Marseille	34	2		
2008–09	Marseille	27	1	122	6
2009–10	Sunderland	31	0	31	0

CARSON, Trevor (G)   18 0
H: 6 0 W: 14 11 b.Downpatrick 5-3-88
Source: Scholar. *Honours:* Northern Ireland Youth, Under-21, B.

2004–05	Sunderland	0	0		
2005–06	Sunderland	0	0		
2006–07	Sunderland	0	0		
2007–08	Sunderland	0	0		
2008–09	Sunderland	0	0		
2008–09	*Chesterfield*	18	0	18	0
2009–10	Sunderland	0	0		

CATTERMOLE, Lee (M)   124 4
H: 5 10 W: 11 13 b.Stockton 21-3-88
Source: Scholar. *Honours:* England Youth, Under-21.

2005–06	Middlesbrough	14	1		
2006–07	Middlesbrough	31	1		
2007–08	Middlesbrough	24	1	69	3
2008–09	Wigan Ath	33	1		
2009–10	Wigan Ath	0	0	33	1
2009–10	Sunderland	22	0	22	0

CHANDLER, Jamie (M)   14 0
H: 5 7 W: 11 02 b.South Shields 24-3-89
Source: Scholar. *Honours:* England Youth.

2007–08	Sunderland	0	0		
2008–09	Sunderland	0	0		
2009–10	Sunderland	0	0		
2009–10	*Darlington*	14	0	14	0

COLBACK, Jack (M)   38 4
H: 5 9 W: 11 05 b.Newcastle 24-10-89
Source: Scholar. *Honours:* England Youth.

2007–08	Sunderland	0	0		
2008–09	Sunderland	0	0		
2009–10	Sunderland	1	0	1	0
2009–10	*Ipswich T*	37	4	37	4

COOK, Jordan (F)   5 0
H: 5 10 W: 10 10 b.Hetton-le-Hole 20-3-90
Source: Scholar.

2007–08	Sunderland	0	0		
2008–09	Sunderland	0	0		
2009–10	Sunderland	0	0		
2009–10	*Darlington*	5	0	5	0

DA SILVA, Paulo (D)   324 16
H: 6 0 W: 13 12 b.Asuncion 1-2-80
Honours: Paraguay 76 full caps, 2 goals.

1996–97	Atlantida SC	29	0	29	0
1997–98	Cerro Porteno	30	1	30	1
1998–99	Perugia	2	0	2	0
1999–2000	Lanus	12	1	12	1
2000–01	Venezia	7	0	7	0
2001–02	Cosenza	2	0	2	0
2002	Libertad	30	2		
2003	Libertad	0	0	30	2
2003–04	Toluca	36	2		
2004–05	Toluca	34	2		
2005–06	Toluca	34	1		
2006–07	Toluca	28	3		
2007–08	Toluca	32	4		
2008–09	Toluca	32	0	196	12
2009–10	Sunderland	16	0	16	0

DOWSON, David (F)   22 4
H: 5 10 W: 12 00 b.Bishop Auckland 12-9-88
Source: Scholar.

2007–08	Sunderland	0	0		
2007–08	*Chesterfield*	12	3	12	3
2008–09	Sunderland	0	0		
2009–10	Sunderland	0	0		
2009–10	*Darlington*	10	1	10	1

EGAN, John (D)   0 0
H: 6 1 W: 11 11 b.Cork
Source: Scholar.

2009–10	Sunderland	0	0

FERDINAND, Anton (D)   193 5
H: 6 2 W: 11 00 b.Peckham 18-2-85
Source: Trainee. *Honours:* England Youth, Under-20, Under-21.

2002–03	West Ham U	0	0		
2003–04	West Ham U	20	0		
2004–05	West Ham U	29	1		
2005–06	West Ham U	33	2		
2006–07	West Ham U	31	0		
2007–08	West Ham U	25	2		
2008–09	West Ham U	0	0	138	5
2008–09	Sunderland	31	0		
2009–10	Sunderland	24	0	55	0

FLETCHER, Matthew (F)   0 0
H: 6 0 b.Sydney
Source: Scholar.

2009–10	Sunderland	0	0

FULOP, Marton (G)   110 0
H: 6 6 W: 14 07 b.Budapest 3-5-83
Source: MTK, Elore, Bodajk. *Honours:* Hungary Under-21, 20 full caps.

2004–05	Tottenham H	0	0		
2004–05	*Chesterfield*	7	0	7	0
2005–06	Tottenham H	0	0		
2005–06	*Coventry C*	31	0	31	0
2006–07	Tottenham H	0	0		
2006–07	Sunderland	5	0		
2007–08	Sunderland	1	0		
2007–08	*Leicester C*	24	0	24	0
2007–08	Stoke C	0	0		
2008–09	Sunderland	26	0		
2009–10	Sunderland	13	0	45	0
2009–10	*Manchester C*	3	0	3	0

GORDON, Craig (G)   210 0
H: 6 4 W: 12 02 b.Edinburgh 31-12-82
Honours: Scotland Under-21, 39 full caps.

2000–01	Hearts	0	0		
2001–02	Hearts	0	0		
2002–03	Hearts	1	0		
2003–04	Hearts	29	0		
2004–05	Hearts	38	0		
2005–06	Hearts	36	0		
2006–07	Hearts	34	0	138	0
2007–08	Sunderland	34	0		
2008–09	Sunderland	12	0		
2009–10	Sunderland	26	0	72	0

HEALY, David (F)   335 84
H: 5 8 W: 10 09 b.Downpatrick 5-8-79
Source: Trainee. *Honours:* Northern Ireland Schools, Youth, Under-21, B, 80 full caps, 35 goals.

1997–98	Manchester U	0	0		
1998–99	Manchester U	0	0		
1999–2000	Manchester U	0	0		
1999–2000	*Port Vale*	16	3	16	3
2000–01	Manchester U	1	0	1	0
2000–01	Preston NE	22	9		
2001–02	Preston NE	44	10		
2002–03	Preston NE	24	5		
2002–03	*Norwich C*	13	2	13	2
2003–04	Preston NE	38	15		
2004–05	Preston NE	11	5	139	44
2004–05	Leeds U	28	7		
2005–06	Leeds U	42	12		
2006–07	Leeds U	41	10	111	29
2007–08	Fulham	30	4		
2008–09	Fulham	0	0	30	4
2008–09	Sunderland	10	1		
2009–10	Sunderland	3	0	13	1
2009–10	*Ipswich T*	12	1	12	1

HENDERSON, Jordan (M) 44 2
H: 6 0 W: 10 07 b.Sunderland 17-6-90
Source: Scholar. *Honours:* England Youth, Under-20.

2008–09	Sunderland	1	0		
2008–09	Coventry C	10	1	10	1
2009–10	Sunderland	33	1	34	1

HOURIHANE, Conor (M) 0 0
H: 5 11 W: 9 11 b.Cork 2-2-91
Source: Scholar.

2008–09	Sunderland	0	0
2009–10	Sunderland	0	0

JONES, Kenwyne (F) 185 55
H: 6 2 W: 13 06 b.Trinidad & Tobago 5-10-84
Source: W Connection. *Honours:* Trindad & Tobago Youth, Under-23, 45 full caps, 5 goals.

2004–05	Southampton	2	0		
2004–05	*Sheffield W*	7	7	7	7
2004–05	*Stoke C*	13	3	13	3
2005–06	Southampton	34	4		
2006–07	Southampton	34	14		
2007–08	Southampton	1	1	71	19
2007–08	Sunderland	33	7		
2008–09	Sunderland	29	10		
2009–10	Sunderland	32	9	94	26

KAY, Michael (D) 0 0
H: 6 0 W: 11 05 b.Consett 12-9-89
Source: Scholar.

2007–08	Sunderland	0	0
2008–09	Sunderland	0	0
2009–10	Sunderland	0	0

KILGALLON, Matthew (D) 197 7
H: 6 1 W: 12 10 b.York 8-1-84
Source: Scholar. *Honours:* England Youth, Under-20, Under-21.

2000–01	Leeds U	0	0		
2001–02	Leeds U	0	0		
2002–03	Leeds U	2	0		
2003–04	Leeds U	8	2		
2003–04	*West Ham U*	3	0	3	0
2004–05	Leeds U	26	0		
2005–06	Leeds U	25	1		
2006–07	Leeds U	19	0	80	3
2006–07	Sheffield U	6	0		
2007–08	Sheffield U	40	2		
2008–09	Sheffield U	40	1		
2009–10	Sheffield U	21	1	107	4
2009–10	Sunderland	7	0	7	0

LAING, Louis (D) 0 0
H: 5 11 W: 12 00 b. 6-9-93
Source: Scholar. *Honours:* England Youth.

2009–10	Sunderland	0	0

LIDDLE, Michael (D) 22 0
H: 5 6 W: 11 00 b.London 25-12-89
Source: Scholar. *Honours:* Eire Under-21.

2007–08	Sunderland	0	0		
2008–09	Sunderland	0	0		
2008–09	*Carlisle U*	22	0	22	0
2009–10	Sunderland	0	0		

LUSCOMBE, Nathan (M) 0 0
H: 5 8 W: 11 07 b.Gateshead 6-11-89
Source: Scholar.

2008–09	Sunderland	0	0
2009–10	Sunderland	0	0

M'VOTO, Jean-Yves (D) 17 1
H: 6 4 W: 14 00 b.Paris 6-9-88
Source: Paris St Germain. *Honours:* France Youth.

2007–08	Sunderland	0	0		
2008–09	Sunderland	0	0		
2009–10	Sunderland	0	0		
2009–10	*Southend U*	17	1	17	1

MADDEN, Daniel (D) 0 0
H: 5 10 W: 14 02 b.Sunderland 10-9-90
Source: Scholar.

2008–09	Sunderland	0	0
2009–10	Sunderland	0	0

MALBRANQUE, Steed (M) 378 44
H: 5 7 W: 11 07 b.Mouscron 6-1-80
Honours: France Under-21.

1997–98	Lyon	2	0
1998–99	Lyon	21	0
1999–2000	Lyon	28	3
2000–01	Lyon	26	2	77	5
2001–02	Fulham	37	8
2002–03	Fulham	37	6
2003–04	Fulham	38	6
2004–05	Fulham	26	6
2005–06	Fulham	34	6	172	32
2006–07	Tottenham H	25	2
2007–08	Tottenham H	37	4	62	6
2008–09	Sunderland	36	1
2009–10	Sunderland	31	0	67	1

McCARTNEY, George (D) 236 1
H: 5 11 W: 11 02 b.Belfast 29-4-81
Source: Trainee. *Honours:* Northern Ireland Schools, Youth, Under-21, 34 full caps, 1 goal.

1998–99	Sunderland	0	0		
1999–2000	Sunderland	0	0		
2000–01	Sunderland	2	0		
2001–02	Sunderland	18	0		
2002–03	Sunderland	24	0		
2003–04	Sunderland	41	0		
2004–05	Sunderland	36	0		
2005–06	Sunderland	13	0		
2006–07	West Ham U	22	0		
2007–08	West Ham U	38	1		
2008–09	West Ham U	1	0	61	1
2008–09	Sunderland	16	0		
2009–10	Sunderland	25	0	175	0

MENSAH, John (D) 162 6
H: 5 9 W: 11 05 b.Obuasi 29-11-82
Honours: Ghana 67 full caps.

1999–2000	Bologne	0	0		
1999–2000	Bellinzona	0	0		
2000–01	Bellinzona	8	0	8	0
2001–02	Genoa	24	3	24	3
2002–03	Verona	11	0		
2003–04	Verona	2	0		
2003–04	Modena	6	0	6	0
2004–05	Verona	9	0	22	0
2005–06	Cremonese	14	0	14	0
2005–06	Rennes	12	1		
2006–07	Rennes	23	0		
2007–08	Rennes	25	1	60	2
2008–09	Lyon	12	0	12	0
2009–10	Sunderland	16	1	16	1

MEYLER, David (M) 12 0
H: 6 3 W: 11 09 b.Cork 29-5-89
Honours: Eire Under-21.

2008	Cork C	2	0	2	0
2008–09	Sunderland	0	0		
2009–10	Sunderland	10	0	10	0

MURPHY, Daryl (F) 132 20
H: 6 2 W: 13 12 b.Waterford 15-3-83
Honours: Eire Youth, Under-21, 9 full caps.

2000–01	Luton T	0	0		
2001–02	Luton T	0	0		
2005–06	Sunderland	18	1		
2005–06	*Sheffield W*	4	0	4	0
2006–07	Sunderland	38	10		
2007–08	Sunderland	28	3		
2008–09	Sunderland	23	0		
2009–10	Sunderland	3	0	110	14
2009–10	*Ipswich T*	18	5	18	5

NOBLE, Liam (M) 0 0
H: 5 9 W: 10 05 b.Newcastle 8-5-91
Source: Scholar.

2009–10	Sunderland	0	0

NOBLE, Ryan (F) 0 0
H: 6 0 W: 11 00 b.Sunderland 11-6-91
Source: Scholar. *Honours:* England Youth.

2009–10	Sunderland	0	0
2009–10	*Watford*	0	0

NOSWORTHY, Nyron (D) 307 5
H: 6 0 W: 12 02 b.Brixton 11-10-80
Source: Trainee.

1998–99	Gillingham	3	0		
1999–2000	Gillingham	29	1		
2000–01	Gillingham	10	0		
2001–02	Gillingham	29	0		
2002–03	Gillingham	39	2		
2003–04	Gillingham	27	2		
2004–05	Gillingham	37	0	174	5
2005–06	Sunderland	30	0		
2006–07	Sunderland	29	0		
2007–08	Sunderland	29	0		
2008–09	Sunderland	16	0		
2009–10	Sunderland	10	0	114	0
2009–10	*Sheffield U*	19	0	19	0

O'DONOVAN, Roy (F) 133 42
H: 5 10 W: 11 07 b.Cork 10-8-85
Source: Scholar. *Honours:* Eire Under-21, B.

2002–03	Coventry C	0	0		
2003–04	Coventry C	0	0		
2004–05	Coventry C	0	0		
2005	Cork C	26	6		
2006	Cork C	29	11		
2007	Cork C	19	14	74	31
2007–08	Sunderland	17	0		
2008–09	Sunderland	0	0		
2008–09	Dundee U	11	1	11	1
2008–09	Blackpool	12	0	12	0
2009–10	Sunderland	0	0	17	0
2009–10	*Southend U*	4	1	4	1
2009–10	*Hartlepool U*	15	9	15	9

REED, Adam (M) 0 0
H: 5 5 W: 10 03 b.Hartlepool 8-5-91
Source: Scholar.

2009–10	Sunderland	0	0

REID, Andy (M) 274 33
H: 5 9 W: 12 08 b.Dublin 29-7-82
Source: Trainee. *Honours:* Eire Youth, Under-21, 27 full caps, 4 goals.

1999–2000	Nottingham F	0	0		
2000–01	Nottingham F	14	2		
2001–02	Nottingham F	29	0		
2002–03	Nottingham F	30	1		
2003–04	Nottingham F	46	13		
2004–05	Nottingham F	25	5	144	21
2004–05	Tottenham H	13	1		
2005–06	Tottenham H	13	0	26	1
2006–07	Charlton Ath	16	0		
2007–08	Charlton Ath	22	5	38	7
2007–08	Sunderland	13	1		
2008–09	Sunderland	32	1		
2009–10	Sunderland	21	2	66	4

RICHARDSON, Kieran (M) 131 13
H: 5 9 W: 11 13 b.Greenwich 21-10-84
Source: Scholar. *Honours:* England Under-21, 8 full caps, 2 goals.

2002–03	Manchester U	2	0		
2003–04	Manchester U	0	0		
2004–05	Manchester U	2	0		
2004–05	WBA	12	3	12	3
2005–06	Manchester U	22	1		
2006–07	Manchester U	15	1	41	2
2007–08	Sunderland	17	3		
2008–09	Sunderland	32	4		
2009–10	Sunderland	29	1	78	8

TAINIO, Teemu (M) 232 19
H: 5 9 W: 11 09 b.Tornio 27-11-79
Honours: Finland Youth, Under-21, 51 full caps, 6 goals.

1997	Haka	20	4	20	4
1997–98	Auxerre	1	0		
1998–99	Auxerre	13	1		
1999–2000	Auxerre	25	3		
2000–01	Auxerre	10	1		
2001–02	Auxerre	28	3		
2002–03	Auxerre	25	1		
2003–04	Auxerre	22	3		
2004–05	Auxerre	0	0	124	12
2005–06	Tottenham H	24	1		
2006–07	Tottenham H	21	2		
2007–08	Tottenham H	16	0	61	3
2008–09	Sunderland	21	0		
2009–10	Sunderland	0	0	21	0
2009–10	*Birmingham C*	6	0	6	0

TOUNKARA, Oumare (F) 0 0
b.France
Source: Sedan.

2009–10	Sunderland	0	0

TURNER, Michael (D) 256 18
H: 6 4 W: 13 05 b.Lewisham 9-11-83
Source: Scholar.

2001–02	Charlton Ath	0	0		
2002–03	Charlton Ath	0	0		
2002–03	*Leyton Orient*	7	1	7	1
2003–04	Charlton Ath	0	0		
2004–05	Charlton Ath	0	0		

2004–05	Brentford	45	1		
2005–06	Brentford	46	2	91	3
2006–07	Hull C	43	3		
2007–08	Hull C	44	5		
2008–09	Hull C	38	4		
2009–10	Hull C	4	0	129	12
2009–10	Sunderland	29	2	29	2

WAGHORN, Martyn (F)   54   13
H: 5 9 W: 13 01 b.South Shields 23-1-90
Source: Scholar. *Honours:* England Youth.

2007–08	Sunderland	3	0		
2008–09	Sunderland	1	0		
2008–09	*Charlton Ath*	7	1	7	1
2009–10	Sunderland	0	0	4	0
2009–10	*Leicester C*	43	12	43	12

WATSON, Jordan (M)   0   0
b.Cyprus
Honours: Northern Ireland Youth.

2009–10	Sunderland	0	0

WEIR, Robbie (M)   0   0
H: 5.9 W: 11 07 b.Belfast 12-12-88
Source: Scholar. *Honours:* Northern Ireland Under-21, B.

2007–08	Sunderland	0	0
2008–09	Sunderland	0	0
2009–10	Sunderland	0	0

ZENDEN, Boudewijn (M)   382   49
H: 5 8 W: 11 01 b.Maastricht 15-8-76
Honours: Holland 54 full caps, 7 goals.

1994–95	PSV Eindhoven	27	5		
1995–96	PSV Eindhoven	25	7		
1996–97	PSV Eindhoven	34	8		
1997–98	PSV Eindhoven	25	3	111	23
1998–99	Barcelona	25	0		
1999–2000	Barcelona	29	2		
2000–01	Barcelona	10	1	64	3
2001–02	Chelsea	22	3		
2002–03	Chelsea	21	1		
2003–04	Chelsea	0	0	43	4
2003–04	Middlesbrough	31	4		
2004–05	Middlesbrough	36	5	67	9
2005–06	Liverpool	7	2		
2006–07	Liverpool	16	0	23	2
2007–08	Marseille	27	2		
2008–09	Marseille	27	4	54	6
2009–10	Sunderland	20	2	20	2

Scholars
Adams, Blair; Armstrong, James; Elliott, Brett; Gorr.n, Alejandro Rodriguez; Harrison, Andrew Ray; King, Lewis Andrew John; Lamb, Michael John; Lynch, Craig Thomas; Marrs, Liam; Wilson, Ben; Wilson, Nathan; Wood, Ben Lewis.

SWANSEA C (80)

ALLEN, Joe (M)   51   1
H: 5 6 W: 9 10 b.Carmarthen 14-3-90
Source: Scholar. *Honours:* Wales Under-21, 2 full caps.

2006–07	Swansea C	1	0		
2007–08	Swansea C	6	0		
2008–09	Swansea C	23	1		
2009–10	Swansea C	21	0	51	1

BAUZA, Guillem (F)   49   9
H: 5 11 W: 12 01 b.Palma de Mallorca 25-10-84
Source: Mallorca, Espanyol.

2007–08	Swansea C	28	7		
2008–09	Swansea C	15	2		
2009–10	Swansea C	6	0	49	9

BEATTIE. Craig (F)   135   26
H: 6 0 W: 11 07 b.Glasgow 16-1-84
Honours: Scotland Under-21, 7 full caps, 1 goal.

2003–04	Celtic	10	1		
2004–05	Celtic	11	4		
2005–06	Celtic	14	6		
2006–07	Celtic	16	2	51	13
2007–08	WBA	21	3		
2007–08	*Preston NE*	2	0	2	0
2008–09	WBA	7	1		
2008–09	*Crystal Palace*	15	5	15	5
2008–09	*Sheffield U*	13	1	13	1
2009–10	WBA	3	0	31	4
2009–10	Swansea C	23	3	23	3

BESSONE, Fede (D)   46   1
H: 5 11 W: 11 13 b.Cordoba 23-1-84
Source: Barcelona B, Espanyol B.

2007–08	*Gimnastic*	10	0	10	0
2008–09	Swansea C	15	0		
2009–10	Swansea C	21	1	36	1

BODDE, Ferrie (M)   215   24
H: 5 10 W: 12 06 b.Delft 4-5-82

2000–01	Den Haag	4	0		
2001–02	Den Haag	27	3		
2002–03	Den Haag	28	2		
2003–04	Den Haag	27	1		
2004–05	Den Haag	29	2		
2005–06	Den Haag	19	2		
2006–07	Den Haag	27	1	161	10
2007–08	Swansea C	33	6		
2008–09	Swansea C	17	7		
2009–10	Swansea C	4	0	54	13

BOND, Chad (F)   1   0
H: 6 0 W: 11 00 b.Neath 20-4-87
Source: Scholar. *Honours:* Wales Youth.

2005–06	Swansea C	0	0		
2006–07	Swansea C	0	0		
2007–08	Swansea C	0	0		
2008–09	Swansea C	0	0		
2009–10	Swansea C	1	0	1	0

BRITTON, Leon (M)   295   10
H: 5 6 W: 10 00 b.Merton 16-9-82
Source: Trainee. *Honours:* England Youth.

1999–2000	West Ham U	0	0		
2000–01	West Ham U	0	0		
2001–02	West Ham U	0	0		
2002–03	West Ham U	0	0		
2002–03	*Swansea C*	25	0		
2003–04	Swansea C	42	3		
2004–05	Swansea C	30	1		
2005–06	Swansea C	38	4		
2006–07	Swansea C	41	2		
2007–08	Swansea C	40	0		
2009–10	Swansea C	36	0	295	10

BURGIN, James (D)   3   0
H: 5 8 W: 10 00 b.Derby 6-9-89
Source: Scholar.

2008–09	Swansea C	0	0		
2009	*Ostersund*	3	0	3	0
2009–10	Swansea C	0	0		

BUTLER, Thomas (M)   214   11
H: 5 7 W: 12 00 b.Dublin 25-4-81
Source: Trainee. *Honours:* Eire Youth, Under-21, 2 full caps.

1998–99	Sunderland	0	0		
1999–2000	Sunderland	1	0		
2000–01	Sunderland	4	0		
2000–01	*Darlington*	8	0	8	0
2001–02	Sunderland	7	0		
2002–03	Sunderland	7	0		
2003–04	Sunderland	12	0	31	0
2004–05	*Dunfermline Ath*	12	0	12	0
2004–05	Hartlepool U	9	1		
2005–06	Hartlepool U	28	1	37	2
2006–07	Swansea C	30	1		
2007–08	Swansea C	42	6		
2008–09	Swansea C	29	1		
2009–10	Swansea C	25	1	126	9

COLLINS, Matty (M)   6   0
H: 5 8 W: 10 10 b.Merthyr 31-3-86
Source: Trainee. *Honours:* Wales Youth, Under-21.

2002–03	Fulham	0	0		
2003–04	Fulham	0	0		
2004–05	Fulham	0	0		
2005–06	Fulham	0	0		
2006–07	Fulham	0	0		
2007–08	Swansea C	0	0		
2007–08	*Wrexham*	2	0	2	0
2008–09	Swansea C	3	0		
2009–10	Swansea C	1	0	4	0

CORNELL, David (G)
H: 5 11 W: 11 07 b.Swansea 28-3-91
Source: Scholar. *Honours:* Wales Under-21.

2009–10	Swansea C	0	0

COTTERILL, David (F)   155   18
H: 5 9 W: 11 02 b.Cardiff 4-12-87
Source: Scholar. *Honours:* Wales Youth, Under-21, 16 full caps.

2004–05	Bristol C	12	0		
2005–06	Bristol C	45	7		
2006–07	Bristol C	5	1	62	8
2006–07	Wigan Ath	16	1		
2007–08	Wigan Ath	2	0	18	1
2007–08	*Sheffield U*	16	0		
2008–09	Sheffield U	24	4		
2009–10	Sheffield U	14	2	54	6
2009–10	Swansea C	21	3	21	3

DE VRIES, Dorus (G)   290   0
H: 6 1 W: 12 08 b.Beverwijk 29-12-80

1999–2000	Telstar	1	0		
2000–01	Telstar	27	0		
2001–02	Telstar	27	0		
2002–03	Telstar	26	0	81	0
2003–04	Den Haag	18	0		
2004–05	Den Haag	32	0		
2005–06	Den Haag	0	0	50	0
2006–07	*Dunfermline Ath*	27	0	27	0
2007–08	Swansea C	46	0		
2008–09	Swansea C	40	0		
2009–10	Swansea C	46	0	132	0

DOBBIE, Stephen (F)   188   71
H: 5 10 W: 11 00 b.Glasgow 5-12-82

2002–03	Rangers	0	0		
2002–03	*Northern Spirit*	3	3	3	3
2003–04	Hibernian	28	2		
2004–05	Hibernian	7	0	35	2
2004–05	*St Johnstone*	8	2		
2005–06	St Johnstone	20	1	28	3
2006–07	*Dumbarton*	17	10	17	10
2006–07	Queen of the S	15	10		
2007–08	Queen of the S	34	6		
2008–09	Queen of the S	32	23	83	49
2009–10	Swansea C	6	0	6	0
2009–10	*Blackpool*	16	4	16	4

DYER, Nathan (M)   125   8
H: 5 5 W: 9 00 b.Trowbridge 29-11-87
Source: Scholar. *Honours:* England Youth.

2005–06	Southampton	17	0		
2005–06	*Burnley*	5	2	5	2
2006–07	Southampton	18	0		
2007–08	Southampton	17	1		
2008–09	Southampton	4	0	56	1
2008–09	*Sheffield U*	7	1	7	1
2008–09	*Swansea C*	17	2		
2009–10	Swansea C	40	2	57	4

GOWER, Mark (M)   293   38
H: 5 11 W: 11 12 b.Edmonton 5-10-78
Source: Trainee. *Honours:* England Schools, Youth.

1996–97	Tottenham H	0	0		
1997–98	Tottenham H	0	0		
1998–99	Tottenham H	0	0		
1998–99	*Motherwell*	9	1	9	1
1999–2000	Tottenham H	0	0		
2000–01	Tottenham H	0	0		
2000–01	Barnet	14	1		
2001–02	Barnet	0	0		
2002–03	Barnet	0	0	14	1
2003–04	Southend U	40	6		
2004–05	Southend U	38	6		
2005–06	Southend U	40	6		
2006–07	Southend U	43	8		
2007–08	Southend U	42	9	203	35
2008–09	Swansea C	36	0		
2009–10	Swansea C	31	1	67	1

GRIMES, Jamie (D)   0   0
H: 6 2 W: 13 00 b.Nottingham 22-12-90
Source: Scholar.

2009–10	Swansea C	0	0

IDRIZAJ, Bezian (F)   18   0
H: 6 2 W: 12 02 b.Austria 12-10-87
Source: LASK Linz.

2005–06	Liverpool	0	0		
2006–07	Liverpool	0	0		
2006–07	*Luton T*	7	1	7	1
2007–08	Liverpool	0	0		
2007–08	*Crystal Palace*	7	0	7	0
2008–09	Liverpool	0	0		
2009–10	Swansea C	4	0	4	0

KUQI, Shefki (F)   496 143
H: 6 2   W: 13 13   b.Vushtrri 10-11-76
Source: Trepka, Miki. *Honours:* Albania 8 full
caps, 1 goal, Finland 60 full caps, 8 goals.

Year	Club				
1995	MP	24	3		
1996	MP	26	7	50	10
1997	HJK Helsinki	25	6		
1998	HJK Helsinki	22	1		
1999	HJK Helsinki	25	11	72	18
2000	Jokerit	33	19	33	19
From Jokerit					
2000–01	Stockport Co	17	6		
2001–02	Stockport Co	18	5	35	11
2001–02	Sheffield W	17	6		
2002–03	Sheffield W	40	8		
2003–04	Sheffield W	7	5	64	19
2003–04	Ipswich T	36	11		
2004–05	Ipswich T	43	19		
2005–06	Blackburn R	33	7		
2006–07	Blackburn R	1	0	34	7
2006–07	Crystal Palace	35	7		
2007–08	Crystal Palace	8	0		
2007–08	Fulham	10	0	10	0
2007–08	Ipswich T	4	0	83	30
2008–09	Crystal Palace	35	10	78	17
2009–10	Koblenz	17	7	17	7
2009–10	Swansea C	20	5	20	5

LOPEZ, Jordi (M)   98 3
H: 6 0   W: 12 02   b.Barcelona 28-2-81

Year	Club				
2003–04	Real Madrid	2	0	2	0
2004–05	Sevilla	18	1		
2005–06	Sevilla	19	1	37	2
2006–07	Mallorca	23	0	23	0
2007–08	Santander	14	0	14	0
2008–09	QPR	10	1	10	1
2009–10	Swansea C	12	0	12	0

MACDONALD, Shaun (M)   59 5
H: 6 1   W: 11 04   b.Swansea 17-6-88
Source: Scholar. *Honours:* Wales Youth,
Under-21.

Year	Club				
2005–06	Swansea C	7	0		
2006–07	Swansea C	8	0		
2007–08	Swansea C	1	0		
2008–09	Swansea C	5	0		
2008–09	Yeovil T	4	2		
2009–10	Swansea C	3	0	24	0
2009–10	Yeovil T	31	3	35	5

MONK, Garry (D)   225 3
H: 6 0   W: 12 10   b.Bedford 6-3-79
Source: Trainee.

Year	Club				
1995–96	Torquay U	5	0		
1996–97	Southampton	0	0		
1997–98	Southampton	0	0		
1998–99	Southampton	4	0		
1998–99	Torquay U	6	0	11	0
1999–2000	Southampton	2	0		
1999–2000	Stockport Co	2	0	2	0
2000–01	Southampton	2	0		
2000–01	Oxford U	5	0	5	0
2001–02	Southampton	2	0		
2002–03	Southampton	1	0		
2002–03	Sheffield W	15	0	15	0
2003–04	Southampton	0	0	11	0
2003–04	Barnsley	17	0	17	0
2004–05	Swansea C	34	0		
2005–06	Swansea C	33	1		
2006–07	Swansea C	2	0		
2007–08	Swansea C	32	1		
2008–09	Swansea C	40	1		
2009–10	Swansea C	23	0	164	0

MORGAN, Kerry (M)   3 0
H: 5 10   W: 11 03   b.Merthyr 31-10-88
Source: Scholar.

Year	Club				
2008–09	Swansea C	0	0		
2009–10	Swansea C	3	0	3	0

O'LEARY, Kristian (M)   292 11
H: 5 11   W: 12 09   b.Port Talbot 30-8-77
Source: Trainee. *Honours:* Wales Youth.

Year	Club		
1995–96	Swansea C	1	0
1996–97	Swansea C	12	1
1997–98	Swansea C	29	0
1998–99	Swansea C	19	2
1999–2000	Swansea C	20	0
2000–01	Swansea C	24	2
2001–02	Swansea C	31	2
2002–03	Swansea C	33	0

Year	Club		
2003–04	Swansea C	34	0
2004–05	Swansea C	32	1
2005–06	Swansea C	15	1
2006–07	Swansea C	23	1
2006–07	*Cheltenham T*	5	1	5	1
2007–08	Swansea C	11	0		
2008–09	Swansea C	0	0		
2009–10	Swansea C	0	0	284	10
2009–10	*Leyton Orient*	3	0	3	0

ORLANDI, Andrea (M)   117 7
H: 6 0   W: 12 01   b.Barcelona 3-8-84

Year	Club				
2005–06	*Alaves*	0	0		
2005–06	*Barcelona*	1	0	1	0
2005–06	*Barcelona B*	32	4		
2006–07	*Barcelona B*	35	1	67	5
2007–08	Swansea C	8	0		
2008–09	Swansea C	11	1		
2009–10	Swansea C	30	1	49	2

PAINTER, Marcos (D)   92 0
H: 5 11   W: 12 04   b.Solihull 17-3-86
Source: Scholar. *Honours:* Eire Youth,
Under-21.

Year	Club				
2005–06	Birmingham C	4	0		
2006–07	Birmingham C	1	0	5	0
2006–07	Swansea C	23	0		
2007–08	Swansea C	30	0		
2008–09	Swansea C	11	0		
2009–10	Swansea C	4	0	68	0
2009–10	*Brighton & HA*	19	0	19	0

PINTADO, Gorka (F)   299 79
H: 5 11   W: 11 11   b.San Sebastian 24-3-78

Year	Club				
2000–01	Union Irun	28	2	28	2
2001–02	Osasuna	35	10	35	10
2002–03	Leganes	12	0		
2003–04	Leganes	4	0	16	0
2003–04	Figures	3	0		
2004–05	Figures	34	7	37	7
2005–06	Gramenet	37	17		
2006–07	Gramenet	36	18	73	35
2007–08	Granada	38	18	38	18
2008–09	Swansea C	40	5		
2009–10	Swansea C	32	2	72	7

PRATLEY, Darren (M)   190 22
H: 6 1   W: 10 12   b.Barking 22-4-85
Source: Scholar

Year	Club				
2001–02	Fulham	0	0		
2002–03	Fulham	0	0		
2003–04	Fulham	1	0		
2004–05	Fulham	0	0		
2004–05	*Brentford*	14	1		
2005–06	Fulham	0	0	1	0
2005–06	*Brentford*	32	4	46	5
2006–07	Swansea C	28	1		
2007–08	Swansea C	42	5		
2008–09	Swansea C	37	4		
2009–10	Swansea C	36	7	143	17

RANGEL, Angel (D)   155 5
H: 5 11   W: 11 09   b.Tortosa 28-10-82
Source: Tortosa, Reus Deportiu, Girona, Sant
Andreu.

Year	Club				
2006–07	Terrassa	34	2	34	2
2007–08	Swansea C	43	2		
2008–09	Swansea C	40	1		
2009–10	Swansea C	38	0	121	3

RICHARDS, Jazz (M)   15 0
H: 6 1   W: 12 04   b.Swansea 12-4-91
Source: Scholar. *Honours:* Wales Under-21.

Year	Club				
2009–10	Swansea C	15	0	15	0

SERRAN, Albert (D)   22 0
H: 6 0   W: 12 10   b.Barcelona 17-7-84

Year	Club				
2006–07	Espanyol	2	0		
2007–08	Espanyol	1	0	3	0
2008–09	Swansea C	13	0		
2009–10	Swansea C	6	0	19	0

TATE, Alan (D)   242 5
H: 6 1   W: 13 05   b.Easington 2-9-82
Source: Scholar.

Year	Club		
2000–01	Manchester U	0	0
2001–02	Manchester U	0	0
2002–03	*Swansea C*	27	0
2003–04	Manchester U	0	0
2003–04	Swansea C	26	1
2004–05	Swansea C	23	0
2005–06	Swansea C	43	0

Year	Club				
2006–07	Swansea C	38	1		
2007–08	Swansea C	21	1		
2008–09	Swansea C	25	1		
2009–10	Swansea C	39	1	242	5

THOMAS, Casey (M)   1 0
H: 5 9   W: 10 09   b.Port Talbot 14-11-90
Source: Scholar. *Honours:* Wales Under-21.

Year	Club				
2009–10	Swansea C	1	0	1	0

VAN DER GUN, Cedric (M)   213 46
H: 5 9   W: 11 00   b.Den Haag 5-5-79

Year	Club				
1999–2000	Den Bosch	10	0	10	0
2000–01	Ajax	33	9		
2001–02	Ajax	2	0		
2002–03	Ajax	0	0	35	9
2002–03	Willem II	30	6	30	6
2003–04	Den Haag	26	6		
2004–05	Den Haag	32	6	58	12
2005–06	Borussia Dortmund	3	0	3	0
2006–07	Utrecht	18	4		
2007–08	Utrecht	13	3		
2008–09	Utrecht	21	10	52	17
2009–10	Swansea C	25	2	25	2

WILLIAMS, Ashley (D)   257 10
H: 6 0   W: 11 02   b.Wolverhampton 23-8-84
Source: Hednesford T. *Honours:* Wales 20 full
caps.

Year	Club				
2003–04	Stockport Co	10	0		
2004–05	Stockport Co	44	1		
2005–06	Stockport Co	36	1		
2006–07	Stockport Co	46	1		
2007–08	Stockport Co	26	0	162	3
2007–08	*Swansea C*	3	0		
2008–09	Swansea C	46	2		
2009–10	Swansea C	46	5	95	7

SWINDON T (81)

AMANKWAAH, Kevin (D)   221 7
H: 6 1   W: 12 12   b.Harrow 19-5-82
Source: Scholar. *Honours:* England Youth.

Year	Club				
1999–2000	Bristol C	5	0		
2000–01	Bristol C	14	0		
2001–02	Bristol C	24	1		
2002–03	Bristol C	1	0		
2002–03	*Torquay U*	6	0	6	0
2003–04	Bristol C	5	0		
2003–04	*Cheltenham T*	12	0	12	0
2004–05	Bristol C	5	0	54	1
2004–05	Yeovil T	15	0		
2005–06	Yeovil T	38	1	53	1
2006–07	Swansea C	29	0		
2007–08	Swansea C	0	0	29	0
2008–09	Swindon T	31	2		
2009–10	Swindon T	36	3	67	5

AUSTIN, Charlie (F)   33 19
H: 6 2   W: 13 03   b.Hungerford 5-7-89
Source: Poole T.

Year	Club				
2009–10	Swindon T	33	19	33	19

BODIN, Billy (M)   0 0
b. 24-3-92
Honours: Wales Under-21.

Year	Club		
2009–10	Swindon T	0	0

CUTHBERT, Scott (D)   72 4
H: 6 2   W: 14 00   b.Alexandria 15-6-87
Honours: Scotland Youth, Under-21, B.

Year	Club				
2004–05	Celtic	0	0		
2005–06	Celtic	0	0		
2006–07	Celtic	0	0		
2006–07	*Livingston*	4	1	4	1
2007–08	Celtic	0	0		
2008–09	Celtic	0	0		
2008–09	*St Mirren*	29	0	29	0
2009–10	Swindon T	39	3	39	3

DOUGLAS, Jonathan (M)   234 15
H: 5 11   W: 11 11   b.Monaghan 22-11-81
Source: Trainee. *Honours:* Eire Under-21, 8
full caps.

Year	Club				
1999–2000	Blackburn R	0	0		
2000–01	Blackburn R	0	0		
2001–02	Blackburn R	0	0		
2002–03	Blackburn R	1	0		
2002–03	*Chesterfield*	7	1	7	1
2003–04	Blackpool	16	3	16	3
2003–04	Blackburn R	14	1		

2004–05	Blackburn R	1	0		
2004–05	*Gillingham*	10	0	**10**	**0**
2005–06	Blackburn R	0	0		
2005–06	*Leeds U*	40	5		
2006–07	Blackburn R	0	0	**16**	**1**
2006–07	Leeds U	35	1		
2007–08	Leeds U	24	3		
2008–09	Leeds U	43	1	**142**	**10**
2009–10	Swindon T	43	0	**43**	**0**

EASTON, Craig (M)   **207 15**
H: 5 11 W: 11 03 b.Bellshill 26-2-79
Source: Dundee U BC. *Honours:* Scotland
Youth, Under-21.

1995–96	Dundee U	0	0		
1996–97	Dundee U	2	0		
1997–98	Dundee U	29	1		
1998–99	Dundee U	30	1		
1999–2000	Dundee U	0	0		
2000–01	Dundee U	0	0		
2001–02	Dundee U	0	0	**61**	**2**
2005–06	Leyton Orient	41	4		
2006–07	Leyton Orient	30	1	**71**	**5**
2007–08	Swindon T	40	6		
2008–09	Swindon T	23	2		
2009–10	Swindon T	12	0	**75**	**8**

FERRY, Simon (M)   **40 2**
H: 5 8 W: 11 00 b.Dundee 11-1-88

2005–06	Celtic	0	0		
2006–07	Celtic	0	0		
2007–08	Celtic	0	0		
2008–09	Celtic	0	0		
2009–10	Celtic	0	0		
2009–10	Swindon T	40	2	**40**	**2**

GREER, Gordon (D)   **217 7**
H: 6 2 W: 12 05 b.Glasgow 14-12-80
Source: Port Glasgow. *Honours:* Scotland B.

2000–01	Clyde	30	0	**30**	**0**
2000–01	Blackburn R	0	0		
2001–02	Blackburn R	0	0		
2002–03	Blackburn R	0	0		
2002–03	*Stockport Co*	5	1	**5**	**1**
2003–04	Kilmarnock	25	0		
2004–05	Kilmarnock	22	1		
2005–06	Kilmarnock	27	2		
2006–07	Kilmarnock	33	0	**107**	**3**
2007–08	Doncaster R	11	1		
2008–09	Doncaster R	1	0	**12**	**1**
2008–09	*Swindon T*	19	1		
2009–10	Swindon T	44	1	**63**	**2**

HUTCHINSON, Ben (F)   **23 2**
H: 5 11 W: 12 07 b.Nottingham 27-11-87
Source: Arnold T.

2005–06	Middlesbrough	0	0		
2006–07	Middlesbrough	0	0		
2007–08	Middlesbrough	8	1	**8**	**1**
2008–09	Celtic	5	0		
2009–10	Celtic	0	0	**5**	**0**

On loan from Celtic.

| 2009–10 | Swindon T | 10 | 1 | **10** | **1** |

JESIONKOWSKI, Jakub (G)   **23 0**
H: 6 3 W: 13 01 b.Poznan 7-3-89
Honours: Poland Youth, Under-21.

2007–08	Zaglebie	1	0		
2008–09	Zaglebie	22	0	**23**	**0**
2009–10	Swindon T	0	0		

KENNEDY, Callum (D)   **12 0**
H: 6 1 W: 12 10 b.Chertsey 9-11-89
Source: Scholar.

2007–08	Swindon T	0	0		
2008–09	Swindon T	4	0		
2009–10	Swindon T	8	0	**12**	**0**

LESCINEL, Jean-Francois (M)   **58 0**
H: 6 2 W: 12 04 b.Cayenne 2-10-86
Source: Paris St Germain, Sedan. *Honours:*
Haiti 1 full cap.

2006–07	Falkirk	8	0	**8**	**0**
2006–07	Guingamp	12	0	**12**	**0**
2008–09	Swindon T	5	0		
2009–10	Swindon T	33	0	**38**	**0**

LUCAS, David (G)   **269 0**
H: 6 1 W: 13 07 b.Preston 23-11-77
Source: Trainee. *Honours:* England Youth.

1995–96	Preston NE	1	0		
1995–96	*Darlington*	6	0		
1996–97	Preston NE	2	0		
1996–97	*Darlington*	7	0	**13**	**0**
1996–97	*Scunthorpe U*	6	0	**6**	**0**
1997–98	Preston NE	6	0		
1998–99	Preston NE	30	0		

1999–2000	Preston NE	6	0		
2000–01	Preston NE	29	0		
2001–02	Preston NE	24	0		
2002–03	Preston NE	21	0		
2003–04	Preston NE	2	0	**121**	**0**
2003–04	*Sheffield W*	17	0		
2004–05	Sheffield W	34	0		
2005–06	Sheffield W	18	0		
2006–07	Sheffield W	0	0	**69**	**0**
2006–07	Barnsley	3	0		
2007–08	Barnsley	0	0	**3**	**0**
2007–08	Leeds U	3	0		
2008–09	Leeds U	13	0	**16**	**0**
2009–10	Swindon T	41	0	**41**	**0**

MACKLIN, Lloyd (M)   **15 0**
H: 5 9 W: 12 03 b.Camberley 2-8-91

2007–08	Swindon T	0	0		
2008–09	Swindon T	2	0		
2009–10	Swindon T	9	0	**11**	**0**
2009–10	*Torquay U*	4	0	**4**	**0**

MARSHALL, Mark (M)   **27 0**
H: 5 7 W: 10 07 b.Manchester, Jam 9-5-86
Source: Carshalton Ath, Grays Ath,
Eastleigh.

2008–09	Swindon T	12	0		
2009–10	Swindon T	7	0	**19**	**0**
2009–10	*Hereford U*	8	0	**8**	**0**

McGOVERN, John-Paul (M)   **227 15**
H: 5 10 W: 12 02 b.Glasgow 3-10-80
Source: Celtic BC.

2001–02	Celtic	0	0		
2002–03	Celtic	0	0		
2002–03	*Sheffield U*	15	1	**15**	**1**
2003–04	Celtic	0	0		
2004–05	Sheffield W	46	6		
2005–06	Sheffield W	7	0	**53**	**6**
2006–07	Milton Keynes D	44	3		
2007–08	Milton Keynes D	3	0	**47**	**3**
2007–08	Swindon T	41	2		
2008–09	Swindon T	26	2		
2009–10	Swindon T	45	1	**112**	**5**

MORRISON, Sean (D)   **39 2**
H: 6 4 W: 14 00 b.Plymouth 8-1-91
Source: Plymouth Arg.

2007–08	Swindon T	2	0		
2008–09	Swindon T	20	1		
2009–10	Swindon T	9	1	**31**	**2**
2009–10	*Southend U*	8	0	**8**	**0**

O'BRIEN, Alan (M)   **66 1**
H: 5 10 W: 10 10 b.Dublin 20-2-85
Source: Scholar. *Honours:* Eire Youth, B,
Under-21, 5 full caps.

2001–02	Newcastle U	0	0		
2002–03	Newcastle U	0	0		
2003–04	Newcastle U	0	0		
2004–05	Newcastle U	0	0		
2005–06	Newcastle U	3	0		
2005–06	*Carlisle U*	5	1	**5**	**1**
2006–07	Newcastle U	2	0	**5**	**0**
2007–08	Hibernian	23	0	**23**	**0**
2008–09	Hibernian	24	0	**24**	**0**
2009–10	Swindon T	9	0	**9**	**0**

PAYNTER, Billy (F)   **310 82**
H: 6 1 W: 14 01 b.Liverpool 13-7-84
Source: Schoolboy.

2000–01	Port Vale	1	0		
2001–02	Port Vale	7	0		
2002–03	Port Vale	31	5		
2003–04	Port Vale	44	13		
2004–05	Port Vale	45	10		
2005–06	Port Vale	16	2	**144**	**30**
2005–06	Hull C	22	3	**22**	**3**
2006–07	Southend U	9	0		
2006–07	*Bradford C*	15	4	**15**	**4**
2007–08	Southend U	0	0	**9**	**0**
2007–08	Swindon T	36	8		
2008–09	Swindon T	42	11		
2009–10	Swindon T	42	26	**120**	**45**

PERICARD, Vincent de Paul (F)   **139 21**
H: 6 1 W: 13 08 b.Efok 3-10-82
Source: Juventus.

2002–03	Portsmouth	32	9		
2003–04	Portsmouth	6	0		
2004–05	Portsmouth	0	0		
2005–06	Portsmouth	6	0	**44**	**9**
2005–06	*Sheffield U*	11	2	**11**	**2**
2005–06	*Plymouth Arg*	15	4	**15**	**4**
2006–07	Stoke C	29	2		
2007–08	Stoke C	5	0		

2007–08	*Southampton*	5	0	**5**	**0**
2008–09	Stoke C	4	0		
2008–09	Millwall	2	0	**2**	**0**
2009–10	Stoke C	0	0	**38**	**2**
2009–10	Carlisle U	10	4	**10**	**4**
2009–10	Swindon T	14	0	**14**	**0**

SCOTT, Mark (G)   **0 0**
H: 5 9 W: 12 04 b.Fleet 3-1-91
Source: Scholar.

2007–08	Swindon T	0	0		
2008–09	Swindon T	0	0		
2009–10	Swindon T	0	0		

SMITH, Phil (G)   **82 0**
H: 6 1 W: 13 11 b.Harrow 14-12-79
Source: Trainee.

| 1997–98 | Millwall | 0 | 0 | | |
| 1998–99 | Millwall | 5 | 0 | **5** | **0** |

From Folkestone, Dover, Margate, Crawley

2006–07	Swindon T	31	0		
2007–08	Swindon T	15	0		
2008–09	Swindon T	25	0		
2009–10	Swindon T	6	0	**77**	**0**

THOMPSON, Nathan (D)   **0 0**
Source: Scholar.

| 2009–10 | Swindon T | 0 | 0 | | |

TIMLIN, Michael (M)   **100 4**
H: 5 8 W: 11 08 b.Lambeth 19-3-85
Source: Trainee. *Honours:* Eire Youth,
Under-21.

2002–03	Fulham	0	0		
2003–04	Fulham	0	0		
2004–05	Fulham	0	0		
2005–06	Fulham	0	0		
2005–06	*Scunthorpe U*	1	0	**1**	**0**
2005–06	*Doncaster R*	3	0	**3**	**0**
2006–07	Fulham	0	0		
2006–07	*Swindon T*	24	1		
2007–08	Fulham	0	0		
2007–08	*Swindon T*	10	1		
2008–09	Swindon T	41	2		
2009–10	Swindon T	21	0	**96**	**4**

TORQUAY U (82)

BENYON, Elliot (F)   **45 11**
H: 5 9 W: 10 01 b.Wycombe 29-8-87
Source: Scholar.

2005–06	Bristol C	0	0		
2006–07	Bristol C	0	0		
2009–10	Torquay U	45	11	**45**	**11**

BEVAN, Scott (G)   **75 0**
H: 6 6 W: 15 10 b.Southampton 16-9-79
Source: Trainee.

1997–98	Southampton	0	0		
1998–99	Southampton	0	0		
1999	*Ayr U*	0	0		
1999–2000	Southampton	0	0		
2000–01	Southampton	0	0		
2001–02	*Stoke C*	0	0		
2002–03	Southampton	0	0		
2002–03	*Huddersfield T*	30	0	**30**	**0**
2003–04	Southampton	0	0		
2003–04	*Wycombe W*	5	0	**5**	**0**
2003–04	Wimbledon	10	0	**10**	**0**
2004–05	Milton Keynes D	7	0		
2005–06	Milton Keynes D	0	0	**7**	**0**

From Kidderminster H.

| 2007–08 | Shrewsbury T | 5 | 0 | **5** | **0** |
| 2009–10 | Torquay U | 18 | 0 | **18** | **0** |

BROUGH, Michael (M)   **90 2**
H: 6 0 W: 12 05 b.Nottingham 1-8-81
Source: Trainee. *Honours:* Wales Under-21.

1999–2000	Notts Co	11	0		
2000–01	Notts Co	16	1		
2001–02	Notts Co	21	0		
2002–03	Notts Co	31	1		
2003–04	Notts Co	10	0	**89**	**2**
2009–10	Torquay U	1	0	**1**	**0**

CAMARA, Mo (D)   **339 2**
H: 5 11 W: 11 03 b.Conakry 25-6-75
Honours: Guinea 79 full caps.

1993–94	Beauvais	19	0		
1994–95	Beauvais	0	0		
1995–96	Troyes	13	0	**13**	**0**

1996–97	Beauvais	35	0	**54**	**0**
1997–98	Le Havre	14	0		
1998–99	Lille	34	2	**34**	**2**
1999–2000	Le Havre	2	0	**16**	**0**
2000–01	Wolverhampton W	18	0		
2001–02	Wolverhampton W	27	0		
2002–03	Wolverhampton W	0	0	**45**	**0**
2003–04	Burnley	45	0		
2004–05	Burnley	45	0	**90**	**0**
2005–06	Celtic	18	0		
2006–07	Celtic	1	0	**19**	**0**
2006–07	Derby Co	19	0		
2007–08	Derby Co	1	0		
2007–08	Norwich C	21	0	**21**	**0**
2008–09	Derby Co	1	0		
2008–09	Blackpool	14	0	**14**	**0**
2008–09	St Mirren	10	0	**10**	**0**
2009–10	Derby Co	0	0	**21**	**0**
2009–10	Torquay U	2	0	**2**	**0**

CARAYOL, Mustapha (F)   **20** **6**
H: 5 10 W: 11 11 b.Gambia 10-4-90
Source: Swindon T, Macclesfield T.

2007–08	Milton Keynes D	0	0		
2009–10	Torquay U	20	6	**20**	**6**

CARLISLE, Wayne (M)   **192** **24**
H: 5 11 W: 11 06 b.Lisburn 9-9-79
Source: Trainee. *Honours:* Northern Ireland
Schools, Youth, Under-21.

1996–97	Crystal Palace	0	0		
1997–98	Crystal Palace	0	0		
1998–99	Crystal Palace	6	0		
1999–2000	Crystal Palace	26	3		
2000–01	Crystal Palace	14	0		
2001–02	Crystal Palace	0	0	**46**	**3**
2001–02	Swindon T	11	2	**11**	**2**
2001–02	Bristol R	5	0		
2002–03	Bristol R	41	7		
2003–04	Bristol R	25	7	**71**	**14**
2004–05	Leyton Orient	28	3		
2005–06	Leyton Orient	12	0	**40**	**3**
From Exeter C.				
2009–10	Torquay U	24	2	**24**	**2**

CHARNOCK, Kieran (D)   **70** **0**
H: 6 1 W: 13 07 b.Preston 3-8-84
Source: Scholar.

2002–03	Wigan Ath	0	0		
From Southport, Northwich Vic.				
2007–08	Peterborough U	10	0		
2008–09	Peterborough U	2	0	**12**	**0**
2008–09	Accrington S	34	0	**34**	**0**
2009–10	Torquay U	24	0	**24**	**0**

ELLIS, Mark (D)   **27** **3**
H: 6 2 W: 12 04 b.Plymouth 30-9-88
Source: Exeter C.

2007–08	Bolton W	0	0		
2009–10	Torquay U	27	3	**27**	**3**

GREEN, Matt (M)   **0** **0**
H: 5 8 W: 10 05 b.Bath 2-1-87

2009–10	Torquay U	0	0		

HALPIN, Saul (M)   **0** **0**
Source: Scholar.

2009–10	Torquay U	0	0		

HARGREAVES, Chris (M)   **480** **28**
H: 6 0 W: 12 13 b.Cleethorpes 12-5-72
Source: Trainee.

1989–90	Grimsby T	19	2		
1990–91	Grimsby T	18	3		
1991–92	Grimsby T	10	0		
1992–93	Grimsby T	4	0		
1992–93	Scarborough	3	0	**3**	**0**
1993–94	Grimsby T	0	0	**51**	**5**
1993–94	Hull C	28	0		
1994–95	Hull C	21	0	**49**	**0**
1995–96	WBA	1	0	**1**	**0**
1995–96	Hereford U	17	2		
1996–97	Hereford U	44	4		
1997–98	Hereford U	0	0	**61**	**6**
From Hereford U.				
1998–99	Plymouth Arg	32	2		
1999–2000	Plymouth Arg	44	3	**76**	**5**
2000–01	Northampton T	31	0		
2001–02	Northampton T	39	3		
2002–03	Northampton T	39	0		
2003–04	Northampton T	42	3	**151**	**6**
2004–05	Brentford	30	2	**30**	**2**

2005–06	Oxford U	35	1		
2006–07	Oxford U	0	0	**35**	**1**
2009–10	Torquay U	23	3	**23**	**3**

HODGES, Lee (M)   **399** **49**
H: 6 0 W: 12 01 b.Epping 4-9-73
Source: Trainee.

1991–92	Tottenham H	0	0		
1992–93	Tottenham H	4	0		
1992–93	Plymouth Arg	7	2		
1993–94	Tottenham H	0	0	**4**	**0**
1993–94	Wycombe W	4	0	**4**	**0**
1994–95	Barnet	34	4		
1995–96	Barnet	40	17		
1996–97	Barnet	31	5	**105**	**26**
1997–98	Reading	24	6		
1998–99	Reading	1	0		
1999–2000	Reading	25	2		
2000–01	Reading	29	2		
2001–02	Reading	0	0	**79**	**10**
2001–02	Plymouth Arg	45	6		
2002–03	Plymouth Arg	39	2		
2003–04	Plymouth Arg	37	3		
2004–05	Plymouth Arg	19	0		
2005–06	Plymouth Arg	13	0		
2006–07	Plymouth Arg	15	0		
2007–08	Plymouth Arg	27	0	**202**	**13**
2009–10	Torquay U	5	0	**5**	**0**

MANSELL, Lee (D)   **175** **15**
H: 5 10 W: 11 10 b.Gloucester 28-10-82
Source: Scholar.

2000–01	Luton T	18	5		
2001–02	Luton T	11	1		
2002–03	Luton T	1	0		
2003–04	Luton T	16	2		
2004–05	Luton T	1	0	**47**	**8**
2005–06	Oxford U	44	1	**44**	**1**
2006–07	Torquay U	45	4		
2009–10	Torquay U	39	2	**84**	**6**

NICHOLSON, Kevin (D)   **130** **3**
H: 5 8 W: 12 05 b.Derby 2-10-80
Source: Trainee. *Honours:* England Schools.

1997–98	Sheffield W	0	0		
1998–99	Sheffield W	0	0		
1999–2000	Sheffield W	0	0		
2000–01	Sheffield W	1	0	**1**	**0**
From Forest Green R.				
2000–01	Northampton T	7	0	**7**	**0**
2001–02	Notts Co	11	2		
2001–02	Notts Co	24	1		
2002–03	Notts Co	37	0		
2003–04	Notts Co	23	0	**95**	**3**
From Scarborough, Forest Green R.				
2009–10	Torquay U	27	0	**27**	**0**

O'KANE, Eunan (M)   **29** **5**
H: 5 8 W: 13 04 b.County Derry 10-7-90
Honours: Northern Ireland Schools, Youth,
Under-21.

2007–08	Everton	0	0		
2008–09	Everton	0	0		
2009–10	Coleraine	13	4	**13**	**4**
2009–10	Torquay U	16	1	**16**	**1**

ROBERTSON, Chris (D)   **55** **3**
H: 6 3 W: 11 08 b.Dundee 11-10-85
Source: Scholar.

2005–06	Sheffield U	0	0		
2005–06	Chester C	1	0	**1**	**0**
2006–07	Sheffield U	0	0		
2006–07	Torquay U	9	1		
2009–10	Torquay U	45	2	**54**	**3**

ROWE-TURNER, Lathanial (D)   **7** **0**
H: 6 1 W: 13 00 b.Leicester 12-11-89
Source: Scholar.

2007–08	Leicester C	0	0		
2008–09	Leicester C	0	0		
2008–09	Cheltenham T	1	0	**1**	**0**
2009–10	Leicester C	0	0		
2009–10	Torquay U	6	0	**6**	**0**

SILLS, Tim (F)   **67** **5**
H: 6 1 W: 14 00 b.Romsey 10-9-79
Source: Camberley T, Basingstoke T,
Kingstonian, Aldershot T.

2005–06	Oxford U	13	1	**13**	**1**
2006–07	Hereford U	36	2	**36**	**2**
2009–10	Torquay U	18	2	**18**	**2**

STEVENS, Danny (F)   **28** **1**
H: 5 5 W: 9 09 b.Enfield 26-11-86
Source: Tottenham H Scholar.

2004–05	Luton T	0	0		
2005–06	Luton T	1	0		
2006–07	Luton T	0	0	**1**	**0**
2009–10	Torquay U	27	1	**27**	**1**

THOMPSON, Tyrone (F)   **27** **0**
H: 5 10 W: 11 00 b.Sheffield 8-5-82
Source: Scholar.

2000–01	Sheffield U	0	0		
2001–02	Sheffield U	0	0		
2002–03	Sheffield U	0	0		
2002–03	Lincoln C	1	0	**1**	**0**
2003–04	Sheffield U	0	0		
2003–04	Huddersfield T	2	0	**2**	**0**
From Scarborough, Halifax T, Crawley T.				
2009–10	Torquay U	24	0	**24**	**0**

TODD, Chris (D)   **64** **5**
H: 6 0 W: 12 09 b.Swansea 22-8-81
Source: Trainee.

2000–01	Swansea C	11	1		
2001–02	Swansea C	32	3	**43**	**4**
2002–03	Exeter C	12	0	**12**	**0**
2009–10	Torquay U	9	1	**9**	**1**

WILLIAMS, Marvin (M)   **114** **8**
H: 5 11 W: 11 06 b.London 12-8-87
Source: Scholar.

2005–06	Millwall	22	4		
2006–07	Millwall	29	3	**51**	**7**
2006–07	Torquay U	2	1		
2007–08	Yeovil T	23	0	**23**	**0**
2008–09	Brentford	34	0	**34**	**0**
2009–10	Torquay U	4	0	**6**	**1**

WROE, Nicky (M)   **99** **10**
H: 5 11 W: 10 02 b.Sheffield 28-9-85
Source: Scholar.

2002–03	Barnsley	1	0		
2003–04	Barnsley	2	1		
2004–05	Barnsley	31	0		
2005–06	Barnsley	12	0		
2006–07	Barnsley	3	0	**49**	**1**
2006–07	Bury	5	0	**5**	**0**
2006–07	Hamilton A	0	0		
From York C.				
2009–10	Torquay U	45	9	**45**	**9**

ZEBROSKI, Chris (F)   **107** **18**
H: 6 1 W: 11 08 b.Swindon 29-10-86
Source: Cirencester T, Scholar.

2005–06	Plymouth Arg	4	0		
2006–07	Plymouth Arg	0	0	**4**	**0**
2006–07	Millwall	25	3		
2007–08	Millwall	0	0	**25**	**3**
2008–09	Wycombe W	33	7		
2009–10	Wycombe W	15	2	**48**	**9**
2009–10	Torquay U	6	0	**30**	**6**

TOTTENHAM H (83)

ALNWICK, Ben (G)   **41** **0**
H: 6 2 W: 13 12 b.Prudhoe 1-1-87
Source: Scholar. *Honours:* England Youth,
Under-21.

2003–04	Sunderland	0	0		
2004–05	Sunderland	3	0		
2005–06	Sunderland	5	0		
2005–06	Sunderland	11	0	**19**	**0**
2006–07	Tottenham H	0	0		
2007–08	Tottenham H	0	0		
2007–08	Luton T	4	0	**4**	**0**
2007–08	Leicester C	8	0	**8**	**0**
2008–09	Tottenham H	0	0		
2008–09	Carlisle U	6	0	**6**	**0**
2009–10	Tottenham H	1	0	**1**	**0**
2009–10	Norwich C	3	0	**3**	**0**

ASSOU-EKOTTO, Benoit (M)   **142** **1**
H: 5 10 W: 10 12 b.Arras 24-3-84
Honours: Cameroon B, 12 full caps.

2003–04	Lens	3	0		
2004–05	Lens	29	0		
2005–06	Lens	34	0	**66**	**0**
2006–07	Tottenham H	16	0		
2007–08	Tottenham H	1	0		
2008–09	Tottenham H	29	0		
2009–10	Tottenham H	30	1	**76**	**1**

BALE, Gareth (D)   **87 10**
H: 6 0 W: 11 10 b.Cardiff 16-7-89
Source: Scholar. *Honours:* Wales Youth, Under-21, 24 full caps, 2 goals.

2005–06	Southampton	2	0		
2006–07	Southampton	38	5	40	5
2007–08	Tottenham H	8	2		
2008–09	Tottenham H	16	0		
2009–10	Tottenham H	23	3	47	5

BASSONG, Sebastien (D)   **137 2**
H: 6 2 W: 11 07 b.Paris 9-7-86
Honours: France Under-21. Cameroon 9 full caps.

2005–06	Metz	23	0		
2006–07	Metz	37	1		
2007–08	Metz	19	0	79	1
2008–09	Newcastle U	30	0		
2009–10	Newcastle U	0	0	30	0
2009–10	Tottenham H	28	1	28	1

BENTLEY, David (F)   **169 18**
H: 5 10 W: 11 03 b.Peterborough 27-8-84
Source: Scholar. *Honours:* England Youth, Under-20, Under-21, B, 7 full caps.

2001–02	Arsenal	0	0		
2002–03	Arsenal	0	0		
2003–04	Arsenal	1	0		
2004–05	Arsenal	0	0		
2004–05	Norwich C	26	2	26	2
2005–06	Arsenal	0	0	1	0
2005–06	Blackburn R	29	3		
2006–07	Blackburn R	36	4		
2007–08	Blackburn R	37	6	102	13
2008–09	Tottenham H	25	1		
2009–10	Tottenham H	15	2	40	3

BLACKWOOD, Anton (D)   **0 0**
b.Edmonton 18-8-91
Source: Northampton T.

2007–08	Arsenal	0	0		
2008–09	Arsenal	0	0		
2009–10	Tottenham H	0	0		

BOSTOCK, John (M)   **13 2**
H: 5 10 W: 11 11 b.Romford 13-10-91
Honours: England Youth.

2007–08	Crystal Palace	4	0	4	0
2008–09	Tottenham H	0	0		
2009–10	Tottenham H	0	0		
2009–10	*Brentford*	9	2	9	2

BUTCHER, Callum (D)   **3 0**
H: 5 11 W: 12 12 b.Rochford 26-2-91
Source: Scholar.

2007–08	Tottenham H	0	0		
2008–09	Tottenham H	0	0		
2009–10	Tottenham H	0	0		
2009–10	*Barnet*	3	0	3	0

BUTTON, David (G)   **43 0**
H: 6 3 W: 13 00 b.Stevenage 27-2-89
Source: Scholar. *Honours:* England Youth.

2005–06	Tottenham H	0	0		
2006–07	Tottenham H	0	0		
2007–08	*Rochdale*	0	0		
2008–09	Tottenham H	0	0		
2008–09	*Bournemouth*	4	0	4	0
2008–09	*Luton T*	0	0		
2008–09	*Dagenham & R*	3	0	3	0
2009–10	Tottenham H	0	0		
2009–10	*Crewe Alex*	10	0	10	0
2009–10	*Shrewsbury T*	26	0	26	0

CAULKER, Steven (D)   **44 0**
H: 6 3 W: 12 00 b.Feltham 29-12-91
Honours: England Youth.

| 2009–10 | Tottenham H | 0 | 0 | | |
| 2009–10 | *Yeovil T* | 44 | 0 | 44 | 0 |

CORLUKA, Vedran (D)   **189 13**
H: 6 3 W: 13 03 b.Zagreb 9-2-86
Honours: Croatia 37 full caps, 1 goal.

2003–04	Dynamo Zagreb	0	0		
2004–05	Inter Zapresic	27	4	27	4
2005–06	Dynamo Zagreb	32	3		
2006–07	Dynamo Zagreb	29	4	61	7
2007–08	Manchester C	35	0		
2008–09	Manchester C	3	1	38	1
2008–09	Tottenham H	34	0		
2009–10	Tottenham H	29	1	63	1

COX, Sam (D)   **4 0**
H: 5 7 W: 10 00 b.Edgware 10-10-90
Source: Scholar.

2009–10	Tottenham H	0	0		
2009–10	*Cheltenham T*	1	0	1	0
2009–10	*Torquay U*	3	0	3	0

CROUCH, Peter (F)   **319 91**
H: 6 7 W: 13 03 b.Macclesfield 30-1-81
Source: Trainee. *Honours:* England Youth, Under-20, Under-21, B, 40 full caps, 21 goals.

1998–99	Tottenham H	0	0		
1999–2000	Tottenham H	0	0		
2000–01	QPR	42	10	42	10
2001–02	Portsmouth	37	18		
2001–02	Aston Villa	7	2		
2002–03	Aston Villa	14	0		
2003–04	Aston Villa	16	4	37	6
2003–04	Norwich C	15	4	15	4
2004–05	Southampton	27	12	27	12
2005–06	Liverpool	32	8		
2006–07	Liverpool	32	9		
2007–08	Liverpool	21	5	85	22
2008–09	Portsmouth	38	11		
2009–10	Portsmouth	0	0	75	29
2009–10	Tottenham H	38	8	38	8

CUDICINI, Carlo (G)   **236 0**
H: 6 1 W: 12 08 b.Milan 6-9-73
Honours: Italy Youth, Under-21.

1991–92	AC Milan	0	0		
1992–93	AC Milan	0	0		
1993–94	Como	6	0	6	0
1994–95	AC Milan	0	0		
1995–96	AC Milan	0	0		
1995–96	Prato	30	0	30	0
1996–97	Lazio	1	0	1	0
1997–98	Castel di Sangro	14	0		
1998–99	Castel di Sangro	32	0	46	0
1999–2000	Chelsea	1	0		
2000–01	Chelsea	24	0		
2001–02	Chelsea	28	0		
2002–03	Chelsea	36	0		
2003–04	Chelsea	26	0		
2004–05	Chelsea	3	0		
2005–06	Chelsea	4	0		
2006–07	Chelsea	8	0		
2007–08	Chelsea	10	0		
2008–09	Chelsea	2	0	142	0
2008–09	Tottenham H	4	0		
2009–10	Tottenham H	7	0	11	0

DAWSON, Michael (D)   **229 12**
H: 6 2 W: 12 02 b.Northallerton 18-11-83
Source: School. *Honours:* England Youth, Under-21, B.

2000–01	Nottingham F	0	0		
2001–02	Nottingham F	1	0		
2002–03	Nottingham F	38	5		
2003–04	Nottingham F	30	1		
2004–05	Nottingham F	14	1	83	7
2004–05	Tottenham H	5	0		
2005–06	Tottenham H	32	0		
2006–07	Tottenham H	37	1		
2007–08	Tottenham H	27	1		
2008–09	Tottenham H	16	1		
2009–10	Tottenham H	29	2	146	5

DEFOE, Jermain (F)   **334 126**
H: 5 7 W: 10 04 b.Beckton 7-10-82
Source: Charlton Ath. *Honours:* England Youth, Under-21, B, 43 full caps, 12 goals.

1999–2000	West Ham U	0	0		
2000–01	West Ham U	1	0		
2000–01	Bournemouth	29	18	29	18
2001–02	West Ham U	35	10		
2002–03	West Ham U	38	8		
2003–04	West Ham U	19	11	93	29
2003–04	Tottenham H	15	7		
2004–05	Tottenham H	35	13		
2005–06	Tottenham H	36	9		
2006–07	Tottenham H	34	10		
2007–08	Tottenham H	19	4		
2007–08	Portsmouth	12	8		
2008–09	Portsmouth	19	7	31	15
2008–09	Tottenham H	8	3		
2009–10	Tottenham H	34	18	181	64

DERVITE, Dorian (D)   **18 0**
H: 6 3 W: 14 01 b.Lille 25-7-88
Honours: France Youth.

2006–07	Tottenham H	0	0		
2007–08	Tottenham H	0	0		
2008–09	Tottenham H	0	0		
2008–09	*Southend U*	18	0	18	0
2009–10	Tottenham H	0	0		

GIOVANI (F)   **43 7**
H: 5 8 W: 12 03 b.Monterrey 11-5-89
Honours: Mexico Youth, 29 full caps, 5 goals.

2006–07	Barcelona B	0	0		
2007–08	Barcelona	28	3	28	3
2008–09	Barcelona	6	0		
2008–09	*Ipswich T*	8	4	8	4
2009–10	Tottenham H	1	0	7	0

GOMES, Heurelho (G)   **252 0**
H: 6 3 W: 12 13 b.Minas Gerais 15-2-81
Source: Democrata. *Honours:* Brazil Under-23, 11 full caps.

2001	Cruzeiro	0	0		
2002	Cruzeiro	14	0		
2003	Cruzeiro	40	0		
2004	Cruzeiro	5	0	59	0
2004–05	PSV Eindhoven	30	0		
2005–06	PSV Eindhoven	32	0		
2006–07	PSV Eindhoven	32	0		
2007–08	PSV Eindhoven	34	0	128	0
2008–09	Tottenham H	34	0		
2009–10	Tottenham H	31	0	65	0

GUDJOHNSEN, Eidur (F)   **369 93**
H: 6 1 W: 14 02 b.Reykjavik 15-9-78
Honours: Iceland Youth, Under-21, 61 full caps, 24 goals.

1994–95	Valur	17	7	17	7
1995–96	PSV Eindhoven	13	3		
1996–97	PSV Eindhoven	0	0	13	3
1998	KR	6	0	6	0
1998–99	Bolton W	14	5		
1999–2000	Bolton W	41	13	55	18
2000–01	Chelsea	30	10		
2001–02	Chelsea	32	14		
2002–03	Chelsea	35	10		
2003–04	Chelsea	26	6		
2004–05	Chelsea	37	12		
2005–06	Chelsea	26	2	186	54
2006–07	Barcelona	25	5		
2007–08	Barcelona	23	2		
2008–09	Barcelona	24	3	72	10
2009–10	Monaco	9	0	9	0

On loan from Monaco.

| 2009–10 | Tottenham H | 11 | 1 | 11 | 1 |

HUDDLESTONE, Tom (M)   **209 7**
H: 6 2 W: 11 02 b.Nottingham 28-12-86
Source: Scholar. *Honours:* England Youth, Under-20, Under-21, 3 full caps.

2003–04	Derby Co	43	0		
2004–05	Derby Co	45	0	88	0
2005–06	Tottenham H	4	0		
2005–06	Wolverhampton W	13	1	13	1
2006–07	Tottenham H	21	1		
2007–08	Tottenham H	28	3		
2008–09	Tottenham H	22	0		
2009–10	Tottenham H	33	2	108	6

HUTTON, Alan (D)   **123 1**
H: 6 1 W: 11 05 b.Glasgow 30-11-84
Honours: Scotland Under-21, 15 full caps.

2004–05	Rangers	10	0		
2005–06	Rangers	19	0		
2006–07	Rangers	33	1		
2007–08	Rangers	20	0	82	1
2007–08	Tottenham H	14	0		
2008–09	Tottenham H	8	0		
2009–10	Tottenham H	8	0	30	0
2009–10	*Sunderland*	11	0	11	0

JANSSON, Oscar (G)   **7 0**
H: 6 0 W: 12 13 b.Orebro 23-12-90
Source: Karlslund.

2007–08	Tottenham H	0	0		
2008–09	Tottenham H	0	0		
2009–10	Tottenham H	0	0		
2009–10	*Exeter C*	7	0	7	0

JENAS, Jermaine (M) 274 34
H: 5 11 W: 11 00 b.Nottingham 18-2-83
Source: Scholar. Honours: England Youth,
Under-21, B, 21 full caps, 1 goal.

1999–2000	Nottingham F	0	0	
2000–01	Nottingham F	1	0	
2001–02	Nottingham F	28	4	29 4
2001–02	Newcastle U	12	0	
2002–03	Newcastle U	32	6	
2003–04	Newcastle U	31	2	
2004–05	Newcastle U	31	1	
2005–06	Newcastle U	4	0	110 9
2005–06	Tottenham H	30	6	
2006–07	Tottenham H	25	6	
2007–08	Tottenham H	29	4	
2008–09	Tottenham H	32	4	
2009–10	Tottenham H	19	1	135 21

KABOUL, Younes (D) 122 10
H: 6 2 W: 13 07 b.St-Julien-en-Genevois
4-1-86
Honours: France Under-21.

2004–05	Auxerre	12	1	
2005–06	Auxerre	9	0	
2006–07	Auxerre	31	2	52 3
2007–08	Tottenham H	21	3	
2008–09	Portsmouth	20	1	
2009–10	Portsmouth	19	3	39 4
2009–10	Tottenham H	10	0	31 3

KEANE, Robbie (F) 422 157
H: 5 9 W: 12 02 b.Dublin 8-7-80
Source: Trainee. Honours: Eire Youth, B, 99
full caps, 43 goals.

1997–98	Wolverhampton W	38	11	
1998–99	Wolverhampton W	33	11	
1999–2000	Wolverhampton W	2	0	73 24
1999–2000	Coventry C	31	12	31 12
2000–01	Internazionale	6	0	6 0
2000–01	Leeds U	18	9	
2001–02	Leeds U	25	3	
2002–03	Leeds U	3	1	46 13
2002–03	Tottenham H	29	13	
2003–04	Tottenham H	34	14	
2004–05	Tottenham H	35	11	
2005–06	Tottenham H	36	16	
2006–07	Tottenham H	27	11	
2007–08	Tottenham H	36	15	
2008–09	Liverpool	19	5	19 5
2008–09	Tottenham H	14	5	
2009–10	Tottenham H	20	6	231 91
2009–10	Celtic	16	12	16 12

KING, Ledley (D) 241 10
H: 6 2 W: 14 05 b.Bow 12-10-80
Source: Trainee. Honours: England Youth, B,
Under-21, 21 full caps, 2 goals.

1998–99	Tottenham H	1	0	
1999–2000	Tottenham H	3	0	
2000–01	Tottenham H	18	1	
2001–02	Tottenham H	32	0	
2002–03	Tottenham H	25	0	
2003–04	Tottenham H	29	1	
2004–05	Tottenham H	38	2	
2005–06	Tottenham H	26	3	
2006–07	Tottenham H	21	0	
2007–08	Tottenham H	4	0	
2008–09	Tottenham H	24	1	
2009–10	Tottenham H	20	2	241 10

KRANJCAR, Niko (M) 242 48
H: 6 1 W: 12 13 b.Zagreb 13-8-84
Honours: Croatia Youth, Under-21, 55 full
caps, 10 goals.

2001–02	Dynamo Zagreb	24	3	
2002–03	Dynamo Zagreb	21	4	
2003–04	Dynamo Zagreb	24	10	
2004–05	Dynamo Zagreb	16	2	85 19
2004–05	Hajduk Split	13	1	
2005–06	Hajduk Split	32	10	
2006–07	Hajduk Split	5	3	50 14
2006–07	Portsmouth	24	2	
2007–08	Portsmouth	34	4	
2008–09	Portsmouth	21	3	
2009–10	Portsmouth	4	0	83 9
2009–10	Tottenham H	24	6	24 6

LENNON, Aaron (M) 177 16
H: 5 6 W: 10 03 b.Leeds 16-4-87
Source: Trainee. Honours: England Youth,
Under-21, B, 19 full caps.

2003–04	Leeds U	11	0	
2004–05	Leeds U	27	1	38 1
2005–06	Tottenham H	27	2	

2006–07	Tottenham H	26	3	
2007–08	Tottenham H	29	2	
2008–09	Tottenham H	35	5	
2009–10	Tottenham H	22	3	139 15

LIVERMORE, Jake (M) 31 2
H: 5 9 W: 12 08 b.Enfield 14-11-89
Source: Scholar.

2006–07	Tottenham H	0	0	
2007–08	Tottenham H	0	0	
2007–08	Milton Keynes D	5	0	5 0
2008–09	Tottenham H	0	0	
2008–09	Crewe Alex	0	0	
2009–10	Tottenham H	1	0	1 0
2009–10	Derby Co	16	1	16 1
2009–10	Peterborough U	9	1	9 1

MASON, Ryan (F) 28 6
H: 5 9 W: 10 00 b.Enfield 13-6-91
Source: Scholar. Honours: England Youth.

2007–08	Tottenham H	0	0	
2008–09	Tottenham H	0	0	
2009–10	Tottenham H	0	0	
2009–10	Yeovil T	28	6	28 6

MODRIC, Luka (M) 170 37
H: 5 8 W: 10 03 b.Zadar 9-9-85
Honours: Croatia Youth, Under-21, 41 full
caps, 7 goals.

2004–05	Inter Zapresic	18	4	18 4
2004–05	Dinamo Zagreb	6	0	
2005–06	Dinamo Zagreb	32	8	
2006–07	Dinamo Zagreb	30	6	
2007–08	Dinamo Zagreb	25	13	93 27
2008–09	Tottenham H	34	3	
2009–10	Tottenham H	25	3	59 6

MPUKU, Paul-Jose (M) 0 0
b.Kinshasa 19-4-92
Source: Scholar.

2008–09	Tottenham H	0	0	
2009–10	Tottenham H	0	0	

NAUGHTON, Kyle (M) 74 1
H: 5 11 W: 11 07 b.Sheffield 11-11-88
Honours: England Under-21.

2006–07	Sheffield U	0	0	
2007–08	Gretna	18	0	18 0
2007–08	Sheffield U	0	0	
2008–09	Sheffield U	40	1	
2009–10	Sheffield U	0	0	40 1
2009–10	Tottenham H	1	0	1 0
2009–10	Middlesbrough	15	0	15 0

O'HARA, Jamie (M) 93 11
H: 5 11 W: 12 04 b.South London 25-9-86
Source: Scholar. Honours: England Youth,
Under-21.

2004–05	Tottenham H	0	0	
2005–06	Tottenham H	0	0	
2005–06	Chesterfield	19	5	19 5
2006–07	Tottenham H	0	0	
2007–08	Millwall	14	2	14 2
2008–09	Tottenham H	15	1	
2009–10	Tottenham H	2	0	34 2
2009–10	Portsmouth	26	2	26 2

OBIKA, Jonathan (F) 44 12
H: 6 0 W: 12 00 b.Enfield 12-9-90
Source: Scholar. Honours: England Youth,
Under-20.

2008–09	Tottenham H	0	0	
2008–09	Yeovil T	10	4	
2009–10	Tottenham H	0	0	
2009–10	Yeovil T	22	6	32 10
2009–10	Millwall	12	2	12 2

PALACIOS, Wilson (D) 88 1
H: 5 10 W: 11 11 b.La Ceiba 29-7-84
Source: Olimpia. Honours: Honduras 73 full
caps, 4 goals.

2007–08	Birmingham C	7	0	7 0
2007–08	Wigan Ath	16	0	
2008–09	Wigan Ath	21	0	37 0
2008–09	Tottenham H	11	0	
2009–10	Tottenham H	33	1	44 1

PARRETT, Dean (M) 4 0
H: 5 10 W: 11 04 b.Hampstead 16-11-91
Source: Scholar. Honours: England Youth.

2008–09	Tottenham H	0	0	
2009–10	Tottenham H	0	0	
2009–10	Aldershot T	4	0	4 0

PAVLYUCHENKO, Roman (F) 281 91
H: 6 2 W: 12 04 b.Mostovskoy 15-12-81
Honours: Russia 34 full caps, 15 goals.

1999	Dinamo Stavropol	31	1	31 1
2000	Rotor Volgograd	11	3	13 3
2000	Rotor Volgograd	16	5	
2001	Rotor Volgograd	28	5	
2002	Rotor Volgograd	22	4	66 14
2003	Spartak Moscow	27	10	
2004	Spartak Moscow	26	10	
2005	Spartak Moscow	25	11	
2006	Spartak Moscow	27	18	
2007	Spartak Moscow	22	14	127 63
2008–09	Tottenham H	28	5	
2009–10	Tottenham H	16	5	44 10

RANIERI, Mirko (G) 0 0
b.Italy 8-2-92
Source: Perugia.

2008–09	Tottenham H	0	0	
2009–10	Tottenham H	0	0	

ROSE, Danny (M) 8 1
H: 5 8 W: 11 11 b.Doncaster 2-6-90
Source: Leeds U. Honours: England Youth,
Under-21.

2007–08	Tottenham H	0	0	
2008–09	Tottenham H	0	0	
2008–09	Watford	7	0	7 0
2009–10	Tottenham H	1	1	1 1

SMITH, Adam (D) 19 0
H: 5 8 W: 10 07 b.Leytonstone 29-4-91
Source: Scholar. Honours: England Youth.

2007–08	Tottenham H	0	0	
2008–09	Tottenham H	0	0	
2009–10	Tottenham H	0	0	
2009–10	Wycombe W	3	0	3 0
2009–10	Torquay U	16	0	16 0

TAARABT, Adel (M) 58 8
H: 5 9 W: 10 12 b.Berre-l'Etang 24-5-89
Honours: France Youth. Morocco 7 full caps,
3 goals.

2006–07	Lens	1	0	1 0
2006–07	Tottenham H	2	0	
2007–08	Tottenham H	6	0	
2008–09	Tottenham H	1	0	
2008–09	QPR	7	1	
2009–10	Tottenham H	0	0	9 0
2009–10	QPR	41	7	48 8

TOWNSEND, Andros (M) 41 5
H: 6 0 W: 12 00 b.Chingford 16-7-91
Source: Scholar. Honours: England Youth.

2008–09	Tottenham H	0	0	
2008–09	Yeovil T	10	1	10 1
2009–10	Tottenham H	0	0	
2009–10	Leyton Orient	22	2	22 2
2009–10	Milton Keynes D	9	2	9 2

WALKER, Kyle (D) 39 0
H: 5 10 W: 11 07 b.Sheffield 28-5-90
Source: Scholar. Honours: England Youth,
Under-21.

2008–09	Sheffield U	2	0	
2008–09	Northampton T	9	0	9 0
2009–10	Tottenham H	2	0	2 0
2009–10	Sheffield U	26	0	28 0

WOODGATE, Jonathan (D) 236 6
H: 6 2 W: 12 06 b.Middlesbrough 22-1-80
Source: Trainee. Honours: England Youth,
Under-21, 8 full caps.

1996–97	Leeds U	0	0	
1997–98	Leeds U	0	0	
1998–99	Leeds U	25	2	
1999–2000	Leeds U	34	1	
2000–01	Leeds U	14	1	
2001–02	Leeds U	13	0	
2002–03	Leeds U	18	0	104 4
2002–03	Newcastle U	10	0	
2003–04	Newcastle U	18	0	28 0
2004–05	Real Madrid	0	0	
2005–06	Real Madrid	9	0	9 0
2006–07	Middlesbrough	30	0	
2007–08	Middlesbrough	16	0	46 0
2007–08	Tottenham H	12	1	
2008–09	Tottenham H	34	1	
2009–10	Tottenham H	3	0	49 2

Scholars
Archer, Jordan Gideon; Byrne, Nathan

William; Carroll, Thomas James; Durojaiye, Olumide Scott; Francis-Angol, Zaine; Fredericks, Ryan; Kane. Harry; Lancaster, Cameron Paul; Lassen, Jesse Waller; McBride, Paul; Miles, Jonathan David; Nicholson, Jake Charlie. Oyenuga, Kudus; Pritchard, Alex David; Tapping, Callum.

TRANMERE R (84)

BAIN, Kithson (F)   10   0
H: 5 8 W: 13 00 b.Grenada 25-5-82
Source: Queens Park Rangers (Grenada), Ball Dogs. *Honours:* Grenada 25 full caps, 9 goals.

2009–10	Tranmere R	10	0	10	0

BAKAYOGO, Zaoumana (D)   44   0
H: 5 9 W: 10 08 b.Paris 11-8-86
Source: Paris St Germain. *Honours:* Ivory Coast Under-23.

2006–07	Millwall	5	0		
2007–08	Millwall	10	0		
2008–09	Millwall	0	0	15	0
2009–10	Tranmere R	29	0	29	0

BARNETT, Charlie (M)   36   4
H: 5 7 W: 11 07 b.Liverpool 19-9-88
Source: Scholar.

2006–07	Liverpool	0	0		
2007–08	Liverpool	0	0		
2008–09	Tranmere R	29	3		
2009–10	Tranmere R	7	1	36	4

BROOMES, Marlon (D)   239   5
H: 6 0 W: 12 12 b.Birmingham 28-11-77
Source: Trainee. *Honours:* England Schools, Youth, Under-21.

1994–95	Blackburn R	0	0		
1995–96	Blackburn R	0	0		
1996–97	Blackburn R	0	0		
1996–97	*Swindon T*	12	1	12	1
1997–98	Blackburn R	4	0		
1998–99	Blackburn R	13	0		
1999–2000	Blackburn R	13	1		
2000–01	Blackburn R	1	0		
2000–01	*QPR*	5	0	5	0
2001–02	*Grimsby T*	0	0	31	1
2001–02	*Grimsby T*	15	0	15	0
2001–02	Sheffield W	19	0	19	0
2002–03	Preston NE	28	0		
2003–04	Preston NE	30	0		
2004–05	Preston NE	11	0	69	0
2005–06	Stoke C	37	2		
2006–07	Stoke C	0	0		
2007–08	Stoke C	0	0	37	2
2008–09	Blackpool	1	0	1	0
2008–09	*Crewe Alex*	19	0	19	0
2009–10	Tranmere R	31	1	31	1

COLLISTER, Joe (G)   3   0
H: 6 0 W: 13 10 b.Wirral 15-12-91
Source: Scholar.

2009–10	Tranmere R	3	0	3	0

CRESSWELL, Aaron (D)   27   1
H: 5 7 W: 10 05 b.Liverpool 15-12-89
Source: Scholar.

2008–09	Tranmere R	13	1		
2009–10	Tranmere R	14	0	27	1

CURRAN, Craig (F)   97   14
H: 5 9 W: 11 09 b.Liverpool 23-9-89
Source: Scholar.

2006–07	Tranmere R	4	4		
2007–08	Tranmere R	35	2		
2008–09	Tranmere R	15	3		
2009–10	Tranmere R	43	5	97	14

EDDS, Gareth (D)   244   16
H: 5 11 W: 11 01 b.Sydney 3-2-81
Source: Trainee. *Honours:* Australia Under-20, Under-23.

1997–98	Nottingham F	0	0		
1998–99	Nottingham F	0	0		
1999–2000	Nottingham F	2	0		
2000–01	Nottingham F	13	1		
2001–02	*Swindon T*	14	0	14	0
2002–03	Bradford C	23	0	23	0
2004–05	Milton Keynes D	39	5		
2005–06	Milton Keynes D	41	3		
2006–07	Milton Keynes D	35	2		
2007–08	Milton Keynes D	7	0	122	10
2008–09	Tranmere R	34	2		
2009–10	Tranmere R	35	3	69	5

FRAUGHAN, Ryan (M)   6   0
H: 5 7 W: 11 02 b.Liverpool 11-2-91
Source: Scholar.

2008–09	Tranmere R	0	0		
2009–10	Tranmere R	6	0	6	0

GOODISON, Ian (D)   323   7
H: 6 1 W: 13 04 b.St James, Jamaica 21-11-72
Source: Olympic Gardens. *Honours:* Jamaica 113 full caps, 9 goals.

1999–2000	Hull C	18	0		
2000–01	Hull C	36	1		
2001–02	Hull C	16	0		
2002–03	Hull C	0	0	70	1

From Seba U.

2003–04	Tranmere R	12	0		
2004–05	Tranmere R	44	1		
2005–06	Tranmere R	38	1		
2006–07	Tranmere R	40	0		
2007–08	Tranmere R	42	0		
2008–09	Tranmere R	33	1		
2009–10	Tranmere R	44	3	253	6

GORNELL, Terry (F)   48   7
H: 5 11 W: 12 04 b.Liverpool 16-12-89
Source: Scholar.

2008–09	Tranmere R	10	1		
2008–09	*Accrington S*	11	4	11	4
2009–10	Tranmere R	27	2	37	3

MAHON, Alan (M)   314   31
H: 5 8 W: 12 03 b.Dublin 4-4-78
Source: Crumplin U. *Honours:* Eire School, Youth, Under-21, 2 full caps.

1994–95	Tranmere R	0	0		
1995–96	Tranmere R	2	0		
1996–97	Tranmere R	25	2		
1997–98	Tranmere R	18	1		
1998–99	Tranmere R	39	6		
1999–2000	Tranmere R	36	4		
2000–01	Sporting Lisbon	1	0	1	0
2000–01	Blackburn R	18	0		
2001–02	Blackburn R	13	1		
2002–03	Blackburn R	0	0		
2002–03	*Cardiff C*	15	2	15	2
2003–04	Blackburn R	3	0	36	1
2003–04	*Ipswich T*	11	1	11	1
2003–04	Wigan Ath	14	1		
2004–05	Wigan Ath	27	7		
2005–06	Wigan Ath	6	1	47	9
2005–06	Burnley	8	0		
2006–07	Burnley	25	2		
2007–08	Burnley	26	1		
2008–09	Burnley	8	1	67	4
2008–09	*Blackpool*	1	0	1	0
2009–10	Tranmere R	16	1	136	14

McLAREN, Paul (M)   492   24
H: 6 0 W: 13 04 b.High Wycombe 17-11-76
Source: Trainee.

1993–94	Luton T	1	0		
1994–95	Luton T	0	0		
1995–96	Luton T	12	1		
1996–97	Luton T	24	0		
1997–98	Luton T	43	0		
1998–99	Luton T	23	0		
1999–2000	Luton T	29	1		
2000–01	Luton T	35	2	167	4
2001–02	Sheffield W	35	2		
2002–03	Sheffield W	36	4		
2003–04	Sheffield W	25	2	96	8
2004–05	Rotherham U	33	1		
2005–06	Rotherham U	39	3	72	4
2006–07	Tranmere R	42	1		
2007–08	Tranmere R	43	4		
2008–09	Bradford C	34	3	34	3
2009–10	Tranmere R	38	0	123	5

RICKETTS, Michael (F)   349   78
H: 6 2 W: 11 12 b.Birmingham 4-12-78
Source: Trainee. *Honours:* England 1 full cap.

1995–96	Walsall	1	1		
1996–97	Walsall	11	1		
1997–98	Walsall	24	1		
1998–99	Walsall	8	0		
1999–2000	Walsall	32	11		
2000–01	Bolton W	39	19		
2001–02	Bolton W	37	12		
2002–03	Bolton W	22	6	98	37
2002–03	Middlesbrough	9	1		
2003–04	Middlesbrough	23	2	32	3
2004–05	Leeds U	21	0		
2004–05	Stoke C	11	0	11	0
2005–06	Leeds U	4	0	25	0
2005–06	*Cardiff C*	17	5	17	5
2005–06	Burnley	13	2	13	2
2006–07	Southend U	2	0	2	0
2006–07	Preston NE	14	1	14	1
2007–08	Oldham Ath	9	2	9	2
2007–08	Walsall	12	3		
2008–09	Walsall	28	9		
2009–10	Walsall	0	0	116	26
2009–10	Tranmere R	12	2	12	2

SAVAGE, Bas (F)   164   22
H: 6 3 W: 13 08 b.London 7-1-82
Source: Walton & Hersham.

2001–02	Reading	1	0		
2002–03	Reading	1	0		
2003–04	Reading	15	0		
2004–05	Reading	0	0	16	0
2004–05	*Wycombe W*	4	0	4	0
2004–05	*Bury*	5	0	5	0
2005–06	Bristol C	23	1		
2006–07	Bristol C	0	0	23	1
2006–07	Gillingham	14	1	14	1
2006–07	Brighton & HA	15	6		
2007–08	Brighton & HA	21	3	36	9
2007–08	Millwall	7	2	11	2
2008–09	Tranmere R	42	9		
2009–10	Tranmere R	13	0	55	9

SHUKER, Chris (M)   270   34
H: 5 5 W: 9 03 b.Liverpool 9-5-82
Source: Scholarship.

1999–2000	Manchester C	0	0		
2000–01	Manchester C	0	0		
2000–01	*Macclesfield T*	9	1	9	1
2001–02	Manchester C	2	0		
2002–03	Manchester C	3	0		
2002–03	*Walsall*	5	0	5	0
2003–04	Manchester C	0	0	5	0
2003–04	*Rochdale*	14	1	14	1
2003–04	*Hartlepool U*	14	1	14	1
2003–04	Barnsley	9	0		
2004–05	Barnsley	45	7		
2005–06	Barnsley	46	10	100	17
2006–07	Tranmere R	46	6		
2007–08	Tranmere R	23	3		
2008–09	Tranmere R	28	3		
2009–10	Tranmere R	26	2	123	14

TAYLOR, Ash (M)   34   1
H: 6 0 W: 12 00 b.Bromborough 2-9-89
Source: Scholar. *Honours:* Wales Youth.

2008–09	Tranmere R	1	0		
2009–10	Tranmere R	33	1	34	1

THOMAS-MOORE, Ian (F)   550   104
H: 5 11 W: 12 00 b.Birkenhead 26-8-76
Source: Trainee. *Honours:* England Youth, Under-21.

1994–95	Tranmere R	1	0		
1995–96	Tranmere R	36	9		
1996–97	Tranmere R	21	3		
1996–97	*Bradford C*	0	0	6	0
1996–97	Nottingham F	5	0		
1997–98	Nottingham F	10	1	15	1
1997–98	*West Ham U*	1	0	1	0
1998–99	Stockport Co	38	3		
1999–2000	Stockport Co	38	10		
2000–01	Stockport Co	17	5	93	20
2000–01	Burnley	27	5		
2001–02	Burnley	46	11		
2002–03	Burnley	44	8		
2003–04	Burnley	40	9		
2004–05	Burnley	35	4	192	37
2004–05	Leeds U	6	0		
2005–06	Leeds U	20	0		
2006–07	Leeds U	33	2	59	2
2007–08	Hartlepool U	24	6	24	6
2007–08	Tranmere R	9	3		
2008–09	Tranmere R	42	10		
2009–10	Tranmere R	43	13	160	38

WELSH, John (M) — 114 7

H: 5 7 W: 12 02 b.Liverpool 10-1-84
Source: Scholar. Honours: England Youth, Under-20, Under-21.

Season	Club				
2000–01	Liverpool	0	0		
2001–02	Liverpool	0	0		
2002–03	Liverpool	0	0		
2003–04	Liverpool	1	0		
2004–05	Liverpool	3	0		
2005–06	Liverpool	0	0	**4**	**0**
2005–06	Hull C	32	2		
2006–07	Hull C	18	1		
2007–08	Hull C	0	0		
2007–08	Chester C	6	0	**6**	**0**
2008–09	Hull C	0	0	**50**	**3**
2008–09	Carlisle U	4	0	**4**	**0**
2008–09	Bury	5	0	**5**	**0**
2009–10	Tranmere R	45	4	**45**	**4**

WALSALL (85)

ADKINS, Sam (M) — 2 0

H: 5 10 W: 11 07 b.Birmingham 3-12-91
Source: Scholar.

Season	Club				
2008–09	Walsall	1	0		
2009–10	Walsall	1	0	**2**	**0**

BRADLEY, Mark (D) — 96 5

H: 6 0 W: 11 05 b.Dudley 14-1-88
Source: Scholar. Honours: Wales Youth, Under-21, 1 full cap.

Season	Club				
2004–05	Walsall	1	0		
2005–06	Walsall	3	0		
2006–07	Walsall	1	0		
2007–08	Walsall	35	3		
2008–09	Walsall	28	2		
2009–10	Walsall	28	0	**96**	**5**

BYFIELD, Darren (F) — 381 96

H: 5 11 W: 12 07 b.Sutton Coldfield 29-9-76
Source: Trainee. Honours: Jamaica 7 full caps.

Season	Club				
1993–94	Aston Villa	0	0		
1994–95	Aston Villa	0	0		
1995–96	Aston Villa	0	0		
1996–97	Aston Villa	0	0		
1997–98	Aston Villa	7	0		
1998–99	Aston Villa	0	0		
1998–99	Preston NE	5	1	**5**	**1**
1999–2000	Aston Villa	0	0	**7**	**0**
1999–2000	Northampton T	6	1	**6**	**1**
1999–2000	Cambridge U	4	0	**4**	**0**
1999–2000	Blackpool	3	0	**3**	**0**
2000–01	Walsall	40	9		
2001–02	Walsall	37	4		
2001–02	Rotherham U	3	2		
2002–03	Rotherham U	13	1		
2003–04	Rotherham U	28	7	**68**	**22**
2003–04	Sunderland	17	5	**17**	**5**
2004–05	Gillingham	38	6		
2005–06	Gillingham	29	13	**67**	**19**
2006–07	Millwall	31	16		
2007–08	Millwall	0	0	**31**	**16**
2007–08	Bristol C	33	8	**33**	**8**
2008–09	Doncaster R	15	0	**15**	**0**
2008–09	Oldham Ath	8	1		
2009–10	Oldham Ath	3	0	**11**	**1**
2009–10	Walsall	37	10	**114**	**23**

DEENEY, Troy (F) — 123 27

H: 5 11 W: 12 00 b.Chelmsley 29-6-88
Source: Chelmsley T.

Season	Club				
2006–07	Walsall	1	0		
2007–08	Walsall	35	1		
2008–09	Walsall	45	12		
2009–10	Walsall	42	14	**123**	**27**

GEDDES, Sean (M) — 0 0

H: 5 6 W: 10 02 b.West Bromwich 13-2-92
Source: Scholar.

Season	Club				
2009–10	Walsall	0	0		

GILMARTIN, Rene (G) — 35 0

H: 6 5 W: 13 06 b.Dublin 31-5-87
Source: St Patrick's BC. Honours: Eire Youth, Under-21.

Season	Club				
2005–06	Walsall	2	0		
2006–07	Walsall	0	0		
2007–08	Walsall	0	0		
2008–09	Walsall	11	0		
2009–10	Walsall	22	0	**35**	**0**

GRAY, Julian (M) — 248 21

H: 6 1 W: 11 00 b.Lewisham 21-9-79
Source: Trainee.

Season	Club				
1998–99	Arsenal	0	0		
1999–2000	Arsenal	1	0	**1**	**0**
2000–01	Crystal Palace	23	1		
2001–02	Crystal Palace	43	2		
2002–03	Crystal Palace	35	5		
2003–04	Crystal Palace	24	2	**125**	**10**
2003–04	Cardiff C	9	0	**9**	**0**
2004–05	Birmingham C	32	2		
2005–06	Birmingham C	21	1		
2006–07	Birmingham C	7	0	**60**	**3**
2007–08	Coventry C	26	3		
2008–09	Coventry C	3	1	**29**	**4**
2008–09	Fulham	1	0		
2009–10	Fulham	0	0	**1**	**0**
2009–10	Barnsley	5	0	**5**	**0**
2009–10	Walsall	18	4	**18**	**4**

GRIGG, Will (M) — 1 0

H: 5 11 W: 11 00 b.Solihull 3-7-91
Source: Stratford T. Honours: Northern Ireland Youth.

Season	Club				
2008–09	Walsall	1	0		
2009–10	Walsall	0	0	**1**	**0**

HUGHES, Mark (D) — 123 6

H: 6 1 W: 12 03 b.Liverpool 9-12-86
Source: Scholar.

Season	Club				
2004–05	Everton	0	0		
2005–06	Everton	0	0		
2005–06	Stockport Co	3	1	**3**	**1**
2006–07	Everton	1	0	**1**	**0**
2006–07	Northampton T	17	2		
2007–08	Northampton T	35	1		
2008–09	Northampton T	41	1	**93**	**4**
2009–10	Walsall	26	1	**26**	**1**

INCE, Clayton (G) — 276 0

H: 6 3 W: 13 03 b.Trinidad 13-7-72
Source: Defence Force. Honours: Trinidad & Tobago 79 full caps.

Season	Club				
1999–2000	Crewe Alex	1	0		
2000–01	Crewe Alex	1	0		
2001–02	Crewe Alex	19	0		
2002–03	Crewe Alex	43	0		
2003–04	Crewe Alex	36	0		
2004–05	Crewe Alex	23	0	**123**	**0**
2005–06	Coventry C	1	0	**1**	**0**
2006–07	Walsall	45	0		
2007–08	Walsall	46	0		
2008–09	Walsall	36	0		
2009–10	Walsall	25	0	**152**	**0**

JONES, Steve (F) — 291 59

H: 5 10 W: 10 05 b.Derry 25-10-76
Source: Leigh RMI. Honours: Northern Ireland B, 29 full caps, 1 goal.

Season	Club				
2001–02	Rochdale	9	1	**9**	**1**
2001–02	Crewe Alex	6	0		
2002–03	Crewe Alex	31	9		
2003–04	Crewe Alex	45	15		
2004–05	Crewe Alex	36	10		
2005–06	Crewe Alex	41	5		
2006–07	Burnley	41	5		
2007–08	Burnley	17	1		
2007–08	Crewe Alex	4	1	**163**	**40**
2008–09	Burnley	0	0	**58**	**6**
2008–09	Huddersfield T	4	0	**4**	**0**
2008–09	Bradford C	27	3	**27**	**3**
2009–10	Walsall	30	9	**30**	**9**

MATTIS, Dwayne (M) — 245 19

H: 6 1 W: 11 12 b.Huddersfield 31-7-81
Source: Trainee. Honours: Eire Youth, Under-21.

Season	Club				
1998–99	Huddersfield T	2	0		
1999–2000	Huddersfield T	0	0		
2000–01	Huddersfield T	0	0		
2001–02	Huddersfield T	5	0		
2002–03	Huddersfield T	33	1		
2003–04	Huddersfield T	5	0	**69**	**2**
2004–05	Bury	39	5		
2005–06	Bury	36	5		
2006–07	Bury	22	1	**97**	**11**
2006–07	Barnsley	3	0		
2007–08	Barnsley	1	0	**4**	**0**
2007–08	Walsall	4	0		
2008–09	Walsall	37	4		
2009–10	Walsall	34	2	**75**	**6**

McDONALD, Clayton (D) — 30 1

H: 6 6 W: 16 05 b.Liverpool 26-12-88
Source: Scholar.

Season	Club				
2007–08	Manchester C	0	0		
2008–09	Manchester C	0	0		
2008–09	Macclesfield T	2	0	**2**	**0**
2008–09	Chesterfield	2	0	**2**	**0**
2009–10	Manchester C	0	0		
2009–10	Walsall	26	1	**26**	**1**

NICHOLLS, Alex (F) — 109 12

H: 5 10 W: 11 00 b.Stourbridge 9-12-87
Source: Scholar.

Season	Club				
2005–06	Walsall	8	0		
2006–07	Walsall	19	2		
2007–08	Walsall	19	2		
2008–09	Walsall	45	6		
2009–10	Walsall	37	4	**109**	**12**

O'KEEFE, Josh (M) — 13 0

H: 6 1 W: 11 05 b.Whalley 22-12-88
Source: Scholar. Honours: Eire Under-21.

Season	Club				
2005–06	Blackburn R	0	0		
2006–07	Blackburn R	0	0		
2007–08	Blackburn R	0	0		
2008–09	Blackburn R	0	0		
2009–10	Walsall	13	0	**13**	**0**

PARKIN, Sam (F) — 295 97

H: 6 2 W: 13 00 b.Roehampton 14-3-81
Honours: England Schools. Scotland B.

Season	Club				
1998–99	Chelsea	0	0		
1999–2000	Chelsea	0	0		
2000–01	Chelsea	0	0		
2000–01	Millwall	7	4	**7**	**4**
2000–01	Wycombe W	8	1	**8**	**1**
2000–01	Oldham Ath	7	3	**7**	**3**
2001–02	Chelsea	0	0		
2001–02	Northampton T	40	4	**40**	**4**
2002–03	Swindon T	43	25		
2003–04	Swindon T	40	19		
2004–05	Swindon T	41	23	**124**	**67**
2005–06	Ipswich T	20	5		
2006–07	Ipswich T	2	0	**22**	**5**
2006–07	Luton T	8	1		
2007–08	Luton T	19	5		
2008–09	Luton T	23	4	**50**	**10**
2008–09	Leyton Orient	13	0	**13**	**0**
2009–10	Walsall	24	3	**24**	**3**

RICHARDS, Matt (D) — 240 13

H: 5 8 W: 11 00 b.Harlow 26-12-84
Source: Scholar. Honours: England Under-21.

Season	Club				
2001–02	Ipswich T	0	0		
2002–03	Ipswich T	13	0		
2003–04	Ipswich T	44	1		
2004–05	Ipswich T	24	1		
2005–06	Ipswich T	38	4		
2006–07	Ipswich T	28	2		
2007–08	Ipswich T	0	0		
2007–08	Brighton & HA	28	0		
2008–09	Brighton & HA	23	1	**51**	**1**
2008–09	Wycombe W	0	0		
2008–09	Notts Co	1	0	**1**	**0**
2008–09	Ipswich T	1	0	**148**	**8**
2009–10	Walsall	40	4	**40**	**4**

ROBERTS, Steve (D) — 239 8

H: 6 1 W: 11 02 b.Wrexham 24-2-80
Source: Trainee. Honours: Wales Youth, Under-21, 1 full cap.

Season	Club				
1997–98	Wrexham	0	0		
1998–99	Wrexham	0	0		
1999–2000	Wrexham	19	0		
2000–01	Wrexham	7	0		
2001–02	Wrexham	24	1		
2002–03	Wrexham	39	2		
2003–04	Wrexham	27	0		
2004–05	Wrexham	34	3	**150**	**6**
2005–06	Doncaster R	27	1		
2006–07	Doncaster R	21	0		
2007–08	Doncaster R	25	0	**73**	**1**
2008–09	Walsall	15	1		
2009–10	Walsall	1	0	**16**	**1**

SANSARA, Netan (D) — 27 0

H: 6 0 W: 12 00 b.Darlaston 3-8-89
Source: Scholar. Honours: England Youth.

Season	Club				
2006–07	Walsall	0	0		
2007–08	Walsall	0	0		
2008–09	Walsall	10	0		
2009–10	Walsall	17	0	**27**	**0**

SMITH, Manny (D) 66 4
H: 6 2 W: 12 03 b.Birmingham 8-11-87
Source: Scholar.

2005–06	Walsall	0	0	
2006–07	Walsall	3	0	
2007–08	Walsall	4	0	
2008–09	Walsall	26	0	
2009–10	Walsall	33	4	66 4

TAUNDRY, Richard (D) 89 3
H: 5 9 W: 12 10 b.Walsall 15-2-89
Source: Scholar.

2007–08	Walsall	21	0	
2008–09	Walsall	38	0	
2009–10	Walsall	30	3	89 3

TILL, Peter (M) 144 5
H: 5 11 W: 11 04 b.Walsall 7-9-85
Source: Scholar.

2005–06	Birmingham C	0	0	
2005–06	*Scunthorpe U*	8	0	8 0
2005–06	*Boston U*	16	1	16 1
2006–07	Birmingham C	0	0	
2006–07	*Leyton Orient*	4	0	4 0
2006–07	Grimsby T	22	0	
2007–08	Grimsby T	34	2	
2008–09	Grimsby T	16	2	72 4
2008–09	*Chesterfield*	16	0	16 0
2009–10	Walsall	28	0	28 0

VINCENT, Jamie (D) 420 10
H: 5 10 W: 11 08 b.Wimbledon 18-6-75
Source: Trainee.

1993–94	Crystal Palace	0	0	
1994–95	Crystal Palace	0	0	
1994–95	*Bournemouth*	8	0	
1995–96	Crystal Palace	25	0	
1996–97	Crystal Palace	0	0	25 0
1996–97	Bournemouth	29	0	
1997–98	Bournemouth	44	3	
1998–99	Bournemouth	32	2	113 5
1998–99	Huddersfield T	7	0	
1999–2000	Huddersfield T	36	2	
2000–01	Huddersfield T	16	0	59 2
2000–01	Portsmouth	14	0	
2001–02	Portsmouth	34	1	
2002–03	Portsmouth	0	0	
2003–04	Portsmouth	0	0	48 1
2003–04	*Walsall*	12	0	
2003–04	Derby Co	7	1	
2004–05	Derby Co	15	1	22 2
2005–06	Millwall	19	0	19 0
2005–06	Yeovil T	0	0	
2006–07	Swindon T	34	0	
2007–08	Swindon T	32	0	
2008–09	Swindon T	18	0	84 0
2009–10	Walsall	38	0	50 0

WESTLAKE, Darryl (D) 22 0
H: 5 9 W: 11 00 b.Sutton Coldfield 1-3-91
Source: Scholar.

2009–10	Walsall	22	0	22 0

WESTON, Rhys (D) 300 3
H: 6 1 W: 12 12 b.Kingston 27-10-80
Source: Trainee. *Honours:* Wales Schools, Youth, Under-21, 7 full caps.

1999–2000	Arsenal	1	0	
2000–01	Arsenal	0	0	1 0
2000–01	Cardiff C	28	0	
2001–02	Cardiff C	37	0	
2002–03	Cardiff C	38	2	
2003–04	Cardiff C	24	0	
2004–05	Cardiff C	25	0	
2005–06	Cardiff C	30	0	182 2
2006–07	Port Vale	15	0	15 0
2007–08	Walsall	44	0	
2008–09	Walsall	31	1	
2009–10	Walsall	27	0	102 1

WATFORD (86)

BENNETT, Dale (D) 10 0
H: 5 11 W: 12 02 b.Watford 6-1-90
Source: Scholar.

2008–09	Watford	0	0	
2009–10	Watford	10	0	10 0

BROOKS, Kurtney (M) 0 0
H: 5 9 W: 10 03 b.Slough 14-9-91
Source: Scholar.

2009–10	Watford	0	0

BRYAN, Michael (M) 7 0
H: 5 8 W: 10 00 b.Wexford 21-2-90
Honours: Northern Ireland Under-21, 2 full caps.

2008–09	Watford	0	0	
2009–10	Watford	7	0	7 0

BUCKLEY, Will (F) 65 14
H: 6 0 W: 13 00 b.Burnley 12-8-88
Source: Curzon Ashton.

2007–08	Rochdale	7	0	
2008–09	Rochdale	37	10	
2009–10	Rochdale	15	3	59 13
2009–10	Watford	6	1	6 1

COWIE, Don (M) 276 34
H: 5 5 W: 8 05 b.Inverness 15-2-83
Honours: Scotland 2 full caps.

2000–01	Ross Co	1	0	
2001–02	Ross Co	18	0	
2002–03	Ross Co	30	1	
2003–04	Ross Co	23	0	
2004–05	Ross Co	34	5	
2005–06	Ross Co	32	4	
2006–07	Ross Co	28	7	166 17
2007–08	Inverness CT	37	9	
2008–09	Inverness CT	22	3	59 12
2008–09	Watford	10	3	
2009–10	Watford	41	2	51 5

DEMERIT, Jay (D) 182 8
H: 6 2 W: 12 13 b.Green Bay 4-12-79
Source: Chicago Fire, Univ of Illinois, Northwood. *Honours:* USA 23 full caps.

2004–05	Watford	24	3	
2005–06	Watford	32	2	
2006–07	Watford	32	2	
2007–08	Watford	35	1	
2008–09	Watford	32	0	
2009–10	Watford	27	0	182 8

DOYLEY, Lloyd (D) 262 1
H: 5 10 W: 12 13 b.Whitechapel 1-12-82
Source: Scholar.

2000–01	Watford	0	0	
2001–02	Watford	20	0	
2002–03	Watford	22	0	
2003–04	Watford	9	0	
2004–05	Watford	29	0	
2005–06	Watford	44	0	
2006–07	Watford	21	0	
2007–08	Watford	36	0	
2008–09	Watford	37	0	
2009–10	Watford	44	1	262 1

ELLINGTON, Nathan (F) 396 116
H: 5 10 W: 13 01 b.Bradford 2-7-81
Source: Walton & Hersham.

1998–99	Bristol R	10	1	
1999–2000	Bristol R	37	4	
2000–01	Bristol R	42	15	
2001–02	Bristol R	27	15	116 35
2001–02	Wigan Ath	3	2	
2002–03	Wigan Ath	42	15	
2003–04	Wigan Ath	44	18	
2004–05	Wigan Ath	45	24	134 59
2005–06	WBA	31	5	
2006–07	WBA	34	9	
2007–08	WBA	3	0	68 14
2007–08	Watford	34	4	
2008–09	Watford	0	0	
2008–09	*Derby Co*	27	3	27 3
2009–10	Watford	17	1	51 5

EUSTACE, John (M) 261 20
H: 5 11 W: 11 12 b.Solihull 3-11-79
Source: Trainee.

1996–97	Coventry C	0	0	
1997–98	Coventry C	0	0	
1998–99	Coventry C	0	0	
1998–99	Dundee U	11	1	11 1
1999–2000	Coventry C	16	1	
2000–01	Coventry C	32	2	
2001–02	Coventry C	6	0	
2002–03	Coventry C	32	4	86 7
2002–03	*Middlesbrough*	1	0	1 0
2003–04	Stoke C	26	5	
2004–05	Stoke C	7	0	
2005–06	Stoke C	0	0	
2006–07	Stoke C	15	0	
2006–07	*Hereford U*	8	0	8 0
2007–08	Stoke C	26	0	74 5

2007–08	Watford	13	0	
2008–09	Watford	17	2	
2008–09	*Derby Co*	9	1	9 1
2009–10	Watford	42	4	72 6

GRAHAM, Danny (F) 191 54
H: 5 11 W: 12 05 b.Gateshead 12-8-85
Source: Trainee. *Honours:* England Youth, Under-20.

2003–04	Middlesbrough	0	0	
2003–04	*Darlington*	9	2	9 2
2004–05	Middlesbrough	11	1	
2005–06	Middlesbrough	3	0	
2005–06	*Derby Co*	14	0	14 0
2005–06	*Leeds U*	3	0	3 0
2006–07	Middlesbrough	1	0	15 1
2006–07	*Blackpool*	4	1	4 1
2006–07	Carlisle U	11	7	
2007–08	Carlisle U	45	14	
2008–09	Carlisle U	44	15	100 36
2009–10	Watford	46	14	46 14

HARLEY, Jon (D) 332 14
H: 5 8 W: 10 03 b.Maidstone 26-9-79
Source: Trainee. *Honours:* England Under-21.

1996–97	Chelsea	0	0	
1997–98	Chelsea	3	0	
1998–99	Chelsea	0	0	
1999–2000	Chelsea	17	2	
2000–01	Chelsea	10	0	30 2
2000–01	*Wimbledon*	6	2	6 2
2001–02	Fulham	10	0	
2002–03	Fulham	11	1	
2002–03	*Sheffield U*	9	1	
2003–04	Fulham	4	0	25 1
2003–04	*Sheffield U*	5	0	
2003–04	*West Ham U*	15	1	15 1
2004–05	Sheffield U	44	2	
2005–06	Sheffield U	4	0	62 3
2005–06	Burnley	41	2	
2006–07	Burnley	45	1	
2007–08	Burnley	33	0	119 3
2008–09	Watford	37	1	
2009–10	Watford	38	1	75 2

HENDERSON, Liam (F) 26 0
H: 5 11 W: 12 02 b.Gateshead 28-12-89
Source: Hartlepool U.

2008–09	Watford	5	0	
2008–09	*Hartlepool U*	8	0	8 0
2009–10	Watford	13	0	18 0

HODSON, Lee (D) 32 0
H: 5 11 W: 11 02 b.Boreham Wood 2-10-91
Source: Scholar. *Honours:* Northern Ireland Under-21.

2008–09	Watford	1	0	
2009–10	Watford	31	0	32 0

HOSKINS, Will (F) 145 32
H: 5 11 W: 11 02 b.Nottingham 6-5-86
Source: Scholar. *Honours:* England Youth, Under-20.

2003–04	Rotherham U	4	2	
2004–05	Rotherham U	22	2	
2005–06	Rotherham U	23	4	
2006–07	Rotherham U	24	15	73 23
2006–07	Watford	9	0	
2007–08	Watford	1	0	
2007–08	*Millwall*	10	2	10 2
2007–08	*Nottingham F*	2	0	2 0
2008–09	Watford	32	4	
2009–10	Watford	18	3	60 7

JENKINS, Ross (M) 53 1
H: 5 11 W: 12 06 b.Watford 9-11-90
Source: Scholar. *Honours:* England Under-20.

2008–09	Watford	29	1	
2009–10	Watford	24	0	53 1

KIERNAN, Rob (M) 0 0
H: 6 1 W: 11 13 b.Rickmansworth 13-1-91
Source: Scholar.

2008–09	Watford	0	0
2009–10	Watford	0	0

LEE, Richard (D) 92 0
H: 6 0 W: 12 06 b.Oxford 5-10-82
Source: Scholar. *Honours:* England Under-20.

2000–01	Watford	0	0
2001–02	Watford	0	0

2002–03	Watford	4	0		
2003–04	Watford	0	0		
2004–05	Watford	33	0		
2005–06	Watford	0	0		
2005–06	*Blackburn R*	0	0		
2006–07	Watford	10	0		
2007–08	Watford	35	0		
2008–09	Watford	10	0		
2009–10	Watford	0	0	92	0

LOACH, Scott (G)   99   0
H: 6 1   W: 13 01   b.Nottingham 27-5-88
Source: Lincoln C. *Honours:* England Under-21.

2006–07	Watford	0	0		
2007–08	Watford	0	0		
2007–08	*Morecambe*	2	0	2	0
2007–08	*Bradford C*	20	0	20	0
2008–09	Watford	31	0		
2009–10	Watford	46	0	77	0

MARIAPPA, Adrian (D)   132   2
H: 5 10   W: 11 12   b.Harrow 3-10-86
Source: Scholar.

2005–06	Watford	3	0		
2006–07	Watford	19	0		
2007–08	Watford	25	0		
2008–09	Watford	39	1		
2009–10	Watford	46	1	132	2

MASSEY, Gavin (F)   1   0
H: 5 11   W: 11 06   b.Watford 14-10-92
Source: Scholar.

2009–10	Watford	1	0	1	0

McGINN, Stephen (M)   82   7
H: 5 9   W: 10 01   b.Glasgow 2-12-88
Honours: Scotland Under-21.

2006–07	St Mirren	4	1		
2007–08	St Mirren	25	2		
2008–09	St Mirren	26	1		
2009–10	St Mirren	18	3	73	7
2009–10	Watford	9	0	9	0

OSHODI, Eddie (D)   1   0
H: 6 3   W: 12 07   b.Brentford 14-1-92
Source: Scholar.

2008–09	Watford	0	0		
2009–10	Watford	1	0	1	0

SADLER, Matthew (D)   108   0
H: 5 11   W: 11 08   b.Birmingham 26-2-85
Source: Scholar. *Honours:* England Youth.

2001–02	Birmingham C	0	0		
2002–03	Birmingham C	2	0		
2003–04	Birmingham C	0	0		
2003–04	*Northampton T*	7	0	7	0
2004–05	Birmingham C	0	0		
2005–06	Birmingham C	8	0		
2006–07	Birmingham C	36	0		
2007–08	Birmingham C	5	0	51	0
2007–08	Watford	15	0		
2008–09	Watford	15	0		
2009–10	Watford	0	0	30	0
2009–10	*Stockport Co*	20	0	20	0

SEVERIN, Scott (D)   324   26
H: 5 11   W: 12 13   b.Stirling 15-2-79
Honours: Scotland 15 full caps.

1998–99	Hearts	7	0		
1999–2000	Hearts	23	2		
2000–01	Hearts	29	4		
2001–02	Hearts	27	3		
2002–03	Hearts	37	4		
2003–04	Hearts	26	1	149	14
2004–05	Aberdeen	31	1		
2005–06	Aberdeen	28	3		
2006–07	Aberdeen	35	4		
2007–08	Aberdeen	35	3		
2008–09	Aberdeen	37	1	166	12
2009–10	Watford	9	0	9	0

SORDELL, Marvin (F)   14   2
H: 5 9   W: 12 06   b.Brent 17-2-91
Source: Scholar.

2009–10	Watford	6	1	6	1
2009–10	*Tranmere R*	8	1	8	1

TAYLOR, Martin (D)   225   10
H: 6 4   W: 15 00   b.Ashington 9-11-79
Source: Trainee. *Honours:* England Youth, Under-21.

1997–98	Blackburn R	0	0		
1998–99	Blackburn R	3	0		
1999–2000	Blackburn R	6	0		
1999–2000	*Darlington*	4	0	4	0
1999–2000	*Stockport Co*	7	0	7	0
2000–01	Blackburn R	16	3		
2001–02	Blackburn R	19	0		
2002–03	Blackburn R	33	2		
2003–04	Blackburn R	11	0	88	5
2003–04	Birmingham C	12	1		
2004–05	Birmingham C	7	0		
2005–06	Birmingham C	21	0		
2006–07	Birmingham C	31	0		
2007–08	Birmingham C	4	0		
2007–08	*Norwich C*	8	1	8	1
2008–09	Birmingham C	24	1		
2009–10	Birmingham C	0	0	99	2
2009–10	Watford	19	2	19	2

TRAVNER, Jure (D)   115   1
H: 5 11   W: 12 08   b.Celje 28-9-85

2004–05	Publikum Celje	2	0		
2005–06	Publikum Celje	20	0		
2006–07	Publikum Celje	31	0	58	0
2007–08	Celje	28	0		
2008–09	Celje	29	1	57	1
2009–10	Watford	0	0		

YOUNG, Lewis (M)   7   0
H: 5 10   W: 11 02   b.Stevenage 27-9-89
Source: Scholar.

2008–09	Watford	1	0		
2009–10	Watford	0	0	1	0
2009–10	*Hereford U*	6	0	6	0

WBA (87)

BARNES, Giles (M)   91   10
H: 6 0   W: 12 10   b.Barking 5-8-88
Source: Scholar. *Honours:* England Youth.

2005–06	Derby Co	19	1		
2006–07	Derby Co	39	8		
2007–08	Derby Co	21	1		
2008–09	Derby Co	3	0		
2008–09	*Fulham*	0	0		
2009–10	Derby Co	0	0	82	10
2009–10	WBA	9	0	9	0

BARNETT, Leon (D)   124   6
H: 6 0   W: 12 04   b.Stevenage 30-11-85
Source: Scholar.

2003–04	Luton T	0	0		
2004–05	Luton T	0	0		
2005–06	Luton T	20	0		
2006–07	Luton T	39	3	59	3
2007–08	WBA	32	3		
2008–09	WBA	11	0		
2009–10	WBA	0	0	45	3
2009–10	*Coventry C*	20	0	20	0

BEDNAR, Roman (F)   147   47
H: 6 3   W: 13 03   b.Prague 26-3-83
Honours: Czech Republic Under-21, 3 full caps.

2001–02	Mlada Boleslav	0	0		
2002–03	Mlada Boleslav	0	0		
2003–04	Mlada Boleslav	0	0		
2004–05	Mlada Boleslav	25	6	25	6
2004–05	Kaunas	0	0		
2005–06	Hearts	22	7		
2006–07	Hearts	18	4	40	11
2007–08	WBA	29	13		
2008–09	WBA	26	6		
2009–10	WBA	27	11	82	30

BORJA VALERO (M)   141   8
H: 5 9   W: 11 07   b.Madrid 12-1-85
Honours: Spain Youth.

2005–06	R M Castilla	0	0		
2005–06	R M Castilla	39	2		
2006–07	R M Castilla	37	2	76	4
2007–08	*Mallorca*	34	4	34	4
2008–09	WBA	30	0		
2009–10	WBA	1	0	31	0

BRUNT, Chris (M)   248   49
H: 6 1   W: 13 04   b.Belfast 14-12-84
Source: Trainee. *Honours:* Northern Ireland Under-21, Under-23, 26 full caps, 1 goal.

2002–03	Middlesbrough	0	0		
2003–04	Middlesbrough	0	0		
2003–04	Sheffield W	9	2		
2004–05	Sheffield W	42	4		
2005–06	Sheffield W	44	7		
2006–07	Sheffield W	44	11		
2007–08	Sheffield W	1	0	140	24
2007–08	WBA	34	4		
2008–09	WBA	34	8		
2009–10	WBA	40	13	108	25

CARSON, Scott (G)   165   0
H: 6 3   W: 14 00   b.Whitehaven 3-9-85
Source: Scholar. *Honours:* England Youth, Under-21, B, 3 full caps.

2002–03	Leeds U	0	0		
2003–04	Leeds U	3	0		
2004–05	Leeds U	0	0	3	0
2004–05	Liverpool	4	0		
2005–06	Liverpool	0	0		
2005–06	*Sheffield W*	9	0	9	0
2006–07	Liverpool	0	0		
2006–07	*Charlton Ath*	36	0	36	0
2007–08	Liverpool	0	0	4	0
2007–08	*Aston Villa*	35	0	35	0
2008–09	WBA	35	0		
2009–10	WBA	43	0	78	0

CECH, Marek (D)   181   5
H: 6 0   W: 11 09   b.Trebisov 26-1-83
Honours: Slovakia 41 full caps, 5 goals.

2000–01	Inter Bratislava	2	0		
2001–02	Inter Bratislava	13	0		
2002–03	Inter Bratislava	30	0		
2003–04	Inter Bratislava	26	1	71	1
2004–05	Sparta Prague	17	0		
2005–06	Sparta Prague	0	0	17	0
2005–06	Porto	14	1		
2006–07	Porto	22	1		
2007–08	Porto	16	0	52	2
2008–09	WBA	8	0		
2009–10	WBA	33	2	41	2

COX, Simon (F)   132   56
H: 5 10   W: 10 12   b.Reading 28-4-87
Source: Scholar.

2005–06	Reading	2	0		
2006–07	Reading	0	0		
2006–07	*Brentford*	13	0	13	0
2006–07	*Northampton T*	8	3	8	3
2007–08	Reading	0	0	2	0
2007–08	Swindon T	36	15		
2008–09	Swindon T	45	29	81	44
2009–10	WBA	28	9	28	9

DANIELS, Luke (G)   77   0
H: 6 1   W: 12 10   b.Bolton 5-1-88
Source: Manchester U Scholar. *Honours:* England Youth.

2006–07	WBA	0	0		
2007–08	*Motherwell*	2	0	2	0
2007–08	WBA	0	0		
2008–09	WBA	0	0		
2008–09	*Shrewsbury T*	38	0	38	0
2009–10	WBA	0	0		
2009–10	*Tranmere R*	37	0	37	0

DORRANS, Graham (M)   144   34
H: 5 9   W: 11 00   b.Glasgow 5-5-87
Honours: Scotland Youth, Under-21, 3 full caps.

2006–07	Livingston	8	0		
2006–07	*Partick T*	15	5	15	5
2006–07	Livingston	34	5		
2007–08	Livingston	34	11	76	16
2008–09	WBA	8	0		
2009–10	WBA	45	13	53	13

DOWNING, Paul (D)   6   0
H: 6 1   W: 12 06   b.Taunton 26-10-91
Source: Scholar.

2009–10	WBA	0	0		
2009–10	*Hereford U*	6	0	6	0

ELFORD-ALLIYU, Lateef (F)   1   0
H: 5 8   W: 10 12   b.Ibadan 1-6-92
Source: Scholar

2009–10	WBA	0	0		
2009–10	*Hereford U*	1	0	1	0

GREENING, Jonathan (M)   357   14
H: 5 11   W: 11 00   b.Scarborough 2-1-79
Source: Trainee. *Honours:* England Youth, Under-21.

1996–97	York C	5	0		

1997–98	York C	20	2	25	2
1997–98	Manchester U	0	0		
1998–99	Manchester U	3	0		
1999–2000	Manchester U	4	0		
2000–01	Manchester U	7	0	14	0
2001–02	Middlesbrough	36	1		
2002–03	Middlesbrough	38	2		
2003–04	Middlesbrough	25	1	99	4
2004–05	WBA	34	0		
2005–06	WBA	38	2		
2006–07	WBA	42	2		
2007–08	WBA	46	1		
2008–09	WBA	34	2		
2009–10	WBA	2	0	196	7
2009–10	*Fulham*	23	1	23	1

HABER, Marcus (F)   5 0
H: 6 3   W: 13 05   b.Vancouver 11-1-89
Source: Vancouver W. *Honours:* Canada Youth.

2009–10	WBA	0	0		
2009–10	*Exeter C*	5	0	5	0

JARA, Gonzalo (D)   155 4
H: 5 10   W: 12 02   b.Chile 29-8-85
Honours: Chile 38 full caps, 3 goals.

2002	Huachipato	0	0		
2003	Huachipato	17	1		
2004	Huachipato	11	0		
2005	Huachipato	23	0		
2006	Huachipato	18	1	69	2
2007	Colo Colo	23	1		
2008	Colo Colo	25	0		
2009	Colo Colo	16	0	64	1
2009–10	WBA	22	1	22	1

KIELY, Dean (G)   664 0
H: 6 1   W: 13 10   b.Salford 10-10-70
Source: WBA School. *Honours:* England Schools, FA Schools, Youth, Eire B, 11 full caps.

1987–88	Coventry C	0	0		
1988–89	Coventry C	0	0		
1989–90	Coventry C	0	0		
1989–90	*Ipswich T*	0	0		
1989–90	*York C*	0	0		
1990–91	York C	17	0		
1991–92	York C	21	0		
1992–93	York C	40	0		
1993–94	York C	46	0		
1994–95	York C	46	0		
1995–96	York C	40	0	210	0
1996–97	Bury	46	0		
1997–98	Bury	46	0		
1998–99	Bury	45	0	137	0
1999–2000	Charlton Ath	45	0		
2000–01	Charlton Ath	25	0		
2001–02	Charlton Ath	38	0		
2002–03	Charlton Ath	38	0		
2003–04	Charlton Ath	37	0		
2004–05	Charlton Ath	36	0		
2005–06	Charlton Ath	3	0	222	0
2005–06	Portsmouth	15	0		
2006–07	Portsmouth	0	0	15	0
2006–07	*Luton T*	11	0	11	0
2006–07	WBA	17	0		
2007–08	WBA	44	0		
2008–09	WBA	3	0		
2009–10	WBA	5	0	69	0

KOREN, Robert (M)   342 68
H: 5 10   W: 11 03   b.Ljubljana 20-9-80
Honours: Slovenia Under-21, 49 full caps, 4 goals.

1999–2000	Dravograd	31	2		
2000–01	Dravograd	31	9	62	11
2001–02	Publikum	31	5		
2002–03	Publikum	32	12		
2003–04	Publikum	15	5	78	22
2004	Lillestrom	23	1		
2005	Lillestrom	26	8		
2006	Lillestrom	26	10	75	19
2006–07	WBA	18	1		
2007–08	WBA	40	9		
2008–09	WBA	35	1		
2009–10	WBA	34	5	127	16

LABADIE, Joss (M)   34 8
H: 5 7   W: 11 02   b.London 31-8-90

2008–09	WBA	0	0		
2008–09	*Shrewsbury T*	1	0		
2009–10	WBA	0	0		
2009–10	*Shrewsbury T*	13	5	14	5
2009–10	*Cheltenham T*	11	0	11	0
2009–10	*Tranmere R*	9	3	9	3

MATTOCK, Joe (D)   95 1
H: 5 11   W: 12 05   b.Leicester 15-5-90
Source: Scholar. *Honours:* England Youth, Under-21.

2006–07	Leicester C	4	0		
2007–08	Leicester C	31	0		
2008–09	Leicester C	31	1		
2009–10	Leicester C	0	0	66	1
2009–10	WBA	29	0	29	0

MEITE, Abdoulaye (D)   214 2
H: 6 1   W: 12 13   b.Paris 6-10-80
Honours: Ivory Coast 48 full caps, 1 goal.

1998–99	Red Star 93	4	1		
1999–2000	Red Star 93	0	0	4	1
2000–01	Marseille	1	0		
2001–02	Marseille	10	0		
2002–03	Marseille	28	0		
2003–04	Marseille	30	0		
2004–05	Marseille	34	1		
2005–06	Marseille	13	0	116	1
2006–07	Bolton W	35	0		
2007–08	Bolton W	21	0	56	0
2008–09	WBA	18	0		
2009–10	WBA	20	0	38	0

MILLER, Ishmael (F)   81 14
H: 6 3   W: 14 00   b.Manchester 5-3-87
Source: Scholar.

2005–06	Manchester C	1	0		
2006–07	Manchester C	16	0		
2007–08	Manchester C	0	0	17	0
2007–08	WBA	34	9		
2008–09	WBA	15	3		
2009–10	WBA	15	2	64	14

MOORE, Luke (F)   150 23
H: 5 11   W: 11 13   b.Birmingham 13-2-86
Source: Trainee. *Honours:* FA Schools, England Youth, Under-21.

2002–03	Aston Villa	0	0		
2003–04	Aston Villa	7	0		
2003–04	*Wycombe W*	6	4	6	4
2004–05	Aston Villa	25	1		
2005–06	Aston Villa	27	8		
2006–07	Aston Villa	13	4		
2007–08	Aston Villa	15	1	87	14
2007–08	*WBA*	10	0		
2008–09	WBA	21	1		
2009–10	WBA	26	4	57	5

MORRISON, James (M)   143 11
H: 5 10   W: 10 06   b.Darlington 25-5-86
Source: Trainee. *Honours:* England Youth, Under-20. Scotland 5 full caps.

2003–04	Middlesbrough	1	0		
2004–05	Middlesbrough	14	0		
2005–06	Middlesbrough	24	1		
2006–07	Middlesbrough	28	2	67	3
2007–08	WBA	35	4		
2008–09	WBA	30	3		
2009–10	WBA	11	1	76	8

MULUMBU, Youssef (M)   82 4
H: 5 9   W: 10 03   b.Kinshasa 25-1-87
Honours: France Youth, Under-21. DR Congo 8 full caps.

2006–07	Paris St Germain	12	0		
2007–08	Paris St Germain	1	0		
2007–08	*Amiens*	23	1	23	1
2008–09	Paris St Germain	0	0	13	0
2008–09	WBA	6	0		
2009–10	WBA	40	3	46	3

OLSSON, Jonas (D)   220 12
H: 6 4   W: 12 08   b.Landskrona 10-3-83
Honours: Sweden Under-21, 1 full cap.

2002	Landskrona	0	0		
2003	Landskrona	22	0		
2004	Landskrona	22	1		
2005	Landskrona	12	0	56	1
2005–06	NEC Nijmegen	34	0		
2006–07	NEC Nijmegen	32	2		
2007–08	NEC Nijmegen	27	3	93	5
2008–09	WBA	28	2		
2009–10	WBA	43	4	71	6

REID, Reuben (F)   95 22
H: 6 0   W: 12 02   b.Bristol 26-7-88

2005–06	Plymouth Arg	1	0		
2006–07	Plymouth Arg	6	0		
2006–07	*Rochdale*	2	0	2	0
2006–07	*Torquay U*	7	2	7	2
2007–08	Plymouth Arg	0	0	7	0
2007–08	*Wycombe W*	11	1	11	1
2007–08	*Brentford*	10	1	10	1
2008–09	Rotherham U	41	18	41	18
2009–10	WBA	4	0	4	0
2009–10	*Peterborough U*	13	0	13	0

ROBINSON, Paul (D)   458 12
H: 5 9   W: 11 12   b.Watford 14-12-78
Source: Trainee. *Honours:* England Under-21.

1996–97	Watford	12	0		
1997–98	Watford	22	2		
1998–99	Watford	29	0		
1999–2000	Watford	32	0		
2000–01	Watford	39	0		
2001–02	Watford	38	3		
2002–03	Watford	37	3		
2003–04	Watford	10	0	219	8
2003–04	WBA	31	0		
2004–05	WBA	30	1		
2005–06	WBA	33	0		
2006–07	WBA	42	2		
2007–08	WBA	43	1		
2008–09	WBA	35	0		
2009–10	WBA	0	0	214	4
2009–10	*Bolton W*	25	0	25	0

SAWYERS, Romaine (M)   0 0
H: 5 9   W: 11 00   b.Birmingham 11-10-90
Source: Scholar.

2009–10	WBA	0	0

SLORY, Andwele (M)   198 54
H: 5 8   W: 11 00   b.Paramaribo 27-9-82

2000–01	Telstar	0	0		
2001–02	Stormvogels	9	0		
2002–03	Stormvogels	2	0		
2003–04	Stormvogels	35	12		
2004–05	Stormvogels	31	9	77	21
2005–06	Excelsior	36	14		
2006–07	Excelsior	29	12	65	26
2007–08	Feyenoord	17	2		
2008–09	Feyenoord	20	1		
2009–10	Feyenoord	13	4	50	7
2009–10	WBA	6	0	6	0

TAMAS, Gabriel (D)   217 12
H: 6 2   W: 12 02   b.Brasov 9-11-83
Honours: Romania 46 full caps, 3 goals.

1998–99	Brasov	1	0		
1999–2000	Brasov	0	0	1	0
2000–01	Tractorul	15	1		
2001–02	Tractorul	19	2	34	3
2002–03	Dinamo Bucharest	19	4		
2003–04	Galatasaray	6	0	6	0
2004	Spartak Moscow	14	0		
2004–05	Dinamo Bucharest	13	0		
2005–06	Dinamo Bucharest	14	1		
2006	Spartak Moscow	3	0	17	0
2006–07	Celta Vigo	29	0	29	0
2007–08	Auxerre	27	0	27	0
2008–09	Dinamo Bucharest	22	0		
2009–10	Dinamo Bucharest	12	2	80	7
2009–10	WBA	23	2	23	2

TEIXEIRA, Felipe (F)   256 31
H: 5 9   W: 10 10   b.Paris 2-10-80
Honours: Portugal Under-21.

1998–99	Felgueiras	27	1		
1999–2000	Felgueiras	27	5		
2000–01	Felgueiras	31	9	85	15
2001–02	Istres	16	2	16	2
2002–03	Paris St Germain	8	2		
2003–04	Paris St Germain	0	0		
2003–04	*Uniao Leiria*	15	3	15	3
2004–05	Paris St Germain	10	0	18	2
2005–06	Academica	30	3		
2006–07	Academica	29	1	59	4
2007–08	WBA	30	5		
2008–09	WBA	10	0		
2009–10	WBA	9	0	49	5
2009–10	*Barnsley*	14	0	14	0

THOMAS, Jerome (M)   143   17
H: 5 9   W: 11 09   b.Wembley 23-3-83
Source: Scholar. *Honours:* England Youth,
Under-20, Under-21.

2001–02	Arsenal	0	0		
2001–02	QPR	4	1		
2002–03	Arsenal	0	0		
2002–03	QPR	6	2	10	3
2003–04	Arsenal	0	0		
2003–04	Charlton Ath	1	0		
2004–05	Charlton Ath	24	3		
2005–06	Charlton Ath	25	1		
2006–07	Charlton Ath	20	3		
2007–08	Charlton Ath	32	0		
2008–09	Charlton Ath	1	0	103	7
2008–09	Portsmouth	3	0		
2009–10	Portsmouth	0	0	3	0
2009–10	WBA	27	7	27	7

THORNE, George (M)   1   0
H: 6 2   W: 13 01   b.Chatham 4-1-93
Source: Scholar. *Honours:* England Youth.

2009–10	WBA	1	0	1	0

WOOD, Chris (F)   20   1
H: 6 3   W: 12 10   b.Auckland 7-12-91
Honours: New Zealand Youth, 12 full caps.

2008–09	WBA	2	0		
2009–10	WBA	18	1	20	1

ZUIVERLOON, Gianni (D)   160   8
H: 5 10   W: 11 00   b.Rotterdam 30-12-86
Honours: Holland Under-21.

2004–05	Feyenoord	9	0	9	0
2005–06	RKC Waalwijk	28	1	28	1
2006–07	Heerenveen	30	1		
2007–08	Heerenveen	30	2	60	3
2008–09	WBA	33	0		
2009–10	WBA	30	4	63	4

WEST HAM U (88)

ABDULLAH, Ahmad (F)   0   0
b.Saudi Arabia 12-11-91
Source: Scholar.

2008–09	West Ham U	0	0
2009–10	West Ham U	0	0

ASHTON, Dean (F)   249   92
H: 6 2   W: 14 07   b.Crewe 24-11-83
Source: Schoolboy. *Honours:* England Youth,
Under-20, Under-21, 1 full cap.

2000–01	Crewe Alex	21	8		
2001–02	Crewe Alex	31	7		
2002–03	Crewe Alex	39	9		
2003–04	Crewe Alex	44	19		
2004–05	Crewe Alex	24	17	159	60
2004–05	Norwich C	16	7		
2005–06	Norwich C	28	10	44	17
2005–06	West Ham U	11	3		
2006–07	West Ham U	0	0		
2007–08	West Ham U	31	10		
2008–09	West Ham U	4	2		
2009–10	West Ham U	0	0	46	15

BEHRAMI, Valon (M)   176   9
H: 6 0   W: 11 02   b.Kosovka Mitrovika
19-4-85
Honours: Switzerland 28 full caps, 2 goals.

2002–03	Lugano	2	0	2	0
2003–04	Genoa	24	0	24	0
2004–05	Verona	33	3	33	3
2005–06	Lazio	26	2		
2006–07	Lazio	17	1		
2007–08	Lazio	23	1	66	4
2008–09	West Ham U	24	1		
2009–10	West Ham U	27	1	51	2

BOA MORTE, Luis (F)   313   47
H: 5 9   W: 12 06   b.Lisbon 4-8-77
Source: Sporting Lisbon, Lourihanense
(loan). *Honours:* Portugal Youth, Under-21,
28 full caps, 1 goal.

1997–98	Arsenal	15	0		
1998–99	Arsenal	8	0		
1999–2000	Arsenal	2	0	25	0
1999–2000	Southampton	14	1		
2000–01	Southampton	0	0	14	1
2000–01	Fulham	39	18		
2001–02	Fulham	23	1		

2002–03	Fulham	29	2		
2003–04	Fulham	33	9		
2004–05	Fulham	31	8		
2005–06	Fulham	35	6		
2006–07	Fulham	15	0	205	44
2006–07	West Ham U	14	1		
2007–08	West Ham U	27	0		
2008–09	West Ham U	27	0		
2009–10	West Ham U	1	1	69	2

COLE, Carlton (F)   185   38
H: 6 3   W: 14 02   b.Croydon 12-11-83
Source: Scholar. *Honours:* England Youth,
Under-20, Under-21, 7 full caps.

2000–01	Chelsea	0	0		
2001–02	Chelsea	3	1		
2002–03	Chelsea	13	3		
2002–03	Wolverhampton W	7	1	7	1
2003–04	Chelsea	0	0		
2003–04	Charlton Ath	21	4	21	4
2004–05	Chelsea	0	0		
2004–05	Aston Villa	27	3	27	3
2005–06	Chelsea	9	0	25	4
2006–07	West Ham U	17	2		
2007–08	West Ham U	31	4		
2008–09	West Ham U	27	10		
2009–10	West Ham U	30	10	105	26

COLLISON, Jack (M)   44   5
H: 6 0   W: 13 13   b.Watford 2-10-88
Source: Scholar. *Honours:* Wales Under-21, 1
full caps.

2007–08	West Ham U	2	0		
2008–09	West Ham U	20	3		
2009–10	West Ham U	22	2	44	5

DA COSTA, Manuel (D)   44   3
H: 6 1   W: 12 12   b.Saint-Max 6-5-86

2005–06	Nancy	10	0	10	0
2006–07	PSV Eindhoven	15	1		
2007–08	PSV Eindhoven	1	0	16	1
2008–09	Fiorentina	1	0	1	0
2008–09	Sampdoria	2	0	2	0
2009–10	West Ham U	15	2	15	2

DAPRELA, Fabio (D)   35   0
H: 5 11   W: 10 03   b.Ticino 19-2-91
Source: YF Juventus. *Honours:* Switzerland
Youth, Under-21.

2007–08	Grasshoppers	16	0		
2008–09	Grasshoppers	12	0	28	0
2009–10	West Ham U	7	0	7	0

DAVENPORT, Calum (D)   144   6
H: 6 4   W: 14 00   b.Bedford 1-1-83
Source: Trainee. *Honours:* England Youth,
Under-20, Under-21.

1999–2000	Coventry C	0	0		
2000–01	Coventry C	1	0		
2001–02	Coventry C	3	0		
2002–03	Coventry C	32	3		
2003–04	Coventry C	33	0		
2004–05	Coventry C	6	0	75	3
2004–05	Southampton	7	0	7	0
2004–05	Tottenham H	1	0		
2004–05	West Ham U	10	0		
2004–05	Tottenham H	4	0		
2005–06	Norwich C	15	1	15	1
2006–07	Tottenham H	10	1	15	1
2006–07	West Ham U	6	0		
2007–08	West Ham U	0	0		
2007–08	Watford	1	0	1	0
2008–09	West Ham U	7	1		
2008–09	Sunderland	8	0	8	0
2009–10	West Ham U	0	0	23	1

DIAMANTI, Alessandro (F)   139   30
H: 5 9   W: 11 09   b.Prato 2-5-83

2002–03	Prato	2	0		
2003–04	Prato	20	4		
2004–05	Albinoleffe	18	0		
2005–06	Prato	13	5		
2005–06	Albinoleffe	8	0	26	0
2006–07	Prato	25	10	60	19
2007–08	Livorno	26	4	26	4
2009–10	West Ham U	27	7	27	7

DYER, Kieron (M)   300   32
H: 5 8   W: 10 01   b.Ipswich 29-12-78
Source: Trainee. *Honours:* England Youth,
Under-21, B, 33 full caps.

1996–97	Ipswich T	13	0		

1997–98	Ipswich T	41	4		
1998–99	Ipswich T	37	5	91	9
1999–2000	Newcastle U	30	3		
2000–01	Newcastle U	26	5		
2001–02	Newcastle U	18	3		
2002–03	Newcastle U	35	2		
2003–04	Newcastle U	25	1		
2004–05	Newcastle U	23	4		
2005–06	Newcastle U	11	0		
2006–07	Newcastle U	22	5		
2007–08	Newcastle U	0	0	190	23
2007–08	West Ham U	2	0		
2008–09	West Ham U	7	0		
2009–10	West Ham U	10	0	19	0

EDGAR, Anthony (M)   3   0
H: 5 8   W: 11 00   b.London 30-9-90
Source: Scholar.

2009–10	West Ham U	0	0		
2009–10	Bournemouth	3	0	3	0

EYJOLFSSON, Holmar (D)   4   0
H: 6 2   W: 11 08   b.Iceland 6-8-90

2008–09	West Ham U	0	0		
2009–10	West Ham U	0	0		
2009–10	Cheltenham T	4	0	4	0

FAUBERT, Julien (M)   203   14
H: 5 10   W: 11 08   b.Le Havre 1-8-83
Honours: France 1 full cap, 1 goal.

2002–03	Cannes	26	1		
2003–04	Cannes	19	3	45	4
2004–05	Bordeaux	36	1		
2005–06	Bordeaux	34	5		
2006–07	Bordeaux	26	3	96	9
2007–08	West Ham U	7	0		
2008–09	West Ham U	20	0		
2008–09	Real Madrid	2	0	2	0
2009–10	West Ham U	33	1	60	1

FRANCO, Guillermo (F)   301   90
H: 5 10   W: 12 08   b.Corrientes 3-11-76
Honours: Mexico 25 full caps, 7 goals.

1995–96	San Lorenzo	3	0		
1996–97	San Lorenzo	6	0		
1997–98	San Lorenzo	10	1		
1998–99	San Lorenzo	5	0		
1999–2000	San Lorenzo	26	10		
2000–01	San Lorenzo	19	7		
2001–02	San Lorenzo	26	5	96	23
2002–03	Monterrey	33	10		
2003–04	Monterrey	30	12		
2004–05	Monterrey	22	17		
2005–06	Monterrey	16	9	101	48
2005–06	Villarreal	12	4		
2006–07	Villarreal	27	2		
2007–08	Villarreal	24	8		
2008–09	Villarreal	18	0	81	14
2009–10	West Ham U	23	5	23	5

FRY, Matt (D)   11   0
H: 6 1   W: 12 02   b.Ebbsfleet 26-9-90
Source: Scholar.

2009–10	West Ham U	0	0		
2009–10	Gillingham	11	0	11	0

GABBIDON, Daniel (D)   287   10
H: 6 0   W: 13 05   b.Cwmbran 8-8-79
Source: Trainee. *Honours:* Wales Youth,
Under-21, 43 full caps.

1998–99	WBA	2	0		
1999–2000	WBA	18	0		
2000–01	WBA	0	0	20	0
2000–01	Cardiff C	43	3		
2001–02	Cardiff C	44	3		
2002–03	Cardiff C	24	0		
2003–04	Cardiff C	41	3		
2004–05	Cardiff C	45	1	197	10
2005–06	West Ham U	32	0		
2006–07	West Ham U	18	0		
2007–08	West Ham U	10	0		
2008–09	West Ham U	0	0		
2009–10	West Ham U	10	0	70	0

GREEN, Rob (G)   363   0
H: 6 3   W: 14 09   b.Chertsey 18-1-80
Source: Trainee. *Honours:* England Youth, B,
11 full caps.

1997–98	Norwich C	0	0
1998–99	Norwich C	2	0
1999–2000	Norwich C	3	0
2000–01	Norwich C	5	0

2001–02	Norwich C	41	0	
2002–03	Norwich C	46	0	
2003–04	Norwich C	46	0	
2004–05	Norwich C	38	0	
2005–06	Norwich C	42	0	223 0
2006–07	West Ham U	26	0	
2007–08	West Ham U	38	0	
2008–09	West Ham U	38	0	
2009–10	West Ham U	38	0	140 0

HINES, Zavon (F)   20 2
H: 5 10   W: 10 07   b.Jamaica 27-12-88
Source: Scholar. *Honours:* England Under-21.

2007–08	West Ham U	0	0	
2007–08	Coventry C	7	1	7 1
2008–09	West Ham U	0	0	
2009–10	West Ham U	13	1	13 1

ILAN (F)   260 79
H: 5 11   W: 11 13   b.Curitiba 18-9-80
Honours: Brazil 3 full caps.

1999	Parana	12	2	12 2
2000	Sao Paulo	12	1	12 1
2001	At Paranense	15	3	
2002	At Paranense	1	0	
2003	At Paranense	30	16	
2004	At Paranense	18	3	64 22
2004–05	Sochaux	27	14	
2005–06	Sochaux	27	10	54 24
2006–07	St Etienne	33	9	
2007–08	St Etienne	31	6	
2008–09	St Etienne	31	9	
2009–10	St Etienne	12	2	107 26
2009–10	West Ham U	11	4	11 4

ILUNGA, Herita (D)   221 2
H: 5 11   W: 11 09   b.Kinshasa 25-2-82
Honours: DR Congo 18 full caps.

2002–03	Espanyol B	0	0	
2003–04	St Etienne	32	0	
2004–05	St Etienne	37	1	
2005–06	St Etienne	30	1	
2006–07	St Etienne	36	0	135 2
2007–08	Toulouse	35	0	35 0
2008–09	West Ham U	35	0	
2009–10	West Ham U	16	0	51 0

JIMENEZ, Luis (M)   164 34
H: 6 0   W: 12 06   b.Santiago 17-6-84
Honours: Chile 20 full caps, 2 goals.

2001	Palestino	5	0	
2002	Palestino	4	0	9 0
2002–03	Temana	6	1	
2003–04	Temana	34	10	
2004–05	Temana	32	11	
2005–06	Temana	16	3	88 25
2005–06	Fiorentina	19	3	19 3
2006–07	Lazio	16	2	16 2
2007–08	Internazionale	15	3	
2008–09	Internazionale	6	0	21 3

On loan from Internazionale.

| 2009–10 | West Ham U | 11 | 1 | 11 1 |

KOVAC, Radoslav (D)   314 18
H: 6 2   W: 12 04   b.Sumperk 27-11-79
Honours: Czech Republic Under-21, 31 full caps, 2 goals.

1997–98	Olomouc	1	0	
1998–99	Olomouc	20	0	
1999–2000	Olomouc	28	0	
2000–01	Olomouc	27	0	
2001–02	Olomouc	23	1	
2002–03	Olomouc	28	2	127 3
2003–04	Sparta Prague	29	3	
2004–05	Sparta Prague	17	0	46 3
2005	Spartak Moscow	27	4	
2006	Spartak Moscow	27	2	
2007	Spartak Moscow	26	1	
2008	Spartak Moscow	21	2	101 9
2008–09	West Ham U	9	1	
2009–10	Sparta Prague	31	2	40 3

KURUCZ, Peter (G)   10 0
H: 6 2   W: 13 09   b.Hungary 30-5-88
Honours: Hungary Under-21.

2008–09	Ujpest	0	0	
2008–09	Tatabanya	9	0	9 0
2009–10	West Ham U	1	0	1 0

LEE, Oliver (M)   0 0
b. 11-7-91
Source: Scholar.

| 2009–10 | West Ham U | 0 | 0 | |

McCARTHY, Benni (F)   358 156
H: 6 0   W: 12 08   b.Ciudad de Cabo 11-12-77
Honours: South Africa 83 caps, 31 goals.

1995–96	Seven Stars	29	27	
1996–97	Seven Stars	20	12	49 39
1997–98	Cape Town Spurs	7	4	7 4
1997–98	Ajax	17	9	
1998–99	Ajax	19	11	36 20
1999–2000	Celta Vigo	31	8	
2000–01	Celta Vigo	19	0	
2001–02	Celta Vigo	2	0	
2001–02	Porto	11	12	
2002–03	Celta Vigo	14	2	66 10
2003–04	Porto	29	20	
2004–05	Porto	23	11	
2005–06	Porto	23	3	86 46
2006–07	Blackburn R	36	18	
2007–08	Blackburn R	31	8	
2008–09	Blackburn R	28	10	
2009–10	Blackburn R	14	1	109 37
2009–10	West Ham U	5	0	5 0

MODELSKI, Filip (D)   0 0
b.Poland 28-9-92
Source: Scholar.

| 2009–10 | West Ham U | 0 | 0 | |

N'GALA, Bondz (D)   14 0
H: 6 0   W: 12 03   b.Newham 13-9-89
Source: Scholar.

2007–08	West Ham U	0	0	
2008–09	West Ham U	0	0	
2008–09	Milton Keynes D	3	0	3 0
2009–10	West Ham U	0	0	
2009–10	Scunthorpe U	2	0	2 0
2009–10	Plymouth Arg	9	0	9 0

NOBLE, Mark (M)   133 11
H: 5 11   W: 12 00   b.West Ham 8-5-87
Source: Scholar. *Honours:* England Youth, Under-21.

2004–05	West Ham U	13	0	
2005–06	West Ham U	5	0	
2005–06	Hull C	5	0	5 0
2006–07	West Ham U	10	2	
2006–07	Ipswich T	13	1	13 1
2007–08	West Ham U	31	3	
2008–09	West Ham U	29	3	
2009–10	West Ham U	27	2	115 10

NOUBLE, Frank (F)   19 0
H: 6 3   W: 12 08   b.Marseille 24-9-91
Source: Chelsea Scholar. *Honours:* France Youth, England Youth.

2009–10	West Ham U	8	0	8 0
2009–10	WBA	3	0	3 0
2009–10	Swindon T	8	0	8 0

PARKER, Scott (M)   281 19
H: 5 9   W: 11 10   b.Lambeth 13-10-80
Source: Trainee. *Honours:* England Schools, Youth, Under-21, 3 full caps.

1997–98	Charlton Ath	3	0	
1998–99	Charlton Ath	4	0	
1999–2000	Charlton Ath	15	1	
2000–01	Charlton Ath	20	1	
2000–01	Norwich C	6	1	6 1
2001–02	Charlton Ath	38	1	
2002–03	Charlton Ath	28	4	
2003–04	Charlton Ath	20	2	128 9
2003–04	Chelsea	11	1	
2004–05	Chelsea	4	0	15 1
2005–06	Newcastle U	26	1	
2006–07	Newcastle U	29	3	55 4
2007–08	West Ham U	18	1	
2008–09	West Ham U	28	1	
2009–10	West Ham U	31	2	77 4

PAYNE, Josh (M)   19 2
H: 6 0   W: 11 09   b.Basingstoke 25-11-90
Source: Scholar.

2008–09	West Ham U	0	0	
2008–09	Cheltenham T	11	1	11 1
2009–10	West Ham U	0	0	2 0
2009–10	Colchester U	3	0	3 0
2009–10	Wycombe W	3	1	3 1

SEARS, Freddie (F)   53 1
H: 5 8   W: 10 01   b.Hornchurch 27-11-89
Source: Scholar. *Honours:* England Youth, Under-21.

2007–08	West Ham U	7	1	
2008–09	West Ham U	17	0	
2009–10	West Ham U	1	0	25 1
2009–10	Crystal Palace	18	0	18 0
2009–10	Coventry C	10	0	10 0

SPECTOR, Jonathan (D)   110 0
H: 6 0   W: 12 08   b.Arlington Heights 1-3-86
Source: Chicago Sockers. *Honours:* USA Youth, 25 full caps.

2003–04	Manchester U	0	0	
2004–05	Manchester U	3	0	
2005–06	Manchester U	0	0	3 0
2005–06	Charlton Ath	20	0	20 0
2006–07	West Ham U	25	0	
2007–08	West Ham U	26	0	
2008–09	West Ham U	9	0	
2009–10	West Ham U	27	0	87 0

SPENCE, Jordan (M)   30 0
H: 6 2   W: 12 07   b.Woodford 24-5-90
Source: Scholar. *Honours:* England Youth.

2007–08	West Ham U	0	0	
2008–09	West Ham U	0	0	
2008–09	Leyton Orient	20	0	20 0
2009–10	West Ham U	1	0	1 0
2009–10	Scunthorpe U	9	0	9 0

STANISLAS, Junior (M)   41 6
H: 6 0   W: 12 00   b.Kidbrooke 26-11-89
Source: Scholar. *Honours:* England Youth, Under-21.

2007–08	West Ham U	0	0	
2008–09	West Ham U	9	2	
2008–09	Southend U	6	1	6 1
2009–10	West Ham U	26	3	35 5

STECH, Marek (G)   3 0
H: 6 3   W: 14 00   b.Prague 28-1-90
Source: Sparta Prague, West Ham U Scholar.
Honours: Czech Republic Youth.

2008–09	West Ham U	0	0	
2008–09	Wycombe W	2,	0	2 0
2009–10	West Ham U	0	0	
2009–10	Bournemouth	1	0	1 0

STREET, Adam (G)   0 0
b.Canada 7-7-91

| 2008–09 | West Ham U | 0 | 0 | |
| 2009–10 | West Ham U | 0 | 0 | |

TOMKINS, James (D)   48 1
H: 6 3   W: 11 10   b.Basildon 29-3-89
Source: Scholar. *Honours:* England Schools, Youth, Under-21.

2005–06	West Ham U	0	0	
2006–07	West Ham U	0	0	
2007–08	West Ham U	6	0	
2008–09	West Ham U	12	1	
2008–09	Derby Co	7	0	7 0
2009–10	West Ham U	23	0	41 1

UPSON, Matthew (D)   271 9
H: 6 1   W: 11 04   b.Stowmarket 18-4-79
Source: Trainee. *Honours:* England Youth, Under-21, 21 full caps, 2 goals.

1995–96	Luton T	0	0	
1996–97	Luton T	1	0	1 0
1996–97	Arsenal	5	0	
1997–98	Arsenal	5	0	
1998–99	Arsenal	5	0	
1999–2000	Arsenal	8	0	
2000–01	Arsenal	2	0	
2000–01	Nottingham F	1	0	1 0
2000–01	Crystal Palace	7	0	7 0
2001–02	Arsenal	14	0	
2002–03	Arsenal	0	0	34 0
2002–03	Reading	14	0	14 0
2002–03	Birmingham C	14	0	
2003–04	Birmingham C	30	0	
2004–05	Birmingham C	36	2	
2005–06	Birmingham C	24	1	
2006–07	Birmingham C	9	2	113 5
2006–07	West Ham U	2	0	
2007–08	West Ham U	29	1	
2008–09	West Ham U	37	0	
2009–10	West Ham U	33	3	101 4

WEAREN, Eoin Patrick (M)   0 0
b. 2-10-92
Source: Scholar.

| 2009–10 | West Ham U | 0 | 0 | |

Scholars
Brown, Jordan; Cowler, Samuel Paul; Craig, Paco; Driver, Callum; McNaughton, Callum James; Mehmet, Deniz Dogan; Moncur, George; Monsergas Sanchez, Sergio; Montano, Cristian; Purdy, Daniel; Smith, Miles Alexander; Subuola, Daniel; Werndly, Jack.

WIGAN ATH (89)

AMAYA, Antonio (D)   163   7
H: 6 3   W: 13 07   b.Madrid 31-5-83

2002–03	Rayo Vallecano B	23	2	23	2
2003–04	SS Reyes	15	0	15	0
2004–05	Rayo Vallecano	22	0		
2005–06	Rayo Vallecano	22	0		
2006–07	Rayo Vallecano	34	1		
2007–08	Rayo Vallecano	29	3		
2008–09	Rayo Vallecano	18	1	125	5
2009–10	Wigan Ath	0	0		

BOYCE, Emmerson (D)   365   14
H: 6 0   W: 12 03   b.Aylesbury 24-9-79
Source: Trainee. *Honours:* Barbados 2 full caps.

1997–98	Luton T	0	0		
1998–99	Luton T	1	0		
1999–2000	Luton T	30	1		
2000–01	Luton T	42	3		
2001–02	Luton T	37	0		
2002–03	Luton T	34	0		
2003–04	Luton T	42	4	186	8
2004–05	Crystal Palace	27	0		
2005–06	Crystal Palace	42	2	69	2
2006–07	Wigan Ath	34	0		
2007–08	Wigan Ath	25	0		
2008–09	Wigan Ath	27	1		
2009–10	Wigan Ath	24	3	110	4

BRAMBLE, Titus (D)   251   9
H: 6 2   W: 13 10   b.Ipswich 31-7-81
Source: Trainee. *Honours:* England Under-21.

1998–99	Ipswich T	4	0		
1999–2000	Ipswich T	0	0		
1999–2000	Colchester U	2	0	2	0
2000–01	Ipswich T	26	1		
2001–02	Ipswich T	18	0	48	1
2002–03	Newcastle U	16	0		
2003–04	Newcastle U	29	0		
2004–05	Newcastle U	19	1		
2005–06	Newcastle U	24	2		
2006–07	Newcastle U	17	0	105	3
2007–08	Wigan Ath	26	2		
2008–09	Wigan Ath	35	1		
2009–10	Wigan Ath	35	2	96	5

CALDWELL, Gary (D)   270   12
H: 5 11   W: 11 10   b.Stirling 12-4-82
Source: Trainee. *Honours:* Scotland Under-21, 37 full caps, 2 goals.

1998–99	Newcastle U	0	0		
1999–2000	Newcastle U	0	0		
2000–01	Newcastle U	0	0		
2001–02	Newcastle U	0	0		
2001–02	Darlington	4	0	4	0
2001–02	Hibernian	11	0	11	0
2002–03	Newcastle U	0	0		
2002–03	Coventry C	36	0	36	0
2003–04	Newcastle U	0	0		
2003–04	Derby Co	9	0	9	0
2003–04	Hibernian	17	1		
2004–05	Hibernian	37	3		
2005–06	Hibernian	34	1	99	5
2006–07	Celtic	21	0		
2007–08	Celtic	35	1		
2008–09	Celtic	36	3		
2009–10	Celtic	14	1	106	5
2009–10	Wigan Ath	16	2	16	2

CHO, Won-Hee (M)   5   0
H: 5 10   W: 11 07   b.South Korea 17-4-83
Honours: South Korea 36 full caps, 1 goal.

2008–09	Wigan Ath	1	0		
2009–10	Wigan Ath	4	0	5	0

On loan to Blue Wings.

CYWKA, Thomasz (M)   9   0
H: 5 10   W: 11 09   b.Gliwice 27-6-88
Source: Gwarek Zabrze. *Honours:* Poland Youth, Under-21.

2006–07	Wigan Ath	0	0		
2006–07	Oldham Ath	4	0	4	0
2007–08	Wigan Ath	0	0		
2008–09	Wigan Ath	0	0		
2009–10	Wigan Ath	0	0		
2009–10	Derby Co	5	0	5	0

DE RIDDER, Daniel (M)   78   4
H: 5 11   W: 10 12   b.Amsterdam 6-3-84
Honours: Holland Under-21.

2003–04	Ajax	15	1		
2004–05	Ajax	15	2	30	3
2005–06	Celta Vigo	17	1		
2006–07	Celta Vigo	3	0	20	1
2007–08	Birmingham C	10	0	10	0
2008–09	Wigan Ath	18	0		
2009–10	Wigan Ath	0	0	18	0

On loan to Hapoel Tel Aviv.

DIAME, Mohamed (M)   100   4
H: 6 1   W: 11 02   b.Creteil 14-6-87

2006–07	Lens	0	0		
2007–08	Linares	31	1	31	1
2008–09	Rayo Vallecano	35	2	35	2
2009–10	Wigan Ath	34	1	34	1

EDMAN, Erik (D)   262   3
H: 5 10   W: 12 04   b.Huskvarna 11-11-78
Source: Habo. *Honours:* Sweden 57 full caps, 1 goal.

1997	Helsingborg	24	0		
1998	Helsingborg	25	0		
1999	Helsingborg	12	1	61	1
1999–2000	Torino	0	0		
1999–2000	Karlsruher	8	0	8	0
2000	AIK Stockholm	8	0		
2001	AIK Stockholm	13	0	21	0
2001–02	Heerenveen	33	1		
2002–03	Heerenveen	30	0	63	1
2004–05	Tottenham H	28	1		
2005–06	Tottenham H	3	0	31	1
2005–06	Rennes	26	0		
2006–07	Rennes	30	0		
2007–08	Rennes	12	0	68	0
2007–08	Wigan Ath	5	0		
2008–09	Wigan Ath	2	0		
2009–10	Wigan Ath	3	0	10	0

FIGUEROA, Maynor (D)   99   4
H: 5 11   W: 12 02   b.Jutiapa 2-5-83
Honours: Honduras 72 full caps, 2 goals.

2000–01	Victoria La Ceiba	2	0		
2001–02	Victoria La Ceiba	22	2	24	2
2007–08	Wigan Ath	2	0		
2008–09	Wigan Ath	38	1		
2009–10	Wigan Ath	35	1	75	2

GOHOURI, Steve (D)   229   37
H: 6 2   W: 13 01   b.Treichville 8-2-81
Honours: Ivory Coast 8 full caps, 3 goals.

1999–2000	Paris St Germain B	1	0	1	0
1999–2000	Bnei Yehuda	13	4	13	4
2000–01	Yverdon	34	9		
2001–02	Yverdon	18	2		
2002–03	Yverdon	20	1	72	12
2002–03	Bologna	0	0		
2003–04	Vaduz	18	5		
2004–05	Vaduz	28	5		
2005–06	Vaduz	7	0	53	10
2005–06	Young Boys	20	5		
2006–07	Young Boys	16	3	36	8
2006–07	Mgladbach	14	0		
2007–08	Mgladbach	17	0		
2008–09	Mgladbach	15	2	46	2
2009–10	Mgladbach II	3	0	3	0
2009–10	Wigan Ath	5	1	5	1

GOMEZ, Jordi (M)   90   13
H: 5 10   W: 11 09   b.Barcelona 24-5-85

2006–07	Espanyol B	21	0	21	0
2007–08	Espanyol	2	0	2	0

On loan from Espanyol.

2008–09	Swansea C	44	12		
2009–10	Swansea C	0	0	44	12
2009–10	Wigan Ath	23	1	23	1

HOLT, Joe (M)   0   0
H: 5 10   W: 10 05   b.Huyton 1-2-90
Source: Scholar.

2008–09	Wigan Ath	0	0		
2009–10	Wigan Ath	0	0		

On loan to Ostersund.

KAPO, Olivier (M)   234   35
H: 6 1   W: 12 06   b.Abidjan 27-9-80
Honours: France 9 full caps, 3 goals.

1999–2000	Auxerre	15	3		
2000–01	Auxerre	29	4		
2001–02	Auxerre	25	4		
2002–03	Auxerre	21	6		
2003–04	Auxerre	29	2	119	19
2004–05	Juventus	14	0	14	0
2005–06	Monaco	25	5	25	5
2006–07	Levante	30	5	30	5
2007–08	Birmingham C	26	5	26	5
2008–09	Wigan Ath	19	1		
2009–10	Wigan Ath	1	0	20	1

On loan to Bologne.

KING, Marlon (F)   345   108
H: 5 10   W: 12 10   b.Dulwich 26-4-80
Source: Trainee. *Honours:* Jamaica 19 full caps, 12 goals.

1998–99	Barnet	22	6		
1999–2000	Barnet	31	8	53	14
2000–01	Gillingham	38	15		
2001–02	Gillingham	42	17		
2002–03	Gillingham	10	4		
2003–04	Gillingham	11	4	101	40
2003–04	Nottingham F	24	5		
2004–05	Nottingham F	26	5		
2004–05	Leeds U	9	0	9	0
2005–06	Nottingham F	0	0	50	10
2005–06	Watford	41	21		
2006–07	Watford	13	4		
2007–08	Watford	27	11	81	36
2007–08	Wigan Ath	15	1		
2008–09	Wigan Ath	0	0		
2008–09	Hull C	20	5	20	5
2008–09	Middlesbrough	13	2	13	2
2009–10	Wigan Ath	3	0	18	1

KIRKLAND, Christopher (G)   186   0
H: 6 5   W: 14 08   b.Leicester 2-5-81
Source: Trainee. *Honours:* England Youth, Under-21, 1 full cap.

1997–98	Coventry C	0	0		
1998–99	Coventry C	0	0		
1999–2000	Coventry C	0	0		
2000–01	Coventry C	23	0		
2001–02	Coventry C	1	0	24	0
2001–02	Liverpool	1	0		
2002–03	Liverpool	8	0		
2003–04	Liverpool	6	0		
2004–05	Liverpool	10	0		
2005–06	Liverpool	0	0		
2005–06	WBA	10	0	10	0
2006–07	Liverpool	0	0	25	0
2007–08	Wigan Ath	26	0		
2007–08	Wigan Ath	37	0		
2008–09	Wigan Ath	32	0		
2009–10	Wigan Ath	32	0	127	0

KOUMAS, Jason (M)   348   62
H: 5 10   W: 11 02   b.Wrexham 25-9-79
Source: Trainee. *Honours:* Wales 34 full caps, 10 goals.

1997–98	Tranmere R	0	0		
1998–99	Tranmere R	23	3		
1999–2000	Tranmere R	23	2		
2000–01	Tranmere R	39	10		
2001–02	Tranmere R	38	8		
2002–03	WBA	4	2	127	25
2002–03	WBA	32	4		
2003–04	WBA	42	10		
2004–05	WBA	10	0		
2005–06	WBA	0	0		
2005–06	Cardiff C	44	12	44	12
2006–07	WBA	39	9	123	23
2007–08	Wigan Ath	30	1		
2008–09	Wigan Ath	16	0		
2009–10	Wigan Ath	8	1	54	2

McCARTHY, James (M)   115   15
H: 5 11   W: 11 05   b.Glasgow 12-11-90
Honours: Eire Youth, Under-21, 1 full cap.

2006–07	Hamilton A	23	1		

2007–08	Hamilton A	35	7		
2008–09	Hamilton A	37	6	95	14
2009–10	Wigan Ath	20	1	20	1

McMANAMAN, Callum (F) 1 0
H: 5 9 W: 11 03 b.Huyton 25-4-91
Source: Everton.

| 2008–09 | Wigan Ath | 1 | 0 | | |
| 2009–10 | Wigan Ath | 0 | 0 | 1 | 0 |

MELCHIOT, Mario (D) 387 9
H: 6 2 W: 11 09 b.Amsterdam 4-11-76
Honours: Holland 22 full caps.

1996–97	Ajax	23	0		
1997–98	Ajax	26	0		
1998–99	Ajax	24	1	73	1
1999–2000	Chelsea	5	0		
2000–01	Chelsea	31	0		
2001–02	Chelsea	37	2		
2002–03	Chelsea	34	1		
2003–04	Chelsea	23	2	130	4
2004–05	Birmingham C	34	1		
2005–06	Birmingham C	23	1	57	2
2006–07	Rennes	30	2	30	2
2007–08	Wigan Ath	31	0		
2008–09	Wigan Ath	34	0		
2009–10	Wigan Ath	32	0	97	0

MORENO, Marcelo (M) 45 9
H: 6 2 W: 12 13 b.Santa Cruz de la Sierra 18-6-87
Source: Vitoria. Honours: Bolivia 17 full caps, 7 goals.

2007	Cruzeiro	13	6		
2008	Cruzeiro	1	1	14	7
2008–09	Shakhtar Donetsk	14	2	14	2
2009–10	Werder Bremen	5	0	5	0
2009–10	Wigan Ath	12	0	12	0

MOSES, Victor (F) 72 12
H: 5 10 W: 11 07 b.Lagos 12-12-90
Source: Scholar. Honours: England Youth.

2007–08	Crystal Palace	13	3		
2008–09	Crystal Palace	27	2		
2009–10	Crystal Palace	18	6	58	11
2009–10	Wigan Ath	14	1	14	1

MUSTOE, Jordan (M) 0 0
b.Wirral 28-1-91
Source: Scholar.

| 2009–10 | Wigan Ath | 0 | 0 | | |

N'ZOGBIA, Charles (M) 166 15
H: 5 9 W: 11 00 b.Le Havre 28-5-86
Honours: France Youth, Under-21.

2004–05	Newcastle U	14	0		
2005–06	Newcastle U	32	5		
2006–07	Newcastle U	22	0		
2007–08	Newcastle U	31	3		
2008–09	Newcastle U	18	1	117	9
2008–09	Wigan Ath	13	1		
2009–10	Wigan Ath	36	5	49	6

NICHOLLS, Lee (G) 0 0
b.Huyton 5-10-92
Source: Scholar.

| 2009–10 | Wigan Ath | 0 | 0 | | |

POLLITT, Mike (G) 502 0
H: 6 4 W: 15 03 b.Farnworth 29-2-72
Source: Trainee.

1990–91	Manchester U	0	0		
1990–91	Oldham Ath	0	0		
1991–92	Bury	0	0		
1992–93	Lincoln C	27	0		
1993–94	Lincoln C	30	0	57	0
1994–95	Darlington	40	0		
1995–96	Darlington	15	0	55	0
1995–96	Notts Co	0	0		
1996–97	Notts Co	8	0		
1997–98	Notts Co	2	0	10	0
1997–98	Oldham Ath	16	0	16	0
1997–98	Gillingham	6	0	6	0
1997–98	Brentford	5	0	5	0
1997–98	Sunderland	0	0		
1998–99	Rotherham U	46	0		
1999–2000	Rotherham U	46	0		
2000–01	Chesterfield	46	0	46	0
2001–02	Rotherham U	46	0		
2002–03	Rotherham U	41	0		
2003–04	Rotherham U	43	0		
2004–05	Rotherham U	45	0	267	0
2005–06	Wigan Ath	24	0		
2006–07	Wigan Ath	3	0		
2006–07	Ipswich T	1	0	1	0
2006–07	Burnley	4	0	4	0
2007–08	Wigan Ath	1	0		
2008–09	Wigan Ath	3	0		
2009–10	Wigan Ath	4	0	35	0

REDMOND, Daniel (D) 0 0
b. 2-3-91
Source: Scholar.

| 2009–10 | Wigan Ath | 0 | 0 | | |

RODALLEGA, Hugo (F) 210 90
H: 5 11 W: 11 05 b.Valle del Cauca 25-7-85
Honours: Colombia 31 full caps, 8 goals.

2004	Quindio	32	31	32	31
2005	Dep Cali	26	12	26	12
2005–06	Monterrey	14	3		
2006–07	Atlas	17	5	17	5
2006–07	Monterrey	15	1	29	4
2007–08	Necaxa	36	16		
2008–09	Necaxa	17	9	53	25
2008–09	Wigan Ath	15	3		
2009–10	Wigan Ath	38	10	53	13

ROUTLEDGE, Jon (M) 1 0
H: 5 7 W: 11 05 b.Liverpool 23-11-89
Source: Liverpool.

| 2008–09 | Wigan Ath | 1 | 0 | | |
| 2009–10 | Wigan Ath | 0 | 0 | 1 | 0 |

On loan to Ostersund.

SCHARNER, Paul (D) 279 27
H: 6 3 W: 12 09 b.Scheibbs 11-3-80
Source: St Polten. Honours: Austria Youth, Under-21, 30 full caps.

1998–99	FK Austria	4	0		
1999–2000	FK Austria	12	0		
2000–01	FK Austria	14	0		
2001–02	FK Austria	16	1		
2002–03	FK Austria	29	1		
2003–04	FK Austria	9	1	84	3
2003–04	Salzburg	13	2		
2004	Brann	7	1		
2004–05	Salzburg	5	1	18	3
2005	Brann	25	6	32	7
2005–06	Wigan Ath	16	3		
2006–07	Wigan Ath	25	3		
2007–08	Wigan Ath	37	4		
2008–09	Wigan Ath	29	0		
2009–10	Wigan Ath	38	4	145	14

SCOTLAND, Jason (F) 238 86
H: 5 8 W: 11 10 b.Morvant 18-2-79
Source: San Juan Jabloteh, Defence Force. Honours: Trinidad & Tobago 41 full caps, 8 goals.

2003–04	Dundee U	21	4		
2004–05	Dundee U	29	3	50	7
2005–06	St Johnstone	31	15		
2006–07	St Johnstone	35	18	66	33
2007–08	Swansea C	45	24		
2008–09	Swansea C	45	21		
2009–10	Swansea C	0	0	90	45
2009–10	Wigan Ath	32	1	32	1

SERRANO, Abian (M) 0 0
Source: Las Palmas.

| 2009–10 | Wigan Ath | 0 | 0 | | |

STOJKOVIC, Vladimir (G) 97 0
H: 6 4 W: 14 07 b.Loznica 28-7-83
Honours: Serbia 36 full caps.

2001–02	Red Star Belgrade	1	0		
2002–03	Red Star Belgrade	1	0		
2003–04	Leotar	4	0	4	0
2003–04	Lemun	5	0		
2004–05	Lemun	28	0	33	0
2005–06	Red Star Belgrade	22	0	24	0
2006–07	Nantes	10	0	10	0
2006–07	Vitesse	8	0	8	0
2007–08	Sporting Lisbon	9	0	9	0
2008–09	Getafe	5	0	5	0
2009–10	Wigan Ath	4	0	4	0

THOMAS, Hendry (M) 31 0
H: 5 11 W: 12 08 b.La Ceiba 23-2-85
Source: Club Olimpija. Honours: Honduras 43 full caps, 2 goals.

| 2009–10 | Wigan Ath | 31 | 0 | 31 | 0 |

WATSON, Ben (M) 207 24
H: 5 10 W: 10 11 b.Camberwell 9-7-85
Source: Scholar. Honours: England Under-21.

2002–03	Crystal Palace	5	0		
2003–04	Crystal Palace	16	1		
2004–05	Crystal Palace	21	0		
2005–06	Crystal Palace	42	4		
2006–07	Crystal Palace	25	3		
2007–08	Crystal Palace	42	5		
2008–09	Crystal Palace	18	5	169	18
2008–09	Wigan Ath	10	2		
2009–10	Wigan Ath	5	1	15	3
2009–10	QPR	16	2	16	2
2009–10	WBA	7	1	7	1

ZAKI, Amr (F) 213 87
H: 6 1 W: 13 05 b.Mansoura 1-4-83
Honours: Egypt 57 full caps, 28 goals.

2001–02	Mansoura	3	1		
2002–03	Mansoura	17	19	20	20
2003–04	ENPPI	22	8		
2004–05	ENPPI	26	10		
2005–06	ENPPI	16	9	64	27
2006	Lokomotiv Moscow	0	0		
2006–07	Zamalek	21	10		
2007–08	Zamalek	23	7		
2008–09	Wigan Ath	29	10		
2008–09	Zamalek	29	10		
2009–10	Zamalek	21	3	94	30
2009–10	Wigan Ath	0	0	29	10
2009–10	Hull C	6	0	6	0

Scholars

Boothman, Steven Geoffrey; Breeze, Jonathan William; Buxton, Adam Mark; Girvan, Michael; Lambert, Daniel Thomas; Langley, Joshua; Morris, Callum Neil; Myler, Sean Francis; Rugg, Jordan; Williams, Callum James; Willis, Liam.

WOLVERHAMPTON W (90)

BATTH, Danny (D) 17 1
H: 6 3 W: 13 05 b.Brierley Hill 21-9-90
Source: Scholar.

| 2009–10 | Wolverhampton W | 0 | 0 | | |
| 2009–10 | Colchester U | 17 | 1 | 17 | 1 |

BENNETT, Elliott (M) 117 12
H: 5 9 W: 10 11 b.Telford 18-12-88
Source: Scholar.

2006–07	Wolverhampton W	0	0		
2007–08	Wolverhampton W	0	0		
2007–08	Crewe Alex	9	1	9	1
2007–08	Bury	19	1		
2008–09	Wolverhampton W	0	0		
2008–09	Bury	46	3	65	4
2009–10	Wolverhampton W	0	0		
2009–10	Brighton & HA	43	7	43	7

BERRA, Christophe (D) 170 4
H: 6 1 W: 12 10 b.Edinburgh 31-1-85
Honours: Scotland Under-21, B, 7 full caps.

2003–04	Hearts	6	0		
2004–05	Hearts	12	0		
2005–06	Hearts	12	1		
2006–07	Hearts	35	1		
2007–08	Hearts	35	2		
2008–09	Hearts	23	0	123	4
2008–09	Wolverhampton W	15	0		
2009–10	Wolverhampton W	32	0	47	0

CRADDOCK, Jody (D) 504 19
H: 6 0 W: 12 04 b.Redditch 25-7-75
Source: Christchurch.

1993–94	Cambridge U	21	4		
1994–95	Cambridge U	38	0		
1995–96	Cambridge U	46	3		
1996–97	Cambridge U	41	1	145	4
1997–98	Sunderland	32	0		
1998–99	Sunderland	6	0		
1999–2000	Sunderland	19	0		
1999–2000	Sheffield U	10	0	10	0
2000–01	Sunderland	34	0		
2001–02	Sunderland	30	1		
2002–03	Sunderland	25	1	146	4
2003–04	Wolverhampton W	32	1		
2004–05	Wolverhampton W	42	1		
2005–06	Wolverhampton W	18	0		
2006–07	Wolverhampton W	34	4		
2007–08	Wolverhampton W	23	1		
2007–08	Stoke C	4	0	4	0
2008–09	Wolverhampton W	17	1		
2009–10	Wolverhampton W	33	5	199	13

DAVIS, David (M) 5 0
H: 5 8 W: 12 03 b.Smethwick 20-2-91
Source: Scholar.
| 2009–10 | Wolverhampton W | 0 | 0 | | |
| 2009–10 | Darlington | 5 | 0 | 5 | 0 |

DOYLE, Kevin (F) 231 84
H: 5 11 W: 12 06 b.Adamstown 18-9-83
Source: Adamstown, Wexford, St Patrick's Ath. Honours: Eire Under-21, 35 full caps, 8 goals.
2004	Cork C	32	13		
2005	Cork C	11	7	43	20
2005–06	Reading	45	18		
2006–07	Reading	32	13		
2007–08	Reading	36	6		
2008–09	Reading	41	18	154	55
2009–10	Wolverhampton W	34	9	34	9

DUNLEAVY, Johnny (D) 0 0
H: 6 0 W: 11 02 b.Donegal 3-7-91
Source: Scholar.
| 2009–10 | Wolverhampton W | 0 | 0 | | |

EBANKS-BLAKE, Sylvan (F) 150 60
H: 5 10 W: 13 04 b.Cambridge 29-3-86
Source: Scholar. Honours: England Under-21.
2004–05	Manchester U	0	0		
2005–06	Manchester U	0	0		
2006–07	Plymouth Arg	41	19		
2007–08	Plymouth Arg	25	11	66	21
2007–08	Wolverhampton W	20	12		
2008–09	Wolverhampton W	41	25		
2009–10	Wolverhampton W	23	2	84	39

EBANKS-LANDELL, Ethan (M) 0 0
Source: Scholar.
| 2009–10 | Wolverhampton W | 0 | 0 | | |

EDWARDS, Dave (M) 196 21
H: 5 11 W: 11 04 b.Shrewsbury 3-2-86
Source: Scholar. Honours: Wales Youth, Under-21, 19 full caps, 3 goals.
2002–03	Shrewsbury T	1	0		
2003–04	Shrewsbury T	0	0		
2004–05	Shrewsbury T	27	5		
2005–06	Shrewsbury T	30	2		
2006–07	Shrewsbury T	45	5	103	12
2007–08	Luton T	19	4	19	4
2007–08	Wolverhampton W	10	1		
2008–09	Wolverhampton W	44	3		
2009–10	Wolverhampton W	20	1	74	5

ELOKOBI, George (D) 85 2
H: 5 10 W: 13 02 b.Cameroon 31-1-86
Source: Dulwich Hamlet.
2004–05	Colchester U	0	0		
2004–05	Chester C	5	0	5	0
2005–06	Colchester U	12	1		
2006–07	Colchester U	10	0		
2007–08	Colchester U	17	1	39	2
2007–08	Wolverhampton W	15	0		
2008–09	Wolverhampton W	4	0		
2009–10	Wolverhampton W	22	0	41	0

FOLEY, Kevin (D) 265 5
H: 5 9 W: 11 11 b.Luton 1-11-84
Source: Scholar. Honours: Eire B, Under-21, 2 full caps.
2002–03	Luton T	2	0		
2003–04	Luton T	33	1		
2004–05	Luton T	39	2		
2005–06	Luton T	38	0		
2006–07	Luton T	39	0		
2007–08	Luton T	0	0	151	3
2007–08	Wolverhampton W	44	1		
2008–09	Wolverhampton W	45	1		
2009–10	Wolverhampton W	25	0	114	2

FRIEND, George (D) 40 2
H: 6 2 W: 13 01 b.Dorchester 19-10-87
2008–09	Exeter C	4	0		
2008–09	Wolverhampton W	6	0		
2009–10	Wolverhampton W	1	.0	7	0
2009–10	Millwall	6	0	6	0
2009–10	Southend U	6	1	6	1
2009–10	Scunthorpe U	4	0	4	0
2009–10	Exeter C	13	1	17	1

GORMAN, Johnny (M) 0 0
H: 5 9 W: 11 00 b.Sheffield 26-10-92
Honours: Northern Ireland 2 full caps.
| 2009–10 | Wolverhampton W | 0 | 0 | | |

GUEDIOURA, Adlene (M) 109 12
H: 6 1 W: 12 08 b.La Roche-sur-Yon 12-11-85
Honours: Algeria 5 full caps.
2004–05	Sedan	0	0		
2005–06	Noisy-Le-Sec	15	1	15	1
2006–07	L'Entente	21	3	21	3
2007–08	Créteil	24	6	24	6
2008–09	Kortrijk	10	0	10	0
2008–09	Charleroi	12	0		
2009–10	Charleroi	13	1	25	1
2009–10	Wolverhampton W	14	1	14	1

HAHNEMANN, Marcus (G) 380 0
H: 6 3 W: 15 03 b.Seattle 15-6-72
Honours: USA 8 full caps.
1997	Colorado Rapids	25	0		
1998	Colorado Rapids	28	0		
1999	Colorado Rapids	13	0	66	0
1999–2000	Fulham	0	0		
2000–01	Fulham	2	0		
2001–02	Fulham	0	0	2	0
2001–02	Rochdale	5	0	5	0
2001–02	Reading	6	0		
2002–03	Reading	41	0		
2003–04	Reading	36	0		
2004–05	Reading	46	0		
2005–06	Reading	45	0		
2006–07	Reading	38	0		
2007–08	Reading	38	0		
2008–09	Reading	32	0		
2009–10	Reading	0	0	282	0
2009–10	Wolverhampton W	25	0	25	0

HALFORD, Greg (D) 219 24
H: 6 4 W: 12 10 b.Chelmsford 8-12-84
Source: Scholar. Honours: England Youth, Under-20.
2002–03	Colchester U	1	0		
2003–04	Colchester U	18	4		
2004–05	Colchester U	44	4		
2005–06	Colchester U	45	7		
2006–07	Colchester U	28	3	136	18
2006–07	Reading	3	0	3	0
2007–08	Sunderland	8	0		
2007–08	Charlton Ath	16	2	16	2
2008–09	Sunderland	0	0		
2008–09	Sheffield U	41	4	41	4
2009–10	Sunderland	0	0	8	0
2009–10	Wolverhampton W	15	0	15	0

HEMMINGS, Ashley (M) 3 0
H: 5 8 W: 11 06 b.Wolverhampton 3-3-91
Source: Scholar.
2008–09	Wolverhampton W	2	0		
2008–09	Cheltenham T	1	0	1	0
2009–10	Wolverhampton W	0	0	2	0

HENNESSEY, Wayne (G) 109 0
H: 6 0 W: 11 06 b.Anglesey 24-1-87
Source: Scholar. Honours: Wales Schools, Youth, Under-21, 25 full caps.
2004–05	Wolverhampton W	0	0		
2005–06	Wolverhampton W	0	0		
2006–07	Wolverhampton W	0	0		
2006–07	Bristol C	0	0		
2006–07	Stockport Co	15	0	15	0
2007–08	Wolverhampton W	46	0		
2008–09	Wolverhampton W	35	0		
2009–10	Wolverhampton W	13	0	94	0

HENRY, Karl (M) 280 8
H: 6 0 W: .2 00 b Wolverhampton 26-11-82
Source: Trainee. Honours: England Youth, Under-20.
1999–2000	Stoke C	0	0		
2000–01	Stoke C	0	0		
2001–02	Stoke C	24	0		
2002–03	Stoke C	18	1		
2003–04	Stoke C	20	0		
2003–04	Cheltenham T	9	1	9	1
2004–05	Stoke C	34	0		
2005–06	Stoke C	24	0	120	1
2006–07	Wolverhampton W	34	3		
2007–08	Wolverhampton W	40	3		
2008–09	Wolverhampton W	43	0		
2009–10	Wolverhampton W	34	0	151	6

HILL, Matt (D) 334 6
H: 5 7 W: 12 06 b.Bristol 26-3-81
Source: Trainee.
1998–99	Bristol C	3	0		
1999–2000	Bristol C	14	0		
2000–01	Bristol C	34	0		
2001–02	Bristol C	40	1		
2002–03	Bristol C	42	3		
2003–04	Bristol C	42	2		
2004–05	Bristol C	23	0	198	6
2004–05	Preston NE	14	0		
2005–06	Preston NE	26	0		
2006–07	Preston NE	38	0		
2007–08	Preston NE	26	0		
2008–09	Preston NE	1	0	105	0
2008–09	Wolverhampton W	13	0		
2009–10	Wolverhampton W	2	0	15	0
2009–10	QPR	16	0	16	0

IKEME, Carl (G) 45 0
H: 6 2 W: 13 09 b.Sutton Coldfield 8-6-86
Source: Scholar.
2005–06	Wolverhampton W	0	0		
2005–06	Stockport Co	9	0	9	0
2006–07	Wolverhampton W	1	0		
2007–08	Wolverhampton W	0	0		
2008–09	Wolverhampton W	12	0		
2009–10	Wolverhampton W	0	0	13	0
2009–10	Charlton Ath	4	0	4	0
2009–10	Sheffield U	2	0	2	0
2009–10	QPR	17	0	17	0

IWELUMO, Chris (F) 363 88
H: 6 3 W: 15 03 b.Coatbridge 1-8-78
Source: Juniors. Honours: Scotland B, 2 full caps.
1996–97	St Mirren	14	0		
1997–98	St Mirren	12	0	26	0
1998–99	Aarhus Fremad	27	4	27	4
1999–2000	Stoke C	3	0		
2000–01	Stoke C	2	1		
2000–01	York C	12	2	12	2
2000–01	Cheltenham T	4	1	4	1
2001–02	Stoke C	38	10		
2002–03	Stoke C	32	5		
2003–04	Stoke C	9	0	84	16
2003–04	Brighton & HA	10	4	10	4
2004–05	Aachen	9	0	9	0
2005–06	Colchester U	46	17		
2006–07	Colchester U	46	18	92	35
2007–08	Charlton Ath	46	10	46	10
2008–09	Wolverhampton W	31	14		
2009–10	Wolverhampton W	15	0	46	14
2009–10	Bristol C	7	2	7	2

JARVIS, Matthew (M) 198 19
H: 5 8 W: 11 10 b.Middlesbrough 22-5-86
Source: Scholar.
2003–04	Gillingham	10	0		
2004–05	Gillingham	30	3		
2005–06	Gillingham	35	3		
2006–07	Gillingham	35	6	110	12
2007–08	Wolverhampton W	26	1		
2008–09	Wolverhampton W	28	3		
2009–10	Wolverhampton W	34	3	88	7

JONES, Daniel (D) 90 4
H: 6 2 W: 13 00 b.Wordsley 14-7-86
Source: Scholar.
2005–06	Wolverhampton W	1	0		
2006–07	Wolverhampton W	8	0		
2007–08	Wolverhampton W	0	0		
2007–08	Northampton T	33	3	33	3
2008–09	Wolverhampton W	0	0		
2008–09	Oldham Ath	23	1	23	1
2009–10	Wolverhampton W	0	0	10	0
2009–10	Notts Co	7	0	7	0
2009–10	Bristol R	17	0	17	0

JONES, David (M) 137 21
H: 5 11 W: 10 10 b.Southport 4-11-84
Source: Trainee. Honours: England Youth, Under-21.
2003–04	Manchester U	0	0		
2004–05	Manchester U	0	0		
2005–06	Manchester U	0	0		
2005–06	Preston NE	24	3	24	3
2005–06	NEC Nijmegen	17	6	17	6
2006–07	Manchester U	0	0		
2006–07	Derby Co	28	6		
2007–08	Derby Co	14	1	42	7

2008–09	Wolverhampton W	34	4	
2009–10	Wolverhampton W	20	1	54 5

KEOGH, Andy (F)   217 42
H: 6 0   W: 11 00   b.Dublin 16-5-86
Source: Scholar. *Honours:* Eire Youth, B, Under-21, 13 full caps, 1 goal.

2003–04	Leeds U	0	0	
2004–05	Leeds U	0	0	
2004–05	Bury	4	2	4 2
2004–05	Scunthorpe U	25	3	
2005–06	Scunthorpe U	45	11	
2006–07	Scunthorpe U	28	7	98 21
2006–07	Wolverhampton W	17	5	
2007–08	Wolverhampton W	43	8	
2008–09	Wolverhampton W	42	5	
2009–10	Wolverhampton W	13	1	115 19

KIGHTLY, Michael (F)   105 20
H: 5 10   W: 10 10   b.Basildon 24-1-86
Source: Scholar. *Honours:* England Under-21.

2002–03	Southend U	1	0	
2003–04	Southend U	11	0	
2004–05	Southend U	1	0	13 0

From Grays Ath.

2006–07	Wolverhampton W	24	8	
2007–08	Wolverhampton W	21	4	
2008–09	Wolverhampton W	38	8	
2009–10	Wolverhampton W	9	0	92 20

LITTLE, Mark (D)   74 0
H: 6 1   W: 12 10   b.Worcester 20-8-88
Source: Scholar. *Honours:* England Youth.

2005–06	Wolverhampton W	0	0	
2006–07	Wolverhampton W	26	0	
2007–08	Wolverhampton W	1	0	
2007–08	*Northampton T*	17	0	
2008–09	Wolverhampton W	0	0	
2008–09	*Northampton T*	9	0	26 0
2009–10	Wolverhampton W	0	0	27 0
2009–10	*Chesterfield*	12	0	12 0
2009–10	*Peterborough U*	9	0	9 0

MAIERHOFER, Stefan (F)   181 84
H: 6 8   W: 14 11   b.Gablitz 16-8-82
Honours: Austria 10 full caps, 1 goal.

2002–03	First Vienna	0	0	
2003–04	Langenrohr	28	10	
2004–05	Langenrohr	25	16	53 26
2005–06	Bayern Munich II	28	10	
2006–07	Bayern Munich II	14	11	42 21
2006–07	Bayern Munich	2	0	2 0
2006–07	Koblenz	14	3	14 3
2007–08	Furth	10	2	10 2
2007–08	Rapid Vienna	11	7	
2008–09	Rapid Vienna	35	23	
2009–10	Rapid Vienna	3	1	49 31
2009–10	Wolverhampton W	8	1	8 1
2009–10	*Bristol C*	3	0	3 0

MALONE, Scott (D)   24 1
H: 6 2   W: 11 11   b.Rowley Regis 25-3-91
Source: Scholar. *Honours:* England Youth.

2008–09	Wolverhampton W	0	0	
2008–09	*Ujpest*	7	1	7 1
2009–10	Wolverhampton W	0	0	
2009–10	*Southend U*	17	0	17 0

McCAREY, Aaron (G)   0 0
Source: Monaghan U.

2009–10	Wolverhampton W	0	0

MENDEZ-LAING, Nathaniel (M)   0 0
H: 5 10   W: 11 12   b.Birmingham 15-4-92
Source: Scholar.

2009–10	Wolverhampton W	0	0

MILIJAS, Nenad (M)   245 57
H: 6 2   W: 13 09   b.Belgrade 30-4-83
Honours: Serbia 18 full caps, 4 goals.

1999–2000	Zemun	2	0	
2000–01	Zemun	10	0	
2001–02	Zemun	28	1	
2002–03	Zemun	27	2	
2003–04	Zemun	26	3	
2004–05	Zemun	22	3	
2005–06	Zemun	15	9	130 18
2005–06	Red Star Belgrade	10	4	
2006–07	Red Star Belgrade	25	5	
2007–08	Red Star Belgrade	28	10	
2008–09	Red Star Belgrade	33	18	96 37
2009–10	Wolverhampton W	19	2	19 2

MUJANGI BIA, Geoffrey (M)   61 9
H: 5 9   W: 11 02   b.Kinshasa 12-8-89
Honours: Belgium 2 full caps.

2006–07	Charleroi	3	0	
2007–08	Charleroi	17	3	
2008–09	Charleroi	28	4	
2009–10	Charleroi	10	2	58 9
2009–10	Wolverhampton W	3	0	3 0

MURRAY, Matt (G)   92 0
H: 6 4   W: 13 10   b.Solihull 2-5-81
Source: Trainee. *Honours:* England Youth, Under-21.

1997–98	Wolverhampton W	0	0	
1998–99	Wolverhampton W	0	0	
1999–2000	Wolverhampton W	0	0	
2000–01	Wolverhampton W	0	0	
2001–02	Wolverhampton W	0	0	
2002–03	Wolverhampton W	40	0	
2003–04	Wolverhampton W	1	0	
2004–05	Wolverhampton W	1	0	
2005–06	Wolverhampton W	1	0	
2005–06	*Tranmere R*	2	0	2 0
2006–07	Wolverhampton W	44	0	
2007–08	Wolverhampton W	0	0	
2008–09	Wolverhampton W	0	0	
2008–09	*Hereford U*	3	0	3 0
2009–10	Wolverhampton W	0	0	87 0

SHACKELL, Jason (D)   166 4
H: 6 4   W: 13 06   b.Stevenage 27-9-83
Source: Scholar.

2002–03	Norwich C	2	0	
2003–04	Norwich C	6	0	
2004–05	Norwich C	11	0	
2005–06	Norwich C	17	0	
2006–07	Norwich C	43	3	
2007–08	Norwich C	39	0	
2008–09	Norwich C	15	0	133 3
2008–09	Wolverhampton W	12	0	
2009–10	Wolverhampton W	0	0	12 0
2009–10	*Doncaster R*	21	1	21 1

SPRAY, James (F)   0 0
H: 6 0   W: 12 01   b.Birmingham 2-12-92
Source: Scholar.

2009–10	Wolverhampton W	0	0

STEARMAN, Richard (D)   169 9
H: 6 2   W: 10 08   b.Wolverhampton 19-8-87
Source: Scholar. *Honours:* England Youth, Under-21.

2004–05	Leicester C	8	1	
2005–06	Leicester C	34	3	
2006–07	Leicester C	35	1	
2007–08	Leicester C	39	2	116 7
2008–09	Wolverhampton W	37	1	
2009–10	Wolverhampton W	16	1	53 2

SURMAN, Andrew (M)   178 23
H: 5 10   W: 11 06   b.Johannesburg 20-8-86
Source: Trainee. *Honours:* England Under-21.

2003–04	Southampton	0	0	
2004–05	Southampton	0	0	
2004–05	*Walsall*	14	2	14 2
2005–06	Southampton	12	2	
2005–06	*Bournemouth*	24	6	24 6
2006–07	Southampton	37	4	
2007–08	Southampton	40	2	
2008–09	Southampton	44	7	
2009–10	Southampton	0	0	133 15
2009–10	Wolverhampton W	7	0	7 0

VOKES, Sam (F)   103 23
H: 6 1   W: 13 10   b.Southampton 21-10-89
Source: Scholar. *Honours:* Wales Under-21, 16 full caps, 2 goals.

2006–07	Bournemouth	13	4	
2007–08	Bournemouth	41	12	54 16
2008–09	Wolverhampton W	36	6	
2009–10	Wolverhampton W	0	0	41 6
2009–10	*Leeds U*	8	1	8 1

WARD, Stephen (D)   183 14
H: 5 11   W: 12 02   b.Dublin 20-8-85
Honours: Eire Youth, Under-21, B.

2003	Bohemians	6	0	
2004	Bohemians	16	2	
2005	Bohemians	29	7	
2006	Bohemians	21	2	72 11
2006–07	Wolverhampton W	18	3	
2007–08	Wolverhampton W	29	0	
2008–09	Wolverhampton W	42	0	
2009–10	Wolverhampton W	22	0	111 3

WINNALL, Sam (F)   0 0
H: 5 9   W: 11 04   b.Wolverhampton 19-1-91
Source: Scholar.

2009–10	Wolverhampton W	0	0

ZUBAR, Ronald (D)   191 5
H: 6 1   W: 12 08   b.Guadeloupe 20-9-85

2002–03	Caen	7	0	
2003–04	Caen	24	1	
2004–05	Caen	34	1	
2005–06	Caen	31	0	96 2
2006–07	Marseille	34	0	
2007–08	Marseille	21	1	
2008–09	Marseille	17	1	72 2
2009–10	Wolverhampton W	23	1	23 1

Scholars
Carvalho-Landell, Andre; East, Daniel Joseph; Gorman, Rory John; Griffiths, Samuel Anthony; Harris, Louis David; McGroary, Brian; Parsonage, James Mitchell; Price, Jack Alexander; Reckord, Jamie; Rooney, Nathan Charles.

WYCOMBE W (91)

AINSWORTH, Gareth (M)   439 91
H: 5 10   W: 12 05   b.Blackburn 10-5-73
Source: Blackburn R Trainee.

1991–92	Preston NE	5	0	
1992–93	Cambridge U	4	1	4 1
1992–93	Preston NE	26	0	
1993–94	Preston NE	38	11	
1994–95	Preston NE	16	1	
1995–96	Preston NE	2	0	
1995–96	Lincoln C	31	12	
1996–97	Lincoln C	46	22	
1997–98	Lincoln C	6	3	83 37
1997–98	Port Vale	40	5	
1998–99	Port Vale	15	5	55 10
1998–99	Wimbledon	8	0	
1999–2000	Wimbledon	2	2	
2000–01	Wimbledon	12	2	
2001–02	Wimbledon	2	0	
2001–02	*Preston NE*	5	1	92 13
2002–03	Wimbledon	12	2	36 6
2002–03	*Walsall*	5	1	5 1
2002–03	*Cardiff C*	9	0	9 0
2003–04	QPR	29	6	
2004–05	QPR	22	2	
2005–06	QPR	43	9	
2006–07	QPR	22	1	
2007–08	QPR	24	3	
2008–09	QPR	0	0	
2009–10	QPR	1	0	141 21
2009–10	Wycombe W	14	2	14 2

ARNOLD, Steven (G)   0 0
H: 6 1   W: 13 02   b.Welham Green 22-8-89
Source: Scholar.

2007–08	Norwich C	0	0	
2008–09	Norwich C	0	0	

From Grays Ath.

2009–10	Wycombe W	0	0

BEAVON, Stuart (F)   33 3
H: 5 7   W: 10 10   b.Reading 5-5-84
Source: Dicot T, Weymouth.

2008–09	Wycombe W	8	0	
2009–10	Wycombe W	25	3	33 3

BETSY, Kevin (M)   350 47
H: 6 1   W: 12 00   b.Woking 20-3-78
Source: Woking.

1998–99	Fulham	7	1	
1999–2000	Fulham	2	0	
1999–2000	*Bournemouth*	5	0	5 0
1999–2000	*Hull C*	2	0	2 0
2000–01	Fulham	5	0	
2001–02	Fulham	1	0	15 1
2001–02	Barnsley	10	0	
2002–03	Barnsley	39	5	
2003–04	Barnsley	45	10	
2004–05	Barnsley	0	0	94 15
2004–05	*Hartlepool U*	6	1	6 1
2004–05	Oldham Ath	36	5	36 5
2005–06	Wycombe W	42	8	
2006–07	Wycombe W	29	5	
2006–07	Bristol C	17	1	

2007–08	Bristol C	1	0	18	1
2007–08	Yeovil T	5	1	5	1
2007–08	Walsall	16	2	16	2
2008–09	Southend U	41	3		
2009–10	Southend U	2	0	43	3
2009–10	Wycombe W	39	5	110	18

BLOOMFIELD, Matt (M) 187 18
H: 5 9 W: 11 00 b.Felixstowe 8-2-84
Source: Scholar. Honours: England Youth, Under-20.

2001–02	Ipswich T	0	0		
2002–03	Ipswich T	0	0		
2003–04	Ipswich T	0	0		
2003–04	Wycombe W	12	1		
2004–05	Wycombe W	26	2		
2005–06	Wycombe W	39	5		
2006–07	Wycombe W	41	4		
2007–08	Wycombe W	35	4		
2008–09	Wycombe W	20	0		
2009–10	Wycombe W	14	2	187	18

COBB, Joe (D) 0 0
H: 5 11 W: 11 06 b.Leicester 13-10-90
Source: Leicester C Scholar.

2009–10	Wycombe W	0	0		

DOHERTY, Tom (M) 300 9
H: 5 8 W: 10 06 b.Bristol 17-3-79
Source: Trainee. Honours: Northern Ireland 9 full caps.

1997–98	Bristol C	30	2		
1998–99	Bristol C	23	1		
1999–2000	Bristol C	1	0		
2000–01	Bristol C	34	1		
2001–02	Bristol C	38	0		
2002–03	Bristol C	33	2		
2003–04	Bristol C	29	1	188	7
2004–05	QPR	15	0		
2005–06	*Yeovil T*	1	0	1	0
2006–07	QPR	0	0		
2006–07	*Wycombe W*	26	2		
2007–08	QPR	0	0	15	0
2007–08	Wycombe W	24	0		
2008–09	Wycombe W	34	0		
2009–10	Wycombe W	12	0	96	2

DUBERRY, Michael (D) 312 6
H: 6 1 W: 13 10 b.Enfield 14-10-75
Source: Trainee. Honours: England Under-21.

1993–94	Chelsea	1	0		
1994–95	Chelsea	0	0		
1995–96	Chelsea	22	0		
1995–96	*Bournemouth*	7	0	7	0
1996–97	Chelsea	15	1		
1997–98	Chelsea	23	0		
1998–99	Chelsea	25	0	86	1
1999–2000	Leeds U	13	1		
2000–01	Leeds U	5	0		
2001–02	Leeds U	3	0		
2002–03	Leeds U	14	0		
2003–04	Leeds U	19	3		
2004–05	Leeds U	4	0	58	4
2004–05	Stoke C	25	0		
2005–06	Stoke C	41	1		
2006–07	Stoke C	29	0	95	1
2006–07	Reading	8	0		
2007–08	Reading	13	0		
2008–09	Reading	27	0	48	0
2009–10	Wycombe W	18	0	18	0

FITCHETT, Dan (F) 0 0
b. 28-3-91
Source: Scholar.

2009–10	Wycombe W	0	0		

GREEN, Stuart (M) 208 33
H: 5 10 W: 11 01 b.Whitehaven 15-6-81
Source: Trainee.

1999–2000	Newcastle U	0	0		
2000–01	Newcastle U	0	0		
2001–02	Newcastle U	0	0		
2001–02	*Carlisle U*	16	3		
2002–03	Newcastle U	0	0		
2002–03	Hull C	28	6		
2002–03	*Carlisle U*	10	2	26	5
2003–04	Hull C	42	6		
2004–05	Hull C	29	8		
2005–06	Hull C	38	4		
2006–07	Hull C	0	0	137	24
2006–07	Crystal Palace	14	2		
2007–08	Crystal Palace	10	2	24	4

2007–08	Blackpool	6	0		
2008–09	Blackpool	0	0	6	0
2008–09	*Crewe Alex*	2	0	2	0
2009–10	Wycombe W	13	0	13	0

HARRIS, Kedeem (M) 2 0
H: 5 9 W: 10 08 b.London 8-6-93
Source: Scholar.

2009–10	Wycombe W	2	0	2	0

HARROLD, Matt (F) 210 33
H: 6 1 W: 11 10 b.Leyton 25-7-84
Source: Harlow T.

2003–04	Brentford	13	2		
2004–05	Brentford	19	0	32	2
2004–05	*Grimsby T*	2	2	6	2
2005–06	Yeovil T	42	9		
2006–07	Yeovil T	5	0	47	9
2006–07	Southend U	36	3		
2007–08	Southend U	16	0		
2008–09	Southend U	0	0	52	3
2008–09	Wycombe W	37	9		
2009–10	Wycombe W	36	8	73	17

HINSHELWOOD, Adam (D) 127 3
H: 5 10 W: 12 10 b.Oxford 8-1-84
Source: Scholar.

2002–03	Brighton & HA	7	0		
2003–04	Brighton & HA	17	0		
2004–05	Brighton & HA	38	1		
2005–06	Brighton & HA	11	0		
2006–07	Brighton & HA	11	0		
2007–08	Brighton & HA	11	0		
2008–09	Brighton & HA	14	1	99	2
2009–10	*Aldershot T*	15	0	15	0
2009–10	Wycombe W	13	1	13	1

HOLT, Gary (M) 461 16
H: 6 0 W: 12 00 b.Irvine 9-3-73
Source: Celtic. Honours: Scotland 10 full caps, 1 goal.

1994–95	Stoke C	0	0		
1995–96	Kilmarnock	26	0		
1996–97	Kilmarnock	12	1		
1997–98	Kilmarnock	27	2		
1998–99	Kilmarnock	33	3		
1999–2000	Kilmarnock	35	0		
2000–01	Kilmarnock	19	3	152	9
2000–01	Norwich C	4	0		
2001–02	Norwich C	46	2		
2002–03	Norwich C	45	0		
2003–04	Norwich C	46	1		
2004–05	Norwich C	27	0	168	3
2005–06	Nottingham F	26	0		
2006–07	Nottingham F	39	1	65	1
2007–08	Wycombe W	43	2		
2008–09	Wycombe W	33	1		
2009–10	Wycombe W	0	0	76	3

HUNT, Lewis (D) 204 7
H: 5 11 W: 12 09 b.Birmingham 25-8-82
Source: Scholar.

2000–01	Derby Co	0	0		
2001–02	Derby Co	0	0		
2002–03	Derby Co	10	0		
2003–04	Derby Co	1	0	11	0
2003–04	Southend U	26	0		
2004–05	Southend U	31	0		
2005–06	Southend U	30	0		
2006–07	Southend U	35	2		
2007–08	Southend U	24	0	146	2
2008–09	Wycombe W	20	1		
2009–10	Wycombe W	27	0	47	1

JOHNSON, Leon (D) 225 7
H: 6 1 W: 13 05 b.Shoreditch 10-5-81
Source: Scholarship.

1999–2000	Southend U	0	0		
2000–01	Southend U	20	1		
2001–02	Southend U	28	2	48	3
2002–03	Gillingham	18	0		
2003–04	Gillingham	20	0		
2004–05	Gillingham	8	0		
2005–06	Gillingham	28	1		
2006–07	Gillingham	24	1	98	2
2007–08	Wycombe W	45	0		
2008–09	Wycombe W	29	2		
2009–10	Wycombe W	5	0	79	2

KEATES, Dean (M) 429 51
H: 5 6 W: 10 06 b.Walsall 30-6-78
Source: Trainee.

1996–97	Walsall	2	0		
1997–98	Walsall	33	1		
1998–99	Walsall	43	2		

1999–2000	Walsall	35	1		
2000–01	Walsall	33	4		
2001–02	Walsall	13	1		
2002–03	Hull C	36	4		
2003–04	Hull C	14	0	50	4
2003–04	Kidderminster H	8	2		
2004–05	Kidderminster H	41	5	49	7
2005–06	Lincoln C	21	4	21	4
2005–06	Walsall	14	2		
2006–07	Walsall	39	13	212	24
2007–08	Peterborough U	40	5		
2008–09	Peterborough U	38	5		
2009–10	Peterborough U	6	1	84	11
2009–10	Wycombe W	13	1	13	1

McLEOD, Kevin (M) 205 20
H: 5 11 W: 11 00 b.Liverpool 12-9-80
Source: Scholar.

1998–99	Everton	0	0		
1999–2000	Everton	0	0		
2000–01	Everton	5	0		
2001–02	Everton	0	0		
2002–03	Everton	0	0		
2002–03	QPR	8	2		
2003–04	Everton	0	0	5	0
2003–04	QPR	35	3		
2004–05	QPR	24	1	67	6
2004–05	Swansea C	11	0		
2005–06	Swansea C	29	7		
2006–07	Swansea C	4	0	44	7
2006–07	Colchester U	24	3		
2007–08	Colchester U	28	4	52	7
2008–09	Brighton & HA	21	0		
2009–10	Brighton & HA	5	0	26	0
2009–10	Wycombe W	11	0	11	0

MONCUR, T J (D) 27 0
H: 5 10 W: 12 08 b.Hackney 23-9-87
Source: Scholar.

2005–06	Fulham	0	0		
2006–07	Fulham	0	0		
2007–08	Fulham	0	0		
2007–08	*Bradford C*	7	0		
2008–09	Fulham	0	0		
2008–09	*Bradford C*	14	0	21	0
2008–09	Wycombe W	2	0		
2009–10	Wycombe W	4	0	6	0

MONTROSE, Lewis (M) 31 0
H: 6 0 W: 12 00 b.Manchester 17-11-88
Source: Scholar.

2006–07	Wigan Ath	0	0		
2007–08	Wigan Ath	0	0		
2008–09	Wigan Ath	0	0		
2008–09	*Cheltenham T*	5	0	5	0
2008–09	Chesterfield	12	0	12	0
2009–10	Wycombe W	14	0	14	0

MOUSINHO, John (D) 137 5
H: 6 1 W: 12 07 b.Buckingham 30-4-86
Source: Univ of Notre Dame.

2005–06	Brentford	7	0		
2006–07	Brentford	34	0		
2007–08	Brentford	23	2	64	2
2008–09	Wycombe W	34	2		
2009–10	Wycombe W	39	1	73	3

OLIVER, Luke (D) 45 2
H: 6 6 W: 14 05 b.Hammersmith 1-5-84
Source: Brook House.

2002–03	Wycombe W	2	0		
2003–04	Wycombe W	2	0		
From Woking					
2005–06	*Yeovil T*	3	0	3	0
From Stevenage B.					
2008–09	Wycombe W	8	0		
2009–10	Wycombe W	23	0	35	0
2009–10	*Bradford C*	7	2	7	2

PHILLIPS, Matthew (M) 75 8
H: 6 0 W: 12 10 b.Aylesbury 13-3-91
Source: Scholar. Honours: England Youth.

2007–08	Wycombe W	2	0		
2008–09	Wycombe W	37	3		
2009–10	Wycombe W	36	5	75	8

PITTMAN, Jon-Paul (F) 70 11
H: 5 9 W: 11 00 b.Oklahoma City 24-10-86
Source: Scholar.

2005–06	Nottingham F	0	0		
2005–06	*Hartlepool U*	3	0	3	0
2006–07	*Bury*	9	1	9	1
2006–07	Doncaster R	0	0		
From Crawley T.					
2008–09	Wycombe W	17	3		
2009–10	Wycombe W	41	7	58	10

REVELL, Alex (F) 175 30
H: 6 3 W: 13 00 b.Cambridge 7-7-83
Source: Scholar.

2000–01	Cambridge U	4	0	
2001–02	Cambridge U	24	2	
2002–03	Cambridge U	1	0	
2003–04	Cambridge U	20	3	57 5

From Braintree T.

2006–07	Brighton & HA	38	7	
2007–08	Brighton & HA	21	6	59 13
2007–08	Southend U	8	0	
2008–09	Southend U	23	4	
2009–10	Southend U	3	0	34 4
2009–10	Swindon T	10	2	10 2
2009–10	Wycombe W	15	6	15 6

SHEARER, Scott (G) 230 0
H: 6 3 W: 12 00 b.Glasgow 15-2-81
Source: Tower Hearts. *Honours:* Scotland B.

2000–01	Albion R	3	0	
2001–02	Albion R	10	0	
2002–03	Albion R	36	0	49 0
2003–04	Coventry C	30	0	
2004–05	Coventry C	8	0	38 0
2004–05	Rushden & D	13	0	13 0
2005–06	Bristol R	45	0	
2006–07	Bristol R	2	0	47 0
2006–07	Shrewsbury T	20	0	20 0
2007–08	Wycombe W	5	0	
2008–09	Wycombe W	29	0	
2009–10	Wycombe W	29	0	63 0

SPENCE, Lewis (M) 32 2
H: 5 9 W: 11 02 b.Lambeth 29-10-87
Source: Scholar.

2006–07	Crystal Palace	2	0	
2007–08	Crystal Palace	0	0	2 0
2008–09	Wycombe W	30	2	
2009–10	Wycombe W	0	0	30 2

WESTLAKE, Ian (M) 208 20
H: 5 10 W: 11 06 b.Clacton 10-7-83
Source: Scholar.

2002–03	Ipswich T	4	0	
2003–04	Ipswich T	39	6	
2004–05	Ipswich T	45	7	
2005–06	Ipswich T	26	2	114 15
2006–07	Leeds U	27	0	
2007–08	Leeds U	20	1	
2007–08	Brighton & HA	11	2	11 2
2008–09	Leeds U	0	0	47 1
2008–09	Cheltenham T	22	2	22 2
2008–09	Oldham Ath	5	0	5 0
2009–10	Wycombe W	9	0	9 0

WESTWOOD, Chris (D) 413 17
H: 5 11 W: 12 10 b.Dudley 13-2-77
Source: Trainee.

1995–96	Wolverhampton W	0	0	
1996–97	Wolverhampton W	0	0	
1997–98	Wolverhampton W	4	1	
1998–99	Wolverhampton W	0	0	4 1
1998–99	Hartlepool U	4	0	
1999–2000	Hartlepool U	37	0	
2000–01	Hartlepool U	46	1	
2001–02	Hartlepool U	35	1	
2002–03	Hartlepool U	46	1	
2003–04	Hartlepool U	45	0	
2004–05	Hartlepool U	37	4	250 7
2005–06	Walsall	29	3	
2006–07	Walsall	40	2	69 5
2007–08	Peterborough U	37	0	
2008–09	Peterborough U	16	0	53 0
2008–09	Cheltenham T	9	2	9 2
2009–10	Wycombe W	28	2	28 2

WOODMAN, Craig (D) 241 5
H: 5 9 W: 10 11 b.Tiverton 22-12-82
Source: Trainee.

1999–2000	Bristol C	0	0	
2000–01	Bristol C	2	0	
2001–02	Bristol C	6	0	
2002–03	Bristol C	10	0	
2003–04	Bristol C	21	0	
2004–05	Bristol C	3	0	
2004–05	Mansfield T	8	1	8 1
2004–05	Torquay U	22	1	
2005–06	Bristol C	37	1	
2005–06	Torquay U	2	0	24 1
2006–07	Bristol C	11	0	90 1
2007–08	Wycombe W	29	0	
2008–09	Wycombe W	46	1	
2009–10	Wycombe W	44	1	119 2

YEOVIL T (92)

ALCOCK, Craig (D) 81 2
H: 5 8 W: 11 00 b.Cornwall 8-12-87
Source: Youth.

2006–07	Yeovil T	1	0	
2007–08	Yeovil T	8	0	
2008–09	Yeovil T	30	1	
2009–10	Yeovil T	42	1	81 2

BOWDITCH, Dean (F) 151 25
H: 5 11 W: 11 05 b.Bishops Stortford 15-6-86
Source: Trainee. *Honours:* FA Schools, England Youth.

2002–03	Ipswich T	5	0	
2003–04	Ipswich T	16	4	
2004–05	Ipswich T	21	3	
2004–05	Burnley	10	1	10 1
2005–06	Ipswich T	21	0	
2005–06	Wycombe W	11	1	11 1
2006–07	Ipswich T	9	1	
2006–07	Brighton & HA	3	1	
2007–08	Ipswich T	0	0	
2007–08	Northampton T	10	2	10 2
2007–08	Brighton & HA	5	0	8 1
2008–09	Ipswich T	1	0	73 8
2008–09	Brentford	9	2	9 2
2009–10	Yeovil T	30	10	30 10

DAVIES, Arron (M) 154 23
H: 5 9 W: 11 00 b.Cardiff 22-6-84
Source: Trainee. *Honours:* Wales Under-21, 1 full cap.

2002–03	Southampton	0	0	
2003–04	Southampton	0	0	
2003–04	Barnsley	4	0	4 0
2004–05	Southampton	0	0	
2004–05	Yeovil T	23	8	
2005–06	Yeovil T	39	8	
2006–07	Yeovil T	39	6	
2007–08	Nottingham F	19	1	
2008–09	Nottingham F	13	0	
2009–10	Nottingham F	0	0	32 1
2009–10	Brighton & HA	7	0	7 0
2009–10	Yeovil T	10	0	111 22

DOWNES, Aiden (F) 34 1
H: 5 8 W: 11 07 b.Dublin 24-7-88
Source: Scholar. *Honours:* Eire Youth, Under-21.

2005–06	Everton	0	0	
2006–07	Everton	0	0	
2007–08	Everton	0	0	
2007–08	Yeovil T	5	1	
2008–09	Yeovil T	24	0	
2009–10	Yeovil T	5	0	34 1

FORBES, Terrell (D) 352 1
H: 5 11 W: 12 07 b.Southwark 17-8-81
Source: Trainee.

1999–2000	West Ham U	0	0	
1999–2000	Bournemouth	3	0	3 0
2000–01	West Ham U	0	0	
2001–02	QPR	43	0	
2002–03	QPR	38	0	
2003–04	QPR	30	0	
2004–05	QPR	3	0	114 0
2004–05	Grimsby T	33	0	33 0
2005–06	Oldham Ath	39	0	39 0
2006–07	Yeovil T	46	0	
2007–08	Yeovil T	41	0	
2008–09	Yeovil T	38	0	
2009–10	Yeovil T	38	1	163 1

HUTCHINS, Daniel (D) 16 0
H: 6 0 W: 11 00 b.London 23-9-89
Source: Scholar.

2007–08	Tottenham H	0	0	
2008–09	Tottenham H	0	0	
2008–09	Yeovil T	9	0	
2009–10	Yeovil T	7	0	16 0

JONES, Nathan (M) 422 11
H: 5 6 W: 10 06 b.Rhondda 28-5-73
Source: Cardiff C Trainee, Maesteg Park, Ton Pentre, Merthyr T.

1995–96	Luton T	0	0	

Badajoz, Numaicia

1997–98	Southend U	39	0	
1998–99	Southend U	17	0	
1998–99	Scarborough	9	0	9 0
1999–2000	Southend U	43	2	99 2
2000–01	Brighton & HA	40	4	
2001–02	Brighton & HA	36	2	
2002–03	Brighton & HA	28	1	
2003–04	Brighton & HA	36	0	
2004–05	Brighton & HA	19	0	159 7
2005–06	Yeovil T	43	0	
2006–07	Yeovil T	42	1	
2007–08	Yeovil T	31	1	
2008–09	Yeovil T	21	0	
2009–10	Yeovil T	18	0	155 2

KALALA, Jean-Paul (M) 136 9
H: 5 10 W: 12 02 b.Lubumbashi 16-2-82
Honours: DR Congo 6 full caps.

2003–04	Nice	2	0	
2004–05	Nice	0	0	2 0
2005–06	Grimsby T	21	5	
2006–07	Yeovil T	38	1	
2007–08	Oldham Ath	20	0	
2008–09	Oldham Ath	0	0	
2008–09	*Grimsby T*	21	2	42 7
2009–10	Oldham Ath	0	0	20 0
2009–10	Yeovil T	34	1	72 2

LINDEGAARD, Andy (M) 156 6
H: 5 8 W: 11 04 b.Taunton 10-9-80
Source: Westland Sp.

2003–04	Yeovil T	23	2	
2004–05	Yeovil T	29	1	
2005–06	Yeovil T	23	0	
2006–07	Yeovil T	14	0	
2007–08	Cheltenham T	41	2	
2008–09	Cheltenham T	15	0	56 2
2008–09	*Aldershot T*	6	1	6 1
2009–10	Yeovil T	5	0	94 2

MARTIN, Richard (G) 3 0
H: 6 2 W: 12 13 b.Chelmsford 1-9-87
Source: Scholar.

2005–06	Brighton & HA	0	0	
2006–07	Brighton & HA	0	0	
2007–08	Manchester C	0	0	
2008–09	Manchester C	0	0	
2009–10	Yeovil T	3	0	3 0

McCOLLIN, Andre (F) 13 1
H: 5 7 W: 10 06 b.Lambeth 26-3-85
Source: Fisher Ath.

2008–09	Yeovil T	11	1	
2009–10	Yeovil T	2	0	13 1

MURRAY, Scott (M) 425 83
H: 5 9 W: 11 00 b.Aberdeen 26-5-74
Source: Fraserburgh. *Honours:* Scotland B.

1993–94	Aston Villa	0	0	
1994–95	Aston Villa	0	0	
1995–96	Aston Villa	3	0	
1996–97	Aston Villa	1	0	
1997–98	Aston Villa	0	0	4 0
1997–98	Bristol C	23	0	
1998–99	Bristol C	32	3	
1999–2000	Bristol C	41	6	
2000–01	Bristol C	46	10	
2001–02	Bristol C	37	8	
2002–03	Bristol C	45	19	
2003–04	Reading	34	5	34 5
2003–04	Bristol C	6	0	
2004–05	Bristol C	42	8	
2005–06	Bristol C	37	10	
2006–07	Bristol C	28	7	
2007–08	Bristol C	14	3	
2008–09	Bristol C	0	0	354 74
2008–09	*Cheltenham T*	13	2	13 2
2009–10	Yeovil T	20	2	20 2

MURTAGH, Kieran (M) 53 3
H: 6 0 W: 12 00 b.Wapping 29-10-88
Source: Charlton Ath Academy, Fisher Ath.

2008–09	Yeovil T	26	0	
2009–10	Yeovil T	27	3	53 3

O'CALLAGHAN, George (M) 208 28
H: 6 1 W: 10 11 b.Cork 5-9-79
Source: Trainee. *Honours:* Eire Youth.

1998–99	Port Vale	4	0	
1999–2000	Port Vale	11	0	
2000–01	Port Vale	8	1	
2001–02	Port Vale	11	3	34 4
2002–03	Cork C	26	6	

2003	Cork C	27	7		
2004	Cork C	35	3		
2005	Cork C	32	6		
2006	Cork C	10	1	130	23
2006–07	Ipswich T	11	1		
2007–08	Ipswich T	1	0	12	1
2007–08	*Brighton & HA*	14	0	14	0
2008–09	Tranmere R	6	0	6	0
2009–10	Yeovil T	12	0	12	0

Transferred to Dundalk February 2009

SMITH, Nathan (D) 74 1
H: 5 11 W: 12 00 b.Enfield 11-1-87
Source: Potters Bar T.

2007–08	Yeovil T	7	0		
2008–09	Yeovil T	33	1		
2009–10	Yeovil T	34	0	74	1

STAM, Stefan (D) 115 2
H: 6 2 W: 13 02 b.Amersfoort 14-9-79
Honours: Holland Under-21.

2004–05	Oldham Ath	13	0		
2005–06	Oldham Ath	13	0		
2006–07	Oldham Ath	22	0		
2007–08	Oldham Ath	36	0		
2008–09	Oldham Ath	13	0	97	1
2009–10	Yeovil T	18	1	18	1

TOMLIN, Gavin (F) 89 14
H: 6 0 W: 12 02 b.Brentford 21-8-83
Source: Staines T, Yeading.

2006–07	Brentford	12	0		
2007–08	Brentford	0	0	12	0

From Fisher Ath

2008–09	Yeovil T	42	7		
2009–10	Yeovil T	35	7	77	14

WELSH, Andy (M) 239 10
H: 5 8 W: 10 03 b.Manchester 24-1-83
Source: Scholar. *Honours:* Scotland Youth.

2001–02	Stockport Co	15	0		
2002–03	Stockport Co	13	2		
2002–03	*Macclesfield T*	6	2	6	2
2003–04	Stockport Co	34	1		
2004–05	Stockport Co	13	0	75	3
2004–05	Sunderland	7	1		
2005–06	Sunderland	14	0		
2005–06	*Leicester C*	10	1		
2006–07	Sunderland	0	0	21	1
2006–07	*Leicester C*	7	0	17	1
2007	Toronto Lynx	20	1	20	1
2007–08	Blackpool	21	0		
2008–09	Blackpool	0	0	21	0
2008–09	Yeovil T	37	0		
2009–10	Yeovil T	42	2	79	2

WILLIAMS, Sam (F) 69 10
H: 5 11 W: 10 08 b.London 9-6-87
Source: Scholar.

2004–05	Aston Villa	0	0		
2005–06	Aston Villa	0	0		
2005–06	Wrexham	15	2	15	2
2006–07	Aston Villa	0	0		
2006–07	*Brighton & HA*	3	1	3	1
2007–08	Aston Villa	0	0		
2008–09	Aston Villa	0	0		
2008–09	Colchester U	1	0	1	0
2008–09	Walsall	5	1	5	1
2008–09	*Brentford*	11	2	11	2
2009–10	Yeovil T	34	4	34	4

BLUE SQUARE PREMIER ROLL-CALL

OXFORD UNITED

Player	H	W	Birthplace	DOB	Source
Billy Turley (G)	6 4	15 06	Wolverhampton	15 7 72	Rushden & D
Damien Batt (D)	5 10	11 07	Hoddesdon	16 9 84	Grays Ath
Kevin Sandwith (D)	5 11	12 06	Workington	30 4 78	Weymouth
Dannie Bulman (M)	5 9	11 11	Ashford	24 1 79	Crawley T
Chris Hargreaves (M)	5 11	12 02	Cleethorpes	12 5 72	Torquay U
Mark Creighton (D)	6 4	12 02	Birmingham	8 10 81	Kidderminster H
Adam Chapman (M)	5 10	11 00	Doncaster	29 11 89	Sheffield U
Adam Murray (M)	5 9	10 01	Birmingham	30 9 81	Macclesfield T
James Constable (F)	6 2	12 13	Malmesbury	4 10 84	Shrewsbury T
Jack Midson (F)	5 8	11 07	Stevenage	21 7 83	Histon
Simon Clist (M)	5 9	11 00	Shaftesbury	13 6 81	Forest Green R
Rhys Day (D)	6 2	13 01	Bridgend	31 8 82	Aldershot T
Anthony Tonkin (D)	5 11	12 02	Newlyn	17 1 80	Cambridge U
Francis Green (F)	5 9	11 05	Derby	23 4 80	Kettering T
Sam Deering (M)	5 6	11 00	London	26 2 91	
Ryan Clarke (G)	6 3	12 13	Bristol	30 4 82	Salisbury C
Jamie Cook (M)	5 10	10 10	Oxford	2 9 79	Crawley T
Aaron Woodley (F)			Oxford	13 10 92	

STEVENAGE

Player	H	W	Birthplace	DOB	Source
Ashley Bayes (G)	6 1	13 05	Lincoln	19 4 72	Crawley T
Lawrie Wilson (D)	5 10	11 02	Collier Row	11 9 87	Colchester U
Scott Laird (D)	5 9	11 09	Taunton	15 5 88	Plymouth Arg
Eddie Odhiambo (M)	5 9	11 02	Arusha	31 8 85	Oxford U
Jon Ashton (D)	6 2	13 05	Nuneaton	4 10 82	Grays Ath
Mark Albrighton (D)	6 1	12 08	Nuneaton	6 3 76	Cambridge U
Darren Murphy (M)	6 0	11 11	Cork	28 7 85	Cork C
Stacy Long (M)	5 8	10 01	Bromley	11 1 85	Ebbsfleet U
Charlie Griffin (F)	6 0	12 08	Bath	25 6 79	Salisbury C
Lee Boylan (F)	5 6	11 05	Witham	2 9 78	Cambridge U
Yemi Odubade (F)	5 7	11 07	Lagos	4 7 84	Oxford U
Joel Byrom (M)	6 0	12 04	Oswaldtwistle	14 9 86	Northwich Vic
Mark Roberts (D)	6 1	11 13	Northwich	16 10 83	Northwich Vic
Chris Day (G)	6 2	13 05	Walthamstow	28 7 75	Millwall
Tim Sills (F)	6 2	12 02	Romsey	10 9 79	Torquay U
David Bridges (M)	6 0	11 13	Huntingdon	22 9 82	Kettering T
Chris Beardsley (F)	6 0	12 02	Derby	28 2 84	Kettering T
Mitchell Cole (M)	5 11	11 05	London	6 10 85	Southend U
Andy Drury (M)	5 11	12 06	Sittingbourne	28 11 83	Lewes
Michael Bostwick (D)			London	17 5 88	Ebbsfleet U
Ronnie Henry (D)	5 11	11 11	Hemel Hempstead	2 1 84	
Peter Vincenti (D)	6 2	12 00	Jersey	7 7 86	Millwall

ENGLISH LEAGUE PLAYERS – INDEX

REFEREEING AND THE LAWS OF THE GAME

Originally little had changed for the coming season but the South Africa World Cup threw up several anomalies not least England's "goal that never was" against Germany so that the original FIFA adamant decision not to consider goal-line technology has been rethought by its President Sepp Blatter and will now be up for future discussion in full. Meanwhile the experiment of two extra Officials on the goal-line one at each end, forced through by UEFA President Michele Platini, in the Europa Cup, which has not been universally applauded, will continue. As to the individual Laws there are very few alterations. However in Law 1, relating to the "Goals" the shape which comprises them, has moved from a "may" to a "must" and so they are now to be definitively of a square, rectangular, round or elliptical shape so as not to be dangerous to players. In the interpretation section of Law 5 which governs Referees there has been a tidying up of the vexatious question of who is to be removed from the field when an injury or collision occurs. There was an unfairness if two players from the same side collided and they both had to go off. leaving their side at a numerical disadvantage. Now if that happens they are included in the exceptions to the ruling. The other two being if the goalkeeper is injured or the goalkeeper and an outfield player have collided and there is a resultant injury. Following on from that change, stretcher bearers are no longer allowed to enter the field until they have received a signal from the referee, in order to avoid unnecessary disruption to the game. There has been an important change to Law 14 which deals with penalty kicks. Now a player taking the kick may employ a feint but must not do so once his/her run up is completed This is now to be considered an act of unsporting behaviour and the kicker must be cautioned. There is still confusion about this change because it was felt that a player stopping in his run up was the one causing most of the problems. In theory if not in practise this had been outlawed as far back as the 1960s, but like many things relating to the penalty kick was observed more in its absence than in its performance (encroachment being one of them). The ubiquitous Fourth Official is now to receive more powers in that his/her original remit which defined what he/she could do has been removed and instead a general power has been afforded. This function is now to read "assists the referee to control the match in accordance with the Laws of the Game". Further support and advice where needed is the intention of this change, but the referee still retains the authority to decide on points connected with play. Other smaller points confirmed were that the authoritative language for the Laws is English and in the event of a divergence between translations of the Laws the English one is to supervene. Contrast that with the dimensions in the Laws which have been for some time metric. Logos and emblems of any nature or kind are still to be banned on the playing field or its football furniture; and finally FIFA have restated that all changes in the Laws and their interpretations are in their remit and no other association or body is allowed to issue their own instructions or recommendations. This obviously cuts out those long overdue experiments and changes relating to sin-bins; a two referee system or codification of the drop ball scenario all of which could prove extremely helpful to discipline in the running of the game.

There has been one major recent change on the domestic front relating to referees at grass roots level. Whereas the Professional Match Officials Limited (PGMOL) was formed to obviously deal with the band of professional referees and assistant referees, the much older Referees' Association (RA) and its subsequent brother society, the Football Association Match Officials Association (FAMOA) has dealt primarily with the bulk of referees who officiate each week. Since FAMOA was formed long after the RA there has sometimes been a certain tension between them. Now however a bond of allegiance has been forged whereby a new entity RA-FA (RA and FA) has been formed to be a partnership for co-operation and joint action between the two. It will not be a members organisation as that will still be the preserve of the RA but FAMOA will be subsumed within the RA-FA. As from the beginning of this season all referees when they register or re-register will automatically become Associate Members of the RA free of charge but will however be strongly encouraged to become full fee-paying members of the RA. The Chairman of the RA-FA Liaison Committee is David Elleray while the FA's Referees Department consists of Neal Barry and Ian Blanchard who head a team of Janie Frampton, Ray Oliver and Roger Vaughan.

Nationally the desire to recruit new referees especially at a young age continues. In May of this year over 170 young referees benefitted from a weekend of further learning at Staverton Park Daventry, at their annual conference, whilst the FA has created a set-up entitled "Become a mini-whistler". That enabled the Derbyshire County FA to construct a June course for students aged 11–14 to help widen the depth and breadth of knowledge to gain experience to become referees.. Earlier in the season the Staverton Park Conference Centre had played host to an International Referee Instructors' Course run by the FA. Thirty instructors from 23 nations attended a one week's course which involved 16 participants on the International Course and 14 on the Advanced Course. The FA also sent Janie Frampton and Lucy May, two of their leading female Referee instructors to Botswana in June, to undertake a five-day referee training workshop, where they carried out both theoretical and practical sessions for a group of 32 intending referees. Back home Over 450 Officials including international guests attended the 10th Annual Conference run by the Professional Game Match Officials Limited which was a two-day event held in the Midlands.

There were also two items of pleasant news in that firstly the former FA head of refereeing John Baker received a 50 year award for services to football and secondly in April 2010 a possibly unique situation occurred when a father and daughter officiated in the same match. Referee Peter Quinn was joined by daughter Alice as Assistant Referee in a match between North and West Riding Ladies.

As to the Referees themselves – Howard Webb refereed the UEFA Champions League Final in Madrid with Assistants Michael Mullarky and Darren Cann, with Martin Atkinson as Fourth Official. The Referee and his two Assistants also went to the World Cup Finals in South Africa as England's representatives and all three were given the honour of officiating the World Cup Final itself between Holland and Spain. This was a singular honour as it was the first time a "team" from the same Country had been chosen together. Webb became the first Englishman to referee the Final since 1974 when Jack Taylor was the man in charge. Webb also became the 4th Englishman to referee the Final.. The Referee for last season's FA Cup Final was Chris Foy; whilst the Referee for the Carling Cup Final was Phil Dowd.

Pat Welton – Remembered
It is with great regret that we announce the death of former Committee Member Pat Welton. Pat was not only a fine goalkeeper whose record is set out here, but an outstanding coach who was appointed an FA Staff Coach at a time when that was a very select list, before that elite structure was surprisingly and unnecessarily torn down. (See also Obituaries page 1021.)

KEN GOLDMAN

NATIONAL LIST OF REFEREES FOR SEASON 2010–11

List as at 2009–10

Atkinson, M (Martin) – W. Yorkshire
Attwell, SB (Stuart) – Warwickshire
Bates, A (Tony) – Staffordshire
Bennett, SG (Steve) – Kent
Booth, R (Russell) – Nottinghamshire
Boyeson, C (Carl) – E. Yorkshire
Bratt, SJ (Steve) – West Midlands
Clattenburg, M (Mark) – Tyne & Wear
Cook, SD (Steven) – Surrey
Crossley, PT (Phil) – Kent
Deadman, D (Darren) – Cambs.
Dean, ML (Mike) – Wirral
Dowd, P (Phil) – Staffordshire
D'urso, AP (Andy) – Essex
East, R (Roger) – Wiltshire
Eltringham, G (Geoff) – Tyne & Wear
Evans, KG (Karl) – Lancashire
Foster, D (David) – Tyne & Wear
Foy, CJ (Chris) – Merseyside
Friend, KA (Kevin) – Leicestershire
Gibbs, PN (Phil) – W. Midlands
Graham, F (Fred) – Essex
Haines, A (Andy) – Tyne & Wear
Hall, AR (Andy) – W. Midlands
Halsey, MR (Mark) – Lancashire
Haywood, M (Mark) – W. Yorkshire
Hegley, GK (Grant) – Hertfordshire
Hill, KD (Keith) – Hertfordshire
Hooper, SA (Simon) – Wiltshire
Horwood, GD (Graham) – Bedfordshire
Ilderton, EL (Eddie) – Tyne & Wear
Jones, MJ (Michael) – Cheshire
Kettle, TM (Trevor) – Rutland
Langford, O (Oliver) – W. Midlands
Laws, G (Graham) – Tyne & Wear
Linington, JJ (James) – Isle of Wight
McDermid, D (Danny) – Middlesex
Marriner, AM (Andre) – W. Midlands

Mason, LS (Lee) – Lancashire
Mathieson, SW (Scott) – Cheshire
Miller, NS (Nigel) – Co. Durham
Miller, P (Pat) – Bedfordshire
Moss, J (Jon) – W. Yorkshire
Oliver, CW (Clive) – Northumberland
Oliver, M (Michael) – Northumberland
Pawson, CL (Craig) – S. Yorkshire
Penn, AM (Andy) – W. Midlands
Phillips, DJ (David) – W. Sussex
Probert, LW (Lee) – Wiltshire
Quinn, P (Peter) – Cleveland
Rushton, SJ (Steve) – Staffordshire
Russell, MP (Mike) – Hertfordshire
Salisbury, G (Graham) – Lancashire
Sarginson, CD (Chris) – Staffordshire
Scott, GD (Graham) – Oxfordshire
Sheldrake, D (Darren) – Surrey
Shoebridge, RL (Rob) – Derbyshire
Singh, J (Jarnail) – Middlesex
Stroud, KP (Keith) – Hampshire
Sutton, GJ (Gary) – Lincolnshire
Swarbrick, ND (Neil) – Lancashire
Tanner, SJ (Steve) – Somerset
Taylor, A (Anthony) – Cheshire
Taylor, P (Paul) – Hertfordshire
Thorpe, M (Mike) – Suffolk
Tierney, P (Paul) – Lancashire
Walton, P (Peter) – Northamptonshire
Ward, GL (Gavin) – Surrey
Waugh, J (Jock) – S. Yorkshire
Webb, D (David) – Co. Durham
Webb, HM (Howard) – S. Yorkshire
Webster, CH (Colin) – Tyne & Wear
Whitestone, D (Dean) – Northamptonshire
Wiley, AG (Alan) – Staffordshire
Williamson, IG (Iain) – Berkshire
Woolmer, KA (Andy) – Northamptonshire
Wright, KK (Kevin) – Cambridgeshire

ASSISTANT REFEREES

List as at 2009–10

Adcock, JG (James) – Nottinghamshire
Akers, C (Chris) – S. Yorkshire
Amey, JR (Justin) – Dorset
Amphlett, MJ (Marvyn) – Worcestershire
Artis, SG (Stephen) – Norfolk
Astley, MA (Mark) – Manchester
Atkin, R (Robert) – Lincolnshire
Atkin, W (Warren) – W. Sussex
Babski, DS (Dave) – Lincolnshire
Bankes, P (Peter) – Merseyside
Bannister, N (Nigel) – E. Yorkshire
Barnes, PW (Paul) – Cambridgeshire
Barratt, W (Wayne) – Worcestershire
Barrow, SJ (Simon) – Staffordshire
Bartlett, R (Richard) – Cheshire
Beck, SP (Simon) – Bedfordshire
Beevor, R (Richard) – Suffolk
Bennett, A (Andrew) – Devon
Bennett, SP (Simon) – Staffordshire
Benton, DK (David) – S. Yorkshire
Berry, CJ (Carl) – Surrey
Beswick, G (Gary) – Co. Durham
Betts, L (Lee) – Norfolk
Blackledge, M (Mike) – Cambridgeshire
Bond, DS (Darren) – Lancashire
Bramley, P (Philip) – W. Yorkshire
Breakspear, CT (Charles) – Surrey
Bristow, M (Matthew) – Manchester
Brown, M (Mark) – E. Yorkshire
Bryan, DS (Dave) – Lincolnshire
Buck, D (David) – Kent
Bull, M (Michael) – Essex
Bull, W (William) – Hampshire
Burt, S (Stuart) – Northamptonshire
Busby, J (John) – Oxfordshire
Bushell, DD (David) – London

Butler, AN (Andrew) – Lancashire
Cairns, MJ (Mike) – Somerset
Cann, DJ (Darren) – Norfolk
Child, SA (Stephen) – Kent
Clark, RM (Richard) – Northumberland
Clayton, S (Simon) – Co. Durham
Collin, J (Jake) – Merseyside
Collins, LM (Lee) – Surrey
Cook, SJ (Steve) – Derbyshire
Cooper, IJ (Ian) – Kent
Coote, DH (David) – Nottinghamshire
Copeland, SJ (Steven) – Merseyside
Cox, JL (James) – Worcestershire
Coy, M (Martin) – Co. Durham
Creighton, SW (Steve) – Berkshire
Crouch, IJ (Ian) – Kent
Curry, PE (Paul) – Northumberland
Daly, SDJ (Stephen) – Middlesex
Davies, A (Andy) – Hampshire
Davies, PP (Peter) – Cheshire
Davison, PA (Paul) – Cleveland
Denton, MJ (Michael) – Lancashire
Dermott, P (Philip) – Cheshire
Dexter, MC (Martin) – Leicestershire
Dicicco, M (Matthew) – Cleveland
Drysdale, D (Darren) – Lincolnshire
Dudley, IA (Ian) – Nottinghamshire
Duncan, SAJ (Scott) – Tyne & Wear
Dunn, C (Carl) – Staffordshire
England, DJH (Darren) – S. Yorkshire
Evetts, GS (Gary) – Hertfordshire
Farries, J (John) – Oxfordshire
Fletcher, R (Russell) – Derbyshire
Flynn, J (John) – Wiltshire
Foley, MJ (Matt) – London
Ford, D (Declan) – Leicestershire
Ganfield, RS (Ron) – Somerset

Garratt, AM (Andy) – West Midlands
George, M (Mike) – Norfolk
Gooch, P (Peter) – Lancashire
Gordon, B (Barry) – Co. Durham
Gosling, IJ (Ian) – Kent
Graham, P (Paul) – Manchester
Gratton, D (Danny) – Staffordshire
Green, RC (Russell) – Lancashire
Greenhalgh, N (Nicholas) – Lancashire
Greenwood, AH (Alf) – Yorkshire
Griffiths, M (Mark) – S. Yorkshire
Grunnill, W (Wayne) – E. Yorkshire
Hair, NA (Neil) – Cambridgeshire
Halliday, A (Andy) – N. Yorkshire
Hambling, GS (Glenn) – Norfolk
Handley, D (Darren) – Lancashire
Harrington, T (Tony) – Cleveland
Hart, G (Glen) – Co. Durham
Harwood, CN (Colin) – Manchester
Haycock, KW (Ken) – W. Yorkshire
Hayward, K (Kevin) – Staffordshire
Hendley, AR (Andy) – W. Midlands
Hewitt, RT (Richard) – N. Yorkshire
Heywood, M (Mark) – Cheshire
Hilton, G (Gary) – Lancashire
Hobbis, N (Nick) – W. Midlands
Hodskinson, P (Paul) – Lancashire
Holderness, BC (Barry) – Essex
Holmes, AR (Adrian) – W. Yorkshire
Hopkins, JD (John) – Essex
Horton, AJ (Tony) – W. Midlands
Hunt, J (Jonathan) – Co. Durham
Hutchinson, AD (Andrew) – Cheshire
Huxtable, B (Brett) – Devon
Ihringova, A (Sasa) – Shropshire
Jerden, GJN (Gary) – Essex
Johnson, KA (Kevin) – Somerset
Johnson, RL (Ryan) – Manchester
Jones, RJ (Robert) – Merseyside
Joyce, R (Ross) – Cleveland
Kavanagh, C (Chris) – Lancashire
Kaye, E (Elliott) – W. Yorkshire
Keane, PJ (Patrick) – W. Midlands
Kendall, R (Richard) – Bedfordshire
Kettlewell, PT (Paul) – Lancashire
Khatib, B (Billy) – Tyne & Wear
Kinseley, N (Nick) – Essex
Kirkup, PJ (Peter) – Northamptonshire
Knapp, SC (Simon) – Gloucestershire
Knight, PJ (Philip) – Kent
Knowles, CJ (Chris) – Northamptonshire
Knowles, J (Jason) – W. Yorkshire
Laver, AA (Andrew) – Hampshire
Law, GC (Geoff) – Leicestershire
Lawson, KD (Keith) – Lincolnshire
Ledger, S (Scott) – S. Yorkshire
Lennard, HW (Harry) – E. Sussex
Lewis, RL (Rob) – Shropshire
Lewis, SD (Sam) – Middlesex
Linden, W (Wes) – Middlesex
Long, SJ (Simon) – Suffolk
Mccallum, DA (Dave) – Tyne & Wear
Mccoy, MT (Michael) – W. Sussex
Mcdonough, M (Mick) – Tyne & Wear
Mclaughlin, M (Mathew) – Bedfordshire
Mackrell, EB (Eric) – Hampshire
Madley, A (Andy) – W. Yorkshire
Madley, RJ (Bobby) – W. Yorkshire
Magill, JP (John) – Essex
Malone, B (Brendan) – Wiltshire
Margetts, DS (David) – Essex
Markham, DR (Danny) – Tyne & Wear
Marsden, PR (Paul) – Lancashire
Martin, PC (Paul) – Northamptonshire
Martin, RJ (Richard) – Somerset
Martin, SJ (Stephen) – Staffordshire
Mason, T (Tony) – Kent
Massey, SL (Sian) – W. Midlands
Massey, T (Trevor) – Cheshire
Matadar, RM (Mo) – Leicestershire
Maton, A (Tony) – Leicestershire
Matthews, A (Adrian) – Wiltshire
Mattocks, KJ (Kevin) – Lancashire
Meeson, DP (Daniel) – Staffordshire
Melin, PW (Paul) – Surrey
Merchant, R (Rob) – Staffordshire

Metcalfe, RL (Lee) – Lancashire
Mohareb, D (Dean) – Cheshire
Muge, G (Gavin) – Bedfordshire
Mullarkey, M (Mike) – Devon
Murphy, ME (Michael) – W. Midlands
Murphy, N (Nigel) – Nottinghamshire
Naylor, D (Dave) – Nottinghamshire
Naylor, MA (Michael) – Sheffield
Newbold, AM (Andy) – Leicestershire
Newell, AC (Andy) – Lancashire
Newman, RP (Ryan) – S. Yorkshire
Norcott, MG (Wade) – Essex
Norris, P (Paul) – Cheshire
Nunn, AJ (Adam) – Wiltshire
Oldham, SA (Scott) – Lancashire
Parker, AR (Alan) – Derbyshire
Peart, T (Tony) – N. Yorkshire
Perry, MS (Marc) – W. Midlands
Philpott, M (Mark) – Cornwall
Phipps, SJ (Stephen) – Oxfordshire
Plowright, DP (David) – Nottinghamshire
Pollock, RM (Bob) – Merseyside
Porter, W (Wayne) – Lincolnshire
Pottage, M (Mark) – Somerset
Powell, CI (Chris) – Dorset
Procter-Green, SRM (Shaun) – Lincolnshire
Radford, N (Neil) – Worcestershire
Rayner, AE (Amy) – Leicestershire
Richards, DC (Ceri) – Carmarthenshire
Richardson, D (David) – W. Yorkshire
Roberts, B (Bob) – Lancashire
Roberts, DJ (Danny) – Manchester
Robinson, TJ (Tim) – W. Sussex
Rock, DK (David) – Hertfordshire
Rodda, A (Andrew) – Devon
Ross, SJ (Stephen) – Lincolnshire
Rowley, MD (Michael) – Berkshire
Rubery, SP (Steve) – Essex
Russell, GR (Geoff) – Northamptonshire
Russell, M (Mark) – Gloucestershire
Sainsbury, A (Andrew) – Wiltshire
Saliy, O (Oleksandr) – Middlesex
Salt, RA (Richard) – N. Yorkshire
Sannerude, A (Adrian) – Suffolk
Scholes, MS (Mark) – Buckinghamshire
Scregg, AJ (Andrew) – Merseyside
Sharp, PR (Phil) – Hertfordshire
Siddall, I (Iain) – Lancashire
Simpson, J (Jeremy) – Lancashire
Simpson, P (Paul) – Co. Durham
Slaughter, A (Ashley) – Sussex
Smallwood, W (William) – Cheshire
Smedley, I (Ian) – Derbyshire
Smith, AN (Andrew) – W. Yorkshire
Smith, EI (Eamonn) – Surrey
Smith, N (Nigel) – Derbyshire
Smith, S (Stephen) – Co. Durham
Stewart, M (Matt) – Suffolk
Stockbridge, SM (Seb) – Tyne & Wear
Storrie, D (David) – S. Yorkshire
Stott, GT (Gary) – Manchester
Street, DR (Duncan) – W. Yorkshire
Stretton, GS (Guy) – Leicestershire
Sutton, MA (Mark) – Derbyshire
Swabey, L (Lee) – Devon
Thompson, MF (Marvin) – Middlesex
Thompson, PI (Paul) – Derbyshire
Tomlinson, SD (Stephen) – Hampshire
Trott, WL (Wayne) – Merseyside
Turner, A (Andrew) – Devon
Turner, GB (Glenn) – Derbyshire
Tyas, J (Jason) – W. Yorkshire
Unsworth, D (David) – Manchester
Vaughan, RG (Roger) – N. Somerset
Waring, J (Jim) – Lancashire
Watts, AS (Adam) – Worcestershire
Weaver, M (Mark) – W. Midlands
West, RJ (Richard) – E. Yorkshire
Whiteley, J (Jason) – W. Yorkshire
Whitton, RP (Rob) – Essex
Wigglesworth, RJ (Richard) – S. Yorkshire
Wright, P (Peter) – Merseyside
Yates, O (Oliver) – Staffordshire
Yeo, KG (Keith) – Essex
Yerby, MS (Martin) – Kent
Young, GR (Gary) – Bedfordshire

TRANSFERS 2009–10

JUNE 2009

	From	To	Fee in £
11 Barry, Gareth	Aston Villa	Manchester City	12,000,000
15 Chapman, Adam	Sheffield United	Oxford United	15,000
16 Dann, Scott	Coventry City	Birmingham City	3,500,000
17 Diagouraga, Toumani	Hereford United	Peterborough United	200,000
30 Doyle, Kevin E.	Reading	Wolverhampton Wanderers	6,500,000
26 Johnson, Glen M.C.	Portsmouth	Liverpool	18,500,000
25 Johnson, Roger	Cardiff City	Birmingham City	5,000,000
30 Kane, Anthony M.	Blackburn Rovers	Carlisle United	undisclosed
29 McGoldrick, David J.	Southampton	Nottingham Forest	1,000,000
5 Morison, Steve	Stevenage Borough	Millwall	130,000
30 Peltier, Lee A.	Yeovil Town	Huddersfield Town	undisclosed
5 Pope, Thomas J.	Crewe Alexandra	Rotherham United	150,000
24 Santa Cruz, Roque	Blackburn Rovers	Manchester City	18,000,000
30 Simpson, Robert	Coventry City	Huddersfield Town	300,000
30 Surman, Andrew R.E.	Southampton	Wolverhampton Wanderers	1,200,000
17 Tudur-Jones, Owain	Swansea City	Norwich City	250,000
16 Williamson, Lee	Watford	Sheffield United	500,000

TEMPORARY TRANSFERS

9 Hatch, Liam M.A. – Peterborough United – Luton Town; 27 Heath, Joseph – Nottingham Forest – Lincoln City; 26 Sears, Fred – West Ham United – Crystal Palace

JULY 2009

	From	To	
24 Adebayor, Emmanuel	Arsenal	Manchester City	25,000,000
27 Allott, Mark S.	Tranmere Rovers	Chesterfield	undisclosed
1 Anderson, Paul	Liverpool	Nottingham Forest	250,000
15 Barker, Shaun	Blackpool	Derby County	900,000
22 Blackstock, Dexter A.	Queens Park Rangers	Nottingham Forest	1,600,000
2 Boyd, Adam	Leyton Orient	Hartlepool United	80,000
30 Boyes, Adam J.	York City	Scunthorpe United	80,000
22 Bromby, Leigh	Watford	Sheffield United	undisclosed
1 Brown, Wayne L.	Hull City	Leicester City	undisclosed
3 Camp, Lee M.J.	Queens Park Rangers	Nottingham Forest	100,000
20 Campbell, Fraizer L.	Manchester United	Sunderland	3,500,000
14 Chopra, Rocky M.	Sunderland	Cardiff City	3,000,000
24 Clingan, Samuel G.	Norwich City	Coventry City	650,000
8 Cox, Simon	Swindon Town	West Bromwich Albion	1,500,000
28 Crouch, Peter J.	Portsmouth	Tottenham Hotspur	10,000,000
9 Delaney, Damien	Queens Park Rangers	Ipswich Town	700,000
15 Dickinson, Liam M.	Derby County	Brighton & Hove Albion	100,000
16 Downing, Stewart	Middlesbrough	Aston Villa	12,000,000
8 Draper, Ross	Hednesford Town	Macclesfield Town	undisclosed
1 Dyer, Nathan A.J.	Southampton	Swansea City	400,000
17 Easter, Jermaine M.	Plymouth Argyle	Milton Keynes Dons	200,00
23 Evans, Chedwyn M.	Manchester City	Sheffield United	3,000,000
10 Evans, Gareth C.	Macclesfield Town	Bradford City	Free
4 Gerken, Dean J.	Colchester United	Bristol City	undisclosed
24 Gerrard, Anthony	Walsall	Cardiff City	undisclosed
1 Gleeson, Stephen M.	Wolverhampton Wanderers	Milton Keynes Dons	undisclosed
21 Gunter, Christopher R.	Tottenham Hotspur	Nottingham Forest	1,750,000
3 Halford, Gregory	Sunderland	Wolverhampton Wanderers	2,000,000
14 Haynes, Danny L.	Ipswich Town	Bristol City	400,000
24 Holt, Grant	Shrewsbury Town	Norwich City	550,000
2 Hudson, Mark A.	Charlton Athletic	Cardiff City	1,075,000
6 Law, Nicholas	Sheffield United	Rotherham United	Free
3 Legge, Leon	Tonbridge Angels	Brentford	undisclosed
22 Lynch, Joel J.	Brighton & Hove Albion	Nottingham Forest	200,000
7 Martin, Lee R.	Manchester United	Ipswich Town	2,000,000
28 McCrae, Romone	Crawley Town	Peterborough United	undisclosed
20 McKenna, Paul S.	Preston North End	Nottingham Forest	750,000
7 Mears, Tyrone	Derby County	Burnley	500,000
23 Mills, Daniel P.	Crawley Town	Peterborough United	undisclosed
1 Moxey, Dean	Exeter City	Derby County	350,000
24 Naughton, Kyle	Sheffield United	Tottenham Hotspur	2,500,000
14 Neal, Christopher M.	Preston North End	Shrewsbury Town	nominal
15 Nyatanga, Lewin J.	Derby County	Bristol City	500,000
8 O'Connor, Michael J.	Crewe Alexandra	Scunthorpe United	250,000
9 Penn, Russell	Kidderminster Harriers	Burton Albion	50,000
2 Robinson, Theo L.R.	Watford	Huddersfield Town	100,000
9 Smith, James D.	Chelsea	Leyton Orient	undisclosed
1 Surman, Andrew R.	Southampton	Wolverhampton Wanderers	1,200,000
31 Talbot, Andrew	Luton Town	Chesterfield	Free
15 Taylor, Andrew	Tranmere Rovers	Sheffield United	400,000

27 Tipton, Matthew J.	Droylsden	Macclesfield Town	undisclosed
31 Toure, Kolo A.	Arsenal	Manchester City	14,000,000
14 Tunnicliffe, James M.	Stockport County	Brighton & Hove Albion	undisclosed
1 Valencia, Luis Antonio	Wigan Athletic	Manchester United	15,250,000
30 Walker, Kyle	Sheffield United	Tottenham Hotspur	1,500,000
14 Wellens, Richard P.	Doncaster Rovers	Leicester City	1,200,000
24 Whaley, Simon	Preston North End	Norwich City	undisclosed
24 Whitehead, Dean	Sunderland	Stoke City	3,000,000
24 Wiggins, Rhoys	Crystal Palace	Norwich City	undisclosed
10 Williams, Benjamin P.	Carlisle United	Colchester United	undisclosed
31 Wright, Jake M.	Crawley Town	Brighton & Hove Albion	undisclosed
9 Yeates, Mark	Colchester United	Middlesbrough	500,000

TEMPORARY TRANSFERS

24 Akurang, Cliff C. – Barnet – Rushden & Diamonds; 24 Alnwick, Ben – Tottenham Hotspur – Norwich City; 24 Archibald-Henville, Troy – Tottenham Hotspur – Exeter City; 14 Bolasie, Yannick – Plymouth Argyle – Barnet; 30 Bunn, Mark – Blackburn Rovers – Sheffield United; 24 Button, David R.E. – Tottenham Hotspur – Crewe Alexandra; 20 Byrne, Mark – Nottingham Forest – Rushden & Diamonds; 16 Caulker, Steven R. – Tottenham Hotspur – Yeovil Town; 29 Craney, Ian T.W. – Accrington Stanley – Morecambe; 21 Daniels, Luke M. – West Bromwich Albion – Tranmere Rovers; 14 Dennehy, Darren J. – Cardiff City – Hereford United; 27 Eastwood, Simon C. – Huddersfield Town – Bradford City; 31 Forster, Fraser G. – Newcastle United – Bristol Rovers; 29 Gazet Du Chattelier, Ryan – Portsmouth – Weymouth; 20 Gowling, Joshua A.I. – Carlisle United – Gillingham; 23 Green, Matthew J. – Torquay United – Oxford United; 1 Hart, Charles J.J. – Manchester City – Birmingham City; 1 Heath, Joseph – Nottingham Forest – Lincoln City; 30 Heath, Matthew P. – Leeds United – Southend United; 29 Jevons, Phillip – Huddersfield Town – Morecambe; 24 Logan, Shaleum – Manchester City – Tranmere Rovers; 23 McCarthy, Alex S. – Reading – Yeovil Town; 19 Mason, Ryan G. – Tottenham Hotspur – Yeovil Town; Moloney, Brendon A. – Nottingham Forest – Notts County; 20 Medley, Luke A.C. – Barnet – Woking; 20 Pearce, Krystian M.V. – Birmingham City – Peterborough United; 3 Potter, Alfie J. – Peterborough United – Oxford United; 10 Price, Lewis P. – Derby County – Brentford; 29 Puddy, Willem J.S. – Cheltenham Town – Bath City; 14 Redmond, Shane P. – Nottingham Forest – Burton Albion; 6 Reid, James A. – Nottingham Forest – Rushden & Diamonds; 28 Rendell, Scott D. – Peterborough United – Torquay United; 27 Reynolds, Callum F. – Portsmouth – Luton Town; 22 Robinson, Paul P. – West Bromwich Albion – Bolton Wanderers; 24 Sawyer, Lee T. – Chelsea – Southend United; 6 Shroot, Robin – Birmingham City – Burton Albion; 27 Taarabt, Adel – Tottenham Hotspur – Queens Park Rangers; 13 Taiwo, Thomas J.W. – Chelsea – Carlisle United; 21 Thornhill, Matthew – Nottingham Forest – Brighton & Hove Albion; 24 Treacy, Keith – Blackburn Rovers – Sheffield United; 30 White, John A. – Colchester United – Southend United

AUGUST 2009

8 Bassong, Sebastian A.	Newcastle United	Tottenham Hotspur	8,000,000
28 Beattie, Craig	West Bromwich Albion	Swansea City	undisclosed
20 Bennett, Elliott	Wolverhampton Wanderers	Brighton & Hove Albion	undisclosed
6 Bent, Darren	Tottenham Hotspur	Sunderland	10,000,000
7 Beye, Habib	Newcastle United	Aston Villa	3,000,000
18 Bikey, Andre S.	Reading	Burnley	2,000,000
31 Boateng, Kevin P.	Tottenham Hotspur	Portsmouth	4,000,000
28 Brown, Michael R.	Wigan Athletic	Portsmouth	nominal
12 Cattermole, Lee B.	Wigan Athletic	Sunderland	6,000,000
6 Charnock, Kieran J.	Peterborough United	Torquay United	undisclosed
27 Chimbonda, Pascal	Tottenham Hotspur	Blackburn Rovers	1,800,000
13 Cranie, Martin J.	Portsmouth	Coventry City	600,000
4 Delph, Fabian	Leeds United	Aston Villa	6,500,000
28 Distin, Sylvain	Portsmouth	Everton	5,000,000
18 Duff, Damien A.	Newcastle United	Fulham	2,500,000
12 Eardley, Neal	Oldham Athletic	Blackpool	undisclosed
7 Elder, Nathan	Brentford	Shrewsbury Town	undisclosed
3 Evans, Chedwyn M.	Manchester City	Sheffield United	3,000,000
27 Flynn, Matthew E.	Macclesfield Town	Rochdale	nominal
21 Gallagher, Paul	Blackburn Rovers	Leicester City	1,000,000
27 Gowling, Joshua A.I.	Carlisle United	Gillingham	undisclosed
24 Gray, Andrew D.	Charlton Athletic	Barnsley	undisclosed
10 Hammill, Adam	Liverpool	Barnsley	undisclosed
18 Hammond, Dean J.	Colchester United	Southampton	undisclosed
11 Hunt, Stephen P.	Reading	Hull City	3,000,000
17 Hurst, Kevan	Scunthorpe United	Carlisle United	undisclosed
28 Huth, Robert	Middlesbrough	Stoke City	5,000,000
14 Knight, Zatyiah	Aston Villa	Bolton Wanderers	2,000,000
10 Lambert, Rickie L.	Bristol Rovers	Southampton	1,000,000
12 Le Fondre, Adam J.	Rochdale	Rotherham United	undisclosed
26 Lescott, Joleon P.	Everton	Manchester City	24,000,000
10 Mattock, Joseph W.	Leicester City	West Bromwich Albion	undisclosed
27 McAnuff, Joel J.F.M.	Watford	Reading	undisclosed
5 McIndoe, Michael	Bristol City	Coventry City	500,000
28 McShane, Paul D.	Sunderland	Hull City	undisclosed
6 Mills, Matthew C.	Doncaster Rovers	Reading	2,000,000
31 Mullin, Paul B.	Accrington Stanley	Morecambe	Free
3 N'Guessen, Diombo	Lincoln City	Leicester City	400,000
6 Olofinjana, Seyi G.	Stoke City	Hull City	3,000,000
7 Parry, Paul I.	Cardiff City	Preston North End	300,000
7 Priskin, Tamas	Watford	Ipswich Town	undisclosed

27 Rasiak, Grzegorz	Southampton	Reading	undisclosed
7 Reid, Reuben J.	Rotherham United	West Bromwich Albion	200,000
14 Ricketts, Sam D.	Hull City	Bolton Wanderers	1,000,000
21 Schmeichel, Kaspar P.	Manchester City	Notts County	800,000
29 Shumulikoski, Veliche	Ipswich Town	Preston North End	300,000
27 Smith, Thomas W.	Watford	Portsmouth	1,200,000
27 Taiwo, Soloman O.	Dagenham & Redbridge	Cardiff City	undisclosed
14 Taylor, Cleveland K.W.	Carlisle United	Brentford	undisclosed
28 Warnock, Stephen	Blackburn Rovers	Aston Villa	6,000,000

TEMPORARY TRANSFERS

26 Adams, Stephen M. – Torquay United – Forest Green Rovers; 5 Ademola, Moses – Brentford – Woking; 20 Alessandra, Lewis P. – Oldham Athletic – Chester City; 28 Artus, Frankie – Bristol City – Cheltenham Town; 4 Bertrand, Ryan – Chelsea – Reading; 7 Bevan, David – Aston Villa – Ilkeston Town; 31 Bignall, Nicholas C. – Reading – Stockport County; 20 Blackman, Nicholas A. – Blackburn Rovers – Oldham Athletic; 28 Blake, Darcy J. – Cardiff City – Plymouth Argyle; 7 Blanchett, Daniel W. – Peterborough United – Stevenage Borough; 28 Boden, Luke – Sheffield Wednesday – Northampton Town; 6 Bozanic, Oliver J. – Reading – Cheltenham Town; 21 Bridcutt, Liam R. – Chelsea – Stockport County; 28 Calver, Craig T. – Southend United – St Albans City; 21 Chambers, Ashley R. – Leicester City – Wycombe Wanderers; 7 Chandler, Jamie – Sunderland – Darlington; 17 Cleverley, Thomas W. – Manchester United – Watford; 19 Clough, Charlie – Bristol Rovers – Chippenham Town; 7 Colback, Jack R. – Sunderland – Ipswich Town; 27 Coleman, Rory C. – Scunthorpe United – Harrogate Town; 28 Cook, Andrew E. – Carlisle United – Workington; 18 Cook, Jordan A. – Sunderland – Darlington; 21 Cork, Jack F.P. – Chelsea – Coventry City; 17 Cummings, Shaun – Chelsea – West Bromwich Albion; 11 Daly, George J. – Wycombe Wanderers – Hayes & Yeading United; 10 Davidson, Ross – Port Vale – Stafford Rangers; 17 Dean, Harlee J. – Dagenham & Redbridge – Braintree Town; 28 Denton, Tom – Huddersfield Town – Cheltenham Town; 28 Dickov, Paul – Leicester City – Derby County; 14 Di Santo, Franco – Chelsea – Blackburn Rovers; 29 Donnelly, Georgie J. – Plymouth Argyle – Luton Town; 7 Dowson, David – Sunderland – Darlington; 6 Doyle, Michael P. – Coventry City – Leeds United; 14 Drinkwater, Daniel N. – Manchester United – Huddersfield Town; 7 Eardley, Neal – Oldham Athletic – Blackpool; 7 Eastham, Ashley – Blackpool – Hyde United; 30 Edward, Daniel G. – Port Vale – Altrincham; 26 Ellis, Marc – Torquay United – Forest Green Rovers; 17 Emmanuel-Thomas, Jay-Aston – Arsenal – Blackpool; 22 Etuhu, Kelvin – Manchester City – Cardiff City; 28 Fairclough, Benjamin M.S. – Notts County – Ilkeston Town; 13 Flynn, Matthew E. – Macclesfield Town – Rochdale; 21 Foley, David J. – Hartlepool United – Barrow; 14 Forecast, Tommy S. – Southampton – Grimsby Town; 28 Forster, Fraser G. – Newcastle United – Norwich City; 14 Friend, George A.J. – Wolverhampton Wanderers – Millwall; 28 Gaughran, Samuel D. – Peterborough United – Grays Athletic; 15 Glover, Daniel – Port Vale – Salisbury City; 6 Godsmark, Jonathan – Newcastle United – Hereford United; 22 Gray, Andrew D. – Charlton Athletic – Barnsley; 21 Green, Michael J. – Bristol Rovers – Gloucester City; 21 Greening, Jonathan – West Bromwich Albion – Fulham; 19 Grimes, Jamie N. – Swansea City – Haverfordwest County; 6 Gunning, Gavin – Blackburn Rovers – Tranmere Rovers; 18 Halstead, Mark J. – Blackpool – Burscough; 15 Heaton, Thomas D. – Manchester United – Queens Park Rangers; 6 Howe, Jermaine R. – Peterborough United – Lincoln City; 25 Jackman, Daniel J. – Northampton Town – Gillingham; 21 Jackson, Marlon M. – Bristol City – Hereford United; 14 Jo – Manchester City – Everton; 6 Judge, Alan – Blackburn Rovers – Plymouth Argyle; 21 Kay, Adam B. – Burnley – Chester City; 4 Kee, Billy R. – Leicester City – Accrington Stanley; 6 Kite, Alexandros – Bristol Rovers – Gloucester City; 14 Krysiak, Artur L. – Birmingham City – Burton Albion; 7 Labadie, Josh C. – West Bromwich Albion – Shrewsbury Town; 21 Lansbury, Henri G. – Arsenal – Watford; 27 Levet, Ciaran A. – Plymouth Argyle – Yeovil Town; 4 Lisbie, Kevin A. – Ipswich Town – Colchester United; 7 Livermore, Jake C. – Tottenham Hotspur – Derby County; 21 Lynch, Christopher M. – Burnley – Chester City; 24 McCrory, Damien P. – Plymouth Argyle – Port Vale; 7 McDermott, Donal – Manchester City – Chesterfield; 31 McGivern, Ryan – Manchester City – Leicester City; 5 Mackay, Michael – Hartlepool United – Gateshead; 14 Mancienne, Michael I. – Chelsea – Wolverhampton Wanderers; 7 Marrow, Alexander J. – Blackburn Rovers – Oldham Athletic; 7 Marshall, Ben – Stoke City – Northampton Town; 4 Martin, Alan – Leeds United – Accrington Stanley; 14 Mellis, Jacob A. – Chelsea – Southampton; 21 Mitchley, Daniel J. – Blackpool – Burscough; 31 Moffatt, Scott L. – Manchester United – Altrincham; 7 Mvoto, Jean – Sunderland – Southend United; 14 Obadeyi, Temitope – Bolton Wanderers – Swindon Town; 3 Obika, Jonathan – Tottenham Hotspur – Yeovil Town; 28 Ojapah, Philip – Oldham Athletic – Stalybridge Celtic; 21 O'Grady, Christopher J. – Oldham Athletic – Rochdale; 31 O'Hara, Jamie – Tottenham Hotspur – Portsmouth; 31 O'Leary, Kristian D. – Swansea City – Leyton Orient; 28 Pack, Marlon – Portsmouth – Wycombe Wanderers; 17 Panther, Emmanuel – Exeter City – Morecambe; 26 Phillips, Steven J. – Bristol Rovers – Shrewsbury Town; 6 Picton, Jake M. – Scunthorpe United – Gainsborough Trinity; 21 Plummer, Tristan D. – Bristol City – Hereford United; 18 Porritt, Nathan J. – Middlesbrough – Darlington; 18 Powell, Darren D. – Brentford – Crawley Town; 15 Prosser, Luke B. – Port Vale – Salisbury City; 7 Puncheon, Jason D.I. – Barnet – Milton Keynes Dons; 22 Rigg, Sean M. – Bristol Rovers – Forest Green Rovers; 14 Robertson, Jordan – Sheffield United – Bury; 7 Rose, Romone A.A. – Queens Park Rangers – Northampton Town; 28 Sappleton, Reneil S.A. – Leicester City – Macclesfield Town; 14 Shackell, Jason – Wolverhampton Wanderers – Doncaster Rovers; 28 Shaw, Jon S. – Rochdale – Barrow; 7 Shumulikoski, Veliche – Ipswich Town – Preston North End; 14 Simpson, Daniel P. – Manchester United – Newcastle United; 27 Simpson, Jay-Alistaire F. – Arsenal – Queens Park Rangers; 6 Sinclair, Scott A. – Chelsea – Wigan Athletic; 7 Smith, Adam J. – Tottenham Hotspur – Wycombe Wanderers; 18 Spence, Jordan – West Ham United – Scunthorpe United; 14 Stephens, Dale C. – Oldham Athletic – Rochdale; 5 St Louis-Hamilton, Danzelle D. – Stoke City – Vauxhall Motors; 7 Taylor, Aaron M. – Morecambe – Barrow; 7 Tejan-Sie, Thomas M. – Dagenham & Redbridge – Braintree Town; 22 Thomas, Simon V. – Crystal Palace – Ebbsfleet United; 21 Threlfall, Robert R. – Liverpool – Northampton Town; 7 Townsend, Andros – Tottenham Hotspur – Leyton Orient; 20 Trotman, Neal A. – Preston North End – Southampton; 28 Trundle, Lee C. – Bristol City – Swansea City; 27 Tuncay – Sanli – Middlesbrough – Stoke City; 14 Tymon, Matthew R. – Hartlepool United – Whitby Town; 31 Tyrrell, James R. – Bristol Rovers – Paulton Rovers; 7 Van Aanholt, Patrick J.M. – Chelsea – Coventry City; 21 Varney, Luke I. – Derby County – Sheffield Wednesday; 10 Verma, Aman – Leicester City – Crewe Alexandra; 7 Waghorn, Martyn T. – Sunderland – Leicester City; 5 Walker, Kyle A. – Tottenham Hotspur – Sheffield United; 31 Walton, Simon W. – Plymouth Argyle – Crewe Alexandra; 21 White, Joseph S. – Bristol Rovers – Yate Town; 21 Wilson, James S. – Bristol City – Brentford; 14 Worley, Harry J. – Leicester City – Crewe Alexandra; 6 Worrall, David R. – West Bromwhich Albion – Bury

SEPTEMBER 2009

1 Ben Haim, Tal	Manchester City	Portsmouth	1,000,000
1 Bromby, Leigh	Sheffield United	Leeds United	undisclosed
1 Colbeck, Philip J.	Bradford City	Oldham Athletic	undisclosed
1 Colins, Daniel L.	Sunderland	Stoke City	2,750,000
1 Cummings, Shaun M.	Chelsea	Reading	undisclosed
3 Diop, Papa B.	Fulham	Portsmouth	undisclosed
1 Dunne, Richard P.	Manchester City	Aston Villa	5,000,000
1 Edwards, Carlos A.	Sunderland	Ipswich Town	1,350,000
1 Howard, Brian R.W.	Sheffield United	Reading	undisclosed
10 Jackman, Daniel J.	Northampton Town	Gillingham	undisclosed
1 Kranjcar, Nico	Portsmouth	Tottenham Hotspur	2,500,000
1 Leadbitter, Grant	Sunderland	Ipswich Town	2,650,000
21 McCombe, Jamie	Lincoln City	Bristol City	undisclosed
10 Myhill, Boaz G.O.	Aston Villa	Hull City	50,000
1 Schofield, Daniel J.	Yeovil Town	Millwall	undisclosed
1 Turner, Michael T.	Hull City	Sunderland	2,000,000
22 Whelan, Glenn D.	Sheffield Wednesday	Stoke City	500,000
1 Williamson, Michael J.	Watford	Portsmouth	3,000,000
8 Wilson, Brian	Cheltenham Town	Bristol City	undisclosed
1 Wright, Mark A.	Brighton & Hove Albion	Bristol Rovers	undisclosed

TEMPORARY TRANSFERS

8 Aldred, Thomas M. – Carlisle United – Workington; 3 Allen-Djilali, Kieran S.L. – Crystal Palace – Crawley Town; 1 Andersen, Mikkel – Reading – Bristol Rovers; 19 Andrew,Daniel K. – Peterborough United – Tamworth; 25 Appiah, Kwesi – Peterborough United – Kings Lynn; 1 Barton, Adam J. – Preston North End – Crawley Town; 17 Batth, Daniel T. – Wolverhampton Wanderers – Colchester United; 29 Bialkowski, Bartosz M. – Southampton – Barnsley; 1 Betsy, Kevin – Southend United – Wycombe Wanderers; 17 Blanchett, Daniel W. – Wigan Athletic – Hereford United; 29 Bogdan, Adam – Bolton Wanderers – Crewe Alexandra; 25 Brough, Michael – Torquay United – Stevenage Borough; 25 Brown, Lee J. – Queens Park Rangers – Salisbury City; 1 Button, David R.E. – Tottenham Hotspur – Crewe Alexandra; 4 Canham, Sean – Notts County – Hayes & Yeading United; 25 Carayol, Mustapha L. – Torquay United – Kettering Town; 14 Cathcart, Craig G. – Manchester United – Watford; 18 Cayford, Daniel – Bristol Rovers – Chippenham Town; 18 Chester, James G. – Manchester United – Plymouth Argyle; 21 Clark, Robert J. – Doncaster Rovers – Boston United; 1 Collins, Dominic – Preston North End – Crawley Town; 1 Collins, Neill – Wolverhampton Wanderers – Preston North End; 11 Convey, Matthew T. – Bradford City – Hyde United; 29 Cresswell, Richard P.W. – Leeds United – Sheffield United; 29 Crook, Billy T. – Peterborough United – Histon; 18 Cumbers, Luis C. – Gillingham – Ebbsfleet United; 1 Cox, Samuel P. – Tottenham Hotspur – Cheltenham Town; 18 Davies, Andrew D. – Stoke City – Sheffield United; 1 Davies, Aaron R. – Nottingham Forest – Brighton & Hove Albion; 25 Davies, Craig M. – Brighton & Hove Albion – Yeovil Town; 17 Devitt, Jamie M. – Hull City – Darlington; 25 Dickinson, Carl M. – Stoke City – Barnsley; 18 Dickson, Christopher A.K. – Charlton Athletic – Bristol Rovers; 19 Doyle, Nathan L.R. – Hull City – Barnsley; 14 Edwards, Declan A. – Stockport County – Northwich Victoria; 18 Elliott, Thomas J. – Leeds United – Bury; 29 Fielding, Francis D. – Blackburn Rovers – Leeds United; 1 Fleetwood, Stuart K.W. – Charlton Athletic – Exeter City; 19 Folan, Caleb C. – Hull City – Middlesbrough; 8 Franks, Oliver C. – Doncaster Rovers – Brigg Town; 19 Francis, Fraser G. – Brentford – Basingstoke Town; 18 Friend, George A.J. – Wolverhampton Wanderers – Southend United; 17 Gobern, Oscar L. – Southampton – Milton Keynes Dons; 18 Gray, David P. – Manchester United – Plymouth Argyle; 1 Haldane, Lewis O. – Bristol Rovers – Port Vale; 25 Harewood, Marlon A. – Aston Villa – Newcastle United; 1 Harper, James A.J. – Reading – Sheffield United; 15 Helguson, Heidar – Queens Park Rangers – Watford; 10 Henry, James – Reading – Millwall; 17 Hoult, Russell – Notts County – Darlington; 3 Howard, Kieran C. – Swansea City – Neath; 11 Huntington, Paul D. – Leeds United – Stockport County; 1 Jansson, Oscar – Tottenham Hotspur – Exeter City; 15 Johnson, Jermaine J. – Derby County – Stafford Rangers; 25 Johnson, John J. – Middlesbrough – Northampton Town; 25 Jones, Daniel J. – Wolverhampton Wanderers – Notts County; 18 Kane, Anthony M. – Carlisle United – Darlington; 25 Keltie, Clark S.B. – Rochdale – Chester City; 18 Khizanishvili, Zurab – Blackburn Rovers – Newcastle United; 1 Kilbey, Thomas C – Portsmouth – Dagenham & Redbridge; 17 King, Craig S. – Leicester City – Hereford United; 24 Knowles, James – Burton Albion – Harrogate Town; 1 Lees, Thomas J. – Leeds United – Accrington Stanley; 1 Lillis, Joshua M. – Scunthorpe United – Grimsby Town; 18 Lowry, Shane T. – Aston Villa – Plymouth Argyle; 25 MacAuley, Joshua – Tranmere Rovers – Colwyn Bay; 21 MacDonald, Shaun B. – Swansea City – Yeovil Town; 28 McManus, Scott H. – Crewe Alexandra – Curzon Ashton; 18 Marshall, Mark A. – Swindon Town – Hereford United; 1 McDonald, Clayton – Manchester City – Walsall; 18 Mills, Daniel P. – Peterborough United – Torquay United; 23 Mills, Gregory A. – Derby County – Solihull Moors; 11 Noone, Craig – Plymouth Argyle – Exeter City; 25 Oastler, Joseph J. – Queens Park Rangers – Salisbury City; 18 Odejayi, Olukayode – Barnsley – Colchester United; 17 O'Donovan, Roy S. – Sunderland – Southend United; 1 O'Toole, John J. – Watford – Colchester United; 18 Parrett, Dean G. – Tottenham Hotspur – Aldershot Town; 4 Plummer, Neikell – Bristol Rovers – Paulton Rovers; 1 Poke, Michael H. – Southampton – Torquay United; 10 Porter, Levi R. – Leicester City – Mansfield Town; 10 Pugh, Andrew J. – Gillingham – Dover Athletic; 1 Revell, Alexander D. – Southend United – Swindon Town; 1 Ritchie, Matthew T. – Portsmouth – Notts County; 1 Rosenior, Liam J. – Reading – Ipswich Town; 1 Rice, Martin – Torquay United – Truro City; 29 Rose, Daniel L. – Tottenham Hotspur – Peterborough United; 28 Rothwell, Josh – Bury – Chorley; 18 Rowe-Turner, Lathaniel A. – Leicester City – Kings Lynn; 15 Scott, Mark J. – Swindon Town – Hungerford Town; 28 Seip, Marcel – Plymouth Argyle – Blackpool; 1 Sharp, Billy L. – Sheffield United – Doncaster Rovers; 1 Sheehan, Alan – Leicester City – Oldham Athletic; 25 Shotton, Ryan C. – Stoke City – Barnsley; 1 Sonko, Ibrahima – Stoke City – Hull City; 11 Spence, Lewwis G. – Crystal Palace – Forest Green Rovers; 15 St Ledger-Hall, Sean P. – Preston North End – Middlesbrough; 26 Stoor, Frederick – Fulham – Derby County; 24 Summerfield, Luke J. – Plymouth Argyle – Leyton Orient; 1 Tainio, Teemu – Sunderland – Birmingham City; 5 Thompson, Stephen – Port Vale – Stafford Rangers; 17 Torres, Sergio R. – Peterborough United – Lincoln City; 1 Uddin, Anwar – Dagenham & Redbridge – Grays Athletic; 18 Vaughan, James C. – Everton – Derby County; 25 Wainwright, Neil – Morecambe – Barrow; 22 Walker, James L.N. – Southend United – Hereford United; 11 Ward, Darren P. – Wolverhampton Wanderers – Millwall; 1 Watson, Ben – Wigan Athletic – Queens Park Rangers; 18 Whaley, Simon – Norwich City – Rochdale; 1 Wilson, James S. – Bristol City – Brentford; 29 Wright, Benjamin M. – Peterborough United – Luton Town; 23 Wright, Matthew J. – Crystal Palace – Maidstone United

OCTOBER 2009

| 1 Tuncay, Sanli | Middlesbrough | Stoke City | 5,000,000 |

TEMPORARY TRANSFERS

12 Adams, Stephen M. – Torquay United – Truro City; 29 Amos, Benjamin P. – Manchester United – Peterborough United; 30 Andrew, Daniel K. – Peterborough United – Kidderminster Harriers; 5 Antonio, Michail G. – Reading – Southampton; 16 Artus, Frankie – Bristol City – Cheltenham Town; 22 Baker, Nathan – Aston Villa – Lincoln City; 9 Barnett, Moses – Everton – Darlington; 16 Begovic, Asmir – Portsmouth – Ipswich Town; 23 Bennett, Ryan – Grimsby Town – Peterborough United; 30 Bent, Marcus N. – Birmingham City – Middlesbrough; 23 Blanchett, Daniel W. – Peterborough United – Hereford United; 16 Boyes, Adam J. – Scunthorpe United – York City; 14 Butcher, Lee A. – Tottenham Hotspur – Leyton Orient; 30 Bryant, Mitchell J. – Reading – Woking; 16 Charles, Elliott G. – Barnet – Ebbsfleet United; 22 Collins, James S. – Aston Villa – Darlington; 9 Cook, Andrew E. – Carlisle United – Barrow; 16 Coulson, Michael J. – Barnsley – Chester City; 16 Dawson, Liam – Oldham Athletic – Nantwich Town; 16 Davies, Scott M.E. – Reading – Wycombe Wanderers; 22 Davis, David L. – Wolverhampton Wanderers – Darlington; 29 Devaney, Martin T. – Barnsley – Milton Keynes Dons; 22 Devitt, Jamie M. – Hull City – Shrewsbury Town; 5 Doran, Aaron B. – Blackburn Rovers – Milton Keynes Dons; 2 Dudley, Mark – Derby County – Alfreton Town; 2 Edgar, Anthony J. – West Ham United – AFC Bournemouth; 6 Eley, Edward D.M. – Grimsby Town – Mansfield Town; 16 Erskine, Emmanuel J. – Gillingham – Bromley; 2 Eyjolfsson, Holmar O. – West Ham United – Cheltenham Town; 23 Fairhurst, Waide S. – Doncaster Rovers – Shrewsbury Town; 24 Frear, Elliott – Exeter City – Tiverton Town; 30 Friend, George A.J. – Wolverhampton Wanderers – Scunthorpe United; 15 Fry, Matthew – West Ham United – Gillingham; 17 Gaughran, Samuel D. – Peterborough United – Tamworth; 5 German, Antonio T. – Queens Park Rangers – Aldershot Town; 12 Gillett, Simon J. – Southampton – Doncaster Rovers; 19 Gradel, Max A. – Leicester City – Leeds United; 23 Griffiths, Scott R. – Dagenham & Redbridge – Peterborough United; 6 Guy, Jamie L. – Colchester United – Port Vale; 13 Hall, Matthew – Leyton Orient – Billericay Town; 9 Hector, Michael – Millwall – Bracknell Town; 9 Hodges, Lee J. – Torquay United – Truro City; 9 Hoyte, Gavin A. – Arsenal – Brighton & Hove Albion; 23 Hughes, Bryan – Hull City – Derby County; 19 Hussey, Christopher I. – AFC Wimbledon – Coventry City; 16 Ide, Lewis B. – Brighton & Hove Albion – Bognor Regis Town; 29 Ikeme, Carl – Wolverhampton Wanderers – Charlton Athletic; 9 Jameson, Arron T. – Sheffield Wednesday – Harrogate Town; 1 Joyce, Ben P. – Swindon Town – Weston-Super-Mare; 2 King, David P. – Milton Keynes Dons – Forest Green Rovers; 24 Lancashire, Oliver J. – Southampton – Grimsby Town; 30 Lavers, Louis J. – Yeovil Town – Dorchester Town; 22 Lichaj, Eric J. – Aston Villa – Lincoln City; 30 Lillis, Joshua M. – Scunthorpe United – Rochdale; 6 Little, Mark D. – Wolverhampton Wanderers – Chesterfield; 30 Lockwood, Matthew D. – Colchester United – Dagenham & Redbridge; 30 McCollin, Andre – Yeovil Town – Dorchester Town; 20 Madine, Gary L. – Carlisle United – Coventry City; 16 Magennis, Joshua B.D. – Cardiff City – Grimsby Town; 2 Makofo, Serge – Grays Athletic – Burton Albion; 16 Martin, David E. – Liverpool – Tranmere Rovers; 2 Mellor, Kelvin – Crewe Alexandra – Nantwich Town; 16 Mendy, Arnaud – Derby County – Grimsby Town; 22 Mills, Daniel P. – Peterborough United – Rushden & Diamonds; 31 Mitchell, Aaron – Nottingham Forest – Ilkeston Town; 16 Mooney, David – Reading – Charlton Athletic; 17 Morgan, Kerry D. – Swansea City – Newport County; 30 Ngala, Bondz – West Ham United – Scunthorpe United; 26 Normington, Grant – Grimsby Town – Frickley Athletic; 30 Omozusi, Elliott – Fulham – Charlton Athletic; 23 Oxley, Mark T. – Hull City – Walsall; 22 Payne, Joshua J. – West Ham United – Colchester United; 2 Perkins, David P. – Colchester United – Chesterfield; 16 Powell, Daniel – Milton Keynes Dons – Forest Green Rovers; 8 Pulis, Anthony J. – Stoke City – Lincoln City; 8 Rose, Romone A.A. – Queens Park Rangers – Cheltenham Town; 16 Smith, Benjamin J. – Doncaster Rovers – Morecambe; 16 Thomas, Casey E. – Swansea City – Newport County; 16 Thomas, Simon V. – Crystal Palace – Darlington; 16 Thompson, David A.R. – Bury – Hyde United; 27 Thomson, Jake S. – Southampton – Torquay United; 16 Titchiner, Alexander – Crewe Alexandra – Chasetown; 15 Vernon, Scott M. – Colchester United – Gillingham; 17 Vokes, Samuel M. – Wolverhampton Wanderers – Leeds United; 2 Watts, Adam – Fulham – Lincoln City; 7 White, Jamie A. – Southampton – Eastleigh; 16 Winn, Peter H. – Scunthorpe United – Gateshead; 7 Winters, Ruairidh T.P. – Morecambe – Kendal Town; 30 Wynter, Thomas L. – Gillingham – Dover Athletic

NOVEMBER 2009 TEMPORARY TRANSFERS

6 Ainsley, Jack W. – Ipswich Town – Rushden & Diamonds; 20 Ainsworth, Gareth – Queens Park Rangers – Wycombe Wanderers; 13 Akinde, John J.A. – Bristol City – Wycombe Wanderers; 13 Allen-Djilali, Kieran S.L. – Crystal Palace – Chesterfield; 19 Atkinson, William H. – Hull City – Rochdale; 6 Bains, Rikki – Darlington – Blyth Spartans; 20 Baldwin, Patrick M. – Colchester United – Bristol Rovers; 20 Balkestain, Pim – Ipswich Town – Brentford; 26 Bannan, Barry – Aston Villa – Blackpool; 4 Barnett, Leon P. – West Bromwich Albion – Coventry City; 9 Benjamin, Joseph J. – Northampton Town – Eastbourne Borough; 27 Bentley, Alexander A. – Dagenham & Redbridge – Aveley; 20 Bingham, Billy C. – Dagenham & Redbridge – Grays Athletic; 5 Bird, Matthew – Grimsby Town – Frickley Athletic; 13 Bostock, John – Tottenham Hotspur – Brentford; 26 Bouzanis, Dean A. – Liverpool – Accrington Stanley; 27 Bozanic, Oliver J. – Reading – Aldershot Town; 18 Bowery, Jordan – Chesterfield – Barrow; 5 Brandy, Febian E. – Manchester United – Gillingham; 23 Brough, Michael – Torquay United – Mansfield Town; 26 Butcher, Callum J. – Tottenham Hotspur – Barnet; 20 Button, David R.E. – Tottenham Hotspur – Shrewsbury Town; 20 Cadogan, Kieron J.N. – Crystal Palace – Burton Albion; 26 Cain, Ashley T. – Coventry City – Luton Town; 26 Campbell, Dudley J. – Leicester City – Derby County; 10 Clark, Jack A. – Charlton Athletic – Bognor Regis Town; 26 Capaldi, Anthony C. – Cardiff City – Leeds United; 2 Clayton, Adam S. – Manchester City – Carlisle United; 20 Cook, Steve A. – Brighton & Hove Albion – Eastleigh; 24 Cotterill, David R.G.B. – Sheffield United – Swansea City; 19 Coulson, Michael J. – Barnsley – Grimsby Town; 16 Cresswell, Richard P.W. – Leeds United – Sheffield United; 18 Cumbers, Luis C. – Gillingham – AFC Wimbledon; 23 Currie, Darren P. – Chesterfield – Dagenham & Redbridge; 26 Davis, Sol S. – Milton Keynes Dons – Kettering Town; 26 Day, Jamie R. – Peterborough United – Dagenham & Redbridge; 20 Dean, Harlee J. – Dagenham & Redbridge – Grays Athletic; 12 Dennis, Kristian – Macclesfield Town – Woodley Sports; 12 Dudley, Mark – Derby County – Hinckley United; 26 Eastham, Ashley – Blackpool – Cheltenham Town; 3 Elding, Anthony L. – Crewe Alexandra – Kettering Town; 26 Ephraim, Hogan – Queens Park Rangers – Leeds United; 26 Facey, Delroy M. – Gillingham – Lincoln City; 19 Featherstone, Nicky L. – Hull City – Grimsby Town; 26 Feeney, Warren J. – Cardiff City – Sheffield Wednesday; 5 Flahavan, Darryl J. – Southend United – Oldham Athletic; 26 Flynn, Jonathan J. – Blackburn Rovers – Accrington Stanley; 26 Franks, Fraser G. – Brentford – Basingstoke Town; 10 Gall, Kevin A. – Darlington – York City; 25 Geohagan, Exodus – Kettering Town – Peterborough United; 26 Glover, Daniel – Port Vale – Rochdale; 26 Goodfellow, Marc D. – Burton Albion – Barrow; 26 Hall, Daniel A. – Chesterfield – Darlington; 26 Harsley, Paul – Chesterfield – Darlington; 13 Heaton, Thomas D. – Manchester United – Rochdale; 9 Hector, Michael A.J. – Reading – Didcot Town; 26 Heffernan, Paul – Doncaster Rovers – Oldham Athletic; 20 Helguson, Heidar – Queens Park Rangers

– Watford; 26 Herd, Christopher – Aston Villa – Lincoln City; 5 Hills, Lee M. – Crystal Palace – Oldham Athletic; 20 Hogg, Jonathan – Aston Villa – Darlington; 26 Ibehre, Jabo O. – Milton Keynes Dons – Southend United; 26 Ikeme, Carl – Wolverhampton Wanderers – Sheffield United; 14 Jackson, Ben – Morecambe – Rossendale United; 26 Jackson, Marlon M. – Bristol City – Aldershot Town; 26 Jameson, Arron T. – Sheffield Wednesday – Matlock Town; 26 John, Stern – Crystal Palace – Ipswich Town; 19 Johnson, Jermaine J. – Derby County – Stafford Rangers; 26 Kabba, Steven – Brentford – Burton Albion; 26 Kallio, Toni – Fulham – Sheffield United; 25 Keltie, Clark S.B. – Rochdale – Gateshead; 10 Kerry, Lloyd – Sheffield United – Alfreton Town; 27 Kite, Alexandrous – Bristol Rovers – Paulton Rovers; 19 Kitson, David B. – Stoke City – Middlesbrough; 20 Labadie, Joss C. – West Bromwich Albion – Cheltenham Town; 26 Lathrope, Damon L. – Norwich City – Bishop Stortford; 26 McAllister, Craig – Exeter City – Barnet; 9 McCrory, Damian P. – Plymouth Argyle – Grimsby Town; 13 McDonald, Clayton – Manchester City – Walsall; 12 McLaggon, Kayne S. – Southampton – Eastbourne Borough; 26 McNamee, Anthony – Swindon Town – Norwich City; 24 Malone, Scott L. – Wolverhampton Wanderers – Southend United; 7 Malton, Russell J. – Colchester United – Heybridge Swifts; 26 Martin, David E. – Liverpool – Leeds United; 26 Martin, Russell K.A. – Peterborough United – Norwich City; 13 Marshall, Ben – Stoke City – Cheltenham Town; 13 Miller, Adam E. – Gillingham – Dagenham & Redbridge; 26 Milne, Andrew A. – Leeds United – Darlington; 23 Mills, Gregory A. – Derby County – Solihull Moors; 26 Morris, Ian – Scunthorpe United – Chesterfield; 26 Morris, Lee – Hereford United – Mansfield Town; 14 Morrison, Sean J. – Swindon Town – Southend United; 24 Murphy, Rhys P.E. – Arsenal – Brentford; 26 Mutch, Jordon J.E.S. – Birmingham City – Hereford United; 13 Nardiello, Daniel A. – Blackpool – Bury; 20 Norwood, James T. – Exeter City – Sutton United; 13 Nwokeji, Mark O. – Dagenham & Redbridge – Luton Town; 26 Ofori-Twumasi, Seth N. – Chelsea – Dagenham & Redbridge; 5 Osbourne, Isaiah G. – Aston Villa – Middlesbrough; 26 Partridge, Richard J. – Milton Keynes Dons – Kettering Town; 13 Pelling, Joshua R.A. – Brighton & Hove Albion – Horsham; 2 Phillips, Steven J. – Bristol Rovers – Crewe Alexandra; 13 Pilkington, Kevin W. – Notts County – Luton Town; 26 Pinney, Nathaniel B. – Crystal Palace – Woking; 26 Pipe, David R. – Bristol Rovers – Cheltenham Town; 19 Puddy, Willem J.S. – Cheltenham Town – Oxford City; 20 Pugh, Andrew J. – Gillingham – Welling United; 24 Quashie, Nigel F. – West Ham United – Milton Keynes Dons; 13 Ranieri, Mirko – Tottenham Hotspur – Ipswich Town; 13 Reed, Stephen L. – Macclesfield Town – Grays Athletic; 19 Reid, Steven J. – Blackburn Rovers – Queens Park Rangers; 20 Ribeiro, Christian M. – Bristol City – Stockport County; 24 Rigg, Sean M. – Bristol Rovers – Port Vale; 26 Rothery, Gavin M. – Carlisle United – Barrow; 3 Rothwell, Josh C. – Bury – Watford; 23 Rundle, Adam – Rochdale – Rotherham United; 13 Scott, Mark J. – Swindon Town – Chippenham Town; 25 Shaw, Jon S. – Rochdale – Gateshead; 26 Sheehan, Alan – Leeds United – Swindon Town; 25 Shephard, Christopher J. – Exeter City – Weston-Super-Mare; 26 Shorey, Nicholas – Aston Villa – Nottingham Forest; 5 Simpson, Joshua R. – Histor – Peterborough United; 26 Sinclair, Dean M. – Charlton Athletic – Barnet; 20 Smith, Adam J. – Tottenham Hotspur – Torquay United; 26 Soares, Thomas J. – Stoke City – Sheffield Wednesday; 14 Sodje, Akpo – Sheffield Wednesday – Charlton Athletic; 24 Sodje, Onome S. – Barnsley – Oxford United; 26 Somma, Davide E. – Leeds United – Chesterfield; 26 Stavrinou, Alexander M. – Charlton Athletic – Ebbsfleet United; 26 Swailes, Daniel – Milton Keynes Dons – Northampton Town; 20 Szczesny, Wojciech T. – Arsenal – Brentford; 13 Tabiri, Joseph O. – Barnet – Havant & Waterlooville; 19 Taylor, Jason J.F. – Rotherham United – Rochdale; 20 Taylor, Rhys F. – Chelsea – Queens Park Rangers; 28 Todd, Christopher R. – Torquay United – Salisbury City; 19 Tonge, Michael W.E. – Stoke City – Preston North End; 20 Walker, Joshua – Middlesbrough – Northampton Town; 26 Ward, Daniel C. – Bolton Wanderers – Swindon Town; 26 Wedderburn, Nathaniel C. – Stoke City – Hereford United; 20 Whaley, Simon – Norwich City – Bradford City; 9 Williams, Thomas A. – Peterborough United – Queens Park Rangers; 19 Wood, Richard M. – Sheffield Wednesday – Coventry City; 26 Wright, Benjamin M. – Peterborough United – Grimsby Town; 26 Wright, Matthew J. – Crystal Palace – Woking; 20 Zebroski, Christopher M. – Millwall – Torquay United

DECEMBER 2009 TEMPORARY TRANSFERS

4 Bryant, Mitchell J. – Reading – Basingstoke Town; 11 Charles, Elliott G. – Barnet – Havant & Waterlooville; 4 Corcoran, Samuel J. – Colchester United – Wealdstone; 4 Davies, Richard P. – Walsall – Solihull Moors; 15 Dean, Luke A. – Bradford City – Halifax Town; 14 Gibson, William M.H. – Watford – Wealdstone; 24 Hall, Grant T. – Brighton & Hove Albion – Bognor Regis Town; 14 Harris, Spencer J. – Huddersfield Town – Curzon Ashton; 10 Harrison, Callum J. – Sheffield Wednesday – Sheffield; 19 Hunt, Ben – Bristol Rovers – Gloucester City; 15 Locke, Simon J. – Reading – Gillingham; 24 Malak, Matthew E. – Chesterfield – Loughborough University; 21 Morris, Aaron J. – Cardiff City – Newport County; 18 Normington, Grant – Grimsby Town – Frickley Athletic; 17 Reed, Stephen L. – Torquay United – Weymouth; 11 Stech, Marek – West Ham United – Bournemouth; 10 Wood, Nicholas J. – Sheffield Wednesday – Sheffield

JANUARY 2010

29 Ademola, Moses	Brentford	Woking	Free
1 Anderson, Joe	Fulham	Lincoln City	undisclosed
8 Baker, Carl P.	Stockport County	Coventry City	undisclosed
22 Barnard, Lee J.	Southend United	Southampton	undisclosed
15 Bennett, Ryan	Grimsby Town	Peterborough United	undisclosed
27 Buckley, William E.	Rochdale	Watford	undisclosed
21 Campbell-Ryce, Jamal J.	Barnsley	Bristol City	undisclosed
6 Collins, Neill	Wolverhampton Wanderers	Preston North End	750,000
28 Conlon, Barry J.	Grimsby Town	Chesterfield	undisclosed
28 Cort, Leon T.A.	Stoke City	Burnley	1,500,000
8 Cotterill, David R.G.B.	Sheffield United	Swansea City	undisclosed
8 Cresswell, Richard P.W.	Stoke City	Sheffield United	500,000
13 Doyle, Nathan L.R.	Hull City	Barnsley	Free
12 Fonte, Jose M.	Crystal Palace	Southampton	800,000
27 Gardner, Craig	Aston Villa	Birmingham City	3,000,000
25 Gradel, Max A.	Leicester City	Leeds United	undisclosed
22 Griffiths, Scott R.	Dagenham & Redbridge	Peterborough United	undisclosed
25 Harper, James A.J.	Reading	Sheffield United	undisclosed
1 Hinshelwood, Adam	Aldershot Town	Wycombe Wanderers	Free
8 Johnson, Oliver T.	Stockport County	Norwich City	undisclosed
30 Kaboul, Younes	Portsmouth	Tottenham Hotspur	5,000,000
21 Kilgallon, Matthew	Sheffield United	Sunderland	2,000,000

4 Martin, Russell K.A.	Peterborough United	Norwich City	undisclosed
1 McDonald, Clayton	Manchester City	Walsall	undisclosed
4 McNamee, Anthony	Swindon Town	Norwich City	undisclosed
1 Odejayi, Olukayode	Barnsley	Colchester United	undisclosed
15 O'Grady, Christopher J.	Oldham Athletic	Rochdale	undisclosed
4 O'Toole, John J.	Watford	Colchester United	undisclosed
14 Otsemobor, Jon	Norwich City	Southampton	undisclosed
22 Paterson, Matthew	Southampton	Southend United	Free
25 Pearce, Krystian M.V.	Birmingham City	Huddersfield Town	Free
28 Robinson, Paul P.	West Bromwich Albion	Bolton Wanderers	undisclosed
26 Routledge, Wayne N.A.	Queens Park Rangers	Newcastle United	undisclosed
13 Seaborne, Daniel A.	Exeter City	Southampton	undisclosed
21 Simpson, Dariel P.	Manchester United	Newcastle United	500,000
14 Taiwo, Thomas J.W.	Chelsea	Carlisle United	undisclosed
1 Ward, Darren P.	Wolverhampton Wanderers	Millwall	Free
4 Watts, Adam	Fulham	Lincoln City	undisclosed
8 Whitbread, Zak B.	Millwall	Norwich City	undisclosed
28 Williamson, Michael J.	Portsmouth	Newcastle United	1,500,000
4 Wood, Richard M.	Sheffield Wednesday	Coventry City	undisclosed
8 Worrall, David R.	West Bromwich Albion	Bury	Free
20 Yeates, Mark S.	Middlesbrough	Sheffield United	undisclosed
8 Zebroski, Christopher M.	Wycombe Wanderers	Torquay United	undisclosed

TEMPORARY TRANSFERS

15 Adams, Nicholas W. – Leicester City – Leyton Orient; 15 Adams, Stephen M. – Torquay United – Truro City; 8 Adelakun, Hakeem A.D. – Crystal Palace – Dover Athletic; 11 Adkins, Sam – Walsall – Hednesford Town; 25 Agyemang, Patrick – Queens Park Rangers – Bristol City; 28 Ainsworth, Lionel G.R. – Huddersfield Town – Brentford; 2 Andersen, Mikkel – Reading – Bristol Rovers; 12 Andrew, Daniel K. – Peterborough United – Cheltenham Town; 5 Antonio, Michail G. – Reading – Southampton; 19 Appiah, Kwesi – Peterborough United – Kettering Town; 21 Artus, Frankie – Bristol City – Chesterfield; 22 Atkins, Ross M. – Derby County – Burton Albion; 21 Bains, Rikki – Darlington – Gateshead; 29 Baldwin, Patrick M. – Colchester United – Southend United; 25 Batt, Shaun A.S.P. – Peterborough United – Millwall; 15 Benjamin, Joseph J. – Northampton Town – Eastbourne Borough; 14 Bentley, Alexander A. – Dagenham & Redbridge – Bishop's Stortford; 5 Bozanic, Oliver J. – Reading – Aldershot Town; 29 Branston, Guy P.B. – Burton Albion – Torquay United; 15 Briggs, Matthew – Fulham – Leyton Orient; 2 Bunn, Mark J. – Blackburn Rovers – Sheffield United; 22 Burns, Michael – Carlisle United – Stafford Rangers; 7 Butler, Andrew P. – Huddersfield Town – Blackpool; 7 Byrne, Mark – Nottingham Forest – Rushden & Diamonds; 22 Chambers, Ashley R. – Leicester City – Grimsby Town; 19 Clayton, Adam S. – Manchester City – Carlisle United; 5 Cleverley, Thomas W. – Manchester United – Watford; 16 Conlon, Barry J. – Grimsby Town & – Chesterfield; 22 Coulson, Michael J. – Barnsley – Grimsby Town; 1 Cowan-Hall, Paris – Portsmouth – Grimsby Town; 22 Cox, Samuel P. – Tottenham Hotspur – Torquay United; 23 Davidson, Ross – Port Vale – Nantwich Town; 15 Davies, Craig M. – Brighton & Hove Albion – Port Vale; 22 Dean, Harlee J. – Dagenham & Redbridge – Grays Athletic; 21 Dennehy, Darren J. – Cardiff City – Gillingham; 21 Diagouraga, Toumani – Peterborough United – Brentford; 1 Dickinson, Carl M. – Stoke City – Barnsley; 29 Donnelly, Georgie J. – Plymouth Argyle – Stockport County; 26 Downing, Paul – West Bromwich Albion – Hereford United; 28 Eccleston, Nathan – Liverpool – Huddersfield Town; 28 Elford-Alliyu, Lateef – West Bromwich Albion – Hereford United; 1 Elliott, Thomas J. – Leeds United – Bury; 12 Facey, Delroy M. – Notts County – Lincoln City; 15 Featherstone, Nicky L. – Hull City – Grimsby Town; 29 Fielding, Francis D. – Blackburn Rovers – Rochdale; 27 Fisher, Oliver C. – Doncaster Rovers – Frickley Athletic; 15 Fletcher, Wesleigh J. – Burnley – Grimsby Town; 5 Forster, Fraser G. – Newcastle United – Norwich City; 22 Franks, Leigh D. – Huddersfield Town – Fleetwood Town; 25 Frear, Elliott – Exeter City – Tiverton Town; 16 Gilbert, Kerrea K. – Arsenal – Peterborough United; 2 Goodwin, James M. – Huddersfield Town – Oldham Athletic; 15 Green, Dominic A. – Peterborough United – Chesterfield; 11 Griffin, Andrew – Stoke City – Reading; 15 Grimes, Jamie N. – Swansea City – Haverfordwest County; 22 Gunning, Gavin – Blackburn Rovers – Rotherham United; 1 Haldane, Lewis O. – Bristol Rovers – Port Vale; 29 Hall, Fitz – Queens Park Rangers – Newcastle United; 29 Hart, Danny – Barnet – Hemel Hempstead Town; 23 Haworth, Andrew A.D. – Blackburn Rovers – Rochdale; 22 Hector, Michael A.J. – Reading – Havant & Waterlooville; 11 Helguson, Heidar – Queens Park Rangers – Watford; 4 Herd, Christopher – Aston Villa – Lincoln City; 25 Hill, Matthew C. – Wolverhampton Wanderers – Queens Park Rangers; 15 Hodges, Lee L. – Torquay United – Truro City; 29 Holroyd, Christopher – Cambridge United – Brighton & Hove Albion; 26 Howard, Kieran C. – Swansea City – Neath; 21 Howe, Jermaine R. – Peterborough United – Gillingham; 12 Hoyte, Gavin A. – Arsenal – Brighton & Hove Albion; 22 Hunt, Jack P. – Huddersfield Town – Grays Athletic; 7 Hunt, Nicholas B. – Bolton Wanderers – Derby County; 19 Ibehre, Jabo O. – Milton Keynes Dons – Stockport County; 7 Ikeme, Carl – Wolverhampton Wanderers – Queens Park Rangers; 25 Jackson, Marlon M. – Bristol City – Aldershot Town; 19 Johnson, Jemal P. – Milton Keynes Dons – Stockport County; 1 Johnson, John J. – Middlesbrough – Northampton Town; 1 Johnson, Lee D. – Bristol City – Derby County; 15 Joyce, Ben P. – Torquay United – Weston-Super-Mare; 15 Kabba, Steven – Brentford – Burton Albion; 19 Kee, Billy R. – Leicester City – Accrington Stanley; 25 Khizanishvili, Zurab – Blackburn Rovers – Reading; 26 King, David P. – Milton Keynes Dons – Wealdstone; 5 Kite, Alexandrous – Bristol Rovers – Chippenham Town; 4 Krysiak, Artur L. – Birmingham City – Burton Albion; 1 Lansbury, Henri G. – Arsenal – Watford; 22 Livermore, Jake C. – Tottenham Hotspur – Peterborough United; 22 Lockwood, Matthew D. – Colchester United – Barnet; 29 Lowry, Shane T. – Aston Villa – Leeds United; 1 MacDonald, Shaun B. – Swansea City – Yeovil Town; 25 Malone, Scott L. – Wolverhampton Wanderers – Southend United; 19 Malton, Russell J. – Colchester United – Billericay Town; 6 Marrow, Alexander J. – Blackburn Rovers – Oldham Athletic; 22 Marshall, Marcus – Blackburn Rovers – Rotherham United; 14 Martin, Richard W. – Yeovil Town – Grays Athletic; 21 McCready, Christopher J. – Northampton Town – Tranmere Rovers; 27 McDermott, Donal – Manchester City – Scunthorpe United; 11 McLeod, Izale M. – Charlton Athletic – Peterborough United; 29 McSheffrey, Gary – Birmingham City – Leeds United; 29 Mills, Gregory A. – Derby County – Macclesfield Town; 27 Moloney, Brendon A. – Nottingham Forest – Scunthorpe United; 13 Mooney, David – Reading – Charlton Athletic; 15 Morgan, Kerry D. – Swansea City – Newport County; 25 Mutch, Jordon J.E.S. – Birmingham City – Doncaster Rovers; 12 Mvoto, Yves O.J. – Sunderland – Southend United; 12 Nwokeji, Mark O. – Dagenham & Redbridge – Luton Town; 29 Obadeyi, Temitope – Bolton Wanderers – Rochdale; 29 O'Hara, Jamie –

Tottenham Hotspur – Portsmouth: 6 Pack, Marlon – Portsmouth – Dagenham & Redbridge; 14 Painter, Marcos – Swansea City – Brighton & Hove Albion; 22 Parkes, Thomas P.W. – Leicester City – Burton Albion; 22 Payne, Joshua J. – West Ham United – Wycombe Wanderers; 19 Pearce, Krystian M.V. – Birmingham City – Huddersfield Town; 19 Perkins, David P. – Colchester United – Stockport County; 6 Phillips, Steven J. – Bristol Rovers – Crewe Alexandra; 21 Plummer, Tristan D. – Bristol City – Gillingham; 3 Poke, Michael H. – Southampton – Torquay United; 17 Powell, Daniel – Milton Keynes Dons – Forest Green Rovers; 26 Prutton, David T. – Leeds United – Colchester United; 13 Puddy, Willem J.S. – Cheltenham Town – Oxford City; 15 Randall, Mark – Arsenal – Milton Keynes Dons; 26 Redmond, Shane P. – Nottingham Forest – Darlington; 15 Reed, Stephen L. – Macclesfield Town – Weymouth; 29 Reid, Kyel R. – Sheffield United – Charlton Athletic; 5 Reid, Reuben J. – West Bromwich Albion – Peterborough United; 29 Revell, Alexander D. – Southend United – Wycombe Wanderers; 22 Ribeiro, Christian M. – Bristol City – Colchester United; 12 Rigg, Sean M. – Bristol Rovers – Port Vale; 29 Riley, Daniel – Darlington – Billingham Town; 29 Rose, Michael – Stockport County – Norwich City; 29 Sadler, Matthew – Watford – Stockport County; 2 Sappleton, Reneil St. A – Leicester City – Macclesfield Town; 1 Saunders, Matthew – Fulham – Lincoln City; 1 Seip, Marcel – Plymouth Argyle – Sheffield United; 25 Senderos, Philippe – Arsenal – Everton; 1 Shackell, Jason – Wolverhampton Wanderers – Doncaster Rovers; 7 Sheehan, Alan – Leeds United – Swindon Town; 1 Shotton, Ryan C. – Stoke City – Barnsley; 28 Sinclair, Dean M. – Charlton Athletic – Grimsby Town; 21 Skarz, Joseph P. – Huddersfield Town – Shrewsbury Town; 8 Smith, Thomas J. – Ipswich Town – Brentford; 26 Soares, Thomas J. – Stoke City – Sheffield Wednesday; 15 Spencer, James C. – Huddersfield Town – Northwich Victoria; 8 Stavrinou, Alexander M. – Charlton Athletic – Ebbsfleet United; 22 Stockdale, David A. – Fulham – Plymouth Argyle; 15 Taylor, Cleveland K.W. – Brentford – Burton Albion; 14 Taylor, Jason J.F. – Rotherham United – Rochdale; 29 Taylor, Martin – Birmingham City – Watford; 29 Thomson, Jake S. – Southampton – Torquay United; 19 Thompson, O'Neil A.M.T. – Barnsley – Burton Albion; 21 Thornhill, Matthew – Nottingham Forest – Cheltenham Town; 1 Timar, Krisztian – Plymouth Argyle – Oldham Athletic; 12 Todd, Christopher R. – Torquay United – Newport County; 14 Townsend, Andros – Tottenham Hotspur – Milton Keynes Dons; 7 Trotter, Liam A. – Ipswich Town – Millwall; 21 Trottman, Neal A. – Preston North End – Huddersfield Town; 1 Trundle, Lee C. – Bristol City – Swansea City; 12 Titchiner, Alexander – Crewe Alexandra – Colwyn Bay; 26 Tudur-Jones, Owain – Norwich City – Yeovil Town; 1 Uwezu, Michael – Fulham – Lincoln City; 29 Van Aanholt, Patrick J.M. – Chelsea – Newcastle United; 21 Varney, Luke I. – Derby County – Sheffield Wednesday; 29 Vernon, Scott M. – Colchester United – Southend United; 25 Weiss, Vladimir – Manchester City – Bolton Wanderers; 25 Welbeck, Daniel – Manchester United – Preston North End; 15 White, Alan – Luton Town – Darlington; 1 White, Joseph S. – Bristol Rovers – Paulton Rovers; 29 Wiggins, Rhoys B. – Norwich City – AFC Bournemouth; 5 Wilkinson, Luke A. – Portsmouth – Northampton Town; 27 Williamson, Michael J. – Portsmouth – Newcastle United; 29 Wilshere, Jack A. – Arsenal – Bolton Wanderers; 26 Wilson, Kyle P. – Macclesfield Town – FC United of Manchester; 4 Worley, Harry J. – Leicester City – Crewe Alexandra; 1 Wright, Jake M. – Brighton & Hove Albion – Oxford United; 23 Wright, Matthew J. – Crystal Palace – Woking

FEBRUARY 2010

1 Archibald-Henville, Troy	Tottenham Hotspur	Exeter City	undisclosed
2 Austin, Charles	Poole Town	Swindon Town	undisclosed
1 Begovic, Asmir	Portsmouth	Stoke City	3,500,000
1 Best, Leon J.	Coventry City	Newcastle United	undisclosed
1 Buchtmann, Christopher	Liverpool	Fulham	100,000
2 Coutts, Paul	Peterborough United	Preston North End	undisclosed
1 Johnson, Adam	Middlesbrough	Manchester City	6,000,000
1 McCarthy, Benedict S.	Blackburn Rovers	West Ham United	2,250,000
5 Johnson, Damien M.	Birmingham City	Plymouth Argyle	Free
1 Martis, Shelton	West Bromwich Albion	Doncaster Rovers	undisclosed
1 McCrory, Damien P.	Plymouth Argyle	Dagenham & Redbridge	undisclosed
1 Moses, Victor	Crystal Palace	Wigan Athletic	2,500,000
1 Puncheon, Jason D.I.	Plymouth Argyle	Southampton	undisclosed
1 Raynes, Michael	Stockport County	Scunthorpe United	Free
1 Rowe-Turner, Lathaniel A.	Leicester City	Torquay United	undisclosed
1 Treacy, Keith	Blackburn Rovers	Preston North End	undisclosed

TEMPORARY TRANSFERS

5 Abnett, Michael M. – Crystal Palace – Dover Athletic; 1 Ainsworth, Lionel G.R. – Huddersfield Town – Brentford; 1 Akinde, John J.A. – Bristol City – Brentford; 1 Atkinson, William H. – Hull City – Rochdale; 19 Bannan, Barry – Aston Villa – Blackpool; 9 Barnes, Ashley L. – Plymouth Argyle – Torquay United; 1 Barnett, Leon P. – West Bromwich Albion – Coventry City; 9 Bartley, Kyle – Arsenal – Sheffield United; 16 Bennett, Alan J. – Brentford – Wycombe Wanderers; 1 Bent, Marcus N. – Birmingham City – Queens Park Rangers; 5 Brough, Michael – Torquay United – Mansfield Town; 16 Broughton, Drewe O. – Rotherham United – Lincoln City; 1 Brown, Wayne J. – Fulham – Bristol Rovers; 1 Bruce, Alex S. – Ipswich Town – Leicester City; 9 Butcher, Richard T. – Lincoln City – Macclesfield Town; 19 Cain, Ashley T. – Coventry City – Oxford United; 9 Calver, Craig T. – Sheffield United – Braintree Town; 1 Campbell, Dudley J. – Leicester City – Blackpool; 1 Clark, Robert J. – Doncaster Rovers – Brigg Town; 1 Cork, Jack F.P. – Chelsea – Burnley; 12 Cumbers, Luis C. – Gillingham – Dover Athletic; 17 Cureton, Jamie – Norwich City – Shrewsbury Town; 11 Davies, Arron R. – Brighton & Hove Albion – Yeovil Town; 17 Devitt, Jamie M. – Hull City – Grimsby Town; 15 Dickinson, Liam M. – Brighton & Hove Albion – Peterborough United; 15 Dickson, Christopher A.K. – Charlton Athletic – Gillingham; 1 Dobbie, Stephen – Swansea City – Blackpool; 22 Doran Cogan, Aaron B. – Bristol Rovers – Leyton Orient; 5 Dudley, Mark – Derby County – Hinckley United; 1 Duffy, Darryl A. – Bristol Rovers – Carlisle United; 12 Durrant, Jack W. – Cheltenham Town – Worcester City; 25 Emmanuel-Thomas, Jay-Aston – Arsenal – Doncaster Rovers; 23 Erskine, Emmanuel J.K. – Dagenham & Redbridge-Bishop's Stortford; 1 Flahavan, Darryl J. – Crystal Palace – Oldham Athletic; 1 Flynn, Jonathan J. – Blackburn Rovers – Accrington Stanley; 27 Folly, Yoann – Plymouth Argyle – Dagenham & Redbridge; 1 Goodfellow, Marc D. – Burton Albion – Kidderminster Harriers; 18 Haber, David – West Bromwich Albion – Exeter City; 1 Harris, Edward G. – Queens Park Rangers – Hayes & Yeading United; 1 Healy, David J. – Sunderland – Ipswich Town; 12 Heaton, Thomas D. – Manchester United – Wycombe Wanderers; 9 Heffernan, Paul – Doncaster Rovers – Bristol Rovers; 1 Henderson, Stephen – Bristol City – Aldershot Town; 1 Hewson, Sam – Manchester United – Bury; 1 Holden, Luke – Charlton Athletic – Wrexham; 1 Hutton, Alan – Tottenham Hotspur – Sunderland; 12 Ireland, Daniel A. – Coventry City – Forest Green Rovers; 12 Iwelumo, Christopher R. – Wolverhampton Wanderers – Bristol City; 18 Jackson, Johnnie A. – Notts County –

Charlton Athletic; 9 James, Matthew – Manchester United – Preston North End; 15 Jones, Daniel J. – Wolverhampton Wanderers – Bristol Rovers; 5 Joyce, Daniel D. – Reading – Bognor Regis Town; 1 Kallio, Toni – Fulham – Sheffield United; 16 Kelly, Julian J. – Reading – Wycombe Wanderers; 15 Knight, Joshua – West Bromwich Albion – Torquay United; 1 Lancashire, Oliver J. – Southampton – Grimsby Town; 12 Leach, Daniel J. – Barnet – Dover Athletic; 16 Lloyd-Weston, Daniel – Port Vale – Nantwich Town; 9 LuaLua, Kazenga – Newcastle United – Brighton & Hove Albion; 1 Lund, Jonathan – Burnley – Rotherham United; 19 Macklin, Lloyd J. – Swindon Town – Torquay United; 12 Madine, Gary L. – Carlisle United – Chesterfield; 12 MacAuley, Joshua L. – Tranmere Rovers – Vauxhall Motors; 1 Marshall, Ben – Stoke City – Carlisle United; 9 Martin, David J. – Millwall – Derby County; 26 McCammon, Mark J. – Gillingham – Bradford City; 19 McCollin, Andre S. – Yeovil Town – Farnborough Town; 5 Medley, Luke A.C. – Barnet – Havant & Waterlooville; 1 Murphy, Daryl – Sunderland – Ipswich Town; 1 Mwaruwari, Benjani – Manchester City – Sunderland; 1 Naughton, Kyle – Tottenham Hotspur – Middlesbrough; 9 Nicholas, Andrew P. – Rotherham United – Mansfield Town; 19 Nolan, Edward W. – Preston North End – Sheffield Wednesday; 2 North, Jonathan P. – Watford – Oxford City; 1 Nosworthy, Nyron – Sunderland – Sheffield United; 9 Nouble, Franck H. – West Ham United – West Bromwich Albion; 1 Nugent, David J. – Portsmouth – Burnley; 12 Obika, Jonathan – Tottenham Hotspur – Millwall; 23 O'Donovan, Roy S. – Sunderland – Hartlepool United; 18 O'Neill, Luke M. – Leicester City – Tranmere Rovers; 26 Oxley, Mark T. – Hull City – Grimsby Town; 9 Pelling, Joshua R.A. – Brighton & Hove Albion – Horsham; 13 Pinney, Nathaniel B. – Crystal Palace – Woking; 26 Preston, Daniel S. – Birmingham City – Hereford United; 1 Price, Jason J. – Millwall – Oldham Athletic; 1 Priskin, Tamas – Ipswich Town – Queens Park Rangers; 19 Putnins, Elvijs – Queens Park Rangers – Hemel Hempstead Town; 12 Ritchie, Matthew T. – Portsmouth – Swindon Town; 1 Rodriguez, Jay E. – Burnley – Barnsley; 26 Scott, Mark J. – Swindon Town – Banbury United; 12 Sears, Fred – West Ham United – Coventry City; 1 Shorey, Nicholas – Aston Villa – Fulham; 8 Smith, Thomas J. – Ipswich Town – Brentford; 1 Sodje, Akpo – Sheffield Wednesday – Charlton Athletic; 25 Somma, Davide E. – Leeds United – Lincoln City; 1 Sordell, Marvin A. – Watford – Tranmere Rovers; 26 Spencer, Damian – Kettering Town – Aldershot Town; 16 Stead, Jonthan G. – Ipswich Town – Coventry City; 26 Steele, Jason – Middlesbrough – Northampton Town; 19 Sunu, Gilles – Arsenal – Derby County; 1 Szczesny, Wojciech T. – Arsenal – Brentford; 5 Tabiri, Joseph O. – Barnet – Havant & Waterlooville; 1 Teixeira, Filipe – West Bromwich Albion – Barnsley; 23 Threlfall, Robert R. – Liverpool – Bradford City; 1 Tonge, Michael W.E. – Stoke City – Derby County; 1 Treacy, Keith – Blackburn Rovers – Preston North End; 9 Trippier, Kieran J. – Manchester City – Barnsley; 11 Tunnicliffe, James – Brighton & Hove Albion – Milton Keynes Dons; 16 Tymon, Matthew R. – Hartlepool United – Spennymoor United; 1 Vidal, Javan – Manchester City – Derby County; 27 Walker, Joshua – Middlesbrough – Rotherham United; 16 Walker, Mitchell C.A. – Brighton & Hove Albion – Eastbourne Borough; 1 Ward, Daniel C. – Bolton Wanderers – Swindon Town; 15 Ward, Elliott L. – Coventry City – Doncaster Rovers; 22 Watson, Ben – Wigan Athletic – West Bromwich Albion; 1 Watt, Herschel O.S. – Arsenal – Southend United; 15 Williams, Thomas A. – Peterborough United – Preston North End; 26 Winters, Ruairidh T.P. – Morecambe – Vauxhall Motors

MARCH 2010 TEMPORARY TRANSFERS

25 Ajdarevic, Astrit – Leicester City – Hereford United; 19 Almond, Louis J. – Blackpool – Cheltenham Town; 2 Arismendi, Hugo D. – Stoke City – Brighton & Hove Albion; 17 Ayling, Luke D. – Arsenal – Yeovil Town; 25 Balkestein, Pim – Ipswich Town – Brentford; 25 Barnes, Ashley L. – Plymouth Argyle – Brighton & Hove Albion; 12 Bell-Baggie, Abdulai H. – Reading – Rotherham United; 25 Bennett, Alan J. – Reading – Wycombe Wanderers; 5 Bolder, Adam P. – Millwall – Bradford City; 18 Borrowdale, Gary I. – Queens Park Rangers – Charlton Athletic; 4 Boyd, George J. – Peterborough United – Nottingham Forest; 1 Boyes, Adam J. – Scunthorpe United – Kidderminster Harriers; 19 Brinkhurst, Steven W. – Brighton & Hove Albion – Lewes; 25 Butcher, Callum J. – Tottenham Hotspur – Exeter City; 2 Button, David R.E. – Tottenham Hotspur – Shrewsbury Town; 19 Chalmers, Lewis J. – Aldershot Town – Oxford United; 16 Clark, Jack A. – Charlton Athletic – Cray Wanderers; 25 Clements, Christopher L. – Crewe Alexandra – Hednesford Town; 19 Coleman, Seamus – Everton – Blackpool; 24 Collins, Neill – Preston North End – Leeds United; 19 Connerton, Jordan – Crewe Alexandra – Lancaster City; 16 Connolly, Paul – Derby County – Sheffield United; 25 Cywka, Tomasz – Wigan Athletic – Derby County; 12 Darby, Stephen – Liverpool – Swindon Town; 25 Darville, Liam T. – Leeds United – Rotherham United; 25 Davidson, Ross – Port Vale – Stafford Rangers; 15 Davies, Scott M.E. – Reading – Yeovil Town; 24 Dawson, Liam – Oldham Athletic – Ashton United; 1 Demetriou, Stephen – Dagenham & RedbridgeT – Aveley; 19 Demontagnac, Ishmel – Blackpool – Chesterfield; 5 Dennehy, Darren J. – Cardiff City – Gillingham; 2 Dennis, Kristian – Macclesfield Town – Woodley Sports; 3 Dickov, Paul – Derby County – Leeds United; 5 Eckersley, Richard J. – Manchester United – Plymouth Argyle; 23 Edgar, David E. – Burnley – Swansea City; 5 Elito, Medy E. – Colchester United – Cheltenham Town; 5 Elliott, Stephen W. – Preston North End – Norwich City; 25 Erskine, Emmanuel J.K. – Gillingham – Croydon Athletic; 25 Forster, Nicholas M. – Brighton & Hove Albion – Charlton Athletic; 4 Friend, George A.J. – Wolverhampton Wanderers – Exeter City; 25 Fry, Matthew – West Ham United – Charlton Athletic; 31 Gaughran, Samuel D. – Peterborough United – Halesowen Town; 25 Glover, Daniel – Port Vale – Stafford Rangers; 25 Gordon, Benjamin L. – Chelsea – Tranmere Rovers; 25 Grabban, Lewis J. – Millwall – Brentford; 19 Grant, John A.C. – Aldershot Town – Oxford United; 4 Grey, Andre A. – Shrewsbury Town – Hinckley United; 16 Guy, Lewis B. – Doncaster Rovers – Oldham Athletic; 8 Hackney, Simon J. – Colchester United – Morecambe; 12 Hall, Grant T. – Brighton & Hove Albion – Lewes; 9 Halstead, Mark J. – Blackpool – Hyde United; 13 Harsley, Paul – Chesterfield – York City; 15 Head, Liam T. – Plymouth Argyle – Tiverton Town; 23 Hendrie, Lee A. – Derby County – Brighton & Hove Albion; 12 Heslop, Simon J. – Barnsley – Luton Town; 25 Hughes-Mason, Kiernan P. – Millwall – Cheltenham Town; 3 Hunt, Ben – Bristol Rovers – Gloucester City; 30 Hunt, Ben – Bristol Rovers – Newport County; 19 Jervis, Jake M. – Birmingham City – Hereford United; 17 Kendall, Ryan P. – Hull City – Bradford City; 25 Kerry, Lloyd – Chesterfield – Kidderminster Harriers; 24 Labadie, Josh C. – West Bromwich Albion – Tranmere Rovers; 18 Leitch-Smith, A-Jay – Crewe Alexandra – Curzon Ashton; 5 Lescott, Aaron A. – Bristol Rovers – Cheltenham Town; 25 Lichaj, Eric J. – Aston Villa – Leyton Orient; 2 Little, Mark D. – Wolverhampton Wanderers – Peterborough United; 24 Lowry, Shane T. – Aston Villa – Leeds United; 13 Lund, Jonathan – Burnley – Barnsley; 16 Maierhofer, Stefan – Wolverhampton Wanderers – Bristol City; 6 Malton, Russell J. – Colchester United – Heybridge Swifts; 2 Marshall, Ben – Stoke City – Carlisle United; 2 Martin, Aaron – Southampton – Salisbury City; 12 Martin, David E. – Liverpool – Derby County; 11 McAllister, Craig – Exeter City – Rotherham United; 9 McCarten, James – Everton – Accrington Stanley; 17 McDermott, Donal – Manchester City – Scunthorpe United; 23 McNulty, Jimmy – Brighton & Hove Albion – Scunthorpe United; 15 Mellor, Kevin – Crewe Alexandra – Newcastle Town; 5 Milne, Andrew A. – Leeds United – Darlington; 25 Mitchley, Daniel J. – Blackpool – Wrexham; 25 Molyneux, Lee R. – Southampton – Port Vale; 25 Morgan, Dean L. – Milton Keynes Dons – Aldershot Town; 19 Morris, Lee – Hereford United – Forest Green Rovers; 25 Naisbitt, Daniel J. – Histon – Brighton & Hove

Albion; 4 Nardiello, Daniel A. – Blackpool – Oldham Athletic; 16 N'Gala, Bondz – West Ham United – Plymouth Argyle; 11 Nightingale, Lewis J. – Huddersfield Town – Salford City; 25 Noble, Ryan – Sunderland – Watford; 19 Nouble, Frank H. – West Ham United – Swindon Town; 3 Oliver, Luke J. – Wycombe Wanderers – Bradford City; 25 O'Shea, James – Birmingham City – Middlesbrough; 18 Parker, Keigan – Oldham Athletic – Bury; 26 Plummer, Neikell – Bristol Rovers – Gloucester City; 25 Poole, James A. – Manchester City – Bury; 10 Price, Jason J. – Millwall – Carlisle United; 25 Prosser, Luke B. – Port Vale – Kidderminster Harriers; 2 Pugh, Andrew J. – Gillingham – Histon; 25 Queudrue, Franck – Birmingham City – Colchester United; 5 Reid, Steven J. – Blackburn Rovers – West Bromwich Albion; 12 Riley, Daniel – Darlington – Billingham Town; 25 Robinson, Andrew M. – Leeds United – Tranmere Rovers; 23 Rodney, Nialle – Nottingham Forest – Ilkeston Town; 16 Rooney, Luke W. – Gillingham – Eastbourne Borough; 17 Saunders, Matthew – Fulham – Lincoln City; 25 Sawyer, Gary D. – Plymouth Argyle – Bristol City; 25 Shephard, Christopher J. – Exeter City – Salisbury City; 19 Simonsen, Steven P.A. – Stoke City – Sheffield United; 23 Spearing, Jay F. – Liverpool – Leicester City; 25 Spicer, John W. – Doncaster Rovers – Leyton Orient; 19 Stephens, David R.R. – Norwich City – Lincoln City; 20 Stirling, Jude B. – Milton Keynes Dons – Grimsby Town; 12 Stokes, Christopher M.T. – Bolton Wanderers – Crewe Alexandra; 13 Tabiri, Joseph O. – Barnet – Dover Athletic; 25 Taylor, Ryan P. – Rotherham United – Exeter City; 25 Thomas, Wesley A.N. – Dagenham & Redbridge – Rushden & Diamonds; 25 Titchiner, Alexander – Crewe Alexandra – Colwyn Bay; 25 Tosic, Dusko – Portsmouth – Queens Park Rangers; 12 Upson, Edward J. – Ipswich Town – Barnet; 12 Vaughan, James O. – Everton – Leicester City; 23 Ward, Elliott L. – Coventry City – Preston North End; 25 Watt, Herschel O.S. – Arsenal – Leeds United; 5 Whing, Andrew J. – Brighton & Hove Albion – Chesterfield; 11 Williams, Gavin J. – Bristol City – Yeovil Town; 11 Wright, Benjamin M. – Peterborough United – Barnet; 19 Young, Lewis J. – Watford – Hereford United

APRIL 2010 TEMPORARY TRANSFERS

7 Bird, Matthew – Grimsby Town – Boston United; 13 Cayford, Daniel – Bristol Rovers – Clevedon Town; 28 Fulop, Marton – Sunderland – Manchester City; 16 Gulacsi, Peter – Liverpool – Tranmere Rovers; 26 Mellor, Kelvin – Newcastle Town – Crewe Alexandra; 2 Oxley, Mark T. – Hull City – Grimsby Town; 13 Tyrrell, James R. – Bristol Rovers – Clevedon Town

MAY 2010

22 Crofts, Andrew L.	Brighton & Hove Albion	Norwich City	undisclosed
18 Mackie, James	Plymouth Argyle	Queens Park Rangers	undisclosed
28 Marney, Dean E.	Hull City	Burnley	undisclosed
13 Sarcevic, Antoni C.	Woodley Sports	Crewe Alexandra	undisclosed
17 Shackell, Jason	Wolverhampton Wanderers	Barnsley	undisclosed
17 Sodje, Akpo	Sheffield Wednesday	Charlton Athletic	undisclosed

TEMPORARY TRANSFERS

6 Bannan, Barry – Aston Villa – Blackpool; 11 Batt, Shaun – Peterborough United – Millwall; 7 Collis, Stephen P. – Bristol City – Torquay United; 10 Trotter, Liam A. – Ipswich Town – Millwall

The biggest managerial transfer saw Roy Hodgson join Liverpool from Fulham on July 1 2010. His in-depth knowledge of European and International Football will be required to boost the reds whose seventh place Premier League finish was their worst since an eighth place finish in 1993–94. (PA Sports)

THE NEW FOREIGN LEGION 2009–10

JULY/AUGUST 2009	From	To	Fee in £
Altidore, Jozy	Villareal	Hull City	Loan
Amaya, Antonio	Rayo Vallecano	Wigan Athletic	1,500,000
Aquilani, Alberto	Roma	Liverpool	18,000,000
Benitez, Christian	Santos Laguna	Birmingham City	8,500,000
Bilyaletdinov, Diniyar	Lokomotiv Moscow	Everton	undisclosed
Cana, Lorik	Marseille	Sunderland	5,000,000
Da Silva, Paulo	Toluca	Sunderland	Free
Diamanti, Alessandro	Livorno	West Ham United	1,500,000
Diame, Mohamed	Rayo Vallecano	Wigan Athletic	2,000,000
Dikgacoi, KIagisho	Golden Arrows	Fulham	undisclosed
Dindane, Aruna	Lens	Portsmouth	Loan
Diouf, Mame Biram	Molde	Manchester United	undisclosed
Elm, David	Kalmar	Fulham	undisclosed
Franco, Guillermo	Villarreal	West Ham United	Free
Ghilas, Kamel	Celta Viga	Hull City	2,000,000
Guerrero, Fernando	Indep del Valle	Burnley	Loan
Heitinga, Johnny	Atletico Madrid	Everton	6,000,000
Jimenez, Luis	Internazionale	West Ham United	Loan
Kakuta, Gael	Lens	Chelsea	undisclosed
Kalinic, Nikola	Hajduk Split	Blackburn Rovers	6,000,000
Klasnic, Ivan	Nantes	Bolton Wanderers	Loan
Kovac, Radoslav	Spartak Moscow	West Ham United	1,800,000
Kyrgiakos, Sotirios	AEK Athens	Liverpool	1,500,000
Lee Chung-Yong	FC Seoul	Bolton Wanderers	2,200,000
Maierhofer, Stefan	Rapid Vienna	Wolverhampton Wanderers	undisclosed
Matic, Nemanja	Kosice	Chelsea	1,500,000
Mensah, John	Lyon	Sunderland	Loan
Milijas, Nenad	Red Star Belgrade	Wolverhampton Wanderers	undisclosed
Mouyokolo, Steven	Bologne	Hull City	2,000,000
N'Zonzi, Steven	Amiens	Blackburn Rovers	400,000
Obertan, Gabriel	Bordeaux	Manchester United	3,000,000
Penny, Diego	Coronel Bolognesi	Burnley	Free
Piquionne, Frederic	Lyon	Portsmouth	Loan
Riise, Bjorn Helge	Lillestrom	Fulham	1,700,000
Salgado, Michel	Real Madrid	Blackburn Rovers	Free
Thomas, Hendry	Dep Olimpia	Wigan Athletic	1,000,000
Vanden Borre, Anthony	Genoa	Portsmouth	Loan
Van Heerden, Elrio	Club Brugge	Blackburn Rovers	Free
Vennegoor of Hesselink, Jan	Celtic	Hull City	Free
Vermaelen, Thomas	Ajax	Arsenal	10,000,000
Yebda, Hassan	Benfica	Portsmouth	Loan
Zhirkov, Yuri	CSKA Moscow	Chelsea	18,000,000
Zubar, Ronald	Marseille	Wolverhampton Wanderers	2,700,000
JANUARY/FEBRUARY 2010			
Basturk, Yildiray	Stuttgart	Blackburn Rovers	Loan
Donovan, Landon	LA Galaxy	Everton	Loan
Gohouri, Steve	Moenchengladbach	Wigan Athletic	undisclosed
Guedioura, Adlene	Charleroi	Wolverhampton Wanderers	Loan
Holden, Stuart	Houston Dynamo	Bolton Wanderers	Free
Ilan	St Etienne	West Ham United	Free
Michel	Gijon	Birmingham City	3,000,000
Moreno, Marcelo	Shakhtar Donetsk	Wigan Athletic	Loan
Mujangi Bia,Geoffrey	Charleroi	Wolverhampton Wanderers	Loan
Okaka Chuka, Stefano	Roma	Fulham	Loan
Rodriguez, Maxi	Atletico Madrid	Liverpool	Free
Stojkovic, Vladimir	Sporting Lisbon	Wigan Athletic	Free

PLAYERS WHO WERE PREVIOUSLY SIGNED BUT DID NOT APPEAR UNTIL 2009–10

Ayala, Daniel	Liverpool
Begovic, Asmir	Stoke City
Borini, Fabio	Chelsea
Bruma, Jeffrey	Chelsea
Degn, Philipp	Liverpool
Fabio	Manchester United
Hines, Zavon	West Ham United
Hoilett, David	Blackburn Rovers
Pacheco, Dani	Liverpool
Nielsen, Gunnar	Manchester City
Weiss, Vladimir	Manchester City

NB: Jordi Gomez and Jason Scotland at Wigan Athletic previously played for Swansea City.

THE THINGS THEY SAID . . .

After the departure of Cristiano Ronaldo to Real Madrid, Sir Alex Ferguson gave his verdict on the £80 million player:
"He is the best player in the world by absolutely miles. He is streets ahead of Messi, streets ahead of Kaka – and, you never know, he may come back."

Ronaldo himself has definite views on his own ability:
"It's true lots of people hate me but there are even more who love and support me. I feel bad only when I play badly. Fortunately that happens rarely."

Thierry Henry reflecting on his "Hand of Frog" action which led to France qualifying for the World Cup in South Africa at the expense of the Republic of Ireland:
"Of course the fairest solution would be to replay the game but it is not in my control."

Previously he had offered a different version:
"The ball hit my hand, I will be honest."

Even Eric Cantona the well-know Frenchman and former Manchester United forward known for nipping into the odd crowd for an "in your face" confrontation, had to have his say in the controversy:
"What shocks me the most is that this player, at the end of the game, went to sit next to an Ireland player to comfort him – when he had just screwed him. If I had been an Irishman he wouldn't have lasted three seconds."

Another French recruit to our shores and no fool by any means is Arsene Wenger the Arsenal supremo, though perhaps the local dialect would have something different:
"If you want to win the title, one thing you need is consistent consistency."

But AW has his priorities correct when it comes to settling down in the country of his footballing adoption:
"My secret is adapting to the country I am in. Here I eat roast beef and Yorkshire pudding."

What a difference a few months make when a manager changes his tune over his attitude to refereeing. Carlo Ancelotti the Chelsea boss said this after his team lost to Wigan Athletic earlier in the season, when Phil Dowd sent off his goalkeeper Petr Cech:
"I don't like to speak about the decisions of the referee."

Sadly when losing to Manchester City in December he put a new slant on the subject:
"We were disappointed because the referee made two important mistakes. I think Richards did handle the ball before the first goal and in the second situation I think it was clear that Ricardo Carvalho took the ball cleanly. I'm surprised because I consider Webb a fantastic referee with experience. I was surprised with his two mistakes."

The World Cup draw for the finals in South Africa produced this comment from England team manager Fabio Capello:
"I think it is one of the most balanced groups; we've already played against the United States and Slovenia and struggled."

Coming on as a sub in the midlands derby with Wolverhampton Wanderers, Birmingham City striker Kevin Phillips aged 36 was asked by a reporter how he managed to keep fit at his age and with only a couple of similar appearances in three months:
"I don't, I'm knackered!"

Soaking wet Charlton Athletic fans in the uncovered end at Yeovil's wind-swept ground:
"Down with pneumonia. We're going down with pneumonia."

Radio Five Live possesses the experts at painting a picture in the mind during matches:
"You can hear the hush of expectancy buzzing around the ground."
(Perhaps something like a pregnant pause?)

Never at any time could you think that Paul Gascoigne was shy about his talents as a player:
"No one is ever going to be as good as I was."

The upbringing and subsequent emergence as an international player was something Emmanuel Adebayor was keen to relate to the world:
"I did not walk for the first four years of my life. Suddenly someone kicked a ball and the first person to stand up and run was me. All of the people in the church who had been praying for me told my mum: – Your son is walking because of football. It is an amazing story but it is true."

Luckily Andrei Arshavin of Arsenal was not around when Emily Pankhurst was on the march:
"If I had it in my power to introduce a ban on women driving cars and to withdraw all of their licences, I would do it without thinking twice. In my opinion a woman and a man are two absolutely different creatures."
(Would you Adam and Eve it!)

Ryan Giggs on receiving the BBC's Sportsman of the Year Award:
"This is a shock. A big shock. If I wasn't nervous enough, just seeing my heroes Seb Coe and Michael Johnson on stage is unbelievable."

One shudders to think what was involved in the advert when David Beckham said he was turning down an Armani advert with Angelina Jolie:
"At the end of the day, I wouldn't do it because I'm married."

Football comes first and the temporary role as house husband can change in a flash, as Ian Holloway discovered:
"One minute I was painting the lounge, the next I'm being asked to manage a Championship side (Blackpool). My wife will have to finish the glossing."

Mohamed Fayed the owner of Fulham Football Club on his thoughts involving football:
"I want to help other clubs. I speak my mind and other chairmen should, too. In fact, they can come and have lunch with me at Harrods, where I can serve them stags' testicles from my Scottish estate. We all need big balls in this business."

Fabio Capello with his own culinary ideas voiced to the England squad:
"I have impressed upon them the advantages of a Mediterranean diet over ketchup and chips."

That amazing moment when Pepe Reina the Liverpool goalkeeper had to do a spot of quick thinking when two balls came into his sight and with no one to kick sand in his face:
"I lost sight of the official ball and stayed on the red one. I went for the red ball instinctively as it was the closest to me and the other went past me."

Sir Alex Ferguson made the referee responsible for Manchester United losing to Chelsea and in particular for allowing Drogba's goal to stand:
"When I saw Mike Dean I was worried. I cannot understand the goal. The linesman is directly in front of him. There is no one near him and there is not a defender in sight, yet he still gets it wrong. In a game of that magnitude we really need quality officials. We did not get them today. It was a poor performance."

Understandably, perhaps, Chelsea manager Carlo Ancelotti had a different view:
"It is only an offside if the assistant referee raises the flag and it is only a penalty when the referee blows his whistle."

Sir Alex Ferguson commenting after Bayern Munich knocked Manchester United out of the Champions League:
"Rafael is a young boy and inexperienced but they (Bayern) got him sent off. Everyone sprinted over to the referee. Typical Germans. It was only a slip, a slight tug, but they saw the opportunity. The ref wasn't going to do anything but they forced him to get a card out. Bayern would never have won that game. With eleven men, there was no problem."

Arsene Wenger talking about that miniscule Merchant of Menace – four-goal Messi after his almost single-handed demolition of Arsenal for Barcelona:
"Messi's like a PlayStation. He can take advantage of every mistake we make. He made the impossible possible. He has something exceptional. He has six or seven years in front of him, touch wood that nothing happens to him and he can reach unbelievable levels."

Fabio Capello on Rooney's injury:
"I don't think Ferguson took an unnecessary risk to play him. It was important psychologically for the whole team."

Fabio Capello on the Spend, Spend, Spend culture in the Premier League:
"If a club is at the top, it should buy one or two high-level players every year."

Fabio Capello on English teams exiting the Champions League:
"All the players will be available for our preparations in Austria."

Fabio Capello on drink:
"Alcohol has always been banned for the players – for myself and my staff, too."

Portsmouth finished a traumatic season with an impassioned speech from manager Avram Grant directed at the club's supporters:
"Thank you. If I could shake the hands of every one of you, I would. If anyone in the world wants a lesson about commitment and passion and loyalty, then Fratton Park is the place. They can take points from us, put an embargo on us but they cannot destroy our spirit."

Failing to read from the same song sheet at Manchester City when Garry Cook explained:
"I think it is important to know that Roberto Mancini was only offered the job after the Spurs game."

But, according to the man himself it was a different version:
"Two weeks before that (the Spurs game) I had met Khaldoon the chairman."

On the final day of the Premier League season the Chelsea manager Carlo Ancelotti gave his opinion of his first season in England:
"After the first year I hope to stay here a long time and win a lot of titles. We had a fantastic season, not only by winning the Premier League but because we showed a good style on the pitch."

Only a point behind, Sir Alex Ferguson's Manchester United spoke his mind:
"I am not going to agonise over where we went wrong. But a refereeing decision at Chelsea was a bad one that swung the title around. I congratulate Carlo Ancelotti on a wonderful achievement. He is a good manager and a good guy."

FA Cup Final referee Chris Foy made an honest and somewhat eyebrow-raising statement about the first match in which he was in charge on a parks pitch in Liverpool:
"The worse thing that happened to me was refereeing my first match and not really understanding what I was doing."

Roy Hodgson the Fulham manager was understandably down following the team's incredible 19-match journey including the final of the first Europa League which ended in extra time defeat at the hands of Atletico Madrid:
"I could never have imagined in my wildest dreams last July that it would end here, but it doesn't help unfortunately at this moment. The players are very

very down. We've suffered a bitter blow and it will take a bit of time before that pain passes over."*

Ahead of the final day in Serie A, rival managers Jose Mourinho (Internazionale) and Claudio Ranieri (Roma) – both Chelsea bosses, too, were each hoping to win the title and clearly not the best of friends:
"He (Mourinho) must hold me close to his heart, seeing as he's always talking about me. He really bores me with the things he says. He's afraid of me."

To this JM responded as follows:
"What is the boredom of Ranieri? I am educated and I only know The Nausea by Jean-Paul Sartre, a philosopher, a Nobel Prize winner, but also a great football fan."

Another fine mess at the FA and exit Lord Triesman – from Communist party member to a Peer following a damaging statement about rivals bidding for the World Cup:
"My assumption is that the Latin Americans, although they've not said so, will vote for Spain. And if Spain drop out, because Spain are looking for help from the Russians to help bribe the referees in the World Cup, their votes may then switch to Russia. I think Russia will cut deals."

Blackpool manager Ian Holloway after his team had won promotion to the Premier League via the play-offs:
"I come from a council house. The money in the Premier League is obscene, but that's the way it is. Let's see what we can do with it."

Upon being installed as Real Madrid manager, Jose Mourinho rendered his usual clear view of what the position meant:
"What's beautiful, beautiful, beautiful isn't working for Real Madrid. What's beautiful, beautiful, beautiful is winning for them."

World Cup news that referees were being given lists of English swearwords prompted former top class official Pierluigi Collina to give his own personal view:
"You do not need a dictionary to know if a player is abusive to you. You just look at his face."

The disallowed goal scored by Frank Lampard in the World Cup against Germany prompted reams of paperwork on the subject of technology and the need to introduce it into football. The man in charge of FIFA, Sepp Blatter was forced to say in the days which followed:
"It is obvious that after the experience so far in this World Cup it would be nonsense not to reopen the file of technology at the business meeting of the International FA Board in July."

Joachim Low the beaten World Cup 2010 manager of Gemany paid fulsome tribute to the Spanish victors:
"Spain is a wonderful team. They have players from Barcelona and Real Madrid and they are masters of the game. You can see that in every pass. Look at how Barca plays – they can hardly be beaten. That's the strength Spain has."

One goal was enough for Spain in Euro 2008. It was the same in South Africa when they won the 2010 World Cup. Match winner Andres Iniesta was modest about his part in the victory:
"I've made a small contribution in a very tough game, a very rough game – there were all sorts of things happening on the pitch – but Spain deserved to win this World Cup. It's something we have to remember and enjoy and should feel very proud of everyone in this squad."

The opposite view of the final was taken by the Dutchman Arjen Robben and his remarks were pointedly made in one direction – at the referee Howard Webb:
"It is wrong when you sit in the dressing-room and you are talking about the referee and his very bad points. If you play a World Cup final you need a world class referee. I didn't know whether that was a world class performance from the referee."

ENGLISH LEAGUE HONOURS 1888 TO 2010

FA PREMIER LEAGUE

MAXIMUM POINTS: a 126; b 114.
Won or placed on goal average (ratio), goal difference or most goals scored. ††Not promoted after play-offs.

	First	Pts	Second	Pts	Third	Pts
1992–93a	Manchester U	84	Aston Villa	74	Norwich C	72
1993–94a	Manchester U	92	Blackburn R	84	Newcastle U	77
1994–95a	Blackburn R	89	Manchester U	88	Nottingham F	77
1995–96b	Manchester U	82	Newcastle U	78	Liverpool	71
1996–97b	Manchester U	75	Newcastle U*	68	Arsenal*	68
1997–98b	Arsenal	78	Manchester U	77	Liverpool	65
1998–99b	Manchester U	79	Arsenal	78	Chelsea	75
1999–2000b	Manchester U	91	Arsenal	73	Leeds U	69
2000–01b	Manchester U	80	Arsenal	70	Liverpool	69
2001–02b	Arsenal	87	Liverpool	80	Manchester U	77
2002–03b	Manchester U	83	Arsenal	78	Newcastle U	69
2003–04b	Arsenal	90	Chelsea	79	Manchester U	75
2004–05b	Chelsea	95	Arsenal	83	Manchester U	77
2005–06b	Chelsea	91	Manchester U	83	Liverpool	82
2006–07b	Manchester U	89	Chelsea	83	Liverpool*	68
2007–08b	Manchester U	87	Chelsea	85	Arsenal	83
2008–09b	Manchester U	90	Liverpool	86	Chelsea	83
2009–10b	Chelsea	86	Manchester U	85	Arsenal	75

FOOTBALL LEAGUE CHAMPIONSHIP

MAXIMUM POINTS: 138

2004–05	Sunderland	94	Wigan Ath	87	Ipswich T††	85
2005–06	Reading	106	Sheffield U	90	Watford	81
2006–07	Sunderland	88	Birmingham C	86	Derby Co	84
2007–08	WBA	81	Stoke C	79	Hull C	75
2008–09	Wolverhampton W	90	Birmingham C	83	Sheffield U††	80
2009–10	Newcastle U	102	WBA	91	Nottingham F††	79

FIRST DIVISION

MAXIMUM POINTS: 138

1992–93	Newcastle U	96	West Ham U*	88	Portsmouth††	88
1993–94	Crystal Palace	90	Nottingham F	83	Millwall††	74
1994–95	Middlesbrough	82	Reading††	79	Bolton W	77
1995–96	Sunderland	83	Derby Co	79	Crystal Palace††	75
1996–97	Bolton W	98	Barnsley	80	Wolverhampton W††	76
1997–98	Nottingham F	94	Middlesbrough	91	Sunderland††	90
1998–99	Sunderland	105	Bradford C	87	Ipswich T††	86
1999–2000	Charlton Ath	91	Manchester C	89	Ipswich T	87
2000–01	Fulham	101	Blackburn R	91	Bolton W	87
2001–02	Manchester C	99	WBA	89	Wolverhampton W††	86
2002–03	Portsmouth	98	Leicester C	92	Sheffield U††	80
2003–04	Norwich C	94	WBA	86	Sunderland††	79

FOOTBALL LEAGUE CHAMPIONSHIP 1

MAXIMUM POINTS: 138

2004–05	Luton T	98	Hull C	86	Tranmere R††	79
2005–06	Southend U	82	Colchester U	79	Brentford††	76
2006–07	Scunthorpe U	91	Bristol C	85	Blackpool	83
2007–08	Swansea C	92	Nottingham F	82	Doncaster R	80
2008–09	Leicester C	96	Peterborough U	89	Milton Keynes D††	87
2009–10	Norwich C	95	Leeds U	86	Millwall	85

SECOND DIVISION

MAXIMUM POINTS: 138

1992–93	Stoke C	93	Bolton W	90	Port Vale††	89
1993–94	Reading	89	Port Vale	88	Plymouth Arg*††	85
1994–95	Birmingham C	89	Brentford††	85	Crewe Alex††	83
1995–96	Swindon T	92	Oxford U	83	Blackpool††	82
1996–97	Bury	84	Stockport Co	82	Luton T††	78
1997–98	Watford	88	Bristol C	85	Grimsby T	72
1998–99	Fulham	101	Walsall	87	Manchester C	82
1999–2000	Preston NE	95	Burnley	88	Gillingham	85
2000–01	Millwall	93	Rotherham U	91	Reading††	86
2001–02	Brighton & HA	90	Reading	84	Brentford*††	83
2002–03	Wigan Ath	100	Crewe Alex	86	Bristol C††	83
2003–04	Plymouth Arg	90	QPR	83	Bristol C††	82

FOOTBALL LEAGUE CHAMPIONSHIP 2

MAXIMUM POINTS: 138

2004–05	Yeovil T	83	Scunthorpe U*	80	Swansea C	80
2005–06	Carlisle U	86	Northampton T	83	Leyton Orient	81
2006–07	Walsall	89	Hartlepool U	88	Swindon T	85
2007–08	Milton Keynes D	97	Peterborough U	92	Hereford U	88
2008–09	Brentford	85	Exeter C	79	Wycombe W*	78
2009–10	Notts Co	93	Bournemouth	83	Rochdale	82

THIRD DIVISION

MAXIMUM POINTS: *a* 126; *b* 138.

	First	Pts	Second	Pts	Third	Pts
1992–93*a*	Cardiff C	83	Wrexham	80	Barnet	79
1993–94*a*	Shrewsbury T	79	Chester C	74	Crewe Alex	73
1994–95*a*	Carlisle U	91	Walsall	83	Chesterfield	81
1995–96*b*	Preston NE	86	Gillingham	83	Bury	79
1996–97*b*	Wigan Ath*	87	Fulham	87	Carlisle U	84

	First	Pts	Second	Pts	Third	Pts
1997–98*b*	Notts Co	99	Macclesfield T	82	Lincoln C	72
1998–99*b*	Brentford	85	Cambridge U	81	Cardiff C	80
1999–2000*b*	Swansea C	85	Rotherham U	84	Northampton T	82
2000–01	Brighton & HA	92	Cardiff C	82	Chesterfield¶	80
2001–02	Plymouth Arg	102	Luton T	97	Mansfield T	79
2002–03	Rushden & D	87	Hartlepool U	85	Wrexham	84
2003–04	Doncaster R	92	Hull C	88	Torquay U*	81

¶9pts deducted for irregularities.

FOOTBALL LEAGUE

MAXIMUM POINTS: *a* 44; *b* 60

	First	Pts	Second	Pts	Third	Pts
1888–89*a*	Preston NE	40	Aston Villa	29	Wolverhampton W	28
1889–90*a*	Preston NE	33	Everton	31	Blackburn R	27
1890–91*a*	Everton	29	Preston NE	27	Notts Co	26
1891–92*b*	Sunderland	42	Preston NE	37	Bolton W	36

FIRST DIVISION to 1991–92

MAXIMUM POINTS: *a* 44; *b* 52; *c* 60; *d* 68; *e* 76; *f* 84; *g* 126; *h* 120; *k* 114.

	First	Pts	Second	Pts	Third	Pts
1892–93*c*	Sunderland	48	Preston NE	37	Everton	36
1893–94*c*	Aston Villa	44	Sunderland	38	Derby Co	36
1894–95*c*	Sunderland	47	Everton	42	Aston Villa	39
1895–96*c*	Aston Villa	45	Derby Co	41	Everton	39
1896–97*c*	Aston Villa	47	Sheffield U*	36	Derby Co	36
1897–98*c*	Sheffield U	42	Sunderland	37	Wolverhampton W*	35
1898–99*d*	Aston Villa	45	Liverpool	43	Burnley	39
1899–1900*d*	Aston Villa	50	Sheffield U	48	Sunderland	41
1900–01*d*	Liverpool	45	Sunderland	43	Notts Co	40
1901–02*d*	Sunderland	44	Everton	41	Newcastle U	37
1902–03*d*	The Wednesday	42	Aston Villa*	41	Sunderland	41
1903–04*d*	The Wednesday	47	Manchester C	44	Everton	43
1904–05*d*	Newcastle U	48	Everton	47	Manchester C	46
1905–06*e*	Liverpool	51	Preston NE	47	The Wednesday	44
1906–07*e*	Newcastle U	51	Bristol C	48	Everton*	45
1907–08*e*	Manchester U	52	Aston Villa*	43	Manchester C	43
1908–09*e*	Newcastle U	53	Everton	46	Sunderland	44
1909–10*e*	Aston Villa	53	Liverpool	48	Blackburn R*	45
1910–11*e*	Manchester U	52	Aston Villa	51	Sunderland*	45
1911–12*e*	Blackburn R	49	Everton	46	Newcastle U	44
1912–13*e*	Sunderland	54	Aston Villa	50	Sheffield W	49
1913–14*e*	Blackburn R	51	Aston Villa	44	Middlesbrough*	43
1914–15*e*	Everton	46	Oldham Ath	45	Blackburn R*	43
1919–20*f*	WBA	60	Burnley	51	Chelsea	49
1920–21*f*	Burnley	59	Manchester C	54	Bolton W	52
1921–22*f*	Liverpool	57	Tottenham H	51	Burnley	49
1922–23*f*	Liverpool	60	Sunderland	54	Huddersfield T	53
1923–24*f*	Huddersfield T*	57	Cardiff C	57	Sunderland	53
1924–25*f*	Huddersfield T	58	WBA	56	Bolton W	55
1925–26*f*	Huddersfield T	57	Arsenal	52	Sunderland	48
1926–27*f*	Newcastle U	56	Huddersfield T	51	Sunderland	49
1927–28*f*	Everton	53	Huddersfield T	51	Leicester C	48
1928–29*f*	Sheffield W	52	Leicester C	51	Aston Villa	50
1929–30*f*	Sheffield W	60	Derby Co	50	Manchester C*	47
1930–31*f*	Arsenal	66	Aston Villa	59	Sheffield W	52
1931–32*f*	Everton	56	Arsenal	54	Sheffield W	50
1932–33*f*	Arsenal	58	Aston Villa	54	Sheffield W	51
1933–34*f*	Arsenal	59	Huddersfield T	56	Tottenham H	49
1934–35*f*	Arsenal	58	Sunderland	54	Sheffield W	49
1935–36*f*	Sunderland	56	Derby Co*	48	Huddersfield T	48
1936–37*f*	Manchester C	57	Charlton Ath	54	Arsenal	52
1937–38*f*	Arsenal	52	Wolverhampton W	51	Preston NE	49
1938–39*f*	Everton	59	Wolverhampton W	55	Charlton Ath	50
1946–47*f*	Liverpool	57	Manchester U*	56	Wolverhampton W	56
1947–48*f*	Arsenal	59	Manchester U*	52	Burnley	52
1948–49*f*	Portsmouth	58	Manchester U*	53	Derby Co	53
1949–50*f*	Portsmouth*	53	Wolverhampton W	53	Sunderland	52
1950–51*f*	Tottenham H	60	Manchester U	56	Blackpool	50
1951–52*f*	Manchester U	57	Tottenham H*	53	Arsenal	53
1952–53*f*	Arsenal*	54	Preston NE	54	Wolverhampton W	51
1953–54*f*	Wolverhampton W	57	WBA	53	Huddersfield T	51
1954–55*f*	Chelsea	52	Wolverhampton W*	48	Portsmouth*	48
1955–56*f*	Manchester U	60	Blackpool*	49	Wolverhampton W	49
1956–57*f*	Manchester U	64	Tottenham H*	56	Preston NE	56
1957–58*f*	Wolverhampton W	64	Preston NE	59	Tottenham H	51
1958–59*f*	Wolverhampton W	61	Manchester U	55	Arsenal*	50
1959–60*f*	Burnley	55	Wolverhampton W	54	Tottenham H	53

	First	Pts	Second	Pts	Third	Pts
1960–61f	Tottenham H	66	Sheffield W	58	Wolverhampton W	57
1961–62f	Ipswich T	56	Burnley	53	Tottenham H	52
1962–63f	Everton	61	Tottenham H	55	Burnley	54
1963–64f	Liverpool	57	Manchester U	53	Everton	52
1964–65f	Manchester U*	61	Leeds U	61	Chelsea	56
1965–66f	Liverpool	61	Leeds U*	55	Burnley	55
1966–67f	Manchester U	60	Nottingham F*	56	Tottenham H	56
1967–68f	Manchester C	58	Manchester U	56	Liverpool	55
1968–69f	Leeds U	67	Liverpool	61	Everton	57
1969–70f	Everton	66	Leeds U	57	Chelsea	55
1970–71f	Arsenal	65	Leeds U	64	Tottenham H*	52
1971–72f	Derby Co	58	Leeds U*	57	Liverpool*	57
1972–73f	Liverpool	60	Arsenal	57	Leeds U	53
1973–74f	Leeds U	62	Liverpool	57	Derby Co	48
1974–75f	Derby Co	53	Liverpool*	51	Ipswich T	51
1975–76f	Liverpool	60	QPR	59	Manchester U	56
1976–77f	Liverpool	57	Manchester C	56	Ipswich T	56
1977–78f	Nottingham F	64	Liverpool	57	Everton	55
1978–79f	Liverpool	68	Nottingham F	60	WBA	59
1979–80f	Liverpool	60	Manchester U	58	Ipswich T	52
1980–81f	Aston Villa	60	Ipswich T	56	Arsenal	53
1981–82g	Liverpool	87	Ipswich T	83	Manchester U	78
1982–83g	Liverpool	82	Watford	71	Manchester U	70
1983–84g	Liverpool	80	Southampton	77	Nottingham F*	74
1984–85g	Everton	90	Liverpool*	77	Tottenham H	77
1985–86g	Liverpool	88	Everton	86	West Ham U	84
1986–87g	Everton	86	Liverpool	77	Tottenham H	71
1987–88h	Liverpool	90	Manchester U	81	Nottingham F	73
1988–89k	Arsenal*	76	Liverpool	76	Nottingham F	64
1989–90k	Liverpool	79	Aston Villa	70	Tottenham H	63
1990–91k	Arsenal†	83	Liverpool	76	Crystal Palace	69
1991–92g	Leeds U	82	Manchester U	78	Sheffield W	75

No official competition during 1915–19 and 1939–46; Regional Leagues operated. †2 pts deducted.

SECOND DIVISION to 1991–92

MAXIMUM POINTS: *a* **44;** *b* **56;** *c* **60;** *d* **68;** *e* **76;** *f* **84;** *g* **126;** *h* **132;** *k* **138.**

	First	Pts	Second	Pts	Third	Pts
1892–93a	Small Heath	36	Sheffield U	35	Darwen	30
1893–94b	Liverpool	50	Small Heath	42	Notts Co	39
1894–95c	Bury	48	Notts Co	39	Newton Heath*	38
1895–96c	Liverpool*	46	Manchester C	46	Grimsby T*	42
1896–97c	Notts Co	42	Newton Heath	39	Grimsby T	38
1897–98c	Burnley	48	Newcastle U	45	Manchester C	39
1898–99d	Manchester C	52	Glossop NE	46	Leicester Fosse	45
1899–1900d	The Wednesday	54	Bolton W	52	Small Heath	46
1900–01d	Grimsby T	49	Small Heath	48	Burnley	44
1901–02d	WBA	55	Middlesbrough	51	Preston NE*	42
1902–03d	Manchester C	54	Small Heath	51	Woolwich A	48
1903–04d	Preston NE	50	Woolwich A	49	Manchester U	48
1904–05d	Liverpool	58	Bolton W	56	Manchester U	53
1905–06e	Bristol C	66	Manchester U	62	Chelsea	53
1906–07e	Nottingham F	60	Chelsea	57	Leicester Fosse	48
1907–08e	Bradford C	54	Leicester Fosse	52	Oldham Ath	50
1908–09e	Bolton W	52	Tottenham H*	51	WBA	51
1909–10e	Manchester C	54	Oldham Ath*	53	Hull C*	53
1910–11e	WBA	53	Bolton W	51	Chelsea	49
1911–12e	Derby Co*	54	Chelsea	54	Burnley	52
1912–13e	Preston NE	53	Burnley	50	Birmingham	46
1913–14e	Notts Co	53	Bradford PA*	49	Woolwich A	49
1914–15e	Derby Co	53	Preston NE	50	Barnsley	47
1919–20f	Tottenham H	70	Huddersfield T	64	Birmingham	56
1920–21f	Birmingham*	58	Cardiff C	58	Bristol C	51
1921–22f	Nottingham F	56	Stoke C*	52	Barnsley	52
1922–23f	Notts Co	53	West Ham U*	51	Leicester C	51
1923–24f	Leeds U	54	Bury*	51	Derby Co	51
1924–25f	Leicester C	59	Manchester U	57	Derby Co	55
1925–26f	Sheffield W	60	Derby Co	57	Chelsea	52
1926–27f	Middlesbrough	62	Portsmouth*	54	Manchester C	54
1927–28f	Manchester C	59	Leeds U	57	Chelsea	54
1928–29f	Middlesbrough	55	Grimsby T	53	Bradford PA*	48
1929–30f	Blackpool	58	Chelsea	55	Oldham Ath	53
1930–31f	Everton	61	WBA	54	Tottenham H	51
1931–32f	Wolverhampton W	56	Leeds U	54	Stoke C	52
1932–33f	Stoke C	56	Tottenham H	55	Fulham	50
1933–34f	Grimsby T	59	Preston NE	52	Bolton W*	51
1934–35f	Brentford	61	Bolton W*	56	West Ham U	56
1935–36f	Manchester U	56	Charlton Ath	55	Sheffield U*	52
1936–37f	Leicester C	56	Blackpool	55	Bury	52
1937–38f	Aston Villa	57	Manchester U*	53	Sheffield U	53
1938–39f	Blackburn R	55	Sheffield U	54	Sheffield W	53
1946–47f	Manchester C	62	Burnley	58	Birmingham C	55
1947–48f	Birmingham C	59	Newcastle U	56	Southampton	52
1948–49f	Fulham	57	WBA	56	Southampton	55
1949–50f	Tottenham H	61	Sheffield W*	52	Sheffield U*	52

	First	Pts	Second	Pts	Third	Pts
1950–51f	Preston NE	57	Manchester C	52	Cardiff C	50
1951–52f	Sheffield W	53	Cardiff C*	51	Birmingham C	51
1952–53f	Sheffield U	60	Huddersfield T	58	Luton T	52
1953–54f	Leicester C*	56	Everton	56	Blackburn R	55
1954–55f	Birmingham C*	54	Luton T*	54	Rotherham U	54
1955–56f	Sheffield W	55	Leeds U	52	Liverpool*	48
1956–57f	Leicester C	61	Nottingham F	54	Liverpool	53
1957–58f	West Ham U	57	Blackburn R	56	Charlton Ath	55
1958–59f	Sheffield W	62	Fulham	60	Sheffield U*	53
1959–60f	Aston Villa	59	Cardiff C	58	Liverpool*	50
1960–61f	Ipswich T	59	Sheffield U	58	Liverpool	52
1961–62f	Liverpool	62	Leyton Orient	54	Sunderland	53
1962–63f	Stoke C	53	Chelsea*	52	Sunderland	52
1963–64f	Leeds U	63	Sunderland	61	Preston NE	56
1964–65f	Newcastle U	57	Northampton T	56	Bolton W	50
1965–66f	Manchester C	59	Southampton	54	Coventry C	53
1966–67f	Coventry C	59	Wolverhampton W	58	Carlisle U	52
1967–68f	Ipswich T	59	QPR*	58	Blackpool	58
1968–69f	Derby Co	63	Crystal Palace	56	Charlton Ath	50
1969–70f	Huddersfield T	60	Blackpool	53	Leicester C	51
1970–71f	Leicester C	59	Sheffield U	56	Cardiff C*	53
1971–72f	Norwich C	57	Birmingham C	56	Millwall	55
1972–73f	Burnley	62	QPR	61	Aston Villa	50
1973–74f	Middlesbrough	65	Luton T	50	Carlisle U	49
1974–75f	Manchester U	61	Aston Villa	58	Norwich C	53
1975–76f	Sunderland	56	Bristol C*	53	WBA	53
1976–77f	Wolverhampton W	57	Chelsea	55	Nottingham F	52
1977–78f	Bolton W	58	Southampton	57	Tottenham H*	56
1978–79f	Crystal Palace	57	Brighton & HA*	56	Stoke C	56
1979–80f	Leicester C	55	Sunderland	54	Birmingham C*	53
1980–81f	West Ham U	66	Notts Co	53	Swansea C*	50
1981–82g	Luton T	88	Watford	80	Norwich C	71
1982–83g	QPR	85	Wolverhampton W	75	Leicester C	70
1983–84g	Chelsea*	88	Sheffield W	88	Newcastle U	80
1984–85g	Oxford U	84	Birmingham C	82	Manchester C	74
1985–86g	Norwich C	84	Charlton Ath	77	Wimbledon	76
1986–87g	Derby Co	84	Portsmouth	78	Oldham Ath††	75
1987–88h	Millwall	82	Aston Villa*	78	Middlesbrough	78
1988–89k	Chelsea	99	Manchester C	82	Crystal Palace	81
1989–90k	Leeds U*	85	Sheffield U	85	Newcastle U††	80
1990–91k	Oldham Ath	88	West Ham U	87	Sheffield W	82
1991–92k	Ipswich T	84	Middlesbrough	80	Derby Co	78

No official competition during 1915–19 and 1939–46; Regional Leagues operated.

THIRD DIVISION to 1991–92

MAXIMUM POINTS: 92; 138 FROM 1981–82.

	First	Pts	Second	Pts	Third	Pts
1958–59	Plymouth Arg	62	Hull C	61	Brentford*	57
1959–60	Southampton	61	Norwich C	59	Shrewsbury T*	52
1960–61	Bury	68	Walsall	62	QPR	60
1961–62	Portsmouth	65	Grimsby T	62	Bournemouth*	59
1962–63	Northampton T	62	Swindon T	58	Port Vale	54
1963–64	Coventry C*	60	Crystal Palace	60	Watford	58
1964–65	Carlisle U	60	Bristol C*	59	Mansfield T	59
1965–66	Hull C	69	Millwall	65	QPR	57
1966–67	QPR	67	Middlesbrough	55	Watford	54
1967–68	Oxford U	57	Bury	56	Shrewsbury T	55
1968–69	Watford*	64	Swindon T	64	Luton T	61
1969–70	Orient	62	Luton T	60	Bristol R	56
1970–71	Preston NE	61	Fulham	60	Halifax T	56
1971–72	Aston Villa	70	Brighton & HA	65	Bournemouth*	62
1972–73	Bolton W	61	Notts Co	57	Blackburn R	55
1973–74	Oldham Ath	62	Bristol R*	61	York C	61
1974–75	Blackburn R	60	Plymouth Arg	59	Charlton Ath	55
1975–76	Hereford U	63	Cardiff C	57	Millwall	56
1976–77	Mansfield T	64	Brighton & HA	61	Crystal Palace*	59
1977–78	Wrexham	61	Cambridge U	58	Preston NE*	56
1978–79	Shrewsbury T	61	Watford*	60	Swansea C	60
1979–80	Grimsby T	62	Blackburn R	59	Sheffield W	58
1980–81	Rotherham U	61	Barnsley*	59	Charlton Ath	59
1981–82	Burnley*	80	Carlisle U	80	Fulham	78
1982–83	Portsmouth	91	Cardiff C	86	Huddersfield T	82
1983–84	Oxford U	95	Wimbledon	87	Sheffield U*	83
1984–85	Bradford C	94	Millwall	90	Hull C	87
1985–86	Reading	94	Plymouth Arg	87	Derby Co	84
1986–87	Bournemouth	97	Middlesbrough	94	Swindon T	87
1987–88	Sunderland	93	Brighton & HA	84	Walsall	82
1988–89	Wolverhampton W	92	Sheffield U*	84	Port Vale	84
1989–90	Bristol R	93	Bristol C	91	Notts Co	87
1990–91	Cambridge U	86	Southend U	85	Grimsby T*	83
1991–92	Brentford	82	Birmingham C	81	Huddersfield T	78

FOURTH DIVISION (1958–1992)

MAXIMUM POINTS: 92; 138 FROM 1981–82.

	First	Pts	Second	Pts	Third	Pts	Fourth	Pts
1958–59	Port Vale	64	Coventry C*	60	York C	60	Shrewsbury T	58
1959–60	Walsall	65	Notts Co*	60	Torquay U	60	Watford	57
1960–61	Peterborough U	66	Crystal Palace	64	Northampton T*	60	Bradford PA	60
1961–62†	Millwall	56	Colchester U	55	Wrexham	53	Carlisle U	52
1962–63	Brentford	62	Oldham Ath*	59	Crewe Alex	59	Mansfield T*	57
1963–64	Gillingham*	60	Carlisle U	60	Workington	59	Exeter C	58
1964–65	Brighton & HA	63	Millwall*	62	York C	62	Oxford U	61
1965–66	Doncaster R*	59	Darlington	59	Torquay U	58	Colchester U*	56
1966–67	Stockport Co	64	Southport*	59	Barrow	59	Tranmere R	58
1967–68	Luton T	66	Barnsley	61	Hartlepools U	60	Crewe Alex	58
1968–69	Doncaster R	59	Halifax T	57	Rochdale*	56	Bradford C	56
1969–70	Chesterfield	64	Wrexham	61	Swansea C	60	Port Vale	59
1970–71	Notts Co	69	Bournemouth	60	Oldham Ath	59	York C	56
1971–72	Grimsby T	63	Southend U	60	Brentford	59	Scunthorpe U	57
1972–73	Southport	62	Hereford U	58	Cambridge U	57	Aldershot*	56
1973–74	Peterborough U	65	Gillingham	62	Colchester U	60	Bury	59
1974–75	Mansfield T	68	Shrewsbury T	62	Rotherham U	59	Chester*	57
1975–76	Lincoln C	74	Northampton T	68	Reading	60	Tranmere R	58
1976–77	Cambridge U	65	Exeter C	62	Colchester U*	59	Bradford C	59
1977–78	Watford	71	Southend U	60	Swansea C*	56	Brentford	56
1978–79	Reading	65	Grimsby T*	61	Wimbledon*	61	Barnsley	61
1979–80	Huddersfield T	66	Walsall	64	Newport Co	61	Portsmouth*	60
1980–81	Southend U	67	Lincoln C	65	Doncaster R	56	Wimbledon	55
1981–82	Sheffield U	96	Bradford C*	91	Wigan Ath	91	Bournemouth	88
1982–83	Wimbledon	98	Hull C	90	Port Vale	88	Scunthorpe U	83
1983–84	York C	101	Doncaster R	85	Reading*	82	Bristol C	82
1984–85	Chesterfield	91	Blackpool	86	Darlington	85	Bury	84
1985–86	Swindon T	102	Chester C	84	Mansfield T	81	Port Vale	79
1986–87	Northampton T	99	Preston NE	90	Southend U	80	Wolverhampton W††	79
1987–88	Wolverhampton W	90	Cardiff C	85	Bolton W	78	Scunthorpe U††	77
1988–89	Rotherham U	82	Tranmere R	80	Crewe Alex	78	Scunthorpe U††	77
1989–90	Exeter C	89	Grimsby T	79	Southend U	75	Stockport Co††	74
1990–91	Darlington	83	Stockport Co*	82	Hartlepool U	82	Peterborough U	80
1991–92†*	Burnley	83	Rotherham U*	77	Mansfield T	77	Blackpool	76

†*Maximum points:* 88 owing to Accrington Stanley's resignation.
†**Maximum points:* 126 owing to Aldershot being expelled (and only 23 teams started the competition).

THIRD DIVISION—SOUTH (1920–1958)

1920–21 SEASON AS THIRD DIVISION. MAXIMUM POINTS: *a* 84; *b* 92.

	First	Pts	Second	Pts	Third	Pts
1920–21*a*	Crystal Palace	59	Southampton	54	QPR	53
1921–22*a*	Southampton*	61	Plymouth Arg	61	Portsmouth	53
1922–23*a*	Bristol C	59	Plymouth Arg*	53	Swansea T	53
1923–24*a*	Portsmouth	59	Plymouth Arg	55	Millwall	54
1924–25*a*	Swansea T	57	Plymouth Arg	56	Bristol C	53
1925–26*a*	Reading	57	Plymouth Arg	56	Millwall	53
1926–27*a*	Bristol C	62	Plymouth Arg	60	Millwall	56
1927–28*a*	Millwall	65	Northampton T	55	Plymouth Arg	53
1928–29*a*	Charlton Ath*	54	Crystal Palace	54	Northampton T*	52
1929–30*a*	Plymouth Arg	68	Brentford	61	QPR	51
1930–31*a*	Notts Co	59	Crystal Palace	51	Brentford	50
1931–32*a*	Fulham	57	Reading	55	Southend U	53
1932–33*a*	Brentford	62	Exeter C	58	Norwich C	57
1933–34*a*	Norwich C	61	Coventry C*	54	Reading*	54
1934–35*a*	Charlton Ath	61	Reading	53	Coventry C	51
1935–36*a*	Coventry C	57	Luton T	56	Reading	54
1936–37*a*	Luton T	58	Notts Co	56	Brighton & HA	53
1937–38*a*	Millwall	56	Bristol C	55	QPR*	53
1938–39*a*	Newport Co	55	Crystal Palace	52	Brighton & HA	49
1939–46	Competition cancelled owing to war. Regional Leagues operated.					
1946–47*a*	Cardiff C	66	QPR	57	Bristol C	51
1947–48*a*	QPR	61	Bournemouth	57	Walsall	51
1948–49*a*	Swansea T	62	Reading	55	Bournemouth	52
1949–50*a*	Notts Co	58	Northampton T*	51	Southend U	51
1950–51*b*	Nottingham F	70	Norwich C	64	Reading*	57
1951–52*b*	Plymouth Arg	66	Reading*	61	Norwich C	61
1952–53*b*	Bristol R	64	Millwall*	62	Northampton T	62
1953–54*b*	Ipswich T	64	Brighton & HA	61	Bristol C	56
1954–55*b*	Bristol C	70	Leyton Orient	61	Southampton	59
1955–56*b*	Leyton Orient	66	Brighton & HA	65	Ipswich T	64
1956–57*b*	Ipswich T*	59	Torquay U	59	Colchester U	58
1957–58*b*	Brighton & HA	60	Brentford*	58	Plymouth Arg	58

THIRD DIVISION—NORTH (1921–1958)

MAXIMUM POINTS: *a* 76; *b* 84; *c* 80; *d* 92.

	First	Pts	Second	Pts	Third	Pts
1921–22*a*	Stockport Co	56	Darlington*	50	Grimsby T	50
1922–23*a*	Nelson	51	Bradford PA	47	Walsall	46
1923–24*b*	Wolverhampton W	63	Rochdale	62	Chesterfield	54
1924–25*b*	Darlington	58	Nelson*	53	New Brighton	53
1925–26*b*	Grimsby T	61	Bradford PA	60	Rochdale	59

	First	Pts	Second	Pts	Third	Pts
1926–27*b*	Stoke C	63	Rochdale	58	Bradford PA	55
1927–28*b*	Bradford PA	63	Lincoln C	55	Stockport Co	54
1928–29*b*	Bradford C	63	Stockport Co	62	Wrexham	52
1929–30*b*	Port Vale	67	Stockport Co	63	Darlington*	50
1930–31*b*	Chesterfield	58	Lincoln C	57	Wrexham*	54
1931–32*c*	Lincoln C*	57	Gateshead	57	Chester	50
1932–33*b*	Hull C	59	Wrexham	57	Stockport Co	54
1933–34*b*	Barnsley	62	Chesterfield	61	Stockport Co	59
1934–35*b*	Doncaster R	57	Halifax T	55	Chester	54
1935–36*b*	Chesterfield	60	Chester*	55	Tranmere R	55
1936–37*b*	Stockport Co	60	Lincoln C	57	Chester	53
1937–38*b*	Tranmere R	56	Doncaster R	54	Hull C	53
1938–39*b*	Barnsley	67	Doncaster R	56	Bradford C	52
1939–46	Competition cancelled owing to war. Regional Leagues operated.					
1946–47*b*	Doncaster R	72	Rotherham U	64	Chester	56
1947–48*b*	Lincoln C	60	Rotherham U	59	Wrexham	50
1948–49*b*	Hull C	65	Rotherham U	62	Doncaster R	50
1949–50*b*	Doncaster R	55	Gateshead	53	Rochdale*	51
1950–51*d*	Rotherham U	71	Mansfield T	64	Carlisle U	62
1951–52*d*	Lincoln C	69	Grimsby T	66	Stockport Co	59
1952–53*d*	Oldham Ath	59	Port Vale	58	Wrexham	56
1953–54*d*	Port Vale	69	Barnsley	58	Scunthorpe U	57
1954–55*d*	Barnsley	65	Accrington S	61	Scunthorpe U*	58
1955–56*d*	Grimsby T	68	Derby Co	63	Accrington S	59
1956–57*d*	Derby Co	63	Hartlepools U	59	Accrington S*	58
1957–58*d*	Scunthorpe U	66	Accrington S	59	Bradford C	57

PROMOTED AFTER PLAY-OFFS

(NOT ACCOUNTED FOR IN PREVIOUS SECTION)

1986–87	Aldershot to Division 3.
1987–88	Swansea C to Division 3.
1988–89	Leyton Orient to Division 3.
1989–90	Sunderland to Division 1; Notts Co to Division 2; Cambridge U to Division 3.
1990–91	Notts Co to Division 1; Tranmere R to Division 2; Torquay U to Division 3.
1991–92	Blackburn R to Premier League; Peterborough U to Division 1.
1992–93	Swindon T to Premier League; WBA to Division 1; York C to Division 2.
1993–94	Leicester C to Premier League; Burnley to Division 1; Wycombe W to Division 2.
1994–95	Huddersfield T to Division 1.
1995–96	Leicester C to Premier League; Bradford C to Division 1; Plymouth Arg to Division 2.
1996–97	Crystal Palace to Premier League; Crewe Alex to Division 1; Northampton T to Division 2.
1997–98	Charlton Ath to Premier League; Colchester U to Division 2.
1998–99	Watford to Premier League; Scunthorpe U to Division 2.
1999–2000	Peterborough U to Division 2
2000–01	Walsall to Division 1; Blackpool to Division 2
2001–02	Birmingham C to Premier League; Stoke C to Division 1; Cheltenham T to Division 2
2002–03	Wolverhampton W to Premier League; Cardiff C to Division 1; Bournemouth to Division 2
2003–04	Crystal Palace to Premier League; Brighton & HA to Division 1; Huddersfield T to Division 2
2004–05	West Ham U to Premier League; Sheffield W to Championship; Southend U to Championship 1
2005–06	Watford to Premier League; Barnsley to Championship; Cheltenham T to Championship 1
2006–07	Derby Co to Premier League; Blackpool to Championship; Bristol R to Championship 1
2007–08	Hull C to Premier League; Doncaster R to Championship; Stockport Co to Championship 1
2008–09	Burnley to Premier League; Scunthorpe U to Championship; Gillingham to Championship 1
2009–10	Blackpool to Premier League; Millwall to Championship; Dagenham & R to Championship 1

LEAGUE TITLE WINS

FA PREMIER LEAGUE – Manchester U 11, Arsenal 3, Chelsea 3, Blackburn R 1.

FOOTBALL LEAGUE CHAMPIONSHIP – Sunderland 2, Newcastle U 1, Reading 1, WBA 1, Wolverhampton W 1.

LEAGUE DIVISION 1 – Liverpool 18, Arsenal 10, Everton 9, Sunderland 8, Aston Villa 7, Manchester U 7, Newcastle U 5, Sheffield W 4, Huddersfield T 3, Leeds U 3, Manchester C 3, Portsmouth 3, Wolverhampton W 3, Blackburn R 2, Burnley 2, Derby Co 2, Nottingham F 2, Preston NE 2, Tottenham H 2; Bolton W, Charlton Ath, Chelsea, Crystal Palace, Fulham, Ipswich T, Middlesbrough, Norwich C, Sheffield U, WBA 1 each.

FOOTBALL LEAGUE CHAMPIONSHIP 1 – Leicester C 1, Luton T 1, Norwich C 1, Scunthorpe U 1, Southend U 1, Swansea C 1.

LEAGUE DIVISION 2 – Leicester C 6, Manchester C 6, Birmingham C (one as Small Heath) 5, Sheffield W 5, Derby Co 4, Liverpool 4, Preston NE 4, Ipswich T 3, Leeds U 3, Middlesbrough 3, Notts Co 3, Stoke C 3, Aston Villa 2, Bolton W 2, Burnley 2, Bury 2, Chelsea 2, Fulham 2, Grimsby T 2, Manchester U 2, Millwall 2, Norwich C 2, Nottingham F 2, Tottenham H 2, WBA 2, West Ham U 2, Wolverhampton W 2; Blackburn R, Blackpool, Bradford C, Brentford, Brighton & HA, Bristol C, Coventry, Crystal Palace, Everton, Huddersfield T, Luton T, Newcastle U, QPR, Oldham Ath, Oxford U, Plymouth Arg, Reading, Sheffield U, Sunderland, Swindon U, Watford, Wigan Ath 1 each.

FOOTBALL LEAGUE CHAMPIONSHIP 2 – Brentford 1, Carlisle U 1, Milton Keynes D 1, Notts Co 1, Walsall 1, Yeovil T 1.

LEAGUE DIVISION 3 – Brentford 2, Carlisle U 2, Oxford U 2, Plymouth Arg 2, Portsmouth 2, Preston NE 2, Shrewsbury T 2; Aston Villa, Blackburn R, Bolton W, Bournemouth, Bradford C, Brighton & HA, Bristol R, Burnley, Bury, Cambridge U, Cardiff C, Coventry C, Doncaster R, Grimsby T, Hereford U, Hull C, Leyton Orient, Mansfield T, Northampton T, Notts Co, Oldham Ath, QPR, Reading, Rotherham U, Rushden & D Southampton, Sunderland, Swansea C, Watford, Wigan Ath, Wolverhampton W, Wrexham 1 each.

LEAGUE DIVISION 4 – Chesterfield 2, Doncaster R 2, Peterborough U 2; Brentford, Brighton & HA, Burnley, Cambridge U, Darlington, Exeter C, Gillingham, Grimsby T, Huddersfield T, Lincoln C, Luton T, Mansfield T, Millwall, Northampton T, Notts Co, Port Vale, Reading, Rotherham U, Sheffield U, Southend U, Southport, Stockport Co, Swindon T, Walsall, Watford, Wimbledon, Wolverhampton W, York C 1 each.

LEAGUE TITLE WINS TO 1957–58

DIVISION 3 (South) – Bristol C 3, Charlton Ath 2, Ipswich T 2, Millwall 2, Notts Co 2, Plymouth Arg 2, Swansea T 2; Brentford, Brighton & HA, Bristol R, Cardiff C, Coventry C, Crystal Palace, Fulham, Leyton Orient, Luton T, Newport Co, Norwich C, Nottingham F, Portsmouth, QPR, Reading, Southampton 1 each.

DIVISION 3 (North) – Barnsley 3, Doncaster R 3, Lincoln C 3, Chesterfield 2, Grimsby T 2, Hull C 2, Port Vale 2, Stockport Co 2; Bradford C, Bradford PA, Darlington, Derby Co, Nelson, Oldham Ath, Rotherham U, Scunthorpe U, Stoke C, Tranmere R, Wolverhampton W 1 each.

RELEGATED CLUBS

1891–92 League extended. Newton Heath, Sheffield W and Nottingham F admitted. *Second Division formed* including Darwen.
1892–93 In Test matches, Sheffield U and Darwen won promotion in place of Notts Co and Accrington S.
1893–94 In Tests, Liverpool and Small Heath won promotion. Newton Heath and Darwen relegated.
1894–95 After Tests, Bury promoted, Liverpool relegated.
1895–96 After Tests, Liverpool promoted, Small Heath relegated.
1896–97 After Tests, Notts Co promoted, Burnley relegated.
1897–98 Test system abolished after success of Stoke C and Burnley. League extended. Blackburn R and Newcastle U elected to First Division. *Automatic promotion and relegation introduced.*

FA PREMIER LEAGUE TO DIVISION 1

1992–93 Crystal Palace, Middlesbrough, Nottingham F	1998–99 Charlton Ath, Blackburn R, Nottingham F
1993–94 Sheffield U, Oldham Ath, Swindon T	1999–2000 Wimbledon, Sheffield W, Watford
1994–95 Crystal Palace, Norwich C, Leicester C, Ipswich T	2000–01 Manchester C, Coventry C, Bradford C
1995–96 Manchester C, QPR, Bolton W	2001–02 Ipswich T, Derby Co, Leicester C
1996–97 Sunderland, Middlesbrough, Nottingham F	2002–03 West Ham U, WBA, Sunderland
1997–98 Bolton W, Barnsley, Crystal Palace	2003–04 Leicester C, Leeds U, Wolverhampton W.

FA PREMIER LEAGUE TO CHAMPIONSHIP

2004–05 Crystal Palace, Norwich C, Southampton	2007–08 Reading, Birmingham C, Derby Co
2005–06 Birmingham C, WBA, Sunderland	2008–09 Newcastle U, Middlesbrough, WBA
2006–07 Sheffield U, Charlton Ath, Watford	2009–10 Burnley, Hull C, Portsmouth

DIVISION 1 TO DIVISION 2

1898–99 Bolton W and Sheffield W	1958–59 Portsmouth and Aston Villa
1899–1900 Burnley and Glossop	1959–60 Luton T and Leeds U
1900–01 Preston NE and WBA	1960–61 Preston NE and Newcastle U
1901–02 Small Heath and Manchester C	1961–62 Chelsea and Cardiff C
1902–03 Grimsby T and Bolton W	1962–63 Manchester C and Leyton Orient
1903–04 Liverpool and WBA	1963–64 Bolton W and Ipswich T
1904–05 League extended. Bury and Notts Co, two	1964–65 Wolverhampton W and Birmingham C
bottom clubs in First Division, re-elected.	1965–66 Northampton T and Blackburn R
1905–06 Nottingham F and Wolverhampton W	1966–67 Aston Villa and Blackpool
1906–07 Derby Co and Stoke C	1967–68 Fulham and Sheffield U
1907–08 Bolton W and Birmingham C	1968–69 Leicester C and QPR
1908–09 Manchester C and Leicester Fosse	1969–70 Sunderland and Sheffield W
1909–10 Bolton W and Chelsea	1970–71 Burnley and Blackpool
1910–11 Bristol C and Nottingham F	1971–72 Huddersfield T and Nottingham F
1911–12 Preston NE and Bury	1972–73 Crystal Palace and WBA
1912–13 Notts Co and Woolwich Arsenal	1973–74 Southampton, Manchester U, Norwich C
1913–14 Preston NE and Derby Co	1974–75 Luton T, Chelsea, Carlisle U
1914–15 Tottenham H and Chelsea*	1975–76 Wolverhampton W, Burnley, Sheffield U
1919–20 Notts Co and Sheffield W	1976–77 Sunderland, Stoke C, Tottenham H
1920–21 Derby Co and Bradford PA	1977–78 West Ham U, Newcastle U, Leicester C
1921–22 Bradford C and Manchester U	1978–79 QPR, Birmingham C, Chelsea
1922–23 Stoke C and Oldham Ath	1979–80 Bristol C, Derby Co, Bolton W
1923–24 Chelsea and Middlesbrough	1980–81 Norwich C, Leicester C, Crystal Palace
1924–25 Preston NE and Nottingham F	1981–82 Leeds U, Wolverhampton W, Middlesbrough
1925–26 Manchester C and Notts Co	1982–83 Manchester C, Swansea C, Brighton & HA
1926–27 Leeds U and WBA	1983–84 Birmingham C, Notts Co, Wolverhampton W
1927–28 Tottenham H and Middlesbrough	1984–85 Norwich C, Sunderland, Stoke C
1928–29 Bury and Cardiff C	1985–86 Ipswich T, Birmingham C, WBA
1929–30 Burnley and Everton	1986–87 Leicester C, Manchester C, Aston Villa
1930–31 Leeds U and Manchester U	1987–88 Chelsea**, Portsmouth, Watford, Oxford U
1931–32 Grimsby T and West Ham U	1988–89 Middlesbrough, West Ham U, Newcastle U
1932–33 Bolton W and Blackpool	1989–90 Sheffield W, Charlton Ath, Millwall
1933–34 Newcastle U and Sheffield U	1990–91 Sunderland and Derby Co
1934–35 Leicester C and Tottenham H	1991–92 Luton T, Notts Co, West Ham U
1935–36 Aston Villa and Blackburn R	1992–93 Brentford, Cambridge U, Bristol R
1936–37 Manchester U and Sheffield W	1993–94 Birmingham C, Oxford U, Peterborough U
1937–38 Manchester U and WBA	1994–95 Swindon T, Burnley, Bristol C, Notts Co
1938–39 Birmingham C and Leicester C	1995–96 Millwall, Watford, Luton T
1946–47 Brentford and Leeds U	1996–97 Grimsby T, Oldham Ath, Southend U
1947–48 Blackburn R and Grimsby T	1997–98 Manchester C, Stoke C, Reading
1948–49 Preston NE and Sheffield U	1998–99 Bury, Oxford U, Bristol C
1949–50 Manchester C and Birmingham C	1999–2000 Walsall, Port Vale, Swindon T
1950–51 Sheffield W and Everton	2000–01 Huddersfield T, QPR, Tranmere R
1951–52 Huddersfield T and Fulham	2001–02 Crewe Alex, Barnsley, Stockport Co
1952–53 Stoke C and Derby Co	2002–03 Sheffield W, Brighton & HA, Grimsby T
1953–54 Middlesbrough and Liverpool	2003–04 Walsall, Bradford C, Wimbledon
1954–55 Leicester C and Sheffield W	**Relegated after play-offs.*
1955–56 Huddersfield T and Sheffield U	**Subsequently re-elected to Division 1 when League was*
1956–57 Charlton Ath and Cardiff C	*extended after the War.*
1957–58 Sheffield W and Sunderland	

FOOTBALL LEAGUE CHAMPIONSHIP TO FOOTBALL LEAGUE CHAMPIONSHIP 1

2004–05 Gillingham, Nottingham F, Rotherham U
2005–06 Crewe Alex, Millwall, Brighton & HA
2006–07 Southend U, Luton T, Leeds U

2007–08 Leicester C, Scunthorpe U, Colchester U
2008–09 Norwich C, Southampton, Charlton Ath
2009–10 Sheffield W, Plymouth Arg, Peterborough U

DIVISION 2 TO DIVISION 3

1920–21 Stockport Co
1921–22 Bradford PA and Bristol C
1922–23 Rotherham Co and Wolverhampton W
1923–24 Nelson and Bristol C
1924–25 Crystal Palace and Coventry C
1925–26 Stoke C and Stockport Co
1926–27 Darlington and Bradford C
1927–28 Fulham and South Shields
1928–29 Port Vale and Clapton Orient
1929–30 Hull C and Notts Co
1930–31 Reading and Cardiff C
1931–32 Barnsley and Bristol C
1932–33 Chesterfield and Charlton Ath
1933–34 Millwall and Lincoln C
1934–35 Oldham Ath and Notts Co
1935–36 Port Vale and Hull C
1936–37 Doncaster R and Bradford C
1937–38 Barnsley and Stockport Co
1938–39 Norwich C and Tranmere R
1946–47 Swansea T and Newport Co
1947–48 Doncaster R and Millwall
1948–49 Nottingham F and Lincoln C
1949–50 Plymouth Arg and Bradford PA
1950–51 Grimsby T and Chesterfield
1951–52 Coventry C and QPR
1952–53 Southampton and Barnsley
1953–54 Brentford and Oldham Ath
1954–55 Ipswich T and Derby Co
1955–56 Plymouth Arg and Hull C
1956–57 Port Vale and Bury
1957–58 Doncaster R and Notts Co
1958–59 Barnsley and Grimsby T
1959–60 Bristol C and Hull C
1960–61 Lincoln C and Portsmouth
1961–62 Brighton & HA and Bristol R
1962–63 Walsall and Luton T
1963–64 Grimsby T and Scunthorpe U
1964–65 Swindon T and Swansea T
1965–66 Middlesbrough and Leyton Orient
1966–67 Northampton T and Bury
1967–68 Plymouth Arg and Rotherham U

1968–69 Fulham and Bury
1969–70 Preston NE and Aston Villa
1970–71 Blackburn R and Bolton W
1971–72 Charlton Ath and Watford
1972–73 Huddersfield T and Brighton & HA
1973–74 Crystal Palace, Preston NE, Swindon T
1974–75 Millwall, Cardiff C, Sheffield W
1975–76 Oxford U, York C, Portsmouth
1976–77 Carlisle U, Plymouth Arg, Hereford U
1977–78 Blackpool, Mansfield T, Hull C
1978–79 Sheffield U, Millwall, Blackburn R
1979–80 Fulham, Burnley, Charlton Ath
1980–81 Preston NE, Bristol C, Bristol R
1981–82 Cardiff C, Wrexham, Orient
1982–83 Rotherham U, Burnley, Bolton W
1983–84 Derby Co, Swansea C, Cambridge U
1984–85 Notts Co, Cardiff C, Wolverhampton W
1985–86 Carlisle U, Middlesbrough, Fulham
1986–87 Sunderland**, Grimsby T, Brighton & HA
1987–88 Huddersfield T, Reading, Sheffield U**
1988–89 Shrewsbury T, Birmingham C, Walsall
1989–90 Bournemouth, Bradford C, Stoke C
1990–91 WBA and Hull C
1991–92 Plymouth Arg, Brighton & HA, Port Vale
1992–93 Preston NE, Mansfield T, Wigan Ath, Chester C
1993–94 Fulham, Exeter C, Hartlepool U, Barnet
1994–95 Cambridge U, Plymouth Arg, Cardiff C, Chester C, Leyton Orient
1995–96 Carlisle U, Swansea C, Brighton & HA, Hull C
1996–97 Peterborough U, Shrewsbury T, Rotherham U, Notts Co
1997–98 Brentford, Plymouth Arg, Carlisle U, Southend U
1998–99 York C, Northampton T, Lincoln C, Macclesfield T
1999–2000 Cardiff C, Blackpool, Scunthorpe U, Chesterfield
2000–01 Bristol R, Luton T, Swansea C, Oxford U
2001–02 Bournemouth, Bury, Wrexham, Cambridge U
2002–03 Cheltenham T, Huddersfield T, Mansfield T Northampton T
2003–04 Grimsby T, Rushden & D, Notts Co, Wycombe W

FOOTBALL LEAGUE CHAMPIONSHIP 1 TO FOOTBALL LEAGUE CHAMPIONSHIP 2

2004–05 Torquay U, Wrexham, Peterborough U, Stockport Co
2005–06 Hartlepool U, Milton Keynes D, Swindon T, Walsall
2006–07 Chesterfield, Bradford C, Rotherham U, Brentford

2007–08 Bournemouth, Gillingham, Port Vale, Luton T
2008–09 Northampton T, Crewe Alex, Cheltenham T, Hereford U
2009–10 Gillingham, Wycombe W, Southend U, Stockport Co

DIVISION 3 TO DIVISION 4

1958–59 Stockport Co, Doncaster R, Notts Co, Rochdale
1959–60 York C, Mansfield T, Wrexham, Accrington S
1960–61 Tranmere R, Bradford C, Colchester U, Chesterfield
1961–62 Torquay U, Lincoln C, Brentford, Newport Co
1962–63 Bradford PA, Brighton & HA, Carlisle U, Halifax T
1963–64 Millwall, Crewe Alex, Wrexham, Notts Co
1964–65 Luton T, Port Vale, Colchester U, Barnsley
1965–66 Southend U, Exeter C, Brentford, York C
1966–67 Swansea T, Darlington, Doncaster R, Workington
1967–68 Grimsby T, Colchester U, Scunthorpe U, Peterborough U (demoted)
1968–69 Northampton T, Hartlepool, Crewe Alex, Oldham Ath
1969–70 Bournemouth, Southport, Barrow, Stockport Co
1970–71 Reading, Bury, Doncaster R, Gillingham
1971–72 Mansfield T, Barnsley, Torquay U, Bradford C
1972–73 Rotherham U, Brentford, Swansea C, Scunthorpe U
1973–74 Cambridge U, Shrewsbury T, Southport, Rochdale

1974–75 Bournemouth, Tranmere R, Watford, Huddersfield T
1975–76 Aldershot, Colchester U, Southend U, Halifax T
1976–77 Reading, Northampton T, Grimsby T, York C
1977–78 Port Vale, Bradford C, Hereford U, Portsmouth
1978–79 Peterborough U, Walsall, Tranmere R, Lincoln C
1979–80 Bury, Southend U, Mansfield T, Wimbledon
1980–81 Sheffield U, Colchester U, Blackpool, Hull C
1981–82 Wimbledon, Swindon T, Bristol C, Chester
1982–83 Reading, Wrexham, Doncaster R, Chesterfield
1983–84 Scunthorpe U, Southend U, Port Vale, Exeter C
1984–85 Burnley, Orient, Preston NE, Cambridge U
1985–86 Lincoln C, Cardiff C, Wolverhampton W, Swansea C
1986–87 Bolton W**, Carlisle U, Darlington, Newport Co
1987–88 Rotherham U**, Grimsby T, York C, Doncaster R
1988–89 Southend U, Chesterfield, Gillingham, Aldershot
1989–90 Cardiff C, Northampton T, Blackpool, Walsall
1990–91 Crewe Alex, Rotherham U, Mansfield T
1991–92 Bury, Shrewsbury T, Torquay U, Darlington

** *Relegated after play-offs.*

APPLICATIONS FOR RE-ELECTION

FOURTH DIVISION
Eleven: Hartlepool U.
Seven: Crewe Alex.
Six: Barrow (lost League place to Hereford U 1972). Halifax T, Rochdale, Southport (lost League place to Wigan Ath 1978), York C.
Five: Chester C, Darlington, Lincoln C, Stockport Cc, Workington (lost League place to Wimbledon 1977).
Four: Bradford PA (lost League place to Cambridge U 1970), Newport Co, Northampton T.
Three: Doncaster R, Hereford U.
Two: Bradford C, Exeter C, Oldham Ath, Scunthorpe U, Torquay U.
One: Aldershot, Colchester U, Gateshead (lost League place to Peterborough U 1960), Grimsby T, Swansea C, Tranmere R, Wrexham, Blackpool, Cambridge U, Preston NE.
Accrington S resigned and Oxford U were elected 1962.
Port Vale were forced to re-apply following expulsion in 1968.
Aldershot expelled March 1992. Maidstone U resigned August 1992.

THIRD DIVISIONS NORTH & SOUTH
Seven: Walsall.
Six: Exeter C, Halifax T, Newport Co.
Five: Accrington S, Barrow, Gillingham, New Brighton, Southport.
Four: Rochdale, Norwich C.
Three: Crystal Palace, Crewe Alex, Darlington, Hartlepool U, Merthyr T, Swindon T.
Two: Aberdare Ath, Aldershot, Ashington, Bournemouth, Brentford, Chester, Colchester U, Durham C, Millwall, Nelson, QPR, Rotherham U, Southend U, Tranmere R, Watford, Workington.
One: Bradford C, Bradford PA, Brighton & HA, Bristol R, Cardiff C, Carlisle U, Charlton Ath, Gateshead, Grimsby T, Mansfield T, Shrewsbury T, Torquay U, York C.

LEAGUE STATUS FROM 1986–87

RELEGATED FROM LEAGUE		PROMOTED TO LEAGUE	
1986–87 Lincoln C	1987–88 Newport Co	1986–87 Scarborough	1987–88 Lincoln C
1988–89 Darlington	1989–90 Colchester U	1988–89 Maidstone U	1989–90 Darlington
1990–91 —	1991–92 —	1990–91 Barnet	1991–92 Colchester U
1992–93 Halifax T	1993–94 —	1992–93 Wycombe W	1993–94 —
1994–95 —	1995–96 —	1994–95 —	1995–96 —
1996–97 Hereford U	1997–98 Doncaster R	1996–97 Macclesfield T	1997–98 Halifax T
1998–99 Scarborough	1999–2000 Chester C	1998–99 Cheltenham T	1999–2000 Kidderminster H
2000–01 Barnet	2001–02 Halifax T	2000–01 Rushden & D	2001–02 Boston U
2002–03 Shrewsbury T, Exeter C		2002–03 Yeovil T, Doncaster R	
2003–04 Carlisle U, York C		2003–04 Chester C, Shrewsbury T	
2004–05 Kidderminster H, Cambridge U		2004–05 Barnet, Carlisle U	
2005–06 Oxford U, Rushden & D		2005–06 Accrington S, Hereford U	
2006–07 Boston U, Torquay U		2006–07 Dagenham & R, Morecambe	
2007–08 Mansfield T, Wrexham		2007–08 Aldershot T, Exeter C	
2008–09 Chester C, Luton T		2008–09 Burton Alb, Torquay U	
2009–10 Grimsby T, Darlington		2009–10 Stevenage B, Oxford U	

Manchester United's Antonio Valencia (centre) closely watched by Carlos Tevez (right) and Craig Bellamy of Manchester City during the epic 4-3 United victory at Old Trafford. Michael Owen's injury-time winner finally killed off City who had fought back to level the scores three times. (Action Images/Jason Cairnduff)

LEAGUE ATTENDANCES SINCE 1946–47

Season	Matches	Total	Div. 1	Div. 2	Div. 3 (S)	Div. 3 (N)
1946–47	1848	35,604,606	15,005,316	11,071,572	5,664,004	3,863,714
1947–48	1848	40,259,130	16,732,341	12,286,350	6,653,610	4,586,829
1948–49	1848	41,271,414	17,914,667	11,353,237	6,998,429	5,005,081
1949–50	1848	40,517,865	17,278,625	11,694,158	7,104,155	4,440,927
1950–51	2028	39,584,967	16,679,454	10,780,580	7,367,884	4,757,109
1951–52	2028	39,015,866	16,110,322	11,066,189	6,958,927	4,880,428
1952–53	2028	37,149,966	16,050,278	9,686,654	6,704,299	4,708,735
1953–54	2028	36,174,590	16,154,915	9,510,053	6,311,508	4,198,114
1954–55	2028	34,133,103	15,087,221	8,988,794	5,996,017	4,051,071
1955–56	2028	33,150,809	14,108,961	9,080,002	5,692,479	4,269,367
1956–57	2028	32,744,405	13,803,037	8,718,162	5,622,189	4,601,017
1957–58	2028	33,562,208	14,468,652	8,663,712	6,097,183	4,332,661

Season	Matches	Total	Div. 1	Div. 2	Div. 3	Div. 4
1958–59	2028	33,610,985	14,727,691	8,641,997	5,946,600	4,276,697
1959–60	2028	32,538,611	14,391,227	8,399,627	5,739,707	4,008,050
1960–61	2028	28,619,754	12,926,948	7,033,936	4,784,256	3,874,614
1961–62	2015	27,979,902	12,061,194	7,453,089	5,199,106	3,266,513
1962–63	2028	28,885,852	12,490,239	7,792,770	5,341,362	3,261,481
1963–64	2028	28,535,022	12,486,626	7,594,158	5,419,157	3,035,081
1964–65	2028	27,641,168	12,708,752	6,984,104	4,436,245	3,512,067
1965–66	2028	27,206,980	12,480,644	6,914,757	4,779,150	3,032,429
1966–67	2028	28,902,596	14,242,957	7,253,819	4,421,172	2,984,648
1967–68	2028	30,107,298	15,289,410	7,450,410	4,013,087	3,354,391
1968–69	2028	29,382,172	14,584,851	7,382,390	4,339,656	3,075,275
1969–70	2028	29,600,972	14,868,754	7,581,728	4,223,761	2,926,729
1970–71	2028	28,194,146	13,954,337	7,098,265	4,377,213	2,764,331
1971–72	2028	28,700,729	14,484,603	6,769,308	4,697,392	2,749,426
1972–73	2028	25,448,642	13,998,154	5,631,730	3,737,252	2,081,506
1973–74	2027	24,982,203	13,070,991	6,326,108	3,421,624	2,163,480
1974–75	2028	25,577,977	12,613,178	6,955,970	4,086,145	1,992,684
1975–76	2028	24,896,053	13,089,861	5,798,405	3,948,449	2,059,338
1976–77	2028	26,182,800	13,647,585	6,250,597	4,152,218	2,132,400
1977–78	2028	25,392,872	13,255,677	6,474,763	3,332,042	2,330,390
1978–79	2028	24,540,627	12,704,549	6,153,223	3,374,558	2,308,297
1979–80	2028	24,623,975	12,163,002	6,112,025	3,999,328	2,349,620
1980–81	2028	21,907,569	11,392,894	5,175,442	3,637,854	1,701,379
1981–82	2028	20,006,961	10,420,793	4,750,463	2,836,915	1,998,790
1982–83	2028	18,766,158	9,295,613	4,974,937	2,943,568	1,552,040
1983–84	2028	18,358,631	8,711,448	5,359,757	2,729,942	1,557,484
1984–85	2028	17,849,835	9,761,404	4,030,823	2,667,008	1,390,600
1985–86	2028	16,488,577	9,037,854	3,551,968	2,490,481	1,408,274
1986–87	2028	17,379,218	9,144,676	4,168,131	2,350,970	1,715,441
1987–88	2030	17,959,732	8,094,571	5,341,599	2,751,275	1,772,287
1988–89	2036	18,464,192	7,809,993	5,887,805	3,035,327	1,791,067
1989–90	2036	19,445,442	7,883,039	6,867,674	2,803,551	1,891,178
1990–91	2036	19,508,202	8,618,709	6,285,068	2,835,759	1,768,666
1991–92	2064*	20,487,273	9,989,160	5,809,787	2,993,352	1,694,974

Season	Matches	Total	FA Premier	Div. 1	Div. 2	Div. 3
1992–93	2028	20,657,327	9,759,809	5,874,017	3,483,073	1,540,428
1993–94	2028	21,683,381	10,644,551	6,487,104	2,972,702	1,579,024
1994–95	2028	21,856,020	11,213,168	6,044,293	3,037,752	1,560,807
1995–96	2036	21,844,416	10,469,107	6,566,349	2,843,652	1,965,308
1996–97	2036	22,783,163	10,804,762	6,931,539	3,195,223	1,851,639
1997–98	2036	24,692,608	11,092,106	8,330,018	3,503,264	1,767,220
1998–99	2036	25,435,542	11,620,326	7,543,369	4,169,697	2,102,150
1999–2000	2036	25,341,090	11,668,497	7,810,208	3,700,433	2,161,952
2000–01	2036	26,030,167	12,472,094	7,909,512	3,488,166	2,160,395
2001–02	2036	27,756,977	13,043,118	8,352,128	3,963,153	2,398,578
2002–03	2036	28,343,386	13,468,965	8,521,017	3,892,469	2,460,935
2003–04	2036	29,197,510	13,303,136	8,772,780	4,146,495	2,975,099

Season	Matches	Total	FA Premier	Championship	Championship 1	Championship 2
2004–05	2036	29,245,870	12,878,791	9,612,761	4,270,674	2,483,644
2005–06	2036	29,089,084	12,871,643	9,719,204	4,183,011	2,315,226
2006–07	2036	29,541,949	13,058,115	10,057,813	4,135,599	2,290,422
2007–08	2036	29,914,212	13,708,875	9,397,036	4,412,023	2,396,278
2008–09	2036	29,881,966	13,527,815	9,877,552	4,171,834	2,304,765
2009–10	2036	30,057,892	12,977,251	9,909,882	5,043,099	2,127,660

*Figures include matches played by Aldershot.
Football League official total for their three divisions in 2001–02 was 14,716,162.

ENGLISH LEAGUE ATTENDANCES 2009–10

FA BARCLAYCARD PREMIERSHIP ATTENDANCES

	Average Gate			Season 2009–10	
	2008–09	2009–10	+/–%	Highest	Lowest
Arsenal	60.040	59,927	–0.19	60,103	59,084
Aston Villa	39.812	38,573	–3.11	42,788	32,917
Birmingham City	19,090	25,246	+32.25	28,958	19,922
Blackburn Rovers	23,479	25,428	+8.30	29,912	21,287
Bolton Wanderers	22,486	21,880	–2.70	25,370	17,849
Burnley	13,082	20,653	+57.87	21,761	18,397
Chelsea	41,589	41,422	–0.40	41,836	40,137
Everton	35,667	36,725	+2.97	39,652	32,163
Fulham	24,344	23,909	–1.79	25,700	20,831
Hull City	24,816	24,389	–1.72	25,030	22,822
Liverpool	43,611	42,863	–1.72	44,392	37,697
Manchester City	42,899	45,512	+6.09	47,370	40,292
Manchester United	75,304	74,864	–0.58	75,316	73,709
Portsmouth	19,830	18,249	–7.97	20,821	16,207
Stoke City	26,960	27,162	+0.75	27,604	25,104
Sunderland	40,168	40,355	+0.47	47,641	34,821
Tottenham Hotspur	35,929	35,794	–0.38	36,041	35,318
West Ham United	33,701	33,683	–0.05	34,989	30,024
Wigan Athletic	18,350	18,006	–1.87	22,113	14,323
Wolverhampton Wanderers	24,153	28,365	+17.44	29,023	26,668

TOTAL ATTENDANCES: 12,977,251 (380 games)
Average 34,151 (–4.07%)
HIGHEST: 75,316 Manchester United v Stoke City
LOWEST: 14,323 Wigan Athletic v Portsmouth
HIGHEST AVERAGE: 74,864 Manchester United
LOWEST AVERAGE: 18,006 Wigan Athletic

FOOTBALL LEAGUE: CHAMPIONSHIP ATTENDANCES

	Average Gate			Season 2009–10	
	2008–09	2009–10	+/–%	Highest	Lowest
Barnsley	13,189	12,964	–1.71	20,079	11,116
Blackpool	7,843	8,611	+9.79	12,296	6,855
Bristol City	16,816	14,600	–13.18	19,144	13,009
Cardiff City	18,044	20,717	+14.81	25,630	17,686
Coventry City	17,451	17,305	–0.84	22,209	14,426
Crystal Palace	15,220	14,770	–2.96	20,643	12,328
Derby County	29,440	29,230	–0.71	33,010	26,186
Doncaster Rovers	11,964	10,991	–8.13	14,850	8,827
Ipswich Town	20,961	20,840	–0.58	27,059	19,283
Leicester City	20,253	23,942	+18.21	31,759	18,928
Middlesbrough	28,429	19,948	–29.83	27,721	16,847
Newcastle United	48,750	43,387	–11.00	52,181	36,944
Nottingham Forest	22,299	23,831	+6.87	29,155	18,332
Peterborough United	7,599	8,913	+17.29	12,877	6,445
Plymouth Argyle	11,533	10,316	–10.55	14,792	7,243
Preston North End	13,426	12,934	–3.66	19,840	10,270
Queens Park Rangers	14,090	13,348	–5.27	17,082	10,940
Reading	19,942	17,495	–12.27	23,163	14,096
Scunthorpe United	4,998	6,463	+29.31	8,921	4,995
Sheffield United	26,023	25,120	–3.47	29,210	22,555
Sheffield Wednesday	21,542	23,179	+7.60	37,121	18,329
Swansea City	15,195	15,407	+1.40	18,794	12,775
Watford	14,858	14,344	–3.46	17,120	12,179
West Bromwich Albion	25,828	22,199	–14.05	25,297	19,390

TOTAL ATTENDANCES: 9,909,882 (552 games)
Average 17,953 (+0.33%)
HIGHEST: 52,181 Newcastle United v Ipswich Town
LOWEST: 4,995 Scunthorpe United v Peterborough United
HIGHEST AVERAGE: 43,387 Newcastle United
LOWEST AVERAGE: 6,463 Scunthorpe United

Premiership and Football League attendance averages and highest crowd figures for 2009–10 are unofficial.

FOOTBALL LEAGUE: DIVISION 1 ATTENDANCES

	Average Gate			Season 2009–10	
	2008–09	2009–10	+/–%	Highest	Lowest
Brentford	5,707	6,017	+5.43	9,031	4,200
Brighton & Hove Albion	6,092	6,466	+6.14	7,784	4,711
Bristol Rovers	7,171	7,042	–1.80	11,448	5,322
Carlisle United	6,268	5,210	–16.88	8,728	3,731
Charlton Athletic	20,894	17,407	–16.69	23,198	14,636
Colchester United	5,084	5,529	+8.75	10,064	3,601
Exeter City	4,939	5,832	+18.08	8,549	4,106
Gillingham	5,307	6,335	+19.37	10,304	3,840
Hartlepool United	3,835	3,443	–10.22	5,115	2,465
Huddersfield Town	13,298	14,381	+8.14	21,764	11,269
Leeds United	23,813	24,817	+4.22	38,234	17,635
Leyton Orient	4,692	4,937	+5.22	8,013	2,669
Millwall	8,940	10,834	+21.19	17,632	6,617
Milton Keynes Dons FC	10,551	10,289	–2.48	16,713	8,528
Norwich City	24,543	24,671	+0.52	25,506	23,041
Oldham Athletic	5,636	4,630	–17.85	8,569	2,833
Southampton	17,858	20,982	+17.49	30,890	16,402
Southend United	7,850	7,718	–1.68	10,329	6,382
Stockport County	6,130	4,420	–27.90	7,768	3,281
Swindon Town	7,499	8,389	+11.87	14,508	6,183
Tranmere Rovers	5,820	5,670	–2.58	8,694	4,317
Walsall	4,572	4,028	–11.90	8,483	2,929
Wycombe Wanderers	5,109	5,544	+8.51	8,400	3,899
Yeovil Town	4,423	4,664	+5.45	7,484	3,469

TOTAL ATTENDANCES: 5,043,099 (552 games)
Average 9,136 (+20.88%)

HIGHEST: 38,234 Leeds United v Bristol Rovers
LOWEST: 2,465 Hartlepool United v Gillingham
HIGHEST AVERAGE: 24,817 Leeds United
LOWEST AVERAGE: 3,443 Hartlepool United

FOOTBALL LEAGUE: DIVISION 2 ATTENDANCES

	Average Gate			Season 2009–10	
	2008–09	2009–10	+/–%	Highest	Lowest
Accrington Stanley	1,414	1,980	+40.03	3,396	1,210
Aldershot Town	3,276	3,085	–5.83	4,506	2,053
Barnet	2,153	2,059	–4.37	4,638	1,298
AFC Bournemouth	4,931	5,719	+15.98	9,055	4,019
Bradford City	12,704	11,422	–10.09	12,403	10,831
Burton Albion	2,401	3,195	+33.07	5,801	2,027
Bury	3,342	3,028	–9.40	6,528	2,123
Cheltenham Town	3,854	3,185	–17.36	4,134	2,331
Chesterfield	3,449	3,849	+11.60	6,196	3,104
Crewe Alexandra	4,537	4,075	–10.18	6,943	3,272
Dagenham & Redbridge	2,048	2,097	+2.39	3,721	1,683
Darlington	2,932	1,943	–33.73	2,744	1,296
Grimsby Town	4,475	4,458	–0.38	7,033	3,090
Hereford United	3,270	2,138	–34.62	3,280	1,208
Lincoln City	3,940	3,670	–6.85	6,012	2,457
Macclesfield Town	1,898	1,928	+1.58	3,449	1,035
Morecambe	2,153	2,262	+5.06	5,268	1,537
Northampton Town	5,200	4,375	–15.87	5,647	3,206
Notts County	4,446	7,352	+65.36	11,331	4,606
Port Vale	5,522	5,079	–8.02	8,467	3,231
Rochdale	3,222	3,443	+6.86	5,371	2,311
Rotherham United	3,587	3,817	+6.41	10,254	2,604
Shrewsbury Town	5,664	5,481	–3.23	7,096	4,328
Torquay United	2,243	2,855	+27.28	5,124	2,122

TOTAL ATTENDANCES: 2,127,660 (552 games)
Average 3,854 (–7.69%)

HIGHEST: 12,403 Bradford City v Northampton Town
LOWEST: 1,035 Macclesfield Town v Northampton Town
HIGHEST AVERAGE: 11,422 Bradford City
LOWEST AVERAGE: 1,928 Macclesfield Town

LEAGUE CUP FINALISTS 1961–2010

Played as a two-leg final until 1966. All subsequent finals at Wembley until 2000, then at Millennium Stadium, Cardiff.

Year	Winners	Runners-up	Score
1961	Aston Villa	Rotherham U	0-2, 3-0 (aet)
1962	Norwich C	Rochdale	3-0, 1-0
1963	Birmingham C	Aston Villa	3-1, 0-0
1964	Leicester C	Stoke C	1-1, 3-2
1965	Chelsea	Leicester C	3-2, 0-0
1966	WBA	West Ham U	1-2, 4-1
1967	QPR	WBA	3-2
1968	Leeds U	Arsenal	1-0
1969	Swindon T	Arsenal	3-1 (aet)
1970	Manchester C	WBA	2-1 (aet)
1971	Tottenham H	Aston Villa	2-0
1972	Stoke C	Chelsea	2-1
1973	Tottenham H	Norwich C	1-0
1974	Wolverhampton W	Manchester C	2-1
1975	Aston Villa	Norwich C	1-0
1976	Manchester C	Newcastle U	2-1
1977	Aston Villa	Everton	0-0, 1-1 (aet), 3-2 (aet)
1978	Nottingham F	Liverpool	0-0 (aet), 1-0
1979	Nottingham F	Southampton	3-2
1980	Wolverhampton W	Nottingham F	1-0
1981	Liverpool	West Ham U	1-1 (aet), 2-1

MILK CUP

1982	Liverpool	Tottenham H	3-1 (aet)
1983	Liverpool	Manchester U	2-1 (aet)
1984	Liverpool	Everton	0-0 (aet), 1-0
1985	Norwich C	Sunderland	1-0
1986	Oxford U	QPR	3-0

LITTLEWOODS CUP

1987	Arsenal	Liverpool	2-1
1988	Luton T	Arsenal	3-2
1989	Nottingham F	Luton T	3-1
1990	Nottingham F	Oldham Ath	1-0

RUMBELOWS LEAGUE CUP

1991	Sheffield W	Manchester U	1-0
1992	Manchester U	Nottingham F	1-0

COCA-COLA CUP

1993	Arsenal	Sheffield W	2-1
1994	Aston Villa	Manchester U	3-1
1995	Liverpool	Bolton W	2-1
1996	Aston Villa	Leeds U	3-0
1997	Leicester C	Middlesbrough	1-1 (aet), 1-0 (aet)
1998	Chelsea	Middlesbrough	2-0 (aet)

WORTHINGTON CUP

1999	Tottenham H	Leicester C	1-0
2000	Leicester C	Tranmere R	2-1
2001	Liverpool	Birmingham C	1-1 (aet)
Liverpool won 5-4 on penalties			
2002	Blackburn R	Tottenham H	2-1
2003	Liverpool	Manchester U	2-0

CARLING CUP

2004	Middlesbrough	Bolton W	2-1
2005	Chelsea	Liverpool	3-2 (aet)
2006	Manchester U	Wigan Ath	4-0
2007	Chelsea	Arsenal	2-1
2008	Tottenham H	Chelsea	2-1 (aet)
2009	Manchester U	Tottenham H	0-0 (aet)
Manchester U won 4-1 on penalties			
2010	Manchester U	Aston Villa	2-1

LEAGUE CUP WINS

Liverpool 7, Aston Villa 5, Chelsea 4, Manchester U 4, Nottingham F 4, Tottenham H 4, Leicester C 3, Arsenal 2, Manchester C 2, Norwich C 2, Wolverhampton W 2, Birmingham C 1, Blackburn R 1, Leeds U 1, Luton T 1, Middlesbrough 1, Oxford U 1, QPR 1, Sheffield W 1, Stoke C 1, Swindon T 1, WBA 1.

APPEARANCES IN FINALS

Liverpool 10, Aston Villa 8, Manchester U 8, Tottenham H 7, Arsenal 6, Chelsea 6, Nottingham F 6, Leicester C 5, Norwich C 4, Manchester C 3, Middlesbrough 3, WBA 3, Birmingham C 2, Bolton W 2, Everton 2, Leeds U 2, Luton T 2, QPR 2, Sheffield W 2, Stoke C 2, West Ham U 2, Wolverhampton W 2, Blackburn R 1, Newcastle U 1, Oldham Ath 1, Oxford U 1, Rochdale 1, Rotherham U 1, Southampton 1, Sunderland 1, Swindon T 1, Tranmere R 1, Wigan Ath 1.

APPEARANCES IN SEMI-FINALS

Arsenal 13, Aston Villa 13, Liverpool 13, Tottenham H 13, Manchester U 12, Chelsea 10, West Ham U 7, Blackburn R 6, Manchester C 6, Nottingham F 6, Leeds U 5, Leicester C 5, Middlesbrough 5, Norwich C 5, Birmingham C 4, Bolton W 4, Burnley 4, Everton 4, Sheffield W 4, WBA 4, Crystal Palace 3, Ipswich T 3, QPR 3, Sunderland 3, Swindon T 3, Wolverhampton W 3, Bristol C 2, Coventry C 2, Derby Co 2, Luton T 2, Oxford U 2, Plymouth Arg 2, Southampton 2, Stoke C 2, Tranmere R 2, Watford 2, Wimbledon 2, Blackpool 1, Bury 1, Cardiff C 1, Carlisle U 1, Chester C 1, Huddersfield T 1, Newcastle U 1, Oldham Ath 1, Peterborough U 1, Rochdale 1, Rotherham U 1, Sheffield U 1, Shrewsbury T 1, Stockport Co 1, Walsall 1, Wigan Ath 1, Wycombe W 1.

CARLING CUP 2009–10

* *Denotes player sent off.*

FIRST ROUND

Monday, 10 August 2009

Darlington (0) 0

Leeds U (0) 1 *(Showunmi 54)*   4487

Darlington: Knight; Arnison, Bower, Chandler, Foster (Plummer), Miller, Smith G, Lumsdon, Thorpe (Main), Dowson, Smith J (Windass).
Leeds U: Higgs; Crowe, Hughes, Doyle, Huntington, Michalik, Snodgrass (Robinson), Howson, Grella (Kilkenny), Showunmi (Becchio), Johnson.

Tuesday, 11 August 2009

Accrington S (0) 2 *(Grant 53, Mullin P 90)*

Walsall (1) 1 *(Nicholls 9)*   1041

Accrington S: Martin; Winnard, King (Grant), Procter, Edwards, Kempson, Ryan, Joyce, Kee (McConville), Mullin P, Miles.
Walsall: Gilmartin; Weston*, Vincent, Richards, Smith, Roberts. Jones (Deeney), Mattis, Parkin, Nicholls, Taundry.

Barnet (0) 0

Watford (0) 2 *(Williamson M 105, Severin 120)*   3139

Barnet: Cole; O'Neill (Devera), Gillet, Hughes (Charles), Yakubu, Leach, Adomah, Hyde M, Furlong, Jarrett, Bolasie (Hyde J).
Watford: Lee; Mariappa, Doyley, Eustace, Severin, Hodson (Harley), McAnuff (Brooks), Williamson M, Graham, Smith, Cowie (Ellington).
aet.

Brentford (0) 0

Bristol C (0) 1 *(Maynard 58)*   3024

Brentford: Bull; Foster, Dickson, O'Connor, Phillips, Bennett, Saunders (Williams), Hunt, Kabba (Osborne), Wood, Weston.
Bristol C: Gerken; Orr, Blackman (Sproule), Skuse, Carey, Fontaine, Elliott, Johnson, Haynes*, Maynard (Akinde), Williams (Wilson B).

Bristol R (1) 2 *(Duffy 37 (pen), 58)*

Aldershot T (0) 1 *(Morgan 60 (pen))*   3644

Bristol R: Evans; Regan, Hughes, Campbell, Anthony, Lescott, Pipe (Blizzard), Lines, Duffy, Osei-Kuffour, Rigg (Swallow).
Aldershot T: Masters; Chalmers, Sandell, Halls, Blackburn, Hinshelwood, Soares, Harding, Morgan M, Donnelly (Hylton), Hudson (Grant).

Bury (0) 0

WBA (2) 2 *(Dorrans 5, Jones 25 (og))*   3077

Bury: Brown; Scott, Buchanan, Dawson, Futcher, Sodje, Racchi (Johnson), Barry-Murphy (Baker), Carlton (Rouse), Lowe, Jones.
WBA: Kiely; Zuiverloon, Mattock, Martis, Barnett, Olsson, Teixeira, Beattie, Cox (Wood), Reid R, Dorrans.

Cardiff C (2) 3 *(Rae 20, Bothroyd 26 (pen), Whittingham 90)*

Dagenham & R (0) 1 *(Scott 81)*   5545

Cardiff C: Enckelman; Quinn, Capaldi, Rae, Hudson, Gerrard, Whittingham, McPhail, Bothroyd, Chopra, Comminges (Wildig).
Dagenham & R: Roberts; Doe (Ogogo), Griffiths, Arber, Antwi, Taiwo, Green (Montgomery), Thurgood, Benson, Thomas (Scott), Gain.

Carlisle U (0) 1 *(Dobie 89)*

Oldham Ath (0) 0   2509

Carlisle U: Pidgeley; Raven, Harte, Taiwo, Livesey, Keogh, Kavanagh, Bridge-Wilkinson (Madine), Dobie, Anyinsah, Robson (Rothery).
Oldham Ath: Brill; Holdsworth, Gilbert, Furman, Gregan, Hazell, Whitaker, Worthington, O'Grady (Parker), Byfield (Abbott), Taylor (Alessandra).

Cheltenham T (1) 1 *(Hammond 45)*

Southend U (0) 2 *(Barnard 77, 88)*   1918

Cheltenham T: Brown SP; Bird (Denton), Ridley, Pook, Duff, Townsend, Richards, Gallinagh, Hammond (Alsop), Hayles, Hutton (Low).
Southend U: Mildenhall; Francis, White, Christophe (Sawyer), Heath, Mvoto, Grant, McCormack, Barnard (Revell), Walker (Freedman), Moussa.

Colchester U (0) 1 *(Hackney 90)*

Leyton Orient (1) 2 *(Patulea 2, Melligan 63)*   3308

Colchester U: Cousins; Maybury, Beevers (Hammond), Izzet, Baldwin, Okuonghae, Vincent, Perkins (Vernon), Platt*, Lisbie, Hackney.
Leyton Orient: Morris; Purches, Daniels, Chorley, Mkandawire, Townsend (Thornton), Melligan, Smith, Patulea (Jarvis), Scowcroft (McGleish), Demetriou.

Crewe Alex (0) 1 *(Zola 73)*

Blackpool (0) 2 *(Nowland 52, Nardiello 79)*   2991

Crewe Alex: Legzdins; Brayford, Jones, Bailey (Verma), Westwood, Ada, Murphy (Donaldson), Mitchel-King, Moore, Zola, Grant (Elding).
Blackpool: Gilks; John-Baptiste, Martin, Nowland, Edwards, Evatt, Clarke, Nardiello, Ormerod, Taylor-Fletcher (Almond), Hudson.

Crystal Palace (0) 2 *(Ambrose 65, 78 (pen))*

Torquay U (0) 1 *(Sills 74)*   3140

Crystal Palace: Speroni; Butterfield, Hill, Derry, McCarthy, Fonte, Moses (Scannell), Danns, Lee (Djilali), Ambrose (Ertl), N'Diaye.
Torquay U: Bevan; Robertson, Nicholson, Thompson (Brough), Charnock, Todd, Carlisle, Wroe, Rendell (Benyon), Sills, Stevens (Carayol).

Exeter C (0) 0

QPR (0) 5 *(Routledge 51, 61, 66 (pen), Pellicori 85, Ephraim 89)*   4614

Exeter C: Jones; Duffy, Golbourne*, Sercombe, Seaborne, Taylor M, Harley, Russell (Logan), Stewart (Tully), McAllister (Norwood), Cozic.
QPR: Cerny; Connolly, Borrowdale, Leigertwood, Stewart, Gorkss, Routledge (Ainsworth), Buzsaky, Agyemang (Mahon), Vine (Pellicori), Ephraim.

Gillingham (2) 2 *(Jackson 42, Barcham 45)*

Plymouth Arg (0) 1 *(Summerfield 49)*   3306

Gillingham: Royce; Fuller, Nutter, Weston, Richards, Gowling, Maher (McCammon), Palmer (Rooney), Jackson, Barcham, Miller.
Plymouth Arg: Larrieu; Sawyer, McNamee, Paterson, Seip, Judge (Clark), Duguid, MacLean (Noone), Fallon, Mackie, Summerfield (Barnes).

Hereford U (0) 1 *(Godsmark 98)*

Charlton Ath (0) 0   2017

Hereford U: Bartlett; Green, Valentine, Rose, Lowe (Dennehy), Lunt, Pugh (Gwynne), Southam (Done), Morris, McQuilkin, Godsmark.
Charlton Ath: Elliot; Solly, Youga, Stavrinou, Semedo, Basey, Spring, Wagstaff (Burton), Gray, McLeod (Fleetwood), Small (Bailey).
aet.

Huddersfield T (1) 3 *(Rhodes 45, 48, Robinson 74)*

Stockport Co (0) 1 *(Poole 88)*   5120

Huddersfield T: Smithies; Peltier, Skarz, Clarke T, Clarke P, Clarke N, Pilkington, Kay, Novak (Robinson), Rhodes (Simpson), Roberts (Ainsworth).
Stockport Co: Gerrard; Mullins, Rose, Tansey, Havern, Raynes, Poole, Turnbull (Pilkington), Thompson P, Johnson (Vincent), Baker (Griffin).

Lincoln C (0) 0

Barnsley (0) 1 *(Bogdanovic 72)*   3635

Lincoln C: Burch; Hughton, Brown, Kovacs, Swaibu, Clarke S, Oakes (Fagan), Butcher, Howe, Connor, Clarke J.

Barnsley: Steele; Hassell, Kozluk, Anderson, Foster, Butterfield, Campbell-Ryce, Potter, Odejayi, Macken (Bogdanovic), Hammill.

Millwall (2) 4 *(Alexander 31, Harris 40, 69, 74)*

Bournemouth (0) 0   3552

Millwall: Forde; Dunne, Barron, Abdou (Laird), Smith, Frampton, Hackett, Fuseini, Morison, Alexander (Grabban), Harris (Grimes).

Bournemouth: Jalal; Bradbury, Cummings, Molesley (Bartley), Pearce, Garry, Igoe (McQuoid), Robinson, Pitman, Goulding (Fletcher), Feeney.

Milton Keynes D (0) 1 *(Easter 53 (pen))*

Swindon T (1) 4 *(McGovern 41, Paynter 56, 72, McCracken 74 (og))*   4812

Milton Keynes D: Gueret; Woodards, Davis (Darren Powell), Howell, Doumbe, McCracken, Gobern L, Carrington (Chadwick), Easter, Bridges (Puncheon), Johnson.

Swindon T: Lucas; Amankwaah, Lescinel, Mackin, Morrison, Greer, McGovern, Douglas, Paynter (Marshall), Timlin, McNamee (Kennedy).

Notts Co (0) 0

Doncaster R (0) 1 *(Coppinger 54)*   4893

Notts Co: Hoult; Moloney, Hunt, Ravenhill, Edwards, Thompson, Hamshaw (Westcarr), Bishop, Hawley, Rodgers (Hughes), Clapham.

Doncaster R: Smith; O'Connor, Roberts, Lockwood, Webster, Wilson, Guy (Hayter), Woods M, Coppinger, Shiels (Spicer), Oster (Chambers).

Preston NE (2) 5 *(Brown 33, Elliott 45, Nicholson 57, Trotman 69, Mellor 90)*

Morecambe (0) 1 *(Twiss 90)*   5407

Preston NE: Lonergan; Hart, Jones, Carter, Chilvers, Mawene (Trotman), Sedgwick, Nicholson, Brown (Mellor), Elliott, Wallace (Parry).

Morecambe: Roche; Moss, Adams, Artell, Hairing, Stanley, Duffy (Wainwright), Drummond (McStay), Twiss, Craney, Wilson (Poole).

Reading (4) 5 *(Mooney 6, 77, Bignall 7, 9, Sigurdsson 27)*

Burton Alb (0) 1 *(Phillips 59)*   5893

Reading: Hamer; Rosenior, Armstrong, Sigurdsson, Pearce, Mills, Matejovsky, Harper, Bignall (Hunt N), Mooney, Henry.

Burton Alb: Poole; Corbett, Boertien, Austin, Branston, McGrath, Simpson, Penn, Walker (Phillips), Pearson, Maghoma.

Rotherham U (1) 2 *(Warne 44, Ellison 65)*

Derby Co (1) 1 *(Teale 11)*   4345

Rotherham U: Warrington; Tonge, Green, Law, Sharps, Fenton, Ellison (Liddell), Mills, Pope, Warne, Taylor J.

Derby Co: Bywater; Connolly, Moxey, Savage, Buxton, Addison, Croft, Pringle (McEveley), Davies (Varney), Pearson, Teale.

Scunthorpe U (1) 2 *(Sparrow 12, Hayes 54)*

Chesterfield (0) 1 *(Currie 72 (pen))*   2501

Scunthorpe U: Lillis; Wright A, Williams, O'Connor (Togwell), Jones, Byrne, Sparrow, Thompson (Forte), Hayes, Hooper, Woolford (Wright J).

Chesterfield: Lee; Gray (Picken), Austin, Harsley (Niven), Hall, Breckin, Talbot, Allott, Gritton (Currie), Bowery, McDermott.

Sheffield U (1) 1 *(Sharp 33)*

Port Vale (2) 2 *(Richards 20, 61)*   7627

Sheffield U: Bennett; France, Taylor, Reid, Bromby, Kilgallon, Little (Treacy), Howard, Henderson, Sharp, Quinn S (Montgomery).

Port Vale: Martin; Stockley, Taylor K, Collins, McCombe, Owen, Griffith, Loft, Richards, Taylor R (Horsfield), Fraser.

Sheffield W (2) 3 *(Esajas 19, Johnson 21, 50)*

Rochdale (0) 0   6696

Sheffield W: Grant; Simek, Spurr (Jeffers), Potter, Beevers, Purse, Miller, McAllister, Johnson (Gray), Tudgay (Hinds), Esajas.

Rochdale: Arthur; Holness (Brizell), Kennedy T, Jones G, Stanton, Dawson, Thompson, Kennedy J, Dagnall, Buckley (Shaw), Rundle (Higginbotham).

Shrewsbury T (2) 3 *(Robinson 18, Hibbert 24, Cansdell-Sherriff 74)*

Ipswich T (2) 3 *(Wickham 11, 59, Quinn 32)*   4184

Shrewsbury T: Neal C; Holden, McIntyre, Murray (Dunfield), Coughlan, Langmead, Cansdell-Sherriff, Disley, Hibbert (Riza), Elder (Bright), Robinson.

Ipswich T: Supple; Ainsley (Upson), Wright D, Garvan (O'Connor), Bruce, Smith, Colback, Healy C, Lambe (Walters), Wickham, Quinn.

aet; Ipswich T won 4-2 on penalties.

Southampton (1) 2 *(Lambert 29, Lallana 68)*

Northampton T (0) 0   10,921

Southampton: Davis; Murty (Thomson), Harding, Wotton, Lancashire, Thomas, Lallana, Schneiderlin, Lambert (Gobern), Paterson (Rasiak), James.

Northampton T: Dunn; McCready, Rose (Akinfenwa), Gilligan (Dyer), Hinton, Beckwith, Marshall, Osman, McKay (Curtis), Guinan, Holt.

Swansea C (1) 3 *(Monk 17, Dobbie 50, 90)*

Brighton & HA (0) 0   6400

Swansea C: De Vries; Collins (Rangel), Bessone, Britton, Tate, Monk, Lopez (Bauza), Orlandi, Dobbie, Dyer, Gower (Morgan).

Brighton & HA: Kuipers; Whing, Virgo, Thornhill, Elphick, Wright J (El-Abd), Cox, Navarro, Dickinson (Murray), Forster, Crofts (Wright M).

Tranmere R (3) 4 *(McLaren 32, Thomas-Moore 37 (pen), Curran 40, Edds 71)*

Grimsby T (0) 0   3527

Tranmere R: Daniels; Logan, Cresswell, McLaren (Taylor), Broomes, Goodison (Edds), Shuker, Welsh, Thomas-Moore (Gornell), Curran, Mahon.

Grimsby T: Colgan; Stockdale, Widdowson, Hegarty, Bennett, Atkinson, Sweeney (Leary), Boshell, Conlon, Proudlock (North), Akpa Akpro.

Wycombe W (0) 0

Peterborough U (2) 4 *(McLean 24, Rowe 33, Boyd 59, Frecklington 68)*   2078

Wycombe W: Young; Green (Zebroski), Woodman, Mousinho, Oliver, Johnson, Spiller, Westwood, Beavon, Pittman, Bloomfield (Phillips).

Peterborough U: Lewis; Lee (Martin), Williams, Diagouraga, Pearce, Zakuani, Rowe, Frecklington, Mackail-Smith (Batt), McLean (Wright), Boyd.

Yeovil T (0) 0

Norwich C (0) 4 *(Hoolahan 55 (pen), Holt 64, 82, 90)*   3860

Yeovil T: McCarthy; Forbes, Jones, O'Callaghan, Caulker, Stam, Murray (Obika), Welsh (Smith), Williams S, Tomlin, Schofield.

Norwich C: Alnwick; Spillane, Drury (Lappin), Whaley, Doherty, Berthel Askou, Gill (Hughes), Adeyemi, McDonald (Maric), Holt, Hoolahan.

Wednesday, 12 August 2009

Coventry C (0) 0

Hartlepool U (0) 1 *(Boyd 105)*   6055

Coventry C: Konstantopoulos; Wright (Wilson), Clarke (Cameron), Osbourne, Turner, Grandison, Cain, Walker, Jeffers, Eastwood, McIndoe (Morrison).

Hartlepool U: Flinders; Haslam, Hartley, Sweeney, Collins, Liddle, Fredriksen (Larkin), Jones, Behan (Boyd), McSweeney (Brown), Monkhouse.

aet.

Macclesfield T (0) 0
Leicester C (0) 2 *(N'Guessan 58, Fryatt 71)*   2197
Macclesfield T: Brain; Brisley, Tremarco, Bolland (Bell), Morgan, Bencherif, Draper, Rooney (Tipton), Wright, Kirk (Reid I), Daniel.
Leicester C: Weale; O'Neill, Powell, Oakley, Morrison, Hobbs, Adams, Wellens, Howard, Fryatt (Waghorn), N'Guessan (Gradel).

Nottingham F (0) 3 *(Anderson 46, Blackstock 60, McGugan 82)*
Bradford C (0) 0   4639
Nottingham F: Smith; McCleary, Lynch, Majewski (McKenna), Morgan, McGugan, Anderson, Davies (Garner), Tyson, Blackstock (McGoldrick), Cohen.
Bradford C: Eastwood; Bateson■, Ramsden, Bullock (O'Brien J), Rehman, Williams, O'Brien L, Flynn, Evans (Boulding M), Hanson, Colbeck.

SECOND ROUND

Monday, 24 August 2009
Norwich C (0) 1 *(Hoolahan 63)*
Sunderland (3) 4 *(Tainio 26, Reid 30, 36, Tudur-Jones 67 (og))*   12,345
Norwich C: Alnwick; Otsemobor, Lappin, Tudur-Jones, Doherty, Spillane■, Whaley (McDonald), Adeyemi (Smith), Daley, Holt (Martin C), Hoolahan.
Sunderland: Gordon; Edwards, McCartney, Tainio (Healy D), Nosworthy, Da Silva, Henderson, Leadbitter, Campbell (Malbranque), Jones (Murphy), Reid.

Tuesday, 25 August 2009
Gillingham (0) 1 *(Jackson 70 (pen))*
Blackburn R (1) 3 *(Dunn 5, Hoilett 47, Pedersen 74)* 7293
Gillingham: Royce; Fuller, Nutter, Weston (Jackman), Gowling, Bentley, Maher (Payne), Barcham, Jackson, McCammon, Oli (Palmer).
Blackburn R: Brown; Reid (Grella), Givet, N'Zonzi, Khizanishvili, Olsson, Andrews, Dunn (Van Heerden), Kalinic (Roberts J), Hoilett, Pedersen.

Hartlepool U (1) 1 *(Boyd 39)*
Burnley (0) 2 *(Fletcher 84, 108)*   3501
Hartlepool U: Flinders; Haslam, Hartley, Sweeney (Fredriksen), Collins, Liddle, McSweeney, Jones, Behan, Boyd (Larkin), Monkhouse.
Burnley: Penny; Eckersley■, Easton, Gudjonsson, Bikey, Edgar, Eagles (Blake), McDonald, Rodriguez (Fletcher), Thompson (Paterson), Guerrero.
aet.

Hull C (2) 3 *(Cairney 7, Altidore 42, Geovanni 75)*
Southend U (1) 1 *(Moussa 45)*   7994
Hull C: Warner; Doyle, Halmosi, Cairney (Kilbane), Mouyokolo, Cooper, Atkinson (Ghilas), Featherstone, Fagan, Altidore, Barmby (Geovanni).
Southend U: Mildenhall; Francis, Mvoto, Christophe, Heath, Barrett, Grant (Betsy), McCormack, Barnard (Walker), Revell, Moussa.

Leeds U (1) 2 *(Snodgrass 38, 98)*
Watford (0) 1 *(Sordell 87)*   14,681
Leeds U: Higgs; Crowe, Hughes, Doyle, Rui Marques, Kisnorbo, Johnson, Howson, Beckford (Showunmi), Grella (Kilkenny), Snodgrass (Becchio).
Watford: Lee; Mariappa, Doyley, Eustace, Hodson, Williamson M, Cleverley, Jenkins (Lansbury), Graham (Henderson), Hoskins (Sordell), Cowie.
aet.

Nottingham F (0) 2 *(Chambers 60, Majewski 103)*
Middlesbrough (1) 1 *(Johnson A 43)*   8838
Nottingham F: Smith; Gunter, Cohen, Majewski, Morgan, Chambers, Anderson (McGoldrick), McKenna, Earnshaw (Adebola), Blackstock, Davies (Tyson).
Middlesbrough: Coyne; Hoyte, Taylor, Williams R, Huth, Wheater, Yeates, Arca (Bennett), Emnes (Lita), Aliadiere (McMahon), Johnson A.

Peterborough U (1) 2 *(Frecklington 32, Boyd 64)*
Ipswich T (1) 1 *(Priskin 14)*   5451
Peterborough U: Lewis; Martin, Rowe (Pearce), Diagouraga, Morgan, Zakuani, Batt (Lee), Frecklington, Mackail-Smith, McLean, Boyd.
Ipswich T: Wright R; Wright D, Delaney, Healy C, Bruce, Balkestein, Colback, Martin (Upson), Priskin (Walters), Counago (Wickham), Quinn.

Port Vale (0) 2 *(Taylor K 63, Taylor R 65)*
Sheffield W (0) 0   6667
Port Vale: Martin; Yates, Taylor K, Collins, McCombe, Owen, Dodds (Jorgensen), Loft (Griffith), Richards (Horsfield), Taylor R, Fraser.
Sheffield W: Grant; Simek, Spurr, McAllister (Johnson), Beevers, Hinds, Esajas (Sodje), Potter, Jeffers■, Tudgay, Miller (O'Connor).

Portsmouth (3) 4 *(Piquionne 20, Utaka 23, Kranjcar 43, Hughes 56)*
Hereford U (0) 1 *(Plummer 62 (pen))*   6645
Portsmouth: Begovic; Vanden Borre, Belhadj, Mokoena, Kaboul, Ward, Basinas, Hughes (Mahoto), Piquionne (Kanu), Utaka (Nugent), Kranjcar.
Hereford U: Bartlett; Green, Rose, Dennehy, Jones D, Lunt (Tolley), Godsmark (Jackson), Southam (Gwynne), Plummer, Constantine, Jones C.

Preston NE (1) 2 *(Brown 14, 65)*
Leicester C (1) 1 *(Adams 6)*   6977
Preston NE: Lonergan; Hart, Nolan, Carter (Chaplow), St Ledger-Hall, Chilvers, Sedgwick, Sumulikoski, Brown, Elliott (Mellor), Parry.
Leicester C: Weale; Neilson, Powell, King A, Morrison, Tunchev, N'Guessan (Dyer), Oakley (Dickov), Gallagher (Kermorgant), Fryatt, Adams.

QPR (0) 2 *(Ephraim 68, Routledge 90)*
Accrington S (0) 1 *(Symes 90)*   5203
QPR: Heaton; Ramage, Connolly, Leigertwood, Stewart, Gorkss (Borrowdale), Mahon (Routledge), Buzsaky, Agyemang (Taarabt), Vine, Ephraim.
Accrington S: Martin; Winnard, Ryan (Turner), Procter, Kempson, Edwards, Murphy (Grant), Joyce, McConville (Kee), Symes, Miles.

Reading (0) 1 *(Kozluk 89 (og))*
Barnsley (0) 2 *(Bogdanovic 56, 90 (pen))*   5576
Reading: Hamer; Kelly (Hunt N), Bertrand (Tabb), Gunnarsson, Pearce, Harper, Henry, Matejovsky, Mooney, Bignall (Antonio), Davies.
Barnsley: Steele; Kozluk, El Haimour, Colace (Butterfield), Foster, Potter, Bogdanovic, Hallfredsson, Odejayi, Macken, Campbell-Ryce (Anderson).

Southampton (0) 1 *(Lallana 51)*
Birmingham C (0) 2 *(Bowyer 77, Carsley 80)*   11,753
Southampton: Davis; Murty (Gillett), Harding, Wotton (Schneiderlin), Perry, Thomas, James, Mellis, Lambert, Saganowski (Paterson), Lallana.
Birmingham C: Maik Taylor; Parnaby, Carr, Carsley, Espinoza, Queudrue, Larsson (O'Connor), O'Shea (McFadden), Benitez, McSheffrey, Bowyer.

Swansea C (0) 1 *(Dobbie 79)*
Scunthorpe U (1) 2 *(Canavan 13, Hooper 111 (pen))* 7321
Swansea C: Cornell; Rangel■, Painter, Britton, Tate, Monk■, Lopez (Idizaj), Morgan (Gower), Pintado■, Bond (Dobbie), Dyer.
Scunthorpe U: Murphy; Mirfin, Williams, Togwell (Hooper), Canavan, Spence, Sparrow, Wright J, Hayes, Forte (O'Connor), Woolford (Thompson).

Tranmere R (0) 0
Bolton W (1) 1 *(Davies M 41)*   5381
Tranmere R: Daniels; Cresswell, Edds, Mahon (Fraughan), Taylor, Goodison, McLaren, Shuker (Barnett), Gornell, Curran (Ricketts), Welsh.
Bolton W: Jaaskelainen; Ricketts, Samuel, Davis, Knight, Cahill, Davies M (Lee), Muamba (McCann), Elmander, Davies K, Taylor.

West Ham U (0) 3 *(Stanislas 87, 98 (pen), Hines 100)*
Millwall (1) 1 *(Harris 26)* 24,492
West Ham U: Green; Faubert, Spector, Parker, Gabbidon, Tomkins, Payne (Hines), Kovac (Nouble), Cole (Upson), Stanislas, Collison.
Millwall: Forde; Dunne, Barron, Laird, Smith, Frampton, Hackett, Fuseini, Alexander (Bolder), Harris (Grimes), Martin (Price).
aet.

Wolverhampton W (0) 0
Swindon T (0) 0 11,415
Wolverhampton W: Hahnemann; Hill, Elokobi (Edwards), David Jones, Collins, Berra, Zubar, Mendez-Laing (Jarvis), Vokes, Doyle (Keogh), Surman.
Swindon T: Lucas; Amankwaah, Kennedy, Douglas, Cuthbert, Greer, McGovern, Easton, Paynter (O'Brien), Obadeyi (Macklin), McNamee (Marshall).
aet; Wolverhampton W won 6-5 on penalties.

Wednesday, 26 August 2009

Blackpool (3) 4 *(Demontagnac 3, Burgess 19, Adam 33, Taylor-Fletcher 67)*
Wigan Ath (0) 1 *(Amaya 90)* 8089
Blackpool: Gilks; Eardley, Crainey, Demontagnac (Taylor-Fletcher), John-Baptiste, Edwards, Bangura (Southern), Clarke, Ormerod, Burgess (Euell), Adam.
Wigan Ath: Pollitt; Boyce, Edman, Watson, Amaya, Scharner, McCarthy (Rodallega), Diame (Thomas), King, Scotland, Sinclair.

Bristol C (0) 0
Carlisle U (0) 2 *(Dobie 61, Madine 77)* 6359
Bristol C: Gerken; Ribeiro, McAllister (Sproule), Skuse, Carey, Fontaine, Elliott, Johnson, Haynes (Blackman), Akinde, Williams (McCombe).
Carlisle U: Pidgeley; Raven, Harte, Thirlwell (Kavanagh), Livesey, Murphy, Hurst, Taiwo, Dobie (Madine), Anyinsah (Rothery), Robson.

Cardiff C (1) 3 *(Chopra 33, Whittingham 66, Magennis 86)*
Bristol R (0) 1 *(Elliott 75)* 9767
Cardiff C: Enckelman; Quinn, Burke (Wildig), Rae (Scimeca), Gerrard, Gyepes, Whittingham, McPhail, Etuhu (Magennis), Chopra, Capaldi.
Bristol R: Evans; Regan, Blizzard (Swallow), Campbell, Elliott, Anthony, Pipe (Reece), Lines, Duffy (Williams), Osei-Kuffour, Hughes.

Doncaster R (0) 1 *(Woods M 61 (pen))*
Tottenham H (3) 5 *(Huddlestone 9, O'Hara 11, Crouch 37, Bentley 52, Pavlyuchenko 69)* 12,923
Doncaster R: Smith; James, Roberts, Lockwood (Webster), Hird, Stock (Fortune), Oster (Fairhurst), Woods M, Hayter, Guy, Spicer.
Tottenham H: Cudicini (Button); Corluka, Naughton, Giovani, Bassong (Boateng), Huddlestone (Rose), Hutton, Bentley, Crouch, Pavlyuchenko, O'Hara.

Leyton Orient (0) 0
Stoke C (0) 1 *(Kitson 94)* 2742
Leyton Orient: Jones (Morris); Purches, Daniels, Chorley, Mkandawire, Smith, Melligan, Townsend (Pires), Patulea (Chambers), Jarvis, Demetriou.
Stoke C: Simonsen; Shotton (Griffin), Dickinson, Amdy Faye, Cort, Sonko (Davies), Pugh, Soares (Moult), Kitson, Cresswell, Tonge.
aet.

Newcastle U (1) 4 *(Guthrie 36, Geremi 48, Ameobi 64 (pen), Nolan 84)*
Huddersfield T (2) 3 *(Robinson 37, 39 (pen), Rhodes 47)* 23,815
Newcastle U: Krul; Simpson, Jose Enrique, Butt (Ameobi) (Vuckic), Kadar, Taylor R, Geremi, Guthrie, Ranger, LuaLua (Gutierrez), Nolan.
Huddersfield T: Smithies; Peltier (Berrett), Skarz, Kay, Clarke P, Butler, Pilkington, Collins, Drinkwater (Ainsworth), Rhodes (Simpson), Robinson.

WBA (1) 4 *(Beattie 10, 101, Dorrans 51, Cox 116)*
Rotherham U (1) 3 *(Cummins 29, Pope 52, 98)* 10,659
WBA: Kiely; Cummings, Cech (Mattock), Reid R (Mulumbu), Meite, Barnett, Borja Valero, Beattie, Bednar (Wood), Cox, Dorrans.
Rotherham U: Warrington; Tonge, Green, Harrison, Joseph, Fenton (Taylor R), Liddell (Ellison), Mills (Nichols), Pope, Law, Cummins.
aet.

Thursday, 27 August 2009

Crystal Palace (0) 0
Manchester C (0) 2 *(Wright-Phillips 50, Tevez 71)* 14,725
Crystal Palace: Speroni; Clyne, Hill, Derry, McCarthy, Fonte, Ambrose (Scannell), Danns, Moses (Carle), Sears (Smith), N'Diaye.
Manchester C: Given; Richards, Bridge, Barry, Toure, Lescott, Wright-Phillips, Ireland, Adebayor, Robinho (Bellamy), Tevez (De Jong).

THIRD ROUND

Tuesday, 22 September 2009

Arsenal (0) 2 *(Watt 68, Vela 76)*
WBA (0) 0 56,592
Arsenal: Szczesny; Gilbert, Gibbs, Traore (Barazite), Senderos, Silvestre, Wilshere, Ramsey, Sunu (Randall), Watt, Coquelin (Vela).
WBA: Kiely; Zuiverloon, Thomas, Barnett, Jara, Olsson (Meite), Teixeira, Koren, Moore (Wood), Cox (Mulumbu), Dorrans.

Barnsley (2) 3 *(Macken 22, Anderson 45, Colace 75)*
Burnley (1) 2 *(Fletcher 21, Eagles 52)* 6270
Barnsley: Preece; Kozluk, Butterfield, Gray J, Moore (Thompson), Foster, Colace, Anderson, Hume, Macken, Hammill.
Burnley: Jensen (Penny); Eckersley (Duff), Kalvenes, Gudjonsson, Carlisle, Bikey, Guerrero, McDonald, Fletcher, Paterson (Rodriguez), Eagles.

Bolton W (0) 3 *(Davies K 86, Cahill 96, Elmander 119)*
West Ham U (0) 1 *(Ilunga 59)* 8050
Bolton W: Jaaskelainen; Ricketts, Samuel, McCann (Cohen), Knight, Cahill, Gardner (Lee), Muamba, Klasnic (Elmander), Davies K, Taylor.
West Ham U: Green; Spector, Ilunga, Kovac, Da Costa (Ngala), Tomkins, Noble, Parker, Hines (Faubert), Diamanti, Dyer (Cole).
aet.

Carlisle U (1) 1 *(Harte 3 (pen))*
Portsmouth (2) 3 *(Dindane 26, Webber 33, Vanden Borre 63)* 7042
Carlisle U: Pidgeley; Raven, Harte, Thirlwell, Livesey (Keogh), Murphy (Bridge-Wilkinson), Hurst, Anyinsah, Offiong, Taiwo (Dobie), Robson.
Portsmouth: Begovic; Vanden Borre, Belhadj, Mullins, Kaboul, Mokoena, Utaka, Basinas, Webber (Piquionne), Dindane (Kanu), Yebda (Brown).

Leeds U (0) 0
Liverpool (0) 1 *(Ngog 66)* 38,168
Leeds U: Higgs; Crowe, Hughes (Kilkenny), Doyle (Showunmi), Michalik, Kisnorbo, Johnson, Howson, Beckford, Becchio (Grella), Snodgrass.
Liverpool: Cavalieri; Kyrgiakos, Dossena, Fabio Aurelio, Carragher, Degen (Johnson), Spearing, Mascherano, Ngog (Gerrard), Babel (Skrtel), Riera.

Nottingham F (0) 0
Blackburn R (1) 1 *(McCarthy 37)* 11,553
Nottingham F: Smith; Gunter, Cohen, Wilson, Morgan, Lynch, Tyson, McKenna (Anderson), Earnshaw, Blackstock (Adebola), Garner (McGugan).
Blackburn R: Brown; Reid (Andrews), Salgado (Jacobsen), Jones, Nelsen, Olsson, Emerton, N'Zonzi, Kalinic, McCarthy (Chimbonda), Hoilett.

Peterborough U (2) 2 *(Mackail-Smith 20, Williams 31)*

Newcastle U (0) 0   10,298

Peterborough U: Lewis; Martin, Williams, Diagouraga, Morgan, Zakuani, Frecklington (Keates), Coutts (Batt), Mackail-Smith (Whelpdale), McLean, Boyd.
Newcastle U: Krul; Taylor R, Tavernier, LuaLua (Smith), Tozer, Taylor S, Guthrie■, Donaldson (Nolan), Ranger, Vuckic (Geremi), Lovenkrands.

Scunthorpe U (0) 2 *(Hayes 92, McCann 95)*

Port Vale (0) 0   3383

Scunthorpe U: Murphy (Slocombe); Canavan, Williams, Wright J, Spence, Mirfin, O'Connor (Togwell), McCann, Hayes (Woolford), Forte, Sparrow.
Port Vale: Martin; Stockley (Yates), Taylor K, Collins, McCombe, Owen, Griffith, Loft (Richman), Richards, Haldane (Taylor R), Fraser.
aet.

Stoke C (0) 4 *(Higginbotham 75, Etherington 78, Fuller 80, Griffin 90)*

Blackpool (1) 3 *(Vaughan 40, Clarke 47, Burgess 81)*
                                                         13,957

Stoke C: Simonsen; Wilkinson, Higginbotham, Griffin, Cort, Pugh, Lawrence, Soares (Fuller), Beattie (Etherington), Tuncay, Arismendi (Tonge).
Blackpool: Gilks; Bangura, John Baptiste, Eastham (Eardley), Edwards, Martin, Adam, Emmanuel-Thomas (Bouazza), Burgess, Clarke, Vaughan.

Sunderland (2) 2 *(Henderson 4, Campbell 23)*

Birmingham C (0) 0   20,576

Sunderland: Gordon; Reid, Mensah, Cana (Nosworthy), Turner, Da Silva, Malbranque (Healy D), Henderson, Campbell, Jones (Murphy), Richardson.
Birmingham C: Maik Taylor; Espinoza, Parnaby (Preston), Ferguson (Bowyer), Dann, Ridgewell, O'Shea (Fahey), Sammons, Phillips, O'Connor, McSheffrey.

Wednesday, 23 September 2009

Aston Villa (1) 1 *(Agbonlahor 3)*

Cardiff C (0) 0   22,527

Aston Villa: Guzan; Beye, Shorey, Delph, Cuellar, James M Collins, Milner, Petrov, Agbonlahor, Carew, Gardner (Albrighton).
Cardiff C: Enckelman; Matthews, Capaldi, Rae (Wildig), Gerrard, Gyepes, Burke, Scimeca (Chopra), Bothroyd, Whittingham, Ledley.

Chelsea (0) 1 *(Kalou 52)*

QPR (0) 0   37,781

Chelsea: Hilario; Belletti, Hutchinson (Terry), Mikel, Ivanovic, Paulo Ferreira, Zhirkov (Cole A), Cole J, Borini, Kalou, Malouda (Lampard).
QPR: Heaton; Borrowdale, Rowlands (Ephraim), Buzsaky, Stewart, Gorkss, Routledge, Faurlin, Simpson (Pellicori), Vine (Taarabt), Leigertwood.

Hull C (0) 0

Everton (3) 4 *(Yakubu 11, Jo 20, Gosling 24, Osman 57)*
                                                         13,558

Hull C: Duke; Mendy, Halmosi, Boateng (Marney), Cooper, Zayatte, Ghilas, Barmby (Kilbane), Cairney, Vennegoor, Featherstone (McShane).
Everton: Howard; Heitinga, Baines (Neill), Bilyaletdinov (Agard), Distin, Hibbert, Gosling, Osman, Jo, Yakubu (Fellaini), Rodwell.

Manchester C (0) 2 *(Barry 52, Toure 111)*

Fulham (1) 1 *(Gera 34)*   24,507

Manchester C: Given; Zabaleta, Bridge, Barry, Lescott, Toure, Wright-Phillips, De Jong (Weiss), Bellamy, Tevez, Ireland (Petrov).
Fulham: Stockdale; Baird, Kelly, Davies (Dikgacoi), Stoor, Smalling, Seol, Greening, Gera (Anderson), Johnson E (Elm), Riise.
aet.

Manchester U (0) 1 *(Welbeck 66)*

Wolverhampton W (0) 0   51,160

Manchester U: Kuszczak; Neville, Fabio■, Carrick, Brown, Evans J, Gibson, Owen (Valencia), Welbeck (King), Macheda (De Laet), Nani.
Wolverhampton W: Hahnemann; Foley, Elokobi, David Jones, Craddock, Berra, Kightly (Keogh), Henry, Ebanks-Blake (Doyle), Maierhofer, Castillo (Milijas).

Preston NE (0) 1 *(Brown 83)*

Tottenham H (2) 5 *(Crouch 14, 77, 90, Defoe 37, Keane 87)*   16,533

Preston NE: Lonergan; Jones, Hart (Chaplow), Nolan, Chilvers, Mawene, Carter, Sumulikoski, Parkin (Mellor), Elliott (Brown), Wallace.
Tottenham H: Gomes; Hutton, Bale, Palacios, Dawson (Corluka), Huddlestone, Bentley, Jenas, Crouch, Defoe (Keane), Giovani (Lennon).

FOURTH ROUND

Tuesday, 27 October 2009

Barnsley (0) 0

Manchester U (1) 2 *(Welbeck 6, Owen 59)*   20,019

Barnsley: Steele; Kozluk, Hammill, Hallfredsson, Moore, Foster, Gray J, Anderson (Campbell-Ryce), Bogdanovich, Macken (Hume), Colace (Butterfield).
Manchester U: Foster; Neville■, Fabio, Anderson, Brown, Evans J, Rafael, Obertan, Owen (De Laet), Welbeck (Tosic), Macheda.

Blackburn R (2) 5 *(Pedersen 4, Reid 45 (pen), Salgado 57, McCarthy 72, Kalinic 74 (pen))*

Peterborough U (1) 2 *(Whelpdale 17, Boyd 50)*   8419

Blackburn R: Brown; Salgado, Givet (Nelsen), Jones, Olsson, Reid (Dunn), Emerton, Hoilett, Kalinic, McCarthy, Pedersen.
Peterborough U: Lewis■; Batt (McKeown), Lee (Martin), Diagouraga, Morgan, Pearce, Whelpdale, Frecklington, Boyd, McLean, Rowe (Day).

Portsmouth (1) 4 *(Piquionne 17, 59, Webber 55, Kanu 81)*

Stoke C (0) 0   11,251

Portsmouth: Ashdown; Vanden Borre, Belhadj, Mullins, Kaboul, Wilson, Yebda (Mokoena), Brown, Piquionne, Dindane (Hughes), Webber (Kanu).
Stoke C: Simonsen; Griffin, Higginbotham, Whelan, Cort, Tonge, Lawrence (Soares), Pugh, Kitson (Sidibe), Tuncay (Moult), Arismendi.

Sunderland (0) 0

Aston Villa (0) 0   27,666

Sunderland: Gordon; Da Silva, McCartney (Ferdinand), Cana, Nosworthy, Turner, Murphy (Reid), Henderson, Campbell (Malbranque), Jones, Richardson.
Aston Villa: Guzan; Cuellar, Warnock, Reo-Coker (Delph), Dunne, James M Collins, Milner, Petrov (Sidwell), Agbonlahor, Heskey (Carew), Young A.
aet; Aston Villa won 3-1 on penalties.

Tottenham H (1) 2 *(Huddlestone 31, Keane 57)*

Everton (0) 0   35,843

Tottenham H: Gomes; Hutton, Assou-Ekotto, Palacios, Bassong, Dawson, Bentley, Huddlestone, Pavlyuchenko, Keane, Bale.
Everton: Howard; Heitinga, Hibbert, Rodwell, Neill, Distin, Gosling, Fellaini, Yakubu, Saha (Jo), Cahill.

Wednesday, 28 October 2009

Arsenal (1) 2 *(Merida 19, Bendtner 50)*

Liverpool (1) 1 *(Insua 26)*   60,004

Arsenal: Fabianski; Gilbert, Gibbs, Eastmond (Randall), Senderos, Silvestre, Merida (Coquelin), Ramsey, Eduardo, Bendtner (Watt), Nasri.
Liverpool: Cavalieri; Kyrgiakos, Insua, Plessis (Aquilani), Degen (Eccleston), Skrtel, Spearing, Voronin, N'Gog (Benayoun), Kuyt, Babel.

Chelsea (2) 4 *(Kalou 15, Malouda 26, Deco 67, Drogba 89)*
Bolton W (0) 0 41,538
Chelsea: Hilario (Turnbull); Belletti, Ivanovic, Deco, Alex, Paulo Ferreira, Ballack, Cole J, Sturridge (Drogba), Kalou (Essien), Malouda.
Bolton W: Al Habsi; Steinsson (Elmander), Samuel, Muamba, Knight, Cahill, Gardner, Ricketts, Klasnic, Taylor (Basham), Davies M.

Manchester C (2) 5 *(Ireland 3, Santa Cruz R 38, Lescott 56, Tevez 71, Johnson M 77)*
Scunthorpe U (1) 1 *(Forte 26)* 36,358
Manchester C: Given; Zabaleta, Sylvinho, Barry (Johnson M), Lescott, Kompany, Wright-Phillips, De Jong, Santa Cruz R, Tevez (Mwaruwari), Ireland (Weiss).
Scunthorpe U: Murphy; Byrne, Williams, Wright J, Mirfin, Jones (Canavan), O'Connor (Hooper), McCann (Togwell), Hayes, Forte, Woolford.

QUARTER-FINALS

Tuesday, 1 December 2009
Manchester U (2) 2 *(Gibson 16, 38)*
Tottenham H (0) 0 57,212
Manchester U: Kuszczak; Neville, De Laet, Anderson (Tosic), Brown, Vidic, Gibson, Obertan (Carrick), Berbatov (Macheda), Welbeck, Park.
Tottenham H: Gomes; Hutton, Bale, Palacios (Huddlestone), Bassong, Dawson, Lennon, Jenas, Keane (Crouch), Defoe, Bentley.

Portsmouth (1) 2 *(Petrov 10 (og), Kanu 87)*
Aston Villa (2) 4 *(Heskey 12, Milner 27, Downing 74, Young A 89)* 17,034
Portsmouth: Begovic; Vanden Borre, Kaboul, Hughes (Wilson), Ben-Haim, Hreidarsson, Yebda, Brown, Webber (Kanu 65), Utaka (Piquionne), Belhadj.
Aston Villa: Guzan; Young L, Warnock, Cuellar, Dunne, Downing, Milner, Petrov, Agbonlahor, Heskey (Delfouneso), Young A.

Wednesday, 2 December 2009
Blackburn R (1) 3 *(Kalinic 9, Emerton 64, McCarthy 93 (pen))*
Chelsea (0) 3 *(Drogba 48, Kalou 52, Paulo Ferreira 120)* 18,136
Blackburn R: Robinson; Salgado, Chimbonda, N'Zonzi (Van Heerden), Nelsen, Samba, Emerton, Kalinic, Roberts (Hoilett), McCarthy, Pedersen (Grella).
Chelsea: Hilario; Belletti (Drogba), Zhirkov, Mikel, Ivanovic, Paulo Ferreira, Ballack, Deco (Bruma), Kalou, Cole J (Kakuta), Malouda.
aet; Blackburn R won 4-3 on penalties.

Manchester C (0) 3 *(Tevez 50, Wright-Phillips 69, Weiss 89)*
Arsenal (0) 0 46,015
Manchester C: Given; Richards, Bridge, Barry, Toure, Lescott, Wright-Phillips (Weiss), Ireland, Adebayor, Tevez (Kompany), Bellamy.
Arsenal: Fabianski; Eboue, Traore, Ramsey, Song Billong, Silvestre, Eastmond (Watt), Merida, Vela, Wilshere, Rosicky.

SEMI-FINALS FIRST LEG

Thursday, 14 January 2010
Blackburn R (0) 0
Aston Villa (1) 1 *(Milner 23)* 18,595
Blackburn R: Robinson; Jacobsen (Olsson), Chimbonda, N'Zonzi, Nelsen, Samba, Salgado (Reid), Emerton, Kalinic, Dunne, Pedersen (McCarthy).
Aston Villa: Guzan; Cuellar, Warnock, Collins JM, Dunne, Downing, Milner, Petrov, Agbonlahor, Heskey (Sidwell), Young A.

Tuesday, 19 January 2010
Manchester C (1) 2 *(Tevez 42 (pen), 65)*
Manchester U (1) 1 *(Giggs 17)* 46,067
Manchester C: Given; Zabaleta, Garrido, Barry, Richards, Kompany, Wright-Phillips (Sylvinho), De Jong, Bellamy, Tevez (Mwaruwari), Boyata (Onuoha).
Manchester U: Van der Sar; Rafael (Diouf), Evra, Carrick, Brown, Evans J, Valencia (Scholes), Anderson (Owen), Fletcher, Rooney, Giggs.

SEMI-FINALS SECOND LEG

Wednesday, 20 January 2010
Aston Villa (1) 6 *(Warnock 30, Milner 40 (pen), N'Zonzi 53 (og), Agbonlahor 58, Heskey 62, Young A 90)*
Blackburn R (2) 4 *(Kalinic 10, 26, Olsson 63, Emerton 84)* 40,406
Aston Villa: Guzan; Cuellar, Warnock, James M Collins, Dunne, Downing (Sidwell), Milner, Petrov, Agbonlahor, Heskey, Young A.
Blackburn R: Robinson; Chimbonda, Givet, N'Zonzi (Reid), Nelsen, Samba, Emerton, Dunn (McCarthy), Kalinic (Di Santo), Pedersen, Olsson.

Wednesday, 27 January 2010
Manchester U (0) 3 *(Scholes 52, Carrick 71, Rooney 90)*
Manchester C (0) 1 *(Tevez 76)* 74,576
Manchester U: Van der Sar; Rafael (Brown), Evra, Carrick, Ferdinand, Evans J, Fletcher, Scholes, Giggs, Rooney, Nani (Valencia).
Manchester C: Given; Richards, Garrido (Ireland), Barry, Boyata, Kompany, Zabaleta, De Jong, Bellamy, Tevez, Wright-Phillips (Adebayor).

CARLING CUP FINAL

Sunday, 28 February 2010

Aston Villa (1) 1   Manchester U (1) 2

(at Wembley Stadium, attendance 88,596)

Aston Villa: Friedel; Cuellar (Carew), Warnock, Collins JM, Dunne, Downing, Milner, Petrov, Agbonlahor, Heskey, Young A.
Scorer: Milner 5 (pen).

Manchester U: Kuszczak; Rafael (Neville), Evra, Carrick, Evans J, Vidic, Valencia, Fletcher, Berbatov, Owen (Rooney), Park (Gibson).
Scorers: Owen 12, Rooney 74.

Referee: P. Dowd (Staffordshire).

JOHNSTONE'S PAINT TROPHY 2009–10

■ *Denotes player sent off.*

NORTHERN SECTION FIRST ROUND
Tuesday, 1 September 2009

Burton Alb (0) 1 *(McGrath 46)*
Chesterfield (1) 5 *(Small 17, 62, Talbot 38, 90, Lowry 87)*
1493

Burton Alb: Krysiak; Austin, Boertien, James (Corbett), Branston, McGrath, Maghoma, Penn, Walker (Phillips), Harrad, Goodfellow (Pearson).
Chesterfield: Lee; Gray, Robertson, Niven (Harsley), Austin (Page), Breckin, Lowry, Allott, Lester (McDermott), Talbot, Small.

Crewe Alex (0) 1 *(Zola 90)*
Stockport Co (3) 4 *(Baker 8, 33, 90, Bignall 41)* 2331
Crewe Alex: Legzdins; Brayford, Jones, Schumacher, Ada, Worley, Verma (Elding), Mitchel-King (Walton), Moore (Miller), Zola, Grant.
Stockport Co: Rigby; Halls (Thompson P), Rose, Turnbull (Tansey), Havern, Mullins, Vincent, Bridcutt, Bignall (Pilkington), Baker, Poole.

Darlington (1) 1 *(Thorpe 27)*
Lincoln C (0) 0 828
Darlington: Knight; Arnison, Bower, Chandler, Plummer, Miller, Smith G, Convery (Bains), Gall (Smith J), Thorpe, Porritt (Dowson).
Lincoln C: Burch; Hughton, Brown, Hone, Swaibu, Kerr, Clarke S, Hutchinson, Howe (Fagan), Connor, Clucas (John-Lewis).

Morecambe (1) 2 *(Hunter 3, Curtis 56)*
Carlisle U (0) 2 *(Kavanagh 48, 90)* 2016
Morecambe: Roche (Davies); Moss (Parrish), Wilson (McStay), Artell, Bentley, Stanley, Wainwright, Hunter, Twiss, Curtis, Duffy.
Carlisle U: Collin; Kane, Horwood, Burns (Harte), Raven, Murphy, Hurst, Kavanagh, Madine, Offiong (Anyinsah), Robson (Rothery).
Carlisle U won 4-2 on penalties.

Oldham Ath (1) 1 *(Whitaker 10)*
Accrington S (0) 2 *(Gregan 60 (og), Edwards 67)* 1619
Oldham Ath: Brill; Holdsworth (Rowney), Sheehan, Furman, Gregan, Hazell, Lee (Bembo-Leta), Marrow, Blackman (Brooke), Abbott, Whitaker.
Accrington S: Dunbavin; Edwards, King G (Richardson), Proctor, Kempson, Lees, Joyce (Ryan) (Murphy), Turner, Grant, Symes, Miles.

Rochdale (0) 1 *(Dawson 59)*
Bradford C (0) 2 *(Flynn 74, Neilson 79)* 1800
Rochdale: Arthur; Flynn (Wiseman), Kennedy T, Flitcroft (Brown), Holness, Dawson, Buckley (Spencer), Kennedy J, Dagnall, Thompson, Rundle.
Bradford C: Eastwood; Bateson, O'Brien L, Flynn, Ramsden, Williams, Neilson, Bullock, Evans, Thorne (Hanson), Brandon (Osborne).

Rotherham U (1) 1 *(Le Fondre 35)*
Huddersfield T (2) 2 *(Clarke P 2, Simpson 7)* 2246
Rotherham U: Warrington; Tonge, Green, Harrison, Joseph, Sharps, Liddell (Taylor R), Cummins (Taylor J), Ellison (Broughton), Le Fondre, Law.
Huddersfield T: Smithies; Peltier, Skarz, Collins, Clarke P, Clarke N, Ainsworth, Goodwin, Novak, Simpson, Pilkington.

Walsall (0) 0
Bury (0) 0 2314
Walsall: Gilmartin; Westlake, Vincent (Jones), Taundry, Smith, McDonald, Till (Parkin), Mattis, Deeney, Byfield (Nicholls), Richards.
Bury: Brown; Scott, Newey, Dawson, Futcher, Sodje, Worrall (Baker), Barry-Murphy, Robertson (Rouse), Bishop, Johnson (Lowe).
Bury won 5-4 on penalties.

SOUTHERN SECTION FIRST ROUND
Tuesday, 1 September 2009

Barnet (1) 2 *(Hyde J 2, Yakubu 65)*
Millwall (0) 0 1623
Barnet: Cole; Devera, Deen, Hughes, Yakubu, Kamdjo, Adomah (Jarrett), Deverdics, O'Flynn (Charles), Hyde J, Bolasie (Hart).
Millwall: Sullivan; Smith, Friend, Abdou, Robinson (Laird), Frampton, Dunne, Fuseini (Bolder), Price (Grimes), Alexander, Martin.

Bournemouth (1) 2 *(Pitman 45, Connell 66)*
Yeovil T (0) 1 *(Obika 87)* 2655
Bournemouth: Jalal; Bradbury, Cummings, Robinson (Molesley), Guyett, Garry, Igoe, Bartley (Webb), Pitman (Tindall), Connell, Feeney.
Yeovil T: Martin; Hutchins, Smith, Murtagh, Stam, Forbes, Murray (Lindegaard), O'Callaghan, Williams S, Tomlin (Obika), Welsh (McCollin).

Cheltenham T (0) 1 *(Low 55)*
Torquay U (3) 3 *(Stevens 6, 45, Benyon 31)* 1397
Cheltenham T: Brown SP; Diallo (Haynes), Tabor, Bird, Gallinagh, Townsend, Watkins (Hayles), Artus, Richards, Denton (Alsop), Low.
Torquay U: Bevan; Robertson, Nicholson, Thompson, Todd, Charnock, Carlisle, Wroe, Benyon (Rendell), Sills, Stevens (Hodges).

Gillingham (0) 1 *(Jackson 77 (pen))*
Colchester U (0) 1 *(Platt 84)* 1725
Gillingham: Julian; Fuller, Palmer, Jackman (Jackson), Richards, Gowling, Rooney (Maher), Barcham, Erskine (Weston), McCammon, Miller.
Colchester U: Cousins; Okuonghae, Lockwood, Fox, White, Heath, Vincent (Thomas), Izzet (Wordsworth), Platt, Vernon, Hackney (Perkins).
Gillingham won 4-3 on penalties.

Hereford U (0) 0
Bristol R (0) 0 970
Hereford U: Bartlett; Rose, Valentine, Dennehy (Lowe), Jones D, Lunt, Pugh, Tolley, Morris (Done), Jackson, Plummer (Southam).
Bristol R: Evans; Regan, Lescott, Campbell, Elliott, Blizzard, Pipe, Lines, Duffy, Swallow (Reece), Hughes.
Hereford U won 4-2 on penalties.

Milton Keynes D (0) 3 *(Lewington 55, Easter 58, 67)*
Dagenham & R (0) 1 *(Scott 90)* 4413
Milton Keynes D: Gueret; Doumbe, Lewington, Woodards (Swailes), Davis, Carrington (Gleeson), Partridge, Johnson, Ibehre, Easter (Leven), Puncheon.
Dagenham & R: Roberts; Ogogo, Griffiths, Arber, Antwi, Kilbey, Nurse (Green), Gain, Benson (Scott), Montgomery, Thomas.

Norwich C (1) 1 *(Martin C 30)*
Brentford (0) 0 12,540
Norwich C: Alnwick; Spillane, Lappin, Russell, Berthel Askou, Nelson, Whaley (Daley), Adeyemi, Martin C, Maric (McDonald), Hughes.
Brentford: Price; Foster, O'Connor, Bean, Osborne, Legge, Taylor, Hunt, Kabba, Saunders (Wood), Weston.

Wycombe W (0) 2 *(Pittman 62 (pen), 90)*
Northampton T (1) 2 *(Gilligan 40 (pen), Guinan 86)* 1035
Wycombe W: Young; Montrose, Woodman (Cobb), Pack, Johnson, Westwood, Westlake, Beavon (Chambers), Pittman, Smith, Phillips (Spence).
Northampton T: Dunn; Hinton, Threlfall, Gilligan, Beckwith, McCready, Osman, Boden (Benjamin), Mulligan (Guinan), Marshall (Dyer), Holt.
Northampton T won 3-0 on penalties.

NORTHERN SECTION SECOND ROUND

Tuesday, 6 October 2009

Bradford C (1) 2 *(Boulding M 20, Brandon 90)*
Notts Co (1) 2 *(Westcarr 10, Facey 85)*   3701
Bradford C: Eastwood; Bateson, O'Brien L, Flynn (Sharry), Ramsden, Clarke, Brandon. Osborne, Boulding M, Neilson (Thorne), O'Brien J.
Notts Co: Schmeichel; Lee■, Jones, Clapham, Edwards, Thompson, Ravenhill, Bishop, Facey, Hawley (Ritchie), Westcarr.
Bradford C won 3-2 on penalties.

Bury (0) 2 *(Worrall 54, Jones 81)*
Tranmere R (1) 1 *(Curran 4)*   1903
Bury: Brown; Buchanan, Newey, Dawson, Futcher, Cresswell, Worrall, Racchi, Jones, Elliott, Baker (Barry-Murphy).
Tranmere R: Daniels; Edds, Taylor, Mahon, Goodison, Cresswell, Carole (Fraughan), Barnett, Bain (Thomas-Moore), Curran, Welsh.

Carlisle U (0) 4 *(Robson 64, Dobie 68, 80, Bridge-Wilkinson 78)*
Macclesfield T (1) 2 *(Brisley 45, Rooney 85)*   1753
Carlisle U: Collin; Raven (Horwood), Harte, Kavanagh, Keogh, Murphy, Rothery (Dobie), Taiwo, Offiong (Anyinsah), Bridge-Wilkinson, Robson.
Macclesfield T: Brain; Reid I, Reed, Brisley, Bollard, Bencherif, Brown, Daniel, Tipton (Rooney), Sappleton, Sinclair.

Chesterfield (0) 3 *(Talbot 57, 74, Bowery 88)*
Huddersfield T (0) 3 *(Pilkington 65, 89, Clarke N 90)*   3003
Chesterfield: Lee; Little, Robertson (Picken), Niven (Gray), Page, Breckin, Lowry, Allott, Lester, Talbot (Bowery), McDermott.
Huddersfield T: Smithies; Goodwin, Skarz (Williams), Collins (Ainsworth), Butler, Clarke N, Pilkington, Kay, Rhodes, Berrett, Roberts (Novak).
Chesterfield won 4-2 on penalties.

Hartlepool U (0) 0
Grimsby T (2) 2 *(Sweeney 6, Proudlock 34)*   1675
Hartlepool U: Flinders; Austin, Haslam, McSweeney (Boyd), Collins, Liddle, Monkhouse, Rowell, Larkin, Bjornsson (Behan), Humphreys.
Grimsby T: Colgan; Fuller (Akpa Akpro), Widdowson, Sweeney, Atkinson, Bennett, Boshell■, Wood, Jarman (Clarke), Proudlock (Leary), Forbes.

Leeds U (2) 2 *(Robinson 25, Kandol 28)*
Darlington (1) 1 *(Convery 45)*   8429
Leeds U: Ankergren; Naylor, Hughes (Johnson), Kilkenny, Bromby, Michalik, Prutton, White, Kandol (Showunmi), Grella (Somma), Robinson.
Darlington: Liversedge■; Arnison, Devitt, Groves (Bennett), Miller, Foster, Smith G, Plummer (Convery), Gall, Barnes (Main), Smith J.

Port Vale (3) 3 *(Haldane 4, Dodds 7, Richards 13)*
Stockport Co (1) 1 *(Bridcutt 22)*   3154
Port Vale: Martin; Stockley, Taylor K, Collins, McCombe, Owen, Griffith, Haldane, Richards (Guy), Dodds (Howland) (Lawrie), Fraser.
Stockport Co: Gerrard; Rose, Havern, Mullins, Rayres, Bridcutt (Vincent), Pilkington (Tansey), Turnbull, Thompson P, Baker, Griffin (Poole).

Tuesday, 20 October 2009

Accrington S (0) 2 *(King G 47, Winnard 52)*
Shrewsbury T (0) 0   819
Accrington S: Martin; Winnard, Lees, Proctor, Edwards, Murphy, King G, Ryan, Grant, Kee (Joyce), Symes.
Shrewsbury T: Neal C; Hooman, Cansdell-Sherriff, Neal L, Coughlan, Langmead, Leslie (Simpson), Labadie (Richards), Elder, Bright (Gray), McIntyre.

SOUTHERN SECTION SECOND ROUND

Tuesday, 6 October 2009

Charlton Ath (2) 4 *(McLeod 15, Tuna 40, Bailey 75, Wagstaff 87)*
Barnet (1) 1 *(O'Flynn 11)*   4522
Charlton Ath: Elliot; Solly (Mambo), Youga, Racon (Stavrinou), Dailly, Basey, Wagstaff, Bailey, Tuna (Shelvey), McLeod, Spring.
Barnet: Cole; Devera, Gillet, Hyde M, Yakubu, Leach, Jarrett, Bolasie (Hart), O'Flynn (Charles), Hyde J, Hughes (Tabiri).

Exeter C (0) 1 *(Fleetwood 90)*
Swindon T (1) 1 *(McNamee 17)*   2006
Exeter C: Marriott; Tully (Saunders), Seaborne, Sercombe, Dunne (Fleetwood), Archibald-Henville, Taylor M, Cozic, Stansfield, Logan, Corr (Golbourne).
Swindon T: Smith; Amankwaah, Lescinel, Douglas, Cuthbert, Greer, McGovern, Timlin, Revell (Peacock), Hutchinson (Austin), McNamee.
Swindon T won 4-3 on penalties.

Gillingham (0) 0
Norwich C (0) 1 *(McDonald 66)*   2814
Gillingham: Julian; Palmer, Nutter Weston, Richards, Bentley, Payne (Lewis), Rooney, Barcham, McCammon (Yussuff), Miller (Erskine).
Norwich C: Forster; Francomb, Wiggins, Hughes, Berthel Askou, Doherty (Stephens), McVeigh (Dawkin), Adeyemi, Martin C (McDonald), Cureton, Daley.

Hereford U (1) 2 *(Walker 42, Manset 89)*
Aldershot T (1) 1 *(Hudson 15, Soares 90)*   897
Hereford U: Bartlett; Gwynne, Rose, Green, Jones D, Lunt, Marshall, King C, Walker (Sonko), Constantine (Manset), Pugh.
Aldershot T: Jaimez-Ruiz; Herd, Straker, Chalmers, Hinshelwood (Winfield), Blackburn, Soares, Hylton, German (Connolly), Donnelly (Hopkinson), Hudson.
Hereford U won 4-3 on penalties.

Leyton Orient (0) 1 *(Patulea 89)*
Brighton & HA (0) 0   1457
Leyton Orient: Jones; Cave-Brown, Daniels, Ashworth, Mkandawire, Smith, Baker (Townsend), Pires, Patulea, Jarvis (Scowcroft), Demetriou.
Brighton & HA: Smith G; Virgo (Tunnicliffe), McNulty (Livermore), Thornhill, Elphick, Wright J, Cox, Navarro, Hart, Murray, Davies A (McLeod).

Milton Keynes D (2) 2 *(Doran 18, Carrington 45)*
Southend U (0) 0   4792
Milton Keynes D: Gueret; Howell, Lewington, Leven (Gobern L), Swailes, McCracken, Doran (Morgan), Carrington, Easter (Baldock S), Wilbraham, Johnson.
Southend U: Mildenhall; Francis Herd, Christophe, Sankofa, Barrett, Sawyer, O'Donovan, Barnard (Freedman), Laurent, Moussa (O'Keefe).

Northampton T (0) 2 *(Guinan 66, Gilligan 90 (pen))*
Bournemouth (1) 1 *(Hollands 33)*   1718
Northampton T: Dunn; Rodgers, Jacobs, Johnson, Hinton, McCready, Gilligan, Dyer (Osman), Mulligan (McKay), Guinan, Marshall (Herbert).
Bournemouth: Thomas; Robinson, Cummings (Stockley), Hollands, Garry, Bartley, McQuoid (Webb), Tindall (Ings), Bradbury, Connell, Edgar.

Southampton (0) 2 *(Papa Waigo 59, 69)*
Torquay U (2) 2 *(Sills 21, Wroe 42 (pen))*   9319
Southampton: Davis; James, Harding, Hammond, Thomas, Perry, Antonio (Mills), Wotton, Lambert, Papa Waigo, Gillett (Saganowski).
Torquay U: Bevan; Mansell, Nicholson, Charnock (Carlisle), Robertson, Ellis, Thompson, Wroe, Benyon, Sills, Rendell (Stevens).
Southampton won 5-3 on penalties.

NORTHERN SECTION QUARTER-FINALS

Tuesday, 10 November 2009

Accrington S (2) 3 *(Symes 2, 40, Grant 82)*
Bury (1) 2 *(Racchi 41, Jones 48)*　　　1637

Accrington S: Dunbavin; Winnard, Lees, Proctor, Kempson, Edwards, Ryan, Joyce, Grant, Symes, Miles.
Bury: Belford; Scott, Newey, Dawson, Cresswell, Futcher, Racchi, Barry-Murphy (Baker), Lowe (Morrell), Jones, Buchanan.

Bradford C (0) 2 *(Flynn 49, Hanson 70)*
Port Vale (1) 2 *(McCombe 27, Taylor R 75)*　　5096

Bradford C: Eastwood; Bateson, O'Brien L, Flynn, Rehman, Clarke, Sharry (Brandon), Williams, Boulding M (O'Brien J), Hanson, Neilson.
Port Vale: Martin; Yates, Taylor K, Collins, McCombe, Owen (Richards), Jarrett (Griffith), Guy (Haldane), Taylor R, Dodds, Fraser.
Bradford C won 5-4 on penalties.

Chesterfield (1) 1 *(Currie 45 (pen))*
Carlisle U (0) 3 *(Robson 62, Murphy 69, Clayton 78)*　2878

Chesterfield: Lee; Picken, Robertson (Currie), Niven (Bowery), Page, Breckin, Austin, Allott, Lester, Talbot (Gray), Boden.
Carlisle U: Collin; Keogh, Horwood, Taiwo, Livesey, Harte (Murphy), Hurst (Bridge-Wilkinson), Anyinsah, Clayton, Pericard (Offiong), Robson.

Leeds U (2) 3 *(Lancashire 40 (og), Kilkenny 45, Beckford 55)*
Grimsby T (0) 1 *(Sweeney 57)*　　　10,430

Leeds U: Ankergren; White, Hughes, Kilkenny, Michalik, Naylor, Gradel, Snodgrass (Robinson), Beckford, Vokes (Showunmi), Johnson (Prutton).
Grimsby T: Colgan; Bore, McCrory, Leary, Lancashire, Atkinson, Clarke (Wood), Sweeney, North (Akpa Akpro), Forbes (Conlon), Shahin.

SOUTHERN SECTION QUARTER-FINALS

Tuesday, 10 November 2009

Leyton Orient (0) 1 *(Demetriou 90)*
Hereford U (1) 1 *(Constantine 25)*　　　1282

Leyton Orient: Jones; Cave-Brown, Daniels, Chorley, Ashworth (Pires), Summerfield, Baker (Patulea), Scowcroft, Jarvis, Townsend (Thornton), Demetriou.
Hereford U: Bartlett; Green, Rose, Blanchett, Lowe, Lunt, Marshall (Tolley), Sonko, McCallum, Constantine (Godsmark), Done.
Hereford U won 3-2 on penalties.

Milton Keynes D (3) 3 *(Wilbraham 6, Baldock 16, 27 (pen))*
Northampton T (0) 1 *(Guinan 51)*　　　8886

Milton Keynes D: Gueret; Howell, Davis, Carrington, McCracken, Darren Powell (Ibehre), Gobern L (Easter), Chadwick (Leven), Baldock S, Wilbraham, Puncheon.
Northampton T: Dunn; Rodgers, Kanyuka (McCready), Guttridge, Hinton, Beckwith (Jacobs), Gilligan, Davis, Mulligan, Guinan (Akinfenwa), Holt.

Swindon (0) 0
Norwich C (0) 0　　　4978

Swindon T: Smith; Amankwaah, Lescinel, Douglas, Cuthbert, Greer, McGovern, Easton, Paynter, Revell (McNamee), Hutchinson (Austin).
Norwich C: Forster; Otsemobor (Dunic), Wiggins, Tudur-Jones, Nelson, Berthel Askou, McVeigh (Hughes), Adeyemi, Cureton, McDonald, Dawkin.
Norwich C won 5-3 on penalties.

Wednesday, 11 November 2009

Southampton (2) 2 *(Thomas 34, Lambert 63)*
Charlton Ath (0) 1 *(McKenzie 90)*　　　13,906

Southampton: Bialkowski; James, Harding, Hammond, Jaidi, Thomas, Antonio (Mellis), Schneiderlin (Trotman), Lambert, Connolly (Papa Waigo), Lallana.

Charlton Ath: Ikeme; Youga, Basey, Spring, Dailly, Llera, Wagstaff (McKenzie), Semedo (Burton), Sam (Holden), Mooney, Shelvey.

NORTHERN SECTION SEMI-FINALS

Tuesday, 15 December 2009

Carlisle U (1) 3 *(Keogh 44, Dobie 68, Robson 74)*
Bradford C (0) 0　　　3176

Carlisle U: Pidgeley; Keogh, Horwood, Murphy, Livesey (Aldred), Harte, Hurst, Taiwo (Dobie), Clayton, Pericard (Bridge-Wilkinson), Robson.
Bradford C: Eastwood; Ramsden[■], O'Brien L, Flynn (Brandon), Rehman, Clarke, Neilson (Daley), Bullock, Evans, Hanson, O'Brien J (Bateson).

Leeds U (1) 2 *(Ephraim 9, Kilkenny 50)*
Accrington S (0) 0　　　12,696

Leeds U: Martin; Crowe, Hughes, Kilkenny, Naylor, Michalik, Prutton, Ephraim, Kandol (Gradel), Grella (Vokes), Snodgrass (Kisnorbo).
Accrington S: Bouzanis; Murphy (Miles), Winnard, Proctor, Kempson, Edwards, Joyce, Ryan, Grant, Symes, Kee (McConville).

SOUTHERN SECTION SEMI-FINALS

Tuesday, 15 December 2009

Hereford U (0) 1 *(Constantine 63)*
Milton Keynes D (1) 4 *(Baldock 6, Puncheon 69, Wilbraham 78, Easter 83)*　　1367

Hereford U: Bartlett; Gwynne, Weir, Jones D, Lowe, Lunt, Pugh (Done), Mutch, King C (Manset), Constantine, McCallum (Godsmark).
Milton Keynes D: Gueret; Woodards, Lewington, Doumbe, McCracken, Quashie, Chadwick (Wilbraham), Gleeson (Leven), Baldock S (Gobern L), Easter, Puncheon.

Southampton (1) 2 *(Papa Waigo 14, Harding 90)*
Norwich C (1) 2 *(Doherty 33, Martin C 55)*　　15,453

Southampton: Bialkowski; James, Harding, Hammond, Perry (Thomas), Trotman, Mellis (Antonio), Schneiderlin (Wotton), Lambert, Lallana, Papa Waigo.
Norwich C: Forster; Martin R, Drury, Russell, Nelson, Doherty, Hoolahan (McDonald), Adeyemi (Otsemobor), Martin C, Holt, Lappin (Gill).
Southampton won 6-5 on penalties.

NORTHERN FINAL FIRST LEG

Tuesday, 19 January 2010

Leeds U (0) 1 *(Crowe 56)*
Carlisle U (1) 2 *(Kavanagh 21, Anyinsah 84)*　　13,011

Leeds U: Ankergren; Crowe, Hughes, Kilkenny, Naylor, Bromby, Johnson, Howson, Beckford, Grella (Becchio), Snodgrass.
Carlisle U: Pidgeley; Keogh, Horwood, Kavanagh (Bridge-Wilkinson), Livesey, Harte, Hurst, Taiwo, Clayton, Dobie (Anyinsah), Robson.

SOUTHERN FINAL FIRST LEG

Wednesday, 20 January 2010

Milton Keynes D (0) 0
Southampton (1) 1 *(Antonio 26)*　　　7918

Milton Keynes D: Gueret; Woodards, Lewington, Doumbe, McCracken, Leven (Randall), Chadwick (Stirling), Gleeson, Easter (Baldock S), Wilbraham, Puncheon.
Southampton: Davis; Thomas, Mills, Wotton, Perry, Fonte, James, Schneiderlin[■], Lambert, Lallana (Holmes), Antonio (Papa Waigo).

NORTHERN FINAL SECOND LEG

Tuesday, 9 February 2010

Carlisle U (1) 2 *(Clayton 33, Hurst 72)*
Leeds U (0) 3 *(Snodgrass 46, Crowe 80, Grella 86)* 9430

Carlisle U: Collin; Keogh, Horwood, Thirlwell, Livesey, Harte, Hurst, Kavanagh (Taiwo), Clayton, Dobie (Madine), Robson.
Leeds U: Ankergren; Crowe, Lowry, Doyle (Kilkenny), Naylor (Grella), Michalik, Snodgrass, Howson (Johnson), Gradel, Becchio, McSheffrey.
Carlisle U won 6-5 on penalties.

SOUTHERN FINAL SECOND LEG

Tuesday, 9 February 2010

Southampton (2) 3 *(Lambert 15, Woodards 30 (og), Lallana 87)*
Milton Keynes D (1) 1 *(Randall 44)* 29,901

Southampton: Davis; Thomas (James), Harding, Hammond, Jaidi, Fonte, Antonio, Schneiderlin (Wotton), Lambert, Lallana, Papa Waigo.
Milton Keynes D: Gueret; Howell (Rae), Lewington, Leven, Woodards (Davis), Stirling, Gleeson, Randall (Gobern L), Morgan, Wilbraham, Chadwick.

JOHNSTONE'S PAINT TROPHY FINAL

Sunday 28 March 2010

(at Wembley Stadium, attendance 73,476)

Carlisle U (0) 1   Southampton (2) 4

Carlisle U: Collin; Keogh, Horwood, Thirlwell (Taiwo), Harte, Murphy, Bridge-Wilkinson (Anyinsah), Kavanagh (Madine), Clayton, Dobie, Robson.
Scorer: Madine 84.

Southampton: Davis; Mills, Harding, Hammond, Jaidi (Perry), Fonte, Lallana, Wotton (Connolly), Lambert, Papa Waigo (Gillett), Antonio.
Scorers: Lambert 15 (pen), Lallana 44, Papa Waigo 50, Antonio 60.
Referee: S. Mathieson (Cheshire).

FOOTBALL LEAGUE COMPETITION ATTENDANCES

LEAGUE CUP ATTENDANCES

Season	Attendances	Games	Average
1960–61	1,204,580	112	10,755
1961–62	1,030,534	104	9,909
1962–63	1,029,893	102	10,097
1963–64	945,265	104	9,089
1964–65	962,802	98	9,825
1965–66	1,205,876	106	11,375
1966–67	1,394,553	118	11,818
1967–68	1,671,326	110	15,194
1968–69	2,064,647	118	17,497
1969–70	2,299,819	122	18,851
1970–71	2,035,315	116	17,546
1971–72	2,397,154	123	19,489
1972–73	1,935,474	120	16,129
1973–74	1,722,629	132	13,050
1974–75	1,901,094	127	14,969
1975–76	1,841,735	140	13,155
1976–77	2,236,636	147	15,215
1977–78	2,038,295	148	13,772
1978–79	1,825,643	139	13,134
1979–80	2,322,866	169	13,745
1980–81	2,051,576	161	12,743
1981–82	1,880,682	161	11,681
1982–83	1,679,756	160	10,498
1983–84	1,900,491	168	11,312
1984–85	1,876,429	167	11,236
1985–86	1,579,916	163	9,693
1986–87	1,531,498	157	9,755
1987–88	1,539,253	158	9,742
1988–89	1,552,780	162	9,585
1989–90	1,836,916	168	10,934
1990–91	1,675,496	159	10,538
1991–92	1,622,337	164	9,892
1992–93	1,558,031	161	9,677
1993–94	1,744,120	163	10,700
1994–95	1,530,478	157	9,748
1995–96	1,776,060	162	10,963
1996–97	1,529,321	163	9,382
1997–98	1,484,297	153	9,701
1998–99	1,555,856	153	10,169
1999–2000	1,354,233	153	8,851
2000–01	1,501,304	154	9,749
2001–02	1,076,390	93	11,574
2002–03	1,242,478	92	13,505
2003–04	1,267,729	93	13,631
2004–05	1,313,693	93	14,216
2005–06	1,072,362	93	11,531
2006–07	1,098,403	93	11,811
2007–08	1,332,841	94	14,179
2008–09	1,329,753	93	14,298
2009–10	1,376,405	93	14,800

CARLING CUP 2009–10

Round	Aggregate	Games	Average
One	146,102	35	4,174
Two	240,613	25	9,625
Three	341,955	16	21,372
Four	241,098	8	30,137
Quarter-finals	138,397	4	34,599
Semi-finals	179,644	4	44,911
Final	88,596	1	88,596
Total	1,376,405	93	14,800

JOHNSTONE'S PAINT TROPHY 2009–10

Round	Aggregate	Games	Average
One	41,005	16	2,563
Two	51,962	16	3,248
Area Quarter-finals	49,093	8	6,137
Area Semi-finals	32,692	4	8,173
Area finals	60,260	4	15,065
Final	73,476	1	73,476
Total	308,488	49	6,296

FA CUP FINALS 1872–2010

1872 and 1874–92	Kennington Oval	1911	Replay at Old Trafford
1873	Lillie Bridge	1912	Replay at Bramall Lane
1886	Replay at Derby (Racecourse Ground)	1915	Old Trafford, Manchester
1893	Fallowfield, Manchester	1920–22	Stamford Bridge
1894	Everton	1923–2000	Wembley
1895–1914	Crystal Palace	1970	Replay at Old Trafford
1901	Replay at Bolton	2001–2006	Millennium Stadium, Cardiff
1910	Replay at Everton	2007 to date	Wembley

Year	Winners	Runners-up	Score
1872	Wanderers	Royal Engineers	1-0
1873	Wanderers	Oxford University	2-0
1874	Oxford University	Royal Engineers	2-0
1875	Royal Engineers	Old Etonians	2-0 (after 1-1 draw aet)
1876	Wanderers	Old Etonians	3-0 (after 1-1 draw aet)
1877	Wanderers	Oxford University	2-1 (aet)
1878	Wanderers*	Royal Engineers	3-1
1879	Old Etonians	Clapham R	1-0
1880	Clapham R	Oxford University	1-0
1881	Old Carthusians	Old Etonians	3-0
1882	Old Etonians	Blackburn R	1-0
1883	Blackburn Olympic	Old Etonians	2-1 (aet)
1884	Blackburn R	Queen's Park, Glasgow	2-1
1885	Blackburn R	Queen's Park, Glasgow	2-0
1886	Blackburn R†	WBA	2-0 (after 0-0 draw)
1887	Aston Villa	WBA	2-0
1888	WBA	Preston NE	2-1
1889	Preston NE	Wolverhampton W	3-0
1890	Blackburn R	The Wednesday	6-1
1891	Blackburn R	Notts Co	3-1
1892	WBA	Aston Villa	3-0
1893	Wolverhampton W	Everton	1-0
1894	Notts Co	Bolton W	4-1
1895	Aston Villa	WBA	1-0
1896	The Wednesday	Wolverhampton W	2-1
1897	Aston Villa	Everton	3-2
1898	Nottingham F	Derby Co	3-1
1899	Sheffield U	Derby Co	4-1
1900	Bury	Southampton	4-0
1901	Tottenham H	Sheffield U	3-1 (after 2-2 draw)
1902	Sheffield U	Southampton	2-1 (after 1-1 draw)
1903	Bury	Derby Co	6-0
1904	Manchester C	Bolton W	1-0
1905	Aston Villa	Newcastle U	2-0
1906	Everton	Newcastle U	1-0
1907	The Wednesday	Everton	2-1
1908	Wolverhampton W	Newcastle U	3-1
1909	Manchester U	Bristol C	1-0
1910	Newcastle U	Barnsley	2-0 (after 1-1 draw)
1911	Bradford C	Newcastle U	1-0 (after 0-0 draw)
1912	Barnsley	WBA	1-0 (aet, after 0-0 draw)
1913	Aston Villa	Sunderland	1-0
1914	Burnley	Liverpool	1-0
1915	Sheffield U	Chelsea	3-0
1920	Aston Villa	Huddersfield T	1-0 (aet)
1921	Tottenham H	Wolverhampton W	1-0
1922	Huddersfield T	Preston NE	1-0
1923	Bolton W	West Ham U	2-0
1924	Newcastle U	Aston Villa	2-0
1925	Sheffield U	Cardiff C	1-0
1926	Bolton W	Manchester C	1-0
1927	Cardiff C	Arsenal	1-0
1928	Blackburn R	Huddersfield T	3-1
1929	Bolton W	Portsmouth	2-0
1930	Arsenal	Huddersfield T	2-0
1931	WBA	Birmingham	2-1
1932	Newcastle U	Arsenal	2-1
1933	Everton	Manchester C	3-0
1934	Manchester C	Portsmouth	2-1
1935	Sheffield W	WBA	4-2

Year	Winners	Runners-up	Score
1936	Arsenal	Sheffield U	1-0
1937	Sunderland	Preston NE	3-1
1938	Preston NE	Huddersfield T	1-0 (aet)
1939	Portsmouth	Wolverhampton W	4-1
1946	Derby Co	Charlton Ath	4-1 (aet)
1947	Charlton Ath	Burnley	1-0 (aet)
1948	Manchester U	Blackpool	4-2
1949	Wolverhampton W	Leicester C	3-1
1950	Arsenal	Liverpool	2-0
1951	Newcastle U	Blackpool	2-0
1952	Newcastle U	Arsenal	1-0
1953	Blackpool	Bolton W	4-3
1954	WBA	Preston NE	3-2
1955	Newcastle U	Manchester C	3-1
1956	Manchester C	Birmingham C	3-1
1957	Aston Villa	Manchester U	2-1
1958	Bolton W	Manchester U	2-0
1959	Nottingham F	Luton T	2-1
1960	Wolverhampton W	Blackburn R	3-0
1961	Tottenham H	Leicester C	2-0
1962	Tottenham H	Burnley	3-1
1963	Manchester U	Leicester C	3-1
1964	West Ham U	Preston NE	3-2
1965	Liverpool	Leeds U	2-1 (aet)
1966	Everton	Sheffield W	3-2
1967	Tottenham H	Chelsea	2-1
1968	WBA	Everton	1-0 (aet)
1969	Manchester C	Leicester C	1-0
1970	Chelsea	Leeds U	2-1 (aet)

(after 2-2 draw, after extra time)

Year	Winners	Runners-up	Score
1971	Arsenal	Liverpool	2-1 (aet)
1972	Leeds U	Arsenal	1-0
1973	Sunderland	Leeds U	1-0
1974	Liverpool	Newcastle U	3-0
1975	West Ham U	Fulham	2-0
1976	Southampton	Manchester U	1-0
1977	Manchester U	Liverpool	2-1
1978	Ipswich T	Arsenal	1-0
1979	Arsenal	Manchester U	3-2
1980	West Ham U	Arsenal	1-0
1981	Tottenham H	Manchester C	3-2

(after 1-1 draw, after extra time)

Year	Winners	Runners-up	Score
1982	Tottenham H	QPR	1-0

(after 1-1 draw, after extra time)

Year	Winners	Runners-up	Score
1983	Manchester U	Brighton & HA	4-0

(after 2-2 draw, after extra time)

Year	Winners	Runners-up	Score
1984	Everton	Watford	2-0
1985	Manchester U	Everton	1-0 (aet)
1986	Liverpool	Everton	3-1
1987	Coventry C	Tottenham H	3-2 (aet)
1988	Wimbledon	Liverpool	1-0
1989	Liverpool	Everton	3-2 (aet)
1990	Manchester U	Crystal Palace	1-0

(after 3-3 draw, after extra time)

Year	Winners	Runners-up	Score
1991	Tottenham H	Nottingham F	2-1 (aet)
1992	Liverpool	Sunderland	2-0
1993	Arsenal	Sheffield W	2-1 (aet)

(after 1-1 draw, after extra time)

Year	Winners	Runners-up	Score
1994	Manchester U	Chelsea	4-0
1995	Everton	Manchester U	1-0
1996	Manchester U	Liverpool	1-0
1997	Chelsea	Middlesbrough	2-0
1998	Arsenal	Newcastle U	2-0
1999	Manchester U	Newcastle U	2-0
2000	Chelsea	Aston Villa	1-0
2001	Liverpool	Arsenal	2-1
2002	Arsenal	Chelsea	2-0
2003	Arsenal	Southampton	1-0
2004	Manchester U	Millwall	3-0
2005	Arsenal	Manchester U	0-0 (aet)

(Arsenal won 5-4 on penalties)

Year	Winners	Runners-up	Score
2006	Liverpool	West Ham U	3-3 (aet)

(Liverpool won 3-1 on penalties)

Year	Winners	Runners-up	Score
2007	Chelsea	Manchester U	1-0 (aet)
2008	Portsmouth	Cardiff C	1-0
2009	Chelsea	Everton	2-1
2010	Chelsea	Portsmouth	1-0

* Won outright, but restored to the Football Association. † A special trophy was awarded for third consecutive win.

FA CUP WINS

Manchester U 11, Arsenal 10, Tottenham H 8, Aston Villa 7, Liverpool 7, Chelsea 6, Blackburn R 6, Newcastle U 6, Everton 5, The Wanderers 5, WBA 5, Bolton W 4, Manchester C 4, Sheffield U 4, Wolverhampton W 4, Sheffield W 3, West Ham U 3, Bury 2, Nottingham F 2, Old Etonians 2, Portsmouth 2, Preston NE 2, Sunderland 2, Barnsley 1, Blackburn Olympic 1, Blackpool 1, Bradford C 1, Burnley 1, Cardiff C 1, Charlton Ath 1, Clapham R 1, Coventry C 1, Derby Co 1, Huddersfield T 1, Ipswich T 1, Leeds U 1, Notts Co 1, Old Carthusians 1, Oxford University 1, Royal Engineers 1, Southampton 1, Wimbledon 1.

APPEARANCES IN FINALS

Manchester U 18, Arsenal 17, Everton 13, Liverpool 13, Newcastle U 13, Aston Villa 10, Chelsea 10, WBA 10, Tottenham H 9, Blackburn R 8, Manchester C 8, Wolverhampton W 8, Bolton W 7, Preston NE 7, Old Etonians 6, Sheffield U 6, Sheffield W 6, Huddersfield T 5, Portsmouth 5, *The Wanderers 5, West Ham U 5, Derby Co 4, Leeds U 4, Leicester C 4, Oxford University 4, Royal Engineers 4, Southampton 4, Sunderland 4, Blackpool 3, Burnley 3, Cardiff C 3, Nottingham F 3, Barnsley 2, Birmingham C 2, *Bury 2, Charlton Ath 2, Clapham R 2, Notts Co 2, Queen's Park (Glasgow) 2, *Blackburn Olympic 1, *Bradford C 1, Brighton & HA 1, Bristol C 1, *Coventry C 1, Crystal Palace 1, Fulham 1, *Ipswich T 1, Luton T 1, Middlesbrough 1, Millwall 1, *Old Carthusians 1, QPR 1, Watford 1, *Wimbledon 1.
* *Denotes undefeated.*

APPEARANCES IN SEMI-FINALS

Arsenal 26, Manchester U 26, Everton 24, Liverpool 22, Aston Villa 20, WBA 20, Chelsea 19, Blackburn R 18, Tottenham H 18, Newcastle U 17, Sheffield W 16, Wolverhampton W 14, Bolton W 13, Derby Co 13, Sheffield U 13, Nottingham F 12, Sunderland 12, Southampton 11, Manchester C 10, Preston NE 10, Birmingham C 9, Burnley 8, Leeds U 8, Leicester C 8, Huddersfield T 7, Portsmouth 7, West Ham U 7, Old Etonians 6, Fulham 6, Oxford University 6, Notts Co 5, The Wanderers 5, Watford 5, Cardiff C 4, Luton T 4, Millwall 4, Queen's Park (Glasgow) 4, Royal Engineers 4, Barnsley 3, Blackpool 3, Clapham R 3, Crystal Palace (professional club) 3, Ipswich T 3, Middlesbrough 3, Norwich C 3, Old Carthusians 3, Oldham Ath 3, Stoke C 3, The Swifts 3, Blackburn Olympic 2, Bristol C 2, Bury 2, Charlton Ath 2, Grimsby T 2, Swansea T 2, Swindon T 2, Wimbledon 2, Bradford C 1, Brighton & HA 1, Cambridge University 1, Chesterfield 1, Coventry C 1, Crewe Alex 1, Crystal Palace (amateur club) 1, Darwen 1, Derby Junction 1, Glasgow R 1, Hull C 1, Marlow 1, Old Harrovians 1, Orient 1, Plymouth Arg 1, Port Vale 1, QPR 1, Reading 1, Shropshire W 1, Wycombe W 1, York C 1.

FA CUP ATTENDANCES 1969–2010

	1st Round	2nd Round	3rd Round	4th Round	5th Round	6th Round	Semi-finals & Final	Total	No. of matches	Average per match
2009–10	147,078	100,476	613,113	335,426	288,604	144,918	254,806	1,884,421	151	12,480
2008–09	161,526	96,923	631,070	529,585	297,364	149,566	264,635	2,131,669	163	13,078
2007–08	175,195	99,528	704,300	356,404	276,903	142,780	256,210	2,011,320	152	13,232
2006–07	168,884	113,924	708,628	478,924	340,612	230,064	177,810	2,218,846	158	14,043
2005–06	188,876	107,456	654,570	388,339	286,225	163,449	177,723	1,966,638	160	12,291
2004–05	161,197	98,702	602,152	477,472	339,082	127,914	193,233	1,999,752	146	13,697
2003–04	162,738	117,967	624,732	347,964	292,521	156,780	167,401	1,870,103	149	12,551
2002–03	189,905	104,103	577,494	404,599	242,483	156,244	175,498	1,850,326	150	12,336
2001–02	198,369	119,781	566,284	330,434	249,190	173,757	171,278	1,809,093	148	12,224
2000–01	171,689	122,061	577,204	398,241	256,899	100,663	177,778	1,804,535	151	11,951
1999–2000	181,483	127,728	514,030	374,795	182,511	105,443	214,921	1,700,913	158	10,765
1998–99	191,954	132,341	609,486	431,613	359,398	181,005	202,150	2,107,947	155	13,599
1997–98	204,803	130,261	629,127	455,557	341,290	192,651	172,007	2,125,696	165	12,883
1996–97	209,521	122,324	651,139	402,293	199,873	67,035	191,813	1,843,998	151	12,211
1995–96	185,538	115,669	748,997	391,218	274,055	174,142	156,500	2,046,199	167	12,252
1994–95	219,511	125,629	640,017	438,596	257,650	159,787	174,059	2,015,249	161	12,517
1993–94	190,683	118,031	691,064	430,234	172,196	134,705	228,233	1,965,146	159	12,359
1992–93	241,968	174,702	612,494	377,211	198,379	149,675	293,241	2,047,670	161	12,718
1991–92	231,940	117,078	586,014	372,576	270,537	155,603	201,592	1,935,340	160	12,095
1990–91	194,195	121,450	594,592	530,279	276,112	124,826	196,434	2,038,518	162	12,583
1989–90	209,542	133,483	683,047	412,483	351,423	123,065	277,420	2,190,463	170	12,885
1988–89	212,775	121,326	690,199	421,255	206,781	176,629	167,353	1,966,318	164	12,173
1987–88	204,411	104,561	720,121	443,133	281,461	119,313	177,585	2,050,585	155	13,229
1986–87	209,290	146,761	593,520	349,342	263,550	119,396	195,533	1,877,400	165	11,378
1985–86	171,142	130,034	486,838	495,526	311,833	184,262	192,316	1,971,951	168	11,738
1984–85	174,604	137,078	616,229	320,772	269,232	148,690	242,754	1,909,359	157	12,162
1983–84	192,276	151,647	625,965	417,298	181,832	185,382	187,000	1,941,400	166	11,695
1982–83	191,312	150,046	670,503	452,688	260,069	193,845	291,162	2,209,625	154	14,348
1981–82	236,220	127,300	513,185	356,987	203,334	124,308	279,621	1,840,955	160	11,506
1980–81	246,824	194,502	832,578	534,402	320,530	288,714	339,250	2,756,800	169	16,312
1979–80	267,121	204,759	804,701	507,725	364,039	157,530	355,541	2,661,416	163	16,328
1978–79	243,773	185,343	880,345	537,748	243,683	263,213	249,897	2,604,002	166	15,687
1977–78	258,248	178,930	881,406	540,164	400,751	137,059	198,020	2,594,578	160	16,216
1976–77	379,230	192,159	942,523	631,265	373,330	205,379	258,216	2,982,102	174	17,139
1975–76	255,533	178,099	867,880	573,843	471,925	206,851	205,810	2,759,941	161	17,142
1974–75	283,956	170,466	914,994	646,434	393,323	268,361	291,369	2,968,903	172	17,261
1973–74	214,236	125,295	840,142	747,909	346,012	233,307	273,051	2,779,952	167	16,646
1972–73	259,432	169,114	938,741	735,825	357,386	241,934	226,543	2,928,975	160	18,306
1971–72	277,726	236,127	986,094	711,399	486,378	230,292	248,546	3,158,562	160	19,741
1970–71	329,687	230,942	956,683	757,852	360,687	304,937	279,644	3,220,432	162	19,879
1969–70	345,229	195,102	925,930	651,374	319,893	198,537	390,700	3,026,765	170	17,805

THE E.ON FA CUP 2009–10

PRELIMINARY AND QUALIFYING ROUNDS

EXTRA PRELIMINARY ROUND

Brandon United v West Auckland Town	2-1
Glossop North End v Formby	3-1
Holbeach United v Shirebrook Town	1-2
Kirkley & Pakefield v Walsham Le Willows	1-0
Calne Town v Downton	1-0
Newport (IW) v Bitton	2-1
Hamworthy United v Buckland Athletic	3-2
Northallerton Town v Shildon	1-2
Esh Winning v Bridlington Town	2-2
Bridlington Town won 4-2 on penalties.	
Birtley Town v Billingham Synthonia	1-3
Atherton LR v Bacup Borough	1-0
Staveley MW v Squires Gate	2-2
Staveley MW won 5-3 on penalties.	
Winsford United v Flixton	4-6
Biddulph Victoria v Cradley Town	0-1
Malvern Town v Highgate United	2-1
Ellistown v Holwell Sports	2-1
Heather St Johns v Gresley	1-0
Bourne Town v Teversal	3-0
Friar Lane & Epworth v Deeping Rangers	3-0
Blackstones v Gedling MW	2-1
Barton Town Old Boys v Gedling Town	2-1
Raunds Town v Great Yarmouth Town	1-3
Haverhill Rovers v Godmanchester Rovers	0-1
Hullbridge Sports v St Margaretsbury	0-1
Southend Manor v Hatfield Town	0-3
Wivenhoe Town v Halstead Town	1-4
Hoddesdon Town v Potton United	2-0
Harringey Borough v Harefield United	1-3
Sevenoaks Town v Tunbridge Wells	2-1
Farnham Town v Raynes Park Vale	0-3
Cobham v Littlehampton Town	2-1
Ringmer v Egham Town	2-0
Pagham v Banstead Athletic	1-1
Pagham won 3-2 on penalties.	
Sandhurst Town v Erith & Belvedere	2-4
Bedfont v Crowborough Athletic	3-2
Horley Town v Dorking	3-0
Westbury United v Wootton Bassett Town	2-3
Wantage Town v Hamble ASSC	4-1
Witney United v Ardley United	2-1
Brislington v Portishead Town	1-2
Dunston UTS v Whitley Bay	0-2
Tow Law Town v Horden CW	1-2
Bristol Manor Farm v Carterton	1-1
Bristol Manor Farm won 3-2 on penalties.	
Street v Willand Rovers	0-1
Leeds Carnegie v Selby Town	1-3
Atherton Colleries v Chadderton	3-1
Whickham v Chester-Le-Street Town	2-0
Whickham removed from the competition for fielding an unregistered player. Chester-Le-Street Town reinstated.	
Scarborough Athletic v Guisborough Town	1-2
Hinckley Downes v Boston Town	1-4
Stansted v Royston Town	2-5
Barkingside v Bowers & Pitsea	1-4
Crawley Green v Cranfield United	3-1
Broxbourne Borough V&E v Enfield 1893	1-4
Spennymoor United v Ashington	5-1
Seaham Red Star v Morpeth Town	1-4
Sunderland RCA v Ryton	1-3
Bedlington Terriers v Thackley	2-0
Hebburn Town v Eccleshill United	7-0
Jarrow Roofing Boldon CA v Armthorpe Welfare	2-1
Consett v Billingham Town	5-0
Team Northumbria v Marske United	4-0
Hall Road Rangers v Bishop Auckland	2-6
Norton & Stockton Ancients v Pickering Town	3-0
South Shields v Newcastle Benfield	1-4
Pontefract Colleries v Penrith	1-4
Stokesley v Crook Town	3-1
West Allotment Celtic v Liversedge	3-2
Silsden v Colne	3-1
Congleton Town v Dinnington Town	3-2
Abbey Hey v Hallam	1-6
Maltby Main v Rossington Main	1-3
Parkgate v St Helens Town	1-3
Folker Old Boys v Padiham	0-2
Maine Road v Alsager Town	3-1
Ashton Athletic v Bootle	1-2
Runcorn Linnets v AFC Emley	4-1
Nostell MW v Oldham Town	2-1
Ramsbottom United v Cheadle Town	5-1
Meir KA v Tipton Town	0-4
Bewdley Town v Alvechurch	0-2
Eccleshall v Tividale	1-3
Westfields v Bolehall Swifts	5-0
Stone Dominoes v Cadbury Athletic	7-0
Causeway United v Wellington	3-1
Studley v Pershore Town	1-0
Coleshill Town v Bridgnorth Town	2-0
Pegasus Juniors v Ellesmere Rangers	5-1
Norton United v Newcastle Town	2-5
Dudley Town v Walsall Wood	3-2
Coventry Sphinx v Bromyard Town	3-2
Heath Hayes v Lye Town	2-1
Brockton v Shifnal Town	5-1
Castle Vale v Goodrich	4-2
Stratford Town v Pilkington XXX	5-0
AFC Wulfrunians v Boldmere St Michaels	2-0
Rocester v Wednesfield	2-1
Nuneaton Griff v Shawbury United	3-1
Borrowash Victoria v Greenwood Meadows	3-0
Barwell v Long Eaton United	1-2
Holbrook Miners Welfare v Heanor Town	5-0
Radford v Rainworth MW	0-3
Oadby Town v Kirby Muxloe	2-3
Bardon Hill Sports v Arnold Town	3-2
Coalville Town v Barrow Town	3-2
Bottisford Town v New Mills	1-5
Dunkirk v Winterton Rangers	1-3
Lincoln Moorlands Railway v St Andrews	2-3
Sleaford Town v Loughborough University	2-0
Long Buckby v Hadleigh United	3-2
Cornard United v Gorleston	0-4
Yaxley v Rothwell Corinthians	1-2
Ely City v Wisbech Town	0-1
Whitton United v Daventry Town	0-5
St Ives Town v Daventry United	6-1
Needham Market v Felixstowe & Walton United	1-0
Wellingborough Town v Wroxham	0-2
Woodbridge Town v St Neots Town	1-4
Desborough Town v Newmarket Town	4-1
Diss Town v Cogenhoe United	2-3
Dereham Town v Leiston	3-1
Stewarts & Lloyds v Norwich United	1-2
Northampton Spencer v March Town United	1-0
Stowmarket Town v Mildenhall Town	0-3
Clapton v Kingsbury London Tigers	2-5
Thame United v Bedford	1-0
Wembley v Basildon United	2-3
Erith Town v Ampthill Town	2-0
Leverstock Green v Burnham Ramblers	2-1
Oxhey Jets v Brimsdown Rovers	0-1
Wootton Blue Cross v Sporting Bengal United	1-0
Bicester Town v Dunstable Town	1-4
FC Clacton v London APSA	2-1
Tiptree United v Colney Heath	3-2
Buckingham Town v Hanwell Town	1-3
Biggleswade United v Stotfold	2-0
Hillingdon Borough v Kentish Town	2-3
London Colney v Harwich & Parkeston	4-1
North Greenford United v Cockfosters	0-2
Chalfont St Peter v Tokyngton Manor	3-2
Witham Town v Saffron Walden Town	2-1
Langford v Aylesbury	0-6
Barking v Tring Athletic	2-3
Hailsham Town v Lingfield	1-7
Worthing United v Badshot Lea	0-3
Hartley Wintney v Holmesdale	1-2
Wick v Frimley Green	4-0
Deal Town v Arundel	3-2
Southwick v Herne Bay	2-1
Chessington & Hook United v Chertsey Town	0-2
Whitehawk v Hythe Town	1-2

Camberley Town v East Preston	1-2
Oakwood v Lordswood	2-4
Croydon v Shoreham	2-5
East Grinstead Town v Feltham	4-1
Eastbourne United v Redhill	3-1
Wealden v Epsom & Ewell	1-3
Cove v Bookham	4-0
Slade Green withdrew v Faversham Town w.o.	
Binfield v Colliers Wood United	3-5
Peacehaven & Telscombe v Mile Oak	1-3
Lancing v Selsey	0-2
Crawley Down v Westfield	4-1
Molesey v Sidley United	2-1
Guildford City v St Francis Rangers	4-1
Three Bridges v Chichester City	1-3
Hassocks v Ash United	1-4
New Milton Town v Cowes Sports	4-1
Petersfield Town v Brockenhurst	0-2
Ringwood Town v Christchurch	2-1
Milton United v Corsham Town	3-0
Bournemouth v Highworth Town	1-2
Fareham Town v Moneyfields	1-2
Romsey Town v Hayling United	3-0
Lydney Town v Totton & Eling	0-5
Arlesford Town v Shaftesbury	8-0
Warminster Town v Amesbury Town	5-1
Laverstock & Ford v Alton Town	1-3
Devizes Town v Shrivenham	0-5
Almondsbury Town v Longwell Green Sports	2-0
Marlow United v Hallen	1-2
Kidlington v Abingdon Town	1-0
Winchester City v Bemerton Heath Harlequins	1-4
Brading Town v Fairford Town	1-0
Shortwood United v Blackfield & Langley	1-0
Reading Town v Melksham Town	2-0
Lymington Town v Harrow Hill	6-0
Wellington Town v Bideford	1-3
Launceston v Clevedon United	1-3
Bridport v Keynsham Town	3-1
Gillingham Town v Cullompton Rangers	5-1
Larkhall Athletic v Shepton Mallet	4-1
Radstock Town v Wimborne Town	0-1
Dawlish Town v Elmore	3-0
Barnstaple Town v Tavistock	3-1
Bishop Sutton v Bodmin Town	1-2
Saltash United v Chard Town	6-2
Ilfracombe Town v Falmouth Town	0-1
Sherborne Town v St Blazey	4-1
Poole Town v Welton Rovers	3-2
Eton Manor v Stanway Rovers	1-2
Hertford Town v Newport Pagnell Town	1-2
Flackwell Heath v Welwyn Garden City	4-0

PRELIMINARY ROUND

Bedlington Terriers v Garforth Town	2-3
Chester-Le-Street Town v Norton & Stockton Ancients	0-5
Morpeth Town v Billingham Synthonia	4-3
Selby Town v Ryton	1-2
Bridlington Town v Shildon	1-0
Wakefield v Guisborough Town	0-0, 0-1
Team Northumbria v Ossett Albion	1-2
Stokesley v Spennymoor Town	1-3
Jarrow Roofing Boldon CA v Penrith	2-0
Hebburn Town v Bishop Auckland	3-4
Horden CW v West Allotment Celtic	2-2, 3-2
Newcastle Benfield v Whitley Bay	1-2
Brandon United v FC Halifax Town	0-6
Consett v Harrogate Railway	0-0, 1-1
Harrogate Railway won 4-3 on penalties.	
Warrington Town v Leigh Genesis	1-0
Clitheroe v Staveley MW	1-1, 3-1
Padiham v AFC Fylde	2-4
Bootle v Woodley Sports	1-4
Silsden v Hallam	1-4
Sheffield v Flixton	4-0
Trafford v Rossendale United	2-2, 1-3
Rossington Main v Glossop North End	1-2
Curzon Ashton v Lancaster City	2-2, 2-3
Chorley v Nostell MW	2-1
Colwyn Bay v St Helens Town	2-4
Cammell Laird v Mossley	2-1
Maine Road v Ramsbottom United	2-1
Atherton LR v Prescot Cables	1-0
Atherton Collieries v Radcliffe Borough	0-1
Bamber Bridge v Runcorn Linnets	6-0

Witton Albion v Congleton Town	0-1
Salford City v Skelmersdale United	3-2
Castle Vale v Studley	5-1
Kidsgrove Athletic v Alvechurch	1-0
Dudley Town v Bromsgrove Rovers	3-3, 0-3
Nuneaton Griff v Stratford Town	1-4
Coventry Sphinx v Stourport Swifts	4-4, 2-0
Heath Hayes v Tividale	0-1
Pegasus Juniors v Willenhall Town	2-2, 2-0
Malvern Town v Cradley Town	1-1, 1-2
Atherstone Town v Romulus	1-2
Stone Dominoes v Market Drayton Town	0-1
Coleshill Town v Causeway United	0-2
Dudley Sports v Rocester	2-0
Chasetown v AFC Wulfrunians	1-1, 2-2
AFC Wulfrunians won 5-4 on penalties.	
Sutton Coldfield Town v Tipton Town	2-1
Leek Town v Bedworth United	2-3
Newcastle Town v Westfields	1-2
Brocton v Rushall Olympic	0-2
Carlton Town v New Mills	4-2
Borrowash Victoria v Quorn	0-0, 1-3
Blackstones v Shepshed Dynamo	3-4
Barton Town Old Boys v Kirby Muxloe	6-3
Brigg Town v Spalding United	4-0
Lincoln United v Friar Lane & Epworth	5-2
Winterton Rangers v St Andrews	6-1
Coalville Town v Bardon Hill Sports	0-1
Glapwell v Ellistown	3-1
Sleaford Town v Stamford	3-1
Rainworth MW v Heather St Johns	3-1
Long Eaton United v Loughborough Dynamo	0-2
Grantham Town v Mickleover Sports	1-1, 1-3
Shirebrook Town v Boston Town	0-2
Belper Town v Holbrook Miners Welfare	1-1, 0-1
Bourne Town v Goole	3-1
Desborough Town v Daventry Town	1-1, 1-2
Norwich United v Long Buckby	0-1
Woodford United v AFC Sudbury	1-2
Rothwell Town v Bury Town	0-1
Needham Market v Wisbech Town	4-0
Lowestoft Town v Great Yarmouth Town	3-0
Kirkley & Pakefield v Cogenhoe United	4-0
Gorleston v Northampton Spencer	1-1, 2-3
Rothwell Corinthians v Godmanchester Rovers	0-0, 0-3
Dereham Town v Wroxham	3-0
Soham Town Rangers v St Ives Town	0-0, 1-2
Mildenhall Town v St Neots Town	3-0
Great Wakering Rovers v Waltham Forest	0-0, 0-1
Windsor & Eton v Bowers & Pitsea	3-1
Northwood v St Margaretsbury	3-1
Potters Bar Town v Cockfosters	1-1, 4-1
Harlow Town v Kingsbury London Tigers	2-2, 1-2
Chesham United v Chalfont St Peter	2-0
Marlow v Ilford	3-0
Witham Town v London Colney	3-6
Newport Pagnell Town v Heybridge Swifts	0-2
Aylesbury United v Tiptree United	2-1
Hanwell Town v Concord Rangers	1-3
Enfield Town v Leverstock Green	2-0
Enfield 1893 v Crawley Green	7-0
Harefield United v Biggleswade Town	2-1
FC Clacton v Hitchin Town	0-1
Barton Rovers v Ware	2-3
Thame United v Wootton Blue Cross	2-0
Thamesmead Town v Tilbury	4-2
Leighton Town v Aylesbury	0-0, 0-1
Burnham v Kentish Town	2-1
Biggleswade United v Halstead Town	1-2
Stanway Rovers v Beaconsfield SYCOB	2-0
Cheshunt v Maldon Town	2-3
Tring Athletic v Slough Town	0-4
Dunstable Town v Wingate & Finchley	0-2
Arlesey Town v Hatfield Town	2-0
Hoddesdon Town v Royston Town	0-1
Erith Town v Basildon United	3-0
Brimsdown Rovers v Flackwell Heath	2-4
East Thurrock United v Brentwood Town	2-0
Redbridge v Romford	0-1
Croydon Athletic v Godalming Town	2-0
Sittingbourne v Horley Town	0-0, 2-1
Worthing v Raynes Park Vale	4-0
Merstham v Faversham Town	2-2, 4-4
Faversham Town won 5-4 on penalties.	
Dulwich Hamlet v Sevenoakes Town	1-1, 2-0
Ashford Town v Mile Oak	6-1

Folkestone Invicta v AFC Hayes	1-0
Selsey v Epsom & Ewell	1-0
Chertsey Town v Metropolitan Police	0-1
Gosport Borough v East Preston	0-1
Lordswood v Whitstable Town	1-1, 1-2
Horsham YMCA v Wick	5-3
Shoreham v Crawley Down	1-2
Chichester City v AFC Totton	1-3
Pagham v Walton Casuals	1-2
Fleet Town v Walton & Hersham	1-1, 2-2
Walton & Hersham won 5-4 on penalties.	
Lingfield v Southwick	0-0, 3-0
Burgess Hill Town v Chipstead	2-3
Andover v Molesey	2-3
Chatham Town v Eastbourne United	1-1, 2-1
East Grinstead Town v Cove	4-2
Cobham v VT	0-6
Leatherhead v Bedfont Green	3-0
Guildford City v Ramsgate	3-1
Hythe Town v Eastbourne Town	4-0
Ash United v Erith & Belvedere	4-0
Bedfont v Colliers Wood United	4-2
Holmesdale v Badshot Lea	1-3
Deal Town v Ringmer	4-1
Corinthian Casuals v VCD Athletic	1-3
Whiteleafe v Uxbridge	0-1
Hallen v Lymington Town	0-0, 4-0
Shortwood United v Romsey Town	5-1
Highworth Town v Bemerton Heath Harlequins	1-0
Totton & Eling v Kidlington	1-4
Wootton Bassett Town v Brockenhurst	0-1
Yate Town v Alton Town	3-1
Mangotsfield United v Bracknell Town	2-0
Calne Town v Shrivenham	0-1
Bishop's Cleeve v Reading Town	3-1
Bristol Manor Farm v Warminster Town	4-4, 4-2
North Leigh v Milton United	2-1
Almondsbury Town v Cinderford Town	2-1
Wantage Town v Newport (IW)	5-0
Moneyfields v Hungerford Town	5-4
Ringwood Town v Abingdon United	1-3
Brading Town v Alresford Town	3-2
Witney United v New Milton Town	3-1
Cirencester Town v Thatcham Town	2-1
Wimborne Town v Sherbourne Town	2-1
Paulton Rovers v Bideford	3-1
Falmouth Town v Willand Rovers	1-1, 1-2
Taunton Town v Bodmin Town	3-1
Poole Town v Barnstaple Town	7-2
Launceston v Bridgwater Town	2-3
Bridport v Dawlish Town	3-3, 2-1
Gillingham Town v Portishead Town	5-0
Larkhall Athletic v Saltash United	0-2
Hamworthy United v Frome Town	3-2

FIRST QUALIFYING ROUND

Horden CW v Durham City	2-2, 3-1
North Ferriby United v Harrogate Railway	2-0
Kendal Town v Guisborough Town	9-1
Spennymoor Town v Ryton	6-0
Morpeth Town v Ossett Town	0-1
Norton & Stockton Ancients v FC Halifax Town	0-4
Bridlington Town v Whitby Town	0-1
Bradford Park Avenue v Bishop Auckland	4-1
Jarrow Roofing Boldon CA v Garforth Town	1-0
Guiseley v Whitley Bay	2-0
Hallam v Burscough	0-4
Cammell Laird v St Helens Town	3-1
Maine Road v Bamber Bridge	1-4
Clitheroe v Stocksbridge Park Steels	0-2
Atherton LR v Congleton Town	1-1, 0-5
Warrington Town v Nantwich Town	1-0
Worksop Town v Frickley Athletic	1-1, 1-2
Lancaster City v Ashton United	0-3
Glossop North End v Chorley	2-3
AFC Fylde v Rossendale United	4-1
Salford City v Marine	2-1
Woodley Sports v Radcliffe Borough	0-1
Sheffield v FC United of Manchester	1-3
Causeway United v Bedworth United	0-0, 0-3
Westfields v Sutton Coldfield Town	0-6
Hednesford Town v Pegasus Juniors	1-4
Evesham United v Tividale	0-0, 2-1
Cradley Town v Stratford Town	0-1
Bromsgrove Rovers v Stourbridge	1-1, 1-3

Kidsgrove Athletic v AFC Wulfrunians	2-3
Coventry Sphinx v Rushall Olympic	1-0
Leamington v Market Drayton Town	0-2
Romulus v Castle Vale	2-1
Rugby Town v Dudley Sports	6-0
Rainworth MW v Holbrook Miners Welfare	2-1
Bourne Town v Boston Town	3-1
Buxton v Winterton Rangers	2-1
Retford United v Lincoln United	1-1, 1-2
Bardon Hill Sports v Barton Town Old Boys	5-0
Blackstones v Hucknall Town	2-4
Quorn v Mickleover Sports	0-2
Brigg Town v Nuneaton Town	0-5
Matlock Town v Sleaford Town	1-1, 2-1
Glapwell v Carlton Town	0-1
Boston United v Loughborough Dynamo	4-2
Lowestoft Town v Dereham Town	3-1
Godmanchester Rovers v Northampton Spencer	1-2
St Ives Town v Kirkley & Pakefield	1-2
Bury Town v King's Lynn	2-0
AFC Sudbury v Needham Market	0-2
Long Buckby v Mildenhall Town	1-1, 3-4
Cambridge City v Daventry Town	2-0
Harefield United v Maldon Town	3-1
Canvey Island v Hitchin Town	3-3, 1-5
Enfield 1893 v Halstead Town	3-3, 0-0
Enfield 1893 won 2-0 on penalties.	
Flackwell Heath v Royston Town	2-1
Chesham United v Harrow Borough	1-1, 2-0
Erith Town v Aylesbury	3-3, 1-2
Heybridge Swifts v Stanway Rovers	1-1, 0-0
Heybridge Swifts won 4-3 on penalties.	
Waltham Abbey v Enfield Town	0-1
Thamesmead Town v Windsor & Eton	1-2
Arlesey Town v Wealdstone	1-2
Thame United v Burnham	0-2
East Thurrock United v Ware	4-1
Northwood v Wingate & Finchley	2-2, 1-3
Hemel Hempstead Town v Slough Town	1-1, 1-2
Marlow v Hendon	0-2
AFC Hornchurch v Billericay Town	0-3
Aylesbury United v Potters Bar Town	0-0, 0-2
London Colney v Aveley	1-1, 2-4
Boreham Wood v Waltham Forest	1-0
Bedford Town v Kingsbury London Tigers	5-1
Romford v Concord Rangers	1-1, 0-6
Guildford City v East Preston	4-4, 2-2
East Preston won 4-3 on penalties.	
Molesey v Bashley	2-3
Walton & Hersham v Cray Wanderers	2-1
Chatham Town v Walton Casuals	0-0, 1-2
Farnborough v Hastings United	2-1
Whitstable Town v Carshalton Athletic	2-1
Crawley Down v Ashford Town (Middlesex)	2-3
Leatherhead v Ashford Town	2-0
Uxbridge v Ash United	4-3
Bognor Regis Town v Kingstonian	1-4
Folkestone Invicta v Sittingbourne	0-1
Maidstone United v Bedfont	2-1
Hythe Town v Faversham Town	2-1
AFC Totton v VCD Athletic	5-0
Lingfield v Badshot Lea	4-4, 1-2
Chipstead v Dartford	1-6
Tooting & Mitcham United v Horsham	4-2
Deal Town v Selsey	1-1, 0-3
VT v Dulwich Hamlet	1-0
Tonbridge Angels v Metropolitan Police	1-0
Croydon Athletic v Worthing	0-1
Horsham YMCA v East Grinstead Town	1-0
Margate v Sutton United	2-2, 2-3
Almondsbury Town v Yate Town	1-1, 2-1
Brading Town v Hallen	1-1, 0-3
Banbury United v Chippenham Town	0-0, 2-3
Brackley Town v Swindon Supermarine	1-0
Bishop's Cleeve v Brockenhurst	5-2
Oxford City v Kidlington	4-2
Mangotsfield United v Wantage Town	3-0
Shortwood United v Witney United	3-3, 1-2
Highworth Town v Abingdon United	0-3
Hungerford Town v Bristol Manor Farm	4-0
Didcot Town v Shrivenham	5-0
Cirencester Town v North Leigh	2-1
Bridgwater Town v Hamworthy United	3-1
Saltash United v Gillingham Town	1-1, 5-6
Truro City v Bridport	1-1, 7-0
Taunton Town v Merthyr Tydfil	0-3

Willand Rovers v Poole Town	1-0
Paulton Rovers v Tiverton Town	1-0
Clevedon Town v Wimborne Town	4-2

Didcot Town v Paulton Rovers	0-2
Evesham United v Stourbridge	0-1

SECOND QUALIFYING ROUND

Whitby Town v Vauxhall Motors	0-5
Warrington Town v Radcliffe Borough	1-1, 1-3
Congleton Town v Frickley Athletic	0-1
Lincoln United v Jarrow Roofing Boldon CA	2-1
Kendal Town v Ossett Town	2-0
Droylsden v FC Halifax Town	0-2
Horden CW v Burscough	1-4
Blyth Spartans v Ossett Albion	7-1
North Ferriby United v FC United of Manchester	0-1
Hyde United v Salford City	2-2, 0-1
Chorley v Ashton United	2-1
Southport v Spennymoor Town	3-1
Bradford Park Avenue v Harrogate Town	4-0
Northwich Victoria v Bardon Hill Sports	8-0
Fleetwood Town v Farsley Celtic	3-1
Workington v Cammell Laird	4-1
Stocksbridge Park Steels v Stalybridge Celtic	2-7
Guiseley v Bamber Bridge	2-0
Buxton v AFC Fylde	5-0
Coventry Sphinx v Stafford Rangers	2-2, 3-2
Matlock Town v Bury Town	2-2, 0-2
Nuneaton Town v Carlton Town	1-1, 3-0
Bedford Town v Romulus	2-1
Alfreton Town v AFC Wulfrunians	6-0
Bedworth United v Rainworth MW	2-1
AFC Telford United v Pegasus Juniors	4-1
Sutton Coldfield Town v Needham Market	3-1
Hinckley United v Kirkley & Pakefield	2-1
Lowestoft Town v Boston United	1-0
Redditch United v Stratford Town	1-1, 2-0
Market Drayton Town v Gainsborough Trinity	1-2
Ilkeston Town v Mildenhall Town	4-1
Eastwood Town v Corby Town	2-1
Worcester City v Bourne Town	3-0
Mickleover Sports v Solihull Moors	3-4
Rugby Town v Hucknall Town	1-3
Cambridge City v Northampton Spencer	4-1
Enfield 1893 v Chelmsford City	0-5
Walton Casuals v Selsey	1-0
Canvey Island v Tooting & Mitcham United	0-2
Heybridge Swifts v St Albans City	1-0
Burnham v Aveley	1-1, 1-3
Chesham United v Billericay Town	4-2
Sutton United v Uxbridge	3-0
Lewes v Leatherhead	1-1, 1-0
Bishop's Stortford v Thurrock	2-3
Hythe Town v Woking	2-2, 1-5
Tonbridge Angels v Horsham YMCA	4-0
Dover Athletic v East Preston	8-0
Boreham Wood v Wealdstone	2-4
Windsor & Eton v Farnborough	0-1
Hendon v Kingstonian	2-1
Potters Bar Town v Whitstable Town	3-0
Bromley v Flackwell Heath	2-0
Braintree Town v Hampton & Richmond Borough	0-0, 1-4
Harefield United v Maidstone United	0-2
Wingate & Finchley v Aylesbury	2-2, 1-2
Sittingbourne v Staines Town	2-3
Worthing v Dartford	1-2
Welling United v East Thurrock United	2-0
Walton & Hersham v Enfield Town	3-2
Ashford Town (Middlesex) v Badshot Lea	10-0
Slough Town v Concord Rangers	2-0
Bishop's Cleeve v Weymouth	3-0
Dorchester Town v Hungerford	4-0
Bashley v Gloucester City	1-2
Gillingham Town v Mangotsfield United	3-3, 0-3
Abingdon United v Cirencester Town	0-0, 1-3
Willand Rovers v Bath City	0-5
Almondsbury Town v AFC Totton	1-4
Weston-Super-Mare v Havant & Waterlooville	0-1
Brackley Town v Basingstoke Town	0-1
Clevedon Town v Newport County	1-3
Chippenham Town v Merthyr Tydfil	4-1
Witney United v Eastleigh	1-6
VT v Oxford City	0-1
Bridgwater Town v Hallen	1-0
Maidenhead United v Truro City	2-5

THIRD QUALIFYING ROUND

Salford City v Blyth Spartans	2-2, 1-2
Fleetwood Town v Vauxhall Motors	3-2
Northwich Victoria v Chorley	4-1
Buxton v Bradford Park Avenue	2-2, 1-0
Guiseley v Kendal Town	1-1, 0-1
Workington v Radcliffe Borough	3-0
Alfreton Town v Southport	2-2, 1-2
FC Halifax Town v Burscough	1-0
Lincoln United v Frickley Athletic	1-1, 1-1
Lincoln United won 3-1 on penalties.	
Cambridge City v Hinckley United	0-5
Solihull Moors v Redditch United	0-2
Stourbridge v Hucknall Town	0-0, 6-1
Ilkeston Town v Eastwood Town	1-1, 3-1
Bury Town v Bedford Town	1-1, 4-3
Coventry Sphinx v Bedworth United	0-1
Lowestoft Town v Sutton Coldfield Town	0-0, 2-1
AFC Telford United v Worcester City	0-0, 1-0
Nuneaton Town v Gainsborough Trinity	1-0
Hampton & Richmond Borough v Aveley	1-1, 2-1
Dartford v Chelmsford City	1-4
Wealdstone v Lewes	3-0
Thurrock v Potters Bar Town	4-2
Hendon v Ashford Town (Middlesex)	0-0, 2-2
Hendon won 9-8 on penalties.	
Tonbridge Angels v Bromley	0-2
Dover Athletic v Welling United	2-0
Tooting & Mitcham United v Slough Town	3-2
Sutton United v Walton & Hersham	1-0
Aylesbury v Chesham United	4-3
Walton Casuals v Staines Town	0-3
Woking v Maidstone United	2-0
Heybridge Swifts v Farnborough	0-0, 0-3
Paulton Rovers v Newport County	1-0
Dorchester Town v Gloucester City	1-2
Oxford City v Cirencester Town	2-0
Eastleigh v Basingstoke Town	2-0
Bishop's Cleeve v Bath City	1-4
Truro City v Mangotsfield United	1-1, 1-1
Mangotsfield United won 4-3 on penalties.	
AFC Totton v Bridgwater Town	3-2
Havant & Waterlooville v Chippenham Town	1-2
FC United of Manchester v Stalybridge Celtic	3-3, 1-0

FOURTH QUALIFYING ROUND

Hinckley United v Histon	2-1
Nuneaton Town v Kendal Town	1-0
FC Halifax Town v Wrexham	0-1
Gateshead v Southport	3-0
Workington v Rushden & Diamonds	0-3
Mansfield Town v Altrincham	3-0
Buxton v Stourbridge	0-4
Blyth Spartans v AFC Telford United	0-0, 0-4
Ilkeston Town v Tamworth	2-0
Lincoln United v Cambridge United	1-3
Kettering Town v Redditch United	1-1, 1-0
Northwich Victoria v FC United of Manchester	3-0
Barrow v Chester City	1-1, 4-0
Kidderminster Harriers v Fleetwood Town	0-0, 1-3
York City v Bedworth United	2-0
Hendon v Woking	0-5
Gloucester City v Lowestoft Town	1-1, 2-4
Farnborough v Salisbury City	0-0, 2-4
Mangotsfield United v Forest Green Rovers	1-2
Crawley Town v AFC Wimbledon	1-1, 1-3
Oxford City v Bury Town	2-1
Bromley v Ebbsfleet United	3-0
Chelmsford City v Stevenage Borough	1-2
Aylesbury v Wealdstone	2-4
Dover Athletic v Eastleigh	3-5
Hayes & Yeading United v Staines Town	0-1
Luton Town v Grays Athletic	3-0
Oxford United v Thurrock	2-0
Bath City v AFC Totton	3-2
Paulton Rovers v Chippenham Town	3-0
Tooting & Mitcham United v Eastbourne Borough	3-3, 4-3
Hampton & Richmond Borough v Sutton United	1-3

THE E.ON FA CUP 2009–10
COMPETITION PROPER

■ *Denotes player sent off.*

FIRST ROUND

Friday, 6 November 2009

Bristol R (0) 2 *(Duffy 73, Hughes 90 (pen))*

Southampton (0) 3 *(Connolly 63, 68, Antonio 70)* 6446

Bristol R: Evans; Regan, Hughes, Campbell, Anthony, Elliott, Lines, Blizzard (Duffy), Wright (Swallow), Osei-Kuffour, Williams.
Southampton: Davis; James, Harding (Gobern O), Hammond, Jaidi, Thomas, Antonio (Wotton), Schneiderlin, Lambert, Lallana, Connolly (Mills).

Huddersfield T (4) 6 *(Williams 9, Roberts 21, 72, Novak 24, 56, Rhodes 44)*

Dagenham & R (0) 1 *(Benson 74)* 5858

Huddersfield T: Smithies; Peltier, Williams, Collins, Clarke P, Clarke N, Pilkington (Ainsworth), Kay (Clarke T), Rhodes, Novak (Robinson), Roberts.
Dagenham & R: Roberts; Doe, Tejan-Sie (Montgomery), Arber, Antwi, Thurgood, Green, Nurse, Benson, Scott (Thomas), Gain.

Notts Co (1) 2 *(Hawley 45, Jackson 46)*

Bradford C (0) 1 *(Boulding M 81)* 4213

Notts Co: Hoult; Bishop, Clapham, Ravenhill, Hunt, Edwards, Jackson, Ritchie (Westcarr), Akinbiyi (Rodgers), Hawley (Facey), Davies.
Bradford C: Eastwood; Bateson, O'Brien L, Bullock, Rehman, Williams, Flynn, Neilson, Evans (Osborne), Hanson, O'Brien J (Boulding M).

Saturday, 7 November 2009

Accrington S (2) 2 *(Ryan 19, Symes 33)*

Salisbury C (0) 1 *(Tubbs 66)* 1379

Accrington S: Dunbavin; Winnard, Lees, Procter, Kempson, Edwards, Joyce, Ryan, Grant, Symes, Miles (McConville).
Salisbury C: Bittner; Clohessy, Turley, Anderson, Tafazolli (Cox), Brown (Gray B), Ruddick (Webb), Clarke, Sinclair, Tubbs, Flood.

AFC Telford U (0) 1 *(Blakeman 49)*

Lincoln C (1) 3 *(Torres 14, Clarke J 65, Brown 76)* 2809

AFC Telford U: Young; Vaughan, Newton, Cowan, Killock, Rodgers, Adams, Blakeman, Thompson, Brown, Trainer.
Lincoln C: Burch; Hughton, Brown, Pulis, Swaibu, Kovacs, Clarke J (John-Lewis), Clarke S, Howe (Pearce), Fagan, Torres.

Aldershot T (2) 2 *(Soares 13, Donnelly 33)*

Bury (0) 0 2519

Aldershot T: Jaimez-Ruiz; Herd, Sandell, Chalmers, Hinshelwood, Charles, Hudson, Soares (Harding), Morgan M (Grant), Donnelly (Hylton), Straker.
Bury: Brown; Buchanan, Newey, Dawson, Cresswell, Sodje, Racchi (Futcher), Barry-Murphy, Lowe, Baker (Scott), Jones.

Barnet (1) 3 *(O'Flynn 18, 66, Hyde M 47)*

Darlington (0) 1 *(Diop 73)* 1654

Barnet: Cole; Deen, Gillet, Hyde M, Yakubu (Kamdjo), Breen, Adomah (Jarrett), Bolasie (Deverdics), Furlong, O'Flynn, Hughes.
Darlington: Liversedge; Barnes, Barnett, Davis, Foster, Plummer, Smith G, Convery (Gray J), Thomas, Collins (Main), Smith J (Diop).

Barrow (1) 2 *(Cook 36, Walker 90)*

Eastleigh (0) 1 *(Forbes 85)* 1655

Barrow: Tomlinson; Spender, Jelleyman, Jones, Pearson, Hulbert, Bond, Kamara, Walker, Cook, Rutherford (Logan).
Eastleigh: Matthews; Goodhind, Poate, Riviere, Jordan, Smith (McAuley), Adeniyi, Forbes, Brown (Taylor), Gillespie, Taggart (White).

Bromley (0) 0

Colchester U (2) 4 *(Hackney 32, Odejayi 35, Platt 71, Gillespie 89)* 4242

Bromley: Williams; Henriques (Dalhouse), Dunk, Corneille, O'Sullivan, Gillman, Carew, L'Anson, McBean (Williams), Erskine, Dolby (Cassius).
Colchester U: Williams; White, Tierney, Fox, Batth, Okuonghae, Ifil, Hackney (Elito), Platt (Thomas), Odejayi (Gillespie), O'Toole.

Cambridge U (1) 4 *(Holroyd 5, Reason 64, Pitt 71, Marriott 86)*

Ilkeston T (0) 0 2395

Cambridge U: Potter; McAuley, Tonkin, Reason, Hatswell, Saah, Willmott, Carden, Holroyd (Marriott), Crow (Phillips), Pitt (Challinor).
Ilkeston T: Lowson; Holmes, Borner, Hooks, Mitchell, Waterfall, Beeckoft (Burge), Dempsey, Mendes (Harris), Morgan-Smith, Duncum.

Carlisle U (1) 2 *(Harte 21, Pericard 55)*

Morecambe (0) 2 *(Jevons 70, Duffy 85)* 4181

Carlisle U: Pidgeley; Keogh, Horwood, Kavanagh, Livesey, Harte, Hurst (Anyinsah), Taiwo (Clayton), Dobie, Pericard, Robson.
Morecambe: Roche; Parrish, Adams (Duffy), Wilson, Bentley, Stanley, Wainwright (Twiss), Drummond■, Mullin (Craney), Jevons, Hunter.

Chesterfield (1) 1 *(Lester 4)*

Bournemouth (2) 3 *(Igoe 8, Connell 28, 76)* 3277

Chesterfield: Lee; Little■, Robertson, Perkins, Hall, Breckin, Small (Niven), Allott, Lester (Bowery), Talbot, Boden.
Bournemouth: Jalal; Bradbury, Cummings, Hollands, Pearce, Garry, Igoe (McQuoid), Robinson, Pitman (Fletcher), Connell (Bartley), Feeney.

Forest Green R (1) 1 *(Hodgkiss 28)*

Mansfield T (0) 1 *(Garner 87)* 1149

Forest Green R: Burton; Hodgkiss, O'Cearuill, Smith, Preece, McDonald, Brown, Ameobi (Davies), Platt, Rigg, Stonehouse.
Mansfield T: Marriott; Silk, Heckingbottom, Mills, Jones, Garner, Istead (Williams), Brough, Duffy (Sturrock), Perry, Speight (Dobson).

Gateshead (0) 2 *(Price 57 (og), Winn 90)*

Brentford (0) 2 *(Cort 61, O'Connor 70)* 1150

Gateshead: Farman; Baxter, Williams, Gate, Curtis, Cave, Harwood (Phillips), Turnbull, Armstrong (One), Clare, Winn.
Brentford: Price; Foster, Dickson, O'Connor, Wilson, Bennett, Saunders (Hunt), Bean, Cort, Weston, Wood (Strevens).

Gillingham (2) 3 *(Weston 25, Brandy 28, Bentley 62)*

Southend U (0) 0 4605

Gillingham: Royce; Fuller, Palmer, Weston, Gowling, Fry, Bentley, Lewis (Maher), Jackson, Barcham (Nutter), Brandy (McCammon).
Southend U: Mildenhall; Francis, Herd (Scannell), Christophe, Barrett, O'Keefe, Grant, Moussa, Freedman, Walker (Asante), Laurent (Okai).

Grimsby T (0) 0
Bath C (1) 2 *(Holland 32, Edwards 52)*   2103
Grimsby T: Colgan; Wood, Widdowson (Fuller), Leary, Linwood, Atkinson, Bore (Jones), Boshell, Akpa Akrpo (North), Conlon, Shahin.
Bath C: Robinson; Jombati, Rollo, Jones, Holland, Connolly, Simpson, Badman, Edwards (Douglas), Mohamed (Perrott), Hogg.

Hartlepool U (0) 0
Kettering T (1) 1 *(Ashikodi 15)*   2645
Hartlepool U: Flinders; Austin, Hartley, Sweeney, Collins, Liddle, Monkhouse, Larkin, Behan (Greulich), Boyd (Jones), Humphreys.
Kettering T: Harper; Eaden, Taylor, Dempster, Roper (Thomas), Geohaghon, Green, Heslop, Elding (Spencer), Ashikodi (Marna), Noubissie.

Hereford U (1) 2 *(Manset 6, Valentine 86 (pen))*
Sutton U (0) 0   1713
Hereford U: Bartlett; Blanchett, Valentine, Jones D, Lowe, Lunt, Godsmark (McCallum), Sonko, King C, Manset[■], Pugh (Done).
Sutton U: Scriven; Hawes B, Bray, Goodliffe, Thomas (Joseph), Cobbs, Hann, Pouton, Gargan, McKimm (Phillips), Hawes J (Perkins).

Luton T (3) 3 *(Basham 4, 29, Newton 21)*
Rochdale (0) 3 *(Dawson 58, Thompson 87, 89)*   3167
Luton T: Gore; Blackett, Murray, Keane (Howells), White, Pilkington G, Newton, Basham (Craddock), Gallen, Burgess, Gnakpa.
Rochdale: Arthur; Holness, Kennedy T, Jones J, McArdle, Dawson, Thompson, Kennedy J, Dagnall, O'Grady (Buckley), Rundle (Higginbotham).

Milton Keynes D (1) 1 *(Gobern L 25)*
Macclesfield T (0) 0   4868
Milton Keynes D: Gueret; Doumbe, Lewington, Leven, McCracken, Daniel Powell, Devaney (Gobern L), Gleeson, Easter (Baldock S), Wilbraham, Chadwick (Puncheon).
Macclesfield T: Veiga; Reid I (Brown), Brisley, Bell, Morgan, Bencherif, Draper, Rooney, Sinclair, Wright (Sappleton), Daniel (Tipton).

Northampton T (1) 2 *(Guttridge 29, 61)*
Fleetwood T (1) 1 *(Clancy 41)*   3077
Northampton T: Dunn; Rodgers, Johnson, Guttridge (Davis), Hinton, Beckwith, Gilligan, Curtis, Guinan, Akinfenwa, Holt.
Fleetwood T: Hurst; Beeley, Wright, Taylor, McNulty, Pond, Clancy, Milligan, Wilde (Cahill), Seddon, Mullan.

Nuneaton T (0) 0
Exeter C (4) 4 *(Taylor M 4, 44, Corr 31, Hadland 38 (og))*
                                                    2452
Nuneaton T: Acton; Oddy, Nisevic, Noon, Dean, Pierpoint, Marsden (Murphey), Spacey, Dillon, Moore, Hadland (Armson).
Exeter C: Marriott; Tully, Golbourne, Russell, Seaborne, Taylor M, Dunne (Sercombe), Cozic, Fleetwood (Stansfield), Corr, Harley.

Oldham Ath (0) 0
Leeds U (1) 2 *(Howson 36, Grella 90)*   5552
Oldham Ath: Flahavan; Holdsworth, Hills, Furman (Brooke), Gregan, Hazell, Colbeck (Whitaker), Taylor, Smalley, Parker (Lee), Marrow.
Leeds U: Ankergren; Naylor, Hughes, Kilkenny, Bromby, Kisnorbo, Doyle (White), Howson, Beckford (Grella), Snodgrass, Johnson.

Oxford U (0) 1 *(Midson 55)*
Yeovil T (0) 0   6144
Oxford U: Clarke; Batt, Kinniburgh, Bulman, Foster, Creighton, Green M (Cook), Murray (Deering), Constable, Midson (Perry), Clist.

Yeovil T: Martin; Alcock, Jones (Hutchins), MacDonald, Caulker, Forbes, Obika, Mason, Williams S, Murtagh, Welsh (O'Callaghan).

Paulton R (0) 0
Norwich C (3) 7 *(Holt 15, 43, Martin C 24, 77, 83, 85, Hoolahan 74)*
                                                    2070
Paulton R: Phillips; Ball, Rich, Plummer (Burborough), Price, Tyrrell, Jefferies, Lane (Cousins), Claridge, Cleverley (Waters), Lacey.
Norwich C: Rudd; Doherty, Drury (Wiggins), Russell, Berthel Askou, Nelson, Hoolahan, Smith, Martin C, Holt (Tudur-Jones), Lappin (McDonald).

Port Vale (1) 1 *(Yates 42)*
Stevenage B (0) 1 *(Griffin 90)*   3999
Port Vale: Martin; Collins, Yates, Griffith, McCombe, Owen, Jarrett, Fraser, Richards, Haldane (Guy), Taylor K.
Stevenage B: Day; Henry, Laird (Vincenti), Roberts, Ashton (Byrom), Bostwick, Drury (Odhiambo), Bridges, Griffin, Odubade, Cole.

Rushden & D (1) 3 *(O'Connor 31, 66, Byrne 82)*
Hinckley U (0) 1 *(Webster 64)*   1540
Rushden & D: Abbey; Osano, Robinson, Porter (Pattison), Stuart, Corcoran, Byrne, Terry, Farrell (Mills), O'Connor (Reid), Tomlin.
Hinckley U: MacKenzie; Taylor (Collins), Giddings, Lavery, Lister, Franklin, Hall, Gooding, Webster, Eribenne (West), Cartwright[■].

Shrewsbury T (0) 0
Staines T (1) 1 *(Chaaban 21)*   3539
Shrewsbury T: Neal C; Hooman (Elder), Cansdell-Sherriff, Neal L, Coughlin, Langmead, Murray, Labadie (Simpson), Hibbert, Robinson (Bright), McIntyre.
Staines T: Wells; Jackson (Scarlett), Sterling, Gordon, Ifura, Brown, Newton, Risbridger, Butler (Thomas), Griffiths, Chaaban (Taylor).

Stockport Co (3) 5 *(Thompson P 13, Poole 20, Baker 38 (pen), Turnbull 67, 72)*
Tooting & M (0) 0   3076
Stockport Co: fon Williams; Vincent, Rose, Mullins, Raynes, Bridcutt (Tansey), Poole, Turnbull, Thompson P (Johnson O), Bignall (Fisher), Baker.
Tooting & M: King; Hamlin, Byatt (Fletcher), Nelson, Vines J, York, McLeod (Pitterson), Goode, Vines P (Haverin), Parker, Hartburn.

Stourbridge (0) 0
Walsall (1) 1 *(Jones 34)*   2014
Stourbridge: Brock; Collins (Drake), Mahon (Dovey), Smith, Canavan, Bennett, Slater, Dyson, Rowe (Rock), Billingham, Evans.
Walsall: Ince; Weston, Hughes, Bradley, Sansara, Smith, Jones, Mattis, Byfield, Deeney (Nicholls), Richards (Till).

Swindon T (1) 1 *(Paynter 36)*
Woking (0) 0   4805
Swindon T: Smith; Amankwaah, Kennedy, Ferry (Peacock), Cuthbert, Greer, McGovern, Timlin, Paynter, Obadeyi (Hutchinson), McNamee (Easton).
Woking: Worner; Sinclair, Nicolau (Hand), Ricketts, Hutchinson, Boardman (Thomas), Anane, Arter, Bryant (Ademola), Sole, Sam-Yorke.

Torquay U (2) 3 *(Wroe 10 (pen), 19 (pen), 70)*
Cheltenham T (1) 1 *(Lewis 8)*   2370
Torquay U: Bevan; Mansell, Nicholson, Hargreaves, Robertson, Charnock, Carlisle, Wroe, Benyon (Rendell), Sills, Thomson (Stevens).
Cheltenham T: Brown SP; Low, Ridley[■], Bird, Diallo, Townsend, Pook (Haynes), Lewis, Hammond (Hayles), Alsop, Richards (Gallinagh).

Tranmere R (0) 1 *(Shuker 51)*
Leyton Orient (1) 1 *(Ashworth 7)* 3180
Tranmere R: Daniels; Logan, Bakayogo, Edds, Goodison, Taylor, Shuker, Welsh, Ricketts, Curran, Mahon.
Leyton Orient: Morris; Purches, Daniels, Chorley, Ashworth, Smith, Pires, Thornton, Patulea (Jarvis), McGleish, Demetriou.

Wrexham (0) 1 *(Taylor G 89)*
Lowestoft T (0) 0 2402
Wrexham: Maxwell; Obeng, Mike Williams (Taylor N), Fleming, Assoumani, Westwood, McCluskey (Cieslewicz), Taboubi (Jones M), Taylor G, Baynes Sakho.
Lowestoft T: Reynolds; Plaskett, Smith, Holt, Crane, Halliday, Godbold (Bussens), Fisk, Nolan, Cockrill (King), Mitchell (McGee).

Wycombe W (2) 4 *(Harrold 18 (pen), 70, Davies 38, Pittman 61)*
Brighton & HA (2) 4 *(Bennett 3, Forster 45 (pen), Murray 51, 83 (pen))* 2749
Wycombe W: Shearer; Hunt, Woodman■, Doherty, Duberry, Johnson, Betsy, Davies, Harrold, Pittman (Zebroski), Phillips (Bloomfield).
Brighton & HA: Smith G; Hoyte■, Virgo, Crofts, Elphick, El-Abd, Cox, Dicker, Murray, Forster (Davies C), Bennett.

York C (1) 3 *(Brodie 39, 88, Pacquette 86)*
Crewe Alex (2) 2 *(Grant 33, Zola 41)* 30¨0
York C: Ingham; Purkiss, Meredith (Pacquette), Barrett, McGurk, Parslow, Lawless, Smith (Graham), Rankine, Brodie, Carruthers (Nelthorpe).
Crewe Alex: Phillips; Brayford, Westwood, Walton, Ada, Mitchel-King, Shelley, Bailey (Donaldson), Moore, Zola (Murphy), Grant (Clements).

Sunday, 8 November 2009
Burton Alb (2) 3 *(Harrad 15 (pen), Maghoma 45, Austin 90)*
Oxford C (1) 2 *(Alexis 6, Brooks 55)* 2207
Burton Alb: Krysiak; Austin, Webster (Brown), Simpson, Branston, James, Maghoma, Penn, Walker (Pearson), Harrad, Phillips (Makofo).
Oxford C: Knight; Clarke, Perpetuini, Savage, Pond, Gunn, Janes (Lyon), Alexis, Ballard■, Steele, Brooks (Bell).

Northwich Vic (0) 1 *(Riley 81)*
Charlton Ath (0) 0 2153
Northwich Vic: Aspden; Aspin, Brown R, Bailey, Kerr, Herring, D'Laryea, O'Connor, Newby (Edwards), Allan (Winter), Elam (Riley).
Charlton Ath: Randolph; Omozusi, Youga, Racon, Dailly, Sodje, Sam, Bailey, Semedo (Wagstaff), McLeod (Burton), Shelvey (McKenzie).

Wealdstone (0) 2 *(Ashe 63, 90)*
Rotherham U (2) 3 *(Le Fondre 33, Ellison 44, Broughton 82)* 1638
Wealdstone: Thomas; McCoy, Chappell, Gray, Massey, Ashe, Forbes, O'Leary, Mpi (Lafayette), Ellerbeck (Spendlove), E'Beyer.
Rotherham U: Warrington; Tonge, Nicholas (Brogan), Harrison, Sharps, Fenton, Law (Warne), Mills, Broughton, Le Fondre, Ellison.

Monday, 9 November 2009
Millwall (0) 4 *(Harris 49, Price 72, 89, Schofield 86)*
AFC Wimbledon (0) 1 *(Taylor 81)* 9453
Millwall: Forde; Dunne, Smith, Laird, Robinson, Craig, Hackett, Abdou, Morison (Price), Harris (Martin), Schofield.
AFC Wimbledon: Pullen; Hatton, Johnson, Godfrey (Duncan), Lorraine, Inns, Gregory, Moore, Kedwell, Main, Taylor.

FIRST ROUND REPLAYS

Wednesday, 11 November 2009
Rochdale (0) 0
Luton T (0) 2 *(Gallen 60, 74)* 1982
Rochdale: Taberner; Holness, Kennedy T, Jones, McArdle, Dawson, Thompson (Higginbotham), Kennedy J, Dagnall, O'Grady, Rundle (Magna).
Luton T: Gore; Asafu-Adjaye, Howells, Hall (Newton), White, Pilkington G, Jarvis, Nicholls, Gallen (Charles), Craddock (Gnakpa), Burgess.

Tuesday, 17 November 2009
Brentford (2) 5 *(Strevens 42, MacDonald 45, 60, Weston 67, 73)*
Gateshead (0) 2 *(Armstrong 58, 81)* 1960
Brentford: Price; Foster, Dickson, O'Connor, Osborne, Legge, Taylor, Bean (Hunt), Strevens (Cort), MacDonald, Weston.
Gateshead: Farman; Baxter, Cave, Gate, Curtis, Williams, Harwood (One), Turnbull (Francis), Armstrong, Clare, Winn.

Leyton Orient (0) 0
Tranmere R (0) 1 *(Taylor 83)* 1518
Leyton Orient: Morris; Purches (Patulea), Daniels, Chorley, Mkandawire, Chambers, Melligan (Jarvis), Thornton, Scowcroft, McGleish, Demetriou.
Tranmere R: Daniels; Logan, Bakayogo, Taylor, Broomes, Goodison, McLaren, Barnett, Thomas-Moore, Curran, Shuker.

Mansfield T (0) 1 *(Perry 71)*
Forest Green R (1) 2 *(Platt 40, 90)* 2496
Mansfield T: Marriott; Silk, Heckingbottom, Mills, Jones, Garner, Brough, Speight (Briscoe), Perry, Sturrock (Duffy), Williams.
Forest Green R: Burton; Hodgkiss, McDonald, Powell, Preece, O'Cearuill, Brown, Smith, Platt, Rigg, Stonehouse.

Morecambe (0) 0
Carlisle U (1) 1 *(Anyinsah 5)* 3307
Morecambe: Roche; Parrish (Duffy), Wilson, Artell, Haining, Craney, Hunter, Stanley, Jevons, Mullin (Curtis), Twiss.
Carlisle U: Pidgeley; Keogh, Horwood, Kavanagh (Hurst), Livesey, Harte, Anyinsah, Taiwo, Clayton, Pericard (Dobie), Robson.

Stevenage B (0) 0
Port Vale (1) 1 *(Dodds 24)* 2914
Stevenage B: Day; Henry, Laird (Byrom), Roberts, Ashton (Murphy), Bostwick, Drury, Bridges (Vincenti), Griffin, Odubade, Cole.
Port Vale: Martin; Loft, Taylor K, Griffith, McCombe, Collins, Haldane (Glover), Jarrett (Howland), Richards, Dodds, Taylor R.

Wednesday, 18 November 2009
Brighton & HA (1) 2 *(Crofts 36, Bennett 61)*
Wycombe W (0) 0 3383
Brighton & HA: Kuipers (Smith G); Whing, Tunnicliffe, Crofts, Elphick, El-Abd, Cox (McLeod), Dicker, Dickinson (Forster), Davies C, Bennett.
Wycombe W: Shearer; Green (Pittman), Woodman, Westwood, Oliver, Doherty, Phillips (Beavon), Mousinho, Harrold (Zebroski), Davies, Betsy.

SECOND ROUND

Saturday, 28 November 2009
Accrington S (1) 2 *(Grant 29, Symes 50)*
Barnet (0) 2 *(Yakubu 47, O'Flynn 90 (pen))* 1501
Accrington S: Dunbavin (Bouzanis); Winnard, Lees (Murphy), Procter, Kempson, Edwards, McConville, Ryan, Grant, Symes, Miles■.
Barnet: Cole; Deen, Gillet, Hyde M (Deverdics), Yakubu, Leach (Hyde), Jarrett, Bolasie (Adomah), Furlong, O'Flynn, Hughes.

Bath C (1) 1 *(Hogg 43)*
Forest Green R (1) 2 *(Smith 24, Preece 48)*   3325
Bath C: Robinson; Jombati (Pelecaci), Rollo, Jones, Holland, Connolly, Simpson, Badman, Edwards (Douglas), Mohamed (Perrott), Hogg.
Forest Green R: Burton; Hodgkiss, McDonald, Smith, Preece, O'Cearuill, Brown, Ameobi, Platt, Joyce (Powell), Stonehouse.

Bournemouth (1) 1 *(Pitman 38)*
Notts Co (0) 2 *(Hughes 49, Westcarr 58)*   6082
Bournemouth: Thomas; Bradbury, Cummings, Bartley (Hollands), Pearce, Garry, Igoe (McQuoid), Robinson, Pitman, Connell (Fletcher), Feeney.
Notts Co: Schmeichel; Thompson, Clapham, Ravenhill (Ritchie), Edwards, Lee, Bishop, Jackson, Hughes, Westcarr, Davies.

Brentford (1) 1 *(Legge 13)*
Walsall (0) 0   2611
Brentford: Price; Foster, Dickson, O'Connor, Bennett, Legge, Bostock (Murphy), Bean, Strevens, MacDonald (Hunt), Wood (Taylor).
Walsall: Ince; Weston (Westlake), Hughes, Bradley, Sansara, Smith, Jones, Mattis, Byfield (Parkin), Deeney, Richards.

Brighton & HA (2) 3 *(Dickinson 3, 86, Forster 22 (pen))*
Rushden & D (2) 2 *(Tomlin 14, O'Connor 40)*   3638
Brighton & HA: Smith G; Hoyte, Virgo, Crofts, Elphick, El-Abd, Navarro (Dicker), McLeod (Hart), Dickinson, Forster, Bennett.
Rushden & D: Abbey; Osano, Robinson, Porter, Stuart, Downer, Byrne, Cousins (Pattison) (Akurang), Farrell, Tomlin, O'Connor (McNamara).

Cambridge U (0) 1 *(Tonkin 84)*
York C (2) 2 *(Rankine 37, Brodie 40 (pen))*   3505
Cambridge U: Potter; Gleeson, Tonkin, McAuley, Hatswell, Saah, Willmott, Ives (Marriott), Holroyd, Crow, Pitt.
York C: Ingham; Parslow, Meredith, Mackin, McGurk, Graham, Lawless, Barrett (Ferrell), Rankine (Gash), Brodie, Carruthers.

Carlisle U (1) 3 *(Pericard 12, Hurst 46, Keogh 72)*
Norwich C (1) 1 *(Holt 26)*   3946
Carlisle U: Collin; Keogh, Horwood, Livesey, Harte, Murphy, Hurst, Kavanagh, Anyinsah, Pericard (Dobie), Robson.
Norwich C: Forster; Otsemobor, Drury, Russell (Hughes), Nelson, Doherty, Hoolahan, Smith, Martin C (McDonald), Holt, Lappin (Dawkin).

Gillingham (0) 1 *(Weston 69)*
Burton Alb (0) 0   4996
Gillingham: Royce; Fuller, Palmer (Nutter), Weston, Gowling, Fry, Bentley, Lewis (Oli) Jackson, Barcham, Brandy (McCammon).
Burton Alb: Redmond; Austin (Brown), Webster, James, Branston, McGrath, Simpson, Penn, Kabba, Harrad (Pearson), Cadogan (Makofo).

Hereford U (0) 0
Colchester U (0) 1 *(O'Toole 90)*   2225
Hereford U: Bartlett; Green, Lowe, Blanchett, Jones D, Lunt (Gwynne), Mutch, McCallum, King C (Pugh), Constantine (Manset), Valentine.
Colchester U: Williams; White, Tierney, Izzet, Reid, Okuonghae, Hackney (Platt), Lisbie, Gillespie (Wordsworth), Odejayi (Ifil), O'Toole.

Milton Keynes D (1) 4 *(Baldock 35, 70, Devaney 75, Easter 86)*
Exeter C (0) 3 *(Corr 50, 54, Stansfield 67)*   4867
Milton Keynes D: Gueret; Woodards (Howell), Lewington, Leven (Devaney), McCracken, Daniel Powell, Gleeson, Chadwick, Baldock S, Wilbraham (Easter), Puncheon.

Exeter C: Marriott; Duffy (Archibald-Henvil.e), Golbourne, Russell, Seaborne, Taylor M, Cozic, Harley, Fleetwood (Stansfield), Corr (Dunne), Stewart.

Northampton T (0) 2 *(Hammond 68 (og), Gilligan 90 (pen))*
Southampton (2) 3 *(Papa Waigo 41, Lallana 43, Hammond 59)*   4858
Northampton T: Dunn; Rodgers, Gilbert, Gilligan, Hinton, Kanyuka, Walker, Guttridge (Dyer), Guinan (McKay), Akinfenwa (Harris), Holt.
Southampton: Bialkowski; Murty, Harding, Wotton, Perry, Jaidi, Papa Waigo, Schneiderlin (Mills), Lambert, Lallana (Antonio), Hammond.

Northwich Vic (0) 1 *(Bailey 47)*
Lincoln C (1) 3 *(Fagan 18, Clarke J 49, 64)*   3544
Northwich Vic: Aspden; Aspin, Brown R, Bailey, Grand, Herring (Riley), D'Laryea, Connor, Newby, Allan (Kerr), Elam (Brown J).
Lincoln C: Burch; Hughton, Heath, Kovacs, Watts, Kerr, Herd, Clarke S, Fagan (Gilmour), Clarke J (Howe), Smith.

Oxford U (1) 1 *(Cook 9)*
Barrow (1) 1 *(Bond 43 (pen))*   6082
Oxford U: Clarke; Chapman, Kinniburgh, Bulman Foster*, Creighton, Potter (Perry), Murray (Deering), Cook, Midson, Clist.
Barrow: Tomlinson; Spender, Jelleyman, Pearson, Bolland, Hulbert (Sheridan), Bond, Boyd, Goodfellow (Logan), Blundell, Rutherford.

Port Vale (0) 0
Huddersfield T (1) 1 *(Clarke N 12)*   5311
Port Vale: Martin; Yates, Taylor K, Collins, McCombe, Prosser (Horsfield), Loft (Dodds), Griffith, Haldane, Richards (Jarrett), Taylor R.
Huddersfield T: Smithies; Peltier, Williams, Collins, Clarke P, Clarke N, Ainsworth (Berrett), Kay, Rhodes (Robinson), Novak, Roberts.

Rotherham U (1) 2 *(Le Fondre 45, Brogan 62)*
Luton T (1) 2 *(Craddock 21 (pen), Nwokeji 74)*   3210
Rotherham U: Warrington; Lynch, Nicholas, Roberts, Sharps, Fenton, Law, Taylor R (Harrison), Pope, Le Fondre, Brogan.
Luton T: Pilkington K; Gnakpa (Nwokeji), Murray, Blackett, White, Pilkington G, Newton, Keane, Gallen (Hall), Craddock (Howells), Nicholls.

Staines T (0) 1 *(Chaaban 79 (pen))*
Millwall (0) 1 *(Robinson 69)*   2753
Staines T: Wells; Jackson, Sterling, Gordon, Ifura, Brown, Newton, Risbridger, Butler, Chaaban, Griffiths.
Millwall: Forde; Dunne, Frampton (Smith), Laird, Robinson, Ward, Hackett, Abdou, Morison (Grimes), Price (Grabban), Martin.

Tranmere R (0) 0
Aldershot T (0) 0   3742
Tranmere R: Daniels; Logan, Bakayogo, Edds, Broomes, Goodison, Welsh, Shuker (Thomas-Moore), Gornell (Ricketts), Curran, Taylor.
Aldershot T: Jaimez-Ruiz; Herd, Sandell, Chalmers, Blackburn, Charles, Jackson (Bozanic), Soares, Morgan M, Donnelly (Halls), Straker (Harding).

Wrexham (0) 0
Swindon T (0) 1 *(Greer 80)*   3011
Wrexham: Maxwell; Obeng, Mike Williams, Fleming, Westwood, Sinclair, Smith*, Baynes, Taylor G, Marc Williams, Taylor N (Cieslewicz).
Swindon T: Lucas; Amankwaah, Lescinel, Douglas (Timlin), Cuthbert, Greer, McGovern, Ferry, Paynter, Hutchinson (Peacock), Sheehan (O'Brien).

Sunday, 29 November 2009

Kettering T (0) 1 *(Roper 63)*

Leeds U (0) 1 *(Beckford 78)* 4837

Kettering T: Harper; Taylor, Davis, Noubissie, Roper, Dempster, Boucaud, Heslop, Elding, Ashikodi (Thomas), Partridge (Marna).
Leeds U: Ankergren; Crowe, Capaldi, Doyle, Bromby, Michalik, Howson, Kilkenny, Beckford, Grella (Becchio), Snodgrass.

Tuesday, 15 December 2009

Stockport Co (0) 0

Torquay U (3) 4 *(Benyon 2, 33, 79, Rendell 28)* 1690

Stockport Co: fon Williams; Mullins, Griffin, Tansey, Vincent, Bridcutt, Poole, Turnbull, Thompson P, Johnson O, Pilkington.
Torquay U: Bevan; Mansell, Smith (Nicholson), Thomson (Stevens), Robertson, Charnock, Carlisle, Wroe, Benyon, Rendell (Sills), Thompson.

SECOND ROUND REPLAYS

Tuesday, 8 December 2009

Aldershot (0) 1 *(Bozanic 90)*

Tranmere R (1) 2 *(Thomas-Moore 43, Gornell 49)* 4060

Aldershot T: Jaimez-Ruiz; Herd, Sandell, Chalmers (Halls), Blackburn, Charles, Jackson (Grant), Soares, Morgan M, Donnelly, Straker (Bozanic).
Tranmere R: Daniels; Logan, Bakayogo, Taylor, Broomes, Goodison, Edds, Welsh (McLaren), Thomas-Moore, Curran, Gornell (Ricketts).

Barnet (0) 0

Accrington S (1) 1 *(Grant 16)* 1288

Barnet: Cole; Deen (Hyde J), Gillet, Hyde M, Yakubu, Butcher, Jarrett, Bolasie, Furlong, O'Flynn, Deverdics (Sinclair).
Accrington S: Bouzanis; Winnard, Joyce, Procter, Kempson, Edwards, Murphy, Ryan, Kee (McConville), Symes, Grant.

Barrow (1) 3 *(Bolland 38, Logan 49, Goodfellow 66)*

Oxford U (0) 1 *(Constable 90)* 2754

Barrow: Tomlinson; Spender, Jelleyman, Pearson, Bolland, Hulbert, Bond, Goodfellow, Walker, Blundell (Rothery), Rutherford (Logan).
Oxford U: Clarke; Chapman, Sandwith, Bulman (Green M), Foster, Creighton, Potter (Midson), Perry, Constable, Cook, Clist.

Leeds U (1) 5 *(Becchio 20, Grella 108, 116, Kandol 109, Beckford 119)*

Kettering T (0) 1 *(Elding 62)* 10,670

Leeds U: Ankergren; White (Capaldi), Hughes (Grella), Doyle, Bromby, Michalik, Kilkenny, Howson, Beckford, Becchio (Kandol), Snodgrass.
Kettering T: Harper; Taylor, Davis, Noubissie (Fowler), Roper, Dempster, Boucaud, Heslop, Elding, Bain (Thomas), Partridge (Wrack).
aet.

Luton T (2) 3 *(Newton 7, White 19, Gnakpa 68)*

Rotherham U (0) 0 2518

Luton T: Pilkington K; Gnakpa (Craddock), Murray, Blackett, White, Pilkington G, Jarvis, Keane, Gallen (Howells), Nicholls (Hall), Newton.
Rotherham U: Warrington; Lynch, Brogan, Roberts, Sharps, Joseph, Law, Harrison, Pope (Taylor R), Le Fondre, Ellison (Broughton).

Wednesday, 9 December 2009

Millwall (1) 4 *(Morison 40, Smith 50, Dunne 79, Schofield 90)*

Staines T (0) 0 3452

Millwall: Forde; Dunne, Smith, Laird, Robinson, Frampton, Hackett (Grimes), Abdou (Boulder), Morison, Grabban, Schofield.
Staines T: Wells; Jackson, Sterling, Gordon, Ifura, Brown (Onochie), Newton (Ahmad), Butler (Taylor), Risbridger, Griffiths, Chaaban.

THIRD ROUND

Saturday, 2 January 2010

Aston Villa (2) 3 *(Delfouneso 12, Cuellar 37, Carew 90 (pen))*

Blackburn R (0) 1 *(Kalinic 55)* 25,453

Aston Villa: Guzan; Beye, Warnock, Delph (Sidwell), James M Collins, Cuellar, Reo-Coker, Downing, Delfouneso (Carew), Heskey, Young A.
Blackburn R: Brown; Chimbonda, Jones, Reid, Givet, Olsson, Salgado (Rigters), Dunn (Khizanishvili), Kalinic, Diouf, Di Santo (Pedersen).

Blackpool (0) 1 *(Ormerod 51)*

Ipswich T (1) 2 *(Colback 3, Garvan 77)* 7332

Blackpool: Rachubka; John Baptiste, Crainey, Southern, Eardley, Evatt, Adam, Euell (Demontagnac), Ormerod, Taylor-Fletcher (Martin), Vaughan (Edwards).
Ipswich T: Lee-Barrett; Wright D, Rosenior (Edwards), Peters, McAuley, Delaney, Norris (Garvan), Leadbitter, Walters, John (Wickham), Colback.

Bolton W (0) 4 *(Swaibu 49 (og), Lee 51, Cahill 83, Davies M 90)*

Lincoln C (0) 0 11,193

Bolton W: Al Habsi; Steinsson, Robinson, Muamba (Davies M), O'Brien A, Cahill, Gardner, Lee (Cohen), Klasnic (Elmander), Davies K, Taylor.
Lincoln C: Burch; Green, Anderson, Watts, Swaibu, Kerr, Herd, Saunders, John-Lewis (Uwezu), Gilmour, Hughton.

Everton (1) 3 *(Vaughan 12, Cahill 82, Baines 90 (pen))*

Carlisle U (1) 1 *(Hurst 18)* 31,196

Everton: Howard; Heitinga, Baines, Neville, Neill, Hibbert (Coleman), Bilyaletdinov, Fellaini, Vaughan (Agard), Cahill, Pienaar.
Carlisle U: Collin; Livesey, Horwood, Kavanagh (Anyinsah), Keogh, Harte, Hurst, Taiwo, Clayton, Pericard (Dobie), Robson.

Fulham (1) 1 *(Zamora 16)*

Swindon T (0) 0 19,623

Fulham: Schwarzer; Kelly, Konchesky, Riise, Hughes, Smalling, Dikgacoi, Greening, Johnson A (Gera), Zamora, Dempsey.
Swindon T: Lucas; Amankwaah, Sheehan, Douglas, Cuthbert, Greer, McGovern, Paynter, Ward (Timlin), Hutchinson (Macklin), Ferry.

Huddersfield T (0) 0

WBA (0) 2 *(Dorrans 77, Wood 82)* 13,472

Huddersfield T: Smithies; Peltier (Drinkwater), Skarz, Collins, Clarke P, Clarke N, Pilkington, Kay, Rhodes, Novak (Clarke R), Roberts (Robinson).
WBA: Carson; Jara, Cech, Mulumbu, Olsson, Martis, Teixeira (Koren), Brunt (Reid R), Bednar, Cox (Wood), Dorrans.

Leicester C (1) 2 *(King A 39, N'Guessan 89)*

Swansea C (1) 1 *(Cotterill 10)* 12,307

Leicester C: Weale; Neilson, McGivern, King A, Morrison, Hobbs, Oakley (N'Guessan), Wellens, Howard (Kermorgant), Fryatt, Dyer (Gallagher).
Swansea C: De Vries; Serran, Painter, Lopez, Tate, Monk, Cotterill, Allen (Gower), Pintado (Trundle), Van der Gun, Pratley (Dobbie).

Middlesbrough (0) 0

Manchester C (1) 1 *(Mwaruwari 45)* 12,474

Middlesbrough: Coyne; McMahon, Hoyte, Williams R, Riggott, Wheater, O'Neil, Arca (Williams L), Franks, Bent, Johnson A (Emnes) (Yeates).
Manchester C: Given; Zabaleta, Sylvinho, De Jong (Barry), Richards (Tevez), Kompany, Garrido, Petrov, Mwaruwari, Boyata, Weiss (Bellamy).

Millwall (0) 1 *(Grabban 49)*
Derby Co (0) 1 *(Commons 52)* 10,531
Millwall: Forde; Smith, Craig, Laird, Robinson, Frampton, Hackett, Abdou, Morison, Grabban (Price), Martin (Schofield).
Derby Co: Bywater; Connolly, Moxey, Green, Buxton, Addison, Hendrie (Johnson), Pearson, Hulse (Davies), Porter, Commons (Teale).

Milton Keynes D (0) 1 *(Morgan 89)*
Burnley (2) 2 *(Alexander 23 (pen), Fletcher 35)* 11,816
Milton Keynes D: Gueret; Doumbe, Lewington, Leven, Woodards, Howell (Stirling), Gleeson, Baldock S (Chadwick), Easter (Morgan), Wilbraham, Puncheon.
Burnley: Jensen; Eckersley, Kalvenes, Alexander, Duff, Bikey, Eagles, McDonald (Gudjonsson), Fletcher (Thompson), Blake, Elliott.

Nottingham F (0) 0
Birmingham C (0) 0 20,975
Nottingham F: Camp; Gunter, Perch, Chambers, Morgan, Majewski, Anderson (Tyson), McKenna, Earnshaw (McCleary), Blackstock (Adebola), Cohen.
Birmingham C: Hart; Parnaby (McSheffrey), Vignal, Ferguson, Ridgewell, Johnson R, Johnson D, Carsley (Bowyer), Jerome, Phillips (Benitez), Fahey.

Plymouth Arg (0) 0
Newcastle U (0) 0 16,451
Plymouth Arg: Larrieu; Duguid, Sawyer, Fletcher, Arnason, Barker, Judge (Noone), Summerfield (McNamee), Fallon, Mackie, Clark.
Newcastle U: Krul; Taylor R, Simpson, Butt, Coloccini, Kadar, Pancrate (Lovenkrands), Guthrie, Ranger (Carroll), Ameobi, Smith (Gutierrez).

Portsmouth (1) 1 *(Boateng 45)*
Coventry C (1) 1 *(Bell 30)* 11,214
Portsmouth: Begovic; Finnan, Kaboul, Brown, Wilson, Hreidarsson, Hughes (Mullins), Boateng, Piquionne (Webber), Smith, Diop (Utaka).
Coventry C: Westwood (Konstantopoulos); Wright, Cranie, Clingan, Wood, McPake, Bell, Gunnarsson, Morrison (Best), Eastwood, McIndoe.

Preston NE (2) 7 *(Brown 13, Sedgwick 27, Parkin 48, 50, 72 (pen), Williams 52 (og), Carter 64)*
Colchester U (0) 0 7621
Preston NE: Lonergan; Nolan, Davidson, Chaplow (Sumulikoski), St Ledger-Hall, Collins, Sedgwick, Carter, Brown (Mellor), Parkin (Elliott), Wallace.
Colchester U: Williams; White (Izzet), Tierney, Fox, Reid, Okuonghae, Ifil, Wordsworth, Gillespie, Odejayi, Hackney (Thomas).

Reading (1) 1 *(Church 24)*
Liverpool (1) 1 *(Gerrard 36)* 23,656
Reading: Federici (Hamer); Gunnarsson, Bertrand, Karacan, Mills, Ingimarsson, McAnuff, Cisse (Howard), Church, Rasiak (Long), Sigurdsson.
Liverpool: Reina; Darby, Insua, Fabio Aurelio (Benayoun), Carragher, Skrtel, Kuyt, Gerrard, Torres, N'Gog (Aquilani), Lucas.

Scunthorpe U (0) 1 *(Hayes 68)*
Barnsley (0) 0 5457
Scunthorpe U: Lillis; Byrne, Williams, Togwell, Mirfin, Jones (Milne), Wright J, Thompson, Hayes, Forte, Woolford (Sparrow).
Barnsley: Steele; Hassell, Dickinson, Butterfield (Hammill), Foster, Shotton, Hallfredsson, Anderson (Campbell-Ryce), Bogdanovic, Gray A (Macken), Colace.

Sheffield W (1) 1 *(Hill 44 (og))*
Crystal Palace (1) 2 *(Danns 19, Andrew 68)* 8690
Sheffield W: Grant; Simek, Spurr, Potter, Beevers (Buxton), Purse, O'Connor, Soares (Johnson), Jeffers, Clarke, Tudgay (Esajas).

Crystal Palace: Speroni; Clyne, Hill, Derry, Davis, Fonte, Ertl, Danns, Ambrose (Wynter), Lee, Scannell (Andrew).

Southampton (1) 1 *(Lambert 36)*
Luton T (0) 0 18,786
Southampton: Davis; James, Harding, Hammond (Lancashire), Perry, Thomas, Lallana, Schneiderlin, Lambert, Papa Waigo (Gobern O), Antonio (Paterson).
Luton T: Pilkington K; Asafu-Adjaye, Howells, Hall, Blackett, Pilkington G, Newton (Watkins), Nicholls (Nwokeji), Gallen (Gnakpa), Craddock, Jarvis.

Stoke C (2) 3 *(Parslow 24 (og), Fuller 25, Etherington 58)*
York C (1) 1 *(Barrett 22)* 15,586
Stoke C: Sorensen (Simonsen); Huth, Higginbotham, Whitehead, Cort, Collins, Lawrence, Delap, Beattie (Tuncay), Fuller (Sidibe), Etherington.
York C: Ingham; Parslow (Purkiss), Meredith (Gall), Mackin, McGurk (Ferrell), Graham, Lawless, Barrett, Rankine, Brodie, Carruthers.

Sunderland (1) 3 *(Malbranque 17, Campbell 52, 58)*
Barrow (0) 0 25,190
Sunderland: Fulop; Bardsley, McCartney (Liddle), Meyler, Da Silva, Cana, Malbranque, Murphy (Healy), Campbell, Bent (Noble), Henderson.
Barrow: Deasy; Spender, Jelleyman, Pearson, Bolland, Hulbert, Bond, Goodfellow (Boyd), Walker, Blundell (Rothery), Rutherford (Logan).

Torquay U (0) 0
Brighton & HA (0) 1 *(Crofts 77)* 4028
Torquay U: Poke; Mansell, Smith (Nicholson), Thomson (Stevens), Ellis, Charnock, Carlisle, Hargreaves, Benyon (Sills), Rendell, Thompson.
Brighton & HA: Kuipers; Hoyte, McNulty, Crofts, Virgo, Tunnicliffe, Cox (Navarro), Dicker, Murray, Forster, Dickinson.

Tottenham H (1) 4 *(Kranjcar 35, 57, Defoe 70, Keane 90 (pen))*
Peterborough U (0) 0 35,862
Tottenham H: Gomes; Hutton, Bale (Naughton), Palacios, Bassong, Dawson, Kranjcar (Pavlyuchenko), Huddlestone, Defoe (Rose), Keane, Modric.
Peterborough U: Lewis; Griffiths, Williams, Coutts, Morgan, Bennett, Whelpdale, Frecklington (Batt), Mackail-Smith, Lee (Green), Boyd.

Wigan Ath (0) 4 *(N'Zogbia 47, 66, McCarthy 63, Sinclair 90)*
Hull C (1) 1 *(Geovanni 35)* 5335
Wigan Ath: Pollitt; Melchiot, Figueroa, Thomas, Bramble, Amaya, Sinclair, McCarthy, Rodallega (Watson), Scotland, Koumas (N'Zogbia).
Hull C: Myhill; Mendy, Kilbane, Cairney, Mouyokolo, Zayatte, Ghilas (Cullen), Garcia, Geovanni, Vennegoor (Altidore), Halmosi (Boateng).

Sunday, 3 January 2010

Chelsea (3) 5 *(Sturridge 5, 68, Eustace 15 (og), Malouda 22, Lampard 64)*
Watford (0) 0 40,912
Chelsea: Hilario; Ivanovic, Cole A (Kakuta), Zhirkov, Terry, Alex, Belletti (Matic), Lampard, Sturridge (Borini), Cole J, Malouda.
Watford: Loach; Mariappa, Doyley, Hodson, DeMerit, Severin (Jenkins), Cleverley, Eustace, Graham (Henderson), Lansbury, Cowie (Harley).

Manchester U (0) 0
Leeds U (1) 1 *(Beckford 19)* 74,526
Manchester U: Kuszczak; Neville, Fabio, Gibson, Brown, Evans J, Welbeck (Giggs), Anderson (Owen), Berbatov, Rooney, Obertan (Valencia).
Leeds U: Ankergren; Crowe, Hughes (White), Doyle, Naylor, Kisnorbo, Kilkenny, Howson (Snodgrass), Beckford, Becchio (Michalik), Johnson.

Sheffield U (1) 1 *(Cresswell 45)*

QPR (1) 1 *(Simpson 39)* 11,461

Sheffield U: Bunn; Geary, Taylor, Montgomery, Morgan, Kilgallon (Seip), Camara, Quinn S (Williamson), Evans, Ward (Little), Cresswell.
QPR: Cerny; Ramage, Borrowdale, Buzsaky (Ephrairn), Stewart, Gorkss, Routledge, Leigertwood, Agyemang (Helguson), Simpson, Faurlin.

Tranmere R (0) 0

Wolverhampton W (0) 1 *(Jarvis 77)* 7476

Tranmere R: Daniels; Logan, Bakayogo, Taylor, Goodison, McLaren, Edds, Welsh (Ricketts), Thomas-Moore, Curran, Gornell (Shuker).
Wolverhampton W: Hennessey; Foley, Ward S, Mancienne, Craddock, Stearman, Jarvis, Henry, Iwelumo (Vokes), Ebanks-Blake (Elokobi), Milijas (Halford).

West Ham U (1) 1 *(Diamanti 45)*

Arsenal (0) 2 *(Ramsey 78, Eduardo 83)* 25 549

West Ham U: Green; Faubert, Daprela, Kovac, Upson, Tomkins, Behrami, Jimenez, Nouble (Sears), Diamanti, Stanislas (Edgar).
Arsenal: Fabianski; Sagna, Silvestre, Song Bilong, Vermaelen, Gallas, Ramsey, Wilshere (Nasri), Eduardo, Vela, Merida (Diaby).

Tuesday, 12 January 2010

Bristol C (0) 1 *(Williams 90)*

Cardiff C (0) 1 *(Chopra 76)* 7289

Bristol C: Gerken; Orr, McAllister (Akinde), Skuse, Fontaine, Carey, Elliott, Clarkson (Saborio), Haynes, Maynard, Hartley (Williams).
Cardiff C: Marshall; Matthews, McNaughton, Rae (Taiwo), Gerrard, Hudson, Wildig, Whittingham, McCormack (Feeney), Chopra, Ledley.

Tuesday, 19 January 2010

Accrington S (0) 1 *(Miles 81)*

Gillingham (0) 0 1322

Accrington S: Bouzanis; Winnard, Lees, Procter, Kempson, Edwards, McConville (Kee), Ryan, Grant, Symes, Miles.
Gillingham: Julian; Fuller, Palmer (Barcham), Weston, Gowling, Wynter, Bentley, Lewis, Jackson, Oli, Nutter.

Brentford (0) 0

Doncaster R (0) 1 *(O'Connor 87)* 2883

Brentford: Price; Foster, Dickson, O'Connor, Bennett, Legge, Wood (Saunders), Bean (Hunt), Strevens, MacDonald, Weston.
Doncaster R: Sullivan; O'Connor, Roberts, Chambers, Shackell, Stock (Hird), Coppinger, Wilson, Shiels (Spicer), Sharp, Oster (Hayter).

Notts Co (0) 2 *(Hunt 50, Hughes 64)*

Forest Green R (0) 1 *(Rankin 63)* 4389

Notts Co: Schmeichel; Thompson, Jackson, Ravenhill, Lee, Hunt, Davies, Bishop, Hughes, Hawley (Rodgers), Westcarr (Hamshaw).
Forest Green R: Burton; Hodgkiss, Stonehouse, Brown, Preece, O'Cearuill, Powell (Berry), Smith, Ameobi, Platt (Else), Rankin.

THIRD ROUND REPLAYS

Tuesday, 12 January 2010

Birmingham C (0) 1 *(Ferguson 62)*

Nottingham F (0) 0 9299

Birmingham C: Hart; Carr, Ridgewell, Ferguson, Dann, Johnson R, Larsson, Bowyer (Fahey), Jerome, Benitez (Phillips), McFadden (Johnson D).
Nottingham F: Camp; Perch, Cohen, Chambers, Morgan, Moussi (Gunter), McCleary (Anderson), McGugan, Adebola, McGoldrick (Garner), Tyson.

Coventry C (1) 1 *(Best 22)*

Portsmouth (0) 2 *(Wright 90 (og), Mokoena 120)* 7097

Coventry C: Westwood; Wright, Cranie, Clingan (Eastwood), Wood, McPake, Bell, Gunnarsson, Morrison, Best (Grandison), McIndoe.
Portsmouth: Begovic; Vanden Borre, Hreidarsson, Mullins (Basinas), Wilson, Mokoena, Boateng (Utaka), Diop, Piquionne, Smith (Webber), Brown.
aet.

Derby Co (0) 1 *(Davies 114)*

Millwall (0) 1 *(Morison 108)* 7183

Derby Co: Bywater; Green, Moxey, Savage, Buxton, Addison (Barker), Croft (Davies), Pearson, Porter, Commons (Teale), Johnson.
Millwall: Forde; Smith, Frampton (Barron), Laird, Robinson, Ward, Hackett (Dunne), Abdou, Morison, Grabban (Schofield), Martin.
aet; Derby Co won 5-3 on penalties.

QPR (0) 2 *(Buzsaky 71 (pen), Stewart 88)*

Sheffield U (1) 3 *(Williamson 19, Ward 68, Cresswell 70)* 5780

QPR: Cerny; Ramage, Borrowdale, Buzsaky, Stewart, Gorkss, Routledge, Leigertwood, Agyemang, Simpson (German), Faurlin (Taarabt).
Sheffield U: Bunn; Geary (Walker), Taylor, Montgomery, Morgan, Seip, Quinn S, Williamson (Ward), Evans, Cresswell (Henderson), Harper.

Wednesday, 13 January 2010

Liverpool (1) 1 *(Bertrand 45 (og))*

Reading (0) 2 *(Sigurdsson 90 (pen), Long 100)* 31,063

Liverpool: Federici; Degen (Skrtel), Insua, Aquilani, Carragher, Agger, Benayoun, Gerrard (Babel), Torres (N'Gog), Kuyt, Lucas.
Reading: Federici; Gunnarsson, Bertrand, Cisse (Howard), Mills, Ingimarsson, McAnuff, Karacan (Long), Church, Rasiak (Kebe), Sigurdsson.
aet.

Newcastle U (2) 3 *(Lovenkrands 10, 40, 72)*

Plymouth Arg (0) 0 15,805

Newcastle U: Krul; Taylor R, Jose Enrique, Butt (Ranger), Coloccini, Taylor S, Gutierrez, Nolan, Carroll, Lovenkrands (Donaldson), Pancrate (Guthrie).
Plymouth Arg: Larrieu; Duguid, Sawyer, Fletcher, Arnason, Barker (McNamee), Judge (Wright-Phillips), Summerfield, Fallon, Barnes (Sheridan), Clark.

Tuesday, 19 January 2010

Cardiff C (0) 1 *(Orr 74 (og))*

Bristol C (0) 0 6731

Cardiff C: Marshall; Matthews (Kennedy), Quinn, Wildig (Chopra), Gerrard, Gyepes, Burke (Blake), Whittingham, Bothroyd, McCormack, Ledley.
Bristol C: Gerken; Orr, McAllister (Elliott), Fontaine, Nyatanga, Carey, Skuse, Sno (Akinde), Sproule, Maynard (Saborio), Hartley.

FOURTH ROUND

Saturday, 23 January 2010

Accrington S (1) 1 *(Symes 25)*

Fulham (1) 3 *(Nevland 21, Duff 59, Gera 80)* 3712

Accrington S: Bouzanis; Winnard, Lees, Procter, Kempson, Edwards, McConville (Kee), Ryan, Grant, Symes, Miles (Joyce).
Fulham: Schwarzer; Kelly, Kallio (Elm), Murphy, Hughes, Hangeland, Duff (Dikgacoi), Baird, Nevland, Riise, Gera (Davies).

Aston Villa (1) 3 *(Delfouneso 5, Young A 48, Delph 63)*

Brighton & HA (1) 2 *(Elphick 41, Forster 90)* 39,725

Aston Villa: Guzan; Young L, Warnock (Davies), Sidwell, Beye, James M Collins, Albrighton (Milner), Downing, Delfouneso, Young A (Lowry), Delph.
Brighton & HA: Kuipers; Calderon, McNulty, Crofts, Elphick, Virgo, Navarro (Cox), Dicker (Carole), Murray, Forster, Bennett (Dickinson).

Bolton W (0) 2 *(Steinsson 48, Elmander 84)*
Sheffield U (0) 0 14,572
Bolton W: Jaaskelainen; Steinsson, Samuel (Basham), Muamba, Knight, Cahill, Ricketts, Lee, Klasnic (Elmander), Davies K (Mustapha), Cohen.
Sheffield U: Bunn; Walker, Taylor, Montgomery, Morgan, Fortune, Quinn S (Ward), Williamson (Cresswell), Camara (Evans), Henderson, Harper.

Cardiff C (1) 4 *(Bothroyd 17, Whittingham 71, Burke 89, McCormack 90)*
Leicester C (2) 2 *(Morrison 34, N'Guessan 39)* 10,961
Cardiff C: Marshall; Quinn (Burke), Kennedy, Blake, Gerrard, Hudson, McCormack, Whittingham, Bothroyd, Chopra, Ledley.
Leicester C: Weale; McGivern, Morrison, Wellens, Brown, Hobbs, N'Guessan, Oakley, Waghorn (Fryatt), Kermorgant, Gallagher.

Derby Co (0) 1 *(McEveley 88)*
Doncaster R (0) 0 11,316
Derby Co: Bywater; Hunt, Moxey (McEveley), Savage, Buxton, Barker, Green, Pearson, Porter (Hulse), Davies (Commons), Johnson.
Doncaster R: Sullivan; Chambers, Roberts, Shackell (Hird), O'Connor, Stock, Coppinger, Wilson (Heffernan), Shiels (Guy), Sharp, Oster.

Everton (0) 1 *(Osman 56)*
Birmingham C (2) 2 *(Benitez 7, Ferguson 40)* 30,875
Everton: Howard; Neville, Baines, Heitinga, Distin, Bilyaletdinov (Osman), Fellaini, Saha (Vaughan), Donovan (Arteta), Cahill, Pienaar.
Birmingham C: Hart; Carr, Ridgewell, Ferguson, Dann, Johnson R, Larsson, Bowyer, McFadden (McSheffrey), Benitez (Jervis), Fahey.

Notts Co (2) 2 *(Hughes 26, Davies 41)*
Wigan Ath (0) 2 *(Scotland 52, Watson 83)* 9073
Notts Co: Schmeichel; Thompson, Clapham, Ravenhill (Rodgers), Lee, Hunt, Bishop, Jackson, Hughes, Davies, Westcarr (Hawley).
Wigan Ath: Stojkovic; Amaya (Gohouri), Figueroa, Diame, Bramble, Boyce, Sinclair (Watson), McCarthy, Rodallega, Scotland, Gomez (N'Zogbia).

Portsmouth (1) 2 *(Utaka 42, 57)*
Sunderland (1) 1 *(Bent 15)* 10,315
Portsmouth: Begovic; Vanden Borre, Kaboul, Mokoena, Wilson, Hreidarsson, Boateng, Diop (Mullins), Utaka, Piquionne (Webber), Brown (Basinas).
Sunderland: Gordon; Bardsley (Healy), Richardson, Turner, Da Silva, Cana, Henderson, Meyler (Reid), Jones (Campbell), Bent, Zenden.

Preston NE (0) 0
Chelsea (1) 2 *(Anelka 37, Sturridge 47)* 23,119
Preston NE: Lonergan; Hart, Davidson, Chaplow, St Ledger-Hall, Mawene, Sedgwick (Mellor), Carter (Parkin), Brown (Mayor), Jones, Wallace.
Chelsea: Hilario; Paulo Ferreira, Zhirkov, Belletti (Malouda), Terry, Alex, Ballack, Lampard (Cole J), Anelka, Sturridge, Deco.

Reading (0) 1 *(Sigurdsson 87)*
Burnley (0) 0 12,910
Reading: Federici; Griffin, Bertrand, Karacan, Mills, Ingimarsson, McAnuff, Gunnarsson (Kebe), Church (Long), Rasiak (Thorvaldsson), Sigurdsson.
Burnley: Jensen; Mears, McCann, Alexander, Duff, Edgar, Eagles, McDonald, Thompson (Paterson), Gudjonsson (Blake), Elliott.

Southampton (1) 2 *(Thomas 31, Antonio 74)*
Ipswich T (0) 1 *(Counago 90)* 20,446
Southampton: Davis; Thomas, Mills, Wotton (Lancashire), Perry, Jaidi, Lallana, James (Gillett), Lambert, Barnard (Antonio), Holmes.
Ipswich T: Lee-Barrett; Rosenior, Delaney, Garvan, McAuley, Peters, Edwards (Martin), Leadbitter, Walters (Counago), John (Priskin), Colback.

Tottenham H (1) 2 *(Crouch 42, Pavlyuchenko 75)*
Leeds U (0) 2 *(Beckford 52, 90 (pen))* 35,750
Tottenham H: Gomes; Hutton, Bale, Rose (Palacios), Bassong, Dawson, Kranjcar (Pavlyuchenko), Jenas, Crouch (Keane), Defoe, Modric.
Leeds U: Ankergren; Crowe, Hughes, Doyle (Becchio), Bromby, Kisnorbo, Kilkenny, Howson, Beckford, Snodgrass, Johnson (White).

WBA (2) 4 *(Olsson 17, Dorrans 31 (pen), 72 (pen), Thomas 76)*
Newcastle U (0) 2 *(Carroll 62, 90)* 16,102
WBA: Carson; Cech, Jara, Mulumbu, Tamas, Olsson, Thomas (Miller), Brunt (Zuiverloon), Bednar (Mattock), Koren, Dorrans.
Newcastle U: Krul; Taylor R[■], Jose Enrique, Nolan, Coloccini, Kadar, Gutierrez, Guthrie (Donaldson), Carroll, Smith, Pancrate (Ameobi (Ranger)).

Wolverhampton W (1) 2 *(David Jones 37, Zubar 84)*
Crystal Palace (1) 2 *(Lee 3, Ambrose 49)* 14,449
Wolverhampton W: Hennessey; Zubar, Elokobi (Ward S), David Jones, Berra, Mancienne, Foley, Henry, Vokes, Ebanks-Blake (Mujangi Bia), Surman (Doyle).
Crystal Palace: Speroni; Butterfield, Clyne, Danns, Davis (Lawrence), Ertl, Ambrose, Derry, Moses, Lee (Andrew), N'Diaye.

Sunday, 24 January 2010
Scunthorpe U (1) 2 *(Hayes 29, Boyata 69 (og))*
Manchester C (2) 4 *(Petrov 3, Onuoha 45, Sylvinho 57, Robinho 84)* 8861
Scunthorpe U: Murphy; Byrne, Williams, Togwell, Mirfin, Jones (Milne), Thompson, McCann (Forte), Hayes (Wright J), Hooper, Woolford.
Manchester C: Taylor; Onuoha, Sylvinho, De Jong (Cunningham), Boyata, Kompany, Ibrahim, Ireland (Zabaleta), Mwaruwari, Robinho (Bellamy), Petrov.

Stoke C (1) 3 *(Fuller 2, 78, Whitehead 86)*
Arsenal (1) 1 *(Denilson 42)* 19,735
Stoke C: Sorensen; Huth, Higginbotham, Whelan, Shawcross, Collins, Whitehead, Delap (Tuncay), Sidibe, Fuller (Diao), Etherington (Pugh).
Arsenal: Fabianski; Coquelin (Eduardo), Traore, Denilson, Campbell, Silvestre, Eastmond, Fabregas, Vela, Emmanuel-Thomas (Ramsey), Walcott (Arshavin).

FOURTH ROUND REPLAYS
Tuesday, 2 February 2010
Crystal Palace (0) 3 *(Butterfield 62, 65, 68)*
Wolverhampton W (0) 1 *(Henry 90)* 10,282
Crystal Palace: Speroni; Clyne, Hill, Derry, Lawrence, Davis, Butterfield (Djilali), Danns, Ambrose, Lee (Andrew), Carle (Comley).
Wolverhampton W: Hennessey; Zubar, Stearman, Berra, Craddock, Mancienne (David Jones), Foley, Henry, Vokes (Iwelumo), Mujangi Bia (Ebanks-Blake), Milijas.

Wigan Ath (0) 0
Notts Co (0) 2 *(Hunt 75, Caldwell 78 (og))* 5519
Wigan Ath: Stojkovic; Bramble, Figueroa, Scharner, Boyce (Rodallega), Caldwell, Sinclair, Gomez, Koumas (McCarthy), Scotland, Diame (N'Zogbia).
Notts Co: Schmeichel; Hunt, Thompson, Ravenhill, Edwards, Clapham, Bishop, Jackson, Hughes (Hawley), Davies (Hamshaw), Westcarr (Rodgers).

Wednesday, 3 February 2010
Leeds U (1) 1 *(Becchio 45)*
Tottenham H (1) 3 *(Defoe 37, 73, 90)* 37,704
Leeds U: Ankergren; Bromby, Hughes (White), Doyle, Naylor, Michalik, Johnson (Crowe), Howson, Beckford, Becchio (Grella), Snodgrass.
Tottenham H: Gomes; Corluka, Bale, Huddlestone, Bassong, Dawson, Bentley, Jenas, Crouch, Defoe, Kranjcar.

FIFTH ROUND

Saturday, 13 February 2010

Chelsea (1) 4 *(Drogba 2, Ballack 51, Sturridge 69, Kalou 86)*

Cardiff C (1) 1 *(Chopra 34)*   40,827

Chelsea: Hilario; Paulo Ferreira, Zhirkov, Mikel, Alex, Ricardo Carvalho, Ballack, Lampard, Sturridge (Malouda), Drogba (Borini), Cole J (Kalou).
Cardiff C: Marshall; McNaughton, Kennedy, Rae (Blake), Gerrard, Gyepes, Burke (McCormack), Wildig (Taiwo), Bothroyd, Chopra, Whittingham.

Derby Co (0) 1 *(McEveley 55)*

Birmingham C (0) 2 *(Dann 73, Ridgewell 90)*   21,043

Derby Co: Bywater; Hunt, McEveley, Savage, Buxton, Barker, Green, Pearson, Hulse, Commons, Tonge.
Birmingham C: Hart; Carr, Ridgewell, Ferguson, Dann, Johnson R, Larsson (Fahey), Bowyer, Jerome, Benitez (Phillips), McFadden (Gardner).

Manchester C (1) 1 *(Wright-Phillips 11)*

Stoke C (0) 1 *(Fuller 57)*   28,019

Manchester C: Given; Zabaleta, Bridge, Barry, Toure, Lescott, Wright-Phillips, De Jong, Adebayor, Ireland (Vieira), Petro (Santa Cruz R).
Stoke C: Sorensen; Wilkinson (Collins), Higginbotham, Whelan, Huth, Shawcross, Diao, Tuncay, Sidibe, Fuller, Etherington (Lawrence) (Delap).

Reading (1) 2 *(Kebe 1, Church 73)*

WBA (1) 2 *(Koren 18, Mattock 87)*   18,008

Reading: Federici; Griffin, Bertrand, Karacan (Tabb), Mills, Ingimarsson, Kebe (Rasiak), Gunnarsson, Long*, Howard (Church), McAnuff.
WBA: Carson; Zuiverloon, Mattock, Meite (Tamas). Jara (Mulumbu*), Olsson, Koren, Brunt (Moore), Bednar, Cox, Dorrans.

Southampton (0) 1 *(Lambert 70)*

Portsmouth (0) 4 *(Owusu-Abeyie 66, Dindane 75, Belhadj 82, O'Hara 85)*   31,385

Southampton: Davis; Thomas, Harding, Hammond, Perry (Holmes), Jaidi, Lallana, Schneiderlin, Lambert, Papa Waigo (Barnard), Antonio.
Portsmouth: James; Mullins, Belhadj, Diop, Wilson, Hreidarsson (Hughes), Yebda, Basinas (Owusu-Abeyie), Utaka (Piquionne), Dindane, O'Hara.

Sunday, 14 February 2010

Bolton W (1) 1 *(Davies K 34)*

Tottenham H (0) 1 *(Defoe 61)*   13,596

Bolton W: Jaaskelainen; Steinsson, Robinson, Muamba, Knight (O'Brien A), Ricketts, Gardner, Lee (Davies M), Elmander, Davies K, Taylor (Cohen).
Tottenham H: Gomes; Corluka, Bale, Palacios, Dawson, King, Bentley, Huddlestone, Crouch, Defoe, Modric (Kranjcar).

Crystal Palace (1) 2 *(Ertl 24, Ambrose 70)*

Aston Villa (1) 2 *(James M Collins 35, Petrov 87)*   20,486

Crystal Palace: Speroni; Clyne, Hill, Derry, Davis, Butterfield, Ertl, Danns, Lee (Andrew), Carle, Ambrose.
Aston Villa: Friedel; Young L, Warnock, Delph (Delfouneso), Dunne, James M Collins, Milner, Petrov, Heskey (Carew), Young A, Downing.

Fulham (2) 4 *(Davies 22, Zamora 41, Duff 73, Okaka Chuka 79)*

Notts Co 0   16,132

Fulham: Schwarzer; Baird, Shorey, Murphy (Greening), Hughes, Hangeland, Duff (Riise), Etuhu, Elm, Zamora (Okaka Chuka), Davies.
Notts Co: Schmeichel; Hunt, Thompson, Ravenhill, Edwards, Clapham (Rodgers), Bishop, Jackson, Hughes (Hamshaw), Westcarr (Hawley), Davies.

FIFTH ROUND REPLAYS

Wednesday, 24 February 2010

Aston Villa (1) 3 *(Agbonlahor 42, Carew 81 (pen), 89 (pen))*

Crystal Palace (0) 1 *(Ambrose 73 (pen))*   31,874

Aston Villa: Guzan; Young L, Warnock, Cuellar, Dunne, Downing, Milner, Delph (Sidwell), Agbonlahor, Carew, Young A.
Crystal Palace: Speroni; Butterfield, Clyne, Derry, Davis, Lawrence, Ertl, Danns (Andrew), Lee (Djilali), Ambrose, Carle (Comley).

Stoke C (0) 3 *(Kitson 79, Shawcross 95, Tuncay 99)*

Manchester C (0) 1 *(Bellamy 81)*   21,813

Stoke C: Sorensen; Whitehead, Collins, Whelan, Huth, Shawcross, Lawrence (Pugh), Diao (Tuncay), Sidibe (Kitson), Fuller, Delap.
Manchester C: Given; Richards, Bridge (Santa Cruz R), Barry (Sylvinho), Onuoha, Lescott, Zabaleta, Kompany, Adebayor*, Bellamy, Ireland (Wright-Phillips).
aet.

Tottenham H (2) 4 *(Pavlyuchenko 23, 87, Jaaskelainen 35 (og), O'Brien A 47 (og))*

Bolton W (0) 0   31,436

Tottenham H: Gomes; Assou-Ekotto, Bale, Palacios (Kranjcar), Bassong, Dawson, Bentley (Rose), Huddlestone, Pavlyuchenko, Defoe (Gudjohnsen), Modric.
Bolton W: Jaaskelainen; Ricketts, Samuel, Muamba, Knight. O'Brien A, Gardner (Lee), Holden, Klasnic (Elmander), Cohen, Taylor (Mustapha).

WBA (1) 2 *(Koren 6, 47)*

Reading (1) 3 *(Kebe 9, Howard 90, Sigurdsson 95)* 13,985

WBA: Carson; Zuiverloon, Mattock, Mulumbu, Tamas, Meite, Koren, Cox, Bednar (Wood), Moore (Cech), Dorrans (Morrison).
Reading: Federici; Griffin, Bertrand, Sigurdsson, Mills (Pearce), Ingimarsson, Tabb (Henry), Kebe, Church (Robson-Kanu), Howard, McAnuff.
aet.

SIXTH ROUND

Saturday, 6 March 2010

Fulham (0) 0

Tottenham H (0) 0   24,533

Fulham: Schwarzer; Baird, Shorey, Greening, Hughes, Hangeland, Duff, Etuhu, Gera, Zamora, Davies (Elm).
Tottenham H: Gomes; Corluka, Assou-Ekotto, Palacios, Bassong, Dawson, Kranjcar, Modric, Crouch, Pavlyuchenko (Defoe), Bale.

Portsmouth (0) 2 *(Piquionne 67, 70)*

Birmingham C (0) 0   20,456

Portsmouth: James; Finnan, Belhadj, Wilson, Ben-Haim, Hreidarsson, Brown, Webber (Diop), Utaka, Piquionne, O'Hara.
Birmingham C: Hart; Carr, Ridgewell, Ferguson, Dann, Johnson R, Larsson (Gardner), Bowyer, Jerome, McFadden (Benitez), Fahey (Phillips).

Sunday, 7 March 2010

Chelsea (1) 2 *(Lampard 35, Terry 67)*

Stoke C (0) 0   41,322

Chelsea: Hilario; Ivanovic, Paulo Ferreira, Mikel, Terry, Alex, Kalou, Lampard, Anelka, Drogba, Malouda.
Stoke C: Sorensen; Wilkinson, Collins, Whelan (Pugh), Huth, Diagne-Faye, Whitehead, Delap, Sidibe (Kitson), Fuller, Tuncay (Lawrence).

Reading (2) 2 *(Long 27, 42)*

Aston Villa (0) 4 *(Young A 47, Carew 51, 57, 90p)* 23,175

Reading: Federici; Griffin, Bertrand, Howard (Gunnarsson), Mills, Ingimarsson, Kebe, Sigurdsson, Church (Rasiak), Long, Tabb.
Aston Villa: Friedel; Cuellar, Warnock, James M Collins, Dunne, Downing (Sidwell), Milner, Petrov, Heskey, Carew, Young A.

SIXTH ROUND REPLAY

Wednesday, 24 March 2010

Tottenham H (0) 3 *(Bentley 47, Pavlyuchenko 60, Gudjohnsen 66)*

Fulham (1) 1 *(Zamora 17)* 35,432

Tottenham H: Gomes; Corluka (Pavlyuchenko), Assou-Ekotto (Huddlestone), Palacios, Bassong, Dawson, Kranjcar (Bentley), Modric, Crouch, Gudjohnsen, Bale.
Fulham: Schwarzer; Kelly (Dempsey), Konchesky, Murphy, Hughes, Hangeland, Duff, Etuhu, Gera, Zamora (Okaka Chuka), Davies.

Sunday, 11 April 2010

Tottenham H (0) 0

Portsmouth (0) 2 *(Piquionne 99, Boateng 117 (pen))*
    84,602

Tottenham H: Gomes; Corluka, Bale, Palacios, Bassong, Dawson, Bentley (Kranjcar), Huddlestone (Gudjohnsen), Crouch, Defoe (Pavlyuchenko), Modric.
Portsmouth: James; Finnan, Wilson, Mokoena, Ricardo Rocha, Mullins (Hughes), Brown, Boateng, Piquionne (Diop), Dindane, Yebda (Utaka).
aet.

SEMI-FINALS (AT WEMBLEY)

Saturday, 10 April 2010

Aston Villa (0) 0

Chelsea (0) 3 *(Drogba 68, Malouda 89, Lampard 90)*
    81,869

Aston Villa: Friedel; Cuellar, Warnock, James M Collins, Dunne, Downing, Milner, Petrov, Agbonlahor, Carew (Heskey), Young A.
Chelsea: Cech; Paulo Ferreira, Zhirkov, Mikel, Terry, Alex, Deco (Ballack), Lampard, Drogba (Anelka), Cole J (Kalou), Malouda.

THE FA CUP FINAL

(Saturday, 15 May 2010 at Wembley Stadium, attendance 88,335)

Chelsea (0) 1 Portsmouth (0) 0

Chelsea: Cech; Ivanovic, Cole A, Ballack (Belletti), Terry, Alex, Kalou (Cole J), Lampard, Anelka (Sturridge), Drogba, Malouda.
Scorer: Drogba 59.

Portsmouth: James; Finnan, Mullins (Belhadj), Boateng (Utaka), Ricardo Rocha, Mokoena, Brown, Diop (Kanu), Piquionne, Dindane, O'Hara.
Referee: C. Foy (Merseyside).

Portsmouth's Ricardo Rocha (left) and Chelsea's Nicolas Anelka battle for the ball during the FA Cup Final at Wembley. The only goal of the game was a Didier Drogba free-kick in the 59th minute. (PA Photos)

BLUE SQUARE PREMIER 2009-10

Had it not been for Chester City's sad demise, Stevenage Borough would have eclipsed Aldershot Town's record-breaking season of two years earlier. The loss of six points from these aborted fixtures deprived them of a new record total.

Yet on 22 August in their fifth game of the season Stevenage lost 2-1 at Oxford United. They had six points compared with United's thirteen. It proved a turning point for the losers, though at the time it had made no appreciable difference to Oxford.

At the end of October, United had lost just once away to Mansfield Town and had an eight point lead over a Stevenage teams in the middle of an undefeated run of seventeen games since their reverse at Oxford.

Moreover in the last third of the season, Stevenage lost just once, the other fourteen ended in victories. Meanwhile Oxford continued to drop points and lost their early momentum. Ironically, Stevenage's one defeat in this period was at home to free-scoring Luton Town who had appeared likely to take over the mantle of Oxford in attempting to catch Stevenage. The Hatters remained unbeaten in their last fourteen including four draws.

Herald the play-offs and a different take on affairs again. Oxford regained form taking out Rushden & Diamonds, then York City, the conquerors of Luton, in the final, to join Stevenage in promotion to the Football League.

York's best run had been a sequence of eleven matches undefeated, dropping just two points in mid-season, followed sadly by just two out of a possible eighteen. Kettering Town were second early in September but had a disappointing second half of the season and overall failed to score in sixteen matches. This was in contrast to Crawley Town who hoisted themselves up from fourteenth in November to seventh.

AFC Wimbledon started slowly, improved noticeably then faded. More had been expected of former Football League clubs Mansfield Town – fourth for a time – Cambridge United with six consecutive defeats at the turn of the year and Wrexham who were unable to string three wins in a row at any time.

Salisbury City, deducted ten points, would have otherwise just missed the play-offs but ended the season unlikely to be allowed to continue in the Blue Square Premier League at all. Kidderminster Harriers needed a stronger second half campaign to reach the cut, but it did not materialize.

Altrincham tailed off with only two wins from mid-February, but Barrow pulled away from the relegation zone after mid-March. Tamworth – third at one stage – would have been disappointed with sixteenth place having lost just once in the opening thirteen matches, yet from late November they were unable to find the net at all in fourteen.

Prone to leak goals at times, Hayes & Yeading United had a purple patch in the middle of the season with just one defeat in ten. Notably, too, they beat Oxford twice and drew both against Stevenage! In contrast, Histon went into almost free-fall from late January having just two wins from that month.

Eastbourne Borough were sucked into the drop zone mid-season after fourteen matches without a win, until four wins from the last six games steered them to safety. With the one point deducted hanging over them, Gateshead won on the last day to escape on goal difference at the expense of Forest Green Rovers, beaten at already-relegated Grays Athletic. FGR had had to wait until the thirteenth game of the season before a victory. But Salisbury's subsequent removal reprieved them once more.

Ebbsfleet won only one of their opening 21 games, scoring just eight goals! The burden proved too much. Grays suffered eight consecutive defeats and their best run was two wins and a draw when already doomed. In addition they used 66 different players!

Chester City, heavily in debt and carrying the weight of twenty-five points deducted, lasted until February before being removed from the competition having refused to fulfil a fixture. Their record was expunged from the table along with the games played against the opposition. They had taken 22 points from 28 matches.

BLUE SQUARE PREMIER ATTENDANCES BY CLUB 2009-10

	Aggregate 2009–10	Average 2009–10	Highest Attendance 2009–10
Luton Town	152,851	6,947	8,860 v Oxford United
Oxford United	132,084	6,003	10,613 v Luton Town
AFC Wimbledon	77,963	3,543	4,688 v Luton Town
Mansfield Town	70,540	3,206	7,261 v Gateshead
Cambridge United	67,701	3,077	4,870 v Luton Town
Wrexham	62,923	2,860	5,672 v Rushden & Diamonds
York City	58,619	2,664	4,587 v Mansfield Town
Stevenage Borough	56,958	2,589	7,024 v Luton Town
Rushden & Diamonds	36,918	1,678	4,820 v Luton Town
Kidderminster Harriers	34,054	1,547	3,569 v Oxford United
Kettering Town	30,506	1,386	3,266 v Luton Town
Barrow	27,580	1,253	1,969 v Altrincham
Eastbourne Borough	26,774	1,217	3,108 v AFC Wimbledon
Tamworth	24,012	1,091	2,246 v Luton Town
Ebbsfleet United	23,505	1,068	2,005 v AFC Wimbledon
Altrincham	23,457	1,066	1,821 v Wrexham
Salisbury City	22,873	1,039	2,677 v Oxford United
Forest Green Rovers	22,269	1,012	1,921 v AFC Wimbledon
Crawley Town	22,061	1,002	2,118 v Luton Town
Histon	18,684	849	2,371 v Cambridge United
Grays Athletic	15,057	684	1,762 v AFC Wimbledon
Gateshead	14,679	667	1,304 v AFC Wimbledon
Hayes & Yeading	13,900	631	1,881 v Luton Town
Chester City	15,087	1,160	1,757 v Cambridge United

BLUE SQUARE PREMIER 2009–10

(P) *Promoted into division at end of 2008-09 season.*   (R) *Relegated into division at end of 2008-09 season.*

		Home						Away					Total						
		P	W	D	L	F	A	W	D	L	F	A	W	D	L	F	A	GD	Pts
1	Stevenage B	44	16	5	1	44	11	14	4	4	35	13	30	9	5	79	24	55	99
2	Luton T (R)	44	14	3	5	54	22	12	7	3	30	18	26	10	8	84	40	44	88
3	Oxford U¶	44	16	4	2	37	10	9	7	6	27	21	25	11	8	64	31	33	86
4	Rushden & D	44	12	6	4	40	21	10	7	5	37	18	22	13	9	77	39	38	79
5	York C	44	13	7	2	40	15	9	5	8	22	20	22	12	10	62	35	27	78
6	Kettering T	44	6	8	8	27	23	12	4	6	24	18	18	12	14	51	41	10	66
7	Crawley T	44	14	3	5	33	24	5	6	11	17	33	19	9	16	50	57	−7	66
8	AFC Wimbledon (P)	44	8	5	9	30	19	10	5	7	31	28	18	10	16	61	47	14	64
9	Mansfield T	44	9	8	5	34	22	8	3	11	35	38	17	11	16	69	60	9	62
10	Cambridge U	44	11	4	7	44	24	4	10	8	21	29	15	14	15	65	53	12	59
11	Wrexham	44	9	7	6	26	17	6	6	10	19	22	15	13	16	45	39	6	58
12	Salisbury C*	44	11	5	6	33	21	10	0	12	25	42	21	5	18	58	63	−5	58
13	Kidderminster H	44	11	3	8	31	21	4	9	9	26	31	15	12	17	57	52	5	57
14	Altrincham	44	7	7	8	29	25	6	8	8	24	26	13	15	16	53	51	2	54
15	Barrow	44	7	9	6	27	29	6	4	12	23	38	13	13	18	50	67	−17	52
16	Tamworth (P)	44	7	6	9	26	30	4	10	8	16	22	11	16	17	42	52	−10	49
17	Hayes & Yeading U (P)	44	7	7	8	38	38	5	5	12	21	47	12	12	20	59	85	−26	48
18	Histon	44	6	9	7	24	28	5	4	13	20	39	11	13	20	44	67	−23	46
19	Eastbourne B	44	8	7	7	26	29	3	6	13	16	43	11	13	20	42	72	−30	46
20	Gateshead* (P)	44	10	3	9	24	23	3	4	15	22	46	13	7	24	46	69	−23	45
21	Forest Green R	44	9	5	8	27	29	3	4	15	23	47	12	9	23	50	76	−26	45
22	Ebbsfleet U	44	7	4	11	25	36	5	4	13	25	46	12	8	24	50	82	−32	44
23	Grays Ath	44	4	5	13	16	41	1	8	13	19	50	5	13	26	35	91	−56	28

Chester City (R) – record expunged.
*Salisbury City deducted 10 points and demoted to the Zamaretto Premier, Gateshead deducted 1 point.
¶Oxford United promoted via play-offs. Forest Green Rovers stay in the division, Grays Ath declined by the Ryman Premier League with Ebbsfleet U joining the Blue Square South.

BLUE SQUARE PREMIER LEADING GOALSCORERS 2009–10

	Club	*League*	*Play-Offs*	*FA Cup*	*Total*
Matt Tubbs	(Salisbury City)	27	0	4	31
Richard Brodie	(York City)	26	1	4	31
James Constable	(Oxford United)	22	3	1	26
Tom Craddock	(Luton Town)	22	0	1	23
Danny Kedwell	(AFC Wimbledon)	21	0	1	22
Danny Crow	(Cambridge United)	19	0	0	19
Jake Speight	(Mansfield Town)	17	0	0	17
Kevin Gallen	(Luton Town)	16	0	2	18
Magno Vieira	(Ebbsfleet United)	16	0	0	16
Chris Senior	(Altrincham)	15	0	0	15

BLUE SQUARE PREMIER LEAGUE PLAY-OFFS

▪ *Denotes player sent off.*

SEMI-FINALS FIRST LEG
Thursday, 29 April 2010
Rushden & D (0) 1 *(Byrne 51)*
Oxford U (1) 1 *(Constable 29)*   4535
Rushden & D: Roberts; Osano, Robinson, Porter, Stuart, Downer (Huke), Byrne, Terry, O'Connor, Tomlin (Akurang), Farrell (Louis).
Oxford U: Clarke; Batt, Tonkin, Bulman, Creighton, Wright, Chapman, Green M (Potter), Constable, Midson (Sandwith), Clist.

York C (0) 1 *(Brodie 90)*
Luton T (0) 0   6204
York C: Ingham; Purkiss, Meredith, Mackin, McGurk, Graham, Lawless, Barrett (Smith A), Rankine (Gash), Brodie, Carruthers.
Luton T: Tyler; Gnakpa (Barnes-Homer), Murray, Keane, Blackett, Pilkington G, Newton, Howells, Gallen, Craddock, Heslop.

SEMI-FINALS SECOND LEG
Monday, 3 May 2010
Luton T (0) 0
York C (0) 1 *(Carruthers 47)*   9781
Luton T: Tyler; Gnakpa, Murray, Keane, Blackett, Pilkington G, Newton▪, Howells (Hatch), Gallen (Barnes-Homer), Craddock, Heslop (Hall).
York C: Ingham; Purkiss, Meredith, Mackin, McGurk, Graham, Lawless (Sangare), Barrett (Parslow), Rankine (Gash), Brodie, Carruthers.

Oxford U (0) 2 *(Green M 53, Constable 57)*
Rushden & D (0) 0   11,963
Oxford U: Clarke; Batt, Tonkin, Bulman, Creighton, Wright, Chapman, Green M (Potter), Constable, Midson (Deering), Clist.
Rushden & D: Roberts; Osano, Huke, Porter, Stuart, Downer (Farrell), Byrne, Terry, Louis (Akurang), Tomlin, O'Connor (Pattison).

FINAL (at Wembley)
Sunday, 16 May 2010

Oxford U (2) 3 *(Green M 15, Constable 21, Potter 90)*   **York C (1) 1** *(Clarke 42 (og))*   38,857
Oxford U: Clarke; Batt, Tonkin, Bulman, Creighton, Wright, Chapman (Day), Midson (Deering), Constable, Green M (Potter), Clist.
York C: Ingham; Purkiss, Meredith, Mackin, McGurk, Graham, Lawless, Barrett (Sangare), Rankine (Gash), Brodie, Carruthers (Pitt).
Referee: M. Naylor (Sheffield).

BLUE SQUARE NORTH & SOUTH 2009–10

(P) Promoted into division at end of 2008-09 season.   (R) Relegated into division at end of 2008-09 season.

BLUE SQUARE NORTH 2009–10

		P	Home W	D	L	F	A	Away W	D	L	F	A	Total W	D	L	F	A	GD	Pts
1	Southport	40	15	4	1	54	19	10	7	3	37	26	25	11	4	91	45	46	86
2	Fleetwood T¶	40	15	4	1	58	21	11	3	6	28	23	26	7	7	86	44	42	85
3	Alfreton T	40	15	3	2	49	20	6	8	6	28	25	21	11	8	77	45	32	74
4	Workington	40	9	7	4	20	14	11	3	6	26	23	20	10	10	46	37	9	70
5	Droylsden	40	11	4	5	47	25	7	6	7	35	37	18	10	12	82	62	20	64
6	Corby T (P)	40	8	6	6	38	31	10	3	7	35	31	18	9	13	73	62	11	63
7	Hinckley U	40	9	7	4	30	20	7	7	6	30	32	16	14	10	60	52	8	62
8	Ilkeston T (P)	40	10	6	4	31	23	6	7	7	22	22	16	13	11	53	45	8	61
9	Stalybridge Celtic	40	8	5	7	34	28	3	2	10	37	36	16	7	17	71	64	7	55
10	Eastwood T (P)	40	5	4	7	22	24	6	5	9	28	31	15	9	16	50	55	–5	54
11	AFC Telford U	40	7	7	6	29	21	7	2	11	23	34	14	9	17	52	55	–3	51
12	Northwich Vic* (R)	40	5	5	6	36	30	6	8	6	26	25	15	13	12	62	55	7	48
13	Blyth Spartans	40	10	3	7	38	30	3	6	11	29	42	13	9	18	67	72	–5	48
14	Gainsborough Trinity	40	9	4	7	29	27	3	7	10	21	30	12	11	17	50	57	–7	47
15	Hyde U	40	9	7	4	28	30	2	5	13	17	42	11	12	17	45	72	–27	45
16	Stafford Rangers	40	6	7	7	28	28	4	7	9	31	42	10	14	16	59	70	–11	44
17	Solihull Moors	40	5	6	9	26	26	6	3	11	21	32	11	9	20	47	58	–11	42
18	Gloucester C (P)	40	7	1	12	23	29	5	5	10	24	30	12	6	22	47	59	–12	42
19	Redditch U	40	6	3	7	28	31	4	1	15	21	52	10	8	22	49	83	–34	38
20	Vauxhall Motors	40	7	7	6	30	34	0	7	13	15	47	7	14	19	45	81	–36	35
21	Harrogate T	40	5	2	12	24	40	2	4	14	17	40	8	6	26	41	80	–39	30

Northwich Victoria deducted 10 points. ¶Fleetwood Town promoted via play-offs. Southport, Fleetwood T promoted to Blue Square Premier League. Vauxhall Motors and Harrogate T not relegated. New clubs for 2009–10 season: Boston U, Guiseley, Nuneaton T and Worcester C from Blue Square South.

BLUE SQUARE SOUTH 2009–10

		P	Home W	D	L	F	A	Away W	D	L	F	A	Total W	D	L	F	A	GD	Pts
1	Newport Co	42	18	3	0	50	8	14	4	3	43	18	32	7	3	93	26	67	103
2	Dover Ath (P)	42	12	4	5	36	20	10	5	6	30	27	22	9	11	66	47	19	75
3	Chelmsford C	42	10	7	4	30	21	12	2	7	32	27	22	9	11	62	48	14	75
4	Bath C¶	42	10	8	3	30	19	10	4	7	36	27	20	12	10	66	46	20	72
5	Woking (R)	42	11	4	6	29	20	10	5	6	28	24	21	9	12	57	44	13	72
6	Havant & Waterlooville	42	10	8	3	40	23	9	6	6	25	21	19	14	9	65	44	21	71
7	Braintree T	42	12	5	4	32	17	6	12	3	24	24	18	17	7	56	41	15	71
8	Staines T (P)	42	10	6	5	37	20	8	7	6	22	20	18	13	11	59	40	19	67
9	Welling U	42	9	4	8	30	23	9	5	7	36	28	18	9	15	66	51	15	63
10	Thurrock	42	9	7	5	37	33	7	6	8	29	27	16	13	13	66	60	6	61
11	Eastleigh	42	8	4	9	37	32	9	5	7	34	34	17	9	16	71	66	5	60
12	Bromley	42	8	5	8	37	27	7	5	9	31	37	15	10	17	68	64	4	55
13	St Albans C	42	9	3	9	25	25	6	7	8	20	30	15	10	17	45	55	–10	55
14	Hampton & Richmond B	42	7	5	9	34	36	7	4	10	22	30	14	9	19	56	66	–10	51
15	Basingstoke T	42	5	5	11	19	33	8	5	8	30	35	13	10	19	49	68	–19	49
16	Maidenhead U	42	6	6	9	24	28	6	6	9	28	31	12	12	18	52	59	–7	48
17	Dorchester T	42	9	4	8	41	26	4	1	16	15	48	13	9	20	56	74	–18	48
18	Bishop's Stortford	42	6	5	10	17	25	6	6	9	31	34	12	11	19	48	59	–11	47
19	Lewes (R)	42	7	7	7	31	28	2	8	11	18	35	9	15	18	49	63	–14	42
20	Worcester C	42	7	4	10	29	28	3	6	12	19	32	10	10	22	48	60	–12	40
21	Weston Super Mare	42	4	5	12	30	42	1	3	17	18	51	5	8	29	48	93	–45	23
22	Weymouth (R)	42	4	3	14	17	51	1	4	16	14	52	5	7	30	31	103	–72	22

¶Bath City promoted via play-offs. Newport Co, Bath C promoted to the Blue Square Premier League. Weston Super Mare not relegated. Worcester C to Blue Square North. New clubs for 2009–10: Boreham Wood, Dartford, Ebbsfleet U, Farnborough.

BLUE SQUARE NORTH & SOUTH PLAY-OFFS

BLUE SQUARE NORTH

SEMI-FINALS FIRST LEG (Wednesday 28 April)

Droylsden 2 *(Meechan 71, Gray 81 (pen))*	
Fleetwood T 0	1104
Workington 0	
Alfreton T 1 *(Hearn 55)*	1483

SEMI-FINALS SECOND LEG (Sunday 2 May)

Fleetwood T 3 *(Seddon 35, Milligan 42, Grand 110)*	
Droylsden 1 *(Roche 113)*	2862
aet; Fleetwood T won 5-4 on penalties.	
Alfreton T 3 *(Ross 37, Clayton 48, 87)*	
Workington 1 *(Arnison 13)*	1475

FINAL (Sunday 9 May)

Fleetwood T 2 *(Pond 8, Thorpe 29)*	
Alfreton T 1 *(Todd 75 (pen))*	3592

BLUE SQUARE SOUTH

SEMI-FINALS FIRST LEG (Tuesday 27 April)

Bath C 2 *(Mohamed 60 (pen), Mackie 87)*	
Chelmsford C 0	1425
Woking 2 *(Ademola 17, Wright 40)*	
Dover Ath 1 *(Shulz 3)*	3080

SEMI-FINALS SECOND LEG (Saturday 1 May)

Chelmsford C 0	
Bath C 1 *(Mohamed 53)*	1650
Dover Ath 0	
Woking 0	2970

FINAL (Sunday 9 May)

Bath C 1 *(Mohamed 56 (pen))*	
Woking 0	4865

AFC WIMBLEDON

Blue Square Premier

Ground: The Cherry Red Records Fans' Stadium, Kingsmeadow, Jack Goodchild Way, 422a Kingston Road, Kingston-Upon-Thames, Surrey KT1 3PB. *Tel:* (0208) 547 3528. *Fax:* (0808) 2800 816. *Year Formed:* 2002.
Record Gate: 4722 (2009 v St Albans City). *Nickname:* The Dons. *Manager:* Terry Brown.
Secretary: David Charles. *Colours:* All blue with gold shirt trimmings.

AFC WIMBLEDON 2009–10 LEAGUE RECORD

Match No.	Date	Venue	Opponents	Result	H/T Score	Lg Pos.	Goalscorers	Atten- dance
1	Aug 8	H	Luton T	D 1-1	0-1	—	Main (pen) 80	4688
2	11	A	Eastbourne Bor	L 0-1	0-0	—		3108
3	15	A	Kettering T	W 2-1	1-0	12	Kedwell 2 (1 pen) 9, 66 (p)	1746
4	18	H	Salisbury C	W 4-0	1-0	—	Moore 2 12, 90, Kedwell 2 (1 pen) 71 (p), 89	3591
5	22	A	Altrincham	W 1-0	0-0	4	Kedwell 82	1438
6	29	H	Oxford U	L 0-1	0-0	7		4304
7	31	A	Grays Ath	W 4-2	2-1	—	Johnson 10, Main 2 (2 pens) 21, 62, Kedwell 90	1762
8	Sept 5	A	Tamworth	D 2-2	0-2	6	Kedwell 2 49, 59	1669
9	12	H	Cambridge U	D 0-0	0-0	10		4128
10	19	A	Ebbsfleet U	D 2-2	1-1	12	Moore 28, Montague 90	2005
11	22	H	Crawley T	D 1-1	0-0	—	Kedwell 76	3408
12	26	H	Histon	W 4-0	1-0	10	Moore 2 13, 75, Taylor 56, Kedwell (pen) 78	3392
13	29	A	Rushden & D	W 1-0	1-0	—	Montague 2	1624
14	Oct 3	H	Kidderminster H	L 0-1	0-0	8		3601
15	10	A	Forest Green R	W 5-2	3-2	6	Taylor 1, Main 2 11, 80, Kedwell 2 23, 58	1921
16	17	A	Kettering T	L 1-2	1-2	8	Main 22	3745
17	Nov 14	A	Barrow	D 2-2	0-1	10	Godfrey 63, Main 76	1614
18	21	H	York C	L 0-1	0-0	12		4016
19	24	H	Ebbsfleet U	W 3-0	1-0	—	Moore 2 42, 73, Kedwell 63	2942
20	28	A	Kidderminster H	W 1-0	1-0	—	Kedwell 20	1788
21	Dec 1	A	Salisbury C	W 2-0	0-0	—	Main 2 63, 69	1157
22	5	H	Gateshead	W 2-0	1-0	6	Gregory 22, Wellard 60	3209
23	26	H	Hayes & Y	W 5-0	4-0	4	Kedwell 2 6, 17, Cumbers 10, Main 2 31, 79	3659
24	28	A	Stevenage Bor	D 0-0	0-0	5		3033
25	Jan 1	A	Hayes & Y	L 0-1	0-0	—		1829
26	16	H	Mansfield T	W 2-0	2-0	—	Elder 3, Taylor 22	3584
27	23	A	Wrexham	L 0-1	0-1	5		3276
28	Feb 6	H	Forest Green R	W 2-0	2-0	5	Elder 8, Hendry 9	3272
29	13	A	Cambridge U	D 2-2	1-1	8	Taylor 2 42, 55	3087
30	20	A	Luton T	W 2-1	1-1	—	Elder 28, Kedwell 64	7736
31	23	A	Oxford U	L 0-2	0-1	—		6250
32	Mar 6	H	Altrincham	D 1-1	0-0	8	Judge 76	3388
33	9	A	Crawley T	L 1-2	1-1	—	Kedwell 1	1569
34	13	H	Eastbourne Bor	W 2-0	1-0	7	Poole 42, Kedwell 85	3358
35	23	H	Barrow	L 0-2	0-0	—		3019
36	27	H	Rushden & D	L 0-1	0-0	8		3640
37	30	A	Wrexham	D 2-2	0-0	—	Sinclair (og) 89, Poole (pen) 90	3149
38	Apr 3	A	Histon	W 3-1	2-0	7	Poole 32, Hatton 36, Kedwell 53	867
39	5	H	Stevenage Bor	L 0-3	0-2	—		3840
40	7	A	York C	L 0-5	0-4	—		2667
41	10	A	Mansfield T	W 1-0	1-0	6	Kedwell 9	2470
42	13	H	Grays Ath	L 0-2	0-0	—		3015
43	20	H	Tamworth	L 0-1	0-1	—		3015
44	24	A	Gateshead	L 0-1	0-1	8		1304

Final League Position: 8

GOALSCORERS

League (61): Kedwell 21 (3 pens), Main 11 (3 pens), Moore 7, Taylor 5, Elder 3, Poole 3 (1 pen), Montague 2, Cumbers 1, Godfrey 1, Gregory 1, Hatton 1, Hendry 1, Johnson 1, Judge 1, Wellard 1, own goal 1.
FA Cup (5): Hatton 1, Kedwell 1, Main 1, Moore 1, Taylor 1.

Pullen 26	Lorraine 37	Hussey 15	Johnson 36+1	Gerrard 5+1	Taylor 29+3	Hatton 34+6	Duncan 13+9	Kedwell 39	Godfrey 7+10	Gregory 35+2	Main 19+8	Moore 25+6	Wellard 21+11	Conroy 21+11	Judge 21+5	Adjei 17+5	Inns 5+2	Drewn 17+1	Montague 5+11	Cumbers 2+2	Hendry 17+2	Rapson —+2	Blanchett 11	Elder 12+6	Poole 12+5	Parker —+2	Stafford —+2	Harmsworth —+3	Jackson 2+1	Turner 1	Stenning —+1	Match No.
1	2	3	4	5	6	7^1	8^2	9	10^3	11	12	13	14																			1
1	2	3	4	5	6	12	8^2	9	7^1	11	10	13																				2
1	2	3	4		6	7	12	9		11	10^1	E			5	13																3
1	2^1	3	4	5	13	7	12	9		11	10^1	E			6^2	14																4
1	2^1	3	4		6	7	10	9	13	11	14	E			5	12^2																5
1	2	3	4		6^2	7	10^1	9	12	11	13	E	14		5^3																	6
1	2	3	4	5		12	14	9	11^2	13	10^3	E	7^1		6																	7
1^6		3	4		12	7		9	13	11^2	10	E			2			6	5^1	15												8
	5	3	4		12	7	10^3	9^2		11	14	E	6^1	2					1	13												9
1	5	3	4		6	7^2	13	9		11^3	10^1	E	2^4			14			12													10
1	5	3	6	2^2	8^1	7	13	9		11			1^m			4			12													11
1	5	3	4^1		6^3	7	14	9		11	10^2	a			2	12			13													12
1		3	4		6	7	12	9		11		9^2		13			2	5	10^1													13
1		3	4		6^2	7	14	9		11	12	a		13			2^3	5	10^1													14
1	5^1	3	6		8	2	4^2	9^3		11	10	a		13				12	14													15
1	6	3		4	7		9		11	10^2	3	12	2^1			5	13															16
	4			8	2		11^3	6	10	7^2	14	13	12		5^1	1	9															17
	5	3		8^3	7		9	11^1	4	10	12	13	2^2	6		1	14															18
	5	3	8			9^2	14	7	10^1	11^3	4	2	6			1	13	12														19
	6		8^3	14			9	13	3	12	11^1	4	2	7		1		10^2														20
	5	3	8	12			9	13		10		7	2^1	6	4^3	1		14	11^2													21
	5	3	8				9	12	4	10^3		7^2	2	6	13	1	14		11^1													22
	5	3	8	13			9^3	14	7^1	10		4^2	2	6	12	1	11															23
	5	3	8	7	2^1		11		10		6	12		4		1	9^2		13													24
	5	3	14	8^2	2			10		7		6	4		1	9^1	11^3	12	13													25
	6		8	2			10			12	13	5	4		1	14		7^2		3	9^3	11^1										26
	5	6^3	8^2	2		9			11	12	14	4		1	13		7^1		3	10												27
1	5	6^1	8^3	2		9		4^2		7	12					11			3	10	13	14										28
1	5		8	2		9		4^3	13	11		6				7^1			3	10^2	12	14										29
1	5		8	2		9		4	13		12	13	6			7^2			3	10^1	11											30
1	5		8^1	2		9		4	13		14	12^4	6			7^3			3	10^2	11											31
1	5		8	2	3	9		4	12	13		6				7				10^1	11^1											32
1	5		8^2	2	3	9	13	4		14	12				6				7		10^3	11^1										33
1	5			7	3	9			8	2	6	4^1								10^2	11		12	13								34
1	5			7	4	9		10^1	8	6	2	3	13							12	11^2											35
1	5	3		2		10		4	9	8		6	12			7^1				13	11^2											36
1	5	6		7^2		10		4		9	8^1	2				11			3	13	12											37
	6			7	8^3	9	12			2^2	5	4		1		14			3	10	11^1			13								38
	5	6		7		9		4	10^2	8	2			1		11^1			3	12	13											39
1	5^1	12		13	14		7^3		9	8	2	6	4						3	10^1	11											40
	5	3		2	8^4	9^3		7		10^2	12	13	6	4	1				11^1		14											41
		5^1		7		9	12	8		10		2	6	4^2	1					3	13	11										42
	5	3			9	7^1	4		13	8		6							11^2		10^3	12			14	2	1					43
		3			10		7		6	8^3	2		4	1					9^1			11^2		13	12	5	14					44

FA Cup
Fourth Qualifying Round   Crawley T   (a)   1-1
                                      (h)   3-1
First Round   Millwall   (a)   1-4

ALTRINCHAM

Blue Square Premier

Ground: Moss Lane, Altrincham WA15 8AP. *Tel:* (0161) 928 1045. *Year Formed:* 1903. *Record Gate:* 10,275 (1991 Altrincham Boys v Sunderland Boys, ESFA Shield). *Nickname:* The Robins. *Manager:* Graham Heathcote. *Secretary:* Graham Heathcote. *Colours:* Red and white striped shirts, black shorts, red stockings.

ALTRINCHAM 2009–10 LEAGUE RECORD

Match No.	Date	Venue	Opponents	Result	H/T Score	Lg Pos.	Goalscorers	Atten-dance
1	Aug 8	H	Ebbsfleet U	D 1-1	1-0	—	Senior [39]	914
2	11	A	Barrow	W 3-0	1-0	—	Kearney [38], Senior [79], Crowell [82]	1969
3	15	A	Hayes & Y	W 2-1	1-0	2	Denham [22], Little [81]	401
4	18	H	Histon	W 2-1	2-1	—	Denham [24], Johnson [41]	698
5	22	H	AFC Wimbledon	L 0-1	0-0	5		1438
6	29	A	Kidderminster H	L 0-3	0-2	9		1415
7	Sept 5	A	Kettering T	L 0-2	0-0	11		1269
8	8	A	Cambridge U	D 0-0	0-0	—		2749
9	12	H	Crawley T	D 0-0	0-0	14		817
10	19	A	Grays Ath	W 3-0	1-0	—	Denham [10], Uddin (og) [62], Senior [65]	674
11	22	H	Tamworth	D 0-0	0-0	—		843
12	26	A	Stevenage Bor	D 1-1	1-0	13	Williams [22]	1200
13	29	H	Gateshead	W 3-2	1-1	—	Danylyk [2], Denham [89], Doughty (pen) [90]	769
14	Oct 3	A	Rushden & D	W 1-0	0-0	7	Kearney [82]	1168
15	10	H	Mansfield T	L 1-2	0-1	10	Burns [64]	1642
16	17	H	Luton T	L 0-1	0-0	11		1762
17	31	A	Oxford U	L 0-1	0-0	13		5609
18	Nov 14	H	Forest Green R	D 2-2	2-1	11	Williams [13], Senior [22]	1119
19	24	A	Tamworth	W 2-0	0-0	—	Doughty [71], McAliskey [88]	630
20	Dec 1	H	Barrow	L 0-1	0-0	—		832
21	5	A	Histon	D 0-0	0-0	11		676
22	Jan 16	A	Ebbsfleet U	W 2-1	1-0	—	Senior [14], Young [53]	873
23	23	H	Hayes & Y	W 3-2	2-2	11	Senior 2 [31, 80], Little [40]	895
24	30	H	Wrexham	L 1-3	0-2	—	Doughty (pen) [87]	1821
25	Feb 6	H	Salisbury C	W 5-0	2-0	11	Young [16], Clee [38], Densmore [61], Senior 2 [80, 90]	777
26	13	A	Crawley T	L 0-1	0-0	11		688
27	16	H	Eastbourne Bor	W 3-0	2-0	—	Doran [17], Denham [28], Senior (pen) [68]	590
28	20	A	Eastbourne Bor	D 2-2	1-1	—	Denham [44], Senior [68]	810
29	23	A	Gateshead	L 0-1	0-0	—		489
30	27	H	Grays Ath	D 1-1	0-0	11	Senior [73]	881
31	Mar 6	A	AFC Wimbledon	D 1-1	0-0	11	Senior (pen) [51]	3388
32	9	A	Wrexham	D 1-1	0-1	—	Young [82]	2114
33	13	H	York C	D 0-0	0-0	11		1236
34	16	H	Kettering T	W 2-0	2-0	—	McAliskey [34], Densmore (pen) [42]	690
35	20	H	Rushden & D	D 2-2	1-1	10	Densmore [34], Denham [90]	1035
36	23	A	Mansfield T	D 1-1	0-0	—	Young [70]	2364
37	27	A	Forest Green R	L 3-4	3-1	10	Senior [12], Williams [39], Densmore (pen) [45]	1043
38	Apr 3	H	Kidderminster H	W 3-2	2-2	10	Denham 2 [26, 43], Young [49]	889
39	5	A	York C	L 1-2	0-0	—	Denham [63]	3005
40	10	H	Oxford U	L 0-1	0-0	12		1356
41	14	A	Stevenage Bor	L 0-1	0-0	—		907
42	17	A	Luton T	D 0-0	0-0	13		7374
43	20	A	Salisbury C	L 1-4	0-0	—	Senior [90]	671
44	24	H	Cambridge U	L 0-2	0-0	14		1546

Final League Position: 14

GOALSCORERS

League (53): Senior 15 (2 pens), Denham 10, Young 5, Densmore 4 (2 pens), Doughty 3 (2 pens), Williams 3, Kearney 2, Little 2, McAliskey 2, Burns 1, Clee 1, Crowell 1, Danylyk 1, Doran 1, Johnson 1, own goal 1.
FA Cup (0).

Coburn 40	Densmore 42	Doughty 23+1	Kearney 29+1	Young 37+3	Smith 34+1	Danylyk 38+2	Crowell 5	Johnson 9+1	Denham 28+10	Senior 40+1	Clee 24+11	Little 12+19	Williams 39+4	Heffernan 3+6	Moffatt 1	Pearson —+5	Thaker —+2	Lawton 20+8	Burns 5+2	Sheridan 4+1	Thornley —+1	Welch 2+10	Dryan 1	Owens —+1	McAliskey 14+6	Saunders 4	Carden 3+12	Doran 14+3	Moyo —+4	Brown 13+4	Match No.
1	2	3	4	5	6	7²	8	9³	10¹	11	12	13	14																		1
1	2	3	4	5	6	7¹	8	9	12	11³		13	14	10²																	2
1	2	3	4	5	6	14	8	9²	7	11³	12	13			10¹																3
1	2	3	4	5	6		8	9¹	7	10²	13	12	11																		4
1	2	3	4	5	6¹		8	9²	7³	10	14	12	11	13																	5
1	2▪	3	4²	5	6		8	9	7	10³	14	12	13	11¹																	6
1		3	4	5	6	11		9²	7		10		8	12				2¹	13												7
1		3¹	4	5	2	11		9²	7		8	10³		6		12		14	13												8
1	7¹	3	4	5	2	11		12	9	8	10⁵			6				13													9
1	2	3	4	5		11		7²	9	8	10¹			6		12		13³	14												10
1	6	3	4		2	8		10	9		5	13						11¹	7²	12											11
1	2	3	4	5		11		9³	8	12	6		14					7²	10¹						13						12
1	2	3	4	5		11³		9	8	7¹	6							12	13			10²			14						13
1	2	3	4	12	5	11³		9	8²	7	13		6					14	10¹												14
1	6	3▪	4	13	2	7³			10¹	11▪	6²	9	5					14	12												15
1	6		4	5	2	8²			11³	9	3					14		7¹	10			13			12						16
1	6	3		5			4		10	9	2					12		7²	8			13			11¹						17
1	6	3		5			4³		10¹	8	13	9	2					7	11²			14			12						18
1	6	3	4³	5	2	8			13	10²	14	9¹	11					7							12						19
1	6	3	4²	14	2	7			10¹	11	13	9³	5					12							8						20
1	6	3	4	5	2	10			12	9			11					7							8¹						21
	6	3²	4¹	5	2	8			10	12	13		11					7							9	1					22
1	3	12	13	5	2	4²		14	10	11¹	9	6						7							8³						23
1	6³	3	4	5	2	8¹			12	10	11²		13					7							9		14				24
1	6	3³	4	5	2	7			10²	9	14		11					8¹							13		12				25
1	6		4	5	2	8²			10	9	11		3												13		7¹	12			26
	6		4	5	2	8			10²	9	11¹	14	3													1	7▪	13	12		27
	6		4	5	2	8			10²	9	11		3					7¹							12	1				13	28
1	6		4³	5	2	7			10	9	11¹	14	3			13									8²					12	29
1	6		4	5	2¹	14			10	8	11	9¹	3					7³							12					13	30
1	6		4	5		8			10¹	9	11		3					12							13			7²		2	31
1	6		4¹	5		8²			10³	9	11	13	3					12										2	14	7	32
1	6			5			4		10²	8	11³	9¹	3									14					13	2	12	7	33
1	6			5			4		12	9	11²	14	3									13			10¹		8³	2		7	34
1	6			5		8¹			13	9			14	3				7				4			10²		12	2³		11	35
1	6			5					10²	11			13	3				7				12			9¹		8	4		2	36
1	6			5	12				10	11			14	3				7				4²			9¹		13	2³		8	37
1	6			5		4			10	11			13	3				7¹				14			9²		8³	12		2	38
1	6			5	2	4			12	10⁵			9¹	3				7				13			14			11²		8	39
1	6			5	2	4			12	13			9²	3				7¹				10³			14			11		8	40
	6			5	2	4			10	9¹		13	3					7²								1	12	8		11	41
1	6			5	2	4			12	10⁶		9²	13	3				7							14			8³		11	42
1	6			5	2	4²			10	11		13	3					7¹							9³		12	14		8	43
1	6			5	2	8¹			10	11		9³	3					7²				13			14		12	4			44

FA Cup
Fourth Qualifying Round
          Mansfield T   (a)   0-3

BARROW

Blue Square Premier

Ground: Holker Street, Wilkie Road, Barrow-in-Furness LA14 5UH. *Tel:* (01229) 828 227. *Year Formed:* 1901.
Record Gate: 16,854 (1954 v Swansea T, FA Cup 3rd rd). *Nickname:* Bluebirds. *Managers:* Dave Bayliss and
Darren Sheridan. *Colours:* White shirts, blue shorts, white stockings.

BARROW 2009–10 LEAGUE RECORD

Match No.	Date	Venue	Opponents	Result	H/T Score	Lg Pos.	Goalscorers	Attendance
1	Aug 8	A	Cambridge U	W 2-0	0-0	—	Logan [62], Walker (pen) [90]	2990
2	11	H	Altrincham	L 0-3	0-1	—		1969
3	15	H	Stevenage Bor	D 0-0	0-0	14		1254
4	18	A	Mansfield T	L 1-4	0-1	—	Walker [61]	3188
5	22	A	Eastbourne Bor	L 1-2	0-2	20	Jones [90]	971
6	29	H	Tamworth	W 1-0	0-0	17	Walker (pen) [77]	1051
7	31	A	Wrexham	D 0-0	0-0	—		3760
8	Sept 5	H	Rushden & D	L 1-6	0-3	17	Bond [53]	1089
9	8	H	York C	D 0-0	0-0	—		1120
10	12	A	Luton T	L 0-1	0-1	17		6264
11	19	H	Forest Green R	D 1-1	0-0	17	Shaw [67]	1065
12	22	A	Kettering T	L 1-2	1-2	—	Shaw [13]	1150
13	26	A	Salisbury C	L 0-3	0-2	17		876
14	29	H	Mansfield T	W 3-1	1-1	—	Walker 2 [7, 50], Kamara [68]	1040
15	Oct 3	A	Oxford U	D 1-1	1-1	18	Shaw [29]	1561
16	10	A	Crawley T	W 1-0	0-0	16	Walker (pen) [75]	1051
17	17	H	Ebbsfleet U	W 2-0	0-0	15	Shaw [76], Cook [86]	1241
18	31	A	Grays Ath	D 3-3	2-1	16	Shaw [33], Kamara [38], Jones [86]	736
19	Nov 14	A	AFC Wimbledon	D 2-2	1-0	16	Lorraine (og) [32], Walker [48]	1614
20	21	A	Oxford U	L 0-1	0-1	16		5629
21	24	H	Grays Ath	D 2-2	1-1	—	Walker [19], Nelthorpe [77]	863
22	Dec 1	A	Altrincham	W 1-0	0-0	—	Nelthorpe [85]	832
23	5	H	Hayes & Y	D 1-1	0-0	16	Walker [52]	1164
24	26	H	Gateshead	D 3-3	1-2	15	Goodfellow [4], Bond [51], Blundell [60]	1727
25	Jan 23	A	Rushden & D	L 1-4	0-1	18	Blundell [82]	1134
26	Feb 6	H	Luton T	L 0-1	0-0	20		1579
27	13	H	Kettering T	L 0-2	0-0	20		1160
28	16	H	Gateshead	L 1-2	1-2	—	Walker [35]	503
29	27	A	Ebbsfleet U	W 4-1	2-0	20	Chadwick 3 [27, 28, 68], Walker (pen) [83]	1146
30	Mar 6	H	Cambridge U	L 0-1	0-0	21		1325
31	9	A	Stevenage Bor	L 0-4	0-2	—		1538
32	16	A	Wrexham	W 2-1	0-0	—	Westwood (og) [67], Chadwick [76]	1066
33	23	A	AFC Wimbledon	W 2-0	0-0	—	Boyd [51], Chadwick [75]	3019
34	27	H	Eastbourne Bor	W 3-2	1-0	17	Chadwick [25], Bond 2 (2 pens) [64, 82]	1302
35	29	H	Histon	D 0-0	0-0	—		994
36	31	H	Forest Green R	L 0-1	0-0	—		786
37	Apr 3	A	Tamworth	L 0-3	0-1	19		817
38	8	H	Kidderminster H	W 1-0	1-0	—	Bolland [4]	1253
39	10	A	Hayes & Y	D 1-1	0-0	17	Bolland [78]	312
40	13	A	York C	L 0-3	0-1	—		2154
41	15	H	Crawley T	W 4-1	1-0	—	Smith (og) [35], Wiles [62], Chadwick [79], Walker [87]	970
42	17	H	Salisbury C	L 0-1	0-0	15		1173
43	20	A	Kidderminster H	W 2-1	2-1	—	Walker 2 [18, 43]	1036
44	24	H	Histon	D 2-2	0-1	15	Chadwick [47], Wiles [54]	753

Final League Position: 15

GOALSCORERS

League (50): Walker 14 (4 pens), Chadwick 8, Shaw 5, Bond 4 (2 pens), Blundell 2, Bolland 2, Jones 2, Kamara 2,
Nelthorpe 2, Wiles 2, Boyd 1, Cook 1, Goodfellow 1, Logan 1, own goals 3.
FA Cup (11): Bond 3 (1 pen), Cook 2, Walker 2 (1 pen), Bolland 1, Goodfellow 1, Logan 1, Rutherford 1.

Tomlinson 20	Spender 41	Newton 4	Jones 30+2	Dugdale 10+1	Hulbert 34+3	Bond 36+4	Rutherford 29+9	Walker 32+4	Green 2	Logan 22+13	Pearson 29+3	Boyd 19+10	Taylor 2+5	Bolland 31+1	Foley 3	Deasy 24	Jelleyman 25+1	Shaw 13+1	Hogan 1+4	Sheridan 7	Morris —+1	Kamara 6	Wainwright 5	Cook 1+2	Neithorpe 6	Bowery 1+3	Blundell 10+9	Rothery —+2	Goodfellow 1+1	Chadwick 17+3	Wiles 9+9	Powell —+2	McEvilly 1+5	Edwards 12	Brown —+2	Owen 1+2	Match No.
1	2	3^8	4	5	6^2	7	8	9^3	10^1	11	12	13	14																								1
1	2		4	5	6	7	8	9	10^2	11	3^1		13	12																							2
1	2	3^1	4		6	7	8	9		10	12	11		5^1																							3
1	2	3	4	12	6	7	8	9		10		11^1		5^1																							4
1	2	3	4	5	6	7^1	13	9		10		12	8^2		11																						5
	2		4		6	13	7^1	9		12		8		5	11^2	1	3	10																			6
	2		4		6		12	9		7		8		5	11^1	1	3	10																			7
	2^8		4		6	12	11	9		7		8^1		5	1	3	10																				8
			4	12	7	11	9			6	2	8	10^1	5	1	3																					9
	2		4	12	7	11	9			6^3	3	8	14	5	1		10^2	13																			10
	2		4	6^1	7	12				9	3	8		5	1		10	11																			11
	2	13	6		7	11				9	4			5^2	1	3	10	12	8^3	14																	12
	2	5^2	4	6		14				13	11				1	3	10	12	8^1		7^3	9															13
1	2		5		6	4	13	9^1		14	11					3	10	12			7^2	8^3															14
1			5	2	6	4		9			11					3	10^1				7	8															15
1	2		5			7^1	11	9			4	12				3	10^1	8		6																	16
1	2		4		6^3	7	8^1	9^2		12	5	14				3	10^1				11	13															17
1			4	2	6^2	7	11^1	9		12	5	13				3	10^3				8	14															18
1	2		4		6	7	13	9			5					3	10^2				8^2		10^1	11													19
1	2		4		6	7	12	9		13	5					3					8^1			11^2	10												20
1	2			6	7	8	9^2	13		4			5			3^1	10^1							11	12												21
1	2			7	6^2			4	3		5			3		9									11	12	10^1	13									22
1	2		12	7	6^3	14			4	8^1		5				9^2									11		10		13								23
1	2		6	7			9			4			5			3									11^2	12	10^1	13	8								24
	2		6	7	8	9^3		11^2	4	12			5		1	3^1								14			10^1	13									25
	2	12		7	6	9^3		11^2	4	8			5^1		1	3								14			10^1	13									26
	2		4	6^8	7	11	9		12	5					1	3								13			10^2	8^1									27
	2		4		7	12	9^3	14	6	8^1			5		1	3		11									10^2		13								28
	2		4	6^3	7	8	9^2	11^1		14			5		1	3								13			10^1	12									29
	2		4		6	7	8	9	11^8				5		1	3											10^1			12							30
	2	4^2		6	7^1	11	9			12			5		1	3								10^3	8	13	14										31
	2	4^1		6	7	11	9^2			12			5		1									10^3		14	8				3	13					32
	2		5		11^3	12		7^2	8	6			4		1									10^1		9	13				3	14					33
	2		6	12	7^3	9^8		11^2	4	8^1			5		1									13		10	14				3						34
	2		4	6	12	13		11^2	4	8^1			5		1									10^3		9	7				14	3					35
	2		6	7	8			11^2	4				5		1									10		9^1	13				12	3					36
	2	4	6^3	7	8			12		14			5		1									13		9	11^1		10^2	3							37
	2	4	6	7		9		12					5		1	3								13		10^2	8^1				11						38
	2	4	6	7		9^2		11^3	10	8^1			5		1									13		12	14				3						39
	2^2	4	6	7	8	12		11	3				5		1									10		9^1	13										40
1	2	4	6^3	7	8	9^2		12		14			5											13		10	11^1				3						41
1	2	4		7	6^2	12	13		8^3	5														10^1		9	11				3		14				42
1	2	4	6	7		9^1		11	8^2				5													12	10				3	13					43
1	2	4					11^2	5	8				12		7									10^3		9	13				14	3^1		6			44

FA Cup

Fourth Qualifying Round	Chester C	(h)	1-1	Second Round	Oxford U	(a)	1-1
		(a)	4-0			(h)	3-1
First Round	Eastleigh	(h)	2-1	Third Round	Sunderland	(a)	0-3

CAMBRIDGE UNITED Blue Square Premier

Ground: Abbey Stadium, Newmarket Road, Cambridge CB5 8LN. *Tel:* (01223) 566 500. *Year Formed:* 1912.
Record Gate: 14,000 (1970 v Chelsea, Friendly). *Nickname:* The U's. *Manager:* Martin Ling.
Secretary: Andrew Pincher. *Colours:* Navy and sky blue shirts, sky blue shorts, sky blue stockings.

CAMBRIDGE UNITED 2009–10 LEAGUE RECORD

Match No.	Date	Venue	Opponents	Result	H/T Score	Lg Pos.	Goalscorers	Atten- dance
1	Aug 8	H	Barrow	L	0-2	0-0	—		2990
2	11	A	Ebbsfleet U	W	3-1	1-0	—	Holroyd 2 [16, 72], Reason [50]	1523
3	18	H	Crawley T	L	0-1	0-1	—		2733
4	22	A	Tamworth	D	0-0	0-0	10		1316
5	29	H	Gateshead	W	3-0	1-0	6	Holroyd 2 (1 pen) [41, 90 (p)], Parkinson [66]	2417
6	31	A	Rushden & D	D	1-1	0-0	—	Hatswell [65]	2344
7	Sept 5	H	Forest Green R	W	7-0	1-0	5	Crow 2 (1 pen) [44, 51 (p)], Holroyd 2 [47, 65], Ives 2 [68, 74], Beesley [90]	2646
8	8	H	Altrincham	D	0-0	0-0	—		2749
9	12	A	AFC Wimbledon	D	0-0	0-0	8		4123
10	19	H	Wrexham	W	2-0	1-0	4	Hatswell [9], Willmott [80]	2823
11	22	A	York C	D	2-2	0-1	—	Reason [79], Beesley [83]	2321
12	26	H	Luton T	L	3-4	2-0	9	Pitt [20], Holroyd 2 (1 pen) [33 (p), 65]	4870
13	29	A	Grays Ath	L	0-2	0-0	—		976
14	Oct 4	A	Histon	D	1-1	0-0	12	Holroyd [81]	2371
15	10	H	Ebbsfleet U	W	4-0	1-0	8	Pitt [45], Holroyd (pen) [53], Willmott [81], Crow [90]	3668
16	17	A	Hayes & Y	L	0-3	0-1	10		744
17	31	H	Kidderminster H	W	2-0	2-0	8	Holroyd [13], Hatswell [31]	3508
18	Nov 14	A	Kettering T	L	0-2	0-1	9		3088
19	21	A	Luton T	D	2-2	0-0	9	Crow 2 (1 pen) [81, 90 (p)]	7456
20	24	H	Rushden & D	D	2-2	0-2	—	Carden [60], Saah [65]	2612
21	Dec 5	A	Eastbourne Bor	D	2-2	1-2	10	Austin (og) [23], Saah [47]	1217
22	26	H	Stevenage Bor	L	1-3	1-1	10	Crow (pen) [5]	4439
23	28	A	Mansfield T	L	1-2	1-1	12	Holroyd [42]	3368
24	Jan 1	A	Stevenage Bor	L	1-4	1-2	—	Crow [38]	3406
25	16	H	Eastbourne Bor	L	0-1	0-0	—		2969
26	23	H	York C	L	0-1	0-0	14		2646
27	Feb 6	A	Crawley T	L	0-1	0-1	15		1108
28	13	H	AFC Wimbledon	D	2-2	1-1	16	Crow [18], Phillips [68]	3087
29	20	A	Forest Green R	D	1-1	1-0	—	Crow [22]	930
30	Mar 2	H	Oxford U	D	1-1	1-1	—	Saah [18]	3002
31	6	A	Barrow	W	1-0	0-0	16	Nielson [73]	1325
32	9	A	Kettering T	W	1-0	0-0	—	Crow [76]	1248
33	13	H	Histon	W	2-1	0-0	15	Nielson [67], Carden [85]	4417
34	16	H	Salisbury C	W	3-1	2-1	—	Coulson [23], Murray [32], Nielson [74]	2028
35	20	A	Wrexham	D	2-2	0-2	13	Crow (pen) [83], Marriott [90]	2105
36	24	H	Tamworth	W	2-0	0-0	—	Crow 2 [51, 68]	2121
37	27	H	Grays Ath	W	3-0	2-0	11	Crow 3 [30, 37, 63]	3125
38	30	A	Kidderminster H	L	0-1	0-1	—		1141
39	Apr 3	A	Gateshead	L	0-2	0-1	11		841
40	5	H	Mansfield T	W	3-2	1-1	—	Coulson [25], Phillips [50], Crow (pen) [90]	2823
41	10	A	Salisbury C	L	1-2	1-0	13	Hudson [31]	1245
42	13	A	Oxford U	D	0-0	0-0	—		5219
43	17	A	Hayes & Y	W	4-1	0-0	10	McAuley [16], Crow 2 [27, 78], Marriott [87]	2940
44	24	A	Altrincham	W	2-0	0-0	10	Marriott 2 [75, 90]	1546

Final League Position: 10

GOALSCORERS

League (65): Crow 19 (5 pens), Holroyd 12 (3 pens), Marriott 4, Hatswell 3, Nielson 3, Saah 3, Beesley 2, Carden 2, Coulson 2, Ives 2, Phillips 2, Pitt 2, Reason 2, Willmott 2, Hudson 1, McAuley 1, Murray 1, Parkinson 1, own goal 1.
FA Cup (8): Hatswell 1, Holroyd 1, McAuley 1, Marriott 1, Pitt 1, Reason 1, Tonkin 1, Willmott 1.

Potter 26	Gleeson 31+1	Coakley 5+2	Reason 31+7	Hatswell 23	Coulson 22+1	Parkinson 15+3	Carden 38	Holroyd 24+1	Beesley 4+13	Willmott 27+2	Pitt 11+5	Ives 9+16	Patrick —+2	McAuley 21+6	Crow 37+4	Tonkin 19+1	Saah 35	Phillips 16+16	Challinor —+2	Palmer 14+1	Hudson 2	Marriott 2+7	Walker 1	Partridge 11	Russell 13+2	Murray 6+6	Brown S 17	Roberts 5+1	Willock 5+8	Nielson 14	Berry —+1	Match No.
1	2	3¹	4²	5	6	7¹	8	9	10	11	12	13	14																			1
1	2	3	4	5	6	7¹	8	9	10²	11	12			13																		2
1	2	3³	4	5	6	7	8	9	10²	11	12					13	14															3
1	2		4	5		7¹	8	9²	13	11		12			10	3	6															4
1	2		4	5		7	8	9	12	11²				13	10¹	3	6															5
1	2		4	5		7¹	8	9²	12	11				13	10	3	6															6
1	2		4¹	5		7	8	9²	13	11		12			10³	3	6	14														7
1	2		4	5		7²	8	9		11				13	10¹	3	6	12														8
1	2		4³	5		7²	8	9	14	11				13	10¹	3	6	12														9
1	2		4	5		7	8	9	12	11²					10¹	3	6		13													10
1	2		4	5		7¹	8	9³	13	11	12				10²	3	6	14														11
1	2		4	5			8	9	10²	7¹	11³	14			13	3	6	12														12
1	2		4²	5			8	9	14	7³	11	13		12	10¹	3	6															13
1	2		4	5			8	9		7	11				10¹	3	6	12														14
1	2		4	5			8³	9¹	13	7²	11	14			10	3	6	12														15
1	2		4	5			8	9		7²	11¹	12			10	3	6	13														16
1	2		4	5		7³	8	9¹		11²		13		14	10	3	6	12														17
1			4³	5			8	9		7¹	11²	14		2	10	3	6	13	12													18
1			4	5		7¹	8	9		11	13			2	12	3	6	10³														19
1	2	3	4	5		7¹	8	9		11				10			6	12														20
1	3	12	5				8	13	14	7	11	4¹		2	10³		6	9²														21
1	2	13	5¹				8	9	14	7³	11¹	4²		12	10	3	6															22
1	2¹	12	4		6²		9	13		7	11	8		5	10	3																23
1	13		4	5	12		9			7¹	11²	8		2	10	3	6¹															24
1	14		4	7¹	8	9	13	11	12	6³				2	10²					3	5											25
1			4	5	12	8		11		7¹				2	10		6	9²		3		13										26
	2		4	5					12	11			8²	10³				9¹		3		14	1		6	7	13					27
	2		4¹	5					12			13	11	10²				9		3		14			6	7	8⁴	1				28
	2		4	5						11¹	12	7	10					9³		3					6	8²		1	13	14		29
	2		13	14			8			7²			4				5	9¹		3					6³	11		1	12			30
			4				8			7			10				5	9¹		3					11	6		1	2	12		31
			4				8						6	10			5	12		3					11		1	2	9¹	7		32
12			4				8						6	10²			5	14		3					11³	13	1	2¹	9³	7		33
	2	14					6			8			4	10²			5	12				13		3		11³	1		9¹	7		34
	2	12					6³			8			4¹	10¹			5	13				14		3		11	1		9²	7		35
	2	4³					6			8			14	10¹			5	9						3	13	11²	1		12	7		36
	2¹		4				6			8			12	10²			5	9³				14		3		11	1		13	7		37
		4¹					6			8			12	10			5	9³						3	13	11²	1	2	14	7		38
							8							4	10		5	13		3		14		6	11³	12	1	2	9²	7¹		39
		11	4				8						6	10			5	9²		12				3⁴	7	13	1			2¹		40
		4	6				8					8³	2				9²			3	5	10¹			11	12	1		13	7	14	41
	2		6				8						4	10			5	9		3	5				11		1			7		42
	2		6				8					12	4	10³			5			3		9			11²	13	1		14	7¹		43
	2	14	6				8					12	4³	10			5	9²		3		13			11		1			7¹		44

FA Cup
Fourth Qualifying Round

	Lincoln U	(a)	3-1
First Round	Ilkeston T	(h)	4-0
Second Round	York C	(h)	1-2

CHESTER CITY Removed from Blue Square Premier

Ground: The Deva Stadium, Bumpers Lane, Chester CH1 4LT. *Tel:* (01244) 371 376. *Year Formed:* 1885. *Record Gate:* 20,500 (1952 v Chelsea, FA Cup 3rd rd replay (at Sealand Road)). *Nickname:* Blues and City. *Manager:* Morell Maison. *Colours:* Blue and white striped shirts, blue shorts and stockings.

CHESTER CITY 2009–10 LEAGUE RECORD

Match No.	Date	Venue	Opponents	Result	H/T Score	Lg Pos.	Goalscorers	Attendance
1	Aug 15	H	Cambridge U	L	2-4	2-2	—	Wilkinson [1], Chadwick [19]	1757
2	18	A	Oxford U	L	0-4	0-0	—		5135
3	22	A	Luton T	D	0-0	0-0	24		6563
4	29	H	Mansfield T	L	0-1	0-1	24		1734
5	31	A	Altrincham	D	1-1	1-1	—	Wilkinson [53]	1737
6	Sept 5	H	Histon	W	2-0	1-0	24	Roberts [44], Chadwick [76]	1171
7	8	H	Tamworth	L	1-2	0-1	—	Chadwick [77]	1199
8	12	A	Eastbourne Bor	D	1-1	1-1	24	Blundell (pen) [45]	968
9	15	H	Gateshead	W	2-1	1-0	—	Blundell (pen) [20], Chadwick [76]	994
10	19	H	Stevenage Bor	L	0-1	0-1	24		1089
11	22	A	Salisbury C	D	1-1	0-0	—	Wilkinson [79]	838
12	27	A	Wrexham	D	0-0	0-0	—		5913
13	29	H	Forest Green R	L	1-2	0-2	—	Roberts [50]	1019
14	Oct 3	A	Hayes & Y	D	0-0	0-0	24		351
15	10	H	Rushden & D	L	0-1	0-1	24		1089
16	17	A	Gateshead	W	1-0	0-0	24	Beesley [57]	631
17	31	H	AFC Wimbledon	W	3-1	2-1	24	Chadwick [10], (og), Blundell [77]	1666
18	Nov 7	A	Grays Ath	W	3-1	2-1	—	Coulson [30], Chadwick 2 [44, 78]	480
19	10	A	York C	L	2-3	0-2	—	Barry [59], Kelly [90]	2164
20	14	A	Tamworth	L	1-3	0-1	24	Beesley [57]	955
21	21	H	Altrincham	L	1-3	0-2	24	Rule [63]	1132
22	24	A	Stevenage Bor	L	0-2	0-1	—		1487
23	Dec 1	A	Cambridge U	L	0-1	0-0	—		2239
24	5	H	Luton T	D	0-0	0-0	24		1352
25	26	A	Kidderminster H	L	0-2	0-1	24		1755
26	Jan 19	H	Salisbury C	L	0-1	0-0	—		425
27	23	A	Mansfield T	L	0-4	0-3	24		2882
28	Feb 6	H	Ebbsfleet U	L	1-2	1-2	24	Rea [30]	460

Final League Position: 24

GOALSCORERS

League (23): Chadwick 7, Blundell 3 (2 pens), Wilkinson 3, Beesley 2, Roberts 2, Barry 1, Coulson 1, Kelly 1, Rea 1, Rule 1, own goal 1.
FA Cup (1): Flynn 1.

Chester City were removed from the Blue Square Conference in February and their records for the season were expunged. This decision was upheld on appeal. Although the records are expunged the above table shows the record of the matches actually played, together with all of the regular statistics for that game. The table below shows the goalscorers for the opposition in these games.

Match No.	Date	Venue	Opponents	Result	H/T Score	Opposition Goalscorers
1	Aug 15	H	Cambridge U	L	2-4	2-2	Holroyd 3 (1 pen) [45 (p), 74, 89], Willmott [45]
2	18	A	Oxford U	L	0-4	0-0	Constable 3 [57, 84, 90], Green M [68]
3	22	A	Luton T	D	0-0	0-0	
4	29	H	Mansfield T	L	0-1	0-1	Duffy [2]
5	31	A	Altrincham	D	1-1	0-1	Little [22]
6	Sept 5	H	Histon	W	2-0	1-0	
7	8	H	Tamworth	L	1-2	0-1	Tait [37], Smith C [59]
8	12	A	Eastbourne Bor	D	1-1	1-1	Atkin [5]
9	15	H	Gateshead	W	2-1	1-0	Mackay [51]
10	19	H	Stevenage Bor	L	0-1	0-1	Bostwick [7]
11	22	A	Salisbury C	D	1-1	0-0	Clohessy [82]
12	27	A	Wrexham	D	0-0	0-0	
13	29	H	Forest Green R	L	1-2	0-2	Platt [18], Rigg [37]
14	Oct 3	A	Hayes & Y	D	0-0	0-0	

Danby 28	Rule 14 + 3	Meynell 11 + 6	Roberts 27 + 1	Ryan 24	Lea 18 + 1	Vaughan S 6	Barry 11 + 3	Wilkinson 19 + 7	Ellams 9 + 7	Ashton 19	Chadwick 21 + 2	Owen 7 + 5	Platt 2 + 3	Rawlinson — + 3	Kay 13 + 3	Lynch 10	Alessandra 4	Blundell 10 + 9	Vaughan J 1	Kelly 15 + 3	Murphy — + 1	Keltie 11	Beesley 8	Flynn 3	Coulson 5	Rea 3 + 1	Freeman 1	Davidson 2 + 3	Jones 4	Coulter 2 + 1	Match No.
1	2	3	4[3]	5	6[2]	7	8[1]	9	10	11	12	13	14																		1
1	13	3[2]	4	5	6	7		8[3]	10[1]	11	9	12			2	14															2
1	13		4	5	6	7		8[2]		11	9	12	14		2[1]	3	10[3]														3
1			4	5	6	7		8		11	9				2[1]	3	10	12													4
1			4	5	6	7		8		11	9				2[1]	3	10	12													5
1			4	5	6	7[3]	13	8[2]		11	9					3	10[1]	12	2	14											6
1			4	5	6	7[2]	8[1]	13		11	9				12			10	2												7
1	2[1]		4	5	6	7	13			11	9				8[2]	3		10		12											8
1	12	14	4	5	6[1]	7[2]	13			11	9				8	3		10	2												9
1[6]	6	13	4	5		7[1]				11	9	12			8[2]	3		10	2												10
1[6]	2[1]	13	4	3	12	7				11	9				8[2]	6		10				5	15								11
1	13		4	5	6	7			14	11	9				8[2]	3[1]		10[3]		12	2										12
1	14		4	5	6		13	7[3]	10[2]	11	9				8[1]			1[2]		3	2										13
1	5		4		6		7[2]	13	14	11	9	12			8[3]			10		3[1]	2										14
1	2[4]	13	6					8		3	12[4]							10[1]				5			4	9					15
1	2		6				8	12[2]	14	3					13			10[1]				5			4	9		7[3]			16
1	2[2]	14	4	5						3		9[3]	13		7[1]			1[2]				8	10	6	11						17
1	3[2]	2	5						13	11	9[1]		8	14				1[2]				4	10	6				7[3]			18
1	11[3]	2	5					12	14	3		9[2]	7[1]					13				6	10	8	4						19
1	3	2	4								9	7						8[1]		13		5	10	6	11						20
1	2	3	5	6							8	12	13					9		7[1]		1[2]	11		4						21
1	3	2	4					8	13	14		11[3]	7[2]					10[1]		12		5	9	6							22
1	3	11	2	4				8		7[1]	10		9	6								5		12							23
1	3	5[8]						8	11[1]	10[2]	9	4	12							6					7	2	13				24
1	3		2	4	6			8		10			11					5				7[2]			12			9[1]	13		25
1	3	11	2	4	6			7		10								5							8	9					26
1	11	3	2		6			7		10								5							8	9	4				27
1	3	11	5		6			7	10[2]			13						2							4	12	9[1]	8			28

FA Cup
Fourth Qualifying Round

Barrow	(a)	1-1	
	(h)	0-4	

Match No.	Date	Venue	Opponents	Result	H/T Score	Opposition Goalscorers
15	10	H	Rushden & D	L 0-1	0-1	Tomlin L [4]
16	17	A	Gateshead	W 1-0	0-0	
17	31	H	AFC Wimbledon	W 3-1	2-1	Main [45]
18	Nov 7	A	Grays Ath	W 3-1	2-1	Onibuje [32]
19	10	A	York C	L 2-3	0-2	Brodie 3 (1 pen) [1, 32 (p), 47]
20	14	A	Tamworth	L 1-3	0-1	MacKenzie [10], Brown [69], Wright [76]
21	21	A	Altrincham	L 1-3	0-2	Little [22], Williams [33], Senior [90]
22	24	A	Stevenage Bor	L 0-2	0-1	Odubade [42], Roberts [66]
23	Dec 1	A	Cambridge U	L 0-1	0-0	Crow [90]
24	5	H	Luton T	D 0-0	0-0	
25	26	A	Kidderminster H	L 0-2	0-1	Caines [16], Courtney [89]
26	Jan 19	H	Salisbury C	L 0-1	0-0	Tubbs (pen) [86]
27	23	A	Mansfield T	L 0-4	0-3	Jones 2 [23, 34], Jones (og) [37], Speight [80]
28	Feb 6	H	Ebbsfleet U	L 1-2	1-2	Vieira 2 [41, 44]

CRAWLEY TOWN · Blue Square Premier

Ground: Broadfield Ground, Broadfield Stadium, Brighton Road, West Sussex RH11 9RX. *Tel:* (01293) 410 000.
Year Formed: 1896. *Record Gate:* 4,522 (2004 v Weymouth, Dr Martens League). *Nickname:* The Reds.
Manager: Steve Evans. *Secretary:* Barry Munn. *Colours:* All red.

CRAWLEY TOWN 2009–10 LEAGUE RECORD

Match No.	Date	Venue	Opponents	Result	H/T Score	Lg Pos.	Goalscorers	Attendance
1	Aug 8	A	Mansfield T	L	0-4	0-3	—		3264
2	11	H	Forest Green R	W	3-1	2-1	—	Cook [3], Hutchinson [21], Ademeno [56]	776
3	15	H	Wrexham	W	1-0	0-0	7	Cook [50]	1014
4	18	A	Cambridge U	W	1-0	1-0	—	Cook [27]	2733
5	22	H	Gateshead	L	1-4	0-3	7	Rents [82]	881
6	29	H	Grays Ath	D	1-1	1-1	10	Louis [6]	846
7	Sept 1	A	Luton T	L	0-3	0-1	—		6389
8	5	A	York C	L	0-2	0-2	16		2139
9	8	H	Histon	W	2-0	0-0	—	Carruthers [87], Louis [90]	798
10	12	A	Altrincham	D	0-0	0-0	13		817
11	19	H	Kettering T	W	2-1	0-0	11	Ademeno [58], Willock [68]	901
12	22	A	AFC Wimbledon	D	1-1	1-0	—	Louis [38]	3408
13	26	H	Rushden & D	W	2-1	1-1	8	Louis [27], Willock [58]	925
14	29	A	Oxford U	L	1-3	1-1	—	Louis [27]	5675
15	Oct 3	A	Ebbsfleet U	D	0-0	0-0	11		987
16	10	H	Barrow	L	0-1	0-0	13		1051
17	17	A	Kidderminster H	L	0-1	0-0	14		1276
18	31	H	York C	W	3-1	0-1	12	Forrest 2 [53, 89], Smith [78]	975
19	Nov 14	A	Mansfield T	L	0-2	0-1	14		883
20	21	A	Hayes & Y	L	1-2	1-1	14	Smith [34]	342
21	24	H	Salisbury C	W	2-0	0-0	—	Smith [50], Killeen [87]	603
22	28	A	Gateshead	L	1-2	1-0	—	Malcolm [29]	467
23	Dec 1	H	Oxford U	L	1-2	1-0	—	Pinault [17]	1319
24	5	A	Tamworth	W	1-0	1-0	13	Killeen [14]	729
25	26	H	Eastbourne Bor	D	2-2	2-1	12	Ademeno [7], Wilson [21]	979
26	28	A	Grays Ath	W	3-2	3-2	10	Ademeno 3 [2, 5, 6]	505
27	Jan 1	A	Eastbourne Bor	W	2-0	2-0	—	Ademeno [3], Wilson [31]	1726
28	23	H	Kidderminster H	D	2-2	1-0	10	Ademeno [13], Cogan [63]	800
29	Feb 6	H	Cambridge U	W	1-0	1-0	10	Cogan [8]	1108
30	13	H	Altrincham	W	1-0	0-0	10	Ademeno [58]	688
31	20	A	Wrexham	L	0-2	0-0	—		2475
32	27	H	Luton T	W	2-1	0-0	10	Smith 2 [55, 87]	2118
33	Mar 2	A	Salisbury C	D	2-2	1-2	—	Cogan [27], Wilson [55]	581
34	6	A	Stevenage Bor	L	0-2	0-0	10		2230
35	9	H	AFC Wimbledon	W	2-1	1-1	—	Forrest [18], Ademeno [52]	1569
36	13	H	Ebbsfleet U	W	2-1	0-0	8	Malcolm [75], Ademeno [86]	983
37	27	H	Stevenage Bor	L	0-3	0-2	9		1229
38	Apr 2	A	Rushden & D	D	1-1	0-1	—	Malcolm [48]	1703
39	5	H	Hayes & Y	W	1-0	0-0	—	Forrest (pen) [57]	860
40	10	A	Histon	W	1-0	0-0	8	Hutchinson [49]	499
41	13	A	Forest Green R	L	0-1	0-0	—		601
42	15	A	Barrow	L	1-4	0-1	—	Smith [58]	970
43	17	H	Tamworth	W	2-0	0-0	7	Forrest (pen) [58], Smith [64]	755
44	20	A	Kettering T	D	1-1	1-0	—	Forrest (pen) [18]	800

Final League Position:

GOALSCORERS

League (50): Ademeno 11, Smith 7, Forrest 6 (3 pens), Louis 5, Cogan 3, Cook 3, Malcolm 3, Wilson 3, Hutchinson 2, Killeen 2, Willock 2, Carruthers 1, Pinault 1, Rents 1.
FA Cup (2): Forrest 1, Louis 1.

Rayner 35	Rents 39	Wilson 28 + 4	Hutchinson 34 + 5	Giles 9	Broadhurst 32 + 2	Powell 1 + 2	Smith 27 + 7	Louis 10 + 8	Ademeno 26 + 6	Cook 6	Rusk 36 + 2	Cogan 31 + 6	Malcolm 22 + 17	Pinault 38 + 2	Killeen 19 + 10	Forrest 17 + 16	Jordan 9 + 1	Carvalhera G + 1	Collins 2	Diilali 5	Barton 1 + 1	Quinn 28	Willock 12 + 4	Carter 2 + 4	Lokanbo 1 + 1	King — + 2	Napper — + 7	Langston 8	Match No.
1	2	3¹	4	5	6	7²	8³	9	10	11	12	¹3	14																1
1	2		4	5	6		8¹	13	10	11²	3	12		7³	9	14													2
1	2		4	5	6		8	14	10²	11	3	12	13	7¹	9³														3
1	2		4	5	6		8	14	10¹	11³	3	7	13		9²	12													4
1	2		4	5	6		8¹	12	10	11³	3	7	13		9²	14													5
	2	3²	4		6	14			9	10¹	11³	13	5	8	7	1	²2												6
	2		4		6			9		12		8¹	10²	7	1	5	3	1'–	13										7
1	3		4			14		9³		2	13		12	7		5²	10¹	1'		8	6								8
1	3		4		6			14	10²	2	12		7¹	13		5	1¹			8	9³								9
1	3		4		6			12	10¹	2			7	13	5²	11				8	9								10
1	3	4			6			13	10²	2		12	7	14	5	11¹				8	9³								11
1	3	7	14		6			9³		2	13	8¹	4		12	‖1				5	10²								12
1	3	4	13		6'			10³		2	11	12	7²	8¹	14					5	9								13
1	3	4³	6			14	10		2¹	11	13	7		8²	12					5	9								14
1	3		4		6		13	10	2	11		7²	8	12						5	9¹								15
1	3	14	8		6'	13	9	12	2	7		4³	11²							5	¹0¹								16
1	3	5	8²			13	14		2	7	12	4	9	11¹						6	10³								17
1		5	8²	2		10	9¹		3	11	13	4		7³						6	12	14							18
1⁶		3		5	6	9		13	2	11¹	12	8		7²	15					4	10								19
1		2	4	5'	6	10			12	11¹	8	7	13							3	9²								20
1		8	4	5'	6	11		12²	2		10	7²	9							3		13	14						21
1		3	4		6	8		10¹	2		11	7	9							5			12	5					22
1	3	7	12		6	8		10¹	2		11	4	9							5									23
1	3	6				8		10¹	2	7	11	4	9							5	12²		13						24
1	3	6	14		13	8²		9	2'	7	11	4³	10							5	12								25
1	3	2	4		6	8			9²		7	11	13	12						5	10¹								26
1	3	2	4		6	8³		10¹		11	9²	7	12							5	14	13							27
1	3	6	4			8		9¹	2	11	10	7		12						5									28
1	3		4		6	11¹		9³	2	7	10²	8	13	12						5			14						29
1	3	6²	4			8³		9	2	11	10	7¹	13	12						5				14					30
1	3		4		6	8			2	11	10	7²	9	12						5				13					31
1	3	14	4		6	8		10	2	11²	12	7³	9¹	13						5									32
1	3	5	4		6			10	2	11	8	7	9¹	12						5									33
1	3	5²	4		6	13		10	2	11	9	7	12	8¹						5									34
1	3	4			6	10		9¹	2	11	12	7	13	8²													5		35
1	3	4			6	10¹		9	2	11	12	7	13	8²													5		36
1	3	4³	14		6	9		10²	2	11¹	13	7	12	8													5		37
	3	2	4²	13		14		12		11	10³	7	9¹	8						5							6		38
	3		4			10¹		12	2	11	9	7		8						5							6		39
	3	14	4		6	8¹		12		11	9	7²	10³	‖						5	2		13						40
	3	10	4			13			2	11	9		8	‖						6¹	7²		12	5					41
	3	6	4¹			10			2	11	9	7		8	1								12	5					42
	3	14	4		6	10²		9	2	11¹	13	7		8³	1								12	5					43
	3	5	4¹		6			10²	2	11	9	7	13	8	1								12						44

FA Cup
Fourth Qualifying Round

AFC Wimbledon	(h)	1-1	
	(a)	1-3	

EASTBOURNE BOROUGH Blue Square Premier

Ground: Langney Sports Club, Priory Lane, Eastbourne, Sussex BN23 7QH.   *Tel:* (01323) 766 265.
Year Formed: 1964.   *Record Gate:* 3,770 (2005 v Oxford U, FA Cup 1st rd).   *Nickname:* The Sports.
Manager: Garry Wilson.   *Secretary:* Myra Stephens.   *Colours:* Red shirts, black shorts, red stockings.

EASTBOURNE BOROUGH 2009–10 LEAGUE RECORD

Match No.	Date	Venue	Opponents	Result	H/T Score	Lg Pos.	Goalscorers	Attendance
1	Aug 8	A	Wrexham	L 0-3	0-1	—		3726
2	11	H	AFC Wimbledon	W 1-0	0-0	—	Jenkins [50]	3108
3	15	H	Rushden & D	D 1-1	1-0	15	Weatherstone [29]	94¹
4	18	A	Grays Ath	L 0-1	0-1	—		487
5	22	H	Barrow	W 2-1	2-0	12	Taylor [42], Atkin [45]	971
6	29	A	Salisbury C	D 1-1	0-0	15	Weatherstone [69]	746
7	31	H	Ebbsfleet U	L 1-2	0-0	—	Taylor [69]	1165
8	Sept 5	A	Kidderminster H	W 2-0	1-0	12	Crabb N [37], Taylor [90]	1307
9	8	A	Stevenage Bor	L 0-2	0-1	—		1660
10	19	A	Oxford U	L 0-4	0-3	14		5688
11	22	H	Hayes & Y	W 3-1	1-0	—	Ruby (og) [44], Enver-Marum 2 [50, 55]	802
12	26	H	Tamworth	D 1-1	0-0	14	Enver-Marum [56]	1053
13	29	A	Histon	L 0-2	0-1	—		633
14	Oct 3	H	Kettering T	L 0-1	0-1	15		884
15	10	A	Gateshead	L 0-3	0-2	17		537
16	17	H	Mansfield T	L 1-2	0-2	18	Enver-Marum [68]	1207
17	31	A	Forest Green R	D 1-1	1-0	18	Crabb M [39]	789
18	Nov 14	H	Salisbury C	L 0-1	0-0	19		756
19	21	A	Mansfield T	D 1-1	1-0	20	McLaggon [44]	2922
20	24	H	Histon	D 1-1	1-0	—	Enver-Marum [42]	703
21	Dec 1	A	Hayes & Y	D 1-1	1-0	—	Taylor [9]	349
22	5	H	Cambridge U	D 2-2	2-1	20	Armstrong [15], Enver-Marum [25]	1217
23	26	A	Crawley T	D 2-2	1-2	20	Enver-Marum [18], Taylor [47]	979
24	28	H	Luton T	L 1-4	1-3	20	Crabb M [6]	6646
25	Jan 1	H	Crawley T	L 0-2	0-2	—		1726
26	16	A	Cambridge U	W 1-0	0-0	—	Taylor [55]	2969
27	23	A	Tamworth	D 1-1	1-1	19	Austin [40]	883
28	Feb 6	H	Wrexham	W 2-1	1-0	19	Taylor [18], Enver-Marum [59]	972
29	9	A	Rushden & D	L 0-2	0-1	—		1038
30	13	H	Luton T	L 0-1	0-1	19		2018
31	16	A	Altrincham	L 0-3	0-2	—		590
32	20	H	Altrincham	D 2-2	1-1	—	Enver-Marum [3], Weatherstone (pen) [83]	810
33	27	A	York C	W 1-0	0-0	19	Enver-Marum [70]	2611
34	Mar 2	H	Stevenage Bor	L 0-6	0-1	—		903
35	6	H	Kidderminster H	D 0-0	0-0	19		913
36	13	A	AFC Wimbledon	L 0-2	0-1	19		3358
37	20	H	Grays Ath	D 2-2	2-0	21	Taylor [2], Rooney [28]	1029
38	27	A	Barrow	L 2-3	0-1	22	Taylor 2 [50, 57]	1302
39	30	H	Gateshead	W 2-1	0-0	—	Weatherstone (pen) [64], Smart [66]	714
40	Apr 3	A	Forest Green R	W 1-0	0-0	20	Rooney [51]	1104
41	5	A	Ebbsfleet U	L 2-3	0-1	—	Crabb N [48], Benjamin [80]	1214
42	10	H	York C	W 3-1	3-1	19	Crabb M [14], Atkin 2 [17, 32]	1144
43	17	A	Kettering T	L 0-4	0-2	20		932
44	24	H	Oxford U	W 1-0	0-0	19	Weatherstone (pen) [84]	2634

Final League Position: 19

GOALSCORERS

League (42): Enver-Marum 10, Taylor 10, Weatherstone 5 (3 pens), Atkin 3, Crabb M 3, Crabb N 2, Rooney 2, Armstrong 1, Austin 1, Benjamin 1, Jenkins 1, McLaggon 1, Smart 1, own goal 1.
FA Cup (6): Elphick 2, Armstrong 1 (pen), Austin 1, Crabb M 1, Taylor 1.

Knowles 33	Baker 27 + 5	Jenkins 27 + 2	Armstrong 27 + 2	Austin 41	Pullan 31 + 2	Johnson 18 + 10	Brown 25 + 5	Taylor 39 + 4	Enver-Marum 28 + 12	Crabb M 40 + 1	Smith 5 + 10	Smart 15 + 13	Treleavan — + 1	Atkin 16 + 16	Weatherstone 23 + 7	Elphick 38 + 1	Crabb N 8 + 14	Jordan 9 + 1	Fraser 2 + 2	Rowe 1 + 3	McLaggon 3	Benjamin 16 + 5	Opinel 2	Walker 1	Rooney 8	Lightwood — + 1	Nessling 1	Match No.
1	2	3	4	5	6	7[1]	8	9[3]	10[2]	11	12	13	14															1
1	2	3	4	5	6	14	8	9[3]	10[2]	11	7[1]	12		13														2
1	2	3[1]	4	5	6		8	9[3]	10[2]	11	14	12		13	7													3
1			4	5	6		8	9	10[1]	11	13	3[2]		12	7	2												4
1	13	3[1]	4	5	6		8	9[3]		11	12	14		10	7	2[2]												5
1				5	6	14	8	9[3]	13	11	4[1]	3		10[2]	7	2	12											6
1[8]	12		4[2]	5	6[1]		8	9		11		13		10	7	2	3[5]	15										7
	2			5	6		8	9	12	11				10[1]	4	3	7[1]	1										8
	2			5[2]	6	13	8	9[3]	12	11	14			10	4	3	7[1]	1										9
		2		3	6	7[2]	8	9	12	11		14		10[1]	4[3]	5	13	1										10
			3		6	14	8[2]	9[3]	10	11[1]	12	13			4	2	7	1										11
		2		3	6		8	9	10	11	12				4	5	7	1										12
12	2			3	6[1]	13	8	9	10	11	14				4[2]	5	7[8]	1										13
8	2	13	3					12	10[1]	11	7[3]	6[2]		9	4	5	14	1										14
	2	3	14	5			8	10	13	11	7	4[2]		9[1]	12	6[3]												15
	2[1]	3	8	5	6			4	10[2]	13	11	7		9		12		1										16
1	12	3	8	5	6[1]		7	14	10	11		13			2[3]	4		9[2]										17
1		3[8]	8	5	6		7	12	10[2]					13	4				2	9[1]	11							18
1	2		8	5		14	7		10[3]	3				13	4	6		12		11[1]	9[8]							19
1	2		8	5	6		11	13	10	3[1]				4				12[8]		9[2]	7							20
1	2		8	5		12	3	9	10	11				4[1]	6						7							21
1	2	3	8	5		4		9[1]	10[3]	11	12			13	6				14		7[2]							22
1	2[1]	3	8	5	12	4	7	9[2]	10[3]	11				14	6	13												23
1		8	5	6	3	2	7[1]	9	10[2]	11				14	13	4	12	7[8]										24
1		3	8	5	6	2	7[1]	9	10[2]	11				12		4	13											25
1		3	8	2	6	4	12	9[2]	10[3]	11				14		5	13				7[1]							26
1		3	8	2	6	4		9[1]	10	11	13	12				5	7[2]											27
1	2	3[8]		8		4[2]		9[3]	10	11		13			5	4		12			7[1]							28
1	2		8		6	4[1]		9	10	11		12			5	13					7[2]	3						29
1	2[1]		8	5	6	3		9	10	11					4	12					7							30
	13		8	2	6[2]	4		9	10[3]	11	12				5	14					7[1]	3[8]	1					31
1	2		8[1]	5	6	7		9[2]	10[3]			4		12	13	3	14				11							32
1	2	12	8	5	6	3		9[2]	10[3]	11				14	13	4					7[1]							33
1	2[8]	12	8	5	6	7[1]		9	10	11[2]		13		14		4[3]					3							34
1		3	8	5	6[1]			9	10[2]	11		7		13		4	14				12	2[3]						35
1	2	3	8[2]	5		7[1]		9[3]		11		4		14	13	6	12					10						36
1		3		5	6	7[2]		9[3]	10[1]	11		8		14	13	4						12		2				37
1	2	3			6[1]	8		10	13	14		4		9	12	5					11[3]			7[2]				38
1	2	3		5			12	9[2]	13	11		4		10[3]	7	6					14			8[1]				39
1	2	3		5			12	9[2]	13	11		4		10[3]	7	6					14			8[1]				40
1	2	3		5			14	9[3]	13			4[1]		10[2]	8	6	11				12			7				41
1	2	3		5			14	13	9[2]	12	11			4[2]	10[1]	8	6							7				42
1[8]	2			5	12	13	3	9		1[1]				4	10[2]	8	6[8]							7[6]	15			43
	2			5			14	3	9[2]	12	11			4	10[8]	8	6[9]					13		7		1		44

FA Cup
Fourth Qualifying Round

Tooting & M   (a) 3-2

                  (h) 3-4

EBBSFLEET UNITED

Blue Square South

Ground : Stonebridge Road, Northfleet, Kent DA11 9BA.   *Tel:* (01474) 533 796.   *Year Formed:* 1946.
Record Gate: 12,036 (1963 v Sunderland, FA Cup 4th rd).   *Nickname:* The Fleet.   *Manager:* Liam Daish.
Secretary: Roly Edwards.   *Colours:* Red shirts, white shorts, red stockings.

EBBSFLEET UNITED 2009–10 LEAGUE RECORD

Match No.	Date	Venue	Opponents	Result	H/T Score	Lg Pos.	Goalscorers	Attendance
1	Aug 8	A	Altrincham	D	1-1	0-1	—	Lindie [59]	914
2	11	H	Cambridge U	L	1-3	0-1	—	Crooks [48]	1523
3	15	H	Kidderminster H	D	0-0	0-0	18		865
4	18	A	Stevenage Bor	L	0-3	0-1	—		1704
5	22	A	Mansfield T	L	0-3	0-1	22		3269
6	29	H	Hayes & Y	L	1-2	1-1	22	Vieira [6]	884
7	31	A	Eastbourne Bor	W	2-1	0-0	—	Vieira (pen) [56], Thomas [90]	1165
8	Sept 5	H	Oxford U	L	0-2	0-2	22		1468
9	8	H	Rushden & D	D	0-0	0-0	—		863
10	12	A	Forest Green R	D	0-0	0-0	21		762
11	19	H	AFC Wimbledon	D	2-2	1-1	18	Cumbers [41], Vieira [79]	2005
12	22	A	Histon	L	0-1	0-0	—		647
13	26	A	Kettering T	L	0-3	0-1	20		1345
14	29	H	Salisbury C	L	1-2	0-0	—	McCarthy [90]	792
15	Oct 3	H	Crawley T	D	0-0	0-0	22		987
16	10	A	Cambridge U	L	0-4	0-1	22		3668
17	17	A	Barrow	L	0-2	0-0	23		1241
18	31	H	Wrexham	L	0-1	0-1	23		969
19	Nov 14	A	York C	L	0-1	0-1	23		2629
20	21	H	Tamworth	L	0-1	0-1	23		867
21	24	A	AFC Wimbledon	L	0-3	0-1	—		2942
22	28	H	Mansfield T	W	2-1	1-1	—	Vieira [3], Holmes [57]	850
23	Dec 1	H	Stevenage Bor	W	2-1	0-1	—	Bailey 2 [49, 55]	836
24	5	A	Oxford U	L	2-4	0-2	23	Vieira [57], Ginty [88]	5188
25	26	H	Grays Ath	W	2-1	1-1	22	Vieira [10], Shakes [79]	937
26	28	A	Hayes & Y	L	2-4	0-1	22	Vieira [84], Ginty [90]	369
27	Jan 1	A	Grays Ath	W	3-0	3-0	—	Holmes [7], Vieira [13], Shakes [42]	793
28	16	H	Altrincham	L	1-2	0-1	—	Ginty [62]	873
29	19	H	Kettering T	L	1-2	0-1	—	Ashikodi (pen) [51]	587
30	23	H	Forest Green R	W	4-3	1-2	20	Vieira 2 [19, 55], Bailey [79], Crooks [90]	790
31	30	A	Luton T	W	3-2	2-1	—	Vieira 2 [41, 45], Ashikodi [67]	6658
32	Feb 9	H	Histon	L	0-1	0-0	—		731
33	13	H	York C	W	1-0	0-0	18	Ashikodi [52]	1226
34	20	A	Gateshead	W	3-1	2-1	—	Shakes [28], Vieira [30], Ashikodi [65]	533
35	27	H	Barrow	L	1-4	0-2	17	Ashikodi [76]	1146
36	Mar 2	A	Kidderminster H	D	2-2	1-1	—	Ashikodi [36], Ginty [69]	1163
37	6	A	Wrexham	D	1-1	0-1	18	Ashikodi [69]	2345
38	13	A	Crawley T	L	1-2	0-0	18	Ashikodi [89]	983
39	20	H	Luton T	L	1-6	1-0	19	Kovacs (og) [24]	1923
40	Apr 2	A	Salisbury C	L	1-3	0-1	—	Vieira [46]	1088
41	5	H	Eastbourne Bor	W	3-2	1-0	—	Bailey [7], Ashikodi 2 [63, 65]	1214
42	10	A	Rushden & D	L	0-2	0-1	19		1440
43	17	H	Gateshead	W	2-0	1-0	22	Vieira [2], Stavrinou [89]	1169
44	24	A	Tamworth	W	4-3	2-2	22	Vieira [12], Shakes [38], Ginty 2 [77, 81]	1694

Final League Position: 22

GOALSCORERS

League (50): Vieira 16 (1 pen), Ashikodi 10 (1 pen), Ginty 6, Bailey 4, Shakes 4, Crooks 2, Holmes 2, Cumbers 1, Lindie 1, McCarthy 1, Stavrinou 1, Thomas 1, own goal 1.
FA Cup (0).

Cronin 44	Salmon 27+4	Collins 16+1	Heeroo 28+4	Crooks 41	Charles D 39	Shakes 35+7	Shulton 8+2	Vieira 38+3	Forshaw 2+11	Welsh 22+8	Lindie 3+3	West 13+9	Wills 13+13	Bailey 30+3	Ginty 2+28	Thomas 6	Pooley 27+1	Cumbers 6	McCarthy 5	Holmes 28	Abbey —+1	Henry 2	Charles E 2+1	Easton 7+2	Smith 6	Stavrinou 19+2	Ashikodi 15	Match No.
1	2	3	4	5	6	7	8	9¹	10²	11³	12	13	14															1
1	2	3	4	5	6	7¹	8²	9	12	11	10	13																2
1	2	3	4	5	6	7	8	9¹	13	11¹²	10		12															3
1	2	3	4	5	6	7	12	9	10²			11		8¹	13													4
1	2³	3	4	5	6		8	9	14	7²		11¹	12		13	10												5
1	2	3	4	5	6	8²		9¹	13	7		12	10	11														6
1	2¹	3	4	5		8¹	11	9	13	7²	14	12	10	6														7
1	2	3	4²	5	6	8¹	12	9	14	7²		13		10	11													8
1		3	4	5	6	13		9	14	7	12	11²	8³	10¹	2													9
1		3	4²	5	6	14		9¹		7	12	13	11	8	10¹	2												10
1	3		4	5	6	14		12	13	7³	9¹	11	8	2	10³													11
1	2		7³	6	5	12		9¹	13	11²	8	4	14	3	10													12
1	2¹		12	5	6	4		9²	7	11	8	13		10	3													13
1			2	5	6	4		9¹	7	11	8	12		10	3													14
1			2	5	6	4²	9³	12	7	13	11	14	8¹	10	3													15
1	2²		6	3	9	8¹		11	12	7	13		10	5	4³	14												16
1		4	2	5	12	3¹	13		11	9²		6	7	8	10													17
1		2	5⁴	6	12	9		11	7¹	13		14		4	8²	10⁸	3³											18
1	12		2	6	10	9		13	11³	7²		4	14	3		8							5¹					19
1		2	6¹	3⁴	10	9¹		11	7	13		4	14			8							12²	5				20
1	3		2		10	9¹	12	11	7			4		6		8							5					21
1	3		2		10	9		7				4		6		8							5	11				22
1		2	6	3	10	9²		11¹	13	4						8							5	7				23
1		2	6	3	10	9²		11¹	7	13		12		4		8							5	8				24
1	2			5	6	10		9¹	11			4	12	3		8								7				25
1	2³			5	6	10		9	11²			14	4¹	13	3	8							12	7				26
1	2			6		10		9²	12	11¹	14	4³	13	5		8							3	7				27
1	2³			6		10		9²	12	11		4¹	13	5		8			14	3	7							28
1	2²			6	4	10			13	11¹	14		12	5		8				3³	7	9						29
1	2	13	6	3	11	10²						4	12	3		8						7¹	9					30
1	2			5	6	11		9¹		12		4				8						3	7	10				31
1	2			5	6	11²		9		13		4	12			8						3	7¹	10				32
1	12	7	5	6	11	9				4	13			2		8						3¹			10²			33
1	12	3¹	2	5	6	11²		9³		13		8	14	4		7								10				34
1	3²			5	6	11		9	12			14	4³	13	2	8						7¹	10					35
1	13	3	14	5²	6	11		9¹				4	12	2		8						7²	10					36
1	2¹	3		5	6							12	4	9	1	8						7	10					37
1	12	3	4²	5	6	11³		9	14			8	13	2¹								7	10					38
1	3	2	5	6	11	9²		12				4	13		8							7¹	10					39
1	2³			5	6	11¹		14	4	13	12	3			8							7²	10					40
1	2	12	5	6	11	9²		7¹	4			3ᵉ		8								13	10					41
1	2	3³	5	6	11¹	9		12	7²	4	14			8								13	10					42
1	2			5	6	12		9²	11¹			4	13	3		8							7	10				43
1	2			5	6	10		9	11¹			4	12	3		8							7					44

FA Cup
Fourth Qualifying Round
      Bromley   (a)   0-3

FOREST GREEN ROVERS Blue Square Premier

Ground: The Lawn, Nympsfield Road, Forest Green, Nailsworth GL6 0ET. *Tel:* (01453) 834 860.
Year Formed: 1890. *Record Gate:* 4,836 (2009 v Derby Co, FA Cup 3rd rd) *Nickname:* Rovers. *Manager:* David
Hockaday. *Secretary:* David Honeybill. *Colours:* Black and white striped shirts, black shorts, red stockings.

FOREST GREEN ROVERS 2009–10 LEAGUE RECORD

Match No.	Date	Venue	Opponents	Result	H/T Score	Lg Pos.	Goalscorers	Attendance
1	Aug 8	H	Kettering T	L	1-2	0-0	—	Davies 68	1074
2	11	A	Crawley T	L	1-3	1-2	—	Smith 37	776
3	15	A	York C	L	0-2	0-0	23		1954
4	18	H	Luton T	L	0-1	0-0	—		1805
5	22	A	Rushden & D	L	2-4	1-2	23	Rigg 6, Stearn 82	1056
6	29	H	Wrexham	L	0-2	0-2	23		1021
7	31	A	Oxford U	D	0-0	0-0	—		6338
8	Sept 5	A	Cambridge U	L	0-7	0-1	23		2646
9	8	H	Hayes & Y	D	0-0	0-0	—		630
10	12	H	Ebbsfleet U	D	0-0	0-0	23		762
11	19	A	Barrow	D	1-1	0-0	23	Rigg 62	1065
12	22	H	Kidderminster H	D	1-1	0-1	—	Rigg 54	707
13	26	H	Grays Ath	W	2-1	1-0	21	Rigg 7, Preece 73	911
14	Oct 3	A	Mansfield T	L	0-1	0-1	20		3022
15	10	A	AFC Wimbledon	L	2-5	2-3	21	Rigg 7, Brown 16	1921
16	17	A	Histon	L	2-5	1-1	22	Smith 9, Brown (pen) 89	823
17	31	H	Eastbourne Bor	D	1-1	0-1	22	Stonehouse 79	789
18	Nov 14	A	Altrincham	D	2-2	1-2	21	Smith 30, Rigg 86	1119
19	21	H	Stevenage Bor	L	0-1	0-1	21		757
20	24	H	Oxford U	L	0-1	0-1	—		1610
21	Dec 1	A	Wrexham	L	0-1	0-0	—		1808
22	5	H	Rushden & D	W	1-0	0-0	22	Preece 64	755
23	26	H	Salisbury C	W	3-1	2-0	21	Rankin 29, Webb (og) 45, Powell 69	1079
24	28	A	Tamworth	D	0-0	0-0	21		868
25	Jan 16	H	Gateshead	W	1-0	0-0	—	Rankin 69	805
26	23	A	Ebbsfleet U	L	3-4	2-1	21	Rankin (pen) 19, Powell 2 23, 71	790
27	26	A	Hayes & Y	W	3-2	1-1	—	Ameobi 22, Styche 2 58, 87	291
28	30	H	Mansfield T	L	1-4	1-0	—	Ameobi 17	817
29	Feb 6	A	AFC Wimbledon	L	0-2	0-2	21		3272
30	13	A	Kidderminster H	L	1-2	0-1	21	Smith 59	1421
31	20	A	Cambridge U	D	1-1	0-1	—	Hodgkiss 72	930
32	Mar 6	H	York C	W	2-1	1-1	22	Powell 22, Thorne 55	892
33	9	A	Luton T	L	1-2	0-1	—	Platt (pen) 81	5884
34	16	A	Gateshead	L	1-3	1-2	—	Powell 39	485
35	20	H	Kettering T	W	2-0	0-0	22	Ameobi 68, Morris 86	1032
36	23	A	Salisbury C	W	3-1	3-0	—	Ameobi 16, Smith 33, Styche 43	665
37	27	H	Altrincham	W	4-3	1-3	20	Smith 19, Styche 69, Brown (pen) 74, Preece 77	1043
38	31	H	Barrow	W	1-0	0-0	—	Morris 84	786
39	Apr 3	A	Eastbourne Bor	L	0-1	0-0	21		1104
40	5	A	Tamworth	L	3-4	2-2	—	Powell 2, Platt 2 (1 pen) 41, 85 (p)	1370
41	10	A	Stevenage Bor	L	0-2	0-1	21		2524
42	13	H	Crawley T	W	1-0	0-0	—	Platt 75	601
43	17	H	Histon	W	2-0	2-0	19	Smith 39, Styche 44	1204
44	24	A	Grays Ath	L	1-2	0-0	21	Brown (pen) 66	940

Final League Position: 21

GOALSCORERS

League (50): Smith 7, Powell 6, Rigg 6, Styche 5, Ameobi 4 (3 pens), Platt 4 (2 pens), Preece 3, Rankin 3 (1 pen), Morris 2, Davies 1, Hodgkiss 1, Stearn 1, Stonehouse 1, Thorne 1, own goal 1.
FA Cup (8): Platt 2, Brown 1 (pen), Davies 1, Hodgkiss 1, Preece 1, Rankin 1, Smith 1.

Burton 25+1	Taylor 6	Stonehouse 40+3	Ayres 6+2	Preece 37	Else 3+3	Stearn 2+5	Smith 39+1	Challinor 7	Brown 33+8	Platt 34+6	Davies 10+8	McDonald 14+2	Armstrong 13	Lloyd 3+10	Pugh 1+2	Fowler —+2	Ellis 7	Adams 7	Morris 1+8	Rigg 15	Pass 1+1	Wilkinson 7	Imudia 3	Spence 6	Palmer —+1	Thorne 18+5	Curran 1+1	Maxwell —+1	Ameobi 25+2	Hodgkiss 31	King 1+3	Powell 19+5	Ford —+1	Rocastle 14+1	O'Cearuill 13+1	Joyce 1+1	Rankin 17+2	Berry —+2	Styche 13+5	Ireland 11	Match No.
1	2	3	4¹	5	6²	13	7	8	9	10	11	12																													1
1	2	3		5	13	6²	7	8	9	10¹	11			4	12																										2
1	2	3		5	6²	13	7	8	9	10³	11		4¹	14	12																										3
1		3		5		12	7¹	8	9	10²	11			13			4	6																							4
1		3		5	2	12	7		9	10¹	11²			13			4	6	8																						5
1		3	2	5		10¹	7		9³	12	14	11	13				4	6²	8																						6
1		3	2	5		13	7		9¹	12	14	11	10²				4	6	8³																						7
1*	5	3	2¹						11	9²	13			7	10⁶	12	4	6	8	15																					8
	5¹	3		2					11	9	12	13	7	10			4	6²	8	1																					9
		3							11		9	10	5	12		4	6¹	8	1	2²	7	13																			10
		3	4						11	6	9²	10		13				8⁸	1	2	7		5	12																	11
1		3	12	6					8²	9	14	7					11		2¹	4		5	10³	13																	12
1		3	2	4					12	6	9	10		13			8			7¹		5²	11																		13
1		3		5					4²	6	9			13			8			7¹		2	11	10	12																14
1		3		5					11	7	9	12					8			4¹		6	10²	2	13																15
1	11	5²							8	9				12	3		10			6			2	4	7¹	13															16
1	3	5							8	10²	9³	12	6				11			13	2	14	4¹		7																17
1	11	5							8	7¹	9		3				1C			2		12	4	6																	18
1	12	5							11	7	9³		3²				1C			13		2	4	8	6¹	14															19
1	3	5							4	7	9	13								6		12	2	11¹	8	10²															20
1	12	5							4	13		10¹	3							6⁸		9²	7	11	8	2															21
1	11	5							4	7²	10¹	3								9		2	12	8	6	13															22
1	3		13						4	12	11									6		9	2	7²	8¹	5	10														23
1	3								4	7	10									6		2	8	11	5	9															24
1	3	5							12	10										6¹		9	4	7	8	2	11														25
1	3	5							4	13										6		9	7	11	8	2	10¹	12													26
	3	5							4		10									6		9	7	11	8	2	8*	2					12							27
	3								4²	13	11³									6		9	2	7¹	8	5	10	14	12											28
		5							4	13	10²	12								6		11	2		8	3¹	9	7												29
	13	5							4	7	11¹	3								14		10	2		12	6	8³	9²	1											30
	11¹	5							4	7	12	3								6		9	2		8	10²	13	1												31
	3	5							8	7³	11						6¹	14		12		9	2	4		10²	13	1												32
	3	5							4	7²	11						6	13		5		9	2	8		10¹	12	1												33
	3		14						4	12	8²	13					6			5³		11	2	7		10¹	9	1												34
	3	5							4	7	8						6		12			11	2			10	9¹	1												35
	3	5							4	7	11						6		12			10	2			8	9¹	1												36
15		5							4	7*	11¹						6					10	2		13	12	8²	9	1⁶												37
	3	5							4		11						7		14	1		13	10³	2	12		6²	8¹	9												38
	3	5							4	7		13					6		12	1		10	2	11²			8¹	9													39
1	3	13	5						4	7²	11						6		12			10	2	8¹				9													40
	3	4¹	5						8	12	11						6		7²			13	2	14			10³	9	1												41
	3	5							4	7	11						6		12			10	2	8¹				9	1												42
	3	5							4	7	11						6		12			10¹	2	8				9	1												43
1	3	5							4	7	11²						6		13			10	2	8¹				12	9												44

FA Cup
Fourth Qualifying Round

Fourth Qualifying Round	Mangotsfield U	(a)	2-1
First Round	Mansfield T	(h)	1-1
		(a)	2-1
Second Round	Bath C	(a)	2-1
Third Round	Notts Co	(a)	1-2

GATESHEAD

Blue Square Premier

Ground: Gateshead International Stadium, Neilson Road, Gateshead NE10 0EF. *Tel:* (0191) 478 3883.
Year Formed: 1889 (Reformed 1977). *Record Gate:* 24,348 (1927 v Swansea T, FA Cup Quarter-Final).
Nickname: The Tynesiders, The Heed. *Manager:* Ian Bogie. *Secretary:* Mike Coulson. *Colours:* White shirts,
black shorts and stockings.

GATESHEAD 2009–10 LEAGUE RECORD

Match No.	Date		Venue	Opponents	Result	H/T Score	Lg Pos.	Goalscorers	Attendance
1	Aug	8	H	Histon	L	0-3	0-1	—	681
2		15	A	Luton T	L	1-2	1-2	22	Mackay [5]	6829
3		18	H	Tamworth	D	1-1	0-1	—	Harwood [87]	429
4		22	A	Crawley T	W	4-1	3-0	18	Gate [19], Brittain 2 (2 pens) [37, 39], Armstrong [90]	881
5		25	H	York C	L	1-2	1-0	—	Francis [45]	1174
6		29	A	Cambridge U	L	0-3	0-1	21		2417
7	Sept	5	H	Hayes & Y	D	0-0	0-0	21		519
8		8	A	Kettering T	L	0-4	0-2	—		1230
9		12	H	Salisbury C	W	2-1	2-0	20	Gate [8], Richardson [39]	478
10		19	A	Kidderminster H	L	2-3	1-2	20	Francis [12], Gate [62]	1286
11		22	H	Rushden & D	D	0-0	0-0	—		409
12		26	H	Oxford U	L	0-1	0-0	19		1144
13		29	A	Altrincham	L	2-3	1-1	—	Armstrong [6], Turnbull [66]	769
14	Oct	3	A	Grays Ath	D	0-0	0-0	21		592
15		10	H	Eastbourne Bor	W	3-0	2-0	19	Armstrong 2 [14, 17], Turnbull [84]	537
16		31	H	Salisbury C	W	1-0	0-0	20	Winn [85]	1050
17	Nov	14	A	Stevenage Bor	L	3-5	1-3	20	Griffin (og) [38], Clare 2 [69, 81]	2203
18		21	H	Grays Ath	W	3-0	1-0	19	Clare 3 [8, 56, 78]	506
19		24	A	York C	L	0-1	0-1	—		2302
20		28	H	Crawley T	W	2-1	0-1	—	Clare [74], Gate [77]	467
21	Dec	1	H	Mansfield T	L	1-3	1-0	—	Mackay [45]	643
22		5	A	AFC Wimbledon	L	0-2	0-1	19		3209
23		26	A	Barrow	D	3-3	2-1	19	McDermott [2], Clare 2 [42, 57]	1727
24	Jan	16	A	Forest Green R	L	0-1	0-0	—		805
25		23	H	Luton T	L	0-1	0-1	22		1218
26		26	H	Kettering T	L	0-2	0-2	—		401
27	Feb	6	A	Mansfield T	W	2-0	1-0	22	Wake 2 [5, 48]	7261
28		13	A	Hayes & Y	L	2-3	2-1	22	Clare 2 (1 pen) [39 (p), 44]	296
29		16	H	Barrow	W	2-1	2-1	—	Winn [7], Turnbull [43]	503
30		20	H	Ebbsfleet U	L	1-3	1-2	—	Winn [41]	533
31		23	H	Altrincham	W	1-0	0-0	—	Baxter [74]	489
32	Mar	2	A	Tamworth	L	0-1	0-0	—		483
33		6	A	Histon	D	0-0	0-0	20		645
34		13	A	Rushden & D	L	0-8	0-2	20		1414
35		16	H	Forest Green R	W	3-1	2-1	—	Armstrong [10], Winn [42], Wake [60]	485
36		23	H	Wrexham	W	1-0	0-0	—	Armstrong [50]	614
37		27	A	Oxford U	L	1-2	0-0	19	Armstrong [56]	5986
38		30	A	Eastbourne Bor	L	1-2	0-0	—	Baxter [72]	714
39	Apr	3	H	Cambridge U	W	2-0	1-0	18	Clare 2 (1 pen) [36, 83 (p)]	841
40		5	A	Wrexham	D	0-0	0-0	—		2380
41		10	H	Kidderminster H	L	0-2	0-0	20		602
42		17	A	Ebbsfleet U	L	0-2	0-1	21		1169
43		20	H	Stevenage Bor	L	0-1	0-1	—		702
44		24	H	AFC Wimbledon	W	1-0	1-0	20	Clare [4]	1304

Final League Position: 20

GOALSCORERS

League (46): Clare 13 (2 pens), Armstrong 7, Gate 4, Winn 4, Turnbull 3, Wake 3, Baxter 2, Brittain 2 (2 pens), Francis
2, Mackay 2, Harwood 1, McDermott 1, Richardson 1, own goal 1.
FA Cup (7): Armstrong 2, Turnbull 2, Baxter 1, Winn 1, own goal 1.

Provett 11	Baxter 42	Robinson 15+2	Gate 30	Curtis 38	Jones 9+1	Brittain 6	Turnbull 36+5	Mackay 14+3	Forsyth 2+3	Phillips 18+17	Francis 7+19	Richardson 9+10	Armstrong 23+15	Harwood 3+3	Swailes 22+1	Pelonde 3	McDermott 4+7	One 7+5	Ascheri 1	Ascheri 1	Cave 17+1	Farman 33	Williams 14+2	Winn 23+1	Clare 26	Haworth 5+1	Keltie 3	Shaw 1	Bains 4+1	Sinclair 3+2	Wake 9+9	Ferrell 14+2	Heckingbottom 15	Buchanan 2	Parkinson 12+2	Hurren 2+4	Match No.
1	2	3	4	5	6	7	8¹	9²	10	11³	12	13	14																								1
1	2	3	4	5	6³		8	9	10¹	11	13	12	14	7²																							2
1	2³	3	4	5		7¹	8	9	12	11²	¹0		14	6																							3
1	2	3	4²	5	6	7³	8	9¹		11	13	10	12	14																							4
1	2	3	4	5	6¹	7	8	9		11	12	10²	13																								5
1	2	3	4	5		7²	13	9		11³	8	¹0¹	12				6⁴	14																			6
1	2	3	4	5		7	13	8¹		11	6²	12						0	9⁴																		7
1	2	3	4	5			8	13	14	11¹	6	12		7²			10	9³																			8
1	2	3	4	5			8³	10		12		11	13				6	14	9²	7¹																	9
1	2¹	3	4				8	10		12	7³		11	14	5		13	9²			6																10
	2		4	5			8	11		7			9		6		10				3	1															11
	2		4	3			8	14		11³	13	10	12		5		9¹				6	1	7²														12
	2	12	4	3			8			14	11	10	9²		5		13				6¹	1	7³														13
	2	13	4	3			8	10¹		11²	14		9³		5		12				6	1	7														14
	2¹		4	5			8	10³	13	11	12		9²		6		14				3	1	7														15
	2		4	5			8	10²		13			9¹		6	14	12				3	1	7	7³	11												16
	2		4	5			8³			14			9²	7¹			13				3	1	11	6	10	12											17
	2	4²	5				8			13			9				12				3	1	6	11	10¹	7											18
	2		4				8	13		12	14				5		10²				3	1	6	11³	9	7¹											19
	2		4	5			8¹			13	12										3	1	6	11²	9	10	7										20
	2		4	5				10		12		13	9³	14							3	1	6²	11¹			7	8									21
	2	3	4	5			8			10		12	14	6							1	13		9³	7²	11¹											22
	2	3	4	5			11			12			6		3						1	7	9¹		10												23
	2		4	5			12			11	14	10²	13		7³						3	1	8¹	9		6											24
	2	3	4¹	5			8			11	¹2	13³	9		7²						¹	14		10		6											25
	2	3		5			8			11²	12		9								¹	4		10		6	7¹	13									26
		3	4	5	6					13			9²				·2				1	2	11				7¹	1C	8								27
		2					8						12				3				1	6	11	9²			4¹	10	7	3	5						28
	2		5				8	14													1		11	9³			12	13	10	4	3	6¹	7²				29
	2		5				8			13			12								1		11	9			6		10²	4	3		7¹				30
	2	4¹	5	6			12						13								1		11	9			13²		8	3	7					31
	2²		5	6			8			12	13	14									1		1?	9			10³		4	3	7¹					32
	2			6			8			13			12		5						1		11	9			10¹		4	3	7²					33
	2			6			8			14	4	12	9		5						1		11³				13	10²	3	7¹						34
	2	5					8			12	13		9³	6							1		11	10			·4		3	7¹	4²					35
	2	5					8			12			9²	6							3	1	11	10³			13	4		7¹	14					36
	2	5					8			14			9³	6							3	1	11²	10			12	4		7¹	13					37
1	2	5					8			12			9	6								1	13	10²			11	7	3		4¹					38
	2	5¹					8			13			9³	6							12	1	11²	10			14	4	3	7						39
	2						8			12			9³	6							3	1	11²	10			14	4	5	7¹	13					40
	2		14				8			12			9	5							3²	1	11²	10			4	6		7¹	13					41
	2	4	5				14			12		7¹	9²	6³							1		11	10			13	8	3							42
	2	4	5				8			7³			9²	6							1		11	10¹			12	13	3	14						43
	2	4¹	5				8			7³			9	6							1		11	10²			13	12	3	14						44

FA Cup
Fourth Qualifying Round
                 Southport   (h)   3-0
First Round   Brentford   (h)   2-2
                                     (ε)   2-5

GRAYS ATHLETIC   Competition undecided

Ground: Recreation Ground, Bridge Road, Grays RM17 6BZ.   *Tel:* (01375) 391 649.   *Year Formed:* 1890.
Record Gate: 9,500 (1959 v Chelmsford City, FA Cup).   *Nickname:* The Blues.   *Manager:* Julian Dicks.
Secretary: Phil O'Reilly.   *Colours:* All sky blue.

GRAYS ATHLETIC 2009–10 LEAGUE RECORD

Match No.	Date	Venue	Opponents	Result	H/T Score	Lg Pos.	Goalscorers	Atten- dance
1	Aug 11	A	Histon	D 0-0	0-0	—		816
2	15	A	Tamworth	L 1-2	1-2	20	Morgan [13]	729
3	18	H	Eastbourne Bor	W 1-0	1-0	—	Graham [16]	487
4	22	H	Kidderminster H	L 1-3	0-2	19	Charge [51]	754
5	29	A	Crawley T	D 1-1	0-1	20	Taylor [85]	846
6	31	H	AFC Wimbledon	L 2-4	1-2	—	Gaughran [29], Charge [47]	1762
7	Sept 5	H	Mansfield T	D 1-1	1-1	20	Slabber [36]	732
8	8	A	Salisbury C	L 0-2	0-1	—		765
9	12	A	Rushden & D	L 4-5	1-1	22	Poole [45], Obersteller [52], Davis [58], Uddin [70]	1192
10	19	H	Altrincham	L 0-3	0-1	21		674
11	22	A	Stevenage Bor	D 1-1	1-1	—	Rnkovic [15]	1803
12	26	A	Forest Green R	L 1-2	0-1	23	Davis [50]	911
13	29	H	Cambridge U	W 2-0	0-0	—	Charge [58], Poole (pen) [90]	976
14	Oct 3	H	Gateshead	D 0-0	0-0	19		592
15	10	A	Oxford U	L 0-5	0-3	20		6150
16	17	A	Wrexham	L 1-2	1-2	21	Slabber [13]	2495
17	31	H	Barrow	D 3-3	1-2	21	Onibuje [14], Slabber 2 [51, 61]	736
18	Nov 14	H	Luton T	L 0-2	0-1	22		1668
19	21	A	Gateshead	L 0-3	0-1	22		506
20	24	A	Barrow	D 2-2	1-1	—	Rnkovic [15], James [72]	863
21	28	H	Tamworth	W 1-0	1-0	—	Rnkovic [32]	496
22	Dec 1	H	Histon	L 0-1	0-1	—		367
23	5	A	Mansfield T	D 0-0	0-0	21		2726
24	26	A	Ebbsfleet U	L 1-2	1-1	23	James [31]	937
25	28	H	Crawley T	L 2-3	2-3	23	Reid (pen) [22], Onibuje [43]	505
26	Jan 1	H	Ebbsfleet U	L 0-3	0-3	—		793
27	23	H	Oxford U	L 0-4	0-1	23		1136
28	26	A	Kidderminster H	L 1-4	1-2	—	Guy (pen) [36]	1109
29	Feb 6	A	Rushden & D	L 0-3	0-1	23		476
30	9	A	Hayes & Y	L 0-4	0-2	—		251
31	13	H	Salisbury C	L 0-2	0-1	23		232
32	27	A	Altrincham	D 1-1	0-0	23	Cissoko [61]	881
33	Mar 6	A	Kettering T	L 0-2	0-2	23		1131
34	13	H	Hayes & Y	D 0-0	0-0	23		308
35	20	A	Eastbourne Bor	D 2-2	0-2	23	Gray [63], Dean [80]	1029
36	23	H	Stevenage Bor	L 1-2	1-0	—	Guy [43]	515
37	27	A	Cambridge U	L 0-3	0-2	23		3125
38	30	H	York C	L 0-4	0-3	—		323
39	Apr 3	H	Kettering T	D 0-0	0-0	23		287
40	5	A	Luton T	L 0-6	0-4	—		7860
41	10	H	Wrexham	L 0-2	0-1	23		298
42	13	A	AFC Wimbledon	W 2-0	0-0	—	Osborn [54], Guy (pen) [73]	3015
43	17	A	York C	D 1-1	0-0	23	Reynolds [90]	2854
44	24	H	Forest Green R	W 2-1	0-0	23	Osborn [75], Cissoko [86]	940

Final League Position: 23

GOALSCORERS

League (35): Slabber 4, Charge 3, Guy 3 (2 pens), Rnkovic 3, Cissoko 2, Davis 2, James 2, Onibuje 2, Osborn 2, Poole 2 (1 pen), Dean 1, Gaughran 1, Graham 1, Gray 1, Morgan 1, Obersteller 1, Reid 1 (1 pen), Reynolds 1, Taylor 1, Uddin 1.
FA Cup (0).

Edwards 19+1	Davis 33+1	Bingham 4+1	Ball 4	Dean 23	Cutler 6+3	Hoyte 27	Mawer 23	Mallmann 1	Robinson 4	Rigoglioso 4	Terry 3	James 5+1	Slabber 11+4	Hudson-Odoi 1+1	Morgan 2	Graham 33+4	Obaze 3	Braham-Barrett 9+3	Hickie 3	Long 1+2	Reid 3	Charge 10+2	Black —+2	Wilson 4+6	Beavan 5+1	Martin 3	Dos Santos —+1	Hunt 4	Harvey 12+2	Rhodes 12+3	Makofo —+1	Guy 15	Gaughran 2	Poole 13+1	Gray 6+7	Taylor 3+8	Baker 4	Butcher 5	Zola 2	Obersteller 3+1	Osborn 3+7	Uddin 11	Conteh —+5	Vernazza 11	Glowacki 3+3	Jeffrey 1+3	Crowther 7+3	Clarey 13	Robson 6+1	Reynolds 14	Rnkovic 6+2	Sweeney —+1	Anderson 1	Garner 12	Onibuje 6+2	Bunce 22+2	Lechmere 2+1	Leahy 1	Logombe 5+1	Bayowa 8+2	Agumbar 6+11	Cissoko 20+1	Reed 1	Match No.
1	2	3	4^1	5	6	7	8	9	10^2	11	12	13																																																				1
1	2	3	4^1	5	6		8	9	10^2	11	12	7^3	13	14																																																2
1	2	3		5	6		8^2	9		11		7^1				10						4	12	13																																							3
1	2	3^3		5	6			9		11^1	7^2	14			10	12					4				8	12																																				4
1	12			7^3	5	6		9^2	14				11		10					4				8^1	2	3	13																																			5
1	8			7	5	6^4	9^2	12	11	14		10				4^3					2^1	3	13																																							6
	8			7	5			9		11^1		10					13					3^1	12	1	2	4	6																																				7
	8			5	3	7^1	9^3	12				11^2				10						1	2	4	6	13	14																																				8
	8		2^3	5	3		9	11				6^1				7	13	1	12	4			10²	14																																							9
1	8			5	3			11	9^2			7	10³			2^1	4	6	13	14	12																																									10
3^3	14		2	6				7	9^2			1	12	1		5	4	13				8	10¹																																								11
	8			5	3		9^2	13	11			7	12	1		4	6			2	10¹																																									12
1	8			5	3			9	11			10¹	7	12		4	6			2																																										13
1	8		14	5	3			12	9^3	11		10²	7	13		4	6			2^1																																										14
1^8	4^1		2	3				12	10	11		9^2	7			5	6	8	13																																										15
3	14		5^1	2				9	11	6		7^3	10²	4				13	1	8	12																																									16
1				2				9	11			13	7			5			6^8	8		10²	3	4^1	12																																						17
1	6			2				9					12			5					10	8		3	4	7	11^1																																				18
1		5	7	2	10								11								9	3		6	4	8																																					19
	11	8	5	3		1	10														6		9	2		4	7																																					20
	11	2	5	3		1	10^3	13	12												6		9^2	14	8	4^1	7																																					21
	11	2	5^1	3		1	10		12												6		9	13	8	4^2	7																																					22
	12	4	5	3		1	8	10²	11												6		9^1	2	13	7																																					23
1	4		7	5				10	11	2	8	9												3	6																																							24
1	4		7	5				12	11	2	8	9												10	3		6^1																																					25
1	4		7	2				11	5	8^1	9	13												10²	3		6		12																																			26
			7	5	6															12	1	2		8^2	9		10^1	11		13	4			3					13																									27
			7	3																11	1	2		10^1	9		8	6		4^2	5				12																													28
			7	5										11						13	1	2		12	9		10	8^1	6	4^2	3																																	29
1			7	5^1										11						4^8	2		13	9		10	8^2			12			3										6																					30
1	2		7											11									8^1	9		10		4			5	12						3			4	5	12		3							6							31
2			7^8											11									4^1	13	9		12		12			5	6			1	3								14	8^1														32
2														11									4^2	10	9	13					5	6		1	3	10²	14	8^1																								33
2			7											11									8^1	9	10						5	6		1	3	7^1		4																							34
2			7^8											11							4	8		9	10						5	6		1	3^1	12	12																								35
2														11								13		7	8^3	9		13		12	5	6		1	3	10³	14	4^1																								36
2														11							14		7	7^8	8^1	9		13			5	6		1	3	10³	12	4																								37
2			7											11^4							12		14		9		12			5		6		1	3	10²	4	8^3																								38
2			7											11						4			8^1	14			13			5	6		1	3	10	9^2																									39
2			7											11						4			9	12	13		12			5	6^1		1	3	10²	8^1																									40
2			7											11						4^1			9		10¹		13	3		5	6		1		10²	14	8^3																									41
2			7											11^2						3	8	9^3	9	14						5	6		1		12	13	4																									42
15	2		7											11^2						3	8^1		9	12						5	6		1^8		10⁶	13	4																									43
1	2		7											11						3	8									5^1	6			13	10²	12	4																									44

FA Cup
Fourth Qualifying Round
        Luton T   (a)   0-3

HAYES AND YEADING UNITED
Blue Square Premier

Ground: Church Road, Hayes, Middlesex UB3 2LE. *Tel:* (0208) 573 2075.   *Year Formed:* 2007.   *Record Gate:* 1,234 (2009 v Histon, Blue Square Premier).   *Nickname:* United.   *Manager:* Garry Haylock.   *Secretary:* Bill Gritt. *Colours:* Red shirts, black shorts, black stockings.

HAYES & YEADING 2009–10 LEAGUE RECORD

Match No.	Date	Venue	Opponents	Result	H/T Score	Lg Pos.	Goalscorers	Attendance
1	Aug 8	A	Kidderminster H	L	0-1	0-1	—	1471
2	11	H	Stevenage Bor	D	1-1	0-0	—	Allen-Page [62]	681
3	15	H	Altrincham	L	1-2	0-1	21	Fitzgerald [90]	401
4	18	A	Rushden & D	L	1-2	0-0	—	Gradwell [89]	1059
5	22	H	York C	D	1-1	0-0	21	Daly (pen) [54]	606
6	29	A	Ebbsfleet U	W	2-1	1-1	19	Daly [3], Little [90]	884
7	31	A	Salisbury C	L	3-4	1-1	—	James [40], Fitzgerald [64], Binns [81]	429
8	Sept 5	A	Gateshead	D	0-0	0-0	19		519
9	8	A	Forest Green R	D	0-0	0-0	—		630
10	12	H	Tamworth	D	2-2	1-0	19	Green [31], Canham S [77]	355
11	19	H	Histon	L	0-2	0-2	19		1234
12	22	A	Eastbourne Bor	L	1-3	0-1	—	Canham S [72]	802
13	26	A	Mansfield T	L	1-3	0-1	22	Canham S (pen) [60]	3180
14	29	H	Kettering T	L	1-2	1-0	—	Canham S (pen) [45]	307
15	Oct 10	A	Stevenage Bor	L	0-4	0-2	23		2120
16	17	H	Cambridge U	W	3-0	1-0	20	Fitzgerald 2 [24, 48], Cadmore [63]	744
17	31	A	Tamworth	W	2-0	2-0	19	Mulley [16], Fitzgerald [28]	919
18	Nov 14	A	Wrexham	W	2-0	2-0	18	Little 2 [9, 11]	2427
19	21	H	Crawley T	W	2-1	1-1	17	Canham S 2 (1 pen) [32, 83 (p)]	342
20	24	A	Kettering T	W	1-0	0-0	—	Watkins [85]	997
21	Dec 1	H	Eastbourne Bor	D	1-1	0-1	—	Basham (pen) [90]	349
22	5	A	Barrow	D	1-1	0-0	17	James [81]	1164
23	26	A	AFC Wimbledon	L	0-5	0-4	17		3659
24	28	H	Ebbsfleet U	W	4-2	1-0	15	Watkins [36], Basham 2 [65, 70], James [86]	369
25	Jan 1	H	AFC Wimbledon	W	1-0	0-0	—	Marwa [59]	1829
26	16	A	York C	L	1-4	0-1	—	Fitzgerald [90]	2403
27	23	A	Altrincham	L	2-3	2-2	15	James [21], Green [28]	895
28	26	H	Forest Green R	L	2-3	1-1	—	Basham 2 [12, 86]	291
29	30	H	Rushden & D	L	1-6	0-3	—	Fitzgerald [80]	377
30	Feb 6	A	Histon	D	3-3	1-2	16	Watkins [33], Stolcers [62], Fitzgerald [81]	617
31	9	H	Grays Ath	W	4-0	2-0	—	Fitzgerald [13], Ruby [26], Allen-Page 2 [55, 61]	251
32	13	H	Gateshead	W	3-2	1-2	14	Cochrane [31], Mulley [63], Basham (pen) [77]	296
33	27	A	Mansfield T	D	1-1	1-0	13	Binns [42]	427
34	Mar 6	H	Luton T	L	2-3	0-2	15	Cochrane [57], Cadmore [88]	1881
35	9	A	Oxford U	W	2-1	2-0	—	Basham 2 [25, 43]	5045
36	13	A	Grays Ath	D	0-0	0-0	14		308
37	27	A	Luton T	L	0-8	0-7	15		6761
38	Apr 2	H	Oxford U	W	2-1	0-1	—	Marwa 2 [46, 65]	1655
39	5	A	Crawley T	L	0-1	0-0	—		860
40	10	H	Barrow	D	1-1	0-0	14	Marwa [64]	312
41	13	A	Salisbury C	L	1-3	0-0	—	Binns [90]	755
42	15	H	Kidderminster H	D	2-2	1-0	—	Fitzgerald 2 [40, 71]	318
43	17	A	Cambridge U	L	1-4	0-2	16	Green [74]	2940
44	24	H	Wrexham	L	0-1	0-1	17		446

Final League Position: 17

GOALSCORERS

League (59): Fitzgerald 11, Basham 8 (2 pens), Canham S 6 (3 pens), James 4, Marwa 4, Allen-Page 3, Binns 3, Green 3, Little 3, Watkins 3, Cadmore 2, Cochrane 2, Daly 2 (1 pen), Mulley 2, Gradwell 1, Ruby 1, Stolcers 1. *FA Cup (0).*

Overland 29 + 1	Mulley 31 + 5	Green 43	Cadmore 39	Ruby 39 + 2	Cochrane 29 + 2	Allen-Page 36	Canham M 30 + 6	Gradwell 4 + 4	Binns 29 + 9	Marwa 32 + 8	Fitzgerald 16 + 13	James 20 + 7	El-Abd 9 + 6	Daly 6 + 10	Little 15 + 8	Preddie — + 1	Canham S 14	Fraser-Allen — + 1	Mehmet — + 1	Palmer — + 3	Watkins 11 + 6	Basham 13 + 1	Masters 15	Harris 13	Stolcers 4 + 5	Wishart 2 + 9	Webb 2 + 2	Ide 2 + 2	Wassmer 1 + 1	Match No.
1	2	3	4	5^2	6	7	8^1	9	10	11	12	13																		1
1	13	3	4	5	6	2		9^1	7	11^2	10		8	12																2
1^0		3	4	5	6^1	2	12	9		11	10		8^2	13	7	15														3
1	7	3	4		6	2	8^2	13	9	11^3	10^1	14	5	12																4
1	7	3	4	5	6^3	2	13	10^1	9		12	8^2		11	14															5
1	7	3	4	5		2^1	6	13	9	12	10	8^2		11^3	14															6
1	2	3	4	5^3	13		6^2	14	9	7	10	8^1		11	12															7
1	7	3		5	8	2		11	6	10^1		4	12				3													8
1	7	3		5	8^2	2^4	6	9	13	14	12	4	11^1				13^3													9
1	7^1	3	2	5	8^2	12		9	6		11	4	13		10															10
1	7	3	4	5^3	13	2	8^1	9	6^2	14	11		12		10															11
1	7^2	3	4	5^1	8	2		11^3	6	13	10		12	14	9															12
1	7	3^3	4	5		2	8	13	6^2	12		14	9^1	11	10															13
1	7	3	4		8^1	2^4	12	11	6	9^2	14	5^3	13		10															14
1	2	3	4		8	14	11		6^1	5	9	7^2					10^3	12	13											15
1	7	3	4	5		2	8	11		10^1		12	6		9															16
1	7	3	4	5		2	8	12	10^2	11^1		13	6		9															17
1	7	3	4	5^1	11	2	8		6^2	12		10			9^3						13	14								18
1	7	3	4	5	8	2		13	12	10^1	6		11^2		9															19
1	10	3	4	5	6	2	8^2	12	13	7^3		11^1		9							14									20
1	2	3	4	5			8^2	11	6	13	7^1				9						10	12								21
1	10	3	4	5^3		2	8^2	12	6	13	7		11^1								14	9								22
1	7		4	5	3^4	2	12	11	14	13	8^3		6								10^2	9^1								23
1	7	3	4	5^1		2	8	13	6		12	14			11^2						10	9								24
1	7^3	3	4	5		2	8	12	6	10	13		9^1								14	11^2								25
1		3	4^4	5		2	8	11^1	6	13	7	12		10^2							14		9^3							26
1	7	3		5	4	2	8	13	14	12	11^1	6			10^2							9^3								27
1	7	3	4	5^2	10	2	8^1	11	6	12											13	9								28
1	7^1	3	4	5^{10}	10	2^2	8	11	13	12		14									6	9								29
		3	4	13	8	2		11^1	6	10^2											9				1	5	7	12		30
		3	4	5	8^3	2	13	11	6^2	10^1			14									1	9	7	12					31
12		3	4	5	8			11	6												2	10	1	9	7^1					32
15	7	3	4	5	10			11	6		8^1										9	1^6	2	12						33
		3	4	5^3	8			11	6		7^2	14	13								9		1	2	10^1	12				34
		3	4	5	7		8	13	6^1	11^4											10	9^1	1	2	12^2	14				35
		3	4	5	7^1	2	8	11	6								12				10	9^2	1				13			36
12		3	4	5^1	7^2	2	8		6	10^3	13												1	11		14		9		37
	7	3		5		2	8	11	6												9^1		1	4	13		10^2	12		38
	7	3		5^2		2	8	11	6^3	9^1													1	4	14	13	12	10		39
	7	3	4	5		2	8	6					11^5								9^1	1	10^2	13	14		12			40
		3	4	5	10^1	2	8	11	6	9											1				12	7^2	13			41
12		3	4	5	11^2	2	8		6	9^8											13	1	7		10^1					42
13		3	4	5^3	10	2	8^2	11	6				1^4								12	1	7		9^1					43
	7	3	4	14	11^1	2^8	8	13	6												9^2	1	5		12			10		44

FA Cup
Fourth Qualifying Round

Staines T	(h)	0-1

HISTON
Blue Square Premier

Ground: Glassworld Stadium, Bridge Road, Impington, Cambridge CB24 9PH. *Tel:* (01223) 237 373. *Year Formed:* 1904. 4,500 (2008 v Leeds U, FA Cup 2nd rd). *Nickname:* The Stutes. *Manager:* John Beck. *Secretary:* Lisa Baldwin. *Colours:* Red shirts, black shorts, black stockings.

HISTON 2009–10 LEAGUE RECORD

Match No.	Date	Venue	Opponents	Result	H/T Score	Lg Pos.	Goalscorers	Atten- dance
1	Aug 8	A	Gateshead	W 3-0	1-0	—	Wright 2 [45, 84], Hudson-Odoi [81]	681
2	11	H	Grays Ath	D 0-0	0-0	—		816
3	15	H	Oxford U	L 3-4	0-1	8	Barker [46], Simpson [81], Langston [88]	1433
4	18	A	Altrincham	L 1-2	1-2	—	Simpson [16]	698
5	22	H	Salisbury C	W 2-0	1-0	9	Frew [33], Wright [81]	684
6	29	A	York C	L 1-3	0-1	16	Wright [90]	1944
7	31	H	Stevenage Bor	L 0-2	0-1	—		1159
8	Sept 8	A	Crawley T	L 0-2	0-0	—		798
9	12	H	Kidderminster H	D 1-1	1-1	18	Hammond [85]	774
10	19	A	Hayes & Y	W 2-0	2-0	15	Knight-Percival [7], Simpson [38]	1234
11	22	H	Ebbsfleet U	W 1-0	0-0	—	Simpson [83]	647
12	26	A	AFC Wimbledon	L 0-4	0-1	15		3392
13	29	A	Eastbourne Bor	W 2-0	1-0	—	Knight-Percival 2 [27, 73]	633
14	Oct 4	H	Cambridge U	D 1-1	0-0	14	Langston [90]	2371
15	10	A	Tamworth	W 3-1	1-0	14	Knight-Percival 2 [27, 77], Simpson [86]	1090
16	17	H	Forest Green R	W 5-2	1-1	12	Knight-Percival [44], Barker [49], Simpson [71], Wright 2 [75, 90]	823
17	31	A	Mansfield T	D 1-1	0-0	11	Simpson (pen) [84]	3162
18	Nov 14	H	Rushden & D	L 1-2	0-1	12	Tidswell [85]	1126
19	21	H	Wrexham	D 0-0	0-0	13		946
20	24	A	Eastbourne Bor	D 1-1	0-1	—	Hudson-Odoi [62]	703
21	Dec 1	A	Grays Ath	W 1-0	1-0	—	Smith [33]	367
22	5	H	Altrincham	D 0-0	0-0	12		676
23	28	H	Kettering T	W 1-0	0-0	11	Tann [59]	716
24	Jan 23	A	Salisbury C	L 0-3	0-1	13		758
25	27	H	Luton T	L 0-2	0-0	—		1543
26	Feb 2	H	York C	D 1-1	1-1	—	Hudson-Odoi [43]	487
27	6	H	Hayes & Y	D 3-3	2-1	14	Wright (pen) [14], Langston [41], Smith [90]	617
28	9	A	Ebbsfleet U	W 1-0	0-0	—	Wright [72]	731
29	13	A	Oxford U	L 0-2	0-0	13		5365
30	27	H	Kidderminster H	L 0-3	0-1	15		1293
31	Mar 3	H	Rushden & D	L 0-1	0-1	—		583
32	6	H	Gateshead	D 0-0	0-0	14		645
33	9	H	Tamworth	W 1-0	1-0	—	Smith [11]	350
34	13	A	Cambridge U	L 1-2	0-0	13	Pugh [61]	4417
35	16	A	Stevenage Bor	L 0-1	0-1	—		2407
36	20	H	Mansfield T	L 0-5	0-1	15		662
37	27	A	Wrexham	L 0-3	0-0	14		2335
38	29	A	Barrow	D 0-0	0-0	—		994
39	Apr 3	H	AFC Wimbledon	L 1-3	0-2	16	Judge (og) [54]	867
40	5	A	Kettering T	D 1-1	0-1	—	Smith [59]	800
41	10	H	Crawley T	L 0-1	0-0	18		499
42	13	A	Luton T	L 3-6	0-2	—	Sparkes [69], Knight-Percival [74], Southam [87]	7083
43	17	A	Forest Green R	L 0-2	0-2	18		1204
44	24	H	Barrow	D 2-2	1-0	18	Southam (pen) [27], Jones (og) [90]	753

Final League Position: 18

GOALSCORERS
League (44): Wright 8 (1 pen), Knight-Percival 7, Simpson 7 (1 pen), Smith 4, Hudson-Odoi 3, Langston 3, Barker 2, Southam 2 (1 pen), Frew 1, Hammond 1, Pugh 1, Sparkes 1, Tann 1, Tidswell 1, own goals 2.
FA Cup (1): Oyebanjo 1.

Naisbitt 27	Oyebanjo 23 + 4	Gwillim 35	Simpson 17	Langston 31	Tann 40 + 1	Barker 21 + 1	Kennedy 15 + 3	Frew 13 + 9	Wright 26	Knight-Percival 43	Andrews 8 + 6	Hudson-Odoi 10 + 9	Pope 10 + 3	Leabon 1 + 3	Welch 5 + 1	Farrell 4 + 1	Bygrave 28 + 5	Hammond + 6	Okay 21 + 4	Joseph-Dubois — + 1	Crook 2 + 3	Long 2 + 4	Cox 2	Tidswell 6 + 11	Smith 24	Stewart 5 + 5	Werndly — + 1	Sparkes 11 + 3	York 1 + 4	Southam 19	Sheringham 10 + 5	Knight 12	Pugh 5 + 1	Verma 7 + 1	Taffe — + 2	Match No.
1	2	3	4	5	6	7³	8¹	9²	10	11	12	13	14																							1
1	2	3	4	5	6	7¹	8²	9¹	10	11		12	13	14																						2
1*	2	3	4	5	6	7²	8¹	9⁶	10	11	12	13			15																					3
	2¹	3	4	5	6	7		9⁸	10	11			13		1		8²	12	14																	4
	2¹	3	4	5	6	7²		9⁸	10	11	8	13	12		1		13																			5
		3	4	5	6²	7¹			10	11	8	9	2	12	1		13																			6
1			4	5	6	7	14			10³	11	8²	9¹	2			13		3			2														7
1	8		4	5	6	7		9		11				2¹			10		3			2														8
1	8		4	5	6	14	12	9²		11	7			2			10¹		3³	13																9
1		3	4	5	6³	8	12	9²		11	7	13		2			10¹		14																	10
1		3	8	5	6	10	7¹	9		11	4			2					12																	11
1		3	4	5	6	8	7¹	9²	10³	11				2			14		12	13																12
1		3	4	5	6⁸	8	7¹	13	10²	11				2			12		9																	13
1		3	4	5		8¹	7²		10	9	12			2			6		11³		13	14														14
1		3	10	5		7²	8³		9	11	14			2			6		4¹		12	13														15
1	2²	3	10	5	13	7¹	8	12	9	11	4						6																			16
1	2	3	4		5	9	7		10¹	11							6							8	12											17
1		3		5	2	7	8	9		11¹							6		12²					4	14	10²	13									18
1	2	3		5	4	9	8²	14		11		12					6		13							7¹	10³									19
1	2	3		6	4²	7	8	12		11	13	9					5								10¹											20
1	2	3³		5	8¹	9	7	13		11	12						6						4²		14	10										21
1	2			5	10	7				11	4				9¹		6								12	8	3									22
1	2			5	3			12	9	11						7²			13					6	4¹	10	8									23
1	2	3		6	4			9¹	10³	11	12						5⁵		7²						8	13	14									24
1	2	3		5	4¹			9²		11	7						10³							8	6	12		13	14							25
1	2	3		5	4			12		11	10³						6		14					9¹	7²			13			8					26
1	2			5	4			9		11	10²						6		12					13	7	3¹			8							27
1	2¹			5	4²			12	9	11	10						6		3					13	7				8							28
1		2		5	4			13	9	11	10²						6⁸		3¹						7				8	12						29
1	13	3		5	4			7¹	9²	11	14						2³		6										8	10						30
		3		5	4			9		11	7						2²		13	6									8	10¹	1	12			31
		3			4										5		7							6	2¹			11	12	8	10	1		9		32
		3			4					11					5		2							7	6			9		8	10	1				33
	12	3			4					11					5		2¹							13	6			9	8²	10	1	7				34
	12	3			4					11					5		2¹							6				7	8	10	1	9				35
	2¹	3			4					11					5		12	6	13					7²	14			8	10	1	9³					36
	13	3			4			9		11					5⁸	2²			8					7				6¹	14	1	10³	12				37
	2	3			4			9		11					5									10				7	8	1				6		38
	2	3			4			9		11					7									5				10		8¹	12	1		6		39
	2	3			4			9⁸		11					5									6				7¹	8	12	1		10		40
	2				4					11					5	3								12	6			9³	14	8¹	10²	1	7	13		41
	2¹				4					11					5	3								13	7	12		9		8	10²	1	6			42
					4					11			1		5	3								10²	7¹	2		9		8	13		6	12		43
			5		4			9		11			1		6¹	2								13	7	12²				8	10		3			44

FA Cup
Fourth Qualifying Round
      Hinckley U   (a)   1-2

KETTERING TOWN

Blue Square Premier

Ground: Rockingham Road, Kettering, Northants NN16 9AW.   *Tel:* (01536) 483 028.   *Year Formed:* 1872.
Record Gate: 11,536 v Peterborough U.   *Nickname:* Poppies.   *Manager:* Lee Harper.   *Colours:* Red shirts, black and white trim, red shorts, black stockings.

KETTERING TOWN 2009–10 LEAGUE RECORD

Match No.	Date	Venue	Opponents	Result	H/T Score	Lg Pos.	Goalscorers	Attendance
1	Aug 8	A	Forest Green R	W 2-1	0-0	—	Marna 2 [71, 81]	1074
2	11	H	Oxford U	D 1-1	1-1	—	Marna (pen) [12]	2240
3	15	H	AFC Wimbledon	L 1-2	0-1	11	Thomas [74]	1746
4	18	A	Kidderminster H	W 1-0	0-0	—	Marna (pen) [86]	1368
5	22	A	Wrexham	W 2-1	1-0	6	Spencer [25], Noubissie [48]	3473
6	29	H	Luton T	D 0-0	0-0	5		3266
7	31	A	Mansfield T	D 0-0	0-0	—		4034
8	Sept 5	H	Altrincham	W 2-0	0-0	4	Ashikodi [84], Green [86]	1269
9	8	H	Gateshead	W 4-0	2-0	—	Thomas [10], Ashikodi [32], Green [73], Spencer [82]	1230
10	12	A	York C	L 0-2	0-0	—		2275
11	19	A	Crawley T	L 1-2	0-0	8	Marna (pen) [85]	901
12	22	H	Barrow	W 2-1	2-1	—	Ashikodi (pen) [28], Dempster [41]	1150
13	26	H	Ebbsfleet U	W 3-0	1-0	2	Ashikodi [34], Green [77], Crooks (og) [87]	1345
14	29	A	Hayes & Y	W 2-1	0-1	—	Fowler [86], Green [90]	307
15	Oct 3	A	Eastbourne Bor	W 1-0	1-0	2	Ashikodi [45]	884
16	17	A	AFC Wimbledon	W 2-1	2-1	3	Taylor [18], Thomas [20]	3745
17	31	H	Stevenage Bor	D 1-1	1-1	3	Ashikodi [29]	1844
18	Nov 3	H	Wrexham	D 2-2	1-2	—	Elding [5], Marna (pen) [90]	1186
19	14	A	Cambridge U	W 2-0	1-0	3	Hatswell (og) [3], Elding [90]	3088
20	21	H	Kidderminster H	L 0-2	0-0	3		1348
21	24	H	Hayes & Y	L 0-1	0-0	—		997
22	Dec 2	A	Luton T	W 1-0	0-0	—	Partridge [64]	6608
23	5	H	Salisbury C	L 1-2	1-1	5	Elding (pen) [19]	1098
24	26	H	Tamworth	D 0-0	0-0	5		1250
25	28	A	Histon	L 0-1	0-0	6		716
26	Jan 19	A	Ebbsfleet U	W 2-1	1-0	—	Dance [30], Marna [63]	587
27	23	H	Stevenage Bor	L 0-2	0-0	6		2136
28	26	A	Gateshead	W 2-0	2-0	—	Appiah [15], Wrack [40]	401
29	Feb 6	H	York C	L 0-1	0-1	8		1375
30	13	A	Barrow	W 2-0	0-0	7	Kelly [53], Marna [77]	1160
31	23	A	Tamworth	W 3-1	2-0	—	Appiah [16], Smith J (og) [20], Dance [50]	473
32	27	A	Rushden & D	D 0-0	0-0	6		2998
33	Mar 6	H	Grays Ath	W 2-0	2-0	6	Roper [10], Jennings [41]	1131
34	9	H	Cambridge U	L 0-1	0-0	—		1248
35	13	A	Oxford U	D 1-1	1-1	5	Dance [42]	5836
36	16	A	Altrincham	L 0-2	0-2	—		690
37	20	H	Forest Green R	L 0-2	0-0	6		1032
38	27	H	Mansfield T	D 2-2	1-2	6	Marna [4], Ebigbo [87]	1188
39	30	H	Rushden & D	L 0-3	0-2	—		2031
40	Apr 3	A	Grays Ath	D 0-0	0-0	6		287
41	5	H	Histon	D 1-1	1-0	—	Jennings [37]	800
42	17	H	Eastbourne Bor	W 4-0	2-0	6	Marna 2 (2 pens) [43, 45], Kelly [59], Jennings [74]	932
43	20	H	Crawley T	D 1-1	0-1	—	Dempster [51]	800
44	24	A	Salisbury C	L 0-2	0-1	6		1123

Final League Position: 6

GOALSCORERS

League (51): Marna 11 (6 pens), Ashikodi 6 (1 pen), Green 4, Dance 3, Elding 3 (1 pen), Jennings 3, Thomas 3, Appiah 2, Dempster 2, Kelly 2, Spencer 2, Ebigbo 1, Fowler 1, Noubissie 1, Partridge 1, Roper 1, Taylor 1, Wrack 1, own goals 3.
FA Cup (5): Ashikodi 2, Elding 1, Marna 1, Roper 1.

Harper 26	Eaden 9	Jennings 34+2	Dempster 39+3	Roper 38	Geoghagan 17+2	Boucaud 29+7	Fowler 16+1	Spencer 10+8	Seddon 4+3	Green 19+1	Marna 15+21	Wrack 17+10	Noubissie 35+3	Thomas 18+16	McPike 1+1	Ashikodi 12+2	Taylor 28+4	Carayol 4+1	Heslop 8	Elding 7+1	Dance 23+1	Davis 3	Kelly 15+2	Partridge 2	Bussey 1	Thelwell 6+2	Bain 2	Dobson 1	Abbey 17	Hadfield 12+3	Appiah 9+6	Robinson —+4	Charles 2+5	Ebigbo 4+5	Carrillo —+2	Pryor 1	Match No.
1	2	3	4	5	6	7	8^2	9^1	10	11	12	13																									1
1	2^3	3	14	5	6	7	8^2	9^8	13	11	10^1		4	12																							2
1	2	3	12	5^1	6	7	8^2			9^3	11	10	4	13	14																						3
1	2	3		5	6	7	8^1	10		9^2	11^3	14	12			4	13																				4
1	2^1	3	12	5	6	7	8	10^2		9	13	14	4^3	11																							5
1		3	2	5	6	7	8	10^2	13	9	12		4	11^1																							6
1		3	2	5	6	7	8	13	10	14		12	4^1	11^2		9^3																					7
1		3^1	2	5	6	7	8	9^2	14	11	10^3		4	12		13																					8
1		3	2	5	6	7	8	9		11^3	13	14	12			4^2			10^1																		9
1		3^3	2	5	6		8	9		11	13	7^1	4	12		10^2	14																				10
1		3	2	5	6	8		9		11	13		4	13		10^1			7^2																		11
1	2		6	5		4^1	8	13		9	14		12	11		10^2	3	7^3																			12
1	2	12	11	5	14		8			9^3	13		4	6		10	3^3	7^1																			13
1	2^2	13	11	5	14		8	12		9			4	6		10	3^3	7^1																			14
1	2	11	5	6		8^2	12			9		13	4	7		10^1	3																				15
1	3	4	5	6	12	8^1	13			9	14		7	11^2		10^3	2																				16
1	3	4	5^1	6	12		9			7			11			10	2		8																		17
1	3	5		6						7^1	14	4	11^2	13		10	$2^{\square}$	12	8	9																	18
1		2	5	6			13			7^1			4	12		10^2	3		8	9	11																19
1		2	5	6		14	13			7^1	12		4	11		10^2	$3^{\square}$		$8^\square$	9																	20
1			6	5		11	8^2	13		1C			4	7^1		12	$3^\square$			9	2																21
1			6	5		4				10^1	13			$2^{\square}$					8	9	12	3	7	11^2													22
			5		13					10^1	4^2	6	14			$5^{\square}$			8	12			7		1	2	9	11^3									23
1			6			7						4	8			$5^{\square}$				10	9^1	2	3	12	11												24
1				7						12	4	8^1				$5^{\square}$				10	9	2	3	13			6	11^2									25
		3	6	5		11				10^2	4	8^1	13								9		7			2			1	12							26
	2	3^3	6	5		11^1				10	4^2	8				14					9		7						1	12	13						27
		3	6	5^1						10^2	4	8	14			1^2					9		7^3			2			1		11	13					28
		3	6	5		13					4^1	11^2				$1\!1$					9		7^3			2			1	8	10	12					29
		3	6	5		13				12	4^1	11				2					9		7^3						1	8	$10^\square$	14					30
		3	6	5		14				12	4	7				2					9^2		11						1	8^3	10	13					31
		3	6	5		14				12	4^3	7	13			2					9		11^2						1	8	$10^\square$						32
		3	6	5		7				13	4^1		14			2					9		11^3						1	8	10^2		12				33
		3	6	5		11				12	13					2					9		7^2						1	8	$1C^3$		4^1	14			34
		3	6	5		11				13	4					2^3					9^2		7			14			1	8	10^1	12					35
		3	6			11				12	4^1	13				2					9^3		7			5			1	8	10^2			14			36
		3^1	6	5		4				10		13	11			2^3					9					12			1	8	14		7^2				37
		3^3	6	5		7				10^2	12	4	11			2					9								1	8^1	13		14				38
		3	6	5		7				12	4^2	2	10^1								9								1	8	13		14	11^3			39
1		3	6	5		$7^\square$				10^2		4	8^3			2					9									12	13		14	11^1			40
1	10	6	5	7						12	4^3	2				3					9									8	13		11^1				41
		3	6^2	5		8^3				10^1	4	2	13			11					9		7						1				12	14			42
		11	6	5^1		7				10^3	4^2	2	12			3					9		8						1				14	13			43
		3	6			7				10		2	11			5					9								1				8	12	4^1		44

FA Cup
Fourth Qualifying Round

	Redditch U	(h)	1-1	
		(a)	1-0	
First Round	Hartlepool U	(a)	1-0	
Second Round	Leeds U	(h)	1-1	
		(a)	1-5	

KIDDERMINSTER HARRIERS Blue Square Premier

Ground: Aggborough Stadium, Hoo Road, Kidderminster DY10 1NB.   *Tel:* (01562) 823 951.   *Year Formed:* 1886.
Record Gate: 9,155 (1948 v Hereford U).   *Nickname:* Harriers.   *Manager:* Steve Burr.   *Secretary:* Roger Barlow.
Colours: Red shirts, white shorts, red stockings.

KIDDERMINSTER HARRIERS 2009–10 LEAGUE RECORD

Match No.	Date	Venue	Opponents	Result	H/T Score	Lg Pos.	Goalscorers	Atten-dance
1	Aug 8	H	Hayes & Y	W 1-0	1-0	—	Barnes-Homer [35]	1471
2	11	A	Salisbury C	L 0-1	0-0	—	—	1034
3	15	A	Ebbsfleet U	D 0-0	0-0	13		865
4	18	H	Kettering T	L 0-1	0-0	—	—	1388
5	22	A	Grays Ath	W 3-1	2-0	11	Bennett [12], Smikle [28], McDermott [90]	754
6	29	H	Altrincham	W 3-0	2-0	8	Smikle 2 [11, 46], Barnes-Homer [23]	1415
7	31	A	Tamworth	L 1-2	0-0	—	McPhee (pen) [73]	1237
8	Sept 5	H	Eastbourne Bor	L 0-2	0-1	15		1307
9	8	H	Mansfield T	W 3-1	1-0	—	Barnes-Homer [14], Caines [47], McPhee [69]	1378
10	12	A	Histon	D 1-1	1-0	11	McPhee [34]	774
11	19	H	Gateshead	W 3-2	2-1	10	Swailes (og) [25], Smikle [40], Barnes-Homer [80]	1286
12	22	A	Forest Green R	D 1-1	1-0	—	McPhee [16]	707
13	26	A	York C	L 2-3	1-2	12	Smikle [2], Barnes-Homer [62]	2509
14	29	H	Wrexham	W 2-0	0-0	—	Smikle [50], Matthews [55]	1585
15	Oct 3	A	AFC Wimbledon	W 1-0	0-0	6	Barnes-Homer [47]	3601
16	10	H	Luton T	L 1-2	1-0	9	Barnes-Homer [13]	2927
17	17	H	Crawley T	W 1-0	0-0	7	Caines [89]	1276
18	31	A	Cambridge U	L 0-2	0-2	9		3508
19	Nov 14	H	Oxford U	W 3-1	2-1	8	Matthews 2 [2, 52], Barnes-Homer [18]	3569
20	21	A	Kettering T	W 2-0	0-0	8	Courtney [70], Barnes-Homer [82]	1348
21	24	A	Wrexham	D 2-2	2-2	—	Smikle [33], McPhee [44]	2086
22	28	H	AFC Wimbledon	L 0-1	0-1	—		1788
23	Dec 1	H	Tamworth	D 0-0	0-0	—		1166
24	5	A	Stevenage Bor	L 0-2	0-1	9		1809
25	28	A	Rushden & D	L 1-2	0-1	9	Matthews [68]	1425
26	Jan 23	A	Crawley T	D 2-2	0-1	9	Finnigan [49], McPhee [85]	800
27	26	H	Grays Ath	W 4-1	2-1	—	Smikle [26], Spencer [30], Finnigan [49], McPhee (pen) [80]	1109
28	Feb 6	A	Oxford U	D 0-0	0-0	9		5802
29	13	H	Forest Green R	W 2-1	1-0	9	Smikle [12], Spencer [90]	1421
30	27	H	Histon	W 3-0	1-0	9	Smikle [4], Finnigan [56], Knights [59]	1293
31	Mar 2	H	Ebbsfleet U	D 2-2	1-1	—	Knights [5], Smikle [77]	1163
32	6	A	Eastbourne Bor	D 0-0	0-0	9		913
33	16	A	Luton T	L 1-3	1-2	—	Lawrie [32]	5908
34	23	H	York C	L 0-1	0-0	—		1127
35	27	H	Salisbury C	L 0-1	0-1	12		1201
36	30	H	Cambridge U	W 1-0	1-0	—	Smikle [18]	1141
37	Apr 3	A	Altrincham	L 2-3	2-2	12	Matthews 2 [15, 44]	889
38	5	H	Rushden & D	D 1-1	0-1	—	Knights [54]	1463
39	8	H	Barrow	L 0-1	0-1	—		1253
40	10	A	Gateshead	W 2-0	0-0	10	McPhee 2 [74, 80]	602
41	15	A	Hayes & Y	D 2-2	0-1	—	McPhee [57], Riley [81]	318
42	17	H	Stevenage Bor	L 0-2	0-1	11		2564
43	20	A	Barrow	L 1-2	1-2	—	Edwards (og) [7]	1036
44	24	A	Mansfield T	D 3-3	0-3	13	Byrne [51], Knights [54], McPhee [74]	2734

Final League Position: 13

GOALSCORERS

League (57): Smikle 12, McPhee 11 (2 pens), Barnes-Homer 9, Matthews 6, Knights 4, Finnigan 3, Caines 2, Spencer 2, Bennett 1, Byrne 1, Courtney 1, Lawrie 1, McDermott 1, Riley 1, own goals 2.
FA Cup (1): Caines 1.

Coleman 29	Dolman 2+5	Baker 33+1	Bennett 36+2	Caines 29+2	Riley 42+1	Smikle 42+1	Knights 31+11	Barnes-Homer 21	McPhee 40	McDermott 13+10	Courtney 39+2	Hadley 3+11	Finnigan 20+3	Sharpe 9+6	Matthews 28+5	Farrell 3+10	Hayward 1+8	Audrew 8	Spencer 5+3	Charles 1+2	Singh 5	Goodfellow 5+5	Atkins 10	Lawrie 3+7	Bignot 2+1	Boyes 1+2	Byrne 10+2	Prosser 9	Kerry 4+5	Match No.
1	2^1	3	4^3	5	6	7	8^2	9	10	11	12	13	14																	1
1		3^3	4	5	6	7	8^1	9	10	11^2	2	12	13	14																2
1		3	4	5	6	7^2	8^1	9	11	13	2	12			10															3
1		3	4	5	6	7	8^1	9	11	12	2				10															4
1	14	3	4^2	5	6	7	13	9	11	12	2			8^1	10^3															5
1		3	4	5	6^4	7	14	9^1	11	13	2			8^3	10^2	12														6
1		3	4	5^3		7	12	9	11	8^1	2		14		10^2	6	13													7
1		3	4	5	6	7	14	9	11		2			8^3	12^2	10^1	13													8
1	12	3	4	5	6	7	10	9	11	8	2																			9
1		3	4	5	6	7	10	9	11	8	2																			10
1		3	4^1	5	6	7	10^3	9	11	8^2	2	13			14	12														11
1		3	4^2	5	6	7	10	9	8	11^1	2	13			12															12
1		3		5^4	6	7	10^1	9	11	8^2	2				4	13	12													13
1	14	3			6	7	10	9	11	8^1	2	12^2	5^3		4	13														14
1	12	3	8	13	6	7	10^1	9^2	11		2		5		4															15
1		3	8^3	12	6	7	10^2	9	5^1		2	14	4		11^4	13														16
1		3	8	5	6	7	10	9	12		2		4^1	13	11^2															17
1			8	5	6	7	10	9	12		2		4^1		11				3											18
1	12		4	5	6	7	10^1	9^1	11^2		2				8	13	14		3											19
1			4^2	5	6	7	10^1	9^3	8	12	2				11	13	14		3											20
1		12	4	5	6	7	13	9^3	8	11^1	2				10	14			3^1											21
1	2^3		4	5	6	7	10^1		8	12					11	14			3			9^2	13							22
1				5	6	7	12		8	11^1	2			4^2	14	13			3			9	10^3							23
1			4	5	6	7	14		8	11^1	2^3				10^2	13			3			9	12							24
1			4	5	6	7	10		8		2				9	11^1			3	12										25
1			3	5	6	7	10^2		8		2		12	4	9^1				11											26
		3	12	5	6^3	7					2	13	4	14		9^2	11		10	1										27
1		3	8	5	6	7	13		10		2		4		9^1				12					11^2						28
1		3	8^2	5	6	7	12		10		2		4		9^1				13					11						29
		3	11	5^4	6	7^2	10		8		2		4	12	9^3									1	13	14				30
		3	8	5	6	7	10		11		2		4^1		9^2							12		1	13					31
		3	4	5	6	7	10^1		8		2				13							12		1	14	11^2	9^3			32
		3			6	7^1	12		8		2		13		5				9			11^2		1	10				4	33
		3	4^1		6	7	10^3		8		2				5				9			^{22}		1	1^{12}	14	13			34
			8^1		6	7	10		13	2^3					5	14			9^2			1	12				11	3	4	35
			4		6^1	7	10		8		2				3				9			1					11	5	12	36
			4		6	7	10^3		8^2	2^1					3				9			13		1	14		11	5	12	37
		3	4		6	7	10		8		2				9									1			11	5		38
		3	4^2		6		10^1			13^3			14		9							1	8		12^2	2	11	11^2	5	7	39
		3	12		6		13	14	8						4	2			9^3			1			10^2		11^1	5	7	40
		3	8^2		6	7	10	9					12		4	2^1	14					1			13		5	11^3		41
		3			6	7	10^1		8		2				4				9^2			1			^{12}		11	5	13	42
		3	8		6	7	10^3	9			2				4^1	13						1			14		11	5^2	12	43
1		3	8^3		12	7	10		6		2		4^2	5	9^1							14					11		13	44

FA Cup
Fourth Qualifying Round

Fleetwood T	(h)	0-0
	(a)	1-3

LUTON TOWN

Blue Square Premier

Ground: Kenilworth Stadium, 1 Maple Road, Luton LU4 8AW. *Tel:* (01582) 411 622. *Year Formed:* 1885.
Record Gate: 30, 869 (1959 v Blackpool, FA Cup 6th rd replay). *Nickname:* The Hatters. *Manager:* Richard Money.
Secretary: Adam Cockfield. *Colours:* Orange shirts, white shorts, orange stockings.

LUTON TOWN 2009–10 LEAGUE RECORD

Match No.	Date	Venue	Opponents	Result	H/T Score	Lg Pos.	Goalscorers	Attendance
1	Aug 8	A	AFC Wimbledon	D 1-1	1-0	—	Craddock (pen) [14]	4688
2	11	H	Mansfield T	W 4-1	1-1	—	Pilkington G 2 [39, 66], Perry (og) [81], Craddock (pen) [90]	7295
3	15	H	Gateshead	W 2-1	2-1	1	Gallen [21], Hall [22]	6829
4	18	A	Forest Green R	W 1-0	0-0	—	Craddock [57]	1805
5	29	A	Kettering T	D 0-0	0-0	3		3266
6	Sept 1	H	Crawley T	W 3-0	1-0	—	Pilkington G 2 [36, 62], Craddock [65]	6389
7	5	A	Salisbury C	D 1-1	1-1	3	Gallen [27]	2044
8	8	A	Oxford U	L 0-2	0-2	—		10,613
9	12	H	Barrow	W 1-0	1-0	2	Newton [21]	6264
10	22	A	Wrexham	L 0-3	0-2	—		3448
11	26	A	Cambridge U	W 4-3	0-2	9	Gallen 2 (1 pen) [48, 75 (p)], Jarvis [60], Howells [61]	4870
12	29	H	Stevenage Bor	L 0-1	0-0	—		8223
13	Oct 3	H	Tamworth	W 2-1	2-0	5	Hall [19], Wright [24]	6297
14	10	A	Kidderminster H	W 2-1	0-1	5	Newton [76], Charles [90]	2927
15	17	A	Altrincham	W 1-0	0-0	5	Newton (pen) [66]	1762
16	20	H	York C	D 1-1	0-1	—	Hall [65]	6387
17	31	H	Rushden & D	L 0-2	0-0	5		7101
18	Nov 14	A	Grays Ath	W 2-0	1-0	5	Craddock [39], Gallen [50]	1668
19	21	H	Cambridge U	D 2-2	0-0	6	Gnakpa [61], Craddock [79]	7458
20	Dec 2	A	Kettering T	L 0-1	0-0	—		6608
21	28	H	Eastbourne Bor	W 4-1	3-1	7	Barnes-Homer [9], Gallen 2 [19, 36], Jarvis [75]	6646
22	Jan 23	A	Gateshead	W 1-0	1-0	7	Farman (og) [29]	1218
23	27	A	Histon	W 2-0	0-0	—	Kovacs [52], Hall [72]	1543
24	30	H	Ebbsfleet U	L 2-3	1-2	—	Hatch [27], Craddock [65]	6658
25	Feb 6	A	Barrow	W 1-0	0-0	7	Hatch [83]	1579
26	9	H	Oxford U	W 2-1	0-0	—	Pilkington G [89], Keane [90]	8860
27	13	A	Eastbourne Bor	W 1-0	1-0	5	Hall [9]	2018
28	16	A	York C	D 0-0	0-0	—		3316
29	20	H	AFC Wimbledon	L 1-2	1-1	—	Craddock [29]	7736
30	27	A	Crawley T	L 1-2	0-0	5	Barnes-Homer [78]	2118
31	Mar 2	A	Mansfield T	D 0-0	0-0	—		3407
32	6	A	Hayes & Y	W 3-2	0-0	5	Hatch [23], Gnakpa (pen) [30], Craddock [74]	1881
33	9	H	Forest Green R	W 2-1	1-0	—	Craddock 2 (1 pen) [38 (p), 90]	5884
34	13	H	Wrexham	W 1-0	1-0	3	Craddock [36]	6538
35	16	H	Kidderminster H	W 3-1	2-1	—	Howells [23], Gallen 2 [30, 57]	5908
36	20	A	Ebbsfleet U	W 6-1	0-1	2	Gnakpa 3 [49, 76, 77], Gallen [50], Craddock [66], Barnes-Homer [90]	1923
37	27	H	Hayes & Y	W 8-0	7-0	3	Gallen 2 [7, 23], Gnakpa 2 [11, 13], Keane [26], Craddock 2 [31, 56], Howells [35]	6761
38	30	H	Salisbury C	W 4-0	2-0	—	Gnakpa [35], Craddock [43], Howells [54], Heslop [74]	6692
39	Apr 3	A	Stevenage Bor	W 1-0	0-0	2	Barnes-Homer [55]	7024
40	5	H	Grays Ath	W 6-0	4-0	—	Craddock 2 [32, 45], Gallen 3 [36, 41, 57], Hatch [80]	7860
41	10	A	Tamworth	D 1-1	1-0	2	Pilkington G [15]	2246
42	13	H	Histon	W 6-3	2-0	—	Howells 2 [29, 56], Craddock 3 (1 pen) [32, 50, 77 (p)], Gallen [84]	7083
43	17	H	Altrincham	D 0-0	0-0	2		7374
44	24	A	Rushden & D	D 1-1	1-1	2	Craddock [9]	4820

Final League Position: 2

GOALSCORERS

League (84): Craddock 22 (4 pens), Gallen 16 (1 pen), Gnakpa 8 (1 pen), Howells 6, Pilkington G 6, Hall 5, Barnes-Homer 4, Hatch 4, Newton 3 (1 pen), Jarvis 2, Keane 2, Charles 1, Heslop 1, Kovacs 1, Wright 1, own goals 2.
FA Cup (13): Basham 2, Gallen 2, Newton 2, Blackett 1, Craddock 1 (pen), Gnakpa 1, Hall 1, Nwokeji 1, White 1, own goal 1.
Play-Offs (0).

Tyler 37	Reynolds 3+2	Emanuel 1+1	Keane 33	Blackett 13+10	Pilkington G 44	Newton 32+3	Hall 27+5	Gallen 30+1	Craddock 40+4	Burgess 5+1	Howells 21+10	Basham —+5	Jarvis 21+6	Murray 38+2	Gnakpa 26+9	White 16	Nicholls 22	Donnelly —+4	Hatch 10+10	Charles —+6	Asafu-Adjaye 18+2	Wright 4+1	Pilkington A 7	Nwokeji —+7	Barnes-Homer 8+14	Nelthorpe —+8	Kovacs 17	Gore —+1	Heslop 11	Match No.
1	2	3^1	4	5	6	7^3	8	9	10^2	11	12	13	14																	1
1	2*		4	5	6	7^3	8	9^1	10	11	13	*2		3^2	14															2
1			4	6	5	2	9	10^1	11	7^2	12	8	3	13																3
1	8		7	6	5	2	9	10^2	11	13	12	3^1	4																	4
1			6	12	5	7^2	9	10^2	11^1	14	3	8	4	2	13															5
1			6	12	5	7^2	13	9^3	10		3	8^1	11	4	2		14													6
1			6	13	5	7	12	9	10^3		14	3	8	11^1	4^2	2														7
1			6	11^1	5	7	8	9	10^2		3	12		4	2*13															8
1			6		5	7	8	9	10		3	11		2^1	4	12														9
1	12			6	7	4	10^2	11			8	3^1	2	5	14	9^3	13													10
1	12			13	5	7	8	9^3	14		3	11	2^1	4			10^8													11
1			5	7	8		9			6^3	3	11	12	4	$1C^2$		14	2^1	13											12
1			5	7	8		13				3	11	12	4	E		9^2	14	2^1 10^5											13
1			6	7	4		9	14			11^8	3^2	12	5	▪		13	2^1 10^2												14
1	13			6	11	4	10				3		7^2	5	3		12	2	9^8											15
1				6	7	4	10				3		11	5	3		12	2	C^1											16
1				6	7	4^2					$11^1$14	12	5^3	8	3	3		2												17
	11		4	6	7		9	10^1	12		3		2^2	5	8			1	13											18
	4		5	6	7^1		9	10	12		3		11	8				2	1											19
	13		4	2^1	6	7		9^2	10		11		3	5	8			1	12											20
	4		12	5	7	13	10	11^3			3		8	2^1	6		14		9^2				1							21
	5		3^1	6	12	4	10^2	7			8	11	2					1	14	$9^3$13										22
	4		6	7	11		9^1	10	14		3		2^2	8^2	12			1	13						5					23
	2		6	7^1	4		10				3		8^2	9	12		$1C$	11	13						5	15				24
1	2		6	7^1	4^2		10				13	3	11^3	8	9			12	14						5					25
1	2*		6	7	4^3		10				11	3	12	8^1	9^2				13	14					5					26
1			6	7	4		10	13			11	3	2^2	8					12	9^1					5					27
1	2	13	6	7	4^1		10				11	3	12	3^2	9^3				14						5					28
1	2		6	7	4^2	9	10	14			11^3	3		8^1	13				12						5					29
1	2		6	7	4^1	9^3	10	11			3	12		8^2	13				14						5					30
1	2		6	7	4	12					8^3	3	11^1	9					13	$10^2$14					5					31
1	2		6	7	4	12					8^2	3	11	9^1					10	13					5					32
1	7		6		4^1	8	10	13			12	3	11					2		9^2	5									33
1	4		6		9	10^2	7	12			3	11^1						2	13							5	8			34
1	4^2		6	13	9	10	8				3	11^1						2		12							7			35
1	4	13	6		9^1	10	8				3	11						2		12					5^2		7			36
1	4	12	6		9^3	10	8				3	11^2	14					2		13					5^1		7			37
1	4	5	6	12	9^1	10	8^1				3	11*		13				2			14						7			38
1	4	5	6	14	9^1	10^5	8^3				3	11		12				2		13							7			39
1	4		6		9^1	10^5	8	3^3			11			13				2		14	12	5					7			40
1	4	5	6	14	10		8^2	13			3	11^1		9^3				2		12							7			41
1	4	5	6	7^1	9^2	10	8				3			13				2		12							11			42
1		5	6	7	4	9	10	8			3^2			13				2^1		12							11			43
1	13		6	2	12	9^1	10^3	4			11	3						14	8						5		7^2			44

FA Cup

Fourth Qualifying Round				
	Grays Ath	(h)	3-0	
First Round	Rochdale	(h)	3-3	
		(a)	2-0	
Second Round	Rotherham U	(a)	2-2	
		(h)	3-0	
Third Round	Southampton	(a)	0-1	

Play-Offs

Semi-Final	York C	(a)	0-1
		(h)	0-1

MANSFIELD TOWN Blue Square Premier

Ground: Field Mill Ground, Quarry Lane, Mansfield, Notts NG18 5DA. *Tel:* (01623) 482 482. *Year Formed:* 1897.
Record Gate: 24,467 (1953 v Nottingham F, FA Cup 3rd rd). *Nickname:* The Stags. *Manager:* David Holdsworth.
Colours: Yellow shirts, blue shorts, blue stockings.

MANSFIELD TOWN 2009–10 LEAGUE RECORD

Match No.	Date	Venue	Opponents	Result	H/T Score	Lg Pos.	Goalscorers	Attendance
1	Aug 8	H	Crawley T	W 4-0	3-0	—	Perry 2 [15, 43], Duffy [40], Speight [82]	3264
2	11	A	Luton T	L 1-4	1-1	—	Garner [18]	7295
3	15	A	Salisbury C	W 1-0	0-0	5	Perry [68]	1147
4	18	H	Barrow	W 4-1	1-0	—	Duffy [27], Speight [66], Clare 2 (2 pens) [78, 90]	3188
5	22	H	Ebbsfleet U	W 3-0	1-0	2	Duffy [30], Briscoe [53], Speight [66]	3269
6	31	H	Kettering T	D 0-0	0-0	—		4034
7	Sept 5	A	Grays Ath	D 1-1	1-1	2	Speight [12]	732
8	8	A	Kidderminster H	L 1-3	0-1	—	Duffy (pen) [88]	1378
9	12	H	Stevenage Bor	L 2-3	2-1	6	Perry 2 [2, 16]	3251
10	19	A	Rushden & D	L 0-1	0-0	9		1822
11	22	H	Oxford U	W 2-1	2-0	—	Williams [21], Speight [25]	3933
12	26	H	Hayes & Y	W 3-1	1-0	4	Duffy 3 (2 pens) [37, 49 (p), 62 (p)]	3180
13	29	A	Barrow	L 1-3	1-1	—	Nix [12]	1040
14	Oct 3	H	Forest Green R	W 1-0	1-0	4	Duffy (pen) [6]	3022
15	10	A	Altrincham	W 2-1	1-0	4	Perry [7], Briscoe [46]	1642
16	17	A	Eastbourne Bor	W 2-1	2-0	4	Perry [6], Duffy [12]	1207
17	31	H	Histon	D 1-1	0-0	4	Williams [90]	3162
18	Nov 14	A	Crawley T	W 2-0	1-0	4	Speight [11], Heckingbottom [77]	883
19	21	H	Eastbourne Bor	D 1-1	0-1	4	Challinor [68]	2922
20	28	A	Ebbsfleet U	L 1-2	1-1	—	Duffy (pen) [16]	850
21	Dec 1	A	Gateshead	W 3-1	1-0	—	Hotchkiss [59], Burgess [69], Morris [90]	643
22	5	H	Grays Ath	D 0-0	0-0	4		2726
23	26	A	York C	L 0-3	0-1	6		4587
24	28	H	Cambridge U	W 2-1	1-1	4	Perry [27], Speight [73]	3368
25	Jan 16	A	AFC Wimbledon	D 0-2	0-2	—		3584
26	30	A	Forest Green R	W 4-1	0-1	—	Jones 2 [63, 86], Duffy [66], Speight [76]	817
27	Feb 2	A	Wrexham	L 1-2	0-1	—	Speight [48]	2689
28	6	H	Gateshead	L 0-2	0-1	4		7261
29	9	A	Stevenage Bor	L 1-3	1-0	—	Shaw [39]	1753
30	13	A	Tamworth	W 4-2	3-1	6	Duffy [17], Shaw [21], Nicholas [42], Sturrock [87]	1389
31	27	A	Hayes & Y	D 1-1	0-1	7	Silk [90]	427
32	Mar 2	H	Luton T	D 0-0	0-0	—		3407
33	6	H	Salisbury C	W 4-2	2-1	7	Challinor [30], Shaw [37], Perry [75], Duffy [90]	2842
34	13	H	Tamworth	D 0-0	0-0	9		2954
35	16	H	York C	L 0-1	0-0	—		2638
36	20	A	Histon	W 5-0	1-0	8	Garner [38], Briscoe [57], Sturrock [64], Burgess [69], Speight [75]	662
37	23	H	Altrincham	D 1-1	0-0	—	Speight [90]	2364
38	27	A	Kettering T	D 2-2	2-1	7	Challinor [10], Sturrock [33]	1188
39	Apr 3	H	Wrexham	L 0-1	0-1	9		2520
40	5	A	Cambridge U	L 2-3	1-1	—	Speight [26], Nix [56]	2823
41	10	H	AFC Wimbledon	L 0-1	0-1	9		2470
42	13	H	Rushden & D	W 3-2	0-1	—	Speight 2 [48, 77], Duffy (pen) [90]	2031
43	17	A	Oxford U	L 0-2	0-0	—		5712
44	24	H	Kidderminster H	D 3-3	3-0	9	Speight 3 [18, 25, 45]	2734

Final League Position: 9

GOALSCORERS

League (69): Speight 17, Duffy 14 (6 pens), Perry 9, Briscoe 3, Challinor 3, Shaw 3, Sturrock 3, Burgess 2, Clare 2 (2 pens), Garner 2, Jones 2, Nix 2, Williams 2, Heckingbottom 1, Hotchkiss 1, Morris 1, Nicholas 1, Silk 1.
FA Cup (5): Duffy 2, Perry 2, Garner 1.

Marriott 44	Armstrong 15+2	Gardner 4	Mills 25+1	Jones 24+1	Garner 31	Briscoe 29+8	Nix 16+7	Duffy 34+3	Perry 28+12	Williams 27+8	Sommer 25+3	Speight 15+19	Clare 3+8	Istead 3+11	Silk 39	Graham 6+1	Sturrock 10+14	Puller 1 2	Heckingbottom 11	Dobson 1+2	Hotchkiss 5+3	Brough 18+2	Challinor 19+1	Burgess 14+3	Morris 2+3	Shaw 6+8	Foster 16	Nicholas 14	Match No.
1	2	3	4^1	5	6	7^2	8	9^3	10	11	12	13	14																1
1	2	3^4		5	6	7^3	8	9	10	11^1	4^2	13	14	12															2
1	2			5	6	7^3	8	9^2	10	11^1	4	12	13	14	3														3
1	2			5	6	7^2	8	9^1	10	11	4	13	12		3														4
1	2			5	6	7^1	8	9^2	10	11^3	4	12	13	14	3														5
1	2^1			5	6	7	8	9^3	10	11^2	4	14	13		3	12													6
1		8	5	6			14	9	10^2	12		4^3	7	11^1	3	2	13												7
1	2	8	5	6	13	4		9	12	11^3		7^2	10^1		3		14												8
1	2	8	5	6	7^2			9^3	10	11^1	4	14			13	3	12												9
1	2	8^4	5	6	7		14	9^2		11^1	4	13			12	3	10^3												10
1	3				6	7	8	9^2		11^3	4	10^1	12	14	2	5	13												11
1	2				6	7^2	8^1	9^3		11	4	10		14	12	3	5	5^3	13										12
1	2				6	7^2	8	9^1	12		4	10		14	3	5^3	13												13
1			4		6		8^3	9^2	13	11	14	12	10		3	5	7^1	2											14
1			4		6	7^3		9	10^1	13	8	12		11^1	2	5	4	3											15
1			4	5	6			9		11^1	13	8	10		7^2	3		2	12										16
1	12		4	5	6			9	10^3	11		13			2		4		14	3^1	8^2	7							17
1	13			5	6		14	10^3	11	8^4		7^2			12	2	9^1			3		4							18
1				5	6	7		9	10^1	11	4	13			3		12^2			2		8							19
1	14	6		5	13			9		11^2		4^3			10	3					2	7	8	12					20
1	3			5	6^4	8^2			10		4				2						12	11^1	7	9	13				21
1				5		8^1		9^3	10	13					2						3	4	6	7	11	12			22
1				5^4	6				10	12	8	14			2						3	13	4^2	11	9^3	7^1			23
1					6	13		9^2	10	11^3	8	12			2						3	4	5	14	7^1				24
1	12				6^1	7		9^3	10		4	13			2						3	8	5	11^2	14				25
1	3			5		13		9^1	12	11^2	8	10			2							8	7			6			26
1	3			5		12		9	13	11^2	8	10			2							14	4^3	7^1		6			27
1	3			5		7^2		9^3	12	11	8	10			2								4^1	13	14	6			28
1			4	5^2			14		11	9^2	8	12			2								13		7^1	10^3	6	3	29
1			4		6	8^1	14	9	11^2			12			2							13	7^3			10	5	3	30
1			4		6			9	11^1	8^2	12				2							13	7^3	14		10	5	3	31
1			4	5^1		8		9	13	11					2							12	7			10^2	6	3	32
1			4			8	12	9	13	11^3					2							5	7^1			10^2	5	3	33
1			4			8	7	9^3	13	11^1					2							6	12			10^2	5	3	34
1			4			8		9^1	13			12			2		10^2						6	7	11		5^1	3	35
1			4^1	5		8^2		9^1		12	13				2		10						6	7	11	14		3	36
1			4		6	8^3	14	9^1		13					2		10						5	7^2	11	12		3	37
1			4			8	12	14	5^3	13					2		10^2						6	7	11^1		5	3	38
1			4			8^1		9	13	12					2		10						6	7	11^2		5	3	39
1			4			13	12	9				8^3			2		10^2						6^1	7	11	14	5	3	40
1			4		6	8^3	12	9		11^1		10			2		13							7^2		14	5	3	41
1			4		6	8	7	9^1		10		13			2^2									11			5	3	42
1			4	5	6	7^1		9^2	13	11	8	10^3			12	2										3	12		43
1			4		6	7^1		9^2	14	11	8	10^3			12	2										3	13	5	44

FA Cup
Fourth Qualifying Round

	Altrincham	(h)	3-0
First Round	Forest Green R	(a)	1-1
		(h)	1-2

OXFORD UNITED

FL Championship 2

Ground: The Kassam Stadium, Grenoble Road, Oxford OX4 4XP. *Tel:* (01865) 337 500. *Year Formed:* 1893.
Record Gate: 22,730 (1964 v Preston NE, FA Cup 6th rd). *Nickname:* The U's. *Manager:* Chris Wilder.
Secretary: Mick Brown. *Colours:* Yellow with navy trim shirts, navy shorts, navy stockings.

OXFORD UNITED 2009–10 LEAGUE RECORD

Match No.	Date	Venue	Opponents	Result	H/T Score	Lg Pos.	Goalscorers	Attendance
1	Aug 8	H	York C	W 2-1	0-1	—	Green M 88, Creighton 90	6403
2	11	A	Kettering T	D 1-1	1-1	—	Sandwith 21	2240
3	15	A	Histon	W 4-3	1-0	3	Green M 16, Clist 47, Constable 2 73, 77	1433
4	22	H	Stevenage Bor	W 2-1	1-0	1	Potter 21, Murray 73	5775
5	29	A	AFC Wimbledon	W 1-0	0-0	1	Conroy (og) 50	4304
6	31	H	Forest Green R	D 0-0	0-0	—		6338
7	Sept 5	A	Ebbsfleet U	W 2-0	2-0	1	Green M 24, Clist 26	1468
8	8	H	Luton T	W 2-0	2-0	—	Constable 5, Cook 16	10,613
9	12	A	Wrexham	W 1-0	1-0	—	Constable 30	3628
10	19	H	Eastbourne Bor	W 4-0	3-0	1	Green M 25, Constable 28, Cook 45, Midson 87	5688
11	22	A	Mansfield T	L 1-2	0-2	—	Constable 74	3933
12	26	A	Gateshead	W 1-0	0-0	—	Green M 62	1144
13	29	H	Crawley T	W 3-1	1-1	—	Chapman 21, Kinninburgh 67, Midson 83	5675
14	Oct 3	A	Barrow	D 1-1	1-1	1	Foster 38	1561
15	10	H	Grays Ath	W 5-0	3-0	1	Constable 2 9, 24, Cook 43, Midson 2 (1 pen) 73, 90 (p)	6150
16	17	A	York C	D 1-1	0-0	1	Clist 81	4302
17	31	H	Altrincham	W 1-0	0-0	1	Batt 85	5609
18	Nov 14	A	Kidderminster H	L 1-3	1-2	—	Constable (pen) 30	3569
19	21	H	Barrow	W 1-0	1-0	1	Constable (pen) 27	5629
20	24	A	Forest Green R	W 1-0	1-0	—	Constable 23	1610
21	Dec 1	A	Crawley T	W 2-1	0-1	—	Chapman 83, Constable 90	1319
22	5	A	Ebbsfleet U	W 4-2	2-0	1	Potter 2 4, 61, Constable 2 9, 68	5188
23	28	A	Salisbury C	D 1-1	0-0	1	Sodje 80	2677
24	Jan 16	H	Tamworth	L 0-1	0-1	—		5690
25	23	A	Grays Ath	W 4-0	1-0	2	Clist 19, Potter 46, Constable 87, Green M 90	1136
26	Feb 6	H	Kidderminster H	D 0-0	0-0	1		5802
27	9	A	Luton T	L 1-2	0-0	—	Green M 74	8860
28	13	H	Histon	W 2-0	0-0	1	Deering 47, Green M 89	5365
29	16	H	Rushden & D	W 1-0	0-0	—	Chapman (pen) 86	7625
30	23	A	AFC Wimbledon	W 2-0	1-0	—	Constable 2 14, 80	6250
31	Mar 2	A	Cambridge U	D 1-1	1-1	—	Green M 42	3002
32	9	H	Hayes & Y	L 1-2	0-2	—	Clist 53	5045
33	13	H	Kettering T	D 1-1	1-1	2	Green F 36	5836
34	21	A	Tamworth	D 0-0	0-0	3		1572
35	24	A	Rushden & D	D 1-1	0-0	—	Deering 57	2970
36	27	H	Gateshead	W 2-1	0-0	2	Constable 52, Green M 90	5986
37	30	A	Stevenage Bor	L 0-1	0-0	—		5744
38	Apr 2	A	Hayes & Y	L 1-2	1-0	—	Constable 45	1655
39	5	H	Salisbury C	W 1-0	0-0	—	Potter 86	5741
40	10	A	Altrincham	W 1-0	0-0	3	Constable 53	1356
41	13	H	Cambridge U	D 0-0	0-0	—		5219
42	17	H	Mansfield T	W 2-0	0-0	3	Constable 2 74, 86	5712
43	20	H	Wrexham	W 1-0	0-0	—	Sandwith 82	4745
44	24	A	Eastbourne Bor	L 0-1	0-0	3		2634

Final League Position: 3

GOALSCORERS

League (64): Constable 22 (2 pens), Green M 10, Clist 5, Potter 5, Midson 4 (1 pen), Chapman 3 (1 pen), Cook 3, Deering 2, Sandwith 2, Batt 1, Creighton 1, Foster 1, Green F 1, Kinninburgh 1, Murray 1, Sodje 1, own goal 1.
FA Cup (5): Clist 1, Constable 1, Cook 1, Creighton 1, Midson 1.
Play-Offs (6): Constable 3, Green M 2, Potter 1.

Clarke R 43	Chapman 21 + 15	Sandwith 16 + 5	Bulman 41 + 1	Foster 20 + 1	Creighton 31 + 3	Murray 21	Clist 40 + 1	Constable 35 + 2	Midson 18 + 17	Kelly 2 + 1	Potter 12 + 10	Green M 26 + 15	Rhodes — + 3	Carruthers 1	Batt 31 + 6	Day 15 + 3	Perry 4 + 4	Kinninmonth 12	Cook 14 + 2	Woodley — + 3	Deering 15 + 8	Sodje 1 + 3	Green F 8 + 3	Tonkin 17	Wright 20	Hargreaves 9 + 1	Grant 4 + 4	Turley 1 + 1	Chalmers 6 + 2	Cain — + 1	Match No.
1	2	3^2	4	5	6	7	8	9	10^3	11^1	12	13	14																		1
1	2	3^2	4	5	6	7	8	12	10^1	11		9	13																		2
1	2^1	3	4	5	6		8	11	10			9			7^2	12	13														3
1	14	3	4	12	6	11^3	8	10			7^2	9	13		2	5^1															4
1	7^2	3	4	5	6	11^3	8	10	9^1	14	2				2		13														5
1	12		4	5	6	11	8	10			7^1	9			2			3													6
1	14	13	4	5	6	11	8	10^1	12			9^2			2			3	7^2												7
1	12		4	5	6	11	8	10^2	13	14		9^1			2			3	7^3												8
1	13		4	5	6	11^1	8	10^2	12			9			2			3^4	7												9
1	14	3	4	5	6	11^3	8	10^1	12		13	9^2			2				7												10
1	13		4	5	6		8^2	11	9		12	7			2			3^1	10												11
1	13		4	5	6	11^3	8	10	12			9^2			2	14		3	7												12
1	2^1	13	4	5	6	11	8	10			7^3	9^2				12		3	14												13
1	2^2		4	5	6	11^1	8	10	12			9			13			3	7												14
1	2		4	5	6		8^3	11	10^1		12	9^2			13			3	7	14											15
1	13		4	5	6	7^1	8	9			12	10			2			3	11^2												16
1			4	5	6		8^2	11	9		10^1	7^2			2	14		3	13		12										17
1	14		4	5	6		8^2	11	9		12	13	7^2		2			3^4			10^1										18
1	12	3	4	5			7^1	11	9		10^3		4		2		6	8^2	13												19
1	12	3	4	5	6			11	9^2		10	8			2^1		7				13										20
1	2	3		5		7^1	11	12	9^2		13	8^3			8^3		6		10	14											21
1	2^1	3	4		6		8	11	9^3		13	7	14		12^2	5			10												22
1	2	3	4	5	6			11	9		10^2	7^1	13						14		12		8^3								23
1	2^1		4		6		8	11	9		13	7^3	14		12^4						10^2		3	5							24
1	13		4	14				11	9		10^3	7^1	12		2	5					8^2		3	6							25
1			4					11^3	9		14	7^1	13		2	5		8^2			10		3	6	12						26
1	13		4					11			10^3	7^2	12		2	5					9^1	14	3	6	8						27
1	13		4					11			10^3	7^1	12		2	5					9^2		3	6	8						28
1	13		4^2					11	9		10^1		12		2	5					3^3	14	3	6	7						29
1^6	2^2		4					11	9		10^1				13	5					8		3	6	7	12	15				30
1	7^1		4	13				11			10^2		14		2	5					12		3^4	6	8	9^3					31
1	4^3				6			11			10		14		2	5^2					7		3	8^1	9^3		12	13			32
1			4					11^1			10^2		12		2	5					7	9	3	6^1		13			8		33
1			4	12				11	9				13		2	5					7	10^3	3	6^1		14			8^2		34
1			4					11	9						2	5					12	10^1	3	6	7	8					35
1	2		4^1					11	9		12		13			5^3			10^2		7		3	6		14	8				36
1	2		6^2					11	9		12	10				13					7		3	5		8^1					37
1	7		6^3					11^1	9		8^2	10^4	14		2						13	12	3	5			4				38
1	7	3^1	4		6				9		10^2		13		2						12	8^2	11	5							39
1	7	14	4		6				9		10^2		12		2						11^3	8^2	3	5					13		40
1	7	3	4	5				11^1	9		15	10^2			2						12	8		6							41
1	7	3	4^2	5^3				11	9		16	12	8^1		2	13					14			6							42
	7	3	12								1	8	9^2		2	5		13	11					6				1	4^1		43
1	12	3			6			13					14		2^1	5			10^3		7		11^2	8	9		4				44

FA Cup

Fourth Qualifying Round

First Round	Yeovil T	(h)	1-0
	Thurrock	(h)	2-0
Second Round	Barrow	(h)	1-1
		(a)	1-3

Play-Offs

Semi-Final	Rushden & D	(a)	1-1
		(h)	2-0
Final	York C		3-1
(at Wembley).			

RUSHDEN & DIAMONDS Blue Square Premier

Ground: Nene Park, Irthlingborough, Northants NN9 5QF.   *Tel:* (01933) 652 000.   *Year Formed:* 1992.
Record Gate: 6,431 (1999 v Leeds U, FA Cup 3rd rd).   *Nickname:* The Diamonds.   *Manager:* Justin Edinburgh.
Secretary: Matt Wild.   *Colours:* White shirts, white shorts, white stockings.

RUSHDEN & DIAMONDS 2009–10 LEAGUE RECORD

Match No.	Date	Venue	Opponents	Result	H/T Score	Lg Pos.	Goalscorers	Attendance
1	Aug 8	H	Salisbury C	L 0-2	0-0	—		1272
2	11	A	York C	D 0-0	0-0	—		2267
3	15	A	Eastbourne Bor	D 1-1	0-1	19	Akurang [58]	941
4	18	H	Hayes & Y	W 2-1	0-0	—	Tomlin L [63], Farrell [85]	1059
5	22	H	Forest Green R	W 4-2	2-1	8	Farrell [13], Byrne [27], Akurang [65], O'Connor [84]	1056
6	29	A	Stevenage Bor	L 1-2	0-1	14	Akurang [58]	1704
7	31	H	Cambridge U	D 1-1	0-0	—	Stuart [58]	2344
8	Sept 5	A	Barrow	W 6-1	3-0	9	Farrell 2 [4, 58], Akurang [14], Pattison [38], Cousins [89], Reid [90]	1089
9	8	A	Ebbsfleet U	D 0-0	0-0	—		863
10	12	H	Grays Ath	W 5-4	1-1	9	Pattison [10], Tomlin L 2 (1 pen) [56, 80 (p)], Reid [63], Akurang [90]	1192
11	19	H	Mansfield T	W 1-0	0-0	5	Akurang [90]	1822
12	22	A	Gateshead	D 0-0	0-0	—		409
13	26	A	Crawley T	L 1-2	1-1	11	Farrell [10]	925
14	29	A	AFC Wimbledon	L 0-1	0-1	—		1624
15	Oct 3	H	Altrincham	L 0-1	0-0	13		1168
16	17	H	Tamworth	W 3-2	2-1	9	Tomlin L 2 [4, 18], O'Connor [78]	1313
17	31	A	Luton T	W 2-0	0-0	6	Tomlin L [84], Byrne [90]	7101
18	Nov 14	A	Histon	W 2-1	1-0	7	Akurang 2 [37, 66]	1126
19	21	A	Salisbury C	W 3-1	0-0	7	Terry [79], O'Connor 2 [83, 90]	840
20	24	A	Cambridge U	D 2-2	2-0	—	Tomlin L [13], Louis [26]	2612
21	Dec 1	H	York C	L 0-1	0-0	—		1117
22	5	A	Forest Green R	L 0-1	0-0	8		755
23	28	A	Kidderminster H	W 2-1	1-0	8	Tomlin L 2 [15, 57]	1425
24	Jan 23	H	Barrow	W 4-1	1-0	8	Louis 2 [14, 46], Farrell [57], Stuart [63]	1134
25	26	H	Wrexham	D 0-0	0-0	—		960
26	30	A	Hayes & Y	W 6-1	3-0	—	Cadmore (og) [4], Tomlin L [18], O'Connor [45], Basham (og) [51], Farrell 2 [71, 76]	377
27	Feb 6	A	Grays Ath	W 3-0	1-0	6	O'Connor [39], Corcoran [72], Louis [81]	476
28	9	H	Eastbourne Bor	W 2-0	1-0	—	Louis [45], Corcoran [52]	1038
29	13	H	Stevenage Bor	W 1-0	0-0	11	Wolleaston [88]	1923
30	16	A	Oxford U	L 0-1	0-0	—		7625
31	27	H	Kettering T	D 0-0	0-0	4		2998
32	Mar 3	A	Histon	W 1-0	1-0	—	Tomlin L (pen) [11]	583
33	6	A	Tamworth	W 1-0	0-0	3	Porter [83]	1016
34	13	H	Gateshead	W 8-0	2-0	4	Stuart [6], Porter [45], Louis 2 [50, 78], Byrne [54], Tomlin L [65], Farrell [81], Downer [85]	1414
35	20	A	Altrincham	D 2-2	1-1	4	Young (og) [40], Terry [73]	1035
36	24	H	Oxford U	D 1-1	0-0	—	Day (og) [69]	2970
37	27	A	AFC Wimbledon	W 1-0	0-0	4	Farrell [55]	3640
38	30	H	Kettering T	W 3-0	2-0	—	Farrell [3], Byrne [12], Tomlin L [64]	2031
39	Apr 2	H	Crawley T	D 1-1	1-0	—	Tomlin L [45]	1703
40	5	A	Kidderminster H	D 1-1	1-0	—	Porter [26]	1463
41	10	H	Ebbsfleet U	W 2-0	1-0	4	O'Connor 2 [27, 70]	1440
42	13	A	Mansfield T	L 2-3	1-0	—	O'Connor [16], Smith [71]	2031
43	17	A	Wrexham	W 1-0	1-0	4	O'Connor [17]	5672
44	24	H	Luton T	D 1-1	1-1	4	Byrne [20]	4820

Final League Position: 4

GOALSCORERS

League (77): Tomlin L 14 (2 pens), Farrell 11, O'Connor 10, Akurang 8, Louis 7, Byrne 5, Porter 3, Stuart 3, Corcoran 2, Pattison 2, Reid 2, Terry 2, Cousins 1, Downer 1, Smith 1, Wolleaston 1, own goals 4.
FA Cup (8): O'Connor 4, Corcoran 2 (1 pen), Byrne 1, Tomlin L 1.
Play-Offs (1): Byrne 1.

Roberts 33	Osano 39 + 2	Robinson 39 + 1	Wolleaston 8 + 9	Stuart 41	Downer 26 + 3	Tomlin L34 + 1	McNamara 7 + 3	O'Connor 29 + 9	Akurang 16 + 17	Reid 4 + 7	Farrell 26 + 15	Smith 3 + 16	Porter 34 + 9	Corcoran 22 + 2	Cousins 4 + 4	Pattison 17 + 8	Byrne 36 + 4	Terry 29 + 2	Abbey 10	Louis 20 + 4	Mills — + 1	Ainsley — + 1	Huke 5 + 2	Day 1	Beecroft 1	McDonald — + 1	Match No.
1	2	3	4	5	6^{8}	7	8^{3}	9	10^{1}	11^{2}	12	13	14														1
1	2	3	4	5		7^{1}		9^{2}	13	12	10		11	6	8												2
1	2		4	5	3	13		9	12	7^{2}	10^{1}		11	6	8												3
1	2		4^{2}	5	3	8	12	9^{3}	10		14		11	6^{1}			7	13									4
1	2			5	3	8^{3}	13	12	10	14	9^{1}		11^{2}	6			7	4									5
1	2	12		5	3	8		9^{1}	10^{3}	13	14		11	6^{8}			7^{2}	4									6
1	2	3		5	6	8		9^{1}	10^{2}		12	13	11				7	4									7
1	2	3		5		8^{1}			13	10	12	9^{2}	11	6	14		7^{3}	4									8
1	2	3		5		8^{1}		9	12	10^{2}	14	13	11	6			7^{3}	4									9
1	2	3		5		8		9^{3}	10	14	12	13	11^{1}	6			7^{2}	4									10
	2	3		5	6	8^{8}		9^{1}	10	11^{3}	12	13	14				7^{2}	4	1								11
	2	3		5	6	11		9	10^{1}		12		4		8		7		1								12
	2	3		5	6			9	10^{1}	11^{2}	12	14	13		8^{3}		7	4	1								13
	2	3		5	6			9	10	11^{1}	12	13			8		7^{2}	4	1								14
	2	3		5	6^{8}			9	10^{1}	11	12	14	13		8^{2}		7^{3}	4	1								15
	2	3		5	6	11		9	10^{1}		12	13	14		8^{3}		7^{2}	4	1								16
	2	3		5	6			9	10^{3}	11^{2}	12	13	14		8		7^{1}	4	1								17
	2	3		5	6	11		9^{3}	10^{1}		12	13	14		8		7	4^{2}	1								18
	2	3		5	6^{2}			9^{3}	10	11^{1}	12		13		8		7	4	1								19
	2	3		5	6^{2}			9^{1}	10	11^{3}	12	14	13		8		7	4	1								20
1	2	3		5	6^{1}				10	11	13	14			8^{2}		7	4		9^{2}	12						21
1	2	3		5	6			9^{1}	10	11^{3}	12	13	14		8		7	4^{2}									22
1	2	3	12	5	6			9	10^{2}	11		13			8		7	4^{1}									23
1	2	3	4^{1}	5	6			9^{3}	10^{2}	11	12	13	14		8		7										24
1	2	3	4^{2}	5	6			9^{1}	10	11^{3}	12	13	14		8		7										25
1	2^{1}	3	14	5	6			9	10^{2}	11^{3}	12	13			8		7	4									26
1	2	3		5	6			9	10^{3}	11^{1}	12	13	14		8^{2}		7	4									27
1	2	3	12	5	6			9	10	11^{2}		13	14		8		7	4^{3}									28
1	2	3	12	5	6			9^{3}	10^{2}	11		13	14		8		7	4^{1}									29
1	12	3	4	5	6^{1}			9^{2}	10	11		13	14		8^{3}		7	2									30
1	2	3		5	6			9^{1}	10	11^{2}	12	13			8		7	4									31
1	2	3					8^{8}	9^{2}	10^{3}	11^{1}	12	13	14	6			7	4									32
1	2	3		5	6			9^{2}	10^{1}	11	12	13	14		8^{2}		7	4									33
1	13	3		5	6			9	10^{3}	11^{1}	12		14	2^{2}			7	4									34
1	2	3		5	6			9	10^{2}	11	12	13					7	4									35
1	2	3		5	6			9^{1}	10	11^{2}	12	13					7	4									36
1	2	3		5	6		8^{1}	9	10^{2}	11^{3}		13	14				7	4		12							37
1	2	3	14	5	6^{1}		8^{3}	9	10^{2}	11		13					7	4		12							38
1	2	3	13	5	6		8^{1}	9	10^{3}	11	12		14				7^{2}	4									39
1	2	3	7	5	6^{3}		8^{1}	9^{2}	10	11	12	13	14					4									40
1	2	3	14	5	6			9^{2}	10^{1}	11	12	13		3			7^{3}	4									41
1	2	3		5	6		9^{8}		10^{1}	11	12	13			8		7	4^{2}									42
	2	3^{2}		5	6^{1}	7		9	10	11^{2}		13	14		8			4	1				5	1	8	12	43
1	2	3		5	6^{3}			9	10^{1}	11	12	13	14		8		7^{2}	4					3				44

FA Cup

Fourth Qualifying Round			
	Workington	(a)	3-0
First Round	Hinckley U	(h)	3-1
Second Round	Brighton & HA	(a)	2-3

Play-Offs

Semi-Final	Oxford U	(h)	1-1
		(a)	0-2

SALISBURY CITY   Zamarreto Premier

Ground: The Raymond McEnhill Stadium, Partridge Way, Old Sarum, Salisbury SP4 6PU. *Tel:* (01722) 326 454.
Year Formed: 1947. *Record Gate:* 8,902 (1948 v Weymouth, Western League). *Nickname:* The Whites.
Coaches: Mikey Harris and Darrell Clarke. *Secretary:* Alec Hayter. *Colours:* White shirts, black shorts, white
stockings.

SALISBURY CITY 2009–10 LEAGUE RECORD

Match No.	Date		Venue	Opponents	Result		H/T Score	Lg Pos.	Goalscorers	Atten- dance
1	Aug	8	A	Rushden & D	W	2-0	0-0	—	Stuart (og) [47], Flood [90]	1272
2		11	H	Kidderminster H	W	1-0	0-0	—	Webb [53]	1034
3		15	H	Mansfield T	L	0-1	0-0	6		1147
4		18	A	AFC Wimbledon	L	0-4	0-1	—		3591
5		22	H	Histon	L	0-2	0-1	16		684
6		29	H	Eastbourne Bor	D	1-1	0-0	18	Clarke [90]	746
7		31	A	Hayes & Y	W	4-3	1-1	—	Tubbs 3 [44, 49, 84], Flood [51]	429
8	Sept	5	H	Luton T	D	1-1	1-1	13	Tubbs [43]	2044
9		8	H	Grays Ath	W	2-0	1-0	—	Flood [25], Tubbs [62]	765
10		12	A	Gateshead	L	1-2	0-2	12	Tubbs (pen) [54]	478
11		19	A	Tamworth	L	0-2	0-2	22		1003
12		26	H	Barrow	W	3-0	2-0	18	Tubbs 2 [13, 75], Flood [39]	876
13		29	A	Ebbsfleet U	W	2-1	0-0	—	Webb [88], Tubbs [89]	792
14	Oct	3	A	Wrexham	W	2-1	2-0	16	Anderson [9], Tubbs [18]	2556
15		10	H	York C	W	1-0	1-0	15	Tubbs (pen) [4]	1266
16		17	A	Stevenage Bor	L	1-3	0-1	17	Flood [53]	2009
17		31	H	Gateshead	L	0-1	0-0	17		1050
18	Nov	14	A	Eastbourne Bor	W	1-0	0-0	17	Flood [90]	756
19		21	H	Rushden & D	L	1-3	0-0	18	Clarke [90]	840
20		24	A	Crawley T	L	0-2	0-0	—		603
21		28	H	Stevenage Bor	L	0-1	0-1	—		851
22	Dec	1	A	AFC Wimbledon	L	0-2	0-0	—		1157
23		5	A	Kettering T	W	2-1	1-1	18	Tubbs [36], Anderson [48]	1098
24		26	A	Forest Green R	L	1-3	0-2	18	Tubbs [83]	1079
25		28	H	Oxford U	D	1-1	0-0	18	Todd [89]	2677
26	Jan	23	H	Histon	W	3-0	1-0	17	Tubbs 2 [37, 75], Adelsbury [63]	758
27	Feb	6	A	Altrincham	L	0-5	0-2	17		777
28		13	A	Grays Ath	W	2-0	1-0	17	Tubbs [28], Clohessy [90]	232
29		16	H	Tamworth	W	1-0	1-0	—	Connolly [2]	586
30		27	H	Wrexham	D	1-1	0-0	16	Tubbs (pen) [89]	948
31	Mar	2	H	Crawley T	D	2-2	2-1	—	Tubbs 2 [16, 35]	581
32		6	A	Mansfield T	L	2-4	1-2	17	Connolly [38], Adelsbury [89]	2842
33		9	A	York C	W	2-1	0-1	—	Connolly [54], Clarke [65]	1867
34		16	A	Cambridge U	L	1-3	1-2	—	Tubbs [6]	2028
35		23	H	Forest Green R	L	1-3	0-3	—	Turley [37]	665
36		27	A	Kidderminster H	W	1-0	1-0	16	Tubbs [24]	1201
37		30	A	Luton T	L	0-4	0-2	—		6692
38	Apr	2	H	Ebbsfleet U	W	3-1	1-0	—	Martin [7], Giles [66], Adelsbury [73]	1088
39		5	A	Oxford U	L	0-1	0-0	—		5741
40		10	A	Cambridge U	W	2-1	0-1	16	Tubbs 2 (1 pen) [60, 89 (p)]	1245
41		13	H	Hayes & Y	W	3-1	0-0	—	Tubbs [67], Reid [78], Shephard [87]	755
42		17	A	Barrow	W	1-0	0-0	14	Reid [81]	1173
43		20	H	Altrincham	W	4-1	0-0	—	Clohessy [49], Reid [51], Tubbs 2 [52, 57]	671
44		24	A	Kettering T	W	2-0	1-0	12	Shephard [19], Tubbs [86]	1123

Final League Position: 12

GOALSCORERS

League (58): Tubbs 27 (4 pens), Flood 6, Adelsbury 3, Clarke 3, Connolly 3, Reid 3, Anderson 2, Clohessy 2, Shephard 2, Webb 2, Giles 1, Martin 1, Todd 1, Turley 1, own goal 1.
FA Cup (5): Tubbs 4, Flood 1.

Bittner 40	Turley 29+2	Clohessy 39+1	Anderson 33+2	Spence 10+1	Webb 22+7	Sinclair 20+3	Clarke 43	Matthews 1	Tubbs 39+3	O'Hara 10+6	Flood 26+16	Cox 10+2	Gray 13+12	Osman T —+11	Glover 2+5	Prosser 10+1	Porter 1	Fereks 1	Ruddick 23+8	Brown 11+2	Oastler 8+3	Tafazolli 5	Lester 1	Todd 4	Adelsbury 19	Robinson 1	Giles 11+1	Bull 8+1	Bush 6+1	Connolly 8+3	Martin 14	Reid 6+6	Pryce 2+1	Shephard 9	Widdrington —+2	Match No.
1	2	3	4	5	6^2	7	8	9	10^3	11^1	12	13	14																							1
1	2	3	4	5	6	7	8		10	11^1	12			9^2	13																					2
1	2	3	4^1	5	6	7	8		10	11^2	12			9^3	13	14																				3
1^4	2	3^1	4	5	12	7	8		10^6	11^2	13			15	9	6																				4
			4	5	3^1	7	8			11	2^2	10	13	9	6		1	12																		5
1	3	2	4	5	9	7^1	8		10	11	12					6																				6
1	3	2	4	5	9^2	7	8		10^3	12	11^1		14	13		6																				7
1	3	2	4	5	9	7^1	8		10^2	12	11^3			13		6			14																	8
1	3	2	4	5	9	7	8		10^2	12	11^1			13		6			12																	9
1	3	2	4^2	5^1	9^6	7	8		10	14	11^3			13		6			12																	10
1	3^2	2	4^3			7	8		10	11^1	9		14			6			13	5	12															11
1	3^1	2^3	4	14	9^2	7	8		10	11					13	6				5	12															12
1	3^2	2	4		9	14	8		13		11	12				6			7^1	5	10^3															13
1	3	2^1	4	13	12	8			10^2	11									7	5	9	6														14
1	3	2	4			7	8		10^1	9									12	5	11	6														15
1	3	2	11		9	7	8		12	13	5^1								10^2	4	6															16
1	3	2	4^2		9^1	8			10	14	11^3	5	12						13	6	7															17
1	5	2	4			9	8		10	11	12								3^1	7		6														18
1	5	2	4	14	13	8			10	11^2	12		9^3						3	7^1		6														19
1	5^1	2^1	4^2	9		8			10	7^3	11	6		14					3	12	13															20
			4			8			10	11^1	9	6	12						3	2	7		1	5^1												21
1	12	4		9^3		8			10	11^2	13	6	14						3	7^1	2	5														22
1		2	4		6		8^2		10	9			11^1	12					3	13	7				5											23
1	5		4		9	8			10	11^1		7	12						3						6	2										24
1	5	2	4		9	8			10		11								3						6	7										25
1	5	2	4^2		6	7^1	8		10	13	12		9^3	14											11	3										26
1	5	2	4			7	8		10	13			9^2						3^1						11		6^3	12	14							27
1		2				4	8		10^3	11	5	9^2	14						12								7^1	6	3	13						28
1		2				10	8			12	4	11^2	13						3								7	6	5	9^1						29
1		2	12			7^1	8		10	11^3	5^2	13	14						3								6			4	9^2					30
1		2	4			8			10	12	9								3								11	5	6^1		7					31
1	2		4			8			10	12	5^1	14							13								11		6	7^2	9^3	3				32
1	5	2	4			8			12										3								7		11^1	10	6	9				33
1		2	4						10^1	11^2	13								3								8	6	7	12	5	9				34
1^4	12	2	4^2	13		8			10	11									3								6		9^6	5^1	7	15		7^2		35
	2	12				8			10	11									3								4^1	6	9	5	13	1		7^2		36
	2					13	8		10^2	11^1									3								4	5	9	6	12	1		7^3		37
1	12	2				13	8		10	11									3								7	12	9^1	6^2	14			7^3		38
1	2	5			6^2	8^3			10	11									3								7	12	13	4^1	14	9				39
1	2	3	4^2			8			10	13									3								7	5	9^1	6	12	11				40
1	5	2		14		8			10	13		9^1															7	6	3^2	4^3	12	11				41
1	5^1	2^1				8^2	10		13	14^4									12								7^1	6	3	4	9	11				42
1	2^1		6			8	10		7										11									3	5	9	4	12				43
1	2^1		6			8	10		7	12									4									3	5	9^2	11	13				44

FA Cup
Fourth Qualifying Round

	Farnborough T	(a)	0-0
		(h)	4-2
First Round	Accrington S	(a)	1-2

STEVENAGE BOROUGH FL Championship 2

Ground: Broadhall Way Stadium, Broadhall Way, Stevenage, Hertfordshire SG2 8RH. *Tel:* (01438) 223 223.
Year Formed: 1976. *Record Gate:* 6,489 (1997 v Kidderminster Harriers, Conference). *Nickname:* The Boro.
Manager: Graham Westley. *Secretary:* Roger Austin. *Colours:* Red and white shirts, black shorts, white stockings.

STEVENAGE BOROUGH 2009–10 LEAGUE RECORD

Match No.	Date	Venue	Opponents	Result	H/T Score	Lg Pos.	Goalscorers	Atten- dance
1	Aug 8	H	Tamworth	D	1-1	1-1	—	Boylan (pen) [13]	2130
2	11	A	Hayes & Y	D	1-1	0-0	—	Drury [49]	681
3	15	A	Barrow	D	0-0	0-0	17		1254
4	18	H	Ebbsfleet U	W	3-0	1-0	—	Beardsley [8], Byrom [75], Wilson [86]	1704
5	22	A	Oxford U	L	1-2	0-1	13	Odubade [90]	5775
6	29	H	Rushden & D	W	2-1	1-0	11	Boylan (pen) [7], Bostwick [74]	1704
7	31	A	Histon	W	2-0	1-0	—	Laird [12], Odubade [62]	1159
8	Sept 8	H	Eastbourne Bor	W	2-0	1-0	—	Ashton [28], Henry [68]	1660
9	12	A	Mansfield T	W	3-2	1-2	3	Beardsley [45], Odubade [59], Griffin [69]	3251
10	22	H	Grays Ath	D	1-1	1-1	3	Boylan [33]	1803
11	26	H	Altrincham	D	1-1	0-1	3	Bostwick [90]	1200
12	29	A	Luton T	W	1-0	0-0	—	Laird [85]	8223
13	Oct 3	A	York C	D	1-1	1-0	—	Parslow (og) [34]	2644
14	10	H	Hayes & Y	W	4-0	2-0	2	Griffin 3 (1 pen) [17, 33, 73 (p)], Bostwick [90]	2120
15	17	H	Salisbury C	W	3-1	1-0	2	Roberts [43], Griffin [60], Beardsley [82]	2009
16	20	A	Wrexham	D	0-0	0-0	—		1763
17	31	A	Kettering T	D	1-1	1-1	2	Byrom [2]	1844
18	Nov 14	H	Gateshead	W	5-3	3-1	2	Griffin 3 [40, 45, 73], Odubade [44], Bostwick [90]	2203
19	21	A	Forest Green R	W	1-0	1-0	2	Boylan [7]	757
20	28	A	Salisbury C	W	1-0	1-0	—	Griffin [45]	851
21	Dec 1	A	Ebbsfleet U	L	1-2	1-0	—	Odubade [21]	836
22	5	H	Kidderminster H	W	2-0	1-0	2	Ashton [37], Cole [46]	1809
23	26	A	Cambridge U	W	3-1	1-1	2	Odubade (pen) [27], Griffin [54], Beardsley [85]	4439
24	28	H	AFC Wimbledon	D	0-0	0-0	2		3033
25	Jan 1	H	Cambridge U	W	4-1	2-1	—	Odubade [25], Boylan 2 [45, 62], Beardsley [50]	3406
26	23	A	Kettering T	W	2-0	0-0	1	Long 2 [63, 90]	2136
27	Feb 6	A	Tamworth	L	0-1	0-1	2		841
28	9	H	Mansfield T	W	3-1	0-0	—	Odubade 2 [53, 69], Drury [73]	1753
29	13	A	Rushden & D	L	0-1	0-0	2		1923
30	24	A	Wrexham	W	1-0	1-0	2	Roberts [45]	2319
31	Mar 2	A	Eastbourne Bor	W	6-0	1-0	—	Roberts [40], Bridges [47], Beardsley [71], Cole 3 (1 pen) [83 (p), 86, 90]	903
32	6	H	Crawley T	W	2-0	0-0	1	Bostwick [47], Boylan [90]	2230
33	9	H	Barrow	W	4-0	2-0	—	Odubade 3 [28, 59, 84], Laird [45]	1538
34	16	H	Histon	W	1-0	1-0	—	Ashton [18]	2407
35	23	A	Grays Ath	W	2-1	0-1	—	Bostwick [65], Griffin [86]	515
36	27	A	Crawley T	W	3-0	2-0	1	Odubade 2 [5, 33], Byrom [69]	1229
37	30	H	Oxford U	W	1-0	0-0	—	Laird (pen) [52]	5744
38	Apr 3	H	Luton T	L	0-1	0-0	1		7024
39	5	A	AFC Wimbledon	W	3-0	2-0	—	Roberts [9], Wilson [11], Odhiambo [90]	3840
40	10	H	Forest Green R	W	2-0	1-0	1	Byrom [10], Laird (pen) [63]	2524
41	14	A	Altrincham	W	1-0	0-0	—	Griffin [83]	907
42	17	A	Kidderminster H	W	2-0	1-0	1	Griffin [2], Byrom [62]	2564
43	20	A	Gateshead	W	1-0	1-0	—	Laird (pen) [21]	702
44	24	H	York C	W	1-0	1-0	1	Bridges [35]	5068

Final League Position: 1

GOALSCORERS

League (79): Odubade 14 (1 pen), Griffin 13 (1 pen), Boylan 7 (2 pens), Beardsley 6, Bostwick 6, Laird 6 (3 pens), Byrom 5, Cole 4 (1 pen), Roberts 4, Ashton 3, Bridges 2, Drury 2, Long 2, Wilson 2, Henry 1, Odhiambo 1, own goal 1.
FA Cup (3): Griffin 2, Vincenti 1.

Day 40	Henry 37	Laird 42	Murphy 20	Roberts 38	Bostwick 42	Drury 21+8	Long 14+7	Griffin 17+9	Boylan 14+7	Byrom 28+11	Cole 19+13	Odubade 24+13	Ashton 32+3	Wilson 7+5	Vincenti 2+19	Bayes 4	Bridges 24+3	Beardsley 30+7	Albrighton 8+6	Annolet —+1	Odhiambo 5+10	Brough 6	Sills 9+8	Anderson 1	Match No.
1	2	3	4	5	6	7^3	8^1	9	10^2	11^4	12	13	14												1
1	2^1	3	4	5	6	7^2 12		9^1 10		11	13			8	14										2
	2	3	4^3	5		7	12		9^1		14	11		6	8	13	1	10^2							3
	2	3	4	5	7	12			10	14	11^2			6^3	8	13	1		9^1						4
	2	3	4^2	5	7					10	11	12	6		8	13	1		9^1						5
1	2	3		5	7		4^3		10	11	12	14	6		8^1 13				9^2						6
1	2	3		5	7				10^3	8^2	9^1 12	6		11^8			13	4	14						7
1	2	3		5	7		4^1	13	10	8	1^{12} 14	6					9^3				12				8
1	2	3		5	7				13	10^2	8	11^1 12	6				9^3 14		4						9
1	5	3		4	7	12			10	8	11^3 14			13			9	6^1			2^2				10
1		3	8^2	5	7	2^3 13	12	10		11			14				9^1			4	6				11
1		3	8	5	7	2^2		10		4	11^1 12		14				9^3			13	6				12
1		3	8	5	7	2^1		10		4	11^2 13						9^3 14			12	6				13
1	2		8	5	6	7^2 12	9	13	11		10^3						14				4^1	3			14
1	2	3	4	5	6	7^1		9^3	8		10^2 13		14				12				11				15
1	2	3	4^2	5	6		9		8	12	11	13		14			10^1				7^3				16
1	2	3		5	6		9		8	12	11^1	4		13			7	10^2							17
1	2^1	3		4	6	7^2	9			11	10^3	5		14			8	13			12				18
1	2	3	8	5	6	7^1		10^3	4	14	11^2			13			9				12				19
1	2	11		3	6	13		9		8	12	10^3	5^2				7		4^1		14				20
1	2	3^3	4	5	6	7	14	9		11	12	10^1					8^6 13								21
1	2	3	4			7		9		13	11^1		5	14			8^6 10^3	6			12				22
1	2	3	7		11			12^2 13	14		10	5					8	9	6^1		4^3				23
1	2	3	4		6		7^1		13	11^3		10	5				6	9^2 12	14						24
1	2	3	4		6		7		10	13		11	5^1	14			8^2	9^3 12							25
1	2			3	6		7		10^3	12	11	9^2	5^1	14			4	8					13		26
1	2^8	3	4^8		6		7	9^3		14	12	11	5				3^1	10^2					13		27
1		3		6	2	12	8		14	4	11^2	7	5				13	9^3					10^1		28
1		3		6	2	13	8		14	4	11^1	12	5				7	9^3					10^2		29
1	2	3		4	7				10^3	11^1	12		5	14			8	9^5	6				13		30
1		3		2	4	12			7^3	13	10^2	5		11^1			8	9	6	14					31
1	2	3		6	4		7		13	11^1	12^2 10^3	5					8	9	14						32
1	2	3		4	6	14	7		10^1	C3	11	5					8^6						12		33
1	2	3	4^1	6		14	7^3			12	11	10	5				8	9^2					13		34
1	2	3		4	6	7		14		11^1	12	10^3	5				8	9^2					13		35
1	2	3		4	6	7^3 14				12	11^1	10	5				8	13					9^2		36
1	2	3		4	6	7^2 13				14	11^1	9	5				8	12					10^3		37
1	2	3		4	6	7		13	14			11^3	5	12			8	9^1					10^2		38
1	2	3		4	6	7^3		12		8			5	11^2				9	14		13		10^1		39
1	2	3		4	6	7		8^2 14		11^3			5	12			13	9^1					10		40
1	2	3		4	6	7		13		8		11^2	5	12	14		9^1						10^3		41
1	2	3		4	6	7		9^3		8^2		11^1	5	12			13						14	10	42
	3	4		6	7	11^2 9^1			12	14			2	13	1	8		5					10^3		43
1	2	3		4	6	7		9^2		11		12	5	14			8^1 10^3						13		44

FA Cup
Fourth Qualifying Round
	Chelmsford C	(a)	2-1
First Round	Port Vale	(a)	1-1
		(h)	0-1

TAMWORTH Blue Square Premier

Ground: The Lamb Ground, Kettlebrook, Tamworth B77 1AA. *Tel:* (01827) 65798. *Fax:* (01827) 62236.
Year Formed: 1933. *Record Gate:* 4,920 (1948 v Atherstone T). *Nickname:* The Lambs. *Manager:* Gary Mills.
Secretary: Rod Hadley. *Colours:* Red shirts with white trim, white shorts, red stockings.

TAMWORTH 2009–10 LEAGUE RECORD

Match No.	Date	Venue	Opponents	Result	H/T Score	Lg Pos.	Goalscorers	Attendance
1	Aug 8	A	Stevenage Bor	D 1-1	1-1	—	Pritchard 29	2130
2	15	H	Grays Ath	W 2-1	2-1	9	Pritchard 20, Sheridan 25	729
3	18	A	Gateshead	D 1-1	1-0	—	Wright 42	429
4	22	H	Cambridge U	D 0-0	0-0	15		1316
5	25	H	Wrexham	W 2-1	1-1	—	Smith C 37, Sheridan 71	1290
6	29	A	Barrow	L 0-1	0-0	13		1051
7	31	H	Kidderminster H	W 2-1	0-0	—	Wright 47, Rodman 63	1237
8	Sept 5	H	AFC Wimbledon	D 2-2	2-0	8	Sheridan 7, Wright 37	1669
9	12	A	Hayes & Y	D 2-2	0-1	7	Benjamin 57, Blackwood 68	355
10	19	H	Salisbury C	W 2-0	2-0	3	Blackwood 13, Briscoe 17	1003
11	22	A	Altrincham	D 0-0	0-0	—		843
12	26	A	Eastbourne Bor	D 1-1	0-0	7	Sheridan 60	1053
13	Oct 3	A	Luton T	L 1-2	0-2	10	Rodman 59	6297
14	6	H	York C	L 2-3	1-1	—	Tait 2 18, 87	1118
15	10	H	Histon	L 1-3	0-1	12	Wylde 48	1090
16	17	A	Rushden & D	L 2-3	1-2	13	Wright 8, Tait 90	1313
17	31	H	Hayes & Y	L 0-2	0-2	14		919
18	Nov 21	A	Ebbsfleet U	W 1-0	1-0	11	Pritchard 27	867
19	24	H	Altrincham	L 0-2	0-0	—		630
20	28	A	Grays Ath	L 0-1	0-1	—		496
21	Dec 1	A	Kidderminster H	D 0-0	0-0	—		1166
22	5	H	Crawley T	L 0-1	0-1	14		729
23	26	H	Kettering T	D 0-0	0-0	14		1250
24	28	H	Forest Green R	D 0-0	0-0	14		868
25	Jan 16	A	Oxford U	W 1-0	1-0	—	Christie 28	5690
26	23	H	Eastbourne Bor	D 1-1	1-1	12	Christie 7	883
27	Feb 6	H	Stevenage Bor	W 1-0	1-0	12	Smith C 23	841
28	9	A	Wrexham	D 0-0	0-0	—		2435
29	13	H	Mansfield T	L 2-4	1-3	12	Wylde 19, Murdock 50	1389
30	16	A	Salisbury C	L 0-1	0-1	—		586
31	23	H	Kettering T	L 1-3	0-2	—	Smith C 83	473
32	Mar 2	H	Gateshead	W 1-0	0-0	—	Christie 56	483
33	6	H	Rushden & D	L 0-1	0-0	13		1016
34	9	A	Histon	L 0-1	0-1	—		350
35	13	A	Mansfield T	D 0-0	0-0	17		2954
36	21	H	Oxford U	D 0-0	0-0	17		1572
37	24	A	Cambridge U	L 0-2	0-0	—		2121
38	27	A	York C	D 1-1	0-0	18	Smith C 82	2863
39	Apr 3	H	Barrow	W 3-0	1-0	15	Mitchell 45, Sheridan 46, Christie 78	817
40	5	A	Forest Green R	W 4-3	2-2	—	Shaw (pen) 6, Pritchard 37, Sheridan 64, Christie 74	1370
41	10	H	Luton T	D 1-1	0-1	15	Lyttle 56	2246
42	17	A	Crawley T	L 0-2	0-0	17		755
43	20	A	AFC Wimbledon	W 1-0	1-0	—	Wylde 26	3015
44	24	H	Ebbsfleet U	L 3-4	2-2	16	Christie 11, Wylde 40, Pritchard 58	1694

Final League Position: 16

GOALSCORERS

League (42): Christie 6, Sheridan 6, Pritchard 5, Smith C 4, Wright 4, Wylde 4, Tait 3, Blackwood 2, Rodman 2,
Benjamin 1, Briscoe 1, Lyttle 1, Mitchell 1, Murdock 1, Shaw 1 (1 pen).
FA Cup (0).

Alcock 43	Tait 41 + 1	Wylde 31 + 2	Smith C 33	Briscoe 29 + 5	MacKenzie 21 + 7	Shaw 33 + 3	Rodman 23	Wright 23 + 2	Sheridan 38 + 3	Pritchard 40 + 1	Blackwood 29 + 4	Benjamin — + 4	Lake-Gaskin 12 + 14	Nicholson — + 4	Lyttle 19 + 4	Hurren 2 + 1	Mills 1 + 1	Russell 10 + 1	Koranteng — + 1	Andrew — + 5	Gaughran 1	Brown 7	Christie 20 + 4	Ulker — + 3	Langdon 3 + 1	Fankem 1	Murdock 3 + 11	Smith J 15 + 1	Mitchell 6 + 2	Match No.
1	2	3	4	5	6	7^2	8	9^1	10	11	12	13																		1
1	2	3^1	4	5	6	7	8	9^2	10^3	11	12		13	14																2
1	2		4	5	6	7	8	9^1	10	11			12	3																3
1	2		4	5	6	7	8	9	10	11		3																		4
1	2		4	5	6	7	8	9^1	10	11		3			12															5
1	2		4	5	6	7	8	9	10^1	11^8		3	12																	6
1	2		4	5	6	7	8	9^1	10			3		12	11															7
1	2		4	5		7	8	9^1	10			3	13	12	11	6^1														8
1	2		4	5		7^2		9	10	8		3		12	11^1	6		13												9
1	2		4	5		7			10	8		3			11^1	6		9		12										10
1	2^2		4	6	12	8		9		11	3		13		7^1	5		10												11
1	2		4	5		7	12		10	8^2	3		13		11^1	6		9												12
1	2		4	5	6	7	8		10^1	11	3				12			9												13
1	2	5	4		8	10	7	9		11^1	3	13			6^2			^{72}												14
1	2	5^1	4		8	10	7^2	9		11^1	3	13			6			^{14}												15
1	2	13	4		10^2	7	8	11	3		6				9^1			12	5											16
1	2	5	4	6	8			10	11	3		9			^{7}															17
1	2	13	4	5	6^2	8^1		9^3	7	11	3							10		12 14										18
1	2	5	4		6			9^1	11	3	13							10		8^2		12								19
1	2	5	4		6			9	11									10		8		3								20
1	2	5	4	13	6^2			7^1	9	11			13							8 12		3								21
1	2	5	4	12	6^3			7^2	9	11		13						10		8		14	3^1							22
1	2	5	4	3	6	8	10		11		12									7^1 9										23
1	2	5	4	3		10	8		7	11										6 9										24
1	2	5	4		6	10		7^1	8^2	11	3						14					9^3 12 13								25
	2	5	4	3	6	10		7^1	8	11										9						1 12				26
1		5	4	2		8		7^1	10	11	3	12^2								9					13 6					27
1		5	4	2	12	7		6	11	3	10^2									9					13		8^1			28
1	13	5	4	2		7		6^2	11	3	10									9					12		8^1			29
1	2		4	6^1	13	7	12		10	3	8^2									14					9 11^3					30
1	2	5	4	6^1		8	10^3	7	11^2	3	13		14							12		9								31
1	2	5	4	6		8	10		11	3	7									9^1					12					32
1	2	5	4	6^2		8	10^1	12	11	3	7									9					13					33
1	2	5	4	12	6^2	10	8		11^2	3^1	7									9					13 14					34
1	2	5	6^1			7	8	11	13	3								9							10^2 4 12					35
1	2	5				8^2	7	11	12	13	3							9							10^1 4 6					36
1	2	5	4		14			10^1	11^3	3	12		8					9^2							13 6 7					37
1	2	5	4		12	10		7	3	14		11^1						9^3							13 8^2 6					38
1	2	5			12	8^1	7	1^1	10	13		3^2						9^3							14 4 6					39
1	2	5	13		12	7	10^2	11		8^1	3							9							4 6					40
1	2	5	4	13	12	7^2	10^1	11^3		6	14	3						9							8					41
1	2	5	4	12	8^3	13	10^1	7	11	14	3							9							6^2					42
1	2	5	4	3	6	13	10^1	8^2	12	11								9									7 4			43
1	2	5	4	6	10^2	8^3	13	11	12	3^1								9									7 14			44

FA Cup
Fourth Qualifying Round
        Ilkeston T   (ε)   0–2

WREXHAM

Blue Square Premier

Ground: Recreation Ground, Mold Road, Wrexham LL11 2AH. Tel: (01978) 262 129.   *Year Formed:* 1872.
Record Gate: 34,445 (1957 v Manchester U, FA Cup 4th rd). *Nickname:* Red Dragons.   *Manager:* Dean Saunders.
Secretary: Geraint Parry.   *Colours:* Red shirts, white shorts, red stockings.

WREXHAM 2009–10 LEAGUE RECORD

Match No.	Date	Venue	Opponents	Result	H/T Score	Lg Pos.	Goalscorers	Attendance
1	Aug 8	H	Eastbourne Bor	W 3-0	1-0	—	Taboubi [34], Taylor G 2 (1 pen) [61 (p), 71]	3726
2	15	A	Crawley T	L 0-1	0-0	16		1014
3	18	H	York C	W 1-0	0-0	—	Taylor G [59]	3371
4	22	H	Kettering T	L 1-2	0-1	14	Assoumani [56]	3473
5	25	A	Tamworth	L 1-2	1-1	—	Taylor G [26]	1290
6	29	A	Forest Green R	W 2-0	2-0	12	Baynes W 2 [29, 32]	1021
7	31	H	Barrow	D 0-0	0-0	—		3760
8	Sept 12	H	Oxford U	L 0-1	0-1	—		3628
9	19	A	Cambridge U	L 0-2	0-1	16		2823
10	22	H	Luton T	W 3-0	2-0	—	Taylor G 2 (1 pen) [6 (p), 21], Mark Jones [86]	3448
11	29	A	Kidderminster H	L 0-2	0-0	—		1585
12	Oct 3	H	Salisbury C	L 1-2	0-2	17	Taylor G [70]	2556
13	17	H	Grays Ath	W 2-1	2-1	16	Smith [5], Taylor G [39]	2495
14	20	A	Stevenage Bor	D 0-0	0-0	—		1763
15	31	H	Ebbsfleet U	W 1-0	1-0	15	Sakho [43]	969
16	Nov 3	A	Kettering T	D 2-2	2-1	—	Harper (og) [14], Westwood [22]	1186
17	14	H	Hayes & Y	L 0-2	0-2	15		2427
18	21	A	Histon	D 0-0	0-0	15		946
19	24	H	Kidderminster H	D 2-2	2-2	—	Mike Williams 2 [26, 35]	2086
20	Dec 1	H	Forest Green R	W 1-0	0-0	—	Baynes W [89]	1808
21	5	A	York C	L 1-2	0-1	15	Fleming A [82]	3006
22	Jan 23	A	AFC Wimbledon	W 1-0	1-0	16	Taylor G [29]	3276
23	26	A	Rushden & D	D 0-0	0-0	—		960
24	30	A	Altrincham	W 3-1	2-0	—	Mangan [4], Baynes W [37], Mark Jones [74]	1821
25	Feb 2	H	Mansfield T	W 2-1	1-0	—	Baynes W [28], Mangan [58]	2689
26	6	A	Eastbourne Bor	L 1-2	0-1	13	Mike Williams [76]	972
27	9	H	Tamworth	D 0-0	0-0	—		2435
28	20	H	Crawley T	W 2-0	0-0	—	Mike Williams [59], Wolfenden [81]	2475
29	24	H	Stevenage Bor	L 0-1	0-1	—		2319
30	27	A	Salisbury C	D 1-1	0-0	12	Smith [69]	948
31	Mar 6	H	Ebbsfleet U	D 1-1	1-0	12	Mangan [15]	2345
32	9	H	Altrincham	D 1-1	1-0	—	Baynes W [33]	2114
33	13	A	Luton T	L 0-1	0-1	12		6538
34	16	A	Barrow	L 1-2	0-0	—	Mark Jones [62]	1066
35	20	H	Cambridge U	D 2-2	2-0	12	Mangan [9], Smith [14]	2105
36	23	A	Gateshead	L 0-1	0-0	—		614
37	27	H	Histon	W 3-0	0-0	13	Holden [54], Mangan 2 (1 pen) [63 (p), 87]	2335
38	30	A	AFC Wimbledon	D 2-2	0-0	—	Pullen (og) [51], Mangan [88]	3149
39	Apr 3	A	Mansfield T	W 1-0	1-0	13	Mark Jones [42]	2520
40	5	H	Gateshead	D 0-0	0-0	—		2380
41	10	A	Grays Ath	W 2-0	1-0	11	Westwood [30], Taylor N [76]	298
42	17	H	Rushden & D	L 0-1	0-1	12		5672
43	20	A	Oxford U	L 0-1	0-0	—		4745
44	24	A	Hayes & Y	W 1-0	1-0	11	Baynes W [23]	446

Final League Position: 11

GOALSCORERS

League (45): Taylor G 9 (2 pens), Baynes W 7, Mangan 7 (1 pen), Mark Jones 4, Mike Williams 4, Smith 3, Westwood 2, Assoumani 1, Fleming A 1, Holden 1, Sakho 1, Taboubi 1, Taylor N 1, Wolfenden 1, own goals 2.
FA Cup (2): Baynes W 1, Taylor G 1.

Russell 18	Spann 24+2	Taylor N 20+3	Fleming A 35+2	Assoumani 38+1	Williams Mike 25+5	Cieslewicz 8+14	Taboubi 10+2	Taylor G 24+3	Wolfenden 4+11	Jones Mark 28+6	Williams Marc 10+6	Smith 7½+4	Baynes W 24+14	Obeng 27+6	Williamson 2	Maxwell 26	Westwood 33	Sinclair 18	Fairhurst 6+3	Tsiakkis 1	Sakho 14+4	McCluskey 6+7	Mangan 23	Anoruo —+6	Holden 13+2	Edwards —+1	Brown 8	O'Leary 8	Mitchley 3+3	Hunt 1+1	Walker 1	Match No.
1	2	3	4^3	5	6	7^2	8	9	10^1	11	12	13	14																			1
1		3	4	5	6	7	8	9	10^1	11				12	2																	2
1	2^3	7	4	5	6	12	8^1	9	10^2	11		3		14	3																	3
1	7^2		5	6	13	8	9	10^1	11	12	4^3	14	2	3																		4
	7	12	8	5	6^1	10		9		11	13	4^2	14	2^3	1	3																5
		10		5		12	7^2			11	9	3	8	2	1	3	4	6														6
		10^2		5		13	7^3	9		11	12	14	8	2	1	3	4	6^1														7
	11	12	5		13	6^1	9		7	10			8	2	1	3^9	4															8
	11		5	4^1	10^3	9		7	13			14	2	1	3		8	6^2	12													9
11	3	4	5		13	9^1		7	10^2	8			2	1	6			12														10
3^8	11	6^2	5		13	14		7	10	8^3	12		2	1	4			9^1														11
	3	12	5		14	6^2	11	7	10	8^1			2	1	4			9^3	13													12
	3	4	5	13		9		11	10	8	12		2	1	6			7^2														13
	3^1	4	5	12	13	9		7	10	8			2	1	6			11^2														14
2		4	5	3		9		7^1		8	10			1	3		12		11^2	13												15
7		4	5	3		9		12		8	10	2		1	6			11^1														16
7^1	13	4	5	3^2	12	9		1^8	8	10	2^3		1	6			11^8															17
	7	5	3	12		9		1^8	8	11	2^1		1	4	6																	18
	11^1	4		3	7			12	8	8	10	2		1	5	6																19
		4		3	13	9	14	7^1	13^3		8	2		1	5	6	12	11^2														20
	11^1	4	5	3	12	9	13			8	2		1		6	7	10^2															21
1	3		4	5	14			9^3		7	8		2	6		11^1	12	10^2	13													22
1	7		4	5				11	8	2^1		6	3		9	12	10^2	13														23
1	2		4	5	12			13	8	7		6	3^1		9	11^2	10^3	14														24
1	2		4	5	3			14	8^1	10	12	6			7^1	9^2	13	11^3														25
1	2		4	5	3			11	10		6		12	7	9	8^1																26
1	2		4	5	3				10	12	6	8^2		7^1	9	13	11															27
1	2		4	5	3			13	12	14	7	10^3		6	11^1	9^2	8															28
1	2		4	5	3			9^1	12	13	8	7^2		6		14	10	11^3														29
1	2^1		4	5	3			10^2		8	7	12		6		9	13	11														30
1	2		4	5	3			13	7^2	11	8^1			6		12	9	10														31
1	2	13	4	5	12			14	7	11	8^2			6	3^8		9	10^3														32
1	2		4^3	5	3			14	7	11	8	13		6		12	9	10^1														33
1	2^1		4	5^8	3			14	7	8^3	11^2	12		6		10	9	13														34
1	2	3	4		6			14	7	8	12		5		1^{12}	10^3	9	13														35
	7^1	3	4		6	14	8			12	2		1	5	13	10^3	9	11^2														36
	3	8				13				12	2		1	5	6		9	11^2	4	7	10^1											37
	4	14			9^1					8^2	12	2	1	5	6^8		10	11^3	3	7	13											38
	11	4	5		12	13	8				2	1	6			9^2		3	8	10^1												39
	11^3	4	5			14	7^2			12	2	1	6			9	13^8	3	8	10^1												40
	11	4	5		9	7					2	1	6			10		3	8													41
12		5	11^2		9^3	14	7^1	8	13	2		1	6			10		3	4													42
13		5	7^1	8^2	9	12				2		1	6			10		3	4	14	11^3											43
		5	6	11^2		7		9		1			8			13	10^3		3^1	4	14	2	2									44

FA Cup
Fourth Qualifying Round

	FC Halifax T	(a)	1-0
First Round	Lowestoft T	(h)	1-0
Second Round	Swindon T	(h)	0-1

YORK CITY
Blue Square Premier

Ground: KitKat Crescent, York YO30 7AQ. *Tel:* (01904) 624 447. *Year Formed:* 1922.
Record Gate: 28,123 (1938 v Huddersfield T, FA Cup 6th rd). *Nickname:* Minster Men.
Manager: Martin Foyle. *Secretary:* Nick Barrett. *Colours:* Red shirts, navy shorts, navy stockings.

YORK CITY 2009–10 LEAGUE RECORD

Match No.	Date	Venue	Opponents	Result	H/T Score	Lg Pos.	Goalscorers	Attendance
1	Aug 8	A	Oxford U	L 1-2	1-0	—	Brodie [33]	6403
2	11	H	Rushden & D	D 0-0	0-0	—		2267
3	15	H	Forest Green R	W 2-0	0-0	10	Rankine (pen) [74], Smith A [90]	1954
4	18	A	Wrexham	L 0-1	0-0	—		3371
5	22	A	Hayes & Y	D 1-1	0-0	17	Pacquette [84]	606
6	25	A	Gateshead	W 2-1	0-1	—	Brodie [55], Gash [80]	1174
7	29	H	Histon	W 3-1	1-0	4	Brodie 2 (1 pen) [12, 65 (p)], Smith A [58]	1944
8	Sept 5	H	Crawley T	W 2-0	2-0	7	Brodie (pen) [6], Gash [10]	2139
9	8	A	Barrow	D 0-0	0-0	—		1120
10	12	H	Kettering T	W 2-0	0-0	—	Brodie 2 [57, 69]	2275
11	22	H	Cambridge U	D 2-2	1-0	—	Gash 2 [33, 89]	2321
12	26	H	Kidderminster H	W 3-2	2-1	5	Brodie 2 (1 pen) [10 (p), 32], Gash [58]	2509
13	Oct 3	H	Stevenage Bor	D 1-1	0-1	9	Sangare [90]	2644
14	6	A	Tamworth	W 3-2	1-1	—	Ferrell [40], Brodie [61], Sangare [78]	1118
15	10	A	Salisbury C	L 0-1	0-1	7		1266
16	17	H	Oxford U	D 1-1	0-0	6	Rankine [71]	4302
17	20	A	Luton T	D 1-1	1-0	—	Barrett [38]	6387
18	31	A	Crawley T	L 1-3	1-0	7	Brodie [28]	975
19	Nov 14	H	Ebbsfleet U	W 1-0	1-0	6	Rankine [38]	2629
20	21	A	AFC Wimbledon	W 1-0	0-0	5	Rankine [64]	4016
21	24	H	Gateshead	W 1-0	1-0	—	Lawless [25]	2302
22	Dec 1	A	Rushden & D	W 1-0	0-0	—	Brodie [73]	1117
23	5	A	Wrexham	W 2-1	1-0	3	Carruthers [6], Brodie [81]	3006
24	26	H	Mansfield T	W 3-0	1-0	3	Brodie 2 (1 pen) [21, 48 (p)], Gash [81]	4587
25	Jan 16	H	Hayes & Y	W 4-1	1-0	—	Carruthers [25], Brodie 2 [47, 58], Gall [83]	2403
26	23	A	Cambridge U	W 1-0	0-0	3	Barrett [48]	2646
27	Feb 2	A	Histon	D 1-1	1-1	—	Purkiss [20]	487
28	6	A	Kettering T	W 1-0	1-0	3	Rankine [16]	1375
29	13	A	Ebbsfleet U	L 0-1	0-0	3		1226
30	16	H	Luton T	D 0-0	0-0	—		3316
31	27	H	Eastbourne Bor	L 0-1	0-0	3		2611
32	Mar 6	A	Forest Green R	L 1-2	1-1	4	Mackin [34]	892
33	9	H	Salisbury C	L 1-2	1-0	—	Sangare [42]	1867
34	13	A	Altrincham	D 0-0	0-0	6		1236
35	16	A	Mansfield T	W 1-0	0-0	—	Pitt [6]	2638
36	23	A	Kidderminster H	W 1-0	0-0	—	Barrett [67]	1127
37	27	H	Tamworth	D 1-1	0-0	5	Graham [57]	2863
38	30	A	Grays Ath	W 4-0	3-0	—	Harsley [31], Brodie 2 [37, 42], Barrett [57]	323
39	Apr 5	H	Altrincham	W 2-1	0-0	—	McGurk [69], Brodie (pen) [90]	3005
40	7	H	AFC Wimbledon	W 5-0	4-0	—	Rankine 2 [17 (p), 22], Brodie 3 (2 pens) [17 (p), 22, 36 (p)]	2667
41	10	A	Eastbourne Bor	L 1-3	1-3	5	Rankine (pen) [45]	1144
42	13	H	Barrow	W 3-0	1-0	—	Brodie 2 [40, 83], Gash [90]	2154
43	17	H	Grays Ath	D 1-1	0-0	5	Brodie [51]	2854
44	24	A	Stevenage Bor	L 0-1	0-1	5		5068

Final League Position: 5

GOALSCORERS

League (62): Brodie 26 (7 pens), Rankine 8 (2 pens), Gash 7, Barrett 4, Sangare 3, Carruthers 2, Smith A 2, Ferrell 1, Gall 1, Graham 1, Harsley 1, Lawless 1, Mackin 1, McGurk 1, Pacquette 1, Pitt 1, Purkiss 1.
FA Cup (8): Brodie 4 (1 pen), Rankine 2, Barrett 1, Pacquette 1.
Play-Offs (3): Brodie 1, Carruthers 1, own goal 1.

Ingham 43	Lawless 31 + 4	Meredith 42 + 1	Mackin 29 + 5	McGurk 28 + 6	Parslow 33	Purkiss 34 + 2	Ferrell 16 + 6	Rankine 29 + 14	Brodie 36 + 4	Barrett 39 + 2	Gash 21 + 15	Neilthorpe — + 6	Smith A 13 + 13	Pacquette 3 + 10	Sangare 18 + 4	McWilliams — + 3	Carruthers 22 + 4	Buyea 1 + 2	Graham 25	Gall — + 5	Pitt 6 + 5	Clarke 7	Harsley 7 + 2	Mimms 1	Match No.
1	2²	3	4	5	6	7	8	9¹	10	11	12	¹3													1
1	2³	3	4	5	6	7	8¹	9²	10	11	13	12	14												2
1	2	3	4	5	6	7	8¹	9³	13	11	10²	12	14												3
1	2¹	3	4	5	6	7	8³	9²	13	11	10	14	12												4
1	2	3	4¹	5	6	7	12	9³	13	11³	10		8	14											5
1	2	3		5¹	6	7	4²	14	8	11	10³			9⁴	12	13									6
1	2	3			6	7	4²	12	8¹	11	10	14		9³	5		13								7
1	2	3	12		6	7	4¹		8	11	10			9	5										8
1	2	3			6	7	4¹	12	8	11	10			9	5										9
1	2	3	13	14	6	7	4²	12	8¹	11	10			9³	5										10
1		3	4²	14	6	2	11¹	12	10	8	9		7³		5		13								11
1		3	2¹	13	6	7	4²	12	8	11	10			9	5										12
1	14	3	2²		6	7	4³	12	8	11	10¹			9	5		13								13
1	13	3²	4		6	7	2		9¹	11	8		10³	12	5		14								14
1	2	3	4	5	6	11		9	10	7					12		8¹								15
1	7	3⁴		12	6	2	4	9¹	10	8		11¹			5		13								16
1	2		13		6	7	4²	9	10	8		11¹			5		3	12							17
1	7	12	13	5	6		4³	9	10	8²		14			2¹		3	11							18
1	7	3	13	5	6	2		9¹	10	4		8²	12				1¹								19
1	7	3	4	5	6			13	9	10¹	8²	12					1·		2						20
1	7¹	3	4	5	2		14	10		8³	3²	12					1↓				6	13			21
1	7³	3	4¹	5	2		14	9²	10	8	13	12					1↓				6				22
1	7	3	4	5	2			9¹	10	8	12						1↓				6				23
1	7²	3	4	5	2		13	9¹	10	8	12						1↓³				6	14			24
1	7	3	4	5	2³	14		9²	10¹	8	·2						11				6	13			25
1		3	4	5	2	7²	14	9	10¹	8			12	13			11³				6				26
1	7	3	4	5	2		8²	9		10¹		12	13				·1				6				27
1	7³	3	4	5	2	8		9	10	14	13		12				1²				6				28
1	7	3	4³	5	2	8¹		9	10⁴	13	12						·12				6	14			29
1	7	3	4	5	2	13		10		8²	9¹			12			11				6				30
1	7¹	3	4	5	2³			9	8	10²	12	13					11				6	3	14		31
1		3	4²	5	2	7³		13	10	8		9¹					11				6	3	14	12	32
1		3				2		9²	10	4	14	13	8³	5		11¹			6	12	7				33
1		3	4¹			2		13	10		9²	8		5			6		11	7	12				34
1		3		13		2		12	10	8	9²	14		5¹			6		11³	4	7				35
1		3				2		13	10	4	9²	12		5		14			6	11¹	8	7			36
1		3				2		12	10	4	9¹	13		5		14			6	11³	8	7²			37
1	13	3		12		2		14	10³	4	9			5¹					6	11	8²	7			38
1	12	3		5		2		13	10	4	9²					14			6	11³	8¹	7			39
1	7³	3	4	5		2		9	10²	8·	12			14			11				6		13		40
1	7	3	4¹	5		2		9	10		14	12					1·²			6³	13	8			41
1	7	3	4	5		2		9¹	10²	8	12			13			11				6				42
1	7	3	4	5		2		9²	10³	8	13			14			11¹				6	12			43
	10	3	4	5	2			9	14	8¹	13			12			11³				6		7²	1	44

FA Cup
Fourth Qualifying Round

	Bedworth U	(h)	2-0
First Round	Crewe Alex	(h)	3-2
Second Round	Cambridge U	(a)	2-1
Third Round	Stoke C	(a)	1-3

Play-Offs

Semi-Final	Luton T	(h)	1-0
		(a)	1-0
Final	Oxford U		1-3
(at Wembley).			

REVIEW OF THE SCOTTISH SEASON 2009–10

Rangers had safely tucked the title away when the last weekend dawned leaving Celtic something of a sorry second in the Scottish Premier League. It had been a traumatic season at Parkhead with Tony Mowbray departing along with many familiar faces on the playing staff. No fewer than 37 different players were called upon in the League alone, none of them ever-present. In contrast at Ibrox just 24 were used in a much more settled squad.

Even so, in early December Celtic were still heading the table. They often scored freely and finished with four players in double figures including Scott McDonald who left later for Middlesbrough and Robbie Keane who topped them all with a dozen goals as a loan star from Tottenham Hotspur in the last third of the season.

Unusually for them, with Celtic four points ahead in late September, Rangers had three successive matches ending in goalless draws – 293 no-goal minutes – but then appeared to be moving towards another championship. Indeed, they lost just three League games throughout, surprisingly 1-0 at Aberdeen (of all places!), St Johnstone (heavily 4-1) and 2-1 at Parkhead in May when it was a fixture for pride alone.

Once again Kris Boyd was the leading goal scorer in the SPL with 23 goals. His outstanding individual performance was hitting five of the seven Rangers goals put past Dundee United at the end of the year. He topped his 150th goal for them and also overhauled Henrik Larsson's all-time SPL record tally.

Not that everything else went the Ibrox way. Dundee United edged them in a sixth round Active Nation Scottish Cup replay at the death and it was only when reduced to nine players did Rangers rally to beat St Mirren in the CIS League Cup final.

However, there was even more embarrassment for Celtic in the Scottish Cup semi-final, beaten by Ross County. The Staggies had earlier hit Stirling Albion for nine goals and appeared at one time to be heading for promotion to the SPL. Perhaps the Cup exertions took their toll. In the final they were beaten by Dundee United, celebrating their centenary with a fitting tribute.

The Tayside Terrors held onto third place but the race for the remaining European berth went down to the wire along with the relegation battle. Hibernian had to win at Tannadice and hope Motherwell did no better than draw at Rangers. Hibs won 2-0 but despite scoring twice at Ibrox in the dying moments to level, Motherwell finished fifth.

At the bottom Falkirk had to win at Kilmarnock to survive, Killie only had to take a point. The Bairns spent the season rooted, their first win arriving in the twelfth match. Kilmarnock had one of their poorest seasons on record and Aberdeen's wretched home record of ten defeats highlighted their problems.

Hamilton Academical recovered from a shaky start – eleven games for three goals at one time – and St Johnstone quietly adjusted to the division's requirements. St Mirren notably hit Celtic for four which actually prompted an eight game winning streak for their victims, though the Ross County cup defeat came in the middle of it.

Half-way through the season the same six clubs to be affected by the cut occupied the top and bottom sections. Hearts after struggling initially improved but were never higher than fifth at any time.

Falkirk's place has been taken over by strongly-finishing Inverness Caley after Dundee again flattered to deceive and Ross had half a mind elsewhere. Dundee had managed to give Caley two goals start in the Alba Challenge Cup final and beat them, but would have wished for a swap of the two prizes. Airdrie United having just caught Ayr United to avoid last place then lost in the play-offs to Brechin City.

Part of the fall-out concerning Livingston affected others of course. Airdrie who had lost out to Ayr in the play-offs had been able to retain their Division One status while Cowdenbeath moved up to Division Two having lost to Stenhousemuir in the Division Three play-off final.

Stirling forgetting their cup disaster judged their 2009–10 Division Two run perfectly and Cowdenbeath joined them from the play-offs. Down came Clyde and Arbroath beaten by Forfar Athletic in their final. Livingston having initially refused to accept demotion to the Division Three won the title though at one stage East Stirling enjoying a fine season looked likely to pip them.

Bad weather played havoc with the Scottish League programme with clubs often having to play three times a week in catch-up, straining their meagre resources.

However, arguably the finest display concerned Irvine Meadow a junior club who achieved the unique feat of beating seniors when they defeated Arbroath from Division Two 1-0 in the third round of the Scottish Cup.

Outside of domestic issues Scottish clubs fared miserably in Europe. Rangers ended bottom of their Champions League group, Celtic beaten in two legs by Arsenal in the same competition managed only third place in the Europa League. They did succeed in beating Dynamo Moscow away after losing at home. Motherwell hit eight goals in one match, but Falkirk lost to Leichtenstein's Vaduz.

Internationally the precarious World Cup position ended as expected but subsequent performances cost George Burley his position. Dundee United's Craig Levein was appointed in his place, Peter Houston taking over at Tannadice. In June, the clan Lennon secured posts. St Mirren appointed Danny Lennon, former Cowdenbeath manager and two days later Celtic upgraded Neil Lennon from his caretaker role. Gordon Smith the Scottish FA's chief executive resigned for personal reasons in April. Now the focus is on Euro 2012.

Scotland have a tough group headed by Spain the holders and closely followed by the Czech Republic. Lithuania and Liechtenstein make up the quintet, respectively old Euro opponents and new ones.

SCOTTISH LEAGUE TABLES 2009–10

CLYDESDALE BANK SCOTTISH PREMIER LEAGUE 2009–10

		P	Home					Away					Total						
		P	W	D	L	F	A	W	D	L	F	A	W	D	L	F	A	GD	Pts
1	Rangers	38	15	4	0	52	13	11	5	3	30	15	26	9	3	82	28	54	87
2	Celtic	38	14	4	1	42	14	11	2	6	33	25	25	6	7	75	39	36	81
3	Dundee U	38	8	4	7	22	21	9	8	2	33	26	17	12	9	55	47	8	63
4	Hibernian	38	9	4	6	29	21	6	5	8	29	34	15	9	14	58	55	3	54
5	Motherwell	38	8	5	5	29	25	5	9	5	23	29	13	14	11	52	54	-2	53
6	Hearts	38	9	4	6	19	20	4	5	10	16	26	13	9	16	35	46	-11	48
7	Hamilton A	38	6	7	6	19	17	7	3	9	20	29	13	10	15	39	46	-7	49
8	St Johnstone (P)	38	6	6	7	31	28	6	5	8	26	33	12	11	15	57	61	-4	47
9	Aberdeen	38	6	4	10	20	31	4	7	7	16	21	10	11	17	36	52	-16	41
10	St Mirren	38	5	9	5	18	18	2	4	13	18	31	7	13	18	36	49	-13	34
11	Kilmarnock	38	5	6	8	23	27	3	3	13	6	24	8	9	21	29	51	-22	33
12	Falkirk	38	3	6	10	17	29	3	7	9	14	28	6	13	19	31	57	-26	31

IRN-BRU SCOTTISH FOOTBALL LEAGUE FIRST DIVISION 2009–10

		P	Home					Away					Total						
		P	W	D	L	F	A	W	D	L	F	A	W	D	L	F	A	GD	Pts
1	Inverness CT (R)	36	11	4	3	36	20	10	6	2	36	12	21	10	5	72	32	40	73
2	Dundee	36	12	4	2	30	13	4	9	5	18	21	16	13	7	48	34	14	61
3	Dunfermline Ath	36	9	3	6	31	23	8	4	6	23	21	17	7	12	54	44	10	58
4	Queen of the S	36	10	4	4	30	15	5	7	6	23	25	15	11	10	53	40	13	56
5	Ross Co	36	9	6	3	28	20	6	5	7	18	24	15	11	10	46	44	2	56
6	Partick Th	36	9	3	6	23	15	5	3	10	20	25	14	6	16	43	40	3	48
7	Raith R (P)	36	6	6	6	20	19	5	3	10	16	28	11	9	16	36	47	-11	42
8	Morton	36	6	4	8	21	24	5	0	13	19	41	11	4	21	40	65	-25	37
9	Airdrie U	36	5	6	7	25	22	3	3	12	16	34	8	9	19	41	56	-15	33
10	Ayr U (P)	36	5	5	8	17	30	2	5	11	12	30	7	10	19	29	60	-31	31

IRN-BRU SCOTTISH FOOTBALL LEAGUE SECOND DIVISION 2009–10

		P	Home					Away					Total						
		P	W	D	L	F	A	W	D	L	F	A	W	D	L	F	A	GD	Pts
1	Stirling Alb	36	7	8	3	30	22	11	3	4	38	26	18	11	7	68	48	20	65
2	Alloa Ath	36	11	2	5	27	21	8	6	4	22	14	19	8	9	49	35	14	65
3	Cowdenbeath (P)¶	36	10	5	3	36	19	6	6	6	24	22	16	11	9	60	41	19	59
4	Brechin C	36	9	6	3	30	20	6	3	9	20	25	15	9	12	50	45	5	54
5	Peterhead	36	8	5	5	23	18	7	1	10	22	31	15	6	15	45	49	-4	51
6	Dumbarton (P)	36	9	4	5	21	32	9	2	7	28	26	14	6	16	49	58	-9	48
7	East Fife	36	6	5	7	23	22	4	6	8	23	31	10	11	15	46	53	-7	41
8	Stenhousemuir	36	5	6	7	16	22	4	7	7	22	20	9	13	14	38	42	-4	40
9	Arbroath	36	4	5	9	22	33	6	5	7	19	22	10	10	16	41	55	-14	40
10	Clyde (R)	36	6	0	12	17	29	2	7	9	20	28	8	7	21	37	57	-20	31

¶Cowdenbeath promoted via play-offs.

IRN-BRU SCOTTISH FOOTBALL LEAGUE THIRD DIVISION 2009–10

		P	Home					Away					Total						
		P	W	D	L	F	A	W	D	L	F	A	W	D	L	F	A	GD	Pts
1	Livingston (R)	36	14	2	2	32	12	10	4	4	31	13	24	6	6	63	25	38	78
2	Forfar Ath¶	36	9	6	3	34	21	9	3	6	25	23	18	9	9	59	44	15	63
3	East Stirling	36	12	2	4	32	19	7	2	9	18	27	19	4	13	50	46	4	61
4	Queen's Park (R)	36	7	2	9	24	27	8	4	6	18	15	15	6	15	42	42	0	51
5	Albion R	36	9	5	4	21	12	4	6	8	14	23	13	11	12	35	35	0	50
6	Berwick R	36	9	3	6	19	18	5	5	8	27	32	14	8	14	46	50	-4	50
7	Stranraer (R)	36	8	5	5	25	23	5	3	10	23	31	13	8	15	48	54	-6	47
8	Annan Ath	36	7	6	5	19	16	4	4	10	22	26	11	10	15	41	42	-1	43
9	Elgin C	36	3	2	13	19	36	6	5	7	27	23	9	7	20	46	59	-13	34
10	Montrose	36	1	6	11	16	35	4	3	11	14	28	5	9	22	30	63	-33	24

¶Forfar Ath promoted via play-offs.
At the end of the 2008–09 season, Livingston were relegated to the Third Division, Airdrie U reinstated in the First Division and Cowdenbeath promoted to the Second Division.

ABERDEEN   Premier League

Year Formed: 1903. *Ground & Address:* Pittodrie Stadium, Pittodrie St, Aberdeen AB24 5QH. *Telephone:* 01224 650400. *Fax:* 01224 644173. *E-mail:* feedback@afc.co.uk *Website:* www.afc.co.uk
Ground Capacity: all seated: 21,421. *Size of Pitch:* 115yd × 72yd.
Chairman: Stewart Milne. *Secretary:* David Johnston.
Manager: Mark McGhee. *Assistant Manager:* Scott Leitch. *U-19 Coach:* Neil Cooper.
Previous Grounds: None.
Record Attendance: 45,061 v Hearts, Scottish Cup 4th rd, 13 Mar 1954.
Record Transfer Fee received: £1.75 million for Eoin Jess to Coventry City (February 1996).
Record Transfer Fee paid: £1m+ for Paul Bernard from Oldham Athletic (September 1995).
Record Victory: 13-0 v Peterhead, Scottish Cup, 9 Feb 1923.
Record Defeat: 0-8 v Celtic, Division 1, 30 Jan 1965.
Most Capped Player: Alex McLeish, 77 (Scotland).
Most League Appearances: 556: Willie Miller, 1973-90.
Most League Goals in Season (Individual): 38: Benny Yorston, Division I, 1929-30.
Most Goals Overall (Individual): 199: Joe Harper, 1969-72; 1976-81.

ABERDEEN 2009–10 LEAGUE RECORD

Match No.	Date	Venue	Opponents	Result	H/T Score	Lg Pos.	Goalscorers	Attendance
1	Aug 15	H	Celtic	L	1-3	0-3	—	Aluko [61]	16,803
2	22	A	Hamilton A	W	3-0	2-0	6	Mulgrew [23], Considine [29], Maguire [63]	3347
3	29	H	Motherwell	D	0-0	0-0	6		11,320
4	Sept 15	A	Falkirk	D	0-0	0-0	—		4724
5	19	A	St Mirren	W	1-0	0-0	5	Mulgrew [88]	10,103
6	26	A	Rangers	D	0-0	0-0	5		47,968
7	Oct 3	A	Kilmarnock	D	1-1	0-0	6	McDonald [84]	4997
8	17	H	Hearts	D	1-1	1-0	6	Miller [42]	11,629
9	24	H	Dundee U	L	0-2	0-2	7		11,766
10	31	A	Hibernian	L	0-2	0-0	7		13,885
11	Nov 7	H	St Johnstone	W	2-1	1-0	6	Aluko [15], Miller (pen) [83]	10,894
12	21	A	Motherwell	D	1-1	0-1	6	McDonald [67]	4668
13	28	H	Rangers	W	1-0	1-0	6	Miller [17]	16,153
14	Dec 5	A	Celtic	L	0-3	0-1	6		56,010
15	12	H	Hamilton A	L	1-2	0-1	6	McDonald [75]	9499
16	19	H	Hibernian	L	0-2	0-1	6		9096
17	Jan 2	A	Dundee U	W	1-0	1-0	—	Mulgrew [15]	10,032
18	12	A	St Mirren	L	0-1	0-0	—		3867
19	23	H	Kilmarnock	W	1-0	0-0	7	Young [49]	12,150
20	27	A	Hearts	W	3-0	1-0	—	Fyvie [12], Mackie [50], Young [75]	14,219
21	30	H	Motherwell	L	0-3	0-1	7		9555
22	Feb 2	A	Falkirk	L	0-1	0-1	—		7741
23	10	A	Hibernian	D	2-2	2-0	—	Paton [25], MacLean [34]	10,469
24	13	H	Celtic	D	4-4	2-2	7	Paton [9], Mackie [37], MacLean 2 (1 pen) [75 (p), 88]	14,898
25	20	A	Falkirk	L	1-3	1-2	7	Mulgrew [5]	4643
26	27	H	Hearts	L	0-0	0-0	7		8316
27	Mar 6	A	Hamilton A	D	1-1	0-0	7	Diamond [76]	2030
28	16	A	St Johnstone	L	0-1	0-1	—		3826
29	20	H	Dundee U	D	2-2	2-2	8	Diamond [32], Paton (pen) [45]	9316
30	27	H	St Mirren	W	2-1	1-0	8	Diamond [37], Aluko [56]	8764
31	Apr 4	A	Kilmarnock	L	0-2	0-1	8		4825
32	7	A	Rangers	L	1-3	0-1	—	Mackie [68]	47,061
33	11	H	St Johnstone	L	1-3	1-2	9	Mackie [17]	7568
34	17	H	Falkirk	W	1-0	1-0	9	MacLean [11]	10,461
35	24	A	St Johnstone	D	1-1	1-0	9	MacLean [16]	3295
36	May 1	H	Hamilton A	L	1-3	0-1	9	Young [85]	7099
37	5	H	Kilmarnock	L	1-2	1-0	—	Kerr [26]	6097
38	8	A	St Mirren	W	1-0	1-0	9	Mair (og) [27]	4022

Final League Position: 9

Honours
League Champions: Division I 1954-55. Premier Division 1979-80, 1983-84, 1984-85; *Runners-up:* Division I 1910-11, 1936-37, 1955-56, 1970-71, 1971-72. Premier Division 1977-78, 1980-81, 1981-82, 1988-89, 1989-90, 1990-91, 1992-93, 1993-94.
Scottish Cup Winners: 1947, 1970, 1982, 1983, 1984, 1986, 1990; *Runners-up:* 1937, 1953, 1954, 1959, 1967, 1978, 1993, 2000.
League Cup Winners: 1955-56, 1976-77, 1985-86, 1989-90, 1995-96; *Runners-up:* 1946-47, 1978-79, 1979-80, 1987-88, 1988-89, 1992-93, 1999-2000.
Drybrough Cup Winners: 1971, 1980.

European: *European Cup:* 12 matches (1980-81, 1984-85, 1985-86); *Cup Winners' Cup:* 39 matches (1967-68, 1970-71, 1978-79, 1982-83 winners, 1983-84 semi-finals, 1986-87, 1990-91, 1993-94); *UEFA Cup:* 56 matches (*Fairs Cup:* 1968-69. *UEFA Cup:* 1971-72, 1972-73, 1973-74, 1977-78, 1979-80, 1981-82, 1987-88, 1988-89, 1989-90, 1991-92, 1994-95, 1996-97, 2000-01, 2002-03, 2007-08). *Europa League:* 2 matches (2009–10).

Club colours: Shirt, Shorts, Stockings: Red.

Goalscorers: *League (36):* MacLean 5 (1 pen), Mackie 4, Mulgrew 4, Aluko 3, Diamond 3, McDonald 3, Miller 3 (1 pen), Paton 3 (1 pen), Young 3, Considine 1, Fyvie 1, Kerr 1, Maguire 1.
Scottish Cup (3): McDonald 1, Mackie 1, Miller 1, own goal 1.
CIS Cup (2): Paton 2.
Europa League (1): Mulgrew 1.

Langfield J 35	Duff S 11+6	Mulgrew C 37	Kerr M 37	Diamond Z 15+1	Ifil J 25+2	Foster R 37	McDonald G 24	Maguire C 5+12	Miller L 18	Aluko S 15+7	Mackie D 21+11	Paton M 22+13	Considine A 15+1	Crawford J 2	Fyvie F 17+9	Grassi D 16+7	Pawlett P 11+3	Megginson M —+2	Ross S 6	Young D 16+4	Wright T —+3	Marshall P 6+3	Low N —+1	Paterson J 7	MacLean S 15+1	Nelson S 3	Grimmer J —+2	Robertson C 1+2	Gibson D 1	Match No.
1	2¹	3	4	5³	6	7	8	9²	10	11	12	13	14																	1
1	13	3	4		6	2		12	10	11	9¹		5		7²	8														2
1		3	4		6	2			10	11	9²	12	5		7¹	8	13													3
1		3	4		6	2	7	14	10	12	9²	11³	5		8³	13														4
1		3	4		6	2	7	12	10	11³	14	9¹	5		8²	13														5
1	12	3	4	6¹	2	7	13	10	14	9³	5	11	8²																	6
1	6	3	4		2	7	11	10		9	5		8¹	12																7
1	2	3	4			7	5	13	10	12	9²	6	8	11¹																8
1		3	4	6	7³		13	10	12	14	9¹	5	8	11²	2															9
1		3	4		6	7	8	9³	10		5	11¹	2³	12																10
1		3	4		2	7	6		10	11¹	12	9	5		8²		13													11
1	13	3	4		2	6	8³		10		14	9³	5		11¹	7²	12													12
1	12	3	4³		2		9¹	10		13	11²		5	8	6	7														13
1	11		5³	2	4	12	10		9¹	6	13³	14	7	3	8²															14
1	6		4		2	8	9²	10	12		11²	5		13	7³	3	14													15
1		3	4		2	8	12	10³		11	9¹	5		6		7														16
1		3	6		2	4	13		10	12	5		9	7⁴	8		11²													17
1		3	4		2	5	12		9	13		10	11	7¹	6²	14	8¹													18
1	13	4	6	5	2	8		9³	14	10²	3	12	7		11¹															19
1	4¹	6	12	5	2	8	13	10		9²			11³	3		7		14												20
1	6		4	5	2	8	13	10		9	13		11²	3¹		7														21
1	3	6	5	4	2	8			9	12		11¹		13			7²	10												22
1	13	3	4	5	12	2	6		11¹		9²	10³	14							7	8									23
1		3	4	5	13	2	7		11¹	9	10²		12							6	8									24
	6	4	5		2	7³		13	9	10²		11	12							14		3¹	8	1						25
1		3	4	5		2	8		12	9	13	11²					6			7¹				10						26
1		3	4	5		2	6		11²12	9				13		7¹								10	8					27
1		3	4	5	6	2	7¹		13	12	9		11											8²	10					28
1	2	3	4	5		6			11³	10	9²		14	12						7				8¹	13					29
1	8	6	4	5		2			11	13	9²		12	3						7¹				10⁴						30
1	8¹	6	4	5		2			11	12	9		10²	3						7	13									31
1		6	8	5	2	4			7²	10	9		14	3³						13				11¹		12				32
1		6²	8	5	2	4			10		9³		13	3						12	7			11¹		14				33
1	11	6	8	5	2	4				9¹	12			3						7				10						34
		4		6		2	5		11¹	10	12		13	3						7	8²			9	1					35
1	6	3	4³	5³	2¹	7⁴			11²				14	10		8								9		1		13		36
	6	5	4		2		8		11¹	9	12			3		7²								10	1		13			37
1	4	3	6		2	5	8		9³	12			13	14										10				7¹	11²	38

AIRDRIE UNITED   Second Division

Year Formed: 1965. *Ground & Address:* Shyberry Excelsior Stadium, Broomfield Park, Craigneuk Avenue, Airdrie ML6 8QZ. *Telephone:* (Stadium) 01236 622000. *Fax:* 01236 626002. *Postal Address:* 60 St Enoch Square, Glasgow G1 4AG.
E-mail: annmarie@airdrieunitedfc.com *Website:* www.airdrieunited.com
Ground Capacity: all seated: 10,171. *Size of Pitch:* 105m × 67m.
Chairman: Jim Ballantyne. *Secretary:* Ann Marie Ballantyne.
Manager: Kenny Black. *Assistant Manager:* Jimmy Boyle.
Record Attendance: 5924 v Motherwell, Scottish Cup 3rd rd, 6 Jan 2007.
Record Victory: 7-0 v Dundee, First Division, 11 March 2006.
Record Defeat: 1-6 v Morton, Second Division, 1 Nov 2003.
Most League Appearances: 101: Mark McGeown, 2002-05.
Most League Goals in Season (Individual): 19: Alan Russell, 2007-08.
Most Goals Overall (Individual): 33: Stephen McKeown, 2002-08.

AIRDRIE UNITED 2009–10 LEAGUE RECORD

Match No.	Date	Venue	Opponents	Result	H/T Score	Lg Pos.	Goalscorers	Attendance
1	Aug 8	A	Ross Co	L	1-2	1-2	—	Baird (pen) 42	1781
2	15	H	Queen of the S	D	1-1	0-0	9	Donnelly 81	1079
3	22	A	Dunfermline Ath	L	0-2	0-1	10		2834
4	29	H	Dundee	D	1-1	1-1	9	Lauchlan (og) 42	1516
5	Sept 12	A	Ayr U	D	1-1	1-0	8	Gemmill 9	1718
6	19	H	Inverness CT	D	1-1	1-0	8	Baird 25	951
7	26	A	Morton	L	0-1	0-0	10		2104
8	Oct 3	A	Partick Th	L	0-2	0-0	10		2639
9	10	H	Raith R	L	1-2	0-1	10	C'Carroll 87	1186
10	17	H	Ross Co	L	0-1	0-0	10		756
11	24	A	Queen of the S	L	0-3	0-2	10		2094
12	31	H	Ayr U	W	3-1	1-1	9	Trouten 2 35, 73, O'Carroll 61	1184
13	Nov 7	A	Dundee	L	1-2	1-2	9	Baird 25	4121
14	14	A	Inverness CT	L	0-2	0-1	10		2780
15	21	H	Morton	L	2-4	2-2	10	Nixon 2, Baird 4	1164
16	Dec 12	H	Partick Th	L	2-5	1-2	10	Baird 2 1, 52	1321
17	15	A	Raith R	D	1-1	0-1	—	Gemmill 84	1247
18	19	A	Ross Co	L	3-5	2-2	—	Waddell 29, O'Carroll 34, McDonald (pen) 78	1823
19	Jan 3	A	Dundee	W	1-0	1-0	—	McDonald (pen) 25	4319
20	23	H	Inverness CT	L	0-1	0-1	10		839
21	Feb 13	A	Partick Th	L	0-2	0-2	10		2404
22	Mar 6	A	Dunfermline Ath	L	0-2	0-0	10		2252
23	9	H	Dunfermline Ath	D	1-1	1-0	—	Waddell 24	703
24	13	H	Ayr U	D	1-1	0-0	—	Keegan 90	1122
25	17	A	Morton	L	1-2	0-1	—	O'Carroll 56	1266
26	20	H	Dundee	W	3-0	0-0	10	McLaughlin 54, O'Carroll 60, Gemmill 75	1172
27	23	A	Inverness CT	L	0-4	0-2	—		2008
28	27	H	Morton	W	3-0	1-0	10	McGuffie (og) 34, Lovering 2 (2 pens) 56, 65	1017
29	Apr 3	A	Partick Th	W	2-0	0-0	10	Lovering (pen) 71, McLaughlin 74	1142
30	12	H	Queen of the S	L	0-1	0-0	—		825
31	14	H	Raith R	W	3-0	1-0	10	Baird 2 5, 65, Waddell 84	815
32	17	H	Ross Co	D	1-1	0-0	10	McDonald (pen) 90	798
33	21	A	Ayr U	W	4-1	0-0	—	Gemmill 47, Baird 3 65, 69, 90	1781
34	24	A	Queen of the S	D	2-2	1-1	10	Gemmill 43, Waddell 50	2541
35	26	A	Raith R	W	1-0	0-0	—	McLaughlin 81	1539
36	May 1	H	Dunfermline Ath	L	0-1	0-1	9		1864

Final League Position: 9

Honours
League Champions: Second Division 2003-04; *Runners-up:* Second Division 2007-08.
League Challenge Cup Winners: 2008-09; *Runners-up:* 2003-04.

Club colours: Shirt: White with red diamond. Shorts: Red. Stockings: Red.

Goalscorers: *League (41):* Baird 11 (1 pen), Gemmill 5, O'Carroll 5, Waddell 4, Lovering 3 (3 pens), McDonald 3 (3 pens), McLaughlin 3, Trouten 2, Donnelly 1, Keegan 1, Nixon 1, own goals 2.
Scottish Cup (7): Baird 2, Donnelly 2, Trouten 2, O'Carroll 1.
CIS Cup (0).
Challenge Cup (0).
Play-Offs (1): Gemmill 1.

Robertson S 34	Smith Darren 11+6	Nixon D 6	McDonald K 21+9	Donnelly B 28+2	Lagana F 14+5	Trouten A 23+3	McLaughlin S 33	Gemmill S 16+8	Baird J 26+5	Waddell R 27+2	McCann R 30+2	Keegan P 4+24	Wuill R 0+10	Lovering P 21+3	Nolan T —+2	Smyth M 24	Keast F —+1	Parratt T 12+1	Storey S 32	Hollis L 2+1	Dain J 1	O'darfl D 1+1	O'Carroll D 28	Match No.
1	2	3³	4¹	5²	6⁸	7	8	9	10	11	12	13	14											1
1	2		4	5		7³	8	12	10	11¹	6	9²	3	14										2
1	2		4	5	9	7²	8		10³		6		3	3¹	12	11	14							3
1	2		4	5	9		8	10²	14		13		1³	12		7		3¹	6					4
1⁶	2		4	5	9¹	13	8	10		12		1	6	7		7		3²		15				5
1			4	5	9¹	6	8		11		2	10	2			7		3						6
1	6³		4	5¹	9²		8			2	10	4	12			7		3		1	13			7
1	12		4	5	9²	7¹	8⁸		10		2		3					6	3		11			8
1	12	6	4	5⁸	10²	7		11		8	3							2¹	3			9		9
1	2²		4¹	5		7	11		10	13	8		2		6			3				9		10
1	8		6			7¹	9		11	13	2³	14	12	3²		4		5				10		11
1	14	6	4	5		7³	8		10²	11	2	12	13					3				9¹		12
1	12	6³	4¹	5		7	8		10	11²	2	14	13					3				9		13
1	12	6³	4	5	13	7	8		10	11²	2	14						3				9		14
1		6¹	12	5	8²	7³	4		11	10	2	13	14					3				9		15
1	4		12	5	8²	7³	6	13	10	11		14		3¹				2				9		16
1	2		4¹	5	8	7		12	10	11		13		3²				6				9		17
1	2		4	5	8²	7⁸		12	10	11		13		3¹				6				9		18
1	12		7	3⁸	8²		6³	13	10	9	2¹		14		4			5				11		19
1		3		14	6²	9	13	11	5³	7	12			4		2	8					10¹		20
1		9²		7³	13⁸	8	12		10	6¹	14		5		4	2	3					11		21
1		8²		12		9	11	6	5	7¹	13			3		4						10		22
1			12	13		7	11	9⁸	8	6²	14		3		4		2¹	5				10		23
1		12	3			8	6	10⁸	9	7	13		5¹		4		2					11²		24
1		8²	3	12	13	7	6		9	2	11	14	5³			4						10		25
1		14	4		6¹	7³	11	12	9	8	13⁸		5		3		2					10²		26
1			4		6	7	11	12	9	8	13	14		3		2¹	5³					10²		27
1			5		7	8	10²		11	4	12	13	3		2		6					5¹		28
1			4		6¹	8	10²	12	9	7	12	14	5		3		2					11³		29
1			4		6	8	11¹	12	9	7			5		3		2					10		30
1	13	3		6	8²		11³	9	7	12	14	5		4		2						10¹		31
1	13	5		7¹	6	12	10	11	8²	14		3³	4			2						9		32
1	13	5¹		6	8	10	11²	7	14		3	4	12²		2							9³		33
1	12			8	6¹	11	9	7	12		5	4	2	3								10²		34
	12			4	8	11¹	9	6		5	3	2	7	1								10		35
		12		6	8²	10	11	7	1³	14	3¹	5	2	4³	1							9		36

ALBION ROVERS Third Division

Year Formed: 1882. *Ground & Address:* Cliftonhill Stadium. Main St, Coatbridge ML5 3RB. *Telephone/Fax:* 01236 606334.
E-mail: general@albionrovers.co.uk *Website:* albionrovers.co.uk
Ground capacity: 1249 (seated 489). *Size of Pitch:* 110yd × 72yd.
Chairman and Secretary: Frank Meade ACMA.
Manager: Paul Martin. *Assistant Manager:* Todd Lumsden. *Physio:* John McMenamy.
Club Nickname(s): The Wee Rovers. *Previous Grounds:* Cowheath Park, Meadow Park, Whifflet.
Record Attendance: 27,381 v Rangers, Scottish Cup 2nd rd, 8 Feb 1936.
Record Transfer Fee received: £40,000 from Motherwell for Bruce Cleland.
Record Transfer Fee paid: £7000 for Gerry McTeague to Stirling Albion, September 1989.
Record Victory: 12-0 v Airdriehill, Scottish Cup, 3 Sept 1887.
Record Defeat: 1-11 v Partick Th, League Cup, 11 Aug 1993.
Most Capped Player: Jock White, 1 (2), Scotland.
Most League Appearances: 399: Murdy Walls, 1921-36.
Most League Goals in Season (Individual): 41: Jim Renwick, Division II, 1932-33.
Most Goals Overall (Individual): 105: Bunty Weir, 1928-31.

ALBION ROVERS 2009–10 LEAGUE RECORD

Match No.	Date	Venue	Opponents	Result	H/T Score	Lg Pos.	Goalscorers	Attendance
1	Aug 8	A	Stranraer	D	1-1	0-1	—	Tyrrell [71]	250
2	15	H	Berwick R	W	2-1	1-1	1	Barr (pen) [7], Walker [62]	322
3	29	H	Livingston	W	1-0	1-0	4	Moyes (og) [27]	485
4	Sept 12	A	Montrose	D	0-0	0-0	3		343
5	19	H	Forfar Ath	D	1-1	1-1	5	O'Byrne [41]	279
6	26	A	Annan Ath	D	0-0	0-0	5		536
7	29	A	Queen's Park	W	1-0	0-0	—	Pollock [56]	376
8	Oct 3	H	East Stirling	W	3-0	3-0	1	Pollock [13], McFarlane 2 [23, 42]	337
9	10	A	Elgin C	W	2-0	2-0	1	McFarlane [31], Canning M [35]	526
10	17	H	Queen's Park	L	0-1	0-0	2		613
11	31	A	Berwick R	L	0-2	0-0	4		471
12	Nov 7	H	Montrose	D	0-0	0-0	3		257
13	21	H	Annan Ath	D	0-0	0-0	5		357
14	24	A	Livingston	L	0-2	0-1	—		726
15	Dec 5	A	Forfar Ath	D	2-2	1-1	5	Donnelly [7], Walker [90]	434
16	12	H	Elgin C	D	1-1	0-0	5	MacAulay (og) [80]	225
17	Jan 23	H	Forfar Ath	L	0-1	0-0	6		227
18	Feb 6	A	Elgin C	L	1-3	0-1	6	McCusker [51]	326
19	9	H	Livingston	L	0-2	0-0	—		587
20	17	A	Annan Ath	W	2-1	1-0	—	Boyle [9], McLeod (pen) [54]	317
21	Mar 2	A	Montrose	D	0-0	0-0	—		249
22	9	H	Berwick R	W	4-1	0-1	—	McLeod [48], Thomson [55], McCusker 2 (1 pen) [59 (d), 69]	227
23	13	H	Montrose	W	1-0	0-0	6	McKeown [79]	217
24	17	A	East Stirling	L	0-2	0-2	—		340
25	20	A	Forfar Ath	D	1-1	1-0	6	Boyle [30]	344
26	23	H	East Stirling	W	2-1	0-0	—	McLeod (pen) [52], Walker [77]	340
27	27	A	Annan Ath	W	1-0	1-0	6	McCusker (pen) [42]	314
28	Apr 3	A	East Stirling	L	1-3	1-2	6	McCusker [29]	325
29	10	H	Elgin C	L	1-2	1-0	6	McCusker [7]	347
30	12	H	Stranraer	W	3-1	1-1	—	Ferry [14], McKeown [62], McLeod [65]	252
31	14	A	Stranraer	L	1-2	0-1	—	McLeod [52]	214
32	17	H	Queen's Park	W	1-0	0-0	6	Donnelly [56]	410
33	20	A	Queen's Park	L	0-1	0-0	—		522
34	24	A	Berwick R	W	2-1	2-0	5	Boyle [7], O'Byrne [33]	460
35	27	A	Livingston	L	0-2	0-2	—		628
36	May 1	H	Stranraer	D	0-0	0-0	5		575

Final League Position: 5

Honours
League Champions: Division II 1933-34, Second Division 1988-89; *Runners-up:* Division II 1913-14, 1937-38, 1947-48.
Scottish Cup Runners-up: 1920.

Club colours: Shirt: Red and yellow stripes. Shorts: Red with yellow flashes. Stockings: Yellow.

Goalscorers: *League (35):* McCusker 6 (2 pens), McLeod 5 (2 pens), Boyle 3, McFarlane 3, Walker 3, Donnelly 2, McKeown 2, O'Byrne 2, Pollock 2, Barr 1 (pen), Canning M 1, Ferry 1, Thomson 1, Tyrrell 1, own goals 2.
Scottish Cup (4): Walker 2, Barr 1, Pollock 1.
CIS Cup (3): Barr 1, McCusker 1, own goal 1.
Challenge Cup (2): Barr 1, McFarlane 1.

Gaston D 21	Reid A 33	McGowan M 36	Canning M 20+2	Benton A 31+1	O'Byrne M 30	McKeown S 17+8	Tyrrell P 26	McFarlane D 18+6	Walker P 15+16	Barr B 11	McCusker M 12+10	Boyle C 21+1	Crozier B —+2	Pollock M 10+3	Stewart P 2+7	Donnelly C 23+2	Ferry D 5+5	O'Boyle J 1+2	Strachan A 4	Gormley D 4	McLeod P 9+8	McGrath P 1	Gilmartin J 2+7	Thomson R 11+4	Lumsden T 8	McLauchin D 7+7	Hoolickin D 7+2	Ewings J 15+1	Bannantyne L 1	Match No.
1	2	3	4¹	5	6	7	8	9²	10	11³	12	13	14																	1
1	2	3	4	5	6		8	9¹	10	11	12	7																		2
1	2	3	4¹	5	6	12	8	9²	10³	11	13	7		14																3
1	2	3	4¹	5	6	12	8	9	10	11		7²				13														4
1	2	3		5	6		8	9	10¹	11		7²			12	13	4													5
1	2	3	4	5	6	7	8	9		11¹					12	10	4													6
1	2¹	3		5	6	12	8	9		11²		7			10	13	4													7
1	2	3	12	5	6	4	8	9²	13	11	7¹	10³	14																	8
1	2	3	4	5	6	7	8	9	13	11¹					12	10²														9
1	2	3	4	5	6		8	9²	12	11		10¹				13														10
1	2¹	3		5	6	4	8	10	11²		9	12	14			13														11
1	2	3		5	6	4¹	8	11²	13		9	7³		10	12	14														12
1	2	3		5	6	8	14	12				10³	11²	4	13	7	3¹													13
1	2	3		5		8	13	12			10	14	4	7³	6	11	9¹													14
1	2	3		5	6	12	8	14	13	7¹		10²		4		11	9³													15
1	2	3		5	6	12	8	13	14	7¹		10²		4		11	9³													16
1	6	5	2	3	4	14	8	12	11²	10¹	9³	7				13														17
1	2	5		4	6	8	12	11	10¹		3	7				9														18
1	2	5	7³	4		9²	8	10¹	11	6						12					3¹		13	14						19
1	2	3	8	5		9¹	11	7²		4	14					12								6	10³	13				20
1⁰	2	5	8	4		10¹	9		6²	7													13	3	11	12	15			21
	2	3	4	5		8	13	9²	11³	7											14		12	6	10¹			1		22
	2	5		3	8	7	11¹	10²	9³							12					14		6	4	13			1		23
	2	5	6		3	7²		14	12	9³		8				11					13		4	10¹				1		24
	2	5		4	9	8	10¹	13	11²	6		7				12							3					1		25
	5	7		3	2	8¹	14	10²	9	13		11³									4		6	12				1		26
	2	5	3	4	12	7	11²	10³	9¹	8		13				6					14		12	7¹		14		1		27
	5	3	6	2	4	8	13	10²	9			11³				12					7¹		14					1		28
	6	4	3	9	8	11³	12	10³	7¹			13				14					2		5					1		29
	2	5	8	3	4	12		14	13							9					11²		7¹	6		10³		1		30
	2	3	13	4		11	9			6						12							10	5		7²	1		8¹	31
	2	5	3	4	8	6		12	13		7	14				11²					9³			10¹				1		32
	2	5	12	3	4			13	11³		8	7				10²					6		14	9¹		1				33
	2	5	8¹	4	3		11³	10	9²		7	12				7					13		6	14				1		34
	2	3		4	5	7	13	10²				8				11							12	6¹		9		1		35
	2	5	3	4	7	6		12				10²	9³			8					14		11¹			13		1		36

ALLOA ATHLETIC   Second Division

Year Formed: 1878. *Ground & Address:* Recreation Park, Clackmannan Rd, Alloa FK10 1RY. *Telephone:* 01259 722695. *Fax:* 01259 210886. *E-mail:* ewen.cameron@scra.gsi.gov.uk *Website:* www.alloaathletic.co.uk
Ground Capacity: total: 3100, seated: 400. *Size of Pitch:* 101m × 69m.
Honorary President: George Ormiston. *Chairman:* Robert Hopkins. *Secretary:* Ewen G. Cameron.
Manager: Allan Maitland. *Assistant Manager:* James Ward. *Coach:* Ronnie Scott. *Physio:* Jim Law.
Club Nickname(s): The Wasps. *Previous Grounds:* West End Public Park, Gabberston Park, Belleview Park.
Record Attendance: 13,000 v Dunfermline Athletic, Scottish Cup 3rd rd replay, 26 Feb 1939.
Record Transfer Fee received: £100,000 for Martin Cameron to Bristol Rovers.
Record Transfer Fee paid: £26,000 for Ross Hamilton from Stenhousemuir.
Record Victory: 9-0 v Selkirk, Scottish Cup First Round, 28 November 2005.
Record Defeat: 0-10 v Dundee, Division II, 8 Mar 1947 v Third Lanark, League Cup, 8 Aug 1953.
Most Capped Player: Jock Hepburn, 1, Scotland.
Most League Goals in Season (Individual): 49: 'Wee' Willie Crilley, Division II, 1921-22.

ALLOA ATHLETIC 2009–10 LEAGUE RECORD

Match No.	Date	Venue	Opponents	Result	H/T Score	Lg Pos.	Goalscorers	Attendance
1	Aug 8	A	Dumbarton	W 3-1	1-0	—	Grant [43], Carrigan [59], Noble [61]	864
2	15	H	Peterhead	W 1-0	0-0	2	Noble [75]	446
3	22	H	Cowdenbeath	D 1-1	1-1	2	Scott [41]	365
4	29	A	Clyde	W 1-0	1-0	1	Carrigan [17]	773
5	Sept 12	H	Stirling A	W 1-0	1-0	1	Scott [13]	1201
6	19	A	Stenhousemuir	L 0-1	0-1	2		698
7	26	H	Arbroath	L 0-1	0-1	2		469
8	Oct 3	H	East Fife	D 0-0	0-0	2		580
9	10	A	Brechin C	L 1-2	1-1	4	Grant [4]	417
10	17	H	Dumbarton	L 1-3	1-2	4	Gilhaney [41]	575
11	24	A	Peterhead	D 0-0	0-0	4		485
12	31	H	Clyde	W 2-0	1-0	4	Carrigan [14], Noble [87]	649
13	Nov 7	A	Stirling A	W 1-0	1-0	4	Scott (pen) [23]	986
14	14	H	Stenhousemuir	L 1-4	0-3	4	Thomson I (og) [67]	544
15	Dec 2	A	Arbroath	D 2-2	1-0	—	Ferguson B [5], Agnew [46]	328
16	5	A	East Fife	W 2-0	1-0	—	Carroll [30], Russell [83]	509
17	12	H	Brechin C	W 2-1	0-0	3	Carrigan (pen) [76], Agnew [89]	394
18	Jan 23	A	Stenhousemuir	W 2-0	2-0	3	Ferguson B [15], Prunty [25]	554
19	30	H	Arbroath	W 1-0	0-0	—	Prunty [90]	535
20	Feb 6	A	Brechin C	D 1-1	0-0	2	Noble [47]	434
21	9	H	Cowdenbeath	W 2-1	1-0	—	Prunty [16], Noble [58]	638
22	13	H	East Fife	W 2-0	1-0	1	Noble 2 [26, 84]	670
23	27	H	Peterhead	W 2-1	1-1	—	Noble [29], MacDonald (og) [79]	448
24	Mar 6	H	Clyde	D 2-2	1-1	1	Scott [35], McClune [90]	628
25	9	A	Dumbarton	L 1-3	0-1	—	Smith (og) [62]	552
26	13	A	Stirling A	W 3-0	1-0	1	Gormley [29], Prunty 2 [71, 88]	1036
27	16	A	Cowdenbeath	D 1-1	0-0	—	Ferguson B [53]	413
28	20	H	Stenhousemuir	W 2-1	0-1	1	Gormley [89], Prunty [90]	550
29	23	H	Stirling A	W 2-1	1-1	—	Carroll [11], Walker [90]	1147
30	27	A	Arbroath	D 0-0	0-0	1		604
31	Apr 3	A	East Fife	W 1-0	0-0	1	McAvoy [55]	637
32	7	A	Clyde	W 2-0	1-0	—	Noble [20], Prunty [85]	465
33	10	H	Brechin C	L 2-3	0-1	1	Walker [83], Noble [68]	626
34	17	H	Dumbarton	L 1-2	0-1	1	Scott (pen) [55]	622
35	24	A	Peterhead	L 0-2	0-1	2		561
36	May 1	H	Cowdenbeath	W 3-1	0-1	2	Prunty [74], Scott 2 (1 pen) [79 (p), 83]	1125

Final League Position: 2

Honours
League Champions: Division II 1921-22; Third Division 1997-98. *Runners-up:* Division II 1938-39. Second Division 1976-77, 1981-82, 1984-85, 1988-89, 1999-2000, 2001-02.
League Challenge Cup Winners: 1999-2000; *Runners-up:* 2001-02.

Club colours: Shirt: Black with gold hoops on front. Shorts: Black. Stockings: Black.

Goalscorers: *League (49):* Noble 10, Prunty 8, Scott 7 (3 pens), Carrigan 4 (1 pen), Ferguson B 3, Agnew 2, Carroll 2, Gormley 2, Grant 2, Walker 2, Gilhaney 1, McAvoy 1, McClune 1, Russell 1, own goals 3.
Scottish Cup (2): Brown 1, Gilhaney 1.
CIS Cup (0).
Challenge Cup (2): Spence 1, own goal 1.
Play-Offs (1): Gormley 1.

Crawford D 36	McClune D 26	Buist S 23+1	Townsley C 18+3	McCafferty M 16+2	Scott A 27+6	Grant J 29+2	Brown M 31+1	Noble S 24+5	Carrigan B 11+2	Agnew S 11+4	Carroll G 19+10	Kerr H 2+11	Spence G —+1	Walker S 31	Gilhaney M 16+3	Ferguson B 25+2	Welsh K 3	Russell I 4+2	Thomson J —+3	Phelps R —+2	Bloom J 5	Prunty B 18	Gormley D 7+10	Philip R —+3	Main D 1+1	Hay J —+5	Stevenson A 5+1	Wilson D —+4	McAvoy D 7+1	Craig C 1+3	Match No.
1	2	3	4	5	6¹	7	8	9²	10³	11	12	13	14																		1
1	2	3		5	6²	7	8	9	10¹	11	12	13		4																	2
1	2	3		5	6	7	8	9¹		11	10²	¹2		4	13																3
1		3		5	6¹	7	8		2	11		¹2		4	9	10															4
1		3			6	7	5		8¹	11²	12			4	9	10		2	¹3												5
1		3	12		8²	7	5	13		11			14	4	9³	10		2¹	6												6
1		3	12		8		6⁸	5¹	7²	11	2³	13		4	9	10			14												7
1	6	3	8		5	7	12	11		2¹				4	9	10															8
1		4	5		9¹	7	8	12	10²	11		13		3	6	2															9
1		4	3¹	11	6		2³	12	9²	10	14			5	7	8		3													10
1	2		4²	3	12	7	6	9		14	13	10¹		5	11³	8															11
1	2	4		3	11	7	6	10²	9¹	12				5		8			13												12
1	4	3	14	2	11³	7	6	10²	9		12	13		5		8¹															13
1	2	4		3¹	11	7	6	10	9		12			5		8															14
1	3	2	4		14	13	6		10	11¹	7²			5	12	8		9³													15
1	5	2	3		9²	7		11³	13	8				4	6¹	12		10	14												16
1	2	4	5	3	12	8	6	10¹	13	14	7²				11³		9														17
1	2		4		9	7²	8⁹	11			13	14		3	6								5	10¹	12						18
1	2	12	3		9	6	8	11			14			4¹		7²							5³	10	13						19
1	2	8¹			10	6	4	9			12			3		7							5	11							20
1	2		13		9²	7	3	11			8			4		6							5	10¹	12						21
1	2				12	6	3	11			7			4	9²	8¹							5	10³	13	14					22
1	2	5¹	4		11	7	8	9			6			3	12								10²	13							23
1	2		3		6	7¹	12	11			8²			4	9²	13	5						10	14							24
1	2	4	3		13	14	6	12			7			5¹	11³	8							9	10²							25
1	2²		5			7	3	11³			6				9¹	8							10	14	13	4	12				26
1				5	10⁸	6	8				7	12²			9¹								9¹	11³		14	13	2			27
	3			5¹			8				7	9¹		4	6²			14					10	11			12	2	13		28
1	2	3		9²			8				7			4					13				10¹	11³	14		12	6	5		29
1	2	3		11			7		12		9			4		6							10¹				8		5		30
1	2	8	3				9				7					6							10			12	4¹	13	5	11²	31
1	2³	3¹	4		6²	8	7	11			13					9							10	14				12	5²		32
1	2		3		9²	6	8	11			7¹			4									10	13			14		5³	12	33
1	2⁸	3	12		9³	8	7¹	11						4		6							10	13				14	5²		34
1		3	2		12	7		10				8¹		4	9								11	6²					5	13	35
1	2	4²	3		6	7		11¹						5	9								10	8					13	12	36

ANNAN ATHLETIC

Third Division

Year Formed: 1942. *Ground & Address:* Galabank, North Street, Annan DG12 5DQ. *Telephone:* 01461 204108.
E-mail: annanathleticfc@aol.com *Website:* www.annanathleticfc
Ground capacity: 3000 (426 seated). *Size of Pitch:* 100m × 69m.
Chairman: Henry McClelland.
Secretary: Alan Irving.
Manager: Harry Cairney.
Assistant Manager: Derek Townsley.
Coaches: George Paterson and Pietro Baldotto.
Club Nickname: Galabankies.
Most League Appearances: 63: Kevin Neilson, 2008-10.
Most League Goals in Season (Individual): 15: Mike Jack, 2008-09.
Most Goals Overall (Individual): 18: Mike Jack, 2008-10.

ANNAN ATHLETIC 2009–10 LEAGUE RECORD

Match No.	Date	Venue	Opponents	Result	H/T Score	Lg Pos.	Goalscorers	Attendance
1	Aug 8	A	Berwick R	L	1-2	1-1	—	Gilfillan [19]	438
2	15	H	East Stirling	L	0-1	0-0	10		525
3	22	A	Stranraer	L	0-2	0-1	10		358
4	29	A	Elgin C	D	1-1	1-0	9	Gilfillan [38]	457
5	Sept 12	H	Forfar Ath	W	1-0	0-0	8	Steele [73]	525
6	19	A	Queen's Park	D	0-0	0-0	8		581
7	26	H	Albion R	D	0-0	0-0	7		536
8	Oct 10	H	Montrose	W	2-0	0-0	7	Sloan L (pen) [66], McBeth [73]	476
9	13	A	Livingston	L	0-2	0-2	—		771
10	17	H	Stranraer	W	1-0	0-0	6	Gilfillan [75]	647
11	31	A	East Stirling	W	3-1	1-1	6	Watson [38], Cox 2 [54, 69]	359
12	Nov 7	A	Forfar Ath	L	1-2	0-2	6	Cox [52]	477
13	14	H	Elgin C	L	0-2	0-0	6		416
14	21	A	Albion R	D	0-0	0-0	6		357
15	Dec 5	H	Queen's Park	W	3-1	1-0	6	Jack 2 [44, 86], Gilfillan [80]	433
16	12	A	Montrose	D	0-0	0-0	6		250
17	Jan 23	A	Queen's Park	L	2-3	1-0	7	McBeth [40], Anson [60]	484
18	Feb 9	H	Berwick R	D	1-1	0-1	—	Bell [58]	382
19	13	A	Livingston	L	2-3	2-0	8	Neilson [17], Cox [45]	1085
20	17	H	Albion R	L	1-2	0-1	—	Watson [72]	317
21	20	A	Berwick R	W	2-0	2-0	7	Jardine [11], Bell [37]	385
22	27	H	East Stirling	W	1-0	0-0	—	Bell [49]	613
23	Mar 2	H	Forfar Ath	D	1-1	0-1	—	Bell [52]	373
24	6	H	Elgin C	D	3-3	2-1	6	Bell 2 [22, 49], Sloan L [37]	364
25	13	A	Forfar Ath	W	5-1	2-1	7	O'Connor [25], Bell [34], Sloan L [72], Anson 2 [83, 87]	424
26	16	H	Livingston	D	0-0	0-0	—		604
27	20	H	Queen's Park	L	0-2	0-1	7		581
28	24	A	Stranraer	L	2-3	0-2	—	Anson [74], Storey [89]	259
29	27	A	Albion R	L	0-1	0-1	7		314
30	Apr 3	H	Livingston	W	2-0	1-0	7	Bell [4], Storey [82]	831
31	6	A	Elgin C	L	0-1	0-1	—		235
32	10	A	Montrose	W	2-1	2-0	7	Jardine [4], Cox [12]	294
33	13	H	Montrose	D	0-0	0-0	—		278
34	17	H	Stranraer	W	3-2	2-0	7	Sloan L [16], Gilfillan [29], Bell [46]	392
35	24	A	East Stirling	L	1-3	0-2	7	Jack [60]	335
36	May 1	H	Berwick R	L	0-1	0-1	8		561

Final League Position: 8

Honours
East of Scotland Premier League: Winners (4).
East of Scotland League Cup: Winners (1).
East of Scotland Div 1: Winners (1).
South of Scotland League: Winners (2).
South of Scotland League Cup: Winners (4).
Scottish Challenge Cup South: Winners (1).
Scottish Qualifying Cup South: Winners (1).

Club colours: Shirt: Black and gold stripes. Shorts: Black. Stockings: Black with gold trim.

Goalscorers: *League (41):* Bell 9, Cox 5, Gilfillan 5, Anson 4, Sloan L 4 (1 pen), Jack 3, Jardine 2, McBeth 2, Storey 2, Watson 2, Neilson 1, O'Connor 1, Steele 1.
Scottish Cup (1): Watson 1.
CIS Cup (0).
Challenge Cup (7): Jack 2 (1 pen), Bell 1, Gilfillan 1, Inglis 1, Storey 1, Watson 1.

Summersgill C 20	Watson P 32+1	McBeth J 30+4	Townsley D 9	Neilson K 30+1	Jack M 20+6	Steele J 27+4	Gilfillan B 33	Cox D 29+1	Bell G 29+4	Sloan L 27+4	Redpath G —+4	Sloan S 18+12	Storey P 11+23	Jardine C 31	Anson S 6+12	Kelly G 15	Muirhead A 22+1	Inglis A 9+3	Adamson R 1	Hoolickin L —+1	O'Connor S 2	Clarke T —+1	Muir N 2	Jamieson J 1+1	Phillips J —+1	Match No.
1	2	3	4	5	6¹	7²	8	9	10³	11	12	13	14													1
1	2	3	4³	5	6²	7		9	10¹	13	14	1	12	8												2
1	2	3		5	12	7²	6	9³	14	11		4¹	13		8	10										3
	2	3		5	7	12	6	9¹	10²	11		4	13			1	8									4
	2			5	7	8	6	9	10					11		1	3	4								5
	2			5	7	6¹	9		8²	13	12	10	11			1	3	4								6
	2	12		5	7	6¹	9	8	10	13				11²		1	3	4								7
1	4	3		5		2	6	9	10¹	12				11²	8	13	7									8
1	4	3		5		12	6	9¹	10			2³	11		8²	13	7	4								9
1	4	3		5			6	9¹	10	12		2	11		7²	13										10
4¹	3			5		2	6	9²	10³	11		12	13		8	14	1	7								11
4	3			5	13	2	6	9	10¹	11³			12		8²	14	1	7								12
4⁴	3²			5		2	6	9	12	11¹		13	10³		8	14	1	7								13
	3	4	5	6¹	2	7	9		11					12	8		1			10²	13					14
	3	4	5	6		2	9³	13	11¹					14	12	8	10²	1	7							15
	5	3	4	7		2	10	9						13	12	8²	11¹	1	6							16
11	7		3	5¹	13		8	10						4	12	6	9²	1	2							17
	4	3		5	6¹		9	10	11					7	12	8		1	7							18
	4	3	2	5		6	9	11	10²					7	13	8¹	1				12					19
	4	3	2	5	12	14	6	9	11²	10³				7	13	8¹	1									20
	3	5		4		2	6	10¹	11²	9				12	13	8	1	7								21
1	2	6		3	14	5²	7	9	11³	10				13	12	8		4								22
1	2	6		3		5	7	9	11	10					8			4								23
1	2	6		7¹	5	3		11	9					12	13	8		4			10²					24
1	3	5		7	2	4		9²	11					13		8	12	6			10¹					25
1	2	6		7	5	3		11²	10					13	12	8	9¹	4								26
1	2¹	6		12	7	5	3	13	11	10				14	8³	9²		4								27
1	13	6¹	2	3	7²	5	4		11	10				12	9	8³	14									28
1	2	8		3		5	4		11	9				6²	10¹	7	12					13				29
1	2	6		3	12	5¹	4	9	11²	10³				7	13	8	14									30
1	2	14		3	6	5³	4	10	11	9¹				8²	12	7	13									31
1	4	13		5	7¹	2	3	10		11²				6	9³	8	14	12								32
1	3	12		4	6¹	5	2	9	13	10²				7	11	8										33
1	2	6		3	13	5	7	9	11¹	10²				12	8		4									34
1⁸	4	5		8¹	2	3	10	9²	11				12	13	7								6	15		35
	2	8	3¹		5		10³	11²	9	6	12	7	13										4	1	14	36

ARBROATH
Third Division

Year Formed: 1878. *Ground & Address:* Gayfield Park, Arbroath DD11 1QB. *Telephone:* 01241 872157. *Fax:* 01241 431125. *E-mail:* afc@gayfield.fsnet.co.uk *Website:* www.arbroathfc.co.uk
Ground Capacity: 4165 (seated 860; standing 3305). *Size of Pitch:* 115yd × 71yd.
Chairman: John D. Christison. *Secretary:* Dr Gary Callon. *Administrator:* Mike Cargill.
Manager: Paul Sheerin. *Assistant Manager:* Robbie Raeside. *Physio:* Jim Crosby.
Club Nickname(s): The Red Lichties. *Previous Grounds:* None.
Record Attendance: 13,510 v Rangers, Scottish Cup 3rd rd, 23 Feb 1952.
Record Transfer Fee received: £120,000 for Paul Tosh to Dundee (Aug 1993).
Record Transfer Fee paid: £20,000 for Douglas Robb from Montrose (1981).
Record Victory: 36-0 v Bon Accord, Scottish Cup 1st rd, 12 Sept 1885.
Record Defeat: 1-9 v Celtic, League Cup 3rd rd, 25 Aug 1993.
Most Capped Player: Ned Doig, 2 (5), Scotland.
Most League Appearances: 445: Tom Cargill, 1966-81.
Most League Goals in Season (Individual): 45: Dave Easson. Division II, 1958-59.
Most Goals Overall (Individual): 120: Jimmy Jack, 1966-71.

ARBROATH 2009–10 LEAGUE RECORD

Match No.	Date	Venue	Opponents	Result	H/T Score	Lg Pos.	Goalscorers	Attendance
1	Aug 8	A	Cowdenbeath	W 2-1	0-0	—	Sellars [80], Scott [84]	302
2	15	H	Dumbarton	W 3-1	1-0	1	Sellars [15], Hislop [46], Ross [90]	605
3	22	A	East Fife	D 1-1	0-0	1	Ross [51]	770
4	29	A	Stenhousemuir	L 0-3	0-0	3		543
5	Sept 12	H	Brechin C	L 1-4	0-0	6	Raeside [70]	649
6	19	H	Peterhead	L 0-1	0-1	8		476
7	26	A	Alloa Ath	W 1-0	1-0	6	Scott (pen) [29]	469
8	Oct 10	A	Stirling A	D 2-2	2-2	6	Scott 2 [7, 18]	689
9	14	H	Clyde	L 0-3	0-1	—		554
10	17	H	Cowdenbeath	L 0-1	0-1	8		479
11	24	A	Dumbarton	L 0-1	0-1	9		696
12	31	H	Stenhousemuir	L 0-3	0-1	10		402
13	Nov 7	A	Brechin C	D 0-0	0-0	9		617
14	14	A	Peterhead	W 2-1	1-0	8	Sellars [45], Dorris [79]	455
15	Dec 2	A	Alloa Ath	D 2-2	0-1	—	Hislop 2 (1 pen) [60, 70 (p)]	328
16	5	A	Clyde	L 0-1	0-1	—		552
17	12	H	Stirling A	L 3-4	0-3	9	Hislop 2 [74, 83], Scott [76]	491
18	Jan 16	A	Stenhousemuir	D 1-1	0-0	—	Hislop [86]	443
19	23	H	Peterhead	L 1-4	1-3	9	Winters [13]	465
20	27	H	East Fife	L 0-1	0-0	—		376
21	30	A	Alloa Ath	L 0-1	0-0	—		535
22	Feb 13	H	Clyde	W 2-0	0-0	9	Ross [79], Dorris [90]	524
23	27	H	Dumbarton	W 3-1	0-1	—	Dorris [55], Redman [74], Booth [88]	521
24	Mar 6	H	Stenhousemuir	D 1-1	1-1	9	Redman [9]	458
25	9	A	Cowdenbeath	L 1-2	1-0	—	Lunan [19]	246
26	13	A	Brechin C	W 2-0	2-0	9	Hislop [1], Ross [31]	637
27	16	A	East Fife	L 1-3	1-1	—	Hislop [6]	480
28	20	A	Peterhead	L 0-3	0-1	9		483
29	24	H	Brechin C	W 1-0	1-0	—	Rattray [14]	386
30	27	A	Alloa Ath	D 0-0	0-0	9		604
31	Apr 3	A	Clyde	W 2-0	2-0	9	Scott [9], Megginson [32]	635
32	10	H	Stirling A	L 2-4	1-1	9	McLean (pen) [45], Megginson [72]	525
33	12	A	Stirling A	D 2-2	1-1	—	Dorris 2 [20, 73]	365
34	17	H	Cowdenbeath	D 1-1	1-0	9	Gibson [41]	488
35	24	A	Dumbarton	W 2-0	1-0	9	Redman [39], Megginson [49]	836
36	May 1	H	East Fife	D 2-2	0-0	9	Dorris [60], Redman [71]	512

Final League Position: 9

Honours
League Runners-up: Division II 1934-35, 1958-59, 1967-68, 1971-72; Second Division 2000-01; Third Division 1997-98, 2007-08.
Scottish Cup: Quarter-finals 1993.

Club colours: Shirt: Maroon with white trim. Shorts: Maroon. Stockings: Maroon.

Goalscorers: *League (41):* Hislop 8 (1 pen), Dorris 6, Scott 6 (1 pen), Redman 4, Ross 4, Megginson 3, Sellars 3, Booth 1, Gibson 1, Lunan 1, McLean 1 (pen), Raeside 1, Rattray 1, Winters 1.
Scottish Cup (0).
CIS Cup (3): Bishop 1, Raeside 1, Sellars 1.
Challenge Cup (1): Redman 1.
Play-Offs (6): McCulloch 1, Megginson 1, Moyes 1, Nimmo 1, Redman 1, Ross 1.

Hill D 36	Rennie S 17+5	Raeside R 6+1	Rattray A 30	McCulloch M 27+1	Lunan P 19+7	Bishop J 12+1	Gibson K 29+3	Dorris S 27+3	Hislop S 24+5	Sellars B 12	Scott B 11+9	Watson P 3+1	Milne K —+10	Dobbins I 11	McMullan K 12+7	Ross R 9+16	Redman J 20+4	McCaffrey D 6	Gates S —+2	McKay D 1	McLean K 15+5	Weir J —+1	Moyes E 16	Faulds K 3	Moffat K —+1	Winters D 2	Jackson A 6+2	McLaughlin J 11	Nimmo 14+5	Booth C 15	McGuire P 7	Megginson M 5	Morrison S —+1	McIlrevey M —+3	Match No.
1	2	3	4	5	6	7	8	9[2]	10[1]	11[3]	12	13	14																						1
1	2		4	5	6	7	8	9[1]	10[2]	11				3	12	13																			2
1	2	7[1]	4	5	6[3]	14	8	12	10	11[2]			9[1]	3	13[4]																				3
1	2	7[1]	4	5	6		8	11	10[2]			12		3		9	13																		4
1	2	5			6		8	11[2]	10				7	13	3	4[1]	12	9[4]																	5
1	12		4[1]	9	7[3]	6		11[2]	10	8	5		14	3	13					2															6
1	5		4	11	7[1]	6		14	10[3]	9[2]				3	12	13	8	2																	7
1	2[3]	12	4[1]	11		5		13	10[2]	9	7			6	14		8	3																	8
1	2		11	13	5	4[1]		8[2]	10	9[3]				6	12	14	7	3																	9
1	5	4		11	7		8[1]		10[2]	9				14	6	2[3]	13	12	3																10
1	2		9[2]	7	4	8		11	10[3]					12	3	6	14	13	5[1]																11
1		5		11	7[2]	6	8		10[1]	9[3]	14	4	2	12	3		13																		12
1	2		4	5	6	3	7	12	11	10[2]					13	9[1]	8																		13
1	2		5	3	7	4	6[2]	12	11	10					13	9[1]	8																		14
1	14		5	3	7	4[3]	6	10	13	9[1]	11[2]			2	12		8																		15
1	3		2		7		4	6		8	10[1]		13		9	11[2]	5		12																16
1	5		4[1]	14		6	7	10	8[2]	13					3		2				9[3]	11	12												17
1			4	5	8		7	11	10		12				2						9[2]		3				6[1]	13							18
1			4	5	13		8[2]	7	10		12				2	14					9[1]		3				6	11[3]							19
1	3		4	5	8		7	6	10		13				2						12						9[1]	11[2]							20
1			3	5	12		8	6	10[4]		13										9[1]		4		7[3]		11[2]	2	14						21
1			4	6			8	11		10[1]					13						9		3				12	2	7[2]	5					22
1			3	5[2]			7	11							13	12					8		4				10	2	6[1]	9					23
1			4	12			7	6	11								8				9		3				10[1]	2		5					24
1			4	5	6[3]		8	10[2]	12			2	13	7							11[1]		3					14		9					25
1			4	12			8	6	11							10[1]	9				7		5						3	2					26
1			4[1]	14	13		8	6	11[3]								12	10[2]	7		9								3	5	2				27
1	13		4	5[3]		7[1]	11	10							6						8[2]						14	2	12	9	3				28
1		2		5			7	6[2]	11[3]	13	14						12				4						10	8		9	3[1]				29
1	13		3	7			6[2]	5	11[1]	12	14						8				4						10[3]	2		9					30
1			5	6			11								9[1]		12	2			8		4				3	7				10[2]	13		31
1	5[1]		3	7[3]			13	10	12				14	8			6[2]	2										9	4	11					32
1	14			8			7	6	11[1]				2[3]	12			9[2]	4										13	5	3	10				33
1	5[2]		3	9			6[1]	11					10[3]	7			12	4										14	8	2			13	34
1			4	5			12	2					6[2]	7			13	3									8	11[1]	9			10[3]	14	35
1			4	5			12	2					6[2]	8			13	3									7	11[1]	9			10[3]	14	36

AYR UNITED   Second Division

Year Formed: 1910. *Ground & Address:* Somerset Park, Tryfield Place, Ayr KA8 9NB. *Telephone:* 01292 263435.
Fax: 01292 281314. *E-mail:* info@ayrunitedfc.co.uk *Website:* ayrunitedfc.co.uk
Ground Capacity: 10,185, seated: 1597. *Size of Pitch:* 101m × 66m.
Chairman and Managing Director: Lachlan Cameron.
Manager: Brian Reid. *Assistant Manager:* Scott MacKenzie. *Physio:* Kevin MacLellan.
Club Nickname(s): The Honest Men. *Previous Grounds:* None.
Record Attendance: 25,225 v Rangers, Division I, 13 Sept 1969.
Record Transfer Fee received: £300,000 for Steven Nicol to Liverpool (Oct 1981).
Record Transfer Fee paid: £90,000 for Mark Campbell from Stranraer (March 1999).
Record Victory: 11-1 v Dumbarton, League Cup, 13 Aug 1952.
Record Defeat: 0-9 in Division I v Rangers (1929); v Hearts (1931); B Division v Third Lanark (1954).
Most Capped Player: Jim Nisbet, 3, Scotland.
Most League Appearances: 459: John Murphy, 1963-78.
Most League League and Cup Goals in Season (Individual): 66: Jimmy Smith, 1927-28.
Most League and Cup Goals Overall (Individual): 213: Peter Price, 1955-61.

AYR UNITED 2009–10 LEAGUE RECORD

Match No.	Date	Venue	Opponents	Result		H/T Score	Lg Pos.	Goalscorers	Attendance
1	Aug 8	H	Partick Th	D	1-1	1-1	—	Roberts [5]	3078
2	15	A	Inverness CT	D	0-0	0-0	7		3297
3	22	H	Morton	L	0-2	0-1	9		2304
4	29	A	Queen of the S	L	0-2	0-1	10		3034
5	Sept 12	H	Airdrie U	D	1-1	0-1	9	Roberts [48]	1718
6	19	A	Ross Co	L	1-2	0-2	9	Roberts [53]	1885
7	26	H	Raith R	W	1-0	1-0	7	Connolly [12]	1783
8	Oct 10	A	Dunfermline Ath	L	1-3	0-0	9	Aitken C (pen) [74]	2460
9	14	H	Dundee	D	2-2	0-1	—	McGowan R [73], Stevenson [86]	1710
10	17	A	Partick Th	L	0-2	0-2	9		3055
11	24	H	Inverness CT	L	1-5	1-4	9	Roberts [13]	1609
12	31	A	Airdrie U	L	1-3	1-1	10	McCann (og) [45]	1184
13	Nov 7	H	Queen of the S	L	0-1	0-1	10		2453
14	14	H	Ross Co	D	1-1	0-1	9	Roberts (pen) [82]	1236
15	21	A	Raith R	D	0-0	0-0	9		1460
16	Dec 5	H	Dunfermline Ath	W	1-0	0-0	9	Stevenson [52]	1625
17	12	A	Dundee	L	1-3	1-1	9	Reynolds [3]	4323
18	Jan 23	A	Ross Co	L	0-1	0-0	9		1935
19	Feb 16	A	Queen of the S	L	0-3	0-1	—		1721
20	20	A	Dunfermline Ath	W	1-0	1-0	—	McManus [37]	2429
21	27	A	Inverness CT	D	3-3	2-1	—	Aitken A [25], Roberts [30], McManus [71]	2843
22	Mar 6	H	Morton	W	2-0	1-0	9	Roberts [26], McManus (pen) [49]	2145
23	10	H	Partick Th	W	1-0	1-0	—	Bowey [35]	1505
24	13	A	Airdrie U	D	1-1	0-0	—	McKay [89]	1122
25	17	H	Dundee	D	1-1	1-1	—	Lafferty [42]	1375
26	20	H	Queen of the S	W	3-0	1-0	8	McManus [25], McKay [79], Roberts (pen) [89]	2139
27	27	A	Raith R	D	1-1	1-0	8	Mitchell [14]	1872
28	30	A	Morton	L	0-1	0-0	—		1289
29	Apr 3	A	Dundee	L	0-3	0-2	9		4270
30	7	H	Raith R	L	0-2	0-2	—		1433
31	10	H	Dunfermline Ath	L	1-2	1-1	—	McManus [45]	1367
32	17	A	Partick Th	W	1-0	0-0	9	McKay [79]	1877
33	21	H	Airdrie U	L	1-4	0-0	—	Keenan [67]	1781
34	24	A	Inverness CT	L	0-7	0-4	9		1804
35	28	H	Ross Co	L	0-1	0-1	—		1032
36	May 1	A	Morton	L	1-2	1-0	10	McKay [20]	3771

Final League Position: 10

Honours
League Champions: Division II 1911-12, 1912-13, 1927-28, 1936-37, 1958-59, 1965-66. Second Division 1987-88, 1996-97;
Runners-up: Division II 1910-11, 1955-56, 1968-69. Second Divison 2008-09.
Scottish Cup: Semi-finals 2002.
League Cup: Runners-up: 2001-02.
B&Q Cup Runners-up: 1990-91, 1991-92.

Club colours: Shirt: White with black hoops. Shorts: White. Stockings: White.

Goalscorers: *League (29):* Roberts 8 (2 pens), McManus 5 (1 pen), McKay 4, Stevenson 2, Aitken A 1, Aitken C 1 (pen), Bowey 1, Connolly 1, Keenan 1, Lafferty 1, McGowan R 1, Mitchell 1, Reynolds 1, own goal 1.
Scottish Cup (3): McManus 1, Roberts 1, Stevenson 1.
CIS Cup (2): Aitken A 1, Easton 1.
Challenge Cup (0).

Grindlay S 4+1	Keenan D 31+3	James K 13+1	Gibson B 19+6	Aitken A 22	Borris R 21+7	Stevenson R 17	Aitken C 12+2	Easton W 19+3	Prunty B 6+4	Roberts M 31+2	Cawley K 3+8	Connolly K 17+14	Gormley D 1+8	Samson C 32	Winters R 1	McGowan N 10+3	Campbell M 24	Winnfhurn A 7+8	McGowan R 28	Mendes J 8+13	Reynolds S 2+2	Mitchell C 14	Connelly A 1+3	Bowey S 17+1	McManus T 17	McKay D 5+8	Visconte R 2+1	Lafferty D 12+2	Match No.
	2	3	4	5	6	7^2	8	9	10^1	11^3	12	13	14																1
	2	3	5	4	7^1	6	8	9^3		11	13	12		1		10^2	14												2
	2	3	5	4	12	6	8^3	9^1	14	11	10^2	7	13																3
	2^1	3	5	4^3	13	6	8	12	11	14	7	9^2		1		10													4
	12	3	5^2		13	6	8^1	9	10	11^3		7	14	1		4	2												5
	8	3	5^1		14	6	12	11^2	9	10	13	2		1		4	3												6
	8	3^1	12		13	6	5	11	9^3	10	14	2		1		4	2												7
	2			4		6	8	3	9^2	10	7^1	11^3	13	1		14	5	1^2											8
	2	3			7	8		9			11	10^1	12	1		5	4	6											9
	2			4	11	6	8	9	13	10^3	14	12		1		3^1	5	7^2											10
	6			2	3	14	7	9^2	10^3	11	12	13		1		5^1	4	8											11
	8			4	3^1	11^3	6	13	9	10	14	2^2		1		12	5	7											12
	6			3	9	7	8	14	11^3	10^2	12	13		1		5	4^1	2											13
	4			3	9	7^8	8^2	12	11	6				1		5^1	14	2	10	13									14
	6	5		4	13	11^2	10	8						1		3	7	2	9^1	12									15
	7			4	3	9	10	12		8				1		5^1	5^2	2	13	11									16
	8	5	12	4^2		11	6	3^1		13	10			1			7^3	2	14	9									17
	8^3			4	11^2	6		10	12	7				1		5	14	2	9^1		3	13							18
15	9		6			3		7^6				8^2	1^8			4	13	2	10					5	11^1	12			19
1	12		3					5^2		11		13				4	7	6					2^1	8	10^5	14	9		20
1	2		3					5^1		10^3		13				4	2	7	9^2				6	8	11	14			21
	7^2			4	11					10		13		1		5		6	14	2				8	9^3	12		3	22
	6			4	9^1					12		1				3		8	13	2				7	10^2	11		5	23
	6^2			4	9^1					13		1				3	4	8	12	2				7^3	10	11		5	24
	13			3	9^3					10		14		1		4	6^1	8		2^2				7	11	12		5	25
	2	5			7^2				9^1	11		12		1		4		6	14					8	10^9	13		3	26
		12		8^1	9					11^2		6		1		3	4		13	2				7	10			5	27
		13		9^1	11					6^8		3^2	12	1		7	14		2					8	10			5	28
		6^3	13	3						12		11		1		4^2		8			2		14	7	10	9^1		5	29
	7	12		4^1	11					10		13		1		5^3		6			2		14	8	9			3^8	30
	6	4	3		9^3					10		12		1			7^1	14	2					8^2	11	13		5	31
9^3	5	4		7			3	11				14		1				6	13		2			8	10^1	12^2			32
2	5	4		11^2			3			10				1				6	14				7^3	8	9^1	12	13		33
8^2		3	5					13				6^1		1		4		7	12		2		14		10^3	11		9	34
	7	14		3^4			6^1	9						1		2	13	5	11^2					4	10	8		12	35
	7	3						9						1		4	6^1	2	11			12			8	10		5	36

BERWICK RANGERS   Third Division

Year Formed: 1881. *Ground & Address:* Shielfield Park, Tweedmouth, Berwick-upon-Tweed TD15 2EF. *Telephone:*
01289 307424. *Fax:* 01289 309424. *Email:* club@berwickrangers.net *Website:* berwickrangers.net
Ground Capacity: 4131, seated: 1366. *Size of Pitch:* 110yd × 70yd.
Chairman: Brian Porteous. *Vice-Chairman:* Moray McLaren. *Football Secretary:* Dennis McCleary.
Manager: Jimmy Crease. *Player-Coach:* Ian Little. *Physio:* Harrison Stevenson. *Ground/Kit:* Ian Oliver.
Club Nickname(s): The Borderers, The Wee Gers. *Previous Grounds:* Bull Stob Close, Pier Field, Meadow Field,
Union Park, Old Shielfield.
Record Attendance: 13,283 v Rangers, Scottish Cup 1st rd, 28 Jan 1967.
Record Victory: 8-1 v Forfar Ath, Division II, 25 Dec 1965; v Vale of Leithen, Scottish Cup, Dec 1966.
Record Defeat: 1-9 v Hamilton A, First Division, 9 Aug 1980.
Most League Appearances: 435: Eric Tait, 1970-87.
Most League Goals in Season (Individual): 33: Ken Bowron, Division II, 1963-64.
Most Goals Overall (Individual): 115: Eric Tait, 1970-87.

BERWICK RANGERS 2009–10 LEAGUE RECORD

Match No.	Date	Venue	Opponents	Result	H/T Score	Lg Pos.	Goalscorers	Attendance
1	Aug 8	H	Annan Ath	W 2-1	1-1	—	Currie [3], Guy [49]	438
2	15	A	Albion R	L 1-2	1-1	6	Brazil [21]	322
3	22	H	Livingston	W 1-0	0-0	2	Brazil [67]	608
4	29	H	Queen's Park	W 1-0	0-0	2	McLaren [89]	519
5	Sept 19	A	Elgin C	D 3-3	2-2	2	Brazil [7], Currie [18], Little [81]	478
6	22	H	Stranraer	W 1-0	0-0	—	Greenhill D [70]	366
7	26	H	Montrose	W 2-0	1-0	1	McLaren [19], Brazil [56]	436
8	Oct 3	H	Forfar Ath	L 0-1	0-0	2		436
9	10	A	East Stirling	L 0-1	0-0	3		464
10	17	A	Livingston	D 1-1	0-0	4	MacDonald (og) [71]	815
11	31	H	Albion R	W 2-0	0-0	2	Currie [70], Gray (pen) [80]	471
12	Nov 7	A	Stranraer	W 4-2	2-0	2	David Mitchell (og) [5], Gray 2 [23, 81], Ewart [80]	274
13	14	H	Queen's Park	D 1-1	1-1	2	McLaren [12]	487
14	Dec 1	A	Montrose	W 3-1	1-0	—	McLean 2 [13, 82], Brazil [74]	265
15	5	H	Elgin C	W 2-0	0-0	2	McLean [64], Little [86]	368
16	12	H	East Stirling	L 0-1	0-0	3		428
17	Jan 16	A	Queen's Park	L 0-2	0-0	—		517
18	23	A	Elgin C	W 5-1	2-1	3	Little [14], Radznski 2 [24, 82], Currie [65], Greenhill D [70]	307
19	30	H	Montrose	L 0-2	0-1	—		392
20	Feb 6	A	East Stirling	L 2-3	0-1	3	Gray 2 [59, 79]	347
21	9	A	Annan Ath	D 1-1	1-0	—	Currie [31]	382
22	13	H	Forfar Ath	L 0-4	0-1	3		386
23	20	H	Annan Ath	L 0-2	0-2	4		385
24	Mar 6	A	Queen's Park	W 3-2	1-1	4	Gray 2 [45, 66], Greenhill D [86]	538
25	9	A	Albion R	L 1-4	1-0	—	McLean [43]	227
26	13	A	Stranraer	L 1-3	0-2	4	Russell [90]	231
27	20	H	Elgin C	W 2-1	2-0	4	Gray [16], Callaghan [42]	317
28	23	A	Forfar Ath	L 0-3	0-0	—		310
29	27	A	Montrose	D 1-1	1-1	4	Greenhill D [45]	376
30	Apr 3	A	Forfar Ath	L 0-2	0-1	5		406
31	6	H	Stranraer	W 1-0	1-0	—	McLaren [12]	289
32	10	H	East Stirling	D 2-2	0-2	5	McMullan [66], Callaghan (pen) [79]	429
33	13	H	Livingston	D 1-1	0-0	—	Gray [76]	604
34	17	A	Livingston	D 0-0	0-0	5		1621
35	24	H	Albion R	L 1-2	0-2	6	Gray [56]	460
36	May 1	A	Annan Ath	W 1-0	1-0	6	Gray [44]	561

Final League Position: 6

Honours
League Champions: Second Division 1978-79. Third Division 2006-07; *Runners-up:* Second Division 1993-94. Third Division 1999-2000.
Scottish Cup: Quarter-finals 1953-54, 1979-80.
League Cup: Semi-finals 1963-64.
League Challenge Cup: Quarter-finals 2004-05.

Club colours: Shirt: Black with gold vertical stripes. Shorts: Black Stockings: Gold.

Goalscorers: *League (46):* Gray 11 (1 pen), Brazil 5, Currie 5, Greenhill D 4, McLaren 4, McLean 4, Little 3, Callaghan 2 (1 pen), Radznski 2, Ewart 1, Guy 1, McMullan 1, Russell 1, own goals 2.
Scottish Cup (3): Brazil 2, Little 1.
CIS Cup (1): Little 1.
Challenge Cup (2): Ewart 1, Little 1.

Peat M 34	Notman S 29	Smith E 32 + 1	Guy G 13 + 5	McLean A 21 + 3	Callaghan S 30 + 2	McMenamin C 1 + 4	Currie P 29 + 2	Brazil A 26 + 1	Little J 22 + 9	Greenhill D 25 + 8	Radznski S 6 + 8	McLaren F 25 + 1	Gray D 22 + 9	Russell O 11 + 6	Ewart J 25 + 1	McMullan P 15 + 7	Horn R 2 + 1	Cropley J — + 2	McGregor H 1 + 2	Gair S 6	Savage J — + 2	McCaldon I 2	Shields J 10 + 3	Kerr G 10	Match No.
1	2	3	4	5	6	7	8	9	10^1	11	12														1
1	2	3	4	5	6*		8	9	10^1	11^2	13	7	12												2
1	2	3	4	5			8	9	10	11^1	13	7^2	12	6											3
1	2	3	4	5^3	13		8	9^1	10	11	12	7	14	6^2											4
1	2	3	4	5	6		8	9	10	12	13	7^2	11^1												5
1	2	3	4		6		8	9	13	11^2	12	7	10^1		5										6
1	2	3	4		6		8^1	9	14	11^3	13	7	10^2	12	5										7
1	2	3	4		6	14		9	12	11	13	7^1	10^2	8^3	5										8
1	2	3	4		6	12	8	9	7^1	11			10^2	13	5										9
1	2	3	4		6		8	9	7^1	11			10	12	5										10
1	2	3	4		6		8	9	7^1	11			10	12	5										11
1	2		4		6	13	8	9		11^3		7^2	10	14	5	3^1	12								12
1		3	2	4	6		8	9	12			7	10	11^1	5										13
1	2	5	14	4	7		8^3	9^1		11	12	6	10^2	3	13										14
1	2	3		5	6		8	9	12	11^2		7	10^1	4	13										15
1	2	3		5	6		8	9^1	12	11^2		7	10	4	13										16
1	2		14	5	13		8		10	11^2		7	9^1	12	6^3	4	3								17
1	2		4					9^3	7	11^1			10	12	6^2	8	3	5	13	14					18
1	2		4			12		9^3	7	11			10^2	13	6	8^1	3	5	14						19
1	2^1			5	12		8	9	7	11			10^2	13	6	3				4					20
1	3		2		6		8	9^1	13	11		7	10^2			4				5	12				21
1		5	2		12		8*	9^3	7	11^2			10	14	6	3					4^1		13		22
	2^3		14				8^2	9		11	12		10	13	6^1	3		5		4		1	7		23
1	2^2	5			13		8	9	12	11^1			10		6	3						4	7		24
1	2	3		5*	6	12		9		11^3	13	7^1	10^2	4	14								8		25
1	2	3	6^1					9^2	7	11			10	14		4	13	5	12				8^3		26
1	2	3	7	5			8	9		11			10		6^1								12	4	27
1	2^3	3	6	5			8^2	9^1	12	11		7	10			13							14	4	28
1	2	3	7	4			8	9		11			10		6									5	29
1	2	3*	8	5				9^2	12	11^3		7	10^1		6	14							13	4	30
1	2	5	14				8	9^2	12	11^3	13		10		6^1	3							7	4	31
1	2	5	7		13			9	12	11^1			10^3	14	6^2	3							8	4	32
1	2	5	7^1		12			9		11			10		6	3							8	4	33
1		3		4	12		8	9^1		11		7	10		6	2							6	5	34
1	2	5			12			9		11	13	7	10		6	3^2							8^1	4	35
	2	3	7		6		8	9		11			10									1	5*	4	36

BRECHIN CITY   Second Division

Year Formed: 1906. *Ground & Address:* Glebe Park, Trinity Rd, Brechin, Angus DD9 6BJ. *Telephone:* 01356 622856.
Fax: 01382 206331. *E-mail:* secretary@brechincityfc.com *Website:* www.brechincity.com
Ground Capacity: total: 3960, seated: 1519. *Size of Pitch:* 110yd × 67yd.
Chairman: Kenneth Ferguson. *Vice-Chairman:* Martin Smith. *Secretary:* Angus Fairlie.
Manager: Jim Weir. *Assistant Manager:* Kevin McAllister. *Physio:* Tom Gilmartin.
Club Nickname(s): The City. *Previous Grounds:* Nursery Park.
Record Attendance: 8122 v Aberdeen, Scottish Cup 3rd rd, 3 Feb 1973.
Record Transfer Fee received: £100,000 for Scott Thomson to Aberdeen (1991) and Chris Templeman to Morton (2004).
Record Transfer Fee paid: £16,000 for Sandy Ross from Berwick Rangers (1991).
Record Victory: 12-1 v Thornhill, Scottish Cup 1st rd, 28 Jan 1926.
Record Defeat: 0-10 v Airdrieonians, Albion R and Cowdenbeath, all in Division II, 1937-38.
Most League Appearances: 459: David Watt, 1975-89.
Most League Goals in Season (Individual): 26: Ronald McIntosh, Division II, 1959-60.
Most Goals Overall (Individual): 131: Ian Campbell, 1977-85.

BRECHIN CITY 2009–10 LEAGUE RECORD

Match No.	Date	Venue	Opponents	Result	H/T Score	Lg Pos.	Goalscorers	Attendance
1	Aug 8	A	East Fife	L	0-2	0-2	—	605
2	15	H	Cowdenbeath	W	3-1	1-1	6	Canning [31], Harty (pen) [67], McAllister [78]	375
3	22	A	Stirling A	L	0-1	0-1	7		608
4	29	H	Dumbarton	W	3-1	2-1	6	Docherty [21], McAllister [36], King (pen) [90]	470
5	Sept 12	A	Arbroath	W	4-1	0-0	3	King [49], McAllister 2 [58, 75], Janczyk [59]	649
6	19	A	Clyde	L	0-1	0-1	4		682
7	26	H	Stenhousemuir	W	1-0	1-0	3	King [23]	418
8	Oct 10	H	Alloa Ath	W	2-1	1-1	2	King (pen) [33], McAllister [90]	417
9	13	A	Peterhead	L	0-1	0-0	—		429
10	17	H	East Fife	W	3-2	1-1	2	King 2 (1 pen) [16 (p), 84], McLean [75]	517
11	24	A	Cowdenbeath	D	0-0	0-0	2		337
12	31	A	Dumbarton	D	0-0	0-0	3		687
13	Nov 7	H	Arbroath	D	0-0	0-0	3		617
14	14	H	Clyde	D	2-2	0-1	3	McAllister [68], King [90]	502
15	21	A	Stenhousemuir	D	1-1	1-1	3	McAllister [29]	551
16	Dec 12	A	Alloa Ath	L	1-2	0-0	4	McAllister [90]	394
17	15	H	Peterhead	W	3-0	1-0	—	McLean [31], McAllister 2 [50, 73]	417
18	Jan 23	A	Clyde	W	3-0	1-0	4	McAllister [38], Docherty [47], Fusco [55]	623
19	30	H	Stenhousemuir	D	2-2	0-0	4	McAllister [59], Docherty [69]	413
20	Feb 6	H	Alloa Ath	D	1-1	0-0	4	McAllister [75]	434
21	13	A	Peterhead	W	3-0	1-0	3	Byers [31], King [75], McAllister [84]	553
22	Mar 6	A	Dumbarton	W	1-0	0-0	4	Byers [67]	751
23	9	H	Stirling A	W	1-0	1-0	—	Docherty [29]	453
24	13	H	Arbroath	L	0-2	0-2	3		637
25	20	H	Clyde	W	3-1	0-1	4	McAllister 2 (1 pen) [66, 77 (p)], King [85]	417
26	24	A	Arbroath	L	0-1	0-1	—		386
27	27	A	Stenhousemuir	W	2-1	1-1	4	McAllister [7], Archdeacon [66]	481
28	30	A	East Fife	L	0-2	0-1	—		213
29	Apr 3	H	Peterhead	L	1-2	1-0	4	Archdeacon [24]	463
30	6	H	Dumbarton	L	0-1	0-0	—		403
31	10	A	Alloa Ath	W	3-2	1-0	4	McLean [42], Archdeacon [77], King (pen) [90]	626
32	14	A	Stirling A	L	2-6	0-2	—	McAllister 2 [49, 71]	357
33	17	H	East Fife	W	1-0	0-0	4	Byers [65]	492
34	20	A	Cowdenbeath	D	3-3	0-3	—	McAllister 2 [51, 54], Vallers [86]	304
35	24	A	Cowdenbeath	L	0-4	0-2	4		391
36	May 1	H	Stirling A	D	1-1	1-1	4	King [25]	1102

Final League Position: 4

Honours
League Champions: C Division 1953-54. Second Division 1982-83, 1989-90, 2004-05. Third Division 2001-02. *Runners-up:* Second Division 1992-93, 2002-03. Third Division 1995-96. Second Division 2004-05.
League Challenge Cup: Runners-up 2002-03. Semi-finals 2001-02.

Club colours: Shirt, Shorts, Stockings: Red with white trim.

Goalscorers: *League (50):* McAllister 21 (1 pen), King 11 (4 pens), Docherty 4, Archdeacon 3, Byers 3, McLean 3, Canning 1, Fusco 1, Harty 1 (pen), Janczyk 1, Vallers 1.
Scottish Cup (8): McAllister 3, King 2, Byers 1, Doherty 1, Fusco 1.
CIS Cup (4): McAllister 2, Byers 1, McKenna 1.
Challenge Cup (1): McAllister 1.
Play-Offs (3): McAllister 2, King 1 (pen).

Nelson C 36	Walker R 35	Nimmo I 1+5	McLean P 33	Dyer W 25	King C 34+2	Janczyk N 27+1	Fusco G 36	Byers K 19+8	McAllister R 34	Harty I 4+3	McKenna S —+4	McGrourty C —+2	Docherty M 30+5	Seeley J 13+2	Canning S 8+14	Cowan M 2+15	Smith B 31	Reuton K 2+0	Murie D 1	Barr B 4	Scott D —+1	Walker A 3	Masson T 1+6	Tulloch B —+2	Archdeacon M 8+1	Kurakins A 2	Vallers K 7	Match No.
1	2	3	4	5	6	7²	8	9³	10	11¹	12	13	14															1
1	2		4	5	6	7¹	8²		10³	11	14		12	3	9	13												2
1	2	14	4	5	6²		8		10	11¹	13		7	3	9¹	12												3
1	2	12	4	5	13	9	8	6¹	10²	11³			7	14		3												4
1	2		4	5²	7¹	9	8	14	10³				13	11	6		3	2										5
1	2	13	4	5	7	9	8	6¹	10				11²				3	2										6
1	2	13	3	5	6¹	9²	8	14	10³				11	4			7	12										7
1	2		4	5	10		8	6		11			9	3			7											8
1	2		3	5	6	7	8¹		10²	12			9		14	11¹	4	13										9
1	2		3	5	6	9	8¹		10³				11²	4	13	14	7	12										10
1	2		7	5	6¹	11		8	13	10²			9²	4		12	3	11										11
1			3	5	6	7	8	12					9²		11	13	4	13¹	2									12
1	2		3	5	10		6		11				9²	4	8¹	13	7	12										13
1	2		4	3	7	6	8		9					12	5	10¹		11										14
1	2		4	3	7	10⁴	8³	13	9				12	5			6	14		1								15
1	2		4	3	10	13	8	6¹	9		12		11²				5		7									16
1⁵	2		3	5	11²	8¹	7		10				9		12		4	³		6	15							17
1	2	14		4	3	10²	6¹	8	7	9³	13		11		12								5					18
1	2			3	5	11²	8	7	6¹	10	12		9		13								4					19
1	2			5	10	4	8	6	11				9			7							3¹	12				20
1	2		4	5	11²	7	8	6	10				9¹	12	13	3												21
1	2		4	5	11³	7	8	6	10¹				9²	14	13	12												22
1	2		3	5	11¹	8	7	6	10				9	12														23
1	2			3	11	9	8	6²	10				7¹	5³	12	13							14					24
1	2		3	5¹	11	9	8	6³	10				12	7²									13	14				25
1	2		4		12	8	7	6	10				5	11²	9¹								13					26
1	2		8		11	4	7		10				9	3									12	6¹				27
1	2			9¹	7	8²	6	10					5	11	13								12					28
1	2		5		11	8	7	12	10				9										6¹	3				29
1	2		3		9	6²	8	14	10				12	13									11³	5¹	7			30
1	2		4		10		8	7	11				5	12	3								9¹	6				31
1	2		4		10²		8	7	9³				3	6	12	14	5							13			11	32
1	2		4		10		8	6	11				5	12	3								9¹	7				33
1	2		4		11		8	6	10				5	12		3²							9	7				34
1	2		3		11		8	6¹	10				5	12	14	7							13	9²	4³			35
1	2			11		8	12						5	4	9¹	13							6	10	7²			36

CELTIC

Premier League

Year Formed: 1888. *Ground & Address:* Celtic Park, Glasgow G40 3RE. *Telephone:* 0871 226 1888. *Fax:* 0141 551 8106.
E-mail: customerservices@celticfc.co.uk *Website:* www.celticfc.net
Ground Capacity: all seated: 60,355. *Size of Pitch:* 105m × 68m.
Chairman: John Reid. *Chief Executive:* Peter Lawwell. *Secretary:* Robert Howat.
Manager: Neil Lennon. *Assistant Manager:* Johan Mjallby. *First Team Coach:* Alan Thompson. *Physio:* Graham Parsons.
Club Nickname(s): The Bhoys. *Previous Grounds:* None.
Record Attendance: 92,000 v Rangers, Division I, 1 Jan 1938.
Record Transfer Fee received: £6,500,000 for Stilian Petrov to Aston Villa (August 2007).
Record Transfer Fee paid: £6,000,000 for Chris Sutton from Chelsea (July 2000).
Record Victory: 11-0 Dundee, Division I, 26 Oct 1895.
Record Defeat: 0-8 v Motherwell, Division I, 30 Apr 1937.
Most Capped Player: Pat Bonner 80, Republic of Ireland.
Most League Appearances: 486: Billy McNeill, 1957-75.
Most League Goals in Season (Individual): 50: James McGrory, Division I, 1935-36.
Most Goals Overall (Individual): 397: James McGrory, 1922-39.

Honours
League Champions: (42 times) Division I 1892-93, 1893-94, 1895-96, 1897-98, 1904-05, 1905-06, 1906-07, 1907-08, 1908-09, 1909-10, 1913-14, 1914-15, 1915-16, 1916-17, 1918-19, 1921-22, 1925-26, 1935-36, 1937-38, 1953-54, 1965-66, 1966-67, 1967-68, 1968-69, 1969-70, 1970-71, 1971-72, 1972-73, 1973-74. Premier Division 1976-77, 1978-79, 1980-81, 1981-82, 1985-86, 1987-88, 1997-98, 2000-01, 2001-02, 2003-04, 2005-06, 2006-07, 2007-08. *Runners-up:* 29 times.
Scottish Cup Winners: (34 times) 1892, 1899, 1900, 1904, 1907, 1908, 1911, 1912, 1914, 1923, 1925, 1927, 1931, 1933, 1937, 1951, 1954, 1965, 1967, 1969, 1971, 1972, 1974, 1975, 1977, 1980, 1985, 1988, 1989, 1995, 2001, 2004, 2005, 2007. *Runners-up:* 18 times.

CELTIC 2009–10 LEAGUE RECORD

Match No.	Date	Venue	Opponents	Result	H/T Score	Lg Pos.	Goalscorers	Attendance
1	Aug 15	A	Aberdeen	W 3-1	3-0	—	McGeady 2 [29, 42], McDonald S [44]	16,803
2	22	H	St Johnstone	W 5-2	2-1	1	Fortune 2 [21, 54], Maloney 2 [28, 53], McDonald S [74]	58,500
3	30	A	Hibernian	W 1-0	1-0	2	Samaras [41]	14,321
4	Sept 12	H	Dundee U	D 1-1	1-1	—	McDonald S [17]	58,500
5	20	H	Hearts	W 2-1	0-1	1	Killen [56], Loovens [90]	58,024
6	26	A	St Mirren	W 2-0	1-0	1	McCourt [27], Maloney [78]	6164
7	Oct 4	A	Rangers	L 1-2	1-2	1	McGeady (pen) [25]	50,276
8	17	H	Motherwell	D 0-0	0-0	1		58,000
9	25	A	Hamilton A	W 2-1	2-0	1	Maloney [15], McDonald S [29]	4689
10	31	H	Kilmarnock	W 3-0	2-0	1	McGeady [13], Samaras [32], McGinn [78]	46,000
11	Nov 8	A	Falkirk	D 3-3	0-1	1	Caldwell [66], McDonald S 2 [72, 79]	6795
12	22	A	Dundee U	L 1-2	0-0	1	Robson (pen) [72]	11,098
13	28	H	St Mirren	W 3-1	2-1	1	McDonald S 2 [39, 61], Samaras [42]	41,000
14	Dec 5	H	Aberdeen	W 3-0	1-0	1	McDonald S [39], Samaras 2 [52, 76]	56,010
15	12	A	Motherwell	W 3-2	1-2	1	Samaras [14], McGeady [52], Fortune [79]	7807
16	20	H	Hearts	L 1-2	1-1	2	Samaras [21]	16,223
17	26	H	Hamilton A	W 2-0	1-0	2	Loovens [13], McGinn [90]	36,827
18	Jan 3	H	Rangers	D 1-1	0-0	—	McDonald S [79]	58,300
19	16	H	Falkirk	D 1-1	1-1	2	Samaras [40]	50,000
20	24	A	St Johnstone	W 4-1	0-1	2	Fortune 2 [64, 81], Samaras [77], McCourt [86]	7743
21	27	H	Hibernian	L 1-2	1-1	—	Fortune [5]	41,000
22	30	A	Hamilton A	W 1-0	0-0	2	Rasmussen [67]	4922
23	Feb 2	A	Kilmarnock	L 0-1	0-0	—		9308
24	10	H	Hearts	W 2-0	0-0	2	Loovens [49], Fortune [50]	44,500
25	13	A	Aberdeen	D 4-4	2-2	2	Kamara [3], Fortune [36], Keane [65], McGeady [72]	14,898
26	20	H	Dundee U	W 1-0	1-0	2	Keane [20]	49,000
27	28	A	Rangers	L 0-1	0-0	2		50,320
28	Mar 7	A	Falkirk	W 2-0	1-0	2	Keane 2 [34, 79]	6792
29	20	H	St Johnstone	W 3-0	1-0	2	Thompson [16], Keane (pen) [67], Samaras [87]	30,000
30	24	A	St Mirren	L 0-4	0-1	—		5018
31	27	H	Kilmarnock	W 3-1	1-0	2	Keane 2 [37, 62], Brown S [66]	41,000
32	Apr 4	A	Hibernian	W 1-0	0-0	2	Keane (pen) [62]	10,523
33	13	H	Motherwell	W 2-1	0-0	2	Thompson 2 [50, 78]	27,750
34	17	H	Hibernian	W 3-2	1-1	2	Keane [4], Fortune [80], Rasmussen [87]	29,650
35	25	A	Dundee U	W 2-0	1-0	2	Kamara [30], Keane (pen) [90]	8638
36	May 1	H	Motherwell	W 4-0	0-0	2	McGeady [48], O'Dea [78], Forrest [87], Keane [90]	24,000
37	4	H	Rangers	W 2-1	2-1	—	Naylor [8], Fortune [45]	58,000
38	9	A	Hearts	W 2-1	1-1	2	Keane [23], Zheng-Zhi [61]	14,389

Final League Position: 2

League Cup Winners: (14 times) 1956-57, 1957-58, 1965-56, 1966-67, 1967-68, 1968-69, 1969-70, 1974-75, 1982-83, 1997-98, 1999-2000, 2000-01, 2005-06, 2008-09; *Runners-up:* 14 times.

European: *European Cup:* 138 matches (1966-67 winners, 1967-68, 1968-69, 1969-70 runners-up, 1970-71, 1971-72, 1972-73, 1973-74 semi-finals, 1974-75, 1977-78, 1979-80, 1981-82, 1982-83, 1986-87, 1988-89, 1998-99, 2001-02, 2002-03, 2003-04, 2004-05, 2005-06, 2006-07, 2007-08, 2008-09, 2009-10). *Cup Winners' Cup:* 28 matches (1963-64 semi-finals, 1965-66 semi-finals, 1975-76, 1980-81, 1984-85, 1985-86, 1989-90, 1995-96). *UEFA Cup:* 75 matches (*Fairs Cup:* 1962-63, 1964-65. *UEFA Cup:* 1976-77, 1983-84, 1987-88, 1991-92, 1992-93, 1993-94, 1996-97, 1997-98, 1998-99, 1999-2000, 2000-01, 2001-02, 2002-03 runners-up, 2003-04 quarter-finals). *Europa League:* 6 matches (2009-10).

Club colours: Shirt: Emerald green and white hoops. Shorts: White with emerald green trim. Stockings: White with emerald green trim.

Goalscorers: *League (75):* Keane 12 (3 pens), Fortune 10, McDonald S 10, Samaras 10, McGeady 7 (1 pen), Maloney 4, Loovens 3, Thompson 3, Kamara 2, McCourt 2, McGinn 2, Rasmussen 2, Brown S 1, Caldwell 1, Forrest 1, Killen 1, Naylor 1, O'Dea 1, Robson 1 (pen), Zheng-Zhi 1.
Scottish Cup (8): Keane 4 (1 pen), Kamara 1, McGinn 1, Rasmussen 1, own goal 1.
CIS Cup (4): McDonald S 2, Killen 1, McCourt 1.
Champions League (3): Donati 1, McDonald S 1, Samaras 1.
Europa League (7): Fortune 2, Samaras 2, McDonald S 1, McGowan 1, Robson 1.

Boruc A 28	Hinkel A 30+1	Fox D 15	Donati M 2	O'Dea D 16+3	Loovens G 20	Maloney S 8+1	N'Guemo L 30	McDonald S 16+2	Fortune M 22+8	McGeady A 35	Brown S 19+2	Samaras G 20+12	Killen C 2+3	Caldwell G 14	Crosas M 14+3	Flood W —+1	Caddis P 3+7	McGinn N 6+11	Mizuno K —+1	McManus S 6+2	McCourt P 3+6	Naylor L 11+1	Wilson M 8+2	Zheng-Zhi 9+7	Robson B 9+1	Zaluska L 10+1	Ki S 5+5	Thompson J 16+2	McGowan P 2+3	Rasmussen M 2+8	Hooiveld J 2	Kamara D 8+1	Keane R 15+1	Braafheid E 9+1	Rogne T 3+1	Forrest J —+2	Match No

CLYDE   Third Division

Year Formed: 1877. *Ground & Address:* Broadwood Stadium, Cumbernauld, G68 9NE. *Telephone:* 01236 451511.
Fax: 01236 733490. *E-mail:* info@clydefc.co.uk *Website:* www.clydefc.co.uk
Ground Capacity: all seated: 8006. *Size of Pitch:* 112yd × 76yd.
Chairman: John Alexander. *Secretary:* John D. Taylor.
Director of Football: Neill Watt. *Head Coach:* Stuart Millar. *Physio:* Ian McKinlay.
Club Nickname(s): The Bully Wee. *Previous Grounds:* Barrowfield Park 1877-97, Shawfield Stadium 1897-1986.
Record Attendance: 52,000 v Rangers, Division I, 21 Nov 1908.
Record Transfer Fee received: £175,000 for Scott Howie to Norwich City (Aug 1993).
Record Transfer Fee paid: £14,000 for Harry Hood from Sunderland (1966).
Record Victory: 11-1 v Cowdenbeath, Division II, 6 Oct 1951.
Record Defeat: 0-11 v Dumbarton, Scottish Cup 4th rd, 22 Nov, 1879; v Rangers, Scottish Cup 4th rd, 13 Nov 1880.
Most Capped Player: Tommy Ring, 12, Scotland.
Most League Appearances: 420: Brian Ahern, 1971-81; 1987-88.
Most League Goals in Season (Individual): 32: Bill Boyd, 1932-33.

CLYDE 2009–10 LEAGUE RECORD

Match No.	Date	Venue	Opponents	Result		H/T Score	Lg Pos.	Goalscorers	Attendance
1	Aug 8	A	Peterhead	L	0-2	0-1	—		627
2	15	H	Stirling A	L	0-1	0-1	9		813
3	22	A	Dumbarton	D	3-3	2-1	8	Lithgow 2 [15, 24], McLauchlan [65]	975
4	29	H	Alloa Ath	L	0-1	0-1	9		773
5	Sept 12	A	Cowdenbeath	L	0-1	0-1	10		401
6	19	H	Brechin C	W	1-0	1-0	9	McLeod [15]	682
7	26	A	East Fife	L	0-1	0-1	10		697
8	Oct 10	H	Stenhousemuir	W	2-1	1-0	10	Howarth [37], Sawyers [83]	755
9	14	A	Arbroath	W	3-0	1-0	—	Sawyers 2 [27, 55], Park [50]	554
10	17	H	Peterhead	L	1-3	0-1	10	McLeod [88]	663
11	24	A	Stirling A	D	1-1	0-0	8	Sawyers [57]	764
12	31	A	Alloa Ath	L	0-2	0-1	9		649
13	Nov 7	H	Cowdenbeath	L	0-1	0-0	10		691
14	14	A	Brechin C	D	2-2	1-0	10	Sawyers [36], McLeod [88]	502
15	21	H	East Fife	L	1-3	0-1	10	Sawyers (pen) [55]	635
16	Dec 5	H	Arbroath	W	1-0	1-0	—	McLauchlan [44]	552
17	12	A	Stenhousemuir	L	0-1	0-0	10		532
18	Jan 23	H	Brechin C	L	0-3	0-1	10		623
19	Feb 6	H	Stenhousemuir	L	0-2	0-1	10		650
20	13	A	Arbroath	L	0-2	0-0	10		524
21	Mar 6	A	Alloa Ath	D	2-2	1-1	10	White [37], Stewart [50]	628
22	9	A	East Fife	D	1-1	1-0	—	Park [45]	463
23	13	H	Cowdenbeath	L	1-2	0-1	10	Borisovs [83]	649
24	16	H	Dumbarton	L	0-2	0-1	—		531
25	20	A	Brechin C	L	1-3	1-0	10	Gramovics [39]	417
26	23	A	Cowdenbeath	L	1-3	1-1	—	White [1]	303
27	27	H	East Fife	W	2-1	0-0	10	Sawyers [49], White [72]	495
28	30	A	Peterhead	D	0-0	0-0	—		303
29	Apr 3	H	Arbroath	L	0-2	0-2	10		635
30	7	H	Alloa Ath	L	0-2	0-1	—		465
31	10	A	Stenhousemuir	W	3-0	1-0	10	Lithgow [27], White [65], Strachan [78]	482
32	13	A	Dumbarton	D	3-3	1-3	—	Strachan 2 (2 pens) [29, 79], McGowan N [63]	601
33	17	H	Peterhead	W	3-1	2-0	10	Sawyers [1], Stewart [11], Lithgow [75]	515
34	20	H	Stirling A	L	1-2	1-1	—	Sawyers [20]	635
35	24	A	Stirling A	L	0-1	0-1	10		796
36	May 1	H	Dumbarton	W	4-2	3-1	10	Sawyers [2], Stewart 2 [15, 19], Strachan [84]	631

Final League Position: 10

Honours
League Champions: Division II 1904-05, 1951-52, 1956-57, 1961-62, 1972-73. Second Division 1977-78, 1981-82, 1992-93, 1999-2000.
Runners-up: Division II 1903-04, 1905-06, 1925-26, 1963-64. Second Division 2003-04.
Scottish Cup Winners: 1939, 1955, 1958; *Runners-up:* 1910, 1912, 1949.
League Challenge Cup Runners-up: 2006-07.

Club colours: Shirt: White with red flashes. Shorts: Black. Stockings: Red.

Goalscorers: *League (37):* Sawyers 10 (1 pen), Lithgow 4, Stewart 4, Strachan 4 (2 pens), White 4, McLeod 3, McLauchlan 2, Park 2, Borisovs 1, Gramovics 1, Howarth 1, McGowan N 1.
Scottish Cup (2): Lithgow 2.
CIS Cup (1): own goal 1.
Challenge Cup (0).

Reidford C 32	Casey M 16+1	Stevenson C 15+6	Gair S 3+1	Lithgow A 32	Doyle J 4	Walker D 1+2	Lang J 4+4	McKay D 4+3	McLeod P 10+5	McLauchlan W 27+2	McFadden A 2+7	Sawyers W 10	Stewart P 24+7	Coakley A 2+3	Boyle C 8+1	Park A 31	Halliday R 11+1	Allon J 2+1	McNeil A 1	Wilson M 13+1	Odunewu S 1+5	Muir G 4+3	Howarth S 5+6	Cassidy C 9+2	Davidson R 2	Bark A 2	Graham L 4+2	White J 17+3	Higgins C 4+5	McGowan N 17	Kinniburgh W 14	Strachan A 18	Findlay S 1+1	Doolan K 9	Gramovics A 14+3	McCulloch W 6	Borisovs D 3+7	Match No.
1	2	3	4	5	6^1	7^2	8	9	10	11	12	13																										1
1	2			4	5	6^3	12	8^2	9	10	11	13			3	7^1	14																					2
1^*	2^1	12	5	6	13			9^2	10	7	11^0		3				4	8	15																			3
	2		5		6^1		14	9	10		12		3		11^2		4	8^5	1	7	13																	4
1	2	6^3	5				12	13	10	9			3	14			4	8		7^1	11^1																	5
1	2		5		6			10^2	9	11^1	3	12					4	8		7	13																	6
1	3	8^1	4				7	11^2	10		6	14					2	5^1				13	12															7
1	4		5				14	13	7	12	9	8^1					2	3^4						6^3					10^2	11								8
1	4	13	5					12	7	14	9	8					2							6^2	11^3	10^1	3											9
1	4	14	5					12	7	13	9^1	8					2	ε						6^5	11^3	10^2												10
1	4	8	5				13	14	6		9	7					2			12	11			3		10^1												11
1	4	8	5						6		9	7					12			11^2				3^1	10^3	2												12
1	4	14	5					10	8		9^1	7					2	3		12^2	13	11^3					6											13
1	4	14	5					12	11	7		9^1						3				8^3		13			2	6	10^2									14
1	4		5					13	11^2	7		9	14					2	3			8^1		12			6	10^1										15
1	6^3		3					12	7	8^1	10	14					2	3						13		5	4	11^2										16
1	12	11	5						7	$14^?$	9	6					2^2							8	3		13	10^3	4^1									17
1^*			5						8	10^1	9		2				6							12	7^6			13	3	4	11^2	15						18
	6^2		5						8	13	9^3		2^1				12										14	11	3	4	7	1	10					19
1			4							10^1			2				7				5			13				3	9		11	6^2	8	12			20
1										12	9^1		4	2													11	5	3	6		$10^?$	7	8				21
1									8	12	10^1		4	2													6	5	3	9		11	7					22
1									8	12	10^2		4	2													6	5	3	9		11	7^1		13		23
1			7^3						8	12	13		5	2													9^1	3	4	11		10^2	6		14		24
	13		6						7	12			4	2	1		8^2										5^4	3	10	11		9^1					25
1			4						7	11^1	10^2		5	2			8^1										6		3	9		12	13		26		
1	8^8		4						12	10^3			5	2													6	7	3^1	9		11	14		13		27
1	7		4						6	10	12		5	2													8	3	9^2			11^1	13				28
1	6									10^2	13		2						4			3					11^3	14	5	7			9^1	8	12		29
1	7	4							2	11	12		3^2										13				9	5	6			8	10^1		30	
1	7	3								10^2	12		8														13	6	5	9		4	2^1	11^1		31
1	8	5							13	9^2			4														11	12	3	7		6	2	10^1		32
1	7	4					13		10^2	11^1			2														6	12	3	5	9	8				33
1	8	4						2	10	11^2											13						12	6^1	5	3	9	7				34
1	8^2	4							11	10^3			2								14	12					6	13	5^1	3		7	9			35
1	12	4						6	11^2	10^3			2	1							13							7^1	5	3	9	8^4		14		36

COWDENBEATH

First Division

Year Formed: 1881. *Ground & Address:* Central Park, Cowdenbeath KY4 9QQ. *Telephone:* 01383 610166. *Fax:* 01383 512132.
E-mail: bluebrazil@cowdenbeathfc.com *Website:* www.cowdenbeathfc.com
Ground Capacity: total: 4370, seated: 1431. *Size of Pitch:* 98m × 59m.
Manager: Jimmy Nicholl.
Previous Grounds: North End Park, Cowdenbeath.
Record Attendance: 25,586 v Rangers, League Cup quarter-final, 21 Sept 1949.
Record Transfer Fee received: £30,000 for Nicky Henderson to Falkirk (March 1994).
Record Victory: 12-0 v Johnstone, Scottish Cup 1st rd, 21 Jan 1928.
Record Defeat: 1-11 v Clyde, Division II, 6 Oct 1951.
Most Capped Player: Jim Paterson, 3, Scotland.
Most League and Cup Appearances: 491 Ray Allan 1972-75, 1979-89.
Most League Goals in Season (Individual): 54, Rab Walls, Division II, 1938-39.
Most Goals Overall (Individual): 127, Willie Devlin, 1922-26, 1929-30.

COWDENBEATH 2009–10 LEAGUE RECORD

Match No.	Date	Venue	Opponents	Result	H/T Score	Lg Pos.	Goalscorers	Atten-dance
1	Aug 8	H	Arbroath	L 1-2	0-0	—	McBride [90]	302
2	15	A	Brechin C	L 1-3	1-1	8	Dempster [40]	375
3	22	H	Alloa Ath	D 1-1	1-1	9	Wardlaw [30]	365
4	29	A	East Fife	D 1-1	1-1	8	Stein [12]	803
5	Sept 12	H	Clyde	W 1-0	1-0	8	Stein [23]	401
6	19	A	Dumbarton	W 3-0	2-0	5	McBride 2 [15, 53], Wardlaw [23]	647
7	26	H	Stirling A	L 1-2	1-2	7	McBride [5]	451
8	Oct 3	A	Stenhousemuir	W 2-0	1-0	4	Robertson [39], McBride (pen) [50]	539
9	10	H	Peterhead	W 5-0	2-0	3	McQuade 2 [24, 39], Wardlaw 2 [48, 85], Robertson [83]	271
10	17	A	Arbroath	W 1-0	1-0	3	Linton [16]	479
11	24	H	Brechin C	D 0-0	0-0	3		337
12	31	H	East Fife	W 2-1	2-1	2	Fairbairn [2], Robertson [14]	733
13	Nov 7	A	Clyde	W 1-0	1-0	1	McBride (pen) [89]	691
14	14	H	Dumbarton	W 2-1	1-1	1	McQuade 2 (1 pen) [18 ipi, 82]	389
15	21	A	Stirling A	D 2-2	1-0	1	Wardlaw [11], Ferguson [90]	682
16	Dec 12	A	Peterhead	W 2-0	1-0	1	Robertson [22], Mbu [55]	494
17	15	H	Stenhousemuir	W 2-1	1-1	—	Fairbairn [23], McQuade [76]	264
18	Jan 16	A	East Fife	D 2-2	1-1	—	Wardlaw 2 [31, 87]	864
19	23	A	Dumbarton	L 1-2	1-0	1	Baxter [29]	659
20	Feb 6	H	Peterhead	L 1-3	0-1	1	Stein [74]	298
21	9	A	Alloa Ath	L 1-2	0-1	—	McQuade [70]	638
22	13	A	Stenhousemuir	D 0-0	0-0	2		443
23	Mar 6	H	East Fife	W 6-2	1-0	2	Stein 2 [35, 70], Wardlaw [53], McQuade [60], McGregor [62], Ramsay [69]	667
24	9	H	Arbroath	W 2-1	0-1	—	McQuade [63], McGregor [66]	246
25	13	A	Clyde	W 2-1	1-0	2	Wardlaw [45], Dempster [68]	649
26	16	A	Alloa Ath	D 1-1	0-0	—	Dempster [84]	413
27	20	H	Dumbarton	D 0-0	0-0	2		349
28	23	H	Clyde	W 3-1	1-1	—	McQuade 2 [32, 72], Robertson [64]	303
29	27	A	Stirling A	L 0-1	0-0	2		575
30	Apr 3	H	Stenhousemuir	W 1-0	0-0	2	Warclaw [72]	438
31	10	A	Peterhead	L 0-1	0-0	2		435
32	17	A	Arbroath	D 1-1	0-1	3	Wardlaw [76]	488
33	20	A	Brechin C	D 3-3	3-0	—	Wardlaw 2 [2, 29], McGregor [6]	304
34	24	H	Brechin C	W 4-0	2-0	3	McQuade 2 [27, 56], McGregor [35], Wardlaw [46]	391
35	27	H	Stirling A	D 3-3	3-0	—	McGregor [5], Wardlaw 2 [23, 38]	1084
36	May 1	A	Alloa Ath	L 1-3	1-0	3	Dempster [28]	1125

Final League Position: 3

Honours
League Champions: Division II 1913-14, 1914-15, 1938-39; *Champions:* Third Division 2005-06. *Runners-up:* Division II 1921-22, 1923-24, 1969-70. Second Division 1991-92. *Runners-up:* Third Division 2000-01, 2008-09.
Scottish Cup: Quarter-finals 1931.
League Cup: Semi-finals 1959-60, 1970-71.

Club colours: Shirt: Royal blue. Shorts: Royal blue. Stockings: Royal blue.

Goalscorers: *League (60):* Wardlaw 16, McQuade 12 (1 pen), McBride 6 (2 pens), McGregor 5, Robertson 5, Stein 5, Dempster 4, Fairbairn 2, Baxter 1, Ferguson 1, Linton 1, Mbu 1, Ramsay 1.
Scottish Cup (0).
CIS Cup (1): McQuade 1 (pen).
Challenge Cup (2): McBride 1, McQuade 1.
Play-Offs (6): Wardlaw 3, Dempster 1, McQuade 1, Mbu 1.

Hay D 34	Baxter M 14+9	Droudge D 25+1	Mbu J 32	Stein J 19+13	Fairbairn B 24+7	Ramsay M 18+13	Adamson K 20+5	McBride S 16+9	Wardlaw G 31	McQuade P 27+4	McCabe N —+4	Dempster J 5+12	Robertson J 29+2	Bradley P 1	Linton S 24+2	Bower K —+1	Veiculis A 1	winner C 28+3	Tomana M —+1	Shields J 3	Ferguson J —+8	Armstrong J 28	MacKay D —+2	McKay C 1	McGregor D 16+1	Robinson M 1	Brett D 1	Wallace D —+1	Match No.
1	2	3^4	4	5	6^2	7^1	8^8	9	10	11^3	12	13	14																1
1^a	2		4	5^3	6^1		14		10^2	11	13	8	3		7	9	12												2
	2	7	4	5	6^1		9		10	12		8^2	3					1	11	13									3
1	2	7	4	5	6^1	13	9		10	3^2		12	8					11											4
1		3	4	9	6^3	14	5	13	10	11^2	12		8					7			2^1								5
1		3	4	9^3	6^2	13	5	11	10^1				8	14				7			2^1	2 12							6
1		3	4	9	6	12	5	10^2	11	13			8	14				7^1			2^1								7
1		3	4	9	6^3	14		10^2	11^1	12			8	5				7			13	2							8
1		3	4	9	6^2	13	12		10	11^3			8	5				7			14	2							9
1^0		5^2	6	11		7	13	12	9	8			10	3				4^4				2 15							10
	2	4	9^1	6	14	12	10		11^2				8	5				7^4			13	3	1						11
1	2	4		6^1	9	13	12	10^2	11				8	5				7				3							12
1	13	5	6		11	7	12	9^2	8				10	3				4^1				2							13
1	2	4	13	12	9^1	6^2	14	10	11^3				8	5				7				3							14
1	5	6	14	7^1	12	11	8^5	9^2	10				3					4			13	2							15
1	12	5^3	6	14	7^2	9	3	8					10	11				4			13	2^1							16
1	2	3	4	8^1	6^2	10	5^{51}		12 13				7	9								2							17
1	3	13	4^1		6	12		9^2 10	7^3				11	5				8			14	2							18
1	5	4		13	10^2	9		12	11^3 7				8	3				6^1				2			14				19
1	3	4^1		13	14	6	5^2		10^3 11					9				12				2			7 8				20
1	4			9	6	12	5		10 11				8					7^1				2			3				21
1	14	3	4	12^2	6	9	5^{81}		11 10				8^1					7^3			13	2							22
1	12	5	6	10	14	7			11^2 8^3	13				3				9^1				2			4				23
1	14	3	4	9	12	6^3			11^1 10^2	13				5				8				2			7				24
1	12	4^2	7^3	9	13	6			10 8^1	14				5				11				2			3				25
1		2	4	13	14	6^1	5^2		10 11^3	12 7				9								3			8				26
1	13	2	4	9	6^3				12 10 11^1	14				5				7^2				3			8				27
1	12	4^1	7	9^1		6	14	13		8				10^2 11				5				2			3				28
1	4		7		13	6^2		12 11	8^1	14 10				5				9^1				2			3				29
1		3	13		6^1 12	5	9 11		10^2 8									7^3				2 14			4				30
1	14	3	12	6	6^2 5	9^1 11	10		13 8									7^3				2			4				31
1	5	8	14		6^2 3^3	9	10 11		13 12									7^1				2			4				32
1	4		3	12	6	5^1	9^2 10 11		8									13				2			7				33
1	7		3	13	6^3		9^2 10 11^1		12 8			5						14				2			4				34
1	6	4	12		7		9^2 10 10^1 11		13 8			5										2			3				35
1			9		6^1 12	8	11^2		10	7		5										2^a			3		4 13		36

DUMBARTON Second Division

Year Formed: 1872. *Ground:* Strathclyde Homes Stadium, Castle Road, Dumbarton G82 1JJ. *Telephone:* 01389 762569.
Fax: 01389 762629. *E-mail:* david_prophet58@hotmail.com *Website:* www.dumbartonfootballclub.com
Ground Capacity: total: 2025. *Size of Pitch:* 110yd × 75yd.
Chairman: Colin Hosie. *Club Secretary:* David Prophet. *Chief Executive Officer:* Gilbert Lawrie.
Manager: Jim Chapman. *Assistant Manager:* Alan Adamson. *Physio:* John Kelly.
Club Nickname(s): The Sons. *Previous Grounds:* Broadmeadow, Ropework Lane, Townend Ground, Boghead Park.
Record Attendance: 18,000 v Raith Rovers, Scottish Cup, 2 Mar 1957.
Record Transfer Fee received: £125,000 for Graeme Sharp to Everton (March 1982).
Record Transfer Fee paid: £50,000 for Charlie Gibson from Stirling Albion (1989).
Record Victory: 13-1 v Kirkintilloch Central. 1st rd, 1 Sept 1888.
Record Defeat: 1-11 v Albion Rovers, Division II; 30 Jan, 1926: v Ayr United, League Cup, 13 Aug 1952.
Most Capped Player: James McAulay, 9, Scotland.
Most League Appearances: 297: Andy Jardine, 1957-67.
Most Goals in Season (Individual): 38: Kenny Wilson, Division II, 1971-72. *(League and Cup):* 46 Hughie Gallacher, 1955-56.
Most Goals Overall (Individual): 169: Hughie Gallacher, 1954-62 (including C Division 1954-55). *(League and Cup):* 202
Hughie Gallacher, 1954-62

DUMBARTON 2009–10 LEAGUE RECORD

Match No.	Date	Venue	Opponents	Result	H/T Score	Lg Pos.	Goalscorers	Attendance
1	Aug 8	H	Alloa Ath	L 1-3	0-1	—	Grant (og) 53	864
2	15	A	Arbroath	L 1-3	0-1	10	Hunter 89	605
3	22	H	Clyde	D 3-3	1-2	10	Dunlop 45, Hunter 63, Chisholm 86	975
4	29	A	Brechin C	L 1-3	1-2	10	Dunlop 26	470
5	Sept 12	H	Stenhousemuir	D 0-0	0-0	9		664
6	19	H	Cowdenbeath	L 0-3	0-2	10		647
7	26	A	Peterhead	W 2-1	0-0	9	Murray 77, Carcary 90	571
8	Oct 3	H	Stirling A	L 2-3	2-1	9	Chaplain 30, Cook 41	654
9	10	A	East Fife	W 1-0	0-0	9	McLaughlin 58	684
10	17	A	Alloa Ath	W 3-1	2-1	7	Geggan 16, Cook 44, Chaplain 62	575
11	24	H	Arbroath	W 1-0	1-0	7	Chaplain 45	696
12	31	H	Brechin C	D 0-0	0-0	6		687
13	Nov 7	A	Stenhousemuir	W 3-0	0-0	6	Hunter 49, Chaplain 64, O'Donoghue 89	568
14	14	A	Cowdenbeath	L 1-2	1-1	6	Geggan 5	389
15	Dec 8	H	Peterhead	W 1-0	1-0	—	Chaplain (pen) 30	397
16	12	H	East Fife	L 0-3	0-1	6		628
17	15	A	Stirling A	D 2-2	0-0	—	Craig C 49, Carcary 84	462
18	Jan 23	H	Cowdenbeath	W 2-1	0-1	5	Hunter 65, Clark 89	659
19	Feb 6	A	East Fife	W 3-2	3-1	5	Gordon 5, Chaplain 15, Carcary 38	581
20	16	H	Stirling A	L 2-4	2-3	—	Gordon 4, Hunter 45	595
21	27	A	Arbroath	L 1-3	1-0	—	Winters 9	521
22	Mar 2	A	Peterhead	L 1-2	1-1	—	Wyness 27	327
23	6	H	Brechin C	L 0-1	0-0	7		751
24	9	H	Alloa Ath	W 3-1	1-0	—	Gordon 17, Cook 47, Clark (pen) 56	552
25	13	A	Stenhousemuir	L 0-1	0-0	6		469
26	16	A	Clyde	W 2-0	1-0	—	Winters 2 27, 62	531
27	20	A	Cowdenbeath	D 0-0	0-0	6		349
28	23	H	Stenhousemuir	W 2-1	1-0	—	Chaplain 2 (1 pen) 45, 68 (p)	486
29	27	H	Peterhead	L 1-3	0-0	6	Chaplain 49	663
30	Apr 3	A	Stirling A	W 2-1	0-0	6	Wyness 2 54, 81	568
31	6	A	Brechin C	W 1-0	0-0	—	Chaplain 56	403
32	10	H	East Fife	L 0-1	0-0	6		728
33	13	H	Clyde	D 3-3	3-1	—	Carcary 2 21, 40, Winters 45	601
34	17	A	Alloa Ath	W 2-1	1-0	5	Winters 33, Wyness 65	622
35	24	H	Arbroath	L 0-2	0-1	6		836
36	May 1	A	Clyde	L 2-4	1-3	6	McStay 33, Wyness 83	631

Final League Position: 6

Honours
League Champions: Division I 1890-91 (shared with Rangers), 1891-92. Division II 1910-11, 1971-72. Second Division 1991-92. Third Division 2008-09; *Runners-up:* First Division 1983-84. Division II 1907-08. Third Division 2001-02.
Scottish Cup Winners: 1883; *Runners-up:* 1881, 1882, 1887, 1891, 1897.

Club colours: Shirt: Amber with thin black stripe. Shorts: Black. Stockings: Black.

Goalscorers: *League (49):* Chaplain 10 (2 pens), Carcary 5, Hunter 5, Winters 5, Wyness 5, Cook 3, Gordon 3, Clark 2 (1 pen), Dunlop 2, Geggan 2, Chisholm 1, Craig C 1, McLaughlin 1, McStay 1, Murray 1, O'Donoghue 1, own goal 1.
Scottish Cup (0).
CIS Cup (0).
Challenge Cup (0).

McEwan D 2	Geggan A 27	Gordon B 34	Dunlop M 34	Smith C 34	Craig C 16 + 1	Clark R 14 + 8	Chaplain S 29 + 5	Murray S 17 + 15	McLaughlin D 10 + 4	Carcary D 9 + 22	Hunter R 14 + 6	Chisholm I 27 + 4	White M 9 + 2	McNiff M 13 + 2	McStay R 19 + 4	Lynch S — + 1	McGeown M 1	O'Donoghue R 1b + 4	Vosachek I 24	Harvey R 1	Strachan A 1 + 2	Cook A 10	Brannan K 5 + 8	Wyness D 16 + 1	Winters D 15	Match No.
1^6	2	3	4	5	6^2	7	8	9^1	10	11	12	13		15												1
	2	3	4	5	7^1	6	8^2	11	9	14	1	10^3	12	13												2
	2	3	4	5	6^3	8	13	11^2	12	9	14	10^1	1	7												3
	2	3	4	5	10^2	6^1	13	14	11	12	9^3	8	7	1												4
	2	5	10^1	6	13	11	9^3	12	4	8	7^2	1^8	3	14												5
1	2	6	5	12	9^2	13	11	10	4	8	7	3^1														6
	2	5	4	3	10^1	8	13	9	12	7	6^3	1	14	11^2												7
	2	5^1	4	3	10^3	8	14	9^2	13	7	12^4	6	1	11												8
	2	4	3	5	11^1	8	10	12	6	7	1	9														9
	2	5	4	3	10^1	8	9	7	6	1	11	12														10
	2^1	4	3	5	11^3	8	14	10	6	7	12	1	9^2	13												11
	4	3	5	11	8	14	10^3	12	13	6	7	2^3	1	9^1												12
	5	4	3	10^1	13	8^2	11	12	9	7	6	2	1													13
	11^2	4	3	5	7	9^1	12	10	6^3	14	8	2	1	13												14
	11	4	3	5	12	8	9	13	10^2	6	7^1	2	1													15
	11^2	4	3	5	13	8	9	12	10	6	7^1	2	1													16
	5	4	3	10	6^3	14	13	9^1	12	7	11	2	1	8^2												17
	5	4	3	9^1	12	7^2	8	11	10	2	6	13														18
	4	3	5	6^1	12	8	9	13	11^3	10^2	2	7	1	14												19
	4	3	5	6^1	14	7	9	10	11^2	2	8^3	12	1	13												20
	3	5	4	9^1	12	6	8	13	2	14	7^3	1												11	10^2	21
	4	5	3	14	9	12	13	2	1	8	7^3	6^2												10	11^1	22
	7^2	5	4	3	8	14	9^3	11	13	2	1	6^1												12	10	23
	8	5	4	3	6	12	11^1	2	13	1	7													10	9^2	24
	8	5	4	3	6^2	13	14	12	11^1	2	1	7^3												10	9	25
	7	5	4	3	12	8^1	11^3	13	2	6	1	14												10	9^2	26
	6^1	4	3	5	8	9^2	13	2	7	1	12													11	10	27
	3	5	4	7^3	12	14	2	6^2	13	8	1	9^1												10	11	28
	6^1	3	5	4	7	9	12	2	8	1														10	11	29
	6	3	8	5	2	7	12	13	1	4	9^1													11	10^2	30
	6	4	3	5	2	8	13	12	1	7	9^1													11	10^2	31
	7	3	5	4	2	6	13	12	14	1	8^3	9^1												10	11^2	32
	6	5	4	3	8	7	11^1	2	1	12														10	9	33
	6	3	5	4	2^1	8	13	12	9	1	7													11	10^2	34
	6	5	2^1	7^2	9	12	13	4	1	3	8													11	10	35
	7	3	5	2^1	6^2	13	12	4	8	1	9	14												10	11^3	36

DUNDEE First Division

Year Formed: 1893. *Ground & Address:* Dens Park Stadium, Sandeman St, Dundee DD3 7JY. *Telephone:* 01382 889966.
Fax: 01382 832284. *E-mail:* laura@dundeefc.co.uk *Website:* www.thedees.co.uk
Ground Capacity: all seated: 11,760. *Size of Pitch:* 101m × 66m.
Chairman: Bob Brannan. *Club Secretary:* Laura Hayes (tel: 01382 826104; mob: 07855 410 929). *Email:*
laura@dundeefc.co.uk
Manager: Gordon Chisholm. *Assistant Manager:* Billy Dodds. *Youth Development Coach:* Gordon Wallace. *Physio:*
Karen Gibson.
Club Nickname(s): The Dark Blues or The Dee. *Previous Grounds:* Carolina Port 1893-98.
Record Attendance: 43,024 v Rangers, Scottish Cup, 1953.
Record Transfer Fee received: £1,200,000 for Robert Douglas to Celtic (2000).
Record Transfer Fee paid: £600,000 for Fabian Caballero (2000).
Record Victory: 10-0 Division II v Alloa, 9 Mar 1947 and v Dunfermline Ath, 22 Mar 1947.
Record Defeat: 0-11 v Celtic, Division I, 26 Oct 1895.
Most Capped Player: Alex Hamilton, 24, Scotland.
Most League Appearances: 400: Barry Smith, 1995-2006.
Most League Goals in Season (Individual): 52: Alan Gilzean, 1960-64.
Most Goals Overall (Individual): 113: Alan Gilzean 1960-64.

DUNDEE 2009–10 LEAGUE RECORD

Match No.	Date	Venue	Opponents	Result	H/T Score	Lg Pos.	Goalscorers	Attendance
1	Aug 8	H	Morton	W 1-0	0-0		Higgins 56	5449
2	15	A	Raith R	D 2-2	1-2	1	Higgins (pen) 5, McMenamin 73	4744
3	22	H	Inverness CT	D 2-2	2-2	2	Harkins 2 9, 29	5507
4	29	A	Airdrie U	D 1-1	1-1	4	McMenamin 36	1516
5	Sept 12	H	Dunfermline Ath	W 1-0	1-0	3	Harkins (pen) 37	5326
6	19	A	Queen of the S	L 0-2	0-1	6		2875
7	26	H	Ross Co	W 2-0	0-0	5	Griffiths 2 59, 77	4682
8	Oct 10	H	Partick Th	W 2-0	1-0	5	Griffiths 4, Harkins 48	5364
9	14	A	Ayr U	D 2-2	1-0	—	Forsyth 13, Griffiths 60	1710
10	17	A	Morton	W 1-0	0-0	2	Griffiths 77	2217
11	24	H	Raith R	W 2-1	2-1	1	McMenamin 15, MacKenzie 35	5156
12	31	A	Dunfermline Ath	D 1-1	0-0	2	Harkins 60	4001
13	Nov 7	H	Airdrie U	W 2-1	2-1	2	Higgins 2 28, 35	4121
14	14	A	Queen of the S	D 0-0	0-0	2		4901
15	Dec 1	A	Ross Co	W 1-0	0-0	—	Harkins 69	2005
16	5	A	Partick Th	W 2-0	1-0	1	McMenamin 44, Harkins 47	4453
17	12	H	Ayr U	W 3-1	1-1	1	Forsyth 23, Griffiths 68, Harkins 90	4323
18	19	H	Morton	W 3-1	0-0	—	Griffiths 54, Harkins 65, Malone 87	4259
19	26	A	Inverness CT	D 1-1	1-0	—	Griffiths (pen) 45	3660
20	Jan 3	H	Airdrie U	L 0-1	0-1	—		4319
21	17	H	Dunfermline Ath	W 3-2	2-1	—	Griffiths 2 2, 82, McMenamin 16	5201
22	23	A	Queen of the S	D 1-1	0-1	1	Griffiths 77	3415
23	30	H	Ross Co	L 0-1	0-1	—		4912
24	Feb 20	H	Partick Th	W 1-0	1-0	—	Paton 6	5216
25	Mar 6	A	Inverness CT	D 2-2	0-0	1	Kerr 78, Harkins 84	4974
26	17	A	Ayr U	D 1-1	1-1	—	Harkins 38	1375
27	20	A	Airdrie U	L 0-3	0-0	1		1172
28	23	H	Queen of the S	D 1-1	1-0	—	Griffiths (pen) 16	4508
29	27	A	Ross Co	D 1-1	0-2	2	Hutchinson 50	3295
30	30	A	Dunfermline Ath	L 1-2	0-2	—	Harkins 90	2134
31	Apr 3	H	Ayr U	W 3-0	2-0	2	McMenamin 2 10, 61, Higgins 22	4270
32	10	A	Partick Th	W 1-0	0-0	—	Clarke 75	2545
33	17	A	Morton	D 2-2	0-1	2	Harkins 67, Griffiths 86	1998
34	21	A	Raith R	L 0-1	0-0	—		1544
35	24	H	Raith R	W 2-0	0-0	2	Higgins 52, Harkins (pen) 65	3187
36	May 1	A	Inverness CT	L 0-1	0-1	2		6031

Final League Position: 2

Honours
League Champions: Division I 1961-62. First Division 1978-79, 1991-92, 1997-98. Division II 1946-47; *Runners-up:* Division I 1902-03, 1906-07, 1908-09, 1948-49, 1980-81. First Division 2007-08.
Scottish Cup Winners: 1910; *Runners-up:* 1925, 1952, 1964, 2003.
League Cup Winners: 1951-52, 1952-53, 1973-74; *Runners-up:* 1967-68, 1980-81, 1995-96.
League Challenge Cup Winners: 2009-10.
B&Q (Centenary) Cup Winners: 1990-91; *Runners-up:* 1994-95.

European: *European Cup:* 8 matches (1962-63 semi-finals). *Cup Winners' Cup:* 2 matches: (1964-65).
UEFA Cup: 22 matches: (*Fairs Cup:* 1967-68 semi-finals. *UEFA Cup:* 1971-72, 1973-74, 1974-75, 2003-04).

Club colours: Shirt: Navy blue. Shorts: White. Stockings: Navy blue.

Goalscorers: *League (48):* Harkins 14 (2 pens), Griffiths 13 (2 pens), McMenamin 7, Higgins 6 (1 pen), Forsyth 2, Clarke 1, Hutchinson 1, Kerr 1, MacKenzie 1, Malone 1, Paton 1.
Scottish Cup (4): Forsyth 1, Griffiths 1, Harkins 1, Hutchinson 1
CIS Cup (13): Griffiths 4, Antoine-Curier 2, Cameron 1, Forsyth 1, Harkins 1, Higgins 1, McMenamin 1, Malone 1, own goal 1.
Challenge Cup (11): Griffiths 3, Forsyth 2, Harkins 2, Antoine-Curier 1, Clarke 1, Higgins 1, own goal 1.

Match	Bullock T 19	Paton E 32	Malone E 33	McHale P 11+3	MacKenzie G 25	Lauchlan J 25	Hart R 20+6	Cameron C 5+9	McMenamin C 24+7	Higgins S 15+11	Harkins G 32+2	Griffiths L 24+5	Ker B 29+4	Forsyth C 21+3	Benedictus K 4+1	Klimpl M 16+2	Cowan D 5+1	Douglas R 15+1	Clarke P 4+13	Young D 2+3	Casement C —+1	Shinnie A 9+3	Hutchinson B 5+4	McKeown C 9+2	Malcolm R 2+1	O'Leary R 8	Geddes R —+1	Soutar D 2
1	1	2	3	4	5	6	7	8[2]	9[1]	10	11[3]	12	13	14														
2	1	2	3	4[3]	5	6	7[1]	8	9	10[2]	11	13	12	14														
3	1	2	3	4	5	6	7[2]	13	9	10[1]	11	12		8														
4	1	2	3	4		6	12	7[1]	9	13	11	10[2]		8		5												
5	1	2	3	4	5	6[1]	14	9	13	11	10[2]	8				7[3]	12											
6	1[2]	2	3	7[2]	4			8[6]	9	12	11	10[1]	13	6	5	15												
7	1	2	3	14	4		13		9[1]	11[2]	10[3]	8	7	6	5	12												
8	1	2	3	14	5		7[3]		13	10[2]	11	9	8	4	6	12												
9	1	2	5	12	3				11[1]	9	10	7	6	8	4													
10	1	2	3	8	5		7[1]		10[2]	14	9[3]	13	11	4	6	12												
11	1	2	3	7	5	6			10	13	12	9[2]	8	11	4[1]													
12	1	3	2	7	5	6	13		12	10[1]	11[2]	9	8	4														
13		2	3	4	5[1]	6	14	13	7	10[3]	12	9	8[2]	11				1										
14		2	3	4[1]	5	6	12	8	13	10	11	7				9[2]		1										
15		2	3		5	6	8[1]		10		11	9[2]	4	7				1	13	12								
16		2	3		5	6	8[1]	12	10		11[2]	4	7			14			9[3]	13								
17		2	3		5	6	8[1]12	10	11		9[2]	4	7					1	13									
18		2	3		5	6	8	10	11[2]	9[1]	4	7	13					1	12									
19		2	3		5	6	8	10[2]	11	9	4	7[1]	12					1	13									
20		2	5	3[4]	4	6	12		11	7	9	8[2]						1	10[1]	13								
21		2	5		4	6[1]	10		11	9[2]12	8	3	7					1	13									
22		2	5		4	9	11		8	10	7	6	3[1]					1	12									
23		2	4[2]	3	6[3]	11	9	12	7	5	13							1	10[1]	8	14							
24		5	4	2	3	12		8	10	6	9	7						1	11[1]									
25		2	5	3	4	13	12		9	10	7	6						1					8[2]	11[1]				
26		2[1]	5	8		11[1]	9	10	7		4	1							6			3	12					
27			5	4[1]		12	10	13	9		8			3		1			6	11[2]		7	2					
28	1	2	5		13		11[1]12	9	10	7	8[2]								6[1]	14	3	4						
29	1	2	3	5		7[1]	13	11	9[3]	8	4								12	10[2]	14	6						
30	1	2[1]	5	3[2]	7		12	9	10	8	4								13	11[3]	14	6						
31	1		5		2	6	12	10	11[2]	9[1]	7								8	13	3	4						
32	1		5		2	9	13	10[3]	11[1]	6	12	7				14			8[2]	3	4							
33	1		5	9	3		14	10[2]	12	7	11	6[3]				13			3[1]	2	4							
34	1[9]	2		4	6		12	11[2]	9		5		8[1]		10				13	3		7	15					
35		5	2			10	11	8		7	9	6							3	4	1							
36			2			10	11[2]	9		8[3]	3	4				12	14		7[1]13	5		6	1					

DUNDEE UNITED

Premier League

Year Formed: 1909 (1923). *Ground & Address:* Tannadice Park, Tannadice St, Dundee DD3 7JW. *Telephone:* 01382 833166. *Fax:* 01382 889398. *E-mail:* enquiries@dundeeunited.co.uk *Website:* www.dundeeunitedfc.co.uk
Ground Capacity: total: 14,223 all seated: stands: east 2868, west 2096, south 2201, Fair Play 1601, George Fox 5151, executive boxes 292. *Size of Pitch:* 110yd × 72yd.
Chairman: Stephen Thompson, OBE. *Vice Chairman:* Cath Thompson. *Secretary:* Spence Anderson.
Manager: Peter Houston. *First Team Coaches:* Paul Hegarty and Gary Kirk. *Coach:* Graeme Liveston. *Physio:* Jeff Clarke.
Club Nickname(s): The Terrors. *Previous Grounds:* None.
Record Attendance: 28,000 v Barcelona, Fairs Cup, 16 Nov 1966.
Record Transfer Fee received: £4,000,000 for Duncan Ferguson from Rangers (July 1993).
Record Transfer Fee paid: £750,000 for Steven Pressley from Coventry C (July 1995).
Record Victory: 14-0 v Nithsdale Wanderers, Scottish Cup 1st rd, 17 Jan 1931.
Record Defeat: 1-12 v Motherwell, Division II, 23 Jan 1954.
Most Capped Player: Maurice Malpas, 55, Scotland.
Most League Appearances: 618, Maurice Malpas, 1980-2000.
Most Appearances in European Matches: 76, Dave Narey (record for Scottish player).
Most League Goals in Season (Individual): 41: John Coyle, Division II, 1955-56.
Most Goals Overall (Individual): 158: Peter McKay, 1947-54.

DUNDEE UNITED 2009–10 LEAGUE RECORD

Match No.	Date	Venue	Opponents	Result	H/T Score	Lg Pos.	Goalscorers	Attendance
1	Aug 17	H	Hearts	W 2-0	1-0	—	Cadamarteri 2 (1 pen) [4 (p), 85]	8253
2	22	A	St Mirren	D 0-0	0-0	5		4775
3	29	H	Falkirk	W 2-1	0-0	3	Cadamarteri [49], Goodwillie [56]	6979
4	Sept 12	A	Celtic	D 1-1	1-1	—	Goodwillie [6]	58,500
5	19	H	Motherwell	L 0-1	0-0	6		7196
6	26	A	St Johnstone	W 3-2	1-1	4	Cadamarteri (pen) [34], Webster [48], Goodwillie [77]	7225
7	Oct 3	A	Hibernian	D 1-1	0-1	4	Webster [72]	13,056
8	17	H	Hamilton A	D 1-1	0-0	4	Kenneth [90]	5944
9	24	A	Aberdeen	W 2-0	2-0	4	Casalinuovo [31], Gomis [36]	11,766
10	Nov 7	A	Kilmarnock	W 2-0	1-0	4	Casalinuovo 2 (1 pen) [22 (p), 57]	4753
11	22	H	Celtic	W 2-1	0-0	4	Daly [83], Dods [90]	11,098
12	28	A	Motherwell	D 2-2	1-2	4	Webster [14], Daly [83]	4593
13	Dec 5	H	St Mirren	W 3-2	2-0	4	Casalinuovo [29], Conway [44], Myrie-Williams [79]	6259
14	12	A	Hearts	D 0-0	0-0	4		14,873
15	15	H	Rangers	L 0-3	0-1	—		10,037
16	26	H	Kilmarnock	D 0-0	0-0	4		6692
17	30	A	Rangers	L 1-7	0-3	—	Casalinuovo [46]	48,721
18	Jan 2	H	Aberdeen	L 0-1	0-1	—		10,032
19	13	A	Hamilton A	W 1-0	0-0	—	Goodwillie [75]	2033
20	16	H	Hibernian	W 1-0	1-0	3	Swanson [39]	7812
21	24	A	Falkirk	W 4-1	2-0	4	Goodwillie [29], Daly 3 [45, 57, 88]	4378
22	27	H	St Johnstone	D 3-3	0-2	—	Daly [52], Swanson [69], Anderson (og) [77]	6600
23	30	A	Kilmarnock	D 4-4	3-2	4	Buaben [16], Conway 2 [28, 33], Daly (pen) [66]	4587
24	Feb 10	A	Hamilton A	L 0-2	0-2	—		5598
25	13	A	St Mirren	W 2-1	0-0	4	Swanson [83], Goodwillie [90]	3944
26	20	A	Celtic	L 0-1	0-1	4		49,000
27	27	H	Falkirk	W 3-0	2-0	3	Goodwillie (pen) [17], Gomis 2 [30, 87]	6352
28	Mar 7	A	Hearts	W 1-0	0-0	3	Gomis [78]	6683
29	20	A	Aberdeen	D 2-2	2-2	3	Daly 2 [8, 24]	9316
30	27	H	Motherwell	W 3-0	2-0	3	Goodwillie [38], Buaben [43], Swanson [72]	7609
31	31	A	Hibernian	W 4-2	2-1	—	Daly (pen) [20], Swanson [26], Goodwillie [60], Sandaza F [88]	9185
32	Apr 5	A	St Johnstone	W 1-0	0-0	—	Daly [83]	5769
33	14	H	Rangers	D 0-0	0-0	—		11,100
34	18	A	Motherwell	W 3-2	2-1	3	Daly 2 [3, 43], Conway [49]	3544
35	25	H	Celtic	L 0-2	0-1	3		8810
36	May 1	H	Rangers	L 1-2	0-2	3	Casalinuovo [80]	10,003
37	5	A	Hearts	D 0-0	0-0	—		12,325
38	9	H	Hibernian	L 0-2	0-1	3		6527

Final League Position: 3

Honours
League Champions: Premier Division 1982-83. Division I: 1924-25, 1928-29; *Runners-up:* Division II 1930-31, 1959-60.
First Division Runners-up 1995-96.
Scottish Cup Winners: 1994, 2010; *Runners-up:* 1974, 1981, 1985, 1987, 1988, 1991, 2005.
League Cup Winners: 1979-80, 1980-81; *Runners-up:* 1981-82, 1984-85, 1997-98, 2007-08.
Summer Cup Runners-up: 1964-65. *Scottish War Cup Runners-up* 1939-40.

European: *European Cup:* 8 matches (1983-84, semi-finals). *Cup Winners' Cup:* 10 matches (1974-75, 1988-89, 1994-95).
UEFA Cup: 86 matches (*Fairs Cup:* 1966-67, 1969-70, 1970-71. *UEFA Cup:* 1975-76, 1977-78, 1978-79, 1979-80, 1980-81,
1981-82, 1982-83, 1984-85, 1985-86, 1986-87 runners-up, 1987-88, 1989-90, 1990-91, 1993-94, 1997-98, 2005-06).

Club colours: Shirts: Tangerine. Shorts: Black. Stockings: Tangerine.

Goalscorers: *League (55):* Daly 13 (2 pens), Goodwillie 9 (1 pen), Casalinuovo 6 (1 pen), Swanson 5, Cadamarteri 4 (2
pens), Conway 4, Gomis 4, Webster 3, Buaben 2, Dods 1, Kenneth 1, Myrie-Williams 1, Sandaza F 1, own goal 1.
Scottish Cup (12): Goodwillie 4, Conway 2, Casalinuovo 1, Kovacevic 1, Robertson D 1, Shala 1, Weaver 1, own goal 1.
CIS Cup (5): Buaben 1, Goodwillie 1, Russell 1, Shala 1, Wilkie 1.

Weaver N 18	Kovacevic M 24 + 1	Dixon P 25	Webster A 26	Dods D 23 + 4	Buaben P 33 + 1	Robertson S 8 + 5	Gomis M 31	Goodwillie D 23 + 10	Cadamarteri D 15 + 6	Swanson D 22 + 9	Conway C 29 + 4	Dillon S 23 + 0	Shala A 2 + 10	Casalinuovo D 16 + 9	Myrie-Williams J 11 + 13	Robertson D 8 + 6	Kenneth G 26 + 2	Wilkie L 1	Fotheringham M 2 + 1	Hitson D — + 2	Daly J 16 + 7	Pernis D 19	Mihadjuks P 3	Smith R — + 1	Sandaza F 1 + 6	Watson K 7 + 1	Smith K 2 + 1	Hill C 1	Dow R — + 2	Banks S 1	Cameron G — + 1	Match No.
1	2²	3	4	5	6	7	8	9	10³	11¹	12	13	14																			1
1	2	3	4	5	6	7	8	9²	10¹	11		13	12²	14																		2
1		3	4	5	6	7¹	8	9²	10	11³	14	2	13		12																	3
	3	4	5	6	7	8²	9³	10	11¹	12	2			13	14																	4
1	12	3¹	4	5	6			9	10	11²	3²	2	14		13	7																5
1	8	3²	4	5	6	7		14	10¹	11⁸		13		9			2³	12														6
1	8	3²	4	5	6⁸	7	11	12	10¹		2	13		9	14																	7
1		3	5			8	12			4²	2	14	10	7³	9¹	6		11	13													8
1	2		5	6		8	12	10¹		3		9	11		4	7																9
1	2	3	4		6		8	9	12	13	1	14		10¹	7²		5															10
1	2	3	4	5	6		8	12	10¹	13	1	2		9³	7				14													11
1	2	3	4	6⁸		8	13	10²	14⁸	1		9¹	7³				12															12
1	2	3	6	5³		12	8⁸	10¹		14	4		9²	7	14		13															13
1	2	3	4		7		12	13	3²	6	14	9¹	11		5		10³															14
1	2¹	3		5	7	12	8³	14	9²		1	4		13	6		10															15
1	7	3	4		6			9¹	12	13	8²	2		14	11		5															16
1	7²	3		5	6		8⁰		9	13	0¹	2		12	11	14	4															17
1	7	3	4		6		8		10²	14	13	2¹		9	12		5		13													18
	2	3	4		6		8	10³		12	11	14		9²		7	5				13	1										19
	2	3	4	5	6		8	10²		7³	11	13		14	12						9³	1										20
	2	3	4¹	12	6³		8	9²		7	11			13		14	5				10	1										21
	2	3		5	6		8	9²		7	11¹			13	12		4				10	1										22
		3		5	6		8	9²		7	11	2		13	12		4				10	1										23
			5	6		9			7	11¹	2	14	13	12		4				10²	1		3³								24
			5	6		8	13			9³	11²	2		14		7³	4				10	1		3¹	12							25
	2³		4	14	6		8	12		7	11	3		9²	13		5				10	1										26
	2	3		5	6		8	10³		7	11²	12		9¹		13	4				14	1										27
	2	3¹	4		6		8	10³		7	11	12		9²			5				13	1			14							28
	2		4		6³		8	9¹		7	11	3			14	2²	5				10	1			13							29
		3¹	11³	14	6			9²			7	8	2	10¹			4				12	1			13	5						30
		3		6		8	9			9¹	11²	2	14			4					10³	1			12	5	13					31
		3	4¹	12	14		8	9²	13	7³	11	2					5				10	1				6						32
	2⁸									12	3			11²	7¹	4				1				10³	13						33
		4	5	6	13	8	9³	12		7²	11¹	2					10	1							14	3						34
	2		5	6		8	9³	14		7	11	3		12⁸		4					10²	1			13							35
			6²	13	8		10			2	14	9		7	5											4	11³	3	12			36
	3¹		6	8³		9²		12	11	2	13		14	7	5					10						4			1		37
			12			7²		2	10	9	11	8	5											1	3¹		4	6³	14	13	38

DUNFERMLINE ATHLETIC First Division

Year Formed: 1885. *Ground & Address:* East End Park, Halbeath Rd, Dunfermline KY12 7RB.
Telephone: 01383 724295. *Fax:* 01383 723468. *Ticket office telephone:* 0870 300 1201. *E-mail:* enquiries@dafc.co.uk
Website: www.dafc.co.uk
Ground Capacity: all seated: 12,509. *Size of Pitch:* 115yd × 71yd.
Chairman: John Yorkston. *Chief Executive:* William Hodgins.
Manager: Jim McIntyre. *Assistant Manager:* Gerry McCabe. *Physio:* Gerry Docherty. *Head of Youth Development:*
Steven Wright.
Club Nickname(s): The Pars. *Previous Grounds:* None.
Record Attendance: 27,816 v Celtic, Division I, 30 Apr 1968.
Record Transfer Fee received: £650,000 for Jackie McNamara to Celtic (Oct 1995).
Record Transfer Fee paid: £540,000 for Istvan Kozma from Bordeaux (Sept 1989).
Record Victory: 11-2 v Stenhousemuir, Division I, 27 Sept 1930.
Record Defeat: 1-11 v Hibernian, Scottish Cup, 3rd rd replay, 26 Oct 1889.
Most Capped Player: Colin Miller 16 (61), Canada.
Most League Appearances: 497: Norrie McCathie, 1981-96.
Most League Goals in Season (Individual): 53: Bobby Skinner, Division II, 1925-26.
Most Goals Overall (Individual): 154: Charles Dickson, 1954-64.

DUNFERMLINE ATHLETIC 2009–10 LEAGUE RECORD

Match No.	Date	Venue	Opponents	Result	H/T Score	Lg Pos.	Goalscorers	Attendance
1	Aug 8	H	Inverness CT	L 0-1	0-0	—		2975
2	15	A	Morton	W 2-0	1-0	4	Kirk [19], Cardle [79]	2661
3	22	H	Airdrie U	W 2-0	1-0	1	Bayne [19], Nolan (og) [58]	2834
4	29	H	Raith R	L 0-2	0-1	5		6289
5	Sept 12	A	Dundee	L 0-1	0-1	7		5326
6	19	A	Partick Th	L 0-2	0-1	7		3263
7	26	H	Queen of the S	L 1-4	1-4	8	Phinn [37]	2624
8	Oct 10	H	Ayr U	W 3-1	0-0	7	Kirk [54], Gibson 2 [55, 63]	2460
9	13	A	Ross Co	D 0-0	0-0	—		1757
10	17	A	Inverness CT	D 1-1	0-1	7	Kirk [69]	3082
11	24	H	Morton	W 3-1	0-0	7	Cardle [62], Graham [71], Bell [86]	2411
12	31	H	Dundee	D 1-1	0-0	7	Bayne [77]	4001
13	Nov 7	A	Raith R	W 2-1	0-1	7	Bayne [54], Wilson (og) [90]	6200
14	14	H	Partick Th	W 3-1	2-0	6	McDougall [4], Gibson 2 [39, 90]	3111
15	Dec 1	A	Queen of the S	W 2-1	2-1	—	McGregor [24], Gibson (pen) [29]	1651
16	5	A	Ayr U	L 0-1	0-0	5		1625
17	12	H	Ross Co	D 3-3	3-2	6	Kirk 2 [22, 35], Gibson [40]	2381
18	19	H	Inverness CT	D 0-0	0-0	—		2280
19	Jan 17	A	Dundee	L 2-3	1-2	—	Graham [10], Kirk [49]	5201
20	23	A	Partick Th	W 4-1	0-0	6	Cardle 3 [48, 71, 82], Woods [83]	1549
21	Feb 13	A	Ross Co	D 2-2	2-0	6	Phinn 2 [10, 32]	2213
22	20	H	Ayr U	L 0-1	0-1	—		2429
23	27	A	Morton	W 2-1	0-0	—	Kirk [70], Mason [77]	1776
24	Mar 6	A	Airdrie U	W 2-0	0-0	6	Kirk (pen) [54], Bell [87]	2252
25	9	A	Airdrie U	D 1-1	0-1	—	Gibson (pen) [87]	703
26	13	H	Queen of the S	W 3-1	2-0	—	McDougall [18], Woods [43], Bell (pen) [86]	2163
27	16	H	Raith R	W 2-1	1-0	—	McDougall [11], Gibson [55]	4549
28	20	A	Raith R	W 2-1	0-0	—	Mason [50], Graham [83]	4098
29	23	H	Partick Th	L 1-2	1-1	—	McDougall [37]	2401
30	27	A	Queen of the S	L 0-2	0-1	3		2298
31	30	H	Dundee	W 2-1	2-0	—	Gibson [6], Bell [34]	2134
32	Apr 3	H	Ross Co	L 1-2	0-2	3	Bell [78]	2641
33	10	A	Ayr U	W 2-1	1-1	—	Campbell R [39], McDougall [53]	1367
34	17	A	Inverness CT	L 0-2	0-0	3		3728
35	24	H	Morton	W 4-1	3-1	4	Phinn [8], Bell 3 (1 pen) [27, 44, 90 (p)]	2532
36	May 1	A	Airdrie U	W 1-0	1-0	3	Phinn [37]	1864

Final League Position: 3

Honours
League Champions: First Division 1988-89, 1995-96. Division II 1925-26. Second Division 1985-86; *Runners-up:* First Division 1986-87, 1993-94, 1994-95, 1999-2000. Division II 1912-13, 1933-34, 1954-55, 1957-58, 1972-73. Second Division 1978-79.
Scottish Cup Winners: 1961, 1968; *Runners-up:* 1965, 2004, 2007.
League Cup Runners-up: 1949-50, 1991-92, 2005-06.
League Challenge Cup Runners-up: 2007-08.

European: *Cup Winners' Cup:* 14 matches (1961-62, 1968-69 semi-finals). *UEFA Cup:* 32 matches (*Fairs Cup:* 1962-63, 1964-65, 1965-66, 1966-67, 1969-70. *UEFA Cup:* 2004-05, 2007-08)

Club colours: Shirt: White and black stripes. Shorts: Black. Stockings: Black.

Goalscorers: *League (54):* Gibson 9 (2 pens), Bell 8 (2 pens), Kirk 8 (1 pen), Cardle 5, McDougall 5, Phinn 5, Bayne 3, Graham 3, Mason 2, Woods 2, Campbell R 1, McGregor 1 own goals 2.
Scottish Cup (11): Kirk 4 (1 pen), Cardle 2, Graham 2, Gibson 1, McDougall 1, Phinn 1.
CIS Cup (9): Kirk 4, Bayne 1, Bell 1, Burke 1, Graham 1, own goal 1.
Challenge Cup (3): Bell 1, Cardle 1, Kirk 1.

Fleming G 25+1	Woods C 25+4	Glass S 1	Bell S 29+2	McGregor N 24	Higgins C 13+4	Gibson W 30+4	Burke A 25+2	Bayne G 15+1	Kirk A 17+4	Graham D 28+1	McCann A 28+2	McDougall S 17+5	Cardle J 16+9	Phinn N 16+17	Dowie A 32	Muirhead S 2+5	Ross G 22+2	Holmes G 6+11	Smith C 8	Paterson G 3	McIntyre J —+2	Campbell R 3+10	Mason G 11+2	Willis P —+2	Match No.
1	2	3	4	5	6	7	8	9	10	11															1
1	2		4	5	6	7^2	8	9	10^3	11^2	3	12	13	14											2
1	2		4	5	6	7	8	9	10^1		3	13	11^2	12											3
1	2		4	5		7^8	8^1	9^2	10		3	13	11	12	6^3	14									4
1	2		4^3	5		8	9	10			3	7	11^2	12	6	14	13								5
1	2		5		7^2	8	9	10		3^1		11	4	6	12			13							6
1		5^1 12	7	8	9	13			11	10	6	4	2	3^1											7
1	12		5		7	11	8	9	10^3		14	4^2	6	3^1	2	13									8
1	3		14 5		7^2	8^1	9		11		13	12	10^1	6			2	4							9
1	3		14 5		7	8	9	13	11^2		12	10^1	6			2	4^3								10
1	3		4	5	14	13	8^1	9^2	10	7		11	12	6			2^3								11
1	3^1		4	5		7	8	13	10	9	12		11^2		6		2								12
1	3		4	5		7	8^3	9	10^1	11	13		14	6			2^2 12								13
1			4	5		7	8^1	9		11	3	10^2	13	6			2 12								14
			6	4^2 13		7	8	10	12	9^3	3	11^1		14	5		2		1						15
			7^3		3	6	8	10^2	12	9	5	11^1		13	4		2 14		1						16
	13		4	5		7	8^1		10	11	3	9^2	12	6			2^2 14		1						17
			4^2 5			7	8		10	11	3	9^1	12	13	6		2		1						18
1			7	3		8^1			10	11	5	9^2	12	6	4		2					13			19
1	13		7	3		9^2			10	11	5	6^1	12	8	4		2								20
1			3	4		7^2	10		11	5	9^1	8	6	13	2	12^4									21
1	14		3	8		6^1	9		10	5		11	7^2	4	2^5					13	12				22
1	4		6	3^1	12	13			11	9	5		8^3	10^2			2					14	7		23
1	2		8		3	12	9		11^2	6	5	13	10^1		4								7		24
1	2		8		5	12			11^1	6	3		10^2	9^3	4		13					14	7		25
1	2^4		8		4	6^1	11^2		9	5	10		14	3			7^3					12	13		26
1	2		7^8		4	6^1	13		11	5	10^3		12	3			9^2					14	8		27
1	2		4	6		9^2			11	5	10^3 13	12	3				7^1					14	8		28
1	2^2	7	4			11^1	5	10	9	6^3	3	14	13				12					12	8		29
	2		4	6			5	11	10^4	9	3	8^1			1		12	7							30
15	7	8	3		9^5			5	10^1		12	4		1				16			11	6	13		31
6		4	3		9		13	5	10	12	14	7	9^1		1							11^4	8^3		32
2	6		3	7		9	5	11		12	4		1									10^1	8		33
4	9		2	8	14	11	5	10^1		7^2	3	13	1									12	6^3		34
4	8		6^2 7		10	5		9^1	11^3	3		2	14	1								12^2	13		35
5	6		7	8^1		10	3		11^2	9	4		2	2^1	1									13	36

EAST FIFE

Second Division

Year Formed: 1903. *Ground & Address:* Bayview Stadium, Harbour View, Methil, Fife KY8 3RW. *Telephone:* 01333 426323. *Fax:* 01333 426376. *E-mail:* office@eastfife.org. *Website:* www.eastfife.org
Ground Capacity: 1992. *Size of Pitch:* 105m × 65m.
Chairman: Sidney Columbine. *Secretary:* John Sharp.
Manager: Stevie Crawford. *Assistant Manager:* Jason Dair. *Physio:* Brian McNeil.
Club Nickname(s): The Fifers. *Previous Ground:* Bayview Park.
Record Attendance: 22,515 v Raith Rovers, Division I, 2 Jan 1950.
Record Transfer Fee received: £150,000 for Paul Hunter from Hull C (March 1990).
Record Transfer Fee paid: £70,000 for John Sludden from Kilmarnock (July 1991).
Record Victory: 13-2 v Edinburgh City, Division II, 11 Dec 1937.
Record Defeat: 0-9 v Hearts, Division I, 5 Oct 1957.
Most Capped Player: George Aitken, 5 (8), Scotland.
Most League Appearances: 517: David Clarke, 1968-86.
Most League Goals in Season (Individual): 41: Jock Wood, Division II; 1926-27 and Henry Morris, Division II, 1947-48.
Most Goals Overall (Individual): 225: Phil Weir, 1922-35.

EAST FIFE 2009–10 LEAGUE RECORD

Match No.	Date	Venue	Opponents	Result	H/T Score	Lg Pos.	Goalscorers	Attendance
1	Aug 8	H	Brechin C	W 2-0	2-0	—	McManus 30, Thomson S 33	605
2	15	A	Stenhousemuir	D 1-1	1-1	3	Muir 43	645
3	22	H	Arbroath	D 1-1	0-0	4	Crawford 54	770
4	29	H	Cowdenbeath	D 1-1	0-1	5	McManus 70	803
5	Sept 12	A	Peterhead	D 1-1	0-1	5	McManus 87	551
6	19	A	Stirling A	L 0-3	0-1	7		678
7	26	H	Clyde	W 1-0	1-0	5	Kerr 5	697
8	Oct 3	A	Alloa Ath	D 0-0	0-0	5		580
9	10	H	Dumbarton	L 0-1	0-0	5		684
10	17	A	Brechin C	L 2-3	1-1	6	Muir 15, McManus (pen) 49	517
11	24	H	Stenhousemuir	W 2-1	0-0	6	Conway 58, McManus 67	509
12	31	A	Cowdenbeath	L 1-2	1-2	7	Crawford 12	733
13	Nov 7	H	Peterhead	L 1-2	1-0	7	McManus 4	574
14	14	H	Stirling A	L 1-2	1-0	9	McManus 21	633
15	21	A	Clyde	W 3-1	1-0	8	McManus 2 9, 68, Linn 80	635
16	Dec 5	A	Alloa Ath	L 0-2	0-1	—		509
17	12	A	Dumbarton	W 3-0	1-0	8	McManus 37, Smart 53, Muir 89	628
18	Jan 16	H	Cowdenbeath	D 2-2	1-1	—	Linn 15, Young 81	864
19	23	A	Stirling A	D 3-3	1-1	7	Young 7, McManus 2 71, 73	665
20	27	A	Arbroath	W 1-0	0-0	—	Linn (pen) 90	376
21	Feb 6	A	Dumbarton	L 2-3	1-3	8	Crawford 2 13, 55	581
22	13	A	Alloa Ath	L 0-2	0-1	8		670
23	27	A	Stenhousemuir	D 1-1	0-1	—	Young 87	476
24	Mar 6	A	Cowdenbeath	L 2-6	0-1	8	Crawford 51, McManus 65	667
25	9	H	Clyde	D 1-1	0-1	—	Cargill 64	463
26	13	H	Peterhead	W 3-0	2-0	8	Crawford 9, Linn 15, Young 81	453
27	16	H	Arbroath	W 3-1	1-1	—	McCunnie 2 25, 81, Murdock 75	480
28	20	H	Stirling A	L 0-3	0-1	8		709
29	23	A	Peterhead	L 1-3	0-0	—	Muir 48	374
30	27	A	Clyde	L 1-2	0-0	8	McManus 78	495
31	30	H	Brechin C	W 2-0	1-0	—	Ovenstone 6, McManus (pen) 63	213
32	Apr 3	H	Alloa Ath	L 0-1	0-0	7		637
33	10	A	Dumbarton	W 1-0	0-0	7	Linn 85	728
34	17	A	Brechin C	L 0-1	0-0	7		492
35	24	H	Stenhousemuir	D 1-1	0-0	7	Cook 54	678
36	May 1	A	Arbroath	D 2-2	0-0	7	Linn 52, Muir 61	512

Final League Position: 7

Honours
League Champions: Division II 1947-48. Third Division 2007-08. *Runners-up:* Division II 1929-30, 1970-71. Second Division 1983-84, 1995-96. Third Division 2002-03.
Scottish Cup Winners: 1938; *Runners-up:* 1927, 1950.
League Cup Winners: 1947-48, 1949-50, 1953-54.

Club colours: Shirt: Gold with black stripes. Shorts: Black Stockings: Gold.

Goalscorers: *League (46):* McManus 15 (2 pens), Crawford 6, Linn 6 (1 pen), Muir 5, Young 4, McCunnie 2, Cargill 1, Conway 1, Cook 1, Kerr 1, Murdock 1, Ovenstone 1, Smart 1, Thomson S 1.
Scottish Cup (1): McManus 1.
CIS Cup (2): Linn 1, Muir 1.
Challenge Cup (0).

Brown M 26	Smart J 27+1	Thomson S 3	Ovenstone J 33	Nugent P 23	Fagan S 9+6	Muir D 36	Linn B 23+10	Campbell R 12+8	McManus P 28+4	Young L 33+2	Staunton M 5+6	Sheerin J 4+5	Crawford S 26+6	Cargill S 7+15	Kerr G 7+4	Conway A 10+15	Thomson D —+1	Baillie S +1	Gourlay D 4+4	McCunnie J 28	Sludden P 4+2	Ridgers M 4	McRae J 1	Watson K 6	Campbell S 3	Lowing A 7	Murdock S 13+1	Cook A 6+3	Match No.
1	2	3	4	5	6³	7	8²	9	10¹	11	12	13	14																1
1	2	3	4	5	6	7	8	9		11			10																2
1	2	3³	4	5	6	7	8¹	9	11²	13	12	10	14																3
1	2		4	5	6	7¹	8	9²	12	11	3	14	10³	13															4
1	2		4¹	5		7	8²	9	10	11³	3	13	6		12	14													5
1	2		5⁴			7	14	9	10	11³	3	8¹	6²		4	13	12												6
			3	7³	2	5	10	8	13	11²	14	9¹	4	6					1	12									7
			3	5	7³	2	10	8	12	11¹	14	13	4	9					1	6²									8
			3	5	7¹	2	10	8	11²	13	14	4	9³						1	12	6								9
			4	5	2	12	8³	6¹	11	13	10	7	9²						1	14	3								10
			3	2	5²	13⁴	11	9	10	12	7³	14	4	8¹					1	6									11
			3	5	2	8	6³	11¹	14	10	13	4	9						1	7	12²								12
			3⁴	4		8	12	11	5¹	13	10²		9					2	6	7	1								13
			4		2	12	10	6	3²	8¹	13		14					5	7	11	1	9³							14
			3			4	12	9	7	5	13	8²		14		11³		2¹	6	10	1								15
			5			3²	9	4³	10	6			14	12		7¹			13	8	11	1		2					16
1	4	5	12	8	9²	3	10³	11¹	6	13		7	14							7				2					17
1	4	5	3	6	9¹	10	7	11	12	8										8				2					18
1	4	5	13	11	9²	10	7	6	12	8										8				2	3¹				19
1	3	4	6	11	13	9³	8	10¹	14	12	7									7				2	5²				20
1	3	5	6	9	12	11	8	10	7											7				2	4¹				21
1	4¹	5	2	12	3	11²	9³	10	8	6	13	14								7									22
1		5	7¹	4	12	3³	10	9	6²	13	14	11								11						2	8		23
	3	4	5	12	9²	11³	8	10	13	14										6						2¹	7		24
1	4⁴	5	3	9²	14	10⁴	8	11³	7¹	12	6									6						2	13		25
1		5	4	3	9	8	13	11²	6¹	12					15					7						2	10		26
1		5	4	3	9¹	14	13	11	10³	6²	12	7								7						2	8		27
1	14	5³	4	3	9	10	11	12	6¹											7²						2	8	13	28
1	3²	5	4	6	9	11	10	12	8											7²						2¹	7	13	29
1		5¹	4	3	9	10	8	11	13	6²										7						2	12		30
1	3	4	5	14	2	12	10¹	8²	11²	13	7									7							6	9	31
1	3	4	2	6	12	13	10	9	11¹	14										7³							8	5²	32
1	2	4	5	3	13	12	11¹	6	10											7							8	9¹	33
1	4³	7	2	3	12	13	10²	9	11	14										6							8	5¹	34
1	3	5	2	4	10	12	9	11¹	8											7							7	6	35
1	4	7	2	3¹	10³	12	13	9	11²	14										6							8	5	36

EAST STIRLINGSHIRE — Third Division

Year Formed: 1880. *Ground & Address:* Ochilview Park, Gladstone Road, Stenhousemuir FK5 4QL. *Telephone:* 01324 562992 (match day only). *Fax:* 01324 562980 (match day only) *E-mail:* paul.marnie@eaststirlingfc.co.uk *Website:* www.eaststirlingfc.com
Ground Capacity: 3776 (626 seated). *Size of Pitch:* 110yd × 72yd.
Chairman: Les Thomson. *Vice Chairman:* Spencer Fearn. *Chief Executive/Secretary:* Leslie G. Thomson.
Head Coach: Jim McInally. *Assistant Coaches:* David Nicholls and John O'Neill. *Physio:* Steve O'Neill.
Club Nickname(s): The Shire. *Previous Grounds:* Burnhouse, Randyford Park, Merchiston Park, New Kilbowie Park, Firs Park.
Record Attendance: 12,000 v Partick Th, *Scottish Cup* 3rd rd, 21 Feb 1921.
Record Transfer Fee received: £35,000 for Jim Docherty to Chelsea (1978).
Record Transfer Fee paid: £6,000 for Colin McKinnon from Falkirk (March 1991).
Record Victory: 11-2 v Vale of Bannock, *Scottish Cup* 2nd rd, 22 Sept 1888.
Record Defeat: 1-12 v Dundee United, Division II, 13 Apr 1936.
Most Capped Player: Humphrey Jones, 5 (14), Wales.
Most League Appearances: 415: Gordon Russell, 1983-2001.
Most League Goals in Season (Individual): 36: Malcolm Morrison, Division II, 1938-39.

EAST STIRLINGSHIRE 2009–10 LEAGUE RECORD

Match No.	Date	Venue	Opponents	Result	H/T Score	Lg Pos.	Goalscorers	Attendance
1	Aug 15	A	Annan Ath	W 1-0	0-0	5	Maquire [52]	525
2	22	H	Elgin C	D 1-1	0-1	6	Stevenson [89]	324
3	29	A	Forfar Ath	L 1-5	1-3	6	Rodgers [23]	425
4	Sept12	H	Queen's Park	W 1-0	0-0	5	Lynch [64]	393
5	19	A	Montrose	W 3-0	2-0	3	Rodgers (pen) [5], Bolochoweckyj [7], Lynch [84]	410
6	26	H	Stranraer	D 1-1	0-1	4	Tully [54]	367
7	30	H	Livingston	W 3-1	2-1	—	Maquire 2 [18, 27], Lynch [82]	567
8	Oct 3	A	Albion R	L 0-3	0-3	4		337
9	10	H	Berwick R	W 1-0	0-0	2	Rodgers [46]	464
10	17	A	Elgin C	W 2-1	1-0	1	Rodgers [5], Richardson [85]	449
11	31	H	Annan Ath	L 1-3	1-1	3	Maquire [3]	359
12	Nov 7	A	Queen's Park	L 0-1	0-0	4		529
13	14	H	Forfar Ath	W 2-1	2-0	3	Rodgers [13], Lynch [43]	365
14	21	A	Stranraer	W 2-1	2-0	2	Rodgers [10], Stevenson [45]	205
15	Dec 6	H	Montrose	W 1-0	0-0	3	Weaver [62]	342
16	12	A	Berwick R	W 1-0	0-0	2	Lynch [61]	428
17	Jan 23	A	Montrose	W 1-0	1-0	2	Bolochoweckyj [19]	310
18	30	H	Stranraer	W 2-0	0-0	—	Rodgers [76], Lynch [78]	348
19	Feb 6	H	Berwick R	W 3-2	1-0	2	Stevenson [40], Maquire 2 [64, 68]	347
20	10	H	Elgin C	W 2-0	1-0	—	Lynch [26], Stevenson [75]	349
21	20	A	Livingston	L 0-2	0-1	2		1062
22	27	A	Annan Ath	L 0-1	0-0	—		613
23	Mar 2	H	Queen's Park	L 0-3	0-3	—		297
24	6	H	Forfar Ath	W 4-0	2-0	2	Lynch 3 [31, 38, 96], Rodgers [83]	436
25	9	A	Livingston	L 0-2	0-1	—		864
26	13	A	Queen's Park	L 0-2	0-0	2		457
27	17	H	Albion R	W 2-0	2-0	—	Bolochoweckyj [21], Richardson [36]	340
28	20	H	Montrose	L 2-3	0-2	2	Stevenson 2 (1 pen) [55, 82 (p)]	306
29	23	A	Albion R	L 1-2	0-0	—	Stevenson [50]	340
30	27	A	Stranraer	D 2-2	0-1	2	Maquire [73], Rodgers [90]	320
31	30	A	Forfar Ath	L 1-4	1-0	—	Stevenson [20]	286
32	Apr 3	H	Albion R	W 3-1	2-1	2	Lynch 2 [13, 57], Stevenson [39]	325
33	10	A	Berwick R	D 2-2	2-0	3	Donaldson [5], Dunn [12]	429
34	17	A	Elgin C	W 1-0	0-0	3	Maquire [51]	398
35	24	H	Annan Ath	W 3-1	2-0	3	Ure [27], Lynch [33], Dunn [61]	335
36	May 1	A	Livingston	L 0-1	0-1	3		1480

Final League Position: 3

Honours
League Champions: Division II 1931-32; C Division 1947-48. *Runners-up:* Division II 1962-63. Second Division 1979-80. Division Three 1923-24.

Club colours: Shirt: All black with white chevrons.

Goalscorers: *League (50):* Lynch 13, Rodgers 9 (1 pen), Stevenson 9 (1 pen), Maquire 8, Bolochoweckyj 3, Dunn 2, Richardson 2, Donaldson 1, Tully 1, Ure 1, Weaver 1.
Scottish Cup (2): Dunn 1, Rodgers 1.
CIS Cup (3): Rodgers 2, McGuire 1.
Challenge Cup (0).
Play-Offs (2): Rodgers 2.

Barclay J 33	Hay P 28+4	Dunn D 14+12	Forrest E 24	King D 12	Weaver P 27+1	Donaldson C 24+2	Tully C 15+2	Maquire S 23+13	Richardson D 31+2	Rodgers A 29+4	McKenzie M 2+27	Stevenson J 32	Lynch S 31+2	Elliot J —+3	Bolochoweckyj M 29+1	Brady C —+4	Johnston S 2+11	Ure D 17+11	Sorley C 3	Harding R 20+2	Match No.
1	2	3	4	5	6	7	8	9	10^1	11	12										1
1	2		4^3	5^2	6	7	8	9^1	10	11	12	3	13	14							2
1	2		4^1	5	6	7^3	8	9	14	11^2	12	3	10	13							3
1	2	13		5	6		8	9^1	7	11^2	12	3	10		4						4
1	2	12		5	6		8	9^1	7	11^2	13	3	10		4^1	14					5
1	2	13		5^2	6		8	9	7	11^1	12	3	10		4						6
1	2	13		5^1	6		8	9^2	7	11^2	12	3	10		4	14					7
1	2	12			6		8	9^3	7^2	11^1	5	3	10	14	4			13			8
1	2		4	7	12	6^1	10^3	3	11^2	14	8	9	5		13						9
1	2	13		4	7^2	6	10^1	3	11^3	12	8	9	5		14						10
1	2^2	12	3	7	6		10	4^1	11^3	14	8	9	5		13						11
1	5	13	2	7^2		4	6	9^1	11	14	8	10^3	3		12						12
	2^3	14	6	7	4		12	3	11	13	8^1	9^2	5		10				1		13
1	14	12	6	7^1	4	2	13	3	11		8^2	9^3	5		10						14
1			4		6	7	2	12	3	11^2	14	8^3	9^1	5	10					3	15
1			6		7	4	2	12	3	11^3	13	8^4	9^1	5	10					14	16
1	8	13	4		6		10^1	5	9^3	14	7	12	3		11			2			17
1	7		3	13	6^1		12	5	11^3		8	10	4		14	9^2		2			18
1	7		3	9		13	6	5	10^3	14	8^1	11^2	4		12			2			19
1	7	14	4		8			9^3	5	11^1	13	6^2	10		3			12		2	20
1	2^1		4		7	13	10^2	3	11^3		8	9	5^3		1			12		6	21
1	7^4	3		6	2		10^2	5	9^1	13	8				12	11				4	22
	5^2	3		6	2	11		9^3	13	8	10	4	14	12	1	7^1					23
1	8	7^1	5		2	9		11^2	14	6^3	10	3	13	12	4						24
1	3^1	4		7^2	2	10	12	11^3	8	9		5	11	13	6						25
1	12				2^3	5		11^2	13	7	10	3	14	6	8						26
1	6	7^1	4		5	12	9		13	10^3	11^2	3	14	8	2						27
1	7	11^3	4		2	13	3	12	14	8	9	5	10^1	6^2							28
1	7^3	8^2	4		6	13	5	12	14	10	11	3^1	9	2							29
1	7^2	9	2		5	13	6	12	14	10	11	4^1	8^3	3							30
1	14	9	3		2	12	5	6	13	8^3	10^2	4^1	11	7							31
1		7	3^2	6	5	12	2^1	11	9	10^3	13	14	8	4							32
1	5^1	9^2	3	6	2	13	12		11^3	10		4	14	8	7						33
1	2	8		7	6		11^1	5	13		10^2	4	12	9	3						34
1	14	11	3		6	2	12	5	13		8^3	10^2	9^1	7	4						35
	2^1	11		7	4	8		9	5	6					13	10	12^2	1	3		36

ELGIN CITY   Third Division

Year Formed: 1893. *Ground and Address:* Borough Briggs, Borough Briggs Road, Elgin IV30 1AP.
Telephone: 01343 551114. *Fax:* 01343 547921. *E-mail:* elgincityfc@ukonline.co.uk *Website:* www.elgincity.com
Ground Capacity: 3927, seated 478, standing 3449. *Size of pitch:* 111yd × 72yd.
Acting Chairman: Graham Tatters. *Secretary:* Ian A. Allan.
Manager: Ross Jack. *Assistant Manager:* David McConachie. *Physio:* Lynda Anderson.
Previous names: 1893-1900 Elgin City, 1900–03 Elgin City United, 1903– Elgin City.
Club Nickname(s): City or Black & Whites. *Previous Grounds:* Association Park 1893-95; Milnfield Park 1895-1909;
Station Park 1909-19; Cooper Park 1919-21.
Record Attendance: 12,608 v Arbroath, Scottish Cup, 17 Feb 1968.
Record Transfer Fee received: £32,000 for Michael Teasdale to Dundee (Jan 1994).
Record Transfer Fee paid: £10,000 to Fraserburgh for Russell McBride (July 2001).
Record Victory: 18-1 v Brora Rangers, North of Scotland Cup, 6 Feb 1960.
Record Defeat: 1-14 v Hearts, Scottish Cup, 4 Feb 1939.
Most League Appearances: 224: David Hind, 2001-09.
Most League Goals in Season (Individual): 20: Martin Johnston, 2005-06.
Most Goals Overall (Individual): 39: Martin Johnston, 2005-07.

ELGIN CITY 2009–10 LEAGUE RECORD

Match No.	Date	Venue	Opponents	Result	H/T Score	Lg Pos.	Goalscorers	Attendance
1	Aug 8	A	Montrose	D	1-1	0-0	—	Frizzel [50]	361
2	15	H	Queen's Park	L	0-1	0-1	—		570
3	22	A	East Stirling	D	1-1	1-0	—	Gunn [15]	324
4	29	H	Annan Ath	D	1-1	0-1	—	Gunn [54]	457
5	Sept 12	A	Livingston	L	2-3	0-1	9	Crooks [73], MacAulay [82]	602
6	19	H	Berwick R	D	3-3	2-2	9	Gunn 2 [40, 43], Nicolson [90]	478
7	26	A	Forfar Ath	D	3-3	2-1	8	Gunn [37], Nicolson 2 [45, 77]	444
8	Oct 3	A	Stranraer	W	2-0	1-0	6	Dunne [5], Crooks (pen) [53]	207
9	10	H	Albion R	L	0-2	0-2	8		526
10	17	H	East Stirling	L	1-2	0-1	9	Gunn [64]	449
11	31	A	Queen's Park	W	3-0	1-0	8	Gunn [5], Tatters [47], Frizzel [73]	538
12	Nov 7	H	Livingston	L	1-6	0-3	9	Gunn [73]	615
13	14	A	Annan Ath	W	2-0	0-0	9	Niven [48], MacAulay [88]	416
14	21	H	Forfar Ath	L	0-2	0-1	9		519
15	Dec 5	A	Berwick R	L	0-2	0-0	9		368
16	12	A	Albion R	D	1-1	0-0	9	MacAulay [62]	225
17	Jan 23	H	Berwick R	L	1-5	1-2	9	Nicolson [26]	307
18	26	A	Livingston	L	0-1	0-0	—		503
19	Feb 6	H	Albion R	W	3-1	1-0	9	Gunn 2 (1 pen) [45 (pl, 55], Cameron [90]	326
20	10	A	East Stirling	L	0-2	0-1	—		349
21	16	A	Forfar Ath	L	0-1	0-0	—		402
22	20	A	Montrose	W	4-0	1-0	9	Sutherland [45], Morrison [49], Gunn 2 [89, 90]	280
23	Mar 6	A	Annan Ath	D	3-3	1-2	9	Sutherland 2 [27, 58], Smith [90]	364
24	13	H	Livingston	L	0-1	0-1	9		433
25	16	A	Stranraer	L	1-2	1-1	—	Frizzel [21]	145
26	20	A	Berwick R	L	1-2	0-2	9	Greenhill D (og) [52]	317
27	23	H	Montrose	L	0-1	0-0	—		295
28	27	H	Forfar Ath	L	0-2	0-0	9		329
29	30	H	Queen's Park	L	0-1	0-1	—		203
30	Apr 3	A	Stranraer	L	1-2	1-0	10	Crocks [37]	375
31	6	H	Annan Ath	W	1-0	1-0	—	Sutherland [32]	235
32	10	A	Albion R	W	2-1	0-1	9	Gunn [69], Morrison [81]	347
33	17	H	East Stirling	L	0-1	0-0	9		398
34	24	A	Queen's Park	W	1-0	0-0	9	Sutherland [85]	644
35	27	H	Stranraer	L	2-3	1-0	—	Gunn [43], Jack A [65]	232
36	May 1	H	Montrose	W	5-2	2-1	9	Smith [26], Gunn 3 [29, 56, 88], MacAulay [46]	504

Final League Position: 9

Honours
Scottish Cup: Quarter-finals 1968.
Highland League Champions: winners 15 times.
Scottish Qualifying Cup (North): winners 7 times.
North of Scotland Cup: winners 17 times.
Highland League Cup: winners 5 times.
Inverness Cup: winners twice.

Club colours: Shirt: Black and white stripes. Shorts: Black. Stockings: Red.

Goalscorers: *League (46):* Gunn 17 (1 pen), Sutherland 5, MacAulay 4, Nicolson 4, Crooks 3 (1 pen), Frizzel 3, Morrison 2, Smith 2, Cameron 1, Dunne 1, Jack A 1, Niver 1, Tatters 1, own goal 1.
Scottish Cup (4): Frizzel 3 (1 pen), Crooks 1 (pen).
CIS Cup (0).
Challenge Cup (8): Crooks 2 (1 pen), Gunn 2, Cameron 1, Edwards 1, Frizzel 1, own goal 1.

Gibson J 36	Dempsie A 20	Kaczan P 28	Craig DW 27	Craig DA 15+7	Gunn C 31+5	McDonald N 21+2	Edwards S 19+8	Nicolson M 32	Frizzel C 33+1	Crooks J 15+12	MacAulay K 27+7	Niven D 25	Calder D 1+11	Cameron B 9+15	Inglis J 9+5	Dunne M 4	Smith D 2+10	Tatters G 9	Sutherland S 17	Morrison G 15	MacLeod D —+3	Jack A 1+2	McConachie M —+1	Fraser S —+1	Match No.
1	2[1]	3	4	5	6	7	8	9	10	11	12														1
1	·	3	4	5[1]	6	7	8[2]	9	10	11[3]	12	2	13	14											2
1		3	4	5[4]	6	7[1]		9	10	11	8	2	12												3
1	5	3	4		6	7		9	10[2]	11[1]	8	2		13	12										4
1	5[1]	3	4		6[1]	7[2]	13	9	10	12	8	2	14	11[3]											5
1		3	4	14	6	7[3]	5	9	10	12	8	2[2]	11[1]	13											6
1	2	3	4[12]	6	7[2]	13		9		10	8	5	14	11[3]											7
1	2	3	14	6[2]	7		9	11[3]	10[1]	8	5	13	12	4											8
1	2	4		7	6[2]	10	9	11[1]	8[3]	3	13	14		5	12										9
1	2	4		6	7		5	10	9	8	3							1[·]							10
1	5[1]	3	4	10	13	6[2]	8	11	12	7	2			14			6[3]								11
1	3	4[1]		13	7	12	6[3]	10	9	14	8	2		5[2]			1								12
1	4			11[2]	7	5[1]	6	10	9		8	2	12	13			3								13
1	4			11[2]	7	5[1]	6[3]	10	9	13	8	2	14	12			3								14
1	5	4[4]		14	7		6	10	9[1]	12	8[3]	2	13	11[2]			3								15
1	2[1]		5	3[2]	7		6[3]	10	9	13	8		12	14	4		11								16
1			4		10[3]	7[1]	2	8[4]	11	12	6	3	14	13					5	9[2]					17
1			5		7	2		9[1]	11[3]	8	4	14	12	13					3	10[2]	6				18
1		3	4	5	10[2]	7[1]		9	12	6	2		13						11	8					19
1		3	4	5[2]	10	8[1]	13	11		6	2		12						9	7					20
1		3	7		10[1]	4[4]		5	8	12	9	2							11	6					21
1		3	5	12		13	7	11[1]	8	9[3]	2[2]		4		14				10	6					22
1	5[2]	3	4		12		13	8	11[3]	10	7[1]		2		14				9	6					23
1	5	3	4		10[1]			8	9[2]	6	13		2		12				11	7					24
1	2	3	7		12			9	10[1]	6		4							5	13	11[2]	8			25
1	2	7	3		6		13	10[1]	11	5[1]	12	4		14	9[3]							8			26
1	5		4	12	6[2]		14	9	11[1]		8	3		7			13		10	2[3]					27
1		3	4	9[2]	13	7[2]	5	6	12		14	2		10[1]					11	8					28
1		4	5	13	7		3	9	14	6[3]	2		10[2]				12		11	3[1]					29
1	5[3]	3	9	10	4[2]		6	8	12	13	2[1]	14							11	7					30
1	5[2]	2	4[1]	12	10	7	13	3	9[3]	6			14						11	3					31
1	4		2	7[2]	6	3	11	9	5[1]	13							12		10	3					32
1	2	4	5	10	8[2]	7[1]	3	9[3]		6			14				12		11		13				33
1	7	5	4	11	2	3	9[2]	8		6[1]			12				10					13			34
1	2[1]	3		10	7	6	9	8		11		4	5[2]						13	12					35
1			5	10	7	2		8		11	4[1]	3[·]	6[·]					12		9[2]	13	14			36

FALKIRK   First Division

Year Formed: 1876. *Ground & Address:* The Falkirk Stadium, Westfield, Falkirk FK2 9DX. *Telephone:* 01324 624121.
Fax: 01324 612418. *Website:* www.falkirkfc.co.uk
Ground Capacity: seated: 8000. *Size of Pitch:* 105m × 68m.
Chairman: Martin Ritchie. *Managing Director:* George Craig. *Secretary:* Alex Blackwood.
Manager: Steven Pressley.
Club Nickname(s): The Bairns. *Previous Grounds:* Randyford 1876-81; Blinkbonny Grounds 1881-83; Brockville Park 1883-2003.
Record Attendance: 23,100 v Celtic, Scottish Cup 3rd rd, 21 Feb 1953.
Record Transfer Fee received: £380,000 for John Hughes to Celtic (Aug 1995).
Record Transfer Fee paid: £225,000 to Chelsea for Kevin McAllister (Aug 1991).
Record Victory: 12-1 v Laurieston, Scottish Cup 2nd rd, 23 Sept 1893.
Record Defeat: 1-11 v Airdrieonians, Division I, 28 Apr 1951.
Most Capped Player: Alex Parker, 14 (15), Scotland and Russell Latapy, Trinidad & Tobago.
Most League Appearances: 450: Tom Ferguson, 1919-32.
Most League Goals in Season (Individual): 43: Evelyn Morrison, Division I, 1928-29.
Most Goals Overall (Individual): 86: Dougie Moran, 1957-61 and 1964-67.

FALKIRK 2009–10 LEAGUE RECORD

Match No.	Date	Venue	Opponents	Result	H/T Score	Lg Pos.	Goalscorers	Attendance
1	Aug 15	A	Rangers	L 1-4	1-2	—	Finnigan [24]	50,239
2	22	H	Hibernian	L 1-3	1-1	11	Flynn [25]	6059
3	29	A	Dundee U	L 1-2	0-0	11	Finnbogason [75]	6979
4	Sept 15	H	Aberdeen	D 0-0	0-0	—		4724
5	19	A	Hamilton A	D 0-0	0-0	12		2640
6	26	H	Kilmarnock	D 0-0	0-0	11		5394
7	Oct 3	A	Motherwell	L 0-1	0-1	12		4337
8	17	H	St Mirren	L 1-3	0-0	12	MacDonald [55]	5084
9	24	A	Hearts	D 0-0	0-0	12		14,127
10	31	A	St Johnstone	L 1-3	0-1	12	Finnigan [49]	4423
11	Nov 8	H	Celtic	D 3-3	0-0	12	Arfield (pen) [61], Moutinho [64], Stewart M [83]	6795
12	21	A	Hamilton A	W 2-0	0-0	12	Mitchell [64], Bullen [79]	5268
13	28	A	Hibernian	L 0-2	0-1	12		13,305
14	Dec 5	H	Rangers	L 1-3	1-2	12	Moutinho [41]	6903
15	12	A	St Mirren	D 1-1	0-0	12	Finnigan [88]	4033
16	19	A	Kilmarnock	W 2-1	1-1	12	Finnigan [3], Flynn [58]	4472
17	26	H	Hearts	L 0-1	0-1	12		6082
18	Jan 16	A	Celtic	D 1-1	1-1	12	Finnigan [19]	50,000
19	24	H	Dundee U	L 1-4	0-2	12	Moutinho [90]	4378
20	27	H	Motherwell	D 0-0	0-0	—		4321
21	30	A	Rangers	L 0-3	0-1	12		45,907
22	Feb 2	A	Aberdeen	W 1-0	1-0	—	Healy [31]	7741
23	10	H	Kilmarnock	L 0-1	0-0	—		7049
24	13	A	Hearts	L 2-3	1-1	12	Kucharski (og) [45], Pele [83]	14,078
25	20	H	Aberdeen	W 3-1	2-1	12	Moutinho [13], Barr [42], Showunmi [70]	4643
26	27	A	Dundee U	L 0-3	0-2	12		6352
27	Mar 7	A	Celtic	L 0-2	0-1	12		6792
28	13	H	St Johnstone	L 1-2	1-1	—	Twaddle [27]	5895
29	20	A	Hamilton A	D 2-2	1-0	12	Arfield [26], Flynn [59]	2461
30	23	A	St Johnstone	D 1-1	1-1	—	Flynn [19]	3107
31	27	H	Hibernian	L 1-3	1-3	12	Stewart M [19]	5460
32	Apr 3	A	Motherwell	W 1-0	1-0	12	Flynn [27]	4268
33	10	H	St Mirren	W 2-1	1-0	12	Moutinho [45], Barr [67]	5671
34	17	A	Aberdeen	L 0-1	0-1	12		10,461
35	24	A	Hamilton A	L 0-1	0-1	12		5118
36	May 1	H	St Mirren	D 1-1	1-0	12	Arfield (pen) [45]	5919
37	5	H	St Johnstone	D 0-0	0-0	—		5502
38	8	A	Kilmarnock	D 0-0	0-0	12		10,662

Final League Position: 12

Honours
League Champions: Division II 1935-36, 1969-70, 1974-75. First Division 1990-91, 1993-94, 2002-03, 2004-05. Second Division 1979-80; *Runners-up:* Division 1907-08, 1909-10. First Division 1985-86, 1988-89. Division II 1904-05, 1951-52, 1960-61.
Scottish Cup Winners: 1913, 1957; *Runners-up:* 1997, 2009. *League Cup Runners-up:* 1947-48. *B&Q Cup Winners:* 1993-94. *League Challenge Cup Winners:* 1997-98, 2004-05.

European: *Europa League:* 2 matches (2009-10).

Club colours: Shirt: Navy blue with white seams. Shorts: White. Stockings: White.

Goalscorers: *League (31):* Finnigan 5, Flynn 5, Moutinho 5, Arfield 3 (2 pens), Barr 2, Stewart M 2, Bullen 1, Finnbogason 1, Healy 1, MacDonald 1, Mitchell 1, Pele 1, Showunmi 1, Twaddle 1, own goal 1.
Scottish Cup (0).
CIS Cup (0).
Europa League (1): Flynn 1.

Olejnik R 38	Barr D 38	Scobbie T 19+1	McNamara J 13	McLean B 36	Twaddle M 30+3	Lima V 22+4	O'Brien B 23+4	Finnigan C 20+7	Arfield S 35+1	Flynn R 36	MacDonald A 4+7	Maraan D 8+7	Mitchell C 5+3	Robertson D —+1	Finnbogason K 7	Stewart M 7+12	Lynch S 3+5	Allison H 4	Moutinho P 20+5	Bullen —+9	Murdoch S —+3	Pele P 7+2	Zerara T 3	Healy C 17+2	Showunmi E 15+6	Compton J 3+10	Duffy K 5+1	Match No.
1	2	3^2	4	5	6	7^1	8	9	10	11^3	12	13	14															1
1	2	3	4^2	5	6		8	9	10	11	7^1	12					13											2
1	2	3^2	4^1	5	6		8	9	7	11^3	14	12			10													3
1	2	3	4	5		12	8	9	7	6^1			^{12}		10^3	13	14											4
1	2	3	4	5			8	9	14	6^3	13	^{12}			10	12	7^1											5
1	2	3^1	4	5	14	13	8	9	6		1^2				10^1	12	7											6
1	2	3	4	5	12	8	9	6	14	1					10^2	13	7^1											7
1	2		5	6	4	11	8^3	9^1	7^2	3	13	0			12	14												8
1	2		3	5	6	4	7		8	11^1	10^3	2^2	13		9	14												9
1	2	4^1	5	6	3		12	8	10^2	11		7			9	13												10
1	2		5		3		7	11^3	8^8	10	6		13					4	9^1	12	14							11
1	2		5	12	3		9	7	8^2		10^1	4						6	11^3	14		13						12
1	2		5	14	3		9^2	7	4	12	11^1	8						6	10^3	13								13
1	2		5		3		9^2	7	11	12	14	8						4	10^3	13		6^1						14
1	2		5	4	7		9	11^2	6^1	13									10	12		8	3					15
1	2		5	4	7		9	11	8^1										10^2	12	13	6	3					16
1	2		5	4	7	14	9	8	11^1	13									10^2	12		6	3^3					17
1	2		5	3	7		9^1	11	8^2										12	14		6			4	10^3	13	18
1	2		5^1	3	7		9^3	11^2	8										13	12		6			4	10	14	19
1	2	5		3			9^3	11				13							14		12	6^6			4^2	10	8	20
1	2	6	5	3	7	12	13	11	8^3																4	10	9^1	21
1	2		5	3	7	13	9^3	11	8^2				12												4	10	6	22
1	2	6	5	3	7^1	12	9^2	11	8	13						14									4	10^3		23
1	2	3	5	6	7		9	11	8								13								4^2	12	10^1	24
1	2	6	5	3	7	4	11	8^2								9^9								12	10	13		25
1	2	6	5	3	7	8^2	11	4								5^1								12	10	13		26
1	2	6	5	3	7^1	4	11	9								12								8	10			27
1	2	6	5	3	7	8		11								9^1								4	10	12		28
1	2	6	5	3	7^1		11	4								9								8	10	12		29
1	2	6	5	3	8	13	7	4				10^1	^{12}			9^2									11			30
1	2	6^1	5	3	8	12	7	4				10				9									11			31
1	2	6		3		5^3	11	8^1				10	14			3^2								7	13	12	4	32
1	2		5	3		6	13	11	8^3			10	14			3^1								7^2	12		4	33
1	2		5	3		6	13^3	7	8			10^1				9^2								11	12	14	4	34
1	2	12	5	3^1		6^2		11	8			10				9								7	13	14	4^3	35
1	2	6	5^1	3	14	4	11	8				10				9^3								7^2	13	12		36
1	2	6	5	3	4		11	8				9				9								7	10			37
1	2	6^1	5	3	4	13	11	8				12				9^3								7^2	10	14		38

FORFAR ATHLETIC — Second Division

Year Formed: 1885. *Ground & Address:* Station Park, Carseview Road, Forfar DD8 3BT. *Telephone:* 01307 463576/462259. *Fax:* 01307 466956. *E-mail:* pat@ramsayladders.co.uk *Website:* www.forfarathletic.co.uk
Ground Capacity: 5177 (739 seated). *Size of Pitch:* 103m × 64m.
Chairman: Neill Wilson. *Vice Chairman:* Jim Farquhar. *Secretary:* David McGregor.
Manager: Dick Campbell.
Club Nickname(s): Loons. *Previous Grounds:* None.
Record Attendance: 10,780 v Rangers, Scottish Cup 2nd rd, 2 Feb 1970.
Record Transfer Fee received: £65,000 for David Bingham to Dunfermline Ath (September 1995).
Record Transfer Fee paid: £50,000 for Ian McPhee from Airdrieonians (1991).
Record Victory: 14-1 v Lindertis, Scottish Cup 1st rd, 1 Sept 1988.
Record Defeat: 2-12 v King's Park, Division II, 2 Jan 1930.
Most League Appearances: 484: Ian McPhee, 1978-88 and 1991-98.
Most League Goals in Season (Individual): 45: Dave Kilgour, Division II, 1929-30.
Most Goals Overall: 124: John Clark, 1978-91.

FORFAR ATHLETIC 2009–10 LEAGUE RECORD

Match No.	Date	Venue	Opponents	Result	H/T Score	Lg Pos.	Goalscorers	Attendance
1	Aug 8	A	Queen's Park	D 2-2	1-1	—	Fotheringham M [2], Campbell I [76]	595
2	15	H	Stranraer	W 1-0	1-0	2	Campbell R (pen) [24]	410
3	22	A	Montrose	W 2-1	1-0	1	Fotheringham K [44], Fotheringham M [75]	548
4	29	H	East Stirling	W 5-1	3-1	1	Campbell R 3 (1 pen) [10 (pl. 30, 61)], Templeman [33], Fotheringham K (pen) [90]	425
5	Sept 12	A	Annan Ath	L 0-1	0-0	1		525
6	19	A	Albion R	D 1-1	1-1	1	Templeman [20]	279
7	26	H	Elgin C	D 3-3	1-2	2	Campbell R 2 [12, 64], Mowat [52]	444
8	Oct 3	A	Berwick R	W 1-0	0-0	2	Campbell R (pen) [65]	436
9	10	H	Livingston	L 0-1	0-1	4		613
10	17	H	Montrose	D 2-2	2-1	5	Campbell R 2 [28, 34]	556
11	31	A	Stranraer	L 0-1	0-0	5		210
12	Nov 7	H	Annan Ath	W 2-1	2-0	5	Campbell R [23], Harty [27]	477
13	14	A	East Stirling	L 1-2	0-2	5	Gordon [74]	365
14	21	A	Elgin C	W 2-0	1-0	4	Fotheringham M [40], Templeman [55]	519
15	Dec 5	H	Albion R	D 2-2	1-1	4	Harty 2 [43, 65]	434
16	12	A	Livingston	W 2-1	1-1	1	Gibson [2], Tulloch [90]	1591
17	Jan 23	A	Albion R	W 1-0	0-0	4	Watson [48]	227
18	Feb 6	H	Livingston	D 2-2	0-0	4	Campbell R [63], Tulloch [90]	510
19	13	A	Berwick R	W 4-0	1-0	4	Campbell R [32], Templeman [47], Tulloch [54], Watson [67]	386
20	16	A	Elgin C	W 1-0	0-0	—	Harty [89]	402
21	20	A	Queen's Park	W 3-1	1-0	3	Sellars [6], Watson [69], Harty [72]	603
22	Mar 2	A	Annan Ath	D 1-1	1-0	3	Harty [4]	373
23	6	A	East Stirling	L 0-4	0-2	3		436
24	9	A	Queen's Park	L 0-1	0-0	—		413
25	13	H	Annan Ath	L 1-5	1-2	3	Harty [15]	424
26	16	A	Montrose	L 0-4	0-2	—		360
27	20	H	Albion R	D 1-1	0-1	3	Campbell R [71]	344
28	23	A	Berwick R	W 3-0	0-0	—	Campbell R [53], Fotheringham K [89], Watson [90]	310
29	27	A	Elgin C	W 2-0	0-0	3	Campbell R [47], Gibson [84]	329
30	30	H	East Stirling	W 4-1	0-1	3	Sellars 3 [48, 66, 75], Harty [70]	286
31	Apr 3	H	Berwick R	W 2-0	1-0	3	Sellars [9], Campbell R [61]	406
32	10	A	Livingston	W 3-2	3-2	2	Harty 2 [13, 21], Campbell I [17]	1500
33	17	H	Montrose	W 2-0	0-0	2	Templeman [47], Fotheringham M [90]	466
34	20	H	Stranraer	W 2-0	1-0	—	Deasley 2 [26, 69]	422
35	24	A	Stranraer	L 0-2	0-2	2		337
36	May 1	A	Queen's Park	D 1-1	0-0	2	Bishop [59]	549

Final League Position: 2

Honours
League Champions: Second Division 1983-84. Third Division 1994-95; *Runners-up:* 1996-97. C Division 1948-49. *Third Division* 2009-10.
Scottish Cup: Semi-finals 1982.
League Cup: Semi-finals 1977-78.
League Challenge Cup: Semi-finals 2004-05.

Club colours: Shirt: Sky and navy blue hoops. Shorts: Navy blue. Stockings: Navy blue.

Goalscorers: *League (59):* Campbell R 16 (3 pens), Harty 10, Sellars 5, Templeman 5, Fotheringham M 4, Watson 4, Fotheringham K 3 (1 pen), Tulloch 3, Campbell I 2, Deasley 2, Gibson 2, Bishop 1, Gordon 1, Mowat 1.
Scottish Cup (5): Campbell R 2, Harty 1 (pen), Templeman 1, Tod 1.
CIS Cup (5): Campbell R 2, Deasley 1, Fotheringham M 1 Tulloch 1.
Challenge Cup (3): Fotheringham M 1, Fotheringham K 1, Templeman 1.
Play-Offs (5): Bishop 1, Campbell R 1 (pen), Deasley 1, Fotheringham M 1, Tulloch 1.

Brown A 28	Malcolm S 5	Tod A 33	Tulloch S 31+1	Mowat D 31+1	Fotheringham M 19+8	Brady D 4+1	Campbell I 32	Campbell R 29+6	Deasley B 9+13	Smith C 3+10	Templeman C 25+7	Gordon K 8+10	Winter C —+1	Divine A 3+1	Smith N 3+3	McCulloch M 23	Gibson G 9+17	McNally S —+5	McGroarty C 1	Harty J 21+5	Grant C 2	Andreoni M 1	Bishop J 17+1	Watson P 12+5	Sellars B 15+3	Fusco S —+1	McLean E 6	Match No.
1	2	3	4	5	6	7	8	9	10¹	11²	12	13																1
1	2²	3	4	5	6	7¹	8	9	10³	11	12	13	14															2
1	2¹	3⁴	14		6	12	8	9		13	10³	11				4	5²											3
1	2		4		6	10³	8	9	5¹	12	13	7	11²			14	3											4
1	2	5			6¹	10²	8	4	9	13	14	7	11³		12	3												5
1		5		2	6		8	4	9	10¹		7	12	11²	13	3												6
1		5	7	2	8¹		10	4	11		12	3²				6³	14	3	1²									7
1		5	7	2	8		10	4	11²		13	9³	6¹			3	13	14										8
1		5	6	8	4		11³	3	14		10²	9	7¹			2	13	13										9
1		5	6	4	7¹		11	3	10		13					2	11	12	8³	9²								10
		5	6	2			11³	3	10	7²		9	13			14	12		8	1	4¹							11
		5	6	2	4		10	3	9²	13		8	12			11		7	1									12
1		5	6	2³	4		10	3	9²	12		8	13			11	14		7									13
1		5	6	2	4¹		11	3	13		14	8³	7			10	12		9²									14
1		5	6	2	4¹		10	3	8	13	14	9³	11²				12		7									15
1		5	6	2	13		10	3	8			9	12			4	11		7²									16
1		3	5	2	14		9³	7	11	13		10¹				6	2						4	8²				17
1	4³	5	7	13			6⁸	8	9²	14		10				2				12			3	11				18
1		4	5²	7	9			6	10	14		11¹				2				12			3	8³	13			19
1		3	5⁴	7	6¹			8	10²			11	14			2				13			4	9²	12			20
1		4	2				7	5	6	13		12				11¹				10			3	9	8²			21
1		5		2	13		6	3	11	14		12				3¹				10			4	7³	8²			22
1		4	3	2³	9²		5		12	14		10				8¹				11			6	7	13			23
1		3	5	13			7²		6			10¹	14			2	12			11			4	9³	8			24
1		4	5	11			13	7³	8	12						2	14			10			3	9²	6¹			25
1		3	4				5		13	6³	14					7¹	8	10²		11			2	12	9			26
1		4	2				5	6	9²	14	10³					8¹				11			3	12	7	13		27
1		5	3	7			14	9	6			11¹				2	13			10²			4	12	8³			28
1		4	2	6			14	9	11			12				5	13			10³			3	8²	6¹			29
1		3	4	9	14		5¹	7	13			10³				2	12			11²				6	8			30
		3	4²	6	14		5¹	8	9³							2	13			11			12	10	7		1	31
		3	5	7	13			8	10²			9¹	14			2	12			11³			4		6		1	32
		4	3	2	14		8³	7	10			11²					12			9¹			5	13	6		1	33
		5	4	2	9			3	13	11		6²	12	7³			10			14				8¹			1	34
		5¹	3	7				9	11	13		6				2	12			10²			4		8		1	35
		4	7	11			5⁸	6³	9²			14				2	10¹			13			3	12	8		1	36

HAMILTON ACADEMICAL   Premier League

Year Formed: 1874. *Ground:* New Douglas Park, Cadzow Avenue, Hamilton ML3 0FT. *Telephone:* 01698 368650.
Fax: 01698 285422. *E-mail:* scott@acciesfc.co.uk *Website:* www.acciesfc.co.uk
Ground Capacity: 6078. *Size of Pitch:* 115yd × 75yd.
Chairman: Ronnie MacDonald. *Vice-Chairman:* Les Gray. *Chief Executive:* George Paterson. *Secretary:* Scott A.
Struthers BA.
Manager: Billy Reid. *First Team Coach:* Stuart Taylor. *Physio:* Alan Rankin.
Club Nickname(s): The Accies. *Previous Grounds:* Bent Farm, South Avenue, South Haugh, Douglas Park, Cliftonhill
Stadium, Firhill Stadium.
Record Attendance: 28,690 v Hearts, Scottish Cup 3rd rd, 3 Mar 1937 (at Douglas Park); 5,895 v Rangers, 28 February
2009 (at New Douglas Park).
Record Transfer Fee received: £380,000 for Paul Hartley to Millwall (July 1996).
Record Transfer Fee paid: £60,000 for Paul Martin from Kilmarnock (Oct 1988) and for John McQuade from Dumbarton
(Aug 1993).
Record Victory: 11-1 v Chryston, Lanarkshire Cup, 28 Nov 1885.
Record Defeat: 1-11 v Hibernian, Division I, 6 Nov 1965.
Most Capped Player: Colin Miller, 29, Canada, 1988-94.
Most League Appearances: 452: Rikki Ferguson, 1974-88.
Most League Goals in Season (Individual): 35: David Wilson, Division I; 1936-37.
Most Goals Overall (Individual): 246: David Wilson, 1928-39.

HAMILTON ACADEMICAL 2009–10 LEAGUE RECORD

Match No.	Date	Venue	Opponents	Result	H/T Score	Lg Pos.	Goalscorers	Atten-dance
1	Aug 15	A	Kilmarnock	L	0-3	0-1	—	5307
2	22	H	Aberdeen	L	0-3	0-2	12	3347
3	29	A	Rangers	L	1-4	0-2	12	McLaughlin [87]	47,633
4	Sept 13	H	Hibernian	W	2-0	2-0	10	Mensing (pen) [9], Antoine-Curier [12]	4023
5	19	H	Falkirk	D	0-0	0-0	10		2640
6	26	A	Hearts	L	1-2	0-0	10	Paixao M [62]	18,025
7	Oct 3	H	St Johnstone	L	0-2	0-1	11		2199
8	17	A	Dundee U	D	1-1	0-0	11	Antoine-Curier [65]	5944
9	25	H	Celtic	L	1-2	0-2	11	Antoine-Curier [83]	4689
10	31	A	St Mirren	W	2-0	2-0	11	Paixao M [3], Canning [41]	4022
11	Nov 7	H	Motherwell	D	2-2	0-0	11	Mensing [61], Paixao M [82]	3583
12	21	A	Falkirk	L	0-2	0-0	11		5268
13	28	A	St Johnstone	D	1-1	1-1	10	Antoine-Curier [24]	3426
14	Dec 6	H	Hearts	W	2-1	2-1	10	McArthur [5], Mensing [24]	2003
15	12	A	Aberdeen	W	2-1	1-0	7	Antoine-Curier [32], Wesolowski [80]	9499
16	26	A	Celtic	L	0-2	0-0	9		36,827
17	Jan 13	H	Dundee U	L	0-1	0-0	—		2033
18	16	H	Rangers	L	0-1	0-0	10		5343
19	23	A	Hibernian	L	1-5	0-3	10	Paixao F [69]	11,481
20	26	H	Kilmarnock	D	0-0	0-0	—		2018
21	30	H	Celtic	L	0-1	0-0	10		4922
22	Feb 6	A	Motherwell	L	0-1	0-0			4777
23	10	A	Dundee U	W	2-0	2-0	—	Paixao F [23], Paixao M [45]	5598
24	13	H	Motherwell	D	0-0	0-0	11		3133
25	21	A	Hearts	L	0-2	0-0	11		13,496
26	27	A	St Mirren	D	0-0	0-0	11		3628
27	Mar 6	H	Aberdeen	D	1-1	0-0	11	Paixao F [62]	2030
28	13	H	St Mirren	W	1-0	0-0	—	Paixao F [90]	2179
29	20	H	Falkirk	D	2-2	0-1	9	Antoine-Curier [50], Mensing (pen) [58]	2461
30	24	A	Kilmarnock	W	2-1	2-0	—	Antoine-Curier [21], Mensing [26]	4068
31	27	H	St Johnstone	W	1-0	1-0	9	Wesolowski [43]	2245
32	Apr 3	A	Rangers	L	0-1	0-1	9		48,068
33	10	H	Hibernian	W	4-1	1-1	8	Mensing 2 (2 pens) [17, 60], Thomas 2 [68, 80]	2520
34	17	H	Kilmarnock	W	3-0	0-0	8	Imrie [72], Paixao F [77], Thomas [87]	2628
35	24	A	Falkirk	W	1-0	1-0	8	Paixao M [19]	5118
36	May 1	A	Aberdeen	W	3-1	0-0	8	Paixao F [1], Wesolowski [49], Mensing (pen) [58]	7099
37	5	H	St Mirren	D	0-0	0-0	—		3102
38	8	A	St Johnstone	W	3-2	2-0	7	McLaughlin [8], Imrie [15], Wesolowski [84]	3188

Final League Position: 7

Honours
League Champions: First Division 1903-04, 1985-86, 1987-88, 2007-08; Third Division 2000-01. *Runners-up:* Division II 1903-04, 1952-53, 1964-65; Second Division 1996-97, 2003-04.
Scottish Cup Runners-up: 1911, 1935. *League Cup:* Semi-finalists three times. *League Challenge Cup*: Runners-up 2006.
B&Q Cup Winners: 1991-92, 1992-93.

Club colours: Shirt: Red and white hoops. Shorts: White. Stockings: White.

Goalscorers: *League (39):* Mensing 8 (5 pens), Antoine-Curier 7, Paixao F 6, Paixao M 5, Wesolowski 4, Thomas 3, Imrie 2, McLaughlin 2, Canning 1, McArthur 1.
Scottish Cup (3): Antoine-Curier 1, Mensing 1 (pen), Paixao M 1.
CIS Cup (1): Mensing 1.

Cerny T 34	Mensing S 37	Rubiales L 3	McQueen B —+1	Andrews M 2	Iriekpen I 2	Evans G 5+4	Wesolowski J 27+2	Paixao F 18+7	Lyle D 4+1	Offiong R 1	Kissock J 2	Louhoungu D —+6	Mills S —+2	Gillespie G —+1	Canning M 37	Wilkie K 3+9	Paixao M 23+10	Knight L —+6	Welch K 1	McLaughlin M 32	Mason G 5	McArthur J 35	Hastings R 17	McClenahan T 23+4	Antoine-Curier M 25+1	Elebert D 15+10	Taylor S —+1	Kirkpatrick J 1+4	Beuzelin G 3+4	Neil A 22	Murdoch S 4+2	Sullivan J 1+1	Elliott S 2+3	Crawford A —+7	Van Zanten D 4+2	Easton B 12	Thomas J 2+9	Imrie D 16	Match No.
1	2	3	4¹	5	6	7³	8	9	10	11²	12	13	14																										1
1	2	3		5	6	7	8³	14				11²	13		4		9¹	10	12																				2
1	11	3				7		9					12		4	14	10²	13	2¹	5	6³	8																	3
1	11					7		9¹					12		4		13		5	6¹	8	2	3	10²	12														4
1	11					7		9¹					12		4		14		5	6²	8	2³	3	10	13														5
1	11¹					12	7²					13			4		9	14	5	6	8	2	3	10³															6
1		5			6	7									4		9	12	11¹	8	2	3²	10	13															7
1	11					7	12								4		9		6	8	3	2	10¹	5														8
1	11					14	7								3		9¹		6	8	2	5³	10	4²	12	13												9
1	11²					13	7	14							3		9		6	8	2	5¹	10³	4	12													10
1	3³					12²	7							14	6		9		4	8	2¹	5	10	13	11▪													11
1	4					7	12								6		9³	14	3	8	2⁵	5	10		13	11¹												12
1	4					7	12								5		9¹		3³	8	2	14	10	6²	13	11												13
1	11					7²									6	12			2	8	3	5	9	13	4¹	10												14
1⁶	11					7									6	12			2	8	3²	5	9	13	4¹	10	15											15
1	4					7²	12								6		9		2	8	3	5	10	13	11³	14												16
1	7					12²									5	11			3	8	2³	4	9		14	10		6¹	13									17
1	7														5	11			6²	8	2	12	9	4		10		13	3¹									18
1	6						9								5	12	8³		4	7	3	2²	10		11¹	14	13											19
1	11														5	12	9¹		4	7	3³	14	10	6	13		8²	2										20
1	8														5	11	13		4	7	2¹	6	9²		14	12	3³	10										21
1	8						12								5	13	9³			7		6		4²	14	2	3	11¹	10									22
1	7						10								5	6	9			8	2	4					3	11										23
1	7						10³								5	13	9²		5	8	2	4		12	14	3¹	11											24
1	6		12			7¹	9								5	10²				8	2	4			11	13	3											25
1	11					7¹	12								5	13			4	8	2²	6	10		3	9												26
1	7						9								5				4	8	12	6	11	2¹	3								21³	3				27
1	4					13	9								5	12			2²	8	7³	6	11										3	14	10¹	28
1	4					7¹	9²								5	13			2	6	11	12	8										3	14	10³	29
1	6					7¹	9								5	13			2	4	8³	12	11										3	14	10²	30
1	6					7	9								5	13			2	4	8¹		11										3	12	10	31
1	3						9								4	12			2	7	8²	5³	11				14		6¹	13	10		32
1	3²		4³			7	9								5	14			2	6	13	8¹	11							12	10		33
1⁶	3		4¹			7	9								5	12			2	6	8²		11	15							13	10		34
	3					7	9								5²	13	10		4¹		2	8³	12			6	1					14	11		35
	3					7³	9²								5	14	10		4¹	8	2	12			13	6	1						11		36
	3					7	9								5	10			4	8	2					6	1						11		37
	3					7	9								5	10¹			4²	8	2	13				6	1					12	11		38

HEART OF MIDLOTHIAN   Premier League

Year Formed: 1874. *Ground & Address:* Tynecastle Stadium, McLeod Street, Edinburgh EH11 2NL. *Telephone:* 0871 663 1874. *Fax:* 0131 200 7222. *E-mail:* hearts@homplc.co.uk *Website:* www.heartsfc.co.uk
Ground Capacity: 17,402. *Size of Pitch:* 100m × 64m.
Chairman: Roman Romanov. *Managing Director:* Campbell Ogilvie.
Manager: Jim Jefferies. *Assistant Managers:* Billy Brown and Werner Burger. *First Team Coach:* Gary Locke. *Fitness Coach:* Tom Ritchie.
Club Nickname(s): Hearts, Jambos. *Previous Grounds:* The Meadows 1874, Powderhall 1878, Old Tynecastle 1881, (Tynecastle Park, 1886).
Record Attendance: 53,396 v Rangers, Scottish Cup 3rd rd, 13 Feb 1932 (57,857 v Barcelona, 28 July 2007 at Murrayfield).
Record Transfer Fee received: £9,000,000 for Craig Gordon to Sunderland (August 2008).
Record of Transfer paid: £850,000 for Mirsad Beslija to Genk (January 2006).
Record Victory: 21-0 v Anchor, EFA Cup, 30 Oct 1880.
Record Defeat: 1-8 v Vale of Leven, Scottish Cup, 1888.
Most Capped Player: Bobby Walker, 29, Scotland.
Most League Appearances: 515: Gary Mackay, 1980-97.
Most League Goals in Season (Individual): 44: Barney Battles, 1930-31.
Most Goals Overall (Individual): 214: John Robertson, 1983-98.

HEART OF MIDLOTHIAN 2009–10 LEAGUE RECORD

Match No.	Date	Venue	Opponents	Result	H/T Score	Lg Pos.	Goalscorers	Attendance
1	Aug 17	A	Dundee U	L	0-2	0-1	—	8253
2	23	H	Rangers	L	1-2	1-0	10	Witteveen [31]	16,284
3	30	A	St Johnstone	D	2-2	0-1	10	Goncalves [59], Obua [86]	5825
4	Sept 15	H	Kilmarnock	W	1-0	1-0	—	Driver [31]	13,328
5	20	A	Celtic	L	1-2	1-0	9	Santana [5]	58,024
6	26	H	Hamilton A	W	2-1	0-0	7	Stewart M (pen) [56], Santana [57]	18,025
7	Oct 3	A	St Mirren	L	1-2	1-1	8	Goncalves [31]	4652
8	17	A	Aberdeen	D	1-1	0-1	8	Driver [62]	11,629
9	24	H	Falkirk	D	0-0	0-0	9		14,127
10	31	A	Motherwell	L	0-1	0-0	8		4830
11	Nov 7	H	Hibernian	D	0-0	0-0	8		16,726
12	21	H	St Johnstone	L	1-2	1-0	9	Nade [38]	13,416
13	28	A	Kilmarnock	W	2-1	0-0	7	Jonsson [66], Nade [76]	4707
14	Dec 6	A	Hamilton A	L	1-2	1-2	7	Jonsson [39]	2003
15	12	H	Dundee U	D	0-0	0-0	8		14,873
16	20	H	Celtic	W	2-1	1-1	7	Stewart M (pen) [32], Bouzid [76]	16,223
17	26	A	Falkirk	W	1-0	1-0	5	Stewart M (pen) [42]	6082
18	30	H	Motherwell	W	1-0	1-0	—	Stewart M [41]	14,411
19	Jan 3	A	Hibernian	D	1-1	1-0	—	Smith [45]	16,949
20	16	H	St Mirren	W	1-0	1-0	5	Stewart M (pen) [24]	12,821
21	23	A	Rangers	D	1-1	0-0	5	Robinson [75]	42,031
22	27	H	Aberdeen	L	0-3	0-1	—		14,219
23	30	A	St Johnstone	L	0-1	0-0	6		4752
24	Feb 10	A	Celtic	L	0-2	0-0			44,500
25	13	H	Falkirk	W	3-2	1-1	6	Wallace L [5], Santana [61], Black [67]	14,078
26	21	H	Hamilton A	W	2-0	0-0	6	Obua [64], Templeton [80]	13,496
27	27	A	Aberdeen	W	1-0	0-0	6	Jonsson [64]	8316
28	Mar 7	A	Dundee U	L	0-1	0-0	6		6683
29	13	A	Motherwell	L	1-3	0-2	—	Templeton [69]	4448
30	20	H	Hibernian	W	2-1	2-0	6	Driver [24], Glen [27]	17,126
31	27	H	Rangers	L	1-4	1-2	6	Santana [16]	16,832
32	Apr 3	A	St Mirren	D	1-1	0-1	11	Zaliukas [47]	4204
33	10	H	Kilmarnock	W	1-0	1-0	6	Santana [31]	14,015
34	18	A	Rangers	L	0-2	0-0	6		47,590
35	24	H	Motherwell	L	0-2	0-2	6		13,447
36	May 1	A	Hibernian	W	2-1	0-0	6	Santana [72], Obua [89]	11,277
37	5	H	Dundee U	D	0-0	0-0	—		12,325
38	9	H	Celtic	L	1-2	1-1	6	Zaliukas [36]	14,389

Final League Position: 6

Honours

League Champions: Division I 1894-95, 1896-97, 1957-58, 1959-60. First Division 1979-80; *Runners-up:* Division I 1893-94, 1898-99, 1903-04, 1905-06, 1914-15, 1937-38, 1953-54, 1956-57, 1958-59, 1964-65. Premier Division 1985-86, 1987-88, 1991-92; *Runners-up:* 2005-06. First Division 1977-78, 1982-83.
Scottish Cup Winners: 1891, 1896, 1901, 1906, 1956, 1998, 2006; *Runners-up:* 1903, 1907, 1968, 1976, 1986, 1996.
League Cup Winners: 1954-55, 1958-59, 1959-60, 1962-63; *Runners-up:* 1961-62, 1996-97.

European: *European Cup:* 8 matches (1958-59, 1960-61, 2006-07). *Cup Winners' Cup:* 10 matches (1976-77, 1996-97, 1998-99). *UEFA Cup:* 47 matches (*Fairs Cup:* 1961-62, 1963-64, 1965-66. *UEFA Cup:* 1984-85, 1986-87, 1988-89, 1990-91, 1992-93, 1993-94, 2000-01, 2003-04, 2004-05, 2006-07). *Europa League:* 2 matches (2009-10).

Club colours: Shirt: Maroon with white trim. Shorts: White. Stockings: White.

Goalscorers: *League (35):* Santana 6, Stewart M 5 (4 pens), Driver 3, Jonsson 3, Obua 3, Goncalves 2, Nade 2, Templeton 2, Zaliukas 2, Black 1, Bouzid 1, Glen 1, Robinson 1, Smith 1, Wallace L 1, Witteveen 1.
Scottish Cup (0).
CIS Cup (3): Stewart M 2 (2 pens), Glen 1.
Europa League (2): Stewart M 1, Zaliukas 1.

Kello M 14	Kucharski D 10+4	Jonsson E 27+1	Bouzid I 26	Goncalves J 19	Palazuelos R 26+1	Santana S 21+6	Stewart M 24+1	Witteveen D 5+5	Nade C 15+8	Obua D 30+2	Black 117+9	Novikovas A 5+8	Balogh J 16	Wallace L 32	Glen G 10+8	Elliot C 6+7	Thomson C 15+5	Driver A 11+1	Zaliukas M 21+1	Robinson E 7+6	Stewart J —+1	Kingston L 10+4	Thomson J 15+1	Mole J 5+2	Mulrooney P 3+3	MacDonald J 8+1	Templeton D 7+9	Cinikas M 1+1	Smith G 2+6	Wallace R —+2	Visconte R 1+1	Stevenson R 9+2	Match No.
1	2	3	4	5	6	7	8^8	9^1	10^2	11	12	13																					1
	2		4	5	6	7		9^1	10^2	11	8	14	1	3	12	13^1																	2
			4	5	14	7^2	6	12	10^3	11	8	13	1	3	9^1		2																3
1	13		4	5	6	7	8		12	9				3	10^1		2	1^2															4
			4	5	10	7	8		9	13	12	1	3		2	1^2	6^1															5
			4	5		7^1	8	9^1	10	3^2	12	1	3		2	11	6	13	14													6
			4	5	6	7^1	8^9	9^2	12	10	13	1	3		2	11		14														7
	14	4	5	6	2^2	8	9^1	12^3	7		1	3	10	11			13															8
			4	5	6	7	8^2	12	10^1	9	13	1	3	14	$5^{..}$	11^3																9
	7^1	4	5	6			14	10^1	9^3	8	13	1	3	12	$2^2$11																	10
			4	5	6		8	10^3	13	7^2	9^1	1	3	12	11			2	14														11
			4	5^4	6		8	12	10	7^3	11^2	1	3	9^1	13			14	2														12
	2	8	4		6		9	10^3	12		1	3^1	13	11			7^2	5	14														13
	2^1	3	4^4	5		8^2	9^8	10	12	6	1^6		13	11			7		15														14
1		2		5	6	8	13	9^1	12	3	14	4		11^3		7	10^2																15
1	14	2	4^2	5	6	8	12			3		7	13	11^1		10^1		9															16
1	14	2	4	5	6	12	8		13	3		7	11^3			10^2	9^1																17
1	14	2	4	5	6	11^2	8		12	3		7	9^3			10^1		13															18
1		2	4		6^8	7^2	9		10	12		3		5							13	8	11^{11}										19
1		2	4		6	14	8		11	7	13		5^2	10^1		3				9^3	12												20
1		6	4			8	9^8	11	7		3		5	10^1		2						12											21
1		8	4		6^2	10	14		7	12		3^1	5	9		2					11^3	13											22
1	3	6	4			8	10	7			9^3	12	5^1		2			13	14	11^2													23
1	2	3				12	10	9^2	11	8		6	13		5						7^1							4					24
1	2	3				7^1		11	8^2	9^3	4	10	12		5				13				14			6							25
1	2	3				11^1		7	9^3	4		10^2		5		14	6	6	14	13			12		13	8							26
	2^1	3					8		7^3	1	4		10			5^2		12^8	6	14	13		11										27
			3		7			12	11	9^2	1	2	8				5	10^1	6^3		13	14			4								28
	2	4		5	14		11			1	3	12	10			7	6	9^3	13							8							29
	2^1	4			6	12		5	8^2	1	3	10	14	11		7^3	5						13										30
			4		6	10		1^1	8^3	3	9^2	12	5	13		7	2^1			1	14												31
			4		6	7		10	8^1	3	9^3	1^4	12	11^2	5		2			1	13												32
			2		6	8^3		10^2	9	4	3			14	11^1	5	13		7			1	12										33
		2^8	4		6	$9^3$13		11	8	3			10^1	5	12		7^2			1	14												34
			4		6	7	8^1	9^3	12	2	10^2	13	3	5			1	11									14						35
			4		6	10		9	11	3	10^1	12	5		7		1	8									2^2						36
		3	4		6	11^3			8^1	2	14	10	5	13		1	9	12									7^2						37
		3	4			11	13			10^2	6^3		5	12		7	7^1	2		1	9	14					8						38

HIBERNIAN Premier League

Year Formed: 1875. *Ground & Address:* Easter Road Stadium, 12 Albion Place, Edinburgh EH7 5QG. *Telephone:* 0131 661 2159. *Fax:* 0131 659 6488. *E-mail:* club@hibernianfc.co.uk *Website:* www.hibernianfc.co.uk
Ground Capacity: total: 17,400. *Size of Pitch:* 112yd × 74yd.
Chairman: Rod Petrie. *Chief Executive:* Scott Lindsay. *Club Secretary:* Garry O'Hagan.
Manager: John Hughes. *Assistant Manager:* Brian Rice. *Physio:* Colin McLelland.
Club Nickname(s): Hibees. *Previous Grounds:* Meadows 1875-78, Powderhall 1878-79, Mayfield 1879-80, First Easter Road 1880-92, Second Easter Road 1892-.
Record Attendance: 65,860 v Hearts, Division I, 2 Jan 1950.
Record Transfer Fee received: £4,400,000 for Scott Brown from Celtic (2007).
Record of Transfer paid: £700,000 to LDU Quito for Ulises de la Cruz (2001).
Record Victory: 22-1 v 42nd Highlanders, 3 Sept 1881.
Record Defeat: 0-10 v Rangers, 24 Dec 1898.
Most Capped Player: Lawrie Reilly, 38, Scotland.
Most League Appearances: 446: Arthur Duncan.
Most League Goals in Season (Individual): 42: Joe Baker, 1959-60.
Most Goals Overall (Individual): 364: Gordon Smith, 1941-1959.

HIBERNIAN 2009–10 LEAGUE RECORD

Match No.	Date	Venue	Opponents	Result	H/T Score	Lg Pos.	Goalscorers	Atten- dance
1	Aug 15	H	St Mirren	W 2-1	1-1	—	Wotherspoon [39], Benjelloun [83]	6350
2	22	A	Falkirk	W 3-1	1-1	3	Bamba [41], Riordan 2 [57, 80]	6059
3	30	H	Celtic	L 0-1	0-1	4		14,321
4	Sept 13	A	Hamilton A	L 0-2	0-2	5		4023
5	19	H	St Johnstone	W 3-0	2-0	3	Stokes 2 [21, 73], Riordan [36]	10,817
6	26	A	Motherwell	W 3-1	1-1	3	Nish [9], Riordan [51], Zemmama [55]	5221
7	Oct 3	H	Dundee U	D 1-1	1-0	3	Zemmama [27]	13,056
8	17	H	Kilmarnock	W 1-0	0-0	3	Benjelloun (pen) [84]	10,922
9	24	A	Rangers	D 1-1	0-1	3	Stokes [63]	46,892
10	31	H	Aberdeen	W 2-0	0-0	2	Nish [88], Miller [90]	13,885
11	Nov 7	A	Hearts	D 0-0	0-0	3		16,726
12	21	A	St Mirren	D 1-1	1-1	3	Riordan [29]	4681
13	28	H	Falkirk	W 2-0	1-0	3	McLean (og) [33], Riordan [86]	13,305
14	Dec 5	H	Motherwell	W 2-0	1-0	3	Stokes 2 [41, 56]	10,398
15	12	A	Kilmarnock	D 1-1	0-0	3	Stokes [60]	5132
16	19	A	Aberdeen	W 2-0	1-0	3	Stokes 2 [40, 55]	9096
17	27	H	Rangers	L 1-4	1-2	3	Stokes [1]	16,894
18	Jan 3	H	Hearts	D 1-1	0-1	—	Stokes [54]	16,949
19	16	A	Dundee U	L 0-1	0-1	4		7812
20	23	H	Hamilton A	W 5-1	3-0	4	Nish [16], Stokes 2 [21, 53], Riordan 2 [30, 49]	11,481
21	27	A	Celtic	W 2-1	1-1	—	Stokes [26], Galbraith [90]	41,000
22	30	H	St Mirren	W 2-1	1-1	3	Miller [33], Ross (og) [90]	11,476
23	Feb 10	H	Aberdeen	D 2-2	0-2	—	Stokes [50], Benjelloun (pen) [88]	10,469
24	14	A	Rangers	L 0-3	0-0	3		48,161
25	17	A	St Johnstone	L 1-5	0-2	—	Stokes [67]	4100
26	20	A	Motherwell	L 0-1	0-0	3		5055
27	27	H	St Johnstone	D 1-1	1-0	4	Stokes (pen) [3]	12,174
28	Mar 6	H	Kilmarnock	W 1-0	0-0	4	Riordan [78]	10,359
29	20	A	Hearts	L 1-2	0-2	5	Riordan [79]	17,126
30	27	A	Falkirk	W 3-1	3-1	4	Riordan [21], Stokes [34], Bamba [43]	5460
31	31	H	Dundee U	L 2-4	1-2	—	Cregg [1], Stokes [90]	9185
32	Apr 4	A	Celtic	L 0-1	0-0	4		10,523
33	10	A	Hamilton A	L 1-4	1-1	4	Nish [34]	2520
34	17	A	Celtic	L 2-3	1-1	4	Riordan [6], Stokes (pen) [54]	29,650
35	25	H	Rangers	L 0-1	0-1	5		10,573
36	May 1	H	Hearts	L 1-2	0-0	5	Stokes (pen) [55]	11,277
37	8	A	Motherwell	D 6-6	4-2	—	Nish 3 [11, 20, 36], Riordan [28], Stokes 2 [56, 65]	6241
38	9	A	Dundee U	W 2-0	1-0	4	Nish 2 [12, 72]	6527

Final League Position: 4

Honours
League Champions: Division I 1902-03, 1947-48, 1950-51, 1951-52. First Division 1980-81, 1998-99. Division II 1893-94, 1894-95, 1932-33; *Runners-up:* Division I 1896-97, 1946-47, 1949-50, 1952-53, 1973-74, 1974-75.
Scottish Cup Winners: 1887, 1902; *Runners-up:* 1896, 1914, 1923, 1924, 1947, 1958, 1972, 1979, 2001.
League Cup Winners: 1972-73, 1991-92, 2006-07; *Runners-up:* 1950-51, 1968-69, 1974-75, 1993-94, 2003-04.

European: *European Cup:* 6 matches (1955-56 semi-finals). *Cup Winners' Cup:* 6 matches (1972-73). *UEFA Cup:* 63 matches (*Fairs Cup:* 1960-61 semi-finals, 1961-62, 1962-63, 1965-66, 1967-68, 1968-69, 1970-71. *UEFA Cup:* 64 matches (1973-74, 1974-75, 1975-76, 1976-77, 1978-79, 1989-90, 1992-93, 2001-02, 2005-06).

Club colours: Shirt: Green with white sleeves. Shorts: White. Stockings: Green.

Goalscorers: *League (58):* Stokes 22 (3 pens), Riordan 13, Nish 9, Benjelloun 3 (2 pens), Bamba 2, Miller 2, Zemmama 2, Cregg 1, Galbraith 1, Wotherspoon 1, own goals 2.
Scottish Cup (11): Nish 3, Riordan 3, Benjelloun 1, Gow 1, Hanlon 1, Stokes 1, Zemmama 1.
CIS Cup (4): Hanlon 1, Riordan 1, Stokes 1, own goal 1.

Ma-Kalambay Y 6+1	McCann K 1	Hanlon P 16+2	Cregg P 10+5	Bamba S 30	Hogg C 33	Wotherspoon D 30+3	McBride K 21+5	Nish C 23+9	Riordan D 35+2	Rankin J 30+3	Benjelloun A 8+20	Galbraith D —+14	Van Zanten D 1	Stokes A 36+1	Stack G 20	McCormack D 7+2	Zemmama M 15+6	Byrne K —+4	Murray J 34	Miller L 37+1	Stevenson L 7+3	Smith G 12	Thicot S 8+2	Gow A 3+4	Match No.
1	2^1	3^2	4	5	6	7	8	9	10	11	12	13													1
1		3	4^1	5	6	12	8	9	10^2	11	13		2	7											2
		3	4^1	5	6	7	8	14	10	11				9^3	1	2^2	12	13							3
		3	4^2	5	6		8^1	9^4	10	11				7^3	1		13	14	2	12					4
		3		5		7	8		10^1	11^2	13	12		9^2	1	4	14		2	6					5
				5	4	7	8	11^1	10^3	14	13	12		9^2	1		3		2	6					6
				5	4	7	8		10		11			9	1	3			2	6					7
		13		5	6	2	8	12	11^3		10^2	14		9^1	1		7		3	4					8
				5	6	7^1	4	14	10^3		11^2	13		9	1	8			3	2	12				9
				5	6	7^2	8	13	10	14	11^3			9	1	$4^?$	12		2	3					10
				2	7	4	10	12	8	1^{11}				9	1		3		6	5					11
				5	6	7^3	8^1	13	10	12	11	14		9^2	1		3	2	4	5					12
15				5	6	7		10	11	8	12			9^2	1^0	13	4^1		3	2					13
1		14	5	6	7		8^3	10^1	11		12			9		4^2	13		3	2					14
1			5	6	7		8	10	11	12				9^1	1		3	2							15
1		14	5	6	2		8^3	10^1	7	13				9		$4^?$	3	11	12						16
1	2		5	6	7		10^3	11^2	8	14	13			9	12	4		3							17
	5		6	7	12		10	11						9	$2^?$	$4^?$	3	8							18
	5	4^2	6	7		14	10	11	12					9^3		$2^?$	Σ	8		1	13				19
	5	13	6	7	2^3	8^1	10	11	12	14				9			4^2	1							20
	5		6	7	4	8^2	10^1	11		13				9			3	2	12	1					21
		5	6	7	4	8	10	11	12					9^1			3	2		1					22
		5	6	$2^?$	7^1	8	10^3	11	13					9		1^2	3	4		1			14		23
	2		5	6	14	13	12	8^3	10					9		4^2	3	11		1			7^1		24
	2		5	6	13		12^4	11	8	10^1				9		4^2	3	7		1					25
	4^1	5	6	7			11							9	1	1^2	3	8^4	2			10			26
		5	6	2	4^1	8	10							9	1	12	3	7	11						27
	13	$5^?$	6	7	4		10		12	14				9	1		3	2	8^3			11^1			28
		5		7	4		10	$11^?$	12					9	1		3	2	8	6					29
	13	5	6	12		11	10	8						9^2	1	7^1	3	2			4				30
	4	5	6		8^2	9	$1C$	13						12	1		3	7	11^1	2					31
	4	5		8^3	10^1	11^2	13	12						9^1	1	7	3	6				2	14		32
	7^2	5		12	11	10	8	13	14					9^3	1	2	3	4^1		6					33
	2	5		7	4	10^2	11^1	8	13	12				9	1	ϵ	3								34
	2	4^2		6^1	7	8	13	10	11	14				9^3	5		3			1	12				35
	5		6	7^1		8	10	11						9			3	4		1	2	12			36
	5		6	7	12	8	10^1	11	13					9^2			3	4		1	2				37
	14		5	6	7	12	8	10	11					9^2			3	2^1		1	4^3	13			38

INVERNESS CALEDONIAN THISTLE
Premier League

Year Formed: 1994. *Ground & Address:* Tulloch Caledonian Stadium, East Longman, Inverness IV1 1FF. *Telephone:* 01463 222880. *Fax:* 01463 227479. *E-mail:* jim.falconer@ictfc.co.uk *Website:* www.ictfc.co.uk
Ground Capacity (seated): 7780. *Size of Pitch:* 115yd × 75yd.
Chairman: George Fraser. *Company Secretary:* Ian MacDonald. *Director of Football:* Graeme Bennett.
Manager: Terry Butcher. *Assistant Manager:* Maurice Malpas. *Physio:* David Brandie.
Record Attendance: 7753 v Rangers, SPL, 20 January 2008.
Record Victory: 8-1, v Annan Ath, Scottish Cup 3rd rd, 24 January 1998.
Record Defeats: 0-5, v Celtic, Premier League, 15 September 2007 and 0-5, v Rangers, Premier League, 1 November 2008.
Most League Appearances: 476: Ross Tokely, 1995-2009.
Most League Goals in Season: 27: Iain Stewart, 1996-97; Denis Wyness, 2002-03.
Most Goals Overall (Individual): 118: Denis Wyness, 2000-03, 2005-08.

INVERNESS CALEDONIAN TH 2009–10 LEAGUE RECORD

Match No.	Date	Venue	Opponents	Result	H/T Score	Lg Pos.	Goalscorers	Attendance
1	Aug 8	A	Dunfermline Ath	W 1-0	0-0	—	Cox [90]	2975
2	15	H	Ayr U	D 0-0	0-0	3		3297
3	22	A	Dundee	D 2-2	2-2	4	Sanchez [20], Cox [38]	5507
4	29	H	Ross Co	L 1-3	0-1	7	Hayes [60]	5846
5	Sept 12	A	Morton	W 3-0	1-0	4	Sanchez [45], Foran [60], Proctor [85]	1946
6	19	A	Airdrie U	D 1-1	0-1	5	Hayes [63]	951
7	26	H	Partick Th	L 2-3	0-3	6	Rooney (pen) [63], Foran [76]	3218
8	Oct 10	H	Queen of the S	L 1-3	1-1	6	Hayes [18]	3011
9	13	A	Raith R	W 1-0	0-0	—	Proctor [83]	2014
10	17	H	Dunfermline Ath	D 1-1	1-0	6	Proctor [45]	3082
11	24	A	Ayr U	W 5-1	4-1	6	Foran 3 [11, 25, 57], Rooney [15], Imrie [21]	1609
12	31	H	Morton	W 4-1	3-1	6	Rooney 3 (1 pen) [19, 42, 51 (p)], Bulvitis [31]	3021
13	Nov 7	A	Ross Co	L 1-2	0-2	6	Rooney [82]	5506
14	14	A	Airdrie U	W 2-0	1-0	4	Sanchez [45], Odhiambo [69]	2780
15	28	A	Partick Th	L 1-2	1-0	—	Tokely [7]	2353
16	Dec 5	A	Queen of the S	D 1-1	1-0	6	Hayes [18]	2196
17	12	H	Raith R	W 1-0	1-0	5	Rooney [23]	2768
18	19	A	Dunfermline Ath	D 0-0	0-0	—		2280
19	26	H	Dundee	D 1-1	0-1	—	Rooney [57]	3660
20	Jan 23	A	Airdrie U	W 1-0	1-0	5	Rooney (pen) [43]	839
21	30	H	Partick Th	W 2-1	1-1	—	Hayes [38], Rooney (pen) [89]	3107
22	Feb 13	A	Raith R	W 4-0	0-0	3	Rooney [67], Hayes [70], Bulvitis [77], Stratford [90]	1568
23	27	A	Ayr U	D 3-3	1-2	—	Foran [45], Hayes [61], Rooney (pen) [90]	2843
24	Mar 6	A	Dundee	D 2-2	0-0	6	Foran [47], Odhiambo [59]	4974
25	9	H	Queen of the S	W 3-1	1-0	—	Rooney 3 (1 pen) [42, 52, 76 (p)]	3003
26	13	H	Morton	W 1-0	0-0	—	Ross [65]	2788
27	20	A	Ross Co	D 0-0	0-0	2		5928
28	23	A	Airdrie U	W 4-0	2-0	—	Rooney [10], Foran [24], Munro [47], Hayes [83]	2008
29	27	A	Partick Th	W 1-0	1-0	1	Rooney [32]	2380
30	30	H	Ross Co	W 3-0	3-0	—	Foran [14], Odhiambo [16], Hayes [40]	5411
31	Apr 3	H	Raith R	W 4-3	2-1	1	Foran 2 [29, 90], Rooney [41], Odhiambo [57]	3562
32	6	A	Morton	W 2-0	1-0	—	Foran [6], Rooney [85]	1277
33	10	A	Queen of the S	W 3-1	1-1	—	Rooney 2 [42, 88], Munro [67]	2093
34	17	H	Dunfermline Ath	W 2-0	0-0	1	Rooney [55], Foran [62]	3728
35	24	A	Ayr U	W 7-0	4-0	1	Hayes [2], Rooney [10], Foran [13], Odhiambo [42], Sanchez [75], Eagle [85], Morrison [89]	1804
36	May 1	H	Dundee	W 1-0	1-0	1	Rooney [28]	6031

Final League Position: 1

Honours
Scottish Cup: Semi-finals 2003, 2004; Quarter-finals 1996.
League Champions: First Division 2003-04, 2009-10. Third Division 1996-97; *Runners-up:* Second Division 1998-99.
League Challenge Cup Winners: 2003-04. *Runners-up:* 1999-2000, 2009-10.

Club colours: All blue.

Goalscorers: *League (72):* Rooney 24 (6 pens), Foran 14, Hayes 10, Odhiambo 5, Sanchez 4, Proctor 3, Bulvitis 2, Cox 2, Munro 2, Eagle 1, Imrie 1, Morrison 1, Ross 1, Stratford 1, Tokely 1.
Scottish Cup (2): Bulvitis 1, Imrie 1.
CIS Cup (10): Eagle 2, Munro 2, Rooney 2, Barrowman 1, Bulvitis 1, Imrie 1, Sanchez 1.
Challenge Cup (8): Foran 2, Sanchez 2, Bulvitis 1, Eagle 1, Rooney 1, own goal 1.

Esson R 36	Proctor D 31 + 3	Bulvitis N 27 + 5	Munro G 35	Djebi-Zadi L 10 + 1	Cox L 27 + 6	Eagle R 7 + 12	Stratford D 8 + 6	Rooney A 27 + 8	Sanchez D 19 + 13	Imrie D 8 + 5	Hayes J 29 + 6	McBain R 2 + 5	Foran R 31	Duncan R 23 + 3	Ross N 3 + 3	Morrison G 1 + 2	Allison K — + 1	Tokely R 27	Golabek S 24	Barrowman A 1 + 4	Shinnie G 1	Odhiambo E 16 + 7	Duff J 3	Match No.
1	2	3	4	5	6	7¹	8	9	10	11²	12	13												1
1	2¹	3	4	5	6	7²	8	13	10		11		9²	12	14									2
1	2³	3	4	5	6	7¹	8		10		11²	13	9			12	14							3
1	2¹	3	4	5¹	6	7	8	12	10²		11		9	13	14									4
1	12	3	4		6	7¹	8	14	10²		11		9³						2	5	13			5
1	12	3	4		6³	7¹	8	13	10²		11		9						2	5	¹4			6
1	2	3	4		6			13	12		11		9	8	7						10¹	5²		7
1		3	4		6	7²		13	10¹	12	11		9	8				2	5					8
1	6	3	4		7		14	13	12	11¹	9		10²	8³				2	5					9
1	7	3	4		6		8	12	13	10²	11³	14	9¹					2	5					10
1	7	3	4		12			11³	6²	9	14		10	8¹				2	5	13				11
1	6	3	4		13			10³	7	11²	12		9¹	8				2	5	14				12
1	6	3³	4		14			10	7¹	11²	12		9	8				2	5			13		13
1	6	3	4		14			10	7²	11¹	12		9³	8				2	5			13		14
1	6²	3	4		13			10	7¹		11		9	8				2	5			12		15
1	5	2	4	3	6			11	12²	14	9³	13	8⁸	7⁸								10¹		16
1	2	3	4	5	6	13	14	9	10²	12	11³										7³	8		17
1	2	3	4	5	6			10	7²	12	¹11¹		9								13	8		18
1	2	3	4	5	6	13		10	7	12			9¹								11²	8		19
1	8	5	7	4	3			11	6¹	9	13		10²	12				2						20
1	2	3	4	5	6			10	7		11		8¹					9				12		21
1	7	4	3				14	11	13		6¹	12	10³	9				2	5			8²		22
1	6	5²	3		13			10	11¹		7		9	8				2	4			12		23
1	12	5	3		8²	13		11			9		10	7				2	4			6¹		24
1	5		3		7	13		11	12		9		10²	8				2	4			6¹		25
1	3		5		6	12	13	11			7			9	8¹			2	4			10²		26
1	8	3¹	4		9	12		11	13		7			6				2	5			10²		27
1	5		3		7	12		11³	6²		9		10¹	8	14			2	4			13		28
1	4	13	3		7			11	12		6²		9	8				2	5			10¹		29
1	2		4		6	13	14	10²	12		11³		9	8				3	5			7¹		30
1	2	13	4		8		5²	11	12		7		10					3	6			9¹		31
1	2	12	3		7		13	11²			6		9	8				4	5			10¹		32
1	2	12	4		6	13		11			8		10²	7				3	5			9¹		33
1	2	4		14			13		10	12		7¹	6	9³	8			3	5			11²		34
1	2	12	3			14		11	13		6	4¹	9²	8				5				10³		35
1		2	4		6	13		10	12		9³			7	8²	13		3	5			11¹		36

KILMARNOCK
Premier League

Year Formed: 1869. *Ground & Address:* Rugby Park, Kilmarnock KA1 2DP. *Telephone:* 01563 545300. *Fax:* 01563 522181. *Website:* www.kilmarnockfc.co.uk
Ground Capacity: all seated: 18,128. *Size of Pitch:* 115yd × 74yd.
Chairman: Michael Johnston. *Secretary:* Kirsten Callaghan.
Manager: Maxu Paatelainen. *Assistant Manager:* Kenny Shiels
Club Nickname(s): Killie. *Previous Grounds:* Rugby Park (Dundonald Road); The Grange; Holm Quarry; Present ground since 1899.
Record Attendance: 35,995 v Rangers, Scottish Cup, 10 Mar 1962.
Record Transfer Fee received: £2,000,000 for Stephen Naismith to Rangers (2007).
Record Transfer Fee paid: £300,000 for Paul Wright from St Johnstone (1995).
Record Victory: 11-1 v Paisley Academical, Scottish Cup, 18 Jan 1930 (15-0 v Lanemark, Ayrshire Cup, 15 Nov 1890).
Record Defeat: 1-9 v Celtic, Division I, 13 Aug 1938.
Most Capped Player: Joe Nibloe, 11, Scotland.
Most League Appearances: 481: Alan Robertson, 1972-88.
Most League Goals in Season (Individual): 34: Harry 'Peerie' Cunningham 1927-28; Andy Kerr 1960-61.
Most Goals Overall (Individual): 148: Willy Culley, 1912-23.

KILMARNOCK 2009–10 LEAGUE RECORD

Match No.	Date	Venue	Opponents	Result	H/T Score	Lg Pos.	Goalscorers	Attendance
1	Aug 15	H	Hamilton A	W 3-0	1-0	—	Kyle 2 [34, 52], Hamill [68]	5307
2	22	A	Motherwell	L 1-3	0-2	7	Hamill [88]	5093
3	29	H	St Mirren	L 1-2	1-0	8	Sammon [4]	5645
4	Sept 15	A	Hearts	L 0-1	0-1	—		13,328
5	19	A	Rangers	D 0-0	0-0	8		10,310
6	26	A	Falkirk	D 0-0	0-0	8		5394
7	Oct 3	H	Aberdeen	D 1-1	0-0	9	Invincibile [78]	4997
8	17	A	Hibernian	L 0-1	0-0	9		10,922
9	24	H	St Johnstone	W 2-1	0-0	8	Kyle 2 [51, 64]	4643
10	31	A	Celtic	L 0-3	0-2	9		46,000
11	Nov 7	H	Dundee U	L 0-2	0-1	10		4753
12	21	A	Rangers	L 0-3	0-3	10		45,358
13	28	H	Hearts	L 1-2	0-0	11	Bryson [90]	4707
14	Dec 5	A	St Johnstone	W 1-0	1-0	11	Kyle [15]	3518
15	12	H	Hibernian	D 1-1	0-0	11	Burchill [54]	5132
16	19	H	Falkirk	L 1-2	1-1	11	Invincibile [8]	4472
17	26	A	Dundee U	D 0-0	0-0	11		6692
18	Jan 2	A	St Mirren	L 0-1	0-0	—		4917
19	16	H	Motherwell	L 0-3	0-0	11		5354
20	23	A	Aberdeen	L 0-1	0-0	11		12,150
21	26	A	Hamilton A	D 0-0	0-0	—		2018
22	30	A	Dundee U	D 4-4	2-3	11	Ford [20], Kyle [41], Pascali [55], Bryson [64]	4587
23	Feb 2	H	Celtic	W 1-0	0-0	—	Maguire [53]	9308
24	10	A	Falkirk	W 1-0	0-0	—	Bryson [58]	7049
25	13	H	St Johnstone	W 3-2	1-1	8	Maguire [44], Hay [64], Kyle [77]	4605
26	20	H	St Mirren	D 1-1	1-0	9	Maguire [33]	5501
27	27	A	Motherwell	L 0-1	0-0	9		4178
28	Mar 6	A	Hibernian	L 0-1	0-0	9		10,359
29	9	H	Rangers	L 0-2	0-0	—		8906
30	24	H	Hamilton A	L 1-2	0-2	—	Maguire [77]	4068
31	27	A	Celtic	L 1-3	0-1	11	Bryson [73]	41,000
32	Apr 4	H	Aberdeen	W 2-0	1-0	10	Grassi (og) [25], Russell [73]	4825
33	10	A	Hearts	L 0-1	0-1	10		14,015
34	17	A	Hamilton A	L 0-3	0-0	11		2628
35	24	A	St Mirren	L 0-1	0-0	11		5639
36	May 1	H	St Johnstone	L 1-2	1-1	11	Wright [38]	4679
37	5	A	Aberdeen	W 2-1	0-1	—	Kelly [69], Kyle [74]	6097
38	8	H	Falkirk	D 0-0	0-0	11		10,662

Final League Position: 11

Honours
League Champions: Division I 1964-65. Division II 1897-98, 1898-99; *Runners-up:* Division I 1959-60, 1960-61, 1962-63, 1963-64. First Division 1975-76, 1978-79, 1981-82, 1992-93. Division II 1953-54, 1973-74. Second Division 1989-90.
Scottish Cup Winners: 1920, 1929, 1997; *Runners-up:* 1898, 1932, 1938, 1957, 1960.
League Cup Runners-up: 1952-53, 1960-61, 1962-63, 2000-01, 2006-07.

European: *European Cup:* 4 matches (1965-66). *Cup Winners' Cup:* 4 matches (1997-98). *UEFA Cup:* 32 matches (*Fairs Cup:* 1964-65, 1966-67, 1969-70, 1970-71. *UEFA Cup:* 1998-99, 1999-2000, 2001-02).

Club colours: Shirt: Blue and white vertical stripes. Shorts: Blue. Stockings: Blue.

Goalscorers: *League (29):* Kyle 8, Bryson 4, Maguire 4, Hamill 2, Invincibile 2, Burchill 1, Ford 1, Hay 1, Kelly 1, Pascali 1, Russell 1, Sammon 1, Wright 1, own goal 1.
Scottish Cup (4): Kelly 2, Pascali 1, Sammon 1.
CIS Cup (4): Kyle 2, Sammon 2 (1 pen).

Bell C 21	Old S 8 + 2	Hay C 27 + 1	Bryson C 33	Wright F 27	Ford S 22 + 1	Taouil M 21 + 6	Hamill J 31 + 4	Kyle K 29 + 3	Sammon G 14 + 9	Skelton G 16 + 4	Flannigan I 3 + 4	Clancy T 19 + 1	Invincibile D 16 + 9	Combe A 3	Pascali M 20 + 2	Fernandez D 9 + 4	Owens G 1 + 5	Brown M 14	U'Leary R 10 + 1	Fowler J 19 + 9	Russell A 6 + 8	Burchill M 9 + 6	Kelly L 13 + 3	Maguire C 12 + 2	Kiernan R 2 + 2	Severin S 13 + 1	Adams J — + 1	Robinson L — + 1	Match No.
1	2	3	4	5	6	7¹	8	9	10	11	12																		1
1	2¹		4	5	6	7	8	9	10	11		3	12																2
		3	4	5	6	7		10	11		2		1	8¹	9	12													3
	3³	4	5	6	8	7	12	10	11²		2	13			9¹	14	1												4
3		4	5		13	7	9	10	12		2¹	11²	8⁴			1	6												5
3	2		5		4	7	9	10	8		11			1	6														6
3¹	2	4	5		7		10	8		11		9²		1	6	12	13												7
	3¹	8	2		6	9	10	11²		7	12		1	5	4	13													8
2	3	4	5		8¹	7	9	10²	11		12		13		6														9
1	12	4	5		8	3	9	10¹	11³	14		7²		13		2	6												10
	3³	4	5		7	8¹	10	12	11	14			9²		1	2	6		13										11
	3	4	5		12	8	10²		11¹			7³	9	14	1	2	6	13											12
2²	3	7	6		11	8	10	13			9¹			1	4	5	12												13
2¹	3	4	11	6	7²	8	9		13					1	12	5	14	10³											14
	2	4	5	6	7	8	9				11			1	3	12	10¹												15
	3	4	2	5	7	8²	9				11¹			12	1	6	13	10											16
	4	3	6¹		12	9		11			7	8	13	1	2	5	10²												17
	4	5		13	3	12	10¹	11		7	8	9²	1	2	6														18
1		3	8	5	6	7	2	9		14		11³	13	12		4²		10¹											19
1	12	3	4		5	8	2¹	13		11		7	6	9			10²												20
1		3	4		5	8	2	9			11	7		5		10¹	12												21
1		3	4		5	6	2	9	12	11¹		8²	7			13		10											22
1		3	4		5	11¹	6	9	12		2²	7						8	10³	13	14								23
1		3	4³		5		12	9	14		2	7¹				13			11	10	6²	8							24
1	14	3	4		5	13	6	9³	12		2¹	11²							8	10		7							25
1		3	4		5¹		2³	9	10²		13		7						8	11	12	6	14						26
1	2	4		13		9	10¹		7²	3	14	6				12				8³	11	5							27
1⁶		3		5	7²	6		8	2		11	9¹			3	12		10	4	15									28
1			5		7	3		8¹	2	12	11			4	9²	13	14	10	6³										29
1		8		14	3	9		2³		7				5³	12	13	11	10	4¹	6									30
1		8	6	5	14	9		2	13					12	4	10¹	7³	11²		3									31
1	3	5¹	6	7	12	9	13		2	11²				4	10³	14			8										32
1	3		5	7¹		10²	13	2	14	4				6	9³	12		11	8										33
1	3	4	5	7			2	13	11					6	9¹	10²	8	12											34
1		4³	5	6		3	9	14	2		7			12		10¹	11	13	8²										35
1	3	4¹	5	6		7	9	13		2		8²		12		11	10												36
		8	5		3	9	11¹		2	12	1	4	13	6²		10		7											37
		4	5	13		3	9	12		2	7¹	1	8²			14		11	10³	6									38

LIVINGSTON
Second Division

Year Formed: 1974. *Ground:* The Braidwood Motor Company Stadium, Almondvale Stadium Road, Livingston EH54 7DN. *Telephone:* 01506 417000. *Fax:* 01506 418888. *Email:* info@livingstonfc.co.uk *Website:* www.livingstonfc.co.uk
Ground Capacity: 10,005 (all seated). *Size of Pitch:* 107yd × 75yd.
Chairman: Gordon McDougall. *Vice Chairman:* Albert Tait.
Manager: Gary Bollan. *Assistant Manager:* Scott Paterson. *Physio:* TJ Johanssen.
Club Nickname: Livi Lions. *Previous Grounds:* None.
Record Attendance: 10,024 v Celtic, Premier League, 18 Aug 2001.
Record Transfer Fee received: £1,000,000 for D. Fernandez to Celtic (June 2002).
Record Transfer Fee paid: £120,000 for Wes Hoolahan from Shelbourne (December 2005).
Record Victory: 7-0 v Queen of the South, Scottish Cup, 29 Jan 2000.
Record Defeat: 0-8 v Hamilton A. Division II, 14 Dec 1974.
Most Capped Player (under 18): I. Little.
Most League Appearances: 446: Walter Boyd, 1979-89.
Most League Goals in Season (Individual): 22: Leigh Griffiths, 2008-09.
Most Goals Overall (Individual): 64: David Roseburgh, 1986-93.

LIVINGSTON 2009–10 LEAGUE RECORD

Match No.	Date	Venue	Opponents	Result	H/T Score	Lg Pos.	Goalscorers	Attendance
1	Aug 15	H	Montrose	W 2-0	1-0	4	Halliday 2 [18, 54]	632
2	22	H	Berwick R	L 0-1	0-0	7		608
3	29	A	Albion R	L 0-1	0-1	7		485
4	Sept 12	H	Elgin C	W 3-2	1-0	6	De Vita [26], Fox 2 (1 pen) [59, 89 (p)]	602
5	19	A	Stranraer	W 3-0	3-0	4	Halliday [3], De Vita 2 [13, 33]	378
6	26	H	Queen's Park	W 2-1	1-1	3	Fox [43], Winters R [55]	961
7	30	A	East Stirling	L 1-3	1-2	—	Winters R [44]	567
8	Oct 10	A	Forfar Ath	W 1-0	1-0	5	Winters R [13]	613
9	13	H	Annan Ath	W 2-0	2-0	—	Winters D [18], Winters R [43]	771
10	17	A	Berwick R	D 1-1	0-0	3	Griffin [88]	815
11	31	A	Montrose	W 3-0	0-0	1	De Vita [53], Halliday [86], McNulty [90]	433
12	Nov 7	A	Elgin C	W 6-1	3-0	1	Keaghan Jacobs 2 [2, 44], Winters D [39], Nicolson (og) [49], Halliday [52], Talbot [68]	615
13	21	A	Queen's Park	W 2-1	0-0	1	Keaghan Jacobs [47], Moyes [65]	620
14	24	H	Albion R	W 2-0	1-0	—	Talbot [5], Keaghan Jacobs [85]	726
15	Dec 5	H	Stranraer	W 3-0	2-0	1	Winters R [14], Mitchell G (og) [35], Halliday [69]	1267
16	12	H	Forfar Ath	L 1-2	1-1	1	Halliday [22]	1591
17	Jan 23	A	Stranraer	D 1-1	0-1	1	Fox [90]	323
18	26	H	Elgin C	W 1-0	0-0	—	Brown [72]	503
19	Feb 2	H	Queen's Park	W 2-0	2-0	—	Fox [7], Halliday [12]	680
20	6	A	Forfar Ath	D 2-2	0-0	1	Winters R [55], Hamilton [61]	510
21	9	A	Albion R	W 2-0	0-0	—	Hamilton (pen) [66], Tosh [90]	587
22	13	H	Annan Ath	W 3-2	0-2	1	De Vita [53], Winters R [74], Halliday [78]	1085
23	20	A	East Stirling	W 2-0	1-0	1	Halliday [14], Winters R [84]	1062
24	Mar 9	H	East Stirling	W 2-0	1-0	—	Halliday [34], Winters R [52]	864
25	13	A	Elgin C	W 1-0	1-0	1	De Vita [42]	433
26	16	A	Annan Ath	D 0-0	0-0	—		604
27	20	H	Stranraer	W 2-1	2-0	1	Fox [27], Winters R [29]	1136
28	27	A	Queen's Park	W 1-0	0-0	1	De Vita [80]	714
29	Apr 3	A	Annan Ath	L 0-2	0-1	1		831
30	6	H	Montrose	W 1-0	0-0	—	Halliday [90]	748
31	10	H	Forfar Ath	L 2-3	2-3	1	De Vita [1], Winters R [33]	1500
32	13	A	Berwick R	D 1-1	0-0	—	Tosh (pen) [71]	604
33	17	H	Berwick R	D 0-0	0-0	1		1621
34	24	A	Montrose	W 5-0	1-0	1	Halliday 2 [40, 53], De Vita [50], Watson [70], Keaghan Jacobs [83]	510
35	27	H	Albion R	W 2-0	2-0	—	Sinclair [15], McGowan (og) [18]	628
36	May 1	H	East Stirling	W 1-0	1-0	1	Keaghan Jacobs [44]	1480

Final League Position: 1

Honours
League Champions: First Division 2000-01. Second Division 1986-87, 1998-99. Third Division 1995-96, 2009-10;
Runners-up: Second Division 1982-83. First Division 1987-33.
Scottish Cup: Semi-finals 2004.
League Cup Winners: 2003-04. Semi-finals 1984-85. *B&Q Cup:* Semi-finals 1992-93, 1993-94, 2001.
League Challenge Cup Runners-up: 2000-01.

European: *UEFA Cup:* 4 matches (2002-03).

Club colours: Shirt: Yellow. Shorts: Black. Stockings: Yellow.

Goalscorers: *League (63):* Halliday 14, Winters R 11, De Vita 9, Fox 6 (1 pen), Keaghan Jacobs 6, Hamilton 2 (1 pen),
Talbot 2, Tosh 2 (1 pen), Winters D 2, Brown 1, Griffin 1, McNulty 1, Moyes 1, Sinclair 1, Watson 1, own goals 3.
Scottish Cup (11): De Vita 2, Fox 3 (1 pen), Halliday 2, Winters R 2, Hamill 1, Keaghan Jacobs 1.
CIS Cup (0).
Challenge Cup (0).

McKenzie R 32	Talbot J 32	Malone C 6+3	Sinclair D 20+10	Watson P 25+1	MacDonald C 21+2	McPartland A 3+1	Hamill J 7+3	Jacobs Keaghan 28+6	One A 1+1	Winters D 10+5	Halliday A 23+9	McKee J —+1	McNeil A 1	Griffin D 23+2	Winters R 34+1	De Vita R 23+6	Brown J 16	Husband C 4+3	Moyes E 6+1	Fox L 30+1	Jacobs Kyle 6+8	McDonald C 3	McNulty M 2+7	Barr B 13+7	Hamilton J 6+5	Tosh S 12+3	Jacobs D 5	McDowall C 2	Hastings N 1	Jamieson D 1	Jacobs S —+1	Match No.
1	2	3	4	5	6	7^2	8	12		9^1	10	11																				1
	2		4	5	6	7^2	8	13	12	10^1	11			16	3	9	15															2
1	2		5				8^1	12		13	11^2				9	10	3	4	6	7												3
1	2	12	5	14			8				11^1				9	10	3	4^3	6^2	7	13											4
1	2			5			8			12	11				9^1	10	3	4	6	7	13											5
1	3	12	14		13		8				11				9^3	10^2	2	4^1	5	7			6^8									6
1	2	5	3	4		11^1	8	13							9^2	10	12	6	7													7
1	3	4		6		12	8	9						5^2	10	11^1				13	7	2										8
1	3	4		6		12	8	9	13					5	10^2	11				7^1	2											9
1	3	4		6		13	8^1	9	12					5	10	11				7^2	2											10
1	5	3		7			8	12			10^3			4	11^1	9^2	2^8			6	13		14									11
1	3	13	4		6		8^1	11	9^2					5	10^3	12				7	2	14										12
1	5	3					8^1	11	9					4	10	2		6	7	12												13
1	3	4		6			8	11	9^1					5	10^2	2		7	12	13												14
1	3	4		6		7^2	8^3	11	9					5	10^1	12	2	13	14													15
1	3	4^3	2	6			8	13	12	9				5	10	11^1				7^2	14											16
1	5			4	3		8	9		11					10	12		6	2^1		7											17
1	3	12	4	5			8^1	6		13					10^3	11^2	2			7		14	9									18
1	5		8	3	4			7		9					11^3		2			6^2		12	13	10^1	14							19
1	5	8^2	3				7			9^1				2	11			6	4		13	10	12									20
1	3	6^1	4	5			12^4	14						2	11	13		8			9	10^2	7									21
1	3	14	4^2	5			8	13						2	10	12		7			11	9^1	6^3									22
1	5			4			8	10^8		11				3	11	9	5	6		12	7											23
1	3	12	6				8	9						5	10^3	11^2	5	7				13	14	4^1								24
1	5	12	3	4			8^1	9						14	10	11^1	5^3	7				6	13									25
1	3^1		4	5			8^2	9						2	10	11		7				13	12	6								26
1	3^2	13	12	4			8	14						5	11			7			9	10^3	6^1	2								27
1	5^2	13	3	4			8	14						2	11	12		7			9	10^1	6^3									28
1	2		3	4^8			8	9						12	11	10		7			5		6^1									29
1	3	6	4				8^1	12						5^2	11	10	2	7			9	13										30
1	5	6^1	3				8							11	10	2	7	4^2			9	13	12									31
1	5	13	3				9							4	11	10	2	8			12	6^1	7									32
1	3		9	4			8	13						5	10^3	9^2	7	11	14			6^1	2									33
	3	9	4				14	1^7						13	10	10^2			12	5^3	6	8	2	1	7							34
	3^1	12	8	4			7							5	10^2	11		6		13	9^3	2	1	14								35
	3	8	4	14			6	9^3						5^2	11^1	10		13		12	7	2	1									36

MONTROSE   Third Division

Year Formed: 1879. *Ground & Address:* Links Park, Wellington St, Montrose DD10 8QD. *Telephone:* 01674 673200.
Fax: 01674 677311. *E-mail:* montrosefootballclub@tesco.net *Website:* www.montrosefc.co.uk
Ground Capacity: total: 3292, seated: 1338. *Size of Pitch:* 113yd × 70yd.
Vice Chairmen: John Crawford and Malcolm J. Watters. *Secretary:* Malcolm J. Watters.
Player Manager: Steven Tweed. *Assistant Manager:* Jim Moffat. *Physios:* Craig Smith and Ashley McCombie.
Club Nickname(s): The Gable Endies. *Previous Grounds:* None.
Record Attendance: 8983 v Dundee, Scottish Cup 3rd rd, 17 Mar 1973.
Record Transfer Fee received: £50,000 for Gary Murray to Hibernian (Dec 1980).
Record Transfer Fee paid: £17,500 for Jim Smith from Airdrieonians (Feb 1992).
Record Victory: 12-0 v Vale of Leithen, Scottish Cup 2nd rd, 4 Jan 1975.
Record Defeat: 0-13 v Aberdeen, 17 Mar 1951.
Most Capped Player: Alexander Keillor, 2 (6), Scotland.
Most League Appearances: 432: David Larter, 1987-98.
Most League Goals in Season (Individual): 28: Brian Third, Division II, 1972-73.

MONTROSE 2009–10 LEAGUE RECORD

Match No.	Date		Venue	Opponents	Result		H/T Score	Lg Pos.	Goalscorers	Attendance
1	Aug	8	H	Elgin C	D	1-1	0-0	—	Hegarty (pen) [67]	361
2		15	A	Livingston	L	0-2	0-1	9		632
3		22	H	Forfar Ath	L	1-2	0-1	9	Gemmell [52]	548
4		29	A	Stranraer	L	0-2	0-1	10		271
5	Sept	12	H	Albion R	D	0-0	0-0	10		343
6		19	H	East Stirling	L	0-3	0-2	10		410
7		26	A	Berwick R	L	0-2	0-1	10		436
8	Oct	10	A	Annan Ath	L	0-2	0-0	10		476
9		13	H	Queen's Park	L	1-2	0-2	—	Tomana [61]	370
10		17	A	Forfar Ath	D	2-2	1-2	10	Anderson [42], Hegarty [90]	556
11		31	H	Livingston	L	0-3	0-0	10		433
12	Nov	7	A	Albion R	D	0-0	0-0	10		257
13		14	H	Stranraer	D	1-1	0-0	10	Anderson [55]	258
14	Dec	1	H	Berwick R	L	1-3	0-1	—	Watson [80]	265
15		6	A	East Stirling	L	0-1	0-0	10		342
16		12	H	Annan Ath	D	0-0	0-0	10		250
17		19	A	Queen's Park	L	2-3	0-1	—	Tosh [82], Nicol [90]	397
18	Jan	16	A	Stranraer	L	4-5	2-2	—	Maitland [43], Campbell [46], Tosh 2 (1 pen) [66 (p), 72]	200
19		23	H	East Stirling	L	0-1	0-1	10		310
20		30	A	Berwick R	W	2-0	1-0	—	Norman (og) [24], Tosh [90]	392
21	Feb	13	H	Queen's Park	L	1-2	1-0	10	Tosh [35]	325
22		20	H	Elgin C	L	0-4	0-1	10		280
23	Mar	2	H	Albion R	D	0-0	0-0	—		249
24		6	A	Stranraer	W	2-0	1-0	10	Tosh [32], Tweed [66]	225
25		13	A	Albion R	L	0-1	0-0	10		217
26		16	H	Forfar Ath	W	4-0	2-0	—	Sinclair [26], Gemmell 2 [45, 88], Milligan [74]	360
27		20	A	East Stirling	W	3-2	2-0	10	Gemmell [16], Sinclair [22], Nicol [72]	306
28		23	A	Elgin C	W	1-0	0-0	—	Tosh [51]	295
29		27	H	Berwick R	D	1-1	1-1	10	Nicol [16]	376
30	Apr	3	A	Queen's Park	L	0-3	0-2	9		487
31		6	A	Livingston	L	0-1	0-0	—		748
32		10	H	Annan Ath	L	1-2	0-2	10	McNalley [89]	294
33		13	A	Annan Ath	D	0-0	0-0	—		278
34		17	A	Forfar Ath	L	0-2	0-0	10		466
35		24	H	Livingston	L	0-5	0-1	10		510
36	May	1	A	Elgin C	L	2-5	1-2	10	Tosh 2 (1 pen) [12, 73 (p)]	504

Final League Position: 10

Honours
League Champions: Second Division 1984-85; *Runners-up:* Second Division 1990-91. Third Division 1994-95.
Scottish Cup: Quarter-finals 1973, 1976.
League Cup: Semi-finals 1975-76.
B&Q Cup: Semi-finals 1992-93.
League Challenge Cup: Semi-finals 1996-97.

Club colours: Shirt: Royal blue. Shorts: Royal blue. Stockings: Royal blue.

Goalscorers: *League (30):* Tosh 9 (2 pens), Gemmell 4, Nicol 3, Anderson 2, Hegarty 2 (1 pen), Sinclair 2, Campbell 1, Maitland 1, McNalley 1, Milligan 1, Tomana 1, Tweed 1, Watson 1, own goal 1.
Scottish Cup (9): Milligan 2, Watson 2, Gemmell 1, Hegarty 1, Maitland 1, Nicholas 1, Nicoll 1.
CIS Cup (0).
Challenge Cup (1): Leyden 1.

Coutts S 7+1	Hegarty C 28	Campbell A 29	Tweed S 31	Pope G 2+2	Maitland J 15+7	Crighton S 29	Davidson H 31+1	Fleming S 7+3	Voigt J 3	Nicol D 15+18	Sinclair A 29+1	Leyden J —+6	Gray N —+6	Adams K 1	Gemmell J 19+3	Anderson S 12+2	Stewart R 4+4	McGowan D 2+1	Hall S —+1	McNeil A 29	Tomana M 15+5	Milligan F 25+3	Deane P 1	Russell M —+1	Watson P 8	Nicholas S 14+1	Tosh P 18	McNalley S 19	Boyle M 1+4	Tresly J —+1	Presly J —+2	Collier J 2+2	Match No.
1	2	3	4	5^1	6	7	8	9^1	10	11	12	13																					1
1	2	3	4		6	7^1	8	9	10^2	11^1	5	13	12																				2
1	2		4		6		8	9^1	10^3	11^2	5	13			3	7	12	14															3
1^6	2		4		6	3	8			11^1	5	13			7	9	12	10^2	15														4
	2	11	4		6^2	3	8	9^1		13	5				7		14			1	10^1	12											5
	2	11	4^1		6	3	8			12	5	14			7^2		13			1	10	9^1											6
	2	3	4		6		8			13	5	12			11^1		7			1	10^2	9											7
2^a		5	4^1		6		8			9	3	13			11		7^2			1	10	12^3	14										8
	2	3			4		8			10^1	5	12	13		6	11	3			1		7											9
	2	4	5		6		8			10	3^2	13			9	12						7^1			11								10
1	2	3	4				8			12	5				10	11					6^1	9			7								11
	2	4	5		13	6	8			12	3^1				9	11^2				1		7			10								12
7		3	4		13		8			12	5				10	11^2				1	6^1	9			2								13
5		3	4		6					12					9	10	11^1			1		2			8	7							14
4		3	5		6		8			12					9^2	11				1	13	2^1			10	7							15
	2	5	3		13	4				7	12				9^2	11					6^1	8			10								16
	2	6	3		13	4				7	12				5^1	9					8^2	11			10								17
	6	4	8^2		5					12		13		14	11	7^3					2^1	10			9	3							18
11		4	7^2		3	8				13					12					6	2	9^1			10		5						19
	3	4			12		8	7				9			11					1		2			6^1		10	5					20
7		3	4		9^1					12	5				11					1	13	6^2			8		10	2					21
7^a		4	3				8				5				11^2	14				1	13	6^3			9^1		10	2	12				22
		5	3		4			7			9^a									1	8	6					11^1	10	2	12			23
7		5	4		3		8				9				11^1					1		6					10	2	12				24
7		5	4		3		8			12	9					13				1	10^1	6^2					11	2					25
7^a		5	4		12	3	8				9				11					1		6^1					10	2					26
		3	5		6	4	8			13	12				11^2					1	10	7^1					9	2					27
		5	4		7^1	3	8			10					9					1	12	6					11	2					28
		3	5		9^1		4								6^2	7				1	11	8				12	10^a	2	13				29
		3	5		9		4			12					11		7^1		13	1	8^2	6^3					10	2		14			30
6		3	5		13	4^1				12					9	10				1		7			8		11	2^2					31
7		4^1	5		13		8			9^2	3				12					1	14	6^2				11	10	2					32
15		6	5		8			7		10	3				11^a					1^9	9^1	2					4				12		33
1	8		5		7^1		4			9	3				6						11^2	10					2	13			12		34
1		4	5		14		9	7^2		12	3^1				11^2							6					10	2		13	8		35
	7	3	5		4		9			12	6									1	13						11	2	10^2		8^1		36

MORTON

First Division

Year Formed: 1874. *Ground & Address:* Cappielow Park, Sinclair St, Greenock PA15 2TY. *Telephone:* 01475 723571.
Fax: 01475 781084. *E-mail:* info@gmfc.net *Website:* www.gmfc.net
Ground Capacity: total: 11,612, seated: 6062. *Size of Pitch:* 110yd × 71yd.
Chairman: Douglas Rae. *Chief Executive:* Gillian Donaldson. *Company Secretary:* Mary Davidson.
Manager: Allan Moore. *Assistant Manager:* Mark McNally. *Physios:* Paul Kelly and John Tierney.
Club Nickname(s): The Ton. *Previous Grounds:* Grant Street 1874, Garvel Park 1875, Cappielow Park 1879, Ladyburn
Park 1882, (Cappielow Park 1883).
Record Attendance: 23,500 v Celtic, 29 April 1922.
Record Transfer Fee received: £350,000 for Neil Orr to West Ham U.
Record Transfer Fee paid: £150,000 for Alan Mahood from Nottingham Forest (August 1998).
Record Victory: 11-0 v Carfin Shamrock, Scottish Cup 1st rd, 13 Nov 1886.
Record Defeat: 1-10 v Port Glasgow Ath, Division II, 5 May, 1894 and v St Bernards, Division II, 14 Oct 1933.
Most Capped Player: Jimmy Cowan, 25, Scotland.
Most League Appearances: 534: Derek Collins, 1987-98, 2001-05.
Most League Goals in Season (Individual): 58: Allan McGraw, Division II, 1963-64.
Most Goals Overall (Individual): 117: Allan McGraw, 1961-66.

MORTON 2009–10 LEAGUE RECORD

Match No.	Date	Venue	Opponents	Result	Score	H/T	Lg Pos.	Goalscorers	Attendance
1	Aug 8	A	Dundee	L	0-1	0-0	—		5449
2	15	H	Dunfermline Ath	L	0-2	0-1	10		2661
3	22	A	Ayr U	W	2-0	1-0	7	Weatherson 2 [23, 85]	2304
4	29	A	Partick Th	L	0-5	0-3	8		2986
5	Sept 12	H	Inverness CT	L	0-3	0-1	10		1946
6	19	A	Raith R	L	0-3	0-0	10		2040
7	26	H	Airdrie U	W	1-0	0-0	9	Graham [79]	2104
8	Oct 3	A	Queen of the S	W	3-2	2-0	7	Graham [13], Weatherson [39], Jenkins [60]	2630
9	10	H	Ross Co	L	0-1	0-0	8		2154
10	17	H	Dundee	L	0-1	0-0	8		2217
11	24	A	Dunfermline Ath	L	1-3	0-0	8	McGuffie [74]	2411
12	31	A	Inverness CT	L	1-4	1-3	8	Paartalu [33]	3021
13	Nov 7	H	Partick Th	L	0-2	0-0	8		2738
14	14	H	Raith R	W	5-0	1-0	8	Paartalu [14], Wake 2 [55, 60], Weatherson 2 [62, 89]	1716
15	21	A	Airdrie U	W	4-2	2-2	8	MacGregor [43], Wake 2 [45, 53], Van Zanten [67]	1164
16	Dec 8	A	Ross Co	L	1-3	1-0	—	Paartalu [29]	1752
17	12	H	Queen of the S	L	1-2	1-1	8	Weatherson [23]	1814
18	19	A	Dundee	L	1-3	0-0	—	Weatherson [60]	4259
19	Jan 4	A	Partick Th	L	0-1	0-0	—		2190
20	23	A	Raith R	W	2-1	1-0	8	Weatherson 2 [33, 52]	1702
21	Feb 13	A	Queen of the S	W	2-1	2-0	8	Masterton 2 (1 pen) [7, 31 (p)]	2611
22	27	H	Dunfermline Ath	L	1-2	0-0	8	McGuffie [55]	1776
23	Mar 6	A	Ayr U	L	0-2	0-1	8		2145
24	13	A	Inverness CT	L	0-1	0-0	—		2788
25	17	H	Airdrie U	W	2-1	1-0	—	Weatherson [20], MacGregor [66]	1266
26	20	H	Partick Th	W	1-0	0-0	9	McAlister [90]	2163
27	23	H	Raith R	D	1-1	0-0	—	Simmons [85]	1415
28	27	A	Airdrie U	L	0-3	0-1	9		1017
29	30	H	Ayr U	W	1-0	0-0	—	Masterton [78]	1289
30	Apr 3	A	Queen of the S	D	3-3	2-1	7	Witteveen 3 [15, 22, 90]	1926
31	6	H	Inverness CT	L	0-2	0-1	—		1277
32	13	H	Ross Co	D	1-1	1-1	8	Monti (pen) [6]	1219
33	17	H	Dundee	D	2-2	1-0	8	Witteveen [41], Monti (pen) [64]	1998
34	24	A	Dunfermline Ath	L	1-4	1-3	8	Monti (pen) [40]	2532
35	26	A	Ross Co	L	1-2	0-1	8	Witteveen [52]	1830
36	May 1	H	Ayr U	W	2-1	0-1	8	Greacen [77], Monti [86]	3771

Final League Position: 8

Honours
League Champions: First Division 1977-78, 1983-84, 1986-87. Division II 1949-50, 1963-64, 1966-67. Second Division 1994-95, 2006-07. Third Division 2002-03. *Runners-up:* Division 1 1916-17, Division II 1899-1900, 1928-29, 1936-37.
Scottish Cup Winners: 1922; *Runners-up:* 1948. *League Cup Runners-up:* 1963-64.
B&Q Cup Runners-up: 1992-93.

European: *UEFA Cup:* 2 matches (*Fairs Cup:* 1968-69).

Club colours: Shirt: Blue and white hoops. Shorts: Blue. Stockings: Blue.

Goalscorers: *League (40):* Weatherson 10, Witteveen 5, Monti 4 (3 pens), Wake 4, Masterton 3 (1 pen), Paartalu 3, Graham 2, MacGregor 2, McGuffie 2, Greacen 1, Jenkins 1, McAlister 1, Simmons 1, Van Zanten 1.
Scottish Cup (1): Graham 1.
CIS Cup (4): Weatherson 2, McFarlane 1, McGuffie 1 (pen).
Challenge Cup (2): Jenkins 1, Masterton 1.

Halliwell B 1	McGuffie R 30 + 2	MacGregor D 21 + 5	McManus A 12	Greacen S 30	Masterton S 11 + 5	Finlayson K 27 + 4	McFarlane M 16	Weatherson P 31 + 2	Monti C 16 + 4	McAlister J 30	Jenkins A 18 + 6	Wake B 6 + 6	Graham B 10 + 12	McWilliams R 3	Grady J 1 + 4	Harding R 2	Stewart C 27 + 1	Walker A 3	Paartalu E 16 + 10	Kane R — + 4	Van Zanten D 7	Reid A 16	Shimmin D 17	Russell I 4 + 1	Tidser M 13	McKinlay K 7 + 1	Simmons D 7 + 7	Cuthbert K 5	Witteveen D 9	Match No.
1	2³	3	4	5	6	7	8	9²	10¹	11	12	13	14																	1
	2	3	4	5	6		8	9	10¹	11	13		12		1	7²														2
	2	12	4	5	6¹		8	9		11	7	13	10²	1		3														3
	2	14	4	5⁸		6	8²	9	14	11	7	12	10¹	1	13	3³														4
	2	5	4			13	8²	9	14	11	7	10¹	12			1	3	6												5
	2		4	5	8¹	7	6²		11	10		9		12		1	5	13												6
	13	4		5	14	7	6	8	12	11	10		9³			1	3	2¹												7
12	2	4	5		7	6	8¹	3	11	10		9				1														8
12	2	4	5		7	6	10	3²	11	8¹		9				1	13													9
3	2	4	5		7	6³	10	14	11	8¹	13	9²				1	12													10
8	2	4	5		7		10	3	11		12	9¹				1	6													11
8	2	4	5		7		10²	3	11		9¹			13		1	6	12												12
8	3		5		7²		10		11		9¹			12		1	6	13	2	4										13
8	3		5		7		10		11		9¹					1	6	12	2	4										14
	8	3	5		7		10²	12	11		9¹	13				1	6		2	4										15
	3		5		7		10	8	11		12	9¹				1	6		2	4⁸										16
10¹	3		5	12	7		9	8²	11			13				1	6		2	4										17
	5		7			9	8	11								1	6	12	2	3	4	10¹								18
	13		4		6	8¹	10		9	12	11					1	7		2	5²	3									19
2			5		7		9		11	8		10²				1	12			3	4	13	6¹							20
2			5	8	6⁸		10¹		9	7	12				1					3	4	11²		13						21
2			4	7			11	6¹	9	8³	14				1		12			5	3	10²			13					22
2	14		5⁸	8	12			9³		11	7¹		13		1					3²	4		6		10					23
2	3			9¹				12		11	8					6				4		7	5	10	1					24
2	4		6				11²		9	7							13				3	10¹	8	5	12	1				25
2	4		6¹	13			10³		9	8		14					12				3		7²	5	11	1				26
2	3		6¹	12			10		9	8							13				4		7²	5	11	1				27
2	5		12	7		6²	13		11	8¹						15					4			3	10	1⁸	9⁶			28
2	4	3	13	6		7	10¹		9								1	14					8⁹	5²	12		11			29
2	4	3	13	6		7³	10²		9	14							1				5		8¹		12		11			30
2			3	6²		7¹	10³		9		14						1	12			5	4	8		13		11			31
2			3	6			10¹		9			12					1	7			5	4	8				11			32
2			3	6			11¹		9								1	7			5	4	8		12		10			33
2			3	6			10¹		9			13					1	4			5	8	7		12		11²			34
2	3		5		7	6		11		8							1					4			9		10			35
2			3	6			9		12	13							1	7¹				4		8	5	11²	10			36

MOTHERWELL

Premier League

Year Formed: 1886. *Ground & Address:* Fir Park Stadium, Motherwell ML1 2QN. *Telephone:* 01698 333333. *Fax:* 01698 338001.
E-mail: info@motherwellfc.co.uk *Website:* www.motherwellfc.co.uk
Ground Capacity: all seated: 13,742. *Size of Pitch:* 110yd × 75yd.
Chairman: John Boyle. *Secretary:* Stewart Robertson.
Manager: Craig Brown. *Assistant Manager:* Archie Knox. *Physio:* John Porteous.
Club Nickname(s): The Well. *Previous Grounds:* Roman Road, Dalziel Park.
Record Attendance: 35,632 v Rangers, Scottish Cup 4th rd replay, 12 Mar 1952.
Record Transfer Fee received: £1,750,000 for Phil O'Donnell to Celtic (September 1994).
Record Transfer Fee paid: £500,000 for John Spencer from Everton (Jan 1999).
Record Victory: 12-1 v Dundee U, Division II, 23 Jan 1954.
Record Defeat: 0-8 v Aberdeen, Premier Division, 26 Mar 1979.
Most Capped Player: Tommy Coyne, 13, Republic of Ireland.
Most League Appearances: 626: Bobby Ferrier, 1918-37.
Most League Goals in Season (Individual): 52: Willie McFadyen, Division I, 1931-32.
Most Goals Overall (Individual): 283: Hugh Ferguson, 1916-25.

MOTHERWELL 2009–10 LEAGUE RECORD

Match No.	Date	Venue	Opponents	Result	H/T Score	Lg Pos.	Goalscorers	Attendance
1	Aug 15	A	St Johnstone	D	2-2	0-1	—	Hutchinson [56], Forbes [66]	5220
2	22	H	Kilmarnock	W	3-1	2-0	4	Sutton [14], Forbes (pen) [45], Hutchinson [68]	5093
3	29	A	Aberdeen	D	0-0	0-0	5		11,320
4	Sept 12	H	Rangers	D	0-0	0-0	4		9355
5	19	A	Dundee U	W	1-0	0-0	4	Forbes (pen) [66]	7196
6	26	H	Hibernian	L	1-3	1-1	6	Reynolds [35]	5221
7	Oct 3	H	Falkirk	W	1-0	1-0	5	Jutkiewicz [18]	4337
8	17	A	Celtic	D	0-0	0-0	5		58,000
9	24	A	St Mirren	D	3-3	0-1	5	Forbes (pen) [49], Jutkiewicz 2 [74, 81]	4327
10	31	H	Hearts	W	1-0	0-0	4	Forbes [55]	4830
11	Nov 7	A	Hamilton A	D	2-2	0-0	5	Murphy [78], Jutkiewicz [87]	3583
12	21	H	Aberdeen	D	1-1	1-0	5	Jutkiewicz [13]	4668
13	28	H	Dundee U	D	2-2	2-1	5	Sutton [16], Jutkiewicz [29]	4593
14	Dec 5	A	Hibernian	L	0-2	0-1	5		10,398
15	12	H	Celtic	L	2-3	2-1	5	Jutkiewicz [26], Reynolds [45]	7807
16	19	A	Rangers	L	1-6	0-1	5	Hutchinson [67]	44,291
17	26	H	St Johnstone	L	1-3	1-0	6	Jennings [39]	4140
18	30	H	Hearts	L	0-1	0-1	—		14,411
19	Jan 16	A	Kilmarnock	W	3-0	0-0	6	O'Brien 2 [55, 70], Jutkiewicz [78]	5354
20	23	H	St Mirren	W	2-0	0-0	6	Murphy [56], Sutton [76]	3621
21	27	A	Falkirk	D	0-0	0-0	—		4321
22	30	A	Aberdeen	W	3-0	1-0	5	Sutton 2 [29, 53], Jutkiewicz [50]	9555
23	Feb 6	H	Hamilton A	W	1-0	0-0	5	Jutkiewicz [68]	4777
24	10	H	Rangers	D	1-1	1-0	—	Hateley [28]	9352
25	13	A	Hamilton A	D	0-0	0-0	5		3133
26	20	H	Hibernian	W	1-0	0-0	5	Murphy [82]	5055
27	27	H	Kilmarnock	W	1-0	0-0	5	Murphy [69]	4178
28	Mar 6	A	St Johnstone	W	2-1	1-1	5	Murphy [12], Sutton [86]	3669
29	9	A	St Mirren	D	0-0	0-0	—		3154
30	13	H	Hearts	W	3-1	2-0	5	Reynolds [2], Sutton [13], O'Brien [68]	4448
31	27	A	Dundee U	L	0-3	0-2	5		7609
32	Apr 3	H	Falkirk	L	0-1	0-1	5		4268
33	13	A	Celtic	L	1-2	0-0	—	Reynolds [49]	27,750
34	18	A	Dundee U	L	2-3	1-2	5	Sutton 2 [28, 81]	3544
35	24	A	Hearts	W	2-0	2-0	4	Saunders [42], Sutton [45]	13,447
36	May 1	A	Celtic	L	0-4	0-0	4		24,000
37	5	H	Hibernian	D	6-6	2-4	—	Coke 2 [16, 67], Sutton 2 [39, 76], Hateley [72], Jutkiewicz [90]	6241
38	9	A	Rangers	D	3-3	0-2	—	Murphy [51], Jennings [89], Jutkiewicz (pen) [90]	50,321

Final League Position: 5

Honours
League Champions: Division I 1931-32. First Division 1981-82, 1984-85. Division II 1953-54, 1968-69; *Runners-up:* Premier Division 1994-95. Division I 1926-27, 1929-30, 1932-33, 1933-34. Division II 1894-95, 1902-03. *Scottish Cup:* 1952, 1991; *Runners-up:* 1931, 1933, 1939, 1951.
League Cup Winners: 1950-51; *Runners-up:* 1954-55, 2004-05. *Scottish Summer Cup:* 1944, 1965.

European: *Cup Winners' Cup:* 2 matches (1991-92). *UEFA Cup:* 8 matches (1994-95, 1995-96, 2008-09). *Europa League:* 6 matches (2009-10).

Club colours: Shirt: Amber with claret hoop and trimmings. Shorts: Amber. Stockings: Amber.

Goalscorers: *League (52):* Jutkiewicz 12 (1 pen), Sutton 12, Murphy 6, Forbes 5 (3 pens), Reynolds 4, Hutchinson 3, O'Brien 3, Coke 2, Hateley 2, Jennings 2, Saunders 1.
Scottish Cup (0).
CIS Cup (3): Forbes 1, McHugh 1, own goal 1.
Europa League (12): Murphy 4, Forbes 3 (1 pen), Sutton 2, Hutchinson 1, McHugh 1, Slane 1.

Ruddy J 34	O'Brien J 29+6	Hammell S 33	Forbes R 22+6	Hutchinson S 4+1	Craigan S 28	Murphy J 24+11	Reynolds M 37	Sutton J 31+4	Coke G 25+7	Hateley T 38	Humphrey C 6+22	McHugh R 2+8	Saunders S 22+3	Jennings S 21+8	Slane P —+2	Jutkiewicz L 27+6	Moutaouakil Y 13	Lasley K 15+5	Halsman J —+1	Fraser M 4+1	Meechan S 1+1	Pollock J —+1	McGarry S —+1	Fitzpatrick M 1+2	McGlinchey M 1+7	Match No.
1	2	3	4	5	6¹	7	8	9²	10	11	12	13														1
1	2³		4	5	6	7¹	8	9	10	11²	12		3	13	14											2
1	2	5¹	4		6	7²	8	12	10	11			14	3	13	9³										3
1	8	5	4²			7¹	2	9²	10	11			3	12		14	6	13								4
1	8	5	4			2	9	10	11				3	7¹		12	6									5
1	8¹	5	4			12	2	9	7³	11	14	13	3			10²	6									6
1	13³	5	9		4	8	2		7	11²	3¹	14	12			10	6									7
1		3	4			9³	6	13	8	11	7¹		5	14		10²	2		12							8
1	2		4	13	7	9	6	14	8¹	11	12		3²			10	5³									9
1	2³	11¹	7		13	6	9	8	4	12			3			10¹	5	14								10
	8³	11²			6¹	12	2	9	3	4	7	14	5	13		10				1						11
1	12	3	11¹			7	2	9	8²	4		14	6	13		10³	5									12
1	13	11	10¹			7²	2	9	6	4			3			8	5	1²								13
1	12	3	11¹			7	6	9²	8	4			5			10	2	1²								14
1		3	14			8¹	6		12	11		9²	5	7³		10	2			4	13					15
1	13	3¹	6			8³	4		11	14	3²	5	7			10	2		12							16
1	8²		6		12	4	9		11	14		5	3	13	10¹	2	7¹									17
1	8	3	9		6	7¹	4	12		11		5³	2²	10	13					14						18
1	2²	3	11¹		6		5	9	8	4	12	14		10³	7					13						19
1	4³	3	11²		6	12	5	9	8	2	13		14	10¹	7											20
1	11³	3	10²		6	4¹	5	9	8⁴	2	14		13	12	7											21
1	8¹	3			6	13	5	9		11	12	14	2	10²	7							4³				22
1	8	3			6		5	9¹	4²	11	12	14	2	10	7							13³				23
1	6	3	8¹		4	12	5	9		11			2	10	7											24
1	6²	3			4	14	5	9	8¹	11	13		2	10³	7								12			25
1	8	3			6	10	5	9	4¹	11	12		2		7											26
1		3			4	8²	5	9	12	11	6		2	10	7								13			27
1	10²	3	13		4	8³	5	9	12	11	6		2	14	7¹											28
1	13	3	10²		4	12	5	9	7¹	11	6³		8	2									14			29
1	8³	3	13		4	6	5	9	12	11			2²	10¹	7								14			30
1	8	3			4	6	5	9¹	13	11	12		2	10³	7²								14			31
1⁰	6	3	10²		4	8	5	9	12	11	13		2		7¹	15										32
	8	3			4⁷	6	5	9	12	11	14	13	2	10³	7¹											33
	8	3			4¹	10²	5	9	6	11	12	7	2	13				1								34
	7²	3	14		4	12	5	9	6	11³	13	8	2	10¹				1								35
1	8³	3	10¹		4	7	5	9²		11	14	6	2	12									13			36
1	8	3	14		4	2²	5	9	7	11³	13	6¹		10									12			37
1	8²	3	14		4	12		9²	7	11	13		5	2		10							6¹			38

PARTICK THISTLE

First Division

Year Formed: 1876. *Ground & Address:* Firhill Stadium, 80 Firhill Rd, Glasgow G20 7AL. *Telephone:* 0141 579 1971. *Fax:* 0141 945 1525. *E-mail:* mail@ptfc.co.uk *Website:* www.ptfc.co.uk
Ground Capacity: total: 13,141, seated: 10,921. *Size of Pitch:* 105yd × 68yd.
Chairman: Allan Cowan. *Secretary:* Antonia Kerr.
Manager: Ian McCall. *Coach:* Ian Cameron. *Head of Youth Development:* Gerry Britton. *Physio:* Kenny Crichton.
Club Nickname(s): The Jags. *Previous Grounds:* Jordanvale Park; Muirpark; Inchview; Meadowside Park.
Record Attendance: 49,838 v Rangers, Division I, 18 Feb 1922. *Ground Record:* 54,728, Scotland v Ireland, 25 Feb 1928.
Record Transfer Fee received: £200,000 for Mo Johnston to Watford.
Record Transfer Fee paid: £85,000 for Andy Murdoch from Celtic (Feb 1991).
Record Victory: 16-0 v Royal Albert, Scottish Cup 1st rd, 17 Jan 1931.
Record Defeat: 0-10 v Queen's Park, Scottish Cup, 3 Dec 1881.
Most Capped Player: Alan Rough, 51 (53), Scotland.
Most League Appearances: 410: Alan Rough, 1969-82.
Most League Goals in Season (Individual): 41: Alex Hair, Division I, 1926-27.

PARTICK THISTLE 2009–10 LEAGUE RECORD

Match No.	Date	Venue	Opponents	Result	H/T Score	Lg Pos.	Goalscorers	Attendance
1	Aug 8	A	Ayr U	D	1-1	1-1	—	Donnelly [21]	3078
2	15	H	Ross Co	D	0-0	0-0	8		2391
3	22	A	Queen of the S	L	0-1	0-0	8		2915
4	29	H	Morton	W	5-0	3-0	6	Buchanan 2 [24, 80], Corcoran 2 [35, 39], Cairney [66]	2986
5	Sept 12	A	Raith R	D	1-1	0-0	6	Doohlan [86]	2370
6	19	H	Dunfermline Ath	W	2-0	1-0	4	Cairney [39], Donnelly [70]	3263
7	26	A	Inverness CT	W	3-2	3-0	3	Buchanan 2 [38, 39], Archibald [45]	3218
8	Oct 3	H	Airdrie U	W	2-0	0-0	1	Hodge [53], Donnelly [67]	2639
9	10	A	Dundee	L	0-2	0-1	3		5364
10	17	H	Ayr U	W	2-0	2-0	3	Corcoran [7], Buchanan [37]	3055
11	24	A	Ross Co	D	2-2	0-1	4	Erskine [62], Buchanan [72]	2369
12	31	H	Raith R	L	1-2	1-1	5	Donnelly [33]	3084
13	Nov 7	A	Morton	W	2-0	0-0	4	Buchanan [53], Donnelly [56]	2738
14	14	A	Dunfermline Ath	L	1-3	0-2	5	Cairney [47]	3111
15	28	H	Inverness CT	W	2-1	0-1	—	Adams [53], Lovell [68]	2353
16	Dec 5	H	Dundee	L	0-2	0-1	3		4453
17	12	A	Airdrie U	W	5-2	2-1	4	Donnelly [26], McKeown [46], Lovell 2 [47, 55], Cairney [66]	1321
18	26	H	Queen of the S	D	2-2	1-0	—	Paton [20], Adams [63]	2500
19	Jan 4	H	Morton	W	1-0	0-0	—	Cairney [74]	2190
20	16	A	Raith R	L	0-1	0-0	—		1951
21	23	H	Dunfermline Ath	L	1-4	0-0	4	Buchanan [87]	1549
22	30	H	Inverness CT	L	1-2	1-1	—	Corcoran [16]	3107
23	Feb 13	A	Airdrie U	W	2-0	2-0	4	Cairney 2 [29, 42]	2404
24	20	A	Dundee	L	0-1	0-1	—		5216
25	27	H	Ross Co	W	2-1	1-0	—	Buchanan [30], Hodge [54]	2192
26	Mar 6	A	Queen of the S	L	0-1	0-0	5		2674
27	10	A	Ayr U	L	0-1	0-1	—		1505
28	20	A	Morton	L	0-1	0-0	6		2163
29	23	A	Dunfermline Ath	W	2-1	1-1	—	Buchanan [27], Donnelly [61]	2401
30	27	H	Inverness CT	L	0-1	0-1	6		2380
31	Apr 3	A	Airdrie U	L	0-2	0-0	6		1142
32	10	H	Dundee	L	0-1	0-0	—		2545
33	17	H	Ayr U	L	0-1	0-0	6		1877
34	19	H	Raith R	D	0-0	0-0	—		1151
35	24	A	Ross Co	W	2-1	0-0	6	Donnelly [80], Grehan [74]	2175
36	May 1	H	Queen of the S	W	1-0	0-0	6	Doohlan [80]	2912

Final League Position: 6

Honours
League Champions: First Division 1975-76, 2001-02; *Runners-up:* 2008-09. Division II 1896-97, 1899-1900, 1970-71;
Second Division 2000-01; *Runners-up:* First Division 1991-92. Division II 1901-02.
Scottish Cup Winners: 1921; *Runners-up:* 1930; *Semi-finals:* 2002.
League Cup Winners: 1971-72; *Runners-up:* 1953-54, 1956-57, 1958-59.
League Challenge Cup: Quarter-finals 2004-05.

European: *Fairs Cup:* 4 matches (1963-64). *UEFA Cup:* 2 matches (1972-73). *Intertoto Cup:* 4 matches 1995-96.

Club colours: Shirt: Red and yellow hoops. Shorts: Black. Stockings: Black.

Goalscorers: *League (43):* Buchanan 10, Donnelly 8, Cairney 7, Corcoran 4, Lovell 3, Adams 2, Doohlan 2, Hodge 2,
Archibald 1, Erskine 1, Grehan 1, McKeown 1, Paton 1.
Scottish Cup (0).
CIS Cup (6): Buchanan 2 (1 pen), Erskine 2, Donnelly 1, Hodge 1
Challenge Cup (8): Buchanan 2, Hamilton 2, Cairney 1, Donnelly 1, Doolan 1, Rowson 1.

Tuffey J 33	Paton P 28+1	Robertson J 34+1	Maxwell I 27	Corrigan M 9+2	McKeown S 9+6	Rowson D 35	Cairney P 30+2	Corcoran M 25+6	Hamilton J 2+7	Donnelly S 27+8	Erskine C 11+23	Hodge B 20+9	Doohlan K 4+13	Archibald A 27	Buchanan L 23+3	Boyle P 5+1	Kinniburgh W 1+1	Adams J 6+1	Lovell S 10+6	Hinchcliffe C 1	Conroy R 15	Shields G 4	McNamara J 4	Grehan M 2+3	Burns K —+5	Halliwell B 2	McGeough R 1+1	MacBeth R 1+2	Match No.
1	2	3	4	5	6	7	8²	9¹	10³	11	12	13	14																1
1	2	3	4	5	6⁴	7	8¹	9¹	12	11²	10	13	14																2
1	2	3	4			7	8	9¹	11²	14	12	6	10³	5	13														3
1	2	3	4		13	7	8¹	9²		12	11			5	10	6													4
1	2	3	4			7³	8	6²	14	9¹	11	12	13	5	10⁴														5
1	2	3	4			7	8	12	14	9¹	11²	6	10¹	5		13													6
1	2	3	4			7	8²	11¹	13	9¹	12	6		5	10		14												7
1	2		4			7	8	12		9¹	11¹	6	13	5	10		3												8
1	2	5	6			8	7¹	11²		10	12	4	13	3	9														9
1	2	5	6			8	7	11¹	14	10²	12	4	13	3	9³														10
1	2	5	6			8	7	11	12	10¹	13	4²	14	3	9³														11
1	2	5	6¹	12		8	7	11	14	10³	13	4²		3	9														12
1	2	5	6			8	7	14		10	11³	4¹		3	9²			12	13										13
	2	5	6			8³	7	11		10²	14	13		3	9			4¹	12	1									14
1		5	6		12	8	7	11³		10²	13	4¹	14	3				2	9										15
1		5	6	13	4¹	8	7³	11		10³	14		12	3				2	9										16
1	2	12	6¹		4³	8	7	11²		10	13	14		3				5	9										17
1	5	3			6¹	8	7	9²		11³	13	12		2	14			4	10										18
1	2	8	3			7	6	12		11³	13	14		4	9²			5¹	10										19
1	2	5				8	7²	11		10	12	13	14	6	9³						3	4¹							20
1	2³	3	4			7	9	10		11²	14			5	13				12		6¹	8							21
1		5	6⁴	2		8		7		11	4			9				10	3										22
1	14	3		2		7⁴	6	9¹		11²	12	8²		4	10			13	5										23
1	5	3		14			6²			12	13	8²		4	10¹			11			9	2	7						24
1		5		2	12	8				13		11¹		6	9				10²		3	4	7						25
1		4		2	7¹	8	12			13	14	9³		5	10				11²		3		6						26
1	2	3			13	8	6³	12		11	9¹			4	10				14		5		7²						27
1	2	4	3			7³	8	6	9⁴		10¹	13		5	.11				14					12					28
1	2	3			13	8	6	9¹		12	14	7³		4	10				11²		5								29
1	2	3	4		8	7	6¹	13		10	12	14		5³	11								9²						30
1	2	3	4		8	7	13	9		11³	6¹				10²	5								12	14				31
1	2	3	4			7	8³	6²		12	14	9	13		11¹	5			10										32
1	5	3	4			7	6¹			12	13	8	11³			2			9					10²	14				33
	2	5		4		7	6¹	11³		10²			13			3			9					14		1	8	12	34
	4	3	2		8		9¹			10	6	7³	11²						5					14	13	1		12	35
	3	4	2		7			11¹	9³	8²	12								5					10	13		14	6	36

PETERHEAD   Second Division

Year Formed: 1891. *Ground and Address:* Balmoor Stadium, Balmoor Terrace, Peterhead AB42 1EU.
Telephone: 01779 478256. *Fax:* 01779 490682. *E-mail:* office@peterheadfc.org.uk *Website:* www.peterheadfc.co.uk
Ground Capacity: 3250, seated 1000.
Chairman: Rodger Morrison. *Vice Chairman:* Les Taylor. *General Manager:* Dave Watson. *Secretary:* Brian McCombie.
Manager: Neale Cooper. *Physio:* Greg Smith.
Club Nickname(s): Blue Toon. *Previous Ground:* Recreation Park.
Record Attendance: 6310 friendly v Celtic, 1948.
Record Victory: 17-0 v Fort William, 1998-99 (in Highland League).
Record Defeat: 0-13 v Aberdeen, Scottish Cup, 1923-24.
Most League Appearances: 135: Martin Johnston, 2000-05.
Most League Goals in Season (Individual): 21: Iain Stewart, 2002-03; 21, Scott Michie, 2004-05.
Most Goals Overall (Individual): 58: Iain Stewart, 2000-05.

PETERHEAD 2009–10 LEAGUE RECORD

Match No.	Date	Venue	Opponents	Result	H/T Score	Lg Pos.	Goalscorers	Attendance
1	Aug 8	H	Clyde	W 2-0	1-0	—	Ross 2 [11, 68]	627
2	15	A	Alloa Ath	L 0-1	0-0	5		446
3	22	H	Stenhousemuir	D 2-2	1-1	5	McVitie [30], Bavidge [48]	519
4	29	A	Stirling A	L 1-2	1-0	7	Cameron [21]	537
5	Sept 12	H	East Fife	D 1-1	1-0	7	Michie [20]	551
6	19	A	Arbroath	W 1-0	1-0	6	Ross [45]	476
7	26	H	Dumbarton	L 1-2	0-0	8	Bruce [52]	571
8	Oct 10	A	Cowdenbeath	L 0-5	0-2	8		271
9	13	H	Brechin C	W 1-0	0-0	—	Stewart [80]	429
10	17	A	Clyde	W 3-1	1-0	5	Ross 2 [6, 62], Stewart [57]	663
11	24	H	Alloa Ath	D 0-0	0-0	5		485
12	31	H	Stirling A	W 3-2	3-1	5	MacDonald [16], Stewart [30], Clark [39]	546
13	Nov 7	A	East Fife	W 2-1	0-1	5	Mann [79], Stewart (pen) [86]	574
14	14	H	Arbroath	L 1-2	0-1	5	Bavidge [60]	455
15	Dec 8	A	Dumbarton	L 0-1	0-1	—		397
16	12	H	Cowdenbeath	L 0-2	0-1	5		494
17	15	A	Brechin C	L 0-3	0-1	—		417
18	Jan 23	A	Arbroath	W 4-1	3-1	6	Ross [11], Wilson (pen) [23], Bavidge [32], Clark [56]	465
19	Feb 6	A	Cowdenbeath	W 3-1	1-0	6	Bavidge 2 [22, 64], Wilson [89]	298
20	13	H	Brechin C	L 0-3	0-1	6		553
21	27	A	Alloa Ath	L 1-2	1-1	—	Clark [34]	448
22	Mar 2	H	Dumbarton	W 2-1	1-1	—	Sharp 2 [13, 79]	327
23	6	A	Stirling A	D 1-1	0-0	5	Clark [86]	497
24	9	A	Stenhousemuir	L 0-2	0-0	—		207
25	13	A	East Fife	L 0-3	0-2	7		453
26	16	A	Stirling A	L 0-2	0-0	—		297
27	20	H	Arbroath	W 3-0	1-0	7	Bruce [13], Bavidge 2 [79, 80]	483
28	23	H	East Fife	W 3-1	0-0	—	Wilson [68], Bavidge [69], Ross [81]	374
29	27	A	Dumbarton	W 3-1	0-0	7	Wilson [55], Bavidge [58], Mann [80]	663
30	30	H	Clyde	D 0-0	0-0	—		303
31	Apr 3	A	Brechin C	W 2-1	0-1	5	Wilson (pen) [52], Bavidge [74]	463
32	6	H	Stenhousemuir	L 0-1	0-1	—		364
33	10	H	Cowdenbeath	W 1-0	0-0	5	Bavidge [70]	435
34	17	A	Clyde	L 1-3	0-2	6	Gethans [65]	515
35	24	H	Alloa Ath	W 2-0	1-0	5	Emslie [22], Gethans [67]	561
36	May 1	A	Stenhousemuir	D 1-1	0-1	5	Emslie [72]	612

Final League Position: 5

Honours
Third Division Runners up: 2004-05.
Scottish Cup: Quarter-finals 2001.
Highland League Champions: winners 5 times.
Scottish Qualifying Cup (North): winners 6 times.
North of Scotland Cup: winners 5 times.
Aberdeenshire Cup: winners 20 times.

Club colours: Shirt: Royal blue with navy sleeves; Shorts: Royal blue; Stockings: Royal blue.

Goalscorers: *League (45):* Bavidge 11, Ross 7, Wilson 5 (2 pens), Clark 4, Stewart 4 (1 pen), Bruce 2, Emslie 2, Gethans 2, Mann 2, Sharp 2, Cameron 1, MacDonald 1, McVitie 1, Michie 1.
Scottish Cup (1): Stewart 1.
CIS Cup (0).
Challenge Cup (1): Bavidge 1.

Bateman J 17+1	Donald D 27	Smith S 35	Mann B 27	MacDonald C 21+1	Strachan R 30+4	Sharp G 24+5	Cameron D 10+4	Sutherland Z 2	Ross D 33+1	Bavidge M 31	Michie S 2+2	Bruce P 8+19	Young P —+2	McVitie N 27+2	Smith J 1+9	Jarvie P 19+1	Clark N 18+5	Stewart J 9+1	Crewford J 14	Wilson B 15+1	Emslie P 12+3	Bowden C —+2	Gethans C 4+9	Moore D 10	Match No.
1	2	3	4	5	6^3	7	8		9^1	10	11^1	12	13	14											1
1	2	3	4	5	6	7	8		9^2	10^1	11	12	13												2
1	2	3	4	5	6^1	7^4	8^2		10	11		13		9		12									3
	2	3	4^8	5	6		8		10	11		12		7^1	9	1									4
	2	3	6^1	9	4				10	11		8	13	7^2		1	12								5
1	2	3	4	5	6	9	7		10^1	11^2		8	13	12											6
1	2	3	4	5	8^1	7	9		11^3	10^2	3	6		14		12									7
1	2	5	3	4	8^1	6	11^2		9	10^3		7	14	13		12									8
1	3	5	2	4	6				10	9		7	8	1											9
1	2	3	4^2	5	13	7	12		8	11^1		6	14	10		9^1									10
1	2	3	4	5		7			9	11		12		6		8	0^1								11
1	2	4		5	13	7	3		9^2	11^1		12		6		8	0								12
1	2		3	4	7		6^1	12	9	10		5		11	8										13
1^8	2	3	4	5	6	7^2	12		9^1	11	13			15		8	10								14
	2	5	3	4^1	7	6			8	9^2	13	12	1	11	10										15
	2	5	4		6	7	3		9^2	11	13	12	1	8	10^1										16
	2	5	3	4	9	6^3	12		8^1	13	7	14	1	11	10^2										17
	2	5	3		9				11^1	10	12	6		1	8		4	7							18
	2	5	3		9^1	13			8	11^3	7			1	10^2		4	6	12	14					19
	2	5		3	9				10^2	11	13	7		1	8^6		4	6	12						20
	2^2	5	3	13	9	14			11	10	7	7^1		1	8^5		4	6	12^8						21
		5	3	4	7^2	9^1			11^3	10	12	14		1	8	2^8	6		13						22
		3	4	5	2	11	9^3	12	14	6^2		1	10	7^8	8	13									23
		5		4	2	9	8^1	10^2	12			1	11	3	6	7	13								24
		5		4	2	12	10^3	11	13	9		1	8	3	6^1	7^2	14								25
	2	5	3	4^8	8	9^2	10	12	7			1	11^{10}	6	14	13									26
	2^2	5	3	13		10	11	7	1		4	6^1	8	12	9										27
	2^1	5	3	12	11^3	10	6^2	7	1	4	13	8	14	9											28
15	5	3	2	11	10	12	8	1^0	4	6^1	7	9													29
1	5	3	2	11	10	6^1	7	4	8	12	9														30
1	3	4^8	2	11^1	12	10	8	5	6	7	9														31
1	5	3	6	11	10	9^1	7	4	2	12	8														32
1	5	3	4	12	6	11	7^1	2	8	10	9														33
1	2	3	4	12	6	10	13	5	7^1	11	8^2	9													34
	2	4	3	6^1	9	11	12	7	1	8	10	5													35
	2	3	4	6	9	11	7	1	8	10	5														36

QUEEN OF THE SOUTH First Division

Year Formed: 1919. *Ground & Address:* Palmerston Park, Dumfries DG2 9BA. *Telephone:* 01387 254853.
Fax: 01387 240470. *E-mail:* admin@qosfc.com *Website:* www.qosfc.com
Ground Capacity: 6412 *Size of Pitch:* 112yd × 73yd.
Chairman: David Rae. *Vice-Chairman:* Craig Paterson. *Club Secretary:* Eric Moffat.
Manager: Kenny Brannigan.
Club Nickname(s): The Doonhamers. *Previous Grounds:* None.
Record Attendance: 26,552 v Hearts, Scottish Cup 3rd rd, 23 Feb 1952.
Record Transfer Fee received: £250,000 for Andy Thomson to Southend U (1994).
Record Transfer Fee paid: £30,000 for Jim Butter from Alloa Athletic (1995).
Record Victory: 11-1 v Stranraer, Scottish Cup 1st rd, 16 Jan 1932.
Record Defeat: 2-10 v Dundee, Division I, 1 Dec 1962.
Most Capped Player: Billy Houliston, 3, Scotland.
Most League Appearances: 731: Allan Ball, 1963-82.
Most League Goals in Season (Individual): 37: Jimmy Gray, Division II, 1927-28.
Most Goals in Season: 41: Jimmy Rutherford, 1931-32.
Most Goals Overall (Individual): 250: Jim Patterson, 1949-63.

QUEEN OF THE SOUTH 2009–10 LEAGUE RECORD

Match No.	Date	Venue	Opponents	Result	H/T Score	Lg Pos.	Goalscorers	Attendance
1	Aug 8	H	Raith R	D 1-1	0-1	—	Holmes [90]	2565
2	15	A	Airdrie U	D 1-1	0-0	6	Kean [70]	1079
3	22	H	Partick Th	W 1-0	0-0	5	Weatherston [82]	2915
4	29	H	Ayr U	W 2-0	1-0	2	McLaren [45], Quinn [53]	3034
5	Sept 12	A	Ross Co	L 2-3	1-0	5	Holmes [5], Kean (pen) [52]	1992
6	19	H	Dundee	W 2-0	1-0	3	Tosh (pen) [6], Holmes [61]	2875
7	26	A	Dunfermline Ath	W 4-1	4-1	1	Wyness [33], Burns 2 [39, 42], Holmes (pen) [45]	2624
8	Oct 3	H	Morton	L 2-3	0-2	2	Wilson [86], Kean [90]	2630
9	10	A	Inverness CT	W 3-1	1-1	3	Holmes 3 [1, 83, 90]	3011
10	17	A	Raith R	L 0-1	0-0	5		2147
11	24	H	Airdrie U	W 3-0	2-0	3	Lilley [27], Kean [31], Wyness [83]	2094
12	31	H	Ross Co	W 2-0	2-0	1	Burns [26], Kean [43]	2245
13	Nov 7	A	Ayr U	W 1-0	1-0	1	Holmes [20]	2453
14	14	A	Dundee	D 0-0	0-0	1		4901
15	Dec 1	H	Dunfermline Ath	L 1-2	1-2	—	Weatherston [16]	1651
16	5	H	Inverness CT	D 1-1	0-1	2	Harris [75]	2196
17	12	A	Morton	W 2-1	1-1	2	Burns [31], Holmes [64]	1814
18	26	A	Partick Th	D 2-2	0-1	—	Quinn [57], Harris [80]	2500
19	Jan 23	H	Dundee	D 1-1	1-0	3	Harris [6]	3415
20	Feb 13	H	Morton	L 1-2	0-2	5	Weatherston [72]	2611
21	16	H	Ayr U	W 3-0	1-0	—	Kean (pen) [19], McKenna [57], Weatherston [70]	1721
22	Mar 6	H	Partick Th	W 1-0	0-0	3	Kean [54]	2674
23	9	A	Inverness CT	L 1-3	0-1	—	Holmes (pen) [61]	3003
24	13	A	Dunfermline Ath	L 1-3	0-2	—	Weatherston [69]	2163
25	20	A	Ayr U	L 0-3	0-1	5		2139
26	23	A	Dundee	D 1-1	0-1	—	Harris [58]	4508
27	27	H	Dunfermline Ath	W 2-0	1-0	5	McLaren [45], Weatherston [71]	2298
28	Apr 3	A	Morton	D 3-3	1-2	5	Quinn 2 [10, 52], Weatherston [85]	1926
29	6	A	Ross Co	D 1-1	0-0	—	Burns [64]	2004
30	10	H	Inverness CT	L 1-3	1-1	—	McLaren [10]	2093
31	12	A	Airdrie U	W 1-0	0-0	—	McLaren [88]	825
32	17	H	Raith R	W 3-0	2-0	4	Holmes [22], Burns [25], McLaren [80]	1827
33	20	H	Ross Co	W 1-0	0-0	—	McLaren [54]	1183
34	24	H	Airdrie U	D 2-2	1-1	3	Holmes [33], Weatherston [90]	2541
35	28	A	Raith R	D 0-0	0-0	—		1030
36	May 1	A	Partick Th	L 0-1	0-0	4		2912

Final League Position: 4

Honours
League Champions: Division II 1950-51. Second Division 2001-02. *Runners-up:* Division II 1932-33, 1961-62, 1974-75. Second Division 1980-81, 1985-86.
Scottish Cup Runners-up: 2007-08.
League Cup: semi-finals 1950-51, 1960-61.
B&Q Cup: semi-finals 1991-92. *League Challenge Cup Winners:* 2002-03; *Runners-up:* 1997-98.

European: *UEFA Cup:* 2 matches (2008-09).

Club colours: Shirt: Royal blue with white flashes. Shorts: White. Stockings: Royal blue.

Goalscorers: *League (53):* Holmes 12 (2 pens), Weatherston 8, Kean 7 (2 pens), Burns 6, McLaren 6, Harris 4, Quinn 4, Wyness 2, Lilley 1, McKenna 1, Tosh 1 (pen), Wilson 1.
Scottish Cup (0).
CIS Cup (7): Weatherston 2, Wilson 2, Burns 1, Harris 1, Quinn 1.
Challenge Cup (3): Kean 1, Tosh 1, Wilson 1.

Hutton D 27+1	Reid C 32	Harris R 32	Lilley D 30	McAusland M 21+4	Burns P 35	Wilson B 5+7	Tosh S 3+2	Quinn R 29+2	Holmes D 35+1	McLaren W 28+6	Kean S 14+15	McGuilken J 1+5	Weatherston D 12+18	Scally N 9+1	McLaughlan G 4+2	Roy L 4	McKenna S 27+1	Wyness D 31+4	McMillan J 16	Andrews M 5+1	McParland A —+4	Knight L 3+3	Fox S 5+1	Hamil J 5+6	Adams J 7	O'Connor S 4+7	Match No.
1	2	3¹	4	5²	6	7	8	9	10	11²	12	13	14														1
1	2¹	3	4	5	11	7²		9	10³	13	14		8	6	12												2
	2	3	4	5	11	7¹	8	10	12	9²	13					1	6										3
	2	3	4	5	11	13	12	7	10³	8²	14		9			1	6¹										4
1	2	3	4	5	11		13	7²	10	8	9¹		12				6										5
	2	3	4	5	11	9¹	7²	13	10	12	8					1	6										6
15	2	3	4	5	11	12		7	10	8						1	6	9¹									7
1	2	3	4	5	11	7		10	8¹	13	12						6	9²									8
1	2	3	5	6²	7			8	9	12	14	11	13³				4	10¹									9
1	2	3	5	6	7²	12		8	9	11¹	10		13				4										10
1	2	3	4		7	13		8	10¹	9²	11				5		6	12									11
1	2	3	4		7	13		8	10¹	9²	11				5		6	12									12
1	2¹	5	4	12	6			7	10	9¹	14	8					13										13
1		3	5	2	7			8	9	11²	10¹	13	12		6		4										14
1		3	4	5	7	14		8	10	9¹	13		11²				6³	12	2								15
1		3	4	5	7	12		8	10	9	13		11²				5¹	2									16
1	5	3			7			8	9	11¹	12		10²	13			4			2	6						17
1			4	9		14	7	5³	11	8²	12		10¹	6				2	3	13							18
1		4	5	3²	13	6		8	10	9			12	7			2				1¹						19
1	2	3	5		6			8	10	9¹	12		13				7			4	11²						20
	5	3	4¹		6			8	11³	10			9²	7		2	2						13	14	1		21
1	5	3	4²		6			10	12	11			9¹	7			8			2	13						22
1	7	5			6			12	10	13	11²		9³	3			8		2¹	4			14				23
1	7	5	4¹		6			8	10	9¹	11²		14	3			2					12	13				24
1	2			4	6			8²	10³	13	12		11				5	9¹				3	7	14			25
1	2	5	4	3	6			7³	11²	10¹			14				8						12	9	13		26
1	3	4	2		5			6	11¹	9³	13		12				7						14	8	10³		27
1	4	5	3		6			10	11²	9⁵			12				2	8				15		7	13		28
	3	4		2	9			8³	11²	10	12		14				7	5					1	6	13		29
	4¹	5	3		9			8	11³	6	10²		13	7			2						1	12	14		30
1		3	4		6³			8	12	9	13		11²				7						2	14	5	10¹	31
1	2	5²	3	4	6			10¹	11³	5	14		12				7						13	8			32
1	2	5	3	4	6¹			10	11²	9	14						7						12	8³	13		33
	2		3	4	9			11²	6¹	10³	14		7				8	12				1	5		13		34
	2		5	3				9	8	11¹	12						4	6				1	7		10		35
1	2	10	3	13				8¹	11	9	12						4	5²						6	7		36

QUEEN'S PARK   Third Division

Year Formed: 1867. *Ground & Address:* Hampden Park, Mount Florida, Glasgow G42 9BA. *Telephone:* 0141 632 1275.
Fax. 0141 636 1612. *E-mail:* secretary@queensparkfc.co.uk *Website:* queensparkfc.co.uk
Ground Capacity: all seated: 52,000. *Size of Pitch:* 115yd × 75yd.
President: Alan Hutchison. *Secretary:* Alistair MacKay. *Treasurer:* David Gordon.
Coach: Gardner Spiers. *Physios:* R. C. Findlay and A. Myles.
Club Nickname(s): The Spiders. *Previous Grounds:* 1st Hampden (Recreation Ground); (Titwood Park was used as an interim measure between 1st & 2nd Hampdens); 2nd Hampden (Cathkin); 3rd Hampden.
Record Attendance: 95,772 v Rangers, Scottish Cup, 18 Jan 1930.
Record for Ground: 149,547 Scotland v England, 1937.
Record Transfer Fee received: Not applicable due to amateur status.
Record Transfer Fee paid: Not applicable due to amateur status.
Record Victory: 16-0 v St. Peters, Scottish Cup 1st rd, 29 Aug 1885.
Record Defeat: 0-9 v Motherwell, Division I, 26 Apr 1930.
Most Capped Player: Walter Arnott, 14, Scotland.
Most League Appearances: 532: Ross Caven, 1982-2002.
Most League Goals in Season (Individual): 30: William Martin, Division I, 1937-38.
Most Goals Overall (Individual): 163: James B. McAlpine, 1919-33.

QUEEN'S PARK 2009–10 LEAGUE RECORD

Match No.	Date	Venue	Opponents	Result	H/T Score	Lg Pos.	Goalscorers	Attendance
1	Aug 8	H	Forfar Ath	D	2-2	1-1	—	Watt [28], Capuano [82]	595
2	15	A	Elgin C	W	1-0	1-0	3	Douglas [19]	570
3	29	A	Berwick R	L	0-1	0-0	5		519
4	Sept 12	A	East Stirling	L	0-1	0-0	7		393
5	19	H	Annan Ath	D	0-0	0-0	7		581
6	26	A	Livingston	L	1-2	1-1	9	Douglas [36]	961
7	29	H	Albion R	L	0-1	0-0	—		376
8	Oct 10	H	Stranraer	L	1-2	1-0	9	Douglas [36]	598
9	13	A	Montrose	W	2-1	2-0	—	Quinn P [11], O'Hara [25]	370
10	17	A	Albion R	W	1-0	0-0	7	Hamilton C [87]	613
11	31	H	Elgin C	L	0-3	0-1	9		538
12	Nov 7	H	East Stirling	W	1-0	0-0	8	Carrol [75]	529
13	14	A	Berwick R	D	1-1	1-1	8	Guy (og) [7]	487
14	21	H	Livingston	L	1-2	0-0	8	Quinn P [62]	620
15	Dec 5	A	Annan Ath	L	1-3	0-1	7	Holmes [57]	433
16	12	A	Stranraer	D	1-1	1-0	7	McBride [22]	255
17	19	H	Montrose	W	3-2	1-0	—	McBride 2 [10, 66], Murray [84]	397
18	Jan 16	H	Berwick R	W	2-0	0-0	—	Douglas [63], Murray [69]	517
19	23	A	Annan Ath	W	3-2	0-1	5	McBride [48], Carrol [68], Douglas (pen) [75]	484
20	Feb 2	A	Livingston	L	0-2	0-2	—		680
21	6	H	Stranraer	L	2-5	1-3	5	McBride [45], Daly [81]	553
22	13	A	Montrose	W	2-1	0-1	5	Murray [51], Quinn T [69]	325
23	20	A	Forfar Ath	L	1-3	0-1	5	Douglas [64]	603
24	Mar 2	A	East Stirling	W	3-0	3-0	—	Murray [14], Daly 2 [24, 28]	297
25	6	H	Berwick R	L	2-3	1-1	5	Henry J [11], Watt [80]	538
26	9	A	Forfar Ath	W	1-0	0-0	—	Watson (og) [76]	413
27	13	H	East Stirling	W	2-0	0-0	5	Stewart [53], Hamilton C [90]	457
28	20	A	Annan Ath	W	2-0	1-0	5	Daly [45], Henry J [90]	581
29	27	H	Livingston	L	0-1	0-0	5		714
30	30	A	Elgin C	W	1-0	1-0	—	Stewart [11]	203
31	Apr 3	H	Montrose	W	3-0	2-0	4	Douglas (pen) [23], McBride [27], Murray [50]	487
32	10	A	Stranraer	D	0-0	0-0	4		365
33	17	A	Albion R	L	0-1	0-0	4		410
34	20	H	Albion R	W	1-0	0-0	—	Douglas [86]	522
35	24	H	Elgin C	L	0-1	0-0	4		644
36	May 1	A	Forfar Ath	D	1-1	0-0	4	Daly [73]	549

Final League Position: 4

Honours
League Champions: Division II 1922-23. B Division 1955-56. Second Division 1980-81. Third Division 1999-2000.
Scottish Cup Winners: 1874, 1875, 1876, 1880, 1881, 1882, 1884, 1886, 1890, 1893; *Runners-up:* 1892, 1900.
FA Cup runners-up: 1884, 1885.

Club colours: Shirt: Black and white. Shorts: White. Stockings: White with black tops.

Goalscorers: *League (42):* Douglas 8 (2 pens), McBride 6, Daly 5, Murray 5. Carrol 2, Hamilton C 2, Henry J 2, Quinn P 2, Stewart 2, Watt 2, Capuano 1, Holmes 1, O'Hara 1, Quinn T 1, own goals 2.
Scottish Cup (1): Quinn T 1.
CIS Cup (1): Douglas 1.
Challenge Cup (0).
Play-Offs (2): Daly 1, own goal 1.

Black S 11	Walker R 17	Sinclair R 9	Brough J 29+1	Douglas B 35	Hamilton C 16+13	Holmes R 14+8	Capuano G 32+1	McBride M 33+1	Daly M 22+5	Watt I 6+13	Ure M 7+1	Green D —+1	Carrol F 9+6	Murray D 15+8	Dunlop R 7+4	Tiernan F —+1	Harkins P 1	Lauchlan G 4	O'Hara M 5+3	Quinn P 9	McGinn P 4+2	Quinn T 24+3	Reilly S 3	Hamilton P 10+1	Little R 24	Burns P 1	McGeown M 15	Stewart P 15	Martin R —+1	Gallagher P 13+1	Henry J 6+6	Match No.
1	2	3¹	4⁸	5	6	7²	8	9	10	11	12	13																				1
1	2	3		5	6¹	7	8	9	10²	11	4		12	13																		2
1		3	2	5	6	7¹	8³	9		11	4		13	12	10²	14																3
1	3		2	5	13		8	9	7	11³	4		14	10²	12		6¹															4
1	3		2	5	6		8	9		11¹	4		12	10	7																	5
1	3		2	5	6¹	13	8	9		11²	4		12	10	7																	6
1	3		2	5	6²	13	8	9		12	4		11	10	7¹																	7
1	3⁸		4	5	6¹		7	9			2²			13				8	10³	1*	12	14										8
1			4	5	6¹		7	11	12²					13				8	9³	10	2	14	3									9
1			5	3	13		6	10	14				8³	2				7¹	11²	3	12	4										10
1			3	5	6	12	13	8	11¹					2				9²	10	7⁸	4											11
	2		4	5	6	9	7	12	13				10²		8¹				14			11³		1	3							12
	2		5	3		11	6	7					8									9		10	1	4						13
	2		4	5	12	9	6	7²					11¹						13	10		8		1	3							14
	2		5	3	12	11	6	7	8				12						10¹	9		9		1	4							15
	2		5	3	13	11	6	7²	8¹				12									9		10	1	4						16
		3	4		12	9²	7	6					10	13					11¹			8		1	2	5						17
	2	4		3	8	11¹	6	7	13				9²	12								10		1	5							18
	2	3		5	9	11¹	7	6	13				10²	12								8		1	4							19
	2	8		5	7¹	9²	4	6	10³	12				13					14			11		1	3							20
	2³	3¹	12	5	10	9²	7	6	14				11	13								8		1	4							21
	2		4	5	6¹			9	10	13			11²									8			3		1	7	12			22
	2²		3	5	9³	14		10					11				6¹					8			4*		1	7		12	13	23
			4	5	13	12	7		10				9²							2		11	15		16	6	3	8¹			24
			5	12			7	10	13				11							2*		8		3	1	6²	4	9¹			25
	3		5			8	6	9					11									10		2	1	7¹	4	12				26
			4	5	12		7	6	10	13			9									8		2	1	11²	3	9¹				27
			5	3			6	7	11				10¹									9		2	1	8	4	12				28
			4	5	14		7³	6	10	13			11²									9		2	1	8¹	3	12				29
			5			13	9	8	11				10²									2	7	3	1	6¹	4	12				30
	5²	7		13	6	3	9³	14					11¹						12			2		1	10		4	8				31
	4	5		12	8	7	10	13					11¹									6		2	1	9²	3					32
	3	5	12	9¹	4²	6	11	13														10		2	1	8	7					33
	3	5	14		7¹	11	10²	13					12									8		2	1	6	4	9³				34
	3	5	14		7¹	11³	10²	13					12									8		2	1	6	4	9				35
	4	5		6	9²	10	12						11¹									8		2	1	7	3	13				36

RAITH ROVERS

First Division

Year Formed: 1883. *Ground & Address:* Stark's Park, Pratt St, Kirkcaldy KY1 1SA. *Telephone:* 01592 263514. *Fax:* 01592 642833. *E-mail:* office@raithroversfc.com *Website:* www.raithroversfc.com
Ground Capacity: all seated: 10,104. *Size of Pitch:* 113yd × 70yd.
Chairman: David Somerville. *General Manager & Secretary:* Bob Mullen.
Manager: John McGlynn. *Assistant Manager:* Paul Smith.
Club Nickname: Rovers. *Previous Grounds:* Robbie's Park.
Record Attendance: 31,306 v Hearts, Scottish Cup 2nd rd, 7 Feb 1953.
Record Transfer Fee received: £900,000 for Steve McAnespie to Bolton Wanderers (Sept 1995).
Record Transfer Fee paid: £225,000 for Paul Harvey from Airdrieonians (1996).
Record Victory: 10-1 v Coldstream, Scottish Cup 2nd rd, 13 Feb 1954.
Record Defeat: 2-11 v Morton, Division II, 18 Mar 1936.
Most Capped Player: David Morris, 6, Scotland.
Most League Appearances: 430: Willie McNaught, 1946-51.
Most League Goals in Season (Individual): 38: Norman Haywood, Division II, 1937-38.
Most Goals Overall (Individual): 154: Gordon Dalziel (League), 1987-94.

RAITH ROVERS 2009–10 LEAGUE RECORD

Match No.	Date	Venue	Opponents	Result	H/T Score	Lg Pos.	Goalscorers	Attendance
1	Aug 8	A	Queen of the S	D 1-1	1-0	—	Walker [45]	2565
2	15	H	Dundee	D 2-2	2-1	5	Williamson [30], Ellis [41]	4744
3	22	A	Ross Co	W 1-0	1-0	3	Hill [32]	2088
4	29	A	Dunfermline Ath	W 2-0	1-0	1	Murray [41], Casalinuovo [60]	6289
5	Sept 12	H	Partick Th	D 1-1	0-0	2	Casalinuovo [69]	2370
6	19	H	Morton	W 3-0	1-0	2	Tade 2 [27, 50], Ferry [85]	2040
7	26	A	Ayr U	L 0-1	0-1	4		1783
8	Oct 10	A	Airdrie U	W 2-1	1-0	4	Davidson [26], Williamson [47]	1186
9	13	H	Inverness CT	L 0-1	0-0	—		2014
10	17	H	Queen of the S	W 1-0	0-0	4	Russell [75]	2147
11	24	A	Dundee	L 1-2	1-2	5	Smith D [20]	5156
12	31	A	Partick Th	W 2-1	1-1	3	Wallas [43], Sloan [62]	3084
13	Nov 7	H	Dunfermline Ath	L 1-2	1-0	5	Campbell [23]	6200
14	14	A	Morton	L 0-5	0-1	7		1716
15	21	H	Ayr U	D 0-0	0-0	6		1460
16	Dec 12	A	Inverness CT	L 0-1	0-1	7		2768
17	15	H	Airdrie U	D 1-1	1-0	—	Corredera [4]	1247
18	Jan 16	H	Partick Th	W 1-0	0-0	—	Smith K [73]	1951
19	23	H	Morton	L 1-2	0-1	7	Smith K (pen) [79]	1702
20	Feb 13	H	Inverness CT	L 0-4	0-0	7		1568
21	Mar 6	A	Ross Co	L 0-1	0-0	7		2033
22	9	H	Ross Co	W 2-1	0-1	—	Walker [53], Tade [83]	1186
23	16	A	Dunfermline Ath	L 1-2	0-1	—	Walker [63]	4549
24	20	H	Dunfermline Ath	L 1-2	0-0	7	Tade [66]	4098
25	23	A	Morton	D 1-1	0-0	—	Murray [72]	1415
26	27	H	Ayr U	D 1-1	0-1	7	Simmons [90]	1872
27	Apr 3	A	Inverness CT	L 3-4	1-2	8	Williamson [12], Tade [66], Mole [74]	3562
28	7	A	Ayr U	W 2-0	2-0	—	Murray [4], Williamson [12]	1433
29	14	A	Airdrie U	L 0-3	0-1	—		815
30	17	A	Queen of the S	L 0-3	0-2	7		1327
31	19	A	Partick Th	D 0-0	0-0	—		1151
32	21	H	Dundee	W 1-0	0-0	—	Hill [64]	1544
33	24	A	Dundee	L 0-2	0-0	7		3187
34	26	H	Airdrie U	L 0-1	0-0	—		1539
35	28	H	Queen of the S	D 0-0	0-0	—		1030
36	May 1	H	Ross Co	W 4-1	3-0	7	Armstrong D [4], Russell 3 [30, 36, 71]	1935

Final League Position: 7

Honours
League Champions: First Division: 1992-93, 1994-95. Second Division: 2008-09. Division II 1907-08, 1909-10 (shared), 1937-38, 1948-49; *Runners-up:* Division II 1908-09, 1926-27. 1966-67. Second Division 1975-76, 1977-78, 1986-87.
Scottish Cup Runners-up: 1913. *League Cup Winners:* 1994-95. *Runners-up:* 1948-49.

European: *UEFA Cup:* 6 matches (1995-96).

Club colours: Shirt: Navy with white. Shorts: Navy. Stockings: Navy with white tops.

Goalscorers: *League (36):* Tade 5, Russell 4, Williamson 4, Murray 3, Walker 3, Casalinuovo 2, Hill 2, Smith K 2 (1 pen), Armstrong D 1, Campbell 1, Corredera 1, Davidson 1, Ellis 1, Ferry 1, Mole 1, Simmons 1, Sloan 1, Smith D 1, Wallas 1.
Scottish Cup (14): Smith K 3, Tade 3, Simmons 2, Smith D 2, Ellis 1, Russell 1 (pen), Williamson 1, own goal 1.
CIS Cup (4): Williamson 2 (1 pen), Tade 1, Walker 1.
Challenge Cup (1): Walker 1.

McGurn D 35	Wilson C 21	Ellis L 29	Campbell M 15+1	Murray G 34	Davidson D 18+2	Walker A 34+1	Simmons S 17+2	Tade G 31+1	Weir G 13+10	Williamson J 25+2	Hill D 26+3	Smith D 17+10	Bryce L —+8	Ferry M 11+17	Sloan R 10+17	Casalinuovo D 3	Wedderburn C —+4	Russell J 10+6	Wallas B 3+1	Gatheussi T 10+4	Cameron G 2	Smith K 4+1	Corredera J 1	Amaya J 1+4	Mackie J —+3	Shields D 3+6	Armstrong D 7+1	Mole J 6+2	Brown K 1	O'Connor G 1	Match No.
1	2	3	4¹	5	6	7	8	9³	10¹	11²	12	13	14																		1
1	2	3		5	6	7	8¹	9	10³	11²	4	12	14	13																	2
1	2	3	6	5		7		9	10¹	11³	4	8²	12	14	13																3
1	2	3	6	5		7		9²		11	4	8¹	13	14	12	10³															4
1	2	3	6¹	5	12	7		9³		11	4¹	8⁵		14	13	10															5
1	2	3³		5	6	7		9	13	8	4		12	11¹	10²	14															6
1	2	3	14	5	6	7		9	10²	8³	4	12		11¹		13															7
1	2	3	4	5	6	8		10⁴	13	7¹		11³	12	14		9²															8
1	2¹	5	3	4	7	8			11³	6	12	9²	14		13	10															9
1		3¹	4	2	6²	8		10	14	7³	5	11		12	13	9															10
1	2		4	3		7		8	10²	5	11¹	13	12	6		9															11
1	2	3	4	6		8		10		5	13	12	11	9⁴	7¹																12
1	2	3	4	6		8²	13	10³	14	5	12		11	9	7¹																13
1	2	3	4⁴			8	6²	10		5	11	13	7³		12	9¹	14														14
1	2	3				8	9	7²		5	11³	14	13	12		10¹	4	6													15
1	2	3	4			7	8	12	14	5⁴	11²					10³	13	6¹	9												16
1	7	3	4	5		14	8	9	13		11²			6³			2	12	10¹												17
1	2	3	4	5		6¹	8	10	14		11	12²		7	13	9¹															18
1	2	3	4	5		6	8	10³	14	12		13	11²		7¹																19
1	2		3	4		7			12	6	5³		8	9²		11		10³		13	14										20
1	2	5		7	8			11³	6	4²	9	13	12					3		14	10¹										21
1	2¹	5		8		6	7	10	11	9²	4³	14						13	3		12										22
1		5	4		8	6	9	10¹	7		14		3	13	11³			2²			12										23
1		4	2			9	7¹	10		8		6		5	13	14	12²	11¹			3³										24
1		4	3	13		6		11		9	5¹	10²		8	7			2³									14	12			25
1		5	3	7²		6	8	11		9¹	4	10³	14	13				2			12										26
1		3	2	5⁴		6	7¹	8	13	9	4		14					12									11¹	10²			27
1		3	4	6	8		7	10³	11¹	5²	13	12						2		14								9			28
1		5		3	9	8	7	6	11		4	13		12														10¹			29
1	5¹		2	3		7	8²	6	10	9¹				4	13			11	12								14				30
1		2	4¹	5			10	11²	7	12	9			3	14			6³									13	8			31
1		2	7²	8			11		6	4	12			5	13			9¹									14	3	10⁵		32
1		2	8	6		12	10	7²	3	14		5		13				9³										4⁴	11¹		33
1		3	7	11²			14	4	9	5	8		13				2				10¹			6³	12					34
1		2	7	6²		10	11³	8³	4		14	9		13				3								12	5				35
	5		2	7		8	10		6²	4¹	13		12	9			14									3	11³			1	36

RANGERS   Premier League

Year Formed: 1873. *Ground & Address:* Ibrox Stadium, 150 Edmiston Drive, Glasgow G51 2XD.
Telephone: 0871 702 1972. *Fax:* 0870 600 1978. *Website:* www.rangers.co.uk
Ground Capacity: all seated: 51,082. *Size of Pitch:* 105m × 68m.
Chairman: Alastair Johnston. *Chief Executive:* Martin Bain.
Manager: Walter Smith. *Assistant Manager:* Ally McCoist. *Physio:* Pip Yeates.
Club Nickname(s): The Gers. *Previous Grounds:* Flesher's Haugh, Burnbank, Kinning Park, Old Ibrox.
Record Attendance: 118,567 v Celtic, Division I, 2 Jan 1939.
Record Transfer Fee received: £9,000,000 for Alan Hutton to Tottenham H (January 2008).
Record Transfer Fee paid: £12,000,000 for Tore Andre Flo from Chelsea (November 2000).
Record Victory: 14-2 v Blairgowrie, Scottish Cup 1st rd, 20 Jan, 1934. *Record Defeat:* 2-10 v Airdrieonians; 1886.
Most Capped Player: Ally McCoist, 60, Scotland.
Most League Appearances: 496: John Greig, 1962-78.
Most League Goals in Season (Individual): 44: Sam English, Division I, 1931-32.
Most Goals Overall (Individual): 355: Ally McCoist; 1985-98.

Honours
League Champions: (53 times) Division I 1890-91 (shared), 1898-99, 1899-1900, 1900-01, 1901-02, 1910-11, 1911-12, 1912-13, 1917-18, 1919-20, 1920-21, 1922-23, 1923-24, 1924-25, 1926-27, 1927-28, 1928-29, 1929-30, 1930-31, 1932-33, 1933-34, 1934-35, 1936-37, 1938-39, 1946-47, 1948-49, 1949-50, 1952-53, 1955-56, 1956-57, 1958-59, 1960-61, 1962-63, 1963-64, 1974-75. Premier Division: 1975-76, 1977-78, 1986-87, 1988-89, 1989-90, 1990-91, 1991-92, 1992-93, 1993-94, 1994-95, 1995-96, 1996-97, 1998-99, 1999-2000, 2002-03, 2004-05, 2008-09, 2009-10; *Runners-up:* 26 times.

RANGERS 2009–10 LEAGUE RECORD

Match No.	Date	Venue	Opponents	Result	H/T Score	Lg Pos.	Goalscorers	Attendance
1	Aug 15	H	Falkirk	W 4-1	2-1	—	McCulloch [14], Miller 2 [34, 72], Naismith [83]	50,239
2	23	A	Hearts	W 2-1	0-1	2	McCulloch [63], Boyd (pen) [90]	16,284
3	29	H	Hamilton A	W 4-1	2-0	1	Whittaker 2 [19, 67], Boyd 2 [27, 65]	47,633
4	Sept 12	H	Motherwell	D 0-0	0-0	1		9355
5	19	A	Kilmarnock	D 0-0	0-0	2		10,310
6	26	H	Aberdeen	D 0-0	0-0	2		47,968
7	Oct 4	H	Celtic	W 2-1	2-1	2	Miller 2 [8, 16]	50,276
8	17	A	St Johnstone	W 2-1	1-1	1	Boyd [40], Papac [83]	7807
9	24	H	Hibernian	D 1-1	1-0	2	Boyd [8]	46,892
10	Nov 7	H	St Mirren	W 2-1	1-0	2	Boyd 2 [1, 57]	45,750
11	21	A	Kilmarnock	W 3-0	3-0	1	Boyd [7], Miller [24], Whittaker [35]	45,358
12	28	A	Aberdeen	L 0-1	0-1	2		16,153
13	Dec 5	A	Falkirk	W 3-1	2-1	2	Boyd 2 [17, 36], Miller (pen) [74]	6903
14	12	H	St Johnstone	W 3-0	2-0	2	Boyd 2 (1 pen) [1, 27 (p)], Novo [51]	44,662
15	15	A	Dundee U	W 3-0	1-0	—	Beasley [26], Miller 2 [58, 75]	10,037
16	19	H	Motherwell	W 6-1	1-0	1	Miller 2 [5, 58], Boyd [53], Lafferty 2 [75, 88], Beasley [84]	44,291
17	27	A	Hibernian	W 4-1	2-1	1	Miller 2 [21, 66], Boyd [37], Novo [53]	16,894
18	30	H	Dundee U	W 7-1	3-0	—	Boyd 5 (1 pen) [20 (p), 25, 29, 75, 80], Whittaker [68], Bougherra [85]	48,721
19	Jan 3	A	Celtic	D 1-1	0-0	—	McCulloch [81]	58,300
20	16	A	Hamilton A	W 1-0	0-0	1	Novo [78]	5343
21	23	A	Hearts	D 1-1	0-0	1	Little [90]	42,031
22	27	A	St Mirren	W 2-0	1-0	—	Davis [2], Novo [86]	5260
23	30	A	Falkirk	W 3-0	1-0	1	Davis [18], Fleck [57], Whittaker [62]	45,907
24	Feb 10	A	Motherwell	D 1-1	0-1	—	Boyd [80]	9352
25	14	H	Hibernian	W 3-0	1-0	1	Whittaker [50], Boyd (pen) [72], Miller [90]	48,161
26	28	H	Celtic	W 1-0	0-0	1	Edu [90]	50,320
27	Mar 6	H	St Mirren	W 3-1	1-1	1	McCulloch 2 [32, 46], Novo [78]	47,474
28	9	A	Kilmarnock	W 2-0	0-0	1	Whittaker [55], Miller [61]	8906
29	27	A	Hearts	W 4-1	2-1	1	Wilson [5], Miller [31], Naismith 2 [49, 77]	16,832
30	30	A	St Johnstone	L 1-4	1-3	—	Papac [16]	6189
31	Apr 3	H	Hamilton A	W 1-0	1-0	1	Edu [11]	48,068
32	7	H	Aberdeen	W 3-1	1-0	—	Davis [24], Lafferty [65], Miller [76]	47,061
33	14	A	Dundee U	D 0-0	0-0	—		11,100
34	18	H	Hearts	W 2-0	0-0	1	Lafferty [54], Miller (pen) [84]	47,590
35	25	A	Hibernian	W 1-0	1-0	1	Lafferty [17]	10,573
36	May 1	A	Dundee U	W 2-1	2-0	1	Boyd [2], Novo [41]	10,003
37	4	A	Celtic	L 1-2	1-2	—	Miller [43]	58,000
38	9	H	Motherwell	D 3-3	2-0	1	Boyd [17], Lafferty 2 [40, 70]	50,321

Final League Position: 1

Scottish Cup Winners: (33 times) 1894, 1897, 1898, 1903, 1928, 1930, 1932, 1934, 1935, 1936, 1948, 1949, 1950, 1953, 1960, 1962, 1963, 1964, 1966, 1973, 1976, 1978, 1979, 1981, 1992, 1993, 1996, 1999, 2000, 2002, 2003, 2008, 2009; *Runners-up:* 17 times.
League Cup Winners: (26 times) 1946-47, 1948-49, 1960-61, 1961-62, 1963-64, 1964-65, 1970-71, 1975-76, 1977-78, 1978-79, 1981-82, 1983-84, 1984-85, 1986-87, 1987-88, 1988-89, 1990-91, 1992-93, 1993-94, 1996-97, 1998-99, 2001-02, 2002-03, 2004-05, 2007-08, 2009-10; *Runners-up:* 7 times.

European: *European Cup:* 153 matches (1956-57, 1957-58, 1959-60 semi-finals, 1961-62, 1963-64, 1964-65, 1975-76, 1976-77, 1978-79, 1987-88, 1989-90, 1990-91, 1991-92, 1992-93 final pool, 1993-94, 1994-95, 1995-96; 1996-97, 1997-98, 1999-2000, 2000-01, 2001-02, 2003-04, 2004-05, 2005-06, 2007-08, 2008-09, 2009-10).
Cup Winners' Cup: 54 matches (1960-61, 1962-63, 1966-67 runners-up, 1969-70, 1971-72 winners, 1973-74, 1977-78, 1979-80, 1981-82, 1983-84).
UEFA Cup: 88 matches (*Fairs Cup:* 1967-68, 1968-69 semi-finals, 1970-71. *UEFA Cup:* 1982-83, 1984-85, 1985-86, 1986-87, 1988-89, 1997-98, 1998-99, 1999-2000, 2000-01, 2001-02, 2002-03, 2004-05, 2006-07, 2007-08 runners-up).

Club colours: Shirt: Royal blue with red and white trim. Shorts: White with red and blue trim. Stockings: Black with red tops.

Goalscorers: *League (82):* Boyd 23 (4 pens), Miller 18 (2 pens), Lafferty 7, Whittaker 7, Novo 6, McCulloch 5, Davis 3, Naismith 3, Beasley 2, Edu 2, Papac 2, Bougherra 1, Fleck 1, Little 1, Wilson 1.
Scottish Cup (9): Boyd 3 (2 pens), Whittaker 3, Miller 2 (1 pen), Novo 1.
CIS Cup (8): Davis 1, Fleck 1, McCulloch 1, Miller 1, Naismith 1, Novo 1, Whittaker 1, own goal 1.
Champions League (4): Bougherra 1, McCulloch 1, Novo 1, own goal 1.

McGregor A 34	Whittaker S 32 + 3	Smith S 7 + 5	McCulloch L 32 + 2	Weir D 38	Bougherra M 16 + 1	Fleck J 8 + 7	Davis S 36	Boyd K 28 + 3	Miller K 29 + 4	Naismith S 20 + 8	Thomson K 20 + 5	Papac S 34	Pedro Mendes 4	Novo N 14 + 21	Wylde G — +2	Rothen J 3 + 1	Little A 2 + 4	Lafferty K 17 + 11	Wilson D 14	Beasley D 6 + 3	Alexander N 4 + 1	Broadfoot K 12	Edu M 8 + 7	Match No.
1	2	3	4	5	6	7	8	9^1	10	11	12													1
1	2	12	4	5	6	7^1	8	13	10^2	9	11^8	3												2
1	2		4	5	6		8	9	10^2	11^1		3		7	12	13								3
1	2		4	5	6^8		8	9	10^2	13		3		7	12			11^1						4
1	2		4	5		7	8	9^2	13	11^1	12	3	6^8	10^1	14									5
1	2	8^2	4	5	6	13		12	9^3	11^1	3			10				7	14					6
1	2	8		5			6	9^2	10	11		3	4	12				7^1	13					7
1	2	6^1	8	5		7		9^1	14	12	4	3		13				11^2	10^1					8
1	2	6	4^1	5	12	7		9	10^2	11	3	13						8^1						9
1	2^1		4	5	8	7		9	13	11	3	10^2						6	12					10
1	2		4	5	14	7		9^2	10^3	11^1	8	3		12				13	6					11
1	2^3		4^2	5	14	8	7	9	12	10	3			13				11^6	6					12
1	2		4	5	6	14	8	9^2	10^3	7	3			11^1				12						13
		12	5	6	13	4		9^3		8^1	3			11				14	7^2	1	2			14
			4	5	6	14	8	9^1	10	13	3			11^3				12	8^2	1	2			15
1			12	5	6		7	9^2	10	14	4^1	3		11^3				13	8	2				16
1	13		4	5	6		7	9	10^2		3		8					1^4			2	12		17
1	13	12	4	5	6		7	9^3	10^8		3^1		8^2		14	1					2			18
1	2		8	5			7	9			3		10^1					1^5	6		4	12		19
1	2			5		12	7			8	3	9					13	1^3	4		6^1	11		20
1	2	11	5		9^2	7				8	3			13			12	1^3	4		6^1			21
1	2		4	5		7			10^2	13	12	3		11				3^1	8		6			22
1	2	13	4	5		9	7			12	8	3^2		11^1			14	13^3	6					23
1	2		4	5	6		8	9	10	11^2		3		12				13				7^1		24
1	2		4	5	6		8	9^2	10		11	3		13				12	7^6					25
1	2	4^1	5		6		7	9	10		8	3		13				11^2				12		26
1	2		4	5			7	9	10^3	14	8^2	3		12					6	11^1		13		27
1	2	11	5				8	9	10^2		6^1	3		13					4	7		12		28
1	2	13	4^1	5			7^2	9	10^3	11	8	3		14					6			12		29
1	2		4	5			7	9^1	10	11	8^2	3		14				3^3	6^3			12		30
1	2		4	5			7	9^1	10^2	11		3		13				2^3	6			8		31
1	2		4	5			7		10	11		3		12				9^1	6			8		32
1	2		4	5	6		7	12	10	11^1	14	3		13				9^2				8^3		33
1	2		4	5	6		7	9^2	10	12	8	3		13				11^1						34
1	2		4	5			7		10^1	11	6	3		12				9				8		35
	13	3^2		5		8		9^1		11	6^1			10			7	14		12	1	2	4	36
16	2	3	4^8	5			7		10	11	6			12				9^1		15			8	37
	2	14		5			7	9	10^1	11	13	3		12				8^3			1	4	6^2	38

ROSS COUNTY   First Division

Year Formed: 1929. *Ground & Address:* Victoria Park Stadium, Jubilee Road, Dingwall IV15 9QW. *Telephone:* 01349 860860. *Fax:* 01349 866277. *E-mail:* donnie@rosscountyfootballclub.co.uk *Website:* www.rosscountyfootballclub.co.uk
Ground Capacity: 6700. *Size of Ground:* 105×68m.
Chairman: David Siegel. *Secretary:* Donnie MacBean.
Manager: Derek Adams. *Director of Football:* George Adams. *Coaches:* Derek Adams and (*Head of Youth*) David Kirkwood. *Physio:* Douglas Sim.
Club Nickname(s): The Staggies.
Record Attendance: 6600, benefit match v Celtic, 31 August 1970.
Record Transfer Fee Received: £200,000 for Neil Tarrant to Aston Villa (April 1999).
Record Transfer Fee Paid: £25,000 for Barry Wilson from Southampton (Oct. 1992).
Record Victory: 11-0 v St Cuthbert Wanderers, Scottish Cup, 11 Dec 1993.
Record Defeat: 1-10 v Inverness Thistle, Highland League.
Most League Appearances: 230: Mark McCulloch, 2002-2009.
Most League Goals in Season: 24: Andrew Barrowman, 2007-08.
Most League Goals (Overall): 44: Steven Ferguson, 1996-2002.

ROSS COUNTY 2009–10 LEAGUE RECORD

Match No.	Date	Venue	Opponents	Result	H/T Score	Lg Pos.	Goalscorers	Attendance
1	Aug 8	H	Airdrie U	W 2-1	2-1	—	Di Giacomo [18], Wood [32]	1781
2	15	A	Partick Th	D 0-0	0-0	2		2391
3	22	H	Raith R	L 0-1	0-1	6		2088
4	29	A	Inverness CT	W 3-1	1-0	3	Di Giacomo [10], Vigurs [53], Brittain [76]	5846
5	Sept 12	H	Queen of the S	W 3-2	0-1	1	Brittain (pen) [46], Craig [48], Gardyne [75]	1992
6	19	H	Ayr U	W 2-1	2-0	1	Brittain [12], Craig [15]	1885
7	26	A	Dundee	L 0-2	0-0	2		4682
8	Oct 10	A	Morton	W 1-0	0-0	2	Wood [68]	2154
9	13	H	Dunfermline Ath	D 0-0	0-0	—		1757
10	17	A	Airdrie U	W 1-0	0-0	1	Wood [78]	756
11	24	H	Partick Th	D 2-2	1-0	2	Gardyne [40], Lawson [69]	2369
12	31	A	Queen of the S	L 0-2	0-2	4		2245
13	Nov 7	H	Inverness CT	W 2-1	2-0	3	Boyd [18], Gardyne [20]	5506
14	14	A	Ayr U	D 1-1	1-0	3	Boyd [41]	1236
15	Dec 1	H	Dundee	L 0-1	0-0	—		2005
16	8	H	Morton	W 3-1	0-1	—	Wood [49], Brittain (pen) [67], Scott [90]	1752
17	12	A	Dunfermline Ath	D 3-3	2-3	3	Brittain (pen) [8], Lawson [24], Vigurs [84]	2381
18	19	H	Airdrie U	W 5-3	2-2	—	Craig [1], Brittain 2 (1 pen) [32, 63 ip], Gardyne [48], Scott [79]	1823
19	Jan 23	H	Ayr U	W 1-0	0-0	2	Boyd [51]	1935
20	30	A	Dundee	W 1-0	1-0	—	Lawson [44]	4912
21	Feb 13	H	Dunfermline Ath	D 2-2	0-2	2	Lawson [54], Watt [85]	2213
22	27	A	Partick Th	L 1-2	0-1	—	Barrowman [76]	2192
23	Mar 6	H	Raith R	W 1-0	0-0	2	Brittain (pen) [76]	2033
24	9	A	Raith R	L 1-2	1-0	—	Barrowman [28]	1186
25	20	H	Inverness CT	D 0-0	0-0	4		5928
26	27	H	Dundee	D 1-1	0-0	4	Craig [87]	3295
27	30	A	Inverness CT	L 0-3	0-3	—		5411
28	Apr 3	A	Dunfermline Ath	W 2-1	2-0	4	Vigurs [15], Barrowman [35]	2641
29	6	H	Queen of the S	D 1-1	0-0	—	Boyd [90]	2004
30	13	A	Morton	D 1-1	1-1	—	Gardyne [39]	1219
31	17	A	Airdrie U	D 1-1	0-0	5	Craig [63]	798
32	20	A	Queen of the S	L 0-1	0-0	—		1183
33	24	H	Partick Th	L 1-2	0-0	5	Di Giacomo [58]	2175
34	26	H	Morton	W 2-1	1-0	—	Brittain [26], Barrowman [90]	1830
35	28	A	Ayr U	W 1-0	1-0	—	Barrowman (pen) [35]	1032
36	May 1	A	Raith R	L 1-4	0-3	5	Morrison [47]	1935

Final League Position: 5

Honours
League Champions: Second Division 2007-08. Third Division 1998-99.
Scottish Cup Runners-up: 2009-10.
League Challenge Cup Winners: 2006-07; *Runners-up:* 2004-05, 2008-09.

Club colours: Shirt: Navy blue with white trim. Shorts: Navy with white flashes. Stockings: White.

Goalscorers: *League (46):* Brittain 9 (5 pens), Barrowman 5 (1 pen), Craig 5, Gardyne 5, Boyd 4, Lawson 4, Wood 4, Di Giacomo 3, Vigurs 3, Scott 2, Morrison 1, Watt 1.
Scottish Cup (24): Wood 5, Craig 4, Gardyne 3, Di Giacomo 2, Morrison 2, Boyd 1, Brittain 1 (pen), Keddie 1, Kettlewell 1, Lawson 1, Miller 1, Scott 1, own goal 1.
CIS Cup (7): Gardyne 2, Brittain 1, Craig 1, Di Giacomo 1, Morrison 1, Stewart 1.
Challenge Cup (7): Gardyne 3, Craig 1, Di Giacomo 1, Lawson 1. Wood 1.

McGovern M 35	Girvan G 3+1	Morrison S 35	Boyd S 29+2	Keddie A 30	Lawson P 25+3	Gardyne M 30+4	Wood G 14+16	Di Giacomo P 20+11	Brittain R 34	Vigurs J 25+10	Miller G 31+1	Kettlewell S 22+9	Watt S 16+3	Moore D —+3	Stewart J —+2	Scott M 20+10	Craig S 12+12	Grant R —+1	Barrowman A 12+2	Smith G 1+3	Stephen R 1	Malin J 1	Match No.
1	2¹	3	4	5	6	7	8	9²	10	11	12	13											1
1		3	4	5			8¹	9²	10	11	2⁸	7	6	12	13								2
1		3	2	5	4¹	7	8	9³	10	11²	12	6				14	13						3
1		3¹	12	5	4	7	14	9²	10	11³	2	8	6			13							4
1		3		5	4	7		9	10	11²	2	8¹	6			13	12						5
1		3	14	5⁴	4	7¹²	9²	10	11	2		6³				13	8						6
1		3	5		4	7	13	9	10¹	11	2		6	12		8²							7
1		3	5	6	12	7²	8	9	10	13	2	4				11							8
1		3		6	8	7	9²	12	10	13	2	4¹	5			11							9
1		3		6	8¹	7³	9	12	10	13	2	4²	5	14		11							10
1		3		6	8²	7³	9¹	13	10	12	2	4	5			11⁴	14						11
1		3		5	7	10²	11	12	8	9³	2	6¹	4			13	14						12
1		3	5	6	8	7	13	9	10	11	2¹	4				12							13
1		3	5	6	8	7	13	9²	10³	11	2	4¹				12	14						14
1		3	5	6	8	7	14	9	10	11²	2	4³				13	12						15
·		3	5	6	8	7³	12	9	10	11¹	2	4				14	13						16
1		3	5	6	8	7³	12	9²	10	14	2	4¹				11	13						17
1		3	5	6	8³	7	11¹	13	10	14	2	12				4	9						18
1		3	5	6	8	7	11²	12	10	14	2³	13				4	9¹						19
1		5³	3	4	7	9²	11¹	10	6	13	2	12	14			8							20
1		5	4		8	7	11³	10¹	9	13	2	12	6			3²			14				21
1	2	3	5		8	7	9²		10³	11		4¹	6			14	12		13				22
1		5	4		8	12	13		9	7	2	6³	3			14	11¹		10²				23
1			4	5	12	13	14		11	9	2	3²	7¹			8	6²		13				24
1		5	3	4	7	10¹	13	12	6	9²	2					8	14		11³				25
1		3	5	6		7	14	12	10	11²	2¹	8				4¹	13		9				26
1		3	5	6⁴		7¹		9	10	11²	2	8²	13			4	12			14			27
1		5	4			12		11¹	10	9	2					7	8		6²	13	3		28
1		3	4	5		9		12	6	8¹	2					7	11		10				29
1		5	3	4	12	9⁵	13		8	6¹	2	14				7	10¹		11				30
1		3	5	6		7¹		13	10	11	2	12				4	9²		8				31
1		5	4	3		12		13	7	9²	2	6				8	11¹		10				32
1		5	4	3		6	13	11	7	12	2	9¹	14				10²						33
1		3	5	4	6³	11	14	10	8	7¹	2²	13				12	9						34
1	14	3	4	5	8	9	12	11				7¹	2³			6	10²	13					35
	2	5	3		7		9		11		6	4				10			8		1		36

ST JOHNSTONE
Premier League

Year Formed: 1884. *Ground & Address:* McDiarmid Park, Crieff Road, Perth PH1 2SJ. *Telephone:* 01738 459090. *Fax:* 01738 625 771. *Clubcall:* 0898 121559. *Email:* karin@perthsaints.co.uk *Website:* www.perthstjohnstonefc.co.uk
Ground Capacity: all seated: 10,673. *Size of Pitch:* 115yd × 75yd.
Chairman: Geoff Brown. *Managing Director:* Grant Cullen.
Manager: Derek McInnes. *Assistant Manager:* Tony Docherty. *Youth Coach:* Tommy Campbell. *Physio:* Nick Summersgill.
Club Nickname(s): Saints. *Previous Grounds:* Recreation Grounds, Muirton Park.
Record Attendance: (McDiarmid Park): 10,545 v Dundee, Premier Division, 23 May 1999.
Record Transfer Fee received: £1,750,000 for Calum Davidson to Blackburn R (March 1998).
Record Transfer Fee paid: £400,000 for Billy Dodds from Dundee (1994).
Record Victory: 9-0 v Albion R, League Cup, 9 Mar 1946.
Record Defeat: 1-10 v Third Lanark, Scottish Cup, 24 Jan 1903.
Most Capped Player: Nick Dasovic, 26, Canada.
Most League Appearances: 298: Drew Rutherford, 1976-85.
Most League Goals in Season (Individual): 36: Jimmy Benson, Division II, 1931-32.
Most Goals Overall (Individual): 140: John Brogan, 1977-83.

ST JOHNSTONE 2009–10 LEAGUE RECORD

Match No.	Date	Venue	Opponents	Result	H/T Score	Lg Pos.	Goalscorers	Attendance
1	Aug 15	H	Motherwell	D	2-2	1-0	—	Davidson [34], Gartland [61]	5220
2	22	A	Celtic	L	2-5	1-2	9	Samuel [36], Morris [76]	58,500
3	30	H	Hearts	D	2-2	1-0	9	Davidson [23], Hardie [90]	5825
4	Sept 12	A	St Mirren	D	1-1	1-1	9	Morris [37]	4543
5	19	A	Hibernian	L	0-3	0-2	11		10,817
6	26	H	Dundee U	L	2-3	1-1	12	Dods (og) [37], Hardie [72]	7225
7	Oct 3	A	Hamilton A	W	2-0	1-0	10	Anderson [45], Grainger [84]	2199
8	17	H	Rangers	L	1-2	1-1	10	Samuel [17]	7807
9	24	A	Kilmarnock	L	1-2	0-0	10	Wright (og) [90]	4643
10	31	H	Falkirk	W	3-1	1-0	10	Samuel [2], Millar [64], Davidson [66]	4423
11	Nov 7	A	Aberdeen	L	1-2	0-1	9	Craig [76]	10,894
12	21	A	Hearts	W	2-1	0-1	8	Samuel [60], Johansson [87]	13,416
13	28	H	Hamilton A	D	1-1	1-1	8	Morais [29]	3426
14	Dec 5	H	Kilmarnock	L	0-1	0-1	8		3518
15	12	A	Rangers	L	0-3	0-2	10		44,662
16	19	H	St Mirren	W	1-0	1-0	8	Millar [19]	2993
17	26	A	Motherwell	W	3-1	0-1	7	MacDonald 3 [54, 57, 70]	4140
18	Jan 24	H	Celtic	L	1-4	1-0	9	Craig (pen) [12]	7743
19	27	A	Dundee U	D	3-3	2-0	—	MacDonald 2 [6, 77], Craig [21]	6600
20	30	H	Hearts	W	1-0	0-0	8	Deuchar [51]	4752
21	Feb 10	A	St Mirren	D	1-1	1-0	—	MacKay [33]	3009
22	13	A	Kilmarnock	L	2-3	1-1	9	MacDonald [36], Gartland [53]	4605
23	17	H	Hibernian	W	5-1	2-0	—	Craig 2 (1 pen) [6, 79 (p)], Sheridan 2 [10, 71], Deuchar [62]	4100
24	27	A	Aberdeen	D	1-1	0-1	8	Craig (pen) [85]	12,174
25	Mar 6	H	Motherwell	L	1-2	1-1	8	Milne [26]	3669
26	13	A	Falkirk	W	2-1	1-1	—	Craig (pen) [45], Deuchar [84]	5895
27	16	H	Aberdeen	W	1-0	1-0	—	Sheridan [22]	3826
28	20	A	Celtic	L	0-3	0-1	7		30,000
29	23	A	Falkirk	D	1-1	1-1	—	Morais [36]	3107
30	27	A	Hamilton A	L	0-1	0-1	7		2245
31	30	H	Rangers	W	4-1	3-1	—	Sheridan [7], Millar [12], Craig [36], Davidson [79]	6189
32	Apr 5	A	Dundee U	L	0-1	0-0	—		5769
33	11	A	Aberdeen	W	3-1	2-1	7	Deuchar [21], Sheridan 2 [26, 65]	7568
34	17	A	St Mirren	D	2-2	0-1	7	Duberry [79], Sheerin (pen) [90]	3557
35	24	H	Aberdeen	D	1-1	0-1	7	Nelson (og) [90]	3295
36	May 1	A	Kilmarnock	W	2-1	1-1	7	Deuchar [44], Samuel [75]	4679
37	5	A	Falkirk	D	0-0	0-0			5502
38	8	H	Hamilton A	L	2-3	0-2	8	Davidson [49], Craig [68]	3188

Final League Position: 8

Honours
League Champions: First Division 1982-83, 1989-90, 1996-97, 2008-09. Division II 1923-24, 1959-60, 1962-63; *Runners-up:* Division II 1931-32. First Division 2005-06, 2006-07. Second Division 1987-88.
Scottish Cup: Semi-finals 1934, 1968, 1989. 1991, 2007, 2008.
League Cup Runners-up: 1969-70, 1998-99.
League Challenge Cup Winners: 2007-08; *Runners-up:* 1996-97.

European: *UEFA Cup:* 10 matches (1971-72, 1999-2000).

Club colours: Shirt: Royal blue. Shorts: Royal blue. Stockings: Royal blue.

Goalscorers: *League (57):* Craig 9 (4 pens), MacDonald 6, Sheridan 6, Davidson 5, Deuchar 5, Samuel 5, Millar 3, Gartland 2, Hardie 2, Morais 2, Morris 2, Anderson 1, Duberry 1, Grainger 1, Johansson 1, MacKay 1, Milne 1, Sheerin 1 (pen). own goals 3.
Scottish Cup (3): Craig 2, Milne 1.
CIS Cup (16): Deuchar 4, Milne 3, Samuel 3, Anderson 1, Millar 1, Morais 1, Morris 1, Swankie 1, own goal 1.

Main A 9	MacKay D 36	Grainger D 35 + 1	Morris J 33 + 1	McCaffrey S 9 + 1	Gartland G 20 + 1	Craig L 22 + 9	Davidson M 30 + 3	Milne S 10 + 6	Deuchar K 25 + 10	Morais F 20 + 10	Hardie M 4 + 6	Samuel C 16 + 11	Irvine G 13 + 4	Millar C 33 + 3	Swankie P 3 + 8	Sheerin P 3 + 8	Anderson S 14 + 3	Reynolds S — + 4	Smith G 29	Rutkiewicz K 7	Johansson J 2 + 4	Moon K 10 + 4	MacDonald P 5 + 2	Sheridan C 12 + 4	Duberry M 17	Connolly M 1	Jackson A — + 2	Falkingham J — + 1	Match No.
1	2	3	4	5	6	7	8	9	10¹	11²	12	13																	1
1	2	3	4	5	6		8		11¹	12	9	7¹	10³	13	14														2
1	2¹	3	4	5	6		8²	14	7	11	13	9	12	10															3
1	2	3	4	5	6		8	10	14	11²	13	9¹		12		7¹													4
1	2	3	4	5	6	11¹	8	13	12		7	3¹		10¹	14														5
1	2	3	4	5	6	12	8		11³	7	14	3²		10¹	13														6
1	2	3	4	13	6	8¹		9¹	10²	14	7	12		11			5												7
1	2	3	4		6	13	8		14	12	10²	9³		7	11¹		5												8
1	2	3	4		6		8³		13		7¹	9		11	10²	12	5	14											9
	2	3	4		6	7	8³		10	11¹	14	9²		12					1	5	13								10
	2	3	4		6¹	7	8		13	14	10³			11		12			1	5	9²								11
	2	3	4	5		13	8³		10	7²		9		11¹					1	6	14	12							12
	2	3	4	5			8²		10	7		9		12					1	6	13	11¹							13
	2	3	4	5		7¹	8³		10²	11		9							1	6	13	12	14						14
	2	3	4		6⁵		8		12	7²			14	11	13		5		1		9¹	10							15
	2	3	4		6	13			12	10	7²			5	11				1			8	9¹						16
	2	3	4		6	12	8	13	10²	14				5	7				1			11¹	9³						17
	2	3	4		6⁴	7	8³	9¹	10²					5	11		12		1			14	13						18
	2	3	4			7¹			13	12				5	10			6	1			1²	8	9²					19
	2	3		6	13	8	9	10¹	7²				5	4			14		1			11³	12						20
	2	3	4			7¹	12	9²		11³			8		14	6		*					10	13	5				21
	2	3	4		6	13	8		12				14		11		7²		1			10¹	9³	5					22
	2					6	7	4³	12	10²			14		8	13		3		1			11	9¹	5				23
	2	3¹				7	8		10	13			12		6			4	1			*1	9²	5					24
	2	12	13		6	7³	4²	9	10	14					9			3¹		1			11		5				25
	2	3	4			7	8²	9¹	10	12				6	11					1			13		5				26
	2	3	4			7			10	12				6	8				13	1			11¹	9²	5				27
	2	3				13	8	9³	10¹	14				6	11	7	4¹		12	1					5				28
	2	3	4			7	8¹			11³			13	6	10	12			14	1				9²	5				29
	2	3	4			7	12		10²	11			12		9			13		1			14	5	6¹				30
	2	3	4			7	12		10	11⁴			13	14	8³			6		1			9²	5					31
	2	3	4			7²			10	11			12		8	13		6		1			9¹	5					32
			4			7	8		10³	11			12	2	6			13	3	1			9²	5		14			33
		3³	4			7¹	12		10	11			13	6	8			11²	2	1			9²	5					34
	2	3	4			14	8		12	7			10¹	5	11					1	6			9²			13		35
	2	3	4		13	7	8		10				9¹		11					1	6²			12	5				36
	2	3	4					8¹	14	10			11⁴		7		*3	6		1				9²	5		12		37
	2	3	4			6¹	7	8	10	12			9³	13	11²		*4			1					5				38

ST MIRREN
Premier League

Year Formed: 1877. *Ground & Address:* St Mirren Park, Greenhill Road, Paisley PA3 1RU. *Telephone:* 0141 889 2558.
Fax: 0141 848 6444. *E-mail:* info@saintmirren.net *Website:* www.saintmirren.net
Ground Capacity: 10,476 (all seated). *Size of Pitch:* 105yd × 68yd.
Chairman: Stewart Gilmour. *Vice-Chairman:* George Campbell. *General Manager:* Brian Caldwell. *Secretary:* Allan Marshall.
Manager: Danny Lennon. *Assistant Manager:* Andy Millen. *Youth Development Officer:* David Longwell. *Physio:* John McCreadie.
Club Nickname(s): The Buddies. *Previous Grounds:* Short Roods 1877-79, Thistle Park Greenhill 1879-83, Westmarch 1883-94, Love Street 1894-2009.
Record Attendance: 47,438 v Celtic, League Cup, 20 Aug 1949.
Record Transfer Fee received: £850,000 for Ian Ferguson to Rangers (1988).
Record Transfer Fee paid: £400,000 for Thomas Stickroth from Bayer Uerdingen (1990).
Record Victory: 15-0 v Glasgow University, Scottish Cup 1st rd, 30 Jan 1960.
Record Defeat: 0-9 v Rangers, Division I, 4 Dec 1897.
Most Capped Player: Godmundor Torfason, 29, Iceland.
Most League Appearances: 371: Hugh Murray, 1997-2010.
Most League Goals in Season (Individual): 45: Dunky Walker, Division I, 1921-22.
Most Goals Overall (Individual): 221: David McCrae, 1923-34.

ST MIRREN 2009–10 LEAGUE RECORD

Match No.	Date	Venue	Opponents	Result	H/T Score	Lg Pos.	Goalscorers	Attendance
1	Aug 15	A	Hibernian	L	1-2	1-1	—	McGinn [38]	6350
2	22	H	Dundee U	D	0-0	0-0	8		4775
3	29	A	Kilmarnock	W	2-1	0-1	7	McGinn 2 [48, 69]	5645
4	Sept 12	H	St Johnstone	D	1-1	1-1	6	Mehmet (pen) [33]	4543
5	19	A	Aberdeen	L	0-1	0-0	—		10,103
6	26	H	Celtic	L	0-2	0-1	9		6164
7	Oct 3	H	Hearts	W	2-1	1-1	7	Thomson [38], Dargo [65]	4652
8	17	A	Falkirk	W	3-1	0-0	7	Dargo [67], Mehmet [71], Brighton [88]	5084
9	24	H	Motherwell	D	3-3	1-0	6	Murray 2 [42, 72], Dorman [59]	4327
10	31	H	Hamilton A	L	0-2	0-2	6		4022
11	Nov 7	A	Rangers	L	1-2	0-1	7	O'Donnell [88]	45,750
12	21	H	Hibernian	D	1-1	1-1	7	Innes [45]	4681
13	28	A	Celtic	L	1-3	1-2	9	Higdon [45]	41,000
14	Dec 5	A	Dundee U	L	2-3	0-2	9	Dods (og) [61], O'Donnell [85]	6259
15	12	H	Falkirk	D	1-1	0-0	9	Higdon [53]	4033
16	19	A	St Johnstone	L	0-1	0-1	10		2993
17	Jan 2	H	Kilmarnock	W	1-0	0-0	—	Innes [81]	4917
18	12	H	Aberdeen	W	1-0	0-0	—	Innes [74]	3867
19	16	A	Hearts	L	0-1	0-1	8		12,821
20	23	A	Motherwell	L	0-2	0-1	8		3621
21	27	H	Rangers	L	0-2	0-1	—		5260
22	30	A	Hibernian	L	1-2	1-1	9	Bamba (og) [9]	11,476
23	Feb 10	H	St Johnstone	D	1-1	0-1	—	Higdon [71]	3009
24	13	A	Dundee U	L	1-2	0-0	10	Higdon [66]	3944
25	20	A	Kilmarnock	D	1-1	0-1	10	Mehmet [82]	5501
26	27	H	Hamilton A	D	0-0	0-0	10		3628
27	Mar 6	A	Rangers	L	1-3	1-1	10	Carey [30]	47,474
28	9	H	Motherwell	D	0-0	0-0	—		3154
29	13	A	Hamilton A	L	0-1	0-0	—		2179
30	24	H	Celtic	W	4-0	1-0	—	Dorman 2 [38, 84], Thomson 2 [56, 87]	5018
31	27	A	Aberdeen	L	1-2	0-1	10	Robb [80]	8764
32	Apr 3	H	Hearts	D	1-1	1-0	11	Carey [44]	4204
33	10	A	Falkirk	L	1-2	0-1	11	Dorman [90]	5671
34	17	A	St Johnstone	D	2-2	1-0	10	Carey [33], Dorman [50]	3557
35	24	H	Kilmarnock	W	1-0	0-0	10	Dorman [74]	5639
36	May 1	H	Falkirk	D	1-1	0-1	10	O'Donnell [86]	5919
37	5	A	Hamilton A	D	0-0	0-0	—		3102
38	8	H	Aberdeen	L	0-1	0-1	10		4022

Final League Position: 10

Honours
League Champions: First Division 1976-77, 1999-2000, 2005-06; *Runners-up:* 2004-05. Division II 1967-68; *Runners-up:* 1935-36.
Scottish Cup Winners: 1926, 1959, 1987; *Runners-up:* 1908, 1934, 1962.
League Cup Runners-up: 1955-56, 2009-10.
League Challenge Cup Winners: 2005-06.
B&Q Cup Runners-up: 1993-94. *Anglo-Scottish Cup:* 1979-80.

European: *Cup Winners' Cup:* 4 matches (1987-88). *UEFA Cup:* 10 matches (1980-81, 1983-84, 1985-86).

Club colours: Shirt: Black and white vertical stripes. Shorts: Black. Stockings: White.

Goalscorers: *League (36):* Dorman 6, Higdon 4, Carey 3, Innes 3, McGinn 3, Mehmet 3 (1 pen), O'Donnell 3, Thomson 3, Dargo 2, Murray 2, Brighton 1, Robb 1, own goals 2.
Scottish Cup (3): Mehmet 2, own goal 1.
CIS Cup (14): Mehmet 7, Higdon 2, Dorman 1, McGinn 1, O'Donnell 1, Ross 1, own goal 1.

Gallacher P 36	Ross J 28	Barron D 34	Dorman A 29+5	Mair L 30+1	Potter J 35	Thomson S 30	Brady G 19+3	Mehmet B 35+2	Higdon M 22+11	McGinn S 18	Brighton T 1+7	Dargo C 13+16	Murray H 35	Robb S 12+8	O'Donnell S 10+12	Innes C 18+3	Johnston A 1+9	Ramsey C +5	Loy R —+8	Carey G 10+5	Howard M 2	Match No.
1	2	3	4	5	6	7^8	8	9	10^1	11^2	12	13										1
1	2	3	4^2	5	6		8	9	12	11	14	10^1	7^3	13								2
1	2	3	4^1	5	6		8	9^1	10	11	13	14	7^2		12							3
1	2	3	4^3	5	6		8	9^2	10^1	11	13	12	7	14								4
1	2	3	12	5^4	6	8	4^2	9	13	11		10^1	7									5
1	2	3	12		6	8	4^1	9^1	14	11	13	10	7^2			5						6
1	2	3	4^3	5^1	6	8		9		11	13	10	7^2		14	12						7
1	2	3	4^3	5	6	7		9		11	13	10^2	8^1		12	14						8
1	2	3	4^2	5	6	7		9	12	11		10^0	8	13								9
1	2	3	4	5^4	6^2		13	9	10	11^2			8		7^1	12	14					10
1	2	3	4		6	7^2	8	9	12	11^1		10	13	5								11
1	2	3	4	5		7		9	10^1	11	12		8^2	6	13							12
1	2	3	4^1	5		7	8	9	12	11^2	14		10^3	6	13							13
1	2	3		5		7^3	8^1	9	10	11	4^2	13	12	6	14							14
	2^1	3	12		6	8		9	10	11	4	13	7^2	5								15
1		3^2		5	6	4	8	9^8	11^1	10		7^3	12	13	2	14						16
1	2	3	4^3	5	6^1		9		11	10		8	14	7^2	12	13						17
1	2	3	4^2		6	7		9	10^1	11	12		8		5	13						18
1	2	3^3	4		6	7		9	12	10	11^2	13	8^1	5		14						19
1	2		4		6	3^2	8^1	9	12	10^3	11	7	13	5	14							20
1	2	3	4		6	7^1	8^2	9	10		13	11	12	5								21
1	2	3	12	5	6	7	8	9	10^2	11			4^1							13		22
1	2	3^2	4	5	6		9	10	12	11			8^1	7						13		23
1	2	3	4^1	5	6	8		9	10	12	11		7^2							13		24
1		3	4	5^3	6	7		9	10	14	11^2	2^1			8	12				13		25
1		3	4^3	5	6		8	9	10^2	13	11	2		7^3	12					14		26
1		3	4	5	6	7	8	9	10^2	13	12	2								11		27
1	2^3	3	13		6	8	12	9^1	10^1	7	14		4^2							11		28
1	2	3	4	5	6		8^1	9	10	7			12							11		29
1	2		4^2	5	6	3	8	9^1	12	10^3	11		7	13					14			30
1	2		4^2	5	6	3^3	8^1	12	9	10	11		7						14	13		31
1	2^2		4	5	6	7		9^1	10	8			13	5					12	11		32
1		3	12	5^2	6	4	8	9	10^3	7^1		13		5					14	11		33
1		3	4	5	6		8	9	10				2	7						11		34
1		3	4	5	6	7	12	9	13	11^1			2	8^2	14					10^3		35
1		3	4	5		7	14	9^3	12	13	11^2	6^1	8	2^8						10		36
1		3		5	6	8^1	9	10	14	13	7^2	2	4						12	11	1	37
		3	4	5	6	7	11^3	9	12	14	2^1	8^2	13							10	1	38

STENHOUSEMUIR Second Division

Year Formed: 1884. *Ground & Address:* Ochilview Park, Gladstone Rd, Stenhousemuir FK5 4QL. *Telephone:* 01324 562992. *Fax:* 01324 562980. *E-mail:* info@stenhousemuirfc.com *Website:* www.stenhousemuirfc.com
Ground Capacity: 3776 (626 seated). *Size of Pitch:* 110yd × 72yd.
Chairman: Martin McNairney. *Vice Chairman:* Bill Darroch. *Secretary:* Margaret Kilpatrick.
Manager: John Coughlin. *Assistant Manager:* Matt Kerr. *Physio:* Alain Davidson.
Club Nickname(s): The Warriors. *Previous Grounds:* Tryst Ground 1884-86, Goschen Park 1886-90.
Record Attendance: 12,500 v East Fife, Scottish Cup 4th rd, 11 Mar 1950.
Record Transfer Fee received: £70,000 for Euan Donaldson to St Johnstone (May 1995).
Record Transfer Fee paid: £20,000 to Livingston for Ian Little (June 1995); £20,000 to East Fife for Paul Hunter (September 1995).
Record Victory: 9-2 v Dundee U, Division II, 16 Apr 1937.
Record Defeat: 2-11 v Dunfermline Ath, Division II, 27 Sept 1930.
Most League Appearances: 434: Jimmy Richardson, 1957-73.
Most League Goals in Season (Individual): 32: Robert Taylor, Division II, 1925-26.

STENHOUSEMUIR 2009–10 LEAGUE RECORD

Match No.	Date	Venue	Opponents	Result	H/T Score	Lg Pos.	Goalscorers	Attendance
1	Aug 8	A	Stirling A	D	0-0	0-0	—	696
2	15	H	East Fife	D	1-1	1-1	7	Scullion [5]	645
3	22	A	Peterhead	D	2-2	1-1	6	Thom [9], Diack [86]	519
4	29	H	Arbroath	W	3-0	0-0	4	Smith J [50], Thomson I [57], Diack [75]	543
5	Sept 12	A	Dumbarton	D	0-0	0-0	4		664
6	19	H	Alloa Ath	W	1-0	1-0	3	Motion [33]	698
7	26	A	Brechin C	L	0-1	0-1	4		418
8	Oct 3	H	Cowdenbeath	L	0-2	0-1	6		539
9	10	A	Clyde	L	1-2	0-1	7	Molloy [84]	755
10	17	H	Stirling A	L	1-2	1-0	9	Motion [40]	584
11	24	A	East Fife	L	1-2	0-0	10	Molloy [90]	509
12	31	A	Arbroath	W	3-0	1-0	8	Motion [19], Love 2 [54, 84]	402
13	Nov 7	H	Dumbarton	L	0-3	0-0	8		568
14	14	A	Alloa Ath	W	4-1	3-0	7	Molloy [22], Motion [34], Dalziel [37], Scullion [74]	544
15	21	A	Brechin C	D	1-1	1-1	7	Motion (pen) [42]	551
16	Dec 12	H	Clyde	W	1-0	0-0	7	Molloy [78]	532
17	15	A	Cowdenbeath	L	1-2	1-1	—	Dalziel [21]	264
18	Jan 16	H	Arbroath	D	1-1	0-0	—	Love [77]	443
19	23	A	Alloa Ath	L	0-2	0-2	8		554
20	30	A	Brechin C	D	2-2	0-0	—	Scullion [67], Dalziel [78]	413
21	Feb 6	A	Clyde	W	2-0	1-0	7	Motion (pen) [20], Smith J [64]	650
22	13	H	Cowdenbeath	D	0-0	0-0	7		443
23	27	H	East Fife	D	1-1	1-0	—	McLeod [8]	476
24	Mar 2	A	Stirling A	D	1-1	1-1	—	Thom [41]	473
25	6	A	Arbroath	D	1-1	1-1	6	Motion (pen) [28]	458
26	9	H	Peterhead	W	2-0	0-0	—	Gibb [73], Dalziel [88]	207
27	13	H	Dumbarton	W	1-0	0-0	5	Quinn [87]	469
28	20	A	Alloa Ath	L	1-2	1-0	5	Dalziel [30]	550
29	23	A	Dumbarton	L	1-2	0-1	—	Lyle [65]	486
30	27	H	Brechin C	L	1-2	1-1	5	Diack [32]	481
31	Apr 3	A	Cowdenbeath	L	0-1	0-0	8		438
32	6	A	Peterhead	W	1-0	1-0	—	Love [3]	364
33	10	H	Clyde	L	0-3	0-1	8		482
34	17	H	Stirling A	L	1-3	0-1	8	Diack [62]	783
35	24	A	East Fife	D	1-1	0-0	8	Quinn [87]	678
36	May 1	H	Peterhead	D	1-1	1-0	8	Dalziel [13]	612

Final League Position: 8

Honours
League Champions: Third Division runners-up: 1998-99.
Scottish Cup: Semi-finals 1902-03. Quarter-finals 1948-49, 1949-50, 1994-95.
League Cup: Quarter-finals 1947-48, 1960-61, 1975-76.
League Challenge Cup Winners: 1995-96.

Club colours: All maroon.

Goalscorers: *League (38):* Motion 7 (3 pens), Dalziel 6, Diack 4, Love 4, Molloy 4, Scullion 3, Quinn 2, Smith J 2, Thom 2, Gibb 1, Lyle 1, McLeod 1, Thomson I 1.
Scottish Cup (6): Bradley 2 (1 pen), Motion 2, Molloy 1, Thompson I 1.
CIS Cup (0).
Challenge Cup (3): Dalziel 2, O'Reilly 1.

McCluskey C 34	Lyle W 24 + 2	Thomson S 27	Thom G 28	Smith J 30	Molloy C 26 + 3	Brand A 5 + 5	Scullion P 27 + 2	Dalziel S 31 + 4	O'Reilly C 4 + 7	Motion K 32 + 1	Bradley K 10 + 10	McLeod C 29 + 1	Diack I 17 + 9	Love R 13 + 10	Thomson I 27 + 3	Stirling A 5 + 10	Reid A 2	Welsh S 2	Currie L 2	Gair S 2	Dickson S — + 2	Gibb S 12 + 1	Quinn P 2 + 10	Smith D 2	Hunter M 1 + 1	Lawson A — + 1	Bennett S 2	Anderson G — + 1	Match No.
1	2	3	4	5	6	7	8	9	10^1	11	12																		1
1	2	3	4	5	6		8	9	10^1	11			7	12															2
1	2	3	4	5	6		8	9	10^1				7^2	12	13														3
1	2^1	3^2	4	5	6		8	9	14	11	12		7	10^3		13													4
1	2	3^1	4	5	6		8^2	9^3	14	11			7	10	13	12													5
1			4	5	6	12	8^1	9^2	13	11	2		7	10^3	14	3													6
1	13		5^1	4	7		8^2		10^3	12	9	6	3	11		2	14												7
1	13		5	4	7	14			10^2	8	9	6^1	3^3	11	12	2													8
1	2	3■	9	5	6	4^1	8^2		14	11^3	13		10		7	12													9
1	2^2		4	5	6^1	14	8	13		11^3	12		9	7	10		3												10
1	2		3	4	7		8^1	12		9	13		10^2	6	11		5												11
1		3^2	4	5	10	13	8	9		11	12	6		7^1	2														12
1		3	4	5	10		8^1	9		11	12	6		7^2	2	13													13
1	2	3		5		7	10	8^1	9^2	13	11		6		4	12													14
1	2	3		5		7	10^1	8	9		11	12	6		4														15
1		3	2	5	6		8	9		11^1	10	4		12	7														16
1		5^1	2	4	7		8^2	10^3	13	9	11	3		12	6	14													17
1		3		9			11	10	8^2	4	12	13	7	6^1			2	5											18
1	2	5		3	14		11		9	10^2	4	12^2	13	6^1			7	8											19
1	2^1	5	8	4		9	3	11^2		6	7^3	14		10	12	13													20
1	2	3	6	5		10^2	9	11		7^1	8		12	4	13														21
1	2	5	4	3^1		10■	11	9		12	6^2	8		7	13														22
1	3		5		10	9		4	11^1	6^2	8		2	12	7	13													23
1	6	5	4		10	8		3	12	11	7		2		9^1														24
1	2■	5	8		10	11^1	9		4	12	6^2	7■		3	13														25
1		5	7		8	13		9	11^1	4	10^3	6^2	12		3	14	2												26
1	2	3^2	6		12		7	9^3		11	5	10	8	13		4	14												27
1	5	9	4	2	13		7^3	10		12	3	11^2	8■	6^1		14													28
	2	5■	4	9		6	13	8	14	3	10^1	7^3		11^2		1	12												29
	2^1		3	4	7^2	10	9		8	11	13	12	6^3		5	14		1											30
1	5	8	4	3	6	14	10^2	9■		2	11	12		7^1	13														31
1	9	3	7		5	10^2	8		2	13	11^1	6	12		4														32
1	2	5		3	8^1	12	11^2		14	9	7	13	6	10						4^3									33
1	5	4	8		6	11	9	3	10^1	7		2	12																34
1	5^1	3	6	14	8^3	11	9	4	10^2	7	12		2	13															35
1	2	5	7	4	9		11	3	12	10	6^1		8																36

STIRLING ALBION

First Division

Year Formed: 1945. *Ground & Address:* Forthbank Stadium, Springkerse Industrial Estate, Stirling FK7 7UJ. *Telephone:* 01786 450399. *Fax:* 01786 448592. *Email:* stirlingalbion@btconnect.com *Website:* www.stirlingalbionfc.co.uk
Ground Capacity: 3808, seated: 2508. *Size of Pitch:* 110yd × 74yd.
Chairman: Peter McKenzie. *Secretary:* Mrs Marlyn Hallam.
Head Coach: John O'Neill. *Assistant Manager:* Roddie Grant. *Physio:* Louise Wilson.
Club Nickname(s): The Binos. *Previous Grounds:* Annfield 1945-92.
Record Attendance: 26,400 (at Annfield) v Celtic, Scottish Cup 4th rd, 14 Mar 1959; 3808 v Aberdeen, Scottish Cup 4th rd, 15 February 1996 (Forthbank).
Record Transfer Fee received: £90,000 for Stephen Nicholas to Motherwell (Mar 1999).
Record Transfer Fee paid: £25,000 for Craig Taggart from Falkirk (Aug 1994).
Record Victory: 20-0 v Selkirk, Scottish Cup 1st rd, 8 Dec 1984.
Record Defeat: 0-9 v Dundee U, Division I, 30 Dec 1967.
Most League Appearances: 504: Matt McPhee, 1967-81.
Most League Goals in Season (Individual): 27: Joe Hughes, Division II, 1969-70.
Most Goals Overall (Individual): 129: Billy Steele, 1971-83.

STIRLING ALBION 2009–10 LEAGUE RECORD

Match No.	Date	Venue	Opponents	Result	H/T Score	Lg Pos.	Goalscorers	Attendance
1	Aug 8	H	Stenhousemuir	D 0-0	0-0	—		696
2	15	A	Clyde	W 1-0	1-0	4	Grehan [38]	813
3	22	H	Brechin C	W 1-0	1-0	3	Grehan [6]	608
4	29	H	Peterhead	W 2-1	0-1	2	McKenna 2 [77, 90]	537
5	Sept 12	A	Alloa Ath	L 0-1	0-1	2		1201
6	19	H	East Fife	W 3-0	1-0	1	Graham [25], Grehan [72], McCord [84]	678
7	26	A	Cowdenbeath	W 2-1	2-1	1	Grehan 2 [16, 43]	451
8	Oct 3	A	Dumbarton	W 3-2	1-2	9	McKenna [32], Devine [51], Robertson [90]	654
9	10	A	Arbroath	D 2-2	2-2	1	Robertson [10], McKenna [33]	689
10	17	A	Stenhousemuir	W 2-1	0-1	1	O'Brian [47], Grehan [55]	584
11	24	H	Clyde	D 1-1	0-0	1	Corr [88]	764
12	31	A	Peterhead	L 2-3	1-3	1	Grehan [37], Devine [65]	546
13	Nov 7	A	Alloa Ath	L 0-1	0-1	2		986
14	14	A	East Fife	W 2-1	0-1	2	O'Brian [50], Grehan [90]	633
15	21	H	Cowdenbeath	D 2-2	0-1	2	Forsyth (pen) [79], McKenna [87]	682
16	Dec 12	A	Arbroath	W 4-3	3-0	2	Murphy [22], O'Brian 2 [37, 44], Mullen [90]	491
17	15	H	Dumbarton	D 2-2	0-0	—	Murphy [61], Devine [88]	462
18	Jan 23	H	East Fife	D 3-3	1-1	2	Smart (og) [25], O'Brian [60], Forsyth [82]	665
19	Feb 16	A	Dumbarton	W 4-2	3-2	—	Robertson 2 [1, 49], Aitken 2 [12, 34]	595
20	Mar 2	H	Stenhousemuir	D 1-1	1-1	—	Aitken [6]	473
21	6	A	Peterhead	D 1-1	0-0	3	O'Brian [81]	497
22	9	A	Brechin C	L 0-1	0-1	—		453
23	13	H	Alloa Ath	L 0-3	0-1	4		1036
24	16	H	Peterhead	W 2-0	0-0	—	McKenna [63], Bowden (og) [78]	297
25	20	A	East Fife	W 3-0	1-0	3	Page 2 [41, 55], Elliott [73]	709
26	23	A	Alloa Ath	L 1-2	1-1	—	Graham [7]	1147
27	27	A	Cowdenbeath	W 1-0	0-0	3	Mullen [78]	575
28	Apr 3	A	Dumbarton	L 1-2	0-0	3	Taggart [51]	568
29	10	A	Arbroath	W 4-2	1-1	3	Gibson [13], Aitken (pen) [75], Graham [81], Russell [83]	525
30	12	A	Arbroath	D 2-2	1-1	—	Graham [38], Russell [50]	365
31	14	H	Brechin C	W 6-2	2-0	—	Aitken (pen) [40], Mullen 3 [45, 53, 57], Russell [55], Colqhoen [90]	357
32	17	A	Stenhousemuir	W 3-1	1-0	2	Graham [20], Forsyth [82], Russell [85]	783
33	20	A	Clyde	W 2-1	1-1	—	Robertson [4], Russell [80]	635
34	24	H	Clyde	W 1-0	1-0	1	Robertson [25]	796
35	27	A	Cowdenbeath	D 3-3	0-3	—	Russell 2 [52, 87], Graham [90]	1084
36	May 1	A	Brechin C	D 1-1	1-1	1	Mullen [8]	1102

Final League Position: 1

Honours
League Champions: Division II 1952-53, 1957-58, 1960-61, 1964-65. Second Division 1976-77, 1990-91, 1995-96, 2009-10; *Runners-up:* Division II 1948-49, 1950-51. Second Division 2006-07. Third Division 2003-04.
League Cup: Semi-finals 1961-62.

Club colours: All red.

Goalscorers: *League (68):* Grehan 8, Russell 7, Graham 6, McKenna 6, Mullen 6, O'Brian 6, Robertson 6, Aitken 5 (2 pens), Devine 3, Forsyth 3 (1 pen), Murphy 2, Page 2, Colqhoen 1, Corr 1, Elliott 1, Gibson 1, McCord 1, Taggart 1, own goals 2.
Scottish Cup (5): Mullen 2, Corr 1, Forsyth 1, Murphy 1.
CIS Cup (1): Devine 1.
Challenge Cup (6): McKenna 2, Devine 1 (pen), Graham 1, Mullen 1, Robertson 1.

Christie S 26	Feaks K 9+1	Forsyth R 32	Roycroft S 10	Graham A 36	Robertson S 27+6	Gibson A 30+5	Murphy P 18+10	McKenna D 19+15	Mullen M 14+14	Devine S 12+3	Grehan M 14+2	O'Brian D 34+2	O'Neil J 10+6	McCord R 4+7	Young C 3+2	Taggart N 11+10	Hogarth M 10	Corr I 1+10	Prunty B 3	McKeown C 2	Allison B 16+1	Aitken C 18+1	Colqhoen D 4+4	Byrne K 2+1	Elliott S 5+2	Page J 16	Russell I 10	Match No.
1	2²	3	4	5	6	7	8³	9	10¹	11	12	13	14															1
1		3	4	5	6³	7	14	13	10²	11	8	9	2¹	12														2
1		3	4	5	6¹	7	12	13	10²	11	8	9	2															3
1		3	4	5	6¹	7¹		13	10²	11	8	9	2	12	14													4
1		3	4	5		7³	12	10	13	11	8	9	2²		6¹	14												5
	4	3		5	14	7	6	10	13	11²	8³	9	2¹	12		1												6
	4	5			2	12	6	3	10	13		11²		9	7¹	8	1											7
	4¹	5			2	13	6	3	10		12	11	9³	7	8²	14	1											8
	14	3	4³		2	6²	7	5	10		8	9	11¹		12	1	13											9
	4	3			2	6¹	7	5²	10³	13	8	9	11	12	14	1												10
	4	3			2	6¹	7	5	10		14	9	11²	12	8³	1	13											11
	4	3⁴			2	13	7	8²	10	12	11	9	14	6¹		5³	1											12
1	4				2		7	5³	10²	13	8	9	11	6	14	3¹		12										13
1		5	3	2	7	6³	4²	11		8¹	10	9		12		14	13											14
1		3	4	2	5	7		13		9³	11	14	6²	12		8¹	10³											15
1	2	3	5	4	6²	7	8³	10	12		11		14		13	9¹												16
1		3	4	2	6	7	8²	13	9¹	14	12	11			10³	5												17
1		5			2	12	7²		11³	14	8¹	9	13								3	4	6				10	18
1		5			3	2	12	7	11²	13		9		6³		14					4	8¹			10			19
1		4			2	8	13	6⁸	10¹			9	14		5²						3	7		11³	12			20
		3			2	6	13		10¹			11		7²	14						4	8	12	9³	5			21
		4			7	6²	13	10²		11	3¹		14	12						2	8	9	5				22
		5			2	13	11	8²	14	10		9		6¹						4	7	12	3³					23
1		5			2	8³	6¹	14	13	10²		9		12						3	7		11	4				24
1		5			2	7²	6	12	10³	14		9			13					3	8		11¹	4				25
1		5			2	8	6¹		10³	13		9		12	4					3	7		11³	4				26
1		5			6		7³	14	12			9²		13						3	8	10¹		4	11			27
1		5			2	8	14		13	12		9		6³						3	7	10¹		4	11²			28
1					2	4	6	5²	14	12		9		13						8	7	10¹		3	11³			29
1					2	8	6	5¹		10²		9		12						3	7	13		4	11			30
1	3				2	6²		13	14	9¹		11		7						4	8	12		5	10³			31
1		5			2	8	4		13	10²		9¹		6							7	12		3	11			32
1		4			2	8	12	13		10		9		5²						6	7¹			3	11			33
1		4			6	8	2	13	12	11¹		9		5							7²			3	10			34
1		9			2	4	6		14	10³		8		5¹						13	7²	12		3	11			35
1		5			2	7	8	13	14	10¹		9		6²						3⁸	12			4	11³			36

STRANRAER

Third Division

Year Formed: 1870. *Ground & Address:* Stair Park, London Rd, Stranraer DG9 8BS. *Telephone and Fax:* 01776 703271.
E-mail: secretary@stranraerfc.org *Website:* www.stranraerfc.org
Ground Capacity: 5600, seated: 1830. *Size of Pitch:* 110yd × 70yd.
Chairman: Alex Connor. *Vice Chairman:* Robert Rice. *Secretary:* Hilde Law.
Manager: Keith Knox. *Assistant Manager:* Stephen Aitken. *Physio:* Walter Cannon.
Club Nickname(s): The Blues. *Previous Grounds:* None.
Record Attendance: 6500 v Rangers, Scottish Cup 1st rd, 24 Jan 1948.
Record Transfer Fee received: £90,000 for Mark Campbell to Ayr U (1999).
Record Transfer Fee paid: £15,000 for Colin Harkness from Kilmarnock (Aug 1989).
Record Victory: 7-0 v Brechin C, Division II, 6 Feb 1965.
Record Defeat: 1-11 v Queen of the South, Scottish Cup 1st rd, 16 Jan 1932.
Most League Appearances: 301: Keith Knox, 1986-90; 1999-2001.
Most League Goals in Season (Individual): 59: Tommy Sloan.

STRANRAER 2009–10 LEAGUE RECORD

Match No.	Date		Venue	Opponents	Result		H/T Score	Lg Pos.	Goalscorers	Attendance
1	Aug	8	H	Albion R	D	1-1	1-0	—	McInnes [40]	250
2		15	A	Forfar Ath	L	0-1	0-1	8		410
3		22	H	Annan Ath	W	2-0	1-0	5	McColm [34], Moore [54]	358
4		29	H	Montrose	W	2-0	1-0	3	Danny Mitchell [17], Montgomerie [73]	271
5	Sept	19	A	Livingston	L	0-3	0-3	6		378
6		22	A	Berwick R	L	0-1	0-0	—		366
7		26	A	East Stirling	D	1-1	1-0	6	Danny Mitchell [39]	367
8	Oct	3	H	Elgin C	L	0-2	0-1	7		207
9		10	A	Queen's Park	W	2-1	0-1	6	Moore [64], Jack [89]	598
10		17	A	Annan Ath	L	0-1	0-0	8		647
11		31	H	Forfar Ath	W	1-0	0-0	7	Moore [68]	210
12	Nov	7	H	Berwick R	L	2-4	0-2	7	McGeouch [55], McColm [72]	274
13		14	A	Montrose	D	1-1	0-0	7	Moore [63]	258
14		21	H	East Stirling	L	1-2	0-2	7	McInnes [57]	205
15	Dec	5	A	Livingston	L	0-3	0-2	8		1267
16		12	H	Queen's Park	D	1-1	0-1	8	Nicoll [75]	255
17	Jan	16	A	Montrose	W	5-4	2-2	—	One 2 [4, 76], Moore (pen) [7], Agnew [85], Bouadii [90]	200
18		23	H	Livingston	D	1-1	1-0	8	Nicoll [12]	323
19		30	A	East Stirling	L	0-2	0-0	—		348
20	Feb	6	A	Queen's Park	W	5-2	3-1	7	McColm [7], Agnew 2 [22, 87], One [36], Danny Mitchell [71]	553
21	Mar	6	A	Montrose	L	0-2	0-1	8		225
22		13	H	Berwick R	W	3-1	2-0	8	McColm 3 [14, 19, 58]	231
23		16	H	Elgin C	W	2-1	1-1	—	Bouadii [26], Montgomerie [87]	145
24		20	A	Livingston	L	1-2	0-2	8	Moore [86]	1136
25		24	H	Annan Ath	W	3-2	2-0	—	One [20], Agnew [22], Moore [90]	259
26		27	H	East Stirling	D	2-2	1-0	8	Noble [10], One [53]	320
27	Apr	3	A	Elgin C	W	2-1	0-1	8	One 2 [67, 78]	375
28		6	A	Berwick R	L	0-1	0-1	—		289
29		10	H	Queen's Park	D	0-0	0-0	8		365
30		12	A	Albion R	L	1-3	1-1	—	Montgomerie [36]	252
31		14	H	Albion R	W	2-1	1-0	—	Noble [6], Agnew [90]	214
32		17	A	Annan Ath	L	2-3	0-2	8	Moore [60], One [70]	392
33		20	A	Forfar Ath	L	0-2	0-1	—		422
34		24	H	Forfar Ath	W	2-0	2-0	8	Henderson [4], Agnew (pen) [34]	337
35		27	A	Elgin C	W	3-2	0-1	—	Cawley 2 [78, 90], Danny Mitchell [84]	232
36	May	1	A	Albion R	D	0-0	0-0	7		575

Final League Position: 7

Honours
League Champions: Second Division 1993-94, 1997-98; *Runners-up:* 2004-05, 2007-08. Third Division 2003-04.
Qualifying Cup Winners: 1937.
Scottish Cup: Quarter-finals 2003
League Challenge Cup Winners: 1996-97.

Club colours: Shirt: Royal blue with white design. Shorts: White. Stockings: Royal blue.

Goalscorers: *League (48):* Moore 8 (1 pen), One 8, Agnew 6 (1 pen), McColm 6, Danny Mitchell 4, Montgomerie 3, Bouadii 2, Cawley 2, McInnes 2, Nicoll 2, Noble 2, Henderson 1, Jack 1, McGeouch 1.
Scottish Cup (1): Moore 1.
CIS Cup (0).
Challenge Cup (4): Danny Mitchell 2 (1 pen), Jack 1, Montgomerie 1.

Mitchell David 35	Agostini D 21 + 2	McInnes P 12 + 4	Nicoll K 26 + 1	Henderson M 26 + 3	Aitken S 3 + 5	McGeouch D 13 + 5	Mitchell Danny 34	Moore M 25 + 6	Jack M 8 + 8	Noble S 34	Montgomerie R 13 + 19	McColm S 15 + 6	McMahon D — + 1	Wright K 4 + 3	Jones R 2 + 4	McGrath P — + 2	Mitchell G 24 + 2	Sharp L 25	Donald B — + 1	McManus S 5 + 6	Bouadii R 21	One A 15 + 4	Agnew S 20	Cawley K 14 + 1	McKillop R — + 1	Carnaghan A — + 1	Marshall R 1	Match No.
1	2	3	4	5	6	7	8	9	10²	11	12	13																1
1	2	3	4	5	6²	7³	8	9	10¹	11	14	12	13															2
1	2	3³	4	5	12	7	8¹	9	13	11		10²		6	14													3
1	2	3³	4	5	14	7¹	8	9	13	11	12	10²		6														4
1	2	3³	4	5		14	8		9²	11	7	13		6¹		12	13											5
1	2	3		5	12	13	8		9³	11	7	10¹		6²		14	4											6
1	2	3³	4	5		13	8	12	9	11	7	10¹		6														7
1		4	5	6²	3¹	8	9	12	11	7	10		13	2														8
1		5	4		8¹	2	10	13	9	7³	11²		12		6	3	14											9
1		6	5		8	2	9	12	11	7¹	10			4	3													10
1	4		5		7	8	9³	10²	11	14	12		6¹		2	3	13											11
1	4¹	12		5¹		7	8	9	10³	11	13	14		6²		2	3											12
1	4	7	14		6³	8	10	13	9		12²				2	5	11¹	3										13
1	5	6¹	7			8	9	12	11	13					2	3	13²	4										14
1	4	6²	10	5		14	8		9¹		12			13		7	3	11³	2									15
1	5¹	6²	7	12		14	8	9		11	¹3					2	3	10	4³									16
1	5		10			6	8	9²	13	3¹	12					2			4	7	11							17
1	4¹		8	5		6	7	10²			14	13		12		2				3³	11	9						18
1		11	4			7	8		3		10					2	5				6	9						19
1		7	4³			6	13		8	12	10¹		14			2	5			3	11²	9						20
1	13	7	4²			8	12		9		11³					2⁴	5		14	3	10	6						21
1³	2	3				5	13		6	12	11						8			4	10²	7	9¹	15				22
1	2	4	12			8			9	13	10						5			3¹	7	6	11²					23
1	2¹	6	13			7	12		10	14	8²						5			4	11	3	9³					24
1	14	6⁴	4			7	12		8	13	11¹						3			2	10¹	5	9					25
1			3			7	11¹		9	12						1	6			2	10	5	8					26
1		4	3			8	11¹		7	13						12	5			2	10²	6	9					27
1		6¹	3			5	11		9	12							4		13	2	10	8	7²					28
1	2	12				9	11²		8	¹3						4	5			3	10	6	7¹					29
1						7	11		9	2						3	5		12	4¹	10	6	8					30
1			4			7	11		6	9						2²	3		13	5¹	10	8	12					31
1			4			7	10		3	11						2	5		13	6¹	12²	3	9					32
1	4		5	13			11¹		9	6				12		3			10	2		7²	8					33
1	4	13	7	3			11¹		9	10						2	5				12	6²	6³		14			34
	2⁴	13	7		14		8	11		9	5²						4				3¹	¹2	6³	10			1	35
1			7	4			8	10		9	11¹						2	5				12	3	6				36

SCOTTISH LEAGUE PLAY-OFFS 2009–10

■ *Denotes player sent off.*

DIVISION 1 SEMI-FINALS FIRST LEG

Wednesday, 5 May 2010

Brechin C (2) 2 *(McAllister 10, King 44 (pen))*

Airdrie U (1) 1 *(Gemmill 15)*   583

Brechin C: Nelson C; Walker, Docherty, Smith B, McLean, Byers, Fusco, Canning, McAllister, King, Archdeacon (Vallers).
Airdrie U: Hollis; Storey, Smyth, Donnelly, Lovering (Trouten), McCann R, McLaughlin, Gemmill, Waddell, O'Carroll (Keegan), Baird.

Cowdenbeath (0) 1 *(Dempster 90)*

Alloa Ath (1) 1 *(Gormley 16)*   578

Cowdenbeath: Hay; Baxter, Adamson, Mbu, Linton, Ramsay (Fairbairn), McGregor, Robertson, McBride (Stein), Wardlaw, McQuade (Dempster).
Alloa Ath: Crawford; McClune, Townsley, Walker, McCafferty, Scott (Thomson), Grant, Hay, McAvoy, Prunty (Carroll), Gormley.

DIVISION 1 SEMI-FINALS SECOND LEG

Saturday, 8 May 2010

Airdrie U (0) 0

Brechin C (0) 1 *(McAllister 61)*   1156

Airdrie U: Hollis; Parratt (Darren Smith), Smyth, Donnelly, Storey (McDonald), Gemmill, McCann R, McLaughlin, Waddell, O'Carroll (Keegan), Baird.
Brechin C: Nelson C; Walker R, McLean, Smith B, Docherty, King (Masson), Fusco, Canning, Byers, McAllister, Vallers (Archdeacon).

Alloa Ath (0) 0

Cowdenbeath (0) 2 *(Wardlaw 59, McQuade 82)*   1234

Alloa Ath: Crawford; McClune, Townsley, Walker, McCafferty, Gormley, Brown (Thomson), Grant, Scott (Hay), Prunty (Craig), Carroll.
Cowdenbeath: Hay; Armstrong, Mbu, Baxter, Adamson, Fairbairn, Winter, McGregor, McBride, Wardlaw (Dempster), McQuade (Ramsay).

DIVISION 1 FINAL FIRST LEG

Wednesday, 12 May 2010

Cowdenbeath (0) 0

Brechin C (0) 0   1119

Cowdenbeath: Hay; Armstrong, Baxter, Mbu, Adamson, Fairbairn (Dempster), Winter, McGregor, McBride, Wardlaw, McQuade (Ramsay).
Brechin C: Nelson C (Scott); Walker R, Smith B, McLean, Docherty, Canning, Fusco, Vallers, Archdeacon (Byers), McAllister, King.

DIVISION 1 FINAL SECOND LEG

Sunday, 16 May 2010

Brechin C (0) 0

Cowdenbeath (3) 3 *(Mbu 17, Wardlaw 25, 45)*   1627

Brechin C: Scott; Walker R, Smith B, McLean, Docherty, Byers (Archdeacon), Vallers (Masson), Fusco, Canning, King (Cowan), McAllister.
Cowdenbeath: Hay; Armstrong (Robertson), Linton, McGregor, Baxter, Mbu, Winter, McQuade (Dempster), Fairbairn, Wardlaw, McBride (Stein).

DIVISION 2 SEMI-FINALS FIRST LEG

Wednesday, 5 May 2010

East Stirling (0) 0

Forfar Ath (0) 1 *(Campbell R 84 (pen))*   487

East Stirling: Barclay; Donaldson, Harding, Bolochoweckyi, Richardson, Weaver, Dunn, Forrest, Ure (Rodgers), Stevenson (Johnston), Lynch.
Forfar Ath: McLean; McCulloch, Bishop, Tod, Tulloch, Harty (Gordon), Campbell R, Fotheringham M (Deasley), Watson, Templeman (Gibson), Mowat.

Queen's Park (0) 0

Arbroath (2) 4 *(Ross 24, Redman 45, Nimmo 53, Moyes 68)*   651

Queen's Park: McGeown; Little, Brough, Gallagher, Douglas, Stewart, Capuano (Watt), Quinn T, Henry (Hamilton C), Daly, McBride.
Arbroath: Hill; Rattray, Moyes, McLaughlin, Doris (Scott), Redman (Gibson), Nimmo, McCulloch, Booth, Megginson, Ross (McLean).

DIVISION 2 SEMI-FINALS SECOND LEG

Saturday, 8 May 2010

Arbroath (2) 2 *(McCulloch 3, Megginson 15)*

Queen's Park (0) 2 *(Daly 57, Rattray 82 (og))*   588

Arbroath: Hill; Booth, Moyes, Rattray, McLaughlin (McGuire), McCulloch, Gibson, Nimmo, Megginson (McLean), Doris (Scott), Ross.
Queen's Park: McGeown; Little, McBride (Henry), Gallagher, Walker, O'Hara, Douglas, Stewart (Hamilton C), Daly, Quinn T, Watt.

Forfar Ath (1) 2 *(Bishop 4, Tulloch 82)*

East Stirling (0) 2 *(Rodgers 49, 76)*   745

Forfar Ath: McLean; McCulloch, Bishop, Tod, Tulloch, Sellars (Fotheringham K), Mowat, Watson, Campbell I, Campbell R (Templeman), Harty (Fotheringham M).
East Stirling: Barclay; Donaldson, Harding (Johnston), Bolochoweckyi, Forrest■, Stevenson, Weaver, Dunn (McKenzie), Richardson, Rodgers, Lynch.

DIVISION 2 FINAL FIRST LEG

Wednesday, 12 May 2010

Arbroath (0) 0

Forfar Ath (0) 0   1027

Arbroath: Hill; McLaughlin, Moyes, Rattray, Doris, Redman, Nimmo (Gibson), McCulloch, Booth, Megginson, Scott (Hislop).
Forfar Ath: McLean; McCulloch, Bishop, Tod, Tulloch, Sellars, Mowat, Watson, Campbell I, Templeman, Gibson.

DIVISION 2 FINAL SECOND LEG

Sunday, 16 May 2010

Forfar Ath (1) 2 *(Fotheringham M 5, Deasley 90)*

Arbroath (0) 0   2207

Forfar Ath: McLean; McCulloch, Tulloch■, Bishop, Tod, Sellars, Watson (Fotheringham K), Mowat, Gibson, Templeman (Gordon), Fotheringham M (Deasley).
Arbroath: Hill; Rattray, McLaughlin, McGuire (Suttie), Doris, Gibson (Nimmo), McCulloch, Booth, McLean, Megginson (McIlravey), Ross.

SCOTTISH LEAGUE HONOURS 1890 to 2010

*On goal average (ratio)/difference. †Held jointly after indecisive play-off. ‡Won on deciding match.
††Held jointly. ¶Two points deducted for fielding ineligible player.
Competition suspended 1940–45 during war; Regional Leagues operating. ‡‡Two points deducted for registration
irregularities. §Not promoted after play-offs.

PREMIER LEAGUE
Maximum points: 108

	First	Pts	Second	Pts	Third	Pts
1998–99	Rangers	77	Celtic	71	St Johnstone	57
1999–2000	Rangers	90	Celtic	69	Hearts	54

Maximum points: 114

	First	Pts	Second	Pts	Third	Pts
2000–01	Celtic	97	Rangers	82	Hibernian	66
2001–02	Celtic	103	Rangers	85	Livingston	58
2002–03	Rangers*	97	Celtic	97	Hearts	63
2003–04	Celtic	98	Rangers	81	Hearts	68
2004–05	Rangers	93	Celtic	92	Hibernian*	61
2005–06	Celtic	91	Hearts	74	Rangers	73
2006–07	Celtic	84	Rangers	72	Aberdeen	65
2007–08	Celtic	89	Rangers	86	Motherwell	60
2008–09	Rangers	86	Celtic	82	Hearts	59
2009–10	Rangers	87	Celtic	81	Dundee U	63

PREMIER DIVISION
Maximum points: 72

	First	Pts	Second	Pts	Third	Pts
1975–76	Rangers	54	Celtic	48	Hibernian	43
1976–77	Celtic	55	Rangers	46	Aberdeen	43
1977–78	Rangers	55	Aberdeen	53	Dundee U	40
1978–79	Celtic	48	Rangers	45	Dundee U	44
1979–80	Aberdeen	48	Celtic	47	St Mirren	42
1980–81	Celtic	56	Aberdeen	49	Rangers*	44
1981–82	Celtic	55	Aberdeen	53	Rangers	43
1982–83	Dundee U	56	Celtic*	55	Aberdeen	55
1983–84	Aberdeen	57	Celtic	50	Dundee U	47
1984–85	Aberdeen	59	Celtic	52	Dundee U	47
1985–86	Celtic*	50	Hearts	50	Dundee U	47

Maximum points: 88

	First	Pts	Second	Pts	Third	Pts
1986–87	Rangers	69	Celtic	63	Dundee U	60
1987–88	Celtic	72	Hearts	62	Rangers	60

Maximum points: 72

	First	Pts	Second	Pts	Third	Pts
1988–89	Rangers	56	Aberdeen	50	Celtic	46
1989–90	Rangers	51	Aberdeen*	44	Hearts	44
1990–91	Rangers	55	Aberdeen	53	Celtic*	41

Maximum points: 88

	First	Pts	Second	Pts	Third	Pts
1991–92	Rangers	72	Hearts	63	Celtic	62
1992–93	Rangers	73	Aberdeen	64	Celtic	60
1993–94	Rangers	58	Aberdeen	55	Motherwell	54

Maximum points: 108

	First	Pts	Second	Pts	Third	Pts
1994–95	Rangers	69	Motherwell	54	Hibernian	53
1995–96	Rangers	87	Celtic	83	Aberdeen*	55
1996–97	Rangers	80	Celtic	75	Dundee U	60
1997–98	Celtic	74	Rangers	72	Hearts	67

FIRST DIVISION
Maximum points: 52

	First	Pts	Second	Pts	Third	Pts
1975–76	Partick Th	41	Kilmarnock	35	Montrose	30

Maximum points: 78

	First	Pts	Second	Pts	Third	Pts
1976–77	St Mirren	62	Clydebank	58	Dundee	51
1977–78	Morton*	58	Hearts	58	Dundee	57
1978–79	Dundee	55	Kilmarnock*	54	Clydebank	54
1979–80	Hearts	53	Airdrieonians	51	Ayr U*	44
1980–81	Hibernian	57	Dundee	52	St Johnstone	51
1981–82	Motherwell	61	Kilmarnock	51	Hearts	50
1982–83	St Johnstone	55	Hearts	54	Clydebank	50
1983–84	Morton	54	Dumbarton	51	Partick Th	46
1984–85	Motherwell	50	Clydebank	48	Falkirk	45
1985–86	Hamilton A	56	Falkirk	45	Kilmarnock	44

Maximum points: 88

	First	Pts	Second	Pts	Third	Pts
1986–87	Morton	57	Dunfermline Ath	56	Dumbarton	53
1987–88	Hamilton A	56	Meadowbank Th	52	Clydebank	49

Maximum points: 78

	First	Pts	Second	Pts	Third	Pts
1988–89	Dunfermline Ath	54	Falkirk	52	Clydebank	48
1989–90	St Johnstone	58	Airdrieonians	54	Clydebank	44
1990–91	Falkirk	54	Airdrieonians	53	Dundee	52

Maximum points: 88

	First	Pts	Second	Pts	Third	Pts
1991–92	Dundee	58	Partick Th*	57	Hamilton A	57
1992–93	Raith R	65	Kilmarnock	54	Dunfermline Ath	52
1993–94	Falkirk	66	Dunfermline Ath	65	Airdrieonians	54

Maximum points: 108

	First	Pts	Second	Pts	Third	Pts
1994–95	Raith R	69	Dunfermline Ath*	68	Dundee	68
1995–96	Dunfermline Ath	71	Dundee U*	67	Morton	67

	First	Pts	Second	Pts	Third	Pts
1996–97	St Johnstone	80	Airdrieonians	60	Dundee*	58
1997–98	Dundee	70	Falkirk	65	Raith R*	60
1998–99	Hibernian	89	Falkirk	66	Ayr U	62
1999–2000	St Mirren	76	Dunfermline Ath	71	Falkirk	68
2000–01	Livingston	76	Ayr U	69	Falkirk	56
2001–02	Partick Th	66	Airdrieonians	56	Ayr U	52
2002–03	Falkirk	81	Clyde	72	St Johnstone	67
2003–04	Inverness CT	70	Clyde	69	St Johnstone	57
2004–05	Falkirk	75	St Mirren*	60	Clyde	60
2005–06	St Mirren	76	St Johnstone	66	Hamilton A	59
2006–07	Gretna	66	St Johnstone	65	Dundee*	53
2007–08	Hamilton A	76	Dundee	69	St Johnstone	58
2008–09	St Johnstone	65	Partick Th	55	Dunfermline Ath	51
2009–10	Inverness CT	73	Dundee	61	Dunfermline Ath	58

SECOND DIVISION
Maximum points: 52

	First	Pts	Second	Pts	Third	Pts
1975–76	Clydebank*	40	Raith R	40	Alloa Ath	35

Maximum points: 78

	First	Pts	Second	Pts	Third	Pts
1976–77	Stirling Alb	55	Alloa Ath	51	Dunfermline Ath	50
1977–78	Clyde*	53	Raith R	53	Dunfermline Ath	48
1978–79	Berwick R	54	Dunfermline Ath	52	Falkirk	50
1979–80	Falkirk	50	East Stirling	49	Forfar Ath	46
1980–81	Queen's Park	50	Queen of the S	46	Cowdenbeath	45
1981–82	Clyde	59	Alloa Ath*	50	Arbroath	50
1982–83	Brechin C	55	Meadowbank Th	54	Arbroath	49
1983–84	Forfar Ath	63	East Fife	47	Berwick R	43
1984–85	Montrose	53	Alloa Ath	50	Dunfermline Ath	49
1985–86	Dunfermline Ath	57	Queen of the S	55	Meadowbank Th	49
1986–87	Meadowbank Th	55	Raith R*	52	Stirling Alb*	52
1987–88	Ayr U	61	St Johnstone	59	Queen's Park	51
1988–89	Albion R	50	Alloa Ath	45	Brechin C	43
1989–90	Brechin C	49	Kilmarnock	48	Stirling Alb	47
1990–91	Stirling Alb	54	Montrose	46	Cowdenbeath	45
1991–92	Dumbarton	52	Cowdenbeath	51	Alloa Ath	50
1992–93	Clyde	54	Brechin C*	53	Stranraer	53
1993–94	Stranraer	56	Berwick R	48	Stenhousemuir*	47

Maximum points: 108

	First	Pts	Second	Pts	Third	Pts
1994–95	Morton	64	Dumbarton	60	Stirling Alb	58
1995–96	Stirling Alb	81	East Fife	67	Berwick R	60
1996–97	Ayr U	77	Hamilton A	74	Livingston	64
1997–98	Stranraer	61	Clydebank	60	Livingston	59
1998–99	Livingston	77	Inverness CT	72	Clyde	53
1999–2000	Clyde	65	Alloa Ath	64	Ross Co	62
2000–01	Partick Th	75	Arbroath	58	Berwick R*	54
2001–02	Queen of the S	67	Alloa Ath	59	Forfar Ath	53
2002–03	Raith R	59	Brechin C	55	Airdrie U	54
2003–04	Airdrie U	70	Hamilton A	62	Dumbarton	60
2004–05	Brechin C	72	Stranraer	63	Morton	62
2005–06	Gretna	88	Morton§	70	Peterhead*§	57
2006–07	Morton	77	Stirling Alb	69	Raith R§	62
2007–08	Ross Co	73	Airdrie U	66	Raith R§	60
2008–09	Raith R	76	Ayr U	74	Brechin C§	62
2009–10	Stirling Alb*	65	Alloa Ath§	65	Cowdenbeath	54

THIRD DIVISION
Maximum points: 108

	First	Pts	Second	Pts	Third	Pts
1994–95	Forfar Ath	80	Montrose	67	Ross Co	60
1995–96	Livingston	72	Brechin C	63	Inverness CT	57
1996–97	Inverness CT	76	Forfar Ath*	67	Ross Co	67
1997–98	Alloa Ath	76	Arbroath	68	Ross Co*	67
1998–99	Ross Co	77	Stenhousemuir	64	Brechin C	59
1999–2000	Queen's Park	69	Berwick R	66	Forfar Ath	61
2000–01	Hamilton A*	76	Cowdenbeath	76	Brechin C	72
2001–02	Brechin C	73	Dumbarton	61	Albion R	59
2002–03	Morton	72	East Fife	71	Albion R	70
2003–04	Stranraer	79	Stirling Alb	77	Gretna	68
2004–05	Gretna	98	Peterhead	78	Cowdenbeath	51
2005–06	Cowdenbeath*	76	Berwick R§	76	Stenhousemuir§	73
2006–07	Berwick R	75	Arbroath§	70	Queen's Park§	68
2007–08	East Fife	88	Stranraer	65	Montrose§	59
2008–09	Dumbarton	67	Cowdenbeath§	63	East Stirling§	61
2009–10	Livingston	78	Forfar Ath	63	East Stirling§	61

FIRST DIVISION to 1974–75
Maximum points: a 36; b 44; c 40; d 52; e 60; f 68; g 76; h 84.

	First	Pts	Second	Pts	Third	Pts
1890–91a	Dumbarton††	29	Rangers††	29	Celtic	21
1891–92b	Dumbarton	37	Celtic	35	Hearts	34
1892–93a	Celtic	29	Rangers	28	St Mirren	20
1893–94a	Celtic	29	Hearts	26	St Bernard's	23
1894–95a	Hearts	31	Celtic	26	Rangers	22
1895–96a	Celtic	30	Rangers	26	Hibernian	24
1896–97a	Hearts	28	Hibernian	26	Rangers	25
1897–98a	Celtic	33	Rangers	29	Hibernian	22
1898–99a	Rangers	36	Hearts	26	Celtic	24
1899–1900a	Rangers	32	Celtic	25	Hibernian	24

	First	Pts	Second	Pts	Third	Pts
1900–01c	Rangers	35	Celtic	29	Hibernian	25
1901–02a	Rangers	28	Celtic	26	Hearts	22
1902–03b	Hibernian	37	Dundee	31	Rangers	29
1903–04d	Third Lanark	43	Hearts	39	Celtic*	38
1904–05d	Celtic‡	41	Rangers	41	Third Lanark	35
1905–06e	Celtic	49	Hearts	43	Airdrieonians	38
1906–07f	Celtic	55	Dundee	48	Rangers	45
1907–08f	Celtic	55	Falkirk	51	Rangers	50
1908–09f	Celtic	51	Dundee	50	Clyde	48
1909–10f	Celtic	54	Falkirk	52	Rangers	46
1910–11f	Rangers	52	Aberdeen	48	Falkirk	44
1911–12f	Rangers	51	Celtic	45	Clyde	42
1912–13f	Rangers	53	Celtic	49	Hearts*	41
1913–14g	Celtic	65	Rangers	59	Hearts*	54
1914–15g	Celtic	65	Hearts	61	Rangers	50
1915–16g	Celtic	67	Rangers	56	Morton	51
1916–17g	Celtic	64	Morton	54	Rangers	53
1917–18f	Rangers	56	Celtic	55	Kilmarnock*	43
1918–19f	Celtic	58	Rangers	57	Morton	47
1919–20h	Rangers	71	Celtic	68	Motherwell	57
1920–21h	Rangers	76	Celtic	66	Hearts	50
1921–22h	Celtic	67	Rangers	66	Raith R	51
1922–23g	Rangers	55	Airdrieonians	50	Celtic	46
1923–24g	Rangers	59	Airdrieonians	50	Celtic	46
1924–25g	Rangers	60	Airdrieonians	57	Hibernian	52
1925–26g	Celtic	58	Airdrieonians*	50	Hearts	50
1926–27g	Rangers	56	Motherwell	51	Celtic	49
1927–28g	Rangers	60	Celtic*	55	Motherwell	55
1928–29g	Rangers	67	Celtic	51	Motherwell	50
1929–30g	Rangers	60	Motherwell	55	Aberdeen	53
1930–31g	Rangers	60	Celtic	58	Motherwell	56
1931–32g	Motherwell	66	Rangers	61	Celtic	48
1932–33g	Rangers	62	Motherwell	59	Hearts	50
1933–34g	Rangers	66	Motherwell	62	Celtic	47
1934–35g	Rangers	55	Celtic	52	Hearts	50
1935–36g	Celtic	66	Rangers*	61	Aberdeen	61
1936–37g	Rangers	61	Aberdeen	54	Celtic	52
1937–38g	Celtic	61	Hearts	58	Rangers	49
1938–39g	Rangers	59	Celtic	48	Aberdeen	46
1946–47e	Rangers	46	Hibernian	44	Aberdeen	39
1947–48e	Hibernian	48	Rangers	46	Partick Th	36
1948–49e	Rangers	46	Dundee	45	Hibernian	39
1949–50e	Rangers	50	Hibernian	49	Hearts	43
1950–51e	Hibernian	48	Rangers*	38	Dundee	38
1951–52e	Hibernian	45	Rangers	41	East Fife	37
1952–53e	Rangers*	43	Hibernian	43	East Fife	39
1953–54e	Celtic	43	Hearts	38	Partick Th	35
1954–55e	Aberdeen	49	Celtic	46	Rangers	41
1955–56f	Rangers	52	Aberdeen	46	Hearts*	45
1956–57f	Rangers	55	Hearts	53	Kilmarnock	42
1957–58f	Hearts	62	Rangers	49	Celtic	46
1958–59f	Rangers	50	Hearts	48	Motherwell	44
1959–60f	Hearts	54	Kilmarnock	50	Rangers*	42
1960–61f	Rangers	51	Kilmarnock	50	Third Lanark	42
1961–62f	Dundee	54	Rangers	51	Celtic	46
1962–63f	Rangers	57	Kilmarnock	48	Partick Th	46
1963–64f	Rangers	55	Kilmarnock	49	Celtic*	47
1964–65f	Kilmarnock*	50	Hearts	50	Dunfermline Ath	49
1965–66f	Celtic	57	Rangers	55	Kilmarnock	45
1966–67f	Celtic	58	Rangers	55	Clyde	46
1967–68f	Celtic	63	Rangers	61	Hibernian	45
1968–69f	Celtic	54	Rangers	49	Dunfermline Ath	45
1969–70f	Celtic	57	Rangers	45	Hibernian	44
1970–71f	Celtic	56	Aberdeen	54	St Johnstone	44
1971–72f	Celtic	60	Aberdeen	50	Rangers	44
1972–73f	Celtic	57	Rangers	56	Hibernian	45
1973–74f	Celtic	53	Hibernian	49	Rangers	48
1974–75f	Rangers	56	Hibernian	49	Celtic	45

SECOND DIVISION to 1974–75

Maximum points: a 76; b 72; c 68; d 52; e 60; f 36; g 44.

	First	Pts	Second	Pts	Third	Pts
1893–94f	Hibernian	29	Cowlairs	27	Clyde	24
1894–95f	Hibernian	30	Motherwell	22	Port Glasgow	20
1895–96f	Abercorn	27	Leith Ath	23	Renton	21
1896–97f	Partick Th	31	Leith Ath	27	Kilmarnock*	21
1897–98f	Kilmarnock	29	Port Glasgow	25	Morton	22
1898–99f	Kilmarnock	32	Leith Ath	27	Port Glasgow	25
1899–1900f	Partick Th	29	Morton	28	Port Glasgow	20
1900–01f	St Bernard's	25	Airdrieonians	23	Abercorn	21
1901–02g	Port Glasgow	32	Partick Th	31	Motherwell	26
1902–03g	Airdrieonians	35	Motherwell	28	Ayr U*	27
1903–04g	Hamilton A	37	Clyde	29	Ayr U	28
1904–05g	Clyde	32	Falkirk	28	Hamilton A	27
1905–06g	Leith Ath	34	Clyde	31	Albion R	27
1906–07g	St Bernard's	32	Vale of Leven*	27	Arthurlie	27

	First	Pts	Second	Pts	Third	Pts
1907–08g	Raith R	30	Dumbarton*‡‡	27	Ayr U	27
1908–09g	Abercorn	31	Raith R*	28	Vale of Leven	28
1909–10g	Leith Ath‡	33	Raith R	33	St Bernard's	27
1910–11g	Dumbarton	31	Ayr U	27	Albion R	25
1911–12g	Ayr U	35	Abercorn	30	Dumbarton	27
1912–13d	Ayr U	34	Dunfermline Ath	33	East Stirling	32
1913–14g	Cowdenbeath	31	Albion R	27	Dunfermline Ath*	26
1914–15d	Cowdenbeath*	37	St Bernard's*	37	Leith Ath	37
1921–22a	Alloa Ath	60	Cowdenbeath	47	Armadale	45
1922–23a	Queen's Park	57	Clydebank¶	50	St Johnstone¶	45
1923–24a	St Johnstone	56	Cowdenbeath	55	Bathgate	44
1924–25a	Dundee U	50	Clydebank	48	Clyde	47
1925–26a	Dunfermline Ath	59	Clyde	53	Ayr U	52
1926–27a	Bo'ness	56	Raith R	49	Clydebank	45
1927–28a	Ayr U	54	Third Lanark	45	King's Park	44
1928–29b	Dundee U	51	Morton	50	Arbroath	47
1929–30a	Leith Ath*	57	East Fife	57	Albion R	54
1930–31a	Third Lanark	61	Dundee U	50	Dunfermline Ath	47
1931–32a	East Stirling*	55	St Johnstone	55	Raith R*	46
1932–33c	Hibernian	54	Queen of the S	49	Dunfermline Ath	47
1933–34c	Albion R	45	Dunfermline Ath*	44	Arbroath	44
1934–35c	Third Lanark	52	Arbroath	50	St Bernard's	47
1935–36c	Falkirk	59	St Mirren	52	Morton	48
1936–37c	Ayr U	54	Morton	51	St Bernard's	48
1937–38c	Raith R	59	Albion R	48	Airdrieonians	47
1938–39c	Cowdenbeath	60	Alloa Ath*	48	East Fife	48
1946–47d	Dundee	45	Airdrieonians	42	East Fife	31
1947–48e	East Fife	53	Albion R	42	Hamilton A	40
1948–49e	Raith R*	42	Stirling Alb	42	Airdrieonians*	41
1949–50e	Morton	47	Airdrieonians	44	Dunfermline Ath*	36
1950–51e	Queen of the S*	45	Stirling Alb	45	Ayr U*	36
1951–52e	Clyde	44	Falkirk	43	Ayr U	39
1952–53e	Stirling Alb	44	Hamilton A	43	Queen's Park	37
1953–54e	Motherwell	45	Kilmarnock	42	Third Lanark*	36
1954–55e	Airdrieonians	46	Dunfermline Ath	42	Hamilton A	39
1955–56b	Queen's Park	54	Ayr U	51	St Johnstone	49
1956–57b	Clyde	64	Third Lanark	51	Cowdenbeath	45
1957–58b	Stirling Alb	55	Dunfermline Ath	53	Arbroath	47
1958–59b	Ayr U	60	Arbroath	51	Stenhousemuir	46
1959–60b	St Johnstone	53	Dundee U	50	Queen of the S	49
1960–61b	Stirling Alb	55	Falkirk	54	Stenhousemuir	50
1961–62b	Clyde	54	Queen of the S	53	Morton	44
1962–63b	St Johnstone	55	East Stirling	49	Morton	48
1963–64b	Morton	67	Clyde	53	Arbroath	46
1964–65b	Stirling Alb	59	Hamilton A	50	Queen of the S	45
1965–66b	Ayr U	53	Airdrieonians	50	Queen of the S	47
1966–67a	Morton	69	Raith R	58	Arbroath	57
1967–68b	St Mirren	62	Arbroath	53	East Fife	49
1968–69b	Motherwell	64	Ayr U	53	East Fife*	48
1969–70b	Falkirk	56	Cowdenbeath	55	Queen of the S	50
1970–71b	Partick Th	56	East Fife	51	Arbroath	46
1971–72b	Dumbarton*	52	Arbroath	52	Stirling Alb	50
1972–73b	Clyde	56	Dunfermline Ath	52	Raith R*	47
1973–74b	Airdrieonians	60	Kilmarnock	58	Hamilton A	55
1974–75a	Falkirk	54	Queen of the S*	53	Montrose	53

Elected to First Division: 1894 Clyde; 1895 Hibernian; 1896 Abercorn; 1897 Partick Th; 1899 Kilmarnock; 1900 Morton and Partick Th; 1902 Port Glasgow and Partick Th; 1903 Airdrieonians and Motherwell; 1905 Falkirk and Aberdeen; 1906 Clyde and Hamilton A; 1910 Raith R; 1913 Ayr U and Dumbarton.

RELEGATED FROM PREMIER LEAGUE

1998–99 Dunfermline Ath
1999–2000 *No relegation due to League reorganization*
2000–01 St Mirren
2001–02 St Johnstone
2002–03 *No relegated team*
2003–04 Partick Th

2004–05 Dundee
2005–06 Livingston
2006–07 Dunfermline Ath
2007–08 Gretna
2008–09 Inverness CT
2009–10 Falkirk

RELEGATED FROM PREMIER DIVISION

1974–75 *No relegation due to League reorganization*
1975–76 Dundee, St Johnstone
1976–77 Hearts, Kilmarnock
1977–78 Ayr U, Clydebank
1978–79 Hearts, Motherwell
1979–80 Dundee, Hibernian
1980–81 Kilmarnock, Hearts
1981–82 Partick Th, Airdrieonians
1982–83 Morton, Kilmarnock
1983–84 St Johnstone, Motherwell
1984–85 Dumbarton, Morton
1985–86 *No relegation due to League reorganization*

1986–87 Clydebank, Hamilton A
1987–88 Falkirk, Dunfermline Ath, Morton
1988–89 Hamilton A
1989–90 Dundee
1990–91 *None*
1991–92 St Mirren, Dunfermline Ath
1992–93 Falkirk, Airdrieonians
1993–94 *See footnote*
1994–95 Dundee U
1995–96 Partick Th, Falkirk
1996–97 Raith R
1997–98 Hibernian

RELEGATED FROM DIVISION 1

1975–76 Dunfermline Ath, Clyde
1976–77 Raith R, Falkirk

1978–79 Montrose, Queen of the S
1979–80 Arbroath, Clyde

1977–78	Alloa Ath, East Fife	1980–81	Stirling Alb, Berwick R
1981–82	East Stirling, Queen of the S	1996–97	Clydebank, East Fife
1982–83	Dunfermline Ath, Queen's Park	1997–98	Partick Th, Stirling Alb
1983–84	Raith R, Alloa Ath	1998–99	Hamilton A, Stranraer
1984–85	Meadowbank Th, St Johnstone	1999–2000	Clydebank
1985–86	Ayr U, Alloa Ath	2000–01	Morton, Alloa Ath
1986–87	Brechin C, Montrose	2001–02	Raith R
1987–88	East Fife, Dumbarton	2002–03	Alloa Ath, Arbroath
1988–89	Kilmarnock, Queen of the S	2003–04	Ayr U, Brechin C
1989–90	Albion R, Alloa Ath	2004–05	Partick Th, Raith R
1990–91	Clyde, Brechin C	2005–06	Stranraer, Brechin C
1992–93	Meadowbank Th, Cowdenbeath	2006–07	Airdrie U, Ross Co
1993–94	*See footnote*	2007–08	Stirling Alb
1994–95	Ayr U, Stranraer	2008–09	Clyde
1995–96	Hamilton A, Dumbarton	2009–10	Airdrie U, Ayr U

RELEGATED FROM DIVISION 2

1994–95	Meadowbank Th, Brechin C	2002–03	Stranraer, Cowdenbeath
1995–96	Forfar Ath, Montrose	2003–04	East Fife, Stenhousemuir
1996–97	Dumbarton, Berwick R	2004–05	Arbroath, Berwick R
1997–98	Stenhousemuir, Brechin C	2005–06	Dumbarton
1998–99	East Fife, Forfar Ath	2006–07	Stranraer, Forfar Ath
1999–2000	Hamilton A**	2007–08	Cowdenbeath, Berwick R
2000–01	Queen's Park, Stirling Alb	2008–09	Stranraer, Queen's Park
2001–02	Morton	2009–10	Arbroath, Clyde

RELEGATED FROM DIVISION 1 (TO 1973–74)

1921–22	*Queen's Park, Dumbarton, Clydebank	1951–52	Morton, Stirling Alb
1922–23	Albion R, Alloa Ath	1952–53	Motherwell, Third Lanark
1923–24	Clyde, Clydebank	1953–54	Airdrieonians, Hamilton A
1924–25	Third Lanark, Ayr U	1954–55	*No clubs relegated*
1925–26	Raith R, Clydebank	1955–56	Stirling Alb, Clyde
1926–27	Morton, Dundee U	1956–57	Dunfermline Ath, Ayr U
1927–28	Dunfermline Ath, Bo'ness	1957–58	East Fife, Queen's Park
1928–29	Third Lanark, Raith R	1958–59	Queen of the S, Falkirk
1929–30	St Johnstone, Dundee U	1959–60	Arbroath, Stirling Alb
1930–31	Hibernian, East Fife	1960–61	Ayr U, Clyde
1931–32	Dundee U, Leith Ath	1961–62	St Johnstone, Stirling Alb
1932–33	Morton, East Stirling	1962–63	Clyde, Raith R
1933–34	Third Lanark, Cowdenbeath	1963–64	Queen of the S, East Stirling
1934–35	St Mirren, Falkirk	1964–65	Airdrieonians, Third Lanark
1935–36	Airdrieonians, Ayr U	1965–66	Morton, Hamilton A
1936–37	Dunfermline Ath, Albion R	1966–67	St Mirren, Ayr U
1937–38	Dundee, Morton	1957–68	Motherwell, Stirling Alb
1938–39	Queen's Park, Raith R	1958–69	Falkirk, Arbroath
1946–47	Kilmarnock, Hamilton A	1969–70	Raith R, Partick Th
1947–48	Airdrieonians, Queen's Park	1970–71	St Mirren, Cowdenbeath
1948–49	Morton, Albion R	1971–72	Clyde, Dunfermline Ath
1949–50	Queen of the S, Stirling Alb	1972–73	Kilmarnock, Airdrieonians
1950–51	Clyde, Falkirk	1973–74	East Fife, Falkirk

*Season 1921–22 – only 1 club promoted, 3 clubs relegated. **15pts deducted for failing to field a team.

Scottish League Championship wins: Rangers 53, Celtic 42, Aberdeen 4, Hearts 4, Hibernian 4, Dumbarton 2, Dundee 1, Dundee U 1, Kilmarnock 1, Motherwell 1, Third Lanark 1.

At the end of the 1993–94 season four divisions were created assisted by the admission of two new clubs Ross County and Caledonian Thistle. Only one club was promoted from Division 1 and Division 2. The three relegated from the Premier joined with teams finishing second to seventh in Division 1 to form the new Division 2. Five relegated from Division 1 combined with those who finished second to sixth to form a new Division 2 and the bottom eight in Division 2 linked with the two newcomers to form a new Division 3. At the end of the 1997–98 season the nine clubs remaining in the Premier Division plus the promoted team from Division 1 formed a breakaway Premier League. At the end of the 1999–2000 season two teams were added to the Scottish League. There was no relegation from the Premier League but two promoted from the First Division and three from each of the Second and Third Divisions. One team was relegated from the First Division and one from the Second Division, leaving 12 teams in each division. In season 2002–03, Falkirk were not promoted to the Premier League due to the failure of their ground to meet League rules. Inverness CT were promoted after a previous refusal in 2003–04 because of ground sharing. At the end of 2005–06 the Scottish League introduced play-offs for the team finishing second from the bottom of Division 1 against the winners of the second, third and fourth finishing teams in Division 2 and with a similar procedure for Division 2 and Division 3.

LEAGUE CHALLENGE FINALS 1991–2010

Year	Winners	Runners-up	Score	Year	Winners	Runners-up	Score
1990–91	Dundee	Ayr U	3-2	2001–02	Airdrieonians	Alloa Ath	2-1
1991–92	Hamilton A	Ayr U	1-0	2002–03	Queen of the S	Brechin C	2-0
1992–93	Hamilton A	Morton	3-2	2003–04	Inverness CT	Airdrie U	2-0
1993–94	Falkirk	St Mirren	3-0	2004–05	Falkirk	Ross Co	2-1
1994–95	Airdrieonians	Dundee	3-2	2005–06	St Mirren	Hamilton A	2-1
1995–96	Stenhousemuir	Dundee U	0-0	2006–07	Ross Co	Clyde	1-1
	(aet; Stenhousemuir won 5-4 on penalties)				*(aet; Ross Co won 5-4 on penalties)*		
1996–97	Stranraer	St Johnstone	1-0	2007–08	St Johnstone	Dunfermline Ath	3-2
1997–98	Falkirk	Queen of the S	1-0	2008–09	Airdrie U	Ross Co	2-2
1998–99	no competition				*(aet; Airdrie U won 3-2 on penalties)*		
1999–2000	Alloa Ath	Inverness CT	4-4	2009–10	Dundee	Inverness CT	3-2
	(aet; Alloa Ath won 5-4 on penalties)						
2000–01	Airdrieonians	Livingston	2-2				
	(aet; Airdrieonians won 3-2 on penalties)						

SCOTTISH LEAGUE CUP FINALS 1946–2010

Season	Winners	Runners-up	Score
1946–47	Rangers	Aberdeen	4-0
1947–48	East Fife	Falkirk	4-1 after 0-0 draw (*aet.*)
1948–49	Rangers	Raith R	2-0
1949–50	East Fife	Dunfermline Ath	3-0
1950–51	Motherwell	Hibernian	3-0
1951–52	Dundee	Rangers	3-2
1952–53	Dundee	Kilmarnock	2-0
1953–54	East Fife	Partick Th	3-2
1954–55	Hearts	Motherwell	4-2
1955–56	Aberdeen	St Mirren	2-1
1956–57	Celtic	Partick Th	3-0 after 0-0 draw
1957–58	Celtic	Rangers	7-1
1958–59	Hearts	Partick Th	5-1
1959–60	Hearts	Third Lanark	2-1
1960–61	Rangers	Kilmarnock	2-0
1961–62	Rangers	Hearts	3-1 after 1-1 draw
1962–63	Hearts	Kilmarnock	1-0
1963–64	Rangers	Morton	5-0
1964–65	Rangers	Celtic	2-1
1965–66	Celtic	Rangers	2-1
1966–67	Celtic	Rangers	1-0
1967–68	Celtic	Dundee	5-3
1968–69	Celtic	Hibernian	6-2
1969–70	Celtic	St Johnstone	1-0
1970–71	Rangers	Celtic	1-0
1971–72	Partick Th	Celtic	4-1
1972–73	Hibernian	Celtic	2-1
1973–74	Dundee	Celtic	1-0
1974–75	Celtic	Hibernian	6-3
1975–76	Rangers	Celtic	1-0
1976–77	Aberdeen	Celtic	2-1
1977–78	Rangers	Celtic	2-1 (*aet.*)
1978–79	Rangers	Aberdeen	2-1
1979–80	Dundee U	Aberdeen	3-0 after 0-0 draw (*aet.*)
1980–81	Dundee U	Dundee	3-0
1981–82	Rangers	Dundee U	2-1
1982–83	Celtic	Rangers	2-1
1983–84	Rangers	Celtic	3-2
1984–85	Rangers	Dundee U	1-0
1985–86	Aberdeen	Hibernian	3-0
1986–87	Rangers	Celtic	2-1
1987–88	Rangers	Aberdeen	3-3
		(*aet; Rangers won 5-3 on penalties*)	
1988–89	Rangers	Aberdeen	3-2 (*aet.*)
1989–90	Aberdeen	Rangers	2-1
1990–91	Rangers	Celtic	2-1
1991–92	Hibernian	Dunfermline Ath	2-0
1992–93	Rangers	Aberdeen	2-1 (*aet.*)
1993–94	Rangers	Hibernian	2-1
1994–95	Raith R	Celtic	2-2
		(*aet; Raith R won 6-5 on penalties*)	
1995–96	Aberdeen	Dundee	2-0
1996–97	Rangers	Hearts	4-3
1997–98	Celtic	Dundee U	3-0
1998–99	Rangers	St Johnstone	2-1
1999–2000	Celtic	Aberdeen	2-0
2000–01	Celtic	Kilmarnock	3-0
2001–02	Rangers	Ayr U	4-0
2002–03	Rangers	Celtic	2-1
2003–04	Livingston	Hibernian	2-0
2004–05	Rangers	Motherwell	5-1
2005–06	Celtic	Dunfermline Ath	3-0
2006–07	Hibernian	Kilmarnock	5-1
2007–08	Rangers	Dundee U	2-2
		(*aet; Rangers won 3-2 on penalties*)	
2008–09	Celtic	Rangers	2-0 (*aet.*)
2009–10	Rangers	St Mirren	1-0

SCOTTISH LEAGUE CUP WINS

Rangers 26, Celtic 14, Aberdeen 5, Hearts 4, Dundee 3, East Fife 3, Hibernian 3, Dundee U 2, Livingston 1, Motherwell 1, Partick Th 1, Raith R 1.

APPEARANCES IN FINALS

Rangers 33, Celtic 27, Aberdeen 12, Hibernian 9, Dundee 6, Dundee U 6, Hearts 6, Kilmarnock 5, Partick Th 4, Dunfermline Ath 3, East Fife 3, Motherwell 3, Raith R 2, St Johnstone 2, St Mirren 2, Ayr U 1, Falkirk 1, Livingston 1, Morton 1, Third Lanark 1.

CIS SCOTTISH LEAGUE CUP 2009–10

■ *Denotes player sent off.*
FIRST ROUND
Saturday, 1 August 2009
Airdrie U (0) 0
Alloa Ath (0) 0 756
Airdrie U: Robertson; Darren Smith, Lovering■, McDonald, Donnelly, Nixon, Trouten (Watt), McLaughlin, Gemmill (Keegan), Baird, Lagana (Waddell).
Alloa Ath: Crawford; McClune, McCafferty (Kerr), Buist, Walker, Grant, Scott, Brown (Townsley), Spence (Anderson■), Agnew, Noble.
aet; Alloa Ath won 4-3 on penalties.

Albion R (1) 3 *(McKenzie 9 (og), Barr 48, McCusker 89)*
Livingston (0) 0 602
Albion R: Caston; Reid, McGowan, Donnelly (Canning M), Benton, O'Byrne, McKeown, Tyrrell, McFarlane (McCusker), Walker P, Barr.
Livingston: McKenzie; Hastings, Talbot, Malone, Fox, McParland, Hamill, Torrance (McKee), Sinclair, Halliday (Keaghan Jacobs), Winters D.

Brechin C (1) 4 *(McAllister 13, 63, Byers 77, McKenna 84)*
Elgin C (0) 0 406
Brechin C: Nelson C; Walker R, Seeley, McLean, Dyer, Byers, Janczyk (Docherty), Fusco (McGroarty), King, McAllister, Harty (McKenna).
Elgin C: Gibson; Dempsie, Kaczan, David W Craig, David A Craig (Cameron), Gunn, McDonald, Edwards, Crooks, Frizzel, Nicolson (Calder).

Clyde (1) 1 *(Tod 28 (og))*
Forfar Ath (0) 3 *(Campbell R 51, Fotheringham M 58, Deasley 65)* 784
Clyde: Reidford; Casey, Stevenson (Park), Gair, Lithgow, Doyle, Stewart, Lang (Fisher), Sawyers (McFadden), McLeod, McKay.
Forfar Ath: Brown; Mowat, Tulloch, Malcolm, Tod, Campbell I, Fotheringham M (Winter), Campbell R (Gordon), Deasley (Smith C), Fotheringham K, Brady.

Cowdenbeath (1) 1 *(McQuade 31 (pen))*
Morton (2) 3 *(Weatherson 7, 51, McFarlane 12)* 486
Cowdenbeath: Hay; Baxter, Mbu (Broudge), Adamson, Linton, Stein, Robertson, McCabe, McBride (Fairbairn), Wardlaw, McQuade (Dempster).
Morton: Halliwell; McGuffie (MacGregor), McManus, Greacen, Monti, Finlayson, MacFarlane, Masterton, McAlister, Weatherson (Graham), Jenkins (Wake).

Dumbarton (0) 0
Dunfermline Ath (3) 5 *(Graham 2, Kirk 9, 56, Burke 45, Bell 65)* 953
Dumbarton: McEwan; Chisholm■, Gordon, Dunlop, McKillen (Geggan), McNiff, Clark (Chaplain), O'Donoghue, Murray (Hunter), McLaughlin, Carcary.
Dunfermline Ath: Fleming; Ross, Bell, McGregor, Glass (McCann), Graham, Higgins, Burke (Holmes), Gibson (McDougall), Bayne, Kirk.

Dundee (3) 5 *(Higgins 23, Harkins 29, Cameron 37, McMenamin 47, Griffiths 67)*
Stranraer (0) 0 2345
Dundee: Bullock; Paton (Casement), Malone, McHale, Benedictus, Lauchlan, Hart, Cameron (Kerr), Higgins, McMenamin (Griffiths), Harkins.
Stranraer: David Mitchell■; McGrath (Mitchell G), Wright, Nicoll, Agostini, Donald (McInnes), McGeoch, Danny Mitchell, Montgomerie, Jack (Moore), Noble.

East Fife (2) 2 *(Linn 5, Muir 19)*
Raith R (0) 3 *(Walker 57, Tade 75, Williamson 90)* 1390
East Fife: Brown; Nugent, Ovenstone, Smart, Thomson S, Linn (Cargill), Fagan (Conway), Muir, Young, McManus, Crawford.
Raith R: McGurn; Wilson, Campbell, Murray, Ellis, Walker, Davidson, Simmons, Tade, Weir, Williamson.

Inverness CT (1) 4 *(Rooney 21, Eagle 52, Imrie 72, Sanchez 88)*
Annan Ath (0) 0 1095
Inverness CT: Allison; Tokely, Bulvitis, Munro, Djebi-Zaci, Cox, Eagle, Stratford (Ross), Rooney (Sutherland), Sanchez, Imrie (Shinnie).
Annan Ath: Summersgill; Muirhead (Sloan S), McBeth, Watson, Neilson, Jack, Steele (Storey), Gilfillan, Cox, Townsley, Sloan L.

Partick Th (1) 5 *(Hodge 29, Buchanan 49, 81 (pen), Erskine 53, 87)*
Berwick R (0) 1 *(Little 69)* 1472
Partick Th: Tuffey; Paton, Corrigan, Hodge (Hamilton), Robertson, Maxwell, McKeown, Cairney (Rowson), Buchanan, Donnelly, Corcoran (Erskine).
Berwick R: Peat; Smith E, McMullan (McMenamin), Ewart, McLean, Callaghan (Guy), Russell (Little), Currie, Brazil, Notman, Greenhill D.

Peterhead (0) 0
Arbroath (1) 3 *(Sellars 6, Bishop 48, Raeside 54)* 499
Peterhead: Jarvie; Donald (Davidson), Smith, Mann, MacDonald, Young, Strachan, Cameron, Ross, Michie (Bruce), Bavidge.
Arbroath: Hill; Rennie, McCulloch, Raeside, Rattray, Bishop, Lunan (Watson), Gibson, Doris (Redman), Hislop (Ross), Sellars.

Queen's Park (0) 1 *(Douglas 82)*
Queen of the S (3) 4 *(Quinn 1, Wilson 10, 14, Burns 70)* 886
Queen's Park: Black; Walker, Sinclair, Brough, Hamilton C (Murray), Capuano (Harkins), Tiernan, McBride, Douglas, Bailey, Watt.
Queen of the S: Hutton; Burns, Lilley, McAusland, Reid, Wilson, Tosh, Quinn (McLaughlan), McQuilken, Holmes (Kean), Weatherston (McLaren).

Ross Co (1) 5 *(Craig 43, Gardyne 56, 75, Morrison 72, Stewart 79)*
Montrose (0) 0 768
Ross Co: McGovern; Girvan, Morrison, Watt, Keddie, Lawson, Gardyne (Moore), Wood (Stewart), Craig, Brittain, Vigurs (Scott).
Montrose: Coutts; Hegarty, Pope (Sinclair), Maitland (Gray), Campbell, Crighton, Nicol, Davidson, Gemmell, Voigt (Leyden), Anderson.

Stenhousemuir (0) 0
St Johnstone (2) 5 *(Milne 22, Deuchar 28, 69, Samuel 67, 74)* 1049
Stenhousemuir: McCluskey; Lyle (Dalziel), Thomson S, Thom, Smith J, McLeod, Bradley (Stirling), Scullion, Diack (Bennett), Molloy, Motion.
St Johnstone: Main; Irvine (MacKay), Grainger, Morris, Gartland, McCaffrey, Davidson, Deuchar, Milne (Samuel), Craig, Morais (Sheerin).

Stirling Alb (1) 1 *(Devine 16)*
Ayr U (0) 2 *(Easton 61, Aitken A 114)* 802
Stirling Alb: Christie; Feaks (McCord), Forsyth■, Roycroft, Graham■, Robertson, Gibson, Murphy, McKenna (Grehan), Mullen (Corr), Devine.
Ayr U: Grindlay; Keenan, Aitken A, James, Campbell (McGowan N), Stevenson, Borris, Aitken C, Prunty (Gormley), Roberts, Easton (Cawley).
aet.

Sunday, 2 August 2009
East Stirling (3) 3 *(McGuire 23, Rodgers 27, 36)*
St Mirren (4) 6 *(Mehmet 6, 13, 17, 44, 67, O'Donnell 73)* 1024
East Stirling: Sorley; Hay, Forrest, Tully (Dunn), King, Weaver, Donaldson (Johnstone), Stevenson, McGuire, Richardson (McKenzie), Rodgers.
St Mirren: Gallacher; Ross, Camara, Brady, Mair, Potter, Dorman (Brighton), Thomson, Mehmet, Higdon (Dargo), Robb (O'Donnell).

SECOND ROUND

Tuesday, 25 August 2009

Alloa Ath (0) 0

Dundee U (2) 2 *(Shala 23, Goodwillie 39)*   1000

Alloa Ath: Crawford; McLune, Buist, Walker, McCafferty, Carroll (Carrigan), Brown, Grant, Agnew (Kerr), Scott, Gilhaney (Ferguson B).
Dundee U: Banks; Dillon, Dixon, Kenneth, Dods, Buaben, Robertson S, Gomis (Myrie-Williams), Goodwillie, Shala (Casalinuovo), Conway (McCord).

Forfar Ath (0) 2 *(Tulloch 55, Campbell R 72)*

Dundee (3) 4 *(Griffiths 11, Antoine-Curier 15, 31, Tod 67 (og))*   1929

Forfar Ath: Brown; Divine (Smith C), Campbell I, Brady, Tod, Fotheringham K, Gordon (Malcolm), Fotheringham M, Templeman, Campbell R, Deasley (Tulloch).
Dundee: Bullock; Casement (Kerr), Malone, Paton, Benedictus, Lauchlan, Cameron, Forsyth, Antoine-Curier, Griffiths, Harkins.

Inverness CT (3) 4 *(Eagle 8, Rooney 16, Bulvitis 41, Munro 57)*

Albion R (0) 0   681

Inverness CT: Esson; Tokely, Bulvitis, Munro, Djebi-Zadi (Proctor), Cox, Eagle (Ross), Stratford, Foran (Sutherland), Rooney, Hayes.
Albion R: Gaston; Reid (Boyle), McGowan, Canning M, Benton, O'Byrne, McKeown, Tyrrell, McCusker (Pollock), Walker P, Barr.

Kilmarnock (1) 3 *(Sammon 24 (pen), 64, Kyle 90)*

Morton (1) 1 *(McGuffie 44 (pen))*   3645

Kilmarnock: Combe; Hamill (Pascali), Clancy, Wright, Ford, Skelton, Bryson, Taouil, Sammon, Kyle, Invincibile (Fernandez).
Morton: McWilliams; McGuffie, Harding, McManus, Greacen, MacFarlane (Wake), Finlayson (Paartalu), Jenkins, Graham, Weatherson, McAlister.

Partick Th (1) 1 *(Donnelly 30)*

Queen of the S (0) 2 *(Weatherston 64, 90)*   1527

Partick Th: Tuffey; Paton, Boyle, Cairney, Robertson, Archibald, Rowson, McKeown (Corrigan), Buchanan (Hamilton), Donnelly, Corcoran (Erskine).
Queen of the S: Roy; Reid, Harris, McKenna (Quinn), Lilley, McAusland, Wilson (McLaren), Tosh, Holmes, Kean (Weatherston), Burns.

Ross Co (1) 2 *(Di Giacomo 32, Brittain 53)*

Hamilton A (0) 1 *(Mensing 90)*   764

Ross Co: McGovern; Miller, Watt, Morrison, Keddie, Kettlewell (Scott), Vigurs, Lawson, Brittain, Gardyne (Wood), Di Giacomo (Stewart).
Hamilton A: Cerny; Rubiales (Louhoungu), McLaughlin, Canning, Iriekpen, Mensing, Wesolowski, McArthur, Evans, Knight (Paixao F), Paixao M (Kissock).

Wednesday, 26 August 2009

Arbroath (0) 0

St Johnstone (4) 6 *(Milne 24, 45, Morais 27, Deuchar 42, 67, Samuel 71)*   1038

Arbroath: Hill; Rennie, Raeside, Bishop, McCulloch, Scott, Dobbins, Gibson (Gates), Watson (McMullan), Hislop (Redman), Doris.
St Johnstone: Main; MacKay, Gartland, McCaffrey, Grainger (Irvine), Morais (Swankie), Sheerin, Hardie, Craig, Milne (Samuel), Deuchar.

Ayr U (0) 0

St Mirren (1) 2 *(Higdon 25, Mehmet 90)*   1652

Ayr U: Samson; Connolly, McGowan N (Gormley), Aitken A, Gibson, Stevenson, Borris (Prunty), Aitken C, Keenan■, Roberts, Easton (Woodburn).
St Mirren: Gallacher; Ross, Barron, McGinn, Mair, Potter, Brighton (Robb), Dorman (O'Donnell), Mehmet, Thomson, Higdon.

Dunfermline Ath (1) 3 *(Kirk 38, 68, Campbell 52 (og))*

Raith R (0) 1 *(Williamson 50 (pen))*   4163

Dunfermline Ath: Fleming; Woods, McCann, Bell, McGregor, Higgins, Gibson (McDougall), Burke (Phinn), Bayne, Kirk, Cardle (Muirhead).
Raith R: McGurn; Wilson, Ellis, Campbell, Hill, Murray, Williamson, Walker R, Tade (Sloan), Weir (Davidson), Smith D (Bryce).

Hibernian (2) 3 *(Nimmo 10 (og), Riordan 16, Hanlon 55)*

Brechin C (0) 0   7047

Hibernian: Stack; Wotherspoon, Hanlon, Hogg, Murray, McBride (Nish), Benjelloun (Byrne), Cregg, Stokes, Riordan, Rankin (Stevenson).
Brechin C: Nelson C; Walker R, Dyer, Seeley, McLean, Janczyk, Nimmo (McGroarty), Fusco, McAllister (Cowan), King (Harty), Docherty.

THIRD ROUND

Tuesday, 22 September 2009

Dundee (1) 3 *(Malone 39, Forsyth 55, Griffiths 105)*

Aberdeen (0) 2 *(Paton 63, 88)*   6131

Dundee: Douglas (Bullock); Paton, MacKenzie, Cowan, Malone, Forsyth, Klimpl, Kerr, Higgins (Griffiths), McMenamin (Clarke), Harkins.
Aberdeen: Langfield; Foster, Mulgrew, Ifil, Considine, Kerr, Crawford (Maguire), McDonald, Miller L, Mackie (Paton), Grassi (Pawlett).
aet.

Hibernian (1) 1 *(Stokes 1)*

St Johnstone (1) 3 *(Swankie 7, Millar 76, Morris 82)*   7078

Hibernian: Stack; McCormack (Zemmama), Hanlon, Miller, Murray, Bamba, Wotherspoon, McBride, Stokes, Riordan, Rankin (Galbraith).
St Johnstone: Main; MacKay, Anderson (McCaffrey), Gartland, Grainger, Morris, Davidson, Craig (Millar), Swankie (Morais), Deuchar, Milne.

Kilmarnock (0) 1 *(Kyle 87)*

St Mirren (0) 2 *(McGinn 64, Dorman 90)*   3561

Kilmarnock: Brown; Old (Invincibile), Hay, O'Leary, Wright, Bryson (Skelton), Hamill, Pascali (Fernandez), Kyle, Sammon, Taouil.
St Mirren: Gallacher; Ross, Barron, Mair, Potter, McGinn, Murray, Thomson, Brady (Dorman), Mehmet, Dargo (Higdon).

Motherwell (1) 3 *(McHugh 33, Bulvitis 94 (og), Forbes 119)*

Inverness CT (0) 2 *(Barrowman 70, Munro 111)*   3905

Motherwell: Ruddy; Moutaouakil, Saunders, Reynolds, Hammell, Hateley, Forbes, Coke, O'Brien (McGarry), McHugh (Murphy), Jutkiewicz (Jennings).
Inverness CT: Esson; Proctor■, Munro, Golabek, Bulvitis, Duncan, Djebi-Zadi (Ross), Cox, Hayes, Stratford (Barrowman), Foran (Rooney).
aet.

Ross Co (0) 0

Dundee U (1) 2 *(Wilkie 36, Russell 77)*   1986

Ross Co: McGovern; Miller, Keddie, Watt, Morrison, Gardyne (Di Giacomo), Lawson, Scott■, Brittain, Craig (Wood), Vigurs.
Dundee U: Banks; Kovacevic, Dixon, Wilkie, Webster, Buaben, Myrie-Williams, Conway, Swanson, Cadamarteri (Russell), Robertson S (Dillon).

Wednesday, 23 September 2009

Falkirk (0) 0

Celtic (1) 4 *(McDonald S 28, 53, McCourt 64, Killen 73)*   5669

Falkirk: Olejnik; Mitchell (Scobbie), McLean, Barr, Twaddle (McNamara), Flynn, Lynch (Stewart M), Arfield, Marceta, Finnbogason, Finnigan.
Celtic: Zaluska; Caddis, Wilson, Crosas, Caldwell, McManus, Flood (McGinn), Robson (Mizuno), McDonald S (McGeady), Killen, McCourt.

Hearts (0) 2 *(Glen 56, Stewart M 73 (pen))*
Dunfermline Ath (1) 1 *(Bayne 15)*   6126
Hearts: Balogh; Thomson C, Wallace (Black), Bouzid, Goncalves, Zaliukas, Santana, Stewart M, Glen (Smith G), Obua, Palazuelos.
Dunfermline Ath: Fleming; Woods (Cardle), McGregor, Dowie, Muirhead, Holmes, Ross (McCann), Phinn (Kirk), Burke, Gibson, Bayne.

Queen of the S (0) 1 *(Harris 90)*
Rangers (1) 2 *(Naismith 16, Novo 79)*   6120
Queen of the S: Roy; Reid, McAusland, Lilley, Harris, Burns, Tosh (Quinn), McKenna, Wilson (McQuilken), Holmes, Weatherston (McLaughlan).
Rangers: Alexander; Whittaker, Papac, Thomson, Weir, Bougherra, Rothen (Novo), Pedro Mendes, Boyd (McCulloch), Naismith, Davis.

QUARTER-FINALS

Tuesday, 27 October 2009
Dundee (0) 1 *(Griffiths 29)*
Rangers (1) 3 *(Whittaker 15, MacKenzie 57 (og), Fleck 85)*   10,654
Dundee: Bullock; Paton, Malone, Forsyth, MacKenzie Lauchlan, McHale, Kerr (Hart), Griffiths (McMenamin) Higgins (Clarke), Harkins.
Rangers: Alexander; McMillan, Smith, Thomson, Papac, Wilson, Whittaker, Fleck, Novo, Lafferty, Beasley (Naismith).

St Johnstone (0) 2 *(Anderson 72, Dods 76 (og))*
Dundee U (0) 1 *(Buaben 82)*   5146
St Johnstone: Smith G; MacKay, Grainger, Davidson, Rutkiewicz (Anderson), Gartland, Millar, Craig, Johansson (Moon), Deuchar, Sheerin (Morais).
Dundee U: Banks; Kovacevic, Dillon, Kenneth, Webster (Dodds), Buaben, Fotheringham (Casalinuovo), Gomis, Goodwillie, Cadamarteri, Swanson (Conway).

St Mirren (1) 3 *(Higdon 23, Ross 61, Craigan 81 (og))*
Motherwell (0) 0   4325
St Mirren: Gallacher; Ross, Barron, Dorman, Mair, Potter, Murray, McGinn, Mehmet, Higdon (Brady), Johnston (O'Donnell).
Motherwell: Ruddy; Moutaouakil (Humphrey), Hutchinson, Reynolds, Saunders, Craigan, Murphy (McHugh), Coke, O'Brien (Forbes), Jutkiewicz, Hateley.

Wednesday. 28 October 2009
Celtic (0) 0
Hearts (0) 1 *(Stewart M 58 (pen))*   18,675
Celtic: Zaluska; Hinkel, Fox, Crosas, Caldwell, McManus, Zheng Zhi (McDonald S), N'Guemo, Maloney (McCourt), Killen (Samaras), McGeady.
Hearts: Balogh; Thomson C, Wallace, Bouzid, Goncalves, Palazuelos, Black (Jonsson), Stewart M, Obua, Nade (Witteveen), Driver.

SEMI-FINALS

Tuesday, 2 February 2010
Hearts (0) 0
St Mirren (0) 1 *(Mehmet 51)*   9170
Hearts: Kello; Thomson J, Wallace, Bouzid (Kucharski), Zaliukas, Jonsson, Smith G (Glen), Black, Nade, Stewart M, Driver.
St Mirren: Gallacher; Ross, Barron, Dorman (O'Donnel), Mair, Innes, Murray, Potter, Mehmet, Higdon (Dargo), Thomson.
at Fir Park.

Wednesday, 3 February 2010
Rangers (2) 2 *(Davis 26, McCulloch 37)*
St Johnstone (0) 0   17,371
Rangers: Alexander; Whittaker, Smith, McCulloch, Weir, Wilson, Davis, Thomson, Fleck, Lafferty (Little), Novo (Naismith).
St Johnstone: Smith G; MacKay, Grainger, Morris, Irvine, Gartland, Millar, Davidson, Sheridan (MacDonald), Craig (Moon), Morais (Milne).
at Hampden Park.

FINAL (at Hampden Park)

Sunday, 21 March 2010
St Mirren (0) 0
Rangers (0) 1 *(Miller 84)*   44,538
St Mirren: Gallacher; Ross, Barron, Potter, Mair, Thomson, Murray (Dorman), Brady (O'Donnell), Mehmet (Dargo), Higdon, Carey.
Rangers: Alexander; Whittaker, Papac, McCulloch, Weir, Wilson, Davis (Edu), Thomson, Boyd (Naismith), Miller, Novo (Smith).
Referee: C. Thomson.

SCOTTISH LEAGUE ATTENDANCES 2009–10

	Average	Highest	Lowest	SECOND DIVISION			
Aberdeen	10,461	16,803	6,097	Alloa Ath	658	1,201	394
Celtic	45,582	58,500	24,000	Arbroath	491	649	328
Dundee U	7,863	11,100	5,598	Brechin C	491	1,102	304
Falkirk	5,634	7,049	4,321	Clyde	632	813	465
Hamilton A	3,005	5,343	2,005	Cowdenbeath	427	1,084	246
Hearts	14,745	18,025	12,325	Dumbarton	671	975	397
Hibernian	11,811	16,949	6,350	East Fife	603	864	213
Kilmarnock	5,919	10,662	4,063	Peterhead	476	627	303
Motherwell	5,307	9,355	3,544	Stenhousemuir	533	783	207
Rangers	47,301	50,321	42,034	Stirling Alb	624	1,036	297
St Johnstone	4,717	7,807	2,993				
St Mirren	4,413	6,164	3,009				
FIRST DIVISION				**THIRD DIVISION**			
Airdrie U	1,080	1,864	703	Albion R	353	613	217
Ayr U	1,783	3,078	1,052	Annan Ath	491	831	278
Dundee	4,759	5,507	3,187	Berwick R	434	608	289
Dunfermline Ath	2,914	6,289	2,154	East Stirling	407	1,062	297
Inverness CT	3,509	6,031	2,008	Elgin C	402	615	203
Morton	1,969	3,771	1,219	Forfar Ath	438	613	286
Partick Th	2,551	4,453	1,151	Livingston	978	1,621	503
Queen of the S	2,364	3,415	1,133	Montrose	341	548	200
Raith R	2,258	6,200	1,080	Queen's Park	541	714	376
Ross Co	2,465	5,928	1,752	Stranraer	268	378	145

ALBA LEAGUE CHALLENGE CUP 2009–10

■ *Denotes player sent off.*

FIRST ROUND NORTH-EAST

Saturday, 25 July 2009
Dunfermline Ath (0) 2 *(Kirk 49, Bell 68)*
Arbroath (0) 1 *(Redman 73)* 1708
Dunfermline Ath: Fleming; Ross, Higgins, McCann, Glass, Graham, Bell (Phinn), Burke, Gibson (Cardle), Kirk (McDougall), Bayne.
Arbroath: Hill; Doris (McMullan), McCulloch, Dobbins■, Bishop, Rattray, Lunan, Gibson, Hislop (Milne), Sellars, Watson (Redman).

East Fife (0) 0
Forfar Ath (1) 2 *(Fotheringham M 38, Fotheringham K 77)*
446
East Fife: Brown; Nugent, Ovenstone, Smart, McRae (Muir), Linn, Thomson S, Crawford, Conway, McManus (Cargill), Staunton (Thomson D).
Forfar Ath: Brown; Mowat, Malcolm, Tod, Campbell I, Fotheringham M, Tulloch, Fotheringham K, Campbell R (Smith N), Templeman (Smith C), Brady (Gordon).

Elgin C (1) 3 *(Crooks 1, Frizzel 61, Edwards 74)*
Brechin C (0) 1 *(McAllister 46)* 381
Elgin C: Gibson; Dempsie, David A Craig, Kaczan, David W Craig, McDonald (Calder), Gunn (Cameron), Edwards, Frizzel (Jack A), Nicolson, Crooks.
Brechin C: Nelson C; Fusco, McGroarty, Seeley, McLean, Janczyk, Canning (Walker R), Nimmo (King), McAllister, Harty (McKenna), Byers.

Inverness CT (1) 1 *(Crighton 45 (og))*
Montrose (0) 1 *(Leyden 87)* 1072
Inverness CT: Esson; Stratford, Djebi-Zadi, Cox, Tokely, Munro, Ross, Duncan, Foran (Hastings), Barrowman (Rooney), Hayes (McBain).
Montrose: Coutts; Hegarty, Fleming (Pope), Maitland (Gray), Campbell, Crighton, Nicol, Davidson, Gemmell, Boitt (Leyden), Anderson.
aet; Inverness CT won 5-3 on penalties.

Peterhead (1) 1 *(Bavidge 12)*
Cowdenbeath (0) 2 *(McBride 52, McQuade 61)* 361
Peterhead: Jarvie; Donald, Smith, Mann, MacDonald, McVitie (Davidson) (Bruce), Sharp, Strachan, Bavidge, Cameron, Ross.
Cowdenbeath: Hay; Baxter, Linton, McCabe, Mbu, Adamson, Fairbairn, Robertson, Wardlaw (Ferguson), McQuade (Tomana), McBride.

Ross Co (0) 3 *(Gardyne 58, 106, 118)*
Alloa Ath (1) 2 *(Watt 4 (og), Spence 99)* 748
Ross Co: McGovern; Garvin, Morrison, Watt, Keddie, Vigurs (Stewart), Scott (Craig), Lawson, Wood, Brittain, Moore (Gardyne).
Alloa Ath: Crawford; McClune, McCafferty, Buist, Walker, Grant (Carroll■), Agnew (Kerr), Brown, Carrigan. Noble (Spence), Scott.
aet.

Stirling Alb (1) 2 *(Graham 45, McKenna 54)*
Raith R (0) 1 *(Walker 90)* 713
Stirling Alb: Christie; Feaks, Forsyth, Roycroft, Graham, Robertson (McCord), Gibson (Taggart), Murphy, McKenna (Grehan), Mullen, Devine.
Raith R: McGurn; Wilson, Ellis, Campbell, Murray, Davidson. Williamson, Simmons, Tade (Bryce), Weir, Smith D (Walker).

FIRST ROUND SOUTH-WEST

Saturday, 25 July 2009
Airdrie U (0) 0
Partick Th (0) 1 *(Buchanan 51)* 1325
Airdrie U: Robertson; Darren Smith, Lovering (Waddell), McDonald, Donnelly, Nixon, Trouten (Watt), McLaughlin, Keegan (Gemmill), Baird, Lagana.
Partick Th: Tuffey; Paton, Boyle, Maxwell, Robertson, Archibald, McKeown (Hamilton), Rowson, Buchanan, Doolan (Erskene), Hodge (Cairney).

Annan Ath (1) 2 *(Jack 27 (pen), 90)*
Queen's Park (0) 0 411
Annan Ath: Summersgill; Muirhead, McBeth, Watson, Neilson, Jack, Steele, Gilfillan, Cox (Sloan S), Storey (Bell), Sloan L.
Queen's Park: Black; Ure (Carrol), Douglas, Reilly■, Brough (Burns), Walker, Hamilton, Capuano, Daly, Harkins, Watt.

Ayr U (0) 0
Albion R (0) 2 *(Barr 79, McFarlane 85)* 979
Ayr U: Samson; Gibson, James, Campbell (Roberts), McGowan, Connolly, Keenan (Aitken C), Stevenson, O'Brien (Easton), Prunty, Cawley.
Albion R: Ewings; Reid, Donnelly (Canning M), Benton, McGowan, McKeown, Tyrrell, O'Byrne, Barr (Boyle), McFarlane, Walker P (McCusker).

Queen of the S (1) 1 *(Wilson 9)*
Livingston (0) 0 1558
Queen of the S: Hutton; Reid, Barr (McLaughlan), Lilley, McAusland, Scally, Wilson, Tosh, Burns, Holmes (McLaren), Weatherston (Kean).
Livingston: McKenzie; Malone, Talbot, MacDonald, Innes, Torrance (Keaghan Jacobs), Hamill, McParland, Halliday (One), Fox, Winters D (Sinclair).

Stenhousemuir (0) 2 *(O'Reilly 75, Dalziel 90)*
Clyde (0) 0 603
Stenhousemuir: McCluskey; Lyle, Thomson S, Thom, Smith J, McLeod, Love (Motion), Scullion (Dalziel, Brand (Bradley), O'Reilly.
Clyde: Allan; Park, Halliday, Gair, Lithgow. Doyle (Stevenson), Stewart, Lang, Sawyers, McLeod (Howarth), McFadden (Boyle).

Stranraer (2) 4 *(Jack 11, Danny Mitchell 18 (pen), 59, Montgomerie 87)*
Berwick R (1) 2 *(Ewart 33, Little 86)* 245
Stranraer: David Mitchell; McGrath, Wright, Nicoll, Henderson, Donald (Aitken), McGeouch (McMahon), Danny Mitchell, McColm (Montgomerie), Jack, Noble■.
Berwick R: Peat; Smith E, Callaghan, Ewart■, McLean, Notman■, Russell (McMahon), Currie, Brazil, Radynski (Little), McMenamin.

Sunday, 26 July 2009
Dumbarton (0) 0
Morton (1) 1 *(Jenkins 25)* 1122
Dumbarton: McEwan; Chisholm, Dunlop, Gordon, McKillen, Geggan, Clark (Chaplain), McStay (O'Donoghue), Murray, McLaughlin, Carcary (Hunter).
Morton: Halliwell; McGuffie, Walker, Greacen, Monti, Finlayson, Masterton (Wake), MacFarlane, McAlister, Weatherson (Graham), Jenkins (Paartalu).

SECOND ROUND

Tuesday, 18 August 2009
Annan Ath (0) 1 *(Watson 90)*
East Stirling (0) 0 357
Annan Ath: Kelly; Sloan S, McBeth, Watson, Neilson, Gilfillan, Steele, Jardine, Cox, Anson, Sloan L.
East Stirling: Barclay; Hay, Forrest, Bolochoweckyi (Tully), King, Weaver, Donaldson (Elliott), Richardson, Maquire (Johnston), Stephenson, McKenzie.

Cowdenbeath (0) 0
Dundee (1) 3 *(Griffiths 20, Harkins 82,*
Antoine-Curier 88) 457
Cowdenbeath: Hay; Baxter (Linton), Mbu, Droudge,
Adamson, Fairbairn (McBride), Robertson, Stein,
McQuade, Dempster (Ferguson), Wardlaw.
Dundee: Bullock; Cowan, Benedictus, Lauchlan, Forsyth,
Casement, McHale (Harkins), Cameron, Kerr, Antoine-
Curier, Griffiths (McMenamin).

Dunfermline Ath (0) 1 *(Cardle 53)*
Queen of the S (1) 2 *(Kean 12, Tosh 90)* 941
Dunfermline Ath: Fleming; Woods, Muirhead, Holmes
(Bell), Dowie, McCann, Gibson, Phinn, McDougall
(Whyte), Kirk, Cardle (Willis).
Queen of the S: Roy; Reid, Harris, McKenna, Lilley,
McAusland, Burns, Quinn (Tosh), Holmes, Kean
(Weatherston), McLaren (McQuilken).

Elgin C (0) 3 *(Crooks 64 (pen), Gunn 80, 90)*
Albion R (0) 0 245
Elgin C: Gibson; Niven (Calder), David A Craig
(MacAulay), Kaczan, David W Craig, McDonald■, Gunn,
Edwards, Frizzel (Cameron), Nicolson, Crooks.
Albion R: Gaston; Reid, McGowan, Canning M■,
Benton, McKeown (Ferry), Boyle, Tyrrell, Pollock
(McCusker), Walker P, Barr.

Forfar Ath (0) 1 *(Templeman 60)*
Partick Th (1) 6 *(Doolan 10, Hamilton 51, 52, Rowson 61,*
Donnelly 74, Cairney 80) 532
Forfar Ath: Brown; Mowat (Smith N), Campbell I,
Brady, Tod, Tulloch (Malcolm), Fotheringham M
(Gordon), Campbell R, Templeman, Fotheringham K,
Deasley.
Partick Th: Tuffey; Paton, Boyle, Hodge, Robertson,
Archibald, Cairney, Rowson (Kinniburgh), Doolan,
Hamilton (Donnelly), Corcoran (Erskine).

Inverness CT (3) 3 *(Foran 12, 32, Sanchez 29)*
Stranraer R (0) 0 665
Inverness CT: Esson; Tokely, Bulvitis, Munro, Shinnie,
Cox, Eagle, Stratford, Foran (Rooney), Sanchez
(McBain), Hayes (Ross).
Stranraer R: David Mitchell; Agostini (Aitken), McInnes,
Nicoll, Henderson, McMahon (McColm), McGeouch,
Danny Mitchell, Moore (Jack), Montgomerie, Wright.

Ross Co (0) 2 *(Lawson 68, Wood 70)*
Morton (0) 1 *(Masterton 63)* 588
Ross Co: McGovern; Boyd, Morrison, Vigurs, Keddie,
Watt, Kettlewell (Gardyne), Wood (Stewart), Di
Giacomo, Brittain, Moore (Lawson).
Morton: Halliwell; McGuffie (MacGregor), Walker,
Harding, Greacen, Masterton, Jenkins, MacFarlane
(Weatherson), Graham, Russell (Finlayson), McAlister.

Stirling Alb (1) 3 *(Mullen 33, Robertson 47, McKenna 80)*
Stenhousemuir (0) 1 *(Dalziel 49)* 275
Stirling Alb: Christie; Graham, Forsyth, O'Neil (Young),
Roycroft, McCord (Murphy), Gibson, Robertson,
Grehan, Mullen (McKenna), Devine.
Stenhousemuir: Bennett; Lyle, Thomson S, Thom,
McLeod, Thomson I, Love, Brand, Diack, Stirling■,
Motion (Dalziel).

QUARTER-FINALS

Sunday, 6 September 2009
Annan Ath (0) 4 *(Gilfillan 56, Bell 75, Inglis 80, Storey 88)*
Elgin C (2) 2 *(Cameron 6, McBeth 43 (og))* 534
Annan Ath: Kelly; Steele, McBeth (Inglis), Watson,
Neilson (Sloan S), Jack, Muirhead, Gilfillan, Cox, Storey,
Sloan L (Bell).
Elgin C: Gibson; Dempsie (David A Craig), Niven,
Kaczan, David W Craig, Edwards, Gunn (Crooks),
MacAulay, Frizzel, Nicolson, Cameron.

Partick Th (0) 1 *(Buchanan 77)*
Inverness CT (1) 1 *(Sanchez 6)* 1746
Partick Th: Tuffey; Paton, Boyle (Hodge), Maxwell,
Robertson, Archibald, Cairney, Rowson, Buchanan,
Corcoran (Donnelly), Erskine (Hamilton).
Inverness CT: Esson; Tokely, Bulvitis, Munro, Golabek,
Cox, Eagle (Rooney), Stratford, Foran, Sanchez
(Barrowman), Hayes (Duncan).
aet; Inverness CT won 4-3 on penalties.

Ross Co (1) 2 *(Di Giacomo 26, Craig 90)*
Queen of the S (0) 0 964
Ross Co: McGovern; Miller, Morrison, Kettlewell,
Keddie, Watt, Gardyne (Craig), Lawson, Di Giacomo
(Wood), Brittain, Vigurs (Scott).
Queen of the S: Roy; Reid, Harris, McKenna (Quinn),
Lilley, McAusland, Wilson (McLaren), Tosh, Holmes,
Weatherston (Kean), Burns.

Stirling Alb (0) 1 *(Devine 89 (pen))*
Dundee (2) 2 *(Griffiths 10, 26)* 1277
Stirling Alb: Christie; Graham, Forsyth, Young (Mullen),
Roycroft, O'Neil, Gibson (McCord), Robertson
(Taggart), Grehan, McKenna, Devine.
Dundee: Bullock; Paton, Malone, Klimpl, MacKenzie
(Forsyth), Benedictus (Lauchlan), Hart (Clarke), Kerr,
McMenamin, Griffiths, Harkins.

SEMI-FINALS

Sunday, 4 October 2009
Dundee (1) 3 *(Higgins 37, Clarke 63, Forsyth 71)*
Annan Ath (0) 0 2321
Dundee: Bullock; Paton (Pasement), Malone, McHale,
MacKenzie, Cowan, Hart (Harkins), Cameron, Clarke,
Higgins, Forsyth (Young).
Annan Ath: Summersgill; Steele, Inglis (McBeth),
Watson, Neilson, Jack (Jardine), Muirhead, Sloan S, Cox,
Bell (Storey), Sloan L.

Inverness CT (1) 1 *(Eagle 44)*
Ross Co (0) 0 2275
Inverness CT: Esson; Proctor, Bulvitis, Munro, Golabek,
Cox (Rooney), Eagle, Duncan, Foran, Sanchez
(Stratford), Hayes.
Ross Co: McGovern; Miller, Morrison, Kettlewell
(Scott), Boyd, Watt, Gardyne (Moore), Lawson, Di
Giacomo, Brittain, Vigurs (Wood).

FINAL (at McDiarmid Park)

Sunday, 22 November 2009
Dundee (0) 3 *(Bulvitis 48 (og), Harkins 53, Forsyth 83)*
Inverness CT (2) 2 *(Rooney 20, Bulvitis 33)* 8031
Dundee: Douglas; Paton (Benedictus), Malone, Kerr,
MacKenzie, Lauchlan, Forsyth, Hart, Griffiths (Clarke),
Higgins (McMenamin), Harkins.
Inverness CT: Esson; Tokely, Bulvitis, Munro, Golabek,
Proctor, Sanchez (Cox), Duncan (Odhiambo), Foran,
Rooney (Imrie■), Hayes.
Referee: C. Richmond.

SCOTTISH CUP FINALS 1874–2010

Year	Winners	Runners-up	Score
1874	Queen's Park	Clydesdale	2-0
1875	Queen's Park	Renton	3-0
1876	Queen's Park	Third Lanark	2-0 after 1-1 draw
1877	Vale of Leven	Rangers	3-2 after 0-0 and 1-1 draws
1878	Vale of Leven	Third Lanark	1-0
1879	Vale of Leven*	Rangers	
1880	Queen's Park	Thornlibank	3-0
1881	Queen's Park†	Dumbarton	3-1
1882	Queen's Park	Dumbarton	4-1 after 2-2 draw
1883	Dumbarton	Vale of Leven	2-1 after 2-2 draw
1884	Queen's Park‡	Vale of Leven	
1885	Renton	Vale of Leven	3-1 after 0-0 draw
1886	Queen's Park	Renton	3-1
1887	Hibernian	Dumbarton	2-1
1888	Renton	Cambuslang	6-1
1889	Third Lanark§	Celtic	2-1
1890	Queen's Park	Vale of Leven	2-1 after 1-1 draw
1891	Hearts	Dumbarton	1-0
1892	Celtic¶	Queen's Park	5-1
1893	Queen's Park	Celtic	2-1
1894	Rangers	Celtic	3-1
1895	St Bernard's	Renton	2-1
1896	Hearts	Hibernian	3-1
1897	Rangers	Dumbarton	5-1
1898	Rangers	Kilmarnock	2-0
1899	Celtic	Rangers	2-0
1900	Celtic	Queen's Park	4-3
1901	Hearts	Celtic	4-3
1902	Hibernian	Celtic	1-0
1903	Rangers	Hearts	2-0 after 1-1 and 0-0 draws
1904	Celtic	Rangers	3-2
1905	Third Lanark	Rangers	3-1 after 0-0 draw
1906	Hearts	Third Lanark	1-0
1907	Celtic	Hearts	3-0
1908	Celtic	St Mirren	5-1
1909	••		
1910	Dundee	Clyde	2-1 after 2-2 and 0-0 draws
1911	Celtic	Hamilton A	2-0 after 0-0 draw
1912	Celtic	Clyde	2-0
1913	Falkirk	Raith R	2-0
1914	Celtic	Hibernian	4-1 after 0-0 draw
1920	Kilmarnock	Albion R	3-2
1921	Partick Th	Rangers	1-0
1922	Morton	Rangers	1-0
1923	Celtic	Hibernian	1-0
1924	Airdrieonians	Hibernian	2-0
1925	Celtic	Dundee	2-1
1926	St Mirren	Celtic	2-0
1927	Celtic	East Fife	3-1
1928	Rangers	Celtic	4-0
1929	Kilmarnock	Rangers	2-0
1930	Rangers	Partick Th	2-1 after 0-0 draw
1931	Celtic	Motherwell	4-2 after 2-2 draw
1932	Rangers	Kilmarnock	3-0 after 1-1 draw
1933	Celtic	Motherwell	1-0
1934	Rangers	St Mirren	5-0
1935	Rangers	Hamilton A	2-1
1936	Rangers	Third Lanark	1-0
1937	Celtic	Aberdeen	2-1
1938	East Fife	Kilmarnock	4-2 after 1-1 draw
1939	Clyde	Motherwell	4-0
1947	Aberdeen	Hibernian	2-1
1948	Rangers	Morton	1-0 after 1-1 draw
1949	Rangers	Clyde	4-1
1950	Rangers	East Fife	3-0
1951	Celtic	Motherwell	1-0
1952	Motherwell	Dundee	4-0
1953	Rangers	Aberdeen	1-0 after 1-1 draw
1954	Celtic	Aberdeen	2-1
1955	Clyde	Celtic	1-0 after 1-1 draw
1956	Hearts	Celtic	3-1
1957	Falkirk	Kilmarnock	2-1 after 1-1 draw
1958	Clyde	Hibernian	1-0
1959	St Mirren	Aberdeen	3-1
1960	Rangers	Kilmarnock	2-0
1961	Dunfermline Ath	Celtic	2-0 after 0-0 draw
1962	Rangers	St Mirren	2-0
1963	Rangers	Celtic	3-0 after 1-1 draw

Year	Winners	Runners-up	Score
1964	Rangers	Dundee	3-1
1965	Celtic	Dunfermline Ath	3-2
1966	Rangers	Celtic	1-0 after 0-0 draw
1967	Celtic	Aberdeen	2-0
1968	Dunfermline Ath	Hearts	3-1
1969	Celtic	Rangers	4-0
1970	Aberdeen	Celtic	3-1
1971	Celtic	Rangers	2-1 after 1-1 draw
1972	Celtic	Hibernian	6-1
1973	Rangers	Celtic	3-2
1974	Celtic	Dundee U	3-0
1975	Celtic	Airdrieonians	3-1
1976	Rangers	Hearts	3-1
1977	Celtic	Rangers	1-0
1978	Rangers	Aberdeen	2-1
1979	Rangers	Hibernian	3-2 after 0-0 and 0-0 draws
1980	Celtic	Rangers	1-0
1981	Rangers	Dundee U	4-1 after 0-0 draw
1982	Aberdeen	Rangers	4-1 (aet)
1983	Aberdeen	Rangers	1-0 (aet)
1984	Aberdeen	Celtic	2-1 (aet)
1985	Celtic	Dundee U	2-1
1986	Aberdeen	Hearts	3-0
1987	St Mirren	Dundee U	1-0 (aet)
1988	Celtic	Dundee U	2-1
1989	Celtic	Rangers	1-0
1990	Aberdeen	Celtic	0-0 (aet)
		(Aberdeen won 9-8 on penalties)	
1991	Motherwell	Dundee U	4-3 (aet)
1992	Rangers	Airdrieonians	2-1
1993	Rangers	Aberdeen	2-1
1994	Dundee U	Rangers	1-0
1995	Celtic	Airdrieonians	1-0
1996	Rangers	Hearts	5-1
1997	Kilmarnock	Falkirk	1-0
1998	Hearts	Rangers	2-1
1999	Rangers	Celtic	1-0
2000	Rangers	Aberdeen	4-0
2001	Celtic	Hibernian	3-0
2002	Rangers	Celtic	3-2
2003	Rangers	Dundee	1-0
2004	Celtic	Dunfermline Ath	3-1
2005	Celtic	Dundee U	1-0
2006	Hearts	Gretna	1-1 (aet)
		(Hearts won 4-2 on penalties)	
2007	Celtic	Dunfermline Ath	1-0
2008	Rangers	Queen of the S	3-2
2009	Rangers	Falkirk	1-0
2010	Dundee U	Ross Co	3-0

*Vale of Leven awarded cup, Rangers failing to appear for replay after 1-1 draw.
†After Dumbarton protested the first game, which Queen's Park won 2-1.
‡Queen's Park awarded cup, Vale of Leven failing to appear.
§Replay by order of Scottish FA because of playing conditions in first match, won 3-0 by Third Lanark.
¶After mutually protested game which Celtic won 1-0.
**Owing to riot, the cup was withheld after two drawn games – between Celtic and Rangers 2-2 and 1-1.

SCOTTISH CUP WINS

Celtic 34, Rangers 33, Queen's Park 10, Aberdeen 7, Hearts 7, Clyde 3, Kilmarnock 3, St Mirren 3, Vale of Leven 3, Dundee U 2, Dunfermline Ath 2, Falkirk 2, Hibernian 2, Motherwell 2, Renton 2, Third Lanark 2, Airdrieonians 1, Dumbarton 1, Dundee 1, East Fife 1, Morton 1, Partick Th 1, St Bernard's 1.

APPEARANCES IN FINAL

Celtic 53, Rangers 50, Aberdeen 15, Hearts 13, Queen's Park 12, Hibernian 11, Dundee U 9, Kilmarnock 8, Vale of Leven 7, Clyde 6, Dumbarton 6, Motherwell 6, St Mirren 6, Third Lanark 6, Dundee 5, Dunfermline Ath 5, Renton 5, Airdrieonians 4, Falkirk 4, East Fife 3, Hamilton A 2, Morton 2, Partick Th 2, Albion R 1, Cambuslang 1, Clydesdale 1, Gretna 1, Queen of the S 1, Raith R 1, Ross Co 1, St Bernard's 1, Thornliebank 1.

ACTIVE NATION SCOTTISH CUP 2009-10

* *Denotes player sent off.*

THIRD ROUND

Saturday, 28 November 2009

Airdrie U (3) 4 *(Trouten 11, 39, Baird 23, O'Carroll 65)*
Queen of the S (0) 0 1141
Airdrie U: Robertson; McCann R (Lagana), Lovering, Darren Smith, Donnelly, Storey, Trouten (Watt), McLaughlin, O'Carroll, Baird (McDonald), Waddell.
Queen of the S: Hutton; McAusland, McQuilken, McKenna, Lilley, McLaughlan (Harris), Burns, Quinn (Wilson), Holmes, Kean (Weatherston), McLaren.

Albion R (0) 1 *(Pollock 62)*
Elgin C (0) 0 275
Albion R: Gaston; Reid, McGowan, Donnelly, Benton, O'Byrne, Boyle (Stewart), Tyrrell, Gormley (McCusker), Pollock (Walker P), Strachan.
Elgin C: Gibson; Dempsie, Inglis, Kaczan, Edwards (Crooks), Niven, Gunn (Cameron), MacAulay, Frizzel, Nicolson, Tatters.

Cowdenbeath (0) 0
Alloa Ath (0) 0 377
Cowdenbeath: Hay; Droudge, Armstrong, Mbu, Adamson, Ramsay, Winter (Ferguson), Robertson, Stein (Linton), Wardlaw, McBride (Fairbairn).
Alloa Ath: Crawford; Buist, Townsley (Carroll), Walker, McClune, Gilhaney (Agnew), Ferguson B, Brown, Noble, Scott, Grant.

Deveronvale (0) 0
Ayr U (0) 1 *(Stevenson 71)* 192
Deveronvale: Blanchard; Milne, Dolan, Chisholm, Fraser, Urquhart (Cowie), McGowan, Brown, Duncanson, McKenzie (Gauld), Smith.
Ayr U: Samson; McGowan R, McGowan N, Gibson, James, Stevenson, Woodburn, Keenan, Connolly, Roberts, Easton (Borris).

Edinburgh C (2) 3 *(Nicol 19 (og), Gair 24, 70)*
Keith (0) 1 *(Harris 90)* 177
Edinburgh C: Montieth; Morrison, Ross (Wilson), Bruce, Harrison, McFarland, Caddow, Gair, Clee, MacNamara (Callandine), Denholn.
Keith: Shearer; Watt (Harris), Lonie, Still, Niddrie, Nicol, Walker, MacKay (Collins), Park (Keith), Lennox, Donaldson.

Irvine Meadow (1) 1 *(Barr 36)*
Arbroath (0) 0 1150
Irvine Meadow: Wardrobe; Swift (Ryan), Wingate, McTowern, Robertson, Crilly, Stain, Turner, Barr (Boyle), McTinty, Lowing.
Arbroath: Hill; Rennie, McCulloch, Bishop, Rattray, Gibson, Lunan, Redman, Sellars (Ross), Hislop (Gates), Scott (Doris).

Montrose (0) 2 *(Watson 57, Gemmell 88)*
East Fife (0) 1 *(McManus 61)* 509
Montrose: McNeil; Hegarty, Tweed, Crighton, Sinclair (Nicol), Milligan, Campbell, Davidson, Watson, Gemmell, Anderson.
East Fife: Ridgers; Gourlay, Muir, Smart, Ovenstone, Young, McCunnie, Cargill (Crawford), Conway (Linn), McManus, Sludden.

Morton (0) 0
Dumbarton (0) 0 1882
Morton: Stewart; Van Zanten, MacGregor, Reid, Greacen, Paartalu, Finlayson, McGuffie, Wake (Graham), Weatherson, McAlister.
Dumbarton: Vojacek; O'Donoghue, Smith, Dunlop, Gordon, McStay, Chisholm, Chaplain, Hunter (Carcary), Geggan (Clark), Murray.

Raith R (0) 0
Peterhead (0) 0 1418
Raith R: McGurn; Wilson, Ellis, Campbell, Hill, Murray, Tade, Walker, Simmons (Weir), Corredera (Smith K), Smith D (Ferry).
Peterhead: Jarvie; Donald, Smith, Mann, MacDonald, Strachan, Sharp (Cameron), Ross, Bavidge, Clark (McVitie), Stewart (Bruce).

Ross Co (3) 5 *(Di Giacomo 38, 40, Lawson 42, Craig 82, Wood 87)*
Berwick R (0) 1 *(Brazil 77)* 819
Ross Co: McGovern; Miller, Morrison, Kettlewell (Scott), Boyd, Keddie, Gardyne (Wood), Lawson, Di Giacomo (Craig), Brittain, Vigurs.
Berwick R: Peat; Notman (Guy), Smith E, McLean, Ewart, Callaghan (Russell), McLaren, Currie, Brazil, Gray, Little (McMullan).

Spartans (0) 0
Forfar Ath (0) 1 *(Templeman 55)* 600
Spartans: Flockhart; Archibald, Fowlie, Gerrard, Sidwright, Malin, King, Manson, Henretty, McLeod, Hoskins (Kader).
Forfar Ath: Brown; McCulloch, Campbell I, Fotheringham M, Tod, Tulloch, Gordon, Harty (Deasley), Templeman (Smith C), Campbell R (Gibson), Fotheringham K.

Stirling Alb (1) 2 *(Corr 10, Forsyth 64)*
Auchinleck Talbot (1) 1 *(McIlroy 35 (pen))* 1185
Stirling Alb: Christie; Feaks, Forsyth, Graham, Robertson, McCord (Murphy), Gibson, Corr, Prunty (Mullen), McKenna (Grehan), O'Brien.
Auchinleck Talbot: Strain; Robb, McVey, Pettergrew, Collins, White, Young, Slavin, McIlroy, Boyle (Gillies), Latta (McKelvie).

Threave R (0) 1 *(Struthers 89)*
Inverurie Locos (1) 2 *(Park 6, Morrison 71)* 520
Threave R: Parker; Wilby, Kerr, Patterson, Fingland, Baty, Green, Dunglinson (Irons), Donley, Nicol (Struthers), Warren.
Inverurie Locos: Reid; Park, Buchan, Wilson, Morrison, Merriman, Singer, Davidson (McLean), Gauld (Broadhurst), Ross, Bisset.

Wick Academy (3) 4 *(Allan 8, 45, Mackay 32, 60 (pen))*
Brechin C (2) 4 *(King 12, 85, Byers 17, McAllister 75)* 177
Wick Academy: Bokas; Campbell, Manson, Ross, MacLeod, Shearer, Farquhar, Mackay, Allan, MacAdie, Cunningham.
Brechin C: Nelson C; Walker R, Dyer, McLean, Seeley, Smith B, King, Janczyk, McAllister, Renton (Fusco), Byers.

Saturday, 5 December 2009

Stenhousemuir (5) 5 *(Motion 1, 34, Molloy 2, Bradley 13, Thomson I 30)*
Cove Rangers (0) 0 409
Stenhousemuir: McCluskey; Lyle, Thomson S, McLeod, Smith J, Molloy, Thomson I, Scullion (Love), Dalziel, Bradley (Halpin), Motion (Stirling).
Cove Rangers: McKenzie; Cruickshank, Black (Lawrie), Bain, Watson, Heads, Henderson, Johnston, Buchan, Webster (Stephen), Milne (McCulloch).

Wednesday, 9 December 2009

Clyde (0) 1 *(Lithgow 63)*
Livingston (0) 1 *(Hamill 48)* 538
Clyde: Reidford; Park, Higgins (Casey), Lithgow, Cassidy, Stewart, McLauchlan, White, Howarth (McFadden), Stevenson, Sawyers.
Livingston: McKenzie; Moyes, Griffin, MacDonald, Talbot, Keaghan Jacobs, Sinclair, Hamill (Fox), Halliday, Winters D (De Vita), Winters R (Watson).

THIRD ROUND REPLAYS

Tuesday, 1 December 2009

Peterhead (0) 1 *(Stewart 87)*

Raith R (0) 4 *(Smith D 46, 73, Smith K 59, Simmons 90)*
537
Peterhead: Jarvie; Donald, Smith S, MacDonald, Mann, McVitie, Ross, Strachan, Cameron, Stewart, Clark.
Raith R: McGurn; Wilson, Ellis, Campbell, Hill, Murray, Tade, Walker, Simmons, Smith K (Bryce), Smith D.

Saturday, 5 December 2009

Dumbarton (0) 0

Morton (0) 1 *(Graham 74)*
1495
Dumbarton: Vojacek; O'Donoghue, Dunlop, Gordon (McNiff), Smith, Chisholm, McStay (Clark), Chaplain[■], Murray (Carcary), Hunter, Geggan.
Morton: Stewart; Van Zanten, Reid, Greacen, MacGregor, Finlayson, Paartalu, Monti, McAlister, Wake (Graham), Weatherson.

Tuesday, 8 December 2009

Alloa Ath (0) 1 *(Gilhaney 88)*

Cowdenbeath (0) 0
423
Alloa Ath: Crawford; Buist, McClune, Townsley, Walker, Brown, Scott (Kerr), Ferguson B, Grant, Carroll, Agnew (Gilhaney).
Cowdenbeath: Hay; Armstrong, Adamson, Ramsay, Droudge, Mbu, Fairbairn, McBride, Wardlaw (Linton), Robertson, Stein (Ferguson).

Brechin C (2) 4 *(Fusco 17, Docherty 42, McAllister 57, 72)*

Wick Academy (1) 2 *(Mackay 39 (pen), MacAdie 82)* 402
Brechin C: Nelson C; Walker, Smith B, McLean, Dyer, Byers, Janczyk, Fusco, Docherty (Cowan), McAllister (McKenna), King.
Wick Academy: Bokas; Campbell, Ross, MacLeod, Manson, Farquhar (Lamb), Shearer, Mackay (Weir), Cunningham (McKiddie), Allan, MacAdie.

Monday, 14 December 2009

Livingston (2) 7 *(Keaghan Jacobs 5, Fox 49, 80, Winters R 50, 67, Halliday 51, 65)*

Clyde (1) 1 *(Lithgow 11)*
690
Livingston: McKenzie (McDowall); Brown, Talbot, Hamill (Kyle Jacobs), Watson, MacDonald, Fox, Keaghan Jacobs, Halliday, Winters R, De Vita (Winters D).
Clyde: Reidford; Stewart, Cassidy, Casey, Lithgow, Stevenson, McLaughlan, Higgins (Lang), Sawyers, White (Boyle), Howarth (McFadden).

FOURTH ROUND

Saturday, 9 January 2010

Aberdeen (0) 2 *(Mackie 60, Miller L 76)*

Hearts (0) 0
8226
Aberdeen: Langfield; Ross, Mulgrew, Young, Ifil, Kerr, Pawlett, Marshall (Maguire); Miller L, Mackie, Fyvie.
Hearts: Kello; Cinikas, Visconte, Bouzid, Zaliukas, Jonsson, Santana (Templeton), Black, Stewart M, Smith G(Nade), Robinson (Obua).

Dunfermline Ath (4) 7 *(Gibson 15, Kirk 17, 83 (pen), Phinn 21, Graham 35, McDougall 63, Cardle 69)*

Stenhousemuir (0) 1 *(Bradley 90)*
1832
Dunfermline Ath: Fleming; Ross (Woods), McGregor Dowie, McCann, Graham, Phinn (Burke), Bell, Gibson (Cardle), Kirk, McDougall.
Stenhousemuir: McCluskey; Lyle, McLeod, Smith J Thomson S (Thom), Thomson I (Welsh), Scullior (Durrie), Molloy, Motion, Bradley, Dalziel.
Dunfermline Ath originally disqualified for fielding an ineligible player; reinstated on appeal, but forced to replay at Stenhousemuir.

Hibernian (2) 3 *(Riordan 32, Zemmama 42, Hanlon 59)*

Irvine Meadow (0) 0
10,197
Hibernian: Smith; Wotherspoon, Hanlon, Zemmama (Cregg), Hogg, Murray, Miller, Rankine (Stevenson), Stokes, Nish (Benjelloun), Riordan.
Irvine Meadow: Wardrobe; Ryan, McGowan (Swift), Robertson, Lowing, Wingate, Strain, Turner (Mclymont), McGinty (Boyle), Hamilton, Barr.

Partick Th (0) 0

Dundee U (1) 2 *(Casalinuovo 26, Goodwillie 90)* 4002
Partick Th: Tuffey; Paton, Robertson, Maxwell (Erskine), Archibald, Cairney, Adams, Rowson, Corcoran, Lovell (Buchanan), Donnelly.
Dundee U: Pernis; Kovacevic, Dixon, Webster, Kenneth, Buaben, Robertson D (Swanson), Gomis, Casalinuovo, Daly (Goodwillie), Conway.

St Mirren (2) 3 *(Crawford 27 (og), Mehmet 45, 87)*

Alloa Ath (1) 1 *(Brown 34)*
2587
St Mirren: Gallacher; Ross, McGinn, Dorman, Innes, Mair, Robb, Johnston (Barron), Mehmet, Dargo (Higdon), Thomson.
Alloa Ath: Crawford; McClune, Walker, Brown (Carroll), Grant, Buist, Ferguson B, Townsley, Gilhaney (Carrigan), Noble (Kerr), Agnew.

Sunday, 10 January 2010

Hamilton A (3) 3 *(Mensing 39 (pen), Paixao M 44, Antoine-Curier 45)*

Rangers (2) 3 *(Whittaker 4, Miller 30, 63 (pen))* 3940
Hamilton A: Cerny; McClenanhan, Hastings[■], McLaughlin, Canning, Elliott (Paixao F), McArthur, Mensing, Paixao M, Neil, Antoine-Curier.
Rangers: McGregor; Whittaker, Papac, Wilson, Weir, Broadfoot, Davis (Thomson), McCulloch, Boyd (Little), Miller, Lafferty.

Monday, 18 January 2010

Albion R (0) 0

Stirling Alb (0) 0
395
Albion R: Gaston; Reid, McGowan, Donnelly, Benton, O'Byrne, McKeown (Dignam), Tyrrell, McCusker (Canning M), Walker P (Ferry), Boyle.
Stirling Alb: Christie; Feaks, Forsyth, Graham, Murphy (Devine), Robertson, Gibson (Taggart), Roycroft, McKenna, Mullen (Grehan), O'Brian.

Ayr U (1) 1 *(Roberts 3)*

Brechin C (0) 0
1139
Ayr U: Samson; Keenan, Aitken A, James (Campbell), Easton, Woodburn (Cawley), Stevenson, Connolly, Borris, Mendes (Connelly), Roberts.
Brechin C: Scott; Walker R, Dyer, McLean, Seeley, Janczyk (Miller), Byers, Fusco, McAllister, King (Canning), Docherty (Cowan).

Edinburgh C (1) 1 *(Gair 37)*

Montrose (1) 3 *(Nicholas 20, Maitland 71, Nichol 84)* 1027
Edinburgh C: Montieth; Harrison, Ross, MacNamara, Bruce, McFarland, Caddow, Gair, MacFarland, Stenhouse (Clee), Denholm (Guthrie).
Montrose: McNeil; Milligan, Fleming (Tomana), Campbell, Tweed, Crighton, Maitland (Nicol), Davidson, Gemmell (Leyden), Hegarty, Nicholas.

Forfar Ath (0) 0

St Johnstone (2) 3 *(Deuchar 23, Craig 43, 58)* 1449
Forfar Ath: Brown; McCulloch, Campbell I, Fotheringham M (Deasley), Tod, Tulloch, Gordon (Smith N), Mowat, Templeman, Campbell R, Gibson (Smith C).
St Johnstone: Smith G; Irvine, Grainger, Mackay, Gartland, Morris, Millar, Craig (Davidson), Milne (Reynolds), Deuchar, MacDonald (Swankie).

Inverness CT (1) 2 *(Bulvitis 42, Imrie 61)*

Motherwell (0) 0   1450

Inverness CT: Esson; Proctor, Bulvitis, Munro, Tokely, Hayes (Imrie), Duncan, Cox, Foran, Rooney, Sanchez (Eagle).
Motherwell: Ruddy; Hammell, Reynolds, Craigan, Coke (Forbes), Humphrey (Sutton), Jutkiewicz, Lasley, O'Brian, Hateley, Saunders (Murphy).

Kilmarnock (0) 1 *(Pascali 83)*

Falkirk (0) 0   3378

Kilmarnock: Bell; Hay, Hamill, Wright (Skelton), Ford, Fowler (Owens), Pascali, Bryson, Kyle (Taouil), Sammon, Russell.
Falkirk: Olejnik; McNamara, Twaddle, Bullen, McLean, Pele, Lima, Flynn (Marceta), Moutinho, Compton (O'Brien), Arfield.

Ross Co (1) 4 *(Craig 37, 56, Morrison 53, Miller 73)*

Inverurie Locos (0) 0   835

Ross Co: McGovern; Miller, Boyd (Watt), Keddie, Morrison, Scott, Lawson, Brittain, Gardyne (Kettlewell), Craig, Wood (Vigurs).
Inverurie Locos: Reid; Park, Merriman, Morrison, Buchan, McLean, Wilson, Davidson R (Neill), Bisset (Broadhurst), Gauld (Djahansovzi), Ross.

Tuesday, 19 January 2010

Morton (0) 0

Celtic (1) 1 *(McGinn 35)*   10,191

Morton: Stewart; McGuffie, Reid, Shimmin, Greacen, MacFarlane (Graham), Finlayson, Jenkins, Weatherson, Wake (Kane), McAlister.
Celtic: Boruc; Hinkel, Naylor, Crosas, Loovens, O'Dea, McGinn, Zheng Zi, Fortune, Samaras, McGeady.

Wednesday, 20 January 2010

Livingston (0) 0

Dundee (1) 1 *(Harkins 33)*   1176

Livingston: McKenzie; Brown, Talbot, Watson, MacDonald, Hamill, Fox (Kyle Jacobs), Keaghan Jacobs, Halliday, Winters R, De Vita (Sinclair).
Dundee: Soutar; Casement (Paton), Benedictus, Lauchlan, Forsyth, Malone, Kerr, Young (Klimpl), Harkins, Griffiths (McMenamin), Clarke.

Monday, 25 January 2010

Raith R (0) 1 *(Smyth 56 (og))*

Airdrie U (1) 1 *(Baird 5)*   1599

Raith R: McGurn; Wilson, Ellis, Campbell, Murray, Walker, Williamson (Sloan), Simmons■, Smith K, Tade (Russell), Smith D (Hill).
Airdrie U: Robertson; Parratt (Watt), Storey, Smyth, Donnelly, McLaughlin (Waddell), McCann R, McDonald, Keegan (Gemmill), Baird, Trouten.

FOURTH ROUND REPLAYS

Tuesday, 19 January 2010

Rangers (0) 2 *(Whittaker 98, 99)*

Hamilton A (0) 0   21,856

Rangers: McGregor; Whittaker, Papac, McCulloch (Edu), Weir, Wilson, Davis, Thomson (Broadfoot), Fleck, Miller, Novo (Little).
Hamilton A: Cerny; McClenahan, Elebert (McLaughlin), Mensing, Canning, McArthur, Evans (Wilkie), Neil, Antoine-Curier, Paixao F, Paixao M (Elliott).
aet.

Wednesday, 20 January 2010

Stirling Alb (3) 3 *(Mullen 9, 33, Murphy 43)*

Albion R (1) 1 *(Walker P 18)*   355

Stirling Alb: Christie; Feaks (Young), Graham, Murphy, Devine, Gibson, Robertson, O'Brian (Taggart), Roycroft, McKenna (Corr), Mullen.
Albion R: Gaston; McGowan, Benton, O'Byrne, Canning M (Ferry), Donnelly, McKeown, Tyrrell, Boyle, McCusker (McFarlane), Walker P.

Tuesday, 26 January 2010

Stenhousemuir (0) 1 *(Bradley 67 (pen))*

Dunfermline Ath (1) 2 *(Cardle 35, Kirk 112)*   1810

Stenhousemuir: McCluskey; Lyle, Thomson S, Gair (Motion), Smith J, Thom, Love (Thomson I), Molloy, Dalziel (Scullion), Bradley, Currie.
Dunfermline Ath: Fleming; Ross, McCann, Bell, McGregor, Dowie, Gibson (Burke), Phinn, Graham, Kirk, Cardle (Holmes).
aet.

Wednesday, 27 January 2010

Airdrie U (1) 1 *(Donnelly 39)*

Raith R (2) 3 *(Smith K 24, Tade 45, Russell 90 (pen))* 852

Airdrie U: Robertson; Storey, Waddell, Smyth, Donnelly, McLaughlin, Trouten (Smith), McDonald (Watt), Baird, Gemmill, McCann R (Lagana).
Raith R: McGurn; Wilson, Ellis, Campbell, Murray, Walker, Williamson, Ferry, Smith K (Weir), Tade, Russell.

FIFTH ROUND

Saturday, 6 February 2010

Dundee (1) 2 *(Hutchinson 41, Griffiths 70)*

Ayr U (1) 1 *(McManus 11)*   2852

Dundee: Douglas; Paton, Malone, Klimpl, MacKenzie, Lauchlan, Forsyth, Kerr, Griffiths, Hutchinson, Harkins.
Ayr U: Samson; McGowan A, Aitken R, Campbell, Easton, Woodburn (Mendes), Keenan, Connolly, Borris, Roberts, McManus.

Hibernian (2) 5 *(Nish 5, 25, Riordan 70, Benjelloun 78, Gow 89)*

Montrose (0) 1 *(Hegarty 74)*   9068

Hibernian: Smith; Wotherspoon, Murray, Hogg, Hanlon, Rankin, McBride (Zemmama), Miller, Nish (Gow), Riordan, Stokes (Benjelloun).
Montrose: McNeil; Milligan, McNalley, Hegarty, Campbell, Crighton, Maitland (Tomana), Davidson, Nicholas (Boyle), Gemmell, Fleming (Sinclair).

Kilmarnock (2) 3 *(Sammon 28, Kelly 36, 59)*

Inverness CT (0) 0   4473

Kilmarnock: Bell; Clancy (Invincibile), Hay, Ford, Bryson, Pascali, Sammon, Kyle (Fernandez), Kelly, Hamill, Severin (Fowler).
Inverness CT: Esson; Tokely, Bulvitis (Duncan), Munro, Djebi-Zadi, Cox, Sanchez (Odhiambo), Proctor, Foran, Rooney, Hayes (Eagle).

Raith R (0) 1 *(Williamson 31)*

Aberdeen (0) 1 *(McDonald 90)*   7045

Raith R: McGurn; Wilson, Ellis (Hill), Campbell, Murray, Walker, Williamson (Ferry), Simmons, Smith K (Weir), Tade, Russell.
Aberdeen: Langfield; Mulgrew, Foster, Ifil, McDonald, Kerr (Diamond), Paterson, MacLean, Mackie (Pawlett), Paton, Young (Aluko).

Ross Co (3) 9 *(Keddie 3, Gardyne 15, 20, Wood 55, 59, 90, Brittain 66 (pen), Kettlewell 83, Morrison 84)*

Stirling Alb (0) 0   1365

Ross Co: McGovern; Miller, Morrison, Scott, Boyd, Keddie (Watt), Gardyne (Barrowman), Lawson, Di Giacomo (Kettlewell), Brittain, Wood.
Stirling Alb: Christie; Feaks, Forsyth, Graham, Roycroft (Mullen), Robertson, Gibson (Corr), Murphy (O'Neil), McKenna, Young, O'Brian.

St Johnstone (0) 0

Dundee U (1) 1 *(Goodwillie 45)*   5636

St Johnstone: Smith G; Irvine, Grainger, Morris, MacKay, Duberry, Millar, Davidson (Sheerin), Milne (MacDonald), Deuchar (Sheridan), Morais.
Dundee U: Pernis; Dillon, Dixon (Cameron), Kenneth, Dods, Buaben, Swanson (Robertson D), Gomis, Goodwillie (Casalinuovo), Daly, Conway.

St Mirren (0) 0

Rangers (0) 0   4909

St Mirren: Gallacher; Ross, Barron, Dorman, Mair, Potter, Thomson, Innes, Mehmet, Higdon (Dargo), Murray.
Rangers: McGregor; Whittaker, Broadfoot, McCulloch, Bougherra, Smith, Davis, Thomson, Naismith (Miller), Lafferty (Boyd), Wilson.

Sunday, 7 February 2010

Dunfermline Ath (2) 2 *(Graham 21, Kirk 28 (pen))*

Celtic (2) 4 *(Kamara 20, Rasmussen 43, Woods 59 (og), Keane 68 (pen))*   8933

Dunfermline Ath: Fleming; Woods (Ross), McCann, Bell. McGregor, Dowie, Gibson, Phinn (Cardle), Graham. Kirk (Nish), Burke.
Celtic: Boruc; Braafheid, Caddis (Zheng Zi), Crosas (Keane), Loovens, Thompson, N'Guemo, Brown S Kamara (McGeady), Samaras, Rasmussen.

FIFTH ROUND REPLAYS

Wednesday, 17 February 2010

Aberdeen (0) 0

Raith R (0) 1 *(Tade 58)*   8153

Aberdeen: Langfield; Ifil, Foster, McDonald, Diamond (Young), Kerr, Paterson, MacLean, Mackie, Paton, Aluko.
Raith R: McGurn; Wilson, Ferry, Murray, Walker, Williamson, Sloan, Simmons, Smith K (Weir), Tade, Russell (Smith D).

Rangers (0) 1 *(Boyd 88)*

St Mirren (0) 0   31,086

Rangers: McGregor; Broadfoot, Smith, Edu, Weir, Bougherra, Davis, Novo (Miller), Boyd (Fleck), Naismith, Lafferty.
St Mirren: Gallacher; Ross (O'Donnell), Barron, Dorman, Innes, Potter, Thomson, Murray (Carey), Mehmet, Higdon (Dargo), Mair.

SIXTH ROUND

Saturday, 13 March 2010

Dundee (0) 1 *(Forsyth 73)*

Raith R (2) 2 *(Simmons 3, Ellis 10)*   7306

Dundee: Douglas; Paton, Malone, Kerr, MacKenzie, Lauchlan (Shinnie), Forsyth, Hart (McMenamin). Griffiths, Higgins (Clarke), Harkins.
Raith R: McGurn; Gathuessi, Ellis, Murray, Hill (Ferry), Simmons, Williamson, Walker, Tade, Weir (Shields), Russell (Smith D).

Hibernian (2) 2 *(Nish 7, Riordan 19)*

Ross Co (1) 2 *(Murray 16 (og), Gardyne 79)*   9857

Hibernian: Stack; Murray, Wotherspoon, Miller, Hogg, Hanlon, McBride, Stokes (Benjelloun), Nish, Riordan, Rankin (Galbraith).
Ross Co: McGovern; Miller, Morrison, Scott, Boyd, Keddie, Gardyne, Lawson, Barrowman, Brittain, Vigurs.

Kilmarnock (0) 0

Celtic (0) 3 *(Keane 64, 81, 82)*   7351

Kilmarnock: Bell; Clancy, Kelly, Fowler, Wright (Kiernan), Severin, Bryson, Taouil, Russell, Burchill (Invincibile), Hamill.
Celtic: Zaluska; Hinkel (Wilson), Braafheid, Crosas (Fortune), O'Dea, Thompson, N'Guemo, Brown S, Rasmussen (Samaras), Keane, McGeady.

Sunday, 14 March 2010

Rangers (2) 3 *(Boyd 34 (pen), 43 (pen), Novo 48)*

Dundee U (1) 3 *(Shala 24, Whittaker 63 (og), Kovacevic 80)*   24,096

Rangers: McGregor; Whittaker, Papac, McCulloch, Weir, Wilson, Davis, Thomson (Edu), Boyd (Lafferty), Novo (Beasley), Miller.
Dundee U: Pernis; Dillon, Kovacevic, Kenneth, Dods, Buaben, Swanson (Robertson D), Gomis (Sandaza), Casalinuovo (Shala), Daly, Conway.

SIXTH ROUND REPLAYS

Tuesday, 23 March 2010

Ross Co (0) 2 *(Wood 70, Boyd 90)*

Hibernian (0) 1 *(Stokes 46)*   5607

Ross Co: McGovern; Miller, Morrison, Scott, Boyd, Keddie, Gardyne (Kettlewell), Lawson (Wood), Barrowman (Craig), Brittain, Vigurs.
Hibernian: Smith; Thicot, Stevenson, McBride, Bamba, Murray, Wotherspoon (Galbraith), Miller, Stokes (Benjelloun), Riordan, Nish.

Wednesday, 24 March 2010

Dundee U (0) 1 *(Robertson D 90)*

Rangers (0) 0   11,898

Dundee U: Pernis; Kovacevic (Watson), Dillon, Kenneth, Dods, Buaben, Robertson D, Gomis (Swanson), Goodwillie, Daly, Conway.
Rangers: McGregor; Whittaker, Papac, Edu, Weir, Wilson, Beasley, Naismith, Fleck (Novo), Little (Boyd), Lafferty (Miller).

SEMI-FINALS (at Hampden Park)

Saturday, 10 April 2010

Celtic (0) 0

Ross Co (0) 2 *(Craig 55, Scott 88)*   24,535

Celtic: Zaluska; Hinkel (Rasmussen), Naylor, Brown S, O'Dea, Thompson, N'Guemo, Samaras, Fortune (McCourt), Keane, McGeady.
Ross Co: McGovern; Miller, Morrison, Scott, Boyd, Keddie, Gardyne (Lawson), Barrowman, Craig, Brittain, Vigurs.

Sunday, 11 April 2010

Dundee U (1) 2 *(Goodwillie 28, Webster 59)*

Raith R (0) 0   17,671

Dundee U: Pernis; Dillon, Dixon (Watson), Webster, Dods, Buaben, Swanson (Myrie-Williams), Gomis, Goodwillie (Cadamarteri), Daly, Conway.
Raith R: McGurn; Gathuessi, Ellis, Murray, Hill (Ferry), Davidson, Walker, Simmons, Mole (Smith D), Tade, Williamson (Weir).

SCOTTISH FA CUP FINAL (at Hampden Park)

Saturday, 15 May 2010 at Hampden Park, attendance 47,122

Dundee U (0) 3 *(Goodwillie 51, Conway 75, 86)*   **Ross Co (0) 0**

Dundee U: Pernis; Kovacevic (Watson), Dillon, Webster, Kenneth, Buaben, Swanson (Robertson S), Gomis, Goodwillie (Robertson D), Daly, Conway.

Ross Co: McGovern; Miller, Morrison, Scott (Wood), Boyd, Keddie, Gardyne (Di Giacomo), Barrowman, Craig (Lawson), Brittain, Vigurs.

Referee: D. McDonald.

WELSH FOOTBALL 2009–10

With a couple of honourable exceptions, Welsh football appears to be in a state of inertia. After the curtain had fallen on another fruitless World Cup qualifying campaign, Cardiff and Swansea both suffered play-off heartbreak as the Premier League tantalisingly beckoned while Wrexham could only tread water – lacking the necessary thrust to propel themselves back into the Football League. But further down the English pyramid, Newport and Colwyn Bay flew the Welsh flag with distinction by winning promotion – The Exiles by a country mile and The Seagulls via the play-offs.

It was always going to be hard for Wales to finish third in their South Africa 2010 group – and so it proved. Defeats by an Andrey Arshavin-inspired Russia at the Millennium Stadium and Finland in Helsinki were followed by an expected 2-0 victory in Vaduz against Liechtenstein. But when another member of the Arsenal midfield, Aaron Ramsey, orchestrated a 3-0 win over Scotland in the first international to be staged at the new Cardiff City stadium in November, spirits were lifted and hopes began to be raised. After scoring the second goal in Liechtenstein, the 19-year-old former Cardiff City starlet set up the first two against the Scots before netting the third with a superb solo effort. Scotland may have been shambolic but Ramsey truly shone. But just as he was starting to establish himself in Arsenal's first team, Ramsey's season was shattered by a double fracture to his lower right leg against Stoke in late February. Four days later, Wales lost 1-0 to Sweden at the Liberty Stadium in Swansea and another friendly against Croatia in Osijek in May ended in a predictable defeat after manager John Toshack had to select from a squad of just 17 players following 15 withdrawals. Depleted yet dogged, his patched-up, makeshift side produced a spirited performance and contained five debutants. 'Disappointing and unfortunate' was Toshack's diplomatic description of the mass no-show by so many of his squad.

There was disappointment of a different kind for Cardiff City. After battling against off-field financial problems which threatened to put the club out of business, they cruised into the Championship's top six. Galvanised by missing out on the 2009 play-offs through a single goal, the Bluebirds finished fourth in the regular season – scoring 73 goals and conceding just 54 in 46 games. But having won 1-0 at Leicester in the first leg of their semi-final, dodgy defending meant they lost 3-2 at home and it took a moment of madness from Leicester's Yann Kermorgant, who inexplicably tried a cheeky chip in the penalty shoot-out, to help them into the final against Blackpool at Wembley. A return to the top flight for the first time in 48 years seemed within their grasp but, on the biggest stage of all, the Bluebirds just couldn't get airborne. A combination of dubious selections and substitutions and inflexible tactics meant that, having led 2-1 seven minutes before half-time though Michael Chopra and Joe Ledley, Cardiff capitulated as Blackpool's highly mobile 4-3-3 formation left their midfield over-run and their defence in tatters just before the break. Despite Cardiff's domination of the second half, the indefatigable Tangerines deservedly held on to win 3-2. At least the £6 million takeover by Dato Chan Tien Ghee and his Malaysian consortium has secured Cardiff's immediate future and, after two successive near-misses, Dave Jones and his coaching staff have another opportunity to make it third time lucky.

One more goal would have taken Swansea into the play-offs at Blackpool's expense but their campaign ended in anti-climax with a 0-0 draw against Doncaster at the Liberty Stadium. Their trademark passing game had kept the Swans in the top six for four months between December and the penultimate match of the season but their lack of firepower, exacerbated by the departure of Jason Scotland to Wigan with former Swans manager Roberto Martinez, proved costly. They hit the net only 40 times in 46 games – with midfielder Darren Pratley finishing as top scorer with just seven goals – and managed only three wins in their last 13 games. Swansea moved up a place to seventh thanks to a solid defence and nice approach play – it was a shame about the end product. Their failure paled into insignificance when their 22-year-old striker, Besian Idrizaj, died from a suspected heart attack at his home in Austria, a fortnight later. His Number 40 shirt was immediately retired by the club.

For a second successive season, and the first with manager Dean Saunders in complete charge, Wrexham struggled to make any impression in the Blue Square Conference, slipping one place to 11th. Like Swansea, they conceded few goals but didn't score enough. The Red Dragons will be joined in the Conference by Newport County as the result of a quite extraordinary achievement by manager Dean Holdsworth. The Exiles moved to the top of the table in September and then stormed to the title in March with seven league matches left to become the first team in the English pyramid to win promotion. They set a Conference South record of 103 points, finishing 28 ahead of runners-up Dover Athletic, to return to the level they played at before going bankrupt in 1989. Seven years after being relegated, Colwyn Bay made good use of their near-miss in 2009 by going one better and winning promotion to the Premier Division of the Northern Premier League by beating Lancaster City in the play-off final. Despite being docked 10 points for spending the season in administration, Merthyr managed to avoid relegation from the Southern League's Premier Division. However, ongoing financial problems ended with the Martyrs going into liquidation. Reformed as Merthyr Town, they will play in the Western League next season, their home games accommodated at Taffs Well.

Sadly, it was business as usual for Welsh clubs playing in Europe. In the Champions League, Rhyl were completely outclassed as they lost 12-0 on aggregate to Partizan Belgrade while it was a case of new competition but same old story for Llanelli, The New Saints and Bangor in the Europa League. The Reds upset the form book by winning 1-0 at Scottish Premier League side Motherwell before going down 3-0 at home, a brace of 2-1 defeats by Iceland's Fram Reykjavik saw off The New Saints while Bangor went out 3-0 on aggregate to FC Honka from Finland. The New Saints regained the Welsh Premier League title – the last one before the competition is reduced to 12 teams – with Llanelli finishing runners-up and Port Talbot Town claiming third place and then losing 3-2 to Bangor City in the Welsh Cup Final.

For the second time this century, Wales will renew their rivalry with The Old Enemy. The two countries were drawn in the same Euro 2012 qualifying group – along with Switzerland, Bulgaria and Montenegro – and England will visit the Millennium Stadium in March with Wales playing at Wembley next September. Those two fixtures in themselves should signal an end to inertia and the team that Toshack built must now step up to the plate. Although Ramsey's talismanic talent will be badly missed during the early part of the campaign, it's to be hoped that, buoyed by a new long-term contract with Arsenal, he will recover in time for the 2011 games. One player, especially one so young, doesn't make a team but the return of a fully fit boy wonder would surely work wonders as Wales try to end so many years of frustration.

GRAHAME LLOYD

PRINCIPALITY BUILDING SOCIETY WELSH PREMIER LEAGUE 2009–10

		P		Home					Away					Total					
			W	D	L	F	A	W	D	L	F	A	W	D	L	F	A	GD	Pts
1	The New Saints	34	14	3	0	49	6	11	4	2	20	7	25	7	2	69	13	56	82
2	Llanelli	34	14	2	1	49	14	11	3	3	30	12	25	5	4	79	26	53	80
3	Port Talbot Town	34	12	3	2	35	8	7	5	5	21	15	19	8	7	56	23	33	65
4	Aberystwyth Town	34	8	4	5	27	25	11	3	3	27	16	19	7	8	54	41	13	64
5	Bangor City	34	11	3	3	43	19	8	3	6	32	26	19	6	9	75	45	30	63
6	Rhyl	34	11	3	3	45	17	7	5	5	29	26	18	8	8	74	43	31	62
7	Airbus UK Broughton	34	6	6	5	25	18	6	7	4	24	19	12	13	9	49	37	12	49
8	Prestatyn Town	34	6	7	4	19	20	6	5	6	34	33	12	12	10	53	53	0	48
9	Neath Athletic	34	6	6	5	25	21	6	5	6	16	17	12	11	11	41	38	3	47
10	Carmarthen Town	34	5	4	8	21	21	7	5	5	24	17	12	9	13	45	38	7	45
11	Bala Town	34	5	6	6	18	23	7	3	7	21	24	12	9	13	39	47	–8	45
12	Haverfordwest County	34	6	6	5	22	20	5	5	7	21	27	11	11	12	43	47	–4	44
13	Newtown	34	6	4	7	29	31	4	7	6	25	26	10	11	13	54	57	–3	41
14	Gap Connah's Quay	34	7	4	6	20	15	4	4	9	11	27	11	8	15	31	42	–11	41
15	CPD Porthmadog	34	2	4	11	10	28	4	2	11	13	38	6	6	22	23	66	–43	24
16	Welshpool Town	34	3	2	12	15	33	3	3	11	15	37	6	5	23	30	70	–40	23
17	Caersws	34	3	2	12	13	37	0	2	15	13	57	3	4	27	26	94	–68	13
18	Elements Cefn Druids	34	1	4	12	8	28	0	2	15	8	49	1	6	27	16	77	–61	9

PREVIOUS WELSH LEAGUE WINNERS

1993	Cwmbran Town	1998	Barry Town	2003	Barry Town	2008	Llanelli
1994	Bangor City	1999	Barry Town	2004	Rhyl	2009	Rhyl
1995	Bangor City	2000	TNS	2005	TNS	2010	The New Saints
1996	Barry Town	2001	Barry Town	2006	TNS		
1997	Barry Town	2002	Barry Town	2007	TNS		

MACWHIRTER WELSH LEAGUE 2009–10

		P	W	D	L	F	A	GD	Pts
1	Goytre United	34	19	12	3	86	47	39	69
2	Cambrian & Clydach Vale	34	19	11	4	73	42	31	68
3	Afan Lido	34	19	6	9	74	37	37	63
4	Caldicot Town	34	16	7	11	78	54	24	55
5	Bryntirion Athletic	34	15	9	10	67	60	7	54
6	Taffs Well	34	15	5	14	72	60	12	50
7	Barry Town	34	12	13	9	46	41	5	49
8	Pontardawe Town	34	13	8	13	59	56	3	47
9	Bridgend Town	34	12	9	13	57	55	2	45
10	Aberaman Athletic	34	12	8	14	56	68	–12	44
11	West End	34	12	8	14	62	84	–22	44
12	Cardiff Corinthians	34	12	7	15	63	69	–6	43
13	Garden Village	34	12	6	16	46	52	–6	42
14	Ton Pentre	34	11	8	15	56	65	–9	41
15	Ely Rangers	34	10	6	18	46	67	–21	36
16	Bettws	34	9	9	16	38	59	–21	36
17	Dinas Powys	34	9	4	21	50	83	–33	31
18	Caerleon	34	8	6	20	37	67	–30	30

HUWS GRAY-FITLOCK CYMRU ALLIANCE LEAGUE 2009–10

		P	W	D	L	F	A	GD	Pts
1	Llangefni Town	32	25	4	3	95	27	68	79
2	Flint Town United	32	23	6	3	84	29	55	75
3	Llandudno Town	32	19	8	5	73	31	42	65
4	Buckley Town	32	17	9	6	57	30	27	60
5	Penrhyncoch	32	16	7	9	51	46	5	55
6	Guilsfield	32	12	9	11	54	54	0	45
7	Ruthin Town	32	13	5	14	48	61	–13	44
8	Holyhead Hotspur*	32	13	4	15	53	52	1	40
9	Bethesda Athletic	32	10	9	13	70	59	11	39
10	Denbigh Town	32	10	9	13	56	56	0	39
11	Llangollen	32	11	3	18	59	78	–19	36
12	Berriew	32	10	5	17	49	74	–25	35
13	Mold Alexandra	32	11	2	19	53	80	–27	35
14	Lex XI	32	9	7	16	45	70	–25	34
15	Llanfairpwll	32	9	5	18	38	60	–22	32
16	Caernarfon Town*	32	8	5	19	50	69	–19	26
17	Gresford Athletic	32	5	5	22	28	87	–59	20

*3 points deducted.

WELSH CUP 2009–10

PRELIMINARY ROUND NORTH

Barmouth & Dyffryn United v Dyffryn Banw	2-0
Blaenau Ffestiniog Amateur v Glan Conwy	0-3
Borras Park Albion v Rhos Aelwyd	4-1
Brickfield Rangers v Hawarden Rangers	0-4
Coedpoeth United bye v Llanllyfni withdrew	
Corwen v Chirk AAA	1-2
Dolgellau Athletic Amateur v Llanfyllin Town	7-2
Halkyn United v Tywyn Bryncrug	1-2
Holywell Town v Llanrug United	0-5
Llandudno Junction v Castell Alun Colts	3-2
Pwllheli v Dyffryn Nantlle Vale	6-0

PRELIMINARY ROUND SOUTH

AFC Llwydcoed v AFC Porth	3-1
Bow Street v Aberbargoed Buds	0-1
Cardiff Bay Harlequins v UWIC	2-0
Cwmamman United v Presteigne St Andrew's	4-5
Garw SGBC v Cwmbran Celtic	0-4
Hay St Mary's v Monmouth Town	1-1
Hay St Mary's won on penalties.	
Llanwern v South Gower	0-5
Maesteg Park v Llantwit Fadre	2-4
Newport YMCA v Croesyceiliog	3-5
Rhayader Town v Newport Civil Service	0-2
Seven Sisters v Briton Ferry Llansawel	2-0
Tredegar Town v Pontyclun	
Tredegar Town disqualified for fielding an ineligible player.	
Troedyrhiw v Cwmbran Town	3-1

FIRST ROUND NORTH

Amlwch Town v Penrhyncoch	2-3
Barmouth & Dyffryn United v Buckley Town	3-2
Berriew v Mold Alexandra	3-1
Brymbo v Llangefni Town	1-6
Carno v Conwy United	2-3
Chirk AAA v Gresford Athletic	1-3
Coedpoeth United v Penparcau	2-0
Glan Conwy v Denbigh Town	2-1
Guilsfield v Llangollen Town	1-3
Hawarden Rangers v Ruthin Town	0-2
Lex XI v Dolgellau Athletic Amateur	5-3
Llanberis v Flint Town United	1-2
Llandudno v Bethesada Athletic	3-1
Llandudno Junction v Llanrhaedr ym Mochnant	1-0
Llanfairpwll v Penycae	2-1
Llanrug United v Nefyn United	4-3
Llanrwst United v Llangeinor	0-2
Llansantffraid Village v Llay Welfare	3-1
Overton Recreational v Holyhead Hotspur	1-2
Pwllheli v Tywyn Bryncrug	2-0
Rhydymwyn v Llandymog United	2-0
Venture Community v Borras Park Albion	3-4

FIRST ROUND SOUTH

Barry Town v Ely Rangers	1-5
Bryntirion Athletic v Cardiff Corinthians	4-2
Caerau Ely v Bettws	2-0
Cambrian & Clydach Vale v Ammanford	4-0
Corus Steel v Garden Village	0-1
Croesyciliog v Risca United	1-0
Cwmaman Institute v Cwmbran Celtic	1-7
Goytre United v Pentwyn Dynamo's	3-1
Hay St Mary's v Dinas Powys	2-1
Llantwit Fadre v Aberbargoed Buds	0-1
Newcastle Emlyn v AFC Llwydcoed	1-2
Penrhiwceiber v Caerleon	3-1
Pontardawe Town v Presteigne St Andrew's	4-1
Pontyclun v Goytre	7-2
Pontypridd Town v Newport Civil Service	3-0
Porthcawl Town v Ton Pentre	2-4
Seven Sisters v Afan Lido	0-7
South Gower v Caldicot Town	0-5
Treharris Athletic Western v Cardiff Bay Harlequins	3-4
Troedyrhiw v Abertillery Bluebirds	2-1
West End v Taffs Well	6-6
Taffs Well won 4-2 on penalties.	

SECOND ROUND NORTH

Bangor City v Elements Cefn Druids	4-1
Borras Park Albion v Bala Town	1-8
Conwy United v The New Saints	0-2
Flint Town United v Barmouth & Dyffryn United	7-1
Gap Connah's Quay v Pwllheli	2-0
Gresford Athletic v Llanrug United	2-3
Holyhead Hotspurs v Newtown	1-1
Holyhead Hotspurs won 4-3 on penalties.	
Lex XI v Airbus UK Broughton	1-3
Llandudno Town v Berriew	3-0
Llanfairpwll v Rhyl	1-3
Llangefni Town v Llandudno Junction	1-2
Llangollen Town v Glan Conwy	1-0
Llansantffraid Village v Coedpoeth United	1-3
Penrhycoch v CPD Porthmadog	0-1
Rhydymwyn v Caernarfon Town	1-0
Ruthin Town v Caersws	1-2
Welshpool v Prestatyn Town	2-3

SECOND ROUND SOUTH

Aberaman Athletic v Penrhiwceiber	3-2
Afan Lido v Croesyceiliog	5-1
Bridgend Town v Ton Pentre	2-0
Bryntirion Athletic v Aberystwyth Town	0-3
Caerau Ely v Hay St Mary's	5-1
Cambrian & Clydach Vale v Troedyrhiw	3-1
Cardiff Bay Harlequins v Aberbargoed Buds	3-2
Carmarthen Town v Pontypridd Town	4-1
Ely Rangers v AFC Llwydcoed	3-2
Garden Village v Caldicot Town	2-6
Goytre United v Pontardawe Town	0-3
Llangeinor v Pontyclun	2-1
Neath v Llanelli	2-2
Llanelli won 3-2 on penalties.	
Port Talbot Town v Cwmbran Celtic	5-0
Taffs Well v Haverfordwest County	0-2

THIRD ROUND

Aberaman Athletic v Ely Rangers	2-0
Bala Town v Llanrug United	1-0
Caerau Ely v Afan Lido	1-2
Caersws v Coedpoeth United	4-1
Caldicot Town v Port Talbot Town	0-3
Cambrian & Clydach Vale v The New Saints	0-2
CPD Porthmadog v Rhydymwyn	3-1
Flint Town United v Bangor City	0-1
Gap Connah's Quay v Airbus UK Broughton	3-2
Haverfordwest County v Aberystwyth Town	1-2
Llanelli v Carmarthen Town	3-1
Llangeinor v Holyhead Hotspurs	1-6
Llangollen Town v Llandudno Junction	1-3
Pontardawe Town v Llandudno Town	2-0
Prestatyn Town v Cardiff Bay Harlequins	3-0
Rhyl v Bridgend Town	4-2

FOURTH ROUND

Aberystwyth Town v Port Talbot Town	0-2
Afan Lido v Gap Connah's Quay	2-1
Bala Town v Caersws	2-0
Bangor City v Aberaman Athletic	3-1
Llandudno Junction v The New Saints	0-6
Llanelli v Holyhead Hotspur	4-0
Prestatyn Town v Porthmadog	1-0
Rhyl v Pontardawe Town	7-0

QUARTER-FINALS

Bala Town v Afan Lido	2-0
Bangor City v Llanelli	2-0
Prestatyn Town v Rhyl	4-4
Prestatyn Town won 5-3 on penalties.	
The New Saints v Port Talbot Town	2-2
Port Talbot Town won 4-3 on penalties.	

SEMI-FINALS

Port Talbot Town v Bala Town	1-0
Prestatyn Town v Bangor City	0-2

FINAL (at Llanelli)   **1303**

1 May 2010

Port Talbot T (0) 2, Bangor C (2) 3

Port Talbot T: Kendall; De Vulgt (Holland 63), Barrow, Phillips, Rees, Surman, Fahiya (John 66), Grist, Rose, McCreesh, Thomas (Lewis 66).
Scorers: Fahiya 57, McCreesh 85.
Bangor C: Smith; Hoy, Roberts, Morley, Brewerton, Garside, Reed (Davies 90), Johnston, Hunt, Jebb (Limbert 80), Smyth (Edwards 69).
Scorers: Hunt 6, Reed 15, Morley 90.
Referee: D. John.

PREVIOUS WELSH CUP WINNERS

1878	Wrexham Town	1909	Wrexham	1950	Swansea Town	1981	Swansea City
1879	White Star Newtown	1910	Wrexham	1951	Merthyr Tydfil	1982	Swansea City
1880	Druids	1911	Wrexham	1952	Rhyl	1983	Swansea City
1881	Druids	1912	Cardiff City	1953	Rhyl	1984	Shrewsbury Town
1882	Druids	1913	Swansea Town	1954	Flint Town United	1985	Shrewsbury Town
1883	Wrexham	1914	Wrexham	1955	Barry Town	1986	Wrexham
1884	Oswestry United	1915	Wrexham	1956	Cardiff City	1987	Merthyr Tydfil
1885	Druids	1920	Cardiff City	1957	Wrexham	1988	Cardiff City
1886	Druids	1921	Wrexham	1958	Wrexham	1989	Swansea City
1887	Chirk	1922	Cardiff City	1959	Cardiff City	1990	Hereford United
1888	Chirk	1923	Cardiff City	1960	Wrexham	1991	Swansea City
1889	Bangor	1924	Wrexham	1961	Swansea Town	1992	Cardiff City
1890	Druids	1925	Wrexham	1962	Bangor City	1993	Cardiff City
1891	Shrewsbury Town	1926	Ebbw Vale	1963	Borough United	1994	Barry Town
1892	Chirk	1927	Cardiff City	1964	Cardiff City	1995	Wrexham
1893	Wrexham	1928	Cardiff City	1965	Cardiff City	1996	TNS
1894	Chirk	1929	Connah's Quay	1966	Swansea Town	1997	Barry Town
1895	Newtown	1930	Cardiff City	1967	Cardiff City	1998	Bangor City
1896	Bangor	1931	Wrexham	1968	Cardiff City	1999	Inter Cable-Tel
1897	Wrexham	1932	Swansea Town	1969	Cardiff City	2000	Bangor City
1898	Druids	1933	Chester	1970	Cardiff City	2001	Barry Town
1899	Druids	1934	Bristol City	1971	Cardiff City	2002	Barry Town
1900	Aberystwyth	1935	Tranmere Rovers	1972	Wrexham	2003	Barry Town
1901	Oswestry United	1936	Crewe Alexandra	1973	Cardiff City	2004	Rhyl
1902	Wellington Town	1937	Crewe Alexandra	1974	Cardiff City	2005	TNS
1903	Wrexham	1938	Shrewsbury Town	1975	Wrexham	2006	Rhyl
1904	Druids	1939	South Liverpool	1976	Cardiff City	2007	Carmarthen Town
1905	Wrexham	1940	Wellington Town	1977	Shrewsbury Town	2008	Bangor C
1906	Wellington Town	1947	Chester	1978	Wrexham	2009	Bangor C
1907	Oswestry United	1948	Lovell's Athletic	1979	Shrewsbury Town	2010	Bangor C
1908	Chester	1949	Merthyr Tydfil	1980	Newport County		

THE LOOSEMORES OF CARDIFF CHALLENGE CUP 2009–10

GROUP 1

	P	W	D	L	F	A	GD	Pts
Port Talbot T	4	3	1	0	8	3	5	10
Neath	4	1	1	2	4	8	–4	4
Carmarthen T	4	0	2	2	3	5	–2	2

GROUP 2

	P	W	D	L	F	A	GD	Pts
Llanelli	4	2	2	0	13	4	9	8
Aberystwyth T	4	1	2	1	5	11	–6	5
Haverfordwest C	4	0	2	2	5	5	–3	2

GROUP 3

	P	W	D	L	F	A	GD	Pts
CPD Porthmadog	4	2	0	2	9	4	5	7
Gap Connah's Quay	4	2	1	1	6	7	–1	7
Caersws	4	0	2	2	2	6	–4	2

GROUP 4

	P	W	D	L	F	A	GD	Pts
Rhyl	4	4	0	0	11	2	9	12
Prestatyn T	4	1	1	2	5	7	–2	4
Airbus UK	4	0	1	3	3	10	–7	1

GROUP 5

	P	W	D	L	F	A	GD	Pts
Welshpool	4	3	1	0	11	5	6	10
Bala T	4	2	1	1	7	3	4	7
Elements Cefn Druids	4	0	0	4	5	15	–10	0

GROUP 6

	P	W	D	L	F	A	GD	Pts
The New Saints	4	3	1	0	13	6	7	10
Bangor C	4	2	0	2	7	8	–1	6
Newtown	4	0	1	3	5	11	–6	1

QUARTER-FINALS

Bala T v Gap Connah's Quay	2-3
CPD Porthmadog v Rhyl	1-4
Port Talbot T v Welshpool	3-1
The New Saints v Llanelli	4-1

SEMI-FINAL FIRST LEG

Gap Connah's Quay v Rhyl	2-1
Port Talbot T v The New Saints	0-0

SEMI-FINAL SECOND LEG

Rhyl v Gap Connah's Quay	4-0
The New Saints v Port Talbot Town	2-0

FINAL (at The Airfield)

27 April 2010

Rhyl (0) 1 *(Turner 65)*

The New Saints (2) 3 *(Seargeant 31, 77, Wood 36)*　　385

Rhyl: Pritchard; Naylor (Heenan 65), Doran, Dowling, Strong, Leah, Williams C, Connolly, Turner, Williams M, Pearson.

The New Saints: Harrison; Jones S, Marriott C, Baker, Holmes T, Murtagh (Edwards 73), Seargeant (Holmes D 80), McKenna, Wood, Marriott R (Jones C 62).

Referee: P. Thomas.

NORTHERN IRISH FOOTBALL 2009–10

The stern reality of the United Kingdom's economic problems, hit Northern Ireland football hard, although the Irish FA reported a £460,000 profit on a turnover of £10m with Sky TV playing a major role.

Some clubs were threatened with bankruptcy as costs spiralled primarily through increased expenditure on players' wages. Now, however, the problem has been grasped in a pragmatic, professional manner by a proposal to apply a wage cap. For years there has been a need for this to be introduced as financial agreements with staff at some clubs proved crippling – certainly much more than they could afford or were generating in income. To make matters worse, the competition turned out so often to be an attempt to keep up with the Joneses.

There has to be a cap not exceeding 55% of income with rigid penalties imposed for contravention. This is a project which will "bite" hard and must be policed properly to ensure there is no deviation from the straight and narrow path. Breeches simply cannot be tolerated.

Playing-wise, this was a season of triumph for Linfield, who achieved an Irish League and Cup double, despite a hic-cup around December when they passed through a phase of poor results, something foreign to their fans who demand constant success.

David Jeffrey was named Manager of the Year, although he reckons his job was in jeopardy during the downturn. "I told the players we were in this together," he said. "Everybody responded magnificently and as a result, we find our-selves again in Europe which is a major cash boost to the club and a fitting reward for endeavour."

Cliftonville, with a corps of highly talented young players, finished second while a serious challenge was also provided by Crusaders and Glentoran, last season's champions, who failed to win a major trophy with manager Alan McDonald resigning and Scott Young, a former player and current coach, taking over. Roy Coyle, Northern Ireland's most success-ful domestic manager, was appointed Director of Football.

Backed by Government funding, UEFA, Irish FA and Sport NI, clubs were able to embark on ground improvements, including the installation of floodlights. Cliftonville, celebrating their 130th anniversary, did a wonderful job at Solitude, with the construction of a new stand, dressing room and medical facilities, a media suite and an elevator to the first tier level boardroom and social suite.

Linfield captain and sweeper Noel Bailie established a world record with his 1000th appearance in April, which earned him plaudits from FIFA and UEFA. An Inland Revenue employee, he is a part-time professional winning every honour in Irish League football as well as being capped at Under-21 level. "He epitomises the Olympian spirit of sport," said Linfield chairman Jim Kerr.

Loughgall won the Ladbrokes.com Division One Championship with Donegal Celtic as the runners-up, but opted not to be promoted so Donegal Celtic met Institute, the Premiership bottom club, in a home and away play-off which they won 1-0 to regain senior status. Major work has also been carried out on Celtic Park in Suffolk, West Belfast.

Internationally, it was a mixed bag and a disappointing end with failure to qualify for the World Cup Finals in South Africa. Draws in Poland (1-1) and the Czech Republic (0-0) and a home defeat to Slovakia meant finishing in fourth place; Slovakia topped the group and Slovenia going through via the play-offs. The Under-21 side's UEFA Championship record was marred by home and away defeats by Iceland.

Northern Ireland now face a formidable European Championship challenge in a qualifying group which includes Italy, due to visit Belfast for the first time in 52 years. What a pity Windsor Park hasn't yet been refurbished, which means a drastically restricted attendance.

And on that point, Irish FA President Raymond Kennedy made some relevant observations in his annual report: "Despite the best efforts of the Association, the refurbishment of Windsor Park remains an elusive goal. Work contin-ues with all the stakeholders, including the Government, Sport NI and Linfield, stadium owners, to try and move this vital and intrinsic project forward.

"There is, of course, no easy fix. Government investment means a level of responsibility for which we are currently striving. No stone will be left unturned until it is achieved.

"Northern Ireland football, given the iconic nature of our national team, deserves this. Nothing must stand in our way to obtaining a fitting stadium to welcome the world's best footballers."   DR MALCOLM BRODIE MBE

CARLING PREMIERSHIP 2009–10

SECTION A	P	W	D	L	F	A	GD	Pts
Linfield	38	22	8	8	78	37	41	74
Cliftonville	38	21	6	11	69	42	27	69
Glentoran	38	19	8	11	58	46	12	65
Crusaders	38	17	9	12	57	52	5	60
Dungannon Swifts	38	16	9	13	56	58	–2	57
Portadown	38	15	10	13	70	55	15	55

SECTION B	P	W	D	L	F	A	GD	Pts
Coleraine	38	16	9	13	76	62	14	57
Glenavon	38	12	7	19	47	67	–20	43
Newry City	38	10	12	16	38	63	–25	42
Ballymena United	38	11	7	20	46	56	–10	40
Lisburn Distillery	38	11	6	21	45	76	–31	39
Institute	38	6	13	19	36	62	–26	31

RELEGATION PLAY-OFFS
Donegal Celtic 0, Institute 0
Institute 0, Donegal Celtic 1
Donegal Celtic promoted; Institute relegated.

MILESTONE
Noel Bailie (Linfield) aged 39 made his 1000th appear-ance for the club on 24 April 2010. In total, he made 1002 appearances, 584 in the League. His 34 European appearances was an Irish League record, he won eight Championships and six Irish Cup medals, was Ulster Young Player of the Year 1990 and Northern Ireland Player of the Year 1994.

LADBROKES.COM CHAMPIONSHIP

DIVISION ONE	P	W	D	L	F	A	GD	Pts
Loughgall	26	19	3	4	60	24	36	60
Donegal Celtic	26	19	2	5	59	21	38	59
Limavady United	26	18	3	5	56	29	27	57
Ards	26	13	6	7	49	27	22	45
Carrick Rangers	26	12	5	9	37	39	–2	41
Ballinamallard United	26	10	8	8	36	29	–7	38
Ballymoney United	26	10	8	8	39	33	6	38
Larne	26	11	4	11	34	37	–3	37
Banbridge Town	26	8	3	15	33	48	–15	27
Glebe Rangers	26	6	13	30	56	–26	27
Bangor	26	7	5	14	36	48	–12	26
Ballyclare Comrades	26	7	5	14	34	46	–12	26
Coagh United*	26	6	4	16	38	62	–24	22
Armagh City*	26	2	4	20	20	62	–42	10#

Loughgall declined promotion.

DIVISION TWO	P	W	D	L	F	A	GD	Pts
H&W Welders	28	23	2	3	73	30	43	71
Dergview	28	20	4	4	77	20	57	64
Dundela	28	18	7	3	66	31	35	61
PSNI	28	15	5	8	54	40	14	50
Knockbreda	28	14	6	8	44	32	12	48
Tobermore United	28	14	4	10	47	39	8	46
Portstewart	28	11	7	10	42	38	4	40
Queen's University	28	11	4	13	43	40	3	37
Moyola Park	28	10	5	13	42	42	0	35
Lurgan Celtic	28	10	4	14	37	49	–12	34
Sport & Leisure Sfts	28	10	4	14	44	60	–16	34
Annagh United	28	7	3	18	28	66	–38	24
Killymoon Rangers	28	7	2	19	38	60	–22	23
Wakehurst	28	5	4	19	33	58	–25	19
Chimney Corner	28	1	7	20	32	95	–63	10

IRISH LEAGUE CHAMPIONSHIP WINNERS

1891	Linfield	1912	Glentoran	1938	Belfast Celtic	1967	Glentoran	1989	Linfield
1892	Linfield	1913	Glentoran	1939	Belfast Celtic	1968	Glentoran	1990	Portadown
1893	Linfield	1914	Linfield	1940	Belfast Celtic	1969	Linfield	1991	Portadown
1894	Glentoran	1915	Belfast Celtic	1948	Belfast Celtic	1970	Glentoran	1992	Glentoran
1895	Linfield	1920	Belfast Celtic	1949	Linfield	1971	Linfield	1993	Linfield
1896	Distillery	1921	Glentoran	1950	Linfield	1972	Glentoran	1994	Linfield
1897	Glentoran	1922	Linfield	1951	Glentoran	1973	Crusaders	1995	Crusaders
1898	Linfield	1923	Linfield	1952	Glenavon	1974	Coleraine	1996	Portadown
1899	Distillery	1924	Queen's Island	1953	Glentoran	1975	Linfield	1997	Crusaders
1900	Belfast Celtic	1925	Glentoran	1954	Linfield	1976	Crusaders	1998	Cliftonville
1901	Distillery	1926	Belfast Celtic	1955	Linfield	1977	Glentoran	1999	Glentoran
1902	Linfield	1927	Belfast Celtic	1956	Linfield	1978	Linfield	2000	Linfield
1903	Distillery	1928	Belfast Celtic	1957	Glentoran	1979	Linfield	2001	Linfield
1904	Linfield	1929	Belfast Celtic	1958	Ards	1980	Linfield	2002	Portadown
1905	Glentoran	1930	Linfield	1959	Linfield	1981	Glentoran	2003	Glentoran
1906	Cliftonville	1931	Glentoran	1960	Glenavon	1982	Linfield	2004	Linfield
	Distillery	1932	Linfield	1961	Linfield	1983	Linfield	2005	Glentoran
1907	Linfield	1933	Belfast Celtic	1962	Linfield	1984	Linfield	2006	Linfield
1908	Linfield	1934	Linfield	1963	Distillery	1985	Linfield	2007	Linfield
1909	Linfield	1935	Linfield	1964	Glentoran	1986	Linfield	2008	Linfield
1910	Cliftonville	1936	Belfast Celtic	1965	Derry City	1987	Linfield	2009	Glentoran
1911	Linfield	1937	Belfast Celtic	1966	Linfield	1988	Linfield	2010	Linfield

LADBROKES.COM CHAMPIONSHIP (Previously First Division)

1996	Coleraine	2001	Ards	2006	Crusaders
1997	Ballymena United	2002	Lisburn Distillery	2007	Institute
1998	Newry Town	2003	Dungannon Swifts	2008	Loughgall
1999	Distillery	2004	Loughgall	2009	Portadown
2000	Omagh Town	2005	Armagh City	2010	Loughgall

SETANTA SPORTS CUP

GROUP 1

Cork City v Cliftonville	1-0
Sligo Rovers v Cork City	2-2
Cliftonville v Sligo Rovers	2-3
Cork City v Sligo Rovers	0-3*
Sligo Rovers v Cliftonville	3-0
Cliftonville v Cork City	3-0*

*Awarded 3-0 wins as Cork City were dismissed from the competition.

	P	W	D	L	F	A	Pts
Sligo Rovers	4	3	1	0	11	4	10
Cork City	4	1	1	2	3	8	4
Cliftonville	4	1	0	3	5	7	3

GROUP 2

Glentoran v Bohemians	1-2
Coleraine v Glentoran	0-0
Bohemians v Coleraine	0-0
Glentoran v Coleraine	3-2
Coleraine v Bohemians	1-3
Bohemians v Glentoran	1-1

	P	W	D	L	F	A	Pts
Bohemians	4	2	2	0	6	3	8
Glentoran	4	1	2	1	5	5	5
Coleraine	4	0	2	2	3	5	2

GROUP 3

Derry City v St Patrick's Ath	1-1
Linfield v Derry City	1-1
St Patrick's Athletic v Derry City	3-0*
St Patrick's Athletic v Linfield	1-1

Linfield v St Patrick's Athletic	1-0
Derry City v Linfield	0-3*

*Awarded 3-0 wins as Derry City were dismissed from the competition.

	P	W	D	L	F	A	Pts
Linfield	4	2	2	0	6	2	8
St Patrick's Athletic	4	1	2	1	5	3	5
Derry City	4	0	2	2	2	8	2

SEMI-FINALS FIRST LEG

Bohemians v Linfield	2-1
St Patrick's Athletic v Sligo Rovers	4-1

SEMI-FINALS SECOND LEG

Linfield v Bohemians	1-0
Sligo Rovers v St Patrick's Athletic	1-2

FINAL

5 May 2010, 3896

(at Tallaght Stadium, Dublin).

Bohemians (1) 1 *(Murphy A 24)*

St Patrick's Athletic (0) 0

Bohemians: Murphy B; Heary, Powell, McGuinness, Shelley, Murphy A (Quigley 71), Keegan, Cronin, Brennan, Byrne (Cretaro 85), Greene (Madden 46).
St Patrick's Athletic: Rogers; Pender, Bermingham, Kenna, Guthrie, Guy, Coughlan (Sinnott 89), Byrne S, Mulcahy (Doyle 89), Byrne P (Williams 67), Faherty.
Referee: A. Black (Antrim).

SETANTA SPORTS CUP WINNERS

2004–05 Linfield	2006–07 Drogheda United	2009–10 Bohemians
2005–06 Drogheda United	2007–08 Cork City	

CO-OPERATIVE INSURANCE IRISH LEAGUE CUP

SEMI-FINALS

Glentoran 1, Portadown 0
Coleraine 2, Dungannon Swifts 0

FINAL

(at Windsor Park)

Coleraine 2 *(Boyce 7, Patterson 31)*

Glentoran 2 *(Martyn 6, Nixon 45)*   4500

Glentoran: James Taylor; McGovern, Nixon, Johnny Taylor, Hill, Gillespie (Fordyce 59), Clarke, Martyn (Fitzgerald 81), Neill, Hamilton, Halliday (Burrows 91).
Coleraine: O'Hare; Beverland (McLaughlin 80), Hegarty, McVey, Boyce, Patterson, McCallion, Carson, Watt (Canning 101), Harkin, Dooley (Tommons 68).
aet; Glentoran won 4-1 on penalties: Hamilton scored; Canning missed; Neill scored; McVey scored; Fordyce scored; Boyce missed; Burrows scored.
Referee: M. Courtney.

JJB SPORTS IRISH CUP 2009–10

FIFTH ROUND

Ballyclare Comrades v Islandmagee	5-1
Ballymena United v Ards	0-0, 1-0
Carrick Rangers v Portadown	1-1, 0-1
Coagh United v Tobermore United	1-0
Crusaders v Bangor	5-1
Donegal Celtic v Linfield	0-4
Dundela v Coleraine	0-2
Dungannon Swifts v Malachians	6-0
Glenavon v H&W Welders	5-1
Glentoran v Omagh United	5-0
Institute v Ballymoney United	1-1, 1-0
Lisburn Distillery v Cliftonville	0-2
Loughgall v Ards Rangers	3-1
Newry City v Larne	2-1
Nortel v Bryansburn Rangers	2-2, 2-2
Bryansburn Rangers won 5-3 on penalties.	
Glebe Rangers v Ballinamallard United	0-3

SIXTH ROUND

Ballyclare Comrades v Glentoran	1-2
Ballymena United v Ballinamallard United	5-2
Coleraine v Nortel	6-0
Crusaders v Coagh United	4-0
Glenavon v Institute	2-1
Linfield v Dungannon Swifts	4-0
Portadown v Cliftonville	2-1
Loughgall v Newry City	1-1, 0-1

QUARTER-FINALS

Glenavon v Ballymena United	3-3, 0-2
Crusaders v Portadown	1-1, 0-1
Glentoran v Linfield	1-3
Coleraine v Newry City	3-2

SEMI-FINALS

Ballymena United v Portadown	1-1
Portadown won 4-3 on penalties.	
Linfield v Coleraine	4-2

FINAL

(at Windsor Park, 8 May 2010)

Linfield 2 *(Thompson 1, Lowry 11)*

Portadown 1 *(Braniff 13)*   8000

Linfield: Blayney; Gault, Murphy, Curran, Lowry (Mulgrew 71), Thompson, Bailie, BT Burns, Garrett, McAllister (Munster 46), JP Gallagher.
Portadown: Miskelly; Redman, Clarke (A Teggart 82), Kelly, Boyle, Braniff, Mouncey, Baker (Lecky 66), Hunter (McCluskey 57), Topley, Mackle.
Referee: M. Courtney.
This was Linfield's 40th Irish Cup triumph – and 4th League and Cup double in five years.

IRISH CUP FINALS (from 1946–47)

1946–47	Belfast Celtic 1, Glentoran 0
1947–48	Linfield 3, Coleraine 0
1948–49	Derry City 3, Glentoran 1
1949–50	Linfield 2, Distillery 1
1950–51	Glentoran 3, Ballymena U 1
1951–52	Ards 1, Glentoran 0
1952–53	Linfield 5, Coleraine 0
1953–54	Derry City 1, Glentoran 0
1954–55	Dundela 3, Glenavon 0
1955–56	Distillery 1, Glentoran 0
1956–57	Glenavon 2, Derry City 0
1957–58	Ballymena U 2, Linfield 0
1958–59	Glenavon 2, Ballymena U 0
1959–60	Linfield 5, Ards 1
1960–61	Glenavon 5, Linfield 1
1961–62	Linfield 4, Portadown 0
1962–63	Linfield 2, Distillery 1
1963–64	Derry City 2, Glentoran 0
1964–65	Coleraine 2, Glenavon 1
1965–66	Glentoran 2, Linfield 0
1966–67	Crusaders 3, Glentoran 1
1967–68	Crusaders 2, Linfield 0
1968–69	Ards 4, Distillery 2
1969–70	Linfield 2, Ballymena U 1
1970–71	Distillery 3, Derry City 1
1971–72	Coleraine 2, Portadown 1
1972–73	Glentoran 3, Linfield 2
1973–74	Ards 2, Ballymena U 1
1974–75	Coleraine 1:0:1, Linfield 1:0:0
1975–76	Carrick Rangers 2, Linfield 1
1976–77	Coleraine 4, Linfield 1
1977–78	Linfield 3, Ballymena U 1
1978–79	Cliftonville 3, Portadown 2
1979–80	Linfield 2, Crusaders 0
1980–81	Ballymena U 1, Glenavon 0
1981–82	Linfield 2, Coleraine 1
1982–83	Glentoran 1:2, Linfield 1:1
1983–84	Ballymena U 4, Carrick Rangers 1
1984–85	Glentoran 1:1, Linfield 1:0
1985–86	Glentoran 2, Coleraine 1
1986–87	Glentoran 1, Larne 0
1987–88	Glentoran 1, Glenavon 0
1988–89	Ballymena U 1, Larne 0
1989–90	Glentoran 3, Portadown 0
1990–91	Portadown 2, Glenavon 1
1991–92	Glenavon 2, Linfield 1
1992–93	Bangor 1:1:1, Ards 1:1:0
1993–94	Linfield 2, Bangor 0
1994–95	Linfield 3, Carrick Rangers 1
1995–96	Glentoran 1, Glenavon 0
1996–97	Glenavon 1, Cliftonville 0
1997–98	Glentoran 1, Glenavon 0
1998–99	*Portadown awarded trophy after Cliftonville were eliminated for using an ineligible player in semi-final.*
1999–2000	Glentoran 1, Portadown 0
2000–01	Glentoran 1, Linfield 0
2001–02	Linfield 2, Portadown 1
2002–03	Coleraine 1, Glentoran 0
2003–04	Glentoran 1, Coleraine 0
2004–05	Portadown 5, Larne 1
2005–06	Linfield 2, Glentoran 1
2006–07	Linfield 2, Dungannon Swifts 2
	(aet; Linfield won 3-2 on penalties).
2007–08	Linfield 2, Coleraine 1
2008–09	Crusaders 1, Cliftonville 0
2009–10	Linfield 2, Portadown 1

PADDY POWER COUNTY ANTRIM SHIELD

FINAL

(at Windsor Park, 20 January 2010)

Linfield 2 *(Burns 6, Ervin 86)*

Crusaders 3 *(Dickson 39, Coates 89, Owens 98)*   1750

Linfield: Addis; Ervin, Douglas, Lindsay, Curran (Tomelty 100), BT Burns (Garrett 90), Gault, Mulgrew, Carville■, McAllister (Allen 78), Munster.
Crusaders: Keenan (Hogg 67); McKeown, Bell (Arthurs 88), Doherty, Magowan, Coates, McMaster, Collins (Caddell 72), Dickson, Owens, Donnelly.
aet.
Referee: T. Mountray .

ULSTER CUP WINNERS

1949 Linfield	1962 Linfield	1975 Coleraine	1988 Glentoran	2001 *No competition*
1950 Larne	1963 Crusaders	1976 Glentoran	1989 Glentoran	2002 *No competition*
1951 Glentoran	1964 Linfield	1977 Linfield	1990 Portadown	2003 Dungannon Swifts
1952 *No competition*	1965 Coleraine	1978 Linfield	1991 Bangor	*(Confined to*
1953 Glentoran	1966 Glentoran	1979 Linfield	1992 Linfield	*First Division clubs)*
1954 Crusaders	1967 Linfield	1980 Ballymena U	1993 Crusaders	2004 *No competition*
1955 Glenavon	1968 Coleraine	1981 Glentoran	1994 Bangor	2005 *No competition*
1956 Linfield	1969 Coleraine	1982 Glentoran	1995 Portadown	2006 *No competition*
1957 Linfield	1970 Linfield	1983 Glentoran	1996 Portadown	2007 *No competition*
1958 Distillery	1971 Linfield	1984 Linfield	1997 Coleraine	2008 *No competition*
1959 Glenavon	1972 Coleraine	1985 Coleraine	1998 Ballyclare Comrades	2009 *No competition*
1960 Linfield	1973 Ards	1986 Coleraine	1999 Distillery	2010 *No competition*
1961 Ballymena U	1974 Linfield	1987 Larne	2000 *No competition*	

ROLL OF HONOUR SEASON 2009–10

Competition	Winner	Runner-up
JJB Sports Premier League	Linfield	Cliftonville
JJB Sports Irish Cup	Linfield	Portadown
Ladbrokes.Com First Division	Loughgall	Donegal Celtic
Ladbrokes.Com Second Division	H&W Welders	Dergview
Ladbrokes.Com League Cup	H&W Welders	Tobermore United
Co-Operative Insurance Cup	Glentoran	Coleraine
County Antrim Shield	Crusaders	Linfield
County Antrim Junior Shield	Crumlin Star	Ardoyne WMC
Steel & Sons Cup	Kilmore Rec	Downpatrick FC
Coca-Cola Irish Junior Cup	Immaculata	Lincoln Court
WKD Intermediate Cup	Donegal Celtic	Loughgall
Irish Reserve League	Linfield Swifts	Cliftonville Olympic
Irish Youth League Section A	Cliftonville Strollers	
Irish Youth League Section B	Carrick Rangers Colts	
Mid Ulster Cup	Glenavon	Loughgall
Youth League Cup Final	Ballymena United III	Glentoran Colts
The Harry Cavan Youth Cup	Linfield Rangers	Dungannon Swifts Youth
George Wilson Memorial Cup	Glentoran II	Cliftonville Olympic
Irish FA League Youth Cup	Ballymena United III	Glentoran Colts
Northwest FA Senior Cup	Coleraine	Limavady United
Northwest FA Craig Cup	Tobermore United	Churchill United
Northwest FA Junior Cup	Newtowne	Greysteel
Fermanagh &Western FA Mulhern Cup	Strathroy Harps	Irvinestown Wanderers
Reihill Cup	Lisbellaw United Res	NFC Kesh III
Mid-Ulster FA Kennedy Cup	Windmill Stars	St Mary's Youth Club
Junior Shield	St Mary's Youth Club	Windmill Stars
Radcliffe Intermediate Cup	Loughgall	Bambridge Town
Senior Cup	Glenavon	Loughgall

AWARDS

ULSTER FOOTBALLER OF THE YEAR
(Castlereagh Glentoran Supporters Award)
Rory Patterson *(Coleraine)*

NORTHERN IRELAND PLAYER OF THE YEAR
(Football Writers Association)
Rory Patterson *(Coleraine).*

YOUNG PLAYER
Liam Boyce *(Cliftonville).*

MANAGER OF THE YEAR
David Jeffrey *(Linfield).*

OUTSTANDING NON SENIOR TEAM
Loughgall

INTERNATIONAL PERSONALITY
Steven Davis *(Rangers).*

CARLING LEADING SCORER
Premier Division
Rory Patterson *(Coleraine)* 41

CARLING TEAM OF THE YEAR (NIFWA)
Alan Rouse *(Dungannon Swifts)*
Billy Jo Burns *(Linfield)*
Colin Coates *(Crusaders)*
David Magowan *(Crusaders)*
Ronan Scannell *(Cliftonville)*
George McMullan *(Cliftonville)*
Kevin Braniff *(Portadown)*
Jamie Mulgrew *(Linfield)*
Neil McCafferty *(Dungannon Swifts)*
Darren Boyce *(Coleraine)*
Rory Patterson *(Coleraine)*

TOP GOALSCORERS 2009–10

All competitions					
Rory Patterson (Coleraine)	41	David Rainey (Crusaders)	19	Richard Lecky (Portadown)	15
Darren Boyce (Coleraine)	23	George McMullan (Cliftonville)	18	Glenn Ferguson	14
Liam Boyce (Cliftonville)	19	Gary McCutcheon (Portadown)	17	(Lisburn Distillery)	
Kevin Braniff (Portadown)	19	Timmy Adamson	16	Paul Munster (Linfield)	14
Trevor Molloy (Glenavon)	19	(Dungannon Swifts)		Chris Scannell (Cliftonville)	14
		Kevin Kelbie (Ballymena United)	16		

CARLING PLAYER OF THE MONTH

Month	Player	Team
August	David Rainey	Crusaders
September	George McMullan	Cliftonville
October	Jamie Mulgrew	Linfield
November	Rory Patterson	Coleraine
December	Niall McCafferty	Dungannon Swifts
January	Rory Patterson	Coleraine
February	Rory Patterson	Coleraine
March	Philip Lowry	Linfield
April	Liam Boyce	Cliftonville

CARLING MANAGER OF THE MONTH

Month	Player	Team
August	Stephen Baxter	Crusaders
September	Marty Quinn	Glentoran
October	David Jeffrey	Linfield
November	Ronnie McFall	Portadown
December	Eddie Patterson	Cliftonville
January	David Platt	Coleraine
February	Ronnie McFall	Portadown
March	Tommy Wright	Lisburn Distillery
April	David Jeffrey	Linfield

EUROPEAN FOOTBALL REVIEW 2009–10

At the quarter-final stage of the two European cup competitions, four English teams remained, albeit facing tough opposition. In the Champions League Manchester United enjoyed an early lead away to Bayern Munich but trailed to a late goal. Arsenal fought back from two goals down to level against Barcelona at the Emirates.

As to the fledgling Europa League, Liverpool – dumped out of the Champions League at the group stage – had to make the long ash-volcano affected journey to Portugal and Benfica. They, too, achieved an early advantage then conceded two penalties. Fulham did well to take a two-goal lead over Wolfsburg before conceding one.

The second legs were entirely different. Four-goal Lionel Messi destroyed Arsenal at the Nou Camp. Manchester United chucked a three goal lead to allow Bayern in on the away goals. In the Europa League, Liverpool ran out 4-1 winners over Benfica. Fulham also produced a strong performance in Germany and led from a first minute Bobby Zamora effort.

Thus ended England's interest in the main tournament, but had two left in the Europa. Liverpool conceded a ninth minute goal to Atletico Madrid's Diego Forlan while Fulham returned from Hamburg with a useful goalless draw. Then despite going behind at Craven Cottage, Fulham scored twice to reach the final, an outstanding performance.

Sadly it was not as fortunate for Liverpool as Atletico forced extra time with Forlan notching the important away goal. Ironically, the Europa League final was also in Hamburg, but though they pushed Atletico to extra time themselves, Forlan's brace, early and late, edged out the London team after its marathon 19 matches.

Meanwhile the Champions League semi-finals presented two fascinating ties. Internazionale faced Barcelona, Bayern met Lyon. The former pair had been involved in the same Group F with Inter hosting Barcelona at the off. It ended goalless, Barca winning the return 2-0. But it was Inter and more importantly Jose Mourinho who learned more. Come the semi-finals and Inter, shrugging off the Catalans' early strike in Milan, led 3-1. Even with ten men for over an hour in Barcelona, Inter conceded just once six minutes from time.

It could be argued, too, that despite these outstanding displays, they had been overshadowed in the knock-out round against Chelsea. This was the tie JM wanted. In three minutes Diego Milito put him ahead at the San Siro and though Chelsea levelled, Inter led 2-1. At Stamford Bridge, Mourinho fashioned a tactical masterpiece with an attacking 4-3-3 formation which puzzled Carlo Ancelotti and his team. It even produced a goal.

As to other English interest, Aston Villa did not make it past the play-off round of the Europa League but battling Everton reached the group stage before Sporting Lisbon edged them out in the knock-out round.

Thus to the Champions League final in Madrid with Inter, conquerors of Chelsea against Bayern Munich, winners against Manchester United. Inter opened cautiously, but ready to spring on the counter attack. Bayern were the more anxious and relied heavily on Robben out on the right wing with his lethal left foot for their cutting edge.

But with two defenders detailed to watch him, Bayern had to switch to alternatives. Yet it was pure Route One for the Special One's team when they took the lead. Julio Cesar's clearance from hand was headed on by Milito to Wesley Sneijder who returned the ball into Milito's path for the Argentine to right-foot past Jorg Butt in the 34th minute. Though Bayern pushed on from both flanks and through the middle, Inter stayed in control and Milito added his second goal, turning his defender to right foot another strike.

Jose Mourinho then prepared to move on to Real Madrid on whose ground the final had been played.

Diego Milito (centre) breaks through the Bayern Munich defence to score Inter Milan's second in their 2-0 Champions League Final triumph in Madrid. (Action Images/Carl Recine)

EUROPEAN CUP FINALS

EUROPEAN CUP FINALS 1956–1992

Year	Winners		Runners-up		Venue	Attendance	Referee
1956	Real Madrid	4	Reims	3	Paris	38,000	Ellis (E)
1957	Real Madrid	2	Fiorentina	0	Madrid	124,000	Horn (Ho)
1958	Real Madrid	3	AC Milan	2 (aet)	Brussels	67,000	Alsteen (Bel)
1959	Real Madrid	2	Reims	0	Stuttgart	80,000	Dutsch (WG)
1960	Real Madrid	7	Eintracht Frankfurt	3	Glasgow	135,000	Mowat (S)
1961	Benfica	3	Barcelona	2	Berne	28,000	Dienst (Sw)
1962	Benfica	5	Real Madrid	3	Amsterdam	65,000	Horn (Ho)
1963	AC Milan	2	Benfica	1	Wembley	45,000	Holland (E)
1964	Internazionale	3	Real Madrid	1	Vienna	74,000	Stoll (A)
1965	Internazionale	1	Benfica	0	Milan	80,000	Dienst (Sw)
1966	Real Madrid	2	Partizan Belgrade	1	Brussels	55,000	Kreitlein (WG)
1967	Celtic	2	Internazionale	1	Lisbon	56,000	Tschenscher (WG)
1968	Manchester U	4	Benfica	1 (aet)	Wembley	100,000	Lo Bello (I)
1969	AC Milan	4	Ajax	1	Madrid	50,000	Ortiz (Sp)
1970	Feyenoord	2	Celtic	1 (aet)	Milan	50,000	Lo Bello (I)
1971	Ajax	2	Panathinaikos	0	Wembley	90,000	Taylor (E)
1972	Ajax	2	Internazionale	0	Rotterdam	67,000	Helies (F)
1973	Ajax	1	Juventus	0	Belgrade	93,500	Guglovic (Y)
1974	Bayern Munich	1	Atletico Madrid	1	Brussels	49,000	Loraux (Bel)
Replay	Bayern Munich	4	Atletico Madrid	0	Brussels	23,000	Delcourt (Bel)
1975	Bayern Munich	2	Leeds U	0	Paris	50,000	Kitabdjian (F)
1976	Bayern Munich	1	St Etienne	0	Glasgow	54,864	Palotai (H)
1977	Liverpool	3	Moenchengladbach	1	Rome	57,000	Wurtz (F)
1978	Liverpool	1	FC Brugge	0	Wembley	92,000	Corver (Ho)
1979	Nottingham F	1	Malmo	0	Munich	57,500	Linemayr (A)
1980	Nottingham F	1	Hamburg	0	Madrid	50,000	Garrido (P)
1981	Liverpool	1	Real Madrid	0	Paris	48,360	Palotai (H)
1982	Aston Villa	1	Bayern Munich	0	Rotterdam	46,000	Konrath (F)
1983	Hamburg	1	Juventus	0	Athens	80,000	Rainea (R)
1984	Liverpool	1	Roma	1	Rome	69,693	Fredriksson (Se)
	(aet; Liverpool won 4-2 on penalties)						
1985	Juventus	1	Liverpool	0	Brussels	58,000	Daina (Sw)
1986	Steaua Bucharest	0	Barcelona	0	Seville	70,000	Vautrot (F)
	(aet; Steaua won 2-0 on penalties)						
1987	Porto	2	Bayern Munich	1	Vienna	59,000	Ponnet (Bel)
1988	PSV Eindhoven	0	Benfica	0	Stuttgart	70,000	Agnolin (I)
	(aet; PSV won 6-5 on penalties)						
1989	AC Milan	4	Steaua Bucharest	0	Barcelona	97,000	Tritschler (WG)
1990	AC Milan	1	Benfica	0	Vienna	57,500	Kohl (A)
1991	Red Star Belgrade	0	Marseille	0	Bari	56,000	Lanese (I)
	(aet; Red Star won 5-3 on penalties)						
1992	Barcelona	1	Sampdoria	0 (aet)	Wembley	70,827	Schmidhuber (G)

UEFA CHAMPIONS LEAGUE FINALS 1993–2010

1993	Marseille*	1	AC Milan	0	Munich	64,400	Rothlisberger (Sw)
1994	AC Milan	4	Barcelona	0	Athens	70,000	Don (E)
1995	Ajax	1	AC Milan	0	Vienna	49,730	Craciunescu (R)
1996	Juventus	1	Ajax	1	Rome	67,000	Vega (Sp)
	(aet; Juventus won 4-2 on penalties)						
1997	Borussia Dortmund	3	Juventus	1	Munich	59,000	Puhl (H)
1998	Real Madrid	1	Juventus	0	Amsterdam	47,500	Krug (G)
1999	Manchester U	2	Bayern Munich	1	Barcelona	90,000	Collina (I)
2000	Real Madrid	3	Valencia	0	Paris	78,759	Braschi (I)
2001	Bayern Munich	1	Valencia	1	Milan	71,500	Jol (Ho)
	(aet; Bayern Munich won 5-4 on penalties)						
2002	Real Madrid	2	Leverkusen	1	Glasgow	52,000	Meier (Sw)
2003	AC Milan	0	Juventus	0	Manchester	63,215	Merk (G)
	(aet; AC Milan won 3-2 on penalties)						
2004	Porto	3	Monaco	0	Gelsenkirchen	52,000	Nielsen (D)
2005	Liverpool	3	AC Milan	3	Istanbul	65,000	González (Sp)
	(aet; Liverpool won 3-2 on penalties)						
2006	Barcelona	2	Arsenal	1	Paris	79,500	Hauge (N)
2007	AC Milan	2	Liverpool	1	Athens	74,000	Fandel (G)
2008	Manchester U	1	Chelsea	1	Moscow	69,552	Michel (Slo)
	(aet; Manchester U won 6-5 on penalties)						
2009	Barcelona	2	Manchester U	0	Rome	62,467	Busacca (Sw)
2010	Internazionale	2	Bayern Munich	0	Madrid	74,954	Webb (E)

*Subsequently stripped of title.

UEFA CHAMPIONS LEAGUE 2009–10

* *Denotes player sent off.*

FIRST QUALIFYING ROUND FIRST LEG

Tuesday, 30 June 2009
Hibernians (0) 0
Mogren (1) 2 *(Cetkovic 32, Grbic 88)*   620
Hibernians: Muscat; Caruana, Pulis, Xuereb, Mintoff (Pearson 62), Callejas (Grech 62), Camilleri B, Herrera, Cohen, Cvetic, Camilleri R.
Mogren: Janjusevic; Pejovic, Belada, Simovic, Cetkovic, Grbic, Bozovic D, Jovanovic, Rakic (Tiodorovic 70), Stojakovic (Kalezic 85), Milic (Bozovic B 63).

Wednesday, 1 July 2009
Tre Fiori (0) 1 *(Andreini 74)*
Sant Julia (1) 1 *(Xinos 42 (pen))*   564
Tre Fiori: Micheletti; Nardone, Macerata, Benedettini, Andreini, Tombetti (Vendemini 85), Lisi, Canarezza (Simoncini 62), Ballanti, Rodriguez, Amici (Giunta 55).
Sant Julia: Perianes; Wagner, Nastri, Varela, Xinos, Peppe, Vicente Munoz*, Mejias (Fernando Goncalves 87), Moreira (Matamala 70), Romero, Machado (Abdian 63).

FIRST QUALIFYING ROUND SECOND LEG

Tuesday, 7 July 2009
Sant Julia (1) 1 *(Moreira 39)*
Tre Fiori (0) 1 *(Canarezza 82)*   600
Sant Julia: Perianes; Wagner, Abdian (Matamala 98), Nastri. Varela, Xinos, Peppe, Mejias, Moreira (Fernando Goncalves 79), Romero (Miraglia 77), Machado.
Tre Fiori: Micheletti; Nardone (Vendemini 75), Macerata, Benedettini, Andreini, Tombetti (Giunta 65), Lisi, Canarezza (Macina 114), Ballanti, Simoncini*, Rodriguez.

Wednesday, 8 July 2009
Mogren (2) 4 *(Milic 41, Grbic 45, 80, Cetkovic 51)*
Hibernians (0) 0   2500
Mogren: Janjusevic; Pejovic, Belada, Simovic, Cetkovic, Grbic, Bozovic D, Jovanovic, Rakic (Tiodorovic 46), Stojakovic (Bozovic B 69), Milic (Kalezic 46).
Hibernians: Muscat; Caruana, Pulis, Xuereb, Pearson (Galabov 34), Mintoff, Camilleri B (Cauchi 72), Herrera, Cohen, Cvetic, Camilleri R (Grech 65).

SECOND QUALIFYING ROUND FIRST LEG

Tuesday, 14 July 2009
EB/Streymur (0) 0
Apoel (1) 2 *(Mirosavljevic 10, Zewlakow 77)*   300
EB/Streymur: Steig; Bo, Djurhuus (Brian Olsen 83), Davidsen, Bardur Olsen, Fridheim, Hanssen, Anghel (Jacobsen 89), Samuelesen, Hansen A (Hansen P 82), Niclasen.
Apoel: Chiotis; Nuno Morais (Grncarov 80), Poursaitidis, Charalambides (Zewlakow 20), Kosowski, Broerse, Helio Pinto, Kontis, Haxhi, Michael (Satsias 84), Mirosavljevic.

Ekranas (0) 2 *(Bicka 52 (pen), Trakys 90)*
Baku (0) 2 *(Felix 78, Batista 89)*   13,000
Ekranas: Cerniauskas; Gleveckas, Matovic, Arlauskas, Galkevicius (Arandjelovic 46), Bicka, Tomkevicius, Ademolu, Trakys, Sidlauskas, Varnas (Pogreban 79).
Baku: Sissokho; Rafael, Bates, Borets, Skulic, Fabio (Mujiri 69), Savinov, Solic, Felix, Soltanov, Adamia (Batista 81).

Makedonija (0) 0
BATE Borisov (1) 2 *(Krivets 40, Skavysh 49)*   3000
Makedonija: Pustinjakovic; Ambourouet, Mojsov, Milevski, Ilievski, Lena, Brnjarchevski, Ivanovski (Koleceski 46), Carlinos (Felipe Montanari 61), Mitrev, Gligorovski (Klechkarovski 52).
BATE Borisov: Veremko; Sosnovskiy, Shitov, Yurevich, Radzov, Likhtarovich (Bordachev 69), Volodzo, Krivets, Nekhaichik (Pavlov 85), Stasevich, Skavysh (Alumona 75).

Pyunik (0) 0
Dinamo Zagreb (0) 0   2500
Pyunik: Hovhannisian; Khachatrian, Hovsepian, Yuspashian (Artur Yedigarian 54), Minasian, Mbola, Mkrtchian, Pizzelli (Aleksanian 68), Malakian, Ghazarian (Tadevosian 78), Manasian.
Dinamo Zagreb: Butina; Lovren (Barbaric 46), Carlos, Vrdoljak, Etto, Sammir, Badelj, Biscan, Mandzukic, Sivonjic (Kramaric 78), Papadopoulos D (Slepicka 65).

Rhyl (0) 0
Partizan Belgrade (3) 4 *(Krstajic 17, Cleo 18, Diarra 45, Dordevic 69)*   1726
Rhyl: Kendall; Naylor, Strong, Horan, Stones, Leah, Owen, Sherbon (Connolly 70), Holden, Roberts, Williams (Hunt 55).
Partizan Belgrade: Bozovic M; Stevanovic (Knezevic 72), Dordevic, Krstajic, Gavrancic, Tomic (Vujovic 72), Petrovic, Almani Moreira, Cleo (Bogunovic 83), Ilic, Diarra.

Wednesday, 15 July 2009
Debrecen (0) 2 *(Varga 76, Kiss 86)*
Kalmar (0) 0   9000
Debrecen: Poleksic; Mate, Bernath, Leandro, Meszaros, Kiss, Varga, Czvitkovics, Rudolf (Katona 90), Szilagyi (Dombi 85), Dudu (Olah 58).
Kalmar: Wasta; Lantz, Larsson, Alander, Nouri, Rydstrom, Sobralense, Elm R, Eriksson, Elm D (Ricardo Santos 84), Mendes (Dauda 84).

FC Copenhagen (3) 6 *(Kristensen 8, Jorgensen M 16, Ailton 24, N'Doye 69, 74, Nordstrand 82)*
Mogren (0) 0   12,226
FC Copenhagen: Christiansen; Pospech, Antonsson, Wendt, Jorgensen M, Norregaard, Kvist, Kristensen (Gronkjaer 59), Vingaard, Ailton (Nordstrand 64), Cesar Santin (N'Doye 64).
Mogren: Janjusevic; Pejovic, Simovic (Novakovic 36), Janicic, Cetkovic, Grbic, Bozovic D, Tiodorovic (Rakic 78), Jovanovic, Bozovic B (Kalezic 62), Milic.

Hafnarfjordur (0) 0
Aktobe (0) 4 *(Tleshev 49, Golovskoy 57, 85, Khayrullin 70)*   2000
Hafnarfjordur: Larusson; Nielsen, Vidarsson P, Gardarsson, Gudmundsson V*, Asgeirsson (Gudmundsson M 54), Vidarsson D, Soderlund (Gudmundsson T 54), Vilhjalmsson, Gudnason, Bjornsson (Sverrisson 71).
Aktobe: Sidelnikov; Smakov, Kenzheisariev, Logvinenko, Chichulin, Khayrullin (Khokhlov 86), Golovskoy, Asanbaev, Lavrik (Mitrofanov 82), Tleshev, Averchenko (Strukov 68).

Inter Turku (0) 0
Sheriff (1) 1 *(Suvorov 42 (pen))*   5108
Inter Turku: Bantamoi; Verino, Nyman, Aho, Lehtonen, Ramirez, Paajanen, Ojala (Nwanganga 69), Furuholm, Purje (Grot 71), Kauko.
Sheriff: Namasco; Tarkhnishvili, Karpovich, Nadson, Corneencov, Balima, Rouamba, Rodriguez, Bulat (Verbetchi 74), Suvorov (Da Costa 90), Diedhiou (Mandricenco 72).

Levski (0) 4 *(Tasevski 50, Hristov 64, 72, Gadzhev 82)*
Sant Julia (0) 0   12,000
Levski: Petkov; Genev, Milanov, Rabeh, Minev, Tasevski, Gadzhev, Yovov (Joaozinho 62), Dimitrov N (Ze Soares 46), Bardon (Mustafa 78), Hristov.
Sant Julia: Burgos; Wagner, Abdian*, Nastri, Varela, Fontan (Miraglia 57), Xinos, Peppe, Mejias (Bernales 77), Romero*, Machado (Vila 69).

Maccabi Haifa (1) 6 *(Rafaelov 36, Katan 52, Dvalishvili 57, 81, Arbeitman 83, Ghadir 89)*

Glentoran (0) 0   11,500

Maccabi Haifa: Davidovitch; Teixeira, Culma (Golasa 55), Masilela, Keinan, Meshumar, Kayal, Rafaelov (Boccoli 61), Dvalishvili, Ghadir, Katan (Arbeitman 72). *Glentoran:* Morris; Nixon, Neill, Leeman, Ward, Taylor, Clarke (Fitzgerald 68), Fordyce (Hall 79), Black, Waterworth (Halliday 68), Hamilton.

Salzburg (1) 1 *(Dudic 25)*

Bohemians (0) 1 *(N'Do 60)*   12,300

Salzburg: Gustafsson; Dudic, Schwegler, Opdam (Jezek 66), Sekagya, Svento, Cziommer (Ilic 64), Leitgeb, Aufhauser, Janko (Nelisse 73), N'Gwat-Mahop. *Bohemians:* Murphy B; Powell, Oman, Shelley, Rossiter, Brennan, Deegan, Keegan, N'Do, Crowe, Byrne (Murphy A 73).

SK Tirana (0) 1 *(Mukaj 50)*

Stabaek (1) 1 *(Kobayashi 34)*   3000

SK Tirana: Nallbani; Dabulla, Lila, Alenchenu, Osmani, Sefa, Mukaj, Devolli, Muzaka (Mohellebi 59), Lilaj (Abilaliaj 85), Xhafaj. *Stabaek:* Knudsen; Segerstrom, Skjonsberg, Olsen, Hauger, Keller, Kobayashi (Hoff 87), Farnerud, Diskerud (Palmason 80), Hedenstad, Berglund (Nannskog 76).

Ventspils (0) 3 *(Butriks 79, Kacanovs 86, Rimkus 87)*

F91 Dudelange (0) 0   2300

Ventspils: Pavlovs; Cilinsek, Astafjevs, Kosmacovs. Kacanovs, Chirkin, Mihadjuks, Tigirlas, Zigajevs (Lazdins 90), Rimkus (Martins 90), Dedov (Butriks 65). *F91 Dudelange:* Joubert; Da Mota, Franceschi, Guthleber, Zeghdane, Diakite, Bendaha (Payal 88), Walter, Hareau, Francoise, Ronny.

Wisla (0) 1 *(Cwielong 90)*

Levadia (1) 1 *(Andrejev 42)*   3000

Wisla: Pawelek; Marcelo, Piotr Brozek, Diaz, Kirm, Jop, Sobolewski, Jirask (Cantoro 73), Lobodzinski (Cwielong 46), Malecki, Pawel Brozek. *Levadia:* Kaalma; Kalimullin, Morozov, Nahk, Malov, Puri S, Teniste, Gussev, Ivanov (Puri E 85), Marmor (Sisov 46), Andrejev (Zelinski 83).

WIT Georgia (0) 0

Maribor (0) 0   7000

WIT Georgia: Bediashvili; Lomaia, Japaridze, Bechvaia, Kvakhadze, Razmadze, Datunaishvili, Lipartia (Zakradze 63), Kakhelishvili (Kvelashvili 90), Kvaratskelia (Beriashvili 68), Klimiashvili[■]. *Maribor:* Ranilovic; Dzinic, Jurkic, Lunder, Mihelic, Bacinovic, Popovic, Pavlovic, Mertelj (Skolnik 69), Tavares, Jelic (Bunderla 70).

Zrinjski (0) 1 *(Kordic 48)*

Slovan Bratislava (0) 0   7400

Zrinjski: Melher; Sunjic, Zurzinov, Susic P (Stanley 54), Ivankovic, Susic M, Stojanovic (Sarac 78), Zadro (Rezdeusek 88), Anicic, Selimovic, Kordic. *Slovan Bratislava:* Bicik; Dobrotka, Salata, Dosoudil, Valachovic, Petras, Bozic (Cernak 78), Slovak, Obzera (Sylvestr 83), Kozak (Gaucho 88), Masaryk.

SECOND QUALIFYING ROUND SECOND LEG

Tuesday, 21 July 2009

Apoel (1) 3 *(Zewlakow 42, Alexandrou 63, Mirosavljevic 75)*

EB/Streymur (0) 0   9054

Apoel: Chiotis; Paulo Jorge, Grncarov, Elia, Broerse, Satsias, Kontis, Zewlakow, Alexandrou, Mirosavljevic (Helio Pinto 80), Breska (Paulista 69). *EB/Streymur:* Steig; Djurhuus, Davidsen, Bardur Olsen, Hansen P (Jacobsen 58), Nielsen (Brian Olsen 70), Hansen, Anghel, Samuelesen (Alex Santos 76), Hansen A, Niclasen.

Baku (0) 4 *(Felix 60, 66, 77, Solic 89)*

Ekranas (0) 2 *(Matovic 81, Gleveckas 90)*   20,000

Baku: Sissokho; Rafael, Bates, Borets, Skulic, Mujiri (Gurbanov 69), Savinov, Solic, Felix (Batista 79), Soltanov, Adamia (Perez 56). *Ekranas:* Cerniauskas; Gleveckas, Sasnauskas, Matovic, Arlauskas, Bicka (Arandjelovic 82), Tomkevicius, Ademolu, Trakys, Sidlauskas, Varnas (Pogreban 71).

BATE Borisov (0) 2 *(Sosnovskiy 83, Rodionov 90)*

Makedonija (0) 0   3000

BATE Borisov: Veremko; Sosnovskiy, Shitov, Yurevich, Radzov, Likhtarovich (Bordachev 72), Volodzo, Krivets, Nekhaichik (Rodionov 77), Stasevich, Skavysh (Alumona 85). *Makedonija:* Pustinjakovic; Ambourouet, Mojsov, Kralevski, Felipe Montanari, Ilievski, Ivanovski (Gjurgjevic 82), Carlinos, Lendoye (Gligorovski 72), Mitrev, Kleckarovski (Koleceski 63).

Dinamo Zagreb (1) 3 *(Mandzukic 31, Badelj 61, Lovren 66)*

Pyunik (0) 0   4000

Dinamo Zagreb: Butina; Lovren, Carlos, Vrdoljak, Etto, Sammir (Chago 75), Badelj, Biscan, Morales (Tomecak 79), Mandzukic, Papadopoulos D (Slepicka 82). *Pyunik:* Hovhannisian; Khachatrian, Hovsepian, Artur Yedigarian (Yuspashian 72), Minasian, Mbola, Mkrtchian, Pizzelli, Malakian, Ghazarian, Sahakian (Artak Yedigarian 66).

Partizan Belgrade (4) 8 *(Diarra 4, Cleo 17, 53, 72 (pen), Dordevic 20, Ilic 38, 65, Petrovic 67)*

Rhyl (0) 0   9321

Partizan Belgrade: Bozovic M; Stevanovic, Dordevic (Jovanovic B 60), Krstajic, Gavrancic, Tomic (Bogunovic 70), Petrovic, Almani Moreira (Brezancic 60), Cleo, Ilic, Diarra. *Rhyl:* Kendall (Pritchard 86); Naylor, Strong, Horan, Stones, Connolly, Leah, Owen, Sherbon (Williams 65), Holden, Roberts.

Sant Julia (0) 0

Levski (3) 5 *(Ognyanov 23, 40, Yovov 34, Tsachev 83, Kirov 87)*   385

Sant Julia: Bergos; Wagner, Fernando Goncalves, Varela, Fontan, Xinos (Matamala 46), Miraglia, Peppe, Mejias, Moreira, Machado (Vila 61) (Perez 82). *Levski:* Petkov; Milanov, Rabeh (Miliev 73), Topuzakov, Minev, Sarmov, Ognyanov, Gadzhev, Yovov (Tsachev 57), Ze Soares (Kirov 46), Mustafa[■].

Sheriff (0) 1 *(Suvorov 69 (pen))*

Inter Turku (0) 0   11,000

Sheriff: Namasco; Tarkhnishvili, Karpovich, Nadson, Corneencov, Balima, Rouamba, Rodriguez, Bulat (Verbetchi 69), Suvorov, Diedhiou. *Inter Turku:* Bantamoi; Gustafsson (Verino 81), Nyman, Aho, Lehtonen, Ramirez, Tumanto (Purje 58), Paajanen, Ojala (Nwanganga 64), Furuholm, Kauko.

Slovan Bratislava (2) 4 *(Halenar 13, 60, Gaucho 19, Sylvestr 90)*

Zrinjski (0) 0   13,850

Slovan Bratislava: Bicik; Dobrotka, Salata, Dosoudil, Valachovic, Petras, Slovak, Kozak, Halenar (Cernak 75), Masaryk (Bozic 89), Gaucho (Sylvestr 84). *Zrinjski:* Melher; Sunjic, Zurzinov, Susic P (Musa 46), Ivankovic, Susic M, Stojanovic, Zadro, Anicic, Selimovic, Kordic.

Stabaek (3) 4 *(Segerstrom 15, 17, Berglund 43, Farnerud 55)*

SK Tirana (0) 0   4783

Stabaek: Knudsen; Segerstrom, Skjonsberg, Olsen, Hauger, Keller (Andersen 76), Kobayashi (Skjelvik 80), Farnerud, Hedenstad, Nannskog, Berglund (Hoff 67). *SK Tirana:* Nallbani; Dabulla, Pashaj, Lila, Alechenu, Osmani, Sefa, Patushi (Abilaliaj 46), Devolli (Mohellebi[■] 63), Lilaj (Hajdari 71), Xhafaj.

Wednesday, 22 July 2009

Aktobe (1) 2 *(Smakov 20, Tleshev 67)*

Hafnarfjordur (0) 0   13,000

Aktobe: Sidelnikov; Smakov, Kenzheisariev, Logvinenko, Chichulin, Khayrullin, Golovskoy, Asanbaev, Lavrik (Badlo 75), Tleshev (Strukov 71), Averchenko (Mitrofanov 84).
Hafnarfjordur: Larusson; Nielsen, Vidarsson P, Gardarsson (Hallfredsson 83), Kristjansson, Gudmundsson M, Sverrisson, Soderlund (Kuld 85), Gudmundsson T, Vilhjalmsson, Gudnason (Benediktsson 85).

Bohemians (0) 0

Salzburg (0) 1 *(Jezek 86)*   6000

Bohemians: Murphy B; Powell, Oman, Shelley, Rossiter (McGuinness 87), Brennan (Murphy A 65), Deegan, Keegan, N'Do, Crowe, Byrne (Cronin 84).
Salzburg: Gustafsson; Dudic, Schwegler, Schiemer, Ulmer (Jezek 58), Augustinussen, Tchoyi, Svento, Ilic (Vladavic 62), Leitgeb (Nelisse 72), Janko.

F91 Dudelange (1) 1 *(Da Mota 15)*

Ventspils (1) 3 *(Astafjevs 27, Butriks 57, Mihadjuks 67)*
     1165

F91 Dudelange: Joubert; Da Mota (Remy 72), Guthleber, Zeghdane, Diakite, Walter (Payal 62), Hareau, Molnar, Francoise■, Ronny (Bendaha 76), Hammami.
Ventspils: Pavlovs; Cilinsek, Astafjevs (Lazdins 71), Kosmacovs, Kacanovs, Chirkin, Mihadjuks, Zigajevs (Martins 63), Rimkus, Dedov (Spakov 46), Butriks.

Glentoran (0) 0

Maccabi Haifa (1) 4 *(Bello 9, 53, Masilela 62, Arbeitman 90)*   872

Glentoran: Morris; Neill, Leeman (Nixon 32), Ward, Taylor, Clarke, McCabe, Fordyce, Black (Gardiner 61), Waterworth (Halliday 67), Hamilton.
Maccabi Haifa: Davidovitch; Teixeira, Culma (Boccoli 46), Masilela, Keinan, Meshumar, Golasa (Ghadir 57), Kayal, Rafaelov, Dvalishvili, Bello (Arbeitman 64).

Kalmar (2) 3 *(Elm R 19, Mendes 32, Elm D 72 (pen))*

Debrecen (1) 1 *(Varga 13)*   3886

Kalmar: Wasta; Lantz, Carlsson (Johansson 56), Larsson, Nouri, Rydstrom, Sobralense (Smylie 69), Elm R (Ricardo Santos 56), Eriksson, Elm D, Mendes.
Debrecen: Poleksic; Mate■, Bernath, Leandro, Meszaros, Kiss, Varga, Szakaly (Dombi 73), Czvitkovics, Rudolf (Komlosi 87), Olah (Szilagyi 64).

Levadia (0) 1 *(Ivanov 90)*

Wisla (0) 0   2000

Levadia: Kaalma; Kalimullin, Morozov, Sisov, Nahk, Malov, Puri S, Teniste, Gussev (Zelinski 90), Ivanov, Andrejev (Leitan 86).
Wisla: Pawelek; Marcelo, Glowacki, Piotr Brozek, Diaz, Kirm, Sobolewski, Jirsak, Malecki, Pawel Brozek, Cwielong (Lobodzinski 73).

Maribor (2) 3 *(Bunderla 9, Tavares 19, Mihelic 85)*

WIT Georgia (1) 1 *(Kvaratskelia 45)*   6500

Maribor: Ranilovic; Dzinic, Jurkic, Lunder, Mihelic, Bacinovic, Pavlovic (Volas 90), Skolnik (Mertelj 63), Mejac, Tavares, Bunderla (Jelic 70).
WIT Georgia: Bediashvili; Lomaia, Japaridze, Bechvaia, Kvakhadze, Razmadze, Datunaishvili, Janelidze, Lipartia (Zakradze 81), Kakhelishvili, Kvaratskelia.

Mogren (0) 0

FC Copenhagen (4) 6 *(N'Doye 11, 40, Nordstrand 16, Vingaard 44, Delaney 47, Ailton 87)*   2000

Mogren: Janjusevic; Pejovic, Simovic (Kapisoda 46), Janicic, Cetkovic, Grbic, Bozovic D, Tiodorovic, Jovanovic (Bozovic B 66), Stojakovic, Milic (Sekulic 56).
FC Copenhagen: Wiland; Jensen N, Laursen, Jorgensen M, Kvist, Kristensen, Vingaard (Ozdogan 46), Sionko, Delaney, Nordstrand (Ailton 66), N'Doye.

Tuesday, 28 July 2009

Aktobe (0) 0

Maccabi Haifa (0) 0   12,850

Aktobe: Sidelnikov; Smakov, Kenzheisariev, Logvinenko, Chichulin, Khayrullin, Golovskoy (Badlo 85), Asanbaev (Strukov 66), Lavrik, Tleshev, Averchenko (Mitrofanov 75).
Maccabi Haifa: Davidovitch; Teixeira, Culma, Masilela, Keinan, Meshumar, Kayal, Rafaelov (Boccoli 64), Dvalishvili (Bello 64), Ghadir, Katan (Golasa 86).

Anderlecht (3) 5 *(De Sutter 17, 76, Boussoufa 22, Chatelle 32, Frutos 90)*

Sivas (0) 0   23,953

Anderlecht: Proto; Deschacht, Van Damme, Juhasz, Wasilewski, Biglia, Polak, Chatelle (Legear 71), Suarez (Frutos 74), Boussoufa, De Sutter (Gillet 78).
Sivas: Petkovic; Sedat, Yasin, Mbemba (Ugur 46), Hayrettin, Onur (Cihan 71), Musa, Ibrahim D, Erman, Abdurrahman, Ersen (Kamanan 46).

Baku (0) 0

Levski (0) 0   29,858

Baku: Sarlija; Rafael, Bates, Borets, Gurbanov (Fabio 82), Skulic, Mujiri (Adamia 68), Savinov, Solic, Felix (Batista 51), Perez.
Levski: Petkov; Milanov, Rabeh, Topuzakov, Minev, Sarmov, Gadzhev, Yovov (Hristov 72), Ortega (Dimitrov N 78), Ze Soares, Bardon (Genev 90).

Sparta Prague (2) 3 *(Holeneder 26, Vacek 31, Kalouda 86)*

Panathinaikos (0) 1 *(Salpingidis 67)*   12,058

Sparta Prague: Blazek; Repka, Hubnik, Kusnir, Pamic, Zofcak, Zeman (Kalouda 76), Vacek, Husek, Wilfried (Strestik 90), Hoheneder (Prudnikov 59).
Panathinaikos: Galinovic; Kante (Sarriegi 69), Bjarsmyr, Gabriel (Leto 59), Simao, Vyntra, Spyropoulos, Gilberto Silva (Katsouranis 84), Karagounis, Cisse, Salpingidis.

Wednesday, 29 July 2009

Apoel (0) 2 *(Mirosavljevic 50, Zewlakow 85)*

Partizan Belgrade (0) 0   15,892

Apoel: Chiotis; Nuno Morais, Poursaitidis, Charalambides, Kosowski (Alexandrou 82), Broerse, Helio Pinto (Zewlakow 73), Kontis, Haxhi, Michael (Satsias 73), Mirosavljevic.
Partizan Belgrade: Bozovic M; Stevanovic (Knezevic 84), Dordevic, Obradovic, Gavrancic, Tomic (Fejsa 61), Petrovic, Almani Moreira, Cleo, Ilic (Bogunovic 72), Diarra.

Celtic (0) 0

Dynamo Moscow (1) 1 *(Kokorin 7)*   54,184

Celtic: Boruc; Hinkel, Naylor, Caldwell, Loovens, N'Guemo, Maloney, Donati (Fox 67), McDonald S (Killen 61), Fortune (Samaras 60), McGeady.
Dynamo Moscow: Gabulov; Kowalczyk, Fernandez, Granat, Kolodin, Kombarov K, Kombarov D, Wilkshire, Svezhov, Kerzhakov, Kokorin (Smolov 74).

FC Copenhagen (2) 3 *(Gronkjaer 11, Cesar Santin 41, 80 (pen))*

Stabaek (0) 1 *(Palmason 58)*   15,383

FC Copenhagen: Christiansen; Pospech, Antonsson, Wendt, Jorgensen M, Norregaard (Vingaard 71), Kvist, Gronkjaer (Kristensen 82), Hutchinson, Ailton (Nordstrand 64), Cesar Santin.
Stabaek: Knudsen; Segerstrom, Skjonsberg, Rogne, Hauger, Kobayashi (Diskerud 90), Palmason, Farnerud, Hedenstad, Nannskog (Andersson 77), Berglund (Hoff 70).

Levadia (0) 0

Debrecen (0) 1 *(Leandro 70)*   4000

Levadia: Kaalma; Kalimullin, Morozov, Sisov, Nahk, Malov (Leitan 74), Puri S (Puri E 89), Teniste, Gussev (Zelinski 86), Ivanov, Andrejev.
Debrecen: Poleksic; Komlosi, Bernath, Leandro, Meszaros, Kiss, Szakaly (Szucs 84), Czvitkovics, Katona (Dombi 67), Rudolf, Szilagyi (Coulibaly 58).

Salzburg (1) 1 *(Zickler 45)*
Dinamo Zagreb (0) 1 *(Mandzukic 63)*   15,800
Salzburg: Gustafsson; Dudic, Schiemer, Ulmer, Sekagya, Augustinussen, Tchoyi, Svento (Jezek 73), Leitgeb, Vladavic (Ilic 85), Zickler (Janko 70).
Dinamo Zagreb: Butina; Lovren, Vrdoljak, Etto, Sammir, Glavina, Badelj, Biscan, Morales (Chago 86), Mandzukic**, Papadopoulos D (Slepicka 71).

Shakhtar Donetsk (0) 2 *(Gladkiy 61, Fernandinho 86)*
Timisoara (1) 2 *(Bucur 20, 80)*   18,000
Shakhtar Donetsk: Pyatov; Hubschman, Kucher, Ilsinho, Shevchuk (Chigrinskiy 46), Ishchenko (Gladkiy 46), Fernandinho, Jadson, Willian, Srna, Luiz Adriano (Aghahowa 80).
Timisoara: Pantilimon; Bonfim, Nibombe, Curtean, Cisovsky, Bourceanu, Alexa (Stancu 71), Art Karamian, Parks (Magera 26), Arm Karamian, Bucur (Ionescu 90).

Sheriff (0) 0
Slavia Prague (0) 0   12,000
Sheriff: Namasco; Tarkhnishvili, Mamah, Nadson, Corneencov, Balima, Rouamba, Arbanas, Rodriguez, Suvorov (Franca 66), Diedhiou (Volkov 90).
Slavia Prague: Hanus; Celustka, Suchy, Vomacka, Ragued, Janda (Volesak 90), Jarolim (Senkerik 66), Cerny M, Cerny J, Vlcek (Belaid 86), Hlousek.

Slovan Bratislava (0) 0
Olympiakos (2) 2 *(Papadopoulos A 2, Leonardo 21)*
                21,250
Slovan Bratislava: Bicik; Salata (Cernak 79), Dobrotka, Valachovic, Petras, Dosoudil, Slovak, Kozak, Halenar, Masaryk (Sylvestr 58), Gaucho (Ivana 74).
Olympiakos: Nikopolidis; Mellberg, Zewlakow, Raul Bravo, Leonardo (Galletti 60), Dudu Cearense, Papadopoulos A, Ledesma, Papadopoulos G (Maresca 70), Zairi, Mitroglou (Diogo 84).

Sporting Lisbon (0) 0
Twente (0) 0   20,000
Sporting Lisbon: Rui Patricio; Daniel Carrico, Anderson Polga, Pedro Silva (Rochemback 77), Caneira (Pereirinha 57), Vukcevic (Yannick Djalo 69), Matias, Miguel Veloso, Joao Moutinho, Helder Postiga, Liedson.
Twente: Boschker**; Wisgerhof, Rajkovic, Douglas, Brama, Stam, Janssen, Stoch (Tiote 74), Ruiz (Rukavytsya 61), Nkufo, Perez (Mihaylov 26).

Ventspils (0) 1 *(Chirkin 64)*
BATE Borisov (0) 0   2950
Ventspils: Pavlovs; Cilinsek, Astafjevs, Kosmacovs (Lazdins 72), Kacanovs, Chirkin (Visnakovs A 83), Mihadjuks, Tigirlas, Zigajevs, Rimkus, Butriks (Spakov 77).
BATE Borisov: Veremko; Sosnovskiy, Shitov, Yurevich, Radzov, Likhtarovich (Volodzo 63), Krivets, Nekhaichik (Bordachev 74), Stasevich, Skavysh, Rodionov (Alumona 88).

Zurich (2) 2 *(Vonlanthen 4, Hassli 29)*
Maribor (2) 3 *(Tavares 12, 22, Pavlovic 50)*   8500
Zurich: Guatelli; Lampi, Rochat, Tihinen, Margairaz (Nikci 64), Aegerter, Okonkwo, Djuric (Alphonse 76), Gajic, Vonlanthen, Hassli.
Maribor: Ranilovic; Dzinic (Kljajevic 77), Lunder, Mihelic, Bacinovic, Popovic, Pavlovic, Mertelj, Mejac (Jurkic 78), Tavares, Volas (Jelic 70).

THIRD QUALIFYING ROUND SECOND LEG

Tuesday, 4 August 2009
Dinamo Zagreb (0) 1 *(Papadopoulos D 47)*
Salzburg (1) 2 *(Svento 34, Nelisse 83)*   20000
Dinamo Zagreb: Butina; Lovren, Carlos (Kramaric 85), Vrdoljak, Sammir (Barbaric 88), Glavina, Chago (Slepicka 46), Badelj, Biscan, Morales, Papadopoulos D.
Salzburg: Gustafsson; Dudic, Schiemer, Ulmer, Sekagya, Tchoyi, Svento (Opdam 90), Leitgeb (Augustinusser 87), Aufhauser, Zickler (Cziommer 79), Nelisse.

Maccabi Haifa (2) 4 *(Katan 26, Golasa 34, Dvalishvili 59, 62)*
Aktobe (3) 3 *(Averchenko 8, Chichulin 13, Khayrullin 15)*   12,000
Maccabi Haifa: Davidovitch; Teixeira, Culma, Masilela, Keinan, Meshumar, Kayal (Arbeitman 58), Rafaelov (Golasa 31), Dvalishvili, Ghadir (Boccoli 65), Katan.
Aktobe: Sidelnikkov; Smakov, Kenzheisariev, Logvinenko, Chichulin, Mitrofanov (Tleshev 60), Khayrullin, Golovskoy (Asanbaev 67), Lavrik, Strukov (Badlo 72), Averchenko.

Panathinaikos (1) 3 *(Sarriegi 45, Katsouranis 54, Salpingidis 89)*
Sparta Prague (0) 0   30,000
Panathinaikos: Galinovic; Moon, Sarriegi, Vyntra, Spyropoulos, Leto (Simao 74), Gilberto Silva, Karagounis (Gabriel 77), Katsouranis, Cisse, Salpingidis.
Sparta Prague: Blazek; Hoheneder, Hubnik, Kusnir, Pamic, Berger, Zofcak, Zeman (Kadlec 58), Vacek, Husek (Kalouda 78), Wilfried (Prudnikov 69).

Sivas (2) 3 *(Ersin 12, Kamanan 19 (pen), Musa 58)*
Anderlecht (1) 1 *(Van Damme 34)*   6000
Sivas: Akin; Sedat, Hayrettin, Ugur, Onur, Murat S, Musa (Ibrahim D 60), Erman (Akeem 58), Cihan, Kamanan, Ersen (Murat E 76).
Anderlecht: Proto; Deschacht, Van Damme, Juhasz, Wasilewski, Polak, Chatelle, Gillet, Sare, Boussoufa (Reynaldo 76), De Sutter (Frutos 57).

Twente (1) 1 *(Douglas 2)*
Sporting Lisbon (0) 1 *(Wisgerhof 90 (og))*   23,700
Twente: Mihaylov; Wisgerhof, Rajkovic, Stam, Douglas, Brama, Janssen, Nkufo, Perez (Tiote 59), Stoch (Rukavytsya 79), Ruiz (Vujicevic 90).
Sporting Lisbon: Rui Patricio; Daniel Carrico, Polga, Andre Marques (Vukcevic 63), Abel, Matias (Pereirinha 46), Miguel Veloso, Joao Moutinho, Yannick Djalo, Helder Postiga (Caicedo 63), Liedson.

Wednesday, 5 August 2009
BATE Borisov (1) 2 *(Krivets 43, 57)*
Ventspils (1) 1 *(Tigirlas 14)*   5500
BATE Borisov: Veremko; Sosnovskiy, Shitov, Yurevich, Bordachev (Alumona 82), Likhtarovich, Volodzo (Pavlov 78), Krivets, Nekhaichik, Stasevich, Rodionov (Skavysh 75).
Ventspils: Pavlovs; Cilinsek, Astafjevs, Kacanovs, Visnakovs A (Lazdins 46), Chirkin**, Mihadjuks, Tigirlas, Zigajevs (Dedov 86), Rimkus, Spakov (Rugins 63).

Debrecen (0) 1 *(Coulibaly 70)*
Levadia (0) 0   9640
Debrecen: Poleksic; Komlosi, Fodor, Bernath (Dombi 54), Meszaros, Kiss, Varga, Szakaly, Czvitkovics, Rudolf (Szucs 89), Coulibaly (Olah 71).
Levadia: Kaalma; Kalimullin, Morozov, Malov**, Saarelma, Puri S, Teniste, Gussev, Ivanov, Marmor (Sisov 21), Andrejev (Zelinski 46).

Dynamo Moscow (0) 0
Celtic (1) 2 *(McDonald S 44, Samaras 90)*   13,753
Dynamo Moscow: Gabulov; Kowalczyk, Fernandez (Ropotan 90), Granat, Kolodin, Kombarov K, Khokhlov, Kombarov D, Wilkshire, Svezhov (Kokorin 84), Kerzhakov.
Celtic: Boruc; Hinkel, Fox, Donati, Caldwell, Loovens, N'Guemo, Maloney, McDonald S (Samaras 79), Fortune (Brown S 69), McGeady.

Levski (0) 2 *(Yovov 64, Hristov 80)*
Baku (0) 0   15,000
Levski: Petkov; Milanov, Rabeh, Topuzakov, Minev, Sarmov, Joaozinho (Tasevski 41), Yovov (Wagner 78), Ze Soares (Ortega 82), Bardon, Hristov.
Baku: Sissokho; Rafael, Bates, Borets, Skulic (Gurbanov 81), Fabio (Mujiri 69), Savinov, Solic, Felix, Perez (Adamia 69), Soltanov.

Maribor (0) 0
Zurich (2) 3 *(Djuric 21, Margairaz 45, Nikci 76)*   12,000
Maribor: Ranilovic; Dzinic, Jurkic, Samardzic, Mihelic, Bacinovic (Bunderla 78), Popovic, Pavlovic, Mertelj (Mezga 65), Tavares, Volas (Jelic 46).
Zurich: Leoni; Lampi, Stahel (Koch 75), Rochat, Tihinen, Margairaz, Aegerter, Djuric (Nikci 65), Gajic, Vonlanthen, Hassli (Okonkwo 82).

Olympiakos (1) 2 *(Maresca 35, Diogo 56)*
Slovan Bratislava (0) 0   26,137
Olympiakos: Nikopolidis; Mellberg, Zewlakow, Raul Bravo, Galletti (Leonardo 69), Dudu Cearense, Papadopoulos A, Maresca (Papadopoulos K 79), Ledesma, Zairi, Mitroglou (Diogo 46).
Slovan Bratislava: Bicik; Salata, Valachovic, Dosoudil, Simao, Slovak, Bozic, Kozak, Halenar (Cernak 85), Masaryk (Obzera 61), Gaucho (Sylvestr 53).

Partizan Belgrade (1) 1 *(Almani Moreira 3)*
Apoel (0) 0   23,867
Partizan Belgrade: Bozovic M; Dordevic, Knezevic, Obradovic, Gavrancic, Tomic (Jovanovic B 85), Petrovic, Almani Moreira, Ljajic (Washington 57), Cleo (Bogunovic 67), Diarra.
Apoel: Chiotis; Nuno Morais, Poursaitidis, Charalambides (Paulo Jorge 90), Kosowski (Alexandrou 86), Broerse■, Satsias, Kontis, Haxhi, Zewlakow (Helio Pinto 67), Mirosavljevic.

Slavia Prague (1) 1 *(Hlousek 15)*
Sheriff (0) 1 *(Nadson 90)*   13,483
Slavia Prague: Hanus; Hubacek, Celustka, Suchy, Vomacka, Ragued, Janda, Jarolim (Vasiljevic 62), Cerny J (Tafat 89), Vlcek, Hlousek (Cerny M 74).
Sheriff: Namasco; Tarkhnishvili, Mamah (Bulat 72), Nadson, Corneencov, Balima, Rouamba, Arbanas, Rodriguez, Suvorov (Volkov 81), Diedhiou (Franca 59).

Stabaek (0) 0
FC Copenhagen (0) 0   12,562
Stabaek: Knudsen; Segerstrom, Skjonsberg (Andersson 80), Rogne, Rauger, Kobayashi (Diskerud 86), Palmason (Hoff 52), Farnerud, Hedenstad, Nannskog, Berglund.
FC Copenhagen: Christiansen; Pospech, Antonsson, Wendt, Jorgensen M, Norregaard, Kvist, Gronkjaer (Kristensen 73), Hutchinson, Ailton (Nordstrand 68), Cesar Santin (N'Doye 86).

Timisoara (0) 0
Shakhtar Donetsk (0) 0   25,000
Timisoara: Pantilimon; Bonfim, Nibombe, Stancu (Ionescu 82), Cisovsky, Alexa (Scutaru 67), Art Karamian, Bourceanu, Parks, Arm Karamian, Bucur (Magera 87).
Shakhtar Donetsk: Pyatov; Hubschman, Kucher, Ilsinho, Rat, Chigrinskiy, Fernandinho, Jadson (Gladkiy 69), Gay (Willian 54), Srna, Luiz Adriano (Aghahowa 32).

PLAY-OFF ROUND FIRST LEG

Tuesday, 18 August 2009
Celtic (0) 0
Arsenal (1) 2 *(Gallas 43, Caldwell 71 (og))*   58,165
Celtic: Boruc; Hinkel, Fox, Donati (McDonald 56), Caldwell, Loovens, N'Guemo (McCourt 76), Brown S, Samaras (Fortune 56), Maloney, McGeady.
Arsenal: Almunia; Sagna, Clichy, Denilson, Vermaelen, Gallas, Song Billong, Fabregas, Bendtner, Van Persie, Arshavin (Diaby 70).

FC Copenhagen (0) 1 *(Pospech 54)*
Apoel (0) 0   16,250
FC Copenhagen: Christiansen; Pospech, Antonsson, Wendt, Jorgensen M, Norregaard, Kvist, Gronkjaer, Hutchinson, Ailton (Nordstrand 75), Cesar Santin (N'Doye 22).
Apoel: Chiotis; Paulo Jorge, Grncarov, Nuno Morais, Charalambides (Alexandrou 77), Kosowski (Breska 86), Satsias (Zewlakow 69), Helio Pinto, Kontis, Haxhi■, Mirosavljevic.

Sheriff (0) 0
Olympiakos (0) 2 *(Dudu Cearense 46, Mitroglou 81)*   12,500
Sheriff: Namasco; Tarkhnishvili, Karpovich, Corneencov, Balima, Erokhin, Rouamba, Arbanas (Bulat 70), Rodriguez, Suvorov (Volkov 55), Diedhiou (Brankovic 81).
Olympiakos: Nikopolidis; Mellberg, Zewlakow, Raul Bravo (Domi 48), Galletti (Leonardo 62), Dudu Cearense, Papadopoulos A, Maresca, Ledesma, Diogo (Mitroglou 80), Zairi.

Sporting Lisbon (0) 2 *(Vukcevic 58, Miguel Veloso 66)*
Fiorentina (1) 2 *(Vargas 6, Gilardino 79)*   27,602
Sporting Lisbon: Rui Patricio; Daniel Carrico, Polga, Pedro Silva (Pereirinha 57), Andre Marques (Caneira 67), Vukcevic■, Matias, Miguel Veloso, Joao Moutinho, Helder Postiga (Yannick Djalo 81), Liedson.
Fiorentina: Frey; Dainelli, Gamberini, Vargas, Comotto, Zanetti, Montolivo (Donadel 80), Gobbi, Marchionni, Mutu (Jovetic 64), Gilardino.

Timisoara (0) 0
Stuttgart (2) 2 *(Gebhart 28 (pen), Hleb 30)*   32,446
Timisoara: Pantilimon; Bonfim, Nibombe, Stancu, Scutaru (Borbely 46), Cisovsky, Alexa, Art Karamian (Latovlevici 77), Arm Karamian, Bucur, Magera (Ionescu 69).
Stuttgart: Lehmann; Tasci, Delpierre, Magnin, Celozzi, Hitzlsperger, Gebhart (Rudy 86), Hleb (Elson 61), Khedira, Marica, Pogrebnyak (Schieber 77).

Wednesday, 19 August 2009
Levski (0) 1 *(Bardon 51)*
Debrecen (1) 2 *(Bodnar 12, Czvitkovics 76)*   14,524
Levski: Petkov; Genev, Topuzakov, Minev, Wagner, Sarmov, Tasevski (Ortega 60), Yovov (Joaozinho 70), Ze Soares, Bardon, Hristov (Krastovchev 85).
Debrecen: Poleksic; Bodnar, Mate (Komlosi 15), Leandro, Meszaros, Kiss, Varga, Szakaly (Dombi 55), Czvitkovics (Ramos 79), Rudolf, Coulibaly.

Lyon (4) 5 *(Pjanic 10, Lisandro Lopez 15 (pen), Bastos 39, Gomis 42, 63)*
Anderlecht (0) 1 *(Suarez 58)*   37,902
Lyon: Lloris; Cris, Reveillere, Cissokho, Bodmer, Kallstrom (Makoun 64), Bastos, Pjanic, Toulalan, Lisandro Lopez (Delgado 71), Gomis (Ederson 82).
Anderlecht: Proto; Deschacht, Van Damme, Juhasz, Wasilewski, Biglia, Polak, Gillet (Legear 46), Suarez, Boussoufa, De Sutter (Lukaku 72).

Panathinaikos (0) 2 *(Salpingidis 47, Leto 74)*
Atletico Madrid (1) 3 *(Maxi Rodriguez 36, Forlan 63, Aguero 70)*   50,540
Panathinaikos: Galinovic; Moon, Simao (Christodoulopoulos 80), Vyntra, Spyropoulos, Marcelo Mattos (Leto 46), Gilberto Silva, Karagounis, Katsouranis, Cisse, Salpingidis.
Atletico Madrid: Sergio Asenjo; Antonio Lopez, Heitinga, Juanito, Ujfalusi, Raul Garcia (Cleber Santana 72), Maxi Rodriguez (Sinama-Pongolle 86), Paulo Assuncao, Simao, Forlan, Aguero (Jurado 75).

Salzburg (0) 1 *(Zickler 57)*
Maccabi Haifa (1) 2 *(Ghadir 22, Arbeitman 84)*   21,260
Salzburg: Gustafsson; Dudic, Schwegler, Schiemer, Ulmer, Augustinussen, Tchoyi, Svento (Jezek 80), Leitgeb, Zickler (Janko 68), Nelisse (Cziommer 60).
Maccabi Haifa: Davidovitch; Maimon, Culma, Masilela, Keinan, Meshumar, Golasa, Kayal (Rafaelov 69), Dvalishvili (Arbeitman 75), Ghadir (Boccoli 65), Katan.

Ventspils (0) 0
Zurich (1) 3 *(Vonlanthen 12, Aegerter 55, Djuric 75)* 7300
Ventspils: Pavlovs; Ndeki, Astafjevs, Kosmacovs, Kacanovs, Visnakovs A (Martins 74), Mihadjuks, Tigirlas, Zigajevs (Cilinsek 69), Rimkus, Dedov (Butriks 60).
Zurich: Leoni; Stahel, Koch, Rochat, Tihinen, Margairaz (Abdi 79), Aegerter, Okonkwo, Djuric, Vonlanthen (Nikci 84), Hassli (Alphonse 73).

PLAY-OFF ROUND SECOND LEG

Tuesday, 25 August 2009

Anderlecht (0) 1 *(Suarez 51 (pen))*
Lyon (3) 3 *(Lisandro Lopez 26, 32, 41)*   16,096
Anderlecht: Schollen; Deschacht, Mazuch, Juhasz, Wasilewski, Polak (Biglia 46), Chatelle (Reynaldo 66), Gillet, Sare, Boussoufa, De Sutter (Suarez 46).
Lyon: Lloris; Cris, Reveillere, Cissokho, Bodmer, Kallstrom (Pjanic 80), Bastos, Makoun, Toulalan (Gonalons 73), Lisandro Lopez (Belfodil 60), Delgado.

Atletico Madrid (1) 2 *(Vyntra 4 (og), Aguero 83)*
Panathinaikos (0) 0   29,910
Atletico Madrid: Sergio Asenjo; Antonio Lopez, Heitinga, Juanito, Ujfalusi, Raul Garcia (Cleber Santana 61), Maxi Rodriguez, Paulo Assuncao, Simao (Reyes 86), Forlan (Jurado 82), Aguero.
Panathinaikos: Galinovic; Moon (Salpingidis 53), Sarriegi, Gabriel, Darlas, Vyntra, Ninis (Christodoulopoulos 63), Leto, Gilberto Silva, Katsouranis (Simao 87), Cisse■.

Debrecen (2) 2 *(Varga 13, Rudolf 35)*
Levski (0) 0   32,000
Debrecen: Poleksic; Bodnar, Komlosi, Leandro, Ramos. Meszaros, Varga, Szakaly (Dombi 58), Czvitkovics (Fodor 81), Rudolf (Olah 88), Coulibaly.
Levski: Petkov; Rabeh, Topuzakov, Minev, Benzoukane Sarmov, Joaozinho (Tasevski 60), Yovov (Dimitrov ℕ 71), Ze Soares, Bardon, Hristov (Ortega 77).

Maccabi Haifa (1) 3 *(Dvalishvili 30, Golasa 56, Ghadir 89*
Salzburg (0) 0   31,70℃
Maccabi Haifa: Davidovitch; Maimon, Teixeira, Culma, Masilela, Meshumar (Harazi 61), Golasa (Boccoli 61⁚, Kayal, Dvalishvili (Rafaelov 71), Ghadir, Katan.
Salzburg: Gustafsson; Dudic (Vladavic 54), Opdam, Schiemer, Ulmer, Tchoyi, Svento, Cziommer (Vladavic 54), Leitgeb, Ilsanker (Ilic 69), Janko.

Zurich (1) 2 *(Vonlanthen 6, Abdi 90)*
Ventspils (1) 1 *(Tigirlas 8)*   905℃
Zurich: Leoni; Lampi, Stahel, Rochat, Tihine∃, Margairaz (Abdi 63), Aegerter, Okonkwo, Djuric (Gajic 78), Vonlanthen, Alphonse (Hassli 83).
Ventspils: Chasnowski; Savcenkovs, Ndeki, Baimatov (Spakov 62), Kosmacovs, Kacanovs, Visnakovs A (Rugins 55), Chirkin, Tigirlas, Rimkus, Butriks (Dedov 72).

Wednesday, 26 August 2009

Apoel (3) 3 *(Kosowski 2, Michael 18 (pen), 41)*
FC Copenhagen (1) 1 *(N'Doye 22)*   21,133
Apoel: Chiotis; Elia, Nuno Morais, Poursaitidis, Charalambides, Kosowski (Alexandrou 81), Broerse, Kontis, Michael, Zewlakow (Helio Pinto 77), Mirosavljevic (Sikora 65).
FC Copenhagen: Christiansen; Pospech, Antonsson, Wendt, Jorgensen M, Norregaard (Sionko 65), Kvist, Hutchinson, Vingaard (Gronkjaer 46), Ailton (Nordstrand 79), N'Doye.

Arsenal (1) 3 *(Eduardo 28 (pen), Eboue 53, Arshavin 74)*
Celtic (0) 1 *(Donati 90)*   59,962
Arsenal: Almunia; Sagna, Clichy, Denilson, Vermaelen, Gallas, Eboue (Wilshere 72), Diaby (Ramsey 61), Eduardo (Arshavin 72), Bendtner, Song Billong.
Celtic: Boruc; Hinkel, Fox, Donati, Caldwell (O'Dea 46), Loovens, Maloney (Flood 61), Brown S, McDonald S, Fortune, McGeady (Naylor 61).

Fiorentina (0) 1 *(Jovetic 54)*
Sporting Lisbon (1) 1 *(Joao Moutinho 35)*   30,821
Fiorentina: Frey; Dainelli, Gamberini, Vargas, Comotto, Zanetti (Donadel 81), Montolivo, Gobbi (Jovetic 46), Marchionni, Mutu (Jorgensen 72), Gilardino.
Sporting Lisbon: Rui Patricio; Daniel Carrico, Polga, Pedro Silva (Tonel 81), Andre Marques, Matias (Saleiro 62), Miguel Veloso, Pereirinha, Joao Moutinho, Yannick Djalo, Liedson.

Olympiakos (0) 1 *(Mitroglou 82)*
Sheriff (0) 0   27,633
Olympiakos: Nikopolidis; Papadopoulos K (Ledesma 46), Mellberg, Zewlakow, Raul Bravo, Leonardo, Galletti (Galitsios 65), Dudu Cearense (Diogo 62), Papadopoulos A, Maresca, Mitroglou.
Sheriff: Namasco; Da Costa, Tarkhnishvili, Tsynya, Corneencov, Balima (Volkov 80), Erokhin (Kuchuk 65), Rouamba, Arbanas, Rodriguez, Diedhiou (Suvorov 58).

Stuttgart (0) 0
Timisoara (0) 0   27,633
Stuttgart: Lehmann; Tasci, Delpierre, Magnin, Celozzi, Hitzlsperger, Gebhart (Elson 90), Rudy (Simak 67), Khedira, Marica (Schieber 79), Pogrebnyak.
Timisoara: Pantilimon; Bonfim (Ionescu 60), Latovlevici, Nibombe, Curtean, Cisovsky (Scutaru 73), Borbely (Stancu 46), Bourceanu, Parks, Arm Karamian, Bucur.

GROUP STAGE

GROUP A

Tuesday, 15 September 2009

Juventus (0) 1 *(Iaquinta 63)*
Bordeaux (0) 1 *(Plasil 75)*   17,513
Juventus: Buffon; Caceres, Cannavaro (Zebina 67), Grosso, Legrottaglie, Felipe Melo, Marchisio, Tiago (Poulsen 81), Iaquinta, Amauri, Giovinco (Camoranesi 73).
Bordeaux: Carrasso (Rame 55); Ciani, Chalme, Planus, Tremoulinas, Diarra, Fernando, Gourcuff, Wendel, Plasil (Gouffran 77), Chamakh.

Maccabi Haifa (0) 0
Bayern Munich (0) 3 *(Van Buyten 65, Muller 85, 88)*   38,789
Maccabi Haifa: Davidovitch; Teixeira, Masilela, Keinan, Meshumar (Rafaelov 74), Boccoli, Golasa, Kayal (Ottman 68), Dvalishvili, Ghadir (Arbeitman 68), Katan.
Bayern Munich: Butt; Van Buyten, Lahm, Badstuber, Ribery (Gomez 64), Pranjic, Schweinsteiger, Tymoshchuk, Robben (Ottl 77), Olic (Sosa 86), Muller.

Wednesday, 30 September 2009

Bayern Munich (0) 0
Juventus (0) 0   66,000
Bayern Munich: Butt; Braafheid, Van Buyten, Lahm, Badstuber, Ribery, Ottl, Schweinsteiger, Robben (Olic 44), Klose (Gomez 74), Muller.
Juventus: Buffon; Chiellini, Grosso, Grygera, Legrottaglie, Felipe Melo, Marchisio, Camoranesi (Tiago 90), Diego (Poulsen 60), Iaquinta, Trezeguet (Amauri 74).

Bordeaux (0) 0 *(Ciani 83)*
Maccabi Haifa (0) 0   28,748
Bordeaux: Carrasso; Ciani, Chalme, Planus, Tremoulinas, Diarra, Gourcuff (Fernando 46), Wendel, Plasil (Sertic 71), Cavenaghi (Bellion 59), Chamakh.
Maccabi Haifa: Davidovitch; Teixeira, Culma, Masilela, Keinan, Meshumar, Golasa (Boccoli 84), Kayal■, Dvalishvili (Arbeitman 57), Ghadir (Rafelov 68), Katan.

Wednesday, 21 October 2009
Bordeaux (2) 2 *(Ciani 29, Planus 41)*
Bayern Munich (1) 1 *(Ciani 6 (og))*   34,000
Bordeaux: Carrasso; Ciani, Chalme, Planus, Tremoulinas, Diarra, Fernando, Gourcuff, Wendel (Jussie 84), Plasil (Gouffran 85), Chamakh.
Bayern Munich: Butt; Van Buyten■, Lahm, Badstuber, Hamit Altintop, Van Bommel (Ottl 78), Schweinsteiger, Tymoshchuk, Toni (Gomez 78), Klose (Pranjic 74), Muller■.

Juventus (0) 1 *(Chiellini 47)*
Maccabi Haifa (0) 0   20,000
Juventus: Buffon; Chiellini, Cannavaro, Grosso, Zebina (Caceres 34), Felipe Melo (Poulsen 62), Camoranesi, Sissoko, Diego, Trezeguet (Amauri 81), Giovinco.
Maccabi Haifa: Davidovitch; Teixeira, Culma, Masilela (Zaguri 46), Keinan, Meshumar, Boccoli, Ottman, Rafaelov (Dutra■ 57), Dvalishvili, Arbeitman (Ghadir 46).

Tuesday, 3 November 2009
Bayern Munich (0) 0
Bordeaux (1) 2 *(Gourcuff 37, Chamakh 90)*   66,000
Bayern Munich: Butt; Braafheid (Gomez 59), Demichelis, Lahm, Badstuber, Van Bommel, Pranjic, Schweinsteiger, Tymoshchuk, Toni, Klose (Robben 46).
Bordeaux: Carrasso; Ciani, Chalme, Planus, Tremoulinas, Diarra, Fernando, Gourcuff, Wendel (Jussie 68), Plasil (Sane 84), Chamakh.

Maccabi Haifa (0) 0
Juventus (1) 1 *(Camoranesi 45)*   39,120
Maccabi Haifa: Davidovitch; Teixeira, Culma (Ghadir 46), Masilela, Keinan, Meshumar, Boccoli (Zaguri 71), Ottman, Dvalishvili (Rafaelov 56), Arbeitman, Katan.
Juventus: Buffon; Caceres, Chiellini, Grosso, Legrottaglie, Felipe Melo, Camoranesi, Poulsen, Diego, Tiago (De Ceglie 60), Amauri (Trezeguet 84).

Wednesday, 25 November 2009
Bayern Munich (0) 1 *(Olic 62)*
Maccabi Haifa (0) 0   58,000
Bayern Munich: Butt; Van Buyten, Demichelis, Lahm, Badstuber, Van Bommel, Pranjic (Ottl 70), Schweinsteiger, Olic (Tymoshchuk 81), Muller, Gomez.
Maccabi Haifa: Davidovitch; Maimon, Culma (Rafaelov 69), Masilela, Keinan, Meshumar, Ottman (Golasa 74), Kayal, Dvalishvili (Arbeitman 63), Ghadir, Katan.

Bordeaux (0) 2 *(Fernando 55, Chamakh 90)*
Juventus (0) 0   32,195
Bordeaux: Carrasso; Ciani, Chalme, Planus, Tremoulinas, Diarra, Fernando, Wendel, Plasil, Gouffran (Traore 75), Chamakh.
Juventus: Buffon; Caceres, Chiellini, Grosso, Legrottaglie, Felipe Melo, Camoranesi, Sissoko (Marchisio 88), Diego, Del Piero (Immobile 68), Amauri (Giovinco 77).

Tuesday, 8 December 2009
Juventus (1) 1 *(Trezeguet 19)*
Bayern Munich (1) 4 *(Butt 30 (pen), Olic 52, Gomez 83, Tymoshchuk 90)*   27,044
Juventus: Buffon; Caceres, Cannavaro, Grosso, Legrottaglie, Felipe Melo (Giovinco 81), Marchisio, Camoranesi, Diego (Amauri 65), Del Piero (Poulsen 46), Trezeguet.
Bayern Munich: Butt; Van Buyten, Demichelis, Lahm, Badstuber, Van Bommel, Pranjic (Robben 73), Schweinsteiger, Olic (Tymoshchuk 79), Muller, Gomez.

Maccabi Haifa (0) 0
Bordeaux (1) 1 *(Jussie 12)*   25,800
Maccabi Haifa: Davidovitch; Teixeira, Culma, Masilela (Twatiha 62), Keinan, Meshumar, Golasa (Harazi 71), Kayal, Rafaelov, Dvalishvili (Arbeitman 54), Ghadir.
Bordeaux: Rame; Jurietti, Placente, Sane, Fernando, Wendel, Traore (Sertic 78), Cavenaghi, Jussie, Bellion, Saivet.

Group A Table	P	W	D	L	F	A	Pts
Bordeaux	6	5	1	0	9	2	16
Bayern Munich	6	3	1	2	9	5	10
Juventus	6	2	2	2	4	7	8
Maccabi Haifa	6	0	0	6	0	8	0

GROUP B

Tuesday, 15 September 2009
Besiktas (0) 0
Manchester U (0) 1 *(Scholes 77)*   26,448
Besiktas: Hakan; Ibrahim K, Ibrahim U, Ferrari. Sivok, Tabata (Tello 69), Dag, Serdar (Yusuf 59), Ernst, Mert, Holosko (Nihat 86).
Manchester U: Foster; Neville, Evra, Carrick (Berbatov 63), Evans J, Vidic, Valencia (Park 86), Scholes, Rooney (Owen 64), Anderson, Nani.

Wolfsburg (2) 3 *(Grafite 35, 41 (pen), 87)*
CSKA Moscow (0) 1 *(Dzagoev 77)*   25,017
Wolfsburg: Benaglio; Schafer, Madlung, Riether, Barzagli, Josue, Misimovic, Gentner (Hasebe 90), Dzeko, Martins (Ziani 65), Grafite (Santana 89).
CSKA Moscow: Akinfeev; Semberas, Ignashevich, Berezutski A, Berezutski V (Necid 84), Shchennikov (Piliev 58), Dzagoev, Krasic, Aldonin (Mamaev 68), Rahimic, Guilherme.

Wednesday, 30 September 2009
CSKA Moscow (1) 2 *(Dzagoev 7, Krasic 61)*
Besiktas (0) 1 *(Dag 90)*   19,750
CSKA Moscow: Akinfeev; Semberas, Ignashevich, Berezutski A (Grigoryev 46), Odiah, Berezutski V, Dzagoev, Mamaev, Gonzalez (Shchennikov 78), Krasic, Necid (Rahimic 64).
Besiktas: Rustu; Ismail, Ibrahim K, Ferrari, Sivok, Tello (Bobo 75), Dag, Ernst, Nihat (Serdar 73), Mert, Holosko (Yusuf 34).

Manchester U (0) 2 *(Giggs 59, Carrick 78)*
Wolfsburg (0) 1 *(Dzeko 56)*   74,037
Manchester U: Kuszczak; O'Shea, Evra, Carrick, Ferdinand, Vidic, Valencia (Fletcher 82), Anderson, Owen (Berbatov 20), Rooney, Giggs.
Wolfsburg: Benaglio; Schafer, Ricardo Costa, Madlung, Riether, Josue, Misimovic, Hasebe (Ziani 73), Gentner, Dzeko, Grafite (Martins 82).

Wednesday, 21 October 2009
CSKA Moscow (0) 0
Manchester U (0) 1 *(Valencia 86)*   45,000
CSKA Moscow: Akinfeev; Semberas, Ignashevich, Berezutski A, Odiah, Berezutski V, Shchennikov (Mamaev 61), Dzagoev, Krasic, Rahimic (Daniel Carvalho 89), Necid (Piliev 73).
Manchester U: Van der Sar; Neville, Fabio (Carrick 88), O'Shea, Ferdinand (Brown 56), Vidic, Valencia, Anderson, Berbatov, Scholes (Owen 70), Nani.

Wolfsburg (0) 0
Besiktas (0) 0   26,490
Wolfsburg: Benaglio; Schafer, Ricardo Costa, Madlung, Riether, Josue, Misimovic, Hasebe (Dejagah 67), Gentner, Dzeko, Grafite■.
Besiktas: Rustu; Ibrahim K, Ibrahim U, Ferrari, Fink (Ugur 87), Sivok, Tello (Tabata 81), Dag, Ernst, Nihat, Bobo (Mert 88).

Tuesday, 3 November 2009
Besiktas (0) 0
Wolfsburg (1) 3 *(Misimovic 14, Gentner 80, Dzeko 87)*
                                                          18,116
Besiktas: Hakan; Ibrahim K, Ibrahim U (Ismail 74), Ferrari, Fink, Sivok, Tabata (Mert 69), Dag, Serdar (Tello 46), Ugur, Bobo.
Wolfsburg: Benaglio; Schafer, Ricardo Costa, Madlung, Riether, Josue, Misimovic (Santana 89), Hasebe (Pekarik 46), Gentner, Dzeko, Martins (Dejagah 69).

Manchester U (1) 3 *(Owen 29, Scholes 84, Valencia 90)*
CSKA Moscow (2) 3 *(Dzagoev 25, Krasic 31,*
Berezutski V 47)   73,718
Manchester U: Van der Sar; Neville, Fabio (Evra 59), Fletcher, Brown, Evans J, Valencia, Scholes, Macheda (Obertan 82), Owen, Nani (Rooney 58).
CSKA Moscow: Akinfeev; Semberas*, Ignashevich, Berezutski A, Berezutski V, Shchennikov, Dzagoev (Daniel Carvalho 72), Mamaev (Rahimic 70), Krasic, Aldonin, Necid (Piliev 85).

Wednesday, 25 November 2009
CSKA Moscow (0) 2 *(Necid 58, Krasic 66)*
Wolfsburg (1) 1 *(Dzeko 19)*   13,478
CSKA Moscow: Akinfeev; Ignashevich, Berezutski A, Berezutski V, Shchennikov, Dzagoev, Mamaev, Krasic, Aldonin, Rahimic, Necid.
Wolfsburg: Benaglio; Schafer, Ricardo Costa, Madlung, Riether, Josue, Misimovic, Hasebe, Gentner, Dzeko, Martins (Ziani 68).

Manchester U (0) 0
Besiktas (1) 1 *(Tello 20)*   74,242
Manchester U: Foster; Neville, Rafael (Evra 74), Anderson, Brown, Vidic, Park (Owen 69), Welbeck, Obertan, Macheda, Gibson (Carrick 74).
Besiktas: Rustu; Ismail, Ibrahim K, Ibrahim U, Ibrahim T (Erhan 67), Ferrari, Fink, Tello (Ugur 75), Dag, Ernst, Bobo (Batuhan 84).

Tuesday, 8 December 2009
Besiktas (0) 1 *(Bobo 86)*
CSKA Moscow (1) 2 *(Krasic 41, Aldonin 90)*   16,129
Besiktas: Rustu; Ibrahim K, Ibrahim U, Ibrahim T, Ferrari, Fink (Ugur 77), Sivok, Tello (Mert 87), Dag (Nihat 68), Ernst, Bobo.
CSKA Moscow: Akinfeev; Semberas, Odiah, Berezutski V, Shchennikov, Dzagoev (Grigoriev 90), Mamaev, Krasic (Oliseh 82), Aldonin, Rahimic, Necid.

Wolfsburg (0) 1 *(Dzeko 56)*
Manchester U (1) 3 *(Owen 44, 83, 90)*   26,490
Wolfsburg: Benaglio; Schafer, Ricardo Costa, Riether, Barzagli, Josue, Misimovic, Hasebe (Ziani 72), Gentner, Dzeko, Grafite (Dejagah 72).
Manchester U: Kuszczak; Park, Evra, Carrick, Fletcher, Anderson, Gibson, Scholes, Welbeck (Valencia 74), Owen, Nani (Obertan 74).

Group B Table	P	W	D	L	F	A	Pts
Manchester U	6	4	1	1	10	6	13
CSKA Moscow	6	3	1	2	10	10	10
Wolfsburg	6	2	1	3	9	8	7
Besiktas	6	1	1	4	3	8	4

GROUP C

Tuesday, 15 September 2009
Marseille (0) 1 *(Heinze 49)*
AC Milan (1) 2 *(Ingazhi 28, 74)*   55,434
Marseille: Mandanda; Taiwo, Heinze, Diawara, Cisse (Morientes 88), Cheyrou, Gonzalez (Ben Arfa 75), Kabore, M'Bia, Brandao, Niang.
AC Milan: Storari; Nesta, Thiago Silva, Oddo, Seedorf (Abate 90), Zambrotta, Flamini, Pirlo, Ambrosini (Gattuso 58), Pato, Inzaghi (Huntelaar 81).

Zurich (0) 2 *(Margairaz 63 (pen), Aegerter 65)*
Real Madrid (3) 5 *(Cristiano Ronaldo 27, 89, Raul 35,*
Higuain 45, Guti 90)   24,424
Zurich: Leoni; Stahel (Gajic 88), Koch, Rochat, Tihinen, Margairaz, Aegerter, Okonkwo (Abdi 65), Vonlanthen, Alphonse, Hassli (Djuric 46).
Real Madrid: Casillas; Arbeloa, Pepe, Drenthe, Albiol, Kaka, Diarra L, Xabi Alonso (Gago 59), Raul, Cristiano Ronaldo, Higuain (Guti 67).

Wednesday, 30 September 2009
AC Milan (0) 0
Zurich (1) 1 *(Tihinen 10)*   32,439
AC Milan: Storari; Kaladze, Nesta (Onyewu 60), Jankulovski, Seedorf (Zambrotta 46), Flamini (Ronaldinho 46), Abate, Pirlo, Ambrosini, Pato, Inzaghi.
Zurich: Leoni; Koch, Rochat (Stahel 80), Barmettler, Tihinen, Margairaz, Aegerter, Okonkwo, Djuric (Alphonse 86), Gajic, Vonlanthen (Nikci 76).

Real Madrid (0) 3 *(Cristiano Ronaldo 58, 64,*
Kaka 61 (pen)
Marseille (0) 0   67,244
Real Madrid: Casillas; Pepe, Sergio Ramos (Garay 72), Marcelo, Albiol, Gago, Kaka (Raul 78), Guti, Xabi Alonso, Cristiano Ronaldo (Higuain 69), Benzema.
Marseille: Mandanda; Taiwo, Heinze, Diawara*, Bonnart, Cheyrou, Gonzalez, M'Bia, Abriel (Rodriguez 62), Niang (Ben Arfa 87), Morientes (Brandao 63).

Wednesday, 21 October 2009
Real Madrid (1) 2 *(Raul 19, Drenthe 76)*
AC Milan (0) 3 *(Pirlo 62, Pato 66, 88)*   80,000
Real Madrid: Casillas; Pepe, Sergio Ramos, Marcelo, Albiol, Kaka, Lassana Diarra, Xabi Alonso, Granero (Drenthe 67), Raul, Benzema.
AC Milan: Dida; Nesta, Zambrotta, Thiago Silva, Oddo, Seedorf, Pirlo, Ambrosini, Ronaldinho (Flamini 90), Pato, Inzaghi (Borriello 60).

Zurich (0) 0
Marseille (0) 1 *(Heinze 69)*   25,000
Zurich: Leoni; Stahel, Koch, Rochat, Tihinen, Margairaz (Nikci 84), Aegerter, Okonkwo, Gajic (Djuric 72), Vonlanthen (Abdi 84), Alphonse.
Marseille: Mandanda; Hilton, Heinze, Bonnart*, Cisse, Cheyrou (Abriel 64), Gonzalez (Kabore 82), M'Bia, Valbuena (Kone 64), Brandao, Niang.

Tuesday, 3 November 2009
AC Milan (1) 1 *(Ronaldinho 35 (pen))*
Real Madrid (1) 1 *(Benzema 29)*   75,092
AC Milan: Dida; Nesta, Zambrotta, Thiago Silva, Oddo, Seedorf, Pirlo, Ambrosini, Ronaldinho, Pato, Borriello (Inzaghi 79).
Real Madrid: Casillas; Arbeloa, Pepe, Sergio Ramos, Marcelo, Albiol, Kaka, Diarra L, Xabi Alonso, Benzema (Van Nistelrooy 82), Higuain (Raul 75).

Marseille (2) 6 *(Aegerter 3 (og), M'Bia 11, Niang 51,*
Hilton 80, Cheyrou 87, Brandao 90)
Zurich (1) 1 *(Alphonse 31)*   56,282
Marseille: Mandanda; Bocaly, Hilton, Heinze, Diawara, Cheyrou, M'Bia (Cisse 84), Abriel (Kabore 68), Brandao, Niang, Kone (Valbuena 61).
Zurich: Leoni; Stahel, Koch, Rochat, Tihinen, Margairaz, Aegerter (Gajic 46), Okonkwo, Djuric, Vonlanthen (Mehmdei 9), Alphonse (Nikci 76).

Wednesday, 25 November 2009
AC Milan (1) 1 *(Borriello 10)*
Marseille (1) 1 *(Gonzalez 16)*   49,063
AC Milan: Dida; Nesta, Zambrotta, Thiago Silva, Oddo (Abate 28), Seedorf, Pirlo, Ambrosini, Ronaldinho, Pato, Borriello.
Marseille: Mandanda; Taiwo, Heinze, Diawara, Bonnart, Cisse, Cheyrou (Morientes 85), Gonzalez (Kone 66), Abriel, Brandao, Niang (Ben Arfa 73).

Real Madrid (1) 1 *(Higuain 21)*
Zurich (0) 0   67,867
Real Madrid: Casillas; Arbeloa (Van der Vaart 58), Pepe, Sergio Ramos, Marcelo, Albiol, Kaka (Granero 89), Diarra L, Xabi Alonso, Raul (Cristiano Ronaldo 70), Higuain.
Zurich: Leoni; Stahel, Koch, Rochat, Barmettler, Tihinen, Margairaz, Aegerter, Djuric (Schonbachler 88), Gajic (Vonlanthen 76), Alphonse (Mehmedi 85).

Tuesday, 8 December 2009
Marseille (1) 1 *(Gonzalez 11)*
Real Madrid (1) 3 *(Cristiano Ronaldo 5, 80, Albiol 60)*
                                        55,722
Marseille: Mandanda; Taiwo, Heinze, Diawara, Bonnart, Cisse (Kone 62), Cheyrou, Gonzalez, Abriel, Brandao (Morientes 78), Niang (Valbuena 68).
Real Madrid: Casillas; Arbeloa, Pepe, Sergio Ramos, Marcelo, Albiol, Cristiano Ronaldo, Diarra L, Xabi Alonso (Diarra 78), Van der Vaart (Raul 72), Higuain (Benzema 63).

Zurich (1) 1 *(Gajic 29)*
AC Milan (0) 1 *(Ronaldinho 64 (pen))*   24,100
Zurich: Leoni; Koch, Rochat■, Barmettler, Tihinen, Aegerter, Okonkwo, Nikci (Vonlanthen 74), Djuric (Lampi 66), Gajic (Margairaz 82), Alphonse.
AC Milan: Dida; Nesta, Thiago Silva (Kaladze 20), Seedorf, Abate, Pirlo, Ambrosini (Flamini 55), Antonini, Ronaldinho, Pato, Borriello (Inzaghi 84).

Group C Table	P	W	D	L	F	A	Pts
Real Madrid	6	4	1	1	15	7	13
AC Milan	6	2	3	1	8	7	9
Marseille	6	2	1	3	10	10	7
Zurich	6	1	1	4	5	14	4

GROUP D

Tuesday, 15 September 2009
Atletico Madrid (0) 0
Apoel (0) 0   30,628
Atletico Madrid: Sergio Asenjo; Ujfalusi, Alvaro Dominguez, Perea (Sinama-Pongolle 67), Ibanez, Jurado, Paulo Assuncao, Simao, Cleber Santana (Maxi Rodriguez 51), Forlan, Aguero.
Apoel: Chiotis; Paulo Jorge (Grncarov 46), Nuno Morais, Poursaitidis, Charalambides (Satsias 67), Kosowski, Helio Pinto, Kontis, Haxhi, Michael, Zewlakow (Paulista 81).

Chelsea (0) 1 *(Anelka 48)*
Porto (0) 0   39,436
Chelsea: Cech; Ivanovic, Cole A, Essien, Terry, Ricardo Carvalho, Ballack, Lampard, Anelka, Kalou (Belletti 77), Malouda.
Porto: Helton; Bruno Alves, Fucile, Rolando, Raul Meireles, Guarin, Cristian Rodriguez (Varela 64), Mariano Gonzalez (Falcao 53), Alvaro Pereira, Fernando■, Hulk.

Wednesday, 30 September 2009
Apoel (0) 0
Chelsea (1) 1 *(Anelka 18)*   21,657
Apoel: Chiotis; Grncarov, Nuno Morais, Poursaitidis, Charalambides (Paulista 85), Helio Pinto, Kontis, Haxhi, Michael (Breska 80), Alexandrou (Kosowski 58), Mirosavljevic.
Chelsea: Cech; Belletti (Deco 68), Cole A, Ivanovic, Terry, Ricardo Carvalho, Essien, Lampard, Anelka, Kalou (Cole J 80), Malouda.

Porto (0) 2 *(Falcao 76, Rolando 82)*
Atletico Madrid (0) 0   37,609
Porto: Helton; Bruno Alves, Fucile, Rolando, Raul Meireles, Belluschi, Mariano Gonzalez (Valeri 90), Alvaro Pereira, Tomas Costa (Guarin 66), Falcao (Farias 88), Hulk.
Atletico Madrid: Roberto (De Gea 25); Juanito, Ujfalusi, Perea, Ibanez, Jurado (Reyes 80), Paulo Assuncao, Simao (Maxi Rodriguez 70), Cleber Santana, Forlan, Aguero.

Wednesday, 21 October 2009
Chelsea (1) 4 *(Kalou 41, 52, Lampard 69, Perea 90 (og))*
Atletico Madrid (0) 0   39,000
Chelsea: Cech; Belletti, Cole A (Malouda 75), Essien, Terry, Ivanovic, Ballack, Lampard, Anelka (Sturridge 78), Kalou (Zhirkov 73), Deco.
Atletico Madrid: Sergio Asenjo; Antonio Lopez, Ujfalusi,

Alvaro Dominguez, Perea, Raul Garcia, Paulo Assuncao (Jurado 54), Simao (Reyes 77), Cleber Santana (Maxi Rodriguez 66), Forlan, Aguero.

Porto (1) 2 *(Hulk 33, 49 (pen))*
Apoel (1) 1 *(Alvaro Pereira 21 (og))*   25,000
Porto: Helton; Bruno Alves, Fucile, Rolando, Raul Meireles (Sapunaru 90), Cristian Rodriguez (Guarin 69), Mariano Gonzalez■, Alvaro Pereira, Fernando, Falcao (Farias 87), Hulk.
Apoel: Chiotis; Grncarov, Elia, Nuno Morais, Charalambides, Kosowski (Breska 38), Broerse, Satsias (Papathanasiou 77), Helio Pinto, Michael (Alexandrou 60), Mirosavljevic.

Tuesday, 3 November 2009
Apoel (0) 0
Porto (0) 1 *(Falcao 84)*   20,825
Apoel: Chiotis; Elia (Grncarov 57), Nuno Morais, Poursaitidis, Charalambides, Broerse, Satsias, Paulista (Alexandrou 61), Helio Pinto, Kontis (Papathanasiou 87), Mirosavljevic.
Porto: Helton; Bruno Alves, Rolando, Sapunaru, Raul Meireles, Guarin (Tomas Costa 83), Cristian Rodriguez (Farias 69), Alvaro Pereira, Fernando, Falcao (Belluschi 90), Hulk.

Atletico Madrid (0) 2 *(Aguero 66, 90)*
Chelsea (0) 2 *(Drogba 82, 88)*   36,284
Atletico Madrid: Sergio Asenjo; Antonio Lopez, Juanito, Perea, Ibanez, Paulo Assuncao, Simao (Jurado 83), Cleber Santana, Forlan, Sinama-Pongolle (Aguero 53), Reyes (Maxi Rodriguez 73).
Chelsea: Cech; Belletti, Cole A, Essien (Ballack 59), Terry, Alex, Cole J (Deco 70), Lampard, Drogba, Kalou (Anelka 70), Malouda.

Wednesday, 25 November 2009
Apoel (1) 1 *(Mirosavljevic 5)*
Atletico Madrid (0) 1 *(Simao 62)*   21,178
Apoel: Chiotis; Paulo Jorge, Elia (Breska 70), Nuno Morais, Poursaitidis, Kosowski (Zewlakow 77), Helio Pinto, Kontis, Michael (Broerse 71), Alexandrou, Mirosavljevic.
Atletico Madrid: Sergio Asenjo; Juanito, Ujfalusi, Alvaro Dominguez, Perea, Camacho, Jurado (Maxi Rodriguez 78), Simao (Antonio Lopez 90), Cleber Santana, Forlan (Reyes 87), Aguero.

Porto (0) 0
Chelsea (0) 1 *(Anelka 69)*   38,410
Porto: Beto; Bruno Alves, Rolando, Sapunaru (Farias 80), Raul Meireles, Belluschi (Guarin 72), Cristian Rodriguez, Alvaro Pereira, Fernando, Falcao, Varela (Hulk 59).
Chelsea: Cech; Ivanovic, Zhirkov, Mikel, Terry, Ricardo Carvalho, Ballack (Essien 68), Deco (Cole J 76), Anelka, Drogba, Malouda.

Tuesday, 8 December 2009
Atletico Madrid (0) 0
Porto (2) 3 *(Bruno Alves 1, Falcao 14, Hulk 76)*   24,603
Atletico Madrid: Sergio Asenjo; Valera (Antonio Lopez 46), Juanito, Alvaro Dominguez, Perea, Maxi Rodriguez (Reyes 68), Paulo Assuncao, Simao, Cleber Santana, Forlan, Aguero (Jurado 48).
Porto: Helton; Bruno Alves, Fucile, Maicon (Sapunaru 59), Raul Meireles, Valeri (Guarin 62), Cristian Rodriguez, Alvaro Pereira, Fernando, Falcao (Varela 70), Hulk.

Chelsea (2) 2 *(Essien 19, Drogba 26)*
Apoel (1) 2 *(Zewlakow 6, Mirosavljevic 87)*   40,917
Chelsea: Turnbull; Belletti, Zhirkov, Mikel, Terry, Ricardo Carvalho, Essien (Lampard 27), Cole J, Kakuta (Borini 73), Drogba, Malouda.
Apoel: Chiotis; Paulo Jorge, Nuno Morais, Poursaitidis, Charalambides, Kosowski (Mirosavljevic 71), Broerse, Helio Pinto, Haxhi (Elia 34), Michael, Zewlakow (Breska 83).

Group D Table

	P	W	D	L	F	A	Pts
Chelsea	6	4	2	0	11	4	14
Porto	6	4	0	2	8	3	12
Atletico Madrid	6	0	3	3	3	12	3
Apoel	6	0	3	3	4	7	3

GROUP E

Wednesday, 16 September 2009

Liverpool (1) 1 *(Kuyt 45)*

Debrecen (0) 0   41,591

Liverpool: Reina; Johnson, Insua, Lucas, Carragher, Skrtel, Benayoun (Mascherano 88), Gerrard, Torres, Kuyt (Fabio Aurelio 90), Riera (Babel 80).
Debrecen: Poleksic; Bodnar, Komlosi, Fodor, Leandro, Ramos (Laczko 67), Meszaros, Kiss, Szakaly (Feczesin 78), Czvitkovics, Coulibaly.

Lyon (0) 1 *(Pjanic 76)*

Fiorentina (0) 0   37,169

Lyon: Lloris; Cris, Reveillere, Cissokho, Kallstrom, Bastos (Govou 26), Pjanic (Ederson 82), Makoun, Toulalan, Lisandro Lopez, Gomis (Delgado 70).
Fiorentina: Frey; Dainelli, Gamberini, Vargas, Comotto Donadel, Montolivo, Gobbi, Marchionni (Santana 73) Mutu (Jovetic 58), Gilardino[a].

Tuesday, 29 September 2009

Debrecen (0) 0

Lyon (3) 4 *(Kallstrom 3, Pjanic 13, Govou 24, Gomis 50)*   41,600

Debrecen: Poleksic; Bodnar, Komlosi, Fodor, Leandro, Kiss, Varga, Szakaly (Dombi 85), Czvitkovics, Laczko (Rudolf 46), Coulibaly.
Lyon: Lloris; Clerc, Cris, Reveillere, Cissokho (Kolodziejczak 78), Kallstrom, Pjanic (Gonalons 57), Makoun, Toulalan, Govou, Gomis (Ederson 54).

Fiorentina (2) 2 *(Jovetic 28, 37)*

Liverpool (0) 0   33,426

Fiorentina: Frey; Dainelli, Gamberini, Vargas (Jorgensen 75), Comotto, Zanetti, Montolivo, Gobbi, Marchionni (De Silvestri 90), Jovetic, Mutu (Donadel 82).
Liverpool: Reina; Johnson, Inusa (Babel 72), Fabio Aurelio, Carragher, Skrtel, Benayoun, Gerrard, Torres, Kuyt (Voronin 80), Lucas.

Tuesday, 20 October 2009

Debrecen (2) 3 *(Czvitkovics 1, Rudolf 28, Coulibaly 87)*

Fiorentina (4) 4 *(Mutu 6, 19, Gilardino 10, Santana 36)*   41,500

Debrecen: Poleksic; Bodnar, Komlosi, Leandro, Meszaros (Szelesi 30), Kiss (Laczko 87), Varga, Szakaly (Dombi 56), Czvitkovics, Rudolf, Coulibaly.
Fiorentina: Frey; Dainelli (Natali 55), Gamberini, Vargas, Pasqual, Comotto, Donadel, Zanetti (Montolivo 46), Santana (Jorgensen 68), Mutu, Gilardino.

Liverpool (1) 1 *(Benayoun 41)*

Lyon (0) 2 *(Gonalons 72, Delgado 90)*   41,562

Liverpool: Reina; Agger, Insua, Mascherano, Carragher, Kelly (Skrtel 74), Benayoun (Voronin 85), Gerrard (Fabio Aurelio 25), N'Gog, Kuyt, Lucas.
Lyon: Lloris; Cris (Gonalons 43), Reveillere, Cissokho, Kallstrom, Pjanic, Ederson (Gomis 61), Makoun, Toulalan, Lisandro Lopez (Delgado 86), Govou.

Wednesday, 4 November 2009

Fiorentina (1) 5 *(Mutu 14, Dainelli 52, Montolivo 59, Marchionni 61, Gilardino 74)*

Debrecen (1) 2 *(Rudolf 38, Coulibaly 70)*   19,576

Fiorentina: Avramov; Dainelli, Gamberini (Kroldrup 33), Vargas (Santana 77), Pasqual, Comotto, Donadel, Zanetti (Montolivo 46), Marchionni, Mutu, Gilardino.
Debrecen: Pantic; Bodnar, Komlosi (Kiss 10), Fodor, Szelesi, Leandro, Ramos (Coulibaly 53), Varga, Czvitkovics, Laczko (Szakaly 65), Rudolf.

Lyon (0) 1 *(Lisandro Lopez 90)*

Liverpool (0) 1 *(Babel 83)*   39,180

Lyon: Lloris; Cris, Reveillere (Gassama 18), Cissokho, Kallstrom, Bastos, Pjanic (Ederson 40), Makoun, Toulalan, Lisandro Lopez, Gomis (Govou 73).
Liverpool: Reina; Kyrgiakos, Insua, Mascherano, Carragher, Agger, Benayoun, Lucas, Torres (N'Gog 87), Voronin (Babel 67), Kuyt.

Tuesday, 24 November 2009

Debrecen (0) 0

Liverpool (1) 1 *(N'Gog 4)*   41,500

Debrecen: Poleksic; Bodnar, Fodor (Dombi 78), Mijadinoski, Szelesi, Meszaros, Kiss, Szakaly (Coulibaly 62), Czvitkovics, Laczko, Rudolf.
Liverpool: Reina; Johnson, Insua, Agger, Carragher, Fabio Aurelio (Dossena 89), Mascherano, Gerrard (Aquilani 90), N'Gog (Benayoun 77), Kuyt, Lucas.

Fiorentina (1) 1 *(Vargas 28 (pen))*

Lyon (0) 0   34,301

Fiorentina: Frey; Kroldrup, Dainelli, Vargas, De Silvestri (Comotto 87), Zanetti (Jorgensen 80), Montolivo, Gobbi, Santana (Donadel 71), Marchionni, Gilardino.
Lyon: Lloris; Cris, Boumsong, Cissokho, Gassama, Kallstrom, Bastos (Lisandro Lopez 67), Pjanic, Makoun, Govou (Delgado 74), Gomis (Ederson 79).

Wednesday, 9 December 2009

Liverpool (1) 1 *(Benayoun 43)*

Fiorentina (0) 2 *(Jorgensen 63, Gilardino 90)*   40,863

Liverpool: Diego; Dossena, Insua, Darby, Agger, Skrtel, Benayoun, Gerrard, Aquilani (Pacheco 76), Kuyt (Torres 65), Mascherano (Fabio Aurelio 86).
Fiorentina: Frey; Kroldrup, Natali, Pasqual, Comotto, De Silvestri (Castillo 83), Donadel, Montolivo, Jorgensen (Marchionni 71), Santana (Vargas 71), Gilardino.

Lyon (2) 4 *(Gomis 25, Bastos 44, Pjanic 59, Cissokho 76)*

Debrecen (0) 0   36,884

Lyon: Lloris; Cris, Boumsong, Reveillere, Cissokho, Bastos, Makoun (Kallstrom 73), Gonalons, Govou (Pjanic 29), Gomis (Lisandro Lopez 67), Delgado.
Debrecen: Pantic; Bodnar (Bernath 52), Mijadinoski, Szelesi, Ramos (Kiss 57), Meszaros, Varga, Szakaly (Feczesin 75), Czvitkovics, Laczko, Coulibaly.

Group E Table

	P	W	D	L	F	A	Pts
Fiorentina	6	5	0	1	14	7	15
Lyon	6	4	1	1	12	3	13
Liverpool	6	2	1	3	5	7	7
Debrecen	6	0	0	6	5	19	0

GROUP F

Wednesday, 16 September 2009

Dynamo Kiev (0) 3 *(Ayila 70, Magrao 79, Gusev 85)*

Rubin (1) 1 *(Dominguez 24)*   15,000

Dynamo Kiev: Shovkovskiy; Khacheridi, Almeida, Vukojevic, Eremenko, Magrao, Ayila, Ninkovic (Ghioane 57), Shevchenko (Betao 90), Milevskiy, Yarmolenko (Gusev 65).
Rubin: Ryzhikov; Ansaldi, Cesar Navas, Kaleshin, Sharonov, Semak, Ryazantsev (Kasaev 83), Noboa, Gokdeniz Karadeniz, Dominguez (Murawski 77), Bukharov.

Internazionale (0) 0

Barcelona (0) 0   76,000

Internazionale: Julio Cesar; Zanetti, Lucio, Maicon, Samuel, Chivu, Thiago Motta, Sneijder (Santon 80), Muntari (Stankovic 62), Eto'o, Milito (Balotelli 85).
Barcelona: Victor Valdes; Dani Alves, Pique, Puyol, Abidal, Xavi, Keita, Yaya Toure, Ibrahimovic, Messi, Henry (Iniesta 77).

Tuesday, 29 September 2009
Barcelona (1) 2 *(Messi 26, Pedro 76)*
Dynamo Kiev (0) 0　　　　　　　　68,221
Barcelona: Victor Valdes; Dani Alves, Pique, Puyol, Abidal, Xavi, Iniesta (Pedro 46), Keita, Yaya Toure (Busquets 68), Ibrahimovic (Jeffren 85), Messi.
Dynamo Kiev: Shovkovskiy; Khacheridi, Almeida, Vukojevic, Eremenko, Gusev (Ninkovic 85), Magrao (Betao 73), Ayila, Shevchenko, Milevskiy, Yarmolenko.

Rubin (1) 1 *(Dominguez 11)*
Internazionale (1) 1 *(Stankovic 28)*　　　23,670
Rubin: Ryzhikov; Ansaldi, Cesar Navas, Salukvadze, Sharonov, Semak, Ryazantsev, Noboa, Gokdeniz Karadeniz, Dominguez (Kasaev 86), Bukharov.
Internazionale: Julio Cesar; Zanetti, Lucio, Maicon, Samuel, Chivu, Stankovic, Cambiasso (Vieira 80), Mancini (Quaresma 64), Eto'o, Balotelli■.

Tuesday, 20 October 2009
Barcelona (0) 1 *(Ibrahimovic 47)*
Rubin (1) 2 *(Ryazantsev 2, Gokdeniz Karadeniz 73)*
　　　　　　　　　　　　　　　　　55,930
Barcelona: Victor Valdes; Dani Alves (Busquets 90), Pique, Marquez (Keita 80), Abidal, Xavi, Iniesta, Yaya Toure, Ibrahimovic, Messi, Pedro (Bojan 66).
Rubin: Ryzhikov; Ansaldi, Cesar Navas, Salukvadze, Kaleshin, Sharonov, Semak (Murawski 43), Ryazantsev (Kasaev 84), Noboa, Gokdeniz Karadeniz (Popov 90), Dominguez.

Internazionale (1) 2 *(Stankovic 35, Samuel 47)*
Dynamo Kiev (2) 2 *(Mikhalik 5, Lucio 40 (og))*　34,721
Internazionale: Julio Cesar; Zanetti (Materazzi 86), Lucio, Maicon, Samuel, Chivu, Stankovic, Sneijder, Ali Muntari (Suazo 46), Cambiasso (Vieira 86), Eto'o.
Dynamo Kiev: Bogush; Mikhalik, Khacheridi, Almeida, Vukojevic, Eremenko, Magrao (Betao 70), Ninkovic (Gusev 69), Shevchenko, Milevskiy (Kravets 90), Yarmolenko.

Wednesday, 4 November 2009
Dynamo Kiev (1) 1 *(Shevchenko 21)*
Internazionale (0) 2 *(Milito 86, Sneijder 89)*　15,900
Dynamo Kiev: Bogush; Mikhalik, Khacheridi, Almeida, Vukojevic, Eremenko, Magrao, Ninkovic, Shevchenko, Milevskiy (Gusev 70), Yarmolenko.
Internazionale: Julio Cesar; Zanetti, Lucio, Maicon, Samuel (Ali Muntari 79), Chivu (Balotelli 46), Stankovic, Sneijder, Cambiasso (Thiago Motta 46), Eto'o, Milito.

Rubin (0) 0
Barcelona (0) 0　　　　　　　　24,600
Rubin: Ryzhikov; Ansaldi, Cesar Navas, Salukvadze, Kaleshin, Sharonov, Semak, Ryazantsev, Noboa, Gokdeniz Karadeniz (Bukharov 62), Dominguez.
Barcelona: Victor Valdes; Dani Alves, Pique, Puyol, Abidal, Xavi, Iniesta, Keita (Henry 83), Yaya Toure, Ibrahimovic, Messi.

Tuesday, 24 November 2009
Barcelona (2) 2 *(Pique 10, Pedro 26)*
Internazionale (0) 0　　　　　　　93,524
Barcelona: Victor Valdes; Dani Alves, Pique, Puyol, Abidal (Maxwell 89), Xavi, Iniesta (Jonathan 90), Keita, Busquets, Henry, Pedro (Bojan 85).
Internazionale: Julio Cesar; Zanetti, Lucio, Maicon, Samuel, Chivu, Stankovic (Balotelli 71), Thiago Motta, Cambiasso (Ali Muntari 46), Eto'o, Milito (Quaresma 81).

Rubin (0) 0
Dynamo Kiev (0) 0　　　　　　　23,185
Rubin: Ryzhikov; Ansaldi, Cesar Navas, Salukvadze, Sharonov (Kaleshin 53), Semak, Ryazantsev, Noboa, Gokdeniz Karadeniz (Bystrov 75), Dominguez, Bukharov.
Dynamo Kiev: Shovkovskiy; Betao, Mikhalik, Vukojevic, Eremenko, Magrao, Ayila, Ninkovic (Ghioane 85), Shevchenko, Milevskiy, Yarmolenko.

Wednesday, 9 December 2009
Dynamo Kiev (1) 1 *(Milevskiy 2)*
Barcelona (1) 2 *(Xavi 33, Messi 86)*　16,300
Dynamo Kiev: Shovkovskiy; Betao, Mikhalik, Almeida, Vukojevic, Eremenko, Magrao (Ninkovic 74), Ayila, Shevchenko, Milevskiy, Yarmolenko.
Barcelona: Victor Valdes; Dani Alves, Pique (Marquez 88), Puyol, Abidal, Xavi, Iniesta (Pedro 82), Keita, Busquets, Ibrahimovic, Messi.

Internazionale (1) 2 *(Eto'o 31, Balotelli 64)*
Rubin (0) 0　　　　　　　　49,539
Internazionale: Julio Cesar; Zanetti, Lucio, Maicon, Samuel (Cordoba 15), Stankovic (Cambiasso 51), Thiago Motta, Sneijder, Eto'o, Milito, Balotelli (Ali Muntari 77).
Rubin: Ryzhikov; Cesar Navas, Salukvadze, Kaleshin, Popov, Semak, Ryazantsev (Balyaykin 84), Noboa (Bystrov 81), Murawski, Gokdeniz Karadeniz (Kasaev 73), Dominguez.

Group F Table	P	W	D	L	F	A	Pts
Barcelona	6	3	2	1	7	3	11
Internazionale	6	2	3	1	6	6	9
Rubin	6	1	3	2	4	7	6
Dynamo Kiev	6	1	2	3	7	9	5

GROUP G

Wednesday, 16 September 2009
Sevilla (1) 2 *(Luis Fabiano 45, Renato 70)*
Unirea (0) 0　　　　　　　　37,500
Sevilla: Palop; Squillaci, Escude, Sergio Sanchez, Fernando Navarro, Jesus Navas, Zokora (Lolo 76), Renato, Diego Capel (Perotti 56), Luis Fabiano, Kanoute (Negredo 63).
Unirea: Arlauskis; Mehmedovic, Galamaz, Brandan, Maftei, Ricardo Vilana (Onofras 81), Balan (Paraschiv 65), Frunza, Apostol, Bilasco, Varga (Semedo 73).

Stuttgart (1) 1 *(Pogrebnyak 18)*
Rangers (0) 1 *(Bougherra 77)*　　　39,000
Stuttgart: Lehmann; Tasci, Boka, Delpierre, Trasch, Hitzlsperger, Hilbert, Hleb (Gebhart 67), Khedira, Cacau (Schieber 88), Pogrebnyak.
Rangers: McGregor; Whittaker, Papac, Thomson, Bougherra, McCulloch, Pedro Mendes, Davis, Miller (Novo 90), Rothen, Naismith.

Tuesday, 29 September 2009
Rangers (0) 1 *(Novo 88)*
Sevilla (0) 4 *(Konko 50, Adriano 64, Luis Fabiano 72, Kanoute 74)*　　　　　　　　40,522
Rangers: McGregor; Whittaker, Papac, Thomson, Weir, Bougherra, Pedro Mendes, Davis, McCulloch (Boyd 73), Naismith, Rothen (Novo 73).
Sevilla: Palop; Squillaci, Escude, Fernando Navarro, Lolo, Adriano (Diego Capel 66), Jesus Navas, Zokora, Konko, Luis Fabiano (Romaric 79), Kanoute (Negredo 75).

Unirea (0) 1 *(Varga 48)*
Stuttgart (1) 1 *(Tasci 5)*　　　　13,557
Unirea: Arlauskis; Galamaz, Nicu, Brandan, Bruno Fernandes, Maftei, Ricardo Vilana, Balan (Frunza 46), Apostol, Bilasco (Rusescu 64), Varga (Paduretu 90).
Stuttgart: Lehmann; Tasci, Boka, Delpierre, Celozzi, Hitzlsperger, Gebhart, Hilbert, Khedira, Marica (Schieber 64), Pogrebnyak.

Tuesday, 20 October 2009
Rangers (1) 1 *(Ricardo Vilana 2 (og))*
Unirea (1) 4 *(Bilasco 32, Lafferty 49 (og), McCulloch 59 (og), Brandan 65)*　　39,476
Rangers: McGregor; Whittaker, Papac, Thomson, Weir, Pedro Mendes (Lafferty 46), Davis, McCulloch, Naismith, Miller, Rothen (Novo 67).
Unirea: Tudor; Galamaz, Nicu (Onofras 19), Brandan, Bruno Fernandes, Maftei, Ricardo Vilana, Balan (Frunza 75), Apostol, Bilasco, Varga (Paduretu 89).

Stuttgart (0) 1 *(Elson 73)*
Sevilla (1) 3 *(Squillaci 23, 72, Jesus Navas 55)*   37,500
Stuttgart: Lehmann; Osorio, Boulahrouz, Tasci, Boka, Trasch (Hitzlsperger 69), Hleb (Elson 69), Khedira, Kuzmanovic, Cacau (Pogrebnyak 69), Schieber.
Sevilla: Javi Varas; Dragutinovic, Squillaci, Sergio Sanchez, Fernando Navarro, Lolo, Adriano (Perotti 37), Jesus Navas, Zokora, Luis Fabiano (Duscher 46), Kanoute (Kone 90).

Wednesday, 4 November 2009
Sevilla (1) 1 *(Jesus Navas 14)*
Stuttgart (0) 1 *(Kuzmanovic 79)*   32,669
Sevilla: Javi Varas; Squillaci, Escude, Fernando Navarro, Jesus Navas, Zokora, Diego Capel (Perotti 58), Romaric (Duscher 62), Konko, Kone (Negredo 31), Luis Fabiano.
Stuttgart: Lehmann; Boulahrouz (Celozzi 46), Tasci, Boka, Delpierre, Hitzlsperger (Schieber 65), Hilbert (Rudy 46), Hleb, Elson, Kuzmanovic, Pogrebnyak.

Unirea (0) 1 *(Onofras 88)*
Rangers (0) 1 *(McCulloch 79)*   9923
Unirea: Arlauskis; Galamaz, Brandan, Bordeanu, Maftei, Ricardo Vilana (Paduretu 81), Balan (Onofras 28), Frunza, Apostol, Bilasco, Varga (Semedo 81).
Rangers: McGregor; Whittaker, Papac, Thomson (Fleck 85), Weir, Wilson, Davis, McCulloch, Lafferty, Miller (Novo 82), Naismith.

Tuesday, 24 November 2009
Rangers (0) 0
Stuttgart (1) 2 *(Rudy 16, Kuzmanovic 59)*   41,468
Rangers: McGregor; Whittaker, Papac, McCulloch, Weir, Wilson, Davis, Thomson (Fleck 76), Boyd, Miller (Novo 68), Lafferty (Beasley 85).
Stuttgart: Lehmann; Osorio, Niedermeier, Boka, Delpierre, Trasch, Rudy (Gebhart 90), Hleb, Kuzmanovic (Hitzlsperger 75), Cacau (Schieber 83), Pogrebnyak.

Unirea (1) 1 *(Dragutinovic 45 (og))*
Sevilla (0) 0   10,007
Unirea: Arlauskis; Mehmedovic, Galamaz, Brandan, Bordeanu, Maftei, Ricardo Vilana (Paduretu 90), Frunza (Balan 64), Apostol, Bilasco, Varga (Semedo 88).
Sevilla: Javi Varas; Dragutinovic, Sergio Sanchez, Fernando Navarro, Lolo (Renato 62), Konko, Jesus Navas, Zokora, Diego Capel (Luis Fabiano 62), Kanoute, Negredo (Perotti 70).

Wednesday, 9 December 2009
Sevilla (1) 1 *(Kanoute 8 (pen))*
Rangers (0) 0   31,550
Sevilla: Palop; Dragutinovic, Fernando Navarro, Konko, Cala, Jesus Navas (Kone 81), Zokora, Renato, Diego Capel, Romaric (Duscher 74), Kanoute (Negredo 60).
Rangers: McGregor; Whittaker, Papac, Thomson, Weir, Bougherra, Davis, Smith (Fleck 84), Beasley (Lafferty 46), Miller (Novo 46), McCulloch.

Stuttgart (3) 3 *(Marica 5, Trasch 8, Pogrebnyak 11)*
Unirea (0) 1 *(Semedo 46)*   37,000
Stuttgart: Lehmann; Tasci, Boka, Delpierre, Celozzi, Trasch, Gebhart, Hleb (Rudy 55), Khedira (Kuzmanovic 59), Marica (Cacau 82), Pogrebnyak.
Unirea: Arlauskis; Mehmedovic, Brandan, Bruno Fernandes, Bordeanu, Paduretu, Balan (Rusescu 62), Apostol (Todoran 85), Bilasco, Onofras (Varga 46), Semedo.

Group G Table	P	W	D	L	F	A	Pts
Sevilla	6	4	1	1	11	4	13
Stuttgart	6	2	3	1	9	7	9
Unirea	6	2	2	2	8	8	8
Rangers	6	0	2	4	4	13	2

GROUP H

Wednesday, 16 September 2009
Olympiakos (0) 1 *(Torosidis 78)*
AZ (0) 0   29,018
Olympiakos: Nikopolidis; Mellberg, Zewlakow, Raul Bravo, Leonardo (Stoltidis 82), Torosidis (Oscar 86), Dudu Cearense, Papadopoulos A, Ledesma, Diogo (Mitroglou 74), Zairi.
AZ: Romero; Jaliens, Moreno, Pocognoli, Moisander, Mendes da Silva (Luijckx 71), Schaars, Martens (Lens 80), Holman, El Hamdaoui (Pelle 77), Dembele.

Standard Liege (2) 2 *(Mangala 2, Jovanovic 5 (pen))*
Arsenal (1) 3 *(Bendtner 45, Vermaelen 78, Eduardo 81)*   23,022
Standard Liege: Bolat; Ricardo Rocha, Camozzato, Sarr, Dalmat (Goreux 80), Mangala, Witsel (Traore 84), Carcela-Gonzalez, Mbokani, De Camargo, Jovanovic (Nicaise 59).
Arsenal: Mannone; Eboue (Sagna 78), Clichy, Song Billong, Vermaelen, Gallas, Diaby, Fabregas, Eduardo (Wilshere 86), Bendtner, Rosicky (Ramsey 70).

Tuesday, 29 September 2009
Arsenal (0) 2 *(Van Persie 78, Arshavin 86)*
Olympiakos (0) 0   59,884
Arsenal: Mannone; Eboue, Clichy, Song Billong, Vermaelen, Gallas, Diaby (Vela 77), Fabregas, Arshavin, Van Persie (Ramsey 85), Rosicky (Eduardo 66).
Olympiakos: Nikopolidis; Mellberg, Zewlakow, Raul Bravo, Leonardo (Oscar 83), Torosidis, Dudu Cearense, Papadopoulos A, Ledesma (Mitroglou 79), Diogo, Zairi (Stoltidis 46).

AZ (0) 1 *(El Hamdaoui 48)*
Standard Liege (0) 1 *(Traore 90)*   16,373
AZ: Romero; Jaliens, Moreno, Pocognoli (Klavan 82), Swerts, Mendes da Silva, Schaars, Martens (Poulsen 71), Holman, El Hamdaoui, Dembele.
Standard Liege: Bolat; Ricardo Rocha (Mulemo 53), Felipe, Camozzato, Sarr (De Camargo 60), Dalmat (Traore 77), Mangala, Witsel, Carcela-Gonzalez, Mbokani, Jovanovic.

Tuesday, 20 October 2009
AZ (0) 1 *(Mendes da Silva 90)*
Arsenal (1) 1 *(Fabregas 35)*   16,666
AZ: Romero; Jaliens, Moreno, Moisander (Wernbloom 85), Mendes da Silva, Schaars, Martens (Lens 69), Poulsen, Holman (Pelle 73), El Hamdaoui, Dembele.
Arsenal: Mannone; Sagna, Clichy, Song Billong, Vermaelen, Gallas, Eboue (Ramsey 83), Fabregas, Arshavin, Van Persie (Vela 74), Diaby.

Olympiakos (1) 2 *(Mitroglou 43, Stoltidis 90)*
Standard Liege (1) 1 *(De Camargo 37)*   29,889
Olympiakos: Nikopolidis; Mellberg, Zewlakow, Raul Bravo, Galletti, Oscar, Dudu Cearense, Papadopoulos A, Maresca, Zairi (Stoltidis 71), Mitroglou.
Standard Liege: Bolat; Ricardo Rocha, Felipe, Camozzato, Sarr, Dalmat (Carcela-Gonzalez 48), Mangala, Witsel, Mbokani, De Camargo (Nicaise 89), Jovanovic.

Wednesday, 4 November 2009
Arsenal (2) 4 *(Fabregas 25, 52, Nasri 43, Diaby 72)*
AZ (0) 1 *(Lens 82)*   59,345
Arsenal: Almunia; Eboue, Gibbs, Song Billong, Vermaelen, Gallas, Diaby, Fabregas (Ramsey 67), Arshavin (Rosicky 75), Van Persie (Eduardo 67), Nasri.
AZ: Romero; Jaliens, Moreno, Moisander, Mendes da Silva (Wernbloom 70), Schaars, Martens, Poulsen (Pocognoli 64), Holman, Dembele (Lens 58), Pelle.

Standard Liege (1) 2 *(Mbokani 31, Jovanovic 88)*
Olympiakos (0) 0 24,787
Standard Liege: Bolat; Ricardo Rocha, Felipe, Camozzato, Sarr (Vitor Ramos 46), Mangala, Witsel, Carcela-Gonzalez (Goreux 87), Mbokani, De Camargo, Jovanovic (Angeli 90).
Olympiakos: Nikopolidis; Mellberg, Zewlakow, Raul Bravo, Galitsios, Galletti (Fetfatzidis 42), Oscar (Stoltidis 78), Dudu Cearense, Papadopoulos A (Papadopoulos G 78), Maresca, Mitroglou.

Tuesday, 24 November 2009
Arsenal (2) 2 *(Nasri 35, Denilson 45)*
Standard Liege (0) 0 59,941
Arsenal: Almunia; Eboue, Gibbs, Denilson (Rosicky 67), Vermaelen, Gallas (Silvestre 46), Song Billong, Fabregas, Vela, Arshavin, Nasri (Walcott 60).
Standard Liege: Bolat; Goreux, Felipe, Mulemo, Camozzato, Sarr, Dalmat (Traore 64), Mangala, Witsel, Carcela-Gonzalez▪, Mbokani (Cyriac 68).

AZ (0) 0
Olympiakos (0) 0 16,213
AZ: Romero; Moreno, Pocognoli, Moisander, Swerts, Mendes da Silva, Schaars (Martens 89), Wernbloom, Holman (Ari 78), Lens, Dembele (Pelle 68).
Olympiakos: Nikopolidis; Mellberg, Zewlakow, Raul Bravo, Leonardo, Galitsios, Oscar, Dudu Cearense, Maresca, Zairi (Pantos 90), Mitroglou.

Wednesday, 9 December 2009
Olympiakos (0) 1 *(Leonardo 47)*
Arsenal (0) 0 30,277
Olympiakos: Nikopolidis; Mellberg, Raul Bravo, Leonardo, Galitsios, Galletti, Oscar (Pantos 90), Dudu Cearense (Domi 85), Papadopoulos A, Maresca, Mitroglou.
Arsenal: Fabianski; Gilbert, Cruise, Song Billong, Bartley, Silvestre, Ramsey, Merida, Vela, Walcott, Wilshere (Sunu 75).

Standard Liege (0) 1 *(Bolat 90)*
AZ (1) 1 *(Lens 42)* 24,359
Standard Liege: Bolat; Felipe (Cyriac 85), Mulemo, Camozzato, Sarr, Dalmat (Traore 80), Nicaise, Witsel, Mbokani, De Camargo, Jovanovic.
AZ: Romero; Jailens, Moreno, Pocognoli, Moisander, Mendes da Silva, Schaars, Holman (Martens 46), Lens (Wernbloom 72), El Hamdaoui (Pelle 90), Dembele.

Group H Table	P	W	D	L	F	A	Pts
Arsenal	6	4	1	1	12	5	13
Olympiakos	6	3	1	2	4	5	10
Standard Liege	6	1	2	3	7	9	5
AZ	6	0	4	2	4	8	4

KNOCK-OUT STAGE

KNOCK-OUT ROUND FIRST LEG

Tuesday, 16 February 2010
AC Milan (1) 2 *(Ronaldinho 3, Seedorf 85)*
Manchester U (1) 3 *(Scholes 36, Rooney 66, 74)* 78,587
AC Milan: Dida; Nesta, Bonera, Thiago Silva, Pirlo, Ambrosini, Beckham (Seedorf 72), Antonini (Favalli 38), Ronaldinho, Pato, Huntelaar (Inzaghi 77).
Manchester U: Van der Sar; Rafael (Brown), Evra, Carrick▪, Ferdinand, Evans J, Park, Scholes, Fletcher, Rooney, Nani (Valencia 65).

Lyon (0) 1 *(Makoun 47)*
Real Madrid (0) 0 40,327
Lyon: Lloris; Cris, Boumsong, Reveillere, Cissokho, Pjanic (Kallstrom 78), Makoun, Toulalan, Lisandro Lopez (Gomis 81), Govou, Delgado (Bastos 89).
Real Madrid: Casillas; Arbeloa, Sergio Ramos, Marcelo (Garay 46), Albiol, Diarra M, Kaka, Cristiano Ronaldo, Xabi Alonso, Granero, Higuain (Benzema 64).

Wednesday, 17 February 2010
Bayern Munich (1) 2 *(Robben 45 (pen), Klose 89)*
Fiorentina (0) 1 *(Kroldrup 50)* 66,000
Bayern Munich: Butt; Van Buyten (Contento 46), Demichelis, Lahm, Badstuber, Ribery, Van Bommel, Schweinsteiger, Robben, Muller (Olic 66), Gomez (Klose 66).
Fiorentina: Frey; Kroldrup, Vargas, Natali (Pasqual 85), De Silvestri, Montolivo (Donadel 84), Gobbi▪, Bolatti, Marchionni, Jovetic (Felipe 75), Gilardino.

Porto (1) 2 *(Varela 11, Falcao 51)*
Arsenal (1) 1 *(Campbell 18)* 45,600
Porto: Helton; Bruno Alves, Fucile, Rolando, Raul Meireles (Tomas Costa 68), Alvaro Pereira, Fernando, Ruben Micael (Belluschi 85), Falcao, Hulk (Mariano Gonzalez 81), Varela.
Arsenal: Fabianski; Sagna, Clichy, Denilson, Vermaelen, Campbell, Rosicky (Walcott 68), Fabregas, Bendtner (Vela 83), Diaby, Nasri (Eboue 88).

Tuesday, 23 February 2010
Olympiakos (0) 0
Bordeaux (1) 1 *(Ciani 45)* 29,773
Olympiakos: Nikopolidis; Mellberg, Raul Bravo, Torosidis, Stoltidis, Datolo, Papadopoulos A, Maresca, Ledesma (Zairi 64), Mitroglou (Derbyshire 77), LuaLua.

Bordeaux: Carrasso; Ciani, Chalme, Sane, Planus, Tremoulinas, Fernando, Gourcuff, Wendel (Jussie 83), Plasil (Gouffran 82), Chamakh.

Stuttgart (1) 1 *(Cacau 25)*
Barcelona (0) 1 *(Ibrahimovic 52)* 40,000
Stuttgart: Lehmann; Tasci, Delpierre, Molinaro, Celozzi, Trasch (Kuzmanovic 58), Gebhart (Rudy 84), Hleb, Khedira, Cacau, Pogrebnyak (Marica 64).
Barcelona: Victor Valdes; Pique, Marquez (Milito 59), Puyol, Maxwell, Xavi, Iniesta, Busquets, Yaya Toure (Henry 53), Ibrahimovic, Messi.

Wednesday, 24 February 2010
CSKA Moscow (0) 1 *(Gonzalez 66)*
Sevilla (1) 1 *(Negredo 25)* 28,600
CSKA Moscow: Akinfeev; Semberas, Ignashevich, Berezutski A, Berezutski V, Shchennikov, Gonzalez, Krasic, Honda (Mamaev 83), Aldonin, Necid.
Sevilla: Palop; Fazio, Escude, Stankevicius, Fernando Navarro, Adriano (Perotti 59), Jesus Navas, Zokora, Renato (Acosta 88), Romaric, Negredo (Kanoute 76).

Internazionale (1) 2 *(Milito 3, Cambiasso 55)*
Chelsea (0) 1 *(Kalou 51)* 78,971
Internazionale: Julio Cesar; Zanetti, Lucio, Maicon, Samuel, Stankovic (Ali Muntari 84), Thiago Motta (Balotelli 58), Sneijder, Cambiasso, Eto'o (Pandev 68), Milito.
Chelsea: Cech (Hilario 61); Ivanovic, Malouda, Mikel, Terry, Ricardo Carvalho, Ballack, Lampard, Anelka, Drogba, Kalou (Sturridge 78).

KNOCK-OUT ROUND SECOND LEG

Tuesday, 9 March 2010
Arsenal (2) 5 *(Bendtner 9, 25, 90 (pen), Nasri 63, Eboue 66)*
Porto (0) 0 59,661
Arsenal: Almunia; Sagna, Clichy, Song Billong, Vermaelen, Campbell, Diaby, Rosicky (Eboue 57), Arshavin (Walcott 76), Bendtner, Nasri (Denilson 73).
Porto: Helton; Bruno Alves, Fucile, Rolando, Nuno Andre (Cristian Rodriguez 46), Raul Meireles, Alvaro Pereira, Ruben Micael (Guarin 76), Falcao, Hulk, Varela (Mariano Gonzalez 76).

Fiorentina (1) 3 *(Vargas 28, Jovetic 54, 64)*
Bayern Munich (0) 2 *(Van Bommel 60, Robben 65)* 45,000
Fiorentina: Frey; Kroldrup, Vargas (Keirrison 82), Natali, Felipe (Pasqual 80), De Silvestri, Zanetti, Montolivo, Marchionni, Jovetic, Gilardino.
Bayern Munich: Butt; Van Buyten, Lahm, Badstuber, Ribery (Pranjic 90), Van Bommel, Muller, Alaba, Schweinsteiger, Robben, Gomez (Klose 30).

Wednesday, 10 March 2010

Manchester U (1) 4 *(Rooney 13, 46, Park 60, Fletcher 88)*
AC Milan (0) 0 74,595
Manchester U: Van der Sar; Neville (Rafael 66), Evra, Fletcher, Ferdinand, Vidic, Valencia, Scholes (Gibson 73), Rooney (Berbatov 66), Park, Nani.
AC Milan: Abbiati; Jankulovski, Bonera (Seedorf 46), Thiago Silva, Flamini, Abate (Beckham 64), Pirlo, Ambrosini, Ronaldinho, Huntelaar, Borriello (Inzaghi 69).

Real Madrid (1) 1 *(Cristiano Ronaldo 5)*
Lyon (0) 1 *(Pjanic 75)* 71,569
Real Madrid: Casillas; Arbeloa (Diarra M 83), Sergic Ramos, Albiol, Garay, Kaka (Raul 76), Cristiano Ronaldo, Diarra L, Guti, Granero (Van der Vaart 62), Higuain.
Lyon: Lloris; Cris, Boumsong (Kallstrom 46), Reveillere, Cissokho, Pjanic (Ederson 83), Makoun (Gonalons 46', Toulalan, Lisandro Lopez, Govou, Delgado.

Tuesday, 16 March 2010

Chelsea (0) 0
Internazionale (0) 1 *(Eto'o 78)* 38,107
Chelsea: Turnbull; Ivanovic, Zhirkov (Kalou 73), Mikel, Terry, Alex, Ballack (Cole J 63), Lampard, Anelka, Drogba■, Malouda.
Internazionale: Julio Cesar; Zanetti, Lucio, Maicon, Samuel, Thiago Motta (Materazzi 90), Sneijder (Mar ga 84), Cambiasso, Eto'o, Milito, Pandev (Stankovic 75).

Sevilla (1) 1 *(Perotti 41)*
CSKA Moscow (1) 2 *(Necid 39, Honda 55)* 40,000
Sevilla: Palop; Fazio, Dragutinovic, Stankevidus, Fernando Navarro (Correia 75), Jesus Navas, Zokora, Renato (Negredo 71), Diego Capel (Kanoute 46), Perotti, Luis Fabiano.
CSKA Moscow: Akinfeev; Semberas, Ignashe▼ich, Berezutski A, Berezutski V, Shchennikov, Gonzalez (Mamaev 88), Krasic (Odiah 72), Honda (Rahimic 82), Aldonin, Necid.

Wednesday, 17 March 2010

Barcelona (2) 4 *(Messi 13, 60, Pedro 22, Bojan 89)*
Stuttgart (0) 0 83,543
Barcelona: Victor Valdes; Dani Alves, Pique, Puyol, Maxwell, Iniesta (Bojan 88), Busquets (Ibrahimovic 66), Yaya Toure, Messi, Henry (Milito 78), Pedro.
Stuttgart: Lehmann; Niedermeier, Delpierre, Molinaro, Celozzi (Gebhart 46), Trasch, Hleb, Khedira, Kuzmanovic, Cacau, Pogrebnyak (Marica 70).

Bordeaux (1) 2 *(Gourcuff 5, Chamakh 88)*
Olympiakos (0) 1 *(Mitroglou 50)* 31,004
Bordeaux: Carrasso; Ciani, Chalme, Sane, Tremoulinas, Diarra■, Fernando, Gourcuff, Wendel (Jussie 90', Plasil (Sertic 84), Chamakh.
Olympiakos: Nikopolidis; Mellberg■, Raul Bravo, Torosidis, Stoltidis (Ledesma 80), Datolo, Papadopoulos A, Maresca, Zairi (Mitroglou 63), Derbyshire■, LuaLua.

QUARTER-FINALS FIRST LEG

Tuesday, 30 March 2010

Bayern Munich (0) 2 *(Ribery 76, Olic 90)*
Manchester U (1) 1 *(Rooney 2)* 66,000
Bayern Munich: Butt; Van Buyten, Demichelis, Lahm, Badstuber, Ribery, Hamit Altintop (Klose 36), Van Bommel, Pranjic (Tymoshchuk 89), Muller (Gomez 73), Olic.

Manchester U: Van der Sar; Neville, Evra, Carrick (Valencia 70), Ferdinand, Vidic, Park (Berbatov 70), Scholes, Fletcher, Rooney, Nani (Giggs 82).

Lyon (2) 3 *(Lisandro Lopez 10, 77 (pen), Bastos 32)*
Bordeaux (1) 1 *(Chamakh 14)* 37,859
Lyon: Lloris; Cris, Reveillere, Cissokho, Bodmer, Bastos (Kallstrom 66), Pjanic (Govou 66), Makoun, Toulalan, Lisandro Lopez, Delgado (Gonalons 86).
Bordeaux: Carrasso; Ciani, Chalme (Henrique 83), Sane, Tremoulinas, Fernando, Gourcuff, Wendel (Jussie 72), Plasil, Gouffran (Bellion 84), Chamakh.

Wednesday, 31 March 2010

Arsenal (0) 2 *(Walcott 69, Fabregas 85 (pen))*
Barcelona (0) 2 *(Ibrahimovic 46, 59)* 59,572
Arsenal: Almunia; Sagna (Walcott 66), Clichy, Song Billong, Vermaelen, Gallas (Denilson 46), Diaby, Fabregas, Bendtner, Arshavin (Eboue 27), Nasri.
Barcelona: Victor Valdes; Dani Alves, Pique, Puyol■, Maxwell, Xavi, Keita, Busquets, Ibrahimovic (Henry 77), Messi (Milito 86), Pedro.

Internazionale (0) 1 *(Milito 65)*
CSKA Moscow (0) 0 69,398
Internazionale: Julio Cesar; Zanetti, Maicon, Materazzi, Samuel, Stankovic, Sneijder, Cambiasso, Eto'o, Milito, Pandev (Mariga 90).
CSKA Moscow: Akinfeev; Semberas, Ignashevich, Berezutski A, Berezutski V, Shchennikov, Mamaev (Gonzalez 73), Krasic, Honda (Dzagoev 70), Aldonin (Rahimic 76), Necid.

QUARTER-FINALS SECOND LEG

Tuesday, 6 April 2010

Barcelona (3) 4 *(Messi 21, 37, 42, 88)*
Arsenal (1) 1 *(Bendtner 18)* 93,330
Barcelona: Victor Valdes; Dani Alves, Marquez, Milito, Abidal (Maxwell 53), Xavi, Keita, Busquets, Messi, Bojan (Yaya Toure 56), Pedro (Iniesta 85).
Arsenal: Almunia; Sagna, Clichy, Denilson, Vermaelen, Silvestre (Eboue 63), Walcott, Diaby, Bendtner, Rosicky (Eduardo 73), Nasri.

CSKA Moscow (0) 0
Internazionale (1) 1 *(Sneijder 6)* 65,000
CSKA Moscow: Akinfeev; Semberas, Ignashevich, Berezutski A, Berezutski V (Odiah■ 14), Shchennikov, Dzagoev, Mamaev, Gonzalez, Honda (Rahimic 77), Necid (Guilherme 71).
Internazionale: Julio Cesar; Zanetti, Lucio, Maicon, Samuel, Stankovic, Sneijder (Ali Muntari 86), Cambiasso, Eto'o, Milito (Balotelli 74), Pandev (Chivu 63).

Wednesday, 7 April 2010

Bordeaux (1) 1 *(Chamakh 45)*
Lyon (0) 0 31,962
Bordeaux: Carrasso; Ciani, Sane, Planus (Cavenaghi 84), Tremoulinas, Diarra (Chalme 70), Gourcuff, Wendel, Plasil, Jussie (Gouffran 77), Chamakh.
Lyon: Lloris; Cris, Boumsong (Bodmer 77), Reveillere, Cissokho, Kallstrom, Bastos (Ederson 88), Toulalan, Gonalons, Gomis (Pjanic 66), Delgado.

Manchester U (3) 3 *(Gibson 3, Nani 7, 41)*
Bayern Munich (1) 2 *(Olic 43, Robben 74)* 74,482
Manchester U: Van der Sar; Rafael■, Evra, Carrick (Berbatov 80), Ferdinand, Vidic, Valencia, Fletcher, Gibson (Giggs 81), Rooney (O'Shea 55), Nani.
Bayern Munich: Butt; Van Buyten, Demichelis, Lahm, Badstuber, Ribery, Van Bommel, Muller (Gomez 46), Schweinsteiger, Robben (Hamit Altintop 76), Olic (Pranjic 84).

Barcelona's Lionel Messi scores his fourth goal of the game during the 4-1 defeat of Arsenal in the Champions League Quarter-Final second leg. The Catalan giants progressed to the Semi-Final with an aggregate score of 6-3. (Action Images/Carl Recine)

SEMI-FINALS FIRST LEG

Tuesday, 20 April 2010

Internazionale (1) 3 *(Sneijder 30, Maicon 48, Milito 61)*

Barcelona (1) 1 *(Pedro 19)* 79,000

Internazionale: Julio Cesar; Zanetti, Lucio, Maicon (Chivu 73), Samuel, Thiago Motta, Sneijder, Cambiasso, Eto'o, Milito (Balotelli 75), Pandev (Stankovic 56).
Barcelona: Victor Valdes; Dani Alves, Pique, Puyol, Maxwell, Xavi, Keita, Busquets, Ibrahimovic (Abidal 62), Messi, Pedro.

Wednesday, 21 April 2010

Bayern Munich (0) 1 *(Robben 69)*

Lyon (0) 0 66,000

Bayern Munich: Butt; Van Buyten, Demichelis, Lahm, Contento, Ribery■, Pranjic (Gomez 63), Muller, Schweinsteiger, Robben (Hamit Altintop 85), Olic (Tymoshchuk 46).
Lyon: Lloris; Cris, Reveillere, Cissokho, Kallstrom, Pjanic (Makoun 56), Ederson (Bastos 70), Toulalan■, Gonalons, Lisandro Lopez, Delgado (Govou 79).

SEMI-FINALS SECOND LEG

Tuesday, 27 April 2010

Lyon (0) 0

Bayern Munich (1) 3 *(Olic 25, 67, 78)* 39,414

Lyon: Lloris; Cris■, Boumsong, Reveillere, Cissokho (Gomis 46), Bastos, Makoun, Gonalons, Lisandro Lopez (Ederson 79), Govou, Delgado (Pjanic 67).
Bayern Munich: Butt; Van Buyten (Demichelis 46), Lahm, Contento, Badstuber, Hamit Altintop, Van Bommel, Muller, Schweinsteiger (Alaba 78), Robben (Klose 76), Olic.

Wednesday, 28 April 2010

Barcelona (0) 1 *(Pique 83)*

Internazionale (0) 0 96,214

Barcelona: Victor Valdes; Dani Alves, Pique, Milito (Maxwell 46), Xavi, Keita, Busquets (Bojan 63), Yaya Toure, Ibrahimovic (Jeffren 63), Messi, Pedro.
Internazionale: Julio Cesar; Zanetti, Lucio, Maicon, Samuel, Chivu, Thiago Motta■, Sneijder (Ali Muntari 66), Cambiasso, Eto'o (Mariga 86), Milito (Cordoba 80).

UEFA CHAMPIONS LEAGUE FINAL

Saturday, 22 May 2010

(in Madrid, 74,954)

Bayern Munich (0) 0   Internazionale (1) 2 *(Milito 35, 70)*

Bayern Munich: Butt; Van Buyten, Demichelis, Lahm, Badstuber, Hamit Altintop (Klose 63), Van Bommel, Muller, Schweinsteiger, Robben, Olic (Gomez 74).

Internazionale: Julio Cesar; Zanetti, Lucio, Maicon, Samuel, Chivu (Stankovic 68), Sneijder, Cambiasso, Eto'o, Milito (Materazzi 90), Pandev (Ali Muntari 79).

Referee: H. Webb (England).

EUROPEAN CUP-WINNERS' CUP
FINALS 1961–99

Year	Winners		Runners-up		Venue	Attendance	Referee
1961	Fiorentina	2	Rangers	0 *(1st Leg)*	Glasgow	80,000	Steiner (A)
	Fiorentina	2	Rangers	1 *(2nd Leg)*	Florence	50,000	Hernadi (H)
1962	Atletico Madrid	1	Fiorentina	1	Glasgow	27,389	Wharton (S)
Replay	Atletico Madrid	3	Fiorentina	0	Stuttgart	38,000	Tschenscher (WG)
1963	Tottenham Hotspur	5	Atletico Madrid	1	Rotterdam	49,000	Van Leuwen (Ho)
1964	Sporting Lisbon	3	MTK Budapest	3 *(aet)*	Brussels	3000	Van Nuffel (Bel)
Replay	Sporting Lisbon	1	MTK Budapest	0	Antwerp	19,000	Versyp (Bel)
1965	West Ham U	2	Munich 1860	0	Wembley	100,000	Szolt (H)
1966	Borussia Dortmund	2	Liverpool	1 *(aet)*	Glasgow	41,657	Schwinte (F)
1967	Bayern Munich	1	Rangers	0 *(aet)*	Nuremberg	69,480	Lo Bello (I)
1968	AC Milan	2	Hamburg	0	Rotterdam	53,000	Ortiz (Sp)
1969	Slovan Bratislava	3	Barcelona	2	Basle	19,000	Van Ravens (Ho)
1970	Manchester C	2	Gornik Zabrze	1	Vienna	8,000	Schiller (A)
1971	Chelsea	1	Real Madrid	1 *(aet)*	Athens	42,000	Scheurer (Sw)
Replay	Chelsea	2	Real Madrid	1 *(aet)*	Athens	35,000	Bucheli (Sw)
1972	Rangers	3	Moscow Dynamo	2	Barcelona	24,000	Ortiz (Sp)
1973	AC Milan	1	Leeds U	0	Salonika	45,000	Mihas (Gr)
1974	Magdeburg	2	AC Milan	0	Rotterdam	4000	Van Gemert (Ho)
1975	Dynamo Kiev	3	Ferencvaros	0	Basle	13,000	Davidson (S)
1976	Anderlecht	4	West Ham U	2	Brussels	58,000	Wurtz (F)
1977	Hamburg	2	Anderlecht	0	Amsterdam	65,000	Partridge (E)
1978	Anderlecht	4	Austria/WAC	0	Paris	48,679	Adlinger (WG)
1979	Barcelona	4	Fortuna Dusseldorf	3 *(aet)*	Basle	58,000	Palotai (H)
1980	Valencia	0	Arsenal	0	Brussels	36,000	Christov (Cz)
	(aet; Valencia won 5-4 on penalties)						
1981	Dynamo Tbilisi	2	Carl Zeiss Jena	1	Dusseldorf	9000	Lattanzi (I)
1982	Barcelona	2	Standard Liege	1	Barcelona	100,000	Eschweiler (WG)
1983	Aberdeen	2	Real Madrid	1 *(aet)*	Gothenburg	17,804	Menegali (I)
1984	Juventus	2	Porto	1	Basle	60,000	Prokop (EG)
1985	Everton	3	Rapid Vienna	1	Rotterdam	50,000	Casarin (I)
1986	Dynamo Kiev	3	Atletico Madrid	0	Lyon	39,300	Wohrer (A)
1987	Ajax	1	Lokomotiv Leipzig	0	Athens	35,000	Agnolin (I)
1988	Mechelen	1	Ajax	0	Strasbourg	39,446	Pauly (WG)
1989	Barcelona	2	Sampdoria	0	Berne	45,000	Courtney (E)
1990	Sampdoria	2	Anderlecht	0	Gothenburg	20,103	Galler (Sw)
1991	Manchester U	2	Barcelona	1	Rotterdam	42,000	Karlsson (Se)
1992	Werder Bremen	2	Monaco	0	Lisbon	16,000	D'Elia (I)
1993	Parma	3	Antwerp	1	Wembley	37,393	Assenmacher (G)
1994	Arsenal	1	Parma	0	Copenhagen	33,765	Krondl (CzR)
1995	Zaragoza	2	Arsenal	1	Paris	42,424	Ceccarini (I)
1996	Paris St Germain	1	Rapid Vienna	0	Brussels	37,500	Pairetto (I)
1997	Barcelona	1	Paris St Germain	0	Rotterdam	45,000	Merk (G)
1998	Chelsea	1	Stuttgart	0	Stockholm	30,216	Braschi (I)
1999	Lazio	2	Mallorca	1	Villa Park	33,021	Benko (A)

INTER-CITIES FAIRS CUP FINALS 1958–71

(Winners in italics)

Year	First Leg	Attendance	Second Leg	Attendance
1958	London 2 Barcelona 2	45,466	*Barcelona* 6 London 0	62,000
1960	Birmingham C 0 Barcelona 0	40,500	*Barcelona* 4 Birmingham C 1	70,000
1961	Birmingham C 2 Roma 2	21,005	*Roma* 2 Birmingham C 0	60,000
1962	Valencia 6 Barcelona 2	65,000	Barcelona 1 *Valencia* 1	60,000
1963	Dynamo Zagreb 1 Valencia 2	40,000	*Valencia* 2 Dynamo Zagreb 0	55,000
1964	*Zaragoza* 2 Valencia 1	50,000	(in Barcelona)	
1965	*Ferencvaros* 1 Juventus 0	25,000	(in Turin)	
1966	Barcelona 0 Zaragoza 1	70,000	Zaragoza 2 *Barcelona* 4	70,000
1967	Dynamo Zagreb 2 Leeds U 0	40,000	Leeds U 0 *Dynamo Zagreb* 0	35,604
1968	Leeds U 1 Ferencvaros 0	25,368	Ferencvaros 0 *Leeds U* 0	70,000
1969	Newcastle U 3 Ujpest Dozsa 0	60,000	Ujpest Dozsa 2 *Newcastle U* 3	37,000
1970	Anderlecht 3 Arsenal 1	37,000	*Arsenal* 3 Anderlecht 0	51,612
1971	Juventus 0 Leeds U 0 *(abandoned 51 minutes)*	42,000		
	Juventus 2 Leeds U 2	42,000	*Leeds U* 1* Juventus 1	42,483

UEFA CUP FINALS 1972–97

(Winners in italics)

Year	First Leg	Attendance	Second Leg	Attendance
1972	Wolverhampton W 1 Tottenham H 2	45,000	*Tottenham H* 1 Wolverhampton W 1	48,000
1973	Liverpool 0 Moenchengladbach 0			
	(abandoned 27 minutes)	44,967		
	Liverpool 3 Moenchengladbach 0	41,169	Moenchengladbach 2 *Liverpool* 0	35,000
1974	Tottenham H 2 Feyenoord 2	46,281	*Feyenoord* 2 Tottenham H 0	68,000
1975	Moenchengladbach 0 Twente 0	45,000	Twente 1 *Moenchengladbach* 5	24,500
1976	Liverpool 3 FC Brugge 2	56,000	FC Brugge 1 *Liverpool* 1	32,000
1977	Juventus 1 Athletic Bilbao 0	75,000	Athletic Bilbao 2 *Juventus* 1*	43,000
1978	Bastia 0 PSV Eindhoven 0	15,000	*PSV Eindhoven* 3 Bastia 0	27,000
1979	Red Star Belgrade 1 Moenchengladbach 1	87,500	*Moenchengladbach* 1 Red Star Belgrade 0	45,000
1980	Moenchengladbach 3 Eintracht Frankfurt 2	25,000	*Eintracht Frankfurt* 1* Moenchengladbach 0	60,000
1981	Ipswich T 3 AZ 67 Alkmaar 0	27,532	AZ 67 Alkmaar 4 *Ipswich T* 2	28,500
1982	Gothenburg 1 Hamburg 0	42,548	Hamburg 0 *Gothenburg* 3	60,000
1983	Anderlecht 1 Benfica 0	45,000	Benfica 1 *Anderlecht* 1	80,000
1984	Anderlecht 1 Tottenham H 1	40,000	*Tottenham H* 1[1] Anderlecht 1	46,258
1985	Videoton 0 Real Madrid 3	30,000	*Real Madrid* 0 Videoton 1	98,300
1986	Real Madrid 5 Cologne 1	80,000	Cologne 2 *Real Madrid* 0	15,000
1987	Gothenburg 1 Dundee U 0	50,023	Dundee U 1 *Gothenburg* 1	20,911
1988	Espanol 3 Bayer Leverkusen 0	42,000	*Bayer Leverkusen* 3[2] Espanol 0	22,000
1989	Napoli 2 Stuttgart 1	83,000	Stuttgart 3 *Napoli* 3	67,000
1990	Juventus 3 Fiorentina 1	45,000	Fiorentina 0 *Juventus* 0	32,000
1991	Internazionale 2 Roma 0	68,887	Roma 1 *Internazionale* 0	70,901
1992	Torino 2 Ajax 2	65,377	Ajax 0* Torino 0	40,000
1993	Borussia Dortmund 1 Juventus 3	37,000	*Juventus* 3 Borussia Dortmund 0	62,781
1994	Salzburg 0 Internazionale 1	47,500	*Internazionale* 1 Salzburg 0	80,326
1995	Parma 1 Juventus 0	23,000	Juventus 1 *Parma* 1	80,750
1996	Bayern Munich 2 Bordeaux 0	62,000	Bordeaux 1 *Bayern Munich* 3	36,000
1997	Schalke 1 Internazionale 0	56,824	Internazionale 1 *Schalke* 0[3]	81,670

*won on away goals   [1]aet; Tottenham H won 4-3 on penalties   [2]aet; Bayer Leverkusen won 3-2 on penalties
[3]aet; Schalke won 4-1 on penalties

UEFA CUP FINALS 1998–2009

Year	Winners		Runners-up		Venue	Attendance	Referee
1998	Internazionale	3	Lazio	0	Paris	42,938	Nieto (Sp)
1999	Parma	3	Marseille	0	Moscow	61,000	Dallas (S)
2000	Galatasaray	0	Arsenal	0	Copenhagen	38,919	Nieto (Sp)
	(aet; Galatasaray won 4-1 on penalties)						
2001	Liverpool	5	Alaves	4	Dortmund	65,000	Veissiere (F)
	(aet; Liverpool won on sudden death)						
2002	Feyenoord	3	Borussia Dortmund	2	Rotterdam	45,000	Pereira (P)
2003	Porto	3	Celtic	2	Seville	52,972	Michel (Slo)
	(aet)						
2004	Valencia	2	Marseille	0	Gothenburg	40,000	Collina (I)
2005	CSKA Moscow	3	Sporting Lisbon	1	Lisbon	48,000	Poll (E)
2006	Sevilla	4	Middlesbrough	0	Eindhoven	36,500	Fandel (G)
2007	Sevilla	2	Espanyol	2	Glasgow	50,670	Busacca (Sw)
	(aet; Sevilla won 3-1 on penalties)						
2008	Zenit St Petersburg	2	Rangers	0	Manchester	43,878	Fröjdfeldt (Se)
2009	Shakhtar Donetsk	2	Werder Bremen	1	Istanbul	40,000	Chantalejo (Sp)

UEFA EUROPA LEAGUE 2010

Year	Winners		Runners-up		Venue	Attendance	Referee
2010	Atletico Madrid	2	Fulham	1 *(aet)*	Hamburg	49,000	Rizzoli (I)

UEFA EUROPA LEAGUE 2009–10

■ *Denotes player sent off.*

FIRST QUALIFYING ROUND FIRST LEG
Thursday, 2 July 2009
Anorthosis (2) 5 *(Da Costa 9 (og), Katsavakis 25, Frousos 62, 90, Cafu 68)*
Kaerjeng (0) 0 8500
Anorthosis: Supic; Katsavakis, Leiwakabessy, Martins, Constantinou, Marangos (Frousos 57), Fernandes (Dellas 79), Laban, Sosin, Cristovao (Garpozis 7'), Cafu.
Kaerjeng: Castellani; Abeid (Leite 79), Shoffner, Ramdedovic, Da Costa, Marinelli, Spinelli, Mukenge (Polidori 71), Rolandi, Zewe (Sagramola 82), Boulafari.

Banants (0) 0
Siroki (1) 2 *(Ivankovic 41, Tiago Rodrigues 66)* 5000
Banants: Ghazarian; Nazarenko, Nasbian (Gyozalyan 46), Grigorian, Voskanian (Romanenko 74), Kasule, Kakosian, Mkhitarian (Stepanian 71), Kavatsiv, Dashiar, Melkonian.
Siroki: Maric; Renato, Topic (Brekalo 77), Wagner Lago, Barisic, Ljubic (Zovko 31), Silic, Diogo, Ivankovic, Martinovic, Peraica (Tiago Rodrigues 52).

Buducnost (0) 0
Polonia (0) 2 *(Koziol 54, Jodlowiec 65)* 5500
Buducnost: Vujadinvoic; Perisic, Vukcevic N (Nikclic 88), Visnjic, Delic (Ajkovic 48), Bmovic, Vukcevic P, Kumedor, Boskovic (Vesovic 62), Vukovic, Beciraj.
Polonia: Przyrowski; Mynar, Skrzynski, Koziol, Jodlowiec, Sokolowski (Maka 85), Zasada, Lato, Majewski, Sarvas (Mierzejewska 55), Ivanowski (Chalbinski 70).

Dinaburg (0) 2 *(Afanasiev 63, Guchashvili 90)*
Kalju (0) 1 *(Haavistu 89)* 780
Dinaburg: Davidovs; Simonov (Zizilev 60), Gabovs, Login, Kryauklis, Danilin, Afanasiev, Kuleshov, Sokolov, Guchashvili, Hong (Kolcov■ 78).
Kalju: Kaas; Haavistu, Balbinot, Felipe Nunes, Pimentel (Novikov 65), Arruda, Tukk, Hurt, Terehhov (Kaukvere 68), Rafael, Shuhanau (Smirnov 73).

Dynamo Minsk (0) 2 *(Kislyak 72 (pen), Strakanovic 88)*
Renova (1) 1 *(Ibraimi 41)* 2643
Dynamo Minsk: Gorbunov; Pavyukovich, Montaroup, Veretilo, Martynovich, Gurenko, Gigevich (Strakanovich 58), Chuhley (Dragun 71), Kislyak, Mbanangoye, Gavryushko (Lebedev 46).
Renova: Kovacevic; Statovci, Memedi, Despctovski, Ibraimi (Ademi 88), Stojanov, Emini, Nuhiu Aliju (Ignjatovski 90), Angjelovski, Ismaili (Gafuri 63).

Fram (1) 2 *(Tillen S 33 (pen), Juzusson 48)*
The New Saints (1) 1 *(Evans 24)* 592
Fram: Halldorsson; Hauksson, Tillen S, Fjolusor, McShane, Olason (Magnusson 87), Jonsson, Gudmundsson, Juliusson (Tillen J 70), Thorarinsson, Ormarsson (Bjornsson 70).
The New Saints: Harrison; Holmes T, Evans, Baker (McKenna 89), Holmes D (Marriott 83), Hogan Ruscoe, Jones C, Murtagh (Darlington 73), Berkeley, Wood.

Grevenmacher (0) 0
Vetra (2) 3 *(Grigaitis 11, 79, Masitsev 26)* 560
Grevenmacher: Pleimling; Schmitt (Thimmesch 72), Habte, Maric, Heinz, Lorig Omerovic (Tejerina 46), Federspiel, Huss, Hoffmann, Boussi (Muller 46).
Vetra: Valinicius; Borovski, Kijanskas, Jankauskas, Paulauskas, Stanaitis, Moroz Masitsev (Vasiliauskas 79), Grigaitis, Eliosius (Vezevicus 57), Grigalevicus (Kubis 81).

Haladas (0) 1 *(Kenesei 79)*
Irtysh (0) 0 4000
Haladas: Rozsa; Guzmics, Euttor, Rajos, Maikel (Skriba 62), Toth, Molnar, Schimmer, Oross, Voros, Kenesei.

Irtysh: Rikhard; Chernyshov, Kolomyts, Shomko, Rimavicius, Nakov, Maltsev (Malinin 64), Yurin (Sobolev 70), Parkhamchuk (Noskov 82), Ivanov, Andreev.

Helsingborg (0) 3 *(Larsson H 50, 86, Sundin 90)*
Mika (0) 1 *(Ulises 65)* 2212
Helsingborg: Hansson; Tambura, Andersson C (Jonsson 36), Nilsson, Sundin, Lantz, Bergholtz (Landgren 74), Holgersson (Wahlstedt 46), Ekstrand, Makondele, Larsson H.
Mika: Harutyunian; Arm Petrosian, Fursin, Lopez, Mikaelian (Ara Hakobian 85), Poghosian, Alex, Mkrtchian, Ednei, Ulises, Demel (Beglarian 89).

Lahti (2) 4 *(Rafael 2, 86, Moilanen 43, Haara 52)*
Dinamo Tirana (1) 1 *(Kuli 28)* 3240
Lahti: Szentpeteri; Haara, Toivomaki, Moilanen, Eerola, Fofana (Hieni 61), Hietanen (Shala 46), Vanninen, Korte, Rafael (Lansitalo 87), Litmanen.
Dinamo Tirana: Kotorri; Vrapi, Pisha, Putincanin (Sina 63), Poci, Allmuca, Diop, Kuli (Sosa 46), Haxhibulic, Bakaj, Brkic (Plaku 46).

Lisburn Distillery (0) 1 *(Whelan 88)*
Zestafoni (4) 5 *(Gelashvili 11, 34, Grigalashvili 22, 38, Aphtsiarui 52)* 600
Lisburn Distillery: Murphy; McShane, Thompson S, Simpson, Callaghan, Melaugh, Gilmartin, Whelan, Shaw (Browne 56), Armour (Kingsberry 69), Thompson G (Corey 55).
Zestafoni: Mamaladze; Oniani, Todua, Khidesheli, Eliava, Daushvili, Dzaria (Benashvili 58), Aphtsiarui, Grigalashvili (Gorgiashvili 74), Gelashvili, Dvali (Kvakhvadze 88).

Motherwell (0) 0
Llanelli (1) 1 *(Jones S 28)* 4307
Motherwell: Fraser; Hammell, Reynolds, Craigan, Saunders, Lasley (Slane 46), Forbes, Sutton, Murphy, O'Brien (McHugh 74), McGarry.
Llanelli: Morris; Jones S, Corbisiero, Venables, Jarman (Thomas 16), Legg (Warlow 51), Phillips, Howard, Mumford, Jones C (Follows 65), Griffiths.

NSI Runavik (0) 0
Rosenborg (1) 3 *(Zahora 21, Joensen M 59 (og), Lustig 89 (pen))* 800
NSI Runavik: Joensen M; Hansen O, Davidsen, Hansen E, Hansen J, Elttor (Olsen 76), Petersen, Lokin, Potemkin (Madsen 79), Frederiksberg (Joensen J 56), Jacobsen.
Rosenborg: Jarstein; Lustig, Stadsgaard (Miller 46), Lago, Nordvik, Annan (Tettey 71), Skjelbred, Konan, Iversen (Olsen 65), Sellin, Zahora.

Olimpi (1) 2 *(Megreladze 10, 88)*
B36 (0) 0 3000
Olimpi: Alavidze; Gilauri, Machavariani, Rekhviashvili (Khubua 46), Gongahadze, Babunashvili■, Seturidze (Chelidze G 72), Dobrovolski, Chelidze Z (Pipia 60), Megreladze, Sirbiladze.
B36: Jakobsen; Ellingsaard, Gunnarsson, Jacobsen H, Faero, Roaldur Jacobsen, Olsen, Matras, Midjord (Hermanson 82), Koroma (Eysturoy 75), Malsom (Borg 46).

Randers (1) 4 *(Berg 36, Sane 47, Nygaard 80, Lorentzen 81)*
Linfield (0) 0 5114
Randers: Stuhr-Ellegaard; Ahmed, Addy, Fenger, Lorentzen, Pedersen S, Grahn (Beckmann 73), Pedersen K (Damborg 82), Sane (Olsen 73), Berg, Nygaard.
Linfield: Blayney; Douglas, Bailie, Burns (Curran 69), Ervin, Lowry (Allen 62), O'Kane, Garrett, Mulgrew, Carvill, McAllister (McHugh 74).

Simurq (0) 0

Bnei Yehuda (0) 1 *(Mori 83)*   11,500

Simurq: Mehdiyev; Sokolov, Malygin, Makhviladze, Bulychev, Solonicins (Calilov 64), Chkhetiani, Bolkvadze, Artyukh (Mammadov E 78), Akhalkatsi (Dolidze 76), Valev.
Bnei Yehuda: Aiyenugba; Mori, Haddad, Raly, Baldout, Radi, Zhairi (Azuz 86), Atar (Biton 76), Galvan (Garrido 90), Abu Zaid, Edri.

Slaven (1) 1 *(Csizmadia 3)*

Birkirkara (0) 0   1500

Slaven: Rodic; Kokalovic, Rogulj, Lapic, Csizmadia, Poldrugac, Juric, Vojnovic, Posavec (Delic 58), Vrucina (Poredski 84), Niverge.
Birkirkara: Borg O; Borg P, Scicluna, Paris, Fenech, Cilia (Muscat 86), Comvalius, Bajada, Zerafa, Tabone, Buhagiar (Sciberras 74).

Sligo Rovers (0) 1 *(Cretaro 89 (pen))*

Vllaznia (0) 2 *(Smajlaj 69, Keane 75 (og))*   2700

Sligo Rovers: Brush; Ventre, Keane, Holmes, Ryan, O'Grady, Feeney (Noctor 64), Cretaro, Boco, Morrison, Cash (Doherty 73).
Vllaznia: Grima■; Mrvaljevic, Osja, Belisha, Hallaci, Beqiri, Smajlaj, Shtubina, Ksapi (Olsi 88), Nallbani, Sinani (Balaj 85).

Spartak Trnava (2) 2 *(Kozuch 20, 26)*

Inter Baku (0) 1 *(Angel Gutierrez 80)*   3948

Spartak Trnava: Kralj; Dolezaj, Prochazka, Duris, Kopunek, Hruska, Hanzel, Kotula, Gueye, Sukennik (Guldan 86), Kozuch (Bernath 68).
Inter Baku: Wilson Junior; Accioly (Zagorac 85), Abbasov, Shukurov, Ismailov, Angel Gutierrez, Cervenka, Zlatinov, Rubins (Mammadov 63), Chertoganov, Huseynov (Mamedov 57).

Sutjeska (0) 1 *(Medjedovic 49)*

MTZ-Ripo (0) 1 *(Bubnov 77)*   4000

Sutjeska: Giljen; Dikanovic, Dzeverdanovic N (Dzeverdanovic M 85), Dubljevic, Delic, Bulatovic, Medjedovic, Bulajic (Markovic 89), Zvicer, Todorovic (Banda 83), Adrovic.
MTZ-Ripo: Sulima; Zrnanovic, Maltsev, Osipovich, Popel, Camara (Makas 74), Kvaratskhelia (Bubnov 77), Tolkanitsa, Shchegrikovich D, Eremchuk, Ryndyuk (Ledenev 71).

Trans (0) 0

Rudar (1) 3 *(Cipot 9 (pen), Omladic 61, Trifkovic 89)* 608

Trans: Storys; Gorshkov, Rimas, Lepik, Kazakov, Tarassenkov (Fyjodorov 90), Bazyukin, Kitto, Ratnikov E, Ratnikov D, Losanov (Starovoitov 77).
Rudar: Savic; Sulejmanovic, Cipot, Golob (Kreft 81), Kolsi, Trifkovic, Pokleka, Tolimir, Dedic (Jesenicnik 66), Prasnikar, Omladic (Mujakovic 61).

Valletta (1) 3 *(Falzon 25, Priso 50, Den Ouden 72)*

Keflavik (0) 0   1000

Valletta: Hogg; Dimech, Bezzina, Scicluna, Briffa, Pace (Agius E 77), Falzon (Sammit 82), Cruyff, Agius G, Den Ouden (Giglio 90), Priso.
Keflavik: Jorgensen L; Sutej, Antoniusson, Jorgensen N, Gudmundsson B (Arnarson 85), Holm, Eysteinsson (Matthiasson 73), Samuelsen, Einarsson, Thorsteinsson, Sveinsson.

Zimbru (0) 1 *(Demerji 48)*

Okzhetpes (0) 2 *(Karakulov 72, Chonkaev 74)*   3100

Zimbru: Calancea; Andronic I, Erhan, Ternavschi, Onila (Andronic G 59), Hvorosteanov, Antoniuc, Clonin, Demerji (Catan 80), Sofroni, Sidorenco (Andronic O 46).
Okzhetpes: Satubaldin; Krutskevich■, Keker, Kuznetsov, Pischulin, Aliyev, Chonkaev (Maymakov 86), Karakulov (Mokrousov 78), Nurgaliyev (Dyak 68), Dosmanbetov, Bekmukhayev.

FIRST QUALIFYING ROUND SECOND LEG

Thursday, 9 July 2009

B36 (0) 0

Olimpi (2) 2 *(Sirbiladze 6, Khubua 28)*   500

B36: Jakobsen; Ellingsgaard, Gunnarsson, Jacobsen H, Faero, Roaldur Jacobsen, Olsen (Hermansen 90), Matras, Midjord (Holmberg 17), Koroma, Malsom (Borg 65).
Olimpi: Alavidze; Gilauri, Machavariani, Lomidze, Gongadze, Seturidze, Dobrovolski, Khubua (Chelidze G 57), Chelidze Z, Chkhetiani (Megreladze 59), Sirbiladze (Pipia 65).

Birkirkara (0) 0

Slaven (0) 0   300

Birkirkara: Borg O; Borg P, Scicluna, Paris (Zammit 89), Fenech (Muscat 85), Cilia, Comvalius, Bajada, Zerafa, Tabone, Buhagiar (Sciberras 76).
Slaven: Rodic; Rogulj, Maras, Csizmadia, Poldrugac, Puric, Juric (Poredski 88), Vojnovic (Delic 60), Posavec (Bilen 74), Vrucina, Niverge.

Bnei Yehuda (1) 3 *(Galvan 27, 66, Biton 86)*

Simurq (0) 0   3000

Bnei Yehuda: Aiyenugba; Mori, Garrido, Raly, Baldout, Radi, Zhairi (Imses 83), Atar, Galvan (Biton 70), Abu Zaid, Edri (Azuz 80).
Simurq: Mehdiyev; Sokolov, Malygin, Bulychev, Chkhetiani, Bolkvadze, Artyukh, Akhalkatsi (Popovici 77), Gunchak, Mammadov E (Solonicins 66), Valev (Mazyar 46).

Dinamo Tirana (1) 2 *(Diop 13, 70)*

Lahti (0) 0   3000

Dinamo Tirana: Kotorri; Vrapi (Ferraj 78), Muca, Pisha, Putincanin, Allmuca, Diop, Malakarne, Kuli (Plaku 46), Haxhibulic, Bakaj.
Lahti: Szentpeteri; Haara (Huuhka 72), Toivomaki, Moilanen, Eerola, Fofana, Vanninen, Korte, Rafael (Kemppinen 26), Litmanen, Shala (Hieni 46).

Inter Baku (1) 1 *(Guglielmone 11)*

Spartak Trnava (2) 3 *(Sukennik 34, Kozuch 40, Prochazka 48)* 12,000

Inter Baku: Wilson Junior; Accioly, Abbasov, Shukurov, Ismailov (Rubins 64), Angel Gutierrez, Cervenka, Zlatinov (Mammadov 65), Chertoganov, Guglielmone (Mamedov 77), Huseynov.
Spartak Trnava: Kralj; Dolezaj, Hanzel, Prochazka, Duris, Kopunek, Hruska (Jakubicka 68), Kotula, Gueye, Sukennik (Zeleznik 74), Kozuch (Bernath 79).

Irtysh (2) 2 *(Yurin 19, Rajos 34 (og))*

Haladas (1) 1 *(Chernyshov 24 (og))*   8000

Irtysh: Rikhard; Chernyshov, Kolomyts, Shomko, Rimavicius, Nakov, Maltsev (Baizhanov 75), Yurin, Noskov (Shabalin 59), Ivanov (Zarechniy 78), Andreev.
Haladas: Rozsa; Guzmics, Kuttor, Rajos, Maikel (Skriba 46), Toth, Molnar, Schimmer, Oross, Voros (Irhas 88), Kenesei (Simon 55).

Kaerjeng (0) 1 *(Fiorani 90)*

Anorthosis (1) 2 *(Sosin 44, Frousos 60)*   567

Kaerjeng: Castellani; Shoffner, Abeid, Ramdedovic, Marinelli, Spinelli (Betorangal 84), Mukenge, Rolandi, Zewe, Carl (Santos Pires 78), Boulahfari (Fiorani 71).
Anorthosis: Supic; Katsavakis, Leiwakabessy, Martins, Constantinou, Georgiou (Dellas 46), Fernandes (Garpozis 61), Laban, Sosin, Cristovao (Frousos 46), Cafu.

Kalju (0) 0

Dinaburg (0) 0   1162

Kalju: Kaas; Haavistu■, Balbinot, Novikov, Felipe Nunes, Arruda, Smirnov (Kaukvere 55), Maccari (Tukk 70), Hurt, Terehhov, Rafael (Shuhanau 64).
Dinaburg: Davidovs; Gabov, Login, Krjauklis, Danilin, Zizilev, Afanasiev, Kuleshov, Sokolov, Guchashvili (Ri 79) (Denisevic 90), Hong (Kortua 59).

Keflavik (0) 2 *(Eysteinsson 55, Gudmundsson J 72)*
Valletta (1) 2 *(Falzon 41, Priso 82)*   900
Keflavik: Johansson; Sutej, Antoniusson, Jorgensen N (Gudmundsson B 46), Holm, Eysteinssen, Samuelsen, Einarsson, Gudnason, Thorsteinsson (Gudmundsson J 70), Sveinsson.
Valletta: Hogg; Dimech, Bezzina, Scicluna (Borg 90), Briffa, Pace, Falzon (Grioli 77), Camilleri, Cruyff, Agius G, Priso (Grima 90).

Linfield (0) 0
Randers (1) 3 *(Olsen 21, Lorentzen 51, Berg 82)*   1000
Linfield: Blayney; Douglas, Bailie, Burns, Ervin, Lowry, O'Kane, Garrett, Mulgrew (Gault 67), Carvill (Allen 59), McAllister (Miskimmin 78).
Randers: Stuhr-Ellegaard; Olesen (Fischer 73), Da Cruz, Jepsen, Damborg, Fenger, Lorentzen, Beckmann (Byskov 77), Berg, Olsen, Nygaard (Konig 63).

Llanelli (0) 0
Motherwell (2) 3 *(Sutton 8, 25, Murphy 71)*   3025
Llanelli: Morris; Jones S (Jenkins 67), Corbisiero, Venables, Legg (Warlow 76), Phillips (Moses 80), Howard, Mumford, Thomas, Griffiths, Follows.
Motherwell: Fraser; Hammell, Reynolds, Craigan, Saunders (Page 78), Lasley, Forbes, Sutton (Archdeacon 76), O'Brien, McGarry (Murphy 69), Slane.

Mika (0) 1 *(Ednei 83 (pen))*
Helsingborg (0) 1 *(Makondele 68)*   6500
Mika: Harutyunian; Arm Petrosian, Fursin, Lopez (Morozov 83), Mikaelian (Ara Hakobian 80), Poghosian, Alex, Mkrtchian, Ulises (Ednei 71), Demel, Voskanian.
Helsingborg: Hansson; Tambura, Patronen, Andersson C (Skulason 74), Wahlstedt, Nilsson, Landgren, Svanback, Bergholtz (Ekstrand 88), Makondele, Jonsson (Unkuri 65).

MTZ-Ripo (0) 2 *(Ryndyuk 67, 111)*
Sutjeska (0) 1 *(Todorovic 63)*   3050
MTZ-Ripo: Sulima; Skshinetskiy, Zrnanovic, Maltsev, Osipovich, Popel, Camara (Sitko 113), Kvaratskheaia, Tolkanitsa (Ryndyuk 60), Shchegrikovich D (Shchegrikovich S 70), Eremchuk.
Sutjeska: Giljen; Dzeverdanovic N (Vukovic 75), Dubljevic, Dikanovic, Delic, Bulatovic, Medjedcvic, Bulajic (Dzeverdanovic M 117), Zvicer, Todorovic (Banda 111), Adrovic.
aet.

Okzhetpes (0) 0
Zimbru (2) 2 *(Andronic O 16, Andronic G 19)*   3500
Okzhetpes: Satubaldin; Keker, Kuznetsov, Pischulin, Aliyev (Ledenev 79), Chonkaev, Karakulov (Dyak 60), Mokrousov (Maymakov 70), Nurgaliyev, Bekmukhayev, Dosmanbetov.
Zimbru: Chririnciuc; Andronic I, Erhan, Ternavschi, Andronic G (Onila 75), Hvorosteanov, Antoniuc (Sidorenco 67), Clonin, Demerji, Sofroni, Andronic O.

Polonia (0) 0
Buducnost (0) 1 *(Vukovic 51)*   5500
Polonia: Przyrowski; Mynar, Skrzynski, Koziol, Jodlowiec, Sokolowski (Mierzejewski 68), Zasada, Lato, Majewski, Sarvas (Piatek 89), Ivanovski (Chalbinski 60).
Buducnost: Vujadinovic; Vukcevic N (Durisic 87), Radulovic, Visnjic, Ajkovic, Brnovic, Vukccvic P, Kumedor■, Boskovic (Delic 74), Vukovic, Becirai (Vesovic 81).

Renova (1) 1 *(Ibraimi 12)*
Dynamo Minsk (1) 1 *(Kislyak 38 (pen))*   4000
Renova: Kovacevic; Statovci, Memedi, Despotovski, Ibraimi, Stojanov, Emini, Nuhiu, Aliju, Angejlovski (Gashi 56) (Ademi 87), Ismaili (Gafuri 81).
Dynamo Minsk: Gorbunov; Pavlyukovich, Mcntaroup, Veretilo, Saraba, Gurenko, Chuhley, Kislyak (Mbanangoye 51), Putilo (Strakanovich 62), Shkabara (Gigevich 31), Lebedev.

Rosenborg (1) 3 *(Iversen 40, Konan 89 (pen), Olsen 90)*
NSI Runavik (1) 1 *(Potemkin 6)*   5654
Rosenborg: Jarstein; Lago, Nordvik, Miller, Annan (Tettey 65), Strand, Olsen, Skjelbred (Traore 76), Konan, Iversen (Sellin 65), Zahora.
NSI Runavik: Joensen M; Hansen O, Davidsen, Hansen E, Hansen J, Eltorr, Petersen, Lokin (Joensen J 89), Potemkin (Olsen 70), Frederiksberg, Jacobsen (Mortensen 61).

Rudar (1) 3 *(Cipot 28, 73, Mahmutovic 70)*
Trans (0) 1 *(Starovoitov 74)*   2000
Rudar: Savic; Sulejmanovic, Cipot, Golob, Kolsi, Trifkovic, Pokleka, Tolimir (Grbic 46), Dedic, Prasnikar (Mahmutovic 65), Omladic (Mujakovic 46).
Trans: Stonys; Gorskov, Rimas, Lepik, Kazakov (Leontovich 75), Tarassenkov, Bazyukin (Ratnikov D 67), Kitto, Ratnikov E, Starovoitov (Éder 76), Losanov.

Siroki (0) 0
Banants (0) 1 *(Balabekian 87)*   4000
Siroki: Maric; Renato, Topic, Wagner Lago, Barisic, Silic, Diogo (Brekalo 64), Ivankovic, Martinovic, Peraica (Pinjuh 89), Zovko (Ljubic 77).
Banants: Ghazarian; Nazarenko, Khachatrian, Kakosian, Romanenko (Oseian 83), Voskanian, Kasule, Mkhitarian, Gyozalian (Balabekian 83), Dashian, Melkonian (Nasibian 85).

The New Saints (1) 1 *(Evans 11)*
Fram (1) 2 *(Ormarsson 16, Tillen S 66 (pen))*   933
The New Saints: Harrison; Marriott, Holmes T, Evans, Baker, Holmes D, Hogan, Ruscoe, Williams (Berkeley 74), Jones C (Sergeant 70), Darlington (Wood 70).
Fram: Halldorsson; Hauksson, Tillen S, Fjoluson, McShane, Olason, Jonsson (Olafsson 90), Gudmundsson, Juliusson (Tillen J 87), Thorarinsson, Ormarsson (Bjornsson 82).

Vetra (3) 3 *(Huss 18 (og), Kijanskas 33, Vezevicius 37)*
Grevenmacher (0) 0   800
Vetra: Valinicius; Borovskij, Kijanskas, Jankauskas, Paulauskas, Stanaitis, Moroz (Kulbis 61), Masitsev, Vezevicius (Eliosius 65), Razanauskas, Grigaitis (Vasiliauskas 82).
Grevenmacher: Diederich; Schmitt (Omerovic 77), Habte, Maric, Heinz, Lorig, Miriem (Stojadinovic 64), Huss, Tejerina, Hoffmann, Muller (Boussi 72).

Vllaznia (1) 1 *(Shtubina 43)*
Sligo Rovers (0) 1 *(Keane 87)*   5000
Vllaznia: Olsi; Mrvaljevic, Belisha, Hallaci, Beqiri (Basic 61), Smajlaj, Shtubina, Kasapi (Sykaj 90), Nallbani, Sinani■, Balaj (Nika 64).
Sligo Rovers: Brush; Holmes, Ventre, Keane, Feeney, Doherty (Morrison 66), Cretaro, Boco, Ryan, O'Grady■, Cash (Kelly 57).

Zestafoni (4) 6 *(Dvali 5, 39, 42, Gelashvili 44, Benashvili 86, 90)*
Lisburn Distillery (0) 0   3100
Zestafoni: Mamaladze; Lobjanidze, Oniani, Khidesheli, Eliava (Benashvili 46), Daushvili (Makaryan 46), Dzaria (Gorgiashvili 60), Aphtsiauri, Grigalashvili, Gelashvili, Dvali.
Lisburn Distillery: Murphy; McShane, Thompson S, Simpson, Callaghan, Melaugh, Gilmartin, Whelan, Kingsberry (Shaw 46), Browne (Corey 46), Armour (Thompson G 73).

SECOND QUALIFYING ROUND FIRST LEG

Tuesday, 14 July 2009

Crusaders (0) 1 *(Rainey 90)*
Rabotnicki (0) 1 *(Bozinovski B 47)*   950
Crusaders: Keenan; McKeown, Magowan, Coates■, McBride, McCann, Doherty (Black 74), Donnelly, Morrow (Owens 63), Dickson, Rainey.
Rabotnicki: Naumovski■; Bojovic, Bozinovski V, Ristov, Sekulovski, Bozinovski B, Savic, Todorovski, Muarem (Carlos 70), Gligorov, Wandeir.

Sliema Wanderers (0) 0
Maccabi Netanya (0) 0   500
Sliema Wanderers: Agius; Muscat (Mintoff 58), Azzopardi, Mifsud[*], Dronca, Fenech, Scerri, Triganza (Baldacchino 74), Ciantar, Woods, Failla (Bartolo 80).
Maccabi Netanya: Lifshitz; Haymovich, Saban, Dgani, Gazal, Cohen, Samia, Menashe, Sabaa, Yampolsky (Weisberg 71), Mugrabi (Gueta 53).

Thursday, 16 July 2009
Aalborg (0) 0
Slavija (0) 0   9175
Aalborg: Zaza; Jakobsen, Gaardsoe, Nielsen, Chanko, Due, Johansson, Enevoldsen (Christensen 70), Curth (Holm 79), Tracy (Dalsgaard 67), Kristensen.
Slavija: Lucic; Lackanovic, Regoje, Stankovic, Simic (Nikolic 88), Radonja, Arsenievic, Todorovic (Radovanovic 57), Kutalija, Scepanovic, Djermanovic (Seslija 75).

Anorthosis (2) 2 _(Fernandes 12, Laban 15)_
Petrovac (0) 1 _(Lakic 84)_   8500
Anorthosis: Supic; Katsavakis, Leiwakabessy, Martins, Constantinou, Skopelitis, Fernandes, Laban, Cristovao (Sosin 72), Cafu, Agali (Frousos 62).
Petrovac: Braic; Radulovic, Graovac, Mikijelj, Lakic, Obradovic, Lopicic, Radovic (Raicevic 46), Dragicevic, Divanovic (Boljevic 89), Duraskovic (Rotkovic 65).

Basle (1) 3 _(Sahin 23, Streller 48, Almerares 59)_
Santa Coloma (0) 0   25,038
Basle: Costanzo; Cagdas, Safari (Shaqiri 68), Inkoom, Ferati, Sahin, Huggel (Gelabert 80), Stocker, Da Silva, Streller (Mustafi 72), Almerares.
Santa Coloma: Fernandez R; Fernandez J, Albanell, Rodriguez V, Leonel Maciel (Maicon Dos Santos 64), Gil, Ayala, Sanchez A, Alvarez, Garcia (Rodriguez A 83), Urbani (Sanchez J 51).

Bnei Yehuda (2) 4 _(Galvan 25, Mori 38, Atar 67, Zhairi 90)_
Dinaburg (0) 0   2500
Bnei Yehuda: Aiyenugba; Mori, Garrido, Raly, Baldout (Imses 78), Radi (Biton 64), Zhairi, Atar, Galvan (Azuz 83), Abu Zaid, Edri.
Dinaburg: Davidovs; Simonov (Kortua 72), Gabov, Login, Krjauklis, Danilin, Afanasijev, Kuleshov, Sokolov, Guchashvili (Ri 56), Hong (Zizilev 46).

Brondby (0) 0
Flora (0) 1 _(Vanna 50)_   6926
Brondby: Andersen; Randrup (Jensen 26), Von Schlebrugge, Rasmussen T, Bischoff, Holmen, Nilsson, Farnerud, Krohn-Dehli, Kristiansen (Agger 65), Jallow (Madsen 84).
Flora: Aksalu; Rooba (Jurgenson 65), Vanna, Kams, Palatu, Kasimir, Vunk, Mosnikov (Kallaste 83), Anniste, Konsa, Zahovaiko (Dupikov 58).

Cherno More (1) 1 _(Manolov 44)_
Iskra-Stal (0) 0   3010
Cherno More: Pirgov; Lazarov M, Bachev (Petkov M 85), Coulibaly, Bornosuzov, Aleksandrov AD, Iliev (Georgiev 68), Yurukov, Aleksandrov A, Lazarov Z (Kakalov 65), Manolov.
Iskra-Stal: Gaiduchevici; Hausi, Feshchenko (Ochinca 86), Zhurka, Stakhiv, Tofan, Osipenco (Romaniuc 85), Rudac, Burcovshi, Stinga, Manaliu (Kilikevych 62).

Differdange (0) 1 _(Piskor 61)_
Rijeka (0) 0   1000
Differdange: Weber; Siebenaler, May, Janisch, Kintziger, Wagner, Soraire, Lebresne, Joachim (Kettenmeyer 61), Mendes (Diop 76), Piskor (Pace 79).
Rijeka: Radman; Cagalj, Cejvanovic, Krizman (Kreilach 81), Budicin, Tadejevic, Anas Sharbini, Strok (Smith 68), Pamic, Fernandez, Ahmad Sharbini.

Dynamo Minsk (0) 0
Tromso (0) 0   4500
Dynamo Minsk: Canovic; Montaroup, Veretilo, Martynovich, Saraba, Gurenko, Dragun (Gigevich 53), Chuhley (Putilo 71), Kislyak, Mbanangoye, Lebedev (Gavryushko 71).
Tromso: Sahlman; Reginiussen T, Larsen, Hogli, Jenssen, Strand (Knudsen 65), Knarvik (Haugen 30), Lindpere (Reginiussen M 86), Sequeira, Moldskred, Rushfeldt.

Elfsborg (0) 3 _(Anders Svensson 61, Ishizaki 83, Avdic 90)_
Szombathelyi (0) 0   3187
Elfsborg: Covic; Floren M, Karlsson, Mobaek, Wikstrom, Lucic, Danielsson, Anders Svensson (Nordmark 88), Ericsson (Ishizaki 46), Bajrami, Keene (Avdic 72).
Szombathelyi: Rozsa; Guzmics, Kuttor, Nagy, Irhas (Lattenstein 67), Toth, Molnar, Schimmer (Csontos 87), Iszlai, Oross, Skriba (Ugrai 66).

Falkirk (0) 1 _(Flynn 50)_
Vaduz (0) 0   5763
Falkirk: Olejnik; Barr, Scobbie, Twaddle, McNamara, McLean, O'Brien, Arfield, Flynn (Mitchell 75), Finnigan (Robertson 77), McDonald (Sludden 89).
Vaduz: Jehle; Steil, Stuckmann (Sutter 84), Cerrone, Stegmayer, Bellon, Koitka (Franjic 79), Burgmeier, Noll, Colocci, Proschwitz.

Flamurtari (0) 1 _(Strati 66)_
Motherwell (0) 0   4012
Flamurtari: Mocka; Guga, Begaj, Veliu, Strati, Beqiri, Alviz, Mema (Galica 78), Ngjele (Beck 46), Zeqiri, Shehaj (Roshi 37).
Motherwell: Fraser; Hammell, Reynolds, Craigan, Saunders (Page 40), Lasley, Forbes (Murphy 75), Sutton, O'Brien, McGarry (Fitzpatrick 65), Slane.

Gorica (1) 1 _(Krsic 38)_
Lahti (0) 0   1800
Gorica: Simcic; Balazic, Dukic, Gorinsek, Krsic (Cvijanovic 63), Skarabot, Demirovic, Rakuscek, Velikonja (Zigon 90), Galesic, Osterc (Arcon 87).
Lahti: Szentpeteri; Toivomaki, Moilanen, Huuhka, Eerola, Fofana (Shala 88), Hietanen (Hieni 46), Vanninen, Korte, Rafael (Kemppinen 68), Litmanen.

Honka (1) 2 _(Perovuo 15, Schuller 74)_
Bangor City (0) 0   1668
Honka: Henriksson; Koskinen, Aalto, Koskimaa, Hakanpaa, Perovuo, Lepola (Vasara 46), Schuller, Vuorinen, Kokko (Puustinen 77), Savage (Otaru 89).
Bangor City: Smith; Johnston, Brewerton, Morley, Roberts, Hoy, Killackey, Limbert (Beattie 87), Stott, Sharp, Smyth (Edwards 77).

Juvenes/Dogana (0) 0
Polonia (1) 1 _(Kokosinski 2)_   519
Juvenes/Dogana: Montanari; Renzi, Marzocchi, Selva, Ceci, Rossi, Tasso, Perrotta, Galli, Nanni (Gasperoni 85), Gamberini.
Polonia: Przyrowski; Mynar, Koziol, Kokosinski, Jodlowiec, Mierzejewski (Piatek 85), Zasada, Lato, Majewski, Sarvas (Golebiewski 46), Ivanovski (Maka 57).

KR Reykjavik (0) 2 _(Sigurdsson B 55, Takefusa 90)_
Larissa (0) 0   1000
KR Reykjavik: Magnusson; Rutgers, Gudjonsson, Saevarsson, Fridgeirsson, Hauksson (Kristjansson 86), Benediktsson (Takefusa 72), Sigurdsson B, Jordao Diogo, Sigurdsson G, Jonsson (Gunnarsson 77).
Larissa: Seremet; Dabizas, Boukouvalas, Aarab, Tripotseris, Vlasopoulos (Labropoulos 59), Toema, Simic (Siatravanis 81), Romeu, Iglesias (Balis 66), Tsigas.

Legia (1) 3 _(Paluchowski 19, Kielbowicz 70, Szalachowski 82)_
Olimpi (0) 0   5000
Legia: Mucha; Szala, Choto, Astiz Ventura, Giza, Iwanski, Kielbowicz, Szalachowski (Borysiuk 83), Radovic (Rybus 46), Ostrowski, Paluchowski (Mieciel 71).

Olimpi: Alavidze; Gilauri, Machavariani (Lomidze 84), Alex Fraga, Gongadze, Seturidze, Dobrovolski, Chelidze Z, Chkhetiani (Chelidze G 61), Jonatas (Sirbiladze 84), Anderson Aquino.

Metalurg Donetsk (2) 3 *(Mguni 34, Mkhitarian 42, Godin 66)*

MTZ-Ripo (0) 0   4000

Metalurg Donetsk: Disljenkovic; Korotetskiy, Checher, China, Mario Sergio, Lazic, Makrides (Tanasa 87), Godin (Danilovskiy 83), Mguni, Mkhitarian, Ekeh (Volovyk 68).

MTZ-Ripo: Sulima; Zrnanovic, Osipovich, Popel, Kvaratskhelia (Sitko 84), Tolkanitsa, Shchegrikovich D, Maevysky (Maltsev 69), Eremchuk, Kharitonchik (Makas 60), Nicolas.

Metalurgs Liepajas (1) 2 *(Karlsons 41, Kirhners 54)*

Dinamo Tbilisi (0) 1 *(Khmaladze 68)*   3500

Metalurgs Liepajas: Spole; Klava, Zirnis, Ivanovs, Jemelins (Kastner 61), Kirhners, Rafalskis, Tamosaukas, Surnins, Karlsons, Grebis (Prohorenkovs 83).

Dinamo Tbilisi: Loria; Tomashvili, Nergadze, Kashia S, Kashia G, Koshkadze, Khmaladze, Merebashvili, Digmelashvili, Vatsadze, Djousse.

Milano (0) 0

Slaven (4) 4 *(Csizmadia 26, Vojnovic 39, 41, 44)*   1000

Milano: Markovski; Cecelija, Shabani B, Brando (Ziba 46), Bogatinov, Limani, Alimi, Aliji (Stojanovic 46), Aziri, Lazarev (Bejuli 66), Trajkovski.

Slaven: Rodic; Rogulj (Lapic 46), Bilen, Maras, Csizmadia, Poldrugac, Puric, Juric, Vojnovic (Poredski 77), Posavec (Safaric 56), Vrucina.

NAC Breda (1) 6 *(Kwakman 24, De Graaf 55, 70, Amoah 57, 61, Lurling 68)*

Gandzasar (0) 0   13,600

NAC Breda: Ten Rouwelaar; Feher, Schilder, Loran Kwakman, Gilissen (Van der Leegte 67), De Graaf (Cairo 71), Kolkka, Lurling, Amoah, Gorter (Snoyl 83).

Gandzasar: Bubuteishvili; Zakarian K, Aleksanian, Simonian (Hayrapetian 71), Tatintsian, Khachatrian, Khanishvili, Antonian, Marshavela (Davtian 58), Leandro Pinto, Avetisian (Sakhokia 64).

Naftan (1) 2 *(Degteryov 21, 66)*

Gent (0) 1 *(Maric 90)*   774⁷

Naftan: Kurskis; Gorbachyov, Politevich, Belousov, Verkhovtsov, Rudik, Degteryov (Zuev 72), Trukhov (Bukatkin 83), Yatskevich, Komarovsky, Stripelyks (Zyuleu 53).

Gent: Jorgacevic; Suler, Hanstveit, Wils, Smolders, Mariz, Grondin, Lepoint, Leye (El Ghanassy 63), Custovic, Ljubijankic.

Omonia (3) 4 *(Karipidis 4, Patsatzoglou 11, Zurawski 34, Efrem 85)*

HB Torshavn (0) 0   12,855

Omonia: Kotsolis; Rasheed Alabi, Karipidis, Caceres, Patsatzoglou, Davidson Morais, Bruno Aguiar, Kaseke (Grammozis 63), Zurawski (Efrem 83), Aloneftis, Christofi (Konstantinou 69).

HB Torshavn: Dawid; Lag, Kuljic, Dam, Olavsstovu (Nolsoe 77), Poulsen, Mortensen, Jespersen, Flotum, Jorgensen B (Joensen 74), Jorgensen P.

Rapid Vienna (1) 5 *(Hofmann 33 (pen), Jelavic 68, 74, Trimmel 83, Hoffer 86)*

Vllaznia (0) 0   13,300

Rapid Vienna: Payer; Patocka, Katzer, Eder, Dober, Heikkinen, Hofmann, Kavlak (Trimmel 74), Pehlivan (Drazan 29), Maierhofer (Jelavic 51), Hoffer.

Vllaznia: Olsi; Mrvaljevic, Osja, Belisha, Hallaci, Beciri, Smajalj, Kasapi (Vajushi 76), Nika, Nallbani, Balaj (Basic 87).

Rosenborg (0) 0

Karabakh (0) 0   6769

Rosenborg: Jarstein; Lustig, Dorsin, Stadsgaard, Lago, Annan (Strand 68), Olsen (Konan 68), Tettey, Skjelbred (Traore 83), Iversen, Prica.

Karabakh: Valiyev; Allahverdiev, Medvedev (Aliyev 89), Kerimov A (Yusifov 72), Teli, Rashad A Sadikhov, Mammadov E, Imamaliev (Gashimov 87), Rashad F Sadikhov, Nadirov, Dzavadov.

Rudar (0) 0

Red Star Belgrade (0) 1 *(Perovic 58)*   3000

Rudar: Savic, Sulejmanovic, Cipot, Golob, Kolsi (Djukic 61), Trifkovic (Grbic 57), Pokleka, Tolimir, Dedic, Prasnikar (Mesic 70), Omladic.

Red Star Belgrade: Pavlovic; Ignjatijevic, Tutoric, Dordevic, Ninkov, Savio, Lazetic (Cvetkovic 90), Issah, Bogdanovic (Nikolic 88), Lekic, Perovic (Jevtic 90).

Sarajevo (1) 1 *(Muminovic 14)*

Spartak Trnava (0) 0   8000

Sarajevo: Alaim; Dudo, Torlak, Rizvanovic, Belosevic, Hadzic (Pliska 90), Muminovic (Hamzagic 85), Dzakmic, Maksumic, Janjos, Jahovik (Avdic 75).

Spartak Trnava: Kralj; Jakubicka, Dolezaj, Prochazka, Duris (Zeleznik 89), Kopunek, Hruska (Danilo 69), Kozula, Gueye, Sukennik, Kozuch (Bernath 82).

Sevojno (0) 0

Kaunas (0) 0   500

Sevojno: Nikolic; Kamberovic, Bulatovic, Rakovic, Stanisavljevic, Jankovic, Maksimovic N (Jovicic 49), Viric, Sunjevaric (Timic 58), Pavicevic, Vujovic (Pejovic 83).

Kaunas: Vertelis L; Vaikasas, Andriuskevicius (Antonovas 55), Fridrikas, Vicius, Vertelis A, Mikklinevicius (Paulius 82), Kochanauskas (Smaryginas 27), Razulis, Cinikas, Pehlic.

Sigma Olomouc (0) 1 *(Rossi 89)*

Fram (1) 1 *(Fjoluson 21)*   5719

Sigma Olomouc: Drobisz; Dreksa, Skerle, Horava (Murin 87), Kascak, Onofrej, Rossi, Otepka, Petr (Hubnik 56), Janotka, Sultes (Caihame 75).

Fram: Halldorsson; Hauksson, Tillen S, Fjoluson, McShane (Tillen J 61), Olason, Jonsson, Gudmundsson, Juliusson, Thorarinsson (Bjornsson 75), Ormarsson (Magnusson 85).

Skonto Riga (1) 1 *(Kozlovs 17)*

Derry City (1) 1 *(McManus 44)*   1950

Skonto Riga: Malins; Hscanovics, Laizans (Agafonovs 77), Juniors, Smirnovs, Golubevs, Gamezardashvili, Kozlovs, Fertovs, Semjonovs (Cauna 62), Tarasovs.

Derry City: Doherty; Hutton, Gray (McCallion 81), O'Brien, Delaney, Higgins, Martyn, McGlynn, Molloy, Farren (Stewart 87), McManus (Morrow 81).

St Patrick's Ath (1) 1 *(O'Brien 38)*

Valletta (0) 1 *(Agius G 65)*   2000

St Patrick's Ath: Rogers; Partridge, Harris, Stevens, Maher, Byrne, Cawley, Ryan B (Fitzpatrick 70), O'Connor, Guy, O'Brien.

Valletta: Hogg; Dimech, Bezzina, Scicluna, Briffa, Pace, Falzon (Sammit 77), Cruyff, Agius G, Den Ouden (Agius E 90), Priso.

Steaua (0) 2 *(Surdu 46, Stancu 71)*

Ujpest (0) 0   19,003

Steaua: Tatarusanu; Goian, Marin, Ghionea, Ninu, Szekely, Toja (Ionescu 83), Ochirosii (Stancu 46), Onicas, Kapetanos, Surdu (Grzelak 88).

Ujpest: Balajcza; Dudic, Lambulic, Vermes, Vasko, Pollak, Sandor, Stokes, Korcsmar, Rajczi (Tisza 81), Kabat.

Sturm Graz (2) 2 *(Haas 11, Holzl 37)*
Siroki (0) 1 *(Ljubic 67)* 10,300
Sturm Graz: Gratzei; Lamotte, Sonnleitner, Feldhofer, Kandelaki, Hlinka, Holzl, Muratovic (Weber 67), Kienzl (Beichler 74), Haas, Jantscher.
Siroki: Maric; Renato, Topic, Wagner Lago, Martinez (Ivankovic 63), Barisic, Ljubic (Krizanovic 75), Silic, Diogo, Martinovic, Peraica (Varea 53).

Suduva (0) 0
Randers (1) 1 *(Beckmann 23)* 3500
Suduva: Klevinskas; Skroblas, Skinderis, Radavicius, Slavickas G (Zagurskas 88), Kozyuberda, Leimonas, Urbsys, Slavickas V, Gardzijauskas (Brokas 46), Luksys.
Randers: Stuhr-Ellegaard; Ahmed, Jepsen, Fenger, Lorentzen (Damborg 82), Pedersen S, Grahn, Beckmann (Konig 76), Pedersen K, Sane (Olsen 68), Berg.

Tobol (1) 1 *(Zhumaskaliyev 2)*
Galatasaray (0) 1 *(Baros 58)* 8320
Tobol: Petukhov; Chelyadinski, Irismetov, Mukanov, Nurgaliev (Baltiyev 70), Zhumaskaliyev (Dimitrov 83), Skorykh, Kharabara, Yakovlev, Golban, Bairamov (Alekperzade 89).
Galatasaray: Orkun; Gokhan, Sabri, Erdem■, Servet, Aydin (Yugur 75), Baris (Arda 46), Mustafa, Yaser, Ayhan, Erhan (Baros 46).

Vetra (0) 0
HJK Helsinki (1) 1 *(Bah 15)* 1200
Vetra: Valinicius; Borovskij, Kijanskas, Jankauskas, Paulauskas, Stanaitis (Ngapounou 56), Masitsev, Vezevicius, Razanauskas, Grigaitis (Moroz 25) (Vasiliauskas 76), Grigalevicius.
HJK Helsinki: Wallen; Hauhia, Sauso, Karkkainen, Raitala, Kamara, Fowler, Sorsa (Taulo 88), Parikka (Popovitch 74), Bah, Pelvas (Makela 61).

Zestafoni (0) 1 *(Benashvili 70)*
Helsingborg (0) 2 *(Jonsson 62, Larsson H 89)* 4100
Zestafoni: Mamaladze; Lobjanidze, Oniani, Khidesheli, Eliava, Daushvili, Dzaria (Benashvili 68), Aphisiauri (Kvakhvadze 85), Grigalashvili, Gelashvili, Dvali (Ionanidze 80).
Helsingborg: Hansson; Tamboura, Andersson C, Wahlstedt, Nilsson, Landgren, Lantz (Skulason 83), Ekstrand, Makondele (Holgersson 80), Larsson H, Jonsson (Unkuri 83).

Zilina (0) 2 *(Oravec 57, Lietava 77)*
Dacia (0) 0 3454
Zilina: Pernis; Angelovic, Guldan, Piacek, Sourek, Mraz, Kobylik (Babatounde 89), Jez, Zlatkovic (Zilak 76), Adauto (Lietava 56), Oravec.
Dacia: Matiughin; Mekang, Negrescu, Caraulan, Demchenko (Buza 85), Bulat, Grosev, Trinitatski, Zgura (Popovici 84), Orbu, Sackey.

Zimbru (0) 0
Pacos de Ferreira (0) 0 7000
Zimbru: Chririnciuc; Andronic I, Erhan, Ternavschi, Andronic G (Onila 74), Hvorosteanov, Antoniuc (Sidorenco 71), Clonin, Demerji (Catan 87), Sofroni, Andronic O.
Pacos de Ferreira: Cassio; Ozeia, Jorginho, Berville, Ricardo, Carlitos (Baiano 90), Pedrinha, William (Torres 86), Leonel Olimpio, Felipe Anunciacao, Leandrinho (Rondon 90).

SECOND QUALIFYING ROUND SECOND LEG

Thursday, 23 July 2009
Bangor City (0) 0
Honka (1) 1 *(Puustinen 39)* 602
Bangor City: Smith; Johnston, Brewerton (Williams 78), Morley, Roberts, Hoy, Killackey, Limbert (Edwards 59), Stott, Sharp (Davies 60), Smyth.
Honka: Henriksson; Koskinen (Haarala 69), Aalto, Koskimaa, Hakanpaa, Perovuo, Schuller, Vuorinen (Kokko 77), Puustinen, Vasara, Savage (Otaru 61).
at Wrexham.

Dacia (0) 0
Zilina (0) 1 *(Oravec 47)* 2500
Dacia: Mosneaga; Mekang, Negrescu (Buza 65), Onica, Demchenko (Zgura 61), Bulat, Grosev (Popovici 46), Caraulan, Trinitatski■, Orbu, Sackey.
Zilina: Pernis; Angelovic, Guldan, Leitner (Zlatkovic 69), Piacek, Sourek, Zilak, Mraz, Kobylik (Adauto 63), Jez, Oravec (Lietava 79).

Derry City (0) 1 *(Deery 57)*
Skonto Riga (0) 0 2500
Derry City: Doherty; McCallion, Hutton, O'Brien, Delaney, McGlynn (Scullion 89), Deery, Molloy, Morrow (Higgins 50), Stewart (Farren 75), McManus.
Skonto Riga: Malins; Hscanovics, Juniors (Agafonovs 84), Smirnovs, Golubevs, Gamezardashvili, Kozlovs, Fertovs (Mingazovs 66), Tarasovs (Laizans 69), Cauna, Blanks.

Dinaburg (0) 0
Bnei Yehuda (1) 1 *(Atar 32)* 850
Dinaburg: Federov; Simonov (Denisevic 59), Gabov, Login (Kortua 63), Kryauklis, Danilin, Afanasijev, Kuleshov, Sokolov, Kokin (Kovaljovs 46), Hong.
Bnei Yehuda: Aiyenugba; Garrido, Azuz, Haddad, Baldout, Rady, Atar (Imses 56), Galvan (Hatari 74), Abu Zaid (Aharonovich 65), Biton, Edri.

Dinamo Tbilisi (1) 3 *(Merebashvili 18, 63, Kashia S 53)*
Metalurgs Liepajas (0) 1 *(Rafalskis 49)* 5000
Dinamo Tbilisi: Loria; Tomashvili, Nergadze, Kashia S, Kashia G, Koshkadze (Lomia 56), Khmaladze, Merebashvili, Digmelashvili, Vatsadze (Kakubava 90), Djousse (Akieremy 71).
Metalurgs Liepajas: Spole; Klava (Prohorenkovs 70), Zirnis (Rakels 87), Ivanovs, Jemelins (Kastner 72), Kirhners, Rafalskis, Tamosauskas, Surnins, Karlsons, Grebis.

Flora (0) 1 *(Kasimir 80)*
Brondby (3) 4 *(Jallow 28, Farnerud 35, Holmen 45, Kristiansen 90)* 3000
Flora: Aksalu; Rooba (Kallaste 46), Vanna, Palatu, Kasimir, Vunk, Jurgenson, Anniste (Tamm 70), Konsa, Anier, Zahovaiko (Dupikov 70).
Brondby: Andersen; Von Schlebrugge, Jonsson, Rasmussen T (Frederiksen 54), Bischoff, Holmen (Kristiansen 73), Nilsson, Farnerud (Agger 62), Krohn-Dehli, Jensen, Jallow.

Fram (0) 1 *(Kasimir 80)*
Sigma Olomouc (0) 2 *(Hubnik 47, Otepka 58)* 1226
Fram: Halldorsson; Hauksson, Helgason, Tillen S, Fjoluson, McShane, Olason (Gudmundsson 68), Jonsson, Juliusson, Thorarinsson, Ormarsson.
Sigma Olomouc: Drobisz; Dreksa, Skerle, Horava (Veprek 88), Kascak (Bajer 80), Onofrej, Rossi, Otepka, Hubnik (Caihame 73), Janotka, Sultes.

Galatasaray (0) 2 *(Mustafa 63, Servet 90)*
Tobol (0) 0 22,000
Galatasaray: Orkun; Gokhan, Hakan Balta, Sabri, Servet, Arda, Mustafa, Yaser (Kewell 46), Ayhan, Serdar (Linderoth 57), Baros (Nonda 90).
Tobol: Petukhov; Chelyadinski, Irismetov, Mukanov, Nurgaliev, Zhumaskaliev (Aubarkov 87), Skorykh, Kharabara, Yakovlev, Golban (Baltiev 70), Bairamov (Alekperzadze 84).

Gandzasar (0) 0
NAC Breda (2) 2 *(Lurling 14, De Graaf 34)* 1000
Gandzasar: Bubuteishvili; Zakarian K, Aleksanian, Simonian (Hayrapetian 55), Tatintsian, Khachatrian■, Khanishvili, Antonian, Marshavela (Sakhokia 62), Davtian, Avetisian (Avagian 73).
NAC Breda: Ten Rouwelaar; Zwaanswijk, Feher, Schilder, Loran, Gilissen (Kwakman 53), De Graaf (Reuser 72), Snoyl (Gorter 61), Lurling, Amoah, Cairo.

Gent (0) 1 *(El Ghanassy 54)*
Naftan (0) 0 6620
Gent: Jorgacevic; Suler, Hanstveit, Wils, Smolders, Azofeifa (Duarte 85), Maric (Custovic 90), Grondin, Lepoint, El Ghanassy (Leye 79), Ljubijankic.
Naftan: Kurskis; Gorbachyov, Politevich, Belousov, Verkhovtsov, Rudik, Degteryov (Volodenkov 74), Trukhov, Yatskevich (Zyuleu 58), Komarovsky, Stripykis (Zuev 61).

Haladas (0) 0
Elfsborg (0) 0 2000
Haladas: Rozsa; Guzmics, Kuttor, Nagy, Irhas (Lattenstein 73), Toth, Molnar, Schimmer, Iszlai, Oross (Simon 70), Skriba (Csontos 89).
Elfsborg: Covic; Floren M, Karlsson, Mobaeck, Wikstrom, Lucic (Andersson 84), Danielsson, Anders Svensson (Floren J 84), Nordmark, Ishizaki, Avdic (Johansson 73).

HB Torshavn (0) 1 *(Jespersen 56)*
Omonia (1) 4 *(Konstantinou 27, 66, 78, Wenzel 90)* 370
HB Torshavn: Dawid; Nolsoe, Kuljic (Poulsen 83), Darr, Benjaminsen, Mouritsen (Nielsen 70), Mortenser, Jespersen, Flotum, Jorgensen P, Joensen (Jorgensen B 67.
Omonia: Kotsolis; Wenzel, Karipidis, Pantic, Efrem, Zlogar, Bruno Aguiar, Kaseke (Panagi 684, Charalambous, Konstantinou, Christofi (Kyriakos 60).

Helsingborg (0) 2 *(Ekstrand 90, Sundin 100)*
Zestafoni (2) 2 *(Dvali 29, Gelashvili 32)* 2580
Helsingborg: Hansson; Andersson C, Wahlstedt, Nilsson, Landgren (Skulason 46), Lantz (Bergholtz 8+), Holgersson, Ekstrand, Makondele (Sundin 64), Larsson H, Jonsson.
Zestafoni: Mamaladze; Lobjanidze, Oniani, Khidesheli, Eliava, Daushvili (Tskhadaia 84), Dzaria (Benashvili 74), Aphtsiauri, Grigalashvili, Gelashvili (Kvakhvadze 50), Dvali.
aet.

HJK Helsinki (1) 1 *(Kamara 3)*
Vetra (2) 3 *(Grigalevicius 28, Jankauskas 30, Moroz 81)* 4261
HJK Helsinki: Wallen; Hauhia (Popovitch 79), Sarso, Karkkainen, Raitala, Kamara, Fowler, Sorsa, Parikka (Oravainen 66), Bah, Pelvas (Makela 46).
Vetra: Valinicius; Borovskij, Kijanskas, Jankauskas, Ngapounou, Paulauskas, Masitsev, Vezevicius (Elicsius 57), Razanauskas, Vasiliauskas (Stanaitis 88), Grigalevicius (Moroz 69).

Iskra-Stal (0) 0
Cherno More (1) 3 *(Manolov 25, 54, Georgiev 60)* 3175
Iskra-Stal: Gaiduchevici; Hausi, Feshchenko (Ochinca 53), Zhurca, Stakhiv, Tofan, Osipenco, Rudac (Romaniuc 62), Kilikevych (Manaliu 57), Burcovshi, Stinga.
Cherno More: Pirgov; Lazarov M (Dyakov 61), Bachev, Coulibaly, Dimov (Petkov M 66), Aleksandrov AD, Iliev, Georgiev, Yurukov (Stoyanov 58), Aleksandrov A, Manolov.

Karabakh (1) 1 *(Rashad F Sadikhov 45)*
Rosenborg (0) 0 29,858
Karabakh: Valiyev; Allahverdiev, Medvedev, Kerimov A (Yusifov 68), Teli, Rashad A Sadikhov, Mammadov E (Gashimov 74), Imamaliev (Aliyev 84), Rashad F Sadikhov, Nadirov, Dzavadov.
Rosenborg: Jarstein; Lustig, Dorsin, Stadsgaard, Lago, Annan, Tettey (Miller 86), Skjelbred (Zahora 76), Konan (Olsen 46), Iversen, Prica.

Kaunas (0) 1 *(Fridrikas 76)*
Sevojno (0) 1 *(Vujovic 48)* 1500
Kaunas: Vertelis L; Vaikasas, Rackus (Smarygicas 71), Andriuskevicius (Juozaitis 82), Fridrikas, Vicus, Vertelis A, Miklinevicius, Razulis (Macezinskas 66), Cinikas, Pehlic.
Sevojno: Nikolic; Kamberovic, Bulatovic, Rakovic, Stanisavljevic, Jankovic, Viric (Sunjevaric 70), Jovicic, Pavicevic, Vujovic, Timic (Maksimovic N 86).

Lahti (0) 2 *(Litmanen 66, Rafael 79)*
Gorica (0) 0 4118
Lahti: Szentpeteri; Toivomaki, Moilanen, Huuhka, Eerola, Fofana (Heini 74), Hietanen (Shala 64), Vanninen, Korte, Rafael (Kemppinen 85), Litmanen.
Gorica: Simcic; Balazic, Dukic, Gorinsek, Krsic, Skarabot, Demirovic, Rakuscek, Velikonja, Galesic, Osterc.

Larissa (1) 1 *(Tsigas 28)*
KR Reykjavik (0) 1 *(Sigurdsson G 75)* 6000
Larissa: Malarz; Dabizas, Boukouvalas, Aarab, Tripotseris, Vlasopoulos (Siatravanis 76), Toema (Muller 83), Metin, Simic (Labropoulos 70), Romeu, Tsigas.
KR Reykjavik: Magnusson; Rutgers, Gudjonsson, Saevarsson, Fridgeirsson, Hauksson, Benediktsson (Takefusa 46), Sigurdsson B (Gunnarsson 86), Jordao Diogo, Sigurdsson G, Jonsson (Jonasson 86).

Maccabi Netanya (0) 3 *(Samia 58, Ezra 83, Sabaa 89)*
Sliema Wanderers (0) 0 500
Maccabi Netanya: Lifshitz; Haymovich, Saban, Dgani, Gazal, Cohen, Gueta, Samia, Menashe (Messika 86), Sabaa, Yampolsky (Ezra 82).
Sliema Wanderers: Agius; Muscat, Azzopardi, Dronca, Baldacchino, Ciantar (Turner 85), Fenech, Scerri, Triganza, Woods, Faillia (Mintoff 79).

Motherwell (6) 8 *(Murphy 16, 19, 34, Slane 25, Forbes 28 (pen), 50, Hutchinson 38, McHugh 72)*
Flamurtari (0) 1 *(Roshi 65)* 4641
Motherwell: Fraser; Reynolds, Craigan, Humphrey (McHugh 67), Jennings (Lasley 68), Forbes, Hutchinson, Sutton, Murphy, O'Brien, Slane (Page 77).
Flamurtari: Mocka; Sakaj, Guga, Begaj, Veliu, Strati, Beqiri (Roshi 38), Alviz, Mema (Galica 46), Ngjele (Shehaj 46), Zeqiri.

MTZ-Ripo (1) 1 *(Nicolas 16)*
Metalurg Donetsk (1) 2 *(Mguni 36, Mkhitarian 85)* 1000
MTZ-Ripo: Sulima; Zrnanovic (Maltsev 46), Osipovich, Camara (Kharitonchik 66), Kvaratskhelia, Tolkanitsa, Shchegrikovich D, Maevyski, Eremchuk, Kendysh (Makas 76), Nicolas.
Metalurg Donetsk: Vorobyov; Korotetskiy (Bilozor 70), Checher, Volovyk, Mario Sergio, Lazic, Makrides, Godin, Mguni (Tanasa 67), Mkhitarian, Ekeh (Tkachenko 81).

Olimpi (0) 0
Legia (1) 1 *(Szalachowski 8)* 3000
Olimpi: Alavidze; Gilauri, Machavariani, Alex Fraga, Gongadze (Geronimo 46), Babunashvili, Seturidze, Dobrovolski, Jonatas, Choco (Chelidze Z 61), Anderson Aquino.
Legia: Mucha; Szala, Choto (Rezzniczak 83), Astiz Ventura, Giza, Iwanski, Kielbowicz, Szalachowski (Borysiuk 46), Rybus, Ostrowski, Paluchowski (Mieciel 59).

Pacos de Ferreira (0) 1 *(Cristiano 84)*
Zimbru (0) 0 1658
Pacos de Ferreira: Cassio; Ozeia (Manuel Jose 77), Jorginho (Pedro Queiros 90), Berville, Ricardo, Carlitos, Pedrinha, Leonel Olimpio, Felipe Anunciacao, Leandrinho (Cristiano 64), Torres.
Zimbru: Chririnciuc; Andronic I, Erhan, Ternavschi, Andronic G (Onila 72), Hvorosteanov, Antoniuc, Clonin (Secrieru 90), Demerji, Sofroni (Sidorenco 61), Andronic O.

Petrovac (1) 3 *(Dragicevic 15, Rotkovic 77, 103)*
Anorthosis (1) 1 *(Katsavakis 45)* 2500
Petrovac: Braic; Radulovic (Raicevic 73), Graovac, Mikijelj, Lakic, Obradovic, Lopicic, Radovic, Dragicevic (Boljevic 113), Divanovic, Duraskovic (Rotkovic 62).
Anorthosis: Supic; Katsavakis, Dellas (Cristovao 95), Leiwakabessy, Martins, Constantinou, Skopelitis, Fernandes (Marangos 71), Laban, Cafu, Agali (Sosin 106).
aet.

Polonia (2) 4 *(Sarvas 10, 66, Mierzejewski 45, Chalbinski 54)*
Juvenes/Dogana (0) 0 3655
Polonia: Przyrowski; Mynar (Piatek 46), Koziol (Tralka 56), Kokosinski, Jodlowiec, Mierzejewski, Zasada, Lato (Golebiewski 56), Sarvas, Chalbinski, Maka.
Juvenes/Dogana: Montanari; Renzi, Marzocchi, Gasperoni (Nanni 46), Selva, Ceci, Rossi, Tasso, Perrotta, Galli, Gamberini (Fantini 50).

Rabotnicki (2) 4 *(Bozinovski B 20, Ze Carlos 35, 79, Petkovski 84)*
Crusaders (0) 2 *(Owens 69, Donnelly 90)* 1900
Rabotnicki: Bogatinov; Bojovic, Bozinovski V, Ristov, Sekulovski, Bozinovski B, Savic (Petkovski■ 67), Ze Carlos (Muarem 79), Todorovski, Gligorov, Wandeir (Carlos 84).
Crusaders: Keenan; McKeown, Black (Caddell 67), Magowan, Magee (Rainey 46), McBride, McCann, Doherty, Donnelly, Morrow (Owens 46), Dickson.

Randers (1) 1 *(Leimonas 17 (og))*
Suduva (0) 1 *(Luksys 58)* 3227
Randers: Stuhr-Ellegaard; Da Cruz, Jepsen, Fenger, Lorentzen, Pedersen S, Grahn (Damborg 82), Pedersen K, Sane (Olsen 71), Berg, Nygaard (Beckmann 58).
Suduva: Klevinskas; Skroblas, Skinderis, Radavicius, Slavickas G (Brokas 71), Kozyuberda, Leimonas, Urbsys (Krasnovkis 81), Slavickas V, Gardzijauskas (Zagurskas 76), Luksys.

Red Star Belgrade (1) 4 *(Bogdanovic 37, Jevtic 74, 90, Cadu 85)*
Rudar (0) 0 25,000
Red Star Belgrade: Pavlovic; Ignajatijevic, Tutoric, Dordevic, Ninkov, Savio, Lazetic (Cadu 76), Issah, Bogdanovic (Nikolic 80), Lekic, Perovic (Jevtic 69).
Rudar: Savic; Sulejmanovic, Cipot, Stojnic (Jesenicnik 53), Golob, Kolsi (Renato 46), Pokleka, Tolimir, Mesic, Prasnikar (Trifkovic 42), Omladic.

Rijeka (2) 3 *(Ceric 20, Anas Sharbini 24, Ahmad Sharbini 64)*
Differdange (0) 0 5000
Rijeka: Mance; Cagalj, Krizman (Matko 77), Budicin, Ceric, Landeka, Anas Sharbini, Strok (Kreilach 69), Pamic, Fernandez (Smith 86), Ahmad Sharbini.
Differdange: Weber; Siebenaler, May (Diop 54), Kettenmeyer (Pace 66), Janisch, Kintziger, Wagner, Soraire, Lebresne, Joachim, Mendes (Piskor 46).

Santa Coloma (1) 1 *(Maicon Dos Santos 43 (pen))*
Basle (3) 4 *(Streller 12, Gelabert 15, Alvarez 40 (og), Almerares 88)* 900
Santa Coloma: Serrano; Fernandez J, Albanell, Rodriguez V (Aguirre 49), Leonel Maciel, Gil, Ayala, Maicon Dos Santos (Da Cunha 76), Alvarez, Garcia, Urbani (Guida 72).
Basle: Costanzo; Ritter, Safari, Sahin (Stocker 71), Gelabert (Da Silva 51), Huggel, Perovic, Shaqiri, Cabral, Aratore, Streller (Almerares 46).

Siroki (0) 1 *(Silic 64)*
Sturm Graz (1) 1 *(Jantscher 41)* 5000
Siroki: Maric; Renato, Topic, Wagner Lago, Martinez (Ivankovic 57), Barisic, Ljubic (Peraica 57), Silic, Diogo (Krizanovic 85), Martinovic, Varea.
Sturm Graz: Gratzei; Lamotte, Sonnleitner, Feldhofer, Kandelaki, Weber (Hassler 90), Hlinka, Holzl, Kienzl, Haas (Beichler 63), Jantscher (Prettenthaler 83).

Slaven (2) 8 *(Poredski 24, Vrucina 45, Tepuric 61, 73, Vojnovic 78, 88, Gregurina 80, Juric 82)*
Milano (0) 2 *(Stojanovic 59, Alimi 75)* 1500
Slaven: Rodic; Rogulj, Maras, Csizmadia, Safaric, Puric, Poredski (Tepuric 46), Vojnovic, Delic (Gregurina 46), Vrucina (Juric 46), Niverge.
Milano: Danic; Cecelija, Puzovic, Shabani B, Brando, Ziba (Shabani F 46), Bogatinov, Limani, Bailozov, Alimi, Trajkovski (Stojanovic 46) (Bejuli 75).

Slavija (1) 3 *(Kutalija 35, Djermanovic 48, Scepanovic 90)*
Aalborg (0) 1 *(Johansson 51)* 4000
Slavija: Lucic; Lackanovic, Regoje, Stankovic, Simic, Radonja, Arsenievic, Todorovic (Vuksanovic 46) (Seslija 90), Kutalija, Scepanovic, Djermanovic (Radovanovic 80).
Aalborg: Zaza; Jakobsen, Bogelund (Christensen 68), Gaardsoe, Nielsen, Chanko, Due (Kristensen 68), Johansson, Enevoldsen, Holm (Tracy 73), Curth.

Spartak Trnava (1) 1 *(Dolezaj 19)*
Sarajevo (0) 1 *(Jahovik 88)* 8215
Spartak Trnava: Hrdina; Jakubicka, Dolezaj, Prochazka, Duris, Kopunek, Hruska (Sukennik 67), Kotula, Gueye, Kozuch (Kone 75), Bernath.
Sarajevo: Alaim; Dudo (Pliska 46), Torlak, Rizvanovic, Belosevic, Hadzic, Dzakmic, Hamzagic (Avdic 76), Maksumic, Janjos, Jahovik (Comor 90).

Tromso (1) 4 *(Knarvik 28, 90, Jenssen 76, Molskred 89)*
Dynamo Minsk (0) 1 *(Mbanangoye 83)* 4019
Tromso: Ramovic; Reginiussen T, Larsen, Hogli, Jenssen, Strand (Haugen 87), Knarvik, Lindpere (Knudsen 80), Sequeira, Moldskred, Rushfeldt (Koppinen 77).
Dynamo Minsk: Canovic; Pavlyukovich, Montaroup■, Martynovich, Saraba■, Gurenko, Dragun (Gigevich 60), Chuhley (Zaleski 72), Kislyak (Strakanovich 79), Mbanangoye, Lebedev.

Ujpest (0) 1 *(Vasko 82)*
Steaua (0) 2 *(Szekely 58, Grzelak 66)* 9678
Ujpest: Balajcza; Dudic, Lambulic, Vermes, Vasko, Pollak (Toth 66), Sandor, Stokes, Rajczi, Tisza, Kabat (Kethevoaema 59).
Steaua: Tatarusanu; Goian, Golanski, Baciu, Marin, Szekely, Toja (Ionescu 83), Nicolita (Grzelak 65), Bicfalvi (Onicas 46), Surdu, Stancu.

Vaduz (1) 2 *(Noll 24, Burgmeier 105)*
Falkirk (0) 0 1810
Vaduz: Jehle; Steil, Stuckmann, Cerrone, Stegmayer, Bellon, Koitka (Kempe 73), Burgmeier, Noll, Colocci (Bader 119), Proschwitz (Franjic 110).
Falkirk: Olejnik; Barr, Scobbie, Twaddle, McNamara, McLean, Mitchell (Sludden 106), O'Brien (Lynch 90), Arfield, Finnigan, McDonald (Flynn 59).
aet.

Valletta (0) 0
St Patrick's Ath (0) 1 *(O'Brien 80)* 1800
Valletta: Hogg; Grioli (Agius E 70), Dimech, Bezzina, Scicluna, Briffa, Pace, Falzon (Sammit 81), Cruyff, Agius G, Den Ouden.
St Patrick's Ath: Rogers; Partridge, Harris, Gavin, Stevens, Maher (Lynch 80), Byrne (Cawley 58), Ryan B (Ryan D■ 73), O'Connor, Guy, O'Brien.

Vllaznia (0) 0
Rapid Vienna (0) 3 *(Hofmann 66, 90, Maierhofer 76)* 2000
Vllaznia: Olsi; Mrvaljevic, Osja (Dibra 90), Belisha, Hallaci, Beqiri, Smajalj (Sykaj 70), Kasapi, Nika (Vajushi 61), Nallbani, Balaj.
Rapid Vienna: Payer; Patocka, Katzer, Eder, Dober, Heikkinen, Hofmann, Drazan (Jelavic 60), Pehlivan, Hoffer (Maierhofer 67), Trimmel (Konrad 78).

THIRD QUALIFYING ROUND FIRST LEG

Tuesday, 28 July 2009

Bnei Yehuda (0) 1 *(Atar 55)*
Pacos de Ferreira (0) 0 3500
Bnei Yehuda: Aiyenugba; Mori, Garrido, Raly, Baldout (Afek 71), Radi, Zhairi, Galvan (Azuz 88), Abu Zaid, Biton (Azuz 52), Edri.
Pacos de Ferreira: Cassio; Ozeia (Andre Leal 86), Jorginho, Baiano, Berville, Ricardo, Pedrinha, Leonel Olimpio, Felipe Anunciacao, Leandrinho (Cristiano 62), Torres (Rondon 82).

Thursday, 30 July 2009

Aberdeen (1) 1 *(Mulgrew 23)*

Sigma Olomouc (1) 5 *(Hubnik 18, Bajer 65, Petr 69, Ordos 83, Horava 90)* 13,973

Aberdeen: Langfield; Foster, Mulgrew, Duff, McDonald, Considine, Miller, Kerr, Mackie (Maguire 60), Young, Aluko (Paton 72).
Sigma Olomouc: Drobisz; Dreksa, Skerle, Horava, Onofrej, Rossi, Otepka (Kascak 57), Bajer, Hubnik (Heidenreich 85), Petr (Ordos 74), Janotka.

Athletic Bilbao (0) 0

Young Boys (1) 1 *(Doumbia 23)* 28,000

Athletic Bilbao: Iraizoz; Amorebeita, Iracla, Aitor Ocio, Castillo, Yeste (David Lopez 46), Orbaiz, Javier Martinez, Toquero (Muniain 59), Llorente, Susaeta (Etxeberria 71).
Young Boys: Wolfli; Ghezal, Dudar, Sutter, Mardassi, Yapi, Degen, Hochstrasser, Regazzoni (Affolter 76), Doumbia (Pasche 90), Schneuwly (Frimpong 84).

Braga (0) 1 *(Meyong 50 (pen))*

Elfsborg (1) 2 *(Danielsson 16, Bajrami 73)* 10,110

Braga: Eduardo; Rodriguez, Paulao, Evaldo, Frechaut, Fernando Alexandre (Yazalde 76), Vandinho, Paulo Cesar (Mossoro 61), Meyong, Alan, Matheus (Diogo Valente 55).
Elfsborg: Covic; Karlsson, Andersson, Mobaek, Lucic, Danielsson, Anders Svensson (Avdic 59), Nordmark (Wikstrom 69), Bajrami, Ishizaki (Johansson 85), Keene.

Brondby (0) 1 *(Farnerud 73 (pen))*

Legia (1) 1 *(Iwanski 40 (pen))* 6955

Brondby: Andersen; Von Schlebrugge, Jonsson (Rasmussen M 60), Rasmussen T, Bischoff (Randrup 33), Holmen, Nilsson, Farnerud, Krohn-Dehli (Kristiansen 81), Jensen, Jallow.
Legia: Mucha; Szala, Astiz Ventura (Jedrzejczyk 83), Rzezniczak, Guerreiro, Giza (Borysiuk 76), Iwanski, Kielbowicz, Szalachowski, Radovic (Rybus 68), Mieciel.

Club Brugge (2) 3 *(Akpala 12, Blondel 35, 90)*

Lahti (1) 1 *(Moilanen 6, Korte 50)* 23,016

Club Brugge: Stijnen; Donk, Alcaraz (Vargas 74), Odjidja-Ofoe, Daerden, Blondel, Simaeys, Vermeulen, Dirar, Sonck (Dahmane 79), Akpala (Geraerts 89).
Lahti: Szentpeteri; Haara, Toivomaki, Moilanen, Eerola, Fofana (Heini 72), Vanninen, Korte, Rafael, Litmanen, Shala (Hietanen 46).

CSKA Sofia (0) 1 *(Stoyanov I 74)*

Derry City (0) 0 10,500

CSKA Sofia: Chavdarov; Vidanov, Kotev, Ivanov, Yanev, Minev, Timonov (Saidhodzha 66), Petrov (Orlinov 58), Marquinhos, Stoyanov I, Rui Miguel (Todorov 80).
Derry City: Doherty; Hutton, Gray, O'Brien, Delaney, Higgins (Martyn 81), McGlynn (McCallion 73), Deery, Molloy, Stewart, McManus (Farren 71).

Dinamo Tbilisi (1) 2 *(Merebashvili 41, Khmaladze 87)*

Red Star Belgrade (0) 0 7500

Dinamo Tbilisi: Loria; Tomashvili, Nergadze, Kashia S, Kakubava (Lomia 63), Kashia G, Koshkadze (Phirtskhalava 78), Khmaladze, Merebashvili (Akieremy 86), Digmelashvili, Batsadze.
Red Star Belgrade: Pavlovic; Ignjatijevic, Tutoric, Dordevic, Ninkov, Savio, Lazetic (Nikolic 73), Issah, Bogdanovic (Cadu 57), Lekic, Jevtic (Perovic 63).

Fenerbahce (3) 5 *(Roberto Carlos 13, Guiza 30, 40, 61, Alex 69)*

Honved (0) 1 *(Zsolnai 78)* 45,000

Fenerbahce: Volkan; Andre Santos, Roberto Carlos (Deivid 17), Onder, Bilica, Gokhan, Cristian, Emre B (Deniz 85), Kazim-Richards, Alex, Guiza (Mehmet 71).
Honved: Nemeth; Angoua, Botis, Debreceni, Vukmir, Hajdu (Moreira 88), Macko, Pastva, Hidi (Horvath 63), Hrepka (Zsolnai 53), Guei-Guei.

Fredrikstad (0) 1 *(Borges 48)*

Lech (3) 6 *(Wilk 10, Arboleda 22, 25, Lewandowski 51, Peszko 54, Bandrowski 56)* 8000

Fredrikstad: Staw; Piiroja, Askar, Ophaug, Wehrman (Elevestad 62), Kvisvik (Tegstrom 46), Thomassen, Gashi, Borges, Barsom (Martinsen 46), Everton.
Lech: Kasprzik; Arboleda, Bosacki, Djurdjevic, Bandrowski, Wilk (Handzic 79), Stilic, Peszko (Chrapek 61), Injac, Lewandowski (Mikolajczak 71), Rengifo.

Helsingborg (1) 2 *(Andersson C 6 (pen), Skulason 58)*

Sarajevo (1) 1 *(Hadzic 22)* 11,136

Helsingborg: Hansson; Tamboura, Patronen, Andersson C, Wahlstedt, Nilsson, Landgren, Skulason, Makondele, Larsson H (Svanback 23), Jonsson (Sundin 75).
Sarajevo: Alaim; Dudo, Torlak, Rizvanovic, Belosevic, Hadzic (Hamzagic 90), Muminovic (Pliska 86), Dzakmic, Maksumic, Janjos*, Jahovik (Avdic 69).

Honka (0) 0

Karabakh (0) 1 *(Mammadov E 69)* 2830

Honka: Henriksson; Koskinen (Aalto 64), Koskimaa (Heilala 72), Hakanpaa, Perovuo, Lepola, Vuorinen, Puustinen (Simpanen 78), Haarala, Vasara, Savage.
Karabakh: Valiyev; Allahverdiev, Medvedev (Gashimov 66), Kerimov A (Yusifov 77), Teli, Rashad A Sadikhov, Mammadov E, Imamaliyev (Ismailov 86), Rashad F Sadikhov, Nadirov, Dzavadov.

IFK Gothenburg (1) 1 *(Hysen 21)*

Hapoel Tel Aviv (0) 3 *(Shechter 73, Yeboah 78, Natcho 90)* 7683

IFK Gothenburg: Christensen; Turunen, Sigurdsson, Jonsson, Lund, Eriksson, Hysen, Olsson (Johansson 70), Svensson G, Bjarnason (Alexandersson 72), Selakovic (Svensson K 89).
Hapoel Tel Aviv: Enyeama; Da Silva. Bondarv, Ben Dayan, Yadin, Zandberg (Menteshashvili 78), Natcho, Badir, Vermouth, Yeboah (Lala 86), Zahavy (Shechter 46).

KR Reykjavik (2) 2 *(Benediktsson 6, Sigurdsson G 9)*

Basle (0) 2 *(Chipperfield 58, Almerares 83)* 1200

KR Reykjavik: Magnusson; Rutgers, Gudjonsson, Fridgeirsson, Johannsson, Hauksson, Benediktsson (Gunnarsson 61), Sigurdsson B, Jordao Diogo, Sigurdsson G, Jonsson (Takefusa 61).
Basle: Costanzo; Atan, Safari, Sahin, Gelabert (Carlitos 85), Huggel, Chipperfield (Almerares 70), Shaqiri (Stocker 61), Cabral, Da Silva, Frei.

Maccabi Netanya (1) 1 *(Yampolsky 25)*

Galatasaray (1) 4 *(Hakan Balta 30, Kewell 47, Sabri 53, Baros 73)* 8000

Maccabi Netanya: Lifshitz; Saban, Dgani, Fransman, Maabi, Gazal, Cohen, Menashe, Sabaa (Awudu Okocha 46), Yampolsky (Ezra 81), Mugrabi (Taga 57).
Galatasaray: Leo Franco; Gokhan, Hakan Balta, Sabri, Servet, Aydin (Baris 71), Arda, Mustafa, Ayhan, Kewell (Keita 66), Baros (Nonda 78).

Metalurg Donetsk (1) 2 *(Godin 20, Sergio 50 (pen))*

Interblock (0) 0 3000

Metalurg Donetsk: Disljenkovic; Korotetskiy, Checher, Volovyk, Mario Sergio, Lazic, Makrides, Godin (Tkachenko 81), Mguni (Tanasa 89), Mkhitarian, Ekeh (Fabinho 76).
Interblock: Rozman; Kokot, Jelecevic, Grabus, Tabot, Brezic, Gill, Horvat (Zadnikar 78), Ilicic (Fink 83), Rakovic, Misura (Geric 50).

Petrovac (1) 1 *(Divanovic 12)*

Sturm Graz (0) 2 *(Haas 63 (pen), Lamotte 75)* 3200

Petrovac: Braic; Radulovic, Mikijelj (Skenderi 90), Lakic, Obradovic, Lopicic, Radovic, Dragicevic (Boljevic 73), Divanovic, Duraskovic, Raicevic.
Sturm Graz: Gratzei; Lamotte, Sonnleitner, Kandelaki, Prettenthaler, Schildenfeld, Weber, Hlinka (Bukva 65), Holzl, Beichler (Hassler 88), Haas (Kienzl 65).

Polonia (0) 0
NAC Breda (1) 1 *(Kwakman 40)*   6500
Polonia: Przyrowski; Mynar■, Koziol (Kulcsar 69), Kokosinski, Jodlowiec, Mierzejewski, Zasada, Tralka (Sokolowski 46), Lato, Sarvas, Chalbinski (Kosmalski 58).
NAC Breda: Ten Rouwelaar; Zwaanswijk, Feher, Schilder, Loran, Kwakman, Gilissen, De Graaf (Gorter 57), Kolkka, Lurling (Cairo 83), Amoah.

PSV Eindhoven (0) 1 *(Marcellis 90)*
Cherno More (0) 0   14,000
PSV Eindhoven: Isaksson; Kromkamp, Salcido, Ooijer, Marcellis, Simons (Bakkal 79), Engelaar, Afellay, Dzsudzsak, Toivonen (Lazovic 62), Amrabat (Koevermans 62).
Cherno More: Pirgov; Lazarov M, Bachev, Coulibaly, Dimov, Aleksandrov A, Iliev (Petkov M 80), Yurukov, Aleksandrov AD (Bornosuzov 90), Lazarov Z (Georgiev 46), Manolov.

Rabotnicki (2) 3 *(Savic 21, Wandeir 24, Ze Carlos 74)*
Odense (2) 4 *(Caca 20, 34, 70, Sorensen 62 (pen))*   1800
Rabotnicki: Naumovski; Bojovic, Bozinovski V (Dimovski 84), Ristov, Sekulovski, Bozinovski B (Carlos 69), Savic, Ze Carlos, Todorovski, Gligorov, Wandeir (Marcio 51).
Odense: Lindegaard; Ruud, Haland, Christensen, Sorensen, Gislason, Hansen H (Andreasen 64), Caca (Utaka 71), Djemba-Djemba, Absalonsen, Demba-Nyren (Hansen E 78).

Randers (0) 0
Hamburg (2) 4 *(Guerrero 11, Boateng 24, Petric 53, Trochowski 80 (pen))*   5755
Randers: Stuhr-Ellegaard; Da Cruz, Addy, Fenger, Lorentzen (Jepsen 60), Pedersen S (Fischer 53), Beckmann (Damborg 76), Pedersen K, Sane, Berg, Olsen.
Hamburg: Rost; Mathijsen, Aogo, Boateng, Ze Roberto, Jarolim (Tesche 66), Trochowski, Demel (Benjamin 7), Pitroipa, Guerrero (Choupo-Moting 66), Petric.

Rapid Vienna (1) 2 *(Maierhofer 25, Jelavic 57)*
APOP (0) 1 *(Semedo 79)*   12,800
Rapid Vienna: Payer; Jovanovic, Katzer, Eder, Dober (Thonhofer 66), Heikkinen, Hofmann, Drazan, Pehlivan (Trimmel 55), Maierhofer, Jelavic (Kulovits 77).
APOP: Fanis; Tall, Galanis, Vitali, Grimaldi, Buyse, Zeljkovic, Grabic, Edgar Marcelino (Gonzalez 70), Semedo (Bengelloun 88), Liri (Filip Da Silva 65).

Rijeka (0) 1 *(Ahmad Sharbini 59)*
Metalist Kharkiv (1) 2 *(Eremenko 43, Lisenko 85)*   7500
Rijeka: Mance; Cagalj, Budicin, Seric, Landeka, Anas Sharbini (Smith 17), Strok (Tadejevic 75), Pamic, Fernandez, Ahmad Sharbini, Matko (Turkalj 80).
Metalist Kharkiv: Goryainov; Pshenichnikh (Berezovchuk 79), Obradovic, Maidana, Gueye, Shelaev, Valyaev■, Edmar, Eremenko (Oleynik 65), Devic (Trisovic 65), Lisenko.

Roma (0) 3 *(Mexes 56, Totti 73 (pen), Vucinic 85)*
Gent (1) 1 *(Leye 23)*   38,000
Roma: Artur; Mexes, Motta (Cassetti 87), Riise, Pizarro, Taddei (Cerci 67), De Rossi, Guberti, Tonetto, Totti, Okaka Chuka (Vucinic 78).
Gent: Jorgacevic; Suler, Thompson■, Duarte, Wils, Smolders, Azofeifa (Lepoint 81), Maric, Grondin, Leye (Harstveit 77), Ljubijankic (Custovic 58).

Sevojno (0) 0
Lille (2) 2 *(Vittek 34, Hazard 39)*   3000
Sevojno: Nikolic; Kamberovic, Bulatovic, Sandulovic, Rakovic, Stanisavljevic, Jankovic, Viric (Maksimovic N 74), Jovicic, Pavicevic, Vujovic (Timic 58).
Lille: Butelle; Emerson, Beria, Rami, Plestan■, Balmont (Debuchy 83), Cabaye, Obraniak, Mavuba, Hazard (Gervinho 74), Vittek (De Melo 67).

Slavija (0) 0
Kosice (1) 2 *(Novak 11, Skutka 60)*   3500
Slavija: Lucic; Lackanovic (Benovic 68), Regoje, Stankovic, Simic, Radonja (Radovanovic 46), Arsenievic, Seslija (Nikolic 67), Kutalija, Scepanovic, Djermanovic.
Kosice: Schreng; Kiss, Kaminsky, Cicman, Basista, Kuzma, Dobias, Viazanko, Milinkovic (Karas 82), Skutka (Janic 61), Novak (Serecin 90).

St Patrick's Ath (0) 1 *(O'Brien 71)*
Krylia (0) 0   3500
St Patrick's Ath: Rogers; Partridge, Harris, Lynch, Gavin, Stevens, Byrne (Dempsey 72), O'Connor, Fitzpatrick (Ryan B 46), Guy, O'Brien.
Krylia: Lobos; Leilton, Shishkin, Belozerov, Kalachev, Bober, Jarosik, Adzhindzhal, Ignatiev, Ivanov O (Kulik 78), Savin.

Steaua (2) 3 *(Craigan 31 (og), Nicolita 45, Stancu 60)*
Motherwell (0) 0   22,000
Steaua: Tatarusanu; Goian, Golanski, Baciu, Ninu, Szekely (Grzelak 26), Nicolita (Ochirosii 87), Ionescu, Onicas, Surdu (Bibishkov 72), Stancu.
Motherwell: Ruddy; Reynolds, Craigan, Saunders, Coke, Humphrey (O'Brien 55), Jennings (Murphy 77), Forbes (Hammell 37), Hutchinson, Sutton, Slane.

Tromso (0) 2 *(Moldskred 67, Rushfeldt 69)*
Slaven (1) 1 *(Safaric 38 (pen))*   3554
Tromso: Sahlman; Reginiussen T, Larsen, Koppinen, Hogli, Jenssen, Strand (Knudsen 87), Knarvik, Lindpere (Yndestad 89), Moldskred, Rushfeldt (Sequeira 75).
Slaven: Rodic; Kokalovic, Rogulj, Maras, Csizmadia, Poldrugac, Safaric (Gregurina 90), Juric, Vojnovic (Delic 70), Vrucina (Tepuric 87), Niverge.

Vaduz (0) 0
Slovan Liberec (1) 1 *(Blazek 43)*   1105
Vaduz: Jehle; Steil, Cerrone, Stegmayer, Bellon, Koitka (Kempe 49), Burgmeier (Ritzberger 85), Noll, Colocci (Petrick 58), Proschwitz, Franjic.
Slovan Liberec: Zlamal; Vulin (Kelic 69), Dejmek, Selassie, Liska, Gecov, Holenak, Dockal (Vacha 76), Coric, Keric, Blazek (Nezmar 81).

Valerenga (1) 1 *(Storbaek 42)*
PAOK Salonika (2) 2 *(Lino 31, Muslimovic 37)*   3470
Valerenga: Perkins; Hagen (Singh 59), Storbaek, Fuenmayor, Leigh (Fellah 46), Nouri, Andresen, Haestad, Zajic, Saeternes, Moa (Berre 75).
PAOK Salonika: Chalkias; Cirillo, Lino, Sznaucner, Bizera, Pablo Garcia, Conceicao, Fotakis, Ivic (Filomeno 64), Sorlin (Malezas 87), Muslimovic (Anastasakos 40).

Vaslui (1) 2 *(Temwanjira 20, 55)*
Omonia (0) 0   8000
Vaslui: Kuciak; Buhus, Zubar, Balace, Canu, Genchev, Ljubinkovic (Pavlovic 68), Wesley, Gerlem (Gangioveanu 78), Burdujan, Temwanjira (Jovanovic 74).
Omonia: Kotsolis; Rasheed Alabi, Patsatzoglou, Davidson Morais, Zlogar, Bruno Aguiar, Kaseke (Konstantinou 77), Charalambous, Zurawski, Aloneftis, Christofi (Efrem 66).

Vetra (0) 0
Fulham (1) 3 *(Zamora 45, Murphy 57 (pen), Seol 85)*   12,000
Vetra: Valinicius; Borovskij, Kijanskas, Jankauskas, Ngapounou (Stanaitis 46), Paulauskas, Masitsev, Vezevicius, Razanauskas, Grigaitis (Eliosius 76), Vasiliauskas (Moroz 58).
Fulham: Schwarzer; Pantsil, Konchesky, Murphy (Riise 87), Hughes, Hangeland, Baird, Dempsey (Seol 81), Johnson A (Nevland 69), Zamora, Gera.

Vojvodina (1) 1 *(Djurovski 45)*
FK Austria (1) 1 *(Jun 40)*   2500
Vojvodina: Brkic; Pekovic, Vulicevic, Karan, Lovric, Ajuru, Stoica (Tumbasovic 46), Djurovski (Grozdanovski 85), Tadic (Maksimovic 62), Stjepanovic, Mrdja.

FK Austria: Almer; Dragovic, Bak Ortlechner, Standfest, Vorisek, Junuzovic Klein 80), Baumgartlinger, Acimovic, Jun, Okotie.

Zilina (0) 1 *(Kobylik 73 (pen))*
Hajduk Split (0) 1 *(Paraiba 52)* 6012
Zilina: Pernis; Angelovic, Guldan, Piacek, Sourek, Zilak (Babatounde 60), Mraz, Kobylik (Zlatkovic 79), Jez, Adauto, Lietava.
Hajduk Split: Subasic; Seric, Pandza, Ibricic, Tomasov (Cernat 57), Gabric, Skoko, Maloca, Rubil, Brkljaca (Strinic 74), Paraiba (Rodic 76).

THIRD QUALIFYING ROUND SECOND LEG

Tuesday, 4 August 2009
Omonia (0) 1 *(Zurawski 84 (pen))*
Vaslui (0) 1 *(Wesley 60)* 20,000
Omonia: Kotsolis; Rasheed Alabi, Wenzel, Patsatzoglou (Zlogar 79), Davidson Morais, Bruno Aguiar, Grammozis (Kyriakos 57), Charalambous**, Zurawski, Konstantinou, Aloneftis (Efrem 62).
Vaslui: Kuciak**; Buhus, Zubar, Balace, Canu, Genchev, Pavlovic, Wesley (Zmeu 87), Bardujan, Gerlem (Gangioveanu 66), Temwanjira (Jovanovic 74).

Thursday, 6 August 2009
APOP (1) 2 *(Marcelino 43 (pen), Gonzalez 80)*
Rapid Vienna (1) 2 *(Konrad 30, Trimmel 111)* 2500
APOP: Fanis; Tall, Galanis, Vitali (Gonzalez 69), Grimaldi, Buyse, Samaras (Liri 56), Zeljkovic, Grabic, Marcelino (Filip Da Silva 78), Semedo.
Rapid Vienna: Payer; Jovanovic, Thonhofer, Katzer, Eder, Heikkinen, Hofmann, Pehlivan (Patocka 120), Jelavic (Maierhofer 67), Trimmel, Konrad (Drazan 105).
aet.

Basle (1) 3 *(Frei 29, 80 (pen), Shaqiri 77)*
KR Reykjavik (1) 1 *(Takefusa 45 (pen))* 13,117
Basle: Costanzo; Inkoom, Ferati, Geabert**, Chipperfield, Shaqiri (Ritter 84), Cabral, Da Silva (Huggel 46), Carlitos (Aratores 82), Streller, Frei.
KR Reykjavik: Magnusson; Ratgers, Gudjonsson, Fridgeirsson, Johannsson (Benediktsson 71), Hauksson, Sigurdsson B, Jordao Diogo, Sigurdsson G, Takefusa, Jonsson (Gunnarsson 75).

Cherno More (0) 0
PSV Eindhoven (1) 1 *(Coulibaly 30 (og))* 9500
Cherno More: Pirgov; Ademar Junior, Lazarov M, Coulibaly, Boronosuzov (Kakalov 65), Aleksandrov AD (Stoyanov 81), Iliev, Petkov M, Georgiev (Lazarov Z 48), Yurukov, Manolov.
PSV Eindhoven: Isaksson; Salcido (Pieters 89), Ooijer, Marcellis, Manolev**, Simons, Engelaar (Bakkal 46), Afellay, Dzsudzsak, Toivonen, Amrabat (Wuytens 46).

Derry City (0) 0 *(Scullion 82)*
CSKA Sofia (0) 1 *(Marquinhos 70)* 2700
Derry City: Doherty; Hutton, Cray, O'Brien, Delaney, Higgins, Deery, Molloy (Scullion 74), Stewart, Farren (McGlynn** 53), McManus (Nash 90).
CSKA Sofia: Chavdarov (Karadzhov 30); Vidanov, Kotev, Ivanov, Yanev, Todorov, Minev, Timonov (Rui Miguel 66), Petrov, Marquinhos (Orlinov 83), Stoyanov I.

Elfsborg (2) 2 *(Keene 15, 31)*
Braga (0) 0 8548
Elfsborg: Covic; Floren M, Karlsson, Andersson, Mobaek, Lucic, Danielsson, Anders Svensson, Bajrami (Nordmark 81), Ishizaki (Johansson 89), Keene (Avdic 76).
Braga: Eduardo; Rodriguez, Evaldo, Frechaut, Joao Pereira, Mossoro (Paulo Cesar 76), Diogo Valente (Matheus 56), Possebon (Kalaba 34), Vandinho Meyong, Alan.

FK Austria (1) 4 *(Jun 45, Sulimani 63, Diabang 81, Okotie 90)*
Vojvodina (1) 2 *(Mrdja 31, Tadic 58)* 8207
FK Austria: Almer; Dragovic, Bak, Ortlechner, Klein, Vorisek (Hattenberger 85), Junuzovic, Baumgartlinger (Sulimani 60), Acimovic, Jun (Diabang 80), Okotie.
Vojvodina: Brkic; Pekovic, Vulicevic, Karan, Ajuru, Grozdanovski, Djurovski (Stoica 84), Tumbasevic (Khutsishvili 84), Tadic, Stjepanovic (Smiljanic 72), Mrcja.

Fulham (0) 3 *(Etuhu 57, Johnson A 80, 84)*
Vetra (0) 0 15,016
Fulham: Schwarzer; Pantsil (Kelly 78), Konchesky, Murphy, Hughes, Hangeland, Gera (Riise 78), Etuhu, Johnson A, Zamora (Johnson E 84), Dempsey.
Vetra: Valinicius; Borovskij, Kijanskas, Jankauskas, Paulauskas, Stanaitis, Vezevicius (Eliosius 46), Razanauskas, Grigaitis, Vasiliauskas (Zulpa 80), Grigalevicius (Moroz 57).

Galatasaray (2) 6 *(Baris 2, 49, Keita 6, Nonda 53, 57, 90)*
Maccabi Netanya (0) 0 25,500
Galatasaray: Leo Franco; Emre G, Ugur, Emre A, Hakan Balta, Linderoth (Ayhan 58), Aydin, Baris, Arda (Serdar 74), Keita (Kewell 46), Nonda.
Maccabi Netanya: Lifshitz; Dgani (Shulkowsky 70), Fransman, Maabi, Gazal, Cohen, Taga, Samia**, Menashe, Sabaa (Weisberg 76), Yampolsky (Ezra 85).

Gent (0) 1 *(Smolders 78)*
Roma (1) 7 *(Totti 35, 56, 64 (pen), De Rossi 58, 74, Menez 80, Okaka Chuka 86)* 11,800
Gent: Jorgacevic; Suler**, Hanstveit, Wils, Smolders, Azofeifa, Maric, Grondin, Leye (Lepoint 63), De Smet (Duarte 46), Ljubijankic (Custovic 46).
Roma: Artur; Andreolli, Mexes, Motta (Cassetti 66), Riise, Pizarro, Taddei (Cerci 70), De Rossi, Brighi, Totti (Okaka Chuka 65), Menez.

Hajduk Split (0) 0
Zilina (0) 1 *(Lietava 76)* 28,000
Hajduk Split: Subasic; Seric, Pandza, Ibricic, Andric, Tomasov (Rodic 80), Gabric, Skoko, Maloca, Rubil (Cernat 85), Paraiba (Brkljaca 64).
Zilina: Pernis; Guldan (Pecalka 74), Leitner, Piacek, Sourek, Mraz, Kobylik (Chupac 84), Jez, Adauto, Oravec, Babatounde (Lietava 54).

Hamburg (0) 0
Randers (1) 1 *(Berg 35)* 41,793
Hamburg: Hesl; Rozehnal, Mathijsen, Jansen, Benjamin (Rincon 46), Jarolim, Tavares, Ben-Hatira (Petric 46), Berg, Castelen, Torun (Pitroipa 63).
Randers: Stuhr-Ellegaard; Ahmed, Jepsen, Addy (Konig 62), Damborg, Arzumanyan, Pedersen S, Beckmann, Pedersen K (Fenger 79), Sane (Olesen 71), Berg.

Hapoel Tel Aviv (1) 1 *(Zandberg 14)*
IFK Gothenburg (0) 1 *(Stiller 52)* 10,000
Hapoel Tel Aviv: Enyeama; Da Silva, Bondarv, Ben Dayan, Yadin, Zandberg (Zahavy 67), Natcho (Menteshashvili 76), Badir, Vermouth, Shechter (Lala 82), Yeboah.
IFK Gothenburg: Christensen; Sigurdsson, Jonsson, Lund, Eriksson, Hysen, Olsson (Bjarnason 56), Svensson G, Selakovic (Svensson K 77), Stiller, Barkroth (Mustafa 69).

Honved (0) 1 *(Fritz 87)*
Fenerbahce (1) 1 *(Andre Santos 9)*
Honved: Nemeth; Fazakas (Zsolnai 46), Angoua, Botis, Debreceni, Takacs (Fritz 82), Hajdu, Macko, Pastva, Horvath, Guei-Guei.
Fenerbahce: Volkan; Onder, Andre Santos (Ugur 80), Bilica**, Wederson (Deniz 69), Alex, Cristian, Ali, Selcuk, Guiza, Deivid (Bekir 75).
Behind closed doors.

Interblock (0) 0

Metalurg Donetsk (0) 3 *(Mkhitarian 67, Mguni 73, Dimitrov 85 (pen))* 450

Interblock: Rozman; Kokot, Ntame, Jelecevic, Tabot, Brezic, Gill, Ilicic, Fink (Milenkovic 46), Rakovic (Majcen 70), Misura (Zadnikar 55).
Metalurg Donetsk: Disljenkovic; Korotetskiy (Bilozor 77), Checher, Volovyk, Mario Sergio, Lazic, Makrides, Godin (Fabinho 72), Mguni, Mkhitarian, Ekeh (Dimitrov 46).

Karabakh (1) 2 *(Mammadov E 32, Rashad F Sadikhov 81)*

Honka (1) 1 *(Koskinen 34)* 24,000

Karabakh: Valiyev; Allahverdiev, Medvedev, Kerimov A (Yusifov 46), Teli, Rashad A Sadikhov, Mammadov E, Rashad F Sadikhov, Ismailov (Gashimov 79), Nadirov (Aliyev 88), Dzavadov.
Honka: Henriksson; Koskinen, Heilala, Hakanpaa, Otaru, Perovuo, Schuller, Vuorinen, Puustinen, Haarala, Vasara (Savage 63).

Kosice (1) 3 *(Novak 2, Basista 55, Cicman 90)*

Slavija (1) 1 *(Djermanovic 17)* 8250

Kosice: Schreng; Kiss, Smrek, Cicman, Basista, Dobias, Viazanko (Karas 81), Janic, Milinkovic (Serecin 84), Skutka, Novak (Hovancik 76).
Slavija: Lucic; Regoje, Benovic, Stankovic, Simic (Nikolic 79), Arsenievic, Seslija, Vuksanovic (Radovanovic 69), Kutalija, Scepanovic (Todorovic 85), Djermanovic.

Krylia (1) 3 *(Bober 43, Savin 54, 57)*

St Patrick's Ath (0) 2 *(Bober 73 (og), O'Brien 79)* 17,000

Krylia: Lobos; Shishkin, Taranov, Belozerov, Kalachev, Bober, Adzhindzhal, Ignatiev (Kulik 39), Budylin (Leilton 68), Ivanov O, Savin.
St Patrick's Ath: Rogers; Partridge, Harris, Lynch, Gavin (Maher 66), Stevens (Ryan D 76), Byrne, Ryan B (Cawley 63), O'Connor, Guy, O'Brien.

Lahti (0) 1 *(Vanninen 87)*

Club Brugge (0) 1 *(Akpala 76)* 8000

Lahti: Szentpeteri; Haara, Toivomaki, Moilanen, Fofana, Hietanen, Vanninen, Korte, Rafael, Litmanen, Heini (Shala 56).
Club Brugge: Stijnen; Donk, Alcaraz, Odjidja-Ofoe (Dahmane 88), Daerden, Blondel, Simaeys, Vargas (Geraerts 75), Vermeulen, Dirar, Akpala (Sonck 83).

Lech (0) 1 *(Lewandowski 64)*

Fredrikstad (2) 2 *(Gashi 31, Piiroja 35)* 5500

Lech: Kotorowski; Arboleda, Bosacki, Kikut, Djurdjevic, Wilk, Stilic (Golik 81), Injac, Lewandowski, Rengifo (Bandrowski 46), Chrapek (Mikolajczak 75).
Fredrikstad: Staw; Piiroja, Askar, Ophaug, Wehrman, Thomassen, Elevstad, Gashi, Barsom, Adiyiah (Trulsen 83), Tegstrom (Johannsson 73).

Legia (1) 2 *(Giza 16, Iwanski 55 (pen))*

Brondby (1) 2 *(Von Schlebrugge 6, Madsen 59)* 5500

Legia: Mucha; Szala, Astiz Ventura, Rzezniczak, Guerreiro (Paluchowski 83), Giza (Borysiuk 90), Iwanski, Kielbowicz, Szalachowski (Radovic 66), Rybus, Mieciel.
Brondby: Andersen; Randrup, Von Schlebrugge, Frederiksen, Jonsson, Holmen, Nilsson, Farnerud (Gislason 77), Krohn-Dehli (Kristiansen 87), Jensen, Madsen (Jallow 61).

Lille (0) 2 *(Cabaye 73, De Melo 85)*

Sevojno (0) 0 15,056

Lille: Butelle; Emerson, Rami, Debuchy, Cabaye (Dumont 77), Chedjou, Mavuba, De Melo, Vittek (Balmont 46), Toure (Aubameyang 64), Gervinho.
Sevojno: Nikolic; Kamberovic (Ljubicic 86), Bulatovic, Sandulovic, Stanisavljevic, Jankovic, Viric (Timic 77), Cosic, Mudrinic (Sunjevaric 64), Pavicevic, Vujovic.

Metalist Kharkiv (1) 2 *(Gueye 12, Oliynik 60)*

Rijeka (0) 0 12,500

Metalist Kharkiv: Goryainov; Pshenichnikh, Obradovic, Maidana, Gueye, Shelaev, Edmar (Zezeto 75), Eremenko, Oliynik (Barilko 87), Devic, Lisenko (Fredes 62).
Rijeka: Mance; Cagalj, Budicin, Seric (Stepcic 73), Turkalj, Tadejevic, Landeka, Strok (Cejvanovic 65), Kreilach, Smith (Datkovic 46), Gerc.

Motherwell (1) 1 *(Forbes 17)*

Steaua (0) 3 *(Marin 55 (pen), Stancu 67, 84)* 4975

Motherwell: Ruddy; Coke (Jennings 71), Hammell, Hutchinson, Reynolds (Humphrey 60), Craigan, Forbes, Murphy (McHugh 60), Sutton, Slane, O'Brien.
Steaua: Zapata; Baciu, Marin, Ghionea (Tudose 76), Ninu, Nicolita, Ionescu, Onicas (Iacob 81), Grzelak, Stancu, Bibishkov 62).

NAC Breda (2) 3 *(Amoah 25, Lurling 45, Kwakman 81)*

Polonia (0) 1 *(Ivanovski 59)* 12,500

NAC Breda: Ten Rouwelaar; Zwaanswijk, Feher, Schilder, Loran, Kwakman (Snoyl 87), Gilissen, De Graaf (Gorter 61), Kolkka, Lurling, Amoah.
Polonia: Przyrowski; Skrzynski, Koziol, Ciach (Kulcsar 77), Jodlowiec, Sokolowski, Zasada, Tralka (Kosmalski 46), Lato, Sarvas (Mierzejewski 59), Ivanovski.

Odense (0) 3 *(Utaka 52, 76, 80)*

Rabotnicki (0) 0 6495

Odense: Lindegaard; Haland, Christensen, Sorensen, Troest, Andreasen (Ruud 78), Hansen H (Gislason 57), Djemba-Djemba, Utaka, Absalonsen, Demba-Nyren (Caca 46).
Rabotnicki: Naumovski; Bojovic, Dimovski, Bozinovski V, Ristov (Rodic 69), Sekulovski, Bozinovski B, Savic (Fabio 88), Ze Carlos, Todorovski, Maurem (Marcio 79).

Pacos de Ferreira (0) 0

Bnei Yehuda (1) 1 *(Atar 31)* 1649

Pacos de Ferreira: Cassio; Ozeia, Jorginho, Baiano, Berville (Rondon 72), Pedrinha, Cristiano, Leonel Olimpio, Felipe Anunciacao (Carlitos 63), Leandrinho (William 46), Torres.
Bnei Yehuda: Aiyenugba; Mori, Garrido, Azuz, Baldout, Rady, Zhairi (Linic 74), Atar, Galvan (Afek 66), Abu Zaid, Edri.

PAOK Salonika (0) 0

Valerenga (0) 1 *(Berre 59)* 28,000

PAOK Salonika: Chalkias; Cirillo, Lino, Sznaucner, Bizera, Pablo Garcia, Conceicao (Papazoglou 77), Fotakis, Ivic (Filomeno 64), Sorlin, Anastasakos (Kotsianikoulis 72).
Valerenga: Perkins; Hagen (Singh 89), Leigh (Fellah 79), Nouri, Andresen, Berre, Haestad, Zajic, Brix, Saeternes, Moa.

Red Star Belgrade (3) 5 *(Perovic 17, Lekic 26, 45, 88, Cadu 76 (pen))*

Dinamo Tbilisi (2) 2 *(Lekic 2 (og), Vatsadze 24)* 25,000

Red Star Belgrade: Pavlovic; Dordevic■, Ninkov, Savic, Savio (Cadu 58), Lazetic, Cvetkovic (Bogdanovic 65), Blazic (Nikolic 73), Issah, Lekic, Perovic.
Dinamo Tbilisi: Loria; Tomashvili (Sikharulidze 90), Neragadze, Kashia S, Kakubava (Phirtskhalava 67), Kashia G, Koshkadze (Lomia 55), Khmaladze, Digmelashvili, Vatsadze, Akieremy■.

Sarajevo (1) 2 *(Hadzic 38, Avdic 78)*

Helsingborg (1) 1 *(Jonsson 2)* 23,000

Sarajevo: Alaim; Dudo (Ihtijarevic 58), Torlak, Rizvanovic, Belosevic (Jahovik 70), Hadzic (Comor 83), Muminovic, Dzakmic, Hamzagic, Maksumic, Avdic.
Helsingborg: Hansson; Tambura, Andersson C (Wahlstedt 105), Nilsson, Svanback, Sundin, Bergholtz (Unkuri 106), Holgersson, Ekstrand, Makondele, Jonsson (Mahlangu 46).
aet; Sarajevo won 5-4 on penalties.

Sigma Olomouc (3) 3 *(Janotka 5, Kascak 12 (pen), Hubnik 45)*
Aberdeen (0) 0 7405
Sigma Olomouc: Drobisz; Dreksa, Skerle, Horava (Ordos 46), Kascak, Onofrej, Rossi, Bajer, Hubnik (Otepka 66), Petr (Sultes 58), Janotka.
Aberdeen: Langfield; Foster, Mulgrew, Duff, Considine, Kerr, McDonald, Maguire (Megginson 85), Miller, Mackie, Aluko.

Slaven (0) 0
Tromso (1) 2 *(Rushfeldt 14, 82)* 3000
Slaven: Rodic; Kokalovic, Rogulj, Maras, Csizmadia, Poldrugac, Safaric, Juric, Vojnovic (Poredski 69), Posavec (Vrucina 46), Delic (Tepuric 55).
Tromso: Ramovic; Reginiussen T, Larsen (Yndestad 72), Koppinen, Hogli, Jenssen, Knarvik (Haugen 62), Knudsen, Lindpere, Moldskred (Sequeira 81), Rushfeldt.

Slovan Liberec (2) 2 *(Keric 16, Nezmar 22)*
Vaduz (0) 0 4822
Slovan Liberec: Hauzr; Vulin, Dejmek, Selassie, Gecov, Holenak, Dockal, Coric (Frejlach 84), Nezmar, Keric, Blazek (Vacha 15).
Vaduz: Jehle; Bader, Steil, Stuckmann, Cerrone, Stegmayer (Rechsteiner 79), Bellon, Kempe (Colocci 46), Proschwitz, Franjic, Rebronja (Loppert 86).

Sturm Graz (2) 5 *(Muratovic 30, Holzl 43, 48, Hassler 55, Weber 83)*
Petrovac (0) 0 11,800
Sturm Graz: Gratzei; Lamotte, Feldhofer, Kandelaki (Prettenthaler 62), Schildenfeld, Weber, Holzl (Bukva 70), Muratovic (Foda 80), Kienzl, Hassler, Jantscher.
Petrovac: Braic; Radulovic (Rotkovic 57), Graovac, Mikijelj, Lakic, Obradovic, Lopicic, Radovic (Raicevic 54), Dragicevic (Boljevic 90), Divanovic, Duraskovic.

Young Boys (0) 1 *(Frimpong 90)*
Athletic Bilbao (1) 2 *(Llorente 26, Muniain 72)* 21,277
Young Boys: Wolfli; Ghezal, Dudar, Sutter (Pasche 78), Mardassi, Yapi*, Degen, Hochstrasser (Traore 80), Regazzoni (Frimpong 74), Doumbia, Schneuwly.
Athletic Bilbao: Iraizoz; Amorebieta, Iraola, Aitor Ocio, Castillo, Yeste (Gurpegui 86), Javier Martinez, Toquero, Llorente, Susaeta (Muniain 70), De Marcos (Orbaiz 80)

PLAY-OFF ROUND FIRST LEG

Thursday, 20 August 2009
Ajax (1) 5 *(Suarez 43, 65, 78, 83, Donald 90)*
Slovan Bratislava (0) 0 20,168
Ajax: Stekelenburg; Van der Wiel, Vertonghen, Alouba (Emanuelson 72), Alderweireld, Enoh, De Jong (Donald 80), De Zeeuw, Sulejmani (Zeegelaar 69), Suarez, Rommedahl.
Slovan Bratislava: Bicik; Salata, Dobrotka, Valachovic, Petras, Slovak, Bozic, Obzera (Gaucho 18), Kozak, Halenar (Cernak 71), Masaryk (Sylvestr 57).

Athletic Bilbao (0) 3 *(Javier Martinez 62 (pen), De Marcos 86, Llorente 90)*
Tromso (1) 2 *(Molskred 42, Lindpere 78)* 25,000
Athletic Bilbao: Iraizoz; Amorebieta, Iraola, Aitor Ocio, Castillo, Yeste (Iturraspe 80), Susaeta (David Lopez 85), Javier Martinez, Llorente, Muniain (Toquero 74), De Marcos.
Tromso: Ramovic; Reginiussen T, Larsen, Koppinen, Hogli, Jenssen, Knarvik, Knudsen (Srand 81), Lindpere (Haugen 90), Moldskred (Reginiussen M 89), Rushfeldt.

Baku (0) 1 *(Perez 49)*
Basle (0) 3 *(Streller 71, 74, Huggel 77)* 13,000
Baku: Sissokho; Bates, Yunisoglu, Borets, Skulic, Mujiri, Savinov, Solic (Adamia 74), Perez, Soltanov, Jaba (Gurbanov 64).
Basle: Costanzo; Atan, Safari (Shaqiri 53), Inkoom (Carlitos 53), Sahin, Huggel, Chipperfield, Cabral, Da Silva, Streller (Almerares 87), Frei.

BATE Borisov (0) 0
Litex (0) 1 *(Sandrinho 81)* 5500
BATE Borisov: Gutor; Sosnovskiy, Skitov, Yurevich, Bordachev, Volodzo, Krivets (Alumona 84), Nekhiychik, Pavlov, Stasevich (Rodionov 64), Skavysh (Goaryan 83).
Litex: Golubovic; Barthe, Nikolov, Zanev, Kishishev, Petkov, Yanev (Todorov S 57), Madureira (Venkov 90), Jelenkovic, Sandrinho, Niflore.

Benfica (1) 4 *(Di Maria 31, Cardozo 54 (pen), Saviola 56, Weldon 77)*
Vorskla (0) 0 34,177
Benfica: Quim; Shaffer, Luisao, David Luiz, Ruben Amorim, Javier Garcia, Aimar, Fabio Coentrao (Ramires 62), Di Maria, Cardozo (Weldon 75), Saviola (Cesar Peixoto 80).
Vorskla: Dolganskiy; Dallku, Krasnoporov, Curri, Yarmash (Bezus 60), Despotovski, Markoski (Chichikov 87), Kulakov, Medvedev, Esin, Sachko (Januzi 46).

Bnei Yehuda (0) 0
PSV Eindhoven (1) 1 *(Afellay 23)* 8000
Bnei Yehuda: Aiyenugba; Mori, Garrido, Azuz, Linic (Imses 81), Raly (Aharanovich 88), Baldout, Radi, Galvan, Biton, Edri.
PSV Eindhoven: Isaksson; Kromkamp (Ojo 78), Salcido, Rodriguez, Pieters, Simons, Afellay, Dzsudzsak, Bakkal, Toivonen (Koevermans 69), Lazovic (Amrabat 61).

Brondby (0) 2 *(Bischoff 51, Pejcinovic 70 (og))*
Hertha Berlin (0) 1 *(Domovchiyski 53)* 12,050
Brondby: Andersen; Randrup, Von Schlebrugge, Rasmussen T, Bischoff, Holmen, Nilsson (Jensen 90), Gislason, Krohn-Dehli, Rasmussen M (Farnerud 80), Madsen (Bernburg 65).
Hertha Berlin: Drobny; Friedrich, Von Bergen, Pejcinovic, Stein, Cicero (Nicu 80), Dardai, Ebert, Kacar (Piszczek 83), Raffael, Wichniarek (Domovchiyski 31).

CSKA Sofia (0) 0
Dynamo Moscow (0) 0 23,000
CSKA Sofia: Karadzhov; Vidanov, Kotev, Ivanov, Yanev (Paskov 70), Todorov, Minev, Yanchev, Timonov (Delev 58), Morozs, Orlinov (Zehirov 62).
Dynamo Moscow: Gabulov; Kowalczyk, Fernandez, Granat, Kolodin, Kombarov K, Knokhlov (Ropotan 85), Kombarov D, Wilkshire, Kerzhakov, Kokorin (Aguiar 68).

Dinamo Bucharest (0) 0
Slovan Liberec (1) 2 *(Liska 5, Blazek 84)* 11,000
Dinamo Bucharest: Dolha; Pulhac, Tamas, Grigore, Scarlatache, Adrian Cristea, Torje, Rus (Zicu 55), N'Doye, Niculae (Niculescu 82), Danciulescu (Andrei Cristea 46).
Slovan Liberec: Hauzr; Vulin, Dejmek, Selassie, Liska, Gecov, Holenak, Dockal, Coric (Blazek 72), Papousek (Vacha 63), Keric.
Abandoned 84 minutes; match forfeited and awarded 3-0 to Slovan Liberec.

Dinamo Zagreb (2) 4 *(Mandzukic 5, Papadopoulos D 35, Vrdoljak 56, Biscan 60)*
Hearts (0) 0 22,000
Dinamo Zagreb: Butina; Carlos, Barbaric, Vrdoljak, Etto (Tomecak 20), Sammir (Kramaric 61), Badelj, Biscan, Morales (Calello 76), Mandzukic, Papadopoulos D.
Hearts: Kello; Jonsson, Wallace, Bouzid (Black 46), Goncalves, Palazuelos, Suso (Novikovas 81), Stewart, Zaliukas, Nade (Glen 58), Obua.

Everton (2) 4 *(Saha 34, 73, Rodwell 40, 54)*
Sigma Olomouc (0) 0 27,433
Everton: Howard; Hibbert, Baines, Yobo, Neville, Rodwell (Gosling 76), Osman, Fellaini, Saha (Jo 78), Cahill, Pienaar (Vaughan 82).
Sigma Olomouc: Drobisz; Dreksa, Skerle, Horava, Kascak, Onofrej, Rossi, Otepka (Bajer 61), Ordos (Sultes 46), Hubnik, Petr (Janotka 74).

Fulham (1) 3 *(Johnson A 4, Dempsey 51, Zamora 75)*
Amkar (0) 1 *(Grishin 77)* 13,000
Fulham: Schwarzer; Pantsil, Konchesky, Murphy, Hughes, Hangeland, Gera (Duff 75), Etuhu (Baird 78), Johnson A (Nevland 68), Zamora, Dempsey.
Amkar: Narubin; Sirakov, Gaal, Belorukov, Peev, Novakovic (Telkiyski 68), Drincic, Cherenchikov, Jean Carlos (Junuzovic 85), Zhilyaev (Grishin 60), Kushev.

Galatasaray (2) 5 *(Keita 21, 45, Baros 56 (pen), Kewell 78, Leitan 88 (og))*
Levadia (0) 0 26,750
Galatasaray: Leo Franco; Gokhan, Hakan Balta, Sabri, Servet, Aydin (Kewell 62), Arda, Mustafa (Mehmet 74), Ayhan, Keita, Baros (Elano 69).
Levadia: Kaalma; Kalimullin, Morozov, Sisov, Leitan, Nahk, Puri S (Saarela 19), Teniste (Puri E 73), Gussev, Ivanov, Zelinski.

Genk (0) 1 *(Tozser 58)*
Lille (1) 2 *(Dumont 40, Vittek 56)* 12,278
Genk: Verhulst; Daeseleire (Matoukou 77), Hubert, Anele, Joao Carlos, Camus (Bakx 60), Tozser, Toth (De Bruyne 77), Pudil, Koita, Barda.
Lille: Butelle; Beria, Rami, Dumont, Debuchy, Balmont (Cabaye 86), Chedjou, Mavuba, Hazard (Obraniak 67), Vittek (Toure 80), Gervinho.

Genoa (1) 3 *(Moretti 9, Figueroa 48, 56)*
Odense (0) 1 *(Gislason 58)* 21,889
Genoa: Amelia; Criscito, Mesto, Moretti, Biava, Bocchetti (Sokratis 74), Juric, Milanetto (Zapater 66), Palacio, Sculli, Figueroa (Kharja 84).
Odense: Carroll; Ruud, Haland, Christensen, Helveg (Utaka 65), Sorensen, Andreasen, Djemba-Djemba, Gislason, Absalonsen, Demba-Nyren (Caca 77).

Guingamp (0) 1 *(Hesl 89 (og))*
Hamburg (3) 5 *(Guerrero 7, Petric 11, 26, 86, Berg 51)* 13,000
Guingamp: Trevisan; Deroff, Kone, Saad, Mathis, Diallo, Bellugou, El Jadeyaoui (Giresse 57), Colleau, Grax (Scarpelli 8), Agunbiyi (Hamroun 68).
Hamburg: Hesl; Mathijsen, Aogo, Boateng, Ze Roberto (Tesche 60), Jarolim, Trochowski, Demel, Guerrero (Berg 46), Petric, Elia (Benjamin 69).

Kosice (1) 3 *(Milinkovic 5, Novak 71 (pen), 81)*
Roma (1) 3 *(Totti 38 (pen), 67, Menez 52)* 8450
Kosice: Schreng; Kiss, Kaminsky (Matic 58), Cicman, Basista, Dobias, Juhar, Viazanko, Milinkovic (Janic 69), Skutka (Karas 69), Novak.
Roma: Artur; Andreolli, Mexes, Motta (Cassetti 84), Riise, Pizarro, De Rossi, Brighi, Totti, Cerci (Taddei 51), Menez (Guberti 74).

Lazio (2) 3 *(Kolarov 23, Zarate 35, Mauri 69)*
Elfsborg (0) 0 18,000
Lazio: Muslera; Lichtsteiner, Kolarov, Siviglia, Cribari, Brocchi, Matuzalem (Dabo 58), Mauri (Diakite 86), Baronio, Zarate (Eliseu 75), Cruz.
Elfsborg: Covic; Floren M, Karlsson, Andersson, Mobaeck, Lucic, Danielsson, Anders Svensson (Floren J 74), Ishizaki, Avdic, Jawo (Johansson 74).

Lech (0) 1 *(Peszko 90)*
Club Brugge (0) 0 6000
Lech: Kasprzik; Gancarczyk, Arboleda, Bosacki, Bandrowski, Wilk (Kikut 71), Stilic (Golik 64), Peszko, Injac, Lewandowski (Mikolajczak 89), Rengifo.
Club Brugge: Stijnen; Klukowski, Alcaraz, Odjidja-Ofoe, Blondel, Simaeys, Vargas (Chavez 81), Vermeulen, Geraerts, Dirar (Sonck 71), Akpala.
Maribor (0) 0
Sparta Prague (1) 2 *(Wilfried 29, 86)* 9000
Maribor: Ranilovic; Dzinic, Jurkic (Aljancic 57), Samardzic, Mihelic (Mertelj 80), Bacinovic, Popovic, Pavlovic (Volas 63), Skolnik, Tavares, Bunderla.
Sparta Prague: Kasper; Repka, Hubnik, Kusnir, Pamic, Zofcak, Zeman, Vacek (Kovba 77), Husek (Hoheneder 74), Wilfried, Kadlec (Kalouda 67).

Metalurg Donetsk (1) 2 *(Ekeh 17, Dimitrov 90)*
FK Austria (1) 2 *(Acimovic 7, Diabang 48)* 3000
Metalurg Donetsk: Disljenkovic; Korotetskiy, Checher, Volovyk (China 68), Mario Sergio, Lazic, Dimitrov, Makrides (Fabinho 72), Godin (Tanasa 57), Mkhitarian, Ekeh.
FK Austria: Safar; Dragovic, Bak, Ortlechner, Standfest, Vorisek, Junuzovic (Klein 46), Baumgartlinger, Acimovic (Suttner 82), Diabang■, Jun.

NAC Breda (1) 1 *(Loran 17)*
Villarreal (1) 3 *(Rossi 15, Ibagaza 49, Llorente 90)* 15,200
NAC Breda: Ten Rouwelaar; Zwaanswijk, Feher, Schilder, Loran, Kwakman, Gilissen (Penders 87), De Graaf (Idabdelhay 76), Kolkka, Reuser (Gorter 66), Lurling.
Villarreal: Diego Lopez; Gonzalo, Godin, Capdevila, Angel, Cazorla, Cani, Ibagaza (Fuster 80), Senna, Nilmar (Pires 75), Rossi (Llorente 66).

Nacional (2) 4 *(Luis Alberto 30, Joao Aurelio 37, Rodrigo Silva 53, Ruben Micael 73)*
Zenit (1) 3 *(Semshov 44, 55, Fatih 90)* 3000
Nacional: Rafael Bracali; Patacas, Felipe Lopes, Wellington (Tomasevic 83), Cleber, Pecnik (Nuno Pinto 55), Ruben Micael, Joao Aurelio, Leandro Salino, Luis Alberto, Rodrigo Silva (Abdou 87).
Zenit: Malafeev; Anyukov, Fernando Meira, Lombaerts, Hubocan, Shirokov, Zyryanov, Semshov, Huszti (Rosina 58), Kornilenko (Fatih 68), Denisov (Ignatovich 76).

PAOK Salonika (0) 1 *(Ivic 54)*
Heerenveen (1) 1 *(Paulo Henrique 45)* 24,000
PAOK Salonika: Chalkias; Cirillo, Malezas, Lino, Savini, Pablo Garcia, Vitolo, Conceicao (Kotsianikoulis 66), Ivic, Muslimovic (Anastasakos 86), Vieirinha (Filomeno 86).
Heerenveen: Lejsal; Breuer, Dingsdag, Svec, Koning, Beerens (Paulo Henrique 20), Grindheim, Popov, Losada (Janmaat 90), Papadopoulos (Sibon 82), Kalou.

Partizan Belgrade (1) 1 *(Cleo 16 (pen))*
Zilina (1) 1 *(Adauto 33 (pen))* 14,143
Partizan Belgrade: Bozovic M; Dordevic, Krstajic, Obradovic, Gavrancic (Knezevic 69), Fejsa (Jovanovic B 46), Tomic (Ilic 63), Almani Moreira, Ljajic, Cleo, Bogunovic.
Zilina: Pernis; Leitner, Piacek, Sourek, Pecalka (Guldan 59), Mraz, Jez, Tsimakuridzde, Adauto (Babatounde 87), Vyskocil (Rilke 82), Oravec.

Rapid Vienna (1) 1 *(Jelavic 1)*
Aston Villa (0) 0 17,800
Rapid Vienna: Payer; Patocka, Jovanovic, Katzer, Dober, Heikkinen, Hofmann, Drazan (Boskovic 83), Pehlivan, Jelavic, Konrad (Trimmel 62).
Aston Villa: Guzan; Beye, Shorey, Sidwell, Davies (Lowry 81), Cuellar, Milner, Reo-Coker, Heskey, Gardner (Agbonlahor 55), Young A.

Sarajevo (0) 1 *(Hadzic 77)*
Cluj (1) 1 *(Dani 19)* 25,000
Sarajevo: Alaim; Dudo, Torlak, Rizvanovic, Belosevic, Hadzic, Ihtijarevic (Jahovik 71), Muminovic, Dzakmic, Janjos (Pliska 82), Avdic (Hamzagic 62).
Cluj: Claro; Da Silva, Panin, Hugo Alcantara, Cadu, Peralta (Andre Leao 73), Culio, Mara (Edimar 63), Dani, Kone, Nei.

Sion (0) 0
Fenerbahce (1) 2 *(Andre Santos 44, Kazim-Richards 84)* 9500
Sion: Vanins; Alioui, Paito, Vanczak, Chihab, Die, Fermino, Obradovic (Yoda 60), Dominguez (Afonso 78), Marin (M'Futi 77), Mpenza.
Fenerbahce: Volkan; Lugano, Roberto Carlos, Deniz (Onder 28), Andre Santos, Gokhan, Emre B (Ugur 76), Kazim-Richards, Cristian, Guiza, Deivid (Semih 62).

Sivas (0) 0
Shakhtar Donetsk (1) 3 *(Gay 6, Ilsinho 76, Kobin 87)*
8500
Sivas: Petkovic■; Sedat, Yasin, Hayrettin, Musa (Martin 46), Ibrahim D, Cihan (Onur 79), Kadir, Ibrahim S, Dereli, Bouazza (Yannick 61).
Shakhtar Donetsk: Pyatov; Hubschman, Kucher, Ilsinho, Rat, Chigrinskiy, Fernandinho, Jadson (Willian 67), Kobin, Gay (Polyanskiy 77), Gladkiy (Aghahowa 71).

Slavia Prague (1) 3 *(Senkerik 34, 65, Vlcek 81)*
Red Star Belgrade (0) 0
12,500
Slavia Prague: Hanus; Hubacek, Celustka (Krajcik 62), Suchy, Vomacka, Ragued, Belaid, Volesak, Cerny J, Hlousek (Janda 89), Senkerik (Vlcek 72).
Red Star Belgrade: Pavlovic; Tutoric, Vilotic, Ninkov, Savic, Savio, Lazetic, Issah (Ignjatijevic 70), Bogdanovic (Nikolic 90), Lekic, Sreckovic (Perovic 46).

Stabaek (0) 0
Valencia (2) 3 *(Pablo Hernandez 29, Villa 35, Joaquin 80)*
9600
Stabaek: Knudsen; Segerstrom, Skjonsberg, Rogne, Hauger, Kobayashi (Diskerud 69), Palmason, Farnerud, Hedenstad, Nannskog (Andersen 63), Berglund (Hoff 63).
Valencia: Cesar; Bruno, Marchena, Dealbert, Alexis, Miguel, Pablo Hernandez (Joaquin 71), Silva (Michel 82), Ever Banega, Villa (Zigic 76), Mata.

Steaua (0) 3 *(Nicolita 55, Stancu 65, 80)*
St Patrick's Ath (0) 0
Steaua: Tatarusanu; Golanski (Tininho 86), Tudose, Baciu, Marin, Nicolita, Ionescu, Ochirosii (Stancu 53), Onicas, Kapetanos (Grzelak 81), Surdu.
St Patrick's Ath: Rogers; Partridge, Harris, Lynch (Cawley 86), Gavin, Stevens, Byrne (Dempsey 70), O'Connor, Fitzpatrick (Quigley 61), Guy, O'Brien.
Behind closed doors.

Sturm Graz (1) 1 *(Beichler 31)*
Metalist Kharkiv (0) 1 *(Oliynik 75)*
11,200
Sturm Graz: Gratzei; Lamotte (Bukva 62), Sonnleitner, Kandelaki, Schildenfeld, Weber, Hlinka, Holzl, Muratovic, Beichler (Weinberger 88), Jantscher (Hassler 81).
Metalist Kharkiv: Goryainov; Pshenichnikh, Obradovic, Maidana, Gueye, Edmar, Eremenko (Bordianu 67), Oliynik (Fredes 88), Devic, Lisenko (Shelaev 46), Jaja.

Teplice (0) 1 *(Vondrasek 89)*
Hapoel Tel Aviv (0) 2 *(Enyeama 73 (pen), Vermouth 90)*
5122
Teplice: Grigar; Klein, Vidlicka, Lukas, Matula, Rosa (Merzic 46), Ljevakovic, Vachousek, Stozicky, Mares (Vondrasek 59), Mahmutovic (Verbir 80).
Hapoel Tel Aviv: Enyeama; Da Silva, Bondarv, Ben Dayan, Yadin, Zandberg (Zahavy 62), Natcho, Eadir, Vermouth, Shechter (Lala 86), Yeboah (Menteshashvili 80).

Trabzonspor (1) 1 *(Song 16)*
Toulouse (1) 3 *(Gignac 12, 59, Mansare 90)*
21,757
Trabzonspor: Sylva; Cale (Kacar 80), Song, Korkmaz, Cora (Alanzinho 65), Tjikuzu (Unal 70), Baytar■, Inan, Colman, Balci, Bulut.
Toulouse: Blondel; Fofana (Congre 83), Cetto, M'Bengue, Ebondo, Machado (Mansare 82), Devaux (Braaten 65), Didot, Sissoko, Capoue, Gignac.

Twente (1) 3 *(Ruiz 38, Nkufo 66, Douglas 81)*
Karabakh (1) 1 *(Nadirov 8)*
23,000
Twente: Boschker; Wisgerhof, Stam, Heubach, Douglas, Brama, Janssen, Nkufo, Perez (Vujicevic 73), Stoch (Tiote 87), Ruiz.
Karabakh: Valiyev; Gashimov, Medvedev, Kerimov A (Yusifov 64), Teli, Rashad A Sadikhov, Mammadov E (Hadjiev 81), Abbasov, Ismailov (Aliyev 84), Nadirov, Dzavadov.

Vaslui (1) 2 *(Wesley 29, 83 (pen))*
AEK Athens (0) 1 *(Blanco 68 (pen))*
9000
Vaslui: Haisan; Akakpo, Zubar, Balace, Farkas, Genchev, Ljubinkovic, Pavlovic (Gangioveanu 75), Wesley, Gerlem (Zmeu 85), Temwanjira (Jovanovic 90).
AEK Athens: Saja; Alves, Majstorovic, Koutromanos, Georgeas, Nsaliwa, Leonardo (Gentsoglou 90), Makos, Djebbour, Manduca, Blanco (Iordache 89).

Werder Bremen (3) 6 *(Boenisch 17, Ozil 28, 67 (pen), Naldo 36, 65, Hugo Almeida 60)*
Aktobe (2) 3 *(Strukov 21, 32, Smakov 87)*
21,446
Werder Bremen: Wiese; Boenisch, Naldo (Pasanen 76), Fritz, Mertesacker, Borowski, Marin (Hugo Almeida 46), Ozil, Frings, Hunt, Pizarro (Marcelo Moreno 82).
Aktobe: Sidelnikov; Badlo, Smakov, Kenzheisariev, Logvinenko, Khayrullin, Golovskoy (Chichulin 72), Asanbaev (Mitrofanov 70), Lavrik, Strukov (Tleshev 84), Averchenko.

PLAY-OFF ROUND SECOND LEG

Tuesday, 25 August 2009
Shakhtar Donetsk (1) 2 *(Jadson 21 (pen), Luiz Adriano 59 (pen))*
Sivas (0) 0
18,000
Shakhtar Donetsk: Khudzhamov; Polyanskiy, Ishchenko, Jadson, Ilsinho (Fernandinho 60), Kobin, Gay (Rakitskiy 60), Willian, Srna, Chizhov, Aghahowa (Luiz Adriano 46).
Sivas: Akim; Yasin, Mbemba, Onur, Murat (Ferhat 72), Ibrahim D, Erman, Cihan (Akeem 62), Kadir, Abdurrahman (Ugur 55), Kamanan.

Thursday, 27 August 2009
AEK Athens (0) 3 *(Manduca 59, Scocco 74, 79)*
Vaslui (0) 0
35,000
AEK Athens: Saja; Araujo, Alves, Majstorovic, Juanfrar, Kafes (Nsaliwa 72), Leonardo (Tachtsidis 67), Makos, Manduca, Blanco, Scocco (Karabelas 85).
Vaslui: Kuciak; Buhus, Zubar, Balace, Farkas, Zmeu (Costin 70), Ljubinkovic (Jovanovic 78), Pavlovic, Wesley, Gerlem, Temwanjira.

Aktobe (0) 0
Werder Bremen (2) 2 *(Pizarro 11, 45)*
11,000
Aktobe: Sidelnikov; Badlo, Smakov, Kenzheisariev■, Logvinenko, Khayrullin, Golovskoy, Asanbaev (Khokhlov 90), Tleshev (Chichulin 46), Strukov, Averchenko (Mitrofanov 74).
Werder Bremen: Wiese; Pasanen, Naldo, Fritz, Mertesacker, Borowski (Bargfrede 59), Ozil (Marin 72), Frings, Niemeyer, Hunt, Pizarro (Marcelo Moreno 82).

Amkar (0) 1 *(Kushev 90)*
Fulham (0) 0
20,000
Amkar: Narubin; Sirakov, Gaal, Belorukov, Grishin (Junuzovic 76), Telkiyski (Novakovic 60), Peev, Drincic, Cherenchikov, Jean Carlos (Zhilyaev 64), Kushev.
Fulham: Schwarzer; Pantsil, Kelly, Riise (Seol 76), Hughes, Hangeland, Baird, Etuhu, Gera, Nevland (Kamara 68), Duff.

Aston Villa (1) 2 *(Milner 38 (pen), Carew 53)*
Rapid Vienna (0) 1 *(Jelavic 76)*
25,563
Aston Villa: Guzan; Beye, Shorey, Delph (Albrighton 86), Davies (Lowry 83), Cuellar, Milner, Petrov, Heskey (Agbonlahor 82), Carew, Young A.
Rapid Vienna: Payer; Patocka, Katzer, Soma, Dober, Heikkinen, Hofmann, Drazan, Pehlivan, Jelavic (Boskovic 87), Trimmel (Maierhofer 56).

Basle (3) 5 *(Almerares 32, Gelabert 36, Frei 63, Shaquiri 74, Mustafi 84)*
Baku (0) 1 *(Felix 33)*
7,100
Basle: Costanzo; Atan (Ritter 64), Abraham (Huggel 46), Inkoom, Gelabert, Chipperfield, Shaquiri, Da Silva, Aratores, Frei (Mustafi 71), Almerares.
Baku: Sissokho; Amirbekov, Bates (Ramir 46), Tomovski, Yunisoglu, Maharramov, Solic, Felix, Perez (Mujiri 73), Soltanov (Adamia 46), Jaba.

Club Brugge (0) 1 *(Sonck 79)*
Lech (0) 0   25,657
Club Brugge: Stijnen; Klukowski, Alcaraz, Odjidja-Ofoe, Blondel (Geraerts 89), Simaeys, Vargas (Dahmane 94), Vermeulen, Dirar, Sonck, Akpala (Chavez 120).
Lech: Kasprzik; Gancarczyk, Arboleda, Bosacki, Kikut, Djurdjevic, Bandrowski, Stilic (Wilk 66), Injac (Golik 120), Lewandowski (Chrapek 116), Rengifo.
aet; Club Brugge won 4-3 on penalties.

Cluj (1) 2 *(Kone 40, Muresan 69)*
Sarajevo (0) 1 *(Avdic 80)*   10,800
Cluj: Claro; Da Silva, Panin, Muresan, Cadu, Peralta (Traore 88), Culio, Dani, Dubarbier (Bus 90), Kone, Nei (Mara 62).
Sarajevo: Alaim; Dudo, Torlak, Rizvanovic, Belosevic (Skoro 55), Hadzic, Ihtijarevic (Pliska 81), Muminovic, Dzakmic, Maksumic, Jahovik (Avdic 71).

Dynamo Moscow (1) 1 *(Kerzhakov 10)*
CSKA Sofia (1) 2 *(Delev 14, Ivanov 55)*   8468
Dynamo Moscow: Gabulov; Kowalczyk (Smolov 61), Fernandez, Granat (Kokorin 56), Kolodin, Kombarov K, Khokhlov, Kombarov D, Aguiar (Dimidko 46), Wilkshire, Kerzhakov.
CSKA Sofia: Karadzhov; Vidanov, Kotev, Ivanov, Todorov (Yanev 75), Minev, Yanchev, Marquinhos (Timonov 21), Morozs, Stoyanov I, Delev (Paskov 85).

Elfsborg (0) 1 *(Avdic 69)*
Lazio (0) 0   11,693
Elfsborg: Covic; Floren M, Karlsson, Andersson, Mobaeck, Lucic, Danielsson (Jawo 84), Anders Svensson, Bajrami, Ishizaki (Nordmark 77), Keene (Avdic 46).
Lazio: Muslera; Lichtsteiner, Siviglia (Kolarov■ 23), Cribari, Radu, Brocchi (Eliseu 52), Matuzalem, Meghni, Baronio, Rocchi, Cruz (Zarate 66).

Fenerbahce (2) 2 *(Andre Santos 2, 41 (pen))*
Sion (2) 2 *(Vanczak 9, Chihab 31 (pen))*   32,000
Fenerbahce: Volkan; Lugano, Onder, Ugur (Emre B 77), Andre Santos, Gokhan, Wederson, Kazim-Richards (Ozer 90), Cristian, Selcuk, Semih (Guiza 77).
Sion: Vanins; Yusuf, Nwaneri, Alioui, Paito (Mpenza 69), Vanczak (Marin 46), Buhler, Chihab, Die, Obradovic, Dabo (M'Futi 73).

FK Austria (1) 3 *(Okotie 36, Acimovic 70 (pen), Sulimani115)*
Metalurg Donetsk (1) 2 *(Tanasa 20, Mkhitarian 54)* 10,400
FK Austria: Safar; Dragovic, Bak, Ortlechner (Suttner 46), Standfest, Klein, Vorisek, Baumgartlinger, Acimovic, Jun (Sulimani 90), Okotie (Topic 64).
Metalurg Donetsk: Disljenkovic; Korotetskiy (Arakelyan 71), Checher, Volovyk (China 88), Mario Sergio, Lazic, Dimitrov■, Makrides, Tanasa, Mkhitarian, Ekeh (Fabinho 109).
aet.

Hamburg (1) 3 *(Tesche 42, 51, Berg 47)*
Guingamp (0) 1 *(Mathis 90)*   25,798
Hamburg: Hesl; Rozehnal, Boateng (Aogo 46), Benjamin, Tesche, Pitroipa, Rincon, Tavares, Guerrero (Torun 46), Berg, Castelen (Elia 73).
Guingamp: Gauclin; Deroff, Saad, Delgado, Bellugou (Mathis 57), Colleau, Djoman (Diallo 62), Giresse (Scarpelli 57), Bazile, Hamroun, Ogunbiyi.

Hapoel Tel Aviv (0) 1 *(Ben Dayan 90)*
Teplice (0) 1 *(Klein 89)*   8000
Hapoel Tel Aviv: Enyeama; Da Silva, Bondarv, Ben Dayan, Yadin, Zandberg (Zahavy 62), Natcho, Badir, Vermouth, Shechter (Menteshashvili 82), Yeboah (Lala 68).
Teplice: Grigar; Klein, Vidlicka, Lukas, Ljevakovic (Dolezal 73), Vachousek, Stozicky, Merzic, Mares (Mahmutovic 82), Hesek (Verbir 46), Vondrasek.

Hearts (1) 2 *(Stewart 17, Zaliukas 55)*
Dinamo Zagreb (0) 0   11,769
Hearts: Balogh; Thomson, Bouzid, Stewart, Goncalves, Palazuelos (Black 82), Suso, Zaliukas, Glen (Driver 60), Nade (Smith 55), Obua.
Dinamo Zagreb: Butina; Lovren, Carlos, Barbaric, Vrdoljak, Sammir (Tomecak 68), Badelj, Biscan, Morales (Calello 87), Mandzukic, Papadopoulos D (Slepicka 89).

Heerenveen (0) 0
PAOK Salonika (0) 0   16,000
Heerenveen: Lejsal; Nielsen K, Breuer, Dingsdag, Koning, Grindheim, Popov, Losada, Papadopoulos, Paulo Henrique (Ingelsten 90), Sibon (Kalou 78).
PAOK Salonika: Chalkias; Cirillo, Lino, Savini (Anastasakos 82), Bizera, Pablo Garcia (Koutsianikoulis 75), Vitolo, Fotakis (Filomeno 61), Ivic, Muslimovic, Vieirinha.

Hertha Berlin (0) 3 *(Kacar 75, 86, Dardai 80)*
Brondby (0) 1 *(Rasmussen M 51)*   10,000
Hertha Berlin: Drobny; Friedrich, Von Bergen, Pejcinovic, Janker, Cicero, Dardai, Ebert (Bengtsson 90), Kacar, Wichniarek (Nicu 67), Domovchiyski (Piszczek 61).
Brondby: Andersen; Randrup, Von Schlebrugge, Rasmussen T (Farnerud 89), Bischoff, Holmen, Nilsson, Gislason, Krohn-Dehli, Rasmussen M (Jensen 79), Madsen (Bernburg 61).

Karabakh (0) 0
Twente (0) 0   12,000
Karabakh: Valiyev; Allahverdiyev, Gashimov, Medvedev, Kerimov A (Yusifov 72), Teli, Rashad A Sadikhov, Mammadov E, Ismailov (Aliyev 67), Nadirov, Dzavadov.
Twente: Boschker; Kuiper, Wisgerhof, Stam, Douglas, Brama, Tiote, Janssen (Perez 46), Nkufo, Stoch (Vujicevic 62), Ruiz (Akram 90).

Levadia (0) 1 *(Puri E 50)*
Galatasaray (0) 1 *(Nonda 64)*   1500
Levadia: Kaalma; Kalimullin, Morozov, Sisov, Leitan (Mones 89), Nahk, Saarela, Teniste, Neemelo (Zelinski 81), Gussev, Puri E.
Galatasaray: Leo Franco; Emre G, Emre A, Sabri, Erdem (Serkan 59), Aydin (Arda 65), Baris, Elano, Mehmet, Serdar, Nonda (Mustafa 74).

Lille (1) 4 *(De Melo 10, 73, Dumont 59, Hazard 70)*
Genk (1) 2 *(Barda 24 (pen), Tozser 86)*   16,055
Lille: Butelle; Emerson, Beria, Dumont, Debuchy (Balmont 51), Cabaye, Chedjou, Mavuba (Vandam 79), De Melo, Aubameyang, Gervinho (Hazard 62).
Genk: Verhulst; Daeseleire, Hubert (Cornelis 67), Joneleit, Anele, Camus (Ogunjimi 74), Tozser, Toth, Pudil■, Koita, Barda (De Bruyne 46).

Litex (0) 0
BATE Borisov (0) 4 *(Sosnovskiy 86, 99, Rodionov 94, Skavysh 118)*   5000
Litex: Golubovic; Barthe, Nikolov, Zanev, Kishishev, Petkov (Yanev 98), Wellington (Milanov 104), Madureira, Jelenkovic, Sandrinho, Niflore (Todorov S 90).
BATE Borisov: Gutor; Sosnovskiy, Shitov, Yurevich, Bordachev, Likhtarovich (Nekhaichik 58), Pavlov (Goaryan 77), Stasevich, Alumona (Krivets 46), Skavysh, Rodionov.
aet.

Metalist Kharkiv (0) 0
Sturm Graz (1) 1 *(Beichler 32)*   25,000
Metalist Kharkiv: Goryainov; Pshenichnikh, Obradovic, Maidana, Gueye, Shelaev (Eremenko 46), Sluysar, Oleynik, Burkhardt (Phantskhava 58), Dedvic (Zezeto 75), Jaja.
Sturm Graz: Gratzei; Sonnleitner, Feldhofer, Kandelaki, Schildenfeld, Weber, Hlinka, Holzl, Muratovic (Hassler 89), Beichler, Jantscher.

Odense (1) 1 *(Figueroa 45 (og))*

Genoa (0) 1 *(Criscito 53)* 10,000

Odense: Carroll; Ruud, Haland (Hansen H 81), Christensen, Sorensen, Andreasen, Caca, Djemba-Djemba, Gislason, Absalonsen, Demba-Nyren (Helveg 79).
Genoa: Amelia; Criscito, Sokratis, Mesto (Palacio 78), Moretti, Biava, Rossi, Zapater, Juric (Milanetto 14), Sculli, Figueroa (Kharja 83).

PSV Eindhoven (1) 1 *(Simons 25 (pen))*

Bnei Yehuda (0) 0 11,000

PSV Eindhoven: Isaksson; Rodriguez, Pieters, Ooijer, Manolev, Simons (Engelaar 46), Afellay, Dzsudzsak, Bakkal, Lazovic, Koevermans (Jonathan 77) (Toivonen 83).
Bnei Yehuda: Aiyenugba; Mori, Azuz, Haddad, Raly (Zhairi 77), Baldout (Biton 71), Radi (Linic 65), Atar, Galvan, Abu Zaid, Edri.

Red Star Belgrade (2) 2 *(Bogdanovic 23 (pen), Perovic 44)*

Slavia Prague (0) 1 *(Vlcek 64)* 35,000

Red Star Belgrade: Stamenkovic; Ignjatijevic (Cadu 38), Vilotic, Ninkov, Savic (Savio 74), Lazetic, Blazic, Issah, Bogdanovic (Nikolic 46), Lekic, Perovic.
Slavia Prague: Vaniak; Hubacek, Celustka, Such, Vomacka, Janda (Trapp 46), Belaid (Krajcik 85), Volesak, Cerny J, Hlousek, Senkerik (Vlcek 57).

Roma (5) 7 *(Totti 1, 6, 86, Guberti 8, Cerci 17, Menez 18, Riise 70)*

Kosice (1) 1 *(Novak 38)* 16,145

Roma: Artur; Mexes, Motta, Riise, Cassetti (Juan 54), Pizarro, De Rossi (Faty 46), Guberti, Totti, Cerci, Menez (Vucinic 56).
Kosice: Schreng; Kiss (Matic 46), Kaminsky (Skutka 46), Smrek, Cicman, Basista, Dobias, Juhar, Viazanko (Serecin 60), Milinkovic, Novak.

Sigma Olomouc (0) 1 *(Sultes 80)*

Everton (1) 1 *(Pienaar 44)* 10,212

Sigma Olomouc: Lovasik; Dreksa, Skerle, Horava, Kascak, Onofrej, Rossi, Bajer (Otepka 73), Ordos, Petr (Stepan 84), Janotka (Sultes 73).
Everton: Howard; Hibbert, Baines, Yobo, Neville, Rodwell, Gosling, Osman (Baxter 66), Jo (Yakubu 76), Fellaini, Pienaar (Wallace 66).

Slovan Bratislava (1) 1 *(Sylvestr 45)*

Ajax (1) 2 *(De Jong 30, Bakircioglu 84)* 5880

Slovan Bratislava: Putnocky; Salata, Dobrotka, Bagayoko, Petras (Simao 59), Dosoudil, Slovak (Serrano 46), Bozic, Halenar, Sylvestr, Gaucho (Masaryk 75).
Ajax: Stekelenburg; Van der Wiel, Vertonghen, Alouba (De Zeeuw 75), Wielaert, Emanuelson, Enoh (Bakircioglu 59), De Jong, Donald, Suarez (Sulejmani 46), Cvitanich.

Slovan Liberec (0) 0

Dinamo Bucharest (1) 3 *(Andrei Cristea 4, Niculae 57, 82)* 7000

Slovan Liberec: Hauzr; Vulin, Dejmek, Selassie, Liska, Gecov, Holenak, Dockal, Coric (Papousek 88), Nezmar (Vacha 61), Keric (Blazek 73).
Dinamo Bucharest: Matache; Diabate, Moti, Melinero, Grigore, Kone, Zicu, Bostina, Adrian Cristea (Torje 64), Danciulescu (Niculae 46), Andrei Cristea (Niculescu 75).
aet; Dinamo Bucharest won 9-8 on penalties.

Sparta Prague (1) 1 *(Wilfried 2)*

Maribor (0) 0 12,710

Sparta Prague: Blazek; Repka, Hubnik, Kusnir Pamic, Zofcak, Zeman (Strestik 81), Kovba, Vacek, Wilfried (Jircus 75), Kadlec (Prudnikov 52).
Maribor: Ranilovic; Aljancic, Lunder, Sandardzic, Mihelic, Popovic, Pavlovic, Skolnik, Mertelj (Crnic 46), Tavares, Jelic (Bunderla 63).

St Patrick's Ath (0) 1 *(O'Connor 49)*

Steaua (0) 2 *(Nicolita 80, Ochirosil 89)* 15,000

St Patrick's Ath: Rogers; Partridge, Harris (Gavin 86), Lynch, Stevens (Ryan B 46), Byrne (Dempsey 79), Cawley, O'Connor, Quigley, Guy, O'Brien.
Steaua: Zapata; Golanski, Tudose, Ghionea, Ninu, Szekely (Ochirosil 86), Ionescu, Onicas, Grzelak (Nicolita 57), Stancu (Surdu 79), Bibishkov.

Toulouse (0) 0

Trabzonspor (0) 1 *(Ceyhun 55)* 15,535

Toulouse: Blondel; Congre, Cetto, Ncunkeu, Ebondo, Devaux (Braaten 74), Sirieix, Sissoko, Capoue, Mansare (M'Bengue 82), Pentecote (Gignac 75).
Trabzonspor: Sylva; Cale, Song, Tayfun (Serkan 73), Remzi, Ceyhun, Selcuk (Tjikuzu 85), Colman, Alanzinho (Umut 54), Gokhan, Baris.

Tromso (0) 1 *(Rushfeldt 61)*

Athletic Bilbao (0) 1 *(Javier Martinez 55 (pen))* 6000

Tromso: Ramovic; Reginiussen T, Koppinen, Hogli, Jenssen, Yndestad (Isaksen 90), Knarvik (Taboga 90), Knudsen (Strand 82), Lindpere, Moldskred, Rushfeldt.
Athletic Bilbao: Iraizoz; Amorebieta, Iraola, Aitor Ocio, Castillo, Yeste (Koikili 90), Susaeta (Gurpegui 90), Javier Martinez, Toquero, Llorente, De Marcos (Iturraspe 69).

Valencia (2) 4 *(Miku 28, 30, 80, Zigic 77)*

Stabaek (1) 1 *(Farnerud 36)* 15,000

Valencia: Moya; David Navarro, Mathieu, Miguel (Bruno 73), Maduro, Albelda (Olcina 57), Joaquin, Michel, Zigic, Mata (Ever Banega 57), Miku.
Stabaek: Austbo; Hoiland (Skjonsberg 74), Segerstrom, Rogne, Hauger, Hoff (Stenvoll 78), Kobayashi, Farnerud, Diskerud, Hedenstad, Andersen (Berglund 69).

Villarreal (3) 6 *(Cazorla 16, Rossi 23 (pen), 37 (pen), San 46, Jonathan Pereira 57, Kiko 61)*

NAC Breda (0) 1 *(De Graaf 80)* 15,200

Villarreal: Diego Lopez; Godin (Kiko 52), Capdevila, Fuentes, Angel, Cazorla, Cani, Ibagaza, Senna (Fuster 58), Llorente, Rossi (Jonathan Pereira 46).
NAC Breda: Ten Rouwelaar; Zwaanswijk, Schilder, Hofstede (Penders 77), Kwakman, De Graaf (Benomar 84), Koikka, Reuser, Snoyl, Gorter, Cairo (Amoah 66).

Vorskla (0) 2 *(Sachko 48, Esin 74)*

Benfica (0) 1 *(Saviola 60)* 12,000

Vorskla: Dolganskiy; Dallku, Krasnoperov, Curri, Yarmash (Brezus 46), Despotovski, Markoski (Chesnakov 88), Kulakov, Medvedev, Esin, Sachko (Chichikov 72).
Benfica: Moreira; Luisao, Felipe Menezes, David Luiz, Sidnei, Javier Garcia, Ramires (Ruben Amorim 71), Fabio Coentrao (Di Maria 63), Cesar Peixoto, Keirrison, Nuno Gomes (Saviola 46).

Zenit (1) 1 *(Fatih 34)*

Nacional (0) 1 *(Ruben Micael 89)* 18,000

Zenit: Contofalsky; Anyukov, Fernando Meira, Kim, Lombaerts, Shirokov (Krizanac 71), Zyryanov, Semshov, Huszti (Ignatovich 90), Fatih, Kornilenko.
Nacional: Rafael Bracali; Patacas, Felipe Lopes, Halliche (Nuno Pinto 46), Wellington Tomasevic 80), Cleber, Luis Alberto, Pecnik, Ruben Micael (Abdou 90), Joao Aurelio, Leandro Salino.

Zilina (0) 0

Partizan Belgrade (0) 2 *(Diarra 59, Ilic 65)* 10,650

Zilina: Pernis; Leitner, Piacek, Sourek, Pecalka, Mraz (Kobylik 72), Jez, Tsimakuridze, Adauto (Lietava 63), Vyskocil (Rilke 64), Oravec.
Partizan Belgrade: Bozovic M; Stevanovic (Gavrancic 85), Dordevic, Krstajic (Knezevic 56), Jovanovic B (Fejsa 67), Obradovic, Tomic, Petrovic, Ljajic, Ilic, Diarra.

GROUP STAGE

GROUP A

Thursday, 17 September 2009

Ajax (0) 0

Timisoara (0) 0   25,391

Ajax: Stekelenburg; Van der Wiel, Vertonghen, Alderweireld, Emanuelson, Aissati (Rommedahl 83), De Jong, De Zeeuw, Suarez, Cvitanich (Pantelic 58), Bakircioglu (Sulejmani 71).

Timisoara: Pantilimon; Bonfim, Nibombe, Mera, Curtean (Ionescu 67), Alexa, Art Karamian, Goga (Poparadu 84), Bourceanu, Parks (Stancu 59), Bucur.

Dinamo Zagreb (0) 0

Anderlecht (0) 2 *(Bernardez 74, Legear 88)*   20,000

Dinamo Zagreb: Butina; Kovac, Lovren, Vrdoljak, Cufre, Etto (Tomecak 85), Sammir (Sivonjic 79), Badelj, Morales, Mandzukic, Papadopoulos D (Slepicka 69).

Anderlecht: Proto; Mazuch, Deschacht, Juhasz, Bernardez, Biglia, Boussoufa (Chatelle 90), Kouyate (Legear 71), Gillet, Sare, Suarez (Lukaku 87).

Thursday, 1 October 2009

Anderlecht (0) 1 *(Legear 85)*

Ajax (0) 1 *(Rommedahl 72)*   17,026

Anderlecht: Proto; Deschacht, Van Damme■, Juhasz, Bernardez, Boussoufa, Gillet, Sare, Suarez (Legear 58), Kanu (De Sutter 79), Lukaku (Kruiswijk 88).

Ajax: Stekelenburg; Van der Wiel, Vertonghen, Alderweireld, Emanuelson, Aissati (Sulejmani 89), Enoh, De Zeeuw, Pantelic, Suarez, Bakircioglu (Rommedahl 58).

Timisoara (0) 0

Dinamo Zagreb (1) 3 *(Badelj 8, Sammir 52, Morales 59)*
     10,000

Timisoara: Pantilimon; Bonfim, Nibombe, Mera, Curtean (Magera 69), Alexa, Art Karamian, Goga, Ionescu (Bourceanu 55), Arm Karamian (Parks 46), Bucur.

Dinamo Zagreb: Loncaric; Kovac, Lovren, Vrdoljak, Cufre (Barbaric 60), Etto, Sammir, Badelj, Morales (Calello 83), Mandzukic, Sivonjic (Papadopoulos D 74).

Thursday, 22 October 2009

Ajax (1) 2 *(Suarez 2 (pen), Rommedahl 81)*

Dinamo Zagreb (0) 1 *(Tomecak 90)*   30,700

Ajax: Stekelenburg; Van der Wiel, Vertonghen, Alderweireld, Emanuelson, Enoh, Anita, De Zeeuw, Pantelic (Rommedahl 74), Sulejmani (Gabri 78), Suarez (Cvitanich 90).

Dinamo Zagreb: Loncaric; Kovac, Lovren, Vrdoljak, Cufre, Etto, Sammir, Badelj, Morales (Sivonjic 62), Mandzukic (Kramaric 88), Papadopoulos D (Tomecak 68).

Timosoara (0) 0

Anderlecht (0) 0   6000

Timosoara: Pantilimon; Bonfim, Nibombe, Scutaru, Mera, Alexa (Magera 81), Art Karamian, Goga, Bourceanu, Arm Karamian (Curtean 72), Bucur (Parks 74).

Anderlecht: Proto; Mazuch, Deschacht, Juhasz, Biglia, Boussoufa, Gillet, Diandy (Kouyate 85), Sare, Kanu (Rnic 46), Lukaku (Suarez 64).

Thursday, 5 November 2009

Anderlecht (1) 3 *(Suarez 29 (pen), Boussoufa 69, Legear 90)*

Timisoara (0) 1 *(Parks 50)*   22,000

Anderlecht: Proto; Mazuch, Deschacht, Juhasz, Biglia, Boussoufa, Gillet, Sare, Suarez (Kouyate 83), Kanu (Legear 62), Lukaku (Frutos 77).

Timisoara: Pantilimon; Bonfim, Nibombe, Scutaru, Maxim, Alexa, Art Karamian (Curtean 80), Bourceanu (Stancu 68), Parks, Bucur (Goga 76), Magera.

Dinamo Zagreb (0) 0

Ajax (2) 2 *(Pantelic 13, De Zeeuw 45)*

Dinamo Zagreb: Butina; Tomecak, Kovac, Lovren, Vrdoljak (Chago 46), Cufre■, Calello■, Etto, Sammir, Morales (Barbaric 42), Sivonjic (Ibanez 78).

Ajax: Stekelenburg; Van der Wiel, Vertonghen (Oleguer 80), Alderweireld, Emanuelson (Sulejmani 77), Enoh (Donald 65), De Jong, Anita, De Zeeuw, Pantelic, Suarez.

Behind closed doors.

Wednesday, 2 December 2009

Anderlecht (0) 0

Dinamo Zagreb (0) 1 *(Slepicka 57)*   16,000

Anderlecht: Proto; Mazuch, Deschacht (Kouyate 85). Van Damme, Juhasz, Biglia, Boussoufa, Legear (Suarez 68), Gillet, Sare (De Sutter 72), Lukaku.

Dinamo Zagreb: Butina; Tomecak (Chago 90), Ibanez, Kovac, Lovren, Vrdoljak, Etto, Sammir (Barbaric 82), Badelj, Mandzukic, Slepicka (Papadopoulos D 67).

Timisoara (1) 1 *(Goga 2)*

Ajax (1) 2 *(Suarez 8, Pantelic 46)*   8085

Timisoara: Pantilimon■; Bonfim■, Stancu, Scutaru, Mera, Alexa, Art Karamian, Goga (Maxim 73), Bourceanu, Bucur (Taborda 65), Magera (Parks 54).

Ajax: Stekelenburg; Van der Wiel (Silva 64), Vertonghen, Alderweireld, Emanuelson (Oleguer 46), Enoh, Anita (Sulejmani 60), Donald, De Zeeuw, Pantelic, Suarez.

Thursday, 17 December 2009

Ajax (0) 1 *(Emanuelson 77)*

Anderlecht (3) 3 *(Lukaku 13, 23, Legear 43)*   36,000

Ajax: Stekelenburg; Van der Wiel, Oleguer, Vertonghen, Emanuelson, Enoh (Rommedahl 59), De Jong (De Zeeuw 83), Anita, Donald (Suarez 80), Pantelic, Sulejmani.

Anderlecht: Proto; Mazuch, Deschacht, Van Damme (Sare 90), Juhasz, Biglia, Boussoufa, Legear (Suarez 80), Kouyate, Gillet, Lukaku (Frutos 63).

Dinamo Zagreb (0) 1 *(Scutaru 80 (og))*

Timisoara (0) 2 *(Bucur 67, Goga 84)*

Dinamo Zagreb: Butina; Ibanez (Tomecak 71), Kovac, Lovren, Vrdoljak, Etto, Sammir, Badelj, Morales (Kramaric 83), Mandzukic, Slepicka (Sivonjic 71).

Timisoara: Taborda; Nibombe, Stancu, Scutaru, Mera, Maxim, Curtean (Goga 75), Alexa, Bourceanu, Parks (Ionescu 90), Bucur (Matei 88).

Behind closed doors.

Group A Table	P	W	D	L	F	A	Pts
Anderlecht	6	3	2	1	9	4	11
Ajax	6	3	2	1	8	6	11
Dinamo Zagreb	6	2	0	4	6	8	6
Timisoara	6	1	2	3	4	9	5

GROUP B

Thursday, 17 September 2009

Genoa (2) 2 *(Zapater 4, Sculli 39)*

Slavia Prague (0) 0   22,000

Genoa: Amelia; Criscito, Moretti, Bocchetti, Tomovic, Kharja (Milanetto 81), Rossi, Zapater (Mesto 85), Palacio, Crespo (Figueroa 82), Sculli.

Slavia Prague: Vaniak; Celustka, Suchy, Vomacka, Ragued, Janda, Vasiljevic (Grajciar 79), Krajcik, Belaid (Volesak 71), Hlousek, Senkerik (Naumov 46).

Lille (0) 1 *(Gervinho 86)*

Valencia (0) 1 *(Mata 78)*   14,676

Lille: Butelle; Emerson, Beria, Rami, Dumont, Balmont (Mavuba 76), Obraniak, Chedjou, Hazard, Aubameyang (Frau 63), Vittek (Gervinho 69).

Valencia: Cesar; Bruno, David Navarro, Mathieu, Maduro, Albelda, Joaquin, Michel, Jordi Alba (Mata 76), Zigic (Villa 82), Miku (Ever Banega 66).

Thursday, 1 October 2009

Slavia Prague (1) 1 *(Belaid 6 (pen))*

Lille (0) 5 *(Suchy 47 (og), Frau 71, Gervinho 85, 90, Souquet 88)* 9158

Slavia Prague: Vaniak; Hubacek, Such⁻, Vomacka, Ragued (Grajciar 62), Janda, Krajcik, Belaid (Vasiljevic 76), Volesak, Hlousek, Senkerik (Vlcek 76).
Lille: Butelle; Vandam, Emerson, Beria, Rami, Dumont, Cabaye (Mavuba 83), Hazard, Souquet. Aubameyang (Gervinho 61), Vittek (Frau 67).

Valencia (0) 3 *(Silva 52, Zigic 56, Villa 82 (pen))*

Genoa (1) 2 *(Floccari 43, Kharja 64 (pen))* 21,333

Valencia: Cesar; David Navarro, Dealbert, Mathieu, Miguel, Albelda (Maduro 79), Pablo Hernandez (Joaquin 79), Silva, Ever Banega, Zigic (Villa 65), Mata.
Genoa: Amelia; Sokratis (Milanetto 74), Mesto, Modesto (Esposito 58), Moretti, Bocchetti, Tomovic (Sculli 57), Kharja, Zapater, Palladino, Floccari.

Thursday, 22 October 2009

Lille (1) 3 *(Obraniak 38, Vittek 63, Hazard 84)*

Genoa (0) 0 16,000

Lille: Butelle; Vandam, Emerson, Rami, Dumont, Cabaye (Beria 81), Obraniak (Hazard 74), Chedjou, Mavuba, Aubameyang (Gervinho 65), Vittek.
Genoa: Amelia; Criscito (Sculli 44), Esposito (Palladino 46), Mesto, Moretti, Bocchetti, Rossi, Juric, Milanetto, Palacio, Floccari (Figueroa 63).

Valencia (0) 1 *(David Navarro 63)*

Slavia Prague (1) 1 *(Naumov 28)* 18,000

Valencia: Moya; David Navarro, Alexis, Mathieu, Miguel, Maduro (Ever Banega 78) Baraja, Pablo Hernandez, Michel (Mata 46), Jordi Alba (Villa 62), Zigic.
Slavia Prague: Vaniak; Hubacek, Celustka, Suchy, Vomacka, Trapp, Ragued, Grajciar (Vlcek 90), Hlousek, Senkerik (Belaid 78), Naumov (Krajcik 36).

Thursday, 5 November 2009

Genoa (1) 3 *(Palacio 14, Crespo 58, Sculli 90)*

Lille (0) 2 *(Frau 76, Gervinho 84)* 34,000

Genoa: Scarpi; Modesto (Sokratis 79), Moretti, Biava, Bocchetti, Tomovic, Rossi, Zapater, Palacio (Figueroa 84), Crespo (Sculli 81), Palladino.
Lille: Landreau; Vandam, Emerson, Beria, Rami, Dumont, Belmont (Cabaye 62), Obraniak, Aubameyang (Gervinho 63), Vittek, Toure (Frau 73).

Slavia Prague (0) 2 *(Janda 79, Grajcia 82)*

Valencia (1) 2 *(Joaquin 22 (pen), Maduro 47)* 10,624

Slavia Prague: Romanovs (Vaniak 28); Hubacek, Celustka, Suchy, Vomacka, Trapp Krajcik, Grajciar (Smicer 86), Hlousek, Senkerik, Naumov (Janda 46).
Valencia: Moya; Bruno, David Navarro, Mathieu (Del Horno 70), Maduro, Baraja, Joaquin, Silva (Pablo Hernandez 58), Zigic, Mata (Jordi Alba 64).

Wednesday, 2 December 2009

Slavia Prague (0) 0

Genoa (0) 0 9443

Slavia Prague: Romanovs; Hubacek, Celustka, Suchy, Ragued, Krajcik, Belaid (Kores 71) Trubila (Mares 81), Grajciar, Vlcek (Naumov 88), Hlousek.
Genoa: Scarpi; Sokratis, Mesto (Palladino 78), Modesto, Biava, Bocchetti, Tomovic, Zapater, Juric (Criscito 52), Crespo (Sculli 52), Floccari.

Valencia (2) 3 *(Joaquin 3, 32, Mata 43)*

Lille (0) 1 *(Chedjou 90)* 20,000

Valencia: Moya; Bruno, Maduro, David Navarro, Marchena (Manuel Fernandes 79), Alexis, Miguel, Joaquin (Jordi Alba 76), Pablo Hernandez, Ever Banega, Mata (Miku 72).
Lille: Landreau; Emerson (Debuchy 46), Beria, Rami, Balmont, Cabaye (Obraniak 71), Chedjou, Mavuba, Hazard, Frau (Vittek 46), Gervinho.

Thursday, 17 December 2009

Genoa (0) 1 *(Crespo 51)*

Valencia (1) 2 *(Bruno 45, Villa 90)* 25,000

Genoa: Scarpi; Criscito, Moretti, Biava, Bocchetti, Rossi, Zapater (Floccari 82), Juric, Palacio, Crespo, Palladino (Sculli 29).
Valencia: Moya; Bruno, David Navarro, Marchena (Maduro 32), Alexis, Miguel, Albelda, Joaquin (Jordi Alba 90), Ever Banega, Villa, Mata (Manuel Fernandes 79).

Lille (2) 3 *(Cabaye 24, Gervinho 39, Obraniak 80)*

Slavia Prague (0) 1 *(Vlcek 56)* 15,358

Lille: Landreau; Vandam, Beria, Rami, Balmont, Cabaye (Dumont 46), Obraniak, Chedjou, Mavuba, Frau (De Melc 81), Gervinho (Hazard 67).
Slavia Prague: Romanovs; Hubacek, Celustka, Hosek, Ragued, Janda (Belaid 84), Krajcik, Trubila (Senkerik 73), Grajciar, Vlcek (Naumov 87), Hlousek.

Group B Table	P	W	D	L	F	A	Pts
Valencia	6	3	3	0	12	8	12
Lille	6	3	1	2	15	9	10
Genoa	6	2	1	3	8	10	7
Slavia Prague	6	0	3	3	5	13	3

GROUP C

Thursday, 17 September 2009

Hapoel Tel Aviv (0) 2 *(Vucicevic 75, Lala 88)*

Celtic (1) 1 *(Samaras 25)* 15,500

Hapoel Tel Aviv: Enyeama; Da Silva, Ben Dayan, Kanada, Yadin, Natcho (Zahavy 68), Badir, Vermouth, Menteshashvili (Lala 54), Vucicevic (Mare 80), Yeboah.
Celtic: Boruc; Hinkel, Fox, Loovens, Caldwell (McDonald S 89), McManus, N'Guemo (McGinn 66), Brown S, Maloney, Samaras (Killen 70), McGeady.

Rapid Vienna (2) 3 *(Hofmann 35, Jelavic 45, Drazan 76)*

Hamburg (0) 0 49,850

Rapid Vienna: Payer; Katzer, Eder, Soma, Kulovits, Heikkinen, Hofmann, Kavlak, Boskovic (Drazan 60), Pehlivan, Jelavic (Salihi 85).
Hamburg: Rost; Rozehnal, Mathijsen, Aogo, Boateng (Demel 46), Ze Roberto, Jarolim, Trochowski (Pitroipa 46), Petric, Elia, Berg (Torun 73).

Thursday, 1 October 2009

Celtic (1) 1 *(McDonald S 21)*

Rapid Vienna (1) 1 *(Jelavic 3)* 40,577

Celtic: Boruc; Wilson, Fox, N'Guemo (Robson 81), Caldwell, McManus, Maloney (Killen 81), Brown S, McDonald S, Samaras, McGeady (McGinn 82).
Rapid Vienna: Payer; Patocka, Katzer, Soma, Dober, Heikkinen, Hofmann, Kavlak, Boskovic (Drazan 63), Pehlivan, Jelavic.

Hamburg (3) 4 *(Berg 5, 11, Elia 40, Ze Roberto 78)*

Hapoel Tel Aviv (1) 2 *(Shechter 37, Yeboah 62)* 29,976

Hamburg: Rost; Mathijsen, Aogo, Boateng, Ze Roberto (Tesche 84), Jarolim, Demel, Petric (Pitroipa 84), Elia (Castelen 46), Berg, Torun.
Hapoel Tel Aviv: Enyeama; Da Silva, Bondarv (Zahavy 84), Ben Dayan, Yadin, Natcho, Badir, Vermouth, Menteshashvili (Shechter 28), Vucicevic (Duani 68), Yeboah.

Thursday, 22 October 2009

Celtic (0) 0

Hamburg (0) 1 *(Berg 63)* 38,821

Celtic: Boruc; Wilson, Naylor, N'Guemo, Caldwell, McManus, Maloney (McGinn 76), Brown S (McCourt 76), McDonald S (Samaras 61), Robson, McGeady.
Hamburg: Rost; Rozehnal, Mathijsen, Aogo, Jansen (Trochowski 77), Ze Roberto, Jarolim, Demel, Pitroipa (Tesche 89), Elia, Berg.

Hapoel Tel Aviv (1) 5 *(Dober 29 (og), Menteshashvili 54, Shechter 60, Vermouth 69, Lala 90)*
Rapid Vienna (1) 1 *(Hofmann 32)*   10,000
Hapoel Tel Aviv: Enyeama; Da Silva, Bondarv, Ben Dayan, Yadin, Natcho, Vermouth, Menteshashvili, Vucicevic (Zahavy 82), Shechter (Mare 87), Yeboah (Lala 77).
Rapid Vienna: Payer; Patocka, Katzer, Soma, Dober (Salihi 66), Hofmann, Kavlak, Boskovic (Jovanovic 70), Pehlivan, Jelavic, Trimmel (Kulovits 73).

Thursday, 5 November 2009
Hamburg (0) 0
Celtic (0) 0   45,037
Hamburg: Rost; Rozehnal, Mathijsen, Aogo, Jansen (Trochowski 83), Ze Roberto, Jarolim, Pitroipa (Torun 88), Rincon, Elia, Berg.
Celtic: Zaluska; Hinkel, Fox, Crosas, Caldwell, Loovens, N'Guemo, Robson (McGinn 75), McDonald S (Fortune 59). Samaras, McGeady (Naylor 59).

Rapid Vienna (0) 0
Hapoel Tel Aviv (1) 3 *(Yadin 13, Vermouth 65, Natcho 70)*
     50,000
Rapid Vienna: Payer; Patocka, Katzer, Soma, Dober, Heikkinen, Hofmann, Kavlak (Dragan 66), Boskovic, Pehlivan (Gartler 57), Jelavic (Salihi 80).
Hapoel Tel Aviv: Enyeama; Da Silva, Bondarv, Ben Dayan, Yadin (Zandberg 88), Natcho, Badir, Vermouth, Vucicevic (Menteshashvili 59), Shechter, Yeboah (Lala 72).

Wednesday, 2 December 2009
Celtic (1) 2 *(Samaras 22, Robson 68)*
Hapoel Tel Aviv (0) 0   32,000
Celtic: Zaluska; Hinkel, Fox, Crosas, Caldwell, Loovens, Robson, N'Guemo, McDonald, Samaras (Fortune 63), McGeady (Naylor 74).
Hapoel Tel Aviv: Enyeama; Da Silva, Bondarv, Ben Dayan, Yadin (Zahavy 79), Natcho, Badir, Vermouth, Menteshashvili (Vucicevic 46), Shechter, Yeboah (Lala 46).

Hamburg (0) 2 *(Jansen 47, Berg 53)*
Rapid Vienna (0) 0   45,737
Hamburg: Rost; Mathijsen, Aogo (Bertram 87), Jansen (Tavares 83), Boateng, Demel, Tesche, Jarolim, Trochowski, Rincon, Berg (Petric 76).
Rapid Vienna: Payer; Jovanovic, Katzer, Soma, Kulovits, Heikkinen (Dober 66), Hofmann (Thonhofer 79), Kavlak, Boskovic, Pehlivan (Salihi 52), Jelavic.

Thursday, 17 December 2009
Hapoel Tel Aviv (1) 1 *(Yeboah 23)*
Hamburg (0) 0   14,500
Hapoel Tel Aviv: Enyeama; Da Silva, Ben Dayan, Kende, Natcho, Badir, Vermouth, Menteshashvili, Shechter (Zandberg 90), Yeboah (Lala 68), Zahavy (Mare 81).
Hamburg: Hesl; Rozehnal, Mathijsen, Jansen, Demel, Tesche, Trochowski (Elia 46), Rincon, Tavares (Torun 46), Petric, Berg.

Rapid Vienna (3) 3 *(Jelavic 1, 8, Salihi 19)*
Celtic (1) 3 *(Fortune 23, 67, McGowan 90)*   45,000
Rapid Vienna: Hedl; Patocka, Katzer, Soma, Dober (Trimmel 30), Kulovits, Hofmann, Kavlak (Drazan 59), Boskovic, Salihi (Ildiz 78), Jelavic.
Celtic: Boruc; Caddis, Wilson, Crosas, Loovens, McManus, Flood, N'Guemo, Fortune (Killen 90), McGowan, McGinn (Carey 78).

Group C Table	P	W	D	L	F	A	Pts
Hapoel Tel Aviv	6	4	0	2	13	8	12
Hamburg	6	3	1	2	7	6	10
Celtic	6	1	3	2	7	7	6
Rapid Vienna	6	1	2	3	8	14	5

GROUP D

Thursday, 17 September 2009
Heerenveen (1) 2 *(Sibon 12, Dingsdag 77)*
Sporting Lisbon (2) 3 *(Liedson 17, 40, 88)*   16,000
Heerenveen: Lejsal; Nielsen K, Breuer, Dingsdag, Svec, Beerens, Grindheim (Assaidi 72), Popov (Elm 51), Losada, Paulo Henrique, Sibon (Papadopoulos 86).
Sporting Lisbon: Rui Patricio; Daniel Carrico, Polga, Caneira, Abel, Vukcevic (Tonel 89), Matias (Miguel Angulo 82), Miguel Veloso, Joao Moutinho, Yannick Djalo (Helder Postiga 62), Liedson.

Hertha Berlin (1) 1 *(Piszczek 34)*
Ventspils (0) 1 *(Gauracs 48)*   13,454
Hertha Berlin: Drobny (Burchert 21); Friedrich, Janker, Stein, Bengtsson, Cicero, Nicu, Piszczek (Cesar 67), Hartmann (Dardai 77), Ramos, Domovchiyski.
Ventspils: Chasnowski; Zamperini, Kosmacovs, Laizans, Visnakovs A (Butriks 72), Chirkin, Mihadjuks, Tigirlas (Astafjevs 75), Gauracs, Zigajevs (Ndeki 86), Solovjovs.

Thursday, 1 October 2009
Sporting Lisbon (1) 1 *(Adrien Silva 18)*
Hertha Berlin (0) 0   16,197
Sporting Lisbon: Rui Patricio; Daniel Carrico, Tonel, Abel, Adrien Silva■, Vukcevic (Grimi 78), Matias (Pereirinha 46), Miguel Veloso, Joao Moutinho, Caicedo (Yannick Djalo 68), Liedson.
Hertha Berlin: Burchert; Kaka, Von Bergen, Pejcinovic, Janker, Dardai, Cesar, Kacar (Nicu 67), Ramos (Piszczek 46), Raffael, Wichniarek (Domovchiyski 80).

Ventspils (0) 0
Heerenveen (0) 0   2000
Ventspils: Kolinko; Ndeki, Zamperini, Hodel, Kosmacovs, Chirkin, Mihadjuks, Tigirlas, Gauracs (Visnakovs A 88), Zigajevs (Butriks 64), Solovjovs (Rugins 90).
Heerenveen: Vandenbussche; Breuer, Dingsdag, Svec (Beerens 54) Janmaat, Elm, Grindheim, Popov, Losada, Paulo Henrique (Assaidi 70), Sibon (Papadopoulos 83).

Thursday, 22 October 2009
Hertha Berlin (0) 0
Heerenveen (1) 1 *(Losada 36)*   13,134
Hertha Berlin: Burchert; Friedrich, Von Bergen, Pejcinovic, Stein, Cicero (Kacar 62), Ebert■, Lustenberger, Bigalke (Raffael 69), Ramos, Wichniarek (Domovchiyski 46).
Heerenveen: Vandenbussche; Nielsen K, Breuer, Dingsdag, Elm, Grindheim (Janmaat■ 73), Popov, Losada, Papadopoulos, Assaidi (Paulo Henrique 83), Sibon (Svec 66).

Ventspils (0) 1 *(Laizans 64 (pen))*
Sporting Lisbon (1) 2 *(Miguel Veloso 6, Joao Moutinho 85)*   4500
Ventspils: Kolinko; Ndeki, Zamperini, Hodel, Kosmacovs (Zigajevs 60), Laizans (Astafjevs 83), Chirkin, Mihadjuks, Tigirlas, Gauracs, Butriks (Visnakovs A 54).
Sporting Lisbon: Rui Patricio; Daniel Carrico, Tonel, Grimi, Abel, Vukcevic (Pereirinha 62), Matias (Miguel Angulo 79), Miguel Veloso, Joao Moutinho, Caicedo (Helder Postiga 72), Liedson.

Thursday, 5 November 2009
Heerenveen (2) 2 *(Papadopoulos 4, 36)*
Hertha Berlin (1) 3 *(Domovchiyski 21, 52, Wichniarek 90)*
     20,000
Heerenveen: Vandenbussche; Nielsen K, Breuer, Svec, Koning, Elm, Beerens (Paulo Henrique 82), Popov, Losada (Vayrynen 66), Papadopoulos, Assaidi.
Hertha Berlin: Drobny; Friedrich, Von Bergen, Pejcinovic, Stein, Cicero, Nicu (Piszczek 72), Lustenberger, Bigalke (Raffael 60), Wichniarek, Domovchiyski (Janker 90).

Sporting Lisbon (1) 1 *(Saleiro 22)*
Ventspils (1) 1 *(Zamperini 15)*   18,103
Sporting Lisbon: Rui Patricio; Daniel Carrico (Grimi 53), Pedro Silva, Tonel, Andre Marques (Miguel Angulo 46), Vukcevic (Helder Postiga 74), Matias, Miguel Veloso, Joao Moutinho, Saleiro, Liedson.
Ventspils: Kolinko; Ndeki, Zamperini, Hodel, Kosmacovs, Laizans, Chirkin, Mihadjuks, Tigirlas (Rugins 90), Gauracs (Butriks 71), Zigajevs (Martins 50).

Thursday, 3 December 2009
Sporting Lisbon (0) 1 *(Grimi 90)*
Heerenveen (0) 1 *(Assaidi 47)*   15,000
Sporting Lisbon: Rui Patricio; Daniel Carrico, Polga, Pedro Silva, Caneira (Grimi 46), Adrien Silva, Matias (Izmailov 46), Miguel Veloso, Joao Moutinho, Helder Postiga (Caicedo 79), Liedson.
Heerenveen: Vandenbussche; Nielsen K, Breuer, Dingsdag, Elm, Beerens, Grindheim (Vayrynen 72), Popov, Losada, Papadopoulos (Paulo Henrique 80), Assaidi (Elyounoussi 85).

Ventspils (0) 0
Hertha Berlin (1) 1 *(Raffael 12)*   7200
Ventspils: Kolinko; Ndeki, Zamperini, Hodel (Gauracs 46), Kosmacovs, Laizans (Butriks 84), Chirkin, Tigirlas, Visnakovs E (Visnakovs A 56), Martins, Solovjovs.
Hertha Berlin: Drobny; Von Bergen, Janker, Radjabali-Fardi, Cicero, Nicu, Piszczek, Lustenberger, Ramos (Kacar 68), Raffael■, Wichniarek.

Wednesday, 16 December 2009
Heerenveen (0) 5 *(Vayrynen 55, Elm 58, Sibon 77, 78, Janmaat 88)*
Ventspils (0) 0   18,000
Heerenveen: Vandenbussche; Nielsen K, Breuer, Janmaat, Elm, Beerens, Vayrynen (Losada 81), Grindheim, Popov, Papadopoulos (Sibon 66), Assaidi (Elyounoussi 79).
Ventspils: Chasnowski; Ndeki, Zamperini, Kosmacovs, Chirkin (Dedov 68), Tigirlas, Zigajevs (Gauracs 59), Rugins (Visnakovs A 55), Visnakovs E, Butriks, Solovjovs.

Hertha Berlin (0) 1 *(Kacar 70)*
Sporting Lisbon (0) 0   14,417
Hertha Berlin: Drobny; Von Bergen, Pejcinovic, Janker, Cicero, Nicu (Kaka 90), Piszczek, Lustenberger, Kacar (Kringe 86), Ramos, Wichniarek (Domovchiyski 69).
Sporting Lisbon: Rui Patricio; Daniel Carrico, Pedro Silva (Abel 67), Tonel, Grimi, Adrien Silva, Izmailov (Vukcevic 46), Matias, Pereirinha, Joao Moutinho (Miguel Veloso 73), Saleiro.

Group D Table	P	W	D	L	F	A	Pts
Sporting Lisbon	6	3	2	1	8	6	11
Hertha Berlin	6	3	1	2	6	5	10
Heerenveen	6	2	2	2	11	7	8
Ventspils	6	0	3	3	3	10	3

GROUP E

Thursday, 17 September 2009
Basle (1) 2 *(Carlitos 11, Almerares 87)*
Roma (0) 0   28,000
Basle: Costanzo; Atan, Abraham, Safari, Inkoom, Chipperfield, Stocker (Ferati 90), Cabral, Ca-litos, Streller (Almerares 85), Frei (Unal 90).
Roma: Julio Sergio; Mexes, Motta, Riise (Tonetto 64), Burdisso, Pizarro, Taddei, De Rossi, Baptista (Vucinic 64), Totti, Menez (Guberti 46).

CSKA Sofia (0) 1 *(Michel 61)*
Fulham (0) 1 *(Kamara 65)*   28,000
CSKA Sofia: Karadzhov; Stoyanov K, Kotev, Ivanov, Yanev (Manchev V 78), Todorov, Minev, Yanchev, Morozs (Marquinhos 46), Stoyanov I (Michel 54), Delev.
Fulham: Stockdale; Kelly, Baird, Riise, Pantsil, Smalling, Greening, Davies, Nevland, Kamara, Gera.

Thursday, 1 October 2009
Fulham (0) 1 *(Murphy 57)*
Basle (0) 0   16,100
Fulham: Schwarzer; Kelly, Konchesky, Murphy, Baird, Smalling, Riise, Greening, Johnson A, Zamora, Dempsey.
Basle: Costanzo; Cagdas, Abraham (Da Silva 69), Safari, Sahin, Gelabert (Chipperfield 86), Huggel, Stocker, Carlitos (Almerares 82), Streller, Frei.

Roma (2) 2 *(Okaka Chuka 20, Perrotta 23)*
CSKA Sofia (0) 0   16,027
Roma: Sergio; Juan (Andreolli 72), Motta, Riise, Burdisso, Pizarro, De Rossi, Perrotta, Vucinic (Menez 46), Cerci (Tonetto 75), Okaka Chuka.
CSKA Sofia: Karadzhov; Stoyanov K, Kotev, Ivanov, Yanev, Todorov (Manchev V 66), Minev, Yanchev (Delev 53), Marquinhos, Morozs (Michel 52), Stoyanov I.

Thursday, 22 October 2009
CSKA Sofia (0) 0
Basle (1) 2 *(Frei 20, 63)*   17,000
CSKA Sofia: Karadzhov; Vidanov, Kotev (Branekov 46), Ivanov, Yanev, Todorov, Minev, Yanchev, Marquinhos (Manchev V 65), Stoyanov I (Rui Miguel 55), Michel.
Basle: Colomba; Atan, Abraham, Safari, Inkoom, Huggel, Stocker, Da Silva, Carlitos (Shaqiri 88), Streller (Almerares 85), Frei (Cabral 81).

Fulham (1) 1 *(Hangeland 24)*
Roma (0) 1 *(Andreolli 90)*   23,561
Fulham: Schwarzer; Kelly■, Konchesky (Pantsil 46), Riise (Duff 75), Hughes, Hangeland, Baird, Greening, Kamara, Zamora (Nevland 62), Gera.
Roma: Doni; Andreolli, Mexes, Riise, Burdisso, Taddei (Vucinic 63), De Rossi, Guberti, Brighi (Perrotta 46), Okaka Chuka (Pizarro 46), Menez.

Thursday, 5 November 2009
Basle (2) 3 *(Gelabert 35, Frei 41 (pen), 67)*
CSKA Sofia (0) 1 *(Yanchev 61)*   15,252
Basle: Colomba; Atan, Safari (Shaquiri 78), Inkoom, Gelabert (Aratores 64), Huggel, Chipperfield, Stocker (Perovic 89), Cabral, Frei, Almerares.
CSKA Sofia: Chavdarov; Baez, Vidarov, Stoyanov K, Branekov, Yanchev, Marquinhos, Morozs (Manchev N 28), Stoyanov I, Manchev V (Rui Miguel 71), Delev (Michel 56).

Roma (0) 2 *(Riise 69, Okaka Chuka 76)*
Fulham (1) 1 *(Kamara 19 (pen))*   20,000
Roma: Doni (Julio Sergio 46); Cicinho (Taddei 46), Andreolli, Mexes, Riise, Cassetti, Pizarro, De Rossi, Baptista, Guberti (Menez 66), Okaka Chuka.
Fulham: Schwarzer; Pantsil, Konchesky■, Riise (Zamora 70), Hughes, Hangeland, Gera, Greening, Kamara (Nevland■ 46), Etuhu (Baird 77), Dempsey.

Thursday, 3 December 2009
Fulham (1) 1 *(Gera 15)*
CSKA Sofia (0) 0   23,604
Fulham: Schwarzer; Pantsil, Kelly, Murphy (Duff 79), Baird, Hangeland (Hughes 46), Smalling, Riise, Gera, Zamora, Davies (Dempsey 70).
CSKA Sofia: Chavdarov; Vidanov, Stoyanov K, Ivanov (Yanev 64), Popov, Todorov (Rui Miguel 72), Minev, Yanchev, Timonov (Michel 54), Morozs, Delev.

Roma (1) 2 *(Totti 32 (pen), Vucinic 58)*
Basle (1) 1 *(Huggel 18)*   27,000
Roma: Sergio; Cicinho, Mexes, Riise, Burdisso, Pizarro, De Rossi, Perrotta, Vucinic (Taddei 59), Totti, Menez (Baptista 59).
Basle: Wessels; Cagdas, Abraham, Safari (Shaquiri 79), Inkoom, Gelabert, Huggel, Stocker, Carlitos, Streller, Frei.

Wednesday, 16 December 2009

Basle (0) 2 *(Frei 64 (pen), Streller 87)*

Fulham (2) 3 *(Zamora 41, 44, Gera 76)*   20,063

Basle: Colomba; Cagdas, Abraham, Safari (Shaqiri 46), Inkoom, Huggel, Stocker, Cabral (Almerares 46), Carlitos (Schurpf 79), Streller, Frei.

Fulham: Schwarzer; Pantsil, Kelly, Murphy, Hughes, Smalling, Riise, Greening (Dempsey 70), Gera, Zamora (Duff 80), Etuhu.

CSKA Sofia (0) 0

Roma (1) 3 *(Cerci 45, 52, Scardina 89)*   12,000

CSKA Sofia: Chavdarov; Vidanov, Stoyanov K, Popov (Rui Miguel 74), Yanev, Minev, Yanchev, Timonov (Manchev N 60), Petrov, Michel, Delev (Todorov 80).

Roma: Lobont; Andreolli, Motta, Riise, Burdisso, Pizarro (Brighi 46), De Rossi, Baptista, Perrotta, Cerci (Pettinari 74), Okaka Chuka (Scardina 81).

Group E Table	P	W	D	L	F	A	Pts
Roma	6	4	1	1	10	5	13
Fulham	6	3	2	1	8	6	11
Basle	6	3	0	3	10	7	9
CSKA Sofia	6	0	1	5	2	12	1

GROUP F

Thursday, 17 September 2009

Panathinaikos (1) 1 *(Salpingidis 77)*

Galatasaray (1) 3 *(Elano 5, Baros 47, Sarriegi 58 (og))*
                                                     46,791

Panathinaikos: Galinovic; Sarriegi, Bjarsmyr, Spyropoulos, Leto, Gilberto Silva, Karagounis, Katsouranis (Ninis 50), Salpingidis, Christodoulopoulos (Petropoulos 50), Marinos.

Galatasaray: Leo Franco; Emre G (Ugur 24), Emre A, Hakan Balta, Sabri, Elano (Arda 62), Mehmet, Mustafa, Kewell, Keita (Baris 72), Baros.

Sturm Graz (0) 0

Dinamo Bucharest (0) 1 *(Tamas 81)*   15,300

Sturm Graz: Gratzei; Sonnleitner, Feldhofer (Bukva 83), Kandelaki, Schildenfeld, Weber (Hassler 83), Hlinka, Holzl, Muratovic, Beichler (Lavric 72), Jantscher.

Dinamo Bucharest: Dolha; Diabate, Tamas, Goian, Scarlatache, Kone (Bostina 90), Alexe, Adrian Cristea (Niculescu 76), Torje (Ze Kalanga 80), N'Doye, Andrei Cristea.

Thursday, 1 October 2009

Dinamo Bucharest (0) 0

Panathinaikos (0) 1 *(Karagounis 79)*

Dinamo Bucharest: Dolha; Diabate, Tamas, Goian, Scarlatache, Kone, Bostina (Rus 74), Alexe (Zicu 52), Adrian Cristea (Niculescu 86), Torje, Andrei Cristea.

Panathinaikos: Tzorvas; Sarriegi, Kante, Bjarsmyr, Simao, Vintra, Leto (Ninis 46), Gilberto Silva, Karagounis (Christodoulopoulos 83), Katsouranis, Salpingidis (Rukavina 67).

Behind closed doors.

Galatasaray (0) 1 *(Baros 63)*

Sturm Graz (1) 1 *(Beichler 45)*   22,400

Galatasaray: Leo Franco; Emre A, Hakan Balta, Sabri, Servet, Elano, Arda, Mehmet (Mustafa 77), Ayhan (Kewell 61), Keita, Baros (Nonda 86).

Sturm Graz: Gratzei; Sonnleitner, Ehrenreich, Kandelaki, Schildenfeld, Weber, Hlinka, Bukva (Prettenthaler 76), Muratovic, Beichler (Lavric 89), Jantscher.

Thursday, 22 October 2009

Galatasaray (2) 4 *(Kewell 33, Nonda 42, 46, Elano 58 (pen))*

Dinamo Bucharest (0) 1 *(Bostina 62)*   25,000

Galatasaray: Leo Franco; Sabri (Ugur 67), Servet, Elano, Mehmet, Mustafa, Ayhan (Baris 75), Kewell, Caner, Keita (Aydin 55), Nonda.

Dinamo Bucharest: Dolha; Diabate, Tamas, Goian, Scarlatache, Alexe (Zicu 59), Adrian Cristea, Torje (Niculescu 75), Rus (Bostina 46), N'Doye, Andrei Cristea.

Panathinaikos (0) 1 *(Salpingidis 60 (pen))*

Sturm Graz (0) 0   30,000

Panathinaikos: Tzorvas; Sarriegi, Gabriel, Vintra, Spyropoulos, Leto (Simao 76), Gilberto Silva, Karagounis (Rukavina 85), Katsouranis (Ninis 46), Cisse, Salpingidis.

Sturm Graz: Gratzei; Sonnleitner, Ehrenreich, Prettenthaler (Feldhofer 48), Schildenfeld, Weber, Hlinka, Holzl (Hassler 80), Bukva (Jantcher 62), Muratovic, Beichler.

Thursday, 5 November 2009

Dinamo Bucharest (0) 0

Galatasaray (2) 3 *(Kewell 23, Nonda 24, Mehmet 55)*

Dinamo Bucharest: Dolha; Pulhac, Moti, Tamas, Scarlatache, Kone (Bostina 60), Alexe, Adrian Cristea (Rus 65), Torje, N'Doye, Niculescu.

Galatasaray: Leo Franco; Gokhan (Emre G 86), Hakan Balta, Sabri, Servet, Baris, Arda, Mehmet, Mustafa (Elano 79), Kewell, Nonda (Keita 73).

Behind closed doors.

Sturm Graz (0) 0

Panathinaikos (0) 1 *(Katsouranis 71)*   13,000

Sturm Graz: Gratzei; Sonnleitner, Ehrenreich (Bukva 80), Kandelaki, Schildenfeld, Weber, Holzl, Muratovic, Beichler (Lavric 60), Foda (Weinberger 53), Jantscher.

Panathinaikos: Tzorvas; Sarriegi, Gabriel, Simao, Vintra, Spyropoulos, Gilberto Silva, Karagounis (Ninis 41), Katsouranis, Cisse (Rukavina 90), Salpingidis (Leto 67).

Thursday, 3 December 2009

Dinamo Bucharest (1) 2 *(Niculae 41, 57)*

Sturm Graz (1) 1 *(Sonnleitner 5)*   3000

Dinamo Bucharest: Dolha; Diabate, Moti, Tamas, Molinero, Bostina, Adrian Cristea, Torje (Kone 58), Rus, Niculae (Niculescu 90), Andrei Cristea (Goian 84).

Sturm Graz: Gratzei; Sonnleitner (Jantscher 61), Feldhofer, Ehrenreich, Prettenthaler, Schildenfeld, Hlinka, Bukva, Muratovic (Beichler 68), Weinberger (Holzl 77), Lavric.

Galatasaray (0) 1 *(Gilberto Silva 50 (og))*

Panathinaikos (0) 0   14,000

Galatasaray: Leo Franco; Gokhan (Baris 30), Hakan Balta, Sabri, Servet, Elano (Ayhan 73), Arda, Mehmet, Mustafa, Kewell (Keita 62), Nonda.

Panathinaikos: Tzorvas; Sarriegi, Kante, Darlas (Spyropoulos 46), Simao, Vintra, Gilberto Silva, Karagounis (Ninis 73), Katsouranis (Christodoulopoulos 62), Rukavina, Cisse.

Wednesday, 16 December 2009

Panathinaikos (0) 3 *(Rukavina 54, Cisse 80, 86)*

Dinamo Bucharest (0) 0   19,617

Panathinaikos: Tzorvas; Kante, Bjarsmyr, Simao, Vyntra, Spyropoulos, Ninis (Leto 68), Gilberto Silva, Karagounis (Katsouranis 56), Rukavina (Salpingidis 82), Cisse.

Dinamo Bucharest: Dolha; Diabate, Moti, Tamas, Molinero, Kone, Alexe (Adrian Cristea 46), Torje (Zicu 60), N'Doye, Niculae, Andrei Cristea (Niculescu 67).

Sturm Graz (1) 1 *(Beichler 21)*

Galatasaray (0) 0   14,800

Sturm Graz: Gratzei; Sonnleitner, Ehrenreich, Kandelaki, Schildenfeld, Weber, Hlinka, Holzl, Beichler (Foda 90), Jantscher (Weinberger 90), Lavric (Bukva 70).

Galatasaray: Aykut; Emre A, Erdem (Emre G 68), Servet (Hakan Balta 74), Linderoth (Mustafa 64), Aydin, Baris, Ayhan, Serdar, Caner, Keita.

Group F Table	P	W	D	L	F	A	Pts
Galatasaray	6	4	1	1	12	4	13
Panathinaikos	6	4	0	2	7	4	12
Dinamo Bucharest	6	2	0	4	4	12	6
Sturm Graz	6	1	1	4	3	6	4

GROUP G

Thursday, 17 September 2009
Lazio (0) 1 *(Foggia 59)*
Salzburg (0) 2 *(Schiemer 82, Janko 90)* 15,000
Lazio: Bizzarri; Lichtsteiner, Cribari, Radu, Diakite, Dabo (Foggia 46), Matuzalem, Meghni (Eliseu 70), Baronio, Zarate, Cruz (Mauri 62).
Salzburg: Gustafsson; Afolabi, Schwegler, Schiemer, Ulmer, Sekagya, Pokrivac (Cziommer 63), Tchoyi, Svento (Nelisse 80), Leitgeb (Vladavic 73), Janko.

Villarreal (0) 1 *(Nilmar 72)*
Levski (0) 0 5000
Villarreal: Diego Lopez; Gonzalo, Capdevila, Javi Venta, Ivan Marcano, Eguren, Pires (Escudero 82), Cani, Bruno (Ibagaza 55), Nilmar, Jonathan Pereira (Rossi 66).
Levski: Petkov; Genev, Rabeh, Minev, Benzoukane, Joaozinho, Tasevski (Simonovic 66), Baltanov, Dimitrov N (Ognyanov 78), Bardon, Hristov (Yovov 62).

Thursday, 1 October 2009
Levski (0) 0
Lazio (2) 4 *(Matuzalem 22, Zarate 45, Meghni 67, Rocchi 73)* 10,000
Levski: Dimitrov T; Rabeh, Topuzakov (Miliev 46), Minev, Benzoukane, Sarmov, Joazinho, Tasevski (Tabakov 46), Ze Soares, Bardon, Hristov (Yovov 72).
Lazio: Bizzarri; Lichtsteiner, Cribari, Radu, Matuzalem (Mauri 74), Meghni, Baronio (Dabo 54), Perpetuini Eliseu, Rocchi, Zarate (Foggia 62).

Salzburg (1) 2 *(Janko 21, Tchoyi 84)*
Villarreal (0) 0 18,800
Salzburg: Gustafsson; Afolabi, Schwegler, Schiemer, Ulmer, Sekagya, Pokrivac, Tchoyi, Svento (Opdam 90", Leitgeb (Cziommer 90), Janko (Zickler 79).
Villarreal: Diego Lopez; Gonzalo (Senna 57), Capdevila, Angel, Ivan Marcano, Eguren, Cazorla, Cani (Escudero 64), Bruno, Llorente (Nilmar 76), Rossi.

Thursday, 22 October 2009
Lazio (1) 2 *(Zarate 20, Rocchi 90)*
Villarreal (1) 1 *(Eguren 40)* 22,000
Lazio: Bizzarri; Lichtsteiner, Kolarov, Cribari, Radu, Dabo (Diakite 46), Matuzalem*, Foggia (Rocchi 76), Baronio, Zarate, Cruz (Mauri 72).
Villarreal: Diego Lopez; Gonzalo, Capdevila, Angel, Ivan Marcano, Eguren, Pires, Cani (Cazorla 75), Senna, Nilmar (Jonathan Pereira 81), Rossi (Llorente 78).

Salzburg (1) 1 *(Svento 45)*
Levski (0) 0 17,888
Salzburg: Gustafsson; Afolabi, Schwegler, Schiemer, Ulmer, Sekagya, Pokrivac, Tchoyi, Svento (Vladavic 90), Leitgeb (Cziommer 80), Zickler (Rakic 75).
Levski: Petkov; Genev, Milanov (Benzoukane 46), Minev, Miliev, Sarmov, Baltanov, Yovov, Ze Soares, Dimitrov N (Joaozinho 65), Bardon (Hristov 53).

Thursday, 5 November 2009
Levski (0) 0
Salzburg (0) 1 *(Schiemer 90)* 5000
Levski: Petkov; Milanov, Rabeh, Minev, Miliev, Sarmov*, Tasevski (Krastovchev 75), Yovov (Baltanov 64), Ze Soares, Dimitrov N (Joaozinho 81), Bardon.
Salzburg: Gustafsson; Afolabi (Jezek 87), Schwegler, Schiemer, Ulmer, Sekagya, Pokrivac, Tchoyi, Svento (Zickler 73), Leitgeb, Janko.

Villarreal (3) 4 *(Pires 2, 15 (pen), Cani 13, Rossi 83 (pen))*
Lazio (0) 1 *(Zarate 73)* 14,000
Villarreal: Diego Lopez (Oliva 52), Gonzalo*, Godin, Capdevila, Angel, Eguren, Pires (Rossi 78), Cani, Bruno, Llorente (Ivan Marcano 57), Nilmar.
Lazio: Bizzarri; Lichtsteiner, Siviglia (Kolarov 54), Radu, Diakite, Mauri, Foggia, Baronio*, Perpetini (Zarate 54), Eliseu, Racchi (Makinwa 64).

Wednesday, 2 December 2009
Levski (0) 0
Villarreal (1) 2 *(Rossi 36, Senna 84)* 5000
Levski: Mitrev; Milanov, Rabeh (Topuzakov 46) (Benzoukane 65), Minev, Miliev, Joaozinho, Tasevski, Simcnovic, Ze Soares, Bardon, Hristov (Krastovchev 52).
Villarreal: Diego Lopez; Godin, Capdevila, Angel, Ivan Marcano, Eguren, Pires (Cani 61), Ibagaza, Fuster (Nilmar 71), Escudero, Rossi (Senna 81).

Salzburg (0) 2 *(Afolabi 52, Tchoyi 78)*
Lazio (0) 1 *(Foggia 57)* 26,270
Salzburg: Gustafsson; Afolabi, Schwegler, Opdam, Ulmer, Sekagya, Pokrivac (Cziommer 87), Tchoyi (Zickler 83), Svento, Leitgeb, Janko (Nelisse 90).
Lazio: Muslera; Lichtsteiner, Kolarov, Cribari, Radu (Rocchi 55), Diakite, Mauri, Foggia, Brocchi (Makinwa 81), Eliseu (Meghni 46), Zarate.

Thursday, 17 December 2009
Lazio (0) 0
Levski (0) 1 *(Yovov 60)* 3000
Lazio: Muslera; Cribari, Sevieri (Cinque 61), Cavanda, Luciani, Diakite, Scaloni, Baronio, Perpetuini, Eliseu, Makinwa.
Levski: Mitrev; Milanov, Rabeh, Minev, Miliev, Sarmov, Tasevski (Hristov 76), Yovov (Simonovic 88), Ze Soares, Dimitrov N (Joaozinho 58), Bardon.

Villarreal (0) 0
Salzburg (1) 1 *(Svento 7)* 7000
Villarreal: Oliva; Gonzalo (Capdevila 46), Angel, Ivan Marcano, Kiko (Matilla 60), Eguren, Bruno, Escudero, Llorente, Nilmar, Jonathan Pereira (Rossi 72).
Salzburg: Gustafsson; Afolabi, Schwegler, Opdam, Ulmer, Sekagya, Augustinussen, Svento, Cziommer (Vladavic 81), Leitgeb (Jezek 84), Nelisse (Rakic 63).

Group G Table	P	W	D	L	F	A	Pts
Salzburg	6	6	0	0	9	2	18
Villarreal	6	3	0	3	8	6	9
Lazio	6	2	0	4	9	10	6
Levski	6	1	0	5	1	9	3

GROUP H

Thursday, 17 September 2009
Fenerbahce (0) 1 *(Mehmet 71)*
Twente (0) 2 *(Nkufo 75, 80)* 36,000
Fenerbahce: Volkan; Lugano, Roberto Carlos (Mehmet 64), Andre Santos, Bilica, Gokhan, Emre B, Kazim-Richards (Semih 81), Alex, Cristian, Guiza (Deivid 81).
Twente: Boschker; Kuiper, Wisgerhof, Stam, Douglas, Brama, Tiote (Janssen 42), Nkufo, Perez (Akram 90), Stoch (Vujicevic 69), Ruiz.

Steaua (0) 0
Sheriff (0) 0
Steaua: Zapata; Rada, Marin, Ghionea, Ninu, Szekely, Nicolita, Ionescu, Onicas (Toja 57), Surdu (Tanase 79), Stancu (Kapetanos 70).
Sheriff: Namasco; Da Costa, Volkov (Diedhiou 63) (Suvorov 90), Verbetchi (Bulat 81), Tarkhnishvili, Tsynya, Balima, Erokhin, Rouamba, Luis Antonio, Kuchuk.
Behind closed doors.

Thursday, 1 October 2009
Sheriff (0) 0
Fenerbahce (0) 1 *(Alex 52)* 11 634
Sheriff: Namasco; Tarkhnishvili, Karpovich, Tsynya (Diedhiou 71), Balima, Erokhin, Rouamba, Arbanas (Corneencov 66), Luis Antonio, Suvorov (Volkov 78), Kuchuk.
Fenerbahce: Volkan; Lugano, Roberto Carlos, Onder, Ugur (Mehmet 70), Bilica, Emre B, Kazim-Richards (Deivid 70), Alex, Cristian, Semih (Wederson 83).

Twente (0) 0

Steaua (0) 0   19,200

Twente: Boschker; Kuiper, Wisgerhof, Stam, Douglas, Brama, Tiote (Janssen 62), Nkufo, Perez (Parker 62), Stoch (Vujicevic 84), Ruiz.
Steaua: Zapata; Rada, Marin, Ghionea, Szekely (Ninu 90), Toja, Nicolita, Bicfalvi, Kapetanos, Surdu (Onicas 77), Stancu (Ionescu 90).

Thursday, 22 October 2009

Sheriff (1) 2 *(Balima 41, Franca 90)*

Twente (0) 0   10,000

Sheriff: Namasco; Tarkhnishvili, Mamah, Nadson, Corneencov, Balima, Erokhin (Arbanas 90), Rouamba, Luis Antonio, Diedhiou (Volkov 66), Kuchuk (Franca 78).
Twente: Boschker; Wisgerhof, Stam, Douglas, Carney, Brama (Tiote 59), Janssen, Nkufo, Perez (Parker 58), Stoch (De Jong 78), Ruiz.

Steaua (0) 0

Fenerbahce (0) 1 *(Kazim-Richards 59)*   8000

Steaua: Zapata; Golanski, Rada, Baciu, Ghionea, Szekely (Moreno 67), Toja, Nicolita, Bicfalvi (Onicas 43), Kapetanos, Surdu.
Fenerbahce: Volkan; Lugano, Roberto Carlos, Andre Santos (Ali 89), Bilica, Gokhan, Emre B, Kazim-Richards (Selcuk 86), Cristian, Ozer (Wederson 71), Mehmet.

Thursday, 5 November 2009

Fenerbahce (1) 3 *(Santos 15, Bilica 51, Alex 67)*

Steaua (1) 1 *(Kapetanos 38)*   28,000

Fenerbahce: Volkan; Lugano, Roberto Carlos, Andre Santos, Bilica, Gokhan, Emre B (Guiza 70), Kazim-Richards (Ozer 70), Alex (Selcuk 85), Cristian, Mehmet.
Steaua: Zapata; Rada, Baciu, Marin, Ghionea, Tanase (Moreno 63), Szekely (Surdu 66), Toja, Nicolita, Bicfalvi (Golanski 72), Kapetanos.

Twente (1) 2 *(Stoch 7, 89)*

Sheriff (0) 1 *(Tiote 67 (og))*   20,200

Twente: Boschker; Wisgerhof, Stam, Douglas, Carney, Brama (Akram 57), Janssen (Parker 79), Nkufo, Perez (Tiote 46), Stoch, Ruiz.
Sheriff: Namasco; Tarkhnishvili, Mamah, Nadson, Corneencov, Balima (Diedhiou 65) (Arbanas 90), Erokhin, Rouamba, Luis Antonio, Suvorov (Volkov 72), Kuchuk.

Wednesday, 2 December 2009

Sheriff (0) 1 *(Diedhiou 83)*

Steaua (0) 1 *(Toja 88)*   12,500

Sheriff: Namasco; Da Costa, Volkov (Diedhiou 77), Tarkhnishvili, Mamah, Franca (Kuchuk 88), Balima, Erokhin, Rouamba, Arbanas, Luis Antonio.
Steaua: Zapata; Rada, Baciu, Ghionea, Tanase (Ionescu 65), Szekely (Marin 20), Toja, Nicolita, Bicfalvi, Surdu, Stancu (Kapetanos 54).

Twente (0) 0

Fenerbahce (0) 1 *(Lugano 70)*   24,000

Twente: Boschker; Wisgerhof, Stam, Douglas, Carney, Brama (De Jong 82), Tiote (Parker 82), Nkufo, Perez, Stoch, Ruiz.
Fenerbahce: Volkan; Lugano, Roberto Carlos (Andre Santos 75), Bilica, Gokhan, Wederson, Alex, Cristian, Selcuk, Mehmet (Deniz 90), Guiza (Semih 82).

Thursday, 17 December 2009

Fenerbahce (1) 1 *(Ugur 15)*

Sheriff (0) 0   15,000

Fenerbahce: Volkan; Lugano, Bekir, Deniz, Ugur (Ali 86), Andre Santos, Balica, Ozer (Mehmet 46), Selcuk, Guiza, Semih (Roberto Carlos 88).
Sheriff: Namasco; Da Costa, Volkov (Luis Antonio 55), Tarkhnishvili, Mamah, Brankovic, Corneencov (Erokhin 66), Franca (Kuchuk 68), Balima, Rouamba, Arbanas.

Steaua (1) 1 *(Kapetanos 17)*

Twente (1) 1 *(Stam 35)*   500

Steaua: Zapata; Golanski (Ninu 63), Rada, Emeghara, Ghionea, Tanase, Szekely (Ochirosii 78), Toja, Nicolita, Bicfalvi (Moreno 73), Kapetanos.
Twente: Boschker; Kuiper, Wisgerhof, Stam, Heubach (Rajkovic 74), Brama, Tiote (Akram 76), Nkufo, Perez, Stoch, Ruiz (Parker 62).

Group H Table	P	W	D	L	F	A	Pts
Fenerbahce	6	5	0	1	8	3	15
Twente	6	2	2	2	5	6	8
Serif	6	1	2	3	4	5	5
Steaua	6	0	4	2	3	6	4

GROUP I

Thursday, 17 September 2009

Benfica (2) 2 *(Nuno Gomes 36, Cardozo 41)*

BATE Borisov (0) 0   34,953

Benfica: Julio Cesar; Luisao, Javier Garcia, Cardozo, Ramires, Maxi Pereira, Di Maria (Ruben Amorim 77), Nuno Gomes (Saviola 66), David Luiz, Felipe Menezes (Fabio Coentrao 59), Cesar Peixoto.
BATE Borisov: Veremko; Likhtarovich (Volodko 64), Sosnovskiy, Yurevich, Krivets, Nekhaichik, Skavysh (Goaryan 56), Pavlov, Bordachev, Rodionov (Alumona 81), Rzhevski.

Everton (3) 4 *(Yobo 10, Distin 17, Pienaar 37, Jo 82)*

AEK Athens (0) 0   26,747

Everton: Howard; Bilyaletdinov (Yakubu 52), Baines, Yobo, Distin, Rodwell, Gosling, Fellaini, Jo, Cahill (Osman 46), Pienaar (Saha[■] 67).
AEK Athens: Saja; Araujo[■], Alves (Nsaliwa 13) (Manduca 48), Juanfran, Jahic, Bianchi, Kafes, Leonardo (Yahaya 71), Makos, Blanco, Scocco.

Thursday, 1 October 2009

AEK Athens (1) 1 *(Majstorovic 43)*

Benfica (0) 0   12,420

AEK Athens: Saja; Majstorovic, Juanfran, Jahic, Georgeas[■], Bianchi, Kafes (Gentsoglou 69), Hersi (Leonardo 78), Manduca, Blanco, Scocco (Karabelas 88).
Benfica: Julio Cesar; Luisao, David Luiz, Javier Garcia, Ramires, Aimar (Nuno Gomes 79), Maxi Pereira (Weldon 59), Di Maria, Cesar Peixoto, Cardozo, Saviola (Fabio Coentrao 59).

BATE Borisov (1) 1 *(Likhtarovich 16)*

Everton (0) 2 *(Fellaini 68, Cahill 76)*   21,200

BATE Borisov: Veremko; Sosnovskiy, Shitov, Yurevich, Bordachev, Likhtarovich (Goaryan 81), Krivets, Nekhaichik, Pavlov (Volodzo 78), Skavysh (Stasevich 28), Rodionov.
Everton: Howard; Hibbert, Baines, Gosling, Distin, Bilyaletdinov (Baxter 90), Osman, Fellaini, Jo, Yakubu (Agard 78), Cahill.

Thursday, 22 October 2009

BATE Borisov (0) 2 *(Pavlov 51, Alumona 85)*

AEK Athens (1) 1 *(Blanco 31 (pen)*   20,000

BATE Borisov: Veremko; Sosnovskiy, Shitov, Yurevich, Bordachev (Alumona 85), Likhtarovich (Goaryan 66), Volodzo, Krivets, Nekhaichik, Pavlov (Skavych 55), Rodionov.
AEK Athens: Saja; Majstorovic[■], Juanfran (Karabelas 62), Jahic, Bianchi[■], Kafes, Nsaliwa, Manduca, Blanco (Makos 59), Nemeth (Leonardo 83), Scocco.

Benfica (1) 5 *(Saviola 14, 83, Cardozo 47, 48, Luisao 52)*

Everton (0) 0   44,534

Benfica: Julio Cesar; Luisao, David Luiz, Ruben Amorim, Javier Garcia, Ramires, Aimar (Carlos Martins 69), Di Maria, Cesar Peixoto, Cardozo (Fabio Coentrao 77), Saviola (Weldon 84).
Everton: Howard; Hibbert, Coleman, Rodwell, Distin, Cahill, Bilyaletdinov (Saha 61), Gosling, Jo, Yakubu (Baxter 71), Fellaini.

Thursday, 5 November 2009

AEK Athens (2) 2 *(Blanco 1, Manduca 38)*

BATE Borisov (2) 2 *(Rodionov 17, Volodzo 26)*   9716

AEK Athens: Saja; Jahic, Karabelas, Georgeas, Gentsoglou, Kafes (Leonardo 83), Nsaliwa (Yahaya 67), Manduca (Hersi 69), Blanco, Nemeth, Scocco.

BATE Borisov: Veremko; Sosnovskiy, Shitov■, Yurevich, Bordachev, Likhtarovich, Volodzo, Krivets (Alumona 68), Nekhaichik (Pavlov 84), Skavysh (Radzov 78), Rodionov.

Everton (0) 0

Benfica (0) 2 *(Saviola 63, Cardozo 76)*   30,790

Everton: Howard; Hibbert, Baines, Yobo, Distin, Rodwell, Bilyaletdinov, Gosling (Jo 69), Yakubu (Agard 81), Fellaini, Cahill.

Benfica: Julio Cesar; Luisao, David Luiz, Sidnei, Ruben Amorim, Javier Garcia, Ramires (Maxi Pereira 46), Fabio Coentrao (Aimar 61), Di Maria, Cardozo, Saviola (Felipe Menezes 87).

Wednesday, 2 December 2009

AEK Athens (0) 0

Everton (1) 1 *(Bilyaletdinov 6)*   15,000

AEK Athens: Saja; Alves, Majstorovic, Juanfran, Georgeas, Kafes, Hersi, Leonardo (Scocco 46), Makos (Manduca 30), Tachtsidis, Pavlis (Blanco 62).

Everton: Howard; Hibbert, Baines, Gosling (Baxter 11), Coleman, Distin (Duffy 18), Bilyaletdinov, Fellaini, Jc (Yakubu 73), Cahill, Pienaar.

BATE Borisov (0) 1 *(Sosnovskiy 68)*

Benfica (0) 2 *(Saviola 46, Fabio Coentrao 63)*   10,000

BATE Borisov: Veremko; Sosnovskiy, Yurevich, Radzov, Bordachev, Likhtarovich (Skavysh 61), Volodzo, Krivets, Nekhaichik, Pavlov (Alumona 57), Rodionov (Goaryan 79).

Benfica: Julio Cesar; David Luiz, Miguel Vitor, Javier Garcia, Ramires, Maxi Pereira (Ruben Amorim 90), Fabio Coentrao (Di Maria 79), Felipe Menezes, Cesar Peixoto, Cardozo, Saviola (Aimar 67).

Thursday, 17 December 2009

Benfica (1) 2 *(Di Maria 45, 73)*

AEK Athens (0) 1 *(Blanco 84)*   15,000

Benfica: Julio Cesar; Shaffer, Roderick Miranda, Luis Filipe, Miguel Vitor, Carlos Martins, Fabio Coentrao (Cesar Peixoto 46), Di Maria, Felipe Menezes (Javier Garcia 65), Weldon, Nuno Gomes (Cardozo 72).

AEK Athens: Saja; Araujo, Alves, Majstorovic (Jahic 45), Georgeas, Gentsoglou, Kafes, Hersi, Makos (Nsaliwa 46), Manduca (Iordache 78), Blanco.

Everton (0) 0

BATE Borisov (0) 1 *(Yurevich 75)*   18,242

Everton: Nash; Hibbert (Mustafi 75), Bidwell, Rodwell (Akpan 9), Coleman, Duffy, Osman (Craig 82), Forshaw, Yakubu, Agard, Baxter.

BATE Borisov: Veremko; Sosnovskiy, Shitov, Yurevich, Bordachev, Likhtarovich (Pavlov 56), Volodzo, Krivets, Nekhaichik (Bulyga 82), Skavysh (Goaryan 74), Rodionov.

Group I Table	P	W	D	L	F	A	Pts
Benfica	6	5	0	1	13	3	15
Everton	6	3	0	3	7	9	9
BATE Borisov	6	2	1	3	9	7	7
AEK Athens	6	1	1	4	5	11	4

GROUP J

Thursday, 17 September 2009

Club Brugge (0) 1 *(Geraerts 63)*

Shakhtar Donetsk (3) 4 *(Gay 11, Willian 19, Srna 35, Kravchenko 75)*   17,770

Club Brugge: De Vlieger; Kulkowski, Alcaraz, Odjidja-Ofoe (Daerden 64), Simaeys, Vermeulen (Hoefkens 46), Geraerts, Perisic, Dirar, Sonck, Akpala (Kouemaha 54).

Shakhtar Donetsk: Pyatov; Kucher, Rat, Fernancinho, Jadson (Polyanskiy 71), Lewandowski, Gay (Kobin 46), Willian (Kravchenko 63), Srna, Rakitskiy, Luiz Adriano.

Partizan Belgrade (1) 2 *(Krstajic 23, Cleo 56)*

Toulouse (2) 3 *(Sirieix 30, 38, Devaux 49)*   11,000

Partizan Belgrade: Bozovic M; Dordevic, Lomic, Krstajic, Knezevic (Stevanovic 46), Gavrancic (Tomic 52), Fejsa, Petrovic, Almani Moreira, Ilic (Cleo 62), Diarra.

Toulouse: Pele; Congre, M'Bengue (Machado 75), Nounkeu, Devaux (Braaten 65), Sirieix, Berson, Sissoko, Tabanou, Capoue, Pentecote (Gignac 61).

Thursday, 1 October 2009

Shakhtar Donetsk (2) 4 *(Lomic 23 (og), Luiz Adriano 38, Jadson 54, Rakitskiy 66)*

Partizan Belgrade (0) 1 *(Ljajic 86)*   49,480

Shakhtar Donetsk: Pyatov; Hubschman (Ishchenko 72), Kucher (Duljaj 72), Rat, Fernandinho. Jadson, Ilsinho, Willian, Srna (Kobin 75), Rakitskiy, Luiz Adriano.

Partizan Belgrade: Radosavljevic; Stevanovic, Dordevic, Lomic (Tomic 70), Krstajic, Gavrancic, Fejsa, Petrovic (Ljajic 46), Almani Moreira, Ilic (Cleo 57), Diarra.

Toulouse (0) 2 *(Sissoko 54, Gignac 84)*

Club Brugge (0) 2 *(Akpala 52, Perisic 90)*   12,275

Toulouse: Pele; Congre, M'Bengue, Nounkeu, Machado (Soukouna 77), Devaux (Sissoko 34), Sirieix, Berson, Capoue, Mansare (Tabanou 46), Gignac.

Club Brugge: Stijnen; Hoefkens, Klukowski, Odjidja-Ofoe, Daerden (Dahmane 87), Blondel (Dirar 63), Vargas, Geraerts, De Mets, Perisic, Akpala (Kouemaha 60).

Thursday, 22 October 2009

Club Brugge (1) 2 *(Perisic 4, Brezancic 58 (og))*

Partizan Belgrade (0) 0   18,903

Club Brugge: Stijnen; Hoefkens (Donk 72), Klukowski, Alcaraz, Odjidja-Ofoe, Blondel (Daerden 83), Geraerts, De Mets, Perisic, Dirar, Akpala (Dahmane 68).

Partizan Belgrade: Radosavljevic; Stevanovic, Krstajic, Jovanovic B (Petrovic 88), Gavrancic (Dordevic 14). Fejsa, Tomic, Almani Moreira (Cleo 46), Ljajic Brezancic, Diarra.

Shakhtar Donetsk (3) 4 *(Fernandinho 8 (pen), Luiz Adriano 24, 56, Hubschman 39)*

Toulouse (0) 0   49,000

Shakhtar Donetsk: Pyatov; Hubschman (Lewandowski 61), Kucher, Rat, Fernandinho, Jadson (Gay 72), Ilsinho, Willian (Aghahowa 72), Srna, Rakitskiy, Luiz Adriano.

Toulouse: Pele; Congre, M'Bengue, Nounkeu, Ebondo, Didot, Luan (Sissoko 46), Sirieix (Tabanou 46), Capoue, Pentecote (Soukouna 88), Braaten.

Thursday, 5 November 2009

Partizan Belgrade (0) 2 *(Ljajic 52, Washington 66)*

Club Brugge (2) 4 *(Perisic 28, Kouemaha 36, 57, Odjidja-Ofoe 74)*   6293

Partizan Belgrade: Radosavljevic; Dordevic, Lomic, Krstajic■, Jovanovic B (Tomic 74), Knezevic, Fejsa, Almani Moreira, Ljajic, Ilic (Bogunovic 46), Diarra (Washington 50).

Club Brugge: Stijnen; Klukowski, Donk, Alcaraz, Odjidja-Ofoe, Blondel, Geraerts, De Mets (Vermeulen 86), Perisic (Simaeys 82), Dirar (Akpala 58), Kouemaha.

Toulouse (0) 0

Shakhtar Donetsk (0) 2 *(Luiz Adriano 50, Gay 63)*   12,046

Toulouse: Pele; Congre, M'Bengue, Nounkeu, Ebondo, Machado (Braaten 66), Didot, Luan, Sineix, Berson (Sissoko 84), Pentecote.

Shakhtar Donetsk: Pyatov; Hubschman, Kucher, Rat, Fernandinho, Jadson (Lewandowski 79), Gay, Willian, Srna (Kobin 74), Rakitskiy, Luiz Adriano (Gladkiy 84).

Thursday, 3 December 2009

Shakhtar Donetsk (0) 0

Club Brugge (0) 0   46,000

Shakhtar Donetsk: Pyatov; Hubschman (Lewandowski 80), Kucher, Rat, Fernandinho, Jadson (Kravchenko 71), Ilsinho, Willian, Srna, Rakitskiy, Luiz Adriano.

Club Brugge: Stijnen; Hoefkens, Klukowski, Donk, Alcaraz, Blondel (Vargas 67), Simaeys, Geraerts, Perisic (Odjidja-Ofoe 69), Sonck (Akpala 84), Dahmane.

Toulouse (0) 1 *(Braaten 54)*
Partizan Belgrade (0) 0   11,123
Toulouse: Blondel; M'Bengue, Nounkeu, Ebondo, Machado, Luan (Tabanou 72), Sirieix, Berson, Capoue, Braaten (N'Gadi Kakou 83), Soukouna.
Partizan Belgrade: Bozovic M; Stevanovic, Dordevic, Jovanovic M, Knezevic, Fejsa, Tomic, Petrovic (Jovanovic B 85), Almani Moreira, Ljajic (Bogunovic 52), Cleo (Washington 74).

Wednesday, 16 December 2009
Club Brugge (0) 1 *(Perisic 90)*
Toulouse (0) 0   23,668
Club Brugge: Stijnen; Hoefkens, Kulkowski, Donk, Alcaraz, Odjidja-Ofoe, Blondel, Geraerts, Perisic, Dirar (Vargas 66), Kouemaha.
Toulouse: Valverde; Fofana, M'Bengue, Nounkeu, Ebondo, Machado (Regattin 82), Didot, Sissoko, Tabanou (Braaten 58), Capoue, Gignac.

Partizan Belgrade (1) 1 *(Diarra 5)*
Shakhtar Donetsk (0) 0   6000
Partizan Belgrade: Bosovic M; Lomic, Jovanovic M, Krstajic, Knezevic, Fejsa, Tomic, Petrovic (Jovanovic B 69), Almani Moreira (Ilic 60), Ljajic, Diarra (Bogunovic 80).
Shakhtar Donetsk: Pyatov; Hubschman, Rat, Ishchenko, Duljaj (Vitsenets 77), Jadson (Gay 77), Fernandinho, Kobin, Willian, Rakitskiy, Luiz Adriano (Gladkiy 81).

Group J Table	P	W	D	L	F	A	Pts
Shakhtar Donetsk	6	4	1	1	14	3	13
Club Brugge	6	3	2	1	10	8	11
Toulouse	6	2	1	3	6	11	7
Partizan Belgrade	6	1	0	5	6	14	3

GROUP K

Thursday, 17 September 2009
Cluj (0) 2 *(Culio 53, Traore 75)*
FC Copenhagen (0) 0   8414
Cluj: Claro; Da Silva, Panin, Muresan, Hugo Alcantara, Cadu, Peralta (Dani 77), Culio, Dubarbier (Mara 54), Kone (Traore 46), Deac.
FC Copenhagen: Wiland; Pospech, Larsson, Antonsson, Wendt, Kvist, Hutchinson, Kristensen (Delaney 78), Vingaard (Sionko 63), Ailton (N'Doye 28), Santin.

Sparta Prague (0) 2 *(Hubnik 76, Zeman 87)*
PSV Eindhoven (0) 2 *(Jonathan 80, 90 (pen))*   16,703
Sparta Prague: Blazek; Repha, Hoheneder, Hubnik, Kusnir, Zofcak, Zeman (Kalouda 90), Vacek (Kucka 85), Husek, Wilfried, Holenda (Kadlec 79).
PSV Eindhoven: Isaksson; Pieters, Ooijer, Manolev, Simons, Engelaar, Dzsudzsak, Bakkal, Toivonen, Lazovic, Koevermans (Jonathan 64).

Thursday, 1 October 2009
FC Copenhagen (1) 1 *(N'Doye 25)*
Sparta Prague (0) 0   15,043
FC Copenhagen: Wiland; Pospech, Larsson, Antonsson, Wendt, Kvist, Gronkjaer, Hutchinson, Vingaard (Norregaard 86), Santin (Ailton 67), N'Doye.
Sparta Prague: Blazek; Repha, Hubnik, Kusnir, Pamic, Zofcak (Strestik 46), Kalouda, Vacek, Husek (Kadlec 79), Prudnikov, Holenda (Wilfried 55).

PSV Eindhoven (1) 1 *(Bakkal 8)*
Cluj (0) 0   13,500
PSV Eindhoven: Isaksson; Rodriguez, Pieters (Salcido 55), Ooijer, Manolev, Engelaar, Afellay, Dzsudzsak, Bakkal (Jonathan 69), Toivonen (Simons 80), Lazovic.
Cluj: Nuno Claro; Da Silva, Panin, Muresan (Dani 9), Hugo Alcantara, Cadu, Peralta, Culio, Dubarbier (Mara 70), Traore, Deac (Nei 78).

Thursday, 22 October 2009
PSV Eindhoven (0) 1 *(Jonathan 72)*
FC Copenhagen (0) 0   18,000
PSV Eindhoven: Isaksson; Rodriguez, Pieters (Vukovic 86), Manolev, Simons (Salcido 61), Engelaar, Afellay, Dzsudzsak, Bakkal (Toivonen 60), Lazovic, Jonathan.
FC Copenhagen: Wiland; Pospech, Laursen, Antonsson, Wendt, Norregaard (Vingaard 77), Kvist, Gronkjaer, Hutchinson, Kristensen (Ailton 76), N'Doye (Santin 76).

Sparta Prague (2) 2 *(Kucka 15, Hubnik 32)*
Cluj (0) 0   10,133
Sparta Prague: Blazek; Repha, Hubnik, Kusnir, Pamic, Kalouda (Strestik 90), Kucka, Kovba, Vacek (Hoheneder 88), Wilfried, Kadlec (Prudnikov 74).
Cluj: Claro; Cabrera, Panin, Cadu, Edimar, Peralta (Mara 46), Culio, Dani, Traore (Bus 72), Deac (Dubarbier 46), Nei.

Thursday, 5 November 2009
Cluj (1) 2 *(Traore 25, Dubarbier 90)*
Sparta Prague (2) 3 *(Holenda 6, 13, Wilfried 90)*   10,000
Cluj: Claro; Da Silva, Panin, Muresan■, Hugo Alcantara, Cadu, Peralta, Culio (Dubarbier 58), Traore, Deac (Mara■ 63), Nei (Bus 83).
Sparta Prague: Blazek; Repha, Hubnik, Kusnir, Pamic, Zofcak (Hoheneder 90), Kucka, Zeman, Vacek (Kalouda 90), Wilfried, Holenda (Kadlec 74).

FC Copenhagen (1) 1 *(Gronkjaer 39 (pen))*
PSV Eindhoven (0) 1 *(Dzsudzsak 72)*   21,605
FC Copenhagen: Wiland; Pospech, Laursen, Antonsson, Wendt, Norregaard (Sionko 84), Kvist, Gronkjaer (Santin 70), Hutchinson, Vingaard, N'Doye.
PSV Eindhoven: Isaksson; Salcido, Rodriguez, Pieters (Vukovic 80), Manolev, Engelaar (Toivanen 71), Afellay, Dzsudzsak, Bakkal, Lazovic, Jonathan (Simons 90).

Thursday, 3 December 2009
FC Copenhagen (2) 2 *(Vingaard 37, N'Doye 43)*
Cluj (0) 0   11,567
FC Copenhagen: Wiland; Pospech, Laursen, Wendt, Jorgensen M, Norregaard (Kristensen 80), Kvist, Gronkjaer (Ailton 72), Hutchinson, Vingaard (Jensen N 90), N'Doye.
Cluj: Claro; Da Silva, Cabrera, Panin, Cadu, Culio, Andre Leao (Nei 67), Dani, Dubarbier, Traore (Deac 46), Kone (Dica 79).

PSV Eindhoven (0) 1 *(Jonathan 90)*
Sparta Prague (0) 0   29,500
PSV Eindhoven: Isaksson; Salcido, Rodriguez (Ooijer 78), Pieters, Manolev, Engelaar, Afellay, Dzsudzsak, Bakkal (Toivonen 61), Lazovic, Jonathan.
Sparta Prague: Blazek; Repha, Hoheneder, Kusnir, Pamic, Zofcak (Kadlec 68), Kucka, Vacek (Kalouda 90), Husek, Wilfried (Prudnikov 90), Holenda.

Wednesday, 16 December 2009
Cluj (0) 0
PSV Eindhoven (1) 2 *(Lazovic 19 (pen), Amrabat 68)*
                                                     3000
Cluj: Peskovic; Da Silva, Cabrera, Panin, Muresan, Culio, Andre Leao (Traore 75), Dica, Dubarbier (Bus 85), Kone (Mara 78), Deac.
PSV Eindhoven: Isaksson; Rodriguez, Pieters, Ooijer, Marcellis, Simons, Afellay (Koevermans 66), Dzsudzsak (Amrabat 46), Bakkal, Toivonen, Lazovic (Vukovic 80).

Sparta Prague (0) 0
FC Copenhagen (2) 3 *(N'Doye 22, 30, Gronkjaer 54 (pen))*
                                                     17,151
Sparta Prague: Blazek; Hoheneder, Kusnir, Pamic■, Zofcak, Kucka (Kladrubsky 78), Zeman, Vacek (Kadlec 52), Husek, Wilfried (Jirous 66), Holenda.
FC Copenhagen: Wiland; Pospech, Laursen, Antonsson, Wendt, Norregaard (Delaney 82), Kvist, Gronkjaer (Ailton 87), Hutchinson, Vingaard (Sionko 71), N'Doye.

Group K Table	P	W	D	L	F	A	Pts
PSV Eindhoven	6	4	2	0	8	3	14
FC Copenhagen	6	3	1	2	7	4	10
Sparta Prague	6	2	1	3	7	9	7
Cluj	6	1	0	5	4	10	3

GROUP L

Thursday, 17 September 2009

Athletic Bilbao (2) 3 *(Llorente 8 (pen), 26, Muniain 54)*
FK Austria (0) 0   38,000

Athletic Bilbao: Iraizoz; Amorebieta, Iraola (Zubiaurre 76), Aitor Ocio, Castillo, Yeste, Susaeta, Gurpegui (San Jose 82), Llorente (David Lopez 59), Etxeberria, Muniain.
FK Austria: Safar; Dragovic, Bak, Ortlechner, Suttner[*], Standfest, Klein, Vorisek (Madl 80), Sulimani (Liendl 31), Diabang (Schumacher 60), Jun.

Nacional (0) 2 *(Felipe Lopes 68, Halliche 75)*
Werder Bremen (1) 3 *(Frings 37 (pen), Pizarro 55, 85)*
                                                         3000
Nacional: Rafael Bracali; Felipe Lopes, Halliche, Wellington (Tomasevic 46), Cleber, Luis Alberto, Pecnik (Mateus 46), Ruben Micael, Joao Aurelio, Leandro Salino (Amuneke 58), Edgar.
Werder Bremen: Wiese; Boenisch, Naldo, Fritz, Mertesacker, Borowski, Marin (Niemeyer 74), Frings, Bargfrede, Hunt, Pizarro (Marcelo Moreno 90).

Thursday, 1 October 2009

FK Austria (0) 1 *(Schumacher 76)*
Nacional (1) 1 *(Ruben Micael 35)*   11,000

FK Austria: Safar; Dragovic, Bak, Ortlechner, Standfest, Klein (Sulimani 70), Vorisek (Junuzovic 46), Baumgartlinger, Acimovic, Diabang (Schumacher 62), Jun.
Nacional: Rafael Bracali; Patacas, Felipe Lopes, Halliche (Pecnik 66), Tomasevic (Joao Aurelio 82), Cleber, Luis Alberto, Ruben Micael, Leandro Salino, Edgar, Mateus (Amuneke 50).

Werder Bremen (2) 3 *(Hunt 18, Naldo 41, Frings 90 (pen))*
Athletic Bilbao (0) 1 *(Llorente 89)*   24,305
Werder Bremen: Wiese; Pasanen, Naldo, Fritz, Mertesacker, Marin (Rosenberg 75), Ozil, Frings, Bargfrede (Niemeyer[*] 60), Hunt (Oehri 89), Pizarro.
Athletic Bilbao: Iraizoz; Amorebieta, Iraola, Aitor Ocio, Castillo, Yeste, Gabilondo (David Lopez 46), Gurpegui, Javier Martinez (Etxeberria 74), Toquero (Muniain 46), Llorente.

Thursday, 22 October 2009

Athletic Bilbao (0) 2 *(Etxeberria 67, Llorente 86)*
Nacional (1) 1 *(Ruben Micael 42)*   35,000
Athletic Bilbao: Iraizoz; Ustaritz, Amorebieta, Iraola, Castillo, Yeste (Javier Martinez 46), Gabilondo (De Marcos 46), Susaeta, Orbaiz, Llorente, Etxeberria (Toquero 72).
Nacional: Rafael Bracali; Patacas, Felipe Lopes, Halliche, Cleber, Luis Alberto (Joao Aurelio 73), Pecnik (Mateus 66), Ruben Micael, Leandro Salino, Nuno Pinto, Edgar (Clebao 79).

FK Austria (0) 2 *(Sulimani 73, Schumacher 87)*
Werder Bremen (1) 2 *(Pizarro 19, 63)*   11,000
FK Austria: Almer; Dragovic, Bak, Ortlechner, Standfest, Klein (Schumacher 64), Junuzovic, Sulimani, Baumgartlinger (Hattenberger 84), Acimovic, Diabarg.
Werder Bremen: Wiese; Boenisch, Naldo, Fritz, Mertesacker, Marin (Rosenberg 59), Ozil, Frings, Bargfrede (Borowski 64), Hunt, Pizarro.

Thursday, 5 November 2009

Nacional (0) 1 *(Edgar 64 (pen))*
Athletic Bilbao (0) 1 *(Etxeberria 85 (pen))*   7500
Nacional: Rafael Braccali; Patacas, Felipe Lopes, Halliche, Tomasevic (Cleber 46), Luis Alberto (Joao Aurelio 69), Pecnik, Ruben Micael, Nuno Pinto[*], Edgar, Mateus (Leandro Salino 46).
Athletic Bilbao: Iraizoz; Ustaritz, Amorebieta, Iraola, Castillo, David Lopez (Diaz de Cerio 60), Gabilondo, Gurpegui, Javier Martinez (Orbaiz 70), Llorente (De Marcos 40), Etxeberria.

Werder Bremen (0) 2 *(Borowski 81, Hugo Almeida 84)*
FK Austria (0) 0   25,000
Werder Bremen: Wiese; Pasanen, Naldo, Fritz, Mertesacker, Borowski, Marin (Rosenberg 60), Ozil, Niemeyer (Jensen 75), Bargfrede (Hugo Almeida 46), Hunt.
FK Austria: Safar (Almer 46); Dragovic, Bak, Leovac, Klein, Hattenberger, Junuzovic, Liendl (Baumgartlinger 74), Sulimani (Diabang 83), Acimovic, Schumacher.

Thursday, 3 December 2009

FK Austria (0) 0
Athletic Bilbao (1) 3 *(Llorente 19, 84, San Jose 62)* 11,000
FK Austria: Safar; Dragovic, Bak, Suttner, Klein, Junuzovic, Liendl (Schumacher 58), Sulimani (Krammer 49), Baumgartlinger, Acimovic, Diabang (Topic 82).
Athletic Bilbao: Iraizoz; Amorebieta, San Jose, Iraola, Castillo, Yeste, Gurpegui (Etxeberria 72), Javier Martinez, Iturraspe, Llorente (Diaz de Cerio 85), Muniain (De Marcos 63).

Werder Bremen (2) 4 *(Rosenberg 31, 34, Marcelo Moreno 84, Marin 90)*
Nacional (0) 1 *(Ruben Micael 61)*   24,784
Werder Bremen: Mielitz; Pasanen, Fritz, Prodl, Mertesacker, Jensen, Frings, Niemeyer (Marin 79), Rosenberg, Hunt (Borowski 46), Marcelo Moreno.
Nacional: Rafael Bracali; Patacas, Felipe Lopes, Tomasevic, Cleber, Luis Alberto, Pecnik, Ruben Micael, Joao Aurelio (Amuneke 74), Leandro Salino (Anselmo 87), Mateus.

Wednesday, 16 December 2009

Athletic Bilbao (0) 0
Werder Bremen (3) 3 *(Pizarro 13, Naldo 20, Rosenberg 36)*   35,000
Athletic Bilbao: Iraizoz; Amorebieta, Etxeita, San Jose, Aurtenetxe, Yeste (Perez 70), Susaeta, Javier Martinez, Toquero (David Lopez 54), Diaz de Cerio (Etxeberria 54), Muniain.
Werder Bremen: Wiese; Pasanen, Naldo, Prodl, Mertesacker, Borowski, Ozil (Marin 76), Jensen, Frings (Niemeyer 69), Rosenberg, Pizarro (Hugo Almeida 62).

Nacional (2) 5 *(Ruben Micael 23, 57, Mateus 32, Tomasevic 61, Felipe Lopes 66)*
FK Austria (1) 1 *(Schumacher 21)*   1500
Nacional: Rafael Bracali; Patacas, Felipe Lopes, Halliche, Tomasevic, Pecnik (Joao Aurelio 60), Ruben Micael (Pacheco 75), Leandro Salino, Nuno Pinto, Edgar (Amuneke 70), Mateus.
FK Austria: Almer; Bak, Ortlechner, Suttner, Klein, Vorisek, Junuzovic (Liendl 80), Baumgartlinger, Acimovic, Diabang (Topic 74), Schumacher (Hattenberger 68).

Group L Table	P	W	D	L	F	A	Pts
Werder Bremen	6	5	1	0	17	6	16
Athletic Bilbao	6	3	1	2	10	8	10
Nacional	6	1	2	3	11	12	5
FK Austria	6	0	2	4	4	16	2

KNOCK-OUT STAGE

SECOND ROUND FIRST LEG

Tuesday, 16 February 2010

Everton (1) 2 *(Pienaar 35, Distin 49)*
Sporting Lisbon (0) 1 *(Miguel Veloso 87 (pen))*   28,131
Everton: Howard; Neville, Baines, Yobo, Distin■, Cahill (Yakubu 62), Osman, Pienaar, Saha (Bilyaletdinov 83), Donovan, Arteta (Rodwell 78).
Sporting Lisbon: Rui Patricio; Daniel Carrico, Tonel, Grimi, Abel, Pedro Mendes, Izmailov, Matias (Saleiro 66), Miguel Veloso, Joao Moutinho (Yannick Djalo 66), Liedson.

Thursday, 18 February 2010

Ajax (1) 1 *(Sulejmani 16)*
Juventus (1) 2 *(Amauri 31, 58)*   51,628
Ajax: Stekelenburg; Van der Wiel, Oleguer, Vertonghen, Alderweireld, Emanuelson (Eriksen 73), Enoh (Jun 85), De Jong, De Zeeuw, Sulejmani (Rommedahl 80), Suarez.
Juventus: Buffon; Chiellini, Zebina (Grygera 46), Legrottaglie, Felipe Melo, Marchisio, Sissoko, Diego (Trezeguet 80), De Ceglie, Del Piero, Amauri (Salihamidzic■ 70).

Athletic Bilbao (0) 1 *(San Jose 58)*
Anderlecht (1) 1 *(Biglia 34)*   39,000
Athletic Bilbao: Iraizoz; Ustaritz, San Jose, Iraola, Castillo, Yeste (Muniain 46), Orbaiz, Gurpegui (Susaeta 55), Javier Martinez, Llorente, De Marcos (Toquero 66).
Anderlecht: Proto; Mazuch, Van Damme, Juhasz, Biglia, Boussoufa (Suarez 90), Legear, Kouyate, Gillet, Kanu, Lukaku (De Sutter 80).

Atletico Madrid (1) 1 *(Reyes 23)*
Galatasaray (0) 1 *(Keita 77)*   30,000
Atletico Madrid: De Gea (Sergio Asenjo 71); Valera, Ujfalusi, Alvaro Dominguez, Perea, Raul Garcia, Paulo Assuncao, Reyes (Salvio 86), Simao, Forlan (Jurado 58), Aguero.
Galatasaray: Leo Franco; Ugur, Neill, Hakan Balta, Servet, Elano (Ayhan 82), Arda (Baris 90), Mehmet, Mustafa, Caner (Giovani 36), Keita.

Club Brugge (0) 1 *(Kouemaha 56)*
Valencia (0) 0   21,657
Club Brugge: Stijnen; Hoefkens, Klukowski, Donk, Alcaraz, Odjidja-Ofoe, Blondel, Geraerts, Perisic, Akpala (Lestienne 79), Kouemaha.
Valencia: Moya; Marchena, Dealbert, Mathieu (Maduro 25), Miguel, Albelda, Baraja, Joaquin (Pablo Hernandez 63), Silva■, Villa, Mata.

FC Copenhagen (0) 1 *(Gronkjaer 79 (pen))*
Marseille (0) 3 *(Niang 72, Ben Arfa 84, Kabore 89)*   26,000
FC Copenhagen: Wiland; Pospech, Antonsson, Wendt, Jorgensen M, Norregaard (Santin 75), Kvist, Gronkjaer, Hutchinson, Vingaard, N'Doye.
Marseille: Mandanda; Taiwo, Diawara, Bonnart, Cisse, Cheyrou (Abriel 73), Gonzalez, M'Bia, Valbuena (Ben Arfa 62), Niang, Kone (Kabore 80).

Fulham (1) 2 *(Gera 3, Zamora 63)*
Shakhtar Donetsk (1) 1 *(Luiz Adriano 32)*   21,832
Fulham: Schwarzer; Kelly, Baird, Murphy, Hughes, Hangeland, Duff, Etuhu, Gera (Elm 89), Zamora, Davies.
Shakhtar Donetsk: Pyatov; Hubschman (Kravchenko 79), Kucher, Rat, Fernandinho, Jadson (Douglas Costa 75), Ilsinho, Willian, Srna, Rakitskiy, Luiz Adriano.

Hamburg (1) 1 *(Jansen 26 (pen))*
PSV Eindhoven (0) 0   35,000
Hamburg: Rost; Rozehnal, Mathijsen, Aogo (Ze Roberto 60), Jansen, Demel (Boateng 81), Tesche, Jarolim, Rincon, Petric, Berg (Van Nistelrooy 65).
PSV Eindhoven: Isaksson; Salcido, Rodriguez, Pieters (Vukovic 81), Manolev (Ooijer 46), Engelaar, Afellay, Dzsudzsak, Bakkal, Toivonen (Koevermans 78), Lazovic.

Hertha Berlin (1) 1 *(Javier Garcia 33 (og))*
Benfica (1) 1 *(Di Maria 4)*   13,684
Hertha Berlin: Drobny; Friedrich, Von Bergen, Janker, Cicero, Ebert, Kobiashvili, Nicu (Kringe 61), Piszczek, Ramos, Raffael (Gekas 88).
Benfica: Julio Cesar; Luisao, David Luiz, Ruben Amorim, Javier Garcia, Ramires (Aimar 63), Carlos Martins (Felipe Menezes 63), Di Maria, Cesar Peixoto, Cardozo, Saviola (Miguel Vitor 83).

Lille (1) 2 *(Balmont 3, Frau 52)*
Fenerbahce (1) 1 *(Wederson 5)*   16,783
Lille: Landreau; Emerson, Beria, Rami, Dumont (Cabaye 60), Balmont, Obraniak, Chedjou, Mavuba, Hazard (Toure 83), Frau (Gervinho 69).
Fenerbahce: Volkan; Lugano (Deniz 10), Andre Santos, Bilica, Gokhan, Emre B, Wederson, Alex (Selcuk 90), Cristian, Ozer (Mehmet 73), Guiza.

Liverpool (0) 1 *(N'Gog 81)*
Unirea (0) 0   40,450
Liverpool: Reina; Carragher, Fabio Aurelio, Mascherano, Agger, Skrtel, Aquilani (Pacheco 75), Gerrard, N'Gog (Lucas 90), Kuyt, Riera (Babel 63).
Unirea: Arlauskis; Galamaz, Brandan, Bruno Fernandes, Maftei, Paraschiv (Viana 86), Paduretu (Rusescu 90), Frunza, Apostol, Bilasco, Onofras (Marinescu 75).

Panathinaikos (0) 3 *(Salpingidis 66, Christodoulopoulos 84, Cisse 89)*
Roma (1) 2 *(Vucinic 29, Pizarro 81 (pen))*   54,274
Panathinaikos: Tzorvas; Sarriegi, Kante, Simao, Vyntra, Spyropoulos, Ninis (Christodoulopoulos 83), Leto (Marinos 85), Karagounis, Katsouranis (Salpingidis 64), Cisse.
Roma: Julio Sergio (Doni 39); Juan, Motta, Riise, Burdisso, Pizarro, Taddei (Cerci 75), De Rossi, Baptista, Brighi, Vucinic (Menez 71).

Rubin (2) 3 *(Bukharov 14, 23, Semak 69)*
Hapoel Tel Aviv (0) 0   7000
Rubin: Ryzhikov; Ansaldi, Cesar Navas, Salukvadze, Kaleshin, Semak, Ryazantsev (Kasaev 40), Noboa, Murawski, Gokdeniz Karadeniz (Gorbanets 88), Bukharov.
Hapoel Tel Aviv: Enyeama; Da Silva, Bondarv, Shish, Yadin (De Ridder 74), Natcho, Badir, Vermouth, Menteshashvili (Mare 46), Shechter, Lala (Zahavy 46).

Standard Liege (0) 3 *(Witsel 66 (pen), 82, De Camargo 80)*
Salzburg (2) 2 *(Janko 4, 45)*   22,000
Standard Liege: Bolat; Goreux, Vitor Ramos, Pocognoli (Gershon 85), Defour, Mangala, Nicaise, Witsel, Mbokani (Traore 90), De Camargo, Jovanovic (Dalmat 90).
Salzburg: Gustafsson; Afolabi, Schwegler, Schiemer, Ulmer, Sekagya, Tchoyi, Svento (Wallner 84), Cziommer (Pokrivac 74), Leitgeb, Janko (Nelisse 88).

Twente (1) 1 *(Janssen 38)*
Werder Bremen (0) 0   24,000
Twente: Boschker; Wisgerhof, Stam, Douglas, Tiendalli, Brama, Janssen, Nkufo, Perez (Tiote 70), Stoch (De Jong 86), Ruiz.
Werder Bremen: Wiese; Pasanen (Abdennour 32), Naldo, Fritz, Mertesacker, Marin, Ozil (Hugo Almeida 67), Frings, Niemeyer (Borowski 77), Hunt, Pizarro.

Villarreal (1) 1 *(Senna 43, Ruben 85)*
Wolfsburg (0) 2 *(Grafite 66, 84 (pen))*   8000
Villarreal: Diego Lopez; Godin, Capdevila, Angel, Ivan Marcano■, Pires (Matilla 77), Ibagaza (Cani 64), Senna, Bruno (Ruben 77), Llorente, Nilmar.
Wolfsburg: Hitz; Schafer, Simunek, Madlung, Pekarik, Riether, Josue, Misimovic, Gentner (Dejagah 58), Dzeko, Grafite.

SECOND ROUND SECOND LEG

Tuesday, 23 February 2010

Benfica (1) 4 *(Aimar 24, Cardozo 48, 62, Javi Garcia 59)*

Hertha Berlin (0) 0   30,401

Benfica: Julio Cesar; Luisao, Maxi Pereira, David Luiz, Ruben Amorim, Javier Garcia, Aimar (Carlos Martins 66), Fabio Coentrao, Di Maria (Nuno Gomes 74, Cardozo, Saviola (Cesar Peixoto 69).
Hertha Berlin: Drobny; Friedrich, Von Bergen, Janker, Cicero, Kringe, Ebert, Nicu, Piszczek (Pejcinovic 72), Ramos (Gekas 63), Raffael (Wichniarek 63).

Thursday, 25 February 2010

Anderlecht (2) 4 *(Lukaku 5, San Jose 26 (og), Juhasz 49, Legear 68)*

Athletic Bilbao (0) 0   24,000

Anderlecht: Proto; Mazuch, Deschacht, Van Damme, Juhasz, Biglia, Boussoufa, Legear (Suarez 81), Kouyate (Sare 74), Gillet, Lukaku (De Sutter 66).
Athletic Bilbao: Iraizoz; Amorebieta, San Jose, Iraola, Castillo, Yeste, Susaeta, Orbaiz (Muniain 46) (Gabilondo 59), Javier Martinez, Toquero (De Marcos 54), Llorente.

Fenerbahce (1) 1 *(Emre B 35)*

Lille (0) 1 *(Rami 85)*   48,000

Fenerbahce: Volkan; Bekir, Onder, Deniz (Semih 79), Bilica, Gokhan, Emre B, Wederson, Alex, Selcuk, Guiza (Cristian 74).
Lille: Landreau; Emerson, Beria, Rami, Dumont (Vandam 79), Obraniak, Chedjou, Mavuba, Hazard, Aubameyang (Toure 68), Frau.

Galatasaray (0) 1 *(Keita 66)*

Atletico Madrid (0) 2 *(Simao 63, Forlan 90)*   22,000

Galatasaray: Leo Franco; Ugur, Neill, Hakan Balta, Servet, Elano (Ayhan 50), Arda, Mehmet, Mustafa (Giovani 90), Caner■, Keita.
Atletico Madrid: Sergio Asenjo; Valera, Antonio Lopez, Ujfalusi, Perea, Raul Garcia, Jurado (Camacho 90), Paulo Assuncao, Reyes (Salvio 90), Simao, Aguero (Forlan 42).

Hapoel Tel Aviv (0) 0

Rubin (0) 0   12,000

Hapoel Tel Aviv: Enyeama; Da Silva, Bondarv (Kende 56), Shish, Yadin (Huta 81), Natcho, Badir, Vermouth, Shechter, Zahavy, Lala (Mare 56).
Rubin: Ryzhikov; Ansaldi, Cesar Navas, Salukvadze, Kaleshin (Balyaykin 51), Semak, Noboa, Murawski, Gokdeniz Karadeniz, Kasaev, Bukharov (Kabze 81).

Juventus (0) 0

Ajax (0) 0   16,441

Juventus: Manninger; Chiellini, Grygera, Legrottaglie, Felipe Melo, Marchisio, Sissoko, Diego (Camoranesi 70), De Ceglie, Del Piero (Candreva 87), Amauri (Trezeguet 15).
Ajax: Stekelenburg; Van der Wiel, Oleguer, Vertonghen, Alderweireld, Enoh (Rommedahl 77), De Jong, De Zeeuw, Eriksen, Pantelic (Emanuelson 75), Sulejmani (Jun 64).

Marseille (1) 3 *(Ben Arfa 43, Kone 62, 78)*

FC Copenhagen (0) 1 *(Ailton 87)*   27,195

Marseille: Mandanda; Taiwo, Hilton, Diawara (Heinze 66), Bonnart, Cheyrou (M'Bow 65), Ben Arfa (Valbuena 79), Kabore, Abriel, Kone, Morientes.
FC Copenhagen: Wiland; Antonsson, Wendt, Jorgensen M, Norregaard, Kvist, Gronkjaer (Ailton 61), Hutchinson, Vingaard, Santin (Kristensen 71), N'Doye (Ozdogan 80).

PSV Eindhoven (2) 3 *(Toivonen 2, Dzsudzsak 43, Koevermans 89)*

Hamburg (0) 2 *(Petric 46, Trochowski 79 (pen))*   28,000

PSV Eindhoven: Isaksson; Salcido, Rodriguez (Koevermans 79) Pieters, Manolev (Ooijer 25., Engelaar, Afellay, Dzsudzsak■, Bakkal (Labyad 71., Toivonen, Lazovic.

Hamburg: Rost; Rozehnal, Mathijsen, Aogo, Demel■, Ze Roberto, Tesche (Pitroipa 46), Trochowski (Berg 89), Rincon, Petric (Boateng 77), Elia.

Roma (1) 2 *(Riise 11, De Rossi 67)*

Panathinaikos (3) 3 *(Cisse 40 (pen), 45, Ninis 43)*   50,000

Roma: Doni; Juan, Mexes, Riise, Cassetti, Taddei, De Rossi, Perrotta, Brighi (Baptista 46), Vucinic, Cerci (Menez 68).
Panathinaikos: Tzorvas; Sarriegi, Kante, Simao, Vyntra, Spyropoulos, Ninis (Gilberto Silva 72), Marinos, Katsouranis■, Cisse (Christodoulopoulos 90), Salpingidis (Leto 87).

Salzburg (0) 0

Standard Liege (0) 0   26,500

Salzburg: Gustafsson; Dudic (Zickler 74), Afolabi, Opdam, Ulmer, Sekagya, Tchoyi, Svento, Cziommer (Wallner 65), Leitgeb, Janko.
Standard Liege: Bolat; Vitor Ramos, Camozzato, Sarr, Pocognoli, Defour, Nicaise (Mangala 81), Witsel, Mbokani (Traore 90), De Camargo, Jovanovic (Carcela-Gonzalez 72).

Shakhtar Donetsk (0) 1 *(Jadson 69)*

Fulham (1) 1 *(Hangeland 33)*   47,509

Shakhtar Donetsk: Pyatov; Hubschman (Kravchenko 46), Kucher, Rat, Fernandinho, Jadson, Ilsinho, Willian (Douglas Costa 53), Srna, Rakitskiy, Luiz Adriano (Gladkiy 76).
Fulham: Schwarzer; Kelly, Baird, Murphy■, Hughes, Hangeland, Duff, Etuhu, Gera, Zamora (Elm 72), Davies (Riise 89).

Sporting Lisbon (0) 3 *(Miguel Veloso 64, Pedro Mendes 76, Matias 90)*

Everton (0) 0   17,609

Sporting Lisbon: Rui Patricio; Daniel Carrico, Tonel, Grimi (Saleiro 62), Abel, Pedro Mendes, Izmailov (Polga 90), Miguel Veloso, Joao Moutinho, Yannick Djalo, Liedson (Matias 90).
Everton: Howard; Neville, Baines, Yobo, Senderos (Jagielka 52), Bilyaletdinov (Rodwell 62), Osman, Pienaar, Saha, Donovan (Yakubu 73), Arteta.

Unirea (1) 1 *(Bruno Fernandes 19)*

Liverpool (2) 3 *(Mascherano 30, Babel 41, Gerrard 57)*   25,000

Unirea: Arlauskis; Galamaz (Mehmedovic 27), Bruno Fernandes, Bordeanu, Maftei, Paraschiv (Ricardo 56), Paduretu, Frunza, Apostol, Bilasco, Onofras (Semedo 62).
Liverpool: Reina; Carragher (Kelly 61), Insua, Mascherano, Agger, Skrtel (Kyrgiakos 66), Benayoun (Fabio Aurelio 77), Gerrard, N'Gog, Lucas, Babel.

Valencia (1) 3 *(Mata 1, Pablo Hernandez 97, 117)*

Club Brugge (0) 0   45,000

Valencia: Cesar; Marchena, Dealbert, Miguel, Albelda, Baraja (Alexis 46), Pablo Hernandez, Ever Banega, Villa, Zigic (Joaquin 57), Mata (Maduro 118).
Club Brugge: Stijnen; Hoefkens, Klukowski, Donk, Alcaraz, Odjidja-Ofoe (Chavez 102), Geraerts, Perisic, Sonck (Akpala 91), Lestienne (Dahmane 82), Kouemaha.
aet.

Werder Bremen (3) 4 *(Pizarro 15, 20, 58, Naldo 27)*

Twente (1) 1 *(De Jong 33)*   20,963

Werder Bremen: Vander; Pasanen, Naldo, Abdennour, Mertesacker, Marin (Ayik 74), Ozil (Borowski 83), Frings, Niemeyer (Bargfrede 57), Hugo Almeida, Pizarro.
Twente: Boschker; Wisgerhof, Stam (Kuiper 62), Douglas, Tiendalli, Brama, De Jong, Janssen, Perez (Tiote 62), Parker, Ruiz (Vujicevic 74).

Wolfsburg (3) 4 *(Dzeko 10, Angel 15 (og), Gentner 41, Grafite 64)*
Villarreal (1) 1 *(Capdevila 30)* 16,613
Wolfsburg: Hitz; Schafer, Simunek (Barzagli 49), Madlung, Pekarik, Riether (Hasebe 79), Josue, Misimovic, Gentner (Schindzielorz 90), Dzeko, Grafite.
Villarreal: Diego Lopez; Gonzalo, Godin (Musacchio 46), Capdevila, Angel, Pires (Montero 70), Cani (Llorente 46), Fuster, Senna, Bruno, Nilmar.

THIRD ROUND FIRST LEG

Thursday, 11 March 2010

Atletico Madrid (0) 0
Sporting Lisbon (0) 0 42,000
Atletico Madrid: De Gea; Antonio Lopez, Ujfalusi, Alvaro Dominguez, Perea (Velera 13), Raul Garcia (Jurado 72), Paulo Assuncao, Reyes, Simao (Salvio 58), Forlan, Aguero.
Sporting Lisbon: Rui Patricio; Polga, Tonel■, Grimi■, Abel, Pedro Mendes, Izmailov, Miguel Veloso (Adrien Silva 85), Pereirinha (Pedro Silva 61), Joao Moutinho, Liedson (Saleiro 90).

Benfica (0) 1 *(Maxi Pereira 76)*
Marseille (0) 1 *(Ben Arfa 90)* 46,635
Benfica: Julio Cesar; Luisao, Maxi Pereira, David Luiz, Javier Garcia, Ramires, Aimar (Carlos Martins 65), Di Maria, Cesar Peixoto (Fabio Coentrao 77), Cardozo, Saviola (Eder Luis 88).
Marseille: Mandanda; Taiwo, Diawara, Bonnart, Cisse, Cheyrou, Gonzalez, M'Bia, Abriel (Valbuena 70), Brandao, Niang (Ben Arfa 75).

Hamburg (2) 3 *(Mathijsen 23, Van Nistelrooy 40, Jarolim 76)*
Anderlecht (1) 1 *(Legear 45)* 34,921
Hamburg: Rost; Rozehnal, Mathijsen, Aogo, Jansen, Ze Roberto, Jarolim, Rincon, Petric, Elia (Trochowski 78), Van Nistelrooy.
Anderlecht: Proto; Mazuch, Deschacht, Van Damme, Juhasz, Biglia, Legear, Kouyate, Gillet, Kanu (Suarez 77), Lukaku.

Juventus (3) 3 *(Legrottaglie 9, Zebina 25, Trezeguet 45)*
Fulham (1) 1 *(Etuhu 36)* 11,406
Juventus: Manninger; Cannavaro, Grosso, Zebina, Legrottaglie, Salihamidzic (Camoranesi 46), Marchisio, Poulsen (Sissoko 76), Candreva, Diego, Trezeguet (Iaquinta 62).
Fulham: Schwarzer; Baird, Konchesky, Greening, Hughes, Hangeland, Duff, Etuhu, Gera, Zamora, Davies (Dempsey 61).

Lille (0) 0 *(Hazard 84)*
Liverpool (0) 0 17,000
Lille: Landreau; Emerson, Beria, Rami, Balmont, Cabaye (Dumont 73), Obraniak (Toure 83), Chedjou, Mavuba, Hazard, Frau (Aubameyang 77).
Liverpool: Reina; Johnson, Insua, Mascherano, Carragher, Agger, Lucas, Gerrard, Torres, Kuyt (El Zhar 88), Babel (Riera 73).

Panathinaikos (0) 1 *(Vyntra 48)*
Standard Liege (2) 3 *(Witsel 8, Jovanovic 16, De Camargo 74)* 55,000
Panathinaikos: Galinovic; Sarriegi, Kante, Darlas, Simao■, Vyntra, Ninis (Karagounis 46), Leto (Salpingidis 46), Gilberto Silva, Rukavina (Christodoulopoulos 71), Cisse.
Standard Liege: Bolat; Vitor Ramos, Camozzato, Sarr, Gershon, Defour (Carcela-Gonzalez 21), Nicaise (Mangala 67), Witsel, Mbokani, De Camargo, Jovanovic (Dalmat 79).

Rubin (1) 1 *(Noboa 29)*
Wolfsburg (0) 1 *(Misimovic 67)* 12,000
Rubin: Ryzhikov; Ansaldi, Cesar Navas, Salukvadze, Orekhov, Sibaya (Murawski 79), Noboa, Gokdeniz Karadeniz (Balyaykin 81), Kasaev (Portnyagin 85), Bukharov, Kabze.
Wolfsburg: Hitz; Schafer, Madlung, Pekarik, Riether, Josue, Misimovic, Hasebe, Gentner, Dzeko, Martins (Dejagah 83).

Valencia (0) 1 *(Mata 57)*
Werder Bremen (1) 1 *(Frings 24 (pen))* 40,000
Valencia: Cesar; David Navarro, Marchena, Dealbert, Alexis (Alba 46), Miguel, Pablo Hernandez, Silva, Ever Banega■, Villa (Baraja 83), Mata (Joaquin 76).
Werder Bremen: Wiese; Pasanen, Naldo, Fritz, Mertesacker, Borowski, Marin (Bargfrede 61), Ozil (Jensen 76), Hunt, Frings, Pizarro.

THIRD ROUND SECOND LEG

Thursday, 18 March 2010

Anderlecht (2) 4 *(Lukaku 44, Suarez 45 (pen), Biglia 59, Boussoufa 66)*
Hamburg (1) 3 *(Boateng 42, Jansen 54, Petric 75)* 23,500
Anderlecht: Proto; Mazuch, Deschacht (De Sutter 62), Van Damme, Juhasz, Biglia, Boussoufa, Kouyate, Gillet, Suarez, Lukaku (Kanu 82).
Hamburg: Rost; Rozehnal, Matijsen, Jansen (Tesche 79), Boateng (Elia 63), Ze Roberto, Jarolim, Rincon, Petric, Van Nistelrooy, Torun (Trochowski 83).

Fulham (2) 4 *(Zamora 9, Gera 39, 49 (pen), Dempsey 83)*
Juventus (1) 1 *(Trezeguet 2)* 23,458
Fulham: Schwarzer; Kelly (Dempsey 72), Konchesky, Baird, Hughes, Hangeland, Duff, Etuhu, Gera (Riise 85), Zamora, Davies.
Juventus: Chimenti; Cannavaro■, Grosso (Del Piero 85), Zebina■, Felipe Melo, Salihamidzic, Camoranesi (De Ceglie 52), Sissoko, Candreva (Grygera 28), Diego, Trezeguet.

Liverpool (1) 3 *(Gerrard 9 (pen), Torres 49, 89)*
Lille (0) 0 38,139
Liverpool: Reina; Johnson, Insua, Mascherano, Carragher, Agger (Kyrgiakos 90), Lucas, Gerrard, Torres (N'Gog 90), Kuyt, Babel (Benayoun 80).
Lille: Landreau; Emerson, Beria, Rami, Balmont (Aubameyang 71), Cabaye, Obraniak, Chedjou, Mavuba, Hazard (Vandam 86), Frau (Toure 59).

Marseille (0) 1 *(Niang 70)*
Benfica (0) 2 *(Maxi Pereira 75, Kardec 90)* 40,000
Marseille: Mandanda; Taiwo, Diawara, Bonnart, Cisse, Cheyrou (Kabore 76), Gonzalez, M'Bia, Abriel (Kone 44) (Ben Arfa■ 90), Brandao, Niang.
Benfica: Julio Cesar; Luisao, Maxi Pereira (Miguel Vitor 90), David Luiz, Javier Garcia, Ramires, Carlos Martins (Kardec 86), Fabio Coentrao, Di Maria, Cardozo, Saviola (Aimar 77).

Sporting Lisbon (2) 2 *(Liedson 19, Anderson Polga 45)*
Atletico Madrid (2) 2 *(Aguero 3, 33)* 45,000
Sporting Lisbon: Rui Patricio; Anderson Polga, Pedro Silva (Vukcevic 54), Caneira, Abel, Pedro Mendes, Miguel Veloso, Pereirinha (Matias 69), Joao Moutinho, Saleiro, Liedson.
Atletico Madrid: De Gea; Antonio Lopez, Ujfalusi, Alvaro Dominguez, Perea, Raul Garcia, Jurado (Camacho 90), Paulo Assuncao, Reyes, Simao (Velera 68), Aguero (Forlan 81).

Standard Liege (1) 1 *(Mbokani 45)*
Panathinaikos (0) 0 29,000
Standard Liege: Bolat; Vitor Ramos, Camozzato, Sarr, Pocognoli, Dalmat (Goreux 72), Witsel, Carcela-Gonzalez, Mbokani (Traore 90), De Camargo, Jovanovic (Mangala 82).
Panathinaikos: Tzorvas; Sarriegi, Kante, Bjarsmyr (Ninis 56), Vyntra, Leto (Christodoulopoulos 82), Gilberto Silva, Karagounis, Katsouranis, Cisse, Salpingidis (Rukavina 69).

Werder Bremen (1) 4 *(Hugo Almeida 26, Frings 57 (pen), Marin 62, Pizarro 84)*

Valencia (3) 4 *(Villa 2, 45, 66, Mata 15)* 24,200

Werder Bremen: Wiese; Pasanen, Naldo, Fritz (Rosenberg 80), Mertesacker, Borowski (Hugo Almeida 22), Marin, Ozil, Hunt, Frings, Pizarro.
Valencia: Cesar; Bruno (Alba 46), Maduro, Marchena (Michel 65), Dealbert, Miguel, Baraja, Joaquin (Manuel Fernandes 55), Silva, Villa, Mata.

Wolfsburg (0) 2 *(Martins 58, Gentner 119)*

Rubin (1) 1 *(Kasaev 21)* 15,412

Wolfsburg: Hitz; Schafer, Simunek (Johnson 75), Madlung, Pekarik (Martins 46), Riether, Josue, Misimovic, Gentner, Dzeko, Degagah.
Rubin: Ryzhikov; Ansaldi (Salukvadze 97), Cesar Navas*, Orekhov, Murawski (Sibaya 97), Noboa, Balyaykin, Gokdeniz Karadeniz, Kasaev (Gorbanets 82), Bukharov, Kabze.
aet.

QUARTER-FINALS FIRST LEG

Thursday, 1 April 2010

Benfica (0) 2 *(Cardozo 59 (pen), 79 (pen))*

Liverpool (1) 1 *(Agger 9)* 62,629

Benfica: Julio Cesar; Luisao, Maxi Pereira (Nuno Gomes 66), David Luiz, Javier Garcia, Ramires, Aimar (Airton 87), Carlos Martins (Ruben Amorim 72), Fabio Coentrao, Di Maria, Cardozo.
Liverpool: Reina; Johnson, Insua, Mascherano, Carragher, Agger, Lucas, Gerrard (Benayoun 90), Torres (N'Gog 82), Kuyt, Babel*.

Fulham (0) 2 *(Zamora 59, Duff 63)*

Wolfsburg (0) 1 *(Madlung 89)* 22,307

Fulham: Schwarzer; Duff, Konchesky, Murphy (Baird 87), Hughes, Hangeland, Dempsey, Etuhu, Gera, Zamora, Davies.
Wolfsburg: Benaglio; Schafer, Madlung, Pekarik (Martins 74), Riether, Barzagli, Josue, Misimovic, Gentner (Dejagah 84), Dzeko, Grafite.

Hamburg (2) 2 *(Petric 42 (pen), Van Nistelrooy 45)*

Standard Liege (1) 1 *(Mbokani 31)* 48,437

Hamburg: Rost; Mathijsen, Aogo, Boateng, Demel, Ze Roberto, Jarolim, Pitroipa, Petric (Trochowski 72), Van Nistelrooy, Torun (Berg 72).
Standard Liege: Bolat; Goreux (Grozav 76), Vitor Ramos, Camozzato, Pocognoli, Mangala, Witsel, Carcela-Gonzalez, Mbokani, De Camargo, Jovanovic (Traore 90).

Valencia (0) 2 *(Manuel Fernandes 67, Villa 82)*

Atletico Madrid (0) 2 *(Forlan 59, Antonio Lopez 72)* 50,000

Valencia: Cesar; Bruno, Maduro, Dealbert, Baraja, Manuel Fernandes (Zigic 81), Pablo Hernandez (Joaquin 70), Silva, Alba, Villa, Mata (Vicente 76).
Atletico Madrid: De Gea; Antonio Lopez, Ujfalusi, Alvaro Dominguez, Perea, Raul Garcia, Jurado (Camacho 90), Paulo Assuncao, Simao, Forlan (Salvio 78), Aguero.

QUARTER-FINALS SECOND LEG

Thursday, 8 April 2010

Atletico Madrid (0) 0

Valencia (0) 0 54,851

Atletico Madrid: De Gea; Antonio Lopez, Juanito, Ujfalusi, Alvaro Dominguez, Raul Garcia, Paulo Assuncao, Reyes (Jurado 46), Simao, Forlan (Camacho 83), Aguero (Salvio 90).
Valencia: Cesar; Maduro, Alexis (David Navarro 80), Baraja, Joaquin (Vicente 70), Manuel Fernandes, Pablo Hernandez, Silva, Alba, Villa, Mata (Zigic 70).

Liverpool (2) 4 *(Kuyt 27, Lucas 34, Torres 58, 82)*

Benfica (0) 1 *(Cardozo 70)* 42,377

Liverpool: Reina; Johnson, Kyrgiakos, Mascherano, Carragher, Agger, Benayoun (El Zhar 90), Gerrard (Aquilani 88), Torres (N'Gog 86), Kuyt, Lucas.
Benfica: Julio Cesar (Moreira 79); Luisao, David Luiz, Sidnei, Ruben Amorim, Javier Garcia, Ramires, Aimar (Fabio Coentrao 86), Carlos Martins (Kardec 67), Di Maria, Cardozo.

Standard Liege (1) 1 *(De Camargo 32)*

Hamburg (2) 3 *(Petric 20, 35, Guerrero 90)* 29,200

Standard Liege: Bolat; Vitor Ramos, Camozzato, Sarr, Pocognoli, Nicaise (Mangala 89), Witsel, Carcela-Gonzalez (Dalmat 76), Mbokani, De Camargo, Jovanovic.
Hamburg: Rost; Mathijsen, Aogo, Boateng, Demel, Ze Roberto, Tesche, Jarolim, Pitroipa (Trochowski 76), Petric (Guerrero 67), Van Nistelrooy (Berg 89).

Wolfsburg (0) 0

Fulham (1) 1 *(Zamora 1)* 25,000

Wolfsburg: Benaglio; Schafer, Simunek (Rever 76), Pekarik (Dejagah 35), Madlung (Martins 62), Misimovic, Gentner (Martins 62), Dzeko, Grafite.
Fulham: Schwarzer; Baird, Konchesky, Murphy, Hughes, Hangeland, Duff, Etuhu, Gera (Nevland 82), Zamora, Davies (Riise 86).

SEMI-FINALS FIRST LEG

Thursday, 22 April 2010

Atletico Madrid (1) 1 *(Forlan 9)*

Liverpool (0) 0 50,000

Atletico Madrid: De Gea; Antonio Lopez, Ujfalusi, Alvaro Dominguez, Perea, Raul Garcia, Jurado, Paulo Assuncao, Reyes (Camacho 90), Simao (Valera 78), Forlan (Salvio 85).
Liverpool: Reina; Johnson, Kyrgiakos, Mascherano, Carragher, Agger, Benayoun (El Zhar 84), Gerrard, N'Gog (Babel 64), Kuyt, Lucas.

Hamburg (0) 0

Fulham (0) 0 49,171

Hamburg: Rost; Mathijsen, Aogo, Boateng, Demel (Rincon 82), Ze Roberto, Jarolim, Trochowski, Pitroipa, Guerrero (Petric 72), Van Nistelrooy.
Fulham: Schwarzer; Baird, Konchesky, Murphy, Hughes, Hangeland, Duff, Etuhu, Gera, Zamora (Dempsey 52), Davies.

SEMI-FINALS SECOND LEG

Thursday, 29 April 2010

Fulham (0) 2 *(Davies 69, Gera 76)*

Hamburg (1) 1 *(Petric 22)* 25,700

Fulham: Schwarzer; Pantsil (Nevland 75), Konchesky, Murphy, Hughes, Hangeland, Duff, Etuhu, Gera, Zamora (Dempsey 58), Davies.
Hamburg: Rost; Mathijsen, Aogo, Boateng, Demel, Ze Roberto, Tesche (Rincon 56) (Guerrero 79), Jarolim (Rozehnal 90), Pitroipa, Petric, Van Nistelrooy

Liverpool (1) 2 *(Aquilani 44, Benayoun 95)*

Atletico Madrid (0) 1 *(Forlan 103)* 42,040

Liverpool: Reina; Mascherano (Degen 110), Johnson, Aquilani (El Zhar 89), Carragher, Agger, Benayoun (Pacheco 114), Gerrard, Babel, Kuyt, Lucas.
Atletico Madrid: De Gea; Valera, Antonio Lopez, Alvaro Dominguez, Perea, Raul Garcia, Paulo Assuncao (Jurado 99), Reyes, Simao, Forlan (Camacho 117), Aguero (Salvio 120).
aet.

UEFA EUROPA LEAGUE FINAL
Wednesday, 12 May 2010
(in Hamburg, attendance 49,000)

Atletico Madrid (1) 2 *(Forlan 32, 116)*   **Fulham (1) 1** *(Davies 37)*

Atletico Madrid: De Gea; Ujfalusi, Perea, Alvaro Dominguez, Antonio Lopez, Reyes (Salvio 78), Paulo Assuncao, Raul Garcia, Simao (Jurado 68), Forlan, Aguero (Valera 119).

Fulham: Schwarzer; Baird, Konchesky, Murphy (Greening 118), Hughes, Hangeland, Duff (Nevland 84), Etuhu, Gera, Zamora (Dempsey 55), Davies.

aet.

Referee: Rizzoli (Italy).

Atletico Madrid's Diego Forlan watches on as his injury-time winner squeezes past Fulham's goalkeeper Mark Schwarzer. A memorable Europa League adventure saw Fulham start their campaign in late July, pass some big-name European opponents, only to be beaten 2-1 after extra time in the final. (PA Photos)

UEFA CHAMPIONS LEAGUE 2010–11

PARTICIPATING CLUBS
This list is provisional and subject to final confirmation from UEFA.

GROUP STAGE
FC Internazionale Milano (ITA)
FC Barcelona (ESP)
Manchester United FC (ENG)
Chelsea FC (ENG)
Arsenal FC (ENG)
FC Bayern München (GER)
AC Milan (ITA)
Olympique Lyonnais (FRA)
Real Madrid CF (ITA)
AS Roma (ITA)
FC Shakhtar Donetsk (UKR)
SL Benfica (POR)
Valencia CF (ESP)
Olympique de Marseille (FRA)
Panathinaikos FC (GRE)
Rangers FC (SCO)
FC Schalke 04 (GER)

FC Spartak Moskva (RUS)
FC Twente (NED)
FC Rubin Kazan (RUS)
CFR 1907 Cluj (ROU)
Bursaspor (TUR)

PLAY-OFF – NON-CHAMPIONS
Sevilla FC (ESP)
Werder Bremen (GER)
Tottenham Hotspur FC (ENG)
UC Sampdoria (ITA)
AJ Auxerre (FRA)

**THIRD QUALIFYING ROUND –
NON-CHAMPIONS**
FC Zenit St. Petersburg (RUS)
AFC Ajax (NED)
Fenerbahçe SK (TUR)
FC Dynamo Kyiv (UKR)
SC Braga (POR)
Celtic FC (SCO)
FC Unirea Urziceni (ROU)

PAOK FC (GRE)
BSC Young Boys (SUI)
KAA Gent (BEL)

**THIRD QUALIFYING ROUND –
CHAMPIONS**
FC Basel 1893 (SUI)
RSC Anderlecht (BEL)
FC København (DEN)

SECOND QUALIFYING ROUND
Hapoel Tel-Aviv FC (ISR)
AC Sparta Praha (CZE)
Rosenborg BK (NOR)
FC Salzburg (AUT)
PFC Litex Lovech (BUL)
NK Dinamo Zagreb (CRO)
FK Partizan (SRB)
FC BATE Borisov (BLR)
KKS Lech Poznań (POL)
MŠK Žilina (SVK)
FC Sheriff (MDA)

Debreceni VSC (HUN)
AC Omonia (CYP)
AIK Solna (SWE)
Bohemian FC (IRL)
FK Ekranas (LTU)
HJK Helsinki (FIN)
FK Aktobe (KAZ)
FC Levadia Tallinn (EST)
SK Liepājas Metalurgs (LVA)

FH Hafnarfjördur (ISL)
FK Željezničar (BIH)
FC Olimpi Rustavi (GEO)
FC Pyunik (ARM)
FC Koper (SVN)
FC Inter Bakı (AZE)
FK Renova (MKD)
KS Dinamo Tirana (ALB)
HB Tórshavn (FRO)

The New Saints FC (WAL)
Linfield FC (NIR)
AS Jeunesse Esch (LUX)

FIRST QUALIFYING ROUND
FC Santa Coloma (AND)
SP Tre Fiori (SMR)
Birkirkara FC (MLT)
FK Rudar Pljevlja (MNE)

UEFA EUROPA LEAGUE 2010–11

PARTICIPATING CLUBS
*This list is provisional and subject to
final confirmation from UEFA.*

GROUP STAGE
Club Atlético de Madrid (ESP)

PLAY-OFFS
FC Porto (POR) [CW]
PFC CSKA Moskva (RUS)
PSV Eindhoven (NED)
FC Steaua Bucureşti (ROU)
LOSC Lille Métropole (FRA)
Bayer 04 Leverkusen (GER)
Paris Saint-Germain FC (FRA) [CW]
Club Brugge KV (BEL)
US Città di Palermo (ITA)
Getafe CF (ESP)
Manchester City FC (ENG)
AEK Athens FC (GRE)
Aston Villa FC (ENG)
FC Lokomotiv Moskva (RUS)
FC Metalist Kharkiv (UKR)
Feyenoord (NED)
RCD Mallorca (ESP)
SSC Napoli (ITA)
BV Borussia Dortmund (GER)
Grasshopper-Club (SUI)
SC Vaslui (ROU)
Trabzonspor (TUR) [CW]
SC Tavriya Simferopol (UKR) [CW]
Dundee United FC (SCO) [CW]

THIRD QUALIFYING ROUND
Liverpool FC (ENG)
Juventus (ITA)
Sporting Clube de Portugal (POR)
VfB Stuttgart (GER)
AZ Alkmaar (NED)
Galatasaray AŞ (TUR)
Maccabi Haifa FC (ISR)
PFC CSKA Sofia (BUL)
Odense BK (DEN)
FC Dnipro Dnipropetrovsk (UKR)
FK Crvena Zvezda (SRB)
Aris Thessaloniki FC (GRE)
FC Timişoara (ROU)
Montpellier Hérault SC (FRA)
FC Sibir Novosibirsk (RUS)
KRC Genk (BEL)
SK Sturm Graz (AUT) [CW]
Hibernian FC (SCO)
FC Luzern (SUI)
FC Nordsjælland (DEN) [CW]
ŠK Slovan Bratislava (SVK) [CW]
PFC Beroe Stara Zagora (BUL) [CW]
FC Viktoria Plzeň (CZE) [CW]
FK Jablonec 97 (CZE)
IFK Göteborg (SWE)

Apollon Limassol FC (CYP) [CW]
Aalesunds FK (NOR) [CW]
HNK Hajduk Split (CRO) [CW]
FC Inter Turku (FIN) [CW]
Jagiellonia Białystok (POL) [CW]

SECOND QUALIFYING ROUND
Olympiacos FC (GRE)
Beşiktaş JK (TUR)
FC Dinamo 1948 Bucureşti (ROU)
PFC Levski Sofia (BUL)
FK Austria Wien (AUT)
Brøndby IF (DEN)
SK Rapid Wien (AUT)
APOEL FC (CYP)
Wisła Kraków (POL)
FC Karpaty Lviv (UKR)
CS Marítimo (POR)
FC Baník Ostrava (CZE)
IF Elfsborg (SWE)
FC Utrecht (NED)
Motherwell FC (SCO)
FC Lausanne-Sport (SUI) [CF]
Cercle Brugge KSV (BEL) [CF]
Stabæk IF (NOR)
FK Ventspils (LVA)
Molde FK (NOR)
Maccabi Tel-Aviv FC (ISR)
FK Dukla Banská Bystrica (SVK)
FC Honka Espoo (FIN)
NK Maribor (SVN) [CW]
FC Dinamo Minsk (BLR)
OFK Beograd (SRB)
FK Spartak Zlatibor Voda (SRB)
FK Bakı (AZE) [CW]
HNK Cibalia (CRO)
FK Sūduva (LTU)
FC WIT Georgia (GEO) [CW]
FC Iskra-Stali (MDA)
Sporting Fingal FC (IRL) [CW]
Shamrock Rovers FC (IRL)
FC Vaduz (LIE) [CW]
ND Gorica (SVN)
FK Borac Banja Luka (BIH) [CW]
KFK Šiauliai (LTU)
FK Jelgava (LVA) [CW]
FC Videoton (HUN)
UE Sant Julià (AND) [CW]
Breidablik (ISL) [CW]
FK Teteks (MKD) [CW]
Bangor City FC (WAL) [CW]
FK Atyrau (KAZ) [CW]
JK Sillamäe Kalev (EST)
FC Mika (ARM)
KS Besa (ALB) [CW]
FC Differdange 03 (LUX) [CW]
Valletta FC (MLT) [CW]
FK Budućnost Podgorica (MNE)

Vikingur (FRO) [CW]
Cliftonville FC (NIR)
SP Tre Penne (SMR)

FIRST QUALIFYING ROUND
Anorthosis Famagusta FC (CYP)
Randers FC (DEN) [FP]
Kalmar FF (SWE)
Bnei Yehuda Tel-Aviv FC (ISR) [CF]
FC Nitra (SVK)
FK Rabotnicki (MKD)
Myllykosken Pallo-47 (FIN) [FP]
Gefle IF (SWE) [FP]
NK Zrinjski (BIH)
FK Qarabag (AZE)
KS Ruch Chorzów (POL)
HNK Šibenik (CRO)
FC Dnepr Mogilev (BLR)
FC Torpedo Zhodino (BLR) [CF]
NK Široki Brijeg (BIH)
Skonto FC (LVA)
FC Dinamo Tbilisi (GEO)
KR Reykjavík (ISL)
FC Dacia Chişinău (MDA) [CW]
Dundalk FC (IRL)
FC TPS Turku (FIN)
KF Tirana (ALB)
FK Tauras (LTU)
FC Zestafoni (GEO)
FC Olimpia Bălţi (MDA)
FK Mogren (MNE)
FC Tobol Kostanay (KAZ)
NK Olimpija Ljubljana (SVN)
FC Flora (EST) [CF]
EB/Streymur (FRO)
Győri ETO FC (HUN)
Zalaegerszegi TE (HUN) [CF]
Glentoran FC (NIR)
F91 Dudelange (LUX)
JK Trans Narva (EST)
FK Khazar Lankaran (AZE)
Fylkir (ISL)
FK Metalurg Skopje (MKD)
FC Shakhtyor Karagandy (KAZ)
FC Banants (ARM) [CF]
KF Laçi (ALB)
Llanelli AFC (WAL)
Sliema Wanderers FC (MLT)
NSÍ Runavík (FRO)
FC Ulysses (ARM)
Port Talbot Town FC (WAL)
CS Grevenmacher (LUX)
FK Zeta (MNE)
Portadown FC (NIR) [CF]
UE Santa Coloma (AND)
FC Lusitans (AND)
SC Faetano (SMR)

SUMMARY OF APPEARANCES

EUROPEAN CUP AND CHAMPIONS LEAGUE (1955–2009)

ENGLISH CLUBS
22 Manchester U
20 Liverpool
14 Arsenal
8 Chelsea
4 Leeds U
3 Everton, Newcastle U, Nottingham F
2 Aston Villa, Derby Co, Wolverhampton W
1 Blackburn R, Burnley, Ipswich T, Manchester C, Tottenham H

SCOTTISH CLUBS
28 Rangers
25 Celtic
3 Aberdeen, Hearts
1 Dundee, Dundee U, Hibernian, Kilmarnock

WELSH CLUBS
6 Barry T
4 TNS
2 Rhyl
1 Cwmbran T, Llanelli

NORTHERN IRELAND CLUBS
24 Linfield
12 Glentoran
3 Crusaders, Portadown
2 Glenavon
1 Ards, Cliftonville, Coleraine, Derry C, Distillery

REPUBLIC OF IRELAND CLUBS
7 Dundalk, Shamrock R
6 Shelbourne, Waterford
5 Bohemians
3 Derry C*, Drumcondra, St Patrick's Ath
2 Athlone T, Cork City, Limerick
1 Celtic, Cork Hibs, Cork Drogheda U, Sligo R

Winners: Celtic 1966–67; Manchester U 1967–68, 1998–99; 2007–08; Liverpool 1976–77, 1977–78, 1980–81, 1983–84, 2004–05; Nottingham F 1978–79, 1979–80; Aston Villa 1981–82
Finalists: Celtic 1969–70; Leeds U 1974–75; Liverpool 1984–85, 2006–07; Arsenal 2005–06; Chelsea 2007–08; Manchester U 2008–09

UEFA EUROPA LEAGUE 2010

ENGLISH CLUBS
1 Aston Villa, Everton, Liverpool, Fulham

SCOTTISH CLUBS
1 Aberdeen, Celtic, Falkirk, Hearts, Motherwell

WELSH CLUBS
1 Bangor C, Llanelli, The New Saints

NORTHERN IRELAND CLUBS
1 Crusaders, Linfield, Lisburn Distillery

REPUBLIC OF IRELAND CLUBS
1 Derry C, St Patrick' Ath, Sligo R

Finalists: Fulham 2009–10

EUROPEAN CUP-WINNERS' CUP (1960–99)

ENGLISH CLUBS
6 Tottenham H 5 Chelsea, Liverpool, Manchester U
4 West Ham U 3 Arsenal, Everton 2 Manchester C
1 Ipswich T, Leeds U, Leicester C, Newcastle U, Southampton, Sunderland, WBA, Wolverhampton W

SCOTTISH CLUBS
10 Rangers 8 Aberdeen, Celtic 3 Dundee U, Hearts
2 Dunfermline Ath 1 Airdrieonians, Dundee, Hibernian, Kilmarnock, Motherwell, St Mirren

WELSH CLUBS
14 Cardiff C 8 Wrexham 7 Swansea C 3 Bangor C
1 Barry T, Borough U, Cwmbran T, Llansantfraid, Merthyr Tydfil, Newport Co

NORTHERN IRELAND CLUBS
9 Glentoran 5 Glenavon 4 Ballymena U, Coleraine
3 Crusaders, Linfield 2 Ards, Bangor
1 Derry C, Distillery, Carrick Rangers, Cliftonville, Portadown,

REPUBLIC OF IRELAND CLUBS
6 Shamrock R 4 Shelbourne 3 Bohemians, Dundalk, Limerick, Waterford
2 Cork City, Cork Hibs, Derry C*, Galway U, Sligo R
1 Bray W, Cork Celtic, Finn Harps, Home Farm, St Patrick's Ath, University College Dublin

Winners: Tottenham H 1962–63; West Ham U 1964–65; Manchester C 1969–70; Chelsea 1970–71, 1997–98; Rangers 1971–72; Aberdeen 1982–83; Everton 1984–85; Manchester U 1990–91; Arsenal 1993–94
Finalists: Rangers 1960–61, 1966–67; Liverpool 1965–66; Leeds U 1972–73; West Ham U 1975–76; Arsenal 1979–80, 1994–95

EUROPEAN FAIRS CUP & UEFA CUP (1955–2009)

ENGLISH CLUBS
13 Leeds U, Liverpool
11 Aston Villa
10 Ipswich T, Newcastle U
9 Arsenal, Everton, Tottenham H
7 Manchester U
6 Blackburn R, Chelsea, Manchester C, Southampton
5 Nottingham F
4 Birmingham C, WBA, Wolverhampton W
3 Sheffield W
2 Bolton W, Derby Co, Leicester C, Middlesbrough, QPR, Stoke C, West Ham U
1 Burnley, Coventry C, Fulham, London Rep XI, Millwall, Norwich C, Portsmouth, Watford

SCOTTISH CLUBS
19 Dundee U
17 Rangers
16 Aberdeen, Celtic, Hibernian
13 Hearts
7 Dunfermline Ath, Kilmarnock
5 Dundee
3 Motherwell, St Mirren
2 Partick T, St Johnstone
1 Gretna, Livingston, Morton, Queen of S, Raith R

WELSH CLUBS
5 Bangor C, TNS
3 Cwmbran T, Inter Cardiff (formerly Inter Cable-Tel), Rhyl
2 Barry T, Carmarthen T, Newtown
1 Afan Lido, Llanelli, Haverfordwest

NORTHERN IRELAND CLUBS
18 Glentoran
9 Coleraine
8 Linfield, Portadown
5 Glenavon
3 Crusaders
1 Ards, Ballymena U, Bangor, Cliftonville, Dungannon Swifts

REPUBLIC OF IRELAND CLUBS
11 Bohemians
7 Shelbourne
6 Dundalk, St Patrick's Ath
5 Cork City, Shamrock R
4 Derry C*
3 Drogheda U, Finn Harps, Longford T
2 Drumcondra
1 Athlone T, Bray Wanderers, Cork Hibs, Galway U, Limerick

Winners: Leeds U 1967–68, 1970–71; Newcastle U 1968–69; Arsenal 1969–70; Tottenham H 1971–72, 1983–84; Liverpool 1972–73, 1975–76, 2000–01; Ipswich T 1980–81
Finalists: London 1955–58, Birmingham C 1958–60, 1960–61; Leeds U 1966–67; Wolverhampton W 1971–72; Tottenham H 1973–74; Dundee U 1986–87; Celtic 2002–03; Middlesbrough 2005–06; Rangers 2007–08
* Now play in League of Ireland

FIFA CLUB WORLD CUP 2009

Formerly known as the FIFA Club World Championship, this tournament is played annually between the champion clubs from all 6 continental confederations, although since 2007 the champions of Oceania must play a qualifying play-off against the champion club of the host country.

FIFA CLUB WORLD CUP 2009

(Finals in Abu Dhabi)

QUARTER-FINAL PLAY-OFF

9 December 2009

Al Ahli (0) 0

Auckland City (1) 2 *(Dickinson 45, Coombes 67)*   14,856

Al Ahli: Yosif Abdalla; Saad Surour, Mohammed (Waleed Ahmed 84), Ali Abbas, Bare, Abd Rabo, Bader Yaqoot, Hassan Ali (Madanchi 54), Yousif Jaber, Salem Khamis, Ali Hussain (Mohamed Rashid 46).
Auckland City: Spoonley; Hogg, Williams, Lee, Coombes, Koprivcic (Jordan 71), Vicelich, Hayne (Feneridis 85), McGeorge, Uhlmann (Campbell 90).

QUARTER-FINALS

11 December 2009

TP Mazembe (1) 1 *(Bedi 28)*

Pohang Steelers (0) 2 *(Denilson 50, 78)*   9627

TP Mazembe: Kidiaba; Nkulukuta, Mputu, Kabangu, Mabele, Bedi, Kaluyituka (Mvete 82), Mihayo, Ekanga (Kanda 83), Tshizeu, Lusadisu (Kasongo 60).
Pohang Steelers: Shin HY; Choi, Kim T, Kim JS, Denilson, Hwang JW, Kim JK, Kim HG, Namkung (Hwang JS 56), Shin HM (Ko 80), No (Song 88).

12 December 2009

Auckland City (0) 0

Atlante (1) 3 *(Arreola 36, Bermudez 69, Silva 90)*   7222

Auckland City: Spoonley; Hogg, Williams, Lee (Nikolic 78), Coombes, Koprivcic (Young 66), Vicelich, Hayne, McGeorge, Uhlmann, Dickinson (Urlovic 88).
Atlante: Vilar; Martinez, Gonzalez, Navarro, Marquez (Pereyra 86), Solari (Silva 74), Guerrero, Bermudez, Rojas, Velasquez, Arreola.

SEMI-FINALS

16 December 2009

Atlante (1) 1 *(Rojas 5)*

Barcelona (1) 3 *(Busquets 35, Messi 55, Pedro 67)*   40,955

Atlante: Vilar; Martinez, Gonzalez, Navarro, Marquez, Solari (Carevic 56), Guerrero, Bermudez, Rojas, Velasquez (Pereyra 63), Arreola.
Barcelona: Victor Valdes; Daniel Alves, Marquez (Pique 54), Puyol, Xavi, Iniesta (Kirkic 76), Ibrahimovic, Busquets, Pedro, Abidal, Toure (Messi 53).

15 December 2009

Pohang Steelers (0) 1 *(Denilson 71)*

Estudiantes (1) 2 *(Benitez 45, 53)*   22,626

Pohang Steelers: Shin HY[■]; Choi, Kim T (Okayama 58), Kim JS[■], Denilson, Hwang JW[■], Kim JK, Kim HG, Namkung (Kim MC 46), Shin HM, No (Park 54).
Estudiantes: Albil; Desabato (Cellay 68), Perez, Veron, Diaz, Re, Boselli, Nunez, Brana, Benitez (Salgueiro 83), Rodriguez.

MATCH FOR THIRD/FOURTH PLACE

19 December 2009

Pohang Steelers (1) 1 *(Denilson 42)*

Atlante (0) 1 *(Marquez 46)*   13,814

aet; Pohang Steelers won 4-3 on penalties.
Pohang Steelers: Song DJ; Choi, Okayama, Kim T, Denilson, Kim MC (Ko 65), Song CH (Ryu 60), Kim JK (Park 54), Kim HG, Shin HM, No.
Atlante: Vilar; Martinez, Gonzalez, Navarro (Peralta 93), Marquez, Pereyra (Solari 93), Guerrero, Bermudez, Rojas, Velasquez, Arreola (Silva 46).

MATCH FOR FIFTH/SIXTH PLACE

16 December 2009

TP Mazembe (0) 2 *(Kasongo 60, Kasusula 67)*

Auckland City (1) 3 *(Hayne 29, 72, Van Steeden 90)*   4200

TP Mazembe: Kidiaba[■]; Kasusula, Mputu, Kabangu (Kaluyituka 74), Mabele, Bedi, Mvete (Bakula 26), Mihayo, Milandu, Ekanga, Kasongo.
Auckland City: Gothard; Hogg (Van Steeden 75), Campbell, Williams, Lee, Pritchett, Coombes, Koprivcic (Young 46), Vicelich, Hayne, Dickinson (Morgan 46).

FIFA CLUB WORLD CUP FINAL 2009

19 December 2009 (attendance 43,050)

Estudiantes (1) 1 *(Boselli 37)*

Barcelona (0) 2 *(Pedro 89, Messi 110)*

Estudiantes: Albil; Desabato, Cellay, Perez (Nunez 79), Veron, Diaz, Re (Rojo 91), Boselli, Brana, Benitez (Sanchez 76), Rodriguez.

Barcelona: Victor Valdes; Daniel Alves, Pique, Puyol, Xavi, Ibrahimovic, Messi, Henry (Jeffren 83), Keita (Pedro 46), Busquets (Toure 79), Abidal.

aet.

PREVIOUS MATCHES

2000 Corinthians beat Vaso de Gama 4-3 on penalties after 0-0 draw
2005 Sao Paulo beat Liverpool 1-0
2006 Internacional beat Barcelona 1-0
2007 AC Milan beat Boca Juniors 4-2
2008 Manchester U beat Liga De Quito 1-0
2009 Barcelona beat Estudiantes 2-1

■ *Denotes player sent off.*

WORLD CLUB CHAMPIONSHIP

Played annually up to 1974 and intermittently since then between the winners of the European Cup and the winners of the South American Champions Cup — known as the Copa Libertadores. In 1980 the winners were decided by one match arranged in Tokyo in February 1981 which remained the venue until 2004, when the match was superseded by the FIFA Club World Championship. AC Milan replaced Marseille who had been stripped of their European Cup title in 1993.

1960 Real Madrid beat Penarol 0-0, 5-1	1985 Juventus beat Argentinos Juniors 4-2 on penalties
1961 Penarol beat Benfica 0-1, 5-0, 2-1	after a 2-2 draw
1962 Santos beat Benfica 3-2, 5-2	1986 River Plate beat Steaua Bucharest 1-0
1963 Santos beat AC Milan 2-4, 4-2, 1-0	1987 FC Porto beat Penarol 2-1 after extra time
1964 Inter-Milan beat Independiente 0-1, 2-0, 1-0	1988 Nacional (Uru) beat PSV Eindhoven 7-6 on
1965 Inter-Milan beat Independiente 3-0, 0-0	penalties after 1-1 draw
1966 Penarol beat Real Madrid 2-0, 2-0	1989 AC Milan beat Atletico Nacional (Col) 1-0 after
1967 Racing Club beat Celtic 0-1, 2-1, 1-0	extra time
1968 Estudiantes beat Manchester United 1-0, 1-1	1990 AC Milan beat Olimpia 3-0
1969 AC Milan beat Estudiantes 3-0, 1-2	1991 Red Star Belgrade beat Colo Colo 3-0
1970 Feyenoord beat Estudiantes 2-2, 1-0	1992 Sao Paulo beat Barcelona 2-1
1971 Nacional beat Panathinaikos* 1-1, 2-1	1993 Sao Paulo beat AC Milan 3-2
1972 Ajax beat Independiente 1-1, 3-0	1994 Velez Sarsfield beat AC Milan 2-0
1973 Independiente beat Juventus* 1-0	1995 Ajax beat Gremio Porto Alegre 4-3 on penalties
1974 Atlético Madrid* beat Independiente 0-1, 2-0	after 0-0 draw
1975 Independiente and Bayern Munich could not agree	1996 Juventus beat River Plate 1-0
dates; no matches.	1997 Borussia Dortmund beat Cruzeiro 2-0
1976 Bayern Munich beat Cruzeiro 2-0, 0-0	1998 Real Madrid beat Vasco da Gama 2-1
1977 Boca Juniors beat Borussia Moenchengladbach*	1999 Manchester U beat Palmeiras 1-0
2-2, 3-0	2000 Boca Juniors beat Real Madrid 2-1
1978 Not contested	2001 Bayern Munich beat Boca Juniors 1-0 after extra
1979 Olimpia beat Malmö* 1-0, 2-1	time
1980 Nacional beat Nottingham Forest 1-0	2002 Real Madrid beat Olimpia 2-0
1981 Flamengo beat Liverpool 3-0	2003 Boca Juniors beat AC Milan 3-1 on penalties after
1982 Penarol beat Aston Villa 2-0	1-1 draw
1983 Gremio Porto Alegre beat SV Hamburg 2-1	2004 Porto beat Once Caldas 8-7 on penalties after 0-0
1984 Independiente beat Liverpool 1-0	draw

*European Cup runners-up; winners declined to take part.

EUROPEAN SUPER CUP 2009

Played annually between the winners of the European Champions' Cup and the European Cup-Winners' Cup (UEFA Cup from 2000). AC Milan replaced Marseille in 1993–94.

EUROPEAN SUPER CUP 2009
28 August 2009, Monaco (attendance 17,000)
Barcelona (0) 1 *(Rodriguez 115)*   Shakhtar Donetsk (0) 0

Barcelona: Victor Valdes; Daniel Alves, Pique, Puyol, Xavi, Ibrahimovic (Rodriguez 81), Messi, Henry (Bojan 96), Keita, Abidal, Toure (Busquets 100).

Shakhtar Donetsk: Pyatov; Hubschman, Kucher, Fernandinho (Jadson 80), Ilsinho, Luiz Adriano, Gay (Kobin 80), Willian (Aghahowa 91), Rat, Chygrynskiy, Srna.

Referee: De Bleeckere (Belgium).

aet.

PREVIOUS MATCHES

1972 Ajax beat Rangers 3-1, 3-2	1991 Manchester U beat Red Star Belgrade 1-0
1973 Ajax beat AC Milan 0-1, 6-0	1992 Barcelona beat Werder Bremen 1-1, 2-1
1974 Not contested	1993 Parma beat AC Milan 0-1, 2-0
1975 Dynamo Kiev beat Bayern Munich 1-0, 2-0	1994 AC Milan beat Arsenal 0-0, 2-0
1976 Anderlecht beat Bayern Munich 4-1, 1-2	1995 Ajax beat Zaragoza 1-1, 4-0
1977 Liverpool beat Hamburg 1-1, 6-0	1996 Juventus beat Paris St Germain 6-1, 3-1
1978 Anderlecht beat Liverpool 3-1, 1-2	1997 Barcelona beat Borussia Dortmund 2-0, 1-1
1979 Nottingham F beat Barcelona 1-0, 1-1	1998 Chelsea beat Real Madrid 1-0
1980 Valencia beat Nottingham F 1-0, 1-2	1999 Lazio beat Manchester U 1-0
1981 Not contested	2000 Galatasaray beat Real Madrid 2-1
1982 Aston Villa beat Barcelona 0-1, 3-0	2001 Liverpool beat Bayern Munich 3-2
1983 Aberdeen beat Hamburg 0-0, 2-0	2002 Real Madrid beat Feyenoord 3-1
1984 Juventus beat Liverpool 2-0	2003 AC Milan beat Porto 1-0
1985 Juventus v Everton not contested due to UEFA ban	2004 Valencia beat Porto 2-1
on English clubs	2005 Liverpool beat CSKA Moscow 3-1
1986 Steaua Bucharest beat Dynamo Kiev 1-0	2006 Sevilla beat Barcelona 3-0
1987 FC Porto beat Ajax 1-0, 1-0	2007 AC Milan beat Sevilla 3-1
1988 KV Mechelen beat PSV Eindhoven 3-0, 0-1	2008 Zenit beat Manchester U 2-1
1989 AC Milan beat Barcelona 1-1, 1-0	2009 Barcelona beat Shakhtar Donetsk 1-0
1990 AC Milan beat Sampdoria 1-1, 2-0	

INTERNATIONAL DIRECTORY

The latest available information has been given regarding numbers of clubs and players registered with FIFA, the world governing body. Where known, official colours are listed. With European countries, League tables show a number of signs. * indicates relegated teams, + play-offs, *+ relegated after play-offs, ++ promoted.
There are 207 member associations. The four home countries, England. Scotland, Northern Ireland and Wales, are dealt with elsewhere in the Yearbook; but basic details appear in this directory. The following countries are not members of FIFA: Gibraltar, Kosovo, and Northern Cyprus.

EUROPE

ALBANIA

The Football Association of Albania, Rruga Labinoti, Pallati Perballe Shkolles 'Gjuhet e Huaja'.
Founded: 1930; *National Colours:* Red shirts, black shorts, red stockings.

International matches 2009
Malta (a) 0-0, Hungary (h) 0-1, Denmark (a) 0-3, Portugal (h) 1-2, Georgia (h) 1-1, Cyprus (h) 6-1, Denmark (h) 1-1, Sweden (a) 1-4, Estonia (a) 0-0.

League Championship wins (1930–37; 1945–2010)
SK Tirana 24 (including 17 Nentori 8); Dinamo Tirana 18; Partizani Tirana 15; Vllaznia 9; Elbasan 2 (including Labinoti 1); Flamurtari 1; Skenderbeu 1; Teuta 1.

Cup wins (1948–2010)
Partizani Tirana 15; Dinamo Tirana 13; SK Tirana 13 (including 17 Nentori 8); Vllaznia 6; Teuta 3; Flamurtari 3; Elbasan 2 (including Labinoti 1); Besa 2; Apolonia 1.

Final League Table 2009–10

	P	W	D	L	F	A	Pts
Dinamo Tirana	33	19	4	10	56	42	61
Besa	33	15	8	10	42	33	53
SK Tirana	33	15	7	11	38	32	52
Laci	33	14	9	10	35	28	51
Vllaznia	33	14	7	12	37	39	49
Flamurtari	33	13	8	12	42	39	47
Shkumbini	33	13	6	14	33	33	45
Teuta	33	13	6	14	33	40	45
Kastrioti+ (–3)	33	13	6	14	33	42	45
Skenderbeu+	33	10	9	14	41	44	39
Apolonia*	33	10	8	15	36	43	38
Gramozi*	33	6	8	19	25	43	26

Top scorer: Xhafaj (Besa) 17.
Cup Final: Besa 2, Vllaznia 1.

ANDORRA

Federacio Andorrana de Futbol, Avinguda Carlemany 67, 3er Pis, Apartado postal 65, Escaldes-Engordany, Principat D'Andorra.
Founded: 1994; *National Colours:* Yellow shirts, red shorts, blue stockings.

International matches 2009
Lithuania (a) 1-3, Croatia (h) 0-2, Belarus (a) 1-5, England (a) 0-6, Ukraine (a) 0-5, Kazakhstan (h) 1-3, Ukraine (h) 0-6.

League Championship wins (1996–2010)
FC Santa Coloma 5; Principat 3; Encamp 2; Ranger's 2; St Julia 2; Constelacio 1.

Cup wins (1991–2010)
FC Santa Coloma 8; Principat 6; St Julia 2; Constelacio 1; Lusitanos 1.

Qualifying League Table 2009–10

	P	W	D	L	F	A	Pts
FC Santa Coloma	14	11	3	0	38	10	36
St Julia	14	10	2	2	59	12	32
UE Santa Coloma	14	10	2	2	41	20	32
Lusitanos	14	7	2	5	30	17	23
Principat	14	7	0	7	27	33	21
Encamp	14	3	1	10	19	50	10
Inter Club	14	1	1	12	10	41	4
Engordany	14	1	1	12	11	52	4

Championship Play-Offs

	P	W	D	L	F	A	Pts
FC Santa Coloma	20	13	7	0	46	14	46
UE Santa Coloma	20	13	4	3	50	26	43
St Julia	20	12	5	3	69	18	41
Lusitanos	20	7	3	10	34	32	24

Relegation Play-Offs

	P	W	D	L	F	A	Pts
Principat	20	8	2	10	42	50	26
Inter Club	20	6	1	13	25	49	19
Encamp+	20	4	3	13	31	67	15
Engordany*	20	4	1	15	22	63	13

Top scorer: Riera (St Julia) 19.
Cup Final: UE Santa Coloma 0, St Julia 1.

ARMENIA

Football Federation of Armenia, Saryan 38, Yerevan, 375 010, Armenia.
Founded: 1992; *National Colours:* Red shirts, blue shorts, orange stockings.

International matches 2009
Latvia (a) 0-0, Estonia (h) 2-2, Estonia (a) 0-1, Moldova (h) 1-4, Bosnia (h) 0-2, Belgium (h) 2-1, Spain (h) 1-2, Turkey (a) 0-2.

League Championship wins (1992–2009)
Pyunik 12 (including Homenetmen 3); Shirak Gyumri 4*; Ararat Yerevan 3*; Araks 2 (including Tsement); FC Yerevan 1.
*Includes one unofficial title.

Cup wins (1992–2010)
Mika 5; Ararat Yerevan 5; Pyunik 4; Tsement 2; Banants 2; Pyunik (including Homenetmen) 1.

Final League Table 2009

	P	W	D	L	F	A	Pts
Pyunik	28	20	5	3	64	13	65
Mika	28	18	4	6	59	34	58
Ulysses	28	16	5	7	47	25	53
Banants	28	13	5	10	40	29	44
Gandzasar	28	12	2	14	32	47	38
Shirak	28	5	8	15	24	55	23
Kilikia	28	5	5	18	22	51	20
Ararat*	28	2	8	18	20	54	14

Top scorer: Kocharyan (Ulysses) 15.
Cup Final: Pyunik 4, Banants 0.

AUSTRIA

Oesterreichischer Fussball-Bund, Ernst-Happel Stadion – Sektor A/F, Postfach 300, Meierestrasse 7, Wien 1021.
Founded: 1904; *National Colours:* White shirts, black shorts, white stockings.

International matches 2009
Sweden (h) 0-2, Romania (h) 2-1, Serbia (a) 0-1, Cameroon (h) 0-2, Faeroes (h) 3-1, Romania (a) 1-1, Lithuania (h) 2-1, France (a) 1-3, Spain (h) 1-5.

League Championship wins (1912–2010)
Rapid Vienna 32; FK Austria (formerly Amateure) 23; Tirol-Svarowski-Innsbruck 10; Admira-Energie-Wacker 8; First Vienna 6; Austria Salzburg 6; Wiener Sportklub 3; Sturm Graz 2; WAC 1; FAC 1; Hakoah 1; Linz ASK 1; WAF 1; Voest Linz 1; Graz 1; WAC 1; Wacker 1.

Cup wins (1919–2010)
FK Austria (formerly Amateure) 27; Rapid Vienna 14; TS Innsbruck (formerly Wacker Innsbruck) 7; Admira-Energie-Wacker (formerly Sportklub Admira & Admira-Energie) 5; Graz 4; Sturm Graz 4; First Vienna 3; WAC 3; Linz ASK 1; Wacker Vienna 1; WAF 1; Wiener Sportklub 1; Kremser 1; Stockerau 1; Ried 1; Karnten 1; WAC 1; Kremser 1, Horn 1.

Final League Table 2009–10

	P	W	D	L	F	A	Pts
Salzburg	36	22	10	4	68	27	76
FK Austria	36	23	6	7	60	34	75
Rapid Vienna	36	21	10	5	80	38	73
Sturm Graz	36	16	10	10	50	36	58

Neustadt	36	13	8	15	54	58	47
Mattersburg	36	12	5	19	45	71	41
Linz	36	9	13	14	59	70	40
Ried	36	10	8	18	39	47	38
Kapfenberger	36	8	9	19	44	67	33
Karnten*	36	2	9	25	29	80	15

Neustadt formally Magna.
Top scorer: Hofmann (Rapid Vienna) 20.
Cup Final: Sturm Graz 1, Neustadt 0.

AZERBAIJAN

Association of Football Federations of Azerbaijan, 42 Gussi Gadjiev Street, Baku 370 009.
Founded: 1992; *National Colours:* White shirts, blue shorts, white stockings.

International matches 2009
Uzbekistan (h) 1-1, Kuwait (a) 1-1, Russia (a) 0-2, Turkey (a) 0-2, Wales (h) 0-1, Spain (h) 0-6, Germany (h) 0-2, Finland (h) 1-2, Germany (a) 0-4, Liechtenstein (a) 2-0, Russia (h) 1-1, Iraq (a) 0-1, Czech Republic (h) 2-0.

League Championship wins (1992–2010)
Neftchi 5; Kapaz 3; Shamkir 3; Baku 2; Inter 2; Karabakh 1; Turan 1; Xazar 1.
Includes one unofficial title for Shamkir in 2002.

Cup wins (1992–2010)
Neftchi 5; Kapaz 4; Karabakh 3; Xazar 2; Baku 2; Inshatchi 1; Shafa 1.

Qualifying League Table 2009–10
	P	W	D	L	F	A	Pts
Inter	22	15	4	3	36	18	49
Xazar	22	12	8	2	29	11	44
Karabakh	22	11	9	2	21	12	42
Baku	22	10	7	5	22	17	37
Kabala	22	10	6	6	24	21	36
Neftchi	22	9	8	5	20	14	35
Simurq	22	9	7	6	26	21	34
Olimpik	22	6	7	9	20	23	25
Turan	22	4	5	13	23	32	17
Mugan	22	3	7	12	12	27	16
Standard	22	2	5	15	16	34	11
Karvan	22	2	5	15	17	36	11

Standard relocated from Baku to Sumkayit; top six for championship, bottom six for relegation play-off.

Final League Table 2009–10
	P	W	D	L	F	A	Pts
Inter	10	2	6	2	11	9	29
Baku	10	4	4	2	11	6	28
Xazar	10	3	3	4	11	10	27
Karabakh	10	3	3	4	10	14	27
Neftchi	10	2	6	2	5	6	23
Kabala	10	3	4	4	12	15	20

Relegation Table 2009–10
	P	W	D	L	F	A	Pts
Olimpik	10	5	3	2	13	5	36
Simurq	10	2	4	4	5	14	31
Turan	10	3	4	3	12	11	29
Mugan	10	5	2	3	12	9	27
Standard*	10	5	1	4	19	10	25
Karvan*	10	1	4	5	5	17	13

Top scorer: Guliyev (Standard) 16.
Cup Final: Xazar 1, Baku 2.

BELARUS

Belarus Football Federation, Kirova Street 8/2, Minsk 220 600, Belarus.
Founded: 1992; *National Colours:* Red shirts, green shorts, red stockings.

International matches 2009
Kazakhstan (a) 5-1, Moldova (h) 2-2, Andorra (h) 5-1, Croatia (h) 1-3, Croatia (a) 0-1, Ukraine (h) 0-0, Kazakhstan (h) 4-0, England (a) 0-3, Saudi Arabia (a) 1-1, Montenegro (a) 0-1.

League Championship wins (1992–2009)
Dynamo Minsk 7; BATE Borisov 6; Slavia Mozyr (formerly MPKC Mozyr) 2; Dnepr Mogilev 1; Belshina 1; Gomel 1; Shakhtyor 1.

Cup wins (1992–2010)
Belshina 3; Dynamo Minsk 3; Slavia Mozyr (formerly MPKC Mozyr) 2; MTZ-RIPA 2; BATE Borisov 2; Neman 1; Dynamo 93 Minsk 1; Lokomotiv 96 1; Gomel 1; Shakhtyor 1; Dynamo Brest 1; Naftan 1.

Final League Table 2009
	P	W	D	L	F	A	Pts
BATE Borisov	26	19	5	2	55	16	62
Dynamo Minsk	26	14	8	4	38	18	50
Dnepr	26	12	4	10	31	26	40
Naftan	26	12	2	12	28	39	38
Dynamo Brest	26	10	8	8	30	24	38
Shakhtyor	26	10	8	8	33	28	38
Neman	26	11	4	11	23	31	37
Torpedo Zhodino	26	10	7	9	31	22	37
Minsk	26	11	3	12	33	26	36
FK Vitebsk	26	10	2	14	26	37	32
MTZ-RIPA	26	8	6	12	34	38	30
Gomel*	26	8	5	13	31	47	29
Granit*	26	6	7	13	27	39	25
Smorgon*	26	2	9	15	17	46	15

Top scorer: Rogerio Silva (Gomel) 15.
Cup Final: BATE Borisov 5, Torpedo Zhodino 0.

BELGIUM

Union Royale Belge Des Societes De Football Association, 145 Avenue Houba de Strooper, B-1020 Bruxelles.
Founded: 1895; *National Colours:* All red.

International matches 2009
Slovenia (h) 2-0, Bosnia (h) 2-4, Bosnia (a) 1-2, Chile (h) 1-1, Japan (a) 0-4, Czech Republic (a) 1-3, Spain (a) 0-5, Armenia (a) 1-2, Turkey (h) 2-0, Estonia (a) 0-2, Hungary (h) 3-0, Qatar (h) 2-0.

League Championship wins (1896–2010)
Anderlecht 30; Club Brugge 13; Union St Gilloise 11; Standard Liege 9; Beerschot 7; RC Brussels 6; FC Liege 5; Daring Brussels 5; Antwerp 4; Mechelen 4; Lierse SK 4; Cercle Brugge 3; Beveren 2; Genk 2; RWD Molenbeek 1.

Cup wins (1912–14; 1927; 1935; 1954–2010)
Club Brugge 10; Anderlecht 9; Standard Liege 6; Racing Genk 3; Gent 3; Beerschot (became Germinal) 2; Waterschei (became Racing Genk) 2; Beveren 2; Antwerp 2; Lierse SK 2; Union St Gilloise 2; Cercle Brugge 2; Mechelen 1; FC Liege 1; Ekeren (became Germinal) 1; Westerlo 1; La Louviere 1; Zulte-Waregem 1; Daring 1; Germinal 1; Tournai 1; Racing 1; Waregem 1.

Qualifying League Table 2009–10
	P	W	D	L	F	A	Pts
Anderlecht	28	22	3	3	62	20	69
Club Brugge	28	17	6	5	52	33	57
Gent	28	14	7	7	49	30	49
Kortrijk	28	12	9	7	39	30	45
St Truiden	28	12	6	10	35	35	42
Waregem	28	10	11	7	39	32	41
Mechelen	28	12	3	13	36	46	39
Standard Liege	28	10	9	9	38	34	39
Cercle Brugge	28	11	5	12	45	40	38
Beerschot	28	9	8	11	30	43	35
Genk	28	8	10	10	33	31	34
Westerlo	28	8	8	12	28	34	32
Charleroi	28	5	8	15	28	45	23
Lokeren	28	5	3	20	22	54	18
Roeselare*+	28	4	6	18	29	58	18

Mouscron excluded after twenty matches.

Championship Play-Off
	P	W	D	L	F	A	Pts
Anderlecht	10	7	3	0	24	9	59
Gent	10	4	4	2	20	13	41
Club Brugge	10	3	3	4	14	15	41
St Truiden	10	3	4	3	9	10	34
Kortrijk	10	3	1	6	9	13	33
Waregem	10	2	1	7	7	23	28

Europa League Qualifying Table A
	P	W	D	L	F	A	Pts
Westerlo*	6	3	1	2	12	9	10
Mechelen	6	3	1	2	10	8	10
CS Brugge	6	2	1	3	9	12	7
Lokeren	6	1	3	2	12	14	6

qualified.

Europa League Qualifying Table B
	P	W	D	L	F	A	Pts
Genk*	6	5	1	0	12	3	16
Standard Liege	6	2	2	2	8	5	8
Beerschot	6	1	2	3	6	12	5
Charleroi	6	1	1	4	4	10	4

qualified.

Final
Genk 2, 3, Westerlo 2, 0.

Play-Off
Genk 2, 3, St Truiden 1, 2.
Genk qualified for Europa League.
Top scorer: Lukaku (Anderlecht) 15.
Cup Final: Gent 3, Cercle Brugge 0.

BOSNIA-HERZEGOVINA

Football Federation of Bosnia & Herzegovina, Ferhadija 30, Sarajevo 71000.
Founded: 1992; *National Colours:* White shirts, blue shorts, white stockings.

International matches 2009
Belgium (a) 4-2, Belgium (h) 2-1, Uzbekistan (a) 0-0, Oman (h) 2-1, Iran (h) 2-3, Armenia (a) 2-0, Turkey (h) 1-1, Estonia (a) 2-0, Spain (h) 2-5, Portugal (a) 0-1, Portugal (h) 0-1.

League Championship wins (1998–2010)
Zeljeznicar 4 Siroki 2; Sarajevo 2; Zrinjski 2; Brotnjo 1; Leotar 1; Modrica 1.

Cup wins (1998–2010)
Sarajevo 3; Zeljeznicar 3; Modrica 1; Orasje 1; Siroki 1; Zrinjski 1; Slavija 1; Borac 1.

Final League Table 2009–10

	P	W	D	L	F	A	Pts
Zeljeznicar	30	18	7	5	52	22	61
Siroki	30	16	7	7	46	27	55
Borac	30	17	2	11	37	29	53
Zrinjski	30	15	6	9	46	33	51
Sarajevo	30	14	8	8	43	25	50
Olimpik	30	12	8	10	30	34	44
Velez	30	13	4	13	42	33	43
Sloboda	30	13	3	14	30	34	42
Travnik	30	11	6	13	40	41	39
Rudar	30	11	5	14	27	32	38
Leotar	30	11	5	14	32	48	38
Zvijezda	30	11	4	15	35	47	37
Celik	30	10	5	15	33	37	35
Slavija	30	10	5	15	32	46	35
Laktasi*	30	10	4	16	38	46	34
Modrica*	30	7	3	20	28	57	24

Top scorer: Dudic (Travnik) 16.
Cup Final: Borac 1, 2, Zeljeznicar 1, 2.

BULGARIA

Bulgarian Football Union, Karnigradska Street 19, BG-1000 Sofia.
Founded: 1923; *National Colours:* White shirts, green shorts, white stockings.

International matches 2009
Switzerland (a) 1-1, Republic of Ireland (a) 1-1, Cyprus (h) 2-0, Republic of Ireland (h) 1-1, Latvia (h) 1-0, Montenegro (h) 4-1, Italy (a) 0-2, Cyprus (a) 1-4, Georgia (h) 6-2, Malta (a) 4-1.

League Championship wins (1925–2010)
CSKA Sofia 31; Levski Sofia 26; Slavia Sofia 7; Vladislav Varna 3; Lokomotiv Sofia 3; Litex 3; Botev Plovdiv (includes Trakija) 2; AC 23 Sofia 1; SC Sofia 1; Sokol Varna 1; Spartak Plovdiv 1; Tichka Varna 1; JSZ Sofia 1; Beroe Stara Zagora 1; Etur 1; Lokomotiv Plovdiv 1.

Cup wins (1946–2010)
Levski Sofia 24; CSKA Sofia 18; Slavia Sofia 7; Lokomotiv Sofia 4; Litex 4; Botev Plovdiv (includes Trakija) 2; Spartak Plovdiv 1; Septemvri Sofia 1; Marek Dupnica 1; Spartak Varna 1; Sliven 1; Beroe 1.

Final League Table 2009–10

	P	W	D	L	F	A	Pts
Litex	30	22	4	4	59	17	70
CSKA Sofia	30	16	10	4	51	25	58
Levski Sofia	30	17	6	7	57	26	57
Locomotiv Sofia	30	15	7	8	47	33	52
Chernomorets	30	15	6	9	44	29	51
Slavia Sofia	30	14	8	8	34	28	50
Cherno More	30	13	9	11	40	28	48
Minjor	30	13	6	9	38	26	45
Pirin	30	11	10	12	34	32	43
Beroe	30	10	8	12	30	36	38
Montana	30	9	9	15	30	37	36
Lokomotiv Plovdiv	30	9	6	16	36	52	33
Sliven	30	9	5	17	29	41	32
Lokomotiv Mezdra	30	7	6	21	30	48	27

Sportist*	30	5	4	21	23	59	19
Botev Plovdiv*	30	1	4	25	12	78	7

Botev Plovdiv excluded during winter break; remaining matches awarded 0-3 against them.
Top scorer: Niflore (Litex) 19.
Cup Final: Beroe 1, Chernomorets 0.

CHANNEL ISLANDS

Guernsey

League Championship wins (1894–2010)
Northerners 29; Rangers 17; Vale Recreation 15; Saint Martin's AC 12; Sylvans 10; Belgrave Wanderers 6; 2nd Batt Manchesters 3; 2nd Batt Royal Irish Regt 2; 2nd Batt Wiltshires 2; 10th Comp W Div Royal Artillery 1; 2nd Batt Leicesters 1; 2nd Batt PA Somerset Light Infantry 1; 2nd Middlesex Regt 1; Athletics 1; Band Comp 2nd Batt Royal Fusiliers 1; G&H Comp Royal Fusiliers 1; Grange 1; Yorkshire Regt (Green Howards) 1.

Final League Table 2009–10

	P	W	D	L	F	A	Pts
Belgrave Wanderers	21	17	1	3	79	30	52
Saint Martin's AC	21	16	2	3	75	28	50
Northerners AC	21	10	3	8	51	42	33
Vale Recreation	21	9	3	9	34	37	30
Guernsey Rangers F&AC	21	9	2	10	42	45	29
Guernsey Athletics	21	8	2	11	31	46	26
Sylvans S&FC	21	4	2	15	23	59	14
Rovers AC	21	3	1	17	13	61	10

Jersey

League Championship wins (1905–2010)
Jersey Wanderers 20; First Tower United 19; Saint Paul's 13; Jersey Scottish 9; Beeches Old Boys 5; Magpies 4; 2nd Batt King's Own Regt 3; Oaklands 3; St Peter 3; 1st Batt Devon Regt 2; 1st Batt East Surrey Regt 2; Georgetown 2; Mechanics 2; YMCA 2; 2nd Batt East Surrey Regt 1; 20th Comp Royal Garrison Artillery 1; National Rovers 1; Sporting Academics 1; Trinity 1.

Final League Table 2009–10

	P	W	D	L	F	A	Pts
Saint Paul's	16	13	3	0	58	7	42
Grouville	16	10	4	2	39	14	34
Trinity	16	7	3	6	30	23	24
Fortuguese Club	16	6	5	5	30	22	23
Saint Ouen	16	5	6	5	24	24	21
Saint Peter	16	5	6	5	17	32	21
Jersey Scottish	16	3	6	7	31	27	15
Rozel Rovers*	16	3	3	10	16	55	12
First Tower United*	16	1	2	13	12	53	5

Upton Park Trophy (For Guernsey & Jersey Winners)
Northerners AC 16; First Tower United 12; Jersey Wanderers 11; Saint Martin's AC 10; Saint Paul's 6; Rangers 5; Jersey Scottish 5; Vale Recreation 4; Belgrave Wanderers 4; Sylvans 3; Beeches Old Boys 3; Old Saint Paul's 3; Magpies 3; Saint Peter 2; Jersey Mechanics 1; Jersey YMCA 1; National Rovers 1; Sporting Academics 1; Trinity 1.

CROATIA

Croatian Football Federation, Rusanova 13, Zagreb, 10 3000, Croatia.
Founded: 1912; *National Colours:* Red & white shirts, white shorts, blue stockings.

International matches 2009
Romania (a) 2-1, Andorra (a) 2-0, Ukraine (h) 2-2, Belarus (a) 3-1, Belarus (h) 1-0, England (a) 1-5, Qatar (h) 3-2, Kazakhstan (a) 2-1, Liechtenstein (h) 5-0.

League Championship wins (1941–46; 1992–2010)
Dinamo Zagreb (formerly Croatia Zagreb) 12; Hajduk Split 8; Gradjanski 1; Concordia 1; Zagreb 1.

Cup wins (1992–2010)
Dinamo Zagreb (formerly Croatia Zagreb) 10; Hajduk Split 5; Rijeka 2; Inker Zapresic 1; Osijek 1.

Final League Table 2009–10

	P	W	D	L	F	A	Pts
Dinamo Zagreb	30	18	8	4	70	20	62
Hajduk Split	30	17	7	6	50	21	58
Cibalia	30	16	9	5	46	20	57
Sibenik	30	14	8	8	34	37	50
Osijek	30	13	8	9	49	36	47
Karlovac	30	12	11	7	32	23	47
Slaven	30	11	10	9	44	45	43
Lokomotiv Zagreb	30	12	6	12	35	38	42

	P	W	D	L	F	A	Pts
Rijeka	30	10	10	10	49	44	40
Varteks	30	9	9	12	36	43	36
Zagreb	30	9	6	15	43	49	35
Istra	30	9	8	13	31	40	35
Zadar	30	9	7	14	27	41	34
Inter*	30	10	3	17	36	50	33
Medimurje*	30	8	5	17	37	61	29
Croatia*	30	3	5	22	30	81	14

Relegations dependent on eligibility of promoted teams.
Top scorer: Vugrinec (Zagreb) 18.
Cup Final: Hajduk Split 2, 2, Sibenik 1, 0.

CYPRUS

Cyprus Football Association, 1 Stasinos Str., Engomi, P.O. Box 25071, Nicosia 2404.
Founded: 1934; *National Colours:* Blue shirts, white shorts, blue stockings.

International matches 2009
Serbia (h) 0-2, Slovakia (h) 3-2, Georgia (h) 2-1, Bulgaria (a) 0-2, Canada (h) 0-1, Montenegro (h) 2-2, Albania (a) 1-6, Republic of Ireland (h) 1-2, Montenegro (a) 1-1, Bulgaria (h) 4-1, Italy (a) 2-3.

League Championship wins (1935–2010)
Apoel 20; Omonia 20; Anorthosis 13; AEL 5; EPA 3; Olympiakos 3; Apollon 3; Pezoporikos 2; Cetinkaya 1; Trast 1.

Cup wins (1935–2010)
Apoel 19; Omonia 12; Anorthosis 10; AEL 6; Apollon 6; EPA 5; Trast 3; Cetinkaya 2; Olympiakos 1; Pezoporikos 1; Salamina 1; AEK 1; APOP 1.

Final League Table 2009–10

	P	W	D	L	F	A	Pts
Omonia	26	19	5	2	52	21	62
Anorthosis	26	18	4	4	45	20	58
Apollon	26	17	6	3	43	15	57
Apcel	26	16	7	3	46	18	55
AEL	26	14	3	9	32	22	45
APOP	26	10	4	12	40	44	34
Ethnikos Achnas	26	8	7	11	23	31	31
ENP	26	7	8	11	29	35	29
Ermis	26	7	8	11	31	34	29
Doxa	26	6	8	12	25	37	26
AEP	26	6	8	12	27	40	26
Aris	26	4	8	14	26	47	20
Nea Salamina*	26	2	8	16	19	45	14
APEP*	26	4	4	18	25	54	10

APEP deducted six points for abandoned match.

Play-Offs League Table 2009–10

Group A	P	W	D	L	F	A	Pts
Omonia	32	22	8	2	60	25	74
Apoel	32	19	8	5	53	24	65
Anorthosis	32	19	7	6	51	27	64
Apollon	32	17	9	6	47	23	60

Group B	P	W	D	L	F	A	Pts
AEL	32	18	4	10	50	33	58
ENP	32	10	10	12	40	42	40
Ethnikos Achnas	32	10	8	14	34	42	38
APOP	32	11	4	17	50	65	37

Group C	P	W	D	L	F	A	Pts
Ermis	32	12	8	12	43	38	44
AEP	32	9	9	14	39	50	36
Doxa	32	9	9	14	36	46	35
Aris*	32	4	9	19	30	63	21

Top scorers: Semedo (APOP), Joeano (Ermis) 22.
Cup Final: Apollon 2, Apoel 1.

CZECH REPUBLIC

Football Association of Czech Republic, Diskarska 100, Prague 6 16017 – Strahov, Czech Republic.
Founded: 1901; *National Colours:* Red shirts, white shorts, blue stockings.

International matches 2009
Morocco (a) 0-0, Slovenia (a) 0-0, Slovakia (h) 1-2, Malta (h) 1-0, Belgium (h) 3-1, Slovakia (a) 2-2, San Marino (h) 7-0, Poland (h) 2-0, Northern Ireland (h) 0-0, UAE (a) 0-0, Azerbaijan (a) 0-2.

League Championship wins (1925–93)
Sparta Prague 19; Dukla Prague (prev. UDA, now Marila Pribram) 11; Slavia Prague 9; Slovan Bratislava (formerly NV Bratislava) 8; Spartak Trnava 5; Banik Ostrava 3; Inter-Bratislava 1; Spartak Hradec Kralove 1; Viktoria Zizkov 1; Zbrojovka Brno 1; Bohemians 1; Vitkovice 1.

Cup wins (1961–93)
Dukla Prague 8; Sparta Prague 8; Slovan Bratislava 5; Spartak Trnava 4; Banik Ostrava 3; Lokomotiva Kosice 2; TJ Gottwaldov 1; Dunajska Streda 1; Kosice 1.
From 1993–94, there were two separate countries; the Czech Republic and Slovakia.

League Championship wins (1994–2010)
Sparta Prague 11; Slavia Prague 3; Slovan Liberec 2; Banik Ostrava 1.

Cup wins (1994–2010)
Sparta Prague 4; Slavia Prague 4; Viktoria Zizkov 2; Teplice 2; Spartak Hradec Kralove 1; Jablonec 1; Slovan Liberec 1; Banik Osrava 1; Viktoria Plzen 1.

Final League Table 2009–10

	P	W	D	L	F	A	Pts
Sparta Prague	30	16	14	0	42	14	62
Jablonec	30	18	7	5	42	24	61
Banik Ostrava	30	17	9	4	47	25	60
Teplice	30	15	10	5	44	25	55
Viktoria Plzen	30	12	12	6	42 · 33	48
Sigma Olomouc	30	14	5	11	49	36	47
Slavia Prague	30	11	8	11	37	35	41
Mlada	30	11	6	13	47	41	39
Slovan Liberec	30	10	7	13	34	39	37
Pribram	30	10	6	14	35	41	36
Brno	30	9	8	13	31	40	35
Bohemians 1905	30	8	10	12	21	29	34
Ceske	30	7	10	13	24	35	31
Slovacko	30	8	6	16	28	42	30
Kladno*	30	7	4	19	24	50	25
Bohemians/Strizkov*	30	4	4	22	27	65	-4

Bohemians/Strizkov deducted 20 points for not playing in round 24.
Top scorer: Ordos (Sigma Olomouc) 12.
Cup Final: Jablonec 1, Viktoria Plzen 2.

DENMARK

Danish Football Association, Idraettens Hus, Brondby Stadion 20, DK-2605, Brondby.
Founded: 1889; *National Colours:* Red shirts, white shorts, red stockings.

International matches 2009
Greece (a) 1-1, Malta (a) 3-0, Albania (h) 3-0, Sweden (a) 1-0, Chile (h) 1-2, Portugal (h) 1-1, Albania (a) 1-1, Sweden (h) 1-0, Hungary (h) 0-1, South Korea (h) 0-0, USA (h) 3-1.

League Championship wins (1913–2010)
KB Copenhagen 15; Brondby 10; B 93 Copenhagen 9; AB (Akademisk) 9; FC Copenhagen 8; B 1903 Copenhagen 7; Frem 6; Esbjerg BK 5; Vejle BK 5; AGF Aarhus 5; Hvidovre 3; OB Odense 3; AaB Aalborg 3; B 1909 Odense 2; Koge BK 2; Lyngby 2; Silkeborg 1; Herfolge 1.

Cup wins (1955–2010)
AGF Aarhus 9; Vejle BK 6; Brondby 6; OB Odense 5; Randers Freja 5; FC Copenhagen 4; Lyngby 3; B 1909 Odense 2; Aab Aalborg 2; Esbjerg BK 2; Frem 2; B 1903 Copenhagen 2; B 93 Copenhagen 1; KB Copenhagen 1; Vanlose 1; Hvidovre 1; B1913 Odense 1, AB (Akademisk) 1, Viborg 1; Silkeborg 1; Nordsjaelland 1

Final League Table 2009–10

	P	W	D	L	F	A	Pts
FC Copenhagen	33	21	5	7	61	22	68
Odense	33	17	8	8	46	34	59
Brondby	33	15	7	11	57	50	52
Esbjerg	33	13	11	9	48	43	50
Aalborg	33	13	9	11	36	30	48
Midtjylland	33	14	5	14	45	48	47
Nordsjaelland	33	12	7	14	40	41	43
Silkeborg	33	12	7	14	47	51	43
Sonderjyske	33	11	8	14	32	37	41
Randers	33	10	10	13	37	43	40
Aarhus*	33	10	8	15	36	47	38
HB Koge*	33	4	7	22	30	69	19

Herfolge and Koge merged to form HB Koge.
Top scorer: Utaka (Odense) 18.
Cup Final: Nordsjaelland 2, Midtjylland 0.

ENGLAND

The Football Association, 25 Soho Square, London W1D 4FA.
Founded: 1863; *National Colours:* White shirts, navy shorts, white stockings.

ESTONIA

Estonian Football Association, Rapia 8/10, Tallinn 11312.
Founded: 1921; *National Colours:* Blue shirts, black shorts, white stockings.

International matches 2009

Kazakhstan (h) 0-2, Armenia (a) 2-2, Armenia (h) 1-0, Wales (a) 0-1, Equatorial Guinea (h) 3-0, Portugal (h) 0-0, Brazil (h) 0-1, Turkey (a) 2-4, Spain (a) 0-3, Bosnia (h) 0-2, Belgium (h) 2-0, Albania (h) 0-0, Angola (a) 1-0.

League Championship wins (1921–40; 1992–2009)

Sport 9; Levadia Tallinn (includes Levadia Maardu) 8; Flora Tallinn 7; Estonia 5; Tallinn JK 2; Norma 2; Lantana (formerly Nikol) 2; Kalev 2; Olimpia 1; VMK Tallinn 1.

Cup wins (1993–2010)

Levadia Tallinn (includes Levadia Maardu) 6; Flora Tallinn 4; Sadam 2; VMV Tallinn 2; Lantana (formerly Nikol) 1; Trans 1; Levadia Tallinn (pre-2004) 1; Norma 1.

Final League Table 2009

	P	W	D	L	F	A	Pts
Levadia Tallinn	36	31	4	1	121	23	97
Kalev Sillamae	36	24	4	8	85	40	76
Trans	36	23	7	6	82	29	76
Flora	36	22	6	8	79	31	72
Kalju	36	15	9	12	65	47	54
Tulevik	36	15	6	15	55	49	51
Tartu	36	7	3	26	29	86	24
Kuressaare	36	7	3	26	21	99	24
Paide+	36	6	4	26	21	97	22
Kalev Tallinn*	36	4	4	28	32	89	15

Maag changed name to Tartu.
Top scorer: Gusev (Levadia Tallinn) 26.
Cup Final: Flora 0, Levadia Tallinn 3.

FAEROE ISLANDS

Fotboltssamband Foroya, The Faeroes' Football Assn., Gundalur, P.O. Box 3028, FR-110, Torshavn.
Founded: 1979; *National Colours:* White shirts, blue shorts, white stockings.

International matches 2009

Iceland (a) 2-1, Serbia (h) 2-0, France (h) 0-1, Austria (a) 1-3, Lithuania (h) 2-1, France (a) 0-5, Romania (a) 1-3.

League Championship wins (1942–2009)

HB Torshavn 20; KI Klaksvik 17; B36 Torshavn 8; TB Tvoroyri 7; GI Gotu 6; B68 Toftir 3; SI Sorvag 1; IF Fuglafjordur 1; B71 Sandur 1; VB Vagur 1; NSI Runavik 1; EB/Streymur 1.

Cup wins (1955–2009)

HB Torshavn 26; GI Gotu 6; KI Klaksvik 5; TB Tvoroyri 5; B36 Torshavn 5; NSI Runavik 2; EB/Streymur 2; VB Vagur 1; B71 Sandur 1; Vikingur 1.

Final League Table 2009

	P	W	D	L	F	A	Pts
HB	27	16	7	4	59	37	55
EB/Streymur	27	15	5	7	56	34	50
Vikingur	27	14	5	8	51	36	47
NSI	27	13	5	9	56	46	44
B68	27	12	7	8	48	41	43
AB	27	9	7	11	29	35	34
IF	27	8	6	13	45	48	30
B36	27	7	7	13	37	53	28
KI*	27	6	6	15	30	57	24
07 Vestur*	27	4	7	16	39	63	19

Top scorer: Justinussen (Vikingur) 19.
Cup Final: Vikingur 3, EB/Streymur 2.

FINLAND

Suomen Palloliitto Finlands Bollfoerbund, Urheilukatu 5, P.O. Box 191, Helsinki 00251.
Founded: 1907; *National Colours:* White shirts, blue shorts, white stockings.

International matches 2009

Japan (a) 1-5, Portugal (a) 0-1, Wales (a) 2-0, Norway (a) 2-3, Liechtenstein (h) 2-1, Russia (h) 0-3, Sweden (a) 0-1, Azerbaijan (a) 2-1, Liechtenstein (a) 1-1, Wales (h) 2-1, Germany (a) 1-1.

League Championship wins (1908–2009)

HJK Helsinki 22; Haka Valkeakoski 9; HPS Helsinki 9; TPS Turku 8; HIFK Helsinki 7; Tampere United (includes IKIssat and Ilves) 5; KuPS Kuopio 5; Kuusysi Lahti 5; KIF Helsinki 4; AIFK Turku 3; Reipas Lahti 3;

VIFK Vaasa 3; Jazz Pori 2; KTP Kotka 2; OPS Oulu 2; VPS Vaasa 2; Unitas Helsinki 1; PUS Helsinki 1; Sudet Viipuri 1; HT Helsinki 1; Pyrkiva Turku 1; KPV Kokkola 1; TPV Tampere 1; MyPa Anjalankoski 1; Inter 1.

Cup wins (1955–2009)

Haka Valkeakoski 12; HJK Helsinki 10; Reipas Lahti 7; KTP Kotka 4; MyPa Anjalankoski 3; Tampere United (includes Ilves) 3; KuPS Kuopio 2; Kuusysi Lahti 2; Mikkeli 2; TPS Turku 2; PPojat 1; Drott (renamed Jaro) 1; HPS Helsinki 1; AIFK Turku 1; RoPS Rovaniemi 1; Jokerit (formerly PK-35) 1; Allianssi (formerly Atlantis) 1; Inter 1.

Final League Table 2009

	P	W	D	L	F	A	Pts
HJK Helsinki	26	14	10	2	45	21	52
Honka	26	13	10	3	65	29	49
TPS Turku	26	13	10	3	46	20	49
Mariehamn	26	10	13	3	30	21	43
Inter	26	11	7	8	38	30	40
Haka	26	10	7	9	40	35	37
Tampere U	26	11	4	11	31	31	37
VPS	26	10	5	11	30	36	35
MyPa	26	9	7	10	32	30	34
Jaro	26	8	8	10	33	34	32
Lahti	26	8	7	11	33	40	31
KuPS	26	6	5	15	29	53	23
Jyvaskyla+	26	3	7	16	25	52	16
RoPS Rovaniemi*	26	4	4	18	21	66	16

Top scorer: Vuorinen (Honka) 16.
Cup Final: Inter 2, Tampere U 1.

FRANCE

Federation Francaise De Football, 60 Bis Avenue d'Iena, Paris 75116.
Founded: 1919; *National Colours:* Blue shirts, white shorts, red stockings.

International matches 2009

Argentina (h) 0-2, Lithuania (a) 1-0, Lithuania (h) 1-0, Nigeria (h) 0-1, Turkey (h) 1-0, Faeroes (a) 1-0, Romania (h) 1-1, Serbia (a) 1-1, Faeroes (h) 5-0, Austria (h) 3-1, Republic of Ireland (a) 1-0, Republic of Ireland (h) 1-1.

League Championship wins (1933–2010)

Saint Etienne 10; Olympique Marseille 9; Nantes 8; AS Monaco 7; Lyon 7; Stade de Reims 6; Girondins de Bordeaux 6; OGC Nice 4; Lille OSC (includes Olympique Lillois) 3; Paris St Germain 2; FC Sete 2; Sochaux 2; Racing Club Paris 1; Roubaix-Tourcoing 1; Strasbourg 1; Auxerre 1; Lens 1.

Cup wins (1918–2010)

Olympique Marseille 10; Paris St Germain 8; Saint Etienne 6; AS Monaco 5; Lille OSC 5; Racing Club Paris 5; Red Star 5; Auxerre 4; Lyon 4; Girondins de Bordeaux 3; OGC Nice 3; Nantes 3; Strasbourg 2; CAS Genereaux 2; Nancy 2; Sedan 2; FC Sete 2; Stade de Reims 2; SO Montpellier 2; Stade Rennes 2; Metz 2; Sochaux 2; AS Cannes 1; Club Français 1; Excelsior Roubaix 1; Le Havre 1; Olympique de Pantin 1; CA Paris 1; Toulouse 1; Bastia 1; Lorient 1; Guingamp 1.

Final League Table 2009–10

	P	W	D	L	F	A	Pts
Marseille	38	23	9	6	69	36	78
Lyon	38	20	12	6	64	38	72
Auxerre	38	20	11	7	42	29	71
Lille	38	21	7	10	72	40	70
Montpellier	38	20	9	9	50	40	69
Bordeaux	38	19	7	12	58	40	64
Lorient	38	16	10	12	54	42	58
Monaco	38	15	10	13	39	45	55
Rennes	38	14	11	13	52	41	53
Valenciennes	38	14	10	14	50	50	52
Lens	38	12	12	14	40	44	48
Nancy	38	13	9	16	46	53	48
Paris St Germain	38	12	11	15	50	46	47
Toulouse	38	12	11	15	36	36	47
Nice	38	11	11	16	41	57	44
Sochaux	38	11	8	19	28	52	41
St Etienne	38	10	10	18	27	45	40
Le Mans*	38	8	8	22	36	59	32
Bologne*	38	7	10	21	31	62	31
Grenoble*	38	5	8	25	31	61	23

Top scorer: Niang (Marseille) 18.
Cup Final: Paris St Germain 1, Monaco 0.

GEORGIA

Georgian Football Federation, 76a Tchavtchavadze Avenue, Tbilisi 380062.
Founded: 1990; *National Colours:* All white.

International matches 2009
Republic of Ireland (a) 1-2, Cyprus (a) 1-2, Montenegro (n) 0-0, Moldova (h) 1-2, Italy (h) 0-2, Malta (a) 0-2, Iceland (a) 1-3, Montenegro (a) 1-2, Bulgaria (a) 2-6, Albania (a) 1-1 .

League Championship wins (1990–2010)
Dinamo Tbilisi 13; Torpedo Kutaisi 3; WIT Georgia 2; Olimpi 2; Sioni 1.

Cup wins (1990–2010)
Dinamo Tbilisi 9; Lokomotivi 3; Torpedo Kutaisi 2; Ameri 2; Dynamo Batumi 1; Guria 1; Zestafoni 1; WIT Georgia 1.

Final League Table 2009–10
	P	W	D	L	F	A	Pts
Olimpi	36	25	7	3	69	26	79
Dinamo Tbilisi	36	22	8	6	62	19	74
Zestafoni	36	19	10	6	58	33	67
WIT Georgia	36	17	13	6	48	31	64
Spartaki	36	11	10	15	44	58	43
Sioni	36	8	14	14	27	43	38
Samtredia	36	10	7	19	43	68	37
Baia	36	7	11	18	29	48	32
Lokomotivi*	36	5	11	20	19	50	26
Gagra*	36	5	9	22	30	59	24

Top scorer: Anderson Aquino (Olimpi) 26.
Cup Final: WIT Georgia 1, Dinamo Tbilisi 0.

GERMANY

Deutscher Fussball-Bund, Otto-Fleck-Schneise 6, Postfach 710265, Frankfurt Am Main 60492.
Founded: 1900; *National Colours:* White shirts, black shorts, white stockings.

International matches 2009
Norway (h) 0-1, Liechtenstein (h) 4-0, Wales (a) 2-0, China (a) 1-1, UAE (a) 7-2, Azerbaijan (a) 2-0, South Africa (h) 2-0, Azerbaijan (h) 4-0, Russia (a) 1-0, Finland (h) 1-1, Ivory Coast (h) 2-2.

League Championship wins (1903–2010)
Bayern Munich 22; 1.FC Nuremberg 9; Schalke 04 7; Borussia Dortmund 6; SV Hamburg 6; Borussia Moenchengladbach 5; VfB Stuttgart 5; 1.FC Kaiserslautern 4; Werder Bremen 4; VfB Leipzig 3; SpVgg Furth 3; 1.FC Cologne 3; Viktoria Berlin 2; Hertha Berlin 2; Hannover 96 2; Dresden SC 2; Munich 1860 1; Union Berlin 1; FC Freiburg 1; Phoenix Karlsruhe 1; Karlsruher FV 1; Holstein Kiel 1; Fortuna Dusseldorf 1; Rapid Vienna 1; VfR Mannheim 1; Rot-Weiss Essen 1; Eintracht Frankfurt 1; Eintracht Brunswick 1;Wolfsburg 1.

Cup wins (1935–2010)
Bayern Munich 15; Werder Bremen 6; 1.FC Cologne 4; Eintracht Frankfurt 4; Schalke 04 4; 1.FC Nuremberg 4; SV Hamburg 3; Moenchengladbach 3; VfB Stuttgart 3; Dresden SC 2; Fortuna Dusseldorf 2; Karlsruhe SC 2; Munich 1860 2; Borussia Dortmund 2; 1.FC Kaiserslautern 2; First Vienna 1; VfB Leipzig 1; Kickers Offenbach 1; Rapid Vienna 1; Rot-Weiss Essen 1; SW Essen 1; Bayer Uerdingen 1; Hannover 96 1; Leverkusen 1.

Final League Table 2009–10
	P	W	D	L	F	A	Pts
Bayern Munich	34	20	10	4	72	31	70
Schalke	34	19	8	7	53	31	65
Werder Bremen	34	17	10	7	71	40	61
Leverkusen	34	15	14	5	65	38	59
Borussia Dortmund	34	16	9	9	54	42	57
Stuttgart	34	15	10	9	51	41	55
Hamburg	34	13	13	8	56	41	52
Wolfsburg	34	14	8	12	64	58	50
Mainz	34	12	11	11	36	42	47
Eintracht Frankfurt	34	12	10	12	47	54	46
Hoffenheim	34	11	9	14	44	42	42
Moenchengladbach	34	10	9	15	43	60	39
Cologne	34	9	11	14	33	42	38
Freiburg	34	9	8	17	35	59	35
Hannover	34	9	6	19	43	67	33
Nuremberg+	34	8	7	19	32	58	31
Bochum*	34	6	10	18	33	64	28
Hertha Berlin*	34	5	9	20	34	56	24

Top scorer: Dzeko (Wolfsburg) 22.
Cup Final: Bayern Munich 4, Werder Bremen 0.

GIBRALTAR

Gibraltar Football Association, 32a Rosia Road, Gibraltar.
Founded: 1905. *National Colours:* Red shirts, white shorts, white stockings.

League Championship wins (1896–2010)
Prince of Wales 19; Glacis United 17; Britannia 14; Gibraltar United 11; Lincoln 10; Manchester United 7; Europa 6; Newcastle (formerly Lincoln) 5; St Theresas 3; Chief Construction 2; Exiles 2; Gibraltar FC 2; Jubilee 2; South United 2; Albion 1; Athletic 1; Commander of the Yard 1; Royal Soverign 1; St Joseph's 1.

Cup wins (1896–2009)
St Joseph's 7; Lincoln 6; Europa 5; Glacis United 5; Newcastle (formerly Lincoln) 4; Britannia 3; Gibraltar United 3; Manchester United 3; AARA 1; Gibraltar FC 1; HMS Hood 1; Lincoln ABG 1; Lincoln Reliance 1; Manchester United Reserves 1; Prince of Wales 1; St Theresas 1; 2nd Battalion RGS 1; 2nd Battalion The King's Regiment 1; 4th Battalion Royal Scots 1; RAF Gibraltar 1; RAF New Camp 1.

Final League Table 2009–10
	P	W	D	L	F	A	Pts
Lincoln	16	15	1	0	60	11	46
St Joseph's	16	8	4	4	33	25	28
Gibraltar U	16	7	3	6	17	29	24
Glacis U	16	5	5	6	27	27	20
Manchester U	18	4	7	7	28	39	19
Laguna	17	4	5	8	20	27	17
College Cosmos	17	0	5	12	12	39	5

Shamrock 101 either withdrew or were excluded.

GOZO

Gozo Football Association.
Founded: 1936.

League Championship wins (1938-2010)
Victoria Hotspurs 11; Nadur Youngsters 10; Sannat Lions 9; Ghajnsielem 6; Salesian Youths 6; Victoria Athletics 4; Xaghra United 4; Xewkija Tigers 4; Calypcians 1; Kercem Ajax 1; Victoria City 1; Victoria Stars 1; Victoria United 1; Xaghra Blue Stars 1; Xaghra Young Stars 1; Zebbug Rovers 1.

Cup wins (1972-2010)
Sannat Lions 9; Xewkija Tigers 7; Nadur Youngsters 6; Ghajnsielem 5; Xaghra United 4; S.K. Calyptians 1; Calypsians Bosco Youths 1; Victoria Hotspurs 1; Kercem Ajax 1; Quala St. Joseph 1.

Final League Table 2009–10
	P	W	D	L	F	A	Pts
Victoria Hotspurs	18	10	4	4	40	16	34
Ghajnsielem	18	9	4	5	40	31	31
Nadur Youngsters	18	6	7	5	40	34	25
Victoria Wanderers	18	7	4	7	34	30	25
Xewkija Tigers	18	7	3	8	21	32	24
Sannat Lions+	18	6	4	8	29	33	22
Kercem Ajax*	18	4	2	12	19	47	14

Cup Final: Sannat Lions 2, Kercem Ajax 1.

GREECE

Hellenic Football Federation, Singrou Avenue 137, Nea Smirni, 17121 Athens.
Founded: 1926; *National Colours:* Blue shirts, white shorts, blue stockings.

International matches 2009
Denmark (h) 1-1, Israel (a) 1-1, Israel (h) 2-1, Poland (a) 0-2, Switzerland (a) 0-2, Moldova (a) 1-1, Latvia (h) 5-2, Luxembourg (h) 2-1, Ukraine (h) 0-0, Ukraine (a) 1-0.

League Championship wins (1928–2010)
Olympiakos 37; Panathinaikos 20; AEK Athens 11; Aris Salonika 3; PAOK Salonika 2; Larisa 1.

Cup wins (1932–2010)
Olympiakos 24; Panathinaikos 17; AEK Athens 13; PAOK Salonika 4; Panionios 2; Larisa 2; Aris Salonika 1; Ethnikos 1; Iraklis 1; Kastoria 1; OFI Crete 1.

Final League Table 2009–10

	P	W	D	L	F	A	Pts
Panathinaikos	30	22	4	4	54	17	70
Olympiakos	30	19	7	4	47	18	64
PAOK Salonika	30	19	5	6	41	16	62
AEK Athens	30	15	8	7	43	31	53
Aris Salonika	30	12	10	8	35	28	46
Kavala	30	10	9	11	31	32	39
Atromitos	30	10	8	12	34	36	38
Larissa	30	10	7	13	31	42	37
Panionios	30	9	10	11	34	35	37
Iraklis	30	10	7	13	39	41	37
Ergotelis	30	9	9	12	37	41	36
Asteras	30	10	6	14	29	36	36
Xanthi	30	10	5	15	27	36	35
Levadiakos*	30	9	7	14	31	44	34
PAS*	30	7	7	16	27	46	28
Panserraikos*	30	3	3	24	21	62	12

Top scorer: Cisse (Panathinaikos) 23.
Cup Final: Panathinaikos 1, Aris 0.

HOLLAND

Koninklijke Nederlandsche Voetbalbond, Woudenbergseweg 56–58, Postbus 515, NL-3700 AM, Zeist.
Founded: 1889; *National Colours:* Orange shirts, black shorts, orange stockings.

International matches 2009
Tunisia (a) 1-1, Scotland (h) 3-0, Macedonia (h) 4-0 Iceland (a) 2-1, Norway (h) 2-0, England (h) 2-2, Japan (h) 3-0, Scotland (a) 1-0, Australia (a) 0-0, Italy (a) 0-0, Paraguay (h) 0-0.

League Championship wins (1898–2010)
Ajax Amsterdam 29; PSV Eindhoven 21; Feyenoord 14; HVV The Hague 8; Sparta Rotterdam 6; Go Ahead Deventer 4; HBS The Hague 3; Willem II Tilburg 3; RAP Amsterdam 2; RCH Heemstede 2; Heracles 2; ADO The Hague 2; AZ 67 Alkmaar 2; Quick The Hague 1; BVV Den Bosch 1; NAC Breda 1; Eindhoven 1; Enschede 1; Volewijckers Amsterdam 1; Limburgia 1; Rapid JC Den Heerlen 1; DOS Utrecht 1; DWS Amsterdam 1; Haarlem 1; SVV Schiedam 1; Be Quick Groningen 1; Twente 1.

Cup wins (1899–2010)
Ajax Amsterdam 18; Feyenoord 11; PSV Eindhoven 8; Quick The Hague 4; AZ 67 Alkmaar 3; Sparta Rotterdam 3; Utrecht 3; HFC Haarlem 3; DFC 2; Fortuna Geleen 2; Haarlem 2; HBS The Hague 2; RCH Haarlem 2; Roda JC 2; VOC 2; Wageningen 2; Willem II Tilburg 2; FC Den Haag (includes ADO) 2; Twente Enschede 2; Concordia Delft 1; CVV 1; Eindhoven 1; HVV The Hague 1; Longa 1; Quick Nijmegen 1; RAP Amsterdam 1; Roermond 1; Schoten 1; Velocitas Breda 1; Velocitas Groningen 1; VSV 1; VUC 1; VVV Groningen 1; ZFC Zaandam 1; NAC Breda 1; Heerenveen 1.

Final League Table 2009–10

	P	W	D	L	F	A	Pts
Twente	34	27	5	2	63	23	86
Ajax	34	27	4	3	106	20	85
PSV Eindhoven	34	23	9	2	72	29	78
Feyenoord	34	17	12	5	54	31	63
AZ	34	19	5	10	64	34	62
Heracles	34	17	5	12	54	49	56
Utrecht	34	14	11	9	39	33	53
Groningen	34	14	7	13	48	47	49
Roda JC	34	14	5	15	56	60	47
NAC Breda	34	12	10	12	42	49	46
Heerenveen	34	11	4	19	44	64	37
VVV	34	8	11	15	43	57	35
NEC Nijmegen	34	8	9	17	35	59	33
Vitesse	34	8	8	18	38	62	32
Den Haag	34	7	9	18	38	59	30
Sparta+	34	6	8	20	30	66	26
Willem II*+	34	7	2	25	36	70	23
RKC Waalwijk*	34	5	0	29	30	80	15

Top scorer: Suarez (Ajax) 35.
Cup Final: Ajax 2, 4, Feyenoord 0, 1.

HUNGARY

Hungarian Football Federation, Robert Karoly krt 61-55, Robert Haz Budapest 1134.
Founded: 1901; *National Colours:* Red shirts, white shorts, green stockings.

International matches 2009
Israel (a) 0-1, Albania (a) 1-0, Malta (h) 3-0, Romania (h) 0-1, Sweden (h) 1-2, Portugal (h) 0-1, Portugal (a) 0-3, Denmark (a) 1-0, Belgium (a) 0-3.

League Championship wins (1901–2010)
Ferencvaros 28; MTK-Hungaria Budapest 23; Ujpest 20; Kispest Honved 13; Vasas Budapest 6; Debrecen 5; Csepel 4; Raba Gyor 3; BTC 2; Nagyvarad 1; Vac 1; Dunaferr 1; Zalaegerszeg 1.

Cup wins (1910–2010)
Ferencvaros 20; MTK-Hungaria Budapest 12; Ujpest 8; Kispest Honved 7; Raba Gyor 4; Vasas Budapest 4; Debrecen 4; Diösgyör 2; Bocskai 1; III Ker 1; Soroksar 1; Szolnoki MAV 1; Siofok Banyasz 1; Bekescsaba 1; Pecsi 1; Matav 1; Fehervar 1.
Cup not regularly held until 1964.

Final League Table 2009–10

	P	W	D	L	F	A	Pts
Debrecen	30	20	2	8	63	37	62
Videoton	30	18	7	5	59	31	61
Gyor	30	15	12	3	38	18	57
Ujpest	30	17	4	9	49	39	55
Zalaegerszeg	30	15	8	7	59	45	53
MTK	30	12	7	11	52	41	43
Ferencvaros	30	10	11	9	34	35	41
Szombathelyi Haladas	30	10	9	11	46	49	39
Honved	30	9	11	10	38	35	38
Kecskemeti	30	10	7	13	50	56	37
Lombard Papa	30	10	5	15	39	50	35
Kaposvari	30	8	8	14	38	50	32
Paksi	30	7	10	13	31	44	31
Vasas	30	8	7	15	39	61	31
Nyiregyhaza*	30	6	9	15	41	60	27
Diosgyor*	30	4	5	21	31	56	17

Top scorer: Rudnevs (Zalaegerszeg) 16.
Cup Final: Debrecen 3, Zalaegerszeg 2.

ICELAND

Knattspyrnusamband Island, Laugardal, 104 Reykjavik.
Founded: 1929; *National Colours:* All blue.

International matches 2009
Liechtenstein (h) 2-0, Faeroes (h) 1-2, Scotland (a) 1-2, Holland (h) 1-2, Macedonia (a) 0-2, Slovakia (h) 1-1, Norway (h) 1-1, Georgia (h) 3-1, South Africa (h) 1-0, Iran (a) 0-1, Luxembourg (a) 1-1.

League Championship wins (1912–2009)
KR 24; Valur 20; Fram 18; IA Akranes 18; Vikingur 5; FH Hafnarfjordur 5; IBK Keflavik 4; IBV Vestmannaeyjar 3; KA Akureyri 1.

Cup wins (1960–2009)
KR 11; Valur 9; IA Akranes 9; Fram 7; IBV Vestmannaeyjar 4; IBK Keflavik 4; Fylkir 2; IBA Akureyri 1; Vikingur 1; FH Hafnarfjordur 1; Breidablik 1.

Final League Table 2009

	P	W	D	L	F	A	Pts
FH	22	15	3	4	57	21	51
KR	22	15	3	4	58	31	48
Fylkir	22	13	4	5	41	26	43
Fram	22	10	4	8	40	32	34
Breidablik	22	10	4	8	38	33	34
Keflavik	22	8	9	5	38	37	33
Stjarnan	22	7	5	10	45	44	26
Valur	22	7	4	11	26	43	25
Grindavik	22	6	4	12	34	44	22
IBV	22	6	4	12	24	45	22
Trottur*	22	4	4	14	23	48	16
Fjolnir*	22	3	6	13	27	47	15

Top scorer: Takefusa (KR) 16.
Cup Final: Breidablik 2, Fram 2.
Breidablik won 5-4 on penalties.

REPUBLIC OF IRELAND

The Football Association of Ireland (Cumann Peile Na H-Eireann), 80 Merrion Square, South Dublin 2.
Founded: 1921; *National Colours:* Green shirts, white shorts, green and white stockings.

League Championship wins (1922–2009)
Shamrock Rovers 15; Shelbourne 13; Bohemians 10; Dundalk 9; Cork Athletic (formerly Cork United) 7; St Patrick's Athletic 7; Waterford 6; Drumcondra 5; St James's Gate 2; Sligo Rovers 2; Limerick 2; Athlone Town 2; Derry City 2; Cork City 2; Dolphin 1; Cork Hibernians 1; Cork Celtic 1; Drogheda United 1.

Cup wins (1922–2009)

Shamrock Rovers 24; Dundalk 9; Bohemians 8; Shelbourne 7; Drumcondra 5; Cork Athletic (formerly Cork United) 4; Derry City 4; Cork City 2; St James's Gate 2; St Patrick's Athletic 2; Cork Hibernians 2; Limerick 2; Waterford 2; Sligo 2; Bray Wanderers 2; Longford Town 2; Alton United 1; Athlone Town 1; Fordsons 1; Cork 1; Transport 1; Finn Harps 1; Home Farm 1; UCD 1; Galway United 1; Drogheda United 1; Sporting Fingal 1.

Final League Table 2009

	P	W	D	L	F	A	Pts
Bohemians	36	24	5	7	62	21	77
Shamrock Rovers	36	21	10	5	51	27	73
Cork City	36	17	9	10	42	28	60
Dundalk	36	12	8	16	46	51	44
Sligo Rovers	36	11	10	15	41	51	43
St Patrick's Ath	36	13	4	19	29	46	43
Galway United	36	12	6	18	36	57	42
Drogheda United+	36	7	11	18	32	50	32
Bray Wanderers+	36	6	10	20	30	56	28
Derry City*	36	18	5	13	49	31	59

Derry City relegated for holding second unofficial contracts with players. Cork City demoted due to financial difficulties.
Top scorer: Twigg (Shamrock Rovers) 24.
Cup Final: Sporting Fingal 2, Sligo Rovers 1.

ISRAEL

Israel Football Association, Ramat-Gan Stadium, 299 Aba Hilell Street, Ramat-Gan 52134.
Founded: 1948; *National Colours:* Blue shirts, white shorts, blue stockings.

International matches 2009

Hungary (h) 1-0, Greece (h) 1-1, Greece (a) 1-2, Northern Ireland (a) 1-1, Latvia (h) 0-1, Luxembourg (h) 7-0, Moldova (h) 3-1, Switzerland (a) 0-0.

League Championship wins (1932–2010)

Maccabi Tel Aviv 18; Maccabi Haifa 11; Hapoel Tel Aviv 11; Hapoel Petah Tikva 6; Beitar Jerusalem 6; Maccabi Netanya 5; Hakoah Ramat Gan 2; Hapoel Beersheba 2; Bnei Yehouda 1; British Police 1; Hapoel Kfar Saba 1; Hapoel Ramat Gan 1; Hapoel Haifa 1.

Cup wins (1928–2010)

Maccabi Tel Aviv 22; Hapoel Tel Aviv 14; Beitar Jerusalem 7; Maccabi Haifa 5; Hapoel Haifa 3; Hapoel Kfar Saba 3; Beitar Tel Aviv 2; Bnei Yehouda 2; Hakoah Ramat Gan 2; Hapoel Petah Tikva 2; Maccabi Petah Tikva 2; Maccabi Hashmonai Jerusalem 1; British Police 1; Gunners 1; Hapoel Jerusalem 1; Hapoel Yehud 1; Hapoel Lod 1; Maccabi Netanya 1; Hapoel Beersheba 1; Hapoel Ramat Gan 1; Hapoel Bnei Sakhnin 1.

Qualifying League Table 2009–10

	P	W	D	L	F	A	Pts
Maccabi Haifa	30	25	2	3	64	12	77
Hapoel Tel Aviv	30	21	8	1	79	25	71
Maccabi Tel Aviv	30	15	7	8	47	33	52
Beitar Jerusalem	30	13	7	10	46	34	46
Bnei Yehouda	30	12	9	9	37	30	45
Ashdod	30	11	10	9	32	31	43
Bnei Sakhnin	30	11	8	11	28	29	41
Hapoel Beersheba	30	10	10	10	44	50	40
Maccabi Netanya	30	9	9	12	41	40	36
Maccabi Petah Tikva	30	8	11	11	37	43	35
Hapoel Ramat Gan	30	8	9	13	26	46	33
Hapoel Haifa	30	8	8	14	39	45	32
Hapoel Petah Tikva	30	6	13	11	23	41	31
Hapoel Acco	30	4	13	13	32	46	25
Maccabi Akhi-Nazrat	30	6	6	18	27	67	24
Hapoel Raanana	30	4	8	18	27	57	20

Championship Play-Off Table 2009–10

	P	W	D	L	F	A	Pts
Hapoel Tel Aviv	35	25	9	1	87	26	49
Maccabi Haifa	35	28	3	4	72	16	49
Maccabi Tel Aviv	35	17	9	9	52	35	34
Bnei Yehouda	35	14	11	10	43	34	31
Beitar Jerusalem	35	14	7	14	50	44	26
Ashdod	35	11	10	14	36	45	22

Middle Play-Off Table 2009–10

	P	W	D	L	F	A	Pts
Bnei Sakhnin	33	13	8	12	31	31	27
Maccabi Petah Tikva	33	10	11	12	44	47	24
Hapoel Beersheba	33	11	10	12	49	55	23
Maccabi Netanya	33	10	9	14	44	47	21

Relegation Table 2009–10

	P	W	D	L	F	A	Pts
Hapoel Haifa	35	10	9	16	44	50	23
Hapoel Acco	35	7	14	14	38	52	23
Hapoel Petah Tikva	35	8	14	13	28	48	23
Hapoel Ramat Gan+	35	9	11	15	34	49	22
Hapoel Raanana*	35	6	10	19	33	58	18
Maccabi Akhi-Nazrat*	35	7	7	21	33	81	16

Top scorer: Arbeitman (Maccabi Haifa) 26.
Cup Final: Hapoel Tel Aviv 3, Bnei Yehouda 1.

ITALY

Federazione Italiana Giuoco Calcio, Via Gregorio Allegri 14, Roma 00198.
Founded: 1898; *National Colours:* Blue shirts, white shorts, blue stockings.

International matches 2009

Brazil (a) 0-2, Montenegro (a) 2-0, Republic of Ireland (h) 1-1, Northern Ireland (h) 3-0, New Zealand (h) 4-3, USA (n) 3-1, Egypt (n) 0-1, Brazil (n) 0-3, Switzerland (a) 0-0, Georgia (a) 2-0, Bulgaria (h) 2-0, Republic of Ireland (a) 2-2, Cyprus (h) 3-2, Holland (h) 0-0, Sweden (h) 1-0.

League Championship wins (1898–2010)

Juventus 27 (excludes two titles revoked); Internazionale 18 (includes one title awarded); AC Milan 17; Genoa 9; Torino 7 (excludes one title revoked); Pro Vercelli 7; Bologna 7; AS Roma 3; Fiorentina 2; Lazio 2; Napoli 2; Casale 1; Novese 1; Cagliari 1; Verona 1; Sampdoria 1.

Cup wins (1928–2010)

AS Roma 9; Juventus 9; Fiorentina 6; Internazionale 6; AC Milan 5; Torino 5; Lazio 5; Sampdoria 4; Napoli 3; Parma 3; Bologna 2; Atalanta 1; Genoa 1; Vado 1; Venezia 1; Vicenza 1.

Final League Table 2009–10

	P	W	D	L	F	A	Pts
Internazionale	38	24	10	4	75	34	82
Roma	38	24	8	6	68	41	80
AC Milan	38	20	10	8	60	39	70
Sampdoria	38	19	10	9	49	41	67
Palermo	38	18	11	9	59	47	65
Napoli	38	15	14	9	50	43	59
Juventus	38	16	7	15	55	57	55
Parma	38	14	10	14	46	51	52
Genoa	38	14	9	15	57	61	51
Bari	38	13	11	14	49	49	50
Fiorentina	38	13	8	17	48	47	47
Lazio	38	11	13	14	39	43	46
Catania	38	10	15	13	44	45	45
Cagliari	38	11	11	16	56	58	44
Udinese	38	11	11	16	54	59	44
Chievo	38	12	8	18	37	42	44
Bologna	38	10	12	16	42	55	42
Atalanta*	38	9	8	21	37	53	35
Siena*	38	7	10	21	40	67	31
Livorno*	38	7	8	23	27	61	29

Top scorer: Di Natale (Udinese) 29.
Cup Final: Internazionale 1, Roma 0.

KAZAKHSTAN

The Football Union of Kazakhstan, Satpayev Street, 29/3 Almaty 480 072, Kazakhstan.
Founded: 1914; *National Colours:* Blue shirts, blue shorts, yellow stockings.

International matches 2009

Estonia (a) 2-0, Belarus (h) 1-5, England (h) 0-4, Ukraine (a) 1-2, Andorra (a) 3-1, Belarus (a) 0-4, Croatia (h) 1-2.

League Championship wins (1992–2009)

Irtysh (includes Ansat) 5; Aqtobe 5; Yelimai 3; Astana (includes Zhenis) 3; Kairat 2; Taraz 1.

Cup wins (1992–2009)

Kairat 5; Astana (includes Zhenis) 3; Dostyk 1; Vostok 1; Yelimai 1; Irtysh 1; Kaisar 1; Taraz 1; Almaty 1; Tobol 1; Aqtobe 1; Atirau 1.

Final League Table 2009

	P	W	D	L	F	A	Pts
Aqtobe	26	21	2	3	65	19	65
Lokomotiv Astana	26	20	0	6	54	24	60
Shakhtyor	26	18	3	5	50	18	57
Tobol	26	14	9	3	54	23	51
Jetisu	26	13	5	8	33	26	44
Atirau	26	11	7	8	37	29	40
Odabasy	26	10	6	10	33	30	36
Taraz	26	9	6	11	37	36	33
Yertis	26	8	5	13	24	31	29

Vostok*	26	7	5	14	32	56	23
Oqjetpes	26	6	4	16	22	48	22
Qazaqmis*	26	7	3	16	32	61	21
Qaysar*	26	3	5	18	15	45	14
Qyzyljar*	26	3	4	19	14	56	6

Qazaqmis and Vostok three points deducted; Qyzyljar seven points deducted. Vostok relegated instead of Oqjetpes.
Top scorers: Tleshev (Aqtobe) 20, Bayramov (Tobol) 20.
Cup Final: Atirau 1, Shakhtyor 0.

KOSOVO

Football Federation Kosova, Agim Ramadani 45, Prishtina, Kosovo 10000.
Founded: 1946; *National Colours:* Blue shirts, white shorts, blue stockings.

League Championship wins (1945–2010)
Prishtina 12; Vellaznimi 9; Trepca 7; Liria 5; Buduqnosti 4; Red Star 3; Rudari 3; Besa 3; Fushe-Kosova 2; Jedinstvo 2; Kosova Prishtina 2; Obiliqi 2; Slloga 2; Besiana 1; Drita 1; Dukagjini 1; KNI Ramiz Sadiku 1; KXEK Kosova 1; Proletari 1; Rudniku 1.

Cup wins (1992–2010)
Liria 3; Flamurtari 2; Prishtina 2; Besa 1; Besiana 1; Drita 1; Gjilani 1; KEK-u 1; Kosova Prishtina 1; Trepca 1; Vellaznimi 1.

Superliga Final League Table 2009–10

	P	W	D	L	F	A	Pts
Trepca	33	16	11	6	46	27	59
Prishtina	33	16	7	10	38	32	55
KEK-u	33	15	8	10	50	33	53
Besa	33	15	6	12	43	28	51
Drenica	33	14	7	12	38	44	49
Hysi	33	14	5	14	51	41	47
Flamurtari	33	12	11	10	42	44	47
Liria	33	12	8	13	38	35	44
Vellaznimi	33	12	6	15	34	42	42
Ferizaj	33	12	6	15	28	42	42
Kosova*	33	9	7	17	28	43	34
Gjilani*	33	5	10	18	28	53	25

Cup Final: Liria 2, Vellaznimi 1.

LATVIA

Latvian Football Federation, Augsiela 1, LV-1009, Riga.
Founded: 1921; *National Colours:* Carmine red shirts, white shorts, carmine red stockings.

International matches 2009
Armenia (h) 0-0, Luxembourg (a) 4-0, Luxembourg (h) 2-0, Bulgaria (a) 0-1, Israel (a) 1-0, Switzerland (h) 2-2, Greece (a) 2-5, Moldova (h) 3-2, Honduras (a) 1-2.

League Championship wins (1922–2009)
Skonto Riga 14; Sarkanais Metalurgs Liepaya 11; ASK Riga 9; RFK Riga 8; Olympija Liepaya 7; VEF Riga 6; Energija Riga 4; Elektrons Riga 3; Torpedo Riga 3; FK Ventspils 3; Daugava Liepaya 2; ODO Riga 2; Khimikis Daugavpils 2; RAF Jelgava 2; Keisermezhs Riga 2; Dinamo Riga 1; Zhmilyeva Team 1; Darba Rezervi 1; RER Riga 1; Starts Brotseni 1; Venta Ventspils 1; Yurnieks Riga 1; Alta Riga 1; Gauja Valmiera 1; Metalurgs Liepaya 1.

Cup wins (1937–2010)
Elektrons Riga 7; Skonto Riga 7; Sarkanais Metalurgs Liepaya 5; FK Ventspils 4; ODO Riga 3; VEF Riga 3; ASK Riga 3; Tseltnieks Riga 3; RAF Jelgava 3; RFK Riga 2; Daugava Liepaya 2; Starts Brotseni 2; Selmash Liepaya 2; Yurnieks Riga 2; Khimikis Daugavpils 2; Rigas Vilki 1; Dinamo Liepaya 1; Dinamo Riga 1; RER Riga 1; Voulkan Kouldiga 1; Baltika Liepaya 1; Venta Ventspils 1; Pilots Riga 1; Lielupe Yurmala 1; Energija Riga 1; Torpedo Riga 1; Daugava SKIF Riga 1; Tseltnieks Daugavpils 1; Olympija Riga 1; FK Riga 1; Metalurgs Liepaya 1; Daugava Daugavpils 1; Jelgava 1.

Final League Table 2009

	P	W	D	L	F	A	Pts
Metalurgs Liepaya	32	25	4	3	96	23	79
FK Ventspils	32	23	5	4	89	21	74
Skonto Riga	32	23	4	5	96	30	73
Jurmala	32	12	4	16	48	60	40
Olimps Riga	32	11	5	16	53	60	38
Blazna	32	7	5	20	30	71	26
Tranzits	32	2	10	20	22	65	16
Daugava Riga*+	32	3	5	24	26	116	14
Dinaburg*	32	5	4	13	31	39	19

FK Riga, Daugava Daugavpils and Vindava withdrew; Dinaburg excluded and relegated in October due to betting on own matches; remaining fixtures awarded 0-3 loss.

Top scorer: Grebis (Metalurgs Liepaya) 30.
Cup Final: Jelgava 2, Jurmala 2.
Jelgava won 6-5 on penalties.

LIECHTENSTEIN

Liechtensteiner Fussball-Verband, Malbuner Huus Altenbach 11, Postfach 165, 9490 Vaduz.
Founded: 1934; *National Colours:* Blue shirts, red shorts, blue stockings.

International matches 2009
Iceland (a) 0-2, Germany (a) 0-4, Russia (h) 0-1, Finland (a) 1-2, Portugal (h) 0-3, Russia (a) 0-3, Finland (h) 1-1, Azerbaijan (h) 0-2, Wales (h) 0-2, Croatia (a) 0-5.
Liechtenstein has no national league. Teams compete in Swiss regional leagues.

Cup wins (1937–2010)
Vaduz 39; Balzers 11; Triesen 8; Eschen/Mauren 4; Schaan 3.
Cup Final: Vaduz 1, Eschen/Mauren 1.
Vaduz won 4-2 on penalties.

LITHUANIA

Lithuanian Football Federation, Seimyniskiu str. 15, 2005 Vilnius.
Founded: 1922; *National Colours:* Yellow shirts, green shorts, yellow stockings.

International matches 2009
Poland (h) 1-1, Andorra (h) 3-1, France (h) 0-1, France (a) 0-1, Romania (h) 0-1, Luxembourg (a) 1-0, Faeroes (a) 1-2, Austria (a) 1-2, Serbia (h) 2-1.

League Championship wins (1990–2009)
FBK Kaunas 8 (including Zalgiris Kaunas 1); Ekranas Panevezys 4; Zalgiris Vilnius 3; Kareda 2; Inkaras Kaunas 2; Sirijus Klaipeda 1; ROMAR Mazeikiai 1.

Cup wins (1990–2010)
Zalgiris Vilnius 5; FBK Kaunas 4; Ekranas Panevezys 3; Kareda 2; Atlantas 2; Suduva 2; Sirijus Klaipeda 1; Lietuvos Makabi Vilnius 1; Inkaras Kaunas 1.

Final League Table 2009

	P	W	D	L	F	A	Pts
Ekranas	28	18	9	1	58	20	63
Vetra	28	16	9	3	55	22	57
Suduva	28	14	11	3	55	22	53
Siauliai	28	13	3	12	40	34	42
Tauras	28	10	8	10	26	22	38
Banga	28	7	6	15	25	49	27
LKKA	28	4	3	21	19	63	15
Kruoja	28	2	7	19	24	70	13

FBK Kaunas and Atlantas withdrew in March; Zalgiris were denied a licence and demoted to the second level; these were replaced by LKKA, Kruoja and Banga as the highest placed 2008 teams. FBK Kaunas and Atlantas were relegated to the third level for "unethical conduct and other irregularities".
Top scorer: Trakys (Ekranas) 18.
Cup Final: Ekranas 2, Vetra 1.

LUXEMBOURG

Federation Luxembourgeoise De Football (F.L.F.), 68 Rue De Gasperich, Luxembourg 1617.
Founded: 1908; *National Colours:* All red.

International matches 2009
Latvia (h) 4-0, Latvia (a) 0-2, Lithuania (h) 0-1, Moldova (a) 0-0, Israel (a) 0-7, Switzerland (h) 0-3, Greece (a) 1-2, Iceland (h) 1-1.

League Championship wins (1910–2010)
Jeunesse Esch 28; Spora Luxembourg 11; Stade Dudelange 10; F91 Dudelange 8; Red Boys Differdange 6; Union Luxembourg 6; Avenir Beggen 6; US Hollerich-Bonnevoie 5; Fola Esch 5; Aris Bonnevoie 3; Progres Niedercorn 3; Sporting Club 2; Racing Club 1; National Schifflange 1; Grevenmacher 1.

Cup wins (1922–2010)
Red Boys Differdange 15; Jeunesse Esch 12; Union Luxembourg 10; Spora Luxembourg 8; Avenir Beggen 7; Stade Dudelange 4; Progres Niedercorn 4; Grevenmacher 4; F91 Dudelange 4; Fola Esch 3; Alliance Dudelange 2; US Rumelange 2; Aris Bonnevoie 1; US Dudelange 1; Jeunesse Hautcharage 1; National Schifflange 1; Racing Club 1; SC Tetange 1; Swift Hesperange 1; Etzella Ettelbruck 1; CS Petange 1; FC Differdange 1.

Final League Table 2009–10

	P	W	D	L	F	A	Pts
Jeunesse Esch	26	17	6	3	45	20	57
F91 Dudelange	26	16	6	4	62	23	54
Grevenmacher	26	13	4	9	46	40	43
Differdange	26	12	6	8	41	30	42
Hamm Benfica	26	11	8	7	50	29	41
Fola Esch	26	11	8	7	49	38	41
Racing	26	12	5	9	39	47	41
Etzella	26	8	8	10	42	43	32
Petange	26	9	5	12	36	42	32
Hesperange	26	8	5	13	33	42	29
Progres	26	6	10	10	39	44	28
Kaerjeng+	26	7	7	12	28	36	28
Rumelange*	26	7	1	18	27	63	22
Mondercange*	26	2	7	17	18	58	13

Top scorer: Huss (Grevenmacher) 22.
Cup Final: FC Differdange 1, Grevenmacher 0.

MACEDONIA

Football Association of Macedonia, VIII-ma Udarna Brigada 31-A, Skopje 1000.
Founded: 1948; *National Colours:* All red.

International matches 2009

Moldova (h) 1-1, Holland (a) 0-4, Norway (h) 0-0, Iceland (h) 2-0, Spain (h) 2-3, Scotland (a) 0-2, Norway (a) 1-2, Qatar (h) 2-1, Canada (h) 3-0, Iran (a) 1-1.

League Championship wins (1993–2010)

Vardar 5; Sileks 3; Sloga Jugomagnat 3; Rabotnicki 3; Pobeda 2; Makedonija 1; Renova 1.

Cup wins (1993–2010)

Vardar 5; Sloga Jugomagnat 3; Sileks 2; Rabotnicki 2; Pelister 1; Pobeda 1; Cement 1; Baskimi 1; Makedonija 1; Teteks 1.

Final League Table 2009–10

	P	W	D	L	F	A	Pts
Renova	26	17	4	5	45	21	55
Rabotnicki	26	15	5	6	38	20	50
Metalurg	26	12	11	3	35	16	47
Pelister	26	11	6	9	28	27	39
Sileks	26	8	8	10	29	33	32
Vardar	26	9	6	11	31	28	30
Teteks	26	8	6	12	31	30	30
Turnovo	26	8	5	13	27	35	26
Milano*+	26	1	3	22	14	81	6
Makedonija	10	5	4	1	23	5	0
Sloga	10	3	2	5	9	14	0
Pobeda	26	8	4	14	29	41	25

Pobeda excluded after round 28. Turnovo and Vardar three points deducted. Sloga and Makedonija disqualified for failing to fulfil two consecutive fixtures.
Top scorer: Bozhinovski (Rabotnicki) 15.
Cup Final: Teteks 3, Rabotnicki 2.

MALTA

Malta Football Association, 280 St Paul Street, Valletta VLT07.
Founded: 1900; *National Colours:* Red shirts, white shorts, red stockings.

International matches 2009

Albania (h) 0-0, Denmark (h) 0-3, Hungary (a) 0-3, Czech Republic (a) 0-1, Sweden (a) 0-4, Georgia (h) 2-0, Cape Verde Islands (h) 0-2, Sweden (h) 0-1, Angola (h) 1-2, Portugal (a) 0-4, Bulgaria (h) 1-4.

League Championship wins (1910–2010)

Sliema Wanderers 26; Floriana 25; Valletta 19; Hibernians 10; Hamrun Spartans 7; Birkirkara 3; Rabat Ajax 2; St George's 1; KOMR 1; Marsaxlokk 1.

Cup wins (1935–2010)

Sliema Wanderers 20; Floriana 18; Valletta 12; Hibernians 8; Hamrun Spartans 6; Birkirkara 4; Gzira United 1; Melita 1; Zurrieq 1; Rabat Ajax 1.

Qualifying League Table 2009–10

	P	W	D	L	F	A	Pts
Valletta	18	12	4	2	45	15	40
Birkirkara	18	12	3	3	40	18	39
Qormi	18	11	2	5	37	22	35
Sliema Wanderers	18	9	2	7	29	21	29
Hibernians	18	7	6	5	31	28	27
Tarxien Rainbows	18	7	5	6	30	29	26
Floriana	18	6	5	7	23	35	23
Hamrun Spartans	18	6	3	9	24	31	21

Msida St Joseph	18	3	2	13	12	34	11
Dingli Swallows	18	1	0	17	13	51	3

Vittoriosa Stars and Marsaxlokk excluded at start of season and replaced by Msida St Joseph and Hamrun Spartans.

Championship Table 2009–10

	P	W	D	L	F	A	Pts
Birkirkara	28	20	4	4	64	32	45
Valletta	28	20	4	4	71	25	44
Qormi	28	15	2	11	53	36	30
Sliema Wanderers	28	14	2	12	41	37	30
Tarxien Rainbows	28	10	6	12	41	50	23
Hibernians	28	8	6	14	40	51	17

Relegation Table 2009–10

	P	W	D	L	F	A	Pts
Floriana	24	10	6	8	35	41	25
Hamrun Spartans	24	10	4	10	41	39	24
Msida St Joseph*	24	4	4	16	24	51	11
Dingli Swallows*	24	2	0	22	23	71	5

Top scorer: Da Silva (Qormi) 17.
Cup Final: Valletta 2, Qormi 1.

MOLDOVA

Football Association of Moldova, 39 Tricolorului Str, 2012, Chisinau.
Founded: 1990; *National Colours:* Red shirts, blue shorts, red stockings.

International matches 2009

Macedonia (a) 1-1, Switzerland (h) 0-2, Switzerland (a) 0-2, Georgia (a) 2-1, Belarus (a) 2-2, Armenia (a) 4-1, Luxembourg (h) 0-0, Greece (h) 1-1, Israel (a) 1-3, Latvia (a) 2-3.

League Championship wins (1992–2010)

Sheriff 10; Zimbru Chisinau 8; Constructorul 1.

Cup wins (1992–2010)

Sheriff 7; Zimbru Chisinau 5; Tiligul 3; Constructorul 2; Comrat 1; Nistru Otaci 1.

Final League Table 2009–10

	P	W	D	L	F	A	Pts
Sheriff	33	27	3	3	75	8	84
Iskra-Stal	33	19	8	6	50	25	65
Olimpia	33	17	9	7	45	23	60
Zimbru Chisinau	33	17	8	8	47	29	59
Dacia	33	16	10	7	54	30	58
Rapid Ghidighici	33	12	9	12	40	39	45
Academia	33	11	9	13	36	37	42
Viitorul	33	10	6	17	32	45	36
Tiraspol	33	8	10	15	20	34	34
Dinamo	33	9	5	19	36	66	32
Sfintul*	33	6	6	21	29	67	24
Nistru*	33	2	5	26	13	74	11

Top scorer: Maximov (Viitorul) 13.
Cup Final: Sheriff 2, Dacia 0.

MONTENEGRO

Football Association of Montenegro.
Founded: 1931.

International matches 2009

Italy (h) 0-2, Georgia (a) 0-0, Cyprus (a) 2-2, Wales (h) 2-1, Bulgaria (a) 1-4, Cyprus (h) 1-1, Georgia (h) 2-1, Republic of Ireland (a) 0-0, Belarus (h) 1-0.

League Championship wins (2006–10)

Buducnost 1; Zeta 1; Mogren; Rudar 1.

Cup wins (2006–10)

Rudar 2; Mogren 1; Petrovac 1.

Final League Table 2009–10

	P	W	D	L	F	A	Pts
Rudar	33	22	5	6	56	26	71
Buducnost	33	21	6	6	67	35	69
Mogren	33	16	9	8	49	34	57
Zeta	33	17	6	10	43	33	57
Grbalj	33	15	8	10	66	42	53
Lovcen	33	15	7	11	32	37	52
Sutjeska	33	11	7	15	33	36	40
Petrovac	33	10	6	17	38	49	36
Decic	33	8	11	14	27	35	35
Mornar+	33	9	8	16	29	49	35
Berane*+	33	8	6	19	28	49	30
Podgorica*	33	5	3	25	16	59	18

Top scorer: Boskovic (Grbalj) 24.
Cup Final: Rudar 2, Buducnost 1.

NORTHERN CYPRUS

Turkish Republic of Northern Cyprus.
Founded: 1955; *National Colours:* All red with white trim.

League Championship wins (1956–63; 1969–74; 1976–2010)
Cetinkaya 12; Gonyeli 9; Magusa 7; Dogan Turk 7; Yenicami 5; BAF Ulku 4; Kucuk 3; Akincilar 1; Binatli 1.

Cup wins (1956-2010)
Cetinkaya 16; Gonyeli 8; Kucuk 6; Magusa 5; Yenicami 5; Turk Ocagi 4; Binatli 1; Dogan Turk 1; Genclik 1; Lefke 1; Yalova 1.

Final League Table 2009–10

	P	W	D	L	F	A	Pts
Dogan Turk	26	19	4	3	76	27	61
Gonyeli	26	19	4	3	75	21	61
Kucuk	26	20	1	5	91	28	61
Magusa	26	14	4	8	52	36	46
Lapta	26	11	4	11	37	55	37
Bostanci	26	10	7	9	43	33	37
Cetinkaya	26	12	1	13	52	63	37
Tatlisu	26	10	6	10	50	48	36
Turk Ocagi	26	10	5	11	46	61	35
Cihangir	26	9	4	13	36	54	31
Ozankoy	26	8	4	14	28	39	28
Turkmenkoy	26	7	6	13	40	55	27
Esentepe*	26	4	5	17	23	59	17
Genclik*	26	1	1	24	29	99	4

Cup Final: Gonyeli 3, Bostanci 1.

NORTHERN IRELAND

Irish Football Association Ltd, 20 Windsor Avenue, Belfast BT9 6EE.
Founded: 1880; *National Colours:* Green shirts, white shorts, green stockings.

NORWAY

Norges Fotballforbund, Ullevaal Stadion, Sognsveien 75J, Serviceboks 1, Oslo 0855.
Founded: 1902; *National Colours:* Red shirts, white shorts, blue stockings.

International matches 2009
Germany (a) 1-0, South Africa (a) 1-2, Finland (h) 3-2, Macedonia (a) 0-0, Holland (a) 0-2, Scotland (h) 4-0, Iceland (a) 1-1, Macedonia (h) 2-1, South Africa (h) 1-0, Switzerland (a) 1-0.

League Championship wins (1938–2009)
Rosenborg Trondheim 21; Fredrikstad 9; Viking Stavanger 8; Lillestrom 5; Valerenga 5; Larvik Turn 3; Brann Bergen 3; Lyn Oslo 2; IK Start 2; Freidig 1; Fram 1; Skeid Oslo 1; Strömsgodset Drammen 1; Moss 1; Stabaek 1.

Cup wins (1902–2010)
Odd Grenland 12; Fredrikstad 11; Rosenborg Trondheim 9; Lyn Oslo 8; Skeid Oslo 8; Rosenborg Trondheim 8; Sarpsborg 6; Brann Bergen 6; Viking Stavanger 5; Lillestrom 5; Orn Horten 4; Strömsgodset Drammen 4; Valerenga 4; Frigg 3; Mjondalen 3; Bodo/Glimt 2; Mercantile 2; Tromso 2; Molde 2; Grane Nordstrand 1; Kvik Halden 1; Sparta 1; Gjovik/Lyn 1; Moss 1; Bryne 1; Stabaek 1; Aalesund 1.
(Known as the Norwegian Championship for HM The King's Trophy).

Final League Table 2009

	P	W	D	L	F	A	Pts
Rosenborg	30	20	9	1	60	22	69
Molde	30	17	5	8	62	35	56
Stabaek	30	15	8	7	52	34	53
Odd	30	12	10	8	53	44	46
Brann	30	12	8	10	51	49	44
Tromso	30	12	10	10	35	36	40
Valerenga	30	12	4	14	47	50	40
Sandefjord	30	10	10	10	39	44	40
Start	30	10	10	10	46	52	40
Viking	30	9	11	10	38	40	38
Lilleström	30	9	10	11	43	50	37
Stromsgodset	30	10	6	14	40	42	36
Aalesund	30	9	9	12	34	43	36
Fredrikstad*+	30	10	4	16	39	44	34
Bodo Glimt*	30	6	10	14	29	53	28
Lyn*	30	2	10	18	29	59	15

Top scorer: Prica (Rosenborg) 16.
Cup Final: Aalesund 2, Molde 2
Aalesund won 5-4 on penalties.

POLAND

Polish Football Association, Polski Zwiazek Pilki Noznej, Miodowa 1, Warsaw 00-080.
Founded: 1919; *National Colours:* White shirts, red shorts, white stockings.

International matches 2009
Lithuania (a) 1-1, Wales (a) 1-0, Northern Ireland (a) 2-3, San Marino (h) 10-0, South Africa (a) 0-1, Iraq (a) 1-1, Greece (h) 2-0, Northern Ireland (h) 1-1, Slovenia (a) 0-3, Czech Republic (a) 0-2, Slovakia (h) 0-1, Romania (h) 0-1, Canada (h) 1-0.

League Championship wins (1921–2010)
Gornik Zabrze 14; Ruch Chorzow 14; Wisla Krakow 13; Legia Warsaw 8; Lech Poznan 6; Cracovia 5; Pogon Lwow 4; Widzew Lodz 4; Warta Poznan 2; Polonia Bytom 2; Stal Mielec 2; LKS Lodz 2; Polonia Warsaw 2; Zaglebie Lubin 2; Garbarnia Krakow 1; Slask Wroclaw 1; Szombierki Bytom 1.

Cup wins (1951–2010)
Legia Warsaw 13; Gornik Zabrze 6; Lech Poznan 5; Zaglebie Sosnowiec 4; GKS Katowice 3; Ruch Chorzow 3; Amica Wronki 3; Wisla Krakow 3; Slask Wroclaw 2; Polonia Warsaw 2; Groclin 2; Gwardia Warsaw 1; LKS Lodz 1; Stal Rzeszow 1; Arka Gdynia 1; Lechia Gdansk 1; Widzew Lodz 1; Miedz Legnica 1; Wisla Plock 1; Jagiellonia 1.

Final League Table 2009–10

	P	W	D	L	F	A	Pts
Lech	30	19	8	3	51	20	65
Wisla	30	19	5	6	48	20	62
Ruch	30	16	5	9	40	30	53
Legia	30	15	7	8	36	22	52
GKS Belchatow	30	9	9	8	37	27	48
Korona	30	9	10	11	35	41	37
Polonia B	30	9	10	11	29	31	37
Lechia	30	9	10	11	30	32	37
Slask	30	8	12	10	32	33	36
Zaglebie	30	8	11	11	30	38	35
Jagiellonia	30	11	11	8	29	27	34
Cracovia	30	9	7	14	25	39	34
Polonia W	30	9	6	15	25	38	33
Arka	30	7	7	16	28	39	28
Odra*	30	7	6	17	27	45	27
Piast*	30	7	6	17	30	50	27

Jagiellonia ten points deducted.
Top scorer: Lewandowski R (Lech) 18.
Cup Final: Jagiellonia 1, Pogon 0.

PORTUGAL

Federacao Portuguesa De Futebol, Praca De Alegria N.25, Apartado 21.100, P-1127, Lisboa 1250-004.
Founded: 1914; *National Colours:* Red shirts, green shorts, red stockings.

International matches 2009
Finland (h) 1-0, Sweden (h) 0-0, South Africa (h) 2-0, Albania (a) 2-1, Estonia (a) 0-0, Liechtenstein (a) 3-0, Denmark (a) 1-1, Hungary (a) 1-0, Hungary (h) 3-0, Malta (h) 4-0, Bosnia (h) 1-0, Bosnia (a) 1-0.

League Championship wins (1935–2010)
Benfica 32; FC Porto 24; Sporting Lisbon 18; Belenenses 1; Boavista 1.

Cup wins (1939–2010)
Benfica 24; Sporting Lisbon 15; FC Porto 15; Boavista 5; Belenenses 3; Vitoria Setubal 3; Academica Coimbra 1; Leixoes 1; Sporting Braga 1; Estrela Amadora 1; Beira Mar 1.

Final League Table 2009–10

	P	W	D	L	F	A	Pts
Benfica	30	24	2	2	78	20	76
Braga	30	22	5	3	48	20	71
Porto	30	21	5	4	70	26	68
Sporting Lisbon	30	13	9	8	42	26	48
Maritimo	30	11	8	11	42	43	41
Guimaraes	30	11	8	11	31	34	41
Nacional	30	10	9	11	36	46	39
Naval	30	10	6	14	20	35	36
Uniao Leiria	30	9	8	13	35	41	35
Pacos de Ferreira	30	8	11	11	32	37	35
Academica	30	8	9	13	37	42	33
Rio Ave	30	6	13	11	22	31	31
Olhanense	30	5	14	11	31	46	29
Setubal	30	5	10	15	29	57	25
Belenenses*	30	4	11	15	23	44	23
Leixoes*	30	5	6	19	25	51	21

Top scorer: Cardozo (Benfica) 26.
Cup Final: Porto 2, Chaves 1.

ROMANIA

Federatia Romana De Fotbal, House of Football, Str. Serg. Serbanica Vasile 12, Bucharest 73412.
Founded: 1909; *National Colours:* All yellow.

International matches 2009
Croatia (h) 1-2, Serbia (h) 2-3, Austria (a) 1-2, Lithuania (a) 1-0, Hungary (a) 1-0, France (a) 1-1, Austria (h) 1-1, Serbia (a) 0-5, Faeroes (h) 3-1, Poland (a) 1-0.

League Championship wins (1910–2010)
Steaua Bucharest 23; Dinamo Bucharest 18; Venus Bucharest 8; Chinezul Timisoara 6; UT Arad 6; Ripensia Timisoara 4; Uni Craiova 4; Petrolul Ploiesti 3; Rapid Bucharest 3; Olimpia Bucharest 2; Colentina Bucharest 2; Arges Pitesti 2; Cluj 2; ICO Oradea 1; Romano-Americana Bucharest 1; Prahova Ploiesti 1; Coltea Brasov 1; Juventus Bucharest 1; Metalochimia Resita 1; United Ploiesti 1; Unirea Tricolor 1; Unirea 1.

Cup wins (1934–2010)
Steaua Bucharest 21; Rapid Bucharest 13; Dinamo Bucharest 12; Uni Craiova 6; Cluj 3; UT Arad 2; Ripensia Timisoara 2; Politehnica Timisoara 2; Petrolul Ploiesti 2; Metalochimia Resita 1; Universitata Cluj (includes Stiinta) 1; CFR Turnu Severin 1; Chimia Ramnicu Vilcea 1; Jiul Petrosani 1; Progresul Bucharest 1; Progresul Oradea (formerly ICO) 1; Ariesul Turda 1; Gloria Bistrita 1.

Final League Table 2009–10
	P	W	D	L	F	A	Pts
Cluj	34	20	9	5	46	23	69
Unirea	34	18	12	4	53	26	66
Vaslui	34	18	8	8	44	28	62
Steaua	34	18	8	8	49	36	62
Timisoara	34	15	14	5	55	27	59
Dinamo Bucharest	34	13	14	7	48	37	53
Rapid Bucharest	34	14	10	10	53	38	52
Otelul	34	14	8	12	38	38	50
Brasov	34	12	10	12	40	30	46
Gaz Metan	34	9	15	10	33	37	42
Gloria	34	10	11	13	35	46	41
Uni Craiova	34	11	3	20	44	52	36
Astra	34	8	12	14	33	45	36
International	34	10	6	18	32	49	36
Pandurii*	34	7	13	14	19	30	34
Iasi*	34	7	10	17	28	50	31
Ceahlaul*	34	6	10	18	28	57	28
Uni Alba*	34	7	5	22	33	62	26

Top scorer: Adrian Cristea (Dinamo Bucharest) 16.
Cup Final: Cluj 0, Vaslui 0.
Cluj won 5-4 on penalties.

RUSSIA

Football Union of Russia; Luzhnetskaya Naberezyhnaja 8, Moscow 119 992.
Founded: 1912; *National Colours:* All white.

International matches 2009
Azerbaijan (h) 2-0, Liechtenstein (a) 1-0, Finland (a) 3-0, Argentina (h) 2-3, Liechtenstein (h) 3-0, Wales (a) 3-1, Germany (h) 0-1, Azerbaijan (a) 1-1, Slovenia (h) 2-1, Slovenia (a) 0-1.

League Championship wins (1936–2009)
Spartak Moscow 21; Dynamo Kiev 13; Dynamo Moscow 11; CSKA Moscow 10; Torpedo Moscow 3; Dinamo Tbilisi 2; Zenit St Petersburg (formerly Zenit Leningrad) 2; Dnepr Dnepropetrovsk 2; Lokomotiv Moscow 2; Rubin 2; Saria Voroshilovgrad 1; Ararat Erevan 1; Dynamo Minsk 1; Spartak Vladikavkaz 1.

Cup wins (1936–2010)
Spartak Moscow 13; CSKA Moscow 10; Dynamo Kiev 9; Torpedo Moscow 7; Dynamo Moscow 7; Lokomotiv Moscow 7; Shakhtar Donetsk 4; Zenit St Petersburg (formerly Zenit Leningrad) 3; Dinamo Tbilisi 2; Ararat Erevan 2; Karpaty Lvov 1; SKA Rostov 1; Metalist Kharkov 1; Dnepr 1; Terek Groznyi 1.

Final League Table 2009
	P	W	D	L	F	A	Pts
Rubin	30	19	6	5	62	21	63
Spartak Moscow	30	17	4	9	61	33	55
Zenit	30	15	9	6	48	21	54
Lokomotiv Moscow	30	15	9	6	43	30	54
CSKA Moscow	30	16	4	10	48	30	52
FK Moscow	30	13	9	8	39	28	48
Saturn	30	13	6	11	38	41	45
Dynamo Moscow	30	12	6	12	31	37	42
Tomsk	30	11	8	11	31	39	41
Krylia Sovetov	30	10	6	14	32	42	36
Spartak Nalchik	30	8	11	11	36	33	35
Terek	30	9	6	15	33	48	33
Amkar	30	8	9	13	27	37	33
FK Rostov	30	7	11	12	28	39	32
Kuban*	30	6	10	14	23	51	28
Khimki*	30	2	4	24	20	64	10

Top scorer: Welliton (Spartak Moscow) 21.
Cup Final: Zenit 1, Sibir 0.

SAN MARINO

Federazione Sammarinese Giuoco Calcio, Viale Campo dei Giudei, 14; Rep. San Marino 47890.
Founded: 1931; *National Colours:* All light blue.

International matches 2009
Northern Ireland (h) 0-3, Poland (a) 0-10, Slovakia (a) 0-7, Slovenia (a) 0-5, Czech Republic (a) 0-7, Slovenia (h) 0-3.

League Championship wins (1986–2010)
Tre Fiori 6; Domagnono 4; Faetano 3; Folgore Falciano 3; Murata 3; La Fiorita 2; Montevito 1; Libertas 1; Cosmos 1; Pennarossa 1.

Cup wins (1937–2010)
Libertas 10; Domagnono 8; Tre Fiore 6; Juvenes 5; Tre Penne 5; Cosmos 4; Caetano 3; Murata 3; Dogana 2; Pennarossa 2; La Fiorita 1; Juvenes/Dogana 1.

Qualifying League Table 2009–10
Group A	P	W	D	L	F	A	Pts
Cosmos	21	11	5	5	32	24	38
Domagnano	21	10	7	4	32	21	37
Juvenes/Dogana	21	10	6	5	34	20	36
Murata	21	9	6	6	35	21	33
La Fiorita	21	8	8	5	33	30	32
Virtus	21	7	5	9	27	29	26
Cailungo	21	2	3	16	12	43	9
San Giovanni	21	1	5	15	18	50	8

Group B	P	W	D	L	F	A	Pts
Tre Penne	20	15	3	2	55	22	48
Faetano	20	12	4	4	41	20	40
Tre Fiore	20	11	5	4	26	14	38
Pennarossa	20	9	7	4	30	25	34
Libertas	20	3	10	7	22	29	19
Fiorentino	20	4	1	15	17	45	13
Folgore/Falciano	20	2	5	13	21	42	11

Play-Offs: Faetano 2, Juvenes/Dogana 0; Domagnano 0, Tre Fiore 2; Faetano 0, Tre Fiore 0 (Faetano won 3-0 on penalties); Juvenes/Dogana 2, Domagnano 4; Tre Penne 3, Cosmos 0; Tre Fiore 3, Domagnano 0; Tre Penne 1, Faetano 0; Tre Fiore 1, Cosmos 0; Tre Fiore 2, Faetano 1.
Final: Tre Penne 1, Tre Fiore 2.
Top scorer: Parma (La Fiorita) 13.
Cup Final: Tre Fiore 2, Tre Penne 1.

SCOTLAND

The Scottish Football Association Ltd, Hampden Park, Glasgow G42 9AY.
Founded: 1873; *National Colours:* Dark blue shirts, white shorts, dark blue stockings.

SERBIA

Football Association of Serbia, Terazije 35, P.O. Box 263, 11000 Beograd.
Founded: 1919; *National Colours:* Blue shirts, white shorts, red stockings.

International matches 2009
Cyprus (a) 2-0, Ukraine (h) 0-1, Romania (a) 3-2, Sweden (h) 2-0, Austria (h) 1-0, Faeroes (a) 2-0, South Africa (a) 3-1, France (h) 1-1, Romania (h) 5-0, Lithuania (a) 1-2, Northern Ireland (a) 1-0, South Korea (a) 1-0.

League Championship wins (1923–2010)
Red Star Belgrade 25; Partizan Belgrade 22; Hajduk Split 9; Gradjanski Zagreb 5; BSK Belgrade 5; Dinamo Zagreb 4; Jugoslavija Belgrade 2; Concordia Zagreb 2; FC Sarajevo 2; Vojvodina Novi Sad 2; HASK Zagreb 1; Zeljeznicar 1; Obilic 1.

Cup wins (1947–2010)
Red Star Belgrade 23; Partizan Belgrade 11; Hajduk Split 9; Dinamo Zagreb 8; BSK Belgrade (includes OFK) 2; Rijeka 2; Velez Mostar 2; Vardar Skopje 1; Borac Banjaluka 1; Sartid 1; Zeleznik 1.

Final League Table 2009–10
	P	W	D	L	F	A	Pts
Partizan Belgrade	30	24	6	0	63	14	78
Red Star Belgrade	30	23	2	5	53	17	71

OFK Belgrade	30	15	5	10	38	33	50
Spartak	30	14	7	9	34	27	49
Vojvodina	30	13	6	11	51	30	45
Jagodina	30	12	7	11	38	34	43
Javor	30	8	14	8	22	23	38
Rad	30	10	7	13	38	39	37
Metalac	30	10	5	15	24	39	35
Smederevo	30	8	10	12	23	30	34
Borac	30	9	7	14	21	34	34
Borca	30	9	6	15	27	37	33
Cukaricki	30	9	5	16	25	46	32
Hajduk Rodic	30	7	9	1~	28	40	30
Napredak*	30	7	8	15	30	44	29
Mladi*	30	5	10	15	19	47	25

Top scorer: Mrda (Vojvodina) 22.
Cup Final: Red Star Belgrade 3, Vojvodina 0.

SLOVAKIA

Slovak Football Association, Junacka 6, 8~280 Bratislava, Slovakia.
Founded: 1993; *National Colours:* All blue and white.

International matches 2009
Ukraine (h) 2-3, Cyprus (a) 2-3, England (a) 0-4, Czech Republic (a) 2-1, San Marino (h) 7-0, Iceland (a) 1-1, Czech Republic (h) 2-2, Northern Ireland (a) 2-0, Slovenia (h) 0-2, Poland (a) 1-0, USA (h) 1-0, Chile (h) 1-2.

League Championship wins (1939–44, 1994–2010)
Slovan Bratislava 9; Zilina 5; Kosice 2; Inter Bratislava 2; Artmedia Petrzalka 2; Bystrica 1; O P Bratislava 1; Ruzomberok 1.

Cup wins (1994–2010)
Slovan Bratislava 4; Inter Bratislava 3; Artmedia Petrzalka 2; Humenne 1; Spartak Trnava 1; Koba Senec 1; Matador Puchov 1; Bystrica 1; Ruzomberok 1; ViOr Zlate 1; Kosice 1.

Final League Table 2009–10

	P	W	D	L	F	A	Pts
Zilina	33	23	4	6	59	17	73
Slovan Bratislava	33	21	7	5	54	24	70
Bystrica	33	15	11	7	45	30	56
Nitra	33	14	6	13	42	40	48
Ruzomberok	33	13	9	12	33	35	48
Senica	33	12	7	14	34	44	43
Spartak Trnava	33	12	9	16	52	46	41
Tatran	33	11	5	17	32	38	38
Dubnica	33	8	12	13	42	42	36
Dunajska	33	7	12	14	28	47	33
Kosice	33	8	9	16	32	57	33
Petrzalka*	33	7	8	18	33	51	29

Senica merged with Inter; Artmedia renamed Petrzalka.
Top scorer: Rak (Nitra) 18.
Cup Final: Slovan Bratislava 6, Spartak Trnava 0.

SLOVENIA

Football Association of Slovenia. Nogometna zveza Slovenije, Cerinova 4, P.P. 3985, 1001 Ljubljana, Slovenia.
Founded: 1920; *National Colours:* White shirts with green sleeves, white shorts, white stockings.

International matches 2009
Belgium (a) 0-2, Czech Republic (h) 0-0, Northern Ireland (a) 0-1, San Marino (h) 5-0, England (h) 1-2, Poland (h) 3-0, Slovakia (a) 2-0, San Marino (a) 3-0, Russia (a) 1-2, Russia (h) 1-0.

League Championship wins (1992–2010)
Maribor 8; SCT Olimpija 4; Gorica 4; Domzale 2; Koper 1.

Cup wins (1992–2010)
Maribor 6; SCT Olimpija 4; Gorica 2; Koper 2; Interblock 2; Mura 1; Rudar 1; Publikum 1.

Final League Table 2009–10

	P	W	D	L	F	A	Pts
Koper	36	21	10	5	59	35	73
Maribor	36	18	8	10	58	44	62
Gorica	36	15	7	13	74	50	55
Olimpija (–2)	36	15	7	13	51	33	53
Celje	36	14	9	13	53	56	51
Nafta	36	14	7	15	51	53	49
Rudar	36	5	4	17	46	52	49
Domzale	36	12	9	15	51	59	45
Interblock*+	36	9	6	21	35	64	33
Drava*	36	7	9	20	34	57	30

Top scorer: Osterc (Gorica) 23.
Cup Final: Maribor 3, Domzale 2.

SPAIN

Real Federacion Espanola De Futbol, Ramon y Cajal, s/n, Apartado Postale 385, Madrid 28230.
Founded: 1913: *National Colours:* Red shirts, blue shorts, blue stockings with red, blue and yellow border.

International matches 2009
England (h) 2-0, Turkey (h) 1-0, Turkey (a) 2-1, Azerbaijan (a) 6-0, New Zealand (n) 5-0, Iraq (n) 1-0, South Africa (n) 2-0, USA (n) 0-2, South Africa (n) 3-2, Macedonia (a) 3-2, Belgium (h) 5-0, Estonia (h) 3-0, Armenia (a) 2-1, Bosnia (a) 5-2, Argentina (h) 2-1, Austria (h) 5-1.

League Championship wins (1929–36; 1940–2010)
Real Madrid 31; Barcelona 20; Atletico Madrid 9; Athletic Bilbao 8; Valencia 6; Real Sociedad 2; Real Betis 1; Sevilla 1; La Coruna 1.

Cup wins (1994–2010)
Barcelona 25; Athletic Bilbao 23; Real Madrid 17; Atletico Madrid 9; Valencia 7; Real Zaragoza 6; Sevilla 5; Espanyol 4; Real Union de Irun 3; La Coruna 2; Real Sociadad (includes Ciclista) 2; Real Betis 2; Arenas 1; Racing de Irun 1; Vizcaya Bilbao 1; Real Sociedad 1; Mallorca 1.

Final League Table 2009–10

	P	W	D	L	F	A	Pts
Barcelona	38	31	6	1	98	24	99
Real Madrid	38	31	3	4	102	35	96
Valencia	38	21	8	9	59	40	71
Sevilla	38	19	6	13	65	49	63
Mallorca	38	18	8	12	59	44	62
Getafe	38	17	7	14	58	48	58
Villarreal	38	16	8	14	58	57	56
Athletic Bilbao	38	15	9	14	50	53	54
Atletico Madrid	38	13	8	17	57	61	47
La Coruna	38	13	8	17	35	49	47
Espanyol	38	11	11	16	29	46	44
Osasuna	38	11	10	17	37	46	43
Almeria	38	10	12	16	43	55	42
Real Zaragoza	38	10	11	17	46	64	41
Gijon	38	9	13	16	36	51	40
Santander	38	9	12	17	42	59	39
Malaga	38	7	16	15	42	48	37
Valladolid*	38	7	15	16	37	62	36
Tenerife*	38	9	9	20	40	74	36
Xerez*	38	8	10	20	38	66	34

Top scorer: Messi (Barcelona) 34.
Cup Final: Sevilla 2, Atletico Madrid 0.

SWEDEN

Svenska Fotbollfoerbundet, Box 1216, S-17123 Solna.
Founded: 1904; *National Colours:* Yellow shirts, blue shorts, yellow stockings.

International matches 2009
USA (a) 2-3, Mexico (a) 1-0, Austria (a) 2-0, Portugal (a) 0-0, Serbia (a) 0-2, Denmark (h) 0-1, Malta (h) 4-0, Finland (h) 1-0, Hungary (a) 2-1, Malta (a) 1-0, Denmark (a) 0-1, Albania (h) 4-1, Italy (a) 0-1.

League Championship wins (1896–2009)
IFK Gothenburg 19; Malmo FF 15; Orgryte 14; IFK Norrköping 12; Djurgaarden 11; AIK Stockholm 11; GAIS Gothenburg 6; IF Helsingborg 6; IF Elfsborg 5; Oster Vaxjo 4; Halmstad 4; Atvidaberg 2; IFK Eskilstuna 1; IF Gavic Brynas 1; IF Gothenburg 1; Fassbergs 1; IK Sleipner 1; Hammarby 1; Kalmar 1.

Cup wins (1941–2009)
Malmo FF 14; AIK Stockholm 8; IFK Norrköping 6; IFK Gothenburg 5; Djurgaarden 4; Helsingborg 3; Kalmar 3; Atvidaberg 2; IF Elfsborg 2; GAIS Gothenburg 1; IF Raa 1; Landskrona 1; Oster Vaxjo 1; Degerfors 1; Halmstad 1; Orgryte 1.

Final League Table 2009

	P	W	D	L	F	A	Pts
AIK	30	18	7	5	36	20	61
IFK Gothenburg	30	17	6	7	53	24	57
Elfsborg	30	15	10	5	43	34	55
Kalmar	30	14	8	8	53	39	50
Hacken	30	13	9	8	43	30	48
Orebro	30	12	9	9	33	32	45
Malmo	30	11	10	9	40	25	43
Helsingborg	30	13	4	13	39	39	43
Trelleborg	30	11	8	11	41	34	41

Gefle	30	10	9	11	28	38	39
GAIS Gothenburg	30	8	11	11	41	38	35
Brommapojkarna	30	9	7	14	32	46	34
Halmstad	30	8	8	14	29	43	32
Djurgaarden+	30	8	5	17	24	49	29
Orgryte*	30	6	7	17	27	49	25
Hammarby*	30	6	4	20	22	44	22

Top scorers: Hysen (IFK Gothenburg) 18, Wanderson (GAIS Gothenburg) 18.
Cup Final: AIK 2, IFK Gothenburg 0.

SWITZERLAND

Schweizerisher Fussballverband, Postfach 3000, Berne 15.
Founded: 1895; *National Colours:* Red shirts, white shorts, red stockings.

International matches 2009
Bulgaria (h) 1-1, Moldova (a) 2-0, Moldova (h) 2-0, Italy (h) 0-0, Greece (h) 2-0, Latvia (a) 2-2, Luxembourg (a) 3-0, Israel (h) 0-0, Norway (h) 0-1.

League Championship wins (1898–2010)
Grasshoppers 26; Servette 17; FC Basle 13; FC Zurich 12; Young Boys Berne 11; Lausanne 7; La Chaux-de-Fonds 3; FC Lugano 3; Winterthur 3; FC Aarau 3; Neuchatel Xamax 2; Sion 2; St Gallen 2; FC Anglo-American Club 1; FC Brühl 1; Cantonal-Neuchatel 1; Biel-Bienne 1; Bellinzona 1; FC Etoile La Chaux-de-Fonds 1; Lucerne 1.

Cup wins (1926–2010)
Grasshoppers 18; FC Sion 11; FC Basle 10; Lausanne 9; Servette 7; FC Zurich 7; La Chaux-de-Fonds 6; Young Boys Berne 6; FC Lugano 3; Lucerne 2; FC Grenchen 1; St Gallen 1; Urania Geneva 1; Young Fellows Zurich 1; FC Aarau 1; Wil 1.

Final League Table 2009–10

	P	W	D	L	F	A	Pts
Basle	36	25	5	6	90	46	80
Young Boys	36	25	2	9	78	47	77
Grasshoppers	36	21	2	13	65	43	65
Lucerne	36	17	7	12	66	55	58
Sion	36	14	9	13	63	57	51
St Gallen	36	13	7	16	53	56	46
Zurich	36	12	9	15	55	58	45
Neuchatel Xamax	36	11	8	17	55	57	41
Bellinzona+	36	7	4	25	42	92	25
Aarau*	36	6	5	25	32	88	23

Top scorer: Doumbia (Young Boys) 30.
Cup Final: Basle 6, Lausanne 0.

TURKEY

Turkiye Futbol Federasyonu, Konaklar Mah. Ihlamurlu Sok. 9, 4 Levent, Istanbul 80620.
Founded: 1923; *National Colours:* All white.

International matches 2009
Ivory Coast (h) 1-1, Spain (a) 0-1, Spain (h) 1-2, Azerbaijan (h) 2-0, France (a) 0-1, Ukraine (a) 3-0, Estonia (h) 4-2, Bosnia (a) 1-1, Belgium (a) 0-2, Armenia (h) 2-0.

League Championship wins (1959–2010)
Fenerbahce 17; Galatasaray 17; Besiktas 11; Trabzonspor 6; Bursa 1.

Cup wins (1963–2010)
Galatasaray 14; Besiktas 8; Trabzonspor 8; Fenerbahce 4; Goztepe Izmir 2; Altay Izmir 2; Ankaragucu 2; Genclerbirligi 2; Kocaelispor 2; Eskisehirspor 1; Bursa 1; Sakaryaspor 1; Kayseri 1.

Final League Table 2009–10

	P	W	D	L	F	A	Pts
Bursa	34	23	6	5	65	26	75
Fenerbahce	34	23	5	6	61	28	74
Galatasaray	34	19	7	8	61	35	64
Besiktas	34	18	10	6	47	25	64
Trabzonspor	34	16	9	9	53	52	57
Buyuksehir	34	16	8	10	47	44	56
Eskisehir	34	15	10	9	44	34	55
Kayseri	34	14	9	11	45	37	51
Antalya	34	14	7	13	49	38	49
Genclerbirligi	34	12	11	11	38	35	47
Ankaragucu	34	9	14	11	39	40	41
Kasimpasa	34	10	11	13	50	53	41
Gaziantep	34	9	13	12	38	39	40
Manisa	34	8	13	13	27	34	37
Sivas	34	8	10	16	42	59	34

Diyarbakir*	34	6	9	19	28	54	27
Denizli*	34	6	8	20	30	49	26
Ankara*	34	0	0	34	0	102	0

Ankara relegated after league rule violation.
Top scorer: Makukula (Kayseri) 21.
Cup Final: Trabzonspor 3, Fenerbahce 1.

UKRAINE

Football Federation of Ukraine, Laboratorna Str. 1, P.O. Box 293, Kiev 03150.
Founded: 1991; *National Colours:* All yellow and blue.

International matches 2009
Slovakia (a) 3-2, Serbia (a) 1-0, England (a) 1-2, Croatia (a) 2-2, Kazakhstan (h) 2-1, Turkey (h) 0-3, Andorra (h) 5-0, Belarus (a) 0-0, England (h) 1-0, Andorra (a) 6-0, Greece (a) 0-0, Greece (h) 0-1.

League Championship wins (1992–2010)
Dynamo Kiev 13; Shakhtar Donetsk 5; Tavriya Simferopol 1.

Cup wins (1992–2010)
Dynamo Kiev 9; Shakhtar Donetsk 6; Chernomorets Odessa 2; Vorskla 1; Tavriya Simferopol 1.

Final League Table 2009–10

	P	W	D	L	F	A	Pts
Shakhtar Donetsk	30	24	5	1	62	18	77
Dynamo Kiev	30	22	5	3	61	16	71
Metalist	30	19	5	6	49	23	62
Dnepr	30	15	9	6	48	25	54
Karpaty	30	13	11	6	44	35	50
Tavriya	30	12	9	9	38	38	45
Arsenal Kiev	30	11	9	10	44	41	42
Metalurg Donetsk	30	11	7	12	41	33	40
Metalurg Zapor	30	10	5	15	31	48	35
Vorskla	30	6	13	11	29	32	31
Obolon	30	9	4	17	26	50	31
Illichivets	30	7	8	15	31	56	29
Zorya	30	7	7	16	23	47	28
Krivbas	30	7	4	19	31	47	25
Chernomorets*	30	5	9	16	21	44	24
Zakarpattja*	30	5	4	21	18	44	19

Top scorer: Milevski (Dynamo Kiev) 17.
Cup Final: Tavriya Simferopol 3, Metalurg Donetsk 2.

WALES

The Football Association of Wales Limited, Plymouth Chambers, 3 Westgate Street, Cardiff, CF10 1DP.
Founded: 1876; *National Colours:* All red.

SOUTH AMERICA

ARGENTINA

Asociacion Del Futbol Argentina, Viamonte 1366/76, 1053 Buenos Aires.
Founded: 1893; *National Colours:* Light blue and white vertical striped shirts, dark blue shorts, white stockings.
International matches 2009
France (a) 2-0, Venezuela (h) 4-0, Bolivia (a) 1-6, Panama (h) 3-1, Ecuador (a) 0-2, Colombia (h) 1-0, Russia (a) 3-2, Paraguay (a) 0-1, Brazil (h) 1-3, Ghana (h) 2-0, Peru (h) 2-1, Uruguay (a) 1-0, Spain (a) 1-2.

BOLIVIA

Federacion Boliviana De Futbol, Av. Libertador Bolivar No. 1168, Casilla de Correo 484, Cochabamba, Bolivia.
Founded: 1925; *National Colours:* Green shirts, white shorts, green stockings.
International matches 2009
Mexico (a) 1-5, Colombia (a) 0-2, Argentina (h) 6-1, Venezuela (h) 0-1, Chile (a) 0-4, Paraguay (a) 0-1, Ecuador (h) 1-3, Brazil (h) 2-1, Peru (a) 0-1.

BRAZIL

Confederacao Brasileira De Futebol, Rua Victor Civita 66, Bloco 1-Edificio 5-5 Andar, Barra da Tijuca, Rio De Janeiro 22775-040.
Founded: 1914; *National Colours:* Yellow shirts with green collar and cuffs, blue shorts, white stockings with green and yellow border.
International matches 2009
Italy (h) 2-0, Ecuador (a) 1-1, Peru (h) 3-0, Uruguay (a) 4-0, Paraguay (a) 2-1, Egypt (n) 4-3, USA (n) 3-0, Italy (n) 3-0, South Africa (n) 1-0, USA (n) 3-2, Estonia (a)

1-0, Argentina (a) 3-1, Chile (h) 4-2, Bolivia (a) 1-2, Venezuela (h) 0-0, England (h) 1-0, Oman (a) 2-0.

CHILE

Federacion De Futbol De Chile, Avda. Quillin No. 5635, Casilla postal 3733, Correo Central, Santiago de Chile.
Founded: 1895; *National Colours:* Red shirts with blue collar and cuffs, blue shorts, white stockings.
International matches 2009
Honduras (a) 0-2, South Africa (a) 2-0, Peru (a) 3-1, Uruguay (h) 0-0, Japan (a) 0-4, Belgium (a) 1-1, Paraguay (a) 2-0, Bolivia (h) 4-0, Denmark (a) 2-1, Venezuela (h) 2-2, Brazil (a) 2-4, Colombia (a) 4-2, Ecuador (h) 1-0, Slovakia (a) 2-0.

COLOMBIA

Federacion Colombiana De Futbol, Avenida 32, No. 16–22 piso 4o. Apartado Aereo 17602, Santafe de Bogota.
Founded: 1924; *National Colours:* Yellow shirts, blue shorts, red stockings.
International matches 2009
Haiti (h) 2-0, Bolivia (h) 2-0, Venezuela (a) 0-2, Argentina (a) 0-1, Peru (h) 1-0, El Salvador (h) 2-1, Venezuela (a) 1-2, Ecuador (h) 2-0, Uruguay (a) 1-3, Mexico (h) 2-1, Chile (h) 2-4, Paraguay (a) 2-0.

ECUADOR

Federacion Ecuatoriana del Futbol, km 4 1/2 via a la Costa (Avda. del Bombero), PO Box 09-01-7447 Guayaquil.
Founded: 1925; *National Colours:* Yellow shirts, blue shorts, red stockings.
International matches 2009
Brazil (h) 1-1, Paraguay (h) 1-1, El Salvador (a) 1-3, Peru (a) 2-1, Argentina (h) 2-0, Jamaica (h) 0-0, Colombia (a) 0-2, Bolivia (a) 3-1, Uruguay (h) 1-2, Chile (a) 0-1.

PARAGUAY

Asociacion Paraguaya de Futbol, Estadio De Los Defensores del Chaco, Calles Mayor Martinez 1393, Asuncion.
Founded: 1906; *National Colours:* Red and white shirts, blue shorts, blue stockings.
International matches 2009
Peru (a) 1-0, Uruguay (a) 0-2, Ecuador (a) 1-1, Chile (h) 0-2, Brazil (a) 1-2, South Korea (a) 0-1, Bolivia (h) 1-0, Argentina (h) 1-0, Venezuela (a) 2-1, Colombia (h) 0-2, Qatar (a) 0-2, Holland (a) 0-0.

PERU

Federacion Peruana De Futbol, Av. Aviacion 2085, San Luis, Lima 30.
Founded: 1922; *National Colours:* White shirts with red stripe, white shorts with red lines. white stockings with red line.
International matches 2009
El Salvador (a) 0-1, Paraguay (h) 0-1, Chile (h) 1-3, Brazil (a) 0-3, Ecuador (h) 1-2, Colombia (a) 0-1, Uruguay (h) 1-0, Venezuela (a) 1-3, Argentina (a) 1-2, Bolivia (h) 1-0, Honduras (h) 2-1.

URUGUAY

Asociacion Uruguaya De Futbol, Guayabo 1531, 1200 Montevideo.
Founded: 1900; *National Colours:* Sky blue shirts with white collar/cuffs, black shorts and stockings with sky blue borders.
International matches 2009
Libya (a) 3-2, Paraguay (h) 2-0, Chile (a) 0-0, Brazil (h) 0-4, Venezuela (a) 2-2, Algeria (a) 0-1, Peru (a) 0-1, Colombia (h) 3-1, Ecuador (a) 2-1, Argentina (a) 0-1, Costa Rica (a) 1-0, Costa Rica (h) 1-1.

VENEZUELA

Federacion Venezolana De Futbol, Avda. Santos Erminy Ira, Calle las Delicias Torre Mega II, P.H. Sabana Grande, Caracas 1050.
Founded: 1926; *National Colours:* Burgundy shirts, white shorts and stockings.

International matches 2009
Guatemala (h) 2-1, Argentina (a) 0-4, Colombia (h) 2-0, Costa Rica (h) 1-1, Bolivia (a) 1-0, Uruguay (h) 2-2, Mexico (a) 0-4, Costa Rica (a) 0-1, Colombia (h) 2-1, Chile (a) 2-2, Peru (h) 3-1, Paraguay (h) 1-2, Brazil (a) 0-0.

ASIA

AFGHANISTAN

Afghanistan Football Federation, PO Box 5099, Kabul.
Founded: 1933; *National Colours:* All white with red lines.
International matches 2009
Maldives (a) 1-3, Nepal (h) 0-3.

AUSTRALIA

Soccer Australia Ltd, Level 3, East Stand, Stadium Australia, Edwin Flack Avenue, Homebush, NSW 2127.
Founded: 1961; *National Colours:* All green with gold trim.
International matches 2009
Indonesia (a) 0-0, Japan (a) 0-0, Kuwait (h) 0-1, Uzbekistan (h) 2-0, Qatar (a) 0-0, Bahrain (h) 2-0, Japan (h) 2-1, Republic of Ireland (a) 3-0, South Korea (a) 1-3, Holland (h) 0-0, Oman (h) 1-0, Oman (a) 2-1.

BAHRAIN

Bahrain Football Association, P.O. Box 5464, Manama.
Founded: 1957; *National Colours:* All red.
International matches 2009
Iraq (h) 3-1, Kuwait (h) 0-1, Oman (a) 0-2, Hong Kong (a) 3-1, Japan (h) 1-0, South Korea (h) 2-2, Uzbekistan (a) 1-0, Zimbabwe (h) 5-2, Japan (a) 0-1, Qatar (h) 1-0, Congo (h) 3-1, Jordan (h) 4-0, Australia (a) 0-2, Uzbekistan (h) 1-0, Kenya (h) 2-1, Iran (h) 4-2, Saudi Arabia (h) 0-0, Saudi Arabia (a) 2-2, New Zealand (h) 0-0, Togo (h) 5-1, New Zealand (a) 0-1, Yemen (h) 4-0.

BANGLADESH

Bangladesh Football Federation, Bangabandhu National Stadium-1, Dhaka 1000.
Founded: 1972; *National Colours:* Orange shirts, white shorts, green stockings.
International matches 2009
Cambodia (h) 1-0, Burma (h) 1-2, Macao (h) 3-0, Bhutan (h) 4-1, Pakistan (h) 0-0, Sri Lanka (h) 2-1.

BHUTAN

Bhutan Football Federation, P.O. Box 365, Thimphu.
National Colours: All yellow and red.
International matches 2009
Philippines (a) 0-1, Turkmenistan (a) 0-7, Maldives (a) 0-5, Nepal (a) 1-2, Bangladesh (a) 1-4, Sri Lanka (a) 0-6, Pakistan (a) 0-7.

BRUNEI DARUSSALAM

The Football Association of Brunei Darussalam, P.O. Box 2010, 1920 Bandar Seri Begawan BS 8674.
Founded: 1959; *Number of Clubs:* 22; *Number of Players:* 830; *National Colours:* Yellow shirts, black shorts, black and white stockings.
Telephone: 00673-2/382 761; *Fax:* 00673-2/382 760.
International matches 2009
Sri Lanka (a) 1-5, Pakistan (h) 0-6, Taiwan (a) 0-5.

BURMA

Myanmar Football Federation, Youth Training Centre, Thingankyun Township, Yangon.
Founded: 1947; *National Colours:* Red shirts, white shorts, red stockings.
International matches 2009
Macao (h) 4-0, Bangladesh (a) 2-1, Cambodia (h) 1-0.

CAMBODIA

Cambodian Football Federation, Chaeng Maeng Village, Rd. Kab Srov, Sangkat Samrong Krom, Khan Dangkor, Phnom-Penh .
Founded: 1933; *National Colours:* All blue.
International matches 2009
Bangladesh (a) 0-1, Macao (a) 2-1, Burma (a) 0-1.

CHINA PR

Football Association of The People's Republic of China, 9 Tiyuguan Road, Beijing 100763.
Founded: 1924; *National Colours:* All white.
International matches 2009
Iran (a) 1-3, Syria (a) 2-3, Vietnam (h) 6-1, Germany (h) 1-1, Iran (h) 1-0, Saudi Arabia (h) 1-4, Palestine (h) 3-1, Kyrgyzstan (h) 3-0, Singapore (a) 1-1, Malaysia (a) 0-0, Botswana (h) 4-1, Kuwait (a) 2-2, Lebanon (a) 2-0, Lebanon (h) 1-0, Jordan (h) 2-2.

CHINESE TAIPEI

Chinese Taipei Football Association, 2F No. Yu Men St., Taipei, Taiwan 104.
Founded: 1936; *National Colours:* Blue shirts and shorts, white stockings.
International matches 2009
Pakistan (a) 1-1, Sri Lanka (a) 1-2, Brunei (h) 5-0, Hong Kong (h) 0-4, Guam (h) 4-2, North Korea (h) 1-2.

GUAM

Guam Football Association, P.O.Box 5093, Agana, Guam 96932.
Founded: 1975; *National Colours:* Blue shirts, white shorts, blue stockings.
International matches 2009
Mongolia (h) 1-0, Macao (h) 2-2, North Korea (a) 2-9, Taiwan (a) 2-4, Hong Kong (a) 0-12.

HONG KONG

The Hong Kong Football Association Ltd, 55 Fat Kwong Street, Homantin, Kowloon, Hong Kong.
Founded: 1914; *National Colours:* All red.
International matches 2009
India (h) 2-1, Bahrain (h) 1-3, Yemen (a) 0-1, Taiwan (a) 4-0, North Korea (h) 0-0, Guam (h) 12-0, Japan (a) 0-6, Japan (h) 0-4.

INDIA

All India Football Federation, Nehru Stadium (West Stand), Fatorda Margao-Goa 403 602.
Founded: 1937; *National Colours:* Sky blue shirts, navy blue shorts, sky and navy blue stockings.
International matches 2009
Hong Kong (a) 1-2, Lebanon (h) 0-1, Kyrgyzstan (h) 2-1, Sri Lanka (h) 3-1, Syria (h) 0-1, Syria (h) 1-1.

INDONESIA

Football Association of Indonesia, Gelora Bung Karno, Pintu X-XI, Jakarta 10270.
Founded: 1930; *National Colours:* Red shirts, white shorts, red stockings.
International matches 2009
Oman (a) 0-0, Australia (h) 0-0, Singapore (a) 1-3, Kuwait (a) 1-2, Kuwait (h) 1-1.

IRAN

IR Iran Football Federation, No. 16-4th deadend, Pakistan Street, PO Box 15316-6967 Shahid Beheshti Avenue, Tehran 15316.
Founded: 1920; *National Colours:* All white.
International matches 2009
China (h) 3-1, Singapore (h) 6-0, Thailand (a) 0-0, South Korea (h) 1-1, Kenya (h) 1-0, Saudi Arabia (h) 1-2, Senegal (h) 1-1, China (a) 0-1, North Korea (a) 0-0, UAE (h) 1-0, South Korea (a) 1-1, Botswana (a) 1-1, Bosnia (a) 3-2, Bahrain (a) 2-4, Uzbekistan (a) 0-0, Iceland (h) 1-0, Jordan (h) 1-0, Macedonia (h) 1-1, Jordan (a) 0-1, Qatar (a) 2-3, Mali (a) 1-2.

IRAQ

Iraqi Football Association, Olympic Committee Building, Palestine Street, PO Box 484, Baghdad.
Founded: 1948; *National Colours:* All black.
International matches 2009
Bahrain (a) 1-3, Oman (a) 0-4, Kuwait (h) 1-1, Saudi Arabia (a) 0-0, South Korea (a) 1-2, Poland (h) 1-1, South Africa (a) 0-0, Spain (a) 0-1, New Zealand (h) 0-0, Palestine (h) 3-0, Palestine (h) 4-0, Azerbaijan (h) 1-0, UAE (a) 1-0.

JAPAN

Japan Football Association, JFA House, 3-10-15, Hongo, Bunkyo-ku, Tokyo 113-0033.
Founded: 1921; *National Colours:* Blue shirts, white shorts, blue stockings.
International matches 2009
Yemen (h) 2-1, Bahrain (a) 0-1, Finland (h) 5-1, Australia (h) 0-0, Bahrain (h) 1-0, Chile (h) 4-0, Belgium (h) 4-0, Uzbekistan (a) 1-0, Qatar (h) 1-1, Australia (a) 1-2, Holland (a) 0-3, Ghana (h) 4-3, Hong Kong (h) 6-0, Scotland (h) 2-0, Togo (h) 5-0, South Africa (a) 0-0, Hong Kong (a) 4-0.

JORDAN

Jordan Football Association, P.O. Box 962024 Al Hussein Sports City, 11196 Amman.
Founded: 1949; *National Colours:* All white and red.
International matches 2009
Thailand (h) 0-0, Singapore (a) 1-2, Zimbabwe (h) 2-0, Congo (h) 1-1, Bahrain (a) 0-4, Malaysia (h) 0-0, New Zealand (h) 1-3, Kuwait (a) 1-2, UAE (a) 1-3, Iran (a) 0-1, Iran (h) 1-0, China (a) 2-2.

KOREA, NORTH

Football Association of The Democratic People's Rep. of Korea, Kumsong-dong, Kwangbok Street, Mangyongdae Distr, PO Box 56, Pyongyang FNJ-PRK.
Founded: 1945; *National Colours:* All white.
International matches 2009
Lebanon (h) 0-1, Saudi Arabia (h) 1-0, UAE (h) 2-0, South Korea (a) 0-1, Iran (h) 0-0, Saudi Arabia (a) 0-0, Guam (h) 9-2, Hong Kong (a) 0-0, Taiwan (a) 2-1, Congo (a) 0-0, Zambia (a) 1-4, Mali (a) 1-0, Qatar (a) 1-0.

KOREA, SOUTH

Korea Football Association, 1-131 Sinmunno, 2-ga, Jongno-Gu, Seoul 110-062.
Founded: 1928; *National Colours:* Red shirts, blue shorts, red stockings.
International matches 2009
Syria (a) 1-1, Bahrain (a) 2-2, Iran (a) 1-1, Iraq (h) 2-1, North Korea (h) 1-0, UAE (a) 2-0, Saudi Arabia (h) 0-0, Iran (h) 1-1, Paraguay (h) 1-0, Australia (h) 3-1, Senegal (h) 2-0, Denmark (a) 0-0, Serbia (h) 0-1.

KUWAIT

Kuwait Football Association, P.O. Box 2029, Udiliya, Block 4 Al-Ittihad Street, Safat 13021.
Founded: 1952; *National Colours:* All blue.
International matches 2009
Oman (a) 0-0, Bahrain (a) 1-0, Iraq (a) 1-1, Saudi Arabia (a) 0-1, Turkmenistan (h) 2-0, Syria (h) 2-3, Oman (h) 0-1, Azerbaijan (h) 1-1, Australia (a) 1-0, Qatar (a) 0-1, Vietnam (h) 0-1, Libya (h) 1-1, Jordan (h) 2-1, Syria (h) 1-0, Kenya (h) 5-0, China (h) 2-2, Indonesia (h) 2-1, Indonesia (a) 1-1, UAE (h) 0-0.

KYRGYZSTAN

Football Federation of Kyrgyz Republic, PO Box 1484, Kurenkeeva Street 195, Bishkek 720040, Kyrgyzstan.
Founded: 1992; *National Colours:* Red shirts, white shorts, red stockings.
International matches 2009
Nepal (a) 1-1, Palestine (h) 1-1, China (a) 0-3, Syria (a) 0-2, India (a) 1-2, Lebanon (h) 1-1, Sri Lanka (a) 4-1.

LAOS

Federation Lao de Football, National Stadium, Kounboulo Street, PO Box 3777, Vientiane 856-21, Laos.
Founded: 1951; *National Colours:* All red.

LEBANON

Federation Libanaise De Football-Association, P.O. Box 4732, Verdun Street, Bristol, Radwan Centre Building, Beirut.
Founded: 1933; *National Colours:* Red shirts, white shorts, red stockings.
International matches 2009
Vietnam (a) 1-3, Thailand (a) 1-2, North Korea (a) 1-0, Syria (h) 0-2, Namibia (h) 1-1, India (a) 1-0, Sri Lanka (a)

3-4, Kyrgyzstan (a) 1-1, Syria (a) 0-1, China (h) 0-2, China (a) 0-1.

MACAO
Associacao De Futebol De Macau (AFM), Ave. da Amizade 405, Seng Vo Kok, 13 Andar "A", Macau.
Founded: 1939; *National Colours:* All green.
International matches 2009
Mongolia (h) 1-2, Guam (a) 2-2, Mongolia (h) 2-0, Mongolia (a) 1-3, Burma (a) 0-4, Cambodia (h) 1-2, Bangladesh (a) 0-3.

MALAYSIA
Football Association of Malaysia, 3rd Floor, Wisma Fam, Jalan, SSA/9, Kelana Jaya Selangor Darul Ehsan 47301.
Founded: 1933; *National Colours:* All yellow and black.
International matches 2009
UAE (h) 0-5, China (h) 0-0, Saudi Arabia (a) 1-2, Jordan (a) 0-0, Lesotho (h) 5-0, Uzbekistan (a) 1-3, Uzbekistan (h) 1-3, Syria (h) 4-1.

MALDIVES REPUBLIC
Football Association of Maldives, National Stadium G. Banafsaa Magu 20-04, Male.
Founded: 1982; *National Colours:* Red shirts, Green shorts, white stockings.
International matches 2009
Sri Lanka (a) 1-1, Turkmenistan (h) 1-3, Philippines (h) 3-2, Bhutan (h) 5-0, Nepal (h) 1-1, Afganistan (h) 3-1, Sri Lanka (h) 5-1.

MONGOLIA
Mongolia Football Federation, PO Box 259 Ulaan-Baatar 210646.
National Colours: White shirts, red shorts, white stockings.
International matches 2009
Guam (a) 0-1, Macao (a) 2-1, Macao (a) 0-2, Macao (h) 3-1.

NEPAL
All-Nepal Football Association, AMFA House, Ward No. 4, Bishalnagar, PO Box 12582, Kathmandu.
Founded: 1951; *National Colours:* All red.
International matches 2009
Palestine (h) 0-0, Kyrgyzstan (h) 1-1, Bhutan (h) 2-1, Maldives (a) 1-1, Afganistan (a) 3-0.

OMAN
Oman Football Association, P.O. Box 3462, Ruwi Postal Code 112.
Founded: 1978; *National Colours:* All white.
International matches 2009
Kuwait (h) 0-0, Iraq (h) 4-0, Bahrain (h) 2-0, Qatar (h) 1-0, Saudi Arabia (h) 0-0, Indonesia (h) 0-0, Kuwait (a) 1-0, Senegal (h) 2-0, Egypt (h) 0-1, Bosnia (a) 1-2, Saudi Arabia (h) 2-1, Qatar (a) 1-1, Australia (a) 0-1, Australia (h) 1-2, Brazil (h) 0-2, Singapore (a) 4-1.

PAKISTAN
Pakistan Football Federation, 6 National Hockey Stadium, Feroze Pure Road, Lahore, Pakistan.
Founded: 1948; *National Colours:* All green and white
International matches 2009
Taiwan (h) 1-1, Brunei (a) 6-0, Sri Lanka (a) 2-2, Sri Lanka (a) 0-1, Bangladesh (a) 0-0, Bhutan (h) 7-0.

PALESTINE
Palestinian Football Federation, Al-Yarmouk, Gaza.
Founded: 1928; *National Colours:* White shirts, black shorts, white stockings.
International matches 2009
Nepal (a) 0-0, Kyrgyzstan (a) 1-1, Iraq (a) 0-3, Iraq (a) 0-4, China (a) 1-3, UAE (a) 1-1.

PHILIPPINES
Philippine Football Federation, Room 405, Building V, Philsports Complex, Meralco Avenue, Pasig City, Metro Manila.
Founded: 1907; *National Colours:* All blue.
International matches 2009
Bhutan (h) 1-0, Maldives (a) 2-3, Turkmenistan (a) 0-5.

QATAR
Qatar Football Association, 7th Floor, QNOC Building, Cornich, P.O. Box 5333, Doha.
Founded: 1960; *National Colours:* All white.
International matches 2009
Saudi Arabia (a) 0-0, UAE (h) 0-0, Yemen (h) 2-1, Oman (a) 0-1, Kuwait (h) 1-0, Syria (a) 2-1, Uzbekistan (a) 0-4, Bahrain (a) 0-1, Saudi Arabia (h) 2-1, Australia (h) 0-0, Japan (a) 1-1, Oman (h) 1-1, Croatia (a) 2-3, Macedonia (a) 1-2, Congo DR (h) 2-2, Paraguay (a) 2-0, Belgium (a) 0-2, Iran (h) 3-2, North Korea (h) 0-1.

SAUDI ARABIA
Saudi Arabian Football Federation, Al Mather Quarter (Olympic Complex), Prince Faisal Bin Fahad Street, P.O. Box 5844, Riyadh 11432.
Founded: 1959; *National Colours:* White shirts, green shorts, white stockings.
International matches 2009
Qatar (h) 0-0, Yemen (h) 6-0, UAE (h) 3-0, Kuwait (h) 1-0, Oman (a) 0-0, Thailand (h) 2-1, North Korea (a) 0-1, Iraq (h) 0-0, Iran (a) 2-1, UAE (h) 3-2, Qatar (a) 1-2, China (a) 4-1, South Korea (a) 0-0, North Korea (h) 0-0, Oman (a) 1-2, Malaysia (h) 2-1, Bahrain (a) 0-0, Bahrain (h) 2-2, Tunisia (a) 1-0, Belarus (h) 1-1.

SINGAPORE
Football Association of Singapore, Jalan Besar Stadium, 100 Tyrwhitt Road, Singapore 207542.
Founded: 1892; *National Colours:* All red.
International matches 2009
Iran (a) 0-6, Jordan (a) 2-1, China (h) 1-1, Turkmenistan (h) 4-2, Vietnam (a) 2-2, Indonesia (h) 3-1, Thailand (h) 1-2, Thailand (a) 1-0, Oman (h) 1-4.

SRI LANKA
Football Federation of Sri Lanka, 100/9, Independence Avenue, Colombo 07.
Founded: 1939; *National Colours:* All white.
International matches 2009
Maldives (h) 1-1, Brunei (h) 5-1, Taiwan (h) 2-1, Pakistan (h) 2-2, Lebanon (h) 4-3, Syria (a) 0-4, India (a) 1-3, Kyrgyzstan (h) 1-4, Pakistan (h) 1-0, Bhutan (h) 6-0, Bangladesh (a) 1-2, Maldives (a) 1-5.

SYRIA
Syrian Football Federation, PO Box 421, Maysaloon Street, Damascus.
Founded: 1936; *National Colours:* All red.
International matches 2009
China (h) 3-2, Turkmenistan (h) 5-1, Kuwait (a) 3-2, Lebanon (a) 2-0, South Korea (h) 1-1, Qatar (h) 1-2, Haiti (a) 2-1, Kyrgyzstan (h) 2-0, Sri Lanka (h) 4-0, Lebanon (h) 1-0, India (a) 1-0, India (h) 1-1, Kuwait (a) 0-1, Thailand (a) 1-1, Vietnam (a) 1-0, Vietnam (h) 0-0, Malaysia (a) 1-4.

TAJIKISTAN
Tajikistan Football Federation, 22 Shotemur Ave., Dushanbe 734 025.
Founded: 1991; *National Colours:* All white.

THAILAND
The Football Association of Thailand, Gate 3, Rama I Road, Patumwan, Bangkok 10330.
Founded: 1916; *National Colours:* All red.
International matches 2009
Jordan (a) 0-0, Lebanon (h) 2-1, Iran (h) 0-0, Saudi Arabia (a) 1-2, New Zealand (h) 3-1, Syria (h) 1-1, Singapore (a) 3-1, Singapore (h) 0-1.

TIMOR-LESTE
Federacao Futebol Timor-Leste, Rua 12 de Novembro Str., Cruz, Dili.
Founded: 2002; *National Colours:* Red shirts, black shorts, red stockings.

TURKMENISTAN
Football Association of Turkmenistan, 32 Belinskiy Street, Stadium Kopetdag, Ashgabat 744 001.
Founded: 1992; *National Colours:* Green shirts, white shorts, green stockings.
International matches 2009
Syria (a) 1-5, Kuwait (a) 0-2, Maldives (a) 3-1, Bhutan (h) 7-0, Philippines (h) 5-0, Vietnam (a) 0-1, Singapore (a) 2-4.

UNITED ARAB EMIRATES

United Arab Emirates Football Association, P.O. Box 916, Abu Dhabi.
Founded: 1971; *National Colours:* All white.
International matches 2009
Yemen (h) 3-1, Qatar (a) 0-0, Saudi Arabia (h) 0-3, Malaysia (a) 5-0, Uzbekistan (h) 0-1, North Korea (a) 0-2, Saudi Arabia (a) 2-3, Germany (h) 2-7, South Korea (h) 0-2, Iran (a) 0-1, Palestine (h) 1-1, Jordan (h) 3-1, Czech Republic (h) 0-0, Iraq (h) 0-1, Kuwait (a) 0-0.

UZBEKISTAN

Uzbekistan Football Federation, Massiv Almazar Furkat Street 15/1, 700003 Tashkent, Uzbekistan.
Founded: 1946; *National Colours:* All white.
International matches 2009
UAE (a) 1-0, Azerbaijan (a) 1-1, Bahrain (h) 0-1, Qatar (h) 4-0, Australia (a) 0-2, Bosnia (h) 0-0, Japan (h) 0-1, Bahrain (a) 0-1, Iran (h) 0-0, Malaysia (h) 3-1, Malaysia (a) 3-1.

VIETNAM

Vietnam Football Federation, 18 Ly van Phuc, Dong Da District, Hanoi 844.
Founded: 1962; *National Colours:* All red.
International matches 2009
Lebanon (h) 3-1, China (a) 1-6, Kuwait (a) 1-0, Turkmenistan (h) 1-0, Singapore (h) 2-2, Syria (h) 0-1, Syria (a) 0-0.

YEMEN

Yemen Football Association, Quarter of Sport – Al Jeraf, Behind the Stadium of Ali Mushsen, Al Moreissy in the Sport, Al-Thawra City.
Founded: 1962; *National Colours:* All green.
International matches 2009
UAE (a) 1-3, Saudi Arabia (a) 0-6, Qatar (a) 1-2, Japan (a) 1-2, Hong Kong (h) 1-0, Tanzania (h) 1-1, Tanzania (h) 2-1, Bahrain (a) 0-4.

CONCACAF

ANGUILLA

Anguilla Football Association, P.O. Box 1318, The Valley, Anguilla, BWI.
National Colours: Turquoise, white, orange and blue shirts and shorts, turquoise and orange stockings.

ANTIGUA & BARBUDA

The Antigua/Barbuda Football Association, Newgate Street, P.O. Box 773, St John's.
Founded: 1928; *National Colours:* Red, black, yellow and blue shirts, black shorts and stockings.
International matches 2009
Guyana (h) 2-1, Grenada (a) 2-2.

ARUBA

Arubaanse Voetbal Bond, Ferguson Street, Z/N P.O. Box 376, Oranjestad, Aruba.
Founded: 1932; *National Colours:* Yellow shirts, blue shorts, yellow and blue stockings.

BAHAMAS

Bahamas Football Association, Plaza on the Way, West Bay Street, P.O. Box N 8434, Nassau, NP.
Founded: 1967; *National Colours:* Yellow shirts, black shorts, yellow stockings.

BARBADOS

Barbados Football Association, Hildor No. 4, 10th Avenue, P.O. Box 1362, Belleville-St. Michael, Barbados.
Founded: 1910; *National Colours:* Royal blue and gold shirts, gold shorts, white, gold and blue stockings.
International matches 2009
Grenada (h) 5-0.

BELIZE

Belize National Football Association, 26 Hummingbird Highway, Belmopan, P.O. Box 1742, Belize City.
Founded: 1980; *National Colours:* Red, white and black shirts, black shorts, red and black stockings.

International matches 2009
Honduras (n) 1-2, El Salvador (n) 1-4, Nicaragua (n) 1-1.

BERMUDA

The Bermuda Football Association, 48 Cedar Avenue, Hamilton HM12.
Founded: 1928; *National Colours:* All blue.

BRITISH VIRGIN ISLANDS

British Virgin Islands Football Association, P.O. Box 29, Road Town, Tortola, BVI.
National Colours: Gold and green shirts, green shorts, and stockings.
International matches 2009
Dominique (a) 0-4.

US VIRGIN ISLANDS

USVI Soccer Federation Inc., 54, Castle Coakley, PO Box 2346, Kingshill, St Croix 00851.
National Colours: Royal blue and gold shirts, royal blue shorts and stockings.

CANADA

The Canadian Soccer Association, Place Soccer Canada, 237 Metcalfe Street, Ottawa, ONT K2P 1R2.
Founded: 1912; *National Colours:* All red.
International matches 2009
Cyprus (a) 1-0, Guatemala (h) 3-0, Jamaica (n) 1-0, El Salvador (n) 1-0, Costa Rica (n) 2-2, Honduras (n) 0-1, Macedonia (a) 0-3, Poland (a) 0-1.

CAYMAN ISLANDS

Cayman Islands Football Association, PO Box 178 GT, Truman Bodden Sports Complex, Olympic Way Off Walkers Rd, George Town, Grand Cayman, Cayman Islands WI.
Founded: 1966; *National Colours:* Red and white shirts, blue and white shorts, white and red stockings.
International matches 2009
Jamaica (h) 1-4.

COSTA RICA

Federacion Costarricense De Futbol, Costado Norte Estatua Leon Cortes, San Jose 670-1000.
Founded: 1921; *National Colours:* Red shirts, blue shorts, white stockings.
International matches 2009
Panama (n) 3-0, Guatemala (n) 3-1, El Salvador (n) 1-0, Panama (n) 0-0, Honduras (h) 2-0, Mexico (a) 0-2, El Salvador (h) 1-0, Venezuela (a) 1-1, USA (h) 3-1, Trinidad & Tobago (a) 3-2, Venezuela (h) 1-0, El Salvador (n) 1-2, Jamaica (n) 1-0, Canada (n) 2-2, Guadeloupe (n) 5-1, Mexico (n) 1-1, Honduras (a) 0-4, Mexico (h) 0-3, El Salvador (a) 0-1, Trinidad & Tobago (h) 4-0, USA (a) 2-2, Uruguay (h) 0-1, Uruguay (a) 1-1.

CUBA

Asociacion de Futbol de Cuba, Calle 13 No. 661, Esq. C. Vedado, ZP 4, La Habana.
Founded: 1924; *National Colours:* All red, white and blue.

DOMINICA

Dominica Football Association, 33 Great Marlborough Street, Roseau.
Founded: 1970; *National Colours:* Emerald green shirts, black shorts, green stockings.
International matches 2009
British Virgin Islands (h) 4-0.

DOMINICAN REPUBLIC

Federacion Dominicana De Futbol, Centro Olimpico Juan Pablo Duarte, Ensanche Miraflores, Apartado De Correos No. 1953, Santo Domingo.
Founded: 1953; *National Colours:* Navy blue shirts, white shorts, red stockings.

EL SALVADOR

Federacion Salvadorena De Futbol, Primera Calle Poniente No. 2025, San Salvador CA1029.
Founded: 1935; *National Colours:* All blue.

International matches 2009
Nicaragua (n) 1-1, Belize (n) 4-1, Honduras (n) 0-2, Costa Rica (n) 1-0, Honduras (n) 0-1, Peru (h) 1-0, Trinidad & Tobago (h) 2-2, USA (n) 2-2, El Salvador (h) 1-0, Ecuador (h) 3-1, Jamaica (h) 0-0, Mexico (h) 2-1, Honduras (a) 0-1, Costa Rica (n) 2-1, Canada (n) 0-1, Jamaica (n) 0-1, Colombia (h) 1-2, Trinidad & Tobago (a) 0-1, USA (a) 1-2, Costa Rica (h) 1-0, Mexico (a) 0-4, Honduras (h) 0-1.

GRENADA

Grenada Football Association, P.O. Box 326, National Stadium, Queens Park, St George's, Grenada, W.I.
Founded: 1924; *National Colours:* Green and yellow striped shirts, red shorts, yellow stockings.
International matches 2009
Barbados (a) 0-5, Antigua & Barbuda (h) 2-2, USA (n) 0-4, Haiti (n) 0-2, Honduras (n) 0-4.

GUADELOUPE

Ligue Guadeloupeenne de Football, Rue de la Ville D'Orly, Bergevin, 97110, Pointe-a-Pitre.
Not affiliated to FIFA.
International matches 2009
Panama (n) 2-1, Nicaragua (n) 2-0, Mexico (n) 0-2, Costa Rica (n) 1-5.

GUATEMALA

Federacion Nacional de Futbol de Guatemala, 2a Calle 15-57, Zona 15, Boulevard Vista Hermosa, Guatemala City 01009.
Founded: 1946; *National Colours:* Blue shirts, white shorts, blue stockings.
International matches 2009
Haiti (h) 1-0, Costa Rica (n) 1-3, Panama (n) 0-1, Nicaragua (n) 0-2, Venezuela (a) 1-2, Mexico (h) 0-0, Canada (h) 0-3.

GUYANA

Guyana Football Federation, 159 Rupununi Street, Bel Air Park, P.O. Box 10727, Georgetown.
Founded: 1902; *National Colours:* Green shirts and shorts, yellow stockings.
International matches 2009
Antigua & Barbuda (h) 1-2, Surinam (a) 1-0, Netherlands Antilles (h) 1-0, Guyane (h) 1-0.

GUYANE

International matches 2009
Netherlands Antilles (h) 4-1, Surinam (a) 0-4, Guyana (h) 0-1.

HAITI

Federation Haitienne De Football, 128 Avenue Christiophe, P.O. Box 2258, Port-Au-Prince.
Founded: 1904; *National Colours:* Blue shirts, red shorts, blue stockings.
International matches 2009
Guatemala (h) 0-1, Colombia (a) 0-2, Panama (a) 0-4, Jamaica (h) 2-2, Panama (h) 1-1, Martinique (h) 0-0, Syria (h) 1-2, Honduras (n) 0-1, Grenada (n) 2-0, USA (n) 2-2, Mexico (n) 0-4.

HONDURAS

Federacion Nacional Autonoma De Futbol De Honduras, Colonia Florencia Norte, Ave Roble, Edificio Plaza America, Ave. Roble 1 y 2 Nivel, Tegucigalpa, D.C.
Founded: 1951; *National Colours:* All white.
International matches 2009
Chile (h) 2-0, Belize (n) 2-1, Nicaragua (n) 4-1, El Salvador (n) 2-0, Panama (n) 0-1, El Salvador (n) 1-0, Costa Rica (a) 0-2, Trinidad & Tobago (a) 1-1, Mexico (h) 3-1, USA (a) 1-2, El Salvador (h) 1-0, Panama (a) 2-0, Haiti (n) 1-0, USA (n) 0-2, Grenada (n) 4-0, Canada (n) 1-0, USA (n) 0-2, Costa Rica (h) 4-0, Trinidad & Tobago (h) 4-1, Mexico (a) 0-1, USA (h) 2-3, El Salvador (a) 1-0, Latvia (h) 2-1, Peru (h) 1-2 .

JAMAICA

Jamaica Football Federation Ltd, 20 St Lucia Crescent, Kingston 5.
Founded: 1910; *National Colours:* Gold shirts, black shorts, gold stockings.
International matches 2009
Nigeria (h) 0-0, Haiti (h) 2-2, El Salvador (h) 0-0, Panama (h) 3-2, Cayman Islands (a) 4-1, Canada (n) 0-1, Costa Rica (n) 0-1, El Salvador (n) 1-0, Ecuador (h) 0-0, St Kitts & Nevis (a) 1-0, South Africa (a) 0-0.

MARTINIQUE

2, Rue Saint John Perse, Nome Tartenson, BP 307, 97203 Fort de France.
Not affiliated to FIFA.
International matches 2009
Haiti (a) 0-0.

MEXICO

Federacion Mexicana De Futbol Asociacion, A.C., Colima No. 373, Colonia Roma Mexico DF 06700.
Founded: 1927; *National Colours:* Green shirts with white collar, white shorts, red stockings.
International matches 2009
Sweden (h) 0-1, USA (a) 0-2, Bolivia (h) 5-1, Costa Rica (h) 2-0, Honduras (a) 1-3, El Salvador (a) 1-2, Trinidad & Tobago (h) 2-1, Venezuela (h) 4-0, Guatemala (h) 0-0, Nicaragua (n) 2-0, Panama (n) 1-1, Guadeloupe (n) 2-0, Haiti (n) 4-0, Costa Rica (n) 1-1, USA (n) 5-0, USA (h) 2-1, Costa Rica (a) 3-0, Honduras (h) 1-0, Colombia (h) 1-2, El Salvador (h) 4-1, Trinidad & Tobago (a) 2-2.

MONSERRAT

Monserrat Football Association Inc., P.O. Box 505, Woodlands, Monserrat.
National Colours: Green shirts with black and white stripes, green shorts with white stripes, green stockings with black and white stripes.

NETHERLANDS ANTILLES

Nederlands Antiliaanse Voetbal Unie, Bonamweg 49, Curacao, NA.
Founded: 1921; *National Colours:* White shirts with red and blue stripes, red shorts with blue and white stripes, white stockings with red stripes.
International matches 2009
Guyane (h) 1-4, Guyana (h) 0-1, Surinam (a) 1-1.

NICARAGUA

Federacion Nicaraguense De Futbol, Hospital Pautista 1, Cuadra avajo, 1 cuada al Sur y 1/2, Cuadra Abajo, Managua 976.
Founded: 1931; *National Colours:* Blue shirts, white shorts, blue stockings.
International matches 2009
El Salvador (n) 1-1, Honduras (n) 1-4, Belize (n) 1-1, Guatemala (n) 2-0, Mexico (n) 0-2, Guadeloupe (n) 0-2, Panama (n) 0-4.

PANAMA

Federacion Panamena De Futbol, Estadio Rommel Fernandez, Puerta 24, Ave. Jose Aeustin Araneo, Apartado Postal 8-391, Zona 8, Panama.
Founded: 1937; *National Colours:* All red.
International matches 2009
Costa Rica (n) 0-3, Guatemala (n) 1-0, Honduras (n) 1-0, Costa Rica (n) 0-0, Trinidad & Tobago (a) 0-1, Haiti (h) 4-0, Argentina (a) 1-3, Jamaica (a) 2-3, Haiti (a) 1-1, Honduras (h) 0-2, Guadeloupe (n) 1-2, Mexico (n) 1-1, Nicaragua (n) 4-0, USA (n) 1-2.

PUERTO RICO

Federacion Puertorriquena De Futbol, P.O. Box 193590 San Juan 00919.
Founded: 1940; *National Colours:* Red, blue and white shirts and shorts, red and blue stockings.

ST KITTS & NEVIS

St Kitts & Nevis Football Association, P.O. Box 465, Warner Park, Basseterre, St Kitts, W.I.
Founded: 1932; *National Colours:* Green and yellow shirts, red shorts, yellow stockings.
International matches 2009
Trinidad & Tobago (h) 2-3, Jamaica (h) 0-1, St Vincent & the Grenadines (a) 3-0, St Vincent & the Grenadines (h) 1-1.

ST LUCIA

St Lucia National Football Association, PO Box 255, Sans Souci, Castries, St Lucia.
Founded: 1979; *National Colours:* White shirts and shorts with yellow, blue and black stripes, white, blue and yellow stockings.

ST MARTIN

Comite de Football des Iles du Nord, PO Box 811, S-M 97059.
Not affiliated to FIFA.

ST VINCENT & THE GRENADINES

St Vincent & The Grenadines Football Federation, Sharpe Street, PO Box 1278, Saint George.
Founded: 1979; *National Colours:* Green shirts with yellow border, blue shorts, yellow stockings.
International matches 2009
St Kitts & Nevis (h) 0-3, St Kitts & Nevis (a) 1-1.

SURINAM

Surinaamse Voetbal Bond, Letitia Vriesde Laan 7, P.O. Box 1223, Paramaribo.
Founded: 1920; *National Colours:* White, green and red shirts, green and white shirts and stockings.
International matches 2009
Guayana (h) 0-1, Guyane (h) 4-0, Netherlands Antilles (h) 1-1.

TRINIDAD & TOBAGO

Trinidad & Tobago Football Federation, 24–26 Dundonald Street, PO Box 400, Port of Spain.
Founded: 1908; *National Colours:* Red shirts, black shorts, white stockings.
International matches 2009
El Salvador (a) 2-2, Panama (h) 1-0, Honduras (h) 1-1, USA (a) 0-3, Costa Rica (h) 2-3, Mexico (a) 1-2, St Kitts & Nevis (a) 3-2, El Salvador (h) 1-0, Honduras (a) 1-4, USA (h) 0-1, Costa Rica (a) 0-4, Mexico (h) 2-2.

TURKS & CAICOS

Turks & Caicos Islands Football Association, P.O. Box 626, Tropicana Plaza, Leeward Highway, Providenciales.
National Colours: All white.

USA

US Soccer Federation, US Soccer House, 1801–1811 S. Prairie Avenue, Chicago, Illinois 60616.
Founded: 1913; *National Colours:* White shirts, blue shorts, white stockings.
International matches 2009
Sweden (h) 3-2, Mexico (h) 2-0, El Salvador (a) 2-2, Trinidad & Tobago (h) 3-0, Costa Rica (a) 1-3, Honduras (h) 2-1, Italy (n) 1-3, Brazil (n) 0-3, Egypt (n) 3-0, Spain (n) 2-0, Brazil (n) 2-3, Grenada (n) 4-0, Honduras (n) 2-0, Haiti (n) 2-2, Panama (n) 2-1, Honduras (n) 2-0, Mexico (n) 0-5, Mexico (a) 1-2, El Salvador (h) 2-1, Trinidad & Tobago (a) 1-0, Honduras (a) 3-2, Costa Rica (h) 2-2, Slovakia (a) 0-1, Denmark (a) 1-3.

OCEANIA

AMERICAN SAMOA

American Samoa Football Association, P.O. Box 282, Pago Pago AS 96799.
National Colours: Navy blue shirts, white shorts, red stockings.

COOK ISLANDS

Cook Islands Football Association, Victoria Road, Tupapa, P.O. Box 29, Avarua, Rarotonga, Cook Islands.
Founded: 1971; *National Colours:* Green shirts with white sleeves, green shorts, white stockings.
International matches 2009
Tonga (a) 1-1, Tonga (a) 2-1.

FIJI

Fiji Football Association, PO Box 2514, Government Buildings, Suva.
Founded: 1938; *National Colours:* White shirts, blue shorts and stockings.

NEW CALEDONIA

Federation Caledonienne de Football, 7 bis, Rue Suffren Quartier latin, BP 760, 99845 Noumea, New Caledonia.
Founded: 1928; *National Colours:* Grey shirts, red shorts, grey stockings.

NEW ZEALAND

New Zealand Soccer Inc., PO Box 301 043, Albany, Auckland, New Zealand.
Founded: 1891; *National Colours:* All white.
International matches 2009
Thailand (a) 1-3, Tanzania (a) 1-2, Botswana (a) 0-0, Italy (a) 3-4, Spain (h) 0-5, South Africa (a) 0-2, Iraq (a) 0-0, Jordan (a) 3-1, Bahrain (a) 0-0, Bahrain (h) 1-0.

PAPUA NEW GUINEA

Papua New Guinea Football Association, PO Box 957, Room II Level I, Haus Tisa, Lae.
Founded: 1962; *National Colours:* Red and yellow shirts, black shorts, yellow stockings.

SAMOA

The Samoa Football Soccer Federation, P.O. Box 960, Apia.
Founded: 1968; *National Colours:* Blue, white and red shirts, blue and white shorts, red and blue stockings.

SOLOMON ISLANDS

Solomon Islands Football Federation, PO Box 854, Honiara, Solomon Islands.
Founded: 1978; *National Colours:* Gold and blue shirts, blue and white shorts, white and blue stockings.

TAHITI

Federation Tahitienne de Football, Rue Coppenrath Stade de Fautana, PO Box 50858 Pirae 98716.
Founded: 1989; *National Colours:* Red shirts, white shorts, red stockings.

TONGA

Tonga Football Association, Tungi Arcade, Taufa'Ahau Road, P.O. Box 852, Nuku'Alofa, Tonga.
Founded: 1965; *National Colours:* Red shirts, white shorts, red stockings.
International matches 2009
Cook Islands (h) 1-1, Cook Islands (h) 1-2.

TUVALU

Not affiliated to FIFA.

VANUATU

Vanuatu Football Federation, P.O. Box 266, Port Vila, Vanuatu.
Founded: 1934; *National Colours:* Gold and black shirts, black shorts, gold and black stockings.

AFRICA

ALGERIA

Federation Algerienne De Foot-ball, Chemin Ahmed Ouaked, Boite Postale No. 39, Dely-Ibrahim-Alger.
Founded: 1962; *National Colours:* Green shirts, white shorts, green stockings.
International matches 2009
Benin (h) 2-1, Rwanda (a) 0-0, Egypt (h) 3-1, Zambia (a) 2-0, Uruguay (h) 1-0, Zambia (h) 1-0, Rwanda (h) 3-1, Egypt (a) 0-2, Egypt (n) 1-0.

ANGOLA

Federation Angolaise De Football, Compl. da Cidadela Desportiva, B.P. 3449, Luanda.
Founded: 1979; *National Colours:* Red shirts, black shorts, red stockings.
International matches 2009
Mali (a) 0-4, Cape Verde Islands (h) 0-1, Morocco (h) 0-2, Namibia (h) 0-0, Guinea (h) 0-0, Togo (h) 2-0, Senegal (h) 1-1, Cape Verde Islands (h) 1-1, Malta (a) 2-1, Cameroon (h) 0-0, Congo (h) 1-1, Ghana (h) 0-0, Estonia (h) 0-1.

BENIN

Federation Beninoise De Football, Stade Rene Pleven d'Akpakpa, B.P. 965, Cotonou 01.
Founded: 1962; *National Colours:* Green shirts, Yellow shorts, red stockings.
International matches 2009
Algeria (a) 1-2, Ghana (a) 0-1, Sudan (h) 1-0, Mali (a) 1-3, Gabon (a) 1-1, Mali (h) 1-1, Ghana (h) 1-0, Sudan (a) 2-1.

BOTSWANA

Botswana Football Association, P.O. Box 1396, Gaborone.
Founded: 1970; *National Colours:* Blue, white and black striped shirts, blue, white and black shorts and stockings.
International matches 2009
Namibia (a) 0-0, Lesotho (a) 0-0, New Zealand (h) 0-0, Iran (h) 1-1, China (a) 1-4, Comoros (a) 0-0, Swaziland (h) 1-0, Seychelles (a) 2-0, Zimbabwe (a) 0-1.

BURKINA FASO

Federation Burkinabe De Foot-Ball, 01 B.P. 57, Ouagadougou 01.
Founded: 1960; *National Colours:* All green, red and white.
International matches 2009
Togo (a) 1-1, Guinea (h) 4-2, Malawi (a) 1-0, Ivory Coast (h) 2-3, Mali (a) 0-3, Ivory Coast (a) 0-5, Guinea (a) 2-1, Malawi (h) 1-0.

BURUNDI

Federation De Football Du Burundi, Bulding Nyogozi, Boulevard de l'Uprona, B.P. 3426, Bujumbura.
Founded: 1948; *National Colours:* Red and white shirts, white and red shorts, green stockings.
International matches 2009
Djibouti (h) 4-0, Zambia (h) 1-1, Sudan (h) 1-0, Kenya (h) 0-1, Uganda (a) 0-5, Tanzania (h) 2-3, Uganda (a) 0-2.

CAMEROON

Federation Camerounaise De Football, B.P. 1116, Yaounde.
Founded: 1959; *National Colours:* Green shirts, red shorts, yellow stockings.
International matches 2009
Guinea (h) 3-1, Togo (a) 0-1, Morocco (h) 0-0, Austria (a) 2-0, Gabon (a) 2-0, Gabon (h) 2-1, Togo (h) 3-0, Angola (a) 0-0, Morocco (a) 2-0.

CAPE VERDE ISLANDS

Federacao Cabo-Verdiana De Futebol, Praia Cabo Verde, FCF CX, P.O. Box 234, Praia.
Founded: 1982; *National Colours:* Blue and white shirts and shorts, blue and red stockings.
International matches 2009
Angola (a) 1-0, Equatorial Guinea (h) 5-0, Malta (a) 2-0, Angola (a) 1-1.

CENTRAL AFRICAN REPUBLIC

Federation Centrafricaine De Football, Immeuble Soca Constructa, B.P. 344, Bangui.
Founded: 1937; *National Colours:* Blue and white shirts, white shorts, blue stockings.

CHAD

Federation Tchadienne de Football, B.P. 886, N'Djamena.
Founded: 1962; *National Colours:* Blue shirts, yellow shorts, red stockings.

COMOROS

Comoros FA, BP 798, Moroni.
Founded: 1979.
International matches 2009
Botswana (h) 0-0, Seychelles (a) 2-1, Swaziland (a) 0-3.

CONGO

Federation Congolaise De Football, 80 Rue Eugene-Etienne, Centre Ville, PO Box 11, Brazzaville.
Founded: 1962; *National Colours:* Green shirts, yellow shorts, red stockings.
International matches 2009
Morocco (a) 1-1, North Korea (a) 0-0, Angola (a) 1-1.

CONGO DR

Federation Congolaise De Football-Association, Av. de l'Enseignemt 210, C/Kasa-Vubu, Kinshasa 1.
Founded: 1919; *National Colours:* Blue and yellow shirts, yellow and blue shorts, white and blue stockings.
International matches 2009
Tanzania (a) 2-0, Namibia (a) 0-4, Senegal (h) 1-2, Qatar (h) 2-2.

DJIBOUTI

Federation Djiboutienne de Football, Stade el Haoj Hassan Gouled, B.P. 2694, Djibouti.
Founded: 1977; *National Colours:* Green shirts, white shorts, blue stockings.
International matches 2009
Burundi (a) 0-4, Sudan (h) 1-1, Kenya (h) 1-5, Ethiopia (h) 0-5, Kenya (a) 0-2, Zambia (a) 0-8.

EGYPT

Egyptian Football Association, 5 Gabalaya Street, Guezira, El Borg Post Office, Cairo.
Founded: 1921; *National Colours:* Red shirts, white shorts, black stockings.
International matches 2009
Kenya (h) 1-0, Ghana (h) 2-2, Zambia (n) 1-1, Oman (a) 1-0, Algeria (a) 1-3, Brazil (n) 2-4, Italy (n) 1-0, USA (n) 0-3, Rwanda (h) 3-0, Guinea (h) 3-3, Rwanda (a) 1-0, Mauritius (h) 4-0, Zambia (a) 1-0, Tanzania (h) 5-1, Algeria (h) 2-0, Algeria (n) 0-1.

ERITREA

The Eritrean National Football Federation, Sematat Avenue 29–31, P.O. Box 3665, Asmara.
National Colours: Blue shirts, red shorts, green stockings.
International matches 2009
Zimbabwe (a) 0-0, Rwanda (h) 1-2, Somalia (h) 3-1.

ETHIOPIA

Ethiopia Football Federation, Addis Ababa Stadium, P.O. Box 1080, Addis Ababa.
Founded: 1943; *National Colours:* Green shirts, yellow shorts, red stockings.
International matches 2009
Djibouti (a) 5-0, Zambia (h) 0-1, Kenya (a) 0-2.

GABON

Federation Gabonaise De Football, B.P. 181, Libreville.
Founded: 1962; *National Colours:* Green, yellow and blue shirts, blue and yellow shorts, white stockings with tri-colour trims.
International matches 2009
Morocco (a) 2-1, Togo (h) 3-0, Benin (h) 1-1, Cameroon (h) 0-2, Cameroon (a) 1-2, Morocco (h) 3-1, Togo (a) 0-1.

GAMBIA

Gambia Football Association, Independence Stadium, Bakau, P.O. Box 523, Banjul.
Founded: 1952; *National Colours:* All red, blue and white.

GHANA

Ghana Football Association, National Sports Council, P.O. Box 1272, Accra.
Founded: 1957; *National Colours:* All yellow.

International matches 2009
Egypt (a) 2-2, Benin (h) 1-0, Uganda (h) 2-1, Mali (a) 2-0, Sudan (a) 2-0, Zambia (h) 4-1, Sudan (h) 2-0, Japan (a) 3-4, Argentina (a) 0-2, Benin (a) 0-1, Mali (h) 2-2, Angola (a) 0-0.

GUINEA
Federation Guineenne De Football, P.O. Box 3645, Conakry.
Founded: 1959; *National Colours:* Red shirts, yellow shorts, green stockings.
International matches 2009
Cameroon (a) 1-3, Burkina Faso (a) 2-4, Ivory Coast (h) 1-2, Angola (a) 0-0, Malawi (h) 2-1, Egypt (a) 3-3, Malawi (a) 1-2, Burkina Faso (h) 1-2, Ivory Coast (a) 0-3.

GUINEA-BISSAU
Federacao De Football Da Guinea-Bissau, Alto Bandim (Nova Sede), PO Box 375 Bissau 1035.
Founded: 1974; *National Colours:* Red, green and yellow shirts, green and yellow shorts, red, green and yellow stockings.

GUINEA, EQUATORIAL
Federacion Ecuatoguineana De Futbol, c/P Patricio Lumumba (Estadio La Paz), Malabo 1071.
Founded: 1986; *National Colours:* All red.
International matches 2009
Cape Verde Islands (a) 0-5, Estonia (a) 0-3.

IVORY COAST
Federation Ivoirienne De Football, 01 PO Box 1202, Abidjan 01.
Founded: 1960; *National Colours:* Orange shirts, black shorts, green stockings.
International matches 2009
Turkey (a) 1-1, Malawi (h) 5-0, Guinea (a) 2-1, Burkina Faso (a) 3-2, Tunisia (a) 0-0, Burkina Faso (h) 5-0, Malawi (a) 1-1, Guinea (h) 3-0, Germany (a) 2-2.

KENYA
Kenya Football Federation, Nyayo National Stadium, P.O. Box 40234, Nairobi.
Founded: 1960; *National Colours:* All red.
International matches 2009
Zambia (a) 0-0, Djibouti (a) 5-1, Burundi (a) 1-0, Tanzania (h) 2-1, Uganda (a) 0-1, Egypt (a) 0-1, Iran (a) 0-1, Tunisia (h) 1-2, Nigeria (a) 0-3, Mozambique (h) 2-1, Bahrain (a) 1-2, Mozambique (a) 0-1, Tunisia (a) 0-1, Kuwait (a) 0-5, Nigeria (h) 2-3, Zambia (h) 0-2, Djibouti (h) 2-0, Ethiopia (h) 2-0, Uganda (h) 0-1.

LESOTHO
Lesotho Football Association, P.O. Box 1879, Maseru-100, Lesotho.
Founded: 1932; *National Colours:* Blue shirts, green shorts, white stockings.
International matches 2009
Botswana (h) 0-0, Swaziland (a) 1-1, Swaziland (a) 1-1, Zimbabwe (a) 1-1, Malaysia (a) 0-5, Zimbabwe (a) 2-2, Mauritius (h) 1-0.

LIBERIA
Liberia Football Association, Broad and Center Streets, PO Box 10-1066, Monrovia 1000.
Founded: 1936; *National Colours:* Blue shirts, white shorts, red stockings.

LIBYA
Libyan Football Federation, Asayadi Street, Near Janat Al-Areet, P.O. Box 5137, Tripoli.
Founded: 1963; *National Colours:* Green and black shirts, black shorts and stockings.
International matches 2009
Uruguay (h) 2-3, Kuwait (a) 1-1.

MADAGASCAR
Federation Malagasy de Football, Immeuble Preservatrice Vie-Lot IBF-9B, Rue Rabearivelo-Antsahavola, PO Box 4409, Antananarivo 101.

Founded: 1961; *National Colours:* Red and green shirts, white and green shorts, green and white stockings.
International matches 2009
South Africa (a) 0-1.

MALAWI
Football Association of Malawi, Mpira House, Old Chileka Road, P.O. Box 865, Blantyre.
Founded: 1966; *National Colours:* Red shirts, white shorts, red and black stockings.
International matches 2009
Mozambique (a) 0-2, Uganda (a) 1-2, Ivory Coast (a) 0-5, Rwanda (h) 2-0, Guinea (a) 1-2, Swaziland (h) 3-1, Guinea (h) 2-1, Ivory Coast (h) 1-1, Mozambique (h) 0-1, Ivory Coast (h) 1-1, Burkina Faso (a) 0-1, Mozambique (a) 1-0.

MALI
Federation Malienne De Football, Avenue du Mali, Hamdallaye ACI 2000, PO Box 1020, Bamako 12582.
Founded: 1960; *National Colours:* Green shirts, yellow shorts, red stockings.
International matches 2009
Angola (h) 4-0, Sudan (a) 1-1, Ghana (h) 0-2, Benin (h) 3-1, Burkina Faso (h) 3-0, Benin (a) 1-1, Sudan (h) 1-0, Ghana (a) 2-2, North Korea (h) 0-1.

MAURITANIA
Federation De Foot-Ball De La Rep. Islamique De Mauritanie, B.P. 566, Nouakchott.
Founded: 1961; *National Colours:* Green and yellow shirts, yellow shorts, green stockings.

MAURITIUS
Mauritius Football Association, Chancery House, 2nd Floor Nos. 303–305, 14 Lislet Geoffroy Street, Port Louis.
Founded: 1952; *National Colours:* All red.
International matches 2009
South Africa (a) 0-2, Egypt (a) 0-4, Zimbabwe (a) 0-3, Lesotho (a) 0-1.

MOROCCO
Federation Royale Marocaine De Football, 51 Bis Av. Ibn Sina, PO Box 51, Agdal, Rabat 10 000.
Founded: 1955; *National Colours:* All green white and red.
International matches 2009
Czech Republic (h) 0-0, Gabon (h) 1-2, Angola (a) 2-0, Cameroon (a) 0-0, Togo (h) 0-0, Congo (h) 1-1, Togo (a) 1-1, Gabon (a) 1-3, Cameroon (h) 0-2.

MOZAMBIQUE
Federacao Mocambicana De Futebol, Av. Samora Machel 11-2, Caixa Postal 1467, Maputo.
Founded: 1978; *National Colours:* Red shirts, black shorts, red and black stockings.
International matches 2009
Malawi (h) 2-0, Nigeria (h) 0-0, Tunisia (a) 0-2, Kenya (a) 1-2, Swaziland (h) 1-0, Kenya (h) 1-0, Nigeria (a) 0-1, Malawi (a) 1-0, Zambia (h) 0-2, Tunisia (h) 1-0, Malawi (h) 0-1.

NAMIBIA
Namibia Football Association, Abraham Mashego Street 8521, Katurua Council of Churches in Namibia, P.O. Box 1345, Windhoek 9000, Namibia.
Founded: 1990; *National Colours:* All red.
International matches 2009
Botswana (h) 0-0, Lebanon (a) 1-1, Angola (a) 0-0, Congo DR (h) 4-0, Swaziland (h) 1-1, Zambia (h) 0-1.

NIGER
Federation Nigerienne De Football, Rue de la Tapoa, PO Box 10299, Niamey.
Founded: 1967; *National Colours:* Orange shirts, white shorts, green stockings.

NIGERIA
Nigeria Football Association, Plot 2033, Olusegun, Obasanjo Way, Zone 7, Wuse Abuja, PO Box 5101 Garki, Abuja, Nigeria.

Founded: 1945; *National Colours:* All green and white.
International matches 2009
Jamaica (h) 0-0, Mozambique (a) 0-0, Republic of Ireland (a) 1-1, France (a) 1-0, Kenya (h) 3-0, Tunisia (a) 0-0, Tunisia (h) 2-2, Mozambique (h) 1-0, Kenya (a) 3-2.

RWANDA

Federation Rwandaise De Football Amateur, B.P. 2000, Kigali.
Founded: 1972; *National Colours:* Red, green and yellow shirts, green shorts, red stockings.
International matches 2009
Uganda (a) 0-5, Somalia (a) 3-0, Tanzania (a) 0-2, Algeria (h) 0-0, Malawi (a) 0-2, Zambia (a) 0-1, Egypt (a) 0-3, Tanzania (h) 1-2, Egypt (h) 0-1, Algeria (a) 1-3, Zambia (h) 0-0, Somalia (a) 1-0, Eritrea (a) 2-1, Zimbabwe (a) 1-0, Zimbabwe (h) 4-1, Uganda (a) 0-2.

SENEGAL

Federation Senegalaise De Football, Stade Leopold Sedar Senghor, Route De L'Aeroport De Yoff, B.P. 130 21, Dakar.
Founded: 1960; *National Colours:* All white and green.
International matches 2009
Oman (a) 0-2, Iran (a) 1-1, Congo DR (a) 2-1, Angola (a) 1-1, South Korea (a) 0-2.

SEYCHELLES

Seychelles Football Federation, P.O. Box 843, People's Stadium, Victoria-Mahe, Seychelles.
Founded: 1979; *National Colours:* Red and green shirts and shorts, red stockings.
International matches 2009
Swaziland (a) 1-2, Comoros (h) 1-2, Botswana (h) 0-2.

ST THOMAS AND PRINCIPE

Federation Santomense De Futebol, Rua Ex-Joao de Deus No. QXXIII-426/26, PO Box 440, Sao Tome.
Founded: 1975; *National Colours:* Green and red shirts, yellow shorts, green stockings.

SIERRA LEONE

Sierra Leone Football Association, 21 Battery Street, Kingtorn, P.O. Box 672, National Stadium, Brookfields, Freetown.
Founded: 1967; *National Colours:* Green and blue shirts, green, blue and white shorts and stockings.
International matches 2009
Syria (a) 0-6.

SOMALIA

Somali Football Federation, PO Box 222, Mogadishu BN 03040.
Founded: 1951; *National Colours:* Sky blue and white shirts and shorts, white and sky blue stockings.
International matches 2009
Tunisia (h) 1-0, Rwanda (a) 0-3, Uganda (a) 0-4, Rwanda (h) 0-1, Zimbabwe (a) 0-2, Egypt (a) 1-3.

SOUTH AFRICA

South African Football Association, First National Bank Stadium, PO Box 910, Johannesburg 2000, South Africa.
Founded: 1991; *National Colours:* White shirts with yellow striped sleeves, white shorts with yellow stripes, white stockings.
International matches 2009
Zambia (h) 1-0, Chile (h) 0-2, Norway (h) 2-1, Portugal (a) 0-2, Mauritius (h) 2-0, Poland (h) 1-0, Serbia (h) 1-3, Iraq (h) 0-0, New Zealand (h) 2-0, Spain (h) 0-2, Brazil (h) 0-1, Spain (h) 2-3, Germany (a) 0-2, Republic of Ireland (a) 0-1, Madagascar (h) 1-0, Norway (a) 0-1, Iceland (a) 0-1, Japan (h) 0-0, Jamaica (h) 0-0.

SUDAN

Sudan Football Association, Bladia Street, Khartoum.
Founded: 1936; *National Colours:* Red shirts, white shorts, black stockings.
International matches 2009
Djibouti (a) 1-1, Burundi (a) 0-1, Zambia (a) 2-0, Uganda (h) 0-2, Mali (h) 1-1, Tunisia (a) 0-4, Benin (a) 0-1, Ghana (h) 0-2, Ghana (a) 0-2, Mali (a) 0-1, Benin (a) 1-2.

SWAZILAND

National Football Association of Swaziland, Sigwaca House, Plot 582, Sheffield Road, PO Box 641, Mbabane H100.
Founded: 1968: *National Colours:* Blue shirts, gold shorts, red stockings.
International matches 2009
Seychelles (h) 2-1, Botswana (a) 0-1, Comoros (h) 3-0, Lesotno (h) 1-1, Lesotho (h) 1-1, Malawi (a) 1-3, Mozambique (a) 0-1, Namibia (a) 1-1.

TANZANIA

Football Association of Tanzania, Uhuru/Shaurimoyo Road, Karume Memorial Stadium, P.O. Box 1574, Ilala/Dar Es Salaam.
Founded: 1930; *National Colours:* Green, yellow and blue shirts, black shorts, green stockings with horizontal stripe.
International matches 2009
Somalia (h) 0-1, Rwanda (a) 2-0, Uganda (a) 1-2, Kenya (a) 1-2, Burundi (h) 3-2, Zimbabwe (h) 0-0, Congo DR (h) 0-2, New Zealand (h) 2-1, Rwanda (a) 2-1, Egypt (a) 1-5, Yemen (a) 0-1, Yemen (a) 1-2.

TOGO

Federation Togolaise De Football, C.P. 5, Lome.
Founded: 1960; *National Colours:* White shirts, green shorts, red stockings with yellow and green stripes.
International matches 2009
Burkina Faso (h) 1-1, Cameroon (h) 1-0, Gabon (a) 0-3, Morocco (a) 0-0, Angola (a) 0-2, Morocco (h) 1-1, Cameroon (a) 0-3, Japan (a) 0-5, Gabon (h) 1-0.

TUNISIA

Federation Tunisienne De Football, Maison des Federations Sportives, Cite Olympique, Tunis 1003.
Founded: 1956; *National Colours:* Red shirts, white shorts, red stockings.
International matches 2009
Holland (h) 1-1, Kenya (a) 2-1, Sudan (h) 4-0, Mozambique (h) 2-0, Nigeria (h) 0-0, Ivory Coast (h) 0-0, Nigeria (a) 2-2, Kenya (h) 1-0, Saudi Arabia (h) 0-1, Mozambique (a) 0-1.

UGANDA

Federation of Uganda Football Associations, Plot No. 879, Kyadondo Block 8, Mengo Wakaliga Road, P.O. Box 22518, Kampala.
Founded: 1924; *National Colours:* All yellow, red and white.
International matches 2009
Rwanda (h) 4-0, Somalia (h) 4-0, Tanzania (h) 2-1, Burundi (h) 5-0, Kenya (h) 1-0, Sudan (a) 2-0, Malawi (h) 2-1, Ghana (a) 1-2, Burundi (a) 2-0, Kenya (a) 1-0, Rwanda (h) 2-0.

ZAMBIA

Football Association of Zambia, Football House, Alick Nkhata Road, P.O. Box 34751, Lusaka.
Founded: 1929; *National Colours:* White and green shirts, green and white shorts, white and green stockings.
International matches 2009
Kenya (h) 0-0, Burundi (a) 1-1, Sudan (h) 0-2, South Africa (a) 0-1, Egypt (a) 1-1, Rwanda (h) 1-0, Algeria (h) 0-2, Ghana (a) 1-4, Algeria (a) 0-1, Egypt (h) 1-1, Namibia (a) 1-0, Mozambique (a) 2-0, Zimbabwe (a) 1-3, Rwanda (a) 0-0, Kenya (a) 2-0, Ethiopia (a) 1-0, Djibouti (h) 8-0, North Korea (h) 4-1.

ZIMBABWE

Zimbabwe Football Association, P.O. Box CY 114, Causeway, Harare.
Founded: 1965; *National Colours:* All green and gold.
International matches 2009
Tanzania (a) 0-0, Jordan (h) 0-2, Lesotho (h) 1-1, Mauritius (h) 3-0, Lesotho (h) 2-2, Botswana (h) 1-0, Zambia (h) 3-1, Eritrea (h) 0-0, Somalia (a) 2-0, Rwanda (h) 0-1, Rwanda (a) 1-4.

WORLD CUP 2010 QUALIFYING COMPETITION

EUROPE

* *Denotes player sent off.*

GROUP 1

Tirana, 6 September 2008, 13,522
Albania (0) 0   Sweden (0) 0
Albania: Beqaj; Vangeli, Dallku, Curri, Beqiri, Skela (Teli 82), Lala, Hyka, Duro, Cana, Salihi (Berisha 75).
Sweden: Isaksson; Wendt (Stoor 78), Mellberg, Majstorovic, Hansson, Nilsson M, Linderoth (Larsson S 6), Kallstrom (Holmen 84), Andersson D, Larsson H, Ibrahimovic.
Referee: Mallenco (Spain).

Budapest, 6 September 2008, 18,984
Hungary (0) 0   Denmark (0) 0
Hungary: Babos; Vanczak, Szelesi, Juhasz, Bodnar, Vadocz, Huszti (Rudolf 90), Hajnal, Dzsudzsak (Torghelle 46), Dardai, Gera.
Denmark: Andersen; Christopher Poulsen, Laursen, Jacobsen L, Agger, Christian Poulsen, Jensen D, Vingaard (Borring 61), Tomasson (Retov 68), Rommedahl, Bendtner (Nygaard 87).
Referee: Hamer (Luxembourg).

Ta'Qali, 6 September 2008, 11,000
Malta (0) 0
Portugal (1) 4 *(Said 25 (og), Hugo Almeida 61, Simao 71, Nani 78)*
Malta: Haber; Said, Dimech, Pace, Briffa, Bajada, Woods (Mallia 59), Scerri (Barbara 70), Sammut, Mifsud, Agius G (Fenech 80).
Portugal: Quim; Ricardo Carvalho, Pepe, Bosingwa, Antunes, Raul Meireles, Nani, Deco, Carlos Martins (Maniche 63), Simao (Joao Moutinho 75), Hugo Almeida (Nuno Gomes 67).
Referee: Blom (Holland).

Tirana, 10 September 2008, 7400
Albania (1) 3 *(Dallku 45, 90, Duro 84)*   **Malta (0) 0**
Albania: Beqaj; Curri, Dallku, Duro (Berisha 86), Hyka, Lala, Skela, Agolli, Cana, Bulku (Beqiri 54), Bogdani (Salihi 73).
Malta: Haber; Dimech, Xuereb, Bajada, Barbara (Frendo 46), Briffa, Pace, Agius G (Scerri 85), Mifsud, Sammut, Schembri.
Referee: Schorgenhofer (Austria).

Lisbon, 10 September 2008, 33,000
Portugal (1) 2 *(Nani 42, Deco 86 (pen))*
Denmark (0) 3 *(Bendtner 63, Christian Poulsen 88, Jensen D 90)*
Portugal: Quim; Bosingwa, Pepe, Ricardo Carvalho, Paulo Ferreira, Raul Meireles, Nani (Joao Moutinho 87), Maniche, Hugo Almeida (Danny 72), Deco, Simao (Nuno Gomes 72).
Denmark: Andersen; Christian Poulsen, Laursen, Agger, Andreasen (Bernburg 87), Jacobsen L (Silberbauer 46), Jensen D, Lovenkrands (Borring 72), Tomasson, Rommedahl, Bendtner.
Referee: Webb (England).

Stockholm, 10 September 2008, 28,177
Sweden (0) 2 *(Kallstrom 55, Holmen 64)*
Hungary (0) 1 *(Rudolf 90)*
Sweden: Isaksson; Hansson, Mellberg, Majstorovic, Holmen, Andersson D, Nilsson M, Larsson S, Kallstrom, Ibrahimovic (Rosenberg 81), Larsson H.
Hungary: Babos; Vanczak, Szelesi, Juhasz, Hajnal, Dardai (Rudolf 70), Bodor (Dzsudzsak 80), Vadocz, Huszti, Gera, Torghelle.
Referee: Meyer (Germany).

Copenhagen, 11 October 2008, 33,124
Denmark (2) 3 *(Larsen 9, 47, Agger 29 (pen))*
Malta (0) 0
Denmark: Sorensen; Bogelund, Laursen, Agger, Kahlenberg (Krohn-Dehli 60), Christian Poulsen, Jensen D (Kristensen 82), Rasmussen T, Rommedahl, Nordstrand, Larsen (Rasmussen M 76).

Malta: Haber; Dimech, Caruana, Azzopardi, Xuereb, Pace, Briffa, Schembri (Barbara 60), Mifsud (Scerri 87), Agius G (Nwoko 80), Woods.
Referee: Paniashvili (Georgia).

Budapest, 11 October 2008, 18,000
Hungary (0) 2 *(Torghelle 49, Juhasz 81)*   **Albania (0) 0**
Hungary: Fulop; Vanczak, Szelesi, Juhasz, Bodnar, Huszti (Vadocz 86), Halmosi, Hajnal (Buzsaky 61), Dzsudzsak, Dardai, Torghelle (Rudolf 90).
Albania: Beqaj; Vangeli (Hyka 54) (Bulku 83), Dallku, Curri, Beqiri (Kapllani 74), Skela, Lala, Duro, Cana, Agolli, Bogdani.
Referee: Circhetta (Switzerland).

Stockholm, 11 October 2008, 33,241
Sweden (0) 0   Portugal (0) 0
Sweden: Isaksson; Majstorovic, Hansson, Safari, Nilsson M, Larsson S, Kallstrom, Holmen, Andersson D, Elmander, Ibrahimovic.
Portugal: Quim; Fernando Meira, Pepe, Paulo Ferreira, Bruno Alves, Bosingwa, Raul Meireles, Nani (Danny 86), Joao Moutinho, Cristiano Ronaldo, Hugo Almeida (Quaresma 65).
Referee: Rosetti (Italy).

Ta'Qali, 15 October 2008, 4797
Malta (0) 0   Hungary (1) 1 *(Torghelle 23)*
Malta: Haber; Xuereb, Dimech, Caruana (Briffa 36), Pace, Barbara (Nwoko 77), Bajada, Woods, Schembri, Scerri (Agius G 63), Mifsud.
Hungary: Fulop; Bodnar, Vanczak, Juhasz, Halmosi, Dzsudzsak (Buzsaky 70), Dardai (Toth 86), Bodor, Huszti, Gera, Torghelle.
Referee: Valgeirsson (Iceland).

Braga, 15 October 2008, 29,500
Portugal (0) 0   Albania (0) 0
Portugal: Quim; Miguel (Maniche 75), Pepe, Paulo Ferreira, Bruno Alves, Manuel Fernandes, Raul Meireles, Joao Moutinho (Quaresma 55), Hugo Almeida, Danny (Nani 55), Cristiano Ronaldo.
Albania: Beqaj; Vangeli, Curri, Beqiri (Teli* 24), Skela, Lala, Duro (Berisha 77), Bulku, Agolli, Cana, Bogdani (Vrapi 46).
Referee: Kircher (Germany).

Ta'Qali, 11 February 2009, 2041
Malta (0) 0   Albania (0) 0
Malta: Haber; Dimech, Muscat A (Failla 81), Bajada, Agius A, Agius G (Fenech 87), Schembri, Scerri (Briffa 69), Sammut, Mifsud, Cohen.
Albania: Hidi; Beqiri, Vrapi, Dallku, Curri, Agolli (Vangeli 46) (Lila 80), Skela, Duro, Bulku, Lika, Bogdani (Berisha 79).
Referee: Deaconu (Romania).

Tirana, 28 March 2009, 12,000
Albania (1) 0   Hungary (1) 1 *(Torghelle 38)*
Albania: Hidi; Dallku, Vangeli, Curri, Skela, Lala, Duro, Cana, Lika (Bakaj 70), Salihi, Berisha.
Hungary: Babos; Vasko, Bodor, Vanczak, Szelesi, Dardai, Huszti, Halmosi (Gera 90), Hajnal (Vadocz 80), Torghelle (Priskin 86), Rudolf.
Referee: Kuipers (Holland).

Ta'Qali, 28 March 2009, 6235
Malta (0) 0
Denmark (2) 3 *(Larsen 12, 23, Nordstrand 89)*
Malta: Haber; Dimech, Caruana (Muscat A 69), Pace, Briffa (Barbara 84), Bajada, Bogdanovic, Schembri (Agius G 72), Mifsud, Agius A, Cohen.
Denmark: Sorensen; Jacobsen L, Kroldrup, Jacobsen M, Agger, Jorgensen, Christian Poulsen, Jensen D (Andreasen 63), Rommedahl, Larsen (Nordstrand 82), Bendtner (Borring 30).
Referee: Mikulski (Poland).

Porto, 28 March 2009, 40,200
Portugal (0) 0   Sweden (0) 0
Portugal: Eduardo; Ricardo Carvalho, Pepe, Bruno Alves, Bosingwa (Rolando 46), Tiago (Deco 62), Duda, Raul Meireles, Simao, Danny (Hugo Almeida 66), Cristiano Ronaldo.
Sweden: Isaksson; Johansson, Mellberg, Majstorovic, Elm R, Anders Svensson (Larsson S 81), Kallstrom, Holmen (Wilhelmsson 58), Nilsson M, Larsson H, Elmander (Berg 86).
Referee: De Bleeckere (Belgium).

Copenhagen, 1 April 2009, 24,320
Denmark (2) 3 *(Andreasen 31, Larsen 38, Christian Poulsen 80)*
Albania (0) 0
Denmark: Sorensen; Jacobsen L, Jacobsen M, Andreasen, Agger, Christian Poulsen, Kahlenberg, Jorgensen (Poulsen J 46), Jensen D (Bendtner 34), Rommedahl (Borring 71), Larsen.
Albania: Hidi; Vangeli, Dallku, Curri, Skela, Bylykbashi, Duro, Bulku (Salihi 46), Agolli, Lika, Berisha (Memelli 85).
Referee: Skomina (Slovenia).

Budapest, 1 April 2009, 35,800
Hungary (1) 3 *(Hajnal 6, Gera 80, Juhasz 90)*   **Malta (0) 0**
Hungary: Fulop; Bodnar, Vanczak, Szelesi, Juhasz, Huszti, Halmosi (Toth 90), Hajnal (Gera 46), Dzsudzsak (Vadocz 79), Bodor, Torghelle.
Malta: Haber; Caruana, Muscat A, Briffa (Fenech 85), Bajada, Agius A, Bogdanovic (Barbara 89), Agius G, Schembri (Scerri 46), Mifsud, Cohen.
Referee: Sukhina (Russia).

Tirana, 6 June 2009, 13,320
Albania (1) 1 *(Bogdani 28)*
Portugal (1) 2 *(Hugo Almeida 27, Bruno Alves 90)*
Albania: Hidi; Vrapi, Vangeli, Curri, Beqiri, Skela (Bylykbashi 90), Duro (Berisha 87), Cana, Bulku, Agolli, Bogdani (Salihi 65).
Portugal: Eduardo; Pepe, Ricardo Carvalho (Nani 76), Bosingwa, Bruno Alves, Raul Meireles, Duda, Deco, Boa Morte (Simao 46), Cristiano Ronaldo, Hugo Almeida (Edinho 69).
Referee: F. Meyer (Germany).

Stockholm, 6 June 2009, 33,619
Sweden (0) 0   Denmark (1) 1 *(Kahlenberg 22)*
Sweden: Isaksson; Johansson, Mellberg, Majstorovic, Elm R, Andersson D (Elm V 68), Wilhelmsson (Elmander 58), Nilsson M (Larsson S 80), Kallstrom, Ibrahimovic, Larsson H.
Denmark: Sorensen; Jacobsen L, Agger, Kjaer, Christian Poulsen (Augustinussen 72), Jorgensen (Gronkjaer 56), Kvist, Kahlenberg, Poulsen J, Bendtner (Bernburg 84), Rommedahl.
Referee: Riley (England).

Gothenburg, 10 June 2009, 25,271
Sweden (1) 4 *(Kallstrom 21, Majstorovic 52, Ibrahimovic 56, Berg 58)*
Malta (0) 0
Sweden: Isaksson; Johansson, Mellberg, Majstorovic, Kallstrom, Elm V (Holmen 80), Elm R (Larsson S 78), Anders Svensson, Safari, Ibrahimovic, Berg (Hysen 78).
Malta: Hogg; Dimech, Caruana, Muscat A (Sammut 89), Briffa, Bajada, Pace, Hutchinson, Agius A (Muscat M 85), Bogdanovic, Schembri (Fenech 78).
Referee: Murray (Scotland).

Copenhagen, 5 September 2009, 37,998
Denmark (1) 1 *(Bendtner 42)*   **Portugal (0) 1** *(Liedson 86)*
Denmark: Andersen; Christensen, Kjaer, Jacobsen L, Silberbauer (Kvist 66), Poulsen J (Gronkjaer 89), Christian Poulsen, Jorgensen (Norregaard 61), Tomasson, Rommedahl, Bendtner.
Portugal: Eduardo; Bosingwa, Ricardo Carvalho, Pepe, Bruno Alves, Tiago (Liedson 46), Raul Meireles (Nuno Gomes 81), Duda, Deco, Simao (Nani 71), Cristiano Ronaldo.
Referee: Busacca (Switzerland).

Budapest, 5 September 2009, 40,169
Hungary (0) 1 *(Huszti 79 (pen))*
Sweden (1) 2 *(Mellberg 8, Ibrahimovic 90)*
Hungary: Babos; Gyepes, Szelesi, Juhasz (Timar 64), Dardai (Torghelle 46), Huszti, Halmosi, Hajnal (Buzsaky 84), Dzsudzsak, Vadocz, Gera.

Sweden: Isaksson; Mellberg, Majstorovic, Nilsson M, Kallstrom, Holmen (Hysen 86), Elm R, Anders Svensson, Safari, Ibrahimovic, Elmander (Berg 75).
Referee: Rizzoli (Italy).

Tirana, 9 September 2009, 6000
Albania (0) 1 *(Bogdani 51)*   **Denmark (1) 1** *(Bendtner 40)*
Albania: Ujkani; Beqiri (Hyka 46), Dallku, Curri, Agolli, Skela (Vila 84), Duro, Cana, Bulku, Bogdani (Lika 78), Salihi.
Denmark: Sorensen; Jacobsen L, Christensen, Kjaer, Jorgensen (Norregaard 69), Poulsen J (Gronkjaer 54), Christian Poulsen, Kvist, Bendtner, Tomasson (Larsen 75), Rommedahl.
Referee: Cuneyt (Turkey).

Budapest, 9 September 2009, 42,000
Hungary (0) 0   Portugal (1) 1 *(Pepe 9)*
Hungary: Babos; Gyepes, Bodnar, Juhasz, Dardai (Hajnal 65), Vadocz, Toth (Buzsaky 83), Huszti (Priskin 65), Halmosi, Dzsudzsak, Torghelle.
Portugal: Eduardo; Liedson (Nani 82), Ricardo Carvalho, Pepe, Bruno Alves, Bosingwa, Tiago (Rolando 89), Raul Meireles, Duda, Deco (Simao 49), Cristiano Ronaldo.
Referee: Lannoy (France).

Ta'Qali, 9 September 2009, 4705
Malta (0) 0   Sweden (0) 1 *(Azzopardi 81 (og))*
Malta: Hogg; Scicluna, Said, Muscat E, Azzopardi, Muscat A (Briffa 62), Pace, Bajada (Failla 73), Agius G, Mifsud, Cohen.
Sweden: Isaksson; Mellberg, Majstorovic, Anders Svensson (Berg 71), Nilsson M, Kallstrom, Holmen (Hysen 58), Elm R, Safari, Ibrahimovic, Elmander (Larsson S 83).
Referee: McCourt (Northern Ireland).

Copenhagen, 10 October 2009, 37,800
Denmark (0) 1 *(Poulsen J 79)*   **Sweden (0) 0**
Denmark: Sorensen; Kjaer, Jacobsen L, Jacobsen M, Agger, Poulsen J, Christian Poulsen, Jorgensen (Silberbauer 46), Tomasson, Rommedahl, Bendtner.
Sweden: Isaksson; Mellberg, Majstorovic, Anders Svensson, Nilsson M (Rosenberg 88), Kallstrom, Holmen (Larsson S 63), Elm R (Berg 80), Safari, Larsson H, Ibrahimovic.
Referee: Gonzalez (Spain).

Lisbon, 10 October 2009, 50,115
Portugal (1) 3 *(Simao 18, 79, Liedson 74)*   **Hungary (0) 0**
Portugal: Eduardo; Ricardo Carvalho, Bruno Alves, Bosingwa, Pedro Mendes, Raul Meireles, Duda, Deco, Simao (Miguel Veloso 80), Cristiano Ronaldo (Nani 27), Liedson (Nuno Gomes 83).
Hungary: Babos; Gyepes, Bodnar, Vanczak, Juhasz, Vadocz (Priskin 56), Toth, Huszti (Buzsaky 67), Dzsudzsak (Varga 84), Torghelle, Gera.
Referee: Hamer (Luxembourg).

Copenhagen, 14 October 2009, 36,956
Denmark (0) 0   Hungary (1) 1 *(Buzsaky 35)*
Denmark: Sorensen; Agger, Christensen, Jacobsen L, Jacobsen M, Poulsen J, Christian Poulsen, Enevoldsen (Larsen 46), Tomasson (Jensen D 62), Rommedahl (Silberbauer 71), Bendtner.
Hungary: Babos; Bodnar, Vanczak, Juhasz, Varga, Buzsaky (Huszti 77), Toth, Halmosi, Dzsudzsak (Priskin 90), Torghelle, Rudolf (Vadocz 87).
Referee: Meyer (Germany).

Guimaraes, 14 October 2009, 29,350
Portugal (2) 4 *(Nani 15, Simao 45, Miguel 52, Edinho 90)*
Malta (0) 0
Portugal: Eduardo; Pepe, Miguel Veloso, Ricardo Carvalho, Bosingwa, Nani (Joao Moutinho 73), Pedro Mendes, Raul Meireles (Nuno Assis 63), Deco, Simao, Liedson (Edinho 63).
Malta: Hogg; Scicluna, Said, Muscat E, Azzopardi, Pace, Hutchinson, Briffa (Sammut 88), Bajada (Fenech 72), Mifsud, Cohen (Failla 23).
Referee: Kelly (Republic of Ireland).

Stockholm, 14 October 2009, 25,342
Sweden (3) 4 *(Mellberg 6, 42, Berg 40, Anders Svensson 86)*
Albania (0) 1 *(Salihi 57)*
Sweden: Isaksson; Mellberg, Majstorovic, Anders Svensson, Nilsson M, Larsson S, Kallstrom (Andersson D 21), Elm R, Safari, Ibrahimovic (Rosenberg 77), Elmander (Berg 37).
Albania: Ujkani; Dallku, Curri, Beqiri, Skela, Haxhi (Hyka 22), Duro, Cana, Bulku, Salihi (Kapllani 79), Bogdani.
Referee: Ivanov (Russia).

Group 1 Table	P	W	D	L	F	A	Pts
Denmark	10	6	3	1	16	5	21
Portugal	10	5	4	1	17	5	19
Sweden	10	5	3	2	13	5	18
Hungary	10	5	1	4	10	8	16
Albania	10	1	4	5	6	13	7
Malta	10	0	1	9	0	26	1

GROUP 2

Tel Aviv, 6 September 2008, 29,600
Israel (0) 2 *(Benayoun 73, Sahar 90)*
Switzerland (1) 2 *(Yakin 45, Nkufo 56)*
Israel: Awat; Kozokin, Ben Haim, Ziv, Strool, Kayal (Ohayon 62), Cohen, Benayoun, Toema, Golan (Barda 60), Colautti (Sahar 46).
Switzerland: Benaglio; Lichtsteiner, Grichting, Djourou, Magnin, Inler, Huggel, Behrami (Spycher 87), Barnetta (Vonlanthen 71), Yakin (Abdi 75), Nkufo.
Referee: Hansson (Sweden).

Luxembourg, 6 September 2008, 4596
Luxembourg (0) 0
Greece (2) 3 *(Torosidis 36, Gekas 45, Charisteas 75 (pen))*
Luxembourg: Joubert; Hoffmann E, Kintziger, Strasser, Peters, Mutsch, Lombardelli (Lang 68), Leweck F (Da Mota 58), Bettmer, Payal, Kitenge (Joachim 81).
Greece: Chalkias; Torosidis, Seitaridis, Kyrgiakos, Dellas, Katsouranis, Karagounis, Basinas (Salpingidis 46), Lyberopoulos (Patsatzoglou 66), Gekas, Charisteas.
Referee: Hermansen (Denmark).

Tiraspol, 6 September 2008, 4300
Moldova (0) 1 *(Alexeev 76)*
Latvia (2) 2 *(Karlsons 8, Astafjevs 22)*
Moldova: Calancea; Rebeja, Lascencov, Golovatenco, Epureanu, Bordian, Corneencov, Andronic (Alexeev 61), Suvorov (Tigirlas 67), Picusciac, Frunza.
Latvia: Vanins; Stepanovs, Klava, Gorkss, Solonicins, Pereplotkins (Kolesnicenko 83), Laizans, Kacanovs (Zirnis 90), Astafjevs, Verpakovskis (Rubins 75), Karlsons.
Referee: Courtney (Northern Ireland).

Riga, 10 September 2008, 8600
Latvia (0) 0   Greece (1) 2 *(Gekas 10, 49)*
Latvia: Vanins; Stepanovs, Gorkss, Klava, Astafjevs, Kacanovs, Laizans, Pereplotkins (Visnakovs 79), Solonicins (Rubins 65), Verkpakovskis, Karlsons (Grebis 60).
Greece: Chalkias; Seitaridis, Torosidis, Dellas, Kyrgiakos, Papadopoulos A, Katsouranis, Karagounis (Basinas 61), Samaras (Lyberopoulos 88), Charisteas, Gekas (Salpingidis 76).
Referee: Chapron (France).

Chisinau, 10 September 2008, 10,500
Moldova (1) 1 *(Picusciac 1)*
Israel (2) 2 *(Golan 39, Saban 45)*
Moldova: Stanislav Namasco; Lascencov, Rebeja, Bordian, Golovatenco[a], Epureanu, Corneencov (Savinov 27), Comlionoc (Andronic 76), Frunza (Alexeev 69), Suvorov, Picusciac.
Israel: Awat; Kozokin (Saban 38), Ziv, Ben Haim, Keinan, Cohen (Kayal 68), Ohayon, Toema, Benayoun, Golan, Sahar (Buzaglo 4).
Referee: Fernandez (Spain).

Zurich, 10 September 2008, 20,500
Switzerland (1) 1 *(Nkufo 43)*
Luxembourg (1) 2 *(Strasser 27, Leweck F 87)*
Switzerland: Benaglio; Nef (Vonlanthen 73), Djourou, Grichting, Magnin, Stocker, Yakin (Abdi 65), Barnetta, Inler, Nkufo, Frei (Lustrinelli 65).
Luxembourg: Joubert; Hoffmann E, Kintziger, Lang (Leweck F 44), Lombardelli (Gerson 76), Mutsch, Payal, Peters, Strasser, Bettmer, Kitenge (Joachim 66).
Referee: Filipovic (Serbia).

Piraeus, 11 October 2008, 13,684
Greece (2) 3 *(Charisteas 31, 51, Katsouranis 40)*
Moldova (0) 0
Greece: Chalkias; Torosidis, Seitaridis, Kyrgiakos, Dellas, Papadopoulos A, Katsouranis (Patsatzoglou 72), Basinas, Samaras (Amanatidis 70), Gekas (Salpingidis 46), Charisteas.

Moldova: Calancea; Epureanu, Rebeja, Bordian, Armas, Tigirlas, Savinov, Corneencov (Andronic 79), Cebotaru, Bugaiov (Suvorov 68), Alexeev (Picusciac 46).
Referee: Berntsen (Norway).

Luxembourg, 11 October 2008, 3562
Luxembourg (1) 1 *(Peters 14)*
Israel (1) 3 *(Benayoun 2 (pen), Golan 54, Toema 81)*
Luxembourg: Joubert; Wagner, Reiter, Kintziger, Peters, Payal, Mutsch, Leweck F, Bettmer, Bensi (Da Mota 67), Bossi (Joachim 67).
Israel: Awat; Ben Dayan, Saban, Keinan, Ben Haim, Toema (Sahar 81), Kayal, Benayoun (Buzaglo 87), Alberman (Ohayon 90), Golan, Barda.
Referee: Egorov (Russia).

St Gallen, 11 October 2008, 18,026
Switzerland (0) 2 *(Frei 63, Nkufo 73)*
Latvia (0) 1 *(Ivanovs 71)*
Switzerland: Benaglio; Spycher, Lichtsteiner, Grichting, Djourou (Eggimann 46), Inler, Huggel, Behrami, Barnetta (Gelson 84), Nkufo, Frei (Yakin 78).
Latvia: Vanins; Ivanovs, Savcenkovs, Gorkss, Cauna (Rubins 59), Solonicins (Visnakovs 81), Pereplotkins (Kolesnicenko 69), Laizans[a], Kacanovs, Astafjevs, Karlsons.
Referee: Baptista (Portugal).

Piraeus, 15 October 2008, 28,810
Greece (0) 1 *(Charisteas 68)*
Switzerland (1) 2 *(Frei 41 (pen), Nkufo 77)*
Greece: Chalkias; Torosidis, Seitaridis, Kyrgiakos (Patsatzoglou 30), Dellas, Papadopoulos A, Katsouranis, Basinas, Samaras (Karagounis 62), Gekas (Lyberopoulos 46), Charisteas.
Switzerland: Benaglio; Spycher, Lichtsteiner, Grichting, Eggimann, Inler, Huggel, Behrami, Barnetta (Gelson 33), Nkufo (Derdiyok 86), Frei (Yakin 75).
Referee: Cantalejo (Spain).

Riga, 15 October 2008, 7100
Latvia (0) 1 *(Kolesnicenko 89)   Israel (0) 1** *(Benayoun 50)*
Latvia: Vanins; Astafjevs, Klava, Ivanovs, Kacanovs, Kolesnicenko, Rubins, Karlsons (Cauna 61), Gorkss, Pereplotkins (Grebis 61), Solonicins (Visnakovs 75).
Israel: Awat; Saban, Ben Haim, Alberman, Toema, Kayal (Ohayon 74), Ben Dayan, Barda (Buzaglo 90), Golan (Sahar 83), Keinan, Benayoun.
Referee: Hrinak (Slovakia).

Luxembourg, 15 October 2008, 2157
Luxembourg (0) 0   Moldova (0) 0
Luxembourg: Joubert; Kintziger, Hoffmann E, Strasser, Peters, Payal (Lombardelli 46), Mutsch, Leweck F (Joachim 69), Bettmer, Kitenge, Bossi (Gerson 46).
Moldova: Calancea; Rebeja, Lascencov, Epureanu, Bordian, Armas, Corneencov (Cebotaru 72), Suvorov, Picusciac (Tigirlas 65), Frunza, Bugaiov (Bulat 53).
Referee: Borski (Poland).

Tel Aviv, 28 March 2009, 38,000
Israel (0) 1 *(Golan 55)   Greece (1) 1** *(Gekas 42)*
Israel: Awat; Saban, Keinan, Ben Haim, Ben Dayan, Cohen (Vermouth 85), Benayoun (Kayal 77), Alberman, Barda (Itzhaki 61), Sahar, Golan.
Greece: Chalkias; Torosidis, Seitaridis, Kyrgiakos, Dellas, Tziolis (Patsatzoglou 88), Papadopoulos A, Karagounis, Basinas (Samaras 62), Gekas, Charisteas.
Referee: Rosetti (Italy).

Luxembourg, 28 March 2009, 2516
Luxembourg (0) 0
Latvia (1) 4 *(Karlsons 25, Cauna 48, Visnakovs 71, Pereplotkins 86)*
Luxembourg: Joubert; Janisch, Hoffmann E, Plein, Strasser, Peters, Payal (Gerson 46), Mutsch, Leweck F (Lombardelli 66), Bettmer, Bensi (Kitenge 70).
Latvia: Vanins; Klava, Ivanovs, Gorkss, Cauna (Rubins 77), Kolesnicenko, Kacanovs, Astafjevs, Zigajevs (Visnakovs 66), Verpakovskis (Pereplotkins 72), Karlsons.
Referee: Whitby (Wales).

Chisinau, 28 March 2009, 10,500
Moldova (0) 0   Switzerland (1) 2 *(Frei 32, Gelson 90)*
Moldova: Stanislav Namasco; Armas (Manaliu 87), Golovatenco, Epureanu, Lascencov, Ionita (Cebotaru 56), Gatcan, Savinov, Calincov, Bugaev, Alexeev.

Switzerland: Benaglio; Senderos, Magnin, Lichtsteiner, Grichting, Padalino (Gelson 79), Inler, Huggel, Barnetta (Djourou 90), Nkufo (Derdiyok 79), Frei.
Referee: McDonald (Scotland).

Iraklion, 1 April 2009, 22,794
Greece (1) 2 *(Salpingidis 32, Samaras 67 (pen))*
Israel (0) 1 *(Golan 59)*
Greece: Chalkias; Torosidis, Seitaridis, Moras, Kyrgiakos, Katsouranis, Karagounis (Patsatzoglou 70), Papadopoulos A, Gekas (Samaras 64), Charisteas (Basinas 84), Salpingidis.
Israel: Awat; Ziv (Barda 40), Saban, Keinan, Ben Haim, Ben Dayan, Kayal, Alberman, Shechter (Itzhaki 74), Sahar (Benayoun 46), Golan.
Referee: Benquerenca (Portugal).

Riga, 1 April 2009, 6700
Latvia (1) 2 *(Zigajevs 44, Verpakovskis 76)*
Luxembourg (0) 0
Latvia: Vanins; Klava, Ivanovs, Gorkss, Kolesnicenko, Kacanovs, Cauna, Astafjeves, Zigajevs (Solonicins 87), Verpakovskis, Karlsons (Pereplotkins 20) (Rubins 69).
Luxembourg: Joubert; Kintziger, Janisch, Hoffmann E (Bensi 80), Strasser, Peters, Payal (Ferreira 83), Mutsch, Lombardelli (Leweck F 60), Bettmer, Kitenge.
Referee: Firat (Turkey).

Geneva, 1 April 2009, 20,100
Switzerland (1) 2 *(Nkufo 21, Frei 52)*   **Moldova (0) 0**
Switzerland: Benaglio; Senderos, Magnin, Lichtsteiner Grichting, Padalino (Abdi 87), Inler, Huggel (Dzemaili 71) Barnetta, Nkufo (Derdiyok 84), Frei.
Moldova: Stanislav Namasco; Lascencov, Golovatenco, Gatcan (Alexeev 57), Onica, Cebotaru, Bulat, Savinov, Calincov (Andronic 78), Manaliu (Tigirlas 79), Bugaev.
Referee: Rocchi (Italy).

Tel Aviv, 5 September 2009, 20,000
Israel (0) 0   Latvia (0) 1 *(Gorkss 59)*
Israel: Awat; Strool, Shpungin, Keinan, Ben Dayan, Kayal, Benayoun (Baruchian 66), Alberman (Cohen 46), Barda, Katan, Golan (Sahar 62).
Latvia: Vanins; Klava, Ivanovs, Gorkss, Rubins (Zirnis 8·), Kolesnicenko, Kacanovs, Cauna (Zigajevs 81), Astafjevs, Karlsons, Verpakovskis (Pereplotkins 90).
Referee: Kircher (Germany).

Chisinau, 5 September 2009, 7820
Moldova (0) 0   Luxembourg (0) 0
Moldova: Stanislav Namasco; Catinsus, Armas, Lascencov, Golovatenco, Onica, Comlionoc (Andronic 81), Gatcan, Sofroni, Calincov, Bugaev (Suvorov 77).
Luxembourg: Joubert; Kintziger, Janisch (Collette 58), Hoffmann E, Blaise, Strasser, Peters, Payal, Lombardelli, Bettmer, Pupovac (Da Mota 84).
Referee: Mazeika (Lithuania).

Basle, 5 September 2009, 38,500
Switzerland (0) 2 *(Grichting 83, Padalino 88)*
Greece (0) 0
Switzerland: Benaglio; Von Bergen, Nef (Vonlanthen 81), Magnin, Grichting, Barnetta, Padalino, Huggel, Gelson (Yakin 67), Nkufo (Derdiyok 81), Frei.
Greece: Chalkias; Papastathopoulos, Vyntra", Spyropoulos, Patsatzoglou, Moras, Kyrgiakos, Katsouranis, Amanatidis (Gekas 81), Salpingidis (Samaras 46), Charisteas (Papadopoulos A 73).
Referee: De Bleeckere (Belgium).

Tel Aviv, 9 September 2009, 7038
Israel (4) 7 *(Barda 9, 21, 44, Baruchian 15, Golan 58, Sahar 63, 84)*   **Luxembourg (0) 0**
Israel: Awat (Davidovitch 46); Strool, Ziv, Ben Haim, Ben Dayan, Baruchian, Cohen, Kayal, Benayoun, Barda (Sahar 58), Golan (Itzhaki 67).
Luxembourg: Oberweis; Hoffmann E, Kintziger, Janisch (Collette 50), Blaise, Bettmer, Peters, Payal (Pedro 46), Mutsch, Lombardelli (Leweck F 65), Pupovac.
Referee: Svendsen (Denmark).

Riga, 9 September 2009, 8600
Latvia (0) 2 *(Cauna 62, Astafjevs 75)*
Switzerland (1) 2 *(Frei 43, Derdiyok 80)*
Latvia: Vanins; Gorkss, Klava, Ivanovs, Cauna (Zirnis 89), Astafjevs, Rubins, Kolesnicenko (Rafalskis 86), Kacanovs, Verpakovskis, Karlsons (Grebis 85).

Chisinau, 9 September 2009, 9870
Moldova (0) 1 *(Andronic 90)*   **Greece (1) 1** *(Gekas 33)*
Moldova: Stanislav Namasco; Armas, Lascencov, Catinsus, Epureanu, Serghei Namasco (Comlionoc 56), Gatcan, Bugaev (Sofroni 46), Bulat, Calincov, Savinov (Andronic 79).
Greece: Chalkias; Patsatzoglou, Spyropoulos, Moras (Papadopoulos A 58), Tziolis, Samaras, Katsouranis, Charisteas, Karagounis (Amanatidis 76), Kyrgiakos, Gekas.
Referee: Stalhammar (Sweden).

Athens, 10 October 2009, 18,981
Greece (1) 5 *(Gekas 3, 46 (pen), 57, 90, Samaras 72)*
Latvia (2) 2 *(Verpakovskis 12, 39)*
Greece: Tzorvas; Papastathopoulos, Moras, Torosidis, Seitaridis, Katsouranis, Karagounis (Pliatsikas 88), Tziolis (Amanatidis 46), Gekas, Samaras, Salpingidis (Patsatzoglou 46)
Latvia: Vanins; Klava, Ivanovs, Gorkss, Rubins (Solonicins 77), Laizans, Kolesnicenko, Kacanovs, Cauna, Verpakovskis (Pereplotkins 84), Karlsons (Grebis 70).
Referee: Ovrebo (Norway).

Tel Aviv, 10 October 2009, 8700
Israel (1) 3 *(Barda 21, 69, Ben Dayan 64)*
Moldova (0) 1 *(Calincov 90)*
Israel: Awat; Yadin, Strool, Ziv (Saban 30), Ben Haim, Ben Dayan, Vermouth, Cohen, Benayoun, Barda (Colautti 72), Sahar (Shechter 60).
Moldova: Stanislav Namasco; Catinsus, Lascencov, Golovatenco, Epureanu, Savinov, Cebotaru (Andronic 67), Bulat, Sofroni (Ovseannicov 79), Calincov, Bugaev (Suvorov 74).
Referee: Blom (Holland).

Luxembourg, 10 October 2009, 8250
Luxembourg (0) 0
Switzerland (3) 3 *(Senderos 6, 7, Huggel 22)*
Luxembourg: Joubert; Kintziger, Blaise, Strasser, Peters, Payal, Mutsch, Bettmer, Laterza (Leweck F 46), Collette (Janisch 73), Kitenge (Pupovac 59).
Switzerland: Benaglio; Von Bergen, Spycher, Senderos, Lichtsteiner, Inler, Huggel, Barnetta (Ziegler 81), Vonlanthen (Yakin 65), Nkufo, Frei (Derdiyok 65).
Referee: Gonzalez (Spain).

Athens, 14 October 2009, 13,932
Greece (2) 2 *(Torosidis 30, Gekas 33)*
Luxembourg (0) 1 *(Papadopoulos A 90 (og))*
Greece: Sifakis; Vyntra (Ninis 82), Torosidis, Spyropoulos, Patsatzoglou, Kyrgiakos (Moras 44), Papadopoulos A, Karagounis, Fotakis (Pliatsikas 46), Salpingidis, Gekas.
Luxembourg: Joubert; Kintziger (Martino 80), Janisch (Leweck F 46), Hoffmann E, Blaise Strasser, Peters, Payal", Mutsch, Bettmer, Kitenge (Pupovac 73).
Referee: Ceferin (Slovenia).

Riga, 14 October 2009, 3800
Latvia (2) 3 *(Rubins 32, 44, Grebis 78)*
Moldova (1) 2 *(Ovsyannikov 25, Sofroni 89)*
Latvia: Vanins; Klava, Ivanovs, Gorkss, Astafjevs, Rubins (Solonicins 63), Kolesnicenko (Laizans 74), Kacanovs, Cauna, Verpakovskis, Karlsons (Grebis 69).
Moldova: Stanislav Namasco; Armas (Andronic 81), Ovseannicov (Sofroni 76), Catinsus, Lascencov", Golovatenco, Epureanu, Serghei Namasco, Savinov, Calincov, Bugaev (Suvorov 70).
Referee: Hyytia (Finland).

Basle, 14 October 2009, 38,500
Switzerland (0) 0   Israel (0) 0
Switzerland: Wolfli; Spycher, Senderos, Lichtsteiner, Grichting, Padalino, Inler, Gelson, Barnetta, Nkufo, Derdiyok (Frei 70).
Israel: Awat; Yadin", Strool, Ziv, Ben Haim, Saban, Cohen, Benayoun, Kayal, Barda (Vermouth 85), Colautti (Shechter 69).
Referee: Tudor (Romania).

Switzerland: Benaglio; Von Bergen, Spycher, Lichtsteiner, Grichting, Gelson (Derdiyok 79), Barnetta (Vonlanthen 76), Padalino (Yakin 76), Huggel, Nkufo, Frei.
Referee: Kralovec (Czech Republic).

Group 2 Table	P	W	D	L	F	A	Pts
Switzerland	10	6	3	1	18	8	21
Greece	10	6	2	2	20	10	20
Latvia	10	5	2	3	18	15	17
Israel	10	4	4	2	20	10	16
Luxembourg	10	1	2	7	4	25	5
Moldova	10	0	3	7	6	18	3

GROUP 3

Wroclaw, 6 September 2008, 8400
Poland (1) 1 *(Zewlakow 17 (pen))*
Slovenia (1) 1 *(Dedic 35)*
Poland: Fabianski; Zewlakow, Wasilewski, Kowalczyk, Bosacki (Jop 50), Roger (Saganowski 71), Piszczek, Murawski (Bandrowski 46), Lewandowski M, Krzynowek, Blaszczykowski.
Slovenia: Handanovic; Suler, Kirm (Birsa 70), Ilic, Cesar, Brecko, Koren, Komac (Zlogar 84), Sisic, Novakovic, Dedic (Matic 90).
Referee: Jakobsson (Iceland).

Bratislava, 6 September 2008, 5445
Slovakia (0) 2 *(Skrtel 46, Hamsik 70)*
Northern Ireland (0) 1 *(Durica 81 (og))*
Slovakia: Senecky; Skrtel, Petras, Pekarik, Durica, Sapara, Kozak, Karhan (Zabavnik 75), Hamsik, Vittek (Mintal 84), Jakubko (Svento 59).
Northern Ireland: Maik Taylor; Baird (Shiels 78), McCartney, Evans, Hughes, Craigan, Davis, Clingan, Gillespie (Feeney 53), Healy, Paterson (Brunt 66).
Referee: Ivanov (Russia).

Belfast, 10 September 2008, 12,882
Northern Ireland (0) 0   Czech Republic (0) 0
Northern Ireland: Maik Taylor; Evans, Hughes, McCartney, Baird, Craigan, Brunt, Clingan (O'Connor 46), Feeney (Paterson 72), Gillespie (Shiels 83), Healy.
Czech Republic: Cech; Jankulovski, Kovac R, Rozehnal, Ujfalusi, Grygera, Plasil, Polak, Sionko (Pospech 67), Sirl, Baros (Slepicka 77).
Referee: Bebek (Croatia).

Serravalle, 10 September 2008, 2374
San Marino (0) 0
Poland (1) 2 *(Smolarek 36, Lewandowski R 68)*
San Marino: Simoncini A (Valentini F 73); Vitaioli F, Albani N, Berretti (Mauro Marani 80), Simoncini D, Valentini C, Bollini (Vannucci 46), Bugli, Michele Marani, Manuel Marani, Selva A.
Poland: Fabianski; Jop, Kowalczyk (Krzynowek 28), Zewlakow, Wojtkowiak, Blaszczykowski, Lewandowski M, Piszczek (Murawski 88), Roger (Saganowski (Lewandowski R 58), Smolarek.
Referee: Zografos (Greece).

Maribor, 10 September 2008, 11,000
Slovenia (1) 2 *(Novakovic 22, 81)*
Slovakia (0) 1 *(Jakubko 83)*
Slovenia: Handanovic; Brecko, Komac, Suler, Cesar, Sisic (Zlogar 85), Koren, Novakovic, Dedic (Ljubijankic 76), Kirm (Matic 90), Ilic.
Slovakia: Senecky; Petras, Skrtel, Pekarik, Karhan (Jakubko 58), Sapara, Vittek, Holosko (Svento 46), Strba, Durica (Kozak 78), Hamsik.
Referee: Moen (Norway).

Chorzow, 11 October 2008, 38,293
Poland (1) 2 *(Pawel Brozek 26, Blaszczykowski 52)*
Czech Republic (0) 1 *(Fenin 87)*
Poland: Boruc; Wawrzyniak (Krzynowek 43), Zewlakow, Wasilewski, Dudka, Roger, Murawski (Jodlowiec 90), Lewandowski M, Blaszczykowski, Smolarek, Pawel Brozek (Lewandowski R 69).
Czech Republic: Cech; Ujfalusi, Rozehnal, Pospech, Kovac R, Jankulovski, Grygera (Sionko 58), Sirl, Plasil, Slepicka (Sverkos 58), Baros (Fenin 80).
Referee: Stark (Germany).

Serravalle, 11 October 2008, 1037
San Marino (1) 1 *(Selva A 45)*
Slovakia (2) 3 *(Sestak 32, Kozak 39, Karhan 50)*
San Marino: Simoncini A; Della Valle, Vannucci, Valentini C, Simoncini D (Vitaioli M 84), Berretti (Bonini 72), Bacciocchi (Albani N 46), Michele Marani, Mauro Marani, Selva A, Manuel Marani.

Slovakia: Kamenar; Jendrisek, Cech, Petras, Kratochvil[#], Krajcik, Borbely (Karhan 46), Mintal (Jakubko 62), Kozak, Vittek, Sestak (Petras 85).
Referee: Kever (Switzerland).

Maribor, 11 October 2008, 12,385
Slovenia (0) 2 *(Novakovic 84, Ljubijankic 85)*
Northern Ireland (0) 0
Slovenia: Handanovic; Suler, Kirm (Matic 90), Ilic, Cesar, Brecko, Koren, Komac, Sisic (Birsa 81), Novakovic, Dedic (Ljubijankic 69).
Northern Ireland: Maik Taylor; Baird, McCartney, McAuley, Hughes, Evans, Gillespie, McCann (McGivern 73), Lafferty, Healy, Davis.
Referee: Gonzalez (Spain).

Teplice, 15 October 2008, 15,220
Czech Republic (0) 1 *(Sionko 62)*   **Slovenia (0) 0**
Czech Republic: Zitka; Ujfalusi, Rozehnal, Rajnoch, Pospech, Jankulovski, Sionko, Plasil, Jarolim (Sirl 66), Fenin (Sverkos 81), Baros (Kladrubsky 90).
Slovenia: Handanovic; Radosavljevic, Moerec, Suler, Kirm, Ilic, Brecko (Mejak 87), Koren, Sisic (Birsa 65), Novakovic, Dedic (Jokic 79).
Referee: Atkinson (England).

Belfast, 15 October 2008, 12,957
Northern Ireland (2) 4 *(Healy 31, McCann 43, Lafferty 56, Davis 75)*
San Marino (0) 0
Northern Ireland: Maik Taylor; Baird, McCartney, McCann (Paterson 73), McAuley (McGivern 61), Hughes, Gillespie, O'Connor, Lafferty (Feeney 82), Healy, Davis.
San Marino: Valentini F; Della Valle, Vannucci, Valentini C, Bacciocchi, Albani N, Michele Marani, Mauro Marani[#], Bonini (Vitaioli F 77), Selva A (Vitaioli M 46), Manuel Marani (Cibelli 86).
Referee: Kari (Finland).

Bratislava, 15 October 2008, 17,650
Slovakia (0) 2 *(Sestak 85, 86)*   **Poland (0) 1** *(Smolarek 70)*
Slovakia: Senecky; Jendrisek (Obzera 80), Petras, Pekarik, Durica, Cech, Zabavnik (Kozak 83), Sapara (Jakubko 73), Hamsik, Vittek, Sestak.
Poland: Boruc; Zewlakow, Wasilewski, Wojtkowiak, Roger (Lewandowski R 89), Murawski (Gargula 65), Lewandowski M, Dudka, Blaszczykowski, Smolarek, Pawel Brozek (Krzynowek 84).
Referee: Layec (France).

Serravalle, 19 November 2008, 1318
San Marino (0) 0
Czech Republic (0) 3 *(Kovac R 48, Pospech 53, Necid 83)*
San Marino: Simoncini A; Della Valle, Vannucci, Simoncini D, Berretti, Bacciocchi, Muccioli (Andreini 70), Michele Marani (Cibelli 81), Bonini, Vitaioli M (Rinaldi 87), Manuel Marani.
Czech Republic: Zitka; Ujfalusi, Rozehnal, Pospech, Kovac R, Jankulovski, Sirl, Sionko, Polak (Jarolim 70), Fenin (Necid 66), Baros (Bednar 81).
Referee: Kaasik (Estonia).

Serravalle, 11 February 2009, 1942
San Marino (0) 0
Northern Ireland (2) 3 *(McAuley 7, McCann 33, Brunt 63)*
San Marino: Valentini F; Della Valle, Berretti, Bacciocchi (Vitaioli F 73), Vannucci, Valentini C, Simoncini D, Muccioli (Bugli 66), Michele Marani, Vitaioli M (Casadei 87), Manuel Marani[#].
Northern Ireland: Maik Taylor; Hughes (McCourt 80), McCartney, McCann, McAuley, Craigan, Johnson, Davis, Lafferty (Brunt 55), Healy, Paterson (Feeney 77).
Referee: Stankovic (Serbia).

Belfast, 28 March 2009, 13,357
Northern Ireland (1) 3 *(Feeney 10, Evans 47, Michal Zewlakow 61 (og))*
Poland (1) 2 *(Jelen 27, Saganowski 90)*
Northern Ireland: Maik Taylor; McAuley, Evans, Craigan, Hughes, Clingan, Johnson, McCann, Feeney (Baird 84), Healy (Little 90), Brunt.
Poland: Boruc; Wasilewski, Michal Zewlakow (Bosacki 65), Wawrzyniak, Roger, Bandrowski (Blaszczykowski 60), Lewandowski M, Krzynowek, Dudka, Jelen (Saganowski 71), Lewandowski R.
Referee: Hansson (Sweden).

Maribor, 28 March 2009, 12,500
Slovenia (0) 0   Czech Republic (0) 0
Slovenia: Handanovic; Mavric, Kirm, Cesar, Filekovic, Koren, Jokic, Komac (Mejac 85), Dedic (Ljubijankic 67), Sisic (Zlogar 83), Novakovic.
Czech Republic: Cech; Ujfalusi, Rozehnal, Jankulovski, Grygera, Sirl (Kadlec 76), Sionko, Polak, Plasil, Sverkos (Necid 79), Baros (Fenin 90).
Referee: Proenca (Portugal).

Prague, 1 April 2009, 20,000
Czech Republic (1) 1 *(Jankulovski 30)*
Slovakia (1) 2 *(Sestak 22, Jendrisek 83)*
Czech Republic: Cech; Rozehnal, Kovac R (Pospech 72), Jankulovski, Grygera, Sionko (Lafata 84), Polak, Plasil, Jarolim, Necid (Fenin 79), Baros.
Slovakia: Mucha; Skrtel, Kadlec, Durica, Strba, Hamsik (Sapara 88), Zabavnik, Karhan, Sestak (Stoch 74), Jendrisek (Vittek 90), Holosko.
Referee: Mallenco (Spain).

Belfast, 1 April 2009, 15,000
Northern Ireland (0) 1 *(Feeney 73)*   **Slovenia (0) 0**
Northern Ireland: Maik Taylor; Hughes, McCartney (McGivern 44), McCann, McAuley (Baird 16), Evans, Davis, Clingan, Feeney, Healy, Johnson.
Slovenia: Handanovic; Mavric, Kirm (Pecnik 77), Cesar, Brecko (Mejac 85), Koren, Komac, Jokic, Filekovic, Novakovic, Dedic (Ljubijankic 64).
Referee: Yefet (Israel).

Kielce, 1 April 2009, 15,200
Poland (4) 10 *(Boguski 1, 28, Smolarek 18, 59, 72, 81, Lewandowski R 43, Jelen 51, Lewandowski M 62, Saganowski 88)*
San Marino (0) 0
Poland: Fabianski; Wasilewski, Bosacki, Roger, Boguski (Saganowski 80), Lewandowski M, Krzynowek, Dudka, Jelen (Blaszczykowski 71), Smolarek, Lewandowski R (Sosin 66).
San Marino: Valentini F; Della Valle, Vitaioli F (Berretti 64), Simoncini D, Bacciocchi, Andreini (Vannucci 82), Albani N, Rinaldi, Michele Marani, Bugli, Bonini (Selva A 53).
Referee: Kulbakou (Belarus).

Bratislava, 6 June 2009, 6652
Slovakia (5) 7 *(Cech 3, 32, Pekarik 12, Stoch 35, Kozak 42, Jakubko 63, Hanzel 69)*
San Marino (0) 0
Slovakia: Mucha; Pekarik, Durica (Salata 46), Cech, Kozak, Hanzel, Hamsik (Novak 46), Karhan, Vittek, Stoch (Borbely 63), Jakubko.
San Marino: Simoncini A; Vitaioli F, Vannucci, Simoncini D, Berretti (Andreini 79), Bacciocchi, Rinaldi (Ciacci 65), Michele Marani (Bonini 86), Mauro Marani, Bugli, Selva A.
Referee: Nzolo (Belgium).

Maribor, 12 August 2009, 4400
Slovenia (2) 5 *(Koren 19, 73, Radosavljevic 38, Kirm 54, Ljubijankic 90)*
San Marino (0) 0
Slovenia: Handanovic; Suler, Radosavljevic (Bacinovic 75), Pecnik (Kirm 46), Cesar, Brecko, Koren, Jokic, Velikonja (Novakovic 72), Ljubijankic, Birsa.
San Marino: Simoncini A; Della Valle, Vitaioli F (Vitaioli M 59), Vannucci, Simoncini D (Albani N 67), Berretti, Bacciocchi, Andreini, Bugli, Ciacci, Manuel Marani (Bonini 80).
Referee: Mekmeckarovski (Macedonia).

Chorzow, 5 September 2009, 38,914
Poland (0) 1 *(Lewandowski M 80)*
Northern Ireland (1) 1 *(Lafferty 38)*
Poland: Boruc; Golanski, Zewlakow, Obraniak (Smolarek 46), Blaszczykowski, Roger, Murawski (Lewandowski R 51), Lewandowski M, Krzynowek, Dudka, Pawel Brozek.
Northern Ireland: Maik Taylor; Hughes, Craigan, Clingan, McAuley, Evans J, Davis, Johnson, Lafferty (Paterson 54), Healy, McCann.
Referee: Gonzalez (Spain).

Bratislava, 5 September 2009, 23,800
Slovakia (0) 2 *(Sestak 60, Hamsik 73 (pen))*
Czech Republic (0) 2 *(Pudil 68, Baros 83)*
Slovakia: Mucha; Skrtel, Pekarik, Durica, Strba, Hamsik[■], Zabavnik, Vittek, Sestak (Cech 82), Holosko (Jendrisek 87), Weiss (Sapara 74).
Czech Republic: Cech; Kadlec, Jankulovski, Grygera, Hubschman, Sivok, Pudil, Plasil, Jarolim (Necid 65), Koller (Baros 55), Stajner (Sverkos 83).
Referee: Ovrebo (Norway).

Uherske Hradiste, 9 September 2009, 8121
Czech Republic (3) 7 *(Baros 28, 44, 45 (pen), 66, Sverkos 47, 90, Necid 86)*   **San Marino (0) 0**
Czech Republic: Cech; Grygera (Stajner 77), Rozehnal, Kadlec (Pudil 46), Hubschman, Rosicky (Jarolim 56), Plasil, Baros, Sverkos, Necid, Bednar.
San Marino: Simoncini A; Della Valle, Berretti, Bacciocchi[■], Andreini, Vitaioli F, Vannucci, Mauro Marani (Bonini 64), Bugli (Cervellini 90), Ciacci (Vitaioli M 75), Selva A.
Referee: Amirkchanian (Armenia).

Belfast, 9 September 2009, 13,019
Northern Ireland (0) 0
Slovakia (1) 2 *(Sestak 15, Holosko 66)*
Northern Ireland: Maik Taylor; Hughes, McAuley, Clingan (Baird 70), Evans J, Craigan, Davis, Johnson, Healy, Paterson (Brunt 76), McCann (McGinn 70).
Slovakia: Mucha; Durica, Skrtel, Pekarik, Kopunek, Strba, Zabavnik, Vittek, Stoch (Jendrisek 80), Sestak (Holosko 65), Weiss (Sapara 90).
Referee: Kuipers (Holland).

Maribor, 9 September 2009, 10,226
Slovenia (2) 3 *(Dedic 12, Novakovic 44, Birsa 62)*
Poland (0) 0
Slovenia: Handanovic; Suler, Radosavljevic (Pecnik 89), Mavric, Kirm, Brecko, Koren, Jokic, Novakovic, Dedic (Ljubijankic 58), Birsa (Komac 71).
Poland: Boruc; Gancarczyk (Lewandowski R 62), Bosacki, Zewlakow, Obraniak (Lobodzinski 46), Blaszczykowski, Roger, Lewandowski M, Krzynowek, Dudka, Pawel Brozek (Smolarek 62).
Referee: Collum (Scotland).

Prague, 10 October 2009, 14,010
Czech Republic (0) 2 *(Necid 51, Plasil 72)*   **Poland (0) 0**
Czech Republic: Cech; Pospech, Jankulovski, Hubschman, Hubnik, Pudil (Stajner 86), Plasil, Sivok, Rosicky (Jarolim 78), Baros, Papadopoulos (Necid 46).
Poland: Kowalewski; Glowacki, Gancarczyk, Polczak, Rzezniczak, Obraniak, Blaszczykowski (Peszko 67), Iwanski, Lewandowski M, Jelen (Lewandowski R 64), Grosicki (Janczyk 81).
Referee: Bo Larsen (Denmark).

Bratislava, 10 October 2009, 23,800
Slovakia (0) 0   Slovenia (0) 2 *(Birsa 56, Pecnik 90)*
Slovakia: Mucha; Skrtel, Pekarik, Durica, Strba (Novak 84), Hamsik, Zabavnik, Vittek (Jendrisek 80), Stoch, Jakubko (Karhan 46), Weiss.
Slovenia: Handanovic; Suler, Radosavljevic, Kirm, Cesar, Brecko, Koren, Jokic, Novakovic, Dedic (Pecnik 78), Birsa (Stevanovic 90).
Referee: Stark (Germany).

Prague, 14 October 2009, 8002
Czech Republic (0) 0   Northern Ireland (0) 0
Czech Republic: Cech; Pospech, Jankulovski, Hubschman, Hubnik, Sivok, Rosicky (Stajner 72), Plasil, Jarolim (Papadopoulos 83), Baros, Necid (Hlousek 58).
Northern Ireland: Maik Taylor; Baird, McGinn, Craigan, Hughes, McAuley, McGivern, McCann (O'Connor 80), Davis, Johnson (Kirk 83), Healy (Feeney 69).
Referee: Duhamel (France).

Chorzow, 14 October 2009, 5000
Poland (0) 0   Slovakia (1) 1 *(Gancarczyk 3 (og))*
Poland: Dudek; Rzezniczak, Glowacki, Gancarczyk, Bienius, Obraniak, Blaszczykowski, Roger (Peszko 60), Lewandowski M, Jelen (Lewandowski R 68), Pawel Brozek (Janczyk 86).
Slovakia: Mucha; Salata, Petras, Pekarik, Strba, Kozak (Karhan 85), Kopunek, Hamsik, Sestak (Svento 75), Jendrisek, Weiss (Novak 67).
Referee: Eriksson (Sweden).

Serravalle, 14 October 2009, 1745
San Marino (0) 0
Slovenia (1) 3 *(Novakovic 24, Stevanovic 67, Suler 81)*
San Marino: Simoncini A; Vitaioli F, Valentini C (Cervellini 77), Simoncini D, Berretti (Bugli 46), Albani N, Michele Marani, Mauro Marani, Vitaioli M, Selva A (Rinaldi 63), Manuel Marani.
Slovenia: Handanovic; Suler, Radosavljevic, Kirm, Cesar, Brecko (Ilic 85), Stevanovic (Krhin 85), Jokic, Novakovic, Dedic (Ljubijankic 52), Birsa.
Referee: Szabo (Hungary).

Group 3 Table	P	W	D	L	F	A	Pts
Slovakia	10	7	1	2	22	10	22
Slovenia	10	6	2	2	18	4	20
Czech Republic	10	4	4	2	17	6	16
Northern Ireland	10	4	3	3	13	9	15
Poland	10	3	2	5	19	14	11
San Marino	10	0	0	10	1	47	0

GROUP 4

Vaduz, 6 September 2008, 7842
Liechtenstein (0) 0
Germany (1) 6 *(Podolski 21, 48, Rolfes 65,*
Schweinsteiger 66, Hitzlsperger 76, Westermann 86)
Liechtenstein: Jehle; Martin Stocklasa, Ritzberger, D'Elia, Polverino (Rohrer 64), Gerster, Burgmeier, Buchel M, Frick M, Fischer (Buchel R 87), Christen (Beck R 74).
Germany: Enke; Westermann, Tasci, Lahm, Fritz, Trochowski, Schweinsteiger, Rolfes (Marin 69), Hitzlsperger, Podolski (Kuranyi 76), Klose (Gomez 64).
Referee: Gomes (Portugal).

Cardiff, 6 September 2008, 17,106
Wales (0) 1 *(Vokes 83)* **Azerbaijan (0) 0**
Wales: Hennessey; Morgan C, Gunter, Williams A, Bale, Edwards D (Vokes 72), Ledley, Fletcher, Earnshaw (Evans C 62). Davies S, Koumas (Robinson 89).
Azerbaijan: Agayev; Yunisoglu, Malikov, Mammadov N (Nduka 78), Abbasov, Rashad Sadikhov, Mammadov E, Fabio[a], Bakhshiyev, Subasic, Huseynov (Nabiyev 46).
Referee: Stavrev (Macedonia).

Baku, 10 September 2008, 25,000
Azerbaijan (0) 0 **Liechtenstein (0) 0**
Azerbaijan: Agayev; Malikov, Yunisoglu, Bakhshiyev, Gurbanov (Zeynalov 71), Chertoganov, Abbasov, Subasic, Javadov (Huseynov 46), Rashad Sadikhov, Mammadov E (Gomesh 65).
Liechtenstein: Jehle; Ritzberger (Oehri 20), D'Elia, Gerster, Martin Stocklasa, Fischer, Frick M, Burgmeier, Buchel M, Christen (Beck T 68), Polverino (Rohrer 46).
Referee: Georgiev (Bulgaria).

Helsinki, 10 September 2008, 37,150
Finland (2) 3 *(Johansson 33, Vayrynen 43, Sjolund 53)*
Germany (2) 3 *(Klose 38, 45, 82)*
Finland: Jaaskelainen; Lampi, Kallio, Hyypia, Pasanen, Kolkka, Heikkinen, Eremenko R, Vayrynen (Kuqi N 75), Johansson, Forssell (Sjolund 41).
Germany: Enke; Tasci, Lahm, Westermann, Fritz (Hinkel 82), Schweinsteiger, Rolfes (Helmes 82), Hitzlsperger (Gomez 68), Trochowski, Podolski, Klose.
Referee: Kassai (Hungary).

Moscow, 10 September 2008, 28,000
Russia (1) 2 *(Pavlyuchenko 22 (pen), Pogrebnyak 81)*
Wales (0) 1 *(Ledley 67)*
Russia: Akinfeev; Anyukov, Ignashevich (Bystrov 90), Kolodin, Semak (Pogrebnyak 74), Semshov, Torbinskiy (Saenko 61), Zhirkov, Zyryanov, Arshavin, Pavlyuchenko.
Wales: Hennessey; Morgan C, Gunter, Bale, Robinson (Ricketts 46), Edwards D (Evans S 76), Fletcher, Ledley, Williams A, Davies S, Vokes (Evans C 62).
Referee: Skomina (Slovenia).

Helsinki, 11 October 2008, 22,124
Finland (0) 1 *(Forssell 61 (pen))* **Azerbaijan (0) 0**
Finland: Jaaskelainen; Tihinen, Pasanen, Kallio, Hyypia, Vayrynen, Tainio (Litmanen 79), Sjolund, Eremenko R (Heikkinen 90), Roiha (Pohja 62), Forssell.
Azerbaijan: Agayev; Shukurov, Yunisoglu, Malikov, Abbasov, Zeynalov, Rashad Sadikhov, Mammadov E (Huseynov 79), Chertoganov (Abdullayev 79), Subasic (Ponomarev 73), Gomesh.
Referee: Collum (Scotland).

Dortmund, 11 October 2008, 65,607
Germany (2) 2 *(Podolski 9, Ballack 28)*
Russia (0) 1 *(Arshavin 51)*
Germany: Adler; Westermann, Mertesacker, Lahm, Friedrich A, Trochowski (Frings 83), Schweinsteiger, Hitzlsperger (Rolfes 90), Ballack, Podolski, Klose (Gomez 71).
Russia: Akinfeev; Berezutski V, Ignashevich, Anyukov, Zhirkov, Yanbaev (Dzagoev 46), Semak (Sychev 84), Zyryanov, Denisov, Pogrebnyak, Arshavin.
Referee: Frojdfeldt (Sweden).

Cardiff, 11 October 2008, 13,356
Wales (1) 2 *(Edwards D 42, Frick M 80 (og))*
Liechtenstein (0) 0
Wales: Hennessey; Morgan C, Gunter, Bale, Williams A, Koumas, Fletcher (Robinson 56), Edwards D, Davies S, Bellamy (Collins J 80), Vokes (Evans C 51).
Liechtenstein: Jehle; Martin Stocklasa, Ritzberger (Christen 67), D'Elia, Polverino (Buchel R 80), Gerster, Burgmeier, Buchel M, Frick M, Fischer, Beck T.
Referee: Vejlgaard (Denmark).

Moenchengladbach, 15 October 2008, 45,000
Germany (0) 1 *(Trochowski 72)* **Wales (0) 0**
Germany: Adler; Westermann, Mertesacker, Lahm, Friedrich A (Fritz 65), Trochowski, Schweinsteiger, Hitzlsperger, Ballack, Podolski (Gomez 82), Klose (Helmes 46).
Wales: Hennessey; Gunter (Ricketts 86), Bale, Fletcher (Robinson 77), Morgan C, Williams A, Davies S, Collins J, Bellamy, Koumas, Edwards D (Evans C 77).
Referee: Duhamel (France).

Moscow, 15 October 2008, 28,000
Russia (1) 3 *(Pasanen 23 (og), Lampi 65 (og), Arshavin 88)*
Finland (0) 0
Russia: Akinfeev; Ignashevich, Berezutski V, Anyukov, Zyryanov, Zhirkov, Semshov, Semak, Pogrebnyak (Saenko 60), Denisov, Arshavin (Dzagoev 90).
Finland: Jaaskelainen; Tihinen, Pasanen, Lampi, Hyypia, Vayrynen (Pohja 69), Sjolund (Litmanen 85), Kolkka, Heikkinen, Eremenko R (Tainio 66), Forssell.
Referee: Vassaras (Greece).

Leipzig, 28 March 2009, 43,368
Germany (2) 4 *(Ballack 4, Jansen 9, Schweinsteiger 48, Podolski 50)*
Liechtenstein (0) 0
Germany: Enke; Tasci, Mertesacker, Lahm, Jansen (Helmes 64), Beck, Schweinsteiger (Rolfes 88), Hitzlsperger (Marin 78), Ballack, Podolski, Gomez.
Liechtenstein: Jehle; Michael Stocklasa, Vogt, Martin Stocklasa, Ritzberger, Oehri, Rohrer, Gerster, Frick M, Buchel R, Beck T (Beck R 74).
Referee: Ishchenko (Ukraine).

Moscow, 28 March 2009, 62,000
Russia (1) 2 *(Pavlyuchenko 32, Zyryanov 71)*
Azerbaijan (0) 0
Russia: Akinfeev; Ignashevich, Berezutski V, Anyukov, Zyryanov, Zhirkov, Semshov, Semak (Dzagoev 56), Pavlyuchenko (Pogrebnyak 72), Denisov, Arshavin.
Azerbaijan: Veliyev; Shukurov, Melikov, Abbasov, Yunisoglu, Rashad Sadikhov, Fabio (Gomesh 61), Bakhshiyev, Maharramov, Subasic (Javadov 46), Nadyrov.
Referee: Gumienny (Belgium).

Cardiff, 28 March 2009, 22,604
Wales (0) 0 **Finland (1) 2** *(Johansson 42, Kuqi S 90)*
Wales: Hennessey; Gunter, Bale, Edwards D (Ramsey 56), Nyatanga, Collins J, Koumas, Fletcher (Robinson 65), Bellamy, Davies S, Ledley (Earnshaw 71).
Finland: Jaaskelainen; Tihinen, Pasanen, Kallio, Hyypia, Eremenko R, Heikkinen, Eremenko A (Sjolund 78), Litmanen (Porokara 90), Johansson, Forssell (Kuqi S 89).
Referee: Gonzalez (Spain).

Vaduz, 1 April 2009, 5679
Liechtenstein (0) 0 **Russia (1) 1** *(Zyryanov 38)*
Liechtenstein: Jehle; Vogt (D'Elia 60), Michael Stocklasa, Martin Stocklasa, Ritzberger, Oehri (Rohrer 46), Polverino, Gerster, Burgmeier, Buchel M (Beck T 75), Frick M.
Russia: Akinfeev; Ignashevich, Berezutski V, Anyukov, Zyryanov, Zhirkov, Torbinskiy (Semak 66), Semchov, Pavlyuchenko (Pogrebnyak 84), Denisov, Arshavin.
Referee: McKeon (Republic of Ireland).

Cardiff, 1 April 2009, 26,064
Wales (0) 0
Germany (1) 2 *(Ballack 11, Williams A 48 (og))*
Wales: Hennessey; Ricketts (Gunter 54), Bale, Williams A,
Nyatanga (Cotterill 75), Collins J, Davies S, Ramsey, Vokes
(Evans C 62), Earnshaw, Ledley.
Germany: Enke; Tasci, Mertesacker, Lahm, Beck,
Schweinsteiger (Helmes 86), Rolfes (Westermann 79),
Hitzlsperger, Ballack, Podolski (Trochowski 72), Gomez.
Referee: Hauge (Norway).

Baku, 6 June 2009, 25,000
Azerbaijan (0) 0 Wales (1) 1 *(Edwards D 41)*
Azerbaijan: Veliyev; Shukurov, Melikov, Levin, Nabiyev
(Huseynov 50), Rashad Sadikhov, Fabio (Subasic 46),
Zeynalov, Bakhshiyev, Javadov, Akhtyamov (Nadyrov 60).
Wales: Hennessey; Gunter, Eardley, Nyatanga, Morgan C,
Williams A, Ramsey, Edwards D, Ledley, Earnshaw (Vokes
70), Church (Tudur-Jones 83).
Referee: Strombergsson (Sweden).

Helsinki, 6 June 2009, 20,319
Finland (1) 2 *(Forssell 33, Johansson 71)*
Liechtenstein (1) 1 *(Frick M 14)*
Finland: Jaaskelainen; Tihinen, Pasanen (Lampi 46), Kallio,
Hyypia, Tainio (Heikkinen 67), Eremenko R, Eremenko A,
Litmanen (Kuqi S 72), Johansson, Forssell.
Liechtenstein: Jehle; Vogt (Rohrer 66), Michael Stocklasa,
Martin Stocklasa, Ritzberger, Polverino, Buchel M
(Christen 58), Burgmeier, Frick M, Fischer, Buchel R
(Buchel S 76).
Referee: Kovarik (Czech Republic).

Helsinki, 10 June 2009, 37,028
Finland (0) 0
Russia (1) 3 *(Kerzhakov 26, 53, Zyryanov 71)*
Finland: Jaaskelainen; Tihinen, Pasanen, Kallio (Moisander
54), Hyypia, Heikkinen, Eremenko R, Eremenko A
(Kolkka 61), Litmanen (Tainio 69), Johansson, Forssell.
Russia: Akinfeev; Kolodin, Ignashevich, Berezutski V,
Zyryanov, Zhirkov, Semshov, Bystrov (Semak 77),
Kerzhakov (Pavlyuchenko 67), Denisov, Arshavin.
Referee: Plautz (Austria).

Baku, 12 August 2009, 22,500
Azerbaijan (0) 0
Germany (1) 2 *(Schweinsteiger 12, Klose 54)*
Azerbaijan: Veliyev; Melikov, Abbasov, Allahverdiev,
Yunisoglu, Shukurov, Rashad Sadikhov, Mammadov E,
Chertoganov, Nadirov (Akhtyamov 75), Dzavadov.
Germany: Enke; Tasci, Schafer, Mertesacker, Lahm,
Trochowski (Jansen 77), Schweinsteiger, Hitzlsperger,
Ballack, Klose (Cacau 75), Gomez (Ozil 83).
Referee: Kelly (Republic of Ireland).

Helsinki, 6 September 2009, 20,319
Finland (1) 2 *(Forssell 33, Johansson 71)*
Liechtenstein (1) 1 *(Frick M 14)*
Finland: Jaaskelainen; Pasanen (Lampi 46), Kallio, Hyypia,
Tihinen, Eremenko R, Eremenko A, Tainio (Heikkinen 67),
Litmanen (Kuqi S 72), Johansson, Forssell.
Liechtenstein: Jehle; Martin Stocklasa, Ritzberger, Vogt
(Rohrer 66), Michael Stocklasa, Polverino, Buchel M
(Christen 58), Burgmeier, Frick M, Fischer, Buchel R
(Buchel S 76).
Referee: Kovarik (Czech Republic).

Hanover, 9 September 2009, 35,369
Germany (1) 4 *(Ballack 14 (pen), Klose 55, 66, Podolski 7.)*
Azerbaijan (0) 0
Germany: Adler; Westermann, Schafer (Beck 46),
Mertesacker, Lahm, Ballack, Schweinsteiger (Trochowski
67), Ozil, Hitzlsperger, Gomez (Klose 46), Podolski.
Azerbaijan: Agayev; Allahverdiev, Abbasov*, Yunisoglu,
Shukurov, Levin, Rashad Sadikhov, Mammadov E (Huseynov
67), Chertoganov, Nadirov (Pereira 57), Dzavadov.
Referee: Kakkos (Greece).

Vaduz, 9 September 2009, 3132
Liechtenstein (0) 1 *(Polverino 75)*
Finland (0) 1 *(Litmanen 73 (pen))*
Liechtenstein: Jehle; Michael Stocklasa, Ritzberger,
Rechsteiner, Oehri, Rohrer (Beck R 85), Buchel M (Polverino
65), Burgmeier, Frick M, Buchel R, Hasler (Beck T 79).

Finland: Jaaskelainen; Tihinen, Pasanen, Moisander,
Hyypia, Heikkinen, Eremenko R, Eremenko A, Sadik
(Kolkka 60), Litmanen (Kuqi 82), Johansson.
Referee: Panic (Bosnia).

Cardiff, 9 September 2009, 14,505
Wales (0) 1 *(Collins J 54)*
Russia (1) 3 *(Semshov 36, Ignashevich 72,
Pavlyuchenko 90)*
Wales: Hennessey; Ricketts, Gunter, Gabbidon (Vokes 75),
Williams A, Collins J, Ramsey, Ledley, Edwards D, Stock,
Bellamy.
Russia: Akinfeev; Ignashevich, Berezutski V, Anyukov,
Zyryanov, Yanbaev, Semshov (Pavlyuchenko 71), Semak,
Bystrov, Kerzhakov (Rebko 84), Arshavin.
Referee: Sousa (Portugal).

Helsirki, 10 October 2009, 14,000
Finland (1) 2 *(Porokara 5, Moisander 77)*
Wales (1) 1 *(Bellamy 17)*
Finland: Jaaskelainen; Tihinen, Pasanen, Moisander,
Hyypia, Sparv, Kolkka (Hamalainen 68), Eremenko R,
Porokara, Litmanen (Eremenko A 90), Johansson (Kuqi S
88).
Wales: Hennessey; Gunter, Bale, Edwards D, Nyatanga
(Eardley 83), Williams A, Collins J, Ramsey, Church (Vokes
63), Bellamy, Cotterill.
Referee: Mazic (Serbia).

Vaduz, 10 October 2009, 1635
Liechtenstein (0) 0
Azerbaijan (0) 2 *(Dzavadov 54, Mammadov E 82)*
Liechtenstein: Jehle; Ritzberger (Christen 81), Rechsteiner,
D'Elia, Oehri, Kieber, Burgmeier, Rohrer (Beck R 58),
Buchel S (Beck T 68), Buchel R, Hasler.
Azerbaijan: Agayev; Levin, Allahverdiyev, Shukurov,
Medvedev (Melikov 90), Mammadov E, Chertoganov,
Abishov, Akhtyamov, Dzavadov (Huseynov 90), Nadirov
(Rashad Sadikhov 46).
Referee: Radovanovic (Montenegro).

Moscow, 10 October 2009, 72,100
Russia (0) 0 Germany (1) 1 *(Klose 35)*
Russia: Akinfeev; Ignashevich, Berezutski V, Anyukov,
Zyryanov, Zhirkov, Semshov (Pogrebnyak 77), Bystrov,
Kerzhakov (Pavlyuchenko 55), Denisov (Torbinsky 46),
Arshavin.
Germany: Adler; Westermann, Mertesacker, Lahm,
Boateng*, Schweinsteiger, Rolfes, Ozil (Friedrich A 72),
Ballack, Podolski (Trochowski 85), Klose (Gomez 90).
Referee: Busacca (Switzerland).

Baku, 14 October 2009, 17,000
Azerbaijan (0) 1 *(Abishov 54)* **Russia (1) 1** *(Arshavin 13)*
Azerbaijan: Agayev; Shukurov, Melikov, Medvedev
(Huseynov 73), Levin, Abbasov, Rashad Sadikhov (Nadirov
46), Mammadov E, Chertoganov, Abishov, Dzavadov.
Russia: Akinfeev; Ignashevich, Berezutski A, Yanbaev,
Torbinsky, Semak, Rebko (Bukharov 64), Dzagoev, Bystrov
(Denisov 64), Bilyaletdinov, Arshavin.
Referee: Webb (England).

Hamburg, 14 October 2009, 51,500
Germany (0) 1 *(Podolski 90)*
Finland (1) 1 *(Johansson 11)*
Germany: Adler; Westermann, Lahm, Friedrich A, Beck,
Trochowski, Hitzlsperger (Gentner 46), Ballack (Ozil 46),
Podolski, Gomez (Klose 77), Cacau.
Finland: Jaaskelainen; Moisander, Lampi, Hyypia,
Eremenko R, Sparv, Heikkinen, Hamalainen (Kolkka 67),
Porokara (Kuqi S 72), Litmanen (Nyman 87), Johansson.
Referee: Atkinson (England).

Vaduz, 14 October 2009, 1858
Liechtenstein (0) 0
Wales (1) 2 *(Vaughan 15, Ramsey 79)*
Liechtenstein: Jehle; Ritzberger, Rechsteiner, D'Elia, Oehri,
Rohrer (Beck R 36), Kieber, Eberle, Frick M, Buchel R
(Polverino 70), Hasler (Christen 72).
Wales: Myhill; Gunter (Eardley 87), Bale (Nyatanga 84),
Collins J, Morgan C, Williams A, Edwards D (King A 82),
Ramsey, Church, Easter, Vaughan.
Referee: Kaldma (Estonia).

Group 4 Table	P	W	D	L	F	A	Pts
Germany	10	8	2	0	26	5	26
Russia	10	7	1	2	19	6	22
Finland	10	5	3	2	14	14	18
Wales	10	4	0	6	9	12	12
Azerbaijan	10	1	2	7	4	14	5
Liechtenstein	10	0	2	8	2	23	2

GROUP 5

Erevan, 6 September 2008, 30,000
Armenia (0) 0   Turkey (0) 2 *(Tuncay 60, Semih 78)*
Armenia: Berezovskiy; Tadevosian, Hovsepian, Arzumanian (Khachatrian 35), Arakelian, Voskanian, Pachajian, Mkrtchian A, Mikhitarian (Zebelian 65), Manucharian (Arm Karamian 76), Art Karamian.
Turkey: Volkan; Gokhan Z, Gokhan G, Servet, Hakan Balta, Arda, Mehmet Aurelio, Emre B, Semih (Gokhan U 82), Tuncay (Ayhan 66), Mevlut (Kazim-Richards 55).
Referee: Ovrebo (Norway).

Liege, 6 September 2008, 17,992
Belgium (1) 3 *(Sonck 40, 80, Defour 75)*
Estonia (0) 2 *(Zenjov 57, Oper 90)*
Belgium: Stijnen; Vermaelen (Van Damme 70), Van Buyten, Kompany, Witsel, Vertonghen, Simons, Fellaini, Defour, Sonck (Huysegems 90), Mirallas (De Sutter 76).
Estonia: Londak; Piiroja (Stepanov 43), Kruglov, Klavan, Jaager, Barengrub, Lindpere, Dmitrijev, Zenjov (Vunk 60), Oper, Kink (Puri 78).
Referee: Dean (England).

Murcia, 6 September 2008, 29,152
Spain (0) 1 *(David Villa 57)*   **Bosnia (0) 0**
Spain: Casillas; Sergio Ramos, Albiol, Puyol, Capdevila, Xavi, Senna, Iniesta, Fabregas (Xabi Alonso 64), Capel (Cazorla 72), David Villa (Guiza 84).
Bosnia: Hasagic; Radeljic, Nadarevic, Berberovic (Ibisevic 65), Salihovic, Rahimic, Muratovic, Mismovic, Damjanovic (Ibricic 80), Vladavic, Dzeko (Pjanic 84).
Referee: Thomson (Scotland).

Zenica, 10 September 2008, 15,000
Bosnia (2) 7 *(Misimovic 24, 30 (pen), 56, Muslimovic 59, Dzeko 60, 72, Ibricic 88)*   **Estonia (0) 0**
Bosnia: Hasagic; Berberovic, Spahic, Muratovic (Ibricic 73), Rahimic, Damjanovic, Muslimovic (Ibisevic 71), Misimovic (Pjanic 66), Dzeko, Nadarevic, Salihovic.
Estonia: Londak (Aksalu 71); Rahn, Barengrub, Dmitrijev (Saag 65), Purje, Oper, Lindpere (Kruglov 65) Vunk, Vassiljev, Klavan, Jaager.
Referee: Balaj (Romania).

Albacete, 10 September 2008, 16,996
Spain (2) 4 *(Capdevila 7, David Villa 16, 79, Senna 83)*
Armenia (0) 0
Spain: Casillas; Capdevila, Sergio Ramos, Albiol, Puyol, Xavi (Fabregas 74), Senna, Iniesta, Cazorla (Krkic 65), Guiza (Xabi Alonso 56), David Villa.
Armenia: Berezovskiy; Tadevosian, Hovsepian, Arzumanian, Arakelian, Aleksanian (Khachatrian 79), Voskanian, Pachajvan, Mkrtchian A, Art Karamian (Arm Karamian 52), Melkonian (Manucharian 46).
Referee: Asumaa (Finland).

Istanbul, 10 September 2008, 25,000
Turkey (0) 1 *(Emre B 74 (pen))*   **Belgium (1) 1** *(Sonck 32)*
Turkey: Volkan; Servet, Caglar, Gokhan Z, Emre B, Gokhan G, Arda, Mehmet Topal (Merlut 69), Semih, Tuncay (Halil Altintop 14), Kazim-Richards (Mehmet Topuz 46).
Belgium: Stijnen; Simons, Kompany, Defour (Mudingayi 46), Witsel (Daems 76), Sonck (De Sutter 85), Vermaelen, Vertonghen, Swertz, Fellaini, Dembele.
Referee: Lannoy (France).

Brussels, 11 October 2008, 20,949
Belgium (2) 2 *(Sonck 21, Fellaini 37)*   **Armenia (0) 0**
Belgium: Stijnen; Van Damme, Kompany, Gillet, Witsel, Vertonghen, Simons, Fellaini, Defour (Huysegems 72), Sonck (De Sutter 87), Dembele.
Armenia: Berezovskiy; Tadevosian, Hovsepian, Arzumanian, Arakelian, Aleksanian (Ara Hakobian 64), Voskanian, Pachajian, Mkrtchian A, Art Karamian (Mikhitarian 85), Zebelian (Melkonian 80).
Referee: Rasmussen (Denmark).

Tallinn, 11 October 2008, 9200
Estonia (0) 0   Spain (2) 3 *(Juanito 34, David Villa 38, Puyol 69)*
Estonia: Londak; Piiroja, Kruglov, Jaager, Barengrub, Vunk, Vassiljev, Lindpere (Klavan 75), Dmitrijev, Voskobionikov (Saag 73), Kink (Puri 59).
Spain: Casillas; Sergio Ramos (Iraola 54), Puyol, Juanito, Capdevila, Xavi, Xabi Alonso, Iniesta (Riera 79), Cazorla, Torres, David Villa (Fabregas 70).
Referee: Eriksson (Sweden).

Istanbul, 11 October 2008, 23,628
Turkey (0) 2 *(Arda 51, Mevlut 86)* **Bosnia (1) 1** *(Dzeko 26)*
Turkey: Volkan; Sabri, Ibrahim K, Servet, Hakan Balta, Ayhan (Halil Altintop 63), Arda, Mehmet Aurelio, Kazim-Richards, Mevlut (Yusuf 79), Batuhan (Nuri 38).
Bosnia: Hasagic (Brasnic 74); Berberovic, Spahic, Radeljic (Ibisevic 63), Salihovic, Rahimic, Muratovic (Pjanic 80), Misimovic, Ibricic, Damjanovic, Dzeko.
Referee: Baskakov (Russia).

Brussels, 15 October 2008, 45,888
Belgium (1) 1 *(Sonck 7)*   **Spain (1) 2** *(Iniesta 36, David Villa 88)*
Belgium: Stijnen; Simons, Kompany, Van Buyten (Daems 46), Defour (Van Damme 73), Witsel, Sonck, Vermaelen, Vertonghen, Vanden Borre (Gillet 87), Fellaini.
Spain: Casillas; Juanito, Puyol, Iniesta (Guiza 84). David Villa, Xavi, Torres (Fabregas 16), Capdevila, Sergio Ramos, Senna, Cazorla (Xabi Alonso 64).
Referee: Michel (Slovakia).

Zenica, 15 October 2008, 13,000
Bosnia (2) 4 *(Spahic 31, Dzeko 39, Muslimovic 56, 89)*
Armenia (0) 1 *(Minasian 85)*
Bosnia: Brasnic; Berberovic (Vladavic 61), Spahic (Vasilic 68), Muratovic, Rahimic, Damjanovic, Misimovic, Dzeko, Mravac, Ibisevic (Muslimovic 46), Salihovic.
Armenia: Berezovskiy; Yedigarian (Minasian 59), Hovsepian, Arzumanian, Voskanian, Zebelian (Ara Hakobian 73), Arm Karamian, Melkonian (Arakelian 41), Pachajian, Mkrtchian A, Tadevosian.
Referee: Kenan (Israel).

Tallinn, 15 October 2008, 6500
Estonia (0) 0   Turkey (0) 0
Estonia: Londak; Shishov, Piiroja, Kruglov, Klavan, Barengrub, Vunk (Puri 77), Vassiljev, Dmitrijev, Voskoboinikov (Zenjov 63), Oper.
Turkey: Volkan; Sabri, Ibrahim K, Servet, Hakan Balta, Arda, Nuri (Mevlut 35), Mehmet Aurelio, Kazim-Richards (Ugur 72), Ayhan (Yusuf 60), Halil Altintop.
Referee: Malek (Poland).

Erevan, 28 March 2009, 3000
Armenia (1) 2 *(Mkhitarian 32, Yedigarian 88)*
Estonia (1) 2 *(Vassiljev 36, Zenjov 67)*
Armenia: Berezovskiy; Minasian, Hovsepian, Arzumanian, Arakelian, Voskanian (Ghazarian 46), Pachajian (Yedigarian 83), Mkrtchian A, Mkhitarian, Art Karamian, Arm Karamian (Manucharian 52).
Estonia: Pareiko; Rahn, Piiroja, Klavan, Jaager, Vunk, Vassiljev (Saag 75), Lindpere (Puri 74), Dmitrijev, Voskoboinikov (Zenjov 63), Kink.
Referee: Wilmes (Luxembourg).

Genk, 28 March 2009, 20,041
Belgium (0) 2 *(Dembele 67, Sonck 89 (pen))*
Bosnia (1) 4 *(Dzeko 11, Jahic 74, Bajramovic 81, Misimovic 86)*
Belgium: Stijnen; Daems (De Sutter 80), Vermaelen, Swerts, Mudingayi, Fellaini, Defour (Pocognoli 60), Simons, Dembele, De Camargo (Hazard 46), Sonck.
Bosnia: Supic; Pandza, Jahic, Spahic (Mravac 60), Nadarevic, Berberovic, Muratovic, Misimovic, Ibricic, Muslimovic (Bajramovic 70), Dzeko (Pjanic 89).
Referee: Ivanov (Russia).

Madrid, 28 March 2009, 73,820
Spain (0) 1 *(Pique 60)*   **Turkey (0) 0**
Spain: Casillas; Capdevila, Pique, Sergio Ramos, Albiol, Cazorla (Silva 78), Xavi, Xabi Alonso, Senna, Torres (Llorente 88), David Villa (Mata 63).
Turkey: Volkan; Ibrahim U, Emre A, Gokhan G, Hakan Balta, Arda (Gokhan U 77), Emre B (Sabri 84), Mehmet Aurelio, Tuncay, Nihat, Semih (Ayhan 57).
Referee: Busacca (Switzerland).

Zenica, 1 April 2009, 13,800

Bosnia (2) 2 *(Dzeko 12, 20)* **Belgium (0) 1** *(Swerts 88)*
Bosnia: Supic; Spahic, Pandza, Nadarevic, Jahic, Berberovic, Rahimic, Muratovic (Bajramovic 87), Misimovic, Ibricic (Pjanic 77), Dzeko (Topic 90).
Belgium: Stijnen; Vermaelen, Kompany, Swerts, Witsel■, Simons, Mudingayi (De Sutter 55), Fellaini, Sonck (Gillet 90), Mirallas (Hazard 73), Dembele.
Referee: Hrinak (Slovakia).

Tallinn, 1 April 2009, 5200

Estonia (0) 1 *(Puri 83)* **Armenia (0) 0**
Estonia: Pareiko; Rahn, Piiroja, Klavan, Jaager, Puri, Vassiljev, Dmitrijev, Viikmae (Zenjov 62), Voskoboinikov (Vunk 87), Kink (Lindpere 69).
Armenia: Kasparov; Yedegarian (Arm Karamian 84), Minasian, Hovsepian, Arzumanian, Arakelian, Manucharian, Pachajian, Mkrtchian A, Mkhitarian, Art Karamian (Ghazarian 89).
Referee: Zimmermann (Switzerland).

Istanbul, 1 April 2009, 19,617

Turkey (1) 1 *(Semih 26)*
Spain (0) 2 *(Xabi Alonso 62 (pen), Riera 90)*
Turkey: Volkan; Ibrahim U, Gokhan G, Hakan Balta, Emre A, Arda (Nuri 88), Mehmet Aurelio, Emre B, Semih (Sabri 81), Tuncay, Nihat (Batuhan 77).
Spain: Casillas; Sergio Ramos, Marchena, Capdevila, Pique, Xavi, Xabi Alonso, Riera, Senna (Cazorla 67), Torres (Guiza 85), David Villa (Busquets 74).
Referee: Riley (England).

Erevan, 5 September 2009, 1800

Armenia (0) 0 Bosnia (1) 2 *(Ibricic 6, Musilmovic 73)*
Armenia: Kasparov; Yedigarian (Yagan 74), Yavruian (Goaryan 46), Arakelian (Minasian 65), Tadevosian Hovsepian, Arzumanian, Mkrtchian A, Mkhitarian, Ar Karamian, Arm Karamian.
Bosnia: Supic; Spahic, Nadarevic, Jahic, Salihovic, Rahimic, Muratovic (Pjanic 64), Ibricic (Bajramovic 84), Vladavic, Dzeko, Ibisevic (Muslimovic 68).
Referee: Braamhaar (Holland).

La Coruna, 5 September 2009, 30,441

Spain (1) 5 *(Silva 41, 68, David Villa 49, 85, Pique 50)*
Belgium (0) 0
Spain: Casillas; Puyol, Pique, Capdevila, Arbeloa (Albiol 83), Xabi Alonso, Silva, Busquets, Xavi (Fabregas 70), Torres (Riera 67), David Villa.
Belgium: Gillet; Vermaelen, Vanden Borre, Van Buyten, Simons, Hazard (Mirallas 59), Fellaini, Defour, Vertonghen (Deschacht 29), Sonck (De Camargo 70), Dembele.
Referee: Layec (France).

Kayseri, 5 September 2009, 28,569

Turkey (2) 4 *(Tuncay 29, 72, Sercan 36, Arda 61)*
Estonia (1) 2 *(Voskoboinikov 7, Vassiljev 52)*
Turkey: Volkan; Gokhan G, Servet, Hakan Balta, Gokhan Z (Onder 34), Arda, Kazim-Richards (Halil Altintop 69), Emre B (Ceyhun 78), Hamit Altintop, Sercan, Tuncay.
Estonia: Pareiko; Piiroja, Kruglov, Klavan, Jaager, Barengrub, Lindpere, Dmitrijev (Vunk 74), Vassiljev, Oper (Kink 73), Voskoboinikov (Zenjov 53).
Referee: Skjerven (Norway).

Erevan, 9 September 2009, 2300

Armenia (0) 1 *(Goaryan 23, Hovsepian 50)*
Belgium (0) 1 *(Van Buyten 90)*
Armenia: Kasparov; Hovsepian, Arzumanian, Arakelian (Mkrtchian K 14), Yedigarian (Kakosian 88), Mkrtchian A, Mkoian, Mkhitarian, Art Karamian, Arm Karamian, Goaryan (Yavruian 32).
Belgium: Gillet; Van Buyten, Deschacht, Swerts, Simons, Martens (De Sutter 54), Defour, Sonck (Lamah 30), Mirallas (Hazard 71), Dembele, De Camargo.
Referee: Stavrev (Macedonia).

Zenica, 9 September 2009, 30,131

Bosnia (1) 1 *(Salihovic 25)* **Turkey (1) 1** *(Emre B 4)*
Bosnia: Supic; Spahic, Nadarevic, Jahic, Salihovic, Rahimic, Muratovic (Pjanic 61), Misimovic, Ibricic (Vladavic 79), Ibisevic (Muslimovic 64), Dzeko.
Turkey: Volkan; Onder (Ismail 46), Gokhan G, Hakan Balta, Arda, Ceyhun, Emre B (Semih 46), Hamit Altintop (Sercan 46), Semih, Tuncay, Oguz.
Referee: Benquerenca (Portugal).

Merida, 9 September 2009, 14,362

Spain (1) 3 *(Fabregas 33, Cazorla 81, Mata 90)*
Estonia (0) 0
Spain: Casillas; Pique, Marchena, Capdevila, Albiol, Xavi, Silva (Mata 79), Senna, Fabregas, David Villa (Cazorla 67), Torres (Guiza 57).
Estonia: Pareiko; Sisov (Jaager 65), Rahn, Piiroja, Kruglov, Klavan, Vunk, Vassiljev, Oper, Zenjov (Voskoboinikov 46), Kink (Lindpere 71).
Referee: Oriekhov (Ukraine).

Erevan, 10 October 2009, 10,500

Armenia (0) 2 *(Arzumanian 58)*
Spain (1) 2 *(Fabregas 33, Mata 64 (pen))*
Armenia: Berezovskiy; Hovsepian, Arzumanian, Yedigarian (Arakelian 74), Pizelli (Dashian 69), Mkrtchian K, Mkrtchian A. Mkoian, Art Karamian, Arm Karamian, Goaryan (Melkonian 60).
Spain: Reina; Sergio Ramos, Puyol, Monreal, Marchena (Pique 46), Xavi, Senna, Fabregas, Cazorla, Torres (Negredo 55), Mata (Iniesta 67).
Referee: Jech (Czech Republic).

Brussels, 10 October 2009, 30,131

Belgium (1) 2 *(Mpenza 8, 84)* **Turkey (0) 0**
Belgium: Bailly; Vermaelen, Van Buyten, Lombaerts, Swerts, Vertonghen, Lamah (Mudingayi 79), Fellaini, Mpenza (De Sutter 90), Mirallas (Hazard 74), Dembele.
Turkey: Volkan; Onder, Gokhan G, Servet, Hakan Balta, Nuri, Ceyhun (Semih 46), Hamit Altintop, Ayhan (Kazim-Richards 61), Tuncay, Nihat (Yusuf 72).
Referee: Trefoloni (Italy).

Tallinn, 10 October 2009, 6450

Estonia (0) 0 Bosnia (1) 2 *(Dzeko 30, Ibisevic 64)*
Estonia: Pareiko; Kruglov, Klavan, Jaager, Barengrub, Rahn, Puri S, Vassiljev, Dmitrijev, Kink (Purje 73), Voskoboinikov (Saag 59).
Bosnia: Hasagic (Begovic 90); Jahic, Spahic, Nadarevic, Muratovic (Berberovic 85), Misimovic, Ibricic, Salihovic, Rahimic, Ibisevic, Dzeko.
Referee: Rizzoli (Italy).

Zenica, 14 October 2009, 13,500

Bosnia (2) 2 *(Dzeko 89, Misimovic 90)*
Spain (2) 5 *(Pique 12, Silva 13, Negredo 50, 55, Mata 88)*
Bosnia: Supic; Spahic, Nadarevic, Jahic, Pjanic, Salihovic (Hrgovic 73), Rahimic (Bajramovic 46), Muratovic (Vladavic 67), Misimovic, Ibisevic, Dzeko.
Spain: Casillas; Pique (Sergio Ramos 77), Iraola, Capdevila, Albiol, Silva (Mata 81), Riera, Iniesta (Senna 67), Busquets, Xabi Alonso, Negredo.
Referee: Plautz (Austria).

Tallinn, 14 October 2009, 4680

Estonia (1) 2 *(Piiroja 30, Vassiljev 67)* **Belgium (0) 0**
Estonia: Pareiko; Rahn, Piiroja (Morozov 62), Kruglov, Jaager, Dmitrijev, Vunk, Vassiljev, Lindpere, Saag (Voskoboinikov 72), Kink (Puri S 59).
Belgium: Bailly; Vermaelen, Van Buyten (Alderweireld 46), Lombaerts, Swerts (De Sutter 76), Vertonghen, Mudingayi (Buffel 46), Lamah, Mpenza, Mirallas, Dembele.
Referee: Vollquartz (Denmark).

Bursa, 14 October 2009, 16,200

Turkey (2) 2 *(Halil Altintop 16, Servet 28)* **Armenia (0) 0**
Turkey: Volkan (Rustu 90); Ismail, Gokhan G, Servet, Arda, Ceyhun■, Emre B, Hamit Altintop (Kazim-Richards 84), Ayhan, Tuncay (Ibrahim K 46), Halil Altintop.
Armenia: Berezovskiy; Hovsepian, Arzumanian, Arakelian (Pizelli 55), Mkrtchian K, Mkrtchian A, Mkoian, Mkhitarian, Art Karamian, Arm Karamian (Kakosian 78), Goaryan.
Referee: Hansson (Sweden).

Group 5 Table

	P	W	D	L	F	A	Pts
Spain	10	10	0	0	28	5	30
Bosnia	10	6	1	3	25	13	19
Turkey	10	4	3	3	13	10	15
Belgium	10	3	1	6	13	20	10
Estonia	10	2	2	6	9	24	8
Armenia	10	1	1	8	6	22	4

GROUP 6

Almaty, 20 August 2008, 7700
Kazakhstan (3) 3 *(Ostapenko 14, 30, Uzdenov 45)*
Andorra (0) 0

Kazakhstan: Loriya; Kuchma, Irismetov, Asanbayev (Baizhanov 78), Baltiyev, Zhumaskaliev, Smakov, Nurdauletov, Skorykh (Karpovich 68), Uzdenov (Byakov 63), Ostapenko.
Andorra: Gomes; Lima T, Lima I, Pujol (Somoza 82), Bernaus, Ayala (Escura 15), Xavi, Vieira, Toscano (Txema 72), Vales, Fernando Silva.
Referee: Banari (Moldova).

Barcelona, 6 September 2008, 10,300
Andorra (0) 0   England (0) 2 *(Cole J 48, 55)*
Andorra: Koldo; Lima T (Juli Fernandez 90), Lima I, Txema, Xavi, Vieira, Pujol (Vales 90), Ayala, Jimenez, Sonejee, Fernando Silva (Toscano 65).
England: James; Johnson G, Cole A, Barry, Terry, Lescott, Walcott, Lampard (Beckham 80), Rooney, Defoe (Heskey 46), Downing (Cole J 46).
Referee: Cuneyt (Turkey).

Zagreb, 6 September 2008, 17,424
Croatia (2) 3 *(Kovac N 13, Modric 36, Petric 81)*
Kazakhstan (0) 0
Croatia: Pletikosa; Kovac R, Corluka, Simunic, Modric (Pokrivac 85), Kovac N, Srna, Rakitic, Pranjic, Olic (Leko 88), Klasnic (Petric 64).
Kazakhstan: Loriya; Kuchma, Irismetov, Zhalmagambetov, Smakov, Byakov, Baizhanov (Chichulin 57), Baltiyev, Zhumaskaliyev, Skorykh (Karpovich 81), Ostapenko (Uzdenov 84).
Referee: Johannesson (Sweden).

Lvov, 6 September 2008, 24,000
Ukraine (0) 1 *(Shevchenko 90 (pen))*   **Belarus (0) 0**
Ukraine: Pyatov; Shevchuk, Rusol, Yarmash, Tymoshchuk, Nazarenko, Mikhalik, Kravchenko, Kalinichenko (Aliev 46), Voronin (Seleznov 58), Milevsky (Shevchenko 74).
Belarus: Zhevnov; Verkhovtsov, Omelyanchuk, Filipenko, Strakanovich, Putsilo (Pavlov 80), Kulchiy, Korytko (Chukhley 67), Hleb A, Kutuzov, Bulyga (Hleb V 72).
Referee: Rizzoli (Italy).

La Vella, 10 September 2008, 200
Andorra (0) 1 *(Pujol 67 (pen))*
Belarus (1) 3 *(Verkhovtsov 37, Rodionov 79, Hleb V 90)*
Andorra: Koldo; Ayala, Escura, Sonejee, Lima T, Lima I, Pujol (Toscano 82), Vieira (Vales 62), Fernando Silva (Moreno 86), Jimenez, Xavi.
Belarus: Veremko; Kulchi, Filipenko, Omelyanchuk, Pavlov (Rodionov 57), Korytko, Bulyga (Hleb V 63), Strakanovich (Sitko 87), Hleb A, Kutuzov, Verkhovtsov.
Referee: Evans (Wales).

Zagreb, 10 September 2008, 35,218
Croatia (0) 1 *(Mandzukic 78)*
England (1) 4 *(Walcott 26, 59, 82, Rooney 63)*
Croatia: Pletikosa; Corluka, Simunic, Kovac R[a], Srna, Rakitic, Pranjic, Modric, Kovac N (Pokrivac 62), Petric (Knezevic 56), Olic (Mandzukic 73).
England: James; Terry (Upson 89), Ferdinand, Cole A, Brown, Lampard, Cole J (Jenas 56), Barry, Walcott (Beckham 85), Rooney, Heskey.
Referee: Michel (Slovakia).

Almaty, 10 September 2008, 17,000
Kazakhstan (0) 1 *(Ostapenko 68)*
Ukraine (1) 3 *(Nazarenko 45, 80, Shevchenko 54)*
Kazakhstan: Loriya; Irismetov, Kuchma, Azovskiy, Karpovich, Smakov, Zhumaskaliyev, Asanbayev (Baizhanov 73), Baltiyev (Uzdenov 88), Skorykh, Ostapenko.
Ukraine: Pyatov; Shevchuk, Yarmash, Kucher, Aliev, Tymoshchuk, Levchenko, Mikhalik, Nazarenko (Kravchenko 81), Seleznov (Homenyuk 87), Shevchenko (Voronin 88).
Referee: Brych (Germany).

Wembley, 11 October 2008, 89,107
England (0) 5 *(Ferdinand 52, Rooney 76, 86, Defoe 90, Kuchma 64 (og))*
Kazakhstan (0) 1 *(Kukeyev 68)*
England: James; Brown, Cole A, Gerrard, Ferdinand, Upson, Walcott (Beckham 79), Lampard, Heskey, Rooney (Defoe 86), Barry (Wright-Phillips 46).
Kazakhstan: Mokin; Kuchma, Kislitsyn, Kirov (Sabalakov 85), Kukeyev, Baltiyev, Logvinenko, Ibrayev, Skorykh, Ostapenko (Maltsev 76), Nusserbayev.
Referee: Allaerts (Belgium).

Kharkiv, 11 October 2008, 38,500
Ukraine (0) 0   Croatia (0) 0
Ukraine: Pyatov; Chigrinskiy, Yarmash, Shevchuk, Aliev, Golaydo, Tymoshchuk, Nazarenko, Mikhalik, Levchenko (Kravchenko 84), Shevchenko.
Croatia: Pletikosa; Krizanac, Corluka, Simunic, Vukojevic, Srna, Rakitic (Mandzukic 84), Pranjic, Modric, Kovac N, Olic.
Referee: Braamhaar (Holland).

Minsk, 15 October 2008, 32,000
Belarus (1) 1 *(Sitko 28)*
England (1) 3 *(Gerrard 11, Rooney 50, 74)*
Belarus: Zhevnov; Verkhovtsov, Filipenko, Omelyanchuk, Molosh, Kulchi, Sitko, Putsilo (Rodionov 67), Stasevich (Hleb V 90), Kutuzov (Strakanovich 77), Bulyga.
England: James; Brown, Bridge, Gerrard, Ferdinand, Upson, Walcott (Wright-Phillips 68), Lampard, Heskey (Crouch 70), Rooney (Beckham 87), Barry.
Referee: Hauge (Norway).

Zagreb, 15 October 2008, 14,441
Croatia (2) 4 *(Rakitic 16, 86 (pen), Olic 32, Modric 75)*
Andorra (0) 0
Croatia: Pletikosa; Krizanac (Knezevic 78), Simunic, Corluka, Vukojevic (Leko 61), Rakitic, Pranjic, Modric, Petric, Olic (Mandzukic 68), Klasnic.
Andorra: Koldo; Rodriguez, Lima I, Escura (Txema 81), Vieira, Pujol, Ayala, Xavi, Vales, Jimenez (Somoza 37), Fernando Silva (Toscano 90).
Referee: Vad (Hungary).

La Vella, 1 April 2009, 1000
Andorra (0) 0   Croatia (2) 2 *(Klasnic 15, Eduardo 35)*
Andorra: Koldo; Lima T, Escura (Rodriguez 90), Vieira, Pujol, Bernaus, Andorra, Vales, Sonejee, Jimenez (Moreno 81), Fernando Silva (Moreira 78).
Croatia: Pletikosa; Vejic, Krizanac, Cale (Vukojevic 69), Corluka, Kranjcar, Juric (Pokrivac 64), Srna, Rakitic, Eduardo, Klasnic (Kalinic 77).
Referee: Trattou (Cyprus).

Wembley, 1 April 2009, 87,548
England (1) 2 *(Crouch 29, Terry 85)*
Ukraine (0) 1 *(Shevchenko 74)*
England: James; Johnson G, Cole A, Barry, Terry, Ferdinand (Jagielka 88), Lennon (Beckham 58), Lampard, Crouch (Wright-Phillips 79), Rooney, Gerrard.
Ukraine: Pyatov; Chigrinskiy, Shevchuk, Yarmash, Mikhalik, Valyaev (Nazarenko 61), Slyusar (Kalinichenko 89), Aliev, Tymoshchuk, Voronin (Shevchenko 55), Milevskiy.
Referee: Bo Larsen (Denmark).

Almaty, 1 April 2009, 19,000
Kazakhstan (1) 1 *(Abdulin 10)*
Belarus (0) 5 *(Hleb A 48, Kalachev 53, 63, Stasevich 57, Kovel 88)*
Kazakhstan: Loriya; Irismetov, Abdulin, Kislitsyn, Smakov, Logvinenko, Kukeev, Karpovich (Ibraev 63), Baltiev (Nurgaliev 81), Ostapenko, Nuserbayev.
Belarus: Zhevnov; Sosnovskiy, Yurevich, Shitov, Stasevich (Kovel 80), Kulchiy (Kashevski 75), Kalachev, Bordachev, Hleb A, Rodionov, Kutuzov (Bliznyuk 86).
Referee: Jech (Czech Republic).

Grodno, 6 June 2009, 8500
Belarus (2) 5 *(Bliznyuk 3, 75, Kalachev 44, Kornilenko 50, 65)*
Andorra (0) 1 *(Lima T 90 (pen))*
Belarus: Zhevnov; Yurevich, Sosnovskiy, Shitov (Rudik 66), Verkhovtsov, Stasevich, Kalachev, Hleb A, Kashevski (Kovel 66), Bliznyuk, Kornilenko (Rodionov 80).

Andorra: Koldo; Lima T (Juli Fernandez 90), Lima I, Escura, Ayala, Andorra (Rodriguez 82), Vales, Sonejee, Fernando Silva, Moreno, Moreira (Jimenez 76).
Referee: Krajnc (Slovenia).

Zagreb, 6 June 2009, 32,073
Croatia (1) 2 *(Petric 2, Modric 68)*
Ukraine (1) 2 *(Shevchenko 13, Gay 54)*
Croatia: Runje; Simunic, Kovac R, Corluka, Juric (Vukojevic 46), Rakitic (Leko 46), Pranjic, Modric, Srna, Petric, Olic (Mandzukic 60).
Ukraine: Pyatov; Chigrinskiy, Mandzyuk, Kucher, Shevchuk, Rotan, Gay, Nazarenko (Kalinichenko 75), Tymoshchuk (Rusol 88), Shevchenko (Seleznov 23), Milevskiy.
Referee: Hauge (Norway).

Almaty, 6 June 2009, 24,000
Kazakhstan (0) 0
England (2) 4 *(Barry 39, Heskey 45, Rooney 72, Lampard 78 (pen))*
Kazakhstan: Mokin; Abdulin, Kirov, Kislitsyn, Karpovich, Logvinenko, Kukeev, Skorykh, Averchenko (Erbes 74), Ostapenko (Ibraev 27), Nuserbaev.
England: Green; Johnson G (Beckham 76), Cole A, Barry, Terry, Upson, Gerrard, Lampard, Heskey (Defoe 81), Rooney, Walcott (Wright-Phillips 46).
Referee: Jakobsson (Iceland).

Wembley, 10 June 2009, 57,897
England (3) 6 *(Rooney 4, 38, Lampard 29, Defoe 73, 75, Crouch 80)*
Andorra (0) 0
England: Green; Johnson G, Cole A (Bridge 63), Beckham, Terry, Lescott, Gerrard (Young A 46), Lampard, Crouch, Rooney (Defoe 46), Walcott.
Andorra: Koldo (Gomes 89); Lima T (Vales 47), Txema, Ayala, Lima I, Andorra, Vieira, Jimenez, Sonejee, Moreno, Fernando Silva (Juli Fernandez 79).
Referee: Nijhuis (Holland).

Kiev, 10 June 2009, 11,500
Ukraine (1) 2 *(Nazarenko 33, 47)*
Kazakhstan (1) 1 *(Nuserbaev 18)*
Ukraine: Bogush; Chigrinskiy, Mandzyuk, Shevchuk, Rusol, Gay, Rotan (Kalinichenko 81), Tymoshchuk, Nazarenko, Milevskiy, Voronin (Seleznov 68).
Kazakhstan: Mokin; Abudlin, Kirov (Irismetov 70), Kislitsyn, Erbes (Averchenko 74), Karpovich, Skorykh, Logvinenko, Kukeev, Khizhinchenko, Nuserbaev (Travin 63).
Referee: Paixao (Portugal).

Minsk, 12 August 2009, 21,651
Belarus (0) 1 *(Verkhovtsov 81)*
Croatia (1) 3 *(Olic 22, 83, Eduardo 68)*
Belarus: Zhevnov; Yurevich, Sosnovskiy, Omelyanchuk, Verkhovtsov, Kulchiy, Kalachev, Kashevski (Kovel 54), Hleb A, Kutuzov (Bliznyuk 85), Kornilenko (Rodionov 71).
Croatia: Runje; Krizanac (Rakitic 46), Simunic, Corluka, Kranjcar (Mandzukic 66), Vukojevic, Srna, Modric, Pranjic, Eduardo (Juric 88), Olic.
Referee: Brych (Germany).

Zagreb, 5 September 2009, 25,628
Croatia (1) 1 *(Rakitic 24)*   **Belarus (0) 0**
Croatia: Runje; Krizanac, Simunic, Corluka*, Kranjcar, Vukojevic, Rakitic (Mandzukic 64), Pranjic, Srna, Eduardo (Juric 81), Olic (Petric 74).
Belarus: Zhevnov; Sosnovskiy, Shitov, Yurevich, Verkhovtsov, Omelyanchuk, Kulchiy, Kalachev, Bordachev (Stasevich 55), Kornilenko (Kovel 77), Hleb V (Krivets 63).
Referee: Plautz (Austria).

Kiev, 5 September 2009, 14,870
Ukraine (2) 5 *(Yarmolenko 18, Milevskiy 45, 89 (pen), Shevchenko 72 (pen), Seleznov 90 (pen))*
Andorra (0) 0
Ukraine: Pyatov; Kobin, Yarmolenko, Chigrinskiy, Mandzyuk, Kucher, Gusev (Gay 70), Tymoschchuk, Shevchenko (Gomenyuk 81), Milevskiy, Voronin (Seleznov 66).
Andorra: Gomes; Toscano (Moreira 84), Pujol, Ayala, Vieira (Escura 75), Sonejee, Jimenez, Vales, Silva, Moreno (Garcia 82), Martinez.
Referee: Sipailo (Latvia).

Andorra la Vella, 9 September 2009, 510
Andorra (0) 1 *(Sonejee 69)*
Kazakhstan (3) 3 *(Khizhinchenko 14, 34, Beltiev 28)*
Andorra: Gomes; Lima I, Bernaus, Ayala, Vieira (Riera 87), Vales (Escura 46), Sonejee, Jimenez (Toscano 54), Silva, Moreno, Martinez.
Kazakhstan: Mokin; Abdulin, Kislitsyn, Kirov, Baltiev, Kukeev (Nurgaliev 87), Logvinenko, Karpovich, Averchenko, Khizhinchenko (Erbes 90), Finonchenko (Skorykh 77).
Referee: Toussaint (Luxembourg).

Minsk, 9 September 2009, 21,727
Belarus (0) 0   **Ukraine (0) 0**
Belarus: Zhevnov; Yurevich, Sosnovskiy, Shitov, Plaskonny (Lentsevich 57), Omelyanchuk, Kalachev, Kulchiy, Hleb A, Kornilenko (Kovel 77), Kutuzov (Hleb V 87).
Ukraine: Pyatov; Chigrinskiy, Mandzyuk, Kucher, Gusev (Nazarenko 59), Gay, Tymoshchuk, Kobir, Yarmolenko, Shevchenko (Voronin 88), Milevskiy.
Referee: Kassai (Hungary).

Wembley, 9 September 2009, 87,319
England (2) 5 *(Lampard 7 (pen), 59, Gerrard 18, 66, Rooney 77)*
Croatia (0) 1 *(Eduardo 71)*
England: Green; Johnson G, Cole A, Barry, Terry, Upson, Lennon (Milner 81), Lampard, Heskey (Defoe 60), Rooney, Gerrard (Beckham 81).
Croatia: Runje; Krizanac, Simunic, Kranjcar, Vukojevic, Srna, Pranjic, Pokrivac (Rakitic 46), Eduardo (Klasnic 73), Olic (Petric 46), Mandzukic.
Referee: Mallenco (Spain).

Brest, 10 October 2009, 9530
Belarus (1) 4 *(Bordachev 23, Kalachev 69, 90, Kovel 86)*
Kazakhstan (0) 0
Belarus: Zhevnov; Yurevich, Sosnovskiy, Shitov, Verkhovtsov, Omelyanchuk, Kulchiy (Rodionov 89), Kalachev, Bordachev (Krivets 83), Kutuzov (Kovel 73), Kornilenko.
Kazakhstan: Mokin; Abdulin, Kislitsyn, Kirov, Skorykh (Erbes 80), Logvinenko, Kukeev, Karpovich, Baltiev (Nuserbaev 62), Khizhinchenko, Averchenko.
Referee: Ennjimi (France).

Dnepr, 10 October 2009, 31,000
Ukraine (1) 1 *(Nazarenko 29)*   **England (0) 0**
Ukraine: Pyatov; Khacheridi, Kucher, Rakitskiy, Gay, Rotan, Tymoshchuk, Nazarenko (Yarmolenko 67), Kobin, Shevchenko (Gusev 90), Milevskiy.
England: Green*; Johnson, Cole A, Carrick, Terry, Ferdinand, Lennon (James 15), Lampard, Rooney, Heskey (Cole C 72), Gerrard (Milner 46).
Referee: Skomina (Slovenia).

Andorra La Vella, 14 October 2009, 820
Andorra (0) 0
Ukraine (1) 6 *(Shevchenko 22, Gusev 61, Lima I 69 (og), Rakitskiy 80, Seleznov 80, Yarmolenko 83)*
Andorra: Gomes; Lima I, Andorra (Garcia 89), Pujol, Ayala, Vales, Jimenez (Moreno 73), Silva, Juli Sanchez (Riera 79), Martinez, Maneiro.
Ukraine: Pyatov; Khacheridi, Mikhalik, Kucher, Gusev, Rakitskiy, Nazarenko (Gay 74), Kobiri, Yarmolenko, Shevchenko (Aliyev 74), Milevskiy (Seleznov 76).
Referee: Thomson (Scotland).

Wembley, 14 October 2009, 76,897
England (1) 3 *(Crouch 3, 75, Wright-Phillips 60)*
Belarus (0) 0
England: Foster; Johnson G, Bridge (Milner 78), Barry, Terry, Ferdinand, Lennon (Beckham 60), Lampard, Crouch, Agbonlahor (Cole C 66), Wright-Phillips.
Belarus: Zhevnov; Yurevich, Sosnovskiy, Shitov, Verkhovtsov, Omelyanchuk, Bordachev (Kashevski 84), Kulchiy, Kalachev, Kutuzov (Rodionov 46), Kornilenko (Kovel 77).
Referee: Batista (Portugal).

Astana, 14 October 2009, 10,250
Kazakhstan (1) 1 *(Khizhinchenko 26)*
Croatia (1) 2 *(Vukojevic 10, Kranjcar 90)*
Kazakhstan: Mokin; Abdulin, Kislitsyn, Kirov, Nurgaliev (Kukeev 54), Erbes (Baltiev 90), Logvinenko, Skorykh, Khizhinchenko, Averchenko, Nuserbaev (Malinin 77).
Croatia: Runje; Lovren, Kovac R, Corluka, Kranjcar, Vukojevic, Rakitic, Pranjic, Srna (Pokrivac 90), Mandzukic (Bilic 63), Klasnic (Jelavic 77).
Referee: Circhetta (Switzerland).

Group 6 Table	P	W	D	L	F	A	Pts
England	10	9	0	1	34	6	27
Ukraine	10	6	3	1	21	6	21
Croatia	10	6	2	2	19	13	20
Belarus	10	4	1	5	19	14	13
Kazakhstan	10	2	0	8	11	29	6
Andorra	10	0	0	10	3	39	0

GROUP 7

Vienna, 6 September 2008, 48,000
Austria (2) 3 *(Janko 8, Aufhauser 41, Ivanschitz 72 (pen))*
France (0) 1 *(Govou 61)*
Austria: Manninger; Scharner, Prodl, Pogatetz, Garics, Stranzl, Ivanschitz (Leitgeb 81), Fuchs, Aufhauser, Janko (Maierhofer 88), Harnik (Standfest 90).
France: Mandanda; Sagna (Gourcuff 71), Mexes, Gallas, Evra, Toulalan, Nasri (Anelka 79), Diarra L, Henry, Govou, Benzema.
Referee: Bo Larsen (Denmark).

Cluj, 6 September 2008, 14,000
Romania (0) 0   Lithuania (1) 3 *(Stankevicius 31, Mikoliunas 69, Kalonas 86)*
Romania: Lobont; Sapunaru, Radu (Niculae M 46), Radoi (Lazar 72), Goian, Contra, Tamas, Dica, Cocis, Niculae D, Marica (Bratu 53).
Lithuania: Karcemarskas; Stankevicius, Semberas, Klimavicius, Dedura, Zelmikas, Pilibaitis (Savenas 74), Mikoliunas, Ksanavicius (Kalonas 62), Cesnauskis D, Danilevicius (Cesnauskis E 80).
Referee: Kelly (Republic of Ireland).

Belgrade, 6 September 2008, 9615
Serbia (1) 2 *(Jacobsen J 30 (og), Zigic 88)*   **Faeroes (0) 0**
Serbia: Disljenkovic; Obradovic, Vidic, Rukavina, Dragutinovic, Tosic (Jankovic 75), Stankovic, Milijas (Ilic 61), Krasic, Pantelic (Lazovic 56), Zigic.
Faeroes: Mikkelsen; Naes■, Jacobsen J, Davidsen, Danielsen, Bo, Thomassen, Samuelsen (Lokin 69), Jacobsen C, Flotum, Borg.
Referee: Nikolaev (Russia).

Torshavn, 10 September 2008, 805
Faeroes (0) 0   Romania (0) 1 *(Cocis 59)*
Faeroes: Mikkelsen; Bo, Danielsen, Davidsen, Jacobsen J, Jacobsen P (Lokin 80), Samuelsen, Thomassen, Borg (Eliasen 90), Flotum (Olsen A 76), Jacobsen C.
Romania: Lobont; Radoi (Ghionea■ 18), Goian, Contra, Nesu, Aliuta (Moti 68), Cocis, Codrea, Lazar, Costea, Niculae M (Bratu 89).
Referee: Strahonja (Croatia).

Paris, 10 September 2008, 53,027
France (0) 2 *(Henry 53, Anelka 63)*
Serbia (0) 1 *(Ivanovic 75)*
France: Mandanda; Abidal, Gallas, Sagna, Clichy, Toulalan, Diarra A, Benzema (Anelka 46), Gourcuff (Flamini 90), Govou (Diarra L 82), Henry.
Serbia: Stojkovic; Krstajic, Vidic, Ivanovic, Stankovic (Kacar 4), Tosic, Ergic (Zigic 56), Jankovic, Kuzmanovic, Sulejmani (Krasic 68), Pantelic.
Referee: Benquerenca (Portugal).

Marijampole, 10 September 2008, 4500
Lithuania (0) 2 *(Danilevicius 52, 58)*   **Austria (0) 0**
Lithuania: Karcemarskas; Semberas, Klimavicius, Dedura, Zelmikas, Stankevicius, Pilibaitis (Cesnauskis E 72), Mikoliunas, Ksanavicius (Zaliukas 75), Cesnauskis D (Kalonas 66), Danilevicius.
Austria: Manninger; Prodl, Pogatetz, Garics, Stranzl, Scharner (Hoffer 86), Ivanschitz, Fuchs, Aufhauser (Saumel 55), Maierhofer, Harnik.
Referee: Tagliavento (Italy).

Torshavn, 11 October 2008, 1890
Faeroes (0) 1 *(Lokin 47)*   **Austria (0) 1** *(Stranzl 49)*
Faeroes: Mikkelsen; Naes, Jacobsen J, Davidsen, Danielsen, Bo, Thomassen (Benjaminsen 37), Hansen A, Holst, Jacobsen C, Borg (Lokin 32) (Flotum 74).
Austria: Manninger; Stranzl, Scharner, Prodl, Pogatetz, Garics (Kienast 67), Ivanschitz, Fuchs, Janko (Arnautovic 80), Hoffer, Harnik (Holzl 25).
Referee: Ceferin (Slovenia).

Constanta, 11 October 2008, 12,800
Romania (2) 2 *(Petre 5, Goian 16)*
France (1) 2 *(Ribery 36, Gourcuff 68)*
Romania: Lobont; Rat, Ogararu, Chivu, Tamas, Goian, Muresan, Cocis, Petre (Costea 75), Mutu (Bucur 75), Marica.
France: Mandanda; Abidal, Boumsong, Sagna, Evra, Malouda (Benzema 37), Toulalan, Ribery (Briand 90), Gourcuff, Diarra A, Henry.
Referee: De Bleeckere (Belgium).

Belgrade, 11 October 2008, 22,000
Serbia (2) 3 *(Ivanovic 6, Krasic 34, Zigic 82)*
Lithuania (0) 0
Serbia: Stojkovic; Obradovic, Dragutinovic (Krstajic 24), Vidic, Ivanovic (Kuzmanovic 57), Stankovic, Milijas, Krasic (Jankovic 72), Jovanovic, Zigic, Pantelic.
Lithuania: Karcemarskas; Zelmikas, Stankevicius, Semberas, Klimavicius■, Dedura, Pilibaitis (Skerla 79), Papeckys (Kalonas 46), Mikoliunas (Jankauskas 46), Ksanavicius, Danilevicius.
Referee: Gonzalez (Spain).

Vienna, 15 October 2008, 48,000
Austria (0) 1 *(Janko 80)*
Serbia (3) 3 *(Krasic 14, Jovanovic 18, Obradovic 24)*
Austria: Manninger; Stranzl (Gercaliu 18), Scharner, Prodl, Pogatetz, Garics, Ivanschitz, Fuchs, Aufhauser (Saumel 60), Janko, Hoffer (Arnautovic 46).
Serbia: Stojkovic; Lukovic, Obradovic, Vidic, Ivanovic, Stankovic (Jankovic 76), Milijas (Kuzmanovic 53), Krasic, Jovanovic, Zigic, Pantelic (Tosic 64).
Referee: Riley (England).

Kaunas, 15 October 2008, 5000
Lithuania (1) 1 *(Danilevicius 20)*   **Faeroes (0) 0**
Lithuania: Karcemarskas; Alunderis, Stankevicius, Skerla, Semberas, Dedura, Pilibaitis (Zaliukas 90), Mikoliunas, Ksanavicius (Kalonas 58), Velicka (Poskus 69), Danilevicius.
Faeroes: Mikkelsen; Naes, Jacobsen J, Davidsen, Danielsen, Bo, Benjaminsen (Jacobsen R 87), Samuelsen (Hojsted 81), Lokin (Hansen A 85), Jacobsen C, Holst.
Referee: Kapitanis (Cyprus).

Kaunas, 28 March 2009, 8700
Lithuania (0) 0   **France (0) 1** *(Ribery 67)*
Lithuania: Karcemarskas; Dedura, Skerla, Semberas, Klimavicius, Cesnauskis E (Mikoliunas 85), Cesnauskis D, Sernas, Panka (Poskus 81), Savenas (Ivaskevicius 65), Danilevicius.
France: Mandanda; Squillaci, Sagna, Gallas, Evra, Toulalan, Ribery, Gourcuff (Nasri 78), Diarra L, Luyindula (Benzema 64), Henry.
Referee: Braamhaar (Holland).

Constanta, 28 March 2009, 12,000
Romania (0) 2 *(Marica 50, Stoica 74)*
Serbia (2) 3 *(Jovanovic 18, Stoica 44 (og), Ivanovic 59)*
Romania: Lobont; Stoica, Tamas, Rat, Radoi, Contra, Cocis (Niculae M 76), Codrea (Tanase 46), Mutu, Marica, Costea (Bucur 63).
Serbia: Stojkovic; Obradovic, Vidic, Ivanovic, Dragutinovic, Stankovic, Milijas, Krasic, Jovanovic (Jankovic 62), Zigic, Pantelic (Subotic 66).
Referee: Trefoloni (Italy).

Klagenfurt, 1 April 2009, 23,000
Austria (2) 2 *(Hoffer 25, 44)*   **Romania (1) 1** *(Tanase 24)*
Austria: Gspurning; Schiemer, Prodl, Pogatetz, Ortlechner, Beichler (Holzl 78), Pehlivan, Scharner, Maierhofer, Hoffer (Okotie 54), Arnautovic (Korkmaz 70).
Romania: Lobont; Tamas, Rat, Radoi (Stoica 46), Goian, Contra, Tanase, Nicolita (Nicu 84), Cocis, Marica, Bucur (Niculae M 68).
Referee: Thomson (Scotland).

Paris, 1 April 2009, 79,543
France (0) 1 *(Ribery 75)* **Lithuania (0) 0**
France: Mandanda; Squillaci, Sagna, Gallas, Evra, Ribery, Gourcuff (Benzema 57), Diarra L, Diarra A, Luyindula (Gignac 68), Henry.
Lithuania: Karcemarskas; Skerla, Semberas, Klimavicius, Alunderis, Zaliukas, Sernas, Pilibaitis (Velicka 82), Mikoliunas (Cesnauskis E 65), Kalonas (Savenas 59), Danilevicius.
Referee: Webb (England).

Marijampole, 6 June 2009, 5850
Lithuania (0) 0   Romania (1) 1 *(Marica 38)*
Lithuania: Karcemarskas; Skerla, Klimavicius (Luksys 84), Stankevicius, Semberas, Cesnauskis E, Kalonas (Mikolunas 64), Zaliukas, Sernas, Pilibaitis (Dedura 81), Danilevicius.
Romania: Coman; Shivu, Apostol, Sapunaru, Rat, Radoi, Tanase, Ghioane (Lazar 90), Marica (Niculae M 85), Mara (Roman 72), Danciulescu.
Referee: Eriksson (Sweden).

Belgrade, 6 June 2009, 50,000
Serbia (1) 1 *(Milijas 7 (pen))*   **Austria (0) 0**
Serbia: Stojkovic; Subotic, Ivanovic, Dragutinovic, Vidic (Rukavina 46), Milijas, Krasic (Kacar 82), Stankovic, Jovanovic, Lazovic (Jankovic 56), Pantelic.
Austria: Gspurning; Ortlechner, Stranzl, Schiemer, Dragovic, Pehlivan, Scharner, Jantscher, Holzl (Lexa 66), Maierhofer (Janko 56), Hoffer (Okotie 56).
Referee: Vink (Holland).

Torshavn, 10 June 2009, 2896
Faeroes (0) 0   Serbia (1) 2 *(Jovanovic 44, Subotic 62)*
Faeroes: Mikkelsen; Gregersen, Naes, Davidsen, Danielsen. Bo, Olsen S (Petersen 78), Benjaminsen, Samuelser (Jacobsen C 68), Lokin, Holst (Flotum 87).
Serbia: Stojkovic; Kolarov, Subotic, Lukovic, Ivanovic Krasic (Kacar 83), Milijas, Kuzmanovic, Jovanovic (Sulejmani 77), Zigic, Pantelic (Lazovic 65).
Referee: Levi (Israel).

Torshavn, 12 August 2009, 2974
Faeroes (0) 0   France (1) 1 *(Gignac 41)*
Faeroes: Mikkelsen; Gregersen, Davidsen, Danielsen (Petersen 43), Bo, Naes, Benjaminsen, Olsen S (Borg 85), Samuelsen, Lokin, Holst (Edmundsson 29).
France: Lloris; Gallas, Evra, Escude, Sagna, Diarra L, Toulalan, Malouda (Ribery 65), Gourcuff, Anelka, Gignac.
Referee: Koukoulakis (Greece).

Graz, 5 September 2009, 12,300
Austria (2) 3 *(Maierhofer 1, Janko 16, 59 (pen))*
Faeroes (0) 1 *(Olsen A 83)*
Austria: Payer; Patocka (Ortlechner 46), Schiemer, Dragovic, Fuchs, Beichler (Wallner 80), Pehlivan, Jantscher, Holzl, Maierhofer (Hoffer 61), Janko.
Faeroes: Mikkelsen; Hansen E, Gregersen, Naes, Danielsen, Bo, Benjaminsen (Petersen 81), Olsen S (Hanssen 68), Lokin, Samuelsen, Holst (Olsen A 72).
Referee: Borg (Malta).

Paris, 5 September 2009, 78,209
France (0) 1 *(Henry 48)*   **Romania (0) 1** *(Escude 56 (og))*
France: Lloris; Sagna, Evra, Diarra L, Toulalan, Gallas, Escude, Gourcuff (Benzema 73), Henry, Anelka, Gignac (Ribery 59).
Romania: Koman; Rat, Radoi, Chivu, Apostol, Maftei, Micu (Bucur 77), Ghioane, Surdu (Codrea 86), Marica, Mara (Roman 61).
Referee: Bebek (Croatia).

Toftir, 9 September 2009, 1942
Faeroes (2) 2 *(Olsen S 15, Hansen A 34)*
Lithuania (1) 1 *(Danilevicius 23)*
Faeroes: Mikkelsen; Hansen E, Gregersen, Eliasen, Davidsen, Petersen, Olsen S, Samuelsen, Hansen A (Olsen A 68), Holst, Borg (Olsen B 90).
Lithuania: Karcemarskas; Stankevicius, Skerla, Semberas, Klimavicius (Mikoliunas 63), Dedura, Sernas, Pilibaitis (Trakys 60), Ivaskevicius (Kalonas 82), Cesnauskis E, Danilevicius.
Referee: Vad (Hungary).

Bucharest, 9 September 2009, 7505
Romania (0) 1 *(Bucur 54)*   **Austria (0) 1** *(Schiemer 82)*
Romania: Coman; Sapunaru, Rat, Radoi, Chivu, Roman, Ghioane, Codrea (Lazar 72), Marica (Mazilu 78), Andrei Cristea (Surdu 86), Bucur.
Austria: Payer; Schiemer, Dragovic, Fehlivan, Fuchs, Beichler (Wallner 72), Scharner, Jantscher (Trimmel 62), Holzl, Baumgartlinger, Hoffer (Maierhofer 46).
Referee: Atkinson (England).

Belgrade, 9 September 2009, 49,256
Serbia (1) 1 *(Milijas 12 (pen))*   **France (1) 1** *(Henry 31)*
Serbia: Stojkovic; Obradovic, Lukovic, Vidic, Ivanovic, Stankovic, Milijas (Kuzmanovic 71), Krasic, Kacar (Ninkovic 46), Zigic, Jovanovic (Lazovic 75).
France: Lloris; Sagna, Evra, Abidal, Toulalan, Gallas, Gourcuff (Diarra A 85), Diarra L, Henry (Ribery 77), Gignac (Mandanda 12), Anelka.
Referee: Rossetti (Italy).

Innsbruck, 10 October 2009, 14,500
Austria (1) 2 *(Janko 16, Wallner 80 (pen))*
Lithuania (0) 1 *(Stankevicius 66)*
Austria: Payer; Ulmer, Schiemer, Dragovic, Prager (Drazan 57), Pehlivan, Kavlak, Beichler (Baumgartlinger 57), Scharner, Wallner, Janko (Maierhofer 73).
Lithuania: Karcemarskas; Stankevicius, Kijanskas, Dedura, Alunderis (Luksys 82), Panka (Trakys 89), Sernas, Razanauskas (Kalonas 46), Semberas, Danilevicius, Cesnauskis E.
Referee: Guminienny (Belgium).

Guingamp, 10 October 2009, 16,755
France (2) 5 *(Gignac 34, 38, Gallas 52, Anelka 86, Benzema 88)*
Faeroes (0) 0
France: Mandanda; Abidal, Evra, Sagna, Gallas, Diarra L, Toulalan (Sissoko 61), Govou (Malouda 62), Gignac (Benzema 73), Anelka, Henry.
Faeroes: Mikkelsen; Gregersen, Danielsen, Bo, Jacobsen R (Olsen A 80), Benjaminsen, Petersen (Naes 64), Olsen S (Olsen B 90), Lokin, Jacobsen C.
Referee: Malek (Poland).

Belgrade, 10 October 2009, 39,839
Serbia (1) 5 *(Zigic 36, Pantelic 50, Kuzmanovic 78, Jovanovic 87, 90)*
Romania (0) 0
Serbia: Stojkovic; Lukovic (Dragutinovic 46), Kolarov, Vidic (Subotic 73), Ivanovic, Stankovic, Milijas (Kuzmanovic 65), Krasic, Zigic, Pantelic, Jovanovic.
Romania: Coman; Rat, Radoi, Maftei, Chivu, Ghioane (Goian 59), Adrian Cristea, Apostol, Varga, Mutu (Andrei Cristea 75), Marica (Bucur 59).
Referee: Kapitanos (Cyprus).

Paris, 14 October 2009, 78,000
France (2) 3 *(Benzema 18, Henry 26 (pen), Gignac 66)*
Austria (0) 1 *(Janko 48)*
France: Lloris; Squillaci, Fanni, Escude, Clichy, Sissoko, Malouda, Diarra A, Henry (Gignac 50), Govou, Benzema (Gomis 79).
Austria: Payer (Gratzei 46); Patocka, Dragovic, Pehlivan, Kavlak, Fuchs (Alaba 80), Scharner, Jantscher, Baumgartlinger, Maierhofer (Hoffer 46), Janko.
Referee: Proenca (Portugal).

Marijampole, 14 October 2009, 2000
Lithuania (1) 2 *(Kalonas 20 (pen), Stankevicius 68 (pen))*
Serbia (0) 1 *(Tosic 59)*
Lithuania: Karcemarskas; Stankevicius, Klimavicius, Kijanskas, Dedura, Sernas (Trakys 89), Pilibaitis, Panka, Kalonas (Razanauskas 82), Ivaskevicius, Mikoliunas (Luksa 66).
Serbia: Disljenkovic; Subotic, Obradovic (Lukovic 60), Ivanovic, Dragutinovic, Petrovic, Krasic (Tosic 46), Kacar, Zigic, Pantelic (Ninkovic 74), Jovanovic.
Referee: Genov (Bulgaria).

Piatra Neamt, 14 October 2009, 13,000
Romania (1) 3 *(Apostol 16, Bucur 64, Mazilu 87)*
Faeroes (0) 1 *(Bo 83)*
Romania: Pantilimon; Rat, Radoi, Panin, Goian (Galamaz 26), Grigore, Apostol, Varga, Marica (Mazilu 81), Mara, Bucur (Andrei Cristea 75).
Faeroes: Mikkelsen; Gregersen, Naes, Danielsen, Bo, Jacobsen R (Hansen A 76), Benjaminsen (Jacobsen C 80), Samuelsen, Olsen A, Holst (Lokin 69), Borg.
Referee: Gvardis (Russia).

Group 7 Table	P	W	D	L	F	A	Pts
Serbia	10	7	1	2	22	8	22
France	10	6	3	1	18	9	21
Austria	10	4	2	4	14	15	14
Lithuania	10	4	0	6	10	11	12
Romania	10	3	3	4	12	18	12
Faeroes	10	1	1	8	5	20	4

GROUP 8

Larnaca, 6 September 2008, 6000
Cyprus (1) 1 *(Aloneftis 29)*　**Italy (1) 2** *(Di Natale 8, 90)*
Cyprus: Georgallides; Christou, Charalambous, Charalambides, Nicolaou, Michael (Yiasoumi 72), Makrides, Garpozis, Aloneftis, Okkas (Pavlou 74), Konstantinou (Christofi 63).
Italy: Buffon; Cannavaro, Grosso (Cassetti 18), Gamberini (Barzagli 4), De Rossi, Camoranesi, Zambrotta, Pirlo, Di Natale, Toni (Gattuso 46), Gilardino.
Referee: Vink (Holland).

Mainz, 6 September 2008, 4500
Georgia (0) 1 *(Kenia 90)*
Republic of Ireland (1) 2 *(Doyle K 13, Whelan 70)*
Georgia: Loria; Shashiashvili, Lobjanidze, Khizanishvili (Asatiani 83), Kaladze, Odikadze, Menteshashvili, Kobiashvili, Kenia, Aleksidze (Siradze 61), Iashvili (Mchedlidze 77).
Republic of Ireland: Given; Finnan (McShane 80), O'Shea, Dunne, Rowlands, Whelan, Kilbane, Hunt, Keane, Doyle K (Miller 77), McGeady (Keogh A 87).
Referee: Szabo (Hungary).

Podgorica, 6 September 2008, 9000
Montenegro (0) 2 *(Vucinic 61, Jovetic 82 (pen))*
Bulgaria (1) 2 *(Petrov S 11, Georgiev 90)*
Montenegro: Poleksic; Pavicevic, Batak, Tanasijevic, Drincic, Bozovic V, Boskovic (Burzanovic 83), Pekovic, Jovetic, Bogavac (Vukcevic 53), Vucinic (Djalovic 86).
Bulgaria: Ivankov; Milanov (Tomasic 48), Iliev, Angelov S**, Tunchev, Genchev (Georgiev 66), Petrov S, Lazarov, Dimitrov, Berbatov, Popov (Yankov 40).
Referee: Oriekhov (Ukraine).

Udine, 10 September 2008, 27,164
Italy (1) 2 *(De Rossi 17, 89)*　**Georgia (0) 0**
Italy: Buffon; Dossena, Cannavaro, Legrottaglie, Zambrotta, Aquilani, Camoranesi, De Rossi, Pirlo (Palombo 46), Di Natale (Del Piero 56), Toni (Iaquinta 70).
Georgia: Loria; Salukvadze, Kaladze, Lobjanidze, Eliava (Kvirkvelia 46), Khmaladze, Menteshashvili (Odikadze 68), Kobiashvili, Kenia, Iashvili, Mchedlidze (Siradze 55).
Referee: Einwaller (Austria).

Podgorica, 10 September 2008, 12,000
Montenegro (0) 0　Republic of Ireland (0) 0
Montenegro: Poleksic; Batak, Jovanovic, Pavicevic, Tanasijevic, Zverotic, Bozovic V (Vukcevic 54), Drincic, Pekovic, Jovetic, Vucinic.
Republic of Ireland: Given; Finnan, Hunt, Dunne, O'Shea, Whelan, Reid A, Doyle K, Keane, Kilbane, McGeady.
Referee: Kaldma (Estonia).

Sofia, 11 October 2008, 35,000
Bulgaria (0) 0　Italy (0) 0
Bulgaria: Ivankov; Wagner (Ivanov I 37), Tunchev, Milanov, Iliev, Petrov M (Popov 90), Yankov, Petrov S, Georgiev, Berbatov, Dimitrov.
Italy: Amelia; Cannavaro, Chiellini, Dossena, Montolivo (Perrotta 68), Zambrotta, Gattuso, De Rossi, Pepe, Gilardino (Toni 73), Di Natale (Rossi 68).
Referee: Lannoy (France).

Tbilisi, 11 October 2008, 40,000
Georgia (0) 1 *(Kobiashvili 73)*
Cyprus (0) 1 *(Konstantinou 67)*
Georgia: Lomaia; Shashiashvili, Salukvadze, Lobjanidze, Khizanishvili, Menteshashvili, Kobiashvili, Kenia (Gotsiridze 65), Razmadze, Iashvili, Mchedlidze (Aleksidze 76).
Cyprus: Georgallides; Elia (Lambrou 83), Constantinou, Charalambides, Michael (Nicolaou 37), Makrides, Charalambous, Aloneftis (Panagi 90), Konstantinou, Garpozis, Okkas.
Referee: Matejek (Czech Republic).

Tbilisi, 15 October 2008, 35,250
Georgia (0) 0　Bulgaria (0) 0
Georgia: Lomaia; Kvakhadze, Shashiashvili, Salukvadze, Lobjanidze, Menteshashvili, Kobiashvili, Razmadze, Mchedlidze (Siradze 32), Iashvili (Merebashvili 71), Gotsiridze (Odikadze 84).
Bulgaria: Petkov; Ivanov I, Tunchev, Milanov, Iliev, Yankov (Angelov S 56), Petrov S, Petrov M (Popov 29), Georgiev, Dimitrov (Rangelov 73), Berbatov.
Referee: Kuipers (Holland).

Lecce, 15 October 2008, 20,162
Italy (2) 2 *(Aquilani 8, 29)*
Montenegro (0) 1 *(Vucinic 19)*
Italy: Amelia; Cannavaro, Zambrotta, Chiellini, Dossena (Bonera 59), Gattuso, De Rossi, Aquilani (Perrotta 65), Di Natale (Quagliarella 76), Gilardino, Pepe.
Montenegro: Poleksic; Jovanovic, Pavicevic, Batak, Zverotic (Novakovic 89), Boskovic (Bozovic V 81), Vukcevic, Drincic, Jovetic, Tanasijevic, Vucinic (Damjanovic 90).
Referee: Proenca (Portugal).

Dublin, 15 October 2008, 55,833
Republic of Ireland (1) 1 *(Keane 5)*　**Cyprus (0) 0**
Republic of Ireland: Given; McShane, Kilbane, Dunne, O'Shea, Whelan, Gibson, Doyle K (Folan 90), Keane, Duff, McGeady.
Cyprus: Georgallides; Elia, Constantinou, Marangos (Panagi 52), Charalambous, Lambrou (Papathanasiou 46), Makrides, Konstantinou (Yiasoumi 79), Garpozis, Christofi, Okkas.
Referee: Tudor (Romania).

Dublin, 11 February 2009, 45,000
Republic of Ireland (0) 2 *(Keane 73 (pen), 78)*
Georgia (1) 1 *(Iashvili 1)*
Republic of Ireland: Given; Kelly, O'Shea, Whelan, Dunne, Andrews, Duff (Hunt S 80), Doyle K, Keane, Kilbane, McGeady.
Georgia: Lomaia; Lobjanidze, Kvirkvelia, Khizanishvili, Kaladze, Siradze (Aleksidze 77), Menteshashvili (Khmaladze 70), Kobiashvili, Razmadze, Iashvili, Gotsiridze (Merebashvili 68).
Referee: Hyytia (Finland).

Larnaca, 28 March 2009, 1500
Cyprus (1) 2 *(Konstantinou 33, Christofi 56)*
Georgia (0) 1 *(Kobiashvili 71 (pen))*
Cyprus: Georgallides; Elia, Christou, Satsias (Avraam 82), Michael, Charalambous (Yiasoumi 90), Garpozis, Alexandrou, Konstantinou, Christofi, Aloneftis (Panagi 69).
Georgia: Lomaia; Shashiashvili, Lobjanidze, Kvakhadze, Khizanishvili, Odikadze, Kobiashvili, Razmadze, Mchedlidze (Siradze 28), Iashvili, Gotsiridze.
Referee: Fautrel (France).

Podgorica, 28 March 2009, 10,500
Montenegro (0) 0　Italy (1) 2 *(Pirlo 11 (pen), Pazzini 73)*
Montenegro: Poleksic; Pavicevic, Batak, Basa, Drincic, Bozovic V, Boskovic, Vukcevic (Zverotic 89), Pekovic (Vujovic 79), Jovetic, Djalovic (Beciraj 71).
Italy: Buffon; Chiellini, Cannavaro, Grosso, De Rossi, Pirlo (Brighi 81), Zambrotta, Palombo, Quagliarella, Iaquinta (Pazzini 59), Di Natale (Pepe 9).
Referee: Atkinson (England).

Dublin, 28 March 2009, 60,002
Republic of Ireland (1) 1 *(Dunne 1)*
Bulgaria (0) 1 *(Kilbane 74 (og))*
Republic of Ireland: Given; McShane, O'Shea, Whelan, Dunne, Andrews, Kilbane, Hunt S, Keane, Doyle K, McGeady (Keogh A 90).
Bulgaria: Ivankov; Manolev, Angelov S, Stoyanov I, Milanov (Kishishev 24), Tomasic, Petrov S, Georgiev (Makriev 66), Telkiyski, Popov I (Dimitrov 46), Rangelov.
Referee: Bebek (Croatia).

Sofia, 1 April 2009, 16,916
Bulgaria (1) 2 *(Popov I 80, Makriev 90)*   **Cyprus (0) 0**
Bulgaria: Ivankov; Manolev, Kishishev, Angelov S, Tomasic, Stoyanov I, Georgiev, Telkiyski (Dimitrov 62), Petrov S, Popov I (Todorov 74), Rangelov (Makriev 90).
Cyprus: Georgallides; Elia, Christou, Satsias, Michael (Marangos 76), Charalambous, Garpozis, Konstantinou, Christofi (Yiasoumi 59), Aloneftis, Alexandrou (Avraam 65).
Referee: Ingvarsson (Sweden).

Tbilisi, 1 April 2009, 16,000
Georgia (0) 0   Montenegro (0) 0
Georgia: Lomaia; Kvirkvelia, Kvakhadze, Kashia, Salukvadze, Kobiashvili, Khmaladze, Odikadze (Klimiashvili 66), Merebashvili, Gotsiridze (Siradze 78), Iashvili.
Montenegro: Poleksic; Batak, Basa, Zverotic (Vujovic 87), Tanasijevic, Pejovic, Drincic, Boskovic, Pekovic, Djalovic (Beciraj 68), Jovetic.
Referee: Malcolm (Northern Ireland).

Bari, 1 April 2009, 41,000
Italy (1) 1 *(Iaquinta 9)*
Republic of Ireland (0) 1 *(Keane 89)*
Italy: Buffon; Grosso, Chiellini, Cannavaro, Zambrotta, Pirlo (Palombo 44), De Rossi, Brighi, Pepe (Dossena 55), Pazzini*, Iaquinta (Quagliarella 90).
Republic of Ireland: Given; McShane, O'Shea, Whelan, Dunne, Andrews (Gibson 54), Kilbane, Hunt S, Keane, Doyle K (Hunt N 63), McGeady.
Referee: Stark (Germany).

Sofia, 6 June 2009, 38,000
Bulgaria (1) 1 *(Telkiyski 29)*
Republic of Ireland (1) 1 *(Dunne 24)*
Bulgaria: Ivankov; Kishishev, Angelov S, Tomasic, Stoyanov I, Milanov, Telkiyski (Dimitrov 81), Petrov S, Petrov M (Georgiev 61), Bojinov (Makriev 59), Berbatov.
Republic of Ireland: Given; O'Shea (Kelly 82), Kilbane, Dunne, St Ledger-Hall, Whelan, Hunt S (McGeady 71), Andrews, Folan, Keane (Best 74), Duff.
Referee: Bo Larsen (Denmark).

Larnaca, 6 June 2009, 3000
Cyprus (2) 2 *(Konstantinou 13, Michael 45 (pen))*
Montenegro (0) 2 *(Damjanovic 65, 78)*
Cyprus: Georgallides (Morfis 34); Elia, Christou, Michael, Makrides, Charalambous, Nicolaou (Charalambides 78), Garpozis (Satsias 68), Konstantinou, Aloneftis, Okkas.
Montenegro: Poleksic; Tanasijevic, Pejovic (Fatic 36), Pavicevic, Djudovic, Batak, Novakovic (Zverotic 19), Kascelan, Drincic (Damjanovic 46), Vujovic, Vucinic.
Referee: Carballo (Spain).

Sofia, 5 September 2009, 7543
Bulgaria (1) 4 *(Kishishev 45, Telkiyski 49, Berbatov 85 (pen), Domovchiyski 90)*
Montenegro (1) 1 *(Jovetic 9)*
Bulgaria: Ivankov; Stoyanov I, Manolev, Kotev (Telkiyski 46), Kishishev, Yankov, Petrov S, Petrov M (Georgiev 76), Angelov, Rangelov (Domovchiyski 83), Berbatov.
Montenegro: Poleksic; Basa (Fatic 73), Pejovic, Pavicevic, Dzudovic, Vukcevic, Pekovic (Vucinic 66), Drincic, Bozovic V (Boskovic 58), Jovetic, Damjanovic.
Referee: Asumaa (Finland).

Nicosia, 5 September 2009, 5191
Cyprus (1) 1 *(Elia 30)*
Republic of Ireland (1) 2 *(Doyle K 5, Keane 83)*
Cyprus: Avgousti; Elia, Christou, Satsias (Marangos 90), Nicolaou, Michael (Alexandrou 71), Makrides, Charalambous, Aloneftis, Okkas (Christofi 90), Avraam.
Republic of Ireland: Given; McShane, O'Shea, Dunne, St Ledger-Hall, Whelan, Hunt S (McGeady 67), Andrews, Doyle K (Folan 75), Keane, Duff.
Referee: Einwaller (Austria).

Teplice, 5 September 2009, 32,000
Georgia (0) 0   Italy (0) 2 *(Kaladze 57 (og), 67 (og))*
Georgia: Lomaia; Ananidze (Vatsadze 59), Lobjanidze, Khizanishvili, Kaladze, Sanaia, Kobiashvili, Khmaladze, Kenia, Razmadze (Tskitshvili 73), Dvalishvili.
Italy: Buffon; Criscito, Chiellini, Cannavaro, Zambrotta, Pirlo, Palombo, Marchionni (D'Agostino 58), Camoranesi (Santon 70), Rossi (Quagliarella 58), Iaquinta.
Referee: Borski (Poland).

Turin, 9 September 2009, 26,122
Italy (2) 2 *(Grosso 11, Iaquinta 39)*   **Bulgaria (0) 0**
Italy: Buffon; Grosso, Chiellini, Cannavaro, De Rossi, Camoranesi, Zambrotta, Pirlo, Marchisio (Pepe 73), Gilardino (Rossi 58), Iaquinta (D'Agostino 84).
Bulgaria: Ivankov; Petkov, Manolev, Kishishev, Stoyanov I, Petrov S, Petrov M (Georgiev 63), Yankov (Domovchiyski 73), Angelov, Berbatov, Rangelov (Bojinov 63).
Referee: Meyer (Germany).

Podgorica, 9 September 2009, 4000
Montenegro (0) 1 *(Vucinic 57 (pen))*
Cyprus (0) 1 *(Okkas 64)*
Montenegro: Poleksic; Pejovic, Pavicevic, Fatic, Basa, Pekovic (Damjanovic 71), Drincic, Boskovic (Kascelan 61), Vukcevic, Jovetic, Vucinic.
Cyprus: Avgousti; Christou, Michael, Makrides, Charalambous, Satsias, Nicolaou (Marangos 85), Konstantinou, Avraam, Alexandrou (Aloneftis 46), Okkas (Efrem 90).
Referee: Zimmermann (Switzerland).

Larnaca, 10 October 2009, 3700
Cyprus (2) 4 *(Charalambides 12, 20, Konstantinou 58, Aloneftis 78)*
Bulgaria (1) 1 *(Berbatov 45)*
Cyprus: Avgousti; Elia (Nicolaou 75), Christou, Dobrasinovic, Makrides, Charalambides, Satsias, Michael, Avraam, Aloneftis (Efrem 86), Konstantinou (Fapathanasiou 90).
Bulgaria: Ivanov; Ivankov (Mihailov 68), Nikolov, Stoyanov K, Minev, Petrov S (Yanev 68), Petrov M, Georgiev, Angelov, Bojinov (Domovchiyski 63), Berbatov.
Referee: Allaerts (Belgium).

Podgorica, 10 October 2009, 5420
Montenegro (1) 2 *(Batak 13, Delibasic 78)*
Georgia (1) 1 *(Dvalishvili 45)*
Montenegro: Poleksic; Zverotic, Pejovic (Jovanovic 46), Batak, Basa, Vukcevic, Novakovic (Kascelan 71), Drincic, Boskovic, Jovetic, Damjanovic (Delibasic 61).
Georgia: Lomaia; Lobjanidze, Khizanishvili, Kaladze, Sanaia (Popkhadze 79), Khmaladze, Razmadze, Merebashvili (Odikadze 73), Iashvili, Gelashvili (Lipartia 67), Dvalishvili.
Referee: Selcuk (Turkey).

Dublin, 10 October 2009, 70,640
Republic of Ireland (1) 2 *(Whelan 8, St Ledger-Hall 87)*
Italy (1) 2 *(Camoranesi 25, Gilardino 90)*
Republic of Ireland: Given; Dunne, O'Shea, Andrews, St Ledger-Hall, Whelan (Rowlands 70), Lawrence, Kilbane, Doyle K (Best 66), Keane, McGeady (Hunt S 78).
Italy: Buffon; Grosso (Bocchetti 76), Chiellini, Zambrotta, Legrottaglie, De Rossi, Camoranesi, Pirlo, Palombo (Pepe 89), Iaquinta, Di Natale (Gilardino 76).
Referee: Hauge (Norway).

Sofia, 14 October 2009, 700
Bulgaria (6) 6 *(Berbatov 6, 23, 35, Petrov M 14, 44, Angelov 31)*
Georgia (2) 2 *(Dvalishvili 34, Kobiashvili 51 (pen))*
Bulgaria: Ivanov; Mihailov, Yanev, Nikolov, Angelov (Bojinov 78), Minev, Petrov M, Rangelov (Stoyanov I 64), Stoyanov K (Bandalovski 46), Berbatov, Georgiev.
Georgia: Lomaia (Mamaladze 29); Lobjanidze, Kaladze, Sanaia (Merebashvili 78), Khmaladze, Iashvili, Kenia (Odikadze 88), Dvalishvili, Khizanishvili, Razmadze, Kobiashvili.
Referee: Jakobsson (Iceland).

Parma, 14 October 2009, 15,009
Italy (0) 3 *(Gilardino 78, 80, 90)*
Cyprus (1) 2 *(Makrides 12, Michael 49)*
Italy: Marchetti, Cannavaro, Bocchetti, Santon, Gamberini, D'Agostino (De Rossi 66), Pepe (Camoranesi 46), Gattuso, Rossi (Di Natale 46), Quagliarella, Gilardino.
Cyprus: Avgousti; Elia, Christou (Satsias 30), Charalambous, Michael, Makrides, Dobrasinovic, Charalambides, Avraam, Aloneftis (Konstantinou 74), Okkas (Alexandrou 85).
Referee: Yefet (Israel).

Dublin, 14 October 2009, 50,212
Republic of Ireland (0) 0   Montenegro (0) 0
Republic of Ireland: Given; McShane, Kilbane, Dunne, St Ledger-Hall, Miller, Rowlands (O'Shea 40), Duff, Hunt N (Best 68), Keane, Hunt S (Keogh A 88).
Montenegro: Poleksic; Zverotic, Batak (Dzudovic 31), Basa, Jovanovic, Vukcevic, Pekovic, Novakovic, Drincic, Boskovic (Kascelan 81), Delibasic (Damjanovic 69).
Referee: Hrinak (Slovakia).

Group 8 Table	P	W	D	L	F	A	Pts
Italy	10	7	3	0	18	7	24
Republic of Ireland	10	4	6	0	12	8	18
Bulgaria	10	3	5	2	17	13	14
Cyprus	10	2	3	5	14	16	9
Montenegro	10	1	6	3	9	14	9
Georgia	10	0	3	7	7	19	3

GROUP 9

Skopje, 6 September 2008, 9000
Macedonia (1) 1 *(Naumoski 5)*   **Scotland (0) 0**
Macedonia: Milosevski; Sedloski, Petrov (Grncarov 79), Noveski, Mitreski, Lazarevski, Sumulikoski, Grozdanovski, Pandev (Tasevski 83), Naumoski (Trajanov 69), Maznov.
Scotland: Gordon; Alexander G, Naysmith, Hartley (Commons 66), Caldwell G, McManus, Fletcher D, Brown S, McFadden, Miller (Boyd 81), Robson (Maloney 76).
Referee: Kralovec (Czech Republic).

Oslo, 6 September 2008, 17,254
Norway (1) 2 *(Iversen 36 (pen), 50)*
Iceland (1) 2 *(Helguson 39, Gudjohnsen E 69)*
Norway: Jarstein; Riise JA, Reginiussen, Hogli, Hangeland, Winsnes, Skjelbred (Grindheim 70), Andresen, Iversen, Helstad, Carew (Pedersen 65).
Iceland: Sturluson; Steinsson, Saevarsson, Hreidarsson, Eiriksson, Sigurdsson K, Hallfredsson (Steinarsson 74), Gunnarsson A (Palmason 68), Gislason S, Helguson (Gunnarsson V 85), Gudjohnsen E.
Referee: Yefet (Israel).

Reykjavik, 10 September 2008, 9767
Iceland (0) 1 *(Gudjohnsen E 77)*
Scotland (1) 2 *(Broadfoot 18, Robson 59)*
Iceland: Sturulson; Eiriksson (Sigurdsson I 46), Hreidarsson, Saevarsson (Gunnarsson V 78), Steinsson, Gislason S, Gunnarsson A (Palmason 64), Sigurdsson K, Hallfredsson, Gudjohnsen E, Helguson.
Scotland: Gordon; Broadfoot, Naysmith, Brown S, Caldwell G, McManus, Fletcher D, Maloney (Alexander G 79), McFadden (Hartley 79), Robson, Commons (Miller 63).
Referee: Gumienny (Belgium).

Skopje, 10 September 2008, 11,000
Macedonia (0) 1 *(Pandev 77)*
Holland (0) 2 *(Heitinga 46, Van der Vaart 60)*
Macedonia: Milosevski; Sedloski, Noveski, Mitreski, Lazarevski (Petrov 58), Trajanov (Ristic 83), Sumulikoski, Grozdanovski, Pandev, Naumoski, Maznov (Tasevski 62).
Holland: Stekelenburg; Ooijer (Boulahrouz 28), Mathijsen, Heitinga, Van der Vaart, Van Bronckhorst, Van Bommel, De Jong, Van Persie (Kuyt 70), Robben (Afellay 82), Huntelaar.
Referee: Gilewski (Poland).

Rotterdam, 11 October 2008, 37,500
Holland (1) 2 *(Mathijsen 15, Huntelaar 64)*   **Iceland (0) 0**
Holland: Van der Sar; Ooijer, Mathijsen, Marcellis, Van der Vaart (Sneijder 81), Van Bronckhorst, Van Bommel, De Jong (De Zeeuw 64), Kuyt, Huntelaar, Babel (Afellay 68).
Iceland: Gunnleifsson; Sigurdsson R (Bjarnason 73), Sigurdsson I, Saevarsson, Hreidarsson, Gunnarsson B (Gunnarsson A 73), Sigurdsson K, Hallfredsson (Smarason 87), Gislason S, Gunnarsson V, Gudjohnsen E.
Referee: Trefoloni (Italy).

Glasgow, 11 October 2008, 50,205
Scotland (0) 0   Norway (0) 0
Scotland: Gordon; Broadfoot, Naysmith, Morrison (Fletcher S 56), Caldwell G, Weir, Robson, Brown, Fletcher D, McFadden (Iwelumo 56), Maloney.
Norway: Knudsen; Hoiland, Waehler, Hangeland, Riise JA, Grindheim, Stromstad (Pedersen 76), Riise BH (Braaten 56), Winsnes, Carew, Iversen.
Referee: Busacca (Switzerland).

Reykjavik, 15 October 2008, 5527
Iceland (1) 1 *(Gunnarsson V 15)*   **Macedonia (0) 0**
Iceland: Gunnleifsson; Steinsson, Sigurdsson I, Saevarsson, Hreidarsson, Gunnarsson B (Gunnarsson A 26), Sigurdsson K, Hallfredsson, Gislason S, Gunnarsson V (Palmason 65), Gudjohnsen E (Bjarnason 80).
Macedonia: Milosevski; Sedloski, Petrov (Trajanov 52), Noveski, Mitreski, Lazarevski, Tasevski (Ristic 78), Sumulikoski, Grozdanovski, Pandev, Maznov (Stojkov 60).
Referee: Selcuk (Turkey).

Oslo, 15 October 2008, 23,840
Norway (0) 0   Holland (0) 1 *(Van Bommel 62)*
Norway: Knudsen; Riise JA, Hangeland, Hoiland, Winsnes, Waehler, Grindheim, Hauger (Helstad 84), Iversen, Carew, Pedersen (Elyounoussi 77).
Holland: Van der Sar; Ooijer, Mathijsen, Marcellis, Van Bronckhorst, Van Bommel, De Zeeuw, Van der Vaart (Sneijder 75), Babel (Afellay 25), Kuyt, Huntelaar (Van Persie 56).
Referee: Plautz (Austria).

Amsterdam, 28 March 2009, 49,552
Holland (2) 3 *(Huntelaar 30, Van Persie 45, Kuyt 76 (pen))*
Scotland (0) 0
Holland: Stekelenburg; Ooijer, Mathijsen, Van der Wiel, De Jong (Afellay 79), Van Bronckhorst, Van Bommel, Kuyt, Huntelaar (Schaars 79), Van Persie (Sneijder 64), Robben.
Scotland: McGregor; Alexander G (Hutton 73), Naysmith, Berra, Caldwell G, Ferguson, Teale (Morrison 84), Fletcher D, McCormack, Miller (Fletcher S 70), Brown S.
Referee: Duhamel (France).

Amsterdam, 1 April 2009, 47,750
Holland (3) 4 *(Kuyt 15, 40, Huntelaar 24, Van der Vaart 87)*
Macedonia (0) 0
Holland: Stekelenburg; Van der Wiel, Ooijer, Mathijsen, Van Bronckhorst, Van Bommel, Sneijder (Van der Vaart 76), De Jong, Robben (Babel 46), Kuyt (Afellay 80), Huntelaar.
Macedonia: Pachovski; Sedloski, Noveski, Mitreski, Popov, Grozdanovski (Lazarevski 57), Trajanov (Polozani 63), Tasevski (Maznov 89), Sumulikoski, Naumoski, Pandev.
Referee: Rasmussen (Denmark).

Glasgow, 1 April 2009, 42,259
Scotland (1) 2 *(McCormack 39, Fletcher S 65)*
Iceland (0) 1 *(Sigurdsson I 54)*
Scotland: Gordon; Hutton, Naysmith, Morrison (Rae 90), Caldwell G, McManus, Fletcher D, Brown S, Fletcher S (Teale 78), Miller, McCormack.
Iceland: Gunnleifsson; Eiriksson, Steinsson, Sigurdsson I (Bjarnason 81), Gunnarsson A (Jonsson E 70), Danielsson, Sigurdsson K, Palmason, Helguson, Gudjohnsen E, Smarason.
Referee: Einwaller (Austria).

Reykjavik, 6 June 2009, 9635
Iceland (0) 1 *(Gudjohnsen K 88)*
Holland (2) 2 *(De Jong 8, Von Bommel 16)*
Iceland: Gunnleifsson; Saevarsson, Steinsson, Sigurdsson I, Hreidarsson, Eiriksson (Smarason 76), Danielsson (Gunnarsson B 46), Sigurdsson K, Palmason, Gislason S (Gunnarsson A 67), Gudjohnsen E.
Holland: Stekelenburg; Ooijer, Mathijsen, Heitinga, Van der Vaart (Babel 75), Van Bommel, De Jong (Mendes 80), Van Bronckhorst, Van Persie, Robben, Kuyt (Huntelaar 67).
Referee: Dean (England).

Skopje, 6 June 2009, 7000
Macedonia (0) 0   Norway (0) 0
Macedonia: Nikolovski; Grncarov, Sedloski, Mitreski, Georgievski, Popov, Despotovski, Sumulikoski (Maznov 63), Naumoski (Ristic 75), Stojkov (Grozdanovski 81), Pandev.
Norway: Knudsen; Waehler, Riise JA, Hoiland, Hangeland, Winsnes, Skjelbred (Riise BH 46), Grindheim (Hauger 73), Pedersen, Carew, Braaten (Huseklepp 57).
Referee: Tagliavento (Italy).

Rotterdam, 10 June 2009, 45,600
Holland (1) 2 *(Ooijer 32, Robben 51)*   **Norway (0) 0**
Holland: Stekelenburg; Ooijer, Mathijsen, Heitinga, Van der Vaart, Van Bommel, Van Bronckhorst (Braafheid 46), Schaars, Robben (Babel 78), Kuyt, Van Persie (Huntelaar 83).

Norway: Knudsen; Hoiland, Waehler, Riise JA, Hauger, Grindheim (Skjelbred 67), Fevang, Pedersen, Winsnes (Tettey 79), Riise BH (Braaten 42), Carew.
Referee: Baskakov (Russia).

Skopje, 10 June 2009, 7000
Macedonia (1) 2 *(Stojkov 9, Ivanovski 86)* **Iceland (0) 0**
Macedonia: Nikolovski (Pachovski 74); Sedloski, Mitreski, Lazarevski, Popov, Georgievski, Despotovski, Sumulikoski (Grozdanovski 80), Naumoski, Stojkov (Ivanovski 66), Pandev.
Iceland: Gunnleifsson; Ottesen, Steinsson, Gunnarsson B, Eiriksson, Sigurdsson K, Palmason (Gudmundsson J 74), Jonsson E (Saevarsson 60), Hallfredsson, Gislason S, Smarason.
Referee: Ennjimi (France).

Oslo, 12 August 2009, 24,493
Norway (2) 4 *(Riise JA 36, Pedersen 45, 90, Huseklepp 60)*
Scotland (0) 0
Norway: Knudsen; Waehler, Riise JA, Hangeland, Hogli, Hoseth, Huseklepp (Iversen 76), Grindheim, Pedersen, Riise BH (Skjelbred 85), Carew (Helstad 84).
Scotland: Marshall; Hutton, Davidson, Caldwell S (McFadden 48), Caldwell G**■**, Alexander G, Fletcher D, Brown S, McCormack (Berra 37) (Whittaker 78), Miller K, Commons.
Referee: Hamer (Luxembourg).

Reykjavik, 5 September 2009, 7321
Iceland (1) 1 *(Gudjohnsen 29)*
Norway (1) 1 *(Riise JA 10)*
Iceland: Gunnleifsson; Steinsson, Sigurdsson I, Ottesen (Sigurdsson R 90), Gunnarsson B, Gislason R, Sigurdsson K, Hallfredsson (Gunnarsson V 89), Gunnarsson A (Gislason S 81), Gudjohnsen, Helguson.
Norway: Knudsen; Moldskred (Helstad 87), Waehler, Riise JA, Hogli, Hangeland, Huseklepp (Riise BH 79), Hoseth (Brenne 46), Grindheim, Pedersen, Carew.
Referee: Tudor (Romania).

Glasgow, 5 September 2009, 50,214
Scotland (0) 2 *(Brown S 56, McFadden 81)*
Macedonia (0) 0
Scotland: Gordon; Alexander G, Hutton, Fletcher D, McManus, Davidson (Whittaker 14), Weir, Brown S (Hartley 73), Fletcher S (Maloney 68), Miller K, McFadden.
Macedonia: Nikolovski; Sedloski, Noveski, Mitreski, Georgievski (Grozdanoski 69), Popov, Despotovski, Sumulikoski, Naumoski (Tasevski 65), Stojkov (Ibraimi 80), Pandev.
Referee: Stark (Germany).

Oslo, 9 September 2009, 14,766
Norway (2) 2 *(Helstad 2, Riise JA 25)*
Macedonia (0) 1 *(Grncarov 79)*
Norway: Knudsen; Waehler, Riise JA, Hoiland, Hangeland, Grindheim (Winsnes 71), Pedersen, Riise BH, Hauger, Carew (Braaten 84), Helstad (Moldskred 76).
Macedonia: Pacovski; Grncarov, Mitreski, Sedloski, Georgievski, Popov, Tasevski (Alimi 65), Sumulikoski, Naumoski (Ivanovski 75), Stojkov (Ibraimi 60), Pandev.
Referee: Paixao (Portugal).

Glasgow, 9 September 2009, 51,230
Scotland (0) 0 Holland (0) 1 *(Elia 81)*
Scotland: Marshall; Hutton, Whittaker, Hartley (Commons 66), Weir, McManus, Maloney (O'Connor 81), Fletcher D, Miller K, Brown S, Naismith.
Holland: Vorm; Ooijer, Mathijsen, Van der Wiel, De Zeeuw, De Jong, Van Bronckhorst, Sneijder (Van der Vaart 77), Robben (Elia 72), Kuyt, Van Persie (Huntelaar 84).
Referee: Bo Larsen (Denmark).

Group 9 Table	P	W	D	L	F	A	Pts
Holland	8	8	0	0	17	2	24
Norway	8	2	4	2	9	7	10
Scotland	8	3	1	4	6	11	10
Macedonia	8	2	1	5	5	11	7
Iceland	8	1	2	5	7	13	5

Denmark, England, Germany, Holland, Italy, Serbia, Slovakia, Spain and Switzerland qualified.
Bosnia, France, Greece, Portugal, Republic of Ireland, Russia, Slovenia and Ukraine play-off for final four places.

SOUTH AMERICA

Buenos Aires, 13 October 2007, 55,000
Argentina (2) 2 *(Riquelme 27, 45)* **Chile (0) 0**
Argentina: Abbondanzieri; Zanetti, Milito, Demichelis, Heinze, Riquelme, Cambiasso, Mascherano, Max Rodriguez (Gago 68), Tevez (Aguero 74), Messi (Saviola 84).
Chile: Bravo; Alvarez**■**, Riffo, Vidal, Ponce, Fernandez, Iturra (Maldonado 63), Gonzalez, Fierro (Droguett 37), Suazo, Rubio (Salas 46).
Referee: Vazquez (Uruguay).

Montevideo, 13 October 2007, 25,200
Uruguay (2) 5 *(Suarez 5, Forlan 38, Abreu 48, Sanchez 68, Bueno 83)*
Bolivia (0) 0
Uruguay: Carini; Fucile, Godin, Garcia, Perez, Scotti, Pereira M, Rodriguez C, Abreu (Bueno 73), Suarez (Regueiro 66), Forlan (Sanchez 66).
Bolivia: Galarza; Raldes, Amador, Soliz (Cabrera 46), Hoyos (Suarez N 75), Alvarez, Lima, Vaca, Garcia F**■**, Martins, Moreno J (Cardozo 59).
Referee: Selman (Chile).

Bogota, 14 October 2007, 41,000
Colombia (0) 0 Brazil (0) 0
Colombia: Agustin; Zuniga, Velez, Mosquera, Moreno W, Amaya, Ferreira (Ramirez 55), Sanchez, Castrillon (Griseles 55), Garcia (Perea 81), Renteria.
Brazil: Julio Cesar; Maicon, Juan, Lucio, Ronaldinho, Kaka (Afonso 84), Gilberto Silva, Gilberto, Mineiro, Vagner Love (Josue 70), Robinho (Julio Baptista 62).
Referee: Amarilla (Paraguay).

Quito, 14 October 2007, 29,644
Ecuador (0) 0 Venezuela (0) 1 *(Rey 68)*
Ecuador: Viteri; Hurtado I, Espinoza, Bagui (Quiroz 76), Mendez, Castillo, Lara (Ayovi 46), Valencia (Borja 71) De La Cruz, Tenorio C, Benitez.

Venezuela: Vega; Rouga, Rojas, Rey, Cichero, Vallenilla, Arango (Guerra 65), Vera, Paez (Gonzalez H 77), Mea Vitali (Vielma 80), Maldonado.
Referee: Ortube (Bolivia).

Lima, 14 October 2007, 50,000
Peru (0) 0 Paraguay (0) 0
Peru: Butron; Acasiete, Vargas (Chiroque 83), Galliquio (Maestri 73), Rodriguez, Vilchez, Solano, De La Haza, Quinteros (Jayo 88), Farfan, Pizarro.
Paraguay: Villar; Morel, Caceres J, Da Silva, Caniza, Vera, Barreto E (Britez 87), Riveros, Caceres V, Cabanas (Achucarro 76), Valdez (Cardozo 69).
Referee: Simon (Brazil).

La Paz, 17 October 2007, 19,469
Bolivia (0) 0 Colombia (0) 0
Bolivia: Galarza; Amador, Ribeiro, Raldes, Verduguez, Reyes L**■**, Mojica, Campos (Cabrera 55), Arce (Gutierrez R 72), Andaveris (Vaca 46), Limberg Gutierrez.
Colombia: Agustin; Arizala, Mosquera, Vallejo, Moreno W, Amaya, Sanchez, Ferreira (Ramirez 55), Anchico (Banguero 85), Valencia (Castrillon 63), Renteria.
Referee: Reinoso (Ecuador).

Maracaibo, 17 October 2007, 10,600
Venezuela (0) 0 Argentina (2) 2 *(Milito 16, Messi 43)*
Venezuela: Vega; Rojas, Vallenilla (Rosales 46), Rey, Cichero, Rouga, Arango, Seijas (Guerra 53), Paez, Mea Vitali, Maldonado (Arismendi 66).
Argentina: Abbondanzieri; Ibarra (Gago 63), Milito, Demichelis, Zanetti, Burdisso (Diaz 73), Riquelme, Cambiasso, Mascherano, Messi, Tevez (Denis 80).
Referee: Simon (Brazil).

Rio de Janeiro, 18 October 2007, 87,000
Brazil (1) 5 *(Vagner Love 19, Ronaldinho 62, Kaka 77, 85, Elano 83)*
Ecuador (0) 0
Brazil: Julio Cesar; Juan, Maicon, Lucio, Mineiro, Gilberto Silva, Gilberto, Ronaldinho, Kaka (Diego 89), Vagner Love (Elano 76), Robinho.
Ecuador: Viteri; Hurtado I, Bagui, Espinoza, Ayovi (Guerron 77), Mendez, De La Cruz, Castillo, Urrutia, Quiroz (Tenorio C 46), Benitez (Lara 82).
Referee: Larrionda (Uruguay).

Santiago, 18 October 2007, 58,000
Chile (1) 2 *(Suazo 11, Fernandez 52)*   **Peru (0) 0**
Chile: Bravo; Droguett, Riffo, Vidal, Ponce, Fernandez, Iturra, Gonzalez, Fierro (Fuentes 89), Suazo (Rubio 83), Salas (Jimenez 87).
Peru: Butron; Vilchez (Bazalar 73), Vargas, Galliquio, Acasiete, Rodriguez, De La Haza (Quinteros 46), Jayo, Solano, Pizarro, Farfan.
Referee: Ruiz (Colombia).

Asuncion, 18 October 2007, 23,200
Paraguay (1) 1 *(Valdez 15)*   **Uruguay (0) 0**
Paraguay: Villar; Morel, Caceres J, Da Silva, Caniza, Riveros, Caceres V, Vera, Barreto E (Santana 86), Cabanas (Achucarro 79), Valdez (Cardozo 66).
Uruguay: Carini; Godin, Fucile, Lugano, Rodriguez C (Bueno 79), Perez (Gonzalez A 68), Garcia, Pereira M, Scotti, Forlan, Suarez (Sanchez 62).
Referee: Baldassi (Argentina).

Buenos Aires, 17 November 2007, 43,308
Argentina (1) 3 *(Aguero 41, Riquelme 57, 74)*
Bolivia (0) 0
Argentina: Abbondanzieri; Milito, Zanetti, Demichelis, Ibarra, Mascherano, Cambiasso (Gago 69), Riquelme, Messi, Tevez (Denis 82), Aguero (Maxi Rodriguez 75).
Bolivia: Arias; Luis Gutierrez, Hoyos, Raldes, Garcia R, Vaca, Mendez, Suarez, Moreno J (Gutierrez R 61), Limberg Gutierrez (Arce 61), Cabrera (Martins 80).
Referee: Rivera (Peru).

Bogota, 17 November 2007, 28,273
Colombia (0) 1 *(Bustos 82)*   **Venezuela (0) 0**
Colombia: Agustin; Mosquera, Bustos, Velez, Moreno W, Ramirez (Torres 46), Castrillon, Amaya, Sanchez (Grisales 71), Renteria, Garcia (Moreno M 50).
Venezuela: Morales; Rojas, Vielma, Rey, Vallenilla, Rouga, Arango, Paez (Gonzalez C 67), Mea Vitali, Maldonado (Guerra 56), Fedor (Cichero 79).
Referee: Selman (Chile).

Asuncion, 18 November 2007, 30,000
Paraguay (2) 5 *(Valdez 10, Riveros 28, 88, Santa Cruz 51, Ayala 83)*
Ecuador (0) 1 *(Kaviedes 80)*
Paraguay: Villar; Da Silva, Caceres J, Morel (Veron 77), Barreto E, Vera, Caceres V, Riveros, Santa Cruz (Ayala 74), Valdez (Bonet 60), Cabanas.
Ecuador: Elizaga; Montano, Guagua, Bagui, Espinoza, Ayovi, Urrutia (Campos 46), Castillo, Mendez, Ordonez (Kaviedes 63), Benitez (Caicedo 74).
Referee: Lopes (Brazil).

Lima, 18 November 2007, 45,847
Peru (0) 1 *(Vargas 72)*   **Brazil (1) 1** *(Kaka 40)*
Peru: Penny; Acasiete, Salas, Rodriguez, Vargas, Lobaton (De La Haza 66), Jayo (Mendoza 63), Solano, Pizarro, Guerrero (Palacios 46), Farfan.
Brazil: Julio Cesar; Maicon, Juan, Lucio, Mineiro, Gilberto, Gilberto Silva, Ronaldinho, Kaka, Robinho (Elano 74), Vagner Love (Luis Fabiano 69).
Referee: Torres (Paraguay).

Montevideo, 18 November 2007, 45,000
Uruguay (1) 2 *(Suarez 42, Abreu 81)*
Chile (0) 2 *(Salas 59, 69 (pen))*
Uruguay: Carini; Godin, Fucile, Lugano, Rodriguez C, Gargano, Perez (Arevalo 46), Scotti (Pereira M 61), Abreu, Sanchez (Gonzalez I 65), Suarez.
Chile: Bravo; Alvarez (Fuentes 60), Jara, Droguett, Riffo, Vidal, Ponce, Fernandez, Suazo (Moya 72), Salas, Rubio (Villanueva 46).
Referee: Pezzotta (Argentina).

San Cristobal, 20 November 2007, 24,000
Venezuela (2) 5 *(Arismendi 20, 40, Guerra 81, Maldonado 89, 90)*
Bolivia (2) 3 *(Arce 27, Martins 19, 77)*
Venezuela: Morales; Rey, Cichero, Rojas, Arango, Vera (Mea Vitali 59), Seijas (Perez 64), Paez (Guerra 74), Rosales, Maldonado, Arismendi.
Bolivia: Arias; Raldes, Luis Gutierrez, Ribeiro, Vaca (Lima 46), Mendez, Garcia R, Gomez, Mojica (Limberg Gutierrez 70), Arce, Martins (Moreno J 79).
Referee: Fagundes (Brazil).

Bogota, 21 November 2007, 45,000
Colombia (0) 2 *(Bustos 62, Moreno D 82)*
Argentina (1) 1 *(Messi 36)*
Colombia: Agustin; Velez, Moreno W, Bustos, Mosquera, Ferreira (Torres 46), Castrillon (Grisales 46), Sanchez, Amaya, Renteria, Moreno M (Moreno D 72).
Argentina: Abbondanzieri; Milito, Demichelis, Zanetti, Ibarra, Gago, Cambiasso (Maxi Rodriguez 74), Mascherano, Riquelme, Messi, Tevez*.
Referee: Larrionda (Uruguay).

Quito, 21 November 2007, 28,557
Ecuador (3) 5 *(Ayovi 10, 48, Kaviedes 24, Mendez 44, 62)*
Peru (0) 1 *(Mendoza 86)*
Ecuador: Elizaga (Villafuerte 66); Espinoza, De Jesus, Ambrosi, Hurtado I, Quiroz, Mendez, Castillo, Ayovi, Kaviedes (Urrutia 68), Benitez (Montero 84).
Peru: Penny; Salas, Vilchez (Solis 9), Acasiete, Gomez, Palacios, Bazalar (Mendoza 58), Lobaton, Garcia, Mostto, Pizarro (Farfan 58).
Referee: Chandia (Chile).

Sao Paulo, 22 November 2007, 70,000
Brazil (1) 2 *(Luis Fabiano 44, 64)*
Uruguay (1) 1 *(Abreu 8)*
Brazil: Julio Cesar; Maicon (Daniel Alves 86), Juan, Alex, Ronaldinho (Josue 60), Mineiro, Kaka, Gilberto Silva, Gilberto, Robinho (Vagner Love 73), Luis Fabiano.
Uruguay: Carini; Lugano, Godin, Fucile, Rodriguez C, Pereira M, Gonzalez I (Bueno 82), Gonzalez A, Gargano, Suarez (Sanchez 71), Abreu.
Referee: Baldassi (Argentina).

Santiago, 22 November 2007, 52,320
Chile (0) 0
Paraguay (2) 3 *(Cabanas 24, Da Silva 45, 57)*
Chile: Bravo; Riffo, Ponce, Droguett, Alvarez, Maldonado, Iturra (Jimenez 46), Fernandez, Suazo, Salas, Rubio (Villanueva 46).
Paraguay: Villa; Morel, Da Silva, Caceres J, Vera, Santana, Riveros (Barreto E 80), Caceres V, Bonet, Valdez (Achucarro 67), Cabanas (Santa Cruz 57).
Referee: Ruiz (Colombia).

Montevideo, 14 June 2008, 25,000
Uruguay (1) 1 *(Lugano 12)*   **Venezuela (0) 1** *(Vargas 56)*
Uruguay: Carini; Caceres, Lugano, Godin, Gargano, Perez, Pereira M (Silva 76), Gonzalez I, Forlan (Sanchez 65), Abreu, Suarez (Bueno 65).
Venezuela: Vega; Hernandez, Rey, Vielma, Rojas (Seijas 79), Mea Vitali, Chacon, Vargas (Rondon 74), Rincon, Arango, Maldonado (Boada 87).
Referee: Intriago (Ecuador).

Buenos Aires, 15 June 2008, 41,167
Argentina (0) 1 *(Palacio 89)*   **Ecuador (0) 1** *(Urrutia 69)*
Argentina: Abbondanzieri; Demichelis, Burdisso, Zanetti, Heinze, Veron (Palacio 85), Maxi Rodriguez (Gago 46), Riquelme, Mascherano (Cruz 63), Aguero, Messi.
Ecuador: Cevallos; De Jesus, Mina, Hurtado I, Espinoza, Castillo, Ayovi (Bolanos 85), Valencia, Urrutia, Tenorio C (De La Cruz 88), Guerron (Benitez 88).
Referee: Artube (Bolivia).

La Paz, 15 June 2008, 27,722
Bolivia (0) 0   Chile (1) 2 *(Medel 28, 76)*
Bolivia: Galarza; Alvarez (Ribeiro 46), Raldes, Hoyos (Saucedo 78), Luis Gutierrez, Reyes A, Reyes L, Campos (Botero 65), Martins, Limberg Gutierrez, Arce.
Chile: Bravo; Cereceda, Medel, Jara, Fuentes, Morales (Villanueva 55), Fuenzalida (Estrada 46), Carmona, Beausejour (Gonzalez 58), Sanchez, Suazo.
Referee: Rivera (Peru).

Asuncion, 15 June 2008, 38,000
Paraguay (1) 2 *(Santa Cruz 26, Cabanas 49)*   **Brazil (0) 0**
Paraguay: Villar; Caniza, Caceres J, Veron■; Da Silva,
Barreto E, Vera, Santana, Cabanas (Torres 74), Valdez
(Caceres V 52), Santa Cruz (Cardozo 81).
Brazil: Julio Cesar; Juan, Maicon, Lucio, Josue (Anderson
46), Gilberto Silva, Gilberto, Diego (Julio Baptista 69),
Mineiro (Adriano 60), Robinho, Luis Fabiano.
Referee: Larrionda (Uruguay).

Lima, 15 June 2008, 25,000
Peru (1) 1 *(Marino 40)*   **Colombia (1) 1** *(Rodallega 8)*
Peru: Butron; Neira (Rengifo 76), Vilchez, Vargas,
Rodriguez, Prado, Hidalgo (Cominges 59), Torres R,
Marino, Solano, Guerrero.
Colombia: Agustin; Bustos, Zapata, Velez (Zuniga 72),
Moreno W, Vargas (Grisales 60), Guarin, Torres
(Portocarrero 86), Sanchez, Rodallega, Perea.
Referee: Torres (Paraguay).

La Paz, 18 June 2008, 8561
Bolivia (2) 4 *(Botero 23, 70, Garcia R 25, Martins 76)*
Paraguay (0) 2 *(Santa Cruz 66, Valdez 82)*
Bolivia: Arias; Ribeiro, Raldes, Luis Gutierrez, Torrico,
Garcia R (Gutierrez R 46), Vaca, Reyes A (Ronald Rivero
67), Reyes L, Martins, Botero (Saucedo 73).
Paraguay: Bobadilla; Morel, Da Silva, Caceres J, Vera
(Zeballos 46), Riveros, Caceres V, Bonet, Barreto E
Cardozo (Valdez 62), Cabanas (Santa Cruz 62).
Referee: Gaciba (Brazil).

Quito, 18 June 2008, 25,000
Ecuador (0) 0   **Colombia (0) 0**
Ecuador: Cevallos; Hurtado I, Ambrosi, Urrutia (Guerron
46), Tenorio C (Caicedo 81), Benitez, De Jesus, Castillo,
Ayovi (Bolanos 72), Valencia, Espinoza.
Colombia: Agustin; Moreno W, Mosquera, Gonzalez,
Escobar (Moreno D 54), Guarin, Rodallega, Amaya, Torres
(Hernandez 63), Soto (Sanchez 80), Zuniga.
Referee: Baldassi (Argentina).

Montevideo, 18 June 2008, 20,016
Uruguay (2) 6 *(Forlan 8, 37 (pen), 56, Bueno 61, 69,
Abreu 90)*
Peru (0) 0
Uruguay: Castillo; Silva, Lugano, Godin, Caceres
Rodriguez C, Perez (Eguren 69), Gonzalez I (Suarez 72),
Gargano, Forlan, Bueno (Abreu 79).
Peru: Butron; Villalta, Vargas (Rengifo 46), Rodriguez C,
Prado, Hidalgo (Salas 67), Cevasco, Torres R, Solano,
Marino (Cruzado 71), Guerrero■.
Referee: Pozo (Chile).

Belo Horizonte, 19 June 2008, 65,000
Brazil (0) 0   **Argentina (0) 0**
Brazil: Julio Cesar; Maicon, Lucio, Juan, Mineiro, Julio
Baptista, Gilberto Silva, Gilberto, Anderson (Diego 34)
(Daniel Alves 79), Adriano (Luis Fabiano 70), Robinho.
Argentina: Abbondanzieri; Zanetti, Heinze, Coloccini,
Burdisso, Riquelme (Battaglia 83), Mascherano, Gutierrez,
Gago, Messi (Palacio 90), Cruz (Aguero 67).
Referee: Ruiz (Colombia).

Puerto La Cruz, 20 June 2008, 38,000
Venezuela (0) 2 *(Maldonado 59, Arango 80)*
Chile (0) 3 *(Suazo 54 (pen), 90, Jara 73)*
Venezuela: Vega; Vielma, Rojas, Rey, Hernandez, Arango,
Vargas (Rincon 59), Mea Vitali (Seijas 80), Chacon, Rondon
(Arismendi 55), Maldonado.
Chile: Bravo; Medel, Jara, Fuentes, Cereceda (Ponce 76),
Beausejor (Gonzalez 59), Morales (Gazale 60), Estrada,
Carmona, Suazo, Sanchez.
Referee: Silvera (Uruguay).

Buenos Aires, 6 September 2008, 46,250
Argentina (0) 1 *(Aguero 60)*
Paraguay (1) 1 *(Heinze 13 (og))*
Argentina: Abbondanzieri (Carrizo 14); Zanetti, Heinze
(Diaz 46), Demichelis, Coloccini, Di Maria (Aguero 46),
Riquelme, Mascherano, Cambiasso, Tevez■, Messi.
Paraguay: Villar; Veron, Morel (Torres 46), Da Silva,
Caceres J, Vera, Santana, Riveros, Barreto E, Valdez,
Cardozo (Lopez 71).
Referee: Simon (Brazil).

Quito, 6 September 2008, 35,000
Ecuador (1) 3 *(Caicedo 21, Mendez 51 (pen), Benitez 72)*
Bolivia (1) 1 *(Botero 40)*
Ecuador: Cevallos; Reasco (De Jesus 28), Hurtado I,
Espinoza, Mendez, Castillo, Ayovi, Guerron, Caicedo
(Palacios 76), Bolanos (Urrutia 75), Benitez.
Bolivia: Arias; Garcia I, Ronald Rivero, Raldes, Hoyos,
Vaca (Saucedo 88), Gomez■, Garcia R, Robles, Escobar
(Pena 67), Botero (Martins 64).
Referee: Pozo (Chile).

Bogota, 7 September 2008, 35,024
Colombia (0) 0   **Uruguay (1) 1** *(Eguren 15)*
Colombia: Agustin; Perea, Zuniga, Velez, Mosquera, Vargas
(Torres 46), Sanchez, Hernandez (Moreno M 63), Guarin,
Rocallega, Garcia (Moreno D 60).
Uruguay: Castillo; Silva (Gonzalez A 80), Lugano, Godin,
Fucile, Rodriguez C, Pereira M, Gargano, Eguren (Scotti
90) Suarez (Sanchez 68), Forlan.
Referee: Gaciba (Brazil).

Lima, 7 September 2008, 25,000
Peru (1) 1 *(Alva Niezen 39)*   **Venezuela (0) 0**
Peru: Butron; Zambrano, Vargas, Rodriguez, Prado, Torres
R, Solano (Quinteros 62), De La Haza, Fano (Rengifo 80),
Chavez (La Rosa 90), Alva Niezen.
Venezuela: Vega; Rojas (Moreno 55), Rey, Hernandez,
Boada, Vargas (Guerra 66), Rincon, Mea Vitali (Vielma
71), Chacon, Arango, Maldonado.
Referee: Maldonado (Bolivia).

Santiago, 8 September 2008, 60,239
Chile (0) 0   **Brazil (2) 3** *(Luis Fabiano 21, 83, Robinho 44)*
Chile: Bravo; Vidal (Cereceda 46), Medel, Jara, Droguett
(Beausejour 46), Gonzalez (Valdivia■ 46), Fernandez,
Estrada, Carmona, Suazo, Sanchez.
Brazil: Julio Cesar; Luisao, Maicon, Lucio, Kleber■,
Ronaldinho (Juan Jr 54), Josue, Gilberto Silva, Diego
(Elano 78), Robinho, Luis Fabiano (Jo 86).
Referee: Torres (Paraguay).

Asuncion, 10 September 2008, 31,867
Paraguay (2) 2 *(Riveros 28, Valdez 45)*   **Venezuela (0) 0**
Paraguay: Villar; Morel, Manzur, Da Silva, Riveros, Caceres
V, Bonet, Barreto E (Torres 79), Santana (Caniza 73),
Valdez (Lopez 63), Santa Cruz.
Venezuela: Vega; Rey, Hernandez (Fuenmayor 55), Boada,
Mea Vitali, Guerra, Chacon (Lucena 35), Arango, Rincon,
Moreno, Maldonado (Torrealba 71).
Referee: Baldassi (Argentina).

Montevideo, 10 September 2008, 45,000
Uruguay (0) 0   **Ecuador (0) 0**
Uruguay: Castillo; Silva, Lugano, Godin, Caceres,
Rodriguez C, Gonzalez I (Suarez 60), Gargano (Pereira M
46), Eguren, Forlan, Bueno (Abreu 70).
Ecuador: Cevallos; Mina, Hurtado I, Espinoza, De Jesus,
Valencia, Mendez, Castillo, Ayovi, Guerron (Cortez 82),
Caicedo (Borja 79).
Referee: Ruiz (Colombia).

Rio de Janeiro, 11 September 2008, 31,422
Brazil (0) 0   **Bolivia (0) 0**
Brazil: Julio Cesar; Maicon, Lucio, Juan Jr, Luisao, Lucas
(Julio Baptista 60), Josue, Diego (Elano 76), Ronaldinho
(Nilmar 76), Robinho, Luis Fabiano.
Bolivia: Arias; Raldes, Ronald Rivero, Hoyos, Garcia I■,
Garcia R, Flores, Vaca (Cabrera 89), Robles, Moreno R
(Luis Gutierrez 56), Martins (Escobar 78).
Referee: Intriago (Ecuador).

Santiago, 11 September 2008, 47,459
Chile (2) 4 *(Jara 26, Suazo 38, Fuentes 48, Fernandez 71)*
Colombia (0) 0
Chile: Bravo; Vidal, Medel, Jara, Fuentes, Cereceda
(Contreras 78), Gonzalez, Fernandez, Estrada, Suazo
(Morales 85), Sanchez (Fierro 81).
Colombia: Agustin; Perea, Portocarrero, Mosquera,
Sanchez, Hernandez (Moreno D 46), Armero, Anchico
(Zuniga 54), Amaya, Rodallega (Rodriguez 75), Moreno M.
Referee: Larrionda (Uruguay).

Lima, 11 September 2008, 40,000
Peru (0) 1 *(Fano 90)*   **Argentina (0) 1** *(Cambiasso 82)*
Peru: Butron; Zambrano, Vilchez, Vargas, Prado, Torres R, Solano, De La Haza, Fano, Chavez (Rengifo 75), Alva Niezen (Salas 66).
Argentina: Carrizo; Zanetti, Diaz, Demichelis, Coloccini, Riquelme, Guttierrez (Battaglia 16), Gago, Cambiasso (Zabaleta 87), Messi, Aguero (Denis 63).
Referee: Amarilla (Paraguay).

Buenos Aires, 11 October 2008, 42,421
Argentina (2) 2 *(Messi 5, Aguero 12)*
Uruguay (1) 1 *(Lugano 39)*
Argentina: Carrizo; Heinze, Demichelis, Burdisso, Zanetti, Mascherano, Cambiasso, Riquelme (Ledesma 72), Messi (Diaz 88), Aguero (Milito 71), Tevez.
Uruguay: Castillo; Lugano, Godin, Fucile (Cavani 23), Caceres, Pereira M, Eguren, Rodriguez C (Bueno 74), Perez, Abreu (Chevanton 73), Suarez.
Referee: Torres (Paraguay).

La Paz, 11 October 2008, 23,147
Bolivia (2) 3 *(Botero 3, 16, Garcia R 81)*   **Peru (0) 0**
Bolivia: Arias; Raldes (Luis Gutierrez 83), Vargas, Ronald Rivero, Reyes A, Garcia R, Flores, Vaca (Torrico 81), Martins (Escobar 64), Botero, Robles.
Peru: Butron; Prado, Zambrano, Vilchez, Vargas, Torres R, Marino, De La Haza, Fano (Rengifo 85), Chavez (Guizasola 46), Alva Niezen (Aguirre 62).
Referee: Buitrago (Colombia).

Bogota, 12 October 2008, 26,000
Colombia (0) 0   Paraguay (1) 1 *(Cabanas 9)*
Colombia: Agustin; Yepes, Bedoya, Zuniga, Perea, Vargas, Hernandez (Ferreira 55), Guarin (Ramos 73), Armero, Montero (Quintero 55), Renteria.
Paraguay: Villar; Vera, Da Silva, Caceres J, Vera, Torres, Riveros, Caceres V, Barreto E (Bonet 82), Valdez (Bogado 76), Cabanas (Cardozo 86).
Referee: Lunati (Argentina).

Quito, 12 October 2008, 33,079
Ecuador (0) 1 *(Benitez 70)*   **Chile (0) 0**
Ecuador: Elizaga; Espinoza, De Jesus, Ambrosi (Bolanos 46), Hurtado I, Castillo (Urrutia 43), Ayovi, Valencia[a], Caicedo (Hidalgo 85), Benitez, Guerron.
Chile: Bravo; Jara[a], Fuentes[a], Cerececeda (Estrada 53), Vidal, Medel, Gonzalez, Fernandez (Contreras 23), Carmona, Suazo (Morales 58), Sanchez.
Referee: Vazquez (Uruguay).

San Cristobal, 12 October 2008, 38,000
Venezuela (0) 0
Brazil (3) 4 *(Kaka 6, Robinho 9, 66, Adriano 19)*
Venezuela: Vega; Rey, Boada, Vielma, Rojas, Mea Vitali (Lucena 70), Guerra (Moreno 61), Chacon, Arango, Vargas (Seijas 55), Maldonado.
Brazil: Julio Cesar; Kleber, Juan (Thiago Silva 46), Maicon, Lucio, Kaka (Alex 71), Josue (Mancini 78), Gilberto Silva, Elano, Adriano, Robinho.
Referee: Rivera (Peru).

La Paz, 14 October 2008, 21,075
Bolivia (2) 2 *(Martins 15, 41)*
Uruguay (0) 2 *(Bueno 64, Abreu 88)*
Bolivia: Arias; Raldes, Vargas, Ronald Rivero, Garcia I, Vaca (Torrico 64), Reyes A, Flores, Robles, Martins (Parada 88), Botero (Escobar 71).
Uruguay: Castillo; Silva, Lugano, Caceres, Arismendi, Scotti, Rodriguez C (Abreu 70), Gonzalez A (Pereira M 55), Gargano, Sanchez, Bueno.
Referee: Baldassi (Argentina).

Asuncion, 15 October 2008, 31,545
Paraguay (0) 1 *(Cardozo 81)*   **Peru (0) 0**
Paraguay: Villar; Morel, Da Silva, Caceres J, Santana (Benitez 87), Riveros, Caceres V, Bonet, Barreto E (Martinez 46), Valdez (Cardozo 67), Cabanas.
Peru: Butron; Contreras, Vilchez, Vargas, Prado, Torres R, Solano, Marino (Alva Niezen 70), De La Haza (Quinteros 84), Rengifo, Fano (Chavez 82).
Referee: Fagundes (Brazil).

Rio de Janeiro, 16 October 2008, 54,910
Brazil (0) 0   Colombia (0) 0
Brazil: Julio Cesar; Maicon, Lucio, Kleber, Juan (Thiago Silva 66), Kaka, Josue, Gilberto Silva, Elano (Mancini 57), Robinho (Alexandre Pato 63), Jo.
Colombia: Agustin; Zuniga, Perea, Bedoya (Aguilar 66), Yepes, Toja, Guarin, Vargas, Armero, Renteria (Ramos 75), Quintero (Moreno D 70).
Referee: Selman (Chile).

Santiago, 16 October 2008, 65,000
Chile (1) 1 *(Orellana 35)*   **Argentina (0) 0**
Chile: Bravo; Medel, Contreras, Ponce (Vidal 87), Gonzalez (Droguett 20), Fernandez, Estrada, Carmona, Beausejour, Orellana (Martinez 87), Suazo.
Argentina: Carrizo; Heinze, Demichelis, Burdisso (Diaz 20), Zanetti, Mascherano, Ledesma, Cambiasso (Sand 85), Aguero, Milito (Bergessio 46), Messi.
Referee: Ruiz (Colombia).

Puerto La Cruz, 16 October 2008, 10,581
Venezuela (0) 3 *(Maldonado 48, Moreno 56, Arango 67)*
Ecuador (1) 1 *(Mina 12)*
Venezuela: Vega; Cichero, Rey, Fuenmayor, Rosales, Rincon, Gonzalez C (Rojas 70), Arango, Lucena, Moreno (Boada 79), Maldonado (Arismendi 74).
Ecuador: Cevallos; Mina, Hurtado I (Castro 36), Espinoza, De Jesus, Cortez, Urrutia, Mendez, Ayovi (Bolanos 60), Guerron (Borja 65), Caicedo.
Referee: Osses (Chile).

Buenos Aires, 28 March 2009, 46,085
Argentina (1) 4 *(Messi 26, Tevez 47, Rodriguez 51, Aguero 73)*
Venezuela (0) 0
Argentina: Carrizo; Angeleri, Zanetti, Heinze, Maxi Rodriguez (Di Maria 75), Mascherano, Gutierrez, Gago, Tevez (Veron 71), Messi, Aguero (Milito 78).
Venezuela: Vega; Rojas (Acosta 84), Fuenmayor, Cichero, Velasquez, Rosales (Moreno 50), Rincon, Gonzalez C, Chacon, Arango, Maldonado (Flores 78).
Referee: Rivera (Peru).

Montevideo, 28 March 2009, 45,000
Uruguay (1) 2 *(Forlan 28, Lugano 57)*   **Paraguay (0) 0**
Uruguay: Viera; Lugano, Godin (Silva 82), Caceres, Pereira M, Eguren, Pereira A, Rodriguez C (Martinez 72), Perez, Forlan (Abreu 78), Suarez.
Paraguay: Villar; Da Silva, Caceres J, Veron, Barreto E, Estigarribia (Aquino 46), Vera (Cardozo 69), Torres (Samudio 58), Riveros, Cabanas, Valdez.
Referee: Simon (Brazil).

Bogota, 29 March 2009, 22,044
Colombia (1) 2 *(Torres 26, Renteria 88)*   **Bolivia (0) 0**
Colombia: Ospina; Marin, Zuniga, Zapata, Yepes, Vargas, Torres (Motta 70), Armero, Aguilar, Quintero (Rodallega 79), Garcia (Renteria 70).
Bolivia: Arias; Ronald Rivero, Pena, Hoyos, Luis Gutierrez, Vaca (Hurtado 77), Garcia R, Flores, Robles (Torrico 46), Escobar, Cabrera (Castillo[a] 67).
Referee: Intriago (Ecuador).

Quito, 29 March 2009, 40,000
Ecuador (0) 1 *(Noboa 89)*   **Brazil (0) 1** *(Julio Baptista 72)*
Ecuador: Cevallos; Reasco, Hurtado I, Espinoza, Valencia, Mendez, Castillo, Ayovi, Guerron (Noboa 75), Caicedo (Palacios 90), Benitez.
Brazil: Julio Cesar; Lucio, Marcelo, Maicon (Daniel Alves 24), Luisao, Gilberto Silva, Elano (Josue 61), Felipe Melo, Ronaldinho (Julio Baptista 71), Robinho, Luis Fabiano.
Referee: Chandia (Chile).

Lima, 30 March 2009, 48,700
Peru (1) 1 *(Fano 34)*
Chile (2) 3 *(Sanchez 2, Suazo 32 (pen), Fernandez 70)*
Peru: Butron; Zambrano, Vargas[a], Rodriguez, Prado, Torres M (De La Haza 46), Ramirez, Torres R, Solano (Sanchez 79), Fano, Chavez (Alva 60).
Chile: Bravo; Ponce, Jara, Cerececeda, Isla (Contreras 63), Gonzalez, Fernandez (Tello 72), Carmona (Estrada 76), Beausejour, Suazo, Sanchez.
Referee: Amarilla (Paraguay).

La Paz, 1 April 2009, 30,487
Bolivia (3) 6 *(Martins 11, Botero 34 (pen), 53, 66, Da Rosa 45, Torrico 87)*
Argentina (1) 1 *(Gonzalez L 25)*
Bolivia: Arias; Ronald Rivero, Ribeiro, Pena, Da Rosa (Saucedo 69), Torrico, Reyes L, Reyes A (Garcia I 53), Martins, Botero, Garcia R (Flores 79).
Argentina: Carrizo; Zanetti, Heinze, Demichelis, Papa, Gonzalez L (Angeleri 69), Maxi Rodriguez (Di Maria■ 57), Mascherano, Gago, Tevez (Montenegro 76), Messi.
Referee: Vazquez (Uruguay).

Quito, 1 April 2009, 36,853
Ecuador (0) 1 *(Noboa 64)* **Paraguay (0) 1** *(Benitez 90)*
Ecuador: Cevallos; Ambrosi, Reasco, Hurtado I, Espinoza, Castillo, Valencia (Urrutia 86), Mendez, Caicedo (Calderon 46), Benitez, Guerron (Noboa 62).
Paraguay: Villar; Veron, Manzur, Da Silva■, Caniza, Vera (Bonet 80), Riveros, Caceres V, Aquino (Martinez 75), Valdez (Benitez 70), Cabanas.
Referee: Roldan (Colombia).

Puerto Ordaz, 1 April 2009, 35,000
Venezuela (0) 2 *(Fedor 78, Arango 82)* **Colombia (0) 0**
Venezuela: Vega; Fuenmayor, Lucena, Gonzalez C (Pena 65), Arango (Acosta 85), Velasquez, Salazar, Rosales, Rincon, Moreno, Maldonado (Fedor 74).
Colombia: Ospina; Marin, Bedoya, Nunez (Mosquera 46), Zuniga, Zapata, Yepes, Aguilar■, Torres (Rodallega 74), Garcia, Quintero (Marrugo 57).
Referee: Pozo (Chile).

Porto Alegre, 2 April 2009, 55,000
Brazil (2) 3 *(Luis Fabiano 18 (pen), 27, Felipe Melo 63)*
Peru (0) 0
Brazil: Julio Cesar; Luisao (Miranda 12), Lucio, Kleber, Daniel Alves, Kaka, Gilberto Silva, Felipe Melo, Elano (Ronaldinho 76), Robinho (Alexandre Pato 70), Luis Fabiano.
Peru: Butron; Zambrano, Vilchez, Rodriguez, Prado, Torres R, Solano (Fernandez 69), Ramirez (Alva 79), La Rosa, Garcia (Sanchez 62), Fano.
Referee: Pezzotta (Argentina).

Santiago, 2 April 2009, 55,000
Chile (0) 0 Uruguay (0) 0
Chile: Bravo; Ponce, Jara, Contreras, Isla■, Gonzalez, Fernandez (Orellana 60), Carmona, Beausejour (Iturra 39) (Cereceda 46), Suazo, Sanchez.
Uruguay: Viera; Lugano, Godin, Caceres, Rodriguez C (Cavani 85), Perez (Fernandez A 41), Pereira M, Pereira A (Abreu 72), Eguren, Suarez, Forlan.
Referee: Baldassi (Argentina).

Buenos Aires, 6 June 2009, 55,000
Argentina (0) 1 *(Diaz 55)* **Colombia (0) 0**
Argentina: Andujar; Diaz, Demichelis, Heinze, Gago (Zanetti 46), Veron, Mascherano, Gutierrez, Aguero (Milito 41), Tevez (Burdisso 84), Messi.
Colombia: Ospina; Marin (Ramos 66), Zuniga, Zapata, Yepes, Perea, Guarin, Armero (Quintero 82), Vargas, Garcia (Rodallega 73), Renteria.
Referee: Ortube (Bolivia).

La Paz, 6 June 2009, 23,427
Bolivia (0) 0 Venezuela (1) 1 *(Rivero 32 (og))*
Bolivia: Arias; Ronald Rivero, Raldes, Hoyos, Da Rosa, Vaca (Escobar 63), Reyes L■, Reyes A, Garcia R (Alvarez 77), Cabrera (Yecerotte 46), Martins■.
Venezuela: Romo; Perozo, Flores, Boada, Yeguez (Salazar 65), Di Giorgi, Velasquez, Seijas, Pena (Fernandez 56), Maldonado, Garcia (Rondon 70).
Referee: Vera (Ecuador).

Montevideo, 6 June 2009, 52,000
Uruguay (0) 0
Brazil (2) 4 *(Daniel Alves 12, Juan 35, Luis Fabiano 51, Kaka 74 (pen))*
Uruguay: Viera; Caceres, Valdez, Godin, Perez (Abreu 46), Pereira M■, Pereira A (Fernandez A 66), Martinez, Eguren, Suarez (Cavani 75), Forlan.
Brazil: Julio Cesar; Daniel Alves, Lucio, Kleber, Juan, Felipe Melo, Elano (Ramirez 66), Kaka (Julio Baptista 85), Gilberto Silva, Robinho (Josue 85), Luis Fabiano■.
Referee: Laverni (Argentina).

Asuncion, 7 June 2009, 34,000
Paraguay (0) 0 Chile (1) 2 *(Fernandez 13, Suazo 51)*
Paraguay: Villar; Caceres M, Manzur, Caniza, Caceres J, Vera (Ledesma 58), Riveros, Caceres V, Barreto E (Martinez 48), Valdez, Cardozo (Benitez 60).
Chile: Bravo; Ponce, Medel, Jara, Gonzalez (Millar 46), Fernandez, Estrada, Carmona, Beausejour, Suazo (Mancilla 72), Sanchez (Orellana 88).
Referee: Pezzotta (Argentina).

Lima, 7 June 2009, 17,050
Peru (0) 1 *(Vargas 51)*
Ecuador (1) 2 *(Montero 37, Tenorio C 58)*
Peru: Fernandez; Zambrano, Vilchez, Vargas, Rodriguez, Prado (Sanchez 72), De La Haza, Torres R (Ballon 80), Ramirez (Merino 46), Guerrero, Fano.
Ecuador: Elizaga; Fleitas, Reasco, Guagua, Castillo, Ayovi, Noboa, Mendez, Montero (Mina 83), Tenorio C (Hidalgo 88), Palacios (Guerron 51).
Referee: Torres (Paraguay).

Quito, 10 June 2009, 36,359
Ecuador (0) 2 *(Ayovi 72, Palacios 83)* **Argentina (0) 0**
Ecuador: Elizaga; Reasco, Hurtado I, Espinoza, Valencia, Noboa (Palacios 46), Mendez, Castillo, Ayovi, Tenorio C (Montero 13), Caicedo (Guerron 79).
Argentina: Andujar; Otamendi, Zanetti, Heinze (Milito 82), Demichelis, Rodriguez, Gutierrez, Gago (Veron 75), Battaglia, Tevez (Bergessio 67), Messi.
Referee: Chandia (Chile).

Recife, 11 June 2009, 56,682
Brazil (1) 2 *(Robinho 41, Nilmar 50)*
Paraguay (1) 1 *(Cabanas 25)*
Brazil: Julio Cesar; Kleber, Lucio, Juan, Daniel Alves, Elano (Ramires 60), Felipe Melo, Kaka, Gilberto Silva, Robinho (Kleberson 85), Nilmar (Alexandre Pato 74).
Paraguay: Villar; Caceres J, Veron, Da Silva, Caniza, Martinez (Lopez 77), Ledesma (Aquino 61), Caceres V, Bonet (Benitez 70), Riveros, Cabanas.
Referee: Ruiz (Colombia).

Santiago, 11 June 2009, 60,214
Chile (1) 4 *(Beausejour 44, Estrada 74, Sanchez 78, 89)*
Bolivia (0) 0
Chile: Bravo; Ponce, Medel, Jara, Millar (Isla 83), Gonzalez, Fernandez (Valdivia 68), Estrada, Beausejour, Suazo (Mancilla 83), Sanchez.
Bolivia: Arias; Vargas, Ronald Rivero, Raldes, Pena, Garcia I■, Torrico (Reyes A 57), Garcia R, Da Rosa (Yecerotte 46), Robles (Vaca 83), Escobar.
Referee: Silvera (Uruguay).

Medellin, 11 June 2009, 32,300
Colombia (1) 1 *(Garcia 26)* **Peru (0) 0**
Colombia: Ospina; Zapata, Marin, Zuniga, Yepes, Perea, Guarin, Vargas (Aguilar 54), Torres (Pino 67), Garcia, Renteria (Rodallega 46).
Peru: Butron; Zambrano, Vilchez, Vargas (Trujillo 21), Rodriguez, De La Haza, Ballon (Sanchez 81), Ramirez, La Rosa, Guerrero (Rengifo 87), Fano.
Referee: Simon (Brazil).

Puerto Ordaz, 11 June 2009, 37,000
Venezuela (1) 2 *(Maldonado 9, Rey 74)*
Uruguay (0) 2 *(Suarez 60, Forlan 72)*
Venezuela: Vega; Fuenmayor, Rey, Gonzalez C (Pena 68), Chacon (Velasquez 61), Arango (Salazar, Rincon, Lucena, Moreno, Maldonado (Fedor 84).
Uruguay: Castillo; Caceres (Cavani 80), Lugano, Godin, Fucile, Fernandez A (Rodriguez C 46), Amado, Perez, Pereira A, Suarez (Abreu 65), Forlan.
Referee: Fagundes (Brazil).

Medellin, 5 September 2009, 42,000
Colombia (0) 2 *(Martinez 82, Gutierrez 90)*
Ecuador (0) 0
Colombia: Julio; Zuniga (Martinez 73), Perea, Yepes, Cordoba I, Guarin, Armero, Moreno G, Vargas (Viafara 46), Gutierrez, Falcao (Fernandez 53).
Ecuador: Cevallos; Reasco, Hurtado I, Espinoza, Ayovi, Valencia, Noboa, Mendez (Montero 87), Castillo, Tenorio C (Palacios■ 23), Benitez.
Referee: Pezzotta (Argentina).

Lima, 5 September 2009, 15,000
Peru (0) 1 *(Rengifo 86)*   **Uruguay (0) 0**
Peru: Butron; Rodriguez, Zambrano, Vilchez, Vargas, Palacios, De la Haza (Prado 46), Ballon, Solano (Torres 80), Rengifo, Chavez (Avila 59).
Uruguay: Castillo; Lugano, Godin■, Fucile, Martinez (Rodriguez J 81), Gargano, Eguren (Fernandez A 61), Rodriguez C, Pereira A, Abreu, Suarez.
Referee: Chandia (Chile).

Rosario, 6 September 2009, 40,000
Argentina (0) 1 *(Datolo 65)*
Brazil (2) 3 *(Luisao 24, Luis Fabiano 30, 67)*
Argentina: Andujar; Dominguez, Zanetti, Otamendi, Heinze, Datolo, Veron, Maxi Rodriguez (Aguero 46), Mascherano, Tevez (Milito 69), Messi.
Brazil: Julio Cesar; Andre Santos, Maicon, Luisao, Lucio, Elano (Dani Alves 69), Kaka, Gilberto Silva, Felipe Melo, Robinho (Ramires 68), Luis Fabiano (Adriano 77).
Referee: Ruiz (Colombia).

Santiago, 6 September 2009, 44,000
Chile (1) 2 *(Vidal 11, Millar 53)*
Venezuela (2) 2 *(Maldonado 34, Rey 45)*
Chile: Bravo; Vidal, Medel, Jara, Cereceda (Orellana 46), Beausejour, Isla, Matias Fernandez, Carmona (Millar 46), Suazo (Valdivia 61), Sanchez.
Venezuela: Vega; Vizcarrondo, Granados, Rey, Seijas (Moreno 67), Rincon, Lucena, Arango, Di Giorgi (Vargas 75), Chacon (Boada 66), Maldonado.
Referee: Ortube (Bolivia).

Asuncion, 6 September 2009, 25,094
Paraguay (1) 1 *(Cabanas 45 (pen))*   **Bolivia (0) 0**
Paraguay: Villar; Morel, Da Silva, Veron, Martinez, Ledesma (Barreto E 70), Bonet, Santana, Riveros, Cabanas (Cardozo 88), Valdez (Benitez 77).
Bolivia: Suarez H; Palacios, Bejarano, Rodriguez, Luis Gutierrez, Parada, Garcia R (Vaca 84), Flores (Pachi 53), Gomez, Escobar (Cabrera 76), Martins.
Referee: Carrillo (Peru).

La Paz, 9 September 2009, 10,200
Bolivia (0) 1 *(Yecerotte 86)*
Ecuador (1) 3 *(Mendez 6, Valencia 47, Benitez 57)*
Bolivia: Suarez; Ronald Rivero, Ribeiro, Rodriguez, Bejarano, Pachi, Garcia R (Gutierrez H 64), Flores (Reyes A 46), Limberg Gutierrez, Cabrera (Yecerotte 52), Martins.
Ecuador: Elizaga; Hurtado I, Fleitas, Espinoza (Guagua 59), Mendez, Castillo, Ayovi, Valencia (Hidalgo 80), Noboa, Montero (Ambrosi 70), Benitez.
Referee: Baldassi (Argentina).

Montevideo, 9 September 2009, 30,000
Uruguay (1) 3 *(Suarez 6, Scotti 77, Eguren 88)*
Colombia (0) 1 *(Martinez 64)*
Uruguay: Castillo; Caceres, Valdez■, Silva, Rodriguez C (Eguren 82), Perez, Pereira A, Gargano, Suarez (Abreu 90), Forlan, Cavani (Scotti 33).
Colombia: Julio; Cordoba I, Yepes, Perea, Armero, Aguilar, Viafara (Hernandez 58), Guarin, Moreno G (Martinez 58), Ramos (Pabon 82), Guttierrez■.
Referee: Torres (Paraguay).

Salvador, 10 September 2009, 30,000
Brazil (2) 4 *(Nilmar 31, 73, 76, Julio Baptista 40)*
Chile (1) 2 *(Suazo 45 (pen), 52)*
Brazil: Julio Cesar; Dani Alves, Andre Santos (Elano 72), Miranda, Maicon, Luisao, Julio Baptista (Sandro Raniere 70), Gilberto Silva, Felipe Melo■, Adriano (Diego Tardelli 69), Nilmar.
Chile: Bravo; Vidal (Cereceda 46), Ponce, Medel, Jara, Carmona, Beausejour, Millar (Isla 68), Matias Fernandez, Suazo (Valdivia 67), Sanchez■.
Referee: Larrionda (Uruguay).

Asuncion, 10 September 2009, 38,000
Paraguay (1) 1 *(Valdez 28)*   **Argentina (0) 0**
Paraguay: Villar; Caceres J, Veron, Da Silva, Barreto E (Caceres V 82), Vera, Torres, Santana (Ledesma 67), Riveros, Cabanas, Valdez (Benitez 81).
Argentina: Romero; Zanetti, Heinze, Dominguez (Schiavi 81), Datolo (Lavezzi 46), Veron■, Papa, Mascherano, Gago, Aguero (Palermo 59), Messi.
Referee: Fagundes (Brazil).

Puerto La Cruz, 10 September 2009, 31,703
Venezuela (1) 3 *(Fedor 30, 52, Vargas 70)*
Peru (1) 1 *(Fuenmayor 41 (og))*
Venezuela: Vega; Fuenmayor, Boada, Vizcarronda, Rey, Vargas, Seijas, Lucena, Arango (Di Giorgi 79), Miku (Del Valle 83), Moreno (Rondon 77).
Peru: Butron; Vilchez, Rodriguez, Prado, Ramos, Torres R (Quinteros 67), Solano (Sanchez 68), Palacios, Ballon, Guerrero (Rengifo 15), Fano.
Referee: Vera (Ecuador).

Buenos Aires, 11 October 2009, 38,019
Argentina (0) 2 *(Higuain 48, Palermo 90)*
Peru (0) 1 *(Rengifo 90)*
Argentina: Romero; Insua E, Schiavi, Heinze, Perez (Palermo 46), Aimar (Insua F 76), Mascherano, Gutierrez, Di Maria, Messi, Higuain (Demichelis 67).
Peru: Butron; Prado, Zambrano, Vilchez, Vargas, Rodriguez, Torres R, Solano (Palacios 65), Ramirez (La Rosa 90), Ballon, Fano (Rengifo 71).
Referee: Ortube (Bolivia).

La Paz, 11 October 2009, 16,557
Bolivia (2) 2 *(Olivares 10, Martins 31)*
Brazil (0) 1 *(Nilmar 70)*
Bolivia: Arias; Zabala, Ronald Rivero, Raldes, Garcia I, Reyes L, Reyes A (Vaca 74), Olivares, Gutierrez H, Martins (Pedriel 81), Arce (Pachi 79).
Brazil: Julio Cesar; Miranda, Maicon, Luisao, Dani Alves, Andre Santos (Elano 67), Diego Souza (Alex 46), Ramires, Josue, Nilmar, Adriano (Diego Tardelli 46).
Referee: Pozo (Chile).

Medellin, 11 October 2009, 18,000
Colombia (1) 2 *(Martinez 14, Moreno G 63)*
Chile (2) 4 *(Ponce 34, Suazo 35, Valdivia 71, Orellana 78)*
Colombia: Ospina; Zuniga, Zapata, Yepes, Fernandez (Marrugo 56), Guarin (Moreno G 56), Armero, Aguilar, Pabon (Rodallega 62), Falcao, Martinez.
Chile: Bravo; Vidal, Ponce, Medel, Orellana■, Millar, Gonzalez (Fierro 63), Matias Fernandez (Valdivia 31), Carmona, Beausejour (Fuentes 46), Suazo.
Referee: Rivera (Peru).

Quito, 11 October 2009, 42,700
Ecuador (0) 1 *(Valencia 68)*
Uruguay (0) 2 *(Suarez 69, Forlan 90 (pen))*
Ecuador: Elizaga; Reasco, Hurtado I, Espinoza (Guagua 79), Valencia, Noboa (Montero 58), Mendez, Castillo, Ayovi, Caicedo (Zura 66), Benitez.
Uruguay: Muslera; Lugano, Caceres, Scotti, Rodriguez J (Fucile 59), Perez (Eguren 73), Pereira M, Pereira A, Gargano, Suarez (Cavani 85), Forlan.
Referee: Fagundes (Brazil).

Puerto Ordaz, 11 October 2009, 41,680
Venezuela (0) 0 *(Rondon 85)*
Paraguay (0) 2 *(Cabanas 56, Cardozo 80)*
Venezuela: Vega; Vizcarrondo, Fuenmayor, Boada, Seijas (Rosales 68), Rincon, Lucena, Gonzalez C (Rondon 81), Arango, Miku, Maldonado (Moreno 63).
Paraguay: Villar; Da Silva, Alcaraz, Veron, Caniza, Vera, Riveros, Martinez (Ledesma 56), Ortigoza, Valdez (Benitez 73), Cabanas (Cardozo 68).
Referee: Chandia (Chile).

Lima, 14 October 2009, 4373
Peru (0) 1 *(Fano 54)*   **Bolivia (0) 0**
Peru: Butron; Zambrano, Vilchez, Vargas, Rodriguez, Prado (Valverde 87), Solano (Quinteros 70), Ramirez (Palacios 62), Ballon, Rengifo, Fano■.
Bolivia: Arias; Zabala, Rodriguez, Ronald Rivero, Garcia I, Rosauro Rivero■, Vaca (Pedriel 81), Reyes L, Olivares (Escobar 77), Gomez (Chavez 82), Martins.
Referee: Soto (Venezuela).

Campo Grande, 15 October 2009, 30,000
Brazil (0) 0   Venezuela (0) 0
Brazil: Julio Cesar; Filipe (Alex 76), Miranda■, Maicon, Luisao, Ramires (Elano 77), Lucas, Kaka, Gilberto Silva, Nilmar, Luis Fabiano (Diego Tardelli 83).
Venezuela: Vega; Vizcarrondo, Rey, Granados, Rincon (Seijas 68), Lucena, Di Giorgi, Chacon, Arango (Miku 84), Moreno (Rondon 74), Maldonado.
Referee: Carrillo (Peru).

Santiago, 15 October 2009, 47,000
Chile (0) 1 *(Suazo 53)* **Ecuador (0) 0**
Chile: Bravo; Ponce, Medel, Cereceda (Fuentes 78), Vidal (Jara 65), Millar, Iturra, Beausejour (Paredes 32), Valdivia, Suazo, Sanchez.
Ecuador: Elizaga; Reasco, Hurtado I, Guagua, Mendez (Zura 77), Lara (Rojas 59), Hidalgo, Castillo**■**, Ayovi, Montero, Benitez.
Referee: Torres (Paraguay).

Asuncion, 15 October 2009, 17,503
Paraguay (0) 0   Colombia (0) 2 *(Ramos 61, Rodallega 80)*
Paraguay: Villar; Da Silva, Caceres J, Marecos (Cardozo 66), Veron, Santana, Riveros, Bonet, Valdez (Benitez 76), Cabanas, Achucarro (Martinez 55).
Colombia: Ospina; Marin, Cordoba I, Zapata, Guarin, Armero, Anchico, Aguilar, Ramos (Cordoba J 83), Falcao (Rodallega 54), Martinez (Gutierrez 76).
Referee: Oliveira (Brazil).

Montevideo, 15 October 2009, 50,000
Uruguay (0) 0   Argentina (0) 1 *(Bolatti 84)*
Uruguay: Muslera; Lugano, Caceres**■**, Scotti, Rodriguez J (Cavani 59), Perez, Pereira M, Pereira A, Gargano (Rodriguez**■** C 71), Suarez (Abreu 78), Forlan.
Argentina: Romero; Schiavi, Otamendi, Heinze, Demichelis, Veron, Mascherano, Gutierrez, Di Maria (Monzon 77), Messi (Tevez 87), Higuain (Bolatti 80).
Referee: Amarilla (Paraguay).

South America Table	P	W	D	L	F	A	Pts
Brazil	18	9	7	2	33	11	34
Chile	18	10	3	5	32	22	33
Paraguay	18	10	3	5	24	16	33
Argentina	18	8	4	6	23	20	28
Uruguay	18	6	6	6	28	20	24
Ecuador	18	6	5	7	22	26	23
Colombia	18	6	5	7	14	18	23
Venezuela	18	6	4	8	23	29	22
Bolivia	18	4	3	11	22	36	15
Peru	18	3	4	11	11	34	13

Brazil, Chile, Paraguay and Argentina qualified. Uruguay play-off with fourth-placed CONCACAF finalist.

EUROPEAN PLAY-OFFS FIRST LEG

Athens, 14 November 2009, 39,045
Greece (0) 0   Ukraine (0) 0
Greece: Tzorvas; Spyropoulos, Mantzios, Samaras, Katsouranis, Karagounis, Vyntra, Salpingidis (Mitroglou 71), Papastathopoulos, Kyrgiakos, Gekas (Charisteas 65).
Ukraine: Pyatov; Rakitskiy, Kucher, Tymoschuk, Shevchenko, Gusev (Aliyev 53), Milevskiy, Yeugen, Kobin, Mikhalik, Rotan (Yarmolenko 46).
Referee: Duhamel (France).

Lisbon, 14 November 2009, 60,588
Portugal (1) 1 *(Bruno Alves 31)* **Bosnia (0) 0**
Portugal: Eduardo; Bruno Alves, Paulo Ferreira, Duca, Ricardo Carvalho, Liedson, Deco (Tiago 84), Simao (Hugo Almeida 88), Pepe, Raul Meireles, Nani (Fabio Coentrao 69).
Bosnia: Hasagic; Spahic, Muratovic (Pjanic 87), Rahimic, Jahic, Misimovic (Muslimovic 81), Dzeko, Nadarevic, Ibisevic, Salihovic, Ibricic.
Referee: Atkinson (England).

Dublin, 14 November 2009, 74,103
Republic of Ireland (0) 0   France (0) 1 *(Anelka 72)*
Republic of Ireland: Given; St Ledger-Hall, Kilbane, O'Shea, Dunne, Whelan, Lawrence (Hunt S 80), Andrews, Doyle K (Best 71), Keane, Duff (McGeady 76).
France: Lloris; Sagna, Abidal, Gallas, Diarra L, Gourcuff, Anelka, Gignac (Malouda 90), Henry, Evra, Diarra A.
Referee: Brych (Germany).

Moscow, 14 November 2009, 71,600
Russia (1) 2 *(Bilyaletdinov 40, 52)*
Slovenia (0) 1 *(Pecnik 88)*
Russia: Akinfeev; Anyukov, Ignashevich, Berezutski V, Bilyaletdinov, Denisov, Pavlyuchenko (Sychev 80), Arshavin, Semak (Bystrov 61), Zyryanov, Zhirkov.
Slovenia: Handanovic; Brecko, Suler, Cesar, Koren, Birsa (Stevanovic 77), Novakovic, Jokic, Dedic (Dzinic 67), Kirm (Pecnik 82), Radosavljevic.
Referee: Bo Larsen (Denmark).

EUROPEAN PLAY-OFFS SECOND LEG

Zenica, 18 November 2009, 12,500
Bosnia (0) 0   Portugal (0) 1 *(Raul Meireles 56)*
Bosnia: Hasagic; Jahic, Pandza, Nadarevic Medunjanin (Muslimovic 46), Ibricic, Bajramovic (Berberovic 82), Salihovic**■**, Pjanic, Ibisevic, Dzeko.
Portugal: Eduardo; Pepe, Paulo Ferreira, Bruno Alves, Ricardo Carvalho, Nani (Edinho 73), Duda, Tiago, Raul Meireles, Liedson (Miguel Veloso 90), Simao (Deco 80).
Referee: Rossetti (Italy).

Paris, 18 November 2009, 79,145
France (0) 1 *(Gallas 102)*
Republic of Ireland (1) 1 *(Keane 32)*
France: Lloris; Evra, Escude (Squillaci 9), Sagna, Gallas, Diarra L, Diarra A, Gourcuff (Malouda 88), Anelka, Henry, Gignac (Govou 57).
Republic of Ireland: Given; St Ledger-Hall, O'Shea (McShane 67), Dunne, Whelan (Gibson 63), Lawrence (McGeady 107), Kilbane, Duff, Andrews, Keane, Doyle K.
Referee: Hansson (Sweden).
aet; France won 2-1 on aggregate.

Maribor, 18 November 2009, 12,510
Slovenia (1) 1 *(Dedic 44)* **Russia (0) 0**
Slovenia: Handanovic; Kirm, Cesar, Brecko, Suler, Radosavljevic, Jokic, Koren, Dedic (Stevanovic 90), Birsa (Pecnik 79), Novakovic.
Russia: Akinfeev; Ignashevich, Berezutski V, Anyukov, Bilyaletdinov (Pogrebnyak 77), Zyryanov, Zhirkov**■**, Yanbaev (Kerzhakov**■** 46), Denisov, Arshavin, Pavlyuchenko (Semak 46).
Referee: Hauge (Norway).

Donetsk, 18 November 2009, 31,648
Ukraine (0) 0   Greece (1) 1 *(Salpingidis 31)*
Ukraine: Pyatov; Mikhalik (Gay 66), Kucher, Khacheridi, Kobin (Gusev 69), Aliyev (Seleznov 57), Tymoshchuk, Rakitskiy, Milevskiy, Yarmolenko, Shevchenko.
Greece: Tzorvas; Papastathopoulos (Pliatsakis 29), Moras, Kyrgiakos, Vyntra, Spyropoulos, Katsouranis, Karagounis, Salpingidis, Charisteas (Tziolis 71), Samaras (Gekas 63).
Referee: Benquerenca (Portugal).
France, Greece, Portugal and Slovenia qualified.

SOUTH AMERICA/CONCACAF PLAY-OFFS FIRST LEG

San Jose, 14 November 2009, 19,500
Costa Rica (0) 0   Uruguay (1) 1 *(Lugano 21)*
Costa Rica: Navas; Sirias, Marin (Fonseca 63), Martinez (Umana 23), Borges, Saborio, Centeno, Ruiz, Miller (Diaz 77), Azofeifa**■**, Bolanos.
Uruguay: Muslera; Lugano, Godin, Victorino, Eguren, Fernandez A, Suarez (Fernandez S 81), Forlan, Pereira A, Lodeiro (Rodriguez J 61), Gonzalez A.
Referee: Undiano (Spain).

SOUTH AMERICA/CONCACAF PLAY-OFFS SECOND LEG

Montevideo, 18 November 2009, 55,000
Uruguay (0) 1 *(Abreu 70)* **Costa Rica (0) 1** *(Centeno 74)*
Uruguay: Muslera; Lugano, Godin, Pereira M, Scotti (Victorino 72), Perez, Pereira A, Lodeiro (Fernandez A 84), Eguren, Suarez (Abreu 65), Forlan.
Costa Rica: Navas; Umana, Miller, Marin (Saborio 69), Herrera, Diaz, Centeno, Borges (Barrantes 58), Bolanos, Ruiz, Nunez (Fonseca 64).
Referee: Busacca (Switzerland).

AFRICA PLAY-OFF

Omdurman (Sudan), 18 November 2009, 30,000
Algeria (1) 1 *(Yahia 40)* **Egypt (0) 0**
Algeria: Chaouchi; Bougherra, Belhadj, Yahia (Zaoui 67), Halliche, Mansouri, Yebda, Ghezzal, Saifi (Ghilas 89), Ziani, Meghni (Matmour 57).
Egypt: El Hadary; Al Muhamadi, El Saqua (Eid 75), Aboutrika, Said, Ahmed Fathi (Zidan 46), Emad Meteab, Moawad, Zaki (Abo Rabo 46), Ahmed Hassan, Gomaa.
Referee: Maillet (Seychelles).

WORLD CUP 2010
OTHER QUALIFYING RESULTS

OCEANIA

GROUP A
Tahiti 0, New Caledonia 1; Fiji 16, Tuvalu 0; New Caledonia 1, Tuvalu 0; Fiji 4, Cook Islands 0; Tahiti 1, Tuvalu 1; New Caledonia 3, Cook Islands 0; Cook Islands 4, Tuvalu 1; Fiji 4, Tahiti 0; Fiji 1, New Caledonia 1; Tahiti 1, Cook Islands 0.

Fiji and New Caledonia qualified.

GROUP B
Solomon Islands 12, American Samoa 1; Samoa 0, Vanuatu 4; Solomon Islands 4, Tonga 0; Samoa 7, American Samoa 0; Vanuatu 15, American Samoa 0; Samoa 2, Tonga 1; Tonga 4, American Samoa 0; Solomon Islands 2, Vanuatu 0; Samoa 0, Solomon Islands 3; Vanuatu 4, Tonga 1.

Solomon Islands and Vanuatu qualified.

SEMI-FINALS
Solomon Islands 2, New Caledonia 3; Fiji 3, Vanuatu 0.

THIRD PLACE
Vanuatu 2, Solomon Islands 0.

FINAL
Fiji 0, New Caledonia 1.

FINAL ROUND
Fiji 0, New Zealand 2; Vanuatu 1, New Zealand 2; Fiji 3, New Caledonia 3; New Zealand 4, Vanuatu 1; New Caledonia 4, Fiji 0; Vanuatu 1, New Caledonia 1; New Caledonia 3, Vanuatu 0; Fiji 2, Vanuatu 0; New Caledonia 1, New Zealand 3; Vanuatu 2, Fiji 1; New Zealand 3, New Caledonia 0; New Zealand 0, Fiji 2.

OCEANIA TABLE	P	W	D	L	F	A	Pts
New Zealand	6	5	0	1	14	5	15
New Caledonia	6	2	2	2	12	10	8
Fiji	6	2	1	3	8	11	7
Vanuatu	6	1	1	4	5	13	4

PLAY-OFF WITH ASIA
Bahrain 0, New Zealand 0; New Zealand 1, Bahrain 0.

New Zealand qualified.

ASIA

FIRST ROUND
Bangladesh 1, Tajikistan 1; Tajikistan 5, Bangladesh 0; Thailand 6, Macao 1; Macao 1, Thailand 7; Vietnam 0, UAE 1; UAE 5, Vietnam 0; Oman 2, Nepal 0; Nepal 0, Oman 2; Syria 3, Afganistan 0; Afganistan 1, Syria 2; Palestine 0, Singapore 4; Singapore v Palestine awarded 3-0; Lebanon 4, India 1; India 2, Lebanon 2; Yemen 3, Maldives 0; Maldives 2, Yemen 0; Cambodia 0, Turkmenistan 1; Turkmenistan 4, Cambodia 1; Uzbekistan 9, Taiwan 0; Taiwan 0, Uzbekistan 2; Kyrgyzstan 2, Jordan 0; Jordan 2, Kyrgyzstan 0 - Jordan won 6-5 on penalties; Mongolia 1, North Korea 4; North Korea 5, Mongolia 1; Timor-Leste 2, Hong Kong 3; Hong Kong 8, Timor-Leste 1; Sri Lanka 0, Qatar 5; Sri Lanka 0, China 7; Myanmar 0, Myanmar 7, China 4; Bahrain 4, Malaysia 1; Malaysia 0, Bahrain 0; Pakistan 0, Iraq 7; Iraq 0, Pakistan 0.

SECOND ROUND
Singapore 2, Tajikistan 0; Tajikistan 1, Singapore 1; Indonesia 1, Syria 4; Syria 7, Indonesia 0; Yemen 1, Thailand 1; Thailand 1, Yemen 0; Hong Kong 0, Turkmenistan 0; Turkmenistan 3, Hong Kong 0.

GROUP 1
Australia 3, Qatar 0; Iraq 1, China 1; China 0, Australia 0; Qatar 2, Iraq 0; Australia 1, Iraq 0; Qatar 0, China 0; China 0, Qatar 1; Iraq 1, Australia 0; China 1, Iraq 2; Qatar 1, Australia 3; Australia 0, China 1; Iraq 0, Qatar 1.

GROUP 2
Japan 4, Thailand 1; Oman 0, Bahrain 1; Thailand 0, Oman 1; Bahrain 1, Japan 0; Japan 3, Oman 0; Thailand 2, Bahrain 3; Oman 1, Japan 1; Bahrain 1, Thailand 1. Thailand 0, Japan 3; Bahrain 1, Oman 1; Japan 1, Bahrain 0; Oman 2, Thailand 1.

GROUP 3
South Korea 4, Turkmenistan 0; Jordan 0, North Korea 1; North Korea 0, South Korea 0; Turkmenistan 0, Jordan 2; South Korea 0, Jordan 2; Turkmenistan 0, North Korea 0; North Korea 1, Turkmenistan 0; Jordan 0, South Korea 1; North Korea 2, Jordan 0; Turkmenistan 1, South Korea 3; South Korea 0, North Korea 0; Jordan 2, Turkmenistan 0.

GROUP 4
Lebanon 0, Uzbekistan 1; Saudi Arabia 2, Singapore 0; Uzbekistan 3, Saudi Arabia 0; Singapore 2, Lebanon 0; Singapore 3, Uzbekistan 7; Saudi Arabia 4, Lebanon 1; Uzbekistan 1, Singapore 0; Lebanon 1, Saudi Arabia 2; Singapore 0, Saudi Arabia 2; Uzbekistan 3, Lebanon 0; Lebanon 1, Singapore 2; Saudi Arabia 4, Uzbekistan 0.

GROUP 5
Iran 0, Syria 0; UAE 2, Kuwait 0; Syria 1, UAE 1; Kuwait 2, Iran 2; Iran 0, UAE 0; Syria 1, Kuwait 0; UAE 0, Iran 1; Kuwait 4, Syria 2; Kuwait 2, UAE 3; Syria 0, Iran 2; Iran 2, Kuwait 0; UAE 1, Syria 3.

GROUP A
Bahrain 2, Japan 3; Qatar 3, Uzbekistan 0; Uzbekistan 0, Australia 1; Qatar 1, Bahrain 1; Australia 4, Qatar 0; Japan 1, Uzbekistan 1; Bahrain 0, Australia 1; Qatar 0, Japan 3; Japan 0, Australia 0; Uzbekistan 0, Bahrain 1; Japan 1, Bahrain 0; Uzbekistan 4, Qatar 0; Australia 2, Uzbekistan 0; Bahrain 1, Qatar 0; Uzbekistan 0, Japan 1; Qatar 0, Australia 0; Japan 1, Qatar 1; Australia 2, Bahrain 0; Bahrain 1, Uzbekistan 0; Australia 2, Japan 1.

Australia and Japan qualified.

GROUP B
UAE 1, North Korea 2; Saudi Arabia 1, Iran 1; North Korea 1, South Korea 1; UAE 1, Saudi Arabia 2; South Korea 4, UAE 1; Iran 2, North Korea 1; UAE 1, Iran 1; Saudi Arabia 0, South Korea 2; North Korea 1, Saudi Arabia 0; Iran 1, South Korea 1; North Korea 2, UAE 0; Iran 1, Saudi Arabia 2; South Korea 1, North Korea 0; Saudi Arabia 3, UAE 2; UAE 0, South Korea 2; North Korea 0, Iran 0; South Korea 0, Saudi Arabia 0; Iran 1, UAE 0; South Korea 1, Iran 1; Saudi Arabia 0, North Korea 0.

North Korea and South Korea qualified.

PLAY-OFFS
Bahrain 0, Saudi Arabia 0; Saudi Arabia 2, Bahrain 2.

PLAY-OFF WITH OCEANIA
Bahrain 0, New Zealand 0; New Zealand 1, Bahrain 0.

New Zealand qualified.

CONCACAF

FIRST ROUND
Dominican Republic v Puerto Rico not played; Puerto Rico 1, Dominican Republic 0; US Virgin Islands v Grenada not played; Grenada 10, US Virgin Islands 0; Surinam v Monserrat not played; Monserrat 1, Surinam 7; Bermuda 1, Cayman Islands 1; Cayman Islands 1, Bermuda 3; Belize 3, St Kitts & Nevis 1; St Kitts & Nevis 1, Belize 1; Nicaragua 0, Netherlands Antilles 1; Netherlands Antilles 2, Nicaragua 0; Dominica 1, Barbados 1; Barbados 1, Dominica 0; Aruba 0, Antigua & Barbuda 3; Antigua & Barbuda 1, Aruba 0; Turks & Caicos 2, St Lucia 1; St Lucia 2, Turks & Caicos 0; El Salvador 12, Anguilla 0; Anguilla 0, El Salvador 4; Bahamas 1, British Virgin Islands 1; British Virgin Islands 2, Bahamas 2.

SECOND ROUND

Honduras 4, Puerto Rico 0; Puerto Rico 2, Honduras 2; Belize 0, Mexico 2; Mexico 7, Belize 0; Surinam 1, Guyana 0; Guyana 1, Surinam 2; Grenada 2, Costa Rica 2; Costa Rica 3, Grenada 0; Guatemala 6, St Lucia 0; St Lucia 1, Guatemala 3; St Vincent & the Grenadines 0, Canada 3; Canada 4, St Vincent & the Grenadines 1; Trinidad & Tobago 1, Bermuda 2; Bermuda 0, Trinidad & Tobago 2; Haiti 0, Netherlands Antilles 0; Netherlands Antilles 0, Haiti 1; USA 8, Barbados 0; Barbados 0, USA 1; Panama 1, El Salvador 0; El Salvador 3, Panama 1; Antigua & Barbuda 3, Cuba 4; Cuba 4, Antigua & Barbuda 0; Jamaica 7, Bahamas 0; Bahamas 0, Jamaica 6.

SEMI-FINAL

GROUP A

Cuba 1, Trinidad & Tobago 3; Guatemala 0, USA 1; Trinidad & Tobago 1, Guatemala 1; Cuba 0, USA 1; USA 3, Trinidad & Tobago 0; Guatemala 4, Cuba 1; USA 6, Cuba 1; Guatemala 0, Trinidad & Tobago 0; Cuba 2, Guatemala 1; Trinidad & Tobago 2, USA 1; USA 2, Guatemala 0; Trinidad & Tobago 3, Cuba 0.

SEMI-FINAL

GROUP B

Canada 1, Jamaica 1; Mexico 2, Honduras 1; Mexico 3, Jamaica 0; Canada 1, Honduras 2; Mexico 2, Canada 1; Honduras 2, Jamaica 0; Jamaica 1, Mexico 0; Honduras 3, Canada 1; Jamaica 1, Honduras 0; Canada 2, Mexico 2; Jamaica 3, Canada 0; Honduras 1, Mexico 0.

SEMI-FINAL

GROUP C

Haiti 2, Surinam 2; Costa Rica 1, El Salvador 0; Costa Rica 7, Surinam 0; El Salvador 5, Haiti 0; Surinam 0, El Salvador 2; Haiti 1, Costa Rica 3; Surinam 1, Costa Rica 4; Haiti 0, El Salvador 0; Costa Rica 2, Haiti 0; El Salvador 3, Surinam 0; El Salvador 1, Costa Rica 3; Surinam 1, Haiti 1.

FINAL ROUND

USA 2, Mexico 0; El Salvador 2, Trinidad & Tobago 2; Costa Rica 2, Honduras 0; Trinidad & Tobago 1, Honduras 1; Mexico 2, Costa Rica 0; El Salvador 2, USA 2; USA 3, Trinidad & Tobago 0; Honduras 3, Mexico 1; Costa Rica 1, El Salvador 0; Costa Rica 2, USA 1; Trinidad & Tobago 2, Costa Rica 3; El Salvador 2, Mexico 1; USA 2, Honduras 1; Mexico 2, Trinidad & Tobago 1; Honduras 1, El Salvador 0; Honduras 4, Costa Rica 0; Trinidad & Tobago 1, El Salvador 0; Mexico 2, USA 1; Honduras 4, Trinidad & Tobago 1; USA 2, El Salvador 1; Costa Rica 0, Mexico 3; El Salvador 1, Costa Rica 0; Mexico 1, Honduras 0; Trinidad & Tobago 0, USA 1; Costa Rica 4, Trinidad & Tobago 0; Mexico 4, El Salvador 1; Honduras 2, USA 3; USA 2, Costa Rica 2; Trinidad & Tobago 2, Mexico 2; El Salvador 0, Honduras 1.

CONCACAF TABLE	P	W	D	L	F	A	Pts
USA	10	6	2	2	19	13	20
Mexico	10	6	1	3	18	12	19
Honduras	10	5	1	4	17	11	16
Costa Rica	10	5	1	4	15	15	16
El Salvador	10	2	2	6	9	15	8
Trinidad & Tobago	10	1	3	6	10	22	6

USA, Mexico and Honduras qualified.

PLAY-OFFS

Costa Rica 0, Uruguay 1; Uruguay 1, Costa Rica 1.

Uruguay qualified.

AFRICA

FIRST ROUND

Madagascar 6, Comoros 2; Comoros 0, Madagascar 4; Sierra Leone 1, Guinea-Bissau 0; Guinea-Bissau 0, Sierra Leone 0; Djibouti 1, Somalia 0; Somalia v Djibouti not played.

GROUP 1

Tanzania 1, Mauritius 1; Cameroon 2, Cape Verde Islands 0; Cape Verde Islands 1, Tanzania 0; Mauritius 0, Cameroon 3; Tanzania 0, Cameroon 0; Mauritius 0 Cape Verde Islands 1; Cameroon 2, Tanzania 1; Cape Verde

Islands 3, Mauritius 1; Mauritius 1, Tanzania 4; Cape Verde Islands 1, Cameroon 2; Tanzania 3, Cape Verde Islands 1; Cameroon 5, Mauritius 0.

GROUP 2

Namibia 2, Kenya 1; Guinea 0, Zimbabwe 0; Kenya 2, Guinea 0; Zimbabwe 2, Namibia 0; Kenya 2, Zimbabwe 0; Namibia 1, Guinea 2; Guinea 4, Namibia 0; Zimbabwe 0, Kenya 0; Kenya 1, Namibia 0; Zimbabwe 0, Guinea 0; Namibia 4, Zimbabwe 2; Guinea 3, Kenya 2.

GROUP 3

Uganda 1, Niger 0; Angola 3, Benin 0; Niger 1, Angola 2; Benin 4, Uganda 1; Uganda 3, Angola 1; Niger 0, Benin 2; Angola 0, Uganda 0; Benin 2, Niger 0; Benin 3, Angola 2; Niger 3, Uganda 1; Uganda 2, Benin 1; Angola 3, Niger 1.

GROUP 4

Equatorial Guinea 2, Sierra Leone 0; Nigeria 2, South Africa 0; South Africa 4, Equatorial Guinea 1; Sierra Leone 0, Nigeria 1; Sierra Leone 1, South Africa 0; Equatorial Guinea 0, Nigeria 1; Nigeria 2, Equatorial Guinea 0; South Africa 0, Sierra Leone 0; South Africa 0, Nigeria 1; Sierra Leone 2, Equatorial Guinea 1; Equatorial Guinea 0, South Africa 1; Nigeria 4, Sierra Leone 1.

GROUP 5

Gabon v Lesotho not played; Ghana 3, Libya 0; Libya 1, Gabon 0; Lesotho 2, Ghana 3; Gabon 2, Ghana 0; Lesotho 0, Libya 1; Ghana 2, Gabon 0; Libya 4, Lesotho 0; Gabon 2, Lesotho 0; Libya 1, Ghana 0; Lesotho 0, Gabon 3; Gabon 1, Libya 0; Ghana 3, Lesotho 0.

GROUP 6

Senegal 1, Algeria 0; Liberia 1, Gambia 1; Algeria 3, Liberia 0; Gambia 0, Senegal 0; Gambia 1, Algeria 0; Liberia 2, Senegal 2; Algeria 1, Gambia 0; Senegal 3, Liberia 1, Algeria 3, Senegal 2; Gambia 3, Liberia 0; Liberia 0, Algeria 0; Senegal 1, Gambia 1.

GROUP 7

Botswana 0, Madagascar 0; Ivory Coast 1, Mozambique 0; Madagascar 0, Ivory Coast 0; Mozambique 1, Botswana 2; Botswana 1, Ivory Coast 1; Madagascar 1, Mozambique 1; Ivory Coast 4, Botswana 0; Mozambique 3, Madagascar 0; Madagascar 1, Botswana 0; Mozambique 1, Ivory Coast 1; Botswana 0, Mozambique 1; Ivory Coast 3, Madagascar 0.

GROUP 8

Rwanda 3, Mauritania 0; Morocco 3, Ethiopia 0; Mauritania 1, Morocco 4; Ethiopia 1, Rwanda 2; Mauritania 0, Ethiopia 1; Rwanda 3, Morocco 1; Ethiopia 6, Mauritania 1; Morocco 2, Rwanda 0; Mauritania 0, Rwanda 1; Morocco 4, Mauritania 1.

GROUP 9

Burundi 1, Seychelles 0; Tunisia 1, Burkina Faso 2; Seychelles 0, Tunisia 2; Burkina Faso 2, Burundi 0; Seychelles 2, Burkina Faso 3; Burundi 0, Tunisia 1; Burkina Faso 4, Seychelles 1; Tunisia 2, Burundi 1; Seychelles 1, Burundi 2; Burkina Faso 0, Tunisia 0; Tunisia 5, Seychelles 0; Burundi 1, Burkina Faso 3.

GROUP 10

Sudan v Chad not played; Mali 4, Congo 2; Chad 1, Mali 2; Congo 1, Sudan 0; Chad 2, Congo 1; Sudan 3, Mali 2; Congo 3, Chad 0; Mali 3, Sudan 0; Sudan 1, Chad 2; Congo 1, Mali 0; Chad 1, Sudan 3; Sudan 2, Congo 0; Mali 2, Chad 1.

GROUP 11

Togo 1, Zambia 0; Swaziland 2, Togo 1; Swaziland 0, Zambia 0; Zambia 1, Swaziland 0; Zambia 1, Togo 0; Togo 6, Swaziland 0.

GROUP 12

Malawi 8, Djibouti 1; Egypt 2, Congo DR 1; Djibouti 0, Egypt 4; Congo DR 1, Malawi 0; Djibouti 0, Congo DR 6; Malawi 1, Egypt 0; Egypt 2, Malawi 0; Congo DR 5, Djibouti 1; Djibouti 0, Malawi 3; Congo DR 0, Egypt 1; Malawi 2, DR Congo 1; Egypt 4, Djibouti 0.

GROUP A

Togo 1, Cameroon 0; Morocco 1, Gabon 2; Cameroon 0, Morocco 0; Gabon 3 Togo 0; Morocco 0, Togo 0; Gabon 0, Cameroon 2; Cameroon 2, Gabon 1; Togo 1, Morocco 1; Cameroon 3, Togo 0; Gabon 3, Morocco 1; Morocco 0, Cameroon 2; Togo 1, Gabon 0.

Cameroon qualified.

GROUP B

Kenya 1, Tunisia 2; Mozambique 0, Nigeria 0; Tunisia 2, Mozambique 0; Nigeria 3, Kenya 0; Tunisia 0, Nigeria 0; Kenya 2, Mozambique 1; Mozambique 1, Kenya 0; Nigeria 2, Tunisia 2; Tunisia 1, Kenya 0; Nigeria 1, Mozambique 0; Kenya 2, Nigeria 3; Mozambique 1, Tunisia 0.

Nigeria qualified.

GROUP C

Rwanda 0, Algeria 0; Egypt 1, Zambia 1; Zambia 1, Rwanda 0; Algeria 3, Egypt 1; Egypt 3, Rwanda 0; Zambia 0, Algeria 2; Algeria 1, Zambia 0; Rwanda 0, Egypt 1; Zambia 0, Egypt 1; Algeria 3, Rwanda 1; Egypt 2, Algeria 0; Rwanda 0, Zambia 0.

PLAY-OFF

Algeria 1, Egypt 0.

Algeria qualified.

GROUP D

Sudan 1, Mali 1; Ghana 1, Benin 0; Benin 1, Sudan 0; Mali 0, Ghana 2; Mali 3, Benin 1; Sudan 0, Ghana 2; Benin 1, Mali 1; Ghana 2, Sudan 0; Benin 1, Ghana 0; Mali 1, Sudan 0; Sudan 1, Benin 2; Ghana 2, Mali 2.

Ghana qualified.

GROUP E

Burkina Faso 4, Guinea 2; Ivory Coast 5, Malawi 0; Malawi 0, Burkina Faso 1; Guinea1, Ivory Coast 2; Burkina Faso 2, Ivory Coast 3; Guinea 2, Malawi 1; Ivory Coast 5, Burkina Faso 0; Malawi 2, Guinea 1; Guinea 1, Burkina Faso 2; Malawi 1, Ivory Coast 1; Burkina Faso 1, Malawi 0; Ivory Coast 3, Guinea 0.

Ivory Coast qualified.

South Africa qualified as hosts.

WORLD CUP 2010
OTHER QUALIFYING TEAMS

AUSTRALIA

■ *Denotes player sent off.*

Melbourne, 6 February 2008, 50,969

Australia (3) 3 *(Kennedy 10, Cahill 18, Bresciano 33)*

Qatar (0) 0

Australia: Schwarzer; Neill, Moore (Holman 77), Cahill (Valeri 67), Culina, Emerton, Wilkshire, Kennedy (Aloisi 70), McDonald, Carney, Bresciano.

Kunming, 26 March 2008, 32,000

China (0) 0

Australia (0) 0

Australia: Schwarzer; Neill, North, Culina, Beauchamp, Valeri, Wilkshire, Thompson (Holman 10), Carney, Grella, Bresciano.

Brisbane, 1 June 2008, 48,678

Australia (0) 1 *(Kewell 47)*

Iraq (0) 0

Australia: Schwarzer; Beauchamp, North, Culina, Emerton, Wilkshire, McDonald (Holman 65), Kewell (Djite 77), Carney, Grella, Bresciano (Valeri 62).

Dubai, 7 June 2008, 8000

Iraq (0) 1 *(Mohammed 27)*

Australia (0) 0

Australia: Schwarzer; Coyne (Kennedy 64), Beauchamp, North, Culina, Valeri, Emerton, Wilkshire, Kewell (McDonald), Carney, Grella (Holman 46).

Doha, 14 June 2008, 12,000

Qatar (0) 1 *(Al Khalfan 90)*

Australia (1) 3 *(Emerton 17, 56, Kewell 75)*

Australia: Schwarzer; Beauchamp, North, Culina, Valeri, Emerton, Wilkshire, Kewell (Djite 85), Carney, Holman, Bresciano.

Sydney, 22 June 2008, 70,054

Australia (0) 0

China (1) 1 *(Sun 11)*

Australia: Petkovic; Topor-Stanley, Spiranovic, North, Zadkovich, Valeri, Jedinak (Kilkenny 79), Holland (Williams), Djite, Kewell, Troisi (Sarkies 83).

Tashkent, 10 September 2008, 34,000

Uzbekistan (0) 0

Australia (1) 1 *(Chipperfield 26)*

Australia: Schwarzer; Neill, Chipperfield, Burns, Emerton, Wilkshire, Kewell (Djite 90), Coyne, Valeri, Holman (Sterjovski 77), Bresciano (Carney 73).

Brisbane, 15 October 2008, 34,320

Australia (2) 4 *(Cahill 8, Emerton 17 (pen), 58, Kennedy 76)*

Qatar (0) 0

Australia: Schwarzer; Neill, Moore, Cahill, Culina, Emerton (Burns 86), Wilkshire, Kennedy, Carney, Chipperfield (Sterjovski 46), McDonald (Holman 68).

Manama, 19 November 2008, 10,000

Bahrain (0) 0

Australia (0) 1 *(Bresciano 90)*

Australia: Schwarzer; Neill, Cahill (Sterjovski 86), Culina, Wilkshire, Kennedy, Kewell (Holman 71), Carney, Coyne (North 69), Valeri, Bresciano.

Yokohama, 11 February 2009, 66,000

Japan (0) 0

Australia (0) 0

Japan: Tsuzuki; Nakazawa, Tanaka MT, Uchida, Endo, Matsui (Okubo 57), Tanaka T (Okazaki 83), Nakamura S, Tamada, Nagatomo, Hasebe.
Australia: Schwarzer; Neill, Moore, Cahill (Kennedy 85), Culina, Wilkshire, Chipperfield, Grella, Holman (Garcia 64), Valeri, Bresciano (Carney 90).

Sydney, 1 April 2009, 57,292

Australia (0) 2 *(Kennedy 66, Kewell 73 (pen))*

Uzbekistan (0) 0

Australia: Schwarzer; Neill, Culina, Beauchamp, Wilkshire, Kewell (Holman 75), Chipperfield, Garcia, Valeri (Jedinak 82), McDonald (Kennedy 61), Bresciano.

Doha, 6 June 2009, 7000

Qatar (0) 0

Australia (0) 0

Australia: Schwarzer; Neill, Cahill (Garcia 90), Culina, Coyne, Kennedy, Kewell, Chipperfield, Grella (North 73), Valeri, Bresciano (Holman 77).

Sydney, 10 June 2009, 39,540

Australia (0) 2 *(Sterjovski 55, Carney 88)*

Bahrain (0) 0

Australia: Schwarzer; Milligan, Carney, Culina, Coyne (North 73), Jedinak (Grella 63), Wilkshire, Kewell, Holman (Carle 84), Sterjovski, McDonald.

Melbourne, 17 June 2009, 69,238

Australia (0) 2 *(Cahill 59, 77)*

Japan (1) 1 *(Tanaka MT 39)*

Australia: Schwarzer; Neill, Stefanutto, Cahill (Vidosic 84), Culina, Kennedy, Carle (Burns 77), Grella, Williams (McDonald 77), Sterjovski, North.
Japan: Narazaki; Abe, Tanaka MT, Uchida, Hashimoto (Kohrogi 84), Konno, Okazaki, Matsui (Yano 67), Tamada, Nakamura K, Nagatomo.

JAPAN

Saitama, 6 February 2008, 35,130

Japan (1) 4 *(Endo 21, Okubo 54, Nakazawa 66, Maki 90)*

Thailand (1) 1 *(Winothai 22)*

Japan: Kawaguchi; Nakazawa, Komano, Abe, Endo, Uchida, Yamase (Maki 68), Suzuki, Nakamura K, Okubo (Hanyu 87), Takahara (Bando 77).

Manama, 26 March 2008, 26,000

Bahrain (0) 1 *(Hubail 78)*

Japan (0) 0

Japan: Kawaguchi; Nakazawa, Komano, Yasuda (Yamagishi 71), Abe (Tamada 81), Maki, Suzuki, Nakamura K, Konno, Okubo.

Yokohama, 2 June 2008, 46,764

Japan (2) 3 *(Nakazawa 10, Okubo 22, Nakamura 49)*

Oman (0) 0

Japan: Narazaki; Nakazawa, Komano, Tanaka MT, Nagatomo (Konno 83), Endo, Matsui, Nakamura S, Tamada (Maki 79), Okubo (Kagawa 72), Hasebe.

Muscat, 7 June 2008, 6500

Oman (1) 1 *(Mubarak 12)*

Japan (0) 1 *(Endo 53 (pen))*

Japan: Narazaki; Nakazawa, Komano, Tanaka MT, Uchida (Konno 90), Endo, Matsui (Yamase 78), Nakamura S, Tamada (Yano 90), Okubo■, Hasebe.

Bangkok, 14 June 2008, 25,000

Thailand (0) 0

Japan (2) 3 *(Tanaka MT 23, Nakazawa 38, Nakamura K 88)*

Japan: Narazaki; Nakazawa, Komano, Tanaka MT, Uchida, Endo, Kagawa (Konno 82), Matsui (Nakamura K 70), Nakamura S (Yano 70), Tamada, Hasebe.

Saitama, 22 June 2008, 51,180

Japan (0) 1 *(Uchida 90)*

Bahrain (0) 0

Japan: Narazaki; Nakazawa, Tanaka MT, Uchida, Endo, Sato (Yamase 64), Nakamura S, Tamada, Nakamura K, Yasuda (Konno 73), Honda (Maki 80).

Manama, 6 September 2008, 20,000

Bahrain (0) 2 *(Isa 87, Tanaka MT 89 (og))*

Japan (2) 3 *(Nakamura S 18, Endo 44 (pen), Nakamura K 85)*

Japan: Narazaki; Nakazawa, Uchida, Tanaka MT, Abe, Endo, Matsui (Nakamura K 70), Nakamura S, Tamada, Tanaka T, Hasebe (Konno 84).

Saitama, 15 October 2008, 55,142

Japan (1) 1 *(Tamada 40)*

Uzbekistan (1) 1 *(Shatskikh 27)*

Japan: Narazaki; Nakazawa, Tanaka MT, Abe, Endo, Nakamura S, Tamada (Kohrogi 81), Kagawa (Inamoto 76), Uchida, Okubo (Okazaki 62), Hasebe.

Doha, 19 November 2008, 13,000

Qatar (0) 0

Japan (1) 3 *(Tanaka T 19, Tamada 47, Tanaka MT 68)*

Japan: Kawaguchi; Terada, Uchida, Tanaka MT, Endo, Tanaka T (Matsui 71), Nakamura S, Tamada (Sato 90), Nagatomo, Okubo (Okazaki 86), Hasebe.

Saitama, 28 March 2009, 57,276

Japan (0) 1 *(Nakamura S 47)*

Bahrain (0) 0

Japan: Narazaki; Nakazawa, Tanaka MT, Uchida, Endo, Tanaka T (Okazaki 86), Nakamura S, Tamada (Matsui 79), Nagatomo, Okubo, Hasebe (Hashimoto 76).

Tashkent, 6 June 2009, 34,000

Uzbekistan (0) 0

Japan (1) 1 *(Okazaki 9)*

Japan: Narazaki; Nakazawa, Komano, Tanaka MT, Endo, Okazaki, Nakamura S (Abe 90), Nakamura K (Honda 66), Nagatomo, Okubo (Yano 69), Hasebe■.

Yokohama, 10 June 2009, 60,256

Japan (1) 1 *(Albinali 3 (og))*

Qatar (0) 1 *(Yahya 53 (pen))*

Japan: Narazaki; Nakazawa, Tanaka MT, Abe (Matsui 58), Uchida, Hashimoto, Okazaki, Nakamura S (Honda 81), Tamada (Kohrogi 67), Nakamura K, Konno.

SOUTH KOREA

Seoul, 6 February 2008, 25,738

South Korea (1) 4 *(Kwak TH 43, Seol 57, 85, Park JS 70)*

Turkmenistan (0) 0

South Korea: Jung; Oh BS, Cho YH (Park WJ 85), Kim N (Lee KW 77), Park JS, Park CY, Seol, Lee YP, Kang, Kwak TH, Yeom (Kim DH 31).

Shanghai, 26 March 2008, 20,000

North Korea (0) 0

South Korea (0) 0

North Korea: Ri MG; Ri J, Ri KH, An YH, Hong, Mun, Jong TS (Pak NC 90), Pak SC, Han (Cha 27), Kim YJ, Nam.
South Korea: Jung; Oh BS, Cho WH, Kim N (Kim DH 27), Park JS, Cho JJ (Yeom 46), Park CY, Seol (Han 81), Lee YP, Kang, Lee JS.

Seoul, 31 May 2008, 50,000

South Korea (1) 2 *(Park JS 39, Park CY 48)*

Jordan (0) 2 *(Mahmoud 73, 81)*

South Korea: Kim YD; Oh BS, Cho WH, Kim N (Cho YH 76), Kwak HJ, Park JS, Park CY, Lee YP, Lee CY (Kim DH 55), Lee JS, Ahn (Ko 86).

Amman, 7 June 2008, 8000

Jordan (0) 0

South Korea (1) 1 *(Park CY 24 (pen))*

South Korea: Jung; Oh BS, Cho WH, Kim N, Kwak HJ, Park JS, Park CY, Seol (Cho YH 46), Lee YP (Lee JS 68), Lee KH (Ahn 80), Kang.

Ashgabat, 14 June 2008, 11,000

Turkmenistan (0) 1 *(Ovekov 77 (pen))*

South Korea (1) 3 *(Kim BH 14, 81, 90 (pen))*

South Korea: Jung; Oh BS (Lee JS 29), Cho WH (Choi HJ 46), Cho YH, Kim N, Lee KH (Lee CY 80), Kim DH, Park CY, Seol, Kim CW, Kang.

Seoul, 22 June 2008, 48,519

South Korea (0) 0

North Korea (0) 0

South Korea: Jung; Kim CW, Oh JE (Lee KH 78), Kim DH, Ahn (Park CY 60), Ko, Choi HJ, Kang, Lee JS, Kim JW (Kim N 71), Lee CY.
North Korea: Ri MG; Cha, Ri J, Ri KC, An YH, Hong (Choe 10), Mun, Jong TS, Pak CJ, Kim YJ (Pak NC 63), Nam.

Shanghai, 10 September 2008, 3000
North Korea (0) 1 *(Hong 64 (pen))*
South Korea (0) 1 *(Ki 69)*

North Korea: Ri MG; Cha, Ri J, Ri KC, An YH, Hong, Mun, Jong TS, Park CJ, Kim YJ (Choe 71) (Kim K 89), Nam.
South Korea: Jung; Oh BS (Choi HJ 79), Kim DJ, Kim N, Kim JK, Choi SK (Lee CS 60), Kim DH, Cho JJ (Seol 60), Kim CW, Kang, Ki.

Seoul, 15 October 2008, 30,000
South Korea (2) 4 *(Lee KH 20, 80, Park JS 26, Kwak TH 89)*
UAE (0) 1 *(Al Hammadi 72)*

South Korea: Jung; Cho YH, Kim DJ, Ki (Cho WH 80), Park JS, Lee CY (Kim HB 55), Lee KH (Shin 88), Lee YP, Kim JW, Jeong, Kwak TH.

Riyadh, 19 November 2008, 60,000
Saudi Arabia (0) 0
South Korea (0) 2 *(Lee KH 76, Park CY 90)*

South Korea: Lee WJ; Oh BS, Cho YH, Ki, Park JS, Kim JW, Jeong (Park CY 74), Lee KH (Yeom 89), Lee YP, Kang, Lee CY (Cho WH 90).

Tehran, 11 February 2009, 75,000
Iran (0) 1 *(Nekounam 58)*
South Korea (0) 1 *(Park JS 81)*

South Korea: Lee WJ; Oh BS, Kang, Cho YH, Park JS (Park CY 84), Kim JW, Jeong (Yeom 41), Lee KH, Lee YP (Kim DJ 70), Ki, Lee CY.

Seoul, 1 April 2009, 48,000
South Korea (0) 1 *(Kim CW 86)*
North Korea (0) 0

South Korea: Lee WJ; Oh BS, Kang, Cho WH, Hwang (Lee JS 53), Park JS, Park CY, Lee KH (Kim CW 77), Lee YP (Kim DJ 59), Ki, Lee CY.
North Korea: Ri MK; Cha, Ri J, Pak NC, Ri KC, Ji (Nam SC 80), Hong, Mun, Jong TS, Pak CJ, Kim YJ (Choe 83).

Dubai, 6 June 2009, 4000
UAE (0) 0
South Korea (2) 2 *(Park CY 9, Ki 37)*

South Korea: Lee WJ; Oh BS, Cho YH, Park JS, Kim JW, Park CY (Bae 82), Lee KH (Cho WH 51), Lee YP (Kim DJ 59), Lee JS, Ki, Lee CY.

Seoul, 10 June 2009, 32,510
South Korea (0) 0
Saudi Arabia (0) 0

South Korea: Lee WJ; Cho WH, Cho YH, Kim DJ, Park JS, Park CY (Yang 73), Lee KH (Choi TU 84), Lee JS, Kim H, Ki, Lee CY.

Seoul, 17 June 2009, 40,000
South Korea (0) 1 *(Park JS 82)*
Iran (0) 1 *(Shojaei 52)*

South Korea: Lee WJ; Oh BS, Cho YH, Kim DJ (Lee YP 70), Park JS, Kim JW, Park CY, Lee KH, Lee JS, Ki (Yang 75), Lee CY (Cho WH 46).

NORTH KOREA

Ulaan-Baatar, 21 October 2007, 4870
Mongolia (0) 1 *(Selenge 90)*
North Korea (3) 4 *(Pak CM 14, Jong CM, 24, 32, 78)*

North Korea: Ri MG (Ju 46); Ri J, Pak NC, Pak CM, Pak SC, Jon, Ri CM (Jong SH 76), Jong CM, Kim KJ, Kim K (So 30), Yun.

Pyongyang, 28 October 2007, 5000
North Korea (3) 5 *(Park CM 3, 74, Kim KJ 10, Jong CM 36, Jon 90)*
Mongolia (1) 1 *(Donorov 41)*

North Korea: Ju; Cha, Ri J (Ri KH 65), Pak NC, Pak CM, Pak SC, Jon, Ri CM■, Jong CM (So 79), Kim KJ (Ri HR 46), Yun.

Amman, 6 February 2008, 16,000
Jordan (0) 0
North Korea (1) 1 *(Hong 44)*

North Korea: Ri MG; Ri J, Ri KC, An YH, Hong, Mun, Jong TS, Pak CJ (Cha 60), Han, Kim YJ (Ryang 40) (Pak NC 90), Nam SC.

Ashgabat, 2 June 2008, 20,000
Turkmenistan (0) 0
North Korea (0) 0

North Korea: Ri MG; Cha (Han 57), Ri J, Ri KC, An YH, Hong, Mun, Jong TS, Pak CJ, Kim YJ (Pak NC 64), Nam SC.

Pyongyang, 7 June 2008, 25,000
North Korea (0) 1 *(Choe 72)*
Turkmenistan (0) 0

North Korea: Ri MG; Cha, Ri J, Pak NC, Ri KC, An YH (Kim YJ 60), Hong (Kim MW 87), Mun, Pak CJ (Han 28), Nam SC, Choe.

Pyongyang, 14 June 2008, 28,000
North Korea (1) 2 *(Hong 44, 72)*
Jordan (0) 0

North Korea: Ri MG; Cha, Ri J, Pak NC (Choe 88), Ri KC, An YH, Hong, Mun, Jong TS, Han, Nam SC.

Abu Dhabi, 6 September 2008, 10,000
UAE (0) 1 *(Basheer Saeed 85)*
North Korea (0) 2 *(Choe 72, An 80)*

North Korea: Ri MG; Cha, Ri J, Ri KC, An YH, Hong (Kim K 71), Mun, Pak CJ, Kim YJ (An CH 29), Nam SC, Choe (Kim MW 86).

Tehran, 15 October 2008, 60,000
Iran (1) 2 *(Mahdavikia 9, Nekounam 63)*
North Korea (0) 1 *(Jong TS 72)*

North Korea: Ri MG; Cha, Ri J, Ri KC, An YH, Hong, Mun (Pak NC 90), Jong TS, Pak CJ, Kim YJ (Choe 46), Nam SC.

Pyongyang, 11 February 2009, 48,000
North Korea (1) 1 *(Mun 29)*
Saudi Arabia (0) 0

North Korea: Ri MG; Cha, Ri J, Pak NC, Ri KC, Ji, An YH (An CH 67) (Kim MW 85), Hong, Mun, Jong TS, Pak CJ.

Pyongyang, 28 March 2009, 50,000
North Korea (0) 2 *(Pak NC 51, Mun 90)*
UAE (0) 0

North Korea: Ri MG; Cha, Ri J, Pak NC, Ri KC, Ji, An YH, Hong (Choe 88), Mun, Jong TS, Pak CJ.

Pyongyang, 6 June 2009, 30,000
North Korea (0) 0
Iran (0) 0

North Korea: Ri MG; Cha, Ri J, Pak NC, Ri KC, Ji, An YH, Hong, Mun (Kim YJ 88), Jong TS, Pak CJ.

Riyadh, 7 June 2009, 65,000
Saudi Arabia (0) 0
North Korea (0) 0

North Korea: Ri MG; Cha, Ri J, Pak NC, Ri KC, Ji, An YH, Hong (An CH 60), Mun (Kim K 74), Jong TS (Kim YJ■ 89), Pak CJ.

CAMEROON

Yaounde, 31 May 2008, 20,000
Cameroon (1) 2 *(Song 8, Eto'o 57 (pen))*
Cape Verde Islands (0) 0

Cameroon: Kameni; Atouba, Song, Mbami, Geremi, Eto'o, Makoun, Nkong (Emana 89), Webo (Bebbe 82), Mbia, Song Billong.

Curepipe, 8 June 2008, 2400
Mauritius (0) 0
Cameroon (2) 3 *(Bikey 11, Eto'o 27, Bebbe 87)*
Cameroon: Kameni; Atouba, Song, Mbami (Binya 81), Geremi, Eto'o (Bebbe 68), Makoun, Webo (Nkong 87), Mbia, Song Billong, Bikey.

Yaounde, 21 June 2008, 25,000
Cameroon (0) 2 *(Eto'o 65, 89)*
Tanzania (0) 1 *(Mrwanda 72)*
Cameroon: Kameni; Atouba (Sadjo 75), Song, Bikey, Song Billong, Mbami, Geremi, Eto'o, Makoun (Emana 65), Webo, Mbia (Epalle 46).

Praia, 6 September 2008, 5000
Cape Verde Islands (1) 1 *(Lito 38)*
Cameroon (0) 2 *(Emana 51, Somen 65)*
Cameroon: Kameni; Atouba, Song, Bikey, Song Billong", Mbami (Emana 46), Makoun, Meyong Ze, Webo (Somen 46), Mbia (Songoo 60), Binya.

Yaounde, 11 October 2008, 12,000
Cameroon (1) 5 *(Eto'o 26, 46 (pen), Meyong Ze 56, 72, Makoun 70)*
Mauritius (0) 0
Cameroon: Kameni; Song, Bikey, Mbami (Essame 70). Geremi, Eto'o, Emana (Meyong Ze 46), Kakoun, Kome Somen (Djemba Djemba 59), Binya.

Accra, 28 March 2009, 26,450
Togo (1) 1 *(Adebayor 11)*
Cameroon (0) 0
Cameroon: Kameni; Assou-Ekotto, Song, Bikey, Mbami (Mbia 59), Geremi, Eto'o, Makoun, Kome (Djemba Djemba 46), Somen, Webo (Aloo 46).

Yaounde, 7 June 2009, 35,000
Cameroon (0) 0
Morocco (0) 0
Cameroon: Kameni; Wome, Song, Nkoulou, Chedjou (Kome 54), Geremi, Eto'o, Emana (Marcus 68), Makoun, Eyong, Aloo (Mbia 77).

Libreville, 5 September 2009, 10,000
Gabon (0) 0
Cameroon (0) 2 *(Emana 65, Eto'o 67)*
Cameroon: Kameni; Assou-Ekotto, Nkoulou, Bassong (Song 27), Geremi, Eto'o, Emana, Makoun, Somen (Aloo 47), Webo (Eyong 77), Mbia.

Yaounde, 9 September 2009, 38,000
Cameroon (1) 2 *(Makoun 25, Eto'o 64)*
Gabon (0) 1 *(Cousin 90)*
Cameroon: Kameni; Assou-Ekotto, Nkoulou, Song Song Billong, Geremi, Eto'o, Emana (Kome 85), Makoun (Chedjou 80), Nguemo, Webo (Aloo 73).

Yaounde, 10 October 2009, 36,401
Cameroon (1) 3 *(Geremi 29, Makoun 46, Emana 54)*
Togo (0) 0
Cameroon: Kameni; Nkoulou, Song, Bedimo, Song Billong, Nguemo (Somen 70). Geremi, Eto'o, Emana, Makoun (Eyong 78), Webo (Mbia 70).

Fes, 14 November 2009, 17,000
Morocco (0) 0
Cameroon (1) 2 *(Webo 19, Eto'o 52)*
Cameroon: Kameni; Assou-Ekotto, Nkoulou, Song, Song Billong, Nguemo (Somen 78), Geremi, Eto'o, Emana (Mbia 68), Makoun, Webo (Eyong 81).

NIGERIA

Freetown, 7 June 2008, 25,000
Sierra Leone (0) 0
Nigeria (0) 1 *(Yobo 89)*
Nigeria: Enyeama; Yobo, Taiwo, Kanu (Uche K 74), Nwaneri, Yussuf, Utaka (Odemwingie 49), Yakubu, Mikel (Olofinjana 67), Uche I, Ayila.

Malabo, 15 June 2008, 15,200
Equatorial Guinea (0) 0
Nigeria (1) 1 *(Yobo 5)*
Nigeria: Enyeama; Yobo, Taiwo, Nwaneri, Yakubu, Odemwingie (Anichebe 59), Odiah, Olofinjana, Uche I (Obinna 56), Uche K, Ayila.

Abuja, 21 June 2008, 20,000
Nigeria (1) 2 *(Yakubu 45, Uche I 84)*
Equatorial Guinea (0) 0
Nigeria: Enyeama; Yobo, Taiwo, Kanu (Mikel 66), Nwaneri, Yakubu (Uche I 80), Odemwingie, Odiah, Uche K, Ayila, Anichebe (Obinna 40).

Abuja, 11 October 2008, 20,000
Nigeria (3) 4 *(Obodo 20, Obinna 34, Odemwingie 45, Odiah 50)*
Sierra Leone (1) 1 *(Yobo 31 (og))*
Nigeria: Aiyenugba; Yobo, Taiwo, Shittu, Obodo, Odemwingie (Ogbuke Obasi 69), Odiah, Kaita, Uche I (Yakubu 83), Uche K, Obinna (Akpala 67).

Maputo, 29 March 2009, 35,000
Mozambique (0) 0
Nigeria (0) 0
Nigeria: Enyeama; Taiwo, Nwaneri, Shittu, Obinna (Ajilore 75), Martins, Mikel, Odemwingie, Odiah (Apam 80), Uche I, Kaita.

Abuja, 7 June 2009, 60,000
Nigeria (1) 3 *(Uche I 2, Obinna 72 (pen), 77)*
Kenya (0) 0
Nigeria: Enyeama; Echiejile, Eneramo (Obinna 54), Odemwingie, Olofinjana, Uche I, Uche K, Adeleye, Sodje (Apam 76), Etuhu (Kanu 46), Yussuf.

Rades, 20 June 2009, 45,000
Tunisia (0) 0
Nigeria (0) 0
Nigeria: Enyeama; Yobo, Taiwo, Mikel, Odemwingie, Adefemi, Olofinjana, Uche I (Utaka 85), Uche K (Kanu 69), Adeleye, Obinna (Eneramo 69).

Abuja, 6 September 2009, 52,000
Nigeria (1) 2 *(Odemwingie 23, Eneramo 80)*
Tunisia (1) 2 *(Nabil 24, Darragi 89)*
Nigeria: Enyeama; Yobo, Taiwo, Adeleye, Ogbuke Obasi (Kanu 68), Mikel, Odemwingie, Adefemi, Olofinjana (Eneramo 56), Uche I (Obinna 65), Uche K.

Abuja, 11 October 2009, 13,000
Nigeria (0) 1 *(Obinna 90)*
Mozambique (0) 0
Nigeria: Enyeama; Yobo, Nwaneri, Ajilore, Yakubu (Martins 56), Eneramo (Obinna 63), Odemwingie, Ayila, Olofinjana, Yussuf (Shittu 32), Echiejile.

Nairobi, 14 November 2009, 20,000
Kenya (1) 2 *(Oliech 15, Wetende 77)*
Nigeria (0) 3 *(Martins 60, 81, Yakubu 64)*
Nigeria: Enyeama; Yobo, Nwaneri, Eneramo (Obinna 61). Yakubu, Mikel, Odemwingie, Olofinjana (Ayila 30), Apam, Echiejile, Ajilore (Martins 46).

ALGERIA

Dakar, 31 May 2008, 50,000
Senegal (0) 1 *(Faye 80)*
Algeria (0) 0
Algeria: Gaouaoui; Belhadj, Yahia (Halliche 82), Mansouri, Hemdani (Djediat 69), Djebbour (Bouazza 76), Saifi, Raho, Lemmouchia, Ziani, Zaoui.

Blida, 6 June 2008, 40,000
Algeria (2) 3 *(Djebbour 16, Ziani 20, 47 (pen))*
Liberia (0) 0
Algeria: Gaouaoui; Belhadj (Zarabi 86), Yahia (Halliche 70), Mansouri, Bezzaz (Djediat 51), Djebbour, Saifi, Raho, Lemmouchia, Ziani, Zaoui.

Banjul, 14 June 2008, 18,000

Gambia (1) 1 *(Jarjue 19 (pen))*

Algeria (0) 0

Algeria: Gaouaoui; Yahia, Mansouri, Lemmouchia, Djebbour (Bezzaz 65), Djediat, Raho, Zarabi, Ziani, Zaoui, Seguer (Hemani 66).

Blida, 20 June 2008, 25,000

Algeria (1) 1 *(Yahia 33)*

Gambia (0) 0

Algeria: Gaouaoui; Bougherra, Yahia, Mansouri, Bezzaz (Djediat 70), Lemmouchia, Djebbour, Saifi (Hemani 82), Raho, Zarabi, Ziani.

Blida, 5 September 2008, 35,000

Algeria (0) 3 *(Gueye 60 (og), Saifi 66, Yahia 72)*

Senegal (0) 2 *(Dia 53, Sougou 90)*

Algeria: Gaouaoui; Bougherra, Belhadj, Yahia, Hemdani, Bezzaz (Zaoui 79), Saifi (Hemani 88), Raho, Abdesslam, Ghilas (Djediat 69), Ziani.

Monrovia, 11 October 2008, 2000

Liberia (0) 0

Algeria (0) 0

Algeria: Gaouaoui; Bougherra, Belhadj, Mansouri, Saifi, Raho, Djediat, Ghilas (Bezzaz 65), Ziani, Zaioui, Abdesslam.

Kigali, 28 March 2009, 22,000

Rwanda (0) 0

Algeria (0) 0

Algeria: Gaouaoui; Bougherra, Belhadj, Mansouri, Matmour, Lemmouchia, Ghezzal (Hadi-Aissa 90), Saifi (Djebbour 61), Raho, Ghilas (Bouazza 61), Halliche.

Blida, 7 June 2009, 26,500

Algeria (0) 3 *(Matmour 60, Ghezzal 64, Djebbour 77)*

Egypt (0) 1 *(Aboutrika 86)*

Algeria: Gaouaoui; Bougherra, Belhadj, Yahia, Halliche, Mansouri, Lemmouchia, Ghezzal (Ghilas 90), Djebbour (Bezzaz 83), Matmour (Bouazza 85), Ziani.

Chililabombwe, 20 June 2009, 9000

Zambia (0) 0

Algeria (1) 2 *(Bougherra 21, Saifi 66)*

Algeria: Gaouaoui; Bougherra, Belhadj, Yahia, Halliche, Mansouri, Lemmouchia, Ghezzal (Saifi 61), Djebbour (Bouazza 81), Matmour, Ziani (Bezzaz 85).

Blida, 6 September 2009, 30,000

Algeria (0) 1 *(Saifi 59)*

Zambia (0) 0

Algeria: Gaouaoui; Bougherra, Belhadj, Yahia (Meghni 46), Halliche, Mansouri, Lemmouchia, Saifi (Ghilas 78), Djebbour (Ghezzal 65), Matmour, Ziani.

Blida, 11 October 2009, 22,000

Algeria (2) 3 *(Ghezzal 22, Belhadj 45, Ziani 90 (pen))*

Rwanda (1) 1 *(Mutesa 19)*

Algeria: Gaouaoui; Bougherra, Belhadj, Yahia, Halliche, Lemmouchia, Ghezzal (Ghilas 85), Saifi (Djebbour 51), Matmour, Ziani, Meghni (Yebda 52).

Cairo, 14 November 2009, 75,000

Egypt (1) 2 *(Zaki 3, Meteab 90)*

Algeria (0) 0

Algeria: Gaouaoui; Bougherra, Belhadj, Yahia, Halliche (Laifaoui 72), Mansouri, Lemmouchia, Saifi (Ghezzal 62), Meghni, Matmour (Bezzaz 46), Ziani.

Omdurman, 18 November 2009, 30,000

Algeria (1) 1 *(Yahia 40)*

Egypt (0) 0

Algeria: Chaquchi; Bougherra, Belhadj, Yahia (Zaoui 67), Halliche, Mansouri, Yebda, Ghezzal, Saifi (Ghilas 89), Ziani, Meghni (Matmour 57).

GHANA

Kumasi, 1 June 2008, 27,908

Ghana (1) 3 *(Tagoe 17, Agogo 54, Kingston 64)*

Libya (0) 0

Ghana: Kingson; Pantsil, John Mensah (Dickoh 78), Annan, Kingston, Essien, Agogo (Bekoe 76), Muntari (Draman 77), Tagoe, Afful, Addo.

Mangaung/Bloemfontein, 8 June 2008, 8000

Lesotho (0) 2 *(Muso 89, Seema 90)*

Ghana (2) 3 *(Kingston 15, Agogo 41, 63)*

Ghana: Kingson; Pantsil, John Mensah, Annan, Kingston, Essien (Agyemang-Badu 83), Agogo, Tagoe (Owusu-Abeyie 71), Draman, Afful, Addo.

Libreville, 14 June 2008, 13,000

Gabon (1) 2 *(Meye 45, Nguema 59)*

Ghana (0) 0

Ghana: Kingson; Pantsil, John Mensah, Annan, Kingston (Draman 66), Essien, Muntari, Tagoe, Bekoe (Agogo 53), Afful, Addo (Dickoh 46).

Accra, 22 June 2008, 29,040

Ghana (1) 2 *(Tagoe 31, Muntari 75)*

Gabon (0) 0

Ghana: Kingson; Pantsil, John Mensah, Annan, Kingston (Owusu-Abeyie 61), Essien, Agogo (Draman 76), Muntari, Tagoe, Issah (Boye 60), Afful.

Tripoli, 5 September 2008, 45,000

Libya (0) 1 *(Osman 86)*

Ghana (0) 0

Ghana: Kingson; Afful, Pantsil (Bekoe 89), Annan, Kingston (Owusu-Abeyie 63), Essien (Appiah 18), Agogo, Muntari, Quartey, Draman, Addo.

Sekondi, 11 October 2008, 20,000

Ghana (2) 3 *(Appiah 19, Agogo 24, Amoah 62)*

Lesotho (0) 0

Ghana: Kingson; Afful, Pantsil, John Mensah, Annan, Agogo (Tagoe 62), Appiah (Bekoe 85), Muntari (Draman 83), Amoah, Yeboah, Addo.

Kumasi, 29 March 2009, 39,000

Ghana (1) 1 *(Tagoe 1)*

Benin (0) 0

Ghana: Kingson; Inkoom, Pantsil, Annan, Essien, Appiah (Gyan 74), Muntari (Vorsah 87), Tagoe, Amoah (Asamoah 60), Quartey, Addo.

Bamako, 7 June 2009, 40,000

Mali (0) 0

Ghana (0) 2 *(Asamoah 66, Amoah 78)*

Ghana: Kingson, Afful, Pantsil, John Mensah, Annan, Agyemang (Vorsah 87), Essien (Narry 90), Asamoah, Tagoe (Draman 88), Amoah, Addo.

Omdurman, 20 June 2009, 30,000

Sudan (0) 0

Ghana (1) 2 *(Amoah 6, 52)*

Ghana: Kingson; Inkoom, Afful, John Mensah, Annan, Agyemang (Vorsah 54), Essien, Asamoah, Tagoe (Draman 80), Amoah (Agogo 85), Addo.

Accra, 6 September 2009, 38,000

Ghana (1) 2 *(Muntari 14, Essien 53)*

Sudan (0) 0

Ghana: Kingson; Inkoom, Afful, John Mensah, Annan, Essien, Appiah (Kingston 74), Muntari (Draman 88), Amoah (Gyan 87), Pantsil, Addo.

Cotonou, 11 October 2009, 20,000

Benin (0) 1 *(Aoudou 89)*

Ghana (0) 0

Ghana: Kingson; Afful, Gyan (Boateng 86), Pantsil, Kingston, Essien, Appiah (Vorsah 80), Yeboah (Draman 70), Amoah, Quartey, Addo.

Kumasi, 11 November 2009, 39,000
Ghana (0) 2 *(Amoah 65, Annan 83)*
Mali (1) 2 *(Fane 23, Ndiaye 68)*
Ghana: Kingson; Inkoom, Gyan, Pantsil, Annan, Essien (Agyemang-Badu 82), Appiah (Asamoah 61), Muntari (Addy 79), Amoah, Quartey, Addo.

IVORY COAST

Abidjan, 1 June 2008, 20,000
Ivory Coast (0) 1 *(Cisse 75)*
Mozambique (0) 0 *Khan*▪
Ivory Coast: Barry; Akale, Boka, Zokora, Demel, Traore K (Cisse 67), Meite (Lolo 46), Eboue, Zoro, Tiene, Sanogo (Fae 85).

Antananarivo, 8 June 2008, 15,000
Madascar (0) 0
Ivory Coast (0) 0
Ivory Coast: Barry; Akale (Traore K 82), Boka, Toure K, Zokora, Fae (Kone 64), Demel (Cisse 74), Meite, Eboue, Sanogo, Tiene.

Gaborone, 14 June 2008, 21,400
Botswana (1) 1 *(Selolwane 25)*
Ivory Coast (0) 1 *(Meite 65)*
Ivory Coast: Barry; Akale (Eboue 77), Boka, Toure K, Zokora, Lolo, Cisse (Traore K 85), Meite, Kone E, Tiene (Fae 89), Sanogo.

Abidjan, 22 June 2009, 15,000
Ivory Coast (2) 4 *(Sanogo 16, Zokora 22, Cisse 46, 70)*
Botswana (0) 0
Ivory Coast: Barry; Akale (Fae 75), Boka, Toure K, Zokora, Cisse (Kalou 71), Meite (Zoro 84), Eboue, Kone E, Tiene, Sanogo.

Maputo, 7 September 2008, 35,000
Mozambique (0) 1 *(Miro 56)*
Ivory Coast (0) 1 *(Kone 48)*
Ivory Coast: Barry; Boka, Toure K, Zokora, Demel, Fae, Kalou (Akale 82), Toure Y (Coulibaly 88), Kone B (Tiene 84), Eboue, Sanogo.

Abidjan, 11 October 2008, 24,000
Ivory Coast (1) 3 *(Sanogo 41, 55, Kalou 65)*
Madagascar (0) 0
Ivory Coast: Barry; Boka, Toure K (Zoro 71), Zokora, Toure Y, Kalou (Akale 88), Lolo, Demel, Kone 3, Eboue, Sanogo.

Abidjan, 29 March 2009, 34,000
Ivory Coast (3) 5 *(Romaric 1, Drogba 6 (pen), 27, Kalou 59, Kone B 70)*
Malawi (0) 0
Ivory Coast: Barry; Toure K, Zokora, Eboue, Kalou, Kone E, Drogba (Sanogo 78), Meite (Bamba 85), Romaric, Kone B (Keita 75), Tiene.

Conakry, 7 June 2009, 14,000
Guinea (0) 1 *(Bangoura 65)*
Ivory Coast (1) 2 *(Kone B 43, Romaric 70)*
Ivory Coast: Barry; Toure K, Zokora, Demel, Eboue, Kalou (Cisse 80), Drogba, Romaric (Angoua 86), Kone B, Toure Y (Kone E 84), Tiene.

Ouagadougou, 20 June 2009, 33,056
Burkina Faso (1) 2 *(Pitroipa 27, Bance 78)*
Ivory Coast (1) 3 *(Toure Y 14, Tall 54 (og), Drogba 77)*
Ivory Coast: Barry; Eboue, Toure K, Zokora, Demel (Tiene 66), Kalou (Cisse 90), Drogba, Meite, Romaric, Kone B (Bamba 82), Toure Y.

Abidjan, 5 September 2009, 78,209
Ivory Coast (1) 5 *(Panandetiguiri 9 (og), Drogba 48, 64, Toure Y 54, Keita 68)*
Burkina Faso (0) 0
Ivory Coast: Barry; Eboue, Boka, Toure K, Zokora, Toure Y, Kalou, Drogba (Sanogo 85), Bamba, Tiene (Kone E 81), Keita (Gervinho 88).

Blantyre, 10 October 2009, 25,000
Malawi (0) 1 *(Ngwira 64)*
Ivory Coast (0) 1 *(Drogba 67)*
Ivory Coast: Barry; Eboue, Boka, Bamba, Zokora, Fae (Gervinho 69), Kalou, Cisse (Drogba 65), Gosso, Demel, Kone E (Toure Y 79).

Abidjan, 14 November 2009, 28,000
Ivory Coast (2) 3 *(Gervinho 16, 31, Tiene 67)*
Guinea (0) 0
Ivory Coast: Zogbo; Eboue, Bamba, Zokora, Toure Y, Angcua, Gervinho, Romaric (Gosso 70), Dindane (Kone 82), Tiene, Keita (Doumbia 78).

USA

Los Angeles, 15 June 2008, 11,500
USA (3) 8 *(Dempsey 1, 62, Bradley 12, Ching 20, 88, Donovan 58, Johnson 82, Ferguson 85 (og))*
Barbados (0) 0
USA: Guzan; Bocanegra, Mastroeni (Adu 26), Onyewu, Cherundolo, Dempsey (Lewis 71), Donovan (Johnson 80), Ching, Bradley, Pearce, Beasley.

Bridgetown, 22 June 2008, 2000
Barbados (0) 0
USA (1) 1 *(Lewis 21)*
USA: Guzan; Califf, Bradley, Moor, Lewis, Szetela (Rolfe 66), Kljestan, Pearce, DeMerit, Adu (Barrett 85), Beasley (Thorrington 78).

Guatemala City, 20 August 2008, 26,000
Guatemala (0) 0 *Cabrera*▪
USA (0) 1 *(Bocanegra 70)*
USA: Howard; Bocanegra, Mastroeni (Edu 78), Onyewu, Cherundolo▪, Lewis (Hejduk 66), Dempsey (Beasley 66), Donovan, Ching, Bradley, Pearce.

Havana, 6 September 2008, 12,000
Cuba (0) 0
USA (1) 1 *(Dempsey 39)*
USA: Howard; Hejduk, Bocanegra, Onyewu, Dempsey (Kljestan 75), Donovan, Ching, Bradley, Edu, Pearce, Beasley.

Bridgeview, 10 September 2008, 11,452
USA (2) 3 *(Bradley 10, Dempsey 18, Ching 57)*
Trinidad & Tobago (0) 0
USA: Howard; Bocanegra, Onyewu, Cherundolo, Dempsey (Lewis 78), Donovan, Ching (Clark 67), Bradley (Johnson 67), Pearce, Kljestan, Beasley.

Washington DC, 11 October 2008, 20,249
USA (2) 6 *(Beasley 10, 30, Donovar 48, Ching 63, Altidore 87, Onyewu 89)*
Cuba (1) 1 *(Munoz 31) Colome*▪
USA: Howard; Bocanegra, Onyewu, Cherundolo, Beasley, Dempsey, Donovan, Ching (Torres 68), Bradley, Pearce (Altidore 68), Kljestan (Adu 76).

Port of Spain, 15 October 2008, 19,000
Trinidad & Tobago (0) 2 *(Latapy 60, Yorke 79)*
USA (0) 1 *(Davies 74)*
USA: Guzan; Hejduk, Orozco, Torres (Szetela 83), Beasley, Altidore, Edu, Califf, Pearce (Rolfe 87), Kljestan, Adu (Davies 69).

Commerce City, 19 November 2008, 9303
USA (0) 2 *(Cooper 53, Adu 68)*
Guatemala (0) 0
USA: Guzan; Bornstein, Goodson, Mastroeni, Thorrington, Cooper (Casey 76), Adu (Arnaud 83), Clark, Altidore (Ching 75), Parkhurst, Kljestan.

Columbus, 11 February 2009, 23,776

USA (1) 2 *(Bradley 43, 90)*

Mexico (0) 0 *Marquez*■

USA: Howard; Hejduk, Bocanegra, Bradley, Onyewu, Beasley, Dempsey, Donovan, Ching (Altidore 82), Pearce, Kljestan (Clark 86).
Mexico: Sanchez; Galindo, Salcido, Marquez■, Osorio, Oldoni, Pardo, Castillo (Martinez 34), Ochoa C, Medina (Zinha 59), Giovani (Bravo 71).

San Salvador, 28 March 2009, 30,350

El Salvador (1) 2 *(Quintanilla 19, Castillo 72)*

USA (0) 2 *(Altidore 77, Hejduk 88)*

USA: Guzan; Hejduk, Bocanegra, Beasley, Dempsey, Donovan, Ching, Bradley (Edu 90), Califf, Pearce (Altidore 61), Kljestan (Torres 71).

Nashville, 1 April 2009, 27,958

USA (1) 3 *(Altidore 13, 71, 89)*

Trinidad & Tobago (0) 0

USA: Howard; Hejduk, Bocanegra, Mastroeni, Onyewu, Beasley, Dempsey (Kljestan 81), Donovan, Ching (Torres 84), Bradley, Altidore.

San Jose, 3 June 2009, 19,200

Costa Rica (2) 3 *(Saborio 2, Borges 13, Herrera 68)*

USA (0) 1 *(Donovan 90)*

USA: Howard; Bocanegra, Mastroeni (Adu 62), Onyewu, Wynne, Beasley, Dempsey (Davies 80), Torres (Kljestan 46), Donovan, Bradley, Altidore.

Chicago, 6 June 2009, 55,647

USA (1) 2 *(Donovan 41 (pen), Bocanegra 67)*

Honduras (1) 1 *(Costly 4)*

USA: Howard; Clark, Bocanegra (DeMerit 71), Mastroeni (Feilhaber 46), Onyewu, Dempsey, Donovan, Casey (Beasley 74), Spector, Bornstein, Altidore.
Honduras: Valladares N; Chavez O, Figueroa, Thomas, Beata, Guevara, Palacios W (Turcios 66), Pavon (Welcome 66), Nunez R (Martinez W 78), Costly, Sabillon.

Mexico City, 12 August 2009, 104,499

Mexico (1) 2 *(Castro 19, Sabah 82)*

USA (1) 1 *(Davies 9)*

Mexico: Ochoa G; Magallon, Salcido, Osorio, Torrado, Castro I, Franco (Sabah 80), Blanco (Vela 55) Juarez, Giovani, Guardado (Castillo 71).
USA: Howard; Bocanegra, Bradley, Onyewu, Cherundolo, Dempsey, Davies (Altidore 77), Donovan, Ching (Holden 57), Clark (Feilhaber 57), DeMerit.

Sandy, 5 September 2009, 19,066

USA (2) 2 *(Dempsey 41, Altidore 45)*

El Salvador (1) 1 *(Castillo 31)*

USA: Howard; Spector, Bocanegra, Bradley, Feilhaber (Beckerman 79), Dempsey, Davies (Holden 72), Donovan, Bornstein, Marshall, Altidore (Torres 84).

Port of Spain, 9 September 2009, 4700

Trinidad & Tobago (0) 0

USA (0) 1 *(Clark 61)*

USA: Howard; Spector, Bocanegra, Bradley, Onyewu, Dempsey (Holden 81), Davies (Ching 76), Donovan, Bornstein, Clark, Altidore (Feilhaber 62).

San Pedro Sula, 10 October 2009, 37,000

Honduras (0) 2 *(De Leon 47, 78)*

USA (0) 3 *(Casey 50, 66, Donovan 71)*

Honduras: Valladares N; Chavez O, Figueroa, Thomas (Nunez R 75), Palacios W, Pavon, De Leon (Martinez W 80), Izaguirre, Costly, Sabillon, Alvarez (Suazo 69).
USA: Howard; Spector, Bocanegra, Bradley, Onyewu, Holden (Cherundolo 90), Casey (Feilhaber 83), Davies (Altidore 78), Donovan, Bornstein, Clark.

Washington DC, 14 October 2009, 26,243

USA (0) 2 *(Bradley 71, Bornstein 90)*

Costa Rica (2) 2 *(Ruiz 20, 23)*

USA: Howard; Bocanegra, Bradley, Onyewu, Cherundolo, Holden (Rogers 68), Casey (Cooper 78), Donovan, Bornstein, Feilhaber (Torres 62), Altidore.

MEXICO

Houston, 15 June 2008, 50,137

Belize (0) 0

Mexico (0) 2 *(Vela 65, Borgetti 90 (pen))*

Mexico: Sanchez; Magallon, Salcido, Galindo, Osorio, Torrado (Pineda 46), Zinha (Villaluz 62), Perez L, Vela (Borgetti 77), Guardado, Arce.

Monterrey, 21 June 2008, 42,000

Mexico (3) 7 *(Vela 8, Borgetti 9, 90, Guardado 33, Arce 45, 47, Lennen 89 (og))*

Belize (0) 0

Mexico: Sanchez; Magallon, Salcido, Galindo, Perez L, Villaluz, Vela, Rojas, Pineda (Zinha 14), Arce (Borgetti 52), Guardado (Osorio 48).

Mexico City, 20 August 2008, 81,100

Mexico (0) 2 *(Pardo 37, 75)*

Honduras (1) 1 *(De Leon 35)*

Mexico: Sanchez; Magallon, Salcido, Marquez, Osorio, Pardo, Vela (Bravo 61), Oldoni, Arce (Blanco 70), Giovani (Franco 56), Guardado.
Honduras: Valladares N; Izaguirre, Figueroa■, Bernardez, Mendoza, Guevara, Palacios W, Suazo, De Leon (Costly 85), Alvarez (Garcia 81), Turcios (Guerrero 69).

Mexico City, 6 September 2008, 96,000

Mexico (2) 3 *(Guardado 3, Arce 33, Magallon 63)*

Jamaica (0) 0

Mexico: Sanchez; Magallon, Salcido, Marquez, Osorio, Perez L, Pardo (Torrado 61), Vela (Vuoso 78), Arce, Giovani (Blanco 71), Guardado.

Tuxtla Gutierrez, 10 September 2008, 26,900

Mexico (0) 2 *(Bravo 59, Marquez 73)*

Canada (0) 1 *(Gerba 78)*

Mexico: Sanchez; Magallon, Pinto, Marquez, Osorio, Torrado, Perez L, Vela (Ochoa C 70), Arce (Blanco 89), Giovani (Bravo 57), Guardado.

Kingston, 11 October 2008, 27,000

Jamaica (1) 1 *(Fuller 34)*

Mexico (0) 0

Mexico: Sanchez; Magallon, Salcido, Marquez, Osorio (Galindo 55), Torrado, Perez L (Arellano 67), Bravo (Vuoso 57), Vela, Arce, Giovani.

Edmonton, 15 October 2008, 14,145

Canada (1) 2 *(Gerba 13, Radzinski 50)*

Mexico (1) 2 *(Salcido 35, Vuoso 64)*

Mexico: Sanchez; Magallon, Salcido, Galindo, Osorio, Torrado, Perez L (Vuoso 55), Vela (Bravo 67), Arce (Ochoa C 82), Giovani, Guardado.

San Pedro Sula, 19 November 2008, 45,000

Honduras (0) 1 *(Osorio 52 (og))*

Mexico (0) 0

Honduras: Valladares N; Figueroa, Thomas (Turcios 46), Bernardez, Mendoza, Guevara, Palacios W, Suazo, Guerrero, Costly, Martinez E (Nunez R 71).
Mexico: Sanchez; Galindo, Salcido, Marquez, Osorio, Torrado■, Zinha (Vela■ 57), Pardo, Vuoso (Bravo 82), Arce (Castillo 73), Guardado.

Mexico City, 28 March 2009, 90,000

Mexico (1) 2 *(Bravo 20, Pardo 53 (pen))*

Costa Rica (0) 0

Mexico: Ochoa G; Pinto, Galindo, Osorio (Magallon 79), Pardo, Bravo, Vuoso (Arellano 85), Oldoni, Arce, Lopez, Guardado (Torrado 79).

San Pedro Sula, 1 April 2009, 28,000
Honduras (2) 3 *(Costly 17, 79, Pavon 43)*
Mexico (0) 1 *(Castillo 82 (pen))*
Honduras: Valladares N; Chavez O, Figueroa, Guevara, Palacios W, Pavon, De Leon (Chavez M 90), Nunez R (Turcios 74), Izaguirre, Costly (Thomas 82). Sabillon.
Mexico: Ochoa G; Magallon, Salcido**■**, Pinto, Perez L (Vuoso 46), Pardo, Bravo (Castillo 70), Vela, Oldoni, Lopez (Galindo 27), Guardado.

San Salvador, 6 June 2009, 33,000
El Salvador (1) 2 *(Martinez 12, Quintanilla 85 (pen))*
Mexico (0) 1 *(Blanco 71 (pen))*
Mexico: Perez O; Rodriguez, Rojas, Galindo, Osorio, Torrado, Pardo (Blanco 46), Castillo, Franco, Arce (Castro I 46), Guardado (Medina 78).

Mexico City, 10 June 2009, 92,000
Mexico (1) 2 *(Franco 2, Rojas 48)*
Trinidad & Tobago (1) 1 *(Tinto 45)*
Mexico: Perez O; Rodriguez, Salcido. Osorio, Rojas, Castro I, Castillo (Sabah 35), Blanco, Franco (Giovani 75), Esquivel (Medina 52), Guardado.

San Jose, 5 September 2009, 20,000
Costa Rica (0) 0
Mexico (1) 3 *(Giovani 45, Franco 62, Guardado 71)*
Mexico: Ochoa G; Magallon, Salcido, Osorio, Torrado, Castro I, Franco (Guardado 70), Blanco (Sabah 74), Castro J, Juarez, Giovani (Castillo 81).

Mexico City, 9 September 2009, 97,897
Mexico (0) 1 *(Blanco 76 (pen))*
Honduras (0) 0
Mexico: Ochoa G; Magallon, Salcido, Osorio, Castro I, Blanco, Sabah (Cacho 71), Castro J (Barrera 62), Juarez, Giovani (Rojas 80), Guardado.
Honduras: Valladares N; Chavez O, Figueroa, Guevara, Palacios W, Pavon, Nunez R (De Leon 71), Izaguirre, Suazo (Costly 59), Sabillon (Garcia 46), Turcios.

Mexico City, 10 October 2009, 104,000
Mexico (1) 4 *(Gonzalez 25 (og), Blanco 71, Palencia 85, Vela 90)*
El Salvador (0) 1 *(Martinez 89)*
Mexico City: Ochoa G; Salcido, Marquez, Osorio, Torrado, Castro I, Franco (Sabah 86), Blanco (Palencia 78), Vela, Juarez, Guardado (Barrera 89).

Port of Spain, 14 October 2009, 2000
Trinidad & Tobago (1) 2 *(Baptiste 23 (pen), 61)*
Mexico (0) 2 *(Esqueda 57, Salcido 65)*
Mexico: Ochoa G; Magallon, Salcido, Moreno, Torrado, Castro I, Vela, Sabah (Esqueda 54), Castro J, Palencia (Blanco 54), Guardado (Barrera 46).

HONDURAS

San Pedro Sula, 4 June 2008, 20,000
Honduras (1) 4 *(De Leon 25, Palacios 51, Suazo 52, 90)*
Puerto Rico (0) 0 *Velez*■
Honduras: Valladares N; Chavez O (Guerrero 79), Figueroa, Bernardez, Mendoza, Guevara (Thomas 88), Palacios W, Suazo, De Leon, Costly (Martinez W 68), Turcios.

Bayamon, 14 June 2008, 5000
Puerto Rico (2) 2 *(Megaloudis 31, Villegas 41)*
Honduras (1) 2 *(Suazo 22, Palacios 52)*
Honduras: Valladares N; Figueroa (Guerrero 72`, Beata, Bernardez, Mendoza, Guevara, Palacios W, Suazo, De Leon (Castillo 79), Costly (Martinez W 65), Turcios.

Montreal, 6 September 2008, 13,032
Canada (1) 1 *(Serioux 5) Bernier*■
Honduras (0) 2 *(Nunez 47, 56)*
Honduras: Valladares N; Chavez O, Thomas, Bernardez, Mendoza (Garcia 84), Guevara, Palacios W, Suazo, Nunez R (Castillo 75), Izaguirre, Costly.

San Pedro Sula, 10 September 2008, 38,000
Honduras (0) 2 *(Nunez R 65, Guevara 73 (pen))*
Jamaica (0) 0
Honduras: Valladares N; Figueroa, Thomas, Bernardez, Mendoza, Guevara (Nunez M 88), Palacios W, Suazo (Turcios 67), Nunez R, Izaguirre, Costly (Martinez S 70).

San Pedro Sula, 11 October 2008, 35,000
Honduras (1) 3 *(Martinez W 8, Costly 60, Thomas 90)*
Canada (0) 1 *(Hainault 52)*
Honduras: Valladares N; Chavez O, Figueroa, Thomas, Bernardez, Mendoza, Guevara, Palacios W, Nunez R (Turcios 46) (Izaguirre 90), Costly, Martinez W (Mejia 70).

Kingston, 15 October 2008, 25,000
Jamaica (1) 1 *(Shelton 16)*
Honduras (0) 0
Honduras: Valladares N; Chavez O, Figueroa, Thomas, Bernardez, Mendoza, Guevara (Nunez R 72), Palacios W, Nunez M (Martinez W 50), Costly, Turcios (Mejia 61).

San Jose, 11 February 2009, 18,000
Costa Rica (0) 2 *(Furtado 48, 59)*
Honduras (0) 0
Honduras: Valladares N; Figueroa, Thomas, Bernardez, Rodriguez (Nunez R 50), Guevara, Suazo, Guerrero, Garcia, Martinez W (Chavez M 40), Martinez E.

Port of Spain, 28 March 2009, 23,500
Trinidad & Tobago (0) 1 *(Hyland 88)*
Honduras (0) 1 *(Pavon 50)*
Honduras: Valladares N; Chavez O, Figueroa, Caballero, Thomas, Guevara, Palacios W, Pavon (Costly 82), De Leon, Nunez R (Chavez M 77), Garcia.

San Pedro Sula, 10 June 2009, 28,000
Honduras (1) 1 *(Pavon 15)*
El Salvador (0) 0
Honduras: Valladares N; Chavez O, Figueroa, Guevara, Palacios W, Pavon, De Leon (Thomas 86), Nunez R (Martinez W 74), Izaguirre, Costly (Bernardez 90), Sabillon.

San Pedro Sula, 12 August 2009, 30,000
Honduras (1) 4 *(Costly 30, 90, Pavon 51, Valladares M 89)*
Costa Rica (0) 0
Honduras: Valladares N; Chavez O, Figueroa, Guevara, Palacios W, Pavon (Valladares M 72), Nunez R (De Leon 60), Izaguirre, Costly, Sabillon, Turcios (Thomas 85).

San Pedro Sula, 5 September 2009, 38,000
Honduras (2) 4 *(Pavon 20, 28, Guevara 62, Suazo 83)*
Trinidad & Tobago (0) 1 *(Baptiste 86)*
Honduras: Valladares N; Norales, Figueroa, Thomas, Guevara (Alvarez 72), Jerry Palacios (Suazo 59), Pavon, Nunez R, Isaguirre, Sabillon, Turcios (Valladares M 77).

San Salvador, 14 October 2009, 28,000
El Salvador (0) 0
Honduras (0) 1 *(Pavon 64)*
Honduras: Valladares N; Jhony Palacios, Alvarez (Turcios 65), Norales, Guevara, Palacios W, Pavon (Costly 76), De Leon, Suazo (Thomas 84), Isaguirre, Sabillon.

SOUTH AFRICA

Abuja, 1 June 2008, 50,000
Nigeria (2) 2 *(Uche I 10, Nwaneri 44)* **South Africa (0) 0**
Nigeria: Enyeama; Yobo, Taiwo, Nwaneri, Yussuf, Utaka, Yakubu (Anichebe 60), Mikel, Uche I, Uche K (Kanu 69), Ayila (Olofinjana 68).
South Africa: Fernandez; Masilela (Mdledle 82), Mokoena, Fransman, Sibaya, Davids, Moriri, Pienaar (Walaza 77), Moon, Dikgacoi, Buckley (Fanteni 60).

Atteridgeville, 7 June 2008, 10,000
South Africa (2) 4 *(Dikgacoi 9, 90, Moriri 33, Fanteni 62)*
Equatorial Guinea (0) 1 *(Edjogo 78 (pen))*
South Africa: Khune; Masilela, Mokoena (Davids 77), Fransman (Khumalo 24), Sibaya, Moriri, Pienaar (Buckley 82), Moon, Modise, Dikgacoi, Fanteni.

Freetown, 14 June 2008, 15,000
Sierra Leone (1) 1 *(Kallon 21 (pen))*   **South Africa (0) 0**
South Africa: Khune; Tsotetsi, Masilela, Khumalo, Sibaya, Moriri, Pienaar, Moon (Mashego 68), Modise, Dikgacoi, Fanteni (Chabangu 81).

Atteridgeville, 21 June 2008, 12,000
South Africa (0) 0   Sierra Leone (0) 0
South Africa: Khune; Masilela, Mokoena, Fransman, Sibaya (Chabangu 70), Moriri, Pienaar (Buckley 83), Moon, Modise, Dikgacoi, Fanteni (Mashego 62).

Port Elizabeth, 6 September 2008, 25,000
South Africa (0) 0   Nigeria (0) 1 *(Uche I 69)*
South Africa: Khune; Carnell, Morris, Sibaya (Moriri 75), Tshabalala (Zuma 75), Modise, Gaxa, Dikgacoi, Mabizela, McCarthy, Nkosi.
Nigeria: Aiyenugba; Taiwo, Nwaneri, Shittu, Utaka, Yakubu, Odiah, Olofinjana, Uche I (Akpala 80), Uche K (Obodo 68), Ayila.

Malabo, 11 October 2008, 6500
Equatorial Guinea (0) 0   South Africa (1) 1 *(Tshabalala 9)*
South Africa: Khune; Carnell, Mokoena, Morris, Davids, Tshabalala, Modise (Tsutsulupa 77), Gaxa, Dikgacoi, McCarthy (Fanteni 88), Nkosi (Parker 71).

CONFEDERATIONS CUP
Johannesburg, 14 June 2009, 48,837
South Africa (0) 0
Iraq (0) 0
South Africa: Khune; Gaxa, Mokoena, Booth, Masilela, Modisi, Sibaya, Mhlongo, Dikgacoi, Parker (Pienaar 85), Fanteni (Mashego 78).

Rustenburg, 17 June 2009, 36,598
South Africa (1) 2 *(Parker 21, 52)*
New Zealand (0) 0
South Africa: Khune; Gaxa, Mokoena, Booth, Masilela, Modisi, Sibaya, Pienaar, Dikgacoi, Parker (Tshabalala 81), Fanteni (Maschego 62).

Bloemfontein, 20 June 2009, 38,212
South Africa (0) 0
Spain (0) 2 *(Villa 52, Llorente 72)*
South Africa: Khune; Gaxa, Mokoena, Booth, Masilela, Modisi, Sibaya (Maschego 83), Pienaar, Dikgacoi, Mhlongo, Parker (Tshabalala 90).

Johannesburg, 25 June 2009, 48,049
South Africa (0) 0
Brazil (0) 1 *(Daniel Alves 87)*
South Africa: Khune; Gaxa, Mokoena, Booth, Masilela, Modisi (Van Heerden 90), Mhlongo, Pienaar (Mphela 90), Dikgacoi, Tshabalala (Mashego 90), Parker.

Rustenburg, 28 June 2009, 31,788
South Africa (0) 2 *(Mphela 73, 90)*
Spain (0) 3 *(Guiza 88, 89, Xabi Alonso 107)*
South Africa: Khune; Gaxa, Mokoena, Booth, Masilela, Modisi (Van Heerden 69), Sibaya, Pienaar (Mphela 65), Dikgacoi, Tshabalala (Malongo 84), Parker.

NEW ZEALAND

Lautoka, 17 October 2007, 6000
Fiji (0) 0
New Zealand (1) 2 *(Vicelich 37, Smeltz 86)*
New Zealand: Paston; Christie, Lochhead, Mulligan (Campbell 58), Boyens (Sigmund 63), Vicelich, Brown, Smeltz, Killen (Smith 87), Bertos, Oughton.

Port Vila, 17 November 2007, 8000
Vanuatu (1) 1 *(Naprapol 26)*
New Zealand (0) 2 *(Smeltz 52, Mulligan 90)*
New Zealand: Paston, Lochhead, Boyens, Vicelich (Mulligan 71), Brown, Smeltz (Ellensohn 84), Bertos, Pritchett, James (Smith 80), Sigmund, Oughton.

Wellington, 21 November 2007, 2500
New Zealand (3) 4 *(Mulligan 14, 81, Smeltz 29 (pen), 34)*
Vanuatu (0) 1 *(Sakama 50)*
New Zealand: Paston, Christie (Pritchett 76), Lochhead, Mulligan (Campbell 87), Boyens, Vicelich, Brown[■], Smeltz (Smith 73), Bertos, Sigmund, Oughton.

Noumea, 6 September 2008, 2589
New Caledonia (0) 1 *(Hmae 55)*
New Zealand (1) 3 *(Sigmund 16, Smeltz 65, Smith 75)*
New Zealand: Moss; Sigmund, Oughton, Nelsen, Mulligan, Lochhead, Pearce (Christie 55), Elliott, Brockie, Smith (James 90), Smeltz.

Auckland, 10 September 2008, 8000
New Zealand (0) 3 *(Smeltz 49, 76, Christie 69)*
New Caledonia (0) 0
New Zealand: Paston, Mulligan, Lochhead, Elliott, Sigmund, Nelsen (Boyens 63), Oughton (Christie 66), Smeltz (Old 84), Smith, Brown, James.

Apia, 19 November 2008, 3700
New Zealand (0) 0
Fiji (0) 2 *(Krishna 63, 90)*
New Zealand: Moss[■], Old, Sigmund, Pritchett, Mulligan, Peverley, Christie, Bertos, Brockie, Barbarouses (Bright 68), Draper (Spoonley 59)

Manama, 10 October 2009, 37,000
Bahrain (0) 0
New Zealand (0) 0
New Zealand: Paston; Lochhead, Sigmund, Vicelich, Nelsen, Elliott, Brown (McGlinchey 68), Smeltz, Killen, Bertos, Fallon (Wood).

Wellington, 14 November 2009, 36,500
New Zealand (1) 1 *(Fallon 45)*
Bahrain (0) 0
New Zealand: Paston, Lochhead, Sigmund, Vicelich, Nelsen, Brown (Boyens 90), Smeltz, Killen (Wood 82), Bertos, McGlinchey (Barron 64), Fallon.

WORLD CUP 2010 REVIEW

Labelled Beauty v The Beast even before the match kicked-off, Spain managed to edge Holland in an entirely unmemorable final unless you add the statistics of one goal for Spain, fourteen yellow cards, one red (John Heitinga) and much ado about very little in the way of football. Mercifully as the last line in King Kong had it "twas beauty killed the beast." Not that there was much for the beautiful game as Andres Iniesta brought justice down on the over-physical Dutch as extra time eroded. Spain added the World Cup crown to its Euro 2008 title. Where was the total football once displayed by Holland? Pity the referee Howard Webb trying his best

Controversy surrounded three things: the case for goal line technology, the irritating Vuvuzelas and the Jabulana ball. No European country had managed to win outside its own sphere. And from the evidence of the group stages there was nothing to suggest a change in such outcome.

The X factor was that the finals were staged for the first time in Africa. However local teams were a disappointment particularly the host nation South Africa. They became the first host nation not to qualify. Algeria, Cameroon and Nigeria were placed last in their respective groups, the Ivory Coast second from bottom in theirs which left just Ghana moving on to the knock-out round.

In contrast all five South American entries emerged from the opening phase virtually unscathed, Argentina, Brazil, Paraguay and Uruguay heading their respective sections, Chile finishing as a runner-up. One should also be mindful of the North and Central American contingent, notably Honduras, Mexico and the USA. Mexico with its long history in the World Cup qualified and Honduras were not disgraced, while the Yanks were something of a revelation. And the Asians put up a decent display, too, with South Korea and Japan leading, though North Korea hit for seven goals by Portugal were clearly out of their depth.

To add to the feeling that it would be something from anywhere, but either Europe or Africa would provide the eventual winners was underlined by some of the early casualties among the so-called elite of Europe. For a start the Euro 2008 finalists Italy and France both finished bottom of their sections. The Italians began by being held by Paraguay and then by a spirited New Zealand who actually retired undefeated from their three matches. Italy then went out losing to Slovakia, only beginning to show form when the game was virtually beyond them.

For France internal strife did nothing to aid their cause. There was equal disappointment for England, too, held by the Americans and Algeria before edging into the second round with a slender win over Slovenia.

The USA actually finished top of Group C while only three European teams achieved a similar standing. In Group D Germany despite losing to Serbia and Spain suffering by the same single goal margin to Switzerland in Group H before recovering were two of them. It was only Holland with three straight victories in Group E who had carried on its impressive form from the World Cup qualifying tournament.

If this was the initial pattern, events in the second round did not derail the earlier Latin American sway. Four of them emerged, Chile only going out to an improving Brazil. But Ghana clipped the USA in extra time with the hopes of an entire continent resting on their shoulders. Germany eventually overran England despite the travesty of a disallowed goal at least a foot over the line which prompted FIFA to hastily have second thoughts about goal line technology. Spain won a tense Iberian derby with Portugal, Paraguay needed penalties to see off Japan and Uruguay came back after South Korea levelled. The Dutch had a slightly easier win than suggested by the score against Slovakia, but Argentina looked to be well into their stride over a battling Mexico – one of their goals clearly off-side.

In the quarter-finals it produced an almost total wipe out for the Latins. Germany thrashed Argentina, Spain left it late over Paraguay and Brazil lost all composure in the second half against the Dutch. Uruguay thankful for a Ghana missed penalty won the subsequent shoot-out to become the sole representatives from South America.

Semi-finals and two goals in three minutes – one off-side – edged the Dutch ahead of Uruguay and Spain patiently wore down the Germans. The match for third place produced five goals and not even Diego Forlan, for many the player of the finals, could save Uruguay at the death as he hit the bar with a free kick to give the Germans third place.

What happened to the stars who failed: Messi, Kaka, Wayne Rooney, Torres and Ronaldo?

Despite a despairing lunge from Holland's Rafael Van der Vaart, Spain's Andres Iniesta scores the winning goal in the 2010 World Cup Final. The 1-0 victory meant Spain lifted the World Cup for the first time.
(Getty Images/Lars Baron)

WORLD CUP 2010 – FINAL RESULTS

Denotes player sent off.

GROUP A

First National Bank Stadium, Johannesburg, 11 June 2010

South Africa (0) 1 *(Tshabalala 55)*

Mexico (0) 1 *(Marquez 79)*   84,490

South Africa: Khune; Gaxa, Mokoena, Thwala (Masilela 46), Khumalo, Tshabalala, Pienaar (Parker 83), Modise, Letsholonyane, Dikgacoi, Mphela.
Mexico: Perez O; Rodriguez, Salcido, Marquez, Osorio, Aguilar (Guardado 55), Torrado, Juarez, Franco (Hernandez 73), Vela (Blanco 69), Giovani.
Referee: Irmatov (Uzbekistan).

Cape Town Stadium, Cape Town, 11 June 2010

Uruguay (0) 0

France (0) 0   64,100

Uruguay: Muslera; Lugano, Godin, Victorino, Pereira M, Ignacio Gonzalez I (Lodeiro■ 63), Pereira A, Perez (Eguren 88), Arevalo, Suarez (Abreu 73), Forlan.
France: Lloris; Sagna, Abidal, Gallas, Evra, Ribery, Gourcuff (Malouda 75), Toulalan, Diaby, Govou (Gignac 85), Anelka (Henry 72).
Referee: Nishimura (Japan).

Loftus Versveld, Pretoria, 16 June 2010

South Africa (0) 0

Uruguay (1) 3 *(Forlan 24, 80 (pen), Pereira A 90)* 42,658

South Africa: Khune■; Gaxa, Masilela, Mokoena, Khumalo, Tshabalala, Pienaar (Josephs 79), Modise, Letsholonyane (Moriri 73), Dikgacoi, Mphela.
Uruguay: Muslera; Lugano, Godin, Fucile (Fernandez A 71), Pereira M, Pereira A, Perez (Gargano 90), Arevalo, Cavani (Sebastian Fernandez 89), Suarez, Forlan.
Referee: Busacca (Switzerland).

Peter Mokaba Stadium, Polokwane, 17 June 2010

France (0) 0

Mexico (0) 2 *(Hernandez 64, Blanco 79 (pen))*   35,370

France: Lloris; Sagna, Abidal, Gallas, Evra, Ribery, Toulalan, Malouda, Diaby, Govou (Valbuena 69), Anelka (Gignac 46).
Mexico: Perez O; Rodriguez, Salcido, Marquez, Osorio, Moreno, Torrado, Juarez (Hernandez 55), Franco (Blanco 62), Vela (Barrera 31), Giovani.
Referee: Al-Ghamdi (Saudi Arabia).

Free State Stadium, Bloemfontein, 22 June 2010

France (0) 1 *(Malouda 70)*

South Africa (2) 2 *(Khumalo 20, Mphela 37)*   39,415

France: Lloris; Sagna, Gallas, Squillaci, Clichy, Ribery, Gourcuff■, Diarra A (Govou 82), Diaby, Cisse (Henry 55), Gignac (Malouda 46).
South Africa: Josephs; Masilela, Mokoena, Ngcongca (Gaxa 55), Khumalo, Sibaya, Tshabalala, Pienaar, Khuboni (Modise 78), Mphela, Parker (Nomvethe 68).
Referee: Ruiz (Colombia).

Royal Bafokeng, Rustenburg, 22 June 2010

Mexico (0) 0

Uruguay (1) 1 *(Suarez 43)*   33,425

Mexico: Perez O; Rodriguez, Salcido, Marquez, Osorio, Moreno (Castro 57), Torrado, Guardado (Barrera 46), Franco, Blanco (Hernandez 63), Giovani.
Uruguay: Muslera; Lugano, Fucile, Victorino, Pereira M, Pereira A (Scotti 77), Perez, Arevalo, Cavani, Suarez (Fernandez A 85), Forlan.
Referee: Kassai (Hungary).

Group A – Final Table	P	W	D	L	F	A	Pts
Uruguay	3	2	1	0	4	0	7
Mexico	3	1	1	1	3	2	4
South Africa	3	1	1	1	3	5	4
France	3	0	1	2	1	4	1

GROUP B

Ellis Park Stadium, Johannesburg, 12 June 2010

Argentina (1) 1 *(Heinze 6)*

Nigeria (0) 0   55,686

Argentina: Romero; Demichelis, Heinze, Samuel, Di Maria (Burdisso 85), Veron (Maxi Rodriguez 74), Mascherano, Gutierrez, Higuain (Milito 79), Messi, Tevez.
Nigeria: Enyeama; Yobo, Taiwo (Uche 74), Shittu, Odiah, Kaita, Haruna, Etuhu, Yakubu, Obinna (Martins 53), Ogbuke Obasi (Odemwingie 60).
Referee: Stark (Germany).

Nelson Mandela Bay, Port Elizabeth, 12 June 2010

South Korea (1) 2 *(Lee J-S 7, Park J-S 52)*

Greece (0) 0   31,513

South Korea: Jung S-R; Cho Y-H, Lee Y-P, Lee J-S, Cha D-R, Park J-S, Kim J-W, Ki S-Y (Kim N-I 75), Lee C-Y (Kim J-S 90), Park C-Y (Lee S-Y 87), Yeom K-H.
Greece: Tzorvas; Seitaridis, Vyntra, Torosidis, Tziolis, Papadopoulos A, Karagounis (Patsatzoglou 46), Katsouranis, Samaras (Salpingidis 59), Charisteas (Kapetanos 61), Gekas.
Referee: Hester (New Zealand).

First National Bank Stadium, Johannesburg, 17 June 2010

Argentina (2) 4 *(Park C-Y 17 (og), Higuain 33, 76, 80)*

South Korea (1) 1 *(Lee C-Y 45)*   82,174

Argentina: Romero; Demichelis, Heinze, Samuel (Burdisso 23), Di Maria, Mascherano, Gutierrez, Maxi Rodriguez, Higuain (Bolatti 82), Messi, Tevez (Aguero 75).
South Korea: Jung S-R; Oh B-S, Cho Y-H, Lee Y-P, Lee J-S, Park J-S, Kim J-W, Ki S-Y (Kim N-I 46), Lee C-Y, Park C-Y (Lee D-G 81), Yeom K-H.
Referee: De Bleeckere (Belgium).

Free State Stadium, Bloemfontein, 17 June 2010

Greece (1) 2 *(Salpingidis 44, Torosidis 71)*

Nigeria (1) 1 *(Uche 16)*   31,593

Greece: Tzorvas; Vyntra, Torosidis, Kyrgiakos, Papastathopoulos (Samaras 37), Tziolis, Papadopoulos A, Karagounis, Katsouranis, Salpingidis, Gekas (Ninis 79).
Nigeria: Enyeama; Yobo, Taiwo (Echiejile 55) (Afolabi 77), Shittu, Odiah, Uche, Kaita■, Haruna, Etuhu, Yakubu, Odemwingie (Ogbuke Obasi 46).
Referee: Ruiz (Colombia).

Peter Mokaba Stadium, Polokwane, 22 June 2010

Greece (0) 0

Argentina (0) 2 *(Demichelis 77, Palermo 89)*   38,891

Greece: Tzorvas; Moras, Vyntra, Torosidis (Patsatzoglou 55), Kyrgiakos, Papastathopoulos, Tziolis, Papadopoulos A, Karagounis (Spyropoulos 46), Katsouranis (Ninis 54), Samaras.
Argentina: Romero; Demichelis, Rodriguez C, Burdisso, Otamendi, Bolatti, Veron, Maxi Rodriguez (Di Maria 63), Messi, Aguero (Pastore 77), Milito (Palermo 80).
Referee: Irmatov (Uzbekistan).

Moses Mabhida, Durban, 22 June 2010

Nigeria (1) 2 *(Uche 12, Yakubu 69 (pen))*

South Korea (1) 2 *(Lee J-S 38, Park C-Y 49)*   61,874

Nigeria: Enyeama; Yobo (Echiejile 46), Afolabi, Shittu, Odiah, Uche, Ayila, Etuhu, Kanu (Martins 57), Yakubu (Obinna 70), Odemwingie.
South Korea: Jung S-R; Cho Y-H, Lee Y-P, Lee J-S, Cha D-R, Park J-S, Kim J-W, Ki S-Y (Kim J-S 87), Lee C-Y, Park C-Y (Kim D-J 90), Yeom K-H (Kim N-I 64).
Referee: Benquerenca (Portugal).

Group B – Final Table	P	W	D	L	F	A	Pts
Argentina	3	3	0	0	7	1	9
South Korea	3	1	1	1	5	6	4
Greece	3	1	0	2	2	5	3
Nigeria	3	0	1	2	3	5	1

GROUP C

Royal Bafokeng, Rustenburg, 12 June 2010

England (1) 1 *(Gerrard 4)*

USA (1) 1 *(Dempsey 40)* 38,646

England: Green; Johnson G, Cole A, Gerrard, King (Carragher 46), Terry, Lennon, Lampard, Heskey (Crouch 79), Rooney, Milner (Wright-Phillips 30).
USA: Howard; Onyewu, Bocanegra, Cherundolo, DeMerit, Bradley, Dempsey, Donovan, Clark, Altidore (Holden 86), Findley (Buddle 77).
Referee: Simon (Brazil).

Peter Mokaba Stadium, Polokwane, 13 June 2010

Algeria (0) 0

Slovenia (0) 1 *(Koren 79)* 30,325

Algeria: Chaouchi; Bougherra, Belhadj, Yahia, Halliche, Lacen, Matmour (Saifi 81), Ziani, Yebda, Kadir (Guedioura 82), Djebbour (Ghezzal■ 58).
Slovenia: Handanovic S; Brecko, Suler, Cesar, Koren, Jokic, Kirm, Radosavljevic (Komac 87), Birsa (Pecnik 84), Novakovic, Dedic (Ljubijankic 53).
Referee: Batres (Guatemala).

Cape Town Stadium, Cape Town, 18 June 2010

England (0) 0

Algeria (0) 0 64,100

England: James; Johnson G, Cole A, Barry (Crouch 84), Carragher, Terry, Lennon (Wright-Phillips 63), Lampard, Heskey (Defoe 74), Rooney, Gerrard.
Algeria: M'Bolhi; Bougherra, Belhadj, Yahia, Halliche, Boudebouz (Abdoun 74), Lacen, Matmour, Ziani (Guedioura 80), Yebda (Mesbah 89), Kadir.
Referee: Irmatov (Uzbekistan).

Ellis Park Stadium, Johannesburg, 18 June 2010

Slovenia (2) 2 *(Birsa 13, Ljubijankic 42)*

USA (0) 2 *(Donovan 48, Bradley 82)* 45,573

Slovenia: Handanovic S; Brecko, Suler, Cesar, Koren, Jokic, Kirm, Radosavljevic, Ljubijankic (Pecnik ˜4) (Komac 90), Birsa (Dedic 87), Novakovic.
USA: Howard; Bocanegra, Onyewu (Gomez 80), Cherundolo, DeMerit, Bradley, Dempsey, Donovan, Torres (Feilhaber 46), Altidore, Findley (Edu 46).
Referee: Coulibaly (Mali).

Nelson Mandela Bay, Port Elizabeth, 23 June 2010

Slovenia (0) 0

England (1) 1 *(Defoe 22)* 36,893

Slovenia: Handanovic S; Brecko, Suler, Cesar, Koren, Jokic, Kirm (Matavz 79), Radosavljevic, Ljubijankic (Dedic 62), Birsa, Novakovic.
England: James; Johnson G, Cole A, Barry, Upson, Terry, Milner, Lampard, Defoe (Heskey 85), Rooney (Cole J 72), Gerrard.
Referee: Stark (Germany).

Loftus Versveld, Pretoria, 23 June 2010

USA (0) 1 *(Donovan 90)*

Algeria (0) 0 35,827

USA: Howard; Bocanegra, Cherundolo, Bornstein (Beasley 80), DeMerit, Bradley, Dempsey, Donovan, Edu (Buddle 64), Gomez (Feilhaber 46), Altidore.
Algeria: M'Bolhi; Bougherra, Belhadj, Yahia■, Halliche, Lacen, Matmour (Saifi 85), Ziani (Guedioura 69) Yebda, Kadir, Djebbour (Ghezzal 65).
Referee: De Bleeckere (Belgium).

Group C – Final Table	P	W	D	L	F	A	Pts
USA	3	1	2	0	4	3	5
England	3	1	2	0	2	1	5
Slovenia	3	1	1	1	3	3	4
Algeria	3	0	1	2	0	2	1

GROUP D

Moses Mabhida, Durban, 13 June 2010

Germany (2) 4 *(Podolski 8, Klose 26, Muller 68, Cacau 70)*

Australia (0) 0 62,660

Germany: Neuer; Friedrich, Badstuber, Lahm, Mertesacker, Khedira, Schweinsteiger, Ozil (Gomez 73), Podolski (Marin 81), Klose (Cacau 68), Muller.
Australia: Schwarzer; Neill, Moore, Chipperfield, Cahill■, Culina, Emerton (Jedinak 74), Wilkshire, Grella (Holman 46), Valeri, Garcia (Rukavytsya 64).
Referee: Rodriguez (Mexico).

Loftus Versveld, Pretoria, 13 June 2010

Serbia (0) 0

Ghana (0) 1 *(Gyan 84 (pen))* 38,833

Serbia: Stojkovic; Kolarov, Vidic, Ivanovic, Lukovic■, Stankovic, Milijas (Kuzmanovic 62), Krasic, Pantelic, Jovanovic (Subotic 76), Zigic (Lazovic 69).
Ghana: Kingson; Sarpei, Pantsil, John Mensah, Annan, Vorsah, Asamoah (Appiah 73), Boateng (Owusu-Abeyie 90), Gyan (Addy 90), Tagoe, Ayew.
Referee: Baldassi (Argentina).

Nelson Mandela Bay, Port Elizabeth, 18 June 2010

Germany (0) 0

Serbia (1) 1 *(Jovanovic 38)* 38,294

Germany: Neuer; Friedrich, Badstuber (Gomez 77), Lahm, Mertesacker, Khedira, Schweinsteiger, Ozil (Marin 70), Podolski, Klose■, Muller (Cacau 70).
Serbia: Stojkovic; Kolarov, Vidic, Ivanovic, Subotic, Stankovic, Krasic, Ninkovic (Kacar 70), Kuzmanovic (Petrovic 75), Jovanovic (Lazovic 79), Zigic.
Referee: Undiano (Spain).

Royal Bafokeng, Rustenburg, 19 June 2010

Ghana (1) 1 *(Gyan 25 (pen))*

Australia (1) 1 *(Holman 11)* 34,812

Ghana: Kingson; Sarpei, Pantsil, Jonathan Mensah, Addy, Annan, Asamoah (Ali Muntari 77), Boateng (Amoah 86), Gyan, Tagoe (Owusu-Abeyie 56), Ayew.
Australia: Schwarzer; Neill, Moore, Culina, Emerton, Wilkshire (Rukavytsya 85), Kewell■, Holman (Kennedy 68), Valeri, Carney, Bresciano (Chipperfield 66).
Referee: Rosetti (Italy).

Mbombela Stadium, Nelspruit, 23 June 2010

Australia (0) 2 *(Cahill 69, Holman 73)*

Serbia (0) 1 *(Pantelic 84)* 37,836

Australia: Schwarzer; Neill, Beauchamp, Cahill, Culina, Emerton, Wilkshire (Garcia 82), Valeri (Chipperfield 66), Carney, Bresciano (Holman 66), Kennedy.
Serbia: Stojkovic; Vidic, Ivanovic, Lukovic, Obradovic, Stankovic, Krasic (Tosic 62), Ninkovic, Kuzmanovic (Lazovic 77), Jovanovic, Zigic (Pantelic 67).
Referee: Larrionda (Uruguay).

First National Bank Stadium, Johannesburg, 23 June 2010

Ghana (0) 0

Germany (0) 1 *(Ozil 60)* 83,391

Ghana: Kingson; Sarpei, Pantsil, John Mensah, Jonathan Mensah, Annan, Asamoah, Boateng (Amoah 81), Tagoe (Ali Muntari 63), Ayew (Adiyiah 90).
Germany: Neuer; Friedrich, Lahm, Mertesacker, Boateng (Jansen 72), Khedira, Schweinsteiger (Kroos 81), Ozil, Podolski, Muller (Trochowski 68), Cacau.
Referee: Simon (Brasil).

Group D – Final Table	P	W	D	L	F	A	Pts
Germany	3	2	0	1	5	1	6
Ghana	3	1	1	1	2	2	4
Australia	3	1	1	1	3	6	4
Serbia	3	1	0	2	2	3	3

GROUP E

First National Bank Stadium, Johannesburg, 14 June 2010

Holland (0) 2 *(Agger 46 (og), Kuyt 85)*
Denmark (0) 0　　　　　　　　　　　　83,465

Holland: Stekelenburg; Van der Wiel, Heitinga, Mathijsen, Van Bronckhorst, Van Bommel, De Jong (De Zeeuw 88), Sneijder, Van der Vaart (Elia 67), Kuyt, Van Persie (Afellay 77).
Denmark: Sorensen; Kjaer, Agger, Jacobsen L, Poulsen S, Poulsen C, Jorgensen, Kahlenberg (Eriksen 73), Enevoldsen (Gronkjaer 56), Bendtner (Beckmann 62), Rommedahl.
Referee: Lannoy (France).

Free State Stadium, Bloemfontein, 14 June 2010

Japan (1) 1 *(Honda 39)*
Cameroon (0) 0　　　　　　　　　　　30,620

Japan: Kawashima; Komano, Tanaka, Nagatomo, Nakazawa, Abe, Endo, Matsui (Okazaki 69), Hasebe (Inamoto 88), Honda, Okubo (Yano 82).
Cameroon: Souleymanou; Assou-Ekotto, N'Koulou, Bassong, Matip (Emana 63), Makoun (Idrissou 74), Enoh, Mbia, Eto'o, Choupo-Moting (Geremi 75), Webo.
Referee: Benquerenca (Portugal).

Loftus Versveld, Pretoria, 19 June 2010

Cameroon (1) 1 *(Eto'o 10)*
Denmark (1) 2 *(Bendtner 33, Rommedahl 61)*　38,074

Cameroon: Souleymanou; Assou-Ekotto, N'Koulou, Bassong (Idrissou 73), Song Billong, Geremi, Emana, Enoh (Makoun 46), Mbia, Eto'o, Webo (Aboubakar 78).
Denmark: Sorensen; Kjaer, Agger, Jacobsen L, Poulsen S, Poulsen C, Gronkjaer (Kahlenberg 67), Jorgensen (Jensen D 46), Tomasson (Poulsen J 86), Bendtner, Rommedahl.
Referee: Larrionda (Uruguay).

Moses Mabhida, Durban, 19 June 2010

Holland (0) 1 *(Sneijder 53)*
Japan (0) 0　　　　　　　　　　　　62,010

Holland: Stekelenburg; Van der Wiel, Heitinga, Mathijsen, Van Bronckhorst, Van Bommel, De Jong, Sneijder (Afellay 82), Van der Vaart (Elia 72), Kuyt, Van Persie (Huntelaar 88).
Japan: Kawashima; Komano, Tanaka, Nagatomo, Nakazawa, Abe, Endo, Matsui (Nakamura 64), Hasebe (Okazaki 77), Honda, Okubo (Tamada 77).
Referee: Baldassi (Argentina).

Cape Town Stadium, Cape Town, 24 June 2010

Cameroon (0) 1 *(Eto'o 65 (pen))*
Holland (1) 2 *(Van Persie 36, Huntelaar 83)*　63,093

Cameroon: Hamidou; Assou-Ekotto, N'Koulou (Rigobert Song 73), Bong (Aboubakar 56), N'Guemo, Geremi, Makoun, Chedjou, Mbia, Eto'o, Choupo-Moting (Idrissou 72).
Holland: Stekelenburg; Heitinga, Mathijsen, Boulahrouz, Van Bronckhorst, Van Bommel, De Jong, Sneijder, Van der Vaart (Robben 73), Kuyt (Elia 66), Van Persie (Huntelaar 59).
Referee: Pozo (Chile).

Royal Bafokeng, Rustenburg, 24 June 2010

Denmark (0) 1 *(Tomasson 81)*
Japan (2) 3 *(Honda 17, Endo 30, Okazaki 87)*　27,967

Denmark: Sorensen; Agger, Jacobsen L, Kroldrup (Larsen 56), Poulsen S, Poulsen C, Jorgensen (Poulsen J 34), Kahlenberg (Eriksen 63), Tomasson, Bendtner, Rommedahl.
Japan: Kawashima; Komano, Tanaka, Nagatomo, Nakazawa, Abe, Endo (Inamoto 90), Matsui (Okazaki 74), Hasebe, Honda, Okubo (Konno 88).
Referee: Damon (South Africa).

Group E – Final Table

	P	W	D	L	F	A	Pts
Holland	3	3	0	0	5	1	9
Japan	3	2	0	1	4	2	6
Denmark	3	1	0	2	3	6	3
Cameroon	3	0	0	3	2	5	0

GROUP F

Cape Town Stadium, Cape Town, 14 June 2010

Italy (0) 1 *(De Rossi 63)*
Paraguay (1) 1 *(Alcaraz 39)*　　　　　62,869

Italy: Buffon (Marchetti 46); Criscito, Chiellini, Cannavaro, Zambrotta, De Rossi, Pepe, Marchisio (Camoranesi 59), Montolivo, Iaquinta, Gilardino (Di Natale 72).
Paraguay: Villar; Morel, Da Silva, Alcaraz, Bonet, Vera, Caceres V, Riveros, Torres (Santana 60), Valdez (Santa Cruz 68), Barrios (Cardozo 76).
Referee: Archundia (Mexico).

Royal Bafokeng, Rustenburg, 15 June 2010

New Zealand (0) 1 *(Reid 90)*
Slovakia (0) 1 *(Vittek 50)*　　　　　　23,871

New Zealand: Paston; Lochhead, Reid, Nelsen, Smith, Vicelich (Christie 78), Elliott, Bertos, Smeltz, Killen (Wood 72), Fallon.
Slovakia: Mucha; Skrtel, Cech, Zabavnik, Durica, Strba, Weiss (Kucka 90), Hamsik, Sestak (Holosko 81), Vittek (Stoch 84), Jendrisek.
Referee: Damon (South Africa).

Mbombela Stadium, Nelspruit, 20 June 2010

Italy (1) 1 *(Iaquinta 29 (pen))*
New Zealand (1) 1 *(Smeltz 7)*　　　　38,229

Italy: Marchetti; Criscito, Chiellini, Cannavaro, Zambrotta, De Rossi, Pepe (Camoranesi 46), Marchisio (Pazzini 61), Montolivo, Iaquinta, Gilardino (Di Natale 46).
New Zealand: Paston; Lochhead, Reid, Nelsen, Smith, Vicelich (Christie 81), Elliott, Bertos, Smeltz, Killen (Barron 90), Fallon (Wood 63).
Referee: Batres (Guatemala).

Free State Stadium, Bloemfontein, 20 June 2010

Slovakia (0) 0
Paraguay (1) 2 *(Vera 27, Riveros 86)*　　26,643

Slovakia: Mucha; Pekarik, Skrtel, Durica, Salata (Stoch 83), Strba, Weiss, Kozak, Hamsik, Sestak (Holosko 70), Vittek.
Paraguay: Villar; Morel, Da Silva, Alcaraz, Bonet, Vera (Barreto E 88), Caceres V, Riveros, Santa Cruz, Valdez (Torres 68), Barrios (Cardozo 82).
Referee: Maillet (Seychelles).

Peter Mokaba Stadium, Polokwane, 24 June 2010

Paraguay (0) 0
New Zealand (0) 0　　　　　　　　　　34,850

Paraguay: Villar; Morel, Caniza, Caceres J, Da Silva, Vera, Caceres V, Riveros, Cardozo (Barrios 66), Santa Cruz, Valdez (Benitez 67).
New Zealand: Paston; Reid, Lochhead, Nelsen, Smith, Vicelich, Elliott, Bertos, Smeltz, Killen (Brockie 79), Fallon (Wood 69).
Referee: Nishimura (Japan).

Ellis Park Stadium, Johannesburg, 24 June 2010

Slovakia (1) 3 *(Vittek 25, 73, Kopunek 89)*
Italy (0) 2 *(Di Natale 81, Quagliarella 90)*　53,412

Slovakia: Mucha; Pekarik, Skrtel, Zabavnik, Durica, Strba (Kopunek 87), Hamsik, Kucka, Vittek (Sestak 90), Stoch, Jendrisek (Petras 90).
Italy: Marchetti; Criscito (Maggio 46), Chiellini, Cannavaro, Zambrotta, De Rossi, Pepe, Gattuso (Quagliarella 46), Montolivo (Pirlo 56), Iaquinta, Di Natale.
Referee: Webb (England).

Group F – Final Table

	P	W	D	L	F	A	Pts
Paraguay	3	1	2	0	3	1	5
Slovakia	3	1	1	1	4	5	4
New Zealand	3	0	3	0	2	2	3
Italy	3	0	2	1	4	5	2

GROUP G

Ellis Park Stadium, Johannesburg, 15 June 2010

Brazil (0) 2 *(Maicon 55, Elano 72)*

North Korea (0) 1 *(Ji Y-N 89)* 54,331

Brazil: Julio Cesar; Maicon, Lucio, Juan, Felipe Melo (Ramires 84), Michel Bastos, Elano (Dani Alves 73), Gilberto Silvo, Kaka (Nilmar 78), Luis Fabiano, Robinho.
North Korea: Ri M-G; Cha J-H, Ri J-I, Ri K-C, Pak C-J, Pak N-C, Ji Y-N, Mun I-G (Kim K-I 80), Ahn Y-H, Jeong T-S, Hong Y-J.
Referee: Kassai (Hungary).

Nelson Mandela Bay, Port Elizabeth, 15 June 2010

Ivory Coast (0) 0

Portugal (0) 0 37,430

Ivory Coast: Barry; Kolo Toure, Eboue (Romaric 88), Zokora, Tiote, Tiene, Yaya Toure, Demel, Kalou (Drogba 66), Gervinho (Keita 82), Dindane.
Portugal: Eduardo; Bruno Alves, Paulo Ferreira, Ricardo Carvalho, Pedro Mendes, Raul Meireles (Ruben Amorim 82), Deco (Tiago 62), Fabio Coentrao, Cristiano Ronaldo, Liedson, Danny (Simao 55).
Referee: Larrionda (Uruguay).

First National Bank Stadium, Johannesburg, 20 June 2010

Brazil (1) 3 *(Luis Fabiano 25, 50, Elano 62)*

Ivory Coast (0) 1 *(Drogba 79)* 84,455

Brazil: Julio Cesar; Maicon, Lucio, Juan, Felipe Melo, Michel Bastos, Elano (Dani Alves 67), Gilberto Silva, Kaka■, Luis Fabiano, Robinho (Ramires 90).
Ivory Coast: Barry; Kolo Toure, Eboue (Romaric 72), Zokora, Tiote, Tiene, Yaya Toure, Demel, Kalou (Keita 68), Drogba, Dindane (Gervinho 54).
Referee: Lannoy (France).

Cape Town Stadium, Cape Town, 21 June 2010

Portugal (1) 7 *(Raul Meireles 29, Simao 53, Hugo Almeida 56, Tiago 60, 89, Liedson 81, Cristiano Ronaldo 87)*

North Korea (0) 0 63,644

Portugal: Eduardo; Bruno Alves, Ricardo Carvalho, Miguel, Pedro Mendes, Raul Meireles (Miguel Veloso 70), Tiago, Fabio Coentrao, Cristiano Ronaldo, Simao (Duda 74), Hugo Almeida (Liedson 77).
North Korea: Ri M-G; Cha J-H (Nam S-C 75), Ri J-I, Ri K-C, Pak C-J, Pak N-C (Kim Y-J 58), Ji Y-N, Mun I-G (Kim K-I 58), Ahn Y-H, Jeong T-S, Hong Y-J.
Referee: Pozo (Chile).

Mbombela Stadium Nelspruit, 25 June 2010

North Korea (0) 0

Ivory Coast (2) 3 *(Yaya Toure 14, Romaric 20, Kalou 82)* 34,763

North Korea: Ri M-G; Cha J-H, Ri J-I, Ri K-C, Pak C-J, Pak N-C, Ji Y-N, Mun I-G (Choe K-C 67), Ahn Y-H, Jeong T-S, Hong Y-J.
Ivory Coast: Barry; Boka, Kolo Toure, Eboue, Zokora, Tiote, Romaric (Doumbia 79), Yaya Toure, Gervinho (Kalou 64), Drogba, Keita (Dindane 64).
Referee: Undiano (Spain).

Moses Mabhida, Durban, 25 June 2010

Portugal (0) 0

Brazil (0) 0 62,712

Portugal: Eduardo; Bruno Alves, Ricardo Carvalho, Pepe (Pedro Mendes 64), Ricardo Costa, Duda (Simao 55), Raul Meireles (Miguel Veloso 84), Tiago, Fabio Coentrao, Cristiano Ronaldo, Danny.
Brazil: Julio Cesar; Maicon, Lucio, Juan, Dani Alves, Felipe Melo (Josue 44), Michel Bastos, Gilberto Silva, Julio Baptista (Ramires 82), Luis Fabiano (Grafite 85), Nilmar.
Referee: Archundia (Mexico).

Group G – Final Table	P	W	D	L	F	A	Pts
Brazil	3	2	1	0	5	2	7
Portugal	3	1	2	0	7	0	5
Ivory Coast	3	1	1	1	4	3	4
North Korea	3	0	0	3	1	12	0

GROUP H

Mbombela Stadium, Nelspruit, 16 June 2010

Honduras (0) 0

Chile (1) 1 *(Beausejour 34)* 32,664

Honduras: Valladares N; Chavez O, Figueroa, Izaguirre, Mendoza, Nunez R (Martinez 78), Palacios W, Alvarez, Guevara (Thomas 66), Pavon (Welcome 60), Espinoza.
Chile: Bravo; Ponce, Isla, Vidal (Contreras 81), Carmona, Valdivia (Gonzalez 87), Fernandez, Beausejour, Medel, Millar (Jara 52), Sanchez.
Referee: Maillet (Seychelles).

Moses Mabhida, Durban, 16 June 2010

Spain (0) 0

Switzerland (0) 1 *(Gelson 52)* 62,453

Spain: Casillas; Pique, Puyol, Capdevila, Sergio Ramos, Iniesta (Pedro 77), Xavi, Xabi Alonso, Busquets (Torres 61), David Silva (Jesus Navas 62), David Villa.
Switzerland: Benaglio; Lichtsteiner, Senderos (Von Bergen 36), Grichting, Ziegler, Huggel, Barnetta (Eggimann 90), Inler, Gelson, Nkufo, Derdiyok (Yakin 79).
Referee: Webb (England).

Nelson Mandela Bay, Port Elizabeth, 21 June 2010

Chile (0) 1 *(Gonzalez 75)*

Switzerland (0) 0 34,872

Chile: Bravo; Ponce, Isla, Vidal (Valdivia 46), Jara, Carmona, Fernandez (Paredes 65), Beausejour, Medel, Sanchez, Suazo (Gonzalez 46).
Switzerland: Benaglio; Lichtsteiner, Von Bergen, Grichting, Ziegler, Huggel, Inler, Behrami■, Gelson (Banjaku 77), Frei (Barnetta 42), Nkufo (Derdiyok 68).
Referee: Al-Ghamdi (Saudi Arabia).

El is Park Stadium, Johannesburg, 21 June 2010

Spain (1) 2 *(David Villa 17, 51)*

Honduras (0) 0 54,386

Spain: Casillas; Pique, Puyol, Capdevila, Sergio Ramos (Arbeloa 77), Xavi (Fabregas 66), Xabi Alonso, Busquets, Jesus Navas, David Villa, Torres (Mata 70).
Honduras: Valladares N; Chavez O, Figueroa, Izaguirre, Mendoza, Palacios W, Turcios (Nunez R 63), Guevara, Suazo (Jerry Palacios 84), Espinoza (Welcome 46), Martinez.
Referee: Nishimura (Japan).

Loftus Versveld, Pretoria, 25 June 2010

Chile (0) 1 *(Millar 47)*

Spain (2) 2 *(David Villa 24, Iniesta 37)* 41,958

Chile: Bravo; Ponce, Isla, Vidal, Jara, Valdivia (Millar 46), Gonzalez (Paredes 46), Estrada■, Beausejour, Medel, Sanchez (Orellana 65).
Spain: Casillas; Pique, Puyol, Capdevila, Sergio Ramos, Iniesta, Xavi, Xabi Alonso (Martinez 73), Busquets, David Villa, Torres (Fabregas 55).
Referee: Rodriguez (Mexico).

Freestate Stadium, Bloemfontein, 25 June 2010

Switzerland (0) 0

Honduras (0) 0 28,042

Switzerland: Benaglio; Lichtsteiner, Von Bergen, Grichting, Ziegler, Huggel (Shaqiri 78), Barnetta, Inler, Gelson (Yakin 46), Nkufo (Frei 69), Derdiyok.
Honduras: Valladares N; Chavez O, Figueroa, Bernardez, Sabillon, Thomas, Nunez R (Martinez 66), Palacios W, Alvarez, Jerry Palacios (Welcome 78), Suazo (Turcios 87).
Referee: Baldassi (Argentina).

Group H – Final Table	P	W	D	L	F	A	Pts
Spain	3	2	0	1	4	2	6
Chile	3	2	0	1	3	2	6
Switzerland	3	1	1	1	1	1	4
Honduras	3	0	1	2	0	3	1

SECOND ROUND

Nelson Mandela Bay, Port Elizabeth, 26 June 2010
Uruguay (1) 2 *(Suarez 8, 80)*
South Korea (0) 1 *(Lee C-Y 68)*   30,597
Uruguay: Muslera; Lugano, Godin (Victorino 46), Fucile, Pereira M, Pereira A (Lodeiro 74), Perez, Arevalo, Cavani, Suarez (Fernandez A 84), Forlan.
South Korea: Jung S-R; Cho Y-H, Lee Y-P, Lee J-S, Cha D-R, Park J-S, Kim J-W, Kim J-S (Lee D-G 61), Ki S-Y (Yeom K-H 85), Lee C-Y, Park C-Y.
Referee: Stark (Germany).

Royal Bafokeng, Rustenburg, 26 June 2010
USA (0) 1 *(Donovan 62 (pen))*
Ghana (1) 2 *(Boateng 6, Gyan 93)*   34,976
USA: Howard; Bocanegra, Cherundolo, Bornstein, DeMerit, Bradley, Dempsey, Donovan, Clark (Edu 31), Altidore (Gomez 91), Findley (Feilhaber 46).
Ghana: Kingson; Sarpei (Addy 73), Pantsil, John Mensah, Inkoom (Ali Muntari 113), Jonathan Mensah, Annan, Asamoah, Boateng (Appiah 78), Gyan, Ayew.
Referee: Kassai (Hungary).
aet.

First National Bank Stadium, Johannesburg, 27 June 2010
Argentina (2) 3 *(Tevez 26, 52, Higuain 33)*
Mexico (0) 1 *(Hernandez 71)*   84,377
Argentina: Romero; Demichelis, Burdisso, Heinze, Otamendi, Di Maria (Gutierrez 79), Mascherano, Maxi Rodriguez (Pastore 87), Higuain, Messi, Tevez (Veron 69).
Mexico: Perez O; Rodriguez, Salcido, Marquez, Osorio, Torrado, Juarez, Guardado (Franco 61), Hernandez, Giovani, Bautista (Barrera 46).
Referee: Rossetti (Italy).

Free State Stadium, Bloemfontein, 27 June 2010
Germany (2) 4 *(Klose 20, Podolski 32, Muller 67, 70)*
England (1) 1 *(Upson 37)*   40,510
Germany: Neuer; Friedrich, Lahm, Mertesacker, Boateng, Khedira, Schweinsteiger, Ozil (Kiessling 83), Podolski, Klose (Trochowski 72), Muller (Gomez 72).
England: James; Johnson G (Wright-Phillips 87), Cole A, Barry, Terry, Upson, Milner (Cole J 64), Lampard, Defoe (Heskey 71), Rooney, Gerrard.
Referee: Larrionda (Uruguay).

Ellis Park Stadium, Johannesburg, 28 June 2010
Brazil (2) 3 *(Juan 34, Luis Fabiano 38, Robinho 59)*
Chile (0) 0   54,096
Brazil: Julio Cesar; Maicon, Lucio, Juan, Dani Alves, Michel Bastos, Gilberto Silva, Kaka (Kleberson 81), Ramires, Luis Fabiano (Nilmar 76), Robinho (Gilberto 85).
Chile: Bravo; Fuentes, Isla (Millar 62), Contreras (Valdivia 46), Vidal, Jara, Carmona, Gonzalez (Tello 46), Beausejour, Sanchez, Suazo.
Referee: Webb (England).

Moses Mabhida, Durban, 28 June 2010
Holland (1) 2 *(Robben 18, Sneijder 84)*
Slovakia (0) 1 *(Vittek 90 (pen))*   61,962
Holland: Stekelenburg; Van der Wiel, Heitinga, Mathijsen, Van Bronckhorst, Van Bommel, De Jong, Sneijder (Afellay 90), Kuyt, Van Persie (Huntelaar 80), Robben (Elia 71).
Slovakia: Mucha; Pekarik, Skrtel, Zabavnik (Sapara 87), Durica, Weiss, Hamsik (Jakubko 87), Kucka, Vittek, Stoch, Jendrisek (Kopunek 71).
Referee: Undiano (Spain).

Loftus Versveld, Pretoria, 29 June 2010
Paraguay (0) 0
Japan (0) 0   36,742
Paraguay: Villar; Morel, Da Silva, Alcaraz, Bonet, Vera, Riveros, Ortigoza (Barreto E 75), Santa Cruz (Cardozo 94), Benitez (Valdez 60), Barrios.

Japan: Kawashima; Komano, Tanaka, Nagatomo, Nakazawa, Abe (Nakamura 81), Endo, Matsui (Okazaki 65), Hasebe, Honda, Okubo (Tamada 106).
Referee: De Bleeckere (Belgium).
aet; Paraguay won 5-3 on penalties: Barreto E scored, Endo scored; Barrios scored, Hasebe scored; Riveros scored, Komano hit bar; Valdez scored, Honda scored; Cardozo scored.

Cape Town Stadium, Cape Town, 29 June 2010
Spain (0) 1 *(David Villa 63)*
Portugal (0) 0   62,955
Spain: Casillas; Pique, Puyol, Capdevila, Sergio Ramos, Iniesta, Xavi, Xabi Alonso (Marchena 90), Busquets, David Villa (Pedro 88), Torres (Llorente 59).
Portugal: Eduardo; Bruno Alves, Ricardo Carvalho, Pepe (Pedro Mendes 72), Ricardo Costa■, Raul Meireles, Tiago, Fabio Coentrao, Cristiano Ronaldo, Simao (Liedson 72), Hugo Almeida (Danny 58).
Referee: Baldassi (Argentina).

QUARTER-FINALS

Nelson Mandela Bay, Port Elizabeth, 2 July 2010
Holland (0) 2 *(Felipe Melo 53 (og), Sneijder 68)*
Brazil (1) 1 *(Robinho 10)*   40,186
Holland: Stekelenburg; Van der Wiel, Heitinga, Ooijer, Van Bronckhorst, Van Bommel, De Jong, Sneijder, Kuyt, Van Persie (Huntelaar 85), Robben.
Brazil: Julio Cesar; Maicon, Lucio, Juan, Dani Alves, Felipe Melo■, Michel Bastos (Gilberto 62), Gilberto Silva, Kaka, Luis Fabiano (Nilmar 77), Robinho.
Referee: Nishimura (Japan).

First National Bank Stadium, Johannesburg, 2 July 2010
Uruguay (0) 1 *(Forlan 55)*
Ghana (1) 1 *(Ali Muntari 45)*   84,017
Uruguay: Muslera; Lugano (Scotti 38), Fucile, Victorino, Pereira M, Perez, Arevalo, Fernandez A (Lodeiro 46), Cavani (Abreu 76), Suarez■, Forlan.
Ghana: Kingson; Sarpei, Pantsil, John Mensah, Inkoom (Appiah 74), Annan, Ali Muntari (Adiyiah 88), Vorsah, Asamoah, Boateng, Gyan.
Referee: Benquerenca (Portugal).
aet; Uruguay won 4-2 on penalties: Forlan scored, Gyan scored; Victorino scored, Appiah scored; Scotti scored, John Mensah saved; Pereira M missed, Adiyiah saved; Abreu scored.

Cape Town Stadium, Cape Town, 3 July 2010
Argentina (0) 0
Germany (1) 4 *(Muller 3, Klose 68, 89, Friedrich 74)*   64,100
Argentina: Romero; Demichelis, Burdisso, Heinze, Otamendi (Pastore 69), Di Maria (Aguero 75), Mascherano, Maxi Rodriguez, Higuain, Messi, Tevez.
Germany: Neuer; Friedrich, Lahm, Mertesacker, Boateng (Jansen 72), Khedira (Kroos 78), Schweinsteiger, Ozil, Podolski, Klose, Muller (Trochowski 84).
Referee: Irmatov (Uzbekistan).

Ellis Park Stadium, Johannesburg, 3 July 2010
Paraguay (0) 0
Spain (0) 1 *(David Villa 83)*   55,395
Paraguay: Villar; Veron, Morel, Da Silva, Alcaraz, Barreto E (Vera 64), Santana, Caceres V (Barrios 85), Riveros, Cardozo, Valdez (Santa Cruz 72).
Spain: Casillas; Pique, Puyol (Marchena 85), Capdevila, Sergio Ramos, Iniesta, Xavi, Xabi Alonso (Pedro 74), Busquets, David Villa, Torres (Fabregas 57).
Referee: Batres (Guatemala).

SEMI-FINALS

Cape Town Stadium, Cape Town, 6 July 2010
Uruguay (1) 2 *(Forlan 41, Pereira M 90)*
Holland (1) 3 *(Van Bronckhorst 18, Sneijder 70,*
Robben 73)   62,479
Uruguay: Muslera; Godin, Victorino, Pereira M, Caceres, Gargano, Pereira A (Abreu 78), Perez, Arevalo, Cavani, Forlan (Fernandez S 84).
Holland: Stekelenburg; Heitinga, Mathijsen, Boulahrouz, Van Bronckhorst, Van Bommel, Sneijder, De Zeeuw (Van der Vaart 46), Kuyt, Van Persie, Robben (Elia 89).
Referee: Irmatov (Uzbekistan).

Moses Mabhida, Durban, 7 July 2010
Germany (0) 0
Spain (0) 1 *(Puyol 73)*   60,960
Germany: Neuer; Friedrich, Lahm, Mertesacker, Boateng (Jansen 52), Khedira (Gomez 81), Schweinsteiger, Ozil, Trochowski (Kroos 62), Podolski, Klose.
Spain: Casillas; Pique, Puyol, Capdevila, Sergio Ramos, Iniesta, Xavi, Xabi Alonso (Marchena 90), Busquets, David Villa (Torres 81), Pedro (Silva 86).
Referee: Kassai (Hungary).

MATCH FOR THIRD PLACE

Nelson Mandela Bay, Port Elizabeth, 10 July 2010
Uruguay (1) 2 *(Cavani 28, Forlan 51)*
Germany (1) 3 *(Muller 18, Jansen 56, Khedira 82)* 36,254
Uruguay: Muslera; Lugano, Godin, Fucile, Pereira M, Caceres, Perez (Gargano 77), Arevalo, Cavani (Abreu 89), Suarez, Forlan.
Germany: Butt; Jansen (Kroos 80), Friedrich, Aogo, Mertesacker, Boateng, Khedira, Schweinsteiger, Ozil (Tasci 90), Muller, Cacau (Kiessling 73).
Referee: Archundia (Mexico).

WORLD CUP FINAL 2010

Sunday, 11 July 2010

Holland (0) 0   Spain (0) 1

First National Bank Stadium, Johannesburg, attendance 84,490

Holland: Stekelenburg; Van der Wiel, Heitingaj, Mathijsen, Van Bronckhorst (Braafheid 105), Van Bommel, De Jong (Van der Vaart 99), Sneijder, Kuyt (Elia 71), Van Persie, Robben.
Spain: Casillas; Pique, Puyol, Capdevila, Sergio Ramos, Iniesta, Xavi, Xabi Alonso (Fabregas 87), Busquets, David Villa (Torres 106), Pedro (Jesus Navas 60).
Scorer: Iniesta 116.
aet.
Referee: Webb (England).

WORLD CUP FINALS 2010 – STATISTICS

- Diego Forlan of Uruguay was named Player of the Tournament in South Africa.
- Although four players finished level with five goals in the 2010 finals, the Golden Boot was awarded to Thomas Muller of Germany because he had contributed three assists. David Villa (Spain) was awarded the Silver for playing fewer minutes than Wesley Sneijder (Holland) whose Bronze was thanks to having played fewer minutes than Diego Forlan (Uruguay)!
- Milestone goals in South Africa: the 37th goal scored by Javier Hernandez for Mexico v France was the 2100th overall goal in the history of the final competition. The 137th goal scored by Arjen Robben was the 2200th.
- Switzerland who defeated Spain in their opening fixture went on to complete a record 559 minutes without conceding a goal having started this sequence in 1994 and continued it in 2006. In the 2006 and 2010 finals they had a record five consecutive clean sheets.
- The longest sequence without conceding a goal was achieved by Walter Zenga the Italian goalkeeper in the 1990 finals when he went 517 minutes without being beaten.
- Spain, the 12th different team to reach the final, became the first country to win the World Cup having lost its opening match.
- Spain became the first European country to win the trophy outside of its own continent.
- Spain needed only eight goals to win the competition in 2010, the fewest on record. The average number of goals per match for them was 1.14.
- David James became the oldest player to make his first appearance in a World Cup final tournament at the age of 39 years 321 days when he played for England against Algeria on 18 June.
- England holds the record for on three occasions being eliminated from the finals without losing an actual match. It happened in 1982, 1990 and 2006.
- In 1954 the winning team West Germany had conceded the most goals of a team being successful (14), while the losers Hungary had recorded the highest average of goals per game at 5.40.
- Hungary's average number of goals scored in 1954 was actually higher than the average total for the tournament at 5.38.
- Brazil is the only country to have featured in all 19 finals. They have won the most times (5), won the most matches (67) and scored the most goals (210). In addition they achieved the most wins with seven in 2002. They remained unbeaten in seven of the tournaments.
- Most goals scored in one final tournament was 171 in 1998. In 2010 the figure was 145.
- There were 260 yellow cards shown in the 2010 World Cup finals.
- Only 17 red cards were shown in South Africa.
- The final between Spain and Holland produced the most cards in a final tournament match: 14 yellow and one red.
- The most red cards issued in a final tournament was 28 in 2006. There was also a record 345 yellow cards.
- A total of 145 goals were scored in the 2010 finals for an average of 2.27 per game.
- The record number of goals scored in a tournament was 171 in 1998.
- New Zealand in 1982 travelled the longest distance in order to qualify for the finals. They covered 55,000 miles.
- Bora Milutinovic coached Mexico in 1986, Costa Rica in 1990, USA in 1994, Nigeria in 1998 and China in 2002. Carlos Alberto Parreira coached Kuwait in 1982, UAE in 1990, Brazil in 1994 and 2006, Saudi Arabia in 1998 and South Africa in 2010.

THE WORLD CUP 1930–2010

Year	Winners		Runners-up		Venue	Attendance	Referee
1930	Uruguay	4	Argentina	2	Montevideo	90,000	Langenus (B)
1934	Italy*	2	Czechoslovakia	1	Rome	50,000	Eklind (Se)
1938	Italy	4	Hungary	2	Paris	45,000	Capdeville (F)
1950	Uruguay	2	Brazil	1	Rio de Janeiro	199,854	Reader (E)
1954	West Germany	3	Hungary	2	Berne	60,000	Ling (E)
1958	Brazi	5	Sweden	2	Stockholm	49,737	Guigue (F)
1962	Brazil	3	Czechoslovakia	1	Santiago	68,679	Latychev (USSR)
1966	England*	4	West Germany	2	Wembley	93,802	Dienst (Sw)
1970	Brazil	4	Italy	1	Mexico City	107,412	Glockner (EG)
1974	West Germany	2	Holland	1	Munich	77,833	Taylor (E)
1978	Argentina*	3	Holland	1	Buenos Aires	77,000	Gonella (I)
1982	Italy	3	West Germany	1	Madrid	90,080	Coelho (Br)
1986	Argentina	3	West Germany	2	Mexico City	114,580	Filho (Br)
1990	West Germany	1	Argentina	0	Rome	73,603	Mendez (Mex)
1994	Brazil*	0	Italy	0	Los Angeles	94,194	Puhl (H)
	(Brazil won 3-2 on penalties)						
1998	France	3	Brazil	0	St-Denis	75,000	Belqola (Mor)
2002	Brazil	2	Germany	0	Yokohama	69,029	Collina (I)
2006	Italy*	1	France	1	Berlin	69,000	Elizondo (Arg)
	(Italy won 5-3 on penalties)						
2010	Spain	1	Holland	0	Johannesburg	84,490	Webb (E)
*(*After extra time)*							

GOALSCORING AND ATTENDANCES IN WORLD CUP FINAL ROUNDS

Venue	Matches	Goals (av)	Attendance (av)
1930 Uruguay	18	70 (3.9)	434,500 (24,138)
1934 Italy	17	70 (4.1)	395,000 (23,235)
1938 France	18	84 (4.6)	483,000 (26,833)
1950 Brazil	22	88 (4.0)	1,337,000 (60,772)
1954 Switzerland	26	140 (5.4)	943,000 (36,270)
1958 Sweden	35	126 (3.6)	868,000 (24,800)
1962 Chile	32	89 (2.8)	776,000 (24,250)
1966 England	32	89 (2.8)	1,614,677 (50,458)
1970 Mexico	32	95 (2.9)	1,673,975 (52,311)
1974 West Germany	38	97 (2.5)	1,774,022 (46,684)
1978 Argentina	38	102 (2.7)	1,610,215 (42,374)
1982 Spain	52	146 (2.8)	2,064,364 (38,816)
1986 Mexico	52	132 (2.5)	2,441,731 (46,956)
1990 Italy	52	115 (2.2)	2,515,168 (48,368)
1994 USA	52	141 (2.7)	3,567,415 (68,604)
1998 France	64	171 (2.6)	2,775,400 (43,366)
2002 Japan/S. Korea	64	161 (2.5)	2,705,566 (42,274)
2006 Germany	64	147 (2.3)	3,354,646 (52,416)
2010 South Africa	64	145 (2.3)	3,178,856 (49,670)

LEADING GOALSCORERS

Year	Player	Goals
1930	Guillermo Stabile (Argentina)	8
1934	Angelo Schiavio (Italy), Oldrich Nejedly (Czechoslovakia), Edmund Conen (Germany)	4
1938	Leonidas da Silva (Brazil)	8
1950	Ademir (Brazil)	9
1954	Sandor Kocsis (Hungary)	11
1958	Just Fontaine (France)	13
1962	Valentin Ivanov (USSR), Leonel Sanchez (Chile), Garrincha, Vava (both Brazil), Florian Albert (Hungary), Drazen Jerkovic (Yugoslavia)	4
1966	Eusebio (Portugal)	9
1970	Gerd Muller (West Germany)	10
1974	Grzegorz Lato (Poland)	7
1978	Mario Kempes (Argentina)	6
1982	Paolo Rossi (Italy)	6
1986	Gary Lineker (England)	6
1990	Salvatore Schillaci (Italy)	6
1994	Oleg Salenko (Russia), Hristo Stoichkov (Bulgaria)	6
1998	Davor Suker (Croatia)	6
2002	Ronaldo (Brazil)	8
2006	Miroslav Klose (Germany)	5
2010	Thomas Muller (Germany), David Villa (Spain), Wesley Sneijder (Holland), Diego Forlan (Uruguay)	5

EUROPEAN FOOTBALL CHAMPIONSHIP
(formerly EUROPEAN NATIONS' CUP)

Year	Winners		Runners-up		Venue	Attendance
1960	USSR	2	Yugoslavia	1	Paris	17,966
1964	Spain	2	USSR	1	Madrid	120,000
1968	Italy	2	Yugoslavia	0	Rome	60,000
	After 1-1 draw					75,000
1972	West Germany	3	USSR	0	Brussels	43,437
1976	Czechoslovakia	2	West Germany	2	Belgrade	45,000
	(Czechoslovakia won on penalties)					
1980	West Germany	2	Belgium	1	Rome	47,864
1984	France	2	Spain	0	Paris	48,000
1988	Holland	2	USSR	0	Munich	72,308
1992	Denmark	2	Germany	0	Gothenburg	37,800
1996	Germany	2	Czech Republic	1	Wembley	73,611
	(Germany won on sudden death)					
2000	France	2	Italy	1	Rotterdam	50,000
	(France won on sudden death)					
2004	Greece	1	Portugal	0	Lisbon	62,865
2008	Spain	1	Germany	0	Vienna	51,428

EURO 2012 FIXTURES

11 AUGUST 2010
Group C Estonia v Faeroe Islands

03 SEPTEMBER 2010
Group A Belgium v Germany
Group A Kazakhstan v Turkey
Group B Slovakia v FYR Macedonia
Group B Armenia v Republic of Ireland
Group B Andorra v Russia
Group C Slovenia v Northern Ireland
Group C Estonia v Italy
Group C Faeroe Islands v Serbia
Group D France v Belarus
Group D Romania v Albania
Group D Luxembourg v Bosnia-Herzegovina
Group E Sweden v Hungary
Group E Moldova v Finland
Group E San Marino v Netherlands
Group F Greece v Georgia
Group F Israel v Malta
Group F Latvia v Croatia
Group G England v Bulgaria
Group G Montenegro v Wales
Group H Portugal v Cyprus
Group H Iceland v Norway
Group I Lithuania v Scotland
Group I Liechtenstein v Spain

07 SEPTEMBER 2010
Group A Germany v Azerbaijan
Group A Turkey v Belgium
Group A Austria v Kazakhstan
Group B Russia v Slovakia
Group B Republic of Ireland v Andorra
Group B FYR Macedonia v Armenia
Group C Italy v Faeroe Islands
Group C Serbia v Slovenia
Group D Bosnia-Herzegovina v France
Group D Belarus v Romania
Group D Albania v Luxembourg
Group E Netherlands v Finland
Group E Sweden v San Marino
Group E Hungary v Moldova
Group F Croatia v Greece
Group F Georgia v Israel
Group F Malta v Latvia
Group G Switzerland v England
Group G Bulgaria v Montenegro
Group H Denmark v Iceland
Group H Norway v Portugal
Group I Czech Republic v Lithuania
Group I Scotland v Liechtenstein

08 OCTOBER 2010
Group A Germany v Turkey
Group A Austria v Azerbaijan
Group A Kazakhstan v Belgium
Group B Republic of Ireland v Russia
Group B Armenia v Slovakia
Group B Andorra v FYR Macedonia
Group C Serbia v Estonia
Group C Northern Ireland v Italy
Group C Slovenia v Faeroe Islands
Group D Albania v Bosnia-Herzegovina
Group D Luxembourg v Belarus
Group E Hungary v San Marino
Group E Moldova v Netherlands
Group F Greece v Latvia
Group F Georgia v Malta

Group G Wales v Bulgaria
Group G Montenegro v Switzerland
Group H Portugal v Denmark
Group H Cyprus v Norway
Group I Spain v Lithuania
Group I Czech Republic v Scotland

09 OCTOBER 2010
Group D France v Romania
Group F Israel v Croatia

12 OCTOBER 2010
Group A Belgium v Austria
Group A Kazakhstan v Germany
Group A Azerbaijan v Turkey
Group B Slovakia v Republic of Ireland
Group B FYR Macedonia v Russia
Group B Armenia v Andorra
Group C Italy v Serbia
Group C Estonia v Slovenia
Group C Faeroe Islands v Northern Ireland
Group D France v Luxembourg
Group D Belarus v Albania
Group E Netherlands v Sweden
Group E Finland v Hungary
Group E San Marino v Moldova
Group F Croatia v Malta
Group F Greece v Israel
Group F Latvia v Georgia
Group G England v Montenegro
Group G Switzerland v Wales
Group H Denmark v Cyprus
Group H Iceland v Portugal
Group I Liechtenstein v Czech Republic
Group I Scotland v Spain

17 NOVEMBER 2010
Group E Finland v San Marino

25 MARCH 2011
Group A Germany v Kazakhstan
Group A Austria v Belgium
Group C Serbia v Northern Ireland
Group C Slovenia v Italy
Group D Luxembourg v France
Group E Hungary v Netherlands
Group I Spain v Czech Republic

26 MARCH 2011
Group B Republic of Ireland v FYR Macedonia
Group B Armenia v Russia
Group B Andorra v Slovakia
Group D Bosnia-Herzegovina v Romania
Group D Albania v Belarus
Group F Israel v Latvia
Group F Georgia v Croatia
Group F Malta v Greece
Group G Bulgaria v Switzerland
Group G Wales v England
Group H Norway v Denmark
Group H Cyprus v Iceland

29 MARCH 2011
Group A Turkey v Austria
Group A Belgium v Azerbaijan
Group C Northern Ireland v Slovenia
Group C Estonia v Serbia

Group D Romania v Luxembourg
Group E Netherlands v Hungary
Group E Sweden v Moldova
Group F Israel v Georgia
Group I Czech Republic v Liechtenstein
Group I Lithuania v Spain

03 JUNE 2011
Group A Austria v Germany
Group A Belgium v Turkey
Group A Kazakhstan v Azerbaijan
Group C Italy v Estonia
Group C Faeroe Islands v Slovenia
Group D Romania v Bosnia-Herzegovina
Group D Belarus v France
Group E Moldova v Sweden
Group E San Marino v Finland
Group I Liechtenstein v Lithuania

04 JUNE 2011
Group B Russia v Armenia
Group B Slovakia v Andorra
Group B FYR Macedonia v Republic of Ireland
Group F Croatia v Georgia
Group F Greece v Malta
Group F Latvia v Israel
Group G England v Switzerland
Group G Montenegro v Bulgaria
Group H Portugal v Norway
Group H Iceland v Denmark

07 JUNE 2011
Group A Azerbaijan v Germany
Group C Faeroe Islands v Estonia
Group D Bosnia-Herzegovina v Albania
Group D Belarus v Luxembourg
Group E Sweden v Finland
Group E San Marino v Hungary

10 AUGUST 2011
Group C Northern Ireland v Faeroe Islands

02 SEPTEMBER 2011
Group A Germany v Austria
Group A Turkey v Kazakhstan
Group A Azerbaijan v Belgium
Group B Russia v FYR Macedonia
Group B Republic of Ireland v Slovakia
Group B Andorra v Armenia
Group C Northern Ireland v Serbia
Group C Slovenia v Estonia
Group C Faeroe Islands v Italy
Group D Belarus v Bosnia-Herzegovina
Group D Albania v France
Group D Luxembourg v Romania
Group E Netherlands v San Marino
Group E Finland v Moldova
Group E Hungary v Sweden
Group F Israel v Greece
Group F Georgia v Latvia
Group F Malta v Croatia
Group G Bulgaria v England
Group G Wales v Montenegro
Group H Norway v Iceland
Group H Cyprus v Portugal
Group I Lithuania v Liechtenstein

03 SEPTEMBER 2011
Group I Scotland v Czech Republic

06 SEPTEMBER 2011
Group A Austria v Turkey
Group A Azerbaijan v Kazakhstan
Group B Russia v Republic of Ireland
Group B Slovakia v Armenia
Group B FYR Macedonia v Andorra
Group C Italy v Slovenia
Group C Serbia v Faeroe Islands
Group C Estonia v Northern Ireland
Group D Romania v France
Group D Bosnia-Herzegovina v Belarus
Group D Luxembourg v Albania
Group E Finland v Netherlands
Group E Moldova v Hungary
Group E San Marino v Sweden
Group F Croatia v Israel
Group F Latvia v Greece
Group F Malta v Georgia
Group G England v Wales
Group G Switzerland v Bulgaria
Group H Denmark v Norway
Group H Iceland v Cyprus
Group I Spain v Liechtenstein
Group I Scotland v Lithuania

07 OCTOBER 2011
Group A Turkey v Germany
Group A Belgium v Kazakhstan
Group A Azerbaijan v Austria
Group E Netherlands v Moldova
Group E Finland v Sweden
Group B Slovakia v Russia
Group B Armenia v FYR Macedonia
Group B Andorra v Republic of Ireland
Group C Serbia v Italy
Group C Northern Ireland v Estonia
Group D France v Albania
Group D Romania v Belarus
Group D Bosnia-Herzegovina v Luxembourg
Group F Greece v Croatia
Group F Latvia v Malta
Group G Wales v Switzerland
Group G Montenegro v England
Group H Portugal v Iceland
Group H Cyprus v Denmark
Group I Czech Republic v Spain

08 OCTOBER 2011
Group I Liechtenstein v Scotland

11 OCTOBER 2011
Group A Germany v Belgium
Group A Turkey v Azerbaijan
Group A Kazakhstan v Austria
Group B Russia v Andorra
Group B Republic of Ireland v Armenia
Group B FYR Macedonia v Slovakia
Group C Italy v Northern Ireland
Group C Slovenia v Serbia
Group D France v Bosnia-Herzegovina
Group D Albania v Romania
Group E Sweden v Netherlands
Group E Hungary v Finland
Group E Moldova v San Marino
Group F Croatia v Latvia
Group F Georgia v Greece
Group F Malta v Israel
Group G Switzerland v Montenegro
Group G Bulgaria v Wales
Group H Denmark v Portugal
Group H Norway v Cyprus
Group I Spain v Scotland
Group I Lithuania v Czech Republic

BRITISH AND IRISH INTERNATIONAL RESULTS 1872–2010

Note: In the results that follow, wc=World Cup, ec=European Championship, ui=Umbro International Trophy. tf = Tournoi de France. For Ireland, read Northern Ireland from 1921. *After extra time.

ENGLAND v SCOTLAND

Played: 110; England won 45, Scotland won 41, Drawn 24. Goals: England 192, Scotland 169.

Year	Date	Venue	E	S	Year	Date	Venue	E	S
1872	30 Nov	Glasgow	0	0	1932	9 Apr	Wembley	3	0
1873	8 Mar	Kennington Oval	4	2	1933	1 Apr	Glasgow	1	2
1874	7 Mar	Glasgow	1	2	1934	14 Apr	Wembley	3	0
1875	6 Mar	Kennington Oval	2	2	1935	6 Apr	Glasgow	0	2
1876	4 Mar	Glasgow	0	3	1936	4 Apr	Wembley	1	1
1877	3 Mar	Kennington Oval	1	3	1937	17 Apr	Glasgow	1	3
1878	2 Mar	Glasgow	2	7	1938	9 Apr	Wembley	0	1
1879	5 Apr	Kennington Oval	5	4	1939	15 Apr	Glasgow	2	1
1880	13 Mar	Glasgow	4	5	1947	12 Apr	Wembley	1	1
1881	12 Mar	Kennington Oval	1	6	1948	10 Apr	Glasgow	2	0
1882	11 Mar	Glasgow	1	5	1949	9 Apr	Wembley	1	3
1883	10 Mar	Sheffield	2	3	wc1950	15 Apr	Glasgow	1	0
1884	15 Mar	Glasgow	0	1	1951	14 Apr	Wembley	2	3
1885	21 Mar	Kennington Oval	1	1	1952	5 Apr	Glasgow	2	1
1886	31 Mar	Glasgow	1	1	1953	18 Apr	Wembley	2	2
1887	19 Mar	Blackburn	2	3	wc1954	3 Apr	Glasgow	4	2
1888	17 Mar	Glasgow	5	0	1955	2 Apr	Wembley	7	2
1889	13 Apr	Kennington Oval	2	3	1956	14 Apr	Glasgow	1	1
1890	5 Apr	Glasgow	1	1	1957	6 Apr	Wembley	2	1
1891	6 Apr	Blackburn	2	1	1958	19 Apr	Glasgow	4	0
1892	2 Apr	Glasgow	4	1	1959	11 Apr	Wembley	1	0
1893	1 Apr	Richmond	5	2	1960	9 Apr	Glasgow	1	1
1894	7 Apr	Glasgow	2	2	1961	15 Apr	Wembley	9	3
1895	6 Apr	Everton	3	0	1962	14 Apr	Glasgow	0	2
1896	4 Apr	Glasgow	1	2	1963	6 Apr	Wembley	1	2
1897	3 Apr	Crystal Palace	1	2	1964	11 Apr	Glasgow	0	1
1898	2 Apr	Glasgow	3	1	1965	10 Apr	Wembley	2	2
1899	8 Apr	Birmingham	2	1	1966	2 Apr	Glasgow	4	3
1900	7 Apr	Glasgow	1	4	ec1967	15 Apr	Wembley	2	3
1901	30 Mar	Crystal Palace	2	2	ec1968	24 Jan	Glasgow	1	1
1902	3 Mar	Birmingham	2	2	1969	10 May	Wembley	4	1
1903	4 Apr	Sheffield	1	2	1970	25 Apr	Glasgow	0	0
1904	9 Apr	Glasgow	1	0	1971	22 May	Wembley	3	1
1905	1 Apr	Crystal Palace	1	0	1972	27 May	Glasgow	1	0
1906	7 Apr	Glasgow	1	2	1973	14 Feb	Glasgow	5	0
1907	6 Apr	Newcastle	1	1	1973	19 May	Wembley	1	0
1908	4 Apr	Glasgow	1	1	1974	18 May	Glasgow	0	2
1909	3 Apr	Crystal Palace	2	0	1975	24 May	Wembley	5	1
1910	2 Apr	Glasgow	0	2	1976	15 May	Glasgow	1	2
1911	1 Apr	Everton	1	1	1977	4 June	Wembley	1	2
1912	23 Mar	Glasgow	1	1	1978	20 May	Glasgow	1	0
1913	5 Apr	Chelsea	1	0	1979	26 May	Wembley	3	1
1914	14 Apr	Glasgow	1	3	1980	24 May	Glasgow	2	0
1920	10 Apr	Sheffield	5	4	1981	23 May	Wembley	0	1
1921	9 Apr	Glasgow	0	3	1982	29 May	Glasgow	1	0
1922	8 Apr	Aston Villa	0	1	1983	1 June	Wembley	2	0
1923	14 Apr	Glasgow	2	2	1984	26 May	Glasgow	1	1
1924	12 Apr	Wembley	1	1	1985	25 May	Glasgow	0	1
1925	4 Apr	Glasgow	0	2	1986	23 Apr	Wembley	2	1
1926	17 Apr	Manchester	0	1	1987	23 May	Glasgow	0	0
1927	2 Apr	Glasgow	2	1	1988	21 May	Wembley	1	0
1928	31 Mar	Wembley	1	5	1989	27 May	Glasgow	2	0
1929	13 Apr	Glasgow	0	1	ec1996	15 June	Wembley	2	0
1930	5 Apr	Wembley	5	2	ec1999	13 Nov	Glasgow	2	0
1931	28 Mar	Glasgow	0	2	ec1999	17 Nov	Wembley	0	1

ENGLAND v WALES

Played: 99; England won 64, Wales won 14, Drawn 21. Goals: England 242, Wales 90.

Year	Date	Venue	E	W	Year	Date	Venue	E	W
1879	18 Jan	Kennington Oval	2	1	1882	13 Mar	Wrexham	3	5
1880	15 Mar	Wrexham	3	2	1883	3 Feb	Kennington Oval	5	0
1881	26 Feb	Blackburn	0	1	1884	17 Mar	Wrexham	4	0

Year	Date	Venue	E	W		Year	Date	Venue	E	W
1885	14 Mar	Blackburn	1	1		1934	29 Sept	Cardiff	4	0
1886	29 Mar	Wrexham	3	1		1936	5 Feb	Wolverhampton	1	2
1887	26 Feb	Kennington Oval	4	0		1936	17 Oct	Cardiff	1	2
1888	4 Feb	Crewe	5	1		1937	17 Nov	Middlesbrough	2	1
1889	23 Feb	Stoke	4	1		1938	22 Oct	Cardiff	2	4
1890	15 Mar	Wrexham	3	1		1946	13 Nov	Manchester	3	0
1891	7 May	Sunderland	4	1		1947	18 Oct	Cardiff	3	0
1892	5 Mar	Wrexham	2	0		1948	10 Nov	Aston Villa	1	0
1893	13 Mar	Stoke	6	0		wc1949	15 Oct	Cardiff	4	1
1894	12 Mar	Wrexham	5	1		1950	15 Nov	Sunderland	4	2
1895	18 Mar	Queen's Club, Kensington	1	1		1951	20 Oct	Cardiff	1	1
1896	16 Mar	Cardiff	9	1		1952	12 Nov	Wembley	5	2
1897	29 Mar	Sheffield	4	0		wc1953	10 Oct	Cardiff	4	1
1898	28 Mar	Wrexham	3	0		1954	10 Nov	Wembley	3	2
1899	20 Mar	Bristol	4	0		1955	27 Oct	Cardiff	1	2
1900	26 Mar	Cardiff	1	1		1956	14 Nov	Wembley	3	1
1901	18 Mar	Newcastle	6	0		1957	19 Oct	Cardiff	4	0
1902	3 Mar	Wrexham	0	0		1958	26 Nov	Aston Villa	2	2
1903	2 Mar	Portsmouth	2	1		1959	17 Oct	Cardiff	1	1
1904	29 Feb	Wrexham	2	2		1960	23 Nov	Wembley	5	1
1905	27 Mar	Liverpool	3	1		1961	14 Oct	Cardiff	1	1
1906	19 Mar	Cardiff	1	0		1962	21 Oct	Wembley	4	0
1907	18 Mar	Fulham	1	1		1963	12 Oct	Cardiff	4	0
1908	16 Mar	Wrexham	7	1		1964	18 Nov	Wembley	2	1
1909	15 Mar	Nottingham	2	0		1965	2 Oct	Cardiff	0	0
1910	14 Mar	Cardiff	1	0		EC1966	16 Nov	Wembley	5	1
1911	13 Mar	Millwall	3	0		EC1967	21 Oct	Cardiff	3	0
1912	11 Mar	Wrexham	2	0		1969	7 May	Wembley	2	1
1913	17 Mar	Bristol	4	3		1970	18 Apr	Cardiff	1	1
1914	16 Mar	Cardiff	2	0		1971	19 May	Wembley	0	0
1920	15 Mar	Highbury	1	2		1972	20 May	Cardiff	3	0
1921	14 Mar	Cardiff	0	0		wc1972	15 Nov	Cardiff	1	0
1922	13 Mar	Liverpool	1	0		wc1973	24 Jan	Wembley	1	1
1923	5 Mar	Cardiff	2	2		1973	15 May	Wembley	3	0
1924	3 Mar	Blackburn	1	2		1974	11 May	Cardiff	2	0
1925	28 Feb	Swansea	2	1		1975	21 May	Wembley	2	2
1926	1 Mar	Crystal Palace	1	3		1976	24 Mar	Wrexham	2	1
1927	12 Feb	Wrexham	3	3		1976	8 May	Cardiff	1	0
1927	28 Nov	Burnley	1	2		1977	31 May	Wembley	0	1
1928	17 Nov	Swansea	3	2		1978	3 May	Cardiff	3	1
1929	20 Nov	Chelsea	6	0		1979	23 May	Wembley	0	0
1930	22 Nov	Wrexham	4	0		1980	17 May	Wrexham	1	4
1931	18 Nov	Liverpool	3	1		1981	20 May	Wembley	0	0
1932	16 Nov	Wrexham	0	0		1982	27 Apr	Cardiff	1	0
1933	15 Nov	Newcastle	1	2		1983	23 Feb	Wembley	2	1
						1984	2 May	Wrexham	0	1
						wc2004	9 Oct	Old Trafford	2	0
						wc2005	3 Sept	Cardiff	1	0

ENGLAND v IRELAND

Played: 98; England won 75, Ireland won 7, Drawn 16. Goals: England 323, Ireland 81.

Year	Date	Venue	E	I		Year	Date	Venue	E	I
1882	18 Feb	Belfast	13	0		1903	14 Feb	Wolverhampton	4	0
1883	24 Feb	Liverpool	7	0		1904	12 Mar	Belfast	3	1
1884	23 Feb	Belfast	8	1		1905	25 Feb	Middlesbrough	1	1
1885	28 Feb	Manchester	4	0		1906	17 Feb	Belfast	5	0
1886	13 Mar	Belfast	6	1		1907	16 Feb	Everton	1	0
1887	5 Feb	Sheffield	7	0		1908	15 Feb	Belfast	3	1
1888	31 Mar	Belfast	5	1		1909	13 Feb	Bradford	4	0
1889	2 Mar	Everton	6	1		1910	12 Feb	Belfast	1	1
1890	15 Mar	Belfast	9	1		1911	11 Feb	Derby	2	1
1891	7 Mar	Wolverhampton	6	1		1912	10 Feb	Dublin	6	1
1892	5 Mar	Belfast	2	0		1913	15 Feb	Belfast	1	2
1893	25 Feb	Birmingham	6	1		1914	14 Feb	Middlesbrough	0	3
1894	3 Mar	Belfast	2	2		1919	25 Oct	Belfast	1	1
1895	9 Mar	Derby	9	0		1920	23 Oct	Sunderland	2	0
1896	7 Mar	Belfast	2	0		1921	22 Oct	Belfast	1	1
1897	20 Feb	Nottingham	6	0		1922	21 Oct	West Bromwich	2	0
1898	5 Mar	Belfast	3	2		1923	20 Oct	Belfast	1	2
1899	18 Feb	Sunderland	13	2		1924	22 Oct	Everton	3	1
1900	17 Mar	Dublin	2	0		1925	24 Oct	Belfast	0	0
1901	9 Mar	Southampton	3	0		1926	20 Oct	Liverpool	3	3
1902	22 Mar	Belfast	1	0		1927	22 Oct	Belfast	0	2

			E	I					E	I
1928	22 Oct	Everton	2	1		1962	20 Oct	Belfast	3	1
1929	19 Oct	Belfast	3	0		1963	20 Nov	Wembley	8	3
1930	20 Oct	Sheffield	5	1		1964	3 Oct	Belfast	4	3
1931	17 Oct	Belfast	6	2		1965	10 Nov	Wembley	2	1
1932	17 Oct	Blackpool	1	0		EC1966	20 Oct	Belfast	2	0
1933	14 Oct	Belfast	3	0		EC1967	22 Nov	Wembley	2	0
1935	6 Feb	Everton	2	1		1969	3 May	Belfast	3	1
1935	19 Oct	Belfast	3	1		1970	21 Apr	Wembley	3	1
1936	18 Nov	Stoke	3	1		1971	15 May	Belfast	1	0
1937	23 Oct	Belfast	5	1		1972	23 May	Wembley	0	1
1938	16 Nov	Manchester	7	0		1973	12 May	Everton	2	1
1946	28 Sept	Belfast	7	2		1974	15 May	Wembley	1	0
1947	5 Nov	Everton	2	2		1975	17 May	Belfast	0	0
1948	9 Oct	Belfast	6	2		1976	11 May	Wembley	4	0
wc1949	16 Nov	Manchester	9	2		1977	28 May	Belfast	2	1
1950	7 Oct	Belfast	4	1		1978	16 May	Wembley	1	0
1951	14 Nov	Aston Villa	2	0		EC1979	7 Feb	Wembley	4	0
1952	4 Oct	Belfast	2	2		1979	19 May	Belfast	2	0
wc1953	11 Nov	Everton	3	1		EC1979	17 Oct	Belfast	5	1
1954	2 Oct	Belfast	2	0		1980	20 May	Wembley	1	1
1955	2 Nov	Wembley	3	0		1982	23 Feb	Wembley	4	0
1956	10 Oct	Belfast	1	1		1983	28 May	Belfast	0	0
1957	6 Nov	Wembley	2	3		1984	24 Apr	Wembley	1	0
1958	4 Oct	Belfast	3	3		wc1985	27 Feb	Belfast	1	0
1959	18 Nov	Wembley	2	1		wc1985	13 Nov	Wembley	0	0
1960	8 Oct	Belfast	5	2		EC1986	15 Oct	Wembley	3	0
1961	22 Nov	Wembley	1	1		EC1987	1 Apr	Belfast	2	0
						wc2005	26 Mar	Old Trafford	4	0
						wc2005	7 Sept	Belfast	0	1

SCOTLAND v WALES

Played: 104; Scotland won 60, Wales won 21, Drawn 23. Goals: Scotland 238, Wales 119.

			S	W					S	W
1876	25 Mar	Glasgow	4	0		1923	17 Mar	Paisley	2	0
1877	5 Mar	Wrexham	2	0		1924	16 Feb	Cardiff	0	2
1878	23 Mar	Glasgow	9	0		1925	14 Feb	Tynecastle	3	1
1879	7 Apr	Wrexham	3	0		1925	31 Oct	Cardiff	3	0
1880	3 Apr	Glasgow	5	1		1926	30 Oct	Glasgow	3	0
1881	14 Mar	Wrexham	5	1		1927	29 Oct	Wrexham	2	2
1882	25 Mar	Glasgow	5	0		1928	27 Oct	Glasgow	4	2
1883	12 Mar	Wrexham	3	0		1929	26 Oct	Cardiff	4	2
1884	29 Mar	Glasgow	4	1		1930	25 Oct	Glasgow	1	1
1885	23 Mar	Wrexham	8	1		1931	31 Oct	Wrexham	3	2
1886	10 Apr	Glasgow	4	1		1932	26 Oct	Edinburgh	2	5
1887	21 Mar	Wrexham	2	0		1933	4 Oct	Cardiff	2	3
1888	10 Mar	Edinburgh	5	1		1934	21 Nov	Aberdeen	3	2
1889	15 Apr	Wrexham	0	0		1935	5 Oct	Cardiff	1	1
1890	22 Mar	Paisley	5	0		1936	2 Dec	Dundee	1	2
1891	21 Mar	Wrexham	4	3		1937	30 Oct	Cardiff	1	2
1892	26 Mar	Edinburgh	6	1		1938	9 Nov	Edinburgh	3	2
1893	18 Mar	Wrexham	8	0		1945	19 Oct	Wrexham	1	3
1894	24 Mar	Kilmarnock	5	2		1947	12 Nov	Glasgow	1	2
1895	23 Mar	Wrexham	2	2		wc1948	23 Oct	Cardiff	3	1
1896	21 Mar	Dundee	4	0		1949	9 Nov	Glasgow	2	0
1897	20 Mar	Wrexham	2	2		1950	21 Oct	Cardiff	3	1
1898	19 Mar	Motherwell	5	2		1951	14 Nov	Glasgow	0	1
1899	18 Mar	Wrexham	6	0		wc1952	18 Oct	Cardiff	2	1
1900	3 Feb	Aberdeen	5	2		1953	4 Nov	Glasgow	3	3
1901	2 Mar	Wrexham	1	1		1954	16 Oct	Cardiff	1	0
1902	15 Mar	Greenock	5	1		1955	9 Nov	Glasgow	2	0
1903	9 Mar	Cardiff	1	0		1956	20 Oct	Cardiff	2	2
1904	12 Mar	Dundee	1	1		1957	13 Nov	Glasgow	1	1
1905	6 Mar	Wrexham	1	3		1958	18 Oct	Cardiff	3	0
1906	3 Mar	Edinburgh	0	2		1959	4 Nov	Glasgow	1	1
1907	4 Mar	Wrexham	0	1		1960	20 Oct	Cardiff	0	2
1908	7 Mar	Dundee	2	1		1961	8 Nov	Glasgow	2	0
1909	1 Mar	Wrexham	2	3		1962	20 Oct	Cardiff	3	2
1910	5 Mar	Kilmarnock	1	0		1963	20 Nov	Glasgow	2	1
1911	6 Mar	Cardiff	2	2		1964	3 Oct	Cardiff	2	3
1912	2 Mar	Tynecastle	1	0		EC1965	24 Nov	Glasgow	4	1
1913	3 Mar	Wrexham	0	0		EC1966	22 Oct	Cardiff	1	1
1914	28 Feb	Glasgow	0	0		1967	22 Nov	Glasgow	3	2
1920	26 Feb	Cardiff	1	1		1969	3 May	Wrexham	5	3
1921	12 Feb	Aberdeen	2	1						
1922	4 Feb	Wrexham	1	2						

			S	W					S	W
1970	22 Apr	Glasgow	0	0		1980	21 May	Glasgow	1	0
1971	15 May	Cardiff	0	0		1981	16 May	Swansea	0	2
1972	24 May	Glasgow	1	0		1982	24 May	Glasgow	1	0
1973	12 May	Wrexham	2	0		1983	28 May	Cardiff	2	0
1974	14 May	Glasgow	2	0		1984	28 Feb	Glasgow	2	1
1975	17 May	Cardiff	2	2		wc1985	27 Mar	Glasgow	0	1
1976	6 May	Glasgow	3	1		wc1985	10 Sept	Cardiff	1	1
wc1976	17 Nov	Glasgow	1	0		1997	27 May	Kilmarnock	0	1
1977	28 May	Wrexham	0	0		2004	18 Feb	Cardiff	0	4
wc1977	12 Oct	Liverpool	2	0		2009	14 Nov	Cardiff	0	3
1978	17 May	Glasgow	1	1						
1979	19 May	Cardiff	0	3						

SCOTLAND v IRELAND

Played: 94; Scotland won 62, Ireland won 15, Drawn 17. Goals: Scotland 257, Ireland 81.

			S	I					S	I
1884	26 Jan	Belfast	5	0		1934	20 Oct	Belfast	1	2
1885	14 Mar	Glasgow	8	2		1935	13 Nov	Edinburgh	2	1
1886	20 Mar	Belfast	7	2		1936	31 Oct	Belfast	3	1
1887	19 Feb	Glasgow	4	1		1937	10 Nov	Aberdeen	1	1
1888	24 Mar	Belfast	10	2		1938	8 Oct	Belfast	2	0
1889	9 Mar	Glasgow	7	0		1946	27 Nov	Glasgow	0	0
1890	29 Mar	Belfast	4	1		1947	4 Oct	Belfast	0	2
1891	28 Mar	Glasgow	2	1		1948	17 Nov	Glasgow	3	2
1892	19 Mar	Belfast	3	2		1949	1 Oct	Belfast	8	2
1893	25 Mar	Glasgow	6	1		1950	1 Nov	Glasgow	6	1
1894	31 Mar	Belfast	2	1		1951	6 Oct	Belfast	3	0
1895	30 Mar	Glasgow	3	1		1952	5 Nov	Glasgow	1	1
1896	28 Mar	Belfast	3	3		1953	3 Oct	Belfast	3	1
1897	27 Mar	Glasgow	5	1		1954	3 Nov	Glasgow	2	2
1898	26 Mar	Belfast	3	0		1955	8 Oct	Belfast	1	2
1899	25 Mar	Glasgow	9	1		1956	7 Nov	Glasgow	1	0
1900	3 Mar	Glasgow	3	0		1957	5 Oct	Belfast	1	1
1901	23 Feb	Glasgow	11	0		1958	5 Nov	Glasgow	2	2
1902	1 Mar	Belfast	5	1		1959	3 Oct	Belfast	4	0
1902	9 Aug	Belfast	3	0		1960	9 Nov	Glasgow	5	2
1903	21 Mar	Glasgow	0	2		1961	7 Oct	Belfast	6	1
1904	26 Mar	Dublin	1	1		1962	7 Nov	Glasgow	5	1
1905	18 Mar	Glasgow	4	0		1963	12 Oct	Belfast	1	2
1906	17 Mar	Dublin	1	0		1964	25 Nov	Glasgow	3	2
1907	16 Mar	Glasgow	3	0		1965	2 Oct	Belfast	2	3
1908	14 Mar	Dublin	5	0		1966	16 Nov	Glasgow	2	1
1909	15 Mar	Glasgow	5	0		1967	21 Oct	Belfast	0	1
1910	19 Mar	Belfast	0	1		1969	6 May	Glasgow	1	1
1911	18 Mar	Glasgow	2	0		1970	18 Apr	Belfast	1	0
1912	16 Mar	Belfast	4	1		1971	18 May	Glasgow	0	1
1913	15 Mar	Dublin	2	1		1972	20 May	Glasgow	2	0
1914	14 Mar	Belfast	1	1		1973	16 May	Glasgow	1	2
1920	13 Mar	Glasgow	3	0		1974	11 May	Glasgow	0	1
1921	26 Feb	Belfast	2	0		1975	20 May	Glasgow	3	0
1922	4 Mar	Glasgow	2	1		1976	8 May	Glasgow	3	0
1923	3 Mar	Belfast	1	0		1977	1 June	Glasgow	3	0
1924	1 Mar	Glasgow	2	0		1978	13 May	Glasgow	1	1
1925	28 Feb	Belfast	3	0		1979	22 May	Glasgow	1	0
1926	27 Feb	Glasgow	4	0		1980	17 May	Belfast	0	1
1927	26 Feb	Belfast	2	0		wc1981	25 Mar	Glasgow	1	1
1928	25 Feb	Glasgow	0	1		1981	19 May	Glasgow	2	0
1929	23 Feb	Belfast	7	3		wc1981	14 Oct	Belfast	0	0
1930	22 Feb	Glasgow	3	1		1982	28 Apr	Belfast	1	1
1931	21 Feb	Belfast	0	0		1983	24 May	Glasgow	0	0
1931	19 Sept	Glasgow	3	1		1983	13 Dec	Belfast	0	2
1932	12 Sept	Belfast	4	0		1992	19 Feb	Glasgow	1	0
1933	16 Sept	Glasgow	1	2		2008	20 Aug	Glasgow	0	0

WALES v IRELAND

Played: 93; Wales won 43, Ireland won 27, Drawn 23. Goals: Wales 187, Ireland 131.

			W	I					W	I
1882	25 Feb	Wrexham	7	1		1886	27 Feb	Wrexham	5	0
1883	17 Mar	Belfast	1	1		1887	12 Mar	Belfast	1	4
1884	9 Feb	Wrexham	6	0		1888	3 Mar	Wrexham	11	0
1885	11 Apr	Belfast	8	2		1889	27 Apr	Belfast	3	1

			W	I
1890	8 Feb	Shrewsbury	5	2
1891	7 Feb	Belfast	2	7
1892	27 Feb	Bangor	1	1
1893	8 Apr	Belfast	3	4
1894	24 Feb	Swansea	4	1
1895	16 Mar	Belfast	2	2
1896	29 Feb	Wrexham	6	1
1897	6 Mar	Belfast	3	4
1898	19 Feb	Llandudno	0	1
1899	4 Mar	Belfast	0	1
1900	24 Feb	Llandudno	2	0
1901	23 Mar	Belfast	1	0
1902	22 Mar	Cardiff	0	3
1903	28 Mar	Belfast	0	2
1904	21 Mar	Bangor	0	1
1905	8 Apr	Belfast	2	2
1906	2 Apr	Wrexham	4	4
1907	23 Feb	Belfast	3	2
1908	11 Apr	Aberdare	0	1
1909	20 Mar	Belfast	3	2
1910	11 Apr	Wrexham	4	1
1911	28 Jan	Belfast	2	1
1912	13 Apr	Cardiff	2	3
1913	18 Jan	Belfast	1	0
1914	19 Jan	Wrexham	1	2
1920	14 Feb	Belfast	2	2
1921	9 Apr	Swansea	2	1
1922	4 Apr	Belfast	1	1
1923	14 Apr	Wrexham	0	3
1924	15 Mar	Belfast	1	0
1925	18 Apr	Wrexham	0	0
1926	13 Feb	Belfast	0	3
1927	9 Apr	Cardiff	2	2
1928	4 Feb	Belfast	2	1
1929	2 Feb	Wrexham	2	2
1930	1 Feb	Belfast	0	7
1931	22 Apr	Wrexham	3	2
1931	5 Dec	Belfast	0	4
1932	7 Dec	Wrexham	4	1
1933	4 Nov	Belfast	1	1
1935	27 Mar	Wrexham	3	1
1936	11 Mar	Belfast	2	3
1937	17 Mar	Wrexham	4	1

			W	I
1938	16 Mar	Belfast	0	1
1939	15 Mar	Wrexham	3	1
1947	16 Apr	Belfast	1	2
1948	10 Mar	Wrexham	2	0
1949	9 Mar	Belfast	2	0
wc1950	8 Mar	Wrexham	0	0
1951	7 Mar	Belfast	2	1
1952	19 Mar	Swansea	3	0
1953	15 Apr	Belfast	3	2
wc1954	31 Mar	Wrexham	1	2
1955	20 Apr	Belfast	3	2
1956	11 Apr	Cardiff	1	1
1957	10 Apr	Belfast	0	0
1958	16 Apr	Cardiff	1	1
1959	22 Apr	Belfast	1	4
1960	6 Apr	Wrexham	3	2
1961	12 Apr	Belfast	5	1
1962	11 Apr	Cardiff	4	0
1963	3 Apr	Belfast	4	1
1964	15 Apr	Swansea	2	3
1965	31 Mar	Belfast	5	0
1966	30 Mar	Cardiff	1	4
EC1967	12 Apr	Belfast	0	0
EC1968	28 Feb	Wrexham	2	0
1969	10 May	Belfast	0	0
1970	25 Apr	Swansea	1	0
1971	22 May	Belfast	0	1
1972	27 May	Wrexham	0	0
1973	19 May	Everton	0	1
1974	18 May	Wrexham	1	0
1975	23 May	Belfast	0	1
1976	14 May	Swansea	1	0
1977	3 June	Belfast	1	1
1978	19 May	Wrexham	1	0
1979	25 May	Belfast	1	1
1980	23 May	Cardiff	0	1
1982	27 May	Wrexham	3	0
1983	31 May	Belfast	1	0
1984	22 May	Swansea	1	1
wc2004	8 Sept	Cardiff	2	2
wc2005	8 Oct	Belfast	3	2
2007	6 Feb	Belfast	0	0

OTHER BRITISH INTERNATIONAL RESULTS 1908–2010

ENGLAND

		v ALBANIA	E	A
wc1989	8 Mar	Tirana	2	0
wc1989	26 Apr	Wembley	5	0
wc2001	28 Mar	Tirana	3	1
wc2001	5 Sept	Newcastle	2	0

		v ALGERIA	E	A
wc2010	18 June	Cape Town	0	0

		v ANDORRA	E	A
EC2006	2 Sept	Old Trafford	5	0
EC2007	28 Mar	Barcelona	3	0
wc2008	6 Sept	Barcelona	2	0
wc2009	10 June	Wembley	6	0

		v ARGENTINA	E	A
1951	9 May	Wembley	2	1
1953	17 May	Buenos Aires	0	0
(abandoned after 21 mins)				
wc1962	2 June	Rancagua	3	1
1964	6 June	Rio de Janeiro	0	1
wc1966	23 July	Wembley	1	0
1974	22 May	Wembley	2	2
1977	12 June	Buenos Aires	1	1
1980	13 May	Wembley	3	1
wc1986	22 June	Mexico City	1	2
1991	25 May	Wembley	2	2
wc1998	30 June	St Etienne	2	2
2000	23 Feb	Wembley	0	0
wc2002	7 June	Sapporo	1	0
2005	12 Nov	Geneva	3	2

		v AUSTRALIA	E	A
1980	31 May	Sydney	2	1
1983	11 June	Sydney	0	0
1983	15 June	Brisbane	1	0
1983	18 June	Melbourne	1	1
1991	1 June	Sydney	1	0
2003	12 Feb	West Ham	1	3

		v AUSTRIA	E	A
1908	6 June	Vienna	6	1
1908	8 June	Vienna	11	1
1909	1 June	Vienna	8	1
1930	14 May	Vienna	0	0
1932	7 Dec	Chelsea	4	3
1936	6 May	Vienna	1	2
1951	28 Nov	Wembley	2	2
1952	25 May	Vienna	3	2
wc1958	15 June	Boras	2	2
1961	27 May	Vienna	1	3
1962	4 Apr	Wembley	3	1
1965	20 Oct	Wembley	2	3
1967	27 May	Vienna	1	0
1973	26 Sept	Wembley	7	0
1979	13 June	Vienna	3	4
wc2004	4 Sept	Vienna	2	2
wc2005	8 Oct	Old Trafford	1	0
2007	16 Nov	Vienna	1	0

		v AZERBAIJAN	E	A
wc2004	13 Oct	Baku	1	0
wc2005	30 Mar	Newcastle	2	0

		v BELARUS	E	B
wc2008	15 Oct	Minsk	3	1
wc2009	14 Oct	Wembley	3	0

		v BELGIUM	E	B
1921	21 May	Brussels	2	0
1923	19 Mar	Highbury	6	1
1923	1 Nov	Antwerp	2	2
1924	8 Dec	West Bromwich	4	0
1926	24 May	Antwerp	5	3
1927	11 May	Brussels	9	1
1928	19 May	Antwerp	3	1
1929	11 May	Brussels	5	1
1931	16 May	Brussels	4	1
1936	9 May	Brussels	2	3
1947	21 Sept	Brussels	5	2
1950	18 May	Brussels	4	1
1952	26 Nov	Wembley	5	0
wc1954	17 June	Basle	4	4*
1964	21 Oct	Wembley	2	2
1970	25 Feb	Brussels	3	1
EC1980	12 June	Turin	1	1
wc1990	27 June	Bologna	1	0*
1998	29 May	Casablanca	0	0
1999	10 Oct	Sunderland	2	1

		v BOHEMIA	E	B
1908	13 June	Prague	4	0

		v BRAZIL	E	B
1956	9 May	Wembley	4	2
wc1958	11 June	Gothenburg	0	0
1959	13 May	Rio de Janeiro	0	2
wc1962	10 June	Vina del Mar	1	3
1963	8 May	Wembley	1	1
1964	30 May	Rio de Janeiro	1	5
1969	12 June	Rio de Janeiro	1	2
wc1970	7 June	Guadalajara	0	1
1976	23 May	Los Angeles	0	1
1977	8 June	Rio de Janeiro	0	0
1978	19 Apr	Wembley	1	1
1981	12 May	Wembley	0	1
1984	10 June	Rio de Janeiro	2	0
1987	19 May	Wembley	1	1
1990	28 Mar	Wembley	1	0
1992	17 May	Wembley	1	1
1993	13 June	Washington	1	1
UI1995	11 June	Wembley	1	3
TF1997	10 June	Paris	0	1
2000	27 May	Wembley	1	1
wc2002	21 June	Shizuoka	1	2
2007	1 June	Wembley	1	1
2009	14 Nov	Doha	0	1

		v BULGARIA	E	B
wc1962	7 June	Rancagua	0	0
1968	11 Dec	Wembley	1	1
1974	1 June	Sofia	1	0
EC1979	6 June	Sofia	3	0
EC1979	22 Nov	Wembley	2	0
1996	27 Mar	Wembley	1	0
EC1998	10 Oct	Wembley	0	0
EC1999	9 June	Sofia	1	1

		v CAMEROON	E	C
wc1990	1 July	Naples	3	2*
1991	6 Feb	Wembley	2	0
1997	15 Nov	Wembley	2	0
2002	26 May	Kobe	2	2

		v CANADA	E	C
1986	24 May	Burnaby	1	0

		v CHILE	E	C
wc1950	25 June	Rio de Janeiro	2	0
1953	24 May	Santiago	2	1
1984	17 June	Santiago	0	0
1989	23 May	Wembley	0	0
1998	11 Feb	Wembley	0	2

		v CHINA	E	C
1996	23 May	Beijing	3	0

		v CIS	E	C
1992	29 Apr	Moscow	2	2

		v COLOMBIA	E	C
1970	20 May	Bogota	4	0
1988	24 May	Wembley	1	1
1995	6 Sept	Wembley	0	0
wc1998	26 June	Lens	2	0
2005	31 May	New Jersey	3	2

		v CROATIA	E	C
1996	24 Apr	Wembley	0	0
2003	20 Aug	Ipswich	3	1
EC2004	21 June	Lisbon	4	2
EC2006	11 Oct	Zagreb	0	2
EC2007	21 Nov	Wembley	2	3
wc2008	10 Sept	Zagreb	4	1
wc2009	9 Sept	Wembley	5	1

		v CYPRUS	E	C
EC1975	16 Apr	Wembley	5	0
EC1975	11 May	Limassol	1	0

		v CZECHOSLOVAKIA	E	C
1934	16 May	Prague	1	2
1937	1 Dec	Tottenham	5	4
1963	29 May	Bratislava	4	2
1966	2 Nov	Wembley	0	0
wc1970	11 June	Guadalajara	1	0
1973	27 May	Prague	1	1
EC1974	30 Oct	Wembley	3	0
EC1975	30 Oct	Bratislava	1	2
1978	29 Nov	Wembley	1	0
wc1982	20 June	Bilbao	2	0
1990	25 Apr	Wembley	4	2
1992	25 Mar	Prague	2	2

		v CZECH REPUBLIC	E	C
1998	18 Nov	Wembley	2	0
2008	20 Aug	Wembley	2	2

		v DENMARK	E	D
1948	26 Sept	Copenhagen	0	0
1955	2 Oct	Copenhagen	5	1
wc1956	5 Dec	Wolverhampton	5	2
wc1957	15 May	Copenhagen	4	1
1966	3 July	Copenhagen	2	0
EC1978	20 Sept	Copenhagen	4	3
EC1979	12 Sept	Wembley	1	0
EC1982	22 Sept	Copenhagen	2	2
EC1983	21 Sept	Wembley	0	1
1988	14 Sept	Wembley	1	0
1989	7 June	Copenhagen	1	1
1990	15 May	Wembley	1	0
EC1992	11 June	Malmo	0	0
1994	9 Mar	Wembley	1	0
wc2002	15 June	Niigata	3	0
2003	16 Nov	Old Trafford	2	3
2005	17 Aug	Copenhagen	1	4

		v ECUADOR	E	Ec
1970	24 May	Quito	2	0
wc2006	25 June	Stuttgart	1	0

		v EGYPT	E	Eg
1986	29 Jan	Cairo	4	0
wc1990	21 June	Cagliari	1	0
2010	3 Mar	Wembley	3	1

		v ESTONIA	E	Es
EC2007	6 June	Tallinn	3	0
EC2007	13 Oct	Wembley	3	0

		v FIFA	E	FIFA
1938	26 Oct	Highbury	3	0
1953	21 Oct	Wembley	4	4
1963	23 Oct	Wembley	2	1

		v FINLAND	E	F
1937	20 May	Helsinki	8	0
1956	20 May	Helsinki	5	1
1966	26 June	Helsinki	3	0
wc1976	13 June	Helsinki	4	1

			E	F
wc1976	13 Oct	Wembley	2	1
1982	3 June	Helsinki	4	1
wc1984	17 Oct	Wembley	5	0
wc1985	22 May	Helsinki	1	1
1992	3 June	Helsinki	2	1
wc2000	11 Oct	Helsinki	0	0
wc2001	24 Mar	Liverpool	2	1

		v FRANCE	E	F
1923	10 May	Paris	4	1
1924	17 May	Paris	3	1
1925	21 May	Paris	3	2
1927	26 May	Paris	6	0
1928	17 May	Paris	5	1
1929	9 May	Paris	4	1
1931	14 May	Paris	2	5
1933	6 Dec	Tottenham	4	1
1938	26 May	Paris	4	2
1947	3 May	Highbury	3	0
1949	22 May	Paris	3	1
1951	3 Oct	Highbury	2	2
1955	15 May	Paris	0	1
1957	27 Nov	Wembley	4	0
EC1962	3 Oct	Sheffield	1	1
EC1963	27 Feb	Paris	2	5
wc1966	20 July	Wembley	2	0
1969	12 Mar	Wembley	5	0
wc1982	16 June	Bilbao	3	1
1984	29 Feb	Paris	0	2
1992	19 Feb	Wembley	2	0
EC1992	14 June	Malmo	0	0
TF1997	7 June	Montpellier	1	0
1999	10 Feb	Wembley	0	2
2000	2 Sept	Paris	1	1
EC2004	13 June	Lisbon	1	2
2008	26 Mar	Paris	0	1

		v GEORGIA	E	G
wc1996	9 Nov	Tbilisi	2	0
wc1997	30 Apr	Wembley	2	0

		v GERMANY	E	G
1930	10 May	Berlin	3	3
1935	4 Dec	Tottenham	3	0
1938	14 May	Berlin	6	3
1991	11 Sept	Wembley	0	1
1993	19 June	Detroit	1	2
EC1996	26 June	Wembley	1	1*
EC2000	17 June	Charleroi	1	0
wc2000	7 Oct	Wembley	0	1
wc2001	1 Sept	Munich	5	1
2007	22 Aug	Wembley	1	2
2008	19 Nov	Berlin	2	1
wc2010	27 June	Bloemfontein	1	4

		v EAST GERMANY	E	EG
1963	2 June	Leipzig	2	1
1970	25 Nov	Wembley	3	1
1974	29 May	Leipzig	1	1
1984	12 Sept	Wembley	1	0

		v WEST GERMANY	E	WG
1954	1 Dec	Wembley	3	1
1956	26 May	Berlin	3	1
1965	12 May	Nuremberg	1	0
1966	23 Feb	Wembley	1	0
wc1966	30 July	Wembley	4	2*
1968	1 June	Hanover	0	1
wc1970	14 June	Leon	2	3*
EC1972	29 Apr	Wembley	1	3
EC1972	13 May	Berlin	0	0
1975	12 Mar	Wembley	2	0
1978	22 Feb	Munich	1	2
wc1982	29 June	Madrid	0	0
1982	13 Oct	Wembley	1	2
1985	12 June	Mexico City	3	0
1987	9 Sept	Dusseldorf	1	3
wc1990	4 July	Turin	1	1*

		v GREECE	E	G
EC1971	21 Apr	Wembley	3	0
EC1971	1 Dec	Piraeus	2	0
EC1983	17 Nov	Salonika	3	0
EC1983	30 Mar	Wembley	0	0

			E	G
1989	8 Feb	Athens	2	1
1994	17 May	Wembley	5	0
wc2001	6 June	Athens	2	0
wc2001	6 Oct	Old Trafford	2	2
2006	16 Aug	Old Trafford	4	0

		v HOLLAND	E	H
1935	18 May	Amsterdam	1	0
1946	27 Nov	Huddersfield	8	2
1964	9 Dec	Amsterdam	1	1
1969	5 Nov	Amsterdam	1	0
1970	14 Jun	Wembley	0	0
1977	9 Feb	Wembley	0	2
1982	25 May	Wembley	2	0
1988	23 Mar	Wembley	2	2
EC1988	15 June	Dusseldorf	1	3
wc1990	16 June	Cagliari	0	0
2005	9 Feb	Villa Park	0	0
wc1993	28 Apr	Wembley	2	2
wc1993	13 Oct	Rotterdam	0	2
EC1996	18 June	Wembley	4	1
2001	15 Aug	Tottenham	0	2
2002	13 Feb	Amsterdam	1	1
2006	15 Nov	Amsterdam	1	1
2009	12 Aug	Amsterdam	2	2

		v HUNGARY	E	H
1908	10 June	Budapest	7	0
1909	29 May	Budapest	4	2
1909	31 May	Budapest	8	2
1934	10 May	Budapest	1	2
1936	2 Dec	Highbury	6	2
1953	25 Nov	Budapest	3	6
1954	23 May	Budapest	1	7
1960	22 May	Budapest	0	2
wc1962	31 May	Rancagua	1	2
1965	5 May	Wembley	1	0
1978	24 May	Wembley	4	1
wc1981	6 June	Budapest	3	1
wc1982	18 Nov	Wembley	1	0
EC1983	27 Apr	Wembley	2	0
EC1983	12 Oct	Budapest	3	0
1988	27 Apr	Budapest	0	0
1990	12 Sept	Wembley	1	0
1992	12 May	Budapest	1	0
1996	18 May	Wembley	3	0
1999	28 Apr	Budapest	1	1
2006	30 May	Old Trafford	3	1

		v ICELAND	E	I
1982	2 June	Reykjavik	1	1
2004	5 June	City of Manchester	6	1
EC2007	24 Mar	Tel Aviv	0	0

		v REPUBLIC OF IRELAND	E	RI
1946	30 Sept	Dublin	1	0
1949	21 Sept	Everton	0	2
wc1957	8 May	Wembley	5	1
wc1957	19 May	Dublin	1	1
1964	24 May	Dublin	3	1
1976	8 Sept	Wembley	1	1
EC1978	25 Oct	Dublin	1	1
EC1980	6 Feb	Wembley	2	0
1985	26 Mar	Wembley	2	1
EC1988	12 June	Stuttgart	0	1
wc1990	11 June	Cagliari	1	1
EC1990	14 Nov	Dublin	1	1
EC1991	27 Mar	Wembley	1	1
1995	15 Feb	Dublin	0	1
	(abandoned after 27 mins)			

		v ISRAEL	E	I
1986	26 Feb	Ramat Gan	2	1
1988	17 Feb	Tel Aviv	0	0
EC2007	24 Mar	Tel Aviv	0	0
EC2007	8 Sept	Wembley	3	0

		v ITALY	E	I
1933	13 May	Rome	1	1
1934	14 Nov	Highbury	3	2
1939	13 May	Milan	2	2
1948	16 May	Turin	4	0
1949	30 Nov	Tottenham	2	0
1952	18 May	Florence	1	1

			E	I
1959	6 May	Wembley	2	2
1961	24 May	Rome	3	2
1973	14 June	Turin	0	2
1973	14 Nov	Wembley	0	1
1976	28 May	New York	3	2
wc1976	17 Nov	Rome	0	2
wc1977	16 Nov	Wembley	2	0
ec1980	15 June	Turin	0	1
1985	6 June	Mexico City	1	2
1989	15 Nov	Wembley	0	0
wc1990	7 July	Bari	1	2
wc1997	12 Feb	Wembley	0	1
tf1997	4 June	Nantes	2	0
wc1997	11 Oct	Rome	0	0
2000	15 Nov	Turin	0	1
2002	27 Mar	Leeds	1	2

v JAMAICA			E	J
2006	3 June	Old Trafford	6	0

v JAPAN			E	J
u11995	3 June	Wembley	2	1
2004	1 June	City of Manchester	1	1
2010	30 May	Graz	2	1

v KAZAKHSTAN			E	K
wc2008	11 Oct	Wembley	5	1
wc2009	6 June	Almaty	4	0

v KUWAIT			E	K
wc1982	25 June	Bilbao	1	0

v LIECHTENSTEIN			E	L
ec2003	29 Mar	Vaduz	2	0
ec2003	10 Sept	Old Trafford	2	0

v LUXEMBOURG			E	L
1927	21 May	Esch-sur-Alzette	5	2
wc1960	19 Oct	Luxembourg	9	0
wc1961	28 Sept	Highbury	4	1
wc1977	30 Mar	Wembley	5	0
wc1977	12 Oct	Luxembourg	2	0
ec1982	15 Dec	Wembley	9	0
ec1983	16 Nov	Luxembourg	4	0
ec1998	14 Oct	Luxembourg	3	0
ec1999	4 Sept	Wembley	6	0

v MACEDONIA			E	M
ec2002	16 Oct	Southampton	2	2
ec2003	6 Sept	Skopje	2	1
ec2006	6 Sept	Skopje	1	0
ec2006	7 Oct	Old Trafford	0	0

v MALAYSIA			E	M
1991	12 June	Kuala Lumpur	4	2

v MALTA			E	M
ec1971	3 Feb	Valletta	1	0
ec1971	12 May	Wembley	5	0
2000	3 June	Valletta	2	1

v MEXICO			E	M
1959	24 May	Mexico City	1	2
1961	10 May	Wembley	8	0
wc1966	16 July	Wembley	2	0
1969	1 June	Mexico City	0	0
1985	9 June	Mexico City	0	1
1986	17 May	Los Angeles	3	0
1997	29 Mar	Wembley	2	0
2001	25 May	Derby	4	0
2010	24 May	Wembley	3	1

v MOLDOVA			E	M
wc1996	1 Sept	Chisinau	3	0
wc1997	10 Sept	Wembley	4	0

v MOROCCO			E	M
wc1986	6 June	Monterrey	0	0
1998	27 May	Casablanca	1	0

v NEW ZEALAND			E	NZ
1991	3 June	Auckland	1	0
1991	8 June	Wellington	2	0

v NIGERIA			E	N
1994	16 Nov	Wembley	1	0
wc2002	12 June	Osaka	0	0

v NORWAY			E	N
1937	14 May	Oslo	6	0
1938	9 Nov	Newcastle	4	0
1949	18 May	Oslo	4	1
1966	29 June	Oslo	6	1
wc1980	10 Sept	Wembley	4	0
wc1981	9 Sept	Oslo	1	2
wc1992	14 Oct	Wembley	1	1
wc1993	2 June	Oslo	0	2
1994	22 May	Wembley	0	0
1995	11 Oct	Oslo	0	0

v PARAGUAY			E	P
wc1986	18 June	Mexico City	3	0
2002	17 Apr	Liverpool	4	0
wc2006	10 June	Frankfurt	1	0

v PERU			E	P
1959	17 May	Lima	1	4
1962	20 May	Lima	4	0

v POLAND			E	P
1966	5 Jan	Everton	1	1
1966	5 July	Chorzow	1	0
wc1973	6 June	Chorzow	0	2
wc1973	17 Oct	Wembley	1	1
wc1986	11 June	Monterrey	3	0
wc1989	3 June	Wembley	3	0
wc1989	11 Oct	Katowice	0	0
ec1990	17 Oct	Wembley	2	0
ec1991	13 Nov	Poznan	1	1
wc1993	29 May	Katowice	1	1
wc1993	8 Sept	Wembley	3	0
wc1996	9 Oct	Wembley	2	1
wc1997	31 May	Katowice	2	0
ec1999	27 Mar	Wembley	3	1
ec1999	8 Sept	Warsaw	0	0
wc2004	8 Sept	Katowice	2	1
wc2005	12 Oct	Old Trafford	2	1

v PORTUGAL			E	P
1947	25 May	Lisbon	10	0
1950	14 May	Lisbon	5	3
1951	19 May	Everton	5	2
1955	22 May	Oporto	1	3
1958	7 May	Wembley	2	1
wc1961	21 May	Lisbon	1	1
wc1961	25 Oct	Wembley	2	0
1964	17 May	Lisbon	4	3
1964	4 June	São Paulo	1	1
wc1966	26 July	Wembley	2	1
1969	10 Dec	Wembley	1	0
1974	3 Apr	Lisbon	0	0
ec1974	20 Nov	Wembley	0	0
ec1975	19 Nov	Lisbon	1	1
wc1986	3 June	Monterrey	0	1
1995	12 Dec	Wembley	1	1
1998	22 Apr	Wembley	3	0
ec2000	12 June	Eindhoven	2	3
2002	7 Sept	Villa Park	1	1
2004	18 Feb	Faro	1	1
ec2004	24 June	Lisbon	2	2*
wc2006	1 July	Gelsenkirchen	0	0

v ROMANIA			E	R
1939	24 May	Bucharest	2	0
1968	6 Nov	Bucharest	0	0
1969	15 Jan	Wembley	1	1
wc1970	2 June	Guadalajara	1	0
wc1980	15 Oct	Bucharest	1	2
wc1981	29 April	Wembley	0	0
wc1985	1 May	Bucharest	0	0
wc1985	11 Sept	Wembley	1	1
1994	12 Oct	Wembley	1	1
wc1998	22 June	Toulouse	1	2
ec2000	20 June	Charleroi	2	3

v RUSSIA			E	R
ec2007	12 Sept	Wembley	3	0
ec2007	17 Oct	Moscow	1	2

v SAN MARINO			E	SM
wc1992	17 Feb	Wembley	6	0
wc1993	17 Nov	Bologna	7	1

v SAUDI ARABIA

			E	SA
1988	16 Nov	Riyadh	1	1
1998	23 May	Wembley	0	0

v SERBIA-MONTENEGRO

			E	S-M
2003	3 June	Leicester	2	1

v SLOVAKIA

			E	S
EC2002	12 Oct	Bratislava	2	1
EC2003	11 June	Middlesbrough	2	1
2009	28 Mar	Wembley	4	0

v SLOVENIA

			E	S
2009	5 Sept	Wembley	2	1
wc2010	23 June	Port Elizabeth	1	0

v SOUTH AFRICA

			E	SA
1997	24 May	Old Trafford	2	1
2003	22 May	Durban	2	1

v SOUTH KOREA

			E	SK
2002	21 May	Seoguipo	1	1

v SPAIN

			E	S
1929	15 May	Madrid	3	4
1931	9 Dec	Highbury	7	1
wc1950	2 July	Rio de Janeiro	0	1
1955	18 May	Madrid	1	1
1955	30 Nov	Wembley	4	1
1960	15 May	Madrid	0	3
1960	26 Oct	Wembley	4	2
1965	8 Dec	Madrid	2	0
1967	24 May	Wembley	2	0
EC1968	3 Apr	Wembley	1	0
EC1968	8 May	Madrid	2	1
1980	26 Mar	Barcelona	2	0
EC1980	18 June	Naples	2	1
1981	25 Mar	Wembley	1	2
wc1982	5 July	Madrid	0	0
1987	18 Feb	Madrid	4	2
1992	9 Sept	Santander	0	1
EC 1996	22 June	Wembley	0	0
2001	28 Feb	Villa Park	3	0
2004	17 Nov	Madrid	0	1
2007	7 Feb	Old Trafford	0	1
2009	11 Feb	Seville	0	2

v SWEDEN

			E	S
1923	21 May	Stockholm	4	2
1923	24 May	Stockholm	3	1
1937	17 May	Stockholm	4	0
1947	19 Nov	Highbury	4	2
1949	13 May	Stockholm	1	3
1956	16 May	Stockholm	0	0
1959	28 Oct	Wembley	2	3
1965	16 May	Gothenburg	2	1
1968	22 May	Wembley	3	1
1979	10 June	Stockholm	0	0
1986	10 Sept	Stockholm	0	1
wc1988	19 Oct	Wembley	0	0
wc1989	6 Sept	Stockholm	0	0
EC1992	17 June	Stockholm	1	2
UI1995	8 June	Leeds	3	3
EC1998	5 Sept	Stockholm	1	2
EC1999	5 June	Wembley	0	0
2001	10 Nov	Old Trafford	1	1
wc2002	2 June	Saitama	1	1
2004	31 Mar	Gothenburg	0	1
wc2006	20 June	Cologne	2	2

v SWITZERLAND

			E	S
1933	20 May	Berne	4	0
1938	21 May	Zurich	1	2
1947	18 May	Zurich	0	1
1948	2 Dec	Highbury	6	0
1952	28 May	Zurich	3	0
wc1954	20 June	Berne	2	0
1962	9 May	Wembley	3	1
1963	5 June	Basle	8	1
EC1971	13 Oct	Basle	3	2
EC1971	10 Nov	Wembley	1	1
1975	3 Sept	Basle	2	1
1977	7 Sept	Wembley	0	0
wc1980	19 Nov	Wembley	2	1
wc1981	30 May	Basle	1	2

			E	S
1988	28 May	Lausanne	1	0
1995	15 Nov	Wembley	3	1
EC1996	8 June	Wembley	1	1
1998	25 Mar	Berne	1	1
EC2004	17 June	Coimbra	3	0
2008	6 Feb	Wembley	2	1

v TRINIDAD & TOBAGO

			E	Tr
wc2006	15 June	Nuremberg	2	0
2008	2 June	Port of Spain	3	0

v TUNISIA

			E	T
1990	2 June	Tunis	1	1
wc1998	15 June	Marseilles	2	0

v TURKEY

			E	T
wc1984	14 Nov	Istanbul	8	0
wc1985	16 Oct	Wembley	5	0
EC1987	29 Apr	Izmir	0	0
EC1987	14 Oct	Wembley	8	0
EC1991	1 May	Izmir	1	0
EC1991	16 Oct	Wembley	1	0
wc1992	18 Nov	Wembley	4	0
wc1993	31 Mar	Izmir	2	0
EC2003	2 Apr	Sunderland	2	0
EC2003	11 Oct	Istanbul	0	0

v UKRAINE

			E	U
2000	31 May	Wembley	2	0
2004	18 Aug	Newcastle	3	0
wc2009	1 Apr	Wembley	2	1
wc2009	10 Oct	Dnepr	0	1

v URUGUAY

			E	U
1953	31 May	Montevideo	1	2
wc1954	26 June	Basle	2	4
1964	6 May	Wembley	2	1
wc1966	11 July	Wembley	0	0
1969	8 June	Montevideo	2	1
1977	15 June	Montevideo	0	0
1984	13 June	Montevideo	0	2
1990	22 May	Wembley	1	2
1995	29 Mar	Wembley	0	0
2006	1 Mar	Liverpool	2	1

v USA

			E	USA
wc1950	29 June	Belo Horizonte	0	1
1953	8 June	New York	6	3
1959	28 May	Los Angeles	8	1
1964	27 May	New York	10	0
1985	16 June	Los Angeles	5	0
1993	9 June	Foxboro	0	2
1994	7 Sept	Wembley	2	0
2005	28 May	Chicago	2	1
2008	28 May	Wembley	2	0
wc2010	12 June	Rustenburg	1	1

v USSR

			E	USSR
1958	18 May	Moscow	1	1
wc1958	8 June	Gothenburg	2	2
wc1958	17 June	Gothenburg	0	1
1958	22 Oct	Wembley	5	0
1967	6 Dec	Wembley	2	2
EC1968	8 June	Rome	2	0
1973	10 June	Moscow	2	1
1984	2 June	Wembley	0	2
1986	26 Mar	Tbilisi	1	0
EC1988	18 June	Frankfurt	1	3
1991	21 May	Wembley	3	1

v YUGOSLAVIA

			E	Y
1939	18 May	Belgrade	1	2
1950	22 Nov	Highbury	2	2
1954	16 May	Belgrade	0	1
1956	28 Nov	Wembley	3	0
1958	11 May	Belgrade	0	5
1960	11 May	Wembley	3	3
1965	9 May	Belgrade	1	1
1966	4 May	Wembley	2	0
EC1968	5 June	Florence	0	1
1972	11 Oct	Wembley	1	1
1974	5 June	Belgrade	2	2
EC1986	12 Nov	Wembley	2	0
EC1987	11 Nov	Belgrade	4	1
1989	13 Dec	Wembley	2	1

SCOTLAND

		v ARGENTINA	S	A
1977	18 June	Buenos Aires	1	1
1979	2 June	Glasgow	1	3
1990	28 Mar	Glasgow	1	0
2008	19 Nov	Glasgow	0	1
		v AUSTRALIA	S	A
wc1985	20 Nov	Glasgow	2	0
wc1985	4 Dec	Melbourne	0	0
1996	27 Mar	Glasgow	1	0
2000	15 Nov	Glasgow	0	2
		v AUSTRIA	S	A
1931	16 May	Vienna	0	5
1933	29 Nov	Glasgow	2	2
1937	9 May	Vienna	1	1
1950	13 Dec	Glasgow	0	1
1951	27 May	Vienna	0	4
wc1954	16 June	Zurich	0	1
1955	19 May	Vienna	4	1
1956	2 May	Glasgow	1	1
1960	29 May	Vienna	1	4
1963	8 May	Glasgow	4	1
(abandoned after 79 mins)				
wc1968	6 Nov	Glasgow	2	1
wc1969	5 Nov	Vienna	0	2
EC1978	20 Sept	Vienna	2	3
EC1979	17 Oct	Glasgow	1	1
1994	20 Apr	Vienna	2	1
wc1996	31 Aug	Vienna	0	0
wc1997	2 Apr	Celtic Park	2	0
2003	30 Apr	Glasgow	0	2
2005	17 Aug	Graz	2	2
2007	30 May	Vienna	1	0
		v BELARUS	S	B
wc1997	8 June	Minsk	1	0
wc1997	7 Sept	Aberdeen	4	1
wc2005	8 June	Minsk	0	0
wc2005	8 Oct	Glasgow	0	1
		v BELGIUM	S	B
1947	18 May	Brussels	1	2
1948	28 Apr	Glasgow	2	0
1951	20 May	Brussels	5	0
EC1971	3 Feb	Liège	0	3
EC1971	10 Nov	Aberdeen	1	0
1974	2 June	Brussels	1	2
EC1979	21 Nov	Brussels	0	2
EC1979	19 Dec	Glasgow	1	3
EC1982	15 Dec	Brussels	2	3
EC1983	12 Oct	Glasgow	1	1
EC1987	1 Apr	Brussels	1	4
EC1987	14 Oct	Glasgow	2	0
wc2001	24 Mar	Glasgow	2	2
wc2001	5 Sept	Brussels	0	2
		v BOSNIA	S	B
EC1999	4 Sept	Sarajevo	2	1
EC1999	5 Oct	Glasgow	1	0
		v BRAZIL	S	B
1966	25 June	Glasgow	1	1
1972	5 July	Rio de Janeiro	0	1
1973	30 June	Glasgow	0	1
wc1974	18 June	Frankfurt	0	0
1977	23 June	Rio de Janeiro	0	2
wc1982	18 June	Seville	1	4
1987	26 May	Glasgow	0	2
wc1990	20 June	Turin	0	1
wc1998	10 June	Saint-Denis	1	2
		v BULGARIA	S	B
1978	22 Feb	Glasgow	2	1
EC1986	10 Sept	Glasgow	0	0
EC1987	11 Nov	Sofia	1	0
EC1990	14 Nov	Sofia	1	1
EC1991	27 Mar	Glasgow	1	1
2006	11 May	Kobe	5	1

		v CANADA	S	C
1983	12 June	Vancouver	2	0
1983	16 June	Edmonton	3	0
1983	20 June	Toronto	2	0
1992	21 May	Toronto	3	1
2002	15 Oct	Easter Road	3	1
		v CHILE	S	C
1977	15 June	Santiago	4	2
1989	30 May	Glasgow	2	0
		v CIS	S	C
EC1992	18 June	Norrkoping	3	0
		v COLOMBIA	S	C
1988	17 May	Glasgow	0	0
1996	30 May	Miami	0	1
1998	23 May	New York	2	2
		v COSTA RICA	S	CR
wc1990	11 June	Genoa	0	1
		v CROATIA	S	C
wc2000	11 Oct	Zagreb	1	1
wc2001	1 Sept	Glasgow	0	0
2008	26 Mar	Glasgow	1	1
		v CYPRUS	S	C
wc1968	17 Dec	Nicosia	5	0
wc1969	11 May	Glasgow	8	0
wc1989	8 Feb	Limassol	3	2
wc1989	26 Apr	Glasgow	2	1
		v CZECHOSLOVAKIA	S	C
1937	22 May	Prague	3	1
1937	8 Dec	Glasgow	5	0
wc1961	14 May	Bratislava	0	4
wc1961	26 Sept	Glasgow	3	2
wc1961	29 Nov	Brussels	2	4*
1972	2 July	Porto Alegre	0	0
wc1973	26 Sept	Glasgow	2	1
wc1973	17 Oct	Prague	0	1
wc1976	13 Oct	Prague	0	2
wc1977	21 Sept	Glasgow	3	1
		v CZECH REPUBLIC	S	C
EC1999	31 Mar	Glasgow	1	2
EC1999	9 June	Prague	2	3
2008	30 May	Prague	1	3
2010	3 Mar	Glasgow	1	0
		v DENMARK	S	D
1951	12 May	Glasgow	3	1
1952	25 May	Copenhagen	2	1
1968	16 Oct	Copenhagen	1	0
EC1970	11 Nov	Glasgow	1	0
EC1971	9 June	Copenhagen	0	1
wc1972	18 Oct	Copenhagen	4	1
wc1972	15 Nov	Glasgow	2	0
EC1975	3 Sept	Copenhagen	1	0
EC1975	29 Oct	Glasgow	3	1
wc1986	4 June	Nezahualcayotl	0	1
1996	24 Apr	Copenhagen	0	2
1998	25 Mar	Glasgow	0	1
2002	21 Aug	Glasgow	0	1
2004	28 Apr	Copenhagen	0	1
		v ECUADOR	S	E
1995	24 May	Toyama	2	1
		v EGYPT	S	E
1990	16 May	Aberdeen	1	3
		v ESTONIA	S	E
wc1993	19 May	Tallinn	3	0
wc1993	2 June	Aberdeen	3	1
wc1997	11 Feb	Monaco	0	0
wc1997	29 Mar	Kilmarnock	2	0
EC1998	10 Oct	Edinburgh	3	2
EC1999	8 Sept	Tallinn	0	0
2004	27 May	Tallinn	1	0

		v FAEROES	S	F
EC1994	12 Oct	Glasgow	5	1
EC1995	7 June	Toftir	2	0
EC1998	14 Oct	Aberdeen	2	1
EC1999	5 June	Toftir	1	1
EC2002	7 Sept	Toftir	2	2
EC2003	6 Sept	Glasgow	3	1
EC2006	2 Sept	Celtic Park	6	0
EC2007	6 June	Toftir	2	0

		v FINLAND	S	F
1954	25 May	Helsinki	2	1
wc1964	21 Oct	Glasgow	3	1
wc1965	27 May	Helsinki	2	1
1976	8 Sept	Glasgow	6	0
1992	25 Mar	Glasgow	1	1
EC1994	7 Sept	Helsinki	2	0
EC1995	6 Sept	Glasgow	1	0
1998	22 Apr	Edinburgh	1	1

		v FRANCE	S	F
1930	18 May	Paris	2	0
1932	8 May	Paris	3	1
1948	23 May	Paris	0	3
1949	27 Apr	Glasgow	2	0
1950	27 May	Paris	1	0
1951	16 May	Glasgow	1	0
wc1958	15 June	Orebro	1	2
1984	1 June	Marseilles	0	2
wc1989	8 Mar	Glasgow	2	0
wc1989	11 Oct	Paris	0	3
1997	12 Nov	St Etienne	1	2
2000	29 Mar	Glasgow	0	2
2002	27 Mar	Paris	0	5
EC2006	7 Oct	Glasgow	1	0
EC2007	12 Sept	Paris	1	0

		v GEORGIA	S	G
EC2007	24 Mar	Glasgow	2	1
EC2007	17 Oct	Tblisi	0	2

		v GERMANY	S	G
1929	1 June	Berlin	1	1
1936	14 Oct	Glasgow	2	0
EC1992	15 June	Norrkoping	0	2
1993	24 Mar	Glasgow	0	1
1998	28 Apr	Bremen	1	0
EC2003	7 June	Glasgow	1	1
EC2003	10 Sept	Dortmund	1	2

		v EAST GERMANY	S	EG
1974	30 Oct	Glasgow	3	0
1977	7 Sept	East Berlin	0	1
EC1982	13 Oct	Glasgow	2	0
EC1983	16 Nov	Halle	1	2
1985	16 Oct	Glasgow	0	0
1990	25 Apr	Glasgow	0	1

		v WEST GERMANY	S	WG
1957	22 May	Stuttgart	3	1
1959	6 May	Glasgow	3	2
1964	12 May	Hanover	2	2
wc1969	16 Apr	Glasgow	1	1
wc1969	22 Oct	Hamburg	2	3
1973	14 Nov	Glasgow	1	1
1974	27 Mar	Frankfurt	1	2
wc1986	8 June	Queretaro	1	2

		v GREECE	S	G
EC1994	18 Dec	Athens	0	1
EC1995	16 Aug	Glasgow	1	0

		v HOLLAND	S	H
1929	4 June	Amsterdam	2	0
1938	21 May	Amsterdam	3	1
1959	27 May	Amsterdam	2	1
1966	11 May	Glasgow	0	3
1968	30 May	Amsterdam	0	0
1971	1 Dec	Rotterdam	1	2
wc1978	11 June	Mendoza	3	2
1982	23 Mar	Glasgow	2	1
1986	29 Apr	Eindhoven	0	0
EC1992	12 June	Gothenburg	0	1

			S	H
1994	23 Mar	Glasgow	0	1
1994	27 May	Utrecht	1	3
EC1996	10 June	Birmingham	0	0
2000	26 Apr	Arnhem	0	0
EC2003	15 Nov	Glasgow	1	0
EC2003	19 Nov	Amsterdam	0	6
wc2009	28 Mar	Amsterdam	0	3
wc2009	9 Sept	Glasgow	0	1

		v HONG KONG XI	S	HK
†2002	23 May	Hong Kong	4	0

†*match not recognised by FIFA*

		v HUNGARY	S	H
1938	7 Dec	Glasgow	3	1
1954	8 Dec	Glasgow	2	4
1955	29 May	Budapest	1	3
1958	7 May	Glasgow	1	1
1960	5 June	Budapest	3	3
1980	31 May	Budapest	1	3
1987	9 Sept	Glasgow	2	0
2004	18 Aug	Glasgow	0	3

		v ICELAND	S	I
wc1984	17 Oct	Glasgow	3	0
wc1985	28 May	Reykjavik	1	0
EC2002	12 Oct	Reykjavik	2	0
EC2003	29 Mar	Glasgow	2	1
wc2008	10 Sept	Reykjavik	2	1
wc2009	1 Apr	Glasgow	2	1

		v IRAN	S	I
wc1978	7 June	Cordoba	1	1

		v REPUBLIC OF IRELAND	S	RI
wc1961	3 May	Glasgow	4	1
wc1961	7 May	Dublin	3	0
1963	9 June	Dublin	0	1
1969	21 Sept	Dublin	1	1
EC1986	15 Oct	Dublin	0	0
EC1987	18 Feb	Glasgow	0	1
2000	30 May	Dublin	2	1
2003	12 Feb	Glasgow	0	2

		v ISRAEL	S	I
wc1981	25 Feb	Tel Aviv	1	0
wc1981	28 Apr	Glasgow	3	1
1986	28 Jan	Tel Aviv	1	0

		v ITALY	S	I
1931	20 May	Rome	0	3
wc1965	9 Nov	Glasgow	1	0
wc1965	7 Dec	Naples	0	3
1988	22 Dec	Perugia	0	2
wc1992	18 Nov	Glasgow	0	0
wc1993	13 Oct	Rome	1	3
wc2005	26 Mar	Milan	0	2
wc2005	3 Sept	Glasgow	1	1
EC2007	28 Mar	Bari	0	2
EC2007	17 Nov	Glasgow	3	1

		v JAPAN	S	J
1995	21 May	Hiroshima	0	0
2006	13 May	Saitama	0	0
2009	10 Oct	Yokohama	0	2

		v LATVIA	S	L
wc1996	5 Oct	Riga	2	0
wc1997	11 Oct	Glasgow	2	0
wc2000	2 Sept	Riga	1	0
wc2001	6 Oct	Glasgow	2	1

		v LITHUANIA	S	L
EC1998	5 Sept	Vilnius	0	0
EC1999	9 Oct	Glasgow	3	0
EC2003	2 Apr	Kaunas	0	1
EC2003	11 Oct	Glasgow	1	0
EC2006	6 Sept	Kaunas	2	1
EC2007	8 Sept	Glasgow	3	1

		v LUXEMBOURG	S	L
1947	24 May	Luxembourg	6	0
EC1986	12 Nov	Glasgow	3	0
EC1987	2 Dec	Esch	0	0

v MACEDONIA

			S	M
wc2008	6 Sept	Skopje	0	1
wc2009	5 Sept	Glasgow	2	0

v MALTA

			S	M
1988	22 Mar	Valletta	1	1
1990	28 May	Valletta	2	1
wc1993	17 Feb	Glasgow	3	0
wc1993	17 Nov	Valletta	2	0
1997	1 June	Valletta	3	2

v MOLDOVA

			S	M
EC2004	13 Oct	Chisinau	1	1
EC2005	4 June	Glasgow	2	0

v MOROCCO

			S	M
wc1998	23 June	St Etienne	0	3

v NEW ZEALAND

			S	NZ
wc1982	15 June	Malaga	5	2
2003	27 May	Tynecastle	1	1

v NIGERIA

			S	N
2002	17 Apr	Aberdeen	1	2

v NORWAY

			S	N
1929	28 May	Oslo	7	3
1954	5 May	Glasgow	1	0
1954	19 May	Oslo	1	1
1963	4 June	Bergen	3	4
1963	7 Nov	Glasgow	6	1
1974	6 June	Oslo	2	1
EC1978	25 Oct	Glasgow	3	2
EC1979	7 June	Oslo	4	0
wc1988	14 Sept	Oslo	2	1
wc1989	15 Nov	Glasgow	1	1
1992	3 June	Oslo	0	0
wc1998	16 June	Bordeaux	1	1
2003	20 Aug	Oslo	0	0
wc2004	9 Oct	Glasgow	0	1
wc2005	7 Sept	Oslo	2	1
wc2008	11 Oct	Glasgow	0	0
wc2009	12 Aug	Oslo	0	4

v PARAGUAY

			S	P
wc1958	11 June	Norrkoping	2	3

v PERU

			S	P
1972	26 Apr	Glasgow	2	0
wc1978	3 June	Cordoba	1	3
1979	12 Sept	Glasgow	1	1

v POLAND

			S	P
1958	1 June	Warsaw	2	1
1960	4 June	Glasgow	2	3
wc1965	23 May	Chorzow	1	1
wc1965	13 Oct	Glasgow	1	2
1980	28 May	Poznan	0	1
1990	19 May	Glasgow	1	1
2001	25 Apr	Bydgoszcz	1	1

v PORTUGAL

			S	P
1950	21 May	Lisbon	2	2
1955	4 May	Glasgow	3	0
1959	3 June	Lisbon	0	1
1966	18 June	Glasgow	0	1
EC1971	21 Apr	Lisbon	0	2
EC1971	13 Oct	Glasgow	2	1
1975	13 May	Glasgow	1	0
EC1978	29 Nov	Lisbon	0	1
EC1980	26 Mar	Glasgow	4	1
wc1980	15 Oct	Glasgow	0	0
wc1981	18 Nov	Lisbon	1	2
wc1992	14 Oct	Glasgow	0	0
wc1993	28 Apr	Lisbon	0	5
2002	20 Nov	Braga	0	2

v ROMANIA

			S	R
EC1975	1 June	Bucharest	1	1
EC1975	17 Dec	Glasgow	1	1
1986	26 Mar	Glasgow	3	0
EC1990	12 Sept	Glasgow	2	1
EC1991	16 Oct	Bucharest	0	1
2004	31 Mar	Glasgow	1	2

v RUSSIA

			S	R
EC1994	16 Nov	Glasgow	1	1
EC1995	29 Mar	Moscow	0	0

v SAN MARINO

			S	SM
EC1991	1 May	Serravalle	2	0
EC1991	13 Nov	Glasgow	4	0
EC1995	26 Apr	Serravalle	2	0
EC1995	15 Nov	Glasgow	5	0
wc2000	7 Oct	Serravalle	2	0
wc2001	28 Mar	Glasgow	4	0

v SAUDI ARABIA

			S	SA
1988	17 Feb	Riyadh	2	2

v SLOVENIA

			S	Sl
wc2004	8 Sept	Glasgow	0	0
wc2005	12 Oct	Celje	3	0

v SOUTH AFRICA

			S	SA
2002	20 May	Hong Kong	0	2
2007	22 Aug	Aberdeen	1	0

v SOUTH KOREA

			S	SK
2002	16 May	Busan	1	4

v SPAIN

			S	Sp
wc1957	8 May	Glasgow	4	2
wc1957	26 May	Madrid	1	4
1963	13 June	Madrid	6	2
1965	8 May	Glasgow	0	0
EC1974	20 Nov	Glasgow	1	2
EC1975	5 Feb	Valencia	1	1
1982	24 Feb	Valencia	0	3
wc1984	14 Nov	Glasgow	3	1
wc1985	27 Feb	Seville	0	1
1988	27 Apr	Madrid	0	0
2004	3 Sept	Valencia	1	1

Match abandoned afer 60 minutes; floodlight failure.

v SWEDEN

			S	Sw
1952	30 May	Stockholm	1	3
1953	6 May	Glasgow	1	2
1975	16 Apr	Gothenburg	1	1
1977	27 Apr	Glasgow	3	1
wc1980	10 Sept	Stockholm	1	0
wc1981	9 Sept	Glasgow	2	0
wc1990	16 June	Genoa	2	1
1995	11 Oct	Stockholm	0	2
wc1996	10 Nov	Glasgow	1	0
wc1997	30 Apr	Gothenburg	1	2
2004	17 Nov	Edinburgh	1	4

v SWITZERLAND

			S	Sw
1931	24 May	Geneva	3	2
1948	17 May	Berne	1	2
1950	26 Apr	Glasgow	3	1
wc1957	19 May	Basle	2	1
wc1957	6 Nov	Glasgow	3	2
1973	22 June	Berne	0	1
1976	7 Apr	Glasgow	1	0
EC1982	17 Nov	Berne	0	2
EC1983	30 May	Glasgow	2	0
EC1990	17 Oct	Glasgow	2	1
EC1991	11 Sept	Berne	2	2
wc1992	9 Sept	Berne	1	3
wc1993	8 Sept	Aberdeen	1	1
wc1996	18 June	Birmingham	1	0
2006	1 Mar	Glasgow	1	3

v TRINIDAD & TOBAGO

			S	TT
2004	30 May	Edinburgh	4	1

v TURKEY

			S	T
1960	8 June	Ankara	2	4

v UKRAINE

			S	U
EC2006	11 Oct	Kiev	0	2
EC2007	13 Oct	Glasgow	3	1

v URUGUAY

			S	U
wc1954	19 June	Basle	0	7
1962	2 May	Glasgow	2	3

			S	U
1983	21 Sept	Glasgow	2	0
wc1986	13 June	Nezahualcoyotl	0	0

v USA			S	USA
1952	30 Apr	Glasgow	6	0
1992	17 May	Denver	1	0
1996	26 May	New Britain	1	2
1998	30 May	Washington	0	0
2005	11 Nov	Glasgow	1	1

v USSR			S	USSR
1967	10 May	Glasgow	0	2
1971	14 June	Moscow	0	1
wc1982	22 June	Malaga	2	2
1991	6 Feb	Glasgow	0	1

v YUGOSLAVIA			S	Y
1955	15 May	Belgrade	2	2
1956	21 Nov	Glasgow	2	0
wc1958	8 June	Vasteras	1	1
1972	29 June	Belo Horizonte	2	2
wc1974	22 June	Frankfurt	1	1
1984	12 Sept	Glasgow	6	1
wc1988	19 Oct	Glasgow	1	1
wc1989	6 Sept	Zagreb	1	3

v ZAIRE			S	Z
wc1974	14 June	Dortmund	2	0

WALES

v ALBANIA			W	A
EC1994	7 Sept	Cardiff	2	0
EC1995	15 Nov	Tirana	1	1

v ARGENTINA			W	A
1992	3 June	Tokyo	0	1
2002	13 Feb	Cardiff	1	1

v ARMENIA			W	A
wc2001	24 Mar	Erevan	2	2
wc2001	1 Sept	Cardiff	0	0

v AUSTRIA			W	A
1954	9 May	Vienna	0	2
EC1955	23 Nov	Wrexham	1	2
EC1974	4 Sept	Vienna	1	2
1975	19 Nov	Wrexham	1	0
1992	29 Apr	Vienna	1	1
EC2005	26 Mar	Cardiff	0	2
EC2005	30 Mar	Vienna	0	1

v AZERBAIJAN			W	A
EC2002	20 Nov	Baku	2	0
EC2003	29 Mar	Cardiff	4	0
wc2004	4 Sept	Baku	1	1
wc2005	12 Oct	Cardiff	2	0
wc2008	6 Sept	Cardiff	1	0
wc2009	6 June	Baku	1	0

v BELARUS			W	B
EC1998	14 Oct	Cardiff	3	2
EC1999	4 Sept	Minsk	2	1
wc2000	2 Sept	Minsk	1	2
wc2001	6 Oct	Cardiff	1	0

v BELGIUM			W	B
1949	22 May	Liège	1	3
1949	23 Nov	Cardiff	5	1
EC1990	17 Oct	Cardiff	3	1
EC1991	27 Mar	Brussels	1	1
wc1992	18 Nov	Brussels	0	2
wc1993	31 Mar	Cardiff	2	0
wc1997	29 Mar	Cardiff	1	2
wc1997	11 Oct	Brussels	2	3

v BOSNIA			W	B
2003	12 Feb	Cardiff	2	2

v BRAZIL			W	B
wc1958	19 June	Gothenburg	0	1
1962	12 May	Rio de Janeiro	1	3
1962	16 May	São Paulo	1	3
1966	14 May	Rio de Janeiro	1	3
1966	18 May	Belo Horizonte	0	1
1983	12 June	Cardiff	1	1
1991	11 Sept	Cardiff	1	0
1997	12 Nov	Brasilia	0	3
2000	23 May	Cardiff	0	3
2006	5 Sept	Cardiff	0	2

v BULGARIA			W	B
EC1983	27 Apr	Wrexham	1	0
EC1983	16 Nov	Sofia	0	1
EC1994	14 Dec	Cardiff	0	3
EC1995	29 Mar	Sofia	1	3
2006	15 Aug	Swansea	0	0
2007	22 Aug	Burgas	1	0

v CANADA			W	C
1986	10 May	Toronto	0	2
1986	20 May	Vancouver	3	0
2004	30 May	Wrexham	1	0

v CHILE			W	C
1966	22 May	Santiago	0	2

v COSTA RICA			W	CR
1990	20 May	Cardiff	1	0

v CROATIA			W	C
2002	21 Aug	Varazdin	1	1
2010	23 May	Osijek	0	2

v CYPRUS			W	C
wc1992	14 Oct	Limassol	1	0
wc1993	13 Oct	Cardiff	2	0
2005	16 Nov	Limassol	0	1
EC2006	11 Oct	Cardiff	3	1
EC2007	13 Oct	Nicosia	1	3

v CZECHOSLOVAKIA			W	C
wc1957	1 May	Cardiff	1	0
wc1957	26 May	Prague	0	2
EC1971	21 Apr	Swansea	1	3
EC1971	27 Oct	Prague	0	1
wc1977	30 Mar	Wrexham	3	0
wc1977	16 Nov	Prague	0	1
wc1980	19 Nov	Cardiff	1	0
wc1981	9 Sept	Prague	0	2
EC1987	29 Apr	Wrexham	1	1
EC1987	11 Nov	Prague	0	2
wc1993	28 Apr	Ostrava†	1	1
wc1993	8 Sept	Cardiff†	2	2

†*Czechoslovakia played as RCS (Republic of Czechs and Slovaks).*

v CZECH REPUBLIC			W	CR
2002	27 Mar	Cardiff	0	0
EC2006	2 Sept	Teplice	1	2
EC2007	2 June	Cardiff	0	0

v DENMARK			W	D
wc1964	21 Oct	Copenhagen	0	1
wc1965	1 Dec	Wrexham	4	2
EC1987	9 Sept	Cardiff	1	0
EC1987	14 Oct	Copenhagen	0	1
1990	11 Sept	Copenhagen	0	1
EC1998	10 Oct	Copenhagen	2	1
EC1999	9 June	Liverpool	0	2
2008	19 Nov	Brondby	1	0

v ESTONIA

			W	E
	1994	23 May	Tallinn	2	1
	2009	29 May	Llanelli	1	0

v FINLAND

			W	F
EC1971	26 May	Helsinki	1	0
EC1971	13 Oct	Swansea	3	0
EC1987	10 Sept	Helsinki	1	1
EC1987	1 Apr	Wrexham	4	0
wc1988	19 Oct	Swansea	2	2
wc1989	6 Sept	Helsinki	0	1
2000	29 Mar	Cardiff	1	2
EC2002	7 Sept	Helsinki	2	0
EC2003	10 Sept	Cardiff	1	1
wc2009	28 Mar	Cardiff	0	2
wc2009	10 Oct	Helsinki	1	2

v FAEROES

			W	F
wc1992	9 Sept	Cardiff	6	0
wc1993	6 June	Toftir	3	0

v FRANCE

			W	F
1933	25 May	Paris	1	1
1939	20 May	Paris	1	2
1953	14 May	Paris	1	6
1982	2 June	Toulouse	1	0

v GEORGIA

			W	G
EC1994	16 Nov	Tbilisi	0	5
EC1995	7 June	Cardiff	0	1
2008	20 Aug	Swansea	1	2

v GERMANY

			W	G
EC1995	26 Apr	Dusseldorf	1	1
EC1995	11 Oct	Cardiff	1	2
2002	14 May	Cardiff	1	0
EC2007	8 Sept	Cardiff	0	2
EC2007	21 Nov	Frankfurt	0	0
wc2008	15 Oct	Moenchengladbach	0	1
wc2009	1 Apr	Cardiff	0	2

v EAST GERMANY

			W	EG
wc1957	19 May	Leipzig	1	2
wc1957	25 Sept	Cardiff	4	1
wc1969	16 Apr	Dresden	1	2
wc1969	22 Oct	Cardiff	1	3

v WEST GERMANY

			W	WG
1968	8 May	Cardiff	1	1
1969	26 Mar	Frankfurt	1	1
1976	6 Oct	Cardiff	0	2
1977	14 Dec	Dortmund	1	1
EC1979	2 May	Wrexham	0	2
EC1979	17 Oct	Cologne	1	5
wc1989	31 May	Cardiff	0	0
wc1989	15 Nov	Cologne	1	2
EC1991	5 June	Cardiff	1	0
EC1991	16 Oct	Nuremberg	1	4

v GREECE

			W	G
wc1964	9 Dec	Athens	0	2
wc1965	17 Mar	Cardiff	4	1

v HOLLAND

			W	H
wc1988	14 Sept	Amsterdam	0	1
wc1989	11 Oct	Wrexham	1	2
1992	30 May	Utrecht	0	4
wc1996	5 Oct	Cardiff	1	3
wc1996	9 Nov	Eindhoven	1	7
2008	1 June	Rotterdam	0	2

v HUNGARY

			W	H
wc1958	8 June	Sanviken	1	1
wc1958	17 June	Stockholm	2	1
1961	28 May	Budapest	2	3
EC1962	7 Nov	Budapest	1	3
EC1963	20 Mar	Cardiff	1	1
EC1974	30 Oct	Cardiff	2	0
EC1975	16 Apr	Budapest	2	1
1985	16 Oct	Cardiff	0	3
2004	31 Mar	Budapest	2	1
2005	9 Feb	Cardiff	2	0

v ICELAND

			W	I
wc1980	2 June	Reykjavik	4	0
wc1981	14 Oct	Swansea	2	2
wc1984	12 Sept	Reykjavik	0	1
wc1984	14 Nov	Cardiff	2	1
1991	1 May	Cardiff	1	0
2008	28 May	Reykjavik	1	0

v IRAN

			W	I
1978	18 Apr	Teheran	1	0

v REPUBLIC OF IRELAND

			W	RI
1960	28 Sept	Dublin	3	2
1979	11 Sept	Swansea	2	1
1981	24 Feb	Dublin	3	1
1986	26 Mar	Dublin	1	0
1990	28 Mar	Dublin	0	1
1991	6 Feb	Wrexham	0	3
1992	19 Feb	Dublin	1	0
1993	17 Feb	Dublin	1	2
1997	11 Feb	Cardiff	0	0
EC2007	24 Mar	Dublin	0	1
EC2007	17 Nov	Cardiff	2	2

v ISRAEL

			W	I
wc1958	15 Jan	Tel Aviv	2	0
wc1958	5 Feb	Cardiff	2	0
1984	10 June	Tel Aviv	0	0
1989	8 Feb	Tel Aviv	3	3

v ITALY

			W	I
1965	1 May	Florence	1	4
wc1968	23 Oct	Cardiff	0	1
wc1969	4 Nov	Rome	1	4
1988	4 June	Brescia	1	0
1996	24 Jan	Terni	0	3
EC1998	5 Sept	Liverpool	0	2
EC1999	5 June	Bologna	0	4
EC2002	16 Oct	Cardiff	2	1
EC2003	6 Sept	Milan	0	4

v JAMAICA

			W	J
1998	25 Mar	Cardiff	0	0

v JAPAN

			W	J
1992	7 June	Matsuyama	1	0

v KUWAIT

			W	K
1977	6 Sept	Wrexham	0	0
1977	20 Sept	Kuwait	0	0

v LATVIA

			W	L
2004	18 Aug	Riga	2	0

v LIECHTENSTEIN

			W	L
2006	14 Nov	Swansea	4	0
wc2008	11 Oct	Cardiff	2	0
wc2009	14 Oct	Vaduz	2	0

v LUXEMBOURG

			W	L
EC1974	20 Nov	Swansea	5	0
EC1975	1 May	Luxembourg	3	1
EC1990	14 Nov	Luxembourg	1	0
EC1991	13 Nov	Cardiff	1	0
2008	26 Mar	Luxembourg	2	0

v MALTA

			W	M
EC1978	25 Oct	Wrexham	7	0
EC1979	2 June	Valletta	2	0
1988	1 June	Valletta	3	2
1998	3 June	Valletta	3	0

v MEXICO

			W	M
wc1958	11 June	Stockholm	1	1
1962	22 May	Mexico City	1	2

v MOLDOVA

			W	M
EC1994	12 Oct	Kishinev	2	3
EC1995	6 Sept	Cardiff	1	0

v MONTENEGRO

			W	M
2009	12 Aug	Podgorica	1	2

v NEW ZEALAND

			W	NZ
2007	26 May	Wrexham	2	2

v NORWAY			W	N
EC1982	22 Sept	Swansea	1	0
EC1983	21 Sept	Oslo	0	0
1984	6 June	Trondheim	0	1
1985	26 Feb	Wrexham	1	1
1985	5 June	Bergen	2	4
1994	9 Mar	Cardiff	1	3
wc2000	7 Oct	Cardiff	1	1
wc2001	5 Sept	Oslo	2	3
2004	27 May	Oslo	0	0
2008	6 Feb	Wrexham	3	0

v PARAGUAY			W	P
2006	1 Mar	Cardiff	0	0

v POLAND			W	P
wc1973	28 Mar	Cardiff	2	0
wc1973	26 Sept	Katowice	0	3
1991	29 May	Radom	0	0
wc2000	11 Oct	Warsaw	0	0
wc2001	2 June	Cardiff	1	2
wc2004	13 Oct	Cardiff	2	3
wc2005	7 Sept	Warsaw	0	1
2009	11 Feb	Vila Real	0	1

v PORTUGAL			W	P
1949	15 May	Lisbon	2	3
1951	12 May	Cardiff	2	1
2000	2 June	Chaves	0	3

v QATAR			W	Q
2000	23 Feb	Doha	1	0

v ROMANIA			W	R
EC1970	11 Nov	Cardiff	0	0
EC1971	24 Nov	Bucharest	0	2
1983	12 Oct	Wrexham	5	0
wc1992	20 May	Bucharest	1	5
wc1993	17 Nov	Cardiff	1	2

v RUSSIA			W	R
EC2003	15 Nov	Moscow	0	0
EC2003	19 Nov	Cardiff	0	1
wc2008	10 Sept	Moscow	1	2
wc2009	9 Sept	Cardiff	1	3

v SAN MARINO			W	SM
wc1996	2 June	Serravalle	5	0
wc1996	31 Aug	Cardiff	6	0
EC2007	28 Mar	Cardiff	3	0
EC2007	17 Oct	Serravalle	2	1

v SAUDI ARABIA			W	SA
1986	25 Feb	Dahran	2	1

v SERBIA-MONTENEGRO			W	SM
EC2003	20 Aug	Belgrade	0	1
EC2003	11 Oct	Cardiff	2	3

v SLOVAKIA			W	S
EC2006	7 Oct	Cardiff	1	5
EC2007	12 Sept	Trnava	5	2

v SLOVENIA			W	Sl
2005	17 Aug	Swansea	0	0

v SPAIN			W	S
wc1961	19 Apr	Cardiff	1	2

			W	S
wc1961	18 May	Madrid	1	1
1982	24 Mar	Valencia	1	1
wc1984	17 Oct	Seville	0	3
wc1985	30 Apr	Wrexham	3	0

v SWEDEN			W	S
wc1958	15 June	Stockholm	0	0
1988	27 Apr	Stockholm	1	4
1989	26 Apr	Wrexham	0	2
1990	25 Apr	Stockholm	2	4
1994	20 Apr	Wrexham	0	2
2010	3 Mar	Swansea	0	1

v SWITZERLAND			W	S
1949	26 May	Berne	0	4
1951	16 May	Wrexham	3	2
1996	24 Apr	Lugano	0	2
EC1999	31 Mar	Zurich	0	2
EC1999	9 Oct	Wrexham	0	2

v TRINIDAD & TOBAGO			W	TT
2006	27 May	Graz	2	1

v TUNISIA			W	T
1998	6 June	Tunis	0	4

v TURKEY			W	T
EC1978	29 Nov	Wrexham	1	0
EC1979	21 Nov	Izmir	0	1
wc1980	15 Oct	Cardiff	4	0
wc1981	25 Mar	Ankara	1	0
wc1996	14 Dec	Cardiff	0	0
wc1997	20 Aug	Istanbul	4	6

v REST OF UNITED KINGDOM			W	UK
1951	5 Dec	Cardiff	3	2
1969	28 July	Cardiff	0	1

v UKRAINE			W	U
wc2001	28 Mar	Cardiff	1	1
wc2001	6 June	Kiev	1	1

v USA			W	USA
2003	27 May	San Jose	0	2

v URUGUAY			W	U
1986	21 Apr	Wrexham	0	0

v USSR			W	USSR
wc1965	30 May	Moscow	1	2
wc1965	27 Oct	Cardiff	2	1
wc1981	30 May	Wrexham	0	0
wc1981	18 Nov	Tbilisi	0	3
1987	18 Feb	Swansea	0	0

v YUGOSLAVIA			W	Y
1953	21 May	Belgrade	2	5
1954	22 Nov	Cardiff	1	3
EC1976	24 Apr	Zagreb	0	2
EC1976	22 May	Cardiff	1	1
EC1982	15 Dec	Titograd	4	4
EC1983	14 Dec	Cardiff	1	1
1988	23 Mar	Swansea	1	2

NORTHERN IRELAND

v ALBANIA			NI	A
wc1965	7 May	Belfast	4	1
wc1965	24 Nov	Tirana	1	1
EC1982	15 Dec	Tirana	0	0
EC1983	27 Apr	Belfast	1	0
wc1992	9 Sept	Belfast	3	0
wc1993	17 Feb	Tirana	2	1
wc1996	14 Dec	Belfast	2	0
wc1997	10 Sept	Zurich	0	1
2010	3 Mar	Tirana	0	1

v ALGERIA			NI	A
wc1986	3 June	Guadalajara	1	

v ARGENTINA			NI	A
wc1958	11 June	Halmstad	1	3

v ARMENIA			NI	A
wc1996	5 Oct	Belfast	1	1
wc1997	30 Apr	Erevan	0	0
EC2003	29 Mar	Erevan	0	1
EC2003	10 Sept	Belfast	0	1

v AUSTRALIA			NI	A
1980	11 June	Sydney	2	1
1980	15 June	Melbourne	1	1
1980	18 June	Adelaide	2	1

v AUSTRIA			NI	A
wc1982	1 July	Madrid	2	2
EC1982	13 Oct	Vienna	0	2
EC1983	21 Sept	Belfast	3	1
EC1990	14 Nov	Vienna	0	0

			NI	A
EC1991	16 Oct	Belfast	2	1
EC1994	12 Oct	Vienna	2	1
EC1995	15 Nov	Belfast	5	3
wc2004	13 Oct	Belfast	3	3
wc2005	12 Oct	Vienna	0	2

		v AZERBAIJAN	NI	A
wc2004	9 Oct	Baku	0	0
wc2005	3 Sept	Belfast	2	0

		v BARBADOS	NI	B
2004	30 May	Waterford	1	1

		v BELGIUM	NI	B
wc1976	10 Nov	Liège	0	2
wc1977	16 Nov	Belfast	3	0
1997	11 Feb	Belfast	3	0

		v BRAZIL	NI	B
wc1986	12 June	Guadalajara	0	3

		v BULGARIA	NI	B
wc1972	18 Oct	Sofia	0	3
wc1973	26 Sept	Sheffield	0	0
EC1978	29 Nov	Sofia	2	0
EC1979	2 May	Belfast	2	0
wc2001	28 Mar	Sofia	3	4
wc2001	2 June	Belfast	0	1
2008	6 Feb	Belfast	0	1

		v CANADA	NI	C
1995	22 May	Edmonton	0	2
1999	27 Apr	Belfast	1	1
2005	9 Feb	Belfast	0	1

		v CHILE	NI	C
1989	26 May	Belfast	0	1
1995	25 May	Edmonton	1	2
2010	30 May	Chillan	0	1

		v COLOMBIA	NI	C
1994	4 June	Boston	0	2

		v CYPRUS	NI	C
EC1971	3 Feb	Nicosia	3	0
EC1971	21 Apr	Belfast	5	0
wc1973	14 Feb	Nicosia	0	1
wc1973	8 May	London	3	0
2002	21 Aug	Belfast	0	0

		v CZECHOSLOVAKIA	NI	C
wc1958	8 June	Halmstad	1	0
wc1958	17 June	Malmo	2	1*

*After extra time

		v CZECH REPUBLIC	NI	C
wc2001	24 Mar	Belfast	0	1
wc2001	6 June	Teplice	1	3
wc2008	10 Sept	Belfast	0	0
wc2009	14 Oct	Prague	0	0

		v DENMARK	NI	D
EC1978	25 Oct	Belfast	2	1
EC1979	6 June	Copenhagen	0	4
1986	26 Mar	Belfast	1	1
EC1990	17 Oct	Belfast	1	1
EC1991	13 Nov	Odense	1	2
wc1992	18 Nov	Belfast	0	1
wc1993	13 Oct	Copenhagen	0	1
wc2000	7 Oct	Belfast	1	1
wc2001	1 Sept	Copenhagen	1	1
EC2006	7 Oct	Copenhagen	0	0
EC2007	17 Nov	Belfast	2	1

		v ESTONIA	NI	E
2004	31 Mar	Tallinn	1	0
2006	1 Mar	Belfast	1	0

		v FAEROES	NI	F
EC1991	1 May	Belfast	1	1
EC1991	11 Sept	Landskrona	5	0

		v FINLAND	NI	F
wc1984	27 May	Pori	0	1
wc1984	14 Nov	Belfast	2	1

			NI	F
EC1998	10 Oct	Belfast	1	0
EC1998	9 Oct	Helsinki	1	4
2003	12 Feb	Belfast	0	1
2006	16 Aug	Helsinki	2	1

		v FRANCE	NI	F
1928	21 Feb	Paris	0	4
1951	12 May	Belfast	2	2
1952	11 Nov	Paris	1	3
wc1958	19 June	Norrkoping	0	4
1982	24 Mar	Paris	0	4
wc1982	4 July	Madrid	1	4
1986	26 Feb	Paris	0	0
1988	27 Apr	Belfast	0	0
1999	18 Aug	Belfast	0	1

		v GEORGIA	NI	G
2008	26 Mar	Belfast	4	1

		v GERMANY	NI	G
1992	2 June	Bremen	1	1
1996	29 May	Belfast	1	1
wc1996	9 Nov	Nuremberg	1	1
wc1997	20 Aug	Belfast	1	3
EC1999	27 Mar	Belfast	0	3
EC1999	8 Sept	Dortmund	0	4
2005	4 June	Belfast	1	4

		v WEST GERMANY	NI	WG
wc1958	15 June	Malmo	2	2
wc1960	26 Oct	Belfast	3	4
wc1961	10 May	Hamburg	1	2
1966	7 May	Belfast	0	2
1977	27 Apr	Cologne	0	5
EC1982	17 Nov	Belfast	1	0
EC1983	16 Nov	Hamburg	1	0

		v GREECE	NI	G
wc1961	3 May	Athens	1	2
wc1961	17 Oct	Belfast	2	0
1988	17 Feb	Athens	2	3
EC2003	2 Apr	Belfast	0	2
EC2003	11 Oct	Athens	0	1

		v HOLLAND	NI	H
1962	9 May	Rotterdam	0	4
wc1965	17 Mar	Rotterdam	2	1
wc1965	7 Apr	Rotterdam	0	0
wc1976	13 Oct	Rotterdam	2	2
wc1977	12 Oct	Belfast	0	1

		v HONDURAS	NI	H
wc1982	21 June	Zaragoza	1	1

		v HUNGARY	NI	H
wc1988	19 Oct	Budapest	0	1
wc1989	6 Sept	Belfast	1	2
2000	26 Apr	Belfast	0	1
2008	19 Nov	Belfast	0	2

		v ICELAND	NI	I
wc1977	11 June	Reykjavik	0	1
wc1977	21 Sept	Belfast	2	0
wc2000	11 Oct	Reykjavik	0	1
wc2001	5 Sept	Belfast	3	0
EC2006	2 Sept	Belfast	0	3
EC2007	12 Sept	Reykjavik	1	2

		v REPUBLIC OF IRELAND	NI	RI
EC1978	20 Sept	Dublin	0	0
EC1979	21 Nov	Belfast	1	0
wc1988	14 Sept	Belfast	0	0
wc1989	11 Oct	Dublin	0	3
wc1993	31 Mar	Dublin	0	3
wc1993	17 Nov	Belfast	1	1
EC1994	16 Nov	Belfast	0	4
EC1995	29 Mar	Dublin	1	1
1999	29 May	Dublin	1	0

		v ISRAEL	NI	I
1968	10 Sept	Jaffa	3	2
1976	3 Mar	Tel Aviv	1	1
wc1980	26 Mar	Tel Aviv	0	0
wc1981	18 Nov	Belfast	1	0

			NI	I
1984	16 Oct	Belfast	3	0
1987	18 Feb	Tel Aviv	1	1
2009	12 Aug	Belfast	1	1

v ITALY			NI	I
wc1957	25 Apr	Rome	0	1
1957	4 Dec	Belfast	2	2
wc1958	15 Jan	Belfast	2	1
1961	25 Apr	Bologna	2	3
1997	22 Jan	Palermo	0	2
2003	3 June	Campobasso	0	2
2009	6 June	Pisa	0	3

v LATVIA			NI	L
wc1993	2 June	Riga	2	1
wc1993	8 Sept	Belfast	2	0
EC1995	26 Apr	Riga	1	0
EC1995	7 June	Belfast	1	2
EC2006	11 Oct	Belfast	1	0
EC2007	8 Sept	Riga	0	1

v LIECHTENSTEIN			NI	L
EC1994	20 Apr	Belfast	4	1
EC1995	11 Oct	Eschen	4	0
2002	27 Mar	Vaduz	0	0
EC2007	24 Mar	Vaduz	4	1
EC2007	22 Aug	Belfast	3	1

v LITHUANIA			NI	L
wc1992	28 Apr	Belfast	2	2
wc1993	25 May	Vilnius	1	0

v LUXEMBOURG			NI	L
2000	23 Feb	Luxembourg	3	1

v MALTA			NI	M
wc1988	21 May	Belfast	3	0
wc1989	26 Apr	Valletta	2	0
2000	28 Mar	Valletta	3	0
wc2000	2 Sept	Belfast	1	0
wc2001	6 Oct	Valletta	1	0
2005	17 Aug	Ta'Qali	1	1

v MEXICO			NI	M
1966	22 June	Belfast	4	1
1994	11 June	Miami	0	3

v MOLDOVA			NI	M
EC1998	18 Nov	Belfast	2	2
EC1999	31 Mar	Chisinau	0	0

v MOROCCO			NI	M
1986	23 Apr	Belfast	2	1

v NORWAY			NI	N
1922	25 May	Bergen	1	2
EC1974	4 Sept	Oslo	1	2
EC1975	29 Oct	Belfast	3	0
1990	27 Mar	Belfast	2	3
1996	27 Mar	Belfast	0	2
2001	28 Feb	Belfast	0	4
2004	18 Feb	Belfast	1	4

v POLAND			NI	P
EC1962	10 Oct	Katowice	2	0
EC1962	28 Nov	Belfast	2	0
1988	23 Mar	Belfast	1	1
1991	5 Feb	Belfast	3	1
2002	13 Feb	Limassol	1	4
EC2004	4 Sept	Belfast	0	3
EC2005	30 Mar	Warsaw	0	1
wc2009	28 Mar	Belfast	3	2
wc2009	5 Sept	Chorzow	1	1

v PORTUGAL			NI	P
wc1957	16 Jan	Lisbon	1	1
wc1957	1 May	Belfast	3	0
wc1973	28 Mar	Coventry	1	1
wc1973	14 Nov	Lisbon	1	1
wc1980	19 Nov	Lisbon	0	1
wc1981	29 Apr	Belfast	1	0
EC1994	7 Sept	Belfast	1	2
EC1995	3 Sept	Lisbon	1	1

			NI	P
wc1997	29 Mar	Belfast	0	0
wc1997	11 Oct	Lisbon	0	1
2005	15 Nov	Belfast	1	1

v ROMANIA			NI	R
wc1984	12 Sept	Belfast	3	2
wc1985	16 Oct	Bucharest	1	0
1994	23 Mar	Belfast	2	0
2006	27 May	Chicago	0	2

v SAN MARINO			NI	SM
wc2008	15 Oct	Belfast	4	0
wc2009	11 Feb	Serravalle	3	0

v ST KITTS & NEVIS			NI	SK
2004	2 June	Basseterre	2	0

v SERBIA			NI	S
2009	14 Nov	Belfast	0	1

v SERBIA-MONTENEGRO			NI	SM
2004	28 Apr	Belfast	1	1

v SLOVAKIA			NI	S
1998	25 Mar	Belfast	1	0
wc2008	6 Sept	Bratislava	1	2
wc2009	9 Sept	Belfast	0	2

v SLOVENIA			NI	S
wc2008	11 Oct	Maribor	0	2
wc2009	1 Apr	Belfast	1	0

v SOUTH AFRICA			NI	SA
1924	24 Sept	Belfast	1	2

v SPAIN			NI	S
1958	15 Oct	Madrid	2	6
1963	30 May	Bilbao	1	1
1963	30 Oct	Belfast	0	1
EC1970	11 Nov	Seville	0	3
EC1972	16 Feb	Hull	1	1
wc1982	25 June	Valencia	1	0
1985	27 Mar	Palma	0	0
wc1986	7 June	Guadalajara	1	2
wc1988	21 Dec	Seville	0	4
wc1989	8 Feb	Belfast	0	2
wc1992	14 Oct	Belfast	0	0
wc1993	28 Apr	Seville	1	3
1998	2 June	Santander	1	4
2002	17 Apr	Belfast	0	5
EC2002	12 Oct	Albacete	0	3
EC2003	11 June	Belfast	0	0
EC2006	6 Sept	Belfast	3	2
EC2007	21 Nov	Las Palmas	0	1

v SWEDEN			NI	S
EC1974	30 Oct	Solna	2	0
EC1975	3 Sept	Belfast	1	2
wc1980	15 Oct	Belfast	3	0
wc1981	3 June	Solna	0	1
1996	24 Apr	Belfast	1	2
EC2007	28 Mar	Belfast	2	1
EC2007	17 Oct	Stockholm	1	1

v SWITZERLAND			NI	S
wc1964	14 Oct	Belfast	1	0
wc1964	14 Nov	Lausanne	1	2
1998	22 Apr	Belfast	1	0
2004	18 Aug	Zurich	0	0

v THAILAND			NI	T
1997	21 May	Bangkok	0	0

v TRINIDAD & TOBAGO			NI	TT
2004	6 June	Bacolet	3	0

v TURKEY			NI	T
wc1968	23 Oct	Belfast	4	1
wc1968	11 Dec	Istanbul	3	0
EC1983	30 Mar	Belfast	2	1
EC1983	12 Oct	Ankara	0	1

			RI	T
wc1985	1 May	Belfast	2	0
wc1985	11 Sept	Izmir	0	0
EC1986	12 Nov	Izmir	0	0
EC1987	11 Nov	Belfast	1	0
EC1998	5 Sept	Istanbul	0	3
EC1999	4 Sept	Belfast	0	3
2010	26 May	New Britain	0	2

v UKRAINE

			NI	U
wc1996	31 Aug	Belfast	0	1
wc1997	2 Apr	Kiev	1	2
EC2002	16 Oct	Belfast	0	0
EC2003	6 Sept	Donetsk	0	0

v URUGUAY

			NI	U
1964	29 Apr	Belfast	3	0
1990	18 May	Belfast	1	0
2006	21 May	New Jersey	0	1

v USSR

			NI	USSR
wc1969	19 Sept	Belfast	0	0
wc1969	22 Oct	Moscow	0	2
EC1971	22 Sept	Moscow	0	1
EC1971	13 Oct	Belfast	1	1

v YUGOSLAVIA

			NI	Y
EC1975	16 Mar	Belfast	1	0
EC1975	19 Nov	Belgrade	0	1
wc1982	17 June	Zaragoza	0	0
EC1987	29 Apr	Belfast	1	2
EC1987	14 Oct	Sarajevo	0	3
EC1990	12 Sept	Belfast	0	2
EC1991	27 Mar	Belgrade	1	4
2000	16 Aug	Belfast	1	2

REPUBLIC OF IRELAND

v ALBANIA

			RI	A
wc1992	26 May	Dublin	2	0
wc1993	26 May	Tirana	2	1
EC2003	2 Apr	Tirana	0	0
EC2003	7 June	Dublin	2	1

v ALGERIA

			RI	A
1982	28 Apr	Algiers	0	2
2010	28 May	Dublin	3	0

v ANDORRA

			RI	A
wc2001	28 Mar	Barcelona	3	0
wc2001	25 Apr	Dublin	3	1

v ARGENTINA

			RI	A
1951	13 May	Dublin	0	1
†1979	29 May	Dublin	0	0
1980	16 May	Dublin	0	1
1998	22 Apr	Dublin	0	2

†*Not considered a full international.*

v AUSTRALIA

			RI	A
2003	19 Aug	Dublin	2	1
2009	12 Aug	Limerick	0	3

v AUSTRIA

			RI	A
1952	7 May	Vienna	0	6
1953	25 Mar	Dublin	4	0
1958	14 Mar	Vienna	1	3
1962	8 Apr	Dublin	2	3
EC1963	25 Sept	Vienna	0	0
EC1963	13 Oct	Dublin	3	2
1966	22 May	Vienna	0	1
1968	10 Nov	Dublin	2	2
EC1971	30 May	Dublin	1	4
EC1971	10 Oct	Linz	0	6
EC1995	11 June	Dublin	1	3
EC1995	6 Sept	Vienna	1	3

v BELGIUM

			RI	B
1928	12 Feb	Liège	4	2
1929	30 Apr	Dublin	4	0
1930	11 May	Brussels	3	1
wc1934	25 Feb	Dublin	4	4
1949	24 Apr	Dublin	0	2
1950	10 May	Brussels	1	5
1965	24 Mar	Dublin	0	2
1966	25 May	Liège	3	2
wc1980	15 Oct	Dublin	1	1
wc1981	25 Mar	Brussels	0	1
EC1986	10 Sept	Brussels	2	2
EC1987	29 Apr	Dublin	0	0
wc1997	29 Oct	Dublin	1	1
wc1997	16 Nov	Brussels	1	2

v BOLIVIA

			RI	B
1994	24 May	Dublin	1	0
1996	15 June	New Jersey	3	0
2007	26 May	Boston	1	1

v BRAZIL

			RI	B
1974	5 May	Rio de Janeiro	1	2
1982	27 May	Uberlandia	0	7
1987	23 May	Dublin	1	0
2004	18 Feb	Dublin	0	0
2008	6 Feb	Dublin	0	1
2010	2 Mar	Emirates	0	2

v BULGARIA

			RI	B
wc1977	1 June	Sofia	1	2
wc1977	12 Oct	Dublin	0	0
EC1979	19 May	Sofia	0	1
EC1979	17 Oct	Dublin	3	0
wc1987	1 Apr	Sofia	1	2
wc1987	14 Oct	Dublin	2	0
2004	18 Aug	Dublin	1	1
wc2009	28 Mar	Dublin	1	1
wc2009	6 June	Sofia	1	1

v CAMEROON

			RI	C
wc2002	1 June	Niigata	1	1

v CANADA

			RI	C
2003	18 Nov	Dublin	3	0

v CHILE

			RI	C
1960	30 Mar	Dublin	2	0
1972	21 June	Recife	1	2
1974	12 May	Santiago	2	1
1982	22 May	Santiago	0	1
1991	22 May	Dublin	1	1
2006	24 May	Dublin	0	1

v CHINA

			RI	C
1984	3 June	Sapporo	1	0
2005	29 Mar	Dublin	1	0

v COLOMBIA

			RI	C
2008	29 May	Fulham	1	0

v CROATIA

			RI	C
1996	2 June	Dublin	2	2
EC1998	5 Sept	Dublin	2	0
EC1999	4 Sept	Zagreb	0	1
2001	15 Aug	Dublin	2	2
2004	16 Nov	Dublin	1	0

v CYPRUS

			RI	C
wc1980	26 Mar	Nicosia	3	2
wc1980	19 Nov	Dublin	6	0
wc2001	24 Mar	Nicosia	4	0
wc2001	6 Oct	Dublin	4	0
wc2004	4 Sept	Dublin	3	0
wc2005	8 Oct	Nicosia	1	0
EC2006	7 Oct	Nicosia	2	5
EC2007	17 Oct	Dublin	1	1
2008	15 Oct	Dublin	1	0
wc2009	5 Sept	Nicosia	2	1

v CZECHOSLOVAKIA

			RI	C
1938	18 May	Prague	2	2
EC1959	5 Apr	Dublin	2	0
EC1959	10 May	Bratislava	0	4

			RI	C
wc1961	8 Oct	Dublin	1	3
wc1961	29 Oct	Prague	1	7
EC1967	21 May	Dublin	0	2
EC1967	22 Nov	Prague	2	1
wc1969	4 May	Dublin	1	2
wc1969	7 Oct	Prague	0	3
1979	26 Sept	Prague	1	4
1981	29 Apr	Dublin	3	1
1986	27 May	Reykjavik	1	0

v CZECH REPUBLIC

			RI	C
1994	5 June	Dublin	1	3
1996	24 Apr	Prague	0	2
1998	25 Mar	Olomouc	1	2
2000	23 Feb	Dublin	3	2
2004	31 Mar	Dublin	2	1
EC2006	11 Oct	Dublin	1	1
EC2007	12 Sept	Prague	0	1

v DENMARK

			RI	D
wc1956	3 Oct	Dublin	2	1
wc1957	2 Oct	Copenhagen	2	0
wc1968	4 Dec	Dublin	1	1
(abandoned after 51 mins)				
wc1969	27 May	Copenhagen	0	2
wc1969	15 Oct	Dublin	1	1
EC1978	24 May	Copenhagen	3	3
EC1979	2 May	Dublin	2	0
wc1984	14 Nov	Copenhagen	0	3
wc1985	13 Nov	Dublin	1	4
wc1992	14 Oct	Copenhagen	0	0
wc1993	28 Apr	Dublin	1	1
2002	27 Mar	Dublin	3	0
2007	22 Aug	Copenhagen	4	0

v ECUADOR

			RI	E
1972	19 June	Natal	3	2
2007	23 May	New Jersey	1	1

v EGYPT

			RI	E
wc1990	17 June	Palermo	0	0

v ENGLAND

			RI	E
1946	30 Sept	Dublin	0	1
1949	21 Sept	Everton	2	0
wc1957	8 May	Wembley	1	5
wc1957	19 May	Dublin	1	1
1964	24 May	Dublin	1	3
1976	8 Sept	Wembley	1	1
EC1978	25 Oct	Dublin	1	1
EC1980	6 Feb	Wembley	0	2
1985	26 Mar	Wembley	1	2
EC1988	12 June	Stuttgart	1	0
wc1990	11 June	Cagliari	1	1
EC1990	14 Nov	Dublin	1	1
EC1991	27 Mar	Wembley	1	1
1995	15 Feb	Dublin	1	0
(abandoned after 27 mins)				

v ESTONIA

			RI	E
wc2000	11 Oct	Dublin	2	0
wc2001	6 June	Tallinn	2	0

v FAEROES

			RI	F
EC2004	13 Oct	Dublin	2	0
EC2005	8 June	Toftir	2	0

v FINLAND

			RI	F
wc1949	8 Sept	Dublin	3	0
wc1949	9 Oct	Helsinki	1	1
1990	16 May	Dublin	1	1
2000	15 Nov	Dublin	3	0
2002	21 Aug	Helsinki	3	0

v FRANCE

			RI	F
1937	23 May	Paris	2	0
1952	16 Nov	Dublin	1	1
wc1953	4 Oct	Dublin	3	5
wc1953	25 Nov	Paris	0	1
wc1972	15 Nov	Dublin	2	1
wc1973	19 May	Paris	1	1
wc1976	17 Nov	Paris	0	2
wc1977	30 Mar	Dublin	1	0
wc1980	28 Oct	Paris	0	2
wc1981	14 Oct	Dublin	3	2
1989	7 Feb	Dublin	0	0
wc2004	9 Oct	Paris	0	0
wc2005	7 Sept	Dublin	0	1
wc2009	14 Nov	Dublin	0	1
wc2009	18 Nov	Paris	1	1

v GEORGIA

			RI	G
EC2003	29 Mar	Tbilisi	2	1
EC2003	11 June	Dublin	2	0
wc2008	6 Sept	Mainz	2	1
wc2009	11 Feb	Dublin	2	1

v GERMANY

			RI	G
1935	8 May	Dortmund	1	3
1936	17 Oct	Dublin	5	2
1939	23 May	Bremen	1	1
1994	29 May	Hanover	2	0
wc2002	5 June	Ibaraki	1	1
EC2006	2 Sept	Stuttgart	0	1
EC2007	13 Oct	Dublin	0	0

v WEST GERMANY

			RI	WG
1951	17 Oct	Dublin	3	2
1952	4 May	Cologne	0	3
1955	28 May	Hamburg	1	2
1956	25 Nov	Dublin	3	0
1960	11 May	Dusseldorf	1	0
1966	4 May	Dublin	0	4
1970	9 May	Berlin	1	2
1975	1 Mar	Dublin	1	0†
1979	22 May	Dublin	1	3
1981	21 May	Bremen	0	3†
1989	6 Sept	Dublin	1	1

†v West Germany 'B'

v GREECE

			RI	G
2000	26 Apr	Dublin	0	1
2002	20 Nov	Athens	0	0

v HOLLAND

			RI	N
1932	8 May	Amsterdam	2	0
1934	8 Apr	Amsterdam	2	5
1935	8 Dec	Dublin	3	5
1955	1 May	Dublin	1	0
1956	10 May	Rotterdam	4	1
wc1980	10 Sept	Dublin	2	1
wc1981	9 Sept	Rotterdam	2	2
EC1982	22 Sept	Rotterdam	1	2
EC1983	12 Oct	Dublin	2	3
EC1988	18 June	Gelsenkirchen	0	1
wc1990	21 June	Palermo	1	1
1994	20 Apr	Tilburg	1	0
wc1994	4 July	Orlando	0	2
EC1995	13 Dec	Liverpool	0	2
1996	4 June	Rotterdam	1	3
wc2000	2 Sept	Amsterdam	2	2
wc2001	1 Sept	Dublin	1	0
2004	5 June	Amsterdam	1	0
2006	16 Aug	Dublin	0	4

v HUNGARY

			RI	H
1934	15 Dec	Dublin	2	4
1936	3 May	Budapest	3	3
1936	6 Dec	Dublin	2	3
1939	19 Mar	Cork	2	2
1939	18 May	Budapest	2	2
wc1969	8 June	Dublin	1	2
wc1969	5 Nov	Budapest	0	4
wc1989	8 Mar	Budapest	0	0
wc1989	4 June	Dublin	2	0
1991	11 Sept	Gyor	2	1

v ICELAND

			RI	I
EC1962	12 Aug	Dublin	4	2
EC1962	2 Sept	Reykjavik	1	1
EC1982	13 Oct	Dublin	2	0
EC1983	21 Sept	Reykjavik	3	0
1986	25 May	Reykjavik	2	1
wc1996	10 Nov	Dublin	0	0
wc1997	6 Sept	Reykjavik	4	2

v IRAN

			RI	I
1972	18 June	Recife	2	1
wc2001	10 Nov	Dublin	2	0
wc2001	15 Nov	Tehran	0	1

v N. IRELAND

			RI	NI
EC1978	20 Sept	Dublin	0	0
EC1979	21 Nov	Belfast	0	1
wc1988	14 Sept	Belfast	0	0
wc1989	11 Oct	Dublin	3	0

v N. IRELAND

			RI	NI
wc1993	31 Mar	Dublin	3	0
wc1993	17 Nov	Belfast	1	1
EC1994	16 Nov	Belfast	4	0
EC1995	29 Mar	Dublin	1	1
1999	29 May	Dublin	0	1

v ISRAEL

			RI	I
1984	4 Apr	Tel Aviv	0	3
1985	27 May	Tel Aviv	0	0
1987	10 Nov	Dublin	5	0
EC2005	26 Mar	Tel Aviv	1	1
EC2005	4 June	Dublin	2	2

v ITALY

			RI	I
1926	21 Mar	Turin	0	3
1927	23 Apr	Dublin	1	2
EC1970	8 Dec	Rome	0	3
EC1971	10 May	Dublin	1	2
1985	5 Feb	Dublin	1	2
wc1990	30 June	Rome	0	1
1992	4 June	Foxboro	0	2
wc1994	18 June	New York	1	0
2005	17 Aug	Dublin	1	2
wc2009	1 Apr	Bari	1	1
wc2009	10 Oct	Dublin	2	2

v JAMAICA

			RI	J
2004	2 June	Charlton	1	0

v LATVIA

			RI	L
wc1992	9 Sept	Dublin	4	0
wc1993	2 June	Riga	2	1
EC1994	7 Sept	Riga	3	0
EC1995	11 Oct	Dublin	2	1

v LIECHTENSTEIN

			RI	L
EC1994	12 Oct	Dublin	4	0
EC1995	3 June	Eschen	0	0
wc1996	31 Aug	Eschen	5	0
wc1997	21 May	Dublin	5	0

v LITHUANIA

			RI	L
wc1993	16 June	Vilnius	1	0
wc1993	8 Sept	Dublin	2	0
wc1997	20 Aug	Dublin	0	0
wc1997	10 Sept	Vilnius	2	1

v LUXEMBOURG

			RI	L
1936	9 May	Luxembourg	5	1
wc1953	28 Oct	Dublin	4	0
wc1954	7 Mar	Luxembourg	1	0
EC1987	28 May	Luxembourg	2	0
EC1987	9 Sept	Dublin	2	1

v MACEDONIA

			RI	M
wc1996	9 Oct	Dublin	3	0
wc1997	2 Apr	Skopje	2	3
EC1999	9 June	Dublin	1	0
EC1999	9 Oct	Skopje	1	1

v MALTA

			RI	M
EC1983	30 Mar	Valletta	1	0
EC1983	16 Nov	Dublin	8	0
wc1989	28 May	Dublin	2	0
wc1989	15 Nov	Valletta	2	0
1990	2 June	Valletta	3	0
EC1998	14 Oct	Dublin	5	0
EC1999	8 Sept	Valletta	3	2

v MEXICO

			RI	M
1984	8 Aug	Dublin	0	0
wc1994	24 June	Orlando	1	2
1996	13 June	New Jersey	2	2
1998	23 May	Dublin	0	0
2000	4 June	Chicago	2	2

v MONTENEGRO

			RI	M
wc2008	10 Sept	Podgorica	0	0
wc2009	14 Oct	Dublin	0	0

v MOROCCO

			RI	M
1990	12 Sept	Dublin	1	0

v NIGERIA

			RI	N
2002	16 May	Dublin	1	2
2004	29 May	Charlton	0	3
2009	29 May	Fulham	1	1

v NORWAY

			RI	N
wc1937	10 Oct	Oslo	2	3
wc1937	7 Nov	Dublin	3	3
1950	26 Nov	Dublin	2	2
1951	30 May	Oslo	3	2
1954	8 Nov	Dublin	2	1
1955	25 May	Oslo	3	1
1960	6 Nov	Dublin	3	1
1964	13 May	Oslo	4	1
1973	6 June	Oslo	1	1
1976	24 Mar	Dublin	3	0
1978	21 May	Oslo	0	0
wc1984	17 Oct	Oslo	0	1
wc1985	1 May	Dublin	0	0
1988	1 June	Oslo	0	0
wc1994	28 June	New York	0	0
2003	30 Apr	Dublin	1	0
2008	20 Aug	Oslo	1	1

v PARAGUAY

			RI	P
1999	10 Feb	Dublin	2	0
2010	25 May	Dublin	2	1

v POLAND

			RI	P
1938	22 May	Warsaw	0	6
1938	13 Nov	Dublin	3	2
1958	11 May	Katowice	2	2
1958	5 Oct	Dublin	2	2
1964	10 May	Kracow	1	3
1964	25 Oct	Dublin	3	2
1968	15 May	Dublin	2	2
1968	30 Oct	Katowice	0	1
1970	6 May	Dublin	1	2
1970	23 Sept	Dublin	0	2
1973	16 May	Wroclaw	0	2
1973	21 Oct	Dublin	1	0
1976	26 May	Poznan	2	0
1977	24 Apr	Dublin	0	0
1978	12 Apr	Lodz	0	3
1981	23 May	Bydgoszcz	0	3
1984	23 May	Dublin	0	0
1986	12 Nov	Warsaw	0	1
1988	22 May	Dublin	3	1
EC1991	1 May	Dublin	0	0
EC1991	16 Oct	Poznan	3	3
2004	28 Apr	Bydgoszcz	0	0
2008	19 Nov	Dublin	2	3

v PORTUGAL

			RI	P
1946	16 June	Lisbon	1	3
1947	4 May	Dublin	0	2
1948	23 May	Lisbon	0	2
1949	22 May	Dublin	1	0
1972	25 June	Recife	1	2
1992	7 June	Boston	2	0
EC1995	26 Apr	Dublin	1	0
EC1995	15 Nov	Lisbon	0	3
1996	29 May	Dublin	0	1
wc2000	7 Oct	Lisbon	1	1
wc2001	2 June	Dublin	1	1
2005	9 Feb	Dublin	1	0

v ROMANIA

			RI	R
1988	23 Mar	Dublin	2	0
wc1990	25 June	Genoa	0	0*
wc1997	30 Apr	Bucharest	0	1
wc1997	11 Oct	Dublin	1	1
2004	27 May	Dublin	1	0

v RUSSIA

			RI	R
1994	23 Mar	Dublin	0	0
1996	27 Mar	Dublin	0	2
2002	13 Feb	Dublin	2	0
EC2002	7 Sept	Moscow	2	4
EC2003	6 Sept	Dublin	1	1

v SAN MARINO

			RI	SM
EC2006	15 Nov	Dublin	5	0
EC2007	7 Feb	Serravalle	2	1

v SAUDI ARABIA

			RI	SA
wc2002	11 June	Yokohama	3	0

v SERBIA

			RI	S
2008	24 May	Dublin	1	1

v SCOTLAND			RI	S
wc1961	3 May	Glasgow	1	4
wc1961	7 May	Dublin	0	3
1963	9 June	Dublin	1	0
1969	21 Sept	Dublin	1	1
EC1986	15 Oct	Dublin	0	0
EC1987	18 Feb	Glasgow	1	0
2000	30 May	Dublin	1	2
2003	12 Feb	Glasgow	2	0

v SLOVAKIA			RI	S
EC2007	28 Mar	Dublin	1	0
EC2007	8 Sept	Bratislava	2	2

v SOUTH AFRICA			RI	SA
2000	11 June	New Jersey	2	1
2009	8 Sept	Limerick	1	0

v SPAIN			RI	S
1931	26 Apr	Barcelona	1	1
1931	13 Dec	Dublin	0	5
1946	23 June	Madrid	1	0
1947	2 Mar	Dublin	3	2
1948	30 May	Barcelona	1	2
1949	12 June	Dublin	1	4
1952	1 June	Madrid	0	6
1955	27 Nov	Dublin	2	2
EC1964	11 Mar	Seville	1	5
EC1964	8 Apr	Dublin	0	2
wc1965	5 May	Dublin	1	0
wc1965	27 Oct	Seville	1	4
wc1965	10 Nov	Paris	0	1
EC1966	23 Oct	Dublin	0	0
EC1966	7 Dec	Valencia	0	2
1977	9 Feb	Dublin	0	1
EC1982	17 Nov	Dublin	3	3
EC1983	27 Apr	Zaragoza	0	2
1985	26 May	Cork	0	0
wc1988	16 Nov	Seville	0	2
wc1989	26 Apr	Dublin	1	0
wc1992	18 Nov	Seville	0	0
wc1993	13 Oct	Dublin	1	3
wc2002	16 June	Suwon	1	1

v SWEDEN			RI	S
wc1949	2 June	Stockholm	1	3
wc1949	13 Nov	Dublin	1	2
1959	1 Nov	Dublin	3	2
1960	18 May	Malmo	1	4
EC1970	14 Oct	Dublin	1	1
EC1970	28 Oct	Malmo	0	1
1999	28 Apr	Dublin	2	0
2006	1 Mar	Dublin	3	0

v SWITZERLAND			RI	S
1935	5 May	Basle	0	1
1936	17 Mar	Dublin	1	0
1937	17 May	Berne	1	0
1938	18 Sept	Dublin	4	0
1948	5 Dec	Dublin	0	1
EC1975	11 May	Dublin	2	1
EC1975	21 May	Berne	0	1
1980	30 Apr	Dublin	2	0
wc1985	2 June	Dublin	3	0
wc1985	11 Sept	Berne	0	0
1992	25 Mar	Dublin	2	1

			RI	S
EC2002	16 Oct	Dublin	1	2
EC2003	11 Oct	Basle	0	2
wc2004	8 Sept	Basle	1	1
wc2005	12 Oct	Dublin	0	0

v TRINIDAD & TOBAGO			RI	TT
1982	30 May	Port of Spain	1	2

v TUNISIA			RI	T
1988	19 Oct	Dublin	4	0

v TURKEY			RI	T
EC1966	16 Nov	Dublin	2	1
EC1967	22 Feb	Ankara	1	2
EC1974	20 Nov	Izmir	1	1
EC1975	29 Oct	Dublin	4	0
1976	13 Oct	Ankara	3	3
1978	5 Apr	Dublin	4	2
1990	26 May	Izmir	0	0
EC1990	17 Oct	Dublin	5	0
EC1991	13 Nov	Istanbul	3	1
EC2000	13 Nov	Dublin	1	1
EC2000	17 Nov	Bursa	0	0
2003	9 Sept	Dublin	2	2

v URUGUAY			RI	U
1974	8 May	Montevideo	0	2
1986	23 Apr	Dublin	1	1

v USA			RI	USA
1979	29 Oct	Dublin	3	2
1991	1 June	Boston	1	1
1992	29 Apr	Dublin	4	1
1992	30 May	Washington	1	3
1996	9 June	Boston	1	2
2000	6 June	Boston	1	1
2002	17 Apr	Dublin	2	1

v USSR			RI	USSR
wc1972	18 Oct	Dublin	1	2
wc1973	13 May	Moscow	0	1
EC1974	30 Oct	Dublin	3	0
EC1975	18 May	Kiev	1	2
wc1984	12 Sept	Dublin	1	0
wc1985	16 Oct	Moscow	0	2
EC1988	15 June	Hanover	1	1
1990	25 Apr	Dublin	1	0

v WALES			RI	W
1960	28 Sept	Dublin	2	3
1979	11 Sept	Swansea	1	2
1981	24 Feb	Dublin	1	3
1986	26 Mar	Dublin	0	1
1990	28 Mar	Dublin	1	0
1991	6 Feb	Wrexham	3	0
1992	19 Feb	Dublin	0	1
1993	17 Feb	Dublin	2	1
1997	11 Feb	Cardiff	0	0
EC2007	24 Mar	Dublin	1	0
EC2007	17 Nov	Cardiff	2	2

v YUGOSLAVIA			RI	Y
1955	19 Sept	Dublin	1	4
1988	27 Apr	Dublin	2	0
EC1998	18 Nov	Belgrade	0	1
EC1999	1 Sept	Dublin	2	1

OTHER BRITISH AND IRISH INTERNATIONAL MATCHES 2009–10

FRIENDLIES

Amsterdam, 12 August 2009, 48,000

Holland (2) 2 *(Kuyt 10, Van der Vaart 38)*

England (0) 2 *(Defoe 49, 77)*

Holland: Stekelenburg; Heitinga, Mathijsen, Ooijer, Braafheid, De Jong, Van der Vaart (Sneijder 46), Schaars (Mendes Da Silva 82), Kuyt (Huntelaar 78), Van Persie (Babel 46), Robben (Afellay 55).
England: Green; Johnson G, Cole A (Bridge 84), Barry (Carrick 46), Ferdinand, Terry, Beckham (Wright-Phillips 46), Lampard, Rooney (Cole C 59), Heskey (Defoe 46), Young A (Milner 68).
Referee: N. Rizzoli (Italy).

Wembley, 5 September 2009, 67,232

England (1) 2 *(Lampard 31 (pen), Defoe 63)*

Slovenia (0) 1 *(Ljubijankic 85)*

England: Green; Johnson G, Cole A, Barry, Terry, Upson (Lescott 64), Wright-Phillips (Lennon 46), Lampard (Milner 46), Heskey (Defoe 46), Rooney (Cole C 80), Gerrard (Carrick 46).
Slovenia: Handanovic; Brecko, Suler, Cesar (Mavric 34), Jokic, Birsa (Komac 64), Radosavljevic (Krhin 77), Koren, Kirm (Stevanovic 77), Dedic (Pecnik 71), Novakovic (Ljubijankic 55).
Referee: J. Eriksson (Sweden).

Doha, 14 November 2009, 50,000

Brazil (0) 1 *(Nilmar 47)*

England (0) 0

Brazil: Julio Cesar; Maicon, Michel Bastos, Felipe Melo, Lucio, Thiago Motta, Elano (Dani Alves 64), Kaka (Eduardo 81), Gilberto Silva, Nilmar (Julio Baptista 81), Luis Fabiano (Hulk 67).
England: Foster; Brown, Bridge, Barry (Huddlestone 82), Upson, Lescott, Wright-Phillips (Crouch 82), Jenas, Rooney, Bent (Defoe 54), Milner (Young A 87).
Referee: A. Abdou (Qatar).

Wembley, 3 March 2010, 80,602

England (0) 3 *(Crouch 56, 80, Wright-Phillips 75)*

Egypt (1) 1 *(Zidan 23)*

England: Green; Brown, Baines, Barry, Upson, Terry, Walcott (Wright-Phillips 57), Lampard (Carrick 46), Rooney (Cole C 86), Defoe (Crouch 46), Gerrard (Milner 73).
Egypt: El Hadari; Al-Muhammadi, Said (Salem 86), Fathi, Gomaa, Ghaly, Moawad (Abdelshafy 76), Hassan (Nagy 64), Abd Rabou, Zidan (Aboutreika 76), Ebdelmaby (Zaki 64).
Referee: C. Torres (Spain).

Wembley, 24 May 2010, 88,638

England (2) 3 *(King 17, Crouch 35, Johnson G 47)*

Mexico (1) 1 *(Franco 45)*

England: Green (Hart 46); Johnson G, Baines, Carrick (Huddlestone 61), Ferdinand (Carragher 46), King, Walcott (Lennon 77), Gerrard, Crouch (Defoe 46), Rooney, Milner (Johnson A 85).
Mexico: Perez; Juarez, Aguilar (Barrera 52), Marquez, Salcido, Osorio, Torrado, Rodriguez, Giovani (Blanco 72), Franco (Hernandez 46), Vela (Guardado 62).
Referee: M. Toma (Japan).

Graz, 30 May 2010, 15,326

Japan (1) 1 *(Tanaka 7)*

England (0) 2 *(Tanaka 72 (og), Nakazawa 83 (og))*

Japan: Kawashima; Nakazawa, Konno, Tanaka, Nagatomo, Endo (Tamada 86), Abe, Hasebe, Honda, Okubo (Matsui 71), Okazaki (Morimoto 65).

England: James (Hart 46); Johnson G (Wright-Phillips 46), Cole A, Huddlestone (Gerrard 46), Ferdinand, Terry, Lennon (Heskey 77), Lampard, Rooney, Bent (Cole J 46), Walcott (Carragher 46).
Referee: R. Eisner (Austria).

Podgorica, 12 August 2009, 5000

Montenegro (2) 2 *(Jovetic 31 (pen), Djalovic 45)*

Wales (0) 1 *(Vokes 52)*

Montenegro: Poleksic (Bozovic M 46); Pavicevic, Batak (Pejovic 68), Dzudovic, Jovanovic, Bozovic V (Nikolic 72), Drincic, Pekovic (Kascelan 62), Vukcevic (Novakovic 86), Djalovic (Beciraj 74), Jovetic.
Wales: Hennessey (Price 46); Gunter, Ricketts (Eardley 57), Williams A (Nyatanga 46), Collins J (Morgan C 63), Gabbidon, Collison, Ramsey (Cotterill 75), Ledley, Church (Vokes 47), Earnshaw.
Refereee: M. Mazic (Serbia).

Cardiff, 14 November 2009, 13,844

Wales (3) 3 *(Edwards 17, Church 32, Ramsey 35)*

Scotland (0) 0

Wales: Hennessey; Ricketts, Nyatanga (Gabbidon 60), Williams A, Morgan C, Bale, Ledley (King 80), Ramsey (Allen 56), Edwards (Cotterill 88), Evans C (Vokes 46), Church (Earnshaw 46).
Scotland: Marshall; Hutton, Fox (Wallace 54), Fletcher D, Caldwell G, McManus, Cowie (Riordan 78), Dorrans (Robson 71), Naismith (McCormack 62), Miller K (Fletcher S 55), McFadden (Kyle 62).
Referee: C. Zimmermann (Switzerland).

Swansea, 3 March 2010, 8258

Wales (0) 0

Sweden (1) 1 *(Elmander 44)*

Wales: Myhill (Hennessey 46); Gunter, Bale (Nyatanga 67), Collins J, Morgan C, Williams A, Davies S (Cotterill 64), Collinson (Crofts 71), Church (Vokes 53), Evans C (Earnshaw 46), Vaughan.
Sweden: Gustafsson; Mellberg, Majstorovic, Safari (Wendt 62), Larsson S, Elm R (Hysen 58), Anders Svensson, Kallstrom (Elm V 80), Elmander (Wernbloom 58), Toivonen, Wilhelmsson (Lustig 73).
Referee: A. Black (Northern Ireland).

Osijek, 23 May 2010, 12,000

Croatia (1) 2 *(Rakitic 44, Gabric 82)*

Wales (0) 0

Croatia: Pletikosa; Strinic, Simunic, Lovren, Srna (Vida 75), Rakitic (Pokrivac 76), Vukojevic (Dujmovic 65), Mandzukic (Badelj 90), Jelavic (Bilic 46), Petric (Gabric 46), Modric.
Wales: Hennessey (Myhill 46); Ricketts, Williams A, Nyatanga, Gunter (Ribeiro 81), Edwards D, Morgan C, Stock (Bradley 57), Dorman (Taylor N 62), Church (Vokes 71), Earnshaw (Robson-Kanu 72).
Referee: S. Vincic (Slovenia).

Belfast, 12 August 2009, 10,250

Northern Ireland (1) 1 *(McCann 18)*

Israel (1) 1 *(Barda 26)*

Northern Ireland: Maik Taylor (Tuffey 46); Baird, Craigan, Hughes (McAuley 46), McCartney, Johnson (McGinn 46), Clingan (McGivern 70), McCann, Brunt (Davis 46), Healy (Paterson 59), Lafferty.
Israel: Awat (Davidovitch 46); Meshumar, Keinan (Ben-Haim 46), Strol (Mori 71), Ben Dayan, Cohen (Kayal 46), Baruchian, Benayoun (Toama 54), Yadin (Ziv 65), Barda, Colautti.
Referee: J. Valgeirsson (Iceland).

Belfast, 14 November 2009, 13,500
Northern Ireland (0) 0
Serbia (0) 1 *(Lazovic 57)*
Northern Ireland: Maik Taylor (Tuffey 77); Evans J (McCann 46), Hughes, Craigan, McCartney, McGinn (McCourt 71), Davis, Baird, Brunt (O'Connor 65), Feeney (Healy 65), Lafferty (Kirk 71).
Serbia: Isailovic; Rukavina, Vidic (Subotic 46), Lukovic, Kolarov (Vukovic 67), Milijas (Ninkovic 46), Kuzmanovic (Kacar 52), Petrovic, Tosic, Jovanovic (Krasic 46), Lazovic (Lekic 76)
Referee: A. Toussaint (Luxembourg).

Tirana, 3 March 2010, 7500
Albania (1) 1 *(Skela 26)*
Northern Ireland (0) 0
Albania: Hidi; Lila, Dallku, Vangjeli, Angolli (Cana 64), Lala (Hyka 64), Curri, Bulku (Kapllani 85), Duro (Bakaj 78), Skela (Vila 81), Bogdani (Salihi 46).
Northern Ireland: Maik Taylor (Tuffey 72); Little, McCartney, Craigan, McGivern, O'Connor (Evans C 46), McGinn (Shiels 46), Davis, Lafferty (Patterson 64), Healy (Kirk 78), McCann.
Referee: E. Pilav (Bosnia).

New Brittain, 26 March 2010, 4000
Turkey (0) 2 *(Sercan 47, Semih 71)*
Northern Ireland (0) 0
Turkey: Onur; Servet, Ibrahim T, Caner, Sabri, Nuri (Mehmet T 46), Selcuk, Inan (Emre B 66), Ozan (Arca 66), Kazim-Richards (Semih 62), Tuncay, Hamit Altintop (Sercan 46).
Northern Ireland: Blayney; Little, McAuley, Craigan, McGivern (Coates 76), Garrett (Lawrie 80), Mulgrew, Evans C, Braniff (McArdle 61), Gorman (Bryan 66) Paterson (Magennis 60).
Referee: T. Vaughn (USA).

Connecticut, 26 May 2010, 4000
Northern Ireland (0) 0
Turkey (0) 2 *(Yildirim 48, Semih 72)*
Northern Ireland: Blayney; Little, McAuley, Craigan, McGivern (Coates 76), Garrett (Lawrie 80), Mulgrew, Evans C, Braniff (McArdle 61), Gorman (Bryar 66), Patterson (Magennis 60).
Turkey: Kivrak; Servet, Caner (Ismail 74), Selcuk (Emre B 67), Ozan (Arda 67), Tuncay, Sabri, Ibrahim T, Hamit Altintop (Mehmet T 46), Nuri (Yildirim 46), Kazim-Richards (Semih 62).
Referee: T. Vaughn (USA).

Chillan, 30 May 2010, 12,000
Chile (1) 1 *(Paredes 30)*
Northern Ireland (0) 0
Chile: Pinto; Vidal (Ross 77), Fuentes, Isla, Cereceda, Contreras, Gonzalez (Orellana 64), Fernandez (Gutierrez 89), Fierro, Estrada, Paredes.
Northern Ireland: Blayney (McGovern 46); Little, McGivern (Coates 56), McAuley, Craigan (McArdle 46), Evans C, Garrett (Braniff 46), Patterson, Mulgrew, Gorman (Magennis 73), Bryan (Lawrie 46).
Referee: L. Prudente (Uruguay).

Limerick, 12 August 2009, 19,428
Republic of Ireland (0) 0
Australia (2) 3 *(Cahill 38, 44, Carney 90)*
Republic of Ireland: Given (Westwood 68); O'Shea, St Ledger-Hall, Dunne, Kilbane (Nolan 63) McGeady (Long 81), Whelan, Gibson (Andrews 62), Duff (Hunt S 46), Keane, Doyle K (Folan 46).
Australia: Schwarzer; Carney, North (Spiranovic 71), Williams, Kisnorbo (Madaschi 46), Jedinak (Holland 89), Wilkshire, Cahill (Holman 46), Bresciano (Carle 78), McDonald (Rukavytsya 46), Kewell.
Referee: A. Burrull (Spain).

Limerick, 8 September 2009, 14,572
Republic of Ireland (1) 1 *(Lawrence 37)*
South Africa (0) 0
Republic of Ireland: Westwood; Kelly, McShane (O'Dea 81), St Ledger-Hall, Nolan, Keogh (Duff 78), Gibson, Andrews, Lawrence, Folan, Doyle K (Best 59).
South Africa: Fernandez; Gaxa, Mokoena, Gould, Masilela (Thwala 78), Van Heerden (Khenyeza 59), Mhlongo, Dikgacoi (Ngobeni 81), Pienaar, Mphela (Henyekane 73), Parker (Tshabalala 63).
Referee: C. Gordon (Scotland).

Emirates Stadium, 2 March 2010, 40,082
Republic of Ireland (0) 0
Brazil (1) 2 *(Andrews 44 (og), Robinho 76)*
Republic of Ireland: Given; Kelly, Kilbane, Whelan (Gibson 56), St Ledger-Hall, McShane, Lawrence (McCarthy 69), Andrews, Doyle K (Best 78), Keane, Duff (McGeady 56).
Brazil: Julio Cesar; Maicon (Carlos Eduardo 84), Lucio (Luisao 82), Juan, Michel Bastos, Ramires (Dani Alves 64), Silva, Felipe Melo, Kaka, Adriano (Grafite 64), Robinho (Nilmar 77).
Referee: M. Dean (England).

Dublin, 25 May 2010, 16,722
Republic of Ireland (2) 2 *(Doyle K 7, Lawrence 39)*
Paraguay (0) 1 *(Barrios 58)*
Republic of Ireland: Westwood; Kelly, McShane, St Ledger-Hall, O'Shea, Lawrence (Foley 82), Whelan (Green 69), Andrews, Duff (Fahey 77), Keane (Sheridan 63), Doyle K (Long 87).
Paraguay: Bobadilla; Da Silva, Caniza, Alcaraz, Morel Rodriguez (Torres 65), Vera (Bonet 66), Riveros (Ortigoza 65), Santana (Aquino 82), Santa Cruz (Martinez 77), Barrios, Gamarra.
Referee: J. Lapperriere (Switzerland).

Dublin, 28 May 2010, 16,800
Republic of Ireland (1) 3 *(Green 31, Keane 52, 85 (pen))*
Algeria (0) 0
Republic of Ireland: Westwood (Murphy 86); Kelly, O'Shea (O'Dea 36), St Ledger-Hall, Cunningham, Lawrence (Long 86), Green, Whelan (Andrews 75), Duff (Fahey 65), Keane, Doyle K (Sheridan 72).
Algeria: Chaouchi (M'Bohli 66); Guedioura, Halliche, Bellaid, Mesbah, Ziani, Lacen, Mansouri (Kadir 66), Belhadj (Boudebouz 66), Djebour (Saifi 58), Ghezzal (Abdoun 77).
Referee: E. Braamhar (Holland).

Yokohama, 10 October 2009, 72,377
Japan (0) 2 *(Berra 83 (og), Honda 90)*
Scotland (0) 0
Japan: Kawashima; Iwamasa, Uchida (Okubo 65), Abe, Hashimoto (Tokunaga 67), Inamoto (Komano 81), Konno, Kengo Nakamura, Ishikawa (Matsui 67), Honda, Maeda (Morimoto 56).
Scotland: Gordon; Berra, Whittaker, Wallace L, Caldwell G, McManus, Adam (Hughes 67), Dorrans, Conway (Riordan 74), Miller L (Cowie 46), Wallace R (Fletcher S 46).
Referee: S.W. Kim (South Korea).

Hampden Park, 3 March 2010, 26,530
Scotland (0) 1 *(Brown 62)*
Czech Republic (0) 0
Scotland: Gordon; Hutton, Wallace L, Brown S, Caldwell G, Webster (Berra 46), Thomson K (Hartley 46), Fletcher D (Whittaker 83), Robson (Adam 69), Miller K (Boyd 63), Dorrans.
Czech Republic: Drobny; Kusnir (Pudil 86), Hubnik, Sivok, Kadlec, Plasil (Moravek 79), Holek, Hubschman (Rajnoch 79), Rosicky (Skacel 66), Necid (Blazek 67), Sverkos (Papadopoulos 67).
Referee: F. Fautrel (France).

INTERNATIONAL APPEARANCES 1872–2010

This is a list of full international appearances by Englishmen, Irishmen, Scotsmen and Welshmen in matches against the Home Countries and against foreign nations. It does not include unofficial matches against Commonwealth and Empire countries. The year indicated refers to the player's international debut season; i.e. 2005 is the 2004–05 season. **Bold type** indicates players who have made an international appearance in season 2009–10.

As at July 2010.

ENGLAND

Abbott, W. 1902 (Everton)	1
A'Court, A. 1958 (Liverpool)	5
Adams, T. A. 1987 (Arsenal)	66
Adcock, H. 1929 (Leicester C)	5
Agbonlahor, G. 2009 (Aston Villa)	**3**
Alcock, C. W. 1875 (Wanderers)	1
Alderson, J. T. 1923 (C Palace)	1
Aldridge, A. 1888 (WBA, Walsall Town Swifts)	2
Allen, A. 1888 (Aston Villa)	1
Allen, A. 1960 (Stoke C)	3
Allen, C. 1984 (QPR, Tottenham H)	5
Allen, H. 1888 (Wolverhampton W)	5
Allen, J. P. 1934 (Portsmouth)	2
Allen, R. 1952 (WBA)	5
Alsford, W. J. 1935 (Tottenham H)	1
Amos, A. 1885 (Old Carthusians)	2
Anderson, R. D. 1879 (Old Etonians)	1
Anderson, S. 1962 (Sunderland)	2
Anderson, V. A. 1979 (Nottingham F, Arsenal, Manchester U)	30
Anderton, D. R. 1994 (Tottenham H)	30
Angus, J. 1961 (Burnley)	1
Armfield, J. C. 1959 (Blackpool)	43
Armitage, G. H. 1926 (Charlton Ath)	1
Armstrong, D. 1980 (Middlesbrough, Southampton)	3
Armstrong, K. 1955 (Chelsea)	1
Arnold, J. 1933 (Fulham)	1
Arthur, J. W. H. 1885 (Blackburn R)	7
Ashcroft, J. 1906 (Woolwich Arsenal)	3
Ashmore, G. S. 1926 (WBA)	1
Ashton, C. T. 1926 (Corinthians)	1
Ashton, D. 2008 (West Ham U)	1
Ashurst, W. 1923 (Notts Co)	5
Astall, G. 1956 (Birmingham C)	2
Astle, J. 1969 (WBA)	5
Aston, J. 1949 (Manchester U)	17
Athersmith, W. C. 1892 (Aston Villa)	12
Atyeo, P. J. W. 1956 (Bristol C)	6
Austin, S. W. 1926 (Manchester C)	1
Bach, P. 1899 (Sunderland)	1
Bache, J. W. 1903 (Aston Villa)	7
Baddeley, T. 1903 (Wolverhampton W)	5
Bagshaw, J. J. 1920 (Derby Co)	1
Bailey, G. R. 1985 (Manchester U)	2
Bailey, H. P. 1908 (Leicester Fosse)	5
Bailey, M. A. 1964 (Charlton Ath)	2
Bailey, N. C. 1878 (Clapham Rovers)	19
Baily, E. F. 1950 (Tottenham H)	9
Bain, J. 1877 (Oxford University)	1
Baines, L. J. 2010 (Everton)	**2**
Baker, A. 1928 (Arsenal)	1
Baker, B. H. 1921 (Everton, Chelsea)	2
Baker, J. H. 1960 (Hibernian, Arsenal)	8
Ball, A. J. 1965 (Blackpool, Everton, Arsenal)	72
Ball, J. 1928 (Bury)	1
Ball, M. J. 2001 (Everton)	1
Balmer, W. 1905 (Everton)	1
Bamber, J. 1921 (Liverpool)	1
Bambridge, A. L. 1881 (Swifts)	3
Bambridge, E. C. 1879 (Swifts)	18
Bambridge, E. H. 1876 (Swifts)	1
Banks, G. 1963 (Leicester C, Stoke C)	73
Banks, H. E. 1901 (Millwall)	1
Banks, T. 1958 (Bolton W)	6

Bannister, W. 1901 (Burnley, Bolton W)	2
Barclay, R. 1932 (Sheffield U)	3
Bardsley, D. J. 1993 (QPR)	2
Barham, M. 1983 (Norwich C)	2
Barkas, S. 1936 (Manchester C)	5
Barker, J. 1935 (Derby Co)	11
Barker, R. 1872 (Herts Rangers)	1
Barker, R. R. 1895 (Casuals)	1
Barlow, R. J. 1955 (WBA)	1
Barmby, N. J. 1995 (Tottenham H, Middlesbrough, Everton, Liverpool)	23
Barnes, J. 1983 (Watford, Liverpool)	79
Barnes, P. S. 1978 (Manchester C, WBA, Leeds U)	22
Barnet, H. H. 1882 (Royal Engineers)	1
Barrass, M. W. 1952 (Bolton W)	3
Barrett, A. F. 1930 (Fulham)	1
Barrett, E. D. 1991 (Oldham Ath, Aston Villa)	3
Barrett, J. W. 1929 (West Ham U)	1
Barry, G. 2000 (Aston Villa, Manchester C)	**39**
Barry, L. 1928 (Leicester C)	5
Barson, F. 1920 (Aston Villa)	1
Barton, J. 1890 (Blackburn R)	1
Barton, J. 2007 (Manchester C)	1
Barton, P. H. 1921 (Birmingham)	7
Barton, W. D. 1995 (Wimbledon, Newcastle U)	3
Bassett, W. I. 1888 (WBA)	16
Bastard, S. R. 1880 (Upton Park)	2
Bastin, C. S. 1932 (Arsenal)	21
Batty, D. 1991 (Leeds U, Blackburn R, Newcastle U, Leeds U)	42
Baugh, R. 1886 (Stafford Road, Wolverhampton W)	2
Bayliss, A. E. J. M. 1891 (WBA)	1
Baynham, R. L. 1956 (Luton T)	3
Beardsley, P. A. 1986 (Newcastle U, Liverpool, Newcastle U)	59
Beasant, D. J. 1990 (Chelsea)	2
Beasley, A. 1939 (Huddersfield T)	1
Beats, W. E. 1901 (Wolverhampton W)	2
Beattie, J. S. 2003 (Southampton)	5
Beattie, T. K. 1975 (Ipswich T)	9
Beckham, D. R. J. 1997 (Manchester U, Real Madrid, LA Galaxy)	**115**
Becton, F. 1895 (Preston NE, Liverpool)	2
Bedford, H. 1923 (Blackpool)	2
Bell, C. 1968 (Manchester C)	48
Bennett, W. 1901 (Sheffield U)	2
Benson, R. W. 1913 (Sheffield U)	1
Bent, D. A. 2006 (Charlton Ath, Tottenham H, Sunderland)	**6**
Bentley, D. M. 2008 (Blackburn R, Tottenham H)	7
Bentley, R. T. F. 1949 (Chelsea)	12
Beresford, J. 1934 (Aston Villa)	1
Berry, A. 1909 (Oxford University)	1
Berry, J. J. 1953 (Manchester U)	4
Bestall, J. G. 1935 (Grimsby T)	1
Betmead, H. A. 1937 (Grimsby T)	1
Betts, M. P. 1877 (Old Harrovians)	1
Betts, W. 1889 (Sheffield W)	1
Beverley, J. 1884 (Blackburn R)	3
Birkett, R. H. 1879 (Clapham Rovers)	1
Birkett, R. J. E. 1936 (Middlesbrough)	1
Birley, F. H. 1874 (Oxford University, Wanderers)	2
Birtles, G. 1980 (Nottingham F)	3
Bishop, S. M. 1927 (Leicester C)	4
Blackburn, F. 1901 (Blackburn R)	3

Blackburn, G. F. 1924 (Aston Villa) 1
Blenkinsop, E. 1928 (Sheffield W) 26
Bliss, H. 1921 (Tottenham H) 1
Blissett, L. L. 1983 (Watford, AC Milan) 14
Blockley, J. P. 1973 (Arsenal) 1
Bloomer, S. 1895 (Derby Co, Middlesbrough) 23
Blunstone, F. 1955 (Chelsea) 5
Bond, R. 1905 (Preston NE, Bradford C) 8
Bonetti, P. P. 1966 (Chelsea) 7
Bonsor, A. G. 1873 (Wanderers) 2
Booth, F. 1905 (Manchester C) 1
Booth, T. 1898 (Blackburn R, Everton) 2
Bould, S. A. 1994 (Arsenal) 2
Bowden, E. R. 1935 (Arsenal) 6
Bower, A. G. 1924 (Corinthians) 5
Bowers, J. W. 1934 (Derby Co) 3
Bowles, S. 1974 (QPR) 5
Bowser, S. 1920 (WBA) 1
Bowyer, L. D. 2003 (Leeds U) 1
Boyer, P. J. 1976 (Norwich C) 1
Boyes, W. 1935 (WBA, Everton) 3
Boyle, T. W. 1913 (Burnley) 1
Brabrook, P. 1958 (Chelsea) 3
Bracewell, P. W. 1985 (Everton) 3
Bradford, G. R. W. 1956 (Bristol R) 1
Bradford, J. 1924 (Birmingham) 12
Bradley, W. 1959 (Manchester U) 3
Bradshaw, F. 1908 (Sheffield W) 1
Bradshaw, T. H. 1897 (Liverpool) 1
Bradshaw, W. 1910 (Blackburn R) 4
Brann, G. 1886 (Swifts) 3
Brawn, W. F. 1904 (Aston Villa) 2
Bray, J. 1935 (Manchester C) 6
Brayshaw, E. 1887 (Sheffield W) 1
Bridge W. M. 2002 (Southampton, Chelsea, Manchester C) **36**
Bridges, B. J. 1965 (Chelsea) 4
Bridgett, A. 1905 (Sunderland) 11
Brindle, T. 1880 (Darwen) 2
Brittleton, J. T. 1912 (Sheffield W) 5
Britton, C. S. 1935 (Everton) 9
Broadbent, P. F. 1958 (Wolverhampton W) 7
Broadis, I. A. 1952 (Manchester C, Newcastle U) 14
Brockbank, J. 1872 (Cambridge University) 1
Brodie, J. B. 1889 (Wolverhampton W) 3
Bromilow, T. G. 1921 (Liverpool) 5
Bromley-Davenport, W. E. 1884 (Oxford University) 2
Brook, E. F. 1930 (Manchester C) 18
Brooking, T. D. 1974 (West Ham U) 47
Brooks, J. 1957 (Tottenham H) 3
Broome, F. H. 1938 (Aston Villa) 7
Brown, A. 1882 (Aston Villa) 3
Brown, A. 1971 (WBA) 1
Brown, A. S. 1904 (Sheffield U) 2
Brown, G. 1927 (Huddersfield T, Aston Villa) 9
Brown, J. 1881 (Blackburn R) 5
Brown, J. H. 1927 (Sheffield W) 6
Brown, K. 1960 (West Ham U) 1
Brown, W 1924 (West Ham U) 1
Brown, W. M. 1999 (Manchester U) **23**
Bruton, J. 1928 (Burnley) 3
Bryant, W. I. 1925 (Clapton) 1
Buchan, C. M. 1913 (Sunderland) 6
Buchanan, W. S. 1876 (Clapham R) 1
Buckley, F. C. 1914 (Derby Co) 1
Bull, S. G. 1989 (Wolverhampton W) 13
Bullock, F. E. 1921 (Huddersfield T) 1
Bullock, H. 1923 (Bury) 3
Burgess, H. 1904 (Manchester C) 4
Burgess, H. 1931 (Sheffield W) 4
Burnup, C. J. 1896 (Cambridge University) 1
Burrows, H. 1934 (Sheffield W) 3
Burton, F. E. 1889 (Nottingham F) 1
Bury, L. 1877 (Cambridge University, Old Etonians) 2

Butcher, T. 1980 (Ipswich T, Rangers) 77
Butler, J. D. 1925 (Arsenal) 1
Butler, W. 1924 (Bolton W) 1
Butt, N. 1997 (Manchester U, Newcastle U) 39
Byrne, G. 1963 (Liverpool) 2
Byrne, J. J. 1962 (C Palace, West Ham U) 11
Byrne, R. W. 1954 (Manchester U) 33

Callaghan, I. R. 1966 (Liverpool) 4
Calvey, J. 1902 (Nottingham F) 1
Campbell, A. F. 1929 (Blackburn R, Huddersfield T) 8
Campbell, S. 1996 (Tottenham H, Arsenal, Portsmouth) 73
Camsell, G. H. 1929 (Middlesbrough) 9
Capes, A. J. 1903 (Stoke) 1
Carr, J. 1905 (Newcastle U) 2
Carr, J. 1920 (Middlesbrough) 2
Carr, W. H. 1875 (Owlerton, Sheffield) 1
Carragher, J. L. 1999 (Liverpool) **38**
Carrick, M. 2001 (West Ham U, Tottenham H, Manchester U) **22**
Carson, S. P. 2008 (Liverpool, WBA) 3
Carter, H. S. 1934 (Sunderland, Derby Co) 13
Carter, J. H. 1926 (WBA) 3
Catlin, A. E. 1937 (Sheffield W) 5
Chadwick, A. 1900 (Southampton) 2
Chadwick, E. 1891 (Everton) 7
Chamberlain, M. 1983 (Stoke C) 8
Chambers, H. 1921 (Liverpool) 8
Channon, M. R. 1973 (Southampton, Manchester C) 46
Charles, G. A. 1991 (Nottingham F) 2
Charlton, J. 1965 (Leeds U) 35
Charlton, R. 1958 (Manchester U) 106
Charnley, R. O. 1963 (Blackpool) 1
Charsley, C. C. 1893 (Small Heath) 1
Chedgzoy, S. 1920 (Everton) 8
Chenery, C. J. 1872 (C Palace) 3
Cherry, T. J. 1976 (Leeds U) 27
Chilton, A. 1951 (Manchester U) 2
Chippendale, H. 1894 (Blackburn R) 1
Chivers, M. 1971 (Tottenham H) 24
Christian, E. 1879 (Old Etonians) 1
Clamp, E. 1958 (Wolverhampton W) 4
Clapton, D. R. 1959 (Arsenal) 1
Clare, T. 1889 (Stoke) 4
Clarke, A. J. 1970 (Leeds U) 19
Clarke, H. A. 1954 (Tottenham H) 1
Clay, T. 1920 (Tottenham H) 4
Clayton, R. 1956 (Blackburn R) 35
Clegg, J. C. 1872 (Sheffield W) 1
Clegg, W. E. 1873 (Sheffield W, Sheffield Albion) 2
Clemence, R. N. 1973 (Liverpool, Tottenham H) 61
Clement, D. T. 1976 (QPR) 5
Clough, B. H. 1960 (Middlesbrough) 2
Clough, N. H. 1989 (Nottingham F) 14
Coates, R. 1970 (Burnley, Tottenham H) 4
Cobbold, W. N. 1883 (Cambridge University, Old Carthusians) 9
Cock, J. G. 1920 (Huddersfield T, Chelsea) 2
Cockburn, H. 1947 (Manchester U) 13
Cohen, G. R. 1964 (Fulham) 37
Cole, A. 2001 (Arsenal, Chelsea) **82**
Cole, A. A. 1995 (Manchester U) 15
Cole, C. 2009 (West Ham U) **7**
Cole, J. J. 2001 (West Ham U, Chelsea) **56**
Colclough, H. 1914 (C Palace) 1
Coleman, E. H. 1921 (Dulwich Hamlet) 1
Coleman, J. 1907 (Woolwich Arsenal) 1
Collymore, S. V. 1995 (Nottingham F, Aston Villa) 3
Common, A. 1904 (Sheffield U, Middlesbrough) 3
Compton, L. H. 1951 (Arsenal) 2
Conlin, J. 1906 (Bradford C) 1
Connelly, J. M. 1960 (Burnley, Manchester U) 20
Cook, T. E. R. 1925 (Brighton) 1

Cooper, C. T. 1995 (Nottingham F)	2
Cooper, N. C. 1893 (Cambridge University)	1
Cooper, T. 1928 (Derby Co)	15
Cooper, T. 1969 (Leeds U)	20
Coppell, S. J. 1978 (Manchester U)	42
Copping, W. 1933 (Leeds U, Arsenal, Leeds U)	20
Corbett, B. O. 1901 (Corinthians)	1
Corbett, R. 1903 (Old Malvernians)	1
Corbett, W. S. 1908 (Birmingham)	3
Corrigan, J. T. 1976 (Manchester C)	9
Cottee, A. R. 1987 (West Ham U, Everton)	7
Cotterill, G. H. 1891 (Cambridge University, Old Brightonians)	4
Cottle, J. R. 1909 (Bristol C)	1
Cowan, S. 1926 (Manchester C)	3
Cowans, G. S. 1983 (Aston Villa, Bari, Aston Villa)	10
Cowell, A. 1910 (Blackburn R)	1
Cox, J. 1901 (Liverpool)	3
Cox, J. D. 1892 (Derby Co)	1
Crabtree, J. W. 1894 (Burnley, Aston Villa)	14
Crawford, J. F. 1931 (Chelsea)	1
Crawford, R. 1962 (Ipswich T)	2
Crawshaw, T. H. 1895 (Sheffield W)	10
Crayston, W. J. 1936 (Arsenal)	8
Creek, F. N. S. 1923 (Corinthians)	1
Cresswell, W. 1921 (South Shields, Sunderland, Everton)	7
Crompton, R. 1902 (Blackburn R)	41
Crooks, S. D. 1930 (Derby Co)	26
Crouch, P. J. 2005 (Southampton, Liverpool, Portsmouth, Tottenham H)	**40**
Crowe, C. 1963 (Wolverhampton W)	1
Cuggy, F. 1913 (Sunderland)	2
Cullis, S. 1938 (Wolverhampton W)	12
Cunliffe, A. 1933 (Blackburn R)	2
Cunliffe, D. 1900 (Portsmouth)	1
Cunliffe, J. N. 1936 (Everton)	1
Cunningham, L. 1979 (WBA, Real Madrid)	6
Curle, K. 1992 (Manchester C)	3
Currey, E. S. 1890 (Oxford University)	2
Currie, A. W. 1972 (Sheffield U, Leeds U)	17
Cursham, A. W. 1876 (Notts Co)	6
Cursham, H. A. 1880 (Notts Co)	8
Daft, H. B. 1889 (Notts Co)	5
Daley, A. M. 1992 (Aston Villa)	7
Danks, T. 1885 (Nottingham F)	1
Davenport, P. 1985 (Nottingham F)	1
Davenport, J. K. 1885 (Bolton W)	2
Davis, G. 1904 (Derby Co)	2
Davis, H. 1903 (Sheffield W)	3
Davison, J. E. 1922 (Sheffield W)	1
Dawson, J. 1922 (Burnley)	2
Day, S. H. 1906 (Old Malvernians)	3
Dean, W. R. 1927 (Everton)	16
Deane, B. C. 1991 (Sheffield U)	3
Deeley, N. V. 1959 (Wolverhampton W)	2
Defoe, J. C. 2004 (Tottenham H, Portsmouth, Tottenham H)	**43**
Devey, J. H. G. 1892 (Aston Villa)	2
Devonshire, A. 1980 (West Ham U)	8
Dewhurst, F. 1886 (Preston NE)	9
Dewhurst, G. P. 1895 (Liverpool Ramblers)	1
Dickinson, J. W. 1949 (Portsmouth)	48
Dimmock, J. H. 1921 (Tottenham H)	3
Ditchburn, E. G. 1949 (Tottenham H)	6
Dix, R. W. 1939 (Derby Co)	1
Dixon, J. A. 1885 (Notts Co)	1
Dixon, K. M. 1985 (Chelsea)	8
Dixon, L. M. 1990 (Arsenal)	22
Dobson, A. T. C. 1882 (Notts Co)	4
Dobson, C. F. 1886 (Notts Co)	1
Dobson, J. M. 1974 (Burnley, Everton)	5
Doggart, A. G. 1924 (Corinthians)	1

Dorigo, A. R. 1990 (Chelsea, Leeds U)	15
Dorrell, A. R. 1925 (Aston Villa)	4
Douglas, B. 1958 (Blackburn R)	36
Downing, S. 2005 (Middlesbrough)	23
Downs, R. W. 1921 (Everton)	1
Doyle, M. 1976 (Manchester C)	5
Drake, E. J. 1935 (Arsenal)	5
Dublin, D. 1998 (Coventry C, Aston Villa)	4
Ducat, A. 1910 (Woolwich Arsenal, Aston Villa)	6
Dunn, A. T. B. 1883 (Cambridge University, Old Etonians)	4
Dunn, D. J. I. 2003 (Blackburn R)	1
Duxbury, M. 1984 (Manchester U)	10
Dyer, K. C. 2000 (Newcastle U, West Ham U)	33
Earle, S. G. J. 1924 (Clapton, West Ham U)	2
Eastham, G. 1963 (Arsenal)	19
Eastham, G. R. 1935 (Bolton W)	1
Eckersley, W. 1950 (Blackburn R)	17
Edwards, D. 1955 (Manchester U)	18
Edwards, J. H. 1874 (Shropshire Wanderers)	1
Edwards, W. 1926 (Leeds U)	16
Ehiogu, U. 1996 (Aston Villa, Middlesbrough)	4
Ellerington, W. 1949 (Southampton)	2
Elliott, G. W. 1913 (Middlesbrough)	3
Elliott, W. H. 1952 (Burnley)	5
Evans, R. E. 1911 (Sheffield U)	4
Ewer, F. H. 1924 (Casuals)	2
Fairclough, P. 1878 (Old Foresters)	1
Fairhurst, D. 1934 (Newcastle U)	1
Fantham, J. 1962 (Sheffield W)	1
Fashanu, J. 1989 (Wimbledon)	2
Felton, W. 1925 (Sheffield W)	1
Fenton, M. 1938 (Middlesbrough)	1
Fenwick, T. W. 1984 (QPR, Tottenham H)	20
Ferdinand, L. 1993 (QPR, Newcastle U, Tottenham H)	17
Ferdinand, R. G. 1998 (West Ham U, Leeds U, Manchester U)	**78**
Field, E. 1876 (Clapham Rovers)	2
Finney, T. 1947 (Preston NE)	76
Fleming, H. J. 1909 (Swindon T)	11
Fletcher, A. 1889 (Wolverhampton W)	2
Flowers, R. 1955 (Wolverhampton W)	49
Flowers, T. D. 1993 (Southampton, Blackburn R)	11
Forman, Frank 1898 (Nottingham F	9
Forman, F. R. 1899 (Nottingham F)	3
Forrest, J. H. 1884 (Blackburn R)	11
Fort, J. 1921 (Millwall)	1
Foster, B. 2007 (Manchester U)	**4**
Foster, R. E. 1900 (Oxford University, Corinthians)	5
Foster, S. 1982 (Brighton & HA)	3
Foulke, W. J. 1897 (Sheffield U)	1
Foulkes, W. A. 1955 (Manchester U)	1
Fowler, R. B. 1996 (Liverpool, Leeds U)	26
Fox, F. S. 1925 (Millwall)	1
Francis, G. C. J. 1975 (QPR)	12
Francis, T. 1977 (Birmingham C, Nottingham F, Manchester C, Sampdoria)	52
Franklin, C. F. 1947 (Stoke C)	27
Freeman, B. C. 1909 (Everton, Burnley)	5
Froggatt, J. 1950 (Portsmouth)	13
Froggatt, R. 1953 (Sheffield W)	4
Fry, C. B. 1901 (Corinthians)	1
Furness, W. I. 1933 (Leeds U)	1
Galley, T. 1937 (Wolverhampton W)	2
Gardner, A. 2004 (Tottenham H)	1
Gardner, T. 1934 (Aston Villa)	2
Garfield, B. 1898 (WBA)	1
Garraty, W. 1903 (Aston Villa)	1
Garrett, T. 1952 (Blackpool)	3
Gascoigne, P. J. 1989 (Tottenham H, Lazio, Rangers, Middlesbrough)	57

Gates, E. 1981 (Ipswich T)	2	Hacking, J. 1929 (Oldham Ath)	3
Gay, L. H. 1893 (Cambridge University, Old Brightonians)	3	Hadley, H. 1903 (WBA)	1
		Hagan, J. 1949 (Sheffield U)	1
Geary, F. 1890 (Everton)	2	Haines, J. T. W. 1949 (WBA)	1
Geaves, R. L. 1875 (Clapham Rovers)	1	Hall, A. E. 1910 (Aston Villa)	1
Gee, C. W. 1932 (Everton)	3	Hall, G. W. 1934 (Tottenham H)	10
Geldard, A. 1933 (Everton)	4	Hall, J. 1956 (Birmingham C)	17
George, C. 1977 (Derby Co)	1	Halse, H. J. 1909 (Manchester U)	1
George, W. 1902 (Aston Villa)	3	Hammond, H. E. D. 1889 (Oxford University)	1
Gerrard, S. G. 2000 (Liverpool)	**84**	Hampson, J. 1931 (Blackpool)	3
Gibbins, W. V. T. 1924 (Clapton)	2	Hampton, H. 1913 (Aston Villa)	4
Gidman, J. 1977 (Aston Villa)	1	Hancocks, J. 1949 (Wolverhampton W)	3
Gillard, I. T. 1975 (QPR)	3	Hapgood, E. 1933 (Arsenal)	30
Gilliat, W. E. 1893 (Old Carthusians)	1	Hardinge, H. T. W. 1910 (Sheffield U)	1
Goddard, P. 1982 (West Ham U)	1	Hardman, H. P. 1905 (Everton)	4
Goodall, F. R. 1926 (Huddersfield T)	25	Hardwick, G. F. M. 1947 (Middlesbrough)	13
Goodall, J. 1888 (Preston NE, Derby Co)	14	Hardy, H. 1925 (Stockport Co)	1
Goodhart, H. C. 1883 (Old Etonians)	3	Hardy, S. 1907 (Liverpool, Aston Villa)	21
Goodwyn, A. G. 1873 (Royal Engineers)	1	Harford, M. G. 1988 (Luton T)	2
Goodyer, A. C. 1879 (Nottingham F)	1	Hargreaves, F. W. 1880 (Blackburn R)	3
Gosling, R. C. 1892 (Old Etonians)	5	Hargreaves, J. 1881 (Blackburn R)	2
Gosnell, A. A. 1906 (Newcastle U)	1	Hargreaves, O. 2002 (Bayern Munich, Manchester U)	42
Gough, H. C. 1921 (Sheffield U)	1	Harper, E. C. 1926 (Blackburn R)	1
Goulden, L. A. 1937 (West Ham U)	14	Harris, G. 1966 (Burnley)	1
Graham, L. 1925 (Millwall)	2	Harris, P. P. 1950 (Portsmouth)	2
Graham, T. 1931 (Nottingham F)	2	Harris, S. S. 1904 (Cambridge University, Old Westminsters)	6
Grainger, C. 1956 (Sheffield U, Sunderland)	7	Harrison, A. H. 1893 (Old Westminsters)	2
Gray, A. A. 1992 (C Palace)	1	Harrison, G. 1921 (Everton)	2
Gray, M. 1999 (Sunderland)	3	Harrow, J. H. 1923 (Chelsea)	2
Greaves, J. 1959 (Chelsea, Tottenham H)	57	**Hart, C. 2008 (Manchester C)**	**3**
Green, F. T. 1876 (Wanderers)	1	Hart, E. 1929 (Leeds U)	8
Green, G. H. 1925 (Sheffield U)	8	Hartley, F. 1923 (Oxford C)	1
Green, R. P. 2005 (Norwich C, West Ham U)	**11**	Harvey, A. 1881 (Wednesbury Strollers)	1
Greenhalgh, E. H. 1872 (Notts Co)	2	Harvey, J. C. 1971 (Everton)	1
Greenhoff, B. 1976 (Manchester U, Leeds U)	18	Hassall, H. W. 1951 (Huddersfield T, Bolton W)	5
Greenwood, D. H. 1882 (Blackburn R)	2	Hateley, M. 1984 (Portsmouth, AC Milan, Monaco, Rangers)	32
Gregory, J. 1983 (QPR)	6	Hawkes, R. M. 1907 (Luton T)	5
Grimsdell, A. 1920 (Tottenham H)	6	Haworth, G. 1887 (Accrington)	5
Grosvenor, A. T. 1934 (Birmingham)	3	Hawtrey, J. P. 1881 (Old Etonians)	2
Gunn, W. 1884 (Notts Co)	2	Haygarth, E. B. 1875 (Swifts)	1
Guppy, S. 2000 (Leicester C)	1		
Gurney, R. 1935 (Sunderland)	1		

England and Liverpool star Steven Gerrard (left) in typical action during the World Cup Qualifier against Croatia at Wembley in September 2009. (Action Images/Andrew Couldridge)

Haynes, J. N. 1955 (Fulham) 56
Healless, H. 1925 (Blackburn R) 2
Hector, K. J. 1974 (Derby Co) 2
Hedley, G. A. 1901 (Sheffield U) 1
Hegan, K. E. 1923 (Corinthians) 4
Hellawell, M. S. 1963 (Birmingham C) 2
Hendrie, L. A. 1999 (Aston Villa) 1
Henfrey, A. G. 1891 (Cambridge University, Corinthians) 5
Henry, R. P. 1963 (Tottenham H) 1
Heron, F. 1876 (Wanderers) 1
Heron, G. H. H. 1873 (Uxbridge, Wanderers) 5
Heskey, E. W. I. 1999 (Leicester C, Liverpool, Birmingham C, Wigan Ath, Aston Villa) 62
Hibbert, W. 1910 (Bury) 1
Hibbs, H. E. 1930 (Birmingham) 25
Hill, F. 1963 (Bolton W) 2
Hill, G. A. 1976 (Manchester U) 6
Hill, J. H. 1925 (Burnley, Newcastle U) 11
Hill, R. 1983 (Luton T) 3
Hill, R. H. 1926 (Millwall) 1
Hillman, J. 1899 (Burnley) 1
Hills, A. F. 1879 (Old Harrovians) 1
Hilsdon, G. R. 1907 (Chelsea) 8
Hinchcliffe, A. G. 1997 (Everton, Sheffield W) 7
Hine, E. W. 1929 (Leicester C) 6
Hinton, A. T. 1963 (Wolverhampton W, Nottingham F) 3
Hirst, D. E. 1991 (Sheffield W) 3
Hitchens, G. A. 1961 (Aston Villa, Internazionale) 7
Hobbis, H. H. F. 1936 (Charlton Ath) 2
Hoddle, G. 1980 (Tottenham H, Monaco) 53
Hodge, S. B. 1986 (Aston Villa, Tottenham H, Nottingham F) 24
Hodgetts, D. 1888 (Aston Villa) 6
Hodgkinson, A. 1957 (Sheffield U) 5
Hodgson, G. 1931 (Liverpool) 3
Hodkinson, J. 1913 (Blackburn R) 3
Hogg, W. 1902 (Sunderland) 3
Holdcroft, G. H. 1937 (Preston NE) 2
Holden, A. D. 1959 (Bolton W) 5
Holden, G. H. 1881 (Wednesbury OA) 4
Holden-White, C. 1888 (Corinthians) 2
Holford, T. 1903 (Stoke) 1
Holley, G. H. 1909 (Sunderland) 10
Holliday, E. 1960 (Middlesbrough) 3
Hollins, J. W. 1967 (Chelsea) 1
Holmes, R. 1888 (Preston NE) 7
Holt, J. 1890 (Everton, Reading) 10
Hopkinson, E. 1958 (Bolton W) 14
Hossack, A. H. 1892 (Corinthians) 1
Houghton, W. E. 1931 (Aston Villa) 7
Houlker, A. E. 1902 (Blackburn R, Portsmouth, Southampton) 5
Howarth, R. H. 1887 (Preston NE, Everton) 5
Howe, D. 1958 (WBA) 23
Howe, J. R. 1948 (Derby Co) 3
Howell, L. S. 1873 (Wanderers) 1
Howell, R. 1895 (Sheffield U, Liverpool) 2
Howey, S. N. 1995 (Newcastle U) 4
Huddlestone, T. A. 2010 (Tottenham H) 3
Hudson, A. A. 1975 (Stoke C) 2
Hudson, J. 1883 (Sheffield) 1
Hudspeth, F. C. 1926 (Newcastle U) 1
Hufton, A. E. 1924 (West Ham U) 6
Hughes, E. W. 1970 (Liverpool, Wolverhampton W) 62
Hughes, L. 1950 (Liverpool) 3
Hulme, J. H. A. 1927 (Arsenal) 9
Humphreys, P. 1903 (Notts Co) 1
Hunt, G. S. 1933 (Tottenham H) 3
Hunt, Rev. K. R. G. 1911 (Leyton) 2
Hunt, R. 1962 (Liverpool) 34
Hunt, S. 1984 (WBA) 2
Hunter, J. 1878 (Sheffield Heeley) 7
Hunter, N. 1966 (Leeds U) 28

Hurst, G. C. 1966 (West Ham U) 49

Ince, P. E. C. 1993 (Manchester U, Internazionale, Liverpool, Middlesbrough) 53
Iremonger, J. 1901 (Nottingham F) 2

Jack, D. N. B. 1924 (Bolton W, Arsenal) 9
Jackson, E. 1891 (Oxford University) 1
Jagielka, P. N. 2008 (Everton) 3
James. D. B. 1997 (Liverpool, Aston Villa, West Ham U, Manchester C, Portsmouth) 53
Jarrett, B. G. 1876 (Cambridge University) 3
Jefferis, F. 1912 (Everton) 2
Jeffers, F. 2003 (Arsenal) 1
Jenas, J. A. 2003 (Newcastle U, Tottenham H) 21
Jezzard, B. A. G. 1954 (Fulham) 2
Johnson, A. 2005 (C Palace, Everton) 8
Johnson, A. 2010 (Manchester C) 1
Johnson, D. E. 1975 (Ipswich T, Liverpool) 8
Johnson, E. 1880 (Saltley College, Stoke) 2
Johnson, G. M. C. 2004 (Chelsea, Portsmouth, Liverpool) 26
Johnson, J. A. 1937 (Stoke C) 5
Johnson, S. A. M. 2001 (Derby Co) 1
Johnson, T. C. F. 1926 (Manchester C, Everton) 5
Johnson, W. H. 1900 (Sheffield U) 6
Johnston, H. 1947 (Blackpool) 10
Jones, A. 1882 (Walsall Swifts, Great Lever) 3
Jones, H. 1923 (Nottingham F) 1
Jones, H. 1927 (Blackburn R) 6
Jones, M. D. 1965 (Sheffield U, Leeds U) 3
Jones, R. 1992 (Liverpool) 8
Jones, W. 1901 (Bristol C) 1
Jones, W. H. 1950 (Liverpool) 2
Joy, B. 1936 (Casuals) 1

Kail, E. I. L. 1929 (Dulwich Hamlet) 3
Kay, A. H. 1963 (Everton) 1
Kean, F. W. 1923 (Sheffield W, Bolton W) 9
Keegan, J. K. 1973 (Liverpool, SV Hamburg, Southampton) 63
Keen, E. R. L. 1933 (Derby Co) 4
Kelly, R. 1920 (Burnley, Sunderland, Huddersfield T) 14
Kennedy, A. 1984 (Liverpool) 2
Kennedy, R. 1976 (Liverpool) 17
Kenyon-Slaney, W. S. 1873 (Wanderers) 1
Keown, M. R. 1992 (Everton, Arsenal) 43
Kevan, D. T. 1957 (WBA) 14
Kidd, B. 1970 (Manchester U) 2
King, L. B. 2002 (Tottenham H) 21
King, R. S. 1882 (Oxford University) 1
Kingsford, R. K. 1874 (Wanderers) 1
Kingsley, M. 1901 (Newcastle U) 1
Kinsey, G. 1892 (Wolverhampton W, Derby Co) 4
Kirchen, A. J. 1937 (Arsenal) 3
Kirkland, C. E. 2007 (Liverpool) 1
Kirton, W. J. 1922 (Aston Villa) 1
Knight, A. E. 1920 (Portsmouth) 1
Knight, Z. 2005 (Fulham) 2
Knowles, C. 1968 (Tottenham H) 4
Konchesky, P. M. 2003 (Charlton Ath, West Ham U) 2

Labone, B. L. 1963 (Everton) 26
Lampard, F. J. 2000 (West Ham U, Chelsea) 82
Lampard, F. R. G. 1973 (West Ham U) 2
Langley, E. J. 1958 (Fulham) 3
Langton, R. 1947 (Blackburn R, Preston NE, Bolton W) 11
Latchford, R. D. 1978 (Everton) 12
Latheron, E. G. 1913 (Blackburn R) 2
Lawler, C. 1971 (Liverpool) 4
Lawton, T. 1939 (Everton, Chelsea, Notts Co) 23
Leach, T. 1931 (Sheffield W) 2
Leake, A. 1904 (Aston Villa) 5

Lee, E. A. 1904 (Southampton) 1
Lee, F. H. 1969 (Manchester C) 27
Lee, J. 1951 (Derby Co) 1
Lee, R. M. 1995 (Newcastle U) 21
Lee, S. 1983 (Liverpool) 14
Leighton, J. E. 1886 (Nottingham F) 1
Lennon, A. J. 2006 (Tottenham H) 19
Lescott, J. P. 2008 (Everton, Manchester C) 9
Le Saux, G. P. 1994 (Blackburn R, Chelsea) 36
Le Tissier, M. P. 1994 (Southampton) 8
Lilley, H. E. 1892 (Sheffield U) 1
Linacre, H. J. 1905 (Nottingham F) 2
Lindley, T. 1886 (Cambridge University, Nottingham F) 13
Lindsay, A. 1974 (Liverpool) 4
Lindsay, W. 1877 (Wanderers) 1
Lineker, G. 1984 (Leicester C, Everton, Barcelona, Tottenham H) 80
Lintott, E. H. 1908 (QPR, Bradford C) 7
Lipsham, H. B. 1902 (Sheffield U) 1
Little, B. 1975 (Aston Villa) 1
Lloyd, L. V. 1971 (Liverpool, Nottingham F) 4
Lockett, A. 1903 (Stoke) 1
Lodge, L. V. 1894 (Cambridge University, Corinthians) 5
Lofthouse, J. M. 1885 (Blackburn R, Accrington, Blackburn R) 7
Lofthouse, N. 1951 (Bolton W) 33
Longworth, E. 1920 (Liverpool) 5
Lowder, A. 1889 (Wolverhampton W) 1
Lowe, E. 1947 (Aston Villa) 3
Lucas, T. 1922 (Liverpool) 3
Luntley, E. 1880 (Nottingham F) 2
Lyttelton, Hon. A. 1877 (Cambridge University) 1
Lyttelton, Hon. E. 1878 (Cambridge University) 1

Mabbutt, G. 1983 (Tottenham H) 16
Macaulay, R. H. 1881 (Cambridge University) 1
McCall, J. 1913 (Preston NE) 5
McCann, G. P. 2001 (Sunderland) 1
McDermott, T. 1978 (Liverpool) 25
McDonald, C. A. 1958 (Burnley) 8
Macdonald, M. 1972 (Newcastle U) 14
McFarland, R. L. 1971 (Derby Co) 28
McGarry, W. H. 1954 (Huddersfield T) 4
McGuinness, W. 1959 (Manchester U) 2
McInroy, A. 1927 (Sunderland) 1
McMahon, S. 1988 (Liverpool) 17
McManaman, S. 1995 (Liverpool, Real Madrid) 37
McNab, R. 1969 (Arsenal) 4
McNeal, R. 1914 (WBA) 2
McNeil, M. 1961 (Middlesbrough) 9
Macrae, S. 1883 (Notts Co) 5
Maddison, F. B. 1872 (Oxford University) 1
Madeley, P. E. 1971 (Leeds U) 24
Magee, T. P. 1923 (WBA) 5
Makepeace, H. 1906 (Everton) 4
Male, C. G. 1935 (Arsenal) 19
Mannion, W. J. 1947 (Middlesbrough) 26
Mariner, P. 1977 (Ipswich T, Arsenal) 35
Marsden, J. T. 1891 (Darwen) 1
Marsden, W. 1930 (Sheffield W) 3
Marsh, R. W. 1972 (QPR, Manchester C) 9
Marshall, T. 1880 (Darwen) 2
Martin, A. 1981 (West Ham U) 17
Martin, H. 1914 (Sunderland) 1
Martyn, A. N. 1992 (C Palace, Leeds U) 23
Marwood, B. 1989 (Arsenal) 1
Maskrey, H. M. 1908 (Derby Co) 1
Mason, C. 1887 (Wolverhampton W) 3
Matthews, R. D. 1956 (Coventry C) 5
Matthews, S. 1935 (Stoke C, Blackpool) 54
Matthews, V. 1928 (Sheffield U) 2
Maynard, W. J. 1872 (1st Surrey Rifles) 2
Meadows, J. 1955 (Manchester C) 1

Medley, L. D. 1951 (Tottenham H) 6
Meehan, T. 1924 (Chelsea) 1
Melia, J. 1963 (Liverpool) 2
Mercer, D. W. 1923 (Sheffield U) 2
Mercer, J. 1939 (Everton) 5
Merrick, G. H. 1952 (Birmingham C) 23
Merson, P. C. 1992 (Arsenal, Middlesbrough, Aston Villa) 21
Metcalfe, V. 1951 (Huddersfield T) 2
Mew, J. W. 1921 (Manchester U) 1
Middleditch, B. 1897 (Corinthians) 1
Milburn, J. E. T. 1949 (Newcastle U) 13
Miller, B. G. 1961 (Burnley) 1
Miller, H. S. 1923 (Charlton Ath) 1
Mills, D. J. 2001 (Leeds U) 19
Mills, G. R. 1938 (Chelsea) 3
Mills, M. D. 1973 (Ipswich T) 42
Milne, G. 1963 (Liverpool) 14
Milner, J. P. 2010 (Aston Villa) 11
Milton, C. A. 1952 (Arsenal) 1
Milward, A. 1891 (Everton) 4
Mitchell, C. 1880 (Upton Park) 5
Mitchell, J. F. 1925 (Manchester C) 1
Moffat, H. 1913 (Oldham Ath) 1
Molyneux, G. 1902 (Southampton) 4
Moon, W. R. 1888 (Old Westminsters) 7
Moore, H. T. 1883 (Notts Co) 2
Moore, J. 1923 (Derby Co) 1
Moore, R. F. 1962 (West Ham U) 108
Moore, W. G. B. 1923 (West Ham U) 1
Mordue, J. 1912 (Sunderland) 2
Morice, C. J. 1872 (Barnes) 1
Morley, A. 1982 (Aston Villa) 6
Morley, H. 1910 (Notts Co) 1
Morren, T. 1898 (Sheffield U) 1
Morris, F. 1920 (WBA) 2
Morris, J. 1949 (Derby Co) 3
Morris, W. W. 1939 (Wolverhampton W) 3
Morse, H. 1879 (Notts Co) 1
Mort, T. 1924 (Aston Villa) 3
Morten, A. 1873 (C Palace) 1
Mortensen, S. H. 1947 (Blackpool) 25
Morton, J. R. 1938 (West Ham U) 1
Mosforth, W. 1877 (Sheffield W, Sheffield Albion, Sheffield W) 9
Moss, F. 1922 (Aston Villa) 5
Moss, F. 1934 (Arsenal) 4
Mosscrop, E. 1914 (Burnley) 2
Mozley, B. 1950 (Derby Co) 3
Mullen, J. 1947 (Wolverhampton W) 12
Mullery, A. P. 1965 (Tottenham H) 35
Murphy, D. B. 2002 (Liverpool) 9

Neal, P. G. 1976 (Liverpool) 50
Needham, E. 1894 (Sheffield U) 16
Neville, G. A. 1995 (Manchester U) 85
Neville, P. J. 1996 (Manchester U, Everton) 59
Newton, K. R. 1966 (Blackburn R, Everton) 27
Nicholls, J. 1954 (WBA) 2
Nicholson, W. E. 1951 (Tottenham H) 1
Nish, D. J. 1973 (Derby Co) 5
Norman, M. 1962 (Tottenham H) 23
Nugent, D. J. 2007 (Preston NE) 1
Nuttall, H. 1928 (Bolton W) 3

Oakley, W. J. 1895 (Oxford University, Corinthians) 16
O'Dowd, J. P. 1932 (Chelsea) 3
O'Grady, M. 1963 (Huddersfield T, Leeds U) 2
Ogilvie, R. A. M. M. 1874 (Clapham R) 1
Oliver, L. F. 1929 (Fulham) 1
Olney, B. A. 1928 (Aston Villa) 2
Osborne, F. R. 1923 (Fulham, Tottenham H) 4
Osborne, R. 1928 (Leicester C) 1
Osgood, P. L. 1970 (Chelsea) 4

Osman, R. 1980 (Ipswich T)	11
Ottaway, C. J. 1872 (Oxford University)	2
Owen, J. R. B. 1874 (Sheffield)	1
Owen, M. J. 1998 (Liverpool, Real Madrid, Newcastle U)	89
Owen, S. W. 1954 (Luton T)	3
Page, L. A. 1927 (Burnley)	7
Paine, T. L. 1963 (Southampton)	19
Pallister, G. A. 1988 (Middlesbrough, Manchester U)	22
Palmer, C. L. 1992 (Sheffield W)	18
Pantling, H. H. 1924 (Sheffield U)	1
Paravicini, P. J. de 1883 (Cambridge University)	3
Parker, P. A. 1989 (QPR, Manchester U)	19
Parker, S. M. 2004 (Charlton Ath, Chelsea, Newcastle U)	3
Parker, T. R. 1925 (Southampton)	1
Parkes, P. B. 1974 (QPR)	1
Parkinson, J. 1910 (Liverpool)	2
Parlour, R. 1999 (Arsenal)	10
Parr, P. C. 1882 (Oxford University)	1
Parry, E. H. 1879 (Old Carthusians)	3
Parry, R. A. 1960 (Bolton W)	2
Patchitt, B. C. A. 1923 (Corinthians)	2
Pawson, F. W. 1883 (Cambridge University, Swifts)	2
Payne, J. 1937 (Luton T)	1
Peacock, A. 1962 (Middlesbrough, Leeds U)	6
Peacock, J. 1929 (Middlesbrough)	3
Pearce, S. 1987 (Nottingham F, West Ham U)	78
Pearson, H. F. 1932 (WBA)	1
Pearson, J. H. 1892 (Crewe Alex)	1
Pearson, J. S. 1976 (Manchester U)	15
Pearson, S. C. 1948 (Manchester U)	8
Pease, W. H. 1927 (Middlesbrough)	1
Pegg, D. 1957 (Manchester U)	1
Pejic, M. 1974 (Stoke C)	4
Pelly, F. R. 1893 (Old Foresters)	3
Pennington, J. 1907 (WBA)	25
Pentland, F. B. 1909 (Middlesbrough)	5
Perry, C. 1890 (WBA)	3
Perry, T. 1898 (WBA)	1
Perry, W. 1956 (Blackpool)	3
Perryman, S. 1982 (Tottenham H)	1
Peters, M. 1966 (West Ham U, Tottenham H)	67
Phelan, M. C. 1990 (Manchester U)	1
Phillips, K. 1999 (Sunderland)	8
Phillips, L. H. 1952 (Portsmouth)	3
Pickering, F. 1964 (Everton)	3
Pickering, J. 1933 (Sheffield U)	1
Pickering, N. 1983 (Sunderland)	1
Pike, T. M. 1886 (Cambridge University)	1
Pilkington, B. 1955 (Burnley)	1
Plant, J. 1900 (Bury)	1
Platt, D. 1990 (Aston Villa, Bari, Juventus, Sampdoria, Arsenal)	62
Plum, S. L. 1923 (Charlton Ath)	1
Pointer, R. 1962 (Burnley)	3
Porteous, T. S. 1891 (Sunderland)	1
Powell, C. G. 2001 (Charlton Ath)	5
Priest, A. E. 1900 (Sheffield U)	1
Prinsep, J. F. M. 1879 (Clapham Rovers)	1
Puddefoot, S. C. 1926 (Blackburn R)	2
Pye, J. 1950 (Wolverhampton W)	1
Pym, R. H. 1925 (Bolton W)	3
Quantrill, A. 1920 (Derby Co)	4
Quixall, A. 1954 (Sheffield W)	5
Radford, J. 1969 (Arsenal)	2
Raikes, G. B. 1895 (Oxford University)	4
Ramsey, A. E. 1949 (Southampton, Tottenham H)	32
Rawlings, A. 1921 (Preston NE)	1
Rawlings, W. E. 1922 (Southampton)	2
Rawlinson, J. F. P. 1882 (Cambridge University)	1

Rawson, H. E. 1875 (Royal Engineers)	1
Rawson, W. S. 1875 (Oxford University)	2
Read, A. 1921 (Tufnell Park)	1
Reader, J. 1894 (WBA)	1
Reaney, P. 1969 (Leeds U)	3
Redknapp, J. F. 1996 (Liverpool)	17
Reeves, K. P. 1980 (Norwich C, Manchester C)	2
Regis, C. 1982 (WBA, Coventry C)	5
Reid, P. 1985 (Everton)	13
Revie, D. G. 1955 (Manchester C)	6
Reynolds, J. 1892 (WBA, Aston Villa)	8
Richards, C. H. 1898 (Nottingham F)	1
Richards, G. H. 1909 (Derby Co)	1
Richards, J. P. 1973 (Wolverhampton W)	1
Richards, M. 2007 (Manchester C)	11
Richardson, J. R. 1933 (Newcastle U)	2
Richardson, K. 1994 (Aston Villa)	1
Richardson, K. E. 2005 (Manchester U)	8
Richardson, W. G. 1935 (WBA)	1
Rickaby, S. 1954 (WBA)	1
Ricketts, M. B. 2002 (Bolton W)	1
Rigby, A. 1927 (Blackburn R)	5
Rimmer, E. J. 1930 (Sheffield W)	4
Rimmer, J. J. 1976 (Arsenal)	1
Ripley, S. E. 1994 (Blackburn R)	2
Rix, G. 1981 (Arsenal)	17
Robb, G. 1954 (Tottenham H)	1
Roberts, C. 1905 (Manchester U)	3
Roberts, F. 1925 (Manchester C)	4
Roberts, G. 1983 (Tottenham H)	6
Roberts, H. 1931 (Arsenal)	1
Roberts, H. 1931 (Millwall)	1
Roberts, R. 1887 (WBA)	3
Roberts, W. T. 1924 (Preston NE)	2
Robinson, J. 1937 (Sheffield W)	4
Robinson, J. W. 1897 (Derby Co, New Brighton Tower, Southampton)	11
Robinson, P. W. 2003 (Leeds U, Tottenham H, Blackburn R)	41
Robson, B. 1980 (WBA, Manchester U)	90
Robson, R. 1958 (WBA)	20
Rocastle, D. 1989 (Arsenal)	14
Rooney, W. 2003 (Everton, Manchester U)	**64**
Rose, W. C. 1884 (Swifts, Preston NE, Wolverhampton W)	5
Rostron, T. 1881 (Darwen)	2
Rowe, A. 1934 (Tottenham H)	1
Rowley, J. F. 1949 (Manchester U)	6
Rowley, W. 1889 (Stoke)	2
Royle, J. 1971 (Everton, Manchester C)	6
Ruddlesdin, H. 1904 (Sheffield W)	3
Ruddock, N. 1995 (Liverpool)	1
Ruffell, J. W. 1926 (West Ham U)	6
Russell, B. B. 1883 (Royal Engineers)	1
Rutherford, J. 1904 (Newcastle U)	11
Sadler, D. 1968 (Manchester U)	4
Sagar, C. 1900 (Bury)	2
Sagar, E. 1936 (Everton)	4
Salako, J. A. 1991 (C Palace)	5
Sandford, E. A. 1933 (WBA)	1
Sandilands, R. R. 1892 (Old Westminsters)	5
Sands, J. 1880 (Nottingham F)	1
Sansom, K. G. 1979 (C Palace, Arsenal)	86
Saunders, F. E. 1888 (Swifts)	1
Savage, A. H. 1876 (C Palace)	1
Sayer, J. 1887 (Stoke)	1
Scales, J. R. 1995 (Liverpool)	3
Scattergood, E. 1913 (Derby Co)	1
Schofield, J. 1892 (Stoke)	3
Scholes, P. 1997 (Manchester U)	66
Scott, L. 1947 (Arsenal)	17
Scott, W. R. 1937 (Brentford)	1
Seaman, D. A. 1989 (QPR, Arsenal)	75

Seddon, J. 1923 (Bolton W)	6
Seed, J. M. 1921 (Tottenham H)	5
Settle, J. 1899 (Bury, Everton)	6
Sewell, J. 1952 (Sheffield W)	6
Sewell, W. R. 1924 (Blackburn R)	1
Shackleton, L. F. 1949 (Sunderland)	5
Sharp, J. 1903 (Everton)	2
Sharpe, L. S. 1991 (Manchester U)	8
Shaw, G. E. 1932 (WBA)	1
Shaw, G. L. 1959 (Sheffield U)	5
Shea, D. 1914 (Blackburn R)	2
Shearer, A. 1992 (Southampton, Blackburn R,	
Newcastle U)	63
Shellito, K. J. 1963 (Chelsea)	1
Shelton A. 1889 (Notts Co)	6
Shelton, C. 1888 (Notts Rangers)	1
Shepherd, A. 1906 (Bolton W, Newcastle U)	2
Sheringham, E. P. 1993 (Tottenham H, Manchester U,	
Tottenham H)	51
Sherwood, T. A. 1999 (Tottenham H)	3
Shilton, P. L. 1971 (Leicester C, Stoke C, Nottingham F,	
Southampton, Derby Co)	125
Shimwell, E. 1949 (Blackpool)	1
Shorey, N. 2007 (Reading)	2
Shutt, G. 1886 (Stoke)	1
Silcock, J. 1921 (Manchester U)	3
Sillett, R. P. 1955 (Chelsea)	3
Simms, E. 1922 (Luton T)	1
Simpson, J. 1911 (Blackburn R)	8
Sinclair, T. 2002 (West Ham U, Manchester C)	12
Sinton, A. 1992 (QPR, Sheffield W)	12
Slater, W. J. 1955 (Wolverhampton W)	12
Smalley, T. 1937 (Wolverhampton W)	1
Smart, T. 1921 (Aston Villa)	5
Smith, A. 1891 (Nottingham F)	3
Smith, A. 2001 (Leeds U, Manchester U, Newcastle U)	19
Smith, A. K. 1872 (Oxford University)	1
Smith, A. M. 1989 (Arsenal)	13
Smith, B. 1921 (Tottenham H)	2
Smith, C. E. 1876 (C Palace)	1
Smith, G. O. 1893 (Oxford University, Old Carthusians,	
Corinthians)	20
Smith, H. 1905 (Reading)	4
Smith, J. 1920 (WBA)	2
Smith, Joe 1913 (Bolton W)	5
Smith, J. C. R. 1939 (Millwall)	2
Smith, J. W. 1932 (Portsmouth)	3
Smith, Leslie 1939 (Brentford)	1
Smith, Lionel 1951 (Arsenal)	6
Smith, R. A. 1961 (Tottenham H)	15
Smith, S. 1895 (Aston Villa)	1
Smith, S. C. 1936 (Leicester C)	1
Smith, T. 1960 (Birmingham C)	2
Smith, T. 1971 (Liverpool)	1
Smith, W. H. 1922 (Huddersfield T)	3
Sorby, T. H. 1879 (Thursday Wanderers, Sheffield)	1
Southgate, G. 1996 (Aston Villa, Middlesbrough)	57
Southworth, J. 1889 (Blackburn R)	3
Sparks, F. J. 1879 (Herts Rangers, Clapham Rovers)	3
Spence, J. W. 1926 (Manchester U)	2
Spence, R. 1936 (Chelsea)	2
Spencer, C. W. 1924 (Newcastle U)	2
Spencer, H. 1897 (Aston Villa)	6
Spiksley, F. 1893 (Sheffield W)	7
Spilsbury, B. W. 1885 (Cambridge University)	3
Spink, N. 1983 (Aston Villa)	1
Spouncer, W. A. 1900 (Nottingham F)	1
Springett, R. D. G. 1960 (Sheffield W)	33
Sproston, B. 1937 (Leeds U, Tottenham H,	
Manchester C)	11
Squire, R. T. 1886 (Cambridge University)	3
Stanbrough, M. H. 1895 (Old Carthusians)	1
Staniforth, R. 1954 (Huddersfield T)	8
Starling, R. W. 1933 (Sheffield W, Aston Villa)	2

Statham, D. J. 1983 (WBA)	3
Steele, F. C. 1937 (Stoke C)	6
Stein, B. 1984 (Luton T)	1
Stephenson, C. 1924 (Huddersfield T)	1
Stephenson, G. T. 1928 (Derby Co, Sheffield W)	3
Stephenson, J. E. 1938 (Leeds U)	2
Stepney, A. C. 1968 (Manchester U)	1
Sterland, M. 1989 (Sheffield W)	1
Steven, T. M. 1985 (Everton, Rangers, Marseille)	36
Stevens, G. A. 1985 (Tottenham H)	7
Stevens, M. G. 1985 (Everton, Rangers)	46
Stewart, J. 1907 (Sheffield W, Newcastle U)	3
Stewart, P. A. 1992 (Tottenham H)	3
Stiles, N. P. 1965 (Manchester U)	28
Stoker, J. 1933 (Birmingham)	3
Stone, S. B. 1996 (Nottingham F)	9
Storer, H. 1924 (Derby Co)	2
Storey, P. E. 1971 (Arsenal)	19
Storey-Moore, I. 1970 (Nottingham F)	1
Strange, A. H. 1930 (Sheffield W)	20
Stratford, A. H. 1874 (Wanderers)	1
Streten, B. 1950 (Luton T)	1
Sturgess, A. 1911 (Sheffield U)	2
Summerbee, M. G. 1968 (Manchester C)	8
Sunderland, A. 1980 (Arsenal)	1
Sutcliffe, J. W. 1893 (Bolton W, Millwall)	5
Sutton, C. R. 1998 (Blackburn R)	1
Swan, P. 1960 (Sheffield W)	19
Swepstone, H. A. 1880 (Pilgrims)	6
Swift, F. V. 1947 (Manchester C)	19
Tait, G. 1881 (Birmingham Excelsior)	1
Talbot, B. 1977 (Ipswich T, Arsenal)	6
Tambling, R. V. 1963 (Chelsea)	3
Tate, J. T. 1931 (Aston Villa)	3
Taylor, E. 1954 (Blackpool)	1
Taylor, E. H. 1923 (Huddersfield T)	8
Taylor, J. G. 1951 (Fulham)	2
Taylor, P. H. 1948 (Liverpool)	3
Taylor, P. J. 1976 (C Palace)	4
Taylor, T. 1953 (Manchester U)	19
Temple, D. W. 1965 (Everton)	1
Terry, J. G. 2003 (Chelsea)	**64**
Thickett, H. 1899 (Sheffield U)	2
Thomas, D. 1975 (QPR)	8
Thomas, D. 1983 (Coventry C)	2
Thomas, G. R. 1991 (C Palace)	9
Thomas, M. L. 1989 (Arsenal)	2
Thompson, A. 2004 (Celtic)	1
Thompson, P. 1964 (Liverpool)	16
Thompson, P. B. 1976 (Liverpool)	42
Thompson T. 1952 (Aston Villa, Preston NE)	2
Thomson, R. A. 1964 (Wolverhampton W)	8
Thornewell, G. 1923 (Derby Co)	4
Thornley, I. 1907 (Manchester C)	1
Tilson, S. F. 1934 (Manchester C)	4
Titmuss, F. 1922 (Southampton)	2
Todd, C. 1972 (Derby Co)	27
Toone, G. 1892 (Notts Co)	2
Topham, A. G. 1894 (Casuals)	1
Topham, R. 1893 (Wolverhampton W, Casuals)	2
Towers, M. A. 1976 (Sunderland)	3
Townley, W. J. 1889 (Blackburn R)	2
Townrow, J. E. 1925 (Clapton Orient)	2
Tremelling, D. R. 1928 (Birmingham)	1
Tresadern, J. 1923 (West Ham U)	2
Tueart, D. 1975 (Manchester C)	6
Tunstall, F. E. 1923 (Sheffield U)	7
Turnbull, R. J. 1920 (Bradford)	1
Turner, A. 1900 (Southampton)	2
Turner, H. 1931 (Huddersfield T)	2
Turner, J. A. 1893 (Bolton W, Stoke, Derby Co)	3
Tweedy, G. J. 1937 (Grimsby T)	1

NORTHERN IRELAND

Addis, D. J. 1922 (Cliftonville)	1
Aherne, T. 1947 (Belfast C, Luton T)	4
Alexander, T. E. 1895 (Cliftonville)	1
Allan, C. 1936 (Cliftonville)	1
Allen, J. 1887 (Limavady)	1
Anderson, J. 1925 (Distillery)	1
Anderson, T. 1973 (Manchester U, Swindon T, Peterborough U)	22
Anderson, W. 1898 (Linfield, Cliftonville)	4
Andrews, W. 1908 (Glentoran, Grimsby T)	3
Armstrong, G. J. 1977 (Tottenham H, Watford, Real Mallorca, WBA, Chesterfield)	63
Baird, C. P. 2003 (Southampton, Fulham)	**44**
Baird, G. 1896 (Distillery)	3
Baird, H. C. 1939 (Huddersfield T)	1
Balfe, J. 1909 (Shelbourne)	2
Bambrick, J. 1929 (Linfield, Chelsea)	11
Banks, S. J. 1937 (Cliftonville)	1
Barr, H. H. 1962 (Linfield, Coventry C)	3
Barron, J. H. 1894 (Cliftonville)	7
Barry, J. 1888 (Cliftonville)	3
Barry, J. 1900 (Bohemians)	1
Baxter, R. A. 1887 (Distillery)	1
Baxter, S. N. 1887 (Cliftonville)	1
Bennett, L. V. 1889 (Dublin University)	1
Best, G. 1964 (Manchester U, Fulham)	37
Bingham, W. L. 1951 (Sunderland, Luton T, Everton, Port Vale)	56
Black, K. T. 1988 (Luton T, Nottingham F)	30
Black, T. 1901 (Glentoran)	1
Blair, H. 1928 (Portadown, Swansea T)	4
Blair, J. 1907 (Cliftonville)	5
Blair, R. V. 1975 (Oldham Ath)	5
Blanchflower, J. 1954 (Manchester U)	12
Blanchflower, R. D. 1950 (Barnsley, Aston Villa, Tottenham H)	56
Blayney, A. 2006 (Doncaster R, Linfield)	3
Bookman, L. J. O. 1914 (Bradford C, Luton T)	4
Bothwell, A. W. 1926 (Ards)	5
Bowler, G. C. 1950 (Hull C)	3
Boyle, P. 1901 (Sheffield U)	5
Braithwaite, R. M. 1962 (Linfield, Middlesbrough)	10
Braniff, K. R. 2010 (Portadown)	**2**
Breen, T. 1935 (Belfast C, Manchester U)	9
Brennan, B. 1912 (Bohemians)	1
Brennan, R. A. 1949 (Luton T, Birmingham C, Fulham)	5
Briggs, W. R. 1962 (Manchester U, Swansea T)	2
Brisby, D. 1891 (Distillery)	1
Brolly, T. H. 1937 (Millwall)	4
Brookes, E. A. 1920 (Shelbourne)	1
Brotherston, N. 1980 (Blackburn R)	27
Brown, J. 1921 (Glenavon, Tranmere R)	3
Brown, J. 1935 (Wolverhampton W, Coventry C, Birmingham C)	10
Brown, N. M. 1887 (Limavady)	1
Brown, W. G. 1926 (Glenavon)	1
Browne, F. 1887 (Cliftonville)	5
Browne, R. J. 1936 (Leeds U)	6
Bruce, A. 1925 (Belfast C)	1
Bruce, W. 1961 (Glentoran)	2
Brunt, C. 2005 (Sheffield W, WBA)	**26**
Bryan, M. A. 2010 (Watford)	**2**
Buckle, H. R. 1903 (Cliftonville, Sunderland, Bristol R)	3
Buckle, J. 1882 (Cliftonville)	1
Burnett, J. 1894 (Distillery, Glentoran)	5
Burnison, J. 1901 (Distillery)	2
Burnison, S. 1908 (Distillery, Bradford, Distillery)	8
Burns, J. 1923 (Glenavon)	1
Burns, W. 1925 (Glentoran)	1
Butler, M. P. 1939 (Blackpool)	1
Campbell, A. C. 1963 (Crusaders)	2
Campbell, D. A. 1986 (Nottingham F, Charlton Ath)	10
Campbell, James 1897 (Cliftonville)	14
Campbell, John 1896 (Cliftonville)	1
Campbell, J. P. 1951 (Fulham)	2
Campbell, R. M. 1982 (Bradford C)	2
Campbell, W. G. 1968 (Dundee)	6
Capaldi, A. C. 2004 (Plymouth Arg, Cardiff C)	22
Carey, J. J. 1947 (Manchester U)	7
Carroll, E. 1925 (Glenavon)	1
Carroll, R. E. 1997 (Wigan Ath, Manchester U, West Ham U)	19
Carson, S. 2009 (Coleraine)	1
Casement, C. 2009 (Ipswich T)	1
Casey, T. 1955 (Newcastle U, Portsmouth)	12
Caskey, W. 1979 (Derby Co, Tulsa R)	8
Cassidy, T. 1971 (Newcastle U, Burnley)	24
Caughey, M. 1986 (Linfield)	2
Chambers, R. J. 1921 (Distillery, Bury, Nottingham F)	12
Chatton, H. A. 1925 (Partick Th)	3
Christian, J. 1889 (Linfield)	1
Clarke, C. J. 1986 (Bournemouth, Southampton, QPR, Portsmouth)	38
Clarke, R. 1901 (Belfast C)	2
Cleary, J. 1982 (Glentoran)	5
Clements, D. 1965 (Coventry C, Sheffield W, Everton, New York Cosmos)	48
Clingan, S. G. 2006 (Nottingham F, Norwich C, Coventry C)	**24**
Clugston, J. 1888 (Cliftonville)	14
Clyde, M. G. 2005 (Wolverhampton W)	3
Coates, C. 2009 (Crusaders)	**3**
Cochrane, D. 1939 (Leeds U)	12
Cochrane, G. 1903 (Cliftonville)	1
Cochrane, G. T. 1976 (Coleraine, Burnley, Middlesbrough, Gillingham)	26
Cochrane, M. 1898 (Distillery, Leicester Fosse)	8
Collins, F. 1922 (Celtic)	1
Collins, R. 1922 (Cliftonville)	1
Condy, J. 1882 (Distillery)	3
Connell, T. E. 1978 (Coleraine)	1
Connor, J. 1901 (Glentoran, Belfast C)	13
Connor, M. J. 1903 (Brentford, Fulham)	2
Cook, W. 1933 (Celtic, Everton)	15
Cooke, S. 1889 (Belfast YMCA, Cliftonville)	3
Coote, A. 1999 (Norwich C)	6
Coulter, J. 1934 (Belfast C, Everton, Grimsby T, Chelmsford C)	11
Cowan, J. 1970 (Newcastle U)	1
Cowan, T. S. 1925 (Queen's Island)	1
Coyle, F. 1956 (Coleraine, Nottingham F)	4
Coyle, L. 1989 (Derry C)	1
Coyle, R. I. 1973 (Sheffield W)	5
Craig, A. B. 1908 (Rangers, Morton)	9
Craig, D. J. 1967 (Newcastle U)	25
Craigan, S. J. 2003 (Partick Th, Motherwell)	**48**
Crawford, A. 1889 (Distillery, Cliftonville)	7
Croft, T. 1922 (Queen's Island)	3
Crone, R. 1889 (Distillery)	4
Crone, W. 1882 (Distillery)	12
Crooks, W. J. 1922 (Manchester U)	1
Crossan, E. 1950 (Blackburn R)	3
Crossan, J. A. 1960 (Sparta-Rotterdam, Sunderland, Manchester C, Middlesbrough)	24
Crothers, C. 1907 (Distillery)	1
Cumming, L. 1929 (Huddersfield T, Oldham Ath)	3
Cunningham, W. 1892 (Ulster)	4
Cunningham, W. E. 1951 (St Mirren, Leicester C, Dunfermline Ath)	30
Curran, S. 1926 (Belfast C)	4
Curran, J. J. 1922 (Glenavon, Pontypridd, Glenavon)	5
Cush, W. W. 1951 (Glenavon, Leeds U, Portadown)	26
Dalrymple, J. 1922 (Distillery)	1

Dalton, W. 1888 (YMCA, Linfield)	11
D'Arcy, S. D. 1952 (Chelsea, Brentford)	5
Darling, J. 1897 (Linfield)	22
Davey, H. H. 1926 (Reading, Portsmouth)	5
Davis, S. 2005 (Aston Villa, Fulham, Rangers)	**40**
Davis, T. L. 1937 (Oldham Ath)	1
Davison, A. J. 1996 (Bolton W, Bradford C, Grimsby T)	3
Davison, J. R. 1882 (Cliftonville)	8
Dennison, R. 1988 (Wolverhampton W)	18
Devine, A. O. 1886 (Limavady)	4
Devine, J. 1990 (Glentoran)	1
Dickson, D. 1970 (Coleraine)	4
Dickson, T. A. 1957 (Linfield)	1
Dickson, W. 1951 (Chelsea, Arsenal)	12
Diffin, W. J. 1931 (Belfast C)	1
Dill, A. H. 1882 (Knock, Down Ath, Cliftonville)	9
Doherty, I. 1901 (Belfast C)	1
Doherty, J. 1928 (Portadown)	1
Doherty, J. 1933 (Cliftonville)	2
Doherty, L. 1985 (Linfield)	2
Doherty, M. 1938 (Derry C)	1
Doherty, P. D. 1935 (Blackpool, Manchester C, Derby Co, Huddersfield T, Doncaster R)	16
Doherty, T. E. 2003 (Bristol C)	9
Donaghey, B. 1903 (Belfast C)	1
Donaghy, M. M. 1980 (Luton T, Manchester U, Chelsea)	91
Donnelly, L. 1913 (Distillery)	1
Donnelly, M. 2009 (Crusaders)	1
Doran, J. F. 1921 (Brighton)	3
Dougan, A. D. 1958 (Portsmouth, Blackburn R, Aston Villa, Leicester C, Wolverhampton W)	43
Douglas, J. P. 1947 (Belfast C)	1
Dowd, H. O. 1974 (Glenavon, Sheffield W)	3
Dowie, I. 1990 (Luton T, West Ham U, Southampton, C Palace, West Ham U, QPR)	59
Duff, M. J. 2002 (Cheltenham T, Burnley)	22
Duggan, H. A. 1930 (Leeds U)	8
Dunlop, G. 1985 (Linfield)	4
Dunne, J. 1928 (Sheffield U)	7
Eames, W. L. E. 1885 (Dublin U)	3
Eglington, T. J. 1947 (Everton)	6
Elder, A. R. 1960 (Burnley, Stoke C)	40
Elleman, A. R. 1889 (Cliftonville)	2
Elliott, S. 2001 (Motherwell, Hull C)	39
Elwood, J. H. 1929 (Bradford)	2
Emerson, W. 1920 (Glentoran, Burnley)	11
English, S. 1933 (Rangers)	2
Enright, J. 1912 (Leeds C)	1
Evans, C. J. 2009 (Manchester U)	**4**
Evans, J. G. 2007 (Manchester U)	**20**
Falloon, E. 1931 (Aberdeen)	2
Farquharson, T. G. 1923 (Cardiff C)	7
Farrell, P. 1901 (Distillery)	2
Farrell, P. 1938 (Hibernian)	1
Farrell, P. D. 1947 (Everton)	7
Feeney, J. M. 1947 (Linfield, Swansea T)	2
Feeney, W. 1976 (Glentoran)	1
Feeney, W. J. 2002 (Bournemouth, Luton T, Cardiff C)	**34**
Ferguson, G. 1999 (Linfield)	5
Ferguson, S. 2009 (Newcastle U)	1
Ferguson, W. 1966 (Linfield)	2
Ferris, J. 1920 (Belfast C, Chelsea, Belfast C)	6
Ferris, R. O. 1950 (Birmingham C)	3
Fettis, A. W. 1992 (Hull C, Nottingham F, Blackburn R)	25
Finney, T. 1975 (Sunderland, Cambridge U)	14
Fitzpatrick, J. C. 1896 (Bohemians)	2
Flack, H. 1929 (Burnley)	1
Fleming, J. G. 1987 (Nottingham F, Manchester C, Barnsley)	31
Forbes, G. 1888 (Limavady, Distillery)	3

Forde, J. T. 1959 (Ards)	4
Foreman, T. A. 1899 (Cliftonville)	1
Forsythe, J. 1888 (YMCA)	2
Fox, W. T. 1887 (Ulster)	2
Frame, T. 1925 (Linfield)	1
Fulton, R. P. 1928 (Larne, Belfast C)	21
Gaffikin, G. 1890 (Linfield Ath)	15
Galbraith, W. 1890 (Distillery)	1
Gallagher, P. 1920 (Celtic, Falkirk)	11
Gallogly, C. 1951 (Huddersfield T)	2
Gara, A. 1902 (Preston NE)	3
Gardiner, A. 1930 (Cliftonville)	5
Garrett, J. 1925 (Distillery)	1
Garrett, R. 2009 (Linfield)	**3**
Gaston, R. 1969 (Oxford U)	1
Gaukrodger, G. 1895 (Linfield)	1
Gault, M. 2008 (Linfield)	1
Gaussen, A. D. 1884 (Moyola Park, Magherafelt)	6
Geary, J. 1931 (Glentoran)	2
Gibb, J. T. 1884 (Wellington Park, Cliftonville)	10
Gibb, T. J. 1936 (Cliftonville)	1
Gibson W. K. 1894 (Cliftonville)	14
Gillespie, K. R. 1995 (Manchester U, Newcastle U, Blackburn R, Leicester C, Sheffield U)	86
Gillespie, S. 1886 (Hertford)	6
Gillespie, W. 1889 (West Down)	1
Gillespie, W. 1913 (Sheffield U)	25
Goodall, A. L. 1899 (Derby Co, Glossop)	10
Goodbody, M. F. 1889 (Dublin University)	2
Gordon, H. 1895 (Linfield)	3
Gordon R. W. 1891 (Linfield)	7
Gordon, T. 1894 (Linfield)	1
Gorman, R. J. 2010 (Wolverhampton W)	**2**
Gorman, W. C. 1947 (Brentford)	4
Gough, J. 1925 (Queen's Island)	1
Gowdy, J. 1920 (Glentoran, Queen's Island, Falkirk)	6
Gowdy, W. A. 1932 (Hull C, Sheffield W, Linfield, Hibernian)	6
Graham, W. G. L. 1951 (Doncaster R)	14
Gray, P. 1993 (Luton T, Sunderland, Nancy, Luton T, Burnley, Oxford U)	26
Greer, W. 1909 (QPR)	3
Gregg, H. 1954 (Doncaster R, Manchester U)	25
Griffin, D. J. 1996 (St Johnstone, Dundee U, Stockport Co)	29
Hall, G. 1897 (Distillery)	1
Halligan, W. 1911 (Derby Co, Wolverhampton W)	2
Hamill, M. 1912 (Manchester U, Belfast C, Manchester C)	7
Hamill, R. 1999 (Glentoran)	1
Hamilton, B. 1969 (Linfield, Ipswich T, Everton, Millwall, Swindon T)	50
Hamilton, G. 2003 (Portadown)	5
Hamilton, J. 1882 (Knock)	2
Hamilton, R. 1928 (Rangers)	5
Hamilton, W. D. 1885 (Dublin Association)	1
Hamilton, W. J. 1885 (Dublin Association)	1
Hamilton, W. J. 1908 (Distillery)	1
Hamilton, W. R. 1978 (QPR, Burnley, Oxford U)	41
Hampton, H. 1911 (Bradford C)	9
Hanna, J. 1912 (Nottingham F)	2
Hanna, J. D. 1899 (Royal Artillery, Portsmouth)	1
Hannon, D. J. 1908 (Bohemians)	6
Harkin, J. T. 1968 (Southport, Shrewsbury T)	5
Harland, A. I. 1922 (Linfield)	2
Harris, J. 1921 (Cliftonville, Glenavon)	2
Harris, V. 1906 (Shelbourne, Everton)	20
Harvey, M. 1961 (Sunderland)	34
Hastings, J. 1882 (Knock, Ulster)	7
Hatton, S. 1963 (Linfield)	2
Hayes, W. E. 1938 (Huddersfield T)	4

McCracken, R. 1921 (C Palace) 4
McCracken, R. 1922 (Linfield) 1
McCracken, W. R. 1902 (Distillery, Newcastle U, Hull C) 16
McCreery, D. 1976 (Manchester U, QPR, Tulsa R, Newcastle U, Hearts) 67
McCrory, S. 1958 (Southend U) 1
McCullough, K. 1935 (Belfast C, Manchester C) 5
McCullough, W. J. 1961 (Arsenal, Millwall) 10
McCurdy, C. 1980 (Linfield) 1
McDonald, A. 1986 (QPR) 52
McDonald, R. 1930 (Rangers) 2
McDonnell, J. 1911 (Bohemians) 4
McElhinney, G. M. A. 1984 (Bolton W) 6
McEvilly, L. R. 2002 (Rochdale) 1
McFaul, W. S. 1967 (Linfield, Newcastle U) 6
McGarry, J. K. 1951 (Cliftonville) 3
McGaughey, M. 1985 (Linfield) 1
McGibbon, P. C. G. 1995 (Manchester U, Wigan Ath) 7
McGinn, N. 2009 (Celtic) **7**
McGivern, R. 2009 (Manchester C) **11**
McGovern, M. 2010 (Ross Co) **1**
McGrath, R. C. 1974 (Tottenham H, Manchester U) 21
McGregor, S. 1921 (Glentoran) 1
McGrillen, J. 1924 (Clyde, Belfast C) 2
McGuire, E. 1907 (Distillery) 1
McGuire, J. 1928 (Linfield) 1
McIlroy, H. 1906 (Cliftonville) 1
McIlroy, J. 1952 (Burnley, Stoke C) 55
McIlroy, S. B. 1972 (Manchester U, Stoke C, Manchester C) 88
McIlvenny, P. 1924 (Distillery) 1
McIlvenny, R. 1890 (Distillery, Ulster) 2
McKeag, W. 1968 (Glentoran) 2
McKeague, T. 1925 (Glentoran) 1
McKee, F. W. 1906 (Cliftonville, Belfast C) 5
McKelvey, H. 1901 (Glentoran) 2
McKenna, J. 1950 (Huddersfield T) 7
McKenzie, H. 1922 (Distillery) 2
McKenzie, R. 1967 (Airdrieonians) 1
McKeown, N. 1892 (Linfield) 7
McKie, H. 1895 (Cliftonville) 3
Mackie, J. A. 1923 (Arsenal, Portsmouth) 3
McKinney, D. 1921 (Hull C, Bradford C) 2
McKinney, V. J. 1966 (Falkirk) 1
McKnight, A. D. 1988 (Celtic, West Ham U) 10
McKnight, J. 1912 (Preston NE, Glentoran) 2
McLaughlin, J. C. 1962 (Shrewsbury T, Swansea T) 12
McLean, B. S. 2006 (Rangers) 1
McLean, T. 1885 (Limavady) 1
McMahon, G. J. 1995 (Tottenham H, Stoke C) 17
McMahon, J. 1934 (Bohemians) 1
McMaster, G. 1897 (Glentoran) 3
McMichael, A. 1950 (Newcastle U) 40
McMillan, G. 1903 (Distillery) 2
McMillan, S. T. 1963 (Manchester U) 2
McMillen, W. S. 1934 (Manchester U, Chesterfield) 7
McMordie, A. S. 1969 (Middlesbrough) 21
McMorran, E. J. 1947 (Belfast C, Barnsley, Doncaster R) 15
McMullan, D. 1926 (Liverpool) 3
McNally, B. A. 1986 (Shrewsbury T) 5
McNinch, J. 1931 (Ballymena) 3
McParland, P. J. 1954 (Aston Villa, Wolverhampton W) 34
McShane, J. 1899 (Cliftonville) 4
McVeigh, P. M. 1999 (Tottenham H, Norwich C) 20
McVicker, J. 1888 (Linfield, Glentoran) 2
McWha, W. B. R. 1882 (Knock, Cliftonville) 7
Madden, O. 1938 (Norwich C) 1
Magee, G. 1885 (Wellington Park) 3
Magennis, J. B. D. 2010 (Cardiff C) **2**
Magill, E. J. 1962 (Arsenal, Brighton & HA) 26
Magilton, J. 1991 (Oxford U, Southampton, Sheffield W, Ipswich T) 52

Maginnis, H. 1900 (Linfield) 8
Mahood, J. 1926 (Belfast C, Ballymena) 9
Mannus, A. 2004 (Linfield) 4
Manderson, R. 1920 (Rangers) 5
Mansfield, J. 1901 (Dublin Freebooters) 1
Martin, C. 1882 (Cliftonville) 3
Martin, C. 1925 (Bo'ness) 1
Martin, C. J. 1947 (Glentoran, Leeds U, Aston Villa) 6
Martin, D. K. 1934 (Belfast C, Wolverhampton W, Nottingham F) 10
Mathieson, A. 1921 (Luton T) 2
Maxwell, J. 1902 (Linfield, Glentoran, Belfast C) 7
Meek, H. L. 1925 (Glentoran) 1
Mehaffy, J. A. C. 1922 (Queen's Island) 1
Meldon, P. A. 1899 (Dublin Freebooters) 2
Mercer, H. V. A. 1908 (Linfield) 1
Mercer, J. T. 1898 (Distillery, Linfield, Distillery, Derby Co) 12
Millar, W. 1932 (Barrow) 2
Miller, J. 1929 (Middlesbrough) 3
Milligan, D. 1939 (Chesterfield) 1
Milne, R. G. 1894 (Linfield) 28
Mitchell, E. J. 1933 (Cliftonville, Glentoran) 2
Mitchell, W. 1932 (Distillery, Chelsea) 15
Molyneux, T. B. 1883 (Ligoniel, Cliftonville) 11
Montgomery, F. J. 1955 (Coleraine) 1
Moore, C. 1949 (Glentoran) 1
Moore, P. 1933 (Aberdeen) 1
Moore, R. 1891 (Linfield Ath) 3
Moore, R. L. 1887 (Ulster) 2
Moore, W. 1923 (Falkirk) 1
Moorhead, F. W. 1885 (Dublin University) 1
Moorhead, G. 1923 (Linfield) 4
Moran, J. 1912 (Leeds C) 1
Moreland, V. 1979 (Derby Co) 6
Morgan, G. F. 1922 (Linfield, Nottingham F) 8
Morgan, S. 1972 (Port Vale, Aston Villa, Brighton & HA, Sparta Rotterdam) 18
Morrison, R. 1891 (Linfield Ath) 2
Morrison, T. 1895 (Glentoran, Burnley) 7
Morrogh, D. 1896 (Bohemians) 1
Morrow, S. J. 1990 (Arsenal, QPR) 39
Morrow, W. J. 1883 (Moyola Park) 3
Muir, R. 1885 (Oldpark) 2
Mulgrew, J. 2010 (Linfield) **2**
Mulholland, T.S. 1906 (Belfast C) 2
Mullan, G. 1983 (Glentoran) 4
Mulligan, J. 1921 (Manchester C) 1
Mulryne, P. P. 1997 (Manchester U, Norwich C, Cardiff C) 27
Murdock, C. J. 2000 (Preston NE, Hibernian, Crewe Alex, Rotherham U) 34
Murphy, J. 1910 (Bradford C) 3
Murphy, N. 1905 (QPR) 3
Murray, J. M. 1910 (Motherwell, Sheffield W) 3

Napier, R. J. 1966 (Bolton W) 1
Neill, W. J. T. 1961 (Arsenal, Hull C) 59
Nelis, P. 1923 (Nottingham F) 1
Nelson, S. 1970 (Arsenal, Brighton & HA) 51
Nicholl, C. J. 1975 (Aston Villa, Southampton, Grimsby T) 51
Nicholl, H. 1902 (Belfast C) 3
Nicholl, J. M. 1976 (Manchester U, Toronto B, Sunderland, Toronto B, Rangers, Toronto B, WBA) 73
Nicholson, J. J. 1961 (Manchester U, Huddersfield T) 41
Nixon, R. 1914 (Linfield) 1
Nolan, I. R. 1997 (Sheffield W, Bradford C, Wigan Ath) 18
Nolan-Whelan, J. V. 1901 (Dublin Freebooters) 5

O'Boyle, G. 1994 (Dunfermline Ath, St Johnstone) 13
O'Brien, M. T. 1921 (QPR, Leicester C, Hull C, Derby Co) 10

O'Connell, P. 1912 (Sheffield W, Hull C)	5
O'Connor, M. J. 2008 (Crewe Alex, Scunthorpe U)	**9**
O'Doherty, A. 1970 (Coleraine)	2
O'Driscoll, J. F. 1949 (Swansea T)	3
O'Hagan, C. 1905 (Tottenham H, Aberdeen)	11
O'Hagan, W. 1920 (St Mirren)	2
O'Hehir, J. C. 1910 (Bohemians)	1
O'Kane, W. J. 1970 (Nottingham F)	20
O'Mahoney, M. T. 1939 (Bristol R)	1
O'Neill, C. 1989 (Motherwell)	3
O'Neill, J. 1962 (Sunderland)	1
O'Neill, J. P. 1980 (Leicester C)	39
O'Neill, M. A. M. 1988 (Newcastle U, Dundee U, Hibernian, Coventry C)	31
O'Neill, M. H. M. 1972 (Distillery, Nottingham F, Norwich C, Manchester C, Norwich C, Notts Co)	64
O'Reilly, H. 1901 (Dublin Freebooters)	3
Parke, J. 1964 (Linfield, Hibernian, Sunderland)	14
Paterson, M. A. 2008 (Scunthorpe U, Burnley)	**11**
Patterson, D. J. 1994 (C Palace, Luton T, Dundee U)	17
Patterson, R. 2010 (Coleraine)	**3**
Peacock, R. 1952 (Celtic, Coleraine)	31
Peden, J. 1887 (Linfield, Distillery)	24
Penney, S. 1985 (Brighton & HA)	17
Percy, J. C. 1889 (Belfast YMCA)	1
Platt, J. A. 1976 (Middlesbrough, Ballymena U, Coleraine)	23
Pollock, W. 1928 (Belfast C)	1
Ponsonby, J. 1895 (Distillery)	3
Potts, R. M. C. 1883 (Cliftonville)	2
Priestley, T. J. M. 1933 (Coleraine, Chelsea)	2
Pyper, Jas. 1897 (Cliftonville)	7
Pyper, John 1897 (Cliftonville)	9
Pyper, M. 1932 (Linfield)	1
Quinn, J. M. 1985 (Blackburn R, Swindon T, Leicester C, Bradford C, West Ham U, Bournemouth, Reading)	46
Quinn, S. J. 1996 (Blackpool, WBA, Willem II, Sheffield W, Peterborough U, Northampton T)	50
Rafferty, P. 1980 (Linfield)	1
Ramsey, P. C. 1984 (Leicester C)	14
Rankine, J. 1883 (Alexander)	2
Rattray, D. 1882 (Avoniel)	3
Rea, R. 1901 (Glentoran)	1
Redmond, R. 1884 (Cliftonville)	1
Reid, G. H. 1923 (Cardiff C)	1
Reid, J. 1883 (Ulster)	6
Reid, S. E. 1934 (Derby Co)	3
Reid, W. 1931 (Hearts)	1
Reilly, M. M. 1900 (Portsmouth)	2
Renneville, W. T. J. 1910 (Leyton, Aston Villa)	4
Reynolds, J. 1890 (Distillery, Ulster)	5
Reynolds, R. 1905 (Bohemians)	1
Rice, P. J. 1969 (Arsenal)	49
Roberts, F. C. 1931 (Glentoran)	1
Robinson, P. 1920 (Distillery, Blackburn R)	2
Robinson, S. 1997 (Bournemouth, Luton T)	7
Rogan, A. 1988 (Celtic, Sunderland, Millwall)	18
Rollo, D. 1912 (Linfield, Blackburn R)	16
Roper, E. O. 1886 (Dublin University)	1
Rosbotham, A. 1887 (Cliftonville)	7
Ross, W. E. 1969 (Newcastle U)	1
Rowland, K. 1994 (West Ham U, QPR)	19
Rowley, R. W. M. 1929 (Southampton, Tottenham H)	6
Rushe, F. 1925 (Distillery)	1
Russell, A. 1947 (Linfield)	1
Russell, S. R. 1930 (Bradford C, Derry C)	3
Ryan, R. A. 1950 (WBA)	1
Sanchez, L. P. 1987 (Wimbledon)	3
Scott, E. 1920 (Liverpool, Belfast C)	31
Scott, J. 1958 (Grimsby)	2

Scott, J. E. 1901 (Cliftonville)	1
Scott, L. J. 1895 (Dublin University)	2
Scott, P. W. 1975 (Everton, York C, Aldershot)	10
Scott, T. 1894 (Cliftonville)	13
Scott, W. 1903 (Linfield, Everton, Leeds City)	25
Scraggs, M. J. 1921 (Glentoran)	2
Seymour, H. C. 1914 (Bohemians)	1
Seymour, J. 1907 (Cliftonville)	2
Shanks, T. 1903 (Woolwich Arsenal, Brentford)	3
Sharkey, P. G. 1976 (Ipswich T)	1
Sheehan, Dr G. 1899 (Bohemians)	3
Sheridan, J. 1903 (Everton, Stoke C)	6
Sherrard, J. 1885 (Limavady)	3
Sherrard, W. C. 1895 (Cliftonville)	3
Sherry, J. J. 1906 (Bohemians)	2
Shields, R. J. 1957 (Southampton)	1
Shiels, D. 2006 (Hibernian, Doncaster R)	**9**
Silo, M. 1888 (Belfast YMCA)	1
Simpson, W. J. 1951 (Rangers)	12
Sinclair, J. 1882 (Knock)	2
Slemin, J. C. 1909 (Bohemians)	1
Sloan, A. S. 1925 (London Caledonians)	1
Sloan, D. 1969 (Oxford U)	2
Sloan, H. A. de B. 1903 (Bohemians)	8
Sloan, J. W. 1947 (Arsenal)	1
Sloan, T. 1926 (Cardiff C, Linfield)	11
Sloan, T. 1979 (Manchester U)	3
Small, J. M. 1887 (Clarence, Cliftonville)	4
Smith, A. W. 2003 (Glentoran, Preston NE)	18
Smith, E. E. 1921 (Cardiff C)	4
Smith, J. E. 1901 (Distillery)	2
Smyth, R. H. 1886 (Dublin University)	1
Smyth, S. 1948 (Wolverhampton W, Stoke C)	9
Smyth, W. 1949 (Distillery)	4
Snape, A. 1920 (Airdrieonians)	1
Sonner, D. J. 1998 (Ipswich T, Sheffield W, Birmingham C, Nottingham F, Peterborough U)	13
Spence, D. W. 1975 (Bury, Blackpool, Southend U)	29
Spencer, S. 1890 (Distillery)	6
Spiller, E. A. 1883 (Cliftonville)	5
Sproule, I. 2006 (Hibernian, Bristol C)	11
Stanfield, O. M. 1887 (Distillery)	30
Steele, A. 1926 (Charlton Ath, Fulham)	4
Stevenson, A. E. 1934 (Rangers, Everton)	17
Stewart, A. 1967 (Glentoran, Derby Co)	7
Stewart, D. C. 1978 (Hull C)	1
Stewart, I. 1982 (QPR, Newcastle U)	31
Stewart, R. K. 1890 (St Columb's Court, Cliftonville)	11
Stewart, T. C. 1961 (Linfield)	1
Swan, S. 1899 (Linfield)	1
Taggart, G. P. 1990 (Barnsley, Bolton W, Leicester C)	51
Taggart, J. 1899 (Walsall)	1
Taylor, M. S. 1999 (Fulham, Birmingham C)	**83**
Thompson, F. W. 1910 (Cliftonville, Linfield, Bradford C, Clyde)	12
Thompson, J. 1897 (Distillery)	1
Thompson, P. 2006 (Linfield, Stockport Co)	8
Thompson, R. 1928 (Queen's Island)	1
Thompson, W. 1889 (Belfast Ath)	1
Thunder, P. J. 1911 (Bohemians)	1
Todd, S. J. 1966 (Burnley, Sheffield W)	11
Toner, C. 2003 (Leyton Orient)	2
Toner, J. 1922 (Arsenal, St Johnstone)	8
Torrans, R. 1893 (Linfield)	1
Torrans, S. 1889 (Linfield)	26
Trainor, D. 1967 (Crusaders)	1
Tuffey, J. 2009 (Partick T)	**5**
Tully, C. P. 1949 (Celtic)	10
Turner, A. 1896 (Cliftonville)	1
Turner, E. 1896 (Cliftonville)	1
Turner, W. 1886 (Cliftonville)	3
Twomey, J. F. 1938 (Leeds U)	2

SCOTLAND

Dailly, C. 1997 (Derby Co, Blackburn R, West Ham U, Rangers) 67
Dalglish, K. 1972 (Celtic, Liverpool) 102
Davidson, C. I. 1999 (Blackburn R, Leicester C, Preston NE) **19**
Davidson, D. 1878 (Queen's Park) 5
Davidson, J. A. 1954 (Partick Th) 8
Davidson, S. 1921 (Middlesbrough) 1
Dawson, A. 1980 (Rangers) 5
Dawson, J. 1935 (Rangers) 14
Deans, J. 1975 (Celtic) 2
Delaney, J. 1936 (Celtic, Manchester U) 13
Devine, A. 1910 (Falkirk) 1
Devlin, P. J. 2003 (Birmingham C) 10
Dewar, G. 1888 (Dumbarton) 2
Dewar, N. 1932 (Third Lanark) 3
Dick, J. 1959 (West Ham U) 1
Dickie, M. 1897 (Rangers) 3
Dickov, P. 2001 (Manchester C, Leicester C, Blackburn R) 10
Dickson, W. 1888 (Dundee Strathmore) 1
Dickson, W. 1970 (Kilmarnock) 5
Divers, J. 1895 (Celtic) 1
Divers, J. 1939 (Celtic) 1
Dobie, R. S. 2002 (WBA) 6
Docherty, T. H. 1952 (Preston NE, Arsenal) 25
Dodds, D. 1984 (Dundee U) 2
Dodds, J. 1914 (Celtic) 3
Dodds, W. 1997 (Aberdeen, Dundee U, Rangers) 26
Doig, J. E. 1887 (Arbroath, Sunderland) 5
Donachie, W. 1972 (Manchester C) 35
Donaldson, A. 1914 (Bolton W) 6
Donnachie, J. 1913 (Oldham Ath) 3
Donnelly, S. 1997 (Celtic) 10
Dorrans, G. 2010 (WBA) **3**
Dougal, J. 1939 (Preston NE) 1
Dougall, C. 1947 (Birmingham C) 1
Dougan, R. 1950 (Hearts) 1
Douglas, A. 1911 (Chelsea) 1
Douglas, J. 1880 (Renfrew) 1
Douglas, R. 2002 (Celtic, Leicester C) 19
Dowds, P. 1892 (Celtic) 1
Downie, R. 1892 (Third Lanark) 1
Doyle, D. 1892 (Celtic) 8
Doyle, J. 1976 (Ayr U) 1
Drummond, J. 1892 (Falkirk, Rangers) 14
Dunbar, M. 1886 (Cartvale) 1
Duncan, A. 1975 (Hibernian) 6
Duncan, D. 1933 (Derby Co) 14
Duncan, D. M. 1948 (East Fife) 3
Duncan, J. 1878 (Alexandra Ath) 2
Duncan, J. 1926 (Leicester C) 1
Duncanson, J. 1947 (Rangers) 1
Dunlop, J. 1890 (St Mirren) 1
Dunlop, W. 1906 (Liverpool) 1
Dunn, J. 1925 (Hibernian, Everton) 6
Durie, G. S. 1988 (Chelsea, Tottenham H, Rangers) 43
Durrant, I. 1988 (Rangers, Kilmarnock) 20
Dykes, J. 1938 (Hearts) 2

Easson, J. F. 1931 (Portsmouth) 3
Elliott, M. S. 1998 (Leicester C) 18
Ellis, J. 1892 (Mossend Swifts) 1
Evans, A. 1982 (Aston Villa) 4
Evans, R. 1949 (Celtic, Chelsea) 48
Ewart, J. 1921 (Bradford C) 1
Ewing, T. 1958 (Partick Th) 2

Farm, G. N. 1953 (Blackpool) 10
Ferguson, B. 1999 (Rangers, Blackburn R, Rangers) 45
Ferguson, D. 1988 (Rangers) 2
Ferguson, D. 1992 (Dundee U, Everton) 7
Ferguson, I. 1989 (Rangers) 9
Ferguson, J. 1874 (Vale of Leven) 6

Ferguson, R. 1966 (Kilmarnock) 7
Fernie, W. 1954 (Celtic) 12
Findlay, R. 1898 (Kilmarnock) 1
Fitchie, T. T. 1905 (Woolwich Arsenal, Queen's Park) 4
Flavell, R. 1947 (Airdrieonians) 2
Fleck, R. 1990 (Norwich C) 4
Fleming, C. 1954 (East Fife) 1
Fleming, J. W. 1929 (Rangers) 3
Fleming, R. 1886 (Morton) 1
Fletcher, D. B. 2004 (Manchester U) **47**
Fletcher, S. 2008 (Hibernian, Burnley) **7**
Forbes, A. R. 1947 (Sheffield U, Arsenal) 14
Forbes, J. 1884 (Vale of Leven) 5
Ford, D. 1974 (Hearts) 3
Forrest, J. 1966 (Rangers, Aberdeen) 5
Forrest, J. 1958 (Motherwell) 1
Forsyth, A. 1972 (Partick Th, Manchester U) 10
Forsyth, C. 1964 (Kilmarnock) 4
Forsyth, T. 1971 (Motherwell, Rangers) 22
Fox, D. J. 2010 (Burnley) **1**
Foyers, R. 1893 (St Bernards) 2
Fraser, D. M. 1968 (WBA) 2
Fraser, J. 1891 (Moffat) 1
Fraser, M. J. E. 1880 (Queen's Park) 5
Fraser, J. 1907 (Dundee) 1
Fraser, W. 1955 (Sunderland) 2
Freedman, D. A. 2002 (C Palace) 2
Fulton, W. 1884 (Abercorn) 1
Fyfe, J. H. 1895 (Third Lanark) 1

Gabriel, J. 1961 (Everton) 2
Gallacher, H. K. 1924 (Airdrieonians, Newcastle U, Chelsea, Derby Co) 20
Gallacher, K. W. 1988 (Dundee U, Coventry C, Blackburn R, Newcastle U) 53
Gallacher, P. 1935 (Sunderland) 1
Gallacher, P. 2002 (Dundee U) 8
Gallagher, P. 2004 (Blackburn R) 1
Galloway, M. 1992 (Celtic) 1
Galt, J. H. 1908 (Rangers) 2
Gardiner, I. 1958 (Motherwell) 1
Gardner, D. R. 1897 (Third Lanark) 1
Gardner, R. 1872 (Queen's Park, Clydesdale) 5
Gemmell, T. 1955 (St Mirren) 2
Gemmell, T. 1966 (Celtic) 18
Gemmill, A. 1971 (Derby Co, Nottingham F, Birmingham C) 43
Gemmill, S. 1995 (Nottingham F, Everton) 26
Gibb, W. 1873 (Clydesdale) 1
Gibson, D. W. 1963 (Leicester C) 7
Gibson, J. D. 1926 (Partick Th, Aston Villa) 8
Gibson, N. 1895 (Rangers, Partick Th) 14
Gilchrist, J. E. 1922 (Celtic) 1
Gilhooley, M. 1922 (Hull C) 1
Gillespie, G. 1880 (Rangers, Queen's Park) 7
Gillespie, G. T. 1988 (Liverpool) 13
Gillespie, Jas 1898 (Third Lanark) 1
Gillespie, John 1896 (Queen's Park) 1
Gillespie, R. 1927 (Queen's Park) 4
Gillick, T. 1937 (Everton) 5
Gilmour, J. 1931 (Dundee) 1
Gilzean, A. J. 1964 (Dundee, Tottenham H) 22
Glass, S. 1999 (Newcastle U) 1
Glavin, R. 1977 (Celtic) 1
Glen, A. 1956 (Aberdeen) 1
Glen, R. 1895 (Renton, Hibernian) 3
Goram, A. L. 1986 (Oldham Ath, Hibernian, Rangers) 43
Gordon, C. S. 2004 (Hearts, Sunderland) **39**
Gordon, J. E. 1912 (Rangers) 10
Gossland, J. 1884 (Rangers) 1
Goudie, J. 1884 (Abercorn) 1
Gough, C. R. 1983 (Dundee U, Tottenham H, Rangers) 61
Gould, J. 2000 (Celtic) 2

Gourlay, J. 1886 (Cambuslang)	2
Govan, J. 1948 (Hibernian)	6
Gow, D. R. 1888 (Rangers)	1
Gow, J. J. 1885 (Queen's Park)	1
Gow, J. R. 1888 (Rangers)	1
Graham, A. 1978 (Leeds U)	11
Graham, G. 1972 (Arsenal, Manchester U)	12
Graham, J. 1884 (Annbank)	1
Graham, J. A. 1921 (Arsenal)	1
Grant, J. 1959 (Hibernian)	2
Grant, P. 1989 (Celtic)	2
Gray, A. 1903 (Hibernian)	1
Gray, A. D. 2003 (Bradford C)	2
Gray, A. M. 1976 (Aston Villa, Wolverhampton W, Everton)	20
Gray, D. 1929 (Rangers)	10
Gray, E. 1969 (Leeds U)	12
Gray, F. T. 1976 (Leeds U, Nottingham F, Leeds U)	32
Gray, W. 1886 (Pollokshields Ath)	1
Green, A. 1971 (Blackpool, Newcastle U)	6
Greig, J. 1964 (Rangers)	44
Groves, W. 1888 (Hibernian, Celtic)	3
Gulliland, W. 1891 (Queen's Park)	4
Gunn, B. 1990 (Norwich C)	6
Haddock, H. 1955 (Clyde)	6
Haddow, D. 1894 (Rangers)	1
Haffey, F. 1960 (Celtic)	2
Hamilton, A. 1885 (Queen's Park)	4
Hamilton, A. W. 1962 (Dundee)	24
Hamilton, G. 1906 (Port Glasgow Ath)	1
Hamilton, G. 1947 (Aberdeen)	5
Hamilton, J. 1892 (Queen's Park)	3
Hamilton, J. 1924 (St Mirren)	1
Hamilton, R. C. 1899 (Rangers, Dundee)	11
Hamilton, T. 1891 (Hurlford)	1
Hamilton, T. 1932 (Rangers)	1
Hamilton, W. M. 1965 (Hibernian)	1
Hammell, S. 2005 (Motherwell)	1
Hannah, A. B. 1888 (Renton)	1
Hannah, J. 1889 (Third Lanark)	1
Hansen, A. D. 1979 (Liverpool)	26
Hansen, J. 1972 (Partick Th)	2
Harkness, J. D. 1927 (Queen's Park, Hearts)	12
Harper, J. M. 1973 (Aberdeen, Hibernian, Aberdeen)	4
Harper, W. 1923 (Hibernian, Arsenal)	11
Harris, J. 1921 (Partick Th)	2
Harris, N. 1924 (Newcastle U)	1
Harrower, W. 1882 (Queen's Park)	3
Hartford, R. A. 1972 (WBA, Manchester C Everton, Manchester C)	50
Hartley, P. J. 2005 (Hearts, Celtic, Bristol C)	**25**
Harvey, D. 1973 (Leeds U)	16
Hastings, A. C. 1936 (Sunderland)	2
Haughney, M. 1954 (Celtic)	1
Hay, D. 1970 (Celtic)	27
Hay, J. 1905 (Celtic, Newcastle U)	11
Hegarty, P. 1979 (Dundee U)	8
Heggie, C. 1886 (Rangers)	1
Henderson, G. H. 1904 (Rangers)	1
Henderson, J. G. 1953 (Portsmouth, Arsenal)	7
Henderson, W. 1963 (Rangers)	29
Hendry, E. C. J. 1993 (Blackburn R, Rangers, Coventry C, Bolton W)	51
Hepburn, J. 1891 (Alloa Ath)	1
Hepburn, R. 1932 (Ayr U)	1
Herd, A. C. 1935 (Hearts)	1
Herd, D. G. 1959 (Arsenal)	5
Herd, G. 1958 (Clyde)	5
Herriot, J. 1969 (Birmingham C)	8
Hewie, J. D. 1956 (Charlton Ath)	19
Higgins, A. 1885 (Kilmarnock)	1
Higgins, A. 1910 (Newcastle U)	4
Highet, T. C. 1875 (Queen's Park)	4

Hill, D. 1881 (Rangers)	3
Hill, D. A. 1906 (Third Lanark)	1
Hill, F. R. 1930 (Aberdeen)	3
Hill, J. 1891 (Hearts)	2
Hogg, G. 1896 (Hearts)	2
Hogg, J. 1922 (Ayr U)	1
Hogg, R. M. 1937 (Celtic)	1
Holm, A. H. 1882 (Queen's Park)	3
Holt, D. D. 1963 (Hearts)	5
Holt, G. J. 2001 (Kilmarnock, Norwich C)	10
Holton, J. A. 1973 (Manchester U)	15
Hope, R. 1968 (WBA)	2
Hopkin, D. 1997 (C Palace, Leeds U)	7
Houliston, W. 1949 (Queen of the South)	3
Houston, S. M. 1976 (Manchester U)	1
Howden, W. 1905 (Partick Th)	1
Howe, R. 1929 (Hamilton A)	2
Howie, H. 1949 (Hibernian)	1
Howie, J. 1905 (Newcastle U)	3
Howieson, J. 1927 (St Mirren)	1
Hughes, J. 1965 (Celtic)	8
Hughes, R. D. 2004 (Portsmouth)	5
Hughes, S. R. 2010 (Norwich C)	**1**
Hughes, W. 1975 (Sunderland)	1
Humphries, W. 1952 (Motherwell)	1
Hunter, A. 1972 (Kilmarnock, Celtic)	4
Hunter, J. 1909 (Dundee)	1
Hunter, J. 1874 (Third Lanark, Eastern, Third Lanark)	4
Hunter, W. 1960 (Motherwell)	3
Hunter, R. 1890 (St Mirren)	1
Husband, J. 1947 (Partick Th)	1
Hutchison, D. 1999 (Everton, Sunderland, West Ham U)	26
Hutchison, T. 1974 (Coventry C)	17
Hutton, A. 2007 (Rangers, Tottenham H)	**15**
Hutton, J. 1887 (St Bernards)	1
Hutton, J. 1923 (Aberdeen, Blackburn R)	10
Hyslop, T. 1896 (Stoke, Rangers)	2
Imlach, J. J. S. 1958 (Nottingham F)	4
Imrie, W. N. 1929 (St Johnstone)	2
Inglis, J. 1883 (Rangers)	2
Inglis, J. 1884 (Kilmarnock Ath)	1
Irons, J. H. 1900 (Queen's Park)	1
Irvine, B. 1991 (Aberdeen)	9
Iwelumo, C.R. 2009 (Wolverhampton W)	4
Jackson, A. 1886 (Cambuslang)	2
Jackson, A. 1925 (Aberdeen, Huddersfield T)	17
Jackson, C. 1975 (Rangers)	8
Jackson, D. 1995 (Hibernian, Celtic)	28
Jackson, J. 1931 (Partick Th, Chelsea)	8
Jackson, T. A. 1904 (St Mirren)	6
James, A. W. 1926 (Preston NE, Arsenal)	8
Jardine, A. 1971 (Rangers)	38
Jarvie, A. 1971 (Airdrieonians)	3
Jenkinson, T. 1887 (Hearts)	1
Jess, E. 1993 (Aberdeen, Coventry C, Aberdeen)	18
Johnston, A. 1999 (Sunderland, Rangers, Middlesbrough)	18
Johnston, L. H. 1948 (Clyde)	2
Johnston, M. 1984 (Watford, Celtic, Nantes, Rangers)	38
Johnston, R. 1938 (Sunderland)	1
Johnston, W. 1966 (Rangers, WBA)	22
Johnstone, D. 1973 (Rangers)	14
Johnstone, J. 1888 (Abercorn)	1
Johnstone, J. 1965 (Celtic)	23
Johnstone, Jas 1894 (Kilmarnock)	1
Johnstone, J. A. 1930 (Hearts)	3
Johnstone, R. 1951 (Hibernian, Manchester C)	17
Johnstone, W. 1887 (Third Lanark)	3
Jordan, J. 1973 (Leeds U, Manchester U, AC Milan)	52
Kay, J. L. 1880 (Queen's Park)	6

Keillor, A. 1891 (Montrose, Dundee)	6
Keir, L. 1885 (Dumbarton)	5
Kelly, H. T. 1952 (Blackpool)	1
Kelly, J. 1888 (Renton, Celtic)	8
Kelly, J. C. 1949 (Barnsley)	2
Kelso, R. 1885 (Renton, Dundee)	7
Kelso, T. 1914 (Dundee)	1
Kennaway, J. 1934 (Celtic)	1
Kennedy, A. 1875 (Eastern, Third Lanark)	6
Kennedy, J. 1897 (Hibernian)	1
Kennedy, J. 1964 (Celtic)	6
Kennedy, J. 2004 (Celtic)	1
Kennedy, S. 1905 (Partick Th)	1
Kennedy, S. 1975 (Rangers)	5
Kennedy, S. 1978 (Aberdeen)	8
Ker, G. 1880 (Queen's Park)	5
Ker, W. 1872 (Queen's Park)	2
Kerr, A. 1955 (Partick Th)	2
Kerr, B. 2003 (Newcastle U)	3
Kerr, P. 1924 (Hibernian)	1
Key, G. 1902 (Hearts)	1
Key, W. 1907 (Queen's Park)	1
King, A. 1896 (Hearts, Celtic)	6
King, J. 1933 (Hamilton A)	2
King, W. S. 1929 (Queen's Park)	1
Kinloch, J. D. 1922 (Partick Th)	1
Kinnaird, A. F. 1873 (Wanderers)	1
Kinnear, D. 1938 (Rangers)	1
Kyle, K. 2002 (Sunderland, Kilmarnock)	**10**
Lambert, P. 1995 (Motherwell, Borussia Dortmund, Celtic)	40
Lambie, J. A. 1886 (Queen's Park)	3
Lambie, W. A. 1892 (Queen's Park)	9
Lamont, W. 1885 (Pilgrims)	1
Lang, A. 1880 (Dumbarton)	1
Lang, J. J. 1876 (Clydesdale, Third Lanark)	2
Latta, A. 1888 (Dumbarton)	2
Law, D. 1959 (Huddersfield T, Manchester C, Torino, Manchester U, Manchester C)	55
Law, G. 1910 (Rangers)	3
Law, T. 1928 (Chelsea)	2
Lawrence, J. 1911 (Newcastle U)	1
Lawrence, T. 1963 (Liverpool)	3
Lawson, D. 1923 (St Mirren)	1
Leckie, R. 1872 (Queen's Park)	1
Leggat, G. 1956 (Aberdeen, Fulham)	18
Leighton, J. 1983 (Aberdeen, Manchester U, Hibernian, Aberdeen)	91
Lennie, W. 1908 (Aberdeen)	2
Lennox, R. 1967 (Celtic)	10
Leslie, L. G. 1961 (Airdrieonians)	5
Levein, C. 1990 (Hearts)	16
Liddell, W. 1947 (Liverpool)	28
Liddle, D. 1931 (East Fife)	3
Lindsay, D. 1903 (St Mirren)	1
Lindsay, J. 1880 (Dumbarton)	8
Lindsay, J. 1888 (Renton)	1
Linwood, A. B. 1950 (Clyde)	1
Little, R. J. 1953 (Rangers)	1
Livingstone, G. T. 1906 (Manchester C, Rangers)	2
Lochhead, A. 1889 (Third Lanark)	1
Logan, J. 1891 (Ayr)	1
Logan, T. 1913 (Falkirk)	1
Logie, J. T. 1953 (Arsenal)	1
Loney, W. 1910 (Celtic)	2
Long, H. 1947 (Clyde)	1
Longair, W. 1894 (Dundee)	1
Lorimer, P. 1970 (Leeds U)	21
Love, A. 1931 (Aberdeen)	3
Low, A. 1934 (Falkirk)	1
Low, J. 1891 (Cambuslang)	1
Low, T. P. 1897 (Rangers)	1
Low, W. L. 1911 (Newcastle U)	5

Lowe, J. 1887 (St Bernards)	1
Lundie, J. 1886 (Hibernian)	1
Lyall, J. 1905 (Sheffield W)	1
McAdam, J. 1880 (Third Lanark)	1
McAllister, B. 1997 (Wimbledon)	3
McAllister, G. 1990 (Leicester C, Leeds U, Coventry C)	57
McAllister, J. R. 2004 (Livingston)	1
Macari, L. 1972 (Celtic, Manchester U)	24
McArthur, D. 1895 (Celtic)	3
McAtee, A. 1913 (Celtic)	1
McAulay, J. 1884 (Arthurlie)	1
McAulay, J. D. 1882 (Dumbarton)	9
McAulay, R. 1932 (Rangers)	2
Macauley, A. R. 1947 (Brentford, Arsenal)	7
McAvennie, F. 1986 (West Ham U, Celtic)	5
McBain, E. 1894 (St Mirren)	1
McBain, N. 1922 (Manchester U, Everton)	3
McBride, J. 1967 (Celtic)	2
McBride, P. 1904 (Preston NE)	6
McCall, A. 1888 (Renton)	1
McCall, A. S. M. 1990 (Everton, Rangers)	40
McCall, J. 1886 (Renton)	5
McCalliog, J. 1967 (Sheffield W, Wolverhampton W)	5
McCallum, N. 1888 (Renton)	1
McCann, N. 1999 (Hearts, Rangers, Southampton)	26
McCann, R. J. 1959 (Motherwell)	5
McCartney, W. 1902 (Hibernian)	1
McClair, B. 1987 (Celtic, Manchester U)	30
McClory, A. 1927 (Motherwell)	3
McCloy, P. 1924 (Ayr U)	2
McCloy, P. 1973 (Rangers)	4
McCoist, A. 1986 (Rangers, Kilmarnock)	61
McColl, I. M. 1950 (Rangers)	14
McColl, R. S. 1896 (Queen's Park, Newcastle U, Queen's Park)	13
McColl, W. 1895 (Renton)	1
McCombie, A. 1903 (Sunderland, Newcastle U)	4
McCorkindale, J. 1891 (Partick Th)	1
McCormack, R. 2008 (Motherwell, Cardiff C)	**5**
McCormick, R. 1886 (Abercorn)	1
McCrae, D. 1929 (St Mirren)	2
McCreadie, A. 1893 (Rangers)	2
McCreadie, E. G. 1965 (Chelsea)	23
McCulloch, D. 1935 (Hearts, Brentford, Derby Co)	7
McCulloch, L. 2005 (Wigan Ath, Rangers)	15
MacDonald, A. 1976 (Rangers)	1
McDonald, J. 1886 (Edinburgh University)	1
McDonald, J. 1956 (Sunderland)	2
MacDougall, E. J. 1975 (Norwich C)	7
McDougall, J. 1877 (Vale of Leven)	5
McDougall, J. 1926 (Airdrieonians)	1
McDougall, J. 1931 (Liverpool)	2
McEveley, J. 2008 (Derby Co)	3
McFadden, J. 2002 (Motherwell, Everton, Birmingham C)	**45**
McFadyen, W. 1934 (Motherwell)	2
Macfarlane, A. 1904 (Dundee)	5
Macfarlane, W. 1947 (Hearts)	1
McFarlane, R. 1896 (Greenock Morton)	1
McGarr, E. 1970 (Aberdeen)	2
McGarvey, F. P. 1979 (Liverpool, Celtic)	7
McGeoch, A. 1876 (Dumbreck)	4
McGhee, J. 1886 (Hibernian)	1
McGhee, M. 1983 (Aberdeen)	4
McGinlay, J. 1994 (Bolton W)	13
McGonagle, W. 1933 (Celtic)	6
McGrain, D. 1973 (Celtic)	62
McGregor, A. 2007 (Rangers)	4
McGregor, J. C. 1877 (Vale of Leven)	4
McGrory, J. 1928 (Celtic)	7
McGrory, J. E. 1965 (Kilmarnock)	3
McGuire, W. 1881 (Beith)	2

McGurk, F. 1934 (Birmingham)	1
McHardy, H. 1885 (Rangers)	1
McInally, A. 1989 (Aston Villa, Bayern Munich)	8
McInally, J. 1987 (Dundee U)	10
McInally, T. B. 1926 (Celtic)	2
McInnes, D. 2003 (WBA)	2
McInnes, T. 1889 (Cowlairs)	1
McIntosh, W. 1905 (Third Lanark)	1
McIntyre, A. 1878 (Vale of Leven)	2
McIntyre, H. 1880 (Rangers)	1
McIntyre, J. 1884 (Rangers)	1
MacKay, D. 1959 (Celtic)	14
Mackay, D. C. 1957 (Hearts, Tottenham H)	22
Mackay, G. 1988 (Hearts)	4
Mackay, M. 2004 (Norwich C)	5
McKay, J. 1924 (Blackburn R)	1
McKay, R. 1928 (Newcastle U)	1
McKean, R. 1976 (Rangers)	1
McKenzie, D. 1938 (Brentford)	1
Mackenzie, J. A. 1954 (Partick Th)	9
McKeown, M. 1889 (Celtic)	2
McKie, J. 1898 (East Stirling)	1
McKillop, T. R. 1938 (Rangers)	1
McKimmie, S. 1989 (Aberdeen)	40
McKinlay, D. 1922 (Liverpool)	2
McKinlay, T. 1996 (Celtic)	22
McKinlay, W. 1994 (Dundee U, Blackburn R)	29
McKinnon, A. 1874 (Queen's Park)	1
McKinnon, R. 1966 (Rangers)	28
McKinnon, R. 1994 (Motherwell)	3
MacKinnon, W. 1883 (Dumbarton)	4
MacKinnon, W. W. 1872 (Queen's Park)	9
McLaren, A. 1929 (St Johnstone)	5
McLaren, A. 1947 (Preston NE)	4
McLaren, A. 1992 (Hearts, Rangers)	24
McLaren, A. 2001 (Kilmarnock)	1
McLaren, J. 1888 (Hibernian, Celtic)	3
McLean, A. 1926 (Celtic)	4
McLean, D. 1896 (St Bernards)	2
McLean, D. 1912 (Sheffield W)	1
McLean, G. 1968 (Dundee)	1
McLean, T. 1969 (Kilmarnock)	6
McLeish, A. 1980 (Aberdeen)	77
McLeod, D. 1905 (Celtic)	4
McLeod, J. 1888 (Dumbarton)	5
MacLeod, J. M. 1961 (Hibernian)	4
MacLeod, M. 1985 (Celtic, Borussia Dortmund, Hibernian)	20
McLeod, W. 1886 (Cowlairs)	1
McLintock, A. 1875 (Vale of Leven)	3
McLintock, F. 1963 (Leicester C, Arsenal)	9
McLuckie, J. S. 1934 (Manchester C)	1
McMahon, A. 1892 (Celtic)	6
McManus, S. 2007 (Celtic, Middlesbrough)	**22**
McMenemy, J. 1905 (Celtic)	12
McMenemy, J. 1934 (Motherwell)	1
McMillan, I. L. 1952 (Airdrieonians, Rangers)	6
McMillan, J. 1897 (St Bernards)	1
McMillan, T. 1887 (Dumbarton)	1
McMullan, J. 1920 (Partick Th, Manchester C)	16
McNab, A. 1921 (Morton)	2
McNab, A. 1937 (Sunderland, WBA)	2
McNab, C. D. 1931 (Dundee)	6
McNab, J. S. 1923 (Liverpool)	1
McNair, A. 1906 (Celtic)	15
McNamara, J. 1997 (Celtic, Wolverhampton W)	33
McNamee, D. 2004 (Livingston)	4
McNaught, W. 1951 (Raith R)	5
McNaughton, K. 2002 (Aberdeen, Cardiff C)	4
McNeill, W. 1961 (Celtic)	29
McNiel, H. 1874 (Queen's Park)	10
McNiel, M. 1876 (Rangers)	2
McPhail, J. 1950 (Celtic)	5
McPhail, R. 1927 (Airdrieonians, Rangers)	17

McPherson, D. 1892 (Kilmarnock)	1
McPherson, D. 1989 (Hearts, Rangers)	27
McPherson, J. 1875 (Clydesdale)	1
McPherson, J. 1879 (Vale of Leven)	8
McPherson, J. 1888 (Kilmarnock, Cowlairs, Rangers)	9
McPherson, J. 1891 (Hearts)	1
McPherson, R. 1882 (Arthurlie)	1
McQueen, G. 1974 (Leeds U, Manchester U)	30
McQueen, M. 1890 (Leith Ath)	2
McRorie, D. M. 1931 (Morton)	1
McSpadyen, A. 1939 (Partick Th)	2
McStay, P. 1984 (Celtic)	76
McStay, W. 1921 (Celtic)	13
McSwegan, G. 2000 (Hearts)	2
McTavish, J. 1910 (Falkirk)	1
McWattie, G. C. 1901 (Queen's Park)	2
McWilliam, P. 1905 (Newcastle U)	8
Madden, J. 1893 (Celtic)	2
Main, F. R. 1938 (Rangers)	1
Main, J. 1909 (Hibernian)	1
Maley, W. 1893 (Celtic)	2
Maloney, S. R. 2006 (Celtic, Aston Villa, Celtic)	**17**
Malpas, M. 1984 (Dundee U)	55
Marshall, D. J. 2005 (Celtic, Cardiff C)	**5**
Marshall, G. 1992 (Celtic)	1
Marshall, H. 1899 (Celtic)	2
Marshall, J. 1885 (Third Lanark)	4
Marshall, J. 1921 (Middlesbrough, Llanelly)	7
Marshall, J. 1932 (Rangers)	3
Marshall, R. W. 1892 (Rangers)	2
Martin, B. 1995 (Motherwell)	2
Martin, F. 1954 (Aberdeen)	6
Martin, N. 1965 (Hibernian, Sunderland)	3
Martis, J. 1961 (Motherwell)	1
Mason, J. 1949 (Third Lanark)	7
Massie, A. 1932 (Hearts, Aston Villa)	18
Masson, D. S. 1976 (QPR, Derby Co)	17
Mathers, D. 1954 (Partick Th)	1
Matteo, D. 2001 (Leeds U)	6
Maxwell, W. S. 1898 (Stoke C)	1
May, J. 1906 (Rangers)	5
Meechan, P. 1896 (Celtic)	1
Meiklejohn, D. D. 1922 (Rangers)	15
Menzies, A. 1906 (Hearts)	1
Mercer, R. 1912 (Hearts)	2
Middleton, R. 1930 (Cowdenbeath)	1
Millar, J. 1897 (Rangers)	3
Millar, J. 1963 (Rangers)	2
Miller, A. 1939 (Hearts)	1
Miller, C. 2001 (Dundee U)	1
Miller, J. 1931 (St Mirren)	5
Miller, K. 2001 (Rangers, Wolverhampton W, Celtic, Derby Co, Rangers)	**47**
Miller, L. 2006 (Dundee U, Aberdeen)	**3**
Miller, P. 1882 (Dumbarton)	3
Miller, T. 1920 (Liverpool, Manchester U)	3
Miller, W. 1876 (Third Lanark)	1
Miller, W. 1947 (Celtic)	6
Miller, W. 1975 (Aberdeen)	65
Mills, W. 1936 (Aberdeen)	3
Milne, J. V. 1938 (Middlesbrough)	2
Mitchell, D. 1890 (Rangers)	5
Mitchell, J. 1908 (Kilmarnock)	3
Mitchell, R. C. 1951 (Newcastle U)	2
Mochan, N. 1954 (Celtic)	3
Moir, W. 1950 (Bolton W)	1
Moncur, R. 1968 (Newcastle U)	16
Morgan, H. 1898 (St Mirren, Liverpool)	2
Morgan, W. 1968 (Burnley, Manchester U)	21
Morris, D. 1923 (Raith R)	6
Morris, H. 1950 (East Fife)	1
Morrison, J. C. 2008 (WBA)	5
Morrison, T. 1927 (St Mirren)	1
Morton, A. L. 1920 (Queen's Park, Rangers)	31

Morton, H. A. 1929 (Kilmarnock)	2
Mudie, J. K. 1957 (Blackpool)	17
Muir, W. 1907 (Dundee)	1
Muirhead, T. A. 1922 (Rangers)	8
Mulhall, G. 1960 (Aberdeen, Sunderland)	3
Munro, A. D. 1937 (Hearts, Blackpool)	3
Munro, F. M. 1971 (Wolverhampton W)	9
Munro, I. 1979 (St Mirren)	7
Munro, N. 1888 (Abercorn)	2
Murdoch, J. 1931 (Motherwell)	1
Murdoch, R. 1966 (Celtic)	12
Murphy, F. 1938 (Celtic)	1
Murray, I. 2003 (Hibernian, Rangers)	6
Murray, J. 1895 (Renton)	1
Murray, J. 1958 (Hearts)	5
Murray, J. W. 1890 (Vale of Leven)	1
Murray, P. 1896 (Hibernian)	2
Murray, S. 1972 (Aberdeen)	1
Murty, G. S. 2004 (Reading)	4
Mutch, G. 1938 (Preston NE)	1
Naismith, S. J. 2007 (Kilmarnock, Rangers)	**4**
Napier, C. E. 1932 (Celtic, Derby Co)	5
Narey, D. 1977 (Dundee U)	35
Naysmith, G. A. 2000 (Hearts, Everton, Sheffield U)	46
Neil, R. G. 1896 (Hibernian, Rangers)	2
Neill, R. W. 1876 (Queen's Park)	5
Neilson, R. 2007 (Hearts)	1
Nellies, P. 1913 (Hearts)	2
Nelson, J. 1925 (Cardiff C)	4
Nevin, P. K. F. 1986 (Chelsea, Everton, Tranmere R)	28
Niblo, T. D. 1904 (Aston Villa)	1
Nibloe, J. 1929 (Kilmarnock)	11
Nicholas, C. 1983 (Celtic, Arsenal, Aberdeen)	20
Nicholson, B. 2001 (Dunfermline Ath)	3
Nicol, S. 1985 (Liverpool)	27
Nisbet, J. 1929 (Ayr U)	3
Niven, J. B. 1885 (Moffat)	1
O'Connor, G. 2002 (Hibernian, Lokomotiv Moscow, Birmingham C)	**16**
O'Donnell, F. 1937 (Preston NE, Blackpool)	6
O'Donnell, P. 1994 (Motherwell)	1
Ogilvie, D. H. 1934 (Motherwell)	1
O'Hare, J. 1970 (Derby Co)	13
O'Neil, B. 1996 (Celtic, Wolfsburg, Derby Co, Preston NE)	7
O'Neil, J. 2001 (Hibernian)	1
Ormond, W. E. 1954 (Hibernian)	6
O'Rourke, F. 1907 (Airdrieonians)	1
Orr, J. 1892 (Kilmarnock)	1
Orr, R. 1902 (Newcastle U)	2
Orr, T. 1952 (Morton)	2
Orr, W. 1900 (Celtic)	3
Orrock, R. 1913 (Falkirk)	1
Oswald, J. 1889 (Third Lanark, St Bernards, Rangers)	3
Parker, A. H. 1955 (Falkirk, Everton)	15
Parlane, D. 1973 (Rangers)	12
Parlane, R. 1878 (Vale of Leven)	3
Paterson, G. D. 1939 (Celtic)	1
Paterson, J. 1920 (Leicester C)	1
Paterson, J. 1931 (Cowdenbeath)	3
Paton, A. 1952 (Motherwell)	2
Paton, D. 1896 (St Bernards)	1
Paton, M. 1883 (Dumbarton)	5
Paton, R. 1879 (Vale of Leven)	2
Patrick, J. 1897 (St Mirren)	2
Paul, H. McD. 1909 (Queen's Park)	3
Paul, W. 1888 (Partick Th)	3
Paul, W. 1891 (Dykebar)	1
Pearson, S. P. 2004 (Motherwell, Celtic, Derby Co)	10
Pearson, T. 1947 (Newcastle U)	2
Penman, A. 1966 (Dundee)	1

Pettigrew, W. 1976 (Motherwell)	5
Phillips, J. 1877 (Queen's Park)	3
Plenderleith, J. B. 1961 (Manchester C)	1
Porteous, W. 1903 (Hearts)	1
Pressley, S. J. 2000 (Hearts)	32
Pringle, C. 1921 (St Mirren)	1
Provan, D. 1964 (Rangers)	5
Provan, D. 1980 (Celtic)	10
Pursell, P. 1914 (Queen's Park)	1
Quashie, N. F. 2004 (Portsmouth, Southampton, WBA)	14
Quinn, J. 1905 (Celtic)	11
Quinn, P. 1961 (Motherwell)	4
Rae, G. 2001 (Dundee, Rangers, Cardiff C)	14
Rae, J. 1889 (Third Lanark)	2
Raeside, J. S. 1906 (Third Lanark)	1
Raisbeck, A. G. 1900 (Liverpool)	8
Rankin, G. 1890 (Vale of Leven)	2
Rankin, R. 1929 (St Mirren)	3
Redpath, W. 1949 (Motherwell)	9
Reid, J. G. 1914 (Airdrieonians)	3
Reid, R. 1938 (Brentford)	2
Reid, W. 1911 (Rangers)	9
Reilly, L. 1949 (Hibernian)	38
Rennie, H. G. 1900 (Hearts, Hibernian)	13
Renny-Tailyour, H. W. 1873 (Royal Engineers)	1
Rhind, A. 1872 (Queen's Park)	1
Richmond, A. 1906 (Queen's Park)	1
Richmond, J. T. 1877 (Clydesdale, Queen's Park)	3
Ring, T. 1953 (Clyde)	12
Rioch, B. D. 1975 (Derby Co, Everton, Derby Co)	24
Riordan, D. G. 2006 (Hibernian)	**3**
Ritchie, A. 1891 (East Stirlingshire)	1
Ritchie, H. 1923 (Hibernian)	2
Ritchie, J. 1897 (Queen's Park)	1
Ritchie, P. S. 1999 (Hearts, Bolton W, Walsall)	7
Ritchie, W. 1962 (Rangers)	1
Robb, D. T. 1971 (Aberdeen)	5
Robb, W. 1926 (Rangers, Hibernian)	2
Robertson, A. 1955 (Clyde)	5
Robertson, D. 1992 (Rangers)	3
Robertson, G. 1910 (Motherwell, Sheffield W)	4
Robertson, G. 1938 (Kilmarnock)	1
Robertson, H. 1962 (Dundee)	1
Robertson, J. 1931 (Dundee)	1
Robertson, J. 1991 (Hearts)	16
Robertson, J. N. 1978 (Nottingham F, Derby Co)	28
Robertson, J. G. 1965 (Tottenham H)	1
Robertson, J. T. 1898 (Everton, Southampton, Rangers)	16
Robertson, P. 1903 (Dundee)	1
Robertson, S. 2009 (Dundee U)	1
Robertson, T. 1889 (Queen's Park)	4
Robertson, T. 1898 (Hearts)	1
Robertson, W. 1887 (Dumbarton)	2
Robinson, R. 1974 (Dundee)	4
Robson, B. 2008 (Dundee U, Celtic, Middlesbrough)	**8**
Ross, M. 2002 (Rangers)	13
Rough, A. 1976 (Partick Th, Hibernian)	53
Rougvie, D. 1984 (Aberdeen)	1
Rowan, A. 1880 (Caledonian, Queen's Park)	2
Russell, D. 1895 (Hearts, Celtic)	6
Russell, J. 1890 (Cambuslang)	1
Russell, W. F. 1924 (Airdrieonians)	2
Rutherford, E. 1948 (Rangers)	1
St John, I. 1959 (Motherwell, Liverpool)	21
Sawers, W. 1895 (Dundee)	1
Scarff, P. 1931 (Celtic)	1
Schaedler, E. 1974 (Hibernian)	1
Scott, A. S. 1957 (Rangers, Everton)	16
Scott, J. 1966 (Hibernian)	1

Scott, J. 1971 (Dundee) — 2
Scott, M. 1898 (Airdrieonians) — 1
Scott, R. 1894 (Airdrieonians) — 1
Scoular, J. 1951 (Portsmouth) — 9
Sellar, W. 1885 (Battlefield, Queen's Park) — 9
Semple, W. 1886 (Cambuslang) — 1
Severin, S. D. 2002 (Hearts, Aberdeen) — 15
Shankly, W. 1938 (Preston NE) — 5
Sharp, G. M. 1985 (Everton) — 12
Sharp, J. 1904 (Dundee, Woolwich Arsenal, Fulham) — 5
Shaw, D. 1947 (Hibernian) — 8
Shaw, F. W. 1884 (Pollokshields Ath) — 2
Shaw, J. 1947 (Rangers) — 4
Shearer, D. 1994 (Aberdeen) — 7
Shearer, R. 1961 (Rangers) — 4
Sillars, D. C. 1891 (Queen's Park) — 5
Simpson, J. 1895 (Third Lanark) — 3
Simpson, J. 1935 (Rangers) — 14
Simpson, N. 1983 (Aberdeen) — 5
Simpson, R. C. 1967 (Celtic) — 5
Sinclair, G. L. 1910 (Hearts) — 3
Sinclair, J. W. E. 1966 (Leicester C) — 1
Skene, L. H. 1904 (Queen's Park) — 1
Sloan, T. 1904 (Third Lanark) — 1
Smellie, R. 1887 (Queen's Park) — 6
Smith, A. 1898 (Rangers) — 20
Smith, D. 1966 (Aberdeen, Rangers) — 2
Smith, G. 1947 (Hibernian) — 18
Smith, H. G. 1988 (Hearts) — 3
Smith, J. 1924 (Ayr U) — 1
Smith, J. 1935 (Rangers) — 2
Smith, J. 1968 (Aberdeen, Newcastle U) — 4
Smith, J. 2003 (Celtic) — 2
Smith, J. E. 1959 (Celtic) — 2
Smith, Jas 1872 (Queen's Park) — 1
Smith, John 1877 (Mauchline, Edinburgh University,
  Queen's Park) — 10
Smith, N. 1897 (Rangers) — 12
Smith, R. 1872 (Queen's Park) — 2
Smith, T. M. 1934 (Kilmarnock, Preston NE) — 2
Somers, P. 1905 (Celtic) — 4
Somers, W. S. 1879 (Third Lanark, Queen's Park) — 3
Somerville, G. 1886 (Queen's Park) — 1
Souness, G. J. 1975 (Middlesbrough, Liverpool,
  Sampdoria) — 54
Speedie, D. R. 1985 (Chelsea, Coventry C) — 10
Speedie, F. 1903 (Rangers) — 3
Speirs, J. H. 1908 (Rangers) — 1
Spencer, J. 1995 (Chelsea, QPR) — 14
Stanton, P. 1966 (Hibernian) — 16
Stark, J. 1909 (Rangers) — 2
Steel, W. 1947 (Morton, Derby Co, Dundee) — 30
Steele, D. M. 1923 (Huddersfield) — 3
Stein, C. 1969 (Rangers, Coventry C) — 21
Stephen, J. F. 1947 (Bradford) — 2
Stevenson, G. 1928 (Motherwell) — 12
Stewart, A. 1888 (Queen's Park) — 2
Stewart, A. 1894 (Third Lanark) — 1
Stewart, D. 1888 (Dumbarton) — 1
Stewart, D. 1893 (Queen's Park) — 3
Stewart, D. S. 1978 (Leeds U) — 1
Stewart, G. 1906 (Hibernian, Manchester C) — 4
Stewart, J. 1977 (Kilmarnock, Middlesbrough) — 2
Stewart, M. J. 2002 (Manchester U, Hearts) — 4
Stewart, R. 1981 (West Ham U) — 10
Stewart, W. G. 1898 (Queen's Park) — 2
Stockdale, R. K. 2002 (Middlesbrough) — 5
Storrier, D. 1899 (Celtic) — 3
Strachan, G. D. 1980 (Aberdeen, Manchester U,
  Leeds U) — 50
Sturrock, P. 1981 (Dundee U) — 20
Sullivan, N. 1997 (Wimbledon, Tottenham H) — 28
Summers, W. 1926 (St Mirren) — 1
Symon, J. S. 1939 (Rangers) — 1

Tait, T. S. 1911 (Sunderland) — 1
Taylor, J. 1872 (Queen's Park) — 6
Taylor, J. D. 1892 (Dumbarton, St Mirren) — 4
Taylor, W. 1892 (Hearts) — 1
Teale, G. 2006 (Wigan Ath, Derby Co) — 13
Telfer, P. N. 2000 (Coventry C) — 1
Telfer, W. 1933 (Motherwell) — 2
Telfer, W. D. 1954 (St Mirren) — 1
Templeton, R. 1902 (Aston Villa, Newcastle U,
  Woolwich Arsenal, Kilmarnock) — 11
Thompson, S. 2002 (Dundee U, Rangers) — 16
Thomson, A. 1886 (Arthurlie) — 1
Thomson, A. 1889 (Third Lanark) — 1
Thomson, A. 1909 (Airdrieonians) — 1
Thomson, A. 1926 (Celtic) — 3
Thomson, C. 1904 (Hearts, Sunderland) — 21
Thomson, C. 1937 (Sunderland) — 1
Thomson, D. 1920 (Dundee) — 1
Thomson, J. 1930 (Celtic) — 4
Thomson, J. J. 1872 (Queen's Park) — 3
Thomson, J. R. 1933 (Everton) — 1
Thomson, K. 2009 (Rangers) — **2**
Thomson, R. 1932 (Celtic) — 1
Thomson, R. W. 1927 (Falkirk) — 1
Thomson, S. 1884 (Rangers) — 2
Thomson, W. 1892 (Dumbarton) — 4
Thomson, W. 1896 (Dundee) — 1
Thomson, W. 1980 (St Mirren) — 7
Thornton, W. 1947 (Rangers) — 7
Toner, W. 1959 (Kilmarnock) — 2
Townsley, T. 1926 (Falkirk) — 1
Troup, A. 1920 (Dundee, Everton) — 5
Turnbull, E. 1948 (Hibernian) — 8
Turner, T. 1884 (Arthurlie) — 1
Turner, W. 1885 (Pollokshields Ath) — 2

Ure, J. F. 1962 (Dundee, Arsenal) — 11
Urquhart, D. 1934 (Hibernian) — 1

Vallance, T. 1877 (Rangers) — 7
Venters, A. 1934 (Cowdenbeath, Rangers) — 3

Waddell, T. S. 1891 (Queen's Park) — 6
Waddell, W. 1947 (Rangers) — 17
Wales, H. M. 1933 (Motherwell) — 1
Walker, A. 1988 (Celtic) — 3
Walker, F. 1922 (Third Lanark) — 1
Walker, G. 1930 (St Mirren) — 4
Walker, J. 1895 (Hearts, Rangers) — 5
Walker, J. 1911 (Swindon T) — 9
Walker, J. N. 1993 (Hearts, Partick Th) — 2
Walker, R. 1900 (Hearts) — 29
Walker, T. 1935 (Hearts) — 20
Walker, W. 1909 (Clyde) — 2
Wallace, I. A. 1978 (Coventry C) — 3
Wallace, L. 2010 (Hearts) — **3**
Wallace, R. 2010 (Preston NE) — **1**
Wallace, W. S. B. 1965 (Hearts, Celtic) — 7
Wardhaugh, J. 1955 (Hearts) — 2
Wark, J. 1979 (Ipswich T, Liverpool) — 29
Watson, A. 1881 (Queen's Park) — 3
Watson, J. 1903 (Sunderland, Middlesbrough) — 6
Watson, J. 1948 (Motherwell, Huddersfield T) — 2
Watson, J. A. K. 1878 (Rangers) — 1
Watson, P. R. 1934 (Blackpool) — 1
Watson, R. 1971 (Motherwell) — 1
Watson, W. 1898 (Falkirk) — 1
Watt, F. 1889 (Kilbirnie) — 4
Watt, W. W. 1887 (Queen's Park) — 1
Waugh, W. 1938 (Hearts) — 1
Webster, A. 2003 (Hearts, Dundee U) — **23**
Weir, A. 1959 (Motherwell) — 6
Weir, D. G. 1997 (Hearts, Everton, Rangers) — **65**
Weir, J. 1887 (Third Lanark) — 1

Weir, J. B. 1872 (Queen's Park)	4
Weir, P. 1980 (St Mirren, Aberdeen)	6
White, John 1922 (Albion R, Hearts)	2
White, J. A. 1959 (Falkirk, Tottenham H)	22
White, W. 1907 (Bolton W)	2
Whitelaw, A. 1887 (Vale of Leven)	2
Whittaker, S. 2010 (Rangers)	5
Whyte, D. 1988 (Celtic, Middlesbrough, Aberdeen)	12
Wilkie, L. 2002 (Dundee)	11
Williams, G. 2002 (Nottingham F)	5
Wilson, A. 1907 (Sheffield W)	6
Wilson, A. 1954 (Portsmouth)	1
Wilson, A. N. 1920 (Dunfermline, Middlesbrough)	12
Wilson, D. 1900 (Queen's Park)	1
Wilson, D. 1913 (Oldham Ath)	1
Wilson, D. 1961 (Rangers)	22
Wilson, G. W. 1904 (Hearts, Everton, Newcastle U)	6
Wilson, Hugh 1890 (Newmilns, Sunderland, Third Lanark)	4
Wilson, I. A. 1987 (Leicester C, Everton)	5
Wilson, J. 1888 (Vale of Leven)	4

Wilson, P. 1926 (Celtic)	4
Wilson, P. 1975 (Celtic)	1
Wilson, R. P. 1972 (Arsenal)	2
Winters, R. 1999 (Aberdeen)	1
Wiseman, W. 1927 (Queen's Park)	2
Wood, G. 1979 (Everton, Arsenal)	4
Woodburn, W. A. 1947 (Rangers)	24
Wotherspoon, D. N. 1872 (Queen's Park)	2
Wright, K. 1992 (Hibernian)	1
Wright, S. 1993 (Aberdeen)	2
Wright, T. 1953 (Sunderland)	3
Wylie, T. G. 1890 (Rangers)	1
Yeats, R. 1965 (Liverpool)	2
Yorston, B. C. 1931 (Aberdeen)	1
Yorston, H. 1955 (Aberdeen)	1
Young, A. 1905 (Everton)	2
Young, A. 1960 (Hearts, Everton)	8
Young, G. L. 1947 (Rangers)	53
Young, J. 1906 (Celtic)	1
Younger, T. 1955 (Hibernian, Liverpool)	24

WALES

Adams, H. 1882 (Berwyn R, Druids)	4
Aizlewood, M. 1986 (Charlton Ath, Leeds U, Bradford C, Bristol C, Cardiff C)	39
Allchurch, I. J. 1951 (Swansea T, Newcastle U, Cardiff C, Swansea T)	68
Allchurch, L. 1955 (Swansea T, Sheffield U)	11
Allen, B. W. 1951 (Coventry C)	2
Allen, J. M. 2009 (Swansea C)	2
Allen, M. 1986 (Watford, Norwich C, Millwall, Newcastle U)	14
Arridge, S. 1892 (Bootle, Everton, New Brighton Tower)	8
Astley, D. J. 1931 (Charlton Ath, Aston Villa, Derby Co, Blackpool)	13
Atherton, R. W. 1899 (Hibernian, Middlesbrough)	9
Bailiff, W. E. 1913 (Llanelly)	4
Baker, C. W. 1958 (Cardiff C)	7
Baker, W. G. 1948 (Cardiff C)	1
Bale, G. 2006 (Southampton, Tottenham H)	24
Bamford, T. 1931 (Wrexham)	5
Barnard, D. S. 1998 (Barnsley, Grimsby T)	22
Barnes, W. 1948 (Arsenal)	22
Bartley, T. 1898 (Glossop NE)	1
Bastock, A. M. 1892 (Shrewsbury T)	1
Beadles, G. H. 1925 (Cardiff C)	2
Bell, W. S. 1881 (Shrewsbury Engineers, Crewe Alex)	5
Bellamy, C. D. 1998 (Norwich C, Coventry C, Newcastle U, Blackburn R, Liverpool, West Ham U, Manchester C)	58
Bennion, S. R. 1926 (Manchester U)	10
Berry, G. F. 1979 (Wolverhampton W, Stoke C)	5
Blackmore, C. G. 1985 (Manchester U, Middlesbrough)	39
Blake, N. A. 1994 (Sheffield U, Bolton W, Blackburn R, Wolverhampton W)	29
Blew, H. 1899 (Wrexham)	22
Boden, T. 1880 (Wrexham)	1
Bodin, P. J. 1990 (Swindon T, C Palace, Swindon T)	23
Boulter, L. M. 1939 (Brentford)	1
Bowdler, H. E. 1893 (Shrewsbury T)	1
Bowdler, J. C. H. 1890 (Shrewsbury T, Wolverhampton W, Shrewsbury T)	4
Bowen, D. L. 1955 (Arsenal)	19
Bowen, E. 1880 (Druids)	2
Bowen, J. P. 1994 (Swansea C, Birmingham C)	2
Bowen, M. R. 1986 (Tottenham H, Norwich C, West Ham U)	41
Bowsher, S. J. 1929 (Burnley)	1

Boyle, T. 1981 (C Palace)	2
Bradley, M. S. 2010 (Walsall)	1
Britten, T. J. 1878 (Parkgrove, Presteigne)	2
Brookes, S. J. 1900 (Llandudno)	2
Brown, A. I. 1926 (Aberdare Ath)	1
Brown, J. R. 2006 (Gillingham, Blackburn R)	2
Browning, M. T. 1996 (Bristol R, Huddersfield T)	5
Bryan, T. 1886 (Oswestry)	2
Buckland, T. 1899 (Bangor)	1
Burgess, W. A. R. 1947 (Tottenham H)	32
Burke, W. 1883 (Wrexham, Newton Heath)	8
Burnett, T. B. 1877 (Ruabon)	1
Burton, A. D. 1963 (Norwich C, Newcastle U)	9
Butler, J. 1893 (Chirk)	3
Butler, W. T. 1900 (Druids)	2
Cartwright, L. 1974 (Coventry C, Wrexham)	7
Carty, T. See McCarthy (Wrexham).	
Challen, J. B. 1887 (Corinthians, Wellingborough GS)	4
Chapman, T. 1894 (Newtown, Manchester C, Grimsby T)	7
Charles, J. M. 1981 (Swansea C, QPR, Oxford U)	19
Charles, M. 1955 (Swansea T, Arsenal, Cardiff C)	31
Charles, W. J. 1950 (Leeds U, Juventus, Leeds U, Cardiff C)	38
Church, S. R. 2009 (Reading)	8
Clarke, R. J. 1949 (Manchester C)	22
Coleman, C. 1992 (C Palace, Blackburn R, Fulham)	32
Collier, D. J. 1921 (Grimsby T)	1
Collins, D. L. 2005 (Sunderland)	7
Collins, J. M. 2004 (Cardiff C, West Ham U, Aston Villa)	34
Collins, W. S. 1931 (Llanelly)	1
Collison, J. D. 2008 (West Ham U)	7
Conde, L. 1884 (Chirk)	3
Cook, F. C. 1925 (Newport Co, Portsmouth)	8
Cornforth, J. M. 1995 (Swansea C)	2
Cotterill, D. R. G. B. 2006 (Bristol C, Wigan Ath, Sheffield U, Swansea C)	16
Coyne, D. 1996 (Tranmere R, Grimsby T, Leicester C, Burnley, Tranmere R)	16
Crofts, A. L. 2006 (Gillingham, Brighton & HA)	13
Crompton, W. 1931 (Wrexham)	3
Cross, E. A. 1876 (Wrexham)	2
Crosse, K. 1879 (Druids)	3
Crossley, M. G. 1997 (Nottingham F, Middlesbrough, Fulham)	8
Crowe, V. H. 1959 (Aston Villa)	16
Cumner, R. H. 1939 (Arsenal)	3

Curtis, A. T. 1976 (Swansea C, Leeds U, Swansea C,
Southampton, Cardiff C) — 35
Curtis, E. R. 1928 (Cardiff C, Birmingham) — 3

Daniel, R. W. 1951 (Arsenal, Sunderland) — 21
Darvell, S. 1897 (Oxford University) — 2
Davies, A. 1876 (Wrexham) — 2
Davies, A. 1904 (Druids, Middlesbrough) — 2
Davies, A. 1983 (Manchester U, Newcastle U,
Swansea C, Bradford C) — 13
Davies, A. O. 1885 (Barmouth, Swifts, Wrexham,
Crewe Alex) — 9
Davies, A. R. 2006 (Yeovil T) — 1
Davies, A. T. 1891 (Shrewsbury T) — 1
Davies, C. 1972 (Charlton Ath) — 1
Davies, C. M. 2006 (Oxford U, Verona, Oldham Ath) — 5
Davies, D. 1904 (Bolton W) — 3
Davies, D. C. 1899 (Brecon, Hereford) — 2
Davies, D. W. 1912 (Treharris, Oldham Ath) — 2
Davies, E. Lloyd 1904 (Stoke, Northampton T) — 16
Davies, E. R. 1953 (Newcastle U) — 5
Davies, G. 1980 (Fulham, Manchester C) — 15
Davies, Rev. H. 1928 (Wrexham) — 1
Davies, Idwal 1923 (Liverpool Marine) — 1
Davies, J. E. 1885 (Oswestry) — 1
Davies, Jas 1878 (Wrexham) — 1
Davies, John 1889 (Wrexham) — 1
Davies, Jos 1888 (Newton Heath, Wolverhampton W) — 7
Davies, Jos 1889 (Everton, Chirk, Ardwick, Sheffield U,
Manchester C, Millwall, Reading) — 11
Davies, J. P. 1883 (Druids) — 2
Davies, Ll. 1907 (Wrexham, Everton, Wrexham) — 13
Davies, L. S. 1922 (Cardiff C) — 23
Davies, O. 1890 (Wrexham) — 1
Davies, R. 1883 (Wrexham) — 3
Davies, R. 1885 (Druids) — 1
Davies, R. O. 1892 (Wrexham) — 2
Davies, R. T. 1964 (Norwich C, Southampton,
Portsmouth) — 29
Davies, R. W. 1964 (Bolton W, Newcastle U,
Manchester C, Manchester U, Blackpool) — 34
Davies, S. 2001 (Tottenham H, Everton, Fulham) — **58**
Davies, S. I. 1996 (Manchester U) — 1
Davies, Stanley 1920 (Preston NE, Everton, WBA,
Rotherham U) — 18
Davies, T. 1886 (Oswestry) — 1
Davies, T. 1903 (Druids) — 4
Davies, W. 1884 (Wrexham) — 1
Davies, W. 1924 (Swansea T, Cardiff C, Notts Co) — 17
Davies, William 1903 (Wrexham, Blackburn R) — 11
Davies, W. C. 1908 (C Palace, WBA, C Palace) — 4
Davies, W. D. 1975 (Everton, Wrexham, Swansea C) — 52
Davies, W. H. 1876 (Oswestry) — 4
Davis, G. 1978 (Wrexham) — 3
Davis, W. O. 1913 (Millwall Ath) — 5
Day, A. 1934 (Tottenham H) — 1
Deacy, N. 1977 (PSV Eindhoven, Beringen) — 12
Dearson, D. J. 1939 (Birmingham) — 3
Delaney, M. A. 2000 (Aston Villa) — 36
Derrett, S. C. 1969 (Cardiff C) — 4
Dewey, F. T. 1931 (Cardiff Corinthians) — 2
Dibble, A. 1986 (Luton T, Manchester C) — 3
Dorman, A. 2010 (St Mirren) — **1**
Doughty, J. 1886 (Druids, Newton Heath) — 8
Doughty, R. 1888 (Newton Heath) — 2
Duffy, R. M. 2006 (Portsmouth) — 13
Durban, A. 1966 (Derby Co) — 27
Dwyer, P. J. 1978 (Cardiff C) — 10

Eardley, N, 2008 (Oldham Ath, Blackpool) — **13**
**Earnshaw, R. 2002 (Cardiff C, WBA, Norwich C,
Derby Co, Nottingham F)** — **49**
**Easter, J. M. 2007 (Wycombe W, Plymouth Arg, Milton
Keynes D)** — **8**

Eastwood, F. 2008 (Wolverhampton W) — 10
Edwards, C. 1878 (Wrexham) — 1
Edwards, C. N. H. 1996 (Swansea C) — 1
Edwards, D. 2008 (Wolverhampton W) — **19**
Edwards, G. 1947 (Birmingham C, Cardiff C) — 12
Edwards, H. 1878 (Wrexham Civil Service, Wrexham) — 8
Edwards, J. H. 1876 (Wanderers) — 1
Edwards, J. H. 1895 (Oswestry) — 3
Edwards, J. H. 1898 (Aberystwyth) — 1
Edwards, L. T. 1957 (Charlton Ath) — 2
Edwards, R. I. 1978 (Chester, Wrexham) — 4
Edwards, R. O. 2003 (Aston Villa, Wolverhampton W) — 15
Edwards, R. W. 1998 (Bristol C) — 4
Edwards, T. 1932 (Linfield) — 1
Egan, W. 1892 (Chirk) — 1
Ellis, B. 1932 (Motherwell) — 6
Ellis, E. 1931 (Nunhead, Oswestry) — 3
Emanuel, W. J. 1973 (Bristol C) — 2
England, H. M. 1962 (Blackburn R, Tottenham H) — 44
Evans, B. C. 1972 (Swansea C, Hereford U) — 7
Evans, C. M. 2008 (Manchester C, Sheffield U) — **12**
Evans, D. G. 1926 (Reading, Huddersfield T) — 4
Evans, H. P. 1922 (Cardiff C) — 6
Evans, I. 1976 (C Palace) — 13
Evans, J. 1893 (Oswestry) — 3
Evans, J. 1912 (Cardiff C) — 8
Evans, J. H. 1922 (Southend U) — 4
Evans, Len 1927 (Aberdare Ath, Cardiff C,
Birmingham) — 4
Evans, M. 1884 (Oswestry) — 1
Evans, P. S. 2002 (Brentford, Bradford C) — 1
Evans, R. 1902 (Clapton) — 1
Evans, R. E. 1906 (Wrexham, Aston Villa, Sheffield U) — 10
Evans, R. O. 1902 (Wrexham, Blackburn R,
Coventry C) — 10
Evans, R. S. 1964 (Swansea T) — 1
Evans, S. J. 2007 (Wrexham) — 7
Evans, T. J. 1927 (Clapton Orient, Newcastle U) — 4
Evans, W. 1933 (Tottenham H) — 6
Evans, W. A. W. 1876 (Oxford University) — 2
Evans, W. G. 1890 (Bootle, Aston Villa) — 3
Evelyn, E. C. 1887 (Crusaders) — 1
Eyton-Jones, J. A. 1883 (Wrexham) — 4

Farmer, G. 1885 (Oswestry) — 2
Felgate, D. 1984 (Lincoln C) — 1
Finnigan, R. J. 1930 (Wrexham) — 1
Fletcher, C. N. 2004 (Bournemouth, West Ham U,
Crystal Palace) — 36
Flynn, B. 1975 (Burnley, Leeds U, Burnley) — 66
Ford, T. 1947 (Swansea T, Aston Villa, Sunderland,
Cardiff C) — 38
Foulkes, H. E. 1932 (WBA) — 1
Foulkes, W. I. 1952 (Newcastle U) — 11
Foulkes, W. T. 1884 (Oswestry) — 2
Fowler, J. 1925 (Swansea T) — 6
Freestone, R. 2000 (Swansea C) — 1

Gabbidon, D. L. 2002 (Cardiff C, West Ham U) — **43**
Garner, G. 2006 (Leyton Orient) — 1
Garner, J. 1896 (Aberystwyth) — 1
Giggs, R. J. 1992 (Manchester U) — 64
Giles, D. C. 1980 (Swansea C, C Palace) — 12
Gillam, S. G. 1889 (Wrexham, Shrewsbury, Clapton) — 5
Glascodine, G. 1879 (Wrexham) — 1
Glover, E. M. 1932 (Grimsby T) — 7
Godding, G. 1923 (Wrexham) — 2
Godfrey, B. C. 1964 (Preston NE) — 3
Goodwin, U. 1881 (Ruthin) — 1
Goss, J. 1991 (Norwich C) — 9
Gough, R. T. 1883 (Oswestry White Star) — 1
Gray, A. 1924 (Oldham Ath, Manchester C,
Manchester Central, Tranmere R, Chester) — 24
Green, A. W. 1901 (Aston Villa, Notts Co,

Nottingham F)	8
Green, C. R. 1965 (Birmingham C)	15
Green, G. H. 1938 (Charlton Ath)	4
Green, R. M. 1998 (Wolverhampton W)	2
Grey, Dr W. 1876 (Druids)	2
Griffiths, A. T. 1971 (Wrexham)	17
Griffiths, F. J. 1900 (Blackpool)	2
Griffiths, G. 1887 (Chirk)	1
Griffiths, J. H. 1953 (Swansea T)	1
Griffiths, L. 1902 (Wrexham)	1
Griffiths, M. W. 1947 (Leicester C)	11
Griffiths, P. 1884 (Chirk)	6
Griffiths, P. H. 1932 (Everton)	1
Griffiths, T. P. 1927 (Everton, Bolton W, Middlesbrough, Aston Villa)	21
Gunter, C. 2007 (Cardiff C, Tottenham H, Nottingham F)	**22**
Hall, G. D. 1988 (Chelsea)	9
Hallam, J. 1889 (Oswestry)	1
Hanford, H. 1934 (Swansea T, Sheffield W)	7
Harrington, A. C. 1956 (Cardiff C)	11
Harris, C. S. 1976 (Leeds U)	24
Harris, W. C. 1954 (Middlesbrough)	6
Harrison, W. C. 1899 (Wrexham)	5
Hartson, J. 1995 (Arsenal, West Ham U, Wimbledon, Coventry C, Celtic)	51
Haworth, S. O. 1997 (Cardiff C, Coventry C)	5
Hayes, A. 1890 (Wrexham)	2
Hennessey, W. R. 2007 (Wolverhampton W)	**25**
Hennessey, W. T. 1962 (Birmingham C, Nottingham F, Derby Co)	39
Hersee, A. M. 1886 (Bangor)	2
Hersee, R. 1886 (Llandudno)	1
Hewitt, R. 1958 (Cardiff C)	5
Hewitt, T. J. 1911 (Wrexham, Chelsea, South Liverpool)	8
Heywood, D. 1879 (Druids)	1
Hibbott, H. 1880 (Newtown Excelsior, Newtown)	3
Higham, G. G. 1878 (Oswestry)	2
Hill, M. R. 1972 (Ipswich T)	2
Hockey, T. 1972 (Sheffield U, Norwich C, Aston Villa)	9
Hoddinott, T. F. 1921 (Watford)	2
Hodges, G. 1984 (Wimbledon, Newcastle U, Watford, Sheffield U)	18
Hodgkinson, A. V. 1908 (Southampton)	1
Holden, A. 1984 (Chester C)	1
Hole, B. G. 1963 (Cardiff C, Blackburn R, Aston Villa, Swansea C)	30
Hole, W. J. 1921 (Swansea T)	9
Hollins, D. M. 1962 (Newcastle U)	11
Hopkins, I. J. 1935 (Brentford)	12
Hopkins, J. 1983 (Fulham, C Palace)	16
Hopkins, M. 1956 (Tottenham H)	34
Horne, B. 1988 (Portsmouth, Southampton, Everton, Birmingham C)	59
Howell, E. G. 1888 (Builth)	3
Howells, R. G. 1954 (Cardiff C)	2
Hugh, A. R. 1930 (Newport Co)	1
Hughes, A. 1894 (Rhos)	2
Hughes, A. 1907 (Chirk)	1
Hughes, C. M. 1992 (Luton T, Wimbledon)	8
Hughes, E. 1899 (Everton, Tottenham H)	14
Hughes, E. 1906 (Wrexham, Nottingham F, Wrexham, Manchester C)	16
Hughes, F. W. 1882 (Northwich Victoria)	6
Hughes, I. 1951 (Luton T)	4
Hughes, J. 1877 (Cambridge University, Aberystwyth)	2
Hughes, J. 1905 (Liverpool)	3
Hughes, J. I. 1935 (Blackburn R)	1
Hughes, L. M. 1984 (Manchester U, Barcelona, Manchester U, Chelsea, Southampton)	72
Hughes, P. W. 1887 (Bangor)	3
Hughes, W. 1891 (Bootle)	3
Hughes, W. A. 1949 (Blackburn R)	5

Hughes, W. M. 1938 (Birmingham)	10
Humphreys, J. V. 1947 (Everton)	1
Humphreys, R. 1888 (Druids)	1
Hunter, A. H. 1887 (FA of Wales Secretary)	1
Jackett, K. 1983 (Watford)	31
Jackson, W. 1899 (St Helens Rec)	1
James, E. 1893 (Chirk)	8
James, E. G. 1966 (Blackpool)	9
James, L. 1972 (Burnley, Derby Co, QPR, Burnley, Swansea C, Sunderland)	54
James, R. M. 1979 (Swansea C, Stoke C, QPR, Leicester C, Swansea C)	47
James, W. 1931 (West Ham U)	2
Jarrett, R. H. 1889 (Ruthin)	2
Jarvis, A. L. 1967 (Hull C)	3
Jenkins, E. 1925 (Lovell's Ath)	1
Jenkins, J. 1924 (Brighton &_HA)	8
Jenkins, R. W. 1902 (Rhyl)	1
Jenkins, S. R. 1996 (Swansea C, Huddersfield T)	16
Jenkyns, C. A. L. 1892 (Small Heath, Woolwich Arsenal, Newton Heath, Walsall)	8
Jennings, W. 1914 (Bolton W)	11
John, R. F. 1923 (Arsenal)	15
John, W. R. 1931 (Walsall, Stoke C, Preston NE, Sheffield U, Swansea T)	14
Johnson, A. J. 1999 (Nottingham F, WBA)	15
Johnson, M. G. 1964 (Swansea T)	1
Jones, A. 1987 (Port Vale, Charlton Ath)	6
Jones, A. F. 1877 (Oxford University)	1
Jones, A. T. 1905 (Nottingham F, Notts Co)	2
Jones, Bryn 1935 (Wolverhampton W, Arsenal)	17
Jones, B. S. 1963 (Swansea T, Plymouth Arg, Cardiff C)	15
Jones, Charlie 1926 (Nottingham F, Arsenal)	8
Jones, Cliff 1954 (Swansea T, Tottenham H, Fulham)	59
Jones, C. W. 1935 (Birmingham)	2
Jones, D. 1888 (Chirk, Bolton W, Manchester C)	14
Jones, D. E. 1976 (Norwich C)	8
Jones, D. O. 1934 (Leicester C)	7
Jones, Evan 1910 (Chelsea, Oldham Ath, Bolton W)	7
Jones, F. R. 1885 (Bangor)	3
Jones, F. W. 1893 (Small Heath)	1
Jones, G. P. 1907 (Wrexham)	1
Jones, H. 1902 (Aberaman)	1
Jones, Humphrey 1885 (Bangor, Queen's Park, East Stirlingshire, Queen's Park)	14
Jones, Ivor 1920 (Swansea T, WBA)	10
Jones, Jeffrey 1908 (Llandrindod Wells)	3
Jones, J. 1876 (Druids)	1
Jones, J. 1883 (Berwyn Rangers)	3
Jones, J. 1925 (Wrexham)	1
Jones, J. L. 1895 (Sheffield U, Tottenham H)	21
Jones, J. Love 1906 (Stoke, Middlesbrough)	3
Jones, J. O. 1901 (Bangor)	2
Jones, J. P. 1976 (Liverpool, Wrexham, Chelsea, Huddersfield T)	72
Jones, J. T. 1912 (Stoke, C Palace)	15
Jones, K. 1950 (Aston Villa)	1
Jones, Leslie J. 1933 (Cardiff C, Coventry C, Arsenal)	11
Jones, M. A. 2007 (Wrexham)	2
Jones, M. G. 2000 (Leeds U, Leicester C)	13
Jones, P. L. 1997 (Liverpool, Tranmere R)	2
Jones, P. S. 1997 (Stockport Co, Southampton, Wolverhampton W, QPR)	50
Jones, P. W. 1971 (Bristol R)	1
Jones, R. 1887 (Bangor, Crewe Alex)	3
Jones, R. 1898 (Leicester Fosse)	1
Jones, R. 1899 (Druids)	1
Jones, R. 1900 (Bangor)	2
Jones, R. 1906 (Millwall)	2
Jones, R. A. 1884 (Druids)	4
Jones, R. A. 1994 (Sheffield W)	1
Jones, R. S. 1894 (Everton)	1

Jones, S. 1887 (Wrexham, Chester) 2
Jones, S. 1893 (Wrexham, Burton Swifts, Druids) 6
Jones, T. 1926 (Manchester U) 4
Jones, T. D. 1908 (Aberdare) 1
Jones, T. G. 1938 (Everton) 17
Jones, T. J. 1932 (Sheffield W) 2
Jones, V. P. 1995 (Wimbledon) 9
Jones, W. E. A. 1947 (Swansea T, Tottenham H) 4
Jones, W. J. 1901 (Aberdare, West Ham U) 4
Jones, W. Lot 1905 (Manchester C, Southend U) 20
Jones, W. P. 1889 (Druids, Wynnstay) 4
Jones, W. R. 1897 (Aberystwyth) 1

Keenor, F. C. 1920 (Cardiff C, Crewe Alex) 32
Kelly, F. C. 1899 (Wrexham, Druids) 3
Kelsey, A. J. 1954 (Arsenal) 41
Kenrick, S. L. 1876 (Druids, Oswestry, Shropshire
    Wanderers) 5
Ketley, C. F. 1882 (Druids) 1
King, A. 2009 (Leicester C) **3**
King, J. 1955 (Swansea T) 1
Kinsey, N. 1951 (Norwich C, Birmingham C) 7
Knill, A. R. 1989 (Swansea C) 1
Koumas, J. 2001 (Tranmere R, WBA, Wigan Ath) 34
Krzywicki, R. L. 1970 (WBA, Huddersfield T) 8

Lambert, R. 1947 (Liverpool) 5
Latham, G. 1905 (Liverpool, Southport Central,
    Cardiff C) 10
Law, B. J. 1990 (QPR) 1
Lawrence, E. 1930 (Clapton Orient, Notts Co) 2
Lawrence, S. 1932 (Swansea T) 8
Lea, A. 1889 (Wrexham) 4
Lea, C. 1965 (Ipswich T) 2
Leary, P. 1889 (Bangor) 1
Ledley, J. C. 2006 (Cardiff C) **32**
Leek, K. 1961 (Leicester C, Newcastle U,
    Birmingham C, Northampton T) 13
Legg, A. 1996 (Birmingham C, Cardiff C) 6
Lever, A. R. 1953 (Leicester C) 1
Lewis, B. 1891 (Chester, Wrexham, Middlesbrough,
    Wrexham) 10
Lewis, D. 1927 (Arsenal) 3
Lewis, D. 1983 (Swansea C) 1
Lewis, D. J. 1933 (Swansea T) 2
Lewis, D. M. 1890 (Bangor) 2
Lewis, J. 1906 (Bristol R) 1
Lewis, J. 1926 (Cardiff C) 1
Lewis, T. 1881 (Wrexham) 2
Lewis, W. 1885 (Bangor, Crewe Alex, Chester,
    Manchester C, Chester) 27
Lewis, W. L. 1927 (Swansea T, Huddersfield T) 6
Llewellyn, C. M. 1998 (Norwich C, Wrexham) 6
Lloyd, B. W. 1976 (Wrexham) 3
Lloyd, J. W. 1879 (Wrexham, Newtown) 2
Lloyd, R. A. 1891 (Ruthin) 2
Lockley, A. 1898 (Chirk) 1
Lovell, S. 1982 (C Palace, Millwall) 6
Lowndes, S. R. 1983 (Newport Co, Millwall, Barnsley) 10
Lowrie, G. 1948 (Coventry C. Newcastle U) 4
Lucas, P. M. 1962 (Leyton Orient) 4
Lucas, W. H. 1949 (Swansea T) 7
Lumberg, A. 1929 (Wrexham, Wolverhampton W) 4

McCarthy, T. P. 1889 (Wrexham) 1
McMillan, R. 1881 (Shrewsbury Engineers) 2
Maguire, G. T. 1990 (Portsmouth) 7
Mahoney, J. F. 1968 (Stoke C, Middlesbrough,
    Swansea C) 51
Mardon, P. J. 1996 (WBA) 1
Margetson, M. W. 2004 (Cardiff C) 1
Marriott, A. 1996 (Wrexham) 5
Martin, T. J. 1930 (Newport Co) 1
Marustik, C. 1982 (Swansea C) 6

Mates, J. 1891 (Chirk) 3
Matthews, R. W. 1921 (Liverpool, Bristol C, Bradford) 3
Matthews, W. 1905 (Chester) 2
Matthias, J. S. 1896 (Brymbo, Shrewsbury T,
    Wolverhampton W) 5
Matthias, T. J. 1914 (Wrexham) 12
Mays, A. W. 1929 (Wrexham) 1
Medwin, T. C. 1953 (Swansea T, Tottenham H) 30
Melville, A. K. 1990 (Swansea C, Oxford U, Sunderland,
    Fulham, West Ham U) 65
Meredith, S. 1900 (Chirk, Stoke, Leyton) 8
Meredith, W. H. 1895 (Manchester C, Manchester U) 48
Mielczarek, R. 1971 (Rotherham U) 1
Millership, H. 1920 (Rotherham Co) 6
Millington, A. H. 1963 (WBA, C Palace,
    Peterborough U, Swansea C) 21
Mills, T. J. 1934 (Clapton Orient, Leicester C) 4
Mills-Roberts, R. H. 1885 (St Thomas' Hospital,
    Preston NE, Llanberis) 8
Moore, G. 1960 (Cardiff C, Chelsea, Manchester U,
    Northampton T, Charlton Ath) 21
Morgan, C. 2007 (Milton Keynes D, Peterborough U) **20**
Morgan, J. R. 1877 (Cambridge University,
    Derby School Staff) 10
Morgan, J. T. 1905 (Wrexham) 1
Morgan-Owen, H. 1902 (Oxford University,
    Corinthians) 4
Morgan-Owen, M. M. 1897 (Oxford University,
    Corinthians) 13
Morley, E. J. 1925 (Swansea T, Clapton Orient) 4
Morris, A. G. 1896 (Aberystwyth, Swindon T,
    Nottingham F) 21
Morris, C. 1900 (Chirk, Derby Co, Huddersfield T) 27
Morris, E. 1893 (Chirk) 3
Morris, H. 1894 (Sheffield U, Manchester C, Grimsby T) 3
Morris, J. 1887 (Oswestry) 1
Morris, J. 1898 (Chirk) 1
Morris, R. 1900 (Chirk, Shrewsbury T) 6
Morris, R. 1902 (Newtown, Druids, Liverpool, Leeds C,
    Grimsby T, Plymouth Arg) 11
Morris, S. 1937 (Birmingham) 5
Morris, W. 1947 (Burnley) 5
Moulsdale, J. R. B. 1925 (Corinthians) 1
Murphy, J. P. 1933 (WBA) 15
Myhill, G. O. 2008 (Hull C) **8**

Nardiello, D. 1978 (Coventry C) 2
Nardiello, D. A. 2007 (Barnsley, QPR) 3
Neal, J. E. 1931 (Colwyn Bay) 2
Neilson, A. B. 1992 (Newcastle U, Southampton) 4
Newnes, J. 1926 (Nelson) 1
Newton, L. F. 1912 (Cardiff Corinthians) 1
Nicholas, D. S. 1923 (Stoke, Swansea T) 3
Nicholas, P. 1979 (C Palace, Arsenal, C Palace, Luton T,
    Aberdeen, Chelsea, Watford) 73
Nicholls, J. 1924 (Newport Co, Cardiff C) 4
Niedzwiecki, E. A. 1985 (Chelsea) 2
Nock, W. 1897 (Newtown) 1
Nogan, L. M. 1992 (Watford, Reading) 2
Norman, A. J. 1986 (Hull C) 5
Nurse, M. T. G. 1960 (Swansea T, Middlesbrough) 12
Nyatanga, L. J. 2006 (Derby Co, Bristol C) **33**

O'Callaghan, E. 1929 (Tottenham H) 11
Oliver, A. 1905 (Bangor, Blackburn R) 2
Oster, J. M. 1998 (Everton, Sunderland) 13
O'Sullivan, P. A. 1973 (Brighton & HA) 3
Owen, D. 1879 (Oswestry) 1
Owen, E. 1884 (Ruthin Grammar School) 3
Owen, G. 1888 (Chirk, Newton Heath, Chirk) 4
Owen, J. 1892 (Newton Heath) 1
Owen, T. 1879 (Oswestry) 1
Owen, Trevor 1899 (Crewe Alex) 2
Owen, W. 1884 (Chirk) 16

Taylor, J. 1898 (Wrexham)	1
Taylor, N. 2010 (Wrexham)	**1**
Taylor, O. D. S. 1893 (Newtown)	4
Thatcher, B. D. 2004 (Leicester C, Manchester C)	7
Thomas, C. 1899 (Druids)	2
Thomas, D. A. 1957 (Swansea T)	2
Thomas, D. S. 1948 (Fulham)	4
Thomas, E. 1925 (Cardiff Corinthians)	1
Thomas, G. 1885 (Wrexham)	2
Thomas, H. 1927 (Manchester U)	1
Thomas, Martin R. 1987 (Newcastle U)	1
Thomas, Mickey 1977 (Wrexham, Manchester U, Everton, Brighton & HA, Stoke C, Chelsea, WBA)	51
Thomas, R. J. 1967 (Swindon T, Derby Co, Cardiff C)	50
Thomas, T. 1898 (Bangor)	2
Thomas, W. R. 1931 (Newport Co)	2
Thomson, D. 1876 (Druids)	1
Thomson, G. F. 1876 (Druids)	2
Toshack, J. B. 1969 (Cardiff C, Liverpool, Swansea C)	40
Townsend, W. 1887 (Newtown)	2
Trainer, H. 1895 (Wrexham)	3
Trainer, J. 1887 (Bolton W, Preston NE)	20
Trollope, P. J. 1997 (Derby Co, Fulham, Coventry C, Northampton T)	9
Tudur-Jones, O. 2008 (Swansea C)	4
Turner, H. G. 1937 (Charlton Ath)	8
Turner, J. 1892 (Wrexham)	1
Turner, R. E. 1891 (Wrexham)	2
Turner, W. H. 1887 (Wrexham)	5
Van Den Hauwe, P. W. R. 1985 (Everton)	13
Vaughan, D. O. 2003 (Crewe Alex, Real Sociedad, Blackpool)	**17**
Vaughan, Jas 1893 (Druids)	4
Vaughan, John 1879 (Oswestry, Druids, Bolton W)	11
Vaughan, J. O. 1885 (Rhyl)	4
Vaughan, N. 1983 (Newport Co, Cardiff C)	10
Vaughan, T. 1885 (Rhyl)	1
Vearncombe, G. 1958 (Cardiff C)	2
Vernon, T. R. 1957 (Blackburn R, Everton, Stoke C)	32
Villars, A. K. 1974 (Cardiff C)	3
Vizard, E. T. 1911 (Bolton W)	22
Vokes, S. M. 2008 (Bournemouth, Wolverhampton W)	**16**
Walley, J. T. 1971 (Watford)	1
Walsh, I. P. 1980 (C Palace, Swansea C)	18
Ward, D. 1959 (Bristol R, Cardiff C)	2
Ward, D. 2000 (Notts Co, Nottingham F)	5
Warner, J. 1937 (Swansea T, Manchester U)	2
Warren, F. W. 1929 (Cardiff C, Middlesbrough, Hearts)	6
Watkins, A. E. 1898 (Leicester Fosse, Aston Villa, Millwall)	5

Watkins, W. M. 1902 (Stoke, Aston Villa, Sunderland, Stoke)	10
Webster, C. 1957 (Manchester U)	4
Weston, R. D. 2000 (Arsenal, Cardiff C)	7
Whatley, W. J. 1939 (Tottenham H)	2
White, P. F. 1896 (London Welsh)	1
Wilcock, A. R. 1890 (Oswestry)	1
Wilding, J. 1885 (Wrexham Olympians, Bootle, Wrexham)	9
Williams, A. 1994 (Reading, Wolverhampton W, Reading)	13
Williams, A. E. 2008 (Stockport Co, Swansea C)	**20**
Williams, A. L. 1931 (Wrexham)	1
Williams, A. P. 1998 (Southampton)	2
Williams, B. 1930 (Bristol C)	1
Williams, B. D. 1928 (Swansea T, Everton)	10
Williams, D. G. 1988 (Derby Co, Ipswich T)	13
Williams, D. M. 1986 (Norwich C)	5
Williams, D. R. 1921 (Merthyr T, Sheffield W, Manchester U)	8
Williams, E. 1893 (Crewe Alex)	2
Williams, E. 1901 (Druids)	5
Williams, G. 1893 (Chirk)	6
Williams, G. E. 1960 (WBA)	26
Williams, G. G. 1961 (Swansea T)	5
Williams, G. J. 2006 (West Ham U, Ipswich T)	2
Williams, G. J. J. 1951 (Cardiff C)	1
Williams, G. O. 1907 (Wrexham)	1
Williams, H. J. 1965 (Swansea T)	3
Williams, H. T. 1949 (Newport Co, Leeds U)	4
Williams, J. H. 1884 (Oswestry)	1
Williams, J. J. 1939 (Wrexham)	1
Williams, J. T. 1925 (Middlesbrough)	1
Williams, J. W. 1912 (C Palace)	2
Williams, R. 1935 (Newcastle U)	2
Williams, R. P. 1886 (Caernarvon)	1
Williams, S. G. 1954 (WBA, Southampton)	43
Williams, W. 1876 (Druids, Oswestry, Druids)	11
Williams, W. 1925 (Northampton T)	1
Witcomb, D. F. 1947 (WBA, Sheffield W)	3
Woosnam, A. P. 1959 (Leyton Orient, West Ham U, Aston Villa)	17
Woosnam, G. 1879 (Newtown Excelsior)	1
Worthington, T. 1894 (Newtown)	1
Wynn, G. A. 1909 (Wrexham, Manchester C)	11
Wynn, W. 1903 (Chirk)	1
Yorath, T. C. 1970 (Leeds U, Coventry C, Tottenham H, Vancouver W)	59
Young, E. 1990 (Wimbledon, C Palace, Wolverhampton W)	21

REPUBLIC OF IRELAND

Aherne, T. 1946 (Belfast C, Luton T)	16
Aldridge, J. W. 1986 (Oxford U, Liverpool, Real Sociedad, Tranmere R)	69
Ambrose, P. 1955 (Shamrock R)	5
Anderson, J. 1980 (Preston NE, Newcastle U)	16
Andrews, K. J. 2009 (Blackburn R)	**15**
Andrews, P. 1936 (Bohemians)	1
Arrigan, T. 1938 (Waterford)	1
Babb, P. A. 1994 (Coventry C, Liverpool, Sunderland)	35
Bailham, E. 1964 (Shamrock R)	1
Barber, E. 1966 (Shelbourne, Birmingham C)	2
Barrett, G. 2003 (Arsenal, Coventry C)	6
Barry, P. 1928 (Fordsons)	2
Beglin, J. 1984 (Liverpool)	15
Bennett, A. J. 2007 (Reading)	2
Bermingham, J. 1929 (Bohemians)	1
Bermingham, P. 1935 (St James' Gate)	1
Best, L. J. B. 2009 (Coventry C, Newcastle U)	**7**
Bonner, P. 1981 (Celtic)	80

Braddish, S. 1978 (Dundalk)	2
Bradshaw, P. 1939 (St James' Gate)	5
Brady, F. 1926 (Fordsons)	2
Brady, T. R. 1964 (QPR)	6
Brady, W. L. 1975 (Arsenal, Juventus, Sampdoria, Internazionale, Ascoli, West Ham U)	72
Branagan, K. G. 1997 (Bolton W)	1
Breen, G. 1996 (Birmingham C, Coventry C, West Ham U, Sunderland)	63
Breen, T. 1937 (Manchester U, Shamrock R)	5
Brennan, F. 1965 (Drumcondra)	1
Brennan, S. A. 1965 (Manchester U, Waterford)	19
Brown, J. 1937 (Coventry C)	2
Browne, W. 1964 (Bohemians)	3
Bruce, A. S. 2007 (Ipswich T)	2
Buckley, L. 1984 (Shamrock R, Waregem)	2
Burke, F. 1952 (Cork Ath)	1
Burke, J. 1929 (Shamrock R)	1
Burke, J. 1934 (Cork)	1
Butler, P. J. 2000 (Sunderland)	1

Butler, T. 2003 (Sunderland) 2
Byrne, A. B. 1970 (Southampton) 14
Byrne, D. 1929 (Shelbourne, Shamrock R, Coleraine) 3
Byrne, J. 1928 (Bray Unknowns) 1
Byrne, J. 1985 (QPR, Le Havre, Brighton & HA,
    Sunderland, Millwall) 23
Byrne, J. 2004 (Shelbourne) 2
Byrne, P. 1931 (Dolphin, Shelbourne, Drumcondra) 3
Byrne, P. 1984 (Shamrock R) 8
Byrne, S. 1931 (Bohemians) 1

Campbell, A. 1985 (Santander) 3
Campbell, N. 1971 (St Patrick's Ath, Fortuna Cologne) 11
Cannon, H. 1926 (Bohemians) 2
Cantwell, N. 1954 (West Ham U, Manchester U) 36
Carey, B. P. 1992 (Manchester U, Leicester C) 3
Carey, J. J. 1938 (Manchester U) 29
Carolan, J. 1960 (Manchester U) 2
Carr, S. 1999 (Tottenham H, Newcastle U) 44
Carroll, B. 1949 (Shelbourne) 2
Carroll, T. R. 1968 (Ipswich T, Birmingham C) 17
Carsley, L. K. 1998 (Derby Co, Blackburn R,
    Coventry C, Everton) 39
Cascarino, A. G. 1986 (Gillingham, Millwall,
    Aston Villa, Celtic, Chelsea, Marseille, Nancy) 88
Chandler, J. 1980 (Leeds U) 2
Chatton, H. A. 1931 (Shelbourne, Dumbarton, Cork) 3
Clarke, C. R. 2004 (Stoke C) 2
Clarke, J. 1978 (Drogheda U) 1
Clarke, K. 1948 (Drumcondra) 2
Clarke, M. 1950 (Shamrock R) 1
Clinton, T. J. 1951 (Everton) 3
Coad, P. 1947 (Shamrock R) 11
Coffey, T. 1950 (Drumcondra) 2
Colfer, M. D. 1950 (Shelbourne) 2
Colgan, N. 2002 (Hibernian, Barnsley) 9
Collins, F. 1927 (Jacobs) 1
Conmy, O. M. 1965 (Peterborough U) 5
Connolly, D. J. 1996 (Watford, Feyenoord,
    Wolverhampton W, Excelsior, Feyenoord,
    Wimbledon, West Ham U, Wigan Ath) 41
Connolly, H. 1937 (Cork) 1
Connolly, J. 1926 (Fordsons) 1
Conroy, G. A. 1970 (Stoke C) 27
Conway, J. P. 1967 (Fulham, Manchester C) 20
Corr, P. J. 1949 (Everton) 4
Courtney, E. 1946 (Cork U) 1
Coyle, O. C. 1994 (Bolton W) 1
Coyne, T. 1992 (Celtic, Tranmere R, Motherwell) 22
Crowe, G. 2003 (Bohemians) 2
Cummins, G. P. 1954 (Luton T) 19
Cuneen, T. 1951 (Limerick) 1
Cunningham, G. R. 2010 (Manchester C) **1**
Cunningham, K. 1996 (Wimbledon, Birmingham C) 72
Curtis, D. P. 1957 (Shelbourne, Bristol C, Ipswich T,
    Exeter C) 17
Cusack, S. 1953 (Limerick) 1

Daish, L. S. 1992 (Cambridge U, Coventry C) 5
Daly, G. A. 1973 (Manchester U, Derby Co, Coventry C,
    Birmingham C, Shrewsbury T) 48
Daly, J. 1932 (Shamrock R) 2
Daly, M. 1978 (Wolverhampton W) 2
Daly, P. 1950 (Shamrock R) 1
Davis, T. L. 1937 (Oldham Ath, Tranmere R) 4
Deacy, E. 1982 (Aston Villa) 4
Delaney, D. F. 2008 (QPR) 2
Delap, R. J. 1998 (Derby Co, Southampton) 11
De Mange, K. J. P. P. 1987 (Liverpool, Hull C) 2
Dempsey, J. T. 1967 (Fulham, Chelsea) 19
Dennehy, J. 1972 (Cork Hibernians, Nottingham F,
    Walsall) 11
Desmond, P. 1950 (Middlesbrough) 4
Devine, J. 1980 (Arsenal, Norwich C) 13

Doherty, G. M. T. 2000 (Luton T, Tottenham H,
    Norwich C) 34
Donnelly, J. 1935 (Dundalk) 10
Donnelly, T. 1938 (Drumcondra, Shamrock R) 2
Donovan, D. C. 1955 (Everton) 5
Donovan, T. 1980 (Aston Villa) 2
Douglas, J. 2004 (Blackburn R, Leeds U) 8
Dowdall, C. 1928 (Fordsons, Barnsley, Cork) 3
Doyle, C. 1959 (Shelbourne) 1
Doyle, Colin 2007 (Birmingham C) 1
Doyle, D. 1926 (Shamrock R) 1
Doyle, K. E. 2006 (Reading, Wolverhampton W) **35**
Doyle, L. 1932 (Dolphin) 1
Doyle, M. P. 2004 (Coventry C) 1
**Duff, D. A. 1998 (Blackburn R, Chelsea, Newcastle U,
    Fulham)** **83**
Duffy, B. 1950 (Shamrock R) 1
Duggan, H. A. 1927 (Leeds U, Newport Co) 5
Dunne, A. P. 1962 (Manchester U, Bolton W) 33
Dunne, J. 1930 (Sheffield U, Arsenal, Southampton,
    Shamrock R) 15
Dunne, J. C. 1971 (Fulham) 1
Dunne, L. 1935 (Manchester C) 2
Dunne, P. A. J. 1965 (Manchester U) 5
**Dunne, R. P. 2000 (Everton, Manchester C,
    Aston Villa)** **58**
Dunne, S. 1953 (Luton T) 15
Dunne, T. 1956 (St Patrick's Ath) 3
Dunning, P. 1971 (Shelbourne) 2
Dunphy, E. M. 1966 (York C, Millwall) 23
Dwyer, N. M. 1960 (West Ham U, Swansea T) 14

Eccles, P. 1986 (Shamrock R) 1
Egan, R. 1929 (Dundalk) 1
Eglington, T. J. 1946 (Shamrock R, Everton) 24
Elliott, S. W. 2005 (Sunderland) 9
Ellis, P. 1935 (Bohemians) 7
Evans, M. J. 1998 (Southampton) 1

Fagan, E. 1973 (Shamrock R) 1
Fagan, F. 1955 (Manchester C, Derby Co) 8
Fagan, J. 1926 (Shamrock R) 1
Fahey, K. D. 2010 (Birmingham C) **2**
Fairclough, M. 1982 (Dundalk) 2
Fallon, S. 1951 (Celtic) 8
Fallon, W. J. 1935 (Notts Co, Sheffield W) 9
Farquharson, T. G. 1929 (Cardiff C) 4
Farrell, P. 1937 (Hibernian) 2
Farrell, P. D. 1946 (Shamrock R, Everton) 28
Farrelly, G. 1996 (Aston Villa, Everton, Bolton W) 6
Feenan, J. J. 1937 (Sunderland) 2
Finnan, S. 2000 (Fulham, Liverpool, Espanyol) 53
Finucane, A. 1967 (Limerick) 11
Fitzgerald, F. J. 1955 (Waterford) 2
Fitzgerald, P. J. 1961 (Leeds U, Chester) 5
Fitzpatrick, K. 1970 (Limerick) 1
Fitzsimons, A. G. 1950 (Middlesbrough, Lincoln C) 26
Fleming, C. 1996 (Middlesbrough) 10
Flood, J. J. 1926 (Shamrock R) 5
Fogarty, A. 1960 (Sunderland, Hartlepools U) 11
Folan, C. C. 2009 (Hull C) **7**
Foley, D. J. 2000 (Watford) 6
Foley, J. 1934 (Cork, Celtic) 7
Foley, K. P. 2009 (Wolverhampton W) **2**
Foley, M. 1926 (Shelbourne) 1
Foley, T. C. 1964 (Northampton T) 9
Foy, T. 1938 (Shamrock R) 2
Fullam, J. 1961 (Preston NE, Shamrock R) 11
Fullam, R. 1926 (Shamrock R) 2

Gallagher, C. 1967 (Celtic) 2
Gallagher, M. 1954 (Hibernian) 1
Gallagher, P. 1932 (Falkirk) 1

Galvin, A. 1983 (Tottenham H, Sheffield W,
Swindon T) 29
Gamble, J. 2007 (Cork C) 2
Gannon, E. 1949 (Notts Co, Sheffield W, Shelbourne) 14
Gannon, M. 1972 (Shelbourne) 1
Gaskins, P. 1934 (Shamrock R, St James' Gate) 7
Gavin, J. T. 1950 (Norwich C, Tottenham H,
Norwich) 7
Geoghegan, M. 1937 (St James' Gate) 2
Gibbons, A. 1952 (St Patrick's Ath) 4
Gibson, D. T. D. 2008 (Manchester U) 9
Gilbert, R. 1966 (Shamrock R) 1
Giles, C. 1951 (Doncaster R) 1
Giles, M. J. 1960 (Manchester U, Leeds U, WBA,
Shamrock R) 59
**Given, S. J. J. 1996 (Blackburn R, Newcastle U,
Manchester C)** 103
Givens, D. J. 1969 (Manchester U, Luton T, QPR,
Birmingham C, Neuchatel X) 56
Gleeson, S. M. 2007 (Wolverhampton W) 2
Glen, W. 1927 (Shamrock R) 8
Glynn, D. 1952 (Drumcondra) 2
Godwin, T. F. 1949 (Shamrock R, Leicester C,
Bournemouth) 13
Golding, J. 1928 (Shamrock R) 2
Goodman, J. 1997 (Wimbledon) 4
Goodwin, J. 2003 (Stockport Co) 1
Gorman, W. C. 1936 (Bury, Brentford) 13
Grace, J. 1926 (Drumcondra) 1
Grealish, A. 1976 (Orient, Luton T, Brighton & HA,
WBA) 45
Green, P. J. 2010 (Derby Co) 2
Gregg, E. 1978 (Bohemians) 8
Griffith, R. 1935 (Walsall) 1
Grimes, A. A. 1978 (Manchester U, Coventry C,
Luton T) 18

Hale, A. 1962 (Aston Villa, Doncaster R, Waterford) 14
Hamilton, T. 1959 (Shamrock R) 2
Hand, E. K. 1969 (Portsmouth) 20
Harrington, W. 1936 (Cork) 5
Harte, I. P. 1996 (Leeds U, Levante) 64
Hartnett, J. B. 1949 (Middlesbrough) 2
Haverty, J. 1956 (Arsenal, Blackburn R, Millwall
Celtic, Bristol R, Shelbourne) 32
Hayes, A. W. P. 1979 (Southampton) 1
Hayes, W. E. 1947 (Huddersfield T) 2
Hayes, W. J. 1949 (Limerick) 1
Healey, R. 1977 (Cardiff C) 2
Healy, C. 2002 (Celtic, Sunderland) 13
Heighway, S. D. 1971 (Liverpool, Minnesota K) 34
Henderson, B. 1948 (Drumcondra) 2
Henderson, W. C. P. 2006 (Brighton & HA,
Preston NE) 6
Hennessy, J. 1965 (Shelbourne, St Patrick's Ath) 5
Herrick, J. 1972 (Cork Hibernians, Shamrock R) 3
Higgins, J. 1951 (Birmingham C) 1
Holland, M. R. 2000 (Ipswich T, Charlton Ath) 49
Holmes, J. 1971 (Coventry C, Tottenham H,
Vancouver W) 30
Hoolahan, W. 2008 (Blackpool) 1
Horlacher, A. F. 1930 (Bohemians) 7
Houghton, R. J. 1986 (Oxford U, Liverpool,
Aston Villa, C Palace, Reading) 73
Howlett, G. 1984 (Brighton & HA) 1
Hoy, M. 1938 (Dundalk) 6
Hughton, C. 1980 (Tottenham H, West Ham U) 53
Hunt, N. 2009 (Reading) 3
Hunt, S. P. 2007 (Reading, Hull C) 25
Hurley, C. J. 1957 (Millwall, Sunderland, Bolton W) 40
Hutchinson, F. 1935 (Drumcondra) 2

Ireland S .J. 2006 (Manchester C) 6
Irwin, D. J. 1991 (Manchester U) 56

Jordan, D. 1937 (Wolverhampton W) 2
Jordan, W. 1934 (Bohemians) 2

Kavanagh, G. A. 1998 (Stoke C, Cardiff C, Wigan Ath)16
Kavanagh, P. J. 1931 (Celtic) 2
**Keane, R. D. 1998 (Wolverhampton W, Coventry C,
Internazionale, Leeds U, Tottenham H, Liverpool,
Tottenham H)** 99
Keane, R. M. 1991 (Nottingham F, Manchester U) 67
Keane, T. R. 1949 (Swansea T) 4
Kearin, M. 1972 (Shamrock R) 1
Kearns, F. T. 1954 (West Ham U) 1
Kearns, M. 1971 (Oxford U, Walsall,
Wolverhampton W) 18
Kelly, A. T. 1993 (Sheffield U, Blackburn R) 34
Kelly, D. T. 1988 (Walsall, West Ham U, Leicester C,
Newcastle U, Wolverhampton W, Sunderland,
Tranmere R) 26
Kelly, G. 1994 (Leeds U) 52
Kelly, J. 1932 (Derry C) 4
Kelly, J. A. 1957 (Drumcondra, Preston NE) 47
Kelly, J. P. V. 1961 (Wolverhampton W) 5
Kelly, M. J. 1988 (Portsmouth) 4
Kelly, N. 1954 (Nottingham F) 1
**Kelly, S. M. 2006 (Tottenham H, Birmingham C,
Fulham)** 18
Kendrick, J. 1927 (Everton, Dolphin) 4
Kenna, J. J. 1995 (Blackburn R) 27
Kennedy, M. F. 1986 (Portsmouth) 2
Kennedy, M. J. 1996 (Liverpool, Wimbledon,
Manchester C, Wolverhampton W) 34
Kennedy, W. 1932 (St James' Gate) 3
Kenny, P. 2004 (Sheffield U) 7
Keogh, A. D. 2007 (Wolverhampton W) 13
Keogh, J. 1966 (Shamrock R) 1
Keogh, S. 1959 (Shamrock R) 1
Kernaghan, A. N. 1993 (Middlesbrough,
Manchester C) 22
Kiely, D. L. 2000 (Charlton Ath, WBA) 11
Kiernan, F. W. 1951 (Shamrock R, Southampton) 5
**Kilbane, K. D. 1998 (WBA, Sunderland, Everton,
Wigan Ath, Hull C)** 103
Kinnear, J. P. 1967 (Tottenham H, Brighton & HA) 26
Kinsella, J. 1928 (Shelbourne) 1
Kinsella, M. A. 1998 (Charlton Ath, Aston Villa,
WBA) 48
Kinsella, O. 1932 (Shamrock R) 2
Kirkland, A. 1927 (Shamrock R) 1

Lacey, W. 1927 (Shelbourne) 3
Langan, D. 1978 (Derby Co, Birmingham C,
Oxford U) 26
Lapira, J. 2007 (Notre Dame) 1
Lawler, J. F. 1953 (Fulham) 8
Lawlor, J. C. 1949 (Drumcondra, Doncaster R) 3
Lawlor, M. 1971 (Shamrock R) 5
Lawrence, L. 2009 (Stoke C) 8
Lawrenson, M. 1977 (Preston NE, Brighton & HA,
Liverpool) 39
Lee, A. D. 2003 (Rotherham U, Cardiff C, Ipswich T) 10
Leech, M. 1969 (Shamrock R) 8
Lennon, C. 1935 (St James' Gate) 3
Lennox, G. 1931 (Dolphin) 2
Long, S. P. 2007 (Reading) 13
Lowry, D. 1962 (St Patrick's Ath) 1
Lunn, R. 1939 (Dundalk) 2
Lynch, J. 1934 (Cork Bohemians) 1

McAlinden, J. 1946 (Portsmouth) 2
McAteer, J. W. 1994 (Bolton W, Liverpool,
Blackburn R, Sunderland) 52
McCann, J. 1957 (Shamrock R) 1
McCarthy, J. 1926 (Bohemians) 3
McCarthy, J. 2010 (Wigan Ath) 1

McCarthy, M. 1932 (Shamrock R)	1
McCarthy, M. 1984 (Manchester C, Celtic, Lyon, Millwall)	57
McConville, T. 1972 (Dundalk, Waterford)	6
McDonagh, Jacko 1984 (Shamrock R)	3
McDonagh, J. 1981 (Everton, Bolton W, Notts Co, Wichita Wings)	25
McEvoy, M. A. 1961 (Blackburn R)	17
McGeady, A. 2004 (Celtic)	**32**
McGee, P. 1978 (QPR, Preston NE)	15
McGoldrick, E. J. 1992 (C Palace, Arsenal)	15
McGowan, D. 1949 (West Ham U)	3
McGowan, J. 1947 (Cork U)	1
McGrath, M. 1958 (Blackburn R, Bradford)	22
McGrath, P. 1985 (Manchester U, Aston Villa, Derby Co)	83
McGuire, W. 1936 (Bohemians)	1
Macken, A. 1977 (Derby Co)	1
Macken J. P. 2005 (Manchester C)	1
McKenzie, G. 1938 (Southend U)	9
Mackey, G. 1957 (Shamrock R)	3
McLoughlin, A. F. 1990 (Swindon T, Southampton, Portsmouth)	42
McLoughlin, F. 1930 (Fordsons, Cork)	2
McMillan, W. 1946 (Belfast C)	2
McNally, J. B. 1959 (Luton T)	3
McPhail, S. 2000 (Leeds U)	10
McShane, P. D. 2007 (WBA, Sunderland, Hull C)	**22**
Madden, O. 1936 (Cork)	1
Maguire, J. 1929 (Shamrock R)	1
Mahon, A. J. 2000 (Tranmere R)	2
Malone, G. 1949 (Shelbourne)	1
Mancini, T. J. 1974 (QPR, Arsenal)	5
Martin, C. 1927 (Bo'ness)	1
Martin, C. J. 1946 (Glentoran, Leeds U, Aston Villa)	30
Martin, M. P. 1972 (Bohemians, Manchester U, WBA, Newcastle U)	52
Maybury, A. 1998 (Leeds U, Hearts, Leicester C)	10
Meagan, M. K. 1961 (Everton, Huddersfield T, Drogheda)	17
Meehan, P. 1934 (Drumcondra)	1
Miller, L. W. P. 2004 (Celtic, Manchester U, Sunderland, Hibernian)	**21**
Milligan, M. J. 1992 (Oldham Ath)	1
Monahan, P. 1935 (Sligo R)	2
Mooney, J. 1965 (Shamrock R)	2
Moore, A. 1996 (Middlesbrough)	8
Moore, P. 1931 (Shamrock R, Aberdeen, Shamrock R)	9
Moran, K. 1980 (Manchester U, Sporting Gijon, Blackburn R)	71
Moroney, T. 1948 (West Ham U, Evergreen U)	12
Morris, C. B. 1988 (Celtic, Middlesbrough)	35
Morrison, C. H. 2002 (C Palace, Birmingham C, C Palace)	36
Moulson, G. 1936 (Lincoln C, Notts Co)	5
Moulson, G. B. 1948 (Lincoln C)	1
Muckian, C. 1978 (Drogheda U)	1
Muldoon, T. 1927 (Aston Villa)	1
Mulligan, P. M. 1969 (Shamrock R, Chelsea, C Palace, WBA, Shamrock R)	50
Munroe, L. 1954 (Shamrock R)	1
Murphy, A. 1956 (Clyde)	1
Murphy, B. 1986 (Bohemians)	1
Murphy, D. 2007 (Sunderland)	9
Murphy, J. 1980 (C Palace)	1
Murphy, J. 2004 (WBA, Scunthorpe U)	**2**
Murphy, P. M. 2007 (Carlisle U)	1
Murray, T. 1950 (Dundalk)	1
Newman, W. 1969 (Shelbourne)	1
Nolan. E. W. 2009 (Preston NE)	**3**
Nolan, R. 1957 (Shamrock R)	10
O'Brien, A. 2007 (Newcastle U)	5

O'Brien, A. J. 2001 (Newcastle U, Portsmouth)	26
O'Brien, F. 1980 (Philadelphia F)	3
O'Brien J. M. 2006 (Bolton W)	3
O'Brien, L. 1986 (Shamrock R, Manchester U, Newcastle U, Tranmere R)	16
O'Brien, M. T. 1927 (Derby Co, Walsall, Norwich C, Watford)	4
O'Brien, R. 1976 (Notts Co)	5
O'Byrne, L. B. 1949 (Shamrock R)	1
O'Callaghan, B. R. 1979 (Stoke C)	6
O'Callaghan, K. 1981 (Ipswich T, Portsmouth)	21
O'Cearuill, J. 2007 (Arsenal)	2
O'Connell, A. 1967 (Dundalk, Bohemians)	2
O'Connor, T. 1950 (Shamrock R)	4
O'Connor, T. 1968 (Fulham, Dundalk, Bohemians)	7
O'Dea, D. 2010 (Celtic)	**1**
O'Driscoll, J. F. 1949 (Swansea T)	3
O'Driscoll, S. 1982 (Fulham)	3
O'Farrell, F. 1952 (West Ham U, Preston NE)	9
O'Flanagan, K. P. 1938 (Bohemians, Arsenal)	10
O'Flanagan, M. 1947 (Bohemians)	1
O'Halloran, S. E. 2007 (Aston Villa)	2
O'Hanlon, K. G. 1988 (Rotherham U)	1
O'Kane, P. 1935 (Bohemians)	3
O'Keefe, E. 1981 (Everton, Port Vale)	5
O'Keefe, T. 1934 (Cork, Waterford)	3
O'Leary, D. 1977 (Arsenal)	68
O'Leary, P. 1980 (Shamrock R)	7
O'Mahoney, M. T. 1938 (Bristol R)	6
O'Neill, F. S. 1962 (Shamrock R)	20
O'Neill, J. 1952 (Everton)	17
O'Neill, J. 1961 (Preston NE)	1
O'Neill, K. P. 1996 (Norwich C, Middlesbrough)	13
O'Neill, W. 1936 (Dundalk)	4
O'Regan, K. 1984 (Brighton & HA)	4
O'Reilly, J. 1932 (Brideville, Aberdeen, Brideville, St James' Gate)	20
O'Reilly, J. 1946 (Cork U)	2
O'Shea, J. F. 2002 (Manchester U)	**62**
Peyton, G. 1977 (Fulham, Bournemouth, Everton)	33
Peyton, N. 1957 (Shamrock R, Leeds U)	6
Phelan, T. 1992 (Wimbledon, Manchester C, Chelsea, Everton, Fulham)	42
Potter, D. M. 2007 (Wolverhampton W)	5
Quinn, A. 2003 (Sheffield W, Sheffield U)	8
Quinn, B. S. 2000 (Coventry C)	4
Quinn, N. J. 1986 (Arsenal, Manchester C, Sunderland)	91
Reid, A. M. 2004 (Nottingham F, Tottenham H, Charlton Ath, Sunderland)	27
Reid, C. 1931 (Brideville)	1
Reid, S. J. 2002 (Millwall, Blackburn R)	23
Richardson, D. J. 1972 (Shamrock R, Gillingham)	3
Rigby, A. 1935 (St James' Gate)	3
Ringstead, A. 1951 (Sheffield U)	20
Robinson, J. 1928 (Bohemians, Dolphin)	2
Robinson, M. 1981 (Brighton & HA, Liverpool, QPR)	24
Roche, P. J. 1972 (Shelbourne, Manchester U)	8
Rogers, E. 1968 (Blackburn R, Charlton Ath)	19
Rowlands, M. C. 2004 (QPR)	**5**
Ryan, G. 1978 (Derby Co, Brighton & HA)	18
Ryan, R. A. 1950 (WBA, Derby Co)	16
Sadlier, R. T. 2002 (Millwall)	1
Savage, D. P. T. 1996 (Millwall)	5
Saward, P. 1954 (Millwall, Aston Villa, Huddersfield T)	18
Scannell, T. 1954 (Southend U)	1
Scully, P. J. 1989 (Arsenal)	1
Sheedy, K. 1984 (Everton, Newcastle U)	46
Sheridan, C. 2010 (Celtic)	**2**

Sheridan, J. J. 1988 (Leeds U, Sheffield W)	34
Slaven, B. 1990 (Middlesbrough)	7
Sloan, J. W. 1946 (Arsenal)	2
Smyth, M. 1969 (Shamrock R)	1
Squires, J. 1934 (Shelbourne)	1
Stapleton, F. 1977 (Arsenal, Manchester U, Ajax, Le Havre, Blackburn R)	71
Staunton, S. 1989 (Liverpool, Aston Villa, Liverpool, Aston Villa)	102
St Ledger-Hall, S. P. 2009 (Preston NE)	**12**
Stevenson, A. E. 1932 (Dolphin, Everton)	7
Stokes, A. 2007 (Sunderland)	3
Strahan, F. 1964 (Shelbourne)	5
Sullivan, J. 1928 (Fordsons)	1
Swan, M. M. G. 1960 (Drumcondra)	1
Synnott, N. 1978 (Shamrock R)	3
Taylor, T. 1959 (Waterford)	1
Thomas, P. 1974 (Waterford)	2
Thompson, J. 2004 (Nottingham F)	1
Townsend, A. D. 1989 (Norwich C, Chelsea, Aston Villa, Middlesbrough)	70
Traynor, T. J. 1954 (Southampton)	8
Treacy, R. C. P. 1966 (WBA, Charlton Ath, Swindon T, Preston NE, WBA, Shamrock R)	42

Tuohy, L. 1956 (Shamrock R, Newcastle U, Shamrock R)	8
Turner, C. J. 1936 (Southend U, West Ham U)	10
Turner, P. 1963 (Celtic)	2
Vernon, J. 1946 (Belfast C)	2
Waddock, G. 1980 (QPR, Millwall)	21
Walsh, D. J. 1946 (Linfield, WBA, Aston Villa)	20
Walsh, J. 1982 (Limerick)	1
Walsh, M. 1976 (Blackpool, Everton, QPR, Porto)	21
Walsh, M. 1982 (Everton)	4
Walsh, W. 1947 (Manchester C)	9
Waters, J. 1977 (Grimsby T)	2
Watters, F. 1926 (Shelbourne)	1
Weir, E. 1939 (Clyde)	3
Westwood, K. 2009 (Coventry C)	**5**
Whelan, G. D. 2008 (Stoke C)	**20**
Whelan, R. 1964 (St Patrick's Ath)	2
Whelan, R. 1981 (Liverpool, Southend U)	53
Whelan, W. 1956 (Manchester U)	4
White, J. J. 1928 (Bohemians)	1
Whittaker, R. 1959 (Chelsea)	1
Williams, J. 1938 (Shamrock R)	1

LANDMARKS

Chelsea: record gap of 71 between goals scored and conceded.

Ashley Cole (Chelsea) collects his sixth FA Cup Winners' Medal (three with Arsenal)

Manchester United's Ryan Giggs is the only player to score at least one Premier League goal in each of its 18 seasons.

Newcastle United record attendance for Football League Championship (since start of the Premier League) 52,181 v Ipswich Town, 24 April 2010.

Portsmouth v Arsenal, 30 December 2009; the first Premier League match to begin with 22 foreign players.

Of 595 Premier League players at the start of 2009–2010, only 41.7% were English and 68 different countries were represented among the remainder.

Shay Given and Kevin Kilbane become the Republic of Ireland's most capped players, each with 103 appearances.

England Under-19's record score for them at this level, beating Slovenia 7-1, 27 July 2009.

On 9 May 2010 Jose Mourinho completed a run of 136 home League matches unbeaten. This began with 38 as Manager of Porto, 60 with Chelsea and 38 with Internazionale.

BRITISH AND IRISH INTERNATIONAL GOALSCORERS SINCE 1872

Where two players with the same surname and initials have appeared for the same country, and one or both have scored, they have been distinguished by reference to the club which appears *first* against their name in the international appearances section.

ENGLAND

Name	Goals
A'Court, A.	1
Adams, T. A.	5
Adcock, H.	1
Alcock, C. W.	1
Allen, A.	3
Allen, R.	2
Amos, A.	1
Anderson, V.	2
Anderton, D. R.	7
Astall, G.	1
Athersmith, W. C.	3
Atyeo, P. J. W.	5
Bache, J. W.	4
Bailey, N. C.	2
Baily, E. F.	5
Baker, J. H.	3
Ball, A. J.	8
Bambridge, A. L.	1
Bambridge, E. C.	11
Barclay, R.	2
Barmby, N. J.	4
Barnes, J.	11
Barnes, P. S.	4
Barry, G.	2
Barton, J.	1
Bassett, W. I.	8
Bastin, C. S.	12
Beardsley, P. A.	9
Beasley, A.	1
Beattie, T. K.	1
Beckham, D. R. J.	17
Becton, F.	2
Bedford, H.	1
Bell, C.	9
Bentley, R. T. F.	9
Bishop, S. M.	1
Blackburn, F.	1
Blissett, L.	3
Bloomer, S.	28
Bond, R.	2
Bonsor, A. G.	1
Bowden, E. R.	1
Bowers, J. W.	2
Bowles, S.	1
Bradford, G. R. W.	1
Bradford, J.	7
Bradley, W.	2
Bradshaw, F.	3
Brann, G.	1
Bridge, W. M.	1
Bridges, B. J.	1
Bridgett, A.	3
Brindle, T.	1
Britton, C. S.	1
Broadbent, P. F.	2
Broadis, I. A.	8
Brodie, J. B.	1
Bromley-Davenport, W.	2
Brook, E. F.	10
Brooking, T. D.	5
Brooks, J.	2
Broome, F. H.	3
Brown, A.	4
Brown, A. S.	1
Brown, G.	5
Brown, J.	3
Brown, W.	1
Brown, W. M.	1
Buchan, C. M.	4
Bull, S. G.	4
Bullock, N.	2
Burgess, H.	4
Butcher, T.	3
Byrne, J. J.	8
Campbell, S. J.	1
Camsell, G. H.	18
Carter, H. S.	7
Carter, J. H.	4
Chadwick, E.	3
Chamberlain, M.	1
Chambers, H.	5
Channon, M. R.	21
Charlton, J.	6
Charlton, R.	49
Chenery, C. J.	1
Chivers, M.	13
Clarke, A. J.	10
Cobbold, W. N.	6
Cock, J. G.	2
Cole, A.	1
Cole, J. J.	10
Common, A.	2
Connelly, J. M.	7
Coppell, S. J.	7
Cotterill, G. H.	2
Cowans, G.	2
Crawford, R.	1
Crawshaw, T. H.	1
Crayston, W. J.	1
Creek, F. N. S.	1
Crooks, S. D.	7
Crouch, P. J.	21
Currey, E. S.	2
Currie, A. W.	3
Cursham, A. W.	2
Cursham, H. A.	5
Daft, H. B.	3
Davenport, J. K.	2
Davis, G.	1
Davis, H.	1
Day, S. H.	2
Dean, W. R.	18
Defoe, J. C.	12
Devey, J. H. G.	1
Dewhurst, F.	11
Dix, W. R.	1
Dixon, K. M.	4
Dixon, L. M.	1
Dorrell, A. R.	1
Douglas, B.	11
Drake, E. J.	6
Ducat, A.	1
Dunn, A. T. B.	2
Eastham, G.	2
Edwards, D.	5
Ehiogu, U.	1
Elliott, W. H.	3
Evans, R. E.	1
Ferdinand, L.	5
Ferdinand, R. G.	3
Finney, T.	30
Fleming, H. J.	9
Flowers, R.	10
Forman, Frank	1
Forman, Fred	3
Foster, R. E.	3
Fowler, R. B.	7
Francis, G. C. J.	3
Francis, T.	12
Freeman, B. C.	3
Froggatt, J.	2
Froggatt, R.	2
Galley, T.	1
Gascoigne, P. J.	10
Geary, F.	3
Gerrard, S. G.	17
Gibbins, W. V. T.	3
Gilliatt, W. E.	3
Goddard, P.	1
Goodall, J.	12
Goodyer, A. C.	1
Gosling, R. C.	2
Goulden, L. A.	4
Grainger, C.	3
Greaves, J.	44
Grovesnor, A. T.	2
Gunn, W.	1
Haines, J. T. W.	2
Hall, G. W.	9
Halse, H. J.	2
Hampson, J.	5
Hampton, H.	2
Hancocks, J.	2
Hardman, H. P.	1
Harris, S. S.	2
Hassall, H. W.	4
Hateley, M.	9
Haynes, J. N.	18
Hegan, K. E.	4
Henfrey, A. G.	2
Heskey, E. W.	7
Hilsdon, G. R.	14
Hine, E. W.	4
Hinton, A. T.	1
Hirst, D. E.	1
Hitchens, G. A.	5
Hobbis, H. H. F.	1
Hoddle, G.	8
Hodgetts, D.	1
Hodgson, G.	1
Holley, G. H.	8
Houghton, W. E.	5
Howell, R.	1
Hughes, E. W.	1
Hulme, J. H. A.	4
Hunt, G. S.	1
Hunt, R.	18
Hunter, N.	2
Hurst, G. C.	24
Ince, P. E. C.	2
Jack, D. N. B.	3
Jeffers, F.	1
Jenas, J. A.	1
Johnson, D. E.	6
Johnson, E.	2
Johnson, G. M. C.	1
Johnson, J. A.	2
Johnson, T. C. F.	5
Johnson, W. H.	1
Kelly, R.	8
Kennedy, R.	3
Kenyon-Slaney, W. S.	2
Keown, M. R.	2
Kevan, D. T.	8
Kidd, B.	1
King, L. B.	2
Kingsford, R. K.	1
Kirchen, A. J.	2
Kirton, W. J.	1
Lampard, F. J.	20
Langton, R.	1
Latchford, R. D.	5
Latheron, E. G.	1
Lawler, C.	1
Lawton, T.	22
Lee, F.	10
Lee, J.	1
Lee, R. M.	2
Lee, S.	2
Le Saux, G. P.	1
Lindley, T.	14
Lineker, G.	48
Lofthouse, J. M.	3
Lofthouse, N.	30
Hon. A. Lyttelton	1
Mabbutt, G.	1
Macdonald, M.	6
Mannion, W. J.	11
Mariner, P.	13
Marsh, R. W.	1
Matthews, S.	11
Matthews, V.	1
McCall, J.	1
McDermott, T.	3
McManaman, S.	3
Medley, L. D.	1
Melia, J.	1
Mercer, D. W.	1
Merson, P. C.	3
Milburn, J. E. T.	10
Miller, H. S.	1
Mills, G. R.	3
Milward, A.	3
Mitchell, C.	5
Moore, J.	1
Moore, R. F.	2
Moore, W. G. B.	2
Morren, T.	1
Morris, F.	1
Morris, J.	3
Mortensen, S. H.	23
Morton, J. R.	1
Mosforth, W.	3
Mullen, J.	6
Mullery, A. P.	1
Murphy, D. B	1
Neal, P. G.	5
Needham, E.	3
Nicholls, J.	1
Nicholson, W. E.	1
Nugent, D. J.	1
O'Grady, M.	3
Osborne, F. R.	3
Owen, M. J.	40
Own goals	31

Page, L. A.	1	Tilson, S. F.	6	Coulter, J.	1	Mahood, J.	2
Paine, T. L.	7	Townley, W. J.	2	Croft, T.	1	Martin, D. K.	3
Palmer, C. L.	1	Tueart, D.	2	Crone, W.	1	Maxwell, J.	2
Parry, E. H.	1			Crossan, E.	1	McAdams, W. J.	7
Parry, R. A.	1	Upson, M. J.	2	Crossan, J. A.	10	McAllen, J.	1
Pawson, F. W.	1			Curran, S.	2	McAuley, G.	1
Payne, J.	2	Vassell, D.	6	Cush, W. W.	5	Mcauley, J. L.	1
Peacock, A.	3	Vaughton, O. H.	6			McCann, G. S.	4
Pearce, S.	5	Veitch, J. G.	3	Dalton, W.	4	McCartney, G.	1
Pearson, J. S.	5	Viollet, D. S	1	D'Arcy, S. D.	1	McCandless, J.	2
Pearson, S. C.	5			Darling, J.	1	McCandless, W.	1
Perry, W.	2	Waddle, C. R.	6	Davey, H. H.	1	McCaw, J. H.	1
Peters, M.	20	Walcott, T. J.	3	Davis, S.	2	McClelland, J.	1
Pickering, F.	5	Walker, W. H.	9	Davis, T. L.	1	McCluggage, A.	2
Platt, D.	27	Wall, G.	2	Dill, A. H.	1	McCracken, W.	1
Pointer, R.	2	Wallace, D.	1	Doherty, L.	1	McCrory, S.	1
		Walsh, P.	1	Doherty, P. D.	3	McCurdy, C.	1
Quantrill, A.	1	Waring, T	4	Dougan, A. D.	8	McDonald, A.	3
		Warren, E.	2	Dowie, I.	12	McGarry, J. K.	1
Ramsay, A. E.	3	Watson, D. V.	4	Dunne, J.	4	McGrath, R. C.	4
Revie, D. G.	4	Watson, V. M.	4			McIlroy, J.	10
Redknapp, J. F.	1	Webb, G. W.	1	Elder, A. R.	1	McIlroy, S. B.	5
Reynolds, J.	3	Webb, N.	4	Elliott, S.	4	McKenzie, H	1
Richards, M.	1	Wedlock, W. J.	2	Emerson, W.	1	McKnight, J.	2
Richardson, K. E.	2	Weller, K.	1	English, S.	1	McLaughlin, J. C.	6
Richardson, J. R.	2	Welsh, D.		Evans, J. G.	1	McMahon, G. J.	2
Rigby, A.	3	Whateley, O.	2			McMordie, A. S.	3
Rimmer, E. J.	2	Wheldon, G. F.	6	Feeney, W.	1	McMorran, E. J.	4
Roberts, F.	2	Whitfield, H.	1	Feeney, W. J.	5	McParland, P. J.	10
Roberts, H.	1	Wignall, F.	2	Ferguson, W.	1	McWha, W. B. R.	1
Roberts, W. T.	2	Wilkes, A.	1	Ferris, J.	1	Meldon, P. A.	1
Robinson, J.	3	Wilkins, R. G.	3	Ferris, R. O.	1	Mercer, J. T.	1
Robson, B.	26	Willingham, C. K.	1	Finney, T.	2	Millar, W.	1
Robson, R.	4	Wilshaw, D. J.	10			Milligan, D.	1
Rooney, W.	25	Wilson, G. P.	1	Gaffkin, J.	4	Milne, R. G.	2
Rowley, J. F.	6	Winterworth, W. N.	1	Gara, A.	3	Molyneux, T. B.	1
Royle, J.	2	Windridge, J. E.	7	Gaukrodger, G.	1	Moreland, V.	1
Rutherford, J.	3	Wise, D. F.	1	Gibb, J. T.	1	Morgan, S.	3
		Withe, P.	1	Gibb, T. J.	1	Morrow, S. J.	1
Sagar, C.	1	Wollaston, C. H. R.	1	Gibson, W.	1	Morrow, W. J.	1
Sandilands, R. R.	3	Wood, H.	1	Gillespie, K. R.	2	Mulryne, P. P.	3
Sansom, K.	1	Woodcock, T.	16	Gillespie, W.	13	Murdock, C. J.	1
Schofield, J.	1	Woodhall, G.	1	Goodall, A. L.	2	Murphy, N.	1
Scholes, P.	14	Woodward, V. J.	29	Griffin, D. J.	1		
Seed, J. M.	1	Worrall, F.	2	Gray, P.	6	Neill, W. J. T.	2
Settle, J.	6	Worthington, F. S.	2			Nelson, S.	1
Sewell, J.	3	Wright, I. E.	9	Halligan, W.	1	Nicholl, C. J.	3
Shackleton, L. F.	1	Wright, M.	1	Hamill, M.	1	Nicholl, J. M.	1
Sharp, J.	1	Wright, W. A.	3	Hamilton, B.	4	Nicholson, J. J.	6
Shearer, A.	30	Wright-Phillips, S. C.	6	Hamilton, W. R.	5		
Shelton, A.	1	Wylie, J. G.	1	Hannon, D. J.	1	O'Boyle, G.	1
Shepherd, A.	2			Harkin, J. T.	2	O'Hagan, C.	2
Sheringham, E. P.	11	Yates, J.	3	Harvey, M.	3	O'Kane, W. J.	1
Simpson, J.	1			Healy, D. J.	35	O'Neill, J.	2
Smith, A.	1	**NORTHERN IRELAND**		Hill, C. F.	1	O'Neill, M. A.	4
Smith, A. M.	2	Anderson, T.	4	Hughes, M. E.	5	O'Neill, M. H.	8
Smith, G. O.	11	Armstrong, G.	12	Humphries, W.	1	Own goals	9
Smith, Joe	1			Hunter, A. (*Distillery*)	1		
Smith, J. R.	2	Bambrick, J.	12	Hunter, A.		Patterson, D. J.	1
Smith, J. W.	4	Barr, H. H.	1	(*Blackburn R*)	1	Peacock, R.	2
Smith, R.	13	Barron, H.	3	Hunter, B. V.	1	Peden, J.	7
Smith, S.	1	Best, G.	9			Penney, S.	2
Sorby, T. H.	1	Bingham, W. L.	10	Irvine, R. W.	3	Pyper, James	2
Southgate, G.	2	Black, K.	1	Irvine, W. J.	8	Pyper, John	1
Southworth, J.	3	Blanchflower, D.	2				
Sparks, F. J.	3	Blanchflower, J.	1	Johnston, H.	2	Quinn, J. M.	12
Spence, J. W.	1	Brennan, B.	1	Johnston, S.	2	Quinn, S. J.	4
Spiksley, F.	5	Brennan, R. A.	1	Johnston, W. C.	1		
Spilsbury, B. W.	5	Brotherston, N.	3	Jones, S.	1	Reynolds, J.	1
Steele, F. C.	8	Brown, J.	1	Jones, S. (*Crewe Alex*)	1	Rowland, K.	1
Stephenson, G. T.	2	Browne, F.	2	Jones, J.	1	Rowley, R. W. M.	2
Steven, T. M.	4	Brunt, C.	1			Rushe, F.	1
Stewart, J.	2			Kelly, J.	4		
Stiles, N. P.	1	Campbell, J.	1	Kernaghan, N.	2	Sheridan, J.	2
Storer, H.	1	Campbell, W. G.	1	Kirwan, J.	2	Sherrard, J.	1
Stone, S. B.	2	Casey, T.	2			Sherrard, W. C.	2
Summerbee, M. G.	1	Caskey, W.	1	Lacey, W.	3	Simpson, W. J.	5
		Cassidy, T.	1	Lafferty, K.	7	Sloan, H. A. de B.	4
Tambling, R. V.	1	Chambers, J.	3	Lemon, J.	2	Smyth, S.	5
Taylor, P. J.	2	Clarke, C. J.	13	Lennon, N. F.	2	Spence, D. W.	3
Taylor, T.	16	Clements, D.	2	Lockhart, N.	3	Sproule, I.	1
Terry, J. G.	6	Cochrane, T.	1	Lomas, S. M.	3	Stanfield, O. M.	11
Thompson, P. B.	1	Condy, J.	1			Stevenson, A. E.	5
Thornewell, G.	1	Connor, M. J.	1	Magilton, J.	5		

Stewart, I.	2	Calderwood, R.	2	Gibson, J. D.	1	Lang, J. J.	2
		Caldow, E.	4	Gibson, N.	1	Latta, A.	2
Taggart, G. P.	7	Cameron, C.	2	Gillespie, Jas.	3	Law, D.	30
Thompson, F. W.	2	Campbell, C.	1	Gillick, T.	3	Leggat, G.	8
Torrans, S.	1	Campbell, John (*Celtic*)	5	Gilzean, A. J.	12	Lennie, W.	1
Tully, C. P.	3	Campbell, John	4	Gossland, J.	2	Lennox, R.	3
Turner, A.	1	(*Rangers*)		Goudie, J.	1	Liddell, W.	6
		Campbell, J.		Gough, C. R.	6	Lindsay, J.	6
Walker, J.	1	(*South Western*)	1	Gourlay, J.	1	Linwood, A. B.	1
Walsh, D. J.	5	Campbell, P.	2	Graham, A.	2	Logan, J.	1
Welsh, E.	1	Campbell, R.	1	Graham, G.	3	Lorimer, P.	4
Whiteside, N.	9	Cassidy, J.	1	Gray, A.	7	Love, A.	1
Whiteside, T.	1	Chalmers, S.	3	Gray, E.	3	Low, J. (*Cambuslang*)	1
Whitley, Jeff	2	Chambers, T.	1	Gray, F.	1	Lowe, J. (*St Bernards*)	1
Williams, J. R.	1	Cheyne, A. G.	4	Greig, J.	3		
Williams, M. S.	1	Christie, A. J.	1	Groves, W.	4	Macari, L.	5
Williamson, J.	1	Clarkson, D.	1			MacDougall, E. J.	3
Wilson, D. J.	1	Clunas, W. L.	1	Hamilton, G.	4	MacFarlane, A.	1
Wilson, K. J.	6	Collins, J.	12	Hamilton, J.	3	MacLeod, M.	1
Wilson, S. J.	7	Collins, R. Y.	10	(*Queen's Park*)		Mackay, D. C.	4
Wilton, J. M.	2	Combe, J. R.	1	Hamilton, R. C.	15	Mackay, G.	1
		Conn, A.	1	Harper, J. M.	2	MacKenzie, J. A.	1
Young, S.	1	Cooper, D.	6	Hartley, P. J.	1	MacKinnon, W. W.	5
N.B. In 1914 Young goal		Craig, J.	1	Harrower, W.	5	Madden, J.	5
should be credited to		Craig, T.	1	Hartford, R. A.	4	Maloney, S.	1
Gillespie W v Wales		Crawford, S.	4	Heggie, C. W	4	Marshall, H.	1
		Cunningham, A. N.	5	Henderson, J. G.	1	Marshall, J.	1
SCOTLAND		Curran, H. P.	1	Henderson, W.	5	Mason, J.	4
Aitken, R. (*Celtic*)	1			Hendry, E. C. J.	3	Massie, A.	1
Aitken, R. (*Dumbarton*)	1	Dailly, C.	6	Herd, D. G.	3	Masson, D. S.	5
Aitkenhead, W. A. C.	2	Dalglish, K.	30	Herd, G.	1	McAdam, J.	1
Alexander, D.	1	Davidson, D.	1	Hewie, J. D.	2	McAllister, G.	5
Allan, D. S.	4	Davidson, J. A.	1	Higgins, A.	1	McAulay, J. D.	1
Allan, J.	2	Delaney, J.	3	(*Newcastle U*)		McAvennie, F.	1
Anderson, F.	1	Devine, A.	1	Higgins, A.	4	McCall, J.	1
Anderson, W.	4	Dewar, G.	1	(*Kilmarnock*)		McCall, S. M.	1
Andrews, P.	1	Dewar, N.	4	Highet, T. C.	1	McCalliog, J.	1
Archibald, A.	1	Dickov, P.	1	Holt, G.J.	1	McCallum, N.	1
Archibald, S.	4	Dickson, W.	4	Holton, J. A.	2	McCann, N.	3
		Divers, J.	1	Hopkin, D.	2	McClair, B. J.	2
Baird, D.	2	Dobie, R. S.	1	Houliston, W.	2	McCoist, A.	19
Baird, J. C.	2	Docherty, T. H.	1	Howie, H.	1	McColl, R. S.	13
Baird, S.	2	Dodds, D.	1	Howie, J.	2	McCormack, R.	1
Bannon, E.	1	Dodds, W.	7	Hughes, J.	1	McCulloch, D.	3
Barbour, A.	1	Donaldson, A.	1	Hunter, W.	1	McCulloch, L.	1
Barker, J. B.	4	Donnachie, J.	1	Hutchison, D.	6	McDougall, J.	4
Battles, B. Jr	1	Dougall, J.	1	Hutchison, T.	1	McFadden, J.	15*
Bauld, W.	2	Drummond, J.	2	Hutton, J.	1	McFadyen, W.	2
Baxter, J. C.	3	Dunbar, M.	1	Hyslop, T.	1	McGhee, M.	2
Beattie, C.	1	Duncan, D.	7			McGinlay, J.	4
Bell, J.	5	Duncan, D. M.	1	Imrie, W. N.	1	McGregor, J.	1
Bennett, A.	2	Duncan, J.	1			McGrory, J.	6
Berry, D.	1	Dunn, J.	2	Jackson, A.	8	McGuire, W.	1
Bett, J.	1	Durie, G. S.	7	Jackson, C.	1	McInally, A.	3
Beveridge, W. W.	1			Jackson, D.	4	McInnes, T.	2
Black, A.	3	Easson, J. F.	1	James, A. W.	4	McKie, J.	2
Black, D.	1	Elliott, M. S.	1	Jardine, A.	1	McKimmie, S.	1
Bone, J.	1	Ellis, J.	1	Jenkinson, T.	1	McKinlay, W.	4
Booth, S.	6			Jess, E.	2	McKinnon, A.	1
Boyd, K	7	Ferguson, B.	3	Johnston, A.	2	McKinnon, R.	1
Boyd, R.	2	Ferguson, J.	6	Johnston, L. H.	1	McLaren, A.	4
Boyd, T.	1	Fernie, W.	1	Johnston, M.	14	McLaren, J.	1
Boyd, W. G.	1	Fitchie, T. T.	1	Johnstone, D.	2	McLean, A.	1
Brackenridge, T.	1	Flavell, R.	2	Johnstone, J.	4	McLean, T.	1
Brand, R.	8	Fleming, C.	2	Johnstone, Jas.	1	McLintock, F.	1
Brazil, A.	1	Fleming, J. W.	3	Johnstone, R.	10	McMahon, A.	6
Bremner, W. J.	3	Fletcher, D.	4	Johnstone, W.	1	McManus, S.	1
Broadfoot, K.	1	Fletcher, S.	1	Jordan, J.	11	McMenemy, J.	5
Brown, A. D.	6	Fraser, M. J. E.	3			McMillan, I. L.	2
Brown, S.	2	Freedman, D. A.	1	Kay, J. L.	5	McNeill, W.	3
Buchanan, P. S.	1			Keillor, A.	3	McNiel, H.	5
Buchanan, R.	1	Gallacher, H. K.	23	Kelly, J.	1	McPhail, J.	3
Buckley, P.	1	Gallacher, K. W.	9	Kelso, R.	1	McPhail, R.	7
Buick, A.	2	Gallacher, P.	1	Ker, G.	10	McPherson, J.	5
Burke, C.	2	Galt, J. H.	1	King, A.	1	McPherson, J.	
Burley, C. W.	3	Gemmell, T. (*St Mirren*)	1	King, J.	1	(*Vale of Leven*)	1
Burns, K.	1	Gemmell, T. (*Celtic*)	1	Kinnear, D.	1	McPherson, R.	1
		Gemmill, A.	8	Kyle, K.	1	McQueen, G.	5
Cairns, T.	1	Gemmill, S.	1			McStay, P.	9
Caldwell, G.	2	Gibb, W.	1	Lambert, P.	1	McSwegan, G.	1
Calderwood, C.	1	Gibson, D. W.	3	Lambie, J.	1		
				Lambie, W. A.	5		

* The Scottish FA officially changed Robsons's goal against Iceland on 10 September 2008 to McFadden.

Meiklejohn, D. D.	3
Millar, J.	2
Miller, K.	11
Miller, T.	2
Miller, W.	1
Mitchell, R. C.	1
Morgan, W.	1
Morris, D.	1
Morris, H.	3
Morton, A. L.	5
Mudie, J. K.	9
Mulhall, G.	1
Munro, A. D.	1
Munro, N.	2
Murdoch, R.	5
Murphy, F.	1
Murray, J.	1
Napier, C. E.	3
Narey, D.	1
Naysmith, G. A.	1
Neil, R. G.	2
Nevin, P. K. F.	5
Nicholas, C.	5
Nisbet, J.	2
O'Connor, G.	4
O'Donnell, F.	2
O'Hare, J.	5
Ormond, W. E.	2
O'Rourke, F.	1
Orr, R.	1
Orr, T.	1
Oswald, J.	1
Own goals	16
Parlane, D.	1
Paul, H. McD.	2
Paul, W.	5
Pettigrew, W.	2
Provan, D.	1
Quashie, N. F.	1
Quinn, J.	7
Quinn, P.	1
Rankin, G.	2
Rankin, R.	2
Reid, W.	4
Reilly, L.	22
Renny-Tailyour, H. W.	1
Richmond, J. T.	1
Ring, T.	2
Rioch, B. D.	6
Ritchie, J.	1
Ritchie, P. S.	1
Robertson, A.	2
Robertson, J.	3
Robertson, J. N.	8
Robertson, J. T.	2
Robertson, T.	1
Robertson, W.	1
Russell, D.	1
Scott, A. S.	5
Sellar, W.	4
Sharp, G.	1
Shaw, F. W.	1
Shearer, D.	2
Simpson, J.	1
Smith, A.	5
Smith, G.	4
Smith, J.	1
Smith, John	13
Somerville, G.	1
Souness, G. J.	4
Speedie, F.	2
St John, I.	9
Steel, W.	12
Stein, C.	10
Stevenson, G.	4
Stewart, A.	1
Stewart, R.	1

Stewart, W. E.	1
Strachan, G.	5
Sturrock, P.	3
Taylor, J. D.	1
Templeton, R.	1
Thompson, S.	3
Thomson, A.	1
Thomson, C.	4
Thomson, R.	1
Thomson, W.	1
Thornton, W.	1
Waddell, T. S.	1
Waddell, W.	6
Walker, J.	2
Walker, R.	7
Walker, T.	9
Wallace, I. A.	1
Wark, J.	7
Watson, J. A. K.	1
Watt, F.	2
Watt, W. W.	1
Webster, A.	1
Weir, A.	1
Weir, D.	1
Weir, J. B.	2
White, J. A.	3
Wilkie, L.	1
Wilson, A.	2
Wilson, A. N.	13
Wilson, D. (*Queen's Park*)	2
Wilson, D. (*Rangers*)	9
Wilson, H.	1
Wylie, T. G.	1
Young, A.	5

WALES

Allchurch, I. J.	23
Allen, M.	3
Astley, D. J.	12
Atherton, R. W.	2
Bale, G.	2
Bamford, T.	1
Barnes, W.	1
Bellamy, C. D.	17
Blackmore, C. G.	1
Blake, N. A.	4
Bodin, P. J.	3
Boulter, L. M.	1
Bowdler, J. C. H.	3
Bowen, D. L.	1
Bowen, M.	3
Boyle, T.	1
Bryan, T.	1
Burgess, W. A. R.	1
Burke, T.	1
Butler, W. T.	1
Chapman, T.	2
Charles, J.	1
Charles, M.	6
Charles, W. J.	15
Church, S. R.	1
Clarke, R. J.	5
Coleman, C.	4
Collier, D. J.	1
Collins, J.	2
Crosse, K.	1
Cumner, R. H.	1
Curtis, A.	6
Curtis, E. R.	3
Davies, D. W.	1
Davies, E. Lloyd	1
Davies, G.	2
Davies, L. S.	6
Davies, R. T.	9
Davies, R. W.	6

Davies, Simon	6
Davies, Stanley	5
Davies, W.	6
Davies, W. H.	1
Davies, William	5
Davis, W. O.	1
Deacy, N.	4
Doughty, J.	6
Doughty, R.	2
Durban, A.	2
Dwyer, P.	2
Earnshaw, R.	14
Eastwood, F.	4
Edwards, D.	3
Edwards, G.	2
Edwards, R. I.	4
England, H. M.	4
Evans, C.	2
Evans, I.	1
Evans, J.	1
Evans, R. E.	2
Evans, W.	1
Eyton-Jones, J. A.	1
Fletcher, C.	1
Flynn, B.	7
Ford, T.	23
Foulkes, W. I.	1
Fowler, J.	3
Giles, D.	2
Giggs, R. J.	12
Glover, E. M.	7
Godfrey, B. C.	2
Green, A. W.	3
Griffiths, A. T.	6
Griffiths, M. W.	2
Griffiths, T. P.	3
Harris, C. S.	1
Hartson, J.	14
Hersee, R.	1
Hewitt, R.	1
Hockey, T.	1
Hodges, G.	2
Hole, W. J.	1
Hopkins, I. J.	2
Horne, B.	2
Howell, E. G.	3
Hughes, L. M.	16
James, E.	2
James, L.	10
James, R.	7
Jarrett, R. H.	3
Jenkyns, C. A.	1
Jones, A.	1
Jones, Bryn	6
Jones, B. S.	2
Jones, Cliff	16
Jones, C. W.	1
Jones, D. E.	1
Jones, Evan	1
Jones, H.	1
Jones, J. L.	1
Jones, J. O.	1
Jones, J. P.	1
Jones, Leslie J.	1
Jones, R. A.	1
Jones, W. L.	6
Keenor, F. C.	2
Koumas, J.	10
Krzywicki, R. L.	1
Ledley, J.	2
Leek, K.	5
Lewis, B.	4
Lewis, W.	8

Lewis, W. L.	3
Llewelyn, C. M	1
Lovell, S.	1
Lowrie, G.	2
Mahoney, J. F.	1
Mays, A. W.	1
Medwin, T. C.	6
Melville, A. K	3
Meredith, W. H.	11
Mills, T. J.	1
Moore, G.	1
Morgan, J. R.	2
Morgan-Owen, H.	1
Morgan-Owen, M. M.	2
Morris, A. G.	9
Morris, H.	2
Morris, R.	1
Morris, S.	2
Nicholas, P.	2
O'Callaghan, E.	3
O'Sullivan, P. A.	1
Owen, G.	2
Owen, W.	4
Owen, W. F.	6
Own goals	14
Palmer, D.	3
Parry, P. I.	1
Parry, T. D.	3
Paul, R.	1
Peake, E.	1
Pembridge, M.	6
Perry, E.	1
Phillips, C.	5
Phillips, D.	2
Powell, A.	1
Powell, D.	1
Price, J.	4
Price, P.	1
Pryce-Jones, W. E.	3
Pugh, D. H.	2
Ramsay A.	2
Reece, G. I.	2
Rees, R. R.	3
Richards, R. W.	1
Roach, J.	2
Robbins, W. W.	4
Roberts, J. (*Corwen*)	1
Roberts, Jas.	1
Roberts, P. S.	1
Roberts, R. (*Druids*)	1
Roberts, W. (*Llangollen*)	2
Roberts, W. (*Wrexham*)	1
Roberts, W. H.	1
Robinson, C. P.	1
Robinson, J. R. C.	3
Rush, I.	28
Russell, M. R.	1
Sabine, H. W.	1
Saunders, D.	22
Savage, R. W.	2
Shaw, E. G.	2
Sisson, H.	4
Slatter, N.	2
Smallman, D. P.	1
Speed, G. A.	7
Symons, C. J.	2
Tapscott, D. R.	4
Taylor, G. K.	1
Thomas, M.	4
Thomas, T.	1
Toshack, J. B.	12
Trainer, H.	2
Vaughan, D. O.	1
Vaughan, John	2

Vernon, T. R.	8	Dempsey, J.	1	Horlacher, A.	2	O'Brien, A. J.	1
Vizard, E. T.	1	Dennehy, M.	2	Houghton, R.	6	O'Callaghan, K.	1
Vokes, S. M.	2	Doherty, G. M. T.	4	Hughton, C.	1	O'Connor, T.	2
		Donnelly, J.	4	Hunt, S. P.	1	O'Farrell, F.	2
Walsh, I.	7	Donnelly, T.	1	Hurley, C.	2	O'Flanagan, K.	3
Warren, F. W.	3	Doyle, K. E.	8			O'Keefe, E.	1
Watkins, W. M.	4	Duff, D. A.	7	Ireland, S. J.	4	O'Leary, D. A.	1
Wilding, J.	4	Duffy, B.	1	Irwin, D.	4	O'Neill, F.	1
Williams, A.	1	Duggan, H.	1			O'Neill, K. P.	4
Williams, D. R.	2	Dunne, J.	13	Jordan, D.	1	O'Reilly, J. (*Brideville*)	2
Williams, G. E.	1	Dunne, L.	1			O'Reilly, J. (*Cork*)	1
Williams, G. G.	1	Dunne, R. P.	7	Kavanagh, G. A.	1	O'Shea, J. F.	1
Williams, W.	1			Keane, R. D.	43	Own goals	10
Woosnam, A. P.	3	Eglington, T.	2	Keane, R. M.	9		
Wynn, G. A.	1	Elliott, S. W.	1	Kelly, D.	9	Quinn, N.	21
		Ellis, P.	1	Kelly, G.	2		
Yorath, T. C.	2			Kelly, J.	2	Reid, A. M.	4
Young, E.	1	Fagan, F.	5	Kennedy, M.	4	Reid, S. J.	2
		Fallon, S.	2	Keogh, A.	1	Ringstead, A.	7
REPUBLIC OF IRELAND		Fallon, W.	2	Kernaghan, A. N.	1	Robinson, M.	4
Aldridge, J.	19	Farrell, P.	3	Kilbane, K. D.	7	Rogers, E.	5
Ambrose, P.	1	Finnan, S.	2	Kinsella, M. A.	3	Ryan, G.	1
Anderson, J.	1	Fitzgerald, P.	2			Ryan, R.	3
Andrews, K.	1	Fitzgerald, J.	1	Lacey, W.	1		
		Fitzsimons, A.	7	Lawrence, L.	2	St Ledger-Hall, S.	1
Barrett, G.	2	Flood, J. J.	4	Lawrenson, M.	5	Sheedy, K.	9
Bermingham, P.	1	Fogarty, A.	3	Leech, M.	2	Sheridan, J.	5
Bradshaw, P.	4	Foley, D.	2	Long, S. P.	3	Slaven, B.	1
Brady, L.	9	Fullam, J.	1			Sloan, J.	1
Breen, G.	7	Fullam, R.	1	McAteer, J. W.	3	Squires, J.	1
Brown, J.	1			McCann, J.	1	Stapleton, F.	20
Byrne, D.	1	Galvin, A.	1	McCarthy, M.	2	Staunton, S.	7
Byrne, J.	4	Gavin, J.	2	McEvoy, A.	6	Strahan, J.	1
		Geoghegan, M.	2	McGee, P.	4	Sullivan, J.	1
Cantwell, J.	14	Giles, J.	5	McGrath, P.	8		
Carey, J.	3	Givens, D.	19	McLoughlin, A. F.	2	Townsend, A. D.	7
Carroll, T.	1	Glynn, D.	1	McPhail, S. J. P.	1	Treacy, R.	5
Cascarino, A.	19	Grealish, T.	8	Mancini, T.	1	Touhy, L.	4
Coad, P.	3	Green, P. J.	1	Martin, C.	6		
Connolly, D. J.	9	Grimes, A. A.	1	Martin, M.	4	Waddock, G.	3
Conroy, T.	2			Miller, L. W. P.	1	Walsh, D.	5
Conway, J.	3	Hale, A.	2	Mooney, J.	1	Walsh, M.	1
Coyne, T.	6	Hand, E.	2	Moore, P.	7	Waters, J.	1
Cummins, G.	5	Harte, I. P.	11	Moran, K.	6	White, J. J.	2
Curtis, D.	8	Haverty, J.	3	Morrison, C. H.	9	Whelan, G. D.	2
		Healy, C.	1	Moroney, T.	1	Whelan, R.	3
Daly, G.	13	Holland, M. R.	5	Mulligan, P.	1		
Davis, T.	4	Holmes, J.	1				

BRITISH & IRISH INTERNATIONAL MANAGERS

England
Walter Winterbottom 1946–1962 (after period as coach); Alf Ramsey 1963–1974; Joe Mercer (caretaker) 1974; Don Revie 1974–1977; Ron Greenwood 1977–1982; Bobby Robson 1982–1990; Graham Taylor 1990–1993; Terry Venables (coach) 1994–1996; Glenn Hoddle 1996–1999; Kevin Keegan 1999–2000; Sven-Goran Eriksson 2001–2006; Steve McClaren 2006–07; Fabio Capello from January 2008.

Northern Ireland
Peter Doherty 1951–1952; Bertie Peacock 1962–1967; Billy Bingham 1967–1971; Terry Neill 1971–1975; Dave Clements (player-manager) 1975–1976; Danny Blanchflower 1976–1979; Billy Bingham 1980–1994; Bryan Hamilton 1994–1998; Lawrie McMenemy 1998–1999; Sammy McIlroy 2000–2003; Lawrie Sanchez 2004–2007; Nigel Worthington from June 2007.

Scotland (since 1967)
Bobby Brown 1967–1971; Tommy Docherty 1971–1972; Willie Ormond 1973–1977; Ally MacLeod 1977–1978; Jock Stein 1978–1985; Alex Ferguson (caretaker) 1985–1986 Andy Roxburgh (coach) 1986–1993; Craig Brown 1993–2001; Berti Vogts 2002–2004; Walter Smith 2004–2007; Alex McLeish 2007; George Burley 2008–2009; Craig Levein from December 2009.

Wales (since 1974)
Mike Smith 1974–1979; Mike England 1980–1988; David Williams (caretaker) 1988; Terry Yorath 1988–1993; John Toshack 1994 for one match; Mike Smith 1994–1995; Bobby Gould 1995–1999; Mark Hughes 1999–2004; John Toshack from November 2004.

Republic of Ireland
Liam Tuohy 1971–1972; Johnny Giles 1973–1980 (after period as player-manager); Eoin Hand 1980–1985; Jack Charlton 1986–1996; Mick McCarthy 1996–2002; Brian Kerr 2003–2006; Steve Staunton 2006–07; Giovanni Trapattoni from February 2008.

SOUTH AMERICA

COPA SUDAMERICANA 2009

FIRST ROUND FIRST LEG
Univ de Chile 2, Dep Cali 1
La Equidad 2, Union Espanola 2
Zamora 0, Emelec 1
Alianza 0, Dep Anzoategui 0
LDU Quito 1, Libertad 0
Blooming v River Plate (Uru) not played.
*Abandoned at 0-1 due to crowd trouble. Match awarded
3-0 to River Plate (Uru).*
Cerro Porteno 2, La Paz 0
Fluminense 0, Flamengo 0
Liverpool (Uru) 0, Cienciano 0
Vitoria 2, Coritiba 0
Tigre 2, San Lorenzo 1
River Plate (Arg) 1, Lanus 2
Boca Juniors 1, Velez Sarsfield 1
Atletico MG 1, Goias 1
Atletico PR 0, Botafogo 0

FIRST ROUND SECOND LEG
Dep Cali 0, Univ de Chile 1
Union Espanola 1, La Equidad 0
Emelec 2, Zamora 1
Dep Anzoategui 1, Alianza 2
Libertad 1, LDU Quito 1
River Plate (Uru) 2, Blooming 1
La Paz 1, Cerro Porteno 2
Flamengo 1, Fluminense 1
Cienciano 2, Liverpool (Uru) 0
Coritiba 2, Vitoria 0
Vitoria won 5-3 on penalties.
San Lorenzo 1, Tigre 0
Lanus 1, River Plate (Arg) 1
Velez Sarsfield 1, Boca Juniors 0
Goias 1, Atletico MG 1
Goias won 6-5 on penalties.
Botafogo 3, Atletico PR 2

SECOND ROUND FIRST LEG
River Plate (Uru) 4, Vitoria 1
Internacional 1, Univ de Chile 1
Botafogo 2, Emelec 0

Velez Sarsfield 3, Union Espanola 2
Alianza 2, Fluminense 2
San Lorenzo 3, Cienciano 0
Cerro Porteno 2, Goias 0
LDU Quito 4, Lanus 0

SECOND ROUND SECOND LEG
Vitoria 1, River Plate (Uru) 1
Univ de Chile 1, Internacional 0
Emelec 2, Botafogo 1
Union Espanola 2, Velez Sarsfield 2
Fluminense 4, Alianza 1
Cienciano 0, San Lorenzo 2
Goias 3, Cerro Porteno 1
Lanus 1, LDU Quito 1

QUARTER-FINALS FIRST LEG
Velez Sarsfield 1, LDU Quito 1
Cerro Porteno 2, Botafogo 1
River Plate (Uru) 0, San Lorenzo 1
Fluminense 2 Univ de Chile 2

QUARTER-FINALS SECOND LEG
LDU Quito 2, Velez Sarsfield 1
Botafogo 1, Cerro Porteno 3
San Lorenzo 0, River Plate (Uru) 1
River Plate (Uru) won 7-6 on penalties.
Univ de Chile 0, Fluminense 1

SEMI-FINALS FIRST LEG
River Plate (Uru) 2, LDU Quito 1
Cerro Porteno 0, Fluminense 1

SEMI-FINALS SECOND LEG
LDU Quito 7, River Plate (Uru) 0
Fluminense 2, Cerro Porteno 1

FINAL FIRST LEG
LDU Quito 5, Fluminense 1

FINAL SECOND LEG
Fluminense 3, LDU Quito 0

COPA LIBERTADORES 2010

PRELIMINARY ROUND FIRST LEG
Dep Tachira 1, Libertad 0
Colon 3, Univ Catolica 2
Juan Aurich 2, Estudiantes (Mex) 0
Real Potosi 1, Cruzeiro 1
Newell's Old Boys 0, Emelec 0
Atletico Junior 2, Racing (Uru) 2

PRELIMINARY ROUND SECOND LEG
Libertad 3, Dep Tachira 1
Univ Catolica 3, Colon 2
Univ Catolica won 5-3 on penalties.
Estudiantes (Mex) 1, Juan Aurich 2
Cruzeiro 7, Real Potosi 0
Emelec 2, Newell's Old Boys 1
Racing (Uru) 2, Atletico Junior 0

GROUP 1	P	W	D	L	F	A	Pts
Corinthians	6	5	1	0	9	3	16
Racing (Uru)	6	2	2	2	4	5	8
Independiente	6	1	3	2	3	4	6
Cerro Porteno	6	0	2	4	3	7	2

GROUP 2	P	W	D	L	F	A	Pts
Sao Paulo	6	4	1	1	9	2	13
Once Caldas	6	3	2	1	8	5	11
Monterrey	6	1	3	2	5	8	5
Nacional (Par)	6	1	0	5	3	10	3

GROUP 3	P	W	D	L	F	A	Pts
Estudiantes (Arg)	6	4	1	1	11	5	13
Alianza	6	4	0	2	12	7	12
Juan Aurich	6	2	0	4	7	13	6
Bolivar	6	1	1	4	3	8	4

GROUP 4	P	W	D	L	F	A	Pts
Libertad	6	3	3	0	10	3	12
Universitario	6	2	4	0	5	2	10
Lanus	6	2	2	2	6	6	8
Blooming	6	0	1	5	3	13	1

GROUP 5	P	W	D	L	F	A	Pts
Internacional	6	3	3	0	8	2	12
Dep Quito	6	3	1	2	5	7	10
Cerro (Uru)	6	2	2	2	5	5	8
Emelec	6	0	2	4	2	6	2

GROUP 6	P	W	D	L	F	A	Pts
Nacional (Uru)	6	3	3	0	9	4	12
Banfield	6	3	2	1	13	8	11
Monarcas	6	1	2	3	4	8	5
Dep Cuenca	6	1	1	4	7	13	4

GROUP 7	P	W	D	L	F	A	Pts
Velez Sarsfield	6	4	1	1	10	5	13
Cruzeiro	6	3	2	1	12	6	11
Colo Colo	6	2	2	2	8	10	8
Dep Italia	6	0	1	5	4	13	1

GROUP 8	P	W	D	L	F	A	Pts
Univ de Chile	6	3	3	0	10	6	12
Flamengo	6	3	1	2	11	9	10
Univ Catolica	6	1	4	1	5	5	7
Caracas	6	0	2	4	5	11	2

SECOND ROUND FIRST LEG
Guadalajara 3, Velez Sarsfield 0
San Luis 0, Estudiantes (Arg) 1
Universitario 0, Sao Paulo 0
Flamengo 1, Corinthians 0
Banfield 3, Internacional 1
Cruzeiro 3, Nacional (Uru) 1
Alianza 0, Univ de Chile 1
Once Caldas 0, Libertad 0

SECOND ROUND SECOND LEG
Velez Sarsfield 2, Guadalajara 0
Estudiantes (Arg) 3, San Luis 1
Sao Paulo 0, Universitario 0
Sao Paulo won 3-1 on penalties.
Corinthians 2, Flamengo 1
Internacional 2, Banfield 0

Nacional (Uru) 0, Cruzeiro 3
Univ de Chile 2, Alianza 2
Libertad 2, Once Caldas 1

QUARTER-FINALS FIRST LEG
Guadalajara 3, Libertad 0
Cruzeiro 0, Sao Paulo 2
Flamengo 2, Univ de Chile 3
Internacional 1, Estudiantes (Arg) 0

QUARTER-FINALS SECOND LEG
Libertad 2, Guadalajara 0
Sao Paulo 2, Cruzeiro 0
Univ de Chile 1, Flamengo 2
Estudiantes (Arg) 2, Internacional 1
Competition still being played.

ASIA

AFC CHALLENGE CUP 2010

QUALIFYING STAGE
India, North Korea, Tajikistan qualified for the semi-final stage; group winners and best runners-up also qualify.

PRELIMINARY ROUND
Macao 2, Mongolia 0
Mongolia 3, Macao 1

GROUP A
Bangladesh 1, Cambodia 0
Myanmar 4, Macao 0
Macao 1, Cambodia 2
Bangladesh 1, Myanmar 2
Cambodia 0, Myanmar 1
Bangladesh 3, Macao 0

GROUP B
Turkmenistan 3, Maldives 1
Philippines 1, Bhutan 0
Maldives 3, Philippines 2
Turkmenistan 7, Bhutan 0
Turkmenistan 5, Philippines 0
Maldives 5, Bhutan 0

GROUP C
Nepal 0, Palestine 0
Nepal 1, Kyrgyzstan 1
Kyrgyzstan 1, Palestine 1

GROUP D
Sri Lanka 5, Brunei 1
Taiwan 1, Pakistan 1

Pakistan 6, Brunei 0
Sri Lanka 2, Taiwan 1
Sri Lanka 2, Pakistan 2
Taiwan 5, Brunei 0
Bangladesh qualified as best runners-up. Afghanistan withdrew.

FINAL TOURNAMENT
(in Sri Lanka).

GROUP A	P	W	D	L	F	A	Pts
Tajikistan	3	2	0	1	7	3	6
Myanmar	3	2	0	1	6	4	6
Sri Lanka	3	1	0	2	4	7	3
Bangladesh	3	1	0	2	3	6	3

GROUP B	P	W	D	L	F	A	Pts
North Korea	3	2	1	0	8	1	7
Turkmenistan	3	2	1	0	3	1	7
Kyrgyzstan	3	1	0	2	6	3	3
India	3	0	0	3	1	6	0

SEMI-FINALS
Tajikistan 0, Turkmenistan 2
North Korea 5, Myanmar 0

MATCH FOR THIRD PLACE
Tajikistan 1, Myanmar 0

FINAL
North Korea 1, Turkmenistan 1
North Korea won 5-4 on penalties.

ASIAN NATIONS CUP 2011

PRELIMINARY ROUND
Lebanon 4, Maldives 0
Maldives 1, Lebanon 2

QUALIFYING ROUND
Top two in each group qualify for final tournament; Qatar, Iraq, Saudi Arabia and South Korea, India plus 2010 AFC Challenge Cup winners also qualify.

GROUP A	P	W	D	L	F	A	Pts
Japan	6	5	0	1	17	4	15
Bahrain	6	4	0	2	12	6	12
Yemen	6	2	1	3	7	9	7
Hong Kong	6	0	1	5	1	18	1

GROUP B	P	W	D	L	F	A	Pts
Australia	6	3	2	1	6	4	11
Kuwait	6	2	3	1	6	5	9
Oman	6	2	2	2	4	4	8
Indonesia	6	0	3	3	3	6	3

GROUP C	P	W	D	L	F	A	Pts
UAE	4	3	0	1	7	1	9
Uzbekistan	4	3	0	1	7	3	9
Malaysia	4	0	0	4	2	12	0

GROUP D	P	W	D	L	F	A	Pts
Syria	6	4	2	0	10	2	14
China	6	4	1	1	13	5	13
Vietnam	6	1	2	3	6	11	5
Lebanon	6	0	1	5	2	13	1

GROUP E	P	W	D	L	F	A	Pts
Iran	6	4	1	1	11	2	13
Jordan	6	2	2	2	4	4	8
Thailand	6	1	3	2	3	3	6
Singapore	6	2	0	4	6	15	6

FINAL TOURNAMENT IN QATAR
To be completed.

NORTH AMERICA

MAJOR LEAGUE SOCCER 2009

EASTERN CONFERENCE

	P	W	D	L	F	A	Pts
Columbus Crew	30	13	10	7	41	31	49
Chicago Fire	30	11	12	7	39	34	45
New England Rev	30	11	9	10	33	37	42
DC United	30	9	13	8	43	44	40
Toronto	30	10	9	11	37	46	39
Kansas City Wizards	30	8	9	13	33	42	33
New York Red Bulls	30	5	6	19	27	47	21

WESTERN CONFERENCE

	P	W	D	L	F	A	Pts
Los Angeles Galaxy	30	12	12	6	36	31	48
Houston Dynamo	30	13	9	8	39	29	48
Seattle Sounders	30	12	11	7	38	29	47
Chivas USA	30	13	6	11	34	31	45
Real Salt Lake	30	11	7	12	43	35	40
Colorado Rapids	30	10	10	10	42	38	40
FC Dallas	30	11	6	13	50	47	39
San Jose Earthquakes	30	7	9	14	36	50	30

EASTERN SEMI-FINALS FIRST LEG

Real Salt Lake v Columbus Crew	1-0
New England Revolution v Chicago Fire	2-1

EASTERN SEMI-FINALS SECOND LEG

Columbus Crew v Real Salt Lake	2-3
Chicago Fire v New England Revolution	2-0

EASTERN FINAL

Chicago Fire v Real Salt Lake	0-0

aet; Real Salt Lake won 5-4 on penalties.

WESTERN SEMI-FINALS FIRST LEG

Seattle Sounders v Houston Dynamo	0-0
Chivas USA v Los Angeles Galaxy	2-2

WESTERN SEMI-FINALS SECOND LEG

Houston Dynamo v Seattle Sounders	1-0
Los Angeles Galaxy v Chivas USA	1-0

WESTERN FINAL

Los Angeles Galaxy v Houston Dynamo	2-0

MLS CUP 2009

Los Angeles Galaxy v Real Salt Lake	1-1

Real Salt Lake won 5-4 on penalties.

AFRICA

AFRICAN NATIONS CUP 2010 (Finals held in Angola)

GROUP A

Angola 4, Mali 4 — Angola 2, Malawi 0
Malawi 3, Algeria 0 — Angola 0, Algeria 0
Mali 0, Algeria 1 — Mali 3, Malawi 1

	P	W	D	L	F	A	Pts
Angola	3	1	2	0	6	4	5
Algeria	3	1	1	1	3	4	4
Mali	3	1	1	1	7	6	4
Malawi	3	1	0	2	4	5	3

GROUP B

Ivory Coast 0, Burkina Faso 0 — Ivory Coast 3, Ghana 1
Togo disqualified. — Burkina Faso 0, Ghana 1

	P	W	D	L	F	A	Pts
Ivory Coast	2	1	1	0	3	1	4
Ghana	2	1	0	1	2	3	3
Burkina Faso	2	0	1	1	0	1	1
Togo disqualified.							

GROUP C

Egypt 3, Nigeria 1 — Egypt 2, Mozambique 0
Mozambique 2, Benin 2 — Benin 0, Egypt 2
Nigeria 1, Benin 0 — Nigeria 3, Mozambique 0

	P	W	D	L	F	A	Pts
Egypt	3	3	0	0	7	1	9
Nigeria	3	2	0	1	5	3	6
Benin	3	0	1	2	2	5	1
Mozambique	3	0	1	2	2	7	1

GROUP D

Cameroon 0, Gabon 1 — Cameroon 3, Zambia 2
Zambia 1, Tunisia 1 — Gabon 1, Zambia 2
Gabon 0, Tunisia 0 — Cameroon 2, Tunisia 2

	P	W	D	L	F	A	Pts
Zambia	3	1	1	1	5	5	4
Cameroon	3	1	1	1	5	5	4
Gabon	3	1	1	1	2	2	4
Tunisia	3	0	3	0	3	3	3

QUARTER-FINALS

Angola 0, Ghana 1
Ivory Coast 2, Algeria 3
Egypt 3, Cameroon 1
Zambia 0, Nigeria 0
aet; Nigeria won 5-4 on penalties.

SEMI-FINALS

Ghana 1, Nigeria 0
Algeria 0, Egypt 4

MATCH FOR THIRD PLACE

Nigeria 1, Algeria 0

FINAL IN LUANDA

Ghana (0) 0
Egypt (0) 1 *(Gedo 85)*   45,000

Ghana: Kingson; Inkoom, Addy, Vorsah, Sarpei, Badu, Annan, Ayew, Asamoah, Opoku (Addo 89), Gyan (Adyiah 87).

Egypt: El Hadary; Gomaa, Said, Fathi (Moatasem 89), El Mohamady, Ghaly, Hosny, Hassan, Moawad (Abdelshafi 57), Zidan, Meteeb (Nagy 70).

Referee: K. Coulibaly (Mali).

FIFA UNDER-20 WORLD CUP

Finals in Egypt

GROUP A
Egypt 4, Trinidad & Tobago 1
Paraguay 0, Italy 0
Italy 2, Trinidad & Tobago 1
Egypt 1, Paraguay 2
Trinidad & Tobago 0, Paraguay 0
Italy 2, Egypt 4

GROUP B
Nigeria 0, Venezuela 1
Spain 8, Tahiti 0
Nigeria 0, Spain 2
Tahiti 0, Venezuela 8
Venezuela 0, Spain 3
Tahiti 0, Nigeria 5

GROUP C
USA 0, Germany 3
Cameroon 2, South Korea 0
South Korea 1, Germany 1
USA 4, Cameroon 1
Germany 3, Cameroon 0
South Korea 3, USA 0

GROUP D
Ghana 2, Uzbekistan 1
England 0, Uruguay 1
Uruguay 3, Uzbekistan 0
Ghana 4, England 0
Uruguay 2, Ghana 2
Uzbekistan 1, England 1

GROUP E
Brazil 5, Costa Rica 0
Czech Republic 2, Australia 1
Australia 0, Costa Rica 3
Brazil 0, Czech Republic 0
Costa Rica 2, Czech Republic 3
Australia 1, Brazil 3

GROUP F
UAE 2, South Africa 2
Honduras 3, Hungary 0
Hungary 4, South Africa 0
UAE 1, Honduras 0
Hungary 2, UAE 0
South Africa 2, Honduras 0

FIRST ROUND
Paraguay 0, South Korea 3
Ghana 2, South Africa 1
Spain 1, Italy 3
Hungary 2, Czech Republic 2
Hungary won 4-3 on penalties
Brazil 3, Uruguay 1
Germany 3, Nigeria 2
Venezuela 1, UAE 2
Egypt 0, Costa Rica 2

QUARTER-FINALS
South Korea 2, Ghana 3
Italy 2, Hungary 3
Brazil 2, Germany 1
UAE 1, Costa Rica 2

SEMI-FINALS
Ghana 3, Hungary 2
Brazil 1, Costa Rica 0

MATCH FOR THIRD PLACE
Hungary 1, Costa Rica 1
Hungary won 2-0 on penalties.

FINAL
Ghana 0, Brazil 0
Ghana won 4-3 on penalties.

UEFA UNDER-19 CHAMPIONSHIP 2009–10

Finals in Ukraine

GROUP A

England v Switzerland	1-1
Ukraine v Slovenia	0-0
Slovenia v Switzerland	1-2
Ukraine v England	2-2
Switzerland v Ukraine	0-1
Slovenia v England	1-7

GROUP B

France v Serbia	1-1
Turkey v Spain	1-2
France v Turkey	1-1
Serbia v Spain	2-1
Spain v France	0-1
Serbia v Turkey	1-0

SEMI-FINALS

England v France	3-1
Serbia v Ukraine	1-3

FINAL

2 Aug
England (0) 0
Ukraine (1) 2 *(Garmash 5, Korkishko 50)*   25,000
England: Steele; Trippier, Mattock, Gosling, Walker, Welbeck (Ranger 63), Drinkwater (Tutte 55), Delfouneso, Lansbury, Bennett, Briggs (Hoyte 56).
Ukraine: Levchenko; Kushnirov, Partsvaniya, Kryvtsov, Korkishko, Petrov (Yeremenko 90), Garmash, Shakhov, Rybalka, Kaverin (Shevchuk 80), Chaykovskiy.

UEFA UNDER-17 CHAMPIONSHIP 2009–10

Finals in Liechtenstein

ELITE ROUND

GROUP A
France 1, Spain 2
Portugal 3, Switzerland 0
Spain 4, Switzerland 0
France 1, Portugal 0
Switzerland 1, France 3
Spain 2, Portugal 0

GROUP B
Greece 1, Turkey 3
England 3, Czech Republic 1
Turkey 1, Czech Republic 1
Greece 0, England 1
Czech Republic 0, Greece 0
Turkey 1, England 2

SEMI-FINALS
England 2, France 1
Spain 3, Turkey 1

FINAL

30 May

England (2) 2 *(Wisdom 30, Wickham 42)*
Spain (1) 1 *(Wisdom 22 (og)* 3990
England: Butland; Chalobah, Garbutt, Pilatos, Wisdom, Coady, Keane (Thorne 67), McEachran (Thorpe 79), Afobe (Hall 73), Wickham, Barkley.
Spain: Ortola; Campabadal (Bernat 73), Ramalho, Alvarez Orti (Hervias 46), Deulofeu, Darder, Rodriguez, Campana, Alcacer, Puerto.

FIFA UNDER-17 WORLD CUP 2009–10

Finals in Nigeria

GROUP A
Nigera 3, Germany 3
Honduras 0, Argentina 1
Argentina 2, Germany 1
Nigeria 1, Honduras 0
Germany 3, Honduras 1
Argentina 1, Nigeria 2

GROUP B
Brazil 3, Japan 2
Mexico 0, Switzerland 2
Switzerland 4, Japan 3
Brazil 0, Mexico 1
Japan 0, Mexico 2
Switzerland 1, Brazil 0

GROUP C
Iran 2, Gambia 0
Colombia 2, Holland 1
Holland 2, Gambia 1
Iran 0, Colombia 0
Gambia 2, Colombia 2
Holland 0, Iran 1

GROUP D
Turkey 1, Burkina Faso 0
Costa Rica 1, New Zealand 1
New Zealand 1, Burkina Faso 1
Turkey 4, Costa Rica 1
Burkina Faso 4, Costa Rica 1
New Zealand 1, Turkey 1

GROUP E
UAE 2, Malawi 0
Spain 2, USA 1
USA 1, Malawi 0
UAE 1, Spain 3
Malawi 1, Spain 4
USA 1, UAE 0

GROUP F
Uruguay 1, South Korea 3
Algeria 0, Italy 1
Italy 2, South Korea 1
Uruguay 2, Algeria 0
South Korea 2, Algeria 0
Italy 0, Uruguay 0

FIRST ROUND
Argentina 2, Colombia 3
Turkey 2, UAE 0
Switzerland 4, Germany 3
Italy 2, USA 1
Spain 4, Burkina Faso 1
Iran 1, Uruguay 2
Mexico 1, South Korea 1
South Korea won 5-3 on penalties.
Nigeria 5, New Zealand 0

QUARTER-FINALS
Colombia 1, Turkey 1
Colombia won 5-3 on penalties.
Switzerland 2, Italy 1
Spain 3, Uruguay 3
Spain won 4-2 on penalties.
South Korea 1, Nigeria 3

SEMI-FINALS
Colombia 0, Switzerland 4
Spain 1, Nigeria 3

MATCH FOR THIRD PLACE
Colombia 0, Spain 1

FINAL
Switzerland 1, Nigeria 0

ENGLAND UNDER-21 RESULTS 1976–2010

EC *UEFA Competition for Under-21 Teams*

Year	Date		Venue		

v ALBANIA — Eng / Alb

				Eng	Alb
EC1989	Mar	7	Shkroda	2	1
EC1989	April	25	Ipswich	2	0
EC2001	Mar	27	Tirana	1	0
EC2001	Sept	4	Middlesbrough	5	0

v ANGOLA — Eng / Ang

				Eng	Ang
1995	June	10	Toulon	1	0
1996	May	28	Toulon	0	2

v ARGENTINA — Eng / Arg

				Eng	Arg
1998	May	18	Toulon	0	2
2000	Feb	22	Fulham	1	0

v AUSTRIA — Eng / Aus

				Eng	Aus
1994	Oct	11	Kapfenberg	3	1
1995	Nov	14	Middlesbrough	2	1
EC2004	Sept	3	Krems	2	0
EC2005	Oct	7	Leeds	1	2

v AZERBAIJAN — Eng / Az

				Eng	Az
EC2004	Oct	12	Baku	0	0
EC2005	Mar	29	Middlesbrough	2	0
2009	June	8	Milton Keynes	7	0

v BELGIUM — Eng / Bel

				Eng	Bel
1994	June	5	Marseille	2	1
1996	May	24	Toulon	1	0

v BRAZIL — Eng / B

				Eng	B
1993	June	11	Toulon	0	0
1995	June	6	Toulon	0	2
1996	June	1	Toulon	1	2

v BULGARIA — Eng / Bul

				Eng	Bul
EC1979	June	5	Pernik	3	1
EC1979	Nov	20	Leicester	5	0
1989	June	5	Toulon	2	3
EC1998	Oct	9	West Ham	1	0
EC1999	June	8	Vratsa	1	0
EC2007	Sept	11	Sofia	2	0
EC2007	Nov	16	Milton Keynes	2	0

v CROATIA — Eng / Cro

				Eng	Cro
1996	Apr	23	Sunderland	0	1
2003	Aug	19	West Ham	0	3

v CZECHOSLOVAKIA — Eng / Cz

				Eng	Cz
1990	May	28	Toulon	2	1
1992	May	26	Toulon	1	2
1993	June	9	Toulon	1	1

v CZECH REPUBLIC — Eng / CzR

				Eng	CzR
1998	Nov	17	Ipswich	0	1
EC2007	June	11	Arnhem	0	0
2008	Nov	18	Bramall Lane	2	0

v DENMARK — Eng / Den

				Eng	Den
EC1978	Sept	19	Hvidovre	2	1
EC1979	Sept	11	Watford	1	0
EC1982	Sept	21	Hvidovre	4	1
EC1983	Sept	20	Norwich	4	1
EC1986	Mar	12	Copenhagen	1	0
EC1986	Mar	26	Manchester	1	1
1988	Sept	13	Watford	0	0
1994	Mar	8	Brentford	1	0
1999	Oct	8	Bradford	4	1
2005	Aug	16	Herning	1	0

v EQUADOR — Eng / E

				Eng	E
2009	Feb	10	Malaga	2	3

v FINLAND — Eng / Fin

				Eng	Fin
EC1977	May	26	Helsinki	1	0
EC1977	Oct	12	Hull	8	1
EC1984	Oct	16	Southampton	1	0
EC1985	May	21	Mikkeli	1	3
EC2000	Oct	10	Valkeakoski	2	2
EC2001	Mar	23	Barnsley	4	0
EC2009	June	15	Halmstad	2	1

v FRANCE — Eng / Fra

				Eng	Fra
EC1984	Feb	28	Sheffield	6	1
EC1984	Mar	28	Rouen	1	0
1987	June	11	Toulon	0	2
EC1988	April	13	Besancon	2	4
EC1988	April	27	Highbury	2	2
1988	June	12	Toulon	2	4
1990	May	23	Toulon	7	3
1991	June	3	Toulon	1	0
1992	May	28	Toulon	0	0
1993	June	15	Toulon	1	0
1994	May	31	Aubagne	0	3
1995	June	10	Toulon	0	2
1998	May	14	Toulon	1	1
1999	Feb	9	Derby	2	1
EC2005	Nov	11	Tottenham	1	1
EC2005	Nov	15	Nancy	1	2
2009	Mar	31	Nottingham	0	2

v GEORGIA — Eng / Geo

				Eng	Geo
EC1996	Nov	8	Batumi	1	0
EC1997	April	29	Charlton	0	0
2000	Aug	31	Middlesbrough	6	1

v GERMANY — Eng / Ger

				Eng	Ger
1991	Sept	10	Scunthorpe	2	1
EC2000	Oct	6	Derby	1	1
EC2001	Aug	31	Frieburg	2	1
2005	Mar	25	Hull	2	2
2005	Sept	6	Mainz	1	1
EC2006	Oct	6	Coventry	1	0
EC2006	Oct	10	Leverkusen	2	0
EC2009	June	22	Halmstad	1	1
EC2009	June	29	Malmo	0	4

v EAST GERMANY — Eng / EG

				Eng	EG
EC1980	April	16	Sheffield	1	2
EC1980	April	23	Jena	0	1

v WEST GERMANY — Eng / WG

				Eng	WG
EC1982	Sept	21	Sheffield	3	1
EC1982	Oct	12	Bremen	2	3
1987	Sept	8	Ludenscheid	0	2

v GREECE — Eng / Gre

				Eng	Gre
EC1982	Nov	16	Piraeus	0	1
EC1983	Mar	29	Portsmouth	2	1
1989	Feb	7	Patras	0	1
EC1997	Nov	13	Heraklion	0	2
EC1997	Dec	17	Norwich	4	2
EC2001	June	5	Athens	1	3
EC2001	Oct	5	Ewood Park	2	1
EC2009	Sept	8	Tripoli	1	1
EC2010	Mar	3	Doncaster	1	2

v HOLLAND — Eng / H

				Eng	H
EC1993	April	27	Portsmouth	3	0
EC1993	Oct	12	Utrecht	1	1
2001	Aug	14	Reading	4	0
EC2001	Nov	9	Utrecht	2	2
EC2001	Nov	13	Derby	1	0
2004	Feb	17	Hull	3	2
2005	Feb	8	Derby	1	2
2006	Nov	14	Alkmaar	1	0
EC2007	June	20	Heerenveen	1	1
2009	Aug	11	Groningen	0	0

			v HUNGARY	Eng	Hun
EC1981	June	5	Keszthely	2	1
EC1981	Nov	17	Nottingham	2	0
EC1983	April	26	Newcastle	1	0
EC1983	Oct	11	Nyiregyhaza	2	0
1990	Sept	11	Southampton	3	1
1992	May	12	Budapest	2	2
1999	April	27	Budapest	2	2

			v REPUBLIC OF IRELAND	Eng	RoI
1981	Feb	25	Liverpool	1	0
1985	Mar	25	Portsmouth	3	2
1989	June	9	Toulon	0	0
EC1990	Nov	13	Cork	3	0
EC1991	Mar	26	Brentford	3	0
1994	Nov	15	Newcastle	1	0
1995	Mar	27	Dublin	2	0
EC2007	Oct	16	Cork	3	0
EC2008	Feb	5	Southampton	3	0

			v ITALY	Eng	Italy
EC1978	Mar	8	Manchester	2	1
EC1978	April	5	Rome	0	0
EC1984	April	18	Manchester	3	1
EC1984	May	2	Florence	0	1
EC1986	April	9	Pisa	0	2
EC1986	April	23	Swindon	1	1
EC1997	Feb	12	Bristol	1	0
EC1997	Oct	10	Rieti	1	0
EC2000	May	27	Bratislava	0	2
2000	Nov	14	Monza*	0	0
2002	Mar	26	Valley Parade	1	1
EC2002	May	20	Basle	1	2
2003	Feb	11	Pisa	0	1
2007	Mar	24	Wembley	3	3
EC2007	June	14	Arnhem	2	2

Abandoned 11 mins; fog.

			v ISRAEL	Eng	Isr
1985	Feb	27	Tel Aviv	2	1

			v LATVIA	Eng	Lat
1995	April	25	Riga	1	0
1995	June	7	Burnley	4	0

			v LITHUANIA	Eng	Lith
EC2009	Nov	17	Vilnius	0	0

			v LUXEMBOURG	Eng	Lux
EC1998	Oct	13	Greven Macher	5	0
EC1999	Sept	3	Reading	5	0

			v MACEDONIA	Eng	M
EC2002	Oct	15	Reading	3	1
EC2003	Sept	5	Skopje	1	1
EC2009	Sept	4	Prilep	2	1
EC2009	Oct	9	Coventry	6	3

			v MALAYSIA	Eng	Mal
1995	June	8	Toulon	2	0

			v MEXICO	Eng	Mex
1988	June	5	Toulon	2	1
1991	May	29	Toulon	6	0
1992	May	25	Toulon	1	1
2001	May	24	Leicester	3	0

			v MOLDOVA	Eng	Mol
EC1996	Aug	31	Chisinau	2	0
EC1997	Sept	9	Wycombe	1	0
EC2006	Aug	15	Ipswich	2	2

			v MONTENEGRO	Eng	M
EC2007	Sept	7	Podgorica	3	0
EC2007	Oct	12	Leicester	1	0

			v MOROCCO	Eng	Mor
1987	June	7	Toulon	2	0
1988	June	9	Toulon	1	0

			v NORWAY	Eng	Nor
EC1977	June	1	Bergen	2	1
EC1977	Sept	6	Brighton	6	0
1980	Sept	9	Southampton	3	0
1981	Sept	8	Drammen	0	0
EC1992	Oct	13	Peterborough	0	2
EC1993	June	1	Stavanger	1	1
1995	Oct	10	Stavanger	2	2
2006	Feb	28	Reading	3	1
2009	Mar	27	Sandefjord	5	0

			v POLAND	Eng	Pol
EC1982	Mar	17	Warsaw	2	1
EC1982	April	7	West Ham	2	2
EC1989	June	2	Plymouth	2	1
EC1989	Oct	10	Jastrzebie	3	1
EC1990	Oct	16	Tottenham	0	1
EC1991	Nov	12	Pila	1	2
EC1993	May	28	Zdroj	4	1
EC1993	Sept	7	Millwall	1	2
EC1996	Oct	8	Wolverhampton	0	0
EC1997	May	30	Katowice	1	1
EC1999	Mar	26	Southampton	5	0
EC1999	Sept	7	Plock	1	3
EC2004	Sept	7	Rybnik	3	1
EC2005	Oct	11	Hillsborough	4	1
2008	Mar	25	Wolverhampton	0	0

			v PORTUGAL	Eng	Por
1987	June	13	Toulon	0	0
1990	May	21	Toulon	0	1
1993	June	7	Toulon	2	0
1994	June	7	Toulon	2	0
EC1994	Sept	6	Leicester	0	0
1995	Sept	2	Lisbon	0	2
1996	May	30	Toulon	1	3
2000	Apr	16	Stoke	0	1
EC2002	May	22	Zurich	1	3
EC2003	Mar	28	Rio Major	2	4
EC2003	Sept	9	Everton	1	2
EC2008	Nov	20	Agueda	1	1
2008	Sept	5	Wembley	2	0
EC2009	Nov	14	Wembley	1	0

			v ROMANIA	Eng	Rom
EC1980	Oct	14	Ploesti	0	4
EC1981	April	28	Swindon	3	0
EC1985	April	30	Brasov	0	0
EC1985	Sept	10	Ipswich	3	0
2007	Aug	21	Bristol	1	1

			v RUSSIA	Eng	Rus
1994	May	30	Bandol	2	0

			v SAN MARINO	Eng	SM
EC1993	Feb	16	Luton	6	0
EC1993	Nov	17	San Marino	4	0

			v SENEGAL	Eng	Sen
1989	June	7	Toulon	6	1
1991	May	27	Toulon	2	1

			v SERBIA	Eng	Ser
EC2007	June	17	Nijmegen	2	0

			v SERBIA-MONTENEGRO	Eng	S-M
2003	June	2	Hull	3	2

			v SCOTLAND	Eng	Sco
1977	April	27	Sheffield	1	0
EC1980	Feb	12	Coventry	2	1
EC1980	Mar	4	Aberdeen	0	0
EC1982	April	19	Glasgow	1	0
EC1982	April	28	Manchester	1	1
EC1988	Feb	16	Aberdeen	1	0
EC1988	Mar	22	Nottingham	1	0
1993	June	13	Toulon	1	0

v SLOVAKIA

				Eng	Slo
EC2002	June	1	Bratislava	0	2
EC2002	Oct	11	Trnava	4	0
EC2003	June	10	Sunderland	2	0
2007	June	5	Norwich	5	0

v SLOVENIA

				Eng	Slo
2000	Feb	12	Nova Gorica	1	0
2008	Aug	19	Hull	2	1

v SOUTH AFRICA

				Eng	SA
1998	May	16	Toulon	3	1

v SPAIN

				Eng	Spa
EC1984	May	17	Seville	1	0
EC1984	May	24	Sheffield	2	0
1987	Feb	18	Burgos	2	1
1992	Sept	8	Burgos	1	0
2001	Feb	27	Birmingham	0	4
2004	Nov	16	Alcala	0	1
2007	Feb	6	Derby	2	2
EC2009	June	18	Gothenburg	2	0

v SWEDEN

				Eng	Swe
1979	June	9	Vasteras	2	1
1986	Sept	9	Ostersund	1	1
EC1988	Oct	18	Coventry	1	1
EC1989	Sept	5	Uppsala	0	1
EC1998	Sept	4	Sundvall	2	0
EC1999	June	4	Huddersfield	3	0
2004	Mar	30	Kristiansund	2	2
EC2009	June	26	Gothenburg	3	3

v SWITZERLAND

				Eng	Swit
EC1980	Nov	18	Ipswich	5	0
EC1981	May	31	Neuenburg	0	0
1988	May	28	Lausanne	1	1
1996	April	1	Swindon	0	0
1998	Mar	24	Brugglifeld	0	2
EC2002	May	17	Zurich	2	1
EC2006	Sept	6	Lucerne	3	2

v TURKEY

				Eng	Tur
EC1984	Nov	13	Bursa	0	0
EC1985	Oct	15	Bristol	3	0
EC1987	April	28	Izmir	0	0
EC1987	Oct	13	Sheffield	1	1
EC1991	April	30	Izmir	2	2
1991	Oct	15	Reading	2	0
EC1992	Nov	17	Orient	0	1
EC1993	Mar	30	Izmir	0	0
EC2000	May	29	Bratislava	6	0
EC2003	April	1	Newcastle	1	1
EC2003	Oct	10	Istanbul	0	1

v UKRAINE

				Eng	Uk
2004	Aug	17	Middlesbrough	3	1

v USA

				Eng	USA
1989	June	11	Toulon	0	2
1994	June	2	Toulon	3	0

v USSR

				Eng	USSR
1987	June	9	Toulon	0	0
1988	June	7	Toulon	1	0
1990	May	25	Toulon	2	1
1991	May	31	Toulon	2	1

v WALES

				Eng	Wales
1976	Dec	15	Wolverhampton	0	0
1979	Feb	6	Swansea	1	0
1990	Dec	5	Tranmere	0	0
EC2004	Oct	8	Blackburn	2	0
EC2005	Sept	2	Wrexham	4	0
2008	May	5	Wrexham	2	0
EC2008	Oct	10	Cardiff	3	2
EC2008	Oct	14	Villa Park	2	2

v YUGOSLAVIA

				Eng	Yugo
EC1978	April	19	Novi Sad	1	2
EC1978	May	2	Manchester	1	1
EC1986	Nov	11	Peterborough	1	1
EC1987	Nov	10	Zemun	5	1
EC2000	Mar	29	Barcelona	3	0
2002	Sept	6	Bolton	1	1

ENGLAND C 2009–10

15 Sept

Hungary 1 *(Srekeres 26)*

England 1 *(Briscoe 41)*

(in Szekesfehervar).
England: Roberts (Welch 80); Reynolds (Vaughan 59), Rents, Garner, Jarvis, Cadmore (McFadzean 70), Briscoe (Simpson 59), Nix, Wright, Holroyd, Knight-Percival (Green 84).

18 Nov

Poland Under-23 1 *(Janczyk 45)*

England 2 *(Holroyd 32, Barnes-Homer 74)*

(in Gradıszk Wielpolski).
England: Roberts (Hedge 86); Densmore, Newton, Cadmore, Charles, Howells, Porter (Reason 73), Jarvis, Wright (Shaw 60), Holroyd, Brodie (Barnes-Homer 66).

26 May

Republic of Ireland Under-23 1 *(Madden 67)*

England 2 *(Fleming 27, Porter 63)*   1570

(in Waterford).
England: Roberts; Densmore, Cadmore, McFadzean, Newton, Morgan-Smith (Obeng 81), Gregory, Fleming (Jarvis 74), Deering (Rodman 90), Barnes-Homer, Porter (Hall 84).
Republic of Ireland: Quigley; Mulcahy, Breen, Browne (Kelly 36), Powell, Finn (Amond 86), O'Donnell (Bolger 63), Chambers, Gaynor (McCabe 59), Byrne (Madden 46), Dennehy.

BRITISH AND IRISH UNDER-21 TEAMS 2009–10

■ *Denotes player sent off.*

ENGLAND

Groningen, 11 August 2009, 6000
Holland (0) 0
England (0) 0
England: Loach (Fielding 46); Richards (Naughton 58), Tomkins, Mancienne, Gibbs (Bertrand 58), Rose, Stanislaus (Sears 83), Cattermole (Carroll 71), Delph (Wilshere 58), Rodwell (Smalling 58), Vaughan (Sturridge 46).

Prilep, 4 September 2009
Macdonia (1) 1 *(Ibraimi 34)*
England (0) 2 *(Sears 68, Cattermole 83 (pen))*
England: Loach; Gibbs, Mancienne, Naughton, Tomkins, Cattermole, Muamba (Sears 46), Rodwell, Rose (Wilshere 72), Sturridge, Stanislaus (Cleverley 83).

Tripoli, 8 September 2009, 2678
Greece (1) 1 *(Ninis 41)*
England (1) 1 *(Sturridge 5)*
England: Loach; Naughton, Gibbs, Muamba, Tomkins, Mancienne, Wilshere, Rodwell (Addison 56), Sturridge (Welbeck 28) (Sears 75), Rose, Cleverley.

Coventry, 9 October 2009, 20,074
England (2) 6 *(Gibbs 22, Richards 29, Carroll 54, 87, Hines 67, 90)*
Macedonia (1) 3 *(Muarem 42, Ibraimi 53, Gibbs 58 (og))*
England: Loach; Richards, Gibbs, Tomkins, Mancienne, Rodwell, Cleverley, Wilshere, Rose (Muamba 69), Carroll (Welbeck 90), Walcott (Hines 46).

Wembley, 14 November 2009, 33,833
England (1) 1 *(Rose 40)*
Portugal (0) 0
England: Loach; Mancienne (Naughton 76), Bertrand, Muamba, Richards, Smalling, Cleverley, Delph (Gosling 90⁺, Carroll, Gibbs, Rose (Cork 76).

Vilnius, 7 November 2009
Lithuania (0) 0
England (0) 0
England. Loach; Gibbs (Bertrand 21), Mancienne, Richards, Smalling, Cleverley, Delph, Muamba (Hines 64), Rose, Carroll, Sturridge (Lansbury 79).

Doncaster, 3 March 2010, 9708
England (0) 1 *(Delfouneso 79)*
Greece (1) 2 *(Papadopoulos K 28, Papadopoulos G 48)*
England: Loach; Walker, Richards, Smalling (Delfouneso 74), Bertrand, Muamba (Sturridge 54), Wilshere, Cattermole, Rodwell, Cleverley (Gosling 87), Carroll.

SCOTLAND

Maria Enzersdorf, 5 September 2009, 1500
Austria (0) 1 *(Weimann 57)*
Scotland (0) 0
Scotland: Martin; Caddis, Mitchell, Hanlon, Scobbie, Coutts (Fleck 64), Arfield, McDonald, Murphy (Loy 86), Maguire, McGinn (Bannan 64).

Paisley, 10 October 2009, 4017
Scotland (0) 1 *(Murphy 90)*
Belarus (0) 0
Scotland: Martin; Caddis, Mitchell, Perry, Hanlon, McGinn, Gray (Murphy 67), McDonald, Maguire, Goodwillie (Loy 90), Bannan.

Baku, 14 November 2009, 500
Azerbaijan (0) 0
Scotland (2) 4 *(Murphy 26, 54, Arfield 36, Loy 83)*
Scotland: Martin; Caddis, Mitchell, Perry, Hanlon, Coutts, Arfield, McDonald, Bannan, Maguire (Loy 79), Murphy (Griffiths 70).

Falkirk, 2 March 2010, 2793
Scotland (1) 2 *(Maguire 32 (pen), Griffiths 66)*
Azerbaijan (1) 2 *(Hajyev 13, Abdullayev 63) Akhumdov■*
Scotland: Martin; Caddis, Easton, Scobbie, Perry, Coutts (McGinn 76), Arfield, McDonald, Maguire, Goodwillie (Griffiths 65), Murphy.

WALES

Wrexham, 12 August 2009, 1403
Wales (3) 4 *(MacDonald 16, Evans C 36, 42, King 90)*
Hungary (1) 1 *(Korcsmar 18)*
Wales: Maxwell; Blake, Taylor N, King, Ribeiro, Morris, Bradley, Evans C, Marc Williams (Thomas C 71), MacDonald, Partington (Richards 58).

Swansea, 4 September 2009, 5366
Wales (1) 2 *(Ribeiro 8, Ramsey 60)*
Italy (1) 1 *(Paloschi 23)*
Wales: Maxwell; Eardley, Taylor N, King, Blake (Morris 50), Ribeiro, Bradley, Ramsey, Vokes, Church (Evans C 46), MacDonald.

Wrexham, 10 October 2009
Wales (0) 2 *(Evans C 56, 90)*
Bosnia (0) 0
Wales: Maxwell; Morris, Taylor N, King, Blake, Ribeiro (Wilson 52), Richards (Chamberlain 56), Craig Bodin 73), Marc Williams, Evans C, MacDonald.

Sarajevo, 18 November 2009, 300
Bosnia (1) 2 *(Haurdic 30, 66)*
Wales (1) 1 *(Allen 5)*
Wales: Maxwell; Taylor N, King, Blake, Ribeiro, Allen, Bradley, Church, Evans C, Matthews (Richards 46), Vokes (MacDonald 57).

Parndorf, 18 May 2010, 750
Austria (0) 1 *(Grunwald 61)*
Wales (0) 0
Wales. Cornell (Maxwell 60); Richards (Craig 71), Taylor N (Alfei 60), Bradley, Morris, Ribeiro, Partington, Robson-Kanu, Vokes, Taylor J (Bodin 46), Chamberlain (Doble 46).

NORTHERN IRELAND

Guarda, 12 August 2009
Portugal (0) 2 *(Ceantrao, Yazlade)*
Northern Ireland (0) 1 *(Duffy 74 (pen))*
Northern Ireland: O'Neill; Casement, Duffy, Flynn■, Magnay, Lowry (Norwood 46), Evans C (Shroot 56), Garrett, Ferguson (Donnelly 46) (Gibb 80), Magennis, McGurk (Lawrie 40).

Jablonec, 4 September 2009
Czech Republic (0) 2 *(Gecov 72, Dockal 83)*
Northern Ireland (0) 0   2723
Northern Ireland: Carson; Hodson, Cathcart (Lowry 82), Duffy, Casement (Lafferty 70), Bryan (Donnelly 67), Weir, Garrett, McQuoid, Kee, Magennis.

Coleraine, 8 September 2009
Northern Ireland (0) 2 *(Magennis 58, 75)*
Iceland (4) 6 *(Vidarsson 14 (pen), Gudmundsson J 32, 57, Finnbogason 42, Gislason 44, 61)*
Northern Ireland: Carson; Hodson, Taylor (Jarvis 73), Weir, Duffy, Casement, Carvill, Garrett, McQuoid, McKay (Magennis 46), Shroot (Donnelly 46).

Grindavik, 13 October 2009
Iceland (0) 2 *(Gudmundsson 56, Josefsson 71)*
Northern Ireland (0) 1 *(Lawrie 80)*   30
Northern Ireland: O'Neill; Flynn, Cathcart, Dudgeon, McClean, McQuoid (McKay 69), Chapman, Evans C, Lawrie, Kee, Magennis.

Oval (Belfast), 12 November 2009
Northern Ireland (0) 1 *(Norwood 90)*
Germany (0) 1 *(Choupo-Moting 89)*
Northern Ireland: Carson; Hodson, McGivern, Evans C, Flynn, Cathcart, Weir, Norwood, Kee (Magennis 69), Lawrie, Dudgeon (McClean 34).

Ballymena, 17 November 2009
Northern Ireland (0) 1 *(Norwood 82)*
Czech Republic (2) 2 *(Zeman 36, Kozak 38)*
Northern Ireland: Carson; Hodson (McQuoid 46), Cathcart, Flynn, McGivern, Weir (Casement 71), Evans C, Norwood, McClean, Kee, Lawrie (Ferguson 80).

Serravale, 2 March 2010
San Marino (0) 0
Northern Ireland (2) 3 *(Norwood 24, 78, Lawrie 38)*   120
Northern Ireland: O'Neill; Hodson, McLaughlin P, Evans C (Boyce 46), Flynn, McLaughlin C, Weir (Jarvis 84), Norwood, Kee (Bryan 58), McKay, Lawrie.

REPUBLIC OF IRELAND

Rakvere, 9 September 2009
Estonia (1) 1 *(Saag 4)*
Republic of Ireland (1) 1 *(Sheridan 7)*
Republic of Ireland: Redmond; Davies, Moloney, Spillane, Bermingham, Gleeson, McCarthy (Collins 67), Garvan, Judge, Sheridan, O'Shea (Scannell 73).

Tallaght (Dublin), 9 October 2009
Republic of Ireland (1) 1 *(Judge 28)*
Georgia (0) 1 *(Ivanischvili 89)*
Republic of Ireland: Redmond; Coleman (Hughton 86), Moloney, Morris, Gunning, Gleeson, Garvan, McCarthy (Collins 90), Judge, Sheridan, Treacy (O'Shea 80).

Waterford, 13 October 2009
Republic of Ireland (0) 1 *(Garvan 90)*
Switzerland (1) 1 *(Frei 58)*   3000
Republic of Ireland: Redmond; Coleman, Conneely (Collins 82), Morris, Hughton, Davies (Clifford C 60), Garvan, McCarthy, Judge, Sheridan, O'Shea (Treacy 60).

Tbilisi, 14 November 2009
Georgia (0) 1 *(Kvaratskhelia 85)*
Republic of Ireland (0) 1 *(Sheridan 48)*   5000
Republic of Ireland: Redmond; Coleman, Morris, Dennehy, Hughton, Gleeson, Meyler, Garvan, Scannell (Carey 42), Collins (Conneely 70), Sheridan (Oyebanjo 86).

Erevan, 17 November 2009
Armenia (1) 4 *(Mkhitarian 31, 61, 84 (pen), Goaryan 75)*
Republic of Ireland (0) 1 *(Sheridan 85)*
Republic of Ireland: Redmond; Oyebanjo, Hughton, Morris, Dennehy, Conneely, Carey (Clifford C 46), Collins (Madden 65), O'Shea, Sheridan, Gleeson.

Dublin, 3 March 2010
Republic of Ireland (0) 1 *(Daly 80)*
Armenia (2) 2 *(Hairapetian 34, Ghazaryan 40)*
Voskanian■
Republic of Ireland: Redmond; Coleman, Morris, Dennehy, Hughton, Clifford C, Garvan, Meyler (Daly 46), Judge, Sheridan, Scannell (Dixon 62).

BRITISH UNDER-21 APPEARANCES 1976–2010

Bold type indicates players who made an international appearance in season 2009–10.

ENGLAND

Ablett, G. 1988 (Liverpool) 1
Adams, N. 1987 (Everton) 1
Adams, T. A. 1985 (Arsenal) 5
Addison, M. 2010 (Derby Co) 1
Agbonlahor, G. 2007 (Aston Villa) 16
Allen, B. 1992 (QPR) 8
Allen, C. 1980 (QPR, C Palace) 3
Allen, C. A. 1995 (Oxford U) 2
Allen, M. 1987 (QPR) 2
Allen, P. 1985 (West Ham U, Tottenham H) 3
Allen, R. W. 1998 (Tottenham H) 3
Alnwick, B. R. 2008 (Tottenham H) 1
Ambrose, D. P. F. 2003 (Ipswich T, Newcastle U, Charlton Ath) 10
Ameobi, F. 2001 (Newcastle U) 19
Anderson, V. A. 1978 (Nottingham F) 1
Anderton, D. R. 1993 (Tottenham H) 12
Andrews, I. 1987 (Leicester C) 1
Ardley, N. C. 1993 (Wimbledon) 10
Ashcroft, L. 1992 (Preston NE) 1
Ashton, D. 2004 (Crewe Alex, Norwich C) 9
Atherton, P. 1992 (Coventry C) 1
Atkinson, B. 1991 (Sunderland) 6
Awford, A. T. 1993 (Portsmouth) 9

Bailey, G. R. 1979 (Manchester U) 14
Baines, L. J. 2005 (Wigan Ath) 16
Baker, G. E. 1981 (Southampton) 2
Ball, M. J. 1999 (Everton) 7
Barker, S. 1985 (Blackburn R) 4
Barmby, N. J. 1994 (Tottenham H, Everton) 4
Bannister, G. 1982 (Sheffield W) 1
Barnes, J. 1983 (Watford) 2
Barnes, P. S. 1977 (Manchester C) 9
Barrett, E. D. 1990 (Oldham Ath) 4
Barry, G. 1999 (Aston Villa) 27
Barton, J. 2004 (Manchester C) 2
Bart-Williams, C. G. 1993 (Sheffield W) 16
Batty, D. 1988 (Leeds U) 7
Bazeley, D. S. 1992 (Watford) 1
Beagrie, P. 1988 (Sheffield U) 2
Beardsmore, R. 1989 (Manchester U) 5
Beattie, J. S. 1999 (Southampton) 5
Beckham, D. R. J. 1995 (Manchester U) 9
Bent, D. A. 2003 (Ipswich T, Charlton Ath) 14
Bent, M. N. 1998 (C Palace) 2
Bentley, D. M. 2004 (Arsenal, Blackburn R) 8
Beeston, C 1988 (Stoke C) 1
Benjamin, T. J. 2001 (Leicester C) 1
Bertrand, R. 2009 (Chelsea) 5
Bertschin, K. E. 1977 (Birmingham C) 3
Birtles, G. 1980 (Nottingham F) 2
Blackstock, D. A. 2008 (QPR) 2
Blackwell, D. R. 1991 (Wimbledon) 6
Blake, M. A. 1990 (Aston Villa) 8
Blissett, L. L. 1979 (Watford) 4
Booth, A. D. 1995 (Huddersfield T) 3
Bothroyd, J. 2001 (Coventry C) 1
Bowyer, L. D. 1996 (Charlton Ath, Leeds U) 13
Bracewell, P. 1983 (Stoke C) 13
Bradbury, L. M. 1997 (Portsmouth, Manchester C) 3
Bramble, T. M. 2001 (Ipswich T, Newcastle U) 10
Branch, P. M. 1997 (Everton) 4
Bradshaw, P. W. 1991 (Wolverhampton W) 4
Breacker, T. 1986 (Luton T) 2
Brennan, M. 1987 (Ipswich T) 5
Bridge, W. M. 1999 (Southampton) 8
Bridges, M. 1997 (Sunderland, Leeds U) 3
Brightwell, I. 1989 (Manchester C) 4
Briscoe, L. S. 1996 (Sheffield W) 1
Brock, K. 1984 (Oxford U) 4
Broomes, M. C. 1997 (Blackburn R) 2
Brown, M. R. 1996 (Manchester C) 4
Brown, W. M. 1999 (Manchester U) 8

Bull, S. G. 1989 (Wolverhampton W) 5
Bullock, M. J. 1998 (Barnsley) 1
Burrows, D. 1989 (WBA, Liverpool) 7
Butcher, T. I. 1979 (Ipswich T) 7
Butt, N. 1995 (Manchester U) 7
Butters, G. 1989 (Tottenham H) 3
Butterworth, I. 1985 (Coventry C, Nottingham F) 8
Bywater, S. 2001 (West Ham U) 6

Cadamarteri, D. L. 1999 (Everton) 3
Caesar, G. 1987 (Arsenal) 3
Cahill, G. J. 2007 (Aston Villa) 3
Callaghan, N. 1983 (Watford) 9
Camp, L. M. J. 2005 (Derby Co) 5
Campbell, A. P. 2000 (Middlesbrough) 4
Campbell, F. L. 2008 (Manchester U) 14
Campbell, K. J. 1991 (Arsenal) 4
Campbell, S. 1994 (Tottenham) 11
Carbon, M. P. 1996 (Derby Co) 4
Carr, C. 1985 (Fulham) 1
Carr, F. 1987 (Nottingham F) 9
Carragher, J. L. 1997 (Liverpool) 27
Carroll, A. T. 2010 (Newcastle U) 5
Carlisle, C. J. 2001 (QPR) 3
Carrick, M. 2001 (West Ham U) 14
Carson, S. P. 2004 (Leeds U, Liverpool) 29
Casper, C. M. 1995 (Manchester U) 1
Caton, T. 1982 (Manchester C) 14
Cattermole, L. B. 2008 (Middlesbrough, Wigan Ath, Sunderland) 16
Chadwick, L. H. 2000 (Manchester U) 13
Challis, T. M. 1996 (QPR) 2
Chamberlain, M. 1983 (Stoke C) 4
Chaplow, R. D. 2004 (Burnley) 1
Chapman, L. 1981 (Stoke C) 1
Charles, G. A. 1991 (Nottingham F) 4
Chettle, S. 1988 (Nottingham F) 12
Chopra, R, M. 2004 (Newcastle U) 1
Clark, L. R. 1992 (Newcastle U) 11
Clarke, P. M. 2003 (Everton) 8
Christie, M. N. 2001 (Derby Co) 11
Clegg, M. J. 1998 (Manchester U) 2
Clemence, S. N. 1999 (Tottenham H) 1
Cleverley, T. W. 2010 (Manchester U) 6
Clough, N. H. 1986 (Nottingham F) 15
Cole, A. 2001 (Arsenal) 4
Cole, A. A. 1992 (Arsenal, Bristol C, Newcastle U) 8
Cole, C. 2003 (Chelsea) 19
Cole, J. J. 2000 (West Ham U) 8
Coney, D. 1985 (Fulham) 4
Connor, T. 1987 (Brighton & HA) 1
Cooke, R. 1986 (Tottenham H) 1
Cooke, T. J. 1996 (Manchester U) 4
Cooper, C. T. 1988 (Middlesbrough) 8
Cork, J. F. P. 2009 (Chelsea) 3
Corrigan, J. T. 1978 (Manchester C) 3
Cort, C. E. R. 1999 (Wimbledon) 12
Cottee, A. R. 1985 (West Ham U) 8
Couzens, A. J. 1995 (Leeds U) 3
Cowans, G. S. 1979 (Aston Villa) 5
Cox, N. J. 1993 (Aston Villa) 6
Cranie, M. J. 2008 (Portsmouth) 16
Cranson, I. 1985 (Ipswich T) 5
Cresswell, R. P. W. 1999 (York C, Sheffield W) 4
Croft, G. 1995 (Grimsby T) 4
Crooks, G. 1980 (Stoke C) 4
Crossley, M. G. 1990 (Nottingham F) 3
Crouch, P. J. 2002 (Portsmouth, Aston Villa) 5
Cundy, J. V. 1991 (Chelsea) 3
Cunningham, L. 1977 (WBA) 6
Curbishley, L. C. 1981 (Birmingham C) 1
Curtis, J. C. K. 1998 (Manchester U) 16

Daniel, P. W. 1977 (Hull C) 7

Dann, S. 2008 (Coventry C) 2
Davenport, C. R. P. 2005 (Tottenham H) 8
Davies, A. J. 2004 (Middlesbrough) 1
Davies, C. E. 2006 (WBA) 3
Davies, K. C. 1998 (Southampton, Blackburn R, Southampton) 3
Davis, K. G. 1995 (Luton T) 3
Davis, P. 1982 (Arsenal) 11
Davis, S. 2001 (Fulham) 11
Dawson, M. R. 2003 (Nottingham F, Tottenham H) 13
Day, C. N. 1996 (Tottenham H, C Palace) 6
D'Avray, M. 1984 (Ipswich T) 2
Deehan, J. M. 1977 (Aston Villa) 7
Defoe, J. C. 2001 (West Ham U) 23
Delfouneso, N. 2010 (Aston Villa) **1**
Delph, F. 2009 (Leeds U, Aston Villa) **4**
Dennis, M. E. 1980 (Birmingham C) 3
Derbyshire, M. A. 2007 (Blackburn R) 14
Dichio, D. S. E. 1996 (QPR) 1
Dickens, A. 1985 (West Ham U) 1
Dicks, J. 1988 (West Ham U) 4
Digby, F. 1987 (Swindon T) 5
Dillon, K. P. 1981 (Birmingham C) 1
Dixon, K. M. 1985 (Chelsea) 1
Dobson, A. 1989 (Coventry C) 4
Dodd, J. R. 1991 (Southampton) 8
Donowa, L. 1985 (Norwich C) 5
Dorigo, A. R. 1987 (Aston Villa) 11
Downing, S. 2004 (Middlesbrough) 8
Dozzell, J. 1987 (Ipswich T) 9
Draper, M. A. 1991 (Notts Co) 3
Driver, A. 2009 (Hearts) 1
Duberry, M. W. 1997 (Chelsea) 5
Dunn, D. J. I. 1999 (Blackburn R) 20
Duxbury, M. 1981 (Manchester U) 7
Dyer, B. A. 1994 (C Palace) 1
Dyer, K. C. 1998 (Ipswich T, Newcastle U) 11
Dyson, P. I. 1981 (Coventry C) 4

Eadie, D. M. 1994 (Norwich C) 7
Ebanks-Blake, S. 2009 (Wolverhampton W) 1
Ebbrell, J. 1989 (Everton) 14
Edghill, R. A. 1994 (Manchester C) 3
Ehiogu, U. 1992 (Aston Villa) 15
Elliott, P. 1985 (Luton T) 1
Elliott, R. J. 1996 (Newcastle U) 2
Elliott, S. W. 1998 (Derby Co) 3
Etherington, N, 2002 (Tottenham H) 1
Euell, J. J. 1998 (Wimbledon) 6
Evans, R. 2003 (Chelsea) 2

Fairclough, C. 1985 (Nottingham F, Tottenham H) 7
Fairclough, D. 1977 (Liverpool) 1
Fashanu, J. 1980 (Norwich C, Nottingham F) 11
Fear, P. 1994 (Wimbledon) 3
Fenton, G. A. 1995 (Aston Villa) 1
Fenwick, T. W. 1981 (C Palace, QPR) 11
Ferdinand, A. J. 2005 (West Ham U) 17
Ferdinand, R. G. 1997 (West Ham U) 5
Fereday, W. 1985 (QPR) 5
Fielding, F. D. 2009 (Blackburn R) **2**
Flitcroft, G. W. 1993 (Manchester C) 10
Flowers, T. D. 1987 (Southampton) 3
Ford, M. 1996 (Leeds U) 2
Forster, N. M. 1995 (Brentford) 4
Forsyth, M. 1988 (Derby Co) 1
Foster, S. 1980 (Brighton & HA) 1
Fowler, R. B. 1994 (Liverpool) 8
Fox, D. J. 2008 (Coventry C) 1
Froggatt, S. J. 1993 (Aston Villa) 2
Futcher, P. 1977 (Luton T, Manchester C) 11

Gabbiadini, M. 1989 (Sunderland) 2
Gale, A. 1982 (Fulham) 1
Gallen, K. A. 1995 (QPR) 4
Gardner, A. 2002 (Tottenham H) 1
Gardner, C. 2008 (Aston Villa) 14
Gascoigne, P. J. 1987 (Newcastle U) 13
Gayle, H. 1984 (Birmingham C) 1
Gernon, T. 1983 (Ipswich T) 1

Gerrard, P. W. 1993 (Oldham Ath) 18
Gerrard, S. G. 2000 (Liverpool) 4
Gibbs, K. J. R. 2009 (Arsenal) **14**
Gibbs, N. 1987 (Watford) 5
Gibson, C. 1982 (Aston Villa) 1
Gilbert, W. A. 1979 (C Palace) 11
Goddard, P. 1981 (West Ham U) 8
Gordon, D. 1987 (Norwich C) 4
Gordon, D. D. 1994 (C Palace) 13
Gosling, D. 2010 (Everton) **2**
Grant, A. J. 1996 (Everton) 2
Grant, L. A. 2003 (Derby Co) 4
Granville, D. P. 1997 (Chelsea) 3
Gray, A. 1988 (Aston Villa) 2
Greening, J. 1999 (Manchester U, Middlesbrough) 18
Griffin, A. 1999 (Newcastle U) 3
Guppy, S. A. 1998 (Leicester C) 1

Haigh, P. 1977 (Hull C) 1
Hall, M. T. J. 1997 (Coventry C) 8
Hall, R. A. 1992 (Southampton) 11
Hamilton, D. V. 1997 (Newcastle U) 1
Harding, D. A. 2005 (Brighton & HA) 1
Hardyman, P. 1985 (Portsmouth) 2
Hargreaves, O. 2001 (Bayern Munich) 3
Harley, J. 2000 (Chelsea) 3
Hart, C. 2007 (Manchester C) 21
Hateley, M. 1982 (Coventry C, Portsmouth) 10
Hayes, M. 1987 (Arsenal) 3
Hazell, R. J. 1979 (Wolverhampton W) 1
Heaney, A. N. 1992 (Arsenal) 6
Heath, A. 1981 (Stoke C, Everton) 8
Heaton, T. D. 2008 (Manchester U) 3
Hendon, I. M. 1992 (Tottenham H) 7
Hendrie, L. A. 1996 (Aston Villa) 13
Hesford, I. 1981 (Blackpool) 7
Heskey, E. W. I. 1997 (Leicester C, Liverpool) 16
Hilaire, V. 1980 (C Palace) 9
Hill, D. R. L. 1995 (Tottenham H) 4
Hillier, D. 1991 (Arsenal) 1
Hinchcliffe, A. 1989 (Manchester C) 1
Hines, Z. 2010 (West Ham U) **2**
Hinshelwood, P. A. 1978 (C Palace) 2
Hirst, D. E. 1988 (Sheffield W) 7
Hislop, N. S. 1998 (Newcastle U) 1
Hoddle, G. 1977 (Tottenham H) 12
Hodge, S. B. 1983 (Nottingham F, Aston Villa) 8
Hodgson, D. J. 1981 (Middlesbrough) 6
Holdsworth, D. 1989 (Watford) 1
Holland, C. J. 1995 (Newcastle U) 10
Holland, P. 1995 (Mansfield T) 4
Holloway, D. 1998 (Sunderland) 1
Horne, B. 1989 (Millwall) 5
Howe, E. J. F. 1998 (Bournemouth) 2
Hoyte, J. R. 2004 (Arsenal) 18
Hucker, P. 1984 (QPR) 2
Huckerby, D. 1997 (Coventry C) 4
Huddlestone, T. A. 2005 (Derby Co, Tottenham H) 33
Hughes, S. J. 1997 (Arsenal) 8
Humphreys, R. J. 1997 (Sheffield W) 3
Hunt, N. B. 2004 (Bolton W) 10

Impey, A. R. 1993 (QPR) 1
Ince, P. E. C. 1989 (West Ham U) 2

Jackson, M. A. 1992 (Everton) 10
Jagielka, P. N. 2003 (Sheffield U) 6
James, D. B. 1991 (Watford) 10
James, J. C. 1990 (Luton T) 2
Jansen, M. B. 1999 (C Palace, Blackburn R) 6
Jeffers, F. 2000 (Everton, Arsenal) 16
Jemson, N. B. 1991 (Nottingham F) 1
Jenas, J. A. 2002 (Newcastle U) 9
Jerome, C. 2006 (Cardiff C, Birmingham C) 10
Joachim, J. K. 1994 (Leicester C) 9
Johnson, A. 2008 (Middlesbrough) 19
Johnson, G. M. C. 2003 (West Ham U, Chelsea) 14
Johnson, M. 2008 (Manchester C) 2
Johnson, S. A. M. 1999 (Crewe Alex, Derby Co, Leeds U) 15

Johnson, T. 1991 (Notts Co, Derby Co) 7
Johnston, C. P. 1981 (Middlesbrough) 2
Jones, D. R. 1977 (Everton) 1
Jones, C. H. 1978 (Tottenham H) 1
Jones, D. F. L. 2004 (Manchester U) 1
Jones, R. 1993 (Liverpool) 2

Keegan, G. A. 1977 (Manchester C) 1
Kenny, W. 1993 (Everton) 1
Keown, M. R. 1987 (Aston Villa) 8
Kerslake, D. 1986 (QPR) 1
Kightly, M. J. 2008 (Wolverhampton W) 7
Kilcline, B. 1983 (Notts C) 2
Kilgallon, M. 2004 (Leeds U) 5
King, A. E. 1977 (Everton) 2
King, L. B. 2000 (Tottenham H) 12
Kirkland, C. E. 2001 (Coventry C, Liverpool) 8
Kitson, P. 1991 (Leicester C, Derby Co) 7
Knight, A. 1983 (Portsmouth) 2
Knight, I. 1987 (Sheffield W) 2
Knight, Z. 2002 (Fulham) 4
Konchesky, P. M. 2002 (Charlton Ath) 15
Kozluk, R. 1998 (Derby Co) 2

Lake, P. 1989 (Manchester C) 5
Lallana, A. D. 2009 (Southampton) 1
Lampard, F. J. 1998 (West Ham U) 19
Langley, T. W. 1978 (Chelsea) 5
Lansbury, H. G. 2010 (Arsenal) **1**
Leadbitter, G. 2008 (Sunderland) 3
Lee, D. J. 1990 (Chelsea) 10
Lee, R. M. 1986 (Charlton Ath) 1
Lee, S. 1981 (Liverpool) 6
Lennon, A. J. 2006 (Tottenham H) 5
Le Saux, G. P. 1990 (Chelsea) 4
Lescott, J. P. 2003 (Wolverhampton W) 2
Lewis, J. P. 2008 (Peterborough U) 5
Lita, L. H. 2005 (Bristol C, Reading) 9
Loach, S. J. 2009 (Watford) **12**
Lowe, D. 1988 (Ipswich T) 2
Lukic, J. 1981 (Leeds U) 7
Lund, G. 1985 (Grimsby T) 3

McCall, S. H. 1981 (Ipswich T) 6
McDonald, N. 1987 (Newcastle U) 5
McEveley, J. 2003 (Blackburn R) 1
McGrath, L. 1986 (Coventry C) 1
MacKenzie, S. 1982 (WBA) 3
McLeary, A. 1988 (Millwall) 1
McLeod, I. M. 2006 (Milton Keynes D) 1
McMahon, S. 1981 (Everton, Aston Villa) 6
McManaman, S. 1991 (Liverpool) 7
Mabbutt, G. 1982 (Bristol R, Tottenham H) 7
Makin, C. 1994 (Oldham Ath) 5
Mancienne, M. I. 2008 (Chelsea) **21**
Marney, D. E. 2005 (Tottenham H) 1
Marriott, A. 1992 (Nottingham F) 1
Marsh, S. T. 1998 (Oxford U) 1
Marshall, A. J. 1995 (Norwich C) 4
Marshall, L. K. 1999 (Norwich C) 1
Martin, L. 1989 (Manchester U) 2
Martyn, A. N. 1988 (Bristol R) 11
Matteo, D. 1994 (Liverpool) 4
Mattock, J. W. 2008 (Leicester C) 5
Matthew, D. 1990 (Chelsea) 9
May, A. 1986 (Manchester C) 1
Merson, P. C. 1989 (Arsenal) 4
Middleton, J. 1977 (Nottingham F, Derby Co) 3
Miller, A. 1988 (Arsenal) 4
Mills, D. J. 1999 (Charlton Ath, Leeds U) 14
Mills, G. R. 1981 (Nottingham F) 2
Milner, J. P. 2004 (Leeds U, Newcastle U, Aston Villa) 46
Mimms, R. 1985 (Rotherham U, Everton) 3
Minto, S. C. 1991 (Charlton Ath) 6
Moore, I. 1996 (Tranmere R, Nottingham F) 7
Moore, L. I. 2006 (Aston Villa) 1
Moran, S. 1982 (Southampton) 2
Morgan, S. 1987 (Leicester C) 2
Morris, J. 1997 (Chelsea) 7
Mortimer, P. 1989 (Charlton Ath) 2

Moses, A. P. 1997 (Barnsley) 2
Moses, R. M. 1981 (WBA, Manchester U) 8
Mountfield, D. 1984 (Everton) 1
Muamba, F. N. 2008 (Birmingham C, Bolton W) **25**
Muggleton, C. D. 1990 (Leicester C) 1
Mullins, H. I. 1999 (C Palace) 3
Murphy, D. B. 1998 (Liverpool) 4
Murray, P. 1997 (QPR) 4
Murray, M. W. 2003 (Wolverhampton W) 5
Mutch, A. 1989 (Wolverhampton W) 1
Myers. A. 1995 (Chelsea) 4

Naughton, K. 2009 (Sheffield U, Tottenham H) **6**
Naylor, L. M. 2000 (Wolverhampton W) 3
Nethercott, S. H. 1994 (Tottenham H) 8
Neville, P. J. 1995 (Manchester U) 7
Newell, M. 1986 (Luton T) 4
Newton, A. L. 2001 (West Ham U) 1
Newton, E. J. I. 1993 (Chelsea) 2
Newton, S. O. 1997 (Charlton Ath) 3
Nicholls, A. 1994 (Plymouth Arg) 1
Noble, M. J. 2007 (West Ham U) 20
Nolan, K. A. J. 2003 (Bolton W) 1
Nugent, D. J. 2006 (Preston NE) 14

Oakes, M. C. 1994 (Aston Villa) 6
Oakes, S. J. 1993 (Luton T) 1
Oakley, M. 1997 (Southampton) 4
O'Brien, A. J. 1999 (Bradford C) 1
O'Connor, J. 1996 (Everton) 3
O'Hara, J. D. 2008 (Tottenham H) 7
Oldfield, D. 1989 (Luton T) 1
Olney, I. A. 1990 (Aston Villa) 10
O'Neil, G. P. 2005 (Portsmouth) 9
Onuoha, C. 2006 (Manchester C) 21
Ord, R. J. 1991 (Sunderland) 3
Osman, R. C. 1979 (Ipswich T) 7
Owen, G. A. 1977 (Manchester C, WBA) 22
Owen, M. J. 1998 (Liverpool) 1

Painter, I. 1986 (Stoke C) 1
Palmer, C. L. 1989 (Sheffield W) 4
Parker, G. 1986 (Hull C, Nottingham F) 6
Parker, P. A. 1985 (Fulham) 8
Parker, S. M. 2001 (Charlton Ath) 12
Parkes, P. B. F. 1979 (QPR) 1
Parkin, S. 1987 (Stoke C) 5
Parlour, R. 1992 (Arsenal) 12
Parnaby, S. 2003 (Middlesbrough) 4
Peach, D. S. 1977 (Southampton) 6
Peake, A. 1982 (Leicester C) 1
Pearce, I. A. 1995 (Blackburn R) 3
Pearce, S. 1987 (Nottingham F) 1
Pennant, J. 2001 (Arsenal) 24
Pickering N. 1983 (Sunderland, Coventry C) 15
Platt, D. 1988 (Aston Villa) 3
Plummer, C. S. 1996 (QPR) 5
Pollock, J. 1995 (Middlesbrough) 3
Pollock, J. 1987 (Watford) 12
Potter, G. S. 1997 (Southampton) 1
Pressman, K. 1989 (Sheffield W) 1
Proctor, M. 1981 (Middlesbrough, Nottingham F) 4
Prutton, D. T. 2001 (Nottingham F, Southampton) 25
Purse, D. J. 1998 (Birmingham C) 2

Quashie, N. F. 1997 (QPR) 4
Quinn, W. R. 1998 (Sheffield U) 2

Ramage, C. D. 1991 (Derby Co) 3
Ranson, R. 1980 (Manchester C) 10
Redknapp, J. F. 1993 (Liverpool) 19
Redmond, S. 1988 (Manchester C) 14
Reeves, K. P. 1978 (Norwich C, Manchester C) 10
Regis, C. 1979 (WBA) 6
Reid, N. S. 1981 (Manchester C) 6
Reid, P. 1977 (Bolton W) 6
Reo-Coker, N. S. A. 2004 (Wimbledon, West Ham U) 23
Richards, D. I. 1995 (Wolverhampton W) 4
Richards, J. P. 1977 (Wolverhampton W) 2
Richards, M. 2007 (Manchester C) **14**

Richards, M. L. 2005 (Ipswich T) 1
Richardson, K. E. 2005 (Manchester U)
Rideout, P. 1985 (Aston Villa, Bari) 5
Ridgewell, L. M. 2004 (Aston Villa) 8
Riggott, C. M. 2001 (Derby Co) 8
Ripley, S. E. 1988 (Middlesbrough) 8
Ritchie, A. 1982 (Brighton & HA) 1
Rix, G. 1978 (Arsenal) 7
Roberts, A. J. 1995 (Millwall, C Palace) 5
Roberts, B. J. 1997 (Middlesbrough) 1
Robins, M. G. 1990 (Manchester U) 6
Robinson, P. P. 1999 (Watford) 3
Robinson, P. W. 2000 (Leeds U) 11
Robson, B. 1979 (WBA) 7
Robson, S. 1984 (Arsenal, West Ham U) 8
Rocastle, D. 1987 (Arsenal) 14
Roche, L. P. 2001 (Manchester U) 1
Rodger, G. 1987 (Coventry C) 4
Rodwell, J. 2009 (Everton) **11**
Rogers, A. 1998 (Nottingham F) 3
Rosario, R. 1987 (Norwich C) 4
Rose, D. L. 2009 (Tottenham H) **8**
Rose, M. 1997 (Arsenal) 2
Rosenior, L. J. 2005 (Fulham) 7
Routledge, W. 2005 (C Palace, Tottenham H) 12
Rowell, G. 1977 (Sunderland) 1
Ruddock, N. 1989 (Southampton) 4
Rufus, R. R. 1996 (Charlton Ath) 6
Ryan, J. 1983 (Oldham Ath) 1
Ryder, S. H. 1995 (Walsall) 3

Samuel, J. 2002 (Aston Villa) 7
Samways, V. 1988 (Tottenham H) 5
Sansom, K. G. 1979 (C Palace) 8
Scimeca, R. 1996 (Aston Villa) 9
Scowcroft, J. B. 1997 (Ipswich T) 5
Seaman, D. A. 1985 (Birmingham C) 10
Sears, F. D. 2010 (West Ham U) **3**
Sedgley, S. 1987 (Coventry C, Tottenham H) 11
Sellars, S. 1988 (Blackburn R) 3
Selley, I. 1994 (Arsenal) 3
Serrant, C. 1998 (Oldham Ath) 2
Sharpe, L. S. 1989 (Manchester U) 8
Shaw, G. R. 1981 (Aston Villa) 4
Shawcross, R. J. 2008 (Stoke C) 2
Shearer, A. 1991 (Southampton) 11
Shelton, G. 1985 (Sheffield W) 1
Sheringham, E. P. 1988 (Millwall) 1
Sheron, M. 1992 (Manchester C) 16
Sherwood, T. A. 1990 (Norwich C) 4
Shipperley, N. J. 1994 (Chelsea, Southampton) 7
Sidwell, S. J. 2003 (Reading) 5
Simonsen, S. P. A. 1998 (Tranmere R, Everton) 4
Simpson, P. 1986 (Manchester C) 5
Sims. S. 1977 (Leicester C) 10
Sinclair, T. 1994 (QPR, West Ham U) 5
Sinnott, L. 1985 (Watford) 1
Slade, S. A. 1996 (Tottenham H) 4
Slater, S. I. 1990 (West Ham U) 3
Small, B. 1993 (Aston Villa) 12
Smalling, C. L. 2010 (Fulham) **4**
Smith. A. 2000 (Leeds U) 11
Smith, D. 1988 (Coventry C) 10
Smith, M. 1981 (Sheffield W) 5
Smith, M. 1995 (Sunderland) 1
Smith, T. W. 2001 (Watford) 1
Snodin, I. 1985 (Doncaster R) 4
Soares, T. J. 2006 (C Palace) 4
Stanislaus, F. J. 2010 (West Ham U) **2**
Statham, B. 1988 (Tottenham H) 5
Statham, D. J. 1978 (WBA) 6
Stead, J. G. 2004 (Blackburn R, Sunderland) 11
Stearman, R. J. 2009 (Wolverhampton W) 4
Stein, B. 1984 (Luton T) 3
Sterland, M. 1984 (Sheffield W) 7
Steven, T. M. 1985 (Everton) 1
Stevens, G. A. 1983 (Brighton & HA, Tottenham H) 8
Stewart, J. 2003 (Leicester C) 1
Stewart, P. 1988 (Manchester C) 1
Stockdale, R. K. 2001 (Middlesbrough) 1

Stuart, G. C. 1990 (Chelsea) 5
Stuart, J. C. 1996 (Charlton Ath) 4
Sturridge, D. A. 2010 (Chelsea) **5**
Suckling, P. 1986 (Coventry C, Manchester C, C Palace) 10
Summerbee, N. J. 1993 (Swindon T) 3
Sunderland, A. 1977 (Wolverhampton W) 1
Surman, A. R. E. 2008 (Southampton) 4
Sutch, D. 1992 (Norwich C) 4
Sutton, C. R. 1993 (Norwich C) 13
Swindlehurst, D. 1977 (C Palace) 1

Talbot, B. 1977 (Ipswich T) 1
Taylor, A. D. 2007 (Middlesbrough) 13
Taylor, M. 2001 (Blackburn R) 1
Taylor, M. S. 2003 (Portsmouth) 3
Taylor, R. A. 2006 (Wigan Ath) 2
Taylor, S. J. 2002 (Arsenal) 3
Taylor, S. V. 2004 (Newcastle U) 29
Terry, J. G. 2001 (Chelsea) 9
Thatcher, B. D. 1996 (Millwall, Wimbledon) 4
Thelwell, A. A. 2001 (Tottenham H) 1
Thirlwell, P. 2001 (Sunderland) 1
Thomas, D. 1981 (Coventry C, Tottenham H) 7
Thomas, J. W. 2006 (Charlton Ath) 2
Thomas, M. 1986 (Luton T) 3
Thomas, M. L. 1988 (Arsenal) 12
Thomas, R. E. 1990 (Watford) 1
Thompson, A. 1995 (Bolton W) 2
Thompson, D. A. 1997 (Liverpool) 7
Thompson, G. L. 1981 (Coventry C) 1
Thorn, A. 1988 (Wimbledon) 5
Thornley, B. L. 1996 (Manchester U) 3
Tiler, C. 1990 (Barnsley, Nottingham F) 13
Tomkins, J. O. C. 2009 (West Ham U) **7**
Tonge, M. W. E. 2004 (Sheffield U) 2

Unsworth, D. G. 1995 (Everton) 8
Upson, M. J. 1999 (Arsenal) 11

Vassell, D. 1999 (Aston Villa) 11
Vaughan, J. O. 2007 (Everton) **3**
Venison, B. 1983 (Sunderland) 10
Vernazza, P. A. P. 2001 (Arsenal, Watford) 2
Vinnicombe, C. 1991 (Rangers) 12

Waddle, C. R. 1985 (Newcastle U) 1
Walcott, T. J. 2007 (Arsenal) **21**
Wallace, D. L. 1983 (Southampton) 14
Wallace, Ray 1989 (Southampton) 4
Wallace, Rod 1989 (Southampton) 11
Walker, D. 1985 (Nottingham F) 7
Walker, I. M. 1991 (Tottenham H) 9
Walker, K. 2010 (Tottenham H) **1**
Walsh, G. 1988 (Manchester U) 2
Walsh, P. A. 1983 (Luton T) 4
Walters, K. 1984 (Aston Villa) 9
Ward, P. 1978 (Brighton & HA) 2
Warhurst, P. 1991 (Oldham Ath, Sheffield W) 8
Watson, B. 2007 (C Palace) 1
Watson, D. 1984 (Norwich C) 7
Watson, D. N. 1994 (Barnsley) 5
Watson, G. 1991 (Sheffield W) 2
Watson, S. C. 1993 (Newcastle U) 12
Weaver, N. J. 2000 (Manchester C) 10
Webb, N. J. 1985 (Portsmouth, Nottingham F) 3
Welbeck, D. 2009 (Manchester U) **4**
Welsh, J. J. 2004 (Liverpool, Hull C) 8
Wheater, D. J. 2008 (Middlesbrough) 11
Whelan, P. J. 1993 (Ipswich T) 3
Whelan, N. 1995 (Leeds U) 2
Whittingham, P. 2004 (Aston Villa, Cardiff C) 17
White, D. 1988 (Manchester C) 6
Whyte, C. 1982 (Arsenal) 4
Wicks, S. 1982 (QPR) 1
Wilkins, R. C. 1977 (Chelsea) 1
Wilkinson, P. 1986 (Grimsby T, Everton) 4
Williams, D. 1998 (Sunderland) 2
Williams, P. 1989 (Charlton Ath) 4
Williams, P. D. 1991 (Derby Co) 6

Williams, S. C. 1977 (Southampton)   14
Wilshere, J. A. 2010 (Arsenal)   5
Wilson, M. A. 2001 (Manchester U, Middlesbrough)   6
Winterburn, N. 1986 (Wimbledon)   1
Wise, D. F. 1988 (Wimbledon)   1
Woodcook, A. S. 1978 (Nottingham F)   2
Woodgate, J. S. 2000 (Leeds U)   1
Woodhouse, C. 1999 (Sheffield U)   4
Woods, C. C. E. 1979 (Nottingham F, QPR, Norwich C) 6
Wright, A. G. 1993 (Blackburn R)   2
Wright, M. 1983 (Southampton)   4

Wright, R. I. 1997 (Ipswich T)   15
Wright, S. J. 2001 (Liverpool)   10
Wright, W. 1979 (Everton)   6
Wright-Phillips, S. C. 2002 (Manchester C)   6

Yates, D. 1989 (Notts Co)   5
Young, A. S. 2007 (Watford, Aston Villa)   10
Young, L. P. 1999 (Tottenham H, Charlton Ath)   12

Zamora, R. L. 2002 (Brighton & HA)   6

NORTHERN IRELAND

Allen, C. 2009 (Lisburn Distillery)   1
Armstrong, D. T. 2007 (Hearts)   1

Bailie, N. 1990 (Linfield)   2
Baird, C. P. 2002 (Southampton)   6
Beatty, S. 1990 (Chelsea, Linfield)   2
Black, J. 2003 (Tottenham H)   1
Black, K. T. 1990 (Luton T)   1
Black, R. Z. 2002 (Morecambe)   1
Blackledge, G. 1978 (Portadown)   1
Blayney, A. 2003 (Southampton)   4
Boyce, L. 2010 (Cliftonville)   1
Boyle, W. S. 1998 (Leeds U)   7
Braniff, K. R. 2002 (Millwall)   11
Brotherston, N. 1978 (Blackburn R)   1
Browne, G. 2003 (Manchester C)   5
Brunt, C. 2005 (Sheffield W)   2
Bryan, M. A. 2010 (Watford)   2
Buchanan, D. T. H. 2006 (Bury)   15
Buchanan, W. B. 2002 (Bolton W, Lisburn Distillery) 5
Burns, L. 1998 (Port Vale)   13

Callaghan, A. 2006 (Limavady U, Ballymena U,
    Derry C)   15
Campbell, S. 2003 (Ballymena U)   1
Capaldi, A. C. 2002 (Birmingham C, Plymouth Arg) 14
Carlisle, W. T. 2000 (C Palace)   9
Carroll, R. E. 1998 (Wigan Ath)   11
Carson, S. 2000 (Rangers, Dundee U)   2
Carson, T. 2007 (Sunderland)   15
Carvill, M. D. 2008 (Wrexham, Linfield)   8
Casement, C. 2007 (Ipswich T, Dundee)   18
Cathcart, C. 2007 (Manchester U)   15
Catney, R. 2007 (Lisburn Distillery)   1
Chapman, A. 2008 (Sheffield U, Oxford U)   7
Clarke, L. 2003 (Peterborough U)   4
Clarke, R. 2006 (Newry C)   7
Clarke, R. D. J. 1999 (Portadown)   5
Clingan, S. G. 2003 (Wolverhampton W, Nottingham F)
                                                                          11
Close, B. 2002 (Middlesbrough)   10
Clyde, M. G. 2002 (Wolverhampton W)   5
Colligan, L. 2009 (Ballymena U)   1
Connell, T. E. 1978 (Coleraine)   1
Coote, A. 1998 (Norwich C)   12
Convery, J. 2000 (Celtic)   4

Davey, H. 2004 (UCD)   3
Davis, S. 2004 (Aston Villa)   3
Devine, D. 1994 (Omagh T)   1
Devine, J. 1990 (Glentoran)   1
Dickson, H. 2002 (Wigan Ath)   1
Doherty, M. 2007 (Hearts)   2
Dolan, J. 2000 (Millwall)   6
Donaghy, M. M. 1978 (Larne)   1
Donnelly, M. 2007 (Sheffield U, Crusaders)   5
Dowie, I. 1990 (Luton T)   1
Dudgeon, J. P. 2010 (Manchester U)   2
Duff, A. 2003 (Cheltenham T)   1
Duffy, S. P. M. 2010 (Everton)   3

Elliott, S. 1999 (Glentoran)   3
Ervin, J. 2005 (Linfield)   2
Evans, C. J. 2009 (Manchester U)   10
Evans, J. 2006 (Manchester U)   3

Feeney, L. 1998 (Linfield, Rangers)   8
Feeney, W. 2002 (Bournemouth)   8
Ferguson, M. 2000 (Glentoran)   2
Ferguson, S. 2009 (Newcastle U)   3
Fitzgerald, D. 1998 (Rangers)   4
Flynn, J. J. 2009 (Blackburn R)   10
Fordyce, D. T. 2007 (Portsmouth, Glentoran)   12
Friars. E. C. 2005 (Notts Co)   7
Friars, S. M. 1998 (Liverpool, Ipswich T)   21

Garrett, R. 2007 (Stoke C, Linfield)   14
Gault, M. 2005 (Linfield)   2
Gibb, S. 2009 (Falkirk, Drogheda U)   2
Gilfillan, B. J. 2005 (Gretna, Peterhead)   9
Gillespie, K. R. 1994 (Manchester U)   1
Glendinning, M. 1994 (Bangor)   1
Graham, G. L. 1999 (C Palace)   5
Graham, R. S. 1999 (QPR)   15
Gray, P. 1990 (Luton T)   1
Griffin, D. J. 1998 (St Johnstone)   10

Hamilton, G. 2000 (Blackburn R, Portadown)   12
Hamilton, W. R. 1978 (Linfield)   1
Harkin, M. P. 2000 (Wycombe W)   9
Harvey, J. 1978 (Arsenal)   1
Hawe, S. 2001 (Blackburn R)   2
Hayes, T. 1978 (Luton T)   1
Hazley, M. 2007 (Stoke C)   3
Healy, D. J. 1999 (Manchester U)   8
Herron, C. J. 2003 (QPR)   2
Higgins, R. 2006 (Derry C)   1
Hodson, L. J. S. 2010 (Watford)   5
Holmes, S. 2000 (Manchester C, Wrexham)   13
Howland, D. 2007 (Birmingham C)   4
Hughes, J. 2006 (Lincoln C)   7
Hughes, M. A. 2003 (Tottenham H, Oldham Ath) 12
Hughes, M. E. 1990 (Manchester C)   21
Hunter, M. 2002 (Glentoran)   1

Ingham, M. G. 2001 (Sunderland)   4

Jarvis, D. 2010 (Aberdeen)   2
Johnson, D. M. 1998 (Blackburn R)   11
Johnston, B. 1978 (Cliftonville)   1
Julian, A. A. 2005 (Brentford)   1

Kane, A. M. 2008 (Blackburn R)   5
Kee, B. R. 2010 (Leicester C)   5
Kee, P. V. 1990 (Oxford U)   1
Kelly, D. 2000 (Derry C)   11
Kelly, N. 1990 (Oldham Ath)   1
Kirk, A. R. 1999 (Hearts)   9

Lafferty, D. 2009 (Celtic)   6
Lafferty, K. 2006 (Burnley)   2
Lawrie, J. 2009 (Port Vale)   8
Lennon, N. F. 1990 (Manchester C, Crewe Alex)   2
Lindsay, K. 2006 (Larne)   1
Little, A. 2009 (Rangers)   4
Lowry, P. 2009 (Institute, Linfield)   6
Lyttle, G. 1998 (Celtic, Peterborough U)   8

Magee, J. 1994 (Bangor)   1
Magee, J. 2009 (Lisburn Distillery)   1
Magennis, J. B. D. 2010 (Cardiff C)   5

Magilton, J. 1990 (Liverpool)	1
Magnay, C. 2010 (Chelsea)	**1**
Matthews, N. P. 1990 (Blackpool)	1
McAllister, M. 2007 (Dungannon Swifts)	4
McArdle, R. A. 2006 (Sheffield W, Rochdale)	19
McAreavey, P. 2000 (Swindon T)	7
McBride, J. 1994 (Glentoran)	1
McCaffrey, D. 2006 (Hibernian)	8
McCallion, E. 1998 (Coleraine)	1
McCann, G. S. 2000 (West Ham U)	11
McCann, P. 2003 (Portadown)	1
McCann, R. 2002 (Rangers, Linfield)	2
McCartney, G. 2001 (Sunderland)	5
McChrystal, M. 2005 (Derry C)	9
McClean, J. 2010 (Derry C)	**3**
McCourt, P. J. 2002 (Rochdale, Derry C)	8
McCoy, R. K. 1990 (Coleraine)	1
McCreery, D. 1978 (Manchester U)	1
McEvilly, L. R. 2003 (Rochdale)	9
McFlynn, T. M. 2000 (QPR, Woking, Margate)	19
McGibbon, P. C. G. 1994 (Manchester U)	1
McGivern, R. 2010 (Manchester C)	**2**
McGlinchey, B. 1998 (Manchester C, Port Vale, Gillingham)	14
McGovern, M. 2005 (Celtic)	10
McGowan, M. V. 2006 (Clyde)	2
McGurk, A. 2010 (Aston Villa)	**1**
McIlroy, T. 1994 (Linfield)	1
McKay, W. 2009 (Leicester C, Northampton T)	**6**
McKenna, K. 2007 (Tottenham H)	6
McKnight, P. 1998 (Rangers)	3
McLaughlin, C. G. 2010 (Preston NE)	**1**
McLaughlin, P. 2010 (Newcastle U)	**1**
McLean, B. S. 2006 (Rangers)	1
McLean, J. 2009 (Derry C)	4
McMahon, G. J. 2002 (Tottenham H)	1
McMenamin, L. A. 2009 (Sheffield W)	4
McQuilken, J. 2009 (Tescoma Zlin)	1
McQuoid, J. J. B. 2009 (Bournemouth)	**8**
McVeigh, A. 2002 (Ayr U)	1
McVeigh, P. M. 1998 (Tottenham H)	11
McVey, K. 2006 (Coleraine)	8
Meenan, D. 2007 (Finn Harps, Monaghan U)	3
Melaugh, G. M. 2002 (Aston Villa, Glentoran)	11
Millar, W. P. 1990 (Port Vale)	1
Miskelly, D. T. 2000 (Oldham Ath)	10
Moreland, V. 1978 (Glentoran)	1
Morgan, M. P. T. 1999 (Preston NE)	1
Morris, E. J. 2002 (WBA, Glentoran)	1
Morrison, O. 2001 (Sheffield W, Sheffield U)	7
Morrow, A. 2001 (Northampton T)	1
Morrow, S. 2005 (Hibernian)	4

Mulgrew, J. 2007 (Linfield)	10
Mulryne, P. P. 1999 (Manchester U, Norwich C)	5
Murray, W. 1978 (Linfield)	1
Murtagh, C. 2005 (Hearts)	1
Nicholl, J. M. 1978 (Manchester U)	1
Nixon, C. 2000 (Glentoran)	1
Norwood, O. J. 2010 (Manchester U)	**4**
O'Connor, M. J. 2008 (Crewe Alex)	3
O'Hara, G. 1994 (Leeds U)	1
O'Kane, E. 2009 (Everton)	3
O'Neill, J. P. 1978 (Leicester C)	1
O'Neill, M. A. M. 1994 (Hibernian)	1
O'Neill, S. 2009 (Ballymena U)	**4**
Paterson, M. A. 2007 (Stoke C)	2
Patterson, D. J. 1994 (C Palace)	1
Quinn, S. J. 1994 (Blackpool)	1
Ramsey, K. 2006 (Institute)	1
Robinson, S. 1994 (Tottenham H)	1
Scullion, D. 2006 (Dungannon Swifts)	8
Shiels, D. 2005 (Hibernian)	6
Shroot, R. 2009 (Harrow B, Birmingham C)	**4**
Simms, G. 2001 (Hartlepool U)	14
Skates, G. 2000 (Blackburn R)	4
Sloan, T. 1978 (Ballymena U)	1
Smylie, D. 2006 (Newcastle U, Livingston)	6
Stewart, S. 2009 (Aberdeen)	1
Stewart, T. 2006 (Wolverhampton W, Linfield)	19
Taylor, J. 2007 (Hearts, Glentoran)	**10**
Taylor, M. S. 1998 (Fulham)	1
Teggart, N. 2005 (Sunderland)	2
Thompson, P. 2006 (Linfield)	4
Toner, C. 2000 (Tottenham H, Leyton Orient)	17
Tuffey, J. 2007 (Partick T)	13
Turner, C. 2007 (Sligo R, Bohemians)	12
Ward, J. J. 2006 (Aston Villa, Chesterfield)	7
Ward, M. 2006 (Dungannon Swifts)	1
Ward, S. 2005 (Glentoran)	10
Waterman, D. G. 1998 (Portsmouth)	14
Waterworth, A. 2008 (Lisburn Distillery, Hamilton A)	7
Webb, S. M. 2004 (Ross Co, St Johnstone, Ross Co)	6
Weir, R. J. 2009 (Sunderland)	**6**
Wells, D. P. 1999 (Barry T)	1
Whitley, J. 1998 (Manchester C)	17
Willis, P. 2006 (Liverpool)	1

SCOTLAND

Adam, C. G. 2006 (Rangers)	5
Adams, J. 2007 (Kilmarnock)	1
Aitken, R. 1977 (Celtic)	16
Albiston, A. 1977 (Manchester U)	5
Alexander, N. 1997 (Stenhousemuir, Livingston)	10
Anderson, I. 1997 (Dundee, Toulouse)	15
Anderson, R. 1997 (Aberdeen)	15
Anthony, M. 1997 (Celtic)	3
Archdeacon, O. 1987 (Celtic)	1
Archibald, A. 1998 (Partick Th)	5
Archibald, S. 1980 (Aberdeen, Tottenham H)	5
Arfield, S. 2008 (Falkirk)	**14**
Bagen, D. 1997 (Kilmarnock)	4
Bain, K. 1993 (Dundee)	4
Baker, M. 1993 (St Mirren)	10
Baltacha, S. S. 2000 (St Mirren)	3
Bannan, B. 2009 (Aston Villa)	**5**
Bannon, E. J. 1979 (Hearts, Chelsea, Dundee U)	7
Beattie, C. 2004 (Celtic)	7
Beattie, J. 1992 (St Mirren)	4
Beaumont, D. 1985 (Dundee U)	1
Bell, D. 1981 (Aberdeen)	2
Bernard, P. R. J. 1992 (Oldham Ath)	15

Berra, C. 2005 (Hearts)	6
Bett, J. 1981 (Rangers)	7
Black, E. 1983 (Aberdeen)	8
Blair, A. 1980 (Coventry C, Aston Villa)	5
Bollan, G. 1992 (Dundee U, Rangers)	17
Bonar, P. 1997 (Raith R)	4
Booth, S. 1991 (Aberdeen)	14
Bowes, M. J. 1992 (Dunfermline Ath)	1
Bowman, D. 1985 (Hearts)	1
Boyack, S. 1997 (Rangers)	1
Boyd, K. 2003 (Kilmarnock)	8
Boyd, T. 1987 (Motherwell)	5
Brazil, A. 1978 (Hibernian)	1
Brazil, A. 1979 (Ipswich T)	8
Brebner, G. I. 1997 (Manchester U, Reading, Hibernian)	18
Brighton, T. 2005 (Rangers, Clyde)	7
Broadfoot, K. 2005 (St Mirren)	5
Brough, J. 1981 (Hearts)	1
Brown, A. H. 2004 (Hibernian)	1
Brown, S. 2005 (Hibernian)	10
Browne, P. 1997 (Raith R)	1
Bryson, C. 2006 (Clyde)	1
Buchan, J. 1997 (Aberdeen)	13

Johnston, A. 1994 (Hearts)	3
Johnston, F. 1993 (Falkirk)	1
Johnston, M. 1984 (Partick Th, Watford)	3
Jordan, A. J. 2000 (Bristol C)	3
Jupp, D. A. 1995 (Fulham)	9
Kennedy, J. 2003 (Celtic)	15
Kenneth, G. 2008 (Dundee U)	8
Kerr, B. 2003 (Newcastle U)	14
Kerr, M. 2001 (Kilmarnock)	1
Kerr, S. 1993 (Celtic)	10
Kinniburgh, W. D. 2004 (Motherwell)	3
Kirkwood, D. 1990 (Hearts)	1
Kyle, K. 2001 (Sunderland)	12
Lambert, P. 1991 (St Mirren)	11
Langfield, J. 2000 (Dundee)	2
Lappin, S. 2004 (St Mirren)	10
Lauchlan, J. 1998 (Kilmarnock)	11
Lavety, B. 1993 (St Mirren)	9
Lavin, G. 1993 (Watford)	7
Lawson, P. 2004 (Celtic)	10
Leighton, J. 1982 (Aberdeen)	1
Lennon, S. 2008 (Rangers)	6
Levein, C. 1985 (Hearts)	2
Leven, P. 2005 (Kilmarnock)	2
Liddell, A. M. 1994 (Barnsley)	12
Lindsey, J. 1979 (Motherwell)	1
Locke, G. 1994 (Hearts)	10
Love, G. 1995 (Hibernian)	1
Loy, R. 2009 (Dunfermline Ath, Rangers)	**5**
Lynch, S. 2003 (Celtic, Preston NE)	13
McAllister, G. 1990 (Leicester C)	1
McAllister, R. 2008 (Inverness CT)	2
McAlpine, H. 1983 (Dundee U)	5
McAnespie, K. 1998 (St Johnstone)	4
McArthur, J. 2008 (Hamilton A)	2
McAuley, S. 1993 (St Johnstone)	1
McAvennie, F. 1982 (St Mirren)	5
McBride, J. 1981 (Everton)	1
McBride, J. P. 1998 (Celtic)	2
McCall, A. S. M. 1988 (Bradford C, Everton)	2
McCann, K. 2008 (Hibernian)	4
McCann, N. 1994 (Dundee)	9
McClair, B. 1984 (Celtic)	8
McCluskey, G. 1979 (Celtic)	6
McCluskey, S. 1997 (St Johnstone)	14
McCoist, A. 1984 (Rangers)	1
McConnell, I. 1997 (Clyde)	1
McCormack, D. 2008 (Hibernian)	1
McCormack, R. 2006 (Rangers, Motherwell, Cardiff C)	13
McCracken, D. 2002 (Dundee U)	5
McCulloch, A. 1981 (Kilmarnock)	1
McCulloch, I. 1982 (Notts Co)	2
McCulloch, L. 1997 (Motherwell)	14
McCunnie, J. 2001 (Dundee U, Ross Co, Dunfermline Ath)	20
MacDonald, J. 1980 (Rangers)	8
MacDonald, J. 2007 (Hearts)	11
McDonald, C. 1995 (Falkirk)	5
McDonald, K. 2008 (Dundee, Burnley)	**14**
McEwan, C. 1997 (Clyde, Raith R)	17
McEwan, D. 2003 (Livingston)	2
McFadden, J. 2003 (Motherwell)	7
McFarlane, J. 2008 (Hamilton A)	3
McGarry, S. 1997 (St Mirren)	3
McGarvey, F. P. 1977 (St Mirren, Celtic)	3
McGarvey, S. 1982 (Manchester U)	4
McGhee, M. 1981 (Aberdeen)	1
McGinn, S. 2009 (St Mirren, Watford)	**4**
McGinnis, G. 1985 (Dundee U)	1
McGlinchey, M. R. 2007 (Celtic)	2
McGregor, A. 2003 (Rangers)	6
McGrillen, P. 1994 (Motherwell)	2
McGuire, D. 2002 (Aberdeen)	2
McInally, J. 1989 (Dundee U)	1
McKenzie, R. 1997 (Hearts)	2
McKimmie, S. 1985 (Aberdeen)	3
McKinlay, T. 1984 (Dundee)	6

McKinlay, W. 1989 (Dundee U)	6
McKinnon, R. 1991 (Dundee U)	6
McLaren, A. 1989 (Hearts)	11
McLaren, A. 1993 (Dundee U)	4
McLaughlin, B. 1995 (Celtic)	8
McLaughlin, J. 1981 (Morton)	10
McLean, E. 2008 (Dundee U, St Johnstone)	2
McLean, S. 2003 (Rangers)	4
McLeish, A. 1978 (Aberdeen)	6
MacLeod, A. 1979 (Hibernian)	3
McLeod, J. 1989 (Dundee U)	2
MacLeod, M. 1979 (Dumbarton, Celtic)	5
McManus, T. 2001 (Hibernian)	14
McMillan, S. 1997 (Motherwell)	4
McNab, N. 1978 (Tottenham H)	1
McNally, M. 1991 (Celtic)	2
McNamara, J. 1994 (Dunfermline Ath, Celtic)	12
McNaughton, K. 2002 (Aberdeen)	1
McNeil, A. 2007 (Hibernian)	1
McNichol, J. 1979 (Brentford)	7
McNiven, D. 1977 (Leeds U)	3
McNiven, S. A. 1996 (Oldham Ath)	1
McParland, A. 2003 (Celtic)	1
McPhee, S. 2002 (Port Vale)	1
McPherson, D. 1984 (Rangers, Hearts)	4
McQuilken, J. 1993 (Celtic)	2
McStay, P. 1983 (Celtic)	5
McWhirter, N. 1991 (St Mirren)	1
Maguire, C. 2009 (Aberdeen)	**7**
Main, A. 1988 (Dundee U)	3
Malcolm, R. 2001 (Rangers)	1
Maloney, S. 2002 (Celtic)	21
Malpas, M. 1983 (Dundee U)	8
Marshall, D. J. 2004 (Celtic)	10
Marshall, S. R. 1995 (Arsenal)	5
Martin, A. 2009 (Leeds U)	**7**
Mason, G. R. 1999 (Manchester C, Dunfermline Ath)	2
Mathieson, D. 1997 (Queen of the South)	3
May, E. 1989 (Hibernian)	2
Meldrum, C. 1996 (Kilmarnock)	6
Melrose, J. 1977 (Partick Th)	8
Millar, M, 2009 (Celtic)	1
Miller, C. 1995 (Rangers)	8
Miller, J. 1987 (Aberdeen, Celtic)	7
Miller, K. 2000 (Hibernian, Rangers)	7
Miller, W. 1978 (Aberdeen)	2
Miller, W. 1991 (Hibernian)	7
Milne, K. 2000 (Hearts)	1
Milne, R. 1982 (Dundee U)	3
Mitchell, C. 2008 (Falkirk)	**7**
Money, I. C. 1987 (St Mirren)	3
Montgomery, N. A. 2003 (Sheffield U)	2
Morrison, S. A. 2004 (Aberdeen, Dunfermline Ath)	12
Muir, L. 1977 (Hibernian)	1
Mulgrew, C. P. 2006 (Celtic, Wolverhampton W, Aberdeen)	14
Murphy J. 2009 (Motherwell)	**8**
Murray, H. 2000 (St Mirren)	3
Murray, I. 2001 (Hibernian)	15
Murray, N. 1993 (Rangers)	16
Murray, R. 1993 (Bournemouth)	1
Murray, S. 2004 (Kilmarnock)	2
Narey, D. 1977 (Dundee U)	4
Naismith, S. J. 2006 (Kilmarnock, Rangers)	15
Naysmith, G. A. 1997 (Hearts)	22
Neilson, R. 2000 (Hearts)	1
Nevin, P. 1985 (Chelsea)	5
Nicholas, C. 1981 (Celtic, Arsenal)	6
Nicholson, B. 1999 (Rangers)	7
Nicol, S. 1981 (Ayr U, Liverpool)	14
Nisbet, J. 1989 (Rangers)	5
Noble, D. J. 2003 (West Ham U)	2
Notman, A. M. 1999 (Manchester U)	10
O'Brien, B. 1999 (Blackburn R, Livingston)	6
O'Connor, G. 2003 (Hibernian)	8
O'Donnell, P. 1992 (Motherwell)	8
O'Leary, R. 2008 (Kilmarnock)	2
O'Neil, B. 1992 (Celtic)	7

O'Neil, J. 1991 (Dundee U) 1
O'Neill, M. 1995 (Clyde) 6
Orr, N. 1978 (Morton) 7

Parker, K. 2001 (St Johnstone) 1
Parlane, D. 1977 (Rangers) 1
Paterson, C. 1981 (Hibernian) 2
Paterson, J. 1997 (Dundee U) 9
Payne, G. 1978 (Dundee U) 3
Peacock, L. A. 1997 (Carlisle U) 1
Pearce, A. J. 2008 (Reading) 2
Pearson, S. P. 2003 (Motherwell) 8
Perry, R. 2010 (Rangers) **3**
Pressley, S. J. 1993 (Rangers, Coventry C, Dundee U) 26
Provan, D. 1977 (Kilmarnock) 1
Prunty, B. 2004 (Aberdeen) 6

Quinn, P. C. 2004 (Motherwell) 3
Quinn, R. 2006 (Celtic) 9

Rae, A. 1991 (Millwall) 8
Rae, G. 1999 (Dundee) 6
Redford, I. 1981 (Rangers) 6
Reid, B. 1991 (Rangers) 4
Reid, C. 1993 (Hibernian) 3
Reid, M. 1982 (Celtic) 6
Reid, R. 1977 (St Mirren) 3
Reilly, A. 2004 (Wycombe W) 1
Renicks, S. 1997 (Hamilton A) 1
Reynolds, M. 2007 (Motherwell) 9
Rice, B. 1985 (Hibernian) 1
Richardson, L. 1980 (St Mirren) 2
Riordan, D. G. 2004 (Hibernian) 5
Ritchie, A. 1980 (Morton) 1
Ritchie, P. S. 1996 (Hearts) 7
Robertson, A. 1991 (Rangers) 1
Robertson, C. 1977 (Rangers) 1
Robertson, D. 1987 (Aberdeen) 7
Robertson, D. 2007 (Dundee U) 4
Robertson, G. A. 2004 (Nottingham F, Rotherham U) 15
Robertson, H. 1994 (Aberdeen) 2
Robertson, J. 1985 (Hearts) 2
Robertson, L. 1993 (Rangers) 3
Robertson, S. 1998 (St Johnstone) 5
Roddie, A. 1992 (Aberdeen) 1
Ross, G. 2007 (Dunfermline Ath) 1
Ross, T. W. 1977 (Arsenal) 1
Rowson, D. 1997 (Aberdeen) 5
Russell, R. 1978 (Rangers) 3

Salton, D. B. 1992 (Luton T) 6
Samson, C. I. 2004 (Kilmarnock) 6
Scobbie, T. 2008 (Falkirk) **7**
Scott, M. 2006 (Livingston) 1
Scott, P. 1994 (St Johnstone) 4
Scrimgour, D. 1997 (St Mirren) 3
Seaton, A. 1998 (Falkirk) 1
Severin, S. D. 2000 (Hearts) 10
Shannon, R. 1987 (Dundee) 7
Sharp, G. M. 1982 (Everton) 1
Sharp, R. 1990 (Dunfermline Ath) 4
Sheerin, P. 1996 (Southampton) 1
Shields, G. 1997 (Rangers) 2
Shinnie, A. 2009 (Dundee) 2
Simmons, S. 2003 (Hearts) 1
Simpson, N. 1982 (Aberdeen) 11
Sinclair, G. 1977 (Dumbarton) 1
Skilling, M. 1993 (Kilmarnock) 2
Smith, B. M. 1992 (Celtic) 5

Smith, C. 2008 (St Mirren) 2
Smith, D. L. 2006 (Motherwell) 2
Smith, G. 1978 (Rangers) 1
Smith, G. 2004 (Rangers) 8
Smith, H. G. 1987 (Hearts) 2
Smith, S. 2007 (Rangers) 1
Sneddon, A. 1979 (Celtic) 1
Snodgrass, R. 2008 (Livingston) 2
Soutar, D. 2003 (Dundee) 11
Speedie, D. R. 1985 (Chelsea) 1
Spencer, J. 1991 (Rangers) 3
Stanton, P. 1977 (Hibernian) 1
Stark, W. 1985 (Aberdeen) 1
Stephen, R. 1983 (Dundee) 1
Stevens, G. 1977 (Motherwell) 1
Stevenson, L. 2008 (Hibernian) 8
Stewart, C. 2002 (Kilmarnock) 1
Stewart, J. 1978 (Kilmarnock, Middlesbrough) 3
Stewart, M. J. 2000 (Manchester U) 17
Stewart, R. 1979 (Dundee U, West Ham U) 12
Stillie, D. 1995 (Aberdeen) 14
Strachan, G. D. 1980 (Aberdeen) 1
Strachan, G. D. 1998 (Coventry C) 7
Sturrock, P. 1977 (Dundee U) 9
Sweeney, P. H. 2004 (Millwall) 8
Sweeney, S. 1991 (Clydebank) 7

Tarrant, N. K. 1999 (Aston Villa) 5
Teale, G. 1997 (Clydebank, Ayr U) 6
Telfer, P. N. 1993 (Luton T) 3
Thomas, K. 1993 (Hearts) 8
Thompson, S. 1997 (Dundee U) 12
Thomson, K. 2005 (Hibernian) 6
Thomson, W. 1977 (Partick Th, St Mirren) 10
Tolmie, J. 1980 (Morton) 1
Tortolano, J. 1987 (Hibernian) 2
Turner, I. 2005 (Everton) 6
Tweed, S. 1993 (Hibernian) 3

Wales, A. 2000 (Hearts) 1
Walker, A. 1988 (Celtic) 1
Wallace, I. A. 1978 (Coventry C) 1
Wallace, L. 2007 (Hearts) 10
Wallace, R. 2004 (Celtic, Sunderland) 4
Walsh, C. 1984 (Nottingham F) 5
Wark, J. 1977 (Ipswich T) 8
Watson, A. 1981 (Aberdeen) 4
Watson, K. 1977 (Rangers) 2
Watt, M. 1991 (Aberdeen) 12
Watt, S. M. 2005 (Chelsea) 5
Webster, A. 2003 (Hearts) 2
Whiteford, A. 1997 (St Johnstone) 1
Whittaker, S. G. 2005 (Hibernian) 18
Whyte, D. 1987 (Celtic) 9
Wilkie, L. 2000 (Dundee) 6
Will, J. A. 1992 (Arsenal) 3
Williams, G. 2002 (Nottingham F) 9
Wilson, M. 2004 (Dundee U, Celtic) 19
Wilson, S. 1999 (Rangers) 7
Wilson, T. 1983 (St Mirren) 1
Wilson, T. 1988 (Nottingham F) 4
Winnie, D. 1988 (St Mirren) 1
Woods, M. 2006 (Sunderland) 2
Wright, P. 1989 (Aberdeen, QPR) 3
Wright, S. 1991 (Aberdeen) 14
Wright, T. 1987 (Oldham Ath) 1

Young, Darren 1997 (Aberdeen) 8
Young, Derek 2000 (Aberdeen) 5

WALES

Adams, N. W. 2008 (Bury, Leicester C) 5
Affei D. M. 2010 (Swansea C) **1**
Aizlewood, M. 1979 (Luton T) 2
Allen, J. M. 2008 (Swansea C) **11**
Anthony, B. 2005 (Cardiff C) 8

Baddeley, L. M. 1996 (Cardiff C) 2

Balcombe, S. 1982 (Leeds U) 1
Bale, G. 2006 (Southampton, Tottenham H) 4
Barnhouse, D. J. 1995 (Swansea C) 3
Basey, G. W. 2009 (Charlton Ath) 1
Bater, P. T. 1977 (Bristol R) 2
Beevers, L. J. 2005 (Boston U, Lincoln C) 7
Bellamy, C. D. 1996 (Norwich C) 8

Birchall, A. S. 2003 (Arsenal, Mansfield T)	12
Bird, A. 1993 (Cardiff C)	6
Blackmore, C. 1984 (Manchester U)	3
Blake, D. J. 2007 (Cardiff C)	**14**
Blake, N. A. 1991 (Cardiff C)	5
Blaney, S. D. 1997 (West Ham U)	3
Bodin, B. P. 2010 (Swindon T)	**2**
Bodin, P. J. 1983 (Cardiff C)	1
Bowen, J. P. 1993 (Swansea C)	5
Bowen, M. R. 1983 (Tottenham H)	3
Boyle, T. 1982 (C Palace)	1
Brace, D. P. 1995 (Wrexham)	6
Bradley, M. S. 2007 (Walsall)	**14**
Brough, M. 2003 (Notts Co)	3
Brown, J. D. 2008 (Cardiff C)	6
Brown, J. R. 2003 (Gillingham)	7
Byrne, M. T. 2003 (Bolton W)	1
Calliste, R. T. 2005 (Manchester U, Liverpool)	15
Carpenter, R. E. 2005 (Burnley)	1
Cegielski, W. 1977 (Wrexham)	2
Chamberlain, E. C. 2010 (Leicester C)	**2**
Chapple, S. R. 1992 (Swansea C)	8
Charles, J. M. 1979 (Swansea C)	2
Church, S. R. 2008 (Reading)	**14**
Clark, J. 1978 (Manchester U, Derby Co)	2
Coates, J. S. 1996 (Swansea C)	5
Coleman, C. 1990 (Swansea C)	3
Collins, J. M. 2003 (Cardiff C)	7
Collins, M. J. 2007 (Fulham, Swansea C)	2
Collison, J. D. 2008 (West Ham U)	7
Cornell, D. J. 2010 (Swansea C)	**1**
Cotterill, D. R. G. B. 2005 (Bristol C, Wigan Ath)	11
Coyne, D. 1992 (Tranmere R)	7
Craig, N. L. 2009 (Everton)	**3**
Critchell, K. A. R. 2005 (Southampton)	3
Crofts, A. L. 2005 (Gillingham)	10
Crowell, M. T. 2004 (Wrexham)	7
Curtis, A. T. 1977 (Swansea C)	1
Davies, A. 1982 (Manchester U)	6
Davies, A. G. 2006 (Cambridge U)	6
Davies, A. R. 2005 (Southampton, Yeovil T)	14
Davies, C. M. 2005 (Oxford U, Verona, Oldham Ath)	9
Davies, D. 1999 (Barry T)	1
Davies, G. M. 1993 (Hereford U, C Palace)	7
Davies, I. C. 1978 (Norwich C)	1
Davies, L. 2005 (Bangor C)	1
Davies, R. J. 2006 (WBA)	4
Davies, S. 1999 (Peterborough U, Tottenham H)	10
Day, R. 2000 (Manchester C, Mansfield T)	11
Deacy, N. 1977 (PSV Eindhoven)	1
De-Vulgt, L. S. 2002 (Swansea C)	2
Dibble, A. 1983 (Cardiff C)	3
Doble, R. A. 2010 (Southampton)	**1**
Doyle, S. C. 1978 (Preston NE, Huddersfield T)	2
Duffy, R. M. 2005 (Portsmouth)	7
Dwyer, P. J. 1979 (Cardiff C)	1
Eardley, N. 2007 (Oldham Ath, Blackpool)	**10**
Earnshaw, R. 1999 (Cardiff C)	10
Easter, D. J. 2006 (Cardiff C)	1
Ebdon, M. 1990 (Everton)	2
Edwards, C. N. H. 1996 (Swansea C)	7
Edwards, D. A. 2006 (Shrewsbury T, Luton T, Wolverhampton W)	9
Edwards, R. I. 1977 (Chester)	2
Edwards, R. W. 1991 (Bristol C)	13
Evans, A. 1977 (Bristol R)	1
Evans, C. 2007 (Manchester C, Sheffield U)	**13**
Evans, K. 1999 (Leeds U, Cardiff C)	4
Evans, P. S. 1996 (Shrewsbury T)	1
Evans, S. J. 2001 (C Palace)	2
Evans, T. 1995 (Cardiff C)	3
Fish, N. 2005 (Cardiff C)	2
Fleetwood, S. 2005 (Cardiff C)	5
Flynn, C. P. 2007 (Crewe Alex)	1
Folland, R. W. 2000 (Oxford U)	1
Foster, M. G. 1993 (Tranmere R)	1

Fowler, L. A. 2003 (Coventry C, Huddersfield T)	9
Freestone, R. 1990 (Chelsea)	1
Gabbidon, D. L. 1999 (WBA, Cardiff C)	17
Gale, D. 1983 (Swansea C)	2
Gall, K. A. 2002 (Bristol R, Yeovil T)	8
Gibson, N. D. 1999 (Tranmere R, Sheffield W)	11
Giggs, R. J. 1991 (Manchester U)	1
Gilbert, P. 2005 (Plymouth Arg)	12
Giles, D. C. 1977 (Cardiff C, Swansea C, C Palace)	4
Giles, P. 1982 (Cardiff C)	3
Graham, D. 1991 (Manchester U)	1
Green, R. M. 1998 (Wolverhampton W)	16
Griffith, C. 1990 (Cardiff C)	1
Griffiths, C. 1991 (Shrewsbury T)	1
Grubb, D. 2007 (Bristol C)	1
Gunter, C. 2006 (Cardiff C, Tottenham H)	8
Haldane, L. O. 2007 (Bristol R)	1
Hall, G. D. 1990 (Chelsea)	1
Hartson, J. 1994 (Luton T, Arsenal)	9
Haworth, S. O. 1997 (Cardiff C, Coventry C, Wigan Ath)	12
Hennessey, W. R. 2006 (Wolverhampton W)	6
Hillier, I. M. 2001 (Tottenham H, Luton T)	5
Hodges, G. 1983 (Wimbledon)	5
Holden, A. 1984 (Chester C)	1
Holloway, C. D. 1999 (Exeter C)	2
Hopkins, J. 1982 (Fulham)	5
Hopkins, S. A. 1999 (Wrexham)	1
Huggins, D. S. 1996 (Bristol C)	1
Hughes, D. 2005 (Kaiserslautern, Regensburg)	2
Hughes, D. R. 1994 (Southampton)	1
Hughes, I. 1992 (Bury)	11
Hughes, L. M. 1983 (Manchester U)	5
Hughes, R. D. 1996 (Aston Villa, Shrewsbury T)	13
Hughes, W. 1977 (WBA)	3
Jackett, K. 1981 (Watford)	2
Jacobson, J. M. 2006 (Cardiff C, Bristol R)	15
James, L. R. S. 2006 (Southampton)	10
James, R. M. 1977 (Swansea C)	3
Jarman, L. 1996 (Cardiff C)	10
Jeanne, L. C. 1999 (QPR)	8
Jelleyman, G. A. 1999 (Peterborough U)	1
Jenkins, L. D. 1998 (Swansea C)	9
Jenkins, S. R. 1993 (Swansea C)	2
Jones, C. T. 2007 (Swansea C)	1
Jones, E. P. 2000 (Blackpool)	1
Jones, F. 1981 (Wrexham)	1
Jones, J. A. 2001 (Swansea C)	3
Jones, L. 1982 (Cardiff C)	3
Jones, M. A. 2004 (Wrexham)	4
Jones, M. G. 1998 (Leeds U)	7
Jones, P. L. 1992 (Liverpool)	12
Jones, R. A. 1994 (Sheffield W)	3
Jones, S. J. 2005 (Swansea C)	1
Jones, V. 1979 (Bristol R)	2
Kendall, L. M. 2001 (C Palace)	2
Kendall, M. 1978 (Tottenham H)	1
Kenworthy, J. R. 1994 (Tranmere R)	3
King, A. 2008 (Leicester C)	**10**
Knott, G. R. 1996 (Tottenham H)	1
Law, B. J. 1990 (QPR)	2
Lawless, A. 2006 (Torquay U)	1
Ledley, J. C. 2005 (Cardiff C)	5
Letheran, G. 1977 (Leeds U)	2
Letheran, K. C. 2006 (Swansea C)	1
Lewis, D. 1982 (Swansea C)	9
Lewis, J. 1983 (Cardiff C)	1
Llewellyn, C. M. 1998 (Norwich C)	14
Loveridge, J. 1982 (Swansea C)	3
Low, J. D. 1999 (Bristol R, Cardiff C)	1
Lowndes, S. R. 1979 (Newport Co, Millwall)	4
MacDonald, S. B. 2006 (Swansea C)	**22**
McCarthy, A. J. 1994 (QPR)	3
McDonald, C. 2006 (Cardiff C)	3

Mackin, L. 2006 (Wrexham)	1
Maddy, P. 1982 (Cardiff C)	2
Margetson, M. W. 1992 (Manchester C)	7
Martin, A. P. 1999 (C Palace)	1
Martin, D. A. 2006 (Notts Co)	1
Marustik, C. 1982 (Swansea C)	7
Matthews, A. J. 2010 (Cardiff C)	**1**
Maxwell, C. 2009 (Wrexham)	**7**
Maxwell, L. J. 1999 (Liverpool, Cardiff C)	14
Meaker, M. J. 1994 (QPR)	2
Melville, A. K. 1990 (Swansea C, Oxford U)	2
Micallef, C. 1982 (Cardiff C)	3
Morgan, A. M. 1995 (Tranmere R)	4
Morgan, C. 2004 (Wrexham, Milton Keynes D)	12
Morris, A. J. 2009 (Cardiff C)	**5**
Moss, D. M. 2003 (Shrewsbury T)	6
Mountain, P. D. 1997 (Cardiff C)	2
Mumford, A. O. 2003 (Swansea C)	4
Nardiello, D. 1978 (Coventry C)	1
Neilson, A. B. 1993 (Newcastle U)	7
Nicholas, P. 1978 (C Palace, Arsenal)	3
Nogan, K. 1990 (Luton T)	2
Nogan, L. M. 1991 (Oxford U)	1
Nyatanga, L. J. 2005 (Derby Co)	10
Oster, J. M. 1997 (Grimsby T, Everton)	9
Owen, G. 1991 (Wrexham)	8
Page, R. J. 1995 (Watford)	4
Parslow, D. 2005 (Cardiff C)	4
Partington, J. M. 2009 (Bournemouth)	**3**
Partridge, D. W. 1997 (West Ham U)	1
Pascoe, C. 1983 (Swansea C)	4
Pearce, S. 2006 (Bristol C)	3
Pejic, S. M. 2003 (Wrexham)	6
Pembridge, M. A. 1991 (Luton T)	1
Perry, J. 1990 (Cardiff C)	3
Peters, M. 1992 (Manchester C, Norwich C)	3
Phillips, D. 1984 (Plymouth Arg)	3
Phillips, G. R. 2001 (Swansea C)	3
Phillips, L. 1979 (Swansea C, Charlton Ath)	2
Pipe, D. R. 2003 (Coventry C, Notts Co)	12
Pontin, K. 1978 (Cardiff C)	1
Powell, L. 1991 (Southampton)	4
Powell, L. 2004 (Leicester C)	3
Powell, R. 2006 (Bolton W)	1
Price, J. J. 1998 (Swansea C)	7
Price, L. P. 2005 (Ipswich T)	10
Price, M. D. 2001 (Everton, Hull C, Scarborough)	13
Price, P. 1981 (Luton T)	1
Pritchard, M. O. 2006 (Swansea C)	4
Pugh, D. 1982 (Doncaster R)	2
Pugh, S. 1993 (Wrexham)	2
Pulis, A. J. 2006 (Stoke C)	5
Ramasut, M. W. T. 1997 (Bristol R)	4
Ramsey, A. J. 2008, (Cardiff C, Arsenal)	**12**
Ratcliffe, K. 1981 (Everton)	2
Ready, K. 1992 (QPR)	5
Rees, A. 1984 (Birmingham C)	1
Rees, J. M. 1990 (Luton T)	3
Rees, M. R. 2003 (Millwall)	4
Ribeiro, C. M. 2008 (Bristol C)	**8**
Richards, A. D. J. 2010 (Swansea C)	**4**
Roberts, A. M. 1991 (QPR)	2
Roberts, C. J. 1999 (Cardiff C)	1
Roberts, G. 1983 (Hull C)	1
Roberts, G. W. 1997 (Liverpool, Panionios, Tranmere R)	11
Roberts, J. G. 1977 (Wrexham)	1
Roberts, N. W. 1999 (Wrexham)	3

Roberts, P. 1997 (Porthmadog)	1
Roberts, S. I. 1999 (Swansea C)	13
Roberts, S. W. 2000 (Wrexham)	3
Robinson, C. P. 1996 (Wolverhampton W)	6
Robinson, J. R. C. 1992 (Brighton & HA, Charlton Ath)	5
Robson-Kanu, K. H. 2010 (Reading)	**1**
Rowlands, A. J. R. 1996 (Manchester C)	5
Rush, I. 1981 (Liverpool)	2
Savage, R. W. 1995 (Crewe Alex)	3
Sayer, P. A. 1977 (Cardiff C)	2
Searle, D. 1991 (Cardiff C)	6
Slatter, D. 2000 (Chelsea)	6
Slatter, N. 1983 (Bristol R)	6
Sommer, M. J. 2004 (Brentford)	2
Speed, G. A. 1990 (Leeds U)	3
Spender, S. 2005 (Wrexham)	6
Stevenson, N. 1982 (Swansea C)	2
Stevenson, W. B. 1977 (Leeds U)	3
Stock, B. B. 2003 (Bournemouth)	4
Symons, C. J. 1991 (Portsmouth)	2
Taylor, G. K. 1995 (Bristol R)	4
Taylor, J. W. T. 2010 (Reading)	**1**
Taylor, N. J. 2008 (Wrexham)	**10**
Taylor, R. F. 2008 (Chelsea)	1
Thomas, C. E. 2010 (Swansea C)	**1**
Thomas, D. G. 1977 (Leeds U)	3
Thomas, D. J. 1998 (Watford)	2
Thomas, J. A. 1996 (Blackburn R)	21
Thomas, Martin R. 1979 (Bristol R)	2
Thomas, Mickey R. 1977 (Wrexham)	2
Thomas, S. 2001 (Wrexham)	5
Tibbott, L. 1977 (Ipswich T)	2
Tipton, M. J. 1998 (Oldham Ath)	6
Tolley, J. C. 2001 (Shrewsbury T)	12
Tudur-Jones, O. 2006 (Swansea C)	3
Twiddy, C. 1995 (Plymouth Arg)	3
Valentine, R. D. 2001 (Everton, Darlington)	8
Vaughan, D. O. 2003 (Crewe Alex)	8
Vaughan, N. 1982 (Newport Co)	2
Vokes, S. M. 2007 (Bournemouth, Wolverhampton W)	**14**
Walsh, D. 2000 (Wrexham)	8
Walsh, I. P. 1979 (C Palace, Swansea C)	2
Walton, M. 1991 (Norwich C.)	1
Ward, D. 1996 (Notts Co)	2
Warlow, O. J. 2007 (Lincoln C)	2
Weston, M. D. 2001 (Arsenal, Cardiff C)	4
Whitfield, P. M. 2003 (Wrexham)	1
Wiggins, R. 2006 (C Palace)	9
Williams, A. P. 1998 (Southampton)	9
Williams, A. S. 1996 (Blackburn R)	16
Williams, D. 1983 (Bristol R)	1
Williams, D. I. L. 1998 (Liverpool, Wrexham)	9
Williams, D. T. 2006 (Yeovil T)	1
Williams, E. 1997 (Caernarfon T)	2
Williams, G. 1983 (Bristol R)	2
Williams, G. A. 2003 (C Palace)	5
Williams, M. 2001 (Manchester U)	10
Williams, M. P. 2006 (Wrexham)	14
Williams, M. R. 2006 (Wrexham)	**4**
Williams, O. fon 2007 (Crewe Alex, Stockport Co)	11
Williams, R. 2007 (Middlesbrough)	10
Williams, S. J. 1995 (Wrexham)	4
Wilmot, R. 1982 (Arsenal)	6
Wilson, J. S. 2009 (Bristol C)	**3**
Worgan, L. J. 2005 (Milton Keynes D, Rushden & D)	5
Wright, A. A. 1998 (Oxford U)	3
Young, S. 1996 (Cardiff C)	5

UEFA UNDER-21 CHAMPIONSHIP 2009–11

QUALIFYING ROUND

GROUP 1
Romania 2, Andorra 0
Russia 4, Andorra 0
Latvia 4, Andorra 0
Faeroes 0, Romania 4
Faeroes 1, Russia 0
Andorra 0, Romania 2
Moldova 1, Latvia 0
Faeroes 1, Moldova 1
Latvia 0, Russia 4
Andorra 0, Russia 4
Romania 3, Moldova 0
Faeroes 1, Latvia 3
Latvia 5, Romania 1
Russia 2, Faeroes 0
Moldova 1, Andorra 0
Romania 3, Faeroes 0
Russia 3, Moldova 1
Romania 4, Latvia 1
Moldova 0, Russia 3
Latvia 0, Faeroes 1
Andorra 1, Faeroes 1
Andorra 1, Moldova 3

GROUP 2
Republic of Ireland 0, Turkey 3
Switzerland 2, Armenia 1
Armenia 2, Turkey 5
Switzerland 0, Estonia 1
Armenia 1, Switzerland 3
Estonia 2, Georgia 0
Georgia 4, Turkey 0
Estonia 1, Republic of Ireland 1
Estonia 1, Switzerland 4
Republic of Ireland 1, Georgia 1
Turkey 1, Armenia 0
Republic of Ireland 1, Switzerland 1
Georgia 1, Republic of Ireland 1
Armenia 1, Estonia 1
Turkey 1, Switzerland 3
Armenia 4, Republic of Ireland 1
Turkey 0, Estonia 0
Switzerland 1, Georgia 0
Georgia 2, Estonia 0
Republic of Ireland 1, Armenia 2
Estonia 2, Armenia 3
Estonia 1, Turkey 0
Switzerland 0, Turkey 2
Georgia 0, Switzerland 0

GROUP 3
Luxembourg 0, Wales 0
Wales 4, Luxembourg 1
Hungary 3, Luxembourg 0
Luxembourg 0, Hungary 1
Wales 4, Hungary 1
Bosnia 0, Luxembourg 1
Wales 2, Italy 1
Italy 2, Luxembourg 0
Wales 2, Bosnia 0
Italy 1, Bosnia 1
Hungary 2, Italy 0

Luxembourg 0, Italy 4
Bosnia 2, Wales 1
Luxembourg 0, Bosnia 1
Italy 2, Hungary 0

GROUP 4
Poland 2, Liechtenstein 0
Spain 2, Poland 0
Holland 2, Finland 0
Liechtenstein 0, Spain 4
Poland 2, Finland 1
Liechtenstein 0, Poland 5
Finland 0, Holland 1
Poland 0, Holland 4
Liechtenstein 0, Finland 4
Spain 1, Finland 0
Holland 3, Liechtenstein 0
Holland 2, Spain 1
Spain 3, Liechtenstein 1
Holland 3, Poland 2

GROUP 5
San Marino 0, Czech Republic 8
Iceland 0, Czech Republic 2
Germany 6, San Marino 0
Czech Republic 2, Northern Ireland 0
Germany 1, Czech Republic 2
Northern Ireland 2, Iceland 6
Iceland 8, San Marino 0
Iceland 2, Northern Ireland 1
San Marino 0, Iceland 6
Northern Ireland 1, Germany 1
San Marino 0, Germany 11
Northern Ireland 1, Czech Republic 2
Germany 2, Iceland 2
San Marino 0, Northern Ireland 3

GROUP 6
Israel 1, Kazakhstan 1
Kazakhstan 2, Bulgaria 0
Kazakhstan 0, Montenegro 2
Bulgaria 3, Israel 4
Bulgaria 3, Kazakhstan 0
Montenegro 0, Sweden 2
Kazakhstan 1, Israel 2
Sweden 2, Bulgaria 1
Bulgaria 1, Montenegro 1
Kazakhstan 1, Sweden 1
Montenegro 3, Kazakhstan 1
Montenegro 1, Israel 0
Sweden 5, Kazakhstan 1
Israel 4, Bulgaria 0
Montenegro 2, Bulgaria 0
Israel 0, Sweden 1
Sweden 2, Montenegro 0

GROUP 7
Croatia 0, Cyprus 2
Norway 2, Slovakia 2
Cyprus 1, Norway 3
Serbia 1, Slovakia 2
Norway 1, Croatia 3

Slovakia 1, Cyprus 0
Norway 0, Serbia 1
Serbia 2, Cyprus 0
Croatia 3, Serbia 1
Cyprus 0, Slovakia 1
Cyprus 1, Croatia 2
Serbia 3, Norway 2
Slovakia 1, Croatia 2
Croatia 1, Slovakia 1

GROUP 8
Malta 0, Slovenia 2
Ukraine 1, Malta 0
Malta 0, Belgium 1
Slovenia 1, France 3
Belgium 2, Slovenia 0
France 2, Ukraine 2
Ukraine 1, Belgium 1
Malta 0, France 2
Belgium 0, France 0
Slovenia 0, Ukraine 2
Slovenia 1, Malta 0
Belgium 0, Ukraine 2
France 1, Slovenia 0
Belgium 1, Malta 0
Malta 0, Ukraine 3

GROUP 9
Greece 3, Macedonia 1
Lithuania 0, Greece 1
Macedonia 1, England 2
Portugal 4, Lithuania 1
Greece 1, England 1
Macedonia 1, Lithuania 1
Greece 2, Portugal 1
England 6, Macedonia 3
Macedonia 1, Portugal 1
Greece 1, Lithuania 0
Lithuania 1, Macedonia 0
England 1, Portugal 0
Lithuania 0, England 0
Portugal 2, Greece 1
England 1, Greece 2

GROUP 10
Albania 0, Scotland 1
Scotland 5, Albania 2
Belarus 2, Austria 1
Albania 1, Azerbaijan 0
Austria 1, Scotland 0
Azerbaijan 2, Belarus 3
Austria 3, Albania 1
Azerbaijan 1, Austria 2
Scotland 1, Belarus 0
Belarus 4, Albania 2
Albania 2, Austria 2
Azerbaijan 0, Scotland 4
Albania 1, Belarus 2
Austria 4, Azerbaijan 0
Scotland 2, Azerbaijan 2

Competition still being played.

FA SCHOOLS & YOUTH GAMES 2009–10

ENGLAND UNDER-16

Ansah (Arsenal); Redmond (Birmingham C); Cotton (Blackburn R); Fielding (Bolton W); Caskey (Brighton & HA); Cousins, Jordan (Charlton Ath); Clayton, Powell (Crewe Alex); Hope (Everton); Arthurworrey (Fulham); Belford, Regan (Liverpool); Evans, Facey, Hutton, Plummer (Manchester C); Barmby, Blackett, Hendrie (Manchester U); Jackson (Middlesbrough); Magri (Portsmouth); Sterling (QPR); McFadzean, Willis (Sheffield U); Callaghan, Pickford (Sunderland); Henshall (Swindon T); Amenku, Nabi (WBA); Fanimo, Turgott (West Ham U).

VICTORY SHIELD

15 Oct (at Yeovil)

England 1 (Ansah 76)   **Wales 0**   3700

England: Pickford; Hendrie, McFadzean (Callaghan 66), Cousins, Magri, Blackett (Henshall 41), Fanimo, Cotton, Hope (Ansah 60), Nabi (Redmond 41), Caskey (Jackson 71).

5 Nov (at Chester)

England 2 (Turgott 50, Fanimo 80)   **Northern Ireland 0**

England: Willis; Facey (Arthurworrey 67), McFadzean, Amenku (Barmby 41), Magri, Jackson, Redmond (Sterling 41), Powell, Ansah (Nabi 71), Fanimo (Jordan 62).

26 Nov (at Tynecastle)

Scotland 1 (Grimmer 26)

England 2 (Ansah 27, Turgott 60)   2870

England: Pickford; McFadzean, Cousins, Magri (Blackett 69), Fanimo, Cotton (Henshall 60), Ansah (Hope 45), Jackson, Powell, Sterling (Amenku 45), Turgott (Hutton 74).

Northern Ireland 1, Scotland 2
Wales 0, Scotland 1
Wales 2, Northern Ireland 0

	P	W	D	L	F	A	Pts
England	3	3	0	0	5	1	9
Scotland	3	2	0	1	4	3	6
Wales	3	1	0	2	2	2	3
Northern Ireland	3	0	0	3	1	6	0

FRIENDLY

9 Feb (in Seraing)

Belgium 1 (Limbombe 77)   **England 1** (Ansah 90)

England: Pickford (Fielding 41); Cousins, Plummer, Hutton (Caskey 41), Magri, Jackson, Powell (Amenku 67), Cotton (Clayton 57), Hope (Sterling 47), Ansah, Henshall (Redmond 41).

THE MONTAIGU INTERNATIONAL TOURNAMENT

31 Mar (in St Gilles)

Ukraine 1   England 3 (Hope 18, 68 (pen), Sterling 48)

England: Pickford; Cousins, Plummer, Magri, Jackson (Barmby), Sterling, Cotton (Clayton), Hope, Fanimo (Regan), Powell (Evans), Turgott (Redmond).

1 Apr (in Venansault)

Gabon 0

England 6 (Barmby 13, 21, Redmond 16, Powell 30, Clayton 45 (pen), Turgott 79)

England: Belford; Cousins (Turgott 54), Evans (Cotton 71), Magri (Jackson 54), Hope (Fanimo 49), Redmond, McFadzean, Powell, Barmby (Sterling 49), Regan, Clayton.

3 Apr (in St Gilles)

England 2 (Fanimo, Clayton)   **Japan 1**

England: Belford; Cousins, Evans (Turgott 60), Jackson, Sterling, Cotton, Fanimo (Hope 66), Redmond (Powell 60), McFadzean (Plummer 60), Regan, Clayton.

5 Apr (in Montaigu)

England 1 (Cotton 29)   **Portugal 1**

Portugal won 3-1 on penalties.

England: Pickford; Cousins, Plummer, Magri, Sterling, Cotton, Hope (Redmond 72), Powell, Turgott (Clayton 72), Barmby (Fanimo 49), Regan.

ENGLAND UNDER-17

Afobe, Aneke, Rees, Yennaris (Arsenal); Butland (Birmingham C); Cousins (Charlton Ath); Blackman, Chalobah, McEachran (Chelsea); Thomas (Coventry C); Barkley, Bidwell, Garbutt (Everton); Wickham (Ipswich T); Moore (Leicester C); Coady, Robinson, Wisdom (Liverpool); Cofie, Johnstone, Keane, Morrison, Thorpe (Manchester U); Atkinson, Fowler, Gibson, Pilatos, Williams (Middlesbrough); Alnwick (Newcastle U); Laing (Sunderland); Kane (Tottenham H); Berahino, Thorne (WBA); Hall (West Ham U); Ismail (Wolverhampton W).

NORDIC TOURNAMENT

28 July (in Trondheim)

Denmark 1 (Rasmussen 36)   **England 1** (Rees 42)

England: Alnwick; Bidwell, Coady (Thomas 71), Wisdom, Chalobah (Gibson 74), Thorne, Pilatos, Berahino, Fowler, Rees, Ismail (Hall 71).

29 July (in Tydal)

England 8 (Hall 11, 21, Wisdom 14, 37, Berahino 22, 32, Fowler 76 (pen), Ismail 79)

Faeroes 0

England: Blackman; Thomas, Bidwell (Fowler 55), Wisdom (Chalobah 55), Pilatos (Coady 55), Berahino (Ismail 55), Hall, Robinson, Cousins, Rees (Thorne 70), Gibson.

31 July

Norway 0   England 1 (Hall 32)

England: Blackman; Bidwell, Coady, Wisdom, Chalobah, Thorne, Pilatos, Berahino, Hall, Robinson, Yennaris.

2 Aug

England 3 (Hall 76, Gibson 79, Bidwell 95)

Scotland 2 (Fyvie 8, Walker 38)

England: Alnwick; Pilatos (Yennaris 74), Wisdom, Chalobah (Thorne 62), Robinson (Bidwell 72), Coady (Cousins 74), Thomas (Ismail 62), Keane (Gibson 53), Hall, Fowler, Berahino.

FA UNDER-17 INTERNATIONAL TOURNAMENT

26 Aug *(at Burton)*

England 1 *(Leali 64 (og))*   **Italy 1** *(Magnaghi 27)*

England: Johnstone; Pilatos, Garbutt, Thorne (Moore 80), Laing, Chalobah, Keane, Aneke (Bidwell 41), Afobe, Morrison (Berahino 58), McEachran (Fowler 80).

28 Aug *(at Northampton)*

England 2 *(Berahino 12, 64)*

Turkey 3 *(Okay 52, Artlin 65, 71)*

England: Butland; Garbutt, Thorne, Chalobah (Laing 41), Keane (Keane 71), Moore, Bidwell (Morrison 41), Thorpe, Rees (Pilatos 61), Berahino, Fowler (Afobe 61).

30 Aug *(at Notts Co.)*

England 1 *(Aneke 69)*   **Portugal 0**

England: Johnstone; Pilatos, Laing, Chalobah (Rees 49), Keane (Fowler 70), Afobe, Morrison, Moore, Bidwell (Garbutt 49), Thorpe, Berahino (Aneke 56).

UEFA UNDER-17 CHAMPIONSHIP

26 Oct *(in Baku)*

England 6 *(Garbutt 2, Keane 16, Afobe 24, 75, Hall 66, 73)*

Kazakhstan 2 *(Kuat 30, Utrobin 32)*

England: Johnstone; Pilatos (Coady 70), Garbutt, Thorpe, Keane, Barkley, Afobe, McEachran (Williams 54), Thorne, Laing, Wickham (Hall 61).

28 Oct *(in Baku)*

England 4 *(Wickham 18, 29 (pen), 39, Afobe 67)*

Azerbaijan 0

England: Butland; Garbutt (Robinson 46), Coady, Chalobah, Thorpe, Keane (Morrison 46), McEachran, Thorne, Laing, Wickham (Afobe 59), Hall.

31 Oct *(in Baku)*

England 1 *(Afobe 58)*

Serbia 0

England: Johnstone; Pilatos, Garbutt, Coady, Chalobah, Keane (Morrison 54), Barkley, Afobe, McEachran (Thorne 76), Robinson, Wickham (Williams 54).

THE ALGARVE INTERNATIONAL TOURNAMENT

13 Feb *(in Parchal)*

France 1 *(Koura 11)*   **England 1** *(Afobe 51)*

England: Johnstone; Atkinson, Coady, Chalobah, Thorne (Pilatos 59), Keane, Thomas (Berahino 63), Afobe, Robinson, Wisdom, Kane (Cofie 63).

14 Feb *(in Algarve)*

England 3 *(Garbutt 30 (pen), Cofie 54, Berahino 75)*

Ukraine 0

England: Butland; Garbutt, ·Coady (Thomas 63), Chalobah (Robinson 70), Thorne, Aneke, Hall, Pilatos, Wisdom, Cofie (Kane 70), Berahino.

16 Feb *(in Ferreiras)*

England 0   **Portugal 0**

England: Johnstone (Butland 40); Garbutt, Coady, Thorne (Atkinson 59), Keane (Thomas 69), Afobe (Cofie 70), Aneke (Berahino 51), Hall (Kane 51), Robinson, Pilatos, Wisdom.

UEFA UNDER-17 QUALIFYING CHAMPIONSHIP

27 Mar *(at Northampton)*

England 4 *(Wickham 21, Afobe 32, Hall 72, Keane 90)*

Sweden 0   1475

England: Johnstone; Garbutt, Coady, Chalobah, Wisdom, Keane, Thorne (Kane 75), Afobe (Butland 51); Pilatos, McEachran (Hall 63), Wickham.

29 Mar *(at Burton)*

England 5 *(Aneke 19, 36, Keane 30, Afobe 37, Kane 72)*

Malta 0   969

England: Butland; Pilatos, Laing, Garbutt (Robinson 41), Coady, Wisdom, Keane, Afobe (Berahino 55), Aneke, Hall, McEachran (Kane 41).

1 Apr *(at Northampton)*

England 2 *(Wickham 60, Kane 76)*   **Slovakia 0**   731

England: Johnstone; Pilatos, Wisdom, Chalobah, Garbutt, Keane (Robinson 68), Thorne, Coady, McEachran (Hall 60), Aneke (Kane 76), Wickham.

UEFA UNDER-17 CHAMPIONSHIP FINALS

18 May *(in Vaduz)*

England 3 *(Barkley 20, McEachran 68, Afobe 69)*

Czech Republic 1 *(Plsek 7)*   550

England: Johnstone; Chalobah, Pilatos, Wisdom, Keane (Hall 59), McEachran (Thorpe 75), Thorne (Williams 75), Afobe, Wickham, Barkley, Garbutt.

21 May *(in Vaduz)*

England 1 *(Barkley 35)*   **Greece 0**   665

England: Johnstone; Pilatos, Garbutt, Coady, Chalobah, Wisdom, Keane (Williams 73), Afobe (Hall 51), McEachran (Thorne 80), Barkley, Wickham.

24 May *(in Vaduz)*

England 2 *(Berahino 35, Hall 62 (pen))*

Turkey 1 *(Okan 31)*   1630

England: Butland; Pilatos, Coady, Wisdom, Thorne, Afobe, Berahino (Garbutt 72), Hall, Gibson, Thorpe, Williams (Barkley 66).

27 May *(in Vaduz)*

England 2 *(Wickham 23, 40)*   **France 1** *(Pogba 56)*   1100

England: Butland; Chalobah, Garbutt, Pilatos, Wisdom, Coady, Keane (Hall 16) (Gibson 80), McEachran (Thorne 68), Afobe, Wickham, Barkley.

30 May *(in Vaduz)*

England 2 *(Wisdom 30, Wickham 42)*

Spain 1 *(Wisdom 22 (og))*   3990

England: Butland; Chalobah, Garbutt, Pilatos, Wisdom, Coady, Keane (Thorne 67), McEachran (Thorpe 79), Afobe (Hall 73), Wickham, Barkley.

ENGLAND UNDER-18

UNDER-18 CENTENARY SHIELD

	P	W	D	L	F	A	Pts
Republic of Ireland	4	3	0	1	7	3	9
England	4	2	1	1	8	3	7
Northern Ireland	4	1	2	1	4	6	5
Scotland	4	1	1	2	7	12	4
Wales	4	0	2	2	3	5	2

ENGLAND UNDER-19

Cruz, Deacon, Hoyte, Lansbury, Murphy, Watt (Arsenal); Baker, Delfouneso, Gardner (Aston Villa); Mutch (Birmingham C); Jones (Blackburn R); Thompson (Celtic); Mellis (Chelsea); Clarke (Coventry C); Clyne (Crystal Palace); Severn (Derby Co); Gosling, Wallace (Everton); Briggs, Foderingham (Fulham); Mattock (Leicester C); Trippier, Tutte (Manchester C); Brown, Drinkwater, James, Stewart, Welbeck (Manchester U); Bennett, Steele (Middlesbrough); Donaldson, Ranger (Newcastle U); Rudd (Norwich C); O'Brien (Portsmouth); Gobern (Southampton); Wedderburn (Stoke C); Noble (Sunderland); Bostock, Caulker, Mason, Parrett, Smith, Townsend, Walker (Tottenham H); Nouble (West Ham U); Malone (Wolverhampton W); Phillips (Wycombe W).

UEFA UNDER-19 QUALIFYING CHAMPIONSHIP

9 Oct *(in Murska Sobota)*

England 3 *(Delfouneso 5, Mellis 16, Parrett 90)*
Finland 1 *(Riski 34)*
England: Rudd; Clarke, Malone, Wallace, Brown, Baker, Parrett, Nouble (Donaldson 72), Delfouneso, Mellis (Caulker 62), Mason (Stewart 54).

11 Oct *(in Murska Sobota)*

Slovenia 1 *(Vrhunc 90)*
England 3 *(Donaldson 41, Mellis 64, Deacon 80 (pen))*
England: Rudd; Malone, Brown, Baker, Parrett (Clarke 24), Nouble (Deacon 57), Delfouneso (Stewart 57), Mellis, Caulker, Wedderburn, Donaldson.

14 Oct *(in Lendava)*

England 2 *(Mason 64, Mellis 90)* **Slovakia 0**
England: Severn; Smith, Brown, Baker, Malone, Wedderburn, Deacon (Delfouneso 72), Mason, Stewart, Donaldson (Mellis 85), Nouble (Wallace 55).

26 May *(in Kiev)*

Republic of Ireland 0 **England 1** *(Parrett)*
England: Caulker; Briggs, Brown, Cruz (Townsend 63), Mellis (Phillips 76), Delfouneso, Donaldson, Parrett (Bostock 86), Rudd, Jones, James.

28 May *(in Kiev)*

England 4 *(Noble 2, Phillips 19, Bostock 69, Delfouneso 80)*
Bosnia 0
England: Caulker; Brown, Bostock (Delfouneso 74), Clyne, Donaldson (Townsend 57), Rudd, Jones (Mellis 65), Phillips, Noble, Thompson, James.

31 May *(in Kiev)*

Ukraine 1 *(Zubko 81)* **England 1** *(Parrett 83)*
England: Caulker; Briggs (Clyne 51), Brown, Cruz, Delfouneso (Townsend 76), Parrett, Rudd, Jones, Noble (Donaldson 60), Thompson, James.

UEFA UNDER-19 CHAMPIONSHIP FINALS

21 July *(in Donetsk)*

England 1 *(Mattock 34)*
Switzerland 1 *(Wutrich 90)*   2000
England: Steele; Mattock, Gosling, Walker, Hoyte, Welbeck (Townsend 69), Ranger, Delfouneso (Drinkwater 84), Lansbury, James, Briggs (Bennett 72).

24 July *(in Donetsk)*

Ukraine 2 *(Petrov 2, 61)*
England 2 *(Lansbury 25 (pen), Gosling 51)*   7438
England: Steele; Mattock, Gosling (Bennett 76), Walker, Hoyte, Welbeck (Delfouneso 84), Drinkwater, Ranger (Murphy 72), Lansbury, James, Briggs.

27 July *(in Donetsk)*

Slovenia 1 *(Dimitrov 50)* *(Jovic⁕)*
England 7 *(Lansbury 10, Briggs 19, Welbeck 25, 32, Delfouneso 38, 70, Ranger 74)*   300
England: Steele; Trippier, Gosling, Walker, Welbeck (Ranger 69), Delfouneso, Lansbury (Townsend 65), Murphy, Bennett, Tutte, Briggs (Hoyte 65).

30 July *(in Donetsk)*

England 3 *(Lansbury 37, Delfouneso 92, 105)*
France 1 *(Gueye 8)*   4200
England: Steele; Trippier, Gosling, Walker, Welbeck (Ranger 75), Drinkwater, Delfouneso, Lansbury, Murphy (Mattock 63), Bennett, Briggs (Hoyte 79).
Sent off: Corchia, El Kaoutari, Boudebouz.

2 Aug *(in Donetsk)*

England 0 **Ukraine 2** *(Garmash 5, Korkishko 50)* 25,100
England: Steele; Trippier, Mattock, Gosling, Walker, Welbeck (Ranger 63), Drinkwater (Tutte 55), Delfouneso, Lansbury, Bennett, Briggs (Hoyte 56).

FRIENDLIES

8 Sept *(at Shrewsbury)*

England 2 *(Ranger 54, Brown 65)*   3043
Russia 1 *(Logua 9)*
England: Rudd (Foderingham 60); Baker, James, Townsend (Wallace 46), Delfouneso, Ranger (Donaldson 60), Watt (Stewart 70), Brown, Clyne (Clarke 46), Malone (Briggs 74), Mellis (Gobern 60).

17 Nov *(at Scunthorpe)*

England 3 *(Parrett 66, Gardner 82, Delfouneso 90)*
Turkey 1 *(Ozgur 40)*   4012
England: Foderingham (Severn 76); Baker, Caulker, Clarke (Clyne 46), Bostock (Gardner 78), Parrett, Stewart (Mason 63), Wedderburn (Watt 46), Delfouneso, Ranger (Nouble 46), Malone (Jones 70).

2 Mar *(in Waalwijk)*

Holland 1 *(Brown 86 (og))* **England 1** *(Mellis)*
England: Foderingham (O'Brien 61); Caulker (Mutch 46), Clyne (Wedderburn 72), Briggs, Cruz (Mason 61), Bostock (Brown 46), Ranger (Noble 61), Watt (Deacon 68), Nouble, Mellis, Malone.

ENGLAND UNDER-20

Hoyte (Arsenal); Albrighton, Clark, Gardner, Parish (Aston Villa); Obadeyi (Bolton W); Cork, Ofori-Twumasi (Chelsea); Briggs (Fulham); Kelly (Liverpool); Clayton, Marshall, Mee, Nimley-Tchuimeni, Trippier, Tutte, Vidal (Manchester C); Brandy, Cleverley, James (Manchester U); Bennett, Walker (Middlesbrough); Baldock (Milton Keynes D); Rudd (Norwich C); Robson-Kanu (Reading); Henderson (Sunderland); Obika (Tottenham H); Jenkins, Parkes (Watford).

FRIENDLY

11 Aug *(at West Bromwich Albion)*

England 5 *(Brandy 13, 45, Cleverley 48, 83, Obadeyi 90)*
Montenegro 0   2150
England: Rudd; Bennett, Kelly, Clark (Mee 58), Vidal, Jenkins (Clayton 46), Albrighton (Henderson 56), Cork, Cleverley, Brandy, Robson-Kanu (Obadeyi 57).

FIFA WORLD UNDER-20 CHAMPIONSHIP

26 Sept *(in Ismailia)*

England 0 **Uruguay 1** *(Viudez 84)*   10,000
England: Parish; Trippier, Clayton, Kelly, Mee, Brandy (Gardner 77), Walker, Marshall (Obika 72), James, Briggs (Ofori-Twumasi 46), Nimley-Tchuimeni.

29 Sept *(in Ismailia)*
Ghana 4 *(Adiyiah 38, 88, Ayew 57, Osei 82)*
England 0   13,000
(in Ismailia).
England: Parish; Trippier, Kelly, Mee, Brandy (Baldock 59), Walker, Nimley-Tchuimeni, Marshall (Tutte 46), James, Ofori-Twumasi, Obika (Gardner 73).

2 Oct *(in Suez)*
Uzbekistan 1 *(Nagaev 77)*
England 1 *(Nimley-Tchuimeni 88)*   27,000
England: Parish; Trippier, Clayton (Hoyte 67), Kelly, Mee, Brandy (Baldock 59), Walker, Nimley-Tchuimeni, Marshall, James, Briggs (Parkes 46).

SCHOOLS FOOTBALL 2009–10

BOODLES INDEPENDENT SCHOOLS FA CUP 2009–10

FIRST ROUND
Aldenham 3 Grange 0
Brentwood 6 Bury GS 1
Cheadle Hulme 2 Wolverhampton GS 3 *(aet.)*
Chigwell 0 Bolton 0
   (aet; Chigwell won 5-4 on penalties)
Colfe's 2 Licensed Victuallers 4
Dover College 0 St. Edmund's Sch., Cantab 4
Eton 0 Latymer Upper 2
Forest 3 Alleyn's 2
Frensham Heights 1 St. Bede's Sch., Hailsham 7
Gramm. Sch., Leeds 0 Bedford Modern 3
Haileybury 5 Ibstock Place 1
Hampton 5 KCS Wimbledon 0
Highgate 3 Kimbolton 0
KES Witley 0 Shrewsbury 4
Millfield 6 John Lyon 1
Norwich 1 King's, Chester 1
   (aet; King's won 5-3 on penalties)
Oldham Hulme GS 2 Malvern 1
QEH Bristol 0 Manchester GS 2
Repton 5 QEGS Blackburn 0
St. Bede's College, Manchester 0 Birkdale 1
St. Columba's College 1 Charterhouse 2
Westminster 1 Ardingly 4

SECOND ROUND
Aldenham 4 Bristol GS 1
Bedford Modern 3 Ardingly 2
Bradfield 4 Birkdale 1
Chigwell 1 RGS Newcastle 2
Dulwich College 0 Manchester GS 1
Ewell Castle 0 City of London 2
Haileybury 0 Hampton 6
King's School, Chester 0 Brentwood 4
Latymer Upper 7 Oldham Hulme GS 0
Millfield 3 Winchester 1
Repton 5 Forest 0
Shrewsbury 2 Lancing 0
St. Bede's Sch. Hailsham 0 Highgate 0
   (aet; St. Bede's won 4-2 on penalties)
St. Edmund's, Cantab 3 Licensed Victuallers 6
Tonbridge 1 St. Mary's Col., Crosby 4 *(aet.)*
Wolverhampton GS 2 Charterhouse 3

THIRD ROUND
Aldenham 3 RGS Newcastle 5 *(aet.)*
Bedford Modern 0 Bradfield 2
Brentwood 1 City of London 0
Hampton 1 Millfield 5
Latymer Upper 2 Repton 2
   (aet; Repton won 11-10 on penalties)
Licensed Victuallers 1 Charterhouse 2
Manchester GS 4 St. Mary's Col., Crosby 0
Shrewsbury 2 St. Bede's Sch., Hailsham 1 *(aet.)*

FOURTH ROUND
RGS Newcastle 1 Shrewsbury 4
Manchester GS 1 Brentwood 0
Millfield 3 Charterhouse 2
Repton 2 Bradfield 0

SEMI-FINALS
Millfield 0 Shrewsbury 0 *(aet.)*
   (Shrewsbury won 7-6 on penalties)
Repton 2 Manchester GS 1

FINAL (at Milton Keynes Dons FC)
Shrewsbury 3 *(Chatterjee 3)*

Repton 0

Shrewsbury: G. Barker, W. Taylor (C. Barrow), A. Blofield, D. Lloyd, C. Pilkington, E. White, R. Williams, T. Elliott (T. Elcock), G. Curtis (A. Dougan), P. White, R. Chatterjee.
Repton: N. Jones, G. Fearn, J. Golding, A. Evans, M. Sanderson, D. Moxham (S. Mullen) (S. Woodhead), S. Graham (W. Byas), L. Duggan, N. Chilaka, H. Rees-Jones, J. Gorman.
Referee: Mr. S. Attwell (Warwickshire).

RENSBURG SHEPPARDS ISFA U15 CUP FINAL
(at Burton Albion FC)
Brentwood 3 Repton 1 *(aet.)*

RENSBURG SHEPPARDS ISFA U13 CUP FINAL
Bolton 2 Forest 1
(at Burton Albion FC)

UNIVERSITY FOOTBALL 2009–10

126th UNIVERSITY MATCH

(at Cambridge United, Friday 30 April 2010)

Oxford 1   Cambridge 1

Oxford: Dwayne Whylly*; Tim Squires* (Alex Biggs), Matthew Flood*, Laurence Ball, Elliot Thomas, Adam Zagajewski (Ben Quigley), James Kelly*, Leon Farr* (c), Julian Austin, Ryan McCrickerd*, Tom Howell (Niko de Walden*).
Substitutes: Jason Adebisi, Reuben Holt.
Scorer: Kelly (89).

Cambridge: Ferguson*; M.J. Johnson, Maynard*, Day*, Gwyther, Hartley*, Baxter*, M.P. Johnson* (c), Stock*, Gotch, Hylands.
Substitutes: Ellis, Kerrigan (72), Rutt* (63), Peacock (28), Broadway.
Scorer: Baxter *(pen 25).*

aet; Oxford won 5-4 on penalties.

*denotes Old Blue
Oxford have won 50 games, Cambridge 48 and 28 drawn.   *Both teams have now scored exactly 198 goals.*

WOMEN'S FOOTBALL 2009–10

The story of the last domestic season was surprisingly not about the continued domination of the game by Arsenal Ladies, but about the rise of several other Clubs and the evening out of the competition for the winning of the domestic prizes. True the Gunners annexed the Premier League Title for an unbelievable seventh successive season, but this time the Women's FA Cup sponsored by E.on went to Everton and the Women's Premier League Cup was won by Leeds Carnegie.

In those Cup competitions the first Final was the League Cup held at Rochdale's Spotland Stadium, on Thursday the 11th February 2010. In something of a surprise the ladies of Leeds Carnegie defeated the favourites Everton Ladies by 3-1. Leeds took a two goal lead before half-time through goals from Kate Holtham on 14 minutes and Ellen White six minutes later; but although Everton pulled one back through Fara Williams four minutes after the break, a third and decisive goal in the 85th minute by Ellen White again, handed the trophy to Leeds.

Everton were however the winners of the Premier League Reserve Section League Cup beating Birmingham City LFC Reserves 2-1 in the Final.

The Women's FA Cup was again contested by Everton but in a great game held at the City Ground home of Nottingham Forest on Monday the 3rd of May 2010 they triumphed over their greatest rivals Arsenal by 3-2. The game went into extra time before the Toffees could hold the Cup aloft and their winner was scored by Natasha Dowie the niece of the then current Director of football at Hull, Ian Dowie. Uncle Ian was unable to be there to celebrate as he was in charge of a Hull fixture. In fact it was Natasha Dowie who had put Everton into the lead in 16 minutes but Arsenal equalised through Kim Little, who netted from the penalty spot on 42 minutes. Everton regained the lead before halftime when Faye White inadvertently headed into her own net. Arsenal pressed strongly in the second period and the dangerous Julie Fleeting equalised for a second time in the 54th minute. However with the anticipation of the dreaded penalty shoot out in view Dowie clinched victory in the 119th minute with a composed solo effort. It was a triumph for Everton's Manager Mo Marley the mastermind of the rise of Everton Ladies, who are now recognised as second only to Arsenal in the Women's football rankings. The victory was also remarkable for the fact that it was Arsenal's first defeat at this stage of the competition having won all 10 of their previous FA Cup Finals.

However in the FA Women's Premier League competition it was business as usual for the Gunners. Their previous Manager Vic Akers led them to victory in achieving 33 trophies in 22 years so it was a big ask of new Manager Laura Harvey in her first season to uphold the tradition, even if Akers was in the background as General Manager. However their 12th League Title was achieved with 20 wins out of 22 matches with one draw and one defeat and a goal difference of 60 having scored 79 goals to achieve 61 points. This was 11 more than nearest rivals Everton, whilst The Toffees total of 50 points was one more than third placed Chelsea another of the up and coming sides. The bottom Club was unfortunately Bristol Academy WFC who achieved only 10 points some 3 less than the other relegated side Nottingham Forest LFC.

In the Leagues below the National Division, promoted Liverpool LFC were the winners of the Northern Division with 59 points which was 10 more than runners up OOH Lincoln LFC and in the Southern Division first place and promotion went to Barnet FC Ladies who had an 8 point margin over second placed Reading FC Women.

The spread of Women's football can be seen in the fact that smaller Clubs in Men's football such as Lincoln City and Barnet FC have very successful Women's teams and the latter also reached the semi-final of the Women's FA Cup whilst several others are flourishing. Likewise there is also a very vibrant Women's Reserve League competition with as many as four Divisions. Thus in the Reserves Mid/North Division One: Blackburn Rovers LFC won the Title with Doncaster Rovers Belles second and in the Reserves Mid/North Division Leicester City WFC were crowned Champions ahead of Manchester City. In the Reserves Southern Section Division One: Arsenal LFC were first with Chelsea LFC second and in Division Two of the same League Cardiff City LFC took the Title ahead of Charlton Athletic WFC.

There is much excitement in the domestic scene over the formation of the FA Women's Super League due to come into existence at its launch in March 2011. The first eight successful clubs for enrolment were in alphabetical order – Arsenal, Birmingham City, Bristol Academy, Chelsea, Doncaster Rovers Belle, Everton, Lincoln Ladies and Liverpool Ladies.

The success of the England Women's National sides has resulted quite correctly in the awarding of a CBE to Hope Powell, England Women's Head Coach, in this year's Queen's Birthday Honours List. She had previously, in 2002, been awarded an OBE and both Honours relate to the very considerable services she has rendered to Women's football particularly in the realms of England's International successes. Hope was the first ever woman to achieve the UEFA Pro Licence and as a player won 66 Caps for England scoring 35 goals.Under her stewardship in the period from August 2009 to May 2010 the senior England Women's team played 14 games 10 of which were won, with two draws and only two defeats; several of these games being important World Cup Qualifying matches. The International structure also encompasses Under 23; Under 19; Under 17 and Under 15 teams.

As Women's football continues to grow at a very fast pace there are initiatives countrywide to raise its awareness and to encourage young girls to become involved. One of these involves the London FA who has launched two new soccer centres in south east London for girls aged 8–12 years of age .These are being linked in with the Centres of Excellence programmes at Millwall and Charlton Athletic. The object is to form small teams which will eventually be entered into local leagues. The funding comes from the London Playing Fields Foundation who has a considerable involvement in the development of Women's football In London. There are also further moves in London to form an innovative London Women's Football Coaching Association as a follow up for those females who have passed their coaching levels and to help others to pass theirs.

KEN GOLDMAN

FA WOMEN'S PREMIER LEAGUE 2009–10

NATIONAL DIVISION

		P	Home					Away					Total					GD	Pts
			W	D	L	F	A	W	D	L	F	A	W	D	L	F	A		
1	Arsenal	22	11	0	0	53	11	9	1	1	26	8	20	1	1	79	19	60	61
2	Everton	22	8	0	3	33	11	8	2	1	34	8	16	2	4	67	19	48	50
3	Chelsea	22	8	0	3	27	16	8	1	2	33	11	16	1	5	60	27	33	49
4	Leeds Carnegie	22	7	1	3	23	9	8	1	2	27	7	15	2	5	50	16	34	47
5	Sunderland	22	6	1	4	18	17	6	0	5	18	18	12	1	9	36	35	1	37
6	Doncaster Rovers Belles	22	3	6	2	18	17	6	1	4	18	20	9	7	6	36	37	-1	34
7	Blackburn Rovers	22	2	2	7	11	25	5	1	5	16	20	7	3	12	27	45	-18	24
8	Millwall Lionesses	22	4	1	6	11	22	2	2	7	13	21	6	3	13	24	43	-19	21
9	Watford	22	3	4	4	10	19	1	1	9	13	41	4	5	13	23	60	-37	17
10	Birmingham City	22	4	0	7	11	16	0	4	7	10	25	4	4	14	21	41	-20	16
11	Nottingham Forest	22	0	2	9	9	34	3	2	6	7	17	3	4	15	16	51	-35	13
12	Bristol Academy	22	2	0	9	5	25	1	1	9	7	33	3	1	18	12	58	-46	10

NORTHERN DIVISION

		P	Home					Away					Total					GD	Pts
			W	D	L	F	A	W	D	L	F	A	W	D	L	F	A		
1	Liverpool	22	9	1	1	31	9	10	1	0	28	10	19	2	1	59	19	40	59
2	OOH Lincoln	22	8	1	2	22	10	7	3	1	24	12	15	4	3	46	22	24	49
3	Leicester City	22	6	3	2	30	17	5	3	3	23	18	11	6	5	53	35	18	39
4	Manchester City	22	3	4	4	20	18	7	2	2	16	7	10	6	6	36	25	11	36
5	Curzon Ashton	22	5	3	3	18	15	4	1	6	19	24	9	4	9	37	39	-2	31
6	Aston Villa	22	4	3	4	15	15	3	5	3	22	20	7	8	7	37	35	2	29
7	Leeds City Vixens	22	4	2	5	21	26	5	0	6	20	22	9	2	11	41	48	-7	29
8	Newcastle United	22	3	3	5	16	20	4	3	4	22	28	7	6	9	38	48	-10	27
9	Preston North End	22	5	2	4	38	27	1	4	6	18	27	6	6	10	56	54	2	24
10	Derby County	22	3	3	5	15	20	2	2	7	15	31	5	5	12	30	51	-21	20
11	Sheffield Wednesday	22	4	3	4	20	22	0	3	8	9	28	4	6	12	29	50	-21	18
12	Luton Town	22	1	1	9	6	23	0	2	9	6	25	1	3	18	12	48	-36	6

SOUTHERN DIVISION

		P	Home					Away					Total					GD	Pts
			W	D	L	F	A	W	D	L	F	A	W	D	L	F	A		
1	Barnet	22	9	2	0	35	8	7	2	2	18	10	16	4	2	53	18	35	52
2	Reading	22	5	5	1	20	14	8	0	3	23	14	13	5	4	43	28	15	44
3	Keynsham Town	22	7	3	1	27	13	5	2	4	28	23	12	5	5	55	36	19	41
4	Portsmouth	22	7	1	3	21	13	4	5	2	21	19	11	6	5	42	32	10	39
5	West Ham United	22	5	4	2	22	12	4	5	2	16	12	9	9	4	38	24	14	36
6	Cardiff City	22	7	2	2	24	17	3	3	5	20	15	10	5	7	44	32	12	35
7	Charlton Athletic	22	6	2	3	11	7	4	2	5	13	13	10	4	8	24	20	4	34
8	Brighton & HA	22	3	4	4	20	19	3	4	4	13	14	6	8	8	33	33	0	26
9	Colchester United	22	4	3	4	10	13	2	2	7	9	27	6	5	11	19	40	-21	23
10	Queens Park Rangers	22	3	2	6	26	20	2	3	6	16	23	5	5	12	42	43	-1	20
11	Fulham	22	0	2	9	8	27	2	0	9	6	36	2	2	18	14	63	-49	8
12	Crystal Palace	22	0	1	10	5	27	1	3	7	7	23	1	4	17	12	50	-38	7

NATIONAL DIVISION LEAGUE – PREVIOUS WINNERS

1992–93	Arsenal	1998–99	Croydon	2004–05	Arsenal
1993–94	Doncaster Belles	1999–00	Croydon	2005–06	Arsenal
1994–95	Arsenal	2000–01	Arsenal	2006–07	Arsenal
1995–96	Croydon	2001–02	Arsenal	2007–08	Arsenal
1996–97	Arsenal	2002–03	Fulham	2008–09	Arsenal
1997–98	Everton	2003–04	Arsenal	2009–10	Arsenal

FA WOMEN'S PREMIER RESERVE LEAGUES 2009–10

MID/NORTH DIVISION ONE

		P	W	D	L	GD	Pts
1	Blackburn Rovers	21	15	1	5	18	46
2	Doncaster Rovers Belles	21	13	1	7	24	40
3	Everton	21	11	7	3	23	40
4	Leeds Carnegie	21	9	2	10	12	29
5	Liverpool	21	9	2	10	-12	29
6	Sunderland	21	7	2	12	5	23
7	Preston North End	21	6	1	14	-47	19
8	Nottingham Forest	21	5	2	14	-23	17

SOUTHERN DIVISION ONE

		P	W	D	L	GD	Pts
1	Arsenal	14	12	0	2	54	36
2	Chelsea	14	11	1	2	41	34
3	Watford	14	9	2	3	14	29
4	Bristol Academy	14	8	1	5	10	25
5	West Ham United	14	6	0	8	-19	18
6	Reading	14	3	2	9	-26	11
7	Millwall Lionesses	14	1	2	11	-35	5
8	Barnet	14	1	2	11	-39	5

MID/NORTH DIVISION TWO

		P	W	D	L	GD	Pts
1	Leicester City	10	6	1	3	17	19
2	Manchester City	10	5	3	2	1	18
3	Birmingham City	10	4	3	3	4	15
4	Derby County	10	3	2	5	-2	11
5	OOH Lincoln	10	2	4	4	-7	10
6	Newcastle United	10	2	3	5	-13	9

SOUTHERN DIVISION TWO

		P	W	D	L	GD	Pts
1	Cardiff City	14	9	4	1	21	31
2	Charlton Athletic	14	9	3	2	24	30
3	Colchester United	14	9	1	4	26	28
4	Brighton & HA	14	5	3	5	8	18
5	Queens Park Rangers	13	4	2	7	-23	14
6	Portsmouth FC	13	4	1	8	-15	13
7	Crystal Palace	13	3	3	7	-15	12
8	Fulham	14	1	3	10	-26	6

THE FA TESCO WOMEN'S PREMIER LEAGUE CUP 2009–10

FIRST ROUND

West Ham United v Millwall Lionesses	0-0
Millwall Lionesses won 4-1 on penalties.	
Keynsham Town v Crystal Palace	7-1
Aston Villa v Derby County	3-0
Birmingham City v Ooh Lincoln Ladies	6-2
Cardiff City v Bristol Academy	0-4
Leicester City v Preston Ladies	3-2
Sunderland v Liverpool	5-1
Sheffield Wednesday v Everton	0-5
Blackburn Rovers v Manchester City	4-2
Chelsea v Barnet	6-2
Leeds Carnegie Ladies v Nottingham Forest	1-0
Doncaster Rovers Belles v Preston North End	4-0
Watford v Arsenal	1-4
Charlton Athletic v Luton Town	1-0
Portsmouth Ladies v Fulham	5-2
QPR v Reading	0-3

SECOND ROUND

Aston Villa v Leeds Carnegie Ladies	2-4
Birmingham City v Blackburn Rovers	1-2
Doncaster Rovers Belles v Leicester City	3-1
Everton v Sunderland	4-0
Bristol Academy v Reading	4-3
Keynsham Town v Charlton Athletic	4-1

Millwall Lionesses v Arsenal	0-2
Portsmouth Ladies v Chelsea	0-1

QUARTER-FINALS

Leeds Carnegie Ladies v Blackburn Rovers	5-0
Chelsea v Bristol Academy	8-0
Arsenal v Keynsham Town	4-0
Everton v Doncaster Rovers Belles	3-0

SEMI-FINALS

Everton v Arsenal	2-1
Chelsea v Leeds Carnegie Ladies	0-2

FINAL (at Rochdale)

Everton (0) 1 (*Williams 46*)   2842

Leeds Carnegie Ladies (2) 3 (*Holtham 14, White 20, 85*)

Everton: Brown; Westwood, Unitt, Williams, Whelan, Johnson, Handley, Scott, Dowie, Hinnigan (Harries 77), Duggan.

Leeds Carnegie Ladies: Telford; Bradley, Walton, Holtham, Smith (Thackary 87), White, Clarke (Allen 71), Cantrell, Metcalfe, Moore, Bassett.

Referee: S. Massey.

THE FA WOMEN'S CUP 2009–10
SPONSORED BY E.ON

PRELIMINARY ROUND

Forest Hall Women's YPC w.o. v Stokesley Ladies withdrew	
Newcastle Medics v Gateshead Rutherford Ravens	0-9
Prudhoe Youth Club v Tynedale Ladies	1-3
Gateshead Cleveland Hall v North Shields Ladies	0-7
Accrington Girls & Ladies v Harraby Catholic Club	0-1
Dearne & District Ladies v Kirklees	2-1
Tipton Town Ladies v Stourport Swifts	16-0
Woodford United v Brackley Sports	0-4
Saffron Walden Town v C&AK Basildon	1-5
Runwell Hospital v Hutton Ladies	4-1
Eastleigh Ladies v Boscombe Albion	5-0
Christchurch v New Forest Ladies	3-3
New Forest Ladies won 4-1 on penalties.	

FIRST QUALIFYING ROUND

Gateshead Rutherford Ravens v Birtley Town Ladies	0-3
Forest Hall Women's YPC v North Shields Ladies	1-5
Whitley Bay Women v Teesside Athletic	7-0
Tynedale Ladies v Brandon United	3-0
Blyth Spartans withdrew v Peterlee Town w.o.	
Abbey Town Women's v Warrington Town	1-2
Birkenhead Ladies v Middleton Athletic	2-3
Whitehaven Ladies v Bury Girls & Ladies	3-1
Chester City v Wigan Athletic Ladies	0-2
Harraby Catholic Club v Dalton United Ladies	1-0
Bolton Wanderers v Preston Rangers	10-1
Barnsley v Hull City	1-2
Dearne & District Ladies v Huddersfield Town	3-1
Steel City Wanderers v Sheffield United Junior Blades Ladies	2-0
Guiseley Ladies v Sheffield Ladies	1-2
Keighley Ladies v Sheffield United Community	1-5
Rolls Royce Leisure v Market Warsop	2-1
Mansfield Town v Peterborough	2-1
Sandiacre Town v Retford United	4-0
Friar Lane & Epworth v Long Eaton United	2-4
Peterborough Azure v West Bridgford	5-0
Hinckley United Ladies v Loughborough Students	1-4
Huntingdon Town Ladies v Oadby & Wigston Girls & Ladies	1-7
Linby CW v Shepshed Dynamo	1-7
Hereford Phoenix Ladies v Cottage Farm Rangers	5-0
Tipton Town Ladies v Scutham United	0-4
Leamington Lions v Carnock Ladies	3-1
Hereford Pegasus v Aliscott	3-2
Worcester City v Stratford Town	0-1
Crusaders Ladies removed v Coventry Ladies Development	
Lichfield Diamonds v Dudley United	1-6
Haverhill Rovers v Stalham Town Ladies	1-0

Cambridge University v West Lynn	1-2
Bungay Town v Woodbridge Town	0-9
AFC Kempston Rovers v Raunds Town	3-0
Daventry Town v Corby S&L	1-3
Bedford Ladies v Kingsthorpe Ladies & Girls	7-0
Leighton Linslade Ladies v Whitwell Ladies	3-0
Brackley Sports v Arlesey Town Ladies	0-3
Kettering Town v Hitchin Hearts	3-0
London Colney withdrew v Brentwood Town w.o.	
C&K Basildon v Barking	0-5
Royston Town v Braintree Town	1-2
Hemel Hempstead Town v Billericay Town	3-2
Tring Athletic v Stevenage Borough	2-1
Runwell Hospital v Chelmsford City	2-5
Sawbridgeworth Town v Garston	2-1
Harringey Borough v Wandgass	4-1
MSA Ladies v Manford Way Ladies	4-1
Leyton Ladies v Panthers	0-4
Tower Hamlets v Westfield Ladies	3-0
AFC Wimbledon Ladies v Horley Town	3-1
Old Actonians v Denham United	2-1
Ashford Girls v Crowborough Athletic	5-1
Rottingdean Village v Canterbury City	0-2
Ramsgate v Maidstone Town	0-9
Bexhill United v Haywards Heath Town	0-3
Eastbourne Town v London Corinthians	5-1
Aldershot Town v Southampton Saints	1-0
Crawley Wasps v Chichester City	3-0
BTC Southampton Ladies withdrew v Shanklin w.o.	
Southampton v University of Portsmouth	1-5
Eastleigh Ladies v Basingstoke Town Ladies	0-5
Littlehampton Town Devils & Ladies v New Forest Ladies	2-1
Bracknell Town v Cheltenham Town Ladies	3-0
Wycombe Wanderers v Forest of Dean	4-1
Chippenham Town Ladies v Stoke Lane Athletic	3-6
Stony Stratford Town v Reading Girls	5-4
MK Wanderers v Oxford United	0-3
Launton v Marlow Ladies	4-1
Maidenhead United Ladies v Banbury United	14-0
Slough v Newent Town Ladies	9-0
Reading v Swindon Supermarine Ladies	1-3
Poole Town v Keynsham Town Development	0-6
Launceston v Saltash United	0-2
Frome Town v Weymouth Ladies	2-0

SECOND QUALIFYING ROUND

Birtley Town Ladies v Whitley Bay Women	2-10
Tynedale Ladies v Peterlee Town	0-2
North Shields Ladies v Harraby Catholic Club	1-5
Warrington Town v Hull City	0-8
Bolton Wanderers v Dearne & District Ladies	3-1

Sheffield Ladies v Middleton Athletic	11-0
Whitehaven Ladies v Wigan Athletic Ladies	0-2
Sheffield United Community v Steel City Wanderers	3-1
Peterborough Azure v Rolls Royce Leisure	2-1
Shepshed Dynamo v Loughborough Students	1-3
Sandiacre Town v Mansfield Town	3-0
Long Eaton United v Oadby & Wigston Girls & Ladies	4-1
Stratford Town v Hereford Phoenix Ladies	1-3
Corby S&L v Coventry Ladies Development	4-0
Leamington Lions v Southam United	3-0
Hereford Pegasus v Dudley United	2-5
Bedford Ladies v Haverhill Rovers	3-0
Kettering Town v Leighton Linslade Ladies	2-1
Woodbridge Town v West Lynn	3-0
AFC Kempston Rovers v Arlesey Town Ladies	1-3
Brentwood Town v Chelmsford City	1-4
Tring Athletic v Sawbridgeworth Town	2-3
MSA Ladies v Barking	2-6
Braintree Town v Hemel Hempstead Town	4-3
Panthers v Harringey Borough	3-4
Tower Hamlets v Maidstone Town	1-3
Canterbury City v Haywards Heath Town	2-3
Aldershot Town v AFC Wimbledon Ladies	5-0
Old Actonians v Ashford Girls	6-0
Crawley Wasps v Eastbourne Town	1-2
Launton v Wycombe Wanderers	1-4
Shanklin v Bracknell Town	5-0
University of Portsmouth v Basingstoke Town Ladies	3-2
Oxford United v Stony Stratford Town	8-0
Littlehampton Town Devils & Ladies v Maidenhead United Ladies	3-2
Slough v Stoke Lane Athletic	8-3
Keynsham Town Development v Swindon Supermarine Ladies	2-4
Frome Town v Saltash United	0-1

THIRD QUALIFYING ROUND

Sheffield Ladies v Whitley Bay Women	1-2
Wigan Athletic Ladies v Peterlee Town	2-6
Harraby Catholic Club v Hull City	1-12
Bolton Wanderers v Sheffield United Community	0-7
Long Eaton United v Peterborough Azure	2-0
Leamington Lions v Corby S&L	4-1
Hereford Phoenix Ladies v Loughborough Students	3-5
Dudley United v Sandiacre Town	2-1
Woodbridge Town v Chelmsford City	3-3
Woodbridge Town won 8-7 on penalties.	
Braintree Town v Sawbridgeworth Town	0-3
Kettering Town v Barking	1-5
Bedford Ladies v Arlesey Town Ladies	2-1
Aldershot Town v Old Actonians	3-5
Haywards Heath Town v Maidstone Town	1-2
Harringey Borough v Eastbourne Town	2-1
Wycombe Wanderers v Littlehampton Town Devils & Ladies	1-7
Slough v Swindon Supermarine Ladies	0-5
Shanklin v Oxford United	1-0
Saltash United v University of Portsmouth	2-0

FIRST ROUND

Liverpool Feds v Peterlee Town	4-0
Salford Ladies w.o. v Darlington RA withdrew	
Stockport County v Bradford City	3-1
Whitley Bay Women v Blackpool Wren Rovers	7-1
Hull City v Rochdale AFC Ladies	0-9
Tranmere Rovers v Rotherham United	1-6
Sheffield United Community v Middlesbrough	1-2
South Durham GSK Royals v Wakefield Ladies	1-2
Wolverhampton Wanderers v Sporting Club Albion	1-3
Stoke City v Loughborough Students	5-4
Long Eaton United v Coventry City	0-2
Leafield Athletic v Leamington Lions	8-0
Copsewood (Coventry) v Scunthorpe United	7-1
Leicester City Ladies v Loughborough Foxes	2-3
Dudley United v TNS	2-1
Littlehampton Town Devils & Ladies v Ebbsfleet United	2-1
Harringey Borough v Barking	3-1
Enfield Town v Maidstone Town	3-1
Tottenham Hotspur v Northampton Town	0-1
Cambridge Women's v Sawbridgeworth Town	5-0
MK Dons Ladies v Old Actonians	3-0
Gillingham v Oxford City	6-0
Lewes v Ipswich Town	5-2

Dagenham & Redbridge withdrew v Norwich City Ladies w.o.	
Welwyn Garden City withdrew v Woodbridge Town w.o.	
Bedford Ladies v Chesham United	0-3
Shanklin v Havant & Waterlooville	0-2
Plymouth Argyle v Swindon Supermarine Ladies	5-1
Saltash United v Yeovil Town	0-3
Cullumpton Rangers withdrew v Forest Green Rovers w.o.	
Swindon Town v Winscombe	3-2
Reading Town v Newquay Ladies	1-7

SECOND ROUND

Whitley Bay Women v Rochdale AFC Ladies	2-3
Salford Ladies v Middlesbrough	0-2
Rotherham United v Liverpool Feds	2-3
Stockport County v Wakefield Ladies	1-0
Coventry City v Leafield Athletic	7-0
Sporting Club Albion v Loughborough Foxes	4-1
Copsewood (Coventry) v Stoke City	2-3
Cambridge Women's v Dudley United	2-3
Norwich City Ladies v Chesham United	3-1
Lewes v Harringey Borough	5-1
Woodbridge Town v Littlehampton Town Devils & Ladies	0-1
Enfield Town v Gillingham	0-3
MK Dons Ladies v Northampton Town	2-0
Newquay Ladies v Swindon Town	2-0
Plymouth Argyle v Havant & Waterlooville	2-5
Yeovil Town v Forest Green Rovers	4-1

THIRD ROUND

Liverpool Feds v Rochdale AFC Ladies	1-0
Liverpool v Preston North End	4-1
Sheffield Wednesday Women v Stockport County	5-2
Middlesbrough v Curzon Ashton	1-2
Leeds City Vixens v Manchester City	1-0
Ooh Lincoln Ladies v Newcastle United	2-2
Ooh Lincoln Ladies won 3-2 on penalties.	
Aston Villa v Sporting Club Albion	3-2
Stoke City v Leicester City	2-6
Luton Town Ladies v Cambridge Women's	4-1
Coventry City v Derby County	1-4
Reading Women v Brighton & Hove Albion	1-0
Charlton Athletic v West Ham United	0-3
Gillingham v Barnet Ladies	1-4
Lewes v Queens Park Rangers	0-5
Yeovil Town v Newquay Ladies	3-1
MK Dons Ladies v Norwich City Ladies	3-5
Keynsham Town v Portsmouth	2-3
Havant & Waterlooville v Cardiff City	2-1
Crystal Palace v Fulham	0-0
Fulham won 5-4 on penalties.	
Colchester United v Littlehampton Town Devils & Ladies	4-0

FOURTH ROUND

Liverpool Feds v Curzon Ashton	0-5
Bristol Academy v West Ham United	1-2
Ooh Lincoln Ladies v Sheffield Wednesday Women	3-1
Portsmouth v Luton Town Ladies	2-1
Fulham v Blackburn Rovers	0-6
Everton v Queens Park Rangers	6-2
Reading Women v Aston Villa	1-1
Aston Villa won 5-4 on penalties.	
Liverpool v Chelsea	1-2
Norwich City Ladies v Yeovil Town	1-3
Nottingham Forest v Leeds City Vixens	3-2
Leeds Carnegie Ladies v Watford	4-1
Leicester City v Millwall Lionesses	0-3
Arsenal v Sunderland	4-1
Doncaster Rovers Belles v Havant & Waterlooville	6-1
Birmingham City v Derby County	4-1
Colchester United v Barnet Ladies	2-3

FIFTH ROUND

Blackburn Rovers v Ooh Lincoln Ladies	1-0
West Ham United v Barnet Ladies	2-3
Everton v Portsmouth	7-0
Arsenal v Leeds Carnegie Ladies	3-2
Birmingham City v Doncaster Rovers Belles	0-1
Curzon Ashton v Aston Villa	1-2
Yeovil Town v Nottingham Forest	0-1
Chelsea v Millwall Lionesses	3-1

Everton's Natasha Dowie (centre) scores the first goal against Arsenal in the Women's FA Cup Final at Nottingham Forest. She was later to make it 3-2 deep into injury time and see Everton lift the cup. (PA Photos)

SIXTH ROUND

Aston Villa v Chelsea	3-4
Barnet Ladies v Nottingham Forest	3-2
Arsenal v Doncaster Rovers Belles	5-0
Everton v Blackburn Rovers	2-1

SEMI-FINALS

Everton v Barnet Ladies	2-0
Chelsea v Arsenal	0-4

FINAL (at Nottingham Forest)

Monday, 3 May 2010

Arsenal (1) 2 (*Little 43(pen), Fleeting 54*)   17,505
Everton (2) 3 (*Dowie 16, 119, White 45 (og)*)

Arsenal: Byrne; Yorston, Flaherty, White, Grant, Fleeting (Carter 70), Yankey, Davison, Beattie, Little, Fahey.
Everton: Brown; Easton, Unitt (Whelan 63), Williams, Westwood, Johnson, Handley, Scott, Dowie, Hinnigan (Chaplen 77), Duggan (Evans 111).
aet.
Referee: U. Hon.

UEFA WOMEN'S CHAMPIONS LEAGUE 2009–10

QUALIFYING ROUND

GROUP 1
Bayern 5, Glasgow 2
Gintra 7, Norchi 1
Bayern 19, Norchi 0
Glasgow 2, Gintra 0
Gintra 0, Bayern 8
Norchi 0, Glasgow 9

GROUP 2
Montpellier 2, KI 0
NSA Sofia 5, Tikvesanka 0
Montpellier 7, Tikvesanka 1
KI 1, NSA Sofia 2
NSA Sofia 0, Montpellier 3
Tikvesanka 2, KI 4

GROUP 3
1st Dezembro 10, Birkirkara 0
Brondby 5, Cardiff 0
Cardiff 0, 1st Dezembro 3
Brondby 6, Birkirkara 0
Birkirkara 1, Cardiff 10
1st Dezembro 0, Brondby 1

GROUP 4
Torres 1, Slovan 0
Krka 0, Trabzonspor 2
Torres 9, Trabzonspor 0

Slovan 2, Krka 2
Krka 0 Torres 3
Trabzonspor 1, Slovan 2

GROUP 5
Clujana 1, Glentoran 0
Linkoping 11, Roma 0
Roma 0, Clujana 9
Linkoping 3, Glentoran 0
Glentoran 2, Roma 0
Clujana 0, Linkoping 6

GROUP 6
Rossiyanka 11, St Francis 0
Maccabi Holon 0, Apollon 4
Rossiyanka 1, Apollon 0
St Francis 0, Maccabi Holon 2
Maccabi Holon 0, Rossiyanka 7
Apollon 2, St Francis 0

GROUP 7
Everton 3, Osijek 1
Strommen 5, Levadia 0
Everton 7, Levadia 0
Osijek 0, Strommen 9
Strommen 0, Everton 1
Levadia 4, Osijek 1

FIRST ROUND FIRST LEG
Alma 1, Sparta Prague 0
Zhilstroy-1 0, Umea 5
Torres 4, Valur 1
Sarajevo 0, Zvezda 3
Unia 1, Neulengbach 3
Roa 3, Everton 0
Masinac 0, Lyon 3
Vitebsk 1, Duisburg 5
PAOK 0, Arsenal 9
Zurich 0, Linkoping 2
Viktoria 0, Bayern 5
Standard 0, Montpellier 0
Honka 1, Potsdam 8
Fortuna 4, Bardolino 0
AZ 1, Brondby 2
Rayo 1, Rossiyanka 3

FIRST ROUND SECOND LEG
Rossiyanka 2, Rayo 1
Sparta Prague 2, Alma 0
Zvezda 5, Sarajevo 0
Neulengbach 0, Unia 1
Arsenal 9, PAOK 0
Everton 2, Roa 0
Valur 1, Torres 2
Linkoping 3, Zurich 0
Bayern 4, Viktoria 2
Montpellier 3, Standard 1

Umea 6, Zhilstroy-1 0
Lyon 5, Masinac 0
Potsdam 8, Honka 0
Brondby 1, AZ 1
Duisburg 6, Vitebsk 3
Bardolino 2, Fortuna 1

SECOND ROUND FIRST LEG
Roa 0, Zvezda 0
Rossiyanka 0, Umea 1
Montpellier 0, Bayern 0
Neulengbach 1, Torres 4
Sparta Prague 0, Arsenal 3
Potsdam 1, Brondby 0
Duisburg 1, Linkoping 1
Fortuna 0, Lyon 1

SECOND ROUND SECOND LEG
Torres 4, Neulengbach 1
Arsenal 2, Sparta Prague 0
Zvezda 1, Roa 1
Umea 1, Rossiyanka 1
Bayern 0, Montpellier 1
Brondby 0, Potsdam 4
Linkoping 0, Duisburg 2
Lyon 5, Fortuna 0

QUARTER-FINALS FIRST LEG
Umea 0, Montpellier 0
Lyon 3, Torres 0
Duisburg 2, Arsenal 1
Potsdam 5, Roa 0

QUARTER-FINALS SECOND LEG
Montpellier 2, Umea 2
Torres1, Lyon 0
Arsenal 0, Duisburg 2
Roa 0, Potsdam 5

SEMI-FINALS FIRST LEG
Lyon 3, Umea 2
Duisburg 1, Potsdam 0

SEMI-FINALS SECOND LEG
Umea 0, Lyon 0
Potsdam 1, Duisburg 0
Potsdam won 3-1 on penalties.

FINAL
Lyon 0, Potsdam 0
Potsdam won 7-6 on penalties.

ENGLAND WOMEN'S INTERNATIONALS 2006–09

EUROPEAN CHAMPIONSHIP 2006–10
Final tournament in Finland

GROUP A
Ukraine 0, Holland 2
Finland 1, Denmark 0
Ukraine 1, Denmark 2
Holland 1, Finland 2
Finland 0, Ukraine 1
Denmark 1, Holland 2

GROUP B
Germany 4, Norway 0
Iceland 1, France 3
France 1, Germany 5
Iceland 0, Norway 1
Germany 1, Iceland 0
Norway 1, France 1

GROUP C
England 1, Italy 2
Sweden 3, Russia 0
Italy 0, Sweden 2
England 3, Russia 2
Russia 0, Italy 2
Sweden 1, England 1

QUARTER-FINALS
Finland 2, England 3
Holland 0, France 0
Holland won 5-4 on penalties.
Germany 2, Italy 1
Sweden 1, Norway 3

SEMI-FINALS
England 2, Holland 1
Germany 3, Norway 1

FINAL IN HELSINKI
England 2, Germany 6

GROUP C – 25 Aug *(in Lahti)*
England 1 *(Williams 38 (pen))*
Italy 2 *(Panico 56, Tuttino 80)*　　　　2950
England: Brown; Scott A, Stoney!, Williams F, Asante (Unitt 73), Carney, Chapman, Aluko (Smith K 46), Smith S (Sanderson 85), Scott J, White F.

GROUP C – 28 Aug *(in Helsinki)*
England 3 *(Carney 24, Aluko 32, Smith K 42)*
Russia 2 *(Tsybutovich 2, Kurochkina 22)*　　1462
England: Brown; Scott A, Williams F, Johnson, Carney, Chapman, Aluko, Smith K, Smith S (Clarke 66), White F, Unitt.

GROUP C – 31 Aug *(in Turku)*
Sweden 1 *(Svensson 40 (pen))*
England 1 *(White 28)*　　　　6142
England: Brown; Scott A, Stoney, Williams F, Johnson, Carney, Chapman, Aluko (Westwood 65), Smith K, Smith S (Clarke 90), White F.

QUARTER-FINAL – 3 Sept *(in Turku)*
Finland 2 *(Sjolund 66, Sallstrom 79)*
England 3 *(Aluko 14, 67, Williams F 49)*　　7247
England: Brown; Stoney, Williams F, Johnson (Bassett 68), Asante, Carney, Chapman, Aluko, Smith K, Smith S, White F(Scott J 41).

SEMI-FINAL – 6 Sept *(in Tampere)*
England 2 *(Smith K 61, Scott J 116)*
Holland 1 *(Pieete 64)*　　　　4621
England: Brown; Scott A, Stoney, Williams F, Johnson, Asante, Chapman, Aluko (Sanderson 70), Smith K, Smith S (Carney 46), Clarke (Scott J 91).

FINAL 10 Sept *(in Helsinki)*
England 2 *(Carney 24, Smith K 55)*
Germany 6 *(Prinz 19, 76, Behringer 22, Kulig 50, Grings 62, 73)*　　　15,877
England: Brown; Scott A, Stoney, Williams F, Asante, White F, Carney, Scott J, Chapman (Westwood 86), Aluko (Sanderson 81), Smith K.

FRIENDLIES

16 July *(at Colchester)*
England 0
Iceland 2 *(Magmusdottir 25, Vidarsodottir 81)*　　4170
England: Chamberlain (Telford 46); Unitt, Yorston (Susi 65), White F, Bassett, Buet, Clarke (Davison 79), Scott J (Williams R 65), Westwood, Aluko, Yankey.

22 July *(at Swindon)*
England 1 *(Handley 87)*　　　　4177
Denmark 0
England: Bardsley; Scott A, Stoney, Chapman, Johnson, Asante, Carney, Scott J (Westwood 90), Sanderson (Handley 46), Williams F, Smith S.

CYPRUS CUP

24 Feb *(in Larnaca)*
England 1 *(Scott J 5)*
South Africa 0
England: Brown (Chamberlain 46); Susi, Stoney, Buet (Bassett 58), White F (Unitt 67), Johnson, Clarke (Yankey 76), Scott J, Westwood, Handley, Smith S.

27 Feb *(in Larnaca)*
England 0
Canada 1 *(Julien 10)*
England: Bardsley; Scott A, Stoney, Williams F, White F, Bassett (Susi 59), Clarke, Scott J, Unitt, Sanderson (Westwood 59), Yankey.

1 Mar *(in Larnaca)*
England 2 *(Stoney 56, Sanderson 76)*
Switzerland 2 *(Dickenmann 27, 84)*
England: Chamberlain; Susi (Clarke 80), Unitt, Buet, Johnson, Stoney, Scott A, Scott J, Handley (Sanderson 46), Westwood (Smith K 73), Smith S.

3 Mar *(in Nicosia)*
England 3 *(Scott A 8, 58, White 90)*
Italy 2 *(Brown 43 (og), Camporese 64)*
England: Brown (Bardsley 68); Susi, White F, Stoney, Unitt, Bassett, Scott J, Smith K (Sanderson 46), Scott A, Clarke, Yankey.

WOMEN'S UNDER-19 CHAMPIONSHIP 2008–09
Final tournament in Belarus

GROUP A
France 1, Germany 2
Belarus 0, France 3
Germany 9, Belarus 0

Belarus 1, Switzerland 4
Switzerland 3, Germany 0
Switzerland 0, France 2

GROUP B
Sweden 0, England 3
Sweden 2, Iceland 1
Norway 1, Sweden 2

Iceland 0, Norway 0
England 0, Norway 0
England 4, Iceland 0

SEMI-FINALS
France 2, Sweden 5

England 3, Switzerland 0

FINAL
Sweden 0 0
England (2) 2 *(Duggan 33, Nobbs 37)*

Sweden: Carlen; Alfsson, Kullberg (Schough 80), Lovgren, Borgstrom (Lyckberg 58), Appelquist, Jakobsson, Heimersson, Johansson, Goransson, Egelryd (Hjolhman 46).
England: Spencer; Weston, Flaherty, Allen, Bronze, Harrop, Christiansen (Holbrook 79), Nobbs, Duggan, Hinnigan (Coombs 67), Moore.
Referee: T. Albon (Romania).

WOMEN'S UNDER-19 CHAMPIONSHIP 2009–10
Final tournament in Macedonia

GROUP A
Scotland 1, England 3
Scotland 1, Germany 5
Italy 3, Scotland 3

Germany 4, Italy 1
England 2, Italy 1
England 1, Germany 2

GROUP B
Holland 2, France 0
Macedonia 0, Holland 7
France 6, Macedonia 1

Macedonia 0, Spain 6
Spain 0, France 1
Spain 0, Holland 2

SEMI-FINALS
Germany 1, France 1
France won 5-3 on penalties.

Holland 0, England 0
England won 5-4 on penalties.

FINAL
France (1) 2 *(Lavaud 29, Crammer 55)*
England (1) 1 *(Holbrook 26)*

France: Philippe; La Villa, Gadea, Rousseau, Rubio, Makanza (Butel 59), Crammer (Catala 80), Barbance (Le Garrec 59), Jaurena, Barbetta, Lavaud.
England: Spencer; Cunningham, Flaherty (Jane 62), Prosser, Bronze, Bonner, Christiansen (Bruton 77), Nobbs, Duggan, Holbrook, Stokes.
Referee: K. Radzik-Johan (Poland).

FIFA 2011 WOMEN'S WORLD CUP

QUALIFYING COMPETITION

25 Oct *(at Blackpool)*
England 8 *(White F 5, Williams F 20, 37, 65, Clarke 35, 75, Westwood 77, Unitt 88)*
Malta 0   3681
England: Bardsley; Scott A, Unitt, Buet, White F (Johnson 59), Bassett, Clarke, Scott J, Sanderson (Handley 53), Williams F (Westwood 68), Smith S.

26 Nov *(in Izmir)*
Turkey 0
England 3 *(Scott A 76, Sanderson 80, Unitt 84)*
England: Bardsley; Scott A, Unitt, Williams F, White F, Bassett, Clarke (Sanderson 76), Buet (Carney 62), Handley (Dowie 84), Westwood, Smith S.

25 Mar *(at QPR)*
England 3 *(Sanderson 15, Aluko 68, White E 90)*.   3980
Austria 0
England: Bardsley; Susi (White E 62), Unitt (Rafferty 87), Chapman, White F, Stoney, Scott A, Williams F, Aluko, Sanderson, Yankey (Smith S 87).

1 Apr *(at Millwall)*
England 1 *(Chapman 29)*
Spain 0   5041
England: Brown; Scott A, Unitt, Chapman, White F, Stoney, Clarke, Williams F, Aluko (White E 69), Smith K (Scott J 59), Yankey (Smith S 83).

20 May *(in Ta'Qali)*
Malta 0
England 6 *(White F 7, Smith K 15, Williams F 29, 82, Clarke 56, White E 67)*
England: Brown; Scott A (Susi 46), Stoney, White F (Dowie 74), Chapman, Williams F, Yankey (Carney 64), Clarke, Smith K, Rafferty, White E.

19 June *(in Aranda de Duero)*
Spain 2 *(Martin 16, Bermudez 67)*
England 2 *(Unitt 78, White F 88)*
England: Brown; Scott A, Stoney, Unitt, White F, Chapman, Williams F, Yankey (Scott J 46), Smith K, Carney, Aluko (White E 73).

NON-LEAGUE TABLES 2009–10

UNIBOND PREMIER DIVISION 2009–10

		Home					Away					Total						
		P	W	D	L	F	A	W	D	L	F	A	W	D	L	F	A	GD	Pts
1	Guiseley	38	12	3	4	32	17	13	1	5	41	24	25	4	9	73	41	32	79
2	Bradford Park Avenue	38	12	2	5	42	25	12	4	3	52	26	24	6	8	94	51	43	78
3	Boston United	38	12	5	2	53	17	11	3	5	37	17	23	8	7	90	34	56	77
4	North Ferriby United	38	11	5	3	38	16	11	4	4	32	22	22	9	7	70	38	32	75
5	Kendal Town	38	12	5	2	38	17	9	3	7	37	30	21	8	9	75	47	28	71
6	Retford United	38	5	8	6	36	27	13	3	3	37	19	18	11	9	73	46	27	65
7	Matlock Town	38	11	3	5	44	23	6	6	7	28	26	17	9	12	72	49	23	60
8	Buxton	38	8	7	4	34	21	8	5	6	32	22	16	12	10	66	43	23	60
9	Marine	38	9	4	6	34	27	8	2	9	26	28	17	6	15	60	55	5	57
10	Nantwich Town	38	10	2	7	40	37	6	4	9	24	32	16	6	16	64	69	-5	54
11	Stocksbridge PS	38	10	3	6	49	33	5	4	10	31	35	15	7	16	80	68	12	52
12	Ashton United	38	7	3	9	25	30	8	3	8	23	33	15	6	17	48	63	-15	51
13	FC United	38	8	3	8	33	31	5	5	9	29	34	13	8	17	62	65	-3	47
14	Whitby Town	38	8	5	6	32	28	4	5	10	24	34	12	10	16	56	62	-6	46
15	Frickley Athletic	38	8	5	6	23	19	4	4	11	27	47	12	9	17	50	66	-16	45
16	Burscough	38	9	1	9	31	23	4	4	11	24	42	13	5	20	55	65	-10	44
17	Hucknall Town	38	8	4	7	42	38	4	4	11	23	43	12	8	18	65	81	-16	44
18	Worksop Town	38	4	5	10	22	34	3	4	12	23	34	7	9	22	45	68	-23	30
19	Ossett Town	38	4	1	14	27	46	2	6	11	19	46	6	7	25	46	92	-46	25
20	Durham City*	38	1	0	18	16	71	1	0	18	11	97	2	0	36	27	168	-141	0

*Durham City deducted 6 points.

ZAMARETTO PREMIER DIVISION 2009–10

		Home					Away					Total						
		P	W	D	L	F	A	W	D	L	F	A	W	D	L	F	A	GD	Pts
1	Farnborough	42	17	2	2	54	20	11	7	3	46	24	28	9	5	100	44	56	93
2	Nuneaton Town	42	13	7	1	47	16	13	3	5	43	21	26	10	6	90	37	53	88
3	Chippenham Town	42	14	2	5	46	24	7	9	5	21	19	21	11	10	67	43	24	74
4	Hednesford Town	42	9	8	4	40	29	11	5	5	39	22	20	13	9	79	51	28	73
5	Brackley Town	42	12	3	6	38	24	9	6	6	45	37	21	9	12	83	61	22	72
6	Cambridge City	42	10	9	2	45	23	8	8	5	28	21	18	17	7	73	44	29	71
7	Bashley	42	12	2	7	41	33	8	9	4	38	28	20	11	11	79	61	18	71
8	Halesowen Town	42	12	8	1	44	24	9	9	3	40	29	21	17	4	84	53	31	70
9	Stourbridge	42	14	4	3	46	22	5	9	7	34	43	19	13	10	80	65	15	70
10	Leamington	42	10	3	8	46	38	9	5	7	38	37	19	8	15	84	75	9	65
11	Truro City	42	7	7	7	39	31	10	4	7	39	34	17	11	14	78	65	13	62
12	Banbury United	42	9	7	5	28	26	5	6	10	25	41	14	13	15	53	67	-14	55
13	Oxford City	42	6	10	5	33	28	7	5	9	32	39	13	15	14	65	67	-2	54
14	Swindon Supermarine	42	4	9	8	30	47	6	5	10	18	29	10	14	18	48	76	-28	44
15	Didcot Town	42	4	7	10	24	31	6	4	11	32	39	10	11	21	56	70	-14	41
16	Evesham United	42	3	10	8	14	21	6	4	11	21	31	9	14	19	35	52	-17	41
17	Merthyr Tydfil	42	8	4	9	30	32	4	7	10	32	41	12	11	19	62	73	-11	37
18	Bedford Town	42	6	5	10	31	38	3	5	13	19	50	9	10	23	50	88	-38	37
19	Tiverton Town	42	4	7	10	16	27	4	5	12	19	34	8	12	22	35	61	-26	36
20	Hemel Hempstead Town	42	6	5	10	32	35	2	5	14	18	46	8	10	24	50	81	-31	34
21	Clevedon Town	42	2	4	15	18	49	4	7	10	30	43	6	11	25	48	92	-44	29
22	Rugby Town	42	3	6	12	26	54	1	2	18	15	60	4	8	30	41	114	-73	20

*Halesowen Town deducted 10 points, Merthyr Tydfil deducted 10 points. Merthyr Tydfil reformed as Merthyr Town and relegated to the Western League.

RYMAN LEAGUE PREMIER DIVISION 2009–10

		Home					Away					Total						
		P	W	D	L	F	A	W	D	L	F	A	W	D	L	F	A	GD	Pts
1	Dartford	42	11	5	5	44	29	18	1	2	57	16	29	6	7	101	45	56	93
2	Sutton United	42	10	5	6	37	26	12	4	5	28	19	22	9	11	65	45	20	75
3	Aveley	42	11	3	7	38	27	10	4	7	45	35	21	7	14	83	62	21	70
4	Boreham Wood	42	10	4	7	32	24	10	4	7	22	20	20	8	14	54	44	10	68
5	Kingstonian	42	11	4	6	41	37	9	4	8	32	32	20	8	14	73	69	4	68
6	Wealdstone	42	10	5	6	29	27	7	9	5	36	38	17	14	11	65	65	0	65
7	Hastings United	42	10	5	6	36	27	8	4	9	32	29	18	9	15	68	56	12	63
8	Tonbridge Angels	42	11	3	7	36	31	7	5	9	33	36	18	8	16	69	67	2	62
9	AFC Hornchurch	42	11	7	3	29	19	5	6	10	22	28	16	13	13	51	47	4	61
10	Hendon	42	10	3	8	30	25	8	3	10	31	34	18	6	18	61	59	2	60
11	Horsham	42	10	2	9	35	33	6	6	9	30	34	16	8	18	65	67	-2	56
12	Tooting and Mitcham	42	7	5	9	33	37	8	5	8	27	27	15	10	17	60	64	-4	55
13	Billericay Town	42	8	6	7	23	23	6	6	9	21	19	14	12	16	44	42	2	54
14	Harrow Borough	42	7	8	6	32	30	6	6	9	34	33	13	14	15	66	63	3	53
15	Cray Wanderers	42	7	3	11	25	33	7	6	8	29	37	14	9	19	54	70	-16	51
16	Canvey Island	42	6	6	9	28	31	7	5	9	29	31	13	11	18	57	62	-5	50
17	Carshalton Athletic	42	8	5	8	27	26	4	8	9	31	38	12	13	17	58	64	-6	49
18	Maidstone United	42	6	4	11	20	34	7	6	8	19	23	13	10	19	39	57	-18	49
19	Margate	42	4	7	10	21	36	7	5	9	28	35	11	12	19	49	71	-22	45
20	Ashford Town (Middx)	42	6	8	7	34	40	5	3	13	28	40	11	11	20	62	80	-18	44
21	Waltham Abbey	42	6	3	12	21	35	6	5	10	28	39	12	8	22	49	74	-25	44
22	Bognor Regis Town	42	5	9	7	27	34	4	5	12	18	35	9	14	19	45	65	-20	41

THE FA TROPHY 2009–10

IN PARTNERSHIP WITH CARLSBERG

PRELIMINARY ROUND

Colwyn Bay v Witton Albion	0-2
Woodley Sports v Harrogate Railway	2-2, 1-2
Clitheroe v Belper Town	1-1, 4-1
Mossley v Bedworth United	5-2
Curzon Ashton v Brigg Town	1-2
Warrington Town v Sheffield	5-2
Rossendale United v Chorley	1-2
Glapwell v Grantham Town	2-2, 3-2
Radcliffe Borough v Mickleover Sports	6-3
Kidsgrove Athletic v Leek Town	0-1
Ossett Albion v Shepshed Dynamo	2-3
Cammell Laird v Stamford	3-1
Lincoln United v Chasetown	1-2
Market Drayton Town v Bamber Bridge	1-1, 0-4
Prescot Cables v Lancaster City	1-2
Trafford v FC Halifax Town	3-4
Wakefield v Carlton Town	1-1, 2-2
Carlton Town won 3-1 on penalties.	
Potters Bar Town v Arlesey Town	0-0, 2-3
Heybridge Swifts v VCD Athletic	0-3
Barton Rovers v Ilford	1-1, 3-2
Leatherhead v Thamesmead Town	3-3, 2-1
Chatham Town v Concord Rangers	1-4
Croydon Athletic v Bury Town	2-2
Burgess Hill Town v Dulwich Hamlet	2-0
Enfield Town v Eastbourne Town	4-0
Corinthian Casuals v Worthing	2-2, 1-0
Folkestone Invicta v Hitchin Town	0-1
Brentwood Town v Great Wakering Rovers	2-0
Whitstable Town v Walton & Hersham	2-2, 5-3
Walton & Hersham won 3-1 on penalties.	
Tilbury v Biggleswade Town	1-2
Waltham Forest v East Thurrock United	2-0
Walton Casuals v Whyteleafe	0-0, 1-2
Romford v AFC Sudbury	0-7
Soham Town Rangers v Cheshunt	3-1
Sittingbourne v Wingate & Finchley	1-1, 2-1
Ramsgate v Leyton	3-2
Chipstead v Horsham YMCA	3-1
Metropolitan Police v Maldon Town	1-0
Lowestoft Town v Redbridge	4-1
Leighton Town v Harlow Town	3-0
Bedfont Green v Chesham United	1-2
North Leigh v Burnham	2-3
AFC Totton v Andover	2-0
Beaconsfield SYCOB v Aylesbury United	2-1
Bishop's Cleeve v Yate Town	1-2
Stourport Swifts v Hungerford Town	0-1
Slough Town v Mangotsfield United	1-1, 1-0
AFC Hayes v Bridgwater Town	1-4
Godalming Town v VT	3-1
Fleet Town v Bromsgrove Rovers	2-0
Rothwell Town v Gosport Borough	0-1
Windsor & Eton v Paulton Rovers	2-1

FC Halifax Town v Romulus	2-0
Stocksbridge Park Steels v Glapwell	1-2
Matlock Town v Loughborough Dynamo	2-1
Ossett Town v Willenhall Town	1-2
Buxton v Hednesford Town	1-0
Frickley Athletic v Bamber Bridge	2-1
Ashton United v FC United of Manchester	1-3
Croydon Athletic v Ashford Town (Middlesex)	2-1
AFC Hornchurch v Brentwood Town	2-1
Wealdstone v Margate	3-1
Aveley v Carshalton Athletic	2-5
Ramsgate v Leatherhead	3-0
Soham Town Rangers v Harrow Borough	2-2, 1-5
Cray Wanderers v Burgess Hill Town	1-2
Corinthian Casuals v Arlesey Town	0-3
Waltham Abbey v Boreham Wood	0-2
Metropolitan Police v Kingstonian	0-1
Biggleswade Town v Chipstead	2-2, 2-2
Chipstead won 4-2 on penalties.	
AFC Sudbury v Billericay Town	3-3, 2-2
Billericay Town won 3-1 on penalties.	
VCD Athletic v Concord Rangers	0-1
Horsham v Barton Rovers	4-4, 3-4
Canvey Island v Hitchin Town	1-2
Tooting & Mitcham United v Walton & Hersham	3-0
Ware v Enfield Town	1-3
Bognor Regis Town v Ashford Town	3-1
Sittingbourne v Dartford	0-1
Waltham Forest v Maidstone United	1-1, 0-1
Leighton Town v Whyteleafe	0-3
Hastings United v Merstham	1-6
Sutton United v Tonbridge Angels	0-2
Hendon v Lowestoft Town	2-0
Cirencester Town v Godalming Town	1-3
Hemel Hempstead Town v Farnborough	0-1
Burnham v Cinderford Town	3-2
Beaconsfield SYCOB v Bashley	1-4
Swindon Supermarine v Fleet Town	2-4
Bracknell Town v Thatcham Town	1-8
Banbury United v Bridgwater Town	2-2, 1-0
AFC Totton v Woodford United	2-2, 4-1
Didcot Town v Cambridge City	0-1
Northwood v Abingdon United	1-0
Yate Town v Bedford Town	2-1
Tiverton Town v Truro City	0-4
Leamington v Stourbridge	1-2
Merthyr Tydfil v Marlow	0-0, 2-4
Hungerford Town v Taunton Town	4-3
Chippenham Town v Frome Town	5-3
Evesham United v Windsor & Eton	1-1, 2-0
Rugby Town v Gosport Borough	0-1
Clevedon Town v Brackley Town	2-4
Uxbridge v Slough Town	1-1, 0-2
Chesham United v Oxford City	2-2, 0-2

FIRST QUALIFYING ROUND

Radcliffe Borough v Quorn	2-2, 3-6
Spalding United v Mossley	1-3
Shepshed Dynamo v Harrogate Railway	2-1
North Ferriby United v Worksop Town	1-1, 4-4
North Ferriby United won 5-4 on penalties.	
Boston United v Chorley	3-2
Cammell Laird v Guiseley	0-3
Retford United v Nantwich Town	0-1
Atherstone Town v Leigh Genesis	1-3
Whitby Town v Warrington Town	5-2
Brigg Town v Burscough	3-2
Leek Town v Kendal Town	2-1
Rushall Olympic v Carlton Town	0-1
Lancaster City v Chasetown	1-1, 4-1
Skelmersdale United v Goole	5-0
Bradford Park Avenue v Clitheroe	0-1
Salford City v Durham City	3-0
Witton Albion v Sutton United	1-1, 3-2
Garforth Town v AFC Fylde	0-3
Marine v King's Lynn	0-1
Nuneaton Town v Hucknall Town	1-1, 3-0

SECOND QUALIFYING ROUND

Salford City v Clitheroe	5-3
Frickley Athletic v Guiseley	0-3
Boston United v Quorn	0-0, 2-3
Willenhall Town v Nuneaton Town	0-6
AFC Fylde v Glapwell	2-1
Whitby Town v King's Lynn	0-2
Carlton Town v North Ferriby United	0-3
Witton Albion v Brigg Town	4-1
Nantwich Town v Leek Town	4-1
Cambridge City v Matlock Town	0-1
Shepshed Dynamo v FC Halifax Town	0-5
Lancaster City v FC United of Manchester	3-3, 0-1
Leigh Genesis v Skelmersdale United	4-1
Brackley Town v Mossley	1-1, 1-3
Buxton v Stourbridge	0-1
Boreham Wood v Slough Town	3-2
Hitchin Town v Gosport Borough	3-1
Concord Rangers v Enfield Town	2-0
Barton Rovers v Billericay Town	2-2, 0-3
Dartford v Chipstead	3-0
Croydon Athletic v Burnham	1-1, 1-2
Carshalton Athletic v AFC Totton	3-1

Fleet Town v Ramsgate	0-2
Bashley v Marlow	2-1
Godalming Town v Banbury United	1-1, 3-1
Kingstonian v Hendon	4-2
Farnborough v Burgess Hill Town	5-2
Tonbridge Angels v Merstham	6-1
Arlesey Town v Oxford City	2-1
Northwood v Evesham United	0-0, 2-1
Harrow Borough v Wealdstone	2-2, 1-2
Yate Town v Hungerford Town	1-1, 0-3
Truro City v Thatcham Town	4-1
Bognor Regis Town v Maidstone United	0-2
Chippenham Town v Tooting & Mitcham United	4-1
Whyteleafe v AFC Hornchurch	1-1, 0-4

THIRD QUALIFYING ROUND

King's Lynn v Salford City	1-0
Ilkeston Town v Mossley	1-1, 2-0
Fleetwood Town v Northwich Victoria	2-0
FC United of Manchester v Harrogate Town	2-3
Farsley Celtic v Droylsden	5-2
Hyde United v Nuneaton Town	3-3, 0-1
North Ferriby United v Gainsborough Trinity	2-2, 2-2
Gainsborough Trinity won 3-2 on penalties.	
Workington v Solihull Moors	1-1, 4-2
Blyth Spartans v Stafford Rangers	2-0
Eastwood Town v Nantwich Town	0-3
Quorn v Vauxhall Motors	2-3
Leigh Genesis v Redditch United	0-1
Stalybridge Celtic v AFC Telford United	1-1, 2-1
Stourbridge v Southport	0-0, 2-4
Witton Albion v Matlock Town	1-1, 3-4
Guiseley v FC Halifax Town	3-1
Corby Town v Alfreton Town	1-1, 2-1
AFC Fylde v Hinckley United	1-1, 3-7
Weston-Super-Mare v Carshalton Athletic	1-1, 1-3
Bromley v Maidstone United	0-1
Billericay Town v Hitchin Town	0-0, 1-0
Eastleigh v Lewes	1-1, 0-1
Truro City v Gloucester City	1-0
Welling United v Tonbridge Angels	3-2
Bashley v Staines Town	2-1
Woking v St Albans City	6-0
Boreham Wood v Hungerford Town	1-0
Thurrock v Havant & Waterlooville	1-4
Maidenhead United v Bath City	1-0
Dover Athletic v Dartford	3-2
Godalming Town v Arlesey Town	0-3
Farnborough v Wealdstone	3-0
Chelmsford City v AFC Hornchurch	4-4, 2-1
Hampton & Richmond Borough v Concord Rangers	3-2
Worcester City v Burnham	2-1
Weymouth v Dorchester Town	3-0
Ramsgate v Bishop's Stortford	0-3
Newport County v Braintree Town	2-1
Kingstonian v Chippenham Town	0-2
Northwood v Basingstoke Town	2-1

FIRST ROUND

Vauxhall Motors w.o. v King's Lynn disbanded.

Mansfield Town v Tamworth	0-2
Gateshead v Harrogate Town	1-1, 2-0
Corby Town v Farsley Celtic	2-0
Workington v Nuneaton Town	2-1
Guiseley v Redditch United	1-0
Hinckley United v York City	0-0, 1-3
Wrexham v Altrincham	0-0, 0-1
Kettering Town v Barrow	0-1
Chester City v Fleetwood Town	0-1
Matlock Town v Kidderminster Harriers	0-2
Nantwich Town v Stalybridge Celtic	0-3
Southport v Gainsborough Trinity	2-2, 0-1
Blyth Spartans v Ilkeston Town	2-0
Welling United v Eastbourne Borough	0-1
Bishop's Stortford v Maidenhead United	1-2

Chelmsford City v Truro City	2-2, 1-0
Stevenage Borough v Ebbsfleet United	2-0
AFC Wimbledon v Boreham Wood	2-1
Hampton & Richmond Borough v Lewes	0-0, 1-3
Rushden & Diamonds v Billericay Town	1-0
Havant & Waterlooville v Dover Athletic	2-3
Bashley v Crawley Town	2-3
Arlesey Town v Chippenham Town	1-1, 0-2
Oxford United v Hayes & Yeading United	1-0
Woking v Forest Green Rovers	1-0
Weymouth v Salisbury City	0-1
Farnborough v Newport County	1-3
Carshalton Athletic v Northwood	1-1, 5-0
Cambridge United v Luton Town	3-1
Worcester City v Grays Athletic	3-1
Maidstone United v Histon	0-3
Tie awarded to Maidstone United; Histon removed from competition.	

SECOND ROUND

AFC Wimbledon v Altrincham	3-1
Worcester City v Carshalton Athletic	1-1, 4-0
Stevenage Borough v Vauxhall Motors	6-0
Blyth Spartans v Guiseley	1-2
Cambridge United v Eastbourne Borough	2-2, 2-0
Gateshead v Chippenham Town	1-0
Oxford United v Woking	1-0
Stalybridge Celtic v Corby Town	1-2
Kidderminster Harriers v Lewes	3-2
Newport County v York City	0-0, 0-1
Workington v Rushden & Diamonds	2-1
Chelmsford City v Crawley Town	2-1
Fleetwood Town v Dover Athletic	0-1
Gainsborough Trinity v Tamworth	0-0, 1-2
Maidenhead United v Barrow	0-1
Salisbury City v Maidstone United	2-0

THIRD ROUND

York City v Corby Town	1-0
Guiseley v Tamworth	0-1
Worcester City v Kidderminster Harriers	0-1
AFC Wimbledon v Workington	2-3
Cambridge United v Salisbury City	0-0, 1-2
Stevenage Borough v Dover Athletic	4-1
Barrow v Gateshead	1-1, 3-2
Chelmsford City v Oxford United	1-3

FOURTH ROUND

Stevenage Borough v Workington	2-1
Salisbury City v Tamworth	2-1
Barrow v York City	2-1
Oxford United v Kidderminster Harriers	1-2

SEMI-FINALS (two legs)

Salisbury City v Barrow	0-1, 1-2
Kidderminster Harriers v Stevenage Borough	1-5, 0-0

FINAL (at Wembley)

Saturday 9 May 2010

Barrow (0) 2 *(McEvilly 79, Walker 107)*

Stevenage Borough (1) 1 *(Drury 10)*   17,500

Barrow: Tomlinson; Spender, Edwards, Jones, Bolland, Hulbert, Bond, Rutherford (Boyd 110), Walker, Blundell (McEvilly 74), Wiles (Logan 64).

Stevenage Borough: Day (Bayes 90); Henry, Laird, Roberts, Ashton, Bostwick, Drury, Bridges, Beardsley (Griffin 66), Odubade, Byrom (Wilson 59).

aet.

Referee: L. Probert (Wiltshire).

THE FA VASE 2009–10

IN PARTNERSHIP WITH CARLSBERG

FIRST QUALIFYING ROUND

Washington v Morpeth Town	1-4
Stokesley v Thackley	5-1
West Auckland Town v Yorkshire Amateur	1-0
Sunderland RCA v Armthorpe Welfare	0-2
Bishop Auckland v Billingham Town	1-0
Esh Winning v Bedlington Terriers	2-4
Billingham Synthonia v Brandon United	3-2
Eccleshill United v Norton & Stockton Ancients	0-7
Glasshoughton Welfare v Tadcaster Albion	1-2
Formby v Chadderton	1-2
Padiham v St Helens Town	4-3
Ashton Athletic v Alsager Town	0-2
Atherton LR v Colne	1-2
Ramsbottom United v Wigan Robin Park	4-1
AFC Blackpool v Maine Road	1-0
Runcorn Linnets v Staveley MW	4-3
Birstall United v Cradley Town	0-2
Anstey Nomads v Coleshill Town	1-2
Dosthill Colts v Barrow Town	1-0
Tipton Town v Rocester	3-0
Coventry Copsewood v Pilkington XXX	1-3

Pilkington XXX removed from the competition for fielding a player under suspension.

Nuneaton Griff v Holwell Sports	1-2
Leek CSOB v Biddulph Victoria	1-2
Heath Hayes v Bartley Green	0-2
Castle Vale JKS v Castle Vale	5-2
Wolverhampton Casuals v Pelsall Villa	3-2
Sporting Kalsa v Goodrich	2-4
Pershore Town v Alvechurch	0-6
Wellington v Eccleshall	2-2, 4-2
Shifnal Town v Wednesfield	0-4
St Andrews v Cadbury Athletic	2-0
Causeway United v Ellesmere Rangers	2-0
Gornal Athletic v Knowle	2-0
Bewdley Town v Warstone Wanderers	6-0
Westfields v Bridgnorth Town	5-4
Bolehall Swifts v Lye Town	1-0
Ashby Ivanhoe v Coventry Sphinx	0-2
AFC Wulfrunians v Dudley Sports	4-1
Gedling MW v Grimsby Borough	1-2
Holbeach United v Newark Town	1-0
Teversal v Sleaford Town	0-1
Ollerton Town v Barton Town Old Boys	1-0
Cambridge Regional College v Huntingdon Town	5-1
Ely City v Cornard United	7-1
Haverhill Rovers v Swaffham Town	4-1
Woodbridge Town v Great Yarmouth Town	2-1
Raunds Town v Daventry Town	1-2
Godmanchester Rovers v Rothwell Corinthians	1-1, 3-3

Rothwell Corinthians won 4-2 on penalties.

Sileby Rangers v March Town United	2-3
Team Bury v Mildenhall Town	3-2
Mauritius Sports Association UK v Eton Manor	2-0

Eton Manor reinstated after Mauritius Sports Association were removed for fielding an ineligible player.

Oxhey Jets v Aylesbury	4-3
Wootton Blue Cross v Wembley	1-3
Buckingham Town v Barking	2-5
Ampthill Town v Bethnal Green United	1-2
Colney Heath v Sporting Bengal United	2-1
Tokyngton Manor v Cockfosters	2-1

Cockfosters reinstated after Tokyngton Manor were removed for fielding an ineligible player.

Leverstock Green v Bowers & Pitsea	3-2
Clapton v Hoddesdon Town	0-1
Brimsdown Rovers v Buckingham Athletic	6-0
AFC Kempston Rovers v Welwyn Garden City	1-0
Kentish Town v Cranfield United	3-1
Erith Town v Canning Town	7-0
Saffron Walden Town v Hanwell Town	1-3
Hatfield Town v Kingsbury London Tigers	3-4
Hullbridge Sports v Hertford Town	1-3
Baldock Town Letchworth v Wivenhoe Town	1-1

Wivenhoe Town won 6-5 on penalties.

Harpenden Town v Harringey Borough	0-0, 2-1
St Margaretsbury v Crawley Green	3-1

Winslow United withdrew v Takeley w.o.

Harwich & Parkeston v Halstead Town	0-6
Beafont v Mile Oak	2-0
Norton Sports v Lingfield	1-2
Three Bridges v Oakwood	4-1
East Preston v Ash United	1-3
Peacehaven & Telscombe v Hailsham Town	2-1
Southwick v Selsey	1-3
Feltham v Holmesdale	1-5

Slade Green withdrew v Frimley Green w.o.

Whitehawk v Littlehampton Town	2-1
Camberley Town v Cobham	4-2
Beckenham Town v Wealden	6-1
Chichester City v Colliers Wood United	4-1
Lordswood v Crawley Down	2-5
Ringmer v Deal Town	2-0
Raynes Park Vale v Horley Town	1-2
Chessington & Hook United v East Grinstead Town	0-1
St Francis Rangers v Egham Town	1-3
Hassocks v Sevenoaks Town	3-1
Badshot Lea v Rye United	2-1
Erith & Belvedere v Sidley United	2-1
Worthing United v Heywoods Heath Town	0-0

Worthing United won 5-4 on penalties.

Newhaven v Cove	0-6
Guildford City v Westfield	3-0
Flackwell Heath v Romsey Town	6-0

Blackfield & Langley w.o. v Harrow Hill withdrew

Melksham Town v Marlow United	3-1
Holyport v Brading Town	4-1
Amesbury Town v Milton United	1-2
Clanfield 85 v Carterton	1-1, 0-1
Henley Town v Abingdon Town	3-4
Westbury United v AFC Wallingford	4-3
Bournemouth v Petersfield Town	1-0
Laverstock & Ford v Lydney Town	4-0
Malmsbury Victoria v Hook Norton	2-1
Calne Town v Ardley United	2-4
Wootton Bassett Town v Hamble ASSC	2-3
Warminster Town v Hayling United	0-5
Binfield v New Milton Town	1-2
Sandhurst Town v Highworth Town	0-2
Cowes Sports v Almondsbury UWE	2-1
Radstock Town v Street	1-2
Ilfracombe Town v Tavistock	0-2
Hamworthy United v Saltash United	0-2
Bodmin Town v Portishead Town	2-1
Wadebridge Town v Penzance	3-4

SECOND QUALIFYING ROUND

Willington v West Auckland Town	1-2
Easington Colliery v Shildon	0-1
Ashington v Armthorpe Welfare	0-1
Northallerton Town v Team Northumbria	2-1
South Shields v Pontefract Collieries	5-0
Brighouse Town v Tadcaster Albion	2-3
Pickering Town v Horden CW	2-1
Hebburn Town v North Shields	1-3
Bedlington Terriers v Jarrow Roofing Boldon CA	3-0
Silsden v Guisborough Town	5-6
Ryton v Crook Town	0-1
Norton & Stockton Ancients v West Allotment Celtic	3-1
Morpeth Town v Thornaby	4-2
Seaham Red Star v Stokesley	1-4
Billingham Synthonia v Tow Law Town	3-3, 2-2

Tow Law Town won 5-4 on penalties.

Liversedge v Chester-Le-Street Town	4-1
Whickham v Darlington Railway Athletic	2-0
Hall Road Rangers v Bishop Auckland	3-0
Birtley Town v Leeds Carnegie	0-3
Ramsbottom United v Nostell MW	1-0
Ashton United v Worsborough Bridge Athletic	1-3
Penrith v Squires Gate	2-0
Daisy Hill v Runcorn Linnets	2-1
Flixton v Hallam	1-3
Rossington Main v Atherton Collieries	1-0
Winsford United v Parkgate	1-0
Whitehaven v Cheadle Town	0-2
AFC Blackpool v Oldham Town	2-4
Chadderton v Padiham	2-2, 0-3

AFC Liverpool v Dinnington Town 1-2
Bacup Borough v Holker Old Boys 2-1
Nelson v Abbey Hey 5-1
Irlam v Colne 1-2
Maltby Main v Hemsworth MW 2-3
AFC Emley v Alsager Town 2-3
Hinckley Downes v Bewdley Town 0-3
Pegasus Juniors v Walsall Wood 2-3
Biddulph Victoria v Bardon Hill Sports 5-0
Shawbury United v Tividale 1-3
Ledbury Town v Friar Lane & Epworth 1-3
St Andrews v Studley 3-6
Brocton v Norton United 0-1
Ellistown v Kirby Muxloe 1-2
Castle Vale JKS v Wolverhampton Casuals 2-5
Causeway United v Coventry Sphinx 4-0
Alvechurch v Tipton Town 1-5
Dudley Town v Loughborough University 1-1, 0-2
Gornal Athletic v Wellington 0-1
Blaby & Whetstone Athletic v Meir KA 2-1
Goodrich v Coleshill Town 1-3
Wednesfield v Holwell Sports 2-1
AFC Wulfrunians v Heather St Johns 4-0
Bartley Green v Bolehall Swifts 2-0
Dosthill Colts v Coventry Copsewood 3-3, 3-2
Westfields v Bromyard Town 3-0
Oadby Town v Cradley Town 3-2
Southam United v Highgate United 0-0, 3-0
Blackstones v Radford 9-0
Calverton MW v Ollerton Town 0-2
Blackwell MW v Louth Town 2-6
Boston Town v Bottisford Town 0-1
Shirebrook Town v Winterton Rangers 2-3
Bourne Town v Graham St Prims 1-0
Gedling Town v Appleby Frodingham 1-1, 3-2
Arnold Town v Kimberley Town 2-1
Borrowash Victoria v Greenwood Meadows 2-1
Grimsby Borough v Holbrook Miners Welfare 3-1
Sleaford Town v Sutton Town 5-0
Lincoln Moorlands Railway v Holbeach United 2-1
Rainworth MW v Radcliffe Olympic 2-0
Heanor Town v Dunkirk 4-4, 1-2
Walsham Le Willows v Kirkley & Pakefield 0-5
Bugbrooke St Michaels v Team Bury 4-2
Long Melford v Whitton United 2-2, 1-3
Fakenham Town v Haverhill Rovers 0-9
Thrapston Town v Wellingborough Town 0-1
Diss Town v Ely City 2-2, 4-5
Gorleston v Wroxham 0-0, 0-3
Daventry Town v Stowmarket Town 5-0
Wisbech Town v Northampton Spencer 0-1
Grantham Athletic v Cambridge Regional College 0-1
Woodbridge Town v Desborough Town 4-0
Newmarket Town v St Neots Town 2-1
Felixstowe & Walton United v Yaxley 2-1
Daventry United v Thetford Town 6-1
Rushton & Higham United v March Town United 1-2
Eynesbury Rovers v Ipswich Wanderers 3-0
Rothwell Corinthians v Hadleigh United 3-2
Norwich United v Long Buckby 1-3
Old Woodstock Town v Bethnal Green United 1-3
Brimsdown Rovers v Colney Heath 4-2
Tiptree United v Barkingside 3-1
Bicester Town v Leverstock Green 1-3
Barking v Basildon United 2-2, 0-1
Hadley v Harpenden Town 2-0
AFC Kempston Rovers v Burnham Ramblers 3-4
Tring Athletic v Stansted 3-4
Kentish Town v London Colney 2-3
Wembley v St Margaretsbury 1-0
Wivenhoe Town v Potton United 2-1
Hoddesdon Town v Oxhey Jets 4-3
London APSA v Royston Town 0-3
Halstead Town v Thame United 1-1, 1-0
Bedford v Hanwell Town 2-1
Langford v Hertford Town 1-0
Biggleswade United v Codicote 7-0
Kingsbury London Tigers v Takeley 5-4
Cockfosters v Bucks University Union (BSU) 3-1
Saltdean United v Peacehaven & Telscombe 0-2
Camberley Town v Selsey 3-2
Farnham Town v Herne Bay 0-4
Pagham v Frimley Green 1-0
Ash United v Tunbridge Wells 3-1
Molesey v Hassocks 2-0
Beckenham Town v Banstead Athletic 2-0

Lancing v Dorking 2-4
Chichester City v South Park 4-4, 4-0
Bedfont v Crawley Down 1-0
Three Bridges v Badshot Lea 1-6
Egham Town v Farnborough North End 1-2
Whitehawk v Lingfield 3-1
Bookham v Redhill 1-2
Worthing United v Shoreham 1-2
Cove v Ringmer 2-3
Hartley Wintney v East Grinstead Town 1-2
Guildford City v Mole Valley SCR 1-2
Horley Town v Erith & Belvedere 1-2
Holmesdale v Greenwich Borough 1-2
Bemerton Heath Harlequins v Blackfield & Langley 1-0
Cheltenham Saracens v Bradford Town 1-4
Malmsbury Victoria v Flackwell Heath 2-4
Alton Town v Longwell Green Sports 0-2
Totton & Eling v Ardley United 2-3
Kidlington v New Milton Town 2-1
Melksham Town v Fairford Town 5-2
Holyport v Fareham Town 2-3
Lymington Town v United Services Portsmouth 0-4
Ringwood Town v Shrivenham 0-1
Hamble ASSC v Milton United 3-0
Westbury United v Devizes Town 3-2
Bournemouth v Brockenhurst 1-2
Cowes Sports v Almondsbury Town 2-3
Carterton v Newport (IW) 3-2
Corsham Town v Hallen 2-1
Wantage Town v Abingdon Town 3-1
Downton v Reading Town 3-2
Bristol Manor Farm v Pewsey Vale 3-0
Alresford Town v Hayling United 2-0
Highworth Town v Laverstock & Ford 1-2
Wells City v Minehead 3-2
Elmore v Liskeard Athletic 2-4
Odd Down v Welton Rovers 0-3
Buckland Athletic v Saltash United 2-4
Sherborne Town v Bishop Sutton 0-5
Torpoint Athletic v Tavistock 1-2
Budleigh Salterton v Barnstaple Town 0-5
Penzance v Wellington Town 1-2
Newquay v Bridport 4-2
Brislington v Street 5-2
Bodmin Town v Shaftesbury 0-1
Tie awarded to Bodmin Town; Shaftesbury removed from the competition.
Shepton Mallet v Porthleven 0-2
Chard Town v St Blazey 0-7
Swanage Town & Herston v Plymouth Parkway 1-1, 0-4
Gillingham Town v Launceston 1-0
Penrith Athletic v Keynsham Town 0-1
Falmouth Town v Clevedon United 0-3
Collompton Rangers v Verwood Town 1-2
Eton Manor v Erith Town 0-2

FIRST ROUND

Bridlington Town v South Shields 2-0
Consett v Bedlington Terriers 0-2
North Shields v Pickering Town 2-3
West Auckland Town v Hall Road Rangers 5-1
Armthorpe Welfare v Liversedge 3-1
Whickham v Tadcaster Albion 1-0
Guisborough Town v Norton & Stockton Ancients 1-2
Crook Town v Northallerton Town 2-0
Stokesley v Morpeth Town 0-2
Newcastle Benfield v Tow Law Town 1-0
Leeds Carnegie v Shildon 2-3
Rossington Main v Alsager Town 0-3
Colne v Hallam 0-4
Padiham v Hemsworth MW 4-2
Ramsbottom United v Bacup Borough 2-4
Penrith v Dinnington Town 4-0
Daisy Hill v Worsborough Bridge Athletic 6-2
Oldham Town v Winsford United 0-1
Cheadle Town v Congleton Town 2-2, 2-5
Nelson v Selby Town 2-0
Loughborough University v Causeway United 1-1, 1-2
Bewdley Town v Coleshill Town 2-1
AFC Wulfrunians v Friar Lane & Epworth 1-5
Southam United v Oadby Town 1-2
Blaby & Whetstone Athletic v Malvern Town 3-1
Wellington v Dosthill Colts 4-1
Walsall Wood v Westfields 0-2
Studley v Boldmere St Michaels 0-1

Tipton Town v Kirby Muxloe	3-1
Tividale v Wolverhampton Casuals	3-2
Wednesfield v Barwell	0-3
Biddulph Victoria v Norton United	2-1
Bartley Green v Newcastle Town	1-2
Bourne Town v New Mills	0-1
Dunkirk v Winterton Rangers	2-0
Grimsby Borough v Gresley	1-3
Blackstones v Lincoln Moorlands Railway	1-2
Louth Town v Sleaford Town	3-4
Bottisford Town v Ollerton Town	0-1
Borrowash Victoria v Gedling Town	0-4
Arnold Town v Long Eaton United	0-1
Rainworth MW v Deeping Rangers	2-1
Ely City v Eynesbury Rovers	3-2
Daventry United v Wellingborough Town	2-3
Cambridge Regional College v March Town United	7-1
Kirkley & Pakefield v Newmarket Town	3-1
Whitton United v Woodbridge Town	1-3
Haverhill Rovers v Bugbrooke St Michaels	2-3
Northampton Spencer v Wroxham	0-3
Daventry Town v Rothwell Corinthians	2-0
Felixstowe & Walton United v Long Buckby	1-1, 1-5
Halstead Town v Dunstable Town	3-0
Burnham Ramblers v Bedford	1-2
Witham Town v Hoddesdon Town	1-2
Broxbourne Borough V&E v Stotfold	1-2
Royston Town v Basildon United	5-0
Hillingdon Borough v Brimsdown Rovers	1-2
Langford v Wembley	1-2
Tiptree United v Harefield United	1-0
Newport Pagnell Town v Erith Town	5-1
London Colney v Bethnal Green United	2-1
Leverstock Green v Hadley	0-1
Enfield 1893 v Southend Manor	1-0
Wivenhoe Town v Stansted	1-3
Cockfosters v North Greenford United	1-2
Biggleswade United v Kingsbury London Tigers	2-1
Ringmer v Crowborough Athletic	2-3
Erith & Belvedere v Pagham	2-1
Ash United v Badshot Lea	5-4
East Grinstead Town v Whitehawk	0-5
Bedfont v Shoreham	1-1, 0-2
Mole Valley SCR v Beckenham Town	0-1
Epsom & Ewell v Farnborough North End	3-2
Eastbourne United v Greenwich Borough	4-3
Molesey v Arundel	1-2
Peacehaven & Telscombe v Chichester City	3-1
Herne Bay v Hythe Town	1-0
Redhill v Camberley Town	3-1
Wick v Faversham Town	3-1
Dorking v Chertsey Town	0-2
Longwell Green Sports v Wantage Town	2-1
Westbury United v Carterton	0-1
Laverstock & Ford v Brockenhurst	1-2
Kidlington v Bradford Town	1-2
Bemerton Heath Harlequins v Arlesford Town	1-1, 5-1
Ardley United v Moneyfields	0-1
Shrivenham v Flackwell Heath	0-2
Almondsbury Town v Melksham Town	3-1
Bristol Manor Farm v Corsham Town	2-1
United Services Portsmouth v Hamble ASSC	0-1
Downton v Fareham Town	2-4
Shortwood United v Winchester City	3-1
Poole Town v Bishop Sutton	4-1
Dawlish Town v Liskeard Athletic	3-0
Willand Rovers v Newquay	5-2
Wellington Town v Barnstaple Town	3-1
Wells City v Verwood Town	3-0
Welton Rovers v Keynsham Town	6-0
Clevedon United v Tavistock	3-5
Brislington v Porthleven	8-0
Bodmin Town v Saltash United	1-2
Plymouth Parkway v St Blazey	4-2
Wimborne Town v Gillingham Town	6-1
Bourne Town v New Mills	2-2
New Mills won 5-4 on penalties.	

SECOND ROUND

Padiham v Norton & Stockton Ancients	2-4
Winsford United v Pickering Town	1-2
Crook Town v Bacup Borough	2-0
Nelson v Morpeth Town	3-1
West Auckland Town v Whickham	4-0
Bedlington Terriers v Spennymoor Town	1-5

Penrith v Hallam	5-2
Daisy Hill v Armthorpe Welfare	2-3
Newcastle Benfield v Marske United	1-2
Glossop North End v Dunston UTS	1-0
Whitley Bay v Alsager Town	2-0
Bootle v Stone Dominoes	2-1
Congleton Town v Shildon	0-2
Scarborough Athletic v Bridlington Town	2-5
Wellington v Stratford Town	3-0
Coalville Town v Oadby Town	4-2
Elaby & Whetstone Athletic v Boldmere St Michaels	0-1
Dunkirk v Lincoln Moorlands Railway	3-1
New Mills v Tividale	6-1
Barwell v Long Eaton United	2-0
Biddulph Victoria v Gedling Town	1-0
Gresley v Ollerton Town	3-1
Causeway United v Newcastle Town	3-2
Friar Lane & Epworth v Tipton Town	1-2
Westfields v Rainworth MW	1-2
Sleaford Town v Bewdley Town	2-1
Long Buckby v Stansted	2-1
Cambridge Regional College v Enfield 1893	4-1
Newport Pagnell Town v Dereham Town	3-2
North Greenford United v Daventry Town	0-1
Kirkley & Pakefield v Biggleswade United	2-0
Ely City v Woodbridge Town	1-1
Tie awarded to Ely City; Woodbridge Town removed.	
Bugbrooke St Michaels v Leiston	0-4
Needham Market v Bedford	5-0
Wellingborough Town v Royston Town	0-4
Stanway Rovers v Hadley	1-0
Wroxham v Halstead Town	0-0, 3-1
FC Clacton v St Ives Town	0-2
Brimsdown Rovers v London Colney	3-2
Wembley v Hoddesdon Town	1-2
Stewarts & Lloyds v Stotfold	2-4
Tiptree United v Cogenhoe United	4-3
Chertsey Town v Croydon	2-0
Eastbourne United v Hamble ASSC	4-2
Whitehawk v Fareham Town	3-2
Herne Bay v Flackwell Heath	0-1
Arundel v Crowborough Athletic	4-0
Badshot Lea v Faversham Town	2-1
Beckenham Town v Carterton	2-1
Witney United v Erith & Belvedere	5-1
Chalfont St Peter v Peacehaven & Telscombe	1-5
Moneyfields v Epsom & Ewell	2-3
Redhill v Shoreham	1-2
Plymouth Parkway v Bitton	3-2
Wellington Town v Bradford Town	3-2
Shortwood United v Bemerton Heath Harlequins	3-0
Tavistock v Brockenhurst	1-3
Wells City v Larkhall Athletic	2-3
Bristol Manor Farm v Saltash United	2-1
Dawlish Town v Wimborne Town	3-1
Christchurch v Almondsbury Town	2-5
Bideford v Welton Rovers	0-2
Longwell Green Sports v Willand Rovers	2-3
Brislington v Poole Town	0-4

THIRD ROUND

Marske United v Nelson	5-0
Whitley Bay v Boldmere St Michaels	3-1
Armthorpe Welfare v Bridlington Town	2-1
Rainworth MW v Norton & Stockton Ancients	1-2
Pickering Town v Dunkirk	1-1, 2-2
Pickering Town won 5-4 on penalties.	
Crook Town v Shildon	2-4
Biddulph Victoria v Causeway United	1-3
New Mills v West Auckland Town	5-1
Penrith v Bootle	1-4
Coalville Town v Tipton Town	0-2
Barwell v Glossop North End	2-0
Gresley v Spennymoor Town	1-0
Tiptree United v Beckenham Town	3-2
Chertsey Town v Sleaford Town	3-2
Brimsdown Rovers v Newport Pagnell Town	3-2
Cambridge Regional College v Needham Market	1-2
Royston Town v Stanway Rovers	2-1
Long Buckby v Wellington	5-2
Stotfold v Badshot Lea	3-1
Hoddesdon Town v Kirkley & Pakefield	0-4
Flackwell Heath v Wroxham	1-3
St Ives Town v Ely City	3-0
Leiston v Daventry Town	3-4

Eastbourne United v Poole Town	3-5
Plymouth Parkway v Arundel	4-2
Willand Rovers v Welton Rovers	6-1
Larkhall Athletic v Whitehawk	0-2
Shortwood United v Shoreham	2-0
Witney United v Almondsbury Town	4-0
Peacehaven & Telscombe v Bristol Manor Farm	0-3
Wellington Town v Epsom & Ewell	2-3
Dawlish Town v Brockenhurst	3-1

FOURTH ROUND

New Mills v Witney United	2-1
Tiptree United v St Ives Town	0-7
Needham Market v Kirkley & Pakefield	5-3
Whitley Bay v Poole Town	3-1
Shortwood United v Barwell	0-3
Brimsdown Rovers v Daventry Town	1-4
Bristol Manor Farm v Whitehawk	1-3
Norton & Stockton Ancients v Bootle	4-2
Pickering Town v Marske United	1-2
Armthorpe Welfare v Wroxham	1-1, 1-1
Wroxham won 3-0 on penalties.	
Willand Rovers v Causeway United	2-0
Long Buckby v Epsom & Ewell	3-2
Dawlish Town v Gresley	4-4, 1-1
Gresley won 7-6 on penalties.	
Royston Town v Tipton Town	2-1
Chertsey Town v Plymouth Parkway	6-0
Stotfold v Shildon	0-2

FIFTH ROUND

St Ives Town v Shildon	1-3
New Mills v Norton & Stockton Ancients	0-2

Whitehawk v Marske United	1-1, 3-2
Long Buckby v Gresley	3-4
Willand Rovers v Barwell	2-2, 1-2
Royston Town v Wroxham	0-5
Needham Market v Daventry Town	2-0
Chertsey Town v Whitley Bay	1-1, 1-2

SIXTH ROUND

Shildon v Whitley Bay	1-5
Needham Market v Wroxham	1-2
Barwell v Norton & Stockton Ancients	3-0
Gresley v Whitehawk	1-3

SEMI-FINAL (two legs)

Barwell v Whitley Bay	3-3, 2-3
Whitehawk v Wroxham	0-2, 1-2

FINAL (at Wembley)

Sunday 9 May 2009

Whitley Bay (2) 6 (*Chow 1, Eastaugh 16 (og), Kerr 46, Johnston 50, Robinson 76, Gillies 85*)

Wroxham (1) 1 (*Cook 12*)   8920

Whitley Bay: Burke; McFarlane, Anderson, Hodgson (Picton 69), Timmons, Ryan, Johnston (Gillies 77), Robson, Kerr, Chow (Bell 62), Robinson.
Wroxham: Howie; Pauling (Durrant 58), Howes, Challen, McNeil (Carus 46), Eastaugh (Paynter 69), Spriggs, Lemmon, Cook, White, Gilmore.
Referee: A. Taylor (Cheshire).

THE FA COUNTY YOUTH CUP 2009–10

FIRST ROUND

Essex v Hampshire	1-7
Cumberland v North Riding	0-2
Herefordshire v Amateur Football Alliance	0-1
Cambridgeshire v Oxfordshire	3-2
Hertfordshire v Cornwall	1-2
Guernsey v Berks & Bucks	3-6
West Riding v Cheshire	0-0
West Riding won 5-4 on penalties.	
Westmoreland v Manchester	2-3
Staffordshire v East Riding	0-4
Gloucestershire v Bedfordshire	1-4
Somerset v Devon	2-1
London v Northamptonshire	3-1
Leicestershire & Rutland v Shropshire	3-1
Norfolk v Suffolk	0-3

SECOND ROUND

Worcestershire v Jersey	5-2
Sussex v Dorset	4-1
Northumberland v West Riding	0-2
Lancashire v Manchester	3-1
Liverpool v North Riding	2-0
Birmingham v Leicestershire & Rutland	4-0
Lincolnshire v East Riding	2-2
East Riding won 4-2 on penalties.	
Sheffield & Hallamshire v Isle of Man	2-0
Nottinghamshire v Durham	1-5
Suffolk v Cambridgeshire	5-4
London v Cornwall	1-4
Middlesex v Huntingdonshire	5-0
Somerset v Kent	1-5
Surrey v Berks & Bucks	3-1
Bedfordshire v Amateur Football Alliance	3-0
Wiltshire v Hampshire	1-0

THIRD ROUND

Middlesex v Lancashire	1-2
Birmingham v Suffolk	3-4
Wiltshire v Cornwall	2-4
East Riding v Durham	1-3
Surrey v Liverpool	1-3
Bedfordshire v West Riding	0-2
Sheffield & Hallamshire v Worcestershire	2-1
Kent v Sussex	1-0

FOURTH ROUND

Durham v Kent	1-2
Sheffield & Hallamshire v West Riding	2-0
Lancashire v Suffolk	1-0
Liverpool v Cornwall	3-0

SEMI-FINALS

Liverpool v Kent	3-5
Sheffield & Hallamshire v Lancashire	1-0

FINAL (at Gillingham FC)
Kent (0) 1 (*Miller 79*)
Sheffield & Hallamshire (0) 0

THE FA YOUTH CUP 2009–10

SPONSORED BY E.ON

PRELIMINARY ROUND

Seaham Red Star v Whitley Bay	8-0
Lancaster City v Salford City	4-0
Nantwich Town v Chester City	0-1
Curzon Ashton v Woodley Sports	0-1
Fleetwood Town v Wrexham	1-2
Southport v Colne	6-1
Cammell Laird v Northwich Victoria	2-0
Formby v Prescot Cables	2-1
Altrincham v Daisy Hill	7-1
Nostell MW v Hemsworth MW	3-2
Pontefract Collieries v Hallam	1-3
Yorkshire Amateur v Glasshoughton Welfare	3-4
Ossett Albion v Goole	0-6
North Ferriby United v Garforth Town	3-0
Farsley Celtic v Eccleshill United	6-0
Barwell v Boston United	1-3
St Andrews v Matlock Town	0-6
Blaby & Whetstone Athletic v Grantham Town	4-2
Hinckley United v Deeping Rangers	1-0
Mansfield Town w.o. v Ilkeston Town withdrew	
Stamford v Lincoln United	1-4
Bedworth United v Chasetown	5-3
Boldmere St Michaels v Willenhall Town	3-0
Kidderminster Harriers v Coventry Sphinx	4-2
Atherstone Town v Sutton Coldfield Town	2-1
Rugby Town v Stratford Town	2-1
Redditch United v Stone Dominoes	0-1
Stourbridge v Newcastle Town	5-0
Lye Town v Pegasus Juniors	1-0
Rocester v Bromyard Town	4-0
Ellesmere Rangers v Eccleshall	7-1
Nuneaton Griff v Stafford Rangers	4-3
Solihull Moors w.o. v Worcester City withdrew	
Nuneaton Town v Malvern Town	3-4
Dosthill Colts v AFC Telford United	1-2
Tipton Town v Dudley Town	2-2
Tipton Town won 5-4 on penalties.	
Gornal Athletic v Pershore Town	2-1
Histon v Long Melford	8-2
Stowmarket Town v Ely City	3-0
Newmarket Town v Kirkley & Pakefield	0-3
Thetford Town v Dereham Town	0-3
Leiston v Wroxham	5-2
Cambridge United v Diss Town	12-0
Hadleigh United v Great Yarmouth Town	2-5
Fakenham Town v Cornard United	1-2
March Town United v King's Lynn	1-6
Ipswich Wanderers v Lowestoft Town	1-5
Huntingdon Town v Stotfold	2-1
Rushden & Diamonds v Stewarts & Lloyds	9-0
Luton Town v Northampton Spencer	6-0
Cranfield United v Yaxley	5-1
Cogenhoe United v AFC Kempston Rovers	2-3
St Ives Town v Rothwell Town	0-3
Corby Town v Raunds Town	0-2
Sileby Rangers v Rothwell Corinthians	4-1
Bugbrooke St Michaels v Wellingborough Town	1-4
Halstead Town v Witham Town	2-1
FC Clacton v Braintree Town	1-2
Chelmsford City v Romford	5-0
Bishop's Stortford v Hoddesdon Town	4-1
St Margaretsbury v Bowers & Pitsea	3-0
Brightlingsea Regent withdrew v Thurrock w.o.	
Boreham Wood v Billericay Town	3-1
Brentwood Town v London Colney	1-2
Grays Athletic v Hemel Hempstead Town	4-2
AFC Hornchurch v Stevenage Borough	3-0
Southend Manor v St Albans City	1-1
St Albans City won 6-5 on penalties.	
Ilford v Harpenden Town	2-0
Corinthian Casuals v Hillingdon Borough	2-1
Tokygnton Manor v Clapton	1-1
Clapton won 5-4 on penalties.	
Staines Town v Harefield United	2-1
Thamesmead Town v Harringey Borough	2-0
Hayes & Yeading United v Welling United	4-0
AFC Wimbledon v Kentish Town	2-1

Hampton & Richmond Borough w.o. v Leyton withdrew	
Kingsbury London Tigers v	
Ashford Town (Middlesex)	0-11
Croydon Athletic v Redbridge	2-0
Hanwell Town v North Greenford United	2-3
Haywards Heath Town v Croydon	0-4
Oakwood v Whyteleafe	1-2
St Francis Rangers v Eastbourne Borough	1-6
Lewes v Folkestone Invicta	4-0
Margate v Merstham	1-0
Eastbourne Town v Redhill	5-3
Three Bridges v Dartford	2-6
Maidstone United v Crawley Down	5-1
Chatham Town v South Park	6-0
Hastings United v Deal Town	4-1
Ramsgate v VCD Athletic	4-3
Tonbridge Angels v Chipstead	1-2
Carshalton Athletic v Burgess Hill Town	8-0
Walton & Hersham v Lancing	5-2
Horsham v Tooting & Mitcham United	1-4
Sutton United v Epsom & Ewell	5-0
Colliers Wood United v Chichester City United	6-0
Wick v Worthing United	1-2
Worthing v Woking	1-4
Thatcham Town v Fleet Town	4-1
Slough Town v Thame United	3-3
Slough Town won 4-2 on penalties.	
Wokingham Town & Emmbrook withdrew v	
Didcot Town w.o.	
Binfield v Basingstoke Town	0-3
Alton Town v Oxford United	0-6
Farnborough w.o. v Aylesbury United withdrew	
Maidenhead United v Newport Pagnell Town	4-0
Windsor & Eton v Abingdon United	4-5
Chesham United v Chalfont St Peter	4-3
Cove v Flackwell Heath	1-3
Buckingham Town v Banbury United	3-0
Winchester City v Salisbury City	0-5
Moneyfields v Bournemouth	4-2
Dorchester Town v Eastleigh	1-3
Christchurch v AFC Totton	3-2
Gosport Borough v VT	1-2
Bishop's Cleeve v Almondsbury	2-1
Weston-Super-Mare v Tiverton Town	4-1
Wootton Bassett Town v Chard Town	1-2
Portishead Town v Clevedon Town	1-2
Elmore w.o. v Bridgwater Town withdrew	
Yate Town v Mangotsfield United	2-1

FIRST QUALIFYING ROUND

Guisborough Town v York City	1-5
Ashton Town v Vauxhall Motors	1-4
Marine v Chester City	0-1
Wrexham v Leigh Genesis	12-0
Woodley Sports v Southport	2-3
Altrincham v Cammell Laird	4-2
Workington v Bootle	1-1
Workington won 6-5 on penalties.	
Warrington Town withdrew v Lancaster City w.o.	
Ashton Athletic v Formby	0-5
Glasshoughton Welfare v Sheffield	2-2
Glasshoughton Welfare won 4-3 on penalties.	
Staveley MW v Wakefield	3-1
Nostell MW v Stocksbridge Park Steels	1-5
Hallam v FC Halifax Town	2-1
Worksop Town v Goole	0-2
Bradford Park Avenue v Thackley	3-4
Carlton Town v Holwell Sports	5-2
Teversal v Matlock Town	1-5
Blaby & Whetstone Athletic v Mansfield Town	0-4
Gresley v Lincoln United	3-1
Gornal Athletic v Malvern Town	2-4
Nuneaton Griff v Bewdley Town	3-0
Pelsall Villa v Highgate United	0-3
Kidderminster Harriers v Wednesfield	2-3
Boldmere St Michaels v Atherstone Town	2-5
Rocester v Bedworth United	5-3

Stourport Swifts v Ellesmere Rangers	1-2
Wellington v Rugby Town	1-0
Kirkley & Pakefield v Great Yarmouth Town	2-2
Kirkley & Pakefield won 5-4 on penalties.	
Felixstowe & Walton United v Needham Market	1-2
Cornard United v Woodbridge Town	2-2
Cornard United won 4-2 on penalties.	
Histon v King's Lynn	3-2
Stowmarket Town v Bury Town	2-3
Lowestoft Town v Dereham Town	1-2
Leiston v Cambridge United	0-6
Soham Town Rangers v Walsham Le Willows	4-3
Luton Town v Raunds Town	7-1
Daventry Town v FCV Reds	3-0
Sileby Rangers v Thrapston Town	3-0
Huntingdon Town v Wellingborough Town	2-1
Rushden & Diamonds v Leighton Town	5-0
Arlesey Town v Cranfield United	2-2
Arlesey Town won 5-4 on penalties.	
AFC Kempston Rovers v Rothwell Town	1-2
Harlow Town v Aveley	0-10
East Thurrock United v Boreham Wood	2-3
London Colney v Ilford	1-0
Chelmsford City v Waltham Abbey	1-1
Chelmsford City won 3-2 on penalties.	
Braintree Town v Bishop's Stortford	1-4
Grays Athletic v Halstead Town	2-2
Halstead Town won 5-4 on penalties.	
Royston Town v AFC Hornchurch	1-5
Enfield Town v Northwood	2-1
Ashford Town (Middlesex) v Wealdstone	1-1
Ashford Town (Middlesex) won 4-2 on penalties.	
Corinthian Casuals v Croydon Athletic	0-2
Clapton v Wingate & Finchley	2-0
North Greenford United v Thamesmead Town	1-2
Hayes & Yeading United v AFC Wimbledon	0-3
Eastbourne Town v Bromley	0-2
Ramsgate v East Grinstead Town	0-4
Dover Athletic v Dartford	3-5
Crawley Town v Whitstable Town	2-3
Maidstone United v Chipstead	3-0
Eastbourne Borough v Horley Town	4-1
Whyteleafe v Lewes	0-4
Chatham Town v Croydon	1-0
Saltdean United v Hastings United	1-4
Lingfield v Margate	0-1
Carshalton Athletic v Chertsey Town	3-2
Walton & Hersham v Molesey	2-3
Cobham v Sutton United	1-2
Colliers Wood United v Worthing United	3-2
Farnborough v Bracknell Town	3-0
Buckingham Town v Kidlington	4-4
Buckingham Town won 4-3 on penalties.	
Burnham v Maidenhead United	0-2
Didcot Town v Andover	2-1
Slough Town v Basingstoke Town	0-2
Chesham United v Thatcham Town	2-4
Witney United v Flackwell Heath	3-2
Eastleigh v Moneyfields	4-1
Christchurch v Salisbury City	3-3
Christchurch won 5-4 on penalties.	
Chard Town v Bitton	2-3
Cheltenham Saracens v Newport County	0-5
Bishop's Cleeve v Cirencester Town	0-3
Weston-Super-Mare v Bath City	1-0
Forest Green Rovers v Clevedon Town	6-0
Elmore v Yate Town	1-5
Gloucester City v Merthyr Tydfil	5-1
Staines Town v Hampton & Richmond Borough	5-0
Scarborough Town v Bedlington Terriers	3-2
Holbeach United withdrew v Glossop North End w.o.	
Hednesford Town v Bromsgrove Rovers	2-4
Tipton Town v Stourbridge	1-5
Lye Town v Solihull Moors	1-2
Thurrock v Burnham Ramblers	9-1
Reading Town v Oxford City	0-1
Stalybridge Celtic v Ashville	7-2
Weymouth v Havant & Waterlooville	0-1
Kingstonian v Pagham	2-0
Ryton v Prudhoe Town	2-3
Sunderland RCA v Gateshead	2-1
Burscough v Congleton Town	0-2
Liversedge v Ossett Town	4-3
Oadby Town v Rainworth MW	2-0

St Albans City v Hitchin Town	3-1
Colney Heath v Tilbury	2-5
Westfield v Mile Oak	3-0
Paulton Rovers v Radstock Town	3-5
Tie awarded to Paulton Rovers; Radstock Town removed.	
North Ferriby United v Farsley Celtic	2-3
Hinckley United v Arnold Town	1-2
New Mills v Long Eaton United	1-2
Retford United v Mickleover Sports	0-3
Dulwich Hamlet v Uxbridge	3-0
Ebbsfleet United v Ashford Town	4-0
Tooting & Mitcham United v Woking	0-5
Marlow v Beaconsfield SYCOB	4-3
Henley Town v Sandhurst Town	6-0
Poole Town v Petersfield Town	1-0
Dunston UTS v Seaham Red Star	2-1
Loughborough Dynamo v Boston United	3-1
Hullbridge Sports v Leverstock Green	1-6
Stone Dominoes v Dosthill Colts	0-2
Dunstable Town v Kettering Town	4-1
Cheshunt v St Margaretsbury	0-6
Camberley Town v Shoreham	2-3
Abingdon United v AFC Wallingford	0-7

SECOND QUALIFYING ROUND

Goole v Farsley Celtic	0-5
Carlton Town v Gresley	6-0
Arnold Town v Long Eaton United	3-1
Arlesey Town v Rothwell Town	1-7
Daventry Town v Dunstable Town	0-1
Leverstock Green v Aveley	3-6
Lewes v Hastings United	3-0
East Grinstead Town v Bromley	1-3
Molesey v Woking	1-4
Paulton Rovers v Gloucester City	1-7
AFC Wallingford v Maidenhead United	2-1
Cirencester Town v Newport County	0-1
Lancaster City v Chester City	0-1
Bromsgrove Rovers v Malvern Town	3-5
Bury Town v Kirkley & Pakefield	5-2
Enfield Town v Dulwich Hamlet	1-4
Oxford City v Marlow	2-3
Basingstoke Town v Witney United	1-0
Weston-Super-Mare v Bitton	1-5
Prudhoe Town v Scarborough Town	0-4
Liversedge v Thackley	0-7
Hallam v Glasshoughton Welfare	3-0
Stocksbridge Park Steels v Staveley MW	2-3
Histon v Cornard United	4-1
Eastbourne Borough v Chatham Town	3-4
Buckingham Town v Farnborough Town	2-2
Farnborough Town won 3-1 on penalties.	
Chelmsford City v Halstead Town	3-1
Dunston UTS v Sunderland RCA	1-0
Formby v Southport	0-3
Wrexham v Stalybridge Celtic	4-5
Glossop North End v Mansfield Town	2-7
Solihull Moors v Stourbridge	2-1
Tilbury v St Margaretsbury	4-1
Clapton v Staines Town	0-0
Clapton won 4-2 on penalties.	
Westfield v Kingstonian	1-3
Congleton Town v Workington	1-0
Atherstone Town v Ellesmere Rangers	4-2
Highgate United v Wellington	10-2
Nuneaton Griff v Dosthill Colts	0-2
Wednesfield v Rocester	2-5
Dereham Town v Cambridge United	0-4
Rushden & Diamonds v Luton Town	2-0
Bishop's Stortford v AFC Hornchurch	2-0
St Albans City v Thurrock	2-1
London Colney v Boreham Wood	1-2
Croydon Athletic v Ashford Town (Middlesex)	0-1
Faversham Town v Ebbsfleet United	2-5
Sutton United v Colliers Wood United	3-1
Carshalton Athletic v Shoreham	3-4
Eastleigh v Sherborne Town	2-0
Poole Town v Havant & Waterlooville	0-1
Chester-Le-Street Town v York City	1-2
Mickleover Sports v Oadby Town	3-2
Whitstable Town v Margate	0-1
Didcot Town v Thatcham Town	0-3
Loughborough Dynamo v Matlock Town	4-1

Needham Market v Soham Town Rangers	5-2
Huntingdon Town v Sileby Rangers	2-1
Thamesmead Town v AFC Wimbledon	1-3
Maidstone United v Dartford	3-2
Henley Town v Oxford United	0-1
Christchurch v VT	2-3
Forest Green Rovers v Yate Town	7-2
Vauxhall Motors v Altrincham	1-2

THIRD QUALIFYING ROUND

Southport v Hallam	8-0
Stalybridge Celtic v Altrincham	3-2
Thackley v Chester City	0-4
Congleton Town v Dunston UTS	3-2
Farsley Celtic v Staveley MW	5-3
York City v Scarborough Town	3-1
Rocester v Rushden & Diamonds	0-5
Loughborough Dynamo v Mansfield Town	1-3
Mickleover Sports v Malvern Town	3-4
Histon v Needham Market	6-1
Bury Town v Huntingdon Town	3-0
Dosthill Colts v Atherstone Town	0-2
Rothwell Town v Cambridge United	0-1
Highgate United v Arnold Town	3-0
Carlton Town v Solihull Moors	5-1
Boreham Wood v Dunstable Town	1-2
Bishop's Stortford v Clapton	2-1
Aveley v St Albans City	2-5
Dulwich Hamlet v Chelmsford City	4-1
Tilbury v AFC Wimbledon	0-2
Shoreham v Marlow	1-4
Sutton United v Margate	2-1
Chatham Town v Bromley	0-3
Kingstonian v Ebbsfleet United	0-3
Ashford Town (Middlesex) v Woking	2-2
Woking won 5-4 on penalties.	
Lewes v Maidstone United	2-3
Bitton v VT	1-3
Newport County v Oxford United	3-4
Forest Green Rovers v AFC Wallingford	1-0
Basingstoke Town v Havant & Waterlooville	2-1
Gloucester City v Thatcham Town	4-2
Farnborough v Eastleigh	2-0

FIRST ROUND

Macclesfield Town v Bury	2-0
Hartlepool United v Lincoln City	3-1
Oldham Athletic v Stalybridge Celtic	4-1
Darlington v Huddersfield Town	1-2
Bradford City v Southport	3-1
Accrington Stanley v Carlisle United	1-1
Carlisle United won 9-8 on penalties.	
Grimsby Town v York City	1-2
Congleton Town v Rochdale	0-3
Leeds United v Crewe Alexandra	0-1
Tranmere Rovers v Farsley Celtic	3-0
Chester City v Morecambe	0-4
Rotherham United v Stockport County	3-3
Stockport County won 4-3 on penalties.	
Bury Town v Walsall	3-2
Rushden & Diamonds v Northampton Town	1-2
Carlton Town v Burton Albion	2-1
Histon v Cambridge United	0-4
Chesterfield v Mansfield Town	4-1
Atherstone Town v Highgate United	2-0
Shrewsbury Town v Port Vale	2-1
Malvern Town v Notts County	0-1
Milton Keynes Dons v Dunstable Town	2-1
Maidstone United v Wycombe Wanderers	3-5
Barnet v Brighton & Hove Albion	0-4
Woking v Dagenham & Redbridge	3-1
AFC Wimbledon v Sutton United	2-1
Charlton Athletic v Gillingham	3-0
Leyton Orient v Bromley	2-1
St Albans City v Colchester United	1-0
Millwall v Southend United	3-1
Bishop's Stortford v Marlow	7-1
Ebbsfleet United v Brentford	2-1
Dulwich Hamlet v Norwich City	1-1
Norwich City won 4-2 on penalties.	
Aldershot Town v Southampton	0-4
Forest Green Rovers v Farnborough	1-2

Bristol Rovers v AFC Bournemouth	1-3
VT v Torquay United	2-3
Basingstoke Town v Hereford United	3-4
Oxford United v Gloucester City	5-2
Exeter City v Cheltenham Town	0-4
Swindon Town v Yeovil Town	6-0

SECOND ROUND

Bradford City v Crewe Alexandra	1-2
Stockport County v Carlton Town	2-0
Oldham Athletic v Rochdale	2-5
Notts County v Hartlepool United	0-2
Northampton Town v Chesterfield	2-1
Shrewsbury Town v Morecambe	5-2
York City v Carlisle United	1-2
Huddersfield Town v Atherstone Town	5-0
Bury Town v Macclesfield Town	1-1
Bury Town won 4-3 on penalties.	
Tranmere Rovers v Cambridge United	3-1
Millwall v Oxford United	1-0
Southampton v Hereford United	6-0
Cheltenham Town v Farnborough	3-2
Swindon Town v Leyton Orient	1-2
Milton Keynes Dons v Bishop's Stortford	2-1
Charlton Athletic v Woking	3-1
AFC Wimbledon v AFC Bournemouth	0-5
Brighton & Hove Albion v Ebbsfleet United	2-0
St Albans City v Wycombe Wanderers	2-2
Wycombe Wanderers won 4-2 on penalties.	
Torquay United v Norwich City	1-0

THIRD ROUND

Manchester United v Birmingham City	2-0
Derby County v Peterborough United	6-1
Middlesbrough v Everton	0-1
Wigan Athletic v Tottenham Hotspur	0-1
Cheltenham Town v Reading	1-2
Nottingham Forest v Bury Town	5-2
Milton Keynes Dons v Leyton Orient	1-3
Shrewsbury Town v Hull City	1-2
Watford v Wycombe Wanderers	3-0
Liverpool v Wolverhampton Wanderers	2-0
Hartlepool United v Sheffield United	2-1
Crystal Palace v Bristol City	3-2
Stockport County v Fulham	1-3
Preston North End v Manchester City	2-1
Cardiff City v Barnsley	1-2
Torquay United v Millwall	0-3
Arsenal v Crewe Alexandra	3-3
Arsenal won 5-4 on penalties.	
Tranmere Rovers v Ipswich Town	0-2
Scunthorpe United v Burnley	1-4
Plymouth Argyle v West Ham United	0-1
Portsmouth v Huddersfield United	1-0
Northampton Town v Brighton & Hove Albion	1-3
Sheffield Wednesday v Sunderland	2-7
Aston Villa v Rochdale	4-0
Carlisle United v Stoke City	0-1
Swansea City v West Bromwich Albion	0-3
Coventry City v Leicester City	2-3
Bolton Wanderers v AFC Bournemouth	3-1
Blackburn Rovers v Blackpool	3-0
Charlton Athletic v Chelsea	1-2
Doncaster Rovers v Newcastle United	0-3
Queens Park Rangers v Southampton	3-1

FOURTH ROUND

Stoke City v Hull City	1-2
West Ham United v Queens Park Rangers	3-0
Millwall v Barnsley	5-4
Blackburn Rovers v Leyton Orient	1-0
Bolton Wanderers v Fulham	2-2
Fulham won 5-3 on penalties.	
Reading v Newcastle United	1-3
Brighton & Hove Albion v Everton	0-2
Tottenham Hotspur v Portsmouth	0-1
Crystal Palace v Derby County	2-0
Leicester City v Liverpool	1-5
West Bromwich Albion v Aston Villa	0-2
Burnley v Manchester United	1-5
Hartlepool United v Watford	0-2

Nottingham Forest v Chelsea	0-4
Sunderland v Preston North End	2-2

Preston North End won 3-0 on penalties.

Arsenal v Ipswich Town	0-2

FIFTH ROUND

Blackburn Rovers v Manchester United	3-0
Preston North End v Everton	0-3
Chelsea v Portsmouth	1-0
Liverpool v Watford	0-1
West Ham United v Newcastle United	0-3
Hull City v Crystal Palace	1-4
Ipswich Town v Fulham	1-3
Aston Villa v Millwall	4-1

SIXTH ROUND

Watford v Chelsea	0-4
Newcastle United v Crystal Palace	4-2
Blackburn Rovers v Everton	2-1
Fulham v Aston Villa	2-2

Aston Villa won 3-1 on penalties.

SEMI-FINALS (two legs)

Aston Villa v Newcastle United	1-1, 1-0
Blackburn Rovers v Chelsea	0-1, 0-4

FINAL FIRST LEG

Thursday 29 April 2010

Aston Villa (1) 1 *(Devine 19)*

Chelsea (0) 1 *(Bruma 64)*   3359

Aston Villa: Siegrist; Berry, Devine, Williams, Deeney, Nelson-Addy, Blythe, Carruthers, Roberts, Simmonds (Halfhuid 82), Poyser (Darkin 79).
Chelsea: Walker; Clifford B, Ince, Bruma, Conteh (Sampayo 90), Djalo, McEachran, Clifford C (Lalkovic 71), Sala, Mitrovic, Tore.
Referee: K. Friend (Leicestershire).

FINAL SECOND LEG

Tuesday 4 May 2010

Chelsea (0) 2 *(Mitrovic 65, Clifford C 86)*

Aston Villa (1) 1 *(Poyser 33)*   10,464

Chelsea: Walker; Clifford B, Ince, Bruma, Conteh, Clifford C, Sala, Djalo (Saville 90), Mitrovic, McEachran, Tore (Lalkovic 89).
Aston Villa: Siegrist; Berry, Deeney, Devine, Williams (Darkin 72), Blythe (Halfhuid 89), Carruthers, Nelson-Addy, Poyser, Simmonds, Roberts.
Referee: K. Friend (Leicestershire).

THE NATIONAL LEAGUE SYSTEMS CUP
2009–10

PRELIMINARY ROUND

Reading Football League v Middlesex County League	4-1
Nottinghamshire Senior League v Teesside Football League	0-1
Midland Football Combination (Div 1) v West Yorkshire Football League	1-0
Brighton Hove & District League v Dorset Premier League	0-3
Northampton Town League v Hampshire Premier League	2-1
Isle of Man League v Manchester Football League	1-0
Wearside League v Cambridgeshire County League	1-2
Guernsey Senior County League v Kent County League	6-0
Jersey Football Combination v Spartan South Midlands League (Div 2)	2-0
Mid Sussex League v Bedfordshire Football League	0-4
Northamptonshire Combination v Peterborough & District League	2-1
Cumberland County League v Yorkshire Old Boys League	4-5

FIRST ROUND

Humber Premier League v West Cheshire League	2-1

Tie awarded to West Cheshire League; Humber Premier League removed.

Northampton Town League v Guernsey Senior County League	0-2
Lancashire Amateur League v Anglian Combination	3-2
Cheshire Football League v Yorkshire Old Boys League	1-3
Northamptonshire Combination v West Riding County Amateur League	1-4
Northern Football Alliance v Liverpool County Premier League	2-3
Dorset Premier League v Sussex County League (Div 3)	5-2
Wiltshire Football League v Jersey Football Combination	0-3
Southern Amateur Football League v Gloucestershire County League	2-0
Somerset County League v Reading Football League	3-4
Bedfordshire Football League v Amateur Football Combination	0-0

Bedfordshire Football League won 4-3 on penalties.

Teesside Football League v Cambridgeshire County League	1-3
Worthing & District League v Essex Olympian League	2-9
Hertfordshire Senior County League v Essex & Suffolk Border League	1-0
Midland Football Combination (Div 1) v Isle of Man League	0-3
Lancashire & Cheshire Amateur League v Birmingham & District Amateur League	4-2

SECOND ROUND

Lancashire & Cheshire Amateur League v Cambridgeshire County League	0-5
West Riding County Amateur League v Yorkshire Old Boys League	0-3
Liverpool County Premier League v Isle of Man League	2-1
Lancashire Amateur League v West Cheshire League	2-3
Essex Olympian League v Jersey Football Combination	0-1
Bedfordshire Football League v Dorset Premier League	1-2
Guernsey Senior County League v Southern Amateur Football League	3-2
Reading Football League v Hertfordshire Senior County League	2-3

THIRD ROUND

Liverpool County Premier League v Cambridgeshire County League	3-1
West Cheshire League v Yorkshire Old Boys League	2-3
Jersey Football Combination v Dorset Premier League	0-1
Guernsey Senior County League v Hertfordshire Senior County League	3-2

SEMI-FINAL

Guernsey Senior County League v Dorset Premier League	3-2
Liverpool County Premier League v Yorkshire Old Boys League	3-2

FINAL

Guernsey Senior County League v Liverpool County Premier League	5-2

THE FA SUNDAY CUP 2009–10

IN PARTNERSHIP WITH CARLSBERG

PRELIMINARY ROUND

Tower v Crossflatts	4-1
Brow v Rawdon Old Boys	4-0
Queens Park v Alder	3-2
Seymour KFCA v Towngate	2-3
Shankhouse United v St Sebastians	3-1
Belt Road v Station Gates	4-0
Hawkins Sports v Warstones Wanderers (Sunday)	0-4
Baldon Sports v London Maccabi Lions	2-3
Broadfields United v Crawley Green (Sunday)	3-1
Dunstable White Swan v AC Sportsman & Ravensborough	3-1
Comets Sports Club v AC Cadoza	3-2
Offley Moat v St Margarets	3-2
Blackwater Valley v Battersea Ironsides	2-3

FIRST ROUND

Bolton Woods v Paddock	0-2
Tower v Salisbury Athletic	0-6
Cleator Moor v West Lee	1-3
Mirehouse v Thirly	3-2
Brow v Thornhill Lees	4-2
Fforde Grene Brazil v Sandstone	1-3
Hetton Lyons Cricket Club v Allerton	7-0
Towngate v Queens Park	1-3
Kelloe WMC v Witton Park Rose & Crown	3-4
Silsden (Sunday) v Salford Celtic	2-1
Britannia v BRNESC	5-0
St Bees Village v Shamrocks	0-4
Shankhouse United v Hartlepool Lion Hillcarter	2-1
East End Park WMC v Canada	1-2
AFC Blackburn Leisure v Obiter	3-0
Huddersfield Irish Centre v Chapeltown Brazil	4-1
Dengo United v Home & Bargain	4-0
Beverley United v Western Approaches	0-4
Lindley WMC v JOB	0-3
Halton Moat v Flat House	
Abandoned 20 minutes; both clubs removed from the competition after mass brawl.	
Ford Motors v Poulton Royal	0-4
Hessle Rangers withdrew v Kempston St Gym w.o.	
Langley Celtic v Dawdon Colliery Welfare	4-2
Sunderland RCA Barnes v Lobster	0-4
Swanfield v Nicosia	3-2
Mariners v Merton Victoria	3-0
Loughborough Saints v Leicester Polska	7-1
Belt Road v Sporting Dynamo	3-2
Barcabullona v Bartley Green Sunday	1-3
Birstall Stamford v Britannia Revolution	2-0
Travellers v Brereton Town	2-0
Anstey Swifts OB withdrew v Barwell Sports Bar w.o.	
Thatch v Harp FC 2003	4-1
Warstones Wanderers (Sunday) v Duke of Rutland	2-0
Robinson's Garage v Magnet Tavern	1-5
Bungay Town v Sawston Keys	2-0
Shelfort Falcons v Wisbech St Mary	0-1
Royal Falcons v London Maccabi Lions	3-2
Greengate v Enfield Rangers	0-2
Sungate v Luton Old Boys	7-1
FC Houghton Centre v Hammer	0-3
Britannia United v North West Neasden	2-4
Club Lewsey v Broadfields United	5-4
Standens Barn v Stanbridge & Tillsworth	0-1
Belstone v Bury Park Saracens	4-5
Gossoms End v Dunstable White Swan	3-2
Unity Nirankari v Silsoe Park Rangers	3-1
St Joseph's (Luton) v Bedfont (Sunday)	2-3
61 FC (Sunday) v Comets Sports Club	0-4
Northampton Trotters v Rumours	1-0
Westoning v CB Hounslow United Sunday	5-0
Wycombe Town v Offley Moat	3-0
Richfield Rovers v Greyhound	0-3
Seven Allstars v Downend	1-3
Brixton United v Ajax LA	6-0
Knighton Arms v Battersea Ironsides	3-1
Totton Town withdrew v Hazelhurst w.o.	
Goring Rangers v Kerria Sports	1-0
Whitenap v Airport Motors	1-1
Whitenap won 4-1 on penalties.	
Sporting Bristol v Lebeq Tavern Courage	0-3
Lakeside Athletic v Hanham Sunday	3-2
Bristol Athletic v Windmill	2-3

SECOND ROUND

West Lee v Silsden (Sunday)	0-0
Silsden (Sunday) won 4-2 on penalties.	
Salisbury Athletic v Paddock	4-1
Sandstone v Mariners	1-0
Brow v Mirehouse	3-3
Mirehouse won 5-4 on penalties.	
Queens Park v Lobster	0-3
Hetton Lions Cricket Club v Canada	6-0
Western Approaches v Langley Celtic	1-4
Huddersfield Irish Centre v Britannia	3-2
Oyster Martyrs v Witton Park Rose & Crown	4-2
Kempston St Gym v Shamrocks	1-3
Shankhouse United received a bye as Halton Moor and Flat House removed from competition.	
Dengo United v AFC Blackburn Leisure	3-3
Dengo United won 6-5 on penalties.	
Swenfield w.o. v Scots Grey withdrew	
Poulton Royal v JOB	6-5
Magnet Tavern v Loughborough Saints	3-0
Belt Road v Wisbech St Mary	2-0
Birstall Stamford v Bartley Green Sunday	4-0
Thatch v Warstones Wanderers (Sunday)	3-2
Barwell Sports Bar v Travellers	0-5
Enfield Rangers v Stanbridge & Tillsworth	1-6
Royal Falcons v Bungay Town	1-2
Bury Park Saracens v Sungate	1-2
North West Neasden v Hammer	4-1
Comets Sports Club v Northampton Trotters	7-2
Unity Nirankari v Club Lewsey	4-1
Bedfont Sunday v Westoning	4-2
Wycombe Town v Gossoms End	3-2
Greyhound v Lakeside Athletic	2-1
Downend v Knighton Arms	0-4
Whitenap v Lebeq Tavern Courage	0-4
Windmill v Goring Rangers	5-3
Hazelhurst v Brixton United	2-0

THIRD ROUND

Sandstone v Silsden (Sunday)	2-1
Salisbury Athletic v Mirehouse	3-2
Langley Celtic v Lobster	1-0
Oyster Martyrs v Huddersfield Irish Centre	2-4
Shankhouse United v Dengo United	2-1
Swanfield v Shamrocks	3-4
Poulton Royal v Hetton Lions Cricket Club	0-2
Birstall Stamford v Thatch	5-0
Travellers v Belt Road	3-1
Stanbridge & Tillsworth v Magnet Tavern	0-4
North West Neasden v Bungay Town	3-1
Sungate v Comets Sports Club	4-1
Wycombe Town v Unity Nirankari	4-1
Bedfont Sunday v Hazelhurst	1-3
Lebeq Tavern Courage v Greyhound	7-0
Knighton Arms v Windmill	2-3

FOURTH ROUND

Salisbury Athletic v Langley Celtic	1-0
Hetton Lions CC v Huddersfield Irish Centre	1-0
Shankhouse United v Shamrocks	2-2
Shankhouse United won 2-1 on penalties.	
Birstall Stamford v Sandstone	3-2
Magnet Tavern v Travellers	3-0
Wycombe Town v Lebeq Tavern Courage	3-5
Hazelhurst v Windmill	6-1
Sungate v North West Neasden	6-4

FIFTH ROUND

Lebeq Tavern Courage v Magnet Tavern	1-3
Hazelhurst v Sungate	4-1
Hetton Lions Cricket Club v Salisbury Athletic	2-1
Shankhouse United v Birstall Stamford	0-1

SEMI-FINALS

Birstall Stamford v Magnet Tavern	1-2
Hazelhurst v Hetton Lions Cricket Club	1-2

FINAL

Hetton Lions Cricket Club v Magnet Tavern	4-2
(at Liverpool FC)	856

FA PREMIER RESERVE LEAGUES 2009–10

FA PREMIER RESERVE LEAGUE – NORTH SECTION

	P	W	D	L	F	A	GD	Pts
Manchester U	18	13	2	3	35	10	25	41
Manchester C	18	10	5	3	34	20	14	35
Liverpool	18	10	2	6	28	20	8	32
Blackburn R	18	8	5	5	35	24	11	29
Sunderland	18	7	1	10	25	32	−7	22
Wigan Ath	18	6	3	9	28	35	−7	21
Burnley	18	6	3	9	22	36	−14	21
Hull C	18	6	2	10	22	26	−4	20
Everton	18	5	3	10	17	30	−13	18
Bolton W	18	5	2	11	24	37	−13	17

Leading Goalscorers

Noble	Sunderland	9
Ball	Manchester C	7
Ward	Bolton W	6
Nimely-Tchuimeni	Manchester C	6
Kupisz	Wigan Ath	6
Wes Fletcher	Burnley	5
Nimani	Burnley	5
Mak	Manchester C	5
Poole	Manchester C	5
Cywka	Wigan Ath	5
Doran Cogan	Blackburn R	4
Rigters	Blackburn R	4
Vaz Te	Bolton W	4
Eccleston	Liverpool	4
Biram Diouf	Manchester U	4
Eikrem	Manchester U	4
Tosic	Manchester U	4
O'Donovan	Sunderland	4

FA PREMIER RESERVE LEAGUE – SOUTH SECTION

	P	W	D	L	F	A	GD	Pts
Aston Villa	16	11	4	1	34	12	22	37
Arsenal	16	10	2	4	28	14	14	32
Fulham	16	8	4	4	25	19	6	28
Chelsea	16	7	1	8	27	26	1	22
Portsmouth	16	6	3	7	21	27	−6	21
West Ham U	16	5	4	7	26	27	−1	19
Birmingham C	16	4	3	9	14	34	−20	15
Wolverhampton W	16	3	4	9	13	24	−11	13

Leading Goalscorers

Weimann	Aston Villa	9
Moult	Stoke C	6
Watt	Arsenal	5
Borini	Chelsea	5
Sturridge	Chelsea	5
Barazite	Arsenal	4
Sunu	Arsenal	4
Clark	Aston Villa	4
Delfouneso	Aston Villa	4
Hoesen	Fulham	4
Piquionne	Portsmouth	4

PREMIER RESERVE LEAGUE PLAY-OFF FINAL

Manchester U (1) (3) *(Diouf 43, 88, Macheda 60 (pen))*

Aston Villa (1) 3 *(Delfouneso 22, 55, Clarke 82)*　　　　2165

Manchester U won 3-2 on penalties.

at Old Trafford.

Manchester U: Foster; Rafael, Dudgeon, Evans C, De Laet, Gill, Stewart (Obertan 56) (Keane 75), Possebon, Diouf, Norwood (Pogba 86), Macheda.

Aston Villa: Marshall; Roome, O'Halloran, Hogg, Clarke, Baker (Collins J 46), Albrighton, Welmann, Delfouneso, Bannan, Hofbauer.

Referee: L. Mason.

TOTESPORT.COM RESERVE LEAGUES 2009–10

TOTESPORT.COM LEAGUE

CENTRAL DIVISION	P	W	D	L	F	A	GD	Pts
Derby Co	16	9	2	5	28	19	9	29
Burton Alb	16	8	4	4	29	28	1	28
WBA	16	7	6	3	38	22	16	27
Port Vale	16	6	5	5	30	24	6	23
Shrewsbury T	16	6	5	5	22	20	2	23
Sheffield U	16	6	2	8	16	22	−6	20
Walsall	16	5	4	7	27	29	−2	19
Macclesfield T	16	5	1	10	19	36	−17	16
Sheffield W	16	4	3	9	16	25	−9	15

WEST DIVISION	P	W	D	L	F	A	GD	Pts
Wrexham	16	9	6	1	35	16	19	33
Carlisle U	16	9	4	3	36	16	20	31
Preston NE	16	8	3	5	30	25	5	27
Rochdale	16	8	2	6	34	31	3	26
Oldham Ath	16	7	2	7	35	33	2	23
Morecambe	16	6	3	7	25	29	−4	21
Blackpool	16	6	1	9	45	45	0	19
Tranmere R	16	6	1	9	27	32	−5	19
Accrington S	16	2	0	14	14	54	−40	6

EAST DIVISION	P	W	D	L	F	A	GD	Pts
Leeds U	18	11	3	4	46	22	24	36
Hartlepool U	18	11	2	5	42	26	16	35
Middlesbrough	18	11	2	5	35	22	13	35
Huddersfield T	18	10	0	8	36	28	8	30
Rotherham U	18	9	0	9	41	41	0	27
Newcastle U	18	7	4	7	31	26	5	25
Lincoln C	18	7	4	7	30	36	−6	25
Grimsby T	18	5	3	10	26	45	−19	18
Bradford C	18	4	3	11	24	39	−15	15
Scunthorpe U	18	3	3	12	30	56	−26	12

TOTESPORT.COM COMBINATION

CENTRAL DIVISION

	P	W	D	L	GD	Pts
Brighton & HA	18	13	4	1	29	43
Crystal Palace	18	13	4	1	25	43
QPR	18	8	8	2	10	32
Aldershot T	18	8	4	6	8	28
Leyton Orient	18	7	5	6	−9	26
Brentford	18	6	3	9	−5	21
Crawley T	18	5	5	8	−4	20
Gillingham	18	3	6	9	−12	15
Millwall	18	2	4	12	−17	10
Eastbourne B	18	1	5	12	−25	8

EAST DIVISION

	P	W	D	L	GD	Pts
Watford	18	13	2	3	30	41
Ipswich T	18	10	3	5	16	33
Norwich C	18	9	3	6	14	30
Wycombe W	18	7	7	4	4	28
Peterborough U	18	8	3	7	10	27
Luton T	18	8	0	10	−5	24
Colchester U	18	5	8	5	8	23
Northampton T	18	5	5	8	−1	20
Stevenage B	18	3	4	11	−35	13
Southend U	18	2	5	11	−32	11

WALES & WEST DIVISION

	P	W	D	L	GD	Pts
Exeter C	18	10	5	3	4	35
Swansea C	18	10	2	6	9	32
Reading	18	10	1	7	14	31
Swindon T	18	9	4	5	12	31
Bristol C	17	9	2	6	23	29
Southampton	18	9	2	7	11	29
Plymouth Arg	17	7	4	6	16	25
Forest Green R	18	4	5	9	−16	17
Salisbury C	18	4	3	11	−38	15
AFC Bournemouth	18	2	2	14	−35	8

TOTESPORT.COM LEAGUE CUP

GROUP ONE

	P	W	D	L	F	A	GD	Pts
Leicester C	3	2	0	1	9	4	5	6
Walsall	3	2	0	1	3	5	−2	6
Sheffield U	3	1	0	2	7	7	0	3
Tranmere R	3	1	0	2	4	7	−3	3

GROUP TWO

	P	W	D	L	F	A	GD	Pts
Preston NE	4	3	0	1	11	8	3	9
Oldham Ath	4	2	1	1	4	4	0	7
Bradford C	4	2	0	2	7	7	0	6
Middlesbrough	4	1	1	2	6	10	−4	4
Morecambe	4	1	0	3	7	6	1	3

GROUP THREE

	P	W	D	L	F	A	GD	Pts
Scunthorpe U	3	2	0	1	8	3	5	6
Sunderland	3	2	0	1	6	5	1	6
Hartlepool U	3	1	1	1	6	6	0	4
Grimsby T	3	0	1	2	1	7	−6	1

SEMI-FINALS

Preston NE v Oldham Ath *(to be played pre-season 2010–11)*.
Leicester C 5, Scunthorpe U 0

FINAL

Leicester C v Preston NE or Oldham Ath *(to be played pre-season 2010–11)*.

FA ACADEMY UNDER 18 LEAGUE 2009–10

GROUP A

	P	W	D	L	F	A	GD	Pts
Arsenal	28	17	5	6	72	41	31	56
Crystal Palace	28	13	8	7	49	31	18	47
Chelsea	28	14	5	9	51	43	3	47
Norwich C	28	11	6	11	50	57	−7	39
West Ham U	28	10	8	10	52	44	8	38
Fulham	28	12	2	14	59	59	0	38
Southampton	28	10	5	13	46	59	−13	35
Charlton Ath	28	10	4	14	41	58	−17	34
Ipswich T	28	8	9	11	39	48	−9	33
Portsmouth	28	4	3	21	31	68	−37	15

GROUP B

	P	W	D	L	F	A	GD	Pts
Leicester C	28	22	6	0	79	31	48	72
Tottenham H	28	19	2	7	94	45	49	59
Aston Villa	28	16	5	7	71	31	40	53
Reading	28	11	7	10	65	63	2	40
Birmingham C	28	11	5	12	39	54	−15	38
Watford	28	10	4	14	53	58	−5	34
Cardiff C	28	10	4	14	37	46	−9	34
Bristol C	28	9	5	14	40	60	−20	32
Coventry C	28	7	9	12	44	54	−10	30
Milton Keynes D	28	2	7	19	27	84	−57	13

GROUP C

	P	W	D	L	F	A	GD	Pts
Manchester U	28	16	7	5	58	31	27	55
Everton	28	15	5	8	55	34	21	50
WBA	28	12	9	7	55	34	21	45
Liverpool	28	14	3	11	43	41	4	45
Wolverhampton W	28	13	5	10	47	46	1	44
Manchester C	28	12	6	10	64	45	19	42
Blackburn R	28	11	9	8	42	44	−2	42
Stoke C	28	9	10	9	32	38	−6	37
Crewe Alex	28	10	6	12	45	54	−9	36
Bolton W	28	5	8	15	28	49	−21	23

GROUP D

	P	W	D	L	F	A	GD	Pts
Nottingham F	28	18	5	5	63	36	27	59
Sunderland	28	17	4	7	66	29	37	55
Newcastle U	28	14	7	7	58	41	17	49
Middlesbrough	28	9	9	10	42	49	−7	36
Leeds U	28	10	5	13	38	53	−15	35
Barnsley	28	8	5	15	31	52	−21	29
Derby Co	28	7	6	15	42	63	−21	27
Sheffield U	28	5	11	12	36	52	−16	26
Huddersfield T	28	4	7	17	30	58	−28	19
Sheffield Wednesday	28	3	8	17	24	57	−33	17

ACADEMY SEMI-FINALS

Manchester United 1, Arsenal 1
Arsenal won 5-3 on penalties.
Leicester City 1, Nottingham Forest 1
Nottingham Forest won 2-1 on penalties.

ACADEMY FINAL

Arsenal 5 *(Afobe 31, 41, 65 (pen), Freeman 72 (pen), 81)*

Nottingham Forest 3 *(Ellict 5, Thompson 61, Mullen 73)*

Arsenal: Shea; Yennaris, Evina, Boateng, Miquel, Frimpong, Ozyakup, Aneke, Henderson, Afobe, Freeman.

Nottingham Forest: Myrides; Sibson, Freeman, Elliot, Diagne, Watson, Meacows, Gibbons (McCashin 72), Thomson, Mullen, Sykes (Bamford 65).

IMPORTANT ADDRESSES

The Football Association: The Secretary, 25 Soho Square, London W1D 4FA. *020 7745 4545*

Scotland: David Taylor, Hampden Park, Glasgow G42 9AY. *0141 616 6000*

Northern Ireland (Irish FA): Chief Executive, 20 Windsor Avenue, Belfast BT9 6EE. *028 9066 9458*

Wales: 11/12 Neptune Court, Vanguard Way, Cardiff CF24 5PJ. *029 2043 5830*

Republic of Ireland National Sports Campus, Abbotstown, Dublin 15. *00 353 1 8999 500*

International Federation (FIFA): P. O. Box 85 8030 Zurich, Switzerland. *00 41 43 222 7777. Fax: 00 411 384 9696*

Union of European Football Associations: Secretary, Route de Geneve 46, Case Postale CH-1260 Nyon, Switzerland. *00 41 848 00 2727. Fax: 0041 22 994 44 88*

THE LEAGUES

The Premier League: M. Foster, 30 Gloucester Place, London W1A 8PL. *0207 864 9000*

The Football League: Secretary, The Football League, Unit 5, Edward VII Quay, Navigation Way, Preston, Lancashire PR2 2YF. *0870 442 0 1888. Fax 0870 442 0 1188*

Scottish Premier League: R. Mitchell, Hampden Park, Somerville Drive, Glasgow G42 9BA. *0141 646 6962*

The Scottish League: P. Donald, Hampden Park, Glasgow G42 9EB. *0141 620 4160*

Football League of Ireland: D. Crowther, 80 Merrion Square, Dublin 2. *00353 16765120*

Football Conference: 3rd Floor, Wellington House, 31–34 Waterloo Street, Birmingham B2 5TJ. *0121 214 1950*

Southern League: J. Mills, Sansome Lodge, 4–6 Sansome Walk, Worcester WR1 1LH. *01905 330 444*

Northern Premier League: R.D. Bayley, 22 Woburn Drive, Hale, Altrincham, Cheshire WA15 8LZ. *0161 980 7007*

Isthmian League: B. Badcock, 14–15 Wisdom Facilities Centre, 42 Hollands Road, Haverhill, Suffolk CB9 8SA. *01449 768 840*

Eastern Counties League: N. Spurling, 16 Thanet Road, Ipswich, Suffolk IP4 5LB. *07952 595 290*

Essex Senior League: J. Taylor, 2 Courage Close, Hornchurch, Essex RM11 2BJ. *07739 996 861*

Hellenic League: B. King, 7 Stoneleigh Drive, Carterton, Oxon OX18 1EE. *0845 260 6644*

Kent League: R. Vinter, Bakery House, The Street, Chilham, Canterbury, Kent CT4 8BX. *01227 730 457*

Midland Alliance: J. Shaw, 176 Springthorpe Road, Erdington, Birmingham B24 0SN. *0121 350 5869*

North West Counties League: J. Deal, 24 The Pastures, Crossens, Southport PR9 8RH. *07713 622210*

Northern Counties East: B. Gould, 42 Thirlmere Drive, Dronfield, Derbyshire S18 2HW. *07773 653 238*

Northern League: T. Golightly, 85 Park Road North, Chester-le-Street, Co. Durham DH3 3SA. *0191 388 2056*

Spartan South Midlands League: M. Mitchell, 26 Leighton Court, Dunstable, Beds LU6 1EW. *07710 455 409*

Sussex County League: P. Beard, 2 Van Gogh Place, Bersted, Bognor Regis, West Sussex PO22 9BG. *07831 497 913*

United Counties League: A. Crick, Daisy Cottage, Shore Road, Freiston, Boston PE22 0LN. *07718 906 053*

Wessex League: I. Craig, 7 Old River, Denmead, Hampshire PO7 6UX. *07733 212 179*

Western League: K.A. Clarke, 32 Westmead Lane, Chippenham, Wilts SN15 3HZ. *01249 464 467*

Suburban League (Formerly Combined Counties): M.J. Bidmead, 55 Grange Road, Chessington, Surrey KT9 1EZ

Midland Combination: N. Wood, 30 Glalsdale Road, Hall Green, Birmingham B28 8PX. *07967 440007*

West Midlands League: N.R. Juggins, 14 Badger Way, Blackwell, Bromsgrove, Worcs B60 1EX. *07977 422 362*

OTHER USEFUL ADDRESSES

Amateur Football Alliance: M. Brown, Unit 3, 7 Wenlock Road, London N1 7SL. *0207 745 4925*

English Schools FA: J. Read, 4 Parker Court, Staffordshire Technology Park, Stafford ST18 0WP. *01785 785 970*

British Universities Sports Association: G. Gregory-Jones, Chief Executive: BUSA, 20–24 King's Bench Street, London SE1 0QX. *0207 633 5050*

The Football Supporters Federation: The Fans Stadium, Kingsmeadow, Jack Goodchild Way, 422a Kingston Road, Kingston-upon-Thames KT1 3PB. *0208 547 3577*

National Playing Fields Association: 57b, 25 Ovington Square, London SW3 1LQ. *0207 584 6445*

Professional Footballers' Association: G. Taylor, 2 Oxford Court, Bishopsgate, Off Lower Moseley Street, Manchester M2 3WQ. *0161 236 0575*

Referees' Association: A. Smith, 1 Westhill Road, Coundon, Coventry CV6 2AD. *024 7660 1701*

Women's Football Alliance: Miss K. Doyle, The Football Association, 25 Soho Square, London W1D 4FA. *020 7745 4545*

Women's Football Conference: M. Appleby, 25 Soho Square, London W1D 4FA. *0207 745 4589*

League Managers Association: The Camkin Suite, 1 Pegasus House, Tachbrook Park, Warwick CV34 6LW. *01926 831 556. Fax: 01926 429 781*

Institute of Football Management and Administration: K. Verity, The Camkin Suite, 1 Pegasus House, Tachbrook Park, Warwick CV34 6LW. *01926 411 884.*

World Cup (1966) Association: Hon. Secretary, David Duncan, 96 Glenlea Road, Eltham, London SE9 1DZ

The Ninety-Two Club: 104 Gilda Crescent, Whitchurch, Bristol BS14 9LD

The Football Trust: Second Floor, Walkden House, 10 Melton Street, London NW1 2EJ. *020 7388 4504*

Association of Provincial Football Supporters Clubs in London: Tina A. Robertson, 45 Durham Avenue, Heston, Middlesex TW5 0HG *0208 843 9854*

World Association of Friends of English Football: Carlisle Hill, Gluck, Habichthof 2, D24939 Flensburg, Germany. *0049 461 4700222*

Football Postcard Collectors Club: PRO: Bryan Horsnell, 275 Overdown Road, Tilehurst, Reading RG31 6NX. *0118 942 4448 (and fax)*

UK Programme Collectors Club: Secretary, John Litster, 46 Milton Road, Kirkcaldy, Fife KY1 1TL. *01592 268718. Fax: 01592 595069*

Programme Monthly & Football Collectable Magazine: P.O. Box 3236 Norwich NR7 7BE

Scottish Football Historians Association: 43 Lady Nairn Avenue, Kirkcaldy KY1 2AW

Phil Gould (Licensed Football Agent), c/o Whoppit Management Ltd, P. O. Box 27204, London N11 2WS. *07071 732 468. Fax: 07070 732 469*

The Scandinavian Union of Supporters of British Football: Postboks, 15 Stovner, N-0913 Oslo, Norway

Football Writers' Association: Executive Secretary, Ken Montgomery, 6 Chase Lane, Barkingside, Essex IG6 1BH. *0208 554 2455 (and fax)*

Programme Promotions: 47 The Beeches, Lampton Road, Hounslow, Middlesex TW3 4DF. Web: www.footballprogrammes.com

Football Safety Officers Association: C/O J. Sidney, Nottingham Forest F.C., City Ground, Pavilion Road, Nottingham NG2 5FG. *0115 952 6000*

Football Foundation: 30 Gloucester Place, London W1U 8FF. *0845 345 4555*

Football Licensing Authority: 27 Harcourt House, 19 Cavendish Square, London W1G 0PL. *0207 491 7191*

Sport England: 16 Upper Woburn Place, London WC1H 0QP. *0207 388 1277.*

FOOTBALL CLUB CHAPLAINCY

Football followers are sometimes heard to enquire "What is it that chaplain's do?" Here are some responses from various chaplains themselves.

"Chaplains are involved in the game they love for the benefit of everyone. A former player of ours, a practising Christian, was supported at a game at our ground by a party from his home church and the pleasure he, they and I took from meeting and encouraging each other was enormous."

"Never forget that chaplains are available to everyone at the stadium. At one match, I popped into the officials' dressing room and was greeted with delight by one of them who had become a Christian a few months before; had been confirmed at his church the previous Sunday and was naturally eager to tell somebody about it!"

"... A player told me that his mother was seriously ill. I was able to visit her with her son and we prayed together at her bedside. When she finally lost her battle against leukaemia, I took the funeral service by invitation and it was attended by several of the players and club officials."

Chaplains may (or may not) be prominent figures at our football clubs, but the three examples given above show just how useful they can be.

THE REV

OFFICIAL CHAPLAINS TO FA PREMIERSHIP AND FOOTBALL LEAGUE CLUBS

Rev Mike Pusey – Aldershot Town; Rev Ken Baker - Aston Villa; Rev Peter Amos – Barnsley; Rev Ken Howles – Blackburn R; Rev Michael Ward – Blackpool; Rev Philip Mason – Bolton W; Rev John Moore – Boston U; Rev Andy Rimmer – Bournemouth; Revs Jimmy Hinton and Paul Deo – Bradford C; Mr Derek Cleave – Bristo C; Rev Dave Jeal – Bristol R; Rev Mark Hirst – Burnley; Rev John O'Dwyer – Bury; Rev Alun Jones – Carlisle U; Rev Matt Baker – Charlton Ath; Mr Paul Bennett – Cheltenham T; Rev Jim McGlade – Chesterfield; Rev Steve Clapham – Crewe Alex; Rev Chris Roe – Crystal Palace; Rev Peter Wyatt – Dagenham & R; Rev Tony Luke – Derby Co; Rev Stephen Clark – Doncaster R; Co-Chaplains Henry Corbett and Harry Ross – Everton; Rev Gary Piper – Fulham; Rev Richard Hayton – Gillingham; Rev Anthony Wareham – Hereford U; Rev Allen Bagshawe – Hull C; Rev Kevan McCormack – Ipswich T; Co-Chaplains Rev Paul C. Welch and Fr Steven Billington – Leeds U; Rev Richard Gamble – Leicester C; Rev Alan Comfort – Leyton Orient; Rev Andrew Vaughan – Lincoln C; Rev Bill Bygroves – Liverpool; Rev Alan West – Luton T; Rev Howard Stringer – Macclesfield T; Rev Chris Howitz – Manchester C; Rev John Boyers – Manchester U; Rev Timothy Mitchell – Mansfield T; Fr Owen Beament – Millwall; Rev Ron Smith – Milton Keynes D; Rev Ken Baker – Northampton T; Co-Chaplains Revs Arthur W. Bowles and Bert Cadmore – Norwich C; Rev Steve Silvester – Nottingham F; Rev Canon Mark Tanner – Notts Co; Rev John Simmons – Oldham Ath; Rev Richard Longfoot – Peterborough U; Rev Jeff Howden – Plymouth Arg; Rev Jonathan Jeffrey – Portsmouth; Rev John M. Hibberts – Port Vale; Rev Chris Nelson – Preston NE; Co-Chaplains Revs Bob Mayo and Cameron Collington – QPR; Rev Steve Prince – Reading; Rev Alan Wright – Scunthorpe U; Rev Peter Allen – Sheffield W; Rev Andy Bowerman – Southampton; Rev Billy Montgomerie – Stockport Co; Rev Stephen Taylor – Sunderland; Rev Kevin Johns – Swansea C; Rev Simon Stevenette – Swindon T; Fr Gerald Courell – Tranmere R; Rev Martin Butt – Walsall; Rev Clive Ross – Watford; Co-Chaplains The Ven Elwin Cockett and Rev Alan Bolding – West Ham U; Co-Chaplains Revs David Wright and Steve Davies – Wolverhampton W; Co-Chaplains Revs John Roberts and Tim O'Brien – Wycombe W; Rev Jim Pearce – Yeovil T.

ENGLISH AND WELSH NON-LEAGUE CLUBS

Mr John Maxwell – Abingdon T; Rev Andrew Barclay-Watt – Altrincham; Rev David Hughes – Barnstaple T; Rev Stuart Wood – Cambridge U; Mr John Maxwell – Cirencester T; The Ven Paul Taylor – Dorchester T; Rev Kevin Johns – Garden Village AFC; Rev Ken Hipkiss – Halesowen T; Paul Barker – Hampton & Richmond B; Rev Ron Day – Histon; Philip Hearn – Kidderminster H; Rev Keith Beardmore – Newport Co AFC; Rev Clive Jones – Nuneaton B; Canon Roger Knight – Rushden & D; Fr Ronald Crane – Solihull Moors; Rev Martin Abrams – Southport; Rev Ken Hawkings – Sutton T; Rev Lee Gilbert – Warrington T; Rev Chris Cullwick – York C; Rev Leo Osborn – Chaplain to the Northern League.

The chaplains hope that those who read this page will see the value and benefit of chaplaincy work in football and will take appropriate steps to spread the word where this is possible. They would also like to thank the editors of the Football Yearbook for their continued support for this specialist and growing area of work.

For further information, please contact: SCORE (Sports Chaplaincy Offering Resources and Encouragement), PO Box 123, Sale, Cheshire M33 4ZA). Telephone 0161 962 6068 or email admin@scorechaplaincy.org.uk.

OBITUARIES

Alan A'Court (Born Rainhill, nr. St Helens, 30 September 1944. Died Nantwich, Cheshire, 14 December 2009.) Alan A'Court was a small but quick and direct winger who made over 350 appearances for Liverpool between 1952 and 1964. He was a member of the England squad for the 1958 World Cup finals and won a total of five full caps. He later spent two seasons with Tranmere before enjoying a successful career in coaching which included posts in Zambia and New Zealand.

Jock Aitken (Born circa 1920. Died 5 February 2010.) Jock Aitken was a powerful centre forward who scored regularly for Airdrie in the closing seasons of the emergency wartime competitions. However, he struggled to break into the line-up when peacetime football returned and later moved on to play for Ayr United and Morton.

Gus Alexander (Born Arbroath, 10 January 1934. Died 1 January 2010.) Gus Alexander was a skilful, scheming inside forward who was on the groundstaff at Burnley without breaking into the first team. The best years of his career were spent with Workington, for whom he played regular first-team football during an 18-month spell in the late 1950s and he also turned out for Southport and York City.

Keith Alexander (Born Nottingham, 14 November 1956. Died Lincoln, 3 March 2010.) Keith Alexander was on Notts County's books as a youngster then played for numerous non-league clubs in the Midlands before making his Football League debut for Grimsby Town at the age of 31. A tall, awkward striker, he also played for Stockport County and Lincoln City. In May 1993 he was appointed as the Lincoln manager, thus becoming the first black manager of a Football League club. He lasted just 12 months but after a spell coaching Mansfield Town he returned to Sincil Bank and led the Red Imps to a place in the end-of-season play-offs on four consecutive occasions. After spells in charge of Peterborough United and as director of football at Bury he was appointed manager of Macclesfield Town in February 2008. He was still in this post when he tragically collapsed after returning home from a game with Notts County and he died shortly afterwards.

Dougie Armstrong (Born Edinburgh, 30 June 1925. Died 6 April 2010.) Dougie Armstrong was a defender who spent eight years on the books of Hearts in the immediate post-war period, making 53 first-team appearances. He also had a brief spell with Third Lanark before leaving the senior game.

Charlie Ashcroft (Born Croston, Lancs, 3 July 1926. Died Preston, 13 March 2010.) Charlie Ashcroft was a goalkeeper who spent nine seasons on the books of Liverpool making 87 Football League appearances and being capped by England B against Netherlands B in March 1952. He later played for Ipswich Town and Coventry before leaving senior football in the summer of 1958.

Archie Baird (Born Rutherglen, Lanarkshire, 8 May 1919. Died Cove, Aberdeen, 3 November 2009.) Archie Baird was a tall inside forward who joined Aberdeen and went on to become a member of the team that defeated Hibs to win the 1947 Scottish Cup final, but his career over the next few seasons was hampered by injury. After a spell with St Johnstone, Archie left the game to focus on his career in teaching.

Sammy Baird (Born Denny, Stirlingshire, 13 May 1930. Died Bangor, Co Down, 21 April 2010.) Sammy Baird was an inside forward who began his career with Clyde before spending a season with Preston. He followed North End manager Scott Symon to Rangers in the summer of 1955. He went on to assist the Ibrox club to successive Scottish League titles in 1955–56 and 1956–57, making over 150 appearances during his stay. Sammy, who was capped seven times for Scotland, also played for Hibernian, Third Lanark and Stirling and had a spell as manager of Albion Rovers.

Michael Barker (Born 1 December 1941. Died 14 June 2010.) Michael Barker was a left back who developed with Shildon Works and Bishop Auckland before becoming one of a group of English-based players to sign for Queen of the South in the 1967–68 season. He stayed five years at Palmerston Park, making 142 competitive appearances. He won six caps for England Amateurs whilst with Bishop Auckland.

Geoff Barrowcliffe (Born Ilkeston, Derbys, 18 October 1931. Died Ilkeston, Derbys, 26 September 2009.) Geoff Barrowcliffe was a skilful full back who made more than 500 first-team appearances for Derby County between 1951 and 1966 and was a near ever-present in the team that lifted the Division Three North title in 1956–57. He eventually left the Rams at the end of the 1965–66 season and later played for Boston United and Heanor Town before managing a number of non-League clubs in the Derby area.

Allen Batsford (Born London, 9 April 1932. Died London, 28 December 2009.) Allen Batsford spent six years as a professional with Arsenal in the early 1950s without making a first-team appearance. As a manager he led Walton & Hersham to victory in the FA Amateur Cup in 1973 and then took over at Wimbledon, taking the Dons on a tremendous FA Cup run in 1973–74 when they defeated top-flight opposition in Burnley and drew with the then mighty Leeds team at Elland Road. He was at the helm when the Dons were elected to the Football League in the summer of 1977 before departing in December of the same year.

Frank Beattie (Born Stirling, 17 October 1933. Died Stirling, 19 November 2009.) Frank Beattie was a legendary figure in the history of Kilmarnock, for whom he made over 500 appearances and captained the side when they won the Scottish League title in 1964–65. Originally an inside forward, he later switched to playing at wing half. He later served Albion Rovers (December 1972 to cs. 1973) and Stirling Albion (cs. 1973 to September 1974) as manager.

Walter Bennett (Born Mexborough, 15 December 1918. Died December 2009.) Walter Bennett signed for Barnsley in April 1938, but it was not until after the war that he played regular first-team football for the club. He went on to make 40 appearances as an inside forward and later also played for Doncaster and Halifax. Walter was from a well known footballing family and his father and two uncles both played in the Football League.

Jim Benson (Born Dalbeattie, Kirkcudbrightshire, 19 March 1925. Died Dalbeattie, Kirkcudbrightshire, 6 November 2009.) Jim Benson was a goalkeeper who spent 18 months as first choice for Kilmarnock, making a total of 63 appearances. He later turned out for Hamilton Academical and Dunfermline Athletic before leaving the game.

Adam Blacklaw (Born Aberdeen, 2 September 1937. Died 28 February 2010.) Adam Blacklaw was a big, powerful goalkeeper who joined Burnley as a youngster and went on to spend six seasons as the club's regular 'keeper. A near ever-present in the Clarets team that won the Football League title in 1959–60, he also won an FA Cup runners-up medal

in 1962. Adam, who won three caps for Scotland, made over 300 Football League appearances for Burnley and also played for Blackburn Rovers and Blackpool before retiring from senior football.

Ernie Blincow (Born Walsall, 9 September 1921. Died 19 February 2010.) Ernie Blincow was an outside left who made a single first-team appearance as an amateur for Walsall, lining up against Brighton in March 1947.

Terry Bly (Born Fincham, Norfolk, 22 October 1935. Died Grantham, 24 September 2009.) Terry Bly shot to fame as a member of the Norwich City team that knocked Manchester United out of the FA Cup in 1958–59 and when he joined Football League newcomers Peterborough United in the summer of 1960 he showed sensational form, netting 52 League goals as Posh raced away with the Fourth Division title in 1960–61. Successful spells at Coventry and Notts County followed before he was appointed as player-manager of Grantham Town in 1964.

Petar Borota (Born Belgrade, Yugoslavia, 5 March 1952. Died Genoa, Italy, 12 February 2010.) Petar Borota began his career in Yugoslavia with OFK and Partizan Belgrade before becoming one of the first European players to star in English football following the relaxation of transfer restrictions in the 1970s. A flamboyant goalkeeper he made over 100 appearances for Chelsea between 1979 and 1982, and also won four full caps for Yugoslavia.

David Boyle (Born North Shields, 24 April 1929. Died November 2009.) David Boyle was a versatile forward who spent time with Newcastle United, Berwick Rangers and Barnsley as a youngster, but it was not until he arrived at Crewe in the summer of 1952 that he made his debut in senior football. David enjoyed two relatively successful seasons with Chesterfield, but it was only at Bradford City that he had a decent run of first-team football, mostly featuring on the wing.

Frank Brady (Died 27 October 2009.) Frank Brady was a centre half who played for Home Farm and Shamrock Rovers in the 1960s. He was a member of the Shamrock team that defeated Waterford to win the FAI Cup in 1968. Frank was one of four brothers to play football professionally, with Pat, Ray and Liam all featuring in the Football League.

Jack Briggs (Born Lincoln, 15 July 1911. Died Grantham, 6 August 2009.) Jack Briggs was a centre forward or inside left who played in the reserve teams of both Tottenham Hotspur and Northampton Town then in non-league football for Peterborough United and Wisbech Town, before spending a brief period with Rochdale, where he made his only Football League appearance, turning out against Chester in March 1939.

Trevor Brissett (Born Stoke-on-Trent, 2 January 1961. Died Birmingham, May 2010.) Trevor Brissett was a defender who began his career with Stoke City, but it was not until he moved on to local rivals Port Vale that he experienced first-team football. A regular for Vale in 1980–81, he made a total of 60 appearances for the club before moving on for a season with Darlington. He subsequently returned to Staffordshire where he was involved in playing and coaching for a number of non-league clubs.

Jack Brownsword (Born Campsall, Yorkshire, 15 May 1923. Died Burton-upon-Stather, Lincs, 19 December 2009.) Jack Brownsword began his career with Hull City, but after just a season with the Tigers he dropped down into the Midland League, signing for Scunthorpe United. He went on to become a legendary figure in the history of the Iron, playing in their first-ever Football League fixture against Shrewsbury in August 1950 and setting a club record of 663 senior appearances. A quick, yet solid defender, he was a member of the team that won the Division Three North title in 1957–58.

Jock Buchanan (Born Leith, Edinburgh, 3 January 1935. Died 1 September 2009.) Jock Buchanan was the first British player to score a goal on home territory in the European Cup, netting for Hibernian in the second leg tie against Germany's Rot Weiss Essen in October 1955. Signed by Hibs as a centre half he was transformed into an effective centre forward at Easter Road. He later played briefly with Raith Rovers before moving south to spend a season with Newport County.

John Burke (Born circa 1918. Died 2010.) John Burke signed for East Stirling when the club resumed activities in the 1945–46 season and he turned out for Shire in the Eastern League and then the C Division in 1945–47. At the time of his death he was believed to be the club's oldest living player.

David Burnside (Born Kingswood, Bristol, 10 December 1939. Died Bristol, 17 October 2009.) David Burnside was a creative inside forward who played over 400 senior games in a career lasting some 16 seasons. An England Youth and U23 international, he won promotion to the top flight with Wolves in 1966–67, while he also enjoyed successful spells with a string of clubs including West Bromwich Albion, Southampton, Crystal Palace and Plymouth. David later embarked on a successful career in coaching and worked with the FA for many years, firstly in the West Region and then with the England Youth team. More recently he had been involved in the academy set-up at Bristol City.

Bill Burtenshaw (Born Portslade, Sussex, 13 December 1925. Died Southwick, Sussex, 23 February 2010.) Bill Burtenshaw came to prominence as a goalscoring centre forward with Sussex League outfit Southwick, but after joining Luton Town in the summer of 1948 he managed just a single first-team outing for the Hatters. The following campaign he moved on to Gillingham, then members of the Southern League, and he remained there for a total of three seasons, helping the club regain Football League status.

Joe Cairney (Born 8 November 1955. Died Glasgow, 6 August 2009.) Joe Cairney was a goalscoring forward who

Adam Blacklaw

signed for Airdrie in the 1975–76 season and scored a hat-trick in his first start for the club, a 6-2 Spring Cup victory over Stranraer, later going on to gain a winners' medal in the competition. He subsequently assisted Kilmarnock to promotion from the Scottish League First Division in 1978–79 before moving to play in Australia.

Gerry Cakebread, OBE (Born Acton, Middlesex, 1 April 1936. Died Taunton, 16 September 2009.) Goalkeeper Gerry Cakebread won representative honours for England Youths and went on to become a mainstay of the Brentford team in the late 1950s and early 1960s. He established a club record of 187 consecutive appearances between November 1958 and August 1962, eventually leaving Griffin Park for non-league football in the summer of 1964.

Tommy Capel (Born Chorlton, Manchester, 27 June 1922. Died 1 October 2009.) Tommy Capel signed for Manchester City during the war but went on to make his name in peacetime as an inside forward for Chesterfield and Nottingham Forest. Tommy became one of Forest's stars of the early 1950s, contributing to the club's success in winning the Division Three South title in 1950–51. He also played for Birmingham City, Coventry and Halifax Town.

Brian Caterer (Born Hayes, Middlesex, 23 January 1943. Died Barnet, 21 January 2010.) Brian Caterer was a big powerful defender who played for the Chesham United team that was defeated by Leytonstone in the 1968 FA Amateur Cup final. He later spent three seasons as an amateur on the books of Brentford, although his contribution was limited to one Football League and one London Challenge Cup game.

Ray Charnley (Born Lancaster, 29 May 1935. Died Fleetwood, 15 November 2009.) Ray Charnley became a prolific scorer in non-league football for Morecambe, earning him a transfer to Blackpool in the summer of 1957. A tall, powerful centre forward he went on to make over 350 appearances for the Seasiders in a decade from 1957 when the club were members of the old First Division, finishing as leading scorer for nine consecutive seasons. After leaving Bloomfield Road, Ray had spells with Preston, Wrexham and Bradford Park Avenue. Ray won a single cap for England, featuring against France in October 1962.

George Christie (Born circa 1946. Died Edinburgh, 24 April 2010.) Centre forward George Christie was a prolific scorer for East Fife and Berwick Rangers in the 1960s, netting 55 goals from 111 appearances. He was one of the stars of Berwick's sensational Scottish Cup victory over Rangers in January 1967, setting up the winning goal for Sammy Reid.

Charlie Church (Born Troon, Ayrshire, 7 July 1929. Died Newton Mearns, Renfrewshire, 11 April 2010.) Charlie Church was a forward who made over 250 first-team appearances for Queen's Park between 1948 and 1961. A one-club man, he was a mainstay of the team during the 1950s and assisted Queen's to promotion to the First Division in 1955–56.

Lew Clayton (Born Royston, Barnsley, 7 June 1924. Died Redcar, 19 January 2010.) Lew Clayton was a reliable wing half who began his career with Barnsley during the war years. He went on to make over 200 Football League appearances in a career that also saw him play for Carlisle, Barnsley, Queen's Park Rangers, Bournemouth and Swindon. At Bournemouth he was a member of the team that reached the quarter-finals of the FA Cup in 1956–57. He later worked on the backroom staff for a number of clubs including Cardiff City and Middlesbrough.

Tommy Clinton (Born Dublin, 13 April 1926. Died Liverpool, 9 August 2009.) Full back Tommy Clinton joined Everton from Dundalk in March 1948 and went on to make 73 League appearances for the Toffees, featuring in the side that reached the FA Cup semi-finals in 1952–53. He later had spells with Blackburn, Tranmere and Runcorn before retiring from the game.

Ben Collins (Born Kislingbury, Northants, 9 March 1928. Died 2 March 2010.) Ben Collins was a solid defender who made over 200 appearances for Northampton Town between 1948 and 1959. Captain of the team for a while, he featured at right back in the team that defeated Arsenal 3-1 in an FA Cup tie in January 1958.

Jack Connor (Born Maryport, Cumberland, 25 July 1934. Died Formby, 9 March 2010.) Jack Connor was a solid and reliable centre half who signed for Huddersfield Town in October 1952. He spent eight years with the Leeds Road club, making 85 League appearances before joining Bristol City, for whom he became a key player in the 1960s, helping the club win promotion to the old Second Division in 1964–65.

Keith Coombs (Born Birmingham, 10 January 1928. Died 22 April 2010.) Keith Coombs was appointed chairman of Birmingham City in 1975 on the death of his father and remained in this post for 11 years. A successful local businessman, during his period at the helm the club transferred Trevor Francis to Nottingham Forest, the first player to be sold for a £1 million fee.

Bobby Cox (Born Dundee, 24 January 1934. Died 20 February 2010.) Bobby Cox was an effective left back who made over 400 first-team appearances for Dundee between 1956 and 1969. Captain of the side that won the Scottish League title in 1961–62, he assisted them to a place in the semi-finals of the European Cup the following season.

George Crawford (Born circa 1928. Died East Kilbride, 5 May 2010.) George Crawford was a centre half who joined Forfar Athletic from Pollok Juniors soon after the start of the 1952–53 season. He went on to make over 90 first-team appearances and captain the team, then spent a season with Albion Rovers before a knee injury brought his career to an end.

Charlie Crowe (Born Walker, Newcastle upon Tyne, 30 October 1924. Died North Shields, 27 February 2010.) Charlie Crowe was a tenacious, industrious wing half who spent 13 years on the books of Newcastle United, making almost 200 first-team appearances. A member of the team that won the FA Cup in 1951, he missed out on the club's two other Wembley trips in the 1950s and eventually left St James' Park in February 1957 to wind down his career at Mansfield.

Tommy Cummings (Born Sunderland, 12 September 1928. Died 12 July 2009.) Tommy Cummings signed for Burnley at the age of 19, soon progressing to the first team and establishing a reputation as one of the country's top young centre halves. He went on to make 23 appearances in the Clarets' 1959–60 League Championship side and also gained an FA Cup runners-up medal in 1962. On leaving Turf Moor he succeeded Jimmy Hill as chairman of the PFA, then took over as manager of Mansfield Town (1963 to July 1967) and followed this with a spell as manager of Aston Villa (July 1967 to November 1968). He was capped on one occasion for the Football League.

George Cummins (Born Dublin, 12 March 1931. Died Southport, 29 November 2009.) George Cummins was a skilful, creative inside forward who crossed the Irish Sea in November 1950 to sign for Everton from League of Ireland outfit St Patrick's. The best years of his career were spent at Luton, for whom he gained an FA Cup runners-up medal in 1959 and made over 150 League appearances. He also played for Cambridge City and Hull, and won a total of 19 caps for the Republic of Ireland.

Bob Curtis (Born Langwith, Notts, 25 January 1950. Died 19 March 2010.) Bob Curtis began his career as a solid defender for Charlton Athletic, signing for the club on schoolboy forms as a 14-year-old and going on to spend over a decade as a professional, making over 300 appearances. Towards the end of his career he moved to a more forward position and during a spell at Mansfield he was used as a striker.

Norman Curtis (Born Dinnington, Yorkshire, 10 September 1924. Died York, 7 September 2009.) Norman Curtis was a powerful and tenacious left back with a cannonball shot who signed for Sheffield Wednesday from Gainsborough Trinity in January 1950. He became a regular in the Owls' defence for a decade or so, making over 300 first-team appearances and featuring in three Division Two championship sides (1951–52, 1955–56 and 1958–59). He later had a spell as player-manager of Doncaster Rovers from August 1960 to August 1961.

George Dick (Died June 2010.) George Dick was a goalscoring outside left who joined Stirling Albion from Hibernian towards the end of the war and featured in the Eastern League during 1945–46. The following season he helped the club win the C Division title and he remained at Annfield until the summer of 1953, making over 100 League appearances.

Norman Dingwall (Born Gateshead, 29 July 1923. Died 22 June 2009.) Norman Dingwall was a centre half who was on Sheffield United's books without featuring in the first team and his only senior football came during the 1947–48 season when he made nine League appearances for Halifax Town.

Tommy Cummings

John Donnelly (Born Broxburn, West Lothian, 17 December 1936. Died Broxburn, West Lothian. 31 July 2009.) John Donnelly was a full back who signed for Celtic from Armadale Thistle and made his name by appearing in the side that defeated Rangers 7-1 to win the Scottish League Cup in October 1957. He later made over 50 appearances for Preston, before moving to play in South Africa in the mid-1960s.

Neil Dougall (Born Falkirk, 7 November 1921. Died Plymouth, 1 December 2009.) Neil Dougall played for Burnley during the war years before moving on to Birmingham City where he featured at inside right in the successful team of 1945–46, when the Blues reached the FA Cup semi-final and won the Football League South. He went on to spend a decade at Plymouth where he was an influential figure in the side that won the Division Three South title in 1951–52 and played in over 250 Football League games He won one full cap for Scotland.

Bobby Dougan (Born Glasgow, 3 December 1926. Died Glasgow, 7 February 2010.) Bobby Dougan was a cultured centre half who made almost 200 Scottish League appearances for Hearts and Kilmarnock between 1947 and 1960. He won a single cap for Scotland against Switzerland in April 1950 and also appeared three times for the Scottish League representative side.

Ralph Dulson (Born Basford, Nottingham, 1925. Died October 2009.) Ralph Dulson joined Nottingham Forest as an amateur in May 1942 and was a regular in the 1943–44 season, when he was the team's leading scorer with 17 goals. He also made one appearance as a guest for Lincoln City in 1944–45.

Fred Durrant (Born Dover, 19 June 1921. Died 5 March 2010.) Fred Durrant was a big, powerful centre forward who played a number of games for Brentford during the war before joining Queen's Park Rangers in September 1946. He featured in the Ranger's team that won the Division Three South title in 1947–48 and later also played for Exeter City.

Charlie Dutton (Born Rugeley, Staffs, 10 April 1934. Died. 30 October 2009.) Charlie Dutton signed for Coventry City in October 1952. A centre forward, he scored eight goals in 27 games during his time at Highfield Road and later had a spell with Northampton Town before leaving the senior game.

Robert Enke (Born Jena, East Germany, 24 August 1977. Died Neustadt am Rübenberge, Germany, 10 November 2009.) Robert Enke was an experienced goalkeeper who was a member of the German national squad at the time of his death, which occurred in tragic circumstances after he was struck by a train on a level crossing. He first came to prominence playing for Carl Zeiss Jena, then, after a spell with Borussia Moenchengladbach he moved around Europe playing for a number of clubs including Benfica and Barcelona. Robert eventually returned to Germany for the 2004–05 season, signing for Hannover 96. He won eight full caps for Germany.

Ray Evans (Born Clipstone. nr. Mansfield, 27 November 1927. Died January 2010.) Ray Evans was a centre forward who spent five seasons on the books of Mansfield Town in the early 1950s, making 39 League appearances. He had earlier been on the books of Coventry City without breaking into the first team.

Ray Evans (Born India, 21 June 1933. Died Chorley, Lancs, 26 June 2009.) Ray Evans was a wing half who signed for Preston North End at the close of the 1950–51 campaign. He played 33 League games for North End, then moved on to Bournemouth in the summer of 1959 where he added a further 39 appearances before dropping into the Lancashire Combination to play for Morecambe.

Alec Farley (Born Finchley, 11 May 1925. Died Southampton, 23 February 2010.) Alec Farley was a left back who made 18 senior appearances for Leyton Orient in the period immediately after the war. He moved on to Bournemouth in the summer of 1948 but soon afterwards suffered a serious injury in a reserve match and this effectively ended his career.

Frank Fidler (Born Middleton, Lancs, 16 August 1924. Died Farnborough, 21 November 2009.) Frank Fidler was on Manchester United's books as a teenager during the war before making his name as a goalscoring centre forward in the Cheshire League with Witton Albion. He scored regularly in his senior career too, netting 55 goals in 119 Football League appearances for Wrexham, Leeds and Bournemouth.

Barry Fitch (Born Brighton, 19 November 1943. Died Durrington, nr. Salisbury, 9 January 2010.) Barry Fitch was a left back who made a single first-team appearance for Brighton against Oxford in September 1963. After leaving the Goldstone Ground he signed for Salisbury City, for whom he went on to establish a club record of 713 appearances.

Ken Flint (Born Nottingham, 12 November 1923. Died Barnet, 21 May 2010.) Ken Flint was a left winger who appeared for Notts County and Leicester during the war, then moved into Southern League football with Bedford before resurrecting his career with a spell at Spurs. However, he is best known for his performances for Aldershot, for whom he played in over 350 first-team games between 1950 and 1958.

Billy Fulton (Born 30 October 1938. Died 11 April 2010.) Billy Fulton made over 500 senior appearances for Ayr United, Falkirk and St Mirren in a career that spanned the period from 1957 to 1972. Initially a versatile forward he eventually dropped back to the half-back line. A highlight of his career came when he helped St Mirren win the Second Division title in 1967–68.

Derek Gibbs (Born Fulham, London, 22 December 1934. Died November 2009.) Derek Gibbs was a tall inside forward who had the distinction of scoring Leyton Orient's first-ever goal in the top flight when he netted against Arsenal in August 1962. He began his career with Chelsea and also played for Queen's Park Rangers before dropping down into the Southern League with Romford.

Brian Gibson (Born Huddersfield, 22 February 1928. Died May 2010.) Brian Gibson was a solid defender who was recruited by Huddersfield Town from local district league football. He went on to establish himself as a regular for the Terriers in the mid-1950s, making over 150 Football League appearances.

Brian Godfrey (Born Flint, 1 May 1940. Died Nicosia, Cyprus, 11 February 2010.) Brian Godfrey began his career with Everton, but it was only when he moved down a division to sign for Scunthorpe that his career began to take off. He went on to play in more than 500 Football League games, captaining the Aston Villa team that reached the Football League Cup final as a Third Division club in 1970–71. Initially a goal scoring inside forward he later switched to wing half, finishing his career at Newport County. He won three full caps for Wales.

Juan Carlos Gonzalez (Born 22 August 1924. Died 15 February 2010.) Juan Carlos Gonzalez was one of the stars of the Penarol team of the 1940s. A defender, he was a member of the Uruguay squad for the 1950 World Cup finals, playing in two of his country's four matches in the tournament although not in the decisive encounter with Brazil.

Alan Gordon (Born Edinburgh, 14 May 1944. Died Edinburgh, 18 February 2010.) Alan Gordon was still a schoolboy when he made his debut for Hearts and he went on to enjoy a 15-year career as a talented, skilful centre forward. After spending eight seasons at Tynecastle he signed for Dundee United, later playing for Hibernian and Dundee. In total he made over 400 senior appearances, helping the Easter Road club win the League Cup and Drybrough Cup in 1972–73.

Stevie Gray (Born Glasgow, 7 February 1967. Died Irvine, Ayrshire, 19 September 2009.) Stevie Gray was a winger with plenty of skill who was capped by Scotland U18s and was still a teenager when he broke into the first team at Aberdeen under manager Alex Ferguson. A substitute for the Dons in the 1985–86 League Cup final victory over Hibs he always remained a fringe first-team player and in the summer of 1989 he moved on to Airdrie where he spent three seasons before leaving senior football.

Ian Green (Born circa 1951. Died 3 July 2009.) Goalkeeper Ian Green spent two seasons on the books of Oldham Athletic, during which time his only senior appearances came when he stepped off the bench to replace broken-leg victim John Platt in an Anglo-Scottish Cup tie against Sheffield United in August 1978 and retained his place for the fixture against Sunderland in the same competition.

Harry Haddington (Born Scarborough, 7 August 1931. Died January 2010.) Harry Haddington was a powerful, traditional-style right back who began his career with the old Bradford Park Avenue club, but it was only when he signed for Walsall that he began to play regular first-team football. Harry went on to captain the Saddlers team to the Fourth Division title in 1959–60, and played 235 first-team games during his stay at Fellows Park before injury ended his career.

John Hagart (Born Edinburgh, November 1937. Died 1 June 2010.) John Hagart enjoyed the briefest of careers in senior football, making a handful of Scottish League appearances for Berwick Rangers during the 1960–61 season. However, he enjoyed much greater success as a coach, serving both Hearts (October 1974 to April 1977) and Falkirk (July 1979 to November 1982) as manager, working on the backroom staff at Motherwell and Rangers and spending time as the Scotland assistant manager when Ally McLeod was in charge.

Les Hall (Born St Albans, 1st October 1921. Died St Albans, 20th March 2010.) Les Hall was a centre half who signed for Luton Town in August 1943 and remained on the club's books for some 13 seasons, making 79 League appearances. A part-time professional, he later played for Hemel Hempstead Town.

Willie Hamilton (Born Hamilton, 1 September 1918. Died Canada, 4 December 2009.) Willie Hamilton was a wing half who joined Preston North End from Blantyre Victoria in September 1937 and went on to play over 100 first-team games during his stay at Deepdale, although many of these were in the emergency wartime competitions. He later returned to Scotland where he turned out for Queen of the South and Hamilton Academical before emigrating to Canada in the 1950s.

Peter Harburn (Born Shoreditch, London, 18 June 1931. Died 13 March 2010.) Peter Harburn was a centre forward who helped Brighton win the Division Three South title in 1957–58 and went on to play for Everton, Scunthorpe and Workington before leaving senior football when he signed for Chelmsford City. He scored a total of 93 Football League goals from 217 appearances.

Don Harnby (Born Hurworth, Co Durham, 20 July 1923. Died Stockton-on-Tees, 24 October 2009.) Don Harnby was on Newcastle United's books during the war when he also guested for Middlesbrough and Hull. A tall full back, he played in the Magpies reserves in 1946–47, then had a brief period attached to York before joining Spennymoor. Don later spent three seasons with Grimsby Town, making 37 appearances before leaving senior football.

Barry Hawkings (Born Birmingham, 7 November 1931. Died 9 May 2010.) Barry Hawkings was a centre forward who developed with Coventry's nursery club before going on to sign professional forms at Highfield Road in January 1949. He went on to make 114 League appearances for Coventry, Lincoln City and Northampton Town scoring 43 goals before leaving the senior game in 1959.

Richard Etim Henshaw (Born 20 February 1926. Died Calabar, Nigeria, 18 November 2009.) Richard Etim Henshaw was the captain of the Nigeria team that toured the UK in 1949. A prolific scorer with the successful Marine club of Lagos, he represented Lagos in inter-colonial fixtures with Gold Coast and also played briefly for the Cardiff Corinthians club.

Dennis Herod (Born Tunstall, Stoke-on-Trent, 27 October 1925. Died Wrinehill, Staffs, 16 December 2009.) Goalkeeper Dennis Herod signed for Stoke City during the war and when peacetime football returned he became the club's regular 'keeper despite fierce competition for his jersey. He made over 200 appearances, scoring against Aston Villa in February 1952 when he suffered a broken arm and was forced to play on the wing. He subsequently spent a season with Stockport County before leaving the game.

Ronnie Hodgson (Born Birkenhead, 2 November 1922. Died 26 August 2009.) Ronnie Hodgson played almost 100 wartime games for Tranmere Rovers before signing for Manchester City. He managed just a single senior outing in peacetime at Maine Road then spent a total of three seasons in Division Three North with Southport and Crewe Alexandra.

Colin Holmes (Born Winchester, 28 March 1939. Died West End, Southampton, 3 September 2009.) Colin Holmes was a centre half who was a member of the Southampton team that reached the semi-final of the FA Youth Cup in 1956–57 and won representative honours for England Youths. He made a single first-team appearance for the Saints in the 1959–60 season before dropping into non-league football. Colin also made a number of appearances for Hampshire 2nd XI at cricket.

Beslan Idrizaj (Born Baden bei Wien, Austria, 12 October 1987. Died Linz Austria, 15 May 2010.) Beslan Idrizaj was a young striker who spent three seasons on the books of Liverpool. He did not make the first team during his stay at Anfield but managed a number of senior appearances during loan spells with Luton, Crystal Palace and Wacker Innsbruck. He signed for Swansea City at the start of the 2009–10 season and made a handful of appearances from the substitutes' bench before his tragic death. He had represented Austria at U21 level.

Billy Ingham (Born Stakeford, Northumberland, 22 October 1952. Died Blackburn, 7 November 2009.) Billy Ingham was a busy, battling midfield player who made over 200 appearances for Burnley, becoming something of a cult figure with the fans. He later spent two seasons with Bradford City where he helped the team win promotion from the old Fourth Division in 1981–82 before switching to then non-league club Accrington Stanley.

Tony Ingham (Born Harrogate, 18 February 1925. Died 21 April 2010.) Full back Tony Ingham began his senior career with Leeds United, but he made just three first-team appearances during his stay at Elland Road before heading south to sign for Queen's Park Rangers. He went on to become a legendary figure for the R's, creating a club record of 555 first-team appearances including a run of 274 consecutive games between February 1956 and September 1961. After retiring as a player in 1963 he served the club as commercial manager, secretary and director.

Frank Jackett (Born Pontadawe, Glamorgan, 5 July 1927. Died 14 April 2010.) Frank Jackett was on Swansea Town's books as a youngster without making a first-team appearance. He went on to play for Watford and Leyton Orient making a total of 18 League appearances before leaving senior football to play for Ramsgate.

Daniel Jarque (Born Barcelona, 1 January 1983. Died Coverciano, Italy, 8 August 2009.) Daniel Jarque was a central defender for Espanyol who had been appointed as club captain shortly before his death, which occurred when he suffered a heart attack while in Italy for pre-season training. He made over 150 first-team appearances for Espanyol and also represented Spain at U21 level.

John Jarman (Born Rhymney, Monmouthshire, 4 February 1931. Died October 2009.) John Jarman spent a lifetime in football, after signing amateur forms for Wolves as a 14-year-old. A strong tackling half back in the 1950s with Barnsley and Walsall he became a top-class coach on retiring as a player. Spells with West Bromwich Albion and both the English and Irish FAs established his reputation and he served as assistant manager to Ian Greaves at Wolves and Mansfield, also working in the academy set-up at Derby for several years.

Kenny Jenkins (Born 28 February 1945. Died November 2009.) Kenny Jenkins began his career as a full back with Johnstone Burgh before successfully converting to centre forward. He went on to make over 250 senior appearances for Albion Rovers and Dumbarton, later reverting to a defensive role. A member of the Dumbarton team that won the Division Two title in 1971–72, he later emigrated to Australia.

Ray John (Born Swansea, 22 November 1932. Died 7 July 2009.) Ray John was a half back or forward who was on the books of both Tottenham Hotspur and Barnsley without playing a first-team game. He then spent four seasons as a regular for Exeter City, making 150 appearances and later played for Oldham Athletic and Margate.

Bert Johnson (Born Stockton, 4 June 1916. Died Evington, Leics, 29 June 2009.) Bert Johnson was a wing half who developed in Northern League football before moving south to sign for Charlton. He became a regular for the Addicks in the 1945–46 season and appeared at wing half in the 1946 and 1947 FA Cup finals, gaining a winners' medal on the latter occasion when Burnley were defeated 1-0. He also won wartime caps for England against Switzerland and France. Bert eventually moved into management and coaching and spent almost a decade as coach for Leicester City up until December 1968.

Dic Jones (Born Llanrwst, Denbighshire, 25 June 1932. Died 15 February 2010.) Dic Jones joined Crewe Alexandra from Holyhead Town in January 1957 and went on to make 80 senior appearances for the Railwaymen during a six-year spell at Gresty Road. He later became well known as manager of a number of North Wales clubs including Bangor City and Rhyl.

Tommy (TE) Jones (Born Liverpool, 11 April 1930. Died 5 June 2010.) Tommy Jones was a reliable defender who made 411 appearances for Everton between 1950 and 1961 before a knee injury brought his career to an end. He succeeded his namesake TG Jones at centre half in the line-up and went on to help the team win promotion from Division Two in 1953–54. He was a member of the FA team that toured West Africa in the summer of 1958.

Jack Keen (Born Barrow, 26 January 1929. Died Barrow, October 2009.) Jack Keen was a wing half who spent a decade on the books of his hometown club, making almost 300 first-team appearances. He featured in two of the club's epic FA Cup ties of the 1950s, lining up against Swansea in January 1954 when a ground record attendance was set, and captaining the team against Wolves in January 1959. He later spent time on the books of Workington and Morecambe.

Keith Kettleborough (Born Rotherham, 29 June 1935. Died Sheffield, 2 November 2009.) Keith Kettleborough was a hard working combative inside forward with excellent distribution skills. After establishing himself at Rotherham he became a key figure at Sheffield United assisting the Blades into the old First Division in 1960–61 and then helping them to stay there. He helped Newcastle avoid relegation in 1965–66 and was considered good enough to be a shadow member of Alf Ramsey's World Cup squad in 1966. He was briefly player-manager at Doncaster then played for Chesterfield before retiring from the game.

Johnny King (Born Great Gidding, Huntingdonshire, 5 November 1926. Died 11 January 2010.) Johnny King was a left half who signed for Leicester City during the war, spending 12 years with the Filbert Street club during which he made almost 200 Football League appearances. He was the youngest member of the team defeated by Wolves in the 1949 FA Cup final. Johnny left the club in the summer of 1955, signing for Kettering Town.

Bobby Kirk (Born Arniston, Midlothian, 12 August 1927. Died 1 February 2010.) Full back Bobby Kirk stepped up to the seniors in January 1948 when he joined Dunfermline Athletic from Arniston Rangers. He enjoyed a 15-year career in the professional game, later playing for Raith Rovers and Hearts and amassing a total of more than 500 competitive appearances. He enjoyed great success during his spell at Tynecastle helping the club to two League titles (1957–58 and 1959–60), as well as victory in the Scottish Cup (1956) and League Cup (1958–59 and 1959–60). He was capped once by Scotland B.

Ray Lambert (Born Bagillt, nr. Holywell, Flintshire, 18 July 1922. Died 22 October 2009.) Ray Lambert made over 100 appearances for Liverpool in the emergency wartime competitions and starred in the successful team of the immediate post-war period, helping the team to the Football League title in 1946–47 and then gaining an FA Cup runners-up medal in 1950. A solid, effective full back, he made over 300 peacetime appearances before eventually leaving the game at the end of the 1955–56 season.

Sam Latter (Born Glasgow, 4 January 1904. Died Edinburgh, 12 June 2010.) Sam Latter signed for Third Lanark in October 1928 and spent four seasons on the books at Cathkin Park. At the time of his death he held the title of Scotland's Oldest Man and was almost certainly the UK's oldest living former professional footballer.

Dai Lawrence (Born Swansea, 18 January 1947. Died Killay, Swansea, 21 July 2009.) Full back Dai Lawrence won amateur international honours for Wales before turning professional with Swansea Town in 1967. He played over 100 senior games for the Swans, featuring regularly in the side that won promotion from the old Fourth Division in 1969–70, before moving on to Chelmsford City in the 1971 close season.

Ian Lawther (Born Belfast, 20 October 1939. Died 25 April 2010.) Ian Lawther was a much-travelled centre forward who came to prominence as a youngster with Irish League club Crusaders. He signed for Sunderland in March 1958 and over the next 18 years he played for Blackburn, Scunthorpe, Brentford, Halifax and Stockport scoring a total of 179 League goals in just over 550 appearances. He won four full caps for Northern Ireland.

Bill Linacre (Born Chesterfield, 10 August 1924. Died January 2010.) Bill Linacre was a talented winger who made over 100 wartime appearances for Chesterfield, but then suffered a broken leg on two occasions. He recovered fitness and in October 1947 he signed for Manchester City where he had two good seasons. He then joined Middlesbrough, where he formed an effective partnership with Wilf Mannion on the right wing, and concluded his career with spells at Hartlepools and at Mansfield.

Joe Livingstone (Born Middlesbrough, 18 June 1942. Died New Marske, Teesside, 1 August 2009.) Joe Livingstone began his senior career as understudy to Brian Clough at Middlesbrough, stepping up to the first team after Clough departed for Sunderland. A big, strapping centre forward he later scored 46 goals from 80 appearances for Carlisle, where he partnered Hugh McIlmoyle up front, before winding down his career with spells at Hartlepools and Stockton.

George Luke (Born Newcastle, 17 December 1933. Died March 2010.) George Luke was an outside left who began his career as a youngster with Newcastle, but it was not until he moved on to Hartlepools in October 1953 that he gained experience of senior football. After six years with Pools he returned to St James's Park where he made a number of first-team appearances in the 1959–60 and 1960–61 seasons before concluding his career with Darlington.

Tommy Lumley (Born Leadgate, Co Durham, 9 December 1924. Died 17 December 2009.) Tommy Lumley was an inside forward who spent four seasons with Charlton after signing from Consett Town, although he had few opportunities to gain an extended run in the line-up for the Addicks. He fared better at Barnsley where he made over 150 appearances, captaining the team to success in Division Three North in 1954–55. He ended his career with a season at Darlington.

Roy Lunnis (Born Islington, London, 4 November 1939. Died January 2010.) Roy Lunnis was a powerful full back who spent three seasons as a professional with Crystal Palace, making 25 appearances. He moved on to Portsmouth, where he was a first-team regular in the 1963–64 and 1964–65 seasons, then had spells with Addington (South Africa), Luton Town and Oakland Clippers (of the NPSL).

Tommy McCabe (Born Dundalk, Irish Free State, October 1932. Died Australia, May 2009.) Tommy McCabe was a quick left winger with a powerful shot who made his first-team debut for Dundalk at the age of 17. He went on to play for Distillery and Glentoran, with whom he won representative honours for the Irish League against the Scottish League in September 1954. He later made five international appearances for New Zealand.

Alex McCrae (Born Stoneyburn, West Lothian, 2 January 1920. Died Livingston, West Lothian, 8 October 2009.) Alex McCrae joined Hearts during the war and was a regular scorer for the Tynecastle club, but he was soon on his way south to Charlton once peacetime football resumed. Next stop on his travels was Middlesbrough, where he excelled as a traditional inside forward with pace, guile and an eye for goal, scoring 49 goals in 130 appearances. He subsequently played for Falkirk, then joined Ballymena United as player-manager, leading the club to success in the Irish Cup in 1958 and a place in the final the following season. Later he served both Stirling Albion (January to March 1960) and Falkirk (April 1960 to May 1965) as manager.

Charlie McDonnell (Born Birkenhead, 15 July 1936. Died 7 June 2010.) Charlie McDonnell was a stocky inside forward who signed for Tranmere in September 1957. A regular goalscorer, he went on to score 83 League goals in 206 appearances in a career that saw him spend two spells at Prenton Park as well as turning out for Stockport County and Southport. He later won an Irish Cup winners' medal as a member of the Glentoran team that defeated Linfield 2-0 in the 1965–66 final.

Willie MacFarlane (Born Edinburgh, 17 March 1930. Died Edinburgh, 11 March 2010.) Willie MacFarlane was a solid full back who spent nine seasons on the books of Hibernian in the 1950s, making a total of 78 League appearances. He later played for Raith Rovers and Morton before turning to management. He had spells in charge of Stirling Albion (March 1968 to September 1969), Hibernian (September 1969 to December 1970) and Meadowbank (1978 to 1980).

John McGinty (Born 1937. Died 22 August 2009.) John McGinty had been active in the movement to save the old Aldershot FC at the time of its demise in 1992 and later that year he was appointed as a director of the newly formed Aldershot Town FC. He went on to become club chairman from November 2006, leading the club back into the Football League two years later. A popular figure at the club, he was still in post at the time of his death.

George McGowan (Born Netherton, Wishaw, Lanarkshire, 30 November 1943. Died 20 November 2009.) George McGowan was a combative inside forward who signed for Preston North End in August 1962, but he was unable to break into the first team and quickly moved on to Chester. Although his Football League career was relatively brief, he played just 23 League games, he continued to coach clubs in the North Wales area and for the last 20 years or so had assisted with the coaching at Wrexham, still being in post at the time of his death.

Paul McGrillen (Born 19 August 1971. Died Hamilton, 29 July 2009.) Paul McGrillen was a striker who came through the ranks at Motherwell and went on to make almost 100 appearances for the club, although many of these were from the subs' bench. The best years of his career were spent at Falkirk, where he scored the winner in the 1997 Scottish Cup semi-final replay against Celtic and gained a runners-up medal when the Bairns went down to Kilmarnock in the final. He was also a member of the team that won the Scottish League Challenge Cup in 1998. Paul later played for Bathgate Thistle and had featured in a friendly encounter with Motherwell shortly before his death.

Harry McIlvenny (Born Bradford, 5 October 1922. Died 29 June 2009.) Harry McIlvenny was a big bustling centre forward who played as an amateur throughout his career. He enjoyed a number of extended runs for Bradford Park Avenue in their Division Two days and later played for Bishop Auckland, featuring in the 1950 and 1951 FA Amateur Cup finals. He won five caps for England Amateurs and appeared in all four of the Great Britain fixtures at the 1948 Olympic Games tournament.

Brian McLaughlin (Born Falkirk, 7 October 1954. Died Falkirk, 13 August 2009.) Brian McLaughlin was a highly promising midfield player as a teenager, making his first-team debut for Celtic at the age of 16, only to suffer a serious knee injury in September 1973. He won the Scottish PFA First Division Player of the Year in both 1979 and 1982 and enjoyed a lengthy career in the game with Ayr, Motherwell, Hamilton and Falkirk, making a total of over 200 League appearances.

Arthur McMillan (Born 2 September 1942. Died Melbourne, Australia, 29 December 2009.) Arthur McMillan signed for Stranraer in December 1967 as a striker after spells with Royal Albert and Stonehouse Thistle. Three years later he moved on to Hamilton where he was converted into a defender and made over 250 appearances. A resolute, no-nonsense player he was a key figure for the Accies in the 1970s, when he was voted as the club's Player of the Year on three occasions.

Eddie Marsh (Born Dundee, 14 December 1927. Died 7 April 2010.) Goalkeeper Eddie Marsh spent almost 12 years on the books of Charlton Athletic, where he was mostly understudy to Sam Bartram. He went on to play for Luton Town and Torquay United, for whom he was the club's regular 'keeper making a total of 61 League appearances.

Don Martin (Born Corby, Northamptonshire, 15 February 1944. Died 14 November 2009.) Don Martin was on the groundstaff at Northampton and won England Youth honours, going on to enjoy a successful career as a goalscoring forward in two spells with the Cobblers separated by seven years at Blackburn. In total he made 452 League appearances, scoring 128 goals. He was joint-top scorer for Northampton in 1964–65 when they won promotion to the old First Division, while at Blackburn he headed the scoring charts in 1974–75 when the Third Division title was won.

Hughie Maxwell (Born Rigghead, Lanarkshire, 14 May 1938. Died Kidlington, Oxfordshire, 25 January 2010.) Hughie Maxwell was an inside forward who began his career with Stirling Albion and Bradford Park Avenue, but it was only when he signed for Falkirk that he became known as a goalscorer. He netted a club record seven goals in the 7-3 win over Clyde in December 1962 and went on to score 46 goals in 84 games for the Bairns. Hughie later had spells with Celtic, St Johnstone and Dunfermline before emigrating to South Africa.

Gil Merrick (Born Sparkhill, Birmingham, 26 January 1922. Died 4 February 2010.) Gil Merrick signed for Birmingham City in August 1939 and he was the club's regular goalkeeper from 1941 until the end of the 1950s, making over 500 peacetime appearances. He assisted Birmingham to two Second Division titles (1947–48 and 1954–55) and gained an FA Cup runners-up medal in 1956 when Blues went down to Manchester City in the Wembley final. Gil also won 23 caps for England, featuring in the 1954 World Cup finals. He went on to spend four years as manager at St Andrew's leading the club to their only major trophy, the Football League Cup in 1962–63.

John Millington (Born Coseley, Staffs, 21 February 1930. Died Dudley, 5 January 2010.) John Millington was a reserve with Aston Villa before signing for Walsall in the summer of 1951. He went on to make 23 League appearances for the Saddlers and also played for Kidderminster Harriers and Stafford Rangers.

Roly Mills (Born Daventry, 22 June 1922. Died Northampton, 8 February 2010.) Roly Mills began his career as a right winger for Northampton Town in the early 1950s, later switching to wing half. A member of the team that defeated Arsenal in the FA Cup third round in January 1958, he made over 300 appearances for the Cobblers. When his playing career was over he remained at the County Ground in a variety of backroom roles, giving the club almost 40 years service.

Gil Merrick

Gerhard Neef (Born Hausham, Germany, 30 October 1946. Died Nürnberg, Germany, 23 February 2010.) Goalkeeper Gerhard Neef was playing amateur football for VfvB Ruhrort/Laar when signed by Rangers. He went on to make 48 appearances for the Ibrox club, featuring as the regular 'keeper between April 1969 and March 1970. He later returned to Germany where he played in the Bundesliga Sud for 1FC Nürnberg.

Jackie Newton (Born Bishop Auckland, 25 May 1925. Died 30 January 2010.) Jackie Newton was a dependable wing half who was a fixture in the Hartlepools United team during the 1950s. Signed from Newcastel United in the summer of 1946, he made over 350 first-team appearances for Pools before moving on in the summer of 1957.

Orlando (Born Niteroi, Brazil, 20 September 1935. Died Rio de Janeiro, Brazil, 10 February 2010.) Orlando was a central defender who was a member of the Brazil team that defeated Sweden to win the 1958 World Cup final. He won a total of 30 caps for Brazil, playing at club level for Vasco de Gama, Boca Juniors and Santos.

Gibby Ormond (Died 5 February 2010.) Gibby Ormond was an outside left who made over 200 senior appearances for Airdrie, Dundee United, Cowdenbeath and Alloa in a career that spanned the period from 1957 to 1965. He also won two caps for the Scottish League in the 1958–59 season.

Dennis Pacey (Born Feltham, Middlesex, 27 September 1928. Died Chertsey, Surrey, 23 September 2009.) Centre forward Dennis Pacey played as an amateur with Woking and Walton & Hersham before turning professional with Leyton Orient. He made a sensational start to his senior career with a hat-trick on his debut in an FA Cup tie with Gorleston. He went on to score 58 goals in 135 appearances for the Os, then made a further century of appearances for Millwall before concluding his senior career with a spell at Aldershot.

Norman Packer (Born Ynysybwl, Glamorgan, 14 June 1931. Died September 2009.) Norman Packer spent six years on the books of Exeter City as a part-time professional, combining football with a career as a schoolteacher. He was mostly a reserve half back for the Grecians, making 18 League appearances.

Chris Palethorpe (Born Maidenhead, 6 November 1942. Died 21 May 2010.) Chris Palethorpe was a winger who made over 100 League appearances for Reading and Aldershot in the early 1960s. A highlight of his career was scoring in the Shots 2-1 win over Aston Villa in an FA Cup third round replay in January 1964.

Stan Palk (Born Liverpool, 28 October 1921. Died Liverpool, 12 October 2009.) Stan Palk was an inside forward or wing half who joined Liverpool during the 1939–40 season and made over 50 wartime appearances for the Reds. He featured in the team that won the Football League title in 1946–47 but was never a first-team regular at Anfield in peacetime. Later he spent four seasons with Port Vale before being released in the summer of 1952.

Alex Parker (Born Irvine, Ayrshire, 2 August 1935. Died Gretna, 7 January 2010.) Alex Parker joined Falkirk as an inside forward from Kello Rovers but was quickly converted to right back, a role in which he continued to play throughout his career. He enjoyed considerable success with the Bairns, featuring regularly at international level, and gaining a Scottish Cup winners' medal in 1957 when he also won the Scottish Player of the Year award. Transferred to Everton in the summer of 1958, he made almost 200 League appearances for the Toffees, gaining a championship winners' medal in 1962–63 and later played for Southport, Ballymena United (as player-manager) and Drumcondra. He won 15 full caps for Scotland.

Jack Parry (Born Pontadarwe, Glamorgan, 11 January 1924. Died 19 January 2010.) Jack Parry was a goalkeeper who joined Swansea Town in June 1946 and went on to feature in the team that won the Division Three South title in 1948–49. He subsequently spent four seasons with Ipswich Town where he was an ever-present in the team that also won the Division Three South championship in 1953–54. He made a total of 256 senior appearances before dropping into the Southern League.

Tony Parry (Born Burton upon Trent, 8 September 1945. Died Burton upon Trent, 23 November 2009.) Tony Parry was a strong, powerful wing half who was playing Southern League football for Burton Albion when he became one of Brian Clough's first signings for Hartlepools. A key figure in the team that won promotion from the old Fourth Division in 1967–68, he made over 200 appearances for Pools before following Clough to Derby. However, he was little more than a squad player with the Rams and later moved on to play for Gresley Rovers for several seasons.

Gordon Pearce (Born circa 1943. Died Bristol, 29 April 2010). Gordon Pearce was a member of the Bristol Rovers Supporters Club who in June 1978 established the Ninety Two Club, a club for those who have attended a first-team competitive fixture played at the current ground of each of the 92 Football/Premier League clubs.

Willie Polland (Born Armadale, 28 July 1934. Died Edinburgh, 10 February 2010.) Willie Polland was a defender who signed for Raith Rovers in the summer of 1955 and quickly became a regular in the line-up. He moved on to Hearts in April 1961 and spent six seasons at Tynecastle before returning to Raith to conclude his career. He played in the Hearts team that defeated Kilmarnock to win the League Cup in 1962–63 and altogether he made almost 550 senior appearances in a career that ended in 1970.

Graham Potter (Born Rutherglen, Lanarkshire, 4 June 1979. Died Co Durham, 26 July 2009.) Goalkeeper Graham Potter featured in Hamilton's Third Division title winning side of 2000–01 and went on to play more than 50 senior games for the Accies before moving on to play for Annan and Pollok Juniors. In 2004 he joined Cumnock Juniors, where he was to remain for the rest of his career, his tragic death occurring during a pre-season tour of Northern England.

Sam Prangley (Born Newport, 30 September 1924. Died Newport, 25 July 2009.) Sam Prangley was a half back who was on the books of Cardiff City and Lovell's Athletic during the war, signing for Newport County soon after the start of the 1946–47 campaign. He went on to make seven appearances for the club in the old Second Division before returning to Lovell's.

Mick Prendergast (Born Denaby Main, Yorkshire, 24 November 1950. Died 29 April 2010.) Mick Prendergast was a brave and fearless striker who joined Sheffield Wednesday as an apprentice in the summer of 1966 and stayed at Hillsborough for more than a decade making over 200 senior appearances and scoring 59 goals. A regular in the line-up from the 1970–71 season, his career was affected by injuries. He later played for Barnsley before leaving the full-time game in 1979.

Robert Rennie (Born Alva, Clackmannanshire, 1914. Died November 2009.) Robert Rennie was a tough tackling right back who joined Dundee from Clydebank Juniors and became a regular in the 1935–36 season, remaining so until the outbreak of war. He served in the Army during the war, when he also appeared as a guest for Third Lanark. He later concluded his career with Montrose in the inaugural season of Division C.

Tony Richards (Born Birmingham, 6 March 1934. Died 4 March 2010.) Tony Richards was prolific centre forward who joined Walsall in September 1954 after a period of National Service and went on to score 185 goals, a club record, from

334 League appearances for the Saddlers. He was leading scorer in the team that won the Division Four title in 1959–60 and netted 36 goals the following season when the club won promotion again. Tony eventually moved on to conclude his career with Port Vale.

Hugh Robertson (Born Auchinleck, Ayrshire, 29 March 1938. Died Edinburgh, 12 March 2010.) Hugh Robertson was an outside left who signed for Dundee in May 1957 and went on to play over 200 Scottish League games during his time at Dens Park. A key figure in the team that won the League title in 1961–62 and reached the semi-final of the European Cup the following season, he went on to gain a Scottish Cup winners' medal with Dunfermline Athletic in 1968 before ending his career at Arbroath. He won a single cap for Scotland, playing against Czechoslovakia in November 1961.

Jimmy Robertson (Born circa 1915. Died Kirkcaldy, 6 September 2009.) Jimmy Robertson was a wing half who featured for Dundee United on a number of occasions in the emergency competitions during World War Two.

Gordon Robinson (Born Chesterfield, 1931. Died Chesterfield. 2010.) Gordon Robinson was on Sheffield United's books as a youngster but failed to make the first team. He spent the 1951–52 and 1952–53 seasons with Motherwell, making a handful of Scottish League appearances before returning south.

Sir Bobby Robson, CBE (Born Sacriston, Co Durham, 18 February 1933. Died Co Durham, 31 July 2009.) Bobby Robson was one of the most important figures in post-war English football. As a player he was a talented inside forward and wing half who joined Fulham soon after leaving school, quickly establishing himself in the line-up at inside right. West Bromwich Albion paid a club record

Bobby Robson

fee for his services in May 1956 and he settled in at The Hawthorns as international honours soon followed. A cultured player, he converted to left half in the 1960–61 season and then returned to Craven Cottage where he gave a further five years of excellent service before retiring as a player at the end of the 1966–67 campaign. In total he made 583 League appearances, winning 20 full caps for England. Bobby became involved in coaching while at Craven Cottage, and after spells in management in Canada and with Fulham he established his reputation at Ipswich, where he gained success in the FA Cup (1978) and the UEFA Cup (1981). In July 1982 Bobby succeeded Ron Greenwood as Head Coach of the England team, a post he held for the next eight years. He proved to be the most successful manager since Alf Ramsey, taking the team to the quarter-finals of the World Cup in 1986 and the semi-finals in 1990. The latter performance remains the best by an England team on foreign soil. After the 1990 tournament Bobby moved on to a series of successful coaching roles with PSV Eindhoven (two spells), Sporting Lisbon, Porto and Barcelona. In September 1999 he returned to Newcastle, where he took the club into the European Champions' League on two consecutive occasions. He left St James' Park in August 2004 and later had a spell as consultant to the Republic of Ireland team under Steve Staunton. A father figure to his players, Bobby always demonstrated great passion for the game and commanded tremendous respect throughout football.

Roberto Rosato (Born Chieri, Italy, 18 August 1943. Died Chieri, Italy, 20 June 2010.) Roberto Rosato was a powerful defender who won 37 caps for Italy between 1965 and 1973, playing in the side defeated by Brazil in the 1970 World Cup final and also gaining a UEFA Championship medal with the Azzurri in 1968. At club level he played for Torino, AC Milan and Genoa, gaining a European Cup winners medal in 1969 and featuring in two successful Cup Winners Cup teams (1968 and 1973).

Albert Scanlon (Born Hulme, Manchester, 10 October 1935. Died Salford, 22 December 2009.) Albert Scanlon was a schoolboy star who went on to become one of the famous Busby Babes of the 1950s. A pacy winger who featured in two FA Youth Cup winning teams for Manchester United, he was seriously injured in the Munich Air Crash, but recovered sufficiently to become an ever-present in the team that finished as runners-up to Wolves in the First Division in 1958–59. He later had spells with Newcastle, Lincoln and Mansfield before leaving the senior game in 1966.

Paul Shirtliff (Born Hoyland, nr. Barnsley, 5 November 1962. Died 13 September 2009.) Paul Shirtliff was a full back or midfield player who began his career as an apprentice with Sheffield Wednesday. Although he graduated to the professional ranks at Hillsborough he was only ever a fringe player for the Owls, although he featured fairly regularly in a season with Northampton. Paul went on to shine in non-League football, winning 15 caps for the England Semi-Professional team between 1986 and 1993.

Billy Simpson (Born 11 July 1945. Died September 2009.) Billy Simpson was on the books of Hibernian for seven seasons in the 1960s, but was mostly a reserve defender. His best season at Easter Road was in 1965–66 when he featured at right back, but it was only when he stepped down to Division Two football with Albion, Alloa and Cowdenbeath that he became a first-team regular. He later went into management, working with Billy Lamont at East Stirling, Dumbarton, Falkirk, Partick Thistle and then Alloa.

Jimmy Simpson (Born Clay Cross, Derbys, 8 December 1923. Died Matlock, 1 May 2010.) Jimmy Simpson was an inside forward who joined Chesterfield from Parkhouse Colliery in May 1945 and played in 10 wartime and three peacetime games. He later had a spell with Buxton before suffering a serious injury in an accident at work, which ended his football career.

Tommy Sloan (Born Barrhead, Lanarkshire, 13 October 1925. Died Paisley, 13 January 2010.) Tommy Sloan signed for Hearts in April 1946. He forged a reputation as a goalscoring winger at Tynecastle, where he made 110 League appearances, but later moved on to Motherwell. He added a further century of appearances at Fir Park and gained personal success as a member of the teams that won the Scottish Cup in 1952 and the B Division title in 1953–54.

Jimmy Smallwood (Born Bearpark, County Durham, 1 September 1925. Died 29 January 2010.) Jimmy Smallwood was an effective wing half who played over 350 games for Chesterfield between December 1949 and January 1961. After retiring as a player Jimmy remained at Saltergate working as trainer, groundsman and club steward until 1986.

Bobby Smith (Born Dalkeith, Midlothian, 21 December 1953. Died Edinburgh, 22 February 2010.) Bobby Smith was an intelligent attacking midfield player for Hibernian before his fellow Scot Jock Wallace persuaded him to sign for Leicester City at the end of 1978. He spent four years at Filbert Street, converting to full back towards the end of his time there. Bobby later returned to Easter Road and then played for Dunfermline, Partick and Berwick, taking his total of senior appearances beyond the 500 mark.

Stan Smith (Born Kidsgrove, Staffs, 24 February 1931. Died 8 April 2010.) Stan Smith joined Port Vale in May 1950 having previously played as a junior for Stoke City and with Chesterton PSA. He made 63 appearances for Vale as a versatile forward, scoring 21 goals and later played for Crewe and Oldham before dropping down to play in the Cheshire League.

Albert Scanlon

Vic Snell (Born Ipswich, 29 October 1927. Died 20 August 2009.) Vic Snell initially signed amateur forms with Ipswich Town from local club football, graduating to the professional ranks in the 1948–49 season. Principally a half back, he remained on the books for well over a decade but was mostly a reserve, making a total of 67 first-team appearances. He later spent time in South Africa where he played for Port Elizabeth City and East London Celtic.

Joe Spence (Born Salford, 13 October 1925. Died Chesterfield, December 2009.) Joe Spence signed for Chesterfield in January 1948, but never made the breakthrough to first-team football at Saltergate and after a season at Buxton he returned to the senior game with York. A cultured defender he made over 100 appearances for the Minstermen before dropping into non-league football with Gainsborough Trinity.

Phil Spruce (Born Chester, 16 November 1929. Died March 2010.) Phil Spruce was a defender who signed for Wrexham in November 1950 and went on to make 24 first-team appearances in a career that was restricted by the requirement to undergo a period of National Service. He later spent several seasons with Rhyl and Colwyn Bay.

Felix Staroscik (Born Poland, 20 May 1920. Died Bedford, 7 August 2009.) Felix Staroscik was a talented winger who came to Britain as a member of the Polish Army after the outbreak of war. After the war he signed for Third Lanark where he became a regular in the first team, scoring 43 goals in 102 appearances before moving south to sign for Northampton. He spent four seasons with the Cobblers then joined Southern League club Bedford Town, where he enjoyed some of his finest moments, playing in the team that defeated Watford and then forced Arsenal to a replay in the FA Cup in 1955–56.

Percy Steele (Born Bootle, 26 December 1923. Died 21 October 2009.) Percy Steele was a full back who signed for Tranmere Rovers during the war. He eventually established himself as a first-team regular at Prenton Park during the 1948–49 campaign and went on to make over 300 appearances for the Wirral club.

Arthur Stenner (Born Yeovil, 7 January 1934. Died Yeovil, 11 March 2010.) Outside left Arthur Stenner spent a season on the books of Bristol City without making the first team and went on to play for Plymouth Argyle, Norwich City and Oldham although he was principally a reserve at all his clubs, making a total of 18 Football League appearances.

John Stevens (Born Forres, Morayshire, 21 August 1941. Died 13 April 2010.) Centre forward John Stevens joined Swindon Town from RAF football and enjoyed a useful run in the line-up towards the end of the 1962–63 campaign when the Robins won promotion from the Third Division. He also played a handful of games the following season before moving on to sign for Guildford City.

George Stillyards (Born Lincoln, 29 December 1918. Died 11 January 2010.) George Stillyards signed for Lincoln City in September 1942, scoring the winner on his debut against Nottingham Forest. In his early days he was a forward, but most of his peacetime appearances were at full back or half back. He was a near ever-present in the Imps team that won the Division Three North title, but left the club at the end of the following season. George also played cricket to a high standard and made two Minor Counties appearances for Lincolnshire.

Sid Storey (Born Darfield, nr. Barnsley, 25 December 1919. Died 6 April 2010.) Sid Storey was a ball-playing inside forward who played a couple of wartime games for Huddersfield Town, later signing for York City from Wombwell in the summer of 1947. He spent almost 10 years as a regular for the Minstermen, making over 350 appearances and assisting the team to a place in the FA Cup semi-final in 1954–55. After leaving Bootham Crescent he had spells with Barnsley, Accrington Stanley and Bradford Park Avenue before retiring from senior football at the age of 40.

Norman Sykes (Born Bristol, 16 October 1936. Died 9 December 2009.) Wing half Norman Sykes won representative honours for England Schools and Youth teams before joining his local club Bristol Rovers. Once he had broken into the first team he quickly established himself as a regular in the line-up at right half, making over 200 appearances and captaining the side for a while. He later played for Plymouth, Stockport and Doncaster before leaving the senior game.

Bobby Thomson (Born Smethwick, 5 December 1943. Died Dudley, West Midlands, 19 August 2009.) Bobby Thomson was a classy full back who joined Wolves on leaving school. Tall and composed, he was just 19 when he made his debut for England, but when Wolves were relegated from the First Division his international prospects faded. Nevertheless he enjoyed a healthy career at Molineux, making almost 300 first-team appearances and helping the side win promotion back to the top flight in 1966–67. Bobby went on to play for Birmingham City, Luton and Port Vale, in addition to spending time in the United States, before retiring from the game.

Mike Tiddy (Born Cadgwith, Cornwall, 4 April 1929. Died 25 November 2009.) Mike Tiddy made his first-team debut for Torquay as a 17-year-old, then went away on National Service. On his return he had a very brief run in the line-up before being sold to Cardiff, where he spent five seasons as a flying winger, making 145 League appearances. He went on to enjoy a spell in the top flight with Arsenal before concluding his senior career at Brighton.

Charlie Timmins (Born Birmingham, 29 May 1922. Died 13 April 2010.) Charlie Timmins was a skilful defender who spent nine years on the books of Coventry City in the immediate post-war period, making a total of 161 League appearances. He left Highfield Road at the end of the 1957–58 season, later turning out for Lockheed Leamington.

Zoltan Varga (Born Val, Hungary, 1 January 1945. Died Budapest, Hungary, 9 April 2010.) Zoltan Varga made his name playing in Hungary in the 1960s, assisting the national team to the gold medal at the 1964 Olympic Games and gaining an Inter Cities Fairs Cup winners medal with Ferencvaros in 1965. He later moved to Western Europe, playing for a string of clubs including Standard Liege and Ajax. He also spent a brief period

Bobby Thomson

with Aberdeen from September 1972 where he impressed as a skilful forward and scored 10 goals in 31 senior appearances.

Richard Walden (Born Hereford, 4 May 1948. Died Frimley, Surrey, 19 November 2009.) Richard Walden was a consistent right back who made over 700 senior appearances in a career that spanned almost two decades. An apprentice with Aldershot, he made his senior debut at the age of 16 and went on to be a near ever-present in the promotion-winning team of 1972–73. After playing 400 games for the Shots he spent time with Sheffield Wednesday and Newport County, where he gained a further promotion in 1979–80 and was a member of the side that reached the quarter-finals of the European Cup Winners Cup the following season.

Ken Watkins (Born Coventry, 7 February 1923. Died 26 November 2009.) Ken Watkins was a wing half who made a number of appearances for Coventry City during World War Two, also featuring as a guest for Port Vale in the 1945–46 season.

George Webber (Born Abercynon, Glamorgan, 28 June 1925. Died Torquay, 7 October 2009.) George Webber was a goalkeeper who was on the books of Cardiff City before signing for Torquay. He spent the best part of three seasons as the Gulls regular 'keeper, making 123 first-team appearances, then ended his career at Northampton.

Pat Welton (Born Eltham, 3 May 1928. Died 28 June 2010.) As a player Pat started his career at Cheshunt and moved to keep goal for Leyton Orient's first team from 1949 to 1957 making 263 appearances for the O's. He then transferred to Queens Park Rangers but only played 3 games for them between 1958 and 1959. Finally he ended his playing career with St Albans City whom he also managed along with Walthamstow Avenue. After that he managed Corinthian Casuals between 1968 and 1969 but in between he was made Manager of the England Youth Team under whose guidance they won the European Youth Championship in 1963 and the Little World Cup in 1964. His good work with youth players led to his being appointed Youth Team Manager at Tottenham Hotspur where he stayed for some time while his teams earned great success winning two FA Youth Cups. He was then appointed Assistant Manager to Keith Burkinshaw at Spurs. His final football stint was as Manager/Coach to Jahra FC in Kuwait. When he returned to England Pat opened a Pub in the Charlton/Grenwich area, where on the opening night the guest of honour was old friend Bill Nicholson and with wife Elsie ran it for some 10 years. Pat served on the LFCA Committee with distinction for some years between the late 1960's and 70's and where he also put on practical sessions for the Association's members.

Phil Whitlock (Born Llanhilleth, Monmouthshire, 1 May 1930. Died January 2010.) Phil Whitlock signed for Chester in August 1950 and went on to become a first-team regular in the mid-1950s, featuring in the side that achieved a famous draw with Chelsea at Stamford Bridge in the third round of the FA Cup in 1951–52 and gaining two Welsh Cup runners-up medals.

Hugh Whyte (Born Kilmarnock, 24 July 1955. Died Dunfermline, 9 November 2009.) Goalkeeper Hugh Whyte joined Hibernian from Hurlford United in September 1972 but only made a handful fo first-team appearances in four seasons at Easter Road. He moved on to Dunfermline in 1976 and in a decade at East End Park he established himself as a legendary figure for the club, making over 300 first-team appearances. A part-time player who was also a GP, he served the Pars as club doctor when his playing days were over and in 2009 he was inducted into the club's Hall of Fame.

David Will, CBE (Born Glasgow, 22 November 1936. Died 25 September 2009.) David Will was a solicitor who entered football administration as chairman of Brechin City in 1966 and went on to become one of the most powerful men in world football. A member of the Scottish FA's Executive Committee from 1970, he later served as a UEFA vice-president, and, from 1990 to 2007, as a vice-president of FIFA.

Jack Wiseman (Born 1917. Died 14 August 2009.) Jack Wiseman spent over 50 years as a key figure in the administration of Birmingham City. Appointed as a director in 1956, he became vice chairman in 1975 and then chairman from 1992 to 1998. He also served on the Football League Management Committee from 1974 to 1983 and on the FA Council from 1974.

Alec Young (Born Glasgow, 20 October 1925. Died Fortrose, Ross-shire, 2 March 2010.) A product of Scottish Junior club Blantyre Victoria, centre half Alec Young signed for Aberdeen in May 1950 and went on to make 222 senior appearances for the Dons. An ever-present in the team that won the Scottish League title in 1954–55, he eventually left to become player-manager of Ross County in the summer of 1958.

Ian Nannestad
www.soccer-history.co.uk

THE FOOTBALL RECORDS

BRITISH FOOTBALL RECORDS

ALL-TIME PREMIER LEAGUE CHAMPIONSHIP SEASONS ON POINTS AVERAGE

	Team	Season	P	W	D	L	F	A	Pts	Pts Av
1	Chelsea	2004–05	38	29	8	1	72	15	95	2.50
2	Manchester U	1999–2000	38	28	7	3	97	45	91	2.39
3	Chelsea	2005–06	38	29	4	5	72	22	91	2.39
4	Arsenal	2003–04	38	26	12	0	73	26	90	2.36
4	Manchester U	2008–09	38	28	6	4	68	24	90	2.36
6	Manchester U	2006–07	38	28	5	5	83	27	89	2.34
7	Arsenal	2001–02	38	26	9	3	79	36	87	2.28
7	Manchester U	2007–08	38	27	6	5	80	22	87	2.28
9	Chelsea	2009–10	38	27	5	6	103	32	86	2.26
10	Manchester U	1993–94	42	27	11	4	80	38	92	2.19
11	Manchester U	2002–03	38	25	8	5	74	34	83	2.18
12	Manchester U	1995–96	38	25	7	6	73	35	82	2.15
13	Blackburn R	1994–95	42	27	8	7	80	39	89	2.11
14	Manchester U	2000–01	38	24	8	6	79	31	80	2.10
15	Manchester U	1998–99	38	22	13	3	80	37	79	2.07
16	Arsenal	1997–98	38	23	9	6	68	33	78	2.05
17	Manchester U	1992–93	42	24	12	6	67	31	84	2.00
18	Manchester U	1996–97	38	21	12	5	76	44	75	1.97

PREMIER LEAGUE EVER-PRESENT CLUBS

	P	W	D	L	F	A	Pts
Manchester U	696	449	147	100	1374	591	1494
Arsenal	696	375	186	135	1199	626	1311
Chelsea	696	362	181	153	1148	662	1267
Liverpool	696	349	177	170	1130	669	1224
Aston Villa	696	264	211	221	888	811	1003
Tottenham H	696	258	181	257	951	933	955
Everton	696	244	192	260	873	894	924

TOP TEN PREMIERSHIP APPEARANCES

1	James, David	572	6	Lampard, Frank	468
2	Giggs, Ryan	548	7	Scholes, Paul	444
3	Speed, Gary	535	8	Shearer, Alan	441
4	Campbell, Sol	496	9	Carragher, Jamie	435
5	Heskey, Emile	469	10	Neville, Phil	429

TOP TEN PREMIERSHIP GOALSCORERS

1	Shearer, Alan	260	6	Owen, Michael	147
2	Cole, Andy	187	7	Sheringham, Teddy	146
3	Henry, Thierry	174	8	Lampard, Frank	129
4	Fowler, Robbie	163	9	Hasselbaink, Jimmy Floyd	127
5	Ferdinand, Les	149	10	Yorke, Dwight	123

PREMIERSHIP GOAL MILESTONES

Goal	Date	Scorer	Match
1	15.8.92	Brian Deane	Sheffield U v Manchester U
100	25.8.92	Mark Walters	Liverpool v Ipswich T
1000	7.4.93	Mike Newell	Blackburn R v Nottingham F
5000	7.12.96	Andy Townsend	Aston Villa v Southampton
10,000	15.12.01	Les Ferdinand	Tottenham H v Fulham
11,000	7.12.02	Jay-Jay Okocha	Bolton W v Blackburn R
12,000	13.12.03	Alan Shearer	Newcastle U v Tottenham H
13,000	28.11.04	Frederic Kanoute	Tottenham H v Middlesbrough
14,000	26.12.05	Jermain Defoe	Tottenham H v Birmingham C
15,000	30.12.06	Moritz Volz	Fulham v Chelsea

EUROPEAN CUP AND CHAMPIONS LEAGUE RECORDS

CHAMPIONS LEAGUE ATTENDANCES AND GOALS FROM GROUP STAGES ONWARDS

Season	Attendances	Average	Goals	Games
1992–93	873,251	34,930	56	25
1993–94	1,202,289	44,529	71	27
1994–95	2,328,515	38,172	140	61
1995–96	1,874,316	30,726	159	61
1996–97	2,093,228	34,315	161	61
1997–98	2,868,271	33,744	239	85
1998–99	3,608,331	42,451	238	85
1999–2000	5,490,709	34,973	442	157
2000–01	5,773,486	36,774	449	157
2001–02	5,417,716	34,508	393	157
2002–03	6,461,112	41,154	431	157
2003–04	4,611,214	36,890	309	125
2004–05	4,946,820	39,575	331	125
2005–06	5,291,187	42,330	285	125
2006–07	5,591,463	44,732	309	125
2007–08	5,454,718	43,638	330	125
2008–09	5,003,754	40,030	329	125
2009–10	5,295,708	42,366	320	125

HIGHEST AVERAGE ATTENDANCE IN ONE EUROPEAN CUP SEASON
1959–60 50,545 from a total attendance of 2,780,000.

HIGHEST SCORE IN A EUROPEAN CUP MATCH
Feyenoord (Holland)12, KR Reykjavik (Iceland) 0
(First Round First Leg 1969–70)

HIGHEST AGGREGATE
Benfica (Portugal) 18, Dudelange (Luxembourg) 0
(Preliminary Round 1965–66)

MOST GOALS OVERALL
66 Raul (Real Madrid) 1995–2010.
60 Ruud Van Nistelrooy (PSV Eindhoven, Manchester United and Real Madrid) 1997–2009.
60 Filippo Inzaghi (Juventus, AC Milan) 1995–2010.
57 Andriy Shevchenko (Dynamo Kiev, AC Milan, Chelsea and Dynamo Kiev) 1994–2010.

CHAMPIONS LEAGUE BIGGEST WINS
Liverpool 8 Besiktas 0 6.11.2007
Juventus 7, Olympiakos 0 10.12.2003
Marseille 6, CKSA Moscow 0 17.9.93

FIRST TEAM TO SCORE SEVEN GOALS
Paris St Germain 7, Rosenborg 2 24.10.2000

HIGHEST AGGREGATE OF GOALS
Monaco 8, La Coruna 3 05.11.2003

HIGHEST SCORING DRAW
Hamburg 4, Juventus 4 13.9.2000

GREATEST COMEBACKS
Werder Bremen beat Anderlecht 5-3 after being three goals down in 33 minutes on 8.12.1993. They scored five goals in 23 second-half minutes.
La Coruna beat Paris St Germain 4-3 after being three goals down in 55 minutes on 7.3.2001. They scored four goals in 27 second-half minutes.
Liverpool after being three goals down in the first half on 25.5.2005 in the Champions League Final. They scored three goals in five second-half minutes and won the penalty shoot-out after extra time 3-2.
Liverpool 3 goals down to Basle in 29 minutes on 12.11.2002. They scored three second half goals in 24 minutes to draw 3-3.

MOST GOALS IN CHAMPIONS LEAGUE MATCH
4, Marco Van Basten, AC Milan v IFK Gothenburg (33, 53 (pen), 61, 62 mins) 4-0 25.11.1992.
4, Simone Inzaghi, Lazio v Marseille (17, 37, 38, 71 mins) 5-1 14.3.2000.
4, Ruud Van Nistelrooy, Manchester U v Sparta Prague (14, 25 (pen), 60, 90 mins) 4-1 3.11.2004.
4, Dado Prso, Monaco v La Coruna (26, 30, 45, 49, 23 mins) 8-3 5.11.2003.
4, Andriy Shevchenko, AC Milan at Fenerbahce (16, 52, 70, 76,60 mins) 4-0 23.11.2005.

MOST WINS WITH DIFFERENT CLUBS
Clarence Seedorf (Ajax) 1995; (Real Madrid) 1998: (AC Milan) 2003, 2007.

MOST WINNERS MEDALS
6 Francisco Gento (Real Madrid) 1956, 1957, 1958, 1959, 1960, 1966.
5 Alfredo Di Stefano (Real Madrid) 1956, 1957, 1958, 1959, 1960.
5 Jose Maria Zarraga (Real Madrid) 1956, 1957, 1958, 1959, 1960.

4 Jose-Hector Rial (Real Madrid) 1956, 1957, 1958, 1959.
4 Marquitos (Real Madrid) 1956, 1957, 1959, 1960
4 Phil Neal (Liverpool) 1977, 1978, 1981, 1984.

MOST GOALS SCORED IN FINALS
7 Alfredo Di Stefano (Real Madrid), 1956 (1), 1957 (1 pen), 1958 (1), 1959 (1), 1960 (3).
7 Ferenc Puskas (Real Madrid), 1960 (4), 1962 (3).

MOST FINAL APPEARANCES PER COUNTRY
Italy 26 (12 wins, 14 defeats)
Spain 21 (12 wins, 9 defeats)
England 17 (11 wins, 6 defeats)
Germany 14 (6 wins, 8 defeats).

MOST CLUB FINAL WINNERS
Real Madrid (Spain) 9 1956, 1957, 1958, 1959, 1960, 1966, 1998, 2000, 2002.
AC Milan (Italy) 7 1963, 1969, 1989, 1990, 1994, 2003, 2007.

MOST APPEARANCES IN FINAL
Real Madrid 12; AC Milan 11.

MOST EUROPEAN CUP APPEARANCES
Paolo Maldini (AC Milan)

Season	European Cup	UEFA Cup	Super Cup	WCC
1985–86	0	6	0	0
1987–88	0	2	0	0
1988–89	7	0	0	0
1989–90	8	0	2	1
1990–91	4	0	1	1
1992–93	10	0	0	0
1993–94	10	0	2	1
1994–95	11	0	1	1
1995–96	0	8	0	0
1996–97	6	0	0	0
1999–2000	6	0	0	0
2000–01	14	0	0	0
2001–02	0	4	0	0
2002–03	19	0	0	0
2003–04	9	0	1	1
2004–05	13	0	0	0
2005–06	9	0	0	0
2006–07	9	0	0	0
2007–08	4	0	0	0
2008–09	2	0	0	0
Total	141	20	7	5

MOST SUCCESSFUL MANAGER
Bob Paisley (Liverpool) 1977, 1978, 1981.

FASTEST GOALS SCORED IN CHAMPIONS LEAGUE
10.2 sec Roy Makaay for Bayern Munich v Real Madrid 7 March 2007.
20.07 sec Gilberto Silva for Arsenal at PSV Eindhoven 25 September 2002.
20.12 sec Alessandro Del Piero for Juventus at Manchester United 1 October 1997.

YOUNGEST CHAMPIONS LEAGUE GOALSCORER
Peter Ofori-Quaye for Olympiakos v Rosenborg at 17 years 195 days in 1997–98.

FASTEST HAT-TRICK SCORED IN CHAMPIONS LEAGUE
Mike Newell, 9 mins for Blackburn R v Rosenborg (4-1) 6.12.95.

MOST SUCCESSIVE CHAMPIONS LEAGUE APPEARANCES
Manchester U (England) 13 1996–97 – 2008–09.

MOST SUCCESSIVE EUROPEAN CUP APPEARANCES
Real Madrid (Spain) 15 1955–56 – 1969–70.

MOST SUCCESSIVE WINS IN THE CHAMPIONS LEAGUE
Barcelona (Spain) 11 2002–03.

LONGEST UNBEATEN RUN IN THE CHAMPIONS LEAGUE
Manchester U (England) 25 2007–08 – 2009 (Final).

REINSTATED WINNERS EXCLUDED FROM NEXT COMPETITION
1993 Marseille originally stripped of title. This was rescinded but they were not allowed to compete the following season.

TOP TEN PREMIER LEAGUE AVERAGE ATTENDANCES 2009–10

1	Manchester U	74,864
2	Arsenal	59,927
3	Manchester C	45,512
4	Liverpool	42,863
5	Chelsea	41,422
6	Sunderland	40,355
7	Aston Villa	38,573
8	Everton	36,725
9	Tottenham H	35,794
10	West Ham U	33,683

TOP TEN FOOTBALL LEAGUE AVERAGE ATTENDANCES 2009–10

1	Newcastle U	43,387
2	Derby Co	29,230
3	Sheffield U	25,120
4	Leeds U	24,817
5	Norwich C	24,671
6	Leicester C	23,942
7	Nottingham F	23,831
8	Sheffield W	23,179
9	WBA	22,199
10	Southampton	20,982

TOP TEN AVERAGE ATTENDANCES

1	Manchester United	2006–07	75,826
2	Manchester United	2007–08	75,691
3	Manchester United	2008–09	75,308
4	Manchester United	2009–10	74,863
5	Manchester United	2005–06	68,765
6	Manchester United	2004–05	67,871
7	Manchester United	2003–04	67,641
8	Manchester United	2002–03	67,630
9	Manchester United	2001–02	67,586
10	Manchester United	2000–01	67,544

TOP TEN AVERAGE WORLD CUP FINAL CROWDS

1	In USA	1994	68,604
2	In Brazil	1950	60,772
3	In Germany	2006	52,416
4	In Mexico	1970	52,311
5	In England	1966	50,458
6	In South Africa	2010	49,670
7	In Italy	1990	48,368
8	In Mexico	1986	46,956
9	In West Germany	1974	46,684
10	In France	1998	43,366

TOP TEN ALL-TIME ENGLAND CAPS

1	Peter Shilton	125
2	David Beckham	115
3	Bobby Moore	108
4	Bobby Charlton	106
5	Billy Wright	105
6	Bryan Robson	90
7	Michael Owen	89
8	Kenny Sansom	86
9	Gary Neville	85
10	Ray Wilkins	84

TOP TEN ALL-TIME ENGLAND GOALSCORERS

1	Bobby Charlton	49
2	Gary Lineker	48
3	Jimmy Greaves	44
4	Michael Owen	40
5	Tom Finney	30
6	Nat Lofthouse	30
7	Alan Shearer	30
8	Vivian Woodward	29
9	Steve Bloomer	28
10	David Platt	27

GOALKEEPING RECORDS
(without conceding a goal)

BRITISH RECORD (all competitive games)
Chris Woods, Rangers, in 1196 minutes from 26 November 1986 to 31 January 1987.

FA PREMIER LEAGUE
Edwin Van der Sar (Manchester U) in 1311 minutes during the 2008–09 season.

FOOTBALL LEAGUE
Steve Death, Reading, 1103 minutes from 24 March to 18 August 1979.

MOST CLEAN SHEETS IN A SEASON
Peter Cech (Chelsea) 24 2004–05

MOST CLEAN SHEETS OVERALL IN PREMIER LEAGUE
David James (Liverpool, Aston Villa, West Ham U, Manchester C and Portsmouth) 171 games.

MOST GOALS FOR IN A SEASON

FA PREMIER LEAGUE		Goals	Games
2009–10	Chelsea	103	38
FOOTBALL LEAGUE			
Division 4			
1960–61	Peterborough U	134	46
SCOTTISH PREMIER LEAGUE			
2003–04	Celtic	105	38
SCOTTISH LEAGUE			
Division 2			
1937–38	Raith R	142	34

MOST GOALS AGAINST IN A SEASON

FA PREMIER LEAGUE		Goals	Games
1993–94	Swindon T	100	42
FOOTBALL LEAGUE			
Division 2			
1898–99	Darwen	141	34
SCOTTISH PREMIER LEAGUE			
1999–2000	Aberdeen	83	36
SCOTTISH LEAGUE			
Division 2			
1931–32	Edinburgh C	146	38

MOST LEAGUE GOALS IN A SEASON

FA PREMIER LEAGUE		Goals	Games
1993–94	Andy Cole (Newcastle U)	34	40
1994–95	Alan Shearer (Blackburn R)	34	42
FOOTBALL LEAGUE			
Division 1			
1927–28	Dixie Dean (Everton)	60	39
Division 2			
1926–27	George Camsell (Middlesbrough)	59	37
Division 3(S)			
1936–37	Joe Payne (Luton T)	55	39
Division 3(N)			
1936–37	Ted Harston (Mansfield T)	55	41
Division 3			
1959–60	Derek Reeves (Southampton)	39	46
Division 4			
1960–61	Terry Bly (Peterborough U)	52	46
FA CUP			
1887–88	Jimmy Ross (Preston NE)	20	8
LEAGUE CUP			
1986–87	Clive Allen (Tottenham H)	12	9
SCOTTISH PREMIER LEAGUE			
2000–01	Henrik Larsson (Celtic)	35	37
SCOTTISH LEAGUE			
Division 1			
1931–32	William McFadyen (Motherwell)	52	34
Division 2			
1927–28	Jim Smith (Ayr U)	66	38

MOST FA CUP FINAL GOALS

Ian Rush (Liverpool) 5: 1986(2), 1989(2), 1992(1)

SCORED IN EVERY PREMIERSHIP GAME

Arsenal 2001–02 38 matches

FEWEST GOALS FOR IN A SEASON

FA PREMIER LEAGUE		Goals	Games
2007–08	Derby Co	20	38
FOOTBALL LEAGUE			
Division 2			
1899–1900	Loughborough T	18	34
SCOTTISH PREMIER LEAGUE			
2001–02	St Johnstone	24	38
SCOTTISH LEAGUE			
New Division 1			
1980–81	Stirling Alb	18	39

FEWEST GOALS AGAINST IN A SEASON

FA PREMIER LEAGUE		Goals	Games
2004–05	Chelsea	15	38
FOOTBALL LEAGUE			
Division 1			
1978–79	Liverpool	16	42
SCOTTISH PREMIER LEAGUE			
2001–02	Celtic	18	38
SCOTTISH LEAGUE			
Division 1			
1913–14	Celtic	14	38

MOST LEAGUE GOALS IN A CAREER

FOOTBALL LEAGUE			
Arthur Rowley	Goals	Games	Season
WBA	4	24	1946–48
Fulham	27	56	1948–50
Leicester C	251	303	1950–58
Shrewsbury T	152	236	1958–65
	434	619	
SCOTTISH LEAGUE			
Jimmy McGrory			
Celtic	1	3	1922–23
Clydebank	13	30	1923–24
Celtic	396	375	1924–38
	410	408	

MOST HAT-TRICKS

Career
34 Dixie Dean (Tranmere R, Everton, Notts Co, England)

Division 1 (one season post-war)
6 Jimmy Greaves (Chelsea), 1960–61

Three for one team one match
West, Spouncer, Hooper, Nottingham F v Leicester Fosse, Division 1, 21 April 1909
Barnes, Ambler, Davies, Wrexham v Hartlepools U, Division 4, 3 March 1962
Adcock, Stewart, White, Manchester C v Huddersfield T, Division 2, 7 Nov 1987
Loasby, Smith, Wells, Northampton T v Walsall, Division 3S, 5 Nov 1927
Bowater, Hoyland, Readman, Mansfield T v Rotherham U, Division 3N, 27 Dec 1932

MOST CUP GOALS IN A CAREER

FA CUP (Pre-Second World war)
Henry Cursham 48 (Notts Co)

FA CUP (post-war)
Ian Rush 43 (Chester, Liverpool)

LEAGUE CUP
Geoff Hurst 49 (West Ham U, Stoke C)
Ian Rush 49 (Chester, Liverpool, Newcastle U)

GOALS PER GAME (Football League to 1991–92)

Goals per game	Division 1		Division 2		Division 3		Division 4		Division 3(S)		Division 3(N)	
	Games	Goals	Games	Goals	Games	Goals	Games	Goals	Games	Goals	Games	Goals
0	2465	0	2665	0	1446	0	1438	0	997	0	803	0
1	5606	5606	5836	5836	3225	3225	3106	3106	2073	2073	1914	1914
2	8275	16550	8609	17218	4569	9138	4441	8882	3314	6628	2939	5878
3	7731	23193	7842	23526	3784	11352	4041	12123	2996	8988	2922	8766
4	6229	24920	5897	23588	2837	11348	2784	11136	2445	9780	2410	9640
5	3752	18755	3634	18170	1566	7830	1506	7530	1554	7770	1599	7995
6	2137	12822	2007	12042	769	4614	786	4716	870	5220	930	5580
7	1092	7644	1001	7007	357	2499	336	2352	451	3157	461	3227
8	542	4336	376	3008	135	1080	143	1144	209	1672	221	1768
9	197	1773	164	1476	64	576	35	315	76	684	102	918
10	83	830	68	680	13	130	8	80	33	330	45	450
11	37	407	19	209	2	22	7	77	15	165	15	165
12	12	144	17	204	1	12	0	0	7	84	8	96
13	4	52	4	52	0	0	0	0	2	26	4	52
14	2	28	1	14	0	0	0	0	0	0	0	0
17	0	0	0	0	0	0	0	0	0	0	1	17
	38164	117061	38140	113030	18768	51826	18631	51461	15042	46577	14374	46466

New Overall Totals (since 1992)		Totals (up to 1991–92)		Complete Overall Totals (since 1888–89)	
Games	36624	Games	143119	Games	179743
Goals	94285	Goals	426421	Goals	520706

Extensive research by statisticians has unearthed seven results from early years of the Football League which differ from the original scores. These are 26 January 1889 Wolverhampton W 5 Everton 0 (not 4-0), 16 March 1889 Notts Co 3 Derby Co 5 (not 2-5), 4 January 1896 Arsenal 5 Loughborough 0 (not 6-0), 28 November 1896 Leicester Fosse 4 Walsall 2 (not 4-1), 21 April 1900 Burslem Port Vale v Lincoln City 2-1 (not 2-0), 25 December 1902 Glossop NE 3 Stockport Co 0 (not 3-1), 26 April 1913 Hull C 2 Leicester C 0 (not 2-1).

GOALS PER GAME (from 1992–93)

Goals per game	Premier		Championship/Div 1		League One/Div 2		League Two/Div 3	
	Games	Goals	Games	Goals	Games	Goals	Games	Goals
0	624	0	836	0	791	0	786	0
1	1333	1333	1868	1868	1857	1857	1887	1887
2	1753	3506	2540	5080	2537	5074	2476	4952
3	1455	4365	2098	6294	2181	6543	2115	6345
4	1008	4032	1365	5460	1385	5540	1282	5128
5	500	2500	751	3755	718	3590	649	3245
6	246	1476	330	1980	287	1722	300	1800
7	105	735	105	735	127	889	116	812
8	49	392	33	264	35	280	39	312
9	10	90	5	45	15	135	11	99
10	2	20	3	30	3	30	3	30
11	1	11	2	22	0	0	2	22
	7086	18460	9936	25533	9936	25660	9666	24632

A CENTURY OF LEAGUE AND CUP GOALS IN CONSECUTIVE SEASONS

George Camsell	*League*	*Cup*	*Season*
Middlesbrough	59	5	1926–27
(101 goals)	33	4	1927–28

(Camsell's cup goals were all scored in the FA Cup.)

Steve Bull			
Wolverhampton W	34	18	1987–88
(102 goals)	37	13	1988–89

(Bull had 12 in the Sherpa Van Trophy, 3 Littlewoods Cup, 3 FA Cup in 1987–88; 11 Sherpa Van Trophy, 2 Littlewoods Cup in 1988–89.)

PENALTIES

Most in a Season (individual)

Division 1		*Goals*	*Season*
Francis Lee (Manchester C)		13	1971–72

Most awarded in one game

Five Crystal Palace (4 – 1 scored, 3 missed)
v Brighton & HA (1 scored), Div 2 1988–89

Most saved in a Season

Division 1
Paul Cooper (Ipswich T)   8 (of 10)   1979–80

MOST GOALS IN A GAME

FA PREMIER LEAGUE
19 Sept 1999 Alan Shearer (Newcastle U)
5 goals v Sheffield W
4 Mar 1995 Andy Cole (Manchester U)
5 goals v Ipswich T
22 Nov 2009 Jermain Defoe (Tottenham H)
5 goals v Wigan Ath

FOOTBALL LEAGUE
Division 1
14 Dec 1935 Ted Drake (Arsenal) 7 goals v Aston V
Division 2
5 Feb 1955 Tommy Briggs (Blackburn R)
7 goals v Bristol R
23 Feb 1957 Neville Coleman (Stoke C) 7 goals v
Lincoln C
Division 3(S)
13 April 1936 Joe Payne (Luton T) 10 goals v Bristol R
Division 3(N)
26 Dec 1935 Bunny Bell (Tranmere R)
9 goals v Oldham Ath

Division 3
16 Sept 1969 Steve Earle (Fulham) 5 goals v Halifax T
24 April 1965 Barrie Thomas (Scunthorpe U)
5 goals v Luton T
20 Nov 1965 Keith East (Swindon T)
5 goals v Mansfield T
2 Oct 1971 Alf Wood (Shrewsbury T)
5 goals v Blackburn R
10 Sept 1983 Tony Caldwell (Bolton W)
5 goals v Walsall
4 May 1987 Andy Jones (Port Vale)
5 goals v Newport Co
3 April 1990 Steve Wilkinson (Mansfield T)
5 goals v Birmingham C
5 Sept 1998 Giuliano Grazioli (Peterborough U)
5 goals v Barnet
6 April 2002 Lee Jones (Wrexham)
5 goals v Cambridge U

Division 4
26 Dec 1962 Bert Lister (Oldham Ath)
6 goals v Southport

FA CUP
20 Nov 1971 Ted MacDougall (Bournemouth)
9 goals v Margate (*1st Round*)

LEAGUE CUP
25 Oct 1989 Frankie Bunn (Oldham Ath)
6 goals v Scarborough

SCOTTISH LEAGUE
Premier Division
17 Nov 1984 Paul Sturrock (Dundee U)
5 goals v Morton
Premier League
23 Aug 1996 Marco Negri (Rangers) 5 goals v
Dundee U
Division 1
14 Sept 1928 Jimmy McGrory (Celtic)
8 goals v Dunfermline Ath
Division 2
1 Oct 1927 Owen McNally (Arthurlie)
8 goals v Armadale
2 Jan 1930 Jim Dyet (King's Park)
8 goals v Forfar Ath
18 April 1936 John Calder (Morton)
8 goals v Raith R
20 Aug 1937 Norman Hayward (Raith R)
8 goals v Brechin C

SCOTTISH CUP
12 Sept 1885 John Petrie (Arbroath)
13 goals v Bon Accord (*1st Round*)

LONGEST SEQUENCE OF CONSECUTIVE SCORING (Individual)

FA PREMIER LEAGUE
Ruud Van Nistelrooy
(Manchester U)   15 in 10 games   2003–04
FOOTBALL LEAGUE RECORD
Tom Phillipson
(Wolverhampton W)   23 in 13 games   1926–27

LONGEST UNBEATEN SEQUENCE

FA PREMIER LEAGUE	Team	Games
May 2003–October 2004	Arsenal	49
FOOTBALL LEAGUE **Division 1**		
Nov 1977–Dec 1978	Nottingham F	42

LONGEST UNBEATEN CUP SEQUENCE

Liverpool	25 rounds	League/Milk Cup	1980–84

LONGEST UNBEATEN SEQUENCE IN A SEASON

FA PREMIER LEAGUE	Team	Games
2003–04	Arsenal	38
FOOTBALL LEAGUE **Division 1**		
1920–21	Burnley	30

LONGEST UNBEATEN START TO A SEASON

FA PREMIER LEAGUE	Team	Games
2003–04	Arsenal	38
FOOTBALL LEAGUE **Division 1**		
1973–74	Leeds U	29
1987–88	Liverpool	29

LONGEST SEQUENCE WITHOUT A WIN IN A SEASON

FA PREMIER LEAGUE	Team	Games
2007–08	Derby Co	32
FOOTBALL LEAGUE **Division 2**	Team	Games
1983–84	Cambridge U	31

LONGEST SEQUENCE WITHOUT A WIN FROM SEASON'S START

FOOTBALL LEAGUE Division 4	Team	Games
1970–71	Newport Co	25

LONGEST SEQUENCE OF CONSECUTIVE DEFEATS

FOOTBALL LEAGUE Division 2	Team	Games
1898–99	Darwen	18

LONGEST WINNING SEQUENCE

FA PREMIER LEAGUE	Team	Games
2001–02 and 2002–03	Arsenal	14
FOOTBALL LEAGUE **Division 2**		
1904–05	Manchester U	14
1905–06	Bristol C	14
1950–51	Preston NE	14
FROM SEASON'S START **Division 3**		
1985–86	Reading	13
SCOTTISH PREMIER LEAGUE		
2003–04	Celtic	25

HIGHEST WINS

Highest win in a First-Class Match
(*Scottish Cup 1st Round*)
Arbroath   36 Bon Accord   0 12 Sept 1885

Highest win in an International Match
England   13 Ireland   0 18 Feb 1882

Highest win in a FA Cup Match
Preston NE   26 Hyde U   0 15 Oct 1887
(*1st Round*)

Highest win in a League Cup Match
West Ham U   10 Bury   0 25 Oct 1983
(*2nd Round, 2nd Leg*)
Liverpool   10 Fulham   0 23 Sept 1986
(*2nd Round, 1st Leg*)

Highest win in an FA Premier League Match
Manchester U 9 Ipswich T   0 4 Mar 1995
Nottingham F 1 Manchester U 8 6 Feb 1999

Highest win in a Football League Match
Division 2 – highest home win
Newcastle U   13 Newport Co 0 5 Oct 1946
Division 3(N) – highest home win
Stockport Co 13 Halifax T   0 6 Jan 1934
Division 2 – highest away win
Burslem Port Vale 0 Sheffield U 10 10 Dec 1892

Highest wins in a Scottish League Match
Scottish Premier League – highest home win
Rangers   7 St Johnstone 0 8 Nov 1998
Celtic   7 Aberdeen   0 16 Oct 1999
Celtic   7 Aberdeen   0 2 Nov 2002
Hibernian   7 Livingston   0 8 Feb 2006
Scottish Division 2 – highest home win
Airdrieonians   15 Dundee Wanderers 1 1 Dec 1894
Scottish Premier League – away win
Hamilton A   0 Celtic   8 5 Nov 1988

MOST HOME WINS IN A SEASON

Brentford won all 21 games in Division 3(S), 1929–30

RECORD AWAY WINS IN A SEASON

Doncaster R won 18 of 21 games in Division 3(N), 1946–47

CONSECUTIVE AWAY WINS

FA PREMIER LEAGUE
Chelsea 9 games 2004–05

FOOTBALL LEAGUE
Division 1
Tottenham H 10 games (1959–60 (2), 1960–61 (8))

MOST WINS IN A SEASON

FA PREMIER LEAGUE		Wins	Games
2004–05	Chelsea	29	38
2005–06	Chelsea	29	38
FOOTBALL LEAGUE			
Division 3(N)			
1946–47	Doncaster R	33	42
SCOTTISH PREMIER LEAGUE			
2001–02	Celtic	33	38
SCOTTISH LEAGUE			
Division 1			
1920–21	Rangers	35	42

MOST POINTS IN A SEASON
(under old system of two points for a win)

FOOTBALL LEAGUE		Points	Games
Division 4			
1975–76	Lincoln C	74	46
SCOTTISH LEAGUE			
Division 1			
1920–21	Rangers	76	42

FEWEST WINS IN A SEASON

FA PREMIER LEAGUE		Wins	Games
2007–08	Derby Co	1	38
FOOTBALL LEAGUE			
Division 2			
1899–1900	Loughborough T	1	34
SCOTTISH PREMIER LEAGUE			
1998–99	Dunfermline Ath	4	36
SCOTTISH LEAGUE			
Division 1			
1891–92	Vale of Leven	0	22

UNDEFEATED AT HOME OVERALL

Liverpool 85 games (63 League, 9 League Cup, 7 European, 6 FA Cup), Jan 1978–Jan 1981

UNDEFEATED AT HOME LEAGUE

Chelsea 86 games, March 2004–October 2008

UNDEFEATED IN A SEASON

FA PREMIER LEAGUE
2003–04   Arsenal   38 games

FOOTBALL LEAGUE
1889–90   Preston NE   22 games

Division 2
1893–94   Liverpool   22 games

UNDEFEATED AWAY

Arsenal 19 games FA Premier League 2001–02 and 2003–04 (only Preston NE with 11 in 1888–89 had previously remained unbeaten away) in the top flight

HIGHEST AGGREGATE SCORES

FA PREMIER LEAGUE
Portsmouth   7 Reading   4 29 Sept 2007

Highest Aggregate Score England
Division 3(N)
Tranmere R   13 Oldham Ath   4 26 Dec 1935

Highest Aggregate Score Scotland
Division 2
Airdrieonians   15 Dundee Wanderers 1 1 Dec 1894

MOST POINTS IN A SEASON
(three points for a win)

FA PREMIER LEAGUE		Points	Games
2004–05	Chelsea	95	38
FOOTBALL LEAGUE			
Championship			
2005–06	Reading	106	46
SCOTTISH PREMIER LEAGUE			
2001–02	Celtic	103	38
SCOTTISH LEAGUE			
New Division 3			
2004–05	Gretna	98	36

FEWEST POINTS IN A SEASON

FA PREMIER LEAGUE		Points	Games
2007–08	Derby Co	11	38
FOOTBALL LEAGUE			
Division 2			
1904–05	Doncaster R	8	34
1899–1900	Loughborough T	8	34
SCOTTISH PREMIER LEAGUE			
2005–06	Livingston	18	38
SCOTTISH LEAGUE			
Division 1			
1954–55	Stirling Alb	6	30

ONE DEFEAT IN A SEASON

FA PREMIER LEAGUE		Defeats	Games
2004–05	Chelsea	1	38

FOOTBALL LEAGUE Division 1			
1990–91	Arsenal	1	38

SCOTTISH PREMIER LEAGUE			
2001–02	Celtic	1	38

SCOTTISH LEAGUE Premier Division Division 1			
1920–21	Rangers	1	42
Division 2			
1956–57	Clyde	1	36
1962–63	Morton	1	36
1967–68	St Mirren	1	36
New Division 2			
1975–76	Raith R	1	26

MOST DEFEATS IN A SEASON

FA PREMIER LEAGUE		Defeats	Games
1994–95	Ipswich T	29	42
2005–06	Sunderland	29	38
2007–08	Derby Co	29	38

FOOTBALL LEAGUE Division 3			
1997–98	Doncaster R	34	46

SCOTTISH PREMIER LEAGUE			
2005–06	Livingston	28	38

SCOTTISH LEAGUE New Division 1			
1992–93	Cowdenbeath	34	44

NO DEFEATS IN A SEASON

FA PREMIER LEAGUE		
2003–04	Arsenal	won 26, drew 12

FOOTBALL LEAGUE Division 1		
1888–89	Preston NE	won 18, drew 4
Division 2		
1893–94	Liverpool	won 22, drew 6

SCOTTISH LEAGUE DIVISION 1		
1898–99	Rangers	won 18

SENDINGS-OFF

SEASON
451 (League alone) 2003–04
(Before rescinded cards taken into account)

DAY
19 (League) 13 Dec 2003

FA CUP FINAL
Kevin Moran, Manchester U v Everton 1985
Jose Antonio Reyes, Arsenal v Manchester U 2005

QUICKEST
FA Premier League
Andreas Johansson Wigan Ath v Arsenal 7 May 2006
and Keith Gillespie Sheffield U v Reading 20 January
2007 both in 10 seconds
Football League
Walter Boyd, Swansea C v Darlington Div 3 as
substitute in zero seconds 23 Nov 1999

MOST IN ONE GAME
Five: Chesterfield (2) v Plymouth Arg (3) 22 Feb 1997
Five: Wigan Ath (1) v Bristol R (4) 2 Dec 1997
Five: Exeter C (3) v Cambridge U (2) 25 Nov 2002

MOST IN ONE TEAM
Wigan Ath (1) v Bristol R (4) 2 Dec 1997
Hereford U (4) v Northampton T (0) 6 Sept 1992

MOST DRAWN GAMES IN A SEASON

FA PREMIER LEAGUE		Draws	Games
1993–94	Manchester C	18	42
1993–94	Sheffield U	18	42
1994–95	Southampton	18	42

FOOTBALL LEAGUE Division 1			
1978–79	Norwich C	23	42
Division 3			
1997–98	Cardiff C	23	46
1997–98	Hartlepool U	23	46
Division 4			
1986–87	Exeter C	23	46

SCOTTISH PREMIER LEAGUE			
1998–99	Dunfermline Ath	16	38

SCOTTISH LEAGUE Premier Division			
1993–94	Aberdeen	21	44
New Division 1			
1985–87	East Fife	21	44

MOST SUCCESSFUL MANAGERS

Sir Alex Ferguson CBE
Manchester U
23 major trophies in 19 seasons:
11 Premier League, 5 FA Cup, 4 League Cup,
2 European Cup, 1 Cup-Winners' Cup.

Aberdeen
1976–86 – 9 trophies:
3 League, 4 Scottish Cup, 1 League Cup, 1 Cup-
Winners' Cup.

Bob Paisley – Liverpool
1974–83 – 13 trophies:
6 League, 3 European Cup, 3 League Cup, 1 UEFA
Cup.

Bill Struth – Rangers
1920–54 – 30 trophies:
18 League, 10 Scottish Cup, 2 League Cup

LEAGUE CHAMPIONSHIP HAT-TRICKS

Huddersfield T	1923–24 to 1925–26
Arsenal	1932–33 to 1934–35
Liverpool	1981–82 to 1983–84
Manchester U	1998–99 to 2000–01
Manchester U	2006–07 to 2008–09

MOST FA CUP MEDALS

Ashley Cole (Arsenal 2002, 2003, 2005, Chelsea 2007, 2009, 2010) 6

MOST LEAGUE MEDALS

Ryan Giggs (Manchester U) 11: 1993, 1994, 1996, 1997, 1999, 2000, 2001, 2003, 2007, 2008 and 2009

MOST SENIOR MATCHES

1390 Peter Shilton (1005 League, 86 FA Cup, 102
League Cup, 125 Internationals, 13 Under-23, 4
Football League XI, 20 European Cup, 7 Texaco Cup,
5 Simod Cup, 4 European Super Cup, 4 UEFA Cup, 3
Screen Sport Super Cup, 3 Zenith Data Systems Cup,
2 Autoglass Trophy, 2 Charity Shield, 2 Full Members
Cup, 1 Anglo-Italian Cup, 1 Football League play-offs,
1 World Club Championship)

MOST LEAGUE APPEARANCES
(750+ matches)

1005 Peter Shilton (286 Leicester City, 110 Stoke City, 202 Nottingham Forest, 188 Southampton, 175 Derby County, 34 Plymouth Argyle, 1 Bolton Wanderers, 9 Leyton Orient) 1966–97

931 Tony Ford (355 Grimsby T, 9 Sunderland (loan), 112 Stoke C, 114 WBA, 68 Grimsby T, 5 Bradford C (loan), 76 Scunthorpe U, 103 Mansfield T, 89 Rochdale) 1975–2002

909 Graeme Armstrong (204 Stirling A, 83 Berwick R, 353 Meadowbank T, 268 Stenhousemuir, 1 Alloa) 1975–2001

863 Tommy Hutchison (165 Blackpool, 314 Coventry City, 46 Manchester City, 92 Burnley, 178 Swansea City, 68 Alloa) 1965–91

824 Terry Paine (713 Southampton, 111 Hereford United) 1957–77

790 Neil Redfearn (35 Bolton W, 10 Lincoln C (loan), 90 Lincoln C, 46 Doncaster R, 57 Crystal Palace, 24 Watford, 62 Oldham Ath, 292 Barnsley, 30 Charlton Ath, 17 Bradford C, 22 Wigan Ath, 42 Halifax T, 54 Boston U, 9 Rochdale) 1982–2004

783 Graham Alexander (Scunthorpe U, 159, Luton T 150, Preston NE 352, Burnley 122).

782 Robbie James (484 Swansea C, 48 Stoke C, 87 QPR, 23 Leicester C, 89 Bradford C, 51 Cardiff C) 1973–94

777 Alan Oakes (565 Manchester C, 211 Chester C, 1 Port Vale) 1959–84

774 Dave Beasant (340 Wimbledon, 20 Newcastle U, 133 Chelsea, 6 Grimsby T (loan), 4 Wolverhampton W (loan), 88 Southampton, 139 Nottingham F, 27 Portsmouth, 1 Tottenham H (loan), 16 Brighton & HA) 1979–2003

771 John Burridge (27 Workington, 134 Blackpool, 65 Aston Villa, 6 Southend U (loan), 88 Crystal Palace, 39 QPR, 74 Wolverhampton W, 6 Derby Co (loan), 109 Sheffield U, 62 Southampton, 67 Newcastle U, 65 Hibernian, 3 Scarborough, 4 Lincoln C, 3 Aberdeen, 3 Dumbarton, 3 Falkirk, 4 Manchester C, 3 Darlington, 6 Queen of the South) 1968–96

770 John Trollope (all for Swindon Town) 1960–80†

764 Jimmy Dickinson (all for Portsmouth) 1946–65

763 Stuart McCall (395 Bradford C, 103 Everton, 194 Rangers, 71 Sheffield U) 1982–2004

761 Roy Sproson (all for Port Vale) 1950–72

760 Mick Tait (64 Oxford U, 106 Carlisle U, 33 Hull C, 240 Portsmouth, 99 Reading, 79 Darlington, 139 Hartlepool U) 1975–97

758 Ray Clemence (48 Scunthorpe United, 470 Liverpool, 240 Tottenham Hotspur) 1966–87

758 Billy Bonds (95 Charlton Ath, 663 West Ham U) 1964–88

757 Pat Jennings (48 Watford, 472 Tottenham Hotspur, 237 Arsenal) 1963–86

757 Frank Worthington (171 Huddersfield T, 210 Leicester C, 84 Bolton W, 75 Birmingham C, 32 Leeds U, 19 Sunderland, 34 Southampton, 31 Brighton & HA, 59 Tranmere R, 23 Preston NE, 19 Stockport Co) 1966–88

752 Wayne Allison (84 Halifax T, 7 Watford, 195 Bristol C, 101 Swindon T, 74 Huddersfield T, 103 Tranmere R, 73 Sheffield U, 115 Chesterfield)

† record for one club

CONSECUTIVE
401 Harold Bell (401 Tranmere R; 459 in all games) 1946–55

YOUNGEST PLAYERS

FA Premier League appearance
Matthew Briggs, 16 years 65 days, Fulham v Middlesbrough, 13.5.2007.

FA Premier League scorer
James Vaughan, 16 years 271 days, Everton v Crystal Palace 10.4.2005

Football League appearance
Reuben Noble-Lazarus 15 years 45 days, Barnsley v Ipswich T, FL Championship 30.9.2008

Football League scorer
Ronnie Dix, 15 years 180 days, Bristol Rovers v Norwich City, Division 3S, 3.3.28.

Division 1 appearance
Derek Forster, 15 years 185 days, Sunderland v Leicester City, 22.8.64.

Division 1 scorer
Jason Dozzell, 16 years 57 days as substitute Ipswich Town v Coventry City, 4.2.84

Division 1 hat-tricks
Alan Shearer, 17 years 240 days, Southampton v Arsenal, 9.4.88
Jimmy Greaves, 17 years 10 months, Chelsea v Portsmouth, 25.12.57

FA Cup appearance (any round)
Andy Awford, 15 years 88 days as substitute Worcester City v Boreham Wood, 3rd Qual. rd, 10.10.87

FA Cup proper appearance
Luke Freeman, 15 years 273 days, Gillingham v Barnet 10.11.2007

FA Cup Final appearance
Curtis Weston, 17 years 119 days, Millwall v Manchester U, 2004

FA Cup Final scorer
Norman Whiteside, 18 years 18 days, Manchester United v Brighton & Hove Albion, 1983

FA Cup Final captain
David Nish, 21 years 212 days, Leicester City v Manchester City, 1969

League Cup appearance
Chris Coward, 16 years 30 days, Stockport Co v Sheffield W, 2005

League Cup Final scorer
Norman Whiteside, 17 years 324 days, Manchester United v Liverpool, 1983

League Cup Final captain
Barry Venison, 20 years 7 months 8 days, Sunderland v Norwich City, 1985

Scottish Premier League appearance
Scott Robinson 16 years 45 days Hearts v Inverness CT 26.4.2008

Scottish Premier League scorer
Fraser Fyvie 16 years 306 days Aberdeen v Hearts 27.1.2010.

OLDEST PLAYERS

FA Premier League appearance
John Burridge 43 years 5 months, Manchester C v QPR 14.5.1995

Football League appearance
Neil McBain, 52 years 4 months, New Brighton v Hartlepools United, Div 3N, 15.3.47 (McBain was New Brighton's manager and had to play in an emergency)

Division 1 appearance
Stanley Matthews, 50 years 5 days, Stoke City v Fulham, 6.2.65

INTERNATIONAL RECORDS

MOST GOALS IN AN INTERNATIONAL

Record/World Cup	Archie Thompson (Australia) 13 goals v American Samoa	11.4.2001
England	Malcolm Macdonald (Newcastle U) 5 goals v Cyprus, at Wembley	16.4.1975
	Willie Hall (Tottenham H) 5 goals v Ireland, at Old Trafford	16.11.1938
	Steve Bloomer (Derby Co) 5 goals v Wales, at Cardiff	16.3.1896
	Howard Vaughton (Aston Villa) 5 goals v Ireland, at Belfast	18.2.1882
Northern Ireland	Joe Bambrick (Linfield) 6 goals v Wales, at Belfast	1.2.1930
Wales	John Price (Wrexham) 4 goals v Ireland, at Wrexham	25.2.1882
	Mel Charles (Cardiff C) 4 goals v Ireland, at Cardiff	11.4.1962
	Ian Edwards (Chester) 4 goals v Malta, at Wrexham	25.10.1978

MOST GOALS IN AN INTERNATIONAL CAREER

		Goals	Games
England	Bobby Charlton (Manchester U)	49	106
Scotland	Denis Law (Huddersfield T, Manchester C, Torino, Manchester U)	30	55
	Kenny Dalglish (Celtic, Liverpool)	30	102
Northern Ireland	David Healy (Manchester U, Preston NE, Leeds U, Fulham, Sunderland)	35	80
Wales	Ian Rush (Liverpool, Juventus)	28	73
Republic of Ireland	Robbie Keane (Wolverhampton W, Coventry C, Internazionale, Leeds U, Tottenham H, Liverpool, Tottenham H)	43	99

HIGHEST SCORES

Record/World Cup Match	Australia	31	American Samoa	0	2001
European Championship	San Marino	0	Germany	13	2006
Olympic Games	Denmark	17	France	1	1908
	Germany	16	USSR	0	1912
Other International Match	Libya	21	Oman	0	1966
European Cup	Feyenoord	12	K R Reykjavik	2	1969
European Cup-Winners' Cup	Sporting Lisbon	16	Apoel Nicosia	1	1963
Fairs & UEFA Cups	Ajax	14	Red Boys	0	1984

GOALSCORING RECORDS

World Cup Final	Geoff Hurst (England) 3 goals v West Germany	1966
World Cup Final tournament	Just Fontaine (France) 13 goals	1958
Career	Artur Friedenreich (Brazil) 1329 goals	1910–30
	Pele (Brazil) 1281 goals	*1956–78
	Franz 'Bimbo' Binder (Austria, Germany) 1006 goals	1930–50
World Cup Finals fastest	Hakan Sukur (Turkey) 10.8 secs v South Korea	2002

*Pele subsequently scored two goals in Testimonial matches making his total 1283.

MOST CAPPED INTERNATIONALS IN THE BRITISH ISLES

England	Peter Shilton	125 appearances	1970–90
Northern Ireland	Pat Jennings	119 appearances	1964–86
Scotland	Kenny Dalglish	102 appearances	1971–86
Wales	Neville Southall	92 appearances	1982–97
Republic of Ireland	Shay Given	103 appearances	1996–2010
	Kevin Kilbane	103 appearances	1998–2010

LONDON INTERNATIONAL VENUES

Eleven different venues in the London area have staged full England international games: Kennington Oval, Richmond Athletic Ground, Queen's Club, Crystal Palace, Craven Cottage, The Den, Stamford Bridge, Highbury, Wembley, Selhurst Park, White Hart Lane and Upton Park.

FOOTBALL TITLES FOR YOUR REFERENCE LIBRARY

THE MEN WHO NEVER WERE by Jack Rollin & Tony Brown
The Football League season of 1939–40 started on August 26th with a
full programme of Football League fixtures. Many clubs had newly
signed players on duty. With the declaration of war on September 2nd
the official League programme came to an end and the records of the
three matches were expunged from the records. Therefore, many of
the new players do not appear in a club's official records. The book
starts with the story of the 1939 close season and recounts the effects
of the outbreak of war on the players and the clubs. Many men
enlisted in the services of course. With many of them based at
Aldershot, the local club enjoyed a succession of star players as guests
in their team! Statistical content includes full results, scorers and line-
ups for the Football League and War Cup games of 1939–40 with details of all the players that
took part. Also included are the results and dates of the regional League competitions.
ISBN 978-1-905891-11-5. £12 plus £1.50 p&p.

THE FORGOTTEN CUP by Jack Rollin & Tony Brown
1945–46 was a transitional season for football. The end of the war in
Europe and the Far East came too late for many professional players
to be demobbed from the services, so the Football League did not
resume until 1946–47. However, a full programme of FA Cup games
took place. The rounds proper featured the only two-legged ties in the
history of the competition. Huge attendances watched the games. *The
Forgotten FA Cup* tells the full story of the 1945–46 competition,
using player reminiscences and contemporary accounts. Other
contents include the full results of the qualifying rounds, complete
line-ups and scorers for the rounds proper and a list of all the players
that took part. The book also includes all Football League results and
dates from the regional competitions that were played in 1945–46.
ISBN 978-1-899468-86-7. £10 plus £1.50 p&p.

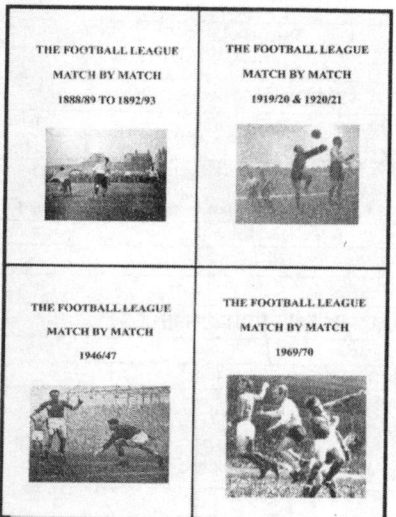

**THE FOOTBALL LEAGUE
MATCH BY MATCH 1888–1970**
The Match by Match series is now complete for
all seasons from 1888–89 to 1969–70. With the
40 editions of the Sky Sports Yearbook (and its
predecessor, the Rothmans Yearbook) there is
now a complete record of every Football
League game since 1888. The 55 Match by
Match volumes include results, attendances,
scorers and line-up grids for League and Cup
ties. The first five seasons are in volume one,
there are two seasons per volume to 1920/21,
then seasons to 1969/70 have a volume each.
Wartime seasons are not included. Sample
pages are available on the Soccerdata web site.
Each book in the series is £12. The 55 volumes
are available at a special price of £500 until
December 2010. Subsets of the series are also
available as follows: 1888 to 1915 (12 books)
£120; 1919 to 1939 (19 books) £190; 1946 to
1970 (24 books): £240. UK postage is free on
these books, but overseas buyers should add
10% to cover the additional cost.

SoccerData publications are available from Tony Brown, 4 Adrian Close, Beeston,
Nottingham NG9 6FL. Cheques should be made payable to Tony Brown.
Please visit the web site at www.soccerdata.com.

THE FA BARCLAYS PREMIERSHIP AND COCA-COLA FOOTBALL LEAGUE FIXTURES 2010-11

Sky Sports   All fixtures subject to change.

Friday, 6 August 2010
npower Football League Championship
Norwich C v Watford* (7.45)

Saturday, 7 August 2010
npower Football League Championship
Bristol C v Millwall
Burnley v Nottingham F
Coventry C v Portsmouth
Crystal Palace v Leicester C
Hull C v Swansea C
Leeds U v Derby Co
Middlesbrough v Ipswich T
Preston NE v Doncaster R
QPR v Barnsley
Reading v Scunthorpe U

npower Football League One
Carlisle U v Brentford
Charlton Ath v Bournemouth
Exeter C v Colchester U
Notts Co v Huddersfield T
Peterborough U v Bristol R
Rochdale v Hartlepool U
Sheffield W v Dagenham & R
Southampton v Plymouth Arg* (12.15)
Swindon T v Brighton & HA
Tranmere R v Oldham Ath
Walsall v Milton Keynes D
Yeovil T v Leyton Orient

npower Football League Two
Accrington S v Aldershot T
Burton Alb v Oxford U
Bury v Port Vale
Chesterfield v Barnet
Crewe Alex v Hereford U
Gillingham v Cheltenham T
Rotherham U v Lincoln C City
Shrewsbury T v Bradford C
Southend U v Stockport Co
Stevenage v Macclesfield T
Torquay U v Northampton T
Wycombe W v Morecambe

Sunday, 8 August 2010
npower Football League Championship
Cardiff C v Sheffield U* (12.35)

Friday, 13 August 2010
npower Football League One
Leyton Orient v Charlton Ath* (7.45)

Saturday, 14 August 2010
Barclays Premier League
Aston Villa v West Ham U
Blackburn R v Everton
Wigan Ath v Blackpool
Bolton W v Fulham
Chelsea v WBA
Sunderland v Birmingham C

Tottenham H v Manchester C* (12.45)
Wolverhampton W v Stoke C

npower Football League Championship
Barnsley v Crystal Palace
Derby Co v Cardiff C
Doncaster R v Bristol C
Ipswich T v Burnley
Leicester C v Middlesbrough
Millwall v Hull C
Portsmouth v Reading
Scunthorpe U v Norwich C
Sheffield U v QPR
Swansea C v Preston NE
Watford v Coventry C

npower Football League One
Bournemouth v Peterborough U
Brentford v Walsall
Brighton & HA v Rochdale
Bristol R v Yeovil T
Colchester U v Sheffield W
Dagenham & R v Exeter C
Hartlepool U v Swindon T
Huddersfield T v Tranmere R
Milton Keynes D v Southampton
Oldham Ath v Notts Co
Plymouth Arg v Carlisle U

npower Football League Two
Aldershot T v Southend U
Barnet v Burton Alb
Bradford C v Stevenage
Cheltenham T v Crewe Alex
Hereford U v Gillingham
Lincoln C City v Torquay U
Macclesfield T v Shrewsbury T
Morecambe v Rotherham U
Northampton T v Accrington S
Oxford U v Bury
Port Vale v Chesterfield
Stockport Co v Wycombe W

Sunday, 15 August 2010
Barclays Premier League
Liverpool v Arsenal* (4.00)

npower Football League Championship
Nottingham F v Leeds U* (1.15)

Monday, 16 August 2010
Barclays Premier League
Manchester U v Newcastle U* (8.00)

Saturday, 21 August 2010
Barclays Premier League
Arsenal v Blackpool
Birmingham C v Blackburn R
Everton v Wolverhampton W
Newcastle U v Aston Villa
Stoke C v Tottenham H
WBA v Sunderland

West Ham U v Bolton W
Wigan Ath v Chelsea* (5.15)

npower Football League Championship
Bristol C v Barnsley
Burnley v Leicester C
Cardiff C v Doncaster R
Coventry C v Derby Co* (12.15)
Crystal Palace v Ipswich T
Hull C v Watford
Leeds U v Millwall
Norwich C v Swansea C
Preston NE v Portsmouth
QPR v Scunthorpe U
Reading v Nottingham F

npower Football League One
Carlisle U v Milton Keynes D
Charlton Ath v Oldham Ath
Exeter C v Bristol R
Notts Co v Dagenham & R
Peterborough U v Huddersfield T
Rochdale v Colchester U
Sheffield W v Brighton & HA
Southampton v Leyton Orient
Swindon T v Brentford
Tranmere R v Bournemouth
Walsall v Plymouth Arg
Yeovil T v Hartlepool U

npower Football League Two
Accrington S v Macclesfield T
Burton Alb v Morecambe
Bury v Northampton T
Chesterfield v Hereford U
Crewe Alex v Barnet
Gillingham v Lincoln C City
Rotherham U v Cheltenham T
Shrewsbury T v Aldershot T
Southend U v Port Vale
Stevenage v Stockport Co
Torquay U v Bradford C
Wycombe W v Oxford U

Sunday, 22 August 2010
Barclays Premier League
Fulham v Manchester U* (4.00)

npower Football League Championship
Middlesbrough v Sheffield U* (1.15)

Monday, 23 August 2010
Barclays Premier League
Manchester C v Liverpool* (8.00)

Saturday, 28 August 2010
Barclays Premier League
Blackburn R v Arsenal* (12.45)
Blackpool v Fulham
Chelsea v Stoke C
Liverpool v WBA
Manchester U v West Ham U
Sunderland v Manchester C

Tottenham H v Wigan Ath
Wolverhampton W v Newcastle U

npower Football League Championship
Barnsley v Middlesbrough
Derby Co v QPR
Doncaster R v Hull C
Ipswich T v Bristol C
Leicester C v Reading* (5.20)
Millwall v Coventry C
Nottingham F v Norwich C
Portsmouth v Cardiff C
Scunthorpe U v Crystal Palace
Sheffield U v Preston NE
Swansea C v Burnley
Watford v Leeds U

npower Football League One
Bournemouth v Notts Co
Brentford v Rochdale
Brighton & HA v Walsall
Bristol R v Southampton
Colchester U v Carlisle U
Dagenham & R v Tranmere R
Hartlepool U v Sheffield W
Huddersfield T v Charlton Ath
Leyton Orient v Exeter C
Milton Keynes D v Swindon T
Oldham Ath v Yeovil T
Plymouth Arg v Peterborough U

npower Football League Two
Aldershot T v Stevenage
Barnet v Bury
Bradford C v Southend U
Cheltenham T v Burton Alb
Hereford U v Rotherham U
Lincoln C City v Crewe Alex
Macclesfield T v Chesterfield
Morecambe v Gillingham
Northampton T v Wycombe W
Oxford U v Accrington S
Port Vale v Torquay U
Stockport Co v Shrewsbury T

Sunday, 29 August 2010
Barclays Premier League
Bolton W v Birmingham C* (1.30)
Aston Villa v Everton* (4.00)

Saturday, 4 September 2010
npower Football League One
Carlisle U v Swindon T
Dagenham & R v Leyton Orient
Exeter C v Charlton Ath
Huddersfield T v Bournemouth
Milton Keynes D v Hartlepool U* (12.15)
Notts Co v Yeovil T
Oldham Ath v Bristol R
Plymouth Arg v Brighton & HA
Southampton v Rochdale
Tranmere R v Peterborough U
Walsall v Colchester U

npower Football League Two
Accrington S v Wycombe W
Aldershot T v Northampton T
Barnet v Cheltenham T
Bradford C v Port Vale
Burton Alb v Hereford U
Bury v Gillingham
Chesterfield v Lincoln C City
Macclesfield T v Stockport Co
Oxford U v Morecambe
Shrewsbury T v Rotherham U
Southend U v Torquay U
Stevenage v Crewe Alex

Sunday, 5 September 2010
npower Football League One
Brentford v Sheffield W* (12.00)

Saturday, 11 September 2010
Barclays Premier League
Arsenal v Bolton W
Fulham v Wolverhampton W
Manchester C v Blackburn R
Newcastle U v Blackpool
WBA v Tottenham H
West Ham U v Chelsea
Wigan Ath v Sunderland

npower Football League Championship
Burnley v Preston NE
Cardiff C v Hull C
Coventry C v Leicester C
Derby Co v Sheffield U
Leeds U v Swansea C
Norwich C v Barnsley
Nottingham F v Millwall
Portsmouth v Ipswich T
QPR v Middlesbrough
Reading v Crystal Palace
Scunthorpe U v Bristol C
Watford v Doncaster R

npower Football League One
Bournemouth v Dagenham & R
Brighton & HA v Milton Keynes D
Bristol R v Brentford
Charlton Ath v Notts Co
Colchester U v Plymouth Arg
Hartlepool U v Exeter C
Leyton Orient v Huddersfield T
Peterborough U v Oldham Ath
Rochdale v Walsall
Sheffield W v Carlisle U
Swindon T v Southampton
Yeovil T v Tranmere R

npower Football League Two
Cheltenham T v Stevenage
Crewe Alex v Bury
Gillingham v Shrewsbury T
Hereford U v Oxford U
Lincoln C City v Barnet
Morecambe v Chesterfield
Northampton T v Southend U
Port Vale v Aldershot T
Rotherham U v Burton Alb
Stockport Co v Bradford C
Torquay U v Accrington S
Wycombe W v Macclesfield T

Sunday, 12 September 2010
Barclays Premier League
Everton v Manchester U* (1.30)
Birmingham C v Liverpool* (4.00)

Monday, 13 September 2010
Barclays Premier League
Stoke C v Aston Villa* (8.00)

Tuesday, 14 September 2010
npower Football League Championship
Barnsley v Leeds U
Bristol C v Watford
Crystal Palace v Portsmouth
Doncaster R v Norwich C
Hull C v Derby Co
Ipswich T v QPR
Leicester C v Cardiff C
Middlesbrough v Burnley
Millwall v Reading
Preston NE v Nottingham F
Sheffield U v Scunthorpe U
Swansea C v Coventry C

Friday, 17 September 2010
npower Football League Championship
Doncaster R v Leeds U* (7.45)

Saturday, 18 September 2010
Barclays Premier League
Aston Villa v Bolton W
Blackburn R v Fulham
Everton v Newcastle U
Stoke C v West Ham U* (12.45)
Sunderland v Arsenal
Tottenham H v Wolverhampton W
WBA v Birmingham C
Wigan Ath v Manchester C

npower Football League Championship
Barnsley v Derby Co
Bristol C v Coventry C
Crystal Palace v Burnley
Hull C v Nottingham F* (5.20)
Ipswich T v Cardiff C
Leicester C v QPR
Middlesbrough v Reading
Millwall v Watford
Preston NE v Norwich C
Sheffield U v Portsmouth
Swansea C v Scunthorpe U

npower Football League One
Brentford v Hartlepool U
Carlisle U v Brighton & HA
Dagenham & R v Bristol R
Exeter C v Peterborough U
Huddersfield T v Yeovil T
Milton Keynes D v Rochdale
Notts Co v Leyton Orient
Oldham Ath v Bournemouth
Plymouth Arg v Sheffield W
Southampton v Colchester U
Tranmere R v Charlton Ath
Walsall v Swindon T

npower Football League Two
Accrington S v Lincoln C City
Aldershot T v Wycombe W
Barnet v Rotherham U
Bradford C v Gillingham
Burton Alb v Crewe Alex
Bury v Hereford U
Chesterfield v Cheltenham T
Macclesfield T v Port Vale
Oxford U v Stockport Co
Shrewsbury T v Northampton T
Southend U v Morecambe
Stevenage v Torquay U

Sunday, 19 September 2010
Barclays Premier League
Manchester U v Liverpool* (1.30)
Chelsea v Blackpool* (4.00)

Friday, 24 September 2010
npower Football League Championship
Portsmouth v Leicester C* (7.45)

Saturday, 25 September 2010
Barclays Premier League
Arsenal v WBA
Birmingham C v Wigan Ath
Blackpool v Blackburn R
Bolton W v Manchester U
Fulham v Everton
Liverpool v Sunderland
Manchester C v Chelsea* (12.45)
West Ham U v Tottenham H

npower Football League Championship
Burnley v Bristol C

Cardiff C v Millwall
Coventry C v Preston NE
Derby Co v Crystal Palace
Leeds U v Sheffield U
Norwich C v Hull C
Nottingham F v Swansea C
QPR v Doncaster R
Reading v Barnsley
Scunthorpe U v Ipswich T
Watford v Middlesbrough

npower Football League One
Bournemouth v Carlisle U
Brighton & HA v Oldham Ath
Bristol R v Notts Co
Charlton Ath v Dagenham & R
Colchester U v Tranmere R
Hartlepool U v Walsall
Leyton Orient v Brentford
Peterborough U v Milton Keynes D
Rochdale v Plymouth Arg
Sheffield W v Southampton
Swindon T v Huddersfield T
Yeovil T v Exeter C

npower Football League Two
Cheltenham T v Bury
Crewe Alex v Oxford U
Gillingham v Burton Alb
Hereford U v Southend U
Lincoln C City v Stevenage
Morecambe v Barnet
Northampton T v Bradford C
Port Vale v Accrington S
Rotherham U v Chesterfield
Stockport Co v Aldershot T
Torquay U v Macclesfield T
Wycombe W v Shrewsbury T

Sunday, 26 September 2010
Barclays Premier League
Wolverhampton W v Aston Villa*
(2.00)
Newcastle U v Stoke C* (4.10)

Tuesday, 28 September 2010
**npower Football League
Championship**
Burnley v Hull C
Cardiff C v Crystal Palace
Coventry C v Doncaster R
Derby Co v Middlesbrough
Leeds U v Preston NE
Norwich C v Leicester C
Nottingham F v Sheffield U
Portsmouth v Bristol C
QPR v Millwall
Reading v Ipswich T
Scunthorpe U v Barnsley
Watford v Swansea C

npower Football League One
Bournemouth v Exeter C
Brighton & HA v Brentford
Bristol R v Tranmere R
Charlton Ath v Milton Keynes D
Colchester U v Dagenham & R
Hartlepool U v Carlisle U
Leyton Orient v Walsall
Peterborough U v Notts Co
Rochdale v Huddersfield T
Sheffield W v Oldham Ath
Swindon T v Plymouth Arg
Yeovil T v Southampton

npower Football League Two
Cheltenham T v Oxford U
Crewe Alex v Macclesfield T
Gillingham v Southend U
Hereford U v Stevenage
Lincoln C City v Burton Alb
Morecambe v Bury

Northampton T v Chesterfield
Port Vale v Shrewsbury T
Rotherham U v Bradford C
Stockport Co v Accrington S
Torquay U v Aldershot T
Wycombe W v Barnet

Saturday, 2 October 2010
Barclays Premier League
Birmingham C v Everton
Liverpool v Blackpool
Manchester C v Newcastle U
Stoke C v Blackburn R
Sunderland v Manchester U
Tottenham H v Aston Villa
WBA v Bolton W
West Ham U v Fulham

**npower Football League
Championship**
Barnsley v Cardiff C
Bristol C v Norwich C
Crystal Palace v QPR
Doncaster R v Nottingham F
Hull C v Coventry C
Ipswich T v Leeds U
Leicester C v Scunthorpe U
Middlesbrough v Portsmouth
Millwall v Burnley
Preston NE v Reading
Sheffield U v Watford
Swansea C v Derby Co

npower Football League One
Brentford v Charlton Ath
Carlisle U v Peterborough U
Dagenham & R v Swindon T
Exeter C v Rochdale
Huddersfield T v Bristol R
Milton Keynes D v Colchester U
Notts Co v Sheffield W
Oldham Ath v Leyton Orient
Plymouth Arg v Hartlepool U
Southampton v Bournemouth
Tranmere R v Brighton & HA
Walsall v Yeovil T

npower Football League Two
Accrington S v Gillingham
Aldershot T v Cheltenham T
Barnet v Hereford U
Bradford C v Morecambe
Burton Alb v Stockport Co
Bury v Rotherham U
Chesterfield v Crewe Alex
Macclesfield T v Northampton T
Oxford U v Port Vale
Shrewsbury T v Torquay U
Southend U v Lincoln C City
Stevenage v Wycombe W

Sunday, 3 October 2010
Barclays Premier League
Chelsea v Arsenal* (4.00)

Monday, 4 October 2010
Barclays Premier League
Wigan Ath v Wolverhampton W*
(8.00)

Saturday, 9 October 2010
npower Football League One
Brentford v Oldham Ath
Brighton & HA v Bournemouth*
(12.15)
Carlisle U v Notts Co
Colchester U v Huddersfield T
Hartlepool U v Peterborough U
Milton Keynes D v Dagenham & R
Plymouth Arg v Charlton Ath
Rochdale v Yeovil T
Sheffield W v Leyton Orient

Southampton v Tranmere R
Walsall v Exeter C

npower Football League Two
Barnet v Bradford C
Burton Alb v Wycombe W
Bury v Accrington S
Cheltenham T v Northampton T
Chesterfield v Southend U
Crewe Alex v Torquay U
Gillingham v Stockport Co
Hereford U v Port Vale
Lincoln C City v Macclesfield T
Morecambe v Shrewsbury T
Oxford U v Aldershot T
Rotherham U v Stevenage

Monday, 11 October 2010
npower Football League One
Swindon T v Bristol R* (7.45)

Saturday, 16 October 2010
Barclays Premier League
Arsenal v Birmingham C
Aston Villa v Chelsea
Bolton W v Stoke C
Fulham v Tottenham H
Manchester U v WBA
Newcastle U v Wigan Ath
Wolverhampton W v West Ham U

**npower Football League
Championship**
Barnsley v Nottingham F
Cardiff C v Bristol C
Crystal Palace v Millwall
Derby Co v Preston NE
Ipswich T v Coventry C
Leicester C v Hull C
Middlesbrough v Leeds U* (5.20)
Portsmouth v Watford
QPR v Norwich C
Reading v Swansea C
Scunthorpe U v Doncaster R
Sheffield U v Burnley

npower Football League One
Bournemouth v Milton Keynes D
Bristol R v Rochdale
Charlton Ath v Brighton & HA
Dagenham & R v Walsall
Exeter C v Carlisle U
Huddersfield T v Swindon T
Leyton Orient v Hartlepool U
Notts Co v Plymouth Arg
Oldham Ath v Colchester U
Peterborough U v Swindon T
Tranmere R v Brentford
Yeovil T v Sheffield W

npower Football League Two
Accrington S v Rotherham U
Aldershot T v Morecambe
Bradford C v Cheltenham T
Macclesfield T v Oxford U
Northampton T v Hereford U
Port Vale v Gillingham
Shrewsbury T v Lincoln C City
Southend U v Crewe Alex
Stevenage v Burton Alb
Stockport Co v Barnet
Torquay U v Bury
Wycombe W v Chesterfield

Sunday, 17 October 2010
Barclays Premier League
Blackpool v Manchester C* (4.00)
Everton v Liverpool* (1.30)

Monday, 18 October 2010
Barclays Premier League
Blackburn R v Sunderland* (8.00)

Tuesday, 19 October 2010
npower Football League Championship
Bristol C v Reading
Burnley v Barnsley
Coventry C v Cardiff C
Doncaster R v Derby Co
Hull C v Sheffield U
Leeds U v Leicester C
Millwall v Portsmouth
Norwich C v Crystal Palace
Nottingham F v Middlesbrough
Preston NE v Scunthorpe U
Swansea C v QPR
Watford v Ipswich T

Friday, 22 October 2010
npower Football League Championship
Bristol C v QPR* (7.45)

Saturday, 23 October 2010
Barclays Premier League
Birmingham C v Blackpool
Chelsea v Wolverhampton W
Liverpool v Blackburn R
Sunderland v Aston Villa
Tottenham H v Everton* (12.45)
WBA v Fulham
West Ham U v Newcastle U* (5.30)
Wigan Ath v Bolton W

npower Football League Championship
Burnley v Reading
Coventry C v Barnsley
Doncaster R v Sheffield U
Hull C v Portsmouth
Leeds U v Cardiff C
Millwall v Derby Co
Norwich C v Middlesbrough
Nottingham F v Ipswich T
Preston NE v Crystal Palace
Watford v Scunthorpe U

npower Football League One
Brentford v Peterborough U
Brighton & HA v Yeovil T
Carlisle U v Charlton Ath
Colchester U v Notts Co
Hartlepool U v Bristol R
Milton Keynes D v Exeter C
Plymouth Arg v Huddersfield T
Rochdale v Dagenham & R
Sheffield W v Bournemouth
Southampton v Oldham Ath
Swindon T v Leyton Orient
Walsall v Tranmere R

npower Football League Two
Barnet v Macclesfield T
Burton Alb v Bradford C
Bury v Southend U
Cheltenham T v Port Vale
Chesterfield v Shrewsbury T
Crewe Alex v Aldershot T
Gillingham v Torquay U
Hereford U v Accrington S
Lincoln C City v Stockport Co
Morecambe v Stevenage
Oxford U v Northampton T
Rotherham U v Wycombe W

Sunday, 24 October 2010
Barclays Premier League
Stoke C v Manchester U* (1.30)
Manchester C v Arsenal* (4.00)

Monday, 25 October 2010
npower Football League Championship
Swansea C v Leicester C* (7.45)

Saturday, 30 October 2010
Barclays Premier League
Arsenal v West Ham U
Aston Villa v Birmingham C
Blackburn R v Chelsea
Everton v Stoke C
Fulham v Wigan Ath
Manchester U v Tottenham H
Wolverhampton W v Manchester C

npower Football League Championship
Barnsley v Hull C* (5.20)
Cardiff C v Norwich C
Crystal Palace v Swansea C
Derby Co v Watford
Ipswich T v Millwall
Leicester C v Preston NE
Middlesbrough v Bristol C
Portsmouth v Nottingham F
QPR v Burnley
Reading v Doncaster R
Scunthorpe U v Leeds U
Sheffield U v Coventry C

npower Football League One
Bournemouth v Colchester U
Bristol R v Carlisle U
Charlton Ath v Sheffield W
Dagenham & R v Hartlepool U
Exeter C v Brentford
Huddersfield T v Walsall
Leyton Orient v Rochdale
Notts Co v Southampton
Oldham Ath v Plymouth Arg
Peterborough U v Brighton & HA
Tranmere R v Milton Keynes D
Yeovil T v Swindon T

npower Football League Two
Accrington S v Cheltenham T
Aldershot T v Bury
Bradford C v Oxford U
Macclesfield T v Burton Alb
Northampton T v Gillingham
Port Vale v Crewe Alex
Shrewsbury T v Barnet
Southend U v Rotherham U
Stevenage v Chesterfield
Stockport Co v Hereford U
Torquay U v Morecambe
Wycombe W v Lincoln C City

Sunday, 31 October 2010
Barclays Premier League
Bolton W v Liverpool* (1.30)
Newcastle U v Sunderland* (4.00)

Monday, 1 November 2010
Barclays Premier League
Blackpool v WBA* (8.00)

Tuesday, 2 November 2010
npower Football League One
Brentford v Bournemouth
Brighton & HA v Exeter C
Carlisle U v Tranmere R
Colchester U v Leyton Orient
Hartlepool U v Notts Co
Milton Keynes D v Yeovil T
Plymouth Arg v Bristol R
Rochdale v Oldham Ath
Sheffield W v Huddersfield T
Southampton v Dagenham & R
Swindon T v Charlton Ath
Walsall v Peterborough U

npower Football League Two
Barnet v Stevenage
Burton Alb v Port Vale
Bury v Bradford C
Cheltenham T v Southend U

Chesterfield v Accrington S
Crewe Alex v Shrewsbury T
Gillingham v Wycombe W
Hereford U v Aldershot T
Lincoln C City v Northampton T
Morecambe v Stockport Co
Oxford U v Torquay U
Rotherham U v Macclesfield T

Saturday, 6 November 2010
Barclays Premier League
Birmingham C v West Ham U
Blackburn R v Wigan Ath
Blackpool v Everton
Bolton W v Tottenham H* (12.45)
Fulham v Aston Villa
Manchester U v Wolverhampton W
Sunderland v Stoke C
WBA v Manchester C

npower Football League Championship
Barnsley v Leicester C
Bristol C v Preston NE
Cardiff C v Swansea C
Coventry C v Leeds U
Derby Co v Portsmouth* (5.20)
Doncaster R v Millwall
Hull C v Scunthorpe U
Middlesbrough v Crystal Palace
Norwich C v Burnley
QPR v Reading
Sheffield U v Ipswich T
Watford v Nottingham F

Sunday, 7 November 2010
Barclays Premier League
Arsenal v Newcastle U* (1.30)
Liverpool v Chelsea* (4.00)

Tuesday, 9 November 2010
Barclays Premier League
Stoke C v Birmingham C
Tottenham H v Sunderland
West Ham U v WBA* (8.00)
Wigan Ath v Liverpool
Wolverhampton W v Arsenal

npower Football League Championship
Burnley v Doncaster R
Crystal Palace v Watford
Ipswich T v Derby Co
Leeds U v Hull C
Leicester C v Sheffield U
Millwall v Norwich C
Nottingham F v Coventry C
Portsmouth v QPR
Preston NE v Barnsley
Reading v Cardiff C
Scunthorpe U v Middlesbrough
Swansea C v Bristol C

Wednesday, 10 November 2010
Barclays Premier League
Aston Villa v Blackpool
Chelsea v Fulham
Everton v Bolton W
Manchester C v Manchester U* (8.00)
Newcastle U v Blackburn R

Friday, 12 November 2010
npower Football League Championship
Preston NE v Hull C* (7.45)

Saturday, 13 November 2010
Barclays Premier League
Aston Villa v Manchester U* (12.45)
Manchester C v Birmingham C
Newcastle U v Fulham

Stoke C v Liverpool
Tottenham H v Blackburn R
West Ham U v Blackpool
Wigan Ath v WBA
Wolverhampton W v Bolton W

**npower Football League
Championship**
Burnley v Watford
Crystal Palace v Coventry C
Ipswich T v Barnsley
Leeds U v Bristol C
Leicester C v Derby Co
Millwall v Sheffield U
Nottingham F v QPR
Portsmouth v Doncaster R
Reading v Norwich C* (5.20)
Scunthorpe U v Cardiff C
Swansea C v Middlesbrough

npower Football League One
Bournemouth v Walsall
Brentford v Milton Keynes D
Bristol R v Leyton Orient
Carlisle U v Southampton
Exeter C v Notts Co
Hartlepool U v Brighton & HA
Oldham Ath v Huddersfield T
Peterborough U v Charlton Ath
Sheffield W v Rochdale
Swindon T v Colchester U
Tranmere R v Plymouth Arg
Yeovil T v Dagenham & R

npower Football League Two
Bury v Stockport Co
Chesterfield v Burton Alb
Gillingham v Crewe Alex
Hereford U v Cheltenham T
Macclesfield T v Aldershot T
Morecambe v Lincoln C City
Northampton T v Port Vale
Rotherham U v Oxford U
Southend U v Accrington S
Stevenage v Shrewsbury T
Torquay U v Barnet
Wycombe W v Bradford C

**Sunday, 14 November 2010
Barclays Premier League**
Everton v Arsenal* (2.00)
Chelsea v Sunderland* (4.10)

**Saturday, 20 November 2010
Barclays Premier League**
Birmingham C v Chelsea
Blackburn R v Aston Villa
Blackpool v Wolverhampton W
Bolton W v Newcastle U
Liverpool v West Ham U
Manchester U v Wigan Ath
WBA v Stoke C

**npower Football League
Championship**
Barnsley v Portsmouth
Bristol C v Leicester C
Cardiff C v Nottingham F
Coventry C v Burnley
Derby Co v Scunthorpe U
Doncaster R v Swansea C
Hull C v Ipswich T
Middlesbrough v Millwall
Norwich C v Leeds U
QPR v Preston NE
Sheffield U v Crystal Palace* (5.20)
Watford v Reading

npower Football League One
Brighton & HA v Bristol R
Charlton Ath v Yeovil T
Colchester U v Hartlepool U

Dagenham & R v Oldham Ath
Huddersfield T v Exeter C
Leyton Crient v Bournemouth
Milton Keynes D v Sheffield W
Notts Co v Tranmere R
Plymouth Arg v Brentford
Rochdale v Swindon T
Southampton v Peterborough U
Walsall v Carlisle U

npower Football League Two
Accrington S v Stevenage
Aldershot T v Chesterfield
Barnet v Northampton T
Bradford C v Macclesfield T
Burton Alb v Bury
Cheltenham T v Morecambe
Crewe Alex v Rotherham U
Lincoln C City v Hereford U
Oxford U v Gillingham
Port Vale v Wycombe W
Shrewsbury T v Southend U
Stockport Co v Torquay U

**Sunday, 21 November 2010
Barclays Premier League**
Arsenal v Tottenham H* (1.30)
Fulham v Manchester C* (4.00)

**Monday, 22 November 2010
Barclays Premier League**
Sunderland v Everton* (8.00)

**Tuesday, 23 November 2010
npower Football League One**
Bournemouth v Yeovil T
Carlisle U v Rochdale
Charlton Ath v Bristol R
Colchester U v Brentford
Huddersfield T v Milton Keynes D
Notts Co v Swindon T
Oldham Ath v Exeter C
Peterborough U v Leyton Orient
Plymouth Arg v Dagenham & R
Sheffield W v Walsall
Southampton v Brighton & HA
Tranmere R v Hartlepool U

npower Football League Two
Barnet v Gillingham
Bradford C v Accrington S
Burton Alb v Aldershot T
Chesterfield v Oxford U
Lincoln C City v Bury
Macclesfield T v Cheltenham T
Morecambe v Crewe Alex
Rotherham U v Northampton T
Shrewsbury T v Hereford U
Stevenage v Southend U
Stockport Co v Port Vale
Wycombe W v Torquay U

**Saturday, 27 November 2010
Barclays Premier League**
Aston Villa v Arsenal* (12.45)
Bolton W v Blackpool
Everton v WBA
Fulham v Birmingham C
Manchester U v Blackburn R
Stoke C v Manchester C
West Ham U v Wigan Ath
Wolverhampton W v Sunderland

**npower Football League
Championship**
Barnsley v Watford
Bristol C v Sheffield U
Burnley v Derby Co
Crystal Palace v Doncaster R
Middlesbrough v Hull C
Norwich C v Ipswich T
Preston NE v Millwall

QPR v Cardiff C
Reading v Leeds U
Scunthorpe U v Coventry C
Swansea C v Portsmouth

**Sunday, 28 November 2010
Barclays Premier League**
Newcastle U v Chelsea* (1.30)
Tottenham H v Liverpool* (4.00)

**Monday, 29 November 2010
npower Football League
Championship**
Leicester C v Nottingham F* (7.45)

**Saturday, 4 December 2010
Barclays Premier League**
Arsenal v Fulham
Birmingham C v Tottenham H
Blackburn R v Wolverhampton W
Blackpool v Manchester U
Chelsea v Everton
Liverpool v Aston Villa
Manchester C v Bolton W
Sunderland v West Ham U
WBA v Newcastle U
Wigan Ath v Stoke C

**npower Football League
Championship**
Cardiff C v Preston NE
Coventry C v Middlesbrough
Derby Co v Norwich C
Doncaster R v Barnsley
Hull C v QPR
Ipswich T v Swansea C
Leeds U v Crystal Palace
Millwall v Scunthorpe U
Nottingham F v Bristol C
Portsmouth v Burnley
Sheffield U v Reading
Watford v Leicester C

npower Football League One
Brentford v Notts Co
Brighton & HA v Colchester U
Bristol R v Bournemouth
Dagenham & R v Huddersfield T
Exeter C v Tranmere R
Hartlepool U v Southampton
Leyton Orient v Carlisle U
Milton Keynes D v Plymouth Arg
Rochdale v Charlton Ath
Swindon T v Sheffield W
Walsall v Oldham Ath
Yeovil T v Peterborough U

npower Football League Two
Accrington S v Shrewsbury T
Aldershot T v Bradford C
Bury v Chesterfield
Cheltenham T v Lincoln C City
Crewe Alex v Wycombe W
Gillingham v Rotherham U
Hereford U v Morecambe
Northampton T v Stockport Co
Oxford U v Barnet
Port Vale v Stevenage
Southend U v Macclesfield T
Torquay U v Burton Alb

**Saturday, 11 December 2010
Barclays Premier League**
Aston Villa v WBA
Bolton W v Blackburn R
Everton v Wigan Ath
Fulham v Sunderland
Manchester U v Arsenal
Newcastle U v Liverpool
Stoke C v Blackpool
Tottenham H v Chelsea

West Ham U v Manchester C
Wolverhampton W v Birmingham C

npower Football League Championship
Barnsley v Sheffield U
Bristol C v Derby Co
Burnley v Leeds U
Crystal Palace v Hull C
Leicester C v Doncaster R
Middlesbrough v Cardiff C
Norwich C v Portsmouth
Preston NE v Ipswich T
QPR v Watford
Reading v Coventry C
Scunthorpe U v Nottingham F
Swansea C v Millwall

npower Football League One
Bournemouth v Hartlepool U
Carlisle U v Dagenham & R
Charlton Ath v Walsall
Colchester U v Yeovil T
Huddersfield T v Brighton & HA
Notts Co v Milton Keynes D
Oldham Ath v Swindon T
Peterborough U v Rochdale
Plymouth Arg v Exeter C
Sheffield W v Bristol R
Southampton v Brentford
Tranmere R v Leyton Orient

npower Football League Two
Barnet v Accrington S
Bradford C v Hereford U
Burton Alb v Southend U
Chesterfield v Torquay U
Lincoln C City v Oxford U
Macclesfield T v Gillingham
Morecambe v Port Vale
Rotherham U v Aldershot T
Shrewsbury T v Cheltenham T
Stevenage v Northampton T
Stockport Co v Crewe Alex
Wycombe W v Bury

Saturday, 18 December 2010
Barclays Premier League
Arsenal v Stoke C
Birmingham C v Newcastle U
Blackburn R v West Ham U
Blackpool v Tottenham H
Chelsea v Manchester U
Liverpool v Fulham
Manchester C v Everton
Sunderland v Bolton W
WBA v Wolverhampton W
Wigan Ath v Aston Villa

npower Football League Championship
Cardiff C v Burnley
Coventry C v Norwich C
Derby Co v Reading
Doncaster R v Middlesbrough
Hull C v Bristol C
Ipswich T v Leicester C
Leeds U v QPR
Millwall v Barnsley
Nottingham F v Crystal Palace
Portsmouth v Scunthorpe U
Sheffield U v Swansea C
Watford v Preston NE

npower Football League One
Brentford v Huddersfield T
Brighton & HA v Notts Co
Bristol R v Colchester U
Dagenham & R v Peterborough U
Exeter C v Sheffield W
Hartlepool U v Charlton Ath
Leyton Orient v Plymouth Arg

Milton Keynes D v Oldham Ath
Rochdale v Bournemouth
Swindon T v Tranmere R
Walsall v Southampton
Yeovil T v Carlisle U

npower Football League Two
Accrington S v Burton Alb
Aldershot T v Lincoln C City
Bury v Stevenage
Cheltenham T v Stockport Co
Crewe Alex v Bradford C
Gillingham v Chesterfield
Hereford U v Macclesfield T
Northampton T v Morecambe
Oxford U v Shrewsbury T
Port Vale v Barnet
Southend U v Wycombe W
Torquay U v Rotherham U

Sunday, 26 December 2010
Barclays Premier League
Arsenal v Chelsea
Aston Villa v Tottenham H
Blackburn R v Stoke C
Blackpool v Liverpool
Bolton W v WBA
Everton v Birmingham C
Fulham v West Ham U
Manchester U v Sunderland
Newcastle U v Manchester C
Wolverhampton W v Wigan Ath

npower Football League Championship
Barnsley v Burnley
Cardiff C v Coventry C
Crystal Palace v Norwich C
Derby Co v Doncaster R
Ipswich T v Watford
Leicester C v Leeds U
Middlesbrough v Nottingham F
Portsmouth v Millwall
QPR v Swansea C
Reading v Bristol C
Scunthorpe U v Preston NE
Sheffield U v Hull C

npower Football League One
Bournemouth v Plymouth Arg
Bristol R v Walsall
Charlton Ath v Southampton
Dagenham & R v Brighton & HA
Exeter C v Swindon T
Huddersfield T v Hartlepool U
Leyton Orient v Milton Keynes D
Notts Co v Rochdale
Oldham Ath v Carlisle U
Peterborough U v Colchester U
Tranmere R v Sheffield W
Yeovil T v Brentford

npower Football League Two
Accrington S v Crewe Alex
Aldershot T v Gillingham
Bradford C v Chesterfield
Macclesfield T v Morecambe
Northampton T v Burton Alb
Port Vale v Lincoln C City
Shrewsbury T v Bury
Southend U v Barnet
Stevenage v Oxford U
Stockport Co v Rotherham U
Torquay U v Cheltenham T
Wycombe W v Hereford U

Tuesday, 28 December 2010
Barclays Premier League
Birmingham C v Manchester U
Chelsea v Bolton W
Liverpool v Wolverhampton W
Manchester C v Aston Villa

Stoke C v Fulham
Sunderland v Blackpool
Tottenham H v Newcastle U
WBA v Blackburn R
West Ham U v Everton
Wigan Ath v Arsenal

npower Football League Championship
Bristol C v Crystal Palace
Burnley v Scunthorpe U
Coventry C v QPR
Doncaster R v Ipswich T
Hull C v Reading
Leeds U v Portsmouth
Millwall v Leicester C
Norwich C v Sheffield U
Nottingham F v Derby Co
Preston NE v Middlesbrough
Swansea C v Barnsley
Watford v Cardiff C

npower Football League One
Brentford v Tranmere R
Brighton & HA v Charlton Ath
Carlisle U v Exeter C
Colchester U v Oldham Ath
Hartlepool U v Leyton Orient
Milton Keynes D v Bournemouth
Plymouth Arg v Notts Co
Rochdale v Bristol R
Sheffield W v Yeovil T
Southampton v Huddersfield T
Swindon T v Peterborough U
Walsall v Dagenham & R

npower Football League Two
Barnet v Stockport Co
Burton Alb v Stevenage
Bury v Torquay U
Cheltenham T v Bradford C
Chesterfield v Wycombe W
Crewe Alex v Southend U
Gillingham v Port Vale
Hereford U v Northampton T
Lincoln C City v Shrewsbury T
Morecambe v Aldershot T
Oxford U v Macclesfield T
Rotherham U v Accrington S

Saturday, 1 January 2011
Barclays Premier League
Birmingham C v Arsenal
Chelsea v Aston Villa
Liverpool v Bolton W
Manchester C v Blackpool
Stoke C v Everton
Sunderland v Blackburn R
Tottenham H v Fulham
WBA v Manchester U
West Ham U v Wolverhampton W
Wigan Ath v Newcastle U

npower Football League Championship
Bristol C v Cardiff C
Burnley v Sheffield U
Coventry C v Ipswich T
Doncaster R v Scunthorpe U
Hull C v Leicester C
Leeds U v Middlesbrough
Millwall v Crystal Palace
Norwich C v QPR
Nottingham F v Barnsley
Preston NE v Derby Co
Swansea C v Reading
Watford v Portsmouth

npower Football League One
Brentford v Dagenham & R
Brighton & HA v Leyton Orient
Carlisle U v Huddersfield T

Colchester U v Charlton Ath
Hartlepool U v Oldham Ath
Milton Keynes D v Bristol R
Plymouth Arg v Yeovil T
Rochdale v Tranmere R
Sheffield W v Peterborough U
Southampton v Exeter C
Swindon T v Bournemouth
Walsall v Notts Co

npower Football League Two
Barnet v Aldershot T
Burton Alb v Shrewsbury T
Bury v Macclesfield T
Cheltenham T v Wycombe W
Chesterfield v Stockport Co
Crewe Alex v Northampton T
Gillingham v Stevenage
Hereford U v Torquay U
Lincoln C City v Bradford C
Morecambe v Accrington S
Oxford U v Southend U
Rotherham U v Port Vale

Monday, 3 January 2011
npower Football League Championship
Barnsley v Coventry C
Cardiff C v Leeds U
Crystal Palace v Preston NE
Derby Co v Millwall
Ipswich T v Nottingham F
Leicester C v Swansea C
Middlesbrough v Norwich C
Portsmouth v Hull C
QPR v Bristol C
Reading v Burnley
Scunthorpe U v Watford
Sheffield U v Doncaster R

npower Football League One
Bournemouth v Brentford
Bristol R v Plymouth Arg
Charlton Ath v Swindon T
Dagenham & R v Southampton
Exeter C v Brighton & HA
Huddersfield T v Sheffield W
Leyton Orient v Colchester U
Notts Co v Hartlepool U
Oldham Ath v Brentford
Peterborough U v Walsall
Tranmere R v Carlisle U
Yeovil T v Milton Keynes D

npower Football League Two
Accrington S v Chesterfield
Aldershot T v Hereford U
Bradford C v Bury
Macclesfield T v Rotherham U
Northampton T v Lincoln C City
Port Vale v Burton Alb
Shrewsbury T v Crewe Alex
Southend U v Cheltenham T
Stevenage v Barnet
Stockport Co v Morecambe
Torquay U v Oxford U
Wycombe W v Gillingham

Tuesday, 4 January 2011
Barclays Premier League
Arsenal v Manchester C
Blackpool v Birmingham C
Bolton W v Wigan Ath
Manchester U v Stoke C
Wolverhampton W v Chelsea

Wednesday, 5 January 2011
Barclays Premier League
Aston Villa v Sunderland
Blackburn R v Liverpool
Everton v Tottenham H

Fulham v WBA
Newcastle U v West Ham U

Saturday, 8 January 2011
npower Football League One
Bournemouth v Sheffield W
Bristol R v Hartlepool U
Charlton Ath v Carlisle U
Dagenham & R v Rochdale
Exeter C v Milton Keynes D
Huddersfield T v Plymouth Arg
Leyton Orient v Swindon T
Notts Co v Colchester U
Oldham Ath v Southampton
Peterborough U v Brentford
Tranmere R v Walsall
Yeovil T v Brighton & HA

npower Football League Two
Accrington S v Bury
Aldershot T v Oxford U
Bradford C v Barnet
Macclesfield T v Lincoln C City
Northampton T v Cheltenham T
Port Vale v Hereford U
Shrewsbury T v Morecambe
Southend U v Chesterfield
Stevenage v Rotherham U
Stockport Co v Gillingham
Torquay U v Crewe Alex
Wycombe W v Burton Alb

Saturday, 15 January 2011
Barclays Premier League
Birmingham C v Aston Villa
Chelsea v Blackburn R
Liverpool v Everton
Manchester C v Wolverhampton W
Stoke C v Bolton W
Sunderland v Newcastle U
Tottenham H v Manchester U
WBA v Blackpool
West Ham U v Arsenal
Wigan Ath v Fulham

npower Football League Championship
Bristol C v Middlesbrough
Burnley v QPR
Coventry C v Sheffield U
Doncaster R v Reading
Hull C v Barnsley
Leeds U v Scunthorpe U
Millwall v Ipswich T
Norwich C v Cardiff C
Nottingham F v Portsmouth
Preston NE v Leicester C
Swansea C v Crystal Palace
Watford v Derby Co

npower Football League One
Brentford v Exeter C
Brighton & HA v Peterborough U
Carlisle U v Bristol R
Colchester U v Bournemouth
Hartlepool U v Dagenham & R
Milton Keynes D v Tranmere R
Plymouth Arg v Oldham Ath
Rochdale v Leyton Orient
Sheffield W v Charlton Ath
Southampton v Notts Co
Swindon T v Yeovil T
Walsall v Huddersfield T

npower Football League Two
Barnet v Shrewsbury T
Burton Alb v Macclesfield T
Bury v Aldershot T
Cheltenham T v Accrington S
Chesterfield v Stevenage
Crewe Alex v Port Vale
Gillingham v Northampton T

Hereford U v Stockport Co
Lincoln C City v Wycombe W
Morecambe v Torquay U
Oxford U v Bradford C
Rotherham U v Southend U

Saturday, 22 January 2011
Barclays Premier League
Arsenal v Wigan Ath
Aston Villa v Manchester C
Blackburn R v WBA
Blackpool v Sunderland
Bolton W v Chelsea
Everton v West Ham U
Fulham v Stoke C
Manchester U v Birmingham C
Newcastle U v Tottenham H
Wolverhampton W v Liverpool

npower Football League Championship
Barnsley v Swansea C
Cardiff C v Watford
Crystal Palace v Bristol C
Derby Co v Nottingham F
Ipswich T v Doncaster R
Leicester C v Millwall
Middlesbrough v Preston NE
Portsmouth v Leeds U
QPR v Coventry C
Reading v Hull C
Scunthorpe U v Burnley
Sheffield U v Norwich C

npower Football League One
Bournemouth v Brighton & HA
Bristol R v Swindon T
Charlton Ath v Plymouth Arg
Dagenham & R v Milton Keynes D
Exeter C v Walsall
Huddersfield T v Colchester U
Leyton Orient v Sheffield W
Notts Co v Carlisle U
Oldham Ath v Brentford
Peterborough U v Hartlepool U
Tranmere R v Southampton
Yeovil T v Rochdale

npower Football League Two
Accrington S v Hereford U
Aldershot T v Crewe Alex
Bradford C v Burton Alb
Macclesfield T v Barnet
Northampton T v Oxford U
Port Vale v Cheltenham T
Shrewsbury T v Chesterfield
Southend U v Bury
Stevenage v Morecambe
Stockport Co v Lincoln C City
Torquay U v Gillingham
Wycombe W v Rotherham U

Saturday, 29 January 2011
npower Football League One
Brentford v Yeovil T
Brighton & HA v Dagenham & R
Carlisle U v Oldham Ath
Colchester U v Peterborough U
Hartlepool U v Huddersfield T
Milton Keynes D v Leyton Orient
Plymouth Arg v Bournemouth
Rochdale v Notts Co
Sheffield W v Tranmere R
Southampton v Charlton Ath
Swindon T v Exeter C
Walsall v Bristol R

npower Football League Two
Barnet v Southend U
Burton Alb v Northampton T
Bury v Shrewsbury T
Cheltenham T v Torquay U

Chesterfield v Bradford C
Crewe Alex v Accrington S
Gillingham v Aldershot T
Hereford U v Wycombe W
Lincoln C City v Port Vale
Morecambe v Macclesfield T
Oxford U v Stevenage
Rotherham U v Stockport Co

Tuesday, 1 February 2011
Barclays Premier League
Arsenal v Everton
Birmingham C v Manchester C
Blackpool v West Ham U
Bolton W v Wolverhampton W
Manchester U v Aston Villa
Sunderland v Chelsea
WBA v Wigan Ath

npower Football League
Championship
Barnsley v Preston NE
Bristol C v Swansea C
Cardiff C v Reading
Coventry C v Nottingham F
Derby Co v Ipswich T
Doncaster R v Burnley
Hull C v Leeds U
Middlesbrough v Scunthorpe U
Norwich C v Millwall
QPR v Portsmouth
Sheffield U v Leicester C
Watford v Crystal Palace

npower Football League One
Bournemouth v Swindon T
Bristol R v Milton Keynes D
Charlton Ath v Colchester U
Dagenham & R v Brentford
Exeter C v Southampton
Huddersfield T v Carlisle U
Leyton Orient v Brighton & HA
Notts Co v Walsall
Oldham Ath v Hartlepool U
Peterborough U v Sheffield W
Tranmere R v Rochdale
Yeovil T v Plymouth Arg

npower Football League Two
Accrington S v Morecambe
Aldershot T v Barnet
Bradford C v Lincoln C City
Macclesfield T v Bury
Northampton T v Crewe Alex
Port Vale v Rotherham U
Shrewsbury T v Burton Alb
Southend U v Oxford U
Stevenage v Gillingham
Stockport Co v Chesterfield
Torquay U v Hereford U
Wycombe W v Cheltenham T

Wednesday, 2 February 2011
Barclays Premier League
Blackburn R v Tottenham H
Fulham v Newcastle U
Liverpool v Stoke C

Saturday, 5 February 2011
Barclays Premier League
Aston Villa v Fulham
Chelsea v Liverpool
Everton v Blackpool
Manchester C v WBA
Newcastle U v Arsenal
Stoke C v Sunderland
Tottenham H v Bolton W
West Ham U v Birmingham C
Wigan Ath v Blackburn R
Wolverhampton W v Manchester U

npower Football League
Championship
Burnley v Norwich C
Crystal Palace v Middlesbrough
Ipswich T v Sheffield U
Leeds U v Coventry C
Leicester C v Barnsley
Millwall v Doncaster R
Nottingham F v Watford
Portsmouth v Derby Co
Preston NE v Bristol C
Reading v QPR
Scunthorpe U v Hull C
Swansea C v Cardiff C

npower Football League One
Bournemouth v Leyton Orient
Brentford v Plymouth Arg
Bristol R v Brighton & HA
Carlisle U v Walsall
Exeter C v Huddersfield T
Hartlepool U v Colchester U
Oldham Ath v Dagenham & R
Peterborough U v Southampton
Sheffield W v Milton Keynes D
Swindon T v Rochdale
Tranmere R v Notts Co
Yeovil T v Charlton Ath

npower Football League Two
Bury v Burton Alb
Chesterfield v Aldershot T
Gillingham v Oxford U
Hereford U v Lincoln C City
Macclesfield T v Bradford C
Morecambe v Cheltenham T
Northampton T v Barnet
Rotherham U v Crewe Alex
Southend U v Shrewsbury T
Stevenage v Accrington S
Torquay U v Stockport Co
Wycombe W v Port Vale

Saturday, 12 February 2011
Barclays Premier League
Arsenal v Wolverhampton W
Birmingham C v Stoke C
Blackburn R v Newcastle U
Blackpool v Aston Villa
Bolton W v Everton
Fulham v Chelsea
Liverpool v Wigan Ath
Manchester U v Manchester C
Sunderland v Tottenham H
WBA v West Ham U

npower Football League
Championship
Barnsley v Ipswich T
Bristol C v Leeds U
Cardiff C v Scunthorpe U
Coventry C v Crystal Palace
Derby Co v Leicester C
Doncaster R v Portsmouth
Hull C v Preston NE
Middlesbrough v Swansea C
Norwich C v Reading
QPR v Nottingham F
Sheffield U v Millwall
Watford v Burnley

npower Football League One
Brighton & HA v Hartlepool U
Charlton Ath v Peterborough U
Colchester U v Swindon T
Dagenham & R v Yeovil T
Huddersfield T v Oldham Ath
Leyton Orient v Bristol R
Milton Keynes D v Brentford
Notts Co v Exeter C
Plymouth Arg v Tranmere R
Rochdale v Sheffield W

Southampton v Carlisle U
Walsall v Bournemouth

npower Football League Two
Accrington S v Southend U
Aldershot T v Macclesfield T
Barnet v Torquay U
Bradford C v Wycombe W
Burton Alb v Chesterfield
Cheltenham T v Hereford U
Crewe Alex v Gillingham
Lincoln C City v Morecambe
Oxford U v Rotherham U
Port Vale v Northampton T
Shrewsbury T v Stevenage
Stockport Co v Bury

Saturday, 19 February 2011
npower Football League
Championship
Burnley v Coventry C
Crystal Palace v Sheffield U
Ipswich T v Hull C
Leeds U v Norwich C
Leicester C v Bristol C
Millwall v Middlesbrough
Nottingham F v Cardiff C
Portsmouth v Barnsley
Preston NE v QPR
Reading v Watford
Scunthorpe U v Derby Co
Swansea C v Doncaster R

npower Football League One
Bournemouth v Huddersfield T
Brighton & HA v Plymouth Arg
Bristol R v Oldham Ath
Charlton Ath v Exeter C
Colchester U v Walsall
Hartlepool U v Milton Keynes D
Leyton Orient v Dagenham & R
Peterborough U v Tranmere R
Rochdale v Southampton
Sheffield W v Brentford
Swindon T v Carlisle U
Yeovil T v Notts Co

npower Football League Two
Cheltenham T v Barnet
Crewe Alex v Stevenage
Gillingham v Bury
Hereford U v Burton Alb
Lincoln C City v Chesterfield
Morecambe v Oxford U
Northampton T v Aldershot T
Port Vale v Bradford C
Rotherham U v Shrewsbury T
Stockport Co v Macclesfield T
Torquay U v Southend U
Wycombe W v Accrington S

Tuesday, 22 February 2011
npower Football League
Championship
Burnley v Middlesbrough
Cardiff C v Leicester C
Coventry C v Swansea C
Derby Co v Hull C
Leeds U v Barnsley
Norwich C v Doncaster R
Nottingham F v Preston NE
Portsmouth v Crystal Palace
QPR v Ipswich T
Reading v Millwall
Scunthorpe U v Sheffield U
Watford v Bristol C

Saturday, 26 February 2011
Barclays Premier League
Aston Villa v Blackburn R
Chelsea v Birmingham C
Everton v Sunderland

Manchester C v Fulham
Newcastle U v Bolton W
Stoke C v WBA
Tottenham H v Arsenal
West Ham U v Liverpool
Wigan Ath v Manchester U
Wolverhampton W v Blackpool

**npower Football League
Championship**
Barnsley v Norwich C
Bristol C v Scunthorpe U
Crystal Palace v Reading
Doncaster R v Watford
Hull C v Cardiff C
Ipswich T v Portsmouth
Leicester C v Coventry C
Middlesbrough v QPR
Millwall v Nottingham F
Preston NE v Burnley
Sheffield U v Derby Co
Swansea C v Leeds U

npower Football League One
Brentford v Bristol R
Carlisle U v Sheffield W
Dagenham & R v Bournemouth
Exeter C v Hartlepool U
Huddersfield T v Leyton Orient
Milton Keynes D v Brighton & HA
Notts Co v Charlton Ath
Oldham Ath v Peterborough U
Plymouth Arg v Colchester U
Southampton v Swindon T
Tranmere R v Yeovil T
Walsall v Rochdale

npower Football League Two
Accrington S v Torquay U
Aldershot T v Port Vale
Barnet v Lincoln C City
Bradford C v Stockport Co
Burton Alb v Rotherham U
Bury v Crewe Alex
Chesterfield v Morecambe
Macclesfield T v Wycombe W
Oxford U v Hereford U
Shrewsbury T v Gillingham
Southend U v Northampton T
Stevenage v Cheltenham T

Saturday, 5 March 2011
Barclays Premier League
Arsenal v Sunderland
Birmingham C v WBA
Blackpool v Chelsea
Bolton W v Aston Villa
Fulham v Blackburn R
Liverpool v Manchester U
Manchester C v Wigan Ath
Newcastle U v Everton
West Ham U v Stoke C
Wolverhampton W v Tottenham H

**npower Football League
Championship**
Burnley v Crystal Palace
Cardiff C v Ipswich T
Coventry C v Bristol C
Derby Co v Barnsley
Leeds U v Doncaster R
Norwich C v Preston NE
Nottingham F v Hull C
Portsmouth v Sheffield U
QPR v Leicester C
Reading v Middlesbrough
Scunthorpe U v Swansea C
Watford v Millwall

npower Football League One
Bournemouth v Oldham Ath
Brighton & HA v Carlisle U

Bristol R v Dagenham & R
Charlton Ath v Tranmere R
Colchester U v Southampton
Hartlepool U v Brentford
Leyton Orient v Notts Co
Peterborough U v Exeter C
Rochdale v Milton Keynes D
Sheffield W v Plymouth Arg
Swindon T v Walsall
Yeovil T v Huddersfield T

npower Football League Two
Cheltenham T v Chesterfield
Crewe Alex v Burton Alb
Gillingham v Bradford C
Hereford U v Bury
Lincoln C City v Accrington S
Morecambe v Southend U
Northampton T v Shrewsbury T
Port Vale v Macclesfield T
Rotherham U v Barnet
Stockport Co v Oxford U
Torquay U v Stevenage
Wycombe W v Aldershot T

Tuesday, 8 March 2011
**npower Football League
Championship**
Barnsley v Scunthorpe U
Bristol C v Portsmouth
Crystal Palace v Cardiff C
Doncaster R v Coventry C
Hull C v Burnley
Ipswich T v Reading
Leicester C v Norwich C
Middlesbrough v Derby Co
Millwall v QPR
Preston NE v Leeds U
Sheffield U v Nottingham F
Swansea C v Watford

npower Football League One
Brentford v Brighton & HA
Carlisle U v Hartlepool U
Dagenham & R v Colchester U
Exeter C v Bournemouth
Huddersfield T v Rochdale
Milton Keynes D v Charlton Ath
Notts Co v Peterborough U
Oldham Ath v Sheffield W
Plymouth Arg v Swindon T
Southampton v Yeovil T
Tranmere R v Bristol R
Walsall v Leyton Orient

npower Football League Two
Accrington S v Stockport Co
Aldershot T v Torquay U
Barnet v Wycombe W
Bradford C v Rotherham U
Burton Alb v Lincoln C City
Bury v Morecambe
Chesterfield v Northampton T
Macclesfield T v Crewe Alex
Oxford U v Cheltenham T
Shrewsbury T v Port Vale
Southend U v Gillingham
Stevenage v Hereford U

Saturday, 12 March 2011
**npower Football League
Championship**
Burnley v Millwall
Cardiff C v Barnsley
Coventry C v Hull C
Derby Co v Swansea C
Leeds U v Ipswich T
Norwich C v Bristol C
Nottingham F v Doncaster R
Portsmouth v Middlesbrough
QPR v Crystal Palace
Reading v Preston NE

Scunthorpe U v Leicester C
Watford v Sheffield U

npower Football League One
Bournemouth v Southampton
Brighton & HA v Tranmere R
Bristol R v Huddersfield T
Charlton Ath v Brentford
Colchester U v Milton Keynes D
Hartlepool U v Plymouth Arg
Leyton Orient v Oldham Ath
Peterborough U v Carlisle U
Rochdale v Exeter C
Sheffield W v Notts Co
Swindon T v Dagenham & R
Yeovil T v Walsall

npower Football League Two
Cheltenham T v Aldershot T
Crewe Alex v Chesterfield
Gillingham v Accrington S
Hereford U v Barnet
Lincoln C City v Southend U
Morecambe v Bradford C
Northampton T v Macclesfield T
Port Vale v Oxford U
Rotherham U v Bury
Stockport Co v Burton Alb
Torquay U v Shrewsbury T
Wycombe W v Stevenage

Saturday, 19 March 2011
Barclays Premier League
Aston Villa v Wolverhampton W
Blackburn R v Blackpool
Chelsea v Manchester C
Everton v Fulham
Manchester U v Bolton W
Stoke C v Newcastle U
Sunderland v Liverpool
Tottenham H v West Ham U
WBA v Arsenal
Wigan Ath v Birmingham C

**npower Football League
Championship**
Barnsley v Reading
Bristol C v Burnley
Crystal Palace v Derby Co
Doncaster R v QPR
Hull C v Norwich C
Ipswich T v Scunthorpe U
Leicester C v Portsmouth
Middlesbrough v Watford
Millwall v Cardiff C
Preston NE v Coventry C
Sheffield U v Leeds U
Swansea C v Nottingham F

npower Football League One
Brentford v Leyton Orient
Carlisle U v Bournemouth
Dagenham & R v Charlton Ath
Exeter C v Yeovil T
Huddersfield T v Swindon T
Milton Keynes D v Peterborough U
Notts Co v Bristol R
Oldham Ath v Brighton & HA
Plymouth Arg v Rochdale
Southampton v Sheffield W
Tranmere R v Colchester U
Walsall v Hartlepool U

npower Football League Two
Accrington S v Port Vale
Aldershot T v Stockport Co
Barnet v Morecambe
Bradford C v Northampton T
Burton Alb v Gillingham
Bury v Cheltenham T
Chesterfield v Rotherham U
Macclesfield T v Torquay U

Oxford U v Crewe Alex
Shrewsbury T v Wycombe W
Southend U v Hereford U
Stevenage v Lincoln C City

Saturday, 26 March 2011
npower Football League One
Bournemouth v Charlton Ath
Brentford v Carlisle U
Brighton & HA v Swindon T
Bristol R v Peterborough U
Colchester U v Exeter C
Dagenham & R v Sheffield W
Hartlepool U v Rochdale
Huddersfield T v Notts Co
Leyton Orient v Yeovil T
Milton Keynes D v Walsall
Oldham Ath v Tranmere R
Plymouth Arg v Southampton

npower Football League Two
Aldershot T v Accrington S
Barnet v Chesterfield
Bradford C v Shrewsbury T
Cheltenham T v Gillingham
Hereford U v Crewe Alex
Lincoln C City v Rotherham U
Macclesfield T v Stevenage
Morecambe v Wycombe W
Northampton T v Torquay U
Oxford U v Burton Alb
Port Vale v Bury
Stockport Co v Southend U

Saturday, 2 April 2011
Barclays Premier League
Arsenal v Blackburn R
Birmingham C v Bolton W
Everton v Aston Villa
Fulham v Blackpool
Manchester C v Sunderland
Newcastle U v Wolverhampton W
Stoke C v Chelsea
WBA v Liverpool
West Ham U v Manchester U
Wigan Ath v Tottenham H

npower Football League Championship
Bristol C v Doncaster R
Burnley v Ipswich T
Cardiff C v Derby Co
Coventry C v Watford
Crystal Palace v Barnsley
Hull C v Millwall
Leeds U v Nottingham F
Middlesbrough v Leicester C
Norwich C v Scunthorpe U
Preston NE v Swansea C
QPR v Sheffield U
Reading v Portsmouth

npower Football League One
Carlisle U v Plymouth Arg
Charlton Ath v Leyton Orient
Exeter C v Dagenham & R
Notts Co v Oldham Ath
Peterborough U v Bournemouth
Rochdale v Brighton & HA
Sheffield W v Colchester U
Southampton v Milton Keynes D
Swindon T v Hartlepool U
Tranmere R v Huddersfield T
Walsall v Brentford
Yeovil T v Bristol R

npower Football League Two
Accrington S v Northampton T
Burton Alb v Barnet
Bury v Oxford U
Chesterfield v Port Vale
Crewe Alex v Cheltenham T

Gillingham v Hereford U
Rotherham U v Morecambe
Shrewsbury T v Macclesfield T
Southend U v Aldershot T
Stevenage v Bradford C
Torquay U v Lincoln C City
Wycombe W v Stockport Co

Saturday, 9 April 2011
Barclays Premier League
Aston Villa v Newcastle U
Blackburn R v Birmingham C
Blackpool v Arsenal
Bolton W v West Ham U
Chelsea v Wigan Ath
Liverpool v Manchester C
Manchester U v Fulham
Sunderland v WBA
Tottenham H v Stoke C
Wolverhampton W v Everton

npower Football League Championship
Barnsley v Bristol C
Derby Co v Coventry C
Doncaster R v Cardiff C
Ipswich T v Crystal Palace
Leicester C v Burnley
Millwall v Leeds U
Nottingham F v Reading
Portsmouth v Preston NE
Scunthorpe U v QPR
Sheffield U v Middlesbrough
Swansea C v Norwich C
Watford v Hull C

npower Football League One
Bournemouth v Tranmere R
Brentford v Swindon T
Brighton & HA v Sheffield W
Bristol R v Exeter C
Colchester U v Rochdale
Dagenham & R v Notts Co
Hartlepool U v Yeovil T
Huddersfield T v Peterborough U
Leyton Orient v Southampton
Milton Keynes D v Carlisle U
Oldham Ath v Charlton Ath
Plymouth Arg v Walsall

npower Football League Two
Aldershot T v Shrewsbury T
Barnet v Crewe Alex
Bradford C v Torquay U
Cheltenham T v Rotherham U
Hereford U v Chesterfield
Lincoln C City v Gillingham
Macclesfield T v Accrington S
Morecambe v Burton Alb
Northampton T v Bury
Oxford U v Wycombe W
Port Vale v Southend U
Stockport Co v Stevenage

Tuesday, 12 April 2011
npower Football League Championship
Barnsley v QPR
Derby Co v Leeds U
Doncaster R v Preston NE
Ipswich T v Middlesbrough
Leicester C v Crystal Palace
Millwall v Bristol C
Nottingham F v Burnley
Portsmouth v Coventry C
Scunthorpe U v Reading
Sheffield U v Cardiff C
Swansea C v Hull C
Watford v Norwich C

Saturday, 16 April 2011
Barclays Premier League
Arsenal v Liverpool
Birmingham C v Sunderland
Everton v Blackburn R
Fulham v Bolton W
Manchester C v Tottenham H
Newcastle U v Manchester U
Stoke C v Wolverhampton W
WBA v Chelsea
West Ham U v Aston Villa
Blackpool v Wigan Ath

npower Football League Championship
Bristol C v Ipswich T
Burnley v Swansea C
Cardiff C v Portsmouth
Coventry C v Millwall
Crystal Palace v Scunthorpe U
Hull C v Doncaster R
Leeds U v Watford
Middlesbrough v Barnsley
Norwich C v Nottingham F
Preston NE v Sheffield U
QPR v Derby Co
Reading v Leicester C

npower Football League One
Carlisle U v Colchester U
Charlton Ath v Huddersfield T
Exeter C v Leyton Orient
Notts Co v Bournemouth
Peterborough U v Plymouth Arg
Rochdale v Brentford
Sheffield W v Hartlepool U
Southampton v Bristol R
Swindon T v Milton Keynes D
Tranmere R v Dagenham & R
Walsall v Brighton & HA
Yeovil T v Oldham Ath

npower Football League Two
Accrington S v Oxford U
Burton Alb v Cheltenham T
Bury v Barnet
Chesterfield v Macclesfield T
Crewe Alex v Lincoln C City
Gillingham v Morecambe
Rotherham U v Hereford U
Shrewsbury T v Stockport Co
Southend U v Bradford C
Stevenage v Aldershot T
Torquay U v Port Vale
Wycombe W v Northampton T

Saturday, 23 April 2011
Barclays Premier League
Aston Villa v Stoke C
Blackburn R v Manchester C
Blackpool v Newcastle U
Bolton W v Arsenal
Chelsea v West Ham U
Liverpool v Birmingham C
Manchester U v Everton
Sunderland v Wigan Ath
Tottenham H v WBA
Wolverhampton W v Fulham

npower Football League Championship
Cardiff C v QPR
Coventry C v Scunthorpe U
Derby Co v Burnley
Doncaster R v Crystal Palace
Hull C v Middlesbrough
Ipswich T v Norwich C
Leeds U v Reading
Millwall v Preston NE
Nottingham F v Leicester C
Portsmouth v Swansea C

Sheffield U v Bristol C
Watford v Barnsley

npower Football League One
Brentford v Colchester U
Brighton & HA v Southampton
Bristol R v Charlton Ath
Dagenham & R v Plymouth Arg
Exeter C v Oldham Ath
Hartlepool U v Tranmere R
Leyton Orient v Peterborough U
Milton Keynes D v Huddersfield T
Rochdale v Carlisle U
Swindon T v Notts Co
Walsall v Sheffield W
Yeovil T v Bournemouth

npower Football League Two
Accrington S v Bradford C
Aldershot T v Burton Alb
Bury v Lincoln C City
Cheltenham T v Macclesfield T
Crewe Alex v Morecambe
Gillingham v Barnet
Hereford U v Shrewsbury T
Northampton T v Rotherham U
Oxford U v Chesterfield
Port Vale v Stockport Co
Southend U v Stevenage
Torquay U v Wycombe W

Monday, 25 April 2011
npower Football League Championship
Barnsley v Doncaster R
Bristol C v Nottingham F
Burnley v Portsmouth
Crystal Palace v Leeds U
Leicester C v Watford
Middlesbrough v Coventry C
Norwich C v Derby Co
Preston NE v Cardiff C
QPR v Hull C
Reading v Sheffield U
Scunthorpe U v Millwall
Swansea C v Ipswich T

npower Football League One
Bournemouth v Bristol R
Carlisle U v Leyton Orient
Charlton Ath v Rochdale
Colchester U v Brighton & HA
Huddersfield T v Dagenham & R
Notts Co v Brentford
Oldham Ath v Walsall
Peterborough U v Yeovil T
Plymouth Arg v Milton Keynes D
Sheffield W v Swindon T
Southampton v Hartlepool U
Tranmere R v Exeter C

npower Football League Two
Barnet v Oxford U
Bradford C v Aldershot T
Burton Alb v Torquay U
Chesterfield v Bury
Lincoln C City v Cheltenham T
Macclesfield T v Southend U
Morecambe v Hereford U
Rotherham U v Gillingham
Shrewsbury T v Accrington S
Stevenage v Port Vale

Stockport Co v Northampton T
Wycombe W v Crewe Alex

Saturday, 30 April 2011
Barclays Premier League
Arsenal v Manchester U
Birmingham C v Wolverhampton W
Blackburn R v Bolton W
Blackpool v Stoke C
Chelsea v Tottenham H
Liverpool v Newcastle U
Manchester C v West Ham U
Sunderland v Fulham
WBA v Aston Villa
Wigan Ath v Everton

npower Football League Championship
Cardiff C v Middlesbrough
Coventry C v Reading
Derby Co v Bristol C
Doncaster R v Leicester C
Hull C v Crystal Palace
Ipswich T v Preston NE
Leeds U v Burnley
Millwall v Swansea C
Nottingham F v Scunthorpe U
Portsmouth v Norwich C
Sheffield U v Barnsley
Watford v QPR

npower Football League One
Brentford v Southampton
Brighton & HA v Huddersfield T
Bristol R v Sheffield W
Dagenham & R v Carlisle U
Exeter C v Plymouth Arg
Hartlepool U v Bournemouth
Leyton Orient v Tranmere R
Milton Keynes D v Notts Co
Rochdale v Peterborough U
Swindon T v Oldham Ath
Walsall v Charlton Ath
Yeovil T v Colchester U

npower Football League Two
Accrington S v Barnet
Aldershot T v Rotherham U
Bury v Wycombe W
Cheltenham T v Shrewsbury T
Crewe Alex v Stockport Co
Gillingham v Macclesfield T
Hereford U v Bradford C
Northampton T v Stevenage
Oxford U v Lincoln C City
Port Vale v Morecambe
Southend U v Burton Alb
Torquay U v Chesterfield

Saturday, 7 May 2011
Barclays Premier League
Aston Villa v Wigan Ath
Bolton W v Sunderland
Everton v Manchester C
Fulham v Liverpool
Manchester U v Chelsea
Newcastle U v Birmingham C
Stoke C v Arsenal
Tottenham H v Blackpool
West Ham U v Blackburn R
Wolverhampton W v WBA

npower Football League One
Bournemouth v Rochdale
Carlisle U v Yeovil T
Charlton Ath v Hartlepool U
Colchester U v Bristol R
Huddersfield T v Brentford
Notts Co v Brighton & HA
Oldham Ath v Milton Keynes D
Peterborough U v Dagenham & R
Plymouth Arg v Leyton Orient
Sheffield W v Exeter C
Southampton v Walsall
Tranmere R v Swindon T

npower Football League Two
Barnet v Port Vale
Bradford C v Crewe Alex
Burton Alb v Accrington S
Chesterfield v Gillingham
Lincoln C City v Aldershot T
Macclesfield T v Hereford U
Morecambe v Northampton T
Rotherham U v Torquay U
Shrewsbury T v Oxford U
Stevenage v Bury
Stockport Co v Cheltenham T
Wycombe W v Southend U

Sunday, 8 May 2011
npower Football League Championship
Barnsley v Millwall
Bristol C v Hull C
Burnley v Cardiff C
Crystal Palace v Nottingham F
Leicester C v Ipswich T
Middlesbrough v Doncaster R
Norwich C v Coventry C
Preston NE v Watford
QPR v Leeds U
Reading v Derby Co
Scunthorpe U v Portsmouth
Swansea C v Sheffield U

Saturday, 14 May 2011
Barclays Premier League
Arsenal v Aston Villa
Birmingham C v Fulham
Blackburn R v Manchester U
Blackpool v Bolton W
Chelsea v Newcastle U
Liverpool v Tottenham H
Manchester C v Stoke C
Sunderland v Wolverhampton W
WBA v Everton
Wigan Ath v West Ham U

Sunday, 22 May 2011
Barclays Premier League
Aston Villa v Liverpool
Bolton W v Manchester C
Everton v Chelsea
Fulham v Arsenal
Manchester U v Blackpool
Newcastle U v WBA
Stoke C v Wigan Ath
Tottenham H v Birmingham C
West Ham U v Sunderland
Wolverhampton W v Blackburn R

BLUE SQUARE PREMIER FIXTURES 20010–11

Saturday, 14 August 2010
Crawley T v Grimsby T
Darlington v Newport Co
Gateshead v Kettering T
Hayes & Yeading U v Bath C
Histon v Barrow
Luton T v Altrincham
Mansfield T v Forest Green R
Rushden & D v Fleetwood T
Southport v AFC Wimbledon
Tamworth v Eastbourne B
Wrexham v Cambridge U
York C v Kidderminster H

Tuesday, 17 August 2010
AFC Wimbledon v Histon
Altrincham v Darlington
Barrow v Gateshead
Bath C v Rushden & D
Cambridge U v Crawley T
Eastbourne B v Hayes & Yeading U
Fleetwood T v Mansfield T
Forest Green R v Wrexham
Grimsby T v York C
Kettering T v Luton T
Kidderminster H v Southport
Newport Co v Tamworth

Saturday, 21 August 2010
AFC Wimbledon v Tamworth
Altrincham v Crawley T
Barrow v Rushden & D
Bath C v York C
Cambridge U v Southport
Eastbourne B v Wrexham
Fleetwood T v Luton T
Forest Green R v Gateshead
Grimsby T v Hayes & Yeading U
Kettering T v Darlington
Kidderminster H v Mansfield T
Newport Co v Histon

Tuesday, 24 August 2010
Crawley T v Bath C
Darlington v Grimsby T
Gateshead v Fleetwood T
Hayes & Yeading U v Forest Green R
Histon v Eastbourne B
Luton T v Newport Co
Mansfield T v Kettering T
Rushden & D v AFC Wimbledon
Southport v Altrincham
Tamworth v Cambridge U
Wrexham v Kidderminster H
York C v Barrow

Saturday, 28 August 2010
Darlington v Gateshead
Eastbourne B v AFC Wimbledon
Forest Green R v Bath C
Hayes & Yeading U v Crawley T
Histon v Kettering T
Mansfield T v Cambridge U
Newport Co v Kidderminster H
Rushden & D v Grimsby T
Southport v Fleetwood T
Tamworth v Luton T
Wrexham v Barrow
York C v Altrincham

Monday, 30 August 2010
AFC Wimbledon v Newport Co
Altrincham v Mansfield T
Barrow v Darlington
Bath C v Wrexham
Cambridge U v Eastbourne B
Crawley T v Forest Green R
Fleetwood T v York C
Grimsby T v Histon
Kettering T v Rushden & D
Kidderminster H v Tamworth
Luton T v Hayes & Yeading U

Saturday, 4 September 2010
Altrincham v Kidderminster H
Bath C v Barrow
Cambridge U v Gateshead
Crawley T v Fleetwood T
Eastbourne B v Darlington
Forest Green R v Southport
Grimsby T v Luton T
Hayes & Yeading U v Histon
Kettering T v AFC Wimbledon
Mansfield T v Tamworth
Newport Co v Wrexham
York C v Rushden & D

Tuesday, 7 September 2010
Gateshead v Southport

Saturday, 11 September 2010
AFC Wimbledon v Bath C
Barrow v Eastbourne B
Darlington v Forest Green R
Fleetwood T v Kettering T
Gateshead v Altrincham
Histon v Crawley T
Kidderminster H v
    Hayes & Yeading U
Luton T v Cambridge U
Rushden & D v Newport Co
Southport v Mansfield T
Tamworth v Grimsby T
Wrexham v York C

Saturday, 18 September 2010
Barrow v Forest Green R
Bath C v Darlington
Crawley T v Gateshead
Eastbourne B v Altrincham
Grimsby T v Fleetwood T
Histon v Tamworth
Kettering T v Wrexham
Kidderminster H v Cambridge U
Luton T v AFC Wimbledon
Newport Co v Mansfield T
Southport v Rushden & D
York C v Hayes & Yeading U

Tuesday, 21 September 2010
AFC Wimbledon v Crawley T
Altrincham v Barrow
Cambridge U v Kettering T
Darlington v Luton T
Fleetwood T v Kidderminster H
Forest Green R v Eastbourne B
Gateshead v Grimsby T
Hayes & Yeading U v Newport Co
Mansfield T v York C
Rushden & D v Histon
Tamworth v Bath C
Wrexham v Southport

Saturday, 25 September 2010
Altrincham v Grimsby T
Cambridge U v Newport Co
Darlington v Southport
Fleetwood T v Bath C
Forest Green R v Kettering T
Gateshead v Luton T
Hayes & Yeading U v Barrow
Kidderminster H v AFC Wimbledon
Mansfield T v Eastbourne B
Rushden & D v Crawley T
Tamworth v York C
Wrexham v Histon

Tuesday, 28 September 2010
AFC Wimbledon v Cambridge U
Barrow v Fleetwood T
Bath C v Kidderminster H
Crawley T v Tamworth
Eastbourne B v Rushden & D
Grimsby T v Wrexham
Histon v Gateshead
Kettering T v Altrincham
Luton T v Mansfield T
Newport Co v Forest Green R
Southport v Hayes & Yeading U
York C v Darlington

Saturday, 2 October 2010
AFC Wimbledon v Forest Green R
Altrincham v Rushden & D
Barrow v Luton T
Cambridge U v Bath C
Crawley T v Kidderminster H
Darlington v Wrexham
Eastbourne B v York C
Fleetwood T v Histon
Gateshead v Mansfield T
Grimsby T v Newport Co
Kettering T v Hayes & Yeading U
Southport v Tamworth

Tuesday, 5 October 2010
Bath C v Altrincham
Forest Green R v Grimsby T
Hayes & Yeading U v Cambridge U
Histon v Southport
Kidderminster H v Gateshead
Luton T v Crawley T
Mansfield T v AFC Wimbledon
Newport Co v Eastbourne B
Rushden & D v Darlington
Tamworth v Barrow
Wrexham v Fleetwood T
York C v Kettering T

Saturday, 9 October 2010
Barrow v Crawley T
Bath C v Eastbourne B
Darlington v Hayes & Yeading U
Fleetwood T v Cambridge U
Gateshead v Tamworth
Histon v Altrincham
Kidderminster H v Grimsby T
Luton T v Forest Green R
Newport Co v York C
Rushden & D v Mansfield T
Southport v Kettering T
Wrexham v AFC Wimbledon

Saturday, 16 October 2010
AFC Wimbledon v Gateshead
Altrincham v Fleetwood T
Cambridge U v Barrow
Crawley T v Newport Co
Eastbourne B v Luton T
Forest Green R v Histon
Grimsby T v Southport
Hayes & Yeading U v Wrexham
Kettering T v Kidderminster H
Mansfield T v Darlington
Tamworth v Rushden & D
York C v Bath C

Saturday, 30 October 2010
AFC Wimbledon v Darlington
Forest Green R v York C
Gateshead v Cambridge U
Grimsby T v Eastbourne B
Hayes & Yeading U v Altrincham
Histon v Wrexham
Luton T v Bath C
Mansfield T v Crawley T
Newport Co v Kettering T
Rushden & D v Barrow
Southport v Kidderminster H
Tamworth v Fleetwood T

Tuesday, 9 November 2010
Altrincham v AFC Wimbledon
Barrow v Newport Co
Bath C v Hayes & Yeading U
Cambridge U v Grimsby T
Darlington v Tamworth
Eastbourne B v Forest Green R
Fleetwood T v Gateshead
Kettering T v Mansfield T
Kidderminster H v Rushden & D
Wrexham v Luton T
York C v Southport

Saturday, 13 November 2010
Altrincham v Luton T
Barrow v AFC Wimbledon
Darlington v Crawley T
Eastbourne B v Newport Co
Fleetwood T v Rushden & D
Forest Green R v Mansfield T
Hayes & Yeading U v Grimsby T
Histon v Kidderminster H
Kettering T v Cambridge U
Southport v Bath C
Tamworth v Gateshead
York C v Wrexham

Saturday, 20 November 2010
AFC Wimbledon v Kettering T
Bath C v Fleetwood T
Cambridge U v Tamworth
Crawley T v Altrincham
Gateshead v Forest Green R
Grimsby T v Barrow
Kidderminster H v Eastbourne B
Luton T v Histon
Mansfield T v Hayes & Yeading U
Newport Co v Southport
Rushden & D v York C
Wrexham v Darlington

Saturday, 27 November 2010
Barrow v Kidderminster H
Cambridge U v Altrincham
Crawley T v Southport
Eastbourne B v Tamworth

Fleetwood T v AFC Wimbledon
Forest Green R v Rushden & D
Histon v Bath C
Kettering T v Gateshead
Luton T v Darlington
Newport Co v Hayes & Yeading U
Wrexham v Mansfield T
York C v Grimsby T

Tuesday, 30 November 2010
AFC Wimbledon v Luton T
Altrincham v Forest Green R
Bath C v Crawley T
Darlington v Histon
Gateshead v Barrow
Grimsby T v Kettering T
Hayes & Yeading U v Eastbourne B
Kidderminster H v York C
Mansfield T v Fleetwood T
Rushden & D v Cambridge U
Southport v Wrexham
Tamworth v Newport Co

Saturday, 4 December 2010
Darlington v Kidderminster H
Eastbourne B v Gateshead
Forest Green R v Luton T
Hayes & Yeading U v Rushden & D
Histon v Fleetwood T
Kettering T v Bath C
Mansfield T v Barrow
Newport Co v Cambridge U
Southport v Grimsby T
Tamworth v Altrincham
Wrexham v Crawley T
York C v AFC Wimbledon

Saturday, 18 December 2010
AFC Wimbledon v Wrexham
Altrincham v Histon
Barrow v Tamworth
Bath C v Southport
Cambridge U v Darlington
Crawley T v Mansfield T
Fleetwood T v Newport Co
Gateshead v Hayes & Yeading U
Grimsby T v Forest Green R
Kidderminster H v Kettering T
Luton T v York C
Rushden & D v Eastbourne B

Sunday, 26 December 2010
Darlington v Fleetwood T
Eastbourne B v Crawley T
Forest Green R v Kidderminster H
Hayes & Yeading U v AFC Wimbledon
Histon v Cambridge U
Mansfield T v Grimsby T
Newport Co v Bath C
Rushden & D v Luton T
Southport v Barrow
Tamworth v Kettering T
Wrexham v Altrincham
York C v Gateshead

Tuesday, 28 December 2010
AFC Wimbledon v Eastbourne B
Altrincham v York C
Barrow v Wrexham
Bath C v Forest Green R
Cambridge U v Mansfield T
Crawley T v Hayes & Yeading U
Fleetwood T v Southport

Gateshead v Darlington
Grimsby T v Rushden & D
Kettering T v Histon
Kidderminster H v Newport Co
Luton T v Tamworth

Saturday, 1 January 2011
AFC Wimbledon v Hayes & Yeading U
Altrincham v Wrexham
Barrow v Southport
Bath C v Newport Co
Cambridge U v Histon
Crawley T v Eastbourne B
Fleetwood T v Darlington
Gateshead v York C
Grimsby T v Mansfield T
Kettering T v Tamworth
Kidderminster H v Forest Green R
Luton T v Rushden & D

Monday, 3 January 2011
Darlington v Barrow
Eastbourne B v Cambridge U
Forest Green R v Crawley T
Hayes & Yeading U v Luton T
Histon v Grimsby T
Mansfield T v Altrincham
Newport Co v AFC Wimbledon
Rushden & D v Kettering T
Southport v Gateshead
Tamworth v Kidderminster H
Wrexham v Bath C
York C v Fleetwood T

Saturday, 8 January 2011
Barrow v Cambridge U
Bath C v Luton T
Crawley T v Kettering T
Darlington v AFC Wimbledon
Eastbourne B v Mansfield T
Forest Green R v Fleetwood T
Gateshead v Kidderminster H
Hayes & Yeading U v Tamworth
Histon v York C
Rushden & D v Altrincham
Southport v Newport Co
Wrexham v Grimsby T

Saturday, 22 January 2011
AFC Wimbledon v Southport
Altrincham v Bath C
Cambridge U v Wrexham
Fleetwood T v Hayes & Yeading U
Grimsby T v Crawley T
Kettering T v Eastbourne B
Kidderminster H v Barrow
Luton T v Gateshead
Mansfield T v Histon
Newport Co v Rushden & D
Tamworth v Darlington
York C v Forest Green R

Tuesday, 25 January 2011
Altrincham v Hayes & Yeading U
Barrow v Histon
Bath C v AFC Wimbledon
Crawley T v Cambridge U
Darlington v Mansfield T
Kettering T v Fleetwood T
Luton T v Grimsby T

Saturday, 29 January 2011
Barrow v Altrincham

Bath C v Cambridge U
Crawley T v Luton T
Darlington v Kettering T
Eastbourne B v Grimsby T
Fleetwood T v Forest Green R
Gateshead v AFC Wimbledon
Hayes & Yeading U v Kidderminster H
Histon v Newport Co
Mansfield T v Wrexham
Rushden & D v Tamworth
Southport v York C

Saturday, 5 February 2011
AFC Wimbledon v Fleetwood T
Altrincham v Southport
Cambridge U v Rushden & D
Forest Green R v Hayes & Yeading U
Grimsby T v Gateshead
Kettering T v Crawley T
Kidderminster H v Bath C
Luton T v Barrow
Newport Co v Darlington
Tamworth v Histon
Wrexham v Eastbourne B
York C v Mansfield T

Saturday, 12 February 2011
AFC Wimbledon v York C
Bath C v Tamworth
Crawley T v Wrexham
Darlington v Eastbourne B
Gateshead v Rushden & D
Grimsby T v Cambridge U
Histon v Hayes & Yeading U
Kettering T v Barrow
Kidderminster H v Altrincham
Luton T v Fleetwood T
Mansfield T v Newport Co
Southport v Forest Green R

Saturday, 19 February 2011
Altrincham v Kettering T
Barrow v Mansfield T
Cambridge U v Kidderminster H
Eastbourne B v Histon
Fleetwood T v Grimsby T
Forest Green R v Darlington
Hayes & Yeading U v Southport
Newport Co v Luton T
Rushden & D v Bath C
Tamworth v AFC Wimbledon
Wrexham v Gateshead
York C v Crawley T

Saturday, 26 February 2011
AFC Wimbledon v Altrincham
Cambridge U v Luton T
Crawley T v Barrow
Fleetwood T v Eastbourne B
Forest Green R v Tamworth
Gateshead v Bath C
Grimsby T v Darlington
Hayes & Yeading U v York C
Histon v Rushden & D
Kettering T v Newport Co
Kidderminster H v Wrexham
Mansfield T v Southport

Tuesday, 1 March 2011
Southport v Histon

Saturday, 5 March 2011
Altrincham v Gateshead

Barrow v York C
Bath C v Kettering T
Crawley T v Histon
Darlington v Cambridge U
Eastbourne B v Southport
Grimsby T v AFC Wimbledon
Luton T v Kidderminster H
Newport Co v Fleetwood T
Rushden & D v Hayes & Yeading U
Tamworth v Mansfield T
Wrexham v Forest Green R

Tuesday, 8 March 2011
Kidderminster H v Crawley T
Rushden & D v Forest Green R

Saturday, 12 March 2011
AFC Wimbledon v Kidderminster H
Fleetwood T v Crawley T
Forest Green R v Barrow
Gateshead v Eastbourne B
Histon v Darlington
Kettering T v Grimsby T
Mansfield T v Bath C
Newport Co v Altrincham
Southport v Cambridge U
Tamworth v Hayes & Yeading U
Wrexham v Rushden & D
York C v Luton T

Saturday, 19 March 2011
Altrincham v Tamworth
Bath C v Grimsby T
Cambridge U v York C
Crawley T v AFC Wimbledon
Eastbourne B v Barrow
Fleetwood T v Wrexham
Forest Green R v Newport Co
Hayes & Yeading U v Gateshead
Histon v Mansfield T
Kidderminster H v Darlington
Luton T v Kettering T
Rushden & D v Southport

Saturday, 26 March 2011
AFC Wimbledon v Rushden & D
Barrow v Bath C
Cambridge U v Forest Green R
Darlington v Altrincham
Eastbourne B v Kettering T
Gateshead v Crawley T
Grimsby T v Tamworth
Hayes & Yeading U v Fleetwood T
Mansfield T v Kidderminster H
Southport v Luton T
Wrexham v Newport Co
York C v Histon

Tuesday, 29 March 2011
Newport Co v Gateshead
Tamworth v Wrexham
York C v Eastbourne B

Saturday, 2 April 2011
AFC Wimbledon v Barrow
Altrincham v Cambridge U
Bath C v Gateshead
Crawley T v Darlington
Fleetwood T v Tamworth
Histon v Forest Green R
Kettering T v York C
Kidderminster H v Luton T
Mansfield T v Rushden & D
Newport Co v Grimsby T

Southport v Eastbourne B
Wrexham v Hayes & Yeading U

Saturday, 9 April 2011
Barrow v Kettering T
Cambridge U v AFC Wimbledon
Darlington v Bath C
Eastbourne B v Fleetwood T
Forest Green R v Altrincham
Gateshead v Histon
Grimsby T v Kidderminster H
Hayes & Yeading U v Mansfield T
Luton T v Southport
Rushden & D v Wrexham
Tamworth v Crawley T
York C v Newport Co

Saturday, 16 April 2011
Eastbourne B v Kidderminster H
Fleetwood T v Altrincham
Forest Green R v Cambridge U
Grimsby T v Bath C
Hayes & Yeading U v Darlington
Histon v AFC Wimbledon
Mansfield T v Luton T
Newport Co v Barrow
Rushden & D v Gateshead
Southport v Crawley T
Wrexham v Kettering T
York C v Tamworth

Saturday, 23 April 2011
AFC Wimbledon v Mansfield T
Altrincham v Newport Co
Barrow v Grimsby T
Bath C v Histon
Cambridge U v Hayes & Yeading U
Crawley T v Rushden & D
Darlington v York C
Gateshead v Wrexham
Kettering T v Forest Green R
Kidderminster H v Fleetwood T
Luton T v Eastbourne B
Tamworth v Southport

Monday, 25 April 2011
Eastbourne B v Bath C
Fleetwood T v Barrow
Forest Green R v AFC Wimbledon
Grimsby T v Altrincham
Hayes & Yeading U v Kettering T
Histon v Luton T
Mansfield T v Gateshead
Newport Co v Crawley T
Rushden & D v Kidderminster H
Southport v Darlington
Wrexham v Tamworth
York C v Cambridge U

Saturday, 30 April 2011
AFC Wimbledon v Grimsby T
Altrincham v Eastbourne B
Barrow v Hayes & Yeading U
Bath C v Mansfield T
Cambridge U v Fleetwood T
Crawley T v York C
Darlington v Rushden & D
Gateshead v Newport Co
Kettering T v Southport
Kidderminster H v Histon
Luton T v Wrexham
Tamworth v Forest Green R

THE SCOTTISH PREMIER LEAGUE AND FOOTBALL LEAGUE FIXTURES 2010–11

Sky Sports   All fixtures subject to change.

Saturday, 7 August 2010
Irn-Bru First Division
Cowdenbeath v Ross Co
Dundee v Queen of the S
Falkirk v Dunfermline Ath
Morton v Stirling Alb
Raith R v Partick Th

Irn-Bru Second Division
Ayr U v Brechin C
East Fife v Airdrie U
Forfar Ath v Dumbarton
Livingston v Alloa Ath
Stenhousemuir v Peterhead

Irn-Bru Third Division
Albion R v Berwick R
Annan Ath v East Stirling
Clyde v Stranraer
Elgin C v Arbroath
Montrose v Queen's Park

Saturday, 14 August 2010
Clydesdale Bank Premier League
Aberdeen v Hamilton A
Hearts v St Johnstone
Inverness CT v Celtic* (12.15)
Motherwell v Hibernian
Rangers v Kilmarnock
St Mirren v Dundee U

Irn-Bru First Division
Dunfermline Ath v Morton
Partick Th v Dundee
Queen of the S v Raith R
Ross Co v Falkirk
Stirling Alb v Cowdenbeath

Irn-Bru Second Division
Airdrie U v Ayr U
Alloa Ath v East Fife
Brechin C v Stenhousemuir
Dumbarton v Livingston
Peterhead v Forfar Ath

Irn-Bru Third Division
Arbroath v Annan Ath
Berwick R v Elgin C
East Stirling v Montrose
Queen's Park v Clyde
Stranraer v Albion R

Saturday, 21 August 2010
Clydesdale Bank Premier League
Celtic v St Mirren
Hamilton A v Hearts
Kilmarnock v Motherwell
St Johnstone v Aberdeen

Irn-Bru First Division
Dundee v Ross Co
Falkirk v Stirling Alb
Morton v Partick Th
Raith R v Dunfermline Ath

Irn-Bru Second Division
Ayr U v Dumbarton
East Fife v Peterhead
Forfar Ath v Brechin C
Livingston v Airdrie U
Stenhousemuir v Alloa Ath

Irn-Bru Third Division
Albion R v Queen's Park
Annan Ath v Stranraer
Clyde v Berwick R
Elgin C v East Stirling
Montrose v Arbroath

Sunday, 22 August 2010
Clydesdale Bank Premier League
Hibernian v Rangers* (12.15)
Dundee U v Inverness CT

Irn-Bru First Division
Cowdenbeath v Queen of the S

Saturday, 28 August 2010
Clydesdale Bank Premier League
Aberdeen v Kilmarnock
Inverness CT v Hamilton A
Motherwell v Celtic
Rangers v St Johnstone

Irn-Bru First Division
Cowdenbeath v Partick Th
Dundee v Falkirk
Queen of the S v Ross Co
Raith R v Morton
Stirling Alb v Dunfermline Ath

Irn-Bru Second Division
Ayr U v Peterhead
Brechin C v Alloa Ath
East Fife v Dumbarton
Livingston v Forfar Ath
Stenhousemuir v Airdrie U

Irn-Bru Third Division
Arbroath v East Stirling
Clyde v Albion R
Elgin C v Stranraer
Montrose v Annan Ath
Queen's Park v Berwick R

Sunday, 29 August 2010
Clydesdale Bank Premier League
St Mirren v Hibernian* (12.15)
Hearts v Dundee U

Saturday, 11 September 2010
Clydesdale Bank Premier League
Celtic v Hearts
Dundee U v Aberdeen
Hamilton A v Rangers
Hibernian v Inverness CT
Kilmarnock v St Mirren
St Johnstone v Motherwell

Irn-Bru First Division
Dunfermline Ath v Dundee
Falkirk v Queen of the S
Morton v Cowdenbeath
Partick Th v Stirling Alb
Ross Co v Raith R

Irn-Bru Second Division
Airdrie U v Brechin C
Alloa Ath v Ayr U
Dumbarton v Stenhousemuir
Forfar Ath v East Fife
Peterhead v Livingston

Irn-Bru Third Division
Albion R v Montrose
Annan Ath v Elgin C
Berwick R v Arbroath
East Stirling v Clyde
Stranraer v Queen's Park

Saturday, 18 September 2010
Clydesdale Bank Premier League
Hibernian v Hamilton A
Inverness CT v Hearts
Motherwell v Aberdeen
Rangers v Dundee U
St Johnstone v St Mirren

Irn-Bru First Division
Dundee v Raith R
Dunfermline Ath v Cowdenbeath
Falkirk v Morton
Queen of the S v Partick Th
Ross Co v Stirling Alb

Irn-Bru Second Division
Airdrie U v Peterhead
Alloa Ath v Dumbarton
Brechin C v Livingston
East Fife v Ayr U
Stenhousemuir v Forfar Ath

Irn-Bru Third Division
Arbroath v Albion R
Berwick R v Stranraer
Clyde v Annan Ath
Elgin C v Montrose
Queen's Park v East Stirling

Sunday, 19 September 2010
Clydesdale Bank Premier League
Kilmarnock v Celtic* (12.15)

Saturday, 25 September 2010
Clydesdale Bank Premier League
Celtic v Hibernian
Dundee U v St Johnstone
Hamilton A v Kilmarnock
Hearts v Motherwell
St Mirren v Inverness CT

Irn-Bru First Division
Cowdenbeath v Dundee
Morton v Ross Co
Partick Th v Dunfermline Ath
Raith R v Falkirk
Stirling Alb v Queen of the S

Irn-Bru Second Division
Ayr U v Stenhousemuir
Dumbarton v Brechin C
Forfar Ath v Airdrie U
Livingston v East Fife
Peterhead v Alloa Ath

Irn-Bru Third Division
Albion R v Elgin C
Annan Ath v Queen's Park
East Stirling v Berwick R
Montrose v Clyde
Stranraer v Arbroath

Sunday, 26 September 2010
Clydesdale Bank Premier League
Aberdeen v Rangers* (12.15)
Will revert to Saturday 25 September
(12.15) if Rangers have a*
Champions League match on Tuesday
28 September

Saturday, 2 October 2010
Clydesdale Bank Premier League
Celtic v Hamilton A
Hearts v Rangers
Inverness CT v Aberdeen
Kilmarnock v Dundee U
Motherwell v St Mirren
St Johnstone v Hibernian

Irn-Bru First Division
Dundee v Morton
Falkirk v Cowdenbeath
Queen of the S v Dunfermline Ath
Raith R v Stirling Alb
Ross Co v Partick Th

Irn-Bru Second Division
Alloa Ath v Forfar Ath
Ayr U v Livingston
Brechin C v Peterhead
Dumbarton v Airdrie U
Stenhousemuir v East Fife

Irn-Bru Third Division
Albion R v East Stirling
Berwick R v Annan Ath
Clyde v Elgin C
Queen's Park v Arbroath
Stranraer v Montrose

Saturday, 16 October 2010
Clydesdale Bank Premier League
Aberdeen v Hearts
Dundee U v Celtic
Hibernian v Kilmarnock
Inverness CT v St Johnstone
Rangers v Motherwell
St Mirren v Hamilton A

Irn-Bru First Division
Cowdenbeath v Raith R
Dunfermline Ath v Ross Co
Morton v Queen of the S
Partick Th v Falkirk
Stirling Alb v Dundee

Irn-Bru Second Division
Airdrie U v Alloa Ath

East Fife v Brechin C
Forfar Ath v Ayr U
Livingston v Stenhousemuir
Peterhead v Dumbarton

Irn-Bru Third Division
Annan Ath v Albion R
Arbroath v Clyde
East Stirling v Stranraer
Elgin C v Queen's Park
Montrose v Berwick R

Sunday, 17 October 2010
Clydesdale Bank Premier League
Dundee U v Celtic* (12.15)
Will revert to Saturday 16 October
(12.15) if Celtic have a Champions*
League match on Tuesday 19 October

Saturday, 23 October 2010
Clydesdale Bank Premier League
Aberdeen v Hibernian
Hamilton A v St Johnstone
Hearts v St Mirren
Kilmarnock v Inverness CT
Motherwell v Dundee U

Irn-Bru First Division
Cowdenbeath v Morton
Dundee v Dunfermline Ath
Queen of the S v Falkirk
Raith R v Ross Co
Stirling Alb v Partick Th

Irn-Bru Second Division
Ayr U v Alloa Ath
Brechin C v Airdrie U
East Fife v Forfar Ath
Livingston v Peterhead
Stenhousemuir v Dumbarton

Sunday, 24 October 2010
Clydesdale Bank Premier League
Celtic v Rangers* (12.00)

Saturday, 30 October 2010
Clydesdale Bank Premier League
Dundee U v Hibernian
Motherwell v Hamilton A
Rangers v Inverness CT
St Johnstone v Celtic
St Mirren v Aberdeen

Irn-Bru First Division
Dunfermline Ath v Stirling Alb
Falkirk v Dundee
Morton v Raith R
Partick Th v Cowdenbeath
Ross Co v Queen of the S

Irn-Bru Second Division
Airdrie U v Stenhousemuir
Alloa Ath v Brechin C
Dumbarton v East Fife
Forfar Ath v Livingston
Peterhead v Ayr U

Irn-Bru Third Division
Albion R v Clyde
Annan Ath v Montrose
Berwick R v Queen's Park
East Stirling v Arbroath
Stranraer v Elgin C

Sunday, 31 October 2010
Clydesdale Bank Premier League
Hearts v Kilmarnock* (12.15)

Saturday, 6 November 2010
Clydesdale Bank Premier League
Celtic v Aberdeen
Hamilton A v Dundee U
Hibernian v Hearts
Inverness CT v Motherwell
St Johnstone v Kilmarnock
St Mirren v Rangers

Irn-Bru First Division
Cowdenbeath v Stirling Alb
Dundee v Partick Th
Falkirk v Ross Co
Morton v Dunfermline Ath
Raith R v Queen of the S

Irn-Bru Second Division
Ayr U v Airdrie U
East Fife v Alloa Ath
Forfar Ath v Peterhead
Livingston v Dumbarton
Stenhousemuir v Brechin C

Irn-Bru Third Division
Arbroath v Berwick R
Clyde v East Stirling
Elgin C v Annan Ath
Montrose v Albion R
Queen's Park v Stranraer

Sunday, 7 November 2010
Clydesdale Bank Premier League
Hibernian v Hearts* (2.15)

Wednesday, 10 November 2010
Clydesdale Bank Premier League
Aberdeen v Inverness CT
Dundee U v St Mirren
Hearts v Celtic
Kilmarnock v Hamilton A
Motherwell v St Johnstone
Rangers v Hibernian

Saturday, 13 November 2010
Clydesdale Bank Premier League
Dundee U v Kilmarnock
Hamilton A v Inverness CT
Hibernian v Motherwell
Rangers v Aberdeen
St Johnstone v Hearts
St Mirren v Celtic

Irn-Bru First Division
Dunfermline Ath v Raith R
Partick Th v Morton
Queen of the S v Cowdenbeath
Ross Co v Dundee
Stirling Alb v Falkirk

Irn-Bru Second Division
Airdrie U v Livingston
Alloa Ath v Stenhousemuir
Brechin C v Forfar Ath
Dumbarton v Ayr U
Peterhead v East Fife

Irn-Bru Third Division
Arbroath v Montrose
Berwick R v Clyde
East Stirling v Elgin C
Queen's Park v Albion R
Stranraer v Annan Ath

Saturday, 20 November 2010
Clydesdale Bank Premier League
Aberdeen v St Johnstone
Celtic v Dundee U
Hearts v Hamilton A
Inverness CT v Hibernian
Kilmarnock v Rangers
St Mirren v Motherwell

Saturday, 27 November 2010
Clydesdale Bank Premier League
Celtic v Inverness CT
Dundee U v Rangers
Hamilton A v St Mirren
Hibernian v St Johnstone
Kilmarnock v Aberdeen

Irn-Bru First Division
Cowdenbeath v Dunfermline Ath
Morton v Falkirk
Partick Th v Queen of the S
Raith R v Dundee
Stirling Alb v Ross Co

Irn-Bru Second Division
Ayr U v East Fife
Dumbarton v Alloa Ath
Forfar Ath v Stenhousemuir
Livingston v Brechin C
Peterhead v Airdrie U

Irn-Bru Third Division
Albion R v Stranraer
Annan Ath v Arbroath
Clyde v Queen's Park
Elgin C v Berwick R
Montrose v East Stirling

Sunday, 28 November 2010
Clydesdale Bank Premier League
Motherwell v Hearts* (2.15)

Saturday, 4 December 2010
Clydesdale Bank Premier League
Aberdeen v Celtic
Hibernian v St Mirren
Inverness CT v Dundee U
Motherwell v Kilmarnock
Rangers v Hearts
St Johnstone v Hamilton A

Irn-Bru First Division
Dundee v Cowdenbeath
Dunfermline Ath v Partick Th
Falkirk v Raith R
Queen of the S v Stirling Alb
Ross Co v Morton

Irn-Bru Second Division
Airdrie U v Forfar Ath
Alloa Ath v Peterhead
Brechin C v Dumbarton
East Fife v Livingston
Stenhousemuir v Ayr U

Irn-Bru Third Division
Arbroath v Stranraer
Berwick R v East Stirling
Clyde v Montrose
Elgin C v Albion R
Queen's Park v Annan Ath

Saturday, 11 December 2010
Clydesdale Bank Premier League
Celtic v Kilmarnock
Dundee U v Motherwell

Hamilton A v Hibernian
Hearts v Aberdeen
Inverness CT v Rangers
St Mirren v St Johnstone

Irn-Bru First Division
Cowdenbeath v Falkirk
Dunfermline Ath v Queen of the S
Morton v Dundee
Partick Th v Ross Co
Stirling Alb v Raith R

Irn-Bru Second Division
Airdrie U v Dumbarton
East Fife v Stenhousemuir
Forfar Ath v Brechin C
Livingston v Ayr U
Peterhead v Brechin C

Irn-Bru Third Division
Albion R v Arbroath
Annan Ath v Clyde
East Stirling v Queen's Park
Montrose v Elgin C
Stranraer v Berwick R

Saturday, 18 December 2010
Clydesdale Bank Premier League
Aberdeen v Motherwell
Hamilton A v Celtic
Hearts v Inverness CT
Kilmarnock v Hibernian
Rangers v St Mirren
St Johnstone v Dundee U

Irn-Bru First Division
Dundee v Stirling Alb
Falkirk v Partick Th
Queen of the S v Morton
Raith R v Cowdenbeath
Ross Co v Dunfermline Ath

Irn-Bru Second Division
Alloa Ath v Airdrie U
Ayr U v Forfar Ath
Brechin C v East Fife
Dumbarton v Peterhead
Stenhousemuir v Livingston

Irn-Bru Third Division
Albion R v Annan Ath
Berwick R v Montrose
Clyde v Arbroath
Queen's Park v Elgin C
Stranraer v East Stirling

Sunday, 26 December 2010
Clydesdale Bank Premier League
Celtic v St Johnstone
Dundee U v Hamilton A
Hibernian v Aberdeen
Inverness CT v St Mirren
Kilmarnock v Hearts
Motherwell v Rangers

Irn-Bru First Division
Dunfermline Ath v Falkirk
Partick Th v Raith R
Queen of the S v Dundee
Ross Co v Cowdenbeath
Stirling Alb v Morton

Irn-Bru Second Division
Airdrie U v East Fife
Alloa Ath v Livingston
Brechin C v Ayr U
Dumbarton v Forfar Ath
Peterhead v Stenhousemuir

Irn-Bru Third Division
Annan Ath v Berwick R
Arbroath v Queen's Park
East Stirling v Albion R
Elgin C v Clyde
Montrose v Stranraer

Wednesday, 29 December 2010
Clydesdale Bank Premier League
Celtic v Motherwell
Hamilton A v Aberdeen
Hibernian v Dundee U
Inverness CT v Kilmarnock
St Johnstone v Rangers
St Mirren v Hearts

Saturday, 1 January 2011
Clydesdale Bank Premier League
Aberdeen v Dundee U
Hamilton A v Motherwell
Hearts v Hibernian
Rangers v Celtic
St Johnstone v Inverness CT
St Mirren v Kilmarnock

Sunday, 2 January 2011
Irn-Bru First Division
Cowdenbeath v Queen of the S
Dundee v Ross Co
Falkirk v Stirling Alb
Morton v Partick Th
Raith R v Dunfermline Ath

Irn-Bru Second Division
Ayr U v Dumbarton
East Fife v Peterhead
Forfar Ath v Brechin C
Livingston v Airdrie U
Stenhousemuir v Alloa Ath

Irn-Bru Third Division
Albion R v Queen's Park
Annan Ath v Stranraer
Clyde v Berwick R
Elgin C v East Stirling
Montrose v Arbroath

Saturday, 8 January 2011
Irn-Bru Third Division
Arbroath v Elgin C
Berwick R v Albion R
East Stirling v Annan Ath
Queen's Park v Montrose
Stranraer v Clyde

Saturday, 15 January 2011
Clydesdale Bank Premier League
Aberdeen v St Mirren
Dundee U v Hearts
Hibernian v Celtic
Kilmarnock v St Johnstone
Motherwell v Inverness CT
Rangers v Hamilton A

Irn-Bru First Division
Dunfermline Ath v Dundee
Falkirk v Queen of the S
Morton v Cowdenbeath
Partick Th v Stirling Alb
Ross Co v Raith R

Irn-Bru Second Division
Airdrie U v Brechin C
Alloa Ath v Ayr U

Dumbarton v Stenhousemuir
Forfar Ath v East Fife
Peterhead v Livingston

Irn-Bru Third Division
Albion R v Montrose
Annan Ath v Elgin C
Berwick R v Arbroath
East Stirling v Clyde
Stranraer v Queen's Park

Saturday, 22 January 2011
Clydesdale Bank Premier League
Celtic v Aberdeen
Hearts v Rangers
Inverness CT v Hamilton A
Kilmarnock v Dundee U
Motherwell v Hibernian
St Johnstone v St Mirren

Irn-Bru First Division
Cowdenbeath v Partick Th
Dundee v Falkirk
Queen of the S v Ross Co
Raith R v Morton
Stirling Alb v Dunfermline Ath

Irn-Bru Second Division
Ayr U v Peterhead
Brechin C v Alloa Ath
East Fife v Dumbarton
Livingston v Forfar Ath
Stenhousemuir v Airdrie U

Irn-Bru Third Division
Arbroath v East Stirling
Clyde v Albion R
Elgin C v Stranraer
Montrose v Annan Ath
Queen's Park v Berwick R

Wednesday, 26 January 2011
Clydesdale Bank Premier League
Celtic v Hearts
Hamilton A v Kilmarnock
Hibernian v Rangers
Inverness CT v Aberdeen
St Johnstone v Motherwell
St Mirren v Dundee U

Saturday, 29 January 2011
Clydesdale Bank Premier League
Aberdeen v Hamilton A
Dundee U v Hibernian
Hearts v St Johnstone
Kilmarnock v Celtic
Motherwell v St Mirren
Rangers v Inverness CT

Irn-Bru First Division
Cowdenbeath v Dundee
Morton v Ross Co
Partick Th v Dunfermline Ath
Raith R v Falkirk
Stirling Alb v Queen of the S

Irn-Bru Second Division
Ayr U v Stenhousemuir
Dumbarton v Brechin C
Forfar Ath v Airdrie U
Livingston v East Fife
Peterhead v Alloa Ath

Irn-Bru Third Division
Albion R v Elgin C
Annan Ath v Queen's Park
East Stirling v Berwick R

Montrose v Clyde
Stranraer v Arbroath

Saturday, 5 February 2011
Irn-Bru Second Division
Airdrie U v Peterhead
Alloa Ath v Dumbarton
Brechin C v Livingston
East Fife v Ayr U
Stenhousemuir v Forfar Ath

Irn-Bru Third Division
Arbroath v Albion R
Berwick R v Stranraer
Clyde v Annan Ath
Elgin C v Montrose
Queen's Park v East Stirling

Saturday, 12 February 2011
Clydesdale Bank Premier League
Hamilton A v Hearts
Hibernian v Kilmarnock
Rangers v Motherwell
St Johnstone v Aberdeen
St Mirren v Inverness CT

Irn-Bru First Division
Dundee v Raith R
Dunfermline Ath v Cowdenbeath
Falkirk v Morton
Queen of the S v Partick Th
Ross Co v Stirling Alb

Irn-Bru Second Division
Alloa Ath v Forfar Ath
Ayr U v Livingston
Brechin C v Peterhead
Dumbarton v Airdrie U
Stenhousemuir v East Fife

Irn-Bru Third Division
Albion R v East Stirling
Berwick R v Annan Ath
Clyde v Elgin C
Queen's Park v Arbroath
Stranraer v Montrose

Sunday, 13 February 2011
Clydesdale Bank Premier League
Dundee U v Celtic

Saturday, 19 February 2011
Clydesdale Bank Premier League
Aberdeen v Kilmarnock
Celtic v Rangers
Hearts v Dundee U
Inverness CT v St Johnstone
Motherwell v Hamilton A
St Mirren v Hibernian

Irn-Bru First Division
Cowdenbeath v Raith R
Dunfermline Ath v Ross Co
Morton v Queen of the S
Partick Th v Falkirk
Stirling Alb v Dundee

Irn-Bru Second Division
Airdrie U v Alloa Ath
East Fife v Brechin C
Forfar Ath v Ayr U
Livingston v Stenhousemuir
Peterhead v Dumbarton

Irn-Bru Third Division
Annan Ath v Albion R
Arbroath v Clyde

East Stirling v Stranraer
Elgin C v Queen's Park
Montrose v Berwick R

Saturday, 26 February 2011
Clydesdale Bank Premier League
Aberdeen v Hearts
Hamilton A v Dundee U
Hibernian v Inverness CT
Kilmarnock v St Mirren
Motherwell v Celtic
Rangers v St Johnstone

Irn-Bru First Division
Dundee v Morton
Falkirk v Cowdenbeath
Queen of the S v Dunfermline Ath
Raith R v Stirling Alb
Ross Co v Partick Th

Irn-Bru Second Division
Ayr U v Brechin C
East Fife v Airdrie U
Forfar Ath v Dumbarton
Livingston v Alloa Ath
Stenhousemuir v Peterhead

Irn-Bru Third Division
Albion R v Berwick R
Annan Ath v East Stirling
Clyde v Stranraer
Elgin C v Arbroath
Montrose v Queen's Park

Saturday, 5 March 2011
Clydesdale Bank Premier League
Celtic v Hamilton A
Dundee U v Aberdeen
Hearts v Kilmarnock
Inverness CT v Motherwell
St Johnstone v Hibernian
St Mirren v Rangers

Irn-Bru First Division
Dunfermline Ath v Morton
Partick Th v Dundee
Queen of the S v Raith R
Ross Co v Falkirk
Stirling Alb v Cowdenbeath

Irn-Bru Second Division
Airdrie U v Ayr U
Alloa Ath v East Fife
Brechin C v Stenhousemuir
Dumbarton v Livingston
Peterhead v Forfar Ath

Irn-Bru Third Division
Arbroath v Annan Ath
Berwick R v Elgin C
East Stirling v Montrose
Queen's Park v Clyde
Stranraer v Albion R

Saturday, 12 March 2011
Irn-Bru First Division
Cowdenbeath v Ross Co
Dundee v Queen of the S
Falkirk v Dunfermline Ath
Morton v Stirling Alb
Raith R v Partick Th

Irn-Bru Second Division
Ayr U v Alloa Ath
Brechin C v Airdrie U
East Fife v Forfar Ath

Livingston v Peterhead
Stenhousemuir v Dumbarton

Irn-Bru Third Division
Arbroath v Berwick R
Clyde v East Stirling
Elgin C v Annan Ath
Montrose v Albion R
Queen's Park v Stranraer

Saturday, 19 March 2011
Clydesdale Bank Premier League
Aberdeen v Rangers
Celtic v Hibernian
Dundee U v Inverness CT
Hamilton A v St Johnstone
Hearts v St Mirren
Kilmarnock v Motherwell

Irn-Bru First Division
Dunfermline Ath v Stirling Alb
Falkirk v Dundee
Morton v Raith R
Partick Th v Cowdenbeath
Ross Co v Queen of the S

Irn-Bru Second Division
Airdrie U v Stenhousemuir
Alloa Ath v Brechin C
Dumbarton v East Fife
Forfar Ath v Livingston
Peterhead v Ayr U

Irn-Bru Third Division
Albion R v Clyde
Annan Ath v Montrose
Berwick R v Queen's Park
East Stirling v Arbroath
Stranraer v Elgin C

Tuesday, 22 March 2011
Irn-Bru First Division
Cowdenbeath v Morton
Dundee v Dunfermline Ath
Queen of the S v Falkirk
Raith R v Ross Co
Stirling Alb v Partick Th

Saturday, 26 March 2011
Irn-Bru First Division
Dundee v Cowdenbeath
Dunfermline Ath v Partick Th
Falkirk v Raith R
Queen of the S v Stirling Alb
Ross Co v Morton

Irn-Bru Second Division
Airdrie U v Forfar Ath
Alloa Ath v Peterhead
Brechin C v Dumbarton
East Fife v Livingston
Stenhousemuir v Ayr U

Irn-Bru Third Division
Arbroath v Stranraer
Berwick R v East Stirling
Clyde v Montrose
Elgin C v Albion R
Queen's Park v Annan Ath

Saturday, 2 April 2011
Clydesdale Bank Premier League
Hibernian v Hearts
Inverness CT v Celtic
Motherwell v Aberdeen
Rangers v Dundee U

St Johnstone v Kilmarnock
St Mirren v Hamilton A

Irn-Bru First Division
Cowdenbeath v Dunfermline Ath
Morton v Falkirk
Partick Th v Queen of the S
Raith R v Dundee
Stirling Alb v Ross Co

Irn-Bru Second Division
Ayr U v East Fife
Dumbarton v Alloa Ath
Forfar Ath v Stenhousemuir
Livingston v Brechin C
Peterhead v Airdrie U

Irn-Bru Third Division
Albion R v Arbroath
Annan Ath v Clyde
East Stirling v Queen's Park
Montrose v Elgin C
Stranraer v Berwick R

Saturday, 9 April 2011
Clydesdale Bank Premier League
Aberdeen v Hibernian
Celtic v St Mirren
Dundee U v St Johnstone
Hamilton A v Rangers
Hearts v Motherwell
Kilmarnock v Inverness CT

Irn-Bru First Division
Falkirk v Partick Th
Queen of the S v Morton
Raith R v Cowdenbeath
Ross Co v Dunfermline Ath

Irn-Bru Second Division
Alloa Ath v Airdrie U
Ayr U v Forfar Ath
Brechin C v East Fife
Dumbarton v Peterhead
Stenhousemuir v Livingston

Irn-Bru Third Division
Albion R v Annan Ath
Berwick R v Montrose
Clyde v Arbroath
Queen's Park v Elgin C
Stranraer v East Stirling

Sunday, 10 April 2011
Irn-Bru First Division
Dundee v Stirling Alb

Saturday, 16 April 2011
Clydesdale Bank Premier League
Hibernian v Hamilton A
Inverness CT v Hearts
Motherwell v Dundee U
Rangers v Kilmarnock
St Johnstone v Celtic
St Mirren v Aberdeen

Irn-Bru First Division
Cowdenbeath v Falkirk
Dunfermline Ath v Queen of the S
Morton v Dundee
Partick Th v Ross Co
Stirling Alb v Raith R

Irn-Bru Second Division
Airdrie U v Dumbarton
East Fife v Stenhousemuir

Forfar Ath v Alloa Ath
Livingston v Ayr U
Peterhead v Brechin C

Irn-Bru Third Division
Annan Ath v Berwick R
Arbroath v Queen's Park
East Stirling v Albion R
Elgin C v Clyde
Montrose v Stranraer

Saturday, 23 April 2011
Irn-Bru First Division
Dunfermline Ath v Raith R
Partick Th v Morton
Queen of the S v Cowdenbeath
Ross Co v Dundee
Stirling Alb v Falkirk

Irn-Bru Second Division
Airdrie U v Livingston
Alloa Ath v Stenhousemuir
Brechin C v Forfar Ath
Dumbarton v Ayr U
Peterhead v East Fife

Irn-Bru Third Division
Arbroath v Montrose
Berwick R v Clyde
East Stirling v Elgin C
Queen's Park v Albion R
Stranraer v Annan Ath

Saturday, 30 April 2011
Irn-Bru First Division
Cowdenbeath v Stirling Alb
Dundee v Partick Th
Falkirk v Ross Co
Morton v Dunfermline Ath
Raith R v Queen of the S

Irn-Bru Second Division
Ayr U v Airdrie U
East Fife v Alloa Ath
Forfar Ath v Peterhead
Livingston v Dumbarton
Stenhousemuir v Brechin C

Irn-Bru Third Division
Albion R v Stranraer
Annan Ath v Arbroath
Clyde v Queen's Park
Elgin C v Berwick R
Montrose v East Stirling

Saturday, 7 May 2011
Irn-Bru First Division
Dunfermline Ath v Falkirk
Partick Th v Raith R
Queen of the S v Dundee
Ross Co v Cowdenbeath
Stirling Alb v Morton

Irn-Bru Second Division
Airdrie U v East Fife
Alloa Ath v Livingston
Brechin C v Ayr U
Dumbarton v Forfar Ath
Peterhead v Stenhousemuir

Irn-Bru Third Division
Arbroath v Elgin C
Berwick R v Albion R
East Stirling v Annan Ath
Queen's Park v Montrose
Stranraer v Clyde

OTHER FIXTURES 2010–11

July 2010
14 Wed   UEFA Champions League 2Q (1)
            UEFA Europa League 2Q (1)
21 Wed   UEFA Champions League 2Q (2)
            UEFA Europa League 2Q (2)
28 Wed   UEFA Champions League 3Q (1)
            UEFA Europa League 3Q (1)

August 2010
04 Wed   UEFA Champions League 3Q (2)
            UEFA Europa League 3Q (2)
11 Wed   International Friendly
            Football League Cup 1
14 Sat   FA Cup EP
18 Wed   UEFA Champions League Play-Off (1)
            UEFA Europa League Play-Off (1)
25 Wed   UEFA Champions League Play-Off (2)
            UEFA Europa League Play-Off (2)
            Football League Cup 2
27 Fri   UEFA Super Cup
28 Sat   FA Cup P
30 Mon   Bank Holiday

September 2010
01 Wed   Football League Trophy 1
03 Fri   England v Bulgaria – Euro 2012 Qualifier
04 Sat   FA Vase 1Q
06 Mon   FA Youth Cup P†
07 Tue   Switzerland v England – Euro 2012 Qualifier
11 Sat   FA Cup 1Q
15 Wed   UEFA Champions League MD1
            UEFA Europa League MD1
18 Sat   FA Vase 2Q
20 Mon   FA Youth Cup 1Q†
22 Wed   Football League Cup 3
25 Sat   FA Cup 2Q
26 Sun   FA Sunday Cup P
29 Wed   UEFA Champions League MD2
            UEFA Europa League MD2

October 2010
02 Sat   FA Trophy P
            FA Vase 1P
04 Mon   FA Youth Cup 2Q†
06 Wed   Football League Trophy 2
09 Sat   International Qualifier
            FA Cup 3Q
12 Tue   England v Montenegro – Euro 2012 Qualifier
16 Sat   FA Trophy 1Q

17 Sun   FA County Youth Cup 1*
            FA Sunday Cup 1
18 Mon   FA Youth Cup 3Q†
20 Wed   UEFA Champions League MD3
            UEFA Europa League MD3
23 Sat   FA Cup 4Q
27 Wed   Football League Cup 4
30 Sat   FA Trophy 2Q

November 2010
03 Wed   UEFA Champions League MD4
            UEFA Europa League MD4
06 Sat   FA Cup 1P
            FA Youth Cup 1P*
10 Wed   Football League Trophy AQF
13 Sat   FA Vase 2P
14 Sun   FA County Youth Cup 2*
17 Wed   International Qualifier
            FA Cup 1P Replay
20 Sat   FA Trophy 3Q
            FA Youth Cup 2P*
21 Sun   FA Sunday Cup 2
24 Wed   UEFA Champions League MD5
27 Sat   FA Cup 2P

December 2010
01 Wed   UEFA Europa League MD5
            Football League Cup 5
            Football League Trophy ASF
04 Sat   FA Vase 3P
08 Wed   UEFA Champions League MD6
            FA Cup 2P Replay
11 Sat   FA Trophy 1P
            FA Youth Cup 3P*
12 Sun   FA Sunday Cup 3
15 Wed   UEFA Europa League MD6
            FIFA World Club Cup
18 Sat   FIFA World Club Cup
19 Sun   FA County Youth Cup 3*

January 2011
08 Sat   FA Cup 3P
12 Wed   Football League Cup SF 1
15 Sat   FA Trophy 2P
            FA Youth Cup 4P*
19 Wed   FA Cup 3P Replay
            Football League Trophy AF1
22 Sat   FA Vase 4P
23 Sun   FA Sunday Cup 4
26 Wed   Football League Cup SF 2
29 Sat   FA Cup 4P
            FA Youth Cup P*
30 Sun   FA County Youth Cup 4*

February 2011

05 Sat	FA Trophy 3P
09 Wed	International Friendly
	FA Cup 4P Replay
	Football League Trophy AF2
12 Sat	FA Vase 5P
	FA Youth Cup 6P*
16 Wed	UEFA Champions League 16 (1)
	UEFA Europa League 32 (1)
19 Sat	FA Cup 5P
20 Sun	FA Sunday Cup 5
23 Wed	UEFA Champions League 16 (1)
	UEFA Europa League 32 (2)
26 Sat	FA Trophy 4P
27 Sun	FA County Youth Cup SF*
	Football League Cup Final

March 2011

02 Wed	FA Cup 5P Replay
05 Sat	FA Vase 6P
	FA Youth Cup SF (1)*
09 Wed	UEFA Champions League 16 (2)
	UEFA Europa League 16 (1)
12 Sat	FA Cup 6P
	FA Trophy SF (1)
16 Wed	UEFA Champions League 16 (2)
	UEFA Europa League 16 (2)
19 Sat	FA Trophy SF (2)
	FA Youth Cup SF (2)*
20 Sun	FA Sunday Cup SF
23 Wed	FA Cup 6p Replay
26 Sat	Wales v England – Euro 2012 Qualifier
	FA Vase SF (1)
29 Tue	International Qualifier

April 2011

02 Sat	FA Vase SF (2)
03 Sun	Football League Trophy Final
06 Wed	UEFA Champions League QF (1)
	UEFA Europa League QF (1)
13 Wed	UEFA Champions League QF (2)
	UEFA Europa League QF (2)
16 Sat	FA Cup SF
17 Sun	FA Cup SF
27 Wed	UEFA Champions League SF (1)
	UEFA Europa League SF (1)
30 Sat	FA County Youth Cup Final (Prov)

May 2011

01 Sun	FA Sunday Cup Final
02 Mon	Bank Holiday
04 Wed	UEFA Champions League SF (2)
	UEFA Europa League SF (2)
07 Sat	FA Trophy Final
	Football League Season Finishes
08 Sun	FA Vase Final
14 Sat	FA Cup Final
18 Wed	UEFA Europa League Final
22 Sun	Premier League Season Finishes
28 Sat	UEFA Champions League Final
	League 2 Play-Off Final
29 Sun	League 1 Play-Off Final
30 Mon	Championship Play-Off Final

June 2011

04 Sat	England v Switzerland – Euro 2012 Qualifier

† *Ties to be played in week commencing.*
* *Closing date of round.*
FA Youth Cup Final 1st and 2nd leg – dates to be confirmed.
FA Women's Cup – dates to be confirmed.

STOP PRESS

Capello's tangled web ... England U-19s start well ... Joe Cole goes to Liverpool ... FIFA backtracks on technology.

Summer transfers completed and pending:

Premier League: Arsenal: Laurent Koscielny (Lorient) undisclosed; Marouane Chamakh (Bordeaux) Free. **Birmingham C:** Nikola Zigic (Valencia) undisclosed; Enric Vales (NAC Breda) Free; Ben Foster (Manchester U) undisclosed. **Bolton W:** Robbie Blake (Burnley) Free; Martin Petrov (Manchester C) Free. **Chelsea:** Yossi Benayoun (Liverpool) undisclosed. **Everton:** Jermaine Beckford (Leeds U) Free. **Fulham:** Philippe Senderos (Arsenal) Free. **Liverpool:** Milan Jovanovic (Standard Liege) Free; Joe Cole (Chelsea) Free. **Manchester C:** Yaya Toure (Barcelona) undisclosed; David Silva (Valencia) undisclosed; Jerome Boateng (Hamburg) undisclosed. **Manchester U:** Chris Smalling (Fulham) undisclosed; Javier Hernandez (*Chicarito*) (Guadalajara) undisclosed. **Newcastle U:** James Perch (Nottingham F) undisclosed. **Stoke C:** Florent Cuvelier (Portsmouth) undisclosed. **Sunderland:** Ahmed Al-Muhammadi (ENPPI) Loan; Simon Mignolet (St Truiden) undisclosed; Christian Riveros (Cruz Azul) Free. **WBA:** Pablo Ibanez (Atletico Madrid) Free; Gabriel Tamas (Auxerre) £800,000; Steven Reid (Blackburn R) Free. **West Ham U:** Thomas Hitzlsperger (Lazio) Free; Frederic Piquionne (Lyon) undisclosed; Pablo Barrera (Univ Nacional) £4,000,000. **Wigan Ath:** Mauro Boselli (Estudiantes) undisclosed; Ali Al-Habsi (Bolton W) Loan. **Wolverhampton W:** Stephen Hunt (Hull C) undisclosed; Steven Mouyokolo (Hull C) undisclosed; Steven Fletcher (Burnley) undisclosed; Jelle van Damme (Anderlecht) undisclosed.

Football League Championship: Barnsley: James McEveley (Derby Co) Free; Goran Lovre (Groningen) undisclosed; Liam Dickinson (Brighton & HA) undisclosed; Diego Arismendi (Stoke C) Loan; Jason Shackell (Wolverhampton W) undisclosed. **Bristol C:** Kalifa Cisse (Reading) undisclosed. **Burnley:** Ross Wallace (Preston NE) undisclosed; Dean Marney (Hull C) undisclosed; Chris Iwelumo (Wolverhampton W) undisclosed. **Cardiff C:** Tom Heaton (Manchester U) Free. **Coventry C:** Roy O'Donovan (Sunderland) Free; Gary McSheffrey (Birmingham C) Free. **Crystal Palace:** Andy Dorman (St Mirren) Free; Adam Barrett (Southend U) Free; David Wright (Ipswich T) Free. **Derby Co:** James Bailey (Crewe Alex) undisclosed: John Brayford (Crewe Alex) undisclosed; Gareth Roberts (Doncaster R) Free; Tomasz Cywka (Wigan Ath) Free. **Doncaster R:** Billy Sharp (Sheffield U) undisclosed; George Friend (Wolverhampton W) Free. **Hull C:** James Harper (Sheffield U) Free; Nolberto Solano (Leicester C) Free. **Ipswich T:** Conor Hourihane (Sunderland) undisclosed; Leeds U: Lloyd Sam (Charlton Ath) Free; Neill Collins (Preston NE) undisclosed; Federico Bessone (Swansea C) Free; Paul Connolly (Derby Co) Free; Billy Paynter (Swindon T) Free; Kasper Schmeichel (Notts Co) Free. **Middlesbrough:** Nicky Bailey (Charlton Ath) £1,400,000; Kris Boyd (Rangers) Free; Andrew Halliday (Livingston) undisclosed; Kevin Thomson (Rangers) £2,000,000; Stephen McManus (Celtic) £1,500,000. **Millwall:** Steve Mildenhall (Southend U) undisclosed. **Norwich C:** John Ruddy (Everton) undisclosed; Andrew Surman (Wolverhampton W) undisclosed; Andrew Crofts (Brighton & HA) undisclosed; Elliott Ward (Coventry C) Free; David Fox (Colchester U) undisclosed; Simeon Jackson (Gillingham) undisclosed. **Preston NE:** Wayne Brown (Leicester C) Free; Craig Morgan (Peterborough U) £400,000; David Gray (Manchester U) Free. **Reading:** Marcus Williams (Scunthorpe U) Free; Andy Griffin (Stoke C) nominal. **Scunthorpe U:** Eddie Nolan (Preston NE) (loan); Michael Collins (Huddersfield T) undisclosed; Chris Dagnall (Rochdale) Free. **Sheffield U:** Simon Walton (Plymouth Arg) Loan; Leon Britton (Swansea C) Free; Daniel Bogdanovic (Barnsley) Free; Robert Kozluk (Barnsley) Free; Steve Simonsen (Stoke C) Free. **Swansea C:** Scott Donnelly (Aldershot T) undisclosed; Neil Taylor (Wrexham) undisclosed; Juanjo (Santander) Loan. **Watford:** Rene Gilmartin (Walsall) undisclosed; Tom Aldred (Carlisle U) undisclosed.

Football League 1: Bournemouth: Steve Lovell (Partick T) Free; Michael Symes (Accrington S) Free; Marc Pugh (Hereford U) Free; Harry Arter (Woking) undisclosed. **Brentford:** Craig Woodman (Wycombe W) undisclosed; Kirk Hudson (Aldershot T) Free; Nicky Forster (Brighton & HA) Free; Toumani Diagouraga (Peterborough U) undisclosed. **Brighton & HA:** Ashley Barnes (Plymouth Arg) undisclosed; Radostin Kishishev (Liteks) undisclosed; Gordon Greer (Swindon T) undisclosed. **Bristol R:** Will Hoskins (Watford) Free; Gary Sawyer (Plymouth Arg) Free; Harry Pell (Charlton Ath) Free; James Tunnicliffe (Brighton & HA) Loan; Luke Daniels (WBA) Loan. **Carlisle U:** Jason Price (Millwall) Free; Sean McDaid (Doncaster R) Free; Craig Curran (Tranmere R) Free. **Charlton Ath:** Johnnie Jackson (Notts Co) Free; Alan McCormack (Southend U) Free; Gary Doherty (Norwich C) Free; Akpo Sodje (Sheffield W) undisclosed; Kyel Reid (Sheffield U) Free. **Colchester U:** Andrew Bond (Barrow) undisclosed. **Dagenham & R:** Luke Wilkinson (Portsmouth) undisclosed; Gavin Tomlin (Yeovil T) Free; Gareth Gwillim (Histon) Free; Stuart Lewis (Gillingham) Free; Alex Osborn (Grays Ath) undisclosed. **Exeter C:** Artur Krysiak (Birmingham C) Free; Daniel Nardiello (Blackpool) undisclosed. **Huddersfield T:** Lee Croft (Derby Co) Loan; Gary Naysmith (Sheffield U) Free; Joey Gudjonsson (Burnley) Free; Graham Carey (Celtic) Loan; Leigh Franks (Fleetwood T) undisclosed. **Leyton Orient:** Elliot Omozusi (Fulham) Free; Aaron Brown (Aldershot T) Free; Terrell Forbes (Yeovil T) Free; Alex Revell (Southend U) Free; Lee Butcher (Tottenham H) undisclosed. **Milton Keynes D:** Angelo Balanta (QPR) Loan; Lewis Guy (Doncaster R) Free; Dietmar Hamann (unattached) Free; Gary MacKenzie (Dundee) Free. **Notts Co:** John Spicer (Doncaster R) Free; Robert Burch (Lincoln C) Free; Ben Burgess (Blackpool) Free. **Oldham Ath:** Paul Dickov (Leeds U) Free; Warren Feeney (Cardiff C) Free. **Peterborough U:** Arron Davies (Brighton & HA) undisclosed; Nathaniel Mendez-Laing (Wolverhampton W) Loan; Grant McCann (Scunthorpe U) Free; Dave Hibbert (Shrewsbury T) Free. **Plymouth Arg:** Rory Patterson (Coleraine) undisclosed; Bondz Ngala (West Ham U) Free. **Rochdale:** Jean-Louis Akpa Akpro (Grimsby T) Free; Josh Lillis (Scunthorpe U) Loan; Brian Barry-Murphy (Bury) Free. **Sheffield W:** Neil Mellor (Preston NE) Loan; Gary Teale (Derby Co) Free; Giles Coke (Motherwell) Free; Paul Heffernan (Doncaster R) Free; Daniel Jones (Wolverhampton W) undisclosed; Clinton Morrison (Coventry C) Free. **Southampton:** Ryan Dickson

(Brentford) undisclosed; Danny Butterfield (Crystal Palace) Free; Frazer Richardson (Charlton Ath) undisclosed. **Swindon T:** David Prutton (Colchester U) Free; Michael Rose (Stockport Co) Free. **Tranmere R:** Timothy Cathalina (Emmen) undisclosed; Joss Labadie (WBA) Free. **Walsall:** Paul Marshall (Manchester C) Free; Oliver Lancashire (Southampton) Free; David Bevan (Torquay U) Free; Aaron Lescott (Bristol R) Free. **Yeovil T:** Edward Upson (Ipswich T) Free; Andy Williams (Bristol R) Free; Luke Ayling (Arsenal) Free; Paul Huntington (Stockport Co) Free.

Football League 2: Accrington S: Craig Lindfield (Macclesfield T) Free. **Aldershot T:** Emmanuel Panther (Exeter C) undisclosed; Jamie Vincent (Walsall) undisclosed; Luke Guttridge (Northampton T) Free; Damien Spencer (Kettering T) undisclosed. **Barnet:** Jordan Parkes (Watford) Free; Danny Kelly (Norwich C) Free; Anwar Uddin (Dagenham & R) Free; Glenn Poole (AFC Wimbledon) Free; Glen Southam (Histon) Free; Ricky Holmes (Chelmsford C) Free; Darren Dennehy (Cardiff C) Free; Mark Byrne (Nottingham F) Loan. **Bradford C:** Shane Duff (Cheltenham T) undisclosed; Luke Oliver (Wycombe W) undisclosed; Robbie Threlfall (Liverpool) undisclosed; Lloyd Saxton (Plymouth Arg) Free; Jake Speight (Mansfield T) £25,000; Tom Adeyemi (Norwich C) Loan; Tommy Doherty (Ferencvaros) Free. **Burton Alb:** Nathan Stanton (Rochdale) Free; Adam Legzdins (Crewe Alex) Free. **Bury:** Steven Schumacher (Crewe Alex) Free; Joe Skarz (Huddersfield T) undisclosed; Andy Haworth (Blackburn R) Free. **Cheltenham T:** John Melligan (Dundalk) Free; Wesley Thomas (Dagenham & R) Free; Frankie Artus (Bristol C) Free; Keith Lowe (Hereford U) Free; Daniel Lloyd-Weston (Port Vale) Free; Jeff Goulding (Bournemouth) Free; Brian Smikle (Kidderminster H) Free; Martin Riley (Kidderminster H) Free; Steve Elliott (Bristol R) Free. **Chesterfield:** Craig Davies (Brighton & HA) Free; Simon Ford (Kilmarnock) Free; Danny Whitaker (Oldham Ath) Free; Ian Morris (Scunthorpe U) Loan. **Crewe Alex:** David Artell (Morecambe) Free; Lee Bell (Macclesfield T) Free. **Gillingham:** Cody McDonald (Norwich C) Loan. **Hereford U:** O'Neill Thompson (Barnsley) Loan; Michael Townsend (Cheltenham T) Free; Daniel Stratford (Inverness CT) undisclosed; Sam Malsom (B36 Torshavn) undisclosed. **Lincoln C:** Gavin McCallum (Hereford U) undisclosed; Mustapha Carayol (Torquay U) undisclosed; Drewe Broughton (Rotherham U) Free; Josh O'Keefe (Walsall) Free; Joe Anyon (Port Vale) Free; Delroy Facey (Notts Co) Free; Jamie Clapham (Ipswich T) undisclosed. **Macclesfield T:** Samuel Wedgbury (Sheffield U) Free; Lewis Chalmers (Aldershot T) Free; Richard Butcher (Lincoln C) Free; Paul Bolland (re-signed). **Morecambe:** Phil Jevons (Huddersfield T) Free; Paul Scott (Bury) Free; Adam Rundle (Chesterfield) Free; James Spencer (Huddersfield T) Loan. **Northampton T:** Nathaniel Wedderburn (Stoke C) Free. **Oxford U:** Jake Wright (Brighton & HA) Free; Mitchell Cole (Stevenage) Free; Simon Eastwood (Huddersfield T) Free; Simon Heslop (Barnsley) Free; Matt Green (Torquay U) undisclosed; Steven Kinniburgh (Rangers) undisclosed; Ben Purkiss (York C) undisclosed. **Port Vale:** Stuart Tomlinson (Barrow) Free; Sean Rigg (Bristol R) Free; Ritchie Sutton (Nantwich T) undisclosed. **Rotherham U:** Johnny Mullins (Stockport Co) Free; Ryan Cresswell (Bury) undisclosed; Tom Newey (Bury) Free; Marcus Marshall (Blackburn R) Free; Tom Elliott (Leeds U) Loan. **Shrewsbury T:** Mat Sadler (Watford) Loan; Ian Sharps (Rotherham U) Free; Mark Wright (Bristol R) Loan. **Southend U:** Peter Gilbert (Northampton T) Free; Barry Corr (Exeter C) Free; Blair Sturrock (Truro C) Free; Ryan Hall (Crystal Palace) Free; Sofiene Zaaboub (Walsall) Free; Craig Easton (Swindon T) Free; Sean Clohessy (Salisbury C) undisclosed. **Stevenage:** Rob Sinclair (Salisbury C) undisclosed; Luke Foster (Mansfield T) Free; Peter Winn (Gateshead) undisclosed; Darius Charles (Ebbsfleet U) undisclosed. **Stockport Co:** Barry Conlon (Chesterfield) Free. **Torquay U:** Lloyd Macklin (Swindon T) Free; Steve Collis (Bristol C) undisclosed.

Scottish Premier League: Aberdeen: Josh Magennis (Cardiff C) Free; Rory McArdle (Rochdale) Free; Mark Howard (St Mirren) Free. **Celtic:** Du-Ri Cha (SC Freiburg) Free; Charlie Mulgrew (Aberdeen) Free; Joe Ledley (Cardiff C) Free; Daryl Murphy (Sunderland) undisclosed. **Hamilton A:** Jack Ross (St Mirren) Free; Gavin Skelton (Kilmarnock) Free. **Hearts:** Kevin Kyle (Kilmarnock) Free. **Hibernian:** Michael Hart (Preston NE) Free; David Stephens (Norwich C) undisclosed; Edwin de Graaf (NAC Breda) undisclosed. **Inverness CT:** Jonathan Tuffey (Partick T) undisclosed. **Motherwell:** Darren Randolph (Charlton Ath) Free. **St Johnstone:** Cleveland Taylor (Brentford) Free; Scott Dobie (Carlisle U) Free; Jamie Adams (Kilmarnock) Free; Sam Parkin (Walsall) Free. **St Mirren:** Paul McQuade (Cowdenbeath) undisclosed; David van Zanten (Hamilton A) Free; Jure Travner (Watford) Loan; Marc McAusland (Q of S) undisclosed; Craig Samson (Ayr U) undisclosed.

Leaving the country: Arsenal: Fran Merida (Atletico Madrid) Free. **Chelsea:** Michael Ballack (Leverkusen) Free. **Fulham:** Christopher Buchtmann (Cologne) undisclosed. **Liverpool:** Mikel San Jose Dominguez (Athletic Bilbao) undisclosed. **Manchester C:** Valeri Bojinov (Parma) undisclosed. **Manchester U:** Zoran Tosic (CSKA Moscow) undisclosed; Ron-Robert Zieler (Hannover 96) Free. **Portsmouth:** Papa Douba Diop (AEK Athens) undisclosed. **Sunderland:** Lorik Cana (Galatasaray) £5,000,000. **Tottenham H:** Dorian Dervite (Villarreal) Free. **WBA:** Borja Valero (Villarreal) Loan. **Wigan Ath:** Tomasz Kupisz (Jagiellonia) Free. **Middlesbrough:** Emanuel Pogatetz (Hannover 96) Free. **Portsmouth:** Nadir Belhadj (Al-Sadd) undisclosed; Lennard Sowah (Hamburg) Free. **Reading:** Marek Matejovsky (Sparta Prague) undisclosed; Oliver Bozanic (Central Coast Mariners) Free. **Aberdeen:** Mark Kerr (Asteras Tripoli) undisclosed. **Celtic:** Artur Boruc (Fiorentina) £1,500,000. **Rangers:** Nacho Novo (Gijon) Free. **St Mirren:** Billy Mehmet (Genclerbirligi) Free.

Managers and Management: Brendan Rodgers appointed manager at Swansea City; Kris Machala is Aldershot Town chairman.

NB: **Huddersfield Town** – Youngest League player was Paul Hart, 16 Years 229 days v Southend U 30 March 1974. (Researched by Alan Hodgson).

Landmarks – First all-foreign Premier League starting line-up was on 30.12.09 not 30.3.10 (see entry for Daily Round-up).

Now you can buy any of these other bestselling sports titles from your bookshop or *direct from the publisher.*

FREE P&P AND UK DELIVERY
(Overseas and Ireland £3.50 per book)

Playfair Football Annual 2010–2011	Glenda Rollin and Jack Rollin	£6.99
My Manchester United Years	Sir Bobby Charlton	£7.99
My England Years	Sir Bobby Charlton	£7.99
1966 and All That	Sir Geoff Hurst	£8.99
Psycho	Stuart Pearce	£7.99
The Autobiography	Niall Quinn	£8.99
Gazza: My Story	Paul Gascoigne	£8.99
Being Gazza	Paul Gascoigne	£6.99
The Doc	Tommy Docherty	£8.99
Black and Blue	Paul Canoville	£7.99
The Autobiography	Alan Mullery	£7.99
Fallen Idle	Peter Marinello	£6.99
Determined	Norman Whiteside	£7.99
Cloughie	Brian Clough	£8.99
Rio: My Story	Rio Ferdinand	£8.99

TO ORDER SIMPLY CALL THIS NUMBER

01235 400 414

or visit our website:
www.headline.co.uk

Prices and availability subject to change without notice.